CANADIAN ALMANAC & DIRECTORY

RÉPERTOIRE ET ALMANACH CANADIEN

2011

CANADIAN ALMANAC & DIRECTORY

RÉPERTOIRE ET ALMANACH CANADIEN

2011

164th YEAR

Grey House Publishing Canada
PUBLISHER: Leslie Mackenzie
GENERAL MANAGER: Bryon Moore
EDITORIAL MANAGER: Robert Lang
ASSOCIATE EDITORS: Janet Hawtin, Terence Martin, Rachel Smeijers
ADMINISTRATIVE ASSISTANTS: Elena Anton, Caitlin Beatty

Grey House Publishing New York
EDITORIAL DIRECTOR: Laura Mars
MARKETING DIRECTOR: Jessica Moody
COMPOSITION: David Garoogian

CONTRIBUTORS: Maj. (Ret.) Richard K. Malott, C.D., M.Sc., B.A., F.R.P.S.C., F.R.P.S.L., A.H.F. (British & Commonwealth Honours), Duy Cuong Nguyen (Astronomical Calculations)

Grey House Publishing Canada
555 Richmond Street West, Suite 301
Toronto, ON M5V 3B1
866-433-4739
FAX 416-644-1904
www.greyhouse.ca
e-mail: info@greyhouse.ca

Grey House Publishing is a wholly owned subsidiary of Grey House Publishing, Inc. USA.

Printed and bound in Canada by Webcom Inc.

Library and Archives Canada has catalogued this publication as follows:
Canadian almanac & directory.
Annual.
v. 101- ; 1948-
Continues: Canadian almanac and legal and court directory, ISSN 0316-227X.
ISSN: 0068-8193
ISBN: 978-1-59237-589-9 (164th edition)

1. Almanacs, Canadian. 2. Canada - Directories. I. Title: Canadian almanac & directory.
AY414.C2 101- 1948- 971'.0025 C75-032392-2

Additional Publications

For more detailed information or to place an order, see the back of the book.

ASSOCIATIONS CANADA 2010

Le Répertoire des Associations du Canada 2010
1880 pages, 8 1/2 x 11, Hardcover
31st edition, February 2010
ISBN 978-1-59237-570-7
ISSN 1186-9798

Nearly 20,000 entries profile Canadian and international organizations active in Canada. Over 2,000 subject classifications index activities, professions and interests served by associations. Includes listings of NGOs, institutes, coalitions, social agencies, federations, foundations, trade unions, fraternal orders, political parties. Fully indexed by subject, geographic location, electronic addresses, executive name, acronym, mailing list availability, conferences and publications.

CANADIAN PARLIAMENTARY GUIDE 2010

1128 pages, 6 x 9, Hardcover
ISBN 978-1-59237-573-8
ISSN 0315-6168

Published annually since before Confederation, this indispensable guide to government in Canada provides information on Federal and Provincial governments, with biographical sketches of government members, descriptions of government institutions, and historical text and charts. With significant bilingual sections, the Guide covers elections from Confederation to the present, including the most recent provincial elections.

CANADIAN ENVIRONMENTAL RESOURCE GUIDE 2010/11

1300 pages, 8 1/2 x 11, Softcover
15th edition, July 2010
ISBN 978-1-59237-569-1
ISSN 1187-1202

Canada's most complete and ONLY national listing of environmental Associations and Organizations, Governmental Regulators and Purchasing Groups, Product and Service Companies, Special Libraries, and more! All indexed and categorized for quick and easy reference. Also included are companies registered by ISO 9001, 9002, 9003 and 14001.

FINANCIAL SERVICES CANADA 2010/2011

1060 pages, 8 1/2 x 11, Softcover
13th edition, May 2010
ISBN 978-1-59237-571-4

This directory of Canadian financial institutions and organizations includes banks and depository institutions, non-depository institutions, investment management firms, financial planners, insurance companies, accountants, major law firms, government and regulatory agencies, and associations. Fully indexed.

LIBRARIES CANADA 2010/11

850 pages, 8 1/2 x 11, Hardcover
25th edition, August 2010
ISBN 978-1-59237-572-1
ISSN 1191-1603

Offers comprehensive information on Canadian libraries, resource centres, business information centres, professional associations, regional library systems, archives, library schools, government libraries, and library technical programs.

Introduction

First published 163 years ago as *Canadian Mercantile Almanac for 1847,* the *Canadian Almanac & Directory* is now published by Grey House Publishing Canada. The 2011 edition of this significant work includes over 48,000 entries covering hundreds of topics, making this the number one reference for collected facts and figures about Canada.

The *Almanac* continues to be widely used by business professionals, government officials, information specialists, researchers, publishers, and anyone needing current, accessible information on all topics relevant to those who live and work in Canada. This latest edition provides the most comprehensive picture of Canada, from physical attributes to economic and business summaries to leisure and recreation. It combines textual material, charts, color photographs and directory listings. This 2011 edition includes hundreds more listings and thousands more details than its predecessor. The comprehensiveness and currency of data is unparalleled.

Each of the 17 sections in this year's *Almanac* includes a detailed Table of Contents, outlining hundreds of subcategories. A *Topical Table of Contents* on the following pages and a comprehensive *Entry Name Index* at the end of the work make navigation of the massive amount of material easier than ever before.

Section 1: Almanac comprises 10 major categories, including History, Geography, Science, Awards & Regulations, Economics, Vital Statistics and more. Readers will find articles, color maps and photographs, charts and tables for a fact-filled snapshot of Canada. This resource section, invaluable for residents, politicians, and the business community, includes a detailed Table of Contents for easy access.

DIRECTORY SECTIONS

Section 2: Arts & Culture includes nine categories: Art Galleries, Aquaria, Botanical Gardens, Museums, Observatories, National Parks, Performing Arts, Science Centres and Zoos. Categories are arranged by province and city. All listings include address, phone, fax, website, email, key executives and a brief description.

Section 3: Associations lists thousands of associations and organizations arranged in 113 topics from Accounting to Writers. Each listing includes valuable descriptions and current contact information. An Association Name Index precedes the listings.

Section 4: Broadcasting begins with Canada's Major Broadcasting Companies, then lists, by Province, all Radio and Television Stations, as well as Cable Companies and Specialty Broadcasters.

Section 5: Business & Finance combines Accounting, Banking, Insurance, and Canada's Major Companies and Stock Exchanges. It includes a separate section for Major Accounting Firms with company descriptions.

Section 6: Education is arranged by Province, and includes Government Agencies, Districts, Specialized and Independent Schools, University and Technical facilities, many with valuable descriptions.

Section 7: Federal Government begins with a Quick Reference Guide to help you find your way around government agencies. The Guide is followed by Federal and Provincial listings, plus information on The Royal Family and Foreign Diplomatic Representation.

Section 8: Municipal Government details all County and Municipal Districts and segregated Major Municipalities. All profiles include date of incorporation, square miles, and population figures. Also included are District Maps for all Provinces.

Section 9: Judicial Government provides thorough coverage for Courts in Canada, including Federal and Provincial. Listings are categorized by type of Court and City within each Province, and include presiding judges.

Section 10: Hospitals and Health Care Facilities is an overview of available facilities by Province. Government agencies, hospitals, community health centers, retirement care and mental health facilities, are all arranged alphabetically by city for easy access.

Originairement publié sous le nom « Canadian Mercantile Almanac for 1847 » il y a plus de 163 ans, le *Répertoire et Almanach Canadien* est maintenant publié par Grey House Publishing Canada. L'édition 2011 comprend plus de 48 500 entrées couvrant des centaines de sujets, faisant de ce répertoire l'*Almanach* le plus complet jamais publié sur les faits et données concernant le Canada.

Le *Répertoire et Almanach Canadien* continu d'être largement consulté par les éditeurs, les gens d'affaires, les bureaux gouvernementaux, les spécialistes de l'information, les chercheurs et par tous ceux qui ont besoin d'une information à jour et facilement accessible sur tous les sujets imaginables concernant le travail et la vie au Canada. La présente édition brosse le tableau le mieux documenté qui soit du Canada en un seul volume, comprenant ses attributs physiques et économiques en passant par les activités commerciales, les divertissements et les loisirs qu'on y pratique. Il constitue un amalgame exceptionnel de textes, de chartes, de photographies couleur et de listes de répertoire. Cette édition comprend un plus grand nombre de données, de profils détaillés et des quantités de mises à jour.

En plus d'offrir un contenu plus riche en information, l'*Almanach* est restructuré de manière à faciliter la recherche. Des tables des matières détaillées pour chacune des 17 sections, une *Table des matières par sujets,* et un *Index par nom* détaillé, rendent la consultation de ces données imposantes plus aisée et accessible que jamais.

La section 1 : Almanach s'étend maintenant sur 10 catégories, dont Histoire, Géographie, Science, Prix et citations, Économies et Mensurations. Il contient plus d'articles, de cartes et de photographies couleur, de chartes et de tableaux qui offrent un portrait juste et à jour des faits et données importants sur le Canada. Elle constitue une source unique de renseignements pour tous les citoyens, les politiciens et les communautés d'affaires. Les tables des matières détaillées de chacune des catégories rendent maintenant la consultation plus facile.

RÉPERTOIRES

La section 2 : Arts et Culture comprend neuf matières principales, des galeries d'art aux parcs zoologiques. Les renseignements y sont regroupés par province et par ville. Chaque entrée comprend des données d'identification, dont l'adresse, numéros de téléphone et télécopieur, site Internet, courriel, cadres, ainsi qu'une brève description.

La section 3 : Associations répertorie des milliers d'associations et d'organismes regroupés sous 113 catégories. Chaque entrée comprend des données d'identification, dont celles de contacts. Un index par nom au début des catégories facilite la recherche.

La section 4 : Radiodiffusion et télédiffusion présente une liste des principales sociétés de radiodiffusion et télédiffusion au pays suivie des listes, par province, des stations de radio et de télévision ainsi que des entreprises de distribution par câble et des émetteurs spécialisés.

La section 5 : Affaires et finance comprend de l'information sur les cabinets comptables, les banques, les compagnies d'assurances, les plus grandes sociétés canadiennes et les bourses. Comprend aussi une liste des principaux cabinets de comptables et une description des sociétés répertoriées.

La section 6 : Éducation est divisée par province et donne des renseignements sur les agences gouvernementales, les commissions scolaires, les écoles privées et spécialisées, les institutions universitaires, collégiales et techniques. Vous y trouverez également plusieurs autres renseignements d'intérêts en matière d'éducation.

La section 7 : Gouvernement fédéral commence par un Guide de références rapide qui vous aidera à trouver votre chemin parmi la multitude d'agences gouvernementales répertoriées, suivi de leurs listes au niveau du pays et des provinces. Cette section comprend également les plus récents résultats d'élection de l'année 2008. Vous y trouverez de plus de l'information sur la Famille royale et les délégations diplomatiques à l'étranger.

La section 8 : Gouvernement municipal fournit de l'information sur les comtés, les municipalités régionales de comté et les principales villes canadiennes. Chaque profil a été revu pour y incorporer la date

Section 11: Law Firms includes a separate section of Major Law Firms with descriptions and Senior Partners. Following the Majors are law firms arranged by Province.

Section 12: Libraries begins with Canada's main Library/Archive and Government Departments for Libraries. Provincial listings follow, with Regional Systems listed first, then Public Libraries and Archives.

Section 13: Publishing includes Publishers—Book, Magazine, Newspapers—and Newspapers by Province. Magazine listings are arranged in six major categories, preceded by a Magazine Name Index for easy searching. Details include frequency and circulation figures.

Section 14: Religion starts off with broad information on religious groups, then lists Associations, arranged alphabetically by 18 denominations, from Anglican to United Church of Christ.

Section 15: Sports provides Associations for 88 single sports, plus detailed League and Team listings for Baseball, Basketball, Football, Hockey Lacrosse and Soccer. You'll also find the major sports venues in Canada, both stadiums and racetracks.

Section 16: Transportation offers comprehensive listings for major transportation modes, plus industry Associations, Government Agencies and Port Authorities.

Section 17: Utilities includes Associations, Government Agencies and Provincial Utility Companies.

In addition, this edition of the *Canadian Almanac & Directory* includes a **Topical Table of Contents** in the front of the book, and a comprehensive **Entry Index** in the back of the book. These documents, used together with the three indexes in the body of the work, and the tables of contents for each individual section, makes easy work of finding exactly what you are looking for.

The *Canadian Almanac & Directory 2011* is also available as part of **Grey House Publishing Canada's Canada Information Resource Center (CIRC)** on the web (www.greyhouse.ca) where subscribers have full access to this rich database right at their computer. Trial subscriptions are available to the CIRC database by calling 866-433-4739.

We acknowledge the valuable contributions of those individuals and organizations that have responded to our information gathering process. Their help and responses to our phone calls, faxes and questionnaires are greatly appreciated.

Every effort has been made to assure the accuracy of the information included in this edition of the *Canadian Almanac & Directory*. Do not hesitate to contact the editorial offices in Toronto with comments, or if revisions are necessary.

d'incorporation, la superficie et la population approximative. Vous trouverez aussi des cartes de comtés de chaque province.

La section 9 : Gouvernement - Juridique dresse la liste de tous les tribunaux judiciaires au Canada, tant fédéraux que provinciaux. Les renseignements y sont regroupés par genre de tribunal et par ville, au niveau de chaque province. On y trouve également le nom des juges actuellement en fonction.

La section 10 : Hôpitaux et soins de santé donne une vue d'ensemble des établissements de santé par province. Pour simplifier la consultation, les agences gouvernementales, les hôpitaux, les centres de santé communautaire, les centres de santé mentale et les établissements de soins de longues durées pour personnes âgées sont regroupés par ville, en ordre alphabétique.

La section 11 : Bureaux d'avocats inclue une sous-section détaillant les principaux cabinets d'avocats au Canada et donnant une brève description de ceux-ci et de leurs principaux associés. Vient ensuite, la liste des bureaux d'avocats regroupés par province.

La section 12 : Bibliothèque présente en premier lieu les principales bibliothèques au Canada et les bibliothèques gouvernementales et d'archives. On y trouve ensuite des renseignements sur les bibliothèques, par province, où sont décrits les systèmes régionaux, suivis des principales bibliothèques publiques et d'archives.

La section 13 : Édition fournit de l'information, détaillé par province, sur les éditeurs des livres, magazines et journaux, ainsi que les quotidiens et autres journaux. La nomenclature des magazines est présentée en six catégories précédées d'un index par nom pour faciliter la recherche. Plusieurs données ont été ajoutées dont celles concernant la fréquence de publication et le tirage.

La section 14 : Religion fournit une vaste quantité d'informations sur les groupements religieux, suivie de celles sur les dix-huit principales confessions, d'Anglicane à United Church of Christ.

La section 15 : Sports fournit des principales informations sur 88 associations de sports individuels et des données sur les ligues et équipes de baseball, basketball, football, hockey, crosse et soccer. Vous y trouverez aussi des renseignements sur les majeures installations sportives du Canada comprenant les stades et les pistes de course.

La section 16 : Transport donne une liste détaillée des principaux modes de transport et organismes œuvrant dans le domaine au pays, ainsi qu'une liste des associations de l'industrie, des agences gouvernementales et des autorités portuaires.

La section 17 : Services publics regroupe sous un même chapitre les associations, les agences gouvernementales et les entreprises œuvrant dans les services publics de chaque province.

De plus, la présente édition du *Répertoire et Almanach Canadien* profite d'une **Table des matières par sujets** au début du volume, et un **Index par nom** à la fin du volume, avec référence au numéro de la page où se trouve l'information. Ces index, qui s'ajoute aux trois autres index contenus dans le répertoire, ont été incorporés pour faciliter davantage votre consultation.

Le *Répertoire et Almanach Canadien 2011* fait partie des vaste données électroniques du **Canada Information Resource Centre (CIRC) de Grey House Publishing Canada** (www.greyhouse.ca) auquel les abonnés peuvent avoir accès de leur ordinateur personnel. Vous pouvez obtenir un abonnement d'essai aux données du CIRC en composant le 866 433-4739.

Nous tenons à souligner la précieuse contribution des personnes et des organismes qui ont collaboré tout au long de l'année à notre procédé de cueillette d'information; votre aide, vos réponses à notre questionnaire dans les délais impartis, vos appels téléphoniques et vos envois par télécopieur sont grandement appréciés.

Nous avons mis tous les efforts pour nous assurer de l'exactitude de l'information contenue dans cette édition du *Répertoire et Almanach Canadien*. N'hésitez pas à communiquer avec le bureau de la rédaction pour faire part de vos commentaires ou si des modifications s'avèrent nécessaires.

Table of Contents

Table des matières

Topical Table of Contents

Table des Matières par Sujets

SECTION 1

ALMANAC

History

Provincial Flags, Coats of Arms, Floral Emblems, Selected Honours

Geography

Science

Economics & Finance

Exhibitions, Shows & Events

Awards & Honours

Government

Governors General

Prime Ministers

Regulations & Abbreviations

Vital Statistics

Weights & Measures

History

History of Canada

Over the past 400 years, Canada has evolved from a sparsely populated trading post to the eighth-richest sovereign power in the world. It stands alone as the only country to separate from its colonial power through peaceful means.

The political boundary of what is now known as Canada recorded thousands of years of history before European colonization, but was one of the last places on Earth to host human habitation. While modern *Homo sapiens* emerged from the eastern region of Africa 200,000 years ago, most scientists agree that it took another 175,000 years for humans to find their way across the ice bridge that once joined Alaska and Eastern Siberia. The land that now constitutes Canada has seen the longest period of human habitation in the New World: from the original migration 25,000 years ago came all the indigenous cultures of North and South America including the Arctic Inuit, Blackfoot, Cree, Algonquin, Dene, and Iroquois League of Five Nations. Estimates put the number of native peoples in the United States and Canada before European contact at about two million.

Columbus may have been given credit for the "discovery" of America in 1492, but proof exists that Vikings voyaged to Greenland and further west as early as 982 A.D. Archeological evidence points to Norse settlements in Newfoundland at L'Anse aux Meadows dating back to approximately 1000 A.D., making Canada the actual site of the European discovery of North America. The Vikings, however, were not concerned with permanent colonization, only Canadian natural resources. By the time Christopher Columbus arrived, the Norse settlements had been abandoned.

With Christopher Columbus came the European fervour of colonizing the New World. Seeking a way to circumvent the long land trade routes to Asian goods by crossing the Atlantic to what he thought was India, Columbus inadvertently began the Age of Discovery. European powers established colonies, seeking spice, gold, slaves, and new crops, as well as the promotion of Christianity among the native peoples. The earlier colonies, mostly Spanish and Portuguese, were concentrated in South America, Central America, and the Caribbean. England and France, however, turned their attention north. John Cabot, an Italian-born English explorer, is credited as being the first European explorer after the Vikings to set foot in North America. Although this exploration occurred only five years after Columbus's discoveries, it was not until 1605 that permanent settlements were established. Many explorers, including Henry Hudson, still attempted to find the Northwest Passage, a reputed waterway through the New World to Asia. The reasons for this 100-year gap have more to do with European affairs than those of the New World.

Two events slowed the colonization of North America: religious unrest and war in Europe. In 1517 Martin Luther distributed his list of 95 grievances against the Catholic Church by means of a new invention, the printing press. Thus began the Protestant Reformation. This schism was to have far-reaching consequences across all of European history, but in the short term, it created rancorous religious strife. Most of Europe turned inward to deal with unrest and religious crisis. Escalating political conflicts enveloped most of Western Europe for decades, drawing resources away from colonization efforts. The French Wars of Religion, the Italian Wars, and popular uprisings combined with new religious uprisings to turn the attention of Europe away from the New World for more than a century.

France looked to North America as the best possible source of wealth and power and as a relief from war debt. When French explorer Jacques Cartier sailed up the St. Lawrence River in 1534, he claimed the territory for France, and gave it the name it still bears today: Canada. Once fur traders arrived in Eastern Canada in the 1500s, France monopolized the fur trade. While the French made an effort to establish friendly trading relations with the native population, the Iroquois in particular proved openly hostile. Conflicts with local tribes soon convinced the crown that if traders were to make a profit in Canada, a permanent military and civilian presence was essential. King Henry IV sent his royal "hydrographer," Samuel de Champlain to map the region.

In 1605, after exploring the coast of North America as far south as Cape Cod, Champlain established the first permanent French settlement at Port Royal, and in 1608 he founded Quebec City. New France, as it was then called, grew slowly, mainly due to disinterest from the mainland and war with the Iroquois. The settlers survived attacks from native peoples through their alliance with the Algonquin, Montagnais, and Huron peoples. These alliances not only secured their survival, but greatly increased France's control of the fur trade. Europeans had little experience in the thick wilderness of the area, an expertise that the native peoples supplied.

Once again religious tensions in Europe interfered with Canada's settlement and growth. By the mid-seventeenth century, while England's American and Caribbean colonies grew self-sufficient, New France remained underpopulated. The struggling colony drained France's resources. The French crown decided to take action by creating land incentives for emigrants to New France. Only one caveat stood in the way: all settlers must be Roman Catholic, or convert to Roman Catholicism before leaving Europe. This change of policy, undertaken at the urging of the fanatical Catholic Cardinal Richelieu, closest advisor to King Louis XIII, created friction. Previously, French Protestants, especially the persecuted sect known as Huguenots, had fled to New France to escape religious persecution. Cardinal Richelieu's new edict would have a lasting impact on the religious and political makeup of modern Canada.

In the late seventeenth century, English and French colonies in the New World began to take a stronger foothold. Both nations finally saw a large-scale financial return on their investments, but a war in Europe again infringed on Canada's nascent growth. New France, already in the middle of brutal intertribal warfare with the Algonquins, conflicted with the Iroquois confederacy opposing them. With the War of the Grand Alliance in 1688, which pitted France against almost all of continual Europe, the Iroquois began to receive English weapons as part of government policy. This escalation by the English heightened the already bloody warfare. English armies and their Iroquois allies captured Port Royal, but were turned back from Quebec City, due mainly to a decimation of forces by disease. The war eventually petered out, and a peace was signed in 1697. The Iroquois, however, continued the fight without British help, and eventually suffered a series of major defeats, forcing them to sue for peace four years later.

New France, and thereby Canada, seemed securely in the mother country's domain following the end of the War of the Grand Alliance. However, France's control of the region was not to last. Queen Anne's War, which began only a year after the French peace with the Iroquois, lead England to claim Nova Scotia and Newfoundland, as well as the rights to the land surrounding Hudson Bay. Fighting broke out again three decades later in 1744, in a battle known as King George's War, but neither side was able to enlarge their colonial positions.

By 1754 the long-standing animosity between the English and French seeped into the New World, culminating in the Seven Years War, known in the Americas as the French and Indian War. The causes of the conflict were threefold. The lucrative fur trade, rich fishing grounds, ample lumber, and mineral deposits all promised great wealth to whoever controlled Canada. Secondly, the fiercely anti-Catholic British felt that the Protestant French were heretics, a feeling that was reciprocated by the French. Thirdly, possession of colonies overseas could be used as diplomatic bargaining chips should the war in Europe go badly.

The Seven Years War was the first worldwide war, fought on five continents: North America, South America, Africa, Europe, and Asia. More than a million died, and the war resulted in a complete change in the power structure of the New World. Britain gained all of France's colonial possessions in North America, and Canada became a British colony. However, 150 years of French colonization didn't disappear overnight. Even today, French-English relations in Canada can be contentious.

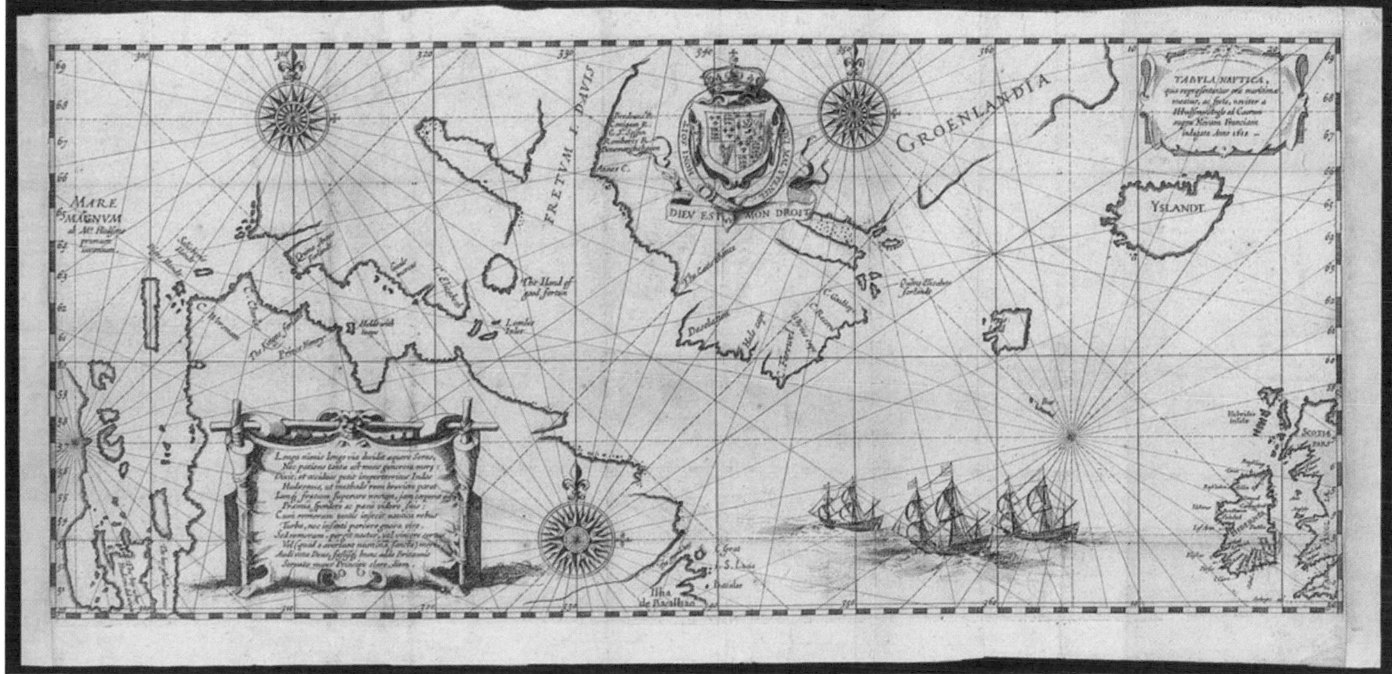

Henry Hudson arrived in Arctic waters in 1610 determined to find the Northwest Passage. He explored Hudson Bay and the mouth of the Bay. His crew mutinied and abandoned him in 1611 and returned to Europe. This map by Dutch cartographer Gerritsz is based on Hudson's discoveries.

Champlain's Map 1632

The British, upon taking control of Canada in 1764, left intact the religious and economic systems already in place, to the relief of the Catholic French colonists. The Quebec Act of 1774 allowed a separate system of French law to continue in Quebec. The British now controlled the entire eastern half of North America, from the eastern seaboard to the Mississippi River. However, George III's mistreatment of the American colonies would soon cause a shift in the balance of power in the New World.

As a base for the British forces, a refuge for fleeing Americans loyal to the British crown, and a source of militia for both the British and American armies, Canada played a large role in the American Revolution. The American army originally attempted to convince Canada to join their revolution but Canadians had just finished rebuilding after the Seven Years War and most did not want no take part in another feud. On June 27, 1775, American troops attacked Quebec and Montreal was taken without a fight. The attack on Quebec City was eventually defeated and in 1776, the American troops evacuated Montreal.

When America gained independence from Britain in 1783, citizens loyal to the British Empire were exiled. Over 35,000 of these loyalists flooded into Nova Scotia. This massive influx prompted the British government to divide Nova Scotia, creating the new colony of New Brunswick. Soon, the loyalists in Quebec were also making demands for their own colony, while the French Canadians were equally determined to have their own elected assembly. In 1791, Quebec was divided into Upper Canada and Lower Canada in order to meet the distinct needs of the English loyalists and the French Canadians.

Tensions between Britain and America remained high in the proceeding decades, and once again a conflict erupted that ensnared Canada. The United States declared war on Britain in 1812 over the arming and supplying of hostile Native American tribes and the forced conscription of American sailors into the British Navy. Canada became one of the primary battlegrounds in this conflict, with the United States planning to seize Canada and use it as leverage against the British. America expected support from the people of Canada, who they assumed were unhappy under English colonial rule. However, many Canadians at that time were children of British loyalists who fled America and saw the United States as invaders and occupiers.

The American army suffered a loss early in the war when they were soundly defeated by General Isaac Brock and his force of Indian allies and local military men at the Battle of Queenston Heights. But the American army did go on to occupy and loot many cities, including York (now Toronto) and Newark (now Niagara-on-the-Lake), eventually controlling much of present day Ontario and Quebec. Ultimately, the American army was driven back, and although the war ended with no real victor, the fact that an attempted American takeover had been thwarted gave Canadians confidence and stimulated national pride.

While Canadians rejected the idea of American invaders on their soil, the political example of the United States resonated throughout the country. Rebellions broke out against the British in 1837. Canadians, angry over the unfair distribution of wealth derived from Canada's natural resources, balked against not being represented in the British government. Based on the opinion of the British that friction between the French and English people was causing conflict in Canada, all of the Canadian colonies were merged together into the United Province of Canada in 1840. In 1849 the United States and the British Empire agreed that the 49th north parallel would be the boundary between the two nations, and the British extended Canada to the western seaboard, encompassing British Columbia.

Canadian independence had been debated in Britain and in Canada almost since the American Revolution. Some advocated violent revolution and total Canadian independence. Others wanted a slower, more gradual autonomy. On July 1st, 1867, the British parliament passed the British North America Act, which established The Dominion of Canada as a separate and self-governing colony. While it was not completely severed from England, especially in matters of foreign policy, domestically, Canada was allowed free reign.

During the next decades, Canada continued to expand westward. With the purchase of two huge northern territories, The North-Western Territory and Rupert's Land, from the Hudson Bay Company, the country more than doubled its size. The sections of Canada west of Ontario housed a large population of French-speaking, Catholic Métis, the children of indigenous people and white settlers. After the sale of Rupert's Land, many settlers from Ontario flooded into the region hoping to claim land. The M,tis became worried that this influx of mostly English Protestant settlers would threaten their rights to language, religion, and land. The Métis leader Louis Riel organized the Red River Resistance in 1869 in order to ensure that these rights were guaranteed. The revolt led to the creation of Manitoba, a province with strong laws protecting the Métis, French-speaking people, and Catholics. By 1905 the founding provinces of Upper and Lower Canada, New Brunswick, and Nova Scotia were soon joined by British Columbia, Saskatchewan, Prince Edward Island, and Alberta.

The construction of a transcontinental railroad, completed in 1885, spurred Canada's expansion. While the railroad enabled additional settlers to move west into the new provinces, it also pushed the Native people aside. Again rebellion flared, resulting in more bloodshed. The sentiment that the Canadian government didn't heed the concerns of French-speaking Catholic citizens caused a political crisis resulting in the resignation of prime minister Mackenzie Bowell in 1896, when the government tried to ban French as an official language of Manitoba, contrary to the laws of the province.

Both Canada and the United States shared a period of western expansion in the late nineteenth century, based on the prominence of the railroad, the promise of free land, and the discovery of mineral deposits. These factors, joined with a large influx of European immigrants, led to Canada becoming the fastest-growing economy in the world between 1896 and 1911. During that time, the Canadian government created the Yukon Territory, a land mass about the size of Germany, Austria, and Switzerland combined, then populated by only 8,500 people.

On the verge of the twentieth century, Canada faced the first serious conflict with its colonial power. When Britain entered the Boer War in 1899, most English-speaking Canadians supported bringing South Africa into the fold of the British Empire. French Canadians, however, had little interest in British imperialism, seeing themselves as a separate concern, only nominally part of the Empire. As a compromise, volunteers were allowed to serve in the Boer War, but the Canadian Army stayed uninvolved. The view of French Canada as a separate entity, exacerbated by rebellion and anti-French laws of the past decades, would continue to play out in Canadian politics in years to come.

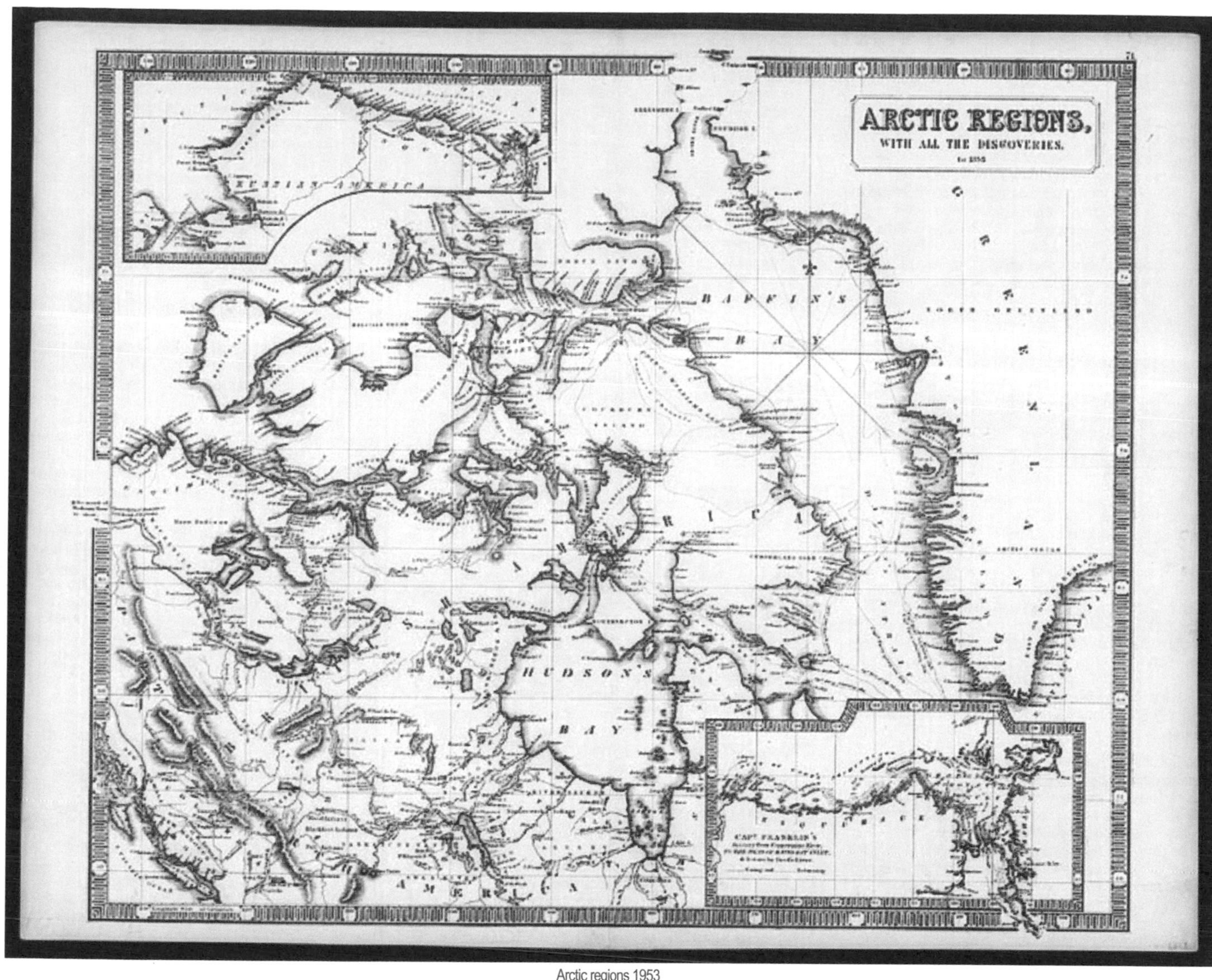

Arctic regions 1953

Although many French Canadians wanted out from under the British Empire's yoke, the country was still obligated to fall in line with British foreign policy. With the assassination of Archduke Ferdinand on June 28, 1914, Canada was swept into the chaotic system of alliances that created the First World War. When Britain declared war on the central powers on August 4th, Canadian troops were called into action. Like most of the allied powers, internal disputes were put aside and support for the war remained high, even among French Canadians. After suffering more than 200,000 dead and wounded casualties out of a population of seven million, support for the war began to wane. By the time the government attempted to introduce conscription in 1917, many Canadians, especially in French Canada, were fiercely anti-war. Despite the popular sentiment, World War I greatly increased the sense of Canadian nationalism and identity, fed by the country's significant role in the largest war mankind had ever known. Massive Canadian casualties in what many Canadians saw as a "British" war also created additional animosity towards the Empire.

The First World War radically changed Canada's political landscape. Soldiers returned home from the horrors of the conflict with altered political ideologies. Socialism, communism, trade unionism and other left-wing progressive movements gained traction in the years immediately after the war, as the influx of soldiers returning home caused high unemployment and wage cuts. The Winnipeg General Strike of 1919, the largest of a wave of strikes that swept the country, was violently crushed by police, killing one man and wounding 30. When women's suffrage was enacted nationwide in 1918, the ruling Conservative Party collapsed, partly because of their actions during the strike. The Liberal Party, upon assuming control of the government, enacted many of the original strike committee's demands, including the right to form unions without government permission. Progressive and socialist parties formed in subsequent years, including the Progressive Party of Canada and the Cooperative Commonwealth Federation.

In 1931, the British Parliament passed the Statute of Westminster, establishing all the colonies and dominions of the British Empire, including Canada, Australia, New Zealand, and Ireland as separate legislative entities. This act allowed these countries to write their own constitutions and removed the power of the British Government to legislate in these areas, effectively making them independent, while still being contained in a worldwide British Commonwealth.

When the American Stock Market crashed on Black Tuesday in 1929 kicking off the Great Depression, the Canadian economy soon felt the effects. By 1933 the Canadian gross national product dropped 40 percent. Manufacturing and farming suffered the most, with the price of wheat, Canada's main export, cut in half. At its worst point in 1933, 30 percent of Canadians were out of work. Newfoundland, deciding that Canadian government policy was the cause of the economic difficulty, voted to leave the Canadian federation and rejoin the British Empire.

When both the Liberal and Conservative parties were unable to produce any solutions to the crisis, many Canadians began to turn to third parties, such as the socialist Cooperative Commonwealth Federation and the Social Credit Party of Canada. After the Conservative government of R.B. Bennett put unemployed men into work camps to offset the great cost of supporting a huge welfare system, the Workers' Unity League put together a massive protest called the "On to Ottawa Trek" in order to call for improved conditions and benefits. Bennett's attempt to repress the Trek resulted in the Regina Riot, and contributed to his defeat in the 1935 election. The new Liberal government did away with the camps and instituted social programs to help lessen the effects of the Depression, but Canada was still severely affected. Almost one-fifth of the population was surviving on government payouts and social support systems. Even after a resurgent boom in Canada's economy, brought on by World War II, these systems remained in place, and continued to evolve.

World War II officially began on September 1, 1939. Canada did not immediately enter the war upon the British declaration as it had in World War I. With its growing independence from England, Canada decided to declare war on its own nine days later. While the Japanese and Nazi onslaught was still in full effect, Canadian supplies and war materiel were instrumental in keeping Britain from succumbing to German invasion. Once the Allies were in a position to counterattack, Canadian troops were deployed all over the world, and served valiantly in some of the major battles including the invasion of Sicily and Italy in 1943, the allied landing at Normandy in 1944, the liberation of the Netherlands, and the drive across France and Germany to end the war. However, Canada endured its own share of loss. A predominantly Canadian raid, at Dieppe, France, resulted in more than 3,000 dead, wounded or captured and German U-boats, which prowled Canadian waters, sank many supply ships. In the end, Canada suffered a total of 42,000 casualties.

When the Japanese bombed Pearl Harbor on December 7, 1941, the 22,000 Japanese Canadians then living in British Columbia took the brunt of the resulting pain and anger. The anti-Asian sentiment in the province was further fueled when thousands of Canadians were killed or captured in the Japanese invasion of Hong Kong. In 1942, all people of Japanese descent were sent to internment camps, and after the war, all Japanese

Canadians were deported from British Columbia. It was not until 1949 that they became free to live anywhere in Canada. Japanese Canadians were finally compensated in 1988, for the wrongs that they had suffered during the war.

At the close of World War II, Canada and the United States alone benefited from never having seen fighting on their home soil. Each country was, therefore, in a unique economic position. Due to a revitalized manufacturing sector, the discovery of oil in Alberta, and as the main trading partner to the economic superpower on their southern border, the Canadian economy exploded. This newfound wealth was put into a radical new program of social support. Based upon the centralized welfare state of the late 1930s and early 1940s, as well as many of the policies of the socialist Cooperative Commonwealth Federation, Canadians enjoyed hospital insurance, old-age pensions, veterans' pensions, and family allowance. These progressive social policies convinced Newfoundland to rejoin Canada in a 1949 referendum.

Canada cemented its position in the Cold War with its founding membership in NATO in 1949. The country's fortunes were firmly rooted with the United States. Canada participated in the Korean War, and Canadian troops were stationed in West Germany, on the border of the communist Eastern Bloc. Canada's voting record in the United Nations was not always aligned with the United States, but there is no question that Canada was an American ally pitted against the Soviet Union.

Canada's treatment of its Native peoples has a sad history. As far back as the late 1800s, when the buffalo were hunted almost to extinction and the expansion of the railroad brought more settlers to native territories, First Nations people were treated as second-class citizens. Starvation, assimilation, and a crushed rebellion largely put an end to the native resistance movement, but it gained strength again after World War II. Decolonialization and a new-found spirit of democracy was being put forth by the Western powers in their opposition to Soviet tyranny, yet most First Nations people could not vote as late as 1950. In order to vote, First Nations people had to gain suffrage by renouncing their status as "Indians". It was not until 1960 (1969 in Quebec) that all First Nations people were allowed to vote freely.

As Canada entered the 1960s, the government faced growing radicalism and organization among its populace. Quebec nationalism had been growing ever since the British took Canada from the French in 1764. French Canadians saw themselves as a separate nation, and frequently found themselves disagreeing with the policies of the Canadian government. The more radical French Canadian factions felt they were being oppressed, and that their language and culture were under attack. Inspired by revolutions around the world, nationalist and left-wing terrorism began to rise, Canada was not unaffected. The Front de Libération du Québec (FLQ), committed more than 200 bombings, and killed five people in pursuit of an independent Quebec. While violence was rejected by a majority of the population, a genuine desire for independence fueled Québécois protests. When Pierre Elliott Trudeau was elected prime minister in 1968, he declared martial law in Quebec, arresting most members of the FLQ.

While the crisis in Quebec worsened throughout the 1970s, the United States became involved in one of the most controversial conflicts in modern history: the war in Indochina. The Vietnam War resulted in over 1,500,000 dead, and radicalized an entire generation. Canada was no exception. Young people throughout the country protested against what they saw as American imperialism. The Canadian government refused to participate in the war, and granted citizenship to as many as 125,000 American draft dodgers over the course of the conflict. This led to serious friction between the governments of Canada and the US. To this day Vietnam and Canada have a close relationship, and hundreds of thousands of Vietnamese have immigrated to Canada's west coast. The period of the Vietnam War also saw the rise of the New Democratic Party (NDP), the successor to the socialist Cooperative Commonwealth Federation. Since its beginning in 1962, the NDP has altered the balance of Canadian politics, regularly receiving between 10 and 20 percent of the national vote, and often having the ability to form a majority coalition by grouping itself with the winning party. It has fought for the continuation of Canada's welfare state, a humanitarian foreign policy, and native rights.

Young people across Canada became increasingly involved in politics as a result of the Vietnam War, and this new political awareness allowed the question of Quebec sovereignty to be addressed. The Parti Québécois was formed in 1968 and elected to govern Quebec in 1976, making French the official language of the province in 1977. Finally, the party made good on its biggest promise and introduced a referendum to decide Quebec's fate. The actual referendum simply said that Quebec would "negotiate a new agreement with the rest of Canada, based on the equality of nations; this agreement would enable Quebec to acquire the exclusive power to make its laws, levy its taxes and establish relations abroad - in other words, sovereignty." The fact that the referendum did not advocate full independence, in combination with a full-out public relations assault from the federal government, doomed the referendum.

While Canada became a sovereign entity in 1867, and had its independence increased in 1931, it was not technically a separate nation. Canada could not make amendments to its own constitution and the power of Canada to act directly against the wishes of the British government was in question. In 1982, Trudeau finally sealed Canada's status as its own unique nation by signing the Canada Act and the Charter of Rights and Freedoms. Although still a member of the British Commonwealth, Canada was now free from control by the British parliament.

With Canada's complete independence from Britain, the question of trade with the United States became central to the Canadian economy. The Canada-United States Free Trade Agreement drafted in 1988 set the model for the subsequent North American Free Trade Agreement and Central American Free Trade Agreement. The criticism of the agreement, as well as later free trade agreements, was that by eliminating trade barriers, Canadian consumers and labour unions would be at the mercy of more powerful US corporations. The agreement was a decisive issue in the 1988 elections, with the Liberal Party and NDP in opposition, and the ruling Progressive Conservatives attempting to pass it. A 57 percent majority voted against the Progressive Conservatives, but because they received the most votes for one single party, they were rewarded with the most seats in parliament, and passed the free trade agreement.

The Parti Québécois, after failing in its referendum of 1980, had formed a national party, the Bloc Québécois, and doggedly pursued its agenda of an independent Quebec. A second referendum, called in 1995, created an even bigger debate than the referendum of 1980, with massive media campaigns on both sides of the issue. When the vote finally came up, it failed by a slim 54,000 votes, but the issue illustrated a true divide in Quebec. Considering that 86,000 ballots were thrown out as invalid, the question of Quebec independence failed by a razor-thin margin, and the probability of it arising again in the future is still possible.

In 1990, in a small town called Oka, west of Montreal, a First Nations revolt led to the intervention of the Canadian Army and three deaths. While this was far from the first violent conflict between First Nations people and the Canadian government, it has marked a new era of militant native resistance. With more than one million people of Aboriginal descent living in Canada, many native organizations have called for more indigenous control over resources in their lands, resulting in violent conflicts between First Nations people and corporations attempting to mine, fish, or harvest lumber. One effect of these protests was the creation of a new territory, Nunavut, in the far north of Canada. While the population is less than 30,000, more than 85 percent of its inhabitants claim Inuit status, and the territory has adopted many laws securing their rights and claims to land and resources.

Today, Canada continues to deal with its internal relations with French speaking Canadians and First Nations people. As a unified country, it also faces other issues such as its position on gay marriage, drug decriminalization, immigration, participation in the Obama Administration's War on Terror, global warming, and control over Arctic seaways.

Histoire du Canada

Au cours des 400 dernières années, le Canada est passé de simple poste de traite peu peuplé au huitième état souverain le plus riche au monde. Il s'agit de plus du seul pays à s'être séparé pacifiquement de sa puissance coloniale.

Malgré que le grand territoire composant aujourd'hui le Canada avait déjà une histoire vieille de plusieurs millénaires au début de la colonisation européenne, il a néanmoins été un des derniers endroits au monde à accueillir des populations humaines. Alors que l'*Homo Sapiens* moderne aurait émergé dans l'est de l'Afrique il y a 200 000 ans, la majorité des scientifiques conviennent qu'il aura fallu 175 000 années de plus pour que les hommes traversent le pont de glace reliant jadis l'Alaska et l'est de la Sibérie. Sur ce nouveau continent, c'est l'espace que délimitent les frontières canadiennes actuelles qui est habité depuis le plus longtemps; la migration originale qui a eu lieu il y a 25 000 ans est la source des cultures indigènes d'Amérique du Nord et du Sud, incluant les Inuits de l'Arctique, les Pieds-Noirs, les Cris, les Algonquins, les Dénés et la Ligue iroquoise des Cinq-Nations. On estime à environ deux millions le nombre d'Autochtones vivant aux États-Unis et au Canada avant l'arrivée des Européens dans le Nouveau Monde.

Christophe Colomb est peut-être celui à qui l'on attribue la « découverte » de l'Amérique en 1492, mais l'on sait aujourd'hui avec certitudes que les Vikings ont atteint et dépassé le Groenland en 982 apr. J.-C. Des traces archéologiques qui dateraient d'environ 1000 ans indiquent la présence à cette époque de peuples norois à L'Anse aux Meadows, à Terre-Neuve, ce qui ferait du Canada le véritable lieu de découverte de l'Amérique du Nord par les Européens. Les Vikings ne visaient pas toutefois à établir une colonisation permanente, mais étaient plutôt intéressés aux ressources naturelles du Canada. Quand Christophe Colomb foula le sol américain pour la première fois, les installations qui y avaient été construites par les peuples norois étaient abandonnées depuis longtemps déjà.

Le voyage de Christophe Colomb déclencha en Europe une course à la colonisation du Nouveau Monde. En traversant l'Atlantique vers ce qu'il croyait être l'Inde pour trouver une voie alternative aux longues routes de commerce terrestres menant à l'Asie et à ses produits, Christophe Colomb donna sans le vouloir le coup d'envoi à l'Ère des grandes découvertes. Les puissances européennes établirent des colonies à la recherche d'épices, d'or, d'esclaves et de nouvelles cultures, ainsi que pour convertir les peuples autochtones au christianisme. Les premières colonies, principalement espagnoles et portugaises, étaient concentrées en Amérique du Sud, en Amérique Centrale et dans les Caraïbes. L'Angleterre et la France ont plutôt tourné leurs efforts vers le Nord. Jean Cabot, un explorateur anglais d'origine italienne, est considéré comme le premier explorateur européen à avoir mis le pied en Amérique du Nord après les Vikings. Bien que cette exploration eut lieu seulement cinq années après les découvertes de Christophe Colomb, il faudra attendre jusqu'en 1605 pour que des installations permanentes soient établies. À cette époque, beaucoup d'explorateurs, dont Henry Hudson, tentaient encore de trouver le passage du Nord-Ouest, la fameuse voie navigable qui devait relier le Nouveau Monde à l'Asie. Si plus de cent ans se sont écoulés avant ces premières installations permanentes, c'est davantage en raison d'événements se déroulant en Europe que de facteurs attribuables au Nouveau Monde.

Deux événements sont venus ralentir la colonisation de l'Amérique du Nord : l'agitation religieuse et la guerre en Europe. En 1517, Martin Luther diffusa sa liste de 95 griefs contre l'Église catholique en utilisant une invention toute nouvelle, la presse à imprimer. Ainsi débuta la réforme protestante. Ce schisme détournera de façon importante le cours de l'Histoire en Europe, mais à court terme, il suscita surtout un conflit religieux tumultueux. Presque toute l'Europe connut un repli sur soi pour faire face à cette agitation ainsi qu'à cette crise religieuse. Des conflits politiques croissants secouèrent la majeure partie de l'Europe de l'Ouest durant des décennies, accaparant les ressources qui auraient dû être attribuées aux efforts de colonisation. Les guerres de religion en France, les guerres en Italie et les révoltes populaires combinées aux soulèvements religieux ont détourné l'attention de l'Europe du Nouveau Monde pendant plus d'un siècle.

La France voyait l'Amérique du Nord comme la meilleure source de richesse et de puissance possible et souhaitait, en exploitant ces contrées, arriver à alléger ses dettes de guerre. Quand l'explorateur français Jacques Cartier navigua sur le fleuve Saint-Laurent en 1534, il revendiqua le territoire au nom de la France et lui donna le nom qu'il porte encore aujourd'hui : le Canada. Après que les commerçants de fourrure se furent implantés dans l'Est du Canada, la France monopolisa le commerce de la fourrure. Bien que les Français tentèrent d'établir des relations commerciales amicales avec les peuples autochtones, certains d'entre eux, dont les Iroquois, se révélèrent particulièrement hostiles. Les conflits avec les tribus locales ont rapidement fait de convaincre la Couronne que pour assurer la rentabilité du commerce au Canada, une présence militaire et civile permanente était essentielle. Le roi Henri IV dépêcha donc sur place son « hydrographe » Samuel de Champlain pour cartographier la région.

En 1605, après avoir exploré la côte de l'Amérique du Nord jusqu'à Cape Cod, Champlain établira un premier peuplement français à Port-Royal et fondera ensuite la ville de Québec en 1608. La Nouvelle-France, comme on l'appelait à l'époque, se développa lentement, principalement en raison du manque d'intérêt de la mère patrie et de la guerre avec les Iroquois. Les colons survécurent aux attaques des Autochtones grâce à leurs alliances avec les Algonquins, les Montagnais et les Hurons. En plus de garantir la survie des colons, ces alliances permirent à la France d'affermir son contrôle du commerce des fourrures. Les Européens n'avaient aucune notion du milieu sauvage de la région, connaissances que les Autochtones leur procureront.

Une fois de plus, des tensions religieuses en Europe vinrent interférer avec le développement des établissements au Canada. Vers le milieu du dix-septième siècle, alors que les colonies anglaises en Amérique et dans les Caraïbes devenaient autosuffisantes, la Nouvelle-France demeurait sous-peuplée. Cette colonie éprouvait des difficultés et épuisait les ressources de la France. La monarchie française décida de prendre les choses en mains en offrant des primes à ceux qui décideraient d'émigrer en Nouvelle-France. Une seule condition s'imposait : tous les colons en partance devaient être catholiques ou se convertir au catholicisme avant de quitter l'Europe. Ce changement de politique, imposé à la demande du fervent cardinal Richelieu, le conseiller le plus proche du roi Louis XIII, créera de nombreuses frictions. Auparavant, les protestants français, particulièrement la secte persécutée connue sous le nom de Huguenots, s'exilaient souvent en Nouvelle-France pour fuir les persécutions religieuses. Ce nouveau décret du cardinal Richelieu aura un effet durable sur la composition politique et religieuse du Canada moderne.

Vers la fin du dix-septième siècle, les assises des colonies anglaises et françaises du Nouveau Monde commençaient enfin à gagner en solidité. Les deux nations avaient remporté leur mise et leurs colonies dégageaient un bon profit, mais une guerre en Europe devait venir gêner une fois de plus la croissance balbutiante du Canada. La Nouvelle-France, déjà au cœur d'une brutale guerre intertribale avec les Algonquins, entra en conflit avec la confédération iroquoise qui s'opposait à elle. Avec la guerre de Neuf Ans, qui débuta en 1688 et vit la France entrer en conflit avec presque tout le reste de l'Europe, les Iroquois commencèrent à recevoir des armes de la part des Anglais, en accord aux politiques de leur gouvernement. Cette escalade de violence des Anglais envenima cette guerre déjà sanglante. L'armée anglaise et ses alliés iroquois capturèrent Port-Royal, mais furent repoussés de Québec, principalement en raison des maladies qui décimaient les forces. La guerre finit par s'essouffler sur le Continent, et un traité de paix fut signé en 1697. Les Iroquois continueront cependant à se battre sans les Britanniques, mais subiront finalement d'importantes défaites qui les forceront à établir la paix quatre ans plus tard.

La Nouvelle-France (et le Canada par le fait même) semblait bien acquise à la mère patrie à la suite de la conclusion de la guerre de Neuf Ans. Toutefois, le contrôle de la région par la France ne durera pas longtemps. La guerre de Succession d'Espagne, qui commencera un an seulement après la signature du traité de paix entre la France et les Iroquois, permettra à l'Angleterre de prendre possession de la Nouvelle-Écosse et de Terre-Neuve, ainsi que des droits sur la région entourant la baie d'Hudson. Un nouveau conflit, nommé la guerre du roi George, débutera trois décennies plus tard, soit en 1744, mais aucun des deux belligérants ne réussira à élargir alors ses positions coloniales.

En 1754, l'animosité de longue date entre les Anglais et les Français gagnera le Nouveau Monde, avec comme point culminant la guerre de Sept Ans, appelée aussi en Amérique guerre franco-indienne. Trois causes principales étaient à la base de ce conflit. D'abord, le lucratif commerce de la fourrure, l'abondance des poissons, la richesse des forêts et les gisements de minerais étaient tous des sources de fortune pour quiconque contrôlerait le Canada. Ensuite, les Anglais, anticatholiques invétérés, croyaient que les Français étaient des hérétiques, un sentiment qui était d'ailleurs réciproque! Enfin, le contrôle des colonies outre-mer pourrait servir comme monnaie d'échange diplomatique si la guerre en Europe devait se détériorer.

La guerre de Sept Ans fut la première guerre à l'échelle mondiale et qui fit rage sur cinq continents : l'Amérique du Nord, l'Amérique du Sud, l'Afrique, l'Europe et l'Asie. Plus d'un million de personnes perdront la vie et la conclusion de cette guerre changera totalement le partage du pouvoir dans le Nouveau Monde. La Grande-Bretagne obtiendra le contrôle de toutes les colonies françaises en Amérique du Nord, faisant ainsi du Canada une colonie britannique. Toutefois, 150 années de colonisation française ne pouvaient disparaître du jour au lendemain. Encore aujourd'hui, les relations entre Anglais et Français au Canada connaissent leurs tensions et contrariétés.

Les Britanniques, suite à leur prise de contrôle du Canada en 1764, ne touchèrent pas aux systèmes religieux et économiques en place, au grand soulagement des colons catholiques français. L'Acte de Québec de 1774 permit qu'un système indépendant de lois françaises continue au Québec. Les Britanniques contrôlaient maintenant complètement la portion est de l'Amérique du Nord, depuis la rive est du fleuve Mississippi jusqu'à la côte Atlantique. Le mauvais traitement réservé aux colonies américaines par George III viendrait cependant bientôt modifier de nouveau l'équilibre du pouvoir dans le Nouveau Monde.

À titre de base pour les forces britanniques, de refuge pour les Américains loyaux à la monarchie britannique qui étaient en fuite et de source de milice pour les armées britanniques et américaines, le Canada joua un rôle important dans la guerre de l'Indépendance américaine. L'armée américaine tenta à l'origine de convaincre le Canada de prendre part à sa révolution, mais les Canadiens se relevaient à peine de la guerre de Sept Ans, et la majorité d'entre eux ne voulaient pas d'un autre conflit. Le 27 juin 1775, les troupes américaines attaquèrent Québec. Montréal fut pris sans résistance, mais l'attaque sur la ville de Québec se solda par une défaite, et en 1776, les troupes américaines évacuèrent Montréal.

Lorsque l'Amérique gagna son indépendance de la Grande-Bretagne en 1783, les citoyens loyaux à l'Empire britannique durent s'exiler. Plus de 35 000 d'entre eux se rendirent en Nouvelle-Écosse. Cet important mouvement de masse força le gouvernement britannique à diviser la Nouvelle-Écosse, créant ainsi la nouvelle colonie du Nouveau-Brunswick. Peu de temps après, les loyalistes établis au Québec commencèrent à présenter des demandes pour obtenir leur propre colonie, alors que les Canadiens français étaient aussi déterminés à avoir leur propre assemblée d'élus. En 1791, le Québec fut divisé en deux parties, le Haut-Canada et le Bas-Canada, afin de répondre aux exigences des loyalistes anglais et des Canadiens français.

Au cours des décennies qui suivirent, les tensions entre la Grande-Bretagne et l'Amérique demeurèrent vives, et encore une fois, un conflit déchira le Canada. Les États-Unis déclarèrent la guerre à la Grande-Bretagne en 1812 en raison de l'approvisionnement en armes des tribus amérindiennes hostiles et du service militaire obligatoire des marins américains à la marine britannique. Le Canada fut un des champs de bataille principaux de ce conflit puisque les États-Unis avaient planifié s'emparer du Canada et l'utiliser comme monnaie d'échange pour négocier avec les Britanniques. Les Américains s'attendaient à gagner le soutien des Canadiens qu'ils croyaient malheureux sous le contrôle colonial des Anglais. Toutefois, beaucoup de Canadiens, descendants de loyalistes britanniques qui avaient fui l'Amérique, percevaient les États-Unis comme des envahisseurs et des occupants.

L'armée américaine subit une défaite tôt dans le conflit lorsqu'elle fut battue par le général Isaac Brock et ses forces d'alliés indiens et de militaires locaux lors de la bataille de Queenston Heights. L'armée américaine en arriva quand même occuper et à piller un grand nombre de villes, incluant York (aujourd'hui Toronto) et Newark (aujourd'hui Niagara-on-the-Lake), jusqu'à contrôler à un certain moment presque tout le territoire correspondant à l'Ontario et au Québec d'aujourd'hui, mais en fin de compte, l'armée américaine fut repoussée, et bien que la guerre finit sans réel vainqueur, le fait qu'une prise de contrôle américaine fut empêchée donna aux Canadiens un regain de confiance et devint source de fierté nationale.

Même si les Canadiens rejetaient l'idée d'un envahisseur américain sur leur sol, l'exemple politique des États-Unis laissait sa marque à travers le pays. Des rébellions éclatèrent contre les Britanniques en 1837. Les Canadiens, insatisfaits de la distribution inéquitable des richesses tirées des ressources naturelles du Canada, s'insurgeaient de ne pas être représentés au sein du gouvernement britannique. Puisque les Britanniques considéraient que les frictions entre les Français et les Anglais étaient la source des conflits qu'ils vivaient avec le Canada, toutes les colonies canadiennes furent réunies en 1840 sous le nom de la Province du Canada, aussi appelée le Canada-Uni. En 1849, les États-Unis et l'Empire britannique se mirent d'accord pour que le 49e parallèle nord serve de frontière entre les deux nations, et les Britanniques étendirent le Canada jusqu'au au littoral ouest, annexant ainsi la Colombie-Britannique.

C'est pratiquement depuis la guerre d'Indépendance américaine que l'indépendance du Canada fait l'objet de débats en Grande-Bretagne comme au Canada. Certains prônaient une révolution violente et une indépendance canadienne totale. D'autres désiraient suivre un processus vers l'autonomie plus lent et graduel. Le 1er juillet 1867, le Parlement britannique édicta l'Acte de l'Amérique du Nord britannique, qui établit le Dominion du Canada comme une colonie distincte et dotée d'un gouvernement autonome. Sans être complètement détaché de l'Angleterre, particulièrement en ce qui a trait à la politique étrangère, sur le plan de la politique intérieure, le Canada gagnait pleine liberté et souveraineté.

Au cours des décennies suivantes, le Canada continua son expansion vers l'Ouest. Grâce à l'achat de deux énormes territoires au nord, les Territoires du Nord-Ouest et la Terre de Rupert, acquis de la Compagnie de la Baie d'Hudson, le pays doubla pratiquement sa superficie. Beaucoup de francophones et de Métis catholiques, les enfants d'Autochtones et de pionniers, vivaient à l'ouest de l'Ontario. Après la vente de la Terre de Rupert, plusieurs colons ontariens affluèrent dans cette région en espérant réclamer ces terres. Les Métis se mirent à craindre que cette arrivée massive de protestants anglais mette en péril leurs droits linguistiques, religieux et territoriaux. Le chef Métis Louis Riel organisa la Rébellion de la rivière Rouge en 1869 dans le but de garantir la protection de ces droits. Cette révolte mena à la création du Manitoba, une province qui mit en place des lois rigoureuses protégeant les Métis, les francophones et les catholiques. En 1905, la Colombie-Britannique, la Saskatchewan, l'Île-du-Prince-Édouard et l'Alberta furent coup sur coup jointes aux provinces fondatrices du Haut et du Bas-Canada, au Nouveau-Brunswick et à la Nouvelle-Écosse.

La construction d'un chemin de fer transcontinental, complété en 1885, stimula l'expansion du Canada. Ce chemin de fer incita de nouveaux colons à déménager dans l'Ouest pour s'établir dans les nouvelles provinces, mais ces nouveaux arrivants voulurent chasser les Autochtones de leurs terres, ce qui, une fois de plus, fit éclater des rébellions qui finirent en bains de sang. Le sentiment que le gouvernement canadien n'écoutait pas les préoccupations des catholiques francophones engendra une crise politique qui entraîna la démission du premier ministre Mackenzie Bowell en 1896 lorsque le gouvernement tenta de retirer au français son statut de langue officielle au Manitoba, ce qui allait à l'encontre des lois de la province.

Le Canada et les États-Unis connurent une période d'expansion vers l'ouest à la fin du dix-neuvième siècle grâce au développement du chemin de fer, à l'attrait qu'exerçaient ses contrées vierges et à la découverte de gisements de minerais. Ces facteurs, additionnés de l'arrivée massive d'immigrants en provenance d'Europe, permirent au Canada d'être le pays présentant la croissance économique la plus forte entre 1896 et 1911. Durant cette période, le gouvernement canadien créa le Yukon, un territoire dont la superficie se compare à celle de l'Allemagne, l'Autriche et la Suisse combinées, et dont la population se chiffrait à seulement 8 500 habitants à ce moment.

À l'aube du vingtième siècle, le Canada connut son premier conflit d'importance avec sa puissance coloniale. Lorsque la Grande-Bretagne entra dans la Guerre des Boers en 1889, la majorité des Anglo-canadiens appuyaient l'annexion de l'Afrique du Sud à l'Empire britannique. Les Canadiens français, toutefois, ne s'intéressaient pas vraiment à l'impérialisme britannique, car ils se considéraient comme un cas à part et considéraient qu'ils faisaient partie de l'Empire britannique uniquement pour la forme. En guise de compromis, tous ceux se portant volontaires purent servir dans la Guerre des Boers, mais l'Armée canadienne comme telle ne s'impliqua pas dans ce conflit. Cette vision du Canada français comme une entité à part, vision exacerbée par les rébellions et par les lois anti-françaises des décennies précédentes, continuera de se manifester dans la politique du Canada des années à venir.

Bien qu'un grand nombre de Canadiens français désirait se départir du joug de l'Empire britannique, le pays devait tout de même se plier à la politique étrangère britannique. Avec l'assassinat de l'Archiduc Ferdinand le 28 juin 1914, le Canada fut pris dans le chaotique système d'alliances que suscita la Première Guerre mondiale. Lorsque la Grande-Bretagne déclara la guerre aux puissances centrales le 4 août, les troupes canadiennes furent appelées en renfort. Comme pour la majorité des puissances alliées, les disputes internes furent temporairement mises de côté, et l'appui à la guerre demeura massif, même chez les Canadiens français. Après plus de 200 000 morts et blessés de guerre, sur une population de 7 millions d'habitants, l'effort de guerre commença à s'essouffler. Au moment où le gouvernement tenta d'introduire le service obligatoire en 1917, beaucoup de Canadiens, et principalement des Canadiens français, s'opposèrent farouchement à la guerre. Malgré l'opinion populaire, la Première Guerre mondiale contribua à alimenter le sentiment de nationalisme et d'identité canadienne, surtout grâce au rôle important que joua le Canada dans la guerre la plus importante de l'histoire de l'humanité. Les très nombreuses victimes canadiennes occasionnées par ce conflit que plusieurs considéraient comme une guerre « britannique » vint aussi augmenter le ressentiment accumulé envers l'Empire.

La Première Guerre mondiale changea radicalement le visage politique du Canada. Après les horreurs vécues pendant ce conflit, les soldats rentrèrent chez eux avec de nouvelles idéologies politiques. Le socialisme, le communisme, le syndicalisme et d'autres courants progressistes de gauche gagnèrent en popularité dans les années suivant la guerre, tandis que le retour massif des soldats faisait augmenter le taux de chômage et diminuer les salaires. La grève générale de Winnipeg de 1919, la plus importante d'une série de grèves qui paralysèrent le pays, fut brutalement mise fin par la police, au prix d'un mort et de 30 blessés. Lorsque le Canada accorda le droit de vote aux femmes en 1918, le Parti conservateur en place s'effondra, en partie en raison de ses actions durant la grève. Le Parti libéral, en prenant le contrôle du gouvernement, acquiesça à une bonne partie des demandes originales du comité de grève, incluant le droit de former des syndicats sans la permission du gouvernement. Des partis progressistes et socialistes se formèrent les années suivantes, incluant le Parti progressiste du Canada et la Fédération du Commonwealth coopératif.

En 1931, le Parlement britannique promulgua le Statut de Westminster, qui donna le statut d'entité législative indépendante à toutes les colonies et à tous les dominions de l'Empire britannique, incluant le Canada, l'Australie, la Nouvelle-Zélande et l'Irlande. Cet acte permit à ces pays de rédiger leur propre constitution et supprima le pouvoir législatif qu'avait le gouvernement britannique dans ces régions, assurant ainsi l'indépendance de celles-ci tout en les incluant dans un Commonwealth britannique à l'échelle mondiale.

Lorsque le marché boursier américain connut son krach lors du mardi noir de 1929, événement qui marqua le début de la Grande dépression, l'économie canadienne ne tarda pas à en ressentir les effets. En 1933, le produit national brut canadien connut une baisse de 40 %. Les secteurs manufacturiers et agricoles furent le plus durement touchés, et le prix de blé, le principal produit d'exportation du Canada, chuta de moitié. Au creux de la vague, 30 % des Canadiens étaient sans emploi. Terre-Neuve, affirmant que les politiques du gouvernement canadien étaient la cause de ce creux économique, vota de quitter la Fédération canadienne pour rejoindre l'Empire britannique.

Après que les partis Libéral et Conservateur se soient montrés incapables de trouver des solutions à cette crise, beaucoup de Canadiens se tournèrent vers d'autres partis, comme la Fédération du Commonwealth coopératif et le Parti Crédit Social du Canada. Après que le gouvernement conservateur de R. B. Bennet ait placé des chômeurs dans des camps de travail pour pallier au coût élevé du système d'aide sociale, la Ligue d'unité ouvrière (LUO) organisa une importante manifestation appelée la « Marche sur Ottawa » dans le but d'obtenir des améliorations aux conditions et avantages dans les camps. La tentative de Bennett pour arrêter cette marche provoquera l'émeute de Regina et contribua en fin de compte à sa défaite aux élections de 1935. Le nouveau gouvernement libéral élimina les camps et institua des programmes sociaux pour diminuer les effets de la Dépression, mais ceci n'empêcha pas le Canada d'être fortement touché par cette dernière. Environ un cinquième de la population dépendait des allocations du gouvernement et du soutien des programmes sociaux. Même après le boom de l'économie canadienne causé par la Seconde Guerre mondiale, ces programmes restèrent en place et continuèrent d'évoluer.

La Seconde Guerre mondiale débuta le 1er septembre 1939. Puisque le Canada était de plus en plus indépendant de l'Angleterre, le pays n'entra pas en guerre immédiatement après la déclaration de la Grande-Bretagne comme il l'avait fait lors de la Première Guerre mondiale, mais décida plutôt de déclarer d'elle-même la guerre neuf jours plus tard. Alors que le massacre japonais et nazi était toujours à son comble, le ravitaillement et le matériel de guerre des Canadiens s'avérèrent d'une importance capitale pour permettre à la Grande-Bretagne de résister à l'invasion allemande. Une fois que les Alliés furent en position de contre-attaquer, les troupes canadiennes furent déployées partout dans le monde, et servirent vaillamment dans plusieurs batailles importantes, incluant l'invasion de la Sicile et de l'Italie en 1943, le débarquement allié en Normandie en 1944, la libération des Pays-Bas et la traversée de la France et de l'Allemagne pour mettre fin à la guerre. Un raid majoritairement canadien à Dieppe en France se solda par 3 000 morts, blessés et captifs, et les sous-marins allemands qui infestaient les eaux canadiennes coulèrent un grand nombre de navires de ravitaillement. En tout et partout, la Seconde Guerre mondiale entraînera la mort de 42 000 canadiens.

Lorsque les Japonais bombardèrent Pearl Harbor le 7 décembre 1941, les 22 000 Canadiens d'origine japonaise vivant alors en Colombie-Britannique durent composer avec les conséquences de la douleur et de la colère qui s'ensuivirent. Le sentiment anti-asiatique dans la province fut davantage attisé lorsque des milliers de Canadiens furent tués ou capturés durant l'invasion de Hong Kong par les Japonais. En 1942, toutes les personnes de descendance japonaise furent envoyées dans des camps d'internement, et après la fin de la guerre, tous les Canadiens d'origine japonaise furent déportés de la Colombie-Britannique. Ce n'est qu'en 1949 qu'ils furent libres de vivre n'importe où au Canada. En 1988, les Canadiens d'origine japonaise furent finalement indemnisés pour le tort qu'ils ont dû subir durant la guerre.

À la conclusion de la Seconde Guerre mondiale, le Canada et les États-Unis étaient les deux seuls pays à n'avoir pas eu de combats liés à cette guerre sur leur territoire. Cela permit à ces deux pays de profiter d'un contexte économique unique. Grâce à un secteur manufacturier en pleine relance, à la découverte de pétrole en Alberta et à sa position de partenaire commercial principal de la superpuissance économique juste au sud de la frontière, le Canada vit son économie exploser. Cette nouvelle prospérité favorisa la création d'un programme d'aide sociale radicalement amélioré. Grâce à l'aide sociale centralisée de la fin des années 1930 et du début des années 1940 ainsi qu'aux nombreuses politiques sociales de la Fédération du Commonwealth coopératif, les Canadiens profiteront de l'assurance-hospitalisation, d'un régime de pensions et des allocations familiales. Ces politiques sociales progressistes convainquirent Terre-Neuve de rejoindre le Canada suite à un référendum en 1949.

Le Canada consolida sa position lors de la Guerre froide grâce à son statut de membre fondateur de l'OTAN en 1949. L'économie du pays était directement liée à celle des États-Unis. Le Canada participa à la guerre de Corée, et ses troupes furent postées en Allemagne de l'Ouest, à la frontière du bloc communiste. Le vote canadien aux Nations Unies ne fut pas toujours identique à celui des États-Unis, mais il n'y avait aucun doute que le Canada était un allié des Américains dans sa guerre contre l'Union soviétique.

Le traitement que le Canada réserva à ses peuples autochtones au fil du temps présente une histoire peu reluisante. Si l'on recule à la fin des années 1800, lorsque le bison fut chassé au point d'être presque totalement exterminé et que les chemins de fer amenèrent davantage de colons dans les territoires autochtones, les membres des Premières nations furent traités comme des citoyens de second ordre. La famine, l'assimilation et une rébellion avortée mirent fin à la résistance autochtone, mais celle-ci reprit vigueur après la Seconde Guerre mondiale. La décolonisation et un esprit de démocratie renouvelé étaient mis de l'avant par les puissances occidentales dans leur lutte contre la tyrannie soviétique, mais la majorité des Premières nations n'obtinrent quand même le droit de vote qu'à la fin des années 1950. Pour pouvoir voter, les gens des Premières nations devaient renoncer à leur statut « d'Indien ». Ce n'est qu'en 1960 (1969 au Québec) que les gens des Premières nations obtinrent le droit de voter librement.

Au début des années 1960, le gouvernement canadien dut faire face à une croissance marquée du radicalisme et d'organisations populaires. Le mouvement nationaliste québécois n'avait cessé de prendre de l'ampleur depuis que les Britanniques avaient pris le contrôle du Canada aux dépens des Français en 1764. Les Canadiens français se considéraient comme une nation distincte, et étaient souvent en désaccord avec les politiques gouvernementales canadiennes. Les factions canadiennes-françaises les plus radicales avaient le sentiment d'être opprimées, et que leur langue et leur culture étaient menacées. Inspirés par les révolutions se déroulant partout dans le monde, les groupes de gauche nationalistes ou terroristes se multiplièrent, et le Canada ne fut pas épargné. Le Front de Libération du Québec commit plus de 200 attentats à la bombe, tuant ainsi cinq personnes dans sa quête d'un Québec indépendant. Bien que les actes de violence furent majoritairement condamnés par la population, un profond désir d'indépendance alimentait les protestations des Québécois. Lorsque Pierre Elliott Trudeau fut élu Premier ministre en 1968, il mit le Québec sous la loi martiale et procéda à l'arrestation de plusieurs membres du FLQ.

Pendant que la crise au Québec s'aggravait durant les années 1970, les États-Unis s'engagèrent dans un des conflits les plus controversés de l'histoire moderne : la guerre en Indochine. La guerre du Vietnam entraîna la mort de 1 500 000 personnes et radicalisa une génération entière. Le Canada ne fit pas exception. Les jeunes de tout le pays protestèrent contre ce qu'ils considéraient être l'impérialisme américain. Le gouvernement canadien refusa de participer à cette guerre, et accorda la citoyenneté à plus de 125 000 Américains réfractaires tout au long du conflit. Ceci mena à d'importantes frictions entre les gouvernements canadien et américain. Aujourd'hui encore, le Vietnam et le Canada jouissent d'une relation privilégiée, et des centaines de milliers de Vietnamiens ont immigré sur la côte Ouest du Canada. La guerre du Vietnam coïncida aussi avec l'ascension du Nouveau Parti Démocratique, le successeur de la Fédération du Commonwealth coopératif. Depuis ses débuts en 1962, le NPD changea le visage de la politique canadienne en obtenant régulièrement entre 10 et 20 % des votes et en formant une coalition majoritaire avec le parti vainqueur. Il a combattu pour la sauvegarde du programme d'aide sociale du Canada, pour une politique étrangère humanitaire ainsi que pour les droits des Autochtones.

Les jeunes de tous les coins du Canada devinrent de plus en plus impliqués en politique après la guerre du Vietnam, et ce nouvel intérêt marqué pour la politique permit d'aborder la question de la souveraineté du Québec. Le Parti québécois fut formé en 1968, remporta les élections au Québec en 1976 et fit du français la langue officielle de la province en 1977. Finalement, le parti tint sa promesse et instaura un référendum pour décider de l'avenir du Québec. Ce référendum stipulait simplement que le Québec « négocierait une nouvelle entente avec le reste du Canada, entente fondée sur l'égalité des peuples, en vertu de laquelle le Québec aurait obtenu le pouvoir exclusif de faire ses lois, autrement dit, la souveraineté ». Le fait que le référendum ne garantissait pas une indépendance complète, combiné à un assaut du service des relations publiques du gouvernement, fit échouer le référendum.

Bien que le Canada devint une entité souveraine en 1867, et que son indépendance s'est accrue en 1931, techniquement, le pays n'était pas encore tout à fait une nation souveraine. Le Canada n'était pas en mesure d'apporter des amendements à sa propre constitution, et la capacité du Canada d'agir à l'encontre des désirs du gouvernement britannique était encore mise en doute. En 1982, Trudeau confirma le statut de nation souveraine du Canada en signant la loi constitutionnelle et la Charte canadienne des droits et libertés. Bien qu'il était encore membre du Commonwealth britannique, le Canada n'était plus sous le contrôle du parlement britannique.

Suite à l'indépendance complète du Canada par rapport à la Grande-Bretagne, la question du commerce avec les États-Unis devint la principale préoccupation de l'économie canadienne. L'Accord de libre-échange Canada-États-Unis rédigé en 1988 devint un modèle pour l'Accord de libre-échange nord-américain et l'Accord de libre-échange de l'Amérique centrale. Cet accord, de même que les accords de libre-échange subséquents, fut critiqué, car on considérait qu'éliminer les barrières commerciales ferait en sorte que les consommateurs canadiens seraient à la merci des puissantes corporations américaines. Cet accord fut au centre des élections de 1988 : le Parti libéral et le NPD s'y opposaient, alors que les progressistes conservateurs tentaient de le faire passer. Une majorité de 57 % vota contre les progressistes conservateurs, mais puisqu'ils reçurent néanmoins le plus grand nombre de votes pour un unique parti, ils obtinrent une majorité de sièges au parlement et conclurent l'accord de libre-échange.

Le Parti Québécois, suite à l'échec du référendum de 1980, forma un parti politique canadien, le Bloc Québécois, et poursuivit avec acharnement son échéancier pour un Québec indépendant. Un deuxième référendum, en 1995, occasionna un débat encore plus virulent que celui du référendum de 1980, avec des campagnes médiatiques massives de part et d'autres des deux camps. Le jour du scrutin, le référendum échoua par une mince marge de 54 000 votes, un résultat qui mit au jour la division du Québec sur cette question. Considérant que 86 000 bulletins avaient été rejetés comme invalides, le résultat sur la question de l'indépendance du Québec a été si près de la ligne décisive qu'il ne serait pas surprenant qu'un autre referendum ait lieu dans le futur.

En 1990, une révolte amérindienne dans une petite ville baptisée Oka, à l'ouest de Montréal, a mené à l'intervention de l'armée canadienne. Trois personnes moururent au cours de cette crise. Bien qu'il y ait précédemment eu de nombreux conflits violents entre les membres des Premières nations et le gouvernement du Canada, la situation à Oka marqua le début d'une nouvelle ère de résistance active des Autochtones. Comme le Canada compte plus d'un million d'habitants de descendance amérindienne, de nombreuses organisations autochtones ont réclamé un meilleur contrôle des ressources sur leurs terres, ce qui a causé des conflits violents entre les membres des Premières nations et les sociétés exploitant les ressources minières, maritimes ou forestières sur leurs territoires. L'une des conséquences de ces manifestations fut la création d'un nouveau territoire, le Nunavut, dans les régions de l'extrême nord du pays. Bien que ce territoire compte moins de 30 000 habitants, près de 85 % de sa population y possède le statut d'Inuit, et le territoire a été en mesure d'adopter de nombreuses lois assurant les droits des Inuits et donnant corps à leurs revendications concernant le territoire et ses ressources.

Aujourd'hui, le Canada doit continuer à gérer ses relations avec le Québec et les membres des Premières nations tout en faisant face à d'autres enjeux, comme le mariage hétérosexuel, les drogues, l'immigration, sa participation à la « guerre contre le terrorisme » de l'administration Obama, le réchauffement de la planète, et le contrôle des bras de mer de l'Arctique.

National Anthem: O Canada

From "Chapter 5, Statutes of Canada 1980; proclaimed July 1, 1980." Composed by Calixa Lavallée; French lyrics written by Judge Adolphe-Basile Routhier; English lyrics written by Robert Stanley Weir (with some changes incorporated in 1967).

O Canada! Our home and native land!
True patriot love in all thy sons command.
With glowing hearts we see thee rise,
The True North strong and free!
From far and wide, O Canada, We stand on guard for thee.
God keep our land glorious and free!
O Canada, we stand on guard for thee.
O Canada, we stand on guard for thee.

O Canada! Terre de nos aïeux!
Ton front est ceint de fleurons glorieux!
Car ton bras sait porter l'épée, Il sait porter la croix!
Ton histoire est une épopée Des plus brillants exploits.
Et ta valeur, de foi trempée,
Protégera nos foyers et nos droits,
Protégera nos foyers et nos droits.

Emblems of Canada

The Beaver
Recognized as a symbol of Canada's sovereignty. Official status as an emblem of Canada as of May 24, 1975.
Maple Tree
Arboreal emblem of Canada, proclaimed April 25, 1996.
Official Colours
Red and white, as proclaimed in 1921.
Official Sports
Hockey (winter); Lacrosse (summer).

Full-colour images of Canadian and provincial flags, coats of arms, floral emblems, and selected honours start on page A-8.

Fathers of Confederation

Three conferences helped to pave the way for Confederation - those held at Charlottetown (September, 1864), Québec City (October, 1864) and London (December, 1866). As all the delegates who were at the Charlottetown conferences were also in attendance at Québec, the following list includes the names of all those who attended one or more of the three conferences.

*Hewitt Bernard was John A. Macdonald's private secretary. He served as secretary of both the Québec and London conferences.

DELEGATES TO THE CONFEDERATION CONFERENCES, 1864-1866

LEGEND:

Charlottetown, 1 September, 1864	C
Québec, 10 October, 1864	Q
London, 4 December, 1866	L

CANADA

John A. Macdonald	C Q L
George E. Cartier	C Q L
Alexander T. Galt	C Q L
William McDougall	C Q L
Hector L. Langevin	C Q L
George Brown	C Q
Thomas D'Arcy McGee	C Q
Alexander Campbell	C Q
Sir Etienne P. Taché	Q
Oliver Mowat	Q
J.C. Chapais	Q
James Cockburn	Q
W.P. Howland	L
*Hewitt Bernard	

NOVA SCOTIA

Charles Tupper	C Q L
William A. Henry	C Q L
Jonathan McCully	C Q L
Adams G. Archibald	C Q L
Robert B. Dickey	Q
J.W. Ritchie	L

NEW BRUNSWICK

Samuel L. Tilley	C Q L
J.M. Johnson	C Q L
William H. Steeves	C Q
E.B. Chandler	C Q
John Hamilton Gray	C Q
Peter Mitchell	Q L
Charles Fisher	Q L
R.D. Wilmot	L

PRINCE EDWARD ISLAND

John Hamilton Gray	C Q
Edward Palmer	C Q
William H. Pope	C Q
A.A. Macdonald	C Q
George Coles	C Q
T.H. Haviland	Q
Edward Whelan	Q

NEWFOUNDLAND

F.B.T. Carter	Q
Ambrose Shea	Q

PARTICIPANTS TO THE FIRST MINISTERS' CONSTITUTIONAL CONFERENCE ON PATRIATION OF THE CONSTITUTION

(Held in Ottawa from September 2 to 5, 1981)

- The Right Honourable Pierre Elliott Trudeau, P.C., Q.C., M.P., Prime Minister of Canada;
- The Honourable William G. Davis, Q.C., Premier of Ontario;
- The Honourable René Lévesque, Premier of Québec;
- The Honourable John M. Buchanan, Q.C., Premier of Nova Scotia;
- The Honourable Richard B. Hatfield, Premier of New Brunswick;
- The Honourable Sterling R. Lyon, Q.C., Premier of Manitoba;
- The Honourable W.R. Bennett, Premier of British Columbia;
- The Honourable J. Angus MacLean, P.C., D.F.C., C.D., Premier of Prince Edward Island;
- The Honourable Allan Blakeney, Q.C., Premier of Saskatchewan;
- The Honourable Peter Lougheed, Q.C., Premier of Alberta;
- The Honourable Brian Peckford, Premier of Newfoundland.

Timeline of Canadian History

- 12000 BC: Migration of natives across the Bering land bridge
- 2000 BC: Inuit arrive in North America
- 1000: Leif Erickson lands on Baffin Island
- 1497: John Cabot reaches Newfoundland
- 1534-1541: Jacque Cartier explores North America
- 1576-1578: Martin Frobisher searches for the Northwest Passage
- 1583: Humphrey Gilbert claims Newfoundland for England
- 1603: Samuel de Champlain's first voyage to New France. The fur trading monopoly Canada & Arcadia Company is formed.
- 1608: Champlain founds Quebec.
- 1609: The Battle of Ticonderoga. France allies with the Hurons to fight the Iroquois.
- 1610: Henry Hudson looks for the Northwest Passage. First European settlement in Newfoundland.
- 1629: Champlain surrenders New France to Great Britain.
- 1641: Village of Ville Marie (Montreal) is formed.
- 1649: The Iroquois destroy the missionary settlement of Huronia.
- 1663: France regains control of New France.
- 1670: Charles II forms the Hudson Bay Company. Fur trade attracts settlers to the Great Lakes area.
- 1682: LaSalle claims Louisiana for France.
- 1701: Peace is declared between native tribes and France.
- 1713: Nova Scotia's Acadian French population forced to swear allegiance to England.
- 1755-6: England deports the Acadians. Seven Years War begins.
- 1763: Seven Years War ends.
- 1766: Pontiac signs peace treaty with Great Britain.
- 1774: America's 13 Colonies urge Canada to join them against the English.
- 1776: American Loyalists flee to Canada.
- 1778: James Cook arrives on Vancouver Island.
- 1784: British divide Nova Scotia and create New Brunswick.
- 1791: King George II divides Quebec into Lower and Upper Canada.
- 1793: Alexander Mackenzie crosses the continent and reaches the Pacific Ocean.
- 1812: The War of 1812 begins when America declares war against Great Britain.
- 1814: The War of 1812 ends.
- 1834: The Patriotes of Lower Canada draw up a list of 92 grievances and deliver them to the government in England.
- 1841: United Canada created.
- 1849: The burning of Parliament in Montreal.
- 1858: Queen Victoria creates British Columbia. The gold rush begins.
- 1867: New Brunswick, Nova Scotia, and the Province of Canada were proclaimed the Dominion of Canada, with John A. Macdonald its first prime minister.
- 1885: Canadian Pacific Railway completed.
- 1896: Canada opens doors to European immigration.
- 1897-1899: Klondike gold rush. Canada enters Boer War.
- 1907: Chinese in Canada encounter violence.
- 1909: Coal miners strike in Cape Breton.
- 1914: Canada enters World War I.
- 1918: Spanish influenza kills millions. World War I ends. Women win vote.
- 1920: Bootlegging flourishes after America declares Prohibition.
- 1929: U.S. stock market crashes. Drought hits prairies.
- 1931: Ottawa outlaws Communist agitation. Socialist Party of Canada created.
- 1933: Unemployment crisis worsens.
- 1938: Canada rejects Jewish refugees escaping Nazi Germany.
- 1939: Canada enters World War II.
- 1945: World War II ends.
- 1947: First major oil find in Alberta.
- 1949: Newfoundland joins Canada.
- 1952: CBC television launched.
- 1956: Suez Canal crisis.
- 1960: Quebec's Quiet Revolution begins.
- 1965: New Maple Leaf flag raised.
- 1967: Expo in Montreal.
- 1970: Alberta aboriginals begin new era of native protests. British trade commissioner kidnapped by radical Quebec separatist group Front de Libération du Québec.
- 1971: Greenpeace begins in Vancouver.
- 1982: Trudeau brings home Canadian constitution.
- 1989: Free Trade with the US begins.
- 1999: New province of Nunavut separated from the Northwest Territories.
- 2001: Canada's border with the United States is on high alert in the aftermath of the September 11 Terrorist Attacks in the USA.
- 2002: G-8 leaders meet at Kananaskis, Alberta
- 2003: Health Canada announces 17 suspected SARS cases in Canada
- 2007: Canada Census data is released; the population of Canada in 2006 was 31,612,897
- 2007: Canadian dollar reaches parity with US greenback
- 2008: 40th Canadian federal election, October 14, 2008. Prime Minister Stephen Harper's Conservative Party re-elected.
- 2009: The 40th Canadian Parliament reopens, January 26, 2009, for its second session after a two-month prorogation.
- 2010: Winter Olympics take place in Vancouver, British Columbia, February 12-28, 2010.
- 2010: Toronto hosts G-20 Summit, June 26-27, 2010

Chronologie de l'histoire du Canada

- 12 000 av. J.-C. : Des peuples en migration traversent le pont continental de Béring.
- 2000 av. J.-C. : Arrivée des Inuits en Amérique du Nord.
- 1000 apr. J.-C. : Leif Erickson débarque sur l'Île de Baffin.
- 1497 : Jean Cabot atteint Terre-Neuve.
- 1534-1541 : Jacques Cartier explore l'Amérique du Nord.
- 1576-1578 : Martin Frobisher recherche le passage du Nord-Ouest.
- 1583 : Humphrey Gilbert revendique Terre-Neuve au nom de l'Angleterre.
- 1603 : Premier voyage de Samuel de Champlain en Nouvelle-France. La Canada & Arcadia Company, qui allait posséder le monopole du commerce des fourrures, voit le jour.
- 1608 : Champlain fonde la ville de Québec.
- 1609 : Bataille de Ticonderoga. La France s'allie aux Hurons pour combattre les Iroquois.
- 1610 : Henry Hudson recherche le passage du Nord-Ouest. Une première colonie européenne en Amérique du Nord est établie à Terre-Neuve.
- 1629 : Champlain cède la Nouvelle-France à la Grande-Bretagne.
- 1641 : Fondation du village de Ville-Marie (Montréal).
- 1649 : Les Iroquois détruisent la mission de Huronie.
- 1663 : La France reprend le contrôle de la Nouvelle-France.
- 1670 : Le roi Charles II forme la Compagnie de la Baie d'Hudson. Le commerce des fourrures attire des colons vers la région des Grands Lacs.
- 1682 : LaSalle revendique la Louisiane au nom de la France.
- 1701 : La paix est déclarée entre les tribus amérindiennes et la France.
- 1713 : La population acadienne francophone de la Nouvelle-Écosse est forcée de prêter serment d'allégeance à l'Angleterre.
- 1755-6 : L'Angleterre ordonne la déportation des Acadiens. Début de la guerre de Sept Ans.
- 1763 : Fin de la guerre de Sept Ans.
- 1766 : Pontiac signe un traité de paix avec la Grande-Bretagne.
- 1774 : Les 13 Colonies américaines recommandent vivement au Canada de se joindre à leur combat contre l'Angleterre.
- 1776 : Les loyalistes américains en fuite se réfugient au Canada.
- 1778 : James Cook découvre l'île de Vancouver.
- 1784 : L'Angleterre divise le territoire de la Nouvelle-Écosse et crée le Nouveau-Brunswick.
- 1791 : Le roi George II divise le Québec en deux parties : le Bas-Canada et le Haut-Canada.
- 1793 : Alexander Mackenzie traverse le continent et atteint l'océan Pacifique.
- 1812 : Les États-Unis déclarent la guerre à la Grande-Bretagne et déclenchent la guerre de 1812.
- 1814 : Fin de la guerre de 1812.
- 1834 : Les Patriotes du Bas-Canada dressent une liste de 92 griefs; elle est ensuite envoyée au gouvernement de l'Angleterre.
- 1841 : Création du Canada-Uni.
- 1849 : Incendie du Parlement à Montréal.
- 1858 : La reine Victoria crée la Colombie-Britannique. Début de la ruée vers l'or.
- 1867 : Le Nouveau-Brunswick, la Nouvelle-Écosse et la province du Canada deviennent le Dominion du Canada, et John A. Macdonald devient le premier Premier ministre du nouveau pays.
- 1885 : Le chemin de fer du Canadien Pacifique est complété.
- 1896 : Le Canada ouvre ses portes aux immigrants européens.
- 1897-1899 : Ruée vers l'or du Klondike. Participation du Canada à la guerre des Boers.
- 1907 : La population chinoise du Canada est victime d'actes de violence.
- 1909 : Grève du charbon au Cap-Breton.
- 1914 : Début de la participation du Canada à la Première Guerre mondiale.
- 1918 : La grippe espagnole fait des millions de victimes. Fin de la Première Guerre mondiale. Les femmes obtiennent le droit de vote.
- 1920 : Le commerce clandestin d'alcool devient florissant avec le début de la Prohibition aux États-Unis.
- 1929 : Aux États-Unis, le marché s'effondre. La sécheresse fait rage dans les Prairies.
- 1931 : Ottawa déclare l'agitation communiste illégale. Le Parti socialiste du Canada voit le jour.
- 1933 : La crise du chômage s'intensifie.
- 1938 : Le Canada refuse d'accueillir des réfugiés juifs ayant fui l'Allemagne nazie.
- 1939 : Début de la participation du Canada à la Deuxième Guerre mondiale.
- 1945 : Fin de la Deuxième Guerre mondiale.
- 1947 : Découverte d'un premier gisement de pétrole important en Alberta.
- 1949 : Terre-Neuve se joint au Canada.
- 1952 : Lancement de la télévision de Radio-Canada.
- 1956 : Crise du Canal de Suez.
- 1960 : Début de la Révolution tranquille au Québec.
- 1965 : Le nouveau drapeau unifolié est hissé pour la première fois.
- 1967 : L'Expo 67 bat son plein à Montréal.
- 1970 : Les Autochtones d'Alberta entament lune nouvelle ère de revendications autochtones. Un délégué commercial britannique est kidnappé par le Front de Libération du Québec, un groupe séparatiste radical.
- 1971 : Fondation de l'organisme Greenpeace à Vancouver.
- 1982 : Trudeau rapatrie la Constitution canadienne.
- 1989 : Début du libre-échange avec les États-Unis.
- 1999 : La nouvelle province du Nunavut se sépare des Territoires-du-Nord-Ouest.
- 2001 : La frontière du Canada et des États-Unis est sur un pied d'alerte par suite des attaques terroristes du 11 septembre chez nos voisins du sud.
- 2002 : Rencontre des dirigeants du G-8 à Kananaskis, en Alberta.
- 2003 : Santé Canada annonce 17 cas soupçonnés de grippe aviaire au Canada.
- 2007 : Les données du recensement de Statistique Canada sont rendues publiques; en 2006, la population du Canada atteignait 31 612 897 habitants.
- 2007 : Le dollar canadien atteint la même valeur que celle du dollar américain.
- 2008 : 40e élection générale fédérale au Canada, le 14 octobre 2008. Le Parti conservateur de Stephen Harper est ré-élu.
- 2009 : Réouverture de la 40e législature du Canada le 26 janvier 2009, après 2 mois de prorogation.
- 2010 : Les Jeux olympiques 2010 se tiennent à Vancouver, Colombie-Britannique, du 12 au 28 février 2010.
- 2010 : Sommet du G20 de Toronto, 26 et 27 juin 2010.

THE ROYAL ARMS OF CANADA BY PROCLAMATION OF KING GEORGE V IN 1921

The Royal Arms of Canada were established by proclamation of King George V on 21 November, 1921. On the advice of the Prime Minister of Canada, Her Majesty the Queen approved, on 12 July, 1994, that the arms be augmented with a ribbon bearing the motto of the Order of Canada, DESIDERANTES MELIOREM PATRIAM - "They desire a better country".

This coat of arms was developed by a special committee appointed by Order in Council and is substantially based on a version of the Royal Arms of the United Kingdom, featuring the historic arms of England and Scotland. To this were added the old arms of Royal France and the historic emblem of Ireland, the harp of Tara, thus honouring many of the founding European peoples of modern Canada. To mark these arms as Canadian, the three red maple leaves on a field of white were added.

The supporters, and the crest, above the helmet, are also versions of elements of the Royal Arms of the United Kingdom, including the lion of England and unicorn of Scotland. The lion holds the Union Jack and the unicorn, the banner of Royal France. The crowned lion holding the maple leaf, which is the The Royal Crest of Canada, has, since 1981, also been the official symbol of the Governor General of Canada, the Sovereign's representative.

At the base of the Royal Arms are the floral emblems of the founding nations of Canada, the English Rose, the Scottish Thistle, the French Lily and the Irish Shamrock.

The motto - A MARI USQUE AD MARE - "From sea to sea" - is an extract from the Latin version of verse 8 of the 72nd Psalm - "He shall have dominion also from sea to sea, and from the river unto the ends of the earth."

THE NATIONAL FLAG

The National Flag of Canada, otherwise known as the Canadian Flag, was approved by Parliament and proclaimed by Her Majesty Queen Elizabeth II to be in force as of February 15, 1965. It is described as a red flag of the proportions two by length and one by width, containing in its centre a white square the width of the flag, bearing a single red maple leaf. Red and white are the official colours of Canada, as approved by the proclamation of King George V appointing Arms for Canada in 1921. The Flag is flown on land at all federal government buildings, airports, and military bases within and outside Canada, and may appropriately be flown or displayed by individuals and organizations. The Flag is the proper national colours for all Canadian ships and boats; and it is the flag flown on Canadian Naval vessels.

The Flag is flown daily from sunrise to sunset. However, it is not contrary to etiquette to have the Flag flying at night. No flag, banner or pennant should be flown or displayed above the Canadian Flag. Flags flown together should be approximately the same size and flown from separate staffs at the same height. When flown on a speaker" platform, it should be to the right of the speaker. When used in the body of an auditorium; it should be to the right of the audience. When two or more than three flags are flown together, the Flag should be on the left as seen by spectators in front of the flags. When three flags are flown together, the Canadian Flag should occupy the central position.

A complete set of rules for flying the Canadian Flag can be obtained from the Department of Canadian Heritage.

THE ROYAL UNION FLAG

The Royal Union Flag, generally known as the Union Jack, was approved by Parliament on December 18, 1964 for continued use in Canada as a symbol of Canada's membership in the Commonwealth of Nations and of her allegiance to the Crown. It will, where physical arrangements make it possible, be flown along with the National Flag at federal buildings, airports, and military bases and establishments within Canada on the date of the official observance of the Queen's birthday, the Anniversary of the Statute of Westminster (December 11th), Commonwealth Day (second Monday in March), and on the occasions of Royal Visits and certain Commonwealth gatherings in Canada.

QUEEN'S PERSONAL CANADIAN FLAG

In 1962, Her Majesty The Queen adopted a personal flag specifically for use in Canada. The design comprises the Arms of Canada with The Queen's own device in the centre. The device - the initial "E" surmounted by the St. Edward's Crown within a chaplet of roses - is gold on a blue background.

When the Queen is in Canada, this flag is flown, day and night, at any building in which She is in residence. Generally, the flag is also flown behind the saluting base when She conducts troop inspections, on all vehicles in which She travels, and on Her Majesty's Canadian ships (HMCS) when the Queen is aboard.

FLAG OF THE GOVERNOR GENERAL

The Governor General's standard is a blue flag with the crest of the Arms of Canada in its centre. A symbol of the Sovereignty of Canada, the crest is made of a gold lion passant imperially crowned, on a wreath of the official colours of Canada, holding in its right paw a red maple leaf. The standard was approved by Her Majesty The Queen on February 23, 1981. The Governor General's personal standard flies whenever the incumbent is in residence, and takes precedence over all other flags in Canada, except The Queen's.

CANADIAN ARMED FORCES BADGE

The Canadian Armed Forces Badge was sanctioned by Her Majesty Queen Elizabeth II in May 1967. The description is as follows:

Within a wreath of ten stylized maple leaves Red, a cartouche medium Blue edge Gold, charged with a foul anchor Gold, surmounted by Crusader's Swords in Saltire Silver and blue, pommelled and hilted Gold; and in front an eagle volant affront head to the sinister Gold, the whole ensigned with a Royal Crown proper.

The Canadian Forces Badge replaces the badges of the Royal Canadian Navy, the Canadian Army, and the Royal Canadian Air Force.

ALBERTA

The Arms of the Province of Alberta were granted by Royal Warrant on May 30, 1907. On July 30th, 1980, the Arms were augmented as follows: Crest: Upon a Helm with a Wreath Argent and Gules a Beaver couchant upholding on its back the Royal Crown both proper; Supporters: On the dexter side a Lion Or armed and langued Gules and on the sinister side a Pronghorn Antelope (Antilocapra americana) proper; the Compartment comprising a grassy mount with the Floral Emblem of the said Province of Alberta the Wild Rose (Rosa acicularis) growing therefrom proper; Motto: FORTIS ET LIBER (Strong and Free) to be borne and used together with the Arms upon Seals, Shields, Banners, Flags or otherwise according to the Laws of Arms.

In 1958, the Government of Alberta authorized the design and use of an official flag. A flag bearing the Armorial Ensign on a royal ultramarine blue background was adopted and the Flag Act proclaimed June 1st 1968. Proportions of the flag are two by length and one by width with the Armorial Ensign seven-elevenths of the width of the flag carried in the centre. The flag may be used by citizens of the Province and others in a manner befitting its dignity and importance but no other banner or flag that includes the Armorial Ensign may be assumed or used.

Floral Emblem: Wild Rose (Rosa Acicularis). Chosen in the Floral Emblem Act of 1930.

Provincial Bird: Great horned owl (budo virginianus). Adopted May 3, 1977.

BRITISH COLUMBIA

The shield of British Columbia was granted by Royal Warrant on March 31, 1906. On October 15th, 1987, the shield was augmented by Her Majesty Queen Elizabeth II. The crest and supporters have become part of the provincial Arms through usage. The heraldic description is as follows: Crest: Upon a Helm with a Wreath Argent and Gules the Royal Crest of general purpose of Our Royal Predecessor Queen Victoria differenced for Us and Our Successors in right of British Columbia with the Lion thereof garlanded about the neck with the Provincial Flower that is to say the Pacific Dogwood (Cornus nuttallii) with leaves all proper Mantled Gules doubled Argent; Supporters: On the dexter side a Wapiti Stag (Cervus canadensis) proper and on the sinister side a Bighorn Sheep Ram (Oviscanadensis) Argent armed and unguled Or; Compartment: Beneath the Shield a Scroll entwined with Pacific Dogwood flowers slipped and leaved proper inscribed with the Motto assigned by the said Warrant of Our Royal Predecessor King Edward VII that is to say SPLENDOR SINE OCCASU, (splendour without diminishment).

The flag of British Columbia was authorized by an Order-in-Council of June 27, 1960. The Union Jack symbolizes the province's origins as a British colony, and the crown at its centre represents the sovereign power linking the nations of the Commonwealth. The sun sets over the Pacific Ocean. The original design of the flag was located in 1960 by Hon. W.A.C. Bennett at the College of Arms in London.

Floral emblem: Pacific Dogwood (Cornus Nuttallii, Audubon). Adopted under the Floral Emblem Act, 1956.

Provincial Bird: Steller's jay. Adopted November 19, 1987.

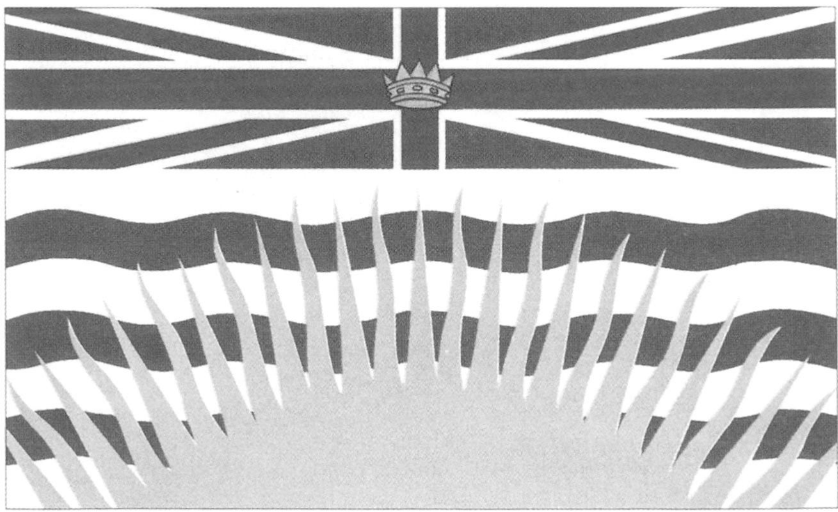

MANITOBA

The Arms of the Province of Manitoba were granted by Royal Warrant on May 10, 1905, augmented by warrant of the Governor General on October 23, 1992. The description is as follows: above the familiar shield of 1905 is a helmet and mantling; above the helmet is the Crest, including the beaver holding a prairie crocus, the province's floral emblem. On the beaver's back is the royal crown. The left supporter is a unicorn wearing a collar bearing a decorative frieze of maple leaves, the collar representing Manitoba's position as Canada's "keystone" province. Hanging from the collar is a wheel of a Red River cart. The right supporter is a white horse, and its collar of bead and bone honours First Peoples. The supporters and the shield rest on a compartment representing the province's rivers and lakes, grain fields and forests, composed of the provincial tree, the white spruce, and seven prairie crocuses. At the base is a Latin translation of the phrase "Glorious and Free."

The flag of the Province of Manitoba was adopted under The Provincial Flag Act, assented to May 11, 1965, and proclaimed into force on May 12, 1966. It incorporates parts of the Royal Armorial Ensigns, namely the Union and Red Ensign; the badge in the fly of the flag is the shield of the arms of the province.

Description: A flag of the proportions two by length and one by width with the Union Jack occupying the upper quarter next the staff and with the shield of the armorial bearings of the province centered in the half farthest from the staff.

Floral Emblem: Pasque Flower, known locally as Prairie Crocus (Anemone Patens). Adopted 1906.

Provincial Bird: Great gray owl. Adopted July 16, 1987.

NEW BRUNSWICK

The Arms of New Brunswick were granted by Royal Warrant on May 26, 1868. The motto SPEM REDUXIT (hope restored) was added by Order-in-Council in 1966. The description is as follows: The upper third of the shield is red and features a gold lion, symbolizing New Brunswick's ties to Britain. The lion is also found in the arms of the Duchy of Brunswick in Germany, the ancestral home of King George III. The lower part of the shield displays an ancient galley with oars in action. It could be interpreted as a reference to the importance of both shipbuilding and seafaring to New Brunswick in those days. It is also based on the design of the province's original great seal which featured a sailing ship on water. The shield is supported by two white-tailed deer wearing collars of Indian wampum. From one is suspended the Royal Union Flag (the Union Jack), from the other the fleur-de-lis to indicate the province's British and French background. The crest consists of an Atlantic Salmon leaping from a coronet of gold maple leaves and bearing St. Edward's Crown on its back. The base, or compartment, is a grassy mound with fiddleheads as well as purple violets, the provincial floral emblem. The motto "Spem Reduxit" is taken from the first great seal of the province.

The flag of New Brunswick, adopted by Proclamation on February 24, 1965, is based on the Arms of the province. The chief and charge occupy the upper one-third of the flag, and the remainder of the armorial bearings occupy the lower two-thirds. The proportion is four by length and two and one half by width.

Floral Emblem: Purple Violet (Viola Cuculata). Adopted by Order-in-Council, December 1, 1936, at the request of the New Brunswick Women's Institute.

Provincial Bird: Black-capped chickadee. Adopted August 1983.

NEWFOUNDLAND & LABRADOR

The Arms of Newfoundland were granted by Royal Letters Patent dated January 1, 1637 by King Charles I. The heraldic description is as follows: Gules, a Cross Argent, in the first and fourth quarters a Lion passant guardant crowned Or, in the second and third quarters an Unicorn passant Argent armed and crined Or, gorged with a Coronet and a Chain affixed thereto reflexed of the last. Crest: on a wreath Or and Gules a Moose passant proper. Supporters: two Savages of the clime armed and apparelled according to their guise when they go to war. The motto reads QUAERITE PRIMEREGNUM DEI (seek ye first the kingdom of God).

The official flag of Newfoundland, adopted in 1980, has primary colours of Red, Gold and Blue, against a White background. The Blue section on the left represents Newfoundland's Commonwealth heritage and the Red and Gold section on the right represents the hopes for the future with the arrow pointing the way. The two triangles represent the mainland and island parts of the province.

Floral Emblem: Pitcher Plant (Sarracenia Purpurea). Adopted June 1954.

Provincial Bird: Atlantic puffin.

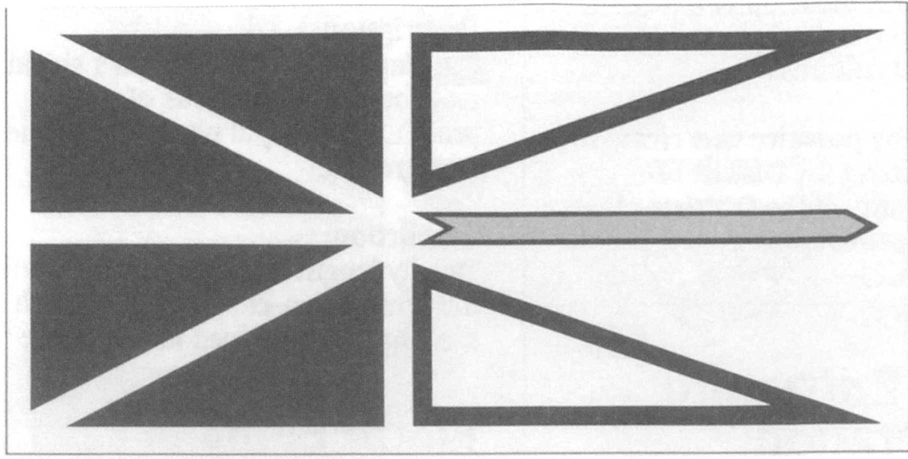

NORTHWEST TERRITORIES

The Arms of the Northwest Territories were approved by Her Majesty Queen Elizabeth II on February 24, 1956. The crest consists of two gold narwhals guarding a compass rose, symbolic of the magnetic north pole. The white upper third of the shield represents the polar ice pack and is crossed by a wavy blue line portraying the Northwest Passage. The tree line is reflected by a diagonal line separating the red and green segments of the lower portion of the shield: the green symbolizing the forested areas south of the tree line, and the red standing for the barren lands north of it. The important bases of northern wealth, minerals and fur, are represented by gold billets in the green portion and the mask of a white fox in the red.

The official flag of the Northwest Territories was adopted by the Territorial Council on January 1, 1969. Blue panels at either side of the flag represent the lakes and waters of the Territories. The white centre panel, equal in width to the two blue panels combined, symbolizes the ice and snow of the North. In the centre of the white portion is the shield from the Arms of the Territories.

Floral Emblem: Mountain Avens (Dryas Integrifolia). Adopted by the Council on June 7, 1957.

Provincial Bird: Gyrfalcon. Adopted June 1990.

NOVA SCOTIA

The Arms of the Province of Nova Scotia were granted to the Royal Province in 1625 by King Charles I. The complete Armorial Achievement includes the Arms, surmounted by a royal helm with a blue and silver scroll or mantling representing the Royal cloak. Above is the crest of heraldic symbols: two joined hands, one armoured and the other bare, supporting a spray of laurel for peace and thistle for Scotland. On the left is the mythical royal unicorn and on the right a 17th century representation of the North American Indian. The motto reads MUNIT HAEC ET ALTERA VINCIT (one defends and the other conquers). Entwined with the thistle of Scotland at the base is the mayflower, added in 1929, as the floral emblem of Nova Scotia.

The flag of the Province of Nova Scotia is a blue St. Andrew's Cross on a white field, with the Royal Arms of Scotland mounted thereon. The width of the flag is three-quarters of the length.

The flag was originally authorized by Charles I in 1625. In 1929, on petition of Nova Scotia, a Royal Warrant of King George V was issued, revoking the modern Arms and ordering that the original Arms granted by Charles I be borne upon (seals) shields, banners, and otherwise according to the laws of Arms.

Floral Emblem: Trailing Arbutus, also known as Mayflower (Epigaea Repens). Adopted April 1901.

Provincial Bird: Osprey. Adopted Spring, 1994.

NUNAVUT

The dominant colours blue and gold are the ones preferred by the Nunavut Implementation Commissioners to symbolize the riches of the land, sea and sky.

Red is a reference to Canada. In the base of the shield, the inuksuk symbolizes the stone monuments which guide the people on the land and mark sacred and other special places. The qulliq, or Inuit stone lamp, represents light and the warmth of family and the community. Above, the concave arc of five gold circles refers to the life-giving properties of the sun arching above and below the horizon, the unique part of the Nunavut year. The star is the Niqirtsuituq, the North Star and the traditional guide for navigation and more broadly, forever remains unchanged as the leadership of the elders in the community.

In the crest, the iglu represents the traditional life of the people and the means of survival. It also symbolizes the assembled members of the Legislature meeting together for the good of Nunavut; with the Royal Crown symbolizing public government for all the people of Nunavut and the equivalent status of Nunavut with other territories and provinces in Canadian Confederation. The tuktu (caribou) and qilalugaq tugaalik (narwhal) refer to land and sea animals which are part of the rich natural heritage of Nunavut and provide sustenance for people. The compartment at the base is composed of land and sea and features three important species of Arctic wild flowers.

Floral Emblem: Purple Saxifrage (Saxifraga oppositifolia). Adopted May 1, 2000.

ONTARIO

The Arms of the Province of Ontario were granted by Royal Warrants on May 26, 1868 (shield), and February 27, 1909 (crest and supporters). The heraldic description is as follows: Vert, a Sprig of three leaves of Maple slipped Or on a Chief Argent the Cross of St. George. Crest: upon a wreath Vert and Or a Bear passant Sable. The supporters are on the dexter side, a Moose, and on the sinister side a Canadian Deer, both proper. The motto reads: UT INCEPIT FIDELIS SIC PERMANET (loyal in the beginning, so it remained).

The flag of the Province of Ontario was adopted under the Flag Act of May 21, 1965. It incorporates parts of the Royal Armorial Ensigns, namely the Union and Red Ensign; the badge in the fly of the flag is the shield of the Arms of the province. The flag is of the proportions two by length and one by width, with the Union Jack occupying the upper quarter next the staff and the shield of the armorial hearings of the province centered in the half farthest from the staff.

Floral Emblem: White Trillium (Trillium Grandiflorum). Adopted March 25, 1937.

Provincial Bird: Common loon. Proposed, but not officially adopted.

PRINCE EDWARD ISLAND

The Arms of the Province of Prince Edward Island were granted by Royal Warrant, May 30, 1905. The heraldic description is as follows: Argent on an Island Vert, to the sinister an Oak Tree fructed, to the dexter thereof three Oak saplings sprouting all proper, on a Chief Gules a Lion passant guardant Or. The motto reads: PARVA SUB INGENTI (the small under the protection of the great).

The flag of the Province of Prince Edward Island was authorized by an Act of the Legislative Assembly, March 24, 1964. The design of the flag is that part of the Arms contained within the shield, but is of rectangular shape, with a fringe of alternating red and white. The chief and charge of the Arms occupies the upper one-third of the flag, and the remainder of the Arms occupies the lower two-thirds. The proportions of the flag are six, four, and one-quarter in relation to the fly, the hoist, and the depth of the fringe.

Floral Emblem: Lady's Slipper (Cypripedium Acaule). Designated as the province's floral emblem by the Legislative Assembly in 1947. A more precise botanical name was included in an amendment to the Floral Emblem Act in 1965.

Provincial Bird: Blue Jay (cyanocitta cristata) was designated as avian emblem by the Provincial Emblems Acts, May 13, 1977.

QUÉBEC

The Arms of the Province of Québec were granted by Queen Victoria, May 26, 1868, and revised by a Provincial Order-in-Council on December 9, 1939. The heraldic description is as follows: Tierced in fess: Azure, three Fleurs-de-lis Or; Gules, a Lion passant guardant Or armed and langued Azure; Or, a Sugar Maple sprig with three leaves Vert veined Or. Surmounted with the Royal Crown. Below the shield a scroll Argent, surrounded by a bordure Azure, inscribed with the motto JE ME SOUVIENS Azure.

The official flag of the Province of Québec was adopted by a Provincial Order-in-Council of January 21, 1948. It is a white cross on a sky blue ground, with the fleur-de-lis in an upright position on the blue ground in each of the four quarters. The proportion is six units wide by four units deep.

Floral Emblem: Iris Versicolor. Adopted November 5, 1999.

Provincial Bird: Snowy owl. Adopted December 17, 1987.

SASKATCHEWAN

The complete armorial bearings of the Province of Saskatchewan were granted by Royal Warrant on September 16, 1986, through augmentation of the original shield of arms granted by King Edward VII on August 25, 1906. The heraldic description is as follows: Shield: Vert three Garbs in fesse Or, on a Chief of the last a Lion passant guardant Gules. Crest: Upon a Helm with a Wreath Argent and Gules a Beaver upholding with its back Our Royal Crown and holding in the dexter fore-claws a Western Red Lily (Lilium philadelphicumandinum) slipped all proper Mantled Gules doubled Argent. Supporters: On the dexter side a Lion Or gorged with a Collar of Prairie Indian beadwork proper and dependent therefrom a six-pointed Mullet faceted Argent fimbriated and garnished Or charged with a Maple Leaf Gules and on the sinister side a White tailed deer (Odocoileus virginianus) proper gorged with a like Collar and dependent therefrom a like Mullet charged with a Western Red Lily slipped and leaved proper. Motto: Beneath the Shield a Scroll entwined with Western Red Lilies slipped and leaved proper inscribed with the motto MULTIS E GENTIBUS VIRES.

The official flag was dedicated on September 22, 1969, and features the Arms of the province in the upper quarter nearest the staff, with the Western Red Lily, in the half farthest from the staff. The upper green portion represents forests, while the gold symbolizes prairie wheat fields. The basic design was adopted from the prize-winning entry of Anthony Drake of Hodgeville from a province-wide flag design competition.

Floral Emblem: Western Red Lily (Lilium philadelphicum var. andinum). Adopted April 8, 1941.

Provincial Bird: Prairie sharp-tailed grouse. Adopted March 30, 1945.

YUKON

The Arms of the Yukon, granted by Queen Elizabeth II on February 24, 1956, have the following explanation: The wavy white and blue vertical stripe represents the Yukon River and refers also to the rivers and creeks where gold was discovered. The red spire-like forms represent the mountainous country, and the gold discs the mineral resources. The St. George's Cross is in reference to the early explorers and fur traders from Great Britain, and the roundel in vair in the centre of the cross is a symbol for the fur trade. The crest displays a Malamute dog, an animal which has played an important part in the early history of the Yukon.

The Yukon flag, designed by Lynn Lambert, a Haines Junction student, was adopted by Council in 1967. It is divided into thirds: green for forests, white for snow, and blue for water.

The flag consists of three vertical panels, the centre panel being one and one-half times the width of each of the other two panels. The panel adjacent to the mast is coloured green, the centre panel is coloured white and has the Yukon Crest disposed above a symbolic representation of the floral emblem of the territory, epilobium angustifolium, (fireweed), and the panel on the fly is coloured blue. The stem and leaves of the floral emblem are coloured green, and the flowers thereof are coloured red. The Yukon Crest is coloured red and blue, with the Malamute dog coloured black.

Floral Emblem: Fireweed (Epilobium Angustifolium). Adopted November 16, 1957.

Provincial Bird: Common raven. Adopted October 28, 1985.

Geography

LAND & FRESHWATER AREAS OF CANADA

Province or Territory	Land (km²)	Freshwater (km²)	Total Area (km²)	Percentage of Total Area
Newfoundland	371,690	34,030	405,720	4.1
Island of Newfoundland*	105,700	5,690	111,390	1.1
Prince Edward Island	5,660	—	5,660	0.1
Nova Scotia	52,840	2,650	55,490	0.6
New Brunswick	72,090	1,350	73,440	0.7
Québec	1,356,790	183,890	1,540,680	15.5
Ontario	891,190	177,390	1,068,580	10.7
Manitoba	548,360	101,590	649,950	6.5
Saskatchewan	570,700	81,630	652,330	6.5
Alberta	644,390	16,800	661,190	6.6
British Columbia	929,730	18,070	947,800	9.5
Yukon Territory	478,970	4,480	483,450	4.8
Northwest Territories	3,293,020	133,300	3,426,320	34.4
Districts of Franklin *	1,423,560	19,430	1,442,990	14.5
Keewatin *	575,470	25,120	600,590	6.0
Mackenzie *	1,293,990	88,750	1,382,740	13.9
Canada	9,215,430	755,180	9,970,610	100.0

*Indicates portion of total.

LARGEST & SELECTED LAKES IN CANADA

Name	Provinces and Territories	Area (square kilometres)
Superior	Ontario (and United States)	82 101 (total); 28 748 in Canada
Huron	Ontario (and United States)	59 569 (total); 36 000 in Canada
Great Bear	Northwest Territories	30 764
Great Slave	Northwest Territories	27 048
Erie	Ontario (and United States)	25 666 (total); 12 768 in Canada
Winnipeg	Manitoba	23 760
Ontario	Ontario (and United States)	19 554 (total); 10 334 in Canada
Athabasca	Saskatchewan and Alberta	7,770
Reindeer	Saskatchewan and Manitoba	6,640
Nettilling	Nunavut	5,699
Winnipegosis	Manitoba	5,370
Nipigon	Ontario	4,848
Manitoba	Manitoba	4,624
Lake of the Woods	Ontario and Manitoba (and US)	4,350 (total); 3,149 in Canada
Dubawnt	Nunavut	3,833
Amadjuak	Nunavut	3,115
Other:		
Wollaston	Saskatchewan	2,681
Mistassini	Québec	2,335
Nueltin	Nunavut	2,279
Southern Indian	Manitoba	2,247
la Martre	Northwest Territories	1,775
Williston	British Columbia	1,760
Claire	Alberta	1,435
Bras d'Or	Nova Scotia	1,099
Kluane	Yukon	409
Grand	New Brunswick	165

LARGEST & SELECTED ISLANDS OF CANADA

Name	Provinces/Territories	Area (square kilometres)
Baffin	Nunavut	507,451
Victoria	Nunavut & Northwest Territories	217,291
Ellesmere	Nunavut	196,236
Island of Newfoundland	Newfoundland and Labrador	108,860
Banks	Northwest Territories	70,028
Devon	Nunavut	55,247
Axel Heiberg	Nunavut	43,178
Melville	Northwest Territories & Nunavut	42,149
Southampton	Nunavut	41,214
Prince of Wales	Nunavut	33,339
Vancouver	British Columbia	31,285
Other:		
Cape Breton Island	Nova Scotia	10,311
Anticosti Island	Québec	7,941
Grand Manan	New Brunswick	137

HIGHEST POINTS BY PROVINCE AND TERRITORY

Provinces and Territories	Name of Highest Point	Height (metres)
Yukon Territory	Mount Logan	5,959
British Columbia	Fairweather Mountain (Alaska-British Columbia border)	4,663
Alberta	Mount Columbia (Alberta-British Columbia border)	3,747
Northwest Territories	Unnamed peak	2,773
Nunavut	Barbeau Peak (Ellesmere Island)	2,616
Quebec	Mont D'Iberville (Quebec-Newfoundland and Labrador boundary)	1,652
Newfoundland and Labrador	Mount Caubvick (Newfoundland and Labrador -Quebec boundary)	1,652
Saskatchewan	Cypress Hills	1,392
Manitoba	Baldy Mountain	832
Ontario	Ishpatina Ridge	693
New Brunswick	Mount Carleton	817
Nova Scotia	White Hill	532
Prince Edward Island	Unnamed hill	142

HIGHEST MOUNTAINS BY PROVINCE AND TERRITORY

Provinces and Territories	Name	Height (metres)
Yukon Territory	Mount Logan	5,959
British Columbia	Fairweather Mountain	4,663
Alberta	Mount Columbia	3,747
Northwest Territories	Unnamed peak (Mackenzie Mountains)	2,773
Nunavut	Barbeau Peak (Ellesmere Island)	2,616
Newfoundland and Labrador	Mount Caubvick (Torngat Mountains)	1,652
Quebec	Mont D'Iberville	1,652
Saskatchewan	Cypress Hills	1,392
Manitoba	Baldy Mountain	832
New Brunswick	Mount Carleton	817
Ontario	Ishpatina Ridge	693
Nova Scotia	White Hill	532
Prince Edward Island	Highest Point	142

LONGEST & SELECTED RIVERS IN CANADA

Name	Length (km)	Location
Mackenzie	4,241	Northwest Territories
Yukon	3,184	British Columbia-Yukon-Alaska
St. Lawrence	3,058	Québec-Ontario
Nelson	2,575	Manitoba
Columbia	2,000	British Columbia-Washington State-Oregon
Peace	1,923	British Columbia-Alberta
Churchill	1,608	Saskatchewan-Manitoba
Fraser	1,370	British Columbia
North Saskatchewan	1,287	Alberta-Saskatchewan
Ottawa	1,271	Québec-Ontario
Athabasca	1,231	Alberta
Back River	1,150	Northwest Territories-Nunavut
Liard	1,115	Yukon-British Columbia-Northwest Territories
Assiniboine	1,070	Saskatchewan-Manitoba
Other:		
Albany	980	Ontario
La Grande Rivière	893	Québec
Coppermine	845	Northwest Territories-Nunavut
St. John River	673	Maine-New Brunswick
Churchill	335	Newfoundland & Labrador
Miramichi	250	New Brunswick
Shubenacadie	52	Nova Scotia
Hillsborough River	45	Prince Edward Island

HIGHEST WATERFALLS IN CANADA

Name of Waterfall	Vertical Drop (metres)	Location
Della Falls	440	Della Lake, BC
Pissing Mare Falls	350	Western Brook Pond, NL
Takakkaw Falls	254	Daly Glacier, BC
Hunlen Falls	253	Atnarko River, BC
Panther Falls	183	Nigel Creek, AB
Helmcken Falls	141	Murtle River, BC
Bridal Veil Falls	122	Bridal Creek, BC
Virginia Falls	90	South Nahanni River, NT
Chute Montmorency	84	Rivière Montmorency, QC
Twin Falls	80	Yoho National Park, BC
Chute Ouiatchouan	79	Rivière Ouiatchouan, QC
Churchill Falls	75	Churchill River, NL
Brandywine Falls	61	Brandywine Creek, BC
Niagara Falls (American Falls)	59	(Niagara River, USA)
Niagara Falls (Horseshoe Falls)	57	Niagara River, ON
Wilberforce Falls	50	Hood River, NU
Dog Falls	47	Kaministiquia River, ON
Chute de Shawinigan	46	Rivière Saint-Maurice, QC
Grand Falls	43	Exploits River, NL
Parry Falls	40	Lockhart River, NT
Kakabeka Falls	40	Kaministiquia River, ON

SYMBOLS OF CANADA

Provinces and Territories	Floral Emblem	Tree	Bird
Alberta	Wild Rose	Lodgepole Pine	Great Horned Owl
British Columbia	Pacific Dogwood	Western Red Cedar	Steller's Jay
Manitoba	Prairie Crocus	White Spruce	Great Gray Owl
New Brunswick	Purple Violet	Balsam Fir	Black-capped Chickadee
Newfoundland and Labrador	Pitcher Plant	Black Spruce	Atlantic Puffin
Northwest Territories	Mountain Avens	Tamarack	Gyrfalcon
Nova Scotia	Mayflower	Red Spruce	Osprey
Nunavut	Purple Saxifrage	Rock Ptarmigan	
Ontario	White Trillium	Eastern White Pine	Loon
Prince Edward Island	Lady's Slipper	Red Oak	Blue Jay
Quebec	Blue Iris Versicolor	Yellow Birch	Snowy Owl
Saskatchewan	Western Red Lily	Paper Birch	Sharp-tailed Grouse
Yukon	Fireweed	Subalpine Fir	Common Raven

Jasper National Park

Moraine Lake near Lake Louise in Canada

Banf Canada

Icefields Parkway in Jasper Canada

Sunwapta Falls in Jasper National Park

North Pole
Polar Ice
Norwegian Sea
Norway
Greenland Sea
UK
Russia
Arctic Ocean
Bering Strait
Ellesmere Island
Alert
North Magnetic Pole
Kalaallit Nunaat
(Grønland)
(Denmark)
Iceland
Arctic Circle
Beaufort Sea
Banks I
Resolute
Baffin Bay
Alaska
(USA)
Inuvik
Victoria Island
Baffin Island
Davis Strait
Arctic Circle
Dawson
Great Bear Lake
Gjoa Haven
Yukon Territory
Mackenzie River
Whitehorse
Northwest Territories
Iqaluit
Labrador Sea
Nunavut
Baker Lake
Atlantic Ocean
Yellowknife
Ungava Bay
Newfoundland and Labrador
Fort Nelson
Great Slave Lake
CANADA
Nain
British Columbia
Kuujjuaq
Fort McMurray
Hudson Bay
Churchill Falls
Prince George
Churchill
St John's
Pacific
Alberta
Saskatchewan
Manitoba
Sept-Îles
Edmonton
L Winnipeg
James Bay
La Grande Rivière
Saint-Pierre et Miquelon
(France)
Fraser River
Vancouver
Kamloops
Calgary
Sandy Lake
Quebec
Prince Edward Island
Charlottetown
Victoria
Saskatoon
New Brunswick
Ocean
Regina
Winnipeg
Thunder Bay
Ontario
Québec
Nova Scotia
Halifax
Fredericton
United States of America
Montréal
LEGEND
National capital
Provincial or Territorial capital
Other populated places
International boundary
Provincial or Territorial boundary
Exclusive 200 nautical mile Economic Zone (EEZ)
Lake Superior
Ottawa
Toronto
Atlantic Ocean
Lake Michigan
Huron
Lake Ontario
Lake Erie
Scale
km 300 0 300 600 900 km
© 2001. Her Majesty the Queen in Right of Canada, Natural Resources Canada.

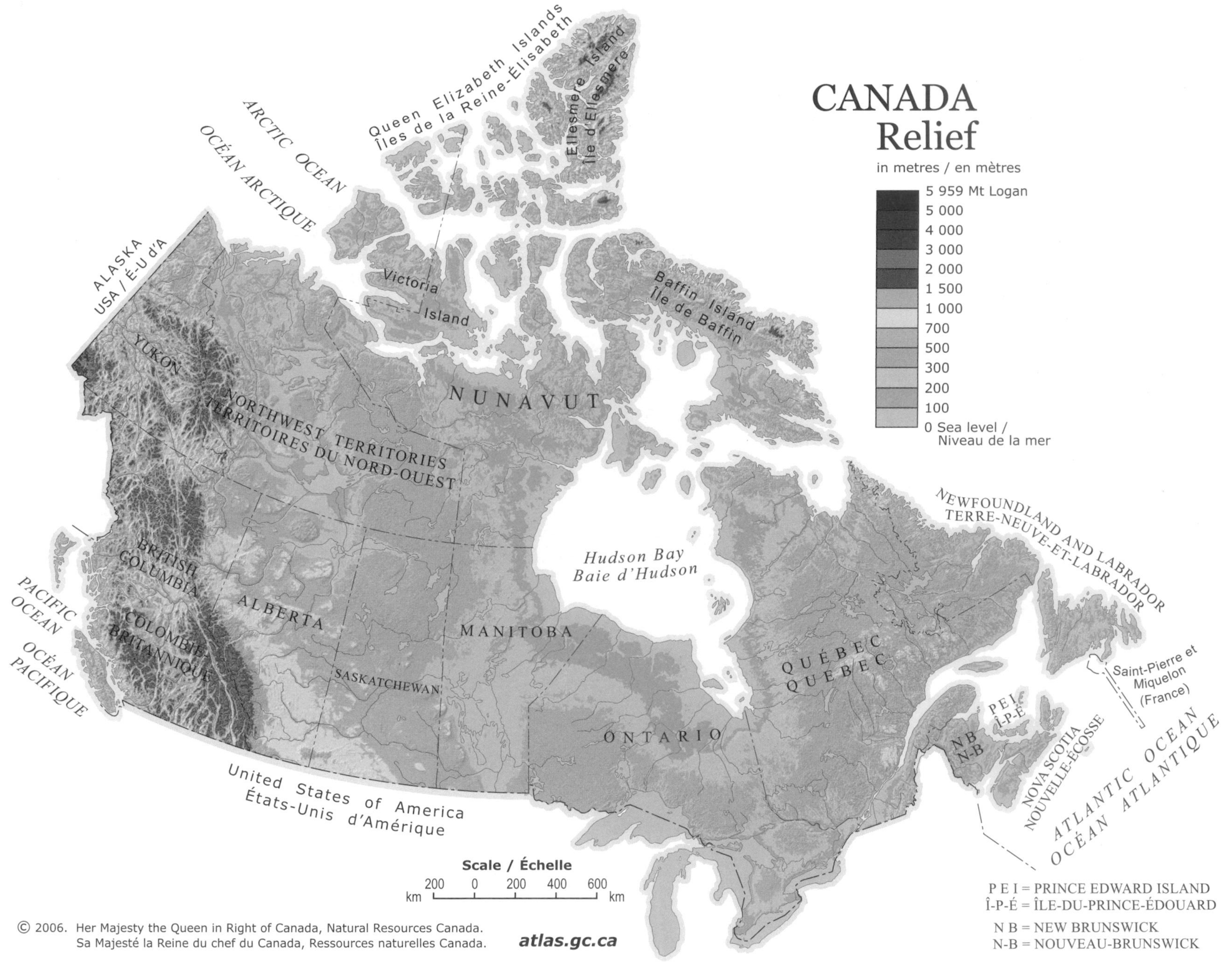

CANADA
Relief
in metres / en mètres
5 959 Mt Logan
5 000
4 000
3 000
2 000
1 500
1 000
700
500
300
200
100
0 Sea level / Niveau de la mer
Queen Elizabeth Islands
Îles de la Reine-Élisabeth
Ellesmere Island
Île d'Ellesmere
ARCTIC OCEAN
OCÉAN ARCTIQUE
Victoria Island
Baffin Island
Île de Baffin
ALASKA
USA / É-U d'A
YUKON
NUNAVUT
NORTHWEST TERRITORIES
TERRITOIRES DU NORD-OUEST
BRITISH COLUMBIA
COLOMBIE-BRITANNIQUE
PACIFIC OCEAN
OCÉAN PACIFIQUE
ALBERTA
SASKATCHEWAN
MANITOBA
Hudson Bay
Baie d'Hudson
ONTARIO
QUÉBEC
QUÉBEC
NEWFOUNDLAND AND LABRADOR
TERRE-NEUVE-ET-LABRADOR
Saint-Pierre et Miquelon (France)
PEI
Î-P-É
NB
N-B
NOVA SCOTIA
NOUVELLE-ÉCOSSE
ATLANTIC OCEAN
OCÉAN ATLANTIQUE
United States of America
États-Unis d'Amérique
Scale / Échelle
km 200 0 200 400 600 km
P E I = PRINCE EDWARD ISLAND
Î-P-É = ÎLE-DU-PRINCE-ÉDOUARD
N B = NEW BRUNSWICK
N-B = NOUVEAU-BRUNSWICK
atlas.gc.ca

CLIMATE

Temperature Data for Representative Stations in Canada

Temperature in Degrees Celsius

Station (Airport)	Elevation (metres)	Mean Daily					Extreme		Days with Measurable Rainfall	Total # of Sunshine Hours
		Annual	Jan.	Apr.	July	Oct.	Max.*	Min.* (m)		
Newfoundland:										
Goose Bay	46	-0.3	-17.3	-1.8	15.5	2.5	37.8	-39.4	109	1607.6
St. John's	134	4.7	-4.3	1.3	15.4	7.0	31.5	-23.8	217	-
Prince Edward Island:										
Charlottetown Int.	48	5.2	-7.7	2.3	18.4	8.0	34.4	-30.5	177	-
Nova Scotia:										
Halifax Int.	126	6.1	-5.8	3.6	18.3	8.5	34.4	-26.1	170	-
Sydney	55	5.5	-5.4	1.9	17.6	8.4	35.0	-25.6	189	1,804.6
Yarmouth	43	6.8	-3.0	4.7	16.3	9.3	30.0	-21.1	161	1,821.8
New Brunswick:										
Chatham	34	4.6	-10.4	2.8	19.1	6.8	37.8	-35.0	161	2,002.2
Fredericton	16	5.2	-9.6	4.1	19.3	7.3	37.2	-37.2	156	-
St. John	103	4.9	-8.2	3.2	16.9	7.5	34.4	-36.7	164	1,893.7
Quebec:										
Inukjuak	3	-6.8	-24.4	-11.2	9.1	-0.1	30.0	-49.4	151	1,457.4
Montréal Int. (Dorval)	31	6.1	-10.3	5.7	20.8	8.3	37.6	-37.8	162	-
Québec	70	4.0	-12.4	3.3	19.1	6.5	35.6	-36.1	178	1,910.4
Schefferville	522	-5.0	-23.4	-7.2	12.4	-1.4	34.3	-50.6	208	-
Sept-Iles	55	0.9	-14.6	0.0	15.2	3.4	32.2	-43.3	166	-
Sherbrooke	238	4.1	-11.6	3.9	18.0	6.4	33.7	-40.0	189	-
Ontario:										
Kapuskasing	226	0.5	-18.5	0.5	17.0	4.2	36.7	-45.3	190	-
Ottawa Int.	116	5.8	-10.8	5.6	20.8	7.9	37.8	-36.7	159	-
Thunder Bay	199	2.4	-15.0	2.7	17.7	5.4	40.3	-41.1	138	2,183.3
Toronto Int.	173	7.2	-6.7	6.0	20.5	8.9	38.3	-31.3	141	2,038.3
Windsor	190	9.1	-5.0	8.1	22.4	10.9	40.2	-27.2	143	-
Manitoba:										
Churchill	28	-7.1	-26.9	-10.0	11.8	-1.4	33.9	-45.4	148	1,820.7
The Pas	271	-0.3	-21.4	0.5	17.7	3.5	36.7	-49.4	127	2,203.2
Winnipeg Int.	239	2.4	-18.3	3.8	19.8	5.7	40.6	-45.0	119	2,377.3
Saskatchewan:										
Regina	577	2.6	-16.5	4.1	19.1	5.1	43.3	-50.0	109	2,364.6
Saskatoon	501	2.0	-17.5	3.9	18.6	4.8	40.6	-50.0	108	-
Alberta:										
Calgary Int.	1,077	3.9	-9.6	4.1	16.4	5.7	36.1	-45.0	111	2,394.6
Edmonton Int.	715	2.1	-14.2	3.7	16.0	4.6	35.0	-48.3	122	2,303.2
Grande Prairie	666	1.6	-15.4	3.3	16.0	4.4	34.5	-52.2	130	-
British Columbia:										
Kamloops	345	8.6	-4.8	9.4	20.8	8.5	40.6	-37.2	74	2,046.8
Prince George	676	3.7	-9.9	4.7	15.3	4.8	36.0	-50.0	107	1,942.4
Prince Rupert	34	6.9	0.8	5.5	12.9	7.8	28.7	-24.4	236	1,211.8
Vancouver Int.	3	9.9	3.0	8.8	17.2	10.0	33.3	-17.8	164	1,919.3
Victoria Int.	20	9.5	3.4	8.4	16.2	9.7	36.1	-15.6	153	2,081.9
Yukon Territory:										
Kamakuk Beach	14	-11.0	-24.0	-17.8	7.6	-9.4	30.0	-51.8	57	-
Whitehorse	703	-1.0	-18.7	0.3	14.1	0.7	34.4	-52.2	122	1,852.4
Northwest Territories:										
Alert	62	-18.1	-31.9	-25.1	3.4	-19.5	20.0	-50.0	100	-
Inuvik	59	-9.5	-28.8	-14.1	13.8	-8.2	31.7	-56.7	129	-
Yellowknife	205	-5.2	-27.9	-6.2	16.5	-1.4	32.5	-51.2	118	-
Nunavut:										
Iqaluit	34	-9.5	-25.8	-14.7	7.7	-4.9	24.4	-45.6	152	1,508.3

*Temperature extremes are for the total period of record 1961-1990.
*1 in. = 25.4 mm. = 2.54 cm.

Precipitation Data for Representative Stations in Canada

Station (Airport)	Average Total Precipitation (mm.)													Aver. Ann. Snowfall (cm)
	Jan.	Feb.	Mar.	Apr.	May	June	July	Aug.	Sept.	Oct.	Nov.	Dec.	Ann.	
Newfoundland:														
Goose Bay	64.9	57.0	68.6	57.1	66.4	100.9	119.4	98.3	90.6	78.8	79.9	77.6	959.5	463.8
St. John's	147.8	133.6	126.7	110.4	100.9	96.9	77.9	121.8	125.0	151.7	144.7	144.2	1481.7	322.1
Prince Edward Island:														
Charlottetown Int.	106.3	91.5	92.2	91.8	96.8	91.1	81.6	88.6	94.1	111.7	121.9	133.2	1200.8	338.7
Nova Scotia:														
Halifax Int.	146.9	119.1	122.6	124.4	110.5	98.4	96.8	109.6	94.9	128.9	154.4	167.0	1473.5	261.4
Sydney	151.6	125.1	131.3	125.3	98.1	91.2	86.2	97.3	103.2	137.6	160.4	172.9	1480.1	329.5
Yarmouth	126.4	106.5	95.3	100.9	96.6	93.6	84.7	82.2	87.5	107.4	134.8	143.5	1259.4	205.3
New Brunswick:														
Chatham	85.2	69.5	86.6	86.3	88.1	84.5	97.8	95.9	87.8	95.2	104.4	105.5	1086.9	323.9
Fredericton	93.3	84.3	90.4	83.4	94.8	86.9	84.5	99.4	92.3	93.1	110.7	118.8	1131.0	294.5
St. John	128.3	102.6	109.9	109.7	123.1	104.8	103.7	103.0	111.3	122.5	146.2	167.6	1432.8	283.2
Quebec:														
Inukjuak	12.6	10.1	12.4	19.2	23.2	36.1	55.1	62.4	64.6	52.4	44.9	25.2	418.1	175.4
Montréal Int. (Dorval)	63.3	56.4	67.6	74.8	68.3	82.5	85.6	100.3	86.5	75.4	93.4	85.6	939.7	214.2
Québec	90.0	74.4	85.0	75.5	99.9	110.2	118.5	119.6	123.7	96.0	106.1	108.9	1207.7	337.0
Schefferville	48.8	38.9	47.8	52.6	51.0	70.0	103.3	89.4	94.3	75.7	68.2	53.4	793.6	415.0
Sept-Iles	86.8	68.9	80.9	93.4	96.3	92.4	90.8	99.6	111.5	100.8	99.6	107.0	1127.9	415.1
Sherbrooke	71.8	59.7	75.2	73.6	94.2	100.5	116.7	130.5	98.6	91.4	100.7	95.8	1108.9	288.2
Ontario:														
Kapuskasing	53.9	41.5	54.8	53.3	71.0	88.6	101.9	91.3	94.6	78.3	76.3	55.6	861.0	325.7
Ottawa Int.	58.0	58.6	64.8	69.0	76.4	76.9	88.1	92.0	82.9	74.8	86.4	82.5	910.5	221.5
Thunder Bay	32.4	25.6	40.9	47.1	69.3	84.0	79.9	88.5	86.4	60.9	49.4	39.3	703.5	195.5
Toronto Int.	45.6	45.5	56.9	64.0	66.0	68.9	76.6	84.2	74.2	63.0	70.3	65.5	780.8	124.2
Windsor	50.3	53.7	72.0	80.3	75.7	97.0	85.3	85.7	86.7	57.9	75.4	81.6	901.6	123.3
Manitoba:														
Churchill	17.3	12.8	18.3	22.6	30.5	44.5	50.7	60.5	52.6	46.5	35.5	19.7	411.6	200.1
The Pas	16.6	15.1	21.0	26.2	33.6	63.1	69.1	65.0	58.3	37.5	26.6	19.8	451.9	170.2
Winnipeg Int.	19.3	14.8	23.1	35.9	59.8	83.8	72.0	75.3	51.3	29.5	21.2	18.6	504.4	114.8
Saskatchewan:														
Regina	14.7	13.0	16.5	20.4	50.8	67.3	58.9	40.0	34.4	20.3	11.7	15.9	364.0	107.4
Saskatoon	15.9	12.9	16.0	19.7	44.2	63.4	58.0	36.8	32.1	16.9	14.1	17.2	347.2	105.4
Alberta:														
Calgary Int.	12.2	9.9	14.7	25.1	52.9	76.9	69.9	48.7	48.1	15.5	11.6	13.2	398.8	135.4
Edmonton Int.	22.9	15.5	15.9	21.8	42.8	76.1	101.0	69.5	47.5	17.7	16.0	19.2	465.8	127.1
Grande Prairie	32.7	20.5	18.6	19.8	35.3	74.2	67.9	61.8	42.2	21.7	28.6	26.9	450.2	174.6
British Columbia:														
Kamloops	26.1	13.8	9.6	14.8	21.8	28.6	27.9	30.2	27.6	14.4	22.0	32.6	269.5	86.2
Prince George	54.4	35.0	34.3	28.3	51.7	64.5	60.0	61.2	59.3	59.4	52.7	53.8	614.7	233.8
Prince Rupert	250.8	216.5	188.2	181.9	142.0	119.5	112.9	162.8	244.7	378.9	284.4	269.8	2551.6	142.6
Vancouver Int.	149.8	123.6	108.8	75.4	61.7	45.7	36.1	38.1	64.4	115.3	169.9	178.5	1167.4	54.9
Victoria Int.	141.1	99.3	71.9	41.9	33.4	27.3	17.6	23.7	36.6	74.4	139.2	151.6	857.9	46.9
Yukon Territory:														
Kamakuk Beach	5.3	4.1	2.9	4.2	4.4	15.5	29.6	36.0	19.7	18.7	8.3	5.4	154.0	68.9
Whitehorse	16.9	11.9	12.1	8.3	14.4	31.2	38.5	39.3	35.2	23.0	18.9	18.9	268.8	145.2
Northwest Territories:														
Alert	7.8	5.2	6.8	9.4	9.9	12.7	25.0	23.8	24.3	13.2	8.8	7.4	154.2	164.9
Inuvik	15.6	11.1	10.8	12.6	19.1	22.2	34.1	43.9	24.2	29.6	17.5	16.8	257.4	175.2
Yellowknife	14.9	12.6	10.6	10.3	16.6	23.3	35.2	41.7	28.8	34.8	23.9	14.7	267.3	143.9
Nunavut:														
Iqaluit	21.8	19.0	22.0	28.4	29.6	36.5	58.2	63.5	51.9	42.4	30.9	19.8	424.1	256.8

 Detailed climate information is available at www.climate.weatheroffice.ec.gc.ca/Welcome_e.html

KILOMETRES

MILES

	BANFF	BRANDON	CALGARY	CHARLOTTETOWN	CHICOUTIMI	CORNER BROOK	DAWSON CREEK	EDMONTON	FLIN FLON	FORT SMITH	FREDERICTON	GANDER	GASPÉ	HALIFAX	HAMILTON	JASPER	KENORA	LETHBRIDGE	LONDON	MONCTON	MONTRÉAL	NIAGARA FALLS	NORTH BAY	OTTAWA	PORT AUX BASQUES	PRINCE ALBERT	PRINCE GEORGE	PRINCE RUPERT	QUÉBEC	REGINA	RIVIÈRE-DU-LOUP	ROUYN	SAINT JOHN	ST. JOHN'S	SASKATOON	SAULT STE. MARIE	SEPT-ÎLES	SHERBROOKE	SUMMERSIDE	SYDNEY	THE PAS	THUNDER BAY	TORONTO	VANCOUVER	VICTORIA	WHITEHORSE	WINDSOR	WINNIPEG	YARMOUTH	YELLOWKNIFE
BANFF	•	782	80	3147	2702	3484	633	266	846	1094	2924	3725	2997	3225	2256	178	1037	216	2327	3047	2406	2299	2059	2288	3356	567	393	853	2574	555	2687	1960	2990	3932	465	1794	2980	2503	3131	3356	920	1354	2214	577	618	1562	2457	910	3055	1205
BRANDON	1259	•	702	2392	1920	2714	1082	715	451	1543	2142	2943	2215	2447	1474	944	255	622	1545	2292	1624	1517	1277	1506	2574	454	1159	1619	1792	227	1905	1178	2208	3152	387	1012	2198	1721	2349	2574	357	572	1432	1359	1400	2011	1677	128	2273	1654
CALGARY	129	1130	•	3055	2622	3404	553	186	766	1011	2832	3633	2917	3133	2176	258	957	136	2247	2955	2326	2219	1979	2208	3264	487	473	933	2494	475	2607	1880	2898	3842	385	1714	2900	2423	3051	3264	840	1274	2134	657	698	1482	2377	830	2963	1125
CHARLOTTETOWN	5065	3850	4917	•	552	368	3442	3075	2787	3903	223	597	516	144	1143	3304	2105	3014	1184	100	736	1147	1083	854	228	2814	3519	3979	587	2587	460	1136	192	804	2747	1348	531	706	39	228	2749	1788	1071	3719	3760	4371	1303	2232	257	4014
CHICOUTIMI	4348	3090	4220	888	•	901	3002	2635	2347	3463	329	1130	402	544	673	2864	1665	2542	744	452	296	716	643	414	761	2374	3079	3539	128	2147	92	696	383	1357	2307	908	385	261	536	761	2277	1348	631	3279	3320	3931	858	1792	460	3574
CORNER BROOK	5607	4368	5478	592	1450	•	3791	3424	3136	4252	572	229	865	402	1462	3653	2454	3336	1534	449	1085	1500	1432	1203	140	3163	3868	4328	936	2936	809	1485	541	436	3096	1697	911	1055	407	140	3071	2137	1420	4068	4109	4720	1652	2581	566	4363
DAWSON CREEK	1019	1741	890	5539	4831	6101	•	367	1020	640	3224	4020	3297	3525	2556	467	1337	689	2627	3342	2706	2599	2359	2588	3651	741	252	712	2874	855	2987	2260	3290	4227	695	2094	3280	2803	3426	3651	1013	1654	2514	747	788	929	2731	1210	3343	751
EDMONTON	428	1151	299	4949	4241	5510	591	•	653	828	2857	3653	2930	3158	2189	299	970	322	2260	2975	2339	2232	1992	2221	3284	374	444	904	2507	488	2620	1893	2923	3860	328	1727	2913	2436	3059	3284	646	1287	2147	773	814	1296	2364	843	2988	939
FLIN FLON	1362	668	1233	4485	3777	5047	1642	1051	•	1481	2569	3365	2642	2870	1901	882	682	862	1972	2687	2051	1944	1704	1933	2996	279	1097	1557	2219	467	2332	1605	2635	3572	381	1439	2625	2148	2771	2996	94	999	1859	1423	1464	1949	2086	555	2700	1592
FORT SMITH	1761	2483	1627	6281	5573	6843	1030	1333	2383	•	3685	4480	3758	3986	3017	995	1798	1150	3083	3803	3167	3055	2820	3049	4112	1202	892	1352	3335	1316	3448	2721	3751	4692	1156	2555	3741	3264	3887	4112	1474	2115	2975	1387	1428	1569	3192	1671	3816	443
FREDERICTON	4706	3447	4558	359	529	921	5189	4598	4134	5930	•	801	435	215	895	3086	1887	2764	966	123	518	938	865	636	432	2596	3301	3761	364	2369	237	918	66	1008	2529	1130	481	483	207	432	2499	1570	853	3501	3542	4153	1080	2014	131	3796
GANDER	5995	4736	5847	961	1819	369	6470	5879	5415	7210	1289	•	1094	631	1691	3882	2683	3560	1762	678	1314	1734	1661	1432	369	3392	4097	4557	1165	3165	1038	1714	770	207	3325	1926	1140	1284	636	369	3300	2366	1649	4297	4338	4949	1881	2810	795	4592
GASPÉ	4823	3565	4694	830	647	1392	5306	4715	4252	6048	700	1761	•	587	968	3159	1960	2837	1039	416	591	1011	938	709	725	2669	3374	3834	437	2442	310	991	501	1301	2602	1203	299	556	500	725	2572	1643	926	3574	3615	4226	1153	2087	566	3869
HALIFAX	5190	3938	5042	232	875	647	5673	5082	4619	6415	346	1015	945	•	1196	3387	2188	3065	1267	171	819	1239	1166	937	262	2897	3602	4062	567	2670	452	1219	149	838	2830	1431	628	698	188	262	2800	1871	1154	3802	3843	4454	1381	2315	217	4097
HAMILTON	3631	2372	3502	1839	1083	2353	4114	3523	3059	4855	1440	2721	1558	1925	•	2418	1219	2096	84	1013	377	43	250	290	1322	1928	2633	3093	545	1701	658	431	961	1898	1861	462	951	474	1097	1322	1831	902	42	2833	2874	3485	198	1346	1026	3128
JASPER	286	1519	415	5317	4609	5879	752	369	1419	1601	4966	6247	5084	5451	3891	•	1199	394	2489	3204	2568	2461	2221	2450	3513	603	215	675	2736	717	2849	2122	3152	4089	557	1956	3142	2665	3288	3513	875	1516	2376	544	585	1396	2635	1072	3217	1106
KENORA	1669	410	1510	3388	2680	3949	2152	1561	1098	2894	3037	4318	3154	3521	1962	1930	•	877	1290	2005	1369	1262	1022	1251	2314	709	1414	1874	1537	482	1650	923	1953	2890	642	757	1943	1466	2089	2314	612	317	1177	1614	1655	2266	1404	127	2018	1909
LETHBRIDGE	384	1001	219	4851	4091	5369	1109	518	1387	1851	4448	5729	4566	4933	3373	634	1411	•	2167	2882	2246	2139	1899	2128	3191	623	609	1069	2414	395	2527	1800	2830	2767	412	1626	2820	2343	2966	3191	768	1194	2054	710	751	1618	2297	750	2902	1261
LONDON	3745	2486	3616	1905	1197	2469	4228	3637	3174	4962	1555	2836	1672	2039	135	4006	2076	3487	•	1084	448	126	321	361	1393	2009	2704	3164	616	1772	729	502	1032	1969	1932	533	1022	545	1166	1393	1902	973	113	2904	2945	3548	126	1417	1097	3199
MONCTON	4904	3689	4756	161	727	723	5378	4788	4324	6120	198	1091	669	275	1630	5156	3227	4638	1745	•	636	1056	983	754	309	2714	3419	3879	487	2487	360	1036	92	885	2647	1248	462	606	84	309	2649	1688	971	3619	3660	4271	1203	2132	157	3914
MONTRÉAL	3872	2614	3743	1184	476	1746	4355	3764	3301	5097	834	2115	951	1318	607	4133	2203	3615	721	1024	•	420	347	118	945	2078	2783	3243	168	1851	281	400	584	1521	2011	612	574	97	720	945	1981	1052	335	2983	3024	3635	562	1496	649	3278
NIAGARA FALLS	3700	2441	3571	1846	1152	2414	4183	3592	3129	4917	1510	2791	1627	1994	69	3961	2031	3442	203	1699	676	•	293	333	1365	1971	2676	3136	588	1744	701	474	1004	1941	1904	505	983	517	1140	1365	1874	945	85	2876	2917	3528	241	1389	1069	3171
NORTH BAY	3314	2055	3185	1743	1035	2305	3796	3206	2742	4538	1392	2673	1510	1876	402	3574	1645	3056	517	1582	558	472	•	229	1292	1731	2436	2896	515	1504	628	181	931	1868	1664	265	921	444	1067	1292	1634	705	208	2636	2677	3280	435	1149	996	2931
OTTAWA	3682	2424	3553	1374	666	1936	4165	3574	3111	4907	1024	2305	1141	1508	467	3943	2013	3425	581	1213	190	536	369	•	1063	1960	2665	3125	286	1733	399	343	702	1639	1893	494	692	215	838	1063	1863	934	248	2865	2906	3517	475	1378	767	3160
PORT AUX BASQUES	5401	4142	5253	367	1225	225	5876	5285	4822	6618	695	594	1167	422	2128	5654	3724	5135	2242	497	1521	2197	2079	1711	•	3023	3728	4188	796	2796	669	1345	401	576	2956	1557	771	915	267	129	2931	1997	1280	3928	3969	4580	1512	2441	426	4223
PRINCE ALBERT	912	731	784	4529	3821	5090	1193	602	449	1934	4178	5459	4295	4662	3103	970	1141	1003	3233	4368	3344	3172	2786	3154	4865	•	818	1278	2246	227	2359	1632	2662	3599	102	1466	2652	2175	2798	3023	272	1026	1896	1144	1185	1670	2082	582	2727	1313
PRINCE GEORGE	632	1865	761	5663	4955	6225	406	715	1765	1436	5312	6593	5430	5797	4237	346	2276	980	4352	5502	4479	4307	3920	4289	6000	1316	•	460	2951	932	3064	2337	3367	4304	772	2163	3357	2880	3503	3728	1090	1731	2591	495	536	1181	2850	1287	3432	1003
PRINCE RUPERT	1373	2606	1502	6404	5695	6965	1146	1455	2506	2176	6053	7334	6170	6537	4978	1086	3016	1720	5092	6243	5219	5047	4661	5029	6740	2057	740	•	3411	1392	3524	2797	3827	4764	1232	2623	3817	3340	3963	4188	1550	2191	3051	955	996	1641	3310	1747	3892	1463
QUÉBEC	4142	2884	4014	945	206	1506	4625	4035	3571	5367	586	1875	703	912	877	4403	2474	3885	991	784	270	946	829	460	1281	3615	4749	5489	•	2019	127	568	418	1372	2179	780	406	133	571	796	2149	1220	503	3151	3192	3803	730	1664	495	3446
REGINA	893	365	764	4163	3455	4725	1376	785	752	2118	3813	5094	3930	4297	2737	1154	776	636	2852	4002	2979	2807	2420	2789	4500	365	1500	2240	3249	•	2132	1405	2435	3372	160	1231	2425	1948	2571	2796	373	799	1659	1132	1173	1784	1902	355	2507	1427
RIVIÈRE-DU-LOUP	4324	3066	4196	740	148	1302	4807	4216	3753	5549	381	1670	499	727	1059	4585	2655	4067	1173	579	452	1128	1011	642	1077	3796	4931	5671	204	3431	•	681	303	1245	2292	893	231	246	444	669	2262	1333	616	3264	3305	3916	843	1777	368	3559
ROUYN	3154	1896	3026	1828	1120	2390	3637	3046	2583	4379	1477	2758	1595	1962	694	3415	1485	2897	808	1667	644	763	291	552	2165	2626	3761	4501	914	2261	1096	•	984	1921	1565	446	974	497	1120	1345	1535	606	389	2537	2578	3189	616	1050	1049	2832
SAINT JOHN	4812	3553	4664	309	616	871	5295	4704	4241	6037	106	1239	806	240	1547	5073	3143	4554	1661	148	940	1616	1498	1130	645	4284	5419	6159	673	3919	488	1584	•	977	2595	1196	547	537	176	401	2565	1636	919	3567	3608	4219	1146	2080	65	3862
ST. JOHN'S	6328	5073	6183	1294	2184	702	6803	6212	5749	7551	1622	333	2094	1349	3055	6581	4651	4453	3169	1424	2448	3124	3006	2638	927	5792	6927	7667	2208	5427	2004	3092	1572	•	3532	2133	1347	1491	843	576	3507	2573	1856	4504	4545	5156	2088	3017	1012	4799
SASKATOON	748	623	620	4421	3713	4983	1118	528	613	1860	4070	5351	4188	4554	2995	896	1033	663	3109	4260	3236	3064	2678	3046	4757	164	1242	1983	3507	257	3689	2519	4176	5684	•	1391	2585	2108	2731	2956	346	959	1819	1042	1083	1624	2036	515	2660	1267
SAULT STE. MARIE	2887	1629	2758	2169	1461	2731	3370	2779	2360	4112	1819	3100	1936	2303	744	3148	1218	2617	858	2008	985	813	426	795	2506	2359	3481	4221	1255	1981	1437	718	1925	3422	2239	•	1186	709	1332	1557	1369	440	420	2363	2404	3015	647	884	1261	2666
SEPT-ÎLES	4796	3537	4667	855	620	1466	5279	4688	4225	6021	774	1835	481	1011	1530	5057	3127	4538	1645	744	924	1582	1482	1114	1241	4268	5403	6143	653	3903	372	1568	880	2168	4160	1909	•	539	515	771	2555	1626	909	3557	3598	4209	1136	2070	612	3852
SHERBROOKE	4028	2770	3899	1136	420	1698	4511	3920	3457	5253	777	2066	895	1123	763	4289	2359	3771	877	975	156	832	715	346	1473	3500	4635	5375	214	3135	396	800	864	2400	3392	1141	867	•	690	915	2078	1149	432	3080	3121	3732	659	1593	614	3375
SUMMERSIDE	5039	3780	4910	63	863	655	5514	4923	4459	6256	333	1024	805	303	1765	5292	3362	4773	1876	135	1159	1835	1717	1349	430	4503	5638	6378	919	4138	715	1802	283	1357	4395	2144	829	1110	•	267	2706	1772	1053	3703	3744	4355	1287	2216	241	3998
SYDNEY	5401	4142	5253	367	1225	225	5876	5285	4822	6618	695	594	1167	422	2128	5654	3724	5135	2242	497	1521	2197	2079	1711	207	4865	6000	6740	1281	4500	1077	2165	645	927	4757	2506	1241	1473	430	•	2931	1997	1280	3928	3969	4580	1512	2441	426	4223
THE PAS	1481	575	1352	4424	3664	4942	1630	1040	151	2372	4022	5311	4139	4506	2947	1408	985	1236	3061	4263	3188	3016	2630	2998	4717	438	1754	2494	3458	600	3640	2470	4128	5644	557	2203	4112	3344	4355	4717	•	929	1789	1388	1429	1942	2008	485	2630	1585
THUNDER BAY	2179	921	2050	2878	2169	3439	2662	2071	1608	3404	2527	3808	2644	3011	1452	2440	510	1922	1566	2717	1693	1521	1135	1503	3214	1651	2786	3526	1963	1286	2145	975	2633	4141	1543	708	2617	1849	2852	3214	1495	•	860	1931	1972	2583	1087	444	741	2226
TORONTO	3563	2305	3434	1724	1015	2285	4046	3455	2992	4788	1373	2654	1490	1857	68	3824	1894	3306	182	1563	539	137	335	399	2060	3051	4170	4910	810	2670	991	626	1479	2987	2927	676	1463	695	1695	2060	2879	1384	•	2791	2832	3435	227	1304	984	3086
VANCOUVER	929	2187	1057	5985	5277	6547	1202	1244	2290	2232	5634	6915	5752	6119	4559	875	2597	1143	4674	5824	4801	4628	4242	4611	6322	1841	797	1537	5071	1822	5253	4083	5741	7248	1677	3803	5724	4957	5959	6322	2234	3108	4492	•	41	1676	3034	1487	3632	1498
VICTORIA	995	2253	1123	6051	5343	6613	1268	1310	2356	2298	5700	6981	5818	6185	4625	941	2663	1209	4740	5890	4867	4694	4308	4677	6387	1907	863	1603	5137	1818	5319	4149	5807	7314	1743	3869	5790	5023	6025	6387	2300	3174	4558	66	•	1717	3053	1528	3673	1539
WHITEHORSE	2514	3236	2385	7034	6326	7596	1495	2086	3137	2525	6684	7965	6801	7168	5609	2247	3647	2604	5710	6874	5850	5678	5279	5660	7371	2688	1901	2641	6120	2871	6302	5132	6790	8298	2614	4852	6774	6006	7009	7371	3125	4157	5528	2697	2763	•	3660	2190	4284	1680
WIINDSOR	3954	2699	3825	2097	1381	2659	4395	3804	3357	5137	1738	3027	1856	2223	319	4241	2260	3697	203	1936	904	388	700	764	2433	3351	4587	5327	1175	3061	1357	991	1844	3360	3277	1041	1828	1061	2071	2433	3232	1749	365	4883	4913	5890	•	1547	1211	3303
WINNIPEG	1465	206	1336	3592	2884	4154	1947	1357	893	2689	3241	4522	3359	3726	2166	1725	204	1207	2280	3431	2408	2235	1849	2218	3928	937	2071	2812	2678	571	2860	1690	3347	4855	829	1423	3331	2564	3566	3928	781	715	2099	2393	2459	3524	2490	•	2145	1782
YARMOUTH	4917	3658	4768	414	740	911	5380	4809	4345	6141	211	1279	911	349	1651	5177	3248	4670	1765	253	1044	1720	1603	1234	686	4389	5523	6264	797	4035	592	1688	105	1629	4281	2029	985	988	388	686	4233	1193	1584	5845	5911	6894	1949	3452	•	3927
YELLOWKNIFE	1939	2662	1811	6460	5752	7022	1209	1511	2562	713	6109	7390	6227	6593	5034	1780	3072	2029	5148	6299	5275	5103	4717	5086	6796	2113	1614	2354	5546	2297	5728	4558	6215	7723	2039	4291	6199	5432	6418	6796	2551	3582	4966	2411	2477	2704	5316	2868	6320	•

Source: National Atlas Service, Natural Resources Canada

CANADIAN HERITAGE — NAVIGATION CANALS

Name	Location	Length of Channel	Locks No.	Minimum Dimensions Length	Width	Depth
Atlantic Area		km		m	m	m
St. Peters	St. Peter's Bay to Bras d'Or Lakes, Cape Breton, NS	0.80	1	91.44	14.45	4.88
Richelieu River						
St-Ours	St. Ours, PQ	0.10	1	99.6	13.41	3.66
Chambly	Chambly to St-Jean, PQ	18.96	9	33.52	6.70	1.98
Ottawa & Rideau/Cataraqui Rivers						
Ste-Anne-de-Bellevue	Junction of St. Lawrence & Ottawa River	0.19	1	54.86	12.9	2.74
Carillon	Carillon Rapids, Ottawa River	0.8	1	54.86	12.9	2.7**
Rideau	Ottawa to Kingston	202.0	45	27.4	8.5	1.22**
	Lower Rideau Lake to Perth (Tay Br.)	10.0	2	27.4	8.5	1.22**
Lake Ontario to Georgian Bay						
Trent-Severn Waterway	Trenton to Rice Lake	91.7	18	46.9	9.75	2.4
	Rice Lake to Kirkfield	180.8	15	31.4	9.75	1.8
	Kirkfield to Gamebridge	18.31	5	36.5	9.75	1.8
	Gamebridge to Port Severn	96.3	5	25.6	7.0	1.8
	Sturgeon Lake to Lindsay (Scugog Br.)	29.19	1	36.5	9.75	1.2
	Lindsay to Port Perry (Scugog Br.)	42.9		—	—	1.2
Murray	Lake Ontario to Bay of Quinte	12.1	—	—	—	2.9

Vessels drawing > 1.5 m must contact the TSW Peterborough (705/742-9267)
Overhead clearance 6.7 m
* Marine railway lift 17.3 m
** Vessels drawing > 1.22 m or with larger dimensions than above, are advised to contact the Rideau Canal (Superintendent, 613/283-5170)

FACTORS GOVERNING THE TRANSIT OF VESSELS THROUGH THE ST. LAWRENCE SEAWAY LOCKS, CANALS & CHANNELS BETWEEN MONTRÉAL & LAKE ERIE

Channel widths vary from a minimum of 61 m between bridge abutments & canals flanked by two embankments, to at least 137 m in open reaches.
Minimum vertical overhead clearance of structures & cables crossing the Seaway is 36 m above high water.

MAXIMUM VESSEL DIMENSIONS

Length	222.50 m overall
Beam	23.15 m extreme breadth excluding permanent fenders

The channels & canals in the deep waterway between Port of Montréal & Lake Erie are designed to a minimum controlling depth of 8.23 m.
In the Seaway canals the maximum permitted draught will be currently prescribed by the St. Lawrence Seaway Authority & the St. Lawrence Seaway Development Corporation.
The present maximum permissible draught is 79.5 dm.

Lock	Normal Lift in Metres	Useable Length in Metres	Widthin Metres	Useable Length Lower Ent. in Metres	Useable Length Upper Ent. in Metres
St-Lambert (Montréal Harbour)	4.5	222.5	24.38	653	458
Côte Ste-Catherine	10.0	222.5	24.38	319	318
Lower Beauharnois	12.2	222.5	24.38	379	503
Upper Beauharnois	11.3	222.5	24.38	503	575
Snell	14.0	222.5	24.38	449	212
Eisenhower	11.8	222.5	24.38	210	330
Iroquois	0.2	222.5	24.38	236	671

Minimum depth on Lock Gate Sills is 9.14 m.

WELLAND CANAL LOCKS

Lock No.	Type	Useable Length in Metres	Width in Metres	Normal Lift in Metres	Mileage From Port Weller (Nautical Miles)*	Useable Length Lower Ent. in Metres	Useable Length Upper Ent. in Metres
1	Single	222.5	24.38	14	1.7	840	448
2	Single	222.5	24.38	14	3.2	458	507
3	Single	222.5	24.38	14	5.5	445	459
4	Double	222.5	24.38	15	6.8	223	—
5	Double	222.5	24.38	15	6.8	—	—
6	Double	222.5	24.38	13	6.8	—	—
7	Single	222.5	24.38	14	7.5	306	601
8	Single	350.0	24.38	2	21.3	342	382.5

*Distances are shown in nautical miles in keeping with an international maritime agreement. One nautical mile equals 1.852 km.

Science

Astronomical Calculations

Prepared for this publication by Duy C. Nguyen, Ph.D., Department of Astronomy and Astrophysics, University of Toronto.

ASTRONOMY IN CANADA

Astronomical research in Canada is carried out in universities, supported by the Natural Sciences and Engineering Research Council (NSERC) of Canada, and by the Canada Foundation for Innovation (CFI), and also in the National Research Council (NRC) — specifically by the Herzberg Institute of Astrophysics (HIA), which operates the following observatories: The Dominion Astrophysical Observatory (DAO) at Victoria, with optical telescopes of 1.8m and 1.2m aperture; and the Dominion Radio Astrophysical Observatory (DRAO) near Penticton, which has a 26m paraboloid and a 7-element array of 9m antennae. The National Research Council also maintains Canada's Time Service in its Institute of National Measurement Standards. The Canadian Astronomy Data Centre (CADC) is housed within HIA.

A number of Canadian universities offer graduate education in astronomy: Victoria, British Columbia (Vancouver), Alberta (Edmonton), Calgary, Saskatchewan (Saskatoon), Manitoba (Winnipeg), Western Ontario (London), Waterloo, McMaster (Hamilton), York (Toronto), Toronto, Queen's (Kingston), Montréal, McGill (Montréal), Laval (Québec), and St. Mary's (Halifax). Most of these have some local facilities for observational and theoretical studies, and all of them have access to national facilities in Canada and elsewhere. Among the major observatories operated by Canadian universities are: a 1.8m infrared telescope opened in 1987 by the University of Calgary; a 1.2m telescope at the University of Western Ontario; a 0.6m telescope now located in, and shared with, Argentina with access through the University of Toronto; and a 1.5m telescope at the Mont Mégantic Observatory operated by the University of Montréal, and Laval University. There is also a Canadian Institute for Theoretical Astrophysics hosted by the University of Toronto. Canadian astronomers have recently established the Association of Canadian Universities for Research in Astronomy (ACURA) to co-ordinate universities' participation in astronomy, especially in the development of large-scale facilities.

Through the National Research Council, Canadian astronomers also have access to excellent international facilities. One of these is the 3.6m Canada-France-Hawaii optical telescope atop Mauna Kea on the island of Hawaii, at an elevation of nearly 4200m. This telescope is shared, both as to cost and operation, by Canada, France, and the state of Hawaii. Canadian astronomers also share (with the Netherlands and the UK) in the operation of the James Clerk Maxwell telescope, a sophisticated millimetre-wave radio telescope at the same site. Canada also is a partner, along with several other countries, in the twin Gemini 8m telescopes, which are in operation in Hawaii and in Chile. Balloon-borne telescopes, Canada's first astronomical satellite MOST (Microvariability and Oscillations of STars), and participation in other space astronomy missions are funded through the Canadian Space Agency, and Canada is a partner in the James Webb Space Telescope, the planned successor to the Hubble Space Telescope. Canada is also a partner in the North American Program in Radio Astronomy, including the Atacama Large Millimetre Array, under contruction high in the Atacama Desert in Chile.

Astronomical education and outreach are carried out in a wide variety of settings. In the formal education system, astronomy is part of the elementary and secondary school science curriculum in most provinces, and is taught in most universities, most commonly in the form of introductory astronomy courses for non-majors. Canada's planetariums, science centres, and public observatories play a major role in communicating the nature and excitement of astronomy, as do science journalists, and the many professional and amateur astronomers who give public lectures, and organize open houses and star parties.

OBSERVATORIES

Observatories are open to the public as follows:

NEW Burke-Gaffney Observatory: St. Mary's University, Halifax NS B3H 3C3 - 902/420-5828; Info line: 902/496-8257; Fax: 902/496-8218; URL: www.smu.ca/academic/science/ap/bgo.html

Free public tours are held, weather permitting, on the 1st and 3rd Saturday of each month, except from June through September when they are held every Saturday. Tours begin at 7pm between November 1 and March 30 and at either 9pm or 10pm (depending on when it gets dark) between April 1 and October 31. On clear evenings, the 40-cm telescope is used to view the planets, the Moon, or other interesting celestial objects.

There will be no tour on cloudy or rainy nights. The decision to hold or cancel a tour is usually made by 6pm on Saturday. Always call the information line after 6pm to find out if the tour is on or off.

Groups wishing special tours can be accommodated on Monday evenings by reservation.

Canada Science & Technology Museum, Helen Sawyer Hogg Observatory: 1867 St. Laurent Blvd., Ottawa ON K1G 5A3 - 613/991-3044; Email: cts@technomuses.ca; URL: www.sciencetech.technomuses.ca

38-cm refractor (from the former Dominion Observatory). See website for details and special programs.

Canada-France-Hawaii Telescope: #65, 1238 Mamalahoa Hwy., Kamuela HI, 96743 - 808/885-7944; Fax: 808/885-7288; E-mail: outreach@cfht.hawaii.edu; URL: www.cfht.hawaii.edu

By appointment only.

Climenhaga Observatory: Dept. of Physics & Astronomy, University of Victoria, PO Box 3055, Station CSC, Victoria BC V8W 3P6 - 250/721-7700; Fax: 250/721-7715; URL: astrowww.phys.uvic.ca/events/

Daytime tours are open from the beginning of April until the end of June. The tour includes an entertaining educational presentation, a look through the big, fully automated telescope in the Climenhaga Observatory and weather permitting, an opportunity to search for sunspots using the smaller telescopes on the roof. The tours are free but space is limited. Interested parties are encouraged to book in-advance.

Night time viewing sessions are open on Wednesdays from 8 p.m. (or sunset) until 10 p.m..

Gordon MacMillan Southam Observatory: H.R. MacMillan Space Centre, 1100 Chestnut St., Vancouver BC V6J 3J9 - 604/738-7827; Fax: 604/736-5665; E-mail: info@spacecentre.ca; URL: www.spacecentre.ca

Open Friday and Saturday 8pm to midnight. Closed December 25. Admission is by donation.

Hume Cronyn Memorial Observatory: Dept. of Physics & Astronomy, University of Western Ontario, London ON N6A 3K7 - 519/661-2111, ext. 86708; URL: www.astro.uwo.ca/~dfgray/pub-nit.html

Public Nights run from late October through mid-December and Mid-January through early April. This activity is oriented toward groups, and reservations must be made in advance.

Open House is run every Saturday evening during the months of June, July, and August. No reservations needed. Start time is 20:30 (8:30 p.m.). Closing time is 23:00 (11:00 p.m.).

National Research Council Canada, Centre of the Universe: Visitor Centre, 5071 West Saanich Rd., Victoria BC V9E 2E7 - 250/363-8262; E-mail: cu@nrc.gc.ca; URL: www.nrc-cnrc.gc.ca/eng/services/hia/centre-universe.html

Open Tuesday to Saturday from 3:30 p.m. to 11:15 p.m. (last admission at 10:15 p.m) during the summer, and 1:00 p.m. to 4:30 p.m. in September. See web pages for admission details.

National Research Council Canada, Dominion Astrophysical Observatory: 5071 West Saanich Rd., Victoria BC V9E 2E7 - 250/363-0001; E-mail: HIA-WWW@nrc-cnrc.gc.ca; URL: www.nrc-cnrc.gc.ca/eng/facilities/hia/astrophysical-observatory.html

Open every evening from April 1 up to and including October 31 to demonstrate the operation the research telescope, regardless of the weather, and to offer a viewing of celestial objects, weather permitting. See web site for details.

National Research Council Canada, Dominion Radio Astrophysical Observatory: 717 White Lake Road, PO Box 248, Penticton BC V2A 6J9 - 250/493-2300; E-mail: HIA-WWW@nrc-cnrc.gc.ca; URL: www.nrc-cnrc.gc.ca/eng/facilities/hia/radio-astrophysical.html

The Observatory grounds and Visitors' Centre are open year-round for self-guided tours between 10 a.m. and 5 p.m., Monday to Friday (except statutory holidays). The grounds are also open on weekends from Easter until Thanksgiving, between 10 a.m. and 5 p.m., with staff on duty in the Visitors' Centre. Guided tours led by Observatory staff are offered on Sundays in July and August, from 2 p.m. until 5 p.m.. Tours typically take about 1 hour.

Observatoire Astronomique Du Mont Mégantic: 189 route du Parc, Notre-Dame-des-Bois QC J0B 2E0 - 819/888-2941; Fax 819/888-2943; E-mail: parc.mont-megantic@sepaq.com; URL: www.astro.umontreal.ca/omm/

The observatory hosts "Festival d'Astronomie Populaire du mont Mégantic" on the weekends in July. For other times of the year, visits including interactive exhibitions, high definition multimedia show, and tours of the observatories can be arranged through AstroLab du Mont Mégantic. See web site for details on dates & times.

PRINCIPAL (MEAN) ELEMENTS OF THE SOLAR SYSTEM

Object	Equatorial Diameter (miles)	Equatorial Diameter (km)	Mass (earth=1)	Axial Rotation (days)	Magnitude at brightest	Mean Dist. from Sun (mill. miles)	Mean Dist. from Sun (mill. km)	Per. of Revol.	Eccentricity	Inclination (deg.)
Sun	865,000	1,392,000	332,946	24.7**	-26.8					
Moon	2,159	3,475	0.0123	27.3217	-12.6					
Mercury	3,032	4,879	0.0553	58.646	-2.0	36.0	57.9	88.0d	0.206	7.0
Venus	7,521	12,104	0.8150	243.019***	-4.7	67.2	108.2	224.7	0.007	3.4
Earth	7,926	12,756	1.0000	0.9973		93.0	149.6	365.3	0.017	(0.0)
Mars	4,222	6,794	0.1074	1.0260	-2.8	141.6	227.9	687.0	0.093	1.8
Jupiter	88,846*	142,984*	317.833	0.410**	-2.8	483.7	778	11.86y	0.048	1.3
Saturn	74,898*	120,536*	95.159	0.44401	-0.4	888	1,429	29.42	0.056	2.5
Uranus	31,763*	51,118*	14.500	0.71833***	5.7	1,786	2,875	83.75	0.046	0.8
Neptune	30,775*	49,528*	17.204	0.67125	7.8	2,799	4,504	163.7	0.009	1.8
Pluto	1,430	2,302	0.0025	6.3872***	13.8	3,676	5,916	248.0	0.249	17.1

at pressure 1 bar (101.325 kPa)   ** at equator * retrograde*

PLANETARY CONFIGURATIONS, 2011

UNIVERSAL (GREENWICH) TIME

	d	h			d	h	
January	2	14	Jupiter 0.6x S. of Uranus	July	1	9	New Moon; Eclipse of Sun (page 22)
	3	19	Earth at perihelion (147.1 million km)		4	15	Earth at Aphelion (152.1 million km)
	4	9	New Moon; Eclipse of Sun (page 22)		6	7	Mars 5x N. of Aldebaran
	8	16	Venus greatest elongation W. (47x)		10	8	Uranus stationary
	9	15	Mercury greatest elongation W. (23x)		20	5	Mercury greatest elongation E. (27x)
	15	22	Venus 8x N. of Antares	August	2	7	Mercury stationary
	27	8	Saturn stationary		16	12	Venus in superior conjunction
February	4	17	Mars in conjunction with Sun		17	1	Mercury in inferior conjunction
	17	10	Neptune in conjunction with Sun		22	23	Neptune at opposition
	25	9	Mercury in superior conjunction		26	4	Mercury stationary
March	16	18	Mercury 2x N. of Jupiter		30	17	Jupiter stationary
	20	23	Vernal Equinox; spring begins in northern hemisphere	September	3	6	Mercury greatest elongation W. (18x)
	21	12	Uranus in conjunction with Sun		9	2	Mercury 0.7x N. of Regulus
	23	1	Mercury greatest elongation E. (19x)		10	2	Mars 6x S. of Pollux
	27	1	Venus 0.2x S. of Neptune		16	12	Pluto stationary
	30	17	Mercury stationary		23	9	Autumnal Equinox; autumn begins in northern hemisphere
April	4	0	Saturn at opposition		26	0	Uranus at opposition
	6	15	Jupiter in conjunction with Sun		28	20	Mercury in superior conjunction
	9	7	Pluto stationary	October	3	12	Venus 3x N. of Spica
	9	20	Mercury in inferior conjunction		13	21	Saturn in conjunction with Sun
	22	5	Mercury stationary		29	2	Jupiter at opposition
	22	19	Venus 0.9x S. of Uranus		31	5	Saturn 5x N. of Spica
May	1	11	Mars 0.4x N. of Jupiter	November	9	21	Neptune stationary
	7	19	Mercury greatest elongation W. (27x)		9	21	Venus 4x N. of Antares
	10	23	Mercury 2x S. of Jupiter		10	5	Mars 1.4x N. of Regulus
	11	9	Venus 0.6x S. of Jupiter		10	5	Mercury 1.9x N. of Antares
	20	1	Mercury 2x S. of Mars		14	9	Mercury greatest elongation E. (23x)
	22	15	Venus 1.1x S. of Mars		24	10	Mercury stationary
June	1	21	New Moon; Eclipse of Sun (page 22)		25	6	New Moon; Eclipse of Sun (page 22)
	3	15	Neptune stationary	December	4	9	Mercury in inferior conjunction
	13	0	Mercury in superior conjunction		10	15	Full Moon; Eclipse of Moon (page 22)
	14	5	Saturn stationary		10	15	Uranus stationary
	15	20	Full Moon; Eclipse of Moon (page 22)		14	2	Mercury stationary
	18	8	Venus 5x N. of Aldebaran		22	6	Winter Solstice; winter begins in northern hemisphere
	21	17	Summer solstice; summer begins in northern hemisphere		22	20	Mercury 7x N. of Antares
	28	5	Pluto at opposition		23	3	Mercury greatest elongation W. (22x)
	28	22	Mercury 5x S. of Pollux		26	11	Jupiter stationary
					29	8	Pluto in conjunction with Sun

This table includes configurations involving the sun, planets, and bright zodiacal stars. The meaning of the terms is as follows:

Aphelion: the point in its orbit at which a planet is furthest from the sun.

Conjunction: in the same direction as another object (the sun, unless otherwise stated). Mercury and Venus can be at inferior conjunction (closer than the sun) or superior conjunction (beyond the sun).

Elongation: the angle between the planet and the sun.

Opposition: opposite another object (the sun, unless otherwise stated).

Perihelion: the point in its orbit at which a planet is closest to the sun.

Stationary: motionless relative to the background stars. Because of the orbital motions of the planet and the earth, the planet normally moves eastward or westward relative to the background stars. At the moment when its motion changes from eastward to westward, or vice versa, the planet is said to be stationary.

Rothney Astrophysical Observatory: Dept. of Physics & Astronomy, University of Calgary, 2500 University Dr. NW, Calgary AB T2N 1N4 - 403/931-2366; E-mail: rao@phas.ucalgary.ca ; URL: www.ucalgary.ca/rao/

Evening programs are available for school groups which involve a grade appropriate presentation, tour of the observatory and skyviewing. Programs run from 7:00 pm to 9:00 pm. Free drop-in visits to the Interpretive Centre are available Monday, Tuesday, and Wednesday from noon - 4pm. Private tours are available on other evenings during the year. School group tours are also available. See web site for details.

Telus World of Science - Edmonton Observatory: 11211 - 142 St., Edmonton AB T5M 4A1 - 780/452-9100; Fax: 780/455-5882; URL: www.edmontonscience.com/pages/PlanVisit/Observatory.aspx

Summer hours (July to Labour Day weekend) 1:00 p.m. - 5:00 p.m. and 6:30 p.m. - 10 p.m. 7 days a week. Fall/Winter/Spring hours (After Labour Day to the following summer) Saturdays, Sundays & Holidays 1:00 p.m. - 4:00 p.m., and Fridays, Saturdays & Sundays 7:00 p.m. - 10:00 p.m.. Open weather permitting.

University of Alberta Observatory: Dept. of Physics, University of Alberta, Edmonton AB T6G 2J1 - 780/492-5286; Email: observatory@phys.ualberta.ca; URL: www.phys.ualberta.ca/research/astro/observ.php

Open to the public Thursday nights from September through April (closed for final exams and winter holidays), weather permitting. See web site for exact hours and details.

University of Saskatchewan Observatory: Dept. of Physics & Engineering Physics, University of Saskatchewan, 116 Science Place, Saskatoon SK S7N 5E2 - 306/966-6396; URL: physics.usask.ca/observatory/

Saturday evening programs year round; times vary. Tours for school and community groups are arranged for Friday evenings (October - March). Special tours may be arranged during the summer months.

University of Toronto, St. George Campus Observatory: Dept. of Astronomy & Astrophysics, University of Toronto, 50 St. George Street, Toronto ON M5S 3H4 - 416/978-2016; URL: www1.astro.utoronto.ca/~gasa/public_talk/iWeb/index.php

Free tours are offered on the first Thursday of every month (excluding January). Tours start at 8 p.m. during winter months and 9 p.m. during summer months. Extra public tours may be also arranged. See web site for details.

York University Observatory: 4700 Keele St., Toronto ON M3J 1P3 - 416/736-2100, ext. 77773 (voice mail); Email: pdelaney@yorku.ca; URL: www.physics.yorku.ca/observatory/

The observatory is open for online viewing Monday nights and public (in-person) viewing on Wednesday nights at the following times: September - October 8:00 p.m. - 10:00 p.m., November - February 6:30 p.m. - 8:30 p.m., March - April 8:00 p.m. - 10:00 p.m., and May - August 9:00 p.m. - 11:00 p.m. See web site for further details.

PLANETARIUMS

A selection of planetaria with URL, phone number & related information:

ASTROLab du parc national du Mont-Mégantic: 189 route du Parc, Notre-Dame-des-Bois, QC J0B 2E0 - Toll Free: 1-800-665-6527; URL: www.astrolab-parc-national-mont-megantic.org

Cosmic Rhythms multimedia show; on-site lodging.

PRINCIPAL ANNUAL METEOR SHOWERS FOR THE NORTHERN HEMISPHERE
(UNIVERSAL TIME)

Shower	Location of Radiant	UT Date of Maximum Frequency	Zenithal Hourly Number	Duration (in days)
Quadrantids (2011)	Bootes	Jan. 4, 0h	90	1
Lyrids	Lyra	Apr. 22, 17h	15	6
Eta Aquarids	Aquarius	May 5, 23h	40	8
Delta Aquarids	Aquarius	July 29, 6h	20	12
Perseids	Perseus	Aug. 13, 5h	100	5
Draconids	Draconis	Oct. 9, 4h	10	1
Orionids	Orion	Oct. 22, 9h	25	8
South Taurids	Taurus	Nov. 4, 22h	10	30
North Taurids	Taurus	Nov. 13, 20h	15	30
Leonids	Leo	Nov. 18, 3h	15	2
Geminids	Gemini	Dec. 14, 4h	95	3
Ursids	Ursa Minor	Dec. 23, 0h	20	2
Quadranids (2012)	Bootes	Jan. 4, 6h	120	1

Doran Planetarium: Laurentian University, 935 Ramsey Lake Rd., Sudbury ON P3E 2C6 - 705/675-1151, ext. 2227, Fax: 705/675-4868; URL: www.oldwebsite.laurentian.ca/physics/planetarium/Planetarium.html

Largest planetarium in northern Ontario; programs.

The Lockhart Planetarium: 500 Dysart Rd., Winnipeg MB R3T 2M8 - 204/474-9785; URL: umanitoba.ca/faculties/science/astronomy/lockhart/

Dome seats 60; open year-round for public groups.

W.J. McCallion Planetarium: Dept. of Physics & Astronomy, McMaster University, 1280 Main St. West, Hamilton ON L8S 4M1 - 905/525-9140, ext. 27777; Fax: 905/546-1252; URL: physwww.physics.mcmaster.ca/planetarium

Planetarium has long history of support from RASC Hamilton Centre; first in Ontario open to the public.

MacMillan Planetarium: 1100 Chestnut St., Vancouver BC V6J 3J9. - 604/738-7827, Fax: 604/736-5665; URL: www.spacecentre.ca

Special laser shows in summer, numerous programs for school groups of all ages, teacher packages online.

Ontario Science Centre: 770 Don Mills Road, North York ON M3C 1T3 - 416/696-1000; URL: www.ontariosciencecentre.ca

OmniMax theatre, school trips & group tours welcome, summer camps & sleepovers available.

Planétarium de Montréal: 1000, rue St-Jacques Ouest, Montréal QC H3C 1G7 - 514/872-4530; Fax: 514/872-8102; E-mail: info@planetarium.montreal.qc.ca; URL: www.planetarium.montreal.qc.ca

Programs, activity sheets, classroom kits, advanced workshop for teachers & educators.

Royal Ontario Museum: Outreach Services, ROM, Royal Ontario Museum, 100 Queens Park, Toronto ON M5S 2C6 - 416/586-5681; Fax: 416/586-5832; E-mail: outreach@rom.on.ca; URL: www.rom.on.ca

Portable Starlab dome available for any location in Ontario.

Telus World of Science - Calgary: PO Box 2100, Station M, #73, Calgary AB T2P 2M5 - 403/268-8300; Fax: 403/237-0186; E-mail: discover@calgaryscience.ca; URL: www.calgaryscience.ca

Join "Seymour Sky" at the Planetarium dome, several programs, multimedia shows & kits available.

Telus World of Science - Edmonton: 11211 - 142 St., Edmonton AB T5M 4A1 - 780/451-3344; Fax: 780/455-5882; URL: www.edmontonscience.com

Mobile planetarium available. Gift shop, IMAX theatre, science programs & computer lab; observatory operated by RASC volunteers.

Winnipeg Planetarium: 190 Rupert Ave., Winnipeg MB R3B 0N2 - 204/956-2830; Fax: 204/942-3679; E-mail: info@manitobamuseum.ca; URL: www.manitobamuseum.ca/main

Science centre, museum & planetarium in one site; mobile planetarium.

Many of Canada's professional astronomers, & most of Canada's enthusiastic amateur astronomers are members of the Royal Astronomical Society of Canada (see index) which has 27 Centres across Canada. An extensive list of astronomy clubs in Canada has been published online by SkyNews and can be found at www.skynewsmagazine.com/pages/clubs.html. Many of these clubs have programs for the general public.

ECLIPSES AND TRANSITS IN 2011

In 2011, there will be six eclipses, four solar, and two lunar. Only one of the solar eclipses, and one of the lunar eclipses will be visible from North America.

1. A **partial eclipse** of the Sun on January 4, not visible from North America.

2. A **partial eclipse** of the Sun on June 1, visible from northern Canada.

3. A **total eclipse** of the Moon on June 15, not visible from North America.

4. A **partial eclipse** of the Sun on July 1, not visible from North America.

5. A **partial eclipse** of the Sun on November 25, not visible from North America.

6. A **total eclipse** of the Moon on December 10, visible from North America except the eastern part.

METEORS, METEORITES, AND METEOR SHOWERS

A *meteor* or "shooting star" appears momentarily in the sky when a particle from beyond the earth enters the earth's atmosphere at a high velocity. Most visible meteors are caused by particles smaller than a grape or marble, and these small particles are completely vaporized in the atmosphere at a height of about 80 km. A spectacular meteor, known as a *fire-ball,* is caused by a larger body which may fall to the earth's surface in one or more pieces. Particles seen thus to fall, or subsequently found by analysis to be of this nature, are called meteorites.

Meteorites may be divided into two main classes-the irons, which are almost pure nickel-iron, and the stones. Any freshly-fallen meteorite is characterized by a dark, smooth crust caused by the fusion of the outer part.

Meteors may be observed on any clear, moonless night at an average rate of about five an hour. At times *meteor showers* occur, when meteors are seen with much greater frequency and appear to radiate from a particular part of the sky which is called the *radiant.* This is an effect of perspective, the radiant being the vanishing point of the parallel tracks of the meteors. Meteor showers usually repeat themselves annually, and in some cases have been associated with the orbits of comets. When the earth passes through or near the orbit of a comet it can intercept the small particles (meteoroids) which cause meteors. The principal meteor showers for the northern hemisphere are listed below. The information is based on that in the annual *Observer's Handbook* of the Royal Astronomical Society of Canada.

The study of meteors and meteorites adds to our knowledge of the nature and origin of the solar system and also to our knowledge of the earth's outer atmosphere.

MAPS OF THE NIGHT SKY

The maps on the next six pages cover the northern sky. Stars are shown down to a magnitude of 4.5 or 5, i.e. those which are readily apparent to the unaided eye on a reasonably dark night.

The maps are drawn for 45°N latitude, but are useful for latitudes several degrees north or south of this. They show the hemisphere of sky visible to an observer at various times of the year. Because the aspect of the night sky changes continuously with both longitude and time, while time zones change discontinuously with both longitude and time of year, it is not possible to state simply when, in general, a particular observer will find that his or her sky fits exactly one of the six maps. The month indicated below each map is the time of year when the map will match the "late evening" sky. On any particular night, successive maps will represent the sky as it appears every four hours later. For example, at 2 or 3 am on a March night, the May map should be used. Just after dinner on a January night, the November map will be appropriate. The centre of each map is the zenith, the point directly overhead; the circumference is the horizon. To identify the stars, hold the map in front of you so that the part of the horizon which you are facing (west, for instance) is downward. (The four letters around the periphery of each map indicate compass directions.)

On the maps, stars forming the usual constellation patterns are linked by straight lines, constellation names being given in upper case letters. The names in lower case are those of first magnitude stars, except Algol and Mira which are famous variable stars, and Polaris which is near the north celestial pole. Small clusters of dots indicate the positions of bright star clusters, nebulae, or galaxies. Although a few of these are just visible to the naked eye, and most can be located in binoculars, a telesope is needed for good views of these objects. The pair of wavy, dotted lines indicates roughly the borders of the Milky Way. Small asterisks locate the directions of the galactic centre (GC), the north galactic pole (NGP), and the south galactic pole (SGP). Two dashed lines appear on each of the six maps. The one with the more dashes is the celestial equator. Tick marks along this indicate hours of right ascension, the odd hours being labelled. The line with fewer dashes is the ecliptic, the apparent annual path of the Sun across the heavens. Letters along this line indicate the approximate position of the Sun at the beginning of each month. Also located along the ecliptic are the vernal equinox (VE), summer solstice (SS), autumnal equinox (AE), and winter solstice (WS). Moon and the other eight planets are found near the ecliptic, but since their motions are not related in a simple way to our year, it is not feasible to show them on a general set of maps.

The text above, and the six star charts on the following pages, were prepared by Professor Roy L. Bishop, former editor of the annual *Observer's Handbook* of the Royal Astronomical Society of Canada (RASC). They are copyright RASC 1996. They are used here with the kind permission of Professor Bishop and the RASC.

AZIMUTH OF THE SUN AT RISING AND SETTING

Only twice a year, namely about March 21 and September 23, does the sun rise and set more or less exactly in the east and west respectively. It is of interest and sometimes of value to know the position of Sunrise and Sunset at other times. The table above tabulates these in degrees east of north and west of north for Sunrise and Sunset respectively for a selection of latitudes and dates. For latitudes and dates other than those tabulated take simple proportions.

STATUS OF PLUTO

In August 2006, the International Astronomical Union officially "demoted" Pluto from planet to dwarf planet, since it is much smaller than the other eight planets, and is only one of many such small bodies in the outer solar system.

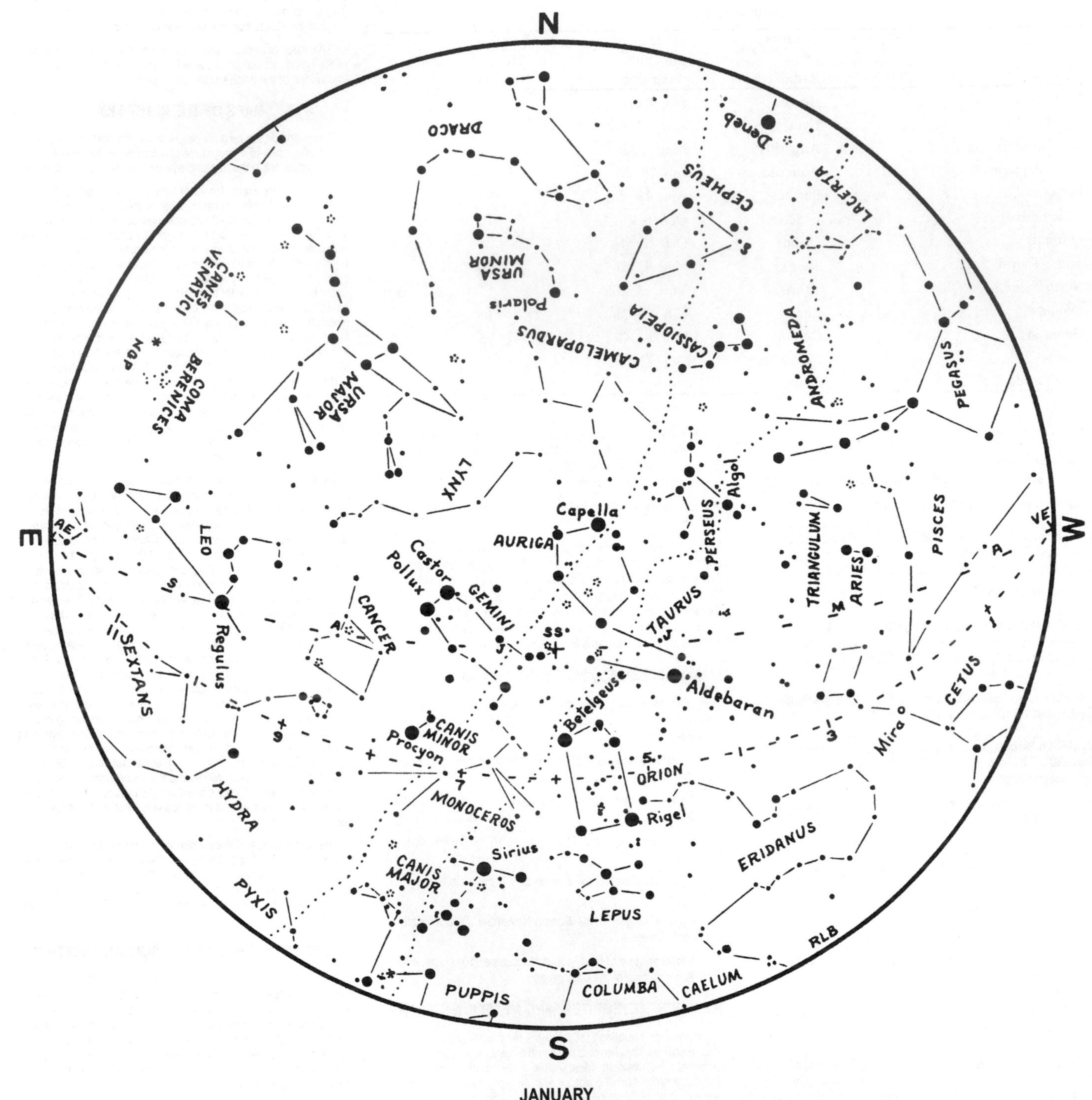

JANUARY

THE NAKED EYE PLANETS IN 2011

January

MERCURY is visible this month, low in the south-east, just before sunrise.

VENUS is a brillant object in the south-east, rising a few hours before sunrise.

MARS is not visible this month.

JUPITER, in Pisces, is visible in the south-west at sunset; it sets a few hours later. It passes just south of Uranus on the 2nd.

SATURN, in Virgo, rises around midnight, and is visible for the rest of the night. It is stationary on the 27th, then moves slowly westward, against the background stars.

February

MERCURY is visible with some difficulty until mid-month, very low in the south-east, just before sunrise.

VENUS is a brillant object in the south-east, just before sunrise.

MARS is not visible this month.

JUPITER, moving from Pisces to Cetus, is visible in the western sky at sunset; it sets a few hours later.

SATURN, in Virgo, rises shortly before midnight, and is visible for the rest of the night.

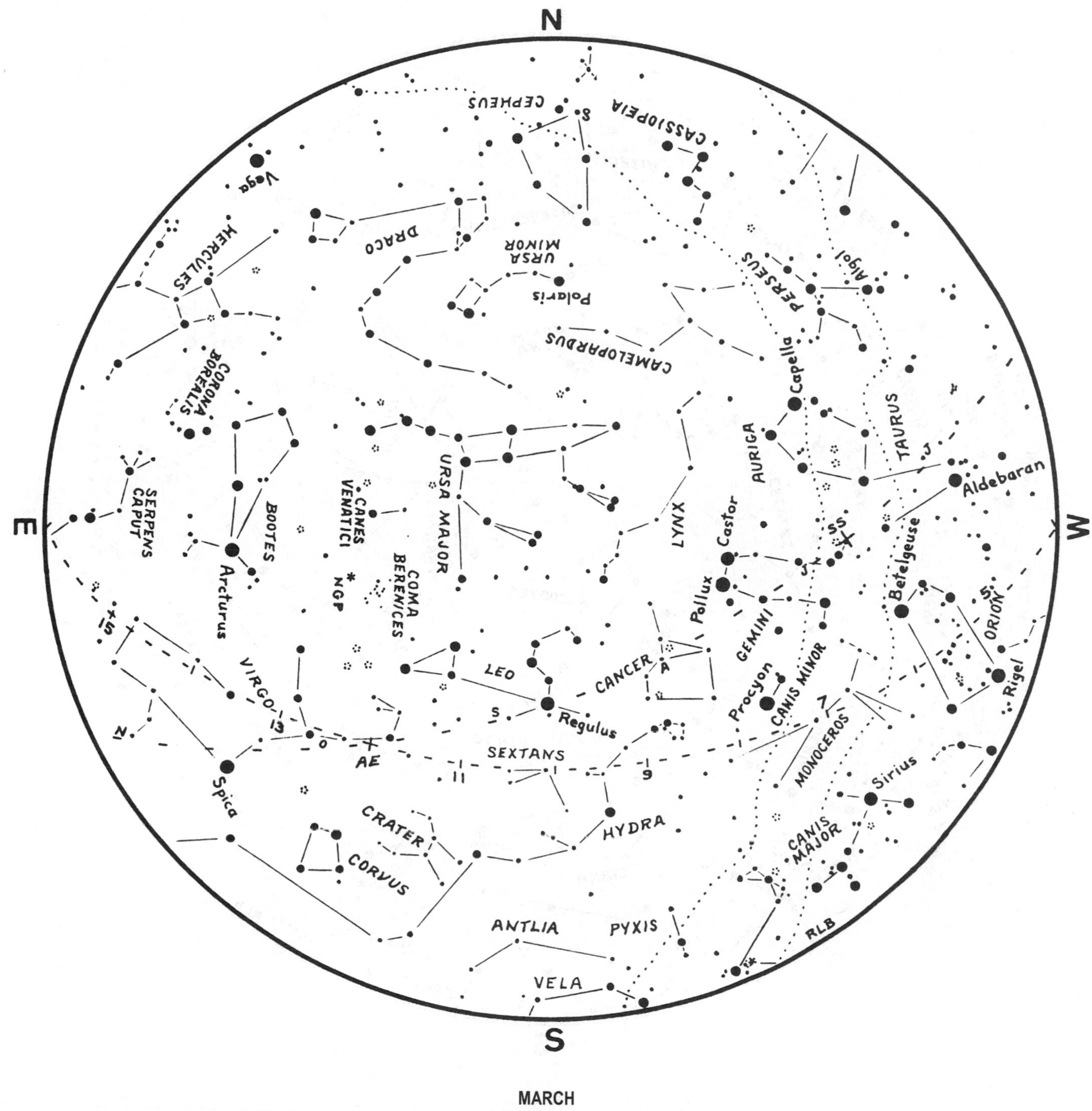

MARCH

THE NAKED EYE PLANETS IN 2011

March

MERCURY is visible by mid-month, in the west, just after sunset. It passes just north of Jupiter on the 16th.

VENUS is visible low in the south-east, just before sunrise. It passes just south of Neptune during the evening of the 26th.

MARS is not visible this month.

JUPITER, moving from Cetus to Pisces, is visible until mid-month, very low in the west at sunset; it sets soon afterwards. It passes just south of Mercury on the 16th. See also Mercury, above.

SATURN, in Virgo, rises shortly after sunset, and is visible for the rest of the night.

April

MERCURY is visible at the beginning of the month, low in the west, just after sunset; it is again visible with some difficulty by the end of the month, very low in the east, just before sunrise.

VENUS is visible, low in the south-east, just before sunrise. It passes just south of Uranus on the 22nd.

MARS, in Pisces, is visible with some difficulty in the eastern sky, just before sunrise.

JUPITER, in Pisces, may be visible by mid-month, very low in the east before sunrise. It is in conjunction with the Sun on the 6th.

SATURN, in Virgo, is visible low in the east at sunset, and sets around sunrise. It is opposite the sun during the evening of the 3rd.

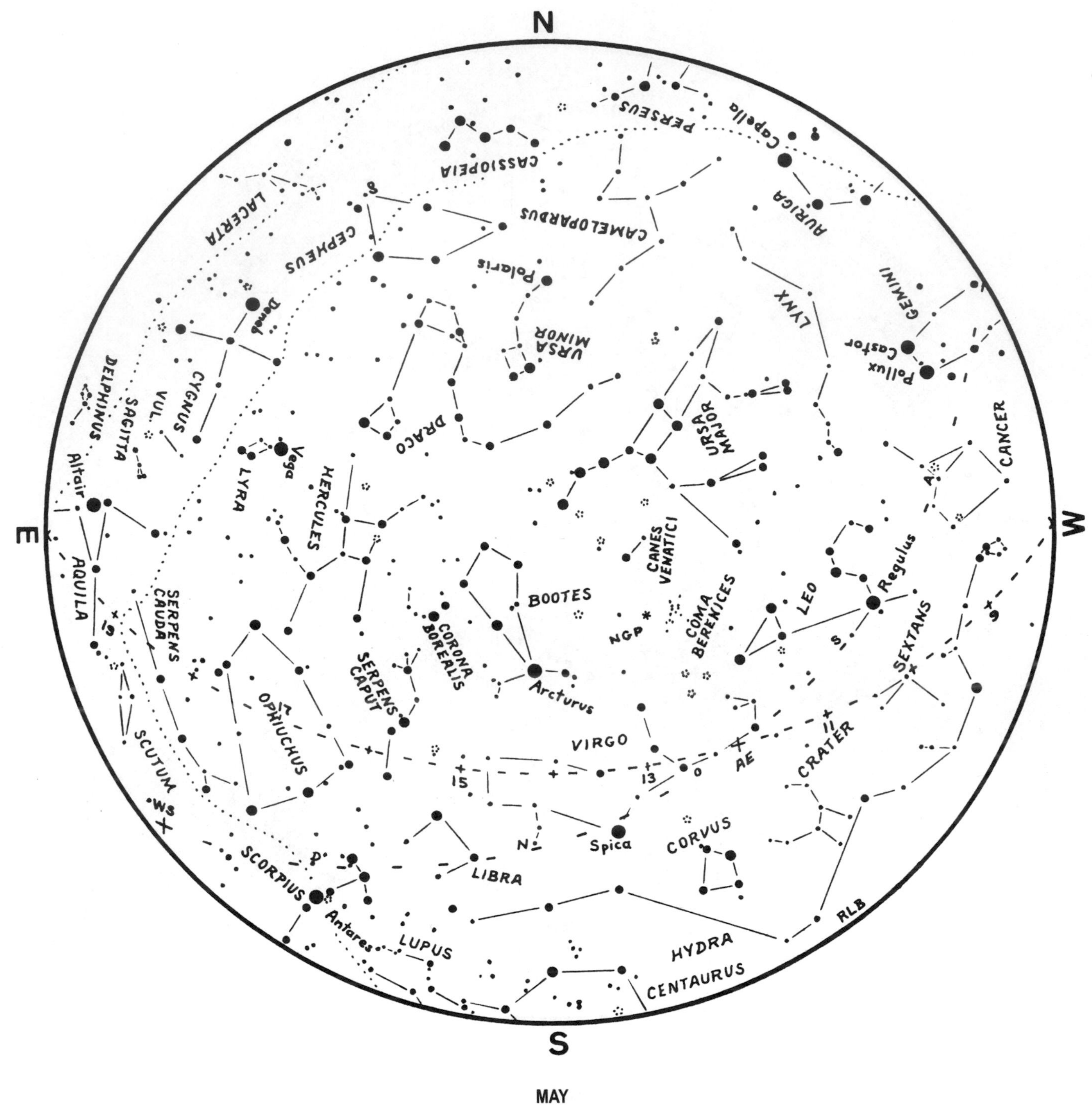

MAY

THE NAKED EYE PLANETS IN 2011

May

MERCURY is visible with some difficulty, very low in the east, just before sunrise. It passes just south of Jupiter on the 10th, and just south of Mars during the evening of the 19th.

VENUS is visible, low in the eastern sky, just before sunrise. It passes just south of Jupiter on the 11th, and just south of Mars on the 22nd.

MARS, moving from Pisces to Aries, is visible in the eastern sky, just before sunrise. It passes just north of Jupiter on the 11th, just north of Mercury during the evening of the 19th, and just north of Venus on the 22nd. See also Mercury and Venus, above.

JUPITER, in Pisces, it rises shortly before the sun, and is visible very low in the east at sunrise. It passes just south of Mars on the 1st, just north of Mercury on the 11th, and just north of Venus on the 11th. See also Mercury, Venus and Mars, above.

SATURN, in Virgo, is well up in the south-east at sunset, and sets a few hours before sunrise.

June

MERCURY may be visible with some difficulty at the beginning of the month, very low in the east, just before sunrise; it is again visible at the end of the month, low in the west, just after sunrise.

VENUS is visible, very low in the eastern sky, just before sunrise. It passes just south of Pollux on the 9th.

MARS, moving from Aries to Taurus, rises a few hours before sunrise, and is visible in the eastern sky.

JUPITER, moving from Pisces to Aries, rises a few hours before sunrise, and is visible in the eastern sky at sunrise.

SATURN, in Virgo, is well up in the southern sky at sunset, and is visible for half of the night. It is stationary during the night of the 13th, then resumes slow eastward motion, relative to the background stars.

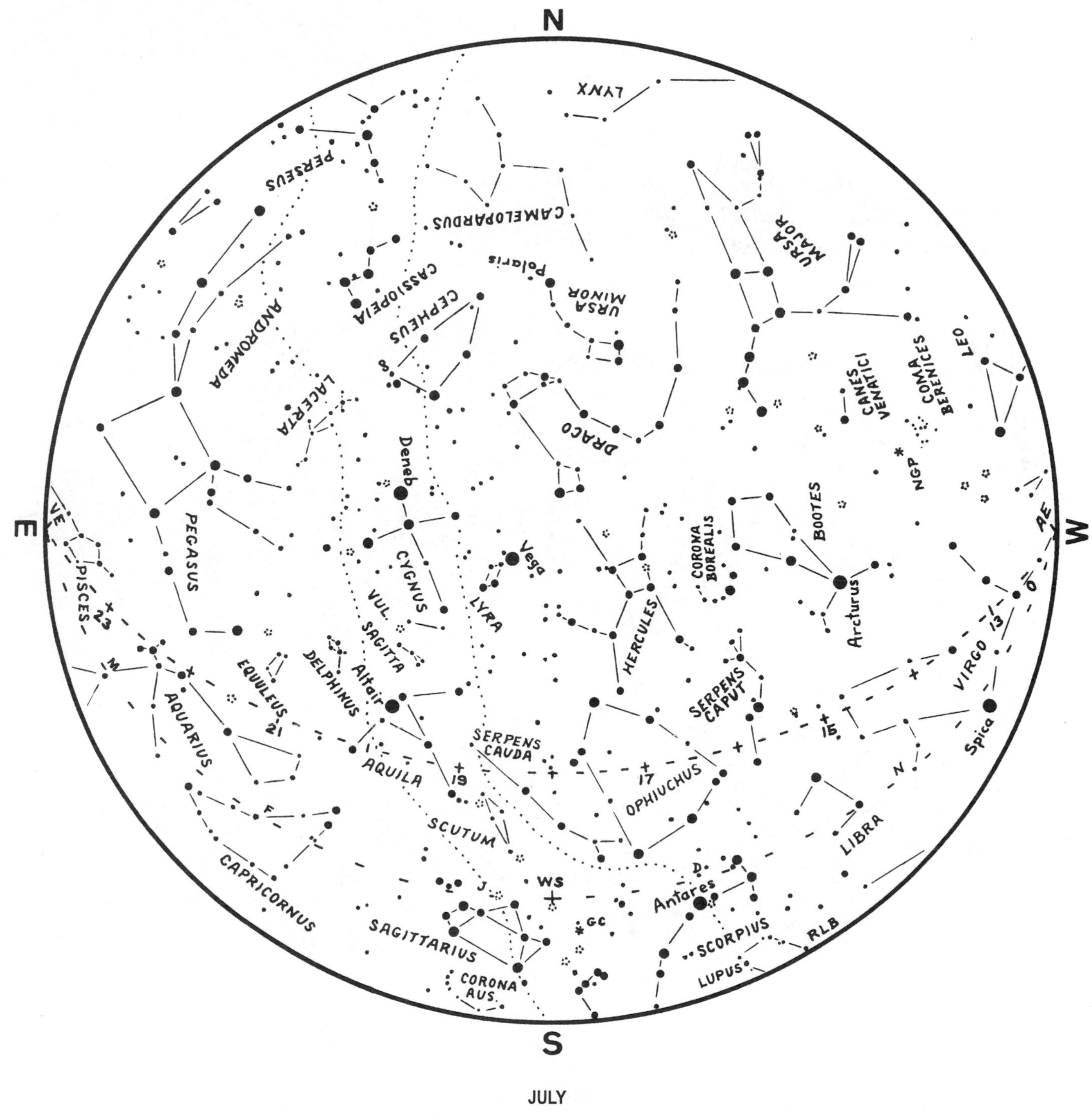

JULY

THE NAKED EYE PLANETS IN 2011

July

MERCURY is visible this month, low in the west, just after sunset.

VENUS is visible with some difficulty until mid-month, very low in the eastern sky, just before sunrise.

MARS, in Taurus, rises a few hours before sunrise, and is visible in the eastern sky.

JUPITER, in Aries, rises a few hours after midnight, and is visible high in the south-eastern at sunrise.

SATURN, in Virgo, is visible in the south-west at sunset; it sets around midnight.

August

MERCURY may be visible with some difficulty at the beginning of the month, very low in the west, just after sunset; it is again visible at the end of the month, low in the east, just before sunrise.

VENUS is not visible this month.

MARS, moving from Taurus to Gemini, rises a few hours before sunrise, and is visible high in the eastern sky by sunrise.

JUPITER, in Aries, rises around midnight, and is visible high in the southern sky at sunrise. It is stationary on the 30th, then moves slowly westward, against the background stars.

SATURN, in Virgo, is visible low in the west at sunset, and sets shortly afterwards.

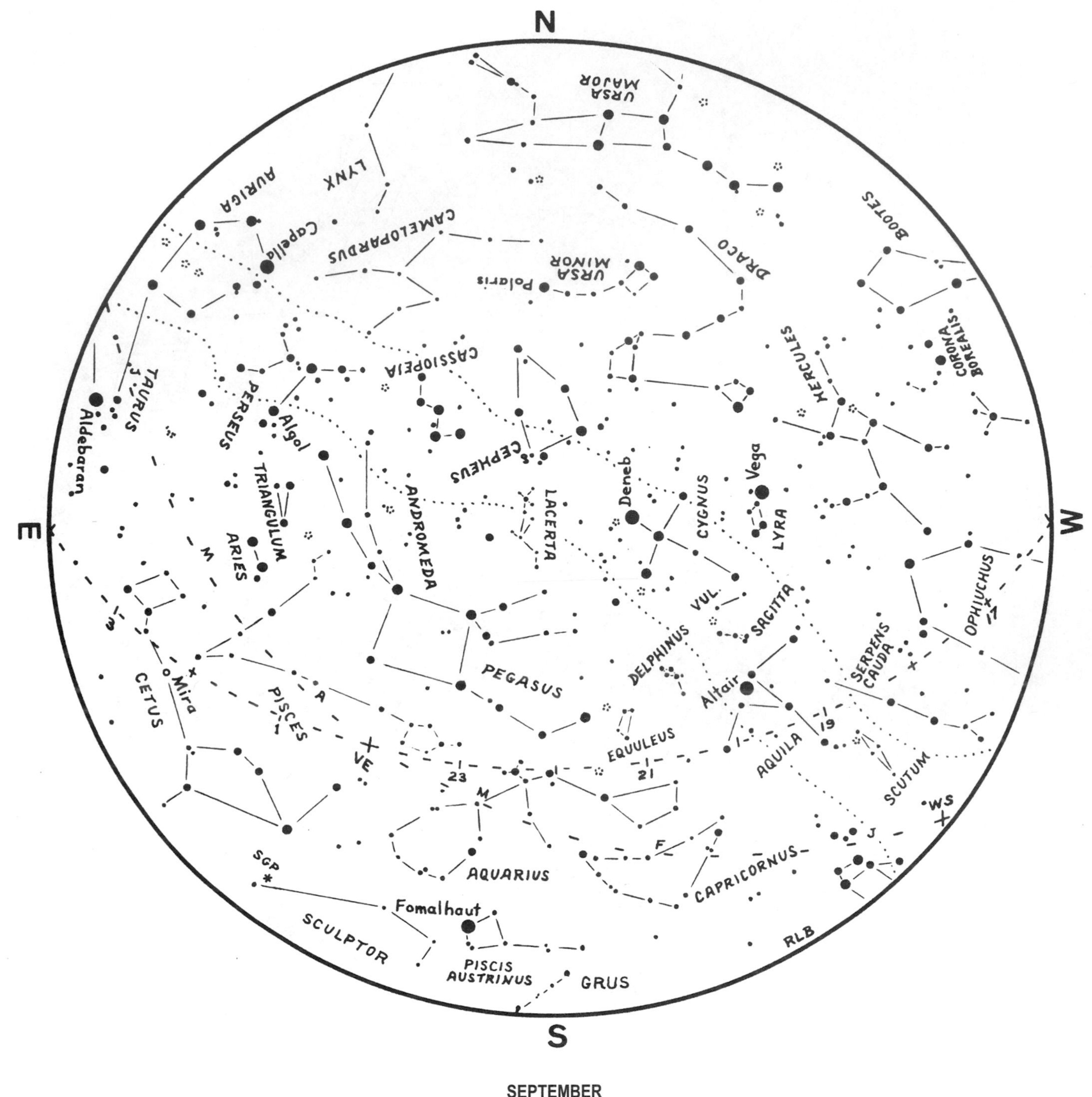

SEPTEMBER

THE NAKED EYE PLANETS IN 2011

September

MERCURY may be visible until mid-month, very low in the east, just before sunrise. It passes just north of Regulus during the evening of the 8th.

VENUS is visible with some difficulty by mid-month, very low in the west, just after sunset; it sets soon afterwards.

MARS, moving from Gemini to Cancer, rises a few hours after midnight, and is visible high in the south-east by sunrise.

JUPITER, in Aries, rises shortly before midnight, and is visible for most of the night.

SATURN, in Virgo, is visible until mid-month, very low in the west, at sunset; it sets soon afterwards.

October

MERCURY may be visible with some difficulty by mid-month, very low in the west, just after sunset.

VENUS is visible, very low in the western sky, just after sunset; it sets soon afterwards.

MARS, in Cancer, rises shortly after midnight, and is visible high in the southern sky at sunrise.

JUPITER, in Aries, rises a few hours after sunset, and is visible for most of the night. It is opposite the sun during the evening of the 28th.

SATURN, in Virgo, may be visible by the end of the month; it rises shortly before the sun. It is in conjunction with the sun on the 13th.

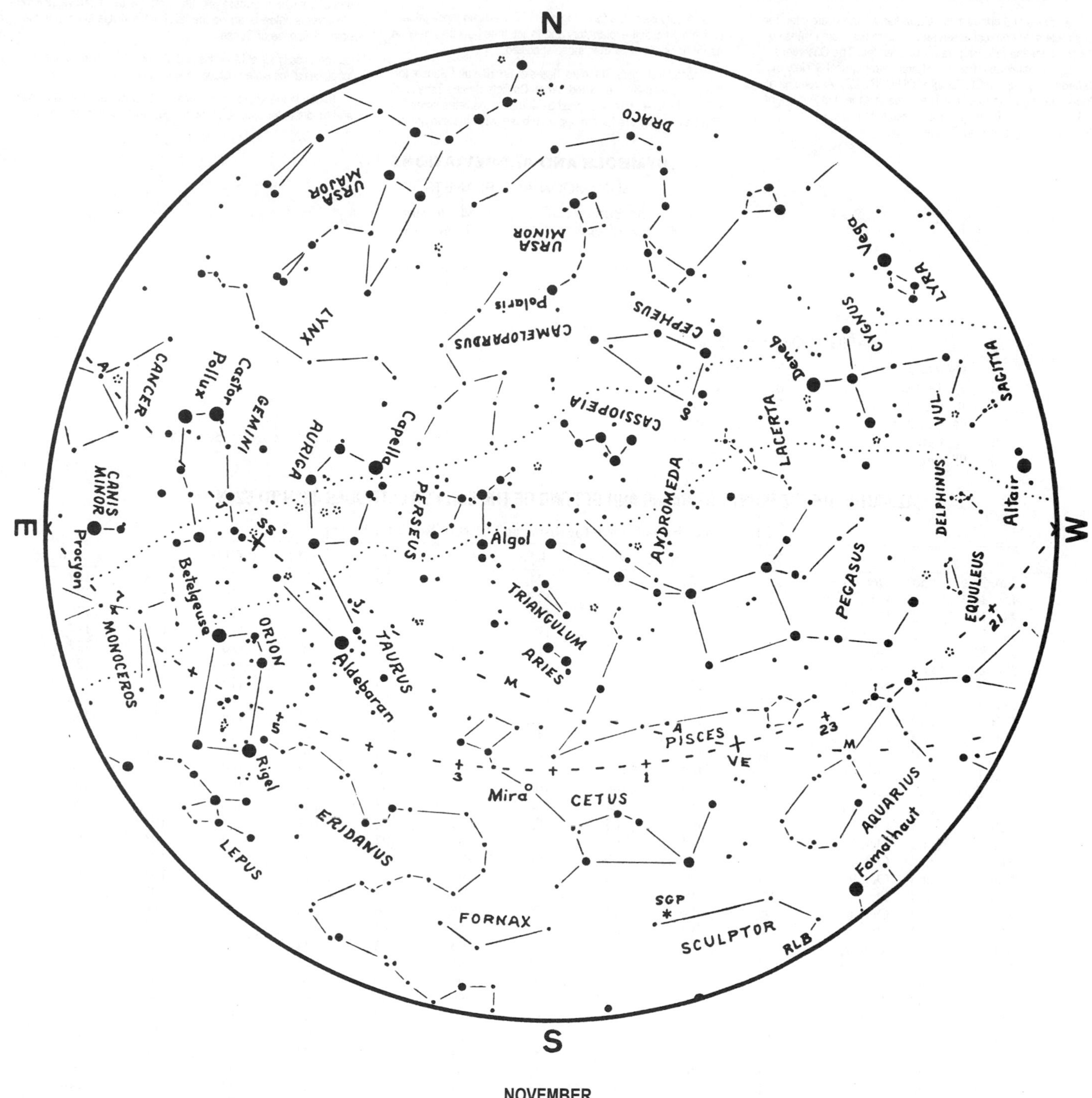

NOVEMBER

THE NAKED EYE PLANETS IN 2011

November

MERCURY may be visible with some difficulty this month, very low in the south-west, just after sunset. It passes north of Antares during the evening of the 9th.

VENUS is visible, very low in the south-west, just after sunset; it sets soon afterwards.

MARS, moving from Cancer to Leo, rises around midnight, and is visible high in the southern sky at sunrise. It passes just north of Regulus during the evening of the 4th.

JUPITER, in Aries, rises shortly after sunset, and is visible for most of the night; it sets shortly before sunrise.

SATURN, in Virgo, rises a few hours before the sun, and is low in the south-east at sunrise.

December

MERCURY is visible by mid-month, low in the south-east, just before sunrise.

VENUS is a brilliant object, low in the south-west, just after sunset; it sets a few hours later.

MARS, in Leo, rises around midnight, and is visible high in the southern sky at sunrise.

JUPITER, moving Aries to Pisces, is up in the eastern sky at sunset; it sets a few hours before sunrise. It is stationary on the 26th, then resumes slow eastward motion, against the background stars.

SATURN, in Virgo, rises a few hours before the sun, and is well up in the south at sunrise.

REFERENCES

The tables and charts in the Canadian Almanac are intended for simple astronomical observations. To make more extensive observations the following are recommended: The Observer's Handbook (obtainable from the Royal Astronomical Society of Canada, 136 Dupont St., Toronto, ON M5R 1V2); Astronomical Phenomena (obtainable from The Superintendent of Documents, U.S. Government Printing Office, Washington, D.C.).
See also "Suggestions for Further Reading".

NOTES ON THE ASTRONOMICAL TABLES

The purpose of the following notes is to explain those tables which are not self-explanatory and to illustrate how they may be used for places other than those specified.

These tables give Standard Times of Sunrise and Sunset for the four Canadian cities listed. When Daylight Saving Time is in effect, of course, one hour must be added to the listed times. The calculations are for the upper limb (edge) of the sun and for the astronomical (sea) horizon. Accordingly, the actual observation of Sunrise or Sunset will differ from the tabulated value if the observer is below or above the level of his visible horizon at the point of Sunrise or Sunset.

The listed times of Moonrise and Moonset have been calculated for places at the stated latitudes and for longitude 5 hours west.

To obtain the approximate times of Sunrise, Sunset, Moonrise and Moonset for other Canadian cities and towns proceed as in-

SYMBOLS AND ABBREVIATIONS

SUN, MOON AND PLANETS

☉	The Sun	♃	Jupiter
☾	The Moon	♄	Saturn
☿	Mercury	⛢	Uranus
♀	Venus	♆	Neptune
⊕	The Earth	♇	Pluto
♂	Mars		

SIGNS OF THE ZODIAC

1.	♈	Aries	7.	♎	Libra	N.	North	′	Minutes of Arc
2.	♉	Taurus	8.	♏	Scorpius	S.	South	″	Seconds of Arc
3.	♊	Gemini	9.	♐	Sagittarius	E.	East	h	Hours
4.	♋	Cancer	10.	♑	Capricornus	W.	West	m	Minutes of Time
5.	♌	Leo	11.	♒	Aquarius	°	Degrees	s	Seconds of Time
6.	♍	Virgo	12.	♓	Pisces				

AZIMUTHS OF THE POINTS OF RISING AND SETTING OF THE SUN FOR LATITUDES 43°N TO 52°N

In Degrees East of North for Rising and West of North for Setting

			43°N	44°N	45°N	46°N	47°N	48°N	49°N	50°N	51°N	52°N
Jan. 2	and	Dec. 11	122	123	124	124	125	126	127	127	128	129
Jan. 10	and	Dec. 3	121	121	122	123	123	124	125	126	127	127
Jan. 16	and	Nov. 27	119	120	120	121	122	122	123	124	125	126
Jan. 21	and	Nov. 22	118	118	119	120	120	121	121	122	123	124
Jan. 25	and	Nov. 17	116	117	117	118	119	119	120	120	121	122
Jan. 29	and	Nov. 14	115	115	116	116	117	118	118	119	119	120
Feb. 2	and	Nov. 10	114	114	114	115	115	116	116	117	118	118
Feb. 5	and	Nov. 6	112	113	113	113	114	114	115	115	116	116
Feb. 9	and	Nov. 3	111	111	111	112	112	113	113	114	114	115
Feb. 12	and	Oct. 31	109	110	110	110	111	111	112	112	113	113
Feb. 15	and	Oct. 28	108	108	109	109	109	110	110	110	111	111
Feb. 18	and	Oct. 25	107	107	107	107	108	108	108	109	109	110
Feb. 20	and	Oct. 22	105	105	106	106	106	106	107	107	108	108
Feb. 23	and	Oct. 19	104	104	104	104	105	105	105	106	106	106
Feb. 26	and	Oct. 17	102	103	103	103	103	104	104	104	104	105
Mar. 1	and	Oct. 14	101	101	101	102	102	102	102	102	103	103
Mar. 3	and	Oct. 11	100	100	100	100	100	100	101	101	101	101
Mar. 6	and	Oct. 9	98	98	98	99	99	99	99	99	100	100
Mar. 8	and	Oct. 6	97	97	97	97	97	97	98	98	98	98
Mar. 11	and	Oct. 4	95	96	96	96	96	96	96	96	96	96
Mar. 13	and	Oct. 1	94	94	94	94	94	94	95	95	95	95
Mar. 16	and	Sept. 28	93	93	93	93	93	93	93	93	93	93
Mar. 18	and	Sept. 26	91	91	91	91	91	92	92	92	92	92
Mar. 21	and	Sept. 23	90	90	90	90	90	90	90	90	90	90
Mar. 23	and	Sept. 21	89	89	89	89	89	88	88	88	88	88
Mar. 26	and	Sept. 18	87	87	87	87	87	87	87	87	87	87
Mar. 28	and	Sept. 16	86	86	86	86	86	86	85	85	85	85
Mar. 31	and	Sept. 13	85	84	84	84	84	84	84	84	84	84
Apr. 3	and	Sept. 10	83	83	83	83	83	83	82	82	82	82
Apr. 5	and	Sept. 8	82	82	82	81	81	81	81	81	80	80
Apr. 8	and	Sept. 5	80	80	80	80	80	80	79	79	79	79
Apr. 11	and	Sept. 2	79	79	79	78	78	78	78	78	77	77
Apr. 13	and	Aug. 30	78	77	77	77	77	76	76	76	76	75
Apr. 16	and	Aug. 28	76	76	76	76	75	75	75	74	74	74
Apr. 19	and	Aug. 25	75	75	74	74	74	73	73	73	72	72
Apr. 22	and	Aug. 22	73	73	73	73	72	72	72	71	71	70
Apr. 25	and	Aug. 19	72	72	71	71	71	70	70	70	69	69
Apr. 28	and	Aug. 16	71	70	70	70	69	69	68	68	67	67
May 1	and	Aug. 12	69	69	69	68	68	67	67	66	66	65
May 5	and	Aug. 9	68	67	67	67	66	66	65	65	64	63
May 8	and	Aug. 5	66	66	66	65	65	64	64	63	62	62
May 12	and	Aug. 2	65	65	64	64	63	62	62	61	61	60
May 16	and	July 28	64	63	63	62	61	61	60	60	59	58
May 21	and	June 24	62	62	61	60	60	59	59	58	57	56
May 26	and	June 19	61	60	60	59	58	58	57	56	55	54
June 1	and	July 12	59	59	58	57	57	56	55	54	53	53
June 10	and	July 3	58	57	56	56	55	54	53	53	52	51

dicated in the table on page 1-6. The errors for Sunrise and Sunset by this approximate method will seldom exceed 10 minutes in winter and summer or 4 minutes in spring and fall, and for Moonrise and Moonset they will seldom exceed 15 minutes.

The tables have been calculated using a computer program written by Duy Cuong Nguyen based on modified algorithms from Astronomical Algorithms (second edition), by Jean Meeus (Willmann-Bell, 1999).

SUGGESTIONS FOR FURTHER READING

There are many excellent astronomy books and materials. Here are some; the books are ones with a Canadian flavour.

Astronomical Society of the Pacific, 390 Ashton Ave., San Francisco CA USA 94112; URL: www.astrosociety.org. Excellent source of astronomical teaching resources, and other useful material; catalogue available. Also publish a free quarterly teachers' newsletter (available on-line).

Astronomy, PO Box 1612, Waukesha WI USA 53187; URL: www.astronomy.com. Popular non-technical monthly magazine for general astronomy readers.

The Backyard Astronomer's Guide, by Terence Dickinson & Alan Dyer. 2nd edition, Camden House Publishing, 2002. The best guide to equipment & techniques.

The Beginner's Observing Guide, by Leo Enright. Royal Astronomical Society of Canada, 136 Dupont St., Toronto ON M5R 1V2. A simple but serious introduction to the night sky. (5th edition: 2005-2010)

The Cold Light of Dawn, by Richard Jarrell. University of Toronto Press, 1988. An authoritative and comprehensive history of Canadian astronomy.

Exploring the Night Sky, by Terence Dickinson. Camden House Publishing, 1987. An award-winning guide, especially for young people.

Looking Up, by Peter Broughton. Dundurn Press, 1993. A history of the Royal Astronomical Society of Canada, illustrated.

Nightwatch, by Terence Dickinson. Camden House Publishing, (3rd revised edition, 1998). Excellent introduction to the night sky.

Observer's Handbook, edited by Patrick Kelly. Royal Astronomical Society of Canada, 136 Dupont St., Toronto ON M5R 1V2. Annual guide to sky phenomena & other astronomical information.

Sky Atlas 2000.0, by Wil Tirion. Sky Publishing. A popular sky atlas for amateur astronomers.

Sky & Telescope, PO Box 9111, Belmont MA USA 02178-9111; URL: skyandtelescope.com. A popular monthly magazine for amateur astronomers.

SkyNews. PO Box 1613, Belleville, ON K8N 9Z9; URL: www.skynews.ca. General astronomy from a Canadian perspective.

SkyWays, by Mary Lou Whitehorne. Royal Astronomical Society of Canada, 2003 (also available in French). A guide for Canadian schoolteachers.

Summer Stargazing, by Terence Dickinson. Firefly Books, 1996. A practical, user-friendly guide.

The Universe and Beyond, by Terence Dickinson, 4th Edition, Firefly Books, 2004. Excellent general book on Astronomy.

The Universe at your Fingertips, and More Universe at Your Fingertips, edited by Andrew Fraknoi et al. Astronomical Society of the Pacific, 390 Ashton Avenue, San Francisco CA USA 94112. An excellent collection of teaching activities & resources.

The Universe on a T-Shirt, by Dan Falk, Arcade Publishing, 2005 (paperback). An excellent short introduction to our understanding of the universe.

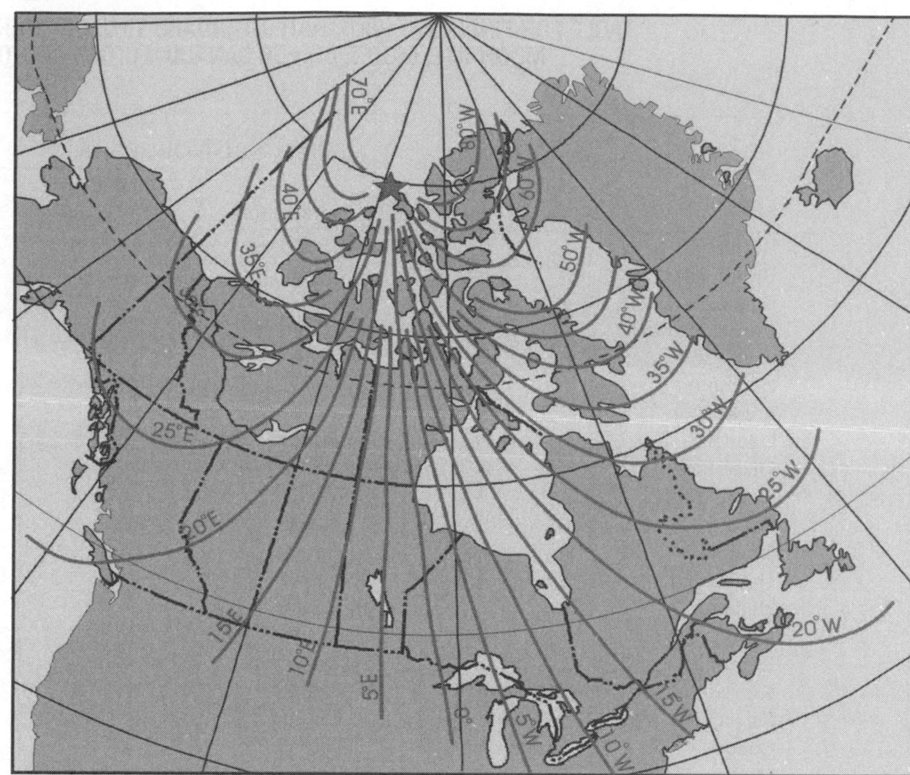

This chart of magnetic declination is © Natural Resources Canada, and was kindly provided by Dr. Larry Newitt, National Geomagnetism Program, Geological Survey of Canada, Natural Resources Canada.

CANADIAN ASTRONOMY WEB SITES

Most astronomical institutions and many of the branches of the Royal Astronomical Society of Canada, have sites on the World Wide Web. They can be accessed from the following key sites:

- Canadian Astronomical Society: www.casca.ca
- Canadian Astronomy Education Website: www.cascaeducation.ca
- Canadian Space Agency: www.space.gc.ca
- Department of Astronomy and Astrophysics, University of Toronto: www.astro.utoronto.ca/home.html
- Herzberg Institute of Astrophysics: www.hia-iha.nrc-cnrc.gc.ca
- National Research Council Astronomy and Space Education: www.nrc-cnrc.gc.ca/education/skies/canadianskies_e.html
- Royal Astronomical Society of Canada: www.rasc.ca. Local branches of the RASC can be accessed through this site.

CHART OF MAGNETIC DECLINATION

A compass needle, even when unaffected by extraneous magnetic fields, does not in general point due north. The amount and direction by which its direction differs from true north is called magnetic declination or variation. The declination varies with the position of the observer and also varies slowly with time. The above chart gives the values of declination over Canada as of 2000. The chart is (c) Natural Resources Canada, and was kindly provided by Dr. Larry Newitt, National Geomagnetism Program, Geological Survey of Canada, Natural Resources Canada.

Example: What is the direction of the compass needle at the southern tip of Lake Manitoba?

That location is on the 5° east line; the declination is 5° east; the compass needle points 5° east of the true north.

For more information, see: http://gsc.nrcan.gc.ca/geomag; on the page http://geomag.nrcan.gc.ca/apps/mdcal-eng.php, you can do an on-line calculation of the magnetic declination for any place at any time.

PROMINENT CANADIAN SCIENTISTS

John F. Allen

Working with Pyotr Leonidovich Kapitsa and Don Misener, Allen discovered the superfluid phase of matter in 1937 at the Royal Society Mond Laboratory in Cambridge, England. A state achieved by a few liquids, such as helium, at extreme temperature where they become able to flow without friction, superfluids are used in high-precision devices, such as gyroscopes, which allow the measurement of some theoretically predicted gravitational effects. Allen along with Harry Jones also discovered the "fountain effect," in which superfluid helium flows up a tube and shoots into the air upon being exposed to a small heat source (the heat source in the original experiment was a flashlight that they were using to look at the apparatus). Allen was born in Winnipeg in 1908 and was professor of physics at St Andrews University, Scotland, from 1947 to 1978, and then emeritus professor until his death in 2001.

Sidney Altman

Born in 1939 in Montreal, the molecular biologist received a Nobel Prize in Chemistry in 1989 for his work with Thomas R. Cech on the catalytic properties of RNA. Their discovery, that ribonucleic acid in living cells is not only a molecule of heredity but also can function as a biocatalyst, affects fundamental aspects of the molecular basis of life. Virtually all chemical reactions taking place in a living cell require catalysts. Such biocatalysts are called enzymes and are determined by hereditary genes. Until the findings of Altman and Cech became known, all enzymes were considered to be proteins. The discovery of catalytic RNA will provide a new tool for gene technology, with potential to create defenses against viral infections. Altman is currently the Sterling Professor of Molecular, Cellular, and Developmental Biology and Chemistry at Yale University.

Frederick G. Banting

A doctor of orthopedic medicine and a decorated World War I veteran, Banting received a Nobel Prize in Medicine in 1923 for his discovery of insulin, a hormone that controls the metabolism of sugar. Early in his medical career, Banting became interested in diabetes, caused by a lack of insulin secreted by the pancreas. Before Banting's work, attempts to supply the missing insulin by feeding patients with fresh pancreas, or extracts of it, had failed. While working with his assistant Charles Best, Banting discovered how to extract insulin from the pancreas before it destroyed itself, thus birthing the first treatment for diabetes suffers. The Banting and Best Diabetes Centre at the University of Toronto continues the work of the two doctors. The cause of diabetes remains a mystery. Banting was killed in an airplane disaster in 1941 in Newfoundland.

Continued on page A-51

TABLE FOR FINDING APPROXIMATE STANDARD TIME OF SUNRISE, SUNSET, MOONRISE, MOONSET, FOR CANADIAN CITIES AND TOWNS

PLACE	Time Zone	FOR SUNRISE OR SUNSET: Take value for	FOR SUNRISE OR SUNSET: and apply correction	FOR MOONRISE OR MOONSET: Take value for	FOR MOONRISE OR MOONSET: and apply correction
Brandon	C	Winnipeg	+11*m*	50°	+40*m*
Brantford	E	Toronto	+ 4	45	+21
Calgary	M	Winnipeg	+ 8	50	+36
Charlottetown	A	Ottawa	+10	45	+13
Cornwall	E	Ottawa	- 4	45	- 1
Edmonton	M	Winnipeg	+ 6	50	+34
Fredericton	A	Ottawa	+24	45	+27
Gander	N	Vancouver	- 4	50	+ 8
Glace Bay	A	Ottawa	- 3	45	0
Goose Bay	A	Winnipeg	-26	50	- 2
Granby	E	Ottawa	-12	45	- 9
Guelph	E	Toronto	+ 3	45	+21
Halifax	A	Ottawa	+11	45	+14
Hamilton	E	Toronto	+ 2	45	+21
Hull	E	Ottawa	0	45	+ 3
Kapuskasing	E	Vancouver	+17	50	+30
Kingston	E	Toronto	-12	45	+ 6
Kitchener	E	Toronto	+ 4	45	+22
London	E	Toronto	+ 8	45	+25
Medicine Hat	M	Winnipeg	- 4	50	+22
Moncton	A	Ottawa	+16	45	+19
Montréal	E	Ottawa	- 9	45	- 6
Moosonee	E	Winnipeg	- 6	50	+23
Moose Jaw	C	Winnipeg	+34	50	+62
Niagara Falls	E	Toronto	- 1	45	+16
North Bay	E	Ottawa	+14	45	+18
Ottawa	E	Ottawa	0	45	+ 3
Owen Sound	E	Ottawa	+21	45	+24
Penticton	P	Vancouver	-14	50	- 2
Peterborough	E	Toronto	- 4	45	+13
Prince Albert	C	Winnipeg	+36	50	+64
Prince Rupert	P	Winnipeg	+12	50	+40
Québec	E	Ottawa	-18	45	-15
Regina	C	Winnipeg	+30	50	+58
St. Catharines	E	Toronto	0	45	+17
St. Hyacinthe	E	Ottawa	-11	45	- 8
Saint John, NB	A	Ottawa	+22	45	+24
St. John's, NL	N	Vancouver	-11	50	+ 1
Sarnia	E	Toronto	+12	45	+30
Saskatoon	C	Winnipeg	+38	50	+66
Sault Ste. Marie	E	Ottawa	+34	45	+37
Shawinigan	E	Ottawa	-12	45	- 9
Sherbrooke	E	Ottawa	-14	45	-12
Stratford	E	Toronto	+ 6	45	+24
Sudbury	E	Ottawa	+21	45	+24
Sydney	A	Ottawa	- 2	45	+ 1
The Pas	C	Winnipeg	+16	50	+44
Trois-Rivières	E	Ottawa	-12	45	- 9
Thunder Bay	E	Vancouver	+44	50	+57
Timmins	E	Vancouver	+13	50	+25
Toronto	E	Toronto	0	45	+18
Trail	P	Vancouver	-22	50	-10
Truro	A	Ottawa	+10	45	+13
Vancouver	P	Vancouver	0	50	+12
Victoria	P	Vancouver	+2	50	+14
Windsor	E	Toronto	+14	45	+32
Winnipeg	C	Winnipeg	0	50	+28

JANUARY 2011

New Moon	4 d	4 h	3 m	Moon's Phases E.S.T.
First Quarter	12 d	6 h	31 m	
Full Moon	19 d	16 h	21 m	
Last Quarter	26 d	7 h	57 m	

Day of Yr.	Day of Mo.	Day of Wk.	SUNRISE AND SUNSET: Ottawa E.S.T. Rises		Sets		Toronto E.S.T. Rises		Sets		Winnipeg C.S.T. Rises		Sets		Vancouver P.S.T. Rises		Sets		MOONRISE AND MOONSET Local Mean Time: Lat. 45° Rises		Sets		Lat. 50° Rises		Sets		Day of Wk.	Day of Mo.
			h	m	h	m	h	m	h	m	h	m	h	m	h	m	h	m	h	m	h	m	h	m	h	m		
1	1	Sat	7	43	16	30	7	51	16	51	8	27	16	38	8	7	16	25	5	11	14	1	5	34	13	37	Sat	1
2	2	Sun	7	43	16	31	7	51	16	52	8	27	16	39	8	7	16	26	6	12	14	56	6	36	14	33	Sun	2
3	3	Mon	7	43	16	32	7	51	16	53	8	26	16	40	8	7	16	27	7	3	15	58	7	25	15	36	Mon	3
4	4	Tue	7	43	16	33	7	51	16	54	8	26	16	41	8	7	16	28	7	45	17	4	8	5	16	45	Tue	4
5	5	Wed	7	43	16	34	7	51	16	55	8	26	16	42	8	7	16	29	8	19	18	10	8	35	17	55	Wed	5
6	6	Thu	7	42	16	35	7	51	16	56	8	26	16	44	8	7	16	30	8	47	19	15	8	59	19	5	Thu	6
7	7	Fri	7	42	16	36	7	51	16	57	8	25	16	45	8	6	16	31	9	11	20	19	9	19	20	12	Fri	7
8	8	Sat	7	42	16	37	7	51	16	58	8	25	16	46	8	6	16	33	9	33	21	21	9	37	21	18	Sat	8
9	9	Sun	7	42	16	39	7	51	16	59	8	25	16	47	8	6	16	34	9	53	22	22	9	53	22	24	Sun	9
10	10	Mon	7	41	16	40	7	50	17	0	8	24	16	49	8	5	16	35	10	14	23	23	10	10	23	29	Mon	10
11	11	Tue	7	41	16	41	7	50	17	1	8	24	16	50	8	5	16	37	10	35	--	--	10	27	--	--	Tue	11
12	12	Wed	7	41	16	42	7	50	17	3	8	23	16	51	8	4	16	38	10	58	0	25	10	47	0	35	Wed	12
13	13	Thu	7	40	16	43	7	49	17	4	8	22	16	53	8	3	16	39	11	25	1	28	11	10	1	42	Thu	13
14	14	Fri	7	40	16	45	7	49	17	5	8	22	16	54	8	3	16	41	11	58	2	33	11	39	2	51	Fri	14
15	15	Sat	7	39	16	46	7	48	17	6	8	21	16	56	8	2	16	42	12	38	3	37	12	17	3	59	Sat	15
16	16	Sun	7	38	16	47	7	48	17	7	8	20	16	57	8	1	16	44	13	29	4	40	13	5	5	3	Sun	16
17	17	Mon	7	38	16	48	7	47	17	9	8	19	16	59	8	0	16	45	14	29	5	37	14	6	6	0	Mon	17
18	18	Tue	7	37	16	50	7	47	17	10	8	18	17	0	8	0	16	46	15	39	6	27	15	19	6	48	Tue	18
19	19	Wed	7	36	16	51	7	46	17	11	8	18	17	2	7	59	16	48	16	56	7	9	16	40	7	26	Wed	19
20	20	Thu	7	36	16	52	7	45	17	12	8	17	17	3	7	58	16	50	18	15	7	45	18	4	7	58	Thu	20
21	21	Fri	7	35	16	54	7	45	17	14	8	16	17	5	7	57	16	51	19	34	8	16	19	28	8	23	Fri	21
22	22	Sat	7	34	16	55	7	44	17	15	8	15	17	6	7	56	16	53	20	52	8	43	20	52	8	46	Sat	22
23	23	Sun	7	33	16	57	7	43	17	16	8	13	17	8	7	55	16	54	22	10	9	9	22	14	9	7	Sun	23
24	24	Mon	7	32	16	58	7	42	17	18	8	12	17	10	7	54	16	56	23	26	9	36	23	36	9	29	Mon	24
25	25	Tue	7	31	16	59	7	41	17	19	8	11	17	11	7	53	16	57	--	--	10	4	--	--	9	53	Tue	25
26	26	Wed	7	30	17	1	7	41	17	20	8	10	17	13	7	51	16	59	0	42	10	36	0	56	10	20	Wed	26
27	27	Thu	7	29	17	2	7	40	17	22	8	9	17	15	7	50	17	1	1	55	11	14	2	14	10	54	Thu	27
28	28	Fri	7	28	17	4	7	39	17	23	8	7	17	16	7	49	17	2	3	4	11	58	3	26	11	35	Fri	28
29	29	Sat	7	27	17	5	7	38	17	24	8	6	17	18	7	48	17	4	4	6	12	50	4	29	12	26	Sat	29
30	30	Sun	7	26	17	6	7	37	17	26	8	5	17	20	7	46	17	6	4	59	13	49	5	22	13	26	Sun	30
31	31	Mon	7	25	17	8	7	36	17	27	8	3	17	21	7	45	17	7	5	43	14	52	6	4	14	32	Mon	31

FEBRUARY 2011

New Moon	2 d	21 h	31 m	Moon's Phases E.S.T.
First Quarter	11 d	2 h	18 m	
Full Moon	18 d	3 h	36 m	
Last Quarter	24 d	18 d	26 m	

Day of Yr.	Day of Mo.	Day of Wk.	SUNRISE AND SUNSET: Ottawa E.S.T. Rises		Sets		Toronto E.S.T. Rises		Sets		Winnipeg C.S.T. Rises		Sets		Vancouver P.S.T. Rises		Sets		MOONRISE AND MOONSET Local Mean Time: Lat. 45° Rises		Sets		Lat. 50° Rises		Sets		Day of Wk.	Day of Mo.
			h	m	h	m	h	m	h	m	h	m	h	m	h	m	h	m	h	m	h	m	h	m	h	m		
32	1	Tue	7	24	17	9	7	35	17	28	8	2	17	23	7	44	17	9	6	20	15	57	6	37	15	41	Tue	1
33	2	Wed	7	23	17	11	7	33	17	30	8	1	17	25	7	42	17	11	6	50	17	3	7	3	16	50	Wed	2
34	3	Thu	7	22	17	12	7	32	17	31	7	59	17	26	7	41	17	12	7	15	18	6	7	25	17	59	Thu	3
35	4	Fri	7	20	17	14	7	31	17	32	7	58	17	28	7	39	17	14	7	38	19	9	7	43	19	5	Fri	4
36	5	Sat	7	19	17	15	7	30	17	34	7	56	17	30	7	38	17	16	7	58	20	11	8	0	20	11	Sat	5
37	6	Sun	7	18	17	17	7	29	17	35	7	55	17	32	7	36	17	17	8	19	21	12	8	17	21	16	Sun	6
38	7	Mon	7	16	17	18	7	28	17	37	7	53	17	33	7	35	17	19	8	39	22	13	8	34	22	21	Mon	7
39	8	Tue	7	15	17	20	7	26	17	38	7	51	17	35	7	33	17	21	9	2	23	15	8	52	23	27	Tue	8
40	9	Wed	7	14	17	21	7	25	17	39	7	50	17	37	7	32	17	22	9	27	--	--	9	13	--	--	Wed	9
41	10	Thu	7	12	17	23	7	24	17	41	7	48	17	38	7	30	17	24	9	57	0	18	9	39	0	34	Thu	10
42	11	Fri	7	11	17	24	7	22	17	42	7	46	17	40	7	28	17	26	10	33	1	21	10	12	1	41	Fri	11
43	12	Sat	7	9	17	25	7	21	17	43	7	45	17	42	7	27	17	27	11	17	2	23	10	54	2	45	Sat	12
44	13	Sun	7	8	17	27	7	20	17	45	7	43	17	44	7	25	17	29	12	11	3	21	11	48	3	44	Sun	13
45	14	Mon	7	6	17	28	7	18	17	46	7	41	17	45	7	23	17	31	13	15	4	14	12	53	4	36	Mon	14
46	15	Tue	7	5	17	30	7	17	17	47	7	39	17	47	7	21	17	32	14	27	4	59	14	9	5	18	Tue	15
47	16	Wed	7	3	17	31	7	15	17	49	7	37	17	49	7	20	17	34	15	44	5	38	15	31	5	53	Wed	16
48	17	Thu	7	2	17	33	7	14	17	50	7	36	17	50	7	18	17	36	17	4	6	12	16	56	6	22	Thu	17
49	18	Fri	7	0	17	34	7	12	17	52	7	34	17	52	7	16	17	37	18	25	6	41	18	22	6	47	Fri	18
50	19	Sat	6	59	17	35	7	11	17	53	7	32	17	54	7	14	17	39	19	46	7	9	19	48	7	10	Sat	19
51	20	Sun	6	57	17	37	7	9	17	54	7	30	17	56	7	12	17	41	21	6	7	37	21	13	7	32	Sun	20
52	21	Mon	6	55	17	38	7	8	17	56	7	28	17	57	7	11	17	42	22	25	8	5	22	37	7	56	Mon	21
53	22	Tue	6	54	17	40	7	6	17	57	7	26	17	59	7	9	17	44	23	41	8	37	23	59	8	23	Tue	22
54	23	Wed	6	52	17	41	7	5	17	58	7	24	18	1	7	7	17	46	--	--	9	14	--	--	8	56	Wed	23
55	24	Thu	6	50	17	43	7	3	17	59	7	22	18	2	7	5	17	47	0	54	9	57	1	15	9	35	Thu	24
56	25	Fri	6	49	17	44	7	1	18	1	7	20	18	4	7	3	17	49	1	59	10	47	2	22	10	24	Fri	25
57	26	Sat	6	47	17	45	7	0	18	2	7	18	18	6	7	1	17	50	2	55	11	44	3	19	11	21	Sat	26
58	27	Sun	6	45	17	47	6	58	18	3	7	16	18	7	6	59	17	52	3	42	12	46	4	4	12	25	Sun	27
59	28	Mon	6	43	17	48	6	56	18	5	7	14	18	9	6	57	17	54	4	21	13	50	4	39	13	33	Mon	28

MARCH 2011

New Moon	4 d	15 h	46 m	Moon's Phases E.S.T.
First Quarter	12 d	18 h	45 m	
Full Moon	19 d	13 h	10 m	
Last Quarter	26 d	7 h	7 m	

Day of Yr.	Day of Mo.	Day of Wk.	SUNRISE AND SUNSET: Ottawa E.S.T. Rises		Sets		Toronto E.S.T. Rises		Sets		Winnipeg C.S.T. Rises		Sets		Vancouver P.S.T. Rises		Sets		MOONRISE AND MOONSET Local Mean Time: Lat. 45° Rises		Sets		Lat. 50° Rises		Sets		Day of Wk.	Day of Mo.
			h	m	h	m	h	m	h	m	h	m	h	m	h	m	h	m	h	m	h	m	h	m	h	m		
60	1	Tue	6	42	17	50	6	55	18	6	7	12	18	11	6	55	17	55	19	32	6	42	19	36	6	41	Mon	1
61	2	Wed	6	40	17	51	6	53	18	7	7	10	18	12	6	53	17	57	20	51	7	7	21	0	7	1	Tue	2
62	3	Thu	6	38	17	52	6	51	18	9	7	8	18	14	6	51	17	58	22	9	7	33	22	23	7	22	Wed	3
63	4	Fri	6	36	17	54	6	50	18	10	7	6	18	16	6	49	18	0	23	23	8	3	23	43	7	47	Thu	4
64	5	Sat	6	34	17	55	6	48	18	11	7	4	18	17	6	47	18	2	--	--	8	37	--	--	8	16	Fri	5
65	6	Sun	6	33	17	56	6	46	18	12	7	2	18	19	6	45	18	3	0	33	9	17	0	56	8	53	Sat	6
66	7	Mon	6	31	17	58	6	44	18	14	7	0	18	21	6	43	18	5	1	35	10	5	2	1	9	39	Sun	7
67	8	Tue	6	29	17	59	6	43	18	15	6	58	18	22	6	41	18	6	2	29	10	59	2	54	10	34	Mon	8
68	9	Wed	6	27	18	0	6	41	18	16	6	56	18	24	6	39	18	8	3	13	11	59	3	37	11	36	Tue	9
69	10	Thu	6	25	18	2	6	39	18	17	6	53	18	25	6	37	18	10	3	49	13	1	4	10	12	42	Wed	10
70	11	Fri	6	23	18	3	6	37	18	19	6	51	18	27	6	35	18	11	4	19	14	4	4	35	13	49	Thu	11
71	12	Sat	6	22	18	4	6	36	18	20	6	49	18	29	6	32	18	13	4	44	15	7	4	56	14	57	Fri	12
72	13	Sun	6	20	18	6	6	34	18	21	6	47	18	30	6	30	18	14	5	6	16	10	5	14	16	4	Sat	13
73	14	Mon	6	18	18	7	6	32	18	22	6	45	18	32	6	28	18	16	5	26	17	13	5	30	17	11	Sun	14
74	15	Tue	6	16	18	8	6	30	18	24	6	43	18	33	6	26	18	17	5	45	18	16	5	45	18	18	Mon	15
75	16	Wed	6	14	18	10	6	29	18	25	6	41	18	35	6	24	18	19	6	4	19	20	6	0	19	27	Tue	16
76	17	Thu	6	12	18	11	6	27	18	26	6	38	18	37	6	22	18	21	6	25	20	26	6	17	20	37	Wed	17
77	18	Fri	6	10	18	12	6	25	18	27	6	36	18	38	6	20	18	22	6	49	21	34	6	36	21	49	Thu	18
78	19	Sat	6	8	18	14	6	23	18	28	6	34	18	40	6	18	18	24	7	17	22	42	7	0	23	2	Fri	19
79	20	Sun	6	7	18	15	6	21	18	30	6	32	18	41	6	16	18	25	7	51	23	50	7	30	--	--	Sat	20
80	21	Mon	6	5	18	16	6	20	18	31	6	30	18	43	6	13	18	27	8	34	--	--	8	10	0	13	Sun	21
81	22	Tue	6	3	18	18	6	18	18	32	6	28	18	45	6	11	18	28	9	28	0	53	9	3	1	18	Mon	22
82	23	Wed	6	1	18	19	6	16	18	33	6	25	18	46	6	9	18	30	10	32	1	49	10	8	2	13	Tue	23
83	24	Thu	5	59	18	20	6	14	18	35	6	23	18	48	6	7	18	31	11	45	2	36	11	24	2	57	Wed	24
84	25	Fri	5	57	18	22	6	12	18	36	6	21	18	49	6	5	18	33	13	3	3	15	12	47	3	32	Thu	25
85	26	Sat	5	55	18	23	6	11	18	37	6	19	18	51	6	3	18	34	14	23	3	47	14	12	3	59	Fri	26
86	27	Sun	5	53	18	24	6	9	18	38	6	17	18	52	6	1	18	36	15	43	4	15	15	38	4	22	Sat	27
87	28	Mon	5	51	18	25	6	7	18	39	6	15	18	54	5	59	18	37	17	2	4	41	17	3	4	43	Sun	28
88	29	Tue	5	49	18	27	6	5	18	41	6	12	18	56	5	56	18	39	18	21	5	6	18	28	5	2	Mon	29
89	30	Wed	5	48	18	28	6	3	18	42	6	10	18	57	5	54	18	40	19	40	5	31	19	52	5	23	Tue	30
90	31	Thu	5	46	18	29	6	2	18	43	6	8	18	59	5	52	18	42	20	58	6	0	21	14	5	46	Wed	31

APRIL 2011

New Moon	3 d	9 h	32 m	Moon's Phases E.S.T.
First Quarter	11 d	7 h	5 m	
Full Moon.	17 d	21 h	44 m	
Last Quarter	24 d	21 h	47 m	

Day of Yr.	Day of Mo.	Day of Wk.	SUNRISE AND SUNSET: Ottawa E.S.T. Rises		Sets		Toronto E.S.T. Rises		Sets		Winnipeg C.S.T. Rises		Sets		Vancouver P.S.T. Rises		Sets		MOONRISE AND MOONSET Local Mean Time: Lat. 45° Rises		Sets		Lat. 50° Rises		Sets		Day of Wk.	Day of Mo.
			h	m	h	m	h	m	h	m	h	m	h	m	h	m	h	m	h	m	h	m	h	m	h	m		
91	1	Fri	5	44	18	31	6	0	18	44	6	6	19	0	5	50	18	43	4	30	16	56	4	31	16	57	Fri	1
92	2	Sat	5	42	18	32	5	58	18	45	6	4	19	2	5	48	18	45	4	51	17	57	4	48	18	2	Sat	2
93	3	Sun	5	40	18	33	5	56	18	47	6	2	19	3	5	46	18	46	5	13	18	58	5	6	19	8	Sun	3
94	4	Mon	5	38	18	34	5	54	18	48	5	59	19	5	5	44	18	48	5	37	20	0	5	26	20	14	Mon	4
95	5	Tue	5	36	18	36	5	53	18	49	5	57	19	6	5	42	18	50	6	4	21	2	5	49	21	20	Tue	5
96	6	Wed	5	34	18	37	5	51	18	50	5	55	19	8	5	40	18	51	6	35	22	4	6	17	22	24	Wed	6
97	7	Thu	5	33	18	38	5	49	18	51	5	53	19	10	5	37	18	53	7	13	23	3	6	52	23	25	Thu	7
98	8	Fri	5	31	18	40	5	47	18	53	5	51	19	11	5	35	18	54	7	58	23	57	7	36	--	--	Fri	8
99	9	Sat	5	29	18	41	5	46	18	54	5	49	19	13	5	33	18	56	8	52	--	--	8	30	0	19	Sat	9
100	10	Sun	5	27	18	42	5	44	18	55	5	47	19	14	5	31	18	57	9	54	0	45	9	33	1	6	Sun	10
101	11	Mon	5	25	18	44	5	42	18	56	5	45	19	16	5	29	18	59	11	1	1	27	10	44	1	45	Mon	11
102	12	Tue	5	23	18	45	5	40	18	57	5	43	19	17	5	27	19	0	12	14	2	3	12	1	2	17	Tue	12
103	13	Wed	5	22	18	46	5	39	18	59	5	41	19	19	5	25	19	2	13	29	2	34	13	20	2	44	Wed	13
104	14	Thu	5	20	18	47	5	37	19	0	5	38	19	21	5	23	19	3	14	45	3	3	14	42	3	8	Thu	14
105	15	Fri	5	18	18	49	5	35	19	1	5	36	19	22	5	21	19	5	16	4	3	31	16	6	3	31	Fri	15
106	16	Sat	5	16	18	50	5	34	19	2	5	34	19	24	5	19	19	6	17	24	3	58	17	31	3	54	Sat	16
107	17	Sun	5	15	18	51	5	32	19	3	5	32	19	25	5	17	19	8	18	45	4	28	18	58	4	19	Sun	17
108	18	Mon	5	13	18	53	5	30	19	4	5	30	19	27	5	15	19	9	20	6	5	2	20	23	4	48	Mon	18
109	19	Tue	5	11	18	54	5	29	19	6	5	28	19	28	5	13	19	11	21	22	5	42	21	43	5	24	Tue	19
110	20	Wed	5	9	18	55	5	27	19	7	5	26	19	30	5	11	19	12	22	31	6	29	22	53	6	8	Wed	20
111	21	Thu	5	8	18	56	5	26	19	8	5	24	19	31	5	9	19	14	23	29	7	24	23	51	7	1	Thu	21
112	22	Fri	5	6	18	58	5	24	19	9	5	22	19	33	5	8	19	15	--	--	8	26	--	--	8	4	Fri	22
113	23	Sat	5	4	18	59	5	22	19	10	5	21	19	35	5	6	19	17	0	16	9	31	0	36	9	12	Sat	23
114	24	Sun	5	3	19	0	5	21	19	12	5	19	19	36	5	4	19	18	0	54	10	37	1	10	10	21	Sun	24
115	25	Mon	5	1	19	1	5	19	19	13	5	17	19	38	5	2	19	20	1	24	11	42	1	37	11	30	Mon	25
116	26	Tue	4	59	19	3	5	18	19	14	5	15	19	39	5	0	19	21	1	51	12	45	2	0	12	38	Tue	26
117	27	Wed	4	58	19	4	5	16	19	15	5	13	19	41	4	58	19	23	2	14	13	47	2	19	13	44	Wed	27
118	28	Thu	4	56	19	5	5	15	19	16	5	11	19	42	4	56	19	24	2	35	14	48	2	37	14	48	Thu	28
119	29	Fri	4	55	19	7	5	13	19	18	5	9	19	44	4	55	19	26	2	56	15	49	2	54	15	53	Fri	29
120	30	Sat	4	53	19	8	5	12	19	19	5	7	19	45	4	53	19	27	3	17	16	50	3	12	16	58	Sat	30

MAY 2011

New Moon.......	3 d	1 h	51 m
First Quarter......	10 d	15 h	33 m
Full Moon........	17 d	6 h	9 m
Last Quarter......	24 d	13 h	52 m

Moon's Phases E.S.T.

Day of Yr.	Day of Mo.	Day of Wk.	SUNRISE AND SUNSET: Ottawa E.S.T.				Toronto E.S.T.				Winnipeg C.S.T.				Vancouver P.S.T.				MOONRISE AND MOONSET Local Mean Time: Lat. 45°				Lat. 50°				Day of Wk.	Day of Mo.
			Rises		Sets		Rises		Sets		Rises		Sets		Rises		Sets		Rises		Sets		Rises		Sets			
			h	m	h	m	h	m	h	m	h	m	h	m	h	m	h	m	h	m	h	m	h	m	h	m		
121	1	Sun	4	52	19	9	5	10	19	20	5	6	19	47	4	51	19	29	3	41	17	52	3	31	18	4	Sun	1
122	2	Mon	4	50	19	10	5	9	19	21	5	4	19	48	4	49	19	30	4	7	18	54	3	53	19	10	Mon	2
123	3	Tue	4	49	19	12	5	8	19	22	5	2	19	50	4	48	19	32	4	37	19	57	4	20	20	16	Tue	3
124	4	Wed	4	47	19	13	5	6	19	23	5	1	19	51	4	46	19	33	5	13	20	57	4	54	21	18	Wed	4
125	5	Thu	4	46	19	14	5	5	19	25	4	59	19	53	4	44	19	35	5	57	21	53	5	35	22	15	Thu	5
126	6	Fri	4	44	19	15	5	4	19	26	4	57	19	54	4	43	19	36	6	48	22	43	6	26	23	4	Fri	6
127	7	Sat	4	43	19	17	5	2	19	27	4	56	19	56	4	41	19	38	7	48	23	26	7	27	23	45	Sat	7
128	8	Sun	4	42	19	18	5	1	19	28	4	54	19	57	4	40	19	39	8	53	--	--	8	35	--	--	Sun	8
129	9	Mon	4	40	19	19	5	0	19	29	4	52	19	59	4	38	19	40	10	3	0	3	9	49	0	19	Mon	9
130	10	Tue	4	39	19	20	4	58	19	30	4	51	20	0	4	37	19	42	11	15	0	35	11	5	0	47	Tue	10
131	11	Wed	4	38	19	22	4	57	19	32	4	49	20	2	4	35	19	43	12	28	1	4	12	23	1	11	Wed	11
132	12	Thu	4	36	19	23	4	56	19	33	4	48	20	3	4	34	19	45	13	43	1	31	13	43	1	33	Thu	12
133	13	Fri	4	35	19	24	4	55	19	34	4	46	20	5	4	32	19	46	15	0	1	58	15	5	1	55	Fri	13
134	14	Sat	4	34	19	25	4	54	19	35	4	45	20	6	4	31	19	47	16	18	2	25	16	28	2	19	Sat	14
135	15	Sun	4	33	19	26	4	53	19	36	4	43	20	7	4	30	19	49	17	37	2	56	17	52	2	45	Sun	15
136	16	Mon	4	32	19	27	4	52	19	37	4	42	20	9	4	28	19	50	18	55	3	33	19	14	3	17	Mon	16
137	17	Tue	4	31	19	29	4	51	19	38	4	41	20	10	4	27	19	52	20	8	4	16	20	30	3	56	Tue	17
138	18	Wed	4	30	19	30	4	50	19	39	4	39	20	12	4	26	19	53	21	12	5	7	21	35	4	45	Wed	18
139	19	Thu	4	29	19	31	4	49	19	40	4	38	20	13	4	24	19	54	22	6	6	7	22	27	5	45	Thu	19
140	20	Fri	4	28	19	32	4	48	19	41	4	37	20	14	4	23	19	55	22	49	7	13	23	7	6	52	Fri	20
141	21	Sat	4	27	19	33	4	47	19	42	4	36	20	16	4	22	19	57	23	23	8	20	23	38	8	3	Sat	21
142	22	Sun	4	26	19	34	4	46	19	43	4	35	20	17	4	21	19	58	23	52	9	28	--	--	9	15	Sun	22
143	23	Mon	4	25	19	35	4	45	19	44	4	33	20	18	4	20	19	59	--	--	10	33	0	2	10	24	Mon	23
144	24	Tue	4	24	19	36	4	44	19	45	4	32	20	19	4	19	20	0	0	16	11	36	0	23	11	31	Tue	24
145	25	Wed	4	23	19	37	4	44	19	46	4	31	20	21	4	18	20	2	0	39	12	38	0	42	12	37	Wed	25
146	26	Thu	4	22	19	38	4	43	19	47	4	30	20	22	4	17	20	3	1	0	13	39	0	59	13	42	Thu	26
147	27	Fri	4	21	19	39	4	42	19	48	4	29	20	23	4	16	20	4	1	21	14	40	1	17	14	47	Fri	27
148	28	Sat	4	21	19	40	4	41	19	49	4	28	20	24	4	15	20	5	1	44	15	42	1	35	15	52	Sat	28
149	29	Sun	4	20	19	41	4	41	19	50	4	28	20	25	4	14	20	6	2	9	16	44	1	57	16	58	Sun	29
150	30	Mon	4	19	19	42	4	40	19	51	4	27	20	26	4	13	20	7	2	37	17	47	2	22	18	5	Mon	30
151	31	Tue	4	19	19	43	4	40	19	52	4	26	20	27	4	13	20	8	3	12	18	48	2	53	19	9	Tue	31

JUNE 2011

New Moon.......	1 d	16 h	3 m
First Quarter......	8 d	21 h	11 m
Full Moon........	15 d	15 h	14 m
Last Quarter......	23 d	6 h	48 m

Moon's Phases E.S.T.

Day of Yr.	Day of Mo.	Day of Wk.	SUNRISE AND SUNSET: Ottawa E.S.T.				Toronto E.S.T.				Winnipeg C.S.T.				Vancouver P.S.T.				MOONRISE AND MOONSET Local Mean Time: Lat. 45°				Lat. 50°				Day of Wk.	Day of Mo.
			Rises		Sets		Rises		Sets		Rises		Sets		Rises		Sets		Rises		Sets		Rises		Sets			
			h	m	h	m	h	m	h	m	h	m	h	m	h	m	h	m	h	m	h	m	h	m	h	m		
152	1	Wed	4	18	19	44	4	39	19	52	4	25	20	28	4	12	20	9	3	53	19	46	3	32	20	9	Wed	1
153	2	Thu	4	17	19	45	4	39	19	53	4	24	20	29	4	11	20	10	4	43	20	39	4	20	21	1	Thu	2
154	3	Fri	4	17	19	45	4	38	19	54	4	24	20	30	4	11	20	11	5	40	21	25	5	19	21	45	Fri	3
155	4	Sat	4	16	19	46	4	38	19	55	4	23	20	31	4	10	20	12	6	45	22	5	6	26	22	21	Sat	4
156	5	Sun	4	16	19	47	4	37	19	55	4	23	20	32	4	9	20	13	7	54	22	39	7	39	22	51	Sun	5
157	6	Mon	4	16	19	48	4	37	19	56	4	22	20	33	4	9	20	14	9	6	23	8	8	55	23	16	Mon	6
158	7	Tue	4	15	19	48	4	37	19	57	4	22	20	34	4	9	20	14	10	19	23	35	10	12	23	39	Tue	7
159	8	Wed	4	15	19	49	4	36	19	57	4	21	20	35	4	8	20	15	11	32	--	--	11	30	--	--	Wed	8
160	9	Thu	4	15	19	50	4	36	19	58	4	21	20	35	4	8	20	16	12	46	0	1	12	49	0	0	Thu	9
161	10	Fri	4	14	19	50	4	36	19	59	4	20	20	36	4	7	20	17	14	1	0	27	14	9	0	22	Fri	10
162	11	Sat	4	14	19	51	4	36	19	59	4	20	20	37	4	7	20	17	15	18	0	56	15	30	0	46	Sat	11
163	12	Sun	4	14	19	52	4	36	20	0	4	20	20	37	4	7	20	18	16	34	1	29	16	51	1	15	Sun	12
164	13	Mon	4	14	19	52	4	35	20	0	4	20	20	38	4	7	20	18	17	48	2	8	18	8	1	49	Mon	13
165	14	Tue	4	14	19	53	4	35	20	1	4	20	20	38	4	7	20	19	18	55	2	54	19	18	2	33	Tue	14
166	15	Wed	4	14	19	53	4	35	20	1	4	20	20	39	4	7	20	19	19	53	3	50	20	15	3	27	Wed	15
167	16	Thu	4	14	19	53	4	35	20	1	4	19	20	39	4	6	20	20	20	41	4	53	21	1	4	31	Thu	16
168	17	Fri	4	14	19	54	4	35	20	2	4	19	20	40	4	6	20	20	21	20	6	0	21	36	5	42	Fri	17
169	18	Sat	4	14	19	54	4	35	20	2	4	19	20	40	4	7	20	21	21	52	7	9	22	4	6	54	Sat	18
170	19	Sun	4	14	19	54	4	36	20	2	4	20	20	41	4	7	20	21	22	18	8	17	22	27	8	6	Sun	19
171	20	Mon	4	14	19	55	4	36	20	3	4	20	20	41	4	7	20	21	22	42	9	22	22	46	9	15	Mon	20
172	21	Tue	4	14	19	55	4	36	20	3	4	20	20	41	4	7	20	21	23	3	10	25	23	4	10	22	Tue	21
173	22	Wed	4	15	19	55	4	36	20	3	4	20	20	41	4	7	20	22	23	25	11	27	23	22	11	28	Wed	22
174	23	Thu	4	15	19	55	4	36	20	3	4	20	20	41	4	7	20	22	23	47	12	28	23	40	12	33	Thu	23
175	24	Fri	4	15	19	55	4	37	20	3	4	21	20	41	4	8	20	22	--	--	13	29	24	0	13	38	Fri	24
176	25	Sat	4	15	19	55	4	37	20	3	4	21	20	41	4	8	20	22	0	10	14	31	0	23	14	44	Sat	25
177	26	Sun	4	16	19	55	4	37	20	4	4	21	20	41	4	9	20	22	0	37	15	33	0	23	15	50	Sun	26
178	27	Mon	4	16	19	55	4	38	20	4	4	22	20	41	4	9	20	22	1	9	16	36	0	52	16	55	Mon	27
179	28	Tue	4	17	19	55	4	38	20	4	4	22	20	41	4	9	20	22	1	47	17	35	1	27	17	57	Tue	28
180	29	Wed	4	17	19	55	4	39	20	3	4	23	20	41	4	10	20	22	2	34	18	31	2	12	18	53	Wed	29
181	30	Thu	4	18	19	55	4	39	20	3	4	24	20	41	4	11	20	21	3	29	19	21	3	7	19	41	Thu	30

JULY 2011

				Moon's Phases E.S.T.
New Moon.......	1 d	3 h	54 m	
First Quarter......	8 d	1 h	29 m	
Full Moon........	15 d	1 h	40 m	
Last Quarter......	23 d	0 h	2 m	
New Moon.......	30 d	13 h	40 m	

Day of Yr.	Day of Mo.	Day of Wk.	SUNRISE AND SUNSET Ottawa E.S.T. Rises		Sets		Toronto E.S.T. Rises		Sets		Winnipeg C.S.T. Rises		Sets		Vancouver P.S.T. Rises		Sets		MOONRISE AND MOONSET Local Mean Time Lat. 45° Rises		Sets		Lat. 50° Rises		Sets		Day of Wk.	Day of Mo.
			h	m	h	m	h	m	h	m	h	m	h	m	h	m	h	m	h	m	h	m	h	m	h	m		
182	1	Fri	4	18	19	55	4	40	20	3	4	24	20	41	4	11	20	21	4	32	20	3	4	12	20	21	Fri	1
183	2	Sat	4	19	19	55	4	40	20	3	4	25	20	40	4	12	20	21	5	41	20	40	5	25	20	54	Sat	2
184	3	Sun	4	19	19	55	4	41	20	3	4	26	20	40	4	13	20	20	6	54	21	11	6	41	21	21	Sun	3
185	4	Mon	4	20	19	54	4	41	20	3	4	26	20	40	4	13	20	20	8	8	21	40	8	0	21	45	Mon	4
186	5	Tue	4	21	19	54	4	42	20	2	4	27	20	39	4	14	20	20	9	22	22	6	9	19	22	7	Tue	5
187	6	Wed	4	21	19	54	4	43	20	2	4	28	20	39	4	15	20	19	10	36	22	32	10	38	22	28	Wed	6
188	7	Thu	4	22	19	53	4	43	20	2	4	29	20	38	4	16	20	19	11	51	23	0	11	57	22	52	Thu	7
189	8	Fri	4	23	19	53	4	44	20	1	4	30	20	37	4	16	20	18	13	6	23	30	13	17	23	18	Fri	8
190	9	Sat	4	24	19	52	4	45	20	1	4	30	20	37	4	17	20	17	14	21	--	--	14	37	23	49	Sat	9
191	10	Sun	4	24	19	52	4	46	20	0	4	31	20	36	4	18	20	17	15	34	0	6	15	54	--	--	Sun	10
192	11	Mon	4	25	19	51	4	46	20	0	4	32	20	35	4	19	20	16	16	42	0	49	17	4	0	28	Mon	11
193	12	Tue	4	26	19	50	4	47	19	59	4	33	20	35	4	20	20	15	17	43	1	40	18	5	1	17	Tue	12
194	13	Wed	4	27	19	50	4	48	19	59	4	34	20	34	4	21	20	15	18	34	2	38	18	55	2	16	Wed	13
195	14	Thu	4	28	19	49	4	49	19	58	4	35	20	33	4	22	20	14	19	16	3	43	19	34	3	23	Thu	14
196	15	Fri	4	29	19	48	4	50	19	57	4	37	20	32	4	23	20	13	19	51	4	51	20	5	4	34	Fri	15
197	16	Sat	4	30	19	48	4	50	19	57	4	38	20	31	4	24	20	12	20	19	5	59	20	30	5	46	Sat	16
198	17	Sun	4	31	19	47	4	51	19	56	4	39	20	30	4	25	20	11	20	44	7	6	20	51	6	57	Sun	17
199	18	Mon	4	32	19	46	4	52	19	55	4	40	20	29	4	27	20	10	21	7	8	10	21	9	8	6	Mon	18
200	19	Tue	4	33	19	45	4	53	19	54	4	41	20	28	4	28	20	9	21	29	9	13	21	27	9	13	Tue	19
201	20	Wed	4	34	19	44	4	54	19	53	4	42	20	27	4	29	20	8	21	50	10	15	21	45	10	18	Wed	20
202	21	Thu	4	35	19	43	4	55	19	53	4	44	20	26	4	30	20	7	22	13	11	16	22	4	11	24	Thu	21
203	22	Fri	4	36	19	42	4	56	19	52	4	45	20	25	4	31	20	6	22	39	12	18	22	26	12	29	Fri	22
204	23	Sat	4	37	19	41	4	57	19	51	4	46	20	23	4	33	20	4	23	8	13	19	22	52	13	34	Sat	23
205	24	Sun	4	38	19	40	4	58	19	50	4	47	20	22	4	34	20	3	23	43	14	21	23	24	14	40	Sun	24
206	25	Mon	4	39	19	39	4	59	19	49	4	49	20	21	4	35	20	2	--	--	15	21	--	--	15	42	Mon	25
207	26	Tue	4	40	19	38	5	0	19	48	4	50	20	20	4	36	20	1	0	25	16	19	0	4	16	41	Tue	26
208	27	Wed	4	41	19	37	5	1	19	47	4	51	20	18	4	38	19	59	1	16	17	11	0	53	17	33	Wed	27
209	28	Thu	4	42	19	36	5	2	19	46	4	53	20	17	4	39	19	58	2	15	17	57	1	54	18	16	Thu	28
210	29	Fri	4	43	19	35	5	3	19	44	4	54	20	15	4	40	19	57	3	22	18	37	3	4	18	53	Fri	29
211	30	Sat	4	44	19	34	5	4	19	43	4	55	20	14	4	42	19	55	4	35	19	11	4	20	19	23	Sat	30
212	31	Sun	4	46	19	32	5	5	19	42	4	57	20	12	4	43	19	54	5	50	19	41	5	40	19	48	Sun	31

AUGUST 2011

				Moon's Phases E.S.T.
First Quarter.....	6 d	6 h	8 m	
Full Moon.......	13 d	13 h	57 m	
Last Quarter......	21 d	16 h	54 m	
New Moon.......	28 d	22 h	4 m	

Day of Yr.	Day of Mo.	Day of Wk.	SUNRISE AND SUNSET Ottawa E.S.T. Rises		Sets		Toronto E.S.T. Rises		Sets		Winnipeg C.S.T. Rises		Sets		Vancouver P.S.T. Rises		Sets		MOONRISE AND MOONSET Local Mean Time Lat. 45° Rises		Sets		Lat. 50° Rises		Sets		Day of Wk.	Day of Mo.
			h	m	h	m	h	m	h	m	h	m	h	m	h	m	h	m	h	m	h	m	h	m	h	m		
213	1	Mon	4	47	19	31	5	6	19	41	4	58	20	11	4	44	19	52	7	6	20	9	7	1	20	12	Mon	1
214	2	Tue	4	48	19	30	5	7	19	40	5	0	20	9	4	46	19	51	8	22	20	36	8	22	20	34	Tue	2
215	3	Wed	4	49	19	28	5	9	19	39	5	1	20	8	4	47	19	49	9	39	21	4	9	43	20	57	Wed	3
216	4	Thu	4	50	19	27	5	10	19	37	5	2	20	6	4	48	19	48	10	55	21	34	11	5	21	23	Thu	4
217	5	Fri	4	51	19	26	5	11	19	36	5	4	20	5	4	50	19	46	12	11	22	8	12	25	21	53	Fri	5
218	6	Sat	4	53	19	24	5	12	19	35	5	5	20	3	4	51	19	44	13	25	22	49	13	43	22	29	Sat	6
219	7	Sun	4	54	19	23	5	13	19	33	5	7	20	1	4	53	19	43	14	34	23	36	14	55	23	14	Sun	7
220	8	Mon	4	55	19	21	5	14	19	32	5	8	20	0	4	54	19	41	15	36	--	--	15	59	--	--	Mon	8
221	9	Tue	4	56	19	20	5	15	19	31	5	10	19	58	4	55	19	39	16	30	0	31	16	51	0	9	Tue	9
222	10	Wed	4	57	19	18	5	16	19	29	5	11	19	56	4	57	19	38	17	14	1	33	17	33	1	12	Wed	10
223	11	Thu	4	58	19	17	5	17	19	28	5	12	19	54	4	58	19	36	17	51	2	39	18	6	2	21	Thu	11
224	12	Fri	5	0	19	15	5	18	19	26	5	14	19	52	5	0	19	34	18	21	3	46	18	33	3	31	Fri	12
225	13	Sat	5	1	19	14	5	20	19	25	5	15	19	51	5	1	19	32	18	48	4	52	18	55	4	42	Sat	13
226	14	Sun	5	2	19	12	5	21	19	23	5	17	19	49	5	3	19	31	19	11	5	57	19	15	5	51	Sun	14
227	15	Mon	5	3	19	11	5	22	19	22	5	18	19	47	5	4	19	29	19	33	7	1	19	33	6	59	Mon	15
228	16	Tue	5	5	19	9	5	23	19	20	5	20	19	45	5	5	19	27	19	55	8	3	19	51	8	5	Tue	16
229	17	Wed	5	6	19	7	5	24	19	19	5	21	19	43	5	7	19	25	20	17	9	4	20	10	9	10	Wed	17
230	18	Thu	5	7	19	6	5	25	19	17	5	23	19	41	5	8	19	23	20	42	10	5	20	31	10	15	Thu	18
231	19	Fri	5	8	19	4	5	26	19	16	5	24	19	39	5	10	19	21	21	9	11	7	20	55	11	20	Fri	19
232	20	Sat	5	9	19	2	5	27	19	14	5	26	19	37	5	11	19	19	21	41	12	8	21	24	12	25	Sat	20
233	21	Sun	5	11	19	1	5	29	19	12	5	27	19	35	5	13	19	18	22	19	13	8	21	59	13	28	Sun	21
234	22	Mon	5	12	18	59	5	30	19	11	5	29	19	33	5	14	19	16	23	5	14	6	22	44	14	27	Mon	22
235	23	Tue	5	13	18	57	5	31	19	9	5	30	19	31	5	15	19	14	--	--	14	59	23	38	15	21	Tue	23
236	24	Wed	5	14	18	55	5	32	19	7	5	32	19	29	5	17	19	12	1	5	15	48	--	--	16	8	Wed	24
237	25	Thu	5	15	18	54	5	33	19	6	5	33	19	27	5	18	19	10	1	2	16	30	0	42	16	47	Thu	25
238	26	Fri	5	17	18	52	5	34	19	4	5	35	19	25	5	20	19	8	2	11	17	7	1	55	17	20	Fri	26
239	27	Sat	5	18	18	50	5	35	19	2	5	36	19	23	5	21	19	6	3	25	17	39	3	13	17	48	Sat	27
240	28	Sun	5	19	18	48	5	36	19	1	5	38	19	21	5	23	19	4	4	42	18	9	4	34	18	13	Sun	28
241	29	Mon	5	20	18	46	5	38	18	59	5	39	19	19	5	24	19	2	5	59	18	37	5	57	18	37	Mon	29
242	30	Tue	5	22	18	45	5	39	18	57	5	41	19	17	5	26	19	0	7	18	19	5	7	20	19	1	Tue	30
243	31	Wed	5	23	18	43	5	40	18	55	5	42	19	15	5	27	18	57	8	37	19	36	8	44	19	26	Wed	31

SEPTEMBER 2011

First Quarter	4 d	12 h	39 m	Moon's Phases E.S.T.
Full Moon	12 d	4 h	27 m	
Last Quarter	20 d	8 h	39 m	
New Moon	27 d	6 h	9 m	

Day of Yr.	Day of Mo.	Day of Wk.	Ottawa E.S.T. Rises h	m	Sets h	m	Toronto E.S.T. Rises h	m	Sets h	m	Winnipeg C.S.T. Rises h	m	Sets h	m	Vancouver P.S.T. Rises h	m	Sets h	m	Moon Lat. 45° Rises h	m	Sets h	m	Moon Lat. 50° Rises h	m	Sets h	m	Day of Wk.	Day of Mo.
244	1	Thu	5	24	18	41	5	41	18	54	5	44	19	13	5	28	18	55	9	55	20	9	10	8	19	56	Thu	1
245	2	Fri	5	25	18	39	5	42	18	52	5	45	19	11	5	30	18	53	11	12	20	49	11	29	20	31	Fri	2
246	3	Sat	5	26	18	37	5	43	18	50	5	47	19	9	5	31	18	51	12	24	21	35	12	45	21	14	Sat	3
247	4	Sun	5	28	18	35	5	44	18	48	5	48	19	6	5	33	18	49	13	30	22	28	13	52	22	6	Sun	4
248	5	Mon	5	29	18	34	5	45	18	47	5	49	19	4	5	34	18	47	14	26	23	28	14	48	23	6	Mon	5
249	6	Tue	5	30	18	32	5	47	18	45	5	51	19	2	5	36	18	45	15	13	--	--	15	33	--	--	Tue	6
250	7	Wed	5	31	18	30	5	48	18	43	5	52	19	0	5	37	18	43	15	52	0	32	16	8	0	13	Wed	7
251	8	Thu	5	32	18	28	5	49	18	41	5	54	18	58	5	38	18	41	16	24	1	38	16	37	1	22	Thu	8
252	9	Fri	5	34	18	26	5	50	18	39	5	55	18	56	5	40	18	39	16	51	2	43	17	0	2	32	Fri	9
253	10	Sat	5	35	18	24	5	51	18	38	5	57	18	53	5	41	18	36	17	16	3	48	17	21	3	40	Sat	10
254	11	Sun	5	36	18	22	5	52	18	36	5	58	18	51	5	43	18	34	17	38	4	51	17	40	4	47	Sun	11
255	12	Mon	5	37	18	20	5	53	18	34	6	0	18	49	5	44	18	32	18	0	5	53	17	58	5	53	Mon	12
256	13	Tue	5	39	18	18	5	54	18	32	6	1	18	47	5	46	18	30	18	22	6	54	18	16	6	59	Tue	13
257	14	Wed	5	40	18	16	5	56	18	30	6	3	18	45	5	47	18	28	18	46	7	56	18	37	8	4	Wed	14
258	15	Thu	5	41	18	14	5	57	18	28	6	4	18	43	5	49	18	26	19	13	8	57	18	59	9	9	Thu	15
259	16	Fri	5	42	18	13	5	58	18	27	6	6	18	40	5	50	18	24	19	43	9	58	19	26	10	13	Fri	16
260	17	Sat	5	43	18	11	5	59	18	25	6	7	18	38	5	51	18	21	20	18	10	58	19	59	11	16	Sat	17
261	18	Sun	5	45	18	9	6	0	18	23	6	9	18	36	5	53	18	19	21	0	11	55	20	39	12	16	Sun	18
262	19	Mon	5	46	18	7	6	1	18	21	6	10	18	34	5	54	18	17	21	50	12	50	21	29	13	11	Mon	19
263	20	Tue	5	47	18	5	6	2	18	19	6	12	18	32	5	56	18	15	22	47	13	39	22	27	14	0	Tue	20
264	21	Wed	5	48	18	3	6	3	18	17	6	13	18	29	5	57	18	13	23	52	14	22	23	34	14	41	Wed	21
265	22	Thu	5	49	18	1	6	5	18	16	6	15	18	27	5	59	18	11	--	--	15	1	--	--	15	16	Thu	22
266	23	Fri	5	51	17	59	6	6	18	14	6	16	18	25	6	0	18	8	1	1	15	34	0	47	15	46	Fri	23
267	24	Sat	5	52	17	57	6	7	18	12	6	18	18	23	6	2	18	6	2	15	16	5	2	5	16	12	Sat	24
268	25	Sun	5	53	17	55	6	8	18	10	6	19	18	21	6	3	18	4	3	31	16	34	3	26	16	36	Sun	25
269	26	Mon	5	54	17	53	6	9	18	8	6	21	18	18	6	4	18	2	4	49	17	3	4	49	17	0	Mon	26
270	27	Tue	5	56	17	51	6	10	18	6	6	22	18	16	6	6	18	0	6	9	17	33	6	14	17	26	Tue	27
271	28	Wed	5	57	17	49	6	11	18	5	6	24	18	14	6	7	17	58	7	29	18	6	7	39	17	54	Wed	28
272	29	Thu	5	58	17	47	6	13	18	3	6	25	18	12	6	9	17	56	8	49	18	44	9	4	18	28	Thu	29
273	30	Fri	5	59	17	46	6	14	18	1	6	27	18	10	6	10	17	53	10	7	19	29	10	26	19	9	Fri	30

OCTOBER 2011

First Quarter	3 d	22 h	15 m	Moon's Phases E.S.T.
Full Moon	11 d	21 h	6 m	
Last Quarter	19 d	22 h	30 m	
New Moon	26 d	14 h	56 m	

Day of Yr.	Day of Mo.	Day of Wk.	Ottawa E.S.T. Rises h	m	Sets h	m	Toronto E.S.T. Rises h	m	Sets h	m	Winnipeg C.S.T. Rises h	m	Sets h	m	Vancouver P.S.T. Rises h	m	Sets h	m	Moon Lat. 45° Rises h	m	Sets h	m	Moon Lat. 50° Rises h	m	Sets h	m	Day of Wk.	Day of Mo.
274	1	Sat	6	1	17	44	6	15	17	59	6	28	18	7	6	12	17	51	11	17	20	21	11	39	20	0	Sat	1
275	2	Sun	6	2	17	42	6	16	17	57	6	30	18	5	6	13	17	49	12	19	21	21	12	41	20	59	Sun	2
276	3	Mon	6	3	17	40	6	17	17	56	6	31	18	3	6	15	17	47	13	10	22	25	13	30	22	5	Mon	3
277	4	Tue	6	4	17	38	6	18	17	54	6	33	18	1	6	16	17	45	13	52	23	31	14	9	23	14	Tue	4
278	5	Wed	6	6	17	36	6	20	17	52	6	34	17	59	6	18	17	43	14	26	--	--	14	40	--	--	Wed	5
279	6	Thu	6	7	17	34	6	21	17	50	6	36	17	57	6	19	17	41	14	55	0	36	15	5	0	24	Thu	6
280	7	Fri	6	8	17	32	6	22	17	48	6	38	17	55	6	21	17	39	15	20	1	41	15	26	1	32	Fri	7
281	8	Sat	6	10	17	31	6	23	17	47	6	39	17	53	6	22	17	37	15	43	2	44	15	46	2	39	Sat	8
282	9	Sun	6	11	17	29	6	24	17	45	6	41	17	50	6	24	17	35	16	5	3	46	16	4	3	45	Sun	9
283	10	Mon	6	12	17	27	6	26	17	43	6	42	17	48	6	25	17	33	16	27	4	47	16	23	4	50	Mon	10
284	11	Tue	6	13	17	25	6	27	17	41	6	44	17	46	6	27	17	31	16	51	5	48	16	42	5	55	Tue	11
285	12	Wed	6	15	17	23	6	28	17	40	6	45	17	44	6	28	17	29	17	17	6	49	17	5	6	59	Wed	12
286	13	Thu	6	16	17	22	6	29	17	38	6	47	17	42	6	30	17	27	17	46	7	50	17	30	8	4	Thu	13
287	14	Fri	6	17	17	20	6	30	17	36	6	48	17	40	6	31	17	25	18	20	8	50	18	1	9	7	Fri	14
288	15	Sat	6	19	17	18	6	32	17	35	6	50	17	38	6	33	17	23	18	59	9	48	18	39	10	8	Sat	15
289	16	Sun	6	20	17	16	6	33	17	33	6	52	17	36	6	35	17	21	19	46	10	43	19	25	11	4	Sun	16
290	17	Mon	6	21	17	14	6	34	17	31	6	53	17	34	6	36	17	19	20	40	11	33	20	19	11	54	Mon	17
291	18	Tue	6	23	17	13	6	35	17	30	6	55	17	32	6	38	17	17	21	40	12	18	21	22	12	37	Tue	18
292	19	Wed	6	24	17	11	6	37	17	28	6	56	17	30	6	39	17	15	22	46	12	57	22	30	13	14	Wed	19
293	20	Thu	6	25	17	9	6	38	17	27	6	58	17	28	6	41	17	13	23	55	13	31	23	43	13	44	Thu	20
294	21	Fri	6	27	17	8	6	39	17	25	7	0	17	26	6	42	17	11	--	--	14	2	--	--	14	11	Fri	21
295	22	Sat	6	28	17	6	6	40	17	23	7	1	17	24	6	44	17	9	1	7	14	31	1	0	14	35	Sat	22
296	23	Sun	6	29	17	4	6	42	17	22	7	3	17	22	6	46	17	7	2	21	14	59	2	19	14	59	Sun	23
297	24	Mon	6	31	17	3	6	43	17	20	7	5	17	20	6	47	17	5	3	38	15	28	3	41	15	23	Mon	24
298	25	Tue	6	32	17	1	6	44	17	19	7	6	17	19	6	49	17	3	4	57	15	59	5	5	15	50	Tue	25
299	26	Wed	6	33	17	0	6	45	17	17	7	8	17	17	6	50	17	2	6	18	16	35	6	30	16	21	Wed	26
300	27	Thu	6	35	16	58	6	47	17	16	7	10	17	15	6	52	17	0	7	38	17	17	7	55	17	0	Thu	27
301	28	Fri	6	36	16	56	6	48	17	14	7	11	17	13	6	54	16	58	8	55	18	8	9	15	17	47	Fri	28
302	29	Sat	6	38	16	55	6	49	17	13	7	13	17	11	6	55	16	56	10	3	19	6	10	25	18	45	Sat	29
303	30	Sun	6	39	16	53	6	51	17	12	7	14	17	10	6	57	16	55	11	1	20	11	11	22	19	51	Sun	30
304	31	Mon	6	40	16	52	6	52	17	10	7	16	17	8	6	58	16	53	11	48	21	19	12	6	21	1	Mon	31

NOVEMBER 2011

First Quarter......	2 d	11 h	38 m
Full Moon........	10 d	15 h	16 m
Last Quarter......	18 d	10 h	9 m
New Moon.......	25 d	1 h	10 m

Moon's Phases E.S.T.

			SUNRISE AND SUNSET								MOONRISE AND MOONSET Local Mean Time					
Day of Yr.	Day of Mo.	Day of Wk.	Ottawa E.S.T.		Toronto E.S.T.		Winnipeg C.S.T.		Vancouver P.S.T.		Lat. 45°		Lat. 50°		Day of Wk.	Day of Mo.
			Rises	Sets	Rises	Sets	Rises	Sets	Rises	Sets	Rises	Sets	Rises	Sets		
			h m	h m	h m	h m	h m	h m	h m	h m	h m	h m	h m	h m		
305	1	Tue	6 42	16 51	6 53	17 9	7 18	17 6	7 0	16 51	12 26	22 26	12 41	22 13	Tue	1
306	2	Wed	6 43	16 49	6 54	17 7	7 19	17 4	7 2	16 50	12 57	23 32	13 8	23 23	Wed	2
307	3	Thu	6 45	16 48	6 56	17 6	7 21	17 3	7 3	16 48	13 24	-- --	13 31	-- --	Thu	3
308	4	Fri	6 46	16 46	6 57	17 5	7 23	17 1	7 5	16 46	13 47	0 36	13 51	0 31	Fri	4
309	5	Sat	6 47	16 45	6 58	17 4	7 24	16 59	7 6	16 45	14 10	1 39	14 10	1 37	Sat	5
310	6	Sun	6 49	16 44	7 0	17 2	7 26	16 58	7 8	16 43	14 32	2 40	14 28	2 42	Sun	6
311	7	Mon	6 50	16 42	7 1	17 1	7 28	16 56	7 10	16 42	14 55	3 40	14 48	3 46	Mon	7
312	8	Tue	6 52	16 41	7 2	17 0	7 29	16 55	7 11	16 40	15 20	4 41	15 9	4 51	Tue	8
313	9	Wed	6 53	16 40	7 4	16 59	7 31	16 53	7 13	16 39	15 48	5 42	15 34	5 55	Wed	9
314	10	Thu	6 54	16 39	7 5	16 58	7 33	16 52	7 14	16 38	16 21	6 43	16 3	6 59	Thu	10
315	11	Fri	6 56	16 37	7 6	16 57	7 34	16 50	7 16	16 36	16 59	7 42	16 39	8 1	Fri	11
316	12	Sat	6 57	16 36	7 8	16 55	7 36	16 49	7 18	16 35	17 44	8 39	17 23	8 59	Sat	12
317	13	Sun	6 59	16 35	7 9	16 54	7 38	16 48	7 19	16 34	18 36	9 30	18 15	9 51	Sun	13
318	14	Mon	7 0	16 34	7 10	16 53	7 39	16 46	7 21	16 32	19 34	10 17	19 15	10 36	Mon	14
319	15	Tue	7 1	16 33	7 12	16 52	7 41	16 45	7 22	16 31	20 37	10 57	20 21	11 14	Tue	15
320	16	Wed	7 3	16 32	7 13	16 52	7 42	16 44	7 24	16 30	21 44	11 32	21 31	11 46	Wed	16
321	17	Thu	7 4	16 31	7 14	16 51	7 44	16 43	7 26	16 29	22 53	12 3	22 44	12 13	Thu	17
322	18	Fri	7 5	16 30	7 15	16 50	7 46	16 42	7 27	16 28	-- --	12 32	23 59	12 38	Fri	18
323	19	Sat	7 7	16 29	7 17	16 49	7 47	16 40	7 29	16 26	0 4	12 59	1 16	13 0	Sat	19
324	20	Sun	7 8	16 28	7 18	16 48	7 49	16 39	7 30	16 25	1 16	13 26	1 17	13 23	Sun	20
325	21	Mon	7 9	16 28	7 19	16 47	7 50	16 38	7 32	16 24	2 31	13 55	2 37	13 48	Mon	21
326	22	Tue	7 11	16 27	7 20	16 47	7 52	16 37	7 33	16 23	3 49	14 27	3 59	14 16	Tue	22
327	23	Wed	7 12	16 26	7 22	16 46	7 53	16 36	7 35	16 23	5 8	15 5	5 22	14 50	Wed	23
328	24	Thu	7 13	16 25	7 23	16 45	7 55	16 35	7 36	16 22	6 26	15 51	6 44	15 32	Thu	24
329	25	Fri	7 15	16 25	7 24	16 45	7 56	16 35	7 38	16 21	7 39	16 46	8 0	16 25	Fri	25
330	26	Sat	7 16	16 24	7 25	16 44	7 58	16 34	7 39	16 20	8 44	17 49	9 5	17 28	Sat	26
331	27	Sun	7 17	16 23	7 26	16 44	7 59	16 33	7 40	16 19	9 37	18 58	9 57	18 39	Sun	27
332	28	Mon	7 18	16 23	7 28	16 43	8 1	16 32	7 42	16 19	10 20	20 8	10 37	19 53	Mon	28
333	29	Tue	7 20	16 22	7 29	16 43	8 2	16 32	7 43	16 18	10 56	21 17	11 8	21 6	Tue	29
334	30	Wed	7 21	16 22	7 30	16 42	8 3	16 31	7 44	16 17	11 25	22 24	11 34	22 16	Wed	30

DECEMBER 2011

First Quarter.....	2 d	4 h	52 m
Full Moon.......	10 d	9 h	36 m
Last Quarter......	17 d	19 h	48 m
New Moon.......	24 d	13 h	6 m

Moon's Phases E.S.T.

			SUNRISE AND SUNSET								MOONRISE AND MOONSET Local Mean Time					
Day of Yr.	Day of Mo.	Day of Wk.	Ottawa E.S.T.		Toronto E.S.T.		Winnipeg C.S.T.		Vancouver P.S.T.		Lat. 45°		Lat. 50°		Day of Wk.	Day of Mo.
			Rises	Sets	Rises	Sets	Rises	Sets	Rises	Sets	Rises	Sets	Rises	Sets		
			h m	h m	h m	h m	h m	h m	h m	h m	h m	h m	h m	h m		
335	1	Thu	7 22	16 21	7 31	16 42	8 5	16 30	7 46	16 17	11 50	23 28	11 55	23 25	Thu	1
336	2	Fri	7 23	16 21	7 32	16 42	8 6	16 30	7 47	16 16	12 14	-- --	12 15	-- --	Fri	2
337	3	Sat	7 24	16 21	7 33	16 41	8 7	16 29	7 48	16 16	12 36	0 30	12 34	0 31	Sat	3
338	4	Sun	7 25	16 20	7 34	16 41	8 9	16 29	7 50	16 15	12 59	1 31	12 53	1 36	Sun	4
339	5	Mon	7 26	16 20	7 35	16 41	8 10	16 28	7 51	16 15	13 23	2 32	13 13	2 40	Mon	5
340	6	Tue	7 27	16 20	7 36	16 41	8 11	16 28	7 52	16 15	13 50	3 33	13 37	3 45	Tue	6
341	7	Wed	7 28	16 20	7 37	16 41	8 12	16 28	7 53	16 14	14 21	4 34	14 4	4 49	Wed	7
342	8	Thu	7 29	16 20	7 38	16 41	8 13	16 28	7 54	16 14	14 57	5 34	14 38	5 52	Thu	8
343	9	Fri	7 30	16 20	7 39	16 41	8 14	16 27	7 55	16 14	15 40	6 32	15 19	6 52	Fri	9
344	10	Sat	7 31	16 20	7 40	16 41	8 15	16 27	7 56	16 14	16 30	7 26	16 9	7 47	Sat	10
345	11	Sun	7 32	16 20	7 41	16 41	8 16	16 27	7 57	16 14	17 27	8 15	17 7	8 35	Sun	11
346	12	Mon	7 33	16 20	7 42	16 41	8 17	16 27	7 58	16 14	18 30	8 57	18 12	9 16	Mon	12
347	13	Tue	7 34	16 20	7 43	16 41	8 18	16 27	7 59	16 14	19 36	9 34	19 22	9 49	Tue	13
348	14	Wed	7 35	16 20	7 43	16 41	8 19	16 27	8 0	16 14	20 44	10 7	20 35	10 18	Wed	14
349	15	Thu	7 36	16 20	7 44	16 41	8 20	16 27	8 1	16 14	21 54	10 36	21 49	10 43	Thu	15
350	16	Fri	7 36	16 20	7 45	16 41	8 21	16 28	8 1	16 14	23 5	11 3	23 4	11 6	Fri	16
351	17	Sat	7 37	16 21	7 46	16 42	8 21	16 28	8 2	16 15	-- --	11 29	-- --	11 28	Sat	17
352	18	Sun	7 38	16 21	7 46	16 42	8 22	16 28	8 3	16 15	0 17	11 56	0 20	11 51	Sun	18
353	19	Mon	7 38	16 21	7 47	16 42	8 23	16 29	8 4	16 15	1 31	12 26	1 39	12 16	Mon	19
354	20	Tue	7 39	16 22	7 47	16 43	8 23	16 29	8 4	16 16	2 46	13 0	2 59	12 46	Tue	20
355	21	Wed	7 39	16 22	7 48	16 43	8 24	16 29	8 5	16 16	4 2	13 40	4 19	13 23	Wed	21
356	22	Thu	7 40	16 23	7 48	16 44	8 24	16 30	8 5	16 17	5 16	14 29	5 36	14 9	Thu	22
357	23	Fri	7 40	16 23	7 49	16 44	8 25	16 31	8 6	16 17	6 24	15 28	6 45	15 6	Fri	23
358	24	Sat	7 41	16 24	7 49	16 45	8 25	16 31	8 6	16 18	7 22	16 34	7 43	16 13	Sat	24
359	25	Sun	7 41	16 25	7 50	16 46	8 26	16 32	8 6	16 19	8 11	17 44	8 29	17 26	Sun	25
360	26	Mon	7 42	16 25	7 50	16 46	8 26	16 33	8 7	16 19	8 51	18 55	9 5	18 42	Mon	26
361	27	Tue	7 42	16 26	7 50	16 47	8 26	16 33	8 7	16 20	9 23	20 5	9 34	19 55	Tue	27
362	28	Wed	7 42	16 27	7 51	16 48	8 26	16 34	8 7	16 21	9 51	21 11	9 58	21 6	Wed	28
363	29	Thu	7 42	16 27	7 51	16 48	8 27	16 35	8 7	16 22	10 16	22 16	10 19	22 15	Thu	29
364	30	Fri	7 42	16 28	7 51	16 49	8 27	16 36	8 7	16 23	10 39	23 18	10 38	23 21	Fri	30
365	31	Sat	7 43	16 29	7 51	16 50	8 27	16 37	8 7	16 24	11 2	-- --	10 58	-- --	Sat	31

Bertram Brockhouse

Brockhouse was born in 1918 to homesteaders in Alberta and attended a one-room schoolhouse in Vancouver. During the Depression, the impoverished Brockhouses moved to Chicago, where, to help out with family finances, Brockhouse learned how to repair radios, and became involved in the socialist democratic movement. During the Second World War, he served six years in the Royal Canadian Navy repairing submarine-tracking equipment. At the war's end he attended the University of British Columbia, where he studied physics and mathematics, and received a PhD from the University of Toronto in the budding field of nuclear physics. In 1994 Brockhouse and Clifford G. Shull received a Nobel Prize in Physics for their contributions to the development of neutron scattering techniques for studies of condensed matter. Neutron scattering techniques are used in widely differing areas such as the study of the new ceramic superconductors, catalytic exhaust cleaning, elastic properties of polymers and virus structure.

H.S.M. Coxeter

Coxeter was born and educated in England. Shortly after finishing his doctoral studies at Cambridge University, he spent two years as a research visitor at Princeton University. In 1936 he joined the Faculty of the University of Toronto, where he remained as a mathematics professor until his death in 2003. Coxeter's work was mainly in geometry. In particular he made contributions of major importance in the theory of non-euclidean geometry, group theory, combinatorics, and polytopes or complicated geometric shapes of any number of dimensions that cannot be constructed in the real world but can be described mathematically and can sometimes be drawn. Much of Coxeter's time was devoted to group theory, or ways of measuring symmetry. This concerns the geometry of, for instance, kaleidoscopes and reflections in different planes, now known as Coxeter groups. Coxeter met the artist M.C. Escher, the master of depicting impossible reality, in 1954 and the two became lifelong friends. Coxeter also influenced Buckminster Fuller who used Coxeter's mathematical concepts of symmetry in his architecture. He attributed his long and productive life to vegetarianism and physical fitness.

J.C. Fields

John Charles Fields was born in Hamilton, Ontario, then Upper Canada, in 1863. He graduated with a degree in mathematics from the University of Toronto and was awarded a PhD from Johns Hopkins University in 1887. Dissatisfied with the state of mathematics in North America, Fields left for Europe, where he met the greatest mathematicians of the time, and changed his mathematical interests to algebraic functions. Fields worked tirelessly to raise the stature of mathematics within academic and public circles. He successfully lobbied the Ontario Legislature for an annual research grant of $75,000 for the university and helped establish the National Research Council of Canada, and the Ontario Research Foundation. Fields is best known for establishing what is now known as the Fields Medal, the premier award in mathematics, often called the Nobel Prize in Mathematics. It is awarded every four years to two to four mathematicians, under the age of 40, who have made important contributions to the field.

Sir Sandford Fleming

Fleming was born in Scotland in 1827, and at the age of 17, he emigrated to Ontario, where he was employed as a surveyor and map maker. In 1851 Fleming designed Canada's first postage stamp, which would do much to publicize the beaver as a distinctly Canadian emblem. In 1855 he became the chief engineer of the Northern Railway of Canada, where he instituted the construction of iron bridges instead of wood for safety reasons. Over the next few years he led a team of surveyors and engineers to investigate the first coast-to-coast railway line. Fleming was present in 1885 when the last spike was driven in Craigellachie, British Columbia. After missing a train in 1876 in Ireland because the printed schedule listed p.m. instead of a.m., he proposed Universal Time, a single 24-hour clock for the entire world, located in Greenwich, England, the center of the Earth and not linked to any surface meridian. He urged that standard time zones be used locally, but they were to be subordinate to his single world time. By 1929 all of the major countries of the world had accepted time zones. Fleming was knighted by Queen Victoria In 1897.

John Kenneth Galbraith

The economist's first major book, published in 1952, was American Capitalism: The Concept of Countervailing Power. In it he argued that giant firms had replaced small ones to the point where the competitive model no longer applied to much of the American economy. But, he argued, the muscle of large firms was offset by the power of large unions, so that consumers were protected by competing centers of power. In his best-selling 1958 book The Affluent Society, Galbraith contrasted the affluence of the private sector with the squalor of the public sector. Galbraith's main argument is that as society becomes relatively more affluent, so private business must "create" consumer wants through advertising, and while this generates artificial affluence through the production of commercial goods and services, the "public sector" becomes neglected as a result. He proposed significant investment in parks, transportation, education, and other public amenities-what we now call infrastructure-to ameliorate these differences and postpone depression and revolution indefinitely. Although born in Canada, Galbraith spent most of his life in the United States, namely as a professor at Harvard University. He was active in politics, serving four US presidents and was the US Ambassador to India under Kennedy. He was awarded the Order of Canada in 1997 and two Presidential Metals of Freedom. He died in 2006 at the age of 97.

William Francis Giauque

Born to American parents on the Canadian side of Niagara Falls, Giauque began his career at the Hooker Electro-Chemical Company in Niagara Falls, NY, as a chemical engineer. Soon after, he received a Ph.D. degree in chemistry with a minor in physics from the University of California, where he became a professor of chemistry in 1934. The principal objective of his was to demonstrate through a variety of accurate tests that the third law of thermodynamics is a basic natural law. In 1927 he proposed a new method of achieving extremely low temperatures using a process called adiabatic demagnetization. By 1933 he had a working apparatus that obtained a temperature within one-tenth of a degree of absolute zero. In the course of his low-temperature studies of oxygen, Giauque discovered with Herrick L. Johnston the oxygen isotopes of mass 17 and 18 in the Earth's atmosphere. He received the Nobel Prize in Chemistry in 1949.

James Gosling

The father of Java programming language was born in 1955 near Calgary, where he attended university. He received his PhD in Computer Science from Carnegie Mellon University. While at the college he built a multi-processor version of Unix, as well as several compilers and computer mail systems.

Since 1984, Gosling has served Sun Microsystems as Vice President and Fellow. In February 2007, he was named an officer of the Order of Canada.

Gerhard Herzberg

Physicist Herzberg was born in Hamburg, Germany in 1904 but was forced to flee Nazi Germany in 1935, when he settled at the University of Saskatchewan. Herzberg's main contributions have enriched the fields of atomic and molecular spectroscopy for which he won a Nobel Prize in Chemistry in 1971. He and his associates determined the makeup of a large number of diatomic and polyatomic molecules, including the structures of many free radicals difficult to determine in any other way. Herzberg has also applied spectroscopic studies to the identification of certain molecules in planetary atmospheres, in comets, and in interstellar space. Herzberg was elected a Fellow of the Royal Society of Canada in 1939 and of the Royal Society of London in 1951. Herzberg died in 1999.

David Hubel

Hubel, along with Torsten Wiesel, greatly expanded the scientific knowledge of sensory processing, describing how signals from the eye are processed by the brain to generate edge detectors, motion detectors, stereoscopic depth detectors and color detectors, the building blocks of the visual scene. These studies opened the door for the understanding and treatment of childhood cataracts and strabismus. For their work the team was awarded the 1981 Nobel Prize in Physiology or Medicine. Hubel was born to American parents in Windsor, but spent his formative years in Montreal.

Rudolph Marcus

Born in Montreal in 1923, Marcus received the 1992 Nobel Prize in Chemistry for his theory of electron transfer. Marcus theory, named after him, provides a thermodynamic and kinetic framework for describing one electron outer-sphere electron transfer. The Marcus theory describes, and makes predictions concerning, such widely differing phenomena as the fixation of light energy by green plants, photochemical production of fuel, chemiluminescence (cold light), the conductivity of electrically conducting polymers, corrosion, the methodology of electrochemical synthesis and analysis, and more.

Marcus developed his theory for what is perhaps the simplest chemical elementary process, the transfer of an electron between two molecules. No chemical bonds are broken in such a reaction, but changes take place in the molecular structure of the reacting molecules and their nearest neighbors. This molecular change enables the electrons to jump between the molecules. He is currently a professor at Caltech and is a member of the International Academy of Quantum Molecular Science.

Sir William Osler

Osler, often dubbed the father of modern medicine, grew up in Ontario, the son of an Anglican minister. After two years at the Toronto School of Medicine, Osler obtained his medical degree in 1872 from McGill University. Upon his death, Osler willed his library to the Montreal university where it forms the nucleus of McGill's Osler Library of the History of Medicine, which opened in 1929. Osler's greatest contribution to medicine was to insist that students learned from seeing and talking to patients and the establishment of the medical residency program. In 1889, Osler accepted the position of Physician-in-Chief at the recently founded Johns Hopkins Hospital in Baltimore where he refined the residency program. He died, at the age of 70, in 1919, during the Spanish influenza epidemic.

Wilder Penfield

The American-born Canadian neurosurgeon studied at Princeton before becoming a Rhodes Scholar at Oxford University where he studied neuropathology, the scientific study of diseases of the nervous system. With his colleague, Herbert Jasper, he invented what is now called the Montreal procedure for treating patients with severe epilepsy by destroying nerve cells in the brain where the seizures originated. Before operating, he stimulated the brain with electrical probes while the patients were conscious on the operating table and observed their responses. In this way he could more accurately target the areas of the brain responsible, reducing the side-effects of the surgery. His technique enabled him to map the sensory and motor parts of the brain, thus showing their connection to the various limbs and organs of the body. After studying epilepsy in New York, Penfield moved to Montreal where he taught at at McGill University and the Royal Victoria hospital, becoming the city's first neurosurgeon. He eventually became the director of the Montreal Neurological Institute and the associated Montreal Neurological Hospital, which was established with funding from the Rockefeller Foundation. In 1967 he was made a Companion of the Order of Canada. In 1994 he was inducted into the Canadian Medical Hall of Fame.

John Polanyi

After completing his undergraduate education at Manchester University, Polanyi moved to Canada in 1952 at the age of 23 to work for the for the National Research Council of Canada before moving to the University of Toronto, where he remains to this day. In 1986 Polanyi shared a Nobel Prize in Chemistry with Dudley R. Herschbach and Yuan T. Lee for their research in reaction dynamics, offering much more understanding into how energy disposal in chemical reactions takes place. Polanyi developed the method of infrared chemiluminescence, in which the extremely weak infrared emission from a newly formed molecule is measured and analyzed.

Arthur Schawlow

Schawlow grew up in Canada in a deeply religious Christian family and studied at the University of Toronto. After the Second World War he studied at Columbia University, spent a decade at Bell Labs, then left to become a professor at Stanford, where he remained as professor emeritus until his retirement in 1996. While at Stanford, he teamed up with Robert Hofstadter, who, like Schawlow, had an autistic child, to help each other find solutions to the condition. Later Schawlow spearheaded an institution to care for people with autism in Paradise, CA, named the Arthur Schawlow Center. Although his research focused on optics, in particular, lasers and their use in spectroscopy, he also pursued investigations in the areas of superconductivity and nuclear resonance. He and Nicolaas Bloembergen shared the 1981 Nobel Prize in Physics by using lasers to study the interactions of electromagnetic radiation with matter.

Myron Scholes

The 1997 winner of the Nobel Memorial Prize in Economics began his early years in Timmins. After the family moved to Hamilton, Scholes attended McMaster University and earned an MBA and PhD from the University of Chicago. He eventually put his name to the Black-Scholes model, which provides the fundamental conceptual framework for valuing options, such as calls or puts, and has become the standard in financial markets globally. All did not go well for Scholes, however. In 2005, Scholes was implicated in the case of Long-Term Capital Holdings v. United States, where he attempted to invest funds from his company, Long-Term Capital Holdings, in an illegal tax shelter in order to avoid having to pay taxes on profits from company investments. It was found that Scholes and his partners were not eligible for US$106 million in tax deductions they had claimed.

They were fined more than US$40 million by the IRS. Scholes now runs the hedge fund Platinum Grove Asset Management.

Michael Smith

Born in 1932 in Blackpool, England, Smith attended the University of Manchester and soon after receiving his PhD accepted a fellowship in Vancouver to work on the synthesis of biologically important organo-phosphates. The 1992 Nobel Prize winner in chemistry didn't keep the money he was granted from the award. He gave half of it to researchers working on the genetics of schizophreniaand shared the other half between Science World BC and the Society for Canadian Women in Science and Technology. Smith could afford to be generous. He had made a small fortune in 1988 when he sold his share of Zymogenetics Incorporated, a Seattle-based biotechnology company that he co-founded in 1981.

Andrew Michael Spence

For his work on the dynamics of information flows and market development, Spence and his colleagues George A. Akerlof and Joseph E. Stiglitz, received the 2001 Nobel Memorial Prize in Economics. In his Job-Market Signaling model, employees convey their respective skills to employers by acquiring a certain degree of education, which is costly to them. Employers will pay higher wages to more educated employees, because they know that the proportion of employees with high abilities is higher among the educated ones, as it is less costly for them to acquire education than it is for employees with low abilities. For the model to work, it is not even necessary for education to have any intrinsic value if it can convey information about the sender (employee) to the recipient (employer) and if the signal is costly. Spence is currently a senior fellow at the Hoover Institution at Stanford University. He grew up in Canada, during and after the war, before leaving for college in the United States.

Henry Taube

For his work on the mechanisms of electron transfer reactions, especially in metal complexes, Taube won the 1983 Novel Prize in Chemistry. Born in Saskatchewan, Taube has published more than 350 articles and a book as a result of his research. A member of the Stanford University faculty since 1962, Taube was "one of the most creative contemporary workers in inorganic chemistry," according to the Nobel committee who rewarded him for his insights into how electrons are transferred from one molecule to another during chemical reactions. Taube maintained a lifelong interest in oxidation-reduction or redox reactions, in which electrons are lost and gained during a chemical reaction. He died in 2005 at the age of 89 at his home on the Stanford campus.

Richard E. Taylor

Born in 1929 in Medicine Hat, Alberta, Taylor received the 1990 Nobel Prize in Physics for his pioneering investigations concerning deep inelastic scattering of electrons on protons and bound neutrons, which have been of essential importance for the development of the quark model in particle physics. He shared the prize with Jerome Friedman and Henry Kendall. Taylor received his undergraduate degree from the University of Alberta and his PhD from Stanford, where he is a professor emeritus.

William Vickrey

Vickrey was born in Victoria, British Columbia, in 1914. His elementary and secondary education was in Europe and the United States, with graduation from Phillips Andover Academy in 1931. He received a B.S. in mathematics from Yale in 1935, followed by graduate work in economics at Columbia University from 1935 to 1937. A conscientious objector during World War II, he spent part of his alternate service designing a new inheritance tax for Puerto Rico. In 1946 he began his teaching career at Columbia University as a lecturer in economics. An essential part of Vickrey's research focused on the properties of different types of auctions, and how they can best be designed to generate economic efficiency. His work provided the basis for a field of research which has also been extended to practical applications such as auctions of treasury bonds and band spectrum licenses. He received the 1996 Nobel Prize in Economics for his endeavors.

John Tuzo Wilson

The Ottawa-born geologist achieved world-wide acclaim for his contributions to study of plate tectonics. Plate tectonics is the idea that the rigid outer layers of the Earth are broken up into numerous pieces that move independently over the weaker soft zone of the upper mantle. Wilson maintained that the Hawaiian Islands were created as a tectonic plate, extending across much of the Pacific Ocean, shifted slowly over a fixed hotspot, spawning a long series of volcanoes. He also conceived of the transform fault, a major plate boundary where two plates move past each other horizontally, such as the San Andreas Fault. The Wilson cycle of seabed expansion and contraction bears his name. He died in 1993 in Toronto.

CANADA'S ENERGY SOURCES

Canada is endowed with an abundant variety of energy resources. It ranks among top countries in the world for production of oil, natural gas, uranium and coal. Most of the country's energy is derived from hydrocarbons-coal, natural gas, and oil. These are used both as direct fuels and in the production of electricity. The only significant non-hydrocarbon energy sources are hydroelectricity and nuclear power. Canadians are the second-highest per capital consumers of energy in the world, doubling Japan and most of Europe. How will Canada cope with future energy needs and consumption?

Oil and Gas

Canada faces the same oil industry challenges as the rest of the world: recent crude oil prices have been high and volatile, and geopolitical uncertainty continues to be a threat to supply around the globe. The impact of severe weather on refining and production has resulted in higher crude oil and gasoline prices. Based on Canada's production rate, they have 10 years or less of proven reserves. This does not mean that Canada will run out of oil in 10 years. It means this is the size of its resource based on the oil pools today, production rates, and the portion that is recoverable using existing technology.

Canadian oil sands -a mixture of sand or clay, water, and extremely heavy crude oil-are estimated to contain 1.7 trillion barrels of oil, and based on today's technology, it's believed that 178 billion barrels can be recovered. To put this in perspective, the size of the recoverable resources ranks second only to Saudi Arabia. The oil sands currently account for approximately one-third of the 3.1 million barrels of oil produced per day in Canada. Conventional oil production in the Western Canada Sedimentary Basin peaked in 1973, but it still accounts for a significant portion of oil supply. There is call to slow the pace of oil sands development in order to allow for better understanding and assessment of the risks to the environment. This could mean temporarily halting further approvals of projects.

Natural Gas

Over the past decade, there has been a trend on the part of large energy consumers and the general public toward increased use of natural gas as the fuel of choice. This has been particularly noteworthy in the electricity generation industry. Canadian production of natural gas has probably already peaked, and will gradually decline as wells mature and become exhausted faster than new discoveries are made. In 2007, Canadian Liquefied Natural Gas production declined, but those deficiencies were offset by higher US imports. Drilling activity was weaker than it was at the same time in past three years. Annual increases in drilling activity and connection of new gas wells are necessary to maintain stable Canadian gas deliverability, because the productivity of new gas wells in the Western Canada Sedimentary Basin has lessened. In 2006, natural gas prices fell below the fuel oil range and competed with coal in the power generation market.

With North American natural gas supply expected to lag future increases in demand, imports of LNG from offshore sources are viewed as the largest source of additional natural gas to the continent. Over 40 import terminal projects have been proposed for North America and development of significant LNG trade could have implications for North American natural gas supply, demand and prices.

Canada will continue to research and develop gas hydrates, a form of natural gas found in the molecular structure of ice, in Northern provinces and offshore on both coasts. Canadian resource estimates are impressive: 1,500 to 28,000 trillion cubic feet of gas in place contained in hydrates, with 311 trillion cubic feet in the Beaufort/Mackenzie Delta region. Both the Pacific and Atlantic margins have confirmed gas hydrates deposits. If there was a system available to transport these deposits, hydrates would be as economical as gas. However, costs are not competitive with conventional gas at this time. Additional testing and modeling is required to ensure results. Plans are to have a full scale production test in about five years and first production by 2020.

Compressed natural gas seems to be a viable transportation option for stranded natural gas offshore Newfoundland, with possible development to occur by 2014 or later. Development still has a number of hurdles to overcome, including safety issues for the delivery to Boston or New York harbours.

Electricity and Coal

The size of Canada's coal resource dwarfs all other energy forms, even the oil sands. Based on current production rates, Canada has a 1,000-year reserve of coal. Currently about 60 percent of Canada's electricity comes from hydro projects, 18 percent from coal combustion, 13 percent from nuclear, 5 percent from natural gas, and the balance from oil and renewables. Coal-based generation became unpopular during the 1980s and 1990s because of its carbon emissions. Canada must develop ways to use coal in a manner that is environmentally acceptable. Until a few years ago, there were two ways to address the challenge of greenhouse gas management: to produce and use energy more efficiently or, to rely increasingly on low-carbon and carbon-free fuels. Unfortunately, energy efficiency and the use of alternative energy may not be enough to stabilize global concentrations of carbon dioxide. Carbon sequestration offers a third option that could, in tandem with the continued development of clean coal generation technologies, prove affordable, effective and environmentally safe.

Canadian metallurgical coal (coal consumed in making steel) is experiencing a comeback in Alberta and British Columbia, and opportunities for Canadian metallurgical coal are driven by demand in China, India and Brazil. Canadian steam coal (all non-metallurgical coal) production remains consistent with some export growth. Steam coal consumption is at risk in Ontario with projected plant shutdowns. Steam coal production remains strong in Alberta, Saskatchewan, New Brunswick and Nova Scotia. The government to build and operate a full-scale clean coal demonstration plant by 2012.

A number of provinces have introduced or are in the process of introducing plans to address electricity needs by way of new generation and transmission projects. For example, British Columbia Transmission Corp. introduced a $3.2-billion 10-year transmission plan, Alberta Electric System Operator began a $3.5 billion 10-year transmission plan, Saskatchewan agreed to address its aging fleet of coal-fired generators, and the Ontario Power Authority moved on its Power System Plan.

Nuclear Energy

Ontario dominates Canada's nuclear industry, containing most of the country's nuclear power generating capacity. Ontario has 16 operating reactors - with another in the planning stage - providing about half of the province's electricity, plus two reactors undergoing refurbishment. Quebec and New Brunswick each have one reactor. Overall, nuclear power provides about 15.5 percent of Canada's electricity. The cost of nuclear power generation has been dropping over the last decade. This is because declining fuel (including enrichment), operating and maintenance costs, while the plant concerned has been paid for, or at least is being paid off. In general the construction costs of nuclear power plants are significantly higher than for coal- or gas-fired plants because of the need to use special materials, and to incorporate sophisticated safety features and back-up control equipment. These contribute much of the nuclear generation cost, but once the plant is built the cost variables are minor. Canada's nuclear plants, however, are quickly reaching the end of their operating lifespans and are entering the long and costly decommissioning phase.

Canada is the world's largest producer of uranium with about one third of world production coming from Saskatchewan mines. The country exports uranium and radioisotopes for medical and industrial purposes. These exports are subject to stringent nuclear non-proliferation policies.

Canada's used reactor fuel is now stored on an interim basis at licensed facilities located where the waste is produced. Like many other countries with nuclear power programs, Canada has yet to decide what to do with this used fuel over the long term. On site storage options are expected to perform well over the near term; however, existing reactor sites were not chosen for their suitability as permanent storage sites. Furthermore, the communities hosting the nuclear reactors have a reasonable expectation that used nuclear fuel will eventually be moved.

Alternative and Renewable Energy

Canadian energy development strategies traditionally focused on low-cost electric power, crude oil, and accessible energy resources. These strategies led to a strong energy industry that has contributed to Canadian prosperity. But today, the world's appetite for cheap energy is counterbalanced by climate change concerns and greenhouse gas emission restrictions. Canada has the potential to become a global leader in renewable energy given its abundant renewable energy resources such as solar, wind, earth, wave, water, tide and biomass. With its large forest and agricultural land base relative to its population, Canada is uniquely positioned to be a world leader in the production and use of biofuels derived from lignocellulose (forestry) biomass. However, renewable energy sources account for less than one percent of the total energy supply today. Utilization of these alternate sources will expand, but they will not become more than small, specialized niche contributors to Canada's energy supply for the foreseeable future.

A recent study by the Pembina Institute, a sustainable-energy think tank, concludes that smart, targeted investments in a diverse array of energy efficiency and renewable energy solutions over the next 20 years will achieve major cuts in greenhouse gas emissions, accelerate the closure of highly-polluting coal plants and avoid the need for new nuclear investments.

THE CALENDAR

The calendar is a method of identifying the passage of time and thereby regulating our civil life and religious observances.

Days, months, and years are based on astronomical periods. The day is the time it takes the earth to make one revolution on its axis, the month is associated with the period of orbiting of the moon around the earth, while the year has to do with the orbiting of the earth around the sun.

Many religious ideas and observances have been connected with the changes of the moon, and in ancient times the calendar took account of the moon rather than the seasons. From new moon to new moon is 29.530 days, and from one spring equinox to the next is 365.24219 days. Since the two are incommensurable, the modern calendar disregards the moon, except insofar as our months are roughly equal to a lunation.

The Week

The division of the week is found only among Aryan nations and in nations and in regions into which they have penetrated. The day is, for convenience, divided into 24 equal parts and is the period of a single rotation of the earth upon its own axis.

A solar or astronomical day commences at midnight, and is divided into two equal portions of 12 hours each - those before noon being termed (A.M.) those after noon (P.M.).

The Chinese week consists of 5 days, which are named after iron, wood, water, feathers and earth; they divide the day into 12 parts of 2 hours each.

The Anglo-Saxons named the days of the week after the following deities: Sunday, the Sun; Monday, the Moon; Tuesday, Tuesco (God of War); Wednesday, Woden (God of Storms); Thursday, Thor (God of Thunder); Friday, Freya (Goddess of Love); Saturday, Saturn (God of Time).

The word week is from Wikon (German); = change, succession.

The Julian Calendar

When Julius Caesar came to power, the Roman Calendar was hopelessly confused. With the advice of the Alexandrian astronomer Sosigenes, Julius Caesar established the Julian Calendar. The length of the year was taken as 365 1/ 4 days, and in order to account for the 1/4 day, an extra day was added every fourth year. From 45 B.C. each month has had its present number of days. In the old Roman Calendar which was based on the moon an extra month was inserted to straighten out the difference between twelve lunations 354.37 days, and 355 days, which they called a year. This was inserted when necessary after February 23rd. In the Julian Calendar the extra day was added by repeating the sixth day before the Kalends (1st) of March, whence comes our word bissextile for leap year.

No very significant change was made till the reform by Pope Gregory XIII in A.D. 1582.

The Julian Calendar is known as the "Old Style" whereas the calendar as improved by Pope Gregory is known as the "New Style". The difference between the two is now 13 days.

The Gregorian Calendar

In that the Solar Year is 11 minutes, 12 seconds less than the Julian Year of 365 1/4 days, it followed in course of years that the Julian Calendar became inaccurate by several days, and in 1582 this difference amounted to 10 days. Pope Gregory XIII, at the suggestion of Aloysius Lilus, an astronomer of Naples, determined to rectify this, and devised the Calendar now known as the Gregorian Calendar. He dropped or cancelled these 10 days - October 5th being called October 15th - and made centurial years leap years only once in 4 centuries; so that whilst 1700, 1800 and 1900 were to be ordinary years, 2000 would be a leap year. This modification brought the Gregorian year into such close exactitude with the solar year that there is only a difference of 26 seconds, which amounts to a day in 3,323 years. This is the "New Style". The Gregorian Calendar was adopted in Italy, France, Spain, Portugal and Poland in 1582, by most of the German Roman Catholic states, Holland and Flanders in 1583, Hungary in 1587. The adoption in Switzerland began in 1584 and was not completed till 1812. The German and Dutch Protestant states generally, along with Denmark adopted it in 1700, British dominions in 1752, Sweden in 1753, Japan in 1873, China in 1912, Bulgaria in 1915, Soviet Russia in 1918, Yugoslavia in 1919, Romania and Greece in 1924, Turkey in 1927. The rules for Easter have not, however, been adopted by those oriental churches that are not subject to the Papacy.

The difference between the two "Styles" will remain 13 days until A.D. 2100.

The Jewish Calendar

The Jewish Calendar from the institution of the Mosaic Law downward was a lunar one, consisting of twelve months. The cycles of religious feasts commencing with the Passover depended not only on the month but on the moon; the 14th of the month of Abid or Nisan was coincident with the full moon; and the new moons themselves were the occasions of regular festivals; the commencement of the month was generally determined by observations of the new moon, but twelve lunar months would make but 354 1/2 days, the years would be short twelve days of the true year and it was necessary that an additional month, Veader, be inserted about every third year.

The modern Jewish Calendar is based on fixed rules and not on observation. A common year may contain 353, 354 or 355 days and the leap year 383, 384 or 385 days. The intercalary month always contains 30 days and is inserted next before the month Adar which name and place it takes, Adar itself called second Adar or Veadar. Tishri 1 is the Jewish New Year and it cannot be a Sunday, Wednesday or Friday. Tishri 1 is not necessarily the day of new moon but is governed by a mean new moon which is calculated from the value of a mean lunation. It is complicated as compared with the Gregorian Calendar. The intercalary month is introduced seven times in every nineteen years.

The identification of the Jewish months with our own cannot be effected with precision on account of the variations existing between the lunar and solar month.

The Muslim Calendar

The Muslim Calendar is called also the calendar of Hegira (i.e. Migration) and is attributed to the primary migration of Mohammed, the Prophet of Islam, on July 16th, 622 A.D. from Mecca, his native city in the land of Hejaz, Arabia, to the city of Medina in the north of the same land. In Medina the Prophet and Founder of the Islamic Faith died and was buried.

Each year consists of 12 lunar months and, since no intercalation is made, the months go round the seasons in between 32 and 33 years.

Far Eastern Calendars

The ancient Chinese calendar is a lunar calendar, divided into 12 months of either 29 or 30 days. It is synchronized with the solar calendar by the addition of extra months as required. The four-day Chinese New Year (Hsin Nien) begins at the first new moon over China after the sun enters Aquarius, and may fall between January 21 and February 19. The calendar runs on a 60-year cycle, and each year has both a number and a name: 2011 (Rabbit), 2012 (Dragon), 2013 (Snake), 2014 (Horse), 2015 (Ram). The three-day Vietnamese New Year (Tet) and the three-to-four-day Korean festival Suhl are set by the same new moon. The Japanese calendar uses the Gregorian date of new year, but with a different epoch.

The Hindu Calendar

The Hindu calendar contains both lunar and solar elements, and is therefore complex. Furthermore, each lunar month is divided into two halves: the dark half (full moon to new moon) and the bright half (new moon to full moon). For some Hindus (primarily South Indian), the lunar month begins on the day following the new moon; for others (primarily North Indian), it begins on the day following the full moon. Likewise, the calculation of the date of New Year varies. There are some holidays which are set by the solar calendar, as well as several which are set by the lunar calendar.

The Indian Calendar

Various religious groups in India have their own calendars (see The Muslim Calendar, and The Hindu Calendar, above). The Indian civil calendar sets the New Year on March 22 in a common year, and on March 21 in a leap year. The years are reckoned according to the native Saka historical era.

The Zoroastrian Calendar

The Zoroastrian calendar is solar, and consists of 12 months of 30 days; five additional days called "gatha" bring the total days in a year to 365. The calculation of the date of the New Year varies among the various Zoroastrian groups.

The Baha'i Calendar

The Baha'i calendar is astronomically fixed, commencing at the vernal equinox. The calendar is solar, and consists of 19 months of 19 days, with the addition of four or five days to bring the total to 365 or 366.

US Civil Calendar 2011

New Year's Day	Fri. Jan. 1
Martin Luther King's Birthday	Mon. Jan. 17
Washington's Birthday	Mon. Feb. 21
Memorial Day	Mon. May 30
Independence Day	Mon. July 4
Labor Day	Mon. Sept. 5
Columbus Day	Mon. Oct. 10
Election Day	Tue. Nov. 8
Veterans' Day	Fri. Nov. 11
Thanksgiving Day	Thu. Nov. 24

United Kingdom Civil Calendar 2011

Accession of Queen Elizabeth II	Sun. Feb. 6
St. David (Wales)	Tue. Mar. 1
Commonwealth Day	Mon. Mar. 14
St. Patrick (Ireland)	Thu. Mar. 17
Birthday of Queen Elizabeth II	Thu. Apr. 21
St. George (England)	Sat. Apr. 23
Coronation Day	Thu. June 2
Birthday of Prince Philip, Duke of Edinburgh	Thu. June 10
The Queen's Official Birthday	Sat. June 11
Remembrance Sunday	Sun. Nov. 13
Birthday of the Prince of Wales	Mon. Nov. 14
St. Andrew (Scotland)	Wed. Nov. 30

For Canadian holidays and festivals, please see inside back cover.

THE SEASONS 2011

Eastern Standard Time

- Spring begins March 20th 18 h 21 m
- Summer begins June 21st 12 h 16 m
- Autumn begins Sept. 23nd 04 h 05 m
- Winter begins Dec. 22st 00 h 30 m

Eastern Standard Time applies in Ontario and Québec. Newfoundland time is 1 1/2 hours later than Eastern Standard time; in the Maritime Provinces, on Atlantic time, time is 1 hour later; in Manitoba and Saskatchewan, on Central time, time is 1 hour earlier; in Alberta and the western half of Saskatchewan, on Mountain time, time is 2 hours earlier; in B.C., on Pacific time, time is 3 hours earlier.

EPOCHS 2011

- The year 7520 of the Byzantine era begins on Wed., Sep. 14, 2011.
- The year 5772 of the Jewish era begins at sunset on Wed., Sep. 28, 2011.
- The New Year of the Chinese (xin mao) era begins on Thu., Feb. 3, 2011.
- The year 2764 of the Roman era begins on Fri., Jan. 14, 2011.
- The year 2760 of the Nabonassar era begins on Thu., Apr. 21, 2011.
- The year 2671 of the Japanese era begins on Sat., Jan. 1, 2011.
- The year 2323 of the Grecian (Seleucidae) era begins on Wed., Sep. 14, 2011 (or Fri., Oct. 14, 2011).
- The year 1933 of the Indian (Saka) era begins on Tue., Mar. 22, 2011.
- The year 1728 of the Diocletian era begins on Mon., Sep. 12, 2011.
- The year 1433 of the Islamic era (Hegira) begins at sunset on Sat., Nov. 26, 2011.
- January 1, 2011 of the Julian Calendar corresponds to Jan. 14, 2011 of the Gregorian Calendar.

PERPETUAL CALENDAR

(Table for Determining the Weekday of a Given Date)

In the YEAR table, locate the first two figures of the given year (lower left) and the last two figures (upper right) and take the number at the intersection.

With that number, enter the MONTH table, and take the number at the intersection with the given month. Note the special columns for January and February in the case of a bissextile (leap) year.

With that number, enter the DAY OF THE MONTH table. The weekday is found at the intersection with the given day of the month.

Example: 1970 March 7

					00	01	02	03	—	04	05
					06	07	—	08	09	10	11
					—	12	13	14	15	—	16
					17	18	19	—	20	21	22
					23	—	24	25	26	27	—
					28	29	30	31	—	32	33
					34	35	—	36	37	38	39
					—	40	41	42	43	—	44
					45	46	47	—	48	49	50
					51	—	52	53	54	55	—
					56	57	58	59	—	60	61
					62	63	—	64	65	66	67
					—	68	69	70	71	—	72
					73	74	75	—	76	77	78
					79	—	80	81	82	83	—
					84	85	86	87	—	88	89
					90	91	—	92	93	94	95
YEAR					—	96	97	98	99		
0	7	14	17	21	6	0	1	2	3	4	5
1	8	15 *J*			5	6	0	1	2	3	4
2	9		18	22	4	5	6	0	1	2	3
3	10				3	4	5	6	0	1	2
4	11	15 *G*	19	23	2	3	4	5	6	0	1
5	12	16	20	24	1	2	3	4	5	6	0
6	13				0	1	2	3	4	5	6

J: until 1582 October 4 inclusively (Julian Calendar)
G: from 1582 October 15 onwards (Gregorian Calendar)
Example: In the first table, we find 5 at the intersection of 19 and 70.

MONTH	May	Feb. *(B)* Aug.	Feb. March Nov.	June	Sept. Dec.	Jan. *(B)* April July	Jan. Oct.
1	2	3	4	5	6	0	1
2	3	4	5	6	0	1	2
3	4	5	6	0	1	2	3
4	5	6	0	1	2	3	4
5	6	0	1	2	3	4	5
6	0	1	2	3	4	5	6
0	1	2	3	4	5	6	0

(B) = Bissextile (leap) year
Example: In the second table, we find 1 at the intersection of 5 and March.

DAY OF MONTH	1 8 15 22 29	2 9 16 23 30	3 10 17 24 31	4 11 18 25	5 12 19 26	6 13 20 27	7 14 21 28
1	Sun.	Mon.	Tue.	Wed.	Thur.	Fri.	Sat.
2	Mon.	Tue.	Wed.	Thur.	Fri.	Sat.	Sun.
3	Tue.	Wed.	Thur.	Fri.	Sat.	Sun.	Mon.
4	Wed.	Thur.	Fri.	Sat.	Sun.	Mon.	Tue.
5	Thur.	Fri.	Sat.	Sun.	Mon.	Tue.	Wed.
6	Fri.	Sat.	Sun.	Mon.	Tue.	Wed.	Thu.
0	Sat.	Sun.	Mon.	Tue.	Wed.	Thu.	Fri.

Example: In the third table, we find *Saturday* at the intersection of 1 and 7.

Reprinted from *Astronomical Tables of the Sun, Moon and Planets*, by Jean Meeus (Willmann-Bell Inc., 1983), with the permission of the publisher.

FIXED AND MOVABLE FESTIVALS AND ANNIVERSARIES

(Gregorian Calendar)

	2011			2012			2013			2014			2015		
JANUARY begins on	Sat.			Sun.			Tue.			Wed.			Thu.		
New Year's Day	Sa	Jan.	1	Su	Jan.	1	Tu	Jan.	1	We	Jan.	1	Th	Jan.	1
Gantan-sai (Shinto New Year)	Sa	Jan.	1	Su	Jan.	1	Tu	Jan.	1	We	Jan.	1	Th	Jan.	1
Mary Mother of God	Sa	Jan.	1	Su	Jan.	1	Tu	Jan.	1	We	Jan.	1	Th	Jan.	1
Epiphany	Th	Jan.	6	Fr	Jan.	6	Su	Jan.	6	Mo	Jan.	6	Tu	Jan.	6
FEBRUARY begins on	Tue.			Wed.			Fri.			Sat.			Sun.		
Lunar New Year (Chinese, etc.)	Th	Feb.	3	Sa	Jan.	23	Su	Feb.	10	Fr	Jan.	31	Th	Feb.	19
MARCH begins on	Tue.			Thu.			Fri.			Sat.			Sun.		
St. David	Tu	Mar.	1	Th	Mar.	1	Fr	Mar.	1	Sa	Mar.	1	Su	Mar.	1
World Day of Prayer	Fr	Mar.	4	Fr	Mar.	2	Fr	Mar.	1	Fr	Mar.	7	Fr	Mar.	6
Ash Wednesday	We		9	We	Feb.	22	We	Feb.	13	We	Mar.	5	We	Feb.	25
Daylight Savings Time begins**	Su	Mar.	13	Su	Mar.	12	Su	Mar.	10	Su	Mar.	9	Su	Mar.	8
	Su	Apr.	3	Su	Apr.	2	Su	Apr.	7	Su	Apr.	6	Su	Apr.	5
St. Patrick	Th	Mar.	17	Sa	Mar.	17	Su	Mar.	17	Mo	Mar.	17	Tu	Mar.	17
St. Joseph (Patron Saint of Canada)	Sa	Mar.	19	Mo	Mar.	19	Tu	Mar.	19	We	Mar.	19	Th	Mar.	19
Naw Ruz (Baha'i New Year)	Mo	Mar.	21	We	Mar.	21	Th	Mar.	21	Fr	Mar.	21	Sa	Mar.	21
Annunciation	Fr	Mar.	25	Su	Mar.	25	Mo	Mar.	25	Tu	Mar.	25	We	Mar.	25
APRIL begins on	Fri.			Sun.			Mon.			Tue.			Wed.		
Hindu New Year***	Mo	Apr.	4	Fr	Mar.	23	Th	Apr.	11	Mo	Mar.	31	Sa	Mar.	21
Baisakhi	We	Apr.	13	Fr	Apr.	13	Sa	Apr.	13	Mo	Apr.	14	Tu	Apr.	14
First Day of Passover (Pesach)	Sa	Apr.	19	Sa	Apr.	7	Tu	Mar.	26	Tu	Apr.	15	Sa	Apr.	4
First Day of Ridvan	Th	Apr.	21	Sa	Apr.	21	Su	Apr.	21	Mo	Apr.	21	Tu	Apr.	21
Good Friday	Fr	Apr.	22	Fr	Apr.	6	Fr	Mar.	29	Fr	Apr.	18	Fr	Apr.	3
St. George	Sa	Apr.	23	Mo	Apr.	23	Tu	Apr.	23	We	Apr.	23	Th	Apr.	23
Easter Sunday	Su	Apr.	24	Su	Apr.	8	Su	Mar.	31	Su	Apr.	20	Su	Apr.	5
MAY begins on	Sun.			Tue.			Wed.			Thu.			Fri.		
Buddha Day (Visakha Puja)	Tu	May	17	Mo	May	6	Fr	May	24	We	May	14	Mo	May	4
Victoria Day	Mo	May	23	Mo	May	21	Mo	May	20	Mo	May	19	Mo	May	18
JUNE begins on	Wed.			Fri.			Sat.			Sun.			Mon.		
Ascension Thursday	Th	June	2	Th	May	17	Th	May	9	Th	May	29	Th	May	7
Ascension Sunday	Su	June	5	Su	May	20	Su	May	12	Su	June	1	Su	May	10
Pentecost (Shavuoth)	We	June	8	Su	May	27	We	May	15	We	June	4	Su	May	24
Pentecost (Whit Sunday)	Su	June	12	Su	May	27	Su	May	19	Su	June	8	Su	May	24
First Nations Day	Tu	June	21	Th	June	21	Fr	June	21	Sa	June	21	Su	June	21
Corpus Christi (Thursday)	Th	June	23	Th	June	7	Th	May	30	Th	June	19	Th	June	4
Sacred Heart of Jesus	Th	June	23	Sa	June	23	Su	June	23	Mo	June	23	Fr	June	19
St. John Baptist	Fr	June	24	Su	June	24	Mo	June	24	Tu	June	24	We	June	24
Corpus Christi (Sunday)	Su	June	26	Su	June	10	Su	June	2	Su	June	22	Su	June	7
St. Peter and St. Paul	We	June	29	Fr	June	29	Sa	June	29	Su	June	29	Mo	June	29
JULY begins on	Fri.			Sun.			Mon.			Tue.			Wed.		
Canada Day	Fr	July	1	Su	July	1	Mo	July	1	Tu	July	1	We	July	1
AUGUST begins on	Mon.			Wed.			Thu.			Fri.			Sat.		
First Day of Ramadan*	Tu	Aug.	2	Fr	July	20	Tu	July	9	Sa	June	28	Th	June	18
Assumption	Mo	Aug.	15	We	Aug.	15	Th	Aug.	15	Fr	Aug.	15	Sa	Aug.	15
Eid al Fitr (Ramadan ends)	We	Aug.	31	Su	Aug.	19	Th	Aug.	8	Tu	July	29	Sa	July	18
SEPTEMBER begins on	Thu.			Sat.			Sun.			Mon.			Tue.		
Labour Day	Mo	Sept.	5	Mo	Sept.	3	Mo	Sept.	2	Mo	Sept.	1	Mo	Sept.	7
Hebrew New Year (Rosh Hashanah)	Th	Sept.	29	Mo	Sept.	17	Tu	Sept.	5	Th	Sept.	25	Fr	Sept.	4
St. Michael	Th	Sept.	29	Sa	Sept.	29	Su	Sept.	29	Mo	Sept.	29	Tu	Sept.	29
OCTOBER begins on	Sat.			Mon.			Tue.			Wed.			Thu.		
Day of Atonement (Yom Kippur)	Sa	Oct.	8	We	Sept.	26	Sa	Sept.	14	Sa	Oct.	4	We	Sept.	23
Thanksgiving	Mo	Oct.	10	Mo	Oct.	8	Mo	Oct.	7	Mo	Oct.	13	Mo	Oct.	12
First Day of Feast of Tabernacles (Sukkoth)	Th	Oct.	13	Mo	Oct.	1	Th	Sept.	19	Th	Oct.	9	Mo	Sept.	28
Diwali	We	Oct.	26	Tu	Nov.	13	Su	Nov.	3	Th	Oct.	23	We	Nov.	11
Daylight Savings Time ends**	Su	Oct.	30	Su	Oct.	28	Su	Oct.	27	Su	Oct.	26	Su	Oct.	25
	Su	Nov.	6	Su	Nov.	4	Su	Nov.	3	Su	Nov.	2	Su	Nov.	1
NOVEMBER begins on	Tue.			Thu.			Fri.			Sat.			Sun.		
All Saints' Day	Tu	Nov.	1	Th	Nov.	1	Fr	Nov.	1	Sa	Nov.	1	Su	Nov.	1
Remembrance Day	Fr	Nov.	11	Su	Nov.	11	Mo	Nov.	11	Tu	Nov.	11	We	Nov.	11
Islamic New Year	Fr	Nov.	26	Th	Nov.	15	Tu	Nov.	5	Sa	Oct.	25	We	Oct.	14
St. Andrew's Day	We	Nov.	30	Fr	Nov.	30	Sa	Nov.	30	Su	Nov.	30	Mo	Nov.	30
DECEMBER begins on	Thu.			Sat.			Sun.			Mon.			Tue.		
First Day in Hanukah	We	Dec.	21	Su	Dec.	9	Th	Nov.	28	We	Dec.	17	Mo	Dec.	7
Christmas Day	Su	Dec.	25	Tu	Dec.	25	We	Dec.	25	Th	Dec.	25	Fr	Dec.	25
Kwanzaa begins on	Mo	Dec.	26	We	Dec.	26	Th	Dec.	26	Fr	Dec.	26	Sa	Dec.	26
Last Day of Year	Sat.			Mon.			Tue.			Wed.			Thu.		

*These are tabular dates; the festival begins at sunset on the day before. According to Islamic custom, the date is actually set by the direct observation of the new crescent moon.
Alberta, British Columbia, Manitoba, New Brunswick, Northwest Territories, Nova Scotia, Ontario, Prince Edward Island and Quebec start Daylight Saving Time on the second Sunday in March and return to standard time on the first Sunday in November. Newfoundland, Nunavut and Yukon start Daylight Saving Time on the first Sunday in April and return to standard time on the last Sunday in October. Saskatchewan doesn't observe Daylight Saving Time. * Different branches of Hinduism celebrate the new year at different times
Jewish holidays begin at sunset the previous evening.

STANDARD HOLIDAYS in Canada include the following: New Year's Day, Good Friday, Victoria Day, Canada Day, Labour Day, Thanksgiving Day, Remembrance Day, Christmas Day, Boxing Day and any other day so proclaimed by the Governor General of Canada, or the Lieutenants Governor of the Provinces. Additionally, Provincial Holidays include: ALBERTA: Alberta Family Day (3rd Monday in February), Heritage Day (1st Monday in August); BRITISH COLUMBIA: British Columbia Day (1st Monday in August); MANITOBA: Louis Riel Day (3rd Monday in February), Civic Holiday (1st Monday in August); NEW BRUNSWICK: New Brunswick Day (1st Monday in August); NEWFOUNDLAND: Regatta Day/Civic Holiday (by municipal orders); following celebrated on nearest Monday: St. Patrick's Day (Mar. 17), St. George's Day (Apr. 23), Discovery Day (June 24), Orangemen's Day (July 12); NORTHWEST TERRITORIES: National Aboriginal Day (June 21), Civic Holiday (1st Monday in August); NOVA SCOTIA: Natal Day (1st Monday in August, varies in Halifax); NUNAVUT: Nunavut Day (July 9), 1st Monday in August (1st Monday in August); ONTARIO: Family Day (3rd Monday in February); PRINCE EDWARD ISLAND: Natal Day (by proclamation, usually 1st Monday in August); QUEBEC: National Day (Fête nationale du Québec) (June 24); SASKATCHEWAN: Family Day (3rd Monday in February), Civic Holiday (1st Monday in August); YUKON: Discovery Day (3rd Monday in August)

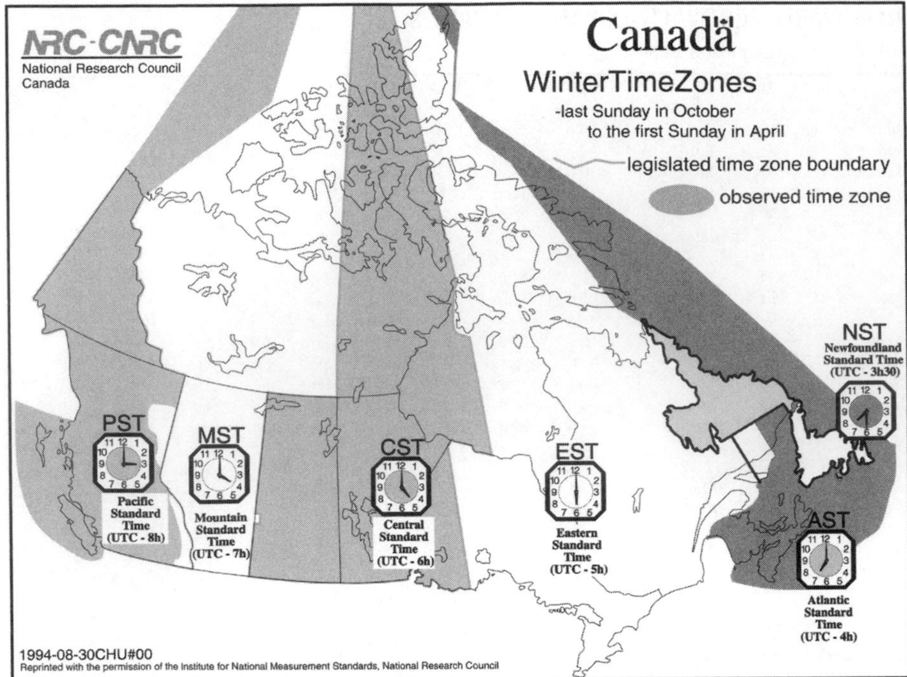

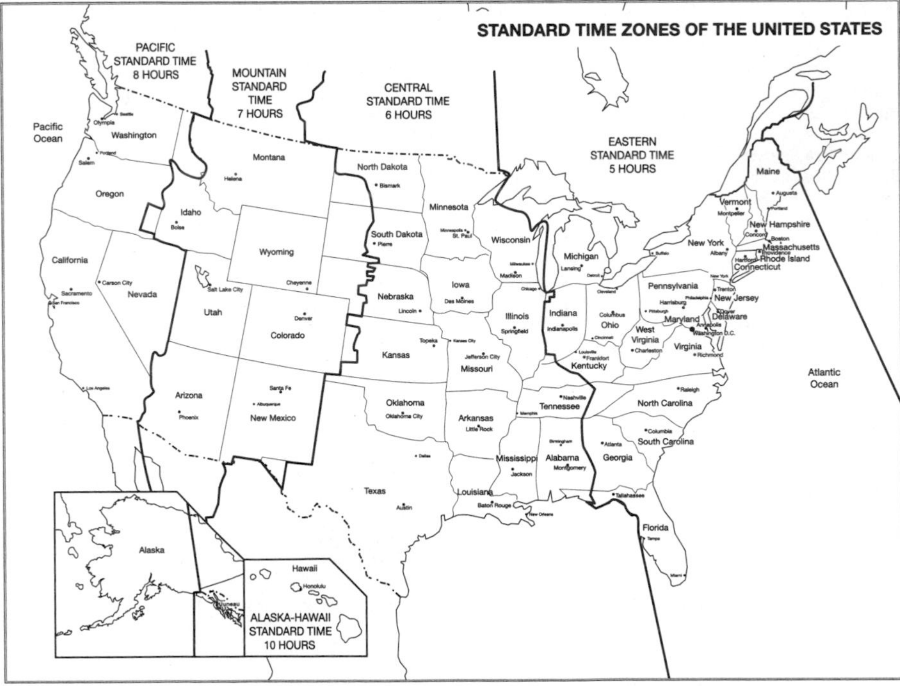

- The 60th year of the reign of Queen Elizabeth II begins on Sun., Feb. 6, 2011.
- The 145th year of the Dominion of Canada begins Fri., July 1, 2011.
- The 236th year of the Independence of the United States of America begins Mon., July 4, 2011.
- The Julian Day 2,455,563 begins at Greenwich noon Jan. 1, 2011, Gregorian Calendar.

STANDARD TIME

Owing to the great breadth of Canada the difference in solar time in various parts of the country is adjusted by the creation of Standard Time Zones, one hour in width, fixed between arbitrary lines running approximately north and south, 15° of longitude apart, the time observed in each zone being an exact, except for Newfoundland, number of hours slow from Greenwich. Example: When it is 8 a.m. by Pacific Time it is 12 noon by Atlantic Time and 4 p.m. at Greenwich.

There are six zones divided as follows, reckoning from Greenwich:

- *Newfoundland Standard Time:* Newfoundland, excluding most of Labrador, 3 1/2 hours slow.
- *Atlantic Standard Time/60th Meridian Time:* most of Labrador, New Brunswick, Nova Scotia, Prince Edward Island, and those parts of Québec and Northwest Territories east of the 63rd Meridian, 4 hours slow.
- *Eastern Standard Time/75th Meridian Time:* Québec west of the 63rd Meridian and Ontario as far west as the 90th Meridian; Northwest Territories between the 68th and 85th Meridian, 5 hours slow.
- *Central Standard Time/90th Meridian Time:* Ontario west of the 90th Meridian, Manitoba, Saskatchewan and Northwest Territories between the 85th and 102nd Meridian, 6 hours slow.
- *Mountain Standard Time/105th Meridian Time:* Throughout Alberta and in Northwest Territories west of the 102nd Meridian, 7 hours slow.
- *Pacific Standard Time/120th Meridian Time:* Throughout most of British Columbia and in the Yukon, 8 hours slow.

Railways and airways make up their schedules according to Standard Time in winter and Daylight Saving Time in summer. Solar time around the globe varies four minutes with each degree of longitude.

INTERNATIONAL TIME ZONES

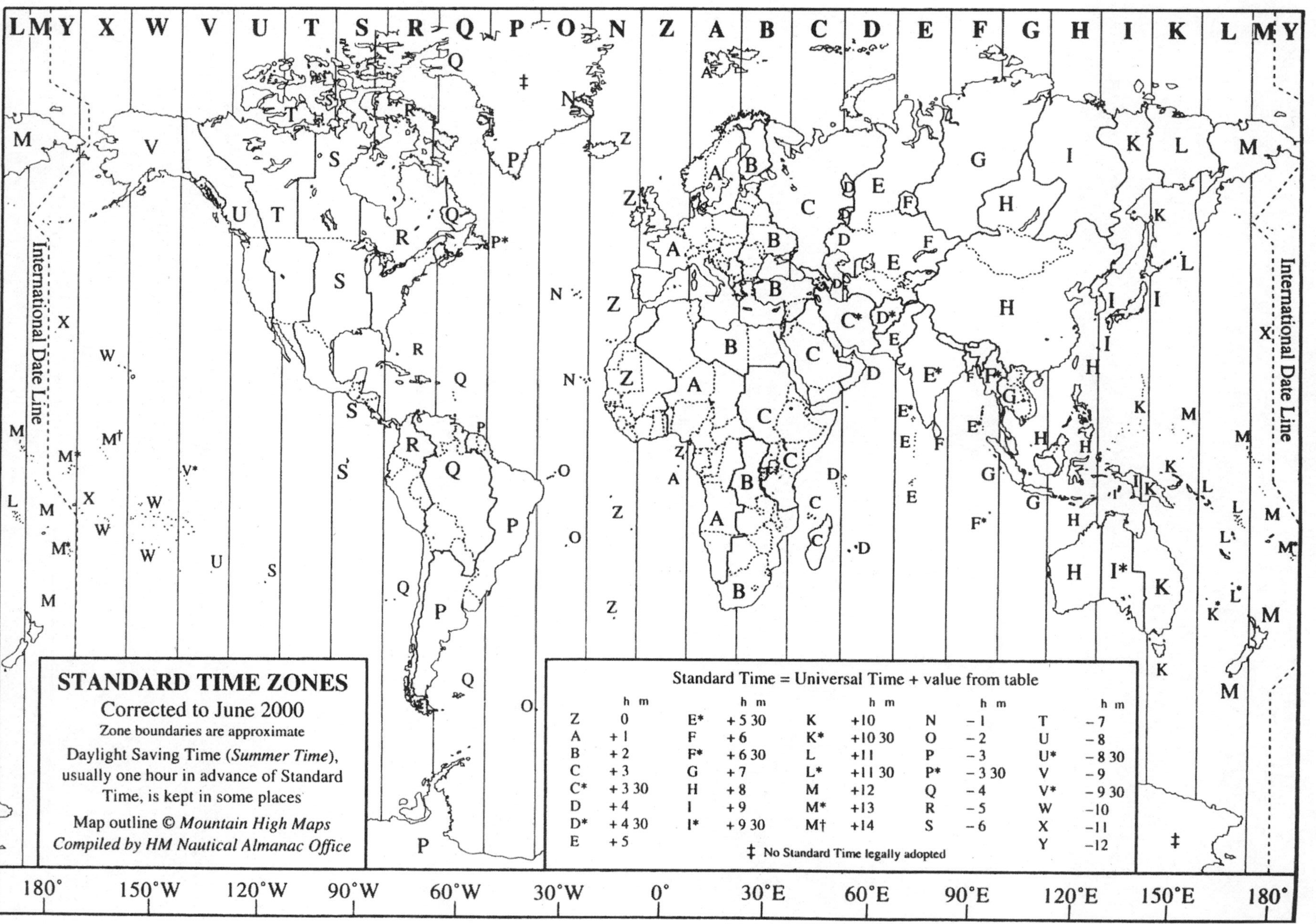

Economics & Finance

Canada's Economy

Since World War II, the growth of Canada's manufacturing, mining, and service sectors has transformed the economy of the world's second-largest nation from a largely rural model into one that is primarily industrial and urban. This transformation has been so progressive that Canada has long enjoyed top-level economic status within the G-7, the international grouping of seven leading industrial countries additionally comprised of the United States, the United Kingdom, France, Germany, Italy, and Japan.

The 1989 U.S.-Canada Free Trade Agreement and the 1994 North American Free Trade Agreement (which also includes Mexico) spurred a dramatic increase in trade and economic integration of the North American continent. Given its significant natural resources, skilled labor force, and modern plants, Canada has benefited tremendously from the free-trade initiatives. Currently, some 85 percent of Canadian exports are absorbed by Canada's principal trading partner, making it the largest foreign supplier of energy, including oil, gas, uranium, and electric power to the US.

In general, Canada's overall economy is operating at full production capacity. Labor markets are tight, with shortages reported in many parts of the country and in a number of sectors. Employment edged up in 2007, with the national unemployment rate remaining unchanged at its 33-year low of 6 percent. Inflation continues to be comfortably under control and the general government and current account balances are in surplus. In addition, efficient fiscal management has produced consecutive balanced budgets since 1997.

The immediate economic future appears equally as positive. However, like any other allied country from World War II, Canada will soon see the baby-boom generation pass into retirement, causing the working-age proportion of its population to diminish. As well, there is continuing public debate regarding the rising cost of Canada's world-famous and well-regarded, publicly funded healthcare system.

In the last few decades, Canada's economic model has moved away from being natural-resource dependant to being service-based. While the production of goods remains significant, accounting for a third of the national economy, three out of four citizens are currently employed in service industries. Maintaining the transportation and storage of goods, along with servicing restaurants, shops, entertainment, healthcare, education, defense, and government now occupies more Canadians than the actual manufacturing of materials. Canada's gross domestic product, being the balance between consumers' expenditures and income, has shown healthy progress, illustrating a growing demand for big-ticket items including houses, cars, furniture, and electronics.

The Canadian dollar continues to be strong and in 2007 reached a 31-year high against the American dollar, achieving one-to-one parity with its neighbour's currency. In October of that same year, Bloomberg reported that the dollar was approaching $1.0412, the currency's all-time high since the information-service company began monitoring it in February 1971 (The Bank of Canada only let the currency float in 1970).

As a major international oil exporter, Canada has benefited from soaring crude prices, more than offsetting its declining conventional oil production. The country has equally profited from the export of nickel, copper, aluminum, and zinc, commodities that all sit at or near record highs. Mineral prices are expected to remain elevated and oil sands production is projected to expand dramatically in coming years to reach close to 3.5 million barrels per day by 2015. With commodities accounting for 35 percent of Canada's exports, the loonie is finally being viewed around the world as a commodity-based currency and has been bid up accordingly. Since January 2002, Canada's dollar-coin has gained more than 40 percent against the buck.

Certainly, some economic sectors could be stronger. Performance in the high-tech sector has been weak, partially due to Canadian companies purchasing much of their software and machinery from the U.S. That said, the recent favourable exchange rate is expected to lead to improvement in this area. The challenges of adjusting to a higher Canadian dollar could additionally benefit other exporters, who have found it necessary to improve efficiency.

A recent decline in the American housing market has caused lumber prices to tumble, hurting British Columbia's forestry industry. However, strong domestic housing starts have boosted the overall production of lumber and other timber products, increasing forestry exports despite U.S. softwood lumber tariffs. (Every one-cent increase in the value of the loonie against the U.S. dollar translates to a loss of more than $150 million in annual revenue for the pulp, paper and forest industry.) Non-residential construction activity also increased in 2005, reflecting multi-billion dollar investments in projects in Canada's energy patch as well as increased investment in commercial building construction.

In May 2003, the discovery of Bovine Spongiform Encephalopathy (BSE), commonly known as mad-cow disease, in one cow from Alberta cause severe harm to Canada's beef-export market. Compounded by the advent of Severe Acute Respiratory Syndrome (SARS) in the late summer of that same year, Canada's growth forecast dampened from 3.4 percent to 2.3 percent, but the current outlook is still improving. In September 2007, the U.S. Department of Agriculture (USDA) agreed to expand cattle trade with Canada, additionally urging beef-importing nations to eliminate unnecessary barriers erected after the mad-cow scare. More trade with the United States will help export-dependent Canadian ranchers recover from trade bans. The impact of the stronger Canadian dollar, if it is maintained, will also result in higher beef-processing costs relative to competitors in the U.S., which could offset more gains.

Canada's commercial ocean fisheries have experienced overall production decline, due in part to the year-2003 closure of northern cod fishing grounds. The volume of production has been adversely affected by an average rate of 4 percent a year as a result of dwindling resources and problems caused by over-exploitation of some major species. West Coast over-fishing has led to a reduction in the size of the salmon fleet, as well as extensive government intervention in the fishing industry on both coasts. Meanwhile aquaculture, or fish farming, continues to thrive. In particular, Eastern Canada boasts extensive operations, growing predominantly Atlantic salmon and mussels. Other key species include bay and sea scallops, brook trout, oysters, bay quahogs, sea urchins, arctic char, haddock, and bar clams, and significant progress has been made in the development of new species such as halibut, sturgeon, abalone and cod. That said, almost every province in Canada, including the Yukon Territory, runs commercial freshwater aquaculture operations, mostly raising rainbow and brook trout. Ontario and Qu,bec are the dominant producers of freshwater fish in Canada, followed by Saskatchewan, Alberta, and New Brunswick. As the Canadian freshwater aquaculture industry is young, it is also ideally poised for growth.

Always historically strong, the Canadian stock market has continued to thrive. The Toronto Stock Exchange (TSX) is the country's largest and the world's sixth largest by market capitalization. In addition, the TSX Group is the international leader in the oil and gas sector, boasting more oil and gas sector listings on the Toronto Stock Exchange and TSX Venture Exchange than any other exchange in the world (in June 2007, 434 oil and gas companies were listed, with a total market capitalization of $544.9 billion). Oil and gas companies continue to raise equity on Canadian exchanges with $5.56 billion raised in the first half of 2007 alone and trading over 10 billion oil and gas shares, valued at $169.2 billion.

Sourcing from China continues to offer an economically viable solution for Canadian companies. This option to reduce costs while growing wealth in major Chinese cities creates vast new opportunities for Canadian firms, particularly exporters of services. With a small domestic market, the steady expansion of multilateral trade is critical to the structure of the country's economy and the continued prosperity of its citizens. Still, while the rapid and ongoing industrialization of China has boosted the world price of Canadian oil, gas, mineral, metal, and farm-product exports, Canada has lagged in terms of taking advantage of Asia's voracious demands. China's imports from the rest of the world currently enjoy double-digit growth, while Canadian exports in 2005 accounted for only 1.1 percent of total Chinese imports, well below the high of 1.7 percent in 2000-01, and substantially out of line with its share of global trade. Canadian sales to Japan have not fared much better. In 1996, Japan received 4.1 percent of Canada's exports, with that figure falling to 2.1 percent a decade later. To complicate matters, China is expected to become the top-ranked destination for U.S. exports within five years, effectively displacing Canada as the No. 1 trading partner to the U.S.

Since the early 1990s, the focus of Canadian monetary policy on low, stable, and predictable inflation has helped to both anchor inflation expectations and reduce the ups and downs in economic activity. Canadians have been able to make spending, saving, and investment decisions with greater certainty, knowing that their central bank will hold the line on future inflation and that the economy will be more stable. Low interest rates and greater confidence about the future have, encouraged Canadian firms to undertake important restructuring initiatives, stepping up to meet the challenges of sweeping worldwide technological change and intensely competitive global markets.

PRINCIPAL TRADING PARTNERS IN 2009

	IMPORTS ($000,000)	EXPORTS ($000,000)
United States (U.S.)	186,815.2	270,128.8
China	39,656.8	11,161.8
Mexico	16,534.8	4,804.9
Japan	12,350.9	8,314.6
Germany	10,658.1	3,738.6
United Kingdom (U.K.)	9,395.0	12,099.5
Korea, South	5,929.6	3,526.2
France (incl. Monaco, French Antilles)	5,630.3	2,682.7
Italy (includes Vatican City State)	4,446.3	1,797.6
Algeria	3,765.0	352.0
Norway	3,570.9	1,764.0
Switzerland	3,445.7	1,187.9
Taiwan (Taipei)	3,343.9	1,109.5
Peru	2,878.1	428.7
Brazil	2,578.6	1,600.1
Malaysia	2,313.3	790.5
Thailand	2,298.6	567.6
Ireland	2,196.3	543.5
India	2,002.4	2,147.6
Netherlands	1,871.8	2,758.6
Sweden	1,797.6	380.9
Chile	1,730.8	644.4
Russia	1,632.7	887.8
Australia	1,625.3	1,780.7
Denmark	1,606.6	618.8
TOTAL ALL COUNTRIES	365,180.3	360,035.1

Source: Industry Canada, August 2010
http://www.ic.gc.ca/sc_mrkti/tdst/tdo/tdo.php?lang=30&headFootDir=/sc_mrkti/tdst/headfoot&productType=HS6&cacheTime=962115865#tag

AVERAGE EARNINGS[1] OF MEN & WOMEN IN CANADA, 1993-2008

	All earners			Full-year full-time workers		
	Average earnings, females (dollars)	Average earnings, males (dollars)	Female-to-male earnings ratio[2] (percent)	Average earnings, females (dollars)	Average earnings, males (dollars)	Female-to-male earnings ratio[2] (percent)
1993	24,800	38,600	64.1	37,900	52,000	72.8
1994	24,800	40,000	61.9	37,600	53,600	70.2
1995	25,300	39,300	64.2	38,300	52,400	73.0
1996	25,400	40,000	63.6	38,600	53,000	72.8
1997	25,400	41,100	61.8	38,200	54,600	70.0
1998	26,500	42,300	62.8	40,500	56,300	71.9
1999	27,000	43,000	62.6	38,900	56,900	68.4
2000	27,500	44,500	61.7	40,200	56,900	70.6
2001	27,600	44,400	62.1	40,600	58,100	69.9
2002	27,900	44,400	62.8	40,800	58,200	70.2
2003	27,600	43,800	62.9	40,700	57,900	70.2
2004	27,900	44,000	63.5	42,000	59,900	70.1
2005	28,600	44,700	64.0	41,800	59,400	70.5
2006	29,000	44,800	64.7	43,200	60,000	71.9
2007	29,900	45,500	65.7	44,100	61,700	71.4
2008	30,200	46,900	64.5	44,700	62,600	71.3

[1] 2008 Constant Dollars [2] Earnings ratio = (female earnings / male earnings) *100

Source: Statistics Canada, CANSIM Table 202-0102, August 2010

AVERAGE HOUSEHOLD EXPENDITURE, CANADA 2002 - 2008

($)

	2002	2003	2004	2005	2006	2007	2008
Total expenditure	59,439	60,088	62,464	65,575	67,736	69,946	71,364
Food	6,553	6,618	6,772	6,978	7,046	7,305	7,435
Shelter	11,079	11,419	11,987	12,376	12,986	13,643	14,183
Household operation	2,741	2,812	2,864	3,027	3,251	3,287	3,345
Household furnishings and equipment	1,810	1,779	1,871	1,954	2,131	1,964	1,967
Clothing	2,421	2,401	2,470	2,538	2,870	2,948	2,856
Transportation	8,337	8,179	8,476	8,914	9,240	9,395	9,722
Health care	1,561	1,553	1,653	1,755	1,867	1,932	2,044
Personal care	820	825	882	1,071	1,158	1,167	1,189
Recreation	3,520	3,533	3,619	3,850	3,975	3,976	4,066
Reading materials and other printed matter	280	278	278	278	264	260	253
Education	907	1,013	1,067	1,214	1,157	1,017	1,179
Tobacco products and alcoholic beverages	1,460	1,455	1,480	1,398	1,475	1,536	1,495
Games of chance (net)	302	262	258	271	258	251	260
Miscellaneous expenditures	875	870	1,000	987	1,087	1,081	1,075

Source: Statistics Canada, CANSIM Table 203-0001, August 2010

AVERAGE FAMILY INCOME[1], 1997- 2008

	1997	1998	1999	2000	2001	2002	2003	2004	2005	2006	2007	2008
Canada	63,400	67,000	69,100	72,300	73,000	72,900	72,200	74,100	74,900	76,300	79,100	80,500
Newfoundland and Labrador	40,000	44,600	47,200	48,700	47,300	48,400	48,600	49,800	51,500	53,700	59,300	61,900
Prince Edward Island	45,700	50,700	51,100	52,400	52,300	53,000	54,100	55,400	55,700	57,600	57,800	60,600
Nova Scotia	48,900	52,900	55,900	57,700	59,600	60,900	57,700	59,700	62,800	64,600	65,200	64,400
New Brunswick	47,300	51,200	53,700	56,100	55,700	55,600	56,000	57,200	55,900	57,000	59,000	59,300
Quebec	55,000	58,600	60,300	63,400	63,900	64,300	63,400	65,500	64,700	65,500	66,100	66,500
Ontario	71,000	75,600	79,400	83,700	83,200	82,500	81,500	82,900	83,000	82,800	85,200	86,300
Manitoba	57,800	61,800	61,000	61,800	64,100	64,800	64,800	66,600	68,300	70,200	74,500	75,200
Saskatchewan	55,000	56,700	58,600	59,500	62,200	62,000	62,900	63,300	67,300	71,300	75,400	80,100
Alberta	72,600	75,900	74,700	78,000	82,100	79,400	82,000	84,400	87,000	93,300	100,000	103,100
British Columbia	65,300	65,900	66,700	67,900	69,100	70,500	68,400	70,900	73,900	76,100	80,100	82,700

[1] Average total income, economic families, 2 persons or more, 2008 contstant dollars.

Source: Statistics Canada, CANSIM Table 202-0202, August 2010

MINIMUM HOURLY WAGE RATES FOR EXPERIENCED ADULT WORKERS IN CANADA[1]

Jurisdiction	Experienced Adult Workers (Including Domestics)	Effective Date
Federal[2]	The minimum wage rate applicable in regard to workers under federal jurisdiction is the general adult minimum rate of the province or territory where the work is performed	18/12/96
Alberta	$8.80	01/04/09
British Columbia	$8.00	01/11/01
Manitoba	$9.00	01/10/09
New Brunswick	$8.25	01/09/09
Newfoundland & Labrador	$9.00	01/07/09
Northwest Territories	$8.25	28/12/03
Nova Scotia	$8.60	01/04/09
Nunavut	$10.00	05/09/08
Ontario	$9.50	31/03/09
Prince Edward Island	$8.40	01/10/09
Québec	$9.00	01/05/09
Saskatchewan	$9.25	01/05/09
Yukon Territory[3]	$8.89	01/04/09

[1]In many jurisdications, these rates also apply to young workers.

[2]Generally, the federal jurisdiction includes labour market sectors coming under federal authority by virtue of the Constitution, such as international and interprovincial transportation, telecommunication & banking.

[3]Effective April 1, 2007, and on April 1 of each subsequent year, this rate will increase by an amount corresponding to the annual increase for the preceding year in the Consumer Price Index for the city of Whitehorse.

CONSUMER PRICE INDEX, CANADA

2005 BASKET, 2002=100

Date	All-items	Food	Shelter	Household operations, furnishings and equipment	Clothing and footwear	Transportation	Health and personal care	Recreation, education and reading	Alcoholic beverages and tobacco products
2000	95.4	93.3	95.6	96.7	100.3	97.2	97.0	97.0	79.0
2001	97.8	97.4	99.1	98.6	100.7	97.3	98.9	98.4	85.0
2002	100.0	100.0	100.0	100.0	100.0	100.0	100.0	100.0	100.0
2003	102.8	101.7	103.2	100.7	98.2	105.2	101.4	100.8	110.1
2004	104.7	103.8	105.8	101.2	98.0	107.7	102.8	101.1	116.0
2005	107.0	106.4	109.2	101.7	97.6	112.0	104.6	100.8	119.1
2006	109.1	108.9	113.1	102.2	95.8	115.2	105.9	100.6	121.7
2007	111.5	111.8	116.9	103.2	95.7	117.1	107.3	101.8	125.5
2008	114.1	115.7	112.0	104.6	93.8	119.5	108.8	102.2	127.5
2009	114.4	121.4	121.6	107.3	93.4	113.1	112.1	103.1	130.7
Jan-10	115.1	122.3	121.8	107.9	90.1	117.2	113.8	101.1	131.1
Feb-10	115.6	122.7	121.8	108.3	91.2	116.7	113.7	104.1	131.4
Mar-10	115.6	123.1	121.7	108.3	93.6	117.1	113.5	102.5	131.5
Apr-10	116	122.8	122.4	108.5	94.1	117.4	114.8	102.9	131.8
May-10	116.3	122.9	123	108.6	92.7	118.1	114.6	103.6	132.1
Jun-10	116.2	123	123.3	108.6	89.7	117.3	114.7	104.2	132.2

Source: Statistics Canada, CANSIM Table #326-0020, August 2010

New Housing Price Indexes, 1992 - 2009, Annual Averages[1]

1997=100

	Canada	Atlantic Region	Quebec	Ontario	Prairie Region	British Columbia
1992	100.9	97.4	98.9	101.0	90.1	109.4
1993	102.2	98.9	99.4	99.3	93.0	117.2
1994	102.4	100.6	99.7	99.0	94.9	116.4
1995	101.2	102.2	100.5	99.0	95.2	110.1
1996	99.3	102.3	100.1	98.0	95.6	103.3
1997	100.0	100.0	100.0	100.0	100.0	100.0
1998	101.0	99.6	100.5	102.5	105.8	94.9
1999	101.9	101.5	102.5	104.2	109.7	91.0
2000	104.1	103.5	106.1	107.4	112.2	89.9
2001	107.0	105.4	111.0	110.8	114.8	90.6
2002	111.3	108.7	117.3	114.9	121.0	92.9
2003	116.7	112.5	126.2	120.0	127.3	96.3
2004	123.2	115.9	134.2	126.7	134.0	101.4
2005	129.4	120.5	140.8	132.6	143.2	106.3
2006	142.0	124.9	147.0	137.5	192.5	113.2
2007	153.0	129.6	153.2	141.1	235.6	120.5
2008	158.2	141.8	160.8	146.1	241.5	123.0
2009	154.6	149.1	165.9	146.1	222.7	115.0

[1]Total (house and land)

Source: Statistics Canada, CANSIM II Table 327-0005, August 2010

HOUSEHOLD USE OF SELECTED MEDIA 2008 [1]

	Canada	N.L.	P.E.I.	N.S.	N.B.	Que.	Ont.	Man.	Sask.	Alb.	B.C.
Telephones (includes business use)	12,060	196	52	367	295	3,091	4,517	421	373	1,207	1,541
Cellular Telephone	9,636	140	40	278	194	2,121	3,660	333	310	1,125	1,435
Compact disc player	10,636	165	46	318	251	2,638	3,916	362	326	1,156	1,458
Cablevision	8,602	128	30	255	168	2,137	3,192	309	211	865	1,306
Satellite dish	3,118	67	23	99	113	752	1,173	112	144	346	289
Colour televisions	13,003	203	55	386	304	3,317	4,821	458	388	1,329	1,743
Video cassette recorders	9,711	155	43	295	232	2,465	3,578	346	290	995	1,313
DVD player	11,372	168	46	335	255	2,820	4,259	391	334	1,198	1,566
Home computer	10,453	143	40	292	223	2,486	3,958	345	303	1,152	1,510
CD writer	6,914	100	29	200	147	1,498	2,601	247	211	822	1,058
DVD writer	5,549	83	22	160	115	1,216	2,050	196	171	713	822
Internet use from home	9,818	134	38	271	201	2,249	3,775	311	286	1,095	1,458
Type of Internet connection:											
Regular telephone connection to a computer	1,018	9	6	23	20	354	393	19	35	72	88
High-speed telephone connection to a computer	3,765	80	23	126	138	750	1,379	177	179	427	486
Cable connection to a computer	4,450	43	5	109	36	1,058	1,772	98	58	485	788

[1] Estimated number of households in thousands

Source: Statistics Canada, 2008 Survey of Household Spending, Table 62F0041

COUNTRIES VISITED BY CANADIANS, 2009

ONE OR MORE NIGHTS

	COUNTRY VISITS	SPENDING LESS FARES
United States	24,913,600	12,483,427,800
MEXICO	1,208,600	1,310,008,500
CUBA	979,100	805,492,000
DOMINICAN REPUBLIC	876,100	789,916,500
UNITED KINGDOM	873,100	986,417,300
FRANCE	734,700	906,129,800
ITALY	361,900	483,774,600
GERMANY	311,800	264,579,900
MAINLAND CHINA	263,800	445,201,000
NETHERLANDS	260,000	195,095,200
SPAIN	218,200	284,055,800
HONG KONG	212,600	243,127,600
REPUBLIC OF IRELAND	173,100	210,115,800
SWITZERLAND	146,700	100,476,800
GREECE	137,300	219,048,900

Source: Statistics Canada, Tourism and the Centre for Education Statistics, http://www40.statcan.gc.ca/l01/cst01/arts37a-eng.htm

LABOUR FORCE ESTIMATES, ANNUAL AVERAGES 1992-2009

	Population 15+ ('000)	Labour Force ('000)	Employment ('000)	Unemployment ('000)	Unemployment rate (%)	Participation rate (%)	Employment rate (%)
1992	21,820	14,336	12,731	1,605	11.2	65.7	58.3
1993	22,093	14,435	12,793	1,642	11.4	65.3	57.9
1994	22,368	14,574	13,059	1,515	10.4	65.2	58.4
1995	22,660	14,689	13,295	1,394	9.5	64.8	58.7
1996	22,967	14,854	13,421	1,432	9.6	64.7	58.4
1997	23,256	15,079	13,706	1,373	9.1	64.8	58.9
1998	23,523	15,316	14,046	1,270	8.3	65.1	59.7
1999	23,787	15,588	14,407	1,182	7.6	65.5	60.6
2000	24,094	15,847	14,764	1,083	6.8	65.8	61.3
2001	24,444	16,110	14,946	1,164	7.2	65.9	61.1
2002	24,797	16,579	15,310	1,269	7.7	66.9	61.7
2003	25,107	16,959	15,672	1,286	7.6	67.5	62.4
2004	25,443	17,182	15,947	1,235	7.2	67.5	62.7
2005	25,806	17,343	16,170	1,173	6.8	67.2	62.7
2006	26,185	17,593	16,484	1,108	6.3	67.2	63.0
2007	26,553	17,946	16,866	1,079	6.0	67.6	63.5
2008	26,924	18,245	17,125	1,119	6.1	67.8	63.6
2009	27,309	18,369	16,849	1,520	8.3	67.3	61.7

Source: Statistics Canada, Labour Force Historical Review Cat. #71F0004XCB, 2009 Edition

LABOUR FORCE BY DETAILED OCCUPATION, CANADA, ANNUAL AVERAGES, 2000-2009

Occupation	2000	2001	2002	2003	2004	2005	2006	2007	2008	2009
Total, all occupations	15,847.0	16,109.8	16,579.3	16,958.5	17,182.3	17,342.6	17,592.8	17,945.8	18,245.1	18,368.7
Management occupations	1,444.3	1,363.6	1,386.2	1,401.0	1,472.8	1,488.0	1,538.6	1,528.4	1,598.4	1,578.7
Senior management occupations	88.1	72.4	72.4	82.1	105.3	92.3	92.8	85.1	78.8	84.5
Other management occupations	1,356.2	1,291.2	1,313.8	1,318.9	1,367.4	1,395.7	1,445.8	1,443.4	1,519.6	1,494.3
Business, finance and administrative occupations	2,689.8	2,802.8	2,846.6	2,909.6	3,003.2	3,007.2	3,091.3	3,141.8	3,237.5	3,200.1
Professional occupations in business and finance	415.9	437.2	468.7	459.4	477.5	489.1	509.2	531.8	548.4	586.8
Financial, secretarial and administrative occupations	780.1	774.2	769.9	793.4	804.4	820.4	823.4	836.5	913.0	862.4
Clerical occupations, including supervisors	1,493.8	1,591.4	1,607.9	1,656.9	1,721.4	1,697.7	1,758.7	1,773.5	1,776.1	1,750.9
Natural and applied sciences and related occupations	1,013.0	1,053.4	1,087.3	1,087.3	1,092.7	1,141.4	1,165.6	1,223.3	1,245.8	1,250.8
Health occupations	797.2	822.5	886.4	907.2	944.4	971.8	1,000.9	1,016.7	1,062.2	1,082.6
Professional occupations in health, nurse supervisors and registered nurses	389.8	395.8	435.9	432.7	450.5	457.6	467.0	484.2	500.4	505.7
Technical, assisting and related occupations in health	407.3	426.7	450.5	474.5	493.9	514.2	533.9	532.5	561.8	576.9
Occupations in social science, education, government service and religion	1,192.5	1,246.6	1,274.0	1,304.3	1,291.6	1,388.8	1,441.3	1,482.1	1,531.5	1,606.2
Occupations in social science, government service and religion	617.3	644.0	669.7	683.4	669.7	722.1	743.7	771.1	816.5	873.6
Teachers and professors	575.2	602.6	604.2	620.9	621.9	666.7	697.6	710.9	715.0	732.5
Occupations in art, culture, recreation and sport	436.5	463.0	469.6	497.9	495.2	525.1	513.5	532.7	555.4	577.2
Sales and service occupations	3,727.9	3,829.8	3,974.8	4,096.1	4,095.9	4,079.2	4,127.2	4,328.0	4,316.4	4,385.9
Wholesale, technical, insurance, real estate sales specialists, and retail, wholesale and grain buyers	479.0	515.0	493.2	527.6	510.7	547.1	546.7	576.5	549.9	592.5
Retail salespersons, sales clerks, cashiers, including retail trade supervisors	934.6	996.2	1,048.3	1,069.8	1,090.1	1,082.3	1,083.5	1,130.0	1,114.7	1,132.0
Chefs and cooks, and occupations in food and beverage service, incl. supervisors	513.3	537.4	554.8	569.3	575.1	536.2	560.8	595.1	583.2	572.4
Occupation in protective services	213.7	223.1	229.0	236.7	243.6	231.1	230.4	244.6	250.2	261.3
Childcare and home support workers	215.1	191.2	202.8	211.6	219.2	197.8	207.0	226.9	223.6	234.2
Sales and service occupations n.e.c.	1,372.2	1,366.9	1,446.7	1,481.2	1,457.3	1,484.6	1,498.8	1,554.9	1,594.8	1,593.5
Trades, transport and equipment operators and related occupations	2,363.0	2,379.9	2,440.7	2,509.0	2,551.1	2,556.4	2,617.6	2,684.0	2,783.3	2,745.3
Contractors and supervisors in trades and transportation	209.1	216.8	227.9	222.2	241.0	249.0	249.1	253.3	277.0	277.4
Construction trades	331.0	337.4	355.6	362.5	358.0	380.3	396.1	409.2	438.3	437.5
Other trades occupations	885.2	900.1	902.8	918.7	929.0	928.0	928.3	955.6	998.4	963.1
Transport and equipment operators	626.0	609.1	628.2	641.5	642.6	623.7	653.8	675.7	663.4	671.0
Trades helpers, construction, and transportation labourers and related occ.	311.7	316.6	326.2	364.1	380.5	375.4	390.4	390.1	406.1	396.3
Occupations unique to primary industry	630.1	583.3	585.7	606.4	613.5	627.1	636.7	628.0	595.7	600.4
Occupations unique to processing, manufacturing and utilities	1,181.5	1,186.7	1,231.3	1,239.4	1,231.5	1,176.9	1,108.0	1,059.4	986.5	907.6
Machine operators and assemblers in manufacturing, including supervisors	964.8	972.6	1,012.6	1,011.1	998.1	938.6	879.5	840.0	788.7	733.7
Labourer in processing, manufacturing and utilities	216.7	214.1	218.7	228.3	233.4	238.3	228.5	219.4	197.8	173.9
Unclassified occupations	371.1	378.2	396.7	400.4	390.4	380.6	352.1	321.5	332.6	433.8

Source: Statistics Canada, Labour Force Historical Review Cat. #71F0004XCB, 2009 Edition

GROWTH STATISTICS: AGRICULTURE/FISHERIES

	Population[1]		Wheat '000 Bushels	Total Canadian Crops[2] '000 Acres	Farm Cash Receipts For Total Crops $000,000	Farm Cash Receipts For Livestock & Livestock Products[3] $000,000	Shipments, Estimated Values Of Goods Of Own Manufacturing, Dairy Products $'000	Fisheries Landed Values $'000
1992	28,371,264	(ID)	1,097,806	100,905	8,551	11,388	7,502,142	1,400,322
1993	28,684,764	(ID)	1,000,387	102,612	9,046	12,300	7,361,334	1,424,056
1994	29,000,663	(ID)	842,154	102,771	11,543	12,514	7,458,679	1,699,372
1995	29,302,311	(ID)	918,197	102,553	13,114	12,704	7,856,580	1,782,957
1996	29,610,218	(ID)	1,095,008	100,567	14,016	13,857	8,228,177	1,565,642 (P)
1997	29,905,948	(ID)	892,846	110,319	14,094	14,633	8,177,141	1,634,285 (P)
1998	30,155,173	(ID)	884,866	100,832	13,642	14,442	8,619,947	1,610,678 (P)
1999	30,401,286	(ID)	990,598	100,902	13,121	15,160	8,756,324	1,924,589
2000	30,685,730	(ID)	975,014	100,727	12,970	17,101	9,068,182	2,061,194
2001	31,019,020	(ID)	755,722	100,016	13,505	18,973	9,876,082	-- -- --
2002	31,353,656	(ID)	595,143	99,791	14,412	18,130	9,748,671	-- -- --
2003	31,639,670	(ID)	865,402	99,485	13,312	16,085	10,725,376	-- -- --
2004	31,940,676	(ID)	950,204	99,715	14,420	17,056	10,897,547	-- -- --
2005	32,245,209	(ID)	983,821	99,006	13,477	18,340	11,365,203	-- -- --
2006	32,576,074	(ID)	1,002,240	99,335	14,686	17,740	12,579,043	-- -- --
2007	32,931,956	(PD)	736,856	96,529	18,414	18,238	12,197,740	-- -- --
2008	33,327,337	(PR)	1,051,282	94,305	22,954	18,802	13,154,135	-- -- --
2009	33,739,859	(PP)	974,249	93,210	22,971	17,903	13,551,866	-- -- --

(ID) Final intercensal estimates

(PD) Final Postcensal estimates

(PR) Updated Postcensal estimates

(PP) Preliminary Postcensal estimates

[1] Period from July 1 to June 30

[2] Includes grains, specialty crops, summerfallow and hay; excludes solin.

[3] Total livestock and livestock products (including poultry and animals on fur farms).

-- -- -- Not available

Sources: Statistics Canada, Field Crop Reporting Series (cat. no. 22-002-XIE Vol. 86 No. 8);
CANSIM Tables # 051-0001, 304-0014 (NAICS 3115) and 002-0001, August 2010 ; Dept. of Fisheries & Oceans Canada.

GROWTH STATISTICS: PRODUCTION OF SELECTED MINERALS/METALS

	Pig Iron Production ('000 metric tonnes)	Crude Oil & Equivalent ('000 cubic metres)	Copper (total production, metal content) ('000 tonnes)	Nickel (production) ('000 tonnes)	Natural Gas ('000,000 cubic metres)	Iron Ore (producer's shipments) ('000 tonnes)	Zinc (total production, metal content) ('000 tonnes)	Asbestos ('000 tonnes)	Cement (Production) ('000 tonnes)	Value of Total Mineral Production[1] ($000,000)
1992	8,621	100,906	761.6	177.6	116,561	32,137.3	1,195.7	587	8,612	35,404
1993	8,633	105,780	711.2	178.4	128,817	33,774.3	990.6	523	9,284	36,564
1994	8,106	110,452	591.0	142.0	138,856	36,728.1	976.4	531	10,457	41,150
1995	8,464	114,372	700.9	172.2	148,203	37,023.6	1,094.9	516	10,600	43,360
1996	8,638	117,621	652.5	182.4	153,578	34,709.3	1,162.8	506	11,003	49,678
1997	8,669	123,827	647.9	180.6	156,171	39,292.9	1,026.8	420	11,790	50,538
1998	8,936	128,401	690.7	197.9	160,651	36,847.0	991.5	321	12,168	44,339
1999	8,856	122,287	581.5	176.9	162,219	33,990.0	963.3	345	12,643	53,466
2000	8,904	127,769	621.7	181.2	167,794	35,246.9	935.7	310	12,753	83,854
2001	8,302	128,951	614.2	184.2	171,351	27,119.3	1,012.2	277	12,793	82,968
2002	8,670	136,970	584.2	179.7	172,197	30,902.0	924.1	241	13,081	76,951
2003	8,554	144,813	541.0	155.4	166,457	33,322.4	757.4	X	13,418	20,077 [1]
2004	8,828	149,425	544.5	177.3	167,503	28,596.4	734.0	X	13,863	24,168 [1]
2005	8,274	146,221	577.2	192.9	170,740	30,386.5	618.8	X	14,179	-
2006	8,305	154,099	586.5	224.6	171,690	33,543.0	601.3	X	14,335	-
2007	8,579	161,276	577.4	244.5	167,195	32,774.2	594.1	X	15,078	-
2008 (R)	8,770	158,881	584.1	246.1	158,209	32,101.5	704.7	X	13,672	-
2009 (P)	4,573 *	158,054	481.4	131.8	147,484	31,703.7	668.9	X	10,985	-

* 2009 Pig Iron Production excludes data for July and August 2009, as the data for these months are suppressed for reasons of confidentiality under the Statistics Act

[1] Excludes oil and gas as of 2003 (R) Revised (P) Preliminary X: suppressed to meet the confidentiality requirements of the Statistics Act - not available

Standard Classification of Goods (SCG) code 7201.00.

Sources: Statistics Canada, Primary Iron and Steel (cat. no. 41-001-XIB) 1992-2004
and Steel, Tubular Products and Steel Wire (cat. no. 41-019); CANSIM tables #152-0001, 152-0004, 303-0001 (1992 - 2003), 303-0048 and 303-0060, August 2010

GROWTH STATISTICS: IMPORTS & EXPORTS

Year	Total Exports + ($000,000)	Total Imports ($000,000)	Imports of Raw Sugar Cane[1] ($,000)	Imports of Natural Rubber[2] ($,000)	Imports of Raw Cotton[3] ($,000)	Imports of Crude Petroleum[4] ($000,000)
1999	355,420	320,409	286,958	160,415	112,487	6,919
2000	413,215	356,992	288,573	164,913	153,731	13,673
2001	404,085	343,111	371,731	136,644	152,600	12,643
2002	396,381	348,957	291,055	189,228	119,890	12,007
2003	381,071	336,141	341,699	195,879	146,027	13,812
2004	412,290	355,886	304,851	228,334	130,528	16,063
2005	436,351	380,858	332,130	241,618	68,067	21,912
2006	440,364	396,773	439,943	301,508	48,696	23,370
2007	450,699	406,998	338,822	287,323	32,854	24,125
2008	483,630	433,519	425,641	341,329	7,793	34,076
2009	360,035	365,180	453,719	202,823	2,733	21,237

Total Exports+ equals Domestic Exports plus Re-exports [1] HS code 1701.11 [2] HS codes 4001.21, 4001.22, 4001.29 [3] HS code 5201.00 [4] HS code 2709.00

Source: Industry Canada, August 2010

http://www.ic.gc.ca/sc_mrkti/tdst/tdo/tdo.php?lang=30&headFootDir=/sc_mrkti/tdst/headfoot&productType=HS6&cacheTime=962115865#tag

GROWTH STATISTICS: TRANSPORT/TRANSPORTATION

	Railway Gross Revenue ($000,000)	Railway Operating Expenses ($000,000)	Tonne Kilometers ('000,000)	Motor Vehicle Registration ('000)
1992	6,907	7,781	250,667	16,581
1993	6,992	6,601	256,134	16,718
1994	7,530	6,699	287,827	16,972
1995	7,210	8,461	280,477	17,048
1996	7,193	6,789	282,018	17,183
1997	7,903	6,719	305,635	17,478
1998	7,610	6,931	297,916	17,988
1999	7,717	6,728	300,140	17,534
2000	8,103	6,426	322,511	17,882
2001	8,156	6,594	323,211	18,102
2002	8,213	6,621	317,807	18,617
2003	8,307	6,713	318,263	18,883
2004	8,862	6,952	338,898	19,156
2005	9,822	7,506	352,140	19,515
2006	10,405	7,794	352,477	20,065
2007	10,481	7,989	358,472	20,593
2008	10,997	8,629	344,903	21,087
2009	N/A	N/A	N/A	21,387

Sources: Statistics Canada, Rail in Canada (cat. no. 52-216-XIB);
CANSIM Tables 404-0016, 405-0001 (1992-1998)and 405-0004 (1999-2009), August 2010

GROWTH STATISTICS: FINANCIAL

	CHARTERED BANKS						LIFE INSURANCE	FEDERAL FINANCE		
Year	Bank of Canada Notes in Circulation $000,000	Assets $000,000	Liabilities Excluding Capital Reserves $000,000	Demand Deposits $000,000	Notice Deposits $000,000	Total Loans $000,000	Net Amount Life Insurance in Force Dec.31 $000,000	Total Revenue[4] $000,000	Total Expenditure[4] $000,000	Net Worth[4,5] $000,000
1992	25,609	676,620	642,382	41,332	136,815	470,464	1,123,191	130,069	165,856	-1,619,360
1993	27,237	753,992	716,795	46,016	142,830	507,394	1,123,619	128,715	168,411	-1,836,651
1994	28,329	841,037	799,279	51,370	140,282	550,444	1,234,746	131,911	166,999	-1,927,463
1995	28,778	911,678	868,796	57,482	135,563	586,591	1,317,184	140,313	172,013	-2,113,483
1996	29,109	1,104,828	1,059,219	68,564	145,589	674,913	1,357,310	147,954	164,911	-2,248,051
1997	30,542	1,321,075	1,266,494	82,674	151,298	803,631	1,446,564	162,556	156,080	-2,253,546
1998	32,638	1,432,114	1,371,371	98,684	152,832	840,929	1,467,479	167,450	159,774	-2,231,509
1999	40,143	1,397,710	1,331,218	113,710	159,567	808,613	1,548,305	177,684	168,914	-2,183,389
2000	36,775	1,550,016	1,476,705	125,453	182,649	884,556	1,606,497	195,726	175,698	-2,078,221
2001	38,821	1,710,431	1,630,333	155,453	216,373	951,927	-- -- --	193,935	181,925	-1,980,901
2002	-- -- --	-- -- --	-- -- --	-- -- --	-- -- --	-- -- --	-- -- --	190,448	181,052	-1,974,943
2003								196,226	192,105	-1,975,074
2004								207,668	196,838	-1,933,707
2005								219,765	218,746	-1,953,126
2006								230,574	218,096	-1,895,417
2007								244,223	228,848	-1,818,295
2008								240,686	241,759	-1,825,557
2009								214,189	254,122	-1,929,825

[4] quarterly data aggregated on a calendar-year basis [5] Total assets minus total liabilities -- Not available
Sources: Bank of Canada; Statistics Canada, CANSIM Tables 385-0032, August 2010
(Federal Finance data produced on a Government Finance Statistics base using quarterly National Accounts data)

GROWTH STATISTICS: INDUSTRIAL/TELEPHONE/POSTAL

			STRIKES AND LOCKOUTS			
Year	Industry Price Index, All Manufacturing Index, All Manufacturing Industries (1997=100)	Average Weekly Earnings[1] ($CDN.)	Employees Affected ('000)	Days Not Worked ('000)	Total Telephone Access Lines ('000)	Revenue from Postal Operations[2] ($'000,000)
1992	83.8	572.41	150	2,110	16,247	3,921
1993	86.8	582.87	102	1,517	16,716	4,118
1994	92.0	592.88	81	1,607	17,250	4,748
1995	98.9	598.67	149	1,583	17,763	4,953
1996	99.3	611.01	282	3,352	18,051	5,103
1997	100.0	623.43	258	3,610	18,660	5,088
1998	100.4	632.72	244	2,444	19,294	5,709
1999	102.2	640.47	159	2,446	19,806	5,638
2000	106.5	655.55	144	1,662	20,317	5,942
2001	107.6	656.74	224	2,240	20,805	4,441 [3]
2002	107.6	672.68			20,301	6,154 [4]
2003	106.2	690.79			20,068	6,344 [4]
2004	109.5	709.41			-	6,651 [4]
2005	111.2	737.29			-	6,945 [4]
2006	113.8	755.48			-	7,265 [4]
2007	115.6	788.06				7,474 [4]
2008	120.6	810.52				7,729 [4]
2009	116.5	823.53				7,312 [4]

1 Average weekly earnings (SEPH), unadjusted for seasonal variation, all employees, including overtime, industrial aggregate excluding unclassified (NAICS)
2 Fiscal year ended March 31. 3Represents 9 months of revenue -- Canada Post's fiscal year now January - December. 4 Fiscal year January - December data - Not Available
Sources: Statistics Canada, CANSIM Tables 329-0038, 281-0027, 356-0001 (1992-1996), August 2010;
Telecommunications Statistics (cat. no. 56-001); Statistics Canada, Public Institutions Division; Human Resources Development Canada.

IMPORTS AND EXPORTS FOR CANADA, 2009

	IMPORTS ($)	EXPORTS ($)		IMPORTS ($)	EXPORTS ($)		IMPORTS ($)	EXPORTS ($)
Afghanistan	1,450,773	59,670,722	France (incl. Monaco, Fr. Ant.)	5,630,247,747	2,682,726,997	Nigeria	458,177,637	223,059,345
Albania	3,962,317	21,473,292	French Polynesia	718,592	10,989,006	Niue	32,921	0
Algeria	3,765,009,473	351,974,566	French Southern Territories	280	272,310	Norfolk Island	6,913	303,780
American Samoa	359,927	1,122,690	Gabon	1,836,100	34,654,688	Norway	3,570,908,743	1,763,949,186
Andorra	196,131	114,201	Gambia	110,056	743,159	Oman (Muscat)	6,187,059	156,636,451
Angola	1,372,994,032	82,674,904	Georgia	134,741,706	17,489,476	Pakistan	242,484,785	408,158,803
Anguilla	307,983	1,936,263	Germany	10,658,124,421	3,738,566,269	Panama	40,709,318	91,460,137
Antartica	9,737	1,758,110	Ghana	27,401,683	161,645,608	Papua New Guinea	2,029,765	42,989,552
Antigua and Barbuda	445,866	21,148,714	Gibraltar	992	17,228,072	Paraguay	9,377,124	12,782,176
Argentina	700,506,253	175,284,209	Greece	140,811,490	111,770,888	Peru	2,878,076,558	428,692,648
Armenia	34,070,220	8,825,562	Greenland	17,411,163	16,364,359	Philippines	735,730,393	526,880,672
Aruba Island	91,341,006	6,345,968	Grenada	508,724	6,029,680	Pitcairn Island	38,517	164,241
Australia	1,625,322,876	1,780,682,491	Guam (U.S.)	269,468	1,929,634	Poland	753,199,399	236,334,607
Austria	1,179,882,405	402,017,100	Guatemala	266,337,997	112,053,876	Portugal	321,868,212	201,104,978
Azerbaijan	1,166,930,624	31,032,321	Guinea	62,747,525	17,420,809	Qatar	53,268,239	224,048,625
Bahamas	30,995,326	151,244,631	Guinea-Bissau	32,619	14,664	Romania	120,958,875	89,537,331
Bahrain	4,770,322	38,975,581	Guyana	300,317,525	29,479,116	Russia	1,632,708,040	887,773,791
Bangladesh	808,339,485	627,473,483	Haiti	21,724,553	41,235,008	Rwanda	314,554	3,418,524
Barbados	8,650,590	60,172,706	Heard/McDonald Island	4,941	100,274	Saint Lucia	2,289,225	10,878,864
Belarus (Byelorussia)	35,408,505	1,467,142	Honduras	139,213,786	36,479,850	Samoa (Western)	4,591	578,009
Belgium	1,447,465,258	1,892,840,522	Hong Kong	363,283,882	1,499,230,077	São Tomé and Principe	42,876	131,242
Belize	7,246,816	6,334,152	Hungary	370,596,519	274,341,966	Saudi Arabia	1,534,197,037	1,159,882,389
Benin	2,957	9,127,654	Iceland	32,691,944	81,149,140	Senegal	1,133,010	35,906,787
Bermuda	10,967,865	66,620,470	India	2,002,386,399	2,147,630,089	Serbia	10,330,971	19,083,335
Bhutan	14,478	171,980	Indonesia	1,009,214,109	971,970,027	Seychelles	633,044	1,107,993
Bolivia	90,956,326	12,483,627	Iran	24,764,578	426,034,182	Sierra Leone	4,040,765	5,524,943
Bosnia-Hercegovina	8,501,604	3,479,024	Iraq	1,279,159,172	489,852,074	Singapore	1,147,622,555	1,091,332,406
Botswana	28,590,578	5,697,055	Ireland	2,196,307,748	543,495,315	Slovakia	165,607,020	27,320,579
Bouvet Island	7,336	8,126	Israel	946,222,327	353,164,115	Slovenia	86,577,739	55,628,484
Brazil	2,578,602,212	1,600,069,375	Italy (includes Vatican City)	4,446,279,087	1,797,568,197	Solomon Islands	102,114	735,384
British Indian Ocean Terr.	2,772	1,172,196	Jamaica	164,762,511	123,146,009	Somalia	39,748	2,884,930
British Virgin Islands	720,216	3,799,702	Japan	12,350,909,258	8,314,567,976	South Africa	631,801,798	454,818,918
Brunei Darussalam	1,916,297	5,697,068	Jordan	16,592,705	65,867,705	Spain	1,328,783,195	1,131,755,324
Bulgaria	119,392,177	70,916,952	Kazakhstan	1,595,930,137	210,703,701	Sri Lanka	115,733,019	334,548,761
Burkina Faso	13,453,711	41,203,567	Kenya	17,023,767	79,634,966	St. Helena	20,735	83,073
Burma (Myanmar)	59,612	153,903	Kiribati (includes Tuvalu)	113,533	74,354	St. Kitts-Nevis	7,032,955	6,703,842
Burundi	248,871	1,221,954	Korea, North	106,309	25,991,787	St.Pierre-Miquelon	306,736	20,447,464
Cambodia (Kampuchea)	289,553,614	7,043,775	Korea, South	5,929,621,908	3,526,200,276	St.Vincent-Grenadines	218,607	12,124,618
Cameroon	4,532,611	34,228,540	Kuwait	37,290,679	107,306,321	Sudan	68,358,926	112,428,926
Cape Verde	139,073	1,450,727	Kyrgyzstan	486,490	6,541,533	Surinam	535,427,956	12,368,927
Cayman Islands	644,610	7,871,634	Laos	6,707,082	3,434,483	Swaziland	1,915,934	11,041,102
Central African Republic	113,812	999,211	Latvia	17,223,686	24,690,089	Sweden	1,797,634,286	380,944,011
Chad	221,389	12,778,832	Lebanon	15,600,660	224,701,236	Switzerland	3,445,712,734	1,187,913,621
Chile	1,730,812,309	644,374,852	Lesotho	8,763,027	204,575	Syria	5,913,224	61,362,680
China	39,656,836,593	11,161,767,191	Liberia	29,107,932	4,867,588	Taiwan (Taipei)	3,343,875,865	1,109,449,157
Christmas Island	31,945	274,960	Libya	4,701,899	263,314,973	Tajikistan	5,415	3,539,419
Cocos (Keeling) Islands	114,571	233,581	Lithuania	154,356,676	41,554,753	Tanzania	4,581,904	37,964,615
Colombia	733,880,341	601,707,771	Luxembourg	138,281,127	70,915,024	Thailand	2,298,638,140	567,608,452
Comoros	88,218	3,154,737	Macau (Macao)	22,271,035	14,952,586	Togo	4,369,532	20,048,319
Congo (Brazzaville)	2,176,185	30,540,253	Macedonia	8,703,062	15,892,104	Tonga	22,458	213,455
Congo (former Zaire)	590,779	18,485,864	Madagascar	41,550,462	71,383,563	Trinidad and Tobago	314,954,661	268,251,730
Cook Islands	46,445	498,636	Malawi	6,720,194	4,447,598	Tunisia	45,671,014	113,723,085
Costa Rica	358,438,560	83,585,699	Malaysia	2,313,288,376	790,505,557	Turkey	632,180,519	891,971,191
Côte-D'Ivoire (Ivory Coast)	223,303,536	28,674,702	Maldives	68,217	11,439,878	Turkmenistan	400,179	7,742,231
Croatia	25,456,341	103,177,125	Mali	346,716	7,119,333	Turks and Caicos Islands	297,374	7,771,733
Cuba	500,428,826	317,895,025	Malta	23,087,445	46,454,969	U.S. Minor Outlying Isl.	5,053,893	13,470,401
Cyprus	2,231,230	12,477,663	Mauritania	850,800	2,927,450	Uganda	2,542,470	14,396,422
Czech Republic	269,221,072	136,636,148	Mauritius	8,961,491	5,526,046	Ukraine	94,302,975	112,105,121
Denmark	1,606,585,669	618,782,717	Mexico	16,534,839,591	4,804,868,257	United Arab Emirates	195,413,299	1,304,540,812
Djibouti	34,161	2,716,530	Moldova	1,895,499	2,668,548	United Kingdom (U.K.)	9,394,995,920	12,099,541,624
Dominica	390,327	4,802,037	Mongolia	158,911,884	4,896,374	United States (U.S.)	186,815,179,767	270,128,776,371
Dominican Republic	147,537,166	134,383,004	Montenegro	294,962	2,939,845	Uruguay	54,538,814	27,365,615
East Timor	4,079,772	90,760	Montserrat	68,984	297,431	Uzbekistan	11,863,387	15,587,841
Ecuador	233,873,216	279,235,054	Morocco	138,291,184	375,133,730	Vanuatu (New Hebrides)	189,763	2,024,949
Egypt	114,198,179	639,358,103	Mozambique	297,545	8,312,000	Venezuela	907,980,354	628,954,365
El Salvador	65,178,901	59,572,501	Namibia	248,309,350	5,997,896	Vietnam	1,053,949,579	219,869,321
Equatorial Guinea	347,936,164	8,281,329	Nauru	135,555	52,654	Wallis & Futuna Islands	4,429	28,923
Eritrea	112,024	2,392,424	Nepal	13,282,122	4,169,711	Western Sahara	1,138	50,000
Estonia	21,627,427	30,578,098	Netherlands	1,871,770,050	2,758,639,277	Yemen	155,081	31,628,026
Ethiopia	16,760,619	12,959,837	Netherlands Antilles	14,655,630	74,849,663	Zambia (Zambi)	809,749	11,027,541
Faeroe Islands	2,073,051	1,043,662	New Caledonia	322,063	13,148,195	Zimbabwe	2,821,174	8,504,151
Falkland Islands	43,030	12,122	New Zealand	454,087,615	303,121,869			
Fiji	6,369,458	5,764,247	Nicaragua	78,669,128	18,160,138			
Finland	941,832,026	331,097,183	Niger	1,132,711	5,553,967	TOTAL (All Countries)	365,180,293,991	360,035,109,759

Source: Industry Canada, August 2010

http://www.ic.gc.ca/sc_mrkti/tdst/tdo/tdo.php?lang=30&headFootDir=/sc_mrkti/tdst/headfoot&productType=HS6&cacheTime=962115865#tag

Exhibitions, Shows & Events

The following list includes Consumer & Trade Shows, Public Events, Conferences & Festivals arranged by category of interest. The addresses given are the addresses of associations/sponsors. Focus is on events of an ongoing annual or biennial nature. The lists are not complete but are fairly representative of shows held throughout Canada. Users are cautioned that dates or venues may vary.

ABORIGINAL *See* MULTICULTURAL

AGRICULTURE *See* FARM BUSINESS/AGRICULTURE

AIR SHOWS/AVIATION

15 Wing Armed Forces Day, 15 Wing, PO Box 5000, Moose Jaw, SK S6H 7Z8 - 306/694-2222; Fax: 306/694-2880; Email: 15wingpao@forces.gc.ca; URL: www.airforce.forces.gc.ca/15wing - Show Organizer, Major John Clowe - Static displays, plus ground & aerial demonstrations - Aug., Moose Jaw SK

17 Wing Manitoba Canadian Forces Day, 17 Wing, CFB Winnipeg, PO Box 17000, Stn. Forces, Winnipeg, MB R3J 3Y5 - 204/833-2500, ext. 6499; Fax: 204-833-2594; Email: Muralt.DA@forces.gc.ca; PubAffairs@forces.gc.ca; URL: www.17wingcfday.com - 17 Wing Public Affairs, Capt. Dave Muralt - Air & static display by Canadian Forces aircraft - May, Southport, MB

19 Wing Comox Armed Forces Day & Airshow, 19 Wing, CFB Comox, PO Box 1000, Stn. Main, Lazo BC V0R 2K0 - 250/339-8211; Fax (Media Information): 250/339-8120 - Celebrates Canadian Forces Day. Biennial - July or Aug.

Abbotsford International Airshow, Abbotsford International Airshow Society, #4, 1276 Tower St., Abbotsford, BC V2T 6H5 - 604/852-8511; Fax: 604/852-6093; Email: info@abbotsfordairshow.com; media@abbotsford airshow.com; URL: www.abbotsfordairshow.com - Large static display. Six hour flying show - Aug., Abbotsford International Airport, BC

Alberta International Airshow, Lethbridge International Airshow Association, PO Box 1315, Stn. Main, Lethbridge, AB T1K 4K1 - 403/380-4245; Toll Free (Ticketing Support): 1-888-695-0888; Email: info@albertaairshow.com; URL: www.albertaairshow.com - July, Lethbridge International Airport, AB

Borden Canadian Forces Day & Airshow, CFSTG/Base Borden Public Affairs Officer, Canadian Forces Base Borden, PO Box 1000 Stn. Main, 400 Cambrai Rd. Borden, ON L0M 1C0 - 705/424-1200, ext. 3162; Fax: 705/ 423-3385; Email: marion.jcn@forces.gc.ca; URL: www.airforce.forces.gc.ca/16wing - Military & civilian air demonstration & acrobatic teams. Ground displays - June, Canadian Forces Base Borden, Borden, ON

Canada Remembers Airshow, Saskatchewan Place, #101, 3515 Thatcher Ave., Saskatoon, SK S7R 1C4 - 306/975-2907; Email: b.swid@creditunioncentre.com; URL: www.canadaremembersairshow.com - Annual. Parade of Veterans. Active & static displays - Aug., Saskatoon, SK

Canadian International Airshow, Press Bldg., Exhibition Place, 210 Princes' Blvd., Toronto, ON M6K 3C3 - 416/263-3650; Fax: 416/263-3654 ; URL: www.cias.org - Annually, three days of the Labour Day Weekend. Best viewed from Canadian National Exhibition grounds - Sept., Over Lake Ontario, Toronto, ON

Festival of Flight, Festival of Flight Staff, Parks, Recreation & Tourism, Town of Gander, 100 Elizabeth Dr., Gander, NL A1V 1G7 - 709/651-5958; URL: www.gandercanada.com - Director, Parks, Recreation & Tourism, Kevin Waterman - Annual. A celebration of Gander's aviation history - 1st weekend in Aug.

Friendship Festival Air Show, Friendship Festival International Air Show, PO Box 1241, Fort Erie ON L2A 5Y2 - 905/871-6454; Fax: 905/871-1266; Tollfree: 1-888-333-1987; Email: info@friendshipfestival.com; URL: www.friendshipfestival.com - Annual - July London Airshow & Balloon Festival, 48 Crampton Dr., Belmont ON N0L 1B0 - 519/473-6444; Fax: 519/644- 1688; Email: info@londonairshow.com; URL: www.londonairshow.com

Nova Scotia International Airshow, Nova Scotia International Air Show Association (NSIASA), PO Box 218, Shearwater, NS B0J 3A0 - 902/465-2725; Fax: 902/484-3222; Email: info@nsairshow.ca; URL: www.nsairshow.ca - Executive Director, Colin Stephenson, Email: colin@nsairshow.ca - Aerial displays, including military & civilian aircraft. Ground displays - Sept., Halifax Stanfield International Airport, Halifax, NS

Saskatchewan Air Show, PO Box 1027, Moose Jaw SK S6H 4P8 - 306/692-4411; Fax: 306/692-2940; Email: info@saskatchewanairshow.com; URL: www.saskatchewanairshow.com - Executive Director, Clive Tolley, July, Moose Jaw SK

Yukon Sourdough Rendezvous Airshow, Yukon Sourdough Rendezvous Society, PO Box 31721, Whitehorse YT Y1A 6L3 - 867/393-4467; Fax: 867/668-6755; Email: ysr@polarcom.com; URL: www.yukonrendezvous.com - Vice-President, Public Relations, Anna Barron - Annual. Aerial & static displays - Feb., Whitehorse Airport, Whitehorse, YT

ANTIQUES

Carswell Collectables Antique Show, Carswell Collectables, PO Box 1036, Red Deer AB T4N 6S5 - 403/343-1614; Fax: 403/342-2943 - Rae Carswell - Nov., Red Deer, AB

The Toronto Toy & Doll Collectors' Show,PO Box 217, Grimsby, ON L3M 4G3 - 905/945-2775; Fax: 905/945-0197; Email: info@antiquetoys.ca; URL: www.antiquetoys.ca - Doug Jarvis, Email: dougjarvis@sympatico.ca - Annual antique & collectible childhood memorabilia - Nov., Mississauga, ON

The Toronto Christmas Train Show, PO Box 217, Grimsby, ON L3M 4G3 - 905/945-2775; Fax: 905/945-0197; Email: info@antiquetoys.ca; URL: www.antiquetoys.ca - Doug Jarvis, Email: dougjarvis@sympatico.ca - Layouts, exhibits, & clinics from railway historical associations & train vendors - Nov., Mississauga, ON

APPAREL *See* FASHION

ARCHITECTURE *See* CONSTRUCTION

ART/ARTS

***See Also* First Night; Crafts; Music; Events**

Arnold Mikelson Festival of Arts, Arnold Mikelson Mind and Matter Gallery, 13743 - 16 Ave., Surrey, BC V4A 1P7 - 604/536-6460; Email: mindandmatterart@aol.com; URL: www.mindandmatterart.com - Mary Mikelson - Featuring new & established artists offering their exhibits for sale - July

Artfocus Artist's Show, Artfocus Indoor Artists' Show, c/o Artfocus Communications, PO Box 1063, Stn F, Toronto ON M4Y 2T7 - 416/925-5564; Fax: 416/925- 2972; Email: info@artfocus.com; URL: www.artfocus.com/artfairs.htm - President, Pat Fleisher - Annual (fall) consumer show. Paintings, photography, sculpture, prints, drawings, electronic art, etc., Metro Hall Rotunda, Toronto ON

Atlantic Theatre Festival, 386 Main St., Wolfville, NS B4P 1C9 - 902/542-1515; Fax: 902/542-1526 - Classical theatre productions - July, Aug. & Sept.

Banff Summer Arts Festival, The Banff Centre, PO Box 1020, Banff AB T1L 1H5 - 403/762-6301; Fax: 403/762-6483; Tollfree: 1-800-413-8368; Email: box_office@banffcentre.ca; URL: www.banffcentre.ca - President & CEO, Mary E. Hofstetter

Bard on the Beach Shakespeare Festival, #301, 601 Cambie St., Vancouver, BC V6B 2P1 - 604/737-0625; Box Office: 604/739-0559; Fax: 604/737-0425; Tollfree: 1-877-739-0559; Email: info@bardonthebeach.org; URL: www.bardonthebeach.org - Artistic Director, Christopher Gaze; General Manager, Robert Barr - May - Sept., Vanier Park waterfront, Vancouver, BC

Blyth Festival, 423 Queen St., PO Box 10, Blyth, ON N0M 1H0 - 519/523-9300; Fax: 519/523-9804; Tollfree: 1-877-862-5984; Email: info@blythfestival.com; URL: www.blythfestival.com - Artistic Director, Eric Coates, Email: ecoates@blythfestival.com - June - Sept., Blyth Memorial Community Hall, Blyth, ON

Charlottetown Festival, Confederation Centre of the Arts, 145 Richmond St., Charlottetown PE C1A 1J1 - 902/628-1864; Fax: 902/566-4648; Tollfree: 1-800-565-0278; Email: info@confederationcentre.com; URL: www.confederationcentre.com - CEO, David MacKenzie, Email: dmack@confederationcentre.com; Artistic Director, Anne Allan, Email: aallan@confederationcentre.com - Annual. Musical & dramatic entertainment - June - Sept.

Dream in High Park, The Canadian Stage Company, 26 Berkeley St., Toronto, ON M5A 2W3 - 416/367-8243; Box Office: 416/368-3110; Fax: 416/367-1768; Email: general@canstage.com ; boxoffice@canstage.com; URL: www.canstage.com - Director, Production, Alistair Hepburn; Artistic Producer, Martin Bragg, July 1 - Labour Day, High Park, Toronto, ON

Edmonton International Fringe Theatre Festival, 10330 - 84 Ave., Edmonton AB T6E 2G9 - 780/448-9000; Box Office: 780/409-1910; Fax: 780/431-1893; URL: www.fringetheatreadventures.ca - Aug.

Festival Antigonish, Bauer Theatre, St. Francis Xavier University, PO Box 5000, Antigonish NS B2G 2W5 - 902/867-3333; Email: boxoffice@festivalantigonish.com; URL: www.festivalantigonish.com - Administrator, Madonna Van Vonderen; Artistic Producer Ed Thomason - July - Sept., Bauer Theatre, Antigonish, NS

Festival by the Sea, PO Box 6157, Saint John NB E2L 4R6 - 506/632-0086; Fax: 506/642-4644; Email: fbts@ nb.aibn.com - General Manager, Amy Wood - Annually, Performing arts - Aug.

Fringe Theatre Event, Fringe Theatre Festival, 10330 - 84 Ave., Edmonton AB T6E 2G9 - 780/448-9000; Fax: 780/431-1893; Email: fta@fringetheatreadventures. ca; URL: www.fringetheatreadventures.ca - Executive Director, Julian Mayne, Office Manager, Geralder Osborn - Aug.

Lunenburg Summer Festival of Crafts, 902/634-8511 - Contact, Robert Black - Annual - Features over 100 Nova Scotian crafters - July, Community Center Grounds, Lunenburg, NS

Manitoba Holiday Festival of the Arts, Margaret Laurence Home, PO Box 147, Neepawa, MB R0J 1H0 - 204/476-2927; Fax: 204/476-2927; Email: mhfa@mts.net; URL: www.mts.net/~mhfa - Administrator, Greg Heschuk - Annual. Programs for children, youth, & adults - July, Neepawa, MB

Nova Scotia Folk Art Festival - 902/640-2113; Email: info@nsfolkartfestival.com; URL: www.nsfolkartfestival.com - Contact, Nancy Wilson - Annual. Juried event, featuring an exhibition, workshops, speaker's corner, & sale of work by Nova Scotia folk artists - Aug., Lunenburg War Memorial Arena, Lunenburg, NS

Open Ears Festival of Music & Sound, c/o Kitchener-Waterloo Symphony, 101 Queen St. North, Kitchener, ON N2H 6P7 - 519/ 579-8564; Fax: 519/743-6773; Toll Free: 1-888-363-3591; Email: info@openears.ca; URL: www.openears.ca - Musical performances, music in alternative venues, sound poetry, sound installations, & conference activity - April / May, Kitchener, ON

Ottawa Fringe Theatre, Ottawa Fringe Festival, #100, 2 Daly Ave., Ottawa ON K1N 6E2 - 613/232-6162; Email: admin@ottawafringe.com; URL: www.ottawafringe.com

Saskatoon Fringe Theatre Festival, #9, 2404 Thayer Ave., Saskatoon, SK S7L 6B4 - 306/664-2239; Fax: 306/653-7701; URL: www.25thstreettheatre.org - Annual - July / Aug., 6 venues, Saskatoon, SK

Shakespeare by the Sea, 5799 Charles St., Halifax NS B3K 1K7 - 902/422-0295; Fax: 902/422-4250; Email: shakespeare@ns.aliantzinc.ca; URL: www.shakespearebythesea.ca - General Manager, Elizabeth Murphy Shakespeare by the Sea Festival, 11 Bavidge St., St. John's NL A1A 5B9 - 709/691-7287; Email: sbts@nfld.com; URL: www.nfld.com/~sbts

Shakespeare on the Saskatchewan Festival, PO Box 1646, Stn Main, Saskatoon SK S7K 3R8 - 306/653-2300; Fax: 306/653-2357; Email: shakespeare@sasktel.net; URL: www.shakespeareonthesaskatchewan.com - Executive & Artistic Director, Mark von Eschen, July/Aug.

Summerworks, 54 Wolseley St, 2nd Fl., PO Box 12, Stn C, Toronto ON M6J 3M7 - 416/410-1048; Email: info@summerworks.ca; URL: www.summerworks.ca - Artistic Producer, Kimahli Powell, Artistic Producer, Keira Loughran

Thunder Bay Fringe Festival, #15, 4A South Court St., Thunder Bay ON P7B 2W4 - 807/344-1343; Fax: 807/346-1855; Email: tbfringe@northroute.net; URL: www.tbfringe.com

Toronto Outdoor Art Exhibition, #264, 401 Richmond St. West, Toronto, ON M5V 3A8 - 416/408-2754; Fax: 416/408-2202; Email: toae@torontooutdoorart.org; URL: www.torontooutdoorart.org - Executive Director, Kelly Rintoul, Email: kelly@torontooutdoorart.org - Canada's largest oudoor art exhibition, held annually. Award program for participating artists - July, Nathan Phillips Square, Toronto ON

Vancouver Fringe Festival, 1398 Cartwright Street, Vancouver BC V6H 3R8 - 604/257-0350; Fax: 604/253-1924; Email: administration@vancouverfringe.com; URL: www.vancouverfringe.com - Executive Director, David Jordan - Annual - Sept.

Winnipeg Fringe Theatre Festival, Manitoba Theatre Centre, 174 Market Ave., Winnipeg MB R3B 0P8 - 204/956-1340; Fax: 204/947- 3741; Email: info@winnipegfringe.com; URL: www.winnipegfringe.com - Executive Producer, Bertram Schneider - Annual, July

World Stage, Harbourfront Centre, 235 Queens Quay West, Toronto ON M5J 2G8 - 416/973-4600; Fax: 416/973- 6055; Email: info@harbourfrontcentre.com; URL: www.harbourfrontcentre.com/worldstage - CEO, William J.S. Boyle - International theatre festival - April - Harbourfront Centre, Toronto ON

York Shakespeare Festival, Resurgence Theatre Company, 211 Main Street South, Newmarket ON L3Y 3Y9 - 905/953-2838;

Email: info@resurgence.on.ca; URL: www.resurgence.on.ca - General Manager, Anthony Leo

AUTOMOTIVE

Air Canada Grand Prix, Grand Prix of Canada, CP 340, Succ B, Montréal QC H3B 3J7 - 514/350-0000; Fax: 514/350-4709; URL: www.grandprix.ca - Vice-Présidente, Services corporatifs, Marie-Josée Labbé, - Annual international auto racing event - June - Gilles-Villeneuve Circuit, Montréal QC

Annual RV Camping & Leisure Show, Recreation Vehicle Dealers Association of Manitoba, 69 Morin Rd., St Francois Xavier MB R4L 1A8 - 204/864-2112; Fax: 204/864-2232; Email: rvdamb@mts.net; URL: www.manitoba.rvda.ca - Manager, Kim Wozniak - Annual consumer show - March, Winnipeg MB

Atlantic Truck Show, Master Promotions Ltd., PO Box 565, 48 Broad St., Saint John NB E2L 3Z8 - 506/658-0018; Fax: 506/658-0750; Tollfree: 1-888-454-7469; Email: info@masterpromotions.ca; URL: www.masterpromotions.ca - Annual - Show Manager, Mark Cusack, June - Coliseum, Moncton NB

Cam-Expo Québec, Pro-Expo Inc., #230, 1400, av St-Jean-Baptiste, Québec QC G2E 5B7 - 418/877-1919; Fax: 418/877-9292; Tollfree: 1-866-858-1919; Email: info@proexpo.qc.ca; URL: http://www.cam-expo.com - President, Roger Desrosiers - Biennial trade & consumer show - Nov.

Canadian International Motorcycle & Powersports Super Show, Bar Hodgson Productions Inc., 8780 Baldwin St., Ashburn ON L0B 1A0 - 905/655-5403; Fax: 905/655- 3812; Email: info@supershowevents.com; URL: www.supershowevents. com - President, Bar Hodgson - Annual consumer & trade show - Jan. - International Centre, Toronto ON

Edmonton Motor Show, Edmonton Motor Dealers' Association, 10310 - 39A Ave. NW, Edmonton AB T6H 5X9 - 780/423-2401; Fax: 780/423-2413; Email: contactemda@emdacars.com; URL: www.emdacars.com - Executive Manager, Robert Vilas - Annual consumer show

Expocam, dmg World Media, 180 Duncan Mills Rd., 4th Fl., Toronto ON M3B 1Z6 - 416/385-1880; Fax: 416/385-1855; Tollfree: 1-888-823-7469; URL: www.dmgworldmedia.com - Show Manager, Glen Chiasson - Biennial trade show. Trucks, trailers, bodies, heavy duty parts & services & accessories, engine & power train components, service shop equipment - Oct., Montréal QC

Halifax RV Show, Master Promotions Ltd., PO Box 565, Saint John NB E2L 3Z8 - 506/658-0018; Fax: 506/658- 0750; Tollfree: 1-888-454-7469; Email: info@masterpromotions. ca; URL: www.masterpromotions.ca - Annual consumer show - Show Manager, Scott Sprague, Feb., Halifax NS

Molson Indy Toronto, Molson Sports & Entertainment Inc., North Tower, #200, 175 Bloor St. East, Toronto ON M4W 3R8 - 416/922-7477; Fax: 416/922-8970; URL: www.molsonindy.com/toronto - President, Jo- Ann McArthur - Annual - July, Toronto ON

Moncton RV Show, Master Promotions Ltd., PO Box 565, Saint John NB E2L 3Z8 - 506/658-0018; Fax: 506/658- 0750; Tollfree: 1-888-454-7469; Email: info@masterpromotions. ca; URL: www.masterpromotions.ca - Annual consumer show - Show Manager, Scott Sprague, Feb., Moncton NB

Montréal International Auto Show, 2335, rue Guénette, Saint-Laurent QC H4R 2E9 - 514/331-6571; Fax: 514/331-7818; Email: communications@ccqm.qc.ca; URL: www.salonautomontreal.com - Executive Director, Francine St-Laurent - Annual consumer show. New cars, light trucks, accessories - Jan. - Palais des Congrès, Montréal QC

Performance World Custom Car Show, Pro-Sho Inc., 298 Sheppard Ave. East, Toronto ON M2N 3B1 - 416/229- 9919; Fax: 416/223-2826; Tollfree: 1-877-950-1500; Email: prosho@meteorshows.com; URL: www.performanceworldcarshow.com; www.llhashows. com - Annual consumer show - Contact, Larry King, March

RV Exposition & Sale, Recreation Vehicle Dealers Association of Alberta, #101, 10340 - 59th Ave., Edmonton AB T6H 1E6 - 780/455-8562; Fax: 780/453-3927; Tollfree: 1-888-858-8787; Email: rvda@rvda-alberta. org; URL: www.rvda-alberta.org - Executive Vice-President, Lori Auld - Annual consumer show held in Calgary, Edmonton & Red Deer

Salon de l'Auto, Club Optimiste de Rivière-du-Loup inc., CP 1344, Rivière-du-Loup QC G5R 4L9 - 418/862- 8454; Fax: 418/862-3366 - Jean-Louis Dorval - Annual. Cars & trucks - April - Motel Universel, Rivièredu-Loup QC

Salon de la Moto de Montréal/de Québec, ExpoMAX Canada Inc., CP 642, Succ B, Montréal QC H3B 3K3 - 514/285-2686; Fax: 514/282-4292; URL: www.salonmotomontreal.com - Executive Vice- President, Roger Saint-Laurent - Annual consumer show - Feb.

Spring Classic Car Auction, RM Classic Car Exhibit, One Classic Car Drive, Blenheim ON N0P 1A0 - 519/352- 2024 - Annual consumer show. Vintage cars, sale of parts & accessories - April - International Centre, Mississauga ON

Toronto International Spring Bike Show, Bar Hodgson Productions Inc., 8780 Baldwin St., Ashburn ON L0B 1A0 - 905/655-5403; Fax: 905/655-3812; Email: info@supershow events. com; URL: www.supershowevents.com - President, Bar Hodgson, April - International Centre, Toronto ON

Vancouver International RV Show, Recreation Vehicle Dealers Association of British Columbia, #201, 17700 - 56th Ave., Surrey BC V3S 1C7 - 604/575-3868; Fax: 604/575-3869; Email: admin@rvda.bc.ca; URL: www.rvda.bc.ca - Annual consumer show - Show Manager, Cathy James, March, Vancouver BC

Wheels, Master Promotions Ltd., PO Box 565, Saint John NB E2L 3Z8 - 506/658-0018; Fax: 506/658-0750; Tollfree: 1-888-454-7469; Email: info@masterpromotions. ca; URL: www.masterpromotions.ca - Marketing & Operations Manager, Jennifer Allaby, President, Wendell Howes - Annual consumer show

BLUEGRASS *See* MUSIC

BOATING

Classic Boat Festival, c/o Victoria Real Estate Board, 3035 Nanaimo St., Victoria BC V8T 4W2 - 250/385-7766; Fax: 250/385-8773; Email: vreb@vreb.org; URL: www.classic boatfestival.ca - Communications Manager, Michael Sampson - Annually, Labour Day weekend, Victoria BC

London International Boat Show, 395 Wellington Rd. South, PO Box 25354, London ON N6C 6B1 - 519/686- 3121; Fax: 519/680-0311; Email: jguy@london.com - General Manager, Jeff Guy - Consumer show - Feb., London ON

New Brunswick Boat & Outdoor Show, Master Promotions Ltd., PO Box 565, Saint John NB E2L 3Z8 - 506/658- 0018; Fax: 506/658-0750; Tollfree: 1-888-454-7469; Email: info@masterpromotions.ca; URL: www.masterpromotions.ca - Annual consumer show - Show Manager, Sydney Peacock, March - Exhibition Harbour Station, Saint John NB

Sudbury Boat & Sportsman Show, DAC Marketing Ltd., PO Box 2837, Stn A, Sudbury ON P3A 5J3 - 705/673- 5588; Fax: 705/525-0626; Email: dac@vianet.on.ca; URL: www.dacshows.com, Mar., Sudbury ON

Toronto International Boat Show, National Marine Manufacturers Association, #E9, 18 King St. East, Bolton ON L7E 1E8 - 905/951-0009; Email: lwaddell@nmma.org; URL: www.discoverboating.com/boatshows/toronto/home.asp - Show Manager, Linda Waddell, Jan. - National Trade Centre, Exhibition Place, Toronto ON

Victoria Boat & Outdoor Show, Canwest Shows Inc., 7 Panorama Bay SW, Calgary AB T3Z 3L6 - 403/686-9699; Fax: 403/246-3856; Email: info@canwestshows.com; URL: www.canwestshows.com - General Manager, Terra Connors - Annual consumer show - Feb. - Pearkes Recreation Centre, Victoria BC

BOOKS

BookExpo Canada, Reed Exhibition Companies Inc., #1, 3761 Victoria Park Ave., Toronto ON M1W 3S2 - 416/491-7565; Fax: 416/491-5088; Email: canada@reedexpo. com; URL: www.reedexpo.com - John Lewinski - Annual trade show - June, Toronto ON

International Festival of Authors, 235 Queen's Quay West, Toronto ON M5J 2G8 - 416/973-4760; Fax: 416/954- 4323; URL: www.readings.org - Director, Geoffrey E. Taylor - Interviews & readings by novelists, poets, playwrights & biographers - Oct. - Harbourfront Centre, Toronto ON

Montréal Book Fair/Salon du livre de Montréal, Salon du livre de Montréal, #403, 480, boul St-Laurent, Montréal QC H2Y 3Y7 - 514/845-2365; Fax: 514/845-7119; Email: slm.info@ videotron.ca; URL: www.salondulivredemontreal.com - Directrice Générale, Francine Bois - Annual consumer show - Nov., Montréal QC

Salon international du Livre de Québec, 26, rue Saint- Pierre, Québec QC G1K 8A3 - 418/692-0010; Fax: 418/692-0029; Email: info@silq.org; URL: www.silq.org - Annual consumer show - avril, Québec QC

The Word on the Street, The Word on the Street Book & Magazine Fair, #142, 67 Mowat Ave., Toronto ON M6K 3E3 - 416/504-7241; Fax: 416/504-7656; Email: toronto@theword onthestreet.ca; URL: www.thewordonthestreet.ca - Festival Coordinator, Maggie Rust - Annual celebration of literacy & the printed word; held in Toronto, Halifax, Calgary & Vancouver - Sept.

BRIDAL

Canada's Bridal Show, #10, 136 Winges Rd., 2nd Fl., Woodbridge ON L4L 6C4 - 905/264-7000; Fax: 905/264-7300; URL: www.canadasbridalshow.com - Lorie Sansone - Annual consumer show. Bridal fashion shows, gifts, florists, photography, entertainment, travel - Jan. & Oct., Toronto ON

Le Salon de la Mariée, Sheldon Kagan International Ltd., 35, McConnell, Dorval QC H9S 5L9 - 514/631-2160; Fax: 514/631-4430; Tollfree: 1-888-524-2648; Email: sheldon@sheldonkagan.com; URL: www.sheldonkagan.com - President, Sheldon Kagan - Annual consumer show - Nov. - Palais des Congrès, Montréal QC

The Total Wedding Show, Ten Star Productions Inc., 155 Castle Cres., Oakville ON L6J 5H4 - 905/845-2644; Fax: 905/845-8050; Email: info@totalweddingshow. com; URL: www.totalweddingshow.com - Janice Fernetti - Annual consumer show - Jan. - International Centre, Mississauga ON

Wedding Dreams, Bingemans Conference & Recreation Centre, 425 Bingemans Centre Dr., Kitchener ON N2B 3X7 - 519/744-1555; Fax: 519/744-1985; Tollfree: 1-800-667-0833; Email: dhauck@ringemans. com - Contact, Doris Hauck - Consumer show. Fashion shows, wedding exhibits; Jan. & Oct.

Wedding Wishes, Thunder Bay Chamber of Commerce Trade Show, #102, 200 Syndicate Ave. South, Thunder Bay ON P7E 1C9 - 807/624-2621; Fax: 807/622-7752; Email: nancy@tb-chamber.on.ca; URL: www.tbchamber. on.ca - Show Manager, Nancy Milani - Annual consumer show - Nov., Thunder Bay ON

BUSINESS

Business Showcase, Greater Saskatoon Chamber of Commerce, 345 - 3 Ave. South, Saskatoon SK S7K 1M6 - 306/244-2151; Fax: 306/244-8366; Email: chamber@ eboardoftrade.com; URL: www.eboardoftrade.com - Executive Director, Kent Smith-Windsor, President, C. Evans, Oct. - Centennial Auditorium, Saskatoon SK

Business World Exhibition, Martin International, #2910, 500, Place des Armes, Montréal QC H2Y 2W2 - 514/288-3931; Fax: 514/288-0641; Email: mbaudard@ martin-intl.com; URL: www.forum-export.ca - General Manager, Marc Baudard - Trade show. International showcase, e-commerce, transportation, export construction, digital office, finance, advertising, small business, home office - Sept.

Canadian Online Investing Forum, Diversified Business Communications Canada, #4, 800 Denison St., Markham ON L3R 5M9 - 905/948-0470; Fax: 905/479- 1364; Tollfree: 1-888-443-6486; URL: www.financialforum.ca/toronto/ visinfo.shtml

Cash & Treasury Management Conference, Treasury Management Association of Canada, #1010, 8 King St. East, Toronto ON M5C 1B5 - 416/367-8500; Fax: 416/367- 3240; Tollfree: 1-800-449-8622; Email: info@tmac.ca; URL: www.tmac.ca - Manager of Administration, Riina Koppel, Email: rkoppel@tmac.ca, President, Mike Whiston, Executive Director, Blair McRobie, Email: bmcrobie@tmac.ca, Director, Finance & Communication, Belinda Espley, Email: bespley@tmac.ca, Coordinator, Membership Development, Rose Ficco, Email: rficco@tmac.ca, Coordinator, Marketing Services, Jennifer Robb - Annual trade show. Bank products, communication systems, financial software, pension management, brokers, dealers, stock exchanges, commercial paper & computers - Oct.

Financial Forum, Diversified Business Communications Canada, #4, 800 Denison St., Markham ON L3R 5M9 - 905/948-0470; Fax: 905/479-1364; Tollfree: 1-888- 443-6786; URL: www.financialforum.ca - Show Manager, Bob McGregor - Annual consumer show

Island Trade Show, Greater Nanaimo Chamber of Commerce, 2133 Bowen Rd., Nanaimo BC V9S 1H8 - 250/756-1191; Fax: 250/756-1584; Email: info@nanaimochamber. bc.ca; URL: www.nanaimochamber.bc.ca - Executive Director, S.D. (Lee) Mason, President, Rick Thurmeier, Oct. - Woodgrove Mall

Quebec City Business & Computer Show, Martin International, #2910, 500, Place des Armes, Montréal QC H2Y 2W2 - 514/288-3931; Fax: 514/288-0641; Email: mbaudard@ martin-intl.com; URL: www.forum-export.ca - General Manager, Marc Baudard - Annual consumer show - May

Salon commerce-vacances de Ville-Marie, c/o Andr, Raymond enr., 147, rue de Montfort, Gatineau QC J8T 8A9 - 819/561-1992; Fax: 819/561-1992; Email: andre@ araymond.qc.ca; URL: araymond.qc.ca - Andr, Raymond - Annual, commercial consumer show - April - Olympia, Ville-Marie QC

Saving & Investment Marketplace, Martin International, #2910, 500, Place des Armes, Montréal QC H2Y 2W2 - 514/288-3931; Fax: 514/288-0641; Email: mbaudard@martin-intl.com; URL: www.forum-export.ca -

General Manager, Marc Baudard - Annual trade & consumer show. RRSPs, mutual funds, real estate tax shelters - Jan.
Sudbury Business & Computer Show, DAC Marketing Ltd., PO Box 2837, Stn A, Sudbury ON P3A 5J3 - 705/673-5588; Fax: 705/525-0626; Email: dac@vianet. on.ca; URL: www.dacshows.com, Sept., Sudbury ON
Thunder Bay Chamber of Commerce Trade Show, #102, 200 Syndicate Ave. South, Thunder Bay ON P7E 1C9 - 807/624-2621; Fax: 807/622-7752; Email: nancy@tbchamber.on.ca; URL: www.tb-chamber.on.ca - Show Manager, Nancy Milani - Annual trade & consumer show - May

CARS *See* AUTOMOTIVE

CHEMISTRY

Canadian Society of Clinical Chemists Annual Meeting, Events & Management Plus Inc., #310, 4 Cataraqui St., Kingston ON K7K 1Z7 - 613/531-9210; Fax: 613/531- 0626; Tollfree: 1-866-560-3838; Email: office@ eventsmgt.com; URL: www.eventsmgt.com - Owner, E. Hooper, June, Hamilton ON

CHILDREN

Calgary International Children's Festival, 205 - 8th Ave. SE, Calgary AB T2G 0K9 - 403/294-7414; Fax: 403/294-7425; Email: admin@calgarychildfest.org; URL: www.calgarychildfest.org - Producer, JoAnne James - Annual - May, Calgary AB
Celebration Jeunesse, Groupe Jeunesse, 7383, rue de la Roche, Montréal QC H2R 2T4 - 514/274-6124; Fax: 514/272-5939; Tollfree: 1-888-274-6124; Email: groupe.jeunesse@ comjeune.com; URL: www.groupejeunesse.com - Ginette Flynn - Children & parents products & services. Annual consumer show - May - Stade Olympique, Montréal QC
Milk International Children's Festival of the Arts, Harbourfront Centre, 235 Queens Quay West, Toronto ON M5J 2G8 - 416/973-3000; Fax: 416/973-6055; Email: info@harbourfront centre.com; URL: www.harbourfrontcentre.com - CEO, William J.S. Boyle - Annual - May - Harbourfront Centre, Toronto ON
Northern Alberta International Children's Festival, 5 St. Anne St., St. Albert AB T8N 3Z9 - 780/459-1542; Fax: 780/459-1726; URL: www.childfest.com - Festival Manager, Paul Moulton - June, St. Albert AB
Northern Saskatchewan International Children's Festival, PO Box 1642, Saskatoon SK S7K 3R8 - 306/664-3378; Fax: 306/664-2344; Email: cozens@sasktel.net; URL: www.saskatoonchildrensfestival.org - Artistic Director, Cass Cozens - Annually, June. Four-day international festival of the performing arts for children
Regina Children's Festival, PO Box 3813, Regina SK S4P 3N8 - 306/352-7655; Fax: 306/525-6947; Email: reginacf@sasktel.net; URL: www.reginachildrensfestival.com - Annually. Three-day festival & cultural activities for children - June
Winnipeg International Children's Festival, #201, One Forks Market Rd.., Winnipeg MB R3C 4L9 - 204/958- 4730; Fax: 204/943-7915; Tollfree: 1-800-527-1515; Email: kidsfest@kidsfest.ca; URL: www.kidsfest.ca - Neal Rempel - Annual - June, Winnipeg MB

CHRISTMAS CRAFTS *See* CRAFTS

COMMUNICATIONS

CTCA Conference & Trade Fair, Canadian Telecommunications Consultants Association, #310, 2175 Sheppard Ave., Toronto ON M2J 1W8 - 416/495-7761; Fax: 416/491-1670; Tollfree: 1-800-463-2569; Email: office@ ctca.ca; URL: www.ctca.ca - Contact, Cheryl Mottershead, 905/451-9819
EXPO COMM Canada Communications, Reed Exhibition Companies Inc., #1, 3761 Victoria Park Ave., Toronto ON M1W 3S2 - 416/491-7565; Fax: 416/491-5088; Email: canada@reedexpo.com; URL: www.reedexpo.com - John Lewinski - Annual trade show - May, Toronto ON

COMPUTERS

Computer Fest, Show Fest Productions Inc., #200, 175 Dufflaw Rd., Toronto ON M6A 2W4 - 416/782-0063; Fax: 416/564-9116; URL: www.compfest.ca - President, David Carter - Consumer show Feb. (Toronto), Apr. (Mississauga), Sept. (Toronto), Nov. (Mississauga). Computers & internet products, services, seminars, demonstrations & information for home, business & education
Exposition industrielle et commerciale, Chambre de Commerce de Sept-Iles, #237, 700, boul Laure, Sept-Iles QC G4R 1Y1 - 418/968-3488; Fax: 418/968-3432; Email: cadoretd@cgocable.ca - Directrice générale, Ginette Lehoux - Computer & small business consumer show
InfoSecurity Canada, Reed Exhibition Companies Inc., #1, 3761 Victoria Park Ave., Toronto ON M1W 3S2 - 416/491-7565; Fax: 416/491-5088; Email: canada@reedexpo. com; URL: www.reedexpo.com - John Lewinski - Annual trade show - June, Toronto ON
Multimedia International Market, Martin International, #2910, 500, Place des Armes, Montréal QC H2Y 2W2 - 514/288-3931; Fax: 514/288-0641; Email: mbaudard@martin-intl.com; URL: www.forum-export.ca - General Manager, Marc Baudard - Annual trade show. Multimedia & digital products
National Factory Automation Show, Reed Exhibition Companies Inc., #1, 3761 Victoria Park Ave., Toronto ON M1W 3S2 - 416/491-7565; Fax: 416/491-5088; Email: canada@reedexpo.com; URL: www.reedexpo.com - John Lewinski - Annual trade show alternating between Toronto & Montréal

CONSTRUCTION & BUILDING PRODUCTS

Atlantic Building Materials Show, Atlantic Building Supply Dealers Association, 70 Englehart St., Dieppe NB E1A 8H3 - 506/858-0700; Fax: 506/859-0064; Tollfree: 1-800-561-7114; Email: absda@nbnet.nb.ca; URL: www.absda.ca - President, Don Sherwood, Chair, David Pritchett - Annual trade show - March
Construct Canada, York Communications, #1000, 5255 Yonge St., Toronto ON M2N 6P4 - 416/512-1215; Fax: 416/512-1993; Tollfree: 1-800-660-7083; Email: jacqui@yorkcom.to; URL: www.yorkcommunications.ca - Principal, Jacqui Peake - Annual trade show. Products, technologies & systems for the design & construction of all building types - Dec. - Metro Toronto Convention Centre, Toronto ON
Homebuilder & Renovation Expo, York Communications, #1000, 5255 Yonge St., Toronto ON M2N 6P4 - 416/512-1215; Fax: 416/512-1993; Tollfree: 1-800-660- 7083; Email: jacqui@yorkcom.to; URL: www.yorkcommunications.ca - Principal, Jacqui Peake - Annual trade show - Dec. - Metro Toronto Convention Centre, Toronto ON

CRAFTS

Art Market, Art Market Productions, PO Box 190, Barriere BC V0E 1E0 - 250/672-2411; Fax: 250/672-9517; Tollfree: 1-877-929-9933; Email: info@artmarketcraftsale. com; URL: www.artmarketcraftsale.com - Marlene Loney - Annual consumer show; art & craft sale - Nov., Calgary AB
Atlantic Craft Trade Show, Nova Scotia Business Inc., PO Box 2374, Halifax NS B3J 3E4 - 902/424-8609; Fax: 902/424-6823; Email: acts@gov.ns.ca; URL: www.actshow.ca - Show Manager, Bernard Burton - Annual trade show. Juried craft & giftware products
Bazaart, MacKenzie Art Gallery, 3475 Albert St., Regina SK S4S 6X6 - 306/584-4250; Fax: 306/569-8191; Email: mackenzie@ uregina.ca; URL: www.mackenzieartgallery.sk.ca - Juried outdoor art show & sale; complete range of crafts - June
Big M Craft & Bake Sale, Manitoba Stampede & Exhibition, PO Box 849, Morris MB R0G 1K0 - 204/746- 2552; Fax: 204/746-2900 - General Manager, Ron Funk Christmas at the Forum - Festival of Crafts, Antiques, Art & Foods,
Christmas at the Forum Crafts Festival, PO Box 34, Annapolis Royal NS B0S 1A0; Tollfree: 1-866- 995-7469; Email: dmsshows@hotmail.com; URL: www.forumcrafts.com - Coordinator, Jason Susnick - Annual consumer show - Nov., Halifax NS
Craft-Ex, DAC Marketing Ltd., PO Box 2837, Stn A, Sudbury ON P3A 5J3 - 705/673-5588; Fax: 705/525-0626; Email: dac@vianet.on.ca; URL: www.dacshows.com - Annual consumer show in Timmins, Sault Ste Marie & Sudbury - April
CraftWorld, Fine Arts & Crafts Show, Cryderman Productions Inc., 136 Thames St., Chatham ON N7L 2Y8 - 519/351-8344; Fax: 519/351-8345; Tollfree: 1-866- 640-9663; Email: john@crydermanproductions.com; URL: www.crydermanproductions.com - John Cryderman - Semi-annual shows in Chatham (March & Oct.) & Kitchener (Mar. & Nov.)
Creative Stitches & Crafting Alive, Canwest Shows Inc., 7 Panorama Bay SW, Calgary AB T3Z 3L6 - 403/686- 9699; Fax: 403/246-3856; Email: info@canwestshows. com; URL: www.canwestshows.com - General Manager, Terra Connors - Annual consumer show in Calgary (Sept.) & Edmonton (April)
Metro Toronto Christmas Gift Show & Sale, Metro Toronto Christmas Show & Sale, Skydome, PO Box 54045, Toronto ON M6A 3B7 - 416/789-1925 - Lawrence Plaza - Annual consumer show - Dec. - Metro Toronto Convention Centre, Toronto ON
Na'Amat Craft & Gift Show, Na'Amat Canada, 272 Codsell Ave., Toronto ON M3H 3X2 - 416/636-5425; Fax: 416/636-5248; Tollfree: 1-888-622-6280; Email: naamatca@aol.com - Executive Director, Lorraine Levene - October
One of a Kind Christmas Canadian Craft Show & Sale, The Canadian Craft Show Ltd., #300, 717 Church St., Toronto ON M4W 2M4 - 416/960-3680; Fax: 416/923- 5624; Email: info@oneofakindshow.com; URL: www.oneofakindshow.com - Show Director, Patti Stewart - Annual consumer show - Nov./Dec. - National Trade Centre, Exhibition Place, Toronto ON
One of a Kind Springtime Canadian Craft Show & Sale, The Canadian Craft Show Ltd., #300, 717 Church St., Toronto ON M4W 2M4 - 416/960-3680; Fax: 416/923- 5624; Email: info@oneofakindshow.com; URL: www.oneofakindshow.com - Show Director, Patti Stewart - Annual consumer show - March/April - Automotive Building, Exhibition Place, Toronto ON
Originals Christmas Craft Show, Signatures Craft Shows Ltd., #810, 325 Dalhousie St., Ottawa ON K1N 7G2 - 613/241-5777; Fax: 613/241-5678; Tollfree: 1-800- 773-4444; Email: inf@signatures.ca; URL: www.signatures.ca, Dec.
Pine Tree Potters Sale, 22 Church St., Aurora ON L4G 1G4 - 905/727-1278 - May & Nov.
Saskatchewan Handcraft Festival, Saskatchewan Craft Council, 813 Broadway Ave., Saskatoon SK S7N 1B5 - 306/653-3616; Fax: 306/244-2711; Tollfree: 1-866- 653-3616; Email: saskcraftcouncil@shaw.ca; URL: www.saskcraftcouncil.org - Chair, Paula Cooley, Executive Director, Glenn Saganace, July, Battleford SK
Saskatchewan Handcraft Festival, 813 Broadway Ave., Saskatoon SK S7N 1B5 - 306/653-3616; Fax: 306/244- 2711; Email: saskcraftcouncil@shaw.ca; URL: www.saskcraft council.org - Marketing Coordinator, Chris Jones - Annual three-day festival - July, Battleford SK
Signatures London, Signatures Craft Shows Ltd., #810, 325 Dalhousie St., Ottawa ON K1N 7G2 - 613/241-5777; Fax: 613/241-5678; Tollfree: 1-800-773-4444; Email: inf@signatures.ca; URL: www.signatures.ca - Annual consumer show - Nov., London ON
Signatures Ottawa, Signatures Craft Shows Ltd., #810, 325 Dalhousie St., Ottawa ON K1N 7G2 - 613/241-5777; Fax: 613/241-5678; Tollfree: 1-800-773-4444; Email: inf@signatures.ca; URL: www.signatures.ca - Annual consumer show - Nov., Ottawa ON
Signatures Toronto, Signatures Craft Shows Ltd., #810, 325 Dalhousie St., Ottawa ON K1N 7G2 - 613/241-5777; Fax: 613/241-5678; Tollfree: 1-800-773-4444; Email: inf@signatures.ca; URL: www.signatures.ca - Annual consumer show - Nov., Toronto ON
Signatures Winnipeg, Signatures Craft Shows Ltd., #810, 325 Dalhousie St., Ottawa ON K1N 7G2 - 613/241- 5777; Fax: 613/241-5678; Tollfree: 1-800-773-4444; Email: inf@signatures.ca; URL: www.signatures.ca - Annual consumer show - Nov., Winnipeg MB
Sundog Handcraft Fair, PO Box 7183, Saskatoon SK S7K 4J1 - 306/384-7364; Fax: 306/384-7364; Email: sundoghand craftfaire@sasktel.net - Coordinator, Diane Boyko-Banda - Juried three-day craft market plus continuous stage acts & gourmet food court. Annually, first weekend of Dec.
Victoria Park Arts/Crafts Fair, PO Box 1394, Moncton NB E1C 8T6 - 506/386-1200; Fax: 506/857-0279; Email: oscar@nb.aibn.com; URL: www.victoriaparkcrafts. com - Annually - Aug.
Wintergreen, Saskatchewan Craft Council, 813 Broadway Ave., Saskatoon SK S7N 1B5 - 306/653-3616; Fax: 306/244-2711; Tollfree: 1-866-653-3616; Email: saskcraftcouncil@shaw.ca; URL: www.saskcraftcouncil.org - Chair, Paula Cooley, Executive Director, Glenn Saganace - Annual. Threeday Christmas craft market - Nov., Regina SK

DANCE *See* MUSIC

DECORATING *See* HOME SHOWS

ELECTRICAL/ELECTRONICS

Audio Thunder, Pro-Sho Inc., 298 Sheppard Ave. East, Toronto ON M2N 3B1 - 416/229-9919; Fax: 416/223- 2826; Tollfree: 1-877-950-1500; Email: prosho@meteorshows. com; URL: www.performanceworldcarshow.com; www.llhashows.com- Contact: Larry King, March - International Centre, Toronto ON
Canadian High Technology Show & Assembly Canada, Reed Exhibition Companies Inc., #1, 3761 Victoria Park Ave., Toronto ON M1W 3S2 - 416/491-7565; Fax: 416/491-5088; Email: canada@reedexpo.com; URL: www.reedexpo.com - John Lewinski - Annual trade show. Electronic components, robotics, communications systems

Electrical Showcase, Manitoba Electrical League, #104, 1780 Wellington Ave., Winnipeg MB R3H 1B3 - 204/783-4125; Fax: 204/783-4216; Email: office@meleague. net; URL: www.meleague.net - General Manager, Dave Foreman - Triennial trade show - April

Eptech, LVP Media Inc., #27, 1200 Aerowood Dr., Mississauga ON L4W 2S7 - 905/624-8100; Fax: 905/624- 1760; Email: info@ept.ca; URL: www.ept.ca - Trade show held in various locations. Electronic components, systems

Mechanical Electical Electronic Technology, Master Promotions Ltd., PO Box 565, Saint John NB E2L 3Z8 - 506/658-0018; Fax: 506/658-0750; Tollfree: 1-888- 454-7469; Email: info@masterpromotions.ca; URL: www.masterpromotions.ca - Marketing & Operations Manager, Jennifer Allaby, President, Wendell Howes - Bienniel show

La Salon de la Technologie Electronique au Québec/Quebec Electronics Technology Show, Reed Exhibition Companies Inc., #1, 3761 Victoria Park Ave., Toronto ON M1W 3S2 - 416/491-7565; Fax: 416/491-5088; Email: canada@ reedexpo.com; URL: www.reedexpo.com - John Lewinski - Biennial trade show

ENERGY

Enercom, York Communications, #1000, 5255 Yonge St., Toronto ON M2N 6P4 - 416/512-1215; Fax: 416/512- 1993; Tollfree: 1-800-660-7083; Email: jacqui@ yorkcom.to; URL: www.yorkcommunications.ca - Principal, Jacqui Peake - Annual conference & exposition focusing on major trends & emerging issues in the procurement, production & distribution of electricity, gas, oil & renewable energy - March - Metro Toronto Convention Centre, Toronto ON

ENVIRONMENT

National Conference on Drinking Water, Canadian Water & Wastewater Association, #11, 1010 Polytek Rd., Ottawa ON K1J 9H9 - 613/747-0524; Fax: 613/747-0523; Email: admin@cwwa.ca; URL: www.cwwa.ca - Executive Director, T. Duncan Ellison - Biennial - April, 2008, Québec QC

ETHNIC *See* MULTICULTURAL

EVENTS

***See Also* specific categories for events such as Winter Carnivals, Music Festivals, Rodeos, Exhibitions, etc.**

Ashkenaz: A Festival of New Yiddish Culture, #303, 455 Spadina Ave., Toronto ON M5S 2G8 - 416/979-9901; Email: info@ashkenazfestival.com; URL: www.ashkenazfestival.com - President, Judy Wolfe - Bienniel; Aug./Sept.

Atlantic Canada Bicycle Rally, c/o Atlantic Canada Cycling, PO Box 1555, Stn M, Halifax NS B3J 2Y3 - 902/423-2453; Fax: 902/423-2452; Email: acbr@atlanticcanadacycling. com; URL: www.atlanticcanadacycling.com - Largest bicycle event in Atlantic Canada - Aug.

Billy Barker Days, PO Box 4441, Quesnel BC V2J 3J4 - 250/992-1234; Fax: 250/992-5083; Email: billyb@ quesnelbc.com; URL: www.pgonline.com/billybarkerdays, July

Blossom Festival, PO Box 329, Creston BC V0B 1G0 - 250/428-2266; Fax: 250/428-3320 - Contact, Bernice Hamilton - May, long weekend

Brockville Riverfest, Waterfront, Brockville Riverfest, Blockhouse Island, PO Box 742, Brockville ON K6V 5V8 - 613/342-8975; Fax: 613/345-6174; Email: riverfest@ripnet.com; URL: www.brockvilleriverfest.ca, June

The Canadian Tulip Festival, Canadian Tulip Festival, #106, 112 Nelson St., Ottawa ON K1N 7R5 - 613/567- 5757; Fax: 613/567-6216; Tollfree: 1-800-668-8547; Email: info@tulipfestival.ca; URL: www.tulipfestival.ca - Executive Director, BemoOt Hubert, May

Canmore Highland Games, Three Sisters Scottish Festival Society, PO Box 8102, Canmore AB T1W 2T8 - 403/678-9454; Fax: 403/678-3385; Email: canmorehighlandgames@telus.net; URL: www.canmorehighlandgames.ca - Annually, Labour Day Sunday - Sept., Canmore AB

Charleswood In-Motion Days, 625 Municipal Rd., Winnipeg MB R3R 1J2 - 204/837-7356 - Annually, June. Business displays, stage performances, carnival, youth soccer tournament

CHIN International Picnic, Exhibition Place, Toronto ON M6K 3C3 - 416/531-9991; Fax: 416/531-5274; Email: info@chinradio.com; URL: www.chinradio.com - June/July

Chocolate Fest, Chocolate Festival, PO Box 5002, St. Stephen NB E3L 2X5 - 506/465-5616; Fax: 506/465- 5610; Email: info@chocolate-fest.ca; URL: www.chocolate-fest.ca - Coordinator, Roxanne Grant - Annual - Aug

Discovery Days, Discovery Days Festival, PO Box 389, Dawson YT Y0B 1G0 - 867/993-5575; Fax: 867/993- 6415; Email: kva@dawsoncity.net; URL: www.dawsoncity.ca - Aug.

Feast of St. Louis, 259 Park Service Rd., Louisbourg NS B1C 2L2 - 902/733-2280; Fax: 902/733-2362; Email: louisbourg.info@pc.gc.ca - Manager, Heritage Presentation, Anne O'Neill, Superintendent, Carol Whitfield - Eighteenth-century celebrations in honour of St. Louis - August, Louisbourg NS

Festival des peches et de l'aquaculture du Nouveau Brunswick, #200, 1 av Hotel de Ville, Shippagan NB E8S 1M1 - 506/336-8726; Fax: 506/336-3901; Email: festival@shippagan.com

Halifax Highland Games, 35 Clearview Cres., Dartmouth NS B3A 2M9 - 902/466-3778; Email: info@halifaxhighlandgames. com; URL: www.halifaxhighlandgames.com, July - Garrison Grounds, Halifax NS

Heritage Canoe Festival, (Lift Lock), c/o Friends of the Trent Severn Waterway, PO Box 572, Peterborough ON K9J 6Z6 - 705/742-2251; Fax: 705/750-4816; Tollfree: 1-800-663-2628; URL: www.ftsw.com - Mark Doherty - Annually, 2nd weekend in May

Icelandic Festival of Manitoba, #107, 94 - 1st Ave., Gimli MB R0C 1B0 - 204/642-7417; Fax: 204/642-9382; Email: icefest@mts.net; URL: www.icelandicfestival.com, Aug., Gimli MB

Just for Laughs Festival, 2101, boul Saint-Laurent, Montréal QC H2X 2T5 - 514/845-3155; Fax: 514/845-4140; Tollfree: 1-888-244-3155; Email: info@hahaha.com; URL: www.hahaha.com, July

Kitchener-Waterloo Oktoberfest, 17 Benton St., PO Box 1053, Kitchener ON N2G 4G1 - 519/570-4267; Fax: 519/742-3072; Tollfree: 1-888-294-4267; Email: info@oktoberfest.ca; URL: www.oktoberfest.ca - Executive Director, Larry Blundell - Annually, October. Bavarian festival: foods, entertainment, parades

Labrador Straits Bakeapple Folk Festival, PO Box 112, Forteau NL A0K 2P0 - 709/931-2013; Email: info@labradorcoastal drive.com - Director, Marketing, Bonnie Goudie - Annually, Aug.

Manitoba Sunflower Festival, PO Box 1630, Altona MB R0G 0B0 - 204/324-9005; Fax: 204/324-1550; Email: info@townofaltona.com; URL: www.town.altona.mb.ca - Annual, last weekend of July

Northern Manitoba Trappers' Festival, Inc., PO Box 475, The Pas MB R9A 1K6 - 204/623-2912; Fax: 204/623- 1974; URL: www.trappersfestival.com - Annually, Feb.; world championship sled dog race

Northwest Territorial Days, PO Box 668, North Battleford SK S9A 2Y9 - 306/445-2024; Fax: 306/445-3352; Email: b.agsociety@sasktel.net; URL: www.agsociety.com - Aug.

Nova Scotia Gaelic Mod, F,is A' MhThe Gaelic Mod, PO Box 80, Englishtown NS B0C 1H0 - 902/295-3411; Fax: 902/295-2912; Email: hector@gaeliccollege.edu; URL: www.gaeliccollege.edu - One-day festival - Aug. - Gaelic College, St. Ann's NS Nova Scotia International Tattoo, 1586 Queen St., Halifax NS B3J 2V1 - 902/420-1114; Fax: 902/423-6629; Tollfree: 1-800-563-1114; Email: info@nstattoo.ca; URL: www.nstattoo.ca - Ian Fraser - Annually, June/July

Penticton Peach Festival, #113, 437 Martin St., S343, Penticton BC V2A 5L1 - 250/492-9830; Fax: 250/492- 7980; Email: info@peachfest.com; URL: www.peachfest.com - Aug.

Peterborough Summer Festival of Lights, 610 Parkhill Rd., Peterborough ON K9J 6N6 - 705/755-1111; Fax: 705/755-0188; Email: info@festivaloflights.ca; URL: www.festivaloflights.ca - Special Events Coordinator, Emily Martin, General Manager, Kathy Kirkland - June to Aug. every Wednesday & Saturday evening at Del Crary Park

Pictou Lobster Carnival, PO Box 1480, Pictou NS B0K 1H0 - 902/485-5150; Fax: 902/485-4915; Email: picoulobstercarnival@hotmail.com; URL: www.townofpictou.com - Annual - July

Québec City Summer Festival, 226, rue St-Joseph est, Québec QC G1K 3A9 - 418/523-4540; Fax: 418/523- 0194; Tollfree: 1-888-992-5200; Email: infofestival@ infofestival.com; URL: www.infofestival.com - Entertainment in the streets & parks of Old Québec, July

Royal St. John's Regatta, PO Box 214, St. John's NL A1C 5J9 - 709/579-8921; Fax: 709/576-3315; Email: stjohnsregatta@nf.aibn.com; URL: www.stjohnsregatta.org - North America's oldest continuing sporting event - Aug., St. John's NL

Sam Steele Days, PO Box 115, Cranbrook BC V1C 4H6 - 250/426-4161; Fax: 250/426-3873; Tollfree: 1-800- 222-6174; Email: info@samsteeledays.org; URL: www.samsteeledays.org, June

Shediac Lobster Festival, 231A Belliveau Ave., Shediac NB E4P 1H4 - 506/532-1122; Fax: 506/532-7986; Tollfree: 1-888-707-1755; Email: lobsterf@ nbnet.nb.ca; URL: www.lobsterfestival.nb.ca - Guy Lavine - Annually, first week of July

Steinbach Pioneer Days, c/o Mennonite Heritage Village, 231, PTH 12 North, Steinbach MB R0A 2A0 - 204/326- 9661

Storytelling Festival, The Storytellers School of Toronto, 43 Queens Park Cres. East, Toronto ON M5S 2C3 - 416/656-2445; Fax: 416/656-8510; Email: admin@storytelling toronto.org; URL: www.storytellingtoronto.org - President, Michael Lobraico, Managing Director, Catherine Melville - Held annually, April

Summerside Lobster Carnival, PO Box 1295, Summerside PE C1N 4K2 - 902/436-4925; Fax: 902/436-0129; URL: www. exhibitions-festivalspeiae.com/summersidelobstercarnival, July

Threshermen's Show & Seniors' Festival, PO Box 98, Yorkton SK S3N 2V6 - 306/783-8361; Fax: 306/782- 1027; Email: yorkton@wdm.ca; URL: www.wdm.ca - Chair, Susan Mandzluk - Annually, Aug.

Trinity Conception Fair, c/o Harbour Grace Stadium, PO Box 365, Harbour Grace NL A0A 2M0 - 709/596-6201; Fax: 709/596-6261; Tollfree: 1-800-596-3233; Email: hgrecdept@nf.aibn.com - Fair Manager, Kevin Bennett - Annually, Sept.

Welland Rose Festival, 800 Niagara St. North, PO Box 23031, Welland ON L3C 5Z4 - 905/735-8696; Fax: 905/735-4832; URL: www.wellandrosefestival.on.ca - Director, Shane Sargant - Annually, June. Rose show, lobsterfest, sporting events, juried art show, seniors' events, day in the park, day-on-the-island, craft show, fishing derby, children's events, grand parade

Winnipeg Oktoberfest, Winnipeg Convention Centre, 375 York Ave., 3rd Fl., Winnipeg MB R3C 3J3 - 204/957- 4535; Fax: 204/943-0310; Email: oktoberfest@ wcc.mb.ca; URL: www.winnipegoktoberfest.com, Sept.

World's Invitational Class A Gold Panning Championships, Taylor Gold Panning Society, District of Taylor, PO Box 300, Taylor BC V0C 2K0 - 250/789-3004; Fax: 250/789-9076; URL: www.districtoftaylor.com - Director, Community Services, Natalie Poole-Moffat - Annually, Aug. long weekend Yukon Gold-Panning Championships, Klondike Visitors Association, PO Box 389, Dawson YT Y0B 1G0 - 867/993-5575; Fax: 867/993-6415; Email: kva@ dawson.net; URL: www.dawsoncity.org - On Canada Day - July, Dawson City YT

Yukon River Bathtub Race, Yukon Sourdough Rendezvous Society, PO Box 31721, Whitehorse YT Y1A 6L3 - 867/393-4467; Fax: 867/668-6755; Email: ysr@polarcom. com; URL: www.yukonrendezvous.com - Executive Director, Harold Sher, President, Marj Eschak - Longest & hardest bathtub race. Two days, 486 miles, Yukon River - Aug.

Yukon Sourdough Rendezvous, Yukon Sourdough Rendezvous Society, PO Box 31721, Whitehorse YT Y1A 6L3 - 867/393-4467; Fax: 867/668-6755; Email: ysr@polarcom.com; URL: www.yukonrendezvous.com - Executive Director, Harold Sher, President, Marj Eschak - Annually. Celebrates the gold rush times. Mad trapper, flour packing, tug-a-truck contests, fiddle show, lip sync & queen contests - Feb.

EXHIBITIONS

***See Also* Farm Business/Agriculture, Rodeos**

Buffalo Days Exhibition, Regina Exhibition Park, PO Box 167, Regina SK S4P 2Z6 - 306/781-9200; Fax: 306/565-3443; Tollfree: 1-888-734-3975; Email: info@reginaexhibition. com - Marketing Manager, Tom Mullin, General Manager, Douglas Cressman, July

Canadian Lakehead Exhibition, 425 Northern Ave., Thunder Bay ON P7C 2V7 - 807/622-6473; Fax: 807/623-5540; Email: clex@btbaytel.net; URL: www.cle.on.ca - Administrative Clerk, Dulcie Prystanski - Annually, Aug.

Canadian National Exhibition, Canadian National Exhibition Association, Exhibition Place, Toronto ON M6K 3C3 - 416/263-3800; Fax: 416/263-3838; Email: info@theex.com; URL: www.theex.com - Annual public show

Edmonton's Klondike Days Exposition, PO Box 1480, Edmonton AB T5J 2N5 - 780/471-7210; Fax: 780/471- 8176; Tollfree: 1-888-800-7275; Email: info@northlands. com; URL: www.northlands.com - Annual consumer show

Expo Québec, ExpoCit,, 250, boul Wilfrid-Hamel, Québec QC G1L 5A7 - 418/691-7110; Fax: 418/691-7249; Email: info@expocite.com - General Manager, Mark Sparrow - Annual exhibition. Industrial, agricultural, food - Aug. - City Fairgrounds, Québec QC

Fredericton Exhibition, PO Box 235, Stn A, Fredericton NB E3B 4Y9 - 506/458-9819; Fax: 506/458-9294; Email: frex@nb.net.nb.ca; URL: brentbriggs_frex@ nb.aibn.com - Annual, begins on Labour Day - Sept.

Home Town Fair, Hometown Fair, c/o Moose Jaw Exhibition Co. Ltd., 250 Thatcher Dr. East, Moose Jaw SK S6J 1L7 - 306/692-2723; Fax: 306/692-2762; Email: moosejawexh@sk.sympatico.ca - General Manager, Glen Lewis - Annually - June

Interior Provincial Exhibition, Interior Provincial Exhibition & Stampede, PO Box 490, Armstrong BC V0E 1B0 - 250/546-9406; Fax: 250/546-6181; Email: ipeandstampede@ telus.net; URL: www.ipeandstampede.com - General Manager, Ken Mather - Annual consumer agricultural fair & show, Aug.-Sept. - Aug.

Lindsay Central Exhibition, 37 Adelaide St. North, Lindsay ON K9V 4K8 - 705/324-5551; Fax: 705/324-8111; Email: info@ lindsayex.com; URL: www.lindsayex.com - Manager, Tom Saunders - Annual consumer agricultural fair & show - Sept.

Markham Agricultural Fair, 10801 McCowan Rd., Markham ON L3P 3J3 - 905/642-3247; Fax: 905/640- 8458; Tollfree: 1-800-450-3557; Email: office@ markhamfair.ca; URL: www.markhamfair.ca - Annual consumer show - Sept./Oct.

Medicine Hat Exhibition & Stampede, 2055 - 21st Ave. SE, PO Box 1298, Medicine Hat AB T1A 7N1 - 403/527- 1234; Fax: 403/529-6553; Email: mhstampede@mhstampede. com; URL: www.mhstampede.com/- General Manager, Jim MacArthur - Annual consumer show - July

New Atlantic National Exhibition, PO Box 284, Saint John NB E2L 3Y2 - 506/633-2020; Fax: 506/636-6958 - Annual - Aug.

Niagara Regional Exhibition, 1100 Niagara St. North, Welland ON L3C 1M6 - 905/735-6413; Fax: 905/735- 2317; Email: nreoffice@nre.ca; URL: www.nre.ca - Annual consumer agricultural fair & show, Sept. - Sept.

Nova Scotia Provincial Exhibition, PO Box 192, Truro NS B2N 5C5 - 902/893-9222; Fax: 902/897-0069; Email: nspe@eastlink.ca - David Coombes - Agricultural exhibition - August, Bible Hill NS

Pacific National Exhibition, 2901 East Hastings St., Stn Hastings Park, Vancouver BC V5K 5J1 - 604/253- 2311; Fax: 604/251-7768; Email: info@pne.ca; URL: www.pne.ca - President & CEO, Michael McDaniel - Annual event; agricultural competitions, parade

Paris Fall Fair, PO Box 124, Paris ON N3L 3E7 - 519/442- 2823; Fax: 519/442-5121; Email: parisfair@ on.aibn.com; URL: www.parisfair.com - Manager, Harry Emmott - Annual Labour Day weekend consumer show

Prince Albert Exhibition, Prince Albert Exhibition Association, PO Box 1538, Prince Albert SK S6V 5T1 - 306/764-1711; Fax: 306/764-5246; Email: paex@ sasktel.net; URL: www.paexhibition.com - Manager, Dave Young - Annual

Red River Exhibition, Red River Exhibition Association, Red River Exhibition Park, 3977 Portage Ave., Winnipeg MB R3K 2E8 - 204/888-6990; Fax: 204/888- 6992; URL: www.redriverex.com - Manitoba's largest fair & single-site entertainment event. Annually, 10 days, last two weeks in June

Thresherman's Reunion & Stampede, Central Canada's Fiddle Festival, PO Box 10, High Bluff MB R0H 0C0 - 204/637-2354; Fax: 204/637-2395; Email: info@agmuseum. mb.ca; URL: www.ag-museum.mb.ca - Contact, Sandra Head - Annual

Western Nova Scotia Exhibition, PO Box 425, Yarmouth NS B5A 4B3 - 902/742-8222; Fax: 902/742-5229; Email: frank@swsda.com; URL: yarmouthexhibition.com/index.html - Frank Anderson - Six-day agricultural fair & talent competition - July or Aug., Yarmouth NS

FARM BUSINESS/AGRICULTURE

See Also **Exhibitions, Rodeos**

Agribition Show & Rodeo, Canadian Western Agribition Show & Rodeo, c/o Public Relations Office, Canadian Western Agribition, PO Box 3535, Regina SK S4P 3J8 - 306/565-0565; Fax: 306/757-9963; Email: info@agribition. com; URL: www.agribition.com - General Manager, Leon Brin - Annually, Nov.

CAAR Convention, Canadian Association of Agri-Retailers, #107, 1090 Waverley St., Winnipeg MB R3T 0P4 - 204/989-9300; Fax: 204/989-9306; Tollfree: 1-800-463-9323; Email: info@caar.org; URL: www.caar.org - Executive Director, Jacqueline Ryrie, President, Bob Evans

Canadian National Hereford Show, c/o Canadian Hereford Association, 5160 Skyline Way NE, Calgary AB T2E 6V1 - 403/275-2662; Fax: 403/295-1333; Email: herefords@ hereford.ca; URL: www.hereford.ca, Nov., Regina SK

Estevan Farmer's Day, c/o Estevan Chamber of Commerce, #303, 1133 Fourth St., Estevan SK S4A 0W6 - 306/634-2828; Fax: 306/634-6729 - Office Manager, Carol Gress - Annually, March

Farmers' Field Day & Open House, c/o St. John's Research Station, Agriculture Canada, Brookfield Rd., PO Box 39088, St. John's NL A1E 5Y7 - 709/772-4619; Fax: 709/772-6064; Email: henderf@em.agr.ca; URL: res.agr.ca/stjohns - Communications Advisor, Lesley Noftall - Annually, 4th Saturday in Aug.

Maritime Fall Fair, 200 Prospect Rd., Goodwood NS B3T 1P2 - 902/876-8221; Fax: 902/876-8551; URL: www.maritimefallfair.com - Annual consumer exhibition, Oct., over the Thanksgiving weekend

Norfolk County Fair & Horse Show, Norfolk County Agricultural Society, 172 South Dr., Simcoe ON N3Y 1G6 - 519/426-7280; Fax: 519/426-7286; URL: www.norfair.com - General Manager, Karen Matthews, Email: kmatthews@norfolkcountyfair.com - Annual consumer show

Northlands Farmfair, Farmfair International, PO Box 1480, Edmonton AB T5J 2N5 - 780/471-7210; Fax: 780/471- 8169; Tollfree: 1-888-800-7275; URL: www.farmfairinternational.com - Annually, Nov.

Nova Scotia 4-H Show, c/o NS Dept. of Agriculture & Fisheries, PO Box 550, Truro NS B2N 5E3 - 902/893-6587; Fax: 902/893-2757; Email: crouseea@gov.ns.ca; URL: www.gov.ns.ca/nsaf/4h - Manager, Elizabeth Crouse - Annual consumer show, Oct.

Poultry Industry Conference & Exhibition, Western Fair Association, 900 King St., PO Box 7550, London ON N5Y 5P8 - 519/438-7203; Fax: 519/679-3124; Tollfree: 1-800-619-4629; Email: gmcrae@westernfair. com; URL: www.westernfair.com - General Manager, Gary McRae - Annual trade show

Regional Potato Festival, #100, 1A Burgess St., Grand Falls NB E3Y 1C6 - 506/475-1816; Fax: 506/473-9091; Email: info@festivalregionaldelapatate.com; URL: www.festivalregionaldelapatate.com - President, John Bellefleur, June

Royal Agricultural Winter Fair, Royal Agricultural Winter Fair Association, The Coliseum, National Trade Centre, Exhibition Place, Toronto ON M6K 3C3 - 416/263- 3400; Fax: 416/263-3488; Email: information@royalfair. org; URL: www.royalfair.org - Annual consumer show. World's largest agricultural fair & equestrian event - Nov., Toronto ON

Salon de l'Agriculteur, #120, 2200, rue Pratte, Saint-Hyacinthe QC J2S 4B6 - 450/771-1226; Fax: 450/771- 6073; Email: info@salonagr.qc.ca; URL: salonagr.qc.ca - Annual trade show. Agricultural products - Jan., St-Hyacinthe QC

Western Canada Farm Progress Show, PO Box 167, Regina SK S4P 2Z6 - 306/781-9200; Fax: 306/781-9396; Tollfree: 1-888-734-3975; Email: wcfps@reginaexhibition. com; URL: www.wcfps.com - Show Manager, Rob O'Connor, Vice-President, Major Event Development, Darrell Komick - Annual consumer & trade show - June - Regina Exhibition Park, Regina SK

Western Fair, Western Fair Association, 900 King St., PO Box 7550, London ON N5Y 5P8 - 519/438-7203; Fax: 519/679-3124; Tollfree: 1-800-619-4629; Email: gmcrae@westernfair.com; URL: www.westernfair.com - General Manager, Gary McRae - Annual consumer show

Western Farm Show, Western Fair Association, 900 King St., PO Box 7550, London ON N5Y 5P8 - 519/438- 7203; Fax: 519/679-3124; Tollfree: 1-800-619-4629; Email: gmcrae@westernfair.com; URL: www.westernfair.com - General Manager, Gary McRae - Annual consumer show

FASHION

Luggage, Leathergoods, Handbags & Accessories, Pro-Sho Inc., 298 Sheppard Ave. East, Toronto ON M2N 3B1 - 416/229-9919; Fax: 416/223-2826; Tollfree: 1-877- 950-1500; Email: prosho@meteorshows.com; URL: www.performanceworldcarshow.com; www.llhashows. com - Annual trade show - Show Manager, Richard Swayze, April - International Centre, Mississauga ON

FESTIVALS *See* EVENTS

FILM & VIDEO FESTIVALS & SPECIAL EVENTS

Alberta Film & Television Awards, Alberta Motion Picture Industries Association, #401, 11456 Jasper Ave., Edmonton AB T5K 0M1 - 780/944-0707; Fax: 780/426- 3057; Email: info@ampia.org; URL: www.ampia.org - President, Connie Edwards, Executive Director, Richard Horne, Feb.

Le Carrousel international du film de Rimouski, 92, 2e rue ouest, Rimouski QC G5L 8B3 - 418/722-0103; Fax: 418/724-9504; Email: cifr@carrousel.qc.ca; URL: www.carrousel.qc.ca - Kathleen Aubry - Films for children. Competition, workshops - Sept., Rimouski QC

Cinéfest - The Sudbury International Film Festival, 45 Durham St., Sudbury ON P3E 3M2 - 705/688-1234; Fax: 705/688-1351; Tollfree: 1-877-212-3222; Email: cinefest@vianet.on.ca; URL: www.cinefest.com - Executive Director, Tammy Frick - Full-length feature festival with over 100 Canadian & international films, animations, shorts, Midnight Madness, documentary & children's film series - Sept., Sudbury ON

Festival du cinéma international en Abitibi-Témiscamingue, 215, av Mercier, Rouyn-Noranda QC J9X 5W8 - 819/762-6212; Fax: 819/762-6762; Email: info@festivalcinema. ca; URL: www.lino. com/festivalcinema - Executive Director, Jacques Matte - Features, mediumlength & short films. Competition; regional jury award for short or medium-length film; people's choice award for feature & animation - Oct., Rouyn-Noranda QC

Festival du film étudiant canadien/Canadian Student Film Festival, Festival du film ,tudiant canadien, 1432, rue de Bleury, Montréal QC H3A 2J1 - 514/848-7186; Fax: 514/848-3886; Email: info@ffm-montreal.org - Films & videos by Canadian students. Film competition - Aug., Montréal QC

Le Festival International du Film Scientifique du Québec, Téléscience, 15, rue de la Commune ouest, Montréal QC H2Y 2C6 - 514/849-1612; Fax: 514/281-0814; Email: dir@telescince.qc.ca; URL: www.telescience.qc.ca - Director, Lise Barrette

Festival international du nouveau Cinéma et des nouveaux M,dias de Montréal, Festival international du nouveau Cin,ma de Montréal, 3530, boul Saint-Laurent, Montréal QC H2X 2V1 - 514/847-9272; Fax: 514/847-0732; Email: info@fcmm.com - Directeur, Claude Chamberlan - New trends in new cinema, video & new media; non-competitive; people's choice award

Film Studies Association of Canada Conference, Film Studies Association of Canada, c/o Global Studies, Wilfrid Laurier Univ., Dr. Alvin Woods Bldg., 75 University Ave. West, Room 3-205, Waterloo ON N2L 3C5; Email: gekoff@contact.net; URL: www.filmstudies.ca - President, Brenda Austin-Smith, Vice-President, Janina Falkowska, Secretary, Christina Stojanowa - May/June annually, held at a different university each year

Flicks: Saskatchewan International Children's Film Festival, Flicks International Children's Film Festival, PO Box 9628, Saskatoon SK S7K 7G1 - 306/956-3456; Fax: 306/664-2344; Email: flicksfilmfestival@sasktel.net; URL: www.flicksfilmfest. org - Artistic Director, Cass Cozens - Annually in March, three day international film festival for children

Images Festival of Independent Film & Video, #448, 401 Richmond St. West, Toronto ON M5V 3A8 - 416/971- 8405; Fax: 416/971-7412; Email: images@imagesfestival. com; URL: www.imagesfestival.com/- Executive Director, Peter Chevrier - Annual. Independent films & videos. Workshops - April, Toronto ON

Les Journées africaines et créoles, Vues d'Afrique, 67, rue Ste-Catherine ouest, 5e étage, Montréal QC H2X 1Z7 - 514/284-3322; Fax: 514/845-0631; Email: info@vuesdafrique. org; URL: www.vuesdafrique.org - Gérard Le Chêne - Competition. Films by & about African & Creole peoples - April, Montréal QC

Les Rendez-vous du cinéma québécois, 1000, rue Fullum, Montréal QC H2K 3L7 - 514/526-9635; Fax: 514/526- 1955; Email: info@rvcq.com; URL: www.rvcq.com - Président, Denis Chouinard - Restrospective of recent Québec productions - Feb., Montréal QC

Ottawa International Animation Festival, #120, 2 Daly Ave., Ottawa ON K1N 6E2 - 613/232-8769; Fax: 613/232-6315; Email: info@animationfestival.ca; URL: www.awn.com/ottawa /- Annual. Animation films & videos. Television animation conference. Workshops & panels - Sept., Ottawa ON

St. John's Women's Film & Video Festival, PO Box 984, St. John's NL A1C 5M3 - 709/754-3141; Fax: 709/754- 3143; Email: womensfilmfest@nfld.net; URL: www.womensfilmfest.com - Festival Director, Katie Nicholson - Women's films & videos. Workshops & panels - Oct., St. John's NL Toronto International Film Festival,

Toronto International Film Festival Group, #1600, 2 Carlton St., Toronto ON M5B 1J3 - 416/967-7371; Fax: 416/967-9477; Email: tiffg@tiffg.ca; URL: www.bell.ca/filmfest - Manager, Development, Sarah Bullick - Features & theatrical shorts. Competition. Awards for excellence in Canadian production. People's choice & film critics awards. Symposium, workshops, sales office - Sept., Toronto ON

Vancouver International Film Festival, #410, 1008 Homer St., Vancouver BC V6B 2X1 - 604/685-0260; Fax: 604/688-8221; Email: viff@viff.org; URL: www.viff.org - Festival Director, Alan Franey - Features, mediumlength & short films. Competition; juried awards for best western Canadian feature film, best young western Canadian director of a short film, best documentary feature & best film by a new director from Pacific Asia; people's choice award for most popular international film & for most popular Canadian film. Trade forum - Sept./Oct., Vancouver BC World Film Festival, Montréal

World Film Festival, 1432, rue de Bleury, Montréal QC H3A 2J1 - 514/848-3883; Fax: 514/848-3886; Email:

info@ffm-montreal.org; URL: www.ffm-montreal.org/- Features, mediumlength & short films. Competition, symposium, markets - Aug., Montréal QC

FIRST NIGHT CELEBRATIONS

First Night Labrador City, PO Box 280, Labrador City NL A2V 2K5 - 709/944-3602; Fax: 709/944-5277 First Night Toronto, 55 Mill St., Case Goods Warehouse 74, Studio 202, Toronto ON M5A 3C4 - 416/603-4778; Fax: 416/595-9651; Email: info@firstnighttoronto.ca; URL: www.firstnighttoronto.ca - Executive Director, Jeffrey Latimer, Dec.

First Night Whistler, 4010 Whistler Way, Whistler BC V0N 1B4 - 604/932-3928; Fax: 604/932-7231

FISHING/AQUACULTURE

Adams River Sockeye Salmon Run, PO Box 1563, Chase BC V0E 1M0 - 250/679-8315; URL: www.salmonsociety.com - Oct.

Atlantic Aquaculture Exposition, Master Promotions Ltd., PO Box 565, Saint John NB E2L 3Z8 - 506/658-0018; Fax: 506/658-0750; Tollfree: 1-888-454-7469; Email: info@masterpromotions.ca; URL: www.masterpromotions.ca - Marketing & Operations Manager, Jennifer Allaby, President, Wendell Howes - Canada's largest aquaculture event - June, St. Andrews NB

Eastern Canada Fisheries Exposition, Master Promotions Ltd., PO Box 565, Saint John NB E2L 3Z8 - 506/658- 0018; Fax: 506/658-0750; Tollfree: 1-888-454-7469; Email: info@masterpromotions.ca; URL: www.masterpromotions.ca - Annual commercial fishing show - Show Manager, Jeff Lacey, Feb - Mariner's Centre, Yarmouth NS

Fish Canada/Workboat Canada West, Master Promotions Ltd., PO Box 565, Saint John NB E2L 3Z8 - 506/658- 0018; Fax: 506/658-0750; Tollfree: 1-888-454-7469; Email: info@masterpromotions.ca; URL: www.masterpromotions.ca - Bienniel commercial fishing/boat show - Show Manager, Sydney Peacock, Nov., Vancouver BC

Flin Flon Trout Festival, PO Box 751, Flin Flon MB R8A 1N6 - 204/687-5166, June, Flin Flon MB

Great Northern Pike Festival, PO Box 863, Nipawin SK S0E 1E0 - 306/862-9866; Fax: 306/862-3076; Tollfree: 1-877-647-2946; Email: events@ nipawin.com; URL: www.nipawinpikefestival.com - June - Sept.

Lunenburg Fishermen's Picnic & Reunion, PO Box 308, Lunenburg NS B0J 2C0 - 902/634-8575; Fax: 902/634- 8575; Email: bacalao@tallships.ca - Chair, Barbara Zwicker, Aug., Lunenburg NS

Nova Scotia Smelt Tournament, 2228 Conquerall Rd., Bridgewater NS B4V 2W3 - 902/543-6453; Email: icefish@tallships.ca - Largest ice fishing tournament, Eastern Canada - Feb.

Salmon Festival, PO Box 24, Campbellton NB E3N 3G1 - 506/759-7997; Fax: 506/759-7403; Tollfree: 1-888- 813-4433; Email: tourism@campbellton.org; URL: www.campbellton.org - Contact, Gilbert Cyr, Email: gilbert.cyr@campbellton.org - June

FLOWERS/LANDSCAPING/GARDENING

Flower, Plant & Garden Show, dmg World Media, 180 Duncan Mills Rd., 4th Fl., Toronto ON M3B 1Z6 - 416/385-1880; Fax: 416/385-1855; Tollfree: 1-888-823- 7469; URL: www.dmgworldmedia.com - Show Manager, Glen Chiasson

Hamilton & Burlington Rose Society Show, Royal Botanical Gardens, 680 Plains Rd. West, Burlington ON L7T 4H4 - 905/527-1158; Fax: 905/577-0375, June Hamilton Orchid Show, Royal Botanical Gardens, 680 Plains Rd. West, Burlington ON L7T 4H4 - 905/527- 1158; Fax: 905/577-0375, March

Ikenobo Ikebana Japanese Flower Show, Royal Botanical Gardens, 680 Plains Rd. West, Burlington ON L7T 4H4 - 905/527-1158; Fax: 905/577-0375, Sept.

Ontario Garden Show, Town Media, 1074 Cooke Blvd., Burlington ON L7T 4A8 - 905/634-8003; Fax: 905/634-7661; URL: www.foodandwineshow.ca; ontariogardenshow. com - Annual - April - Royal Botanical Gardens Centre, Burlington ON

Provincial Rose Show, 1747 Summer St., Halifax NS B3H 3A6 - 902/423-4458 - Ann-Marie Clifford - Competitive show for rose growers in Nova Scotia - July - Nova Scotia Museum of Natural History, Halifax NS

Saskatoon Horticultural Society Annual Show, PO Box 161, Saskatoon SK S7K 3K4 - 306/373-7075; Email: sasktoonhortsociety@sasktel.net - Elsie, Aug.

FOOD & BEVERAGE

***See Also* Hospitality Industry**

Canadian Natural Product Spring/Fall Show, Canadian Health Food Association, #205, 550 Alden Rd., Markham ON L3R 6A8 - 905/479-6939; Fax: 905/479- 1516; Tollfree: 1-800-661-4510, fax 1-888-2927; Email: admin@chfa.ca; URL: www.chfa.ca - Organic & natural products; homeopathy, food supplements & herbs. April & Oct.

The Good Food Festival & Market, 117 Evelyn Ave., Toronto ON M6J 4G7 - 416/766-2084; Fax: 416/762-9942; Email: info@goodfoodfestival.net; URL: www.goodfoodfestival.net - General Manager, Lynda Chubak - Annual consumer festival - April - International Centre, Hall 5, Mississauga ON

Gourmet Food & Wine Expo, Town Media, 1074 Cooke Blvd., Burlington ON L7T 4A8 - 905/634-8003; Fax: 905/634-7661; URL: www.foodandwineshow.ca; ontariogardenshow.com - Consumer show - Nov. - Metro Toronto Convention Centre, Toronto ON

Ottawa Wine & Food Show, Player Expositions International, 255 Clemow Ave., Ottawa ON K1S 2B5 - 613/567-6408; Fax: 613/567-2718; Email: rplayer@sympatico. ca; URL: www.playerexpo.com - Show Organizer, Halina Player - Annual trade & consumer show - Oct./Nov.

Salon des vins et spiritueux de Montréal, AFLD Consultants Inc., 3565, rue Edgar Leduc, Lachine QC H8T 3L5 - 514/639-6806; Fax: 514/639-6629; Email: afld@ videotron.ca - Show Manager, Lucie Desharnais, CDE - Biennial trade & public show

Salon Distal, Distal, 414, boul Raymond, Beauport QC GIC 7S4 - 418/666-5575; Fax: 418/666-8005 - Michel Renaud - Annual trade show. Food products & distributors. Held in Montréal & Québec - April

SSA International - Super Salon de l'alimentation, SIAL Montréal - Salon international de l'alimentation, #1100, 300, rue Léo Pariseau, CP 159, Montréal QC H2W 2M9 - 514/289-9669; Fax: 514/289-1034; Tollfree: 1-800- 281-7425; Email: info@sialmontreal.ca; URL: www.sial-montreal.com/- Directeur général, Alain Bellefeuille - Annual trade show for the food retail industry including food & beverage products & store equipment - April

Toronto Wine & Cheese Show, Premier Publications & Shows, 467 Speers Rd., Oakville ON L6K 3S4; Fax: 905/337-5570; Tollfree: 1-800-265-3673; URL: www.towineandcheese.com - Marti Milks, 905/815-0017, ext.426, Email: marti.milks@ sympatico.ca, Brad Dean, 416/365-1500, ext.41, Email: bdean@travelweek. ca, Christine Wong, 905/815-0017, ext.447, Email: cwong@metroland.com - Annual consumer show - March - International Centre, Toronto ON

FOREST INDUSTRY

DEMO International, Master Promotions Ltd., PO Box 565, Saint John NB E2L 3Z8 - 506/658-0018; Fax: 506/658- 0750; Tollfree: 1-888-454-7469; Email: info@masterpromotions. ca; URL: www.masterpromotions.ca - Active demonstrations of all types of industrial woodlands equipment. Harvesting, silviculture, transportation & handling, Sept. - Show Manager, Mark Cusack, Sept. - Laval University, Laval QC

Forest Expo, 850 River Rd., Prince George BC V2L 5S8 - 250/563-8833; Fax: 250/563-3697; Email: info@forestexpo. bc.ca; URL: www.forestexpo.bc.ca - General Manager, Trudy Swaan - Biennial - June 5-7, 2008, Prince George BC

InterSaw, Master Promotions Ltd., PO Box 565, Saint John NB E2L 3Z8 - 506/658-0018; Fax: 506/658-0750; Tollfree: 1-888-454-7469; Email: info@masterpromotions. ca; URL: www.masterpromotions.ca - Biennial show - Show Manager, Mark Cusack, May - Centre de foires, Québec QC

LogFor, Master Promotions Ltd., PO Box 565, Saint John NB E2L 3Z8 - 506/658-0018; Fax: 506/658-0750; Tollfree: 1-888-454-7469; Email: info@masterpromotions. ca; URL: www.masterpromotions.ca - Marketing & Operations Manager, Jennifer Allaby, President, Wendell Howes - Biennial logging & forestry show - Sept.

FUNERALS

Canadian Funeral Trade Show, PO Box 97507, Toronto ON M1C 4Z1 - 416/281-5460; Fax: 416/282-9095; Email: info@canadianfuneraltradeassociation.com; URL: www.canadianfuneraltradeassociation.com - Executive Director, Brenda Broughton - Annual trade show - June

FURNITURE *See* HOME SHOWS

GARDENING *See* FLOWERS

GIFTS & JEWELLERY

Expo Prestige, Corporation des bijoutiers du Québec, 868, rue Brisette, Sainte-Julie QC J3E 2B1 - 514/485-3333; Fax: 450/649-8984; Email: info@cbq.qc.ca; URL: www.cbq.qc.ca - Président, André Marchand, Directrice générale, Lise Petitpas, août - Palais des Congrès, Montréal QC

Jewellery World Expo, Reed Exhibition Companies Inc., #1, 3761 Victoria Park Ave., Toronto ON M1W 3S2 - 416/491-7565; Fax: 416/491-5088; Email: canada@ reedexpo.com; URL: www.reedexpo.com - John Lewinski - Annual trade show - Aug., Toronto ON

The Last Minute Christmas Show & Sale, Metro Toronto Christmas Show & Sale, Skydome, PO Box 54045, Toronto ON M6A 3B7 - 416/789-1925 - Lawrence Plaza - Annual consumer show - Dec. - Metro Toronto Convention Centre, Toronto ON

Montréal Gift Show/Le Salon du Cadeau - Montréal, dmg World Media, 180 Duncan Mills Rd., 4th Fl., Toronto ON M3B 1Z6 - 416/385-1880; Fax: 416/385-1855; Tollfree: 1-888-823-7469; URL: www.dmgworldmedia.com - Show Manager, Glen Chiasson - Annual trade show. Giftware, stationery, kitchenware, luggage & leathergoods, pottery, china, glass, jewellery - March, Montréal QC

North Bay Gift Show, North Bay & District Chamber of Commerce, 1375 Seymour St., PO Box 747, North Bay ON P1B 8J8 - 705/472-8480; Fax: 705/472-8027; Tollfree: 1-888-249-8998; Email: nbcc@northbaychamber. com; URL: www.northbay chamber.com - Manager, Patti Alcorn-Carr - Annual trade show. Giftware, fashion, food services & furniture - April - West Ferris Community Centre, North Bay ON

Toronto International Gift Fair, dmg World Media, 180 Duncan Mills Rd., 4th Fl., Toronto ON M3B 1Z6 - 416/385-1880; Fax: 416/385-1855; Tollfree: 1-888-823- 7469; URL: www.dmgworldmedia.com - Show Manager, Glen Chiasson

Vancouver Spring/Fall Gift Show, dmg World Media (Canada) Inc., #402, 4601 Canada Way, Burnaby BC V5G 4X7 - 604/433-5121; Fax: 604/434-6853; Tollfree: 1-800-633-8332; URL: www.dmgworldmedia.com - Exec. Vice-President, Gifts Sector, Fred Barnes - Annual trade show. Giftwares, housewares, luggage & leathergoods, jewellery. March & Sept.

GRAPHIC ARTS

Print Ontario, Print World, #8, 1606 Sedlescomb Dr., Mississauga ON L4X 1M6 - 905/625-7070; Fax: 905/625-4856; Tollfree: 1-800-331-7408 - Biennial trade show - Nov. - Exhibition Place, Toronto ON

HAIRDRESSING

Allied Beauty Show, Allied Beauty Association, #46/47, 450 Matheson Blvd. East, Mississauga ON L4Z 1R5 - 905/568-0158; Fax: 905/568-1581; Email: abacan@idirect. com; URL: www.abacanada.com - Executive Director, Marc Speir - Held in various locations

HEATING, PLUMBING & AIR CONDITIONING

***See Also* Hardware**

CIPHEX, CIPH, #330, 295 The West Mall, Toronto ON M9C 4Z4 - 416/695-0447; Fax: 416/695-0450; Tollfree: 1-800-639-2474; Email: info@ciph.com; URL: www.ciph.com - Elizabeth McCullugh - Biennial trade show. Plumbing, heating, cooling & piping exhibits & conference (Calgary, Toronto & Montreal)

CMX, Shield Associates Ltd., 25 Bradgate Rd., Toronto ON M3B 1J6 - 416/444-5225; Fax: 416/444-8268; Tollfree: 1-800-282-0003; Email: sal@salshow.com; URL: www.cmxshow.com; www.windoorshow.com - Show Coordinator, Patrick Shield - Biennial trade show. Heating, ventilation, plumbing, air conditioning, ventilation & refrigeration - March

HOBBIES

***See Also* Crafts**

Gem, Mineral & Fossil Show, Calgary Rock & Lapidary Club, 110 Lissington Dr. SW, Calgary AB T3E 5E3 - 403/287-1570; Email: martintm@telus.net; URL: www.crlc.ca - Director, Public Relations, Trudy Martin - Annual

Toronto Model Railway Show, 2938 Dundas St. West, PO Box 70618, Toronto ON M6P 4E7 - 416/249-4563 - Show Co-ordinator, Jack Bell - Annual consumer show held 3rd weekend of March

HOME ENTERTAINMENT *See* ELECTRICAL/ELECTRONICS

HOME SHOWS

Atlantic National Home Show, Master Promotions Ltd., PO Box 565, Saint John NB E2L 3Z8 - 506/658-0018; Fax: 506/658-0750; Tollfree: 1-888-454-7469; Email: info@masterpromotions.ca; URL: www.masterpromotions.ca -

Annual consumer show - Show Manager, Brian McKiel, March, Saint John NB

BC Home & Garden Show, dmg World Media (Canada) Inc., #402, 4601 Canada Way, Burnaby BC V5G 4X7 - 604/433-5121; Fax: 604/434-6853; Tollfree: 1-800- 633-8332; URL: www.dmgworldmedia.com - Annual consumer show - Show Manager, Trish Almeida, Feb.

Bridgewater Home & Leisure Show, Master Promotions Ltd., PO Box 565, Saint John NB E2L 3Z8 - 506/658- 0018; Fax: 506/658-0750; Tollfree: 1-888-454-7469; Email: info@masterpromotions.ca; URL: www.masterpromotions.ca - Annual consumer show. Home products, services & leisure products - Show Manager, Brian McKeil, April - Bridgewater Arena, Bridgewater NS

Burlington Fall Lifestyle Home Show, Jenkins Show Productions, 1076 Skyvalley Cres., Oakville ON L6M 3L2 - 905/827-4632; Fax: 905/827-8139; Tollfree: 1-800- 465-1073; Email: djenkins2@cogeco.ca; URL: www.jenkinsshow.com - President, Dave Jenkins - Annual consumer show - Sept., Burlington ON

Burlington Lifestyle Home Show, Jenkins Show Productions, 1076 Skyvalley Cres., Oakville ON L6M 3L2 - 905/827-4632; Fax: 905/827-8139; Tollfree: 1-800- 465-1073; Email: djenkins2@cogeco.ca; URL: www.jenkinsshow.com - President, Dave Jenkins - Annual consumer show - April, Burlington ON

Calgary Home & Interior Design Show, dmg World Media, #605, 999 - 8 St. SW, Calgary AB T2R 1N7 - 403/209- 3555; Fax: 403/245-8649; Tollfree: 1-888-799-2545; URL: www.dmgworldmedia.com - Annual consumer show - Show Manager, Lisa Macintosh, Sept. - Stampede Park, Calgary AB

Canadian Spa & Pool Conference & Expo, Pool & Hot Tub Council of Canada, #10B, 242 Applewood Cres., Vaughan ON L4K 4E5 - 905/761-7920; Fax: 905/761- 8837; Tollfree: 1-800-879-7066; Email: office@poolcouncil. ca; URL: www.poolcouncil.ca - Executive Director, Ken Tomihiro - Annual trade & consumer show - Dec. - Toronto Congress Centre, Toronto ON

Colchester County Home Show, Master Promotions Ltd., PO Box 565, Saint John NB E2L 3Z8 - 506/658-0018; Fax: 506/658-0750; Tollfree: 1-888-454-7469; Email: info@masterpromotions.ca; URL: www.masterpromotions.ca - Annual consumer show - Show Manager, Scott Sprague, April - Legion Stadium, Truro NS

Edmonton Home & Interior Design Show, dmg World Media, #605, 999 - 8 St. SW, Calgary AB T2R 1N7 - 403/209-3555; Fax: 403/245-8649; Tollfree: 1-888- 799-2545; URL: www.dmgworldmedia.com - Annual consumer show - Show Manager, Lisa Macintosh, Sept. - Northlands AgriCom, Edmonton AB

Expo Habitat de St-Hyacinthe, DBC Communications Inc. (Division Ev,nements), 655, av Ste-Anne, Saint-Hyacinthe QC J2S 5G4 - 450/773-3976, Fax: 450/773 3115 - Personne ressource, Pierre Charbonneau - Annual consumer show. Home construction & renovation products & services - April - Pavillion de Pionnieres, St-Hyacinthe QC

Fall Home & Outdoor Recreation Show, DAC Marketing Ltd., PO Box 2837, Stn A, Sudbury ON P3A 5J3 - 705/673-5588; Fax: 705/525-0626; Email: dac@vianet. on.ca; URL: www.dacshows.com, Sept., Sudbury ON

Fall Home Show, dmg World Media, 180 Duncan Mills Rd., 4th Fl., Toronto ON M3B 1Z6 - 416/385-1880; Fax: 416/385-1855; Tollfree: 1-888-823-7469; URL: www.dmgworldmedia.com - Show Manager, Glen Chiasson

Fredericton Lifestyles Show, Master Promotions Ltd., PO Box 565, Saint John NB E2L 3Z8 - 506/658-0018; Fax: 506/658-0750; Tollfree: 1-888-454-7469; Email: info@masterpromotions.ca; URL: www.masterpromotions.ca - Annual consumer show - Show Manager, Brian McKeil, March - Capital Exhibit Centre, Fredericton NB

Home - Health & Lifestyles Show, Cryderman Productions Inc., 136 Thames St., Chatham ON N7L 2Y8 - 519/351- 8344; Fax: 519/351-8345; Tollfree: 1-866-640-9663; Email: john@crydermanproductions.com; URL: www.crydermanproductions.com - John Cryderman - Annual - Jan. - Kinsmen Auditorium, Chatham ON

Home Show, Thunder Bay Chamber of Commerce Trade Show, #102, 200 Syndicate Ave. South, Thunder Bay ON P7E 1C9 - 807/624-2621; Fax: 807/622-7752; Email: nancy@tb-chamber.on.ca; URL: www.tbchamber. on.ca - Show Manager, Nancy Milani, Sept., Thunder Bay ON

Home, Garden & Leisure Show, Medicine Hat & District Chamber of Commerce, 413 - 6th Ave. SE, Medicine Hat AB T1A 2S7 - 403/527-5214; Fax: 403/527-5182; Email: mhchamber@monarch.net; URL: www.medicinehatchamber. com - President, Jason Mutschler, Executive Director, Mary Lou Hansen - Consumer show - March - Cypress Centre, Stampede Park, Medicine Hat AB

Home, Garden & Renovation, Cryderman Productions Inc., 136 Thames St., Chatham ON N7L 2Y8 - 519/351- 8344; Fax: 519/351-8345; Tollfree: 1-866-640-9663; Email: john@ crydermanproductions.com; URL: www.cryderman productions.com - John Cryderman - Annual - Feb. - Kinsmen Auditorium, Chatham ON

International Home & Garden Show, Showcase Marketing Ltd., #410, 1110 Sheppard Ave. East, Toronto ON M2K 2W2 - 416/512-1305; Email: homeshow@idirect. com - Paul Newdick - Annual consumer show - March - International Centre, Toronto ON

International Home Show, Showcase Marketing Ltd., #410, 1110 Sheppard Ave. East, Toronto ON M2K 2W2 - 416/512-1305; Email: homeshow@idirect.com - Paul Newdick - Annual consumer show - Oct. - International Centre, Toronto ON

London Home & Garden Show, London Show Productions, 2326 Fanshawe Park Rd. East, London ON N5X 4A2 - 519/455-5888; Fax: 519/455-7780 - Consumer show - April, London ON

Mall Home Shows, Jenkins Show Productions, 1076 Skyvalley Cres., Oakville ON L6M 3L2 - 905/827-4632; Fax: 905/827-8139; Tollfree: 1-800-465-1073; Email: djenkins2@cogeco.ca; URL: www.jenkinsshow.com - President, Dave Jenkins - Shows at shopping centres throughout Ontario in Feb., Mar., June, Oct., Nov.

Metro Home Show, dmg World Media, 180 Duncan Mills Rd., 4th Fl., Toronto ON M3B 1Z6 - 416/385-1880; Fax: 416/385-1855; Tollfree: 1-888-823-7469; URL: www.dmgworldmedia.com - Show Manager, Glen Chiasson - Annual consumer show - Jan. - National Trade Centre, Exhibition Place, Toronto ON

Miramichi Lifestyles Show, Master Promotions Ltd., PO Box 565, Saint John NB E2L 3Z8 - 506/658-0018; Fax: 506/658-0750; Tollfree: 1-888-454-7469; Email: info@masterpromotions.ca; URL: www.masterpromotions.ca - Annual consumer show - Show Manager, Brian McKeil, April - Miramichi Civic Centre, Miramichi NB

Moncton Kiwanis Lifestyles Show, Master Promotions Ltd., PO Box 565, Saint John NB E2L 3Z8 - 506/658- 0018; Fax: 506/658-0750; Tollfree: 1-888-454-7469; Email: info@masterpromotions.ca; URL: www.masterpromotions.ca - Annual consumer show - Show manager, Brian McKiel, April, Moncton NB

Montréal National Home Show, dmg World Media, 180 Duncan Mills Rd., 4th Fl., Toronto ON M3B 1Z6 - 416/385-1880; Fax: 416/385-1855; Tollfree: 1-888-823- 7469; URL: www.dmgworldmedia.com - Show Manager, Glen Chiasson

National Home Show, dmg World Media, 180 Duncan Mills Rd., 4th Fl., Toronto ON M3B 1Z6 - 416/385- 1880; Fax: 416/385-1855; Tollfree: 1-888-823-7469; URL: www.dmgworldmedia.com - Show Manager, Glen Chiasson - Annual consumer show - April - Coliseum Bldg., Exhibition Place, Toronto ON

Niagara Lifestyle Home Show, Jenkins Show Productions, 1076 Skyvalley Cres., Oakville ON L6M 3L2 - 905/827 4632; Fax: 905/827-8139; Tollfree: 1-800-465- 1073; Email: djenkins2@cogeco.ca; URL: www.jenkinsshow.com - President, Dave Jenkins - Annual consumer show - April - Garden City/Rex Stimers Arena, St Catharines ON

Nova Scotia Fall Ideal Home Show, Master Promotions Ltd., PO Box 565, Saint John NB E2L 3Z8 - 506/658- 0018; Fax: 506/658-0750; Tollfree: 1-888-454-7469; Email: info@masterpromotions.ca; URL: www.masterpromotions.ca - Annual consumer show - Show Manager, Bev Campbell, Oct., Halifax NS

Nova Scotia Spring Ideal Home Show, Master Promotions Ltd., PO Box 565, Saint John NB E2L 3Z8 - 506/658- 0018; Fax: 506/658-0750; Tollfree: 1-888-454-7469; Email: info@masterpromotions.ca; URL: www.masterpromotions.ca - Annual consumer show - Show Manager, Bev Campbell, April, Halifax NS

Oakville Lifestyle Home Show, Jenkins Show Productions, 1076 Skyvalley Cres., Oakville ON L6M 3L2 - 905/827-4632; Fax: 905/827-8139; Tollfree: 1-800-465- 1073; Email: djenkins2@cogeco.ca; URL: www.jenkinsshow.com - President, Dave Jenkins - Annual consumer show - April - Glen Abbey Recreation Centre, Oakville ON

Ottawa Spring/Fall Home Show, dmg World Media, #302, 260 Dalhousie St., Ottawa ON K1N 7E4 - 613/241- 2888; Fax: 613/241-4827; Tollfree: 1-877-241-0007; URL: www.ottawahomeshows.com - Show Manager, Chantale Boisvert - Annual consumer show. March & Sept.

PEI Provincial Home Show, Master Promotions Ltd., PO Box 565, Saint John NB E2L 3Z8 - 506/658-0018; Fax: 506/658-0750; Tollfree: 1-888-454-7469; Email: info@masterpromotions.ca; URL: www.masterpromotions.ca - Annual consumer show - Show Manager, Brian McKeil, March, Charlottetown PE

Red Deer Home Ideas, Home Ideas & Lifestyles, #10, 7895 - 49 Ave., Red Deer AB T4P 2B4 - 403/346-5321; Fax: 403/342-1301; Email: admin@cahb.ca; URL: www.cahba.ca - Contact, Joan Butler - Annual, Feb./March

Showcase, Medicine Hat & District Chamber of Commerce, 413 - 6th Ave. SE, Medicine Hat AB T1A 2S7 - 403/527-5214; Fax: 403/527-5182; Email: mhchamber@monarch.net; URL: www.medicinehatchamber.com - President, Jason Mutschler, Executive Director, Mary Lou Hansen - Annual consumer show - Nov.

Success With Gardening, Showcase Marketing Ltd., #410, 1110 Sheppard Ave. East, Toronto ON M2K 2W2 - 416/512-1305; Email: homeshow@idirect.com - Paul Newdick - Annual consumer show - Mar. - International Centre, Toronto ON

Sudbury Spring Home Show, DAC Marketing Ltd., PO Box 2837, Stn A, Sudbury ON P3A 5J3 - 705/673-5588; Fax: 705/525-0626; Email: dac@vianet.on.ca; URL: www.dacshows.com, March, Sudbury ON

Vancouver Home & Interior Design Show, dmg World Media (Canada) Inc., #402, 4601 Canada Way, Burnaby BC V5G 4X7 - 604/433-5121; Fax: 604/434-6853; Tollfree: 1-800-633-8332; URL: www.dmgworldmedia.com - Annual consumer show - Show Manager, Trish Almeida, Oct.

Western Canada Kitchen, Bath & Renovation Show, Manitoba Home Builders' Association, #1, 1420 Clarence Ave., Winnipeg MB R3T 1T6 - 204/925-2560; Fax: 204/925-2567; Email: mbhomebd@mb.sympatico. ca; URL: www.homebuilders.mb.ca - Show Manager, Danita Brisson - Annual consumer show

Win Door, Shield Associates Ltd., 25 Bradgate Rd., Toronto ON M3B 1J6 - 416/444-5225; Fax: 416/444-8268; Tollfree: 1-800-282-0003; Email: sal@salshow.com; URL: www.cmxshow.com; www.windoorshow.com - Show Coordinator, Patrick Shield - Trade, Windows & doors show, new products & technologies - Nov.

Windsor Home & Leisure Show, Cryderman Productions Inc., 136 Thames St., Chatham ON N7L 2Y8 - 519/351- 8344; Fax: 519/351-8345; Tollfree: 1-866-640-9663; Email: john@crydermanproductions.com; URL: www.crydermanproductions.com - John Cryderman - Annual - Feb. - University of Windsor, Windsor ON

Yarmouth Lifestyles Show, Master Promotions Ltd., PO Box 565, Saint John NB E2L 3Z8 - 506/658-0018; Fax: 506/658-0750; Tollfree: 1-888-454-7469; Email: info@masterpromotions.ca; URL: www.masterpromotions.ca - Marketing & Operations Manager, Jennifer Allaby, President, Wendell Howes, April, Yarmouth NS

HORSES

The Masters Show Jumping Tournament, Spruce Meadows, RR#9, Calgary AB T2J 5G5 - 403/974-4200; Fax: 403/974-4270; Email: information@sprucemeadows.com; URL: www.sprucemeadows.com - Annual tournament. Includes consumer/trade show Equi-Fair, & the Festival of Nations - Sept.

North American Tournament, RR#9, Calgary AB T2J 5G5 - 403/974-4249; Fax: 403/947-4266; Email: jack.hugill@ sprucemeadows.com; URL: www.sprucemeadows.com - Coordinator, Sales, Jack Hugill - Annual. Showcased through Sun Life Financials at Fort Meadows - July

Royal Red Arabian Horse Show, PO Box 167, Regina SK S4P 2Z6 - 306/781-9200; Fax: 306/781-9396; Email: roconnor@reginaexhibition.com - Facility Contact, Rob O'Connor - Annual - Aug.

HORTICULTURE *See* **FLOWERS**

HOSPITALITY INDUSTRY (HOTEL, MOTEL, RESTAURANT)

See Also **Food & Beverage**

ApEx, Canadian Restaurant & Foodservices Association, 316 Bloor St. West, Toronto ON M5S 1W5 - 416/923- 8416; Fax: 416/923-1450; Tollfree: 1-800-387-5649; Email: info@crfa.ca; URL: www.crfa.ca - President, Douglas C. Needham, Senior Exec. Vice-President, David Harris - Annual trade show - April

ARFEX - Alberta Restaurant & Foodservices Exposition, Alberta Restaurant & Foodservices Association, #1003, 10080 Jasper Ave., Edmonton AB T5J 1V9 - 780/444- 9496; Fax: 780/481-8727; Tollfree: 1-800-461-9762; Email: lrollingson@arfa.net; URL: www.arfa.net - President, Lindy Rollingson, CPM CAE - Annual trade show - April - Northlands Agricom, Edmonton AB

Canadian Convenience Store Expo, Reed Exhibition Companies Inc., #1, 3761 Victoria Park Ave., Toronto ON M1W 3S2 - 416/491-7565; Fax: 416/491-5088; Email:

canada@reedexpo.com; URL: www.reedexpo.com - John Lewinski - Annual trade show - Sept., Mississauga ON

Grocery Showcase Canada, Canadian Federation of Independent Grocers, #902, 2235 Sheppard Ave. East, Toronto ON M2J 5B5 - 416/492-2311; Fax: 416/492-2347; Tollfree: 1-800-661-2344; Email: info@cfig.ca; URL: www.cfig.ca - President, John F.T. Scott, Chair, Mike Coleman, Vice-President, Gary Sanos - Annual trade show - Oct.

Grocery Showcase West, Canadian Federation of Independent Grocers, #902, 2235 Sheppard Ave. East, Toronto ON M2J 5B5 - 416/492-2311; Fax: 416/492-2347; Tollfree: 1-800-661-2344; Email: info@cfig.ca; URL: www.cfig.ca - President, John F.T. Scott, Chair, Mike Coleman, Vice-President, Gary Sanos - Annual trade show - March - Vancouver Trade & Convention Centre, Vancouver BC

HostEx, Canadian Restaurant & Foodservices Association, 316 Bloor St. West, Toronto ON M5S 1W5 - 416/923- 8416; Fax: 416/923-1450; Tollfree: 1-800-387-5649; Email: info@crfa.ca; URL: www.crfa.ca - President, Douglas C. Needham, Senior Exec. Vice-President, David Harris - Annual trade show

INDUSTRIAL

Atlantic Industrial Exhibition - Halifax, Reed Exhibition Companies Inc., #1, 3761 Victoria Park Ave., Toronto ON M1W 3S2 - 416/491-7565; Fax: 416/491-5088; Email: canada@reedexpo.com; URL: www.reedexpo.com - John Lewinski - Biennial trade show - Sept., Halifax NS

Atlantic Industrial Exhibition - Moncton, Reed Exhibition Companies Inc., #1, 3761 Victoria Park Ave., Toronto ON M1W 3S2 - 416/491-7565; Fax: 416/491-5088; Email: canada@reedexpo.com; URL: www.reedexpo.com - John Lewinski - Biennial trade show - Sept., Moncton NB

Montréal Fabricating & Machine Tool Show/Le Salon du Travail des M,taux et de la Machine Outil de Montréal, Reed Exhibition Companies Inc., #1, 3761 Victoria Park Ave., Toronto ON M1W 3S2 - 416/491-7565; Fax: 416/491-5088; Email: canada@reedexpo.com; URL: www.reedexpo.com - John Lewinski - Biennial trade show

Plant Maintenance & Engineering Show/Le Salon Industriel de la Maintenance et de l'Ingenierie, Reed Exhibition Companies Inc., #1, 3761 Victoria Park Ave., Toronto ON M1W 3S2 - 416/491-7565; Fax: 416/491- 5088; Email: canada@reedexpo.com; URL: www.reedexpo.com - John Lewinski - Bienniel trade show

Salon industriel de L'Estrie, Les Promotions André Pageau Inc., 1627, boul Bastien, Québec QC G2K 1H1 - 418/623-3383; Fax: 418/623-5033; Tollfree: 1-800-387- 3383; Email: info@promoapageau.com; URL: www.promoapageau.com - Pr,sident, Andr, Pageau, Sept., St-Hyacinthe QC

Salon Industriel de Québec, Les Promotions Andr, Pageau Inc., 1627, boul Bastien, Québec QC G2K 1H1 - 418/623-3383; Fax: 418/623-5033; Tollfree: 1-800-387- 3383; Email: info@promoapageau.com; URL: www.promoapageau.com - Président, André Pageau - Biennial trade show - Oct., Québec QC Salon Industriel du Saguenay/Lac-St-Jean, Les Promotions André Pageau Inc., 1627, boul Bastien, Québec QC G2K 1H1 - 418/623-3383; Fax: 418/623-5033; Tollfree: 1-800-387-3383; Email: info@promoapageau. com; URL: www.promoapageau.com - Président, André Pageau - Biennial - May, Chicoutimi QC

Weld Expo Canada, Reed Exhibition Companies Inc., #1, 3761 Victoria Park Ave., Toronto ON M1W 3S2 - 416/491-7565; Fax: 416/491-5088; Email: canada@reedexpo. com; URL: www.reedexpo.com - John Lewinski - Biennial trade show - Oct.

Western Manufacturing Technology Show - Edmonton, Reed Exhibition Companies Inc., #1, 3761 Victoria Park Ave., Toronto ON M1W 3S2 - 416/491-7565; Fax: 416/491-5088; Email: canada@reedexpo.com; URL: www.reedexpo.com - John Lewinski - Biennial trade show - June, Edmonton AB

Western Manufacturing Technology Show - Vancouver, Reed Exhibition Companies Inc., #1, 3761 Victoria Park Ave., Toronto ON M1W 3S2 - 416/491-7565; Fax: 416/491-5088; Email: canada@reedexpo.com; URL: www.reedexpo.com - John Lewinski - Biennial trade show - June, Abbotsford BC

JEWELLERY *See* GIFTS

LANDSCAPING *See* FLOWERS

LEGAL

Canadian Association of Law Libraries, Events & Management Plus Inc., #310, 4 Cataraqui St., Kingston ON K7K 1Z7 - 613/531-9210; Fax: 613/531-0626; Tollfree: 1-866-560-3838; Email: office@ eventsmgt.com; URL: www.eventsmgt.com - Owner, E. Hooper, May

LEISURE *See* SPORTS & RECREATION

MACHINERY & MANUFACTURING

***See Also* Industrial**

Assembly Québec, Reed Exhibition Companies Inc., #1, 3761 Victoria Park Ave., Toronto ON M1W 3S2 - 416/491-7565; Fax: 416/491-5088; Email: canada@reedexpo. com; URL: www.reedexpo.com - John Lewinski - Biennial trade show - April, Montréal QC

Atlantic Heavy Equipment Show, Master Promotions Ltd., PO Box 565, Saint John NB E2L 3Z8 - 506/658-0018; Fax: 506/658-0750; Tollfree: 1-888-454-7469; Email: info@masterpromotions.ca; URL: www.masterpromotions.ca - Biennial - Show Manager, Mark Cusack, April - Coliseum, Moncton NB

Canadian Machine Tool Show, Reed Exhibition Companies Inc., #1, 3761 Victoria Park Ave., Toronto ON M1W 3S2 - 416/491-7565; Fax: 416/491-5088; Email: canada@reedexpo.com; URL: www.reedexpo.com - John Lewinski - Biennial trade show - Sept., Toronto ON

Canadian Manufacturing Week, Reed Exhibition Companies Inc., #1, 3761 Victoria Park Ave., Toronto ON M1W 3S2 - 416/491-7565; Fax: 416/491-5088; Email: canada@reedexpo.com; URL: www.reedexpo.com - John Lewinski - Biennial trade show - Sept., Mississauga ON

National Heavy Equipment Show, Master Promotions Ltd., PO Box 565, Saint John NB E2L 3Z8 - 506/658-0018; Fax: 506/658-0750; Tollfree: 1-888-454-7469; Email: info@masterpromotions.ca; URL: www.masterpromotions.ca - Biennial - Show Manager, Mark Cusack, March - International Centre, Toronto ON

Toronto ISA Show, dmg World Media, 180 Duncan Mills Rd., 4th Fl., Toronto ON M3B 1Z6 - 416/385-1880; Fax: 416/385-1855; Tollfree: 1-888-823-7469; URL: www.dmgworldmedia.com - Show Manager, Glen Chiasson

MAGAZINES

Magazines, Print World, #8, 1606 Sedlescomb Dr., Mississauga ON L4X 1M6 - 905/625-7070; Fax: 905/625- 4856; Tollfree: 1-800-331-7408 - Annual conference & trade show for publishing professionals - June, Toronto ON

MARKETING *See* ADVERTISING

MATERIALS HANDLING *See* LOGISTICS

MEDICAL

Canadian Congress of Neurological Sciences, Venue West Conference Services Ltd., #645, 375 Water St., Vancouver BC V6B 5C6 - 604/681-5226; Fax: 604/681- 2503; Email: congress@venuewest.com; URL: www.venuewest.com

COS Annual Meeting & Exhibition, Canadian Ophthalmological Society, #610, 1525 Carling Ave., Ottawa ON K1Z 8R9 - 613/729-6779; Fax: 613/729-7209; Email: cos@eyesite.ca; URL: www.eyesite.ca - Executive Director, Hubert Drouin, June

Mayfest, The Canadian Hearing Society, 271 Spadina Rd., Toronto ON M5R 2V3 - 416/928-2500; Fax: 416/928- 2506; Tollfree: 1-877-347-3427; Email: info@chs.ca; URL: www.chs.ca - Executive Assistant, Mary Lumgair, President/CEO, Kelly Duffin, Vice-President, Regional Operations, Maribeth Meijer, President, Access, Counselling & Training, Katherine Hum-Antonopoulus, Vice-President Finance/CFO, Fred Enzel, Director, Human Resources, Lisa Smecca, Director, Marketing Communications, Susan Main, Director, External Affairs & Employment Development, Gary Malkowski - Latest innovations & access for deaf, deafened & hard of hearing people - May, Toronto ON

MINING & MINERALS

CIM Conference & Exhibition, Canadian Institute of Mining, Metallurgy & Petroleum, #855, 3400, boul de Maisonneuve ouest, Montréal QC H3Z 3B8 - 514/939- 2710; Fax: 514/939-2714; Email: cim@cim.org; URL: www.cim.org - Executive Director, Jean Vavrek - Annual consumers show. Mining industry, equipment & services - April-May - Palais des congrSs de Montréal, Montréal QC

Mines & Minerals Symposia, Ministry of Northern Development & Mines, 933 Ramsey Lake Rd., 6th Fl., Sudbury ON P3E 6B5 - 705/670-5838; Fax: 705/670-5807; URL: www.mndm.gov.on.ca/mndm/mines/- Annual trade show & seminar in April (Northern Ontario) & Dec. (Toronto)

MOTORCYCLES *See* AUTOMOTIVE

MULTICULTURAL

Canada's National Ukrainian Festival, 1550 Main St. South, PO Box 368, Dauphin MB R7N 2V2 - 204/622-4600; Fax: 204/622-4606; Tollfree: 1-877-474-2683; Email: cnuf@mts.net; URL: www.cnuf.ca - Annual. Three days of song, dance, music, costume, cuisine, culture - Aug.

Caravan, #503, 263 Adelaide St. West, Toronto ON M5H 1Y2; Email: kirk@caravan-org.com; URL: www.caravan-org.com - President, Kirk Jensen - Annual, mid-June. Nine days. Forty international pavilions

Celebration Multicultural Festival, Multicultural Association of Nova Scotia, 1113 Marginal Rd., Halifax NS B3H 4P7 - 902/423-6534; Fax: 902/422-0881; Email: admin@mans.ns.ca; URL: www.mans.ns.ca - Executive Director, Alexandra McCallum, President, Dr. Bridglal Pachai - Annual festival - June, Dartmouth NS

Le Festival de l'Escaouette, a/s Les Trois Pignons, PO Box 430, Cheticamp NS B0E 1H0 - 902/224-2612; Fax: 902/224-1579; Email: lestroispignons@ns.sympatico. ca; URL: www.lestroispignons.com - Assistant Manager, Daniel Aucoin - Annually. Acadian folklore, traditions, culture - Aug.

Foire Brayonne, 95 Victoria St., Edmundston NB E3V 3K8 - 506/739-6608; Fax: 506/739-9578; Email: info@ foirebrayonne.com; URL: www.foirebrayonne.com - July/Aug. Brayon heritage festival

Folkfest, #303, 506 - 25th St. East, Saskatoon SK S7K 4A7 - 306/931-0100; Fax: 306/665-3421; Email: info@ saskatoonfolkfest.com; URL: www.saskatoon.com/folkfest/- Coordinator, Deneen Gudjonson, Terri Rau - Annual. Three days. Twenty or more ethnic pavilions - Aug.

Folklorama - Canada's Cultural Celebration, 183 Kennedy St., Winnipeg MB R3C 1S6 - 204/982-6210; Fax: 204/943-1956; Tollfree: 1-800-665-0234; Email: folkarts@ folklorama.ca; URL: www.folklorama.ca - Executive Director, Ron Gauthier, Email: gauthierr@folklorama. ca - Annual. Fourteen days. More than forty ethnic pavilions - Aug.

Manitoba Highland Gathering, PO Box 59, Selkirk MB R1A 2B1 - 204/269-1304; Fax: 204/269-1304; Email: ccox@mts.net - Treasurer, John Cox - Annual - July

MOSAIC - Regina's Annual Festival of Cultures, Regina Multicultural Council, 2144 Cornwall St., Regina SK S4P 2K7 - 306/757-5990; Fax: 306/352-1977; Email: rmc.pa@sasktel.net; URL: www.reginamulticulturalcouncil.ca/mosaic.htm - Executive Director, Vivian Molnar - Annual. First weekend in June. Twenty ethno-cultural pavilions

Vesna Festival, PO Box 1592, Saskatoon SK S7K 3R3 - 306/657-4412; Fax: 306/657-4410; Email: dlalach@ wellwest.ca; URL: www.vesnafestival.com - Annual Spring celebration. Two days of entertainment, dancing, cultural demonstrations & displays. The World's Largest Ukrainian Cabaret - May

MUSIC

Atlantic Jazz Festival, PO Box 33043, Halifax NS B3L 4T6 - 902/492-2225; Fax: 902/425-7946; Tollfree: 1-800- 567-5277; Email: info@jazzeast.com; URL: www.jazzeast.com - Manager, Operations, Geoff Barnes - July

Beaches International Jazz Festival, 1998 Queen St. East, Toronto ON M4L 1G8 - 416/698-2152; Fax: 416/698- 2064; Email: infobeachesjazz@rogers.com; URL: www.beachesjazz.com - Executive Producer, Lido Chilelli, July, Toronto ON

Biennial Canada Dance Festival, Canada Dance Festival Society, PO Box 1376, Stn B, Ottawa ON K1P 5R4 - 613/947-7000, ext.576; Fax: 613/943-1399; Email: cdffdc@nac-cna.ca; URL: www.canadadance.ca - Artistic Producer, Brian H. Webb, Email: webb@shaw.ca, Chair, Myrna Barwin

Big Valley Jamboree, 4238 -37th St., Camrose AB T4V 4L6 - 780/672-0224; Fax: 780/672-9530; Tollfree: 1-888-404-1234; Email: bvj@bigvalleyjamboree. com; URL: www.bigvalleyjamboree.com - Country music - Aug.

Brandon Folk Music & Arts Festival, PO Box 22091, Brandon MB R7A 6Y9 - 204/727-3928; Fax: 204/571- 9243; Email: info@brandonfolkfestival.com; URL: www.brandonfolkfestival.com - Music Director, Jody Weger - Annually, last weekend in July

Canadian Open Old Time Fiddler's Contest, Canadian Open Old Time Fiddle Championship, Sports Complex, c/o, PO Box 27, Shelburne ON L0N 1S0 - 519/925- 3551; Fax: 519/925-1105; Email: cindy.sabo@sympatico. ca; URL: www.shelburnefiddlecontest.on.ca/, Aug.

Central Canada's Fiddle Festival, PO Box 10, High Bluff MB R0H 0C0 - 204/637-2354; Fax: 204/637-2395; Email: info@ag-museum.mb.ca; URL: www.ag-museum. mb.ca - Contact, Sandra Head - Held annually last weekend of July

Classical Music Festival, 4010 Whistler Way, Whistler BC V0N 1B0 - 604/932-3928; Fax: 604/932-7231 - Aug.

Dawson City Music Festival, PO Box 456, Dawson YT Y0B 1G0 - 867/993-5584; Fax: 867/993-5510; Email: info@dcmf.com; URL: www.dcmf.com - Producer, Dylan Griffith - Annually, second last weekend in July

Dockside Ceilidh, 89 King St., North Sydney NS B2A 2T3 - 902/794-3772; Fax: 902/539-7210; Email: 7batherson@ns.sympatico.ca - President, Northside Highland Dancers' Association, Kay Batherson, Secretary, Sheila Hall, Treasurer, Jeannie Niesten - Daily, July-Sept. Cultural music & entertainment at Marine Atlantic Ferry Terminal Downtown Jazz (Toronto), Toronto

Downtown Jazz Society, 82 Bleecker St., Toronto ON M4X 1L8 - 416/928- 2033; Fax: 416/928-0533; Email: tdjs@tojazz.com; URL: www.torontojazz.com - President/Executive Producer, Patrick Taylor, Artistic Director, Jim Galloway

Downtown Oakville Jazz Festival,Downtown Oakville BIA, 146 Lakeshore Rd. East, Oakville ON L6J 1H4 - 905/844-4520; Fax: 905/844-1154; Email: info@ oakvilledowntown.com; URL: www.oakvillejazz.com, Aug., Oakville ON

Edgefest, Edge 102, #1600, 1 Dundas St. West, Toronto ON M5T 1Z3 - 416/408-3343; Fax: 416/408-3300; URL: www.edge102.com, July

Elora Festival, 33 Henderson St., PO Box 370, Elora ON N0B 1S0 - 519/846-0331; Fax: 519/846-5947; Tollfree: 1-800-265-8977; Email: info@elorafestival. com; URL: www.elorafestival.com - Artistic Director, Noel Edison - July - Aug. Choral & contemporary Canadian & international music

Enbridge Symphony Under the Sky, Edmonton Symphony Orchestra, 9720 - 102 Ave., Edmonton AB T5J 4B2 - 780/428-1108; Fax: 780/425-0167; Tollfree: 1-800- 563-5081; Email: info@winspearcentre.com; URL: www.edmonton symphony.com - Managing Director, Elaine Calder, Music Director, Bill Eddins - Aug.-Sept.

Festival de LanaudiSre, 1500, boul Base-de-Roc, Joliette QC J6E 3Z1 - 450/759-7636; Fax: 450/759-3082; Email: festival@lanaudiere.org; URL: www.lanaudiere.org - Annually June-Aug.; biggest mostly classical festival in Canada

Festival International de Jazz de Montréal, 822, rue Sherbrooke est, Montréal QC H2L 1K4 - 514/523-3378; Fax: 514/525-8033; Tollfree: 1-888-515-0515; URL: www.montrealjazzfest.com - Senior Director, Communications & Advertising, Nathalie Carriere - Annual. Over 2,000 musicians & 450 shows - July, Montréal QC

Le Festival International du Domaine Forget, Le Festival International de Domaine Forget, 5, rang Saint-Antoine, Saint-Irénée QC G0T 1V0 - 418/452-8111; Fax: 418/452-3503; Tollfree: 1-888-336-7438; Email: info@domaineforget. com; URL: www.domaineforget.com - June-Aug.

Festival International Nuits d'Afrique de Montréal, 4374, boul St-Laurent, 1e ,tage, Montréal QC H2W 1Z5 - 514/499-9239, 9520; Fax: 514/499-9215; Email: info@festivalnuitsdafrique. com; URL: www.festivalnuitsdafrique.com, juil.

Festival of the Sound, 42 James St., PO Box 750, Parry Sound ON P2A 2Z1 - 705/746-2410; Fax: 705/746- 5639; Tollfree: 1-866-364-0061; Email: info@festivalofthesound. on.ca; URL: www.festivalofthesound.on.ca - July-Aug.

Festival Vancouver, The Vancouver Summer Festival Society, #400, 873 Beatty St., Vancouver BC V6B 2M6 - 604/688-1152; Fax: 604/688-8441; Email: music@festival vancouver. bc.ca; URL: www.festivalvancouver.bc.ca - Program Director, George Laverock, Administrative Director, Morna Edmundson

FFIDA Fringe Festival of Independent Dance Artists, FFIDA - 416/214-5854; Email: info@ffida.org; URL: www.ffida.org - Artistic Director, Michael Menegon

Folk on the Rocks, PO Box 326, Yellowknife NT X1A 2N3 - 867/920-7806; Fax: 867/873-6535; Email: info@ folkonthe rocks.com; URL: www.folkontherocks.com - Annual. Two days. Inuit, Dene, other northern & southern folk groups - July

Guelph Jazz Festival, 123 Woolwich St., 2nd Fl., Guelph ON N1H 3V1 - 519/763-4952; Fax: 519/763-3155; Email: info@guelphjazzfestival.com; URL: www.guelphjazz festival.com, Sept., Guelph ON

Harvest Jazz & Blues Festival, 65 York St., PO Box 20139, Fredericton NB E3B 6Y8 - 506/454-2583; Fax: 506/457-1815; Tollfree: 1-888-622-5837; Email: info@harvestjazzandblues. com; URL: www.harvestjazzandblues.com, Sept.

International Festival of Baroque Music, International Baroque Music Festival, #2, 28, rue de l'H"pital, Lameque NB E8T 1C3 - 506/344-5846; Fax: 506/344-5741; Tollfree: 1-800-320-2276; Email: baroque@ nbnet.nb.ca; URL: www.festivalbaroque.com - Executive Director, Claire Guimond - Early music festival with five productions, last week of July (Northeastern New Brunswick, on Lameque Island)

Jazz City International Music Festival, Jazz City Festival Society, #202, 10518 - 82 Ave. NW, Edmonton AB T6E 2A4 - 780/432-7166; Fax: 780/433-3779; Email: info@jazzcity.ca; URL: www.jazzcity.ca - Manager, Festival & Sponsorships, Lynda Jones, Contact, Media & Musicians, Kent Sutherland

JazzFest International, Victoria Jazz Society, #250, 727 Johnson St., PO Box 8542, Victoria BC V8W 3S2 - 250/388-4423; Fax: 250/388-4407; Tollfree: 1-888-671- 2112; Email: vicjazz@pacificcoast.net; URL: www.vicjazz.bc.ca/jazzfest/

Kinsmen International Band & Choral Festival, Moose Jaw Kinsmen Club, PO Box 883, Moose Jaw SK S6H 4P5 - 306/692-1291; Fax: 306/692-2091; Email: bl.mcdonald@ sasktel.net; URL: www.mjkinsmenfestival.com - Bill McDonald - 3,000 musicians, evening concerts. Annual - May, Moose Jaw SK

Kiwanis Music Festival of Greater Toronto, 330 Walmer Rd., Toronto ON M5R 2Y4 - 416/487-5885; Fax: 416/487-5784; Email: kiwanismusic@bellnet.ca; URL: www3.sympatico.ca/ kiwanismusicfest.toronto - Festival Coordinator, Pam Allen, General Manager, Pam Allen, Feb., Toronto ON

L'OFF Festival de Jazz, L'OFF Festival de Jazz de Montréal, 5101, rue St-Denis, CP 60150, Montréal QC H2J 4E1 - 514/570-0722; Email: info@lofffestivaldejazz. com; URL: www.lofffestivaldejazz.com

Mariposa Folk Festival, Mariposa Folk Foundation, 23 Peter St. South, PO Box 383, Orillia ON L3V 6J8 - 705/329-2333; Fax: 705/329-4099; Email: info@mariposafolk. com; URL: www.mariposafolkfestival.com - President, Chris Lusty Maritime Fiddle Fest,

Maritime Fiddle Festival, PO Box 3037, Stn DEPS, Dartmouth NS B2W 4Y3 - 902/434- 5466; Fax: 902/434-5466; Email: marfiddlefest@ ns.sympatico.ca; URL: www3.ns.sympatico.ca/marfiddlefest - Hon. Chair, James Delaney, Co-Chair, Betty Ann Chennell, 902/835-5988, Email: babm@ns.sympatico. ca, Co-Chair, Doug Morash, 902/435-4168, Email: rdouglas@ns.sympatico.ca, July

Markham Jazz Festival, #281, 4261 A-145, Hwy.#7, Unionville ON L3R 9W6 - 905/471-5299; Fax: 905/471- 7764; Email: info@guidingstar.ca; URL: www.guidingstar.ca/Markham_Jazz_Festival.htm, Aug., Markham ON

Miramichi Folk Song Festival, PO Box 13, Miramichi NB E1V 3M2 - 506/623-2150; Fax: 506/623-2261; Email: bb2@nb.sympatico.ca; URL: www.miramichifolksongfestival.com/- Susan Butler - Aug.

Newfoundland & Labrador Folk Festival, PO Box 6283, St. John's NL A1C 6J9 - 709/576-8508; Fax: 709/757- 8500; Tollfree: 1-866-576-8508; Email: office@ sjfac.nf.net; URL: www.sjfac.nf.net - Contact, Erin McArthur - Traditional Newfoundland & Labrador music & dance - Aug.

Northern Lights Festival BorSal, Northern Lights Festival Bor,al, 109 Elm St., Sudbury ON P3C 1T4 - 705/674- 5512; Fax: 705/671-1998; Email: info@nlfb.on.ca; URL: www.nlfb.on.ca - July

Nova Scotia Bluegrass Oldtime Music Festival, Annual Nova Scotia Bluegrass/Oldtime Music Festival, 1455 Hwy. 2, Lantz NS B2S 2A2 - 902/883-7189; Email: jerry@rushcomm.ca - Correspondent, Jerry Murphy - Annually, last weekend in July

Nova Scotia Kiwanis Music Festival, PO Box 22039, Halifax NS B3L 4T7 - 902/423-6147; Fax: 902/423-8668; URL: www.hfxmusicfest.com - Executive Director, Nancy Keating, Chair, Art Hood - Adjudicated music festival & closing concert - Feb., Halifax NS

Old Time Fiddle & Step Dancing Championships, PO Box 1329, Deep River ON K0J 1P0 - 613/584-3962 - Labour Day weekend, annually

Orford Festival, 3165, Parc Orford Rd., Orford QC J1X 7A2 - 819/843-9871; Fax: 819/843-7274; Tollfree: 1-800-567-6155; Email: centre@arts-orford. org; URL: www.arts-orford.org - June-Aug. Ottawa Bluesfest,

Ottawa BluesFest, 1810 St. Laurent Blvd., Ottawa ON K1G 1A2 - 613/247-1188; Fax: 613/247-2220; Tollfree: 1-866-258-3748; URL: www.ottawa-bluesfest.ca - Executive Director, Mark Monahan - Annual blues music & gospel festival - July

Ottawa Folk Festival, #107A, 858 Bank St., Ottawa ON K1S 3W3 - 613/230-8234; Fax: 613/230-7887; Email: festival@ottawafolk.ca; URL: www.ottawafolk.org, Aug.

Ottawa International Chamber Music Festival, Ottawa Chamber Music Society, PO Box 20583, Ottawa ON K1N 1A3 - 613/234-8008; Fax: 613/234-7692; Email: info@chamberfest. com; URL: www.chamberfest.com, July-Aug.

Ottawa International Jazz Festival, 61A York St., Ottawa ON K1N 5T2 - 613/241-2633; Fax: 613/241-5774; Email: info@ottawajazzfestival.com; URL: www.ottawajazzfestival.com - Manager, Programming, Jacques Emond - June-July

Regina Folk Festival, #101, 1855 Scarth St., PO Box 1203, Regina SK S4P 3B4 - 306/757-7684; Fax: 306/757- 7688; Email: info@reginafolkfestival.com; URL: www.reginafolk festival.com - Artistic Director, Sandra Butel - Annual three day folk-based music festival - Aug.

Scotia Festival of Music, 6181 Lady Hammond Rd., Halifax NS B3K 2R9 - 902/429-9467; Fax: 902/425-6785; Email: admin@scotiafestival.ns.ca; URL: www.scotiafestival.ns.ca - Contact, Christopher Wilcox - Annually, May. Chamber music

Stan Rogers Folk Festival, PO Box 46, Canso NS B0H 1H0 - 902/366-2475; Fax: 902/366-2978; Tollfree: 1-888- 554-7826; Email: info@stanfest.com; URL: www.stanfest.com - Artistic Director, Troy Greencorn

Summerfolk Music & Crafts Festival, Georgian Bay Folk Society, PO Box 521, Owen Sound ON N4K 5R1 - 519/371-2995; Fax: 519/371-2973; Email: gbfs@bmts.com; URL: www.summerfolk.org - President, David McLeish

Vancouver Chamber Music Festival, Vancouver Recital Society, #304, 873 Beatty St., Vancouver BC V6B 2M6 - 604/602-0363; Fax: 604/602-0364; URL: www.vanrecital.com - Artistic Director, Leila Getz, July

Vancouver Folk Music Festival, #1114, 207 West Hastings St., Vancouver BC V6B 1H7 - 604/602-9798; Fax: 604/602-9790; Tollfree: 1-800-883-3655; Email: info@ thefestival.bc.ca; URL: www.thefestival.bc.ca - Artistic Director, Dugg Simpson - Annual festival - July, Vancouver BC

Vancouver International Jazz Festival, Vancouver International Jazz Festival/Coastal Jazz & Blues Society, 316 West 6th Ave., Vancouver BC V5Y 1K9 - 604/872- 5200; Fax: 604/872-5250; Tollfree: 1-888-438-5200; Email: cjbs@coastaljazz.ca; URL: www.coastaljazz.ca - Executive Director, Robert Kerr, Artistic Director, Ken Pickering - June-July

Vancouver Island Music Fest, PO Box 338, Cumberland BC V0R 1S0 - 250/336-7981; Email: dougcox@shaw.ca; URL: www.islandmusicfest.com - Artistic Director, Doug Cox, July

Victoriaville International Festival of New Music, 82, rue Notre-Dame est, CP 460, Victoriaville QC G6P 6T3 - 819/752-7912; Fax: 819/758-4370; Email: info@ fimav.qc.ca; URL: www.fimav.qc.ca - 25 concerts in 5 days, musicians from 12 different countries - May

Western Canada Olde Tyme Fiddling Championship, Western Canada Amateur Olde Tyme Fiddling Championship, PO Box 2406, Swift Current SK S9H 4J8 - 306/773-4387; Fax: 306/773-9055 - Secretary, Alvina Kantrud - Annual - Sept.

Winnipeg Folk Festival, #203, 211 Bannatyne Ave., Winnipeg MB R3B 3P2 - 204/231-0096; Fax: 204/231- 0076; Email: info@winnipegfolkfestival.ca; URL: www.winnipegfolkfestival.ca - Annually, July

Winnipeg Jazz Festival, #501, 100 Arthur St., Winnipeg MB R3B 1H3 - 204/989-4650; Fax: 204/956-5280; URL: www.jazzwinnipeg.com, June

OKTOBERFESTS *See* EVENTS

PACKAGING

Pacex International, Packaging Association of Canada, #E330, 2255 Sheppard Ave. East, Toronto ON M2J 4Y1 - 416/490-7860; Fax: 416/490-7844; Email: info@ pac.ca; URL: www.pac.ca - President/CEO, Alan M. Robinson, Chair, Sylvia MacVey - Biennial trade show - May - National Trade Centre, Exhibition Place, Toronto ON

PARENTS *See* CHILDREN

PETROLEUM

Go-Expo Show, dmg World Media, #605, 999 - 8 St. SW, Calgary AB T2R 1N7 - 403/209-3555; Fax: 403/245- 8649; Tollfree: 1-888-799-2545; URL: www.dmgworldmedia.com - Pat Atkinson - Biennial trade show. Petroleum & natural gas products, services & technology; exploration, production, transmission, processing, marketing

Offshore Newfoundland Petroleum Show, dmg World Media, #605, 999 - 8 St. SW, Calgary AB T2R 1N7 - 403/209-3555; Fax: 403/245-8649; Tollfree: 1-888- 799-2545; URL: www.dmgworldmedia.com - Pat Atkinson

PETS

L'Exposition canine internationale de Montréal/Montreal International Dog Show, United Kennel Club Inc., c/o 1562, route 203, Howick QC J0S 1G0 - 450/825-2824; Email: info@ukc.ca; URL: www.ukc.ca - Show Secretary, Diana Edwards - Annual all breed dog exhibition

PetExpo Calgary, Canwest Shows Inc., 7 Panorama Bay SW, Calgary AB T3Z 3L6 - 403/686-9699; Fax: 403/246-3856; Email: info@canwestshows.com; URL: www.canwestshows. com - General Manager, Terra Connors - Annual consumer trade show - Sept. - Stampede Park, Calgary AB

Salon Canin Rive-Sud de Montréal, Club Canin de l'Estrie, 121, rue des Hirondelles, Sherbrooke QC J1R 0P3 - 819/346-4745

- Annual. All breed dog exhibition - April - Aréna régional, Iberville QC

Vancouver PetExpo, Canwest Shows Inc., 7 Panorama Bay SW, Calgary AB T3Z 3L6 - 403/686-9699; Fax: 403/246-3856; Email: info@canwestshows.com; URL: www.canwestshows.com - General Manager, Terra Connors - Annual consumer trade show - March - Vancouver Convention & Exhibition Centre, Vancouver BC

PLASTICS & RUBBER

Expoplast, Canadian Plastics Industry Association, #712, 5915 Airport Rd., Mississauga ON L4V 1T1 - 905/678- 7748; Fax: 905/678-0774; Email: national@cpia.ca; URL: www.plastics.ca - President & CEO, Serge Lavoie, Show Director, Sally Damstra - Triennial international trade show: plastics machinery, raw materials suppliers, mold makers, processors, fabricators, auxiliary equipment

Plast-Ex, Canadian Plastics Industry Association, #712, 5915 Airport Rd., Mississauga ON L4V 1T1 - 905/678- 7748; Fax: 905/678-0774; Email: national@cpia.ca; URL: www.plastics.ca - Triennial international trade show: plastics machinery, raw materials suppliers, mold makers, processors, fabricators, auxiliary equipment - Show Director: Sally Damstra, May - International Centre, Toronto ON

PSYCHIC PHENOMENA

ESP Psychic Expo, Impact Event Management, 358 Danforth Ave., PO Box 65060, Toronto ON M4K 3Z2 - 416/461-5306; Fax: 416/461-8460; Email: impactevent@ sympatico.ca - Donald Nausbaum - Annual consumer show. Psychics, astrologers, natural healing, crystals, books, tapes, computers - Feb. - International Centre, Toronto ON

Toronto Psychic Expo, Impact Event Management, 358 Danforth Ave., PO Box 65060, Toronto ON M4K 3Z2 - 416/461-5306; Fax: 416/461-8460; Email: impactevent@sympatico.ca - Donald Nausbaum - Consumer show. Psychics, astrologers, tarot card readers, holistic health, computers - Oct. - Exhibition Place, Toronto ON

REAL ESTATE

Leadership Conference, The Canadian Real Estate Association, Minto Place, The Canada Bldg., #1600, 344 Slater St., Ottawa ON K1R 7Y3 - 613/237-7111; Fax: 613/234-2567; Tollfree: 1-800-842-2732; Email: info@ crea.ca; URL: www.crea.ca - Annual trade show - Coordinator, Sherry Watson, March

Property Management Today, Master Promotions Ltd., PO Box 565, Saint John NB E2L 3Z8 - 506/658-0018; Fax: 506/658-0750; Tollfree: 1-888-454-7469; Email: info@masterpromotions.ca; URL: www.masterpromotions.ca - Annual trade show - Show Manager, Brian McKiel, Oct. - Trade & Convention Centre, Saint John NB

RECREATIONAL VEHICLES *See* AUTOMOTIVE

RODEOS

***See Also* Exhibitions, Farm Business/Agriculture**

Calgary Exhibition & Stampede, PO Box 1060, Stn M, Calgary AB T2P 2K8 - 403/261-0101; Fax: 403/265-7197; Tollfree: 1-800-661-1260; URL: www.calgarystampede.com - COO, Vern Kimball, Senior Manager, Corporate Communications, Lindsey Galloway - Annual city-wide festival; agricultural exhibits

CCA Finals Rodeo, RR#4, Site 412, PO Box 287, Saskatoon SK S7K 3J8 - 306/931-2700; Fax: 306/931-4480; Email: canadiancowboy@yourlink.ca; URL: www.canadiancowboys.sk.ca - Office Coordinator, Charlene Symington - Annually, Oct. Four days

Maple Creek Cowtown Rodeo, PO Box 1091, Maple Creek SK S0N 1N0 - 306/662-2673 - Tom Boychuk - Annually, May

Williams Lake Stampede, Williams Lake Stampede Association, PO Box 4076, Williams Lake BC V2G 2V2 - 250/392-6585; Fax: 250/398-7701; Tollfree: 1-800- 717-6336; Email: info@williamslakestampede.com; URL: www.williams lakestampede.com - President, Bob Breitkreutz, July

RVS *See* AUTOMOTIVE; SPORTS & RECREATION

SEWING *See* CRAFTS

SEX

The Everything to Do with Sex Show, Canwest Shows Inc., 7 Panorama Bay SW, Calgary AB T3Z 3L6 - 403/686- 9699; Fax: 403/246-3856; Email: info@canwestshows. com; URL: www.canwestshows.com - General Manager, Terra Connors

SPORTS & RECREATION

***See Also* Boating; Automotive, for combined auto/RV shows**

24 Hours of Adrenalin, #4, 160 Gibson Dr., Markham ON L3R 1K1 - 416/640-0824; Fax: 416/640-0825; Email: info@twenty4sports.com; URL: www.twenty4sports.com - Team & solo mountain biking events that take place in Alberta, Ontario & BC in June, July & Aug.

Atlantic Outdoor Sports & RV Show, PO Box 2968, Dartmouth NS B2W 4Y2 - 902/827-7469; Fax: 902/827- 1247; Email: dhubley@ns.sympatico.ca; URL: www.sportsandrvshow.com - Manager, Darrelyn Hubley - Annual consumer show. Trailer & motor homes, 4x4s, tent trailers, boats, motors, hunting, fishing & camping, tourism & sporting goods - March, Halifax NS

Bicycle Fall Blowout Sale, #1801, One Yonge St., Toronto ON M5E 1W7 - 416/363-1292; Fax: 416/369-0515; Email: josie@telsec.net; URL: www.bicycleshowtoronto.com - Marketing & Sales Manager, Josie Graziosi - Annual; fall - Oct., Toronto ON

Canadian Power Toboggan Championship, PO Box 22, Beausejour MB R0E 0C0 - 204/268-2049; Fax: 204/268-4209; URL: www.cptcracing.com/- Annual - March

Country Living Show, Square Feet Northwest Event Management Inc., PO Box 82550, Stn N, Burnaby BC V5C 5Z1 - 604/683-4766; Fax: 604/688-0270; Tollfree: 1-877-888-7111; Email: mgmt@ sqftevent.com; URL: www.reel-shows.com - Blaine Woit - Annual consumer show - March - Tradex, Abbotsford BC

Ironman Canada Triathlon Championship, 416 Westminster Ave. West, Penticton BC V2A 1K5 - 250/490-8787; Fax: 250/490-8788; Email: ironman@vip.net; URL: www.ironman.ca - Race Director, Dave Bullock - Annual four-day trade expo staged as part of the events prior to the Ironman race - Aug.

London Boat & Cottage Show, Western Fair Association, 900 King St., PO Box 7550, London ON N5Y 5P8 - 519/438-7203; Fax: 519/679-3124; Tollfree: 1-800-619- 4629; Email: gmcrae@westernfair.com; URL: www.westernfair.com - General Manager, Gary McRae - Annual consumer show

Motorhead Snowmobile, Watercraft & ATV Show, Marketer Shows Inc., 78 Main St. South, Newmarket ON L3Y 3Y6 - 905/898-8585; Fax: 905/898-8071; Tollfree: 1-888-661-7469; Email: rkehoe@bellnet.ca; URL: www.torontosnowmobile shows.com - Richard Kehoe - Annual consumer show - March - Toronto International Centre, Toronto ON

National Outfitter's Hunting & Fishing Show, Mobilvision Inc., 9200, boul Henri-Bourassa ouest, Montréal QC H4S 1L5 - 514/334-7277; Fax: 514/334-1180; Tollfree: 1-800-668-3976; Email: mobilvision@pourvoirie. net; URL: www.pourvoirie.net - Président, Jacques Forest, Feb. - Montréal Congress Centre

Ontario PGA Golf Merchandise Show, Reed Exhibition Companies Inc., #1, 3761 Victoria Park Ave., Toronto ON M1W 3S2 - 416/491-7565; Fax: 416/491-5088; Email: canada@reedexpo.com; URL: www.reedexpo.com - John Lewinski - Annual trade show - Oct., Toronto ON

Salon Camping, Plein Air, Chasse et Pêche de Montréal/Montréal Sportsmen's Show, Canadian National Sportsmen's Shows (1989) Ltd., #222, 980, St-Antoine ouest, Montréal QC H3C 1A8 - 514/866-5409; Fax: 514/866-4092; URL: www.sportsmensshows.com - Regional Manager, Francine St-Laurent - Annual consumer show: camping, fishing, hunting, RVs, tourism

Salon Camping, Plein Air, Chasse et Pêche de Québec/Québec City Sportsmen's Show, Canadian National Sportsmen's Shows (1989) Ltd., #222, 980, St-Antoine ouest, Montréal QC H3C 1A8 - 514/866-5409; Fax: 514/866-4092; URL: www.sportsmensshows.com - Regional Manager, Francine St-Laurent - Annual consumer show: camping, fishing, hunting, RVs, tourism

Sport Compact Challenge, Pro-Sho Inc., 298 Sheppard Ave. East, Toronto ON M2N 3B1 - 416/229-9919; Fax: 416/223-2826; Tollfree: 1-877-950-1500; Email: prosho@ meteorshows.com; URL: www.performanceworldcarshow. com; www.llhashows. com, Mar. - International Centre, Toronto ON

Supertrax International Snowmobilers Show, Marketer Shows Inc., 78 Main St. South, Newmarket ON L3Y 3Y6 - 905/898-8585; Fax: 905/898-8071; Tollfree: 1-888-661-7469; Email: rkehoe@bellnet.ca; URL: www.torontosnowmobile shows.com - Richard Kehoe - Annual consumer show - Oct. - Toronto International Centre, Toronto ON

Toronto Ski & Snowboard Show, Canadian National Sportsmen's Shows (1989) Ltd., #202, 703 Evans Ave., Toronto ON M5C 5E9 - 416/695-0311; Fax: 416/695- 0381; Email: oster@sportshow.ca; URL: www.sportshow.ca - Annual consumer show - Show Manager, Harley Austin, Oct. - National Trade Centre, Exhibition Place, Toronto ON

Toronto Sportsmen's Show, Canadian National Sportsmen's Shows (1989) Ltd., #202, 703 Evans Ave., Toronto ON M5C 5E9 - 416/695-0311; Fax: 416/695- 0381; Email: oster@sportshow.ca; URL: www.sportshow.ca - Annual consumer show - Show Manager, Harley Austin, March - National Trade Centre, Exhibition Place, Toronto ON

The Toronto Star Golf & Travel Show, Premier Consumer Shows, 467 Speers Rd., Oakville ON L6K 3S4 - 905/815-0017; Fax: 905/337-5570; Tollfree: 1-800-265- 3673 - Show Manager, Jane Hills - Annual consumer show - March

STAMPEDES *See* RODEOS

THEATRE *See* ARTS

TOYS & GAMES

The Toronto Christmas Train Show, Toronto Show Promotions, PO Box 217, Grimsby ON L3M 4G3 - 905/945- 2775; Fax: 905/945-0197; Email: info@antiquetoys.ca; URL: www.antiquetoys.ca - Doug Jarvis - Annual; operating train layouts, memorabilia - Nov., Mississauga ON

TRANSPORTATION

***See Also* Automotive**

Annual Convention & Trade Show, Ontario School Bus Association, #304, 1 Eva Rd., Toronto ON M9C 4Z5 - 416/695-9965; Fax: 416/695-9977; Email: info@ osba.on.ca; URL: www.osba.on.ca - Coordinator of Communications, Jackie Laurie, Executive Director, Richard Donaldson - Annual conference & trade show. Safety, fuel economy, buses & accessories, computers

TRAVEL & TOURISM

Canadian Meetings & Incentive Travel Symposium & Trade Show, 1 Mount Pleasant Rd., Toronto ON M4Y 2Y5 - 416/764-1635; Fax: 416/764-1419; URL: www.meetingscanada.com - Annual trade show & conference - Aug.

Salon Industriel et Commercial, Chambre de Commerce de Manicouagan, #302, 67, Place Lasalle, Baie-Comeau QC G4Z 1K1 - 418/296-2010; Fax: 418/296-5397 - Directeur général, François Desy - Annual show. Recreational products & services - avril - Centre Léonard, Baie-Comeau QC

Summer Holiday Show, dmg World Media, 180 Duncan Mills Rd., 4th Fl., Toronto ON M3B 1Z6 - 416/385- 1880; Fax: 416/385-1855; Tollfree: 1-888-823-7469; URL: www.dmgworldmedia.com - Show Manager, Glen Chiasson

The Travel & Vacation Show, Player Expositions International, 255 Clemow Ave., Ottawa ON K1S 2B5 - 613/567-6408; Fax: 613/567-2718; Email: rplayer@sympatico. ca; URL: www.playerexpo.com - Show Organizer, Halina Player - Annual consumer & trade show - May - Lansdowne Park, Ottawa ON

Travel Technology Conference & Trade Show, Baxter Travel Group, 310 Dupont St., Toronto ON M5R 1V9 - 416/968-7252; Fax: 416/968-2377; Email: baxgroup@ baxter.net; URL: www.baxter.net - Annual. Travel industry - March - Toronto Convention Centre, Toronto ON

TRUCKS *See* AUTOMOTIVE

TVS, STEREOS *See* ELECTRICAL/ELECTRONICS

VIDEO *See* COMMUNICATIONS

WINTER CARNIVALS

Banff/Lake Louise Winter Festival, PO Box 1298, Banff AB T0L 0C0 - 403/762-8421; Fax: 403/762-8163; Email: info@ banfflakelouise.com; URL: www.banfflakelouise.com, Feb.

Carnaval de Québec M. Christie/Mr. Christie's Queb,c Winter Carnival, Carnaval de Québec, 290, rue Joly, Québec QC G1L 1N8 - 418/626-3716; Fax: 418/626- 7252; Tollfree: 1-866-422-7628; Email: comm@carnaval. qc.ca; URL: www.carnaval.qc.ca - Directeur général, Jean Pelletier, Directeur du marketing et des communications, Annick Marchand - 17 days, major winter event

Carnaval-Souvenir de Chicoutimi, 49, rue Lafontaine, CP 567, Chicoutimi QC G7H 5C8 - 418/543-4438; Fax: 418/543-4884; Tollfree: 1-877-543-4439; Email: info@carnavalsouvenir. qc.ca; URL: www.reseau.qc.ca/carnaval - Ten days, major winter event - Feb.

Charlottetown Winter Carnival, PO Box 98, Charlottetown PE C1A 7K2 - 902/892-5708, Feb.

Conception Bay South Winterfest, Conception Bay South NL - 709/834-6534, 834-6548, 682-0453; Fax: 709/834-8337, Feb.

Corner Brook Winter Carnival, PO Box 886, Corner Brook NL A2H 6H6 - 709/632-5343; Fax: 709/632-5344; Email: cbwc@nf.aibn.com; URL: www.cornerbrookwinercarnival.ca - General Manager, Shirley M. Brake - Annually, 10 days - Feb.

Elliot Lake Winterfest, Lester B. Pearson Civic Centre, Hwy.#108, Elliot Lake ON P5A 2T1 - 705/848-2084; Fax: 705/848-7121 - Donna Hennessy, Feb.

Fête des Neiges, Parc Jean-Drapeau, 1, circuit Gilles-Villeneuve, Montréal QC H3C 1A9 - 514/872-6120; Fax: 514/872-6779; Email: webmaster@fetedesneiges. com; URL: www.fetedesneiges.com - Marcel Caron - 6 day major winter event. Sports, cultural, ice sculptures - Jan.

Hamilton Winterfest, Culture & Recreation Division, Public Health & Community Services, 71 Main St. West, Hamilton ON L8P 4Y5 - 905/546-2424, ext.2747; Fax: 905/546-2338; URL: www.city.hamilton.on.ca/culture-and-rec/winterfest - Special Events Coordinator, Jim Moore, Feb.

Jasper in January, PO Box 98, Jasper AB T0E 1E0 - 780/852-3858; Fax: 780/852-4932; URL: www.jasperadventures.com, Jan.

Kapuskasing Winter Carnival, 88 Riverside Dr., Kapuskasing ON P5N 1B3 - 705/335-2341; URL: kapuskasing.com - Feb. & March

Kirkland Lake Winter Carnival, Kirkland Lake Festivals Committee, PO Box 277, Kirkland Lake ON P2N 3H7, March

Mount Pearl Frosty Festival, 3 Centennial St., Mount Pearl NL A1N 1G4 - 709/748-1008; Fax: 709/748-1150; Email: smoothsaleing@nl.rogers.com; URL: www.mtpearl.nf.ca - Contact, Karen Bowering, Feb.

Prince Albert Winter Festival, 1211 - 1 Ave. West, Prince Albert SK S6V 4T8 - 306/764-7595; Fax: 306/763- 3311; Email: pa.winterfestival@sasktel.net - Jane Smith, Feb.

Red Deer Family Winter Fest, c/o City of Red Deer, Recreation, Parks & Culture Dept., PO Box 5008, Red Deer AB T4N 3T4 - 403/309-8409; Fax: 403/342-6073; Email: suzanne.jubb@reddeer.ca; URL: www.reddeer.ca - Suzanne Jubb, Feb.

Regina Waskimo Winter Festival, City Hall, 2476 Victoria Ave., Regina SK S4N 6M5 - 306/777-7262; Email: cityhelp@regina.ca; URL: www.regina.ca - Executive Director, J.B. Paterson - Annual, third weekend in Feb.

Riverview Winter Carnival, 30 Honour House Court, Riverview NB E1B 3Y9 - 506/387-2028; Fax: 506/387- 7455 - Gina McNeil, Feb.

Vernon Winter Carnival, 3401 - 35th Ave., Vernon BC V1T 2T5 - 250/545-2236; Fax: 250/545-0006; Email: carnival@junction.net; URL: www.vernonwintercarnival.com - Chairman, Donna Hall, Feb.

Winterlude, #202, 40 Elgin St., Ottawa ON K1P 1C7 - 613/239-5555; Fax: 613/239-5063; Tollfree: 1-800-704- 8227; Email: info@ncc-ccn.ca; URL: www.canadascapital.gc.ca - Sr. Program Manager, Thérèse St-Onge, 613/239-5278 - Major winter festival, first three weekends of February. Skating on Rideau Canal, international ice & snow sculpture competitions, musical & figure skating shows, North America's largest winter playground for kids, various sporting & social events, fireworks, stage performances & buskers - Feb.

Winterlude, PO Box 439, Grand Falls-Windsor NL A2A 2J8 - 709/489-0450; Fax: 709/489-0454; URL: www.grandfalls windsor.com/centennial/events - Contact, Dave Nichols, Feb.

WOMEN

Calgary Woman's Show, The Calgary Woman's Show Ltd., #224, 1982 Kensington Rd. NW, Calgary AB T2N 3R5 - 403/270-7274; Fax: 403/270-3037; Email: calgary.woman.show@home.com; URL: www.calgarywomansshow.com - President, Judy Markle - Semi-annual consumer show in April & Oct.; Products & services.

Women's Conferences, PO Box 25125, London ON N6C 6A9 - 519/668-5677; Fax: 519/668-6883; Email: dianvail@execulink.com - Contact, Diann Vail - Bi-annual conference, spring & fall for business professional & corporate women

World of Women, 29 Fern Cres., Sylvan Lake AB T4S 1Y4 - 403/887-0111; Fax: 403/887-0133; Email: ptkennedy@shaw.ca; URL: www.worldofwomenshow.com - Event Marketing, Sherall Kennedy, Sept.

WOOD/WOODWORKING

Chatham Woodworking Show, Cryderman Productions Inc., 136 Thames St., Chatham ON N7L 2Y8 - 519/351- 8344; Fax: 519/351-8345; Tollfree: 1-866-640-9663; Email: john@cryder manproductions.com; URL: www.crydermanproductions.com - John Cryderman - Annual - Jan. - Kinsmen Auditorium

Salon Industriel du Bois Ouvre, Reed Exhibition Companies Inc., #1, 3761 Victoria Park Ave., Toronto ON M1W 3S2 - 416/491-7565; Fax: 416/491-5088; Email: canada@reed expo.com; URL: www.reedexpo.com - John Lewinski - Biennial trade show - Sept., Montréal QC

Woodworking & Tool Show, Canwest Shows Inc., 7 Panorama Bay SW, Calgary AB T3Z 3L6 - 403/686-9699; Fax: 403/246-3856; Email: info@canwestshows.com; URL: www.canwestshows.com - General Manager, Terra Connors - Annual consumer show - Oct.

Awards & Honours

Canadian Awards

(Including Scholarships, Grants, Bursaries)
Awards are listed under the following categories:

ADVERTISING & PUBLIC RELATIONS

The Advertising & Design Club of Canada
#318, 160 Pears Ave., Toronto ON M5R 3P8
416/423-4113; Fax:416/423-3362
Email:info@theadcc.ca; URL:www.theadcc.ca

The Advertising & Design Club of Canada Awards
Main categories of awards are: Advertising Print, Advertising Broadcast, Advertising Multiple Media, Graphic Design, Editorial Design & Interactive Design; winners receive gold, silver or merit awards

Association of Canadian Advertisers Inc. / Association canadienne des annonceurs
#1103, 95 St. Clair Ave. West, Toronto ON M4V 1N6
416/964-3805; Fax:416/964-0771; Toll Free:1-800-565-0109
Email:info@aca-online.com; URL:www.aca-online.com

ACA Gold Medal
Established in 1941 to encourage high standards of personal achievement in advertising - for introducing new concepts or techniques, for significantly improving existing practices, or for enhancing the stature of advertising

Canadian Marketing Association / Association canadienne du marketing
#607, One Concorde Gate, Toronto ON M3C 3N6
416/391-2362; Fax:416/441-4062
Email:info@the-cma.org; URL:www.the-cma.org

CMA Awards
Celebrating the art and science of marketing, CMA has restructured its judging breakdown to 40%-Results, 40%-Creative, 20%-Production. Entries can be submitted under type of business, type of program or specialty, representing particularly innovative solutions. CMA also offers Student Awards to post secondary students enrolled in direct marketing, marketing or business programs.

Institute of Communication Agencies & Advertising / Institut des communications et de la publicité
#500, 2300 Yonge St., Toronto ON M4P 1E4
416/764-1608; Fax:416/482-1856
Email:ica@ica-ad.com; URL:www.ica-ad.com

CASSIES Awards
Established 1993; CASSIES (Canadian Advertising Success Stories) are open to all channels of marketing communications. Eligible submissions must show impressive business results and convincingly prove results were a result of the advertising.

Marketing Magazine
1 Mount Pleasant Rd., 7th floor Toronto ON M4Y 2Y5
416/764-2000; Fax:416/764-1519
URL:www.marketingmag.ca

The Marketing Awards
Annual advertising awards offering 40 Gold Awards in the following categories: television/cinema, radio, magazine, newspaper, transit, business press, direct mail, outdoor, point-of-purchase/interior store design, multimedia campaign, non-traditional & public service. Silver Awards, Bronze Awards, & Certificates of Excellence are also awarded. Entries must have run in the previous year & must have been conceived & created by people working in English in the Canadian advertising business

Publicité Club de Montréal
#200, 4316, boulevard St.-Laurent, Montréal QC H2W 1Z3
514/499-1391; Fax:514/842-4886
Email:info@amm-pcm.ca; URL:www.pcm.qc.ca
Le Concourse Stratégics vise à mettre en valeur les réalisations des professionnels de l'industrie des communications et du marketing au Québec. Un jury selectionne une finalist pour chacune des cinq catégories du concours: Innovation, Créativité, Audace, Impacte et Efficience.

AGRICULTURE & FARMING

Canadian Society of Animal Science / Société canadienne de science animale
c/o Agriculture & Agri-Food Canada Research Station, PO Box 90, Lennoxville QC J1M 1Z3
819/565-9171; Fax:819/564-5507
Email:info@csas.net; URL:www.csas.net
CSAS offers five prestigious awards:

Fellowship Award
Awarded to members who have made an outstanding contribution in any field of animal contribution

Award for Excellence in Nutrition and Meat Sciences

Award for Technical Innovation in Enhancing Production of Safe Affordable Food

Young Scientist Award

Animal Indutries Award in Extension & Public Service

International Development Research Centre / Centre de recherches pour le développement international
PO Box 8500, Ottawa ON K1G 3H9
613/236-6163; Fax:613/238-7230
Email:info@idrc.ca; URL:www.idrc.ca
IRDC has five special awards awarded at the discretion of its Board of Governors. They are:

Journalism Award

Professional Development Award

Centre Sabbatical Award

Project-Related Award

Pearson Fellowship

Provincial Exhibition of Manitoba
#3, 1175 - 18 St., Brandon MB R7A 7C5
204/726-3590; Fax:204/725-0202; Toll Free:1-877-729-0001
Email:info@brandonfairs.com; URL:www.brandonfairs.com

Royal Manitoba Winter Fair Awards
Prizes given in various categories for best of show for agricultural products, animals & crops; several equestrian events offer prizes for best in competition

Royal Agricultural Winter Fair Association / Foire agricole royale d'hiver
The Ricoh Coliseum, Direct Energy Centre
Exhibition Place, Toronto ON M6K 3C3
416/263-3400; Fax:416/263-3488
Email:info@royalfair.org; URL:www.royalfair.org

Agricultural Awards
Grand Champion is the highest honour in the following categories: dairy, beef, sheep, goats, swine, market livestock, field crops, vegetables, honey & maple, poultry, jams/jellies/pickles, dairy products, square dancing, fiddling, fleece wool, rabbits, & eight youth activities

Breeding Horse Awards
17 sections award prizes in this category

Performance Horse Awards
35 divisions & classes offer prizes; Leading International Rider is the highest honour in the horse show

BROADCASTING & FILM

Academy of Canadian Cinema & Television / Académie canadienne du cinéma et de la télévision
172 King St. East, Toronto ON M5A 1J3
416/366-2227; Fax:416/366-8454; Toll Free:1-800-644-5194
Email:info@academy.ca; URL:www.academy.ca

Gemini Awards
The nationally telecast awards for excellence & achievement in Canadian English-language television production are awarded annually & presented to winners in more than 80 categories covering Best Program, Best Performance & Best Craft, as well as special awards following nomination & voting by a peer group

Genie Awards
The nationally telecast Genie Awards celebrate excellence in Canadian cinema. The annual awards cover 21 categories from Best Picture to Best Sound, as well as the Golden Reel award for the top Canadian box office gross. Special achievement awards are voted by members of the Academy.

Prix Gémeaux
For excellence & achievement in French-language television production; held annually & presented in 70 categories covering Programs, Performance & Crafts; nominations & voting by peer groups composed of academy members

Alberta Motion Picture Industries Association
#318, 8944 - 182 Street NW, Edmonton AB T5T 2E3
780/944-0707; Fax:780/426-3057
URL:www.ampia.org

Alberta Film & Television Awards
Awarded annually, the "Rosie Awards", are presented to producers and craftpeople, who reside in Alberta, in recognition of their outstanding film & television works. Awards are given in 22 class categories (ie. Best Documentary, Best Drama, Best Movie, Best Musical etc.) and 22 craft categories (ie. Best Director; Best Screenwriter, Cinematography etc.)

David Billington Awards
Awarded to a special individual in recognition of their incomparable dedication and contribution to the growth of Alberta's film and television industry.

The Alliance for Children & Television / Alliance pour l'enfant et la télévision
#713, 1400, boul René-Lévesque est, Montréal QC H2L 2M2
514/597-5417; Fax:514/597-5205
Email:alliance@act-aet.tv; URL:www.act-aet.tv

The Award of Excellence
The Alliance for Children & Television has been recognizing the importance of quality television for Canadian children for over 30 years. This award is presented to a person or team for their exceptional work on a children's television show produced in Canada, which stands out for its excellence.

Banff World Television Festival
c/o Achilles Media Ltd., #202, 102 Boulder Cres., Canmore AB T1W 1L2
403/678-1216; Fax:403/678-3357
Email:info@achillesmedia.com; URL:www.bwtvf.com/

Banff Rockie Awards
Annual television awards for: made-for-TV-movies; mini-series; continuing series; short dramas; comedies; social & political documentaries; original webcasts; popular science programs & natural history; arts documentaries; performance specials; animation; sports; children's programs; history & biography programs; & information programs. Also a grand prize winner, two special jury awards & best HDTV program. All entries must be made for television & either in English or French

Canadian Association of Broadcasters / Association canadienne des radiodiffuseurs
PO Box 627, Stn B, Ottawa ON K1P 5S2
613/233-4035; Fax:613/233-6961
Email:cab@cab-acr.ca; URL:www.cab-acr.ca

Astral Media Scholarship
Established in 1975 by Astral Media with the association; awarded annually to French Canadian students who are members of a of visible minority or who are Aboriginals with broadcasting experience who are enrolled in, or wish to begin or complete a program of studies in communications at the university level
$5,000

BBM Scholarship
Established in 1986; awarded annually to a student in a graduate study program, or final year of an Honours degree with the intention of entering a graduate program at a Canadian university or post-secondary institution, who has demonstrated achievement in & knowledge of statistical &/or quantitative research methodology
$4,000

Jim Allard Broadcast Journalism Scholarship
Established 1983; awarded annually to an aspiring broadcaster enrolled in a broadcast journalism program at a Canadian col-

lege or university, who best combines academic achievement with natural talent
$2,500

Ruth Hancock Memorial Scholarships
Award established jointly in 1975 by the association, the Broadcast Executives Society & Canadian Association of Broadcast Representatives; presented annually to three Canadian students enrolled in recognized communications courses
$1,500 (x3)

Canadian Ethnic Media Association
24 Tarlton Rd., Toronto ON M5P 2M4
416/260-3625; Fax:416/260-3810
Email:canscene@rogers.com;
URL:www.canadianethnicmedia.com

Awards of Achievement
Up to nine plaques are offered annually to jounalists in print, radio, & television; awards are given to journalists for excellence in their field; competition is open to all journalists, in any language, whether or not they are members of the Club; a single award is also given to writers of a published work of fact, fiction or poetry in book form

Sierhey Khmara Ziniak Award
In honour of the Club's founder, award is presented to a single person, based on a body or work celebrating Canada's diversity

Canadian Film & Television Production Association / Association canadienne de production de film et télévision
#902, 151 Slater St., Ottawa ON K1P 5H3
613/233-1444; Fax:613/233-0073; Toll Free:1-800-656-7440
Email:ottawa@cftpa.ca; URL:www.cftpa.ca

CFTPA Producer's Award
Awarded to an independent producer of a Canadian feature being screened at the Toronto International Film Festival
The CFTDA - Kodak Canada Lifetime Achievement Award
Presented to an individual who has contributed to the success & progress of the Canadian film & television industry

The CFTPA Entrepreneur of the Year Award
Presented to an individual or company that has demonstrated private sector entrepreneurial achievement in the Canadian film & television industry

Canadian Society of Cinematographers
#131, 3007 Kingston Rd., Toronto ON M1M 1P1
416/266-0591; Fax:416/266-3996
Email:admin@csc.ca; URL:www.csc.ca

Canadian Society of Cinematography Awards
16 Awards given annually for various genres and contributions.

Media Communications Association International - Toronto Chapter
PO Box 5822, Stn A, Toronto ON M5W 1P2
416/910-4776
Email:execdirect@mca-i.org; URL:www.mca-i.org

The Chuck Webb Award
This award recognizes and honours individuals who have demonstrated the highest level of involvement in, dedication and commmitment to the Association without regard for personal profit of gain. Candidates are nominated by the Board of Directors.

The Board of Directors Award
This award recognizes and honours members who have demonstrated outstanding service to the Association on a regional or national level. Candidates are nominated by the Board of Directors.

The President's Award
This prestigious recognition is not given annually, but allows the President to recognize individuals who have been of particular significance during his or her term.

Shining Star Award
This award was developed to recognize the special volunteers who give freely of their time and talents to the Association. The International Shining Star award recognizes chapter leaders who standout above all other member with their significant contributions to the chapter. The Chapter Shining Star recognizes chapter members who have gone above and beyond for the chapter.

G. Warren Scholarship Award
Presented annually, this $500 scholarship program was developed in memory of G. Warren. The only requirement is that the student will be returning for at least one more term of school

Société Saint-Jean-Baptiste de Montréal
82, rue Sherbrooke ouest, Montréal QC H2X 1X3
514/843-8851; Fax:514/844-6369
Email:mbeaulieu@ssjb.com; URL:www.ssjb.com
Prix André-Guérin
Créé en 1990; décerné à une personnalité canadienne-française qui s'illustre dans le domaine du cinéma et vidéo

Toronto International Film Festival Group
2 Carlton St., Suite 1600., Toronto ON M5B 1J3
416/967-7371; Fax:416/967-9477
Email:customerrelations@tiffg.ca; URL:www.tiffg.ca

AGF People's Choice Award
Sponsored by AGF & voted best film of the festival by festival audiences

Award for Best Canadian Short Film
CityTV Award for Best Canadian First Feature Film
Established by CityTV; awarded to a Canadian filmmaker whose first feature film is considered exemplary; award acknowledges the fresh new talent emerging within Canadian cinema
$15,000

FIPRESCI Award
Selected by an international FIPRESCI jury, awarded to a feature film by an emerging filmmaker having its world premiere at the festival

Toronto-City Award for Best Canadian Feature Film
Jointly sponsored by the City of Toronto & CityTV; awarded to the Best Canadian Feature Film
$25,000

BUSINESS & TRADE

Business Development Bank of Canada (BDC)
5, Place Ville-Marie, Suite 400, Montréal QC H3B 5E7
Fax:1-877-329-9232; Toll Free:1-877-232-2269
Email:yea@bdc.ca; URL:www.bdc.ca

BDC Ongoing Achievement Award
Introduced in 2003, this award is offered to an entrepreneur who received the a Yong Entrepreneur Award between 1988 and 2002 and whose business has since undergone sustained growth.

Laurentian Bank Export Achievement Award
This award is presented to the entrepreneurs to have most distinguished himself in the area of exports.

Bell Creative Mind Award
This award is presented to a company, in recognition of it's original approach and initiative that allows it to successfully differentiate itself from its competitors.

BDC Young Entrepreneur Awards
Awarded annually; honours outstanding entrepreneurs representing each province & territory

The Caldwell Partners
165 Avenue Rd., Toronto ON M5R 3S4
416/920-7702; Fax:416/922-8646
Email:leaders@caldwell.ca; URL:www.caldwell.ca

Canada's Outstanding CEO of the Year
Sponsored by The Caldwell Partners, this annual award takes into consideration the candidate's leadership, innovation, business achievements, corporate performance, social responsibility, sense of vision & global competitiveness

Canada's Top 40 Under 40
Established & managed by The Caldwell Partners, celebrates Canadian leaders who have demonstrated remarkable success before the age of 40.

Canada's CFO of the Year
Founded in 2003 and sponsored by Financial Executives International, PricewaterhouseCoopers LLP and in association with The Caldwell Partners International, this annual award is designed to recognize the very highest level of financial leadership in the country. Winners are chosen by a distinguished panel of business leaders.

Certified General Accountants Association of Canada
#800, 1188 West Georgia St., Vancouver BC V6E 4A2
604/669-3555; Fax:604/689-5845; Toll Free:1-800-663-1529
Email:public@cga-canada.org; URL:www.cga-online.org/canada

Fellowship Award
This annual award was designed to recognize members who provide exemplary service to the Association, the profession or the public, or achiever prominence through a variety of means. Only members in good standing, who have been admitted into membership at least two year prior are eligible.

John Leslie Award
Given to a member who has achieved national recognition for exceptional service to business, the community, politics, & the arts, or who has overcome physical adversity

The Conference Board of Canada
255 Smyth Rd., Ottawa ON K1H 8M7
613/526-3280; Fax:613/526-4857; Toll Free:1-866-711-2262
Email:infoserv@conferenceboard.ca;
URL:www.conferenceboard.ca

National Awards for Excellence in Business-Education Partnership
Awarded to partnerships that have a demonstrated record of success in promoting the importance of science, technology &/or mathematics; linking education & the world of work, promoting teacher development, encouraging students to stay in school, expanding vocational &/or apprenticeship training
- Mary Ann McLaughlin

National Awards in Governance
Awarded to boards of directors that have demonstrated excellence in governance & have implemented successful innovations in their governance practices; overall award for innovation & sector specific awards for public, private & not for profit sectors

Ernst & Young Entrepreneur of the Year Award
Ernst & Young Tower, TD Centre, 222 Bay St., PO Box 251, Toronto ON M5K 1J7
416/943-3785; Fax:416/943-2207; Toll Free:1-888-946-3694
Email:linda.moss@ca.ey.com; URL:www.eoy.ca

Ernst & Young Entrepreneur of the Year Award
Best entrepreneurs in 5 regions nationwide (Pacific Canada, The Prairies, Ontario, Québec, Atlantic Canada); other awards include Master Entrepreneur, Emerging Entrepreneur, Turnaround Entrepreneur, Young Entrepreneur, Supporter of Entrepreneurship. Awarded annually

Heritage Canada Foundation / Fondation Héritage Canada
5 Blackburn Ave., Ottawa ON K1N 8A2
613/237-1066; Fax:613/237-5987
Email:heritagecanada@heritagecanada.org;
URL:www.heritagecanada.org

The Prince of Wales Prize for Municipal Heritage Leadership
Established in 1999, The Prince of Wales agreed to lend his title to this annual award in recognition of the government of a municipality, which has demonstrated a strong and sustained commitment to the conservation of its historic places.

Gabrielle Léger Award for Lifetime Achievement in Heritage Conservation
Founded in 1978, this annual award is Canada's premier hounour fo individual achievement in heritage conservation

The Journalism Award
Presented annually to a journalist whose work has brought profile to Canadian communities' historic places.

Corporate Price
This annual award recognizes Canadian corporations, which have invested in the conservation of historic property of the purposes of restoration, rehabilitation, or reuse.

Achievement Awards
These awards honour individuals or groups for their achievement in heritage advocacy and volunteerism, and for projects that demonstrate a community's commitment to heritage conservation.

Information Highways Magazine
#102, 1999 Avenue Rd., Toronto ON M5M 4A5
416/488-7372; Fax:416/488-7078
Email:info@econtentinstitute.org; URL:www.econtentinstitute.org

Canadian Online Product Awards
Honours online products designed for Canadian organizations & consumers; open to companies & individuals who develop or market products to Canadians in the following categories: general business, finance, legal, engineering, scientific, medical, consumer, library, internet search & retrieval technology & internet-enabled decision support products. Entry fee of $160.50 for each entry required

International Trade Canada
Canada Export Award Program, Team Canada Inc, 125 Sussex Dr., Ground Fl., Ottawa ON K1A 0G2
613/944-2395; Fax:613/994-0120

Email:cea-peec@international.gc.ca;
URL:www.infoexport.gc.ca/awards-prix

Canada Export Award
Honours those firms from across Canada who have demonstrated superior performance in the export arena. Open to all firms or divisions of firms resident in Canada, that have been exporting goods or services for three or more years; this includes trading houses & banks, as well as transport, market research, packaging & promotion firms; selection is based on but not limited to the extent to which the firm has shown significant increases in its export sales, success in breaking into new markets, success in introducing export products into world markets; other achievements by firms in export markets that contribute to Canada's economic well-being or to the reputation of the organization as a world-class exporter will also be considered.

National Quality Institute / Institut national de la qualité

#307, 2275 Lakeshore West Blvd., Toronto ON M8V 3Y3
416/251-7600; Fax:416/251-9131; Toll Free:1-800-263-9648
Email:info@nqi.ca; URL:www.nqi.ca

Canada Awards for Excellence
Previously called the Canada Awards for Business Excellence & established by the Government of Canada in 1984, the awards recognize outstanding continuous achievement in seven key areas: Leadership, Customer Focus, Planning for Improvement, People Focus, Process Optimization, Supplier Focus & Organizational Performance

National Transportation Week Inc.

Crowchild Square, #201, 5403 Crowchild Trail NW
Calgary AB T3B 4Z1
403/247-4115; Fax:403/541-0915
Email:ntwsnt@igs.net

Transportation Person of the Year
This award is given annually to an individual who has assumed a leadership role that has contributed to significant improvements or advancements in the transportation industry in Canada.

Award of Achievement
Established 1987; awarded to those who have brought about positive & measurable developments of significant & lasting benefit to transportation in Canada

Award of Excellence
Established 1975; for an outstanding contribution to the betterment of the transportation industry

Skills/Compétences Canada

#205, 260, boul Saint Raymond, Gatineau QC J9A 3G7
819/771-7545; Fax:819/771-5575; Toll Free:1-877-754-5226
Email:skillscanada@skillscanada.com;
URL:www.skillscanada.com

Canadian Skills Competition
Awarded annually; is an olympic-style skills competition in over 40 skilled trades, technology & leadership contests, representing 6 industry sectors, designed to test skills required in technology & trade occupations; allows students access to newest technologies & communicate with industry experts who serve as mentors Students compete at the local, regional & provincial levels to win the right to represent their province at the national level
Gold, silver & bronze medals

University of Alberta

School of Business, 3-23 Business Bldg.
Edmonton AB T6G 2R6
780/492-7676; Fax:780/492-3325
URL:www.business.ualberta.ca

Canadian Business Leader Award
Annual award recognizes distinguished professional achievements & contributions to the community

CITIZENSHIP & BRAVERY

Alberta Order of Excellence

Executive Secretary, Alberta Order of Excellence Council
c/o Policy Coordination Office
Executive Council
1201 Legislature Annex
9718 - 107 Street., Edmonton AB T5K 1E4
780/427-7243; Fax:780/427-0305
Email:aoe@gov.ab.ca; URL:www.lieutenantgovernor.ab.ca/aoe/

Alberta Order of Excellence
Established in 1979, the award recognizes those persons who have rendered service of the greatest distinction & of singular excellence for or on behalf of Albertans.

Bridgestone/Firestone Canada Inc.

#400, 5770 Hurontario St., Mississauga ON L5R 3G5
905/890-1990; Fax:905/890-1991; Toll Free:1-800-267-1318
URL:www.truckhero.ca

National Truck Hero Award
Established 1956; endorsed by the Canada Safety Council, the Traffic Injury Research Foundation & the trucking industry; designed to promote highway safety by focusing public attention on acts of bravery performed by professional Canadian truck drivers in the course of their daily work

The Canadian Council of Christians & Jews / Conseil canadien des chrétiens et des juifs

4211 Yonge St., PO Box 17, Toronto ON M2P 2A9
416/597-9693; Fax:416/597-9775; Toll Free:1-800-663-1848
Email:info@cccj.ca; URL:www.cccj.ca

Human Relations Award
This prestigious annual award recognizes outstanding contributions to Canadian society crossing cultural, religious, racial and ethnic lines.

Good Servant Medal
Created to commemorate the retirement of Richard D. Jones, O.C., LL.D., after 30 years of continuous service to CCCJ, as founder & principal officer, 1947-1977; recognizes individuals who have rendered extraordinary service to their community beyond the call of duty without seeking public recognition

Discovering Diversity Award
Established in 2004, this award is given to a student and his/her school who have made an outstanding effort to build community understanding and respect for others or different faiths and ethnic backgrounds.

The Canadian Council of the Blind / Le Conseil canadien des aveugles

#401, 396 Cooper St., Ottawa ON K2P 2H7
613/567-0311; Fax:613/567-2728; Toll Free:1-877-304-0968
Email:ccb@ccbnational.net; URL:ccbnational.net

Award of Merit
This award is bestowed in recognition of service to Canadians who are blind and vision impaired.

Book of Fame Citation
The Book of Fame was donated to the Council in 1958 by the disbanded Comrades Club of Toronto; it contains the names & citations of outstanding blind Canadians selected yearly by the eight divisions & the National Board of Directors of the Council; each recipient of a citation is presented with a framed photograph of the appropriate page in the book

Canadian Decorations for Bravery

c/o The Chancellory, Rideau Hall, One Sussex Drive
Ottawa ON K1A 0A1
613/991-0895; Fax:613/991-1681; Toll Free:1-800-465-6890
URL:www.gg.ca/honours/decorations/bra/bd-info_e.asp

Canadian Decorations for Bravery
Presented by the Governor General, Bravery decorations recognize people who have risked their lives to save or protect others; Three levels - the Cross of Valour, the Star of Courage & the Medal of Bravery - reflect the varying degrees of risk involved in any act of bravery

The Duke of Edinburgh's Award

#450, 207 Queen's Quay West, PO Box 124
Toronto ON M5J 1A7
416/203-0674; Fax:416/203-0676
Email: sanderson@dukeofed.org; URL:www.dukeofed.org

Young Canadians Challenge
Established in Canada in 1963 with His Royal Highness Prince Philip as Patron, the award recognizes personal achievement in a voluntary program of activities by young people in the age range of 14-25.
Open to all Canadian youth; young people participate independently or through youth groups, clubs, schools, etc.; program is operated throughout Canada, with divisional offices located in each of the ten provinces.
Award is in the form of a pin & an inscribed certificate representing Gold, Silver, & Bronze levels; Gold awards are presented by Her Excellency The Governor General of Canada, or a member of the Royal Family, at national awards ceremonies

National Aboriginal Achievement Foundation

#450, 215 Spadina Ave., Toronto ON M5T 2C7
416/926-0775; Fax:416/926-7554; Toll Free:1-800-329-9780
Email:info@naaf.ca; URL:www.naaf.ca

National Aboriginal Achievement Awards
Established in 1993, this award recognizes the outstanding career achievemennts of First Nations, Inuit and Métis people, in diverse occupations.

Ontario Ministry of Citizenship & Immigration

Ontario Honours & Awards
400 University Ave. West, 6th Fl., Toronto ON M7A 2R9
416/327-2422; Fax:416/314-4965; Toll Free:1-800-267-7329

June Callwood Outstanding Achievement Award
Created in 2007 to commemorate the life of June Callwood CC, O.Ont, LL.D, a Canadian journalist whose life was marked by a strong concern for social justice, especially on issues affecting children and women. This annual award is given to 20 individual volunteers, volunteer groups, businesses and other organizations in recognition of their outstanding contributions to their communities ad the province.

Lieutenant Governor's Community Volunteer Award for Students
This award honours one graduating student from each of Ontario's post secondary schools who not only completed the number of volunteer hours required to graduate, but have gone above and byond.

Ontario Medal for Good Citizenship
This award recognizes residents of Ontario for outstanding achievement, whose lives serve as an example to all Ontarians. They are individuals who have made their communities better places to live.

Ontario Medal for Young Volunteers
Recognizes the outstanding achievements of 10 young volunteers, 15-24 who have made a difference to their communities

The Lincoln M. Alexander Award
Recognizes young people who have demonstrated exemplary leadership in eliminating racial discrimination; 3 student awards & 1 community award are offered yearly

The Ontario Medal for Firefighters Bravery
Established 1976 to recognize acts of superlative courage & bravery performed in the line of duty by members of Ontario's firefighting forces

The Ontario Medal for Good Citizenship
Established 1973 to recognize people who, through exceptional long-term efforts have made outstanding contributions to the well being of their communities

The Ontario Medal for Police Bravery
Established 1975 to recognize acts of superlative courage & bravery performed in the line of duty by members of Ontario's police forces

The Order of Ontario
Established 1986 to recognize those men & women who have rendered service of the greatest distinction & of singular excellence in all fields of endeavour benefiting society in Ontario & elsewhere

The Order of British Columbia

Honours & Awards Secretariat, PO Box 9422, Stn Prov Govt, Victoria BC V8W 9V1
250/387-1616; Fax:250/356-2814
Email:protocol@gov.bc.ca; URL:www.protocol.gov.bc.ca

The Order of British Columbia
Established in 1989 to recognize individuals who have served with the greatest distinction & excelled in any field of endeavour benefiting the people of British Columbia or elsewhere.

Order of New Brunswick / Ordre du Nouveau-Brunswick

Intergovernmental & International Relations,
Office of Protocol
#274, 670 King St., PO Box 6000, Fredericton NB E3B 5H1
506/453-2671; Fax:506/453-2995
URL:www.gnb.ca/lg/ONB/index-e.asp

Order of New Brunswick
Established in December, 2000 to recognize individuals who have demonstrated excellence & achievement & who have made outstanding contributions to the social, cultural or economic well-being of New Brunswick & its residents. Maximum of 10 recipients annually

The Order of Prince Edward Island

Legislative Assembly, Province House, PO Box 2000, Charlottetown PE C1A 7N8
902/368-5970; Fax:902/368-5175
Email:chmackay@gov.pe.ca; URL:www.assembly.pe.ca

The Order of Prince Edward Island
Highest provincial honour that can be bestowed on a resident of the province; it is awarded in public recognition of individual Islanders whose efforts & accomplishments have been exemplary An enameled medallion, which incorporates the Provincial emblem against a blue background worn with a ribbon of rust, green & white. Recipients receive a stylized lapel pin & miniature medal, an official certificate & are entitled to use O.P.E.I. after their names

The Saskatchewan Order of Merit
Saskatchewan Honours & Awards Program
Office of Protocol & Honours
#1530 - 1855 Victoria Ave., Regina SK S4P 3T2
306/787-8965; Fax:306/787-1269; Toll Free:1-877-427-5505
Email:honours@gr.gov.sk.ca; URL:www.gr.gov.sk.ca/Protocol/Honours/SOM.htm

The Saskatchewan Order of Merit
This is a prestigious recognizes of excellence, achievement and contributions to the social, cultural and economic well-being of the province and its residence.

Secrétariat de l'Ordre national du Québec
Ministère du Conseil exécutif, #3.221, 875, Grande Allée Est, Québec QC G1R 4Y8
418/643-8895; Fax:418/646-4307
Email:ordre-national@mce.gouv.qc.ca; URL:www.ordre-national.gouv.qc.ca/index.htm

Ordre national du Québec
L'Ordre national du Québec est la plus haute distinction décernée par le gouvernement du Québec. Il a été institué par la Loi sur l'Ordre national du Québec (L.R.Q., c. 0-7.01) sanctionnée le 20 juin 1984 par le Parlement de Québec. L'Ordre national du Québec est composé de personnes à qui le gouvernement a conféré le titre de Grand Officier (G.O.) ou d'Officier (O.Q.) ou de Chevalier de l'Ordre national du Québec (C.Q.). La loi prévoit qu'une nomination puisse être faite à titre posthume. Elle accorde aussi au premier ministre du Québec le privilège exclusif de procéder à des nominations étrangères

Société Saint-Jean-Baptiste de Montréal
82, rue Sherbrooke Ouest, Montréal QC H2X 1X3
514/843-8851; Fax:514/844-6369
Email:mbeaulieu@ssjb.com; URL:www.ssjb.com

Prix Bene Merenti De Patria
Créée en 1923, cette médaille souligne les mérites d'un compatriote ayant rendu des services exceptionnels à la patrie. La maquette est l'oeuvre d'un artiste qui a préparé les chars allégoriques de nos grands défilés pendant de nombreuses années
Médaille d'argent

Prix Chomedey-de-Maisonneuve
Créé en 1983; décerné à une personnalité dont les réalisations contribuent au rayonnement de Montréal

Prix Patriote de l'année
Décerné à une personnalité qui s'est distinguée dans la défense des intérêts du Québec et de la démocratie des peuples, en mémoire des Patriotes des années 1830; créé en 1975

Prix Séraphin-Marion
Créé en 1984; décerné à une personnalité qui défend les droits de la francophonie hors-Québec

St. John Ambulance / Ambulance Saint-Jean
#400, 1900 City Park Dr., Ottawa ON K1J 1A3
613/236-7461; Fax:613/236-2425
Email:nhq@sja.ca; URL:www.sja.ca

Life-saving Awards of the Order of St. John
Instituted in 1874, recognizes those who risk their lives in unselfish acts of bravery & heroism when saving or attempting to save a life.

United Nations Association in Canada / Association canadienne pour les Nations-Unies
#300, 309 Cooper St., Ottawa ON K2P 0G5
613/232-5751; Fax:613/563-2455
Email:info@unac.org; URL:www.unac.org

Pearson Peace Medal
Awarded to a Canadian who has contributed significantly to humanitarian causes

CULTURE, VISUAL ARTS & ARCHITECTURE

The Canada Council for the Arts / Conseil des Arts du Canada
350 Albert St., PO Box 1047, Ottawa ON K1P 5V8
613/566-4414; Fax:613/566-4390; Toll Free:1-800-263-5588
Email:info@canadacouncil.ca; URL:www.canadacouncil.ca

Bell Canada Award in Video Art
$10,000 awarded annually to a Canadian video artist who has made an exceptional contribution to the advancement of video art in Canada through his/her video tapes or video installations; candidates are nominated by three professional curators &/or critics who are specialists in Canadian video art; the winner is selected by the committee of professional video artists

Duke & Duchess of York Prize in Photography
Endowed by the Government of Canada in 1986 on the occasion of Prince Andrew's marriage; $8,000 prize awarded annually to the best candidate in the competition for the Grants to Professional Artists in visual arts; prize is given in addition to the arts grant received

Governor General's Medals in Architecture
Awarded every two years; recognizes excellence in the art of architecture in completed projects; Canada Council adminsters the jurying of the awards & contributes $20,000 to the Royal Architectural Institute of Canada towards the publication of a book/catalogue on the winning projects

Governor-General's Awards for Visual & Media Arts
Six $15,000 prizes awarded annually for distinguished career achievement in visual & media arts, plus one $15,0000 prize for distinguished contributions to the visual & media arts through voluntarism, philanthropy, board governance or community outreach activities.
Nominees must be Canadian Citizens or permanent residents of Canada, & they may not apply for an award. They must be nominated by specialist in the field. To be nominated for one of the six awards in the artistic category, candidates must have created an outstanding, distinguished body of work in visual or media arts & have made a substantial contribution to the development of visual or media arts in Canada over a significant period of time. A peer assessment committee selects the winners

J.B.C. Watkins Award
A bequest from the estate of the late John B.C . Watkins, provides special fellowships of $5,000 to Canadian artists in any field, who are graduates of a Canadian university or post-secondary art institution or training school. Preference is given to those who wish to carry out their post-graduate studies in Denmark, Norway, Sweden or Iceland, but applications are accepted for studies in any country other than Canada. Post-graduate schools include post-secondary institutions or training schools, whether or not these are degree-granting institutions; fellowships are normally awarded in music, visual arts (architecture only), theatre & media arts

Joseph S. Stauffer Prizes
Each year the Canada Council designates up to three Canadians who have been awarded an arts grant in the fields of music, visual arts or literature as winners; the prizes, which provide an additional $5,000 each, honour the memory of the benefactor whose bequest to the Canada Council enables it to "encourage young Canadians of outstanding promise or potential"
Molson Prizes.
Two prizes of $50,000 each are awarded annully to distinguished Canadians, one in the arts and the other in the social sciences and humanities.

Petro-Canada Award in New Media
Endowed by Petro-Canada in 1987 to celebrate the centenary of engineering in Canada, $10,000 awarded approximately every three years to a professional Canadian artist. The recipient must demonstrate outstanding & innovative use of new technology in the media arts. Candidates are nominated by a committee of three professional curators &/or critics who are specialists in new media & audio arts; winner is selected by a committee of professional new media & audio artists

Prix de Rome in Architecture
Established 1987; designed to recognize the work of a Canadians actively engaged in the field of contemporary architecture whose career is well under way & whose personal work shows exceptional talent. Winner is chosen by a peer asessment committee convened by the Canada Council for the Arts

Ronald J. Thom Award for Early Design Achievement
$10,000 awarded every two years to a Canadian in the early stages of his/her career in architecture who must demonstrate both outstanding creative talent & exceptional potential in architectural design.
Sensitivity to architecture's allied arts, crafts & professions in the context of the integrated building environment must be evident in all work. Winner is chosen by the peer assessment committee for the Creation/Production Grants to Professional Artists in architecture

Saidye Bronfman Awards
Funded by the Samuel & Saidye Bronfman Family Foundation, $25,000 prize is awarded annually to an exceptional craftsperson for excellence in the fine crafts; in addition to the cash award, works by the recipient are acquired by the Canadian Museum of Civilization.
Candidates must be nominated by the national or provincial crafts council, a previous recipient of the awards, a member association of the Canadian Craft Council or a single media guild. Laureates are chosen by a peer assessment committee of distinguished craftspersons & experts in the fine crafts

Victor Martyn Lynch-Staunton Awards
Each year the Canada Council designates several Canadian artists who have been awarded grants in music & visual arts as holders of Victor Martyn Lynch-Staunton Awards; this designation is made to honour the memory of the benefactor whose bequest to the Council enables it to increase the number of grants available to senior or established artists; the awards provide each recipient with $4,000 in addition to the arts grant, which is also provided by the income from this bequest

York Wilson Endowment Awards
$30,000 awarded annually; enables Canadian art museums & public art galleries to purchase original works by living, contemporary Canadian painters & sculptors; awarded through a Canada Council for the Arts competition, to an eligible Canadian institution to allow it to purchase an original artwork that would significantly enhance its collection of contemporaray Canadian painting or sculpture. Winner is chosen by a peer assessment committee of Canadian curators of contemporary art or other appropriate peers

Canadian Conference of the Arts / Conférence canadienne des arts
#804, 130 Albert St., Ottawa ON K1P 5G4
613/238-3561; Fax:613/238-4849
Email:info@ccarts.ca; URL:www.ccarts.ca

Diplôme d'honneur
Established in 1954; presented annually to Canadians who have contributed outstanding service to the arts; recipients have included Vincent Massey, Wilfrid Pelletier, Maureen Forrester, Floyd Chalmers, Gabrielle Roy, Glenn Gould, Alfred Pellan, Bill Reid, Antonine Maillet

Canadian Historical Association / Société historique du Canada
395 Wellington St., Ottawa ON K1A 0N3
613/233-7885; Fax:613/567-3110
Email:cha-shc@lac-bac.bc.ca; URL:www.cha-shc.ca

Albert B. Corey Prize
Established 1966 & jointly sponsored by the CHA & the American Historical Association; awarded every two years to the best book dealing with the history of Canadian-American relations or the history of both countries
$1,000

The Wallace K. Ferguson Prize
Established 1979; awarded annually for outstanding work in a field of history other than Canadian
$1,000

The City of Toronto
Chief Administrator's Office, City Hall, 100 Queen St. West, 11th Fl., East Tower, Toronto ON M5H 2N2
416/392-8592; Fax:416/696-3645

Architecture & Urban Design Awards
Awarded every two years, this award recognizes and celebrates design excellence and in turn elevates public awareness of the vital role that design plays in Toronto

Conseil de la vie française en Amérique
#201, 5350, boul Henri-Bourassa, Québec QC G1H 6Y8
418/626-5665; Fax:418/626-5663
Email:cvfa@cvfa.ca; URL:www.cvfa.ca/

L'Ordre du Conseil de la vie française en Amérique
Destiné à reconnaître les mérites exceptionnels d'un francophone ayant apporté une contribution significative au progrès des francophones et à la promotion des facteurs de vie et de la culture française en Amérique du Nord

Prix littéraire Champlain
1 500 $; vise à encourager en Amérique du Nord la production littéraire chez les francophones qui vivent à l'extérieur du Québec, d'une part, et à susciter chez les Québécois un intérêt pour les francophones qui sont en situation de minorité hors du Québec en Amérique du Nord

Fondation Émile-Nelligan

261, rue Bloomfield, Outremont QC H2V 3R6
514/278-4657; Fax:514/271-6369
Email:info@fondation-nelligan.org;
URL:www.fondation-nelligan.org

Prix Émile-Nelligan
Ce prix annuel date de 1979, année de la création de la Fontation Émile-Nelligan. C'est un prix de poésie décerné à des poètes de 35 ans ou moins, pour un recueil publié au cours de l'année.
7 500$

Prix Ozias-Leduc
Prix triennal en arts visuels (peinture, sculpture, gravure, installations, 'land art'). Décerné à un artiste citoyen du Canada né au Québec ou à un artiste citoyen du Canada ayant sa résidence principale au Québec depuis au moins dix ans
25 000$

Prix Gilles-Corbeil
Le prix Gilles-Corbeil est un prix de littérature. C'est un prix triennal et is al été décerné pour la première fois en 1990.
100 000$

Prix Serge-Garant
Le prix Serge-Garant est un prix de compostiion musicale. C'est un prix triennal qui a été décerné pour le première fois en 1991.
25 000$

The Gershon Iskowitz Foundation

#302, 862 Richmond St. West, Toronto ON M6J 1C9
416/351-0216; Fax:416/351-0217

Gershon Iskowitz Prize
$25,000 to recognize achievements in visual art

Heritage Canada Foundation / Fondation Héritage Canada

5 Blackburn Ave., Ottawa ON K1N 8A2
613/237-1066; Fax:613/237-5987
Email:heritagecanada@heritagecanada.org;
URL:www.heritagecanada.org

Achievement Awards
Established 1989, these awards honour individuals or groups for their achievement in heritage advocacy and volunteerism, and for projects that demonstrate a community's commitment to heritage conservation. Local Heritage organizations are encouraged to submit nominations within prescribed criteria and eligibility rules. Each award is given jointly by the Heritage Canada Foundation and the heritage organization making the nomination. In this way, the Heritage Canada Foundation also recognizes the nominating organizations for their dedication and commitment to excellence in heritage conservation.

Gabrielle Léger Award
Recognizes outstanding work in architectural conservation in Canada; this is an annual national award to an individual who has contributed outstanding community service in the cause of heritage conservation

Lieutenant Governor's Award
Established 1979 to recognize outstanding work in architectural conservation on a provincial level by an individual or group
It must be demonstrated that the applicant's continuous efforts in the field of heritage conservation have benefited the province where the foundation's annual meeting is being held; applicants must be sponsored by an organized heritage group &/or elected officials at any level of government

Prince of Wales Prize
Established in 1999, awarded annually to a municipal government which has shown exemplary commitment to heritage preservation within its jurisdiction

Ontario Arts Council / Conseil des arts de l'Ontario

151 Bloor St. West, 5th Fl., Toronto ON M5S 1T6
416/961-1660; Fax:416/961-7796; Toll Free:1-800-387-0058
Email:info@arts.on.ca; URL:www.arts.on.ca
The Ontario Arts Council provides a variety of Funds and Scholarships for different studies and careers in the arts. For more information visit their website.

PEI Council of the Arts

115 Richmond St., Charlottetown PE C1A 1H7
902/368-6176; Fax:902/368-4418 Toll Free: 1-888-734-2784
Email:info@peiartscouncil.com; URL:www.peica.ca

Father Adrien Arsenault Senior Arts Awards
The Price Edward Island Council of the Arts recognizes the achievements of artists on Prince Edward Island through a program of annual and bi-annual awards and prizes.

Island Literary Awards
These awards are given annually to Prince Edward Island's writers. Awards are made to all levels of the discipline from students, through senior memebers of the writing community.

Québec Ministère de la culture et des communications

225, Grande Allée est, Québec QC G1R 5G5
418/380-2300; Fax:418/080-2364
Email:DC@mcc.gouv.qc.ca; URL:www.mcc.gouv.qc.ca

Les Prix du Québec:

Prix d'excellence en architecture
Ce prix souligne, depuis 1978, la contribution essentielle des architectes québecois au cadre bâti. Les prix accordés par l'Order des architectres du Québec permettent d'identifier et de valoriser les meilleures réalisations architecturales au Québec et ailleurs dans le monde.

Prix Paul-Émile-Borduas
Accordée à un artisan ou un artiste pour l'ensemble de son oeuvre dans le domaine des arts visuels, des métiers d'art, de l'architecture et du design

Royal Architectural Institute of Canada / Institut royal d'architecture du Canada

#330, 55 Murray St., Ottawa ON K1N 5M3
613/241-3600; Fax:613/241-5750
Email:info@raic.org; URL:www.raic.org

Awards of Excellence
These awards are bestowed every two years, recognizing the greatest achievement in several different categories.

RAIC Gold Medal
Established 1930; this medal is awarded annually in recognition of an individual whose personal work has demonstrated exceptional excellence in the design and practice of architecture; and/or, whose work related to architecture, has demonstrated exceptional excellence in research or education.

The Royal Society of Canada / La Société royale du Canada

170 Waller St., Ottawa ON K1N 9B9
613/991-6990; Fax:613/991-6996
Email:info@rsc.ca; URL:www.rsc.ca

Centenary Medal
Established 1982; awarded at irregular intervals in recognition of outstanding contributions to the object of the society & to recognize links to international organizations

Sir John William Dawson Medal
Established 1985; awarded for important & sustained contributions by one individual in at least two different fields in the general areas of interest of the Society or in a broad domain that transcends the usual disciplinary boundaries
$2,500 & a silver medal

The J.B. Tyrrell Historical Medal
Established 1927; awarded at least every two years for outstanding work in the history of Canada

Sobey Art Foundation

c/o Art Gallery of Nova Scotia
1723 Hollis Street, PO Box 2262, Halifax NS B3J 3C8
902/424.5169;
Email: fillmose@gov.ns.ca URL: www.sobeyartaward.ca

Sobey Art Award
Awarded every year to an artist 39 years old or younger who has shown their work in a public or commercial art gallery in Canada in the past 18 monthe.
$50 000

Social Sciences & Humanities Research Council of Canada

350 Albert St., PO Box 1610, Ottawa ON K1P 6G4
613/992-0691; Fax:613/992-1787
Email:info@sshrc.ca; URL:www.sshrc.ca

Doctoral Fellowships
Must have completed one year of doctoral study or a master's degree leading to a Ph.D. or equivalent; disciplines include: Geography, Health Studies, Applied Health Studies & Environmental Studies
Approx. $14,400 per year

Postdoctoral Fellowships
To support a core of the most promising new scholars in the social sciences & humanities & to assist them in establishing a research base at an important time in their research career; provides stipendiary support to non-tenured PhD graduates who are undertaking new research, publishing research findings, developing & expanding personal research networks, broadening teaching experience & preparing to become competitive in national research competitions.
Approximately $38,000 per year (for a maximum of two years) plus a $5,000 accountable research allowance

The Bora Laskin National Fellowship in Human Rights Research
To support interdisciplinary or multidisciplinary research & the development of expertise in the field of human rights, with emphasis on Canadian human rights issues
$45,000 stipend plus $10,000 for research & research-related travel expenses

The Jules & Gabrielle Léger Fellowship
Awarded to promote research & writing on the historical contribution of the Crown & its representatives, federal & provincial, to the political, constitutional, cultural, intellectual & social life of the country.
Award is for $40,000, plus $10,000 for research & research -travel expenses

Société Saint-Jean-Baptiste de Montréal

82, rue Sherbrooke Ouest, Montréal QC H2X 1X3
514/843-8851; Fax:514/844-6369
Email:mbeaulieu@ssjb.com; URL:www.ssjb.com

Prix Esdras-Minville
Créé en 1978; décerné à une personnalité canadienne-française qui s'illustre dans le domaine des sciences humaines

Prix Louis Philippe-Hébert
Créé en 1971; décerné à une personnalité canadienne-française qui s'illustre dans le domaine des arts plastiques

Prix Victor-Morin
Créé en 1962; décerné à une personnalité canadienne-française qui s'illustre dans le domaine des arts de la scène

Toronto Arts Council Foundation

141 Bathurst St., Toronto ON M5V 2R2
416/392-6800; Fax:416/392-6920
Email:mail@torontoartscouncil.org;
URL:www.torontoartscouncil.org

Margo Bindhardt Award
$10,000 cash prize presented every second year to Toronto artist or administrator whose leadership & vision, whether through their creative work or cultural activism, have had a significant impact on the arts in Toronto & for whom the cash prize will make a difference

Marilyn Lastman Award
$5,000 cash prize presented to a professional artist or arts administrator who is a Toronto resident & who has made a significant contribution in the field of arts education. Awarded every second year

Muriel Sherrin Award
$10,000 cash prize presented to an artist or creator who has made a contribution to the cultural life ot Toronto through outstanding achievement in music. The recipient will also have participated in international initiatives, including touring, study abroad & artist exchanges. Awarded every second year

Rita Davies Award
$5,000 cash prize presented to a Toronto artist, volunteer or administrator who has demonstrated creative leadership in the development of arts & culture in Toronto. Awarded every second year

William Kilbourn Award
$5,000 cash prize presented to an individual performer, teacher, administrator or creator in any arts discipline, including architecture & design, whose work is a celebration of life through the arts in Toronto. Awarded every second year

Ville de Montréal

Service du développement culturel
5650, d'Iberville, 4e étage, Montréal QC H2G 3E4
514/872-1156
URL:www.ville.montreal.qc.ca/culture/culture.htm

Prix François-Houdé
La Ville de Montréal, en collaboration avec le Conseil des métiers d'art du Québec décerne annuellement ce Prix afin de promouvoir l'excellence de la nouvelle création montréalaise en métiers d'art et de favoriser la diffusion d'oeuvres des jeunes artisans créateurs. Bourse de 3000$ et 2 500$ pour organiser une exposition

Prix Louis-Comtois
La Ville de Montréal, en collaboration avec l'Association des galeries d'art contemporain, décerne annuellement ce Prix qui vient apppuyer et promouvoir le travail d'un artiste en mi-carrière qui s'est distingué dans le domaine de l'art contemporain à Montréal depuis les 15 dernières années. Bourse 5000$ et 2 500$ pour organiser une exposition solo

Prix Pierre-Ayot
La Ville de Montréal, en collaboration avec l'Association des galeries d'art contemporain, décerne annuellement ce Prix qui souligne la facture exceptionnelle et l'apport original de la production des jeunes artistes en peinture, en estampe, en dessin, en illustration, en photographie ou tout autre médium. Bourse 3000$ et 2 500$ pour organiser une exposition solo

EDUCATIONAL

Alberta Scholarship Programs
PO Box 28000, Stn Main, Edmonton AB T5J 4R4
780/427-8640; Fax:780/427-1288
Email:scholarships@gov.ab.ca; URL:www.alis.gov.ab.ca/scholarships/main.asp

Alberta Scholarships Program
32 scholarships & awards are available in various fields of study

Association for Media & Technology in Education in Canada / Association des médias et de la technologie en éducation au Canada
#1318, 3-1750 The Queensway, Etobicoke ON M9C 5H5
URL:www.amtec.ca

AMTEC Leadership Award
Two awards recognize outstanding individual achievement & leadership in the field of educational media & technology
Association of Canadian Universities for Northern Studies / Association universitaire canadienne d'études nordiques
#405, 17 York St., Ottawa ON K1N 9J6
613/562-0515; Fax:613/562-0533
Email:awards@acuns.ca; URL:www.acuns.ca/

Studentships in Northern Studies
Research culminating in a thesis or similar document involving direct northern experience; for students enrolled in graduate & undergraduate degree programs or other courses of study recognized at a Canadian university with special relevance to Canada's northern territories & adjacent regions
$10,000

Association of Universities & Colleges of Canada / Association des universités et collèges du Canada
#600, 350 Albert St., Ottawa ON K1R 1B1
613/563-1236; Fax:613/563-9745
Email:awards@aucc.ca; URL:www.aucc.ca

AUCC Scholarship for Students with Disabilities
Scholarships open to students entering full-time studies leading to a first undergraduate degree
Up to ten $5,000

Bowater Maritimes Scholarship Program
Scholarships open to grade 12 New Brunswick students
Three $1,500 for undergraduate studies

CATSA - Brian Flemming Research Fellowship and Security Award
Scholarship open to doctoral or post-doctoral research relating to tactical and strategic issues of Canadian aviation security screening
$15,000

C.D. Howe Memorial Foundation Engineering Awards
(One male, one female) for students who have completed the first year of an engineering program
Two $7,500 scholarships

C.D. Howe Scholarship Program
Scholarships open to all disciplines but for students from Thunder Bay or the following school boards: Lakehead, Lakehead District R.C., Lake Superior, North of Superior District R.C., Geraldton, Geraldton District R.C., Nipigon-Red Rock, & Hornepayne
Two $5,500

Cable Telecommunications Research Fellowship (Canadian Cable Telecommunications Association)
Scholarship awarded annually to students pursuing a master's degree in any discipline directly related to the development & delivery of cable in Canada
$5,000

CIBC Youthvision Scholarship
Must be enrolled in Big Brothers/Big Sisters of Canada
30 scholarships: $4,000 or actual tuition fees, plus paid summer employment with YMCA Canada

Conocophillips Canada Centennial Scholarship
Scholarship program encourages individuals with academic excellence and demonstrated leadership.
Three scholarships of up to $10,000 per year for a maximum of 2 consecutive years

Department of National Defence Security & Defence Forum
Eight $8,000 (master's), four $16,000 (doctorate) scholarships & two $35,000 (post-doctoral) fellowships in studies relating to current & future Canadian natural security & defence issues. Three internships of up to 12 months worth $32,000 to help recent MA graduates obtain work experience in security & defence studies by working in this field in the non-governmental or private sectors.

Fessenden-Trott Awards
Scholarships open to all disciplines; restricted to Ontario in 2005
Four $9,000

Frank Knox Memorial Fellowship Program
Awards, plus tuition fees & health insurance for Canadian citizens or permanent residents who have graduated from a AUCC member institution before Sept. 2005 & wish to study at Harvard in the following disciplines: arts & sciences (including engineering), business administration, design, divinity studies, education, law, public administration, medicine, dental medicine & public health; applications for students currently studying in the US will not be considered
Up to three US$18,500

Mattinson Endowment Fund Scholarship for Disabled Students
For undergraduate study, all disciplines
$2,500

Programme canadien de bourses de la Francophonie
Scholarship based on merit for especially deserving and motivated applicants, funded by the Canadian International Development Agency. Awarded by competition for professional training in leading-edge technologies at the college level (certificate or diploma) or for undergraduate, master's or doctoral studies at a university

Public Safety & Emergency Preparedness Canada Research Fellowship in Honour of Stuart Nesbitt White
For research in the area of disaster/emergency research & planning; preference is given to applicants who hold a Master's degree & who are planning research in the following fields: Urban & Regional Planning, Economics, Earth Sciences, Risk Analysis & Management, Systems Science, Social Sciences, Business Administration & Health Administration
Eight up to $19,250

Queen Elizabeth Silver Jubilee Endowment Fund for Study in a Second Official Language Award Program
Scholarships open to all disciplines, except translations, for students studying in their second language
Three $5,000 (plus travel costs)

TD Canada Trust Scholarship for Outstanding Community Leadership
All disciplines, undergraduate degrees
20 renewable scholarships for $5,000 living stipend, plus all tuition & compulsory fees, plus summer employment

BC Ministry of Advanced Education
PO Box 9173, Stn Prov Govt, Victoria BC V8W 9H7
250/387-6100; Fax:250/356-9455; Toll Free:1-800-561-1818
URL:www.bcsap.bc.ca

Governor General's Academic Medal Award
Awards medals to college & university students achieving the highest academic standing upon graduation

Irving K. Barber Scholarship
Up to 150 scholarships worth $5,000 annually; open to students who have completed two years at a BC community college, university college or institute & must transfer to a public degree-granting institution in BC in order to complete their degrees

Lieutenant Governor's Silver Medal Award
Honours students registered in a vocational or career program of less than two years duration, who have excelled academically, & have contributed to the life of the college or institute or their community

Premier's Excellence Award
Recognizes the top all-around graduating secondary students, from the 15 college regions in BC, who are proceeding to full-time post secondary education in BC

United World College Scholarships
Valued at approximately $60,000, the award covers full tuition & residence for two years at the Lester B. Pearson College of the Pacific; the International Baccalaureate allows students to finish their final year of high school & earn credit towards the first year of university

Black Business & Professional Association
#210, 675 King St. West, Toronto ON M5V 1M9
416/504-4097; Fax:416/504-7343
Email:bbpa@bellnet.ca; URL:www.bbpa.org

Harry Jerome Scholarships
Scholarship celebrates excellence in achievement in the Black community. Award recipients are selected from among Canada-wide nominees recommended by business and professional colleagues, teachers, relatives and friends.
Five $2,000 annual awards

The Canada Council for the Arts / Conseil des Arts du Canada
350 Albert St., PO Box 1047, Ottawa ON K1P 5V8
613/566-4414; Fax:613/566-4390; Toll Free:1-800-263-5588
Email:info@canadacouncil.ca; URL:www.canadacouncil.ca

Coburn Fellowships
Up to three $20,000 fellowships are awarded annually to a Canadian student (at Victoria University or the University of Toronto) & an Israeli student, in the fields of fine arts or humanities, to study on a reciprocal basis; they are intended to cover travel expenses, tuition & accommodation costs for a year; winners are chosen by Victoria University

John G. Diefenbaker Award
Funded by the Government of Canada, this annual award honours the memory of former Prime Minister John G. Diefenbaker; it enables a German scholar to spend up to 12 months in Canada to pursue research in any of the disciplines in the social sciences & humanities; candidates must be nominated by university departments or research institutes in Canada. Value of full award is $75,000; in addition, the Social Sciences & Humanities Research Council of Canada provides a travel allowance of up to $20,000

Canadian Association of University Business Officers / Association canadienne du personnel administratif universitaire
#320, 350 Albert St., Ottawa ON K1R 1B1
613/230-6760; Fax:613/563-7739
Email:cworkman@caubo.ca; URL:www.caubo.ca

CAUBO Quality & Productivity Awards
Designed to recognize, reward & share university achievements in improving the quality & reducing the cost of higher education programs & services; National & Regional categories
Awards evaluated on portability, originality, quality impact, productivity impact, & involvement
National: first prize $10,000; second prize $5,000; third prize $3,000

Canadian Mathematical Society / Société mathématique du Canada
#109, 577 King Edward St., Ottawa ON K1N 6N5
613/562-5702; Fax:613/565-1539
Email:office@cms.math.ca; URL:www.cms.math.ca

Canadian Mathematical Olympiad
Annual mathematics competition established to provide an opportunity for students to perform well on the Canadian Open Mathematics Challenge & to complete on a national basis.
Fifteen cash prizes

Canadian Merit Scholarship Foundation
#502 - 460 Richmond Street West St., Toronto ON M5V 1Y1
416/646-2120; Fax:416/646-0846; Toll Free:1-866-544-2673
URL:www.cmsf.ca

Finalist Award
Given to every finalist who is selected for & attends, National Selections
$2,500 awarded to outstanding students from across the country as one-time entrance awards to be used at any accredited Canadian university

National Award
Up to $8,000 per year plus a tuition stipend, for up to four years of full-time undergraduate study at any one of our participating Canadian universities

Provincial Award
One-time entrance award tenable at any accredited university in Canada at which the recipient gains admission & enrolls in a full-time program of study

$1,500

Regional Award
One-time entrance award tenable at any accreditied university in Canada at which the recipient gains admission & enrolls in a full-time program of study
$1,500

Canadian Sociology & Anthropology Association / Société canadienne de sociologie et d'anthropologie
Université Concordia University SB-323
1455, De Maisonneuve Ouest, Montréal QC H3G 1M8
514/848-8780; Fax:514/848-8780
Email:info@csaa.ca; URL:www.csaa.ca

John Porter Award
Recognizes outstanding published scholarly contributions within the "John Porter Tradition" to the advancement of sociological and/or anthropological knowledge in Canada
Outstanding Contribution Award
Given to recognize the work of eminent sociologists & anthropologists

Best Student Paper Award
Recognizes the best paper among those received for adjudication, written by a graduate student

CIDA Awards Program
Canadian Bureau for International Education
#1550, 220 Laurier Ave. West, Ottawa ON K1P 5Z9
613/237-4820; Fax:613/237-1073
Email:info@cbie.ca; URL:www.cbie.ca

Awards for Canadians
A program funded by CIDA & managed by the Canadian Bureau for International Education; CIDA wishes to increase the number of Canadian professionals capable of working in the international arena by providing funding up to $15,000 for short-term, overseas work experiences
Must possess a university degree, college diploma or professional designation, have substantial work experience, two years of which have involved using specific skills necessary to undertake the proposed project. For information on fields of specialization & eligible countries, contact CIDA Communications Branch, 200 Promenade du Portage, Hull PQ K1A 0G4; 819/997-5006; Fax: 819/953-6088. Other information & applications should be sent to the CBIE at the above address

Foundation for Educational Exchange Between Canada & the United States of America
#2015, 350 Albert St., Ottawa ON K1R 1A4
613/688-5540; Fax:613/237-2029
Email:info@fulbright.ca; URL:www.fulbright.ca

Canada-US Fulbright Program
To expand research, teaching & study opportunities for Canadian & American faculty & students engaged in the study of Canada, the United States & the relationship between the two countries; based on academic excellence & the merit of the applicant's proposed project, awards given annually for study in a number of different fields including conservation, ecology, environmental management, resource analysis & environmental policy. Applicants must relocate from the U.S. to Canada, or Canada to the U.S.
$15,000 US for graduate students; $25,000 US for faculty

International Development Research Centre / Centre de recherches pour le développement international
250 Albert St., Ottawa ON K1G 3H9
613/236-6163; Fax:613/238-7230
Email:info@idrc.ca; URL:www.idrc.ca

Canadian Window on International Development Awards
Award offered for doctoral research that explores the relationship between Canadian aid, trade, immigration & diplomatic policy, & international development & the alleviation of global policy
Applicants must hold Canadian citizenship or permanent residency status; be registered at a Canadian university; be conducting the proposed research for a doctoral dissertation & have completed course work & passed comprehensive examinations by the time of the award tenure
$20,000 per year - Centre Training & Awards Unit, 613/236-6163 ext 2098; Fax: 613/563-0815; Email: cta@idrc.ca

Centre Internships
These awards provide exposure to research for international development through program work & research under the guidance of IDRD program staff. Internships will be considered for a program of work & research responding to IDRC's current Program Initiatives
The program is aimed at candidates who, through demonstrated achievements in academic studies, work or research, have shown interest in the creation & utilization of knowledge from an international perspective. Candidates can be both Canadians (or permanent residents) or citizens of developing countries, & will have had some training at the master's level. Candidates need not be affiliated with an institution. They may participate in internships as part of an academic requirement
Stipend $2,500 - $28,000 per year - Centre Training & Awards Unit, 613/236-6163 ext 2098; Fax: 613/563-0815; Email cta@irdc.ca

The Japan Foundation, Toronto / Kokosai Koryu Kikin Toronto Nihon Bunka Centre
#213, 131 Bloor St. West, Toronto ON M5S 1R1
416/966-1600; Fax:416/966-9773
Email:info@jftor.org; URL:www.japanfoundationcanada.org

The Japan Foundation Fellowships
Scholars, researchers, artists & other professionals are provided an opportunity to conduct research or pursue projects in Japan. Term of award is from two to 14 months, depending on category; annual application deadline is Dec. 1 for funding year beginning the following April 1

The Japan Foundation Scholarships & Programs
The Foundation offers a wide range of programs in more than 180 countries, including the following: exchange of persons (fellowships); support for Japanese-language instruction; support for Japanese studies; support for arts-related exchange; support for media exchange

National Aboriginal Achievement Foundation
#450 - 215 Spadina Ave., Toronto ON M5T 2C7
416/926-0775; Fax:416/926-7554; Toll Free:1-800-329-9780
Email:info@naaf.ca; URL:www.naaf.ca

National Aboriginal Achievement Foundation Scholarships
Established 1985; provides scholarships to Aboriginal students for post-secondary education

Northern Enterprise Fund Inc.
PO Box 220, Beauval SK S0M 0G0
306/288-2258; Fax:306/288-4667; Toll Free:1-800-864-3022
Email:info@nefi.ca; URL: www.nefi.ca

Northern Spirit Scholarship Program
To promote entrepreneurial spirit in Northern Saskatchewan by providing scholarships to students enrolled in courses related to business or based on occupational shortages in the north
Ten $2,500 scholarships are awarded to full-time students who are permanent northern residents of the Northern Administration District; priority will be given to applicants showing intention of returning to, or remaining in the north; with an academic record of 70% average in most recent year completed

Ontario Council on Graduate Studies / Conseil ontarien des études supérieures
#1100, 180 Dundas St. West, Toronto ON M5G 1Z8
416/979-2165; Fax:416/595-7392
Email:kpanesar@cou.on.ca; URL:ocgs.cou.on.ca/

John Charles Polanyi Prizes
In honour of the achievement of John Charles Polanyi, co-recipient of the 1986 Nobel Prize in Chemistry, the Government of Ontario has established a fund to provide annually up to five prizes to persons continuing to post-doctoral studies at an Ontario university; prizes available in the areas of Physics, Chemistry, Physiology or Medicine, Literature & Economic Science
$15,000

Ordre des conseillers en ressources humaines et en relations industrielles agréés du Québec
#1400, 1200, av McGill College, Montréal QC H3B 4G7
514/879-1636; Fax:514/879-1722; Toll Free: 1 (800) 214-1609
Email:info@orhri.org; URL:www.orhri.org

EXCALIBUR: Le tournoi universitaire canadien en ressources humaines
Promouvoir un enseignement de la gestion des ressources humaines dans les universités canadiennes préparant les étudiants au marché du travail
3 000$; 2 250$; 1 500$

The Royal Society of Canada / La Société royale du Canada
170 Waller St., Ottawa ON K1N 9B9
613/991-6990; Fax:613/991-6996
Email:info@rsc.ca; URL:www.rsc.ca

Innis-Gérin Medal
Established 1966; awarded every two years for a distinguished & sustained contribution to the literature of the social sciences including human geography & social psychology

Pierre Chauveau Medal
Established 1951; awarded every two years (since 1966) for a distinguished contribution to knowledge in the humanities other than Canadian literature & Canadian history

Social Sciences & Humanities Research Council of Canada
350 Albert St., PO Box 1610, Ottawa ON K1P 6G4
613/992-0691; Fax:613/992-1787
Email:info@sshrc.ca; URL:www.sshrc.ca

The Thérèse F.-Casgrain Fellowship
$40,000 stipend awarded every second year (2004, 2006, etc.) to support research on women & social change in Canada

Yukon Government
PO Box 2703, Whitehorse YT Y1A 2C6
867/667-5811; Fax:867/393-6339
Email:information@gov.yk.ca

Excellence in Education Award
Awarded to individuals or groups that have demonstrated innovation, superior dedication or outstanding service to public school education in the Yukon; winners receive a specially commissioned artwork created by Ted Harrison

ENVIRONMENTAL

Alberta Emerald Foundation for Environmental Excellence
c/o McLennan Ross LLP, #400, 12220 Stony Plain Rd., Edmonton AB T5N 3Y4
780/413-9629; Fax:780/482-9100; Toll Free:1-800-219-8329
Email:info@emeraldawards.com; URL:www.emeraldawards.com

Emerald Awards
Awarded to Albertans who have made a significant contribution to the protection or enhancement of the environment
Nominations are open to individual, not-for-profit organizations, business & industry, communities & government, educational institutions & volunteer organizations excelling in environmental achievements

Alberta Sustainable Resource Development
Fish & Wildlife Division
Information Centre, Main Floor, 9920 - 108 St. Edmonton AB T5K 2M4
780/944-0313; Fax:780/427-4407
URL:www.srdgov.ab.ca

Order of the Bighorn
Fish & wildlife conservation awards presented every other year, to individuals, organizations & corporations for their outstanding contributions to fish & wildlife conservation in Alberta - Program Manager, Dave England

Association of Universities & Colleges of Canada / Association des universités et collèges du Canada
#600, 350 Albert St., Ottawa ON K1R 1B1
613/563-1236; Fax:613/563-9745
Email:info@aucc.ca; URL:www.aucc.ca

Cement Association of Canada Environmental Scholarship Program
Open to students in Alberta, British Columbia, Newfoundland, Nova Scotia, Ontario & Quebec who have fully completed the two years of course work in an environmental science or environmental engineering program that is required to continue a third year of their eligible program
Six $2,000

Atlantic Salmon Federation / Fédération du saumon atlantique
15 Rankine Mill Road, Chamcook NB E5B 3A9
506/529-1033; Fax:506/529-4438; Toll Free:1-800-565-5666
Email:tiffinic@nb.aibn.com; URL:www.asf.ca

Affiliate of the Year
Recognizes outstanding leadership & achievement in Atlantic salmon conservation within the federation's affiliate structure
Engraved plaque & a cheque for $500 to be used toward its conservation programs - Muriel Ferguson, Manager, Public Information

Olin Fellowship
Fellowships offered annually to individuals seeking to improve their knowledge or skills in fields dealing with current problems in biology, management, or conservation of Atlantic salmon & its habitat; the fellowship may be applied toward a wide range of endeavours such as salmon management, graduate study, & research.

Applicants need not be enrolled in a degree program, but must be legal residents of the US or Canada
$1,000-$3,000 - Ellen Merrill

Roll of Honour
Presented annually to individuals who exhibit outstanding commitment to salmon conservation at the grassroots level
ASF member in good standing - Muriel Ferguson, Manager, Public Information

T.B. (Happy) Fraser Award
Presented annually to an individual who has made outstanding long-term contributions to Atlantic salmon conservation in Canada. The award reflects efforts on a regional or national level - Muriel Ferguson, Manager, Public Information

BC Ministry of Environment
PO Box 9339, Stn Prov Govt, Victoria BC V8W 9M1
250/387-9422
URL:www.gov.bc.ca/wlap/

Minister's Environmental Awards
Awarded for identifying, reducing, solving or avoiding an environmental problem; demonstrating consistently responsible environmental management practices; &/or promoting public awareness, understanding & active concern for the enhancement & protection of the environment
Categories include individual citizen, youth, government, community or non-profit organization, business, industry or labour, environmental educator, scientist or innovator, environmental steward by nomination

Canadian Land Reclamation Association / Association canadienne de réhabilitation des sites dégradés
PO Box 61047, RPO Kensington, Calgary AB T2N 4S6
403/289-9435; Fax:403/289-9435
Email:clra@telusplanet.net; URL:www.clra.ca

Dr. Edward M. Watkin Award
Presented annually to an association member in recognition of outstanding contribution to the field of reclamation, through research, field work, teaching or innovation, or distinguished service to the association through active participation & leadership

The Noranda Land Reclamation Award
Presented annually by the association on behalf of Noranda Mines Inc. in recognition of superior research or field work in reclamation; not restricted to members

Canadian Wildlife Federation / Fédération canadienne de la faune
350 Michael Cowpland Dr., Kanata ON K2M 2W1
613/599-9594; Fax:613/599-4428; Toll Free:1-800-563-9453
Email:info@cwf-fcf.org; URL:www.cwf-fcf.org

Canadian Conservation Achievement Awards Program:

Roderick Haig-Brown Memorial Award
Awarded annually to an individual who has made a significant contribution to furthering the sport of angling &/or conservation & wise use of Canada's recreational fisheries resources

Roland Michener Conservation Award
A trophy is given annually in recognition of an individual's outstanding achievement in the field of conservation in Canada

Stan Hodgkiss Outdoorsman of the Year Award
Presented annually to an outdoorsperson who has demonstrated an active commitment to conservation in Canada

Centre for Environment
University of Toronto, #1016, 33 Wilcocks St.
Toronto ON M5S 3E8
416/978-7077; Fax:416/978-3884
Email:centre.environment@utoronto.ca; URL:www.environment.utoronto.ca/

Adaptation & Impacts Research Group (AIRG) Annual Prize
Awarded to a qualified graduate student for the best research paper addressing one or more of AIRG's reseach directions. This includes impacts of, & adaptation to, climate change/variabililty & extreme events; atmospheric natural hazards/disasters & societal adjustment; & integrated assessment of multiple atmospheric issues (climate change, stratospheric ozone depletion, acidic deposition & air quality), particularly in terms of their cumulative effects on human health

Energy Probe Research Foundation
225 Brunswick Ave., Toronto ON M5S 2M6
416/964-9223; Fax:416/964-8239
Email: webadmin@eprf.ca; URL:www.eprf.ca/eprf/index.html

The Margaret Laurence Fund
Grants & scholarships are made to foster an understanding of peace & the environment upon which the fate of the planet rests
Recipients of the grants & scholarships are limited to students, authors, researchers, & publishers, working with the foundation in collaborative projects approved by the directors

Environment Canada
70 Crémazie St., Gatineau QC K1A 0H3
819/997-2800; Fax: 819/994-1412; Toll Free:1-800-668-6767
Email: enviroinfo@ec.gc.ca; URL:www.ec.gc.ca

Canadian Environment Awards
Annual awards to honour initiatives in the areas of clean air, environmental learning, sustainable living, climate change, clean water, environmental health, lands & forests, wildlife & nature

International Development Research Centre / Centre de recherches pour le développement international
250 Albert St., Ottawa ON K1P 6M1
613/236-6163; Fax:613/238-7230
Email:info@idrc.ca; URL:www.idrc.ca

Ecosystem Approaches to Human Health Training Awards
Supports research that focuses on ecosystem management interventions leading to the improvement of human health & well-being while simultaneously maintaining or improving the condition of the ecosystem as a whole. Awards will be granted for training & research linked to the Ecosystem Approaches to Human Health Program Initiatives of the Centre. Priority will be give to proposals for research on ecosystems that are stressed through agriculture, urbanization or mining activities.
Citizens of developing countries &/or Canadian citizens or landed immigrants students currently enrolled in a graduate programme at a recognized university in Canada or in a developing country. Relevant language proficiency for site of study
Up to 6 awards for a maximum of $15,000 - Centre Training & Awards Unit, 613/236-6163 ext 2098; Fax: 563-0815; Email: cta@idrc.da

IDRC Doctoral Research Awards (IDRA)
Supports the field research of Canadian graduate students enrolled in a Canadian university for doctoral research on a topic of relevance to sustainable & equitable development
Applicants must hold Canadian citizenship or permanent residency status; be registered at a Canadian university; research proposal is for a doctoral thesis; provide evidence of affiliation with an institution or organization in the region in which the research will take place; have completed course work & passed comprehensive examinations by the time of award tenure
Maximum of $20,000 per year - Centre Training & Awards Unit, 613/236-6163 ext 2098; Fax: 613/563-0815; Email: cta@irdc.ca

John G. Bene Fellowship: Community Forestry, Trees & People
Contributes to the expenses of Canadian graduate students undertaking field research in social forestry in a developing country
Applicants must be Canadian citizens or hold permanent residency status; be registered in a Canadian university at the master's or doctoral level; have an academic background that combines forestry or agroforestry with social sciences. Applicants from interdisciplinary programs (e.g. environmental studies) may also be eligible, provided their programs contain the specified elements
$15,000 per year - Centre Training & Awards Unit, 613/236-6163 ext. 2098; Fax: 613/563-0815; Emails cta@irdc.ca

Newfoundland & Labrador Department of Environment & Conservation
Confederation Bldg., West Block, 4th Fl., PO Box 8700, St. John's NL A1B 4J6
709/729-2664; Fax:709/729-6639
Email: info@gov.nl.ca; URL:www.env.gov.nl.ca/env/

The Newfoundland & Labrador Environmental Awards Program
Established in partnership with the Newfoundland & Labrador Women's Institutes Multi-Materials Stewardship Board & the Dept. of Environment to create public awareness for the proactive environmental actions being taken by Newfoundlanders & Labradorians; the object is to demonstrate the contributions people are making to create a healthier environment & through their efforts, encourage others to do the same; awards are given in seven categories: individual, citizen's group or organization, educator, youth, school, business, & municipal - Newfoundland & Labrador Women's Institutes, Executive Director, Sylvia Manning, 709/753-8780; email nlwi@nfld.com

Recycling Council of Ontario / Conseil du recyclage de l'Ontario
#407 - 215 Spadina Av., Toronto ON M5T 2C7
416/657-2797; Fax:416/960-8053
Email:rco@rco.on.ca; URL:www.rco.on.ca

Ontario Waste Minimization Awards
A series of awards for outstanding achievement in recycling: includes 3Rs initiatives in commercial, industrial & institutional settings; Outstanding Municipal, Non-profit Organization, Recycling Program Operator; Outstanding School Program, & Media Contribution Award - Tracy Sakamoto

The Royal Society of Canada / La Société royale du Canada
170 Waller St., Ottawa ON K1N 9B9
613/991-6990; Fax:613/991-6996
Email:info@rsc.ca; URL:www.rsc.ca

Miroslaw Romanowski Medal
Established in 1994; awarded every year in recognition of significant contributions to the resolution of scientific aspects of environmental problems or for important improvements to the quality of an eco-system in all aspects, terrestrial, atmospheric & aqueous brought about by scientific means.
$3,000 & a medal - Geneviève Gouin, Awards Coordinator, 613/991-5760

HEALTH & MEDICAL

Canadian Association of Medical Radiation Technologists / Association canadienne des technologues en radiation médicale
#500, 1095 Carling Ave., Ottawa ON K1Y 4P6
613/234-0012; Fax:613/234-1097; Toll Free:1-800-463-9729
Email:lgoulet@camrt.ca; URL:www.camrt.ca

CAMRT Awards
Administers awards for students & registered technologists including: Dr. M. Mallett Student Award, Dr. Petrie Memorial Award, George Reason Memorial Cup, E.I. Hood Award, CAMRT Student Achievement Award, Philips Rose Bowl, PACS Technology Award

Canadian Association on Gerontology / Association canadienne de gérontologie
#106 - 222 College St., Toronto ON M5T 3J1
416/978-7977; Fax:416/978-4771
Email:contact@cagacg.ca; URL:www.cagacg.ca

CAG Award for Contribution to Gerontology
To recognize an individual who has recently made an outstanding contribution to the field of aging
Certificate

Canadian Federation for Sexual Health / Fédération canadienne pour la santé sexuelle
#430, One Nicholas St., Ottawa ON K1N 7B7
613/241-4474; Fax:613/241-7550; Toll Free:1-888-270-7444
Email:admin@cfsh.ca; URL:www.cfsh.ca

John & Lois Lamont Scholarship
Established 2004; awarded to a full-time graduate student in the field of sexual & reproductive health
$2,600

Phyllis P. Harris Scholarship
Endowed in the memory of Phyllis P. Harris, who for over thirty years was an inspiring presence in the world of family planning. This scholarship is awarded to a volunteer or individual currently enrolled in undergraduate studies in the general field of human sexuality, family planning or population including: biology, education, history, medicine, political science, psychology.
$2,600

Canadian Institutes of Health Research
160 Elgin St., 9th Floor; Address Locator 4809A,
Ottawa ON K1A 0W9
613/941-2672; Fax:613/954-1800; Toll Free:1-888-603-4178
Email:info@cihr-irsc.gc.ca; URL:www.cihr-irsc.gc.ca

Michael Smith Prize in Health Research
A medal plus $50,000 research grant awarded annually to an outstanding Canadian researcher who has demonstrated innovation, creativity & dedication to health research

Canadian Nurses Association / Association des infirmières et infirmiers du Canada
50 Driveway, Ottawa ON K2P 1E2
613/237-2133; Fax:613/237-3520; Toll Free:1-800-361-8404
Email:info@cna-aiic.ca; URL:www.cna-aiic.ca

Jeanne Mance Awards
Established in 1971, this award is named after one of Canada's most inspirational nurses. Awarded every other year, Nurses nominated for this have have made significant and innovative contributions to the health of Canadians.

Canadian Orthopaedic Foundation / Fondation orthopédique du Canada

PO Box 7029, Innisfil ON L9S 1A8
416/410-2341; Toll Free:1-800-461-3639
Email:mailbox@canorth.org; URL:www.canorth.org

I. Edouard Samson Award
Medal & $15,000 awarded for outstanding orthopaedic research by a young investigator; paper presented at the annual meeting of the Canadian Orthopaedic Research Society

Canadian Society for Medical Laboratory Science / Société canadienne de science de laboratoire médical

PO Box 2830, Stn LCD 1, Hamilton ON L8N 3N8
905/528-8642; Fax:905/528-4968; Toll Free:1-800-263-8277
Email:michellee@csmls.org; URL:www.csmls.org

CSMLS Student Scholarship Program
Awarded to the best students who are enrolled in general medical laboratory technology, cytotechnology, or cytogenetics studies
Five scholarships of $500 each

E.V. Booth Scholarship Award
Awarded to certified medical laboratory technologists who are enrolled in studies leading to a degree in medical laboratory science
Two awards of $500

Canadian Veterinary Medical Association / Association canadienne des médecins vétérinaires

339 Booth St., Ottawa ON K1R 7K1
613/236-1162; Fax:613/236-9681; Toll Free:1-800-567-2862
Email:admin@cvma-acmv.org;
URL:www.canadianveterinarians.net;
www.veterinairesaucanada.net

The CVMA Humane Award
Established 1986 to encourage care & well-being of animals; awarded to an individual (veterinarian or non-veterinarian) whose work is judged to have contributed significantly to the welfare & well-being of animals; $1,000 & a plaque awarded

The Schering Veterinary Award
Established 1985 to enhance progress in large animal medicine & surgery; award made to a veterinarian whose work in large animal practice, clinical research or basic sciences is judged to have contributed significantly to the advancement of large animal medicine, surgery & theriogenology, including herd health management; $1,000 & a plaque awarded

The Small Animal Practitioner Award
Established 1987 to encourage progress in the field of small animal medicine & surgery; awarded to a veterinarian whose work in small animal practice, clinical research or basic sciences is judged to have contributed significantly to the advancement of small animal medicine, surgery, or the management of small animal practice, including the advancement of the public's knowledge of the responsibilities of pet ownership; $1,000 & a plaque awarded

Catholic Health Association of Canada / Association catholique canadienne de la santé

1247 Kilborn Pl., Ottawa ON K1H 6K9
613/731-7148; Fax:613/731-7797
Email:info@chac.ca; URL:www.chac.ca

Performance Citation Award
Established 1981; awarded annually to an individual who makes an outstanding contribution to health care in a Christian context, who exhibits exemplary leadership of a national effort at building the Christian community & unselfish dedication to others

College of Family Physicians of Canada / Collège des médecins de famille du Canada

2630 Skymark Ave., Mississauga ON L4W 5A4
905/629-0900; Fax:905/629-0893; Toll Free: 800/387-6197
Email:info@cfpc.ca; URL:www.cfpc.ca

D.I. Rice Merit Award
Awarded annually to a renowned leader in family medicine to allow travel for a period of approximately one month in order to engage in educational activities
$10,000 plus travel expenses

Family Physician of the Year Award
Sponsored by Janseen Ortho; awarded to physicians who have been in family practice for a minimum of 15 years & members of the college for at least 10 years, & who have made outstanding contributions to family medicine, to their communities & to the college

Family Medicine Researcher of the Year Award
Sponsored by the CFPC'S Research & Education Foundation, this award recognizes a Family Medicine researcher who has been a pivotal force in the definition, development and dissemination of concepts central to the discipline of family medicine.

Easter Seals Canada / Timbres de Pâques Canada

#208, 90 Eglinton Ave. East, Toronto ON M4P 2Y3
416/932-8382; Fax:416/932-9844
Email:info@easterseals.ca; URL:www.easterseals.ca

The Easter Seals Canada Leadership Award
Established in 1959 as the Timmy Award, is intended to celebrate & recognize outstanding leadership & dedication by a volunteer to children with disabilities, through involvement with Easter Seals

Epilepsy Canada / Épilepsie Canada

#336, 2255B Queen St. East, Toronto ON M4E 1G3
Toll Free:1-877-734-0873
Email:epilepsy@epilepsy.ca; URL:www.epilepsy.ca

Epilepsy Canada Research Fellowships
To develop expertise in clinical or basic epilepsy research & to enhance the quality of care for epilepsy patients in Canada; awarded annually to a Ph.D. or M.D. for clinical research at a Canadian institution; designed as a training program & not intended for those holding faculty appointments

The Royal College of Physicians & Surgeons of Canada / Le Collège royal des médecins et chirurgiens du Canada

774 Echo Dr., Ottawa ON K1S 5N8
613/730-8177; Fax:613/730-8830; Toll Free:1-800-668-3740
Email:infos@rcpsc.edu; URL:medical.org
The Office of Fellowship Affairs administers an annual competition for five Fellowship grants, three Awards that recognize original research, and three faculty development projects.

The Royal Society of Canada / La Société royale du Canada

170 Waller St., Ottawa ON K1N 9B9
613/991-6990; Fax:613/991-6996
Email:info@rsc.ca; URL:www.rsc.ca

Jason A. Hannah Medal
Established 1976; awarded annually for an important publication in the history of medicine
$1,500 & a bronze medal

The McLaughlin Medal
Awarded annually for important research of sustained excellence in any branch of medical science
$2,500 & a medal

JOURNALISM

Atlantic Journalism Awards

46 Swanton Dr., Dartmouth NS B3W 2C5
902/425-2727; Fax:902/462-1892
Email:office@ajas.ca; URL:ajas.ca

Atlantic Journalism Awards
Originally a program of the University of King's College School of Journalism established in 1981, is now a non-profit organization to recognize excellence & achievement in work by Atlantic Canadian journalists; covers work in English or French; 23 award categories featuring work published or broadcast in the news media of Atlantic Canada.
Winners in individual categories will receive framed certificate presented at the Awards dinner.

Journalistic Achievement Award
An award which recognizes outstanding work in Atlantic Canada by an individual journalist, team of journalists, or a media organization, presented at the Awards dinner

Canadian Association of Journalists / L'Association canadienne des journalistes

c/o Algonquin College, #B224, 1385 Woodroffe Ave.,
Ottawa ON K2G 1V8
613/526-8061; Fax:613/521-3904
Email:canadianjour@magma.ca; URL:www.caj.ca

The CAJ Awards
Awards presented for the top investigative report published or broadcast in the following media: Newspaper/Newswire (open category), Newspaper (circulation under 25,000), Magazine, TV, Radio, Faith & Spirituality, Photojournalism, Computer assisting reporting & the Don McGillivray award for Best Investigative Report
$1,000 - John Dickins

Canadian Business Press / La Presse spécialisée du Canada

#346, 4195 Dundas St. West, Toronto ON M8X 1Y4
416/239-1022; Fax:416/239-1076
Email:admin@cbp.ca; URL:www.cbp.ca

Kenneth R. Wilson Awards
Recognize excellence in writing & graphic design (17 categories) in specialized business/professional publications; open to all business publications, regardless of CBP membership, that are published in English &/or French; all awards, except the Harvey Southam Editorial Career Award, require an entry fee - krwawards@cbp.ca

Canadian Newspaper Association / Association canadienne des journaux

#200, 890 Yonge St., Toronto ON M4W 3P4
416/923-3567; Fax:416/923-7206
Email:info@cna-acj.ca; URL:www.cna-acj.ca

National Newspaper Awards/Concours canadien de journalisme
Awards are presented annually in early spring in 16 categories: Spot News Reporting, Enterprise Reporting, Special Project, Layout & Design, Critical Writing, Sports Writing, Feature Writing, Cartooning, Columns, Business Reporting, International Reporting, Spot News Photography, Feature Photography, Sports Photography, Editorial Writing, Local Reporting.
Eligible are those employed by or freelance for daily newspapers or wire services in French or English; awards are governed by an independent board of governors consisting of newspaper & public representatives.
Winners receive $2,500 plus certificates; two runners-up in each category receive citations of merit & $250

Canadian Science Writers' Association / Association canadienne des rédacteurs scientifiques

PO Box 75, Stn A, Toronto ON M5W 1A2
Toll Free:1-800-796-8595
Email:office@sciencewriters.ca; URL:www.sciencewriters.ca

Canadian Forest Service-Ontario Journalism Award
Open to print journalists who have published an article concerning some aspect of forestry in Ontario during the previous calendar year in either a newspaper or magazine published in Ontario

Science in Society Journalism Awards
Open to Canadian journalists in all media for work appearing in the previous calendar year; 14 categories include newspapers, magazines, trade publications, radio, television, children's books & general books; awards total $14,000

L'Oreal Excellence In Science Journalism Award

Heritage Canada Foundation / Fondation Héritage Canada

5 Blackburn Ave., Ottawa ON K1N 8A2
613/237-1066; Fax:613/237-5987
Email:heritagecanada@heritagecanada.org;
URL:www.heritagecanada.org

The Heritage Canada Journalism Prize
Awarded annually to a journalist, working in either the print or electronic media, whose coverage of heritage issues is judged to be outstanding

National Magazine Awards Foundation / Fondation nationale des prix du magazine canadien

#700, 425 Adelaide St. West, Toronto ON M5V 3C1
416/828-9011; Fax:416/504-0437
Email:staff@magazine-awards.com; URL:www.magazine-awards.com

National Magazine Awards
Awards are presented annually in 26 categories including Personal Journalism, Arts & Entertainment, Humour, Business, Science, Health & Medicine, Sports & Recreation, Fiction, Poetry, Travel, Magazine Illustration, Photojournalism, Art Direction, Magazine Covers, & Photography; all above awards go to individual magazine writers, photographers, illustrators, or art directors; Magazine of the Year recognizes continual overall excellence, The President's Medal is awarded to an article from the text categories & offers a prize of $3,000; The Foundation Award for Outstanding Achievement was introduced in 1990 & recognizes an individual's innovation & creativity through career-long contributions to the magazine industry
Awards are gold or silver scrolls with $1,500 & $500 cash prizes respectively; President's Medal $3,000

Ontario Newspaper Awards
c/o The Record, 160 King St. East, Kitchener ON N2G 4E5
519/894-2231
Email:lwilson@therecord.com
Celebrated annually and available in a variety of journalism categories such as: Novice Reporting; Sports Writing; Sports Photography, Humour Writing.

Société Saint-Jean-Baptiste de Montréal
82, rue Sherbrooke Ouest, Montréal QC H2X 1X3
514/843-8851; Fax:514/844-6369
Email:mbeaulieu@ssjb.com; URL:www.ssjb.com

Prix Olivar-Asselin
Established 1955; $1,500 & a medal awarded annually to a French Canadian in recognition of outstanding achievement in journalism in serving the higher interests of the French Canadian people

Western Magazine Awards Foundation
1506 East 11th Ave., Garden Unit, Vancouver BC V5N 1Y7
604/669-3717;
URL:www.westernmagazineawards.com

The Western Magazine Awards
Editorial excellence in western Canadian magazine writing, photography, illustration & art direction

LEGAL, GOVERNMENTAL, PUBLIC ADMINISTRATION

Alberta Solicitor General and Public Security
Communications, 10365 - 97 St., 10th Fl., Edmonton AB T5J 3W7
780/427-3441; Fax:780/427-1903
URL:www.solgen.gov.ab.ca/crime_prev/awards.aspx

Crime Prevention Awards
Awards highlight the activities & accomplishments of special Albertans who prove that preventing crime is everyone's responsibility; awards are presented to an individual, for youth leadership, business, community program or organization & police member for efforts beyond regular duties

Canadian Society of Association Executives / Société canadienne des directeurs d'association
#1100, 10 King St. East, Toronto ON M5C 1C3
416/363-3555; Fax:416/363-3630; Toll Free:1-800-461-3608
Email:csae@csae.com; URL:www.csae.com

Pinnacle Award
Recognizes the association executive who has demonstrated exceptional & outstanding leadership qualities within their organization, has contributed to other voluntary organizations & the community at large, to CSAE at local & national levels

Institute of Public Administration of Canada / Institut d'administration publique du Canada
#401, 1075 Bay St., Toronto ON M5S 2B1
416/924-8787; Fax:416/924-4992
URL:www.ipac.ca

IPAC Award for Innovative Management
Awarded in recognition of outstanding organizational achievement in the public sector

Vanier Medal
A gold medal is awarded annually as a mark of distinction & exceptional achievement to a person who has shown outstanding leadership in public administration in Canada

Justice Canada
Legal Studies for Aboriginal People Program, Department of Justice Canada, Programs Branch, 284 Wellington St., 6th Fl., Ottawa ON K1A 0H8
613/941-0388; Fax:613/941-2269; Toll Free:1-888-606-5111
Email:LSAP@justice.gc.ca; URL:canada.justice.gc.ca/en/ps/pb/prog/legal_sap.html

Legal Studies for Aboriginal People Program
A scholarship program to encourage Métis & Non-Status Indians to enter the legal profession by providing financial assistance through a pre-law orientation course & an annual scholarship program for a maximum of 3 years
Open to Aboriginal People (Métis & Non-Status Indians)

The Professional Institute of the Public Service of Canada / Institut professionnel de la fonction publique du Canada
250 Tremblay Rd., Ottawa ON K1G 3J8
613/228-6310; Fax:613/228-9048; Toll Free:1-800-267-0446
URL:www.pipsc.ca

Gold Medal Awards
Established 1937; the gold medals are presented biennially. Those eligible are scientific, professional, or technical workers or groups of workers employed by the federal, provincial, or municipal government services of Canada who have made a contribution of outstanding importance to national or world well-being in either pure or applied science or in some field outside pure or applied science

LITERARY ARTS, BOOKS & LIBRARIES

Book Publishers Association of Alberta
10523 - 100 Ave., Edmonton AB T5J 0A8
780/424-5060; Fax:780/424-7943
Email:info@planet.eon.net; URL:www.bookpublishers.ab.ca

Alberta Book Awards
To recognize outstanding achievements in Alberta publishing; nine awards are given - Alberta Publisher of the Year, Alberta Trade Book of the Year, Alberta Book Design Award, Alberta Book Cover Design Award, Alberta Educational Book of the Year, Alberta Childrens' Book of the Year, Alberta Book Illustration Award, Alberta Scholarly Book, Alberta Emerging Publisher of the Year.
Stone carvings by Brian Clark are presented & kept by the winner in the award year & exchanged for plaques the following year.

Lois Hole Award for Editorial Excellence
Established in honour of Lois Hole's dedication to books, libraries, literacy and respect for editors.

Alberta Book Publishing Achievement Award
Established to recognize long-standing contributions made to Alberta book publishing.

British Columbia Historical Federation
PO Box 5254, Stn B, Victoria BC V8R 6N4
604/277-2627; Fax:604/277-2657
Email:info@bchistory.ca; URL:www.bchistory.ca
W. Kaye Lamb Essay Scholarships
Awarded for essays written by students at BC colleges or universities on a topic related to BC history

Writing Awards
Established 1983; Lieutenant-Governor's Medal for Historical Writing, three Certificates of Merit, & cash awards given annually to authors of best books on any facet of BC history

The Canada Council for the Arts / Conseil des Arts du Canada
350 Albert St., PO Box 1047, Ottawa ON K1P 5V8
613/566-4414; Fax:613/566-4390; Toll Free:1-800-263-5588
Email:info@canadacouncil.ca; URL:www.canadacouncil.ca

Canada-Japan Literary Awards
Two awards valued at $10,000 awarded every two years in recognition of literary excellence by Canadian writers writing about Japan, Japanese themes or themes that promote mutual understanding between Japan & Canada, or by Canadian translators of such books from Japanese into English or French

CBC Literary Awards
A joint presentation of CBC, enRoute magazine & the Canada Council for the Arts; two prizes of $6,000 & $4,000 given in each of three categories in English & French: poetry, travel literature & short fiction. CBC selects the jury & administers the adjudication process, enRoute publishes the winning entries & the Canada Council provides the cash prizes to the six winners in French & English

The Governor General's Literary Awards
$15,000 each awarded annually to the best English-language & best French-language work in each of the following categories: children's literature (text & illustration), drama, fiction, poetry, literary non-fiction, & translation.
Books must be by Canadian authors, illustrators & translators, published in Canada or abroad. In the case of translation, the original work must also be a Canadian-authored title. Peer assessment committees select the winning titles from the books formally nominated by publishers.

Canadian Association for School Libraries
c/o Canadian Library Association, 328 Frank St., Ottawa ON K2P 0X8
613/232-9625; Fax:613/563-9895
URL:www.cla.ca/casl.html

The Angela Thacker Memorial Award
Established in memory of Angela Thacker, teacher-librarian, library coordinator, this award honours teacher-librarians who have made contributions to the profession through publications, productions or professional development activities that deal with topics relevant to teacher-librarianship and/or information literacy.

Margaret B. Scott Award of Merit
Awarded annually to recognize outstanding achievement in school librarianship in Canada

National Book Service Teacher-Librarian of the Year Award
To honour a school-based teacher-librarian who has made an outstanding contribution to school librarianship by planning & implementing an exemplary school library program based on a collaborative model; award is sponsored by National Book Service

Canadian Association of Children's Librarians
c/o Canadian Library Association, 328 Frank St., Ottawa ON K2P 0X8
613/232-9625; Fax:613/563-9895
Email:info@cla.ca; URL:www.cla.ca/divisions/capl/cacl.htm

Amelia Frances Howard-Gibbon Illustrators Medal
Established 1971; a silver medal awarded annually for outstanding illustrations in a children's book published in Canada; the illustrator must be a Canadian or a Canadian resident - Brenda Shield

Book of the Year for Children Medal
A silver medal awarded annually for the outstanding children's book published during the calendar year; book must have been written by a Canadian or a resident of Canada - Brenda Shield

Canadian Association of College & University Libraries
c/o Canadian Library Association, 328 Frank St., Ottawa ON K2P 0X8
613/232-9625; Fax:613/563-9895
Email:info@cla.ca; URL:www.cla.ca/divisions/cacul/ctcl.htm

Innovation Achievement Award
To recognize academic libraries which, through innovation in ongoing programs/services or in a special event/project, have contributed to academic librarianship & library development; a framed acknowledgement & a $1,500 gift certificate is offered for the vendor of the institution's choice

Miles Blackwell Award for Outstanding Academic Librarian
Awarded to a librarian who has made a notable contribution to the field of academic librarianship

Canadian Association of Public Libraries
c/o Canadian Library Association, 328 Frank St., Ottawa ON K2P 0X8
613/232-9625; Fax:613/563-9895
Email:info@cla.ca; URL:www.cla.ca/divisions/capl/

CAPL/Brodart Outstanding Public Library Service Award
The Canadian Association of Public Libraries, in partnership with Brodart, is please to offer this prestigious award offered annually for outstanding service in the field of Canadian public librarianship.

Canadian Authors Association
320 South Shores Rd., PO Box 419, Campbellford ON K0L 1L0
705/653-0323; Fax:705/653-0593; Toll Free:1-866-216-6222
Email:admin@canauthors.org; URL:www.canauthors.org

CAA Award for Fiction
$2,500 & a silver medal

CAA Carol Bolt Award
$1,000 & a silver medal

CAA Jack Chalmers Poetry Award
$1,000 & a silver medal

Lela Common Award for Canadian History
$2,500 & a silver medal

The Canadian Children's Book Centre
#101, 40 Orchard View Blvd., Toronto ON M4R 1B9
416/975-0010; Fax:416/975-8970
Email:info@bookcentre.ca; URL:www.bookcentre.ca

The Geoffrey Bilson Award for Historical Fiction
Rewards excellence in outstanding work of historical fiction for young people by a Canadian author, published in previous calendar year; judges are: a writer, bookseller, children's books specialist, historian, librarian
$1,000

The Norma Fleck Award for Non-Fiction
Rewards excellence in outstanding work of non-fiction for young people by a Canadian author, published in previous calendar year; jury members include a teacher, a librarian, a reviewer & a bookseller
$10,000

Canadian Historical Association / Société historique du Canada
395 Wellington St., Ottawa ON K1A 0N3
613/233-7885; Fax:613/567-3110
Email:cha-shc@lac-bac.gc.ca; URL:www.cha-shc.ca
10 Awards available for outstanding nonfiction publications in the field of history.
Prizes also available for High School and University levels as well as Research Work and Popular Work.

Canadian Library Association
328 Frank St., Ottawa ON K2P 0X8
613/232-9625; Fax:613/563-9895
Email:info@cla.ca; URL:www.cla.ca

Dafoe Scholarship
$3,000 awarded annually to a student entering an accredited Canadian library school

H.W. Wilson Scholarship
$2,500 presented annually to a student entering an accredited Canadian library school

World Book Scholarship in Library Science & Information Studies
$2,500 scholarship given annually to be used for a program of study or series of courses either leading to a further library degree or related library work in which the candidate is currently engaged

Young Adult Canadian Book Award
Presented to recognize the best English-language fiction for young adults by a Canadian author

Canadian Library Trustees Association
c/o Canadian Library Association, 328 Frank St., Ottawa ON K2P 0X8
613/232-9625; Fax:613/563-9895
Email:info@cla.ca; URL:www.cla.ca/divisions/clta/clta.htm

CLTA/Stan Heath Achievement in Literacy Award
Through this award, CLTA endorses the initiatives of the public library systems, which have structured literacy programs as a component of library services to the community

CLTA Merit Award for Distinguished Service as a Public Library Trustee
The CLTA Merit Award is presented annually to a library trustee who has demonstrated outstanding leadership in the advancement of trusteeship and public library service in Canada.

CBC Literary Awards/Prix Littéraires Radio-Canada
CBC Radio, PO Box 6000, Montréal QC H3C 3A8
Toll Free:1-877-888-6788
URL:www.radio-canada.ca/prixlitteraires/

CBC Literary Awards/Prix Littéraires Radio-Canada
The only literary competition that celebrates original, unpublished works, in Canada's two official languages. Prizes are available in three categories: short story, poetry and creative nonfiction. Winning entries are published in Air Canada's enRoute magazine.

Corporation des bibliothécaires professionnels du Québec / Corporation of Professional Librarians of Québec
#103, 353, rue St. Nicolas, Montréal QC H2Y 2P1
514/845-3327; Fax:514/845-1618
Email:info@cbpq.qc.ca; URL:www.cbpq.qc.ca

Annuel de la CBPQ - Bibliothécaire de l'année
Stimuler et reconnaître l'excellence parmi les membres; attirer l'attention des médias sur les récipiendaires de cette distinction honorifique et sur la nature des réalisations primées; orienter des perceptions; le prix comporte les volets suivants: distinction honorifique, remise d'une épinglette en or, publicité entourant l'événement

The Crime Writers of Canada
3007 Kingston Rd., PO Box 113, Toronto ON M1M 1P1
416/597-9938
Email:info@crimewriterscanada.com;
URL:www.crimewriterscanada.com

The Arthur Ellis Awards
Established 1984; awarded annually in the following categories: best crime novel (by a previously published novelist), best crime non-fiction, best first crime novel (by a previously unpublished novelist), best crime short story, best juvenile crime book, & best crime writing in French

Donner Canadian Foundation
c/o Meisner Publicity & Promotion, 394A King St. East, Toronto ON M5A 1K9
416/368-8253; 368-3763; Fax:416/363-1448
Email:meisnerpublicity@sympatico.ca;
URL:www.donnerbookprize.com

The Donner Prize
Award of $35,000 for the best book on Canadian public policy; five runners-up prizes of $5,000 each

Fondation Émile-Nelligan
261, rue Bloomfield, Outremont QC H2V 3R6
514/278-4657; Fax:514/271-6369
Email:info@fondation-nelligan.org;
URL:www.fondation-nelligan.org

Prix Émile-Nelligan
Prix annuel. Il s'agit d'un prix de poésie décerné à un poète de moins de 35 ans, pour un recueil publié au cours de l'année
7 500$ et une médaille en bronze frappée à l'effigie d'Émile Nelligan

Prix Gilles-Corbeil
Prix triennal en littérature (poésie, roman, nouvelles, récits, théâtre ou essai littéraire). Décerné à un écrivain citoyen du Canada ou des États-Unis, pour une oeuvre écrite en langue française
100 000$

Fondation Les Forges
1497, rue Laviolette, CP 335, Trois-Rivières QC G9A 5G4
819/379-9813; Fax:819/376-0774
Email:info@fiptr.com; URL:www.fiptr.com

Grand Prix du Festival International de la Poésie
Le Festival International de la Poésie remet une bourse de 5 000 $ au lauréat lors de l'ouverture officielle du festival; le candidat doit: être de citoyenneté canadienne et avoir déjà publié trois ouvrages de poésie chez un éditeur reconnu

Prix Félix-Antoine-Savard de poésie
Décerné annuellement lors des cérémonies d'ouverture du Festival International de la Poésie; vise à honorer, tout en les respectant, la mémoire, l'esprit et l'oeuvre poétique de cet écrivain; une bourse de 250$ y est rattachée et le contenant de 100 feuilles de papier Saint-Gilles sont remis à St-Joseph-de-la-Rive, le jour de l'Action de Grâce
Prix Félix-Leclerc de poésie
Créé en octobre 1997, à l'occasion du 10e anniversaire de la mort du poète; décerné tous les 2 ans lors des cérémonies d'ouverture du Festival International de la Poésie; prix de 1000$
Prix Piché de poésie
Les bourses sont offertes par le Festival International de la Poésie; 1er prix, 2 000 $, 2e prix, 500 $; le candidat doit être de citoyenneté canadienne et n'avoir jamais publié d'ouvrage de poésie chez un éditeur reconnu
The Griffin Trust for Excellence in Poetry
6610 Edwards Blvd., Mississauga ON L5T 2V6
905/565-5993
Email:info@griffinpoetryprize.com;
URL:www.griffinpoetryprize.com/home.php
The Griffin Prize
Established in 2000, two prizes of $50,000 each awarded annually for collections of poetry published in English during the preceding year; one will go to a living Canadian poet; the other to a living poet or translator from any other country which may include Canada
International Board on Books for Young People - Canadian Section / Union internationale pour les livres de jeunesse
c/o Canadian Children's Book Centre, #101, 40 Orchard View Blvd., Toronto ON M4R 1B9
416/975-0010; Fax:416/975-8970
Email:info@ibby-canada.org; URL:www.ibby-canada.org
Claude Aubry Award
Awarded biennially for distinguished contributions to Canadian children's literature by a librarian, teacher, author, illustrator, publisher, bookseller, or editor
$1,000
Elizabeth Mrazik-Cleaver Picture Book Award
Awarded for distinguished Canadian picture book illustration; submissions to Children's Literature Service, National Library of Canada, 395 Wellington St., Ottawa, ON K1A 0N4
$1,000
Frances E. Russell Award
Awarded to initiate & encourage research in children's literature in Canada
$1,000
The League of Canadian Poets
#608, 920 Yonge St., Toronto ON M4W 3C7
416/504-1657; Fax:416/504-0096
Email:info@poets.ca; URL:www.poets.ca
Gerald Lampert Memorial Award
Established 1979; awarded annually for excellence in a first book of poetry, written by a Canadian citizen or landed immigrant, & published in the preceding year
$1,000
Pat Lowther Memorial Award
$1,000 awarded annually for excellence in a book of poetry, written by a Canadian female citizen or landed immigrant, & published in the preceding year
The Lionel Gelber Prize
c/o Prize Administrator, Munk Centre for International Studies, University of Toronto, 1 Devonshire Pl., Toronto ON M5S 3K7
416/946-8901; Fax:416/946-9815
Email:gelberprize.munk@utoronto.ca;
URL:www.utoronto.ca/mcis/gelber
The Lionel Gelber Prize
This $15,000 prize is the largest of its kind in the world; a legacy of Lionel Gelber, international writer who died in 1989 & who was much acclaimed for his service to Canada; the prize is "designed to stimulate authors of any nationality who write about international relations, & to encourage the audience for these books to grow"
Books published in English or English translation, must be copyrighted in the year in which the prize is awarded; books must be published or distributed in Canada; submissions by publishers only
Literary Translators' Association of Canada / Association des traducteurs et traductrices littéraires du Canada
Concordia University LB 631, 1455, boul de Maisonneuve ouest, Montréal QC H3G 1M8
514/848-2424, ext. 8702; Fax:514/848-4514
Email:info@attlc-ltac.org; URL:www.attlc-ltac.org
Glassco Translation Prize
Awarded annually for a translator's first work in book-length literary translation into French or English, published in Canada during the previous calendar year
$1,000 & one year's membership in the association

Manitoba Writers' Guild Inc.
#206, 100 Arthur St., Winnipeg MB R3B 1H3
204/942-6134; Fax:204/942-5754; Toll Free:1-888-637-5802
Email:info@mbwriter.mb.ca; URL:www.mbwriter.mb.ca

Alexander Kennedy Isbister Award for Non-Fiction
Presented to the Manitoba writer whose book is judged the best book of adult non-fiction written in English
$3,500

Carol Shields City of Winnipeg Award
To honour books that evoke the special caracter of & contribute to the appreciation & understanding of the City of Winnipeg
$5,000

Eileen McTavish Sykes Award for Best First Book
Awarded annually to a Manitoba author whose first professionally published book is deemed the best written
Must have been written in the previous year
$1,500

John Hirsch Award for Most Promising Manitoba Writer
Awarded annually to the most promising Manitoba writer working in poetry, fiction, creative non-fiction or drama
$2,500

Le Prix littéraire Rue des Chambeault
Biennial award presented to the author whose published book or play is judged to be the best French language work by a Manitoba author
$3,500

Manitoba Book Design of the Year Awards
For the best overall design in Manitoba book publishing in two categories: book design & best illustration

Margaret Laurence Award for Fiction
Presented to the Manitoba writer whose book is judged the best book of adult fiction written in English
$3,500

Mary Scorer Award for Best Book by a Manitoba Publisher
Awarded to the best book published by a Manitoba publisher & written for the trade, bookstore, educational, academic or scholarly market
$1,000

McNally Robinson Book for Young People Awards
Awarded annually to the writer whose young person's book is judged the best written by a Manitoba author; two categories: children's & young adult
$2,500

McNally Robinson Book of the Year
To the Manitoba author judged to have written the best book in the calendar year
$5,000

McClelland & Stewart
c/o McClelland & Stewart Ltd., #900 - 481 University Ave., Toronto ON M5G 2E9
416/598-1114; Fax:416/598-7764
Email:journeyprize@mcclelland.com;
URL:www.mcclelland.com/jpa

The Writers' Trust of Canada/McClelland & Stewart Journey Prize
$10,000 awarded annually to a new & developing writer of distinction for a short story published in a Canadian literary journal. The shortlisted stories are selected from journal submissions & published annually by McClelland & Stewart as The Journey Prize Anthology. M&S presents its own award of $2,000 to the literary journal that originally published the winning story. Only submissions from Canadian literary journals are accepted. Stories must have had original publication in the nominating journal during the previous year.

The Municipal Chapter of Toronto IODE
#205, 40 St. Clair Ave. East, Toronto ON M4T 1M9
Phone:416/925-5078; Fax:416/925-5127
Email:iodetoronto@bellnet.ca

IODE Book Award
Established in 1975; an inscribed scroll & not less than $1,000 awarded annually to the author or illustrator of the best children's book written or illustrated by a Canadian resident in Toronto or surrounding area & published by a Canadian publisher within the preceding 12 months

The National Chapter of Canada IODE
#254, 40 Orchard View Blvd., Toronto ON M4R 1B9
416/487-4416; Fax:416/487-4417; Toll Free:1-866-827-7428
Email:iodecanada@bellnet.ca

The National Chapter of Canada IODE Violet Downey Book Award
Awarded annually for the best English-language book, containing at least 500 words of text, preferably with Canadian content, in any category suitable for children aged 13 & under
$3,000

Nova Scotia Library Association
c/o Nova Scotia Provincial Library, 3770 Kempt Rd., Halifax NS B3K 4X8
902/742-2486; Fax:902/742-6920
Email:mlandry@nsme.library.ns.ca; URL:www.nsla.ns.ca

Ann Connor Brimer Award
Awarded to the author of fiction or non-fiction books published in Canada currently in print & intended for children up to the age of 15; writer must be residing in Atlantic Canada
$1,000 - Heather Mackenzie, Halifax Regional Library, 5381 Spring Garden Rd., Halifax NS B3J 1E9; Email: mahm1@nsh.library.ns.ca

Norman Horrocks Award for Library Leadership
Honours leadership in the Nova Scotia Library community & is awarded for distinguished contributions to the promotion & development of library service in Nova Scotia - Trudy Amirault, Western Counties Regional Library, 405 Main St., Yarmouth NS B5A 1G3, Email: tamiraul@nsy.library.ns.ca

Ontario Arts Council / Conseil des arts de l'Ontario
151 Bloor St. West, 5th Fl., Toronto ON M5S 1T6
416/961-1660; Fax:416/961-7796; Toll Free:1-800-387-0058
Email:info@arts.on.ca; URL:www.arts.on.ca

Ruth Schwartz Children's Book Award
Two awards presented annually; $3,000 for best picture book & $2,000 for best young adult/middle reader book; in conjunction with the Canadian Booksellers Association

Ontario Library Association
50 Wellington St. East, Suite 201, Toronto, ON M5E 1C8
416/363-3388; Fax: 416/941-9581
Email:info@accessola.com; URL: www.accessola.com

Blue Spruce™ Award Program
The Blue Spruce Award™ is a provincial primary reading program which brings recently published Canadian children's picture books to Ontario children ages 4 to 7 in kindergarten through to grade two. Award given out in May every year.

Silver Birch® Fiction, Non-Fiction And Express Award Program
The Silver Birch Award® is given by Grade 3, 4, 5 and 6 students in a spectacular ceremony held annually in May before fifteen hundred of their peers. The children choose winners in Fiction, Non-Fiction and Express when they cast their ballots on the province-wide Voting Day earlier in the same month. It is the most democratic and unbiased process possible when the children make their choice. The program is administered by the Ontario Library Association and run by teacher-librarians and teachers in schools and by children's librarians in public libraries. But the choice belongs to the children. And, in their tens of thousands, they know what they are doing.

Red Maple™ Award Program
The Red Maple Award™ reading program is offered for the enjoyment of students in Grades 7 and 8. The program, like the Association's Silver Birch Awards™ reading program, gives students who have read a minimum number of nominated titles the opportunity to vote with a large group of their peers for the nominated title that they feel should win the Red Maple Award™ each year.

White Pine™ Award Program
The White Pine Award™ reading program offers high school-aged teens at all grade levels the opportunity to read the best of Canada's recent young adult fiction titles. All of these 10 books for Young Adults on this list are accessible and will allow all readers to be successful participants/voters. As in all of the independent reading programs, a reader only needs to read 5 books out of a list of 10 to qualify to vote. Based on student voting across the province, the most popular book is then selected and author is honoured with the White Pine Award™.

The Evergreen® Award Program
The Evergreen Award™ is OLA's newest addition to the Forest of Reading®. It was introduced at Super Conference 2005 for adults of any age. It gives adult library patrons the opportunity to vote for a work of Canadian fiction or non-fiction that they have liked the most.

Ontario Media Development Corporation
c/o OMDC, North Tower, #501, 175 Bloor St. East, Toronto ON M4W 3R8
416/314-6858; Fax:416/314-6876
Email:mail@omdc.on.ca; URL:www.omdc.on.ca

Trillium Book Award for Poetry
Awarded in both English & French
$10,000

Trillium Book Award/Prix Trillium
Awarded annually to an Ontario author of a book of excellence; the winning book must have been published within the preceding 12 months; books in English or French in any genre are eligible; winner receives $12,000 & the publisher receives $2,500

PEI Council of the Arts
115 Richmond St., Charlottetown PE C1A 1A7
902/368-4410; Fax:902/368-4418; Toll Free:1-888-734-2784
Email:info@peiartscouncil.com; URL:www.peiartscouncil.com

Island Literary Awards
Established in 1987 in recognition of Island writers in six categories: Short Story, Poetry, Children's Literature, Feature Article, Creative Writing for Children, Playwriting; an additional award is made "for distinguished contribution to the literary arts"
$500, $200 & $100

Periodical Marketers of Canada
South Tower, #1007, 175 Bloor St. East, Toronto ON M4W 3R8
416/968-7311; Fax:416/968-6281

Canadian Letters Awards
Established 1996; recognizes an individual who has made an outstanding contribution to writing, publishing, teaching or literary administration; award consists of a statuette & a $5,000 donation to the charitable literary organization or educational institution of the winner's choice

Phoenix Community Works Foundation
316 Dupont St., Toronto ON M5R 1V9
416/964-7919; Fax:416/964-8516
Email:info@pcwf.ca; URL:www.pcwf.ca

The Chap-Book Award
Awarded for the best poetry chap-book in English, published in Canada; entries must be from 10-48 pages in length
$1,000

PriceWaterhouseCoopers
Royal Trust Tower, #3000, 77 King St. West,
Toronto ON M5K 1G8
416/869-1130; Fax:416/941-8345
URL:www.pwcglobal.com/ca/eng/about/events/nbba.html

National Business Book Award
Established 1985; annual prize of $20,000 awarded to author of book containing key material on business in Canada - Mary Ann Freedman

Prism International
Creative Writing Program, UBC, Buch. E462 - 1866 Main Mall, Vancouver BC V6T 1Z1
604/822-2514; Fax:604/822-3616
Email:prism@interchange.ubc.ca; URL:prism.arts.ubc.ca

Earle Birney Prize for Poetry
Awarded annually to an outstanding poetry contributor published in Prism International
$500

Literary Non-Fiction Contest
$1,500

Prism Short Fiction Contest
$3,000 in prizes for annual short fiction contest

Prix Aurora Awards
#501, 88 Bruce St., Kitchener ON N2B 1Y8
Email:prix.aurora.awards@gmail.com;
URL:www.sentex.net/~dmullin/aurora

Prix Aurora Awards
Awards presented annually for the best in Canadian Science Fiction & Fantasy; 10 categories: six professional awards (three English & three French), three fan awards & the artistic achievement award

Québec Ministère de la culture et des communications
225, Grande Allée est, Québec QC G1R 5G5
418/380-2300; Fax:418/080-2364
Email:DC@mcc.gouv.qc.ca; URL:www.mcc.gouv.qc.ca

Les Prix du Québec
Founded in 1977, these awards are given annually by the Government of Quebec to individuals for cultural and scientific achievements. There are six awards in the cultural field.

Québec Ministère des Relations internationales
Édifice Hector-Fabre, 525, boul René-Lévesque est,
Québec QC G1R 5R9
418/649-2300; Fax:418/649-2656
Email:francine.marcotte@mri.gouv.qc.ca;
URL:www.mri.gouv.qc.ca

Prix Québec Wallonie-Bruxelles de littérature de jeunesse
Créé en 1978; vise à encourager le développement de la littérature de jeunesse de langue fran‡aise et à faire la promotion des lauréats. Décerné conjointement par le ministère des Relations internationales et ministère de la Culture et des Communications

Québec Writers' Federation / Fédération des Écrivaines et Écrivains du Québec
1200 Atwater av., Montréal QC H3Z 1X4
514/933-0878; Fax:514/933-0878
Email:info@qwf.org; URL:www.qwf.org

QWF Prizes
Established 1988; awards five annual prizes of $2,000 each to honour literary excellence: The A.M. Klein poetry prize, The Hugh MacLennan fiction prize, Mavis Gallant prize for non-fiction, The McAuslan First Book Award & Translation award Books can be submitted for prizes in five categories by publishers or authors; four copies, accompanied by entry form & $10 registration fee per submission; authors must have lived in Québec three of the past five years

The Royal Society of Canada / La Société royale du Canada
170 Waller St., Ottawa ON K1N 9B9
613/991-6990; Fax:613/991-6996
Email:info@rsc.ca; URL:www.rsc.ca

Lorne Pierce Medal
Established 1926; awarded every two years for an achievement of special significance & conspicuous merit in imaginative or critical literature written in either English or French, preferably dealing with a Canadian subject

Salon International du livre de Québec
26, rue Saint-Pierre, Québec QC G1K 8A3
418/692-0010; Fax:418/692-0029
Email:info@silq.org; URL:www.silq.org

Prix des libraires du Québec
Ce prix fut créé en 1994 par l'Association des libraires du Québec et le Salon international du livre de Québec; il souligne

l'excellence d'un roman québécois par sa qualité d'écriture et son originalité; une bourse de 2 000 $ est offerte en 2005 par le Conseil des Arts et des Lettres du Québec

Saskatchewan Book Awards
#205B, 2314 - 11th Ave., Regina SK S4P 0K1
306/569-1585; Fax:306/569-4187
Email:director@bookawards.sk.ca; URL:www.bookawards.sk.ca

Anne Szumigalski Poetry Award
$2,000 awarded for the best book of poetry by a Saskatchewan author; sponsored by the Saskatchewan Arts Board

Award for Publishing
A commemorative plaque for the publisher & a certificate for the author presented to the best book published in Saskatchewan; judged on overall quality of design, production, content & significance; sponsored by Saskatchewan Culture, Youth & Recreation

Book of the Year Award
$2,000 awarded for the best book (any genre) by a Saskatchewan author

Brenda MacDonald Riches First Book Award
$2,000 for the best first book by a Saskatchewan writer; sponsored by Agrium Inc.

Children's Literature Award
$2,000 awarded for the best book of children's literature by a Saskatchewan author; sponsored by SaskEnergy

Fiction Award
$2,000 awarded for the best book of fiction (novel or short fiction) by a Saskatchewan author; sponsored by SaskPower

First Peoples Publishing Award
Commemorative certificate for the publisher & for the writer of the best book with First Nations, Metis, or non-status Indian content written, or in the case of an anthology, edited by a person of First Nations, Metis, or non-status Indian descent; based on the quality of publisher's craft, editing, & literary or artistic value; sponsored by the University of Saskatchewan

Non-Fiction Award
$2,000 award awarded for the best book of non-fiction by a Saskatchewan author; sponsored by the University of Saskatchewan

Prix du livre français
$2,000 awarded biennially for the best book written in French by a Saskatchewan author; sponsored by Fondation fransaskoise

Publishing in Education Award
Commemorative plaque for the publisher & certificates for the writer or editor & publisher of the best book produced as an educational resource, judged on the quality of the publisher's craft, editing & its value to educators at primary, secondary or post secondary levels; sponsored by the University of Regina Bookstore

Regina Book Award
$2,000 to the author of the best book by a Regina writer; sponsored by the City of Regina & Regina Public Library

Saskatoon Book Award
$2,000 awarded to the best book written by a Saskatoon author; sponsored jointly by the Saskatoon Public Library & the City of Saskatoon

Scholarly Writing Award
$2,000 awarded for the book making the best contribution to scholarship by a Saskatchewan author; sponsored by Luther College

Saskatchewan Library Association
#15, 2010 - 7th Ave., Regina SK S4R 1C2
306/780-9413; Fax:306/780-9447
Email:slaexdir@sasktel.net; URL:www.lib.sk.ca/sla/

The Mary Donaldson Award of Merit
Awarded for excellence to a student studying at a library education institution in Saskatchewan

The SLA Frances Morrison Award
Awarded for outstanding service to libraries

Saskatchewan Writers Guild Inc.
#205, 2314 - 11th Ave., Regina SK S4P 0K1
306/757-6310; Fax:306/565-8554; Toll Free:1-800-667-6788
Email:swg@sasktel.net; URL:www.skwriter.com

City of Regina Writing Award
To a Regina writer to reward merit & enable a writer to work on a specific writing project; funded by the City of Regina Arts Commission & administered by the SWG
$4,000

The Scotiabank Giller Prize
c/o Elana Rabinovitch, 576 Davenport Rd., Toronto ON M5R 1K9
416/934-0755
Email:contact@scotiabankgillerprize.ca;
URL:www.scotiabankgillerprize.ca/

The Giller Prize
$25,000 award to the author of the best Canadian novel or collection of short stories published in English

Société Saint-Jean-Baptiste de Montréal
82, rue Sherbrooke ouest, Montréal QC H2X 1X3
514/843-8851; Fax:514/844-6369
Email:mbeaulieu@ssjb.com; URL:www.ssjb.com

Prix Ludger-Duvernay
Le prix a été crée en 1944 afin de signaler les mérites d'un compatriote dont la compétence et le rayonnement dans le domaine intellectuel et littéraire servent les intérêts supérieurs de la nation québécoise; le prix est de 3 000 $, accompagne une médaille, et est attribué à tous les trois ans

Stephen Leacock Association Inc.
PO Box 854, Orillia ON L3V 6K8
705/835-7061; Fax:705/835-7062
Email:info@leacock.ca; URL:www.leacock.ca

Stephen Leacock Memorial Medal
Established 1946 to encourage the writing & publishing of humorous works in Canada; given annually for the best Canadian book of humour published in the preceding year
Winner receives the medal & a cash award of $10,000 donated by TD Canada Trust

The Order of Mariposa
Awarded occasionally to someone who has contributed significantly to humour in Canada, in other than the written word

University of British Columbia
President's Office, 6328 Memorial Rd., Vancouver BC V6T 1Z2
604/822-4439; Fax:604/822-6906
Email:jflick@interchange.ubc.ca

Medal for Canadian Biography
Established 1952; awarded annually for the best biography written either about or by a Canadian & published in the preceding year - Jane Flick

Ville de Montréal
Service du développement culturel
5650, d'Iberville, 4e étage, Montréal QC H2G 3E4
514/872-1156
URL:www.ville.montreal.qc.ca/culture/culture.htm

Grand Prix du livre de Montréal
Le prix est offert par la Ville de Montréal à l'auteur ou aux co-auteurs d'un ouvrage de langue française ou anglaise, pour la facture exceptionnelle et l'apport original de cette publication; le prix consiste en une bourse de 15 000 $, ount admissibles un auteur ou un éditeur qui habite sur le territoire de la Ville de Montréal

West Coast Book Prize Society
#902, 207 West Hastings St., Vancouver BC V6B 1H7
604/687-2405; Fax:604/669-3701
Email:info@bcbookprizes.ca; URL:www.bcbookprizes.ca

BC Book Prizes:
Established 1985; awards of $2,000 presented to winners in each of six categories; the book may have been published anywhere in the world; $25 fee per entry:

Dorothy Livesay Poetry Prize
Awarded to the author of the best work of poetry; the writer must have lived in BC for three of the preceding five years

Lieutenant Governor's Award of Literary Excellence

The Bill Duthie Booksellers' Choice Prize
Awarded for the best book in terms of public appeal, initiative, design, production & content; the book must have been published in BC
The Christie Harris Illustrated Children's Literature Prize

The Ethel Wilson Fiction Prize
Awarded to the author of the best work of fiction; the writer must have lived in BC for three of the preceding five years

The Hubert Evans Non-Fiction Prize
Awarded to the author of the best original non-fiction literary work (philosophy, belles lettres, biography, history, etc.); the writer must have lived in BC for three of the preceding five years

The Haig-Brown Regional Prize
Awarded to the author of the book that contributes most to the enjoyment & understanding of BC; the book may deal with any aspect of the province & should epitomize the BC experience

The Sheila A. Egoff Children's Prize
Awarded to the author of the best book for young people aged 16 & under; the author or illustrator must have lived in BC for three of the preceding five years

Writers Guild of Alberta
11759 Groat Rd., Edmonton AB T5M 3K6
780/422-8174; Fax:780/422-2663; Toll Free:1-800-665-5354
Email:mail@writersguild.ab.ca; URL:www.writersguild.ab.ca

Annual Awards Program
Established 1982 to recognize excellence in writing by Alberta authors; published books may be entered in any of the following categories: Children's Literature (any genre), Drama, Novel, Non-Fiction, Poetry, Short Fiction, Best First Book; winners receive $1000 cash award

Writers' Federation of Nova Scotia
1113 Marginal Rd., Halifax NS B3H 4P7
902/423-8116; Fax:902/422-0881
Email:talk@writers.ns.ca; URL:www.writers.ns.ca

Atlantic Poetry Prize
$2,000

Evelyn Richardson Memorial Literary Trust Award
Award was established in 1978 to recognize outstanding work in non-fiction by a Nova Scotian writer (native or resident)
$2,000

Thomas H. Raddall Atlantic Fiction Prize
Honours the best fiction writing by an Atlantic Canadian writer
$10,000

The Writers' Trust of Canada
#200, 90 Richmond St. East, Toronto ON M5C 1P1
416/504-8222; Fax:416/504-9090
Email:info@writerstrust.com; URL:www.writerstrust.com

The Bronwen Wallace Memorial Award
Awarded annually to a Canadian writer under the age of 35 who is not yet published in book form; award alternates each year between poetry & short fiction
$1,000

McClelland & Stewart Journey Prize
Awarded annually to a new & developing writer
$10,000

The Marian Engel Award
Established 1986; awarded annually to a female Canadian writer, for a body of work & in hope of future contributions
$15,000

Matt Cohen Award
For a lifetime of distinguished work by a Canadian writer, working in either poetry or prose, writing in either French or English who has dedicated their life to writing as a primary pursuit
$20,000

Rogers Writers' Trust Fiction Prize
Annually to the author of the work of fiction published in the previous year that in the opinion of the judges, shows the best literary merit
$15,000

Nereus Writers' Trust Non-Fiction Prize
Awarded annually to the author of the work of non-fiction published in the previous year that, in the opinion of the judges, shows the best literary merit
$15,000

The Writers Trust of Canada's Shaughnessy Cohen Award for Political Writing
Sponsored by CTV awarded to a non-fiction book of outstanding literary merit that enlarges our understanding of contemporary Canadian political & social issues
$10,000

The Timothy Findley Award
Awarded annually to a male Canadian writer for a body of work & in hope of future contributions
$15,000

Vicky Metcalf Prize for Children's Literature
Awarded annually to an author of children's literature, either fiction, non-fiction, picture books or poetry, not for a single book, but for a body of work, unless, in the opinion of the jury, there is no author worthy of the award that year
$15,000

The W.O. Mitchell Literary Prize
Presented annually to a writer who has produced an outstanding body of work, has acted during his/her career as a "caring mentor" for writers, & has published a work of fiction or had a new stage play produced during the three-year period specified for each competition; every third year the prize will be awarded to a writer who works in French
$15,000

The Writers' Union of Canada
#200, 90 Richmond St. East, Toronto ON M5C 1P1
416/703-8982; Fax:416/504-9090
Email:info@writersunion.ca; URL:www.writersunion.ca

Danuta Gleed Literary Award
Awarded to a Canadian writer for the best first collection of published short stories in the English language
$10,000

Postcard Story Competition
$500

Short Prose Competition for Developing Writers
$2,500

Writing for Children Competition
$1,500

PERFORMING ARTS

Alberta Scholarship Programs
PO Box 28000, Stn Main, Edmonton AB T5J 4R4
780/427-8640; Fax:780/427-1288
Email:scholarships@gov.ab.ca; URL:www.alis.gov.ab.ca/scholarships/main.asp

Arts Graduate Scholarships
Five awards of $5,000 at graduate level for study in music, drama, dance & the visual arts & up to $50,000 is available to assist Alberta artists to further their training through non-academic short-term courses & internship or apprenticeship programs

Association québécoise de l'industrie du disque, du spectacle et de la vidéo
6420, rue Saint-Denis, Montréal QC H2S 2R7
514/842-5147; Fax:514/842-7762
Email:info@adisq.com; URL:www.adisq.com

ADISQ Awards
The event honours the best musical achievement produced in Québec during the past year

The Banff Centre
PO Box 1020, Banff AB T1L 1H5
403/762-6180; Fax:403/762-6345
Email:arts_info@banffcentre.ca; URL:www.banffcentre.ca

The Clifford E. Lee Choreography Award
Established 1978; awarded annually in recognition of outstanding Canadian choreography & jointly sponsored by the Banff Centre & the Edmonton-based Clifford E. Lee Foundation. Winner receives a $5,000 cash prize & a commission to mount a new work for premiere at the Banff Festival of the Arts - George Ross.

The Canada Council for the Arts / Conseil des Arts du Canada
350 Albert St., PO Box 1047, Ottawa ON K1P 5V8
613/566-4414; Fax:613/566-4390; Toll Free:1-800-263-5588
Email:info@canadacouncil.ca; URL:www.canadacouncil.ca

Bernard Diamant Prize
Offers professional Canadian classical singers under 35 an opportunity to pursue their career through further studies. $5,000 awarded in addition to the regular grant to an outstanding young classical singer in the annual competition for Grants to Professional Musicians

Canada Council for the Arts Grand Prize for the CBC Young Composers Competition
$10,000 grand prize awarded every two years to the winner of the CBC Young Composers Competition

Canada Council for the Arts/CBC First Prizes for the CBC Radio National Young Performers Competition
Every two years; two first prizes of $15,000 is awarded to the winners of each of the two categories

Canada Council Musical Instrument Bank
Created in 1987 as a means of acquiring exceptional instruments to be loaned to established Canadian musicians or gifted young musicians who are about to embark on an international solo career, following a national jured competition; collection includes the 1827 McConnel Nicolaus Gagliano cello & the 1717 Windsor-Weinstein Stradivarius violin

Eckhardt-Gramatté National Music Competition
Provides assistance in the amount of $9,000 towards the cost of administering the competiton

Healey Willan Prize
$5,000 awarded every two years to the Canadian amateur choir that gives the best performance in terms of musicianship, technique & program in the CBC National Radio Competition for Amateur Choirs

Jacqueline Lemieux Prize
$6,000 awarded annually to the most talented Canadian candidate in the Grants to Dance Professionals competition

Japan-Canada Fund
Supports performance, exhibitions, distribution networks, etc. of Japanese performing artists, media artists, visual artists through established, professional Canadian presenters, as well as for the translations of Canadian & Japanese literary works

Jean-Marie Beaudet Award in Orchestra Conducting
$1,000 awarded annually to a young Canadian conductor, is adjudicated by a committee of music professionals convened by the Canada Council

John Hirsh Prize
$6,000 awarded to a new & developing theatre director who has demonstrated great potential for future excellence & exciting artistic vision; awarded every two years, one in each of the Anglophone & Francophone theatre communites; nominations are made by the professional theatre community & the winners are chosen by a peer assessment committee for the Canada Council Grants to Theatre Artists program

Jules Léger Prize for New Chamber Music
Established in 1978; annual $7,500 prize designed to encourage Canadian composers to write for chamber music groups & to foster the performance of Canadian chamber music by these groups; the Canadian Music Centre administers the award, the Canada Council funds the award & selects the assessment committee of musicians to study the submitted scores; the CBC Radio Two & La Chaîne culturelle de Radio-Canada broadcasts the winning work on the English- & French-language stereo networks

Robert Fleming Prizes
The annual $2,000 prize in memory of Robert Fleming is intended to encourage the career development of young composers & is awarded to the most talented Canadian music composer in the competition for Canada Council Grants to Professional Musicians in classical music

Sylva Gelber Foundation Award
Established 1981; $15,000 awarded annually to the most talented Canadian artist under the age of 30 in the "Grants to Musicians" competition for performers in classical music

Virginia Parker Award
Approximately $25,000 awarded annually to a young Canadian classical musician, instrumentalist, or conductor who has received at least one Canada Council grant awarded by a peer assessment committee; the prize is intended to assist a young performer in furthering his/her career

Peter Dwyer Scholarships
Annual scholarships totalling $20,000 awarded to the most promising Canadian students at the National Ballet School & the National Theatre School; each school is awarded $10,000 & chooses the winner on behalf of the Canada Council

Walter Carsen Prize for Excellence in the Performing Arts
Awarded annually, $50,000 prize recognizes the highest level of artistic excellence & distinguished career in the performing arts; awarded to a Canadian artist who is actively performing or who has spent the major part of his/her career in Canada in dance, theatre, or music - in creation or interpretation; prize will be presented on a four-year cycle - dance, theatre, dance, music

Canadian Academy of Recording Arts & Sciences / Académie canadienne des arts et des sciences de l'enregistrement
345 Adelaide Street West, 2nd Floor, Toronto ON M5V 1R5
416/485-3135, ext.227; Fax:416/485-4978; Toll Free:1-888-440-5866
Email: info@carasonline.ca; URL:www.carasonline.ca

Juno Awards
Annual awards for: Canadian Hall of Fame Award, Walt Grealis Special Achievement Award, Juno Fan Choice (presented by Doritos), Single of the Year, International Album of the Year, Francophone Album of the Year, Artist of the Year, Group of the Year, Instrumental Album of the Year, New Artist of the Year (sponsored by FACTOR & Canada's Private Radio Broadcasters), New Group of the Year (sponsored by FACTOR & Canada's Private Radio Broadcasters), Songwriter of the Year, Country Recording of the Year, Rap Recording of the Year, Pop Album of the Year, Rock Album of the Year, Vocal Jazz Album of the Year, Contemporary Jazz Album of the Year, Traditional Jazz Album of the Year, Children's Album of the Year, Classical Album of the Year: Solo or Chamber Ensemble, Classical Album of the Year: Large Ensemble or Soloist(s) with Large Ensemble Accompaniment, Classical Album of the Year: Vocal or Choral Performance, Classical Composition of the Year, Alternative Album of the Year, Dance Recording of the Year,
Also: Reggae Recording of the Year, Roots & Traditional Album of the Year-Solo, Roots & Traditional Album of the Year-Group, Blues Album of the Year, Jack Richardson Producer of the Year, Recording Engineer of the Year, Album Design of the Year (sponsored by Ever-Reddy Packaging Ltd.), Video of the Year, Music DVD of the Year

Canadian Broadcasting Corporation
CBC Radio Music, PO Box 500, Stn A, Toronto ON M5W 1E6
416/205-3311; Fax:416/205-6040
URL:www.radio.cbc.ca

National Radio Competition for Amateur Choirs
Established 1975; awarded biennially; prizes offered in following categories: Children's, Youth, Large, Adult Mixed Chamber, Adult Equal Voice, Church, Traditional & Ethno-Cultural, & Contemporary Choral Music.
Eight first prizes of $3,000 each; eight 2nd prizes of $2,000 each; $1,000 for best performance of a Canadian work.

National Radio Competition for Young Composers
Established 1973; competition sponsored every two years by CBC & the Canada Council; entrants must be Canadian citizens or landed immigrants, 30 years of age or under, & must not be employees of the CBC.
Up to 10 prizes are given: three 1st prizes of $5,000 each; three 2nd prizes of $4,000 each; three 3rd prizes; a $5,000 Grand Prize; a performance of the winning works is given on CBC English & French radio networks.

National Radio Competition for Young Performers
Established 1960; competition sponsored every two years by CBC/Radio-Canada & the Canada Council for the Arts; entrants must be Canadian citizens or landed immigrants, 30 years of age or under (32 for singers); categories rotate among strings, piano, voice, winds & brass; finals of competiton heard live on CBC Radio Two & La Chaîne culturelle.
First prize $15,000; 2nd prize $10,000; 3rd prize $5,000; prizes also include recital & concert engagements across Canada - URL: www.cbc.ca/ypc.

Canadian Country Music Association / Association de la musique country canadienne
#203, 626 King St. West, Toronto ON M5V 1M7
416/947-1331; Fax:416/947-5924
Email:country@ccma.org; URL:www.ccma.org

Music Awards
Awards in 10 categories are presented annually to outstanding performers; 35 citations honour individuals & organizations which, have made a significant contribution to country music

Canadian Theatre Critics Association / Association des critiques de théâtre du Canada
#700, 250 Dundas St. West, Toronto ON M5T 2Z5
416/782-0966; Fax:416/782-0366
Email:aruprech@ccs.carleton.ca;
URL:www.canadiantheatrecritics.ca

The Herbet Whittaker/Drama Bench Award for Outstanding Contribution to Canadian Theatre
Presented annually to Canadian citizen or permanent resident working in any theatrical discipline who has demonstrated distinguished contribution in playwriting, performance, direction or design; named after Herbert Whittaker Founding Chairman of the Canadian Theatre Critics Assoc.

Council for Business & the Arts in Canada / Conseil pour le monde des affaires et des arts du Canada
#903, 165 University Ave., Toronto ON M5H 3B8
416/869-3016; Fax:416/869-0435
Email:info@businessforarts.org; URL:www.businessforarts.org

Globe and Mail Business for the Arts Awards
These awards honour businesses in the categories of Best Arts/Entrepreneur Partnership, Most Effective Corporate Program, Most Innovative Marketing Sponsorship and The First Dance Award.

Edmund C. Bovey Award
To recognize individual members of the business community who contribute leadership, time, money & expertise to the arts
A sculpture to the winner & $20,000 distributed to the arts in a way specified by the winner

Dance Ontario Association / Association Ontario Danse
Case Goods Bldg., #304, 55 Mill St., Toronto ON M5A 3C4
416/204-1083; Fax:416/204-1085
Email:contact@danceontario.ca; URL:www.danceontario.ca

Dance Ontario Award
Recognizes a lifetime commitment to dance - Peter Ryan

Dancer Transition Resource Centre / Centre de ressources et transition pour danseurs
The Lynda Hamilton Centre, #500, 250 The Esplanade, Toronto ON M5A 1J2
416/595-5655; Fax:416/595-0009; Toll Free:1-800-667-0851
Email:nationaloffice@dtrc.ca; URL:www.dtrc.ca

Anne M. Delicaet Bursary
To help fund tuition, books &/or supplies for applicant in their third year of full-time retraining/grants received from the DTRC
Award amount is discretionary

Karen Kain Award
Given to a dancer entering a second or subsequent year of full-time retraining
Award is discretionary

Lynda Hamilton Award
Awarded annually to a dancer in transition who has completed two years of study & requires a third to complete or continue the proposed course of study
$18,000 subsistence & $4,000 for tuition & supplies

Peter F. Bronfman Memorial Award
It is earmarked for a second or third year of retraining & subsistence & may be only awarded for the full amount
$18,000 subsistence & $4,000 for tuition & supplies

Sara Symons Bursary
Open to all recipients of at least one year of funding under type C grant who are continuing their studies
Amount is discretionary

Zella Wolofsky/Doug Wright Bursary
Awarded to a dancer with a degree from a recognized university & who is in second or subsequent year of professional program or doing graduate studies or second degree
$2,000 for any purpose

East Coast Music Association / Association de la musique de la côte est
145 Richmond St., Charlottetown PE C1A 1J1
902/892-9040; Fax:902/892-9041
Email:ecma@ecma.ca; URL:www.ecma.ca

East Coast Music Awards
General Categories: Male Artist of the Year, Female Artist of the Year, Group of the Year, Songwriter of the Year, Single of the Year, Video of the Year, Album of the Year, New Artist(s) of the Year, Entertainer of the Year; Genre Specific Categories: Country Recording of the Year, Pop Recording of the Year, Rock Recording of the Year, Instrumental Recording of the Year, Alternative Recording of the Year, Jazz Recording of the Year, Blues Recording of the Year, Gospel Recording of the Year, Children's Recording of the Year, Bluegrass Recording of the Year, Urban Recording of the Year, Classical Recording of the Year, Roots/Traditional Recording of the Year, Folk Recording of the Year; Cultural Categories: Francophone Recording of the Year, Aboriginal Recording of the Year, African-Canadian Recording of the Year

Elinore & Lou Siminovitch Prize in Theatre
c/o BMO Financial Group, 55 Bloor St. West, 4th Fl., Toronto ON M4W 3N5
(416) 9927-2771
Email: andrew.soren@bmo.com; URL:www.siminovitchprize.com

Elinore & Lou Siminovitch Prize
Awarded annually; honours a director, playwright, or designer who in mid-career has made a significant contribution through a body of work to the theatre in Canada; direction, playwriting & design will be honoured on a three year cycle.
$100,000; the winner will receive an immediate cash prize of $75,000, in addition the honoured artist will be invited to designate $25,000 to a protegé of his/her choice who is involved in direction, playwriting or design in theatre in Canada or to an institution (theatre or educational facility) that contributes to better & more successful theatre in Canada

Fondation Émile-Nelligan
261, rue Bloomfield, Outremont QC H2V 3R6
514/278-4657; Fax:514/278-1943
Email:info@fondation-nelligan.org;
URL:www.fondation-nelligan.org

Prix Serge-Garant
Prix triennal de composition musicale décerné à un compositeur citoyen du Canada né au Québec ou à un compositeur citoyen du Canada ayant sa résidence principale au Québec depuis au moins dix ans
25 000$

Governor General's Performing Arts Awards Foundation
#113, 24 York St., Ottawa ON K1N 1K2
613/241-5297; Fax:613/241-4677
URL:www.bce.ca/ggawards

Governor General's Performing Arts Awards
Established in 1992; honours six performing artists for their lifetime achievement & contribution to the cultural enrichment of Canada; each recipient is awarded $15,000 & a commemorative medal

Ramon John Hnatyshyn Award for Voluntarism in the Performing Arts
Recognizes outstanding service to the performing arts; the recipient is presented with a specially commissioned artwork by Canadian glass artist Naoko Takenouchi

The Jazz Report
#7, 592 Markham St., Toronto ON M6G 2L8
Email:jazzreport@sympatico.ca;
URL:www.nationaljazzawards.com

The National Jazz Awards
Established in 2001; annual awards in 26 categories determined by readers & contributors to the quarterly; voting done online, through website
Open to all Canadian residents

Ontario Arts Council / Conseil des arts de l'Ontario
151 Bloor St. West, 5th Fl., Toronto ON M5S 1T6
416/969-7422; Fax:416/961-7796;
Toll Free:1-800-387-0058 ext. 7422
Email:mwarren@arts.on.ca; URL:www.arts.on.ca

John Adaskin Memorial Fund
Established in memorial of the Canadian Music Centre's first executive secretary; supports a project that encourages the promotion & development of Canadian music in the school system

Colleen Peterson Songwriting Award
Established in 2003, in honour of Colleen Peterson's contribution to Canadian folk and country music. This annual award was designed to support and promote the work of an emerging professional singer/songwriter in the genres of roots, traditional, folk and country music
$1,000

Heinz Unger Award for Conducting
Awarded every two years; Established 1968 & awarded biennially to honour the memory of the York Concert Society music director; administered by the Music Office of the Ontario Arts Council in cooperation with the Association of Canadian Orchestras
Up to $9,000

John Hirsch Director's Award
Established by a bequest to the Ontario Arts Council from the late John Hirsch; presented every three years to a promising theatre director in Ontario
$5,000

Leslie Bell Scholarship for Choral Conducting
Established 1973; awarded biennially in competition; the purpose of the award is to help young emerging choral conductors in Ontario further their studies in the choral music field either in Canada or abroad; competition organized by the Ontario Choral Federation
Up to $2,000

Pauline McGibbon Award
Annual award alternates between designers, directors & production crafts persons
$7,000

Premier's Award for Excellence in the Arts
Established in 2006, the Government of Ontario created this award to recognize outstanding achievement in the professional arts by an individual and a group.
Up to $50,000

The Vida Peene Fund
Provides assistance to projects which benefit the orchestra community as a whole

Tim Sims Encouragement Fund Award
Established in 1995; to be awarded annually to a promising young comedic performer or troupe
$1,000

Québec Ministère de la culture, des communications et de la condition féminine
Direction générale du secrétariat et des sociétés d'Etat
225, Grande Allée est, Québec QC G1R 5G5
418/380-2358 ext. 7220; Fax:418/080-2364
Email:claude.janelle@mcc.gouv.qc.ca;
URL:www.prixduquebec.gouv.qc.ca

Prix Denise-Pelletier
Prix réservé aux domaines de la chanson, de la musique, de l'art lyrique, du théâtre et de la danse

Québec Ministère des Relations internationales
Édifice Hector-Fabre, 525, boul René-Lévesque est, Québec QC G1R 5R9
418/649-2300; Fax:418/649-2656
URL:www.mri.gouv.qc.ca

Prix Québec-Flandre de musique contemporaine
Créé en 1988; récompense les compositeurs flamands et interprètes québecois; décerné aux deux ans et en alternance, ce prix est constitué d'une bourse pour le compositeur et l'exécution de l'ouvre devant le public de l'autre communauté

Prix Rapsat-Lelièvre du disque de chanson
Initialement connu sous le nom Prix Québec/Wallonie-Bruxelles du disque de chanson; vise à encourager le développement et la promotion de la langue française, à stimuler la production et la diffusion de disques francophones

Société Saint-Jean-Baptiste de Montréal
82, rue Sherbrooke ouest, Montréal QC H2X 1X3
514/843-8851; Fax:514/844-6369
Email:mbeaulieu@ssjb.com; URL:www.ssjb.com

Prix Calixa-Lavallée
Established 1959; $1,500 & a medal awarded annually to a French Canadian in recognition of outstanding achievement in music in serving the higher interests of the French Canadian people

Toronto Alliance for the Performing Arts
#210, 215 Spadina Ave., Toronto ON M5T 2C7
416/536-6468; Fax:416/536-3463; Toll Free:1-800-541-0499
URL:www.tapa.ca

Dora Mavor Moore Awards
Established 1979; celebrating excellence in Toronto theatre, 33 awards in large, medium & small theatre divisions, Theatre for Young Audiences & New Choreography

Western Canadian Music Alliance
#637, 776 Corydon Ave., Winnipeg MB R3M 0Y1
204/943-8485; Fax:204/453-1594
Email:info@wcmw.ca; URL:www.wcmw.ca

Prairie Music Awards
Annual Awards in the following categories: Recording Engineer of the Year, Record Producer of the Year, Recording Studio of the Year, Record Company of the Year, Publishing Company of the Year, Best Compilation Album of the Year, Best Album Design of the Year, Best Music Score of the Year, Best Music Video, Best Booking Agent, Manager of the Year, & Musician of the Year; also Annual Awards for Prairie artists in the following categories: People's Choice Award, Female/Male Recording Artist of the Year, Group Recording of the Year, Most Promising Artist, Best Pop/Light Rock, Best Rock/Heavy Metal, Best Alternative, Best Country, Best Blues/R&B/Soul, Best Roots/Traditional/Ethnic, Best Rap/Dance/Rhythm, Best Jazz, Best Classical Performance

PUBLIC AFFAIRS

B'nai Brith Canada
15 Hove St., Toronto ON M3H 4Y8
416/633-6224; Fax:416/630-2159
Email:bnb@bnaibrith.ca; URL:www.bnaibrith.ca

Award of Merit & Humanitarian Awards
Established 1981; presented annually at gala events in major communities across Canada
Selection of honourees based on outstanding achievement in their chosen fields as well as personal commitment to the overall betterment of Canadian society - Sharon Anisman

Canadian Association on Gerontology / Association canadienne de gérontologie

#106, 222 College St., Toronto ON M5T 3J1
416/978-7977; Fax:416/978-4771
Email:contact@cagacg.ca; URL:www.cagacg.ca

The CAG Donald Menzies Bursary
To support post-baccalaureate students registered in a program of study focused on aging or the aged
$1,500

The CAG Margery Boyce Bursary
To support post-baccalaureate students who have made a significant contribution to their community through volunteer activities with or on behalf of seniors & who are registered in a program of study focused on aging or the aged
$500

The Canadian Council of Christians & Jews / Conseil canadien des chrétiens et des juifs

4211 Yonge St., PO Box 17, Toronto ON M2P 2A9
416/597-9693; Fax:416/597-9775; Toll Free:1-800-663-1848
Email:info@cccj.ca; URL:www.cccj.ca

Human Relations Award
Made to outstanding Canadians who have made a significant contribution towards bringing people together regardless of race, religion, or social status, in an atmosphere of understanding & respect; the award is made annually & is approved by a National Nominating Committee from the Board of Directors of CCCJ

Canadian Council of Professional Engineers / Conseil canadien des ingénieurs

#1100, 180 Elgin St., Ottawa ON K2P 2K3
613/232-2474; Fax:613/230-5759
Email:info@engineerscanada.ca; URL:www.engineerscanada.ca

Meritorious Service Award for Community Service
Awarded for exemplary voluntary contribution to a community organization or humanitarian endeavour

The Canadian Council of the Blind / Le Conseil canadien des aveugles

#401, 396 Cooper St., Ottawa ON K2P 2H7
613/567-0311; Fax:613/567-2728; Toll Free:1-877-304-0968
Email:ccb@ccbnational.net; URL:ccbnational.net

Award of Merit
Established 1952; presented to a Canadian, blind or sighted, who has rendered outstanding work for the blind
A gold medal & clasp, a specially printed & bound citation & honorary life membership in the CCB

Canadian Federation for Sexual Health / Fédération canadienne pour la santé sexuelle

#430, One Nicholas St., Ottawa ON K1N 7B7
613/241-4474; Fax:613/241-7550
Email:admin@cfsh.ca; URL:www.cfsh.ca

Phyllis P. Harris Scholarship
For students who have worked or volunteered in the general field of human sexuality who intend to work for a degree in the field of family planning or population issues
$2,500 towards full-time study at a Canadian university

The City of Toronto

Diversity Management and Community Engagement, Strategic and Corporate Policy/Healthy City Office, Manager's Office, City Hall, 100 Queen St. West, 11th Fl., East Tower, Toronto ON M5H 2N2
416/392-8592; Fax:416/696-3645
Email: diversity@toronto.ca; URL:www.toronto.ca/civicawards/

Aboriginal Affairs Award
Est. 2003, given to a person(s) or organization whose volunteer efforts have made or are making a significant or ongoing contribution to the well-being & advancement of the Aboriginal community in Toronto

Access Award for Disability Issues
Established 1982; honours people or organizations that have made or are making a significant or ongoing contribution, beyond legislated requirements, to the well-being & advancement of people with disabilities; the award honours those who are sensitive to the access needs of persons with disabilities when planning structures or programs (this could include consideration of access requirements in the design of new or renovated buildings, a job creation campaign, a transportation system, recreational program, etc.)

Constance E. Hamilton Award on the Status of Women
This award commemorates the Privy Council of Great Britain granting women status as persons in 1929; award is named after the first woman member of City Council; recipients are persons who have made a significant contribution to securing equitable treatment for Toronto women

Pride Award for Lesbian Gay Bisexual Transgender Transsexual Two Spirited Issues
Est. 2003, the Pride Award honours individuals &/or organizations that have made or are making a significant or ongoing contribution to the well-being & advancement of these communities in Toronto

William P. Hubbard Race Relations Award
Named for Toronto's first visible minority Member of Council & Acting Mayor, this award honours persons with outstanding achievement & commitment to this field in Toronto; award was presented for the first time in 1990

Ethics in Action Awards

c/o VanCity, 183 Terminal Ave., PO Box 2120, Stn Terminal, Vancouver BC V6B 5R8
604/877-7000; Toll Free:1-800-826-2489
Email:eia@ethicsinaction.com; URL:www.ethicsinaction.com

Ethics in Action Awards
Awards recognize businesses & individuals in business, whose actions & decisions have made a positive impact on our communities

Ontario Ministry of Citizenship & Immigration

Ontario Honours & Awards
Secretariat Ministry of Citizenship and Immigration, 400 University Ave., 4th Fl., Toronto ON M7A 2R9
416/314-7526; Fax:416/314-7743
Email:ontariohonoursandawards@ontario.ca; URL:www.citizenship.gov.on.ca/english/honours

Ontario Senior Achievement Award
Presented annually to Ontario residents who have made a significant contribution to their communities after reaching 65 years of age; nominations may be made by any individual or organization

Status of Women Canada

Ottawa ON K1P 1H9
613/995-7835; Fax:613/943-2386
URL:www.swc-cfc.gc.ca

Governor General's Award in Commemoration of Persons Case
Established 1979 to celebrate the 50th anniversary of the "Persons Case" which resulted in women being declared eligible for appointment to the Senate; annual awards recognize contributions by individuals toward promoting the equality of women in Canada

SCIENTIFIC, ENGINEERING, TECHNICAL

Association of Universities & Colleges of Canada / Association des universités et collèges du Canada

#600, 350 Albert St., Ottawa ON K1R 1B1
613/563-1236; Fax:613/563-9745
Email:awards@aucc.ca; URL:www.aucc.ca

Fairfax Financial Holdings Limited Program
Undergraduate students of all disciplines
36 university undergraduate scholarships of $5,000; 24 college diploma scholarships of $3,500

BC Innovation Council

1188 West Georgia St., 9th Fl., Vancouver BC V6E 4A2
604/438-2752; Fax:604/438-6564; Toll Free:1-800-665-7222
Email:info@bcinnovationcouncil.com;
URL:www.bcinnovationcouncil.com

BC Innovation Council Awards
Up to six gold medals awarded each year for outstanding achievements by BC scientists, engineers, industrial innovators & science communicators. The awards are: BC Science & Technology Champion of the Year, Young Innovator Award, Frontiers in Research, Cecil Green Award for Technology Entrepreneurship, Chairman's Award for Career Achievement, Lieutenant Govenor's Technology Innovation Award & Eve Savory Award for Science Communication

The Canada Council for the Arts / Conseil des Arts du Canada

350 Albert St., PO Box 1047, Ottawa ON K1P 5V8
613/566-4414; Fax:613/566-4390; Toll Free:1-800-263-5588
Email:info@canadacouncil.ca; URL:www.canadacouncil.ca

Killam Prizes
Up to five prizes of $100,000 each are given annually to eminent Canadian scholars in recognition of a distinguished career achievement in the natural sciences, health sciences, engineering, social sciences & humanities. Candidates must be nominated by three experts in their field. Chosen by Killam Selection

Killam Research Fellowships
Fellowships offered on a competitive basis to support specific research projects by distinguished Canadian researchers in any of the following broad fields: humanities, social sciences, natural sciences, health sciences, engineering & studies linking any of the disciplines within these broad fields; provide release time to individual scholars, normally full professors in Canadian universitites, who wish to pursue individual research; provides two years of teaching replacement to a maximum of $53,000 per year, plus the cost of fringe benefits of the Fellow, based on actual salary for the year before the tenure of the award; application must be made by individuals, not by institutions, universities or organizations

Canadian Aeronautics & Space Institute / Institut aéronautique et spatial du Canada

#104, 350 Terry Fox Drive., Kanata ON K2K 2W5
613/591-8787; Fax:613/591-7291
Email:casi@casi.ca; URL:www.casi.ca

C.D. Howe Award
Established 1966; a silver plaque presented annually for achievement in the fields of planning, policy making & overall leadership in Canadian aeronautics & space activities

McCurdy Award
Established 1954; a silver medal & trophy presented annually for outstanding achievement in art, science & engineering relating to aeronautics & space

Romeo Vachon Award
Established 1969; bronze plaque awarded annually for outstanding contribution of a practical nature to the art, science, & engineering of aeronautics & space in Canada

Trans-Canada (McKee) Trophy
Canada's oldest aviation award established 1927; presented annually except when no qualified recipient is nominated for outstanding achievement in the field of air operations

Canadian Council of Professional Engineers / Conseil canadien des ingénieurs

#1100, 180 Elgin St., Ottawa ON K2P 2K3
613/232-2474; Fax:613/230-5759

Email:info@engineerscanada.ca; URL:www.engineerscanada.ca
Gold Medal Award
Awarded for exceptional individual achievement & distinction in a field of engineering

Medal for Distinction in Engineering Education
Awarded for exemplary contribution to engineering teaching at a Canadian University

The Young Engineer Achievement Award
Awarded for outstanding contribution in a field of engineering by an engineer 35 years of age or younger

Canadian Institute of Forestry / Institut forestier du Canada

#504, 151 Slater St., Ottawa ON K1P 5H3
613/234-2242; Fax:613/234-6181
Email:cif@cif-ifc.org; URL:www.cif-ifc.org

Canadian Forest Management Group Achievement Award
Established 1998; to recognize outstanding achievement by teams in groups of Natural Resource managers, researchers and NGO groups in forest resources related activities in Canada.

Canadian Forestry Achievement Award
Established 1966 & presented annually in recognition of superior accomplishments in forestry research &/or in recognition of outstanding administrative leadership in management, education, research & affairs of professional & scientific societies

Canadian Forestry Scientific Achievement Award
Established 1980; presented annually in recognition of superior accomplishments in scientific forestry

International Forestry Achievement Award
Established 1980; presented in recognition of outstanding achievement in international forestry

James M. Kitz Award
Awarded to a person who has made outstanding contributions to the practice of forestry, including: superior personal accomplishments; outstanding leadership in education, management research or professional association work; promotion of forestry to various audiences
Open to anyone involved in forestry

Canadian Institute of Mining, Metallurgy & Petroleum / Institut canadien des mines, de la métallurgie et du pétrole

#855, 3400, boul de Maisonneuve ouest, Montréal QC H3Z 3B8
514/939-2710; Fax:514/939-2714
Email:cim@cim.org; URL:www.cim.org

CIM Awards
The institute administers 26 awards recognizing achievement in mining, metallurgy & petroleum industries

CANARIE Inc.: Canada's Advanced Internet Development Organization

110 O'Connor St., Ottawa ON K1P 1H1
613/943-5454; Fax:613/943-5443
Email:info@canarie.ca; URL:www.canarie.ca

Iway Awards
The Canarie IWAY Awards honors individuals or group & organizations who have made outstanding contributions to Canada's information society; focuses on R&D, advancements in internet technology providing cultural, social & economic benefits; five categories: New Technology Development; Application of Technology; Public Leadership; Community Service; Adaptive Technologies; Judges Award

The Chemical Institute of Canada / Institut de chimie du Canada

#550, 130 Slater St., Ottawa ON K1P 6E2
613/232-6252; Fax:613/232-5862; Toll Free:1-888-542-2242
Email:info@cheminst.ca; URL:www.cheminst.ca

Chemical Institute of Canada Awards
The institute administers several awards & scholarships in chemistry, chemical engineering, & macromolecular science or engineering

E.W.R. Steacie Memorial Fund / Fondation E.W.R. Steacie

100 Sussex Dr., Ottawa ON K1A 0R6
613/993-1212; Fax:613/954-5242
Email:PrixSteaciePrize.SIMS@nrc-cnrc.gc.ca;
URL:www.steacieprize.ca/index_e.html

The Steacie Prize
Canada's most prestigious award for young scientists & engineers; named to honour the memory of Edgar William Richard Steacie, a physical chemist & former President of the National Research Council of Canada; established 1963; awarded annually to a young scientist or engineer up to 40 years of age for outstanding scientific work in a Canadian context; winner receives a certificate & $10,000
$15,000

The Engineering Institute of Canada / Institut canadien des ingénieurs

1295 Hwy. 2 East, Kingston ON K7L 4V1
613/547-5989; Fax:613/547-0195
Email:jplant1@cogeco.ca; URL:www.eic-ici.ca

The Sir John Kennedy Medal
Established in 1927 in commemoration of the great services rendered in the field of engineering by Sir John Kennedy, a past president of the EIC; medal is awarded every two years by the council in recognition of outstanding merit in the profession or of noteworthy contributions to the science of engineering or to the benefit of the institute

Ernest C. Manning Awards Foundation

#421 - 7th Ave. SW, 38th floor, Calgary AB T2P 4K9
403/645-8277; Fax:403/645-8320
Email:manning@encana.com; URL:www.manningawards.ca

The Manning Awards
Given annually to Canadian innovators who have conceived & developed new concepts, procedures, processes or products of benefit to Canada; awards may be in any area of activity.
One $100,000 Principal Award; one $25,000 Award of Distinction; two $10,000 Innovation prizes, & four $4,000 Young Canadian Innovation Awards.

Natural Sciences & Engineering Research Council of Canada / Conseil de recherches en sciences naturelles et en génie

350 Albert St., Ottawa ON K1A 1H5
613/995-5992; Fax:613/992-5337
URL:www.nserc.ca

Gerhard Herzberg Gold Medal for Science & Engineering
Awarded annually to an individual who has made outstanding & sustained contributions to Canadian research in natural sciences & engineering; the gold medal will be awarded for any activity of exceptional importance & impact that leads to the enhancement of the research enterprise in Canada - such activities may include contributions to knowledge, the application of existing knowledge, to the novel solution of practical problems, the promotion or management of research activity, the leadership in the transfer of knowledge.
The accomplishments for which the award is given must have been carried out in Canada & achieved over a substantial period of time; persons from any sector (academic, business & industry, or government) are eligible; current members of council are not eligible; awardee's performance in relation to the cited achievement must demonstrate an unusually high degree of ability & the application of such qualities as expertise, creativity, imagination, leadership, perseverance & dedication.

The E.W.R. Steacie Memorial Fellowships
Awarded to enhance the career development of outstanding & highly promising scientists & engineers who are staff members of Canadian universities; successful fellows are relieved of any teaching & administrative duties, enabling them to devote all their time & energy to research; up to four fellowships are awarded annually for a one or two-year period; fellowships are held at a Canadian university or affiliated research institution
Set at $90,000 to be paid to the university by NSERC to cover the cost of replacing the Steacie Fellow's teaching & administrative responsibilities

Prix Galien Canada

#800, 1200, av McGill College, Montréal QC H3B 4G7
514/843-2535; Fax:514/843-2183
Email:christiane.bordeleau@groupesante.rogers.com;
URL:htt://fgic-gfci.scitech.gc.ca/

Belleau-Nickerson Prize
Awarded in recognition of a drug that has been on the market for the past 10 years anywhere in the world & for at least three years in Canada

MacLean Hunter Health Fellowship
Awarded to a deserving young Canadian researcher
$15,000

Prix Galien - Innovative Drug
Awarded to a company that has developed & marketed a drug that has made the most significant contribution to the well-being of the general public, in terms of efficacy, safety & innovation

Prix Galien - Research
Awarded to a scientist who is known for his/her contribution to pharmaceutical research In Canada

Québec Ministère du Développement économique, de l'Innovation et de l'Exportation

710, place D'Youville, 3e étage, Québec QC G1R 4Y4
418/691-5950; Fax:418/644-0118
URL:www.mdeie.gouv.qc.ca/

Prix Armand-Frappier
Décerné pour la création ou le développement d'institutions de recherche, ou pour l'administration et la promotion de recherche

Prix Lionel-Boulet
Décerné au chercheur qui s'est distingué par ses inventions, ses innovations scientifiques et technologiques, son leadership dans le développement scientifique et sa contribution à la croissance économique du Québec

Prix Marie-Victorin
Décerné aux chercheurs de sciences exactes et naturelles, les sciences de l'ingénierie et technologiques ainsi que les sciences agricoles

Prix Wilder-Penfield
Décerné aux scientifiques dont l'objet de recherche appartient au domaine biomédical

Royal Astronomical Society of Canada / Société royale d'astronomie du Canada

136 Dupont St., Toronto ON M5R 1V2
416/924-7973; Fax:416/924-2911; Toll Free:1-888-924-7272
Email:nationaloffice100000@rasc.ca; URL:www.rasc.ca

Chant Medal
Established 1940 in appreciation of the great work of the late Prof. C.A. Chant in furthering the interests of astronomy in Canada; silver medal is awarded no more than once a year to an amateur astronomer resident in Canada on the basis of the value of the work which he/she has carried out in astronomy & closely allied fields of original investigation

Ken Chilton Prize
Established 1977; plaque awarded annually to an amateur astronomer resident in Canada, in recognition of a significant piece of work carried out or published during the year

Simon Newcomb Award
Established 1978; trophy awarded annually for the best article on astronomy, astrophysics or space sciences submitted by a member of the society during the year

The Plaskett Medal
Presented jointly with CASCA for an outstanding doctoral thesis

The Royal Canadian Geographical Society / Société géographique royale du Canada

39 McArthur Ave., Vanier ON K1L 8L7
613/745-4629; Fax:613/744-0947; Toll Free:1-800-267-0824
Email:rcgs@rcgs.org; URL:www.rcgs.org

The Gold Medal
Established 1972; to recognize a particular achievement of one or more individuals in the field of geography, or a significant national or international event - Coordinator, Society Programs, Carolyn Milano

The Massey Medal
Established 1959; awarded annually for outstanding personal achievement in the exploration, development, or description of the geography of Canada

The Royal Society of Canada / La Société royale du Canada

170 Waller St., Ottawa ON K1N 9B9
613/991-6990; Fax:613/991-6996
Email:info@rsc.ca; URL:www.rsc.ca

Bancroft Award
Established 1968; awarded every two years for publication, instruction & research in the earth sciences that have conspicuously contributed to public understanding & appreciation of the subject
$2,500 & a presentation scroll - Geneviève Gouin, Awards Coordinator, 613/991-5760

Eadie Medal
Established 1975; awarded annually in recognition of major contributions to any field in engineering or applied science with preference given to those having an impact on communications.
$3,000 & a bronze medal - Génèvieve Gouin, Awards Coordinator, 613/991-5760

John L. Synge Award
Established 1986; awarded at irregular intervals for outstanding research in any of the branches of mathematics
$2,500 & a diploma

Rutherford Memorial Medals: Chemistry & Physics
Established 1980; awarded annually for outstanding research, one in chemistry, one in physics
Two medals & $2,500 each

The Flavelle Medal
Established 1924; awarded every two years (since 1966) for an outstanding contribution to biological science during the preceding 10 years or for significant additions to a previous outstanding contribution to biological science

The Henry Marshall Tory Medal
Established 1941; awarded every two years (since 1947) for outstanding research in a branch of astronomy, chemistry, mathematics, physics, or an allied science

The McNeil Medal
Awarded to encourage communication of science to students & the public
$1,500 bursary & a medal

Willet G. Miller Medal
Established 1943; awarded every two years for outstanding research in any branch of the earth sciences - Géneviève Gouin, Awards Coordinator, 613/991-5760

Société Saint-Jean-Baptiste de Montréal

82, rue Sherbrooke ouest, Montréal QC H2X 1X3
514/843-8851; Fax:514/844-6369
Email:mbeaulieu@ssjb.com; URL:www.ssjb.com

Prix Léon-Lortie
Established 1987; awarded for achievement in the area of pure & applied sciences

Society of Chemical Industry - Canadian Section

#550, 130 Slater St., Ottawa ON K1P 6E2
Email:communications@soci.org; URL:www.soci.org

Canada Medal Award
Established 1939; awarded every two years for outstanding services in the Canadian chemical industry; recipient delivers an address at a meeting of the society

International Award
Established 1976; award is presented in recognition of outstanding service in the chemical industry in the international sphere, preferably to Canadians or persons who have contributed measurably to the Canadian chemical scene

Le Sueur Memorial Award
Established 1955 to commemorate Ernest A. Le Sueur; award is presented in recognition of outstanding innovation in the Canadian chemical industry

SPORTS & RECREATION

Canadian Association for Health, Physical Education, Recreation & Dance / Association canadienne pour la santé, l'éducation physique, le loisir et la danse
#301, 2197 Riverside Dr., Ottawa ON K1H 7X3
613/523-1348; Fax:613/523-1206; Toll Free:1-800-663-8708
Email:info@cahperd.ca; URL:www.cahperd.ca

R. Tait McKenzie Award of Honour
Instituted at the Montreal Convention in 1948, this is the most prestigious award presented by CAHPERD; named after the distinguished Canadian physician, sculptor & physical educator, Dr. Robert Tait McKenzie; candidate shall have performed distinguished, meritorious service as a recognized leader regionally & nationally in his/her field

Canadian Association for the Advancement of Women & Sport & Physical Activity / Association canadienne pour l'avancement des femmes du sport et de l'activité physique
#N202, 801 King Edward Ave., Ottawa ON K1N 6N5
613/562-5667; Fax:613/562-5668
Email:caaws@caaws.ca; URL:www.caaws.ca

Breakthrough Awards
Presented annually to outstanding nominees who have used innovative ideas & alternative approaches to encourage & enable more girls & women to participate/lead/coach in sport & physical activity - Karin Lofstrom

CAAWS/Nike Girls@Play MVP Grant
Monthly grant awarded to a female athlete, coach, official or sport/recreation organization to help make their sporting goals & dreams - URL: www.caaws.ca/girlsatplay/grants/index.htm

Girls@Play Nike Youth Award

Stacey Levitt Scholarships
Awarded each year on behalf of the Levitt family & in memory of Stacey Levitt, who was killed while jogging in 1995 after being hit by a car.
$500 & a copy of "I am a Rose," a collection of poetry written by Stacey is given to a young woman, a girl's team or a sport organization that exemplifies Stacey's ideals & qualities.

Canadian Curling Association / Association canadienne de curling
1660 Vimont Ct., Cumberland ON K4A 4J4
613/834-2076; Fax:613/834-0716; Toll Free:1-800-550-2875
Email:info@curling.ca; URL:www.curling.ca

Award of Achievement
Commemorative plaque presented in recognition of individuals who have contributed significantly to any aspect of Canadian curling operations

Ray Kingsmith Award
Awarded to an individual who parallels the level of involvement & commitment exemplified by Ray Kingsmith

Volunteer of the Year Award
Based on contributions from the previous curling season; national volunteer of the year receives an all-expense paid weekend trip to Nokia Brier or Scott Tournament of Hearts, where they will be recognized during a playoff game

Ontario Ministry of Tourism & Recreation
Ontario Sport Awards
900 Bay St., 9th Fl., Toronto ON M7A 2R9
416/326-9326
URL:www.tourism.gov.on.ca/english/sportdiv/sport/sports-awards.htm

Ontario Sports Awards
Awards for Athlete of the Year (Male & Female), Coach of the Year (Male & Female), Athlete with a Disability of the Year (Male & Female), Team of the Year, Special Achievement Award for Volunteers, Corporate Sport Citation

Société Saint-Jean-Baptiste de Montréal
82, rue Sherbrooke ouest, Montréal QC H2X 1X3
514/843-8851; Fax:514/844-6369
Email:mbeaulieu@ssjb.com; URL:www.ssjb.com

Prix Maurice-Richard
Established 1979; $1,500 & a medal awarded annually to a French Canadian in recognition of outstanding achievement in sports & athletics in serving the higher interests of the French Canadian people

Swimming/Natation Canada
#700, 2197 Riverside Dr., Ottawa ON K1H 7X3
613/260-1348; Fax:613/260-0804
Email:natloffice@swimming.ca; URL:www.swimming.ca

Administrator of the Year Award
Annual award presented to a volunteer, who has demonstrated outstanding commitment to the organization

Club of the Year Award
Awards presented annually to three clubs

Coach of the Year
Annual awards recognize coaches of swimmers in the following categories: 1) able-bodied athletes; 2) athletes with a disability, & 3) long distance competitors; each winner receives a plaque & gift

Female/Male Swimmer of the Year
Annual awards recognize best international swimmers in the following categories: 1) able-bodied athletes, 2) athletes with a disability, & 3) long distance competitors; each winner receives a plaque & gift

Official of the Year Award
Annual award recognizes outstanding service to Canadian swimming

Victor Davis Memorial Award
Annual awards from the Victor Davis Memorial Fund assist young Canadian swimmers to continue their training, education & pursuit of excellence at the international level of competition; recipients are determined by the Victor Davis Memorial Fund Awards Committee

Canadian Honours System

For some years after Confederation, awards were made of a few hereditary honours and some knighthoods and companionships in orders of chivalry, and this policy continued until the end of the first World War.

From 1919 until 1933 no titular honours were granted. There was a brief revival of the defunct honours policy during the Conservative administration of R.B. Bennett, and several distinctions were awarded from 1934 to 1935, but the prohibition was reinstated with the return of the Liberals to office in 1935. Consequently, at the outset of the second World War, Canadians in the armed services were not entitled to receive awards in the order of chivalry for which other Commonwealth personnel were eligible. A parliamentary committee appointed in 1943 recommended that the ban on nontitular honours be lifted, clearing the way for members of the military and civilians to receive recognition for wartime services.

The hundredth anniversary of Confederation, July 1st, 1967, was the occasion on which the Order of Canada was created as the first component of a distinctly Canadian honours system. More information concerning Orders, Decorations and Medals (as well as various Governor General's awards) may be obtained by writing to: Public Information Directorate, Government House, 1 Sussex Dr., Ottawa ON K1A 0A1.

HERALDRY
Coats-of-arms, flags, badges and other heraldic devices are marks of honour and symbols of identity, authority and, in some cases, sovereignty. Each is granted by the Crown under an exercise of the Sovereign's prerogative to create heraldic honours.

Until June 4, 1988, Canadian corporations and individuals wishing to bear lawful arms petitioned the Sovereign's traditional heraldic officers in London and Edinburgh. On that date, by Royal Letters Patent, the Queen transferred the exercise of her heraldic prerogative, as Queen of Canada, to the Governor General who now heads a new office, the Canadian Heraldic Authority. With the act, heraldry, which has a long history in Canada, has been fully patriated.

These vice-regal responsibilities are administered by Canadian officers of arms appointed by commission under the Governor General's privy seal: the Herald Chancellor (the Secretary to the Governor General), the Deputy Herald Chancellor (the Deputy Secretary, Chancellery) and the Chief Herald of Canada (Director, Heraldry). He is assisted by three officers of arms: Saint-Laurent, Athabaska, and Fraser heralds, and one officer of arms extraordinary, Dauphin Herald.

New heraldic emblems are granted, and existing ones registered, by the Chief Herald upon receipt of an enabling Warrant from the Herald Chancellor or the Deputy Herald Chancellor acting on behalf of the Governor General. Grants and registrations are made by Letters Patent, documents that set out the Governor General's heraldic responsibilities, describe the emblem granted, and feature a representation of the Governor General's personal arms. To ensure a lasting record, the newly granted and registered emblems are entered in Canada's national armorial, the Public Register of Arms, Flags and Badges of Canada. Since the Authority was created, hundreds of petitions have been received from every part of the country, most for new grants of arms.

Canadian Honours List

ORDER OF CANADA
As mentioned above, the Order of Canada was created July 1, 1967. Her Majesty The Queen is Sovereign of the Order of Canada and the Governor General is, by virtue of that office, Chancellor and Principal Companion. He/She is assisted in the administration of the Order by an Advisory Council which comprises of:

a) the Chief Justice of Canada (Chair)
b) the Clerk of the Privy Council
c) the Deputy Minister, Canadian Heritage
d) the Chair of the Canada Council
e) the President of the Royal Society of Canada
f) the Chair of the Board of the Association of Universities and Colleges of Canada
g) not more than five other members, when considered appropriate by the Governor General, can be appointed for three-year terms.

The Secretary to the Governor General is, by his/her office, Secretary General of the Order.

The Order of Canada is designed to honour Canadian citizens for outstanding achievement and service to the country or to humanity at large and also for distinguished service in particular localities and fields of activity. The Order comprises three levels of membership: Companion, Officer, and Member. Up to 15 Companions may be appointed annually, but the total number of living Companions may not exceed 165. Up to 64 Officers and 136 Members may be appointed annually with no over-all limit.

The Order includes no titles of honour and confers no special privileges, hereditary or otherwise. Awards are made solely on the basis of merit. Members of the Order are entitled to place after their names the letters "C.C." for Companions, "O.C." for Officers, and "C.M." for Members.

Any person or organization may make nominations for appointment to the Order by writing to the Chancellery, Rideau Hall, Ottawa. The Advisory Council submits to the Governor General lists of those nominees who, in the opinion of the Council, are of greatest merit. Appointments to the Order are made by the Sovereign of the Order on the recommendation of the Governor General as Chancellor of the Order, under an instrument sealed with the Seal of the Order.

Non-Canadians whom the Government desires to honour may be accorded honourary membership in the Order.

Companions of the Order of Canada/ Compagnons de l'Ordre du Canada (C.C.)
(Announced August 31, 2010)
The Right Honourable Kim Campbell, P.C., C.C., Paris, France & Vancouver, BC
Ben Heppner, C.C., Toronto, ON
Chantal Petitclerc, C.C., C.Q., M.S.M., Montréal, QC

(Announced June 30, 2010)
Willard Sterling Boyle, C.C., Wallace, NS
Joseph A. Rouleau, C.C., G.O.Q., Montréal, QC*
The Honourable Michael H. Wilson, P.C., C.C., Toronto, ON
** indicates a promotion within the Order*

(Announced June 16, 2010)
Peter Munk, C.C., Toronto, ON

(Announced March 31, 2010)
The Honourable Michel Bastarache, C.C., Moncton, NB & Ottawa, ON

(Announced October 30, 2009)
Harley N. Hotchkiss, C.C., A.O.E., Calgary, AB
Stephen A. Jarislowsky, C.C., G.O.Q., Westmount, QC
Raymond Moriyama, C.C., O.Ont., Toronto, ON

Officers of the Order of Canada/ Officiers de l'Ordre du Canada (O.C.)
(Announced August 31, 2010)
George Beaton, O.C., Willowdale, ON

Clark Blaise, O.C., San Francisco, CA, U.S.A. & Montréal, QC
Pierre Boivin, O.C., Montréal, QC
Burton Cummings, O.C., O.M., Los Angeles, CA, U.S.A. & Winnipeg, MB
The Honourable Gary Filmon, P.C., O.C., O.M., Winnipe, MB
The Honourable John F. Hamm, O.C., Halifax, NS
Yves Jacques, O.C., Montréal, QC
Donald K. Johnson, O.C., Toronto, ON
Mario Lemieux, O.C., C.Q.,Pittsburgh, PA, U.S.A. & Montréal, QC
Jonathan Lomas, O.C., Ottawa, ON
Alexa McDonough, O.C., Halifax, NS
The Honourable R. Roy McMurtry, O.C., O.Ont., Toronto, ON
Pierre Nadeau, O.C., C.Q., Montréal, QC
Gordon W. Perkin, O.C., Seattle, WA, U.S.A. & Minden, ON
Bruce Phillips, O.C., Okanagan Falls, BC
Guylène Proulx, O.C. (Deceased), Gatineau, QC
Jack Rabinovitch, O.C., O.Ont., Toronto, ON
Ivan Reitman, O.C., Montecito, CA, U.S.A. & Toronto, ON
Donald (Don) Thompson, O.C., Toronto, ON

(Announced June 30, 2010)
The Honourable David A. Anderson, P.C., O.C., Victoria, BC
Raymonde April, O.C., Montréal, QC
Richard B. Baltzan, O.C., Saskatoon, SK
Raymond Chrétien, O.C., Montréal, QC
Claudio Cuello, O.C., Montréal, QC
Hélène Dorion, O.C., C.Q., Montréal, QC
Gwynne Dyer, O.C., London, U.K. & St. John's, NL
The Honourable Jake Epp, P.C., O.C., Calgary, AB & St. Boniface, MB
Michael J. Fox, O.C., New York, NY, U.S.A. & Burnaby, BC
John Furlong, O.C., Vancouver, BC
R. Brian Haynes, O.C., Dundas, ON
Margaret Lock, O.C., O.Q., Montréal, QC
John Mighton, O.C., Toronto, ON
Earl Muldon, O.C., Hazelton, BC
Julie Payette, O.C., C.Q., Montréal, QC. & Houston, TX, U.S.A.
Alvin C. Segal, O.C., Montréal, QC*
Nahum Sonenberg, O.C., Montréal, QC
Mladen Vranic, O.C., O.Ont., Toronto, ON
** indicates a promotion within the Order*

(Announced June 16, 2010)
Ian Bruce, O.C., Dorval, QC
Paul Georges Buissonneau, O.C., Montréal, QC
Mel Cappe, O.C., Toronto, ON
Nellie J. Cournoyea, O.C., Inuvik, NT
John W. Crow, O.C., Etobicoke, ON
Clémence DesRochers, O.C., C.Q., Austin, QC
Stanley C. (Buzz) Holling, O.C., Nanaimo, BC
Peter Jaffe, O.C., London, ON
The Honourable Michael Kirby, O.C., Ottawa, ON
Anita Kunz, O.C., Toronto, ON
The Honourable John P. Manley, P.C., O.C., Ottawa, ON
Cornelia Hahn Oberlander, O.C., Vancouver, BC

(Announced March 31, 2010)
Gary Birch, O.C., Vancouver, BC
The Honourable Iona Campagnolo, O.C., O.B.C., Courtenay, BC
Paul Garfinkel, O.C., Toronto, ON
Clara Hughes, O.C., O.M., Glen Sutton, QC & Winnipeg, MB
Dave Joe,O.C., Vancouver, BC
Arvind Koshal, O.C., Edmonton, AB
Louise Lecavalier, O.C., Montréal, QC
Allan P. Markin, O.C., Calgary, AB
David P. O'Brien, O.C., Calgary, AB & Montréal, QC
Ian C.P. Smith, O.C., Winnipeg, MB
The Honourable Barry L. Strayer, O.C., Ottawa, ON

(Announced February 23, 2010)
The Honourable Sterling R. Lyon, P.C., O.C., O.M., Winnipeg, MB

(Announced December 30, 2009)
Peter Hinton, O.C., Ottawa, ON
The Honourable Philippe Kirsch, O.C., The Hague, Netherlands, & Montréal, QC
James Orbinski, O.C., M.S.C., Toronto, ON
Carol L. Richards, O.C., Québec, QC
Carol Stephenson, O.C., London, ON
Neil Young, O.C., O.M., La Honda, CA, U.S.A. & Winnipeg, MB

(Announced October 30, 2009)
Gail Asper, O.C., O.M., Winnipeg, MB
Robin W. Boadway, O.C., Kingston, ON
AA Bronson, O.C., New York, NY, U.S.A. & Toronto, ON
Victor S. Buffalo, O.C., A.O.E., Hobbema, AB
William J. Commanda, O.C., Maniwaki, QC
Basil (Buzz) Hargrove, O.C., Mississauga, ON
The Honourable Donald J. Johnston, P.C., O.C., Glen Sutton, QC
Peter Mansbridge, O.C., Stratford, ON
The Honourable Frank McKenna, P.C., O.C., O.N.B., Cap-Pelé, N.B. & Toronto, ON
Clayton H. Riddell, O.C., Calgary, AB
Françoise Sullivan, O.C., C.Q., Montréal, QC

Honorary Officer of the Order of Canada/ Officier honorifique de l'Ordre du Canada (Invested July 1, 2009)
Sima Samar, O.C., Kabul, Afghanistan

Honorary Member of the Order of Canada/ Membre honorifique de l'Ordre du Canada (Invested July 1, 2009)
Zachary Richard, C.M., Montréal, QC

Members of the Order of Canada/ Membres de l'Ordre du Canada (C.M.) (Announced August 31 2010)
The Honourable Jean Augustine, P.C., Toronto, ON
The Honourable Lise Bacon, C.M., G.O., Montréal, QC
Lyle R. Best, C.M., Edmonton, AB
Sandra Birdsell, C.M., Regina, SK
Tantoo Cardinal, C.M., Vancouver, BC
Gail Cook-Bennett, C.M., Toronto, ON
Max Cynader, C.M., O.B.C., West Vancouver, BC
James J. Douglas, C.M., West Vancouver, BC
John C. Godel, C.M., Heriot Bay, BC
Dan Hanganu, C.M., O.Q., Montréal, QC
Jack Hodgins, C.M., Victoria, BC
Stanley J. Hughes, C.M., Ottawa, ON
Jay Ingram, C.M., Toronto, ON
Margaret Lyons, C.M., Toronto, ON
Matilda Murdoch, C.M., O.N.B., Miramichi, NB
Guy Nadon, C.M., Montréal, QC
Gordon M. Nixon, C.M., O.Ont., Toronto, ON
Jean O'Neil, C.M., C.Q., Paris, France & Montréal, QC
Patricia Parr, C.M., Toronto, ON
Ross E. Petty, C.M., Vancouver, BC
David Adams Richards, C.M., O.N.B., Fredericton, NB
Sister Simone Roach, C.M, Antigonish, NS
Bruce Sanford, C.M., Ottawa, ON
Roméo Savoie, C.M., Moncton, NB
Joseph A. (Joe) Sealy, C.M, Toronto, ON
Raoul Sosa, C.M., Montréal, QC
Wayne Strongman, C.M., Toronto, ON
Paul Stubbing, C.M., Ottawa, ON & Iqaluit, NU
Bob White, C.M., Calgary, AB
Jeanne M. Wolfe, C.M. (Deceased), Westmount, QC

(Announced June 30, 2010)
Georges A. Arès, C.M., Little Current, ON & Edmonton, AB
The Honourable Lise Bacon, C.M., G.O.Q., Laval, QC
Herbert C. Belcourt, C.M., Edmonton, AB
Michel G. Bergeron, C.M., O.Q., Québec, QC
Sandra Birdsell, C.M., Regina, SK
Alice Chan-Yip, C.M., Montréal, QC
W. Edmund Clark, C.M., Toronto, ON
Stephen Clarkson, C.M., Toronto, ON
Phil Comeau, C.M., Montréal, QC & Saulnierville, NS
Adriana A. Davies, C.M., Edmonton, AB
Abraham (Braam) de Klerk, C.M., Inuvik, NT
Marq de Villiers, C.M., Port Medway, NS
René Derouin, C.M., C.Q., Val-David, QC
Marlys A. Edwardh, C.M., Toronto, ON
James Ehnes, C.M.,Bradenton, FL, U.S.A. & Brandon, MB
Étienne Gaboury, C.M., Winnipeg, MB
Clarence A. Guenter, C.M., Canmore, AB
Mary Jo Haddad, C.M., Toronto, ON
Garry Hilderman, C.M., Dugald, MB
Stanley J. Hughes, C.M., Ottawa, ON
Patrick Jarvis, C.M., Calgary, AB
Mary Ellen Jeans, C.M., Ottawa, ON
Donald M. Julien, C.M., O.N.S., Truro, NS
Claude Laberge, C.M., Montréal, QC
Andrée Lortie, C.M., Ottawa, ON
Pierre Lucier, C.M., Québec, QC
James C. MacDougall, C.M., Montréal, QC
F. Richard Matthews, C.M., Calgary, AB
Alex C. Michalos, C.M., Brandon, MB & Prince George, BC
Karen Minden, C.M., Toronto, ON
Rita Mirwald, C.M., Saskatoon, SK
Aftab A. Mufti, C.M., Winnipeg, MB
Matilda Murdoch, C.M., O.N.B., Miramichi, NB
Guy Nadon, C.M., Montréal, QC
Gordon M. Nixon, C.M., O.Ont., Toronto, ON
Harold (Hal) O'Leary, C.M., Winter Park CO, U.S.A. & Fredericton, NB
Gilles G. Patry, C.M., Ottawa, ON
Bonnie M. Patterson, C.M., O.Ont., Toronto, ON
Ross H. Paul, C.M., Vancouver, BC & Windsor, ON
Chesley D. Penney, C.M., Conception Bay South, NL
Gordon L. Porter, C.M., Woodstock, NB
Rosalind Prober, C.M., Winnipeg, MB
Simone Roach, C.M., Antigonish, NS
Pierre Rolland, C.M., Montréal, QC
Walter Rosser, C.M., Kingston, ON
Ernesto L. Schiffrin, C.M., Montréal, QC
Glen Sorestad, C.M., Saskatoon, SK
Ann Southam, C.M., Toronto, ON
Orysia (Irene) Sushko, C.M., Hamilton, ON
Louis Taillefer, C.M., Sherbrooke, QC
Robert Holmes (R.H.) Thomson, C.M., Toronto, ON
David Turpin, C.M., Victoria, BC
Kue Young, C.M., Toronto, ON

(Announced June 16, 2010)
Carroll Baker, C.M., Guelph, ON. & Port Medway, NS
Elsie C. Basque, C.M., Saulnierville, NS
Stan Bevington, C.M., Toronto, ON
Émile Bouchard, C.M., C.Q., Saint-Lambert, QC
Melvin J. Boutilier, C.M., O.N.S., Halifax, NS
Deane Cameron, C.M., Toronto, ON
Savvas Chamberlain, C.M., Waterloo, ON
Victor Cicansky, C.M., Regina, SK
Joan Clark, C.M., St. John's, NL
Ian D. Clark, C.M., Toronto, ON
Maureen & Patrick Doherty, C.M., Bragg Creek, AB
Fred S. Fountain, C.M., Head of St. Margaret's Bay, NS
George Gate, C.M., Pointe-Claire, QC
Alan Giachino, C.M., Ottawa, ON
Susan J. Glass, C.M., Winnipeg, MB
Shirley E. Greenberg, C.M., Ottawa, ON
David G. Helwig, C.M., Charlottetown, PEI
Winston S. L. Kassim, C.M., Toronto, ON
Krishna Kumar, C.M., S.O.M., Regina, SK
Jean-Claude Labrecque, C.M., C.Q., Montréal, QC
Roderick R. McInnes, C.M., O.Ont., Mount Royal, QC
Father Sylvio Michaud, C.M., Montréal, QC
Mahmood A. Naqvi, C.M., O.N.S., Sydney, NS
Roland Priddle, C.M., Ottawa, ON. & Victoria, BC
Peter R. Taylor, C.M., Vancouver, BC
Ian M. Thom, C.M., Victoria, BC
Réjean Thomas, C.M., C.Q., Montréal, QC
Marvin Tile, C.M., Toronto, ON
Nancy Turner, C.M., O.B.C., Victoria, BC
Donald A. Young, C.M., Fredericton, NB
Madeline Ziniak, C.M., O.Ont., Toronto, ON

(Announced March 31, 2010)
Elsa Bolam, C.M., Montréal, QC
David Bouchard, C.M., Victoria, BC
David A. Brown, C.M., Kettleby, ON
Frederick J. Carmichael, C.M., Inuvik, NT
Renée Claude, C.M., Montréal, QC
Hélène Desmarais, C.M., Montréal, QC
Daniel Germain, C.M., C.Q., M.S.M., Boucherville, QC
Kenneth Kernaghan,C.M., Fenwick, ON
Marc Kielburger, C.M., Toronto, ON
Claude Le Bouthillier, C.M., Bas-Caraquet, NB
Frank L. Lovsin, C.M., Peace River, AB
David Matas, C.M., Winnipeg, MB
Gordon A. McBean, C.M., London, ON
Barbara McInnes, C.M., Ottawa, ON
Don McKay, C.M., St. John's, NL
K. Alexander Nilsson, C.M., Creston, BC
Allison D. O'Brien,C.M., Barrhead, AB
Willie E. O'Ree, C.M., O.N.B., La Mesa, U.S.A. & Fredericton, NB
Lata Pada, C.M., Mississauga, ON
Brian Paisley, C.M., Victoria, BC
Douglas Pollard, C.M. (Deceased), Cobalt, ON
Elinor G. Ratcliffe, C.M., O.N.L., Kingston, ON. & St. John's, NL
Angela Rebeiro, C.M., Toronto, ON
Henry A. Regier, C.M., Elmira, ON
Zachary Richard, C.M., Louisiana, U.S.A. & Montréal, QC
The Honourable Edward Roberts, C.M., O.N.L., St. John's, NL
Byron P. Rourke, C.M., Windor, ON
Donald W. Storch, C.M., Victoria, BC
David Thauberger,C.M., Regina, SK
Pierre Théroux, C.M., Montréal, QC
Shirley Westeinde, C.M., Ottawa, ON

(Announced December 30, 2009)
Murray Angus, C.M., Ottawa, ON
Calixte Duguay, C.M., Caraquet, NB
Janet C. Gardiner, C.M., St. John's, NL
Judy Gingell, C.M., Whitehorse, YT
Joan Glode, C.M., Shubenacadie, NS

S. Larry Goldenberg, C.M., O.B.C., Vancouver, BC
Bernard S. Goldman, C.M., Toronto, ON
Patrick J. Gullane, C.M., Toronto, ON
Louise Lévesque, C.M., C.Q., Hudson, QC
Jeffrey C. Lozon, C.M., Toronto, ON
David K. Pecaut, C.M. (deceased), Toronto, ON
Robert W. Slater, C.M., Ottawa, ON
John Stanton, C.M., Edmonton, AB
Richard B. Wright, C.M., St. Catharines, ON

(Announced October 30, 2009)
M. Azhar Ali Khan, C.M., O.Ont., Ottawa, ON
Gordon E. Arnell, C.M., Calgary, AB
Michael A. Baker, C.M., O.Ont., Toronto, ON
Robert E. Brown, C.M., O.Q., Westmount, QC
Dinu Bumbaru, C.M., Montréal, QC
Douglas Cole, C.M., Port Sydney, ON
Robert G. Glossop, C.M., Ottawa, ON
Arlene Haché, C.M., Yellowknife, NT
Dezsö J. Horváth, C.M., Toronto, ON
Rudolph J. Kriegler, C.M., Ottawa, ON
John F. Lewis, C.M., St. John's, N.L
H. Wade MacLauchlan, C.M., West Covehead, PEI
Michael R. Marrus, C.M., Toronto, ON
Ian W. McDougall, C.M., Victoria, BC
James H. Morrison, C.M., Halifax, NS
Victor M. Power, C.M., Timmins, ON
The Honourable Herbert O. Sparrow, C.M., North Battleford, SK
Ian Vorres, C.M., Athens, Greece & Toronto, ON
Henry H. Wakabayashi, C.M., O.B.C., Vancouver, BC
William J. Wall, C.M., London, ON
Michael R. Weir, C.M., O.Ont., Draper, UT, U.S.A. & Bright's Grove, ON

(Announced August 31, 2009)
Archie Charles, C.M., Seabird Island, BC

(Announced August 25, 2009)
Joyce Barkhouse, C.M., O.N.S., Bridgewater, NS

ORDER OF MILITARY MERIT

The Order of Military Merit was created on July 1, 1972 to recognize meritorious service and devotion to duty by members of the Canadian Forces. The Order has three grades of membership: Commander (C.M.M.), Officer (O.M.M.) and Member (M.M.M.). The annual number of appointments is limited to one-tenth of one percent of the number of persons in the Canadian Forces in the preceding year.

Commanders of the Order of Military Merit/ Commandeurs de l'Ordre du mérite militaire (C.M.M.)
(Invested February 24, 2010)
Major-General Christopher Davis, C.M.M., C.D., Brussels, Belgium
Major-General André Deschamps, C.M.M., C.D., Ottawa, ON
Vice-Admiral Bruce Donaldson, C.M.M., C.D., Ottawa, ON
Major-General Glynne Hines, C.M.M., C.D., Ottawa, ON*
** indicates a promotion within the Order*

(Invested January 21, 2010)
Rear-Admiral Robert Andrew Davidson, C.M.M., C.D., Ottawa, ON
Lieutenant-General Joseph Paul André Deschamps, C.M.M., C.D., Ottawa, ON
Major-General Peter John Devlin, C.M.M., M.S.C., C.D., Ottawa, ON
Vice-Admiral Alistair Bruce Donaldson, C.M.M., C.D., Ottawa, ON
Major-General David Allison Fraser, C.M.M., M.S.C., M.S.M., C.D., Kingston, ON
Brigadier-General David Charles Kettle, C.M.M., C.D., Ottawa, ON

Officers of the the Order of Military Merit/ Officiers de l'Ordre du mérite militaire (O.M.M.)
(Invested February 24, 2010)
Col. Lawrence Aitken, O.M.M.,C.D., Kingston, ON
Col. Scott Becker, O.M.M., C.D., Ottawa, ON
Col. David Belovich, O.M.M., C.D., Ottawa, ON
L.Col. Troy Crosby, O.M.M., C.D., Ottawa, ON
Maj. Daniel Gagnon, O.M.M., C.D., Ottawa, ON
Commodore Roger MacIsaac, O.M.M., C.D., Ottawa, ON
Col. David Marshall, O.M.M., C.D., Ottawa, ON
Col. Bruce McQuade, O.M.M., C.D., Ottawa, ON
Brigadier-General Gary O'Brien, O.M.M., M.S.C., C.D., Ottawa, ON
Col. Alain Parent, O.M.M., C.D.,Kingston, ON
Col. Jonathan Vance, O.M.M., C.D., Edmonton, AB
Maj. Eileen Vaughan, O.M.M., C.D., Borden, ON
Col. Kelly Woiden, O.M.M., C.D., Edmonton, AB

(Invested January 21, 2010)
Col. David Morris Belovich, O.M.M., C.D., Ottawa, ON
Capt. (Navy) Joseph John Robert Richard Bergeron, O.M.M., C.D., Washington, DC, USA
Maj. Kevin Linus Caldwell, O.M.M., C.D., Ottawa, ON
Maj. Steven Mark Card, O.M.M., C.D., Kingston, ON
Col. Christopher John Coates, O.M.M., C.D., Kingston, ON
L.Col. Dalton James Côté, O.M.M., C.D., Kingston, ON
Col. Francis Paul Crober, O.M.M., C.D., Victoria, BC
Col. Michael Donald Day, O.M.M., C.D., Ottawa, ON
Commander Christopher John Deere, O.M.M., C.D., Ottawa, ON
Maj. Joseph François Daniel Gagnon, O.M.M., C.D., Ottawa, ON
Col. Derek William Joyce, O.M.M., C.D., Greenwood, NS
L.Col. James Gérard Kile, O.M.M., C.D., Toronto, ON
Col. Charles Adrien Lamarre, O.M.M., C.D., Edmonton, AB
Col. Patrice Joseph Roger Laroche, O.M.M., C.D., Belleville, ON
Commodore James Roger MacIsaac, O.M.M., C.D., Ottawa, ON
Col. Douglas Alan Maclean, O.M.M., C.D., Halifax, NS
Col. Dean James Milner, O.M.M., C.D., North York, ON
Brigadier-General Gary James Patrick O'Brien, O.M.M., M.S.C., C.D., Ottawa, ON
Capt. (Navy) Colin Wallace Plows, O.M.M., C.D., Ottawa, ON
Col. Joseph Pierre Julien St-Amand, O.M.M., C.D., Ottawa, ON
Col. Christopher Calvin Thurrott, O.M.M., M.S.M., C.D.,Ottawa, ON
Col. Robert Schuman Williams, O.M.M., M.S.M., C.D., North York, ON

Members of the Order of Military Merit/ Membres de l'Ordre du mérite militaire (M.M.M.)
(Invested February 24, 2010)
Master Warrant Officer Douglas Badgerow, M.M.M., C.D., London, ON
Maj. William Beaudoin, M.M.M., C.D., Oromocto, NB
Warrant Officer Leonard R. Canam, M.M.M., C.D., Oromocto, NB
Chief Petty Officer 2nd Class Richard Clark-McKay, M.M.M., C.D., Victoria, BC
Sgt. Allan Comé, M.M.M., C.D., Astra, ON
Chief Warrant Officer David Coxall, M.M.M., C.D., Edmonton, AB
Master Warrant Officer Derek Curtis, M.M.M., M.S.M., C.D., Gander, NL
Chief Warrant Officer David Ells, M.M.M., C.D., Meaford, ON
Chief Warrant Officer Charles Fortin, M.M.M., C.D., Kandahar, Afghanistan
Lieutenant-Commander Pierre Godin, M.M.M., C.D., Richelain, QC
Warrant Officer Luc Guillemette, M.M.M., C.D., Courcelette, QC
Chief Warrant Officer Tom Hennessey, M.M.M., C.D., Victoria, BC
Capt. Paul Hillier, M.M.M., C.D., Oromocto, NB
Master Warrant Officer Glenn Innis, M.M.M., C.D., Edmonton, AB
Chief Petty Officer 2nd Class Patrick Jacobs, M.M.M., C.D., Halifax, NS
Master Warrant Officer Jerry Juraszko, M.M.M., C.D., London, ON
Capt. Rock Labrecque, M.M.M., C.D., Ste-Foy, QC
Sgt. Manon Langlois, M.M.M., C.D., Ottawa, ON
Master Warrant Officer Kevin Lewis, M.M.M., C.D., Richelain, QC
Chief Warrant Officer Daniel Libby, M.M.M., C.D., Ottawa, ON
Master Warrant Officer Jean-Guy Lizotte, M.M.M., C.D., Oromocto, NB
Maj. Leslie Mader, M.M.M., C.D., Ottawa, ON
Master Warrant Officer Michele Manoukarakis, M.M.M., C.D., Kingston, ON
Warrant Officer John Murphy, M.M.M., C.D., Victoria, BC
Chief Warrant Officer Donald Noël, M.M.M., C.D., Québec, QC
Maj. David Parker, M.M.M., C.D., Ottawa, ON
Chief Petty Officer 2nd Class Sharon Rideout, M.M.M., C.D., Ottawa, ON
Chief Warrant Officer Pedro Rosa, M.M.M., C.D., Toronto, ON
Master Warrant Officer David Steiger, M.M.M., C.D., Halifax, NS
Sgt. Albert Sutherland, M.M.M., Borden, ON
Lieutenant-Commander Ian Torrie, M.M.M., C.D., Ottawa, ON
Chief Petty Officer 1st Class Luc Tremblay, M.M.M., C.D., Ottawa, ON
Maj. Roger Tremblay, M.M.M., C.D., Ottawa, ON
Warrant Officer Daniel Verreault, M.M.M., C.D., Courcelette, QC
Chief Warrant Officer Glenn Wallace, M.M.M., C.D., Winnipeg, MB
Master Warrant Officer Peter Whipps, M.M.M., C.D., Edmonton, AB
Capt. Jeff Willis, M.M.M., C.D., Kingston, ON

(Invested January 21, 2010)
Master Warrant Officer Jeffrey Charles Lorne Aman, M.M.M., C.D., Petawawa, ON
Capt. Dwayne William Atkinson, M.M.M., C.D., Kingston, ON
Master Warrant Officer John Gerard Barnes, M.M.M., C.D., Kingston, ON
Sgt. Alain André Joseph Barriault, M.M.M., C.D., Courcelette, QC
Petty Officer 1st class Stephen Beastall, M.M.M., C.D., London, ON
Chief Warrant Officer Gary Bradley Biggar, M.M.M., C.D., Oromocto, NB
Warrant Officer Charles David Brady, M.M.M., C.D., Toronto, ON
Chief Petty Officer 2nd class Cheryl Dawn Bush, M.M.M., C.D., Ottawa, ON
Master Warrant Officer Dale William Coble, M.M.M., C.D., Edmonton, AB
Chief Petty Officer 2nd class Austin Joseph Collett, M.M.M., C.D., Shearwater, NS
Master Warrant Officer Edward William Dallow, M.M.M., C.D., Petawawa, ON
Master Warrant Officer Thaddeous Bernard D'Andrade, M.M.M., C.D., Edmonton, AB
Master Warrant Officer André Joseph Lucien Demers, M.M.M., C.D., Montréal, QC
Chief Warrant Officer Joseph Léopold Mario Dion, M.M.M., C.D., Cold Lake, AB
Master Warrant Officer Dany Joseph Joël Dubuc, M.M.M., C.D., Courcelette, QC
Master Warrant Officer Elizabeth Marguerite Dunsmore, M.M.M., C.D., Lazo, BC
Capt. Jason Brent English, M.M.M., C.D., Winnipeg, MB
Chief Petty Officer 2nd class Michael David Fairfex, M.M.M., C.D., North York, ON
Master Warrant Officer Pierre Joseph Frenette, M.M.M., C.D., Québec, QC
Warrant Officer Kelly Todd Grant, M.M.M., C.D., Oromocto, NB
Chief Petty Officer 2nd class Gilles André Grégoire, M.M.M., C.D., Halifax, NS
Chief Warrant Officer Joseph René Raoul Stéphane Guy, M.M.M., C.D., Kingston, ON
Chief Warrant Officer Joseph Sandor Gyuk, M.M.M., C.D., Ottawa, ON
Warrant Officer Thomas William Hale, M.M.M., C.D., Oromocto, NB
Maj. Marie Gisèle Carmen Hamel, M.M.M., C.D., Richelain, QC
Capt. Peter William Hamilton, M.M.M., C.D., Kingston, ON
Chief Warrant Officer Stuart Gordon Hartnell, M.M.M., C.D., Petawawa, ON
Chief Warrant Officer Tom Carl Hennessey, M.M.M., C.D., Ottawa, ON
Maj. Lewis Edwin Irvine, M.M.M., C.D., Halifax, NS
Master Warrant Officer James Robert Jeckell, M.M.M., C.D., Astra, ON
Capt. Lennard Mark Johnston, M.M.M., C.D., Borden, ON
Master Warrant Officer Lewis Harry Johnstone, M.M.M., C.D., Winnipeg, MB
Master Warrant Officer Raymond Chester King, M.M.M., C.D., Kingston, ON
Master Warrant Officer Roger William King, M.M.M., C.D., Kingston, ON
Sgt. Manon Gina Langlois, M.M.M., C.D., Ottawa, ON
Master Warrant Officer Michel Joseph Sylva Lavallée, M.M.M., C.D., Oromocto, NB
Capt. Patrick Joseph Lee, M.M.M., C.D., Halifax, NS
Chief Petty Officer 2nd class Thomas Allan Lizotte, M.M.M., C.D., Halifax, NS
Warrant Officer Patrick Timothy Love, M.M.M., C.D., Denwood, AB
Chief Warrant Officer Kenneth Charles Lutz, M.M.M., C.D., St-John's, NL
Capt. Donna Anne MacAulay, M.M.M., C.D., Ottawa, ON
Chief Warrant Officer Donald Alexander MacIsaac, M.M.M., C.D., Belleville, ON
Maj. Leslie Robert Mader, M.M.M., C.D., Ottawa, ON
Chief Petty Officer 2nd class Bradley James Main, M.M.M., C.D., Victoria, BC
Master Warrant Officer Kevin James Mathers, M.M.M., C.D., Petawawa, ON
Chief Warrant Officer Michael Lawrence McDonald, M.M.M., M.S.C., C.D., Kingston, ON
Warrant Officer Sandra Ann Melanson M.M.M., C.D., Astra, ON
Chief Petty Officer 2nd class Eric Rudyard Meredith, M.M.M., C.D., Victoria, BC
Master Warrant Officer Marie Carole Fernande Monsigneur, M.M.M., C.D., Richelain, QC
Master Warrant Officer Lawrence Russell Mullen, M.M.M., C.D., Denwood, AB
Master Warrant Officer Sean Joseph Murphy, M.M.M., C.D., Vandenberg, California, USA

Petty Officer 1st class Peter Francis Neville, M.M.M., C.D., Halifax, NS
Chief Warrant Officer André Joseph Gérald Normandin, M.M.M., C.D., Courcelette, QC
Chief Warrant Officer Marc André Joseph Pelletier, M.M.M., C.D., Ottawa, ON
Master Warrant Officer David Charles Phillips, M.M.M., C.D., Denwood, AB
Warrant Officer Stephen Glen Piccolo, M.M.M., C.D., Cold Lake, AB
Capt. Peter Joseph Pitcher, M.M.M., C.D., Aldergrove, BC
Maj. Lorne Benedict Plemel, M.M.M., C.D., Belleville, ON
Sgt. Markussie Qinuajuak, M.M.M., C.D., Richelain, QC
Chief Warrant Officer Joseph Ramsay, M.M.M., C.D., Edmonton, AB
Chief Warrant Officer Glen Richard Rideout, M.M.M., C.D., Winnipeg, MB
Chief Warrant Officer Pedro Eduardo Rosa, M.M.M., C.D., Toronto, ON
Warrant Officer Claudette Jacqueline Saunders, M.M.M., C.D., Yellowknife, NT
Petty Officer 1st class Patrick James Johannes Saunders, M.M.M., C.D., Halifax, NS
Chief Warrant Officer Michael Gerald Scarcella, M.M.M., C.D., Lazo, BC
Petty Officer 1st class Cavel Thomas Shebib, M.M.M., C.D., Halifax, NS
Chief Warrant Officer Anthony James Slack, M.M.M., C.D., Kingston, ON
Master Warrant Officer Roland Wavel Smith, M.M.M., C.D., Petawawa, ON
Master Warrant Officer Jennifer Lynne Ste-Croix, M.M.M., C.D., Winnipeg, MB
Sgt. Yan St-Pierre, M.M.M., C.D., Courcelette, QC
Maj. Jean-Yves Taschereau, M.M.M., C.D., Happy Valley-Goose Bay, NL
Master Warrant Officer Sharman Patrick Thomas, M.M.M., C.D., Trail, BC
Chief Petty Officer 1st class Luc Joseph Royal Tremblay, M.M.M., C.D., Ottawa, ON
Master Warrant Officer Pierre Joseph Richard Tremblay, M.M.M., C.D., Courcelette, QC
Chief Petty Officer 2nd class Charles Melvin Frederick Trombley, M.M.M., C.D., Shearwater, NS
Master Warrant Officer Donald Wellesley Tupper, M.M.M., C.D., Oromocto, NB
Maj. Darren Edward Turner, M.M.M., C.D., Petawawa, ON
Warrant Officer Michael Bernard Vandepol, M.M.M., C.D., Petawawa, ON
Chief Warrant Officer Armand Joseph Simon Vinet, M.M.M., C.D., Belleville, ON
Warrant Officer Leslie James Wilson, M.M.M., C.D., Edmonton, AB
Chief Petty Officer 2nd class Kevin Allen Woods, M.M.M., C.D., Victoria, BC
Maj. John Garnet Zoellner, M.M.M., C.D., Montréal, QC
Roland Gregory Zwicker, M.M.M., C.D., Edmonton, AB

(Invested July 6, 2009)

Chief Warrant Officer George Hughes, M.M.M., C.D., Edmonton, AB

ORDER OF MERIT OF THE POLICE FORCES

In October 2000, Her Majesty The Queen approved the creation of the Order as a means of recognizing conspicuous merit and exceptional service by members and employees of the Canadian police forces whose contributions extend beyond protection of the community. There are three levels of membership - Commander, Officer and Member - that reflect long-term, outstanding service in varying degrees of responsibility. Each level has corresponding nominal letters: C.O.M., O.O.M. and M.O.M.

Commander of the Order of Merit of the Police Forces/ Commandeur de l'Ordre du mérite des corps policiers (C.O.M.) (Invested May 21, 2010)

Assistant Director General Steven Chabot, C.O.M., Montréal, QC*

** indicates a promotion within the Order*

Officers of the the Order of Merit of the Police Forces/ Officiers de l'Ordre du mérite des corps policiers (O.O.M.) (Invested May 21, 2010)

Deputy Commissioner Lawrence Graham Beechey, O.O.M., Orillia, ON
Chief Constable Jamie Hamilton Graham, O.O.M., Victoria, BC
Deputy Commissioner J. V. N. (Vincent) Hawkes, O.O.M., Orillia, ON
Deputy Commissioner Christopher D. Lewis, O.O.M., Orillia, ON*
Assistant Commissioner Robert Wilfred Paulson, O.O.M., Ottawa, ON*
Inspector Joseph Lance Valcour, O.O.M., Ottawa, ON

** indicates a promotion within the Order*

Members of the the Order of Merit of the Police Forces/ Membres de l'Ordre du mérite des corps policiers (M.O.M.) (Invested May 21, 2010)

Chief Keith John Atkinson, M.O.M., Brandon, MB
Superintendent Bradley Blair, M.O.M., Orillia, ON
Staff Sgt. Murray Elijah Brown, M.O.M., Halifax, NS
Chief Constable Douglas James Cessford, M.O.M., Delta, BC
Sgt. G. Shawn Coady, M.O.M., C.D., Vancouver, BC
Deputy Chief Constable John Alexander Ducker, M.O.M., Victoria, BC
Staff Superintendent Michael Federico, M.O.M., Toronto, ON
Chief Inspector André Fortin, M.O.M., Montréal, QC
Corporal Christopher G. Gosselin, M.O.M., Chilliwack, BC
Sgt. Stewart C. Kellock, M.O.M., C.D., Toronto, ON
Assistant Commissioner Wayne Alexander Lang, M.O.M., Fredericton, NB
Ms. Brenda Lawson, M.O.M., Ottawa, ON
Chief Barry D. MacKnight, M.O.M., Fredericton, NB
Chief Superintendent William Fraser MacRae, M.O.M., Surrey, BC
Deputy Chief Michael S. Mann, M.O.M., Cambridge, ON
Superintendent H. Alfred Niedtner, M.O.M., Vancouver, BC
Inspector André Péloquin, M.O.M., Montréal, QC
Deputy Chief John Allan Redford, M.O.M., Calgary, AB
Inspector Ronald 'Dean' Robinson, M.O.M., Vancouver, BC
Constable Tom Stamatakis, M.O.M., Vancouver, BC
Director Marc St-Laurent, M.O.M., Longueuil, QC
Deputy Chief Constable Stephen C. Sweeney, M.O.M., Vancouver, BC
Detective Sergeant James Arthur Van Allen, M.O.M., Orillia, ON

CANADIAN BRAVERY DECORATIONS/DÉCORATIONS CANADIENNES POUR ACTES DE BRAVOURE

The Decorations for Bravery, consisting of the Cross of Valour, the Star of Courage, and the Medal of Bravery, were instituted and created on May 10, 1972. They may be awarded to Canadian citizens or to non-Canadians who have performed an act of bravery in Canada, or outside Canada if the act was in Canada's interest. The Decorations for Bravery may be awarded posthumously.

The Cross of Valour is awarded for acts of the most conspicuous courage in circumstances of extreme peril. The Star of Courage is awarded for acts of conspicuous courage in circumstances of great peril. The Medal of Bravery is awarded for acts of bravery in hazardous circumstances.

Cross of Valour/Croix de Valeur (C.V.)

None awarded since last edition.

Star of Courage/Étoile du courage (S.C.) (Announced September 24, 2010)

Miranda Suggitt, S.C., Lindsay, ON
Michael Thomas Westwell, S.C., C.D., Pukatawagan, MB

(Announced August 27, 2010)

Miguel Gonzalez, S.C., Montréal, QC
Luc Paquette, S.C., Montréal, QC

(Announced August 3, 2010)

Casey Marie Peirce, S.C., Calgary, AB
Alexander Bruce Scott, S.C., Saint John, NB

(Announced February 2, 2010)

Petty Officer 2nd Class Drew D. Dazzo, S.C., Elizabeth City, North Carolina, USA

(Announced November 23, 2009)

Sgt. Bryant Wood, S.C., M.B., Port Hope, ON

Medal of Bravery/Médaille de la bravoure (M.B.) (Announced September 24, 2010)

L.Co. Douglas Wynn Baird, M.B., C.D., Aylesford Lake, NS
Constable Robert Bérubé, M.B., Montréal, QC
Scott Borlase, M.B., Winnipeg, MB
Joseph Henry Roland Bouliane, M.B., Winnipeg, MB
Constable Benoit Brissette, M.B., Montréal, QC
Sgt. Steve Desgagné, M.B., Montréal, QC
Richard Frauley, M.B., Saint John, NB
Isabelle Gagnon, M.B., Saint-Hubert, QC
Master-Corporal Julien Gauthier, M.B., Greenwood, NS
Maj. William Robertson Green, M.B., C.D., Moose Jaw, SK
Blair William Allan Hockin, M.B., Portage La Prairie, MB
Sgt. André Joseph Hotton, M.B., C.D., Greenwood, NS
Tim Kautaq, M.B., Hall Beach, NU
RCMP Constable Alfred Douglas Lavallee, M.B., Winnipeg, MB
Pascale Pelletier, M.B., Mercier, QC
Sgt. Joseph Kenneth Penman, M.B., Winnipeg, MB
Stephen Power, M.B., Charlottetown, PEI
Master Warrant Officer Hamish Seggie, M.B., C.D., Winnipeg, MB
Warrant Officer Shaun Spence, M.B., C.D., Ottawa, ON
Tami Elizabeth Strickland, M.B., Charlottetown, PEI
Abebe Yohannes, M.B., Brandon, MB
Herman Zarbel, M.B., Winnipeg, MB

(Announced August 27, 2010)

Constable Nicholas Bell, M.B., Vancouver, BC
John Peter Chatterton, M.B., Richmond, ON
Daisy Flamand, M.B. Manawan, QC
Jared Douglas Gagen, M.B., Cobble Hill, BC
Ernest Jean, M.B., Montréal, QC
Marjorie Jean-Baptiste, M.B., Montréal, QC
Thomas Manuel, M.B., Fort Good Hope, NT
Warren Bruce Miller, M.B., Victoria, BC
Michaël Perreault Giroux, M.B., Rivière-Rouge, QC
Edward Stirling, M.B., Ladysmith, BC
Constable Wayne Thompson, M.B., Vancouver, BC
Philippe Tremblay, M.B., Bathurst, NB
Art Unruh, M.B., Abbotsford, BC
Chad Verch, M.B., Victoria, BC
William Watt, M.B., Victoria, BC

(Announced August 3, 2010)

Sgt. B. John Ayers, M.B., Victoria, BC
Leading Seaman Robert T. Binder, M.B. (deceased), Toronto, ON
Steve Blake, M.B., Jasper, AB
Dale Brady, M.B., Valemount, BC
Shane Michael Doucette, M.B., Red Deer, AB
Constable Lionel Girault, M.B., Montréal, QC
Sgt. Michael Johnston, M.B., Victoria, BC
Master Corporal David Frederick Taylor King, M.B., C.D., Victoria, BC
Sgt. Patrick Lalonde, M.B., Montréal, QC
Guy Lavoie, M.B., Saint-Narcisse, QC
Able Seaman Jaret A. McQueen, M.B., Hamilton, ON
Constable Jean Milliard, M.B., Montréal, QC
Constable Cal Traversy, M.B., Delta, BC
Constable Clifford Watson, M.B., Victoria, BC
Andrea Wiznuk, M.B., Enderby, BC

(Announced March 18, 2010)

David H. R. Byrd, M.B., Belleville, ON
Michael D. Byrd, M.B., Belleville, ON
Thomas James Dodd, M.B. (Posthumous), Chilliwack, BC
Robert Edward Dorie, M.B., Long Creek, NB
Robin Fabiani, M.B., Montréal, QC
Constable Michael Verney Gallant, M.B., Windsor, ON
Constable Phillip Kolody, M.B., Windsor, ON
Doug Knill, M.B., Scotland, ON
Samantha-Joe Larose, M.B., Noëlleville, ON
Bruce Lavallee, M.B., Alban, ON
Donald Morrison, M.B., Dutch Valley, NB
Marc Patterson, M.B., Kamloops, BC
Stuart Pringle, M.B., Chesterville, ON
Corporal Gabriel Proulx, M.B., Belleville, ON
Francis Quevillon, M.B., Laval, QC
Constable Dale George Sleightholme, M.B., Victoria, BC
Constable Paul Allan Spencelayh, M.B., Victoria, BC
Mike André Toupin, M.B., Miramichi, NB
Daniel White, M.B., Paris, ON

(Announced February 2, 2010)

Ryan Cecil Atwin, M.B., Oromocto, NB
Provincial Constable Daniel Bailey, M.B., Fort Frances, ON
Mark Barnard, M.B., Regina, SK
Jerrica Lynn Bartlett, M.B., St. Stephen, NB
Capt. Denis Beaulieu, M.B., Bushell Park, SK
Gerard Beernaerts, M.B., Winnipeg, MB
Gary Victor Brown, M.B., Bella Coola, BC
Benjamin Loren Correos, M.B. (posthumous), Whitehorse, YT
Constable Aaron Courtney, M.B., Abbotsford, BC
Constable Frédéric Couture, M.B., Montréal, QC
Michael Cruz, M.B., Holyoke, Massachusetts, USA
Master Corporal Jonas Denechezhe, M.B., Lac Brochet, MB
Robert Joseph Kyle Donelle, M.B., Fredericton, NB
Kimpton Gagnon-Després, M.B., Whitehorse, YT
Evan John Michael Green, M.B., Oromocto, NB
Robert Hardy, M.B., Conception Bay South, NL
Shaun Harper, M.B., West Vancouver, BC
Michel Harvey, M.B., Saint-Constant, QC
Raphaël Harvey Bérard, M.B., Saint-Constant, QC

Andrew Douglas Hilderman, M.B., Regina, SK
Gerry Kuczek, M.B., Winnipeg, MB
Wayne Kuczek, M.B., Winnipeg, MB
Michael David Landry, M.B., Regina, SK
Constable Martin Langlois, M.B., Montréal, QC
Nicholas Levi Francis Lannigan, M.B., Oromocto, NB
G. Gregory Lawlor, M.B., Conception Bay South, NL
Scott Lee Joseph Moody, M.B. (deceased), Bella Coola, BC
RCMP Corporal James Allan Munro, M.B., Dauphin, MB
Provincial Constable Gino Nolet, M.B., Hearst, ON
Provincial Constable James D. Orser, M.B., Campbellford, ON
Harry Prymak, M.B., St. Clements, MB
Daniel Reynolds, M.B., Hamilton, ON
Robert Ringuette, M.B., Hearst, ON
Kelsey Jessica Roy, M.B., Carleton Place, ON
Sharanjit (Shawn) Sangha, M.B., Abbotsford, BC
Tanya Silveira, M.B., Vancouver, BC
Cody Brian Sloot, M.B., Castlegar, BC
Provincial Constable Bruce A. Thompson, M.B., Campbellford, ON
Tony Niels Tingskou, M.B., Surrey, BC
Clifford Tsessasze, M.B., Lac Brochet, MB
David Glenn Virgoe, M.B., (posthumous), Angus, ON
Provincial Constable Darrell Wagner, M.B., Pembroke, ON
Tanya Lee Waldriff, M.B., Arnstein, ON
Robert A. Walker, M.B.Dundas, ON
Caroline Young, M.B., Conception Bay South, NL
Constable Kevin Wade Zeh, M.B., Calgary, AB

(Announced November 23, 2009)
Jimmy Victor Beardy, M.B., Manitoba
Constable Patrick Benoit, M.B., Kingston, ON
Ryan Sterling Burry, M.B., St. John's, NL
Elaine Dare, M.B., Port Loring, ON
Frédéric Dufresne, M.B., Trois-Rivières, QC
Kimberly Friesen, M.B., Quesnel, BC
Paul Linklater, M.B., Thompson, MB
Gillian Irene MacAulay, M.B., Trenton, NS
Sylvain Joseph Marcoux, M.B., Montréal, QC
Constable Sean Ralph, M.B., Ottawa, ON
Constable Alain Rochette, M.B., Ottawa, ON
Bryant Wood, S.C., M.B., Port Hope, ON (honored with two Bravery Decorations)

(Announced September 11, 2009)
Terry Bratton, M.B., Verdun, QC
Louis-Paul Courbron, M.B., Québec, QC
Frédérick Dionne, M.B., Saint-Nicolas, QC
James Donovan, M.B., Montréal, QC
Yves Pilotte, M.B., (posthumous), Notre-Dame-de-Lourdes, QC
Tommy Thériault, M.B., Québec, QC
Alexis Laliberté, M.B., Montréal, QC
Constable François Lavoie, M.B., Jonquière, QC
Constable Yves Rousseau, M.B., Jonquière, QC
Philippe O. Murphy, M.B., Brossard, QC

(Announced September 1, 2009)
Dean R. DeJoseph, M.B., Windsor, ON
Norbert Hébert, M.B., Lacolle, QC
Shawn Joseph Lahey, M.B., Kilbride, NL
Leading Seaman Roxanne Anneke Lalonde, M.B. (posthumous), Merrickville, ON
Sgt. Roger Chadwick Lane, M.B., Gagetown, NB
Chris MacLeod, M.B., Sydney, NS
Guillaume Massé, M.B., La Minerve, QC
Hady Quan, M.B. (posthumous), Vancouver, BC
Michael Braden Walker, M.B., North York, ON

MERITORIOUS SERVICE DECORATIONS/DÉCORATIONS POUR SERVICE MÉRITOIRE

Approved by Her Majesty the Queen on July 10, 1991, the Meritorious Service Decorations were created to honour Canadians & foreigners (military & civil) for commendable actions performed on or after June 11, 1984.

The Meritorious Service Cross (Military Division) is awarded for the performance of a military deed or a military activity in an outstandingly professional manner or of a rare high standard that brings considerable benefit or great honour to the Canadian Forces.

The Meritorious Service Cross (Civil Division) is awarded for the performance of a deed or activity in an outstandingly professional manner or of an uncommonly high standard that brings considerable benefit or great honour to Canada.

The Meritorious Service Medal (Military Division) is awarded for the performance of a military deed or a military activity in a highly professional manner or of a very high standard that brings benefit or honour to the Canadian Forces.

The Meritorious Service Medal (Civil Division) is awarded for the performance of a deed or activity in a highly professional manner or of a very high standard that brings benefit or honour to Canada.

Meritorious Service Cross/M.S.C. (Civil)/
La Croix du service méritoire (civile)
None awarded since last edition.

Meritorious Service Cross/M.S.C. (Military)/
La Croix du service méritoire (militaire)
(Announced September 29, 2010)
Sgt. Joseph Martin Brink, M.S.C., Sylvan Lake, AB

(Announced May 31, 2010)
Sgt. Nicholas Samuel James Deriger, M.S.C., C.D., Petawawa and Ottawa, ON
Sgt. Darrell Lawrence Spence, M.S.C., C.D., Deep River, ON. & Springhill, NS
L.Col. Dana Jeffrey Woodworth, M.S.C., C.D., Edmonton, AB

(Announced March 19, 2010)
Commander Craig Alan Baines, M.S.C., C.D., Victoria & Comox, BC
General Bantz John Craddock, M.S.C., Myrtle Beach, South Carolina, USA
Rear-Admiral Robert Andrew Davidson, M.S.C., C.D., Ottawa, ON
Sgt. Shawn E. Harrison, M.S.C., C.D., Winnipeg, MB, & Gander, NL
Warrant Officer Bryan Keith Pierce, C.V., M.S.C., C.D., Winnipeg, MB
General Victor Eugene Renuart, Jr., M.S.C., Colorado Springs, Colorado, & Miami, Florida, USA

(Announced November 11, 2009)
Master Warrant Officer Rodney Albert Dearing, M.S.C., C.D., Denwood, AB, & Armstrong, BC
Commander Pierre Christophe Dickinson, M.S.C., C.D., Ottawa, ON, & Sillery, QC
General Raymond Roland Joseph Henault, C.M.M., M.S.C., C.D. (Retired), Headingley & Winnipeg, MB
L.Col. Darryl Albert Mills, M.S.C., C.D., Meaford, ON., & Oromocto, NB
Chief Warrant Officer Giovanni Moretti, M.M.M., M.S.C., C.D., Petawawa & Toronto, ON, and St-Anicet, QC
Brigadier-General Denis William Thompson, O.M.M., M.S.C., C.D., Ottawa & Stayner, ON

(Announced October 21, 2009)
Lieutenant-General Joseph Guy Marc Lessard, C.M.M., M.S.C., C.D., Ottawa, ON
Warrant Officer John Robert McNabb, M.S.C., C.D., Lancaster Park & Edmonton, AB

Meritorious Service Medal/M.S.M. (Civil)/
La Médaille du service méritoire (civile)
None awarded since last edition.

Meritorious Service Medal M.S.M. (Military)/
La Médaille du service méritoire (militaire)
(Announced September 29, 2010)
Maj. Geoffrey Arthur Abthorpe, M.S.M., C.D., Thunder Bay, ON
Petty Officer 2nd Class Barbara Agnes Benson, M.S.M., C.D., Isle aux Morts, NL
Maj. Timothy Charles Byers, M.S.M., C.D., Belleisle Creek, NB
Chief Warrant Officer Robert Daly, M.S.M., C.D., Lincoln, NB
Chief Warrant Officer Patrick Joseph Earles, M.S.M., C.D., Mount Pearl, NL
Col. Martin Girard, M.S.M., C.D., Gatineau, QC
Sgt. Marie Renay Groves, M.S.M., C.D., St. John's, NL
Master Warrant Officer John William Hooyer, M.S.M., C.D., Brantford, ON
Chief Warrant Officer Michael Raymond Lacharite, M.S.M., C.D., Edmonton, AB
Capt. Tyler Lavigne, M.S.M., Bathurst, NB
Corporal Derick Lewis, M.S.M., Kings-Hants, NS
Maj. Martin Andre Lipcsey, M.S.M., C.D., Ottawa, ON
Capt. Steven E. Luce, M.S.M. (United States Navy), Cleveland, Ohio & Las Vegas, Nevada, U.S.A.
Maj. Gilbert Joseph William McCauley, M.S.M., C.D., Sherbrooke & Gatineau, QC
Chief Warrant Officer Mark Henry Miller, M.S.M., C.D., Minto, NB
Master Warrant Officer Robert Joseph Montague, M.S.M., C.D., Ottawa, ON
Maj. Steven John Vincent Nolan, M.S.M., C.D., Whitby & Scarborough, ON
Corporal Curtis J. Stephens, M.S.M., Victoria, BC
L.Col. Duart Paul Townsend, M.S.M., C.D., Toronto, ON
Sgt. Christopher Stuart Whalen, M.S.M., St. John's, NL

(Announced July 26, 2010)
Col. Michael McLean, O.M.M., C.D., Summerside, PEI & Ottawa, ON

(Announced July 5, 2010)
Col. Jean-Michel Désiré Verney, M.S.M., Paris, France

(Announced June 7, 2010)
Col. Philip M. L. Napier, M.S.M., Salisbury & London, UK

(Announced May 31, 2010)
Warrant Officer Russell Keith Arsenault, M.S.M., C.D., Petawawa, ON. & O'Leary, PEI
Maj. Orest Babij, M.S.M., C.D., Ottawa & St. Catharines, ON
L.Col. Roger Ronald Barrett, M.S.M., C.D., Ottawa, ON
L.Col. James Frederick Camsell, M.S.M., C.D., St. John's, NL
L.Col. Frances Chilton-Mackay, O.M.M., M.S.M., C.D., Ottawa, ON
Col. Christopher John Coates, M.S.M., C.D., Kingston, ON. & Calgary, AB
Master Warrant Officer Kevin Joseph Ralph Donovan, M.S.M., C.D., Petawawa, ON
Warrant Officer Richard Dubé, M.S.M., C.D., Edmonton, AB. & Brossard, QC
Master Warrant Officer Luc Emond, M.S.M., C.D., Ottawa, ON & Lévis, QC
Capt. David Fearon, M.S.M., C.D., Ottawa & Elmvale, ON
Master Warrant Officer David Eugene Fisher, M.S.M., C.D., Petawawa, ON. & Stephenville Crossing, NL
Col. Richard Joseph Delphis Gervais, M.S.M., C.D., Ottawa, ON
Chief Warrant Officer Ernest Joseph Hall, M.M.M., M.S.M., C.D., Petawawa & Perth, ON
Master Corporal William Thomas Hoggarth, M.S.M., C.D., Amherstview, ON & Portage la Prairie, MB
Brigadier-General Alan John Howard, M.S.M., C.D., Ottawa, ON
L.Col. Daniel S. Hurlbut, M.S.M., Fort Benning, Georgia and Salt Lake City, Utah, USA
Master Warrant Officer Lewis Duthie Joseph Lavoie, M.S.M., C.D., Petawawa & Marathon, ON
Maj. Robert Walter McBride, M.S.M., C.D., North York & Petawawa, ON
Master Warrant Officer Shawn Anthony Mercer, M.S.M., C.D., Petawawa, ON
L.Col. Scott Miller, M.S.M., Las Vegas, Nevada & Los Angeles, California, USA
Col. Theodore E. Osowski, M.S.M., Las Vegas, Nevada & Flushing, Michigan, USA
Master Warrant Officer Eric John Rolfe, M.S.M., C.D., Oromocto, NB & New Glasgow, NS
L.Col. Joseph Stephen Shipley, M.S.M., C.D., Windsor Junction & Halifax, NS
Maj. Dean Dwayne Tremblay, M.S.M., C.D., Bath, ON. & Halifax, NS
Maj. Russell Neal Washburn, M.S.M., C.D., Ottawa, ON & St. George, NB

(Announced April 23, 2010)
Vice Admiral Robert B. Murrett, M.S.M., Bethesda, Maryland, & Buffalo, New York, USA

(Announced April 13, 2010)
General Victor Eugene Renuart, Jr., M.S.C. (United States Air Force)

(Announced March 19, 2010)
Chief Warrant Officer Sheila Alaine Blair, M.M.M., M.S.M., C.D., Enfield & Greenwood, NS
Col. Joseph Patrick Breen, M.S.M., Washington, D.C., USA
Col. Gordon David Corbould, M.S.M., C.D., Belleville, ON, & Bella Coola, BC
Maj.-Gen. Jonkheer J. Harmen de Jonge, M.S.M., Münster, Germany
Col. Sean G. Friday, M.S.M., C.D., Ottawa & Stoney Creek, ON
L.Col. Kerry William Horlock, M.S.M., C.D., Ottawa & Simcoe, ON
Chief Warrant Officer Christopher Avard Kaye, M.M.M., M.S.M., C.D., Victoria, BC, & Moncton, NB
Col. Paul Keddy, M.S.M., C.D., Bushell Park, SK, & St. Catharines, ON
Capt. Peter Paul Kleinschmidt, M.S.M., C.D., Belleville & Hamilton, ON
Col. Thomas J. McGrath, M.S.M., Burke, Virginia, & Boston, Massachusetts, USA
Col. Scott Andrew McLeod, M.S.M., C.D., Greely, ON, & Regina, SK
Maj.-Gen. Christopher D. Miller, M.S.M., Washington, D.C., & Colorado Springs, Colorado, USA
Commandant Yves Minjollet, M.S.M., Paris, France
Vice Admiral Robert B. Murrett, M.S.M., Bethesda, Maryland, & Buffalo, New York, USA

ORDER OF CANADA

Companions of the Order of Canada

Members of the Order of Canada

Officers of the Order of Canada

ORDER OF MILITARY MERIT

Officers of the Order of Military Merit

Commanders of the Order of Military Merit

Members of the Order of Military Merit

Col. Philip M. L. Napier, M.S.M., Salisbury & London, UK
Maj. Eric Jean Perey, M.S.M., C.D., St-Luc & St-Jean-sur-Richelieu, QC
Col. Joseph Paul Jacques Ricard, M.S.M., Ottawa, ON, & Drummondville, QC
Maj.-Gen. Dennis Charles Tabbernor, C.M.M., M.S.M., C.D., Winnipeg, MB
Chief Warrant Officer Christopher Arnold White, M.M.M., M.S.M., C.D., Harrowsmith & Collingwood, ON
Maj. Mark G. Wuennenberg, M.S.M., C.D., Ottawa, ON, & Chilliwack, BC

(Announced November 26, 2009)
Col. Colin P. Richardson, M.S.M. (New Zealand Army)

(Announced November 11, 2009)
Maj. James Edward Allen, M.S.M., C.D., Fort Leavenworth, Kansas, & Platte City, Missouri, USA, and St. John's, NL
Warrant Officer Todd Barry Buchanan, M.S.M., C.D., Shilo & Carberry, MB, and New Denver, BC
Col. Jamieson Cade, M.S.M., C.D., Kingston, ON, & Coquitlam, BC
Maj. Michael Roy Deutsch, M.S.M., C.D., Dartmouth & Kingston, NS, and Edson, AB
Warrant Officer Michael Patrick Forest, M.S.M., C.D., Shilo, MB, & Sherbrooke, QC
Maj. Trevor Patrick Gosselin, M.S.M., C.D., Oromocto, NB & Dawson Creek, BC
Chief Petty Officer 1st Class Michael Paul Gourley, M.M.M., M.S.M., C.D., Dartmouth & Halifax, NS
Maj. Stacy Allan Grubb, M.S.M., C.D., Shilo, Hamiota & Brandon, MB
Maj. Joseph Antonio Marcel Louis Hamel, M.S.M., C.D., Alouette, La Baie & Montréal, QC
Maj. Christopher Robin Henderson, M.S.M., C.D. / Ottawa, ON & Halifax, NS
Col. Yann John Hidiroglou, M.S.M., C.D. (Retired), Ottawa, ON
Col. Bernd Horn, O.M.M., M.S.M., C.D., Ottawa & Kingston, ON
Warrant Officer Kevin Thomas Johnson, M.S.M., C.D., Shilo, MB, & Sault Ste. Marie, ON
Col. Vihar Govind Joshi, M.S.M., C.D., Ottawa, ON
Commander Kelly Brian Larkin, M.S.M., C.D., Victoria, Vancouver & Langley, BC
Maj. John Robert Prudent Latulippe, M.S.M., C.D., Astra & Ameliasburgh, ON, and Shannon, QC
Corporal Marc L. S. Murray, M.S.M., Shilo & Brandon, MB, and Ottawa, ON
Commander Steven Paget, M.S.M., C.D., Halifax & Lucasville, NS
Master Corporal Jacob N. Petten, M.S.M., Edmonton, AB, & Victoria, BC
Warrant Officer Jason Guy Pickard, M.S.M., C.D., Oromocto, Burton & Bathurst, NB
Maj. Catherine Enid Potts, M.S.M., C.D., Kingston, ON
Corporal John Clifton Wayne Prior, M.S.M., Edmonton, AB, & Victoria, BC
Col. Jean-François Riffou, M.S.M., C.D., Toronto & Ottawa, ON, and Québec, QC
Maj. Robert Tennant Ritchie, M.S.M., C.D., Toronto & Ottawa, ON
Capt.(N) Brendan Ryan, M.S.M., C.D., Halifax, NS, & Placentia, NL
Corporal Cameron M. Smithers, M.S.M., Edmonton, AB, & Dundas, ON
Commander Joseph Honoré Patrick St-Denis, M.S.M., C.D. (Retired), Victoria, BC
L.Col. Martha-Anne Paule Stouffer, M.S.M., C.D., Ottawa, ON
Corporal Rory E. Swanson, M.S.M., Lazo, BC, & Thunder Bay, ON
Commander John Aubrey Williston, M.S.M., C.D., Ottawa, ON, & Moncton, NB
Warrant Officer Terence Charles Wolaniuk, M.S.M., C.D., Edmonton & Spruce Grove, AB

(Announced October 21, 2009)
Col. Charles Mark Hazleton, O.M.M., M.S.M., C.D., Kingston, ON
Master Corporal Tyler J. Latta, M.S.M., Edmonton, AB, Rutherglen & London, ON

(Announced July 7, 2009)
Col. Jean-Pierre Duran, M.S.M. (French Army), Bry-sur-Marne, France

GENERAL SERVICE AWARDS

Rather than creating a new honour for each new Canadian Forces operation as it arises, in July of 2004, Her Majesty the Queen approved the creation of the following:

The General Campaign Star (G.C.S.) recognizes military service in a theatre of operations in the presence of an armed enemy.

The General Service Medal (G.S.M.) acknowledges civilian and military service in direct support of operations in the presence of an armed enemy.

General Campaign Star/Étoile de campagne générale (G.C.S.)
None awarded since last edition.

General Service Medal/Médaille du service général (G.S.M.)
None awarded since last edition.

British & Commonwealth Honours

In earlier times Canadians could receive hereditary titles, knighthoods and other such honours under the British system of honours, and this is still the case with Canadians who pursue careers in the United Kingdom. Furthermore, the Canadian military system of decorations was based on the British system and many Canadians hold British honours as a result of service in Canadian, British or other Commonwealth forces. While Canada

CANADIAN BRAVERY DECORATIONS

Star of Courage

Cross of Valour

Medal of Bravery

MERITORIOUS SERVICE DECORATIONS

Meritorious Service Cross
Obverse (Military Version)

Meritorious Service Medal
Reverse (Civil Version)

has developed its own honours system, honours are still from time to time granted by the Sovereign to Canadians for, among other things, service to the Commonwealth.

VICTORIA CROSS (V.C.)

The Victoria Cross was founded by Queen Victoria at the close of the Crimean War in 1856, but made retroactive to 1854. It is described as a Maltese cross, made of gun metal, with a Royal Crest in the centre and underneath it an escroll bearing the inscription "For Valour". It is awarded, irrespective of rank, to members of any branch of Her Majesty's services, either in the British Forces or those of any Commonwealth realm, dominion, colony or dependency, the Mercantile Marine, nurses or staffs of hospitals, or to civilians of either sex while serving in either regular or temporary capacity during naval, military, or air force operations. It is awarded only "for most conspicuous bravery or some daring or pre-eminent act of valour or self-sacrifice or extreme devotion to duty in the presence of the enemy." For additional conduct of similar bravery, a Bar is added. The ribbon was formerly red for the Army and blue for the Navy, but it is now red (a dull crimson) for all services. Since June 17th, 1943, the financial responsibility for a stipend to Canadian recipients has been assumed by the Canadian Government. Ninetysix V.C.s have been awarded to Canadians or to foreigners serving in Canadian or Commonwealth forces.

GEORGE CROSS (G.C.)

Arthur Richard Cecil Butson, G.C., O.M.M., C.St.J., C.D., M.A., M.D., F.R.C.S. (Eng.), F.R.C.S.C.C. In 1940, King George VI instituted the George Cross for civilians and members of the services alike, male or female, who performed "acts of the greatest heroism or of the most conspicuous courage in circumstances of extreme danger." This decoration - the second highest Commonwealth award for bravery - is a plain silver cross bearing in the centre a representation of Saint George slaying the dragon and the words: "For Gallantry". The ribbon is garter blue. Eleven Canadians, and a Bermudian serving in a Canadian unit, have won the G.C. Not all were members of the armed forces.

ALBERT MEDAL (A.M.)

Ernest Alfred Wooding, A.M., R.C.N.V.R. Queen Elizabeth II requested that all living Albert Medal recipients convert their Albert Medal to a George Cross. For some reason Mr. Wooding did not convert his Albert Medal.

ROYAL HONOURS (COMMONWEALTH)

The Order of Baronets, the lowest Hereditary rank, was instituted in 1611; a Baronet is designated "Sir John Smith, Baronet." The abbreviation Bt. is used in Court Circulars and has been generally adopted in lieu of "Bart." Taking precedence to Baronets are members of The Most Honourable Privy Council, who are addressed "Right Honourable."

The Most Noble Order of the Garter, instituted 1349. - K.G.

The Most Ancient and Most Noble Order of the Thistle, instituted 1687. - K.T.

The Most Honourable Order of the Bath, instituted in 1399, and revived in 1725, is divided into three classes - Knights Grand Cross, G.C.B.; Knights Commanders, K.C.B.; and Companions, C.B.

The Order of Merit, O.M., carries no title.

The Most Distinguished Order of St. Michael and St. George, instituted in 1818, has three classes - Knights Grand Cross, G.C.M.G.; Knights Commanders, K.C.M.G.; Companions, C.M.G.

The Most Eminent Order of the Indian Empire instituted 1877, has three classes - Knights Grand Commanders, G.C.I.E.; Knights Commanders, K.C.I.E.; Companions, C.I.E. (This Order has not been conferred since 1947.)

The Royal Victorian Order, instituted in 1896, has five classes - Knights Grand Cross, G.C.V.O.; Knights Commanders, K.C.V.O.; Commanders, C.V.O.; Members 4th and 5th classes - M.V.O. Ribbon, blue with red and white edges.

The Most Excellent Order of the British Empire, instituted in 1917, has five classes - Knights (or Dames) Grand Cross, G.B.E.; Knights Commanders, K.B.E.; Dames Commanders, D.B.E.; Commanders, C.B.E.; Officers, O.B.E.; and Members, M.B.E. Ribbon (Military) rose pink, pearl grey edging, vertical pearl stripe in centre; (Civil) rose pink, pearl grey edging, and no central vertical stripe.

Knights Bachelors are gentlemen unconnected with any order who have received the honour of Knighthood, and are entitled to the prefix "Sir". They rank immediately after Knights Commanders of the British Empire.

The Companions of Honour, C.H., instituted in 1917 rank immediately after Knights (Dames) Grand Cross of the Order of the British Empire. Membership is limited and carries no title.

In all Orders of Knighthood the Knights Grand Cross and the Knights Commanders have the prefix "Sir" with the initials of their class following the name. Companions and Members bear no title, but have the letters C.B., C.M.G., L.V.O., M.V.O., as the case may be, attached to their names.

The Garter, the Thistle, The Order of Merit and the Royal Victorian Order are all in the personal bestowal of the Sovereign. Appointments to the other Orders are made by Her Majesty on recommendation of the Prime Ministers of Commonwealth countries who wish to secure such appointments. Premiers of individual Australian states may also make recommendations.

MARQUESS

The Most Hon. the Marquess of Exeter, Michael Anthony Cecil, 8th Marquess

The Most Hon. the Marquess of Ely, Charles John Tottenham, 9th Marquess

EARLS

The Right Hon. the Earl of Egmont, Thomas Frederick Gerald Perceval, 12th Earl and 16th Baronet
The Right Hon. the Earl Grey, Richard Fleming George Charles Grey, 6th Earl
The Right Hon. the Earl of Orkney, Peter St. John, 9th Earl
The Right Hon. the Earl Winterton, Donald David Turnour, 8th Earl

VISCOUNTS

The Right Hon. the Viscount Charlemont, John Dodd Caulfield, 15th Viscount
The Right Hon. the Viscount Galway, L.Cdr. George Rupert Monckton, R.C.N. (Ret'd), 12th Viscount
The Right Hon. the Viscount Hardinge, Andrew Hartland Hardinge, 7th Viscount

OLD CANADIAN TITLE

The title of Baron de Longueuil existed prior to the Treaty of Paris (1763), and was duly recognized by Queen Victoria pursuant to that treaty.

BARONS

The Right Hon. the Lord Beaverbrook, Maxwell William Henry Aitken, 3rd Baron and 3rd Baronet
The Right Hon. the Lord Cullen of Ashbourne, Edmund Willoughby Marsham Cokayne, 3rd Baron
The Right Hon. the Lord Lucas of Chilworth, Simon William Lucas, 3rd Baron
The Right Hon. the Lord Martonmere, John Stephen Robinson, 2nd Baron
The Right Hon. the Lord Morris, Michael David Morris, 3rd Baron
The Right Hon. the Lord Rodney, George Brydges Rodney, 10th Baron and 10th Baronet
The Right Hon. the Lord Sanford, James, John, Mowbray Edmonton Sanford, 3rd Baron
The Right Hon. The Lord Shaughnessy, Charles George Patrick Shaughnessy, 5th Baron
The Right Hon. the Lord Strathcona and Mount Royal, Hon. Col. Donald Euan Palmer Howard, 4th Baron
The Right Hon. the Lord Thomson of Fleet David Kenneth Roy Thomson, 3rd Baron

BARONETS

Sir Richard Aylmer (16th Bt.)
Sir Christopher Hilaro Barlow (7th Bt.)
Sir James Barlow (4th Bt.)
Sir Benjamin Barrington (8th Bt.)
Sir James Bates (7th Bt)
Sir John Irving Bell, (1st Bt.)
Sir Alexander Boyd (3rd Bt.)
Sir Theodore Brinckman (6th Bt.)
Sir James Brunton (4th Bt.)
Sir Peter Burbidge (6th Bt.)
Sir Michael Butler (3rd Bt.)
Sir Robert Cave-Brown-Cave (16th Bt.)
Sir Bruce Chaytor (9th Bt.)
Sir Robin Chetwynd (9th Bt.)
Sir John Davis (3rd Bt.)
Sir David Dyke (10th Bt.)
The Revd. Sir Christopher Gibson, Bt., C.P. (4th Bt.)
Sir James Grant-Suttie (9th Bt.)
Sir Philip Grotrian (3rd Bt.)
Sir Charles Gunning C.D., (8th Bt.)
Sir Wayne King (8th Bt,)
Sir Charles Knowles (7th Bt.)
Sir Colpoys Johnson (8th Bt.)
Sir Peter Lambert (10th Bt.)
Sir Richard Latham (3rd Bt.)
Sir Ian McGregor (8th Bt.)
Sir Roderick McQuhae MacKenzie (12th Bt.)
Sir Allan Morris (11th Bt.)
Sir Christopher Oakes (3rd Bt.)
Sir Mathew Philipson-Stow (6th Bt.)
Sir James Piers (11 Bt.)
Sir Francis Price, Bt. (7th Bt.)
Sir Christopher Robinson (8th Bt.)
Sir John James Michael Laud Robinson (11th Bt.)
Sir Julian Rose (5th Bt.)
Sir James Rugge-Price (10th Bt.)
Sir John Samuel (5th Bt.)
Sir Adrian Sharp (4th Bt.)
Sir Richard Simeon (8th Bt.)
The Rev. Sir Michael Stonhouse (19th Bt.)
Sir Adrian Stott (4th Bt.)
Sir John Stracey (9th Bt.)
Sir Philip Stuart (9th Bt.)
Sir Richard Sullivan (9th Bt.)
Sir Robert Synge (8th Bt.)
Sir Rodney Touche (2nd Bt.)
Sir Charles Hibbert Tupper (5th Bt.)
Sir Christopher Wells, M.D. (3rd Bt.)
Sir Donald Williams (10th Bt.)

Knight Grand Cross of the Most Honourable Order of the Bath (G.C.B.)

Air Chief Marshal Sir David Evans, G.C.B., C.B.E.

The Order of Merit (O.M.)

The Right Honourable Jean Chrétien, PC, OM, CC.

Knight Grand Cross or Dame Grand Cross of the Most Excellent Order of the British Empire (G.B.E.)

Member of the Order of the Companions of Honour (C.H.)

General John de Chastelaine, O.C., C.M.M., C.H., E.D.
Dr. Anthony Pawson, C.H., O.C., O.Ont.

Knight Commander of the Most Distinguished Order of St. Michael and St. George (K.C.M.G.)

Knight Commander of the Royal Victorian Order (K.C.V.O.)
Sir Conrad Swan, K.C.V.O.

Knight Commander of the Most Excellent Order of the British Empire (K.B.E.)

Sir David Bate, K.B.E.

Knight Commander or Dame Commander of the Most Excellent Order of the British Empire (K.B.E. or D.B.E.)

Dame Clara Furse, D.B.E.

KNIGHT BACHELOR

Sir George Bain
Sir Graham Day
Sir John Reginald Gorman, C.V.O., C.B.E., M.C
Sir Terence Matthews, O.B.E.
Sir Christopher Ondaatje, C.B.E.
Sir Neil Shaw

Companion of the Most Honourable Order of the Bath (C.B.)

Air Vice-Marshal George Brookes, C.B., O.B.E.

Companion of the Most Distinguished Order of St. Michael and St. George (C.M.G.)

H.J. Carmichael, C.M.G.
Edmond Cloutier, C.M.G., B.A., L.Ph.
Donovan Bartley Finn, C.M.G., M.Sc., Ph.D., F.R.S.C., F.C.I.C.
George H. McIvor, C.M.G.
Hector Brown McKinnon, C.C., C.M.G.
William Andrew O'Neil, C.M.G.
Alexander Ross, C.M.G.
Joseph Emile St. Laurent, C.M.G.
Ivor Otterbein Smith, C.M.G., O.B.E.

Companion of the Most Eminent Order of the Indian Empire (C.I.E.)

Maj. Frederick Wernham Gerrard, C.I.E.
Capt. John Ryland, C.I.E., R.C.N.
Maj. Frederick Augustus Berrill Sheppard, C.I.E., O.B.E.

Commander of the Royal Victorian Order (C.V.O.)

Leopold Henry Amyot, C.V.O.
Dr. Michael Jackson, C.V.O., C.D.
The Hon. David C. Lam, C.V.O., C.M., K.St.J., O.B.C., B.A.(Econ.), M.B.A., L.L.D., D.Mil.Sc., D.H.L., D.H.
Veronica Jane Langton, C.V.O.
Judith A. LaRocque, C.V.O.
Kevin Stewart MacLeod, C.V.O.
Cdr. G.J. Manson, C.V.O., C.D., R.C.N.
John Crosbie Perlin, C.V.O.
Peter Michael Pitfield, C.V.O., P.C., Q.C.
M.Gen. Roy A. Reid, C.V.O., C.M., M.C., C.D.
L.Cdr. Lawrence James Wallace, C.V.O., O.C., O.B.C., R.C.N.V.R.

Commander of the Order of the British Empire (C.B.E.)

William Eric Adams, C.B.E.
James Pomeroy Anderson, C.B.E.
Brig. Gerald Gardiner Anglin, C.B.E., M.C., E.D.
Brig. Walter A. Bean, C.B.E., E.D., C.D.
Brig. John Arthur Watson Bennett, C.B.E., C.D.
Brig. John Francis Bingham, C.B.E.
Brig. Dudley Kingdon Black, C.B.E., D.S.O.
George Herbert Bowler, C.B.E.
Garrett Brownrigg, C.B.E.
John Burke, C.B.E.
Alfred Charpentier, C.B.E.
Howard Brown Chase, C.B.E.
Brig. Frederick Graham Coleman, C.B.E.
Brig. J. A. de Lalanne, C.B.E., M.C., E.D.
Conrad Trelawny Fitz-Gerald, C.B.E., M.D.
Charles Gavsie, C.B.E., Q.C.
Gerald Godsoe, C.B.E., Q.C.
Alexander Grant, C.B.E.
Joseph Ernest Gregoire, C.B.E.
Frank Sydney Grisdale, C.B.E.
Raymond Gushue, O.C., C.B.E., Q.C.
Wallace Bruce Haughan, C.B.E.
Brig. Robert James Henderson, C.B.E.
Harold Ferguson Hodgson, C.B.E.
Capt. Francis Deschamps Howie, C.B.E., D.S.O., R.N.
Alexander George Irvine, C.B.E.
Lester Millman Keachie, C.B.E., Q.C.
Capt. Thomas Douglas Kelly, C.B.E., R.C.N.R.
Allan Collingwood Travers Lewis, C.B.E., Q.C.
Col. Edward Raymond Lewis, C.B.E.
Wilfrid Bennett Lewis, C.O., C.B.E., Ph.D
Gordon Clapp Lindsay, C.B.E.
John Struthers McNeil, C.B.E.
E.J. Mackie, C.B.E.
Raymond Charles Manning, C.B.E.
Walter Melvill Marshall, C.B.E.
James Matson, C.B.E.
Ronald Henry Moray Mavor, C.B.E.
Air Vice-Marshal Walter Alyn Orr, C.B.E., C.D., R.C.A.F.
Luke William Pearsall, C.B.E.
M.Gen. Matthew Howard Somers Penhale, C.B.E., C.D.
Cyril Horace Frederick Pierrepont, C.B.E., E.D.
M.Gen. Norman Elliott Rodger, C.B.E.
James Joseph Alexander Ross, C.B.E., C.D.
T.H. Savage, C.B.E.
Lynn Seymour, C.B.E.
Air Vice-Marshal Douglas McCully Smith, C.B.E., C.D.
Brig. Gerald Lucian Morgan Smith, C.B.E., C.D.
George Spence, C.B.E., LL.D.
William Leonard O'Brien Stallard, C.B.E.
Basil Otto Stevenson, C.B.E.
Air Cdre. Stanley Gibson Tackaberry, C.B.E.
Kenneth Wiffin Taylor, O.C., C.B.E.
George Gamlin Thomas, C.B.E.
Lyman Trumbull, C.B.E.
M.Gen. Arthur Egbert Wrinch, C.B.E., C.D.
Henry Wrong, C.B.E.

IMPERIAL SERVICE ORDER (I.S.O.)

George Clayton Anderson
Robert Albert Andison
Arthur Barnstead
Avila Bedard
Peter Cooligan
Henri Fortier
Frank Henry French
Arthur Leigh Jolliffe
Edward Jost
Louis MacMillan
Walter Clifton Ronson
David John Scott
Ivan Vallee

ROYAL VICTORIAN CHAIN

Bestows no precedence; currently not held by anyone.

Order of Precedence for Orders, Decorations and Medals

The following is the approved order of prededence as of April 2, 1998. The asterisk indicates honours added since that date.

SEQUENCE 1

1. The sequence for wearing the insignia of Canadian orders, decorations and medals, and the post-nominal letters associated with such orders, decorations and medals are the following:
Victoria Cross (V.C.)
Cross of Valour (C.V.)

NATIONAL ORDERS

Companion of the Order of Canada (C.C.)
Officer of the Order of Canada (O.C.)
Member of the Order of Canada (C.M.)
Commander of the Order of Military Merit (C.M.M.)
*Commander of the Order of Merit of the Police Forces (C.O.M.)
Commander of the Royal Victorian Order (C.V.O.)
Officer of the Order of Military Merit (O.M.M.)
*Officer of the Order of Merit of the Police Forces (O.O.M.)
Lieutenant of the Royal Victorian Order (L.V.O.)
Member of the Order of Military Merit (M.M.M.)
*Member of the Order of Merit of the Police Forces (M.O.M.)
Member of the Royal Victorian Order (M.V.O.)
The Most Venerable Order of the Hospital of St. John of Jerusalem (all grades) (post-nominal letters only for internal use by the Order of St. John)

PROVINCIAL ORDERS
*Ordre national du Québec (G.O.Q., O.Q., C.Q.)
Saskatchewan Order of Merit (S.O.M.)
Order of Ontario (O.Ont.)
Order of British Columbia (O.B.C.)
Alberta Order of Excellence (A.O.E.)
Order of Prince Edward Island (O.P.E.I.)
Order of Manitoba (O.M.)
Order of New Brunswick (O.N.B.)
Order of Nova Scotia (O.N.S.)
Order of Newfoundland & Labrador (O.N.L.)

DECORATIONS
Star of Military Valour (S.M.V.)
Star of Courage (S.C)
Meritorious Service Cross (M.S.C.)
Medal of Military Valour (M.M.V.)
Medal of Bravery (M.B.)
Meritorious Service Medal (M.S.M.)
Royal Victorian Medal (R.V.M.)

WAR AND OPERATIONAL SERVICE MEDALS
Korea Medal
Canadian Volunteer Service Medal for Korea
Gulf and Kuwait Medal
Somalia Medal
*South-West Asia Service Medal
*General Campaign Star
*General Service Medal

SPECIAL SERVICE MEDALS (S.S.M.)
S.S.M. with bars for:
Pakistan (1989-1990)
Alert
Humanitas
NATO/OTAN
Peace/Paix
*Ranger
*Canadian Peacekeeping Service Medal (C.P.S.M.)

UNITED NATIONS MEDALS
Service (Korea) (1950-1954)
Emergency Force (Egypt/Sinai) (1956-67)
Truce Supervision Organization in Palestine (1948-) and Observer Group in Lebanon (1958)
Military Observation Group in India and Pakistan (1948-)
Operation in Congo (1960-64)
Temporary Executive Authority in West New Guinea (1962-63)
Yemen Observation Mission (1963-64)
Force in Cyprus (1964-)
India/Pakistan Observation Misison (1965-66)
Emergency Force Middle East (1973-79)
Disengagement Observation Force Golan Heights (1974-)
Interim Force in Lebanon (1978-)
Military Observation Group in Iran/Iraq (1988-91)
Transition Assistance Group (Namibia) (1989-90)
Observer Group in Central America (1989-92)
Iraq/Kuwait Observer Mission (1991-)
Angola Verification Mission (1988-97)
Mission for the Referendum in Western Sahara (1991-)
Observer Mission in El Salvador (1991-95)
Protection Force (Yugoslavia) (1992-95)
Advance Mission in Cambodia (1991-92)
Transitional Authority in Cambodia (1992-93)
Operation in Somalia (1992-93)
Operation in Mozambique (1992-94)
Observation Mission in Uganda/Rwanda (1993-94)
Assistance Mission in Rwanda (1993-96)
Mission in Haïti (1993-)
Verification of Human Rights and Compliance with the Comprehensive Agreement on Human Rights in Guatemala (1997-98)
*Mission in the Central African Republic (1998-2000)
*Preventive Deployment Force (Macedonia) (1995- 99)
*Mission in Bosnia and Herzegovina (1995-) *Mission of Observers in Prevlaka (Croatia) (1996-)
*Interim Administration Mission in Kosovo (1999-)
*Observer Mission in Sierra Leone (1999-)
*Mission in East Timor and Transitional Administration in East Timor (1999-)
*Mission in the Democratic Republic of the Congo (1999-)
*Mission in Ethiopia and Eritrea (2000-)
Special Service (1995-)
*Headquarters

NATO MEDALS
*North Atlantic Treaty Organization (NATO) Medal for the Former Yugoslavia (1992-2002)
*NATO Medal for Kosovo (1999-)
*NATO Medal for the Former Yugoslav Republic of Macedonia (2001-02)
*Article 5 NATO Medal for Operation "Eagle Assist" (2001-02)
*Article 5 NATO Medal for Operation "Active Endeavour" (2001-)
*Non-Article 5 NATO Medal for Operations in the Balkans (2003-)

INTERNATIONAL MISSION MEDALS
International Commission for Supervision and Control (Indo-China) (1954-74)
International Commission for Control and Supervision (Vietnam) (1973)
Multinational Force and Observers (Sinai) (1982-)
European Community Monitor Mission (Yugoslavia) (1991-)
*International Force East Timor (1999-)
*European Security and Defence Policy Service Medal

COMMEMORATIVE MEDALS
Canadian Centennial Medal (1967)
Queen Elizabeth II's Silver Jubilee Medal (1977)
125th Anniversary of the Confederation of Canada Medal (1992)
*Queen Elizabeth II's Golden Jubilee Medal (2002)

LONG SERVICE AND GOOD CONDUCT MEDALS
R.C.M.P. Long Service Medal
Canadian Forces Decoration (C.D.)

EXEMPLARY SERVICE MEDALS
Police Exemplary Service Medal
Corrections Exemplary Service Medal
Fire Services Exemplary Service Medal
Canadian Coast Guard Exemplary Service Meda
Emergency Medical Services Exemplary Service Medal
*Peace Officer Exemplary Service Medal

SPECIAL MEDAL
Queen's Medal for Champion Shot

OTHER DECORATIONS AND MEDALS
Ontario Medal for Good Citizenship (O.M.C.)
Ontario Medal for Police Bravery
Ontario Medal for Firefighters Bravery
Saskatchewan Volunteer Medal (S.V.M.)
Ontario Provincial Police Long Service and Good Conduct Medal
Service Medal of the Most Venerable Order of the Hospital of St. John of Jerusalem
Commissionaire Long Service Medal
*Newfoundland and Labrador Bravery Award
*Newfoundland and Labrador Volunteer Service Medal
*British Columbia Fire Services Long Service and Bravery Medals
*Commemorative Medal for the Centennial of Saskatchewan
*Alberta Centennial Medal

2. The Bar to the Special Service Medal is worn centred on the ribbon. If there is more than one Bar, they are spaced evenly on the ribbon with the most recent uppermost.

3. Commonwealth orders, decorations and medals, the award of which is approved by the Government of Canada, are worn after Canadian orders, decorations and medals listed in Section 1, the precedence in each category being set by the date of appointment or award.

4. Foreign orders, decorations and medals, the award of which is approved by the Government of Canada, are worn after those referred to in Sections 1 and 3, the precedence in each category being set by the date of appointment or award.

5. Notwithstanding Sections 1, 3 and 4, a person who, **prior to 1 June, 1972,** was a member of a British Order or the recipient of a British decoration or medal referred to in this section, may wear the insignia of the decoration or medal together with the insignia of any Canadian order, decoration or medal that the person is entitled to wear, the proper sequence being the following:
Victoria Cross (V.C.)
George Cross (G.C.)
Cross of Valour (C.V.)
Order of Merit (O.M.)
Order of the Companions of Honour (C.H.)
Companion of the Order of Canada (C.C.)
Officer of the Order of Canada (O.C.)
Member of the Order of Canada (C.M.)
Commander of the Order of Military Merit (C.M.M.)
*Commander of the Order of Merit of the Police Forces (C.O.M.)
Companion of the Order of the Bath (C.B.)
Companion of the Order of St. Michael and St. George (C.M.G.)
Commander of the Royal Victorian Order (C.V.O.)
Commander of the Order of the British Empire (C.B.E.)
Distinguished Service Order (D.S.O.)
Officer of the Order of Military Merit (O.M.M.)
*Officer of the Order of Merit of the Police Force (O.O.M.)
Lieutenant of the Royal Victorian Order (L.V.O.)
Officer of the Order of the British Empire (O.B.E.)
Imperial Service Order (I.S.O.)
Member of the Order of Military Merit (M.M.M.)
*Member of the Order of the Police Forces (M.O.M.)
Member of the Royal Victorian Order (M.V.O.)
Member of the Order of the British Empire (M.B.E.)
Member of the Royal Red Cross (R.R.C.)
Distinguished Service Cross (D.S.C.)
Military Cross (M.C.)
Distinguished Flying Cross (D.F.C.)
Air Force Cross (A.F.C.)
Star of Military Valour (S.M.V.)
Star of Courage (S.C.)
Meritorious Service Cross (M.S.C.)
Medal of Military Valour (M.M.V.)
Medal of Bravery (M.B.)
Meritorious Service Medal (M.S.M.)
Associate of the Royal Red Cross (A.R.R.C.)
The Most Venerable Order of St. John of Jerusalem (all grades) (post-nominal letters only for internal use by the Order of St. John)
Provincial Orders (order of precedence as set out in Section 1)
Distinguished Conduct Medal (D.C.M.)
Conspicuous Gallantry Medal (C.G.M.)
George Medal (G.M.)
Distinguished Service Medal (D.S.M.)
Military Medal (M.M.)
Distinguished Flying Medal (D.F.M.)
Air Force Medal (A.F.M.)
Queen's Gallantry Medal (Q.G.M.)
Royal Victorian Medal (R.V.M.)
British Empire Medal (B.E.M.)

WAR AND OPERATIONAL SERVICE MEDALS
Africa General Service Medal (1902-1956)
India General Service Medal (1908-1935)
Naval General Service Medal (1915-1962)
India General Service Medal (1936-39)
General Service Medal - Army and Air Force (1918- 1962)
General Service Medal (1962-)
1914 Star
1914-15 Star
British War Medal (1914-18)
Mercantile Marine War Medal (1914-18)
Victory Medal (1914-18)
Territorial Force War Medal (1914-19)
1939-45 Star
Atlantic Star
Air Crew Europe Star
Africa Star
Pacific Star
Burma Star
Italy Star
France and Germany Star
Defence Medal
Canadian Volunteer Service Medal
Newfoundland Second World War Volunteer Service Medal (see Section 6)
War Medal (1939-45)
Korea Medal
Canadian Volunteer Service Medal for Korea
Gulf and Kuwait Medal Somalia Medal
*South-West Asia Service Medal
*General Campaign Medal
*General Service Medal

SPECIAL SERVICE MEDALS
(The order of precedence is as set out for Special Service Medals in Section 1.)

UNITED NATIONS MEDALS
(The order of precedence is as set out for United Nations Medals in Section 1.)

INTERNATIONAL COMMISSION AND ORGANIZATION MEDALS
(The order of precedence is as set out for International Commission and Organization Medals in Section 1.)

POLAR MEDALS
(The order of precedence is by order of date awarded.)

COMMEMORATIVE MEDALS
King George V's Silver Jubilee Medal (1935)
King George VI's Coronation Medal (1937)
Queen Elizabeth II's Coronation Medal (1953)
Canadian Centennial Medal (1967)
Queen Elizabeth II's Silver Jubilee Medal (1977)
125th Anniversary of the Confederation of Canada Medal (1992)

*Queen Elizabeth II's Golden Jubilee Medal (2002)

LONG SERVICE AND GOOD CONDUCT MEDALS

Army Long Service and Good Conduct Medal
Naval Long Service and Good Conduct Medal
Air Force Long Service and Good Conduct Medal
RCMP Long Service Medal
Volunteer Officer's Decoration (V.D.)
Volunteer Long Service Medal
Colonial Auxiliary Forces Officer's Decoration (V.D.)
Colonial Auxiliary Forces Long Service Medal
Efficiency Decoration (E.D.)
Efficiency Medal
Naval Volunteer Reserve Decoration (V.R.D.)
Naval Volunteer Reserve Long Service and Good Conduct Medal
Air Efficiency Award Canadian Forces Decoration (C.D.)

EXEMPLARY SERVICE MEDALS

(The order of precedence is as set out for Exemplary Service Medals in Section 1.)

SPECIAL MEDAL

Queen's Medal for Champion Shot

OTHER DECORATIONS AND MEDALS

(The order of precedence is as set out for Other Decorations and Medals in Section 1.)

6. The Newfoundland Volunteer War Service Medal has the same precedence as the Canadian Volunteer Service Medal.

7. The insignia of orders, decorations and medals not listed above, as well as foreign awards, the award of which has not been approved by the Government of Canada, shall not be mounted or worn in conjunction with orders, decorations and medals listed above.

8. The insignia of orders, decorations and medals shall not be worn by anyone other than the recipient of the orders, decorations or medals.

NOTE: Policy regarding the wearing on non-authorized awards Only the insignia of orders, decorations and medals officially awarded under the authority of the Crown or that the wearing of which has been authorized by the Crown may be worn. Only the actual recipient of an honour can wear its insignia; no family member or any person other than the original recipient may wear the insignia of an order, decoration or medal. Insignia that are purchased or otherwise acquired may be used for display purpose only and cannot be worn on the person in any form or manner.

Abbreviations Indicating Honours and Decorations

A.F.C. - Air Force Cross. Ribbon, wide diagonal stripes of white and red.
A.F.M. - Air Force Medal. Ribbon, narrow diagonal stripes of white and red.
A.M. - Albert Medal, gold (Sea). Ribbon, nine alternate narrow stripes of blue and white.
Albert Medal, gold (Land). Ribbon, nine alternate narrow stripes of red and white.
Albert Medal, bronze (Sea). Ribbon, blue ground with two wide stripes of white.
Albert Medal, bronze (Land). Ribbon, red ground with two wide stripes of white.
B.E.M. - British Empire Medal.
Bt. - Baronet
C.B. - Companion of the Most Honourable Order of the Bath.
C.B.E. - Commander of the Order of the British Empire.
C.C. - Companion of the Order of Canada.
C.D. - Canadian Forces Decoration.
C.G.M. - Conspicuous Gallantry Medal; Navy and Air Force. It carries a cash grant. The Navy Medal ribbon is white with dark blue edges; the Air Force ribbon is light blue with dark blue edges.
C.H. - Member of the Order of the Companions of Honour.
C.I.E. - Companion of the Most Eminent Order of the Indian Empire.
C.M. - Member of the Order of Canada. C.M.G. - Companion of the Most Distinguished Order of St. Michael and St. George.
C.M.M. - Commander of the Order of Military Merit.
C.P.S.M. - Canadian Peacekeeping Service Medal.
C.S.I. - Companion of the Most Exalted Order of the Star of India.
C.V. - Cross of Valour. C.V.O. - Commander of the Royal Victorian Order.
D.C.M. - Distinguished Conduct Medal. Ribbon, red ground, dark blue stripe in centre.
D.F.C. - Distinguished Flying Cross. Ribbon, wide diagonal stripes of violet and white.
D.F.M. - Distinguished Flying Medal. Ribbon, narrow diagonal stripes of white and violet.
D.S.C. - Distinguished Service Cross. Ribbon, three broad bands, dark blue, white, dark blue.
D.S.M. - Distinguished Service Medal.
D.S.O. - Companion of the Distinguished Service Order. Instituted 1886. Ribbon, dark red with dark blue stripe at each end.
E.D. - Canadian Efficiency Decoration for Officers of Military Auxiliary Forces.
E.M. - Edward Medal. Posthumous award.
E.M. - Efficiency Medal.
G.B.E. - Knight Grand Cross or Dame Grand Cross of the Most Excellent Order of the British Empire.
G.C. - George Cross.
G.C.B. - Knight Grand Cross of the Most Honourable Order of the Bath.
G.C.I.E. - Knight Grand Commander of the Most Eminent Order of the Indian Empire.
G.C.M.G. - Knight Grand Cross of the Most Distinguished Order of St. Michael and St. George.
G.C.S.I. - Knight Grand Commander of the Most Exalted Order of the Star of India.
G.C.V.O. - Knight Grand Cross of the Royal Victorian Order.
G.M. - George Medal.
I.S.M. - Imperial Service Medal.
I.S.O. - Companion of the Imperial Service Order. Instituted 1902.
K.B.E. - Knight Commander of the Most Excellent Order of the British Empire.
K.C.B. - Knight Commander of the Most Honourable Order of the Bath.
K.C.I.E. - Knight Commander of the Most Eminent Order of the Indian Empire.
K.C.M.G. - Knight Commander of the Most Distinguished Order of St. Michael and St. George.
K.C.S.I. - Knight Commander of the Most Exalted Order of the Star of India.
K.C.V.O. - Knight Commander of the Royal Victorian Order.
K.G. - Knight of the Most Noble Order of the Garter.
K.P. - Knight of the Most Illustrious Order of St. Patrick.
Kt. - Knight Bachelor.
K.T. - Knight of the Most Ancient and Most Noble Order of the Thistle.
L.V.O. - Lieutenant of the Royal Victorian Order.
M.B. - Medal of Bravery.
M.B.E. - Member of the Order of the British Empire.
M.C. - Military Cross. Instituted 1915. Ribbon, white with broad band of blue in centre.
M. du C. - Canada Medal.
M.M. - Military Medal.
M.M.M. - Member of the Order of Military Merit.
M.V.O. - Member of the Royal Victorian Order.
M.S.C. - Meritorous Service Cross.
M.S.M. - Meritorious Service Medal.
O.B.E. - Officer of the Order of the British Empire.
O.B. - Order of the Beaver (Award of the BNAPS).
O.C. - Officer of the Order of Canada.
O.M. - Member of the Order of Merit.
O.M.M. - Officer of the Order of Military Merit.
P.C. - Privy Counsellor.
R.R.C. - Royal Red Cross. Instituted 1883. Ribbon, dark blue with narrow band of dark red at each end.
R.V.M. - Royal Victorian Medal.
S.C. - Star of Courage.
S.S.M. - Special Service Medal
U.E. - Unity of Empire. Descendants of United Empire Loyalists.
V.C. - Victoria Cross.
V.D. - Auxiliary Forces (Volunteer) Officers' Decoration.
V.R.D. - Naval Volunteer Reserve Decoration.

Government

Table of Precedence for Canada

1. The Governor General of Canada or the Administrator of the Government of Canada. (Notes 1, 2 & 2.1).
2. The Prime Minister of Canada. (Note 3).
3. The Chief Justice of Canada. (Note 4).
4. The Speaker of the Senate.
5. The Speaker of the House of Commons.
6. Ambassadors, High Commissioners, Ministers Plenipotentiary. (Note 5).
7. Members of the Canadian Ministry:
   a. Members of the Cabinet; and
   b. Secretaries of the State; with relative precedence within sub-categories (a) and (b) governed by the date of their appointment to the Queen's Privy Council for Canada.
8. The Leader of the Opposition. (Subject to Note 3).
9. The Lieutenant Governor of Ontario;
   The Lieutenant Governor of Québec;
   The Lieutenant Governor of Nova Scotia;
   The Lieutenant Governor of New Brunswick;
   The Lieutenant Governor of Manitoba;
   The Lieutenant Governor of British Columbia;
   The Lieutenant Governor of Prince Edward Island;
   The Lieutenant Governor of Saskatchewan;
   The Lieutenant Governor of Alberta;
   The Lieutenant Governor of Newfoundland
   (Note 6).
10. Members of the Queen's Privy Council for Canada, not of the Canadian Ministry, in accordance with the date of their appointment to the Privy Council.
11. Premiers of the Provinces of Canada in the same order as Lieutenant Governors. (Note 6).
12. The Commissioner of the Northwest Territories; The Commissioner of the Yukon Territory; The Commissioner of Nunavut
13. Government Leader of the Northwest Territories; The Government Leader of the Yukon Territory; The Government Leader of Nunavut
14. Representatives of faith communities. (Note 7).
15. Puisne Judges of the Supreme Court of Canada.
16. The Chief Justice and the Associate Chief Justice of the Federal Court of Canada.
17. (a) Chief Justices of the highest court of each Province and Territory; and
    (b) Chief Justices and Associate Chief Justices of the other superior courts of the Provinces and Territories; with precedence within sub-categories (a) and (b) governed by the date of appointment as Chief Justice.
18. (a) Judges of the Federal Court of Canada.
    (b) Puisne Judges of the superior courts of the Provinces and Territories.
    (c) the Chief Judge of the Tax Court of Canada;
    (d) the Associate Chief Judge of the Tax Court of Canada; and
    (e) Judges of the Tax Court of Canada; with precedence within each sub-category governed by date of appointment.
19. Senators of Canada.
20. Members of the House of Commons.
21. Consuls General of countries without diplomatic representation.
22. The Chief of the Defence Staff and the Commissioner of the Royal Canadian Mounted Police.
    (Note 8).
23. Speakers of Legislative Assemblies, within their Provinces and Territory.
24. Members of the Executive Councils, within their Provinces and Territory.
25. Judges of Provincial and Territorial Courts, within their Province and Territory.
26. Members of Legislative Assemblies, within their Provinces and Territory.

NOTES

1. The presence of the Sovereign in Canada does not impair or supersede the authority of the Governor General to perform the functions delegated to him under the Letters Patent constituting the office of the Governor General. The Governor General, under all circumstances, should be accorded precedence immediately after the Sovereign.
2. Precedence to be given immediately after the Chief Justice of Canada to former Governors General, with relative precedence among them governed by the date of their leaving office.

2.1 Precedence to be given immediately after the former Governors General to surviving spouses of deceased former Governors General (applicable only where the spouse was married to the Governor General during the latter's term of office), with relative precedence among them governed by the dates on which the deceased former Governor General left office.

3. Precedence to be given immediately after the surviving spouses of deceased former Governors General referred to in Note 2.1 to former Prime Ministers, with relative precedence among them governed by the dates of their first assumption of office.
4. Precedence to be given immediately after former Prime Ministers to former Chief Justices of Canada, with relative precedence among them governed by the dates of their appointment as Chief Justice of Canada.
5. Precedence among Ambassadors and High Commissioners, who rank equally, to be determined by the date of the presentation of their credentials. Precedence to be given to Chargés d'Affaires immediately after Ministers Plenipotentiary.
6. This provision does not apply to such ceremonies and occasions which are of a provincial nature.
7. The religious dignitaries will be senior Canadian representatives of faith communities having a significant presence in a relevant jurisdiction. The relevant precedence of the representatives of faith communities is to be governed by the date of their assumption in their present office, their representatives being given the same relative precedence.
8. This precedence to be given to the Chief of the Defence Staff and the Commissioner of the R.C.M.P. on occasions when they have official functions to perform, otherwise they are to have equal precedence with Deputy Ministers, with their relative position to be determined according to the respective dates of their appointments to office. The relative precedence of Deputy Ministers and other high officials of the public service of Canada is to be determined from time to time by the Minister of Canadian Heritage in consultation with the Prime Minister.

Table of Titles to be Used in Canada

1. The Governor General of Canada to be styled "Right Honourable" for life and to be styled "His Excellency" and his wife "Her Excellency", or "Her Excellency" and her husband "His Excellency", as the case may be, while in office.
2. The Lieutenant Governor of a Province to be styled "Honourable" for life and to be styled "His Honour" and his wife "Her Honour", or "Her Honour" and her husband "His Honour", as the case may be, while in office.
3. The Prime Minister of Canada to be styled "Right Honourable" for life.
4. The Chief Justice of Canada to be styled "Right Honourable" for life.
5. Privy Councillors of Canada to be styled "Honourable" for life.
6. Senators of Canada to be styled "Honourable" for life.
7. The Speaker of the House of Commons to be styled "Honourable" while in office.
8. The Commissioner of a Territory to be styled "Honourable" while in office.
9. Puisne Judges of the Supreme Court of Canada and Judges of the Federal Courts and the Tax Court of Canada as well as the Judges of the undermentioned Courts in the Provinces and Territories:
   Ontario - Court of Appeal and the Ontario Court of Justice (General Division)
   Québec - The Court of Appeal and the Superior Court of Québec
   Nova Scotia - The Court of Appeal and the Supreme Court of Nova Scotia
   New Brunswick - The Court of Appeal and the Court of Queen's Bench of New Brunswick
   Manitoba - The Court of Appeal and the Court of Queen's Bench of Manitoba
   British Columbia - The Court of Appeal and the Supreme Court of British Columbia
   Prince Edward Island - The Supreme Court of Prince Edward Island

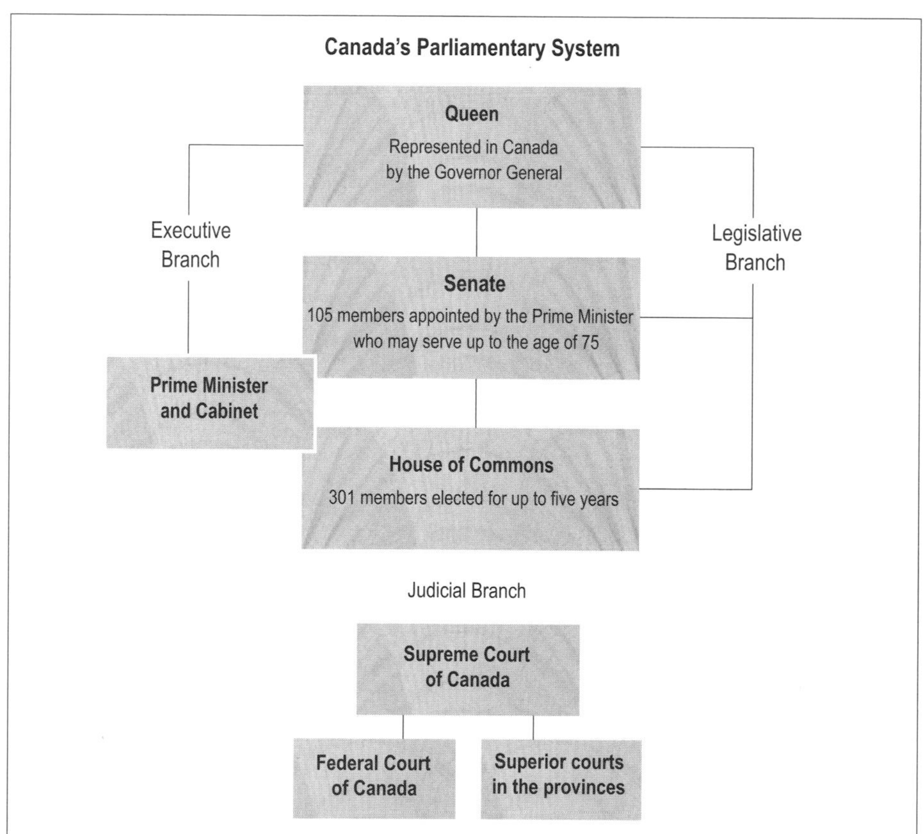

Parliament as a legislative body functions as an instrument of government within a broader structure that includes the Executive Branch and the Judicial Branch. In the Westminster-based model of parliamentary government, the Executive, comprised of the Prime Minister and the Cabinet, is incorporated into Parliament, while retaining a separate sphere of authority and autonomy. The Judiciary, consisting of the Supreme Court and all the other courts of the land, is the third branch of government that is also independent of either Parliament or the Executive.

Saskatchewan - The Court of Appeal and the Court of Queen's Bench of Saskatchewan
Alberta - The Court of Appeal and the Court of Queen's Bench of Alberta
Newfoundland - The Supreme Court of Newfoundland
Northwest Territories - The Supreme Court of Northwest Territories
Yukon Territory - The Supreme Court of Yukon
Nunavut Territory - The Nunavut Court of Justice

10. Presidents and Speakers of the Legislative Assemblies of the Provinces and Territories to be styled "Honourable" while in office.
11. Members of the Executive Councils of the Provinces and Territories to be styled "Honourable" while in office.
12. Judges of Provincial and Territorial Courts (appointed by the Provincial and Territorial Governments) to be styled "Honourable" while in office.
13. The following are eligible to be granted permission by the Governor General, in the name of Her Majesty The Queen, to retain the title of "Honourable" after they have ceased to hold office: (a) Speakers of the House of Commons; (b) Commissioners of Territories; (c) Judges designated in item 9.
14. The title "Right Honourable" is granted for life to the following eminent Canadians: The Right Honourable Martial Asselin The Right Honourable Ellen L. Fairclough The Right Honourable Francis Alvin George Hamilton The Right Honourable Donald F. Mazankowski The Right Honourable Robert Lorne Stanfield The Right Honourable Herb Eser Grey

GOVERNORS GENERAL OF CANADA SINCE CONFEDERATION

(WITH DATE APPOINTED)

The Viscount Monck, G.C.M.G.
June 1, 1867

Lord Lisgar, G.C.M.G.
Dec. 29, 1868

The Earl of Dufferin, K.P., G.C.B., G.C.S.I., G.C.M.G., G.C.I.E
May 22, 1872

The Marquess of Lorne, K.T., G.C.M.G., G.C.V.O.
Oct. 5, 1878

The Marquess of Lansdowne, K.G., G.C.S.I., G.C.M.G., G.C.I.E.
Aug. 18, 1883

Lord Stanley of Preston, K.G., G.C.B., G.C.V.O.
May 1, 1888

The Earl of Aberdeen, K.T., G.C.M.G., G.C.V.O.
May 22, 1893

The Earl of Minto, K.G., G.C.S.I., G.C.M.G., G.C.I.E.
July 30, 1898

The Earl Grey, G.C.B., G.C.M.G., G.C.V.O.
Sept. 26, 1904

H.R.H. The Duke of Connaught, K.G., K.T., K.P., G.M.B., G.C.S.I., G.C.M.G., G.C.I.E., G.C.V.O., G.B.E., T.D.
Mar. 21, 1911

The Duke of Devonshire, K.G., G.C.M.G., G.C.V.O., T.D.
Aug.. 19, 1916

Lord Byng of Vimy, G.C.B., G.C.M.G., M.V.O.
Aug. 2, 1921

The Viscount Willingdon of Ratton, G.C.S.I., G.C.M.G., G.C.I.E., G.B.E.
Aug. 5, 1926

The Earl of Bessborough, G.C.M.G.
Feb. 9, 1931

Baron Tweedsmuir of Elsfield, G.C.M.G., G.C.V.O., C.H.
Aug. 10, 1935

Major-General The Earl of Athlone, K.G., G.C.B., G.C.M.G., G.C.V.O., D.S.O.
Apr. 3, 1940

Field Marshal The Viscount Alexander of Tunis, K.G., G.C.B., O.M., G.C.M.G., C.S.I., D.S.O., M.C., A.D.C.
Aug. 1, 1945

The Rt. Hon. Vincent Massey, P.C., C.C., C.H.
Jan. 24, 1952

Major General The Rt. Hon. Georges-P. Vanier, D.S.O., M.C., C.D.
Aug. 1, 1959

The Rt. Hon. Roland Michener, P.C., C.C., C.M.M., C.D., Q.C.
Mar. 25, 1967

The Rt. Hon. Jules Léger P.C., C.C., C.M.M., C.D.
Oct. 5, 1973

The Rt. Hon. Edward Richard Schreyer, P.C., C.C., C.M.M., C.D.
Dec. 7, 1978

The Rt. Hon. Jeanne Sauvé, P.C., C.C., C.M.M., C.D.
Dec. 23, 1983

The Rt. Hon. Ramon John Hnatyshyn, P.C., C.C., C.M.M., C.D., Q.C.
Oct. 6, 1989

The Rt. Hon. Roméo LeBlanc, P.C., C.C., C.M.M., C.D.
Nov. 22, 1994

Her Excellency, the Rt. Hon. Adrienne Clarkson, C.C., C.M.M., C.O.M., C.D.
Oct. 7, 1999

Her Excellency, the Rt. Hon. Michaëlle Jean, C.C., C.M.M., C.O.M., C.D.
Sept. 27, 2005

His Excellency, the Rt. Hon. David Johnston, C.C., C.M.M., C.O.M.
Oct. 1, 2010

CANADIAN PRIME MINISTERS

(WITH PARTY AFFILIATION AND TIME IN OFFICE)

Rt. Hon. Sir John A. Macdonald (Conservative)
July 1, 1867 to Nov. 5, 1873
Oct. 17, 1878 to June 6, 1891
Photo credit: William James Topley/National Archives of Canada/PA-027013

Hon. Alexander MacKenzie (Liberal)
Nov. 7, 1873 to Oct. 16, 1878
Photo credit: William James Topley/National Archives of Canada/PA-026308

Hon. Sir John J. Abbott (Conservative)
June 16, 1891 to Nov. 24, 1892
Photo credit: William James Topley/National Archives of Canada/PA-033933

Rt. Hon. Sir John S. D. Thompson (Conservative)
Dec. 5, 1892 to Dec. 12, 1894
Photo Credit: National Archives of Canada/C-000698

Hon. Sir Mackenzie Bowell (Conservative)
Dec. 21, 1894 to April 27, 1896
Photo Credit: William James Topley/National Archives of Canada/PA-027159

Rt. Hon. Sir Charles Tupper (Conservative)
May 1, 1896 to July 8, 1896
Photo Credit: National Archives of Canada/PA-027743

Rt. Hon. Sir Wilrid Laurier (Liberal)
July 11, 1896 to Oct. 6, 1911
Photo Credit: William James Topley/National Archives of Canada/C-001971

Rt. Hon. Sir Robert L. Borden
Oct. 10, 1911 to Oct. 12, 1917
(Conservative Administration)
Oct. 12, 1917 to July 10, 1920
(Unionist Administration)
Photo Credit: William James Topley/National Archives of Canada/PA-028128

Rt. Hon. Arthur Meighen
July 10, 1920 to Dec. 29, 1921
(Unionist "National Liberal and Conservative Party")
June 29, 1926 to Sept. 25, 1926
(Conservative)
Photo Credit: William James Topley/National Archives of Canada/PA-026987

Rt. Hon. William Lyon Mackenzie King (Liberal)
Dec. 29, 1921 to June 28, 1926
Sept. 25, 1926 to Aug. 6, 1930
Oct. 23, 1935 to Nov. 15, 1948
Photo Credit: National Archives of Canada/C-027645

Rt. Hon. Richard Bedford Bennett (Conservative) (Became Viscount Bennett, 1941)
Aug. 7, 1930 to Oct. 23, 1935
Photo Credit: National Archives of Canada/C-000687

Rt. Hon. Louis Stephen St. Laurent
(Liberal)
Nov. 15, 1948 to June 21, 1957
Photo Credit: National Archives of Canada/C-010461

Rt. Hon. John G. Diefenbaker
(Progressive Conservative)
June 21, 1957 to April 22, 1963
Photo Credit: Paul Horsdal/National Archives of Canada/PA-130070

Rt. Hon. Lester Bowles Pearson
(Liberal)
April 22, 1963 to April 20, 1968
Photo Credit: Ashley-Crippen Studio/National Archives of Canada/PA-126393

Rt. Hon. Pierre Elliott Trudeau
(Liberal)
April 20, 1968 to June 4, 1979
Mar. 3, 1980 to June 30, 1984
Photo Credit: National Archives of Canada/C-046600

Rt. Hon. Charles Joseph Clark
(Progressive Conservative)
June 4, 1979 to Mar. 3, 1980
Photo Credit: Mia & Klaus

Rt. Hon. John Napier Turner
(Liberal)
June 30, 1984 to Sept. 17, 1984
Photo Credit: Courtesy of the Liberal Party of Canada

Rt. Hon. Martin Brian Mulroney
(Progressive Conservative)
Sept 17, 1984 to June 25, 1993
Photo Credit: Robert Cooper/National Archives of Canada/PA-152416

Rt. Hon. Kim Campbell
(Progressive Conservative)
June 25, 1993 to Nov. 4, 1993
Photo Credit: Courtesy of the National Speakers Bureau

Rt. Hon. Jean Chrétien
(Liberal)
Nov. 4, 1993 to Dec. 11, 2003
Photo Credit: Courtesy of the Prime Minister's Office

Rt. Hon. Paul Edgar Philippe Martin
(Liberal)
Dec. 12, 2003 to Feb. 6, 2006
Photo Credit: Courtesy of the Liberal Party of Canada

Rt. Hon. Stephen Joseph Harper
(Conservative)
Feb. 6, 2006 to —
Photo Credit: Courtesy of the Prime Minister's Office

PORTRAITS OF PRIME MINISTERS IN THE HOUSE OF COMMONS

Reproduced with the permission of the Curator, House of Commons

Sir John Alexander Macdonald
Credit: Henry Sandham
National Archives of Canada C-025743

Hon. Alexander Mackenzie
Credit: John Wycliffe Lowes Forster
National Archives of Canada C-116811

Hon. Sir John J. Abbott
Credit: Muli Tang
House of Commons Collection

Sir John Thompson
Credit: John Wycliffe Lowes Forster
National Archives of Canada C-116812

Hon. Sir Mackenzie Bowell
Credit: Joanne Tod
House of Commons Collection

Sir Charles Tupper
Credit: Victor A. Long
National Archives of Canada C-116813

Sir Wilfrid Laurier
Credit: John Wentworth Russell
National Archives of Canada C-116814

Sir Robert Borden
Credit: Kenneth Keith Forbes
National Archives of Canada C-116815

Rt. Hon. Arthur Meighen
Credit: George Ernest Fosbery
National Archives of Canada C-116816

Rt. Hon. William Lyon Mackenzie King
Credit: Frank O. Salisbury
National Archives of Canada C-116818

Rt. Hon. Richard Bedford Bennett
Credit: Kenneth Keith Forbes
National Archives of Canada C-116817

Rt. Hon. Louis St. Laurent
Credit: Audrey Watts McNaughton
National Archives of Canada C-116819

Rt. Hon. John G. Diefenbaker
Credit: Arthur Edward Cleeve Horne
National Archives of Canada C-116820

Rt. Hon. Lester Bowles Pearson
Credit: Hugh Seaforth MacKenzie
National Archives of Canada C-116821

Rt. Hon. Pierre Elliott Trudeau
Credit: Myfanwy Pavelic
House of Commons Collection

Rt. Hon. John Napier Turner
Credit: Brenda Bury
House of Commons Collection

Rt. Hon. Brian Mulroney
Credit: Igor Babailov
House of Commons Collections

Rt. Hon. Kim Campbell
Credit: David Goatley
House of Commons Collections

Regulations & Abbreviations

Forms of Address

The following are reprinted with the permission of Canadian Heritage.

The Royal Family/La Famille Royale

THE QUEEN:

Her Majesty The Queen, Buckingham Palace, London SW1A 1AA United Kingdom
Salutation - Your Majesty:
Final Salutation - I remain Your Majesty's faithful and devoted servant,
In Conversation - "Your Majesty" first then "Ma'am"
Note: The Queen's full title is "Her Majesty Queen Elizabeth II, Queen of Canada" Normally one refers to "Her Majesty The Queen" or "The Queen"

LA REINE:

Sa Majesté la Reine, Palais de Buckingham, Londres SW1A 1AA Royaume-Uni
Appel - Majesté,
Salutation - Je prie Votre Majesté d'agréer l'expression de ma très haute considération.
Conversation - ‹‹Majesté››
Remarques: Le titre complet de la Reine est le suivant: ‹‹Sa Majesté la reine Ellizabeth II, Reine du Canada›› On parle normalement de ‹‹Sa Majesté›› ou de ‹‹la Reine››

THE PRINCE OF WALES:

His Royal Highness The Prince of Wales, St. James's Palace, London SW1A 1BS United Kingdom
Salutation - Your Royal Highness:
Final Salutation - Yours very truly,
In Conversation - "Your Royal Highness" first then "Sir"
Note: Should never be referred to as: "Charles, Prince of Wales" or Prince Charles.

LE PRINCE DE GALLES:

Son Altesse Royale le prince de Galles, Palais de St. James, Londres SW1A 1BS Royaume-Uni
Appel - Altesse Royale,
Saluation - Je prie Votre Altesse Royal d'agréer l'expression de ma très haute considération.
Conversation - ‹‹Altesse Royale››
Remarques: Il ne faut jamais dire: ‹‹Charles, prince de Galles›› ou ‹‹le prince Charles››

Government/Gouvernement

GOVERNOR GENERAL OF CANADA:

His/Her Excellency the Right Honourable (full name), C.C., C.M.M., C.D., Governor General of Canada, Rideau Hall, 1 Sussex Dr., Ottawa ON K1A 0A1
Salutation - Excellency:
Final Salutation - Yours truly,
In Conversation - "Your Excellency" or "Excellency" first then "Sir" or "Madam"
Note: The Governor General may have other postnominal letters, such as P.C., Q.C.

GOVERNEUR GÉNÉRAL DU CANADA:

(homme) Son Excellence le très honorable (prénom et nom), C.C., C.M.M., C.O.M., C.D., Gouverneur général du Canada, Rideau Hall, 1, promenade Sussex, Ottawa ON K1A 0A1
(femme) Son Excellence la très honorable (prénom et nom), C.C., C.M.M., C.O.M., C.D., Gouverneure générale du Canada, Rideau Hall, 1, promenade Sussex, Ottawa ON K1A 0A1
Appel - (homme) Monsieur le Gouverneur général,
(femme) Madame la Gouverneure générale,
Saluation - (homme) Je vous prie d'agréer, Monsieur le Gouverneur général, l'expression de ma très haute considération.
(femme) Je vous prie d'agréer, Madame la Gouverneure générale, l'hommage de mon profond respect.
Remarques: D'autres initiales peuvent suivre le nom du gouverneur général, comme C.P. et C.R.

LIEUTENANT GOVERNOR OF A PROVINCE:

His/Her Honour the Honourable (full name) Lieutenant Governor of (Province), Address
Salutation - Your Honour or My dear Lieutenant Governor:
Final Salutation - Yours sincerely,
In Conversation - "Your Honour" first then "Sir" or "Madam" or "Mr./Mrs./Ms./Miss (name)"
Note: The Lieutenant Governor of a province has the title "Honourable" for life; the courtesy title "His/ Her Honour" is used only while in office.

LIEUTENANT-GOUVERNEUR

(homme) Son Honneur l'honorable (prénom et nom) Lieutenant-gouverneur de (province), Adresse
(femme) Son Honneur l'honorable (prénom et nom) Lieutenante-gouverneure de (province), Adresse
Appel - (homme) Monsieur le Lieutenant-Gouverneur,
(femme) Madame la Lieutenante-Gouverneure,
Salutation - (homme) Je vous prie d'agréer, Monsieur le Lieutenant-Gouverneur, l'expression de ma haute considération.
(femme) Je vous prie d'agréer, Madame la Lieutenante-Gouverneure, l'hommage de mes respectueux hommages.
Conversation - On commence par ‹‹Votre Honneur››. On poursuit avec ‹‹Monsieur›› ou ‹‹Madame››
Remarques: Le titre ‹‹honorable›› est accordé à vie au lieutenant-gouverneur; le titre de courtoisie ‹‹Son Honneur›› n'est utilisé que pendant la durée du mandat.

THE PRIME MINISTER OF CANADA:

The Right Honourable (full name), P.C., M.P., Prime Minister of Canada, Langevin Block, Ottawa, ON K1A 0A2
Salutation - Dear Prime Minister: or Prime Minister:
Final Salutation - Yours sincerely,
In Conversation - "Prime Minister" first then "Mr./ Mrs./Ms./Miss (name)"
Note: The term "Mr. Prime Minister" should not be used. The Prime Minister may have other post-nominal letters, such as Q.C.

PREMIER MINISTRE DU CANADA

(homme) Le très honorable (prénom et nom), C.P., député Premier Ministre du Canada, Édifice Langevin, Ottawa ON K1A 0A2
(femme) La très honorable (prénom et nom), C.P., députée Première Ministre du Canada, Édifice Langevin, Ottawa ON K1A 0A2
Appel - (homme) Monsieur le Premier Ministre,
(femme) Madame la Première Ministre,
Salutation -
(homme) Je vous prie d'agréer, Monsieur le Premier Ministre, l'expression de ma très haute considération.
(femme) Je vous prie d'agréer, Madame la Première Ministre, l'hommage de mon profond respect. Conversation -
(homme) On commence par ‹‹Monsieur le Premier Ministre››. On poursuit avec ‹‹Monsieur››
(femme) On commence par ‹‹Madame la Première Ministre››. On pousuit avec ‹‹Madame››
Remarques: D'autres initiales peuvent suivre le nom, comme C.R.

THE PREMIER OF A PROVINCE OF CANADA:

The Honourable (full name), M.L.A. or (M.P.P., M.N.A., or M.H.A.), Premier of (Province), Address
Salutation - Dear Premier:
Final Salutation - Yours sincerely,
In Conversation - "Premier" first then "Mr./Mrs./Ms./ Miss (name)"
Note: The title "Honourable" is used only while in office, unless he/she is a member of the Privy Council. The term "Mr./Madam Premier" should not be used.

LE PREMIER MINISTRE D'UNE PROVINCE

(homme) L'honorable (prénom et nom) M.A.L ou (M.A.N., M.P.P. ou M.C.A) Premier Ministre de (province), Adresse
(femme) L'honorable (prénom et nom) M.A.L ou (M.A.N., M.P.P. ou M.C.A) Première Ministre de (province), Adresse
Appel - (homme) Monsieur le Premier Ministre,
(femme) Madame la Première Ministre,
Salutation - (homme) Je vous prie d'agréer, Monsieur le Premier Ministre, l'expression de ma haute considération.
(femme) Je vous prie d'agréer, Madame la Première Ministre, l'hommage de mon profond respect.
Conversation - On commence par ‹‹Monsieur le Premier Ministre››. On poursuit avec ‹‹Monsieur››
(femme) On commence par ‹‹Madame la Première Ministre››. On pousuit avec ‹‹Madame››
Remarques: Les premiers ministres ne conservent pas le titre ‹‹honorable›› après la fin de leur mandat, à moins qu'ils ne soient membres du Conseil privé.

COMMISSIONER OF A TERRITORY:

The Honourable (full name), Commissioner of (Territory), Address
Salutation - Commissioner (name):
Final Salutation - Yours sincerely,
In Conversation - "Sir" or "Madam" or "Mr./Mrs./ Ms./Miss (name)"

COMMISSAIRE DU TERRITOIRE

(homme/femme) L'honorable (prénom et nom) Commissaire du (territoire), Adresse
Appel - (homme) Monsieur le Commissaire,
(femme) Madame la Commissaire,
Salutation - Je vous prie d'agréer, Monsieur le Commissaire, l'expression de ma haute considération.
(femme) Je vous prie d'agréer, Madame la Commissaire, l'expression de mes respectueux hommages. Conversation -
(homme) ‹‹Monsieur››
(femme) ‹‹Madame››
Remarques: Le titre ‹‹honorable›› n'est utilisé que pendant la durée de ses fonctions.

GOVERNMENT LEADER OF A TERRITORY:

The Honourable (full name), M.L.A., Government Leader of (Territory), Address
Salutation - Dear Mr./Mrs./Ms./Miss (name):
Final Salutation - Yours sincerely,
In Conversation - "Mr./Mrs./Ms./Miss (name)"
Note: The title "Honourable" is used only while in office, unless he/she is a member of the Privy Council. The term "Mr./Madam Leader" should not be used.

LE LEADER DU GOUVERNEMENT D'UN TERRITOIRE

(homme/femme) L'honorable (prénom et nom), M.A.L. Leader du gouvernement du (territoire), Adresse
Appel - (homme) Monsieur le leader du gouvernement,
(femme) Madame la leader du gouvernement,
Salutation - (homme) Je vous prie d'agréer, Monsieur le Leader du gouvernement, l'expression de ma haute consideration.
(femme) Je vous prie d'agréer, Madame la Leader du gouvernement, l'hommage de mon profond respect.
Conversation - On commence par ‹‹Monsieur le Leader du gouvernement››. On poursuit avec ‹‹Monsieur››
(femme) On commence par ‹‹Madame la Leader du gouvernement››. On poursuit avec ‹‹Madame››
Remarques: Les leaders ne conservent pas le titre ‹‹honorable›› après la fin de leur mandat, à moins qu'ils ne soient membres du Conseil privé.

CABINET MINISTERS:

Member of the House of Commons: The Honourable (full name), P.C., M.P., Minister of ________, House of Commons, Ottawa ON K1A 0A6
Salutation - Dear Minister: or Dear Colleague: (between colleagues)
Final Salutation - Yours sincerely,
In Conversation - "Minister" first then "Mr./Mrs./ Ms./Miss (name)"
For a Senator: Senator the Honourable (full name), P.C., Minister of ________ , The Senate, Ottawa, ON K1A 0A4
Salutation - Dear Minister: or Dear Colleague: (between colleagues)
Final Salutation - Yours sincerely,
In Conversation - "Minister" first then "Mr./Mrs./ Ms./Miss (name)"

CONSEIL DES MINISTRES DU CANADA

(homme) L'honorable (prénom et nom), C.P. député Ministre de ________, Chambre de communes, Ottawa ON K1A 0A6
(femme) L'honorable (prénom et nom), C.P. députée Ministre de ________, Chambre de communes, Ottawa ON K1A 0A6
Appel - (homme) Monsieur le Ministre, ou Cher collègue, (Entre collègues)
(femme) Madame la Ministre, ou Chère collègue, (Entre collègues)
Salutation -
(homme) Je vous prie d'agréer, Monsieur le Ministre, l'expression de ma considération respectueuse.
(femme) Je vous prie d'agréer, Madame la Ministre, l'hommage de mon profond respect. Conversation -
(homme) On commence par ‹‹Monsieur le Ministre››. On poursuit avec ‹‹Monsieur››
(femme) On commence par ‹‹Madame la Ministre››. On poursuit avec ‹‹Madame››
Remarques: Les ministres fédéraux sont membres du Conseil privé de la Reine pour le Canada et conservent le titre ‹‹honorable›› à vie. On place les initiales C.P. après leur nom.

SECRETARIES OF STATE:

The Honourable (full name), P.C., M.P., Secretary of State (Portfolio), House of Commons, Ottawa, ON K1A 0A6
Salutation - Dear Secretary of State: or Dear Colleague: (between colleagues)
Final Salutation - Yours sincerely,
In Conversation - "Secretary of State" first then "Mr./ Mrs./Ms./Miss (name)"
Note: Members of the Ministry are members of the Queen's Privy Council for Canada and retain the title "Honourable" for life, using the initials P.C. after their name. The term "Mr. Minister" or "Madame Minister" should not be used. The term "Mr. Secretary of State" or "Madame Secretary of State" should not be used.

SECRÉTAIRES D'ÉTAT
(homme) L'honorable (prénom et nom), C.P. député Secrétaire d'État (Portefeuille), Chambre des communes, Ottawa ON K1A 0A6
(femme) L'honorable (prénom et nom), C.P. députée Secrétaire d'État (Portefeuille), Chambre des communes, Ottawa ON K1A 0A6
Appel - (homme) Monsieur le Secrétaire d'État, ou Cher collègue, (Entre collègues)
(femme) Madame la Secrétaire d'État, ou Chère collègue, (Entre collègues)
Salutation - (homme) Je vous prie d'agréer, Monsieur le Secrétaire d'État, l'expression de ma considération respectueuse. Ou Je vous prie, cher collègue, de recevoir mes cordiales salutations. (Entre collègues)
(femme) Je vous prie d'agréer, Madame la Secrétaire d'État, l'hommage de mon profond respect. Ou Je vous prie, chère collègue, de recevoir mes cordiales salutations. (Entre collègues) Conversation -
(homme) On commence par «Monsieur le Secrétaire d'État». On poursuit avec «Monsieur»
(femme) On commence par «Madame la Secrétaire d'État». On poursuit avec «Madame»
Remarques: Les secrétaires d'État sont membres du Conseil privé de la Reine pour le Canada et conservent le titre «honorable» à vie. On place les initiales C.P. aprés leur nom.

SPEAKER OF THE SENATE:
The Honourable (full name), Senator, Speaker of State, The Senate, Ottawa, ON K1A 0A4
Salutation - Dear Mr./Madam Speaker:
Final Salutation - Yours sincerely,
In Conversation - "Mr. Speaker" or "Madam Speaker"
Note: A senator who is a member of the Canadian Privy Council is addressed as "Senator the Honourable (name), P.C. " After a Senator retires, he/she retains the title "Honourable" but the salutation is "Dear Sir/ Madam" or "Dear Mr./Mrs./Ms./Miss (name)"

PRÉSIDENT OU PRÉSIDENTE DU SÉNAT
(homme) L'honorable (prénom et nom), sénateur Président du Sénat, Le Sénat, Ottawa ON K1A 0A4
(femme) L'honorable (prénom et nom), sénatrice Présidente du Sénat, Le Sénat, Ottawa ON K1A 0A4
Appel - (homme) Monsieur le Président,
(femme) Madame la Présidente,
Salutation - (homme) Je vous prie d'agréer, Monsieur le Président, l'expression de ma haute considération.
(femme) Je vous prie d'agréer, Madame la Présidente, l'hommage de mon profond respect. Conversation -
(homme) «Monsieur le Président»
(femme) «Madame la Présidente»
Remarques: Dans le cas d'un sénateur ou d'une sénatrice qui est membre du Conseil privé, la formule d'appel à utiliser est «L'honorable (nom), C.P., sénateur(trice)». Après leur retraite, les sénateurs conservent le titre «honorable» mais la formule d'appel devient: «Monsieur/Madame».

SPEAKER OF THE HOUSE OF COMMONS:
The Honourable (full name), M.P., Speaker of the House of Commons, House of Commons, Ottawa, ON K1A 0A6
Salutation - Dear Mr./Madam Speaker:
Final Salutation - Yours sincerely,
In Conversation - "Mr. Speaker" or "Madam Speaker"

PRÉSIDENT OU PRÉSIDENTE DE LA CHAMBRE DES COMMUNES
(homme) L'honorable (prénom et nom) député Président de la Chambre des communes, Chambre des communes, Ottawa ON K1A 0A6
(femme) L'honorable (prénom et nom) députée Présidente de la Chambre des communes, Chambre des communes, Ottawa ON K1A 0A6
Appel - (homme) Monsieur le Président,
(femme) Madame la Présidente,
Salutation - (homme) Je vous prie d'agréer, Monsieur le Président, l'expression de ma haute considération.
(femme) Je vous prie d'agréer, Madame la Présidente, l'hommage de mon profond respect. Conversation -
(homme) «Monsieur le Président»
(femme) «Madame la Présidente»

SENATORS:
The Honourable (full name), Senator, The Senate, Ottawa, ON K1A 0A1
Salutation - Dear Senator (name):
Final Salutation - Yours sincerely,
In Conversation - "Senator (name)"
Note: A senator who is a member of the Queen's Privy Council is addressed as "Senator the Honourable (full name), P.C." After a Senator retires, he/she retains the title "Honourable" for life but the salutation is "Dear Sir/Madam" or "Dear Mr./Mrs./Ms./Miss (name)".

SÉNATEURS:
(homme) L'honorable (prénom et nom) sénateur, Le Sénat, Ottawa ON K1A 0A4
(femme) L'honorable (prénom et nom) sénatrice, Le Sénat, Ottawa ON K1A 0A4
Appel - (homme) Monsieur le Sénateur,
(femme) Madame la Sénatrice,
Salutation - (homme) Je vous prie d'agréer, Monsieur le Sénateur, l'expression de mes meilleurs sentiments.
(femme) Je vous prie d'agréer, Madame la Sénatrice, mes hommages respectueux. Conversation -
(homme) «Monsieur le Sénateur». On poursuit avec «Monsieur»
(femme) «Madame la Sénatrice». On poursuit avec «Madame»
Remarques: Après leur retraite, les sénateurs conservent le titre «honorable», mais la formule d'appel devient: «Monsieur» ou «Madame».

MEMBERS OF THE HOUSE OF COMMONS:
Mr. John Smith, M.P. or The Honourable John Smith, P.C., M.P., House of Commons, Ottawa, ON K1A 0A6
Salutation - Dear Mr./Mrs./Ms./Miss (name):
Final Salutation - Yours sincerely,
In Conversation - "Mr./Mrs./Ms./Miss (name)"
Note: The members of the House of Commons who are members of the Queen's Privy Council retain the title "Honourable" for life and use the initials "P.C." after their name. M.P.: Member of the House of Commons P.C., M.P.: Member of the Privy Council and Member of the House of Commons

DÉPUTÉS FÉDÉRAUX
(homme) Monsieur (prénom et nom), député ou L'honorable (prénom et nom), C.P., député Chambre des communes, Ottawa ON K1A 0A6
(femme) Madame (prénom et nom), députée ou L'honorable (prénom et nom), C.P., députée Chambre des communes, Ottawa ON K1A 0A6
Appel - (homme) Monsieur le Député,
(femme) Madame la Députée,
Salutation - (homme) Je vous prie d'agréer, Monsieur le Député, l'expression de mes meilleurs sentiments.
(femme) Je vous prie d'agréer, Madame la Députée, mes respectueux hommages. Conversation -
(homme) On commence par «Monsieur le Député». On poursuit avec «Monsieur»
(femme) On commence par «Madame la Députée». On poursuit avec «Madame»
Remarques: Les députés qui sont membres du Conseil privé de la Reine pour le Canada ont le «honorable» à vie et portent les initiales «C.P.» après leur nom.

MEMBER OF THE PROVINCIAL/TERRITORIAL CABINET:
The Honourable (full name), M.L.A. or (M.P.P., M.N.A. or M.H.A.), Minister of ________, Address
Salutation - Dear Minister: or Dear Colleague: (between colleagues)
Final Salutation - Yours sincerely,
In Conversation - "Minister" first then "Mr./Mrs./ Ms./Miss (name)"
Note: A provincial/territorial cabinet minister does not retain the title "Honourable" after tenure of office unless he/she is a member of the Privy Council. M.L.A.: all provinces/territories except for: Ontario (M.P.P.); Québec (M.N.A.); Newfoundland (M.H.A.). The term "Mr./Madam Minister" should not be used.

MINISTRES PROVINCIAUX/TERRITORIAUX
(homme/femme) L'honorable (prénom et nom), M.A.L. ou (M.A.N., M.P.P. ou M.C.A.) Ministre de ________, Adresse
Appel - (homme) Monsieur le Ministre, ou Cher collègue, (Entre collègues)
(femme) Madame la Ministre, ou Chère collègue, (Entre collègues)
Salutation - (homme) Je vous prie d'agréer, Monsieur le Ministre, l'expression de ma considération respectueuse. Ou Je vous prie, cher collègue, de recevoir mes cordiales salutations. (Entre collègues)
(femme) Je vous prie d'agréer, Madame la Ministre, l'expression de ma considération respectueuse. Ou Je vous prie, chère collègue, de recevoir mes cordiales salutations. (Entre collègues) Conversation -
(homme) On commence par «Monsieur le Ministre». On poursuit avec «Monsieur»
(femme) On commence par «Madame la Ministre». On poursuit avec «Madame»
Remarques: Les ministres provinciaux/territoriaux ne conservent pas le titre «honorable» après la fin de leur mandat à moins qu'ils ne soient membres du Conseil privè. M.A.L.: toutes les provinces et les territoires, sauf: - l'Ontario (M.P.P.) - le Québec (M.A.N.) - Terre- Neuve (M.C.A.)

MEMBER OF A PROVINCIAL/TERRITORIAL LEGISLATIVE ASSEMBLY:
Mr. John Smith, M.L.A. or (M.P.P., M.N.A., or M.H.A.)
Salutation - Dear Mr./Mrs./Ms./Miss (name),
Final Salutation - Yours sincerely,
In Conversation - "Mr./Mrs./Ms./Miss (name)"
Note: Members of the Queen's Privy Council retain the title "Honourable" for life and use the initials "P.C." after their name. M.L.A.: all provinces/territories except for: Ontario (M.P.P.); Quebec (M.N.A.); Newfoundland (M.H.A.) P.C., M.L.A.: Member of the Privy Council and Member of the Legislative Assembly

DÉPUTÉS PROVINCIAUX/TERRITORIAUX
(homme) Monsieur (prénom et nom), M.A.L. ou (M.P.P., M.A.N. ou M.C.A.), Adresse
(femme) Madame (prénom et nom), M.A.L. ou (M.P.P., M.A.N. ou M.C.A.), Adresse
Appel - (homme) Monsieur le Député,
(femme) Madame la Députée,
Salutation - (homme) Je vous prie d'agréer, Monsieur le Député, l'expression de mes meilleurs sentiments.
(femme) Je vous prie d'agréer, Madame la Députée, mes respectueux hommages. Conversation -
(homme) «Monsieur»
(femme) «Madame»
Remarques: Les membres du Conseil privé de la Reine conservent le titre «honorable» à vie et placent les initiales C.P. après leur nom. M.A.L.: toutes les provinces et les territoires sauf: - l'Ontario (M.P.P.) - le Québec (M.A.N.), Terre-Neuve (M.C.A.) C.P., M.A.L.: Membre du Conseil privé et membre de l'Assemblée législative.

MAYOR OF A CITY OR TOWN:
His/Her Worship (full name), Mayor of (name), Address
Salutation - Dear Sir/Madam: or Dear Mr./Madam Mayor:
Final Salutation - Yours sincerely,
In Conversation - "Your Worship" first then "Mayor (name)"

MAIRE/MAIRESSE
(homme) Son Honneur monsieur (prénom et nom), Maire de (Ville), Adresse
(femme) Son Honneur madame (prénom et nom), Mairesse de (Ville), Adresse Appel - Monsieur le Maire,
(femme) Madame la Mairesse,
Salutation - (homme) Je vous prie d'agréer, Monsieur le Maire, l'expression de mes meilleurs sentiments.
(femme) Je vous prie d'agréer, Madame la Mairesse, mes hommages respectueux. Conversation -
(homme) On commence par «Votre Honneur». On poursuit avec «Monsieur le Maire»
(femme) On commence par «Votre Honneur». On poursuit avec «Madame la Mairesse»

JUDGES/JUGES
CHIEF JUSTICE: The Right Honourable (full name), P.C., Chief Justice of Canada, Supreme Court of Canada, Ottawa, ON K1A 0J1
Salutation - Dear Chief Justice:
Final Salutation - Yours sincerely,
In Conversation - "Mr./Madam Chief Justice" first then "Sir/Madam" or "Mr./Mrs./Ms./Miss (name)"

JUGE EN CHEF DU CANADA
(homme) Le très honorable (prenom et nom), C.P. Juge en chef du Canada, Cour suprême du Canada, Ottawa ON K1A 0J1
(femme) La très honorable (prenom et nom), C.P. Juge en chef du Canada, Cour suprême du Canada, Ottawa ON K1A 0J1
Appel - (homme) Monsieur le Juge en chef,
(femme) Madame la Juge en chef,
Salutation - (homme) Je vous prie d'agréer, Monsieur le Juge en chef, l'expression de ma très haute considération.
(femme) Je vous prie d'agréer, Madame la Juge en chef, l'hommage de mon profond respect. Conversation -
(homme) On commence par «Monsieur le Juge en chef». On poursuit avec «Monsieur»
(femme) On commence par «Madame la Juge en chef». On poursuit avec «Madame»

JUDGES OF SUPERIOR COURTS:
Supreme Court of Canada & Federal Court of Canada: The Honourable (full name), Judge of the ________ Court of Canada, Address.
Salutation - Dear Mr./Madam Justice (name):
Final Salutation - Yours sincerely,
In Conversation - "Mr./Madam Justice" Appeal Court, Superior Court, Court of the Queen's Bench: The Honourable (full name), Judge of ________, Address
Salutation - Dear Mr./Madam Justice (name):
Final Salutation - Yours sincerely,
In Conversation - "Mr./Madam Justice (name)"

JUGES DES COURS SUPÉRIEURES

Cour suprême, Cour fédérale et Cour de l'impôt: L'honorable (prénom et nom), Titre, Adresse
Appel - (homme) Monsieur le Juge,
(femme) Madame la Juge,
Salutation - (homme) Je vous prie d'agréer, Monsieur le Juge, l'expression de ma haute considération.
(femme) Je vous prie d'agréer, Madame la Juge l'hommage de mon profond respect. Conversation -
(homme) «Monsieur le Juge»
(femme) «Madame la Juge» Cour d'appel, Cour supérieure, Cour du Banc de la Reine, L'honorable (prénom et nom) Juge de ________, Adresse
Appel - (homme) Monsieur le Juge,
(femme) Madame la Juge,
Salutation -
(homme) Je vous prie d'agréer, Monsieur le Juge, l'expression de ma haute considération.
(femme) Je vous prie d'agréer, Madame la Juge, l'hommage de mon profond respect. Conversation -
(homme) «Monsieur le Juge»
(femme) «Madame la Juge»

JUDGES OF THE TAX COURT:

The Honourable (full name), Judge of the Tax Court of Canada, Address
Salutation - Dear Chief Judge/Judge (name):
Final Salutation - Yours sincerely,
In Conversation - "Chief Judge/Judge (name)"
Remarques: En français, voir ci-dessus.

CHIEF JUDGES/JUDGES OF PROVINCIAL/TERRITORIAL COURTS:

The Honourable (full name), Provincial/Territorial Court of ________, Address
Salutation - Dear Chief Judge/Judge (name):
Final Salutation - Yours sincerely,
In Conversation - "Judge (name)"
Note: The titles to be used in Canada now recognize the title"Honourable" for provincially/territorially appointed judges. The courtesy title "His/Her Honour" is no longer appropriate given an official title has been granted.

JUGES EN CHEF/JUGES DES COURS PROVINCIALES/ TERRITORIALES

L'honorable (prénom et nom), Cour provinciale de ________, Adresse
Appel - (homme) Monsieur le Juge en chef/le Juge,
(femme) Madame la Juge en chef/la Juge,
Salutation -
(homme) Je vous prie d'agréer, Monsieur le Juge en chef/le Juge, l'expression de mon profond respect.
(femme) Je vous prie d'agréer, Madame la Juge en chef//la Juge, l'hommage de mon profond respect. Conversation -
(homme) «Monsieur le Juge en chef/ le Juge»
(femme) «Madame la Juge en chef/la Juge»
Remarques: Le tableau des titres pour le Canada reconnaît le titre «honorable» aux juges des cours provinciales/ territoriales; le titre de courtoisie «Son Honneur» n'est plus de mise maintenant qu'un titre officiel est utilisé.

Religion

Anglican Church of Canada/ Église anglicane du Canada

PRIMATE:

The Most Reverend (full name), Primate of the Anglican Church of Canada, Address
Salutation - Dear Archbishop (name):
Final Salutation - Yours sincerely,
In Conversation - "Archbishop"

PRIMAT:

Le révérendissime (prénom et nom), Primate de l'Église anglicane du Canada, Adresse Appel - Monsieur le Primat,
Salutation - Je vous prie d'agréer, Monsieur le Primat, l'expression de mes sentiments les plus respectueux.
Conversation - «Monsieur l'Archevêque»

ARCHBISHOP:

The Most Reverend (full name), D.D., Archbishop of (name of Diocese), Address
Salutation - Dear Archbishop (name):
Final Salutation - Yours very truly,
In Conversation - "Archbishop"
ARCHEVÊQUE:
Le révérendissime (prénom et nom), Archevêque de (nom du diocèse), Adresse Appel - Monsieur l'Archevêque,
Salutation - Je vous prie d'agréer, Monsieur l'Archevêque, l'expression de mes sentiments les plus respectueux.
Conversation - «Monsieur l'Archevêque»

BISHOP:

The Right Reverend (full name), Bishop of (name of Diocese), Address
Salutation - Dear Bishop (name):
Final Salutation - Yours very truly,
In Conversation - "Bishop (name)" or "Bishop"

ÉVÊQUE:

(homme) Le très révérend (prénom et nom), Évêque de (nom du diocèse), Adresse
(femme) La très révérende (prénom et nom), Évêque de (nom du diocèse), Adresse
Appel - (homme) Monsieur l'Évêque,
(femme) Madame l'Évêque,
Salutation - (homme) Je vous prie d'agréer, Monsieur l'Évêque, l'expression de mes sentiments les plus respectueux.
(femme) Je vous prie d'agréer, Madame l'Évêque, l'hommage de mon profond respect. Conversation -
(homme) «Monsieur l'Évêque»
(femme) «Madame l'Évêque»

ARCHDEACON:

The Venerable (full name), Archdeacon, Address
Salutation - Dear Archdeacon (name):
Final Salutation - Yours sincerely,
In Conversation - "Archdeacon (name)"

ARCHIDIACRE:

(homme) Le vénérable (prénom et nom), Archidiacre, Adresse
(femme) La vénérable (prénom et nom), Archidiacre, Adresse
Appel - (homme) Monsieur l'Archidiacre,
(femme) Madame l'Archidiacre,
Salutation - (homme) Je vous prie d'agréer, Monsieur l'Archidiacre, l'expression de mes sentiments les plus respectueux.
(femme) Je vous prie d'agréer, Madame l'Archidacre, l'hommage de mon profond respect. Conversation -
(homme) «Monsieur l'Archidiacre»
(femme) «Madame l'Archidiacre»

DEAN:

The Very Reverend (full name), Dean of (name of Cathedral), Address
Salutation - Dear Dean (name):
Final Salutation - Yours sincerely,
In Conversation - "Dean (name)" or "Mr./Mrs./Ms./ Miss (name)"

DOYEN:

(homme) Le très révérend (prénom et nom), Doyen de (nom de la cathédrale), Adresse
(femme) La très révérende (prénom et nom), Doyenne de (nom de la cathédrale), Adresse
Appel - (homme) Monsieur le Doyen,
(femme) Madame la Doyenne,
Salutation - (homme) Je vous prie d'agréer, Monsieur le Doyen, l'expression de mes sentiments les plus respectueux.
(femme) Je vous prie d'agréer, Madame la Doyenne, l'hommage de mon profond respect. Conversation -
(homme) «Monsieur le Doyen» ou «Monsieur»
(femme) «Madame la Doyenne» ou «Madame»

CANON:

The Reverend Canon (full name), Address
Salutation - Dear Canon (name):
Final Salutation - Yours sincerely,
In Conversation - "Canon (name)"

CHANOINE:

(homme) Le chanoine, (prénom et nom), Adresse
(femme) La chanoinesse, (prénom et nom), Adresse
Appel - (homme) Monsieur le Chanoine,
(femme) Madame la Chanoinesse,
Salutation - (homme) Je vous prie d'agréer, Monsieur le Chanoine, l'expression de mes sentiments les plus respectueux.
(femme) Je vous prie d'agréer, Madame La Chanoinesse, l'hommage de mon profond respect. Conversation -
(homme) «Monsieur le Chanoine»
(femme) «Madame la Chanoinesse»

PRIEST:

The Reverend (full name), Address
Salutation - Dear Father (name) or Dear Mr. (name): or Dear Mrs./Ms./Miss (name)
Final Salutation - Yours sincerely,
In Conversation - "Father" or "Father (name) or "Mrs./Ms./Miss (name)"
Note: "Reverend" is an adjective which is never used without the full name.

PRÊTRE:

(homme) Le révérend père (prénom et nom), Adresse
(femme) La révérende (prénom et nom), Adresse
Appel - (homme) Monsieur le Curé, Monsieur l'Abbé,
(femme) Madame,
Salutation - (homme) Je vous prie d'agréer, Monsieur le Curé, l'expression de mes sentiments respectueux.
(femme) Je vous prie d'agréer, Madame, l'expression de mes sentiments respectueux. Conversation -
(homme) «Monsieur le Curé/Monsieur l'Abbé»
(femme) « Madame)»

RELIGIOUS:

(man) The Reverend Father (full name), Address
Salutation - Dear Father (name):
Final Salutation - Yours sincerely,
In Conversation - "Reverend Father" (woman) Reverend Mother (full name)/Reverend Sister (full name)
Salutation - Dear Reverend Mother/Sister:
Final Salutation - Yours sincerely,
In Conversation - "Reverend Mother (name)/Reverend Sister (name)"

RELIGIEUX/RELIGIEUSE:

(homme) Le révérend père (prénom et nom), Adresse
(femme) La révérende mère/ soeur (prénom et nom), Adresse
Appel - (homme) Révérend père/Mon père,
(femme) Révérende mère/Ma soeur
Salutation - (homme) Je vous prie d'agréer, Révérend père/Mon père, l'expression de mes sentiments les plus respectueux.
(femme) Je vous prie d'agréer, Révérende mère/ Ma soeur, l'hommage de mon profond respect. Conversation -
(homme) «Révérend père/Mon père»
(femme) «Révérende mère/Ma soeur»

Roman Catholic/Église catholique romaine

THE POPE:

His Holiness Pope Benedict XVI, Address
Salutation - Your Holiness:
Final Salutation - I have the honour to remain Your Holiness's obedient servant,
In Conversation - "Your Holiness"

LE PAPE:

Sa Sainteté le pape Benedict XVI, Adresse Appel - Très Saint-Père,
Salutation - Je vous prie d'agréer, Très Saint-Père, l'expression de mon profond respect et de ma très haute considération.
Conversation - «Votre Sainteté» ou «Très Saint- Père»

CARDINAL:

His Eminence John Cardinal Smith, Address
Salutation - Your Eminence: or Dear Cardinal (name):
Final Salutation - Yours very truly,
In Conversation - "Your Eminence"

CARDINAL:

Son Éminence le cardinal (prénom et nom), Adresse Appel - Monsieur le Cardinal,
Salutation - Je vous prie d'agréer, Monsieur le Cardinal, l'expression de mon profond respect.

Conversation - «Éminence»

ARCHBISHOP/BISHOP:
The Most Reverend (full name), Archbishop/Bishop of (name of Diocese). Address
Salutation - Dear Archbishop/Bishop (name):
Final Salutation - Yours very truly,
In Conversation - "Archbishop/Bishop"
Note: The Holy See accorded the courtesy title "His Excellency" to Roman Catholic Archbishops and Bishops; that title is not recognized by Canadian civil authorities.

ARCHEVÊQUE/ÉVÊQUE:

Monseigneur (prénom et nom), Archevêque ou Évêque de (nom du diocèse), Adresse Appel - Monseigneur,
Salutation - Je vous prie d'agréer, Monseigneur , l'expression de mes sentiments les plus respectueux.
Conversation - «Monseigneur»
Remarques: Le titre «Son Excellence» est utilisé par le Saint-Siège pour les archevêques et évêques catholiques; il n'est toutefois pas reconnu par les autorités civiles canadiennes.

ABBOT:

The Right Reverend (full name), Abbot of (name of ________), Address
Salutation - Right Reverend Father: or Dear Abbott (name):
Final Salutation - Yours sincerely,
In Conversation - "Father Abbott"

ABBÉ:

Le révérend père (prénom et nom), Adresse Appel - Monsieur l'Abbé,

Salutation - Je vous prie d'agréer, Monsieur l'Abbé, l'expression de mes sentiments les plus respectueux.
Conversation - «Monsieur l'Abbé»

CANON:
The Very Reverend (full name), Address
Salutation - Dear Canon (name):
Final Salutation - Yours sincerely,
In Conversation - "Canon (name)"

CHANOINE:
Le chanoine (prénom et nom), Adresse Appel - Monsieur le Chanoine,
Salutation - Je vous prie d'agréer, Monsieur le Chanoine, l'expression de mes sentiments respectueux.
Conversation - «Monsieur le Chanoine»

PRIEST
The Reverend (full name), Address
Salutation - Dear Father:
Final Salutation - Yours sincerely,
In Conversation - "Father" or "Father (name)"
Note: "Reverend" is an adjective which is never used without the full name.

PRÊTRE:
Le révérend père (prénom et nom), Adresse Appel - Monsieur le Curé/l'Abbé,
Salutation - Je vous prie d'agréer, Monsieur le Curé, l'expression de mes sentiments respectueux.
Conversation - «Monsieur le Curé/l'Abbé»

SULPICIAN:
Mr. (full name), Address
Salutation - Dear Mr. (name):
Final Salutation - Yours truly,
In Conversation - "Mr. (name)"

SULPICIEN:
Monsieur (prénom et nom), Adresse Appel - Monsieur,
Salutation - Je vous prie d'agréer, Monsieur, l'expression de mes sentiments respectueux.
Conversation - «Monsieur»

RELIGIOUS:
(man) The Reverend Father (full name), Address
Salutation - Dear Father (name):
Final Salutation - Yours sincerely,
In Conversation - "Reverend Father" (woman) Reverend Mother (full name)/Reverend Sister (full name)
Salutation - Dear Reverend Mother/Sister:
Final Salutation - Yours sincerely,
In Conversation - "Reverend Mother/Sister (name)"

RELIGIEUX/RELIGIEUSE:
(homme) Le révérend père (prénom et nom), Adresse
(femme) La révérende mère/soeur (prénom et nom), Adresse
Appel - (homme) Révérend père/Mon père,
(femme) Révérende mère/Ma soeur,
Salutation - (homme) Je vous prie d'agréer, Révérend père/Mon père, l'expression de mes sentiments respectueux.
(femme) Je vous prie d'agréer, Révérende mère/Ma soeur, l'hommage de mon profond respect. Conversation -
(homme) «Révérend père ou Mon père»
(femme) «Révérende mère/Ma soeur»

Jewish/Juif

RABBI:
Rabbi (full name), Address
Salutation - Dear Rabbi (name):
Final Salutation - Yours sincerely,
In Conversation - "Rabbi (name)"

RABBIN:
Le rabbin (prénom et nom), Adresse Appel - Monsieur le Rabbin,
Salutation - Je vous prie d'agréer, Monsieur le Rabbin, l'expression de mes sentiments respectueux.
Conversation - «Monsieur le Rabbin»

Other Religious Denominations/ Autres dénominations:

MODERATOR:
(United Church of Canada and Presbyterian Church in Canada) A present ordained Moderator: The Right Reverend (full name), Moderator of (name of Church), Address
Salutation - Dear Mr./Mrs./Ms./Miss (name):
Final Salutation - Yours sincerely,
In Conversation - "Mr./Mrs./Ms./Miss (name)" A past ordained Moderator: The Very Reverend (full name), Moderator of (name of Church), Address
Salutation - Dear Mr./Mrs./Ms./Miss (name):
Final Salutation - Yours sincerely,
In Conversation - "Mr./Mrs./Ms./Miss (name)"

MODÉRATEURS:
(Église unie du Canada et Église presbytérienne au Canada)
(homme) Le très révérend (prénom et nom), Modérateur de (nom de l'Église), Adresse
(femme) La très révérende (prénom et nom), Modératrice de (nom de l'Église), Adresse
Appel - (homme) Monsieur le Modérateur,
(femme) Madame la Modératrice,
Salutation - (homme) Je vous prie d'agréer, Monsieur le Modérateur, l'expression de mes sentiments respectueux.
(femme) Je vous prie d'agréer, Madame la Modératrice, l'hommage de mon profond respect. Conversation -
(homme) «Monsieur le Modérateur»
(femme) «Madame la Modératrice»

MINISTER:
The Reverend (full name), Address
Salutation - Dear Mr./Mrs./Ms./Miss (name):
Final Salutation - Yours sincerely,
In Conversation - "Mr./Mrs./Ms./Miss (name)"
Note: "Reverend" is an adjective which is never used without the full name.

MINISTRE:
(homme) Le révérend (prénom et nom), Adresse
(femme) La révérende (prénom et nom), Adresse
Appel - (homme) Monsieur le Pasteur,
(femme) Madame,
Salutation - (homme) Je vous prie d'agréer, Monsieur le Pasteur, l'expression de mes sentiments respectueux.
(femme) Je vous prie d'agréer, Madame, l'hommage de mon profond respect.
Conversation - (homme) «Monsieur le Pasteur»
(femme) «Madame»

Diplomatic/Diplomates

AMBASSADORS/HIGH COMMISSIONERS of foreign countries in Canada:
His/Her Excellency (full name), Ambassador of Canada to ________/High Commissioner for ________, Address
Salutation - Dear Ambassador/High Commissioner:
Final Salutation - Yours sincerely,
In Conversation - "Your Excellency" or "Excellency"
Note: British High Commissioner and not High Commissioner for Britain

AMBASSADEURS/HAUTS-COMMISSAIRES de pays étrangers au Canada:
(homme) Son Excellence monsieur (prénom et nom), Ambassadeur de ________/Haut-Commissaire de ________, Adresse
(femme) Son Excellence madame (prénom et nom), Ambassadrice de ________/Haute-Commissaire de ________, Adresse
Appel - (homme) Monsieur/l'Ambassadeur/le Haut - Commissaire,
(femme) Madame l'Ambassadrice/la Haute-Commissaire,
Salutation - (homme) Je vous prie d'agréer, Monsieur l'Ambassadeur/le Haut-Commissaire, l'expression de ma haute considération.
(femme) Je vous prie d'agréer, Madame l'Ambassadrice/ la Haute-Commissaire, l'expression de mes respectueux hommages.
Conversation - «Excellence»

CANADIAN AMBASSADORS/HIGH COMMISSIONERS abroad:
Mr./Mrs. (full name), Ambassador of Canada to ________/High Commissioner for Canada to ________, Address
Salutation - Dear Ambassador/High Commissioner:
Final Salutation - Yours sincerely,
In Conversation - "Mr./Madam Ambassador/High Commissioner"
AMBASSADEURS DU CANADA/HAUTS-COMMISSAIRES à l'étranger
(homme) Monsieur (prénom et nom) Ambassadeur du Canada/Haute-commissaire du Canada au ________, Adresse
(femme) Madame (prénom et nom) l'Ambassadrice du Canada/Haute-commissaire du Canada au ________, Adresse
Appel - (homme) Monsieur l'Ambassadeur/le Haut-Commissaire,
(femme) Madame l'Ambassadrice/la Haute-Commissaire,
Salutation - (homme) Je vous prie d'agréer, Monsieur l'Ambassadeur/le Haut-commissaire, l'expression de ma haute considération.
(femme) Je vous prie d'agréer, Madame l'Ambassadrice/ la Haute-commissaire, l'expression de mes respectueux hommages.
Conversation - (homme) «Monsieur l'Ambassadeur/ le Haut-Commissaire»
(femme) «Madame l'Ambassadrice/la Haut-Commissaire»
Remarques: Si un ambassadeur du Canada ou un haut-commissaire du Canada se trouve au Canada ou à l'étranger, la formule à employer est simplement «Ambassadeur» ou «Haut-commissaire». Le titre «Excellence» n'est pas accordé par un citoyen canadien à un ambassadeur du Canada ou à un haut-commissaire du Canada, mais par le gouvernement et les citoyens du pays auprès duquel l'ambassadeur ou le haut-commissaire est accédité.

Armed Forces/Forces Armées

OFFICER RANK:
Brigadier General/Major General/Lieutenant General/General (full name), Address
Salutation - Dear General:
Final Salutation - Yours sincerely,
In Conversation - "General (name)"
Colonel (full name), Address
Salutation - Dear Colonel:
Final Salutation - Yours sincerely,
In Conversation - "Colonel (name)"
Lieutenant Colonel (full name), Address
Salutation - Lieutenant Colonel:
Final Salutation - Yours sincerely,
In Conversation - "Lieutenant Colonel (name)"
Major (full name), Address
Salutation - Dear Major:
Final Salutation - Yours sincerely,
In Conversation - "Major (name)"
Captain (full name), Address
Salutation - Dear Captain:
Final Salutation - Yours sincerely,
In Conversation - "Captain (name)"
Lieutenant (full name), Address
Salutation - Dear Lieutenant:
Final Salutation - Yours sincerely,
In Conversation - "Lieutenant (name)"

AVEC GRADE:
(homme) Le brigadier-général/major-général/lieutenant- général (prénom et nom), Adresse
(femme) La brigadière-générale/majore-générale/lieutenante-générale (prénom et nom), Adresse
Appel - (homme) Général,
(femme) Générale,
Salutation - (homme) Je vous prie d'agréer, Général, l'expression de mes meilleurs sentiments.
(femme) Je vous prie d'agréer, Générale, l'expression de mes hommages respectueux.
Conversation - (homme) «Général»
(femme) «Générale»
(homme) Le colonel (prénom et nom), Adresse
(femme) La colonelle (prénom et nom), Adresse
Appel - (homme) Colonel,
(femme) Colonelle,
Salutation - (homme) Je vous prie d'agréer, Colonel, l'expression de mes meilleurs sentiments.
(femme) Je vous prie d'agréer, Colonelle, l'expression de mes hommages respectueux.
Conversation - (homme) «Colonel»
(femme) «Colonelle»
(homme) La lieutenant-colonel, (prénom et nom), Adresse
(femme) La lieutenante-colonelle, (prénom et nom), Adresse
Appel - (homme) Lieutenant-Colonel,
(femme) Lieutenante-Colonelle,
Salutation - (homme) Je vous prie d'agréer, Lieutenant- Colonel, l'expression de mes meilleurs sentiments.
(femme) Je vous prie d'agréer, Lieutenante-Colonelle, l'expression de mes meilleurs hommages respectueux.
Conversation - (homme) «Lieutenant-Colonel»
(femme) «Lieutenante-Colonelle»
(homme) Le major (prénom et nom), Adresse
(femme) La majore (prénom et nom), Adresse
Appel - (homme) Major,
(femme) Majore,
Salutation - (homme) Je vous prie d'agréer, Major, l'expression de mes meilleurs sentiments.
(femme) Je vous prie d'agréer, Majore, l'expression de mes hommages respectueux.
Conversation - (homme) «Major»
(femme) «Majore»
(homme) Le capitaine (prénom et nom), Adresse
(femme) La capitaine (prénom et nom), Adresse
Appel - Capitaine,
Salutation - (homme) Je vous prie d'agréer, Capitaine, l'expression de mes meilleurs sentiments.
(femme) Je vous prie d'agréer, Capitaine, l'expression de mes

hommages respectueux.
Conversation - «Capitaine»
(homme) Le lieutenant (prénom et nom), Adresse
(femme) La lieutenante (prénom et nom), Adresse
Appel - (homme) Lieutenant,
(femme) Lieutenante,
Salutation - (homme) Je vous prie d'agréer, Lieutenant, l'expression de mes meilleurs sentiments.
(femme) Je vous prie d'agréer, Lieutenante, l'expression de mes hommages respectueux.
Conversation - (homme) «Lieutenant»
(femme) «Lieutenante»

NCO and other ranks:
Chief Warrant Officer (full name)
Salutation - Dear Chief Warrant (name)
Final Salutation - Yours sincerely,
In Conversation - "Mr./Mrs./Ms./Miss (name)"
Master Warrant Officer (full name)
Salutation - Dear Master Warrant (name):
Final Salutation - Yours sincerely,
In Conversation - "Mr./Mrs./Ms./Miss (name)"
Warrant Officer (full name)
Salutation - Dear Warrant (name):
Final Salutation - Yours sincerely,
In Conversation - "Mr./Mrs./Ms./Miss (name)"
Sergeant (full name)
Salutation - Dear Sergeant (name):
Final Salutation - Yours sincerely,
In Conversation - "Mr./Mrs./Ms./Miss (name)"
Corporal (full name)
Salutation - Dear Corporal (name):
Final Salutation - Yours sincerely,
In Conversation - "Mr./Mrs./Ms./Miss (name)"
Private (full name)
Salutation - Dear Private (name):
Final Salutation - Yours sincerely,
In Conversation - "Mr./Mrs./Ms./Miss (name)"

SOUS OFFICIERS ET AUTRES GRADES:
(homme) L'adjudant-chef (prénom et nom)
(femme) L'adjudante-chef (prénom et nom)
Appel - (homme) Adjudant-chef,
(femme) Adjudante-chef,
Salutation - (homme) Je vous prie d'agréer, Adjudant-chef, l'expression de mes meilleurs sentiments.
(femme) Je vous prie d'agréer, Adjudante-chef, l'expression de mes hommages respectueux.
Conversation - Le qualificatif du grade «Monsieur/ Madame/Mademoiselle»
(homme) L'adjudant-maître (prénom et nom)
(femme) L'adjudante-maîtresse (prénom et nom)
Appel - (homme) Adjudant-maître,
(femme) Adjudante-maîtresse,
Salutation - (homme) Je vous prie d'agréer, Adjudant-maître, l'expression de mes meilleurs hommages respectueux.
(femme) Je vous prie d'agréer, Adjudantemaîtresse, l'expression de mes hommages respectueux.
Conversation - Le qualificatif du grade «Monsieur/ Madame/Mademoiselle»
(homme) L'adjudant (prénom et nom)
(femme) L'adjudante (prénom et nom)
Appel - (homme) Adjudant,
(femme) Adjudante,
Salutation - (homme) Je vous prie d'agréer, Adjudant, l'expression de mes meilleurs sentiments.
(femme) Je vous prie d'agréer, Adjudante, l'expression de mes hommages respectueux.
Conversation - Le qualificatif du grade «Monsieur/ Madame/Mademoiselle»
(homme) Le sergent (prénom et nom)
(femme) La sergente (prénom et nom)
Appel - (homme) Sergent,
(femme) Sergente,
Salutation - (homme) Je vous prie d'agréer, Sergent, l'expression de mes meilleurs sentiments.
(femme) Je vous prie d'agréer, Sergente, l'expression de mes hommages respectueux.
Conversation - Le qualificatif du grade «Monsieur/ Madame/Mademoiselle»
(homme) Le caporal (prénom et nom)
(femme) La caporale (prénom et nom)
Appel - (homme) Caporal,
(femme) Caporale,
Salutation - (homme) Je vous prie d'agréer, Caporal, l'expression de mes meilleurs sentiments.
(femme) Je vous prie d'agréer, Caporale, l'expression de mes hommages respectueux.
Conversation - Le qualificatif du grade «Monsieur/ Madame/Mademoiselle»
(homme) Le soldat (prénom et nom)
(femme) La soldate (prénom et nom)
Appel - Monsieur/Madame/Mademoiselle,
Salutation - (homme) Je vous prie d'agréer, Monsieur, l'expression de mes meilleurs sentiments.
(femme) Je vous prie d'agréer, Madame/Mademoiselle, l'expression de mes hommages respectueux.
Conversation - Le qualificatif du grade «Monsieur/ Madame/Mademoiselle»

Foreign Dignitaries/Les Dignitaires Étrangers

AN EMPEROR:
His Imperial Majesty Akihito, Emperor of Japan, Address
Salutation - Your dignified Majesty:
Final Salutation - I have the honour to remain, Your Imperial Majesty's obedient servant,
In Conversation - "Your Majesty" first then "Sire"

EMPEREUR:
Sa Majesté Impériale (Nom) ________, Empereur du ________, Adresse Appel - Votre Majesté Impériale,
Salutation - Je prie Votre Majesté Impériale d'agréer l'hommage de mon profond respect et de ma très haute considération.
Conversation - On commence par «Majesté». On poursuit avec «Sire»

A KING:
His Majesty Juan Carlos, King of Spain, Address
Salutation - Your Majesty/Sire:
Final Salutation - I have the honour to remain, Your Majesty's obedient servant,
In Conversation - "Your Majesty" first then "Sire"

UN ROI:
Sa Majesté (Nom) ________, Roi de ________, Adresse Appel - Majesté/Sire,
Salutation - Je prie Votre Majesté d'agréer l'hommage de mon profond respect et de ma très haute considération.
Conversation - On commence par «Majesté». On poursuit avec «Sire»

A QUEEN:
Her Majesty Queen Sophia, Queen of Spain, Address
Salutation - Your Majesty/Madame:
Final Salutation - I have the honour to remain, Your Majesty's obedient servant,
In Conversation - "Your Majesty" first then "Ma'am"

UNE REINE:
Sa Majesté la reine (Nom) ________, Reine de ________, Adresse Appel - Majesté/Madame,
Salutation - Je vous prie d'agréer Madame, l'hommage de mon profond respect et de ma très haute considération.
Conversation - On commence par «Majesté». On poursuit avec «Madame»

A PRESIDENT OF A REPUBLIC:
His/Her Excellency (full name), President of the Republic of (name), Address
Salutation - Excellency:
Final Salutation - Yours sincerely
In Conversation - "Excellency" first then "President" or "Sir/Madam"
UN PRÉSIDENT DE RÉPUBLIQUE:
(homme) Son Excellence monsieur (prénom et nom) Président de la République (nom), Adresse
(femme) Son Excellence madame (prénom et nom) Présidente de la République (nom), Adresse
Appel - (homme) Monsieur le Président,
(femme) Madame la Présidente,
Salutation - (homme) Je vous prie d'agréer Monsieur le Président, l'expression de ma très haute considération.
(femme) Je vous prie d'agréer Madame la Présidente, l'hommage de mon profond respect. Conversation -
(homme) On commence par «Excellence». On poursuit avec «Monsieur le Président» ou «Monsieur»
(femme) On commence par «Excellence». On poursuit avec «Madame la Présidente» ou «Madame»

THE PRESIDENT OF THE UNITED STATES:
The Honourable (full name), President of the United States, The White House, Washington, D.C.
Salutation - Dear Mr. President:
Final Salutation - Yours sincerely,
In Conversation - "Mr. President" first then "Sir"

PRÉSIDENT DES ÉTATS-UNIS D'AMÉRIQUE:
Son Excellence l'honorable (prénom et nom) Président de États-Unis d'Amérique, The White House, Washington D.C. Appel - Monsieur le Président,
Salutation - Je vous prie d'agréer Monsieur le Président, l'expression de ma très haute considération.
Conversation - On commence par «Monsieur le Président» ou «Excellence»

A PRIME MINISTER:
His/Her Excellency (full name), Prime Minister of (name), Address
Salutation - Dear Prime Minister:
Final Salutation - Yours sincerely,
In Conversation - "Prime Minister" or "Excellency" first then "Sir/Madam" or "Mr./Mrs./Ms./Miss (name)"

PREMIER MINISTRE:
(homme) Son Excellence monsieur (prénom et nom) Premier Ministre de ________, Adresse
(femme) Son Excellence madame (prénom et nom) Première Ministre de ________, Adresse
Appel - (homme) Monsieur le Premier Ministre,
(femme) Madame la Première Ministre,
Salutation - (homme) Je vous prie d'agréer Monsieur le Premier Ministre, l'expression de ma haute considération.
(femme) Je vous prie d'agréer Madame la Première Ministre, l'hommage de mon profond respect. Conversation -
(homme) On commence par «Monsieur le Premier Ministre» ou «Excellence». On poursuit par «Monsieur»
(femme) On commence par «Madame la Première Ministre» ou «Excellence». On poursuit par «Madame»

Others/Autres

LAWYERS/NOTARIES:
Mr./Mrs./Ms./Miss (full name) or Mr./Mrs./Ms./Miss, Q.C.
Salutation - Dear Mr./Mrs./Ms./Miss (name):
Final Salutation - Yours sincerely,
In Conversation - "Mr./Mrs./Ms./Miss (name)"

AVOCATS/NOTAIRES:
Me (prénom et nom) Appel - Maître,
Salutation - Je vous prie d'agréer, Maître, l'expression de mes meilleurs sentiments.
Conversation - «Maître»

AIDE-DE-CAMP:
Military: (See Armed Forces) Civilian (according to their title), Mr./Mrs./Ms./Miss (full name)
Salutation - Dear Mr./Mrs./Ms./Miss (name):
Final Salutation - Yours sincerely,
In Conversation - "Mr./Mrs./Ms./Miss (name)"
Note: Post nominals "A. de C." have been authorized for Aides-de-camps to the Governor General and Lieutenant Governors. Militaire: (voir la rubrique «Forces armées») Civil (selon le titre), Monsieur/Madame/Mademoiselle (prénom et nom) Appel - Monsieur/Madame/Mademoiselle,
Salutation - Je vous prie d'agréer, Monsieur/Madame/ Mademoiselle, l'expression de mes sentiments les meilleurs.
Conversation - «Monsieur/Madame/Mademoiselle» Remarque: Les initiales «A. de C.» sont autorisées pour les aides de camp du Governeur général et des lieutenants-gouverneurs.

INDIAN CHIEFS:
Chief (full name), Chief of (name), Address
Salutation - Chief (name):
Final Salutation - Yours sincerely,
In Conversation - "Chief (name)"

CHEFS INDIENS:
Chef (prénom et nom), Chef de (nom), Adresse Appel - Chef,
Salutation - Je vous prie d'agréer, Chef, l'expression de mes sentiments les meilleurs.
Conversation - «Chef»

BAND COUNCILLORS:
Mr./Mrs./Ms./Miss (full name):
Salutation - Mr./Mrs./Ms./Miss (name):
Final Salutation - Yours sincerely,
In Conversation - "Mr./Mrs./Ms./Miss (name)"

CONSEILLERS DE BANDES:
Monsieur/Madame/Mademoiselle (prénom et nom), Adresse Appel - Monsieur/Madame/Mademoiselle,
Salutation - Je vous prie d'agréer, Monsieur/Madame/ Mademoiselle, l'expression de mes sentiments les meilleurs.
Conversation - «Monsieur/Madame/Mademoiselle»

Abbreviations

Indicating Academic, Ecclesiastical and other Degrees, membership in Societies and Institutions, military ranks, etc., appearing in the Canadian Almanac and Directory. For other lists of abbreviations, see Index.

AACCA	Associate of Association of Certified Accountants & Corporate Accountants (British)
AACI	Accredited Appraiser Canadian Institute
AAE	Associate of Accountants' & Executives' Corp. of Canada
AAGO	— of the American Guild of Organists
AASA	— of the Alberta Society of Artists
AB	Bachelor of Arts, American (Artium Baccalaureus)
AC	"Advanced Certification" Canadian Association of Medical Radiation Technologists
ACA	Associate of Institute of Chartered Accountants (Eng.)
ACAM	Associate Certified Administrative Manager
ACCO	— of Canadian College of Organists
AccSCRP	— of Canadian Public Relations Society Inc.
ACD	Archaeologiae Christianae Doctor
ACGI	Associate of the City & Guilds of London Institute
ACIC	— of Canadian Institute of Chemistry
ACInstM	— of the Institute of Marketing
ACIS	— of Chartered Institute of Secretaries (British)
ACSM	— of Cambourne School of Mines
Adm.	Admiral
Adm. A. Pl.Fin.	Administrateur agréé en planification financière
AFC	Accredited Financial Counsellor
AFRAS (AFRAeS)	Fellow of the Royal Aeronautical Society
Ag de l'U (Paris)	Honorary Professor of University of Paris (Agrégé de l'Université Paris)
Ag. de Phil.	Professor of Philosophy (Agrégé en Philosophie Louvain)
AGSM	Associate of the Guildhall School of Music (British)
AIC	— of the Institute of Chemistry (British)
AICB	Associate of the Institute of Canadian Bankers
AIIC	— of the Insurance Institute of Canada
AKC	— of King's College (London)
ALCM	— of London (Canada) Conservatory of Music
ALS	Commissioned Alberta Land Surveyor
AM	Master of Arts (Artium Magister)
AMEIC	Associate Member of the Engineering Institute of Canada
AMICE	— Member of the Institution of Civil Engineers (British)
AMIEE	— Member of the Institute of Electrical Engineers
AMIMechE	— Member of the Institution of Mechanical Engineers (British)
A.Mus.	— of Music
APA	— Member of the Institute of Accredited Public Accountants (British)
APHA	— Member of the Public Health Association (British)
APR	Accredited Member of the Canadian Public Relations Society
ARA	Associate of the Royal Academy (honorary)
ARCD	— of the Royal College of Dancing
ARCM	— of the Royal College of Music
ARCO	— of the Royal College of Organists (Canadian)
ARCS (A.R.C.Sc.)	— of the Royal College of Science
ARCT	— of the Royal Conservatory of Music of Toronto
ARCVS	— of the Royal College of Veterinary Surgeons
ARDIO	— of Registered Interior Designers of Ontario
ARDS	— of the Royal Drawing Society (London, Eng.)
ARIBA	— of the Royal Institute of British Architects
ARIC	— of the Royal Institute of Chemistry
ARSH	— of the Royal Society of Health
ARSM	— of the Royal School of Mines
ARSM	— of the Royal School of Music
AScT	Applied Science Technologist
Assoc. Inst. M.M.	Associate of the Institute of Mining and Metallurgy (British)
ATCL	— of Trinity College, London (Eng.)
ATCM	— of the Toronto Conservatory of Music
A.Th.	— in Theology
BA	Bachelor of Arts
BAA	— of Applied Arts
B.Acc.	— of Accountancy
B.Adm. (B.Admin.)	— of Administration
B.Adm.Pub.	— Baccalauréat spécialisé en administration publique
BAeE (BAeroE)	Bachelor of Aeronautical Engineering
BAI	— of Engineering (U. of Dublin)
BALS	— of Arts in Library Science
BAO	— of Obstetrics
B.Arch.	— in Architecture
BAS (B.A.Sc.)	— of Applied Science
BASM	— of Arts, Master of Science
B.A.Theo.	— of Arts in Theology
BBA	— of Business Administration
BCD	Bachelier en Chirurgie Dentale
BCE	Bachelor of Civil Engineering
B.Ch. (ChB)	— in Surgery (British)
BChE	— in Chemical Engineering (American)
BCL	— of Civil Law (or Canon Law)
B.Com. (B. Comm.)	— of Commerce
B.Comp.Sc.	— of Computer Science
BD	— of Divinity
BDC	Bachelier en droit canonique
B.Des.	Bachelor of Design
BDS	— of Dental Surgery (British)
BE (B.Eng.)	— of Engineering
B.Ed. (BEAD)	— of Education
BEDS	— of Environmental Design Studies
BEE	— of Electrical Engineering (American)
B. en Ph.	Bachelier en Philosophie
B. en Sc. Com.	— en Science Commerciale
BES	Bachelor of Environmental Sciences (or Studies)
B ès A	Bachelier ès Arts
B ès L.	— ès Lettres
B. ès Sc.	— ès Science
B. ès Sc. App.	— ès Science Appliquée
BF	Bachelor of Forestry (American)
BFA	— of Fine Arts
B.Gen.	Brigadier-General
BHE (B.H.Ec.)	Bachelor of Home Economics
B.H.Sc.	— of Household Science
BJ	— of Journalism
BJC	— in Canon Law
BL	— in Literature (or of Laws)
BLA	— of Landscape Architecture
B.Litt.	— of Literature (American & British)
BLS	— of Library Science
BM	— of Medicine
B.Mus.	— of Music
BMV	Bachelier en Médecine Vetérinaire
BN	Bachelor of Nursing
B.N.Sc.	— of Nursing Science
B. Paed. (Péd.)	— of Pedagogy
BPA	— of Public Administration
BPE	— of Physical Education
B.Ph. (B.Phil.)	— of Philosophy
BPHE	— of Physical & Health Education
B.Ps.	Baccalauréat en Psychologie
Br.	Brother
BS	Bachelor of Science (or of Surgery) (American)
BSA	— of Science in Agriculture (or in Accounting, or in Administration)
B.Sc.	— of Science
BScA	Bachelier ès science appliquées
BScB	— en Bibliothéconomie
B.Sc.(CE)	Bachelor of Science in Civil Engineering
B.Sc.Com.	— of Commercial Science
B.Sc.Dom.	Baccalauréat en Sciences Domestiques
BScF (BSF)	Bachelor of Science in Forestry
BScFE	— of Science in Forestry Engineering
BScH	Bachelier en Sciences Hospitalières
BScN	Bachelor of Science in Nursing
B.Sc.(Nurs.)	— of Science in Nursing
B.Sc.(Occ.Ther.)	— of Science in Occupational Therapy
B.Sc.(OT)	— of Science in Occupational Therapy
B.Sc.Phm.(BSP)	— of Science in Pharmacy
B.Sc.Soc.	— of Social Science
BSCE	— of Science in Civil Engineering
B.S.Ed.	— of Science in Education
BSEE	— of Science in Electrical Engineering
BSN	— of Science in Nursing
BSS	— of Social Sciences
BSW.	— of Social Work (or Welfare)
B.Tech.	— of Technology
B.Th.	— of Theology
BTS	— of Technological Science (Edinburgh)
B.V.Sc.	— of Veterinary Science
CA	Chartered Accountant
C. Adm., F.P.	Chartered Administrator in Financial Planning
CAAP	Certified Advertising Agency Practitioner
CAE	— Association Executive
CAE/c.a.é.	Chartered Account Executive
CAM	Certified Administrative Manager
CAP	Certificat d'Aptitude Pedagogique
Capt. (or Capt.(N))	Captain (or Captain (Naval))
CBE	Commander, Order of the British Empire
CBV	Chartered Business Valuator

CC .... Chartered Cartographer
CC .... Companion, Order of Canada
CD .... Canadian Forces Decoration
Cdr. .... Commander
CE .... Civil Engineer
CEA .... Certified Environmental Administrator
CEA .... Certified Environmental Auditor
CEBS .... Certified Employee Benefit Specialist
Cer.E. .... Ceramic Engineer
Cert. Bus. Admin. ..... Doctor of Applied Science Diploma Business Administration
CES .... Certificat d'Études Secondaires (La Sorbonne)
CFA .... Chartered Financial Analyst
CFP .... Chartered Financial Planner
CGA .... Certified General Accountant
CHA .... Certified Housing Administrator
Chan. .... Chanoine (Canon)
Ch.E. .... Chartered Executive
CHE .... Certified Health Executive
Chem. Ing. .... Ingénieur Chimiste Diplomé (Swiss Fed. Inst. Technology)
CHFC .... Chartered Financial Consultant
CIF .... Canadian Institute of Forestry
CIM .... Certificate in Management
CIM .... Certified Industrial Manager
CIM .... Certified Investment Manager
CIS&P .... Canadian Inst. of Surveying & Photogrammetry
CLA .... Canadian Library Association
CLS .... Canada Land Surveyor
CLU .... Chartered Life Underwriter
CM .... Master in Medicine (British)
CM .... Member, Order of Canada
CMA .... Certified Management Accountant (or Canadian Medical Association or Canadian Management Association)
CMC .... Certified Management Consultant
CmdO .... Commissioned Officer
Cmdre. .... Commodore
CMM .... Certified Municipal Manager (Ontario)
CMM .... Commander, Order of Military Merit
COM .... Commander of the Order of Merit (Police Forces)
Col. .... Colonel
CPA .... Certified Public Accountant
CPC .... — Personnel Consultant
CPM .... Certificate in Personnel Management
CPPMA .... — in Public Personnel Management Association
CPPO .... Certified Public Purchasing Officer
CPP .... — Professional Purchaser
CR (c.r.) .... Conseiller de la Reine (Queen's Counsel)
CRA .... Canadian Residential Appraiser
CSC .... Canadian Securities Course
CSR .... Chartered Stenographic Reporter
CTC .... Certified Travel Counsellor
C.Tech. .... — Technician
CWO .... Chief Warrant Officer
DA .... Doctor of Arts (honorary)
DA .... — of Archaeology (Laval)
D.Arch. .... — of Architecture
D.A.Sc. .... — in Applied Sciences
DC .... — of Chiropractic
DCD .... Docteur en Chirurgie Dentale
D.Ch. .... Doctor of Surgery (British)
DChE .... — of Chemical Engineering (American)
DCL .... — of Civil Law (or Canon Law)
DD .... — of Divinity
DDC .... Doctorat Droit Canonique
D. de l'Un. .... — Docteur de l'Université
DDS .... Doctor of Dental Surgery (British)
DDT .... — of Drugless Therapy
D.Ed. .... — of Education
D.Eng. .... — of Engineering
D. en Méd. Vet. .... Docteur en Médecine Vetérinaire
D. en Ph. .... — en Philosophie
D ès L .... — ès Lettres (Doctor of Letters)
D. ès Sc. App. .... Doctor of Applied Science
DF .... — of Forestry (American)
DFA .... — of Fine Arts (often honorary)
D.F.Sc. .... — of Financial Science (Laval)
DIC .... Diploma of Membership of Imperial College of Science & Technology (British)
Dip. Bact. .... — in Bacteriology
Dip d'É .... Diplome d'Études
Dip de l'U (P) .... Diploma of the U. of Paris
Dip. d'É. Sup. or DipES .. Diplome d'Études Supérieures, Paris
Dip. Ing. .... Diploma in Engineering
Dipl. Bus. Admin. ..... Diploma Business Administration
D.Jour .... Doctor of Journalism
D. Lit. (D. Litt.) .... — of Letters (or Literature)
DLO .... Diploma in Laryngology & Otology
DLS .... Dominion Land Surveyor (or Doctor of Library Science)
DM .... Doctorat Médecine
DMD .... Doctor of Dental Medicine
D.Ms. .... — in Missionology
D.Mus. .... Doctorat en Musique
DMR (D or T) .... Diploma in Medical Radiology (Royal Coll. of Surgeons, London)
DMT .... — in Tropical Medicine
DMT & H (Eng.) .... — in Tropical Medicine & Hygiene
D.N.S (D.N.Sc.) .... Doctor of Nursing Science
DO .... — of Osteopathy
Doct.Arch. .... — of Christian Archaeology (Pontifical Institute, Rome)
D.Paed. (Péd.) .... — of Paedagogy
DPE .... Diploma in Physical Education
D.Ph. (D.Phil. or PhD) .. Doctor of Philosophy
D.P.Ec. .... — of Political Economy
DPH .... — (or Diploma) in Public Health
D.Ps. (D.Psy.) .... — of Psychologie
D.P.Sc. .... — of Political Science
D.Psych. .... — (or Diploma) in Psychiatry
DPT .... — of Physio-Therapy
Dr. .... Doctor
DR .... Doctor of Radiology
Dr.Com.Sc. .... — of Commercial Science
Dr de l'U (P) .... — of the U. of Paris
Dr. ès Lettres .... — of Letters (History of Literature)
Dr. jur. .... — of Law (Dr. Juris)
Dr. rer. pol. .... — of Political Economy (Dr. Rerum Politicarum) (Docteur des Sciences Politiques)
DSA (DScA) .... Docteur ès science appliqués
D.Sc. .... Doctor of Science
D.Sc.Mil. .... — of Military Science
DSL .... — of Sacred Letters
D.Sc.Com. .... — of Commercial Science
D.Sc.Fin. .... — of Financial Science
D.Sc.Nat. .... — in Natural Science
D.Sc.Soc. .... — of Social Science
D.Th. .... — of Theology
DVM (DMV) .... — of Veterinary Medicine
D.V.Sc. .... — of Veterinary Science
E.C.E. .... Early Childhood Educator
EdD .... Doctor of Education
EdM .... Master of Education (Harvard)
EE .... Electrical Engineer
EM .... Mining Engineer
ETCM .... Graduate of Eastern Townships Conservatory of Music
FAAO .... Fellow of the American Academy of Optometry
F.A.A.O.Dip. .... Diplomatic Fellow of the American Academy of Optometry
FACD .... Fellow of the American College of Dentists
FACO .... — of the American College of Organists
FACP .... — of the American College of Physicians
FACR .... — of the American College of Radiology
FACS .... — of the American College of Surgeons
FAE .... — of the Accountants' & Executives' Corp. of Canada
FAGS .... — of the American Geographical Society
FAIA .... — of the American Institute of Actuaries
.... — of the American Institute of Architects
FAIA .... Association of International Accountants
FAOU .... Fellow of the American Ornithologists Union
FAPHA .... — of the American Public Health Association
FAPS .... — of the American Physical Society
FAS .... — of the Actuarial Society
FBA .... — of the British Academy (honorary)
FBOA .... — of British Association of Optometrists
FCA .... — of the Institute of Chartered Accountants (British)
FCAM. .... — of the Certified Administrative Manager
FCBA .... — of Canadian Bankers' Association
FCCA .... — of the Association of Certified Accountants
FCCO .... — of the Canadian College of Organists
FCCT .... — of the Canadian College of Teachers
FCCUI .... — of the Canadian Credit Union Institute
FCGI .... — of the City & Guilds of London Institute
FCI .... — of the Canadian Credit Institute
FCIC .... — of the Chemical Institute of Canada
FCII .... — of the Chartered Insurance Institute (British)

FCIS	— of the Chartered Institute of Secretaries (British)
FCOG	— of the College of Obstetricians & Gynaecologists (British)
FCAMRT	— of Canadian Association of Medical Radiation Technologists
FCIA	— of the Canadian Institute of Actuaries
FCMA	— of the Society of Management Accountants of Canada
FCSI	— of the Canadian Securities Institute
FCTC	— of the Canadian Institute of Travel Counsellors
FCUIC	— of the Credit Union Institute of Canada
FE	Forest Engineer
FEIC	Fellow of the Engineering Institute of Canada
FFA	— of the Faculty of Actuaries (Scotland)
FFR	— of the Faculty of Radiologists (British)
FGS	— of the Geological Society (British)
FGSA	— of the Geological Society of America
FIA	— of the Institute of Actuaries (British)
FIC	— of the Institute of Chemistry
FICB	— of the Institute of Canadian Bankers
FICE	— of the Institution of Civil Engineers
FIEE	— of the Institution of Electrical Engineers
FIIC	— of the Insurance Institute of Canada
FIL	— of the Institute of Linguists (British)
FLA	— of the Library Association (England)
FMA	Financial Management Advisor
FMSA	— of the Mineralogical Society of America
Fr.	Father
FRAI	Fellow of the Royal Anthropological Institute
FRAIC	— of the Royal Architectural Institute of Canada
FRAM	— of the Royal Academy of Music
FRAS	— of the Royal Astronomical Society
FRCCO	— of the Royal Canadian College of Organists
FRCM	— of the Royal College of Music
FRCO	— of the Royal College of Organists
FRCOG	— of the Royal College of Obstetricians & Gynaecologists
FRCP	— of the Royal College of Physicians of London
FRCP(C)	— of the Royal College of Physicians of Canada
FRCP(E)	— of the Royal College of Physicians of Edinburgh
FRCP(I)	— of the Royal College of Physicians of Ireland
FRCP(Glas)	— of the Royal College of Physicians of Glasgow
FRCS	— of the Royal College of Surgeons of England
FRCS(C)	— of the Royal College of Surgeons of Canada
FRCS(E)	— of the Royal College of Surgeons of Edinburgh
FRCS(I)	— of the Royal College of Surgeons of Ireland
FRCS(Glas)	— of the Royal College of Surgeons of Glasgow
FRGS	— of the Royal Geographical Society
FRHistS	— of the Royal Historical Society
FRHortS	— of the Royal Horticultural Society
FRIBA	— of the Royal Institute of British Architects
FRIC	— of the Royal Institute of Chemistry
FRICS	— of the Royal Institution of Chartered Surveyors
FRMCM	— of Royal Manchester College of Music
FRMS (FRMetS)	— of the Royal Meteorological Society
FRS	— of the Royal Society (honorary)
FRSA	— of the Royal Society of Arts
FRSC	— of the Royal Society of Canada
FRSE	— of the Royal Society of Edinburgh
FRSH	— of the Royal Society of Health
FRSL	— of the Royal Society of Literature
FSA	— of the Society of Actuaries (or of Antiquaries) (honorary)
FSMAC	— of the Society of Management Accountants of Canada
FSS	— of the Royal Statistical Society
FTCL	— of Trinity College of Music (London)
FZS	— of the Zoological Society (British)
Gen.	General
GJ	Graduate Jeweller
HARCVS	Honorary Associate of Royal College of Veterinary Surgeons
IA	Investment Advisor
IC	Investment Counsellor
IngETP	Diplome de l'École Spéciale des Travaux Publiques
JCB	Bachelor of Canon Law
JCD	Doctor of Canon Law (or of Civil Law)
JCL	Licentiate in Canon Law (Juris Canonici Licentiatus)
JD	Doctor of Jurisprudence
JDS	— of Jurisdical Science
Jr.	Junior
JUL	Licentiate of Law in Utroque (both Civil & Canon Law)
JurM	Master of Jurisprudence
Jur. utr. Dr.	Juris utriusque doctor, Equiv. to LL.D.
LAB	Licentiate of the Assoc. Bd. of Royal Schools of Music (London, Eng.)
L.Cdr.	Lieutenant-Commander
LCL	Licentiate in Canon Law
LCMI	— of the Cost & Management Institute
L.Col.	Lieutenant-Colonel
LDC	Licencié ès Droit Canonique
LDS	Licentiate in Dental Surgery (British)
L ès L	Licencié ès Lettres
L. ès Sc.	— ès Sciences
L.Gen.	Lieutenant-General
LGSM	Licentiate of the Guildhall School of Music & Drama (London, Eng.)
LittD	Doctor of Letters (or Literature)
LittL	Licence ès Lettres
Litt.M.	Master of Letters (or Literature)
LJC	Licentiatus Juris Canonici
LL	License in Civil Law
LLB	Bachelor of Laws (Legum Baccalaureus)
LLD	Doctor of Laws (usually honorary)
LLL	Licence en droit
LLM	Master of Law
L. Mus.	Licentiate in Music
LMUS	— in Music of the Univ. of Saskatchewan
L Mus TCL	— in General Musicianship of Trinity College, London
L.Péd.	Licence en Pédagogie
L.Ph.	— en Philosophie
L.Psych.	Licencié en Psychologie
LRAM	Licentiate of the Royal Academy of Music (London)
LRCM	— of the Royal College of Music (London)
LRCP	— of the Royal College of Physicians
LRCS	— of the Royal College of Surgeons
LRCT	— of the Royal Conservatory of Toronto
LRE	— in Religious Education
LRSM	— of the Royal Schools of Music (London)
LS	Land Surveyor
LSA	Licentiate in Agricultural Science
L.Sc.Com.	— in Commercial Science
LScO	Licence en optométrie
L.S.Sc.	Licentiate in Sacred Scriptures
L.Sc.Soc.	Licence in Social Science
LST	Licentiate in Sacred Theology
Lt. (or Lt(N))	Lieutenant (or Lieutenant (Naval))
LTCL	Licentiate of Trinity College of Music (London)
LTCM	— of the Toronto Conservatory of Music
L.Th	Licentiate in Theology
M.	Monsieur
MA	Master of Arts
M.Acc.	— of Accountancy
MACF	Membre de l'Académie canadiennefrançaise
MAeE	Master of Aeronautical Engineering
MAIEE	Member of American Institute of Electrical Engineers
MAIME	— of American Institute of Mining Engineers
Maj.	Major
MALS	Master of Arts in Library Science
MAP	Maîtrise en administration publique
M.Arch.	Master of Architecture
MAS	— of Archival Studies
M.A.Sc. (MAS)	— of Applied Science
MASCE	Member of the American Society of Civil Engineers
MASME	— of the American Society of Mechanical Engineers
MAust IM	— of the Australian Institute of Mining & Metallurgy
MB	Bachelor of Medicine (British)
MBA	Master in Business Administration
MCE	— of Civil Engineering
M.Ch. (ChM)	— of Surgery (British)
MChE	— of Chemical Engineering (American)
MCI	Member of the Credit Institute
MCIC	— of the Chemical Institute of Canada
MCIF	— of the Canadian Institute of Forestry
MCIM	— of the Canadian Institute of Mining
MCIMM	— of the Canadian Institute of Mining & Metallurgy
MCInstM	— of the Canadian Institute of Marketing
MCL	Master of Civil Law
M.Com.	— of Commerce
M.Comp.	— of Canon Law
M.Comp.Sc.	— of Computer Science
MD	Doctor of Medicine
MDC	Master of Canon Law
MDCM	Doctor of Medicine & Master of Surgery
M.Des.	Master of Design
M.Div.	— of Divinity
MDS	— of Dental Surgery (British)
MDV	Doctor of Veterinary Medicine
Me	Maître

ME .... Master of Mechanical Engineering
M.Ed. (M.A.Ed.) .... — of Education
MEDS .... — of Environmental Design Studies
MEE................ — of Electrical Engineering (American)
MEIC .... Member of the Engineering Institute of Canada
M.Eng. .... Master of Engineering
MF .... — of Forestry
MFA .... — of Fine Arts
M.Gen. .... Major-General
Mgr. .... Monsignor (or Manager or Monseigneur)
MHA .... Master of Health (or Hospital) Administration
MHE (M.H.Ec.)........ — of Home Economics
MICE .... Member of the Institution of Civil Engineers (British)
MICIA............... — of Industrial, Commercial & Institutional Accountants
MIEE .... — of the Institution of Electrical Engineers (British)
MIMM............... — of the Institute of Mining & Metallurgy (British)
MINA .... — of the Institute of Naval Architects
MIRE .... — of the Institute of Radio Engineers
M.I.St. .... Master of Information Studies
MJ .... — of Journalism
M.Litt................ — of Letters (or Literature)
MLIS .... — of Library & Information Science
MLS................. — of Library Science (or Licentiate in Medieval Studies)
MM (M.Mus.) .... — of Music
MMM .... Member, Order of Military Merit
MOM .... Member of the Order of Merit (Police Forces)
MN (M.Nurs.) .... Master of Nursing
MP................. — of Planning
MP .... Member of Parliament
MPE .... Master of Physical Education
M.Ph. (M.Phil.)........ — of Philosophy
MPM .... — of Pest Management
MPP .... Member of Provincial Parliament
M.Ps. (M.Psy.) .... Master of Psychology
MRAIC .... Member of the Royal Architectural Institute of Canada
MRCOG............. — of the Royal College of Obstetricians & Gynaecologists
MRCP .... — of the Royal College of Physicians
MRCP(E)............ — of the Royal College of Physicians of Edinburgh
MRCP(I)............. — of the Royal College of Physicians of Ireland
MRCP(Glas).......... — of the Royal College of Physicians of Glasgow
MRCS .... — of the Royal College of Surgeons
MRCS(E)............ — of the Royal College of Surgeons of Edinburgh
MRCVS .... — of the Royal College of Veterinary Surgeons
MRM .... Master of Resource Management
MRSC .... Member of the Royal Society of Canada
MRSH .... — of the Royal Society of Health
MRST............... — of the Royal Society of Teachers
MS .... Master of Surgery (British)
MSA................ — of Science in Agriculture
M.Sc................ — of Science
MScA............... — of Applied Science
MSCE .... — of Science in Civil Engineering
MScF............... — of Science in Forestry
M.Sc.(Med.).......... — of Science in Medicine
MScN (MSN) .... — of Science in Nursing
M.Sc.Phm............ — of Science in Pharmacy
M.Sc.Soc. .... — in Social Sciences
M.S.Ed. .... — of Science in Education
M.S.Litt.............. — of Sacred Letters
MSPE .... McGill School of Physical Education
MSRC .... Membre Société Royale du Canada
MSS .... Master of Social Science
MSW .... — of Social Work
MTCI .... Member of Trust Companies Institute
M.U.Dr. .... Medecinae Universae Doctor (Prague) (Dentistry & Medicine)
MUP .... Master of Planning
MURP .... — of Urban & Rural Planning
Mus. Bac. (Mus.B.) .... Bachelor of Music
Mus. Doc. (Mus.D.) .... Doctor of Music
Mus. G. Paed. .... Musicae Graduatus Paedagogus (Graduate Teacher in Music)
MusM .... Master of Music
MV .... Médécin Vétérinaire
M.V.Sc. .... Master of Veterinary Science
NDA .... National Diploma in Agriculture (Royal Ag. Soc. of Engineering)
NDD .... National Diploma in Dairying (Scotland)
NP................. Notary Public
OA................. Officier d'Académie (France)
OC .... Order of Canada
OD .... Doctor of Optometry
OIP .... Officier de l'Instruction Publique
OLS................ Ontario Land Surveyor
OMM .... Officer, Order of Military Merit
OOM .... Officer of the Order of Merit (Police Forces)
OSA .... Ontario Society of Artists
PC................. Privy Councillor
PD................. Doctor of Parapsychology
PE................. Professional Engineer
P.Eng. .... Registered Professional Engineer
PFC................ Planificateur Financier Certifié
PFP................ Personal Financial Planner
PhB................ Bachelor of Philosophy
PhC................ Philosopher of Chiropractic
PhD................ Doctor of Philosophy
PhTD............... Physical Therapy Doctor
PhL .... Licentiate in Philosophy
PLS .... Professional Legal Secretary
P.Mgr................ — Manager
PP .... — Purchaser
PPB................ — Public Buyer
Prof. .... Professor
PTIC .... Patent & Trade Mark Institute of Canada
QAA .... Qualified Administrative Assistant
QC .... Queen's Counsel
QLS................ Québec Land Surveyor
RA................. Royal Academy (honorary)
R.Adm. .... Rear-Admiral
RAM .... Royal Academy of Music (Budapest)
RAS .... Royal Aeronautical Society
RBA................ Royal Society of British Artists
RCA .... Royal Canadian Academy of Arts
RCAM .... Royal College & Academy of Music (Budapest)
RCM .... Royal Conservatory of Music (Leipzig)
RE................. Royal Engineers
REBC .... Registered Employee Benefits Consultant
Rev................. Reverend
RFP................ Registered Financial Planner
RHU .... Registered Health Underwriter
RMS .... Royal Society of Miniature Painters
RMT .... Registered Music Teacher
RN................. — Nurse
ROI .... Royal Institute of Oil Painters
RP................. Member of the Royal Society of Portrait Painters
RP................. Révérend Père (Reverend Father)
RPA................ Registered Professional Accountant
R.P.Bio. .... — Professional Biologist
R.P.Dt............... — Professional Dietitian
RPF................ — Professional Forester
RRL................ — Record Librarian
RSH .... Royal Society of Health
RSW .... Registered Specification Writer
RT................. — Technician of the Cdn. Association of Medical Radiation Technologists
SC................. Senior Counsel (Eire) equivalent of Q.C.
ScD .... Doctorat ès Sciences
ScL .... Licence ès Sciences
Sc Soc B .... Bachelier Science Sociale
Sc Soc D .... Doctor of Social Science
Sc Soc L .... License in Social Science
SFC................ Specialist in Financial Counselling
SJ .... Society of Jesus
SLS .... Saskatchewan Land Surveyor
S.Lt. .... Sub-Lieutenant
SM .... Master of Science
Sr. .... Senior
Sr. .... Sister
SSB................ Bachelier en Science Sacrée
SSC .... Sculptors' Society of Canada
SSL................ Licentiate in Sacred Scripture
STB (SThB) .... Bachelor of Sacred Theology
STD (SThD) .... Doctor of Sacred Theology
STL (SThL) .... Sacrae Theologiae Licentiatus (Licentiate in Sacred Theology)
STM .... Master of Sacred Theology
TCL................ Trinity College, London
TMMG.............. Teacher, Massage & Medical Gymnastics
ThD .... Doctor of Theology
V.Adm. .... Vice-Admiral
VG .... Vicar-General
VS................. Veterinary Surgeon

Business & Shipping Abbreviations

As shipping terms vary in different countries, insurance or shipping agents should be consulted. For other lists of abbreviations, academic, etc., see Index.

a/c .... Account
Ad val. .... Ad valorem
avoir .... Avoirdupois
bbl. .... Barrel
B/L. .... Bill of Lading
b.m. .... Board Measure
B.O. .... Buyer's Option
B/P. .... Bills Payable
B/R. .... Bills Receivable
B/S. .... Bill of Sale
c. .... Hundred
C or Cent. ..... Centigrade
cf. .... Compare
C. and F. ...... Cost & Freight
Cie .... Compagnie
c.i.f. .... Cost insurance & freight
C.L. .... Car Load (of freight)
Co. .... Company
C.O.D. .... Cash on Delivery
C. of F. .... Cost of Freight
Cr. .... Credit
C.W.O. .... Cash with Order
Cwt. .... Hundredweight
D/A. .... Documents Attached, also Deposit Account
Dis. (Disct.) .... Discount
Dl. (or Tl.) ...... Double (or triple) first class
D.O.A. .... Deliver Documents on Acceptance of Draft
D.O.P. .... Deliver Documents on Payment of Draft
Dr. .... Debit
D.V. .... God willing (Deo volente)
e.g. .... For example (exempli gratia)
E.&.O.E. .... Errors & omissions excepted
Est. Wt. .... Estimated Weight
et seq. .... And the following (et sequens)
Ex. Div. .... Without Dividend
Ex-Warehouse .. Purchaser pays carriage charges & assumes risks from seller's warehouse
F. .... Fahrenheit
F.a.a. .... Free of Average (marine insurance)
F.A.S. .... Free Alongside (Seller assumes risks & delivers goods to alongside of steamer free of carriage charges)
F.O.B. .... Free on Board (Purchaser pays carriage charges & assumes risks from point specified)
F.P.A. .... Free of Particular Average (Insured can recover only for a total loss, subject to other conditions of the contract)
Franco. .... Pre-paid free of expense to point specified
G.A. .... General Average (All owners of cargo & vessel share in any loss arising from expense incurred to preserve ship & contents from greater loss)
gm. .... Grammes
gr. .... Grain; grains, or gross
ibid. .... In the same place (ibidem)
i.e. .... That is (id est)
Inc. .... Incorporated
Int. .... Interest
K.D. .... Knocked down
lb. (libra) ...... Pound
L/C. .... Letter of Credit
L.C.L. .... Less than Car Load (of freight)
Limited; Ltd. .... Limited Liability (Shareholders are "limited" in liability to the amount of their subscribed stock in certain companies)
L.P. .... List Price
M. .... Thousand (Mille)
MS., MSS. ..... Manuscript(s)
N.E.S. (N.O.P.) .. Not Otherwise Provided For (Customs)
N.O.S. .... Not Otherwise Specified
N.S.F. .... Not Sufficient Funds (re cheques)
Nstd. .... Nested
O.K. .... Correct
op. cit. .... In the work quoted (opere citato)
O.R. .... At Owner's Risk
O.R.B. .... At Owner's Risk of Breakage
oz. .... Ounce
P.A. .... Particular Average (As used in Marine Insurance, means damage to the goods caused by perils insured against & named in the contract. This form is often written with a Franchise Clause, & means there will be no claim unless the loss exceeds the percentage named)
P/A. .... Power of Attorney
P & D. .... Pick Up & Deliver
pp. .... Pages
Pro forma ...... As a Matter of Form
P.S. .... Postscript
q.v. .... Which see (quod vide)
R.R. .... Rural Route (Postal delivery)
S.B. .... Shipping Bill
s.s. .... Steamship
s/o .... Ship's Option, weight or measurement
S.U. .... Set Up (meaning article is complete)
T.B.L. .... Through Bill of Lading
Tare .... Weight of Container (Deducting tare from "gross weight" gives "net weight")
Ton .... 2,000 (short ton) or 2,240 (long ton) lbs. avoirdupois. A cubic ton in marine freight = 40 cubic feet
Ton wt/M. ...... Ton, weight or measurement (ship's option)
vide .... See
viz .... Namely; to wit (videlicet)

Border Services, Customs Regulations for Canadians Returning from Abroad

Note: The Canada Border Services Agency (CBSA) operates as an agency under the Public Safety and Emergency Preparedness (PSEP) portfolio, and its mission is to ensure the security and prosperity of Canada by managing the access of people and goods to and from Canada. With a workforce of approximately 12,000 public servants, the Canada Border Services Agency (CBSA) provides services at 1,200 points across Canada and over 30 locations abroad. At over 100 land border crossings and nine international airports, we operate on a 24/7 basis. We administer more than 90 acts and regulations on behalf of other Government of Canada departments and agencies, and international agreements.

It integrates several key functions previously spread among three organizations: the Customs program from the Canada Customs Revenue Agency, the Intelligence, Interdiction and Enforcement program from Citizenship and Immigration Canada, and the Import Inspection at Ports of Entry program from the Canadian Food Inspection Agency.

If you have information about suspicious cross-border activity, please call the CBSA Border Watch tollfree line at 1-888-502-9060.

Canadians returning to Canada may bring any amount of goods into the country subject to duties and any provincial or territorial assessments, with the exception of restricted items. This applies even if you do not qualify for a personal exemption. The term duty can include Goods and Services. Duties represent duty, excise taxes and the Goods & Services Tax (GST) or Harmonized Sales Tax (HST). In addition to duties, provincial and territorial taxes (PST) are assessed if an agreement has been signed between the federal government and a province or territory whereby the federal government collects the PST, levies and fees on their behalf.

Goods included in personal exemptions must be for personal or household use, souvenirs or gifts. Goods brought in for commercial use, or on behalf of another person do not qualify and are subject to full duties.

On your return to Canada, you must declare to the Canada Border Services Agency (CBSA) all goods acquired (purchases, gifts, awards, prizes, and purchases made at Canadian or foreign duty-free shops and still in your possession) and repairs or modifications you made to your vehicle, vessel or aircraft while outside Canada.

Personal Exemptions

To qualify for personal exemptions you must be:

- Canadian resident returning from a trip abroad;
- former resident of Canada returning to live in Canada; or
- temporary resident of Canada.

Children and infants qualify for personal exemptions as long as the goods are for the use of the child or infant. The parent or guardian makes the customs declaration for the child.

Personal exemptions are applicable after the following minimum absences:

1. After an absence of 24 hours but less than 48 hours: up to a value of $50 (Canadian) in total (with the exception of tobacco products and alcoholic beverages) any number of times a year. If the value of the goods exceeds $50, you pay duties and PST on the full value (exemption cannot be claimed). The goods must accompany you on your return to Canada.

2. After an absence of 48 hours but less than seven days: up to $400 (Canadian) in total any number of times in a year. The goods must accompany you on your return to Canada.

3. After an absence of seven days or more: up to $750 (Canadian) any number of times in a year. You may have to make a written declaration. Goods you claim under this exemption may follow you by mail or other means, with the exception of alcoholic beverages and tobacco products. You require a Form E24, Personal Exemption Customs Declaration, which is to be completed at the time of arrival and can be obtained from a customs officer. To claim your goods when they arrive, present your copy of the E24 to the CBSA for clearance. Goods must be claimed within 40 days of their arrival in Canada; duties and taxes are then payable, along with a Canada Post Corporation processing fee. You may pay the duties and then apply to the CBSA for a refund (if the personal exemption applies) or refuse delivery; following a review that determines if the goods are eligible for free importation, the goods will be released to you without an assessment.

Persons residing outside Canada for part of the year are considered to be residents of Canada and are entitled to the above personal exemptions.

Exemptions cannot be transferred to another person or combined with another person's personal exemption. You cannot combine a 24-hour ($50) or 48- hour ($400) or the seven-day ($750) exemption when claiming an exemption, nor can you carry over an unused portion of an exemption for another period of absence.

Tobacco & Alcohol

Tobacco products and alcoholic beverages must accompany you in your hand or checked luggage and may be included in the 48-hour ($400) or the seven-day ($750) exemptions, but not in the 24-hour ($50) exemption. You must meet the age requirements set by the province or territory where you enter Canada. In addition the following conditions apply:

1. You may bring in up to 200 cigarettes, 50 cigars or cigarillos, 200 tobacco sticks **and** 200 grams of manufactured tobacco. Duties must be paid on anything above this allowance, plus any applicable provincial or territorial limits or assessments.

If you include cigarettes, tobacco sticks, or manufactured tobacco in your personal allowance, only a partial exemption will apply. You will have to pay a special duty on these products **unless** they are marked "CANADA DUTY-PAID — DROIT ACQUITTÉ." You will find Canadian-made products sold at a duty-free shop marked this way. You can speed up your clearance by having your tobacco products available for inspection when you arrive.

2. You may include up to 1.5 litres of wine, or 1.14 litres (40 ounces) of liquor, or a total of 1.14 litres (40 ounces), or 24 x 335 ml (12-ounce) cans or bottles (8.5 litres) of beer or ale. Wine coolers are classified as wine; beer coolers are classified as beer. Beer or wine that contains 0.5% alcohol by volume or less is not classified as an alcoholic beverage, so no quantity limits apply. You may bring in more than this allowance of alcohol anywhere in Canada (with the exception of the Northwest Territories and Nunavut) as long as the quantities are within the limits set by the province or territory. If bringing in more than the free allowance, you must pay customs and provincial/territorial assessments. For more information, check with the appropriate provincial/ territorial liquor control agency prior to leaving Canada.

Gifts

While abroad, you may send gifts duty- and tax-free to recipients in Canada. To qualify, the gift must be valued at $60 CAN or less and cannot be an alcoholic beverage, tobacco product, or advertising material. Gifts in excess of $60 CAN require duty payment by the recipient on the excess amount. Gifts that accompany you on your return to Canada must be included in your personal exemption, while gifts you send from abroad are not included. Some conditions apply - for additional information, contact the CBSA Border Information Service (BIS) at one of the numbers listed at the end of this section.

Prizes & Awards

In most cases, you pay regular duties on prizes or awards received outside Canada. Contact the BIS line for more information.

Paying Duties

Duties may be paid by cash or travellers' cheques. Personal cheques are also acceptable (for amounts of $2,500 or less and with proper identification); VISA, American Express and MasterCard are accepted at most border services locations and Debit Cards at many locations.

For information on duty rates for particular items, contact the BIS line.

Special Duty Rate

After any trip abroad of 48 hours or longer you are entitled to a special duty rate on goods worth up to $300 more than your personal exemption of $400 or $750. The goods must accompany you. The special duty rate does not apply to tobacco or alcoholic beverages. The special duty rate for goods not eligible under NAFTA, when combined with the GST, is about 14% or 22% when combined with the HST.

NAFTA Special Duty Rate

Goods qualify for a lower U.S. duty rate under NAFTA if they are:

- for personal use; and
- marked as made in the U.S. or Canada; or
- not marked or labelled to indicate they were made anywhere other than in the U.S. or Canada.

Your goods qualify for the lower Mexican duty rate in a similar way.

If you do not qualify for a personal exemption, or if you exceed your exemption limit, you will have to pay GST or HST over and above applicable duties or taxes on the portion not eligible under your exemption. The rates vary according to the goods, their country of origin, and the country from which you are importing them.

For information on goods eligible for the special duty rate under NAFTA, contact your nearest CBSA office and ask for a copy of Memorandum D11-4-13, Rules of Origin for Casual Goods Regulations.

Regular Duty Rates

If you do not qualify for a personal exemption, or you exceed your exemption limit, you will pay GST or HST over and above all duties, taxes, and assessments that apply on the portion not eligible under your exemption. The rates vary according to the goods, their country of origin, and the country from which you are importing them. You may also have to pay provincial sales tax if you live in a province where we have an agreement to collect the tax and you return from your trip through your province.

World Trade Organization (WTO) Agreement

The duty on a wide range of products originating in non-NAFTA countries has been eliminated or will be reduced to zero within the next few years. NAFTA goods also qualify for the WTO rate, so if the rate on the goods you are importing is lower under WTO than under NAFTA, the lower rate will automatically be applied.

Value for Duty/Foreign Sales Tax

Value for duty is the amount used to calculate duty and is generally the price you paid for the item. Foreign sales tax is included in the price and forms part of the value of the item.

Some foreign governments will refund sales tax to you if you export the items you bought. If this is the case, you do not include the amount of the foreign sales tax that was or will be refunded to you.

Declaration

When returning to Canada by commercial aircraft, a Canada Border Services Agency (CBSA) declaration card is distributed for completion before arrival. The cards are also used at some locations for people arriving by train, vessel or bus. If arriving by a private vehicle (e.g., automobile), you must make an oral declaration unless you are claiming goods that preceded or will follow your arrival in Canada as part of your $750 exemption. If this is the case, ask the border services officer for Form E24, Personal Exemption Customs Declaration. You will need your copy of this form to claim your goods. Otherwise, you may have to pay regular duty on them.

CBSA officers are legally entitled to examine luggage; you are responsible for opening, unpacking and repacking the luggage. Retain receipts of purchases and repairs made to verify length of stay and value of goods or repairs. Failure to declare or a false declaration may result in the seizure of goods. Penalties range from 25 to 80% of the value of the seized goods. Vehicles used to transport unlawfully imported goods may also be seized, with a penalty imposed before the vehicle can be returned. Commodities such as alcohol and tobacco are seized and not returned.

Currency and Monetary Instruments

If you are importing or exporting monetary instruments equal to or greater than CAN$10,000 (or its equivalent in a foreign currency), whether in cash or other monetary instruments, you must report it to the CBSA when you arrive or before you leave Canada. For more information, ask for a copy of the publication called "Crossing the Border with $10,000 or More?" or select "Publications and forms" on our Web site at www.cbsa.gc.ca.

Restrictions

Firearms: Contact the Canada Firearms Centre at: 1-800-731-4000 (toll-free in Canada and the United States); (506) 624-5380 (from all other countries), Fax: (613) 825-0297, E-mail: cfc-cafc@cfc-cafc.gc.ca, Website: www.cfc-cafc.gc.ca.

Replica firearms are designed or intended to resemble a firearm with near precision. They are classified as prohibited devices and you cannot import them into Canada.

Mace or pepper spray that is used for the purpose of injuring, immobilizing or otherwise incapacitating any person is considered a prohibited weapon. You cannot import it into Canada. Aerosol or similar dispensers that contain substances capable of repelling or subduing animals are not considered weapons if the label of the container specifically indicates that they are for use against animals.

Explosives, fireworks, certain types of ammunition: You require written authorization and permits. Contact Chief Inspector of Explosives Regulatory Division, Natural Resources Canada, 1431 Merivale Rd., Ottawa ON K1A 0G1, 613/948-5200.

Vehicles: Vehicles must meet the requirements of the CBSA, Transport Canada and the Canadian Food Inspection Agency before they can be imported. Transport Canada defines a vehicle as any vehicle that is capable of being driven or drawn on roads, by any means other than muscular power exclusively, but does not run exclusively on rails. It considers trailers such as recreational, camping, boat, horse and stock trailers as vehicles, as well as woodchippers, generators and any other equipment mounted on rims and tires.

CBSA import restrictions apply to most used or second- hand vehicles that are not manufactured in the current year. Transport Canada requirements apply to vehicles that are less than fifteen years old. All imported vehicles less than fifteen years old must comply with Canadian federal safety and emission standards. The person importing the vehicle is responsible for ensuring it meets the Canadian safety standards.

If you have acquired a vehicle from the United States, you must contact the Transport Canada's Registrar of Imported Vehicle (RIV) before you import your vehicle, to ensure that it is admissible for importation and can be modified to meet the Canadian standards after you import it.

Registrar of Imported Vehicles: Telephone: 1-888- 848-8240 (toll free in Canada, the United States and Mexico); (416) 626-6812 (from all other countries), Fax: 1-888-346-8235, Website: www.riv.ca.

Import restrictions apply to most used or secondhand cars, generally from countries other than the United States. Under NAFTA, restrictions do not apply to vehicles imported from the U.S., however, not all vehicles that are manufactured for sale in the U.S. can be imported because they do not meet the Transport Canada requirements; special duty rates, as outlined above, apply. Excise tax and GST continue to apply in the usual way. Under NAFTA, customs restrictions continue to apply to vehicles imported from Mexico until 2009, when you will be able to import vehicles ten years or older. The age restriction will drop every second year until the restriction is dropped altogether in 2019.

In most instances, Canadian residents are not allowed to import vehicles into Canada that have been purchased or obtained in countries other than the United States. If you have acquired a vehicle from a country other than the United States, before importing it, contact: Transport Canada, Road Safety & Motor Vehicle Regulation, Place de Ville, Tower C, 330 Sparks St., 8th Fl., Ottawa ON K1A 0N5, 613/998-8616, or 1-800-333- 0371 (toll free from Canada and the U.S.); Fax: 613/998- 4831; Website: www.tc.gc.ca.

Your vehicle may be subject to provincial or territorial sales tax; contact your provincial or territorial department of motor vehicles for information. In addition, you may need to meet some requirements in the country which the vehicle is being exported.

Import Controls: Importations of certain goods are controlled. You may need a permit to import, even for personal and household use. For information, contact: Export & Import Controls Bureau, International Trade Canada (ITCan) , Tower C, 4th Floor, 125 Sussex Drive, Ottawa ON K1A 0G2, Website: www.international. gc.ca.

Meat, dairy products, wheat, barley, and their products: Complex requirements and restrictions exist; importation of certain meat and dairy products from certain U.S. states is allowed. All meat and meat products have to be identified as products of the United States. Limits exist for amounts or dollar value in certain foodstuffs you can import for personal use; if above those limits, duty ranges from 150 to 300% and you may also require an agricultural inspection certificate. For more information, contact the CBSA BIS line.

Agricultural products: Restrictions exist on live animals and animal products, meat and poultry products, dairy products, egg and egg products, honey and fresh fruits and vegetables, seeds and grains, animal feeds, plant and plant products, forestry products, soil and fertilizers, pest control products, biological products. For information on these products, refer to the Automated Import Reference System (AIRS) on the CFIA Website at www.inspection.gc.ca or call the CBSA BIS line.

Cultural property: Antiquities or cultural objects of significance in the country of origin cannot be imported into Canada. For information, contact Movable Cultural Property, Canadian Heritage, 15 Eddy St., 3rd Fl., Gatineau, QC K1A 0M5, 819/997-7761, Fax: 613/997- 7757.

Endangered species: Canada has signed an international agreement restricting the sale, trade or movement of endangered animals, birds, reptiles, fish, insects and certain forms of plant life; the restrictions also apply to their parts or products made from their parts. Before you bring back any of these products, you should contact CITES Administrator, Canadian Wildlife Service, Environment Canada, Ottawa ON K1A 0H3, 1-800-668-6767 (toll-free number in Canada), 819/ 997-1840 (local calls and from all other countries).

Appeals

If you disagree with the amount of duty and taxes that you had to pay, please ask to speak with the superintendent on duty. A consultation can often resolve the issue quickly and without cost. If you are still not satisfied, our officers can tell you how to make a formal appeal. If you do not declare goods, or if you falsely declare them, we can seize the goods. This means that you may lose the goods permanently, or that you may have to pay a penalty to get them back.

If you do not declare tobacco products and alcoholic beverages at the time of importation, we will seize them permanently.

Depending on the type of goods and the circumstances involved, we may impose a penalty that ranges from 25% to 80% of the value of the seized goods.

In addition, the *Customs Act* provides CBSA officers with the authority to seize all vehicles that were used unlawfully to import goods. When this happens, we impose a penalty you have to pay before we return the vehicle.

If goods have been seized and you disagree with the action taken, you must notify the CBSA in writing within 90 days of the seizure date of your intention to appeal. You should send your appeal to the CBSA Office where the seizure took place. You can find more information about this process on the front of your seizure receipt form.

In addition to the activities mentioned above, designated CBSA officers may arrest for a criminal offence under the *Criminal Code* or any other Act of Parliament. This includes the offences of impaired driving, outstanding arrest warrants, stolen property, and abductions/kidnappings. If you are arrested, you may be compelled to attend court in Canada. You should note that all persons arrested in Canada are protected by, and will be treated in accordance with, the *Canadian Charter of Rights and Freedoms.*

A record of infractions is kept in the CBSA computer system. If you have an infraction record, you may have to undergo a more detailed examination on future trips.

Precautions

Carry proper identification.

Traveling with Children

Border services officers are on alert for children who need protection. Children under the age of 18 are classified as minors and are subject to the same entry requirements as any other visitor to Canada.

We will conduct a more detailed examination of minors entering Canada without proper identification or those traveling in the company of adults other than their parents or legal guardian(s). This additional scrutiny helps ensure the safety of the children.

Minors traveling alone must have proof of citizenship and a letter from both parents detailing the length of stay, providing the parents' telephone number and authorizing the person waiting for them to take care of them while they are in Canada.

If you are traveling with minors, you must carry proper identification for each child such as a birth certificate, passport, citizenship card, permanent resident card or Certificate of Indian Status.

If you are a parent traveling alone with your child, it is recommended that you have a letter of authorization from your spouse. If you are divorced or separated, you should carry with you copies of the legal custody agreements for your children. If you are traveling with minors and you are not their parent/guardian, you should have written permission from the parent/guardian authorizing the trip. The letter should include addresses and telephone numbers of where the parents or guardian can be reached and identify a person who can confirm that the children are not being abducted or taken against their will.

If you are traveling with a group of vehicles, make sure you arrive at the border in the same vehicle as your children, to avoid any confusion.

"Identification of Articles for Temporary Exportation": CBSA offices offer a free identification program for valuables; a list of your valuables (excluding jewellery) and their serial numbers on a wallet-sized form will show border services officers that the items were previously purchased in Canada or that you lawfully imported them prior to your current time abroad. In the case of jewellery, carry an appraisal of the item(s) from a gemmologist, jeweller or insurance agent, together with a signed and dated photograph and a written declaration that the items in the photograph are those described in the appraisal report. If previously imported, carry a copy of the customs receipt.

If you take any item outside Canada and modify it, it is considered to be a new item and its full value will need to be declared. Similarly, under Canadian law, any repairs or modifications to a vehicle that increase its value, improve its condition or modify it while abroad may require that you pay duties on its full value on your return to Canada. This does not apply to incidental repairs to keep the car in operational condition while abroad, although you may be required to pay duties on the repairs and parts. A special provision is available that waives duties payable in such cases. Contact the CBSA for information.

Additional Information

If you have any other questions, contact the Border Information Service (BIS) line. This is a 24-hour telephone service that automatically answers all incoming calls and provides general border services information. If you call during regular business hours (8:00 a.m. to 4:00 p.m. local time, Monday to Friday, except holidays), you can speak directly to an agent by pressing "0" at any time.

English Enquiries: 1-800-461-9999 (toll-free in Canada)
French Enquiries: 1-800-959-2036 (toll-free in Canada)
Out-of-Canada callers can reach BIS by calling:

Western Sites
English: . . . . . . 204/983-3500 (long-distance charges will apply)
French . . . . . . : 204/983-3700 (long-distance charges will apply)

Eastern Sites
English: . . . . . . 506/636-5064 (long-distance charges will apply)
French . . . . . . : 506/636-5067 (long-distance charges will apply)
Website: . . . . www.cbsa-asfc.gc.ca

Election Regulations

According to the Canada Elections Act, and subject to certain exceptions, the general rule as to the franchise of electors at a federal election is that every person is qualified as an elector if such person

(a) is of the full age of 18 years on election day;

(b) is a Canadian citizen.

Among persons disqualified are certain officials charged with administering the elections, and, individuals who have lost their right to vote for a specified period for the commission of an election-related offence.

Writs for an election (general or by-election) are issued at least 36 days before the date fixed for election day.

Similar qualifications apply in the Provinces and Territories, although for provincial and territorial elections there is usually a residence requirement of either six or twelve months before the date of the issue of the writ of election. The age requirement is 18 years.

To contact election officers see Index, "Elections, Govt. Info. Sources".

Elections Canada - 613/993-2975; Toll Free: 1-800-463-6868; TTY: 1-800-361-8935; Fax: 1-888-524-1444; URL: www.elections.ca.

Liquor Regulations

For names of personnel of the various Liquor Control Boards see index "Liquor Board, Commission, or Control."

Alberta

- Ensure integrity, transparency, disclosure, public consultation & accountability in Alberta's gaming & liquor industries;
- Administer the Alberta Lottery Fund with full public disclosure & continue to support communities & charitable organizations;
- License, regulate & monitor liquor & gaming activities, as well as certain aspects of tobacco sales;
- Implement & account for specific lottery fund programs administered by Alberta Gaming;
- Develop & communicate provincial gaming & liquor policy;
- Responsible for the Department of Gaming, the Alberta Gaming & Liquor Commission (AGLC), the Alberta Gaming Research Council.

Alberta Gaming & Liquor Commission, 50 Corriveau Ave., St. Albert AB T8N 3T5 - 780/447-8600; Fax: 780/447-8918; Toll Free: 1-800-272-8876; URL: www.aglc.gov.ab.ca

British Columbia

The Liquor Control & Licensing Branch is responsible for issuing licences to:

- pubs, bars, lounges, stadiums, nightclubs & restaurants to sell liquor by the glass, & cold beer & wine stores to sell liquor by the bottle
- breweries, distilleries & wineries to manufacture liquor, &
- UBrews/UVins to sell their customers the ingredients, equipment & advice they need to make their own beer, wine cider or coolers

In addition, the branch:

- regulates both Serving It Right: The Responsible Beverage Service Program & Special Occasion Licences for the events such as community celebrations, weddings or banquets
- educates those who hold liquor licences (called licensees) about the laws & rules that may affect them inspects licensed establishments, &
- takes enforcement action when licensees do not follow the *Liquor Control & Licensing Act,* Regulations, &/or the specific terms & conditions of their licences British Columbia Liquor Control & Licensing

Branch, PO Box 9292, Stn Prov Govt, Victoria BC V8W 9J8; street address: 1019 Wharf St., 250/387-1254; Fax: 250/387-9184; Toll Free: 1-866-209-2111; Email: lclb.lclb@gems4.gov.bc.ca; URL: www.pssg.gov.bc.ca/lclb

Manitoba

Persons over the age of 18 years and who are not otherwise prohibited may purchase and consume spirits, wine and beer in premises licensed by the Liquor Control Commission. Further, those persons may purchase from a MLCC liquor mart, liquor vendor or specialty wine store for consumption in a residence.

Beer may also be purchased from beer vendor depots located in most hotels throughout the province.

Parents dining with their children may purchase alcoholic beverages for the latter, for consumption with meals, only in licensed restaurants, dining rooms, cocktail lounges or cabarets.

Beverage rooms and cocktail rooms must be vacated within 30 minutes after the hour at which sale of liquor must cease.

Manitoba Liquor Control Commission, 1555 Buffalo Place, PO Box 1023, Winnipeg MB R3C 2X1 - 204/ 284-2501; Fax: 204/453-5254; URL: www.liquormartsonline.com

New Brunswick

Intoxicating liquor is sold in sealed packages at Liquor Stores and agency stores. Where a permit and/or a license has been obtained, liquor may be sold by the glass in dining rooms, restaurants, taverns, cabarets, lounges, beverage rooms, and clubs. Age of majority is 19.

New Brunswick Liquor Corp., PO Box 20787, Fredericton NB E3B 5B8 - 506/452-6826; Fax: 506/462- 2024; Email: info@anbl.com; URL: www.anbl.com

Newfoundland & Labrador

The importation, manufacture, and sale of alcoholic beverages through Retail Liquor outlets is the responsibility of the Newfoundland Liquor Corp.

The Newfoundland Liquor Corporation is also responsible for the issuing of all licenses, including those to manufacture and to sell packaged beer, and enforcement of regulations including, but not limited, to the following:

- All liquor sold upon licensed premises shall be consumed thereon.
- All liquor served in licensed premises shall be dispensed from the original container in which the liquor is purchased from or under the authority of the Liquor Corp.
- The drinking age in Newfoundland is 19 years.

Nfld. Liquor Corp., PO Box 8750, Stn A, St. John's NL A1B 3V1 - 709/724-1100; Fax: 709/754-0321

Northwest Territories

The *Northwest Territories Act,* Chapter 331 of the Revised Statutes of Canada, 1952, authorizes the Commissioner in Council of the Northwest Territories to make acts respecting intoxicants.

The Liquor Licensing Board, established under Part I of the *Liquor Act,* controls the conduct of licensees and operation of licensed premises; grants, renews and transfers licenses and, after a hearing, may cancel or suspend licenses. There are presently twelve types of licenses issued by the Board. Part I also provides for plebiscites to be held concerning new liquor license applications and also concerning restriction or prohibition in a community.

Part II of the *Liquor Act* establishes a Liquor Commission. The Minister responsible for this Part may designate his powers to the Liquor Commission to operate liquor stores and to purchase, sell and distribute liquor in the Northwest Territories. Through agency agreements, private contractors operate retail liquor stores on behalf of the Liquor Commission in Fort Simpson, Fort Smith, Hay River, Inuvik, Yellowknife, Norman Wells and liquor warehouses in Hay River and Yellowknife.

Northwest Territories Liquor Commission, #201, 31 Capital Dr., Hay River NT X0E 1G2 - 867/874-2100; Fax: 867/874-2180; URL: www.fin.gov.nt.ca

Northwest Territories Liquor Licensing Board, #210, 31 Capital Dr., Hay River NT X0E 1G2 - 867/874- 2906; Fax: 867/874-6011

Nova Scotia

All liquor is sold through Government Stores.

Generally local option vote applies.

Eating establishment liquor licenses, lounges, clubs and cabarets serve spirits, draught beer, bottled beer and wine.

The legal minimum drinking age is 19 years.

Nova Scotia Alcohol & Gaming Authority, PO Box 545, Alderney Gate, 40 Alderney Dr., Dartmouth NS B2Y 3Y8 - 902/424-6160; Fax: 902/424-4942; Toll Free: 1-877-565-0556; URL: www.gov.ns.ca/aga

Nova Scotia Liquor Corporation, PO Box 8720, Stn A, Halifax NS B3K 5M4 - 902/450-6752; Fax: 902/453-1153

Nunavut

Nunavut Liquor Management is a Branch of the Department of Finance within the Government of Nunavut. Nunavut Liquor Management has two sections, referred to as the Nunavut Liquor Commission and the Nunavut Liquor Licensing Board.

The Nunavut Liquor Commission is responsible for, as first receiver, the purchasing, storage and distribution of alcohol products within the Nunavut Territory.

The Nunavut Liquor Licensing Board deals with the issuance of liquor licenses, liquor permits, inspection and enforcement under the *Nunavut Liquor Act.*

Communities in Nunavut are empowered and are enabled to establish their own liquor controls through the *Nunavut Liquor Act.* They are prohibited, restricted (variety) and unrestricted (only Liquor Act applies). The age of majority in Nunavut is nineteen.

Nunavut Liquor Commission, Bag 002, Rankin Inlet, NU X0C 0G0 - 867/645-3148; 867/645-3327

Nunavut Liquor Licensing Board, Bag 002, Rankin Inlet, NU X0C 0G0 - 867/645-3302; 867/645-3327

Ontario

In accordance with the provisions of the *Liquor Control Act* of Ontario, the Liquor Control Board buys wine, spirits and beer from all over the world for distribution and sale to Ontario consumers and licensed establishments. To provide this service, the

LCBO operates five major regional storage and distribution centres which supply more than 600 retail liquor stores.

In the interests of consumer protection, the LCBO also regularly tests all alcoholic beverages sold in Ontario. This "quality control" testing ensures that all products carried by LCBO stores, Ontario winery stores and Brewers Retail outlets comply with the standards required under the Federal *Food & Drug Act* and Regulations.

The Alcohol and Gaming Commission of Ontario (AGCO) is a Provincial agency that was established on February 23, 1998 after legislation was tabled to merge the Liquor Licence Board of Ontario (LLBO) with the Gaming Control Commission (GCC). The AGCO is responsible for administering the *Liquor Licence Act*, the *Gaming Control Act*, 1992, and the *Wine Content Act*. The AGCO conducts hearings as required: to determine the eligibility for liquor licences or gaming registration; to determine the eligibility for, or the revocation of liquor licences in public interest cases; and, in disciplinary cases involving liquor licensees or gaming registrants.

Liquor-related responsibilities include: licensing of public places which serve beverage alcohol for on-premises consumption; licensing of Ontario liquor manufacturers and the sales representatives of foreign manufacturers; promoting moderation and the responsible use of beverage alcohol.

Gaming-related responsibilities include: regulating charitable and casino gambling in Ontario; ensuring that games of chance are conducted fairly in compliance with the *Gaming Control Act*, regulations, and the terms and conditions that are imposed with charity gaming licences; ensuring that the people and the companies involved in casino and charitable gaming satisfy high standards of honesty, integrity and financial responsibility; registering commercial suppliers and gaming assistants of charitable gaming events and administering the issuance of charity gaming licences in partnership with municipalities.

Alcohol and Gaming Commission of Ontario, 20 Dundas St. W., Toronto ON M5G 2N6; Enquiries: 416/326-8700, or 1-800-522-2876 (toll-free in Ontario); Fax: 416/326-5555 (liquor), 416/326-8711 (gaming); URL:www.agco.on.ca

Prince Edward Island

Beverage alcohol sealed packages may be purchased at Commission Stores throughout the Province by any person 19 or older who is not otherwise disqualified.

Spirits by the glass, and beer and wine by the open bottle or glass, may be purchased in dining rooms, lounges, clubs and military canteens licensed by the Commission.

Prince Edward Island Liquor Control Commission, 3 Garfield St., PO Box 967, Charlottetown, PE C1A 7M4 - 902/368-5710; Fax: 902/368-5735

Québec

Spirits and wines are sold by Québec Liquor Corporation (Société des alcools du Québec) stores only.

Spirits, beer and wine may be sold to the public by restaurants, bars and clubs under permit for consumption on the premises. Taverns may sell beer and cider. Pubs may sell beer, draught wine and cider.

A licensed grocery store may sell beer and certain designated wines and the product must not be consumed on the premises.

Persons under the age of 18 years old cannot be admitted into bars, pubs and taverns and at no time may alcoholic beverages be sold to them in other establishments.

Régie des Alcools, des courses et des jeux, 1, rue Notre-Dame est, Montréal PQ H2Y 1B6 - 514/873- 3577; 560, boul Charest est, Québec PQ G1K 3J3 - 418/643-7667

Saskatchewan

The Saskatchewan Liquor & Gaming Authority, a Treasury Board Crown corporation, regulates liquor and gaming activities and conducts and manages gaming in the Saskatchewan Indian Gaming Authority Casinos and the Video Lottery Terminals throughout the province. It is responsible for the control, sale and distribution of liquor in the province, and also licenses and regulates bingos, raffles, casinos, and breakopen tickets.

The minimum drinking age is 19.

Saskatchewan Liquor & Gaming Authority, PO Box 5054, Regina SK S4P 3M3 -306/787-4213; Fax: 306/798-2252

Yukon Territory

The *Yukon Act*, Chapter Y-2 of the Revised Statutes of Canada, 1970, authorizes the Commissioner in Executive Council, Yukon Territory, to make acts respecting intoxicants.

By virtue of Chapter 105 cited as the *Liquor Act*, established the laws governing the importation, distributing, licensing and retailing of alcoholic beverages in Yukon.

The formation of the Yukon Liquor Corporation by means of amendments to the *Liquor Act* came into force on April 1st, 1977. The separation as a Corporate entity resulted in increased responsibility and full accountability in all areas except major government policy.

The five members of the Board of Directors are appointed by the Commissioner in executive council to hold office at pleasure.

The President and Chief Executive Officer of the Corporation, is charged with the general direction, supervision and control of the Corporation and the administration of the Act.

Yukon Liquor Corp., 9031 Quartz Road, Whitehorse YT Y1A 4P9 - 867/667-5245; Fax: 867/393-6306; URL: www.ylc.yk.ca

Legal Age of Consent to Sexual Activity

Age of Consent, under the *Tackling Violent Crime Act, 2008*:

Raises the age at which youths can consent to non-exploitative sexual activity from 14 to 16 years of age;

Maintains the existing age of protection of 18 years for exploitative sexual activity (i.e. sexual activity involving prostitution, pornography, or a relationship of trust, authority or dependency or that is otherwise exploitative); and

Includes a close-in-age exception which permits 14- and 15-year old youths to engage in consensual, non-exploitative sexual activity with a partner who is less than five years older. Another exception will be available for marriages and for pre-existing common-law relationships.

Marriage Regulations

Divorce Act in Canada

Divorce grounds in Canada, under the *Divorce Act, 1985:*

Breakdown of marriage, established by:
- Spouses intentionally living separate and apart at least one year with the idea that the marriage is over, or

Since the marriage, either spouse has:
- Committed adultery, or
- Treated the other spouse with physical or mental cruelty rendering continued cohabitation intolerable.

Alberta

Marriageable age:
- Without parental consent: 18 years
- With parental consent: 16 years
- A female, under the age of 16, may be married with parental consent & proof that she is the mother of a living child or proof that she is expecting a child.

Blood Test: not required
Waiting Period: None. Marriage Licence is valid immediately & is valid for 3 months (from date of issuance).
Licence fee: $40 + agent
Civic Marriage ceremony fee: uncapped

British Columbia

Marriageable age:
- Without parental consent: 19 years
- With parental consent: 16 to 18 years
- A court order of consent: under 16 years

Blood test: not required
Waiting period for licence: none
Marriage Licence: $100
Civil Marriage Ceremony: $80.25

Manitoba

Marriageable age:
- Without parental consent: 18 years
- With parental consent: 16 years (Persons under 16 years of age can be married only with the consent of a judge of the Family Court.)

Blood test: not required
Waiting period for licence: none
Waiting period after issuance of licence: 24 hours (This may be waived in exceptional circumstances by person performing ceremony.)
Licence fee: $90. Licence valid for 3 months (from date of issuance).

New Brunswick

Marriageable age:
- Without parental consent: 18 years
- With parental consent: under 18 years
- Under 16 years: a declaration of a Judge of the Court of Queen's Bench that the proposed marriage may take place is necessary.

Blood test: not required
Waiting period for licence: none
Licence fee: none
Vital Statistics, Dept. of Health & Wellness - 506/ 453-7411; Fax: 506/453-3245; URL: www.gov.nb.ca/en/ index.htm

Newfoundland & Labrador

Marriageable age:
- Greater than or equal to 19 years: without parental consent
- Greater than or equal to 18 years: without parental consent in certain circumstances
- Greater than or equal to 16 years and less than 19 years: with the applicable parental, guardian or Director of Child Welfare consent (Consent may be dispensed within exceptional cases.)
- Less than 16 years: where by reason of pregnancy a judge issues a licence

Blood test: not required
Licence fee: $50

Northwest Territories

Marriageable age:
- Without parental consent: 19 years
- Under the age of 19 years and declares via statutory declaration that:
  - (a) that no person has lawful custody of the minor; or
  - (b) that any person who has lawful custody of the minor not a resident of the Territories & that the minor has been a resident of the Territories for not less than 12 months immediately preceding the date of the declaration; or
  - (c) that any person who has lawful custody of the minor is unable to consent by reason of disability; or
  - (d) that the minor has, for not less than six months immediately preceding the date of the declaration, withdrawn from the charge of the persons who have lawful custody of the minor & that the minor has not returned to such charge
- With parental consent: 15 years, or under 15 years & pregnant

Blood test: not required
Waiting period for licence: none
Licence fee: $50

Nova Scotia

Marriageable age:
- Without parental consent: 19 years or over
- With parental consent, or if a widow, widower, or divorcee: 16 years
- With court order: under 16 years

Blood test: not required
Waiting period for licence: 5 days
Licence fee: $106.50

Nunavut

Marriageable age:
- Without parental consent: 19 years
- At least 18 years of age

Blood test: not required
Waiting period for licence: none
Licence fee: $25

Ontario

Marriageable age:
- Without parental consent: 18 years
- With parental consent: 16 years

Blood test: not required
Waiting period after issuance of licence: none
Licence fee: $75-$100
Fee for solemnization of marriage by judge or justice of the peace: $75
Purchased marriage licence must be used within 3 months.

Prince Edward Island

Marriageable age:
- Without parental consent: 18 years
- With parental consent: under 18 years

Other requirements: birth certificates and Social Insurance Numbers; in the case of a widow or widower, death certificate; in the case of a divorced person, certified copy of the Decree Absolute or Certificate of Divorce
Waiting period for licence: none
Licence fee: $100

Québec

Marriageable age:

- Minimum age: 16 years (ref.: art. 373, Code Civil du Québec)
- Moreover, a minor (under 18 years of age) must have the authorization of his or her parent(s) or tutor to get married.

Blood test: not required
Waiting period for licence: none
Fee for civil marriage: $186.89 (taxes included)

Saskatchewan

Marriageable age:

- Without parental consent: 18 years
- With parental consent: 16 to 18 years
- With parental and court consent: under 16 years

Blood test: not required
Licence fee: $50

Yukon Territory

Marriageable age:

- Without parental consent: 19 years (In the case of an 18 year old person who has lived apart from his parents/ guardians for at least 6 months & received no financial aid from them during that time, no consent is needed.)

A certificate of divorce or death must be produced if previously married
Blood test: not required
Waiting period for licence: none
Waiting period after issuance of licence: 24 hours
Licence fee: $20
Vital Statistics - Email: vital.statistics@gov.yk.ca; URL: www.hss.gov.yk.ca

Postal Information

Services and rates quoted are subject to change. For complete and up-to-date information you may: consult a local Canada Post retail outlet; call 1-800-267-1177, TTD 1-800-267-2797; or refer to the Canada Post website at www.canadapost.ca. For distribution services, call 1-888-550-6333, and for Postal Code information (fees apply) call 1-900-565-2633 (English) or 1-900-565- 2634 (French).

Communications Services

LETTERMAIL RATES FOR DELIVERY IN CANADA

Includes letters, postcards, greeting cards and business correspondence.

Standard Lettermail:

Up to 30 g	$0.57
Over 30 g to 50 g	$1.00

Other Lettermail Incl. Non-Standard & Oversize:

Up to 100 g	$1.22
Over 100 g to 200 g	$2.00
Over 200 g to 300 g	$2.75
Over 300 g to 400 g	$3.00
Over 400 g to 500 g	$3.25

Oversize Letter Rates apply to all letters with any dimension greater than 24.5 cm (length) x 15 cm (width) x .5 mm (thickness), but not greater than 38 cm (length) x 27 cm (width) x 2 cm (thickness). Maximum weight for Lettermail is 500g. Items with any dimension exceeding the maximum dimension for Oversize Lettermail or exceeding 500g must be paid at parcel rates. Incentive Rates are available under sales agreements for customers whose mailing meets standard volume, frequency and preparation conditions. For details, please contact a Canada Post Corp. representative. Canada Post is committed to consistently deliver properly prepared lettermail as follows: two business days within the same metropolitan area/community; three business days within the same province; four business days between provinces.

Distribution Services

PRIORITY COURIER™

Priority Courier is an overnight domestic courier service providing next business day noon delivery of your items for local and regional destinations and next business day noon to three day delivery nationally between major Canadian centres. This service comes with an on-time delivery guarantee, an acceptance scan, delivery confirmation, free insurance up to $100 and a no-charge signature-on-delivery option. Prepaid envelopes are available in two sizes and prepaid labels are available to business customers in 4 weight increments. For item delivery status or product information, customers can call 1-888-550-6333 or visit the website at www.canadapost.ca.

XPRESSPOST™

XPRESSPOST is an affordable, simple to use delivery service for packages and documents which provides an on-time service guarantee and confirmation of delivery. Positioned right in the middle between Priority Courier and Regular Post in terms of price, service and features, XPRESSPOST offers next business day locally and regionally, and 2 days national between most major urban centres. Customers can verify delivery of their items or obtain product information by calling 1- 888-550-6333, or by accessing the Internet.

EXPEDITED PARCEL™

Expedited Parcel is the fastest ground service providing next business day local, 1-3 business day regional and 2-7 business day national delivery and a no-charge delivery confirmation/guarantee option. A full range of prepaid labels are also available to business customers.

REGULAR PARCEL™

Regular Parcel is the most economical, domestic, ground parcel service. Service is 3 business days local, 4-6 business days regional and 5-10 business days national between most major urban centres.

ADVICE OF RECEIPT (USA/INTERNATIONAL ONLY)

The Advice of Receipt (AR) service provides mailers with the actual signature of the addressee. An Advice of Receipt card is purchased at the time of mailing. The addressee's signature is obtained on the AR card and returned to the sender, thus providing the mailer with a Delivery Confirmation.

To international and USA destinations, AR can be used only with Registered Mail and only at the time of mailing, for a fee of $1.65.

AIR STAGE SERVICE (LESS THAN 5 ITEMS)

Canada Post services many communities where the only access to the community is by air. These communities are called Air Stage Offices.

The casual mailer who sends the occasional letter and parcel to these isolated communities pays the normal rate outlined in the various rate charts for Lettermail, Parcel Post, XPRESSPOST & Priority Courier.

Any customer (individual or business) who ships more than 5 parcels or more than 20 kg of parcels on any day or more than 20 parcels or more than 80 kg of parcels in any month is considered an Air Stage Service Shipper and must pay Air Stage Freight Service rates. These shippers must also sign an agreement with CPC in order to use this service. An infrequent mailer who meets the volume or weight criteria can use the Air Stage Freight Service rates providing the goods shipped are not for resale. There are various rate levels based on the type of goods shipped.

Air Stage Freight Service rates apply whether the mailer is a business or an individual. Appropriate Regular Post zoned parcel rates apply for all other shippers, and appropriate Priority Courier or Xpresspost Rates apply.

CANADIAN FORCES MAIL SERVICE

Canadian Forces Mail is mail sent to or by Canadian Forces personnel, their dependents and the civilians attached to the Canadian Forces served through the Canadian Forces Post Office (CFPO) or the Fleet Mail Office (FMO).

The rate charged for domestic mail is applicable for mail sent to Canadian Forces personnel providing it is sent through a CFPO or an FMO.

All parcels must include an International Customs Declaration form (CP72) and are subject to customs inspection in the country of destination. Oversize parcels and parcels over 20 kg are not acceptable.

COLLECT ON DELIVERY (COD)

COD is a service for domestic mail for which an amount due to the sender, up to $1,000 where the amount to be collected is in cash and $25,000 where the amount to be collected is by cheque, is collected from the addressee before delivery and returned to the mailer. It is a service available to consumer and business mailers. COD is available for parcels only or items mailed at parcel rates. The amount collected from the addressee can include:

1. Amount representing the value of the item.
2. Service charge in the case of repairs.
3. Sales tax.
4. Postage.
5. COD fee & special service fees.

COD cannot be used to collect on items not ordered or requested by the addressee or to collect money owing on previous accounts. Insurance is available up to $5,000. Items sent COD must abide by Canada Post mail preparation requirements. The amount of the COD collected from the addressee will be forwarded to the sender by Postal Money Order when payment is made by cash or by cheque drawn up by the addressee payable to the sender.

PUROLATOR™

Purolator Overnight is a domestic service provided by Canada Post on behalf of Purolator Courier Ltd. It allows customers to buy PuroLetter or PuroPak prepaid labels at a postal counter. Canada Post provides PuroLetter and PuroPak convenience packaging which must be used in conjunction with PuroLetter and Puro- Pak prepaid labels.

DEFICIENT POSTAGE FEE

Unpaid or shortpaid mail is mail for which the postage or fees have not been paid or have been partially paid. Lettermail and Parcelmail is returned to the sender for the collection of the postage.

When there is no return address on the item, the item is forwarded to the addressee for the collection of the postage plus an administrative charge. All postage due charges must be paid before delivery.

DO NOT FORWARD SERVICE

Do Not Forward is a service for Lettermail, mailed in Canada for delivery in Canada. Mail that cannot be delivered as addressed because the addressee has filed a Change Of Address Notification will be returned to the sender rather than being forwarded to the addressee.

The customer who requires this service:

1. Must complete an agreement form with Canada Post.
2. Should establish a deposit account with Canada Post with a prescribed minimum amount to cover postage & fees.
3. Must print the approved "Do Not Forward" artwork on the Lettermail items for which the service will be provided.

The fee to return Lettermail to sender is the appropriate rate of postage plus a per item fee.

FRANKED MAIL

Canada Post provides free mailing privileges to the following:

1. Governor General or Secretary to the Governor General;
2. Speaker or Clerk of the Senate or House of Commons;
3. Parliamentary Librarian or Associate Parliamentary Librarian;
4. Members of the Senate;
5. Members of the House of Commons.

In addition, anyone mailing an item to the above in Canada receives free postage. As a general rule, only Lettermail, Publications Mail and Addressed Admail are acceptable. Parcels and add-on services are not acceptable as part of this service. As long as the letters M.P. appear on the mailing, it can be sent free of postage.

COLLECTION OF THE GST

The Goods & Service Tax (GST) is a value added consumption tax instituted by the Federal Government. By law, businesses must charge 5% on most goods and services provided.

Most postal services and products are subject to the GST, such as stamps, Advance Purchase Products, all add-on options (e.g., Insurance, Trace Mail, COD), optional Postal Box rentals, and postage meter fill-ups.

There are certain items sold by Canada Post that are not taxable such as Postal Money Orders, the fee on a Money Order and the exchange on a Money Order. Provincial governments are exempt from paying the GST.

Mail addressed to foreign destinations requiring total shipping charges of $5 or more (single item or a cumulative purchase) and products ordered from and shipped directly by Canada Post to a foreign destination, such as Philatelic and Retail products, are not subject to the GST. The 5% tax is calculated on the total taxable purchased and rounded up or down to the nearest cent.

HOLD MAIL

Many Canadians wish to have their mail held because they are going on an extended holiday or will be away from their home or their business for a period of time. Customers must complete a "Hold Mail" form which can be obtained from a postal outlet, or online. The completed card, which indicates the period of time that the mail should be held, is sent to the customer's normal delivery office to inform the postal employees to hold the mail. The held mail will be delivered on the "resume service" date indicated on the card.

HUNTING PERMITS

Prior to hunting season, hunting permits can be purchased from a postal outlet. The rules, regulations and fees pertaining to these permits are provided to the outlets by the Provincial and Federal bodies responsible for these permits. Unsold permits can be returned by the postal outlet to the depot from where they were originally ordered at the end of the hunting season for a refund.

INSURANCE

Insurance is available from Canada Post to provide compensation for the loss or damage of mailable items if the requirements are met. Coverage for up to $100 is included for Registered Mail services; however, Canada Post shall have no liability for loss or damage of Registered Mail items containing:

1. Bank notes, travellers' cheques & coins;
2. Stocks, bonds, coupons, & other securities negotiable by bearer;
3. Lottery tickets;
4. Jewellery;
5. Manufactured & non-manufactured precious metals, precious stones, gold bullion & gold dust;
6. Canceled or uncanceled postage stamps.

Additional coverage is available, for a fee, for domestic Registered Mail items up to $5,000.

To USA destinations, coverage for up to $100 is included for Registered Mail services, with the same exceptions as above; there is no additional coverage available for USA Registered Mail.

KEY SERVICE™

Hotel, motel and automobile keys can be mailed without postage at any postal outlet in Canada for delivery in Canada if the keys have a tag clearly showing the complete address of the addressee. They can also be dropped in a street letter box.

LIBRARY BOOKS

Available to Public Libraries, University Libraries, and Libraries maintained by non-profit organizations for use by the general public in Canada to mail library books to their Canadian patrons. This service is for books only (not tapes, videos or records). The library completes an "Application for Mail Privileges" form and be authorized by Canada Post to use this service. The maximum weight per shipment is 5 kg.

The maximum weight for sewn or bound books is 5 kg and 3 kg for books that are not sewn or bound. The rates are based on a per item cost plus weight and destination. Postage paid by the library at the time of mailing covers both the outgoing and the return postage.

LITERATURE FOR THE BLIND

Literature for the Blind is a service available free of charge from Canada Post allowing blind persons and recognized institutions for the blind to mail free of postage specific items used by blind persons.

Admissible items in Canada include items impressed in Braille or similar raised type, plates for printing literature for the blind, tapes and records posted by the blind in Canada for delivery in Canada and recording tapes, records and special writing paper intended solely for the use of the blind-when mailed by or addressed to a recognized institution for the blind.

The maximum weight in Canada is 7 kg. Add on services such as Registered (500 g), and Advice of Receipt (USA/International only), which should be endorsed "Braille Free" can be applied to Literature for the Blind at no charge.

This service is available to the USA and to international destinations at no charge. There is a charge for Literature for the Blind mailed to international destinations using Air mail service. Although the objective of the service is the same for Canada, the USA, and international destinations, some minor variations exist in the rules and conditions.

MAILING LISTS

Some Canadians may object to receiving Addressed Admail and would like their name removed from all mailing lists. Canadians are advised to contact the sender of the Admail to request that his or her name be removed from their mailing list.

If any recipient of this type of mail wishes to have all Addressed Admail stopped, the customer should write to the following addresses asking them to have their members delete his or her name from their mailing lists.

In Canada:
Canadian Direct Marketing Association
Do Not Mail Service
#607, 1 Concorde Gate, Don Mills ON M3C 3N6
416/391-2362; Fax: 416/441-4062

In the United States:
Direct Marketing Association
Mail Preference Service
PO Box 9008, Farmingdale NY 11735-9008, USA.
212/768-7277

PHILATELIC PRODUCTS

Canada Post offers stamp collectors, ranging from the person with a passing interest in stamps to a very serious collector, a complete range of philatelic products. Stamp collectors are concerned with product quality. It is for this reason that we have set up philatelic centres within specific postal outlets across the country. It is from these centres that the philatelist can more easily obtain the product and information required. There is also a National Philatelic Centre in Antigonish, Nova Scotia, from which any collector can get access to information and products by mail or by telephone.

POSTAL BOXES/CONTAINERS/BAG SERVICE/GENERAL DELIVERY

A postal box is a numbered compartment in a post office that is kept locked, and to which the boxholder and postal employee have access.

The container/bag service is a service whereby containers or bags are assigned to a customer for the delivery of mail, either because postal boxes are not available or because the size of the postal boxes cannot accommodate the volume of mail addressed to this particular customer.

The General Delivery service at post offices is offered to the travelling public, customers with no fixed address within the letter carrier delivery area, or to anyone who cannot receive their mail from the normal delivery modes.

MONEY ORDERS

A Money Order is a secured cashable document, guaranteed by Canada Post, which is used to transfer funds anywhere in Canada and to most countries. The service guarantee offers free replacement of lost or destroyed money orders and/or photocopies of paid money orders upon enquiry from the purchaser.

Postal money orders can be purchased by consumers and businesses, and constitute a guaranteed payment. They can be used for financial or retail transactions.

Postal money orders can be sent to most countries in the world. To several countries, customers may send Canadian postal money orders in Canadian, U.S. or British funds directly. To other countries there is an advice system, meaning that CPC will forward the amount to the recipient in the local currency via the respective Postal Administration.

The maximum value of a single postal money order is $999.99 (Canadian and U.S. dollars) and £100. (British currency). The fee is $5.50 for a Canadian postal money order. and for US/International postal money orders.

PROHIBITED MAIL

Prohibited Mail is defined as any mail which is prohibited by law or may contain products or substances that could harm postal employees or damage other mail or postal equipment. The mail service cannot be used for criminal activities or for the transportation of dangerous goods. Animals and plants are generally not acceptable except under certain well-defined conditions in Canada. Prohibitions and restrictions on mail sent to the USA and to international destinations exists and are wide-ranging.

REDIRECTION OF MAIL (PERMANENT)

Canada Post provides a redirection of mail service. When a customer is permanently moving, he or she should complete a "Request for Redirection of Mail" form available at postal facilities and pay the appropriate fee. The form is used to advise the appropriate people at CPC of the need to redirect the mail. The completed form is sent to the postal supervisor responsible for the mail at the customer's old address from where the mail is redirected.

Change of Address announcement cards are available at postal facilities for customers to use to notify their correspondents of their new address. The announcement cards require the Lettermail rate of postage when addressed for delivery in Canada. Customers can also change their address on-line, and must do so at least 3 business days before their move date.

Mail can be redirected from any Canadian address to any other address in Canada, the USA and most international destinations. The service is available for a six-month period. The service can be extended, providing the extension is requested before the expiry date of the service. There are no limitations on the additional periods of extension, although the extension price will be the current price at the time the application is filed.

Redirection of mail to the USA and to international destinations is also available for six-month renewable periods for both consumers and businesses.

REDIRECTION OF MAIL (TEMPORARY)

Temporary redirection of mail is also available from a Canadian address to another address in Canada, the USA and international destinations. The customer must complete a "Request for Temporary Redirection of Mail" card and pay the required fee. The card is sent by the postal authorities to the postal supervisor responsible for the mail at the customer's old address.

For consumers: The customer must pay the initial fee for a three-month period and can renew for up to six months for a monthly fee. The same process is applicable for the U.S. and international destinations.

For businesses: The initial fee is not required but a monthly charge is levied for the service. The same process is applicable for temporary redirection to the USA or to other international destinations.

UNDELIVERABLE MAIL

Undeliverable Mail is mail that fails delivery and does not bear a return address. Mail is considered undeliverable if:

1. the address is incomplete or does not exist
2. the addressee has moved without providing a change of address or the Change of Address Notification (COAN) has expired
3. it is refused by the addressee
4. it is refused by the addressee, bears a return address, & is refused by the sender
5. the addressee refuses to pay postage due charges
6. it is prohibited by law
7. it is an item found loose in the mail
8. it is an empty wrapper or carton.

PROOF OF DELIVERY/HARD COPY SIGNATURE - REGISTERED MAIL

A hard copy of the signature can be obtained at a later date, if required, by calling 1-888-550-6333. There is a fee for this service. The Signature Copy will be sent via Lettermail or Fax within three business days of your request.

Other Services

SELECTED RATES TO THE UNITED STATES (its Territories & Possessions):

LETTERMAIL

Weight Steps:

Up to & including 30 g	$ 1.00
Over 30 g to 50 g	1.22
Oversize letter rates (max. 500g)	
Up to & including 100 g	2.00
100 g to 200 g	3.50
Over 200 g to 500 g	7.00

Lettermail more than 27 cm (width) x 38 cm (length) x 2 cm (thickness) up to 90 cm length plus width plus thickness (longest side may not exceed 60 cm).

USA Incentive Lettermail offers Canadian mailers significant postage savings and improved service performance linked to volume, and quality of mail preparation. For various USA Incentive Lettermail rates, please inquire at a postal outlet.

XPRESSPOST™ - USA

Xpresspost service is now available to the USA providing 3-5 days service for documents and packages to major centres.

REGISTERED MAIL

Available for airmail lettermail items. Fees to the USA- $12.95 plus the applicable postage.

SELECTED INTERNATIONAL RATES

All countries except the USA, its Territories and Possessions, Canadian Forces post offices and Fleet Mail Offices.

LETTERMAIL

Weight Steps	Air Mail
Up to & including 30 g	$ 1.70
Over 30 g to 50 g	2.44
Other letter rates, including Oversize (max. 500g)	
Up to & including 100g	4.00
Over 100 g to 200 g	7.00
Over 200 g to 500 g	14.00

POSTCARDS

All countries .... $ 1.49 each

General Information

POSTAL CODE DIRECTORY

The Canadian Postal Code Directory is available for $49.95 (plus applicable taxes) and may be purchased at selected postal outlets or ordered from the National Philatelic Centre at 1-800-565-4362. Canada Post postal data products are available on CD-ROM or by download from the Canada Post FTP site on a 12-month subscription basis, which includes monthly updates.

PROVINCIAL SYMBOLS

Standard two-letter postal abbreviations for the provinces and territories are as follows:

Alberta	AB
British Columbia	BC
Manitoba	MB
New Brunswick	NB
Newfoundland & Labrador	NL
Northwest Territories	NT
Nova Scotia	NS
Nunavut	NU
Ontario	ON
Prince Edward Island	PE
Québec	QC
Saskatchewan	SK
Yukon Territory	YT

STAMP & COLLECTOR SERVICES

Canada Post offers a wide selection of postage stamps, stationery, supplies and philatelic products such as Official First Day Covers, Annual Souvenir Collections and Commemorative Stamp Packs. The National Philatelic Centre also sells stamps from several other postal administrations, including the U.S., Great Britain and the United Nations.

Philatelic products are available at postal outlets and through authorized stamp sales agents across Canada. Customers may visit the Stamps and Gifts On-line store or the National Philatelic Centre, Canada Post Corporation, 75 St. Ninian St., Antigonish NS B2G 2R8; from Canada and the USA call toll-free 1-800-565-4362, and from other countries call 902/863-6550.

CUSTOMER SERVICE

Further information on Canada Post's products and services can be obtained through your local postal outlets, postal directory, your local customer service representative, or by calling one of the following numbers:

Toll Free (Canada) (8 a.m. to 6 p.m. local time)	1-866-607-6301
Outside of Canada	416/979-8822
Hearing Impaired with TTY-Teletyping	1-800-267-2797

Customers may also contact Canada Post via the Internet: www.canadapost.ca or mail: Canada Post Corporation, 2701 Riverside Dr., Ottawa ON K1A 0B1.

Vital Statistics

CANADIAN POPULATION AND PERCENTAGE DISTRIBUTION PROVINCES AND TERRITORIES, 1971-2006 (CENSUS)

Province/Territory	1971 %	1981 %	1991 %	2001 %	2006 %
Newfoundland & Labrador	522,104 2.42	567,681 2.33	568,474 2.08	512,930 1.71	505,469 1.60
Prince Edward Island	111,641 0.52	122,506 0.50	129,765 0.46	135,294 0.45	135,851 0.43
Nova Scotia	788,960 3.66	847,442 3.48	899,942 3.30	908,007 3.03	913,462 2.89
New Brunswick	634,557 2.94	696,403 2.86	723,900 2.65	729,498 2.43	729,997 2.31
Québec	6,027,764 28.00	6,438,403 26.40	6,895,963 25.30	7,237,479 24.10	7,546,131 23.87
Ontario	7,703,106 35.70	8,625,107 35.40	10,084,885 36.90	11,410,046 38.00	12,610,282 38.47
Manitoba	988,247 4.58	1,026,241 4.21	1,091,942 4.00	1,119,583 3.73	1,148,401 3.63
Saskatchewan	926,242 4.29	968,313 3.97	988,928 3.62	978,933 3.26	968,157 3.06
Alberta	1,627,874 7.55	2,237,724 9.19	2,545,553 9.33	2,974,807 9.91	3,290,350 10.41
British Columbia	2,184,621 10.10	2,744,467 11.30	3,282,061 12.00	3,907,738 13.00	4,113,487 13.01
Yukon	18,388 0.09	23,153 0.09	27,797 0.10	28,674 0.10	30,372 0.10
Northwest Territories	34,807 0.16	45,741 0.18	57,649 0.21	37,360 0.13	41,464 0.13
Nunavut	- -	- -	- -	26,745 0.09	29,474 0.09
Totals	21,568,311 100.00	24,343,181 100.00	27,296,859 100.00	30,007,094 100.00	31,612,897 100.00
Rural	5,157,525 23.90	5,907,254 24.30	6,389,724 23.40	6,098,883 20.30	6,262,154 19.81
Urban	16,410,785 76.10	18,435,927 75.70	20,907,135 76.60	23,908,211 79.70	25,350,743 80.19

Source: Statistics Canada: A National Overview, 2006 Census (cat. no. 92-200-XPB)

POPULATION OF CANADA, PROVINCES AND TERRITORIES, BY AGE GROUPS

2006 CENSUS OF POPULATION

Province/Territory	Total	< 5 years	5 to 9	10 to 14	15 to 24	25 to 34	35 to 44	45 to 54	55 to 64	65 to 74	75 to 84	85 +
Canada	31,612,895	1,690,540	1,809,370	2,079,925	4,220,875	4,005,805	4,818,730	4,977,905	3,674,490	2,288,360	1,526,280	520,605
Newfoundland & Labrador	505,465	22,860	25,905	29,460	65,295	58,370	78,200	85,575	69,540	39,685	22,930	7,645
Prince Edward Island	135,850	6,690	7,920	9,375	18,530	15,205	19,435	21,070	17,440	10,810	6,685	2,690
Nova Scotia	913,460	42,040	48,145	56,245	118,210	105,235	136,660	148,910	119,805	73,300	46,310	18,610
New Brunswick	729,995	34,430	38,875	44,945	92,330	87,495	109,445	120,070	94,760	56,845	36,685	14,105
Quebec	7,546,130	375,270	398,980	478,255	947,175	960,190	1,121,420	1,232,120	952,425	583,710	377,300	119,285
Ontario	12,160,285	670,770	721,590	818,440	1,630,370	1,535,645	1,916,400	1,861,370	1,356,510	868,190	589,180	191,810
Manitoba	1,148,400	68,100	73,835	83,235	161,575	140,970	161,740	171,570	125,480	78,930	59,045	23,910
Saskatchewan	968,155	57,495	61,070	69,135	142,145	113,180	127,875	146,015	101,935	70,885	54,595	23,820
Alberta	3,290,350	202,600	204,110	224,810	489,285	474,830	506,135	512,205	322,970	189,330	121,795	42,295
British Columbia	4,113,485	201,880	220,700	257,020	539,465	499,855	625,480	664,255	505,010	313,400	210,365	76,050
Yukon Territory	30,370	1,740	1,830	2,145	4,160	3,785	4,960	5,820	3,635	1,475	635	180
Northwest Territories	41,460	3,220	3,095	3,605	6,725	6,445	6,905	6,150	3,345	1,235	580	165
Nunavut	29,475	3,430	3,315	3,260	5,615	4,590	4,070	2,760	1,630	580	180	45

Source: Statistics Canada, 2006 Census of Population, 97-551XCB06005

POPULATION OF CANADA, PROVINCES AND TERRITORIES, BY SEX
2006 CENSUS OF POPULATION

	Total	Male	Female
Canada	31,612,895	15,475,970	16,136,930
Newfoundland and Labrador	505,465	245,730	259,735
Prince Edward Island	135,850	65,595	70,255
Nova Scotia	913,460	439,830	473,630
New Brunswick	729,995	355,500	374,495
Quebec	7,546,130	3,687,695	3,858,435
Ontario	12,160,285	5,930,705	6,229,580
Manitoba	1,148,400	563,275	585,125
Saskatchewan	968,155	475,235	492,920
Alberta	3,290,350	1,646,795	1,643,550
British Columbia	4,113,485	2,013,985	2,099,500
Yukon Territory	30,370	15,280	15,090
Northwest Territories	41,460	21,225	20,235
Nunavut	29,475	15,110	14,365

Source: Statistics Canada, 2006 Census of Population, 97-551XCB06005

POPULATION OF CENSUS METROPOLITAN AREAS
1996 – 2006

	1996	2001	2006
Abbotsford, BC	136,480	147,370	159,020
Calgary, AB	821,628	951,395	1,079,310
Edmonton, AB	862,597	937,845	1,034,945
Greater Sudbury, ON	165,618[A]	155,601	158,258
Halifax, NS	342,966[A]	359,183	372,858
Hamilton, ON	624,360	662,401	692,911
Kingston, ON	144,528	146,838	152,358
Kitchener, ON	382,940[A]	414,284	451,235
London, ON	416,546[A]	432,451	457,720
Montréal, PQ*	3,326,447[A]	3,426,350	3,635,571
Oshawa, ON	268,773	296,298	330,594
Ottawa-Gatineau[2], ON, PQ	998,718[A]	1,063,664	1,130,761
Ontario (part)	751,646[A]	806,096	-
Québec (part)	247,072	257,568	-
Québec, PQ	671,889	682,757	715,515
Regina, SK	193,652	192,800	194,971
Saguenay[1], PQ	160,454	154,938	151,643
Saskatoon, SK	219,056	225,927	233,923
Sherbrooke, PQ	149,569[A]	153,811	186,952
St. Catharines-Niagara, ON	372,406	377,009	390,317
St. John, NB	125,705	122,678	122,389
St. John's, NF	174,051	172,918	181,113
Thunder Bay, ON	126,643[A]	121,986	122,907
Toronto, ON	4,263,759[A]	4,682,897	5,113,149
Trois-Rivières, PQ	139,956	137,507	141,529
Vancouver, BC	1,831,665	1,986,965	2,116,581
Victoria, BC*	304,287	311,902	330,088
Windsor, ON	286,811[A]	307,877	323,342
Winnipeg, MB	667,093[A]	671,274	694,668
New 2006 Census CMAs:			
Barrie, ON	-	148,480	177,061
Brantford, ON	-	118,086	124,607
Guelph, ON	-	117,344	127,009
Kelowna, BC	-	147,739	162,276
Moncton, NB	-	118,678	126,424
Peterborough, ON	-	110,876	116,570

* Excludes census data for one or more incompletely enumerated Indian reserves or Indian settlements;
[A] Adjusted figure due to boundary change; 1 Formerly Chicoutimi-Jonquière; 2 Formerly Ottawa-Hull
Source: Statistics Canada, A National Overview, 2006 Census (cat no 92-200-XPB)

Estimates of Population by Age & Sex for Canada, 1996 - 2009

	1996	1997	1998	1999	2000	2001	2002	2003	2004	2005	2006	2007	2008	2009
Both Sexes														
All ages	29,610,218	29,905,948	30,155,173	30,401,286	30,685,730	31,019,020	31,353,656	31,639,670	31,940,676	32,245,209	32,576,074	32,931,956	33,327,337	33,739,859
0 to 14 years	5,985,792	5,977,731	5,958,400	5,918,977	5,883,508	5,854,321	5,829,983	5,795,726	5,754,660	5,698,605	5,651,798	5,619,669	5,609,116	5,611,606
0 to 17 years	7,198,564	7,202,273	7,189,688	7,157,153	7,137,692	7,121,079	7,095,985	7,053,939	7,023,932	7,005,983	6,996,462	6,970,503	6,943,362	6,924,460
15 to 64 years	20,045,149	20,273,661	20,472,300	20,696,249	20,950,263	21,242,401	21,532,363	21,779,619	22,044,570	22,326,765	22,599,461	22,878,899	23,161,347	23,440,807
18 years and over	22,411,654	22,703,675	22,965,485	23,244,133	23,548,038	23,897,941	24,257,671	24,585,731	24,916,744	25,239,226	25,579,612	25,961,453	26,383,975	26,815,399
18 to 64 years	18,832,377	19,049,119	19,241,012	19,458,073	19,696,079	19,975,643	20,266,361	20,521,406	20,775,298	21,019,387	21,254,797	21,528,065	21,827,101	22,127,953
18 to 24 years	2,798,097	2,810,699	2,834,012	2,875,149	2,909,950	2,956,778	2,999,724	3,044,806	3,081,998	3,100,719	3,118,696	3,158,753	3,210,074	3,260,706
25 to 44 years	9,713,951	9,729,837	9,697,095	9,650,065	9,616,676	9,605,618	9,581,708	9,525,469	9,479,900	9,438,961	9,393,924	9,380,284	9,380,799	9,397,356
45 to 64 years	6,320,329	6,508,583	6,709,905	6,932,859	7,169,453	7,413,247	7,684,929	7,951,131	8,213,400	8,479,707	8,742,177	8,989,028	9,236,228	9,469,891
65 years and over	3,579,277	3,654,556	3,724,473	3,786,060	3,851,959	3,922,298	3,991,310	4,064,325	4,141,446	4,219,839	4,324,815	4,433,388	4,556,874	4,687,446
Males														
All ages	14,650,326	14,806,491	14,925,201	15,048,761	15,193,958	15,365,609	15,533,158	15,675,460	15,825,754	15,979,800	16,147,873	16,325,702	16,524,504	16,732,476
0 to 14 years	3,068,454	3,065,381	3,054,035	3,032,746	3,012,946	2,997,037	2,985,215	2,968,334	2,947,720	2,919,903	2,898,453	2,883,552	2,878,978	2,880,952
0 to 17 years	3,691,878	3,694,527	3,686,460	3,669,084	3,658,463	3,649,014	3,636,266	3,614,557	3,599,729	3,592,181	3,589,283	3,575,349	3,560,904	3,551,583
15 to 64 years	10,068,025	10,189,782	10,285,595	10,400,140	10,532,534	10,684,572	10,829,898	10,952,582	11,084,776	11,226,895	11,363,110	11,500,157	11,640,674	11,780,434
18 years and over	10,958,448	11,111,964	11,238,741	11,379,677	11,535,495	11,716,595	11,896,892	12,060,903	12,226,025	12,387,619	12,558,590	12,750,353	12,963,600	13,180,893
18 to 64 years	9,444,601	9,560,636	9,653,170	9,763,802	9,887,017	10,032,595	10,178,847	10,306,359	10,432,767	10,554,617	10,672,280	10,808,360	10,958,748	11,109,803
18 to 24 years	1,427,462	1,437,061	1,450,030	1,472,328	1,490,651	1,514,524	1,535,879	1,559,934	1,579,333	1,588,650	1,599,104	1,621,263	1,648,486	1,675,286
25 to 44 years	4,877,603	4,890,769	4,872,381	4,852,544	4,841,436	4,843,176	4,833,847	4,805,459	4,781,919	4,759,831	4,734,782	4,725,178	4,723,317	4,729,687
45 to 64 years	3,139,536	3,232,806	3,330,759	3,438,930	3,554,930	3,674,895	3,809,121	3,940,966	4,071,515	4,206,136	4,338,394	4,461,919	4,586,945	4,704,830
65 years and over	1,513,847	1,551,328	1,585,571	1,615,875	1,648,478	1,684,000	1,718,045	1,754,544	1,793,258	1,833,002	1,886,310	1,941,993	2,004,852	2,071,090
Females														
All ages	14,959,892	15,099,457	15,229,972	15,352,525	15,491,772	15,653,411	15,820,498	15,964,210	16,114,922	16,265,409	16,428,201	16,606,254	16,802,833	17,007,383
0 to 14 years	2,917,338	2,912,350	2,904,365	2,886,231	2,870,562	2,857,284	2,844,768	2,827,392	2,806,940	2,778,702	2,753,345	2,736,117	2,730,138	2,730,654
0 to 17 years	3,506,686	3,507,746	3,503,228	3,488,069	3,479,229	3,472,065	3,459,719	3,439,382	3,424,203	3,413,802	3,407,179	3,395,154	3,382,458	3,372,877
15 to 64 years	9,977,124	10,083,879	10,186,705	10,296,109	10,417,729	10,557,829	10,702,465	10,827,037	10,959,794	11,099,870	11,236,351	11,378,742	11,520,673	11,660,373
18 years and over	11,453,206	11,591,711	11,726,744	11,864,456	12,012,543	12,181,346	12,360,779	12,524,828	12,690,719	12,851,607	13,021,022	13,211,100	13,420,375	13,634,506
18 to 64 years	9,387,776	9,488,483	9,587,842	9,694,271	9,809,062	9,943,048	10,087,514	10,215,047	10,342,531	10,464,770	10,582,517	10,719,705	10,868,353	11,018,150
18 to 24 years	1,370,635	1,373,638	1,383,982	1,402,821	1,419,299	1,442,254	1,463,845	1,484,872	1,502,665	1,512,069	1,519,592	1,537,490	1,561,588	1,585,420
25 to 44 years	4,836,348	4,839,068	4,824,714	4,797,521	4,775,240	4,762,442	4,747,861	4,720,010	4,697,981	4,679,130	4,659,142	4,655,106	4,657,482	4,667,669
45 to 64 years	3,180,793	3,275,777	3,379,146	3,493,929	3,614,523	3,738,352	3,875,808	4,010,165	4,141,885	4,273,571	4,403,783	4,527,109	4,649,283	4,765,061
65 years and over	2,065,430	2,103,228	2,138,902	2,170,185	2,203,481	2,238,298	2,273,265	2,309,781	2,348,188	2,386,837	2,438,505	2,491,395	2,552,022	2,616,356

Source: Statistics Canda, CANSIM Table # 051-0001, August 2010

Population of Canada, Projections, 2010-2061 (in thousands)

Year	Projection scenario L: low-growth	Projection scenario M1: medium-growth, historical trends (1981 to 2008)	Projection scenario M2: medium-growth, 2006 to 2008 trends	Projection scenario M3: medium-growth, 1988 to 1996 trends	Projection scenario M4: medium-growth, 2001 to 2006 trends	Projection scenario H: high-growth	Projection scenario A1: replacement fertility	Projection scenario A2: zero immigration	Projection scenario A3: 1% immigration
2010	34,103.4	34,138.2	34,138.2	34,138.1	34,138.2	34,163.9	34,161.4	33,883.1	34,224.5
2011	34,454.5	34,532.2	34,532.4	34,532.0	34,532.4	34,594.6	34,596.3	34,016.8	34,711.9
2012	34,792.4	34,921.9	34,922.3	34,921.4	34,922.3	35,031.8	35,044.8	34,141.1	35,202.1
2013	35,086.3	35,317.5	35,318.1	35,316.8	35,318.2	35,527.5	35,518.4	34,255.6	35,695.0
2014	35,367.6	35,711.7	35,712.5	35,710.6	35,712.5	36,035.2	36,009.5	34,360.2	36,190.3
2015	35,643.2	36,103.9	36,105.0	36,102.4	36,105.1	36,545.2	36,500.4	34,454.6	36,687.7
2016	35,912 8	36,493.8	36,495.3	36,491.9	36,495.4	37,057.1	36,990.3	34,538.5	37,186.7
2017	36,176.1	36,881.0	36,882.8	36,878.6	36,882.9	37,570.6	37,478.8	34,611.8	37,686.9
2018	36,432.5	37,264.8	37,266.9	37,261.8	37,267.0	38,084.8	37,965.0	34,674.1	38,187.7
2019	36,681.7	37,644.6	37,647.2	37,641.1	37,647.3	38,599.2	38,448.4	34,725.0	38,688.5
2020	36,928.1	38,025.1	38,028.0	38,021.0	38,028.1	39,118.2	38,933.2	34,769.4	39,193.7
2021	37,171.2	38,405.5	38,408.9	38,400.9	38,409.0	39,641.2	39,418.8	34,806.8	39,702.9
2022	37,410.6	38,785.5	38,789.2	38,780.3	38,789.3	40,167.4	39,904.6	34,837.1	40,215.3
2023	37,645.6	39,164.3	39,168.4	39,158.5	39,168.4	40,696.3	40,389.8	34,859.7	40,730.5
2024	37,875.9	39,541.3	39,545.7	39,535.0	39,545.8	41,227.1	40,873.7	34,874.2	41,247.7
2025	38,100.7	39,915.9	39,920.7	39,909.1	39,920.7	41,759.4	41,355.9	34,880.3	41,766.5
2026	38,319.6	40,287.7	40,292.8	40,280.4	40,292.7	42,292.6	41,835.7	34,877.5	42,286.2
2027	38,532.3	40,656.2	40,661.5	40,648.4	40,661.5	42,826.5	42,313.2	34,865.6	42,806.5
2028	38,738.3	41,021.1	41,026.8	41,012.8	41,026.6	43,360.9	42,788.1	34,844.5	43,327.3
2029	38,937.5	41,382.4	41,388.3	41,373.6	41,388.1	43,895.8	43,260.9	34,814.0	43,848.3
2030	39,129.6	41,740.0	41,746.1	41,730.7	41,745.9	44,431.3	43,732.1	34,774.2	44,369.6
2031	39,314.5	42,093.9	42,100.3	42,084.1	42,100.0	44,968.0	44,202.3	34,725.2	44,891.3
2032	39,492.5	42,444.6	42,451.1	42,434.2	42,450.8	45,506.4	44,672.6	34,667.4	45,413.8
2033	39,664.0	42,792.2	42,799.0	42,781.3	42,798.6	46,046.6	45,144.0	34,601.1	45,937.5
2034	39,829.3	43,137.3	43,144.4	43,125.8	43,143.9	46,589.4	45,617.6	34,526.6	46,462.9
2035	39,988.7	43,480.4	43,487.6	43,468.2	43,487.1	47,135.7	46,094.6	34,444.5	46,990.6
2036	40,142.4	43,821.7	43,829.3	43,808.9	43,828.7	47,686.0	46,576.1	34,355.3	47,521.0
2037	40,290.8	44,162.0	44,169.8	44,148.4	44,169.2	48,241.2	47,063.2	34,259.2	48,054.6
2038	40,434.6	44,501.4	44,509.5	44,487.0	44,508.9	48,801.5	47,557.0	34,156.7	48,592.1
2039	40,573.9	44,840.5	44,848.9	44,825.3	44,848.3	49,367.6	48,058.6	34,048.2	49,133.8
2040	40,708.9	45,179.6	45,188.3	45,163.4	45,187.6	49,940.2	48,568.9	33,933.9	49,680.3
2041	40,839.8	45,518.8	45,527.9	45,501.7	45,527.2	50,519.6	49,088.5	33,814.1	50,231.7
2042	40,966.6	45,858.5	45,868.0	45,840.3	45,867.2	51,106.4	49,617.9	33,688.8	50,788.4
2043	41,089.4	46,198.7	46,208.6	46,179.5	46,207.9	51,700.8	50,157.3	33,558.3	51,350.7
2044	41,208.5	46,539.6	46,550.0	46,519.3	46,549.2	52,302.8	50,706.7	33,422.6	51,918.7
2045	41,324.2	46,881.3	46,892.1	46,859.8	46,891.3	52,912.5	51,265.8	33,282.0	52,492.7
2046	41,436.5	47,224.0	47,235.2	47,201.1	47,234.4	53,529.9	51,834.0	33,136.6	53,072.7
2047	41,546.0	47,567.5	47,579.3	47,543.4	47,578.5	54,154.9	52,411.1	32,986.5	53,659.0
2048	41,652.9	47,912.3	47,924.5	47,886.8	47,923.7	54,787.3	52,996.3	32,832.0	54,251.7
2049	41,757.8	48,258.3	48,271.1	48,231.4	48,270.2	55,427.2	53,589.3	32,673.5	54,851.0
2050	41,860.9	48,605.9	48,619.2	48,577.6	48,618.3	56,074.4	54,189.5	32,511.3	55,457.2
2051	41,962.9	48,955.2	48,969.1	48,925.4	48,968.2	56,729.1	54,796.8	32,345.8	56,070.5
2052	42,064.1	49,306.6	49,320.9	49,275.2	49,320.0	57,391.3	55,410.7	32,177.6	56,691.1
2053	42,164.9	49,660.2	49,675.1	49,627.3	49,674.2	58,061.2	56,031.3	32,007.0	57,319.5
2054	42,265.7	50,016.5	50,032.0	49,982.0	50,031.0	58,739.1	56,658.8	31,834.8	57,955.9
2055	42,367.1	50,375.9	50,391.9	50,339.8	50,390.9	59,425.5	57,293.6	31,661.6	58,600.9
2056	42,469.4	50,738.9	50,755.5	50,701.1	50,754.4	60,121.0	57,936.0	31,487.9	59,254.8
2057	42,572.9	51,105.8	51,122.9	51,066.3	51,121.8	60,826.1	58,586.8	31,314.5	59,918.1
2058	42,677.8	51,477.1	51,494.8	51,435.8	51,493.5	61,541.5	59,246.5	31,141.9	60,591.2
2059	42,784.4	51,853.2	51,871.4	51,810.1	51,870.1	62,267.8	59,915.9	30,970.7	61,274.5
2060	42,892.8	52,234.3	52,253.1	52,189.4	52,251.7	63,005.7	60,595.9	30,801.4	61,968.4
2061	43,003.1	52,620.8	52,640.2	52,573.9	52,638.6	63,755.9	61,287.2	30,634.5	62,673.2

Source: Statistics Canada, CANSIM Table # 052-0005, August 2010

VITAL STATISTICS COMPARED WITH MACROREGIONS & REGIONS 1995-2000

MACRO REGIONS AND REGIONS	BIRTH RATE 0/000	DEATH RATE 0/000
World	**22**	**9**
Africa	**38**	**14**
Eastern Africa	42	18
Middle Africa	45	15
Northern Africa	28	7
Southern Africa	28	12
Western Africa	40	15
Northern America	**14**	**8**
Latin America	**23**	**6**
Caribbean	21	8
Central America	27	5
South America	22	7
Asia	**22**	**8**
Eastern Asia	16	7
South Central Asia	27	9
South Eastern Asia	23	7
Western Asia	30	7
Europe	**10**	**11**
Eastern Europe	10	13
Northern Europe	12	11
Southern Europe	10	10
Western Europe	11	10
Oceania	**18**	**8**
Australia and New Zealand	14	8
Melanesia	31	9
Micronesia	36	5
Polynesia	25	5

Source: United Nations Statistical Yearbook, 45th issue

BIRTHS & DEATHS, NUMBER AND RATES, 2007

PROVINCE	LIVE BIRTHS Number	LIVE BIRTHS Rate[2]	DEATHS Number	DEATHS Rate[2]	INFANT DEATHS[1] Number	INFANT DEATHS[1] Rate[3]
Newfoundland and Labrador	4,553	9.0	4,505	8.9	34	7.5
Prince Edward Island	1,389	10.1	1,147	8.3	7	5.0
Nova Scotia	8,868	9.5	8,353	8.9	29	3.3
New Brunswick	7,146	9.6	6,324	8.5	31	4.3
Quebec	84,387	11.0	56,521	7.4	379	4.5
Ontario	138,436	10.9	87,340	6.8	723	5.2
Manitoba	15,285	12.9	9,958	8.3	111	7.3
Saskatchewan	13,248	13.3	9,062	9.1	77	5.8
Alberta	49,028	14.0	20,202	5.8	296	6.0
British Columbia	43,649	10.2	31,308	7.3	176	4.0
Yukon	355	10.9	192	5.9	3	8.5
Northwest Territories	725	16.7	174	4.0	3	4.1
Nunavut	794	25.4	129	4.1	12	15.1
TOTALS	367,864	11.2	235,217	7.1	1,881	5.1

[1] Children under one year of age. [2] Rate per 1,000 population. [3] Rate per 1,000 live births.
Source: Statistics Canada, CANSIM Tables 102-4502, 102-4505, 102-0504, 102-0507, August 2010

DEATHS, CANADA, 2007

	Number of deaths			Crude rate*		
	Both sexes	Males	Females	Both sexes	Males	Females
Canada	235,217	118,681	116,536	7.1	7.3	7.0
Newfoundland and Labrador	4,505	2,332	2,173	8.9	9.4	8.4
Prince Edward Island	1,147	582	565	8.3	8.6	8.0
Nova Scotia	8,353	4,124	4,229	8.9	9.1	8.8
New Brunswick	6,324	3,203	3,121	8.5	8.8	8.2
Quebec	56,521	28,093	28,428	7.4	7.4	7.3
Ontario	87,340	43,814	43,526	6.8	6.9	6.7
Manitoba	9,958	5,014	4,944	8.3	8.4	8.2
Saskatchewan	9,062	4,504	4,558	9.1	9.1	9.0
Alberta	20,202	10,569	9,633	5.8	5.9	5.6
British Columbia	31,308	16,138	15,170	7.3	7.6	7.0
Yukon Territory	192	117	75	5.9	7.0	4.7
Northwest Territories	174	102	72	4.0	4.5	3.4
Nunavut	129	89	40	4.1	5.5	2.6

*per 1,000 population
Source: Statistics Canada, CANSIM Table 102-0504, August 2010

LEADING CAUSES OF DEATH, CANADA, 2006

(in rank order)

MALES	Number of deaths	Mortality rate*	FEMALES	Number of deaths	Mortality rate*
Malignant neoplasms	35,624	220.3	Major cardiovascular diseases	34,501	209.4
Major cardiovascular diseases	34,214	211.6	Malignant neoplasms	32,183	195.3
All other diseases (residual)	9,954	61.6	All other diseases (residual)	14,506	88.0
Accidents (unintentional injuries)	5,749	35.6	Chronic lower respiratory diseases	4,659	28.3
Chronic lower respiratory diseases	5,127	31.7	Alzheimer's disease	3,996	24.2
Diabetes mellitus	3,775	23.3	Accidents (unintentional injuries)	3,891	23.6
Intentional self-harm (suicide)	2,695	16.7	Diabetes mellitus	3,486	21.2
Influenza and pneumonia	2,320	14.3	Influenza and pneumonia	2,832	17.2
Nephritis, nephrotic syndrome and nephrosis	1,857	11.5	Nephritis, nephrotic syndrome and nephrosis	1,829	11.1
Symptoms...not elsewhere classified	1,647	10.2	Symptoms...not elsewhere classified	1,445	8.8
Chronic liver disease and cirrhosis	1,592	9.8	Other diseases of respiratory system	1,147	7.0
Other diseases of respiratory system	1,345	8.3	Septicaemia	985	6.0
Parkinson's disease	955	5.9	Chronic liver disease and cirrhosis	821	5.0
Septicaemia	867	5.4	Intentional self-harm (suicide)	817	5.0
Pneumonitis due to solids and liquids	787	4.9	Parkinson's disease	731	4.4
Total, all causes of death	115,149	712.1	Total, all causes of death	112,930	685.3

*per 100,000 population

Source: Statistics Canada, CANSIM Table #102-0551, August 2010

IMMIGRANTS TO CANADA, BY CLASS, 1992 - 2008

Year	Economic	Family	Refugees	Others[1]	Total
1992	95,806	101,128	52,351	5,544	254,829
1993	105,667	112,679	30,629	7,751	256,726
1994	102,313	94,194	20,438	7,455	224,400
1995	106,635	77,386	28,087	761	212,869
1996	125,371	68,359	28,478	3,865	226,073
1997	128,351	59,979	24,308	3,400	216,038
1998	97,911	50,896	22,843	2,547	174,197
1999	109,251	55,277	24,396	1,031	189,955
2000	136,292	60,614	30,092	460	227,458
2001	155,719	66,794	27,919	206	250,638
2002	137,864	62,287	25,116	3,782	229,049
2003	121,046	65,112	25,984	9,207	221,349
2004	133,748	62,260	32,687	7,128	235,823
2005	156,313	63,360	35,776	6,790	262,240
2006	138,252	70,508	32,503	10,380	251,643
2007	131,250	66,229	27,955	11,325	236,759
2008	149,072	65,567	21,860	10,742	247,243
			%		
1992	37.6	39.7	20.5	2.2	100.0
1993	41.2	43.9	11.9	3.0	100.0
1994	45.6	42.0	9.1	3.3	100.0
1995	50.1	36.4	13.2	0.4	100.0
1996	55.5	30.2	12.6	1.7	100.0
1997	59.4	27.8	11.3	1.6	100.0
1998	56.2	29.2	13.1	1.5	100.0
1999	57.5	29.1	12.8	0.5	100.0
2000	59.9	26.6	13.2	0.2	100.0
2001	62.1	26.6	11.1	0.1	100.0
2002	60.2	27.2	11.0	1.7	100.0
2003	54.7	29.4	11.7	4.2	100.0
2004	56.7	26.4	13.9	3.0	100.0
2005	59.6	24.2	13.6	2.6	100.0
2006	54.9	28.0	12.9	4.1	100.0
2007	55.4	28.0	11.8	4.8	100.0
2008	60.3	26.5	8.8	4.3	100.0

[1] Includes defered removal order class, post determination refugee claimant class, temporary resident permit holders and humanitarian and compassionate/public policy cases.

Source: Statistics Canada, Report on the Demographic Situation in Canada (cat. no. 91-209XIE) and the "2009 Annual Report to Parliament on Immigration", Citizensip and Immigration Canada

Net Migration for Provinces and Territories, 1992-2009

Year [1]	N.L.	P.E.I.	N.S.	N.B.	Que.	Ont.	Man.	Sask.	Alta.	B.C.	Y.T.	N.W.T.	Nvt.
1992/1993	-3,078	654	96	-1,402	-8,420	-14,189	-5,544	-6,348	-1,181	40,099	-265	-330	-92
1993/1994	-4,952	622	-1,887	-671	-8,758	-9,420	-4,614	-5,431	-1,630	37,871	-1,094	-19	-17
1994/1995	-6,974	349	-2,741	-813	-8,947	-2,841	-3,220	-3,652	-556	29,291	269	78	-243
1995/1996	-7,436	638	-1,245	-369	-12,626	-2,822	-3,566	-2,161	7,656	22,025	564	-554	-104
1996/1997	-8,134	136	-1,648	-1,263	-17,436	1,977	-5,873	-2,794	26,282	9,880	-54	-696	-377
1997/1998	-9,490	-416	-2,569	-3,192	-16,958	9,231	-5,276	-1,940	43,089	-10,029	-1,024	-1,316	-110
1998/1999	-5,695	193	201	-1,244	-13,065	16,706	-2,113	-4,333	25,191	-14,484	-747	-555	-55
1999/2000	-4,263	104	-270	-1,183	-12,146	22,369	-3,456	-7,947	22,674	-14,610	-691	-651	70
2000/2001	-4,493	165	-2,077	-1,530	-9,442	18,623	-4,323	-8,410	20,457	-8,286	-572	-160	48
2001/2002	-3,352	62	-898	-1,218	-4,350	5,354	-4,344	-8,820	26,235	-8,556	-221	84	24
2002/2003	-1,683	165	510	-843	-1,829	637	-2,875	-5,141	11,903	-1,037	149	242	-198
2003/2004	-2,027	144	-772	-760	-822	-6,935	-2,565	-4,521	10,606	7,865	27	-105	-135
2004/2005	-3,710	-139	-3,041	-2,074	-4,963	-11,172	-7,227	-9,515	34,423	8,214	53	-668	-181
2005/2006	-4,342	-639	-3,024	-3,487	-9,411	-17,501	-7,881	-7,083	45,795	8,800	-73	-954	-200
2006/2007	-4,067	-849	-4,126	-2,632	-12,865	-20,047	-5,500	1,549	33,809	15,005	101	-221	-157
2007/2008 (Final)	-528	-291	-1,794	-908	-11,682	-14,750	-3,703	4,171	15,317	14,643	235	-420	-290
2008/2009 (Preliminary)	2,332	-559	-1,255	-537	-10,666	-18,738	-1,541	4,108	23,006	4,673	126	-850	-99
Average (1998/99 - 2008/09)	-2,893	-149	-1,504	-1,492	-8,295	-2,314	-4,139	-4,177	24,492	1,112	-147	-387	-107
Total (1992/93 - 2008/09)	-71,892	339	-26,540	-24,126	-164,386	-43,518	-73,621	-68,268	343,076	141,364	-3,217	-7,095	-2,116

[1] the period beginning July 1 of a given year and ending June 30 of the following year.

Source: Statistics Canada, CANSIM Table #051-0018 annual (persons), August 2010

MARRIAGES, 2004

	Canada	Nfld	P.E.I.	N.S.	N.B.	Que.	Ont.	Man.	Sask.	Alta	B.C.	Yukon	N.W.T.	Nvt
Marriages	146,242	2,848	851	4,609	3,589	21,281	62,425	5,706	5,050	17,457	22,076	150	131	69
Crude Marriage Ratio [1]	4.6	5.5	6.2	4.9	4.8	2.8	5.0	4.9	5.1	5.4	5.3	4.9	3.1	2.3
Mean age at marriage														
Grooms	34.9	33.9	34.1	35.1	34.7	36.8	*	33.3	32.5	33.0	35.8	37.7	35.8	32.3
Brides	32.4	31.4	31.8	32.8	32.2	34.0	*	30.9	30.2	30.6	33.3	33.8	32.7	30.1

* Data not available for this reference period [1] Per 1,000 population.

Source: Statistics Canada, CANSIM Tables 101-1001, 101-1004, 101-1002, August 2009

MOTHER TONGUE[1]

2006 Census of Population (Top 25)

Language	Total Responses
English	18,232,200
French	6,970,405
Italian	476,905
Chinese, n.o.s.	467,235
German	466,655
Panjabi (Punjabi)	382,585
Cantonese	369,645
Spanish	362,120
Arabic	286,790
Tagalog (Pilipino, Filipino)	266,445
Portuguese	229,280
Polish	217,605
Mandarin	173,730
Urdu	156,420
Vietnamese	146,410
Ukrainian	141,805
Persian (Farsi)	138,075
Russian	136,235
Dutch	133,240
Korean	128,120
Greek	123,575
Tamil	122,020
Gujarati	86,285
Hindi	85,500
Cree	84,905

[1] Total Single and Multiple Responses

Source: Statistics Canada, 2006 Census, 97-555-X2006007

RELIGION

	2001 CENSUS		1991 CENSUS[1]	
	POPULATION	% OF TOTAL POPULATION	POPULATION	% OF TOTAL POPULATION
All religions	29,639,030	100.0	26,994,040	100.0
Catholic[2]	12,936,910	43.6	12,335,255	45.7
Protestant[3]	8,654,850	29.2	9,780,715	36.2
United Church	2,839,125	9.6	3,093,120	11.5
Anglican	2,035,500	6.9	2,188,110	8.1
Baptist	729,475	2.5	663,360	2.5
Lutheran	606,590	2.0	636,205	2.4
Protestant, n.o.s.	549,205	1.9	-- -- --	-- -- --
Presbyterian	409,830	1.4	636,295	2.4
Pentecostal	369,480	1.2	436,435	1.6
Christian, n.i.e.[4]	780,450	2.6	-- -- --	-- -- --
Eastern religions[5]	37,545	0.1	747,455	2.8
Muslim	579,640	2.0	253,260	0.9
Buddhist	300,345	1.0	163,415	0.6
Hindu	297,200	1.0	157,010	0.6
Sikh	278,410	0.9	147,440	0.5
Jewish[6]	329,995	1.1	318,070	1.2
Christian Orthodox[7]	479,620	1.6	387,390	1.4
Para-religious[8]	63,975	0.2	28,160	0.1
No religious affiliation	4,900,095	16.5	3,386,365	12.5

1. 1991 data from Statistics Canada, Religions in Canada (cat. no. 93-319-XPB), 1991 census of population.
2. Catholic includes Eastern Catholic groups in 2001, which were previously included in the "Eastern Orthodox" group in 1991.
3. in 2001, Protestant does not include "Other Christian" and "Christian n.o.s." as it did in 1999.
4. Christian, n.i.e. is separate in 2001, but was previously included in "Protestant" in 1991.
5. in 1991, "Eastern non-Christian" included Hindu, Islam, Sikh and Buddhist. They are reported separately in 2001.
6. Jewish includes Kalabarian or Kabbalah which were included in Para-religious groups in 1991.
7. was "Eastern Orthodox" in 1991. Does not include Eastern Catholic groups, which were reassigned to "Other Catholics" in 2001.
8. Religions listed in "Para-religions groups" in 1991 are listed separately in 2001, but aggregated here for comparision.

-- Not available

Source: Statistics Canada, 2001 Census of Population tabulation 97F0022XCB01001

EDUCATION STATISTICS, CANADA

Elementary and Secondary Education (public institutions)	2001/2002	2002/2003	2003/2004	2004/2005	2005/2006	2006/2007	2007/2008	2008/2009
Enrolment	5,099,142	5,076,369	5,010,649	4,976,197	4,936,313	4,885,921	4,833,402	
Graduates	288,713	307,063	285,597	288,658	285,065	293,175	302,195	
Educators	350,206	349,766	350,704	354,839	361,296	377,924	383,478	
Expenditure (current $ per student)	7,897	8,238	8,658	9,124	9,739	10,284	10,678	
University Institutions								
Enrolment[1]	886,665	936,393	993,714	1,021,521	1,050,225	1,066,905	1,072,488	1,112,370
Graduates[1]	178,098	186,462	199,137	211,902	216,240	227,085	242,787	244,380
Educators	35,112	36,054	37,203	38,574	39,615	40,567	41,304	41,955
Domestic Tuition Fees[2]	3,577	3,711	3,975	4,141	4,211	4,400	4,558	4,747
Number of Institutions (reporting based on enrolment - parent institutions)	80	81	82	83	84	84	83	81

[1] Excludes University of Regina for 2005/2006, 2006/2007, 2007/2008 and 2008/2009.

[2] Weighted average undergraduate domestic tuition fees for full-time students in current dollars

Source: Statistics Canada, Tourism and the Centre for Education Statistics Division

Selected Criminal Code Incidents, Canada, 2008 to 2009

	2008[r]		2009	
	Number	Rate[1]	Number	Rate[1]
Homicide	611	2	610	2
Assault (Levels 1, 2, & 3)	239,432	719	238,670	708
Sexual Assault (Levels 1, 2 & 3)	21,472	64	20,931	62
Robbery	32,372	97	32,239	96
Total Crimes of Violence	443,608	1,331	443,284	1,314
Breaking and Entering	211,078	633	205,710	610
Motor Vehicle Theft	125,568	377	108,172	321
Total Property Crimes	1,415,572	4,247	1,376,895	4,081
Mischief Under $5,000 (property damage)	373,064	1,119	362,767	1,075
Total Other Criminal Code Offences	345,463	1,037	341,134	1,011
TOTAL - CRIMINAL CODE OFFENCES (Excluding Traffic	2,204,643	6,615	2,161,313	6,406

[1] per 100,000 population [r] - revised 2008 data

Source: Statistics Canada, Canadian Centre for Justice Statistics, Uniform Crime Reporting Survey, Juristat Cat. No. 85-002-X, Vol. 30 No. 2, Summer 2010

Weights & Measures

THE INTERNATIONAL SYSTEM OF UNITS (SI) (BASE & SUPPLEMENTARY UNITS)

With the permission of the Canadian Standards Association, material is reproduced from CSA Standard CAN/CSA-Z234.1-89 (Canadian Metric Practice Guide), which is copyrighted by CSA, 178 Rexdale Blvd., Etobicoke, ON M9W 1R3. While use of this material has been authorized, CSA shall not be responsible for the manner in which the information is presented, nor for any interpretations thereof.

BASE UNITS

The International System of Units includes two classes of units: seven base units, and derived units. The base units are seven precisely defined units used internationally for teaching and scientific research.

SI BASE UNITS

Quantity	Name	Symbol
length	metre	m
mass	kilogram	kg
time	second	s
electric current	ampere	A
thermodynamic temperature	kelvin	K
amount of substance	mole	mol
luminous intensity	candela	cd

SI PREFIXES

Multiplying Factor	Prefix	Symbol
1 000 000 000 000 000 000 = 10^{18}	exa	E
1 000 000 000 000 000 = 10^{15}	peta	P
1 000 000 000 000 = 10^{12}	tera	T
1 000 000 000 = 10^{9}	giga	G
1 000 000 = 10^{6}	mega	M
1 000 = 10^{3}	kilo	k
100 = 10^{2}	hecto	h
10 = 10^{1}	deca	da
0.1 = 10^{-1}	deci	d
0.01 = 10^{-2}	centi	c
0.001 = 10^{-3}	milli	m
0.000 001 = 10^{-6}	micro	µ
0.000 000 001 = 10^{-9}	nano	n
0.000 000 000 001 = 10^{-12}	pico	p
0.000 000 000 000 001 = 10^{-15}	femto	f
0.000 000 000 000 000 001 = 10^{-18}	atto	a

SI Prefixes and their symbols given in the above table are used to form names and symbols of decimal multiples or sub-multiples of SI units.

SI DERIVED UNITS WITH SPECIAL NAMES

Name	Symbol	Typical Form [1]	In Base Units	Quantity
becquerel	Bq	s^{-1}	s^{-1}	activity of radionuclides
coulomb	C	s•A	s•A	quantity of electricity, electric charge
degree Celsius	°C	K	K	Celsius Temperature [2]
farad	F	C/V	$m^{-2}•kg^{-1}•s^{4}•A^{2}$	electric capacitance
gray	Gy	J/kg	$m^{2}•s^{-2}$	absorbed dose of ionizing radiation
henry	H	Wb/A	$m^{2}•kg•s^{-2}•A^{-2}$	inductance
hertz	Hz	s^{-1}	s^{-1}	frequency [3]
joule	J	N•m	$m^{2}•kg•s^{-2}$	energy, work, quantity of heat
lumen	lm	cd•sr	cd	luminous flux
lux	lx	lm/m^{2}	$m^{-2}•cd$	illuminance
newton	N	$m•kg/s^{2}$	$m•kg•s^{-2}$	force
ohm	Ω	V/A	$m^{2}•kg•s^{-3}•A^{-2}$	electric resistance
pascal	Pa	N/m^{2}	$m^{-1}•kg•s^{-2}$	pressure, stress
radian	rad	m/m	$m•m^{-1} = 1$	plane angle
siemens	S	A/V	$m^{-2}•kg^{-1}•s^{3}•A^{2}$	electric conductance
sievert	Sv	J/kg	$m^{2}•s^{-2}$	dose equivalent of ionizing radiation
steradian	sr	m^{2}/m^{2}	$m^{2}•m^{-2} = 1$	solid angle
tesla	T	Wb/m^{2}	$kg•s^{-2}•A^{-1}$	magnetic flux density
volt	V	W/A	$m^{2}•kg•s^{-3}•A^{-1}$	electric potential, potential difference, electromotive force
watt	W	J/s	$m^{2}•kg•s^{-3}$	power, radiant flux
weber	Wb	V•s	$m^{2}•kg•s^{-2}•A^{-1}$	magnetic flux

1. The formulae for derived units are not necessarily unique. For example, the volt may be defined as one joule per coulomb.
2. The Celsius temperature scale (previously called Centigrade, but renamed to avoid confusion with "centigrade", associated with the centesimal system of angular measurement) is the commonly used scale, except for certain scientific and technological purposes where the thermodynamic temperature scale is preferred. Note the use of uppercase C for Celsius.
3. The SI unit of frequency, the hertz, is one cycle per second. The reciprocal of the frequency is the period. The hertz should not be used as a measure of discrete items per unit of time, e.g. 5 boxes per second on an assembly line would not be referred to as 5 hertz, but may be referred to in terms of the reciprocal second i.e. $5s^{-1}$.

EXAMPLE OF SI DERIVED UNITS WITHOUT SPECIAL NAMES

Name	Typical Form	In Base Units	Quantity
ampere per metre	A/m	$A \cdot m^{-1}$	magnetic field strength
ampere per square metre	A/m^2	$A \cdot m^{-2}$	current density
candela per square metre	cd/m^2	$cd \cdot m^{-2}$	luminance
coulomb per cubic metre	C/m^3	$m^{-3} \cdot s \cdot A$	electric charge density
coulomb per kilogram	C/kg	$A \cdot s \cdot kg^{-1}$	exposure
coulomb per square metre	C/m^2	$m^{-2} \cdot s \cdot A$	surface density of charge, flux density
cubic metre	m^3	m^3	volume
cubic metre per kilogram	m^3/kg	$m^3 \cdot kg^{-1}$	specific volume
farad per metre	F/m	$m^{-3} \cdot kg^{-1} \cdot s^4 \cdot A^2$	permittivity
gray per second	Gy/s	$m^2 \cdot s^{-3}$	absorbed dose rate
henry per metre	H/m	$m \cdot kg \cdot s^{-2} \cdot A^{-2}$	permeability
joule per cubic metre	J/m^3	$m^{-1} \cdot kg \cdot s^{-2}$	energy density
joule per kelvin	J/K	$m^2 \cdot kg \cdot s^{-2} \cdot K^{-1}$	heat capacity, entropy
joule per kilogram kelvin	J/(kg•K)	$m^2 \cdot s^{-2} \cdot K^{-1}$	specific heat capacity, specific entropy
joule per kilogram	J/kg	$m^2 \cdot s^{-2}$	specific energy
joule per mole	J/mol	$m^2 \cdot kg \cdot s^{-2} \cdot mol^{-1}$	molar energy
joule per mole kelvin	J/(mol•K)	$m^2 \cdot kg \cdot s^{-2} \cdot K^{-1} \cdot mol^{-1}$	molar entropy, molar heat capacity
kilogram per cubic metre	kg/m^3	$kg \cdot m^{-3}$	density, mass density
metre per second	m/s	$m \cdot s^{-1}$	speed - linear
metre per second squared	m/s^2	$m \cdot s^{-2}$	acceleration - linear
mole per cubic metre	mol/m^3	$mol \cdot m^{-3}$	concentration (of amount of substance)
newton metre	N•m	$m^2 \cdot kg \cdot s^{-2}$	moment of force
newton per metre	N/m	$kg \cdot s^{-2}$	surface tension
pascal second	Pa•s	$m^{-1} \cdot kg \cdot s^{-1}$	dynamic viscosity
radian per second	rad/s	s^{-1}	speed- angular
radian per second squared	rad/s^2	s^{-2}	acceleration- angular
reciprocal metre	m^{-1}	m^{-1}	wave number*
square metre	m^2	m^2	area
square metre per second	m^2/s	$m^2 \cdot s^{-1}$	kinematic viscosity
volt per metre	V/m	$m \cdot kg \cdot s^{-3} \cdot A^{-1}$	electric field strength
watt per metre kelvin	W/(m•K)	$m \cdot kg \cdot s^{-3} \cdot K^{-1}$	thermal conductivity
watt per square metre	W/m^2	$kg \cdot s^{-3}$	heat flux density, irradiance
watt per square metre steradian	$W/(m^2 \cdot sr)$	$kg \cdot s^{-3}$	radiance
watt per steradian	W/sr	$m^2 \cdot kg \cdot s^{-3}$	radiant intensity

UNITS PERMITTED FOR USE WITH THE SI

Quantity	UNIT Name	Symbol	Definition [1]
time	minute	min	1 min = **60** s [2]
	hour	h	1 h = **3600** s [2]
	day	d	1 d = **86 400** s [2]
	year	a	
plane angle	degree	°	1° = (π/**180**) rad [3]
	minute	'	1' = (π/**10 800**) rad [3]
	second	"	1" = (π/**648 000**) rad [3]
	revolution	r	1 r = **2**π rad [4]
area	hectare	ha	1 ha = **1** hm^2 = **10 000** m^2 [5]
volume	litre	L	1 L = **1** dm^3 [6]
mass	metric ton or tonne	t	1 t = **1000** kg [7] = **1** Mg
linear density	tex	tex	1 tex = **1 x** 10^{-6} kg/m [8]
energy	electronovolt	eV	* [9]
mass of atom	unified atomic mass unit	u	* [10]
length	astronomical unit parsec	pc	* [11, 12]

1. Conversion factors that are exact are shown in boldface.
2. These sysmbols are used only in the sense of duration of time & not for expressing the time of day.
3. No space is left between these symbols & the last digit of a number. The unit "degree", with its decimal subdivisions, is used when the unit "radian" is not suitable.
4. The designations revolution per minute (r/min) and revolution per second (r/s) are widely used in connection with rotating machinery.
5. Because of the need for a unit similar to the acre, the hectare will continue to be recognized as a unit for use in surveying & agriculture.
6. The international symbol for litre is L or l. In order to avoid possible confusion with the number one, the "L" is preferred in Canada.
7. Care must be taken in the interpretation of the word "tonne" when it occurs in French text of Canadian origin, where the meaning may be a "ton of 2000 pounds".
8. The tex is used only in the textile industry.
9. One electronvolt is the kinetic energy acquired by an electron in passing through a potential difference of 1V in vacuum.
10. The unified atomic mass unit is equal to the fraction 1/12 of the mass of an atom of the nuclide ^{12}C.
11. The astronomical symbol does not have an international symbol; abbreviations are used (e.g. AU in English, UA in French). The astronomical unit of distance is the length of the radius of the unperturbed circular orbit of a body of negligible mass moving around the sun with a sidereal angular velocity of 0.017 202 098 950 radian per day of 86 400 ephemeris seconds.
12. 1 parsec (pc) is the distance at which 1 astronomical unit subtends an angle of 1 second of arc.

CONVERSION OF UNITS TO THE INTERNATIONAL SYSTEM OF UNITS (SI)

Area

1 acre	=0.404 685 6 ha
1 arpent (French measure)*	=0.341 889 4 ha
1 circular mil	=506.7 x 10^{-6} or μm^2
1 legal subdivision (40 acres)	=0.161 874 2 km^2
1 perch (French measure)*	=34.188 94 m^2
1 rood (1210 square yards)	=0.101 171 4 ha
1 section (1 mile square, 640 acres)	=2.589 988 km^2
1 square foot	=929.030 4 cm^2
1 square foot (French measure)*	=1 055.214 cm^2
1 square inch	=645.16 mm^2
1 square mile	=2.589 988 km^2
1 square yard	=0.836 127 4 m^2
1 township (36 sections)	=93.239 57 km^2

* Measures formerly used to describe certain land in the Province of Québec

Energy

1 British thermal unit (Btu) (International Table)	= 1.055 056 kJ
1 British thermal unit (Btu) (mean)	= 1.055 87 kJ
1 British thermal unit (Btu) (thermochemical)	= 1.054 35 kJ
1 British thermal unit (Btu) (39° F)	= 1.059 67 kJ
1 British thermal unit (Btu) (59° F, 15° C)	= 1.054 80 kJ
1 British thermal unit (Btu) (60.5° F)	= 1.054 615 kJ
1 Calorie (dietetic)	= 4.185 5 kJ
1 calorie (International Table)	= 4.186 8 J
1 calorie (thermochemical)	= 4.184 J
1 calorie (15° C)	= 4.185 5 J
1 calorie (15° C)	= 4.185 8 J
1 electronovolt	= 0.160 217 7 aJ
1 erg	= 0.1 μJ
1 foot poundal	= 42.140 11 mJ
1 foot pound-force	= 1.355 818 J
1 horsepower hour	= 2.684 520 MJ
1 kilowatt hour	= 3.6 MJ
1 therm	= 105.506 MJ
1 ton (nuclear equivalent of TNT)	= 4.2 GJ
1 watt hour	= 3.6 kJ
1 watt second	= 1 J

Force

1 dyne	=10 μN
1 kilogram-force	= 9.806 65 N
1 kilopond	= 9.806 65 N
1 kip (thousand pounds force)	= 4.448 222 kN
1 ounce-force	= 0.278 013 9 N
1 poundal	= 0.138 255 0 N
1 pound-force	= 4.448 222 N

Length

1 angstrom	=0.1 nm
1 arpent (French measure)*	=58.471 31 m
1 astronomical unit	=149.597 870 Gm
1 chain (66 feet)	=20.116 8 m
1 ell (45 inches)	=1.143 m
1 fathom	=1.828 8 m
1 fermi	=1 fm
1 foot	=0.304 8 m
1 foot (French measure)*	=0.324 840 6 m
1 foot (US survey, limited usage)	=0.304 800 6 m
1 furlong	=0.201 168 km
1 inch	=25.4 mm
1 league (Intl. nautical)	=5.556 km
1 league (UK nautical)	=5.559 552 km
1 league (US)	=4.828 032 km
1 light year	=9.460 528 Pm
1 link (1/100 chain)	=0.201 168 m
1 microinch	=25.4 nm
1 micron	=1 μm
1 mil (0.001 inch)	=25.4 μm
1 mile	=1.609 344 km
1 mile (Intl. nautical)	=1.852 km
1 mile (UK nautical)	=1.853 184 km
1 mile (US nautical)	=1.852 km
1 parsec	=30.856 78 Pm
1 perch	=5.029 2 m
1 perch (French measure)*	=5.847 130 8 m
1 pica (printers)	=4.217 518 mm
1 point (printers)	=0.351 459 8 mm
1 pole	=5.029 2 m
1 rod	=5.029 2 m
1 yard	=0.914 4 m

Mass

1 carat	=200 mg
1 cental (100 lb)	=45.359 237 kg
1 coal tub (100 lb, Newfoundland)	=45.359 237 kg
1 drachm (apothecary)	=3.887 935 g
1 dram (apothecary, US)	=3.887 935 g
1 dram (avoirdupois)	=1.771 845 g
1 gamma	=1 μg
1 grain	=64.798 91 mg
1 hundredweight (100 lb)	=45.359 237 kg
1 hundredweight (long 112 lb, UK)	=50.802 35 kg
1 ounce (avoirdupois)	=28.349 523 g
1 ounce (troy or apothecary)	=31.103 476 8 g
1 metric carat	=200 mg
1 pennyweight	=1.555 174 g
1 pound (avoirdupois)	=0.453 592 37 kg
1 pound (troy or apothecary)	=373.241 721 6 g
1 quarter (28 lb, UK)	=12.700 58 kg
1 scruple (apothecary, 20 grains)	=1.295 978 g
1 slug	=14.593 90 kg
1 stone (14 lb, UK)	=6.350 293 kg
1 ton (2240 lb, UK)	=1.016 046 908 8 Mg
1 ton (short, 2000 lb)	=0.907 184 74 Mg
1 unified atomic mass	=1.660 540 x 10^{-27} kg

Power

1 Btu (IT) per hour	=0.293 071 1 W
1 Btu (thermochemical) per hour	=0.292 875 1 W
1 Btu (thermochemical) per minute	=17.572 50 W
1 Btu (thermochemical) per second	=1.054 350 kW
1 foot pound-force per hour	=0.376 616 1 mW

1 foot pound-force per second	=1.355 818 W
1 horsepower (boiler)	=9.809 50 kW
1 horsepower (electric)	=746 W
1 horsepower (metric, cheval vapeur)	=735.498 75 W
1 horsepower (water)	=746.043 W
1 horsepower (550 ft•lbf/s)	=745.699 9 W

Pressure or Stress (Force per Area)

1 atmosphere, standard	=101.325 kPa (=760 torr)
1 atmosphere, technical	=98.066 5 kPa (=1 kgf/cm^2)
1 bar	=100 kPa
1 foot of water (39.2° F, 4° C)	=2.988 98 kPa
1 inch of mercury (conventional 32° F)	=3.386 39 kPa
1 inch of mercury (60° F)	=3.376 85 kPa
1 inch of mercury (68° F, 20° C)	=3.374 11 kPa
1 inch of water (conventional)	=249.088 9 Pa
1 inch of water (39.2° F, 4° C)	=249.082 Pa
1 inch of water (60° F)	=248.843 Pa
1 inch of water (68° F, 20° C)	=248.641 Pa
1 ksi (1000 lbf/in^2)	=6.894 757 MPa
1 poundal /square foot	=1.488 164 Pa
1 pound-force/square foot	=47.880 26 Pa
1 pound-force/square inch (psi)	=6.894 757 kPa
1 ton-force/square inch	=13.789 514 MPa
1 ton-force (UK)/square inch	=15.444 3 MPa
1 torr	=133.322 4 Pa

Temperature

Celsius temperature	= temperature in kelvins - 273.15
Fahrenheit temperature	= 1.8 (Celsius temperature) + 32
Fahrenheit temperature	= 1.8 (temperature in kelvins) - 459.67
Rankine temperature	= 1.8 (temperature in kelvins)

Velocity (Speed)

1 foot per hour	=84.666 67 μm/s
	=304.8 mm/h
1 foot per minute	=5.08 mm/s
	=304.8 mm/min
1 foot per second	=304.8 mm/s
1 inch per minute	=25.4 mm/min
1 inch per second	=25.4 mm/s
1 knot (International)	=1.852 km/h
	=0.514 444 4 m/s
1 knot (UK)	=1.853 184 km/h
1 mile per hour	=0.447 04 m/s
	=1.609 344 km/h
1 mile per minute	=26.822 4 m/s

Volume

1 acre foot	=1233.482 m^3
1 barrel (oil, 42 US gallons)	=0.158 987 3 m^3
1 barrel (US dry, 7056 in^3)	=0.115 627 1 m^3
1 barrel (US dry, cranberries, 5826 in^3)	=95.471 03 dm^3
1 barrel (36 UK gallons)	=0.163 659 2 m^3
1 board foot [a]	=2.359 737 dm^3
1 bushel	=36.368 72 dm^3
1 bushel (US dry, 2150.42 in^3)	=35.239 07 dm^3
1 cord (128 ft^3, 4 ft x 4 ft x 8 ft, stacked wood)	=3.624 556 m^3
1 cubic foot	=28.316 85 dm^3
1 cubic inch	=16.387 064 cm^3
1 cubic yard	=0.764 554 9 m^3
1 cunit (100 ft^3, solid wood)	=2.831 685 m^3
1 cup	=250 cm^3
1 demiard	=0.284 130 6 dm^3
1 drop (1/100 teaspoon)	=0.05 cm^3
1 fluid dram	=3.551 633 cm^3
1 fluid dram (US measure)	=3.696 691 cm^3
1 fluid ounce	=28.413 062 cm^3
1 fluid ounce (US)	=29.573 53 cm^3
1 gallon	=4.546 09 dm^3
1 gallon (US)	=3.785 412 dm^3
1 gill	=0.142 065 dm^3
1 gill (US)	=0.118 294 dm^3
1 herring barrel	=145.474 9 dm^3
1 herring tub	=72.737 44 dm^3
1 hogshead	=245.488 9 dm^3
1 lambda	=1 mm^3
1 minim	=59.193 9 mm^3
1 minim (US)	=61.611 52 mm^3
1 peck	=9.092 180 dm^3
1 peck (US dry)	=8.809 768 dm^3
1 Petrograd standard (165 ft^3, sawn timber)	=4.672 280 m^3
1 pint	=0.568 261 2 dm^3
1 pint (US dry)	=0.550 610 5 dm^3
1 pint (US liquid)	=0.473 176 5 dm^3
1 quart	=1.136 522 dm^3
1 quart (US dry)	=1.101 221 dm^3
1 quart (US liquid)	=0.946 352 9 dm^3
1 salt cart	=490.977 7 dm^3
1 salt tub	=81.829 62 dm^3
1 sand barrel	=81.829 62 dm^3
1 tablespoon	=15 cm^3
1 teaspoon	=5 cm^3
1 ton (register)	=2.831 685 m^3

a. The board foot is nominally 1x12x12 = 144 in^3. However, the actual volume of wood is about 2/3 of the nominal quality.

b. This applies to stacked wood, comprising wood, bark, & arispace, to a total volume of 128 ft^3.

c. Also referred to as the "imperial gallon".

MEASURES HAVING FORMER HOUSEHOLD USAGE

1 cup (Canadian, 8 fluid ounces)	=227 cm^3
1 cup (US, 8 fluid ounces)	=236 cm^3
1 cup (UK, 10 fluid ounces)	=284 cm^3
1 tablespoon (Canadian, 1/2 fluid ounce)	=14.21 cm^3
1 tablespoon (UK, 5/8 fluid ounce)	=17.8 cm^3
1 tablespoon (US, 1/2 fluid ounce)	=14.8 cm^3
1 teaspoon (1/6 fluid ounce)	=4.74 cm^3
1 teaspoon (UK, 5/24 fluid ounce)	=5.92 cm^3
1 teaspoon (US, 1/6 fluid ounce)	=4.93 cm^3
*1 cm^3	=1 ml

SECTION 2
ARTS & CULTURE

Many of the following categories are also represented in Section 3: Associations.

Art Galleries

National Art Galleries

National Gallery of Canada (NGC/MBAC) / Musée des beaux-arts du Canada
PO Box 427 A, 380 Sussex Dr., Ottawa, ON K1N 9N4
613-990-1985, Fax: 613-993-4385, 800-319-2787
info@gallery.ca
national.gallery.ca
The permanent collection of the National Gallery comprises paintings, sculpture, prints & drawings, photographs, film & video art from the Canadian, European, American & Asian schools. Special exhibitions as well as permanent installations of the gallery's collections are on display. The gallery also sends its exhibitions on tour across the country & participates in international exhibitions.
Marie Claire Morin, Director, Development
Mayo Graham, Director, Outreach & International Relations
Dr. David Franklin, Deputy Director/Chief Curator
Alain Boivert, Chief, Communications & Marketing
Lise Labine, Director, Human Resources
Daniel Amadei, Director, Exhibitions & Installations
Charles Hill, Curator, Canadian Art
Ann Thomas, Curator, Photographs
Graham Larkin, Curator, European Art
Stephen Gritt, Chief, Restoration & Conservation Laboratory
Murray Waddington, Chief Librarian
Serge Thériault, Chief, Publications
Louise Filiatrault, Chief, Education & Public Programs
Delphine Bishop, Chief, Collections Management
Pierre Théberge, Director O.C., C.Q.
David Baxter, Deputy Director, Administration & Finance
Joanne Charette, Director, Public Affairs
Kitty Scott, Curator, Contemporary Art

Alberta

Provincial Art Galleries

The Edmonton Art Gallery (EAG)
2 Sir Winston Churchill Sq., Edmonton, AB T5J 2C1
780-422-6223, Fax: 780-426-3105,
info@artgalleryalberta.com
www.artgalleryalberta.com
Collections include: Canadian & international contemporary & historical paintings, sculpture, photography, video & graphic art. Research fields: Western Canadian art, historical & contemporary art; painting; sculpture; photography; graphics. Activities: Guided tours; lectures; films; gallery talks; art rental & sales gallery; studio art classes for children & adults; program workshops & seminars
Catherine Crowston, Deputy Director & Senior Curator
Ron Gregg, Director, Administration
Tony Luppino, Executive Director
Catrin Owen, Director, Development & Marketing

Other Art Galleries in Alberta

***Banff:* Walter Phillips Gallery (WPG)**
The Banff Centre, PO Box 1020 14, 107 Tunnel Mountain Dr., Banff, AB T1L 1H5
403-762-6281, Fax: 403-762-6659,
walter_phillipsgallery@banffcentre.ca
www.banffcentre.ca/WPG
Contemporary, national & international fine arts; open year round
Anthony Kiendl, Director
Sylvie Gilbert, Senior Curator

***Brocket:* Oldman River Cultural Centre**
PO Box 70, Brocket, AB T0K 0H0
403-965-3939,
oldmancc@telusplanet.net
Aboriginal history
Jo-Ann Yellow Horn, Director

***Calgary:* Art Gallery of Calgary**
117 - 8th Ave. SW, Calgary, AB T2P 1B4
403-770-1350, Fax: 403-264-8077,
artinfo@artgallerycalgary.org
www.artgallerycalgary.org
Non-profit public gallery, exhibiting works by contemporary Canadian artists; travelling exhibitions & education programs
Valerie Cooper, President and CEO

***Calgary:* Illingworth Kerr Gallery (IKG)**
Alberta College of Art & Design, 1407 - 14 Ave. NW, Calgary, AB T2N 4R3
403-284-7680, Fax: 403-289-6682,
gallery@acad.ab.ca
www.acad.ca
Contemporary art exhibitions, publications, lectures, screenings & related events
Ron Moppett, Director/Curator
Richard Gordon, Curator

***Calgary:* Leighton Foundation Collection**
Box 9, Site 31, RR#8, Calgary, AB T2J 2T9
403-931-3633, Fax: 403-931-3633,
www.sharecom.ca/leighton
A.C. Leighton's paintings; open year round
Lorna Johnson, Director

***Edmonton:* Front Gallery**
12312 Jasper Ave., Edmonton, AB T5N 3K5
780-488-2952,

***Edmonton:* Latitude 53**
10248 - 106 St., Edmonton, AB T5J 1H5
780-423-5353, Fax: 780-424-9117,
info@latitude53.org
www.latitude53.org
Contemporary artistic projects, experimental cultural development; performance art; literary projects; interdisciplinary art
Todd Janes, Executive Director

***Edmonton:* West End Gallery**
12308 Jasper Ave., Edmonton, AB T5N 3K5
780-488-4892, Fax: 780-488-4893,
info@westendgalleryltd.com
www.westendgalleryltd.com
Fine art gallery representing Canadian paintings & sculpture; the largest representation of glass artists in Canada
Daniel Hudon
Lana Hudon

***Grande Prairie:* The Prairie Art Gallery**
#103, 9856-97 Ave., Grande Prairie, AB T8V 7K2
780-532-8111, Fax: 780-539-9522,
info@prariegallery.com
www.prairiegallery.com
Public art gallery. The Gallery's collection currently stands at approximately 600 works of art, almost exclusively created in Alberta in the midto late 20th Century.
Robert Steven, Curator

***Lethbridge:* Southern Alberta Art Gallery (SAAG)**
601 - 3 Ave. South, Lethbridge, AB T1J 0H4
403-327-8770, Fax: 403-328-3913,
info@saag.ca
www.saag.ca
Fosters the work of contemporary visual artists who challenge the boundaries of their discipline & advance their work in a larger public realm
Joan Stebbins, Curator
Marilyn Smith, Director

***Lethbridge:* University of Lethbridge Art Gallery**
W600, Centre for the Arts, 4401 University Dr., Lethbridge, AB T1K 3M4
403-329-2666, Fax: 403-382-7115,
www.uleth.ca/artgallery/
Josephine Mills, Director & Curator

British Columbia

Provincial Art Galleries

Vancouver Art Gallery
750 Hornby St., Vancouver, BC V6Z 2H7
604-662-4700, Fax: 604-682-1086,
www.vanartgallery.bc.ca
Other contact information: Info Line: 604/662-4719
Largest gallery in western Canada; presents major exhibitions from contemporary art to historical masters; founded in 1931, has over 7,800 works in its collection, 41,400 sq. ft. of exhibition space & is located in the former provincial courthouse in downtown Vancouver; collection includes acclaimed Canadian artists such as Stan Douglas, Jeff Wall & Ian Wallace; also holds the world's most signifi
Kathleen Bartels, Director
Paul Larocque, Associate Director

Other Art Galleries in British Columbia

***Burnaby:* The Simon Fraser University Gallery**
AQ 3004, Simon Fraser University, 8888 University Dr., Burnaby, BC V5A 1S6
604-291-4266, Fax: 604-291-3029,
gallery@sfu.ca
www.sfu.ca/gallery
Hosts six or seven exhibitions a year, both historical & contemporary, covering the full range of media; serves the SFU community directly by providing an occasional platform for student, staff & faculty work to be shown; The Gallery also administers the Teck Gallery at the SFU Vancouver Campus, a small space used to show work that deals with social & environmental issues
Bill Jeffries, Director/Curator
Veronika Klaptoez, Coordinator

***Burnaby:* Burnaby Art Gallery**
***Also known as:* Visual Arts Burnaby**
6344 Deer Lake Ave., Burnaby, BC V5G 2J3
604-205-7332, Fax: 604-205-7339,
darrin.martens@city.burnaby.bc.ca
www.city.burnaby.bc.ca
Services include educational programs for children, adults & seniors; community projects & exhibitions in libraries & recreational centres; school programs support the exhibitions & take works of art into the schools
Darrin Martens, Director/Curator

***Campbell River:* Campbell River & District Public Art Gallery**
1235 Shoppers Row, Campbell River, BC V9W 2C7
250-287-2261, Fax: 250-287-2268,
art.gallery@crcn.net
crartgal.ca
Contemporary work from both local & visiting artists; classes, lectures & workshops throughout the year; open Tue.-Sat., 12-5; June & Aug. Mon.-Sat., 10-5
Jeanette Taylor, Director
Manon Staiger, Curator

***Castlegar:* Kootenay Gallery of Art, History & Science**
***Also known as:* Kootenay Gallery**
120 Heritage Way, Castlegar, BC V1N 4M5
250-365-3337, Fax: 250-365-3822,
info@kootenaygallery.com
www.kootenaygallery.com
Exhibits on art, history & science, from international to local sources; offers workshops, performances, lectures & classes; gift shop
Val Field, Executive Director
Marilyn Luscombe, Chair

***Dawson Creek:* Dawson Creek Art Gallery**
#101, 816 Alaska Ave., Dawson Creek, BC V1G 4T6
250-782-2601, Fax: 250-782-8801,
www.dcartgallery.ca
Open year round
Ellen Corea, Curator

***Grand Forks:* Grand Forks Art Gallery**
PO Box 2140, Grand Forks, BC V0H 1H0
250-442-2211, Fax: 250-442-0099,
gfagchin@direct.ca
www.galleries.bc.ca/grandforks
Historical & contemporary works by established & emerging regional, national & international artists
Paul Crawford, Director

***Hope:* John Weaver Sculpture Museum**
PO Box 1723, 19225 Silverhope Rd., Hope, BC V0X 1L0
604-869-5312, Fax: 604-869-5117,
johnweaver@johnweaverfinearts.com
Founded: 1977 John Weaver's work of bronzes based on historical, anthropological, & charity-work themes can be viewed by those wishing to learn about bronze sculpture & by those who wish to be commissioners of work; collection of over 60 years of work
Henry Weaver, Director
Sara M. Lesztak, Chief Information Officer & Director
Elizabeth Lesztak, Director
Richard Roles, Computer Expert

***Kamloops:* Kamloops Art Gallery**
#101, 465 Victoria St., Kamloops, BC V2C 2A9
250-377-2400, Fax: 250-828-0662,
kamloopsartgallery@kag.bc.ca
www.kag.bc.ca
Changing exhibits of contemporary & historical art; permanent collection of Canadian art
Jann L.M. Bailey, Director

***Kaslo:* Langham Cultural Centre**
***Parent:* The Langham Cultural Society**
PO Box 1000, Kaslo, BC V0G 1M0
250-353-2661, Fax: 250-353-2671,
langham@netidea.com
www.thelangham.ca
Founded: 1975 Art exhibits; theatre; music; workshops; The Japanese Canadian Museum. Street address: 447 A Ave., Kaslo, BC
Alice Windsor, Executive Director

***Kelowna:* Kelowna Art Gallery**
1315 Water St., Kelowna, BC V1Y 9R3
250-762-2226, Fax: 250-762-9875,
kelowna.artgallery@shaw.ca
www.kelownaartgallery.com
Historical & contemporary fine art; extensive education programs; open year round
Dona Moore, Executive Director
Ms Liz Wylie, Curator

***Maple Ridge:* Maple Ridge Art Gallery Society**
11944 Haney Pl., Maple Ridge, BC V2X 6G1
604-467-5855, Fax: 604-466-5852,
gallery@mrag.ca
www.theactmapleridge.org
Exhibition of local, amateur & professional artists; art rental program for patrons
Ms Laura Moodie, Curator

***Nakusp:* Bonnington Arts Centre**
6th Ave. West & 4th St. North, Nakusp, BC V0G 1R0
250-265-4234, Fax: 250-265-3808,
Open Sept. - June

***Nanaimo:* Nanaimo Art Gallery**
c/o Malaspina University College, 900 - Fifth St., Nanaimo, BC V9R 5S5
250-740-6350, Fax: 250-740-6475,
Info@nanaimogallery.ca
www.nanaimogallery.ca
Celebrating art on the west coast; art central & sales program; gift shop full of elegant & eclectic gifts; inspiring & thought provoking exhibitions
Chris Kuderle, Administrative Director
Gregory Ball, Curator

***New Westminster:* Amelia Douglas Gallery**
PO Box 2503, New Westminster, BC V3L 5B2
604-527-5465, Fax: 604-527-5528,
lmccallum@douglas.bc.ca
www.douglas.bc.ca/artscomm
A non-profit organization run by members of the Arts Exhibition Committee at Douglas College; mandate is to feature new & established BC artists & to enhance the educational offerings of the College
Lorna McCallum, Representative

***North Vancouver:* Presentation House Museum Galleries**
209 West 4th St., North Vancouver, BC V7M 1H8
604-987-5612, Fax: 604-987-5609,
www.presentationhousegall.com
Celebrates & preserves North Vancouver's social, industrial & cultural history
Robin Inglis, Director

***North Vancouver:* Seymour Art Gallery**
4360 Gallant Ave., North Vancouver, BC V7G 1L2
604-924-1378, Fax: 604-924-3786,
seymourartgallery@shawcable.com
seymourartgallery.com
Open year round
Jacquie Morgan, Director/Curator

***Osoyoos:* Osoyoos Art Gallery**
PO Box 256, 8713 Main St., Osoyoos, BC V0H 1V0
250-495-2800,
Ivana Zita, Director

***Penticton:* Penticton Art Gallery (AGSO)**
199 Marina Way, Penticton, BC V2A 1H3
250-493-2928, Fax: 250-493-3992,
agso@shawbiz.ca
www.galleries.bc.ca/agso
Founded: 1972 The Penticton Art Gallery offers in-house & touring exhibitions from local, regional & national sources.

***Port Alberni:* Rollin Art Centre**
***Also known as:* Community Arts Council of the Alberni Valley**
3061 - 8th Ave., Port Alberni, BC V9Y 2K5
250-724-3412, Fax: 250-724-3472,
communityarts@alberni.net
www.alberni.net/communityarts
Gareth Flostrand, Arts Administrator
Liisa McInnis, Co-ordinator, Gallery & Gift Shop

***Prince George:* Two Rivers Gallery**
Prince George Art Gallery Association, 725 Civic Plaza, Prince George, BC V2L 5T1
250-614-7800, Fax: 250-563-3211, 888-221-1155
art@tworiversartgallery.com
www.tworiversartgallery.com
The Two Rivers Gallery is a vital centre for visual art in Prince George and the central interior of British Columbia, Canada. It is run by the nonprofit Prince George Regional Art Gallery Association with a mission to: encourage lifelong learning through the arts, create an environment for vigorous artistic and cultural expression, provide opportunities for diverse experiences through participation and exhibition.
George Harris, Curator
Peter L. Thompson, Managing Director

***Prince Rupert:* CHTK**
***Also known as:* Standard Radio Inc.**
#212, 215 Cow Bay Rd., Prince Rupert, BC V8J 1A2
250-624-9111, Fax: 250-624-3100, 800-668-6330
smenhinick@srt.ca
wwww.themix.com
Brian Langston

***Qualicum Beach:* The Old School House Arts Centre (TOSH)**
PO Box 791, 122 Fern Rd. West, Qualicum Beach, BC V9K 1T2
250-752-6133, Fax: 250-752-2600, 800-661-3211
qbtosh@shaw.ca
www.theoldschoolhouse.org
Fifteen resident artists; 3 exhibition galleries; concert series; classrooms; gift shop
Greg Sabo, President

***Richmond:* Richmond Art Gallery**
#180, 7700 Minoru Gate, Richmond, BC V6Y 1R9
604-247-8300, Fax: 604-247-8301,
gallery@richmond.ca
www.richmondartgallery.org
Presents a diverse program of exhibitions, workshops, lectures & special events, as well as outreach programs which focus on contemporary art & art issues
Corinne Currie, Director/Curator

***Smithers:* Smithers Gallery Association & Public Art Gallery**
Central Park Bldg., PO Box 122, Smithers, BC V0J 2N0
250-847-3898,
Public gallery, admission by donation; monthly exhibition rotation; workshops & artcamps for young & old, all artisan levels & mediums; call for a current listing
Sue Brookes, President
Pam Allen, Secretary

***South Surrey:* Arnold Mikelson Mind & Matter Gallery**
13743 -16 Ave., South Surrey, BC V4A 1P7
604-536-6460,
mindandmatterart@aol.com
www.mindandmatterart.com
Wood sculptures of the late Arnold Mikelson
Mary Mikelson, Owner/Director

***Vancouver:* Charles H. Scott Gallery**
Emily Carr College of Art & Design, 1399 Johnston St., Granville Island, Vancouver, BC V6H 3R9
604-844-3809, Fax: 604-844-3801,
scottgal@eciad.ca
www.eciad.ca/www/whatson/chs_index.html
Greg Bellerby, Curator

***Vancouver:* Circle Craft Gallery**
1-1666 Johnston St., Net Loft Granville Island, Vancouver, BC V6H 3S2
604-669-8021, Fax: 604-669-8585,
shop@circlecraft.net
www.circlecraft.net
Features over 200 works of BC artists
Ron Kong, Store Manager

***Vancouver:* Contemporary Art Gallery**
555 Nelson St., Vancouver, BC V6B 6R5
604-681-2700, Fax: 604-683-2710,
info@contemporaryartgallery.ca
www.contemporaryartgallery.ca
Promotes knowledge & understanding of contemporary visual art through: exhibitions that address current issues in contemporary art; educational programs in the form of artist & curator talks, student tours, high school projects, public symposia; publications; visiting artist/curator programs; information & resource services; The City of Vancouver Art Collection of 3,000 works of art
Christina Ritchie, Director/Curator

***Vancouver:* grunt gallery**
#116, 350 - East 2nd Ave., Vancouver, BC V5T 4R8
604-875-9516, Fax: 604-877-0073,
grunt@telus.net
www.grunt.bc.ca
Open Wed. - Sat., 12-6
Glenn Alteen, Director

***Vancouver:* Heffel Gallery Limited**
2247 Granville St., Vancouver, BC V6H 3G1
604-732-6505, Fax: 604-732-4245,
mail@heffel.com
www.heffel.com
Fine art auction house.
Mr David Heffel, Director

***Vancouver:* Marion Scott Gallery**
308 Water St., Vancouver, BC V6B 1B6
604-685-1934, Fax: 604-685-1890,
art@marionscottgallery.com
www.marionscottgallery.com
Established in 1975, & one of the leading galleries dealing with Canadian Inuit art
Judy Kardosh, Director

***Vancouver:* Morris & Helen Belkin Art Gallery**
University of British Columbia, 1825 Main Mall, Vancouver, BC V6T 1Z2
604-822-2759, Fax: 604-822-6689,
belkin@interchange.ubc.ca
www.belkin-gallery.ubc.ca
Specializes in exhibiting contemporary work by national & international artists; programming includes exhibitions, artists' talks, publications & collaborative projects with other galleries/organizations; masters program in Critical Curatorial Studies; archival collections focus on Vancouver Canadian avant garde in 1960s-70s
Scott Watson, Director/Curator

***Vancouver:* Exposure Gallery (VAPA)**
***Also known as:* Vancouver Association for Photographic Art**
851 Beatty St., Vancouver, BC V6B 2M6
604-688-9501,
exposuregallery@shaw.ca
www.exposure-gallery.com
Photographic & photo-based medium
Ian McGuffie, President/Curator

***Vancouver:* Wickaninnish Gallery**
#14, 1166 Johnston St., Vancouver, BC V6H 3S2
604-681-1057,
info@wickaninnishgallery.com
www.wickaninnishgallery.com
Patricia Rivard, Owner

***Vernon:* Vernon Public Art Gallery (VPAG)**
3228 - 31st Ave., Vernon, BC V1T 2H3
250-545-3173, Fax: 250-545-9096,
vernonartgallery@shawbiz.ca
www.galleries.bc.ca/vernon
Community programming; local, regional, national & international exhibitions; gift shop; art & video rentals; group tours
Paula Burns Resch, Executive Director
Marion Morrison, President

***Victoria:* Art Gallery of Greater Victoria (AGGV)**
1040 Moss St., Victoria, BC V8V 4P1
250-384-4101, Fax: 250-361-3995,
aggv@aggv.bc.ca
aggv.bc.ca
Canadiana 1860 to present; work of Emily Carr; one of Canada's finest collections of Asian art
Donna McAlear, Director/CEO

***Victoria:* Maltwood Art Museum & Gallery (MAMAG)**
PO Box 3025 CSC, Victoria, BC V8W 3P2
250-721-8298, Fax: 250-721-8997,
msegger@uvic.ca
www.maltwood.uvic.ca
Named after the collection of fine, decorative & applied arts of English sculptress & antiquarian Katherine Emma Maltwood, F.R.S.A. (1878-1961); over 6,000 items representing the work of contemporary Western Canadian artists
Martin Segger, Director

***Wells:* Island Mountain Gallery**
PO Box 65, Wells, BC V0K 2R0
250-994-3466, Fax: 250-994-3433, 800-442-2787
info@imarts.com
www.imarts.com
Provides visual, literary & performing arts instruction; presents contemporary art exhibitions; concert venue in summer; also holds workshops
Julie Fowler, Artistic Director

***Williams Lake:* Stationhouse Gallery & Gift Shop**
1 North Mackenzie Ave., Williams Lake, BC V2G 1N4
250-392-6113, Fax: 250-392-6184,
manager@stationhousegallery.com
www.stationhousegallery.com
Monthly exhibitions; gift shop
Diane Koebel, Gallery Manager

Manitoba

Provincial Art Galleries

The Winnipeg Art Gallery (WAG)
300 Memorial Blvd., Winnipeg, MB R3C 1V1
204-786-6641, Fax: 204-788-4998,
inquiries@wag.mb.ca
www.wag.mb.ca
Founded in 1912, the WAG is Western Canada's oldest civic art gallery. With over 23,000 works in its collection, the WAG features 9 galleries of contemporary & historical works (fine arts, decorative arts & photography) by Manitoba, Canadian & international artists. A highlight is the Gort Collection of Northern Gothic & Renaissance paintings & altar panels. A portion of the Inuit art collection (
Eva Rempel, Deputy Director

Pierre Arpin, Director

Other Art Galleries in Manitoba

Brandon: **The Art Gallery of Southwestern Manitoba / Le Musé D'art du Sud-ouest du Manitoba**
Also known as: **Art Gallery of Southwestern Manitoba**
#2, 710 Rosser Ave., Brandon, MB R7A 0K9
204-727-1036, Fax: 204-726-8139,
info@agsm.ca
www.agsm.ca
Contemporary Manitoban art; approximately 16 exhibitions a year; open year round
Jenny Western, Curator, Contemporary & Aboriginal Art

Saint Boniface: **Centre culturel franco-manitobain (CCFM)**
340, boul Provencher, Saint Boniface, MB R2H 0G7
204-233-8972, Fax: 204-233-3324,
ccfm@ccfm.mb.ca
www.ccfm.mb.ca
Le Centre culturel franco-manitobain a un rôle de premier plan comme maison de la culture et carrefour de la vie culturelle et artistique en français à Winnipeg et au Manitoba/The Centre culturel franco-manitobain is the focal point of French cultural life in Winnipeg & Manitoba
Agnès Champagne, Executive Director

Winnipeg: **aceartinc.**
290 McDermot Ave., 2nd Fl., Winnipeg, MB R3B 0T2
204-944-9763, Fax: 204-944-9101,
gallery@aceart.org
www.aceart.org
aceartinc. is an artist-run centre dedicated to the development, exhibition & dissemination of contemporary art by cultural producers; dedicated to cultural diversity
Theo Sims, Programmer

Winnipeg: **Gallery 1.1.1.**
211 FitzGerald Bldg., School of Art, University of Manitoba, Winnipeg, MB R3T 2N2
204-474-9322, Fax: 204-474-7605,
umanitoba.ca/schools/art/galleryoneoneone/info111.html
Prof. Cliff Eyland, Gallery Director, eylandc@cc.umanitoba.ca
Robert Epp, Coordinator, epp@ms.umanitoba.ca

Winnipeg: **University of Winnipeg Fine Art Collection & Gallery 1C03**
515 Portage Ave., Winnipeg, MB R3B 2E9
204-786-9253, Fax: 204-774-4134,
j.gibson@uwinnipeg.ca
gallery1c03.uwinnipeg.ca
19th & 20th century paintings, drawings, prints, photographs & sculptures; open year round

Winnipeg: **Upstairs Gallery**
266 Edmonton St., Winnipeg, MB R3C 1R9
204-943-2734, Fax: 204-943-7726,
upstairs@mts.net
Inuit Contemporary & early 20th-century Canadian art; prints, sculptures, wall-hangings & drawings
Faye Settler, Director

New Brunswick

Provincial Art Galleries

Owens Art Gallery
c/o Mount Allison University, 61 York St., Sackville, NB E4L 1E1
506-364-2574, Fax: 506-364-2575,
owens@mta.ca
www.mta.ca/owens
Permanent collection of over 2500 works, dating from the 18th century; 30 exhibitions yearly
Gemey Kelly, Director

Other Art Galleries in New Brunswick

Campbellton: **Galerie Restigouche Gallery**
PO Box 674, 39 Andrew St., Campbellton, NB E3N 3H1
506-753-5750, Fax: 506-759-9601,
rgaleri@nbnet.nb.ca
Charline Lanteigne, Director

Edmundston: **Gallerie Colline**
195, boul Hébert, Edmundston, NB E3V 2S8
506-737-5282, Fax: 506-737-5373,
galerie@umce.ca
www.umce.ca/galerie
Trente ans d'expositions d'artistes amateurs et professionnels qui ont aidé à l'appréciation de l'art dans notre milieu.
Ms Elisabeth Hubault, Présidente

Fredericton: **The Beaverbrook Art Gallery / La galerie d'art Beaverbrook**
PO Box 605, 703 Queen St., Fredericton, NB E3B 5A6
506-458-8545, Fax: 506-459-7450, 888-458-8545
emailbag@beaverbrookartgallery.org
www.beaverbrookartgallery.org
Founded: 1959 Atlantic Canadian art & historical British art; open year round
Bernard Riordon, Director/CEO O.C., briordon@beaverbrookartgallery.org, 506-458-2030

Fredericton: **Gallery Connexion**
Justice Bldg. Annex, PO Box 696, 453 Queen St., Fredericton, NB E3B 5B4
506-454-1433, Fax: 506-454-1401,
connex@nbnet.nb.ca
galleryconnexion.ca
Artist-run centre, non-profit & non commercial; gallery exists for the purpose of exhibiting, supporting, & promoting the development & understanding of all forms of contemporary art practice of local, national & international significance
Ms Meredith Snider, Director

Fredericton: **UNB Art Centre**
Memorial Hall, PO Box 4400, University of New Brunswick, Fredericton, NB E3B 5A3
506-453-4623, Fax: 506-453-5012,
mem@unb.ca
www.unb.ca/web/FineArts
Historical & contemporary exhibitions; interpretive programs; Atlantic art collection
Marie Maltais, Director

Moncton: **Atelier IMAGO**
#35, 140 Botsford St., Moncton, NB E1C 4X5
506-388-1431, Fax: 506-857-2064,
imago@nb.aibn.com
www.atelierimago.com
Artist-run not-for-profit printmaking studio

Moncton: **Galerie d'art de l'Université de Moncton (GAUM)**
Also known as: **Galerie d'art Louise-et-Reuben-Cohen**
Pavillon Clément-Cormier, Centre universitaire de Moncton, 10, av Université, Moncton, NB E1A 3E9
506-858-4088, Fax: 506-858-4043,
galrc@umoncton.ca
www.umoncton.ca/gaum/
Founded: 1964 La Galerie a pour mission encourager la créativité des artistes acadiens/acadiennes, et collectioner et documenter les oeuvres d'art; centre de documentation; programmation.
Luc A. Charette, Directeur-conservateur

Moncton: **Galerie Sans Nom Coop Ltée**
Also known as: **GSN Coopérative**
Centre Culturel Aberdeen, #16, 140 Botsford St., Moncton, NB E1C 4X4
506-854-5381, Fax: 506-857-2064,
ash@fundy.net
www.galeriesansnom.org
Galerie Sans Nom (GSN) is a non-profit, artist-run centre involved in the promotion, production & exhibition of contemporary art. GSN is a venue for creative expression of the artistic community & acting as a vital communication vehicle, provides an impetus for innovation & creativity
Nisk Imbeault, Directrice
André Gorin, Président

Moncton: **Galerie Georges-Goguen SRC**
Also known as: **Mini Galerie Radio-Canada**
CP 950, 250, av Université, Moncton, NB E1C 8N8
506-382-8326, Fax: 506-853-6739,
ghg@nbnet.nb.ca
Primarily promotes the works of Atlantic artists
Georges Goguen

Sackville: **Struts Gallery & Faucet Media Arts Centre: An Artist-Run Centre**
7 Lorne St., Sackville, NB E4L 3Z6
506-536-1211, Fax: 506-536-4565,
info@strutsgallery.ca
www.strutsgallery.ca
Presenting local, regional & national contemporary artist-initiated activities: expositions, performances, demonstrations, workshops, symposia, residencies & digital video production facilities
Paul Henderson, Faucet Manager
John Murchie, Coordinator

Saint John: **City of Saint John Gallery**
Saint John Arts Centre, 20 Hazen Ave., Saint John, NB E2L 3G8
506-649-6040, Fax: 506-632-6118,
info@saintjohnartscentre.com
www.saintjohnartscentre.com
First municipally funded art gallery in Atlantic Canada; features monthly exhibitions of local & regional art works
Bernard J. Cormier

St Andrews: **Sunbury Shores Arts & Nature Centre**
139 Water St., St Andrews, NB E5B 1A7
506-529-3386, Fax: 506-529-4779,
info@sunburyshores.org
www.sunburyshores.org
Provides facilities for the study, practice & appreciation of the art, crafts & environmental sciences; stresses the aesthetic appreciation of nature & the importance of its use
Debbie Nielsen, Director

Newfoundland & Labrador

Provincial Art Galleries

The Rooms Provincial Art Gallery
The Rooms Corporation of Newfoundland & Labrador, PO Box 1800 C, 9 Bonaventure Ave., St. John's, NL A1C 5P9
709-757-8040, Fax: 709-757-8041,
www.therooms.ca/artgallery/
Regularly changing exhibitions of all media, chiefly contemporary Canadian, with some international, historic Canadian & Newfoundland folk art & traditional crafts; permanent collection of contemporary Canadian art in many media, with strong holdings of Newfoundland work; art slide library. Extensive public programming & special projects with emphasis on collaboration with professional artists & p
Dr. Shauna McCabe, Director

Other Art Galleries in Newfoundland & Labrador

Corner Brook: **Sir Wilfred Grenfell College Art Gallery (SWGC)**
Memorial University of Newfoundland, Corner Brook, NL A2H 6P9
709-637-6209, Fax: 709-637-6203,
gtuttle@swgc.ca
www.swgc.ca/artgallery
Contemporary art
Gail Tuttle, Director

St. John's: **Eastern Edge Art Gallery**
72 Harbour Dr., PO Box 2641 C, St. John's, NL A1C 6K1
709-739-1882, Fax: 709-739-1866,
egallery@nfld.net
www.easternedge.ca
Not-for-profit, artist-run centre dedicated to exhibiting contemporary art in diverse media; exhibitions include work by Newfoundland artists & artists from the rest of Canada
Michelle Bush, Director

Northwest Territories

Territorial Art Galleries

Gallery of the Midnight Sun
5005 Bryson Dr., Yellowknife, NT X1A 2A3
867-873-8064, Fax: 867-873-8065,
galleryofthemidnightsun@canada.com
www.gallerymidnightsun.com
NWT's largest selection of Inuit & Dene arts & crafts
Lisa Seagrave, Contact

Nova Scotia

Provincial Art Galleries

Art Gallery of Nova Scotia (AGNS)
PO Box 2262, 1723 Hollis St., Halifax, NS B3J 3C8
902-424-7542, Fax: 902-424-7359,
spaldijj@gov.ns.ca
www.agns.gov.ns.ca
Housed in 1868 heritage building. The Gallery has over 13,000 peices in its permanent collection.
Jeffrey Spalding, Director/Chief Curator

Other Art Galleries in Nova Scotia

Chéticamp: **Les Trois Pignon**
La Société St-Pierre, CP 430, 15584 Cabot Trail, Chéticamp, NS B0E 1H0
902-224-2642, Fax: 902-224-1579,
lestroispignons@ns.sympatico.ca
www.lestroispignons.com
Les tapisseries du Dr. Elizabeth LeFort ainsi que d'autres tapis historiques de la région; le musée d'antiquité à Marguerite Gallant est attaché sur la Galerie aussi que centre généalogique
Lisette Aucoin-Bourgeois, Director

Halifax: **Centre for Art Tapes**
#207, 5600 Sackville St., Halifax, NS B3J 1L2
902-420-4002, Fax: 902-420-4581,
www.centreforarttapes.ca
An artist-run centre that facilitates & supports emerging, intermediate & established artists working with electronic media,

such as video, audio & new media; strives to provide production facilities, ongoing programming & training to a diverse membership whose creative abilities contribute to social & artistic goals
Ilan Sandler, Executive Director,
cfat.operations@ns.sympatico.ca

***Halifax:* Dalhousie Art Gallery (DAG)**
6101 University Ave., Halifax, NS B3H 3J5
902-494-2403, Fax: 902-423-0591,
art.gallery@Dal.ca
www.artgallery.Dal.ca
The Dalhousie Art Gallery is a public art gallery, an academic support unit within the educational and research context of Dalhousie University, and a cultural resource for the whole community.
Susan Gibson Garvey, Director/Curator

***Halifax:* Eye Level Gallery**
2128 Gottingen St., Halifax, NS B3K 3B3
902-425-6412, Fax: 902-425-0019,
director@eyelevelgallery.ca
www.eyelevelgallery.ca
Eryn Foster, Director

***Halifax:* MSVU Art Gallery, Mount Saint Vincent University**
166 Bedford Hwy., Halifax, NS B3M 2J6
902-457-6160, Fax: 902-457-2447,
info@msvuart.ca
msvuart.ca
Open daily except Mondays; exhibition program emphasizes women as cultural subjects & producers, new Nova Scotia artists, & themes relevant to the university's academic programs; admission free
Stephen Fisher, Gallery Technician
Ingrid Jenkner, Director

***Halifax:* Nova Scotia Centre for Craft & Design & Maray E. Black Gallery (NSCCD)**
1683 Barrington St., Halifax, NS B3J 1Z9
902-424-4062, Fax: 902-492-2526,
info@craft-design.ns.ca
www.craft-design.gov.ns.ca
Develops & promotes crafts & design in Nova Scotia; includes the Mary E. Black Gallery, a craft showroom, an info. centre, & 5 studios; open year round
Susan MacAlpine Foshay, Director

***Halifax:* Saint Mary's University Art Gallery**
Saint Mary's University, Halifax, NS B3H 3C3
902-420-5445, Fax: 902-420-5060,
gallery@smu.ca
www.smu.ca/administration/externalaffairs/artgallery
Contemporary visual arts by artists within & outside the region; lectures, publications & performing arts program; permanent collection of over 1,800 works
Robin Metcalfe, Director/Curator

***Lunenburg:* Lunenburg Art Gallery (L.A.G.S)**
PO Box 1418, 79-81 Pelham St., Lunenburg, NS B0J 2C0
902-640-4044, Fax: 902-640-3035,
lag@eastlink.ca
www.lunenburgartgallery.com
Founded: 1972 The gallery promotes the works of local, provincial & international artists, sponsors workshops & raises funds; houses the Meldrum collection by the late Earl Bailly; month-long solo exhibitions & ongoing Members Gallery; open seasonally: Mar.-Oct., Tues-Sat 10-5 & Sun 1-5.
Doug Cooke, President
Jim Hannaford, Treasurer
Christine Hurlburt, Gallery Attendant

***Pictou:* Hector Exhibit Centre**
***Also known as:* Hector Centre**
PO Box 1210, 86 Haliburton Rd., Pictou, NS B0K 1H0
902-485-4563, Fax: 902-485-5213,
pcghs@gov.ns.ca
www.rootsweb.com/~nspcghs/
Genealogical & historical archives for Pictou County - census records, cemetery records, shipping lists, newspapers, etc.; local historical, cultural, genealogical & craft exhibits
Katherine Chaisson, Site Manager

***Sydney:* Cape Breton University Art Gallery**
PO Box 5300, Sydney, NS B1P 6L2
902-563-1342, Fax: 902-563-1142,
suzanne_crowdis@captebretonu.ca
capebretonartgallery.blogspot.com;
www.capebretonu.ca/artgalley/
First & only full-time public art gallery on Cape Breton Island; acquires & presents art with emphasis on contemporary Canadian works & the artistic traditions of Cape Breton Island; offers educational & research facilities; a major cultural resource within the educational & research context of the university
Suzanne A. Crowdis, Director/Curator

***Wolfville:* Acadia University Art Gallery**
Highland Ave., Wolfville, NS B4P 2R6
902-585-1373, Fax: 902-585-1070,
fran.kruschen@acadiau.ca
ace.acadiau.ca/arts/artgal/home.htm
The University Gallery serves both as a public gallery and as a teaching facility within Acadia's Faculty of Arts. Its purpose in the community and on the campus is to enrich visual experience through showcasing original works of historical or contemporary importance. The Gallery looks after Acadia's collection of art.
Franziska Kruschen, Director

Ontario

Provincial Art Galleries

Art Gallery of Hamilton (AGH)
123 King St. West, Hamilton, ON L8P 4S8
905-527-6610, Fax: 905-577-6940,
larissa@artgalleryofhamilton.com
www.artgalleryofhamilton.com
Collection of 8,000 art objects; holds one of Canada's most comprehensive collections of Canadian historical, modernist & contemporary art; British, American & European works
Louise Dompierre, President/CEO

Art Gallery of Ontario (AGO)
317 Dundas St. West, Toronto, ON M5T 1G4
416-979-6648, Fax: 416-204-2713, 877-225-4246
ticketing@ago.net
www.ago.net
Visit the AGO, located in the heart of Toronto, for an experience of art that includes European Old Masters, Group of Seven, & Canadian & international contemporary works — plus the world's largest public collection of sculptures by Henry Moore. Now in the midst of a Frank Gehry-designed building expansion, the AGO is poised to become a preeminent art museum of our time
Dennis Reid, Chief Curator
Matthew Teitelbaum, Director/CEO

Art Gallery of Windsor (AGW)
401 Riverside Dr. West, Windsor, ON N9A 7J1
519-977-0013, Fax: 519-977-0776,
email@artgalleryofwindsor.com
www.artgalleryofwindsor.com
One of the larger, non-government run galleries in Ontario; focus is on Canadian art in an international context; permanent collection of 2,500 paintings & sculptures; resource centre & gift shop; closed Mon., Tue.
Merry Ellen Scully Mosna, President

McMichael Canadian Art Collection
10365 Islington Ave., Kleinburg, ON L0J 1C0
905-893-1121, Fax: 905-893-0692, 888-213-1121
info@mcmichael.com
www.mcmichael.com
Founded: 1965 The collection features works of art created by First Nations & Inuit artists, the artists of the Group of Seven & their contemporaries, & other artists who have contributed to the development of Canadian art. Comprehensive education program at kindergarten, elementary & secondary school levels; guided group tours by appt.; extension program & temporary exhibition program. Also programs for adults
Thomas Smart, Executive Director/CEO
Mary Benvenuto, CFO

Other Art Galleries in Ontario

***Bancroft:* The Art Gallery of Bancroft**
PO Box 1360, 8 Hastings Heritage Way, Bancroft, ON K0L 1C0
613-332-1542, Fax: 613-332-2119,
artgallerybancroftont@bellnet.ca
www.algonquinarts.ca
Local & other Ontario artists; gift shop for area artists only; open year round
Diana Gurley, Director
Mr Wayne Link, Curator

***Barrie:* MacLaren Art Centre**
37 Mulcaster St., Barrie, ON L4M 3M2
705-721-9696, Fax: 705-735-6935,
maclaren@maclarenart.com
www.maclarenart.com
Open Tue.-Fri. 10-5, Sat. 10-4
John Lister, Interim Director

***Bracebridge:* Chapel Gallery**
c/o Muskoka Arts & Crafts Inc., PO Box 376, 15 King St., Bracebridge, ON P1L 1T7
705-645-5501, Fax: 705-645-0385,
info@muskokaartsandcrafts.com
www.muskokaartsandcrafts.com
Open Tue.-Sat.
Elene J. Freer, Curator

***Bracebridge:* Ziska Gallery Muskoka**
RR#1, Bracebridge, ON P1L 1W8
705-645-2587,
The beauty of nature in paintings & sculpture; open June to Oct.
Jack MacCallum, Curator

***Brampton:* Art Gallery of Peel**
Peel Heritage Complex, 9 Wellington St. East, Brampton, ON L6W 1Y1
905-791-4055, Fax: 905-451-4931,
david.somers@peelregion.ca
www.peelheritagecomplex.org
Located within a cluster of 19th century buildings; features the works of local artists in Peel & contemporary art from across Canada; collection of over 1,500 works consists of contemporary & historic Canadian works with a special emphasis on artists from Peel
David Somers, Curator

***Brantford:* Glenhyrst Art Gallery of Brant**
20 Ava Rd., Brantford, ON N3T 5G9
519-756-5932, Fax: 519-756-5910,
info@glenhyrstartgallery.ca
www.glenhyrst.ca
Permanent collection comprises contemporary works on paper & paintings by Robert Reginald Whale & his descendants; offers a rotating schedule of art exhibitions, an art rental & sales showroom, giftshop & a variety of classes & programmes
James M. Stowe, President, Board of Govenors

***Burlington:* Burlington Art Centre (BAC)**
1333 Lakeshore Rd., Burlington, ON L7S 1A9
905-632-7796, Fax: 905-632-0278,
info@BurlingtonArtCentre.on.ca
www.BurlingtonArtCentre.on.ca
Exhibitions of regional & nationally recognized Canadian artists; a permanent collection of contemporary Canadian ceramic art & a gallery shop, art rental & sales & studios; open daily
Ian D. Ross, Executive Director MFA

***Caledon East:* Yaneff International Art**
18949 Centreville CRK. Rd., Caledon East, ON L0N 1E6
905-584-9398, Fax: 905-584-9569,
posters@yaneff.com
www.yaneff.com
Specializes in rare, 19th-century, 20th century & modern posters online
Chris Yaneff, Director R.C.A., R.GDC, F.GDC
Greg Yaneff, Director/Curator

***Cambridge:* Cambridge Galleries**
Queen's Square, 1 North Square, Cambridge, ON N1S 2K6
519-621-0460, Fax: 519-621-2080,
mmisner@cambridge.galleries.ca
www.cambridgegalleries.ca
Exhibitions offered at 3 locations within Cambridge reflect a range of local & international developments in contemporary & historical visual arts & architecture; collection of contemporary Canadian fibre art; studio courses for all ages; concerts; Canadian international film series
Mary Misner, Gallery Director
Ivan Jurakic, Curator
Sascha Hastings, Curator, Design at Riverside

***Chatham:* Thames Art Gallery (TAG)**
Chatham Cultural Centre, 75 William St. North, Chatham, ON N7M 4L4
519-360-1998, Fax: 519-354-4170,
carll@chatham-kent.ca
www.chatham-kent.ca/ccc
Historical & contemporary artwork by local, national & international artists; hosts 12-15 exhibitions a year; guided tours available with advanced bookings; art lectures & workshops for children & adults; open daily 1-5; admission by donation
Carl L. Lavoy, Curator

***Cobourg:* Art Gallery of Northumberland**
55 King St. West, Cobourg, ON K9A 2M2
416-372-0333, Fax: 416-372-1587,
agn@eagle.ca
www.artgalleryofnorthumberland.com
Maintains a permanent collection of more than 600 works of art; changing exhibitions are displayed throughout the year; lectures; education trips; workshops & special events
Dorette E. Carter, Director/Curator

***Cornwall:* Cornwall Regional Art Gallery (CRAG) / Galerie régionale des arts de Cornwall**
168 Pitt St., Cornwall, ON K6J 6P4
613-938-7387, Fax: 613-938-9619,
info@cornwallregionalartgallery.ca
www.cornwallregionalartgallery.ca
Promotes and stimulates interest in and the study of the visual arts; advances knowledge and appreciation of the visual arts;

provides improved opportunities for Canadian artistic talent; advances the development of the visualarts in Canada.

Curve Lake: **Whetung Craft Centre & Art Gallery**
Curve Lake, ON K0L 1R0
705-657-3661, Fax: 705-657-3412,
mwhetung@whetung.com
www.whetung.com
Authentic works by Indian artists from across Canada.
Michael Whetung, Owner

Durham: **Durham Art Gallery**
PO Box 1021, Durham, ON N0G 1R0
519-369-3692, Fax: 519-369-3120,
info@durhamart.on.ca
www.durhamart.on.ca
Located at 251 George St. East
Ilse Gassinger, Executive Director

Etobicoke: **The Art Gallery, Neilson Park Creative Centre**
56 Neilson Dr., Etobicoke, ON M9C 1V7
416-622-5294, Fax: 416-622-0892,
info@neilsonparkcreativecentre.com
www.neilsonparkcreativecentre.com
Provides a community focus for creative visual arts; variety of exhibitions with strong emphasis on local & contemporary artists
Denise Rainville, Executive Director

Grimsby: **Grimsby Public Art Gallery**
18 Carnegie Lane, Grimsby, ON L3M 1Y1
905-945-3246, Fax: 905-945-1789,
gpag@town.grimsby.on.ca
www.grimsby.ca
Permanent collection of 1,000+ works; contemporary exhibitions & programmes year round
Rhona Wenger, Director

Guelph: **Macdonald Stewart Art Centre (MSAC)**
358 Gordon St., Guelph, ON N1G 1Y1
519-837-0010, Fax: 519-767-2661,
info@msac.ca
www.uoguelph.ca/msac
Permanent collection of over 4,000 works; contemporary Inuit drawings & the Donald Forster Sculpture Park
Judith Nasby, Director

Haileybury: **Temiskaming Art Gallery**
Hailebury Public Library Bldg., PO Box 1090, 545 Lakeshore Rd., Haileybury, ON P0J 1K0
705-672-3706, Fax: 705-672-5966,
tag@ntl.sympatico.ca
www.museumnorth.org/temiskaming_art_gallery
Public gallery; open year round
Maureen Steward, Director/Curator

Haliburton: **Rails End Gallery & Arts Centre**
PO Box 912, 23 York St., Haliburton, ON K0M 1S0
705-457-2330, Fax: 705-457-2338,
hhgfa.railsend@on.aibn.com
www.railsendgallery.com
Open year round
Saskiatent Rees, Executive Director

Kingston: **Agnes Etherington Art Centre (AEAC) / Centre d'art Agnes Etherington**
Queen's University, Kingston, ON K7L 3N6
613-533-2190, Fax: 613-533-6765,
aeac@post.queensu.ca
www.queensu.ca/ageth/
Contemporary & historical art collections & exhibitions; gallery shop, art rental & sales gallery, facility rentals; open year round
Janet M. Brooke, Director

Kingston: **St. Lawrence College Art Gallery**
Portsmouth Ave., Kingston, ON K7L 5A6

D. Gordon, Director

Kitchener: **Homer Watson House & Gallery**
1754 Old Mill Rd., Kitchener, ON N2P 1H7
519-748-4377, Fax: 519-748-6808,
programs@homerwatson.on.ca
www.homerwatson.on.ca
Open Jan. - Dec.
Faith Hieblinger, Director/Curator

Kitchener: **Kitchener-Waterloo Art Gallery (KWAG)**
101 Queen St. North, Kitchener, ON N2H 6P7
519-579-5860, Fax: 519-578-0740,
mail@kwag.on.ca
www.kwag.ca
Founded: 1956 Open year round; Monday - Wednesday: 9:30-5:00; Thursday: 9:30-9:00; Saturday: 10:00-5:00; Sunday 1:00-5:00.
Alf Bogusky, Director General
Caroline Oliver, Director, Development & Marketing

Leamington: **Leamington Art Centre**
72 Talbot St. West, Leamington, ON N8H 1M4
519-326-2711, Fax: 519-326-6491,
artcentr@mnsi.net
www.leamingtonartscentre.com
The Leamington Arts Centre, run by the South Essex Arts Association, is a charitable, not-for-profit organization. Its purpose is to serve the community through arts & culture. The Leamington Arts Centre includes a main gallery, which exhibits the work of local artists. Heinz Memorabilia explains the history of the Heinz Co.. The Centre also features the Marine Heritage Interpretive Centre, Signature Gifts, & several educational programs throughout the year for both adults & children.
Tamsen Dippel, Gallery Coordinator

Lindsay: **The Lindsay Gallery**
190 Kent St. West, Lindsay, ON K9V 2Y6
705-324-1780, Fax: 705-324-1780,
lind.gall@on.aibn.com
www.thelindsaygallery.com
Not-for-profit gallery offering regular exhibitions, art classes & a boutique
Margot J. Fawcett, Marketing Co-chair
Janet Smith, Chair

London: **McIntosh Gallery**
The University of Western Ontario, London, ON N6A 3K7
519-661-3181, Fax: 519-661-3059,
akenned4@uwo.ca
www.mcintoshgallery.ca
Exhibitions featuring local, national, & international artists working in various media; exhibitions change every 6 weeks & are accompanied by art-related videos, films & lectures; art collection & gallery's records, some artist archives & periodical library available as resources to students for research purposes; open 6 days/week
Arlene Kennedy, Director

Minden: **Agnes Jamieson Gallery**
PO Box 648, 176 Bobcaygeon Rd. North, Minden, ON K0M 2K0
705-286-3763, Fax: 705-286-4917,
gallery@minden.on.ca
Laurie Carmount, Administrator

Mississauga: **Art Gallery of Mississauga (AGM)**
300 City Centre Dr., Mississauga, ON L5B 3C1
905-896-5088, Fax: 905-615-4167,
fred.troughton@mississauga.ca
www.artgalleryofmississauga.com
A public art gallery providing state of the art exhibitions by local, national & international artists; exhibits change every 7 weeks; admission is free; open Mon.-Fri. 9 am to 5 pm, weekends: noon to 4 pm
Fred Troughton, Executive Director

Mississauga: **Blackwood Gallery**
University of Toronto, 3359 Mississauga Rd. North, Mississauga, ON L5L 1C6
905-828-3789, Fax: 905-569-4262,
blackwood.gallery@utoronto.ca
www.blackwoodgallery.ca
Founded: 1992 Presents exhibitions of contemporary art in all media.
Carmen Victor, Curatorial Assistant
Christof Migone, Director/Curator

Mississauga: **Harbour Gallery**
1697 Lakeshore Rd. West, Mississauga, ON L5J 1J4
905-822-5495, Fax: 905-822-5578,
info@harbourgallery.com
www.harbourgallery.com
Rotating collection of over 30 accredited Canadian artists in a variety of mediums.
Jacqueline Bryant, Director

Niagara on the Lake: **RiverBrink: Home of the Weir Collection**
116 Queenston St., RR#1, Niagara on the Lake, ON L0S 1J0
905-262-4510, Fax: 905-262-4477,
weirlib@becon.org
www.riverbrink.org
Open Victoria Day - Thanksgiving
Karin Jahnke-Haslam, Managing Director
Gary Essar, Curator/Artistic Director

North Bay: **W.K.P. Kennedy Gallery**
150 Main St. East, North Bay, ON P1B 1A8
705-474-1944, Fax: 705-474-8431,
gallery@capitolcentre.ca
www.kennedygallery.org
A changing program of historical & contemporary visual art; free
Dermot Wilson, Director/Curator

North Bay: **White Water Gallery**
PO Box 1491, 147 Worthington St. East, North Bay, ON P1B 8K6
705-476-2444, Fax: 705-476-9243,
info@whitewatergallery.com
whitewatergallery.com
Artist-run centre for contemporary art

Oakville: **Oakville Galleries**
1306 Lakeshore Rd. East, Oakville, ON L6J 1L6
905-844-4402, Fax: 905-844-7968,
info@oakvillegalleries.com
www.oakvillegalleries.com
Contemporary art gallery with 2 exhibition spaces: Oakville Galleries at Centennial Square, 120 Navy St. & Oakville Galleries in Gairloch Gardens, 1306 Lakeshore Rd. East
Francine Périnet, Director
Marnie Fleming, Curator, Contemporary Art

Orillia: **Orillia Museum of Art & History**
30 Peter St. South, Orillia, ON L3V 5A9
705-326-2159, Fax: 705-326-7828,
info@orilliamuseum.org
www.orilliamuseum.org
Public art gallery & museum; gift shop; open Mon. - Sat.
Sim Salata, Director/Curator

Orton: **Burdette Gallery Ltd.**
111212 - 11th Line, East Garafraxa, RR#2, Orton, ON L0N 1N0
519-928-5547, Fax: 519-928-2349,
art@burdettegallery.com
www.burdettegallery.com
The Gallery represents approximately 100 artists who are locally, nationally, and internationally renowned.
Dr. George R. Cormack, Owner

Oshawa: **The Robert McLaughlin Gallery**
Civic Centre, 72 Queen St., Oshawa, ON L1H 3Z3
905-576-3000, Fax: 905-576-9774,
communications@rmg.on.ca
www.rmg.on.ca
Permanent exhibitions include masterpieces of Canadian Art: Emily Carr, members of the Group of Seven, Painters Eleven
David Aurandt, Executive Director

Oshweken: **Two Turtle Iroquois Fine Art Gallery**
Middleport Plaza, 1180 Hwy. 54, Oshweken, ON N3W 2G9
519-751-2774, 877-264-6651
arnold@twoturtle.com
www.twoturtle.com
Showcasing the art of the Hodenosaunee and Arnold Jacobs.
Arnold Aron Jacobs, Owner

Ottawa: **Carleton University Art Gallery (CUAG)**
Carleton University, St. Patrick's Bldg., 1125 Colonel By Dr., Ottawa, ON K1S 5B6
613-520-2120, Fax: 613-520-4409,
www.carleton.ca/gallery
27,000 works in contemporary Canadian art, European prints & drawings from the 16th to 19th centuries, Inuit prints & sculpture
Sandra Dyck, Curator

Ottawa: **Artists' Centre d'Artistes Ottawa Inc.**
Also known as: **Gallery 101**
236 Nepean St., Ottawa, ON K2P 0B8
613-230-2799, Fax: 613-230-3253,
info@gallery101.org
www.gallery101.org
A non-profit artist operated centre dedicated to the professional presentation & circulation of visual & media arts; solo & curated group exhibitions by local Canadian & international contemporary artists
Leanne L'Hirondelle, Director

Owen Sound: **Tom Thomson Memorial Art Gallery**
840 First Ave. West, Owen Sound, ON N4K 4K4
519-376-1932, Fax: 519-376-3037,
ttmag@city.owen-sound.on.ca
www.tomthomson.org
Public art gallery featuring an extensive collection of Canadian art, historical & contemporary, with a focus on Thomson & the Group of Seven; full range of educational activities including lectures, workshops, & tours; gallery shop
Stuart Reid, Director/Curator

Peterborough: **Art Gallery of Peterborough**
250 Crescent St., Peterborough, ON K9J 2G1
705-743-9179, Fax: 705-743-8168,
gallery@agp.on.ca
www.agp.on.ca
Public art gallery with changing exhibitions
Curtis Joseph Collins, Director
Pamela Edmonds, Curator/Arts Coordinator

Peterborough: **Artspace**
PO Box 1748, 378 Aylmer St. North, Peterborough, ON K9J 7X6

705-748-3883, Fax: 705-748-3224,
info@artspace-arc.org
www.artspace-arc.org
Committed to supporting the growth & development of contemporary artists & related-art practices; dedicated to artistic freedom & exploration
Iga Janik, Director

***Peterborough:* The Russell Gallery of Fine Art**
165 King St., Peterborough, ON K9J 2R8
705-743-0151,
info@russellgallery.com
www.russellgallery.com
Representing leading Canadian & international contemporary artists
Bruce Rapp, Co-Director
Sally Rapp, Co-Director

***St Catharines:* Rodman Hall Arts Centre**
109 St. Paul Cres., St Catharines, ON L2S 1M3
905-684-2925, Fax: 905-682-4733,
rodmanhall@brocku.ca
www.brocku.ca/rodmanhall/
Collection of about 1000 works of art, contemporary & historical, majority by Canadian artists; closed Mon.
Gordon Hatt, Director

***St Thomas:* St Thomas-Elgin Public Art Centre**
301 Talbot St., St Thomas, ON N5P 1B5
519-631-4040, Fax: 519-631-4057,
info@stepac.ca
www.stepac.ca
Promotion of visual arts by a permanent collection of over 800 artworks, exhibitions by current artists, & a variety of art education programs; volunteers & new members welcome; facility rental available; open Tue. - Sun.
David Bobier, Executive Director
Barbara Hodge, Admin. Asst/Volunteer Coordinator
Sherri Howard, Education Coordinator/Events Coordinator

***Sarnia:* Gallery Lambton**
Bayside Mall, 150 Christina St. North, Sarnia, ON N7T 2M6
519-336-8127, Fax: 519-336-8128,
david.talyor@county-lambton.on.ca
www.lclmg.org
Other contact information:
holly.rutherford@county-lambton.on.ca
Exhibitions of contemporary art, featuring some of the best artists working in Ontario today, many with national & international reputations; collection contains paintings by the Group of Seven, & others, which are important to Canadian art history & are considered national treasures; wide range of changing exhibitions, tours for adults & school groups, education services, artist talks, films, pub
David G. Taylor, Curator

***Sault Ste Marie:* Art Gallery of Algoma**
10 East St., Sault Ste Marie, ON P6A 3C3
705-949-9067, Fax: 705-949-6261,
aga@shaw.ca
www.artgalleryofalgoma.on.ca
Dedicated to cultivating & advancing the awareness of visual arts in Sault Ste Marie & the district of Algoma
Michael Burtch, Director/Curator

***Simcoe:* Norfolk Arts Centre**
Lynnwood National Historic Site, PO Box 67, 21 Lynnwood Ave., Simcoe, ON N3Y 4K8
519-428-0540, Fax: 519-428-0549,
artscentre@norfolkcounty.on.ca
www.norfolkcounty.on.ca
Norfolk county's only arts centre, located in downtown Simcoe; programming includes exhibitions, kids studio, adult art workshops, Lynnwood's Film Simcoe, annual drive-thru art gallery exhibition
Robert Missen, Curator/Director

***Stouffville:* The Latcham Gallery**
PO Box 3, 6240 Main St., Stouffville, ON L4A 7Z4
905-640-8954, Fax: 905-640-6246,
Public art gallery
Roz Pritchard, Director
Maura Broadhurst, Curator

***Stratford:* Gallery Stratford**
54 Romeo St. South, Stratford, ON N5A 4S9
519-271-5271, Fax: 519-271-1642,
clee@gallerystratford.on.ca
www.gallerystratford.on.ca
A non-profit, public art gallery open year round; contemporary, historical, local, national & international artists are highlighted annually in the heritage building; offers educational programs, workshops & fundraisers
Jennifer Rudder, Executive Director

***Sudbury:* Art Gallery of Sudbury / Galerie d'art de Sudbury**
251 John St., Sudbury, ON P3E 1P9
705-675-4871, Fax: 705-674-3065,
gallery@artsudbury.org
www.artsudbury.org
Historical & contemporary Canadian art; open Tue.-Sat. 10-5, Sun. 12-5
Celeste Scopelites, Director/Curator

***Thunder Bay:* Thunder Bay Art Gallery**
***Also known as:* Thunder Bay National Exhibition Centre & Centre for Indian Art**
PO Box 10193 F, 1080 Keewatin St., Thunder Bay, ON P7B 6T7
807-577-6427, Fax: 807-577-3781,
info@tbag.ca
www.tbag.ca
Collection & exhibition of contemporary First Nations art, regional & international exhibits
Sharon Godwin, Director
Glenn Allison, Curator

***Toronto:* Academy of Spherical Arts**
38 Hanna Ave., Toronto, ON M6K 1X5
416-532-2782, Fax: 416-532-3075, 866-532-2782
info@sphericalarts.com
www.sphericalarts.com
Four room gallery displaying Canada's oldest collection of billiard tables, as well as billiard related accessories. Also hosts yearly art exhibitions for emerging Canadian artists, and includes Canadian art in its permanent collection.
Rick Williams, Founder

***Toronto:* Angell Gallery**
890 Queen St. West, Toronto, ON M6J 1G3
416-530-0444,
info@angellgallery.com
www.angellgallery.com
Wed.-Sat. 12-5
Jamie Angell, Director

***Toronto:* Annex Art Centre**
1073 Bathurst St., Toronto, ON M5R 3G8
416-516-0110,
info@annexartcentre.com
www.annexartcentre.com
An art gallery and teaching studio located in Toronto's Annex. We offer visual art, drama for kids, teens, and adults.

***Toronto:* Art Dialogue Gallery**
#501, 900 Yonge St., Toronto, ON M4W 3P5
416-928-5904, Fax: 416-928-6515,
Provides educated information & guidance in acquiring fine art; exhibitions & consultations for the display of artwork; lectures on various topics of contemporary art
Luciana Benzi, Director

***Toronto:* Art Gallery of York University**
Accolade East, 4700 Keele St., Toronto, ON M3J 1P3
416-736-5169, Fax: 416-736-5985,
AGYU@yorku.ca
www.yorku.ca/agyu
Devoted to the presentation of innovative contemporary art; aims to situate Canadian art within an international context & to introduce Canadian audiences to important artists working abroad
Philip Monk, Director

***Toronto:* Art Metropole**
***Also known as:* Art Official Inc.**
788 King St. West, Toronto, ON M5V 1N6
416-703-4400, Fax: 416-703-4404,
info@artmetropole.com
www.artmetropole.com
Specializes in contemporary art in multiple formats; offers artists' products for sale on premises & through web site as well as publishes, promotes, exhibits & distributes artists' products in various formats
Ann Dean, Director

***Toronto:* The Bluffs Gallery**
Scarborough Arts Council, 1859 Kingston Rd., Toronto, ON M1N 1T3
416-698-7322, Fax: 416-698-7972,
info@scarborougharts.com
www.scarborougharts.com
Founded: 1979 The Bluffs Gallery is dedicated to the exhibition & sale of artwork by Scarborough Arts Council members. The Gallery offers solo & group exhibitions of all arts media, special events, workshops, & city-wide programs to promote the arts. Open Monday - Saturday; Closed on long weekends.
Tim Whalley, Executive Director

***Toronto:* Corkin Shopland Gallery**
Bldg. 61, 55 Mill St., Toronto, ON M5A 3C4
416-979-1980, Fax: 416-979-7018,
info@corkinshopland.com
www.corkinshopland.com
Eclectic works by contemporary artists in all media
Jane Corkin

***Toronto:* Creative Spirit Art Centre (CSAC)**
PO Box 16 P, 122 Wells St., Toronto, ON M5S 2S6
416-588-8801, Fax: 416-588-8966,
csac@creativespirit.on.ca
creativespirit.on.ca
Founded: 1992 Arts & Disabilities - Public Art Gallery/Studio, resource and information centre. Monthly exhibitions - Special area of collection of Art Brut, Outsider Art, Folk Art - Integrated exhibitions of Art produced by Artists with disabilities and Artists without disabilities. Closed August; Closed between Dec. 24, 2009 and Jan. 4, 2010
Ellen Anderson, Director

***Toronto:* Drabinsky Gallery**
122 Scollard St., Toronto, ON M5R 1G2
416-324-5766, Fax: 416-324-5770,
info@drabinskygallery.com
www.drabinskygallery.com
Presents & promotes contemporary Canadian art in all media, representing the estate of Harold Town; located in Toronto's Yorkville district
Linda Book, Director
Garth Drabinsky, Principal

***Toronto:* Edward Day Gallery**
952 Queen St. West, Toronto, ON M6J 1G8
416-921-6540, Fax: 416-921-6624,
eddaygal.toronto@sympatico.ca
www.edwarddaygallery.com
Mary Sue Rankin, Director

***Toronto:* Gabor Mezei Studio**
587 Markham St., Toronto, ON M6G 2L7
416-534-9800,
www.gallerygabor.com
Other contact information: Mobile: 416/319-0914
Small art gallery showing mainly the owner's work & a small selection of Canadian & international artists; approximately four exhibitions per year; by appt.
Gabor P. Mezei, Director/Curator

***Toronto:* Gallery Arcturus**
80 Gerrard St. East, Toronto, ON M5B 1G6
416-977-1077, Fax: 416-977-1066,
ob-art@arcturus.ca
www.arcturus.ca
Contemporary art gallery.
Cathy Stilo, Curator

***Toronto:* Glendon Gallery / Galerie Glendon**
Glendon College, York University, 2275 Bayview Ave., Toronto, ON M4N 3M6
416-487-6721, Fax: 416-487-6779,
gallery@glendon.yorku.ca
www.glendon.yorku.ca/gallery
University-affiliated public art gallery that focuses on contemporary Canadian art of merit with an added interest in francophone artistic expression; literature in French & English; guided tours & lectures
Martine Rheault, Director, 416/487-6859

***Toronto:* The Isaacs/Innuit Gallery**
PO Box 84, 401 Richmond St. West, Toronto, ON M5V 3A8
416-921-9985, Fax: 416-921-9530,
Contemporary Inuit art, Inuit antiquities & early North American Indian art; contemporary Canadian artists
A. Isaacs

***Toronto:* Joseph D. Carrier Art Gallery**
Columbus Centre, 901 Lawrence Ave. West, Toronto, ON M6A 1C3
416-789-7011, Fax: 416-789-3951,
jdcarrier@villacharities.com
www.villacharities.com
Flavio Belli, Curator/Director

***Toronto:* The Justina M. Barnicke Gallery**
Hart House, University of Toronto, 7 Hart House Circle, Toronto, ON M5S 3H3
416-978-8398, Fax: 416-978-8387,
barbara.fischer@utoronto.ca
www.utoronto.ca/gallery/
Each year, 8-10 exhibitions are mounted featuring contemporary Canadian artists as well as historical exhibitions
Barbara Fischer, Director/Curator

***Toronto:* Knight Galleries International**
472 Coldstream Ave., Toronto, ON M5N 1Y5
416-923-0836, Fax: 416-923-8985,
knight@knightgall.com
www.knightgall.com
Julian Liknaitzky, President

***Toronto:* Koffler Gallery/Koffler Centre of the Arts**
4588 Bathurst St., Toronto, ON M2R 1W6

416-636-1880, Fax: 416-636-5813,
koffler@bjcc.ca
www.bjcc.ca
The Koffler Gallery maintains a year-round exhibition program of contemporary art; programming emphasizes new work by mid-career & more senior Canadian artists, & within this context, work of special interest to the Jewish community
Carolyn Bell Farrell, Senior Curator
Diane Uslaner, Director

***Toronto:* The Market Gallery**
South St. Lawrence Market, 95 Front St. East, Toronto, ON M5E 1C2
416-392-7604, Fax: 416-392-0572,
marketgallery@toronto.ca
www.toronto.ca/culture/the_market_gallery.htm
A focus on the art & history of Toronto
Pamela Wachna, Curator

***Toronto:* Mercer Union, A Centre for Contemporary Visual Art**
37 Lisgar St., Toronto, ON M6J 3T3
416-536-1519,
info@mercerunion.org
www.mercerunion.org
An artist-run centre dedicated to the existence of contemporary art; provides a forum for the production & exhibition of Canadian & international conceptually & aesthetically engaging art & related cultural practices; pursues primary concerns through critical activities that include exhibitions, lectures, screenings, performances, publications, events & special projects; non-profit, charitable org
Dave Dyment, Co-Director

***Toronto:* Museum of Contemporary Canadian Art**
952 Queen St. West, Toronto, ON M6J 1G8
416-395-0067, Fax: 416-395-7598,
mocca@toronto.ca
www.mocca.toronto.ca
Contemporary Canadian artists' works, including traditional & new media; six exhibitions a year showcase established & emerging artists from across Canada; exhibition based programming; open Tue.-Sun., 11-6; free admission; groups & tours by appt.
David Liss, Director/Curator

***Toronto:* Odon Wagner Gallery**
196 Davenport Rd., Toronto, ON M5R 1J2
416-962-0438, Fax: 416-962-1581, 800-551-2465
info@odonwagnergallery.com
www.odonwagnergallery.com
Fine art gallery featuring masterpieces of past & present; sale & purchase of quality paintings, restoration, appraisal, consultation & framing services
Odon Wagner, Director

***Toronto:* Odon Wagner Gallery & Odon Wagner Contemporary**
172 Davenport Rd., Toronto, ON M5R 1J2
416-962-0438, Fax: 416-962-1581, 800-551-2465
info@odonwagnergallery.com
www.odonwagnergallery.com
Features an ensemble of historic, modern & contemporary painting, representing the many periods & schools from the last three centuries
Odon Wagner, Director

***Toronto:* Olga Korper Gallery**
17 Morrow Ave., Toronto, ON M6R 2H9
416-538-8220, Fax: 416-538-8772,
info@olgakorpergallery.com
www.olgakorpergallery.com
Established in 1973, the gallery is committed to the exhibition & promotion of Canadian & international contemporary art
Olga Korper, Director

***Toronto:* A Space Gallery**
#110, 401 Richmond St. West, Toronto, ON M5V 3A8
416-979-9633, Fax: 416-979-9683,
info@aspacegallery.org
www.aspacegallery.org
A Space has a thirty year history of multi-disciplinary artist-run activity. The organizations' mandate encompasses the investigation, presentation and interpretation of contemporary art forms, different disciplines and theories. A Space maintains a politically engaged issue oriented programming that is inclusive of a wide range of media, disciplines and views.
Michelle LaVallee, Curatorial Resident

***Toronto:* Susan Hobbs Gallery**
137 Tecumseth St., Toronto, ON M6J 2H2
416-504-3699, Fax: 416-504-8064,
info@susanhobbs.com
www.susanhobbs.com
Exhibition & sales of contemporary Canadian art; artists represented include Ian Carr-Harris, Magdalen Celestino, Robin Collyer, Max Dean, Brian Groombridge, Scott Lyall, Arnaud Maggs, Liz Magor, Sandra Meigs, Colette Whiten, Robert Wiens, Shirley Wiitasalo, & Kevin Yates
Susan Hobbs

***Toronto:* Gallery TPW**
***Also known as:* Toronto Photographers Workshop**
56 Ossington Ave., Toronto, ON M6J 2Y7
416-645-1066, Fax: 416-645-1681,
info@gallerytp.ca
gallerytpw.ca
Contemporary photography by Canadian & international artists.
Gary Hall, Executive Director
Kim Simon, Programming Director

***Toronto:* University of Toronto Art Centre**
University College, 15 King's College Circle, Toronto, ON M5S 3H7
416-978-1838, Fax: 416-971-2059,
niamh.olaoghaire@utoronto.ca
www.utoronto.ca/artcentre
Housing galleries with selections from university collections as well as a schedule of changing exhibitions
Dr. Niamh O'Laoghaire, Director, 416/946-7015
Dr. Dawn Cain, Malcove Curator, 416/978-6596
Liz Wylie, University of Toronto Art Curator, 416/946-3029

***Toronto:* Ydessa Hendeles Art Foundation (YHAF)**
778 King St. West, PO Box 757 F, Toronto, ON M4Y 2N6
416-413-9400, Fax: 416-969-9889,
ydessa@yhaf.org
Contemporary art collection; features work of international artists; works on display include paintings, photography, and multimedia projects.
Ydessa Hendeles

***Toronto:* York Quay Gallery**
Harbourfront Centre, 235 Queen's Quay West, Toronto, ON M5J 2G8
416-973-4000, Fax: 416-973-4859,
info@harbourfront.on.ca
www.harbourfront.on.ca
Contemporary art.

***Toronto:* YYZ Artists' Outlet**
#140, 401 Richmond St. West, Toronto, ON M5V 3A8
416-598-4546, Fax: 416-598-2282,
yyz@yyzartistsoutlet.org
www.yyzartistsoutlet.org
YYZ is dedicated to the support of work by contemporary artists working in all media, and to the provision of a venue for the exhibition of this work through on-going programs in both visual and time-based arts - video, film and performance.
Gregory Elgstrand, Director of Programming
Jeffrey Matt, Director of Operations

***Waterloo:* Canadian Clay & Glass Gallery / Galerie Canadienne de la Céramique et du Verre**
25 Caroline St. North, Waterloo, ON N2L 2Y5
519-746-1882, Fax: 519-746-6396,
info@canadianclayandglass.ca
www.canadianclayandglass.ca
Exhibits contemporary artworks executed in clay, glass, stained glass & enamel for public education & enjoyment
Robert Achtemichuk, Director

***Waterloo:* Robert Langen Gallery**
Wilfrid Laurier University, Waterloo, ON N2L 3C5
519-884-1970, Fax: 519-888-9721,
sluke@wlu.ca
www.wlu.ca
The University's visual arts centre, since 1989; provides knowledge, stewardship, appreciation & enjoyment of Canadian art & culture to members of the Laurier community & the community at large
Suzanne Luke, Curator/Art Gallery Coordinator
Deborah Currie, Manager, Cultural Affairs

***Waterloo:* University of Waterloo Art Gallery**
University of Waterloo, 200 University Ave. West., ECH, Waterloo, ON N2L 3G1
519-888-4567, Fax: 519-746-4982,
cpodedwo@uwaterloo.ca
www.artgallery.uwaterloo.ca
Produces exhibitions of contemporary Canadian art in all media; holds a collection of contemporary Canadian art since 1960; open Tue. - Sat. during academic year at two sites: Modern Languages Building & the main gallery in East Campus Hall
Andrew Hunter, Director/Curator
Bruce Taylor, Chair, Board

***Whitby:* The Station Gallery**
1450 Henry St., Whitby, ON L1N 0A8
905-668-4185, Fax: 905-668-1934,
stationgallery@whitby.ca
www.whitbystationgallery.com
The gallery's Permanent Collection exceeds 300 original prints, paintings, sculpture, and mixed media works.
Donna Raetsen-Kemp, Director

***Woodstock:* Woodstock Art Gallery (WAG)**
447 Hunter St., Woodstock, ON N4S 4G7
519-539-2382, Fax: 519-539-2564,
gallery@city.woodstock.on.ca
www.city.woodstock.on.ca
Features contemporary & historical exhibitions; wide range of classes & workshops for adults & children; focuses on local painter Florence Carlyle through an extensive permanent collection & family artifacts
Maria Ricker, Curator

Prince Edward Island

Provincial Art Galleries

Confederation Centre Art Gallery (CCAG) / Le Musée d'Art du Centre de la Confédération
145 Richmond St., Charlottetown, PE C1A 1J1
902-628-6111, Fax: 902-566-4648,
jsimpson@confederationcentre.com
www.confederationcentre.com
Critical inquiry into 200 years of Canadian art; 28 annual exhibitions; 15,000 work collection
Jon L. Tupper, Director

Quebec

Provincial Art Galleries

Musée d'art contemporain de Montréal (MACM)
185, rue Ste-Catherine ouest, Montréal, QC H2X 3X5
514-847-6226, Fax: 514-847-6292,
info@macm.org
www.macm.org
Collection of over 6,000 works dating from 1939 by artists from Québec, Canada & around the world; a specialized reference centre is available for research; various performances, lectures & educational programs are offered by the museum throughout the year; restaurant, boutique & bookstore
Marc Mayer, Directeur
Paulette Gagnon, Curator-in-Chief

Musée des beaux-arts de Montréal / Montreal Museum of Fine Arts
CP 3000 A, #1379, 1380, rue Sherbrooke ouest, Montréal, QC H3G 2T9
514-285-2000, Fax: 514-844-6042, 800-899-6873
webmaster@mbamtl.org
www.mmfa.qc.ca
The Museum houses an encyclopaedic collection that includes Canadian Art, Contemporary Art, European Art, Decorative Arts, Ancient Cultures, & Mediterranean Archeology; access to the permanent collection is free
Guy Cogeval, Director
Wanda Palma, Public Relations

Musée national des beaux-arts du Québec
Parc des Champs-de-Bataille, Québec, QC G1R 5H3
418-643-2150, Fax: 418-646-3330, 866-220-2150
info@mnba.qc.ca
www.mnba.qc.ca
Founded: 1933 The museum, situated on the Plains of Abraham, houses prestigious collections of 17th, 18th, & 19th century art, plus a collection of contemporary art. Various temporary exhibitions are also held. Open year round, the museum also features a library, a bookstore, & an educational service.
Esther Trépanier, Director

Other Art Galleries in Quebec

***Alma:* Langage Plus**
CP 518, #102, 414, rue Collard, Alma, QC G8B 5W1
418-668-6635, Fax: 418-668-3263,
langageplus@cgocable.ca
www.langageplus.com

***Amos:* Centre d'exposition d'Amos**
222, 1e av est, Amos, QC J9T 1H3
819-732-6070, Fax: 819-732-3242,
exposition@ville.amos.qc.ca
www.ville.amos.qc.ca
L'art actuel et traditionnel; les sciences et l'histoire
Marianne Trudel, Directrice

***Aylmer:* Centre d'exposition l'Imagier**
9, rue Front, Aylmer, QC J9H 4W8
819-684-1445, Fax: 819-684-4058,
info@limagier.qc.ca
www.limagier.qc.ca
Gallery & sculpture garden

Yvette Debain, Directrice

***Baie-Saint-Paul:* Centre d'Art**
4, boul Fafard, Baie-Saint-Paul, QC G3Z 2J3
418-435-3681, Fax: 418-435-6269,
cartbstp@charlevoix.net
www.centredart-bsp.qc.ca

***Baie-Saint-Paul:* Centre d'Exposition de Baie-St-Paul**
23, rue Ambroise-Fafand, Baie-Saint-Paul, QC G3Z 2J2
418-435-3681, Fax: 418-435-6269,
cexpo@bellnet.ca
centredart-bsp.qc.ca/cexpo/centrexpo.htm
Françoise Labbé

***Carleton:* Centre d'Artistes Vaste et Vague**
774, boul Perron est, Carleton, QC G0C 1J0
418-364-3123, Fax: 418-364-6822,
cvaste.communication@globetrotter.net
Centre de production et de diffusion en art actuel et contemporain Expositions, résidences d'artiste, atelier de production, production d'événements majeurs (Symposium)
Guylaine Langlois

***Chicoutimi:* Espace Virtuel**
534, rue Jacques-Cartier est, Chicoutimi, QC G7H 1Z6
418-698-3873, Fax: 418-698-3874,
espacevirtuel@cybernaute.com
espacevirtuel.ca/centre.html

***Drummondville:* Galerie d'art l'Union-Vie du Centre Culturel de Drummondville**
175, rue Ringuet, Drummondville, QC J2C 2P7
819-477-5416, Fax: 819-477-5723,
nblanchette@centre-culturel.qc.ca
www.centre-culturel.qc.ca
Open year round
Normand Blanchette, Directeur

***Gatineau:* Axe Néo-7 Art Contemporain**
80, rue Hanson, Gatineau, QC J8Y 3M5
819-771-2122, Fax: 819-771-0696,
axeneo7@axeneo7.qc.ca
www.axeneo7.qc.ca
Artist run centre; contemporary art gallery

***Gatineau:* Centre d'exposition Art-Image et espace Odyssée**
Maison de la Culture de Gatineau
855, boul de la Gappe, Gatineau, QC J8T 8H9
819-243-2325, Fax: 819-243-2527,
art_image@gatineau.ca
www.ville.gatineau.qc.ca/artimage
To increase communication between the artistic fields & the general public

***Gatineau:* Galerie Montcalm**
Maison du Citoyen, CP 1970 Hull, 25, rue Laurier, Gatineau, QC J8X 3Y9
819-595-7488, Fax: 819-595-7492,
galeriemontcalm1@gatineau.ca
www.gataineau.ca/galerie
Open year round; free
Dominique Laurent, Responsable

***Jonquière:* Centre national d'exposition**
CP 605 A, 4160, rue du Vieux Pont, Jonquière, QC G7X 7W4
418-546-2177, Fax: 418-546-2180,
cne@videotron.ca
pages.infinit.net/cne
Presents exhibitions of the works of professional artists & several travelling shows; demonstrates richness of the collections of Québec & other Canadian & international museums; guided tours, workshops, demonstrations & edukits available
Jacqueline Caron, Directrice

***Laval:* Salle Alfred Pellan, Maison des arts de Laval**
1395, boul de la Concorde ouest, Laval, QC H7N 5W1
450-662-4440, Fax: 450-662-4428,
sallealfredpellan@ville.laval.qc.ca
www.ville.laval.qc.ca
Arts visuels à caractère contemporain
Ginette Beaunoyer, Contact

***Lennoxville:* Foreman Art Gallery of Bishop's University**
***Also known as:* Galerie d'art Foreman de l'Université Bishop's**
Bishop's University, 2600 College St., Lennoxville, QC J1M 0C8
819-822-9600, Fax: 819-822-9703,
gallery@ubishops.ca
www.ubishops.ca/artgallery.htm
To serve as a forum for the presentation & examination of the visual arts through the programming of contemporary & historical exhibitions as well as lecture series , workshops & films; open Tues. - Sat. 12-5, evenings when Centennial Theatre open; admission free
Vicky Chainey Gagnon, Curator

***Longueuil:* Plein sud, centre d'exposition en art actuel à Longueuil**
100, rue de Gentilly est, espace D-0626, Longueuil, QC J4H 4A9
450-679-2966, Fax: 450-679-4480,
plein-sud@plein-sud.org
www.plein-sud.org
Diffuse la production d'artistes professionnels dont les recherches s'inscrivent en art actuel; présente des expositions temporaires et offre des activités qui visent à familiariser le public avec les différentes avenues proposées par cet art

***Matane:* Galerie d'art de Matane**
#3, 520, av Saint-Jérôme, Matane, QC G4W 3B5
418-566-6687, Fax: 418-562-6675,
gartm@globetrotter.qc.ca
www.rcaaq.org/membres/profil/34
Présenter environ 8 expositions d'artistiques du Québec, du Canada et de l'étranger

***Mont-Laurier:* Centre d'exposition Mont-Laurier**
CP 323, 385, rue Du Pont, Mont-Laurier, QC J9L 3N7
819-623-2441, Fax: 819-623-3007,
ceml@lino.sympatico.ca
Le Centre d'exposition de Mont-Laurier est une institution muséale dont la mission est la diffusion, l'éducation et l'action culturelle en arts visuels et en patrimoine

***Montréal:* Artothèque**
5720, rue St-André, Montréal, QC H2S 2K1
514-278-8181, Fax: 514-278-3044,
info@artotheque.ca
www.artotheque.ca/

***Montréal:* La Centrale (Galerie Powerhouse)**
4296, boul Saint-Laurent, Montréal, QC H2W 1Z3
514-871-0268, Fax: 514-871-9830,
galerie@lacentrale.org
www.lacentrale.org
Artist-run centre dedicated to the presentation of women's contemporary art

***Montréal:* Centre international d'art contemporain de Montréal**
CP 760 Place du Parc, Montréal, QC H2X 4A6
514-288-0811, Fax: 514-288-5021,
ciac@ciac.ca
www.ciac.ca
Centre international d'art contemporain de Montréal is an office for contemporary art producing exhibitions, La Biennale de Montréal, an electronic art magazine, publications, & events.
Claude Gosselin, Director

***Montréal:* Galerie de l'UQAM**
Université du Québec à Montréal, CP 8888 Centre-ville, Montréal, QC H3C 3P8
514-987-6150, Fax: 514-987-6897,
galerie@uqam.ca
www.galerie.uqam.ca

***Montréal:* Leonard & Bina Ellen Art Gallery / Galerie Leonard et Bina Ellen**
Concordia University, 1455, boul de Maisonneuve ouest, Montréal, QC H3G 1M8
514-848-2424,
ellengallery.concordia.ca
Committed to researching, collecting & interpreting Canadian art; programming centres on exhibitions that help advance knowledge in the visual arts; in keeping with Concordia's academic mission, the Gallery is committed to the enhancement of the University's educational programmes & cultural environment
Michèle Thériault, Director

***Montréal:* Segal Centre for Performing Arts**
5170, côte Sainte-Catherine, Montréal, QC H3W 1M7
514-739-2301, Fax: 514-739-9340,
info@segalcentre.org
www.segalcentre.org
Alvin Segal, President
Joel Segal, Vice-President
Bryna Wasserman, Artistic & Executive Director
Barry Taggart, Director, Finance & Operations
Michael Blumenstein, Secretary
Tasso Lagios, Treasurer

***Mont-Saint-Hilaire:* Musée d'art de Mont-Saint-Hilaire**
150, rue du Centre-Civique, Mont-Saint-Hilaire, QC J3H 5Z5
450-536-3033, Fax: 450-536-3032,
mamsh@mamsh.qc.ca
mamsh.qc.ca
Promotes work of local artists Ozias Leduc, Paul-Émile Borduas & Jordi Benet; works of contemporary artists

***Pointe-Claire:* La Galerie d'art Stewart Hall Art Gallery**
Centre culturel de Pointe-Claire Stewart Hall, 176, ch Bord-du-Lac, Pointe-Claire, QC H9S 4J7
514-630-1254, Fax: 514-630-1285,
millarj@ville.pointe-claire.qc.ca
Open year round; exhibitions from local, national & international sources; paintings, photographs, sculptures, graphics & theme exhibitions; free admission; wheelchair access

***Québec:* VU centre de diffusion et de production de la photographie**
***Also known as:* Centre VU**
523, Saint-Vallier est, Québec, QC G1K 3P9
418-640-2558, Fax: 418-640-2586,
vuphoto@meduse.org
www.meduse.org/vuphoto/
VU se consacre à la promotion et au développement de la photographie d'auteur. Son mandat vise principalement le soutien aux activités de recherche et de création en photographie à travers des expositions, des résidences d'artistes, des publications et des événements spéciaux. VU offre un accès privilégié à une vaste gamme d'équipements de production en photographie argentique et numérique
André Gilbert, Directeur

***Rimouski:* Galerie Coup d'Oeil**
CP 710, Rimouski, QC G5L 7C7
418-724-3235, Fax: 418-724-3139,

***Rouyn-Noranda:* Centre d'exposition de Rouyn-Noranda inc.**
Cégep de l'Abitibi-Témiscamingue, CP 415, 425, boul du Collège, Rouyn-Noranda, QC J9X 6C4
819-762-6600, Fax: 819-762-9425,
cern@cegepat.qc.ca
www.cern.ca
Louise Boudreault, Directrice générale

***Saint-Hyacinthe:* Expression, Centre d'exposition de Saint-Hyacinthe**
495, rue Saint-Simon, Saint-Hyacinthe, QC J2S 5C3
450-773-4209, Fax: 450-773-5270,
expression@expression.qc.ca
www.expression.qc.ca
Une institution muséale dont la mission est de promouvoir et de diffuser l'art contemporain et actuel. Depuis 1985, Expression présente au public, dans une salle magnifique et spacieuse, des expositions réputées pour leur qualité artistique. A ces expositions, s'ajoutent un service d'animation, des conférences et des publications. De plus, Expression insère ponctuellement des activités satellites

***Saint-Jean-Port-Joli:* Maison Médard-Bourgault**
322, av de Gaspé ouest, Saint-Jean-Port-Joli, QC G0R 3G0
418-598-3880,

***Saint-Laurent:* Musée des maîtres et artisans du Québec (MMAQ)**
615, av Sainte-Croix, Saint-Laurent, QC H4L 3X6
514-747-7367, Fax: 514-747-8892,
m.dube@mmaq.qc.ca
www.mmaq.qc.ca
Chefs d'oeuvres de grands maîtres et pièces exceptionnelles d'artisans anonymes présentent un panorama de la culture traditionnelle québécoise dans une église néo-gothique de 1867
Pierre Wilson, Directeur-conservateur

***Saint-Léonard:* Galerie Port-Maurice**
8420, boul Lacordaire, Saint-Léonard, QC H1R 3G5
514-328-8514,
Crée en 1979; sensibilise la population aux différents courants contemporains d'arts visuels

***La Sarre:* Centre d'art Rotary**
195, rue Principale, La Sarre, QC J9Z 1Y3
819-333-2294, Fax: 819-333-2296,
llafreniere@ville.lasalle.qc.ca
www.ville.lasarre.qc.ca/Loisir/Plan.htm
Susy Tousignant

***Shawinigan:* Centre d'exposition de Shawinigan**
***Also known as:* Centre des Arts de Shawinigan**
c/o Corporation culturelle de Shawinigan, 2100, boul Des Hêtres, Shawinigan, QC G9N 8R8
819-539-1888, Fax: 819-539-2400,
corporationculturelle@shawinigan.ca
www.cdas.ca
Louise Martin, Directrice générale

***Sherbrooke:* Galerie d'art du Centre culturel de l'Université de Sherbrooke**
2500, boul Université, Sherbrooke, QC J1K 2R1
819-821-7000,
www.usherbrooke.ca/galerie/

***Sherbrooke:* Musée des beaux-arts de Sherbrooke**
241, rue Dufferin, Sherbrooke, QC J1H 4M3
819-821-2115, Fax: 819-821-4003,
mbas@interlinx.qc.ca
www.mbas.qc.ca

Plusieurs expositions temporaires ainsi que la collection du Musée, notamment les oeuvres de Frederick Simpson Coburn et la collection Luc LaRochelle
Cécile Gèlinas, Directrice

***St-Georges:* Centre d'Art de St-Georges**
c/o Centre culturel Marie-Fitzbach., 250, 18e rue ouest, St-Georges, QC G5Y 4S9
418-226-2271, Fax: 418-228-1321,
Open year round
Marie Tanguay, Chef de division

***Trois-Rivières:* Galerie d'art du Parc et Manoir de Tonnancour**
CP 871, 864, rue des Ursulines, Trois-Rivières, QC G9A 5J9
819-374-2355, Fax: 819-374-1758,
www.galeriedartduparc.qc.ca
Drawings, paintings, sculptures, stamps, photos, videos & mixed-media exhibitions; permanent exhibition on the history of the Manoir de Tonnancour

***Valcourt:* Centre culturel Yvonne L. Bombardier**
1002, av J.-A.-Bombardier, Valcourt, QC J0E 2L0
450-532-3033,
ccylb@fjab.qc.ca
www.centreculturelbombardier.com/accueil.htm

***Val-d'Or:* Centre d'exposition de Val d'Or inc.**
600, 7e rue, Val-d'Or, QC J9P 3P3
819-825-0942, Fax: 819-825-3062,
expovd@ville.valdor.qc.ca
membres.lycos.fr/centreexpositionvd/
Ginette Vézina, Présidente

***Verdun:* Centre culturel de Verdun**
5955, rue Bannantyne, Verdun, QC H4H 1H6
514-765-7170, Fax: 514-765-7263,
nancy.raymond@verdun.ca

Saskatchewan

Provincial Art Galleries

MacKenzie Art Gallery (MAG)
T.C. Douglas Bldg., 3475 Albert St., Regina, SK S4S 6X6
306-584-4250, Fax: 306-569-8191,
mackenzie@uregina.ca
www.mackenzieartgallery.sk.ca
Founded: 1953 Historical & contemporary Canadian, American & European works; special emphasis on western Canadian art; works on paper, contemporary photography, major touring exhibits; facilities include learning centre, studios, theatre, gift shop; sculpture court; outdoor sculpture garden; open daily year round
Stuart Reid, Director
Timothy Long, Curator

Mendel Art Gallery & Civic Conservatory (MAG)
PO Box 569, 950 Spadina Cres. East, Saskatoon, SK S7K 3L6
306-975-7610, Fax: 306-975-7670,
info@mendel.ca
www.mendel.ca
Historical & contemporary Canadian & international art; 5 exhibition periods/year; open year-round
Terry Graff, Director

Other Art Galleries in Saskatchewan

***North Battleford:* Allen Sapp Gallery**
***Also known as:* Allen Sapp Gallery - The Gonor Collection**
PO Box 460, 1 Railway Ave. East, North Battleford, SK S9A 2Y6
306-445-1760, Fax: 306-445-1694,
sapp@accesscomm.ca
www.allensapp.com
Cree art & interpretive centre; open year round
Dean Bauche, Curator

***North Battleford:* The Chapel Gallery**
PO Box 460, 891 - 99 St., North Battleford, SK S9A 2Y6
306-445-1757, Fax: 306-445-1009,
chapelgallery@sasktel.net
www.nbleisure.com/galleries
Exhibition of local to international artists, permanent collection of the city of North Battleford
Michael Brukop, Curator
Dean Bauche, Director

***Prince Albert:* Grace Campbell Gallery**
c/o John M. Cuelenaere Public Library, 125 - 12 St. East, Prince Albert, SK S6V 1B7
306-763-8496, Fax: 306-763-3816,
bmazurkewich@jmcpl.ca
www.jmcpl.ca
Local, provincial & national exhibitions; no permanent collection
Eleanor Acorn, Library Director
Beverley Mazurkewich, Gallery Coordinator

***Regina:* Dunlop Art Gallery**
Regina Public Library, PO Box 2311, 2311 - 12th Ave., Regina, SK S4P 3Z5
306-777-6040, Fax: 306-949-7264,
bantal@rpl.regina.sk.ca
www.dunlopartgallery.org
Permanent art collection of contemporary & historical significance by Saskatchewan artists

***Regina:* McIntyre Gallery**
2347 McIntyre St., Regina, SK S4P 2S3
306-757-4323,
mcintyre.gallery@sasktel.net
www.mcintyregallery.com
Contemporary Saskatchewan art; open year round
Louise Durnford, Director

***Regina:* Rosemont Art Gallery**
Neil Balkwill Civic Arts Centre, PO Box 1790, 2420 Elphinstone St., Regina, SK S4P 3C8
306-522-5940,

***Saskatoon:* A.K.A. Gallery**
424 - 20th St. West, Saskatoon, SK S7M 0X4
306-652-0044, Fax: 306-652-0534,
aka@sasktel.net
www.akagallery.org
Artist-run centre; membership open to all
Clark Ferguson, Administrative Coordinator
Cindy Baker, Programme Coordinator

***Saskatoon:* Gordon Snelgrove Art Gallery**
191 Murray Bldg., University of Saskatchewan, 3 Campus Dr., Saskatoon, SK S7N 5A4
306-966-4208, Fax: 306-966-4266,
gary.young@usask.ca
www.usask.ca/snelgrove
The gallery, managed by the Univ. of Sask. department of Art & Art History, supports program & course instruction, student shows & exhibitions, & community outreach.
Gary Young, Coordinator

***Saskatoon:* Kenderdine Art Gallery/University of Saskatchewan Permanent Art Collection**
University of Saskatchewan, #12, College Bldg., 107 Administration Pl., Saskatoon, SK S7N 5A2
306-966-4571, Fax: 306-978-8340,
kenderdine.artgallery@usask.ca
www.usask.ca/kenderdine
Open year round
Kent Archer, Director/Curator

***Saskatoon:* St. Thomas More Art Gallery**
St. Thomas More College, 1437 College Dr., Saskatoon, SK S7N 0W6
306-966-8900, Fax: 306-966-8904, 800-667-2019
lstark@stmcollege.ca
www.stmcollege.ca
Founded: 1964 Located on the 2nd floor of the College, next to the Library. Exhibitions from Sept. through April, featuring local & regional artists with a university level studio background or extensive formal training. Submissions accepted year round.
Linda Stark, Curator

***Weyburn:* Allie Griffin Art Gallery (AGAG)**
45 Bison Ave., Weyburn, SK S4H 1L8
306-848-3278, Fax: 306-848-3271,
weyburnartscouncil@live.ca
www.weyburnartscouncil.ca
Founded: 1964 Features touring exhibitions from the Mendel Art Gallery, the Mackenzie Art Gallery, the Saskatchewan Craft Council, the Saskatchewan Arts Board through OSAC, and many locally curated shows. The exhibitions feature the work of well-known as well as emerging Saskatchewan artists.
Marnie Bernard, Gallery Curator
Alice Neufeld, Arts Director

***Weyburn:* Signal Hill Arts Centre**
424 - 10 Ave. South, Weyburn, SK S4H 2A1
306-848-3278, Fax: 306-848-3271,
aneufeld@weyburn.ca
Founded: 1985 The Signal Hill Arts Centre is located in a five storey multi-purpose civic heritage facility, which also houses a pottery studio, gallery, gift shop, kitchen, dance studio, an office, & meeting rooms.
Alice Neufeld, Arts & Cultural Director

***Yorkton:* Godfrey Dean Art Gallery**
Yorkton Arts Council, 49 Smith St. East, Yorkton, SK S3N 0H4
306-786-2992, Fax: 306-782-2767,
gdag@sasktel.net
www.deangallery.ca
Founded: 1981 Devoted to the exhibition of visual art that reflects contemporary issues relevant to the Yorkton region; classes & special events programming.
Donald Stein, Director

Yukon Territory

Territorial Art Galleries

Yukon Arts Centre
Yukon Place, PO Box 16, 300 College Dr., Whitehorse, YT Y1A 5X9
867-667-8485, Fax: 867-393-6300,
info@yac.ca
www.yukonartscentre.org
Yukon Arts Centre is the territory's premier venue for performing and visual arts. The Gallery hosts 10-14 contemporary art exhibitions per year. Emphasis is to showcase work of professional Yukon artists & to bring exhibitions of national importance to the Yukon. The Theatre is a 428-seat proscenium theatre, boasting outstanding acoustics and top-of-the-line technical support.
Scott Marsden, Curator, Public Art Gallery
Al Cushing, Executive Director

Aquaria

British Columbia

***Sidney:* Marine Ecology Station**
Port Sidney Marina, 9835 Seaport Pl., Sidney, BC V8L 4X3
250-655-1555, Fax: 250-655-1573,
info@mareco.org
mareco.org
Dedicated to marine education, awareness & stewardship; open year round
Dr. Bill Austin, Director

***Vancouver:* Vancouver Aquarium**
Stanley Park, PO Box 3232, Vancouver, BC V6B 3X8
604-659-3474, Fax: 604-659-3515, 800-931-1186
information@vanaqua.org
www.vanaqua.org
The largest in Canada & one of the five largest in North America; a self-sufficient, non-profit organization, the Aquarium is internationally recognized for display & interpretation excellence & was the first facility to incorporate professional Naturalists into the galleries to complement interpretive graphics; research projects extend world wide & it is internationally recognized for its success
Dr. John Nightingale, President
His Excellency Gary Doer, Ambassador

New Brunswick

***St Andrews:* Huntsman Marine Science Centre**
1 Lower Campus Rd., St Andrews, NB E5B 2L7
506-529-1200, Fax: 506-529-1212,
aquarium@huntsmanmarine.ca
www.huntsmanmarine.ca
Public aquarium/museum with local flora & fauna, & the Atlantic Reference Centre which houses a zoological & botanical museum reference collection; research & teaching in marine sciences & coastal biology; marine education courses for elementary, high school & university groups; aquaculture research & development facilities
William Robertson, Executive Director

***Shippagan:* Aquarium et Centre Marin de Shippagan (ACM)**
100, rue Aquarium, Shippagan, NB E8S 1H9
506-336-3013, Fax: 506-336-3057,
aquarium@gnb.ca
www.gnb.ca/aquarium
Aquarium publique qui expose un nombre impressionnant d'espèces de poissons qui vivent dans les eaux du golfe St-Laurent ainsi que dans les lacs et rivières de l'est du Canada. L'Attraction vedette est une famille de phoque communs; présentation audio-visuelle; bassin touchez-y; ouvert de mai á sept.; acceptons réservations de groups hors saison
Robert Rioux, Directeur

Newfoundland & Labrador

***St. John's:* The Fluvarium**
Nagle's Place, Box 5, St. John's, NL A1B 2Z2
709-754-3474, Fax: 709-754-5947,
info@fluvarium.ca
www.fluvarium.ca
Delivers an environmental education program to over 10,000 school children annually; houses interactive fresh water exhibits & nine underwater viewing windows into Nagle's Hill Brook
Jane Smith-Parsons, Executive Director

Ontario

Niagara Falls: **Marineland**
7657 Portage Rd., Niagara Falls, ON L2E 6X8
905-356-9565,
www.marinelandcanada.com
Interactive marina and amusement park; facility for animal and marine mammal care, where guests can learn about animals through an exciting mix of entertainment and education. Contains the largest whale habitat in the world. Open May - Oct.
John Holer, President

Prince Edward Island

Stanley Bridge: **Stanley Bridge Marine Aquarium**
Rte. 6, Stanley Bridge, PE C0A 1E0
902-886-3355,
www.kata.pe.ca/attract/marine/marine.htm
With live fish aquariums and touch tanks, North America's largest collection of mounted birds - over 700 specimens - the World of Butterflies display, and a history of Malpeque oysters, the Irish moss and shellfish industries, it's an educational experience for the whole family. Open June - Oct.
John Holer, President

Quebec

Sainte-Flavie: **Parc de la rivière Mitis (CISA)**
900, route de la Mer, Sainte-Flavie, QC G0J 2L0
418-775-2969, Fax: 418-775-9466,
info@parcmitis.com
www.parcmitis.com
Le Parc de la riviére Mitis est situé à Saint-Flavie et se veut un site écotouriste qui améne les gens à porter un nouveau regard sur l'interprétation et la préservation du patrimonie naturel et culturel. Ouvert mi-juin - sept.
Julie Isabel

Sainte-Foy: **Parc aquarium du Québec**
1675, av des Hôtels, Sainte-Foy, QC G1W 4S3
418-659-5264, Fax: 418-646-9238, 866-659-5264
aquarium@sepaq.com
www.sepaq.com
16 hectare park encompassing aspects of the northern ecosystem and marine life. Observe and interact with over 10,000 fresh and salt-water fish specimens, reptiles, amphibians, invertebrates, as well as marine mammals, such as Atlantic and Pacific walruses, seals and polar bears.

Saskatchewan

Fort Qu'appelle: **Fish Culture Station**
PO Box 190, Fort Qu'appelle, SK S0G 1S0
306-332-3200, Fax: 306-332-3203,
Jerry Banks, Manager

Botanical Gardens

Alberta

Brooks: **Golden Prairie Arboretum**
Alberta Agriculture, Food & Rural Development, Crop Diversification Centre South, SS#4, Brooks, AB T1R 1E6
403-362-1300, Fax: 403-362-1306,
christine.murray@gov.ab.ca
Collection of deciduous trees & shrubs
Dr. Christine Murray
Nigel Seymour

Calgary: **University of Calgary Herbarium**
Dept. of Biological Sciences, 2500 University Dr. NW, Calgary, AB T2N 1N4
403-220-5262, Fax: 403-289-9311,
ccchinna@ucalgary.ca
Vascular plants
C.C. Chinnappa, Curator

Edmonton: **Devonian Botanic Garden**
University of Alberta, Edmonton, AB T6G 2E1
780-987-3054, Fax: 780-987-4141,
www.devonian.ualberta.ca
80 acres of cultivated gardens & 110 acres of natural area; native & alpine plants, ecological reserves, Kurimoto Japanese Garden & Orchid House & a Butterly House; picnic area, patio cafe & gift shop; open daily, Apr.-Dec.
Dr. Michael Hickman, Associate Director
Bruce Dancik, Director
Dionne Allen, General Manager

Edmonton: **Muttart Conservatory**
9626 - 96A St., Edmonton, AB T6C 4L8
780-496-8735, Fax: 780-496-8747,
muttartquestions@edmonton.ca
www.edmonton.ca/muttart
Four pyramids house flora of different world climatic zones, including arid, temperate, & tropical; Show Pyramid features 6 different floral shows per year; species orchid greenhouse; outdoor trail gardens in summer
Judith Rohovie, Director

Lethbridge: **Nikka Yuko Japanese Garden**
c/o Lethbridge & District Japanese Garden Society, PO Box 751, Lethbridge, AB T1J 3Z6
403-328-3511, Fax: 403-328-0511,
info@nikkayuko.com
www.japanesegarden.ab.ca
The Nikka Yuko Japanese Garden is a mature four acre garden providing a quiet, serene place for the appreciation of nature and discovery of inner peace. Includes dry rock garden, mountain and waterfall, streams and bridges, ponds and islands, flat prarie garden.

Trochu: **Trochu Arboretum & Gardens**
Also known as: **The Arboretum at Trochu**
PO Box 340, Trochu, AB T0M 2C0
403-442-2111, Fax: 403-442-2528,
Open Victoria Day to Thanksgiving
Roy Ashcroft, President
Judy Reeds, Curator

British Columbia

Burnaby: **Simon Fraser University Arboretum**
Dept. of Biological Sciences, Simon Fraser University, Burnaby, BC V5A 1S6
604-291-4475, Fax: 604-291-3496,

Kimberley: **Cominco Gardens**
340 Spokane St., Kimberley, BC V1A 2E8
250-427-5160,
kcds@kimberley.ca
Open May - Oct.
Ginnesa Clive, Manager

North Vancouver: **Park & Tilford Gardens**
Park & Tilford Centre, #440, 333 Brookbank Ave., North Vancouver, BC V7J 3S8
604-984-8200, Fax: 604-984-6099,
bfielding@bentall.com
www.parkandtilford.ca
10 themed public gardens; free admission; open dawn to dusk
Bernice Fielding, Garden Director

Richmond: **Fantasy Garden World**
10800 No. 5 Rd., Richmond, BC V7A 4E5
604-277-7777, Fax: 604-274-1212,
An amusement park with gardens, rides, a miniature train, a "castle" from Coevorden, Holland and an Olde World Village

Rosedale: **Minter Gardens**
52892 Bunker Rd., Rosedale, BC V0X 1X0
604-792-3799, 888-646-8377
mail@mintergardens.com
www.mintergardens.com
Founded: 1980 Open Apr. - mid-Oct.; located at 52892 Bunker Rd., Rosedale BC; take exit #135 of the Trans Canada Hwy #1
Brian Minter
Faye Minter

Surrey: **Surrey Art Gallery**
Surrey Arts Centre, 13750 - 88 Ave., Surrey, BC V3W 3L1
604-501-5566, Fax: 604-501-5581,
artgallery@city.surrey.bc.ca
www.arts.surrey.ca
Promotes contemporary BC & Canadian artists; exhibitions & public programs encourage community appreciation of contemporary visual art; open year round
Liane Davison, Curator, Exhibitions
Ingrid Kolt, Curator, Visual Arts Programs

Vancouver: **Bloedel Conservatory**
Queen Elizabeth Park, c/o Van. Bd. of Parks & Recreation, 2099 Beach Ave., Vancouver, BC V6G 1Z4
604-257-8584, Fax: 604-257-8427,
www.vancouver.parks.ca
Canada's largest single-structure tropical conservatory featuring over 500 species in simulated rain-forest, subtropic & desert environments; also features tropical birds, parrots & a Japanese Koi fish collection

Vancouver: **Dr. Sun Yat-Sen Classical Chinese Garden**
578 Carrall St., Vancouver, BC V6B 5K2
604-662-3207, Fax: 604-682-4008,
sunyatsen@telus.net
www.vancouverchinesegarden.com
The first authentic, full-scale, classical Chinese garden built outside China; museum, garden & cultural attraction
Kathy Gibler, Executive Director

Vancouver: **Nitobe Memorial Garden**
c/o UBC Botanical Garden and Centre for Plant Research, 6804 Southwest Marine Dr., Vancouver, BC V6T 1Z4
604-822-9666, Fax: 604-822-2016,
botg@interchange.ubc.ca
www.nitobe.org
Authentic Japanese tea & stroll garden; cherry blossoms; Japanese Irises, Japanese Maples; Koi; lanterns & much more
Quentin Cronk, Director
Douglas Justice, Associate Director

Vancouver: **Queen Elizabeth Park & Arboretum**
30 East 30th Ave., Vancouver, BC V5V 2T9
604-257-8373,
A 125 acre public park with extensive floral display gardens, naturalized areas, arboretum, golf course, tennis courts, roller hockey rinks & basketball courts

Vancouver: **UBC Botanical Garden**
University of British Columbia, 6804 Southwest Marine Dr., Vancouver, BC V6T 1W5
604-822-9666, Fax: 604-822-2016,
botg@interchange.ubc.ca
www.ubcbotanicalgarden.org
Living museum of plants in 110 acres of BC coastal native forest; over 10,000 assorted trees, shrubs, flowers; divided into various components
Quentin Cronk, Director
Douglas Justice, Associate Director

Vancouver: **VanDusen Botanical Garden**
5251 Oak St., Vancouver, BC V6M 4H1
604-878-9274, Fax: 604-266-2436,
jill.cherry@vancouver.ca
www.vandusengarden.org
22-hectare garden comprised of over 255,000 plants. Open year-round.
Chris Woods, Garden Director

Victoria: **The Butchart Gardens Ltd.**
PO Box 4010, Victoria, BC V8X 3X4
250-652-4422, Fax: 250-652-7751, 866-652-4422
email@butchartgardens.com
www.butchartgardens.com
55 acres of manicured gardens on a 130 acre private estate; open year-round

Victoria: **Royal Roads Botanical Garden**
Also known as: **Hatley Park Gardens**
c/o Royal Roads University, 2005 Sooke Rd., Victoria, BC V9B 5Y2
250-391-2617, Fax: 250-391-2622,
www.hatleypark.ca
Native coastal forest & formal gardens

Victoria: **Horticulture Centre of the Pacific**
505 Quayle Rd., Victoria, BC V6E 2J7
250-479-6162, Fax: 250-479-6047,
info@hcp.bc.ca
www.hcp.bc.ca
A nonprofit organization founded in 1979 as The Horticulture Centre of the Pacific or HCP, it manages 103 acres to demonstrate sound gardening practices using the diversity of plants that can be grown in this area, to preserve natural plant and animal habitat, and to provide a unique environment for preparing students for careers in horticulture. It relies on public funding, on local businesses, and on its own fundraising activities to support these activities.

Manitoba

Boissevain: **International Peace Garden**
PO Box 419, Boissevain, MB R0K 0E0
204-534-2510, 888-432-6733
kathy@peacegarden.com
www.peacegarden.com
2300-acre park located on the North Dakota & Manitoba boarders; tribute to peace & friendship between the people of Canada & the United States of America; maintains extensive gardens containing a wide variety of shrubs, perennials, & annual plants; souvenir shop, interpretative centre, picnic sites, hiking trails, International music camp, Royal Canadian Legion sports camp, 9/11 Memorial Site
Doug Hevenor, CEO

Leaf Rapids: **Leaf Rapids National Exhibition Centre**
Also known as: **Societé des Arts of Leaf Rapids, Inc.**
Town Centre Complex, PO Box 220, Leaf Rapids, MB R0B 1W0
204-473-8682, Fax: 204-473-2707,
excentre@mts.net
The Exhibition Centre features traveling displays and local and regional artists exhibits. Each year, two to four live performances are offered for youth and adults.
Joan Seddon, Director

Morden: **Morden Arboretum**
Morden Research Centre, Agriculture & Agri-Food Canada, #100-101, Rte. 100, Morden, MB R6M 1Y5

204-822-4471, Fax: 204-822-7207, res2.agr.ca/winnipeg/index_e.htm
A federal government research centre; variety of programs including breeding & development of trees, shrubs, roses & herbaceous perennials; improvement & agronomic research programs carried out on linseed flax, field peas & dry edible beans
Dr. Campbell G. Davidson

***Winnipeg:* Assiniboine Park**
***Also known as:* City Park**
c/o Community Services Dept., 395 Main St., 6th Fl., Winnipeg, MB R3B 3N8
204-986-4208, Fax: 204-986-8112, www.winnipeg.ca/cms/ape
Includes Assiniboine Park Zoo, Assiniboine Park Conservatory, Leo Mol Sculpture Garden, Pavillion Art Gallery, English & Formal Gardens, Assiniboine Forest Natural Area
Patti Sullivan, COO, Assiniboine Park Enterprise, City of Winnipeg Community Services Dept.

***Winnipeg:* Living Prairie Museum**
2795 Ness Ave., Winnipeg, MB R3J 3S4
204-832-0167, Fax: 204-986-4172, www.winnipeg.ca/publicworks/naturalist/livingprairie/
38-hectare preserve of original tall grass; interpretive centre; open Apr. 15 - Aug.; Sept - April by appt.

***Winnipeg:* Sandilands Forest Centre, Hadashville, MB**
c/o 900 Corydon Ave., Winnipeg, MB R3M 0Y4
204-453-3182, Fax: 204-477-5765, mfainc@mts.net
www.mbforestryassoc.ca
125 hectares of forests; artifacts in the museum; open May - Oct.
Dianne Beaven, President

New Brunswick

***Saint-Jacques:* New Brunswick Botanical Garden**
PO Box 1629, 33 Principale St., Saint-Jacques, NB E7B 1A3
506-737-4444, Fax: 506-737-5389, jardin@umce.ca
www.umce.ca/jardin
7 hectares; over 50,000 plants.

Newfoundland & Labrador

***St. John's:* The Memorial University of Newfoundland Botanical Garden**
306 Mt. Scio Rd., St. John's, NL A1C 5S7
709-737-8590, Fax: 709-737-8596, garden@mun.ca
www.mun.ca/botgarden
The Memorial University of Newfoundland Botanical Garden maintains cultivated gardens and natural habitats for public display and is a centre for botanical, horticultural and environmental research and education.
Dr. K. Wilf Nicholls, Director

Nova Scotia

***Annapolis Royal:* Annapolis Royal Historic Gardens**
PO Box 278, 441 Saint George St., Annapolis Royal, NS B0S 1A0
902-532-7018, Fax: 902-532-7445, www.historicgardens.com
Theme gardens, collections & displays reflect historical periods - Open May - Oct.
Dr. K.W. Nicholls, Director

***Halifax:* Halifax Public Gardens**
1606 Bell Rd., Halifax, NS B3H 2Z3
902-423-9865, Fax: 902-446-4002, www.halifaxpublicgardens.ca
Formal Victorian Garden, located at Summer St. & Spring Garden Rd.
, Parks

Ontario

***Burlington:* Royal Botanical Gardens (RBG)**
680 Plains Rd. West, Burlington, ON L7T 4H4
905-527-1158, Fax: 905-577-0375, 800-694-4769
info@rbg.ca
www.rbg.ca
A living museum which serves local, regional and global communities while developing and promoting public understanding of the relationship between the plant world, humanity and the rest of nature. 1,100 hectares of land: 120 cultivated hectares, while the rest remains a managed natural area including marshlands and walking trails.
Mark Runciman, Director

***Guelph:* The Arboretum**
University of Guelph, Guelph, ON N1G 2W1
519-824-4120, Fax: 519-763-9598, arbor@uoguelph.ca
www.uoguelph.ca/arboretum
Environmental education & research activities; plant collections; formal gardens; recreational workshops; dinner theatre; meeting & banquet facilities
Prof. Alan Watson, Director, awatson@uoguelph.ca

***Hamilton:* Centre for Canadian Historical Horticultural Studies (CCHHS)**
PO Box 399, Royal Botanical Gardens, Hamilton, ON L8N 3H8
905-527-1158, Fax: 905-577-0375, 800-668-9449
library@rbg.ca
Vicki DeNardis, Contact

***Kingsville:* Colasanti's Tropical Gardens**
1550 Rd. 3 East, Kingsville, ON N9Y 2E5
519-326-3287, Fax: 519-322-2302, tropical@colasanti.com
www.colasanti.com
Founded: 1941 Colasanti's Tropical Gardens features over 3.5 acres of tropical greenhouses. It is open 363 days each year. Attractions include exotic plants, animals, indoor miniature golf, children's rides, an indoor playground, an arcade, a restaurant, plus home decor & collectables.
Joe Colasanti, Contact
Terry Colasanti

***London:* Sherwood Fox Arboretum**
University of Western Ontario, Richmond St. North, London, ON N6A 5B7
519-661-2111, Fax: 519-661-3935, arboretum@uwo.ca
www.uwo.ca/biology/arboretum
The arboretum includes the trees planted on the campus of the university
Dr. Jane Bowles

***Miller Lake:* Larkwhistle Garden**
191 Lindsay Rd. 40, Miller Lake, ON N0H 1Z0
519-795-7763, larkwhistle@amtelecom.net

***Niagara Falls:* Niagara Parks Botanical Gardens & School of Horticulture**
c/o Niagara Parks Commission, PO Box 150, Niagara Falls, ON L2E 6T2
905-356-8554, Fax: 905-356-5488, schoolofhorticulture@niagaraparks.com
www.schoolofhorticulture.com
Includes the Niagara Parks Butterfly Conservatory
Tom Laviolette, Superintendent, Botanical Gardens & Butterfly Conservatory
Liz Klose, Superintendent, School of Horticulture

***Ottawa:* Central Experimental Farm**
c/o Bldg. 72, Arboretum, Ottawa, ON K1A 0C6
613-230-3276, Fax: 613-230-1238, thefarm@cyberus.ca
www.friendsofthefarm.ca

***Ridgetown:* J.J. Neilson Arboretum**
120 Main Street East, Ridgetown, ON N0P 2C0
519-674-1570, Fax: 519-674-1600, arboretu@ridgetownc.uoguelph.ca
www.ridgetownc.uoguelph.ca
Includes upwards of 500 taxa., including Carolinian trees & shrubs, & collections of Viburnum & Dogwood, along with perennial & annual displays, & theme landscape areas
Mike Gladstone, Contact

***Sault Ste Marie:* Great Lakes Forestry Centre Arboretum**
Canadian Forest Service, 1219 Queen St. East, Sault Ste Marie, ON P6A 2E5
705-949-9461, Fax: 705-541-5700, www.glfc.cfs.nrcan.gc.ca/arboretum/index_e.html
Two hectares of natural land and forest.
D.J. Kennington, Arboretum Manager

***Thunder Bay:* Centennial Conservatory**
c/o Parks & Recreation Dept., 1601 Dease St. North, Thunder Bay, ON P7B 4A2
807-622-7036, Fax: 807-622-7602, 807-622-7036
Four seasonal flower displays; cactus & tropical displays year round; open year round, 1-4 pm daily; free admission

***Thunder Bay:* Soroptimist International Friendship Garden**
Parks Division, Victoriaville Civic Centre, 111 South Syndicate Ave., Thunder Bay, ON P7E 6S4
807-625-3166, Fax: 807-625-3258,
Soroptimist International Friendship Garden was created by Canadians of varied ethnic origins as a centennial gift to Canada & the community. Individual gardens have been planned, designed, constructed, & financed by the respective groups; Each group has created a garden typical of their culture & homeland.
Don Vezina, Coordinator, Parks Services, dvezina@thunderbay.ca

***Toronto:* Allan Gardens Conservatory**
19 Horticultural Ave., Toronto, ON M5A 2P2
416-392-7288, Fax: 416-392-0318, ckenned1@toronto.ca
collections.ic.gc.ca/gardens
Permanent plant collection of tropical & sub-tropical plants; seasonal plant displays; open daily 10-5
Chris Kennedy, Superintendent

***Toronto:* Edwards Gardens**
Civic Garden Centre, 777 Lawrence Ave. East, Toronto, ON M3C 1P2
416-392-8188,
A former Estate garden featuring perennials and roses on the uplands and wildflowers, rhododendrons and an extensive rockery in the valley.

***Toronto:* Humber Arboretum**
205 Humber College Blvd., Toronto, ON M9W 5L7
416-675-6622, Fax: 416-255-6876, steve.bodsworth@humber.ca
www.humberarboretum.on.ca
100 hectares of ornamental gardens & green space on the west branch of the Humber River
Stephen Bodsworth, Director

***Toronto:* The Power Plant Contemporary Art Gallery at Harbourfront Centre**
231 Queens Quay West, Toronto, ON M5J 2G8
416-973-4949, Fax: 416-973-4933, thepowerplant@harbourfrontcentre.com
www.thepowerplant.org
New work by today's best artists
Helena Reckitt, Curator

***Toronto:* Toronto Sculpture Garden**
#713, 38 Avenue Rd., Toronto, ON M5R 2G2
416-515-9658, Fax: 416-515-9655, www.torontosculpturegarden.com
Semi-annual exhibitions of contemporary sculpture in a park, 115 King St. East
Rina Greer, Director

***Windsor:* Fogolar Furlan Botanic Garden**
1800 E.C. Row, North Service Rd., Windsor, ON N8W 1Y3

***Windsor:* Jackson Park Queen Elizabeth II Garden**
c/o Parks & Recreation Dept., 2450 McDougall Rd., Windsor, ON N8X 3N6
519-253-2300, Fax: 519-255-7990, parkrec@city.windsor.on.ca
www.city.windsor.on.ca
More than 10,000 plants, formal gardens, fountains, and sports park.

Prince Edward Island

***Kensington:* Malpeque Gardens**
RR#1, Blue Heron Dr., Kensington, PE C0B 1M0
Open June 15 - Aug. 15
George MacKay

Quebec

***Grand-Métis:* Jardin de Métis / Reford Gardens**
200, rte 132, Grand-Métis, QC G0J 1Z0
418-775-2222, Fax: 418-775-6201, reford@refordgardens.com
www.jardinsmetis.com
3,000 species; native & exotic plants
Brigitte Bourdages, Office Co-ordinator

***Montréal:* Jardin botanique de Montréal / Montréal Botanical Garden**
4101, rue Sherbrooke est, Montréal, QC H1X 2B2
514-872-1400, Fax: 514-872-4917, jardin_botanique@ville.montreal.qc.ca
www.ville.montreal.qc.ca/jardin
Collection of 22,000 plant species & varieties, 10 exhibition greenhouses & 30 thematic gardens from around the world; Insectarium; covers 75 hectares
Gilles Vincent, Director

***Sainte-Anne-de-Bellevue:* Morgan Arboretum**
Macdonald Campus, McGill University, PO Box 186, Sainte-Anne-de-Bellevue, QC H9X 3V9
514-398-7811, Fax: 514-398-7959, morgan.arboretum@mcgill.ca
www.morganarboretum.org
Situated at the western tip of the island of Montreal; trees grow in forests, experimental plantations & ornamental collections
Leslie Ann LaDuke, Financial Administrator

Christina Idziak, Curator

***Sainte-Foy:* Jardin Roger-Van den Hende**
Université Laval, Pavillon de L'Envirotron, 2480 Hochelaga, Sainte-Foy, QC G1K 7P4
418-656-3742, Fax: 418-656-3515,
jardin@fsaa.ulaval.ca
www.jardin.ulaval.ca
More than 4000 species and cultivars arranged in order of botanical family. Open April - Oct.; free admission
Simon Chrétien
Hélène Corriveau

Saskatchewan

***Estevan:* Shand Greenhouse**
PO Box 280, Estevan, SK S4A 2A3
306-634-9771, Fax: 306-634-6682, 866-778-7337
greenhouse@saskpower.com
www.saskpower.com
Greenhouse, shade houses, nursery, display area; uses by-products of energy generation from the Shand Power Station; open year round
Martin Lelliott, Manager

***Indian Head:* Prairie Farm Rehabilitation Administration (PFRA)**
***Also known as:* Shelterbelt Centre**
PO Box 940, Hwys. 1 & 56, Indian Head, SK S0G 2K0
306-695-2284, Fax: 306-695-2568,
pfratree@agr.gc.ca
www.agr.ca/pfra/shelterbelt.htm
Arboretum, nursery, horticultural displays; open daily
Dr. G.B. Neill, Manager

***Saskatoon:* Patterson Gardens**
Dept. of Plant Sciences, University of Saskatchewan, 51 Campus Dr., Saskatoon, SK S7N 5A8
306-966-5855, Fax: 306-966-5015,
www.usask.ca/agriculture/plantsci/facilities.html
Patterson Gardens are a 5 acre plot of mature trees & shrubs which are open to the public at anytime; it represents many of our hardy good quality landscape materials
B. E. Coulman, Dept. Head

***Swift Current:* Art Gallery of Swift Current NEC**
411 Hebert St. East, Swift Current, SK S9H 1M5
306-778-2736, Fax: 306-773-8769,
k.houghtaling@swiftcurrent.ca
www.artgalleryofswiftcurrent.org
Non-profit public art gallery & national standard art museum offering exhibitions of provincial, national & international artwork; provides access to & education in visual art culture for Southwest Saskatchewan
Laurie Wagner, Education Coordinator,
l.wagner@swiftcurrent.ca
Kim Houghtaling, Director/Curator,
k.houghtaling@swiftcurrent.ca

Museums

National Museums

Canada Aviation Museum / Musée de l'aviation du Canada
PO Box 9724 T, 11 Aviation Pkwy., Ottawa, ON K1G 5A3
613-993-2010, Fax: 613-990-3655, 800-463-2038
aviation@technomuses.ca; member@technomuses.ca
www.aviation.technomuses.ca
Other contact information: TTY: 613-990-7530; Phone, Library & Archives: 613-993-2303
As a component of the Canada Science and Technology Museum Corporation, the Canada Aviation Museum collects, preserves, & displays aviation-related objects, from the pioneer era, through war & peace, & to the present time.
Denise Amyot, President & Chief Executive Officer, Canada Science & Technology Museum Corporation
Anthony P. Smyth, Director General, Canada Aviation Museum

Canada Science & Technology Museum Corporation (CSTMC/SMSTC) / Société du Musée des Sciences et de la technologie du Canad
PO Box 9724 T, 1867 St. Laurent Blvd., Ottawa, ON K1G 5A3
613-991-3044, Fax: 613-990-3636, 866-442-4416
info@technomuses.ca
www.sciencetech.technomuses.ca
Other contact information: TTY: 613-991-9207; E-mail, Library: library@technomuses.ca
Exhibits at the Canada Science & Technology Museum include astronomy, space, marine & land transportation, communications, computer technology, & domestic technology. The library of the Canada Science & Technology Museum contains material about the history & development of science & technology, with an emphasis upon Canada.
Denise Amyot, President & Chief Executive Officer
James Paul, Chair
Michèle Desloges, Corporate Secretariat, 613-990-6352

The Canadian Museum of Civilization Corporation (CMCC) / Société du Musée canadien des civilisations
PO Box 3100 B, 100, rue Laurier, Gatineau, QC J8X 4H2
819-776-7000, Fax: 819-776-8300, 800-555-5621
web@civilization.ca
www.civilization.ca
The Canadian Museum of Civilization conducts research in Canadian studies & collects, preserves & displays objects which reflect Canada's cultural heritage. Its activities extend across the country through field research programs, publications & loans to various groups & institutions. Through permanent & changing exhibitions, public programs, film & theatre programs, the museum unfolds the storie
Victor Rabinovitch, President & CEO,
victor.rabinovitch@civilization.ca
Chantal Schryer, Vice-President, Public Affairs & Publishing,
chantal.schryer@civilization.ca

Canadian Museum of Contemporary Photography (CMCP / MCPC) / Musée canadien de la photographie contemporaine
PO Box 465 A, 380 Sussex Dr., Ottawa, ON K1N 9N6
613-990-1985, Fax: 613-993-4385, 800-319-2787
cmcp@gallery.ca
www.cmcp.gallery.ca
Other contact information: TDD: 613-990-0777
Founded: 1985 Affiliated with the National Gallery of Canada, the collection of the Canadian Museum of Contemporary Photography dates from the early 1960s to the present. Photographic works include prints, negatives, transparencies, books, filmstrips, video art, audio-visual presentations, mixed media works, assemblages, & installation pieces.
Martha Hanna, Director
Joanne Charette, Director, Public Affairs, 613-990-5050, Fax: 613-990-9824, jcharette@gallery.ca

Canadian Museum of Nature / Musée canadien de la nature
PO Box 3443 D, Ottawa, ON K1P 6P4
613-566-4700, Fax: 613-364-4021, 800-263-4433
questions@mus-nature.ca; cmnlib@mus-nature.ca
www.nature.ca
Other contact information: TTY: 613-566-4770; 1-866-600-8801
The natural sciences & natural history museum features specimens, such as fossils, horned dinosaurs, fish, freshwater mussels, tropical beetles, animals, lichens, plants, & minerals from Canada & around the world.
Joanne DiCosimo, President & Chief Executive Officer, 613-566-4733, Fax: 613-364-4020, jdicosimo@mus-nature.ca
Maureen Dougan, Vice-President & Chief Operating Officer, 613-566-4732, Fax: 613-364-4020, mdougan@mus-nature.ca
Roger Baird, Director, Collection Services, 613-364-4138, Fax: 613-364-4022, rbaird@mus-nature.ca
Kim Curran, Director, Development & Fundraising Services, 613-566-4790, Fax: 613-364-4021, kcurran@mus-nature.ca
Mark S. Graham, Director, Research, 613-566-4743, Fax: 613-364-4022, mgraham@mus-nature.ca
Denyse Jomphe, Director, Human Resources Management Services, 613-566-4294, Fax: 613-364-4028, djomphe@mus-nature.ca
Lynne Ladouceur, Director, Financial Management Services, 613-566-4253, Fax: 613-364-4025, lladouceur@mus-nature.ca
Marie Lasnier, Director, Community Services, 613-364-4101, Fax: 613-566-4746, mlasnier@mus-nature.ca
Jennifer Doubt, Chief Collection Manager, Botany, 613-364-4076, Fax: 613-364-4027, jdoubt@mus-nature.ca
Jean-Marc Gagnon, Chief Collection Manager, Invertebrates, 613-364-4066, Fax: 613-364-4027, jmgagnon@mus-nature.ca
Kamal Khidas, Chief Collection Manager, Vertebrates, 613-364-4098, Fax: 613-364-4027, kkhidas@mus-nature.ca
Kieran Shepherd, Chief Collection Manager, Earth Sciences, 613-364-4054, Fax: 613-364-4027, kshepherd@mus-nature.ca
Elizabeth McCrea, Manager, Communications Services, 613-566-4249, Fax: 613-364-4021, emccrea@mus-nature.ca

The Canadian War Museum (CWM) / Musée canadien de la guerre
1 Vimy Place, Ottawa, ON K1R 1C2
819-776-8600, Fax: 819-776-8623, 800-555-5621
info@warmuseum.ca
www.warmuseum.ca
Affiliated museum of the Canadian Museum of Civilization; war art; uniforms & accoutrements; medals; weapons & small arms; archives; the Hartland Molson library; vast collection of military vehicles & artillery
Mark O'Neill, Director General, mark.oneill@warmuseum.ca
Morgan Wright, Public Relations Officer

Currency Museum of the Bank of Canada / Musée de la monnaie de la Banque du Canada
245 Sparks St., Ottawa, ON K1A 0G9
613-782-8914, Fax: 613-782-7761,
museum-musee@bank-banque-canada.ca
www.currencymuseum.ca; www.museedelamonnaie.ca
The most complete collection of Canadian notes & coins in the world, plus representative collections of world coins & paper money, including whales' teeth, glass pearls, elephant-hair bracelets, shells & copper axes
Paul S. Berry, Chief Curator
Henriette Riegel, Director, Visitor Services
Enrica Schwilden, Manager, Marketing & Communications

National Museums

***Cardston:* Courthouse Museum**
89 - 3rd Ave. West, Cardston, T0K 0K0
403-653-4322,
Other contact information: Phone, Off Season: 403-653-3366
The Courthouse is a Provincial Historic Site, which was constructed in 1907 from local sandstone. Court artifacts are on display, including the witness stand, judge's bench, & orginal jail cells. The musuem is open during July & August. During the off season, appointments may be arranged.

Alberta

Provincial Museums

Glenbow Museum, Art Gallery, Library & Archives
130 - 9 Ave. SE, Calgary, AB T2G 0P3
403-268-4100, Fax: 403-265-9769,
glenbow@glenbow.org
www.glenbow.org
Glenbow documents the settlement of western Canada with exhibits tracing the lives & traditions of native peoples, the development of the railway, ranching, farming & growing up in the West. A large art gallery highlights historical & contemporary art from Glenbow's own collections as well as from national & international collections. Books, maps, photographs & manuscripts relating to southern Alb

Kristin Evenden, President & CEO

Lauchlan Currie, Chair

Royal Alberta Museum
12845 - 102 Ave., Edmonton, AB T5N 0M6
780-453-9100, Fax: 780-454-6629,
www.royalalbertamuseum.ca
Major collections & exhibits of Alberta's natural & human history, including habitat groups, geology, palaeontology, archaeology, & western Canadian history & the Syncrude Gallery of Aboriginal Culture; feature exhibitions, museum shop, café, films, lectures, live demonstrations & cultural performances; special programs for schools & other groups; discovery room
Chris Robinson, Acting Executive Director, 780-453-9168, chris.robinson@gov.ab.ca
Albert Finnamore, Director, Curatorial & Collections Preservation, 780-453-9177, Fax: 780-454-6629, albert.finnamore@gov.ab.ca
Chris Robinson, Director, Marketing, Communications & Education, 780-453-9168, chris.robinson@gov.ab.ca
Bruce Bolton, Director, Business Operations, 780-453-9130, Fax: 780-454-6629, bruce.bolton@gov.ab.ca
Tom Thurston, Director, Renewal Project, 780-453-9105, Fax: 780-454-9105, tom.thurston@gov.ab.ca

Royal Tyrrell Museum
PO Box 7500, Drumheller, AB T0J 0Y0
403-823-7707, Fax: 403-823-7131, 888-440-4240
tyrrell.info@gov.ab.ca
www.tyrrellmuseum.com
Founded: 1985 Located in Midland Provincial Park, on Hwy #838 in Drumheller, the internationally recognized Royal Tyrrell Museum is in the heart of one of the richest fossil localities in the world. The Museum is Canada's only museum dedicated exclusively to palaeontology & showcases Alberta's abundant & diverse fossil record, featuring more than 800 fossils & 35 dinosaur skeletons on display. Other highlights include dramatic dioramas, interactive exhibits, computer stations & mini-theatre, special events & programming, gift shop & cafeteria

Andrew Neuman, Executive Director M.Sc.

Other Museums in Alberta

Airdrie: **Nose Creek Valley Museum**
1701 Main St. SW, Airdrie, AB T4B 1C5
403-948-6685,
ncvm@telus.net
www.nosecreekvalleymuseum.com
Nose Creek Valley Museum offers the history of Airdrie & the surrounding region. Visitors will learn about the geology & natural history of the area, the First Nations & pioneers, farming, antique automobiles, & military history. A Canadian Pacific caboose is also on display. The museum is open year-round.
Laurie Harvey, Curator

Alberta Beach: **Alberta Beach & District Museum**
PO Box 68, 4823 - 50 Ave., Alberta Beach, AB T0E 0A0
780-924-2140,
abmuseum@netscape.ca
History of the Lac Ste Anne area; open year round, weekends only in winter
Leanne Knysh, President

Alberta Beach: **Garden Park Farm Museum**
PO Box 639, Alberta Beach, AB T0E 0A0
780-924-3391,
David Oselies

Alix: **Alix Wagon Wheel Museum**
PO Box 245, Alix, AB T0C 0B0
403-747-3119,
alixwagonwheelmuseum@live.ca
alixwagonwheelmuseum.wordpress.com
Local history and artifacts; souvenir shop. Open year round, but by appointment from Oct. through May.
Eve Keates, Curator

Andrew: **Andrew & District Local History Museum**
PO Box 180, Andrew, AB T0B 0C0
403-365-3687,
Local artifacts & records; open year round

Banff: **Banff Park Museum National Historic Site**
PO Box 900, Banff, AB T1L 1K2
403-762-1558, Fax: 403-762-1565,
banff.vrc@pc.gc.ca
www.pc.gc.ca/lhn-nhs/ab/banff/index_e.asp
Founded: 1895 The Banff Park Museum is a natural history museum. The collection is located in a 1903 building.

Banff: **Buffalo Nations Luxton Museum**
PO Box 850, 1 Birch Ave., Banff, AB T1L 1A8
403-762-2388, Fax: 403-760-2803,
buffalonations@telus.net
www.buffalonationsmuseum.ca
The Buffalo Nations Luxton Museum depicts the cultures & traditions of the First Nations people of the Plains. Artifacts date back over 100 years.
Joseph Yellowhorn, President
Anthony Starlight, Vice-President
Roy Louis, Secretary
Stewart Breaker, Treasurer
Estelle Guthro, General Manager
Ray Cowley, Head, Buildings & Installations

Banff: **Whyte Museum of the Canadian Rockies**
PO Box 160, 111 Bear St., Banff, AB T1L 1A3
403-762-2291, Fax: 403-762-8919,
info@whyte.org; archives@whyte.org
www.whyte.org
Other contact information: Phone, Archives: 403-762-2291, ext. 335
Visitors to the Whyte Museum discover the history, art, & social & cultural past of the Canadian Rockies. Guided tours are provided of the heritage gallery, the art gallery, heritage homes, the Luxton home & garden, & historic Banff. The Archives & Library, located at the museum, collects books, journals, maps, newspaper clippings, microforms, textual records, photographs, & audio-visual materials related to the Canadian Rockies.
Michale Lang, Executive Director & Chief Curator
Graeme Nunn, Chief Financial & Operating Officer & Executive Director, Whyte Foundation
Natalie Fedrau, Manager, Visitor Services
Elizabeth Kundert-Cameron, Manager, Archives & Library, Fax: 403-762-2339, archives@whyte.org
Craig Richards, Curator, Photography
Jennifer Rutkair, Archivist
Lena Goon, Reference Archivist
Catherine Hawkins, Coordinator, Education & Interpretation
Katie Daniel, Specialist, Marketing & Communications

Barrhead: **Barrhead Centennial Museum & Visitor Information Center**
PO Box 4122, 5629 - 49th St., Barrhead, AB T7N 1A1
780-674-5203,
barrheadmuseum@lycos.ca
Other contact information: Phone, Appointments: 780-674-3513
Founded: 1967 The Barrhead Centennial Museum is operted by the Barrhead & District Historical Society. Exhibits at the Barrhead Centennial Museum & Visitor Information Center include Barrhead settlers' furniture, pioneer farm equipment, & tools. The complete local newspaper is also available at the museum, plus a large collection of African artifacts. The museum is open from the Victoria Day weekend in May to the Labour Day weekend in September.

Beaverlodge: **South Peace Centennial Museum**
PO Box 493, Beaverlodge, AB T0H 0C0
780-354-8869, Fax: 780-354-8068,
sitemanager@spcm.ca
www.spcm.ca
Pioneer equipment & buildings; open mid-May - Sept. 1
Lois Dueck, President

Bowden: **Bowden Pioneer Museum**
PO Box 576, 2201 - 19th Ave., Bowden, AB T0M 0K0
403-224-2122,
bhs@shawbiz.ca
museum.anwc.net
Founded: 1967 Goverened by the Bowden Historical Society, the Bowden Pioneer Museum is located in the old Bowden curling rink. The museum contains the following artifacts & exhibits: The Bob Hoare Photography Exhibit; The Eastern Star Exhibit; The Irene M. Wood Avon Collection, The Women of Aspenland Lives & Works; a hardware & general store display; military artifacts; geological collections, decorative arts, such as musical instruments; fine arts of First Nations & European origins; & human hisotry artifacts, such as religious objects, household items, & sports equipment. The museum also conducts research services. It is open from the long weekend in May to September.

Brooks: **Brooks Aqueduct National & Provincial Historic Site**
c/o Eastern Irrigation District, PO Box 8, 550 Industrial Rd., Brooks, AB T1R 1B2
403-653-5139,
eid@eid.ab.ca; darren.marty@gov.ab.ca
www.eidnet.org/local/aqueduct
Other contact information: Phone, Information Kiosk: 403-362-4451
The Brooks Aqueduct is located 8 km southeast of Brooks, Alberta. The structure was completed in 1914 by the irrigation division of the Canadian Pacific Railway. It has been preserved by the Government of Alberta, Environment Canada, the Prairie Farm Rehabilitation Administration, & the Eastern Irrigation District. The interpretive center at the aqueduct is open from May 15th to Labour Day.

Brownvale: **Brownvale North Peace Agricultural Museum**
PO Box 186, Brownvale, AB T0H 0L0
780-597-3934, Fax: 780-597-3950,
The Brownvale North Peace Agricultural Museum features artifacts such as historic farm machinery, horse-powered equipment, & construction equipment. The museum is open during July & August.

Calgary: **Aero Space Museum of Calgary**
4629 McCall Way NE, Calgary, AB T2E 8A5
403-250-3752, Fax: 403-250-8399,
info@asmac.ab.ca
www.asmac.ab.ca
With over 20 historical aircrafts on display, guests can explore Canadian achievements in aviation & space. Aircraft engines, extensive aviation library & interactive exhibits; educational programs & tours; gift shop; meeting/function room rentals. Open year round.
Steven Ogle, CEO
Jennifer Herrick, Executive Director
Sara Bateman, Marketing & Development
Anthony Worman, Curator

Calgary: **Calgary Chinese Cultural Centre**
197 - First St. SW, Calgary, AB T2P 4M4
403-262-5071, Fax: 403-232-6387,
info@culturalcentre.ca
www.culturalcentre.ca
Founded: 1992 The Calgary Chinese Cultural Centre promotes Chinese heritage, history, & culture, as well as cultural diversity.
Victor Mah, Chair
Malcolm Chow, Vice-President
Samantha Yang, Executive Administrator
Tony Wong, Secretary
Leonard Chow-Wah, Treasurer

Calgary: **The Calgary Highlanders Museum & Archives**
4520 Crowchild Trail SW, Calgary, AB T3E 1T8
403-974-2855, Fax: 403-974-2855,
highrs@nucleus.com
www.calgaryhighlanders.com
A history and recollection of the Calgary Highlanders
Barry Agnew, Curator Lt. Ret'd

Calgary: **Fort Calgary**
Also known as: **Fort Calgary Historic Park**
PO Box 2100 M, #106, 750 - 9th Ave. SE, Calgary, AB T2P 2M5
403-290-1875, Fax: 403-265-6534,
info@fortcalgary.com
www.fortcalgary.com
40-acre park; interpretive centre; 1875 fort reconstruction project; guided tours; open year round
Sara Jane Gruetzner, Executive Director

Calgary: **The Grain Academy**
Plus 15 Level, Roundup Centre, Stampede Park, PO Box 1060 M, Calgary, AB T2P 2K8
403-263-4594, Fax: 403-233-9500,
grainacademy@nucleus.com
www.grainacademymuseum.com
Founded: 1981 Grain elevator; grain transportation exhibit

Calgary: **Heritage Park Historical Village**
1900 Heritage Dr. SW, Calgary, AB T2V 2X3
403-268-8500, Fax: 403-268-8501,
info@heritagepark.ab.ca
www.heritagepark.ca
Founded: 1964 Billed as a living history museum, the expansive site offers a wide range of exhibits and activities, most notably the exploration of a village of historical, "old west" buildings replete with antiques, artifacts and costumed guides. Gasoline Alley Museum focuses on the history of the automobile. There is a steam train, antique midway and Haskayne Mercantile Block of shops. Open May - Sept.
MS Alida Visbach, President/CEO

Calgary: **Lord Strathcona's Horse (Royal Canadians) Regimental Museum**
4520 Crowchild Trail SW, Calgary, AB T2T 5J4
403-974-2854, Fax: 403-974-2858,
museum@strathconas.ca; archives@strathconas.ca
www.strathconas.ca
Founded: 1990 Museum relates the history of the Regiment from 1900 to present. The collection holds many artifacts yet undisplayed. The Archives store photographs, records, documents and diaries and research is conducted for personal and professional institutions. Open year round.
Warrant Officer D.E. (Ted) MacLeod, Curator

Calgary: **King's Own Calgary Regiment (RCAC) Museum**
Also known as: **Museum of the Regiments**
CFB Calgary, 4520 Crowchild Trail South West, Calgary, AB T2P 5J4
403-974-2856,
Robertson.DB@kingsown.org
www.kingsown.org
Depicts the history of the four regiments of Calgary; art gallery; open all year. Artifacts and pictures of regimental "family tree"; permanent displays of the 50th Battalion C.E.F. which deature The Deadly Sniper; Cpl. Henry Norwest; M.M. Vimy; Pte. John George Pattison V.C.; non-permanent active militial Dieppel The Prisoner of War Room; Sicily, Italy, including the Kingsmill Bridge and the Battle of Cassino. Special film and military documentaties in the Amoco Theatre.
Col. Ian Gray, Executive Director CD (Ret'd)
Jan Roseneder, Librarian/Archivist
Noel Ratch, Curator

Calgary: **Naval Museum of Alberta**
1820 - 24 St. SW, Calgary, AB T2T 0G6
403-242-0002, Fax: 403-240-1966,
info@navalmuseum.ab.ca
www.navalmuseum.ab.ca
Other contact information: Information line: 403/974-2853
Collection includes one each of the 3 naval aircraft (fighter planes) used by RCN; naval armament including guns, torpedos, anti-submarine equipment, clothing etc. Part of The Military Museums
Glen Hardie, President

Calgary: **The Nickle Arts Museum**
The University of Calgary, 2500 University Dr. NW, Calgary, AB T2N 1N4
403-220-7234, Fax: 403-282-4742,
nickle@ucalgary.ca
www.ucalgary.ca/~nickle
Founded in 1979 through a donation from Sam Nickle & a Province of Alberta grant; champions contemporary Canadian art, numismatics & Oriental carpets; changing exhibitions & programs
Dr. Ann Davis, Director

Calgary: **Olympic Hall of Fame & Museum**
c/o Canada Olympic Park, 88 Canada Olympic Rd. SW, Calgary, AB T3B 5R5
403-247-5452,
info@winsportcanada.ca; groups@winsportcanada.ca

www.winsportcanada.ca/cop
Other contact information: Phone, School Department, Outdoor Education Programming: 403-202-6577
The Olympic Hall of Fame & Museum honours past & present Canadian Olympians & Paralympians. A large collection of Olympic artifacts is featured, such as Olympic torches. Visitors can test their skills with interactive simulators of Olympic sports, including alpine skiing. The Olympic Hall of Fame & Museum is open year-round.
Gordon Ritchie, Chair, WinSport Canada Board of Directors
Tracy Cobb, National Director, Communications & Fund Development, WinSport Canada, 403-247-5954, tracy.cobb@winsportcanada.ca

***Calgary:* Princess Patricia's Canadian Light Infantry Regimental Museum & Archives**
4520 Crowchild Trail SW, Calgary, AB T2T 5J4
403-974-2862, Fax: 403-974-2864, ppcli@nucleus.com
www.archivesalberta.org/place/ppcli.htm
Other contact information: Phone, Archives: 403-974-2867
Princess Patricia's Canadian Light Infantry Regimental Museum & Archives collects & preserves items that cover the dates from 1914, when Princess Patricia's Canadian Light Infantry was founded, to the present day. The Infantry is known for its service in both World Wars, Korea, & Afghanistan, & during other operations for the United Nations & NATO. Holdings include war journals, photographs, training manuals, cartographic materials, & audio-visual resources, especially related to the Princess Patricia's Canadian Light Infantry, & to the Canadian Army in general. The museum is open year-round.
Ronald B. Gallant, Curator
Bruce A. Graham, Archivist

***Calgary:* Sarcee Tsuu T'ina People's Museum**
#135, 3700 Anderson Rd. SW, Calgary, AB T2W 3C4
403-238-2677,
Located on Sarcee (Tsuu T'ina) Reserve, the museum features artifacts such as headdresses from around 1938 & a model tipi.

***Calgary:* University of Calgary, Museum of Zoology**
2500 University Dr., Calgary, AB T2N 1N4
403-220-5269, Fax: 403-289-9311, fitch@ucalgary.ca
Teaching museum used for zoology & ecology courses
Warren Fitch, Curator

***Calgary:* Youthlink Calgary: Calgary Police Service Interpretive Centre**
133 - 6th Ave. SE, Calgary, AB T2G 4Z1
403-206-4566,
www.youthlinkcalgary.com
Interactive exhibits & programs educate youth about life, crime, & law enforcement.
Janet Pieschel, Executive Director, janet.pieschel@calgarypolice.ca
Gail Niinimaa, Administrator, 403-206-8927, gail.niinimaa@calgarypolice.ca
Lindsie Bruns, Technician, Historical Collections, 403-206-8691, lbruns@calgarypolice.ca
Colleen Acheson, Coordinator, Booking, 403-206-8950, colleen.acheson@calgarypolice.ca
Rachel Joo, Coordinator, Outreach Programs, 403-206-8691, rachel.joo@calgarypolice.ca

***Camrose:* Camrose & District Centennial Museum**
PO Box 1622, Camrose, AB T4V 1X6
780-672-3298,
www.camrosemuseum.ca
Founded: 1967 Buildings on the museum grounds include a pioneer home, The Likeness School, the St. Dunstan's Church, a firehall, the local newspaper building, a blacksmith shop, the Mona Sparling Building, the Oldtimers Hut, & the R.C.M.P. Machine Building. The musuem is open from Victoria Day weekend to Labour Day weekend. Appointments may be arranged at other times of the year.

***Canmore:* Canmore Museum & Geoscience Centre**
Civic Centre, 902B - 7th Ave., Canmore, AB T1W 3K1
403-678-2462, Fax: 403-678-2216, info@cmags.org
www.cmags.org
Other contact information: Phone, 1893 North West Mounted Police Barracks: 403-678-1955
The Canmore Museum & Geoscience Centre features historical artifacts, geological collections, & information about the heritage of Canmore & the surrounding mountainous area. The museum also operates the 1893 North West Mounted Police Barracks, which is situated on 609 Main Street.
V. Richard (Rick) Green, President
Ian Schofield, Vice-President, Heritage
Edward van Vliet, Director & Curator
Lindsay Walker, Coordinator, Earth Science
David Moore, Treasurer

***Cardston:* C.O. Card Pioneer Home & Museum**
PO Box 1830, 337 Main St., Cardston, AB T0K 0K0
403-653-4322,
Other contact information: Phone, Off Season: 403-653-3366
C.O. Card Home & Museum is a Provincial Historic Site. It features the log cabin built by Charles Ora Card, who was the founder of Cardston. The museum is open during July & August. During the off season, appointments may be arranged.

***Cardston:* Remington Carriage Museum**
PO Box 1649, Cardston, AB T0K 0K0
403-653-5139, Fax: 403-653-5160, info@remingtoncentre.com
www.remingtoncarriagemuseum.com
Founded: 1993 The Remington Carriage Museum features the largest collection of horse-drawn vehicles in North America, such as carriages, sleighs, & wagons. The facility also contains a working stable, a carriage factory, & a restoration shop. Educational programs are offered. The museum is open year-round.

***Carstairs:* Roulston Museum**
***Also known as:* Carstairs Museum**
***Parent:* Carstairs & District Historical Society**
PO Box 1067, Carstairs, AB T0M 0N0
403-337-3710, Fax: 403-337-3343,
Founded: 1988 Located at 1138 Nanton St. in Carstairs. Main collection housed in the hall of Knox Presbyterian Church (1901), a registered historic site; church records; pictures & artifacts of local life from early settlement to present; McCaig House (1901); archives; new library research room; new farm implement display building
Betty Ayers, Curator
Robert Disney, President

***Cereal:* Cereal Prairie Pioneer Museum**
PO Box 131, Cereal, AB T0J 0N0
403-326-3899,
Museum of artifacts from Pioneer days; pictures, papers & cards of the period; museum was once old CN Railway Station with living quarters; yard includes old jail house & restoration of old Cereal Town Office

***Claresholm:* Appaloosa Horse Club of Canada Senior Citizens Museum & Archives**
PO Box 940, Claresholm, AB T0L 0T0
403-625-3326, Fax: 403-625-2274, museum@appaloosa.ca
www.appaloosa.ca/museum.htm
History of Appaloosa horse

***Claresholm:* Claresholm Museum**
PO Box 1000, 5126 1st St. W., Claresholm, AB T0L 0T0
403-625-3131, Fax: 403-625-3869, claresholmmuseum@gmail.com
www.town.claresholm.ab.ca
Founded: 1969 Local history museum in the old Sandstone Railway Station; Claresholm was home to Louise C. McKinney, a social activist for the cause of women's welfare and legal status, and the first woman parliamentarian in the British Empire; open daily May-Sept; admission by donation
Jo-Ann Peach, Collections Assistant

***Cochrane:* Cochrane Ranche Historic Site**
PO Box 1522, Cochrane, AB T4C 1A7
403-932-2902, Fax: 403-932-2578,
www.cochrane.ca
Located off Hwy #22, north of downtown Cochrane, The Cochrane Ranche is Alberta's first large-scale livestock ranch, comprising approx. 136 acres; open May 15 - Labour Day; hiking & picnic areas open year round

***Coleman:* Crowsnest Museum**
PO Box 306, 7701 - 18 Ave., Coleman, AB T0K 0M0
403-563-5434, Fax: 403-563-5434, cnmuseum@shaw.ca
www.crowsnestmuseum.ca
Over 25,000 artifacts on display interpreting the history of the Crowsnest Pass & its people; themed galleries include pioneers, underground mining, general store/blacksmith shop, Legends of Prohibition, Gushul Studio. Veterans' exhibit, wildlife diorama; open year round
Wendy Zack, Operations Manager

***Crowsnest Pass:* The Frank Slide Interpretive Centre (FSIC)**
PO Box 959 Blairmore, Crowsnest Pass, AB T0K 0E0
403-562-7388, Fax: 403-562-8635, info@frankslide.com
www.frankslide.com
Site of the 1903 rockslide avalanche; visual presentation "In the Mountain's Shadow" shown daily; open year-round.
Monica Field, Manager

***Crowsnest Pass:* Leitch Collieries Provincial Historic Site**
PO Box 959 Blairmore, c/o Frank Slide Interpretive Centre, Crowsnest Pass, AB T0K 0E0
403-562-7388, Fax: 403-562-8635, 310-000-0 in info@frankslide.com
tprc.alberta.ca/museums/historicsiteslisting/leitchc ollieries
Ruin of coal mining operation; staffed May 15 - Labour Day
Monica Field, Manager

***Czar:* Prairie Panorama Museum**
PO Box 149, Czar, AB T0B 0Z0
780-857-3778, Fax: 782-857-2239,
Displays many historical artifacts; includes a school section
Julie Anne Adams, Sec.-Treas.

***DeBolt:* DeBolt & District Pioneer Museum**
311 - 1st St. West, DeBolt, AB T0H 1B0
780-957-3957, Fax: 780-957-2934,
www.albertasource.ca/spiritofthepeace/collections/
Founded: 1975 The museum comprises 8 heritage buildings with displays: in Hubert Memorial Park on Viriginia Ave., in the community church & Legion Hall; collections include the Bickell Fossil Collection. Open summer.
Fran Moore, Curator, franmoore@iwantwireless.ca

***Delburne:* Anthony Henday Museum**
PO Box 374, Delburne, AB T0M 0V0
403-749-2711, Fax: 403-749-2800,
Housed in the former CNR train station; water tank tower, caboose, machine shed & pioneer cabin replica on site; depicts history of Delburne & district with emphasis on agriculture, households & coal mining. Open June M-F, 9-5. From July to Labour Day open daily 9-5.

***Didsbury:* Didsbury & District Museum**
PO Box 1175, 2118 - 21st Ave., Didsbury, AB T0M 0W0
403-335-9295, ddhs@telusplanet.net
1906 building; local history; open year round; Tue.-Wed. 1-4:30; Sat. 1-5
Tyrone Patten, President
Joan Court, Secretary

***Donalda:* Donalda & District Museum**
PO Box 179, Donalda, AB T0B 1H0
403-883-2100, Fax: 403-883-2022, info@donaldamuseum.com
www.donaldamuseum.com
Over 850 lamps; Whitford Collection of Métis artifacts from the late 1800's; native tools; artifacts; open year round
Gail Kerr, Manager

***Drayton Valley:* Drayton Valley & District Historical Society**
PO Box 5099, Drayton Valley, AB T7A 1R3
780-542-5482,
Local history; open Wed. & Sat. 1-4
Fred Cox, Vice-President
Vi Koehmstedt, President
Charlie Miner, Secretary

***Drumheller:* Drumheller & District Museum**
PO Box 2135, 335 - 1st St., Drumheller, AB T0J 0Y0
403-823-2593, Fax: 403-823-4737, stego@telusplanet.net
Fossil remains; interpretive displays; Aboriginal artifacts & items of local historical interest

***Drumheller:* Homestead Pioneer Museum**
PO Box 3154, 901 North Dinosaur Trail, Drumheller, AB T0J 0Y0
403-823-2600, Fax: 403-823-5411,
www.traveldrumheller.com/homestead-museum.html
Founded: 1965 Situated in the Canadian Badlands, the Homestead Pioneer Museum presents exhibits from the Drumheller Valley, including farm machinery & tools, vehicles, & a 1919 house. The museum is open from mid May to mid October.

***East Coulee:* Atlas Coal Mine National Historic Site**
PO Box 521, 110 Century Ave., East Coulee, AB T0J 1B0
403-822-2220, Fax: 403-822-2225, info@atlascoalmine.ab.ca
www.atlascoalmine.ab.ca
Founded: 1989 Located in the Canadian Badlands, the Atlas Coal Mine National Historic Site offers tours & educational programs. Visitors can go underground, explore the last wooden tipple in Canada, see the blacksmith shop, & ride an authentic mine locomotive. The site is open from the beginning of May to mid-October.
Linda Digby, Director

***East Coulee:* East Coulee School Museum**
PO Box 539, East Coulee, AB T0J 1B0
403-822-3970, Fax: 403-922-2111, info@ecsmuseum.ca
www.ecsmuseum.ca
Open year round
Heather Farquherson, Museum Administrator

***Edmonton:* Alberta Aviation Museum**
11410 Kingsway Ave., Edmonton, AB T5G 0X4

780-451-1175, Fax: 780-451-1607,
info@albertaaviationmuseum.com
www.albertaaviationmuseum.com
Tells & interprets the story of aviation & its importance to Edmonton & Northern Alberta; displays & exhibits allow visitors to embrace the spirit of those involved in early aviation endeavours that helped Edmonton establish its title as "Gateway to the North". Flight simulators, aircraft restoration area, activities for children, guided tours, special events. Space rentals, with theatre projection & sound system, wireless Internet available. Open year round.
Jim Salzman, President

***Edmonton:* Alberta Railway Museum**
PO Box 70014 LRPO, 24215 - 34th St., Edmonton, AB T5C 3R6
780-472-6229, Fax: 780-968-0167,
hdixon@incentre.net
www.railwaymuseum.ab.ca
Founded: 1968 The Alberta Railway Museum features over sixty railway cars & locomotives, interpretive displays, a Morse telegraph demonstration, tours, & train rides on selected long weekends. The museum is open on weekends only from Victoria Day (the long weekend in May) to Labour Day (the long weekend in September).

***Edmonton:* Calgary & Edmonton (1891) Railway Museum**
10447 - 86th Ave., Edmonton, AB T6E 2M4
780-433-9739, Fax: 780-431-0138,
jledm@ecn.ab.ca
Visitors to the Calgary & Edmonton (1891) Railway Museum can see a replica railway station, which served the area from 1891 to 1907. Train & station artifacts are on display, including a working telegraph service. The museum is open from June to August. At other times, appointments may be arranged.

***Edmonton:* College & Association of Registered Nurses Of Alberta Museum & Archives**
11620 - 168 St., Edmonton, AB T5M 4A6
780-453-0534, Fax: 780-482-4459, 800-252-9392
www.nurses.ab.ca
Items related to the founding & development of the AARN, as well as the early history of professional nursing in Alberta; Collection includes caps, pins, uniforms, yearbooks, original diplomas, & photographs from early days of nurses' education in Alberta to present; Scrapbooks, uniforms, & military medals (WWI & WWII) from the Nursing Sisters Association; Records of various nursing interest groups
Lorraine Mychajlunow, Curator & Archivist, 780-453-0534, lmychajlunow@nurses.ab.ca

***Edmonton:* Edmonton Public Schools Archives & Museum**
10425 - 99 Ave., Edmonton, AB T5K 0E5
780-422-1970, Fax: 780-426-0192,
archives@epsb.ca
archives.epsb.net
Located in historic McKay Ave. School, site of the first session of the Alberta Legislature; 1905 restored brick building & features the restored 1906 legislative Chamber; holdings include Edmonton Public School Board District #7 & individual school records from 1885 to present
Catherine Luck, Supervisor

***Edmonton:* Edmonton Radial Railway Society**
PO Box 45040 Lansdowne PO, Edmonton, AB T6H 5Y1
780-437-7721, Fax: 780-437-3095,
info@edmonton-radial-railway.ab.ca
edmonton-radial-railway.ab.ca
Other contact information: Park Line: 780/496-1464
Vintage 3 km streetcar ride from Strathcona to downtown Edmonton along former CPR right of way & across the High Level Bridge; restored streetcar rides for visitors to Fort Edmonton Park
Robert Clark, President

***Edmonton:* Father Lacombe Chapel - Provincial Historic Site / La Chapelle du Père Lacombe**
8820 -112 St., Edmonton, AB T6G 2P8
780-459-7663, Fax: 780-427-0808,
father-lacombe@gov.ab.ca
www.cd.gov.ab.ca/flc
Alberta's oldest building; Located on St. Vital Ave., St. Albert; open May 15 - Labour Day
Marianne Mack, Facility Supervisor

***Edmonton:* Fort Edmonton Park**
c/o City of Edmonton Community Services, PO Box 2359, Edmonton, AB T5J 2R7
780-442-5311, Fax: 780-496-8797,
attractions@edmonton.ca
www.fortedmontonpark.ca
Canada's largest living history park; a complete 1846 fur-trading fort & 1885, 1905 & 1920 costumed interpreters; steam train & street car; giftshops & restaurants; fully operational hotel on site
Roger Jevne, Director

***Edmonton:* John Janzen Nature Centre**
PO Box 2359, Edmonton, AB T5J 2R7
780-428-7900, Fax: 780-496-4701,
Sandra Opdenkamp

***Edmonton:* John Walter Museum**
10661 - 91A Ave., Edmonton, AB T5K 0B3
780-496-8787, Fax: 780-496-4701,
attractions@edmonton.caton.ca
www.edmonton.ca/johnwalter
Other contact information: E-mail, School Programs: cmsschoolbookings@edmonton.ca
The museum consists of houses from 1874, 1886, & 1901. A variety of group programs are available. John Walter Museum is open from mid March to mid December.

***Edmonton:* The Loyal Edmonton Regiment Military Museum**
Prince of Wales Armouries, #118, 10440 - 108 Ave., Edmonton, AB T5H 3Z9
780-421-9943, Fax: 780-421-9943,
lermus1@telus.net
www.lermuseum.org
Military museum focusing on history of The Loyal Edmonton Regiment & other military service branches from Northern Alberta
David Haas, Curator

***Edmonton:* Rutherford House Provincial Historic Site**
11153 Saskatchewan Dr., Edmonton, AB T6G 2S1
780-427-3995, Fax: 780-422-4288,
info@rutherfordhouse.ca
www.rutherfordhouse.ca
Home of Alberta's first premier; gift shop, tea room, tours & special events; open year round

***Edmonton:* Stephansson House Provincial Historic Site**
8820 - 112 St., Edmonton, AB T6G 2P8
780-427-3995,
Icelandic poet's pioneer home; open May 15 - Labour Day; located 7 km. north of Markerville off Hwy. 592 or 781

***Edmonton:* The Telephone Historical Centre (THC)**
PO Box 188 Main, 10440 - 108 Ave., Edmonton, AB T5J 2J1
780-433-1010, Fax: 780-426-1876,
bertyeudall@hotmail.com
www.telephonehistoricalcentre.com
Open year round; Canada's largest independent telephone museum
Bert Yeudall, Executive Director

***Edmonton:* Ukrainian Canadian Archives & Museum of Alberta**
9543 - 110 Ave., Edmonton, AB T5H 1H3
780-424-7580, Fax: 780-420-0562,
ucama@shaw.ca
www.ucama.ca
The Ukrainian Canadian Archives & Museum of Alberta is dedicated to preserving Ukrainian-Canadian history & culture. Collections include Ukrainian-Canadian military memorabilia such as uniforms, textiles made by Ukrainian pioneers in Alberta, as well as ecclesiastical artifacts. The museum is open year-round, from Tuesday to Friday.
Khrystyna Kohut, President
Michelle Tracy, Vice-President
Christina Scharabun, Secretary

***Edmonton:* Ukrainian Catholic Women's League of Canada Arts & Crafts Museum**
10825 - 97th St., Edmonton, AB T5H 2M4
780-474-0846,
cyncarno@shaw.ca
Open by appt.
Nadia Cyncark, President
Elizabeth Holinaty, Corresponding Secretary

***Edmonton:* Ukrainian Cultural Heritage Village**
8820 - 112 St. NW, Edmonton, AB T6G 2P8
780-662-3640, Fax: 780-662-3273,
uchv@gov.ab.ca
www.ukrainianvillage.ca
The provincial historic site presents Ukrainian settlement in east central Alberta between 1892 & 1930. The Ukrainian Cultural Heritage Village has over thiry historic buildings for visitors to explore, including a grain elevator, a budei (a sod hut), & three churches of Eastern Byzantine Rite. The village is open from the May long weekend to Labour Day. School groups may book a tour at other times of the year.
Arnold Grandt, Acting Director, Arnold.Grandt@gov.ab.ca
Becky Dahl, Curator, Becky.Dahl@gov.ab.ca
Shirley Hauck, Head, Special Events, Shirley.Hauck@gov.ab.ca
Pamela Trischuk, Head, Education & Interpretation Services, Pamela.Trischuk@gov.ab.ca
Radomir Bilash, Senior Historian & Project Manager, Alberta-Ukraine Genealogical Project, Radomir.Bilash@gov.ab.ca

Bruce McGregor, Coordinator, Historic Farm Program, Bruce.McGregor@gov.ab.ca

***Edmonton:* University of Alberta Dental Museum**
Dentistry Pharmacy Centre, University of Alberta, Edmonton, AB T6G 2N8
780-492-5194, Fax: 780-492-1624,
gsperber@ualberta.ca
Collection of antique dental instruments & furniture; natural history collection of animal skulls & fossil hominid models
Dr. G. Sperber, Curator

***Edmonton:* University of Alberta Museum of Paleontology**
University of Alberta - B-01 Earth Sciences Building, Edmonton, AB T6G 2E3
780-492-3265, Fax: 780-492-8190,
eas-inquiries@ualberta.ca
www.ualberta.ca/EAS
The museum presents the history of life over the course of geological time, starting with PreCambrian stromatolites and ending with Pleistocene megafauna; open during business hours Mon.-Fri.
M. Sharp, Chair
A. Locock, Collections Manager

***Edmonton:* University of Alberta Museum of Zoology**
#Z1011, Biological Sciences Bldg., University of Alberta, Edmonton, AB T6G 2E9
780-492-4622, Fax: 780-492-9234,
uamz@odum.biology.ualberta.ca
www.biology.ualberta.ca/uamz.hp/uamz.html
Open year round

***Edmonton:* University of Alberta Museums**
c/o Museums & Collections Services, Ring House #1, Edmonton, AB T6G 2E1
780-492-5834, Fax: 780-492-6185,
museums@ualberta.ca
www.museums.ualberta.ca
Museum services & expertise are provided to more than 35 teaching & research collections at the University; human history, fine art, natural & applied science collections, public programs, educational outreach & other community service programs offered
Janine Andrews, Executive Director
Frannie Blondheim, Manager, Communications Program
Pauline Rennick, Manager, Collections Program
Jim Corrigan, Curator, Univ. of Alberta Art & Artifact Collection

***Edmonton:* University of Alberta Vascular Plant Herbarium**
Dept. of Biological Sciences, University of Alberta, B-414, Biological Sciences, Edmonton, AB T6G 2E1
780-492-3308, Fax: 780-492-9234,
dorothy.fabijan@ualberta.ca
www.biology.ualberta.ca
Dorothy Fabijan, Assistant Curator

***Edmonton:* Victoria School Archives & Museum**
10210 - 108 Ave., Edmonton, AB T5H 1A8
780-426-3010, Fax: 780-498-8727,
jack.calkins@epob.ca
www.virtualmuseum.ca
Artifacts that relate to the school from 1903 to present; student & teacher records from 1911; books, playbills, posters, uniforms, photos, sweaters
Jack Calkins, Director, Cell: 780-862-0644
Michael Calkins, Archivist

***Edson:* Galloway Station Museum**
5425A - 3 Ave., Edson, AB T7E 1L5
780-723-5696,
Forestry; coal mining; railway
Jean Hatlen

***Edson:* Red Brick Arts Centre & Museum**
4818 - 7 Ave., Edson, AB T7E 1K8
780-723-3582, Fax: 780-723-3582,
Art gallery, theatre, school room museum, dance studio & gift shop
Betty Stitzenberger, President

***Elk Point:* Fort George Museum**
PO Box 66, Elk Point, AB T0A 1A0
780-645-6256, Fax: 780-645-4760,
Historical & archaeological material of a local nature; located 13 km SE of Elk Point on Secondary Rd. #646

***Etzikom:* Heritage Museum & Historic Windmill Centre**
PO Box 585, Etzikom, AB T0K 0W0
403-666-3737, Fax: 403-666-2002,
Canadian national historic windmill centre; open May long weekend - Sept. long weekend Mon-Sat 10-5, Sun. 12-6
June Mitzel, Director
Harold Halvorson, President

***Evansburg:* Pembina Lobstick Historical Museum**
PO Box 85, Evansburg, AB T0E 0T0

Artifacts of local historical interest

***Fairview:* RCMP Centennial Celebration Museum**
PO Box 1994, Fairview, AB T0H 1L0
780-835-4815,
Original barracks; also 2nd museum on a 10-acre site; open summer
Jean Bartlett, 780/835-4715
Robert Keddie, 780/835-2847
Marshall Rolling, 780/835-2392

***Forestburg:* Forestburg & District Museum**
PO Box 46, 4707 - 50 St., Forestburg, AB T0B 1N0
780-582-2165, Fax: 780-582-4203,
Housed in former Masonic Hall; displays relevant to the area; open by appt.

***Fort Chipewyan:* Fort Chipewyan Bicentennial Museum**
PO Box 203, Fort Chipewyan, AB T0P 1B0
780-697-3844, Fax: 780-697-2389,
fortchipmuseum@telus.net
www.woodbuffalo.ab.ca
Founded: 1991 The museum is a replica of the Hudson's Bay Store; local artifacts & archives; library reference collection; classes. Located on Mackenzie Ave. in Fort Chipewyan.
Oliver Glanfield, Chair
Maureen Clarke, Vice-Chair

***Fort MacLeod:* The Fort Museum**
PO Box 776, Fort MacLeod, AB T0L 0Z0
403-553-4703, Fax: 403-553-3451, 866-273-6841
info@nwmpmuseum.com
www.nwmpmuseum.com
Tells the story of the arrival of the NWMP into Western Canada, & the Natives & Pioneers of that time

***Fort MacLeod:* Head-Smashed-In Buffalo Jump**
PO Box 1977, Fort MacLeod, AB T0L 0Z0
403-553-2731, Fax: 403-553-3141,
info@head-smashed-in.com
www.head-smashed-in.com
Founded: 1987 Designated a UNESCO World Heritage Site in 1981, this jump is a testimony to the hunting customs of native peoples, particularly the Blackfoot, for thousands of years. The Interpretive Centre, blending into a sandstone cliff, explores the lives of the Blackfoot peoples from the geography of the region to the family life and ceremonies. Open year round.
Terry Malone, Facility Manager

***Fort McMurray:* Fort McMurray Oil Sands Discovery Centre**
515 MacKenzie Blvd., Fort McMurray, AB T9H 4X3
780-743-7167, Fax: 780-791-0710,
osdc@gov.ab.ca
www.oilsandsdiscovery.com
Open year round
Nancy Dodsworth, Facility Supervisor

***Fort McMurray:* Heritage Park**
1 Tolen Dr., Fort McMurray, AB T9H 1G7
780-791-7575, Fax: 780-791-5180,
heritage@fortmcmurrayhistory.com
www.fortmcmurrayhistory.com
Founded: 1974 The park is a village of 17 historic buildings from a trapper's cabin to a Catholic Mission celebrating the history of Ft. McMurray and the region. On site are 2 railway cars. Exhibits cover the logging, fishing and trapping industries. There is an extensive archive of photographs and historical documents.
MS Roseann Davidson, Executive Director, 780-791-7575, X-228

***Fort Saskatchewan:* Fort Saskatchewan Museum**
10006 - 101 St., Fort Saskatchewan, AB T8L 1V9
780-998-1783,
info@fortsask.ca
www.fortsask.ca
Kris Nygren, Curator

***Girouxville:* Musée Girouxville Museum**
Village of Girouxville, PO Box 276, Girouxville, AB T0H 1S0
780-323-4252, Fax: 780-323-4110,
Located in the heart of Girouxville, museum offers visitors a glimpse back into a time when pioneers first settled in the Smoky River Region; more than 6,000 pieces on display; collections includes: Religion, Native history, Natural history, Pioneer life, Hunting & Trapping, Transportation, Fur trade, Domestic history, Communications, Agriculture, Photography, Education, Geology & Palaeontology

***Grande Prairie:* Grande Prairie Museum**
Pioneer Museum Society of Grande Prairie & District, PO Box 687, Grande Prairie, AB T8V 3A8
780-532-5482, Fax: 780-831-7371,
info@grandeprairiemuseum.org
www.grandeprairiemuseum.org
Dinosaur bones; arrowheads; wildlife exhibits; pioneer artifacts; heritage village; archives; open daily, closed on holidays
Peter Goertzen, Manager/Curator

***Grande Prairie:* The Heritage Discovery Centre (HDC)**
Centre 2000 Building, PO Box 687, Grande Prairie, AB T8V 3A8
780-532-5790, Fax: 780-831-7371,
pgoertzen@grandeprairiemuseum.org
Located at Centre 2000 in the Tourist Information Bldg.; includes a main exhibit gallery, a Rotary Learning Theatre, & the Kin Gallery. Also includes dinosaur exhibit, survivor games, mini-theatres, and hands-on display.
Peter Goertzen

***Hanna:* Hanna Museum & Pioneer Village**
***Parent:* Hanna & District Historical Society**
PO Box 1528, Pioneer Trail, Hanna, AB T0J 1P0
403-854-4244,
www.hanna.ca
Historic buildings at the pioneer village include a ranch house, a one room schoolhouse, a store, a church, a hospital, a dental office, & a power mill. Archives are also available for research. The museum & pioneer village is open from June to August, & in May & September by appointment.
Vic Mohl, Secretary-Treasurer

***High Prairie:* High Prairie & District Museum & Historical Society**
PO Box 1442, High Prairie, AB T0G 1E0
780-523-2601, Fax: 780-523-2633,
hpdmhs@telusplanet.net
www.highprairiemuseum.com
Founded: 1967 The museum preserves the history of High Prairie & surrounding area by conserving artifacts used by homesteaders from the early 1900s. Stories of the settlers are also archived. Programs offered to children include butter-making, bread-making and sewing lessons. Open year round, with summer & winter hrs.

***High River:* Museum of the Highwood**
309B Macleod Trail SW, High River, AB T1V 1Z5
403-652-7156, Fax: 403-652-2396,
museumofthehighwood@highriver.ca
www.highriver.ca
Located in the historic sandstone Canadian Pacific Railway Station on 1st Street Southwest in High River, the Museum of the Highwood exhibits the history of the Highwood River basin. The museum features a family discovery room, which is a hands-on space with old fashioned games & toys. Programs & tours are available upon request.

***Hines Creek:* End of Steel Heritage Society**
PO Box 686, Hines Creek, AB T0H 2A0
403-494-3522,
Former Northern Alberta Railway cars; homes & church circa. 1930; pioneering artifacts; trapper's cabin; community hall

***Hinton:* Alberta Forest Service Museum**
1176 Switzer Dr., Hinton, AB T7V 1V3
780-865-8200, Fax: 780-865-8266,
envtrain@gov.ab.ca
tpr.alberta.ca/parks/switzer/attractions
Established to preserve a history of forestry in the province of Alberta; displays reflect work performed by the early rangers & provide an appreciation of their accomplishments achieved without benefit of modern transportation, tools & technology; "compact disk" guided tour; ranger headquarters cabin built in 1922; open daily; weekends by appt
Rob Thorburn

***Holden:* Holden Historical Society Museum**
PO Box 32, 4920 - 50 Holden Ave., Holden, AB T0B 2C0
780-688-2464, Fax: 780-688-2464,
dmarus@telus.net
The collection is of the local farming community with objects pertaining to pioneer life. Open Wed., Fri., & Sun. in summer, 2-4
Dave Maruszeczka

***Iddesleigh:* Rainy Hills Historical Society Pioneer Exhibits (RHHS)**
***Also known as:* Rainy Hills Historical Society**
c/o Margaret Harahue, Iddesleigh, AB T0J 1T0
403-898-2443,
Community museum exhibiting homestead items including furnishings, clothing, farm equipment & photographs; also features a blacksmith shop, school room, general store, an old-time kitchen & the original Iddlesleigh Alberta Wheat Post Office building
Margaret Harahue, Sec.-Treas.

***Innisfail:* Innisfail Historical Village**
52nd Ave. & 42nd St., Innisfail, AB T0M 1A0
403-227-2906, Fax: 403-227-2901,
idhs@telus.net
www.innisfailhistory.com
Promote the preservation, interpretation, enjoyment of the history of Innisfail & District; village is made up of seventeen buildings on two acres of land; farm machinary and picnic area.

***Irvine:* Prairie Memories Museum**
PO Box 245, Irvine, AB T0J 1V0
403-834-2646,
Local history; open June 30 - Sept.

***Islay:* Morrison Museum of the Country School**
PO Box 120, Islay, AB T0B 2J0
780-744-2271,
Contains a collection of the artifacts to be found in a western Canadian country school of the 1930s & 1940s
Allen Ronaghan, Curator

***Jasper:* Jasper Yellowhead Museum & Archives (JYHS)**
PO Box 42, 400 Pyramid Lake Rd., Jasper, AB T0E 1E0
780-852-3013,
webadministrator@jaspermuseum.org
www.jaspermuseum.org
Other contact information: Phone, Archives: 780-852-3240
The Jasper Yellowhead Museum & Archives collects, preserves, & exhibits artifacts & documents related to the human history of Jasper National Park & the Yellowhead corridor. Displays in the historical gallery tell the story of the fur trade, the railway, & early tourism. The area has been designated as part of a World Heritage Site. The Jasper Yellowhead Museum & Archives is open year-round. Visits to the archives are by appointment only.
B. Bell, President
Karen Byers, Manager, manager@jaspermuseum.org
J. Couture, Historian
Dee Dee Bartlett, Contact, Collections, collections@jaspermuseum.org
Val Delill, Contact, Exhibits, exhibits@jaspermuseum.org
Lucie Doucet, Contact, Gift Shop, giftshop@jaspermuseum.org
Meghan Power, Contact, Archives, archives@jaspermuseum.org

***Leduc:* Dr. Woods House Museum**
4801 - 49 Ave., Leduc, AB T9E 6L6
780-986-1517,
Restored 1920s house with attached garage & medical wing

***Lethbridge:* Fort Whoop-Up**
***Also known as:* Fort Hamilton**
PO Box 1074, Lethbridge, AB T1J 4A2
403-329-0444, Fax: 403-329-0645,
info@fortwhoopup.ca
www.fortwhoopup.ca
Located in Indian Battle Park, west end of 3rd Ave. As an Interpretive Centre, "the Fort" has been reconstructed and interpreted to be the norotirious whiskey fort: as such is has electronic displays, historical sights, and sounds to pay tribute to and commentorate the legact of the NMMP, Aboriginal People, and pioneers that shaped Western Canada. Open year round
Doran Degenstein, Curator and Director, 403-329-0444

***Lethbridge:* Sir Alexander Galt Museum & Archives**
910 - 4 Ave. South, Lethbridge, AB T1J 0P6
403-320-3898, Fax: 403-329-4958,
info@galtmuseum.com
www.galtmuseum.com
The human history of Lethbridge & southern Alberta in 5 galleries & an outdoor courtyard; free admission
Wendy Aitkens, Curator

***Lloydminster:* Barr Colony Heritage Cultural Centre**
4420 - 50th Ave., Lloydminster, AB T9V 0W2
306-825-5655, Fax: 306-825-9070,
bchcc@lloydminster.ca
142.179.207.186/bchcc
Other contact information: Phone, City of Lloydminster: 780-875-6184; Fax: 780-871-8345
Located at Highway 16 & 45th Avenue, the Barr Colony Heritage Cultural Centre consists of an antique museum, the Imhoff art collection, the OTS Heavy Oil Science Centre, & the Fuchs wildlife exhibit. The Richard Larsen Museum presents antiques of the Barr Colonists. Artifacts include funiture & agricultural equipment. Visitors can also see Lloydminster's first church, a log cabin, a filling station, & a 1906 schoolhouse. The centre is open year round.

***Longview:* Bar U Ranch National Historic Site of Canada**
PO Box 168, Longview, AB T0L 1H0
403-395-2212, Fax: 403-395-2331, 888-773-8888
BarU.info@pc.gc.ca
www.pc.gc.ca/lhn-nhs/ab/baru/index_e.asp
Other contact information: TTY: 866-787-6221
With 35 buildings & structures, the Bar U Ranch commemorates the history of ranching in Canada. The Ranch is open from late May to the end of September. Visits can be arranged during the off season.

Lougheed: **Iron Creek Museum**
PO Box 249, Lougheed, AB T0B 2V0
780-386-3787,
Two one-room school houses; church; blacksmith & shoe repair shop; log hall housing artifacts & farm machinery

Markerville: **Historic Markerville Creamery**
PO Box 837, Markerville, AB T0M 1M0
403-728-3006, Fax: 403-728-3225,
creamery@touralberta.com
Creamery museum restored to 1930s profiles Icelandic settlement of central Alberta; "Kaffistofa" features Icelandic menu
Kathleen Raines, Manager

Medicine Hat: **Esplanade Arts & Heritage Centre (MHM&AG)**
401 First St. SE, Medicine Hat, AB T1A 8W2
403-502-8580, Fax: 403-502-8589,
esplanade@medicinthat.ca
www.esplanade.ca
Museum: Permanent Gallery featuring the history of Medicine Hat & area using pieces from vast collection, including pioneer home funishings, Victorian period artifacts, archaeological artifacts, military, sporting & Native artifacts, business & industry equipment, clothing & more; Archives: database of manuscripts, extensive black & white photographic collection, genealogical information & more; A
Carol Beatty, Manager

Medicine Hat: **Medicine Hat Clay Industries National Historic District**
713 Medalta Ave. SE, Medicine Hat, AB T1A 3K9
403-529-1070, Fax: 403-580-5868, 866-526-2777
info@medalta.org
www.medalta.org
The 150-acre Historic Clay District preserves the history of the region's pottery industry. With working, circular kilns and original factory, it is living museum. The Medalta International Artists in Residence (MIAIR) program hosts contemporary ceramic artists. An interactive clay area and education programs are available for children.
MR Barry G. Finkelman, General Manager/Executive Director, barry@medalta.org

Millet: **Millet & District Museum & Archives**
PO Box 178, 5120 - 50 St., Millet, AB T0C 1Z0
780-387-5558, Fax: 780-387-5548,
info@milletmuseum.ca
www.milletmuseum.ca
Founded: 1985 Exhibits incude archives on local history, home settings from 1900-1950 and portraits of over 200 local veterans of World Wars I, II. Building also houses the Millet Visitor Information Centre; open to the public Tues. - Sat. in summer
MS Tracey Leavitt, Executive Director/Curator

Mirror: **Mirror & District Museum**
PO Box 246, 4910 - 53 St., Mirror, AB T0B 3C0
403-788-3828,
mmuseum@telus.net
Other contact information: Phone, Off season: 403-788-3094
Settler & railway artifacts are presented at the Mirror & District Museum. The museum if open from mid May to the beginning of September. Appointments may be arranged at other times.

Mundare: **Basilian Fathers Museum**
PO Box 386, Mundare, AB T0B 3H0
780-764-3887, Fax: 780-764-3825,
curator@basilianmuseum.org
www.basilianmuseum.org
Ukrainian culture & religion
Karen Lemiski, Associate Director/Curator

Nanton: **Bomber Command Museum of Canada**
PO Box 1051, Nanton, AB T0L 1R0
403-646-2270, Fax: 403-646-2214,
office@bombercommandmuseum.ca
www.bombercommandmuseum.ca
Other contact information: Twitter:
www.twitter.com/BCMofCanada
The Bomber Command Museum of Canada honours persons associated with Bomber Command during World War II. It also commemorates the operations of the British Commonwealth Air Training Plan. The Museum's library & archives may be contacted at the following e-mail address: library@bombercommandmuseum.ca. School & group visits may be organized by contacting the following e-mail address: visitorservices@bombercommandmuseum.ca.
Bob Evans, Curator, curator@bombercommandmuseum.ca
Robert Pedersen, President

Olds: **Mountain View Museum & Archives**
Parent: **Olds Historical Society**
PO Box 3882, 5038 - 50th St., Olds, AB T4H 1P6
403-556-8464,
info@oldsmuseum.ca
www.oldsmuseum.ca
Founded: 1972 The Olds Historical Society preserves artifacts, textual documents, & photographs, which depict the history & heritage of Olds & its surrounding area. Items are displayed & research services are available at the Mountain View Museum & Archives, which is located in the 1920 Olds AGT building. The museum is open from Monday to Friday. Guided tours & educational programs are offered.
Michael Dougherty, Museum Manager, manager@oldsmuseum.ca
Jeffery Kearney, Archivist, archives@oldsmuseum.ca

Oyen: **Crossroads Museum**
PO Box 563, 310 1st Avenue East, Oyen, AB T0J 2J0
403-664-2330,
www.virtualmuseum.ca
Buildings include a period house (1918); cook car; blacksmith shop; tractor & truck building; a 120x40 Quonset; 1912 schoolhouse; former community hall; "teepee" type building containing archaeological artifacts; season May-Aug.
Nellie Eaton, President

Peace River: **Peace River Centennial Museum & Archives (PRMCAA)**
Also known as: **Peace River Museum**
10302 - 99 St., Peace River, AB T8S 1K1
780-624-4261, Fax: 780-624-2470,
prcma@telusplanet.net
Displays include: Sir Alexander Mackenzie, fur trade, town of Peace River

Pincher Creek: **Kootenai Brown Pioneer Village**
PO Box 1226, Pincher Creek, AB T0K 1W0
403-627-3684, Fax: 403-627-5850, 888-298-5855
kootenai@telusplanet.net
telusplanet.net/public/kootenai
Open year round
George Sinnott, President

Plamondon: **Plamondon & District Museum**
c/o Emilie Chevigny, PO Box 119, Plamondon, AB T0A 2T0
403-798-3193,
www.plamondonalberta.ca
Operated by the Plamondon & District Museum Society, the Plamondon & District Museum features local cultural artifacts from early pioneers. The museum is open from June to August.
Bonita Marchand, Contact

Ponoka: **Fort Ostell Museum**
5320 - 54 St., Ponoka, AB T4J 1L8
403-783-5224,
fomol@telus.net
www.ponoka.org
Founded: 1967 Open May 24-Sept. 4, winter special occasions or by appt.
Barb Greshner, Chair

Red Deer: **Alberta Sports Hall of Fame & Museum**
30 Riverview Park, Red Deer, AB T4N 1E3
403-341-8614, Fax: 403-341-8619,
postmaster@albertasportshalloffame.com
www.albertasportshalloffame.com
Founded: 1957 To preserve artifacts & archival material that are significant in Alberta's sporting history; 7 Honoured Members are inducted into the Sports Hall of Fame each year, plus 3 award recipients; interactive multisport virtual game system & a curriculum based education program; theatre; boardroom rental.
Donna Hately, Managing Director

Red Deer: **Kerry Wood Nature Centre**
6300 - 45 Ave., Red Deer, AB T4N 3M4
403-346-2010, Fax: 403-347-2550,
general@waskasoopark.ca
www.waskasoopark.ca
Central Alberta's year-round home of entertaining & informative nature activities & exhibits; gateway to Gaetz Lakes Sanctuary; features art gallery, bookshop, A/V theatre, meeting rooms, children's Discovery Room & exhibits; extensive programs, courses, field trips for all ages; open daily except Christmas; admission by donation
Jim Robertson, Manager
Paul Gowans, Executive Director

Red Deer: **Red Deer Museum & Art Gallery**
4525 - 47A Ave., Red Deer, AB T4N 6Z6
403-309-8405, Fax: 403-342-6644,
museum@reddeer.ca
www.reddeermuseum.com
Founded: 1973 The Red Deer Museum & Art Gallery tells the story of the people, history, & culture of central Alberta, through its collections, exhibitions, & programs. The museum's more than 85,000 objects include clothing & First Nations & Inuit art. A library on the site houses artifact books, catalogues, & other printed material.
Lorna Johnson, Executive Director BFA, M.ED, lorna.johnson@reddeer.ca
Michael Dawe, Curator, History, michael.dawe@reddeer.ca
Valerie Miller, Coordinator, Collections, valerie.miller@reddeer.ca
Lynn Norman, Coordinator, Communications & Marketing, lynn.norman@reddeer.ca

Redcliff: **Redcliff Historical & Museum Society**
Also known as: **Redcliff Museum**
PO Box 758, Redcliff, AB T0J 2P0
403-548-6260,
Exhibits showing the commercial & recreational aspect of Redcliff citizens; extensive drug store, domestic, school, toy & organizational exhibits; history of past industries with manufactured artifacts; weekly newpaper on microfilm 1910-1939; open May-Aug., Tue.-Sat., Sun., Oct.-Apr. by appt.

Rocky Mountain House: **Rocky Mountain House National Historic Site of Canada**
Comp. 6, Site 127, RR#4, Rocky Mountain House, AB T4T 2A4
403-845-2412, Fax: 403-845-5320,
rocky.info@pc.gc.ca
www.pc.gc.ca/rockymountainhouse
Site of four fur trading posts dating back to 1799; Commemorates the fur trade & the role of Native peoples in the fur trade & western exploration (David Thompson); Over 500 acres; Hiking trails, displays, herd of bisons; Exhibits; 3/4 size playfort; Eight trailside listening stations; Heritage demonstrations & presentations; Open Victoria Day weekend - Labour Day
Scott Whiting, Site Operations Supervisor

Rosebud: **Rosebud Historical Society**
PO Box 601, Rosebud, AB T0J 2T0
403-677-2208, Fax: 403-533-2243,
A collection of pioneer tools, etc. that have been donated to the museum; open year round

Rowley: **Yester-Year Artifacts Museum**
General Delivery, Rowley, AB T0J 2X0
403-368-3816, Fax: 403-368-2239,
Early settlers artifacts housed in original buildings

St Albert: **Musée Héritage Museum & Archives**
Also known as: **St. Albert Museum**
5 Ste-Anne St., St Albert, AB T8N 3Z9
780-459-1528, Fax: 780-459-1546,
museum@compusmart.ab.ca
History of St. Albert & surrounding area
Alexandra Hatcher, Director

St Paul: **Fort George & Buckingham House Provincial Historic Site (FGBH)**
#318, Provincial Bldg., 5025, 49th Ave., St Paul, AB T0A 3A4
403-645-6256, Fax: 403-645-4760,
ross.stromberg@gov.ab.ca
Archaeological remains of 2 fur trade forts; interpretive centre & gift shop; open May 15 - Labour Day; located 13 km SE of Elk Point on Hwy. 646

St Paul: **Victoria Settlement Provincial Historic Site**
Also known as: **Fort Victoria**
#318, Provincial Bldg., St Paul, AB T0A 3A4
403-645-6256, Fax: 403-645-4760,
Located 10 km south of Smoky Lake on Hwy. 855, 6 km east along Victoria Trail; Hudson Bay Company post & settlement; open May 15-Labour Day

Saint-Paul: **Musée historique de Saint-Paul**
CP 1925, Saint-Paul, AB T0A 3A0
780-645-4800, Fax: 780-645-5959,
Founded: 1984 Relever l'histoire de la communauté de Saint-Paul; expositions; cours d'histoire aux élèves; projets spécials.
Jeannette Létourneau, Trésorière

Sangudo: **Lac Ste-Anne Historical Society Pioneer Museum**
PO Box 525, Sangudo, AB T0E 2A0
403-785-2674,
Ed Liss, President

Seba Beach: **Seba Beach Heritage Museum**
General Delivery, Seba Beach, AB T0E 2B0
403-420-6704,
Summer resort themed artifacts, such as regatta trophies & photographs; historical material related to Seba Beach; located at Main Ave. & 101 St. North

Sedgewick: **Sedgewick Archives, Gallery & Museum**
PO Box 538, Sedgewick, AB T0B 4C0
780-384-3741,
www.sedgewick.ca
Founded: 1989 Clothing, jewelry, books, photographs, tools; open Tues-Fri, 1:30-4:30; located in the historic Bank of Montreal building on Main St. in Sedgewick
Lorne Abre, President
Myrtle Matthews, Secretary

Sherwood Park: **Strathcona County Heritage Museum**
913 Ash St., Sherwood Park, AB T8A 2G3
780-467-8189, Fax: 780-467-8189,
Local history; open year round

Siksika: **Siksika Nation Museum**
PO Box 1730, Siksika, AB T0J 3W0
403-734-5361, Fax: 403-264-9659,
Floria Duckchief, Manager

Stettler: **Stettler Town & Country Museum**
PO Box 2118, Stettler, AB T0C 2L0
403-742-4534,
stcmuse@telus.net
A village replica housing artifacts from the local & surrounding areas; includes a courthouse, schools, church, CN station, pioneer homes & barns, agricultural items as well as a local sports museum; also an original Estonian Grist mill & log cabin of the early twenties constructed by early Estonian pioneers; situated on 10 acres in SW Stettler; open daily May-Aug. or by appt.
Wilda V. Gibbon, Curator
Karen Wahlund, Assistant

Stony Plain: **Multicultural Heritage Centre**
PO Box 5411, 51 Street, Stony Plain, AB T7Z 1X7
780-963-2777, Fax: 780-963-0233,
The Heritage Centre includes restored buildings including a 1925 high school, a settler's cabin, and a homestead's kitchen. This living history museum offers entertainment and weekend demos. Open M-Sa 10-6, Su 10-6:30
Judy Unterschultz, Executive Director

Stony Plain: **Stony Plain & District Pioneer Museum**
5120 - 43 Ave., Stony Plain, AB T7Z 1X2
780-963-9825,
Open April 1 - Oct. 31

Strome: **Sodbuster Archives Museum**
PO Box 151, Strome, AB T0B 4H0
780-376-3546,
sodbustersarchivesmuseum@telus.net
Other contact information: Tel. 780/376-3688 (summer)
Shows the development of the West & of the Strome & district community from 1900 to the 1950s
Joan Brockhoff, Sec.-Treas., joanbl@telusplanet.net

Sundre: **Sundre Pioneer Village Museum**
PO Box 314, 211, 1st Ave. SW, Sundre, AB T0M 1X0
403-638-3233,
sundremuseum@telus.net
www.museum.sundre.com
Located at 130 Centre St. South; open May-Sept.
Darleen Smee, Secretary

Taber: **Taber & District Museum**
4702 - 50 St., Taber, AB T1G 2B6
403-223-5708, Fax: 403-223-0529,
tiimchin@telusplanet.net
Open year round, closed in Aug.

Three Hills: **Knee Hill Historical Museum**
PO Box 653, 1301-2nd St.N, Three Hills, AB T0M 2A0
403-443-2092, Fax: 403-443-7941,
www.threehills.ca
Pioneer Museum and tourist information centre.

Tofield: **Beaverhill Lake Nature Centre & Tofield Museum**
PO Box 30, 5020 - 48th Ave., Tofield, AB T0B 4J0
780-662-3269,
Founded: 1985 The Beaverhill Lake Nature Centre presents information about Beaverhill Lake & its wildlife. The lake is a federally recognized bird sanctuary. Located in the Beaverhill Lake Nature Centre facility is the Tofield Museum. The museum features the history of the community since 1882. The Tofield Museum is open from mid-April to Labour Day. Appointments may be arranged at other times of the year.

Trochu: **Trochu & District Museum**
PO Box 538, Trochu, AB T0M 2C0
403-442-2220,
Displays on the early pioneers including a kitchen, blacksmith shop, general store, schools, coal mining & an extensive collection of WW I & II pictures & uniforms; open May to Aug.
George O. Braham

Two Hills: **Two Hills & District Historical Museum**
PO Box 566, 5910-51 St., Two Hills, AB T0B 4K0
403-657-2461,
Houses 4,000 artifacts pertaining to the area; collection of steamers, automobiles, farm equipment, farm tools, early household artifacts, buildings, railways caboose, etc.

Valhalla Centre: **Melsness Mercantile**
PO Box 52, Valhalla Centre, AB T0H 3M0
780-356-2403, Fax: 780-356-2007,
loberg@gpwins.ca
Provincial historic site; museum displays, deli café, gift shop
E. Loberg, President

Vegreville: **Vegreville Regional Museum**
PO Box 328, Vegreville, AB T9C 1R3
780-632-7650,
museum@digitalweb.net
www.vegreville.com
Located on the site of the solonetzic soils research station of Agriculture Canada, The Vegreville Regional Museum depicts the history of Vegreville & its agricultural & business development. A special collection is The Right Honourable Donald Mazankowski, P.C. Collection. Mazankowski was the former Deputy Prime Minister of Canada. The regional museum also houses the Vegreville & District Sports Hall of Fame. The museum is open year-round.

Viking: **Viking Historical Museum**
PO Box 270, Viking, AB T0B 4N0
780-336-3066,
Displays various facets of pioneer life; includes 1907 school, 1903 log store, 1938 church & 1919 farm house; open summer; May 15 - Thanksgiving
J.H. Roddick, Director

Wainwright: **Wainwright Museum**
PO Box 2994, Wainwright, AB T9W 1S9
403-842-3115, Fax: 403-842-4910,
battleriverhs@cablerocket.com
Open year round
Billie Patterson

Wanham: **Grizzly Bear Prairie Museum**
PO Box 68, Wanham, AB T0H 3P0
780-694-3933,
jesather@telusplanet.net
Several buildings including 1920s log house, Presbyterian church & storage building; displays of agricultural machinery & artifacts used by the pioneers of the area; forestry tower; forestry cabin containing schoolroom, toolroom & pioneer kitchen displays; 1920 era hiproof barn; CNR rail display: building to store two handcars; two handcars; various tools related to work on CNR
Stan Sather

Warner: **Devil's Coulee Dinosaur Heritage Museum**
PO Box 156, 300 County Rd., Warner, AB T0K 2L0
403-642-2118, Fax: 403-642-3660,
dinoegg@telusplanet.net
www.devilscoulee.com
Dinosaur eggs; local fossils; local history
Suzanne Lodermeier, Manager

Wetaskiwin: **Alberta Central Railway Museum**
RR#2, Wetaskiwin, AB T9A 1W9
780-352-2257, Fax: 780-352-3202,
abcentral@incentre.net
www.abcentralrailway.com
Collection of early heavy weight cars from the passenger era, as well as fright equipment, cabooses, freight cars, and a snowplow. They also house the second oldest standing grain elevator in Alberta built by the Alberta Grain Company in 1906. Located southeast of Westaskiwin. Open from Victoria Day until Labour Day.
W.G. Wilson, Operations Manager
Ellen Wilson, Customer Services Manager

Wetaskiwin: **Canada's Aviation Hall of Fame / Panthéon de l'Aviation du Canada**
PO Box 6360, Hwy. 13, Wetaskiwin, AB T9A 2G1
780-361-1351,
cahf@telusplanet.net
www.cahf.ca
Founded: 1973 Canada's Aviation Hall of Fame collects, preserves, & exhibits material related to individuals & organizations that have made outstanding contributions to aviation & aerospace in Canada.
John Holding, Chair
Brian Fowler, Chair, Operations
Rosella Bjornson, Secretary-Treasurer

Wetaskiwin: **Reynolds Museum Ltd.**
4110 - 57 St., Wetaskiwin, AB T9A 2B6
780-352-5201, Fax: 780-352-4666,
rml@incentre.net
800 surplus antique cars, trucks, fire engines, tractors plus machinery for sale to allow for expansion of our displays of aircraft & military vehicles
Stanley G. Reynolds, President
Bruce A. Olson, Manager

Wetaskiwin: **Wetaskiwin & District Heritage Museum**
5007 - 50th Ave., Wetaskiwin, AB T9A 0S3
780-352-0227, Fax: 780-352-0226,
wdhm@persona.ca
www.wetaskiwinmuseum.com
Founded: 1986 The Wetaskiwin & District Heritage Museum presents the history of Westaskiwin, Alberta & the surrounding area, from dinosaur fossils, to First Nations' history, to the war years. Visitors can also learn about life on a Hutterite colony. A resource library is part of the museum. The museum is open year-round.
Sylvia Larson, Chief Executive Officer & Manager
Brianne Stone, Museum Administrator
Gillian Furuness, Manager, Collections
Helmer Larson, Manager, Projects

Willingdon: **Historic Village & Pioneer Museum at Shandro**
PO Box 102, Willingdon, AB T0B 4R0
780-367-2452,
mereska@vegnet.com
Ukrainian architecture & artifacts; open summer, other seasons by appt.

British Columbia

Provincial Museums

Museum of Anthropology
University of British Columbia, 6393 Marine Dr. NW, Vancouver, BC V6T 1Z2
604-822-5950, Fax: 604-822-2974,
jenwebb@interchange.ubc.ca
www.moa.ubc.ca
Art & objects from around the world, with emphasis on First Nations cultures of the Northwest Coast; displayed in architect Arthur Erickson's award-winning building overlooking Howe Sound
Dr. Anthony A. Shelton, Director

Museum of Vancouver (MOV)
1100 Chestnut St., Vancouver, BC V6J 3J9
604-736-4431,
guestservices@museumofvancouver.ca
www.museumofvancouver.ca
The Museum of Vancouver offers permanent displays, exhibitions, & educational programs about the human, cultural, & natural history of the city of Vancouver & the surrounding area. The Local History Lab & the Archaeology Education Centre contribute to the museum's school programs. The museum is open year-round.
Nancy Noble, Chief Executive Officer, 604-730-5323, nnoble@museumofvancouver.ca
Amanda Gibbs, Director, Audience Engagement, 604-730-5317, agibbs@museumofvancouver.ca
Joan Seidl, Director, Collections & Exhibitions, 604-730-5316, jseidl@museumofvancouver.ca
Viviane Gosselin, Curator, Contemporary Issues, 604-730-5318, vgosselin@museumofvancouver.ca
Wendy Nichols, Curator, Collections, 604-730-5312, wnichols@museumofvancouver.ca
Genny Krikorian, Officer, Marketing, 604-730-5309, gkrikorian@museumofvancouver.ca
Jane Lougheed, Officer, Education Program, 604-730-5307, jlougheed@museumofvancouver.ca

Royal BC Museum Corp.
675 Belleville St., Victoria, BC V8W 9W2
250-356-7226, Fax: 250-387-5674, 888-447-7977
reception@royalbcmuseum.bc.ca
www.royalbcmuseum.bc.ca
Founded in 1886, the RBCM specializes in the natural & human history of British Columbia
Pauline Rafferty, CEO
Grant Hughes, Director, Curatorial Services
Cynthia Wrate, Director, Marketing & Communications
Angela Williams, Director, Visitor & Human Resource Services
Gary Mitchell, Director, Access & Information Management
Faye Zinck, CFO

Other Museums in British Columbia

108 Mile Ranch: **100 Mile & District Historical Society**
PO Box 225, 108 Mile Ranch, BC V0K 2Z0
250-791-5288, Fax: 250-791-1947,
historical@bcinternet.net
www.historical.bc.ca
The 108 Mile Ranch Heritage Site comprises 11 historical buildings dating from the Gold Rush era; largest log barn in Canada; open May long weekend to Labour Day
Tom Rutledge, President

108 Mile Ranch: **108 Mile House Heritage Site & Museum**
100 Mile & District Historical Society, Hwy. 97, Box 225, 108 Mile Ranch, BC V0K 2Z0
250-791-5288, Fax: 250-791-1947,
historical@bcinternet.net
www.historical.bc.ca
Original 105 Mile Roadhouse along the Cariboo Gold Rush Trail, 10 other historical buildings including the largest log barn in Canada (circa 1908), also mill equipment display

Marianne Rutledge, Director

Abbotsford: **Matsqui-Sumas-Abbotsford Museum - Trethewey House**
Also known as: **MSA Museum**
2313 Ware St., Abbotsford, BC V2S 3C6
604-853-0313, Fax: 604-853-0326,
mail@MSA.Museum.bc.ca
www.abbotsford.net/msamuseum
Trethewey House was built in 1920 by B.C. timber baron, J.O. Trethewey and has been restored to period style, incuding its gardens and grounds. Also on site are the Playhouse and the Carriage House with the museum offices. Exhibits include an extensive collection of historical photographs of the region, in addition to an array of artifacts from local home life and businesses, particularly, the lumber industry. Tours are available.
MS Dorothy Van der Ree, Executive Director
MS Christina Reid, Collections Manager

Ainsworth Hot Springs: **Silver Ledge Hotel Museum**
PO Box 1314, Ainsworth Hot Springs, BC V0G 1A0
403-243-6302, Fax: 403-243-3672,
silverledge@shaw.ca
www.members.shaw.ca/silverledge
Photographic history of the first community in the west Kootenays & the Ainsworth Mining District housed in the Silver Ledge Hotel built in 1896
J.E Duff, President, 604/221-7605

Alert Bay: **Alert Bay Library & Museum**
PO Box 440, 118 Fir St., Alert Bay, BC V0N 1A0
250-974-5721, Fax: 250-974-5026,
abplb@island.net
www.alertbay.bclibrary.ca; www.alertbay.ca
Ethnographic material; artifacts related to the fishing industry, local history; gift shop
Joyce Wilby, Head Librarian/Archivist

Alert Bay: **U'Mista Cultural Centre**
PO Box 253, Front St., Alert Bay, BC V0N 1A0
250-974-5403, Fax: 250-974-5499,
umista@north.island.net
Kwakwaka'wakw masks depicting the Potlatch ceremony; traditional & contemporary arts & crafts

Armstrong: **Armstrong Spallumcheen Museum & Arts Society**
PO Box 308, 3415 Pleasant Valley Rd., Armstrong, BC V0E 1B0
250-546-8318,
www.asmas.ca
Other contact information: asmas@telus.net
Founded: 1974 The Armstrong Spallumcheen Museum and Arts Society features a museum, archives, & an art gallery. Visitors are educated about the history of the local region. Genealogy & art workshops are conducted.

Ashcroft: **Ashcroft Museum & Archives**
PO Box 129, Ashcroft, BC V0K 1A0
250-453-9161, Fax: 250-453-9664,
admin@village.ashcroft.bc.ca
www.village.ashcroft.bc.ca
Founded: 1935 History of the Southern Cariboo region, & the farming & ranching communities of Hat Creek Valley. Open 5 days a week, Apr.-Nov.; open 7 days a week July & Aug. Admission by donation. Located at the corner of Brink & Fourth streets in Ashcroft.
Kathy Paulos, Curator

Atlin: **Atlin Historical Museum (AHS)**
Also known as: **Atlin Historical Society**
PO Box 111, Atlin, BC V0W 1A0
250-651-7522, Fax: 250-651-7522,
heritage@atlin.net
Open May 15 - Labour Day. Closed on Mondays.

Barkerville: **Barkerville Historic Town**
PO Box 19, Barkerville, BC V0K 1B0
250-994-3332, Fax: 250-994-3435, 888-994-3332
barkerville@barkerville.ca
www.barkerville.ca
Other contact information: Info Email:
barkerville@gems8.gov.bc.ca
Restored Cariboo Gold Rush town; Blessing's Grave; Richfield Court House; open year round; peak season from early May to late Sept.
William Quackenbush, Curator
Judy Campbell, CEO
Reuben Berlin, Manager, Operations

Bella Coola: **Bella Coola Museum**
PO Box 726, 269 Hwy. 20, Bella Coola, BC V0T 1C0
250-799-5767,
info@bellacoolamuseum.ca
www.bellacoolamuseum.ca
Other contact information: Phone, Archives: 250-982-2130
Founded: 1963 Owned & operated by the Bella Coola Valley Museum Society, the Bella Coola Valley Museum depicts the human history of the Bella Coola Valley. Exhibits present the history of the area from European contact to 1955. The museum's historic building is open from June to September. School presentations can be arranged at other times of the year. The British Columbia Central Coast Archives ia open year round, from Tuesday to Thursday.
Wendy Kingsley, Manager

Bralorne: **Bralorne Pioneer Museum**
PO Box 40, 400 Hawkes Ave., Bralorne, BC V0K 1P0
250-238-2349, Fax: 250-238-2349,
bralornepioneermuseum@telus.net
Founded: 1977 Bralorne Pioneer Museum depicts the history of a community which is known as the home of the Bralorne Mine, a productive gold mine during the gold mining era. Mining artifacts are part of the museum's collection, as well as general historical information about the local Bridge River Valley area. The museum is situated in the industrial education shop of the Bralorne High School. It is open during the summer & on weekends.

Britannia Beach: **British Columbia Museum of Mining**
PO Box 188, Britannia Beach, BC V0N 1J0
604-896-2233, Fax: 604-896-2260, 800-896-4044
general@bcmuseumofmining.org
www.bcmuseumofmining.org
Founded: 1971 Governed by the Britannia Beach Historical Society, the British Columbia Museum of Mining preserves the material & social history of mining in British Columbia.
Mark Germyn, President, Britannia Beach Historical Society, mark@bcmuseumofmining.org
Kirsten Clausen, Executive Director, kclausen@bcmuseumofmining.org
Diane Mitchell, Curator, Education & Collections, diane@bcmuseumofmining.org
Henry Gottardi, Site Manager & Coordinator, Filming, henry@bcmuseumofmining.org
Carol Watts, Manager, Visitor Services, Retail Operations, & Tour Buses, carol@bcmuseumofmining.org
Katherine Flett, Director, Marketing, 604-924-5542
Robin MacDonald, Coordinator, Bookings & Communications, robin@bcmuseumofmining.org
Rory Odenbach, Coordinator, Programmes & Head Tour Guide, rory@bcmuseumofmining.org

Burnaby: **Burnaby Village Museum**
6501 Deer Lake Ave., Burnaby, BC V5G 3T6
604-297-4565, Fax: 604-297-4557,
bvm@burnaby.ca
www.burnabyvillagemuseum.ca
Other contact information: Phone, Schools: 604-297-4558;
Phone, Rentals: 604-297-4552
The Burnaby Village Museum consists of heritage & replica buildings from the 1920s, such as a blacksmith shop, a general store, a print shop, a farmhouse, a restored interurban tram & a carousel.
Lisa Codd, Curator, lisa.codd@burnaby.ca
Elisabeth Czerwinski, Conservator, elisabeth.czerwinski@burnaby.ca
Maurice Guibord, Coordinator, Programs, maurice.guibord@burnaby.ca
Nancy Stagg, Coordinator, Marketing, nancy.stagg@burnaby.ca

Burnaby: **Canadiana Costume Society of British Columbia & Western Canada**
6501 Deer Lake Ave., Burnaby, BC V8Z 1G1
604-293-6520, Fax: 604-293-6525,
CanadianaCostume@hotmail.com
www.vcn.bc.ca/ccs
Founded: 1976 The Canadiana Costume Society of British Columbia & Western Canada collects, conserves, researches, & displays British Columbia's costume heritage. The collection dates from the late 1700s to the 1980s. The Society's members create displays & provide lectures.

Burnaby: **Simon Fraser University Museum of Archaeology & Ethnology**
c/o Dept. of Archaeology, Simon Fraser University, 8888 University Dr., Burnaby, BC V5A 1S6
604-291-3325, Fax: 604-291-5666,
bwinter@sfu.ca
www.sfu.museum
Major emphasis on the Pacific Northwest coast; open year round
Dr. Barbara J. Winter, Curator

Burns Lake: **Lakes District Museum Society**
PO Box 266, Burns Lake, BC V0J 1E0
250-692-7450,
Artifacts, archival records, and historical reference material relation to the Lakes District of northwestern B.C., including Burns Lake, Palling, Francois Lake, Babine Lake, Ootsa Lake, and Tweedsmuir Provinvial Park. Includes interviews with early settlers (and descendants) in the Lakes District.

Cache Creek: **Historic Hat Creek Ranch**
PO Box 878, Junction Hwy. 97-99, Cache Creek, BC V0K 1H0
250-457-9722, Fax: 250-457-9311, 800-782-0922
contact@hatcreekranch.com
www.hatcreekranch.com
Founded: 1984 Offering a blend of cultures, on site are an 1860 roadhouse with gold rush era artifacts and a traditional kekuli, or pit house, used as a winter home by people of the Shuswap Nation. Costumed guides explain the life of area's history & culture and visitors can experience firsthand a stagecoach ride. Other activities include gold panning and archery. There are a gift shop, food services, as well as cabins & campground facilities. Open daily, May to Sept.
MR Ken Mather, General Manager, kenm@hatcreekranch.com

Campbell River: **Museum at Campbell River (MCR)**
Also known as: **Campbell River Museum & Archives**
PO Box 70 A, 470 Island Hwy., Campbell River, BC V9W 4Z9
250-287-3103, Fax: 250-286-0109,
general.inquiries@crmuseum.ca
www.crmuseum.ca
Founded: 1958 Exhibits include First Nations ceremonial masks & regalia, coastal logging, fishing history & settler development; archives & research centre; gift shop
Lesia Davis, Executive Director, lesia.davis@crmuseum.ca

Castlegar: **Castlegar & District Heritage Society**
400 - 13th Ave., Castlegar, BC V1N 1G2
250-365-6440,
www.stationmuseum.ca/museum/
The Society operates the CPR Museum, housed in a 99 year old station, and Zuckerberg Island park; newspaper archives; gift shop featuring local artisans; special events and programming.

Chetwynd: **Little Prairie Heritage Museum**
PO Box 1777, Chetwynd, BC V0C 1J0
250-788-3358,
lphs@pris.ca
Open July & Aug.
Shirley Weeks, President

Chilliwack: **Chilliwack Museum & Archives**
45820 Spadina Ave., Chilliwack, BC V2P 1T3
604-795-5210, Fax: 604-795-5291,
cm_chin@smartt.com
www.chilliwack.museum.bc.ca/museum
Founded: 1957 The Archives are located at 9291 Corbould St. in Chilliwack, phone 604-795-9255; newspapers, photographs, books, DVDs, maps relating to the flood history of Chilliwack; special exhibits; programming; gift shop; open year round.
Ron Denman, Director
Brenda Paterson, Education Co-ordinator
Paul Ferguson, Manager, Heritage Collections

Clearbrook: **Fraser Valley Antique Farm Machinery Association**
PO Box 2234, Clearbrook, BC V2T 3X8
604-856-4571,
johnbateman@telus.net
To collect & restore to working condition antique farm & household machinery; displays annually at Agrifair; visitors welcome to building any time of year; call for appt.
Phil Chapman, President

Clinton: **South Cariboo Historical Museum Society**
1419 Cariboo Hwy., Clinton, BC V0K 1K0
250-459-2442, Fax: 250-459-0058,
Open daily June - Sept.

Courtenay: **Courtenay & District Museum & Palaeontology Centre**
207 - 4th St., Courtenay, BC V9N 1G7
250-334-0686, Fax: 250-338-0619,
museum@island.net
www.courtenaymuseum.ca
Includes archives; open year round
Deborah Griffiths, Curator

Cowichan Bay: **Cowichan Bay Maritime Centre**
PO Box 22, 1761 Cowichan Bay Rd., Cowichan Bay, BC V0R 1N0
250-746-4955, Fax: 250-746-9989,
cwbs@island.net
www.classicboats.org
Exhibits housed in unique pods designed to reflect the surrounding landspace & reveal the rich maritime history of Cowichan Bay; offers classic wooden boat building programs & undertakes restoration projects; open daily
Eric Sandilands, Manager

Cranbrook: **Aasland Museum Taxidermy**
3700 Collinson Rd., Cranbrook, BC V1C 7B8

250-426-3566, Fax: 250-426-3574,
www.aasland@shaw.ca
Small natural history museum displaying mounted birds & animals for the public; admission free; a lecture accompanies the visit if prior arrangements are made; school groups, handicapped, adult groups & individual visitors welcome; Mon.-Sat.
Odd Aasland, Director

Cranbrook: **Canadian Museum of Rail Travel**
Also known as: **The Cranbrook Archives, Museum & Landmark Foundation**
PO Box 400, 57 Van Horne St. South, Cranbrook, BC V1C 4H9
250-489-3918, Fax: 250-489-5744,
mail@trainsdeluxe.com
www.trainsdeluxe.com
The Canadian Museum of Rail Travel depicts the story of rail travel in Canada, through the collection, restoration, & display of historic rail equipment from various eras. The museum features a large historic railcar collection. Other sights at the museum include the Royal Alexandra Hall, which was the former cafe from the Canadian Pacific Railway's 1906 Royal Alexandra Hotel in Winnipeg, an 1898 railway freight shed, & a wooden railway water tower.
Garry W. Anderson, Executive Director
Brian Dees, Office Manager

Creston: **Creston & District Museum**
Also known as: **Stone House Museum**
219 Devon St., Creston, BC V0B 1G3
250-428-9262, Fax: 250-428-3324,
mail@creston.museum.bc.ca
www.creston.museum.bc.ca
Guided tours, permanent & temporary exhibits; open spring, summer, fall; in winter by appt.
Fred Ryckman, President
Tammy Hardwick, Manager

Crofton: **Old Crofton School Museum Society**
Also known as: **Crofton Old School Museum Society**
PO Box 49, 1507 Joan St., Crofton, BC V0R 1R0
250-246-2456, Fax: 250-246-2778,
History of old schools, Crofton & area; open June-Sept.
Pat Montgomery, President

Cumberland: **Cumberland Museum & Archives**
Also known as: **Cumberland & District Historical Society**
PO Box 258, 2680 Dunsmuir Ave., Cumberland, BC V0R 1S0
250-336-2445, Fax: 250-336-2321,
info@cumberland.museum.bc.ca
www.museum.bc.ca/cma
Open year round

Dawson Creek: **Dawson Creek Station Museum**
900 Alaska Ave., Dawson Creek, BC V1G 4T6
250-782-9595, Fax: 250-782-9538, 866-645-3022
frontoffice@tourismdawsoncreek.com
www.pris.bc.ca/dcsm/
Two galleries, the Northern Alberta Railway and the Natural History Gallery. Open year round
Dan Bastiansen, President, 250-782-5408, museum@pris.ca

Dawson Creek: **Walter Wright Pioneer Village & Sudeten Hall**
1901 Alaska Hwy., Dawson Creek, BC V1G 1P7
250-782-7144,
info@tourismdawsoncreek.com
www.dawsoncreek.ca/life/recreation/walter.asp
The Walter Wright Pioneer Village presents life in Dawson Creek, before the construction of the Alaska Highway. Historic buildings include the Pouce Coupe School, the W.O. Harper General Store, & the St. Paul's Anglican Church. The Sudeten Hall honours Germany's Sudeten people who arrived in the area in 1939.

Delta: **Delta Museum & Archives**
4858 Delta St., Delta, BC V4K 2T8
604-946-9322, Fax: 604-946-5791,
info@deltamuseum.ca
www.deltamuseum.ca
1912 heritage building; archives; exhibitions on pioneer homelife, village life, farming, fishing, duck decoys, First Nations archeology, basketry
Mark Sakai, Executive Director
Jordana Feist, Curator
Carol Ballard, Program Coordinator
Kathy Bossort, Archivist

Denman Island: **Denman Island Museum**
PO Box 28, Denman Island, BC V0R 1T0
250-335-0880,
Collection houses NW Coast artifacts from the Salish; natural history specimens; European settlement items; photographs & maps

Duncan: **British Columbia Forest Discovery Centre**
2892 Drinkwater Rd., Duncan, BC V9L 6C2
250-715-1113, Fax: 250-715-1170,
info.bcfdc@shawlink.ca; manager.bcfdc@shawlink.ca
www.discoveryforest.com
Other contact information: E-mail, Volunteering & Education: education.bcfdc@shawlink.ca
The BC Forest Discovery Centre is a 100-acre, open air museum, which features forest & marsh trails, logging artifacts, & heritage buildings.
Vicki Holman, Manager
Aimee Greenaway, Coordinator, Program & Collections

Duncan: **Cowichan Valley Museum**
PO Box 1014, Duncan, BC V9L 3Y2
250-746-6612, Fax: 250-746-6612,
cvmuseum.archives@shaw.ca
www.cowichanvalleymuseum.bc.ca
Local history museum; includes archives; open year round
Priscilla Lowe, Curator/Manager

Enderby: **Enderby & District Museum Society**
901 George St., Enderby, BC V0E 1V0
250-838-7170, Fax: 250-838-9641,
edms@jetstream.net
www.enderbymuseum.ca
Founded: 1973 Open year round
Joan Cowan, Curator, 250-838-7171

Fernie: **Fernie & District Historical Society Museum**
PO Box 1527, Fernie, BC V0B 1M0
250-423-7016, Fax: 250-423-7461,
history@ferniemuseum.com
www.ferniemuseum.com
Coal mining history museum; local history & early families research

Fort Langley: **British Columbia Farm Machinery & Agricultural Museum Association**
PO Box 279, 9131 King St., Fort Langley, BC V1M 2R6
604-888-2273,
bcfm@telus.net
www.bcfma.com
British Columbia Farm Machinery & Agricultural Museum Association presents the history of farming in British Columbia. Displays include horse drawn carriages & wagons, steam, gas & diesel powered grinders & tractors, an 1890s sawmill, a blacksmith shop, & British Columbia's first crop duster, the Tiger Moth airplane. The museum is open seven days a week from April 1st to Thanksgiving Day.

Fort Langley: **Fort Langley National Historic Site of Canada (FLNHSC) / Lieu historique national du Canada Fort-Langley**
PO Box 129, 23433 Mavis Ave., Fort Langley, BC V1M 2R5
604-513-4777, Fax: 604-513-4798,
fort.langley@pc.gc.ca
www.pc.gc.ca/fortlangley
Birthplace of British Columbia; 19th century Hudson's Bay Co. trading post; open year round
John Aldag

Fort Langley: **Langley Centennial Museum & National Exhibition Centre**
PO Box 800, 9135 King St., Fort Langley, BC V1M 2S2
604-888-3922, Fax: 604-888-7291,
info@langleymuseum.org
www.langleymuseum.org
Art, history & science exhibits; open year round
John Robertson, Manager, Community & Heritage Services

Fort Nelson: **Fort Nelson Heritage Museum**
PO Box 716, Fort Nelson, BC V0C 1R0
250-774-3536,
info@fortnelsonmuseum.ca
www.fortnelsonmuseum.ca
Artifacts related to the construction of the Alaska Highway; open mid-May - mid-Sept.
Marlin Brown, Curator

Fort St. James: **Fort St. James National Historic Site of Canada**
280 Kwah Rd. West, Fort St. James, BC V0J 1P0
250-996-7191, Fax: 250-996-8566,
bob_grill@pch.gc.ca
The Fort St James National Historic Site offers the largest collection of original wooden buildings, representing the fur trade in Canada. The following buildings are located at the site: Fur WareHouse (1888-1889); Fish cache (1889); Men's House (1884); Trade Store & Office (1884); Murray House (1883-1884); Dairy (1884); & Wharf & Tramway (1894-1914). The Historic Site is open daily from 9:00 to 5:00 from the long weekend in May to the end of September.
Alan Latourelle, Chief Officer

Fort St John: **Fort St. John-North Peace Museum**
9323 - 100 St., Fort St John, BC V1J 4N4
250-787-0430, Fax: 250-787-0405,
fsjnpmuseum@solarwinds.com
Open year round
Larry Evans, President

Fort Steele: **Fort Steele Heritage Town**
9851 Hwy. 93/95, Fort Steele, BC V0B 1N0
250-417-6000, Fax: 250-489-2624,
info@FortSteele.bc.ca
www.FortSteele.bc.ca
Restored 1890s mining boom town of the East Kootenay; open year round with varying program levels each season, call for details
David Stokes, General Manager

Fraser Lake: **Fraser Lake Museum**
PO Box 430, Fraser Lake, BC V0J 1S0
250-699-6257, Fax: 250-699-6469,
village@fraserlake.ca
Open summer
Donna Ward, Clerk/Treas.

Gibsons: **Sunshine Coast Museum & Archives**
PO Box 766, 716 Winn Rd., Gibsons, BC V0N 1V0
604-886-8232, Fax: 604-886-8232,
scm_a@dccnet.com
www.sunshinecoastmuseum.ca
Collection of historical documents & artifacts pertaining to the Sunshine Coast of BC; open year round; closed Sun. & Mon.

Golden: **Golden & District Museum**
PO Box 992, 1302 - 11 Ave., Golden, BC V0A 1H0
250-344-5169, Fax: 250-344-5169,
museum@redshift.bc.ca
Open May-Sept.
Colleen Palumbo, Curator

Grand Forks: **Boundary Museum**
Boundary Museum Society, PO Box 817, 6145 Reservoir Rd., Grand Forks, BC V0H 1H0
250-442-3737, Fax: 250-442-3737,
boundarymuse@shaw.ca
www.boundarymuseum.com
The Boundary Museum is situated in a former schoolhouse, which was built in 1929 by the Christian Communities of Universal Brotherhood Doukhobors. The grounds of the restored schoolhouse feature a fruit drying facility & a bread oven which were also built by the society.

Grand Forks: **Mountain View Doukhobor Museum**
PO Box 1235, 3655 Hardy Mountain Rd., Grand Forks, BC V0H 1H0
250-442-8855,

Greenwood: **Greenwood Heritage Society**
PO Box 399, 214 South Copper St., Greenwood, BC V0H 1J0
250-445-6355, Fax: 250-445-6355,
museum@shaw.ca
www.greenwoodmuseum.com
Mining, forestry, ranching & the internment of Japanese Canadians; Greenwood was an internment camp during WW II
Marge Maclean, Chair

Groundbirch: **Groundbirch Museum**
PO Box 124, Groundbirch, BC V0C 1T0
250-780-2383,
Open summer

Harrison Mills: **Kilby Museum & Farm**
PO Box 55, 215 Kilby Rd., Harrison Mills, BC V0M 1L0
604-796-9576, Fax: 604-796-9592,
info@kilby.ca
www.kilby.ca
Open daily May-Sept. 11-5, then seasonal hours

Hope: **Hope Museum**
PO Box 26, 919 Water Ave., Hope, BC V0X 1L0
604-869-7322, Fax: 604-869-2160, 866-467-3842
destinationhope@telus.net
Open summer; off-season tours by request
Inge Wilson, Manager

Horsefly: **Jack Lynn Memorial Museum**
c/o Horsefly Historical Society, PO Box 11, Horsefly, BC V0L 1L0
250-620-3440,
www.horsefly.bc.ca/community/virtualvillage/museum.html
Open daily July to Aug. anually; Sept. to June by appointment only; small museum run by volunteers; features artifacts, photos & paper archives, all relating to Horsefly

Hudson's Hope: **Hudson's Hope Museum & Historical Society**
PO Box 98, 9510 Beattie Dr., Hudson's Hope, BC V0C 1V0
250-783-5735, Fax: 250-783-5770,
hhmuseum@pris.ca
www.hhmuseum.com

Hudson's Bay Company store of 1942; archives; fossil collection; Aboriginal display; North West & Hudson's Bay Company artifacts; North West Mounted Police, trapping, coal mining, gold mining, pioneer, logging & World War memorabilia & photographic history of W.A.C. Bennett dam
Melodie Godsma, Coordinator/Administrator
Fay Lavallee, President

***Invermere:* Windermere Valley Museum & Archives**
PO Box 2315, Invermere, BC V0A 1K0
250-342-9769,
wvmuseum@cyberlink.bc.ca
Open Mon. - Fri. June & Sept.; Tue.-Sat. July & Aug.; Oct. - May by appt.
Jaryl McIsaac, Archivist
Dorothy Blunden, Curator, 250/342-2005

***Kamloops:* Kamloops Museum & Archives**
207 Seymour St., Kamloops, BC V2C 2E7
250-828-3576, Fax: 250-314-2016,
museum@city.kamloops.bc.ca
Open year round

***Kamloops:* Rocky Mountain Rangers Museum & Archives**
PO Box 3250, 1221 McGill Rd., Kamloops, BC V2C 6B8
250-372-7424,

***Kamloops:* Secwepemc Museum & Heritage Park (SCES)**
***Parent:* Secwepemc Cultural Education Society**
#311, 355 Yellowhead Hwy., Kamloops, BC V2H 1H1
250-828-9778, Fax: 250-372-1127,
museum@secwepemc.org
www.secwepemc.org
Museum is located on 12 acres & exhibits artifacts, photographs & histories of the Secwepemc people; displays include canoes, hunting & fishing objects, clothing, games; the Heritage Park complements the Museum with outdoor displays & reconstructed winter pit houses. lean-tos, smoke house & traditional plant foods; trails, gardens; giftshop (seasonal); museum open year round
Daniel Saul, Museum Manager

***Kaslo:* Kaslo Village**
PO Box 576, 413 - 4th St., Kaslo, BC V0G 1M0
250-353-2311, Fax: 250-353-7767,
village@netidea.com
www.kaslo.ca
Designated National Historic Site; open Mon. - Fri.
Rae Sawyer, CAO

***Kaslo:* S.S. Moyie National Historic Site**
PO Box 537, Kaslo, BC V0G 1M0
250-353-2525, Fax. 250-353-2525,
ssmoyie@klhs.bc.ca
www.klhs.bc.ca
Moored in the town of Kaslo, this is the oldest intact passenger sternwheeler in the world; gift shop; operated by the Kootenay Lake Historical Society; open daily mid-May to mid-Oct.
Ken Butler, Manager
Jack Morris, President
Mark Gordon, Manager

***Kelowna:* Benvoulin Heritage Park & Benvoulin Heritage Church**
c/o Central Okanagan Heritage Society, 1060 Cameron Ave., Kelowna, BC V1Y 8V3
250-861-7188, Fax: 250-868-1392,
cohs@telus.net
www.okheritagesociety.com
Located at 2279 Benvoulin Road in Kelowna, the Benvoulin Church was built in 1892 in the Gothic Revival style. The pioneer church was restored by the Central Okanagan Heritage Society, which owns & operates Benvoulin Heritage Park.
Janice Henry, Executive Director, Central Okanagan Heritage Society

***Kelowna:* British Columbia Orchard Industry Museum**
1304 Ellis St., Kelowna, BC V1Y 1Z8
250-763-0433, Fax: 250-868-9272,
orchard@kelownamuseum.ca
www.kelownamuseum.ca
Founded: 1989 The BC Orchard Industry Museum is located in the historic, restored Laurel Packinghouse. The museum features exhibits about the Okanagan Valley's orchard industry, including picking, processeing, packing, preserving, & marketing. The museum is open year round.
Wayne Wilson, Director
Nathalie Limbos-Bomberg, Associate Director
Colleen Cornock, Program Assistant

***Kelowna:* Central Okanagan Heritage Society**
1060 Cameron Ave., Kelowna, BC V1Y 8V3
250-861-7188, Fax: 250-868-0391,
cohs@telus.net
www.okheritagesociety.com
Founded: 1982 The Society promotes & participates in the preservation of the Central Okanagan region's natural, cultural & horticultural heritage; operates the Guisachan Heritage Park, the Benvoulin Heritage Park, Brent's Grist Mill Park.
Janice Henry, Executive Director

***Kelowna:* Father Pandosy Mission**
Box 22105, Capri PO, Kelowna, BC V1Y 9N9
250-860-8369,
www.okanaganhistoricalsociety.org/pandosy_mission.html
Oblate Mission, 1859
John Sugars, Contact

***Kelowna:* Kelowna Museum**
470 Queensway, Kelowna, BC V1Y 6S7
250-763-2417, Fax: 250-763-5722,
info@kelownamuseum.ca
www.kelownamuseum.ca
Open Tue.-Sat. 10-5; admission by donation
Nathalie Limbos-Bomberg, Associate Director
Wayne Wilson, Director

***Kelowna:* Silver Lake Forestry Centre**
***Parent:* Silver Lake Forest Education Society**
PO Box 20023, Kelowna, BC V1Y 9H2
250-717-0033, Fax: 250-717-3231,
info@silverlakekidscamp.com
www.silverlakekidscamp.com/society.html
Other contact information: E-mail, Board of Directors: directors@silverlakekidscamp.com
Founded: 1971 The Silver Lake Forestry Centre is owned & managed by the Silver Lake Forest Education Society. Year-round outdoor environmental education is available for youth, adults, & educators. The society is also engaged in the collection, restoration, & display of logging & forestry artifacts.

***Keremeos:* The Grist Mill at Keremeos**
Upper Bench Rd., RR#1, Keremeos, BC V0X 1N0
250-499-2888,
Designated British Columbia Heritage Site; open May - Oct & by appt.

***Keremeos:* South Similkameen Museum**
PO Box 135, Keremeos, BC V0X 1N0
250-499-5445, Fax: 250-499-5746,
Restored gaol-house with B.C. provincial police displays, pioneer artifacts

***Kimberley:* Kimberley Heritage Musuem**
PO Box 144, 105 Spokane St., Kimberley, BC V1A 2Y5
250-427-7510,
kdhs@telus.net
Early Kimberley History; Sullivan Mine display; open year round; admission by donation; archives available for research, by request, at a nominal fee
Marie Stang, Administrator

***Kitimat:* Kitimat Centennial Museum**
293 City Centre, Kitimat, BC V8C 1T6
250-632-8950, Fax: 250-632-7429,
kitimatmuseum@telus.net
www.kitimatmuseum.ca
Natural history; homesteader & Haida histories; Kemano-Kitimat Project history; temporary exhibitions; giftshop; open year round
Louise Avery, Curator

***Kitwanga:* Meanskinisht Village Historical Association, Cedarvale**
***Also known as:* Cedarvale Museum**
PO Box 183, Kitwanga, BC V0J 2A0
250-849-5732,
Houses the history & remnants of ancient village of Gitlusec, Meanskinisht village & Cedarvale; also looks after the graveyard (private); Cedarvale Museum open by appt.
Mary G. Dalen, Director

***Ladysmith:* Black Nugget Museum**
PO Box 1449, 12 Gatacre St., Ladysmith, BC V0R 2E0
250-245-4846,
Formerly the Jones Hotel, the Black Nugget Museum depicts the history of Ladysmith, through antiques & memorabilia dating back to the late 1800s. The hotel's barroom & lobby have been restored. The museum is open during the summer, and at other times when requested by groups.
Kurt Guilbride, Owner

***Lake Cowichan:* Kaatza Station Museum & Archives**
PO Box 135, Lake Cowichan, BC V0R 2G0
250-749-6142, Fax: 250-749-3900,
kaatzamuseum@shaw.ca
Open year round

***Langley:* Canadian Museum of Flight (CMF)**
Hangar 3, Langley Airport, 5333 - 216th St., Langley, BC V2Y 2N3
604-532-0035, Fax: 604-532-0056,
cmflight@telus.net
www.canadianflight.org
Founded: 1977 The Canadian Museum of Flight restores, preserves, & displays Canada's aviation heritage. The museum & restoration site features more than twenty-five aircraft, such as a World War II Handley Page Hampden & a T-33 Silver Star. The Millennium Kids Room ia a "hands-on" facility for young visitors.
Gord Wintrup, President
George Miller, Vice-President
Terry Brunner, General Manager, tbrunner@telus.net
Paul de Lange, Treasurer
Matt Offer, Secretary

***Lazo:* Comox Air Force Museum (CAFM)**
PO Box 1000 Forces, 19 Wing Comox, Lazo, BC V0R 2K0
250-339-8162, Fax: 250-339-8162,
info@comoxairforcemuseum.ca
www.comoxairforcemuseum.ca
History of CFB Comox & West Coast aviation
Capt. John Low, Executive Director
Lorraine Analy, Curator

***Lillooet:* Lillooet District Historical Society & Museum**
PO Box 441, Lillooet, BC V0K 1V0
250-256-4308, Fax: 250-256-0043,
lillmuseum@cablelan.net
www.lillooetbc.com
Open May-Oct., Tue.-Sat., 10-4; daily July & Aug. 9-7
Susan H. Bell, Manager

***Lytton:* Lytton Museum & Archives**
420 Fraser St., Lytton, BC V0K 1Z0
250-455-2254, Fax: 250-455-2394,
curator@lyttonmuseum.ca
www.botaniecreek.com/museum
Founded: 1995 Built by the Canadian National Railway as a residence in 1942, the museum is filled with local artifacts and archives, including pieces formally used at the C.N. station.
MR Richard Forrest, President, Lytton Museum and Archives Commission
Dorothy Dodge, Curator

***Mackenzie:* Mackenzie & District Museum**
PO Box 934, Mackenzie, BC V0J 2C0
250-997-3021,
museum@mackbc.com

***Maple Ridge:* Haney House Museum**
11612 - 224th St., Maple Ridge, BC V2X 5Z7
604-463-1377, Fax: 604-463-5317,
haneyhouse@telus.net
www.mapleridgemuseum.org
Founded: 1981 Haney House was the residence of pioneer Thomas Haney, who came to Maple Ridge, British Columbia in 1876. Guided tours are available year-round.

***Maple Ridge:* Maple Ridge Museum & Archives**
22520 - 116th Ave., Maple Ridge, BC V2X 0S4
604-463-5311, Fax: 604-463-5317,
mrmuseum@telus.net
Open year round

***Mayne Island:* Mayne Island Museum**
Comp. 4, Site 1, RR#1, Mayne Island, BC V0N 2J0
250-539-5286,

***McBride:* Valley Museum & Archives**
PO Box 775, 241 Dominion St., McBride, BC V0J 2E0
250-569-2411,
Displays within McBride & District Public Library

***Merritt:* Nicola Valley Museum & Archives**
PO Box 1262, 1675 Tutill Court, Merritt, BC V1K 1B8
250-378-4145, Fax: 250-378-4145,
nvm@uniserve.com
www.nicolavalleymuseum.org
Founded: 1976 The museum houses an extensive collection of artifacts & photographs of various aspects of Nicola Valley's history, including churches, the general hospital, rail travel & other transportation, Craigmont mine history, Judge Henry Castillou, ranching & mining displays; James Teit Gallery & First Nations displays; Merritt Model Railway club display; the Archives preserves the James Teit First Nations reference material, early newspapers, mining reports, cemetery information, early maps & hundreds of photopgraphs. Open year round.
Barbara Watson, Office Manager

***Midway:* Kettle River Museum Society**
PO Box 149, Midway, BC V0H 1M0
250-449-2614, Fax: 250-449-2614,
midwaybc@sunshinecable.com
Mile of Kettle Valley Railway; restored 1900s CPR Station; B.C. Provincial Police display
Tannis Killough, President
Helen Schultheiss, Manager

***Mission:* Fraser River Heritage Park**
PO Box 3341, 7494 Mary St., Mission, BC V2V 4J5
604-826-0277, Fax: 604-826-0333,
mhadmin@direct.ca
www.heritagepark-mission.ca

Original site of St. Mary's Mission & Indian Residential School, founded in 1861; park features foundations of mission

***Mission:* Mission District Historical Society & Museum**
33201 - 2nd Ave., Mission, BC V2V 1J9
604-826-1011, Fax: 604-826-1017,
muse@mission.museum.bc.ca
www.mission.museum.bc.ca
Founded: 1972 Permanent exhibits include Sto:lo First Nations display, the history of settlement with pioneers, rails, rivers, and items from business and home life, notably period 1920s rooms. Also featured are items from Mission's old Chinatown. Museum is housed in a 1907 B.C. Mills, prefabricated, Canadian Bank of Commerce Bldg. Gift shop offers books on Mission's history. There is a selection of school tours.
Kim Allen, Curator

***Mission:* Xá:ytem Longhouse Interpretive Centre**
***Parent:* Sto:lo Heritage Trust Society**
35087 Lougheed Hwy., Mission, BC V2V 6T1
604-820-9725, Fax: 604-820-9735,
info@xaytem.ca
www.xaytem.ca
On the coast of British Columbia, Xá:ytem has been an important Salish spiritual site. Today, Xá:ytem is a National Historic Site, where visitors discover a traditional Salish cedar longhouse & two pit houses. The site is open year-round.

***Nanaimo:* The Bastion**
#211, 450 Stewart Ave., Nanaimo, BC V9S 5E9
250-755-1047, Fax: 250-740-0125,
www.nanaimomuseum.ca
1853 Hudson's Bay Co. log fortification

***Nanaimo:* Centennial Museum of the Nanaimo Regional General Hospital**
Nanaimo Regional General Hospital, 1200 Dufferin Cres., Nanaimo, BC V9S 2B7
250-755-7637, Fax: 250-755-7947,
www.viha.ca
Health care records & artifacts
Lynne Tourond, Manager, Volunteer Resources,
lynne.tourond@viha.ca

***Nanaimo:* Nanaimo District Museum (NDM)**
100 Cameron Rd., Nanaimo, BC V9R 2X1
250-753-1821, Fax: 250-740-0125,
debbie@nanaimomuseum.ca
www.nanaimomuseum.ca
Open year round
Debbie Trueman, General Manager

***Naramata:* Naramata Heritage Museum**
PO Box 95, Naramata, BC V0H 1N0
250-496-5866,
Local history; 3 permanent displays
Berte Berry, Chair

***Nelson:* Touchstones Nelson: Museum of Art & History**
***Also known as:* Nelson & District Museum, Archives, Art Gallery & Historical Soc.**
502 Vernon St., Nelson, BC V1L 4E7
250-352-9813, Fax: 250-352-9810,
info@touchstonesnelson.ca
www.touchstonesnelson.ca
Other contact information: E-Mail, Exhibitions:
exhibitions@touchstonesnelson.ca
The museum displays the history & culture of Nelson, British Columbia. Archives & an art gallery are also part of the museum.
Best Leah, Executive Director,
director@touchstonesnelson.ca
Rod Taylor, Co-Curator, rod@touchstonesnelson.ca
Deborah Thompson, Co-Curator,
deborah@touchstonesnelson.ca
Alex Dudley, Manager, Visitor Services,
shop@touchstonesnelson.ca
Laura Fortier, Archivist & Manager, Collections,
collections@touchstonesnelson.ca

***New Denver:* Sandon Historical Society Museum & Visitors' Centre**
***Parent:* Sandon Historical Society**
PO Box 52, New Denver, BC V0G 1S0
250-358-7920,
shs@slocanlake.com
www.slocanlake.com/sandon/
Historic museum & archives of Sandon & area; heritage photographs, artifacts, guided tours
Lorna Obermayr, Contact, 250-358-7965

***New Denver:* Silvery Slocan Historical Museum**
PO Box 301, New Denver, BC V0G 1S0
250-358-2201, Fax: 250-358-7251,
sgn@netidea.com
Cultural & economic history of the Slocan Lake area; open July & Aug.
Webb Cummings, President

***New Westminster:* Canadian Lacrosse Hall of Fame**
PO Box 308, 302 Royal Ave., New Westminster, BC V3L 4Y6
604-527-4640, Fax: 604-527-4641,
allan@lacrosse.ca
www.lacrosse.ca
Founded: 1965 Inductees to the Canadian Lacrosse Hall of Fame are featured in the following categories: builders, box players, field players, veteran players, & teams.

***New Westminster:* Museum of the Royal Westminster Regiment Historical Society**
The Armouries, 530 Queens Ave., New Westminster, BC V3L 1K3
604-526-5116, Fax: 604-666-4042,
Permanent collection of military artifacts & memorabilia from the experience of The Royal Westminster Regiment & its antecedents; open every Tue. & Thurs.
Lt.Col. B.V. Morgan, Curator (Ret'd)
B. Gen. H.E. Hamm, Chair C.D., (Ret'd)

***New Westminster:* New Westminster Museum & Archives**
302 Royal Ave., New Westminster, BC V3L 1H7
604-527-4640, Fax: 604-527-4641,
www.nwpr.bc.ca
The New Westminster Museum, with more than 30,000 items in its collection, depicts the history of British Columbia's first capital. The New Westminster Archives, which contains 13,000 archival items, preserves the documentary heritage of the city from its time as a Royal Engineers' settlement camp. Irving House is an 1865 colonial period house. Guided tours are given of the home.
Colin Stevens, Manager, cstevens@newwestcity.ca
Cynthia Bronaugh, Coordinator, Tour Groups,
cbronaugh@city.new-westminster.bc.ca
Barry Dykes, Archivist, 604-527-4642,
bdykes@newwestcity.ca

***New Westminster:* Samson V Maritime Museum**
c/o Royal Agricultural & Industrial Society of BC, PO Box 42516, #105, 1005 Columbia St., New Westminster, BC V3M 6H5
604-522-6894, Fax: 604-522-6094,
hyackfst@direct.ca
www.nwheritage.org/heritagesite/orgs/samson/
A restored sternwheel snagpuller, moored on the Fraser River at the Westminster Quay Market; history of the vessel, educational programming
Valerie Francis, Manager

***North Vancouver:* Lynn Canyon Ecology Centre**
3663 Park Rd., North Vancouver, BC V7J 3G3
604-981-3103, Fax: 604-981-3154,
kissings@district.north-van.bc.ca
Open year round

***North Vancouver:* North Vancouver Museum & Archives Community History Centre, 3203 Institute Rd., North Vancouver, BC V7K 3E5**
604-990-3700, Fax: 604-987-5688,
nvmac@dnv.org
www.dnv.org/nvma
Celebrates & preserves North Vancouver's social, industrial & cultural history; WWII shipbuilding; P.G.E. Railway; logging; Archives Reading Room & Archives Collection
Nancy L. Kirkpatrick, Director

***North Vancouver:* Pacific Great Eastern Railway Station**
107 Carrie Cates Ct., North Vancouver, BC V7M 3J4
604-984-8588,
Restored station building with railway exhibits
Robin Inglis, Director

***Okanagan:* Lake Country Museum**
11255 Okanagan Centre Rd. West, Okanagan, BC V4V 2J7
250-766-0111, Fax: 250-766-2844,
lcmuseum@cablelan.net
www.lakecountrymuseum.com/
Open Mid-May - Aug.
Felena Sigal

***Okanagan Falls:* Okanagan Falls Heritage House & Museum**
***Also known as:* Bassett House**
Okanagan Falls Heritage & Museum Society, PO Box 323, 1145 Main St., Okanagan Falls, BC V0H 1R0
250-497-7047,
ofhms@uniserve.com
www3.telus.net/okmuseum
The Bassett House is a prefabricated house. Ordered from the T. Eaton & Company catalogue, the house was shipped by rail from the east, and then by sternwheeler, & horse-drawn wagon to Okanagan Falls. The pioneer Bassett family lived in the home from 1909.

***Osoyoos:* Osoyoos Desert Society & Osoyoos Desert Centre**
PO Box 123, Osoyoos, BC V0H 1V0
250-495-2470, Fax: 250-495-2474,
mail@desert.org
www.desert.org
Founded: 1991 The Osoyoos Desert Society is a non-profit society that was founded in 1991 to conserve the biologically rich and diverse habitats of British Columbia's southern interior. The south Okanagan is home to one of the largest concentrations of rare and at-risk species in all of Canada. Through conservation and education, the society strives to generate public knowledge, respect and active concern for these fragile and endangered ecosystems. In 1998, as part of it's effort to conserve the Southern Okanagan's unique habitats, the Desert Society opened an interpretive facility - the Osoyoos Desert Centre. In addition to an interpetive centre with hands-on exhibits, the Desert Centre also features a 1.5 km elevated wooden walkway. Visitors are invited to explore Canada's desert while enjoying a guided or self-guided tour along the boardwalk. The Desert Centre, located 3 km north of Osoyoos off Highway 97, is open annually from April through October
Marlin Clapson, Treasurer
Leslie Plaskett, President

***Parksville:* Craig Heritage Park Museum**
PO Box 1452, Parksville, BC V9P 2H4
250-248-6966,
parksvillemuseum@shaw.ca
www.parksvillemuseum.ca
Open mid-May - Sept. 30
J. Tryon, Museum Manager
P. Cardwell, Archives

***Pemberton:* Pemberton & District Museum**
PO Box 267, Pemberton, BC V0N 2L0
604-894-6765,
Three heritage buildings decorated with artifacts depicting local history dating back to 1850s

***Penticton:* Penticton R.N. Atkinson Museum & Archives**
785 Main St., Penticton, BC V2A 5E3
250-490-2451, Fax: 250-490-2442,
museum@city.penticton.bc.ca
Museum & archives open July & Aug. Mon.-Sat. 10-5; Oct., Apr., May & June Tue.-Sat. 10-5; Nov., Dec., Jan., Feb. & Mar. Tue.-Sat. 10-4
R. Manuel, Director

Jeanne Boyle, Museum Assistant

***Pitt Meadows:* Pitt Meadows Museum**
12294 Harris Rd., Pitt Meadows, BC V3Y 2E9
604-465-4322, Fax: 604-465-4322,
pittmeadowsmuseum@telus.net
www.pittmeadows.bc.ca
Founded: 1997 Located in an 1885 general store, which was later used as a post office & a residence, the Pitt Meadows Museum relates the pioneer & agricultural history of the Pitt Meadows community. An archives is also situated at the museum. The Hoffmann & Son machine shop & ditching business was donated to the Pitt Meadows Heritage & Museum Society. Hoffmann & Son Ltd. had been in business since the 1920s. The museum is open year round.

***Port Alberni:* Alberni Valley Museum**
4255 Wallace St., Port Alberni, BC V9Y 3Y6
250-723-2181, Fax: 250-723-1035,
info@alberniheritage.com
www.alberniheritage.com
History & culture of Alberni Valley & West Coast of Vancouver Island; exhibits include aboriginal artifacts, particularly the Nuu chah Nulth basketry; clothing and textiles; household implements and tools; agricultural equipment; local memorabilia; and 17,0000 historic photographs available for research purposes or reproduction on request. Open year round

***Port Alberni:* McLean Mill National Historic Site**
5633 Smith Rd., Comp. 14, Site 125, Port Alberni, BC V9Y 7L5
250-723-1376, Fax: 250-723-5910,
email@alberniheritage.com
www.alberniheritage.com/mill/
Founded: 1989 Operated by R.B. McLean and his three sons from 1926 to 1965, the site commemorates the history of logging and saw milling in British Columbia. As well as the steam sawmill, typical remote coastal lumber camp buildings are being restored. A resident troupe of interpretive actors called the Tin Pants Theatre Company perform original stage shows and offer guided tours. There is also a cafe and gift shop.
MR Neil Malbon, General Manager

***Port Clements:* Port Clements Museum**
PO Box 417, Port Clements, BC V0T 1R0
250-557-4576, Fax: 250-557-4576,
pcmuseum@island.net
www.portclementsmuseum.org
The Port Clements Museum contains artifacts of pioneer life on the Queen Charlotte Islands, including information &

photographs about the logging, farming, fishing, & mining industries. The museum grounds display early machinery from the logging industry.

***Port Edward:* North Pacific Cannery Historic Site and Museum**
PO Box 1109, 1889 Skeena Dr., Port Edward, BC V0V 1G0
250-628-3538, Fax: 250-628-3540,
northpac@citytel.net
www.cannery.ca
National historic site; oldest & most complete cannery village in BC; guided tours, gift shop, café; open May-Sept.

***Port Hardy:* Port Hardy Museum & Archives**
c/o Port Hardy Heritage Society, PO Box 2126, 7110 Market St, Port Hardy, BC V0N 2P0
250-949-8143,
phmachin@island.net
www.northislandmuseums.org
The Port Hardy Museum & Archives houses geological & First Nations displays, as well as exhibits of settlers' history. The story of the fishing & logging industries in Port Hardy, Port Alice, Cape Scott, & Quatsino is also depicted at the museum. The museum is open year round.

***Port McNeill:* Port McNeill Museum**
351 Shelley Cres., Port McNeill, BC V0N 2R0
250-956-9898,
Hornsby steam tractor located at Seven Hills Golf Course
Margaret Hanuse, Chair

***Port Moody:* Port Moody Station Museum**
2734 Murray St., Port Moody, BC V3H 1X2
604-939-1648, Fax: 604-939-1647,
pmmuseum@telus.net
www.vcn.bc.ca/pmmuseum
Exhibits & programs about the heritage of Port Moody & the surrounding area are presented at the Port Moody Station Museum. The museum is located in the Port Moody Station, which was built by the Canadian Pacific Railway Company in 1905. The Port Moody Heritage Society is the owner & operator of the museum.
Jim Millarn, Manager & Curator
Rebecca Clarke, Coordinator, Events
Deb Naso, Bookkeeper

***Pouce Coupe:* Pouce Coupe Museum**
PO Box 293, 49th Ave., Pouce Coupe, BC V0C 2C0
250-786-5555, Fax: 250-786-5216,
Pioneer artifacts & archives
Ellen DeWetter, President

***Powell River:* Powell River Historical Museum & Archives**
PO Box 42, 4798 Marine Ave., Powell River, BC V8A 4Z5
604-485-2222, Fax: 604-485-2327,
museum@powellrivermuseum.ca
www.powellrivermuseum.ca
Open year-round, exhibits at the Powell River Historical Museum & Archives include the local First Nation culture, logging at the Powell River Mill, & the war years.
Don Allan, President
Teedie Kagume, Coordinator
Debbie Dan, Curator
Frances Cudworth, Bookkeeper

***Prince George:* The Exploration Place at the Fraser-Fort George Regional Museum (FFGRM)**
PO Box 1779, 333 Becott Pl., Prince George, BC V2L 4V7
250-562-1612, Fax: 250-562-6395, 866-562-1612
info@theexplorationplace.com
www.theexplorationplace.com
Children's gallery; hands-on Explorations Gallery of Science & Natural History; History Hall of regional development; photo archives; motion simulator ride; Nature Exchange; Sports Hall of Fame Gallery with interactive sports machine
Tracy Calogheros, Executive Director

***Prince George:* Huble Homestead/Giscome Portage Heritage Society**
#202, 1685 Third Ave., Prince George, BC V2L 3G5
250-564-7033, Fax: 250-564-7040,
hublehomestead@shaw.ca
www.huble.ca
A living heritage site with over one dozen historic buildings

***Prince George:* The Railway & Forestry Museum, Prince George & Region**
850 River Rd., Prince George, BC V2L 5S8
250-563-7351, Fax: 250-563-3697,
trains@pgrfm.bc.ca
www.pgrfm.bc.ca
1913 100-tonne steam wrecking crane; wooden 1903 Ruissell snowplow

***Prince Rupert:* Kwinitsa Station Railway Museum**
PO Box 669, Prince Rupert, BC V8J 3S1
250-624-3207, Fax: 250-627-8009,
mnbc@citytel.net
www.museumofnorthernbc.com
Depicts the life of early station agents & linemen who worked the Grand Trunk Railway at the turn of the 20th century; located at the Prince Rupert waterfront next to Rotary Waterfront Park; June - Aug.
Susan Marsden, Curator

***Prince Rupert:* Museum of Northern British Columbia**
100 First Ave. West, Prince Rupert, BC V8J 1A8
250-624-3207, Fax: 250-627-8009,
mnbc@citytel.net
www.museumofnorthernbc.com
Exhibits artifacts depicting 12,000 years of human & natural history of the Northwest Coast of BC
Robin R. Weber, Director
Susan Marsden, Curator

***Prince Rupert:* Prince Rupert Fire Museum Society**
200 - 1st Ave. West, Prince Rupert, BC V8J 1A8
250-624-2211, Fax: 250-624-3407,
Firefighting in Prince Rupert since 1908; restored 1925 fire engine; old fire alarm system

***Princeton:* Princeton & District Museum & Archives Society**
PO Box 281, 167 Vermilion Ave., Princeton, BC V0X 1W0
250-295-7588, Fax: 250-295-3477,
Founded: 1958 The museum's collection features fossils & mining artifacts, as well as Aboriginal, Chinese, & pioneer items. Archives collected include records of Princeton & surrounding area organizations, land assessment rolls, court information, photographs, historical newspapers, postcards, posters, & personal papers.

***Qualicum Beach:* Vancouver Naval Museum & Heritage Society**
771 Chartwest Ct., Qualicum Beach, BC V9K 2P9
250-752-1291, Fax: 250-752-1292,
fosterdennison@shaw.ca
Depicts the history of the Royal Canadian Navy since its inception: uniforms, medals & decorations, 3D artifacts, pictorial displays, including naval library & archives
Foster K. Dennison, Curator/Director
Roderick H. Macloy, President

***Quathiaski Cove:* Kwagiulth Museum & Cultural Centre**
PO Box 8, Quathiaski Cove, BC V0P 1N0
250-285-3733, Fax: 250-285-3753,
kmccchin@island.net
Potlatch collection of Kwakwaka'wakw (Kwagiulth) ceremonial artifacts

***Queen Charlotte:* Kitwanga Fort National Historic Site**
c/o Gwaii Haanas National Park Reserve, Haida Heritage Site, PO Box 37, Queen Charlotte, BC V0T 1S0
250-559-8818, Fax: 250-559-8366,
gwaii.haanas@pc.gc.ca
www.pc.gc.ca/lhn-nhs/bc/kitwanga/index_e.asp
Other contact information: TDD: 250/559-8139
Commemorates the culture of the Tsimshian people & their history; located near an important native trade route between the Skeena & Nass Rivers; Battle Hill features archaeological evidence from the 1750-1835 period
Ernie Gladstone, Field Unit Superintendent

***Quesnel:* Quesnel & District Museum & Archives (QDMA)**
705 Carson Ave., Quesnel, BC V2J 2B6
250-992-9580, Fax: 250-992-9680,
ehunter@city.quesnel.bc.ca
www.quesnelmuseum.ca
Artifacts & archival items include Chinese artifacts, pioneer items, medical instruments, World War II letters from service men & women, & photographs from Quesnel & the surrounding area. Quesnel & District Museum & Archives is open year round.
Elizabeth Hunter, Manager, Museum & Heritage

***Revelstoke:* Revelstoke Court House**
1123 - 2nd St. West, Revelstoke, BC V0E 2S0
250-837-6981, Fax: 250-837-4669,
Courthouse built in 1913; no tours & no collections

***Revelstoke:* Revelstoke Museum & Archives**
PO Box 1908, 315 First St. West, Revelstoke, BC V0E 2S0
250-837-3067, Fax: 250-837-3094,
Revelstokemuseum@telus.net
www.revelstoke-museums-gallery.com
The Revelstoke Museum & Archives is situated in Revelstoke's former post office & customs building, where the history of Revelstoke & the surrounding district is presented. The museum organizes exhibits, programs, heritage walks, & cemetery tours. The archives, consisting of photographs, newspapers, assessment rolls, & records of local businesses & organizations, are housed on the second floor of the building. There, visitors will find a microform reader/printer to facilitate their research.
Cathy English, Curator

***Revelstoke:* Revelstoke Railway Museum (RRM)**
***Parent:* The Revelstoke Heritage Railway Society**
PO Box 3018, 719 Track St. West, Revelstoke, BC V0E 2S0
250-837-6060, Fax: 250-837-3732, 877-837-6060
railway@telus.net; finance.railway@telus.net
www.railwaymuseum.com
Other contact information: E-mail, Gift Shop:
giftshop.railway@telus.net
Visitors to the Revelstoke Railway Museum will learn about the challenges of building the Canadian Pacific Railway through British Columbia. Displays include survey & railway tools, CPR china & silverware, a locomotive, a car, a CPR telegraph service office, & a CPR weight scale shack. The museum also collects & organizes photographic archives. The museum is open year-round.
Jennifer Dunkerson, Executive Director,
director.railway@telus.net

***Revelstoke:* Rogers Pass Information Centre**
Glacier National Park, PO Box 350, Revelstoke, BC V0E 2S0
250-837-6274,
Natural & human history of Mount Revelstoke & Glacier National Park

***Revelstoke:* Three Valley Gap Heritage Ghost Town**
PO Box 860, Revelstoke, BC V0E 2S0
250-837-2109, Fax: 250-837-5220, 888-667-2109
hello@3valley.com; 3valley@revelstoke.net
www.3valleyroundhouse.com
Guided tours of historic town of late 1800s; open mid April - mid Oct.

***Richmond:* 12 (Vancouver) Service Battalion Museum**
The Sherman Armoury, 5500 - No. 4 Rd., Richmond, BC V6X 3L5
604-666-4097, Fax: 604-666-4040,
info@12servicebattalion.com
www.12servicebattalion.com/museum.htm
Founded: 1990 An accredited Canadian Forces museum; military artifacts, with particular emphasis on the 12 Service Battalion and it's predecessor corps; small reference library of military-related materials; open Tue. & Thu. evenings
J.B. Dutton C.W.O.(R), 604/940-9812, jdutt@oanet.com

***Richmond:* Britannia Heritage Shipyard**
Britannia Heritage Shipyard Site Office, 5180 Westwater Dr., Richmond, BC V7E 6P3
604-718-8050, Fax: 604-718-8040,
britannia@richmond.ca
www.britannia-hss.ca
Britannia Heritage Shipyard is a National Historic Site, which depicts Canada's west coast marine history. It is an example of a village which served the fishing industry. Many buildings date back to 1885. The Britannia Heritage Shipyard Society works to preserve the history of commercial boat building in Steveston. The shipyard is open from the beginning of May to the end of September. From October to April, the shipyard is open on weekends.
Bryan Klassen, Site Supervisor, 604-718-8044
Brooke Lees, Coordinator, Heritage, 604-718-8043
Angela Soon, Coordinator, Special Projects, 604-718-8037

***Richmond:* Deeley Motorcycle Exhibition**
1875 Boundary Rd., Richmond, BC V6V 1V2
604-293-2221, Fax: 604-909-6232,
info@deeleymotorcycleexhibition.ca
www.deeleymotorcycleexhibition.ca
Display of over 250 classic & antique motorcycles; open year round Mon.-Fri., 10-4. Also a

***Richmond:* Gulf of Georgia Cannery National Historic Site**
12138 - 4th Ave., Richmond, BC V7E 3J1
604-664-9009, Fax: 604-664-9008,
gog.info@pc.gc.ca
www.gulfofgeorgiacannery.com
History of the west coast fishing industry; open May-Oct..
Mark Sakai, Manager

***Richmond:* Richmond Museum**
Richmond Cultural Centre, 7700 Minoru Gate, Richmond, BC V6Y 1R9
604-247-8300, Fax: 604-247-8341,
museum@richmond.ca
www.richmond.ca
The mission of the Richmond Musuem is to collect, research, document, preserve, exhibit, & interpret items of significance to the history of the community.
Connie Baxter, Supervisor, Museum & Heritage Services
Rebecca Forrest, Curator
Peter Harris, Coordinator, Exhibits & Programs
Emily So, Coordinator, Educational Programs
Bill Jones, Treasurer

***Richmond:* Steveston Museum**
3811 Moncton St., Richmond, BC V7E 3A7

604-271-6868,
steveston@telus.net
www.steveston.bc.ca/online/museum.html
Founded: 1976 Housed in a 1905 bank building, currently a post office; summer music series on the museum grounds; music & craft programs; museum tours; walking tours of Steveston Village.
Karen Schiefner, Chair

***Rossland:* Rossland Historical Museum**
PO Box 26, Rossland, BC V0G 1Y0
250-362-7722, Fax: 250-362-5379, 888-448-7444
museum@rossland.com
www.rosslandmuseum.ca
Local pioneer & mining history; Western Canada Ski Hall of Fame; underground mine tour; open daily mid-May - mid-Sept.; in winter by appt.
Joyce Austin, Manager

***Saanichton:* Log Cabin Museum & Archives**
c/o Saanich Pioneer' Society, 7910 East Saanich Rd., Saanichton, BC V8M 1T4
250-658-8347, Fax: 250-479-8580,
spsma@shaw.ca; bbjohnson@shaw.ca
victoria.tc.ca/Community/Spsma
Artifacts & archives from the early days of the Saanich Peninsula pioneer families; operates in the log cabin built for this purpose in 1933
Beatrice Johnson, President
Edna Ralston, Secretary

***Saanichton:* Saanich Historical Artifacts Society (SHAS)**
7321 Lochside Dr., Saanichton, BC V8M 1W4
250-652-5522, Fax: 250-652-5999,
heritageacres@shas.ca
www.shas.ca
Collects & preserves artifacts from Saanich's rural past, including household & industrial objects, working steam engines, tractors & other agricultural machinery; chapel, school house & other buildings on site; trails & picnic area; open year round
Brian Bevan, President

***Salmo:* Salmo Museum**
PO Box 69, 100 - 4th St., Salmo, BC V0G 1Z0
250-357-2200, Fax: 250-357-2596,
salmomus@telus.net
www.virtualmuseum.ca; www.salmovillage.ca
Local histories, photographs, mining/logging/farming artifacts; household objects & clothing; tours; educational programming; annual Heritage Tea & annual Dinner Evening; admission by donation; open May-Sept.

***Salmon Arm:* R.J. Haney Heritage Village & Museum (SAM)**
***Parent:* Salmon Arm Museum & Heritage Association**
PO Box 1642, 751 Hwy. 97B NE, Salmon Arm, BC V1E 4P7
250-832-5243, Fax: 250-832-5291,
hpark@sunlite.ca
www.salmonarmmuseum.org
Other contact information: Archives phone: 250/832-5289;
Email: samha@sunlite.ca
40-acre parcel of land with a municipally designated heritage home; 10 relocated, replicated & restored buildings from the village depict thematic displays on the history of Salmon Arm; 2 km nature trail; majority of collection housed in Salmon Arm Museum; Ernie Doe Archives Room also on site, with 111 linear feet of records dating from turn of 20th century; open May-Sept., Oct.-Apr., Tue.-Fri. 10
Gary Cruikshank, General Manager
Colleen McLellan, Coordinator, Visitor Services

***Scotch Creek:* Shuswap Lake Provincial Park Nature House**
PO Box 24108, Scotch Creek, BC V0E 3L0
250-955-0861,
peg@mail.ocis.net
Natural history

***Sechelt:* Têms Swiya Museum**
PO Box 740, Sechelt, BC V0N 3A0
604-885-2273, Fax: 604-885-3490,
Bee Jackson, Curator

***Sicamous:* Sicamous & District Museum & Historical Society**
PO Box 944, Sicamous, BC V0E 2V0
250-836-4456,
Museum & archives; collects, preserves, records, exhibits & promotes information, of artifacts & archival, historical & cultural value associated with the Columbia Shuswap Regional District Electoral Area E; open July & Aug.; located in Finlayson Park
Betty Durocher, President

***Sidney:* A.N.A.F. Vets Sidney No. 302 Museum Unit**
9831 4th St., Sidney, BC V8L 3S3
250-656-3777, Fax: 250-656-6410,
info@unit302.ca
www.unit302.ca
Military artifacts
Shane Holwell, President, Unit 302

***Sidney:* British Columbia Aviation Museum**
1910 Norseman Rd., Sidney, BC V8L 5V5
250-655-3300, Fax: 250-655-1611,
bcam@bcam.net
www.bcam.net
Located beside Victoria International Airport, the British Columbia Aviation Museum preserves & displays aircraft & aviation artifacts, with an emphasis on the history of aviation in British Columbia. Aircraft on display include the Avro Anson MK II, the Eastman E2 Sea Rover, & the Bristol Bolingbroke MK IV. The museum is open year-round.

***Silverton:* Silverton Outdoor Mining Exhibit**
PO Box 69, Silverton, BC V0G 1S0
250-358-2485, Fax: 250-358-2485,
Open May - Sept.

***Skidegate:* Haida Gwaii Museum at Qay'llnagaay**
PO Box 1373, Skidegate, BC V0T 1S1
250-559-4643, Fax: 250-559-4662,
muse@haidagwaii.net
www.haidagwaiimuseum.com
History collections of the Queen Charlotte Islands; open year round
Nathalie Macfarlane, Director
Nika Collison, Curator

***Smithers:* Adams Igloo Wildlife Museum**
11955 Yellowhead Hwy., Smithers, BC V0J 2N2
250-847-3188, Fax: 250-847-3188,
Display of area wildlife, including bear & cougar.

***Smithers:* Bulkley Valley Museum**
***Also known as:* BV Museum**
PO Box 2615, 1425 Main St., Smithers, BC V0J 2N0
250-847-5322, Fax: 250-847-5363,
info@bvmuseum.com
www.bvmuseum.com
Founded: 1976 The Bulkley Valley Museum's collection showcases the social & technological development of the Bulkley Valley. Exhibits include the Bulkley Valley First Nations, the Grand Trunk Pacific Railway in Smithers, & the forestry & mining industries in the area. The museum, operated under the Bulkley Valley Historical & Museum Society, is open year round.

***Sooke:* Sooke Region Museum, Gallery, Historic Cottage & Lighthouse**
PO Box 774, 2070 Phillips Rd., Sooke, BC V0S 1N0
250-642-6351, Fax: 250-642-7089, 866-888-4748
info@sookeregionmuseum.com
www.sookeregionmuseum.com
Extensive archive and significant collection of photographs from Sooke's past. Aritfacts include a restored steam engine yarder, blacksmith shop, and a rotating lighthouse light.
Elida Peers, Executive Director

***Squamish:* West Coast Railway Heritage Park**
***Parent:* West Coast Railway Association**
39645 Government Rd., Squamish, BC V8B 0B6
604-898-9336, 800-722-1233
park@wcra.org; info@wcra.org; tours@wcra.org
www.wcra.org
Other contact information: E-mail, Archives: archives@wcra.org;
Twitter: twitter.com/WCRailway
The mission of the West Coast Railway Association is the collection & preservation of British Columbia's railway heritage. Visitors to the West Coast Railway Heritage Park have the opportunity to view authentic railway equipment, including seventy locomotives & cars. The site also features the 1914 Pacific Great Eastern carshop & a railway station, built to 1915 Pacific Great Eastern plans. The heritage park is open year-round.

***Stewart:* Stewart Historical Museum**
PO Box 402, 603 Columbia St., Stewart, BC V0T 1W0
250-636-2568,

***Summerland:* Summerland Museum & Heritage Society**
PO Box 1491, 9521 Wharton St., Summerland, BC V0H 1Z0
250-494-9395, Fax: 250-494-9326,
info@summerlandmuseum.org
www.summerlandmuseum.org
Collections and displays devoted to Summerland's history.

***Surrey:* Historic Stewart Farmhouse**
13723 Crescent Rd., Surrey, BC V4A 2W3
604-592-6956, Fax: 604-591-4789,
heritage@surrey.ca
www.surrey.ca/Living+in+Surrey/Heritage/default.htm
This restored Victorian farmhouse was originally built in 1894 and features a parlor, dining room and kitchen with working wood-burning stove. Also on site are a circa-1900 pole barn which used to house 6 draft horses and other animals, as well as a fully loaded hay wagon. A team of staff and volunteers tend the heritage gardens of period flowers, vegetables and herbs, and to the orchards with trees of apple, pear and plum. Tours and school programs are also available. Open mid-Feb. - mid-Dec.

***Surrey:* Surrey Museum**
17710 - 56A Ave., Surrey, BC V3S 5H8
604-592-6956, Fax: 604-592-6957,
City Museum; Local history collections; Textile studio; open Tuesdays to Saturdays; admission free
Jacqueline O'Donnell, Manager
Robert McCullough, Public Programs
Oana Capota, School Programs
Dennis Oomen, Exhibits Technician

***Telkwa:* Telkwa Museum**
PO Box 595, Telkwa, BC V0J 2X0
250-846-9656,
Open May - Sept.
Joanne Cattle

***Terrace:* Heritage Park Museum**
PO Box 512, 4702 Kerby Ave., Terrace, BC V8G 4B5
250-635-4546, Fax: 250-635-4536,
hpmuseum@telus.net
Contains historic log buildings, depicting the history of the pioneers in the region; guided tours offered; open May - Aug.

***Trail:* Trail Museum**
PO Box 405, 1051 Victoria St., Trail, BC V1R 4L7
250-364-1262, Fax: 250-364-0830,
jforbes@trail.ca
www.trailhistory.com
Open June - Aug.
Jamie Forbes, Curator

***Valemount:* Valemount Museum & Archives**
***Parent:* Valemount Historic Society**
1090 Main St., Valemount, BC V0E 2Z0
250-566-4177, Fax: 250-566-8428,
museum@valemount.com
www.valemountmuseum.ca
Founded: 1992 The Valemount Museum & Archives is housed in the original train station, where visitors learn about about the history of the community. Exhibits include information about trapping, the railroad, early settlers, & the Japanese internment camps. The museum is open from May to September.

***Vancouver:* 15th Field Artillery Regiment Museum & Archives Society**
2025 - 11th Ave. West, Vancouver, BC V6J 2C7
604-666-4370, Fax: 604-666-4083,
Equipment of artillery units from Vancouver area; open year round

***Vancouver:* Biblical Museum of Canada**
#70, 3180 East 58th Ave., Vancouver, BC V5S 3S8
604-432-6122,
fwmetzger@telus.net
www.biblicalmuseum.com
The Biblical Museum of Canada is a teaching museum. It features items from Sumerian, Egyptian, Biblical, & classical times. Also part of the museum's collections are documentations & art objects from the Middle Ages, the Renaissance, the Industrial Revolution, & modern history.
Hon. Garde G. Gardom, Honorary Chair
Rev. John Opmeer, President
Rev. Dr. Frederick W. Metzger, Executive Director & Curator
Florence Metzger, Secretary

***Vancouver:* British Columbia Golf Museum & Hall of Fame**
University Golf Club, 2545 Blanca St., Vancouver, BC V6R 4N1
604-222-4653,
office@bcgolfmuseum.org
www.bcgolfmuseum.org
Founded: 1986 The BC Golf Museum & Hall of Fame collects, preserves, & displays the history of golf & golfers in British Columbia. A collection of golf clubs dates back to 1790. The reference library houses a collection of over 5,000 books, plus player biographies & tournament records. The museum is open year round.
Barrie McWha, Executive Director
Peter Young, Treasurer

***Vancouver:* British Columbia Medical Association Medical Museum**
c/o British Columbia Medical Association Archives Department, #1665, 1665 West Broadway, Vancouver, BC V6J 5A4
604-736-5551, Fax: 604-736-4566,
museum@bcma.bc.ca
www.bcmamedicalmuseum.org
Founded: 1962 The BCMA Medical Museum holdings include instruments & other equipment used by physicians in British Columbia throughout the past 150 years.

***Vancouver:* British Columbia Sports Hall of Fame & Museum**
Gate A, BC Place Stadium, 777 Pacific Blvd. South, Vancouver, BC V6B 4Y8
604-687-5520, Fax: 604-687-5510,
sportinfo@bcsportshalloffame.com
www.bcsportshalloffame.com
The BC Sports Hall of Fame & Museum contains interactive displays about British Columbia's world-class athletes. In addition to its history galleries, the Hall of Fame & Museum features galleries devoted to Terry Fox & Rick Hansen, a Greg Moore gallery, & a participation gallery.
Bill Maclagan, Chair
Jason Beck, Curator
John Ormiston, Treasurer

***Vancouver:* Cowan Vertebrate Museum**
Dept. of Zoology, University of British Columbia, #4349, 6270 University Blvd., Vancouver, BC V6T 1Z4
604-822-4665, Fax: 604-822-2416,
vertmus@zoology.ubc.ca
www.zoology.ubc.ca/~vertmus
Natural history collection with bird, mammal & herpetological specimens; open year round, by appt.
Dr. D. Irwin, Director
Dr. R. Kenner, Curator

***Vancouver:* Old Hastings Mill Store Museum**
1575 Alma Rd., Vancouver, BC V6R 3P3
604-734-1212, Fax: 604-876-9779,
eandelockhart@shaw.ca
www.findfamilyfun.com/hastingsmill.htm
Founded: 1919 Oldest building in Vancouver owned by The Native Daughters of British Columbia Post No. 1; houses artifacts pertaining to the pioneers of the city and Native peoples; open Tue.-Sun., June 15 - Sept. 15, 1-4; weekends in winter months, closed Dec. & Jan.
Jacqui Underwood, Chief Factor
Elsie Lockhart, Corresponding Secretary

***Vancouver:* The Pacific Museum of the Earth**
Dept. of Earth & Ocean Sciences, University of British Columbia, 6339 Stores Rd., Vancouver, BC V6T 1Z4
604-822-6992, Fax: 604-228-6088,
mparker@eos.ubc.ca
www.eos.ubc.ca/resources/museum
Includes mounted dinosaur, insects in amber, wide variety of fossils & minerals
Kirsten Parker, Curator

***Vancouver:* Roedde House Museum**
***Parent:* Roedde House Preservation Society**
1415 Barclay St., Vancouver, BC V6G 1J6
604-684-7040,
roeddehs@roeddehouse.org
www.roeddehouse.org
Founded: 1990 Roedde House is a late-Victorian home, built in 1893. Today, the house reflects the life of an immigrant, middle class family around 1900. The museum provides guided tours & educational & cultural programs.
Anthony Norfolk, President
Helene Perndl, Manager
Susan Erb, Secretary
Sharon Sprinkhuysen, Treasurer

***Vancouver:* St. Roch National Historic Site**
c/o Vancouver Maritime Museum, 1095 Ogden Ave., Vancouver, BC V6J 1A3
604-257-8300, Fax: 604-737-2621,
info@vancouvermaritimemuseum.com
www.vancouvermaritimemuseum.com
Arctic patrol vessel & 1944 RCMP memorabilia
Simon Robinson, Executive Director

***Vancouver:* Seaforth Highlanders Regimental Museum**
Seaforth Armoury, 1650 Burrard St., Vancouver, BC V6J 3G4
604-733-3836, Fax: 604-666-4078,
seaforthmuseum@gmail.com
bcoy1cpb.pacdat.net/museum.htm
Founded: 1972 Artifacts pertaining to the Seaforth Highlanders of Canada & affiliated regiments
Colin Stevens, Curator

***Vancouver:* Spencer Entomological Museum (SEM)**
Dept. of Zoology, University of British Columbia, 6270 University Blvd., Vancouver, BC V6T 1Z4
604-822-3379, Fax: 604-822-2416,
needham@zoology.ubc.ca
www.insecta.com
Largest collection of BC insects in the world containing 700,000 specimens; museum closed to public
Karen Needham, Curator
G.G.E. Scudder, Director

***Vancouver:* Vancouver Holocaust Education Centre (VHEC)**
***Parent:* Vancouver Holocaust Centre Society**
#50, 950 - 41st Ave. West, Vancouver, BC V5Z 2N7
604-264-0499, Fax: 604-264-0497,
info@vhec.org; library@vhec.org
www.vhec.org
Founded: 1994 The Vancouver Holocaust Education Centre is a teaching museum which provides Holocaust based anti-racism education. It aims to promote human rights, genocide awareness, & social justice. The causes & consequences of discrimination, racism, & antisemitism are explored. The centre includes a museum collection, archives, a library, & a resource centre. The education centre is also engaged in a survivor testimony project. School programs & outreach speakers are available. Exhibits are not recommended for children under the age of ten. The education centre is open year-round.
Frieda Miller, Executive Director
Nina Krieger, Education Director
Shannon LaBelle, Librarian
Elizabeth Shaffer, Archivist
Gisella Levitt, Coordinator, Suvivivor Services
Marla Guralnick Pekarsky, Secretary
Robbie Waisman, Treasurer

***Vancouver:* The Vancouver Maritime Museum Society (VMM)**
1905 Ogden Ave., Vancouver, BC V6J 1A3
604-257-8300, Fax: 604-737-2621,
info@vancouvermaritimemuseum.com
www.vancouvermaritimemuseum.com
Includes National Historic Site St. Roch, RCMP Schooner
Simon Robinson, Executive Director

***Vancouver:* Vancouver Police Museum**
***Parent:* Vancouver Police Historical Society**
240 Cordova St. East, Vancouver, BC V6A 1L3
604-665-3346, Fax: 604-665-3585,
info@vancouverpolicemuseum.ca
www.vancouverpolicemuseum.ca
Other contact information: Twitter:
www.twitter.com/policemuseum
Founded: 1986 Located in the historic City Morgue & Coroner's Court in Vancouver, the Vancouver Police Museum presents a collection of artifacts, papers, photographs, & published materials related to the history of the Vancouver Police Department. The museum is open year-round.

***Vanderhoof:* Vanderhoof Heritage Museum**
c/o Nechako Valley Historical Society, PO Box 1515, Vanderhoof, BC V0J 3A0
250-567-2991, Fax: 250-567-2931,
1920's heritage village & community museum with restaurant café serving old-fashioned food
Stephen Flagg, President
Shelley Olson, Curator/Manager

***Vernon:* Greater Vernon Museum & Archives**
3009 - 32 Ave., Vernon, BC V1T 2L8
250-542-3142, Fax: 250-542-5358,
mail@vernonmuseum.ca
www.vernonmuseum.ca
Open year round
Ron Candy, Curator

***Vernon:* O'Keefe Ranch**
***Also known as:* Historic O'Keefe Ranch**
9380 Hwy. 97, Vernon, BC V1H 1W9
250-542-7868,
www.okeeferanch.ca
Founded: 1867 Founded in 1867, the O'Keefe Ranch operated when thousands of cattle grazed in the Okanagan, Thompson, & Cariboo regions. Today, Historic O'Keefe Ranch depicts the story of early ranching in British Columbia. The ranch offers an informative & entertaining school program. Each summer the ranch hosts a Cowboy Festival.

***Victoria:* Canadian Forces Base Esquimalt Naval & Military Museum**
Canadian Forces Base Esquimalt, PO Box 17000 Forces, Victoria, BC V9A 7N2
250-363-4312, Fax: 250-363-4252,
info@NavalandMilitaryMuseum.org
www.navalandmilitarymuseum.org
Other contact information: E-mail, Curator:
curator@NavalandMilitaryMuseum.org
The CFB Esquimalt Naval & Military Museum collects, preserves, & displays the history of naval presence on the Canadian west coast. In addition, the history of the military on southern Vancouver Island is also depicted. The musuem features an archive & research library. Reproductions of photographs in the archive are available.
Debbie Towell, Curator, nadenmuseum@pacificcoast.net
Joseph Lenarcik, Assistant Curator, 250-363-5655
Clare Sugrue, Coordinator, Museum Volumteers

***Victoria:* The Canadian Scottish Regiment (Princess Mary's) Regimental Museum**
Bay Street Armoury, 715 Bay St., Victoria, BC V8T 1R1
250-363-8753, Fax: 250-363-3593,
csrmuse@islandnet.com
www.islandnet.com/~csrmuse
Items of historical significance to the regiment; located in the Bay Street Armoury, a National Historic Site built in 1915

***Victoria:* Craigdarroch Castle**
1050 Joan Cres., Victoria, BC V8S 3L5
250-592-5323, Fax: 250-592-1099,
info@thecastle.ca
www.craigdarrochcastle.com
Historic house museum, built in 1890 by Robert Dunsmuir, wealthy coal baron; 39 rooms, 87 stairs to tower, lavish Victorian era furnishings, woodwork, stained glass
C. Williams, Executive Director

***Victoria:* Emily Carr House**
207 Government St., Victoria, BC V8V 2K8
250-383-5843, Fax: 250-356-7796,
ecarr@shaw.ca
www.emilycarr.com
Birthplace of Emily Carr; People's Gallery; open May-Oct. & Dec. or by appointment

***Victoria:* Fort Rodd Hill & Fisgard Lighthouse National Historic Sites**
603 Fort Rodd Hill Rd., Victoria, BC V9C 2W8
250-478-5849, Fax: 250-478-2816,
fort.rodd@pc.gc.ca
www.fortroddhill.com
Turn of the century coastal defence gun batteries & first permanent lighthouse (1860) on Canada's west coast

***Victoria:* Goldstream Regional Museum**
#2, 697 Goldstream Ave., Victoria, BC V9B 2X2
250-474-6113,
History of region; WWI & WWII displays; open year round

***Victoria:* Helmcken House**
Royal BC Museum, 675 Belleville St., Victoria, BC V8W 9W2
250-356-7226, Fax: 250-387-5674, 888-447-7977
reception@royalbcmuseum.bc.ca
www.royalbcmuseum.bc.ca
Home of Dr. John Sebastian Helmcken built in 1852; medical & domestic collections; managed by the Royal BC Museum
Pauline Rafferty, CEO

***Victoria:* Lt. General Ashton Armoury Museum**
724 Vanalman Ave., Victoria, BC V8Z 3B5
250-363-8346, Fax: 250-363-8326,
Army service support
Maj. Derek Brown

***Victoria:* Maritime Museum of British Columbia**
28 Bastion Sq., Victoria, BC V8W 1H9
250-385-4222, Fax: 250-382-2869,
info@mmbc.bc.ca
www.mmbc.bc.ca
Founded: 1954 This extensive museum of 3 floors covers the history of marine navigation on the BC coast from First Nation cultures through to European explorers and territorial tussles. Interactive displays include a mock-up of a ship's deck complete with climbable crow's nest & ratlines. The 2nd floor offers model ships for viewing, while the 3rd floor houses a library. Open all year, with winter & summer hrs.
MS Shirley Vickers, Executive Director, 250-385-4222, X-104, svickers@mmbc.bc.ca

***Victoria:* Metchosin School Museum**
4475 Happy Valley Rd., Victoria, BC V9C 3Z3
250-478-3451,
roper@pacificcoast.net
www.metchosinmuseum.org
Founded: 1972 School, household & agricultural exhibits/archives pertaining to the School and the area; operated by a society of volunteers; open April-Oct.

***Victoria:* Museum & Archives of 5 (BC) Regiment, Royal Canadian Artillery**
The Armoury, #304, 715 Bay St., Victoria, BC V8T 1R1
250-363-3814, Fax: 250-363-3512,
info@5rcamuseum.ca; curator@5rcamuseum.ca
www.5rcamuseum.ca
Other contact information: E-mail, Archives:
archivist@5rcamuseum.ca; Gifts: shop@5rcamuseum.ca
Founded: 1996 The Museum & Archives of 5 (BC) Regiment depicts the history of coast artillery & associated units. Displays date from 1861 to the present. Examples of artifacts include a rifled muzzle loading gun & a vintage cannon. An archives & reference library are also available for reserach. The museum is open year round, two days each week. For visits outside regular hours, please call 250-363-8270.

***Victoria:* Point Ellice House & Gardens**
2616 Pleasant St., Victoria, BC V8T 4V3
250-380-6506, Fax: 250-381-2338, reservations@pointellicehouse.ca
www.tca.gov.bc.ca/heritage/historic_sites/point_ellice_house.htm
Other contact information: Alternative URL: www.pointellicehouse.ca
Point Ellice House was owned by Magistrate & Gold Commissioner Peter O'Reilly, starting in 1867. The home & garden are open from May to September.

***Victoria:* Royal London Wax Museum**
470 Belleville St., Victoria, BC V8V 1W9
250-388-4461, Fax: 250-388-4493, 877-929-3228
info@waxmuseum.bc.ca
www.waxmuseum.bc.ca
Houses over 300 wax sculptures; group tours available; open daily
Dr. Arne H. Lane, President
Ken H. Lane, General Manager

***Victoria:* Victoria Police Historical Society**
850 Caledonia Ave., Victoria, BC V8T 5J8
250-995-7654, Fax: 250-995-7450, museum@police.victoria.bc.ca
History of the Victoria police, est. 1858; exhibits include 1921 "Commerce" Patrol Wagon, 1938 UL Harley Davidson motorcycle & sidecar, 1940 Dodge police car
Cst. Bob Raappana, Curator

***Wells:* Wells Museum**
***Parent:* Wells Historical Society**
PO Box 244, Wells, BC V0K 2R0
250-994-3422, museum@wellsbc.come
www.wellsmuseum.ca
Wells Museum is located within the Island Mountain Mine office, which was built during the 1930s when Wells was established as a company town for the Cariboo Gold-Quartz Mine. The museum features displays about the mining history in the area. It is open from May to September.
William (W.G) (W.G) Quackenbush, Contact

***West Vancouver:* West Vancouver Museum**
680 - 17th St., West Vancouver, BC V7V 3T2
604-925-7295, www.westvancouvermuseum.ca
The West Vancouver Museum offers exhibitions & educational programs to increase awareness of the history, culture, & art of the West Vancouver region & the country. The museum is open year-round.
Darrin Morrison, Curator, 604-925-7296, dmorrison@westvancouver.ca
Carol Howie, Coordinator, Collections, 604-925-7294, chowie@westvancouver.ca
Isaac Vanderhorst, Coordinator, Education, 604-925-7297, ivanderhorst@westvancouver.ca

***White Rock:* White Rock Museum & Archives**
14970 Marine Drive, White Rock, BC V4B 1C4
604-541-2222, Fax: 604-541-2223, whiterockmuseum@telus.net
www.whiterock.museum.bc.ca
Located in the White Rock Train Station; collections include artifacts relating to the history & families of White Rock, documentation relating to the civic, political & business life of the community, objects relating to the Great Northern Railway & rail history of the area, and natural history objects of the locality.
Shelly Copping, Manager

***Williams Lake:* Museum of the Cariboo-Chilcotin**
113 - 4th Ave. North, Williams Lake, BC V2G 2C8
250-392-7404, Fax: 250-392-7404, mccwl@uniserve.com
cowboy-museum.com
Displays focusing on the ranching & rodeo history of the Cariboo Chilcotin area; home of the BC Cowboy Hall of Fame; Shuswap First Nation, Chinese & Chilcotin materials; open June-Aug., Mon.-Sat. 10-4; Sept.-May, Tues.-Sat. 11-4
Pat Skoblanuik, Manager

***Yale:* Historic Yale Museum**
PO Box 74, 31187 Douglas St., Yale, BC V0K 2S0
604-863-2324, Fax: 604-863-2495, yahs@uniserve.com
First Nations; Gold Rush; Railway Era

***Ymir:* Ymir Arts & Museum Society**
PO Box 65, Ymir, BC V0G 2K0
250-357-9262, ymirartsandmuseumsociety@hotmail.com
www.ymirbc.com/yams
The Ymir Arts & Museum Society preserves the Ymir Schoolhouse, where arts & culture in Ymir are promoted.
Located in the West Kootenays of British Columbia, Ymir was an active mining town in the late 1800s.
Robyn Balaski, Arts & Museum Contact, rainspirit13@hotmail.com

Manitoba

Provincial Museums

The Manitoba Museum / Le Musée du Manitoba
190 Rupert Ave., Winnipeg, MB R3B 0N2
204-956-2830, Fax: 204-942-3679, 888-231-9739
info@manitobamuseum.ca
www.manitobamuseum.ca
Other contact information: Info Line: 204/943-3139
Nine permanent galleries & Alloway Hall which houses temporary & travelling exhibitions. Permanent galleries are: Orientation (in which the main theme of the Museum is explained), Earth History, Grasslands, Urban (a section of Winnipeg, reconstructed as it might have been in 1920), Nonsuch (a replica of the 17th-century Ketch), Arctic-Subarctic & Boreal Forest. The Hudson's Bay Company Gallery reflects the legacy of the Company & the people whose daily activities & legendary deed bring to life the drama & history of Canada's fur trade. The all new Parklands/mixed woods Gallery, representing the most natural & culturally diverse region of the province. The Planetarium provides educational & entertaining programs for the general public & school groups in the 287-seat Star Theatre; feature presentations touch all aspects of astronomy, science facts/science fiction, as well as present day space programs & technology
Claudette Leclerc, Chief Executive Officer
C. Ellis, Director, Operations
J. Schwersensky, Director, Marketing
Mike Jensen, Supervisor, Planetarium Programs

Other Museums in Manitoba

***Alonsa:* Alex Robertson Museum**
Alonsa, MB R0H 0A0
204-767-2101, Fax: 204-767-2004, alonsa@mts.net
Antique guns; pioneer tools & artifacts; 1939 fire engine; open year round

***Anola:* Anola & District Museum**
PO Box 153, Anola, MB R0E 0A0
204-866-2922,
Open May - Sept., Sun. or by appt.
Jack Mavins, Treasurer

***Ashern:* Ashern Pioneer Museum**
PO Box 642, 36 - 1st St. South, Ashern, MB R0C 0E0
204-768-3147, Fax: 204-768-3051,
Other contact information: Phone, appointments: 204-768-2394
The Ashern Museum features the following restored buildings: St Michael's Anglican Church, the CNR station, the Ashern Post Office, the Hoffman Log House, the Darwin School House, & Ashern's first Rural Municipality of Siglunes Office. Artifacts include a threshing machine, tractor, bailer, & plow. The museum is open from May to September. At other times, tours can be arranged.

***Austin:* Manitoba Agricultural Museum**
PO Box 10, Austin, MB R0H 0C0
204-637-2354, Fax: 204-637-2395, agmuseum@mts.net; info@ag-museum.mb.ca
www.ag-museum.mb.ca
Founded: 1953 Located 3 km south of Hwys. 1 & 34, the site boasts Canada's largest collection of vintage agricultural equipment from 1900 on. There is also a pioneer village with over 20 buildings from log cabins to mills & mansions. The Manitoba Amateur Radio Museum is also housed on site. Events include the annual Thresherman's Reunion & Stampede last week in July. Open daily 9:00-5:00, May 12 - Oct. 5.
Diane Nesbitt, Administrator

***Austin:* Manitoba Amateur Radio Museum Inc. (MARM)**
PO Box 10, Austin, MB R0H 0C0
204-728-2463, Fax: 204-728-2463, ve4arm@mts.net
www.marminc.ca
Located on the grounds of the Manitoba Agricultural Museum, Hwy. #34 in Austin; Canada's only amateur radio museum; home of amateur radio station VE4ARM/VE4MTR.
Dave Snydal, Curator, dsnydal@mts.net

***Beausejour:* Pioneer Village Museum**
PO Box 310, 7th St. North, Beausejour, MB R0E 0C0
204-268-3048, Fax: 204-268-3048,
Open July & Aug.
Peter H. Kozyra, President

***Belmont:* Belmont & District Museum**
PO Box 69, 202 - 5th St., Belmont, MB R0K 0C0
204-528-3300,
Other contact information: Phone, Off-season: 204-537-2405; 204-537-2474
The Belmont & District Museum features a CNR caboose, plus displays of medical equipment, sports memorabilia, military uniforms, & printing equipment for the Belmont News. The museum is open during July & August, & by appointment at other times of the year.

***Belmont:* Evergreen Firearms Museum Inc.**
PO Box 57, Belmont, MB R0K 0C0
204-537-2647,
www.museumsmanitoba.com/dir/western/95.html
Military & non-military historical firearms; open year round

***Binscarth:* Binscarth & District Gordon Orr Memorial Museum**
PO Box 239, 162 - 2nd Ave., Binscarth, MB R0J 0G0
204-532-2217, Fax: 204-532-2153, vilbins@mts.net
www.binscarthmb.com/museum.html
The Binscarth & District Gordon Orr Memorial Museum contains displays such as Native artifacts, a chapel, a general store, a school room, & large agricultural machinery. The museum is open during July & August.
Rita Wasslen, Contact

***Birtle:* Birdtail Country Museum**
PO Box 508, 738 Main St., Birtle, MB R0M 0C0
204-842-5342, birdtailcm@hotmail.com
Other contact information: Alternative Phone: 204-842-3363; 204-842-5350
The Birdtail Country Museum is housed in the former Union Bank Building in Birtle. It contains a variety of objects from pioneer days in the Birtle area. The museum also holds local newspapers on microfilm. Birdtail Country Museum is open from mid-May to the end of August.

***Boissevain:* Beckoning Hills Museum**
PO Box 389, 425 Mill Rd. South, Boissevain, MB R0K 0E0
204-534-6544, bhmuseum@mts.net
The Beckoning Hills Museum presents historical displays from Boissevain & the surrounding area. Exhibits include pioneer household items, agricultural tools & implements, native artifacts, & military items. The museum is open from June until September. Appointments can be arranged at other times of the year.

***Boissevain:* Moncur Gallery**
PO Box 1241, Civic Centre, Boissevain, MB R0K 0E0
204-534-6478, Fax: 204-534-3710, info@moncurgallery.org
www.moncurgallery.org
Founded: 1984 Gallery showcases an extensive collection of ancient artifacts portraying the earliest history of the Turtle Mountain and surrounding prairie area in southwestern Manitoba. Exhibits include lifestyle artifacts of nomadic peoples which predate the written record, such as ceremonial items, food preparation utensils & tools. Open Tue.-Sat., 10:00-5:00.
Shannon Moncur, Chair
Phyllis Hallett, Secretary

***Brandon:* B.J. Hales Museum of Natural History**
George T. Richardson Library, Lower Level, Brandon University, 270 - 18th St., Brandon, MB R7A 6A9
204-727-7307, Fax: 204-728-7346, jacksonk@brandonu.ca
www2.brandonu.ca/bjhales
The B.J. Hales Museum of Natural History collects, preserves, & presents artifacts of the natural heritage of Manitoba. Collections include bird & mammal specimens & a geological display. The museum is open year-round, Monday to Friday.

***Brandon:* Chapman Museum**
PO Box 43, RR#2, Brandon, MB R7A 5Y2
204-728-7396,
www.brandon.com; www.virtualmuseum.ca
Village-type museum setting with 16 historic buildings, among them the Roseville Church, Harrow School, Pendennis Rail Station, Robinville School, and various shops; guided tours; special needs facilities & wheelchair access; picnic area; open during the summer, free admission or donations appreciated.
Albert T. Chapman, Director

***Brandon:* Commonwealth Air Training Plan Museum**
PO Box 3, Group 520, RR#5, Brandon, MB R7A 5Y5
204-727-2444, Fax: 204-725-2334, airmuseum@inetlink.ca
www.airmuseum.ca
Canada's only air museum dedicated to those who trained & fought for the British Commmonwealth during WW II; artifacts include photographs, uniforms & clothing, personal papers, logbooks, station magazines, tools, equipment, trade badges, & medals; display of training aircraft

Stephen Hayter, Executive Director
John McNarry, President

***Brandon:* Daly House Museum & Steve Magnacca Research Centre**
122 - 18 St., Brandon, MB R7A 5A4
204-727-1722, Fax: 204-727-1722,
dalymus@mts.net
www.mts.net/~dalymus
Period home of the 1880s; 1903 grocery store; 1892 council chambers; open daily in the summer; Tue.-Sun. winter
Eileen Trott, Curator

***Brandon:* Manitoba Agricultural Hall of Fame**
1129 Queens Ave., Brandon, MB R7A 1L9
204-728-3736, Fax: 204-726-6260,
info@manitobaaghalloffame.com
www.manitobaaghalloffame.com
Recognizing those who improved agricultural & rural living; plaques are at the Keystone Centre in Brandon (1175 - 18th St.); open daily
Robert G. (Bob) Roehle, President
Allan Chambers, Treasurer
Patricia Bailey, Office Manager,
info@manitobaaghalloffame.com

***Brandon:* XII Manitoba Dragoons/26 Field Regiment Museum**
Brandon Armoury, 1116 Victoria Ave., Brandon, MB R7A 1B2
204-726-3498, Fax: 204-725-1766,
sim.gordo@gmail.com
www.12mbdragoons.com
Founded: 1979 The museum has a wide range of military memorabilia and artifacts on display, including photos, uniforms and equipment; small research library; archival materials; regimental button collection; open Tuesdays throughout the year
Mr. Ed McArthur, Curator

***La Broquerie:* Musée Saint Jachim**
PO Box 66, La Broquerie, MB R0A 0W0
204-424-5232,

***Carberry:* Carberry Plains Museum**
PO Box 1072, 520 - 4th Ave., Carberry, MB R0K 0H0
204-834-6609, Fax: 204-834-2795,
www.townofcarberry.ca
Other contact information: Phone, Off Season: 204-834-2284
The Carberry Plains Museum reflects early prairie life, through its collections from former residents, including a First World War pilot & Ernest Thompson Seton, a well-known naturalist. The museum is open during July & August. Appointments may be made during June & September.
Rae Anderson, Contact, 204-834-2284

***Carberry:* The Seton Centre**
PO Box 408, 116 Main St., Carberry, MB R0K 0H0
204-834-2509,
Materials by & about Ernest Thompson Seton, 1860-1946; open June - Sept. long weekend
Cheryl Orr, Contact

***Carberry:* Spruce Woods Provincial Heritage Park**
Park Centre, PO Box 900, Carberry, MB R0K 0H0
204-827-8950, Fax: 204-827-8852,
swppterp@mts.net
Northwest Co. fur-trading artifacts
Madelyn Robinson, Interpreter

***Carman:* Dufferin Historical Museum**
PO Box 1646, 44 King's Park Ed., Carman, MB R0G 0J0
204-745-3597, Fax: 204-828-3698,
www.cici.mb.ca/mmedia/dufferin.html
Other contact information: Off-season phone: 204/745-2443
An early 20th century home. Open Mid-June - September.
Shirley Snider, President

***Carman:* Heaman's Antique Autorama**
PO Box 105, Hwy. 3, Carman, MB R0G 0J0
204-745-2981,
Canadian & American automobiles dating back to 1902

***Cartwright:* Heritage Village Museums**
PO Box 9, Cartwright, MB R0K 0L0
204-529-2047,
edocart@hotmail.com
www.cartwrightmb.ca
This is a collection of historic buildings representing village life in pioneer days. The Blacksmith Museum is a fully restored, functional smithy. Todds Shoe Repairs has authentic cobbling equipment. Badger Creek Museum conserves artifacts of rural family life. There are also a schoolhouse, post office and telephone office.

***Churchill:* Eskimo Museum**
PO Box 10, 242 La Verendrye Ave., Churchill, MB R0B 0E0
204-675-2030, Fax: 204-675-2140,
chhbay@mts.net
Open Mon.-Sat., year-round

Lorraine Brandson, Curator
Cathy Widdowson, Asst. Curator

***Churchill:* Manitoba North National Historic Sites & Wapusk National Park of Canada**
Parks Canada Visitor Centre, PO Box 127, 1 Manteyo Seepee, Churchill, MB R0B 0E0
204-675-8863, Fax: 204-675-2026,
mannorth.nhs@pc.gc.ca; wapusk.np@pc.gc.ca
www.pc.gc.ca/eng/lhn-nhs/mb/prince/index.aspx
Guided tours are offered to Prince of Wales Fort, Cape Merry Battery, Sloop Cove & York Factory by contacting the Parks Canada Visitor Centre in Churchill which houses exhibits introducing the history of the Hudson's Bay Company and the fur trade of the 1700s. Open year round.

***Crystal City:* Crystal City Community Printing Museum**
PO Box 302, 218 Broadway, Crystal City, MB R0K 0N0
204-873-2260,
btreble@mts.net
Newspaper print shop started by Thomas Greenway (7th premier of Manitoba) in 1881; tours on request
B. Treble

***Darlingford:* Darlingford School Heritage Museum**
PO Box 98, 197 Bradburn St., Darlingford, MB R0G 0L0
204-246-2015,
School built in 1910; open by appointment
Robert Jordan

***Dauphin:* Fort Dauphin Museum**
PO Box 181, 140 Jackson Ave., Dauphin, MB R7N 2V1
204-638-6630, Fax: 204-629-2327,
fortdphn@mts.net
www.dauphin.ca; fortdauphinmuseum.wordpress.com
Fur trade history, pioneer history, local history, the Parkland Archaeological Laboratory; open mid-May - early Sept. & by appt. early Sept.-mid May
Heidi Husband, Curator/Manager

***Dauphin:* Cross of Freedom Historical Site & Museum**
***Also known as:* Trembowla Cross of Freedom**
121 - 7 Ave. SE, Dauphin, MB R7N 2E3
204-638-9641, Fax: 204-638-9963,
The history & culture of Ukrainian pioneers; Cross of Freedom site of first Ukrainian Catholic Divine Liturgy & first Ukrainian Catholic Church St. Michael's, the oldest such church in Canada & dedicated as an Heritage site building in 2000; monuments include a large granite cross, bronze bust of Rev. Nestor Dmytriw, a grotto & monument of the first Ukrainian Catholic Bishop in Canada, Bishop Nyky
Kay Slobodzian, Secretary
Stella Sapach, Treasurer
John Slobodzian, President

***Dufresne:* Aunt Margaret's Museum of Childhood Inc.**
Trans-Canada Hwy., Dufresne, MB R0A 0J0
204-422-8426,
Aunt Margaret's Museum of Childhood includes a collection of antique furniture & artifacts.

***Dugald:* Cook's Creek Heritage Museum**
Group 22, Box 6, RR#2, Dugald, MB R0E 0K0
204-444-4448, Fax: 204-444-4224,
cchm@mts.net
www.stmichaelsrc.mb.ca
Open daily, except Wed. May-Aug. 11-5
Jane Burpee, President

***Elkhorn:* Manitoba Antique Automobile Museum**
PO Box 477, Elkhorn, MB R0M 0N0
204-845-2604, Fax: 204-845-2312,
info@elkhorn.mb.ca
www.mbautomuseum.com
Founded: 1961 Donated to the community by local farmer, Isaac "Ike" Clarkson, the collection began with a hand-restored 1909 Hupmobile to a sizeable array of vintage automobiles. The site also includes exhibits of agricultural machinery and household articles. Open May - Sept., 9:00-6:00.
Agnes Wolfe, Curator
Roland Gagnon, Chair
Garth Mitchell, Sec.-Treas.

***Erickson:* The Erickson Museum**
Erickson, MB R0J 0P0
204-636-2431,
The Parsonage, built in 1897-98 & the Nedrob School feature period artifacts; open by appt.

***Eriksdale:* Eriksdale Museum**
PO Box 71, Eriksdale, MB R0C 0W0
204-739-2621, Fax: 204-739-2073,
dmysmith@mts.net
www.eriksdale.com
Open mid-May - Sept., excluding Thurs. & Sun.; Eriksdale Creamery Museum now open
Elaine Henrotte, Secretary

Donna Smith, Chair

***Flin Flon:* Flin Flon Station Museum**
CN Building, PO Box 160, Highway 10, Flin Flon, MB R8A 1M6
204-687-2946, Fax: 204-687-4456,
www.cityofflinflon.com
Household artifacts from the late 1920s; mining; open Victoria Day - Labour Day
Ron Dodds

***Gardenton:* Ukrainian Museum & Village Society**
***Also known as:* Gardenton Park**
Gardenton, MB R0A 0M0
204-425-3501,
Clothing, icons & many articles from the early settlers; an exhibit of churches & photos of early pioneer life; clay thatched roof house & a one-room school; picnic facilities; tours & meals upon request
Linda Shewchuk, President

***Gilbert Plains:* Gilbert Plains & District Historical Society**
PO Box 662, Gilbert Plains, MB R0L 0X0
204-548-4448, Fax: 204-548-2564,
rmofgilbertplains@mts.net
10 log buildings; Ukrainian artifacts; open July & Aug.
Susan Boyachek, Sec.-Treas.
Eugene Dedio, President
Jim Michaluk, Vice-President

***Gimli:* New Iceland Heritage Museum**
The Waterfront Centre, #108, 94 - 1st Ave., Gimli, MB R0C 1B1
204-642-4001, Fax: 204-642-9382,
nihm@mts.net
www.nihm.ca
The New Iceland Heritage Museum preserves & interprets the history of New Iceland & Lake Winnipeg & its fishing industry.
Tammy Axelsson, Executive Director

***Gladstone:* Gladstone & District Museum**
PO Box 651, 49 - 6th St., Gladstone, MB R0J 0T0
204-385-2551, Fax: 204-385-2391,
Local pioneer artifacts

***Grandview:* The Watson Crossley Community Museum**
PO Box 396, Grandview, MB R0L 0Y0
204-546-2661, Fax: 204-546-3310,
guards45@mts.net
Facility includes museum display of local area pioneer artifacts, shedded display of antique farm machinery, tractors & automobiles; also included is a pioneer homestead building (1896), pioneer house (1918), rural one-room schoolhouse & a pioneer Ukrainian Orthodox church; open June-Sept. & year round by appt.
Gerald Morran
Mervin Mitchell
Allan Yuihl

***Hamiota:* Hamiota Pioneer Club Museum**
PO Box 279, Hamiota, MB R0M 0T0
204-764-2552,
Open Sundays in July & Aug. & by appt.
R. Neil McDonald, Secretary
John L. Rankin, President

***Hartney:* Hart-Cam Museum**
PO Box 399, Hartney, MB R0M 0X0
204-858-2590, Fax: 204-858-2681,
hartney@mts.net
Artifacts from Aboriginal to post-settlement times

***Inglis:* St. Elijah 1908 Pioneer Church Museum**
Inglis, MB R0J 0X0
204-564-2228, Fax: 204-564-2643,
Designated provincial historic site
Barry Sawchuk, President

***Killarney:* J.A.V. David Museum**
PO Box 1451, 414 Williams Ave., Killarney, MB R0K 1G0
204-523-8836, Fax: 204-523-8740,
Museum of artifacts, clothing & memorabilia associated with Killarney & area history
Mark Witherspoon, Chair

***Lac du Bonnet:* Lac du Bonnet & District Historical Society**
PO Box 658, 578 Riverland, Lac du Bonnet, MB R0E 1A0
204-345-2726, Fax: 204-345-9787,
memories@granite.mb.ca
Louis Bruneau, President

***Ladywood:* Atelier Ladywood Museum**
PO Box 14, RR#3, Ladywood, MB R0E 0C0
204-265-3226,
Atelier Ladywood Museum features the former H. Gabel's General Store, with items from the 1930s to the 1950s.

***Lundar:* Lundar Museum Society**
PO Box 265, Lundar, MB R0C 1Y0

204-739-0147,
Open mid-June - Sept.
Harold Hallson, Director

***Lynn Lake:* Lynn Lake Mining Town Museum**
PO Box 847, 470 Cobalt Pl., Lynn Lake, MB R0B 0W0
204-356-8302,
Open May 24 - Aug. 31

***Melita:* Antler River Historical Society Museum**
Townsend Dr., Melita, MB R0M 1L0
204-522-3103, Fax: 204-522-8387,
Local history
W.H. Critchlow, President

***Miami:* Miami Museum**
PO Box 153, Miami, MB R0G 1H0
204-435-2305, Fax: 204-435-2067,
Fossils; souvenirs of WWI & WWII; wedding dresses from 1896-1900

***Miniota:* Miniota Municipal Museum Inc.**
PO Box 59, 110 Stewart Ave., Miniota, MB R0M 1M0
204-567-3675, Fax: 204-567-3505,
Open May - Oct.; pioneer & Aboriginal artifacts
R. Moorehead, President
S. Moorehead, Secretary

***Minnedosa:* Minnedosa Heritage Museum**
PO Box 2005, 100 Heritage Park Cres., Minnedosa, MB R0J 1E0
204-867-3542,
Local history includes Cadurcis House, Hunterville Church, Havelock School, McManus Trappers' Cabin, Munro Blacksmith Shop, Minnedosa Power House, Hopkins Log Barn & operating windmill & waterwheel; museum open July 1st - Sept. long weekend; group tours by appt.
Earl Thompson, Vice-President, 204/867-2050
Charlie Kingdon, President, 204/867-2027

***Moosehorn:* Moosehorn Heritage Museum Inc.**
PO Box 28, Moosehorn, MB R0C 2E0
204-768-3305,
Local pioneer history; radar equipment

***Morden:* Canadian Fossil Discovery Centre**
111B Gilmour St., Morden, MB R6M 1N9
204-822-3406, Fax: 204-272-3303,
info@discoverfossils.com
www.discoverfossils.com
Housing an extensive collection of marine reptile fossils, the galleries of the Canadian Fossil Discovery Centre interpret life in the Western Interior Seaway during the cretaceous period. The museum is open year round.
Tyler Schroeder, General Manager, gm@discoverfossils.com
Anita-Maria Janzic, Curator, curator@discoverfossils.com

***Morris:* Morris & District Centennial Museum Inc.**
PO Box 344, Morris, MB R0G 1K0
204-746-2169,
morrismuseum@mts.net
Exhibits artifacts which depict pioneer life in the Red River Valley
Larry McCrady, Director

***Neepawa:* Beautiful Plains Museum**
PO Box 1732, 91 Hamilton St. West, Neepawa, MB R0J 1H0
204-476-3896,
www.neepawa.ca/museum
Other contact information: Phone, September - May: 204-476-3232
The Beautiful Plains Museum features the following attractions: a military room; costume rooms; a medical hall; jewellery & general store displays; a post office exhibit; a local history room; office equipment; farm & home tools; information about local lodges; sports memorabilia; information about the local Ukranian Polish culture; & a chapel room, which depicts the history of religious settlement in the Neepawa area. The museum is house in the CNR station, which was built in 1902. Neepawa's Beautiful Plains Museum is open from Victoria Day to Labour Day.

***Neepawa:* The Margaret Laurence Home**
PO Box 2099, 312 - 1st Ave., Neepawa, MB R0J 1H0
204-476-3612,
mlhome@mts.net
www.mts.net/~mlhome/
Birthplace of Margaret Laurence; includes research area, meeting room & modern artwork; open daily in summer, other times by appt.
Lane England

***Notre Dame de Lourdes:* Pioneers & Chanoinesses Museum / Musée des Pionniers et des Chanoinessess**
PO Box 186, 55 Rogers St., Notre Dame de Lourdes, MB R0G 1M0
204-248-2687, Fax: 204-248-2049,
museend@mts.net
The first pioneers in Notre Dame de Lourdes arrived from Quebec in 1880, & soon after pioneers came from France & Switzerland. The Chanoinesses Regulieres des Cinq-Plaies du Sauveur came to Notre Dame de Lourdes from Lyon, France in 1895. The Pioneers & Chanoinesses Museum houses artifacts of the pioneers & Chanoinesses in the community. The museum is open year round.

***The Pas:* The Sam Waller Museum**
PO Box 185, 306 Fischer Ave., The Pas, MB R9A 1K4
204-623-3802, Fax: 204-623-5506,
samwallermuseum@mts.net
www.samwallermuseum.ca
Permanent collection comprises some 70,000 items of natural history specimens, historical artifacts, books & other library materials, photographs & negatives, fine art objects, & archival resources of the Town of The Pas; temporary exhibits; special events & programming
David Raitt, Director
Sharain Jones, Curator

***Pilot Mound:* Marringhurst Pioneer Park Museum**
PO Box 58, RR#2, Pilot Mound, MB R0G 1P0
204-825-2102, Fax: 204-825-2391,
Schoolhouse with original furnishings; open year round

***Pilot Mound:* Pilot Mound Museum**
Centennial Bldg., PO Box 126, Broadway St., Pilot Mound, MB R0G 1P0
204-825-2035,
amdata@hotmail.com
Pioneer household & agricultural items; natural history artifacts; open year round

***Plum Coulee:* Plum Coulee & District Museum**
PO Box 36, 277 Main Ave., Plum Coulee, MB R0G 1R0
204-829-3419, Fax: 204-829-3436,
pcoulee@mts.net
Artifacts & photographs portray the Ukrainian, Mennonite, Jewish, & Ukrainian pioneer history of Plum Coulee & the surrounding area. The Plum Coulee & District Museum is open during the summer, or by appointment.

***Portage la Prairie:* The Fort-La-Reine Museum & Pioneer Village**
PO Box 744, 2652 Saskatchewan Ave. East, Portage la Prairie, MB R1N 3C2
204-857-3259, Fax: 204-239-4917,
enquiries@fortlareinemuseum.ca
www.fortlareinemuseum.ca
Depicts native & pioneer life in the 1800s & includes a fort, trading post, village store, country church, schoolhouse, print shop, fire hall, stable, trapper's cabin & several heritage homes; also includes a railway display of a caboose, 1882 official private railcar of Sir William Van Horne, several maintenance railroad vehicles & railway crossing; Muskateer Aircraft & Allis Chalmers Museum hous
John L. Bjore, Sec.-Manager/Curator

***Rapid City:* Rapid City Museum**
PO Box 271, Rapid City, MB R0K 1W0
204-826-2043,
hhaslen@yahoo.ca
Cundy watch display; Frederick Philip Grove display; old school building; old Rapid City Reporter building with press & back copies; open July & Aug., other times by appt.
Howard Haslen, Contact

***Reston:* Reston & District Historical Museum**
PO Box 304, Reston, MB R0M 1X0

Local artifacts & archival material

***Riverton:* Hecla Island Heritage Home Museum**
c/o Manitoba Conservation, Riverton, MB R0C 2R0
204-279-2056,
Depiction of the life of an Icelandic family, 1920-1940s

***La Riviere:* Archibald Historical Museum**
***Also known as:* Archibald Museum**
PO Box 97, La Riviere, MB R0G 1A0
204-242-2825,
1878 log house furnished as it was during Nellie McClung's residency plus large frame home (furnished) where she lived, had the first of her family & wrote her first books; also La Rivière C.P.R. Station & more; open mid-May - Labour Day, closed Wed. & Thu. unless by appt.
R.K. Wallcraft, President

***Roblin:* Keystone Pioneers Museum Inc.**
PO Box 10, Roblin, MB R0L 1P0
204-937-2935,
Agricultural equipment & artifacts; Elaschuk House; Makaroff Church; Sawmill
Len Curle, President, 204/934-2602
Gladys Ludwig, Sec.-Treas., 204/937-2863
Art McIntyre, Director

***Rossburn:* Rossburn Museum**
c/o Town of Rossburn, PO Box 70, 43 Main St. North, Rossburn, MB R0J 1V0
204-859-2762, Fax: 204-859-2959,
town.rsb@mts.net
www.town.rossburn.mb.ca
The Rossburn Museum features rooms representing a pioneer kitchen, a classroom, a hospital room, a print shop, & a hairdressing salon. The museum also displays a miniature Ukrainian village, plus Ukrainian artifacts.

***St Andrews:* Lower Fort Garry National Historic Site of Canada**
5925 Hwy. 9, St Andrews, MB R1A 4A8
204-785-6050, Fax: 204-482-5887, 888-773-8888
LFGNHS.Info@pch.gc.ca
pc.gc.ca/garry
1830s stone Hudson's Bay Co. fort; costumed interpreters, visitor centre, gift store, restaurant; open May 15 - Labour Day, daily from 9-5
Tom Kynman, Superintendent

***Saint-Boniface:* Le Musée de Saint-Boniface / Saint Boniface Museum**
494, av Taché, Saint-Boniface, MB R2H 2B2
204-237-4500, Fax: 204-986-7964,
info@msbm.mb.ca
www.msbm.mb.ca
Logé dans l'ancien couvent des Soeurs Grises, le musée a pour mission d'effectuer des recherches sur des objets reliés au patrimoine canadien-français et métis de l'Ouest canadien; préservation et interprétation; expositions thématiques; plus de 30 000 objets historiques et ethnologiques dans la collection; programmation; boutique.
Dr. Philippe R. Mailhot, Directeur
Pierrette Boily, Conservatrice

***St Claude:* Manitoba Dairy Museum**
PO Box 131, St Claude, MB R0G 1Z0
204-379-2156, Fax: 204-379-2156,
Artifacts from settlers, many of whom came from France; variety of dairy artifacts
Raymond Philippot, Contact

***St George:* Musée St-Georges**
CP 171, St George, MB R0E 1V0
204-367-8801,
Open May - Sept.
Jean Dupont, Conservateur

***St Joseph:* Musée St-Joseph Museum Inc.**
PO Box 8096, St Joseph, MB R0G 2C0
204-737-2397, Fax: 204-737-2248,
stm@stjosephmuseum.org
Domestic & agricultural artifacts; the oldest timber house in southern Manitoba; antique tractors. Open May 15 - Sept. 15
George Perron, Vice-President
Renald Parent, President

***Saint-Pierre-Jolys:* Musée de St-Pierre-Jolys**
CP 321, 432, rue Joubert nord, Saint-Pierre-Jolys, MB R0A 1V0
204-433-7635,
froy@hsd.ca
www.museestpierrejolys.ca
Le musée est un ancien couvent et sert à se rappeler le patrimoine et les contributions des religieuses au développement du village de Saint-Pierre-Jolys; on retrouve aussi la Maison Goulet, et un cabane à sucre.

***Sandy Lake:* Ukrainian Cultural Heritage Museum**
Sandy Lake, MB R0J 1X0
204-585-2168,
1899 Ukrainian settlement; traditional Ukrainian arts & crafts; open June - Sept. & by appt.
S. Liebing, President
H. Lewandoski, Secretary
M. Solonyczny, Treasurer

***Selkirk:* Marine Museum of Manitoba (Selkirk) Inc.**
PO Box 7, 490 Eveline St., Selkirk, MB R1A 2B1
204-482-7761,
marinemuseum@mts.net
www.marinemuseum.ca
Founded: 1973 The museum gathers and restores marine vessels related to Manitoba's Lake Winnipeg and the Red River from about 1850 to the present. Storehouses of artifacts and records are located aboard historic vessels, including the S.S. Keenora and the C.G.S. Bradbury. Open May - Sept.; school/group tours available.
MS Shaylene Nordal, Museum Manager
Don Gordon, Chair

***Selkirk:* St. Andrews' Rectory National Historic Site**
374 River Rd., Selkirk, MB R1A 2Y1
204-785-6050, Fax: 204-482-5887, 800-442-0600
Collection of panels & antiques; open May - Sept.

Seven Sisters: **Whiteshell Natural History Museum**
c/o Manitoba Conservation, Seven Sisters, MB R0E 1Y0

www.gov.mb.ca/conservation/parks/popular_parks/whiteshell
Founded: 1960 Located in the Whiteshell Provincial Park, the natural history museum contains informative displays about the wildlife in the park, the boreal forest, sturgeon & the Winnipeg River, petroforms, & the Aborignal people. The Whiteshell Natural History Museum, located in a log building at Nutimik Lake, is open from the long weekend in May to the long weekend in September.

Shilo: **Royal Canadian Artillery Museum / Le Musée national de l'Artillerie du Canada; Le Musée de l'**
Also known as: **The National Artillery Museum of Canada; The RCA Museum**
CFB Shilo, Shilo, MB R0K 2A0
204-765-3000, Fax: 204-765-5289,
stag@mts.net
www.rcamuseum.com
Three permanent galleries, one temporary exhibits gallery; archives; library; kit shop; 109 major pieces of equipment; largest collection of Canadian military-pattern vehicles; open year round
K. Christensen, Curator
R. Sanderson, Director

Shoal Lake: **The Clack Family Heritage Museum**
c/o Don Yanick, PO Box 568, Shoal Lake, MB R0J 1Z0
204-759-2368, Fax: 204-759-2484,
dsyanick@inethome.ca
www.shoallake.ca/prairiemountain
Antique cars, tractors, trucks & farm implements; Victorian china & clothing; railway, RCMP military & native artifacts; open June-Sept.

Shoal Lake: **Clegg Carriage Museum**
c/o Prairie Mountain Regional Museums Collection Inc., PO Box 568, Shoal Lake, MB R0J 1Z0
204-759-2368, Fax: 204-759-2484,
dsyanick@inethome.ca
www.shoallake.ca/prairiemountain;
www.museumsmanitoba.com
Located 3 miles south of Hwy #24 in Arrow River; collection of 90 completely restored horse-drawn vehicles, including a WW1 ambulance, a covered wagon, peddlar's wagon and hearse
Don Yanick, President, Prairie Mountain Regional Museums Collection Inc.

Shoal Lake: **Shoal Lake Police & Pioneer Museum**
PO Box 233, Shoal Lake, MB R0J 1Z0
204-759-2429, Fax: 204-759-2704,
Other contact information: Summer phone: 204/759-3326
A replica of an 1875 NWMP building; it houses a collection of North West Mounted Police & Royal Canadian Mounted Police displays; official Museum for the Mounted Police in Manitoba; open June-Sept. by summer staff, other times by appt.; school talks & presentations available
Ewen Booth, Museum Manager
Barb Pettinger, Secretary/Treasurer

Snowflake: **Star Mound School Museum Park**
General Delivery, Snowflake, MB R0G 2K0
204-876-4749,
One-room country school c. 1886

Souris: **Hillcrest Museum**
PO Box 662, Souris, MB R0K 2C0
204-483-2008,
souris.cimnet.ca
Includes agricultural museum & CPR caboose; open May - Sept.; collection of over 5000 butterflies on display
Donna Russell, President
Laura Horn, Secretary

Ste Anne des Chênes: **Musée Pointe des Chênes**
208 Centrale Ave., Ste Anne des Chênes, MB R5H 1C9
204-422-5639, Fax: 204-422-5514,
Situated in a park next to the Villa Youville; museum features old pioneer artifacts of the region
Louis Bernardin, Responsable

Steinbach: **Mennonite Heritage Village (Canada) Inc.**
231 PTH 12 N, Steinbach, MB R5G 1T8
204-326-9661, Fax: 204-326-5046, 866-280-8741
info@mhv.ca
www.mennoniteheritagevillage.com
Includes J.J. Reimer Historical Library & Archives; historical village with traditional housebarns, semlin, blacksmith shop, printery, general store, operating windmill, farm fields, exihibition gallery; livery barn restaurant serving ethnic Mennonite food; library; gift shop; special events throughout the summer; educational programming; online bookstore on the website. Open May through September.
Barry Dyck, Executive Director, barryd@mhv.ca
Dr. Roland Sawatzky, Senior Curator, rolands@mhv.ca
John Milinkovic, Manager, Fundraising, johnm@mhv.ca
Anne Toews, Program Director, annet@mhv.ca

St-Malo: **Le Musée Pionnier St Malo**
PO Box 328, Hwy. 59 South, St-Malo, MB R0A 1T0
204-347-5102, Fax: 204-347-5307,
pmaynard@conexe.ca
Depiction of early settlers' lives

Stonewall: **Stonewall Quarry Park**
PO Box 250, Stonewall, MB R0C 2Z0
204-467-5354, Fax: 204-467-5260,
stoneqp@stonewall.ca
www.stonewall.ca
Exhibits pertain to the limestone quarries & their role in the development of the community of Stonewall

Strathclair: **Strathclair Museum**
PO Box 383, Main St., Strathclair, MB R0J 2C0
204-365-5201,
www.museumsmanitoba.com/dir/western/68.html
In a restored CPR station and residence, the museum contains material relating to the district, which includes geneaology and information on Lord Elphinstone; replica blacksmith shop and machine shed; Open July & August or by appt.
Helga Gerrard, Sec.-Treas.

Swan River: **Swan Valley Historical Museum & Archives**
PO Box 2078, Swan River, MB R0L 1Z0
204-734-3585,
History of Swan River Valley, Ice Age to settlement; open mid-May - mid-Sept.; archives open by appt. Tues. 9-2, summer
Niel Brown, President
Gwen Palmer, Secretary

Teulon: **Teulon & District Museum**
PO Box 44, Teulon, MB R0C 3B0
204-886-2098, Fax: 204-886-3787,
jtrombo@mts.net
Site includes a log house, a caboose, two schoolhouses, a small church, a large machine shed, old shoe shop, outside bake oven & the Dr. Hunter Home, 1918 Ford car, doll house with over 300 dolls; open June - Sept., Tues. to Sun., or by appt.
Joan Trombo, Treasurer

Thompson: **Heritage North Museum**
162 Princeton Dr., Thompson, MB R8N 2A4
204-677-2216, Fax: 204-677-8953,
hnmuseum@mts.net
www.heritagenorthmuseum.ca
Founded: 1990 The museum preserves the heritage & history of Thompson & area, where in 1956 nickel was discovered. One of the log buildings displays a taxidermy array of animals native to the region, hides, furs and fossils, while the other building focuses on the mining industry. There is a gift shop.
Tanna Teneycke, Executive Director
Sharon McLeod, President
Valerie Little, Vice-President

Treherne: **Treherne Museum**
PO Box 30, 183 Vanzile St., Treherne, MB R0G 1H0
204-723-2621,

Virden: **Currahee Military Museum**
PO Box 729, Virden, MB R0M 2C0
204-748-1461, Fax: 204-748-1805,
john@wolverinesupplies.com
Open by appt. only
John Hipwell

Virden: **River Valley School Museum**
PO Box 2048, Virden, MB R0M 2C0
204-748-3920, Fax: 204-748-3920,
Country school furnishings & library 1896-1955
Lawrence Anderson, President
Alene R. Welch, Treasurer

Virden: **Pioneer Home Museum of Virden & District**
Also known as: **Virden Pioneer Home Museum Inc.**
PO Box 29, 390 King St. West, Virden, MB R0M 2C0
204-748-1659,
virden.cimnet.ca/cim/187C1_4T421T3T168.dhtm
Open summer daily
F. Eleanor McIntosh, Secretary
Helen Boulton-Elliott, President

Wabowden: **Wabowden Historical Museum**
c/o Wabowden Community Council, PO Box 130, Wabowden, MB R0B 1S0
204-689-2362, Fax: 204-689-2355,
wabcouncil@digistar.mb.ca
wabowden.cimnet.ca/cim/83C150_239T6744T238T6136.dhtm
The Wabowden Historical Museum preserves & displays artifacts from Wabowden & the surrounding region, such as mining, logging, fishing, & trapping items. The museum is open from Canada Day until the Labour Day weekend.

Wasagaming: **Riding Mountain Historical Society & Pinewood Museum**
PO Box 254, Wasagaming, MB R0J 2H0
204-848-2310,
Records & preserves the history of humans in the Riding Mountain National Park; open daily 2-5pm in July & Aug.
Cathy Chalmers, President

Wasagaming: **Riding Mountain National Park of Canada (RMNPC) / Parc national du Canada du Mont-Riding**
General Delivery, Wasagaming, MB R0J 2H0
204-848-7275, Fax: 204-848-2596,
rmnp.info@pc.gc.ca
www.pc.gc.ca/ridingmountain
Other contact information: TTY: 1-866-787-6221; E-mail, Friends of RMNP: friends.rmnp@pc.gc.ca
The Riding Mountain National Park of Canada covers 3,000 km2 of the Manitoba prairie & escarpment. The park provides a variety of school & interpretation programs. The Visitor Centre is open from mid May to mid October.
Scot Shellborn, Officer, Visitor Experiences, 204-848-7284

Waskada: **Waskada Museum**
c/o Village of Waskada, PO Box 40, 103 - 2nd St., Waskada, MB R0M 2E0
204-673-2503,
www.waskada.ca/pages/Museum.htm
Other contact information: Phone, Appointments: 204-673-2557
The Waskada Museum features the following buildings: the 1914 Anglican Church, the 1906 Union (Royal) Bank, a 1927 blacksmith shop, the 1896 Menota country school, a vehicle display building, & a display building. The museum is open during July & August.

Wawanesa: **Sipiweske Museum**
PO Box 116, 102 - 4th St., Wawanesa, MB R0K 2G0
204-824-2289, Fax: 204-824-2008,
wawanesacap@yahoo.com
www.wawanesa.ca/Sipiweske Museum.htm
Memorabilia from pioneers, Nellie McClung, Native people & 1903 insurance company; open July-Aug.; by appointment other times

Whitemouth: **Whitemouth Municipal Museum**
PO Box 294, Whitemouth, MB R0E 2G0
204-348-2641, Fax: 204-348-7731,
Museum depicting the different ways of life in the area - farming, railway, forestry, trapping, peat moss plants, hydro, AECL, fishing, brickyard, flour mill; artifacts housed in six buildings & two pole sheds; cairn honouring Dr. Charlotte Ross (The Iron Rose), first female to practice medicine in Manitoba; turn of the century house; 1905 Anglican Church; CPR Caboose; open July-Aug. Sat.-Thu., op
Sheilagh Wardrop, Secretary
Gloria Henderson, Treasurer
David King, President

Winkler: **Pembina Threshermen's Museum Inc.**
PO Box 1103, Winkler, MB R6W 4B2
204-325-7497, Fax: 204-331-3733,
info@threshermensmuseum.com
www.threshermensmuseum.com
The Pembina Threshermen's Museum preserves the area's agricultural & Mennonite heritage. The grounds of the museum feature several heritage buildings, such as the 1909 Pomeroy School, the 1905-1906 Morden CPR Sation, an 1885 log house, plus a sawmill, windmill, blacksmith shop, barbershop, & post office. The museum is open from the beginning of May to the end of September.

Winnipeg: **402 Squadron Association**
PO Box 42202 St. James, Winnipeg, MB R3J 0X7
204-786-5503,
Archives, photographs of #402 City of Winnipeg Squadron
Jim Bell, Director

Winnipeg: **Air Force Heritage Museum & Air Park / Le Musée du patrimoine de la force aérienne et du parc aéri**
1 Canadian Air Division Headquarters, PO Box 17000 Forces, 17 Wing, Winnipeg, MB R3J 3Y5
204-833-2500, Fax: 204-833-2512,
pearsons@mts.net
www.airforce.dnd.ca
The museum, located in the Billy Bishop building, is part of a complex that consists of an outdoor air park showcasing 14 aircraft. The air park is open year round. Museum is open daily Mon-Fri throughout the summer from 8:00-4:00 BY APPOINTMENT. Guided tours, with services in English and French; wheelchair accessible; food service and restrooms. Located on Air Force Way, north off Ness Ave. on Sharp Blvd.
Maj. Guy Trudeau, Contact
Don Pearsons, Contact

Winnipeg: **Aquatic Hall of Fame & Museum of Canada, Inc.**
25 Poseidon Way, Winnipeg, MB R3M 3E4
204-986-5890,

Aquatic art & memorabilia on display; Olympics, Commonwealth, Pan-Am & posters; open year round
Vaughan L. Baird, President/Chair

Winnipeg: **Costume Museum of Canada**
109 Pacific Ave., Winnipeg, MB R3B 0M1
204-989-0072, Fax: 204-853-2077, 866-853-2166
info@costumemuseum.com
www.costumemuseum.com
Over 35,000 artifacts spanning over 400 years; collection of costumes, textiles & related accessories
Brenda Hamer, Curator
Garth Rogerson, Executive Director

Winnipeg: **Dalnavert Museum**
61 Carlton St., Winnipeg, MB R3C 1N7
204-943-2835, Fax: 204-943-2565,
dalnavert@mhs.mb.ca
www.mhs.mb.ca/info/museums/dalnavert/index.shtml
1895 restored Victorian home of Hugh John Macdonald, son of Sir John A. Macdonald
Tim Worth, Curator

Winnipeg: **Fort Garry Horse Regimental Museum & Archives Inc.**
c/o McGregor Armoury, 551 Machray Ave., Winnipeg, MB R2W 1A8
204-586-6298, Fax: 204-582-0370,
museum12009@fortgarryhorse.ca
www.fortgarryhorse.ca
Depicts the history of the Fort Garry Horse from 1912 to present; open Mon. evenings 7:30-10:30; other times by appt.
Larry Lajeunesse, Chair

Winnipeg: **Fort Whyte Centre**
1961 McCreary Rd., Winnipeg, MB R3P 2K9
204-989-8355, Fax: 204-895-4700,
info@fortwhyte.org
www.fortwhyte.org
74 hectares of lakes, marshes aspen parkland for environmental education; exhibit building

Winnipeg: **Historical Museum of St. James-Assiniboia**
3180 Portage Ave., Winnipeg, MB R3K 0Y5
204-888-8706,
bonitah@mts.net
Open year round

Winnipeg: **Ivan Franko Museum**
200 Mc Gregor St., 595 Pritchard Ave., Winnipeg, MB R2W 2K4
204-589-4397, Fax: 204-589-3404,
History of Ivan Franko, Ukrainian poet, novelist, and social activist & Ukrainian pintings; ceramics, woodcarving, glassware, embroidery, and weaving.

Winnipeg: **J.B. Wallis Museum of Entomology**
Dept. of Entomology, University of Manitoba, Winnipeg, MB R3T 2N2
204-474-9257, Fax: 204-474-7628,
head_entomo@umanitoba.ca
250,000 species of insects

Winnipeg: **Manitoba Children's Museum**
The Forks, 45 Forks Market Rd., Kinsmen Building, Winnipeg, MB R3C 4T6
204-924-4000, Fax: 204-956-2122,
general@childrensmuseum.com
www.childrensmuseum.com
Founded: 1983 Catering to children, the site includes such hands-on exhibits as a 1950s train station with CNR diesel locomotive. Open daily, year round.
Diane Doth, Executive Director

Winnipeg: **Manitoba Crafts Museum & Library**
#1B, 183 Kennedy St., Winnipeg, MB R3C 1S6
204-487-6117,
mcml1@mts.net
www.mts.net/~mcml
Founded: 1986 The museum's collection focuses on the development of Canadian, and particularly Manitoban, crafts since the 1920s. The library houses about 2,500 titles pertaining to crafts, including scrapbooks and design patterns. Open year round
MS Andrea Reichert, Curator

Winnipeg: **Manitoba Electrical Museum & Education Centre**
PO Box 815, 680 Harrow St., Winnipeg, MB R3C 2P4
204-477-7905,
www.hydro.mb.ca/about_us/electrical_museum.shtml
Founded: 1971 The museum explores the history of electricity in Manitoba from the 1800s. Exhibits include archival photographs, documents and electrical artifacts, including vintage household appliances and an electric streetcar. In the lower level is an interactive section with Hazard Hamlet where, children can learn about potentially hazardous situations if electricity is not used properly.

Winnipeg: **Manitoba Sports Hall of Fame & Museum Inc. (MSHOF)**
Offices, #210, 200 Main St., Winnipeg, MB R3C 4M2
204-925-5736, Fax: 204-925-5792,
halloffame@sport.mb.ca
www.halloffame.mb.ca
Founded: 1993 The museum aims to honour those people who have contributed significantly to Manitoba's rich sports history. The exhibits use various memorabilia and photos to cover such sports as athletics, basketball, baseball/softball, curling, football, golf, hockey, and the Winter Olympics. The museum is closed until Nov., 2010, when it will open in a new location at in the Sport for Life Centre, 145 Pacific Ave.
Rick D. Brownlee, Sport Heritage Manager, Sport Manitoba

Winnipeg: **Ogniwo Polish Museum Society Inc.**
1417 Main St., Winnipeg, MB R2W 3V3
204-586-5070,
ogniwo@mb.sympatico.ca
Artifacts related to Polish immigrants in Canada; open year round
Christine Tabbernor

Winnipeg: **Ukrainian Cultural & Educational Centre**
Also known as: **Oseredok Archives and Museum**
184 Alexander Ave. East, Winnipeg, MB R3B 0L6
204-942-0218, Fax: 204-943-2857,
uce@mts.net
www.oseredok.org
Library & historical & archival collections dealing with the history of Ukrainians in Canada & the history of Ukraine; open Tues. - Sat. year round

Winnipeg: **Queen's Own Cameron Highlanders of Canada Regimental Museum Inc.**
Minto Armoury, #230, 969 St. Matthew's Ave., Winnipeg, MB R3G 0J7
204-786-4330,
Regimental dress, equipment & archives from 1910 to present

Winnipeg: **Riel House National Historic Site of Canada / Parc historique national du Canada de la Maison-Riel**
PO Box 73, Winnipeg, MB R2M 4A5
204-257-1783, Fax: 204-254-8331,
Riel family home, depicts life of Métis family in St. Vital during the 1880s; open daily mid-May - Labour Day
Vania Gagnon

Winnipeg: **Ross House Museum**
Joe Zuken Heritage Park, 140 Meade St. North, Winnipeg, MB R2W 3K5
204-943-3958,
rosshouse@mhs.mb.ca
www.mhs.mb.ca
Ross House was the first post office in western Canada. It is now a museum, owned by the City of Winnipeg & operated by the Manitoba Historical Society. The museum depicts the operation of early postal service & the life of the Ross family around 1850. Ross House is open from the beginning of June to the end of August. Schools & large groups may arrange appointments at other times of the year.
Dr. Simon Lucy, Chair, Ross House Community Committee
Victor Sawelo, Museum Manager

Winnipeg: **Royal Canadian Mint - Winnipeg Facility**
520 Lagimodiere Blvd., Winnipeg, MB R2J 3E7
204-983-6400, Fax: 204-255-5203,
www.mint.ca
Tours of the mint available year round; call for reservations
Christian Robin, Supervisor, Tour Operations, robin@mint.ca

Winnipeg: **Royal Winnipeg Rifles Regimental Museum**
Minto Armoury, #208, 969 St. Matthews Ave., Winnipeg, MB R3G 0J7
204-786-4300, Fax: 204-786-4384,
riflesmuseum@shaw.ca
www.mts.net
Founded: 1970 Collects & preserves the history of the Regiment, & also houses displays relevant to the Winnipeg Light Infantry & the Winnipeg Grenadiers; military artifacts & memorabilia, pictures, books & other documents; open Tues. & by appt.; closed Sat. June - Aug
Dave Wawryk, Archivist
Win Anders, Curator

Winnipeg: **St. Norbert Provincial Heritage Park**
PO Box 53, 200 Saulteaux Cres., Winnipeg, MB R3J 3W3
204-945-4375, Fax: 204-945-0012,
kporteous@gov.mb.ca
manitobaparks.com
Illustrates how a natural landscape used for hunting, fishing & camping by Aboriginal peoples evolved into a French-speaking Métis settlement, then a French-Canadian agricultural community of the pre-World War I period; guided tours of restored Turenne & Bohémier houses; open daily May long weekend to Labour Day weekend.
Ken Porteous

Winnipeg: **St. Vital Historical Society**
600 St. Mary's Rd., Winnipeg, MB R2M 3L5
204-255-2864, Fax: 204-256-6892,
info@svhs.ca
www.svhs.ca/
Educational centre, bringing "the history of St. Vital" to the community by way of shows & displays; museum holds artifacts
Lorna Miner, President

Winnipeg: **Sandilands Forest Centre**
c/o The Manitoba Forestry Association, 900 Corydon Ave., Winnipeg, MB R3M 0Y4
204-453-3182, Fax: 204-477-5765,
mfainc@mts.net
www.mbforestryassoc.ca
The Centre is sited on 122 hectares of land granted to the Manitoba Forestry Ass'n, and located near Hadashville, just south of the Trans Canada Hwy, east of Winnipeg; information on biodiversity, forest ecology, sustainable management of forest resources, fire prevention and management; nature trails, museum, fire tower & picnic area; educational programming; commemorative tree planting
Bill Baker, Education Director

Winnipeg: **Seven Oaks House Museum**
PO Box 25176, 1650 Main St., Winnipeg, MB R2V 4C8
204-339-7429, Fax: 204-334-8516,
Seven Oaks House is a log residence, which was built between 1851 & 1853. It has been restored to reflect life during the Red River settlement in the 19th century. The museum is open from mid May to Labour Day.

Winnipeg: **Stewart Hay Memorial Museum**
Duff Roblin Bldg., Dept. of Zoology, University of Manitoba, Winnipeg, MB R3T 2N2
204-474-9245, Fax: 204-474-7588,
hann@ms.umanitoba.ca
Mounted & study specimens of mammals, birds, fish, reptiles, amphibians, crustaceans, mollusks & other invertebrates; casts of fossils; open year round

Winnipeg: **Transcona Historical Museum**
141 Regent Ave. West, Winnipeg, MB R2C 1R1
204-222-0423, Fax: 204-222-0208,
info@transconamuseum.mb.ca
www.transconamuseum.mb.ca
Archives, photographs, rare books, reference files, natural history (including an 8,000 specimen lepidoptera collection), First Nations cultural artifacts (3,500 items), Euro-Canadian cultural artifacts & a clothing & textile collection
Alanna Horejda, Curator

Winnipeg: **University of Manitoba: Fitzgerald Study Collection**
School of Art, Fitzgerald Bldg., Main Fl., Winnipeg, MB R3T 2N2
204-474-9367,
Papers, drawings & watercolours of L.L. Fitzgerald; open year round

Winnipeg: **University of Winnipeg Geography Museum**
515 Portage Ave., Winnipeg, MB R3B 2E9
204-786-9485, Fax: 204-774-4134,
kmonson@uwinnipeg.ca
Teaching & reference collection of rocks, minerals & fossils, with a Manitoba focus; open year round

Winnipeg: **UVAN Historical Museum & Archives**
#203, 456 Main St., Winnipeg, MB R3B 1B6
204-942-5861,
Historical, ethnological & archival material

Winnipeg: **Western Canada Aviation Museum (WCAM) / Musée de l'aviation de l'ouest du Canada**
Hangar T-2, 958 Ferry Rd., Winnipeg, MB R3H 0Y8
204-786-5503, Fax: 204-775-4761,
info@wcam.mb.ca; events@wcam.mb.ca
www.wcam.mb.ca
Other contact information: E-mail, School Tours: programs@wcam.mb.ca; Gifts: giftshop@wcam.mb.ca
The Western Canada Aviation Museum's recovery & restoration department works to prepare aircraft for display. The museum features sights such as Canada's first helicopter, bushplanes, historic military jets, & commercial aircraft. The museum also contains an aviation reference library, with collections of books, magazines, manuals, photographs, drawings, & audio-visual materials. The library is open to the public by appointment. The museum is open year-round.

Winnipeg: **Winnipeg Police Museum**
Parent: **Winnipeg Police Museum & Historical Society Inc.**
PO Box 1680, 130 Allard Ave., Winnipeg, MB R3C 2Z7
204-986-3976,
wps-museum@winnipeg.ca
www.winnipeg.ca

Founded: 1974 The Winnipeg Police Museum exhibits items related to the Winnipeg Police Force, which formed in 1874. Objects on display include early handcuffs,& identification cameras, & a jail cell which was built in 1911. There are also exhibits surrounding the 1919 Winnipeg General Strike & Earle "The Strangler" Nelson. Located at the Winnipeg Police Academy, the Winnipeg Police Museum is open daily. Conducted group tours can be arranged.

***Winnipeg Beach:* Winnipeg Beach Ukrainian Homestead**
PO Box 396, Winnipeg Beach, MB R0C 3G0
204-389-4079,
Artifacts of Ukrainian origin & tradition; historic house with furnishings; clay-bake oven; grist mill; open weekends Victoria Day - July 1; daily, July 1 - Labour Day weekend; closed Wed.
Vic Siran

***Winnipegosis:* Winnipegosis Museum**
Winnipegosis, MB R0L 2G0
204-656-4791, Fax: 204-656-4947,
Housed in former CNR Railway Station (c.1897); 65-foot freighter, the "Myrtle M"; artifacts; CNR historical material; War Memorial items; native handiwork
Edna Medd, Curator

***Woodlands:* Woodlands Pioneer Museum**
General Delivery, Woodlands, MB R0C 3H0
204-383-5554,
Post office; municipal office; doctor's office; church; school; log house; open July-Aug.

New Brunswick

Provincial Museums

Kings Landing Historical Settlement
20 Kings Landing Rd., Kings Landing Historical, NB E6K 3W3
506-363-4999, Fax: 506-363-4989,
info@kingslanding.nb.ca
www.kingslanding.nb.ca
Historical settlement on the St. John River with more than 100 costumed interpreters depicting rural life from 1790-1910; 65,000 artifacts; open June - Oct.

Musée Acadien (MAUM)
c/o Pavillon Clément-Cormier, Université de Moncton, Moncton, NB E1A 3E9
506-858-4088, Fax: 506-858-4043,
maum@umoncton.ca
www.umoncton.ca/maum
Founded: 1886 Le plus ancien musée acadien au monde est fondé par le père Camille Lefebvre. La collection dépasse 35,000 objets et photographies et représente tous les aspects de la vie acadienne. Exposition permanente; expositions temporaires; expositions virtuelles.
Isabelle Cormier, Directrice
Nicole LeBlanc, Secrétaire administrative
Jeanne Mance Cormier, Conservatrice
Bernard LeBlanc, Conservateur

New Brunswick Museum (NBM/MNB) / Musée du Nouveau-Brunswick
277 Douglas Ave., Saint John, NB E2K 1E5
506-643-2300, Fax: 506-643-2360, 888-268-9595
nbmuseum@nbm-mnb.ca
www.nbm-mnb.ca
Founded: 1934 Collections at the provincial museum of New Brunswick include human history, marine & technology, prints, fine & decorative arts, botany, zoology, & geology; A full range of exhibitions & programs are offered daily; Closed Christmas Day & Good Friday
Jane Fullerton, Director & Chief Executive Officer, 506-643-2346

Other Museums in New Brunswick

***Aulac:* Fort Beauséjour National Historic Site**
111 Fort Beauséjour Rd., Aulac, NB E4L 2W5
506-364-5080, Fax: 506-536-4399,
fort.beausejour@pc.gc.ca
www.pc.gc.ca/lhn-nhs/nb/beausejour/index_E.asp
Built in 1751 by the French; star-shaped fort overlooking the Bay of Fundy
Pierrette Robichaud, Manager

***Boiestown:* Central New Brunswick Woodmen's Museum Inc.**
6342 Rte. 8, Boiestown, NB E6A 1Z5
506-369-7214, Fax: 506-369-9081,
woodmen@nb.aibn.com
www.woodmenmuseum.com
Founded: 1979 16 exhibit buildings, depicts life of Central New Brunswick lumberjack & culture of Miramichi people
Megan Scammell, Executive Director

***Caraquet:* Musée Acadien de Caraquet/Caraquet Acadian Museum**
15, boul St-Pierre est, Caraquet, NB E1W 1B6
506-726-2682, Fax: 506-726-2660,
Promotes the history & culture of the Acadian people from the Acadian Peninsula using its own collection as well as other collections & regional archives
Mrs. Graham LeBlanc, Trésorière

***Clair:* Société historique de Clair Inc.**
724, rue Principale, Clair, NB E7A 2H4
506-992-3637, Fax: 506-992-6247,
sochclair@nb.aibn.com
Museum & historic site guided tours; Beaux-arts, Historie humaine; visites guidées; open June to Labour Day
Betty Levasseur, Président
Lyne Bard, Trésorière

***Connors:* Connors Museum**
3614 Rte. 205, Connors, NB E7A 1S3
506-992-2500, Fax: 506-992-2500,
armandb@nb.sympatico.ca
Items used in general store; blacksmith shop; Victorian mansion
Rachel Bernier, Director

***Dalhousie:* Musée Restigouche Regional Museum**
115 George St., Dalhousie, NB E8C 1R6
506-684-7490, Fax: 506-684-7613,
qurrm@nbnet.nb.ca
Local history museum, archives, gallery
Bill Clarke, Director

***Doaktown:* Doak House Historic Site**
386 Main St., Doaktown, NB E9C 1E4
506-453-2324, Fax: 506-453-2416,
guy.tremblay@gnb.ca
Open end June - Early Sept.
Glen Harding, Site Manager

***Doaktown:* Atlantic Salmon Museum**
***Also known as:* Miramichi Salmon Museum**
263 Main St., Doaktown, NB E9C 1A9
506-365-7787, Fax: 506-365-7359,
museum@nbnet.nb.ca
www.atlanticsalmonmuseum.com
Founded: 1982 Through interpretive displays, the Atlantic Salmon Museum shows the history of the life of the Atlantic salmon, as well as the cultural & economic value of the Atlantic salmon to the Miramichi River & New Brunswick. Conservation is also emphasized. The museum is open from June to October. Appointments for rentals can be made during other times.
Linda Gaston, Executive Director

***Dorchester:* Dorchester Heritage Properties Committee**
#5, 3497 Cape Rd., Dorchester, NB E4K 2X2
506-379-6633, Fax: 506-379-3033, 800-822-6633
keillorhouse@nb.aibn.com
www.keillorhousemuseum.com
Operating: The Keillor House (Westmorland Centennial Museum, c. 1813), 506/379-6633; open June - Sept. or by appt.; Bell Inn (c.1811), 506/379-2580; open Apr. - Oct.; St. James Presbyterian Church Museum, 506/379-6633; Beachkirk Collection (c. 1884); open June - Sept. or by appt.; The Maritime Penetentiary Museum, 506/379-6633; open June - Sept.
Alice Folkins, Manager

***Edmundston:* Antique Automobile Museum**
35, Principale St., Edmundston, NB E7B 1V6
506-737-2637,
Open June - Sept.
Jocelyne Michaud

***Edmundston:* Musée historique du Madawaska**
195, boul Hébert, Edmundston, NB E3V 2S8
506-737-5282, Fax: 506-737-5373,
Gilbert Lavoie, Director

***Fredericton:* Brydone Jack Observatory Museum**
University of New Brunswick, PO Box 4400, Fredericton, NB E3B 5A3
506-453-4723,
The first astronomical observatory in Canada was built in 1851. The building is now a Nnational Historic Site & a museum on the campus of the University of New Brunswick. It houses tools & equipment used by Dr. William Brydone Jack, who was a professor of mathematics, natural philosophy, & astronomy.

***Fredericton:* Electrical Engineering Museum**
University of New Brunswick, Dept. of Electrical Engineering, Fredericton, NB E3B 5A3
506-453-4561, Fax: 506-453-3589,

***Fredericton:* Guard House & Soldiers' Barracks**
c/o Fredericton Tourism, PO Box 130, 11 Carleton St., Fredericton, NB E3B 4Y7
506-460-2041, Fax: 506-460-2474, 888-888-4768
tourism@fredericton.ca
www.tourismfredericton.ca
Historic military buildings 1828-1866

***Fredericton:* New Brunswick Sports Hall of Fame / Temple de la renommée sportive du Nouveau-Brunswick**
PO Box 6000, 503 Queen St., Fredericton, NB E3B 5H1
506-453-3747, Fax: 506-459-0481,
deborah.williams@gnb.ca
www.nbsportshalloffame.nb.ca
Open year round, hours vary; recognizes, collects, preserves, exhibits & promotes New Brunswick's sports heroes & sports heritage. Street address is 503 rue Queen St., Frederiction, NB, E3B 1B8.
Jamie Wolverton, Executive Director, jamie.wolverton@gnb.ca
Deborah Williams, Executive Assistant, deborah.williams@gnb.ca
Kelly Ross, Curator/Exhibits Director, curator@gnb.ca

***Fredericton:* Old Government House**
PO Box 6000, 51 Woodstock Rd., Fredericton, NB E3B 5H1
506-453-2505, Fax: 506-453-2416,
ogh@gnb.ca
www.gnb.ca/lg/ogh/index-e.asp
Constructed from 1826 to 1828, Government House was the residence of New Brunswick's Governors & Lieutenant-Governors. Government House also served as a school for hearing impaired students, a military barracks during World War I, a hospital for returning soldiers, & an RCMP headquarters. Since 1999, the House has been open to the public, featuring restored rooms, exhibits, & bilingual tours during the summer. Government House still contains the Lieutenant-Governor's office & residence.

***Fredericton:* Wulastook Museums**
PO Box 700, 108 Queen St., Fredericton, NB E3B 5B4
506-451-7777, Fax: 506-451-1029,
Francis Atkinson, Owner

***Fredericton:* York Sunbury Museum**
PO Box 1312, Fredericton, NB E3B 5C8
506-455-6041, Fax: 506-458-8741,
yorksun@nbnet.nb.ca

***Fredericton Junction:* Currie House**
110 Currie Lane, Fredericton Junction, NB E5L 1X7
506-368-2818, Fax: 506 368-1900,
ddupl@nbnet.nb.ca
www.tourismnewbrunswick.ca/en-CA/Product/Museum.htm?pid=401
Museum with displays of antiques and artifacts, history of area and local families. Large picnic area, nature trails through woods and by river.
Don Duplisea, Contact, 506-368-2818, Fax: 506-422-1223, ddupl@nbnet.nb.ca

***Gagetown:* Queens County Museum**
69 Front St., Gagetown, NB E5M 1A4
506-488-2966,
Gagetown's Queens County Museum is located in the Tilley Home, which was the home of Sir Leonard Tilley, a Father of Confederation, & the 1836 Queens County Courthouse. The museum contains furnishings of the Loyalist & Victorian periods, plus historical exhibits. It is open from mid June to mid September.

***Grand Falls:* Grand Falls Museum / Musée de Grand-Sault**
#103, 142 Court St., Grand Falls, NB E3Z 2R2
506-473-5265, Fax: 506-473-7160,
Local artifacts; Extensive collection of church records, genealogies, etc.; Open mid-June to end of Aug. or by appt.
Patrick McCooey, President

***Grand Manan:* Grand Manan Museum**
1141 Rte. 776, Grand Manan, NB E0G 1X0
506-662-3524,
gmadmin@grandmananmuseum.ca
www.grandmananmuseum.ca
Open June - Sept.; in winter by appt.

***Grand-Anse:* Musée des Papes**
184 Acadie St., Grand-Anse, NB E8N 1A6
506-732-3003, Fax: 506-732-5491,
museedespapes@nb.aibn.com
Relates the evolution of Christianity to the present religious congregations; open mid-June to end of Aug.
Edmond Landry, Directeur

***Hampton:* Kings County Museum**
c/o Kings County Historical & Archival Society Inc., PO Box 1813, 27 Centennial Rd., Hampton, NB E5N 6N3

506-832-6009, Fax: 506-832-6409,
kingscm@nbnet.nb.ca
www3.nbnet.nb.ca/kingscm
Founded: 1968 Artifacts include textiles, clothing, china, guns, glassware, military, royalty, art & archival material
A. Faye Pearson, Director

***Hillsborough:* Hon. William Henry Steeves House**
40 Mill St., Hillsborough, NB E4H 2Z8
506-734-3102, Fax: 506-734-3452,
steevesmuseum@nb.aibn.com
www.steeveshousemuseum.ca
Founded: 1971 Operated by Heritage Hillsborough Inc.; birthplace of William Henry Steeves, a Father of Confederation; open every day July 1 to Labour Day
Lois Snider, President

***Hillsborough:* New Brunswick Railway Museum**
2847 Main St., Hillsborough, NB E4H 2X7
506-734-3195, Fax: 506-734-3711,
info@nbrm.ca
www.nbrm.ca/en/index.shtml
Founded: 1993 Dedicated to preserving the history of train travel in New Brunswick, the museum has on site an extensive collection of full-sized railway cars. This is the province's only operating railway museum, with excursion trains 4 days a week along the Petitcodiac River & southeastern New Brunswick. Displays of equipment & artifacts highlight the local & area railway history. There is a gift shop. Open daily, June - Sept.
Patrick McKinley, President
J.A. Clowes, Secretary & Director

***Hopewell Cape:* Albert County Museum**
3940 Rte 114, Hopewell Cape, NB E4H 3J8
506-734-2003, Fax: 506-734-3291,
albertcountymuseum@nb.aibn.com
www.albertcountymuseum.ca
The museum is located in the UNESCO Fundy Biosphere Reserve. Experience early life in Albert County & the Shepody Bay region by visiting the original Shire Town buildings, circa 1845. Explore the former County Jail complete with cells, displays & collections relating to the early history of the area. Visit the magnificent County Courthouse & ask about the project to commemorate R.B. Bennett, Canada's 11th Prime Minister. Displays on shipbuilding, farming; gift shop; meeting rooms; research resources room.
Donald Alward, Manager/Curator

***Kingston:* John Fisher Memorial Museum**
129 Gorhams Bluff Rd., Kingston, NB E5N 1A7
506-763-2561, Fax: 506-763-2632,
gbaxter@nb.sympatico.ca
macdonald.nbed.nb.ca/johnfisher1.htm
Located in MacDonald Consolidated School

***Kouchibouguac:* Saint Croix Island International Historic Site / Lieu historique international de l'Ile-Sainte-Croix**
c/o Kouchibouguac National Park of Canada, 186, Rte. 117, Kouchibouguac, NB E4X 2P1
506-876-2443, Fax: 506-876-4802,
kouch.info@pc.qc.ca
www.pc.gc.ca
Founded: 1984 Located on Rte. 127 Bayside, with a view of Saint Croix Island; site of Pierre Dugua's first attempt to found a settlement in N. America; viewing deck & self-guided interpretive trail; picnic area. The site is also a U.S. National Monument
Carole Loiselle, Unit Superintendent

***Lower Newcastle:* MacDonald Farm Historic Site**
600 Rte. 11, Lower Newcastle, NB E1V 7G1
506-453-2324, Fax: 506-453-2416,
www.gnb.ca/0007/heritage/Macdonald.asp
Founded: 1970 Constructed by Scottish settler, Lt. Col. Alexander MacDonald of Bartibog, between 1815 and 1820 in Georgian style, the site includes a barn, 4 outbuildings, as well as a wharf and boat house. Costumed guides demonstrate cooking, crafts and care of animals.
MR Guy Tremblay, Manager, Museum Services, Government of New Brunswick, 506-444-5892, guy.tremblay@gnb.ca

***Memramcook:* Monument Lefebvre National Historic Site / Lieu historique national du Monument-Lefebvre**
480, rue Centrale, Memramcook, NB E4K 3S6
506-758-9783, Fax: 506-758-9813, 877-765-1896
monument@nbnet.nb.ca
www.pc.gc.ca/lhn-nhs/nb/lefebvre/index_e.asp
Founded: 1982 Located in the Monument LeFebvre building, in cooperation with Parks Canada, the centre focuses on the survival of the Acadian people from 1755 to present. Shows are performed in the theatre. There is a gift shop with a variety of Acadian products. Guided tours are offered.
Conrad LeBlanc, President, Monument LeFebvre Society
Hermance LeBlanc, Directrice générale

***Minto:* Minto Museum & Information Centre**
420 Pleasant Dr., Minto, NB E4B 2T3
506-327-3383, Fax: 506-327-3041,
Open July 1 - Sept. 1
Rose Collette, Clerk Administrator

***Minto:* New Brunswick Internment Camp Heritage Museum**
#1, 420 Pleasant Dr., Minto, NB E4B 2T3
506-327-3573, Fax: 506-327-6008,
Artifacts & model of the Ripples Internment Camp
Ed Caissie, Director, 506/450-9666

***Miramichi:* Miramichi Natural History Museum**
PO Box 162, 149 Wellington St., Miramichi, NB E1N 2B5
506-773-7305,
Natural history museum built in 1909, the oldest museum of its kind in New Brunswick and the third oldest in Canada; houses the Dr. Henri Marc Ami Collection; leased to the Miramichi Natural History Association

***Miramichi:* Rankin House Museum**
2224 King George Hwy., Miramichi, NB E1V 6N3
506-773-3448,
1837; example of mansions built by the early lumber & shipping barons; unique collection of historic items; tourist information centre; open July & Aug.
Jack Ullock, Director

***Miramichi:* St. Michael's Museum Association Inc.**
PO Box 368, 10 Howard St., Miramichi, NB E1N 3A7
506-778-5152, Fax: 506-778-5156,
mmuseum@nbnet.nb.ca; connejof@nbed.nb.ca
www.saintmichaelsmuseum.com
Miramichi history & extensive civil & church records for most denominations; geneology; tours in June-Aug.
John Connell, Curator

***Miramichi:* W.S. Loggie Cultural Centre**
222 Wellington St., Miramichi, NB E1N 1M9
506-773-7645,

***Moncton:* Free Meeting House**
c/o Moncton Museum, 20 Mountain Rd., Moncton, NB E1C 2J8
506-856-4383, Fax: 506-856-4355,
info.museum@moncton.ca
www.moncton.ca

***Moncton:* Lutz Mountain Meeting House**
Lutz Mountain Heritage Foundation, 3143 Mountain Rd., Moncton, NB E1G 2X1
506-384-7719, Fax: 506-854-8051,
lutzmtnheritage@rogers.com
www.lutzmtnheritage.ca
Founded: 1975 The Lutz Mountain Meeting House is open during the summer only, or by appointment.
Gerry Gillcash, President

***Moncton:* Moncton Museum / Musée de Moncton**
20 Mountain Rd., Moncton, NB E1C 2J8
506-856-4383, Fax: 506-856-4355,
info.museum@moncton.org
www.moncton.ca/Residents/Recreation_Parks_and_Culture/Museums_and_Heritage
Founded: 1974 The permanent exhibits showcase Moncton's history from the time of the Micmacs to the period preceding the Deportation of Acadians, when agriculture was Moncton's primary economic engine, to the golden shipbuilding years and the railway era. There are also temporary and travelling exhibits. A research library and educational programs are offered. Open year round.
Brenda Orr, Sr. Heritage Officer, Recreation, Parks & Culture Dept., City of Moncton, 506-856-4383, brenda.orr@moncton.ca

***New Denmark:* New Denmark Memorial Museum**
***Parent:* New Denmark Historical Society**
6 Main Rd., New Denmark, NB E7G 2B7
506-553-6724,
newdenmarkmuseum@live.com
www.republiquemadawaska.com
New Denmark Memorial Museum honours the Danish immigrants who settled in the New Denmark area of New Brunswick in 1872. It is the oldest Danish settlement in Canada. Exhibits include books, china, & farm machinery. The museum is open from mid June to the beginning of September.

***Oromocto:* Canadian Forces Base Gagetown Military Museum / Musée militaire de la BFC Gagetown**
Bldg. A-5, PO Box 17000 Forces, Oromocto, NB E2V 4J5
506-422-1304, Fax: 506-422-1304,
museumgagetown@nb.aibn.com
www.museumgagetown.ca
Visitors to the Canadian Forces Base Gagetown Military Museum may visit the following rooms: Royal Canadian Dragoons \ 8th Canadian Hussars; 403 Squadron Air Force; Black Watch; MacGillivray; Naval; Barrack; & Weapons.

***Oromocto:* Canadian Military Engineering Museum**
***Also known as:* CME Museum**
Canadian Forces School of Military Engineering, CFB / ASG Gagetown, #J-10, D215, Mitchell Bldg., Oromocto, NB E2V 4J5
506-422-2000, Fax: 506-422-1220,
cmemuseum@forces.gc.ca (Museum Staff)
www.cmemuseum.ca
Other contact information: E-mail, Research Inquiries: cme.research@sympatico.ca
Founded: 1957 Displays at the Canadian Military Engineering Museum date back before the 1800s, with drawings, plans, & photographs of forts built by engineers, such as the Citadel in Nova Scotia. Displays also depict trench life during World War I. Weapons & uniforms from World War II, artifacts from the Korean War, & a United Nations display are also part of the museum. A research library houses photographs, reference books, training manuals, & personal diaries. The museum is open year round.
Col. John Tattersall, Chair
Maj. Joe Gale, Museum Executive Officer
CWO Blaine Thurston, Vice-President, History & Heritage
Sgt John Wilt, Curator & Treasurer

***Oromocto:* Fort Hughes Military Blockhouse**
1 Wharf Rd., Oromocto, NB E2V 1S2
506-357-3333, Fax: 506-357-2266,
bjarratt@town.oromocto.nb.ca
Located in Sir Douglas Hazen Park
James Arbeau, Director

***Petit-Rocher:* New Brunswick Mining & Mineral Interpretation Centre (CIMMNB) / Centre d'interprétation des mines & minerais du Nouveau-Bru**
397, rue Principale, Petit-Rocher, NB E8J 1L9
506-542-2672, Fax: 506-542-2708,
The Mining & Mineral Interpretation Centre features exhibitions about the mining heritage of New Brunswick, plus a simulation of an underground descent.
Marc-André Godin, Contact

***Plaster Rock:* Plaster Rock Museum & Information Centre**
81 Ridgewell St., Plaster Rock, NB E7G 2N6
506-356-6077,
Plaster Rock Museum & Information Centre features exhibits about the community's past, including the lumbering & farming activities in Plaster Rock & the surrounding region.

***Riverside-Albert:* Old Bank Museum**
***Also known as:* Albert County Heritage Trust**
5985 Rte. 114, Riverside-Albert, NB E4H 4B8
506-882-2015,
maryspt@nbnet.nb.ca
Historic bank building now a museum & information centre
Mary Majka, President

***Sackville:* Mary's Point Shorebird Reserve & Interpretive Centre**
***Also known as:* Shepody National Wildlife Area, Mary's Point Section**
PO Box 6227, Sackville, NB E4L 1G6
506-882-2544,
maryspt@nbnet.nb.ca
www.naturenb.ca/Eng/maryspoint.aspx
Founded: 1992 Located in the Shepody National Wildlife Area and administered by both Nature NB and Environment Canada's Canadian Wildlife Service, these wetlands protect large numbers of shorebird species. The Interpretation Centre educates the public on the shorebirds' habitats and their hemispheric migrations over the Bay of Fundy region.

***Sackville:* Struts Gallery**
7 Lorne St., Sackville, NB E4L 3Z6
506-536-1211, Fax: 506-536-4565,
info@strutsgallery.ca
www.strutsgallery.ca
An artist-run centre dedicated to presenting regional & national contemporary artist-initiated activities
Leah Garnett, President

***Saint John:* Barbour's General Store**
St. Andrew's Sq., PO Box 1971, King St., Saint John, NB E2L 4L1
506-658-2939,
www.tourismsaintjohn.com
Other contact information: Phone, Off season: 506-658-2855
Artifacts housed at Barbour's General Store include authentic grocery items, pharmaceutical items, cooking utensils, china, farm implements, & yard goods. The restored nineteenth-century country general stored is open from mid-June to mid-September.

***Saint John:* Loyalist House Museum**
***Also known as:* Merritt House**
120 Union St., Saint John, NB E2L 1A3

506-652-3590, Fax: 506-637-9163,
info@loyalisthouse.com
www.loyalisthouse.com
Founded: 1960 Operated by the New Brunswick Historical Society as a national historic site, Loyalist House was built in 1817 by David Daniel Merritt, a United Empire Loyalist from Rye, NY. The house remains very much as it was built & still displays its original furniture: piano-organ, swooning divans, 'yoke-back' chairs, four-poster bed, etc. This buiding is one of the few surviving buildings of the Great Saint John Fire in 1877.
MS Kathy Wilson, President, New Brunswick Historical Society

***Saint John:* Saint John Firefighters Museum**
24 Sydney St., Saint John, NB E2L 3X1
506-633-1840, Fax: 506-633-1840,
www.tourismsaintjohn.com
The museum is the site of the No. 2 Engine house, built in 1840; a collection of firefighting artifacts & photographs; includes an entire room dedicated to the Great Saint John Fire of 1877, an authentic hand pump, a 1956 LaFrance Fire Engine, a Junior Firefighters play room & much more!

***Saint John:* Saint John Jewish Historical Museum**
91 Leinster St., Saint John, NB E2L 1J2
506-633-1833, Fax: 506-642-9926,
sjjhm@nbnet.nb.ca
personal.nbnet.nb.ca/sjjhm
Founded: 1986 Housed in the same building with the Shaarei Zedek Synagogue, the museum collects, displays & preserves articles related specifically to the Saint John Jewish community; provides a research facility for genealogists, historians & religious scholars; 7 display areas; Jewish education outreach kits, membership program
Katherine Biggs-Craft, Curator

***Saint John:* Saint John Sports Hall of Fame**
PO Box 1971, Saint John, NB E2L 4L1
506-658-2909, Fax: 506-658-2902,
recandparks@saintjohn.ca
www.cityofsaintjohn.com/services_recreation_hall-of-fame.cfm
Located in Harbour Station
Ian Polley, Chair

***Saint John:* St. Andrews Blockhouse National Historic Site**
454 Whipple St., Saint John, NB E2M 2R3
506-529-4270, Fax: 506-636-4574,
fundy.info@pc.gc.ca
www.pc.gc.ca
Other contact information: Off-season Tel: 506/636-4011
Blockhouse built for border defence during the War of 1812; contains elements of the oldest blockhouse in New Brunswick; located at 23 Joe's Point Rd., St. Andrews NB E5B 2J7
Anne Bardou

***St Andrews:* Ross Memorial Museum / Musée mémorial Ross**
188 Montague St., St Andrews, NB E5B 1J2
506-529-5124, Fax: 506-529-5183,
rossmuse@nb.aibn.com
www.townsearch.com/rossmuseum
Decorative arts museum in one of St. Andrews' finest early houses; open June - Oct.
Margot Magee Sackett, Director

***St Martins:* Quaco Museum & Archives**
236 Main St., St Martins, NB E5R 1B8
506-833-4740, Fax: 506-833-2594,
quaco@nbnet.nb.ca
www.quaco.ca
Founded: 1970 Displays the history & heritage of the Quaco-St. Martins area with a specific focus on the shipbuilding heritage of the region; archives available for historical/genealogical research; the Carson Memorial Library, located behind the museum, is a volunteer-run public reading/lending library; gift shop. Museum & archives open June-Sept., other times by apppointment. Library is open Wednesdays & Saturdays throughout the year.
Barbara McIntyre, Curator, 506-833-4768, curator@quaco.ca
Faye Marks, Archivist, 506-833-2553, archivist@quaco.ca
Elizabeth Thibodeau, Librarian, 506-833-2553, librarian@quaco.ca

***St Stephen:* Charlotte County Museum Inc.**
443 Milltown Blvd., St Stephen, NB E3L 1J9
506-466-3295, Fax: 506-466-6606,
charlotteco.museum@nb.aibn.com
www.town.ststephen.nb.ca
Founded: 1977 Exhibits on 3 floors of the 1864 James Murchie Home; collection includes china, including early Chinese porcelain dating to the 17th century; hand-crafted articles, quilts, samplers; costumes; early tools & furniture; theme rooms portray area from the late 18th - early 20th century.
Irene Ritch, Executive Director

***Shippagan:* Societé historique Nicolas-Denys**
218, boul J.D. Gauthier, Shippagan, NB E8S 1P6
506-336-3461, Fax: 506-336-3478,
shnd@umcs.ca
www.acadie.net/guide/organismes3.cfm?id=40
Heures d'ouvertures et les différentes coordonnées comment nous joindre pour le centre de documentation: mardi, mercredi et jeudi de 8 h 30 à 12 h et de 13 h à 16 h 30, mercredi soir de 19 à 21 h.
Ivan Robichaud, Contact

***St-Isidore:* St-Isidore Museum Inc.**
3942, boul des Fondateurs, St-Isidore, NB E8M 1C2
506-358-2983, Fax: 506-358-6610,
Exhibits depict agricultural & forestry background of the region; open in July & Aug., Thu.-Sun.

***Sussex:* Agricultural Museum of New Brunswick**
28 Perry St., Sussex, NB E4E 2N7
506-433-6799, Fax: 506-433-2829,
www.agriculturalmuseumofnb.com
The museum houses agricultural equipment, military memorabilia, and furniture and housewares. Open mid-June - mid-Sept.
Judy Ross, Secretary

***Tabusintac:* Tabusintac Centennial Memorial Library & Museum**
4490 Rte. 11, Tabusintac, NB E9H 1J3
506-779-9261,
Houses historical artifacts & memorabilia from the Tabusintac area

***Tracadie-Sheila:* Musée Historique de Tracadie Inc.**
#399, 222, rue du Couvent, Tracadie-Sheila, NB E1X 1E1
506-393-6366, Fax: 506-395-6355,
museehis@nb.sympatico.ca
Founded: 1978 Leprosy in the 19th century; also history of Tracadie, artifacts dating several centuries before the arrival of the white colonists, articles relating to the life of the Acadians
Zélica Daigle, President, 506-393-6366, museums@nb.sympatico.ca

***Welshpool:* Roosevelt Campobello International Park / Parc international Roosevelt de Campobello**
459 Rte. 774, Welshpool, NB E5E 1A4
506-752-2922, Fax: 506-752-6000,
info@fdr.net
www.fdr.net
The Roosevelt Campobello International Park, located on Campobello Island in New Brunswick's Bay of Fundy, features the 34-room summer residence of Franklin D. Roosevelt & his wife Eleanor. Guided tours are given of the home. The park also contains the Edmund S. Muskie Visitor Center, where visitors learn the story of the former president of the United States, through displays & a film. The Roosevelt Cottage & Visitor Centre are open from mid May to mid October. The park is open year-round.

***Woodstock:* Old Carleton County Court House**
c/o Carleton County Historical Society, 128 Connell St., Woodstock, NB E7M 1L5
506-328-9706, Fax: 506-328-2942,
cchs@nb.aibn.com
www.cchs-nb.ca
Founded: 1986 The Carleton County Historical Society restored the Old County Court House which was built in 1833. The court house originally served as the County seat of justice & was also the meeting place for the first County Council in New Brunswick. Guided tours are available during the summer & by appointment at other times.

Newfoundland & Labrador

Provincial Museums

The Rooms
PO Box 1800 C, 9 Bonaventure Ave., St. John's, NL A1C 5P9
709-757-8000, Fax: 709-757-8017,
information@therooms.ca
www.therooms.ca
Other contact information: Archives: 709-757-8030; Museum: 709-757-8020; Gallery: 709-757-8040
The Rooms consists of the Newfoundland & Labrador Provincial Archives, Art Gallery, & Museum. The Archives collects records of the Government of Newfoundland & Labrador, as well as records from private sources which have value to the history of the province. Permanent exhibits at the museum depict Newfoundland & Labrador's early people, as well as Fort Townsend, the home of British soldiers &, since 1870, the Royal Newfoundland Constabulary. One level of the museum is dedicated to the birds of Newfoundland & Labrador. The Rooms Provincial Art Gallery presents more than 7,000 historical & contemporary works.
Dean Brinton, Chief Executive Officer, 709-757-8012, Fax: 709-757-8017
Anne Chafe, Director, The Rooms Provincial Museum, 709-757-8077, Fax: 709-757-8021, annechafe@therooms.ca
Deanne Fisher, Director, Marketing & Development, 709-757-8070, Fax: 709-757-8017, deannefisher@therooms.ca
Penny Houlden, Director, The Rooms Regional Museums, 709-757-8022, Fax: 709-757-8021, phoulden@therooms.ca
Vicky Lewis, Director, Finance & General Operations, 709-757-8015, Fax: 709-757-8017, vlewis@therooms.ca
Sheila Perry, Director, The Rooms Provincial Art Gallery, 709-757-8042, Fax: 709-757-8041, sheilaperry@therooms.ca
Greg Walsh, Director, Provincial Archives, 709-757-8032, Fax: 709-757-8031
Gillian Davidge, Manager, Education & Public Programming, 709-757-8109, gilliandavidge@therooms.ca

Other Museums in Newfoundland & Labrador

***L'Anse au Loup:* Labrador Straits Museum**
PO Box 98, L'Anse au Loup, NL A0K 3L0
709-927-5659,
Hunting & fishing collections, household communication & religious items

***Baie Verte:* Baie Verte Peninsula Miners' Museum**
PO Box 122, Hwy. 410, Baie Verte, NL A0K 1B0
709-532-8090, Fax: 709-532-4166,
baievertpeda@nf.aibn.com
Founded: 1975 The Miners' Museum presents a replica of life & work during the mining years (1860 - 1864 & 1901-1915) on the Baie Verte Peninsula.
Frank Clarke, President
Gail Goudie, Administrator
Jennifer Whelan, Treasurer

***Bonavista:* Bonavista Historical Society Museum**
Ryan Premises National Historic Site, PO Box 295, 10 Ryan's Hill, Bonavista, NL A0C 1B0
709-468-2920, Fax: 709-468-2495,
Founded: 1969 The Bonavista Historical Society Museum is situated in the restored turn-of-the-century Ryan Retail Store at the Ryan Premises National Historic Site. The collection reflects local life in the late 19th century in one of Newfoundland's inshore fishing communities. The musuem also holds a collection of medical artifacts from the early twentieth century. Bonavista Museum is open from mid-June to mid-October.

***Bonne Bay:* Wiltondale Pioneer Village**
PO Box 159, Woody Point, Bonne Bay, NL A0K 1P0
709-453-2470, Fax: 709-453-7214,
Recreated turn-of-the-century logging community; museum; one-room schoolhouse; church; log barn; original home; general store, craft store & tearoom

***Botwood:* Botwood Heritage Centre**
12 Airbase Pl., Botwood, NL A0H 1E0
709-257-4612, Fax: 709-257-3022,
bhsa@nf.aibn.com
town.botwood.nl.ca
The Botwood Heritage Centre depicts the time of the Beothuk, the European exploration era in the Exploits Valley, & the early railway & shipping period of Abitibi.

***Burin:* Burin Heritage House**
***Also known as:* Reddy House**
PO Box 500, Seaview Dr., Burin, NL A0E 1E0
709-891-2217, Fax: 709-891-2358,
burinheritagemuseum@nf.aibn.com
www.burincanada.com
Other contact information: Phone, Off Season: 709-891-1760; Fax, Off Season: 709-891-2069
The Burin Heritage House features artifacts related to the history of Burin, including the fishery & the tidal wave. The museum is open from mid May to the beginning of October.
Claudine Prior, Contact

***Carbonear:* Baccalieu Trail Heritage Corporation**
#2, 4 Pike's Lane, Carbonear, NL A1Y 1A7
709-596-1906,
www.baccalieudigs.ca
Founded: 1993 The corporation preserves, protects, & promotes the heritage of the Baccalieu Trail Region, which consists of approximately seventy communities along 240 km of coastline on Newfoundland & Labrador's Avalon Peninsula.

***Carbonear:* Carbonear C.N. Railway Station**
PO Box 64, Water St. West, Carbonear, NL A1Y 1B5
709-596-2532, Fax: 709-596-2582,
www.heritage.nf.ca/society/rhs
Other contact information: Phone, Off Season: 709-596-2849
The Carbonear Railway Station is one of Newfoundland & Labrador's Resgistered Heritage Structures. Built around 1917, the building exemplifies a station during the one hundred year era of the Newfoundland railroad. Operated by the Carbonear

Heritage Society, the station contains railway artifacts, exhibits about the history of Carbonear, genealogical information, & a tourist information centre. The Carbonear C.N. Railway Station is open from June to September. Appointments may be arranged during the off season.

***Cow Head:* Dr. Henry N. Payne Community Museum Conservation & Heritage Inc., PO Box 238, Cow Head, NL A0K 2A0**
709-243-2466,
cowhead.ca/heritage/index.htm
Restored theme home; artifacts tell story of Dr. Henry N. Payne & cultural heritage of area; gift shop. Located at the northern tip of Gros Morne National Park.
MS Glenda Reid Bavis, Staff contact, 709-243-2466, g.bavis@nf.sympatico.ca

***Cupids:* Cupids Museum**
PO Box 200, Cupids, NL A0A 2B0
709-528-3500,
cupidshistorical@nf.sympatico.ca
www3.nf.sympatico.ca/cupidshistorical
Located on Seaforest Dr.; open June 15-Sept. 30
Linda Kane, Curator

***Deer Lake:* Heritage Museum**
PO Box 989, Rte. 1, Deer Lake, NL AOK 2E0
709-635-4440, Fax: 709-635-5103,
www.town.deerlake.nf.ca
Founded: 1988 The museum preserves the local history with displays related to logging, agriculture and the settlers' lives in the Humber Valley. Open May-Dec.

***Durrell:* Durrell Museum & Crafts**
PO Box 83, Durrell, NL A0G 1Y0
709-884-2780,
lbulgin@nf.sympatico.ca
Other contact information: 709/884-5391/5537
Open end of May - end of Sept.; mounted polar bear exhibit & crafts
Lloyd Bulgin, President

***Ferryland:* Historic Ferryland Museum**
PO Box 7, Ferryland, NL A0A 2H0
709-432-2711,
Other contact information: Off Season: 709/432-2155
Located in the old Courthouse; exhibits depicting community life & Ferryland's role in colonization of North America; open mid-June - Labour Day
Maxine Dunne, Curator

***Flatrock:* Flat Rock Museum**
663 Windgap Rd., Flatrock, NL A1K 1C7
709-437-6312, Fax: 709-437-6311,
Open July - Sept. or by appt.

***Fogo:* Bleak House Museum**
PO Box 57, Fogo, NL A0G 2B0
709-266-2237,
Other contact information: Alternative Phone: 709-266-2487
Founded: 1988 Bleak House was built around 1816 for the Slade family, who were involved in the Fogo Island fish trade. The home was restored & made into a museum. The home features items that belonged to owners of the home, plus artifacts that depict the history of Fogo. Bleak House Museum is open from July to September.

***Forteau:* Point Amour Lighthouse**
c/o Labrador Straits Historical Development Corporation, PO Box 112, Forteau, NL A0K 2P0
709-927-5825, Fax: 709-656-3150, 800-563-6353
lshdc@labradorstraits.net; tourisminfo@gov.nl.ca
www.pointamourlighthouse.ca
Other contact information: Alternative Phone: 709-931-2013; 709-927-5826
Consisting of several buildings, the Point Amour Light station dates back to the 1850s. The Provincial Historic Site in Newfoundland & Labrador has been restored, & now features displays that depict the maritime history of the Labrador Straits. An interpretive trail at the site takes visitors to the site of the HMS Raleigh & HMS Lily shipwrecks. The site is open from mid May to the beginning of October.
Linda Badcock, Historic Sites Officer, 709-729-0592, Fax: 709-729-7989, lbadcock@gov.nl.ca

***Gander:* North Atlantic Aviation Museum**
***Parent:* North Atlantic Aviation Museum Association**
PO Box 234, Trans Canada Hwy., Gander, NL A1V 1W6
709-256-2923,
naam@nf.aibn.com
www.naam.ca
Founded: 1996 The North Atlantic Aviation Museum depicts important aviation moments over the North Atlantic, from the war years to commercial flying. The focus is upon Gander's involvement in aviation history. The Museum features six aircraft.
Bob Briggs, President
Brian Williams, Vice-President
Jonathan Waterman, Secretary
Harold Penney, Treasurer

***Grand Bank:* Southern Newfoundland Seamen's Museum (SNSM)**
PO Box 1109, 54 Marine Dr., Grand Bank, NL A0E 1W0
709-832-1484, Fax: 709-832-2053,
gwcrews@nf.aibn.com
Artifacts pertaining to the banks fishery

***Grand Falls-Windsor:* Beothuk Village**
PO Box 222, Grand Falls-Windsor, NL A2A 2J7
709-489-3559, Fax: 709-489-0465, 888-491-9453
evta@nf.sympatico.ca
Other contact information: Phone, Off Season: 709-489-9629
Beothuk Village is a replica of a Beothuk village, where visitors can discover the lifestyle of people who lived in the Exploits Valley. The village features reconstructed mamateek dwellings, a smokehouse, a storage pit, & a burial place. The site is open from mid June to early September.

***Grand Falls-Windsor:* Logger's Life Provincial Museum Provincial Bldg., Grand Falls-Windsor, NL A2A 1W9**

Logging exhibit is a replica of 1920s logging camp; displays tools & clothing representative of that era; located west of Grand Falls-Windsor on Trans Canada Hwy.

***Grand Falls-Windsor:* Mary March Provincial Museum Provincial Building, Cromer Ave., Grand Falls-Windsor, NL A2A 1W9**
709-292-4522, Fax: 709-292-4526,
information@therooms.ca
www.therooms.ca/museum/mary_march_museum.asp
Founded: 1988 From the European name of one of the last Beothuks, the aboriginal people of the island of Newfoundland, the Mary March Museum traces the Aboriginal, European, natural & geological history of the Central Newfoundland Region. Open daily 9am-4:45pm, May-Oct. The museum is located at 24 St. Catherine St. It is part of The Rooms Regional Museums network.
MS Deanne Fisher, Director, Marketing and Development, The Rooms, 709-757-8070, deannefisher@therooms.ca

***Greenspond:* Greenspond Court House**
PO Box 119, Greenspond, NL A0G 3L0
709-536-3220,
lindaw@morgan.ucs.mun.ca
Open June - Sept.
Frank E. Blackwood, Director
Roland Burry

***Happy Valley-Goose Bay:* Northern Lights Military Museum**
PO Box 2168 B, Happy Valley-Goose Bay, NL A0P 1E0
709-896-5939,

***Harbour Grace:* Conception Bay Museum**
PO Box 298, Water St., Harbour Grace, NL A0A 2M0
709-596-5465, Fax: 709-596-5465,
pfahey@conceptionbaymuseum.nf.ca
Open June - Aug; off season by appt.

***Hopedale:* National Historic Site: Agvituk Historical Society Museum**
PO Box 12, Hopedale, NL A0P 1G0
709-933-3777, Fax: 709-933-3746,
Moravian Mission House; archaeology artifacts from 1500-2000 years ago; items related to Labrador Inuit; European medical supplies & furniture

***Lewisporte:* By The Bay Museum & Craft Shop**
PO Box 569, 235 Main Rd., Lewisporte, NL A0G 3A0
709-535-8555,
lada@nf.aibn.com; btbmuseum@nf.aibn.com
Other contact information: Alternative Phone: 709-535-3900
Founded: 1872 Exhibits at the Bye The Bay Museum show the history of Lewisporte & its surrounding region, including Beothuk artifacts, the shipbuilding & logging industries & World War I & World War II. Owned & operated by the Lewisporte Area Development Association, the museum is open from the end of May to the end of August.
Pat Martin, Contact
Barry Porter, Contact

***Little Catalina:* Mockbeggar Plantation Provincial Historic Site**
***Also known as:* Bradley House**
PO Box 128, Little Catalina, NL A0C 1W0
709-468-7300, Fax: 709-468-5044, 800-563-6353
mockbeggar@nf.aibn.com
www.tcr.gov.nl.ca/tcr/heritage/historicsites/mock beggar.html
Other contact information: In Season Tel: 709/468-7300; Fax: 709/468-5044
Founded: 1990 Built in the 1870s, the museum was the home of Newfoundland statesman, Senator F. Gordon Bradley and is restored to that 1939 period. Other buildings include a carpenter shop, fish store and cod-liver oil factory from the 18 century. Museum is located on Roper St., Bonavista, NL, A0C 1B0.
MS Linda Badcock, Historic Sites Officer, 709-729-0592, Fax: 709-729-7989
Don Johnson, Site Supervisor

***Marystown:* Marystown Heritage Museum Corporation**
PO Box 688, Ville Marie Dr., Marystown, NL A0E 2M0
709-279-2463, Fax: 709-276-5116,
heritagemuseum@nf.aibn.com
www.marystownheritagemuseum.com/
The museum exhibits include everyday articles from the town's historic past, from squid jiggers to priests. Open daily mid-June - Aug.; Jan.-May, Sept.-Dec. Mon.-Fri 9-5
Albert Dober

***Moreton's Harbour:* Moreton's Harbour Community Museum**
PO Box 28, Main Rd., Moreton's Harbour, NL A0G 3H0
709-684-2355,
Operated by the Moreton's Harbour Women's Institute, the Moreton's Harbour Community Museum is situated in a house which was built in 1916. The museum features various artifacts, including agricultural implements & equipment used during the inshore fishery. Archives include census records, diaries, & school minute books. The community museum is open from mid June to the beginning of September. Tours may be arranged during the off season.

***Mount Arlington Heights:* St. Bartholomew's Church**
c/o Mt. Arlington Hts., PO Box 25, Mount Arlington Heights, NL A0B 2L0
709-228-2583,
Church built in 1930 by parishoners

***Musgrave Harbour:* Fishermen's Museum**
PO Box 159, 4 Marine Dr., Musgrave Harbour, NL A0G 3J0
709-655-2162,
Ship models, engines, photographs, accounts of local shipwrecks

***Nain:* Piulimatsivik - Nain Museum**
c/o Moravian Mission, General Delivery, Nain, NL A0P 1L0
709-922-2821,
Moravian & Inuit artifacts are on display at Piulimatsivik, the Nain Museum.

***North West River:* Labrador Heritage Museum**
PO Box 99, North West River, NL A0P 1M0
709-492-8282, Fax: 709-497-8856,
lab.heritage@nf.sympatico.ca
www3.nf.sympatico.ca/lab.heritage/museum .htm
Exhibit includes arifacts & infomation about the Hudson Bay Company store, trapping, exploration of Labrador & the International Grenfell Association in North West River

***Old Perlican:* Howard House of Artifacts**
PO Box 100, Old Perlican, NL A0A 3G0
709-587-2022,
Located 3 miles from Old Perlican on Shore Line country road at Daniel's Cove; artifacts represent the 1890s & 1900 to 1945; collection of Newfoundland homemade furniture of the 1930s; open daily
Jerome Howard, Owner

***Placentia:* O'Reilly House Museum**
c/o Placentia Area Historical Society, PO Box 233, 48 Orcan Dr., Placentia, NL A0B 2Y0
709-227-5568,
pahs37@hotmail.com
www.placentia.20m.com/mainframe2.htm
Founded: 1989 Built in 1902 as a residence for magistrate, William O'Reilly, O'Reilly House is now a museum operated by the Placentia Area Historical Society. The Victorian home displays many items from Placemtia' past. The museum is open from the beginning of June to mid October.

***Placentia Bay:* Castle Hill National Historic Site of Canada**
PO Box 10 Jerseyside, Placentia Bay, NL A0B 2G0
709-227-2401, Fax: 709-227-2452,
castle.hill@pc.gc.ca
www.pc.gc.ca
17th & 18th century remains of French & English fortifications; picnic areas & hiking trails; special events & programming; Visitor Centre with gift shop
Jewel Cunningham, Acting Superintendent

***Port au Choix:* Port au Choix National Historic Park Site**
PO Box 140, Port au Choix, NL A0K 4C0
709-861-3522, Fax: 709-861-3827,
pac-historic-site@pch.gc.ca
parkscanada.pch.gc.ca
Commemorates area's rich aboriginal history dating back 5400 years; visitors can view artifacts & exhibits on the four prehistoric cultures that occupied area; walking trails, archaeological sites, lighthouse & fossils
Millie Spence, Site Supervisor

***Port au Port:* Our Lady of Mercy Museum**
PO Box 239, Port au Port, NL A0N 1T0
709-648-2632,
Open May - Sept.
Margaret Lawler, Chair

***Port aux Basques:* Gulf Museum**
c/o South West Coast Historical Society, PO Box 1299, Port aux Basques, NL A0M 1C0
709-695-7604,
Nautical items & the astrolabe (dated 1628) an instrument used by early navigators to determine latitude; society operates a refurbished train site facility consisting of a railway station & nine rail cars

***Port aux Basques:* Port aux Basques Railway Heritage Centre**
PO Box 1299, Port aux Basques, NL A0M 1C0
709-695-7560,
The Port aux Basques Railway Heritage Centre depicts the significance of the railway to Newfoundland's history. In the late 1890s, Port aux Basques became the western terminus of the Newfoundland Railway, where the railway schedule connected with steamers. Open from June to October, the heritage centre features the train station & various rail cars.

***Port de Grave:* Fishermen's Museum, Porter House & School**
Port de Grave, NL A0A 3J0
709-786-3912,
hermanporter@personainternet.com
Founded: 1979 Museum contains artifacts depicting life & times of Newfoundland fishermen; Porter House is a traditional fisherman's house restored to early 1900s; Hibbs' Hole Schoolhouse, a restored one-room school
Herman Porter, Curator

***Port Union:* Port Union Museum**
PO Box 98, Port Union, NL A0C 2J0
709-469-2304,
thebungalow@nf.aibn.com
Includes estate of the late Sir Wm. F. Coaker, founder of Port Union & Sir Wm. F. Coaker Memorial Cemetery; open mid June - Sept.; small admission fees apply
Rosella Hiscock, Curator

***Pouch Cove:* Pouch Cove Museum**
PO Box 59, 660 Main Rd., Pouch Cove, NL A0A 3L0
709-335-2848, Fax: 709-335-2840,
pouchcove@nf.aibn.com
pouchcove.ca
Open year round
Wavy Ellsworth, Town Clerk/Manager

***Red Bay:* Red Bay National Historic Site of Canada**
PO Box 103, Red Bay, NL A0K 4K0
709-920-2142, Fax: 709-920-2144,
redbay.info@pc.gc.ca
www.pc.gc.ca/lhn-nhs/nl/redbay/natcul/basque.aspx
Other contact information: Phone, Summer: 709-920-2051
During the 16th century, Basque merchants & ship owners from France & Spain planned seasonal expeditions to the south coast of Labrador & the north shore of Quebec to hunt whales. The port they used most often was called Butus, which is now Red Bay. Red Bay is now a National Historic Site with a Visitor Centre. The Visitor Centre features discoveries from a marine archaeology project in the Red Bay area. Visitors learn about Labrador's 16th century history, through displays of original artifacts recovered from archaeological excavations, plus reproductions. The site is open from June to October.

***Rocky Harbour:* L'Anse aux Meadows National Historic Site**
Parks Canada, PO Box 70, Rocky Harbour, NL A0K 4N0
709-623-2608, Fax: 709-623-2028,
viking_lam@pch.gc.ca
www.pc.gc.ca/lhn-nhs/nl/meadows/index_E.asp
Other contact information: TTD: 709/772-4564
UNESCO World Heritage Site depicting first authenticated European presence in North America; the focal point are the reconstructions of three Norse buildings of this archaeological site. There are also exhibits the Viking lifestyle, artifacts, and the archaeological discovery of the site. Visitor centre open mid-June - early Oct.

***Rocky Harbour:* Gros Morne National Park Visitor Reception Centre**
PO Box 130, Rocky Harbour, NL A0K 4N0
709-458-2417, Fax: 709-458-2059,
grosmorner.info@pc.gc.ca
www.parkscanada.gc.ca/grosmorne
Other contact information: TDD: 709/772-4564
Gros Morne was declared a UNSESCO World Heritage site in 1987. GM discovery centre looks at the forces of nature. The centre looks at geology, plant and animal life, marine story and human history. It is located on the south side of Bonne Bay, one hour from Deer Airport and the Trans Canada Highway.

***St Anthony:* Grenfell House Museum**
PO Box 93, St Anthony, NL A0K 4S0
709-454-4010, Fax: 709-454-4047,
info@grenfell-properties.com
www.grenfell-properties.com
Dr. Wilfred Grenfell's former home restored circa 1920; open May to Oct.

***St. John's:* Anglican Cathedral of St. John the Baptist**
Parish House, 9 Cathederal St., St. John's, NL A1C 3Y4
709-726-5677, Fax: 709-726-2053,
cathedral@nf.aibn.com
www.infonet.st-johns.nf.ca/cathedral
Pictures, artifacts, records, documents & books related to the history of the Cathedral & Parish; established in 1699, the parish is the oldest non-Roman Catholic religious foundation in Canada; Cathedral building is one of the finest examples of English neo-Gothic architecture in North America
Donna Hiscock, Cathederal Archivist
Very Rev. Josiah Noel, Dean

***St. John's:* Boyd's Cove Beothuk Site & Interpretation Centre**
PO Box 8700, St. John's, NL A1B 4J6
709-656-3114, Fax: 709-656-3150, 800-563-6353
boydscove@nf.aibn.com
Founded: 1981 The Beothuk site at Boyd's Cove dates back to the late 17th & early 18th centuries. The site features the archaeological remains of Beothuk life, including their house pits. Visitors can learn about these extinct people at the interpretive centre, where several artifacts from the site are displayed & on the interpretive trail. The centre is open from mid June to mid October.
Linda Badcock, Historic Sites Officer
Karen Le Drew Day, Site Supervisor

***St. John's:* Cape Bonavista Lighthouse Provincial Historic Site**
Department of Tourism, Culture & Recreation, Heritage Division, PO Box 8700, Hwy. 230, St. John's, NL A1B 4J6
800-563-6353
tourisminfo@gov.nl.ca
www.tcr.gov.nl.ca/tcr/heritage/historicsites/capebonavista.html
The Cape Bonavista Lighthouse was built in 1843. The site features guided tours & a walking trail. The lighthouse is open from mid May to the beginning of October.
Linda Badcock, Historic Sites Officer (Year Round Contact), 709-729-0592, Fax: 709-729-7989, lbadcock@gov.nl.ca
Don Johnson, Site Supervisor (Seasonal Contact), 709-468-7444, Fax: 709-468-5426, capebonavista@nf.aibn.com

***St. John's:* Cape Spear National Historic Site of Canada / Lieu historique national du Canada du Cap-Spear**
PO Box 1268 C, St. John's, NL A1C 5M9
709-772-5367, Fax: 709-772-6302,
cape.spear@pc.gc.ca
www.pc.gc.ca/eng/lhn-nhs/nl/spear/index.aspx
Located at most easterly point in North America, the Cape Spear lighthouse is the oldest in Newfoundland & Labrador. The lighthouse has been restored to reflect 1839. Visitors can view displays about the history of lighthouses & lightkeeping. The grounds are open year round, & the lighthouse, Visitor Interpretation Centre & the Heritage Gift Shop are open from mid May to mid October.

***St. John's:* Commissariat House Provincial Historic Site, St. John's, NF**
Dept. of Tourism, Culture & Recreation, Culture & Heritage Division, PO Box 8700, King's Bridge Rd., St. John's, NL A1B 4J6
709-729-6730, Fax: 709-729-6745, 800-563-6353
commissariat@nf.aibn.com
www.explorenewfoundlandandlabrador.com
Other contact information: Year-round Email: tourisminfo@gov.nl.ca
This building, one of the oldest buildings in NFLD, was built especially for the Commissariat to supply the city's garrison and has been restored back to the 1830's era complete with tradtionally dressed maids and clerks to help answer questions.
Linda Badcock, Historic Sites Officer

***St. John's:* Heart's Content Cable Station Provincial Historic Site, Heart's Content NF**
Provincial Historic Sites, Arts & Culture Centre, PO Box 8700, St. John's, NL A1B 4J6
709-583-2160, Fax: 709-583-2373, 800-563-6353
heartscontent@nf.aibn.com
www.tcr.gov.nl.ca/tcr/heritage/historicsites/heartscontentcablestation.html
Other contact information: Year-round Email: tourisminfo@gov.nf.ca
Founded: 1974 Located on Hwy. 80, this cable station marks the first successful transatlantic telegraph cable landing in 1866. Displays focus on the history of cable, with equipment and instrumentation on exhibit. Open May-Oct., 10:00-5:30 daily.
MR Scott Andrews, Historic Sites Officer, Tourism, Culture and Recreation, 709-729-0592, Fax: 709-729-7989, tourisminfo@gov.nl.ca
Bob Balsom, Site Supervisor

***St. John's:* James J. O'Mara Pharmacy Museum**
Apothecary Hall, 488 Water St., St. John's, NL A1E 1B3
709-753-5877, Fax: 709-753-8615,
jomara@nlpb.ca
www.nlpb.ca
Drug store c. 1895; open end-June - end-Aug. or by appt.
Donald F. Rowe, Secretary-Registrar

***St. John's:* Hiscock House Provincial Historic Site, Trinity NL**
***Also known as:* Mountain Ash Villa**
Dept. of Tourism, Culture & Recreation, PO Box 8700, St. John's, NL A1B 4J6
709-464-2042, Fax: 709-464-2349, 800-563-6353
trinity@nf.aibn.com
www.tcr.gov.nl.ca/tcr/heritage/historicsites/thehisc ockhouse.html
Other contact information: In Season Tel: 709/464-2042; Fax: 709/464-2349
Founded: 1982 Owned solely by the Hiscock family until it was reborn as a museum, the house has been restored to its 1910 style. Located on Church St., it is open late spring to early autumn, 10:00-5:30 daily.
MS Linda Badcock, Historic Sites Officer, Tourism, Culture & Recreation, 709-729-0592, Fax: 709-729-7989, tourisminfo@gov.nl.ca
Joan Kane, Site Supervisor

***St. John's:* Quidi Vidi Battery Provincial Historic Site**
PO Box 8700, St. John's, NL A1B 4J6
709-729-0592, Fax: 709-729-6745,
commissariat@nf.aibn.com
The Quidi Vidi Battery was built by the French in the 1700s. It was later taken over by the British, who rebuilt the guardhouse. The site is now restored to the era of 1812, when it was used to ward off a possible American attack. The Quidi Vidi Battery is located on Cuckhold's Cove Road in Quidi Vidi Village, Newfoundland & Labrador. Tours are available from guides dressed in period costumes, from late June until September.
Andrea van Nostrand, Seasonal Contact, 709-729-6745, quidividi@nf.aibn.com

***St. John's:* Royal Newfoundland Constabulary Historical Society Archives & Museum**
Royal Newfoundland Constabulary Bldg., 1 Fort Townshend, St. John's, NL A1C 2G2
709-729-8000, Fax: 709-729-8214,
contactrnc@rnc.gov.nl.ca
www.rnc.gov.nl.ca
Collects & preserves early police records; 48+ audio tapes of oral history interviews, as well as 10,000+ photographs; researchers may contact the office of the Chief of Police, indicating their area of interest, to arrange for access to the archives; photocopying available upon request, subjet to copyright protocols; open year round

***St. John's:* The Royal St. John's Regatta Museum**
PO Box 214, Clancy Dr., St. John's, NL A1C 5J2
709-576-8921, Fax: 709-576-3315,
stjohnsregatta@nf.aibn.com
www.stjohnsregatta.org
The long history of rowing competition in St. John's, dating back to the early 1800s, is depicted at the Regatta Museum, through photographs, trophies, & other memorabilia. Please contact the Regatta Museum to arrange an appointment to visit.
Wayne Young, President, Regatta Committte
Paul Rogers, Secretary, Regatta Committte

***St. John's:* Lester-Garland Premises Provincial Historic Site, Trinity NL**
***Also known as:* The Ryan Shop**
c/o Dept of Tourism, Culture & Recreation, Culture & Heritage, PO Box 8700, St. John's, NL A1B 4J6
709-464-2042, Fax: 709-729-7989, 800-563-6353
trinity@nf.aibn.com
www.tcr.gov.nl.ca/tcr/historicsites
Mercantile bldg. including counting house restored to 1820 & retail shop restored to 1910; open daily June - Sept.
Linda Badcock, Historic Sites Officer
Joan Kane, Site Supervisor

***St. John's:* St. Thomas' Old Garrison Church Museum**
8 Military Rd., St. John's, NL A1C 2C4
709-576-6632, Fax: 709-576-2541,
office@st-thomaschurch.com
www.st-thomaschurch.com
c. 1836
Jean E.C. Lewis, Archival Committee Member
David Edwards, Archival Committee Member
Rev. Robert Chafe, Archival Committee Member

***St. John's:* Signal Hill National Historic Site of Canada / Lieu historique national du Canada de Signal Hill**
PO Box 1268, St. John's, NL A1C 5M9
709-772-5367, Fax: 709-772-6302, 888-773-8888
signal.hill@pc.gc.ca
www.pc.gc.ca/lhn-nhs/nl/signalhill/index.aspx
In 1901, Signal Hill was the reception point of the first transatlantic wireless signal. From the 18th century to World War II, Signal Hill was also the site of harbour defence for St. John's, Newfoundland. Today, visitors can tour the Visitor Interpretation Centre & visit Cabot Tower to view the Marconi exhibit. The site is open year-round.

***St. John's:* Trinity Interpretation Centre, Trinity NL**
Dept. of Tourism, Culture & Recreation, Culture & Heritage Division, PO Box 8700, St. John's, NL A1B 4J6
709-464-2042, Fax: 709-729-7989, 800-563-6353
trinity@nf.aibn.com
www.tcr.gov.nl.ca/tcr/heritage/historicsites/index.h tml
Exhibits on the commercial & social history of Trinity; open June - Sept.
Linda Badcock, Historic Sites Officer
Joan Kane, Site Supervisor

***St Lawrence:* St. Lawrence Miner's Memorial Museum**
PO Box 128, St Lawrence, NL A0E 2V0
709-873-2222, Fax: 709-873-3352,
townofstlawrence@nf.aibn.com
Open daily in summer
Mayor Wayde Rowsell
Gregory Quirke, Clerk/Manager

***Salvage:* Salvage Fishermens' Museum**
General Delivery, Salvage, NL A0G 3X0
709-677-2414,
gmheffen@hotmail.com
www.explorenewfoundlandandlabrador.com
The museum building, a home once owned by the Lane family, dates from 1860 and is the oldest dwelling in the area; collection of fishing & domestic artifacts relates to the history and cultural life of Salvage, from the late 19th c. to the present; open daily, mid-June to Labour Day; wheelchair accessible; archive; gift shop
Marion Heffern, Contact

***Springdale:* Harvey Grant Heritage Centre Community Museum**
***Also known as:* H.C. Grant Heritage Museum**
PO Box 57, 50 Main St., Springdale, NL A0J 1T0
709-673-4313, Fax: 709-673-4969,
Artifacts from 1940s, 50s & 60s, related to life of Harvey Grant; open July & Aug.

***Torbay:* Torbay Museum**
Torbay Municipal Centre, PO Box 1160, 1288 Torbay Rd., Torbay, NL A1K 1K4
709-437-6534, Fax: 709-437-1309,
torbayheritage@nfmail.net
torbay.museum.tripod.com
Over 500 artifacts dating from early 1800s; the collection is dedicated to produce a display of historical artifacts for public viewing, and the preservation and promotion of the heritage of Torbay. Open Mon. - Fri. 9-4, Tues. & Thu. 6:30-8:30 in summer; Tue. & Thu. 6:30-8:30 off season; otherwise by appt.
Jerri Pellegrinetti, Curator

***Trepassey:* Trepassey Area Museum**
PO Box 63, Trepassey, NL A0A 4B0
709-436-2044,
Open July & Aug.

***Trinity:* Trinity Museum**
***Parent:* Trinity Historical Society**
PO Box 8, Trinity, NL A0C 2S0
709-464-3599, Fax: 709-464-3599,
info@trinityhistoricalsociety.com
www.trinityhistoricalsociety.com
Founded: 1967 The artifacts of Trinity Museum are displayed in a salt box style house, which was built in the 1880s. The collection reflects the history of Trinity, & includes fishing, boat building, commercial, & domestic items. The site also features a fire engine shed, which displays an 1811 fire pump. Trinity Museum is owned & operated by the Trinity Historical Society. The museum is open from mid June to mid October, & by appointment at other times during the year.

***Twillingate:* Twillingate Museum & Craft Shop**
PO Box 369, Twillingate, NL A0G 4M0
709-884-2825,
info@tmacs.ca
www.tmacs.ca
Other contact information: Phone, After Hours: 709-884-2044
Founded: 1973 Twillingate Museum is located in the former Anglican Church Rectory, which was built around 1900. Furnishings in the museum reflect the Victorian era. Examples of exhibits include Inuit, Dorset, & Beothuk First Nations artifacts. Archives include photographs, family histories, & cemetery data. The museum is open from May to October.
Linda Blondin, Contact

***Wesleyville:* Bonavista North Museum & Gallery**
PO Box 257, 12 Memorial Dr, Wesleyville, NL A0G 4R0
709-536-2110,
museum@nf.aibn.com
www.bonavistanorth.blogspot.com
The Bonavista North Museum & Gallery contains photographs, artifacts, & artwork from the local area. The museum is open daily from the beginning of July to the end of August. Appointments can be arranged during the off season.

***Whitbourne:* Whitbourne Heritage Society, Inc.**
PO Box 166, Station Rd., Whitbourne, NL A0B 3K0
709-759-2345, Fax: 709-759-2242,
Founded: 1991 Open July 1 - Labour Day.
Judy Gosse, President
Curtis Sheppard, Vice-President
Susan George, Secretary
Mary Gosse, Treasurer

Northwest Territories

Territorial Museums

Prince of Wales Northern Heritage Centre (PWNHC)
PO Box 1320, 4750 48th St., Yellowknife, NT X1A 2L9
867-873-7551, Fax: 867-873-0205,
www.pwnhc.ca
Other contact information: Phone, NWT Archives: 867-873-7698; Fax, NWT Archives: 867-873-0660
Located on the shores of Frame Lake, the Prince of Wales Northern Heritage Centre is open year-round. Visitors to the centre will discover various exhibits about the people, places, & natural history of the Northwest Territories.
Barb Cameron, Director, 867-873-7551, barb_cameron@gov.nt.ca
Joanne Bird, Curator of Collections, 867-873-7668, joanne_bird@gov.nt.ca
Rosalie Scott, Conservator, 867-873-7664, rosalie_scott@gov.nt.ca
Richard Valpy, Territorial Archivist, 867-873-7657, richard_valpy@gov.nt.ca

Other Museums in Northwest Territories

***Colville Lake:* Colville Lake Museum**
General Delivery, Colville Lake, NT X0E 1L0
867-709-2500, Fax: 867-709-2500,
www.virtualmuseum.ca
Museum housing ethnographic artifacts, art gallery & archives; discovery centre; guided tours; gift shop; part of Colville Lake Lodge, a log cabin facility in a Dene community
Bern Will Brown, Curator

***Fort Smith:* Northern Life Museum**
PO Box 420, Fort Smith, NT X0E 0P0
867-872-2859, Fax: 867-872-5808,
nlmmanager@hughes.net
Collection, preservation & presentation of NWT culture & history; open year round
Kevin Brunt, Curator

***Norman Wells:* Norman Wells Historical Centre**
PO Box 56, Norman Wells, NT X0E 0V0
867-587-2415, Fax: 867-587-2469,
Dene cultural artifacts; geological history; WWI & Canol Project interpretation; Great Bear Lake & MacKenzie River explorers; local archives

Nova Scotia

Provincial Museums

Fisheries Museum of the Atlantic
Lunenburg Waterfront, PO Box 1363, 68 Bluenose Dr., Lunenburg, NS B0J 2C0
902-634-4794, Fax: 902-634-8990, 866-579-4909
fma@gov.ns.ca
museum.gov.ns.ca/fma/
Historic buildings featuring 3 floors of exhibits & activities: Millenium Aquarium; Bluenose Memorabilia; Fishermen's Memorial Room; August Gales 1926-1927; Bank Fishery Gallery; Rum Running; life in fishing communities; Hall of Inshore Fisheries; fisherman's store; Marine Engine Room, whales, boat shop; schooner Theresa E. Connor; side trawler Cape Sable; part of the Nova Scotia Museum
Jim Tupper, General Manager
Felicia Knock, Secretary-Bookkeeper
Ralph Getson, Curator, Education

Maritime Museum of the Atlantic (MMA) / Musée Maritime d'Atlantique
1675 Lower Water St., Halifax, NS B3J 1S3
902-429-7490, Fax: 902-424-0612,
hennigsj@gov.ns.ca
museum.gov.ns.ca/mma/
Marine history branch of the Nova Scotia Museum; on waterfront; marine artifacts, memorabilia from the Titanic, Halifax explosion exhibit, restored ship chandlery, extensive small craft collection; library & gift shop; Vessel CSS Acadia at museum wharf; open year round
John Hennigar-Shuh, General Manager

Nova Scotia Museum
Heritage Division, NS Dept. of Tourism, Culture & Heritage, 1747 Summer St., Halifax, NS B3H 3A6
902-424-7344, Fax: 902-424-0560, 800-632-1114
museum.gov.ns.ca
The Nova Scotia Museum family includes 27 museums across the province: Museum of Natural History, Halifax; Maritime Museum of the Atlantic, Halifax; Haliburton House, Windsor; Uniacke Estate Museum Park, Mount Uniacke; Prescott House, Starr's Point; Lawrence House, Maitland; Balmoral Grist Mill, Balmoral; Sutherland Steam Mill, Denmark; Fisherman's Life Museum, Jeddore; Shand House, Windsor; Museu
Bill Greenlaw, Executive Director

Other Museums in Nova Scotia

***Amherst:* Cumberland County Museum & Archives**
150 Church St., Amherst, NS B4H 3C4
902-667-2561, Fax: 902-667-0996,
ccmuseum@ns.aliantzinc.ca
www.cumberlandcountymuseum.com
Founded: 1973 Exhibits & archives on the natural, social & industrial heritage of Cumberland County; located in the 1838 heritage home of Robert Barry Dickey, a Father of Confederation; the archives houses genealogical & other material; fine art collection by County artists; well maintained gardens surround the museum. Open year round.
Shirley Nickerson, Manager/Curator

***Annapolis Royal:* Fort Anne National Historic Site / Lieu historique national du Fort-Anne**
PO Box 9, Annapolis Royal, NS B0S 1A0
902-532-2397, Fax: 902-532-2232,
information@pc.gc.ca
www.pc.gc.ca
Other contact information: Off-Season Phone: 902/532-2321
French & English period fortifications, 1629-1854; exhibits; open May 15 - Oct. 15
Theresa Bunbury, Supt., Operations

***Annapolis Royal:* Fort Edward National Historic Site / Lieu historique national du Fort Édouard**
PO Box 9, Annapolis Royal, NS B0S 1A0
902-532-2321, Fax: 902-532-2232,
www.parkscanada.gc.ca
Built in 1750 by Major Charles Lawrence, this Fort protected the route from Halifax to the Annaplos Valley and remains one of Nova Scotia's oldest builings.
Theresa Bunbury, Director

***Annapolis Royal:* North Hills Museum**
PO Box 503, 5065 Granville Rd., Annapolis Royal, NS B0S 1A0
902-532-7754, Fax: 902-532-0700,
scrantrg@gov.ns.ca
museum.gov.ns.ca/nhm/
Other contact information: Tel.: 902/532-7754 (late Oct.-late May)
Late 18th-century farmhouse which serves as the setting for the collection of Georgian furniture, ceramics, glass, silver & paintings of former owner Robert Patterson
Ryan Scranton, Executive Director

***Annapolis Royal:* O'Dell House Museum**
136 Saint George St., Annapolis Royal, NS B0S 1A0
902-532-7754,
historic@ns.aliantzinc.ca
www.annapolisheritagesociety.com/odell.htm
The museum is housed in a stagecoach inn & tavern from around 1869. O'Dell House is the former home of Nova Scotia Pony Express rider, Corey O'Dell & his family. Among the displays are items from Annapolis Royal's ship-building & sea-faring history. The Annapolis Heritage Society's Genealogy Centre's Archives & Collections Centre is also located at O'Dell House Museum. The Centre contains local histories, vital statistics for Annapolis & Digby counties, deeds, & church, cemetery, & probate records.
Barry Moody, Chair, Annapolis Heritage Society
Frances Rafuse, Secretary, Annapolis Heritage Society
Jane Dewolfe, Treasurer, Annapolis Heritage Society

***Annapolis Royal:* Port-Royal National Historic Site of Canada / Lieu historique national de Port-Royal**
PO Box 9, Annapolis Royal, NS B0S 1A0
902-532-2898, Fax: 902-532-2232, information@pc.gc.ca
www.pc.gc.ca/lhn-nhs/ns/portroyal/index.aspx
Other contact information: Phone, Off-Season: 902-532-2321 (mid October to mid May)
The national historic site on the coast of Nova Scotia is a reconstruction of early 17th-century buildings. The buildings represent a French colony from the era. The site features costumed interpreters & demonstrations to reflect life in one of the earliest settlements in North America.

***Antigonish:* Antigonish Heritage Museum**
20 East Main St., Antigonish, NS B2G 2E9
902-863-6160, antheritage@auracom.com
Open year round

***Arichat:* Lenoir Forge Museum**
PO Box 223, General Delivery, Arichat, NS B0E 1A0
902-226-9364, Fax: 902-226-1919,
Community museum; local artifacts; local artisan blacksmith

***Baddeck:* Alexander Graham Bell National Historic Site of Canada / Lieu historique national Alexander-Graham-Bell du Canada**
PO Box 159, Baddeck, NS B0E 1B0
902-295-2069, Fax: 902-295-3496, information@pc.gc.ca
www.parkscanada.gc.ca; capebretonisland.com/AGBell.html
Presents Dr. Bell's life & work, with emphasis on his accomplishments in Baddeck; open year round; Nov. 1 - Apr. 30 site visits by arrangement. The site is located on Chebucto St. (Rte 205), on the eastern edge of Baddeck.
Aynsley MacFarlane, Site Manager
Carol Whitfield, Field Unit Supt.

***Baddeck:* Canso Islands & Grassy Island Fort National Historic Sites of Canada / Iles-Canso et Fort-de-l'Ile-Grassy Lieux historiques du Can**
PO Box 159, Baddeck, NS B0E 1B0
902-295-2069, Fax: 902-295-3496, information@pc.gc.ca; atlantic.parksinfo@pc.gc.ca
www.pc.gc.ca/eng/lhn-nhs/ns/canso/index.aspx
Other contact information: Alternative Phone, Summer: 902-366-3136
The Canso Islands were a fishing base for the French during the 16th & 17th centuries. The British used the fishing port during the first half of the 18th century. The Islands were the scene of several battles between the French & English & the Mi'kmaq. In 1744, the Canso settlement was destroyed by the French. The visitor centre & interpretive trail are open from June 1st to September 15th.

***Baddeck:* Marconi National Historic Site of Canada / Lieu historique national Marconi du Canada**
c/o Alexander Graham Bell National Historic Site, PO Box 159, Baddeck, NS B0E 1B0
902-295-2069, Fax: 902-295-3496, information@pc.qc.ca
parkscanada.gc.ca/marconi
The site marks where Guglielmo Marconi initiated the age of global communications in 1902 by transmitting the first wireless message across the Atlantic Ocean. Visitors can see the Wireless Hall of Fame and walk to the original transmission station. Open June 1 - Sept.
Aynsley MacFarlane, Site Manager
Carol Whitfield, Field Unit Supt.

***Barrington:* Cape Sable Historical Society Centre**
Old Court House, PO Box 67, 2401 Hwy. 3, Barrington, NS B0W 1E0
902-637-2185, Fax: 902-637-2185, barmusuemcomplex@eastlink.ca
Founded: 1937 The Cape Sable Historical Society illustrates the history of Shelburne & Yarmouth Counties by collecting historical documents, genealogical records, & other items, & preserving historical sites. The Cape Sable Historical Society Centre is open year round.
Brenda Maxwell, Manager

***Barss Corners:* Parkdale Maplewood Community Museum**
3005 Barss Corner Rd., RR#1, Barss Corners, NS B0R 1A0
902-644-2893, Fax: 902-644-3422, p-mcm@hotmail.com.ca
parkdale.ednet.ns.ca
Founded by Thomas I. Spidell, a missionary-salesman for the New & Latter House of Israel
Donna M. Smith, Administrator

***Bear River:* Riverview Ethnographic Museum**
18 Chute Rd., Box 3, RR#1, Bear River, NS B0S 1B0
902-467-4321,
Folk costumes & early Americana, open year round

Sarah Elizabeth Glover, Owner & Curator

***Bedford:* Atlantic Canada Aviation Museum (ACAM) / Musée D'aviation des provinces Atlantique**
PO Box 44006, 1658 Bedford Hwy., Bedford, NS B4A 3X5
902-873-3773, info@atlanticcanadaaviation.com
www.atlanticcanadaaviation.com
Founded: 1977 Located at the Halifax International Airport (20 Sky Blvd.), the Atlantic Canada Aviation Museum preserves the aviation heritage of Atlantic Canada. The aircraft collection includes the Bell 47-J-2 Ranger Helicopter, the CF-5A Freedom Fighter, a Harvard Mk II, & a CF-104 Starfighter. The museum is open from mid-May to mid-October. At other times, tours can be arranged.
Michael White, Public Affairs Officer, 902-446-7606, mga1937@hotmail.com

***Bridgetown:* James House**
c/o The Bridgetown & Area Historical Society, PO Box 645, 12 Queen St., Bridgetown, NS B0S 1C0
902-665-4530, james.house.museum@gmail.com
Founded: 1979 James House was built in 1835 by Richard James, a member of the British Army who served in England & India. The house was donated to the Bridgetown & Area Historical Society. It became a Provincial Heritage Building, & now operates as the museum for the town of Bridgetown. James House features the Memorial Military Museum, which is sponsored by the Royal Canadian Legion, Branch 33. The museum is open from June to October.

***Bridgetown:* Tupperville School Museum**
RR#3, Bridgetown, NS B0S 1C0
902-665-2427, Fax: 902-665-4890,
Open daily mid-May - mid-Sept.
Marion Inglis, Chair

***Bridgewater:* DesBrisay Museum & Exhibition Centre**
c/o 60 Pleasant St., Bridgewater, NS B4V 3X9
902-543-4033, Fax: 902-543-4713, museum@bridgewater.ca
www.bridgewater.ca/desbrisay-museum
Founded: 1902 Home of famed porcupine quill-decorated cradle; parkland & trails; open year round; located 130 Jubilee Rd., Bridgewater; admission fee
Linda Bedford, Curator
Barbara Thompson, Director

***Bridgewater:* Wile Carding Mill**
c/o 60 Pleasant St., Bridgewater, NS B4V 3X9
902-543-8233, Fax: 902-543-4713, museum@town.bridgewater.ns.ca
cardingmill.museum.gov.ns.ca
Other contact information: Off season: 902/543-4033
Last surviving plant of a 19th-century water-powered industrial park; part of Nova Scotia Museum; open June 1 - Sept. 30; located at 242 Victoria Rd., Bridgewater; admission fee
Gary Selig, Manager

***Canso:* Whitman House Museum & Tourist Bureau**
Canso Historical Society, PO Box 128, 1297 Union St., Canso, NS B0H 1H0
902-366-2170, Fax: 902-366-3093, cansotouristbureau@ns.sympatico.ca
Founded: 1975 Whitman House was built in 1885. The first resident was C.H. Whitman, a Baptist minister. The operation of the Whitman House Museum is now overseen by the Canso Historical Society. Exhibits at the Whitman House Museum depict the history of the town of Canso & eastern Guysborough County, & Canso Harbour. The museum is open from June 1st to September 30th. At other times of the year, appointments may be arranged.

***Cheticamp:* Musée Acadien**
CP 98, Cheticamp, NS B0E 1H0
902-224-3463, Fax: 902-224-2170,
Open May - Oct.

***Church Point:* Le Musée Sainte-Marie**
PO Box 28, Church Point, NS B0W 1M0
902-769-2832, Fax: 902-769-0048, stmarysmuseum@hotmail.com
Largest wooden church in North America; open June - Oct.
André Valotaire, Président

***Clarks Harbour:* Archelaus Smith Museum & Historical Society**
PO Box 190, Clarks Harbour, NS B0W 1P0
902-745-3361, bryant.newell@ns.sympatico.ca
Portrays the history of Cape Sable Island including fishing techniques & gear, the Cape Island boat, shipwrecks, lives of sea captains, items from old kitchens, paintings by local artists, geneological & other historical records. The collection illustrates the background & growth of a pre-Loyalist fishing community
Bryant Newell, Secretary

***Clementsport:* Old St. Edward's Anglican Loyalist Church**
PO Box 171, Clementsport, NS B0S 1E0
Original Loyalist, Old St. Edward's Anglican Church & Cemetery consecrated 1797; managed by volunteers; situated at 34 Old Post Rd., Clementsport, Annapolis County, NS

***Cole Harbour:* Cole Harbour Heritage Farm Museum**
471 Poplar Dr., Cole Harbour, NS B2W 4L2
902-434-0222, farm.museum@ns.aliantzinc.ca
www.coleharbourfarmmuseum.ca
Open daily from May 15 - Oct.15; or by appt.
Elizabeth Corser

***Dartmouth:* Black Cultural Centre for Nova Scotia**
1149 Main St., Dartmouth, NS B2Z 1A8
902-434-6223, Fax: 902-434-2306, 800-465-0767
contact@bccns.com
www.bccns.com
Founded: 1983 Programs at the cultural education centre have include guided tours, music, plays, workshops, & lectures.
Dr. Henry V. Bishop, Chief Curator
Russell Grosse, Manager, Operations

***Digby:* Admiral Digby Museum**
PO Box 1644, 95 Montague Row, Digby, NS B0V 1A0
902-245-6322, Fax: 902-245-5196, admuseum@ns.sympatico.ca
www.admuseum.ns.ca
Museum is housed in a Georgian-style home and is named for Rear Admiral Robert Digby. On display are period rooms, furnishings and artifacts relating to the history of Digby; costumes; Marine Room with charts, ship models, and navigational equipment; photographs; online gift shop; online archives which include family registers and other items of interest to genealogical and historical researchers. Open mid-June - mid-Oct.; two days a week in winter
Sheryl Stanton, Curator

***Dingwall:* North Highlands Community Museum & Culture Centre**
PO Box 3, Dingwall, NS B0C 1G0
902-383-2579, community@northhighlandsmuseum.ca
www.northhighlandsmuseum.ca
The history & culture of northern Cape Breton Island is celebrated at the North Highlands Community Museum & Culture Centre, through artifacts & documents. The collection includes maritime artifacts, such as shipwreck booty, schoolroom materials, doctor's instruments, & farming tools.
Rob Macdonald, Co-Chair
David Rasmussen, Co-Chair
Deidre Fraser, Coordinator
Esther Danielson, Secretary
Maureen Grover, Treasurer

***Englishtown:* Great Hall of The Clans, Highland Pioneers Museum**
PO Box 80, Englishtown, NS B0C 1H0
902-295-3411, Fax: 902-295-2912, info@gaeliccollege.edu
www.gaeliccollege.edu
Open daily June - Sept.
Beth Anne MacEachen, Manager

***Glace Bay:* Cape Breton Miners' Museum**
PO Box 310, 42 Birkley St., Glace Bay, NS B1A 5T8
902-849-4522, Fax: 902-849-8022, info@minersmuseum.com
www.minersmuseum.com
The Cape Breton Miners' Museum tells the story of the area's history of coal mining. Visitors may tour the Ocean Deeps Colliery, which is a coal mine situated beneath the museum building. Exhibits include coal mining equipment. Research inquiries will be responded to by museum staff. The museum also features the Men of the Deeps Theatre.

***Grand Pre:* Grand-Pré National Historic Site of Canada**
PO Box 150, Grand Pre, NS B0P 1M0
902-542-3631, Fax: 902-542-1691, 866-542-3631
contact@grand-pre.com
www.grand-pre.com
Bilingual guides interpret history of the Acadians; open daily May 1 - Oct. 30; entrance fee
Victor Tétrault, Executive Director

***Greenwood:* Greenwood Military Aviation Museum**
PO Box 786, Greenwood, NS B0P 1N0
902-765-1494, Fax: 902-765-1261, gmam001@hotmail.com
gmam.ca
Founded: 1995 Recording the history of RAF/RCAF/CF station 1942 to present
Maj. R. Leblanc, General Manager
Bryan Nelson, Curator

***Guysborough:* Old Court House Museum**
PO Box 232, Guysborough, NS B0H 1N0
902-533-4008,
guysborough.historical@ns.sympatico.ca
Open June - Oct.

***Halifax:* Africville National Historic Site**
PO Box 392 CBO, Halifax, NS B3J 3P8
902-492-0253, Fax: 902-420-2816,
Accessible year round
Irvine Carvery, President

***Halifax:* Army Museum**
Cavalier Bldg., Halifax Citadel National Historic Site, PO Box 9080 A, Halifax, NS B3K 5M7
902-422-5979, Fax: 902-426-4228,
armymuseum@ns.aliantzinc.ca
Founded: 1953 The Army Museum preserves & promotes the military heritage of Atlantic Canada. Displays, including uniforms, decorations, weapons, & firearms, are related to the British, Canadian Regular Force, & Militia. The museum is open from May to October.

***Halifax:* HMCS Sackville**
***Also known as:* Canadian Naval Memorial Trust (CNMT)**
PO Box 99000 Forces, Halifax, NS B3K 5X5
902-429-2132, Fax: 902-427-1346,
rasoucie@ns.sympatico.ca
www.hmcssackville-cnmt.ns.ca
Canada's Naval Memorial; WWII corvette museum; open summer, downtown Halifax, open winter, HMCS Dockyard
Vice-Admiral Duncan Miller, Chair
Cdr. Wendall Brown, Commanding Officer

***Halifax:* Fisherman's Life Museum (FLM)**
Jeddore, Oyster Pond, 58 Navy Pool Loop, Halifax, NS B0J 1W0
902-772-2344, Fax: 902-772-2344,
monkma@gov.ns.ca
museum.gov.ns.ca/flm/
Other contact information: Summer Tel: 902/889-2053, Fax: 902/889-2053
Open daily June 1 - Oct. 15
Martha Monk, Site Manager
Judith Shiers Milne, Public Information Officer, 902/424-7398, shiersjl@gov.ns.ca

***Halifax:* Halifax Citadel National Historic Site of Canada**
PO Box 9080 A, Halifax, NS B3K 5M7
902-426-5080, Fax: 902-426-4228,
denise.graham@pc.gc.ca
www.pc.gc.ca/lhn-nhs/ns/halifax/index_e.asp
Present Citadel was completed in 1856 & was the fourth in a series of British forts on this site; a national landmark commemorating Halifax's role as a key naval station in the British Empire; living history program featuring the 78th Highlanders & the precision of the Royal Artillery
Linda Frank, Field Unit Superintendent

***Halifax:* Halifax Police Museum**
1975 Gottingen St., Halifax, NS B3J 2H1
902-421-6595,

***Halifax:* Maritime Command Museum / Musée du Commandement Maritime**
***Also known as:* Marcom Museum**
Admiralty House, PO Box 99000 Forces, 2725 Gottingen St., Halifax, NS B3K 5X5
902-721-8250, Fax: 902-721-8541,
marcommuseum@forces.gc.ca
www.pspmembers.com/marcommuseum
Founded: 1974 Of the Dept. of National Defence's 55 museums, this is the largest. Housed within 30 rooms of Admiralty House, a Georgian mansion, are displays representing facets of the Canadian Military. The collection consists of a research library, uniforms, model ships, medals, badges, ships' bells and other memorabilia associated with naval life. Open year round
Marilyn Gurney, Director

***Halifax:* Nova Scotia Sport Hall of Fame**
#446, 1800 Argyle St., Halifax, NS B3J 3N8
902-421-1266, Fax: 902-425-1148,
sporthalloffame@eastlink.ca
www.novascotiasporthalloffame.com
The Hall of Fame honours Nova Scotians who have made an impact on sports during the past 100 years. Inductees are addeed to the Hall of Fame each year, during The Hall of Fame Induction Night.
Bill Robinson, Executive Director, billr@eastlink.ca
Shane Mailman, Manager, Facility & Communications
Karolyn Sevcik, Coordinator, Administration & Special Events, halloffameevents@eastlink.ca
Rob Randall, Treasurer

***Halifax:* Prince of Wales Tower National Historic Site of Canada**
c/o Halifax Citadel National Historic Site, PO Box 9080 A, Halifax, NS B3K 5M7
902-426-5080, Fax: 902-426-4228,
halifax.citadel @pc.gc.ca
www.pc.gc.ca/lhn-nhs/ns/prince/index.aspx
The Prince of Wales Tower was built in 1796 & 1797. Its purpose was to protect the British from Fench attack. Over 200 years later, visitors will discover exhibits which show the tower's history. The Tower is open from the beginning of July to the end of August.
Linda Frank, Field Unit Superintendent, Mainland Nova Scotia Field Unit, Parks Canada
Dave Danskin, Manager, Heritage Presentation & Visitor Services, Mainland Nova Scotia Field Unit, Parks Canada
Tanya Taylor White, Manager, External Relations, Mainland Nova Scotia Field Unit, Parks Canada

***Halifax:* Thomas McCulloch Museum**
Biology Dept., Dalhousie University, 1355 Oxford St., Halifax, NS B3H 4J1
902-494-3515, Fax: 902-494-3736,
biology@dal.ca
biotype.biology.dal.ca/museum/
Founded: 1883 Collection of mounted birds, artifacts, Lorenzen ceramic mushrooms, shells & insects; marine & freshwater aquaria; occasional temporary exhibits; open weekdays; free admission
Stephen Fry, Chief Curator, 902-494-3530, steve.fry@dal.ca
Karen Smith, Curator, 902-494-2785, karen.smith@dal.ca
Julie Walker, Director

***Halifax:* York Redoubt National Historic Site of Canada**
c/o Halifax Citadel National Historic Site, PO Box 9080 A, Halifax, NS B3K 5M7
902-426-5080, Fax: 902-426-4228,
halifax.citadel@pc.gc.ca
www.pc.gc.ca/lhn-nhs/ns/york/index.aspx
York Redoubt was established in 1793 to defend the Halifax Harbour. Today, it is a National Historic Site of Canada, which is part of the Halifax Defence Complex. The site is open year-round.
Linda Frank, Field Unit Superintendent, Mainland Nova Scotia Field Unit

***Hantsport:* Churchill House & Marine Memorial Room**
c/o Town of Hantsport, PO Box 399, Hantsport, NS B0P 1P0
902-684-3461, Fax: 902-684-3227,
susan@hantsportnovascotia.com
www.hantsportnovascotia.com;
nsgna.ednet.ns.ca/hantsport/churchl.htm
Other contact information: (off season) 902/684-9068
Located at 6 Main St., Hantsport; open daily July - Sept., or by appt.; classic Victorian architecture; documents local shipbuilding history
Susan Carey, Tourism Manager, Hantsport

***La Have:* Fort Point Museum**
c/o Lunenburg County Historical Society, PO Box 99, La Have, NS B0R 1C0
902-688-2696,
lchs-fortpoint@ns.sympatico.ca
www3.ns.sympatico.ca/lchs-fortpoint/
On National Historic Site of Fort Ste. Marie de Grâce, 1632

***La Have:* La Have Island Marine Museum**
PO Box 69, La Have, NS B0R 1C0
902-688-3192,
limms@auracom.com
www.lahaveislandsmarinemuseum.ca
Historical treasures from a community that derived its life & livelihood from the sea
Douglas Berrigan, President
Sheila Chambers, Contact

***Inverness:* Inverness Miners Museum**
PO Box 598, Inverness, NS B0E 1N0
902-258-3822,
invhistsoc@ns.sympatico.ca
Location: 62 Lower Railway St.
Ned MacDonald, Director

***Iona:* Highland Village Museum / An Clachan Gàidhealach**
4119 Hwy. 223, Iona, NS B2C 1A3
902-725-2272, Fax: 902-725-2227, 866-442-3542
highlandvillage@gov.ns.ca
www.museum.gov.ns.ca/hv
Founded: 1959 The museum's mission is to collect & preserve the Gaelic heritage of Nova Scotia, with a focus on advancing the language. Included on site are: interpretation centre & museum, carding mill, 1880-1900 frame house, schoolhouse, forge, country store, barn, frame house (1830-1875), log cabin, stone (black) house, outdoor performance centre. There is also an extensive database of genealogical information. The museum is open June - Oct., 9:30-5:30 daily.
MR Rodney Chaisson, Director, chaissrs@gov.ns.ca

***Kentville:* Blair House Museum**
c/o N.S. Fruit Growers' Association, Kentville Agricultural Centre, 32 Main St., Kentville, NS B4N 1J5
902-678-1093, Fax: 902-678-1567,
www.nsapples.com/museumb.htm
Founded: 1981 The Blair House Museum was opened by the Nova Scotia Fruit Growers' Association. The purpose of the museum is the preservation & presentation of the history of the apple growing industry. The Agriculture Canada wing of the museum displays past & present research conducted at the station. The museum is located in a 1911 building, which was the residence of the research station's first superintendent, Dr. William Saxby Blair.
Dela Erith, Executive Director, Nova Scotia Fruit Growers' Association, derith@nsapples.com
Helen Arenburg, Inspector, & Contact, Public Relations, harenburg@nsapples.com

***Kentville:* Kings County Museum**
37 Cornwallis St., Kentville, NS B4N 2E2
902-678-6237, Fax: 902-678-2764,
curator@okcm.ca
www.okcm.ca
Cultural & natural history of Kings County; Parks Canada commemorative exhibit to the New England Planters; genealogy & community history archives
Cathy Margeson, Office Manager
Bria Stokesbury, Curator

***Liverpool:* Hank Snow Country Music Centre**
PO Box 1419, 148 Bristol Ave., Liverpool, NS B0T 1K0
902-354-4675, Fax: 902-354-5199, 888-450-5525
info@hanksnow.com
www.hanksnow.com
Founded: 1996 A tribute to Hank Snow, legendary country/folk singer from "down east," the displays include a plethora of photos and memorabilia, from his guitar strings to his iconic toupées to his yellow 1947 Cadillac. The centre also houses the Nova Scotia Country Music Hall of Fame.

***Liverpool:* Perkins House**
Queen's County Museum, PO Box 1078, 105 Main St., Liverpool, NS B0T 1K0
902-354-4058, Fax: 902-354-2050,
rafusela@gov.ns.ca
museum.gov.ns.ca/peh/
Connecticut style cottage built by merchant & diarist Simeon Perkins in 1766; open June - Oct. 15
Linda Rafuse, Curator, rafusel@gov.ns.ca

***Liverpool:* Queens County Museum**
PO Box 1078, 109 Main St., Liverpool, NS B0T 1K0
902-354-4058, Fax: 902-354-2050,
www.queenscountymuseum.com
Founded: 1980 The Queens County Museum depicts the cultural history of Nova Scotia's Queens County. The south shore of the province has a strong history related to the Mi'kmaq culture, fishing, & the forest. Programs are available for schools & the public.
Linda Rafuse, Director, rafusela@gov.ns.ca

***Lockeport:* Little School Museum**
PO Box 69, Lockeport, NS B0T 1L0
902-656-2238,
townoflockeport@aura.com
Replica of a former school room & a marine room; historical artifacts of local area

***Louisbourg:* Fortress of Louisbourg National Historic Site / Forteresse-de-Louisbourg, Lieu historique national**
259 Park Service Rd., Louisbourg, NS B1C 2L2
902-733-2280, Fax: 902-733-2423,
lhs.library@pc.gc.ca
fortress.uccb.ns.ca/parks/gal_e.html
Other contact information: TDD: 902/733-3607
Carol Whitfield, Field Unit Manager, Parks Canada, Cape Breton District

***Louisbourg:* Louisbourg Marine Interpretive Centre**
7548 Main St., Louisbourg, NS B1C 1J4
902-733-2252, Fax: 902-733-2053,
e.p@seascape.ns.ca
Open June- Sept.
Ernie Parsons, Director

***Louisbourg:* S&L (Sydney & Louisburg) Railway Museum**
7330 Main St., Louisbourg, NS B1C 1P5
902-733-2720,
fortress.uccb.ns.ca/historic/s_l.html
Exhibits include railroad artifacts, models, photographs & other documentation; paintings; rolling stock, model railroad, souvenirs; open June 1 - Oct. 15; tourist information centre
Eugene Magee, Curator

Lower Sackville: **Fultz House Museum**
PO Box 124, 33 Sackville Dr., Lower Sackville, NS B4C 2S8
902-865-3794, Fax: 902-865-6940,
fultz.house@ns.sympatico.ca
www.fultzhouse.ca
1860s home which belonged to the Fultz family of Sackville, NS; contains many artifacts & photographs from the Sackville area; blacksmith shop & cooperage shop from 1800s
Gail Hagee, Vice-President
Wilma Treen, President

Mabou: **An Drochaid**
PO Box 175, Mabou, NS B0E 1X0
902-945-2311,
androchaid@ns.sympatico.ca
Mabou Gaelic and Historical Society. Open July & Aug.
Margie Beaton, Director, 902/945-2790
Effie Rankin, Director, 902/945-2279

Mahone Bay: **Mahone Bay Settlers Museum**
PO Box 583, 578 Main St., Mahone Bay, NS B0J 2E0
902-624-6263, Fax: 902-624-0646,
info@settlersmuseum.ns.ca
www.settlersmuseum.ns.ca
Community Museum which provides vistors with a local history of the area; Open June to Sept.
Wilma Stewart-White, Curator

Maitland: **East Hants Historical Museum**
PO Box 51, Maitland, NS B0N 1C0
902-261-2796,
ehhs.weebly.com
Small museum containing historical Nova Scotian artifacts with local connections, historical documents, military records & cemetary records
Nancy Doane, President, East Hants Historical Society
Glenys Leck, Secretary
Olive Terris, Treasurer

Maitland: **Lawrence House Museum**
8660 rte. 215, RR #1, Maitland, NS B0N 1T0
902-424-6478, Fax: 902-424-0560,
lawrence.museum.gov.ns.ca
c.1865 home of William D. Lawrence, shipwright; open June 1 - Oct. 15
Marvan Moore, Director

Middleton: **Annapolis Valley Macdonald Museum**
PO Box 925, 21 School St., Middleton, NS B0S 1P0
902-825-6116, Fax: 902-825-0531,
info@macdonaldmuseum.ca
www.macdonaldmuseum.ca
Features antique clocks and pocket watches; Art Gallery featuring local artists; historical artifacts, household items, tools; recreated classroom and general store; sports heritage wall of fame; gift shop.
Sherry Griffin, Director

Milton: **Milton Blacksmith Shop Museum**
PO Box 572, 351 West St., Milton, NS B0T 1P0
902-350-0268,
www.qcis.ns.ca/blacksmith
Managed by the Milton Heritage Society, the museum is a 1903 smithy, complete with forge, ox sling & original workbenches, as well as a wide array of tools of the trade; also large display of photographs of historical Milton, NS
MS Christine Tupper, Curator, 902-354-2550

Mount Uniacke: **Uniacke Estate Museum Park**
PO Box 12, 758 Hwy. #1, Mount Uniacke, NS B0N 1Z0
902-866-0032, Fax: 902-866-2560,
c.1813; open June - Oct. 15
Martina Murphy, Supervisor

Musquodoboit Harbour: **Musquodoboit Railway Museum**
PO Box 303, Musquodoboit Harbour, NS B0J 2L0
902-889-2689,
Open May 16 - Oct.

New Glasgow: **Carmichael Stewart House**
86 Temperance St., New Glasgow, NS B2H 3A7
902-752-5583,
pictoucounty@ns.sympatico.ca
www.parl.ns.ca/csmuseum
Founded: 1965 Operated by the Pictou County Historical Society, the Carmichael Stewart House Museum is a late Victorian home which contains collections such as photographs, clothing, & Trenton Glassware. The museum is open during the summer.
Fergie MacKay, President
Jessica MacNeil, Treasurer
George McKay, Secretary

New Glasgow: **Pictou County Historical Museum**
86 Temperance St., New Glasgow, NS B2H 3A7
902-752-5583,
pictoucounty@ns.sympatico.ca
Fergie MacKay, President

New Ross: **Ross Farm Museum**
4568 Hwy. 12, New Ross, NS B0J 2M0
902-689-2210, Fax: 902-689-2264,
rossfarm@gov.ns.ca
rossfarm.museum.gov.ns.ca
Ross family farm 1817
Lisa Wolfe, Director

North East Margaree: **Margaree Salmon Museum**
PO Box 21, North East Margaree, NS B0E 2H0
902-248-2848,
Exhibits relate to salmon angling on the Margaree River. In a former schoolhouse excellent collections of fishing tackle, phots & memorabilia of famous anglers

Orangedale: **Orangedale Railway Museum**
PO Box 16, Orangedale, NS B0E 2K0
902-756-3384, Fax: 902-756-2547,
Open June - mid-Oct.; railway station built in 1911
Martin Boston

Parrsboro: **Fundy Geological Museum**
PO Box 640, 162 Two Island Rd., Parrsboro, NS B0M 1S0
902-254-3814, Fax: 902-254-3666, 866-856-9466
fundygeo@gov.ns.ca
fundygeo.museum.gov.ns.ca
Open daily in summer; Tues.-Sat. in winter
Carol Corbett, Education Coordinator
Kenneth Adams, Director/Curator

Pictou: **McCulloch House Museum (MCH)**
PO Box 1210, 100 Old Haliburton Rd., Pictou, NS B0K 1H0
902-485-4563, Fax: 902-485-5213,
nsmwebmaster@gov.ns.ca
www.rootsweb.ancestry.com/~nspcghs
Founded: 1972 Administered by the Pictou County Genealogy and Heritage Society, the museum was built in 1805 as home to Rev. Dr. McCulloch, the founder of Pictou Academy & first president of Dalhousie University. The exhibits reflect the life & times of the Scottish immigrants and their influence on today's Nova Scotia.
MS Dayle Crouse, Director

Pictou: **Northumberland Fisheries Museum & Heritage Association (NFM)**
PO Box 1489, 71 Front St., Pictou, NS B0K 1H0
902-485-4972, Fax: 902-485-6586,
northumberlandmuseum@ns.sympatico.ca
www.northumberlandfisheriesmuseum.c om
Founded: 1978 Located in the historic C.N. Station; fishing artifacts from the late 1800s to present day; original fisherman's Bunkhouse; The "Silver Bullet"; photographs; boat models; fishing tools; artifacts on lobster processing; shell fish/live fish displays; sea heritage education for schools & seniors; education is based on fact & scientific data from Northumberland Strait area; local research conducted on fishing & sea heritage; recent additions to the museum include a lobster hatchery & lighthouse museum & research centre.
David MacKeil, Chairman, dave_mackeil@hotmail.com
Michelle Davey, Business Manager

Port Hastings: **Port Hastings Museum & Archives**
9 Church St., Port Hastings, NS B9A 1N5
902-625-1295,
gutofcanso@ns.sympatico.ca
fortress.uccb.ns.ca/historic/port.html
Located in 100-year-old Cape Breton house; displays include pioneer artifacts, photographic displays & exhibits on construction of causeway; genealogical records available
Dernie Gillis, President
Beryl MacDonald-MacLeod, Curator

Port Hood: **Chestico Museum & Historical Society**
PO Box 144, Port Hood, NS B0E 2W0
902-787-2244,
chesticoplace.com
Founded: 1986 Located in Harbourview, on Rte 19 on the outskirts of Port Hood, the museum houses artifacts from the local community; house histories, historical events, people of the Port Hood area; gift shop; tea room; special programming. The museum will be housed in a new facility, Chestico Place, located in the centre of Port Hood, in the near future.
Susan Mallette, Director

Port Williams: **Prescott House**
1633 Starr's Point Rd., Port Williams, NS B0P 1T0
902-542-3984, Fax: 902-542-3984,
mortonnl@gov.ns.ca
museum.gov.ns.ca/prh/
c.1814 Georgian house, open June 1 - Oct. 15; museum shop; bus tours welcome
Nancy Morton, Caretaker

Pubnico-Ouest: **Musée des Acadiens des Pubnicos et Centre de recherche**
CP 92, Pubnico-Ouest, NS B0W 3S0
902-762-3380, Fax: 902-762-0726,
musee.acadien@ns.sympatico.ca
www.museeacadien.ca
Le Musée: #898, autoroute 335; consacré au patrimoine des Acadiens/Acadiennes de Pubnico-Ouest; articles de maison; documents; photographies; archives; potager traditionnel; boutique de souvenirs.
Paul d'Entremont, Président

Riverport: **Ovens Natural Park & Museum**
326 Ovens Rd., Riverport, NS B0J 2W0
902-766-4621, Fax: 902-766-4344,
info@ovenspark.com
www.ovenspark.com
Located on the Atlantic ocast of Nova Scotia, Ovens Natural Park is a reserve of coastal forest, featuring the sea caves or "Ovens". The area became known internationally during th 1861 gold rush. The Gold Rush Museum contains artifacts from that era.
Angel Chapin, Director

St Peters: **Nicolas Denys Museum**
PO Box 249, St Peters, NS B0E 3B0
902-535-2175,
nicolasdenysmuseum@ns.aliantzinc.ca
fortress.uccb.ns.ca/historic/denys.html
Micmac, Acadien, Scottish & Irish artifacts

Shag Harbour: **Chapel Hill Museum**
PO Box 46, 5492 Hwy #3, Shag Harbour, NS B0W 3B0
902-723-1313,
chapelhillhistory@aliantzinc.ns.ca
chapelhill.webs.com
Located in former Baptist Church; features various displays related to local area including tools for ship building, genealogical research materials, various fishing exhibits; able to view 4 local lighthouses from observation tower; open June 1 - Sept. 15 daily; rest of the year by appt.
Douglas Shand, President, Chapel Hill Historical Society, 902-723-2949, shawimm@ns.sympatico.ca
Veronica Hopkins, Vice President/Treasurer, Chapel Hill Historical Society, vhopkins@ns.sympatico.ca

Shelburne: **John C. Williams Dory Shop**
PO Box 39, 11 Dock St., Shelburne, NS B0T 1W0
902-875-4003, Fax: 902-875-4141,
shelburne.museum@ns.sympatico.ca
www.historicshelburne.com
Restored dory factory, est. 1880; open June 1 - Sept. 30; dories still built to order
Kim Truchan, Complex Manager, shs.kimtruchan@ns.aliantzinc.ca

Shelburne: **Ross Thomson House & Store Museum**
PO Box 39, Shelburne, NS B0T 1W0
902-875-3141, Fax: 902-875-4141,
shelburne.museum@ns.sympatico.ca
www.historicshelburne.com
Located on Charlotte St. in Shelburne; 1785 Loyalist house & garden; 18th-century store & chandlery; 19th-century military artifacts; open June 1 - Oct. 15
Kim Truchan, Complex Manager, shs.kimtruchan@ns.aliantzinc.ca

Shelburne: **Shelburne County Museum**
PO Box 39, 20 Dock St., Shelburne, NS B0T 1W0
902-875-3219, Fax: 902-875-4141,
shelburne.museum@ns.sympatico.ca
www.historicshelburne.com
Cultural & economic history of Shelburne from 1783; genealogy information; open year round
Finn Bower, Curator

Sherbrooke: **Sherbrooke Village**
PO Box 295, 42 Main St., Sherbrooke, NS B0J 3C0
902-522-2400, Fax: 902-522-2974,
svillage@gov.ns.ca
sherbrookevillage.museum.gov.ns.ca
Open June - mid-Oct.
Craig MacDonald, Project Director

Smiths Cove: **Old Temperance Hall Museum**
Smiths Cove, NS B0S 1S0
902-245-4315,
Exhibits of the 19th and 20th century pertaining to the local community including the earliest inhabitants, the Mi'kmaq; history of the Sons of Temperance.
Dorothy Gray, President, 902/245-4665

Springhill: **The Anne Murray Centre**
36 Main St., Springhill, NS B0M 1X0
902-597-8614, Fax: 902-597-2001,
info@annemurraycentre.com
www.annemurraycentre.com

Founded: 1989 Pays tribute to the achievements of Springhill's internationally acclaimed singing superstar; open May - Oct., otherwise by appt. or by chance.

***Springhill:* Springhill Miner's Museum**
PO Box 610, Black River Rd., Springhill, NS B0M 1X0
902-597-3449, Fax: 902-597-2001,
museum.gov.ns.ca/musdir/springhillminersmuseum.htm
Tours of the Springhill coal mine, famous in song & legend; gift shop & picnic area; open May - Oct.

***Stellarton:* The Museum of Industry**
PO Box 2590, 147 North Foord St., Stellarton, NS B0K 1S0
902-755-5425, Fax: 902-755-7045,
industry@gov.ns.ca
museum.gov.ns.ca/moi/index.html
Atlantic Canada's largest museum; chronicles the impact of industrialization on the people, economy & landscape of Nova Scotia; features Canada's oldest steam locomotives, an historic model railway layout, a belt-driven working machine shop & a collection of Nova Scotia's Trenton glass
Debra McNabb, Director

***Sydney:* Cape Breton Centre for Heritage & Science**
***Also known as:* The Lyceum Museum**
225 George St., Sydney, NS B1P 1J5
902-539-1572, Fax: 902-539-1572,
fortress.uccb.ns.ca/historic/oldsyd.html
The Lyceum was built in 1904 by the Roman Catholic diocese. The Opera House contained a 900 seat theatre, as well as a library, gymnasium, billiards room, & clubrooms. Today, the Lyceum houses the Cape Breton Centre for Heritage & Science. The Old Sydney Society provides tours of the Colonial Town of Old Sydney, which was first the home to Mi'Kmaq people, then Basque fishermen, Loyalists, & later immigrating Scots. In the Cape Breton Centre for Heritage & Science, visitors will discover the natural & social histories of Cape Breton County. The museum is open year round.
Dr. Robert Morgan, President, 902-539-3951
J. Peyton Chisholm, Curator
Elaine Hummer, Bookkeeper

***Tatamagouche:* Balmoral Grist Mill**
RR#4, Tatamagouche, NS B0K 1V0
902-657-3016, Fax: 902-657-2606,
www.museum.gov.ns.ca/bgm
Located at 660 Matheson Brook Road in Balmoral Mills, the 1874 three-storey grist mill is still operational. The grist mill is open from June 1st to October 15th.
Darrell Burke, Site Manager, 902-657-3016, burked@gov.ns.ca

***Tatamagouche:* Sunrise Trail Museum**
216 Main St., Tatamagouche, NS B0K 1V0
902-657-2689,
Open daily mid-June - Labour Day

***Tatamagouche:* Sutherland Steam Mill Museum**
RR#5, Tatamagouche, NS B0K 1V0
902-657-3365, Fax: 902-657-3016,
museum.gov.ns.ca/ssm/
Open June 1 - Oct. 15
John Taylor, Superintendent, 902/657-3016

***Truro:* Colchester Historical Society Museum**
***Also known as:* Colchester Historical Museum**
PO Box 412, 29 Young St., Truro, NS B2N 5C5
902-895-6284, Fax: 902-895-9530,
colchestermuseum@ns.aliantzinc.ca
www.genealogynet.com/Colchester/
Founded: 1954 Open year round
Aidan Norton, Curator
Nan Harvey, Archivist, colchesterarchives@ns.aliantzinc.ca

***Truro:* The Little White Schoolhouse**
PO Box 1252, 20 Arthur St., Truro, NS B2N 5N2
902-895-5170,
lwsm1979@msn.com
lwsm.ednet.ns.ca
Original Riverton School; commemorates schoolhouses in Nova Scotia from Confederation to the 1950s; contains books & artifacts from the era of one-room schoolhouse; requests for research on the graduates of the Provincial Normal School & College & in old copies of the NS Journal of Education, accepted; open early June - Aug. & by appt.
Tom Acker, Curator

***Wallace:* Wallace Area Museum**
***Parent:* Wallace & Area Museum Society**
PO Box 179, 13440 Rte. 6, Wallace, NS B0K 1Y0
902-257-2191, Fax: 902-257-2191,
wallacemuseum@ns.aliantzinc.ca
www.wallaceandareamuseum.com
Founded: 1984 The museum collect, preserves, & displays the history of Wallace & the surrounding region. Artifacts include nineteenth century marine charts & maps, the United Empire Loyalist grant, pre-Confederation letters, & items about shipbuilding in Wallace & the Wallace sandstone quarries.
Doris Purdy, President
Glenda Waugh, Vice-President
David Dewar, Curator
Doug Perry, Secretary

***West Bay:* Marble Mountain Library & Museum**
RR#1, West Bay, NS B0E 3K0
902-756-3289,
Wendy MacDonald, Curator

***Windsor:* The Haliburton**
PO Box 2683, 414 Clifton Ave., Windsor, NS B0N 2T0
902-798-2915,
dauphiar@gov.ns.ca
museum.gov.ns.ca/hh/
Open June 1 - Oct. 15
Alan Dauphinee, Superintendent

***Windsor:* Shand House**
PO Box 2683, 389 Avon St., Windsor, NS B0N 2T0
902-798-8213, Fax: 902-798-5619,
dauphiar@gov.ns.ca
museum.gov.ns.ca/sh/
Open June 1 - Oct. 15
Alan Dauphinee, Superintendent

***Windsor:* West Hants Historical Society Museum**
PO Box 2335, 281 King St., Windsor, NS B0N 2T0
902-798-4706,
whhs@ns.aliantzinc.ca
www.westhantshistoricalsociety.ca
Artifacts related to the history of Hants County in Nova Scotia are collected & preserved by the West Hants Historical Society & displayed at its museum. Visitors will find information about the Mi'kmaq, the Acadians, the Loyalists, the Great Windsor Fire of 1897, & the local shipbuilding industry. The society also operates a genealogy department. The museum is open five days a week from mid June to the end of August, & one day a week from September to June. Summer tours are available of the Fort Edward Blockhouse. Appointments may be arranged for times when the museum is closed.

***Wolfville:* Randall House Museum**
c/o Wolfville Historical Society, 259 Main St., Wolfville, NS B4P 1C6
902-542-9775,
randallhouse@live.ca
www.wolfvillehs.ednet.ns.ca
The Randall House is an historic farmhouse, from around 1800, which is owned & operated by the Wolfville Historical Society. The Randall House Museum reflects life in Wolfville & the surrounding area during the 18th & 19th centuries. On display are furniture, clothing, china, & a collection of Victorian greeting cards. A library is located in The Randall House for persons researching local history & genealogy.
John Whidden, President
Heather Watts, Archivist, 902-542-0307
William Bishop, Historian

***Yarmouth:* Firefighters' Museum of Nova Scotia**
Nova Scotia Museum Complex, 451 Main St., Yarmouth, NS B5A 1G9
902-742-5525,
darbydl@gov.ns.ca
museum.gov.ns.ca/fm/
Artifacts date to the early 1800s; open year round
David Darby, Curator

***Yarmouth:* Yarmouth County Museum & Archives**
c/o Yarmouth County Historical Society, 22 Collins St., Yarmouth, NS B5A 3C8
902-742-5539, Fax: 902-749-1120,
ycmuseum@eastlink.ca
yarmouthcountymuseum.ednet.ns.ca
Also operates the Pelton-Fuller House in Yarmouth, the historic summer home of A.C. Fuller, the Fuller Brush Man & the Killam Brothers' shipping office, the oldest in Canada, during the summer months
Nadine Gates, Curator
Adèle Hampel, Director
J. Stuart McLean, Archivist MLIS

Nunavut

Other Museums in Nunavut

***Arctic Bay:* Sod House Museum**
c/o Innumariit Committee, Arctic Bay, NU X0A 0A0
History & traditions of the Inuit of Admiralty Inlet

***Iqaluit:* Nuantta Sunaqutangit Museum**
PO Box 1900, Iqaluit, NU X0A 0H0
867-979-5537, Fax: 867-979-4533,
museum@nunanet.com
Founded in 1969; housed in a historic Hudson Bay Company warehouse building; collections focus on Inuit culture & history from the Baffin region, including historical & archeological artifacts, tools, clothing, & equipment as well as arts & crafts; also maintains a collection of archival photographs, publications & documents for exhibition & research purposes; open Tues.-Sun.
Brian Lunger, Manager/Curator

***Pangnirtung:* Auyuittuq National Park of Canada (ANPR)**
Parks Canada, PO Box 353, Pangnirtung, NU X0A 0R0
867-473-3500, Fax: 867-473-8612,
nunavut.info@pch.gc.ca
www.pc.gc.ca/pn-np/nu/auyuittuq/index_e.asp
Other contact information: Phone, Communications: 867-975-4673; Fax: 867-975-4674
Founded: 1976 Located in the eastern Arctic, on Baffin Island, Auyuittuq National Park of Canada protects 19,089 km2 of terrain.
Maryse Mahy, Planner, Nunavut Field Unit, 867-975-4673, Fax: 867-975-4674, Maryse.Mahy@pc.gc.ca

***Pangnirtung:* Sipalaseequtt Museum Society**
Angmarlik Visitor Centre, PO Box 227, Pangnirtung, NU X0A 0R0
867-473-8737, Fax: 867-473-8685,
oarnaqaq1@gov.nu.ca
Inuit artifacts; whaling history in Cumberland Sound Baffin Island; Elders' meetings; craft production; tours
Ooleepeela Arnaqaq, Manager

Ontario

Provincial Museums

Hockey Hall of Fame (HHOF) / Le Temple de la Renommée du Hockey
Brookfield Place, 30 Yonge St., Toronto, ON M5E 1X8
416-360-7765, Fax: 416-360-1501,
info@hhof.com
www.hhof.com
Founded: 1961 The museum holds a veritable treasure of artifacts, memorabilia, films and photos, displayed in multi-media exhibits, all on a hockey theme. Also on site is the D.K. (Doc) Seaman Hockey Resource Centre which stores a vast archive. The museum offers a variety of educational programs. Visitors can also enjoy interactive games. This is the home of hockey's ultimate trophy, Lord Stanley's Cup.
MR William C. Hay, Chair/CEO, Board of Directors, bhay@hhof.com
MR Philip Pritchard, Vice-President/Curator, ppritchard@hhof.com

Royal Ontario Museum (ROM)
100 Queen's Park, Toronto, ON M5S 2C6
416-586-8000,
info@rom.on.ca
www.rom.on.ca
Founded: 1912 Recently renovated & expanded, The Royal Ontario Museum (ROM) is Canada's largest museum, an internationally renowned facility & popular public attraction. Created in 1912, the ROM has an unusually broad dual mandate of collecting & preserving in the areas of natural history & human cultures, & communicating its research to the world. Today, the ROM holds in excess of 6 million objects in its collections, which include galleries of art, archaeology & science.
William Thorsell, Director & CEO
Glenn Dobbin, Deputy Director, Operations
Dr. Mark Engstrom, Deputy Director, Collections & Research
James Temerty, Chair, Board of Governors

Other Museums in Ontario

***Alliston:* Museum on the Boyne**
PO Box 910, Alliston, ON L9R 1A1
705-435-0167, Fax: 705-434-3006,
boynemuseum@town.newtecumseth.on.ca
www.town.newtecumseth.on.ca/museum.c fm
Community museum displaying household, agricultural & industrial artifacts from 1840's to present; site features 1850's log cabin, 1860 English barn & 1915 fair building
Rachelle Clayton, Curator

***Almonte:* J.H. Naismith Museum & Hall of Fame**
c/o Dr. James Naismith Basketball Foundation, PO Box 1991, 14 Bridge St., Almonte, ON K0A 1A0
613-256-0492,
info@naismithmuseum.com
www.naismithmuseum.com
Artifacts related to life of Dr. James Naismith, originator of game of basketball; Canadian Basketball Hall of Fame exhibits & archives

John Gosset, Executive Director
Phil Wood, President

Almonte: Mill of Kintail Conservation Area
4175 Hwy 511, RR#2, Almonte, ON K0G 1K0
613-259-2421, Fax: 613-259-3468, info@mvc.on.ca
www.mvc.on.ca/index.php/conservation-areas/mill-of-kintail
Kintail Museum, housed in a heritage grist mill, is a collection and a conservation site on the Indian River in Lanark County. The museum showcases the life and works of Robert Tait McKenzie as the mill was his summer home and sculpture studio; the museum showcases the largest collection of McKenzie's sculptures and memorabilia in Canada.
Stephanie Kolsters, Museum Manager, 613-256-3610, ext. 2, skolsters@mvc.on.ca

Almonte: Mississippi Valley Textile Museum
PO Box 784, 3 Rosamond St. East, Almonte, ON K0A 1A0
613-256-3754, Fax: 613-256-3754, mvtm@magma.ca
www.textilemuseum.mississippimills.com
Founded: 1985 Museum is located in the annex of the former Rosamond Woolen Company constructed in 1867; houses information on the early mills & their owners, displays of period offices, artifacts & machinery related to the beginnings of the textile industry, and a gift shop.
MR Martin Ruben, President

Almonte: North Lanark Regional Museum
Appleton Ramsay Township, Almonte, ON K0A 1A0
613-256-1805, jeandawn@comnet.ca
Operates a small regional museum; open May 22nd to Thanksgiving, Wed.-Sun., 10-4; admission $2
Dawn Leduc, Curator

Ameliasburg: Ameliasburgh Historical Museum
PO Box 67, Ameliasburg, ON K0K 1A0
613-968-9678, Fax: 613-966-1599, amelmuseum@pecounty.on.ca
www.pec.on.ca/ameliasburghmuseum/index.html
Founded: 1968 Household items, quilts, crafts, agricultural machinery & tools & a 1910 Goldie Corlis engine with an 18-foot flywheel in a village setting; lots of events during season; tea room. Located at 517 County Rd. 19, Ameliasburgh.
Janice Hubbs, Curator

Ameliasburgh: Quinte Educational Museum & Archives
14 Coleman St., Ameliasburgh, ON K0K 1A0
613-966-5501, qema@bellnet.ca
www.pec.on.ca/victoriaschoolhouse
The history of education in Prince Edward County & Ontario is preserved at the Quinte Educational Museum & Archives, through educational artifacts & archival material.

Amherstburg: Fort Malden National Historic Site of Canada (FMNHS) / Lieu historique national du Canada du Fort-Malden
PO Box 38, 100 Laird Ave., Amherstburg, ON N9V 2Z2
519-736-5416, Fax: 519-736-6603, ont.fort-malden@pc.gc.ca
www.parkscanada.gc.ca/malden
Riverfront site includes original earthworks, a restored soldier's barrack & a museum
John MacLeod, Resource Centre Specialist
Jennifer Duquette, Site Manager

Amherstburg: North American Black Historical Museum
277 King St., Amherstburg, ON N9V 2C7
519-736-5433, Fax: 866-622-4672, 800-713-6336
nabhm@mnsi.net
www.blackhistoricalmuseum.org
The Museum allows visitors to experience Black history through the Taylor Log Cabin, a home of escaped slaves from the United States, the Nazrey African Methodist Episcopal Church, & a Cultural Centre.
Kenn Stanton, Curator & Administrator
Lyle Browning, President
Paul Hertel, Secretary
Wava Jackson, Treasurer

Amherstburg: Park House Museum
Kings Navy Yard, 214 Dalhousie St., Amherstburg, ON N9V 1W4
519-736-2511, Fax: 519-736-2511, info@ParkHouseMuseum.com
www.parkhousemuseum.com
Other contact information: E-mail, Tours: order@ParkHouseMuseum.com
Built during the 1790s by a family of Loyalists, Park House is an example of Pièce sur Pièce log construction. The Park House Museum is open year-round to display items of historical significance to the town of Amherstburg & the surrounding area.
During the summer, tinsmithing is demonstrated in the pensioner's cottage.

Ancaster: Fieldcote Memorial Park & Museum
64 Sulphur Springs Rd., Ancaster, ON L9G 1L8
905-648-8144, Fax: 905-648-4857, fieldcote@hamilton.ca
Collection, preservation & exhibition of local history; landscaped gardens & walking trails
Lois Corey

Ancaster: Ingledale
c/o Hamilton Region Conservation Authority, PO Box 7099, Ancaster, ON L9G 3L3
416-643-2103,
c. 1812 home of Inglehart family; located at Fifty Point Conservation Area, Stoney Creek

Ancaster: Sulpher Springs Station/Dundas Valley Trail Centre
c/o Hamilton Conservation Authority, PO Box 7099, Ancaster, ON L9G 3L3
905-627-1233, Fax: 905-627-9722, 888-319-4722
dvalley@conservationhamilton.ca
www.conservationhamilton.ca
Centre is a replica of an 1800-era train station; displays/exhibits on the Niagara Escarpment, local cultural heritage & trail etiquette governing the valley's extensive, multi-use trail network; bird watching, cycling or historical tours
Paul Piett, Supt.

Ancaster: Valens Log Cabin Museum
PO Box 7099, Ancaster, ON L9G 3L3
905-659-7715,
C. 1836 restored homestead located at Valens Conservation Area, 1691 Regional Rd. 97, RR#6, Cambridge ON N1R 5S7

Appin: Ekfrid Community Museum
48 Wellington St., Appin, ON N0L 1A0
519-289-2015, Fax: 519-287-2359,
Located in the former Appin Post Office & Orange Hall; artifacts from late 1800s; open May-Aug., weekends & by request

Arnprior: Arnprior & District Museum / Musée d'Arnprior et Région
35 Madawaska St., Arnprior, ON K7S 1R6
613-623-4902, Fax: 613-623-4902,
www.arnpriormuseum.org/Museum.htm
Located in the former post office, which was built in 1896, the Arnprior & District Museum features local artifacts & photograpsh, a 1928 fire engine, a lumbering exhibit, & an early 19th century canon. The museum is open Monday to Saturday.
Janet Carlile, Curator, jcarlile@arnprior.ca

Astra: RCAF Memorial Museum / ARC Musée Commémoratif
PO Box 1000 Forces, Astra, ON K0K 3W0
613-965-7223, Fax: 613-965-7352, 866-701-7223
director@rcafmuseum.on.ca
rcafmuseum.on.ca
Social history museum dedicated to the airmen & airwomen who served in Canada's Air Force; features daily viewing of the on-going restoration of the world's only fully restored Halifax bomber aircraft; an Air Park displays 14 aircraft, 21 commemorative cairns & 5,600 "ADASTRA" granite stones; a large collection of artifacts; & a specialty gift shop; open daily May 1 - Sept. 30 Wed. - Sun.
Jodi Ann Eskritt, Curator
Chris Colton, Executive Director

Atikokan: Atikokan Centennial Museum & Historical Park
204 East Main St., Atikokan, ON P0T 1C0
807-597-6585, Fax: 807-597-6585,
atikokancentennialmuseum@bellnet.ca
Restored logging engine & train; mining & logging exhibits; Steep Rock & Caland Iron Ore Mines; local archival & art collections
Catherine Reilly, Museum Curator
Janis McIntyre, Museum Assistant

Aurora: Aurora Historical Society & Hillary House, National Historic Site
15372 Yonge St., Aurora, ON L4G 1N8
905-727-8991, ahs@aurorahs.com
www.hhahs.space4art.biz
Founded: 1963 Heritage artifacts held by the Aurora Historical Society date back over 200 years. The collections are related to the history of Aurora & to Hillary House. Hillary House, the Koffler Museum of Medicine, contains a significant collection of medical instruments.
Jennifer Steen, Manager & Curator, jennifer@aurorahs.com

Aurora: Hillary House, Koffler Museum of Medicine
15372 Yonge St., Aurora, ON L4G 1N8
905-727-8991, ahs@aurorahs.com
www.hillaryhouse.ca
Built in 1862, the house was home to 3 generations of medical doctors and their families, covering the evolution of medicine from the era of leeches and bleeding to the discovery of penicillin. Exhibits include: medicial instruments, books, papers, household furnishings, and equipment dating from the early 19th century. Open May - Aug., 9:30-4:30 daily; Sept. - Apr. by appointment only.

Aylmer: Aylmer & District Museum Association
14 East St., Aylmer, ON N5H 1W2
519-773-9723, Fax: 519-773-3445, aylmermuseum@amtelecom.net
www.amtelecom.net/~aylmermuseum
The Aylmer & District Museum Association preserves & promotes the history of Aylmer & Malahide. The museum is open from the beginning of March to the end of November.
Pat Zimmer, Curator
Jacquie Jeffery, Chair

Aylmer: Ontario Police College Museum
PO Box 1190, 10716 Hacienda Rd., Aylmer, ON N5H 2T2
519-773-5361, Fax: 519-773-5762,
Founded: 1962 Small display of police related items including speed measuring devices, breath collection & testing equipment, handcuffs & batons, police uniforms & hats, First Nations Police display, Forensics Investigative display
Rudy Gheysen, Director, 519-773-4200, rudy.gheysen@ontario.ca
Bill Stephens, Deputy Director, 519-773-4516, bill.stephens@ontario.ca

Bancroft: Bancroft Mineral Museum
c/o Bancroft and District Chamber of Commerce, PO Box 539, Bancroft, ON K0L 1C0
613-332-1513, Fax: 613-332-2119,
Located at 30 Station Street in Bancroft, the Bancroft Mineral Museum is a natural science museum which features mineral specimens collected from the local area. The museum is open year-round.

Bancroft: North Hastings Heritage Museum
PO Box 239, Station Street, Bancroft, ON K0L 1C0
613-332-1884,
Log house built in 1859; documents of North Hastings area

Barriefield: Frontenac County Schools Museum
Also known as: Schools Museum
414 Regent St., Barriefield, ON K7K 5R1
613-544-9113,
www.fcsmuseum.com/MuseumInfo.html
This community museum and archives has a geographical focus on Frontenac County and the City of Kingston, with a heritage schoolroom (1900-1920), a late 19th- and 20th-century archival collection and public elementary school records. Public programming includes costumed interpretive tours, educational programs and research assistance.

Bath: United Empire Loyalist Heritage Centre & Park
Parent: Bay of Quinte Br., United Empire Loyalist Association of Canada
54 Adolphustown Park Rd., Bath, ON K0K 2S0
613-373-2196, 1784@uel.ca
www.uel.ca
The United Empire Loyalist Heritage Centre houses the H.C. Burleigh Archives. The Heritage Centre is owned & operated by the Bay of Quinte Branch of the United Empire Loyalist Association of Canada. It is open from April to October, & by appointment at other times of the year.
Brian Tackaberry, Bay of Quinte Branch President, United Empire Loyalist Association
June Dafoe, Bay of Quinte Branch Board Governor, United Empire Loyalist Association, adafoe1@cogeco.ca
Tom Riddolls, Curator, tom@uel.ca

Beachville: Beachville District Museum
PO Box 220, 584371 Beachville Rd., Beachville, ON N0J 1A0
519-423-6497, Fax: 519-423-6935, bmchin@execulink.com
www.beachvilledistrictmuseum.ca
The Beachville District Museum features artifacts, such as Mastadon bones found on the O.J. Bond farm. The history of limestone quarries is also depicted at the museum, since the area is home to the largest open face quarries in Canada. A baseball display is featured because Beachville is the place where the first recorded baseball game in North America took place. The museum is open year round.

Beaverton: Beaver River Museum
PO Box 314, 284 Simcoe St., Beaverton, ON L0K 1A0
705-426-9641, bte.hist.soc@on.aibn.com
www.btehs.com
Founded: 1976 The Beaver River Museum consists of the Old Stone Jail, a settlers' log cabin (c.1850), & a brick house

(c.1900). The museum is open during weekends in May, June, & September, & daily, except on Tuesdays, in July & August.
Julie Everett, Curator
Ken Alsop, Archivist

Belleville: **Glanmore National Historic Site**
257 Bridge St. East, Belleville, ON K8N 1P4
613-962-2329, Fax: 613-962-6340,
mwakeling@city.belleville.on.ca
www.quinte.net/glanmore/
The restored Victoria home of the Phillips-Burrows-Faulkner families; original & period furnishings displayed in principal rooms; paintings & decorative art from the Couldery Collection on permanent exhibit; lamps from the Paul Lamp Collection, as well as other exhibits; special exhibits/events held throughout the year
Rona Rustige, Curator

Blind River: **Timber Village Museum**
PO Box 628, 180 Leacock St., Blind River, ON P0R 1B0
705-356-7544, Fax: 705-356-7343,
museum@blindriver.ca
www.blindriver.com/museum
Other contact information: Year round: 705/356-2251
Provides guest with a sense of what a lumberjack's life was like at the turn of the last century; displays include axes, saws, logging tools & a portable forge; art gallery which exhibits works of contemporary local artists & artisans; workshops, children's educational programmes; lumberjack dinner, 1st Sat. in Oct.; open all year round.
Christine Clark, Curator/Manager
Ken Corbiere, Clerk Administrator/Treasurer

Bobcaygeon: **Kawartha Settlers' Village**
85 Dunn St., Bobcaygeon, ON K0M 1A0
705-738-6163,
settlersvillage@nexicom.net
www.kawartha.net/~bobcom/ksv.htm
Twelve historic homes & buildings collected on former Kawartha farm; regional arts & heritage centre offering courses in the Arts
Shane Maclean, President

Borden: **Base Borden Military Museum**
Canadian Forces Base Borden, PO Box 1000 Main, 27 Ram St., Borden, ON L0M 1C0
705-423-3531, Fax: 705-423-3623,
beaton.sl@forces.gc.ca
www.borden.forces.gc.ca/998/89/46/91-eng.asp
The Base Borden Military Museum consists of several buildings & a memorial park. It features the history of CFB Borden, with a collection of armoured vehicles, artillery pieces, trucks, & aircraft from World War I, World War II, & the present. As the birthplace of the Canadian Air Force, Base Borden also displays the Avro 504 K aircraft, a Tiger Moth, a Silver Star, & a Tutor aricraft.

Bothwell: **Fairfield Museum**
14878 Longwoods Rd., RR#3, Bothwell, ON K0P 1C0
519-692-4397,
fairfield.museum@sympatico.ca
Site of Moravian Delaware mission, est. 1792, destroyed 1813 by US soldiers; artifacts from burnt village

Bowmanville: **Clarington Museums & Archives**
Municipality of Clarington, 62 Temperance St., Bowmanville, ON L1C 3A8
905-623-2734, Fax: 905-623-5684,
info@claringtonmuseums.com
www.claringtonmuseums.com
Comprised of Bowmanville Museum, Clarke Museum, Sarah Jane Williams Heritage Centre; depicts the early urban & rural roots of the Municipality of Clarington; special collections including Dominion Pianos & Organs; one of the largest doll collections in Canada
Martha Rutherford Conrad, Administrator,
claringtonmuseums@rogers.com

Bracebridge: **Woodchester Villa**
PO Box 376, 15 King St., Bracebridge, ON P1L 1T7
705-645-5501, Fax: 705-645-0385,
info@octagonalhouse.com
www.octagonalhouse.com
Woodchester Villa is an octagonal house museum, which dates back to 1882. The house is designated as a historic site, under the Ontario Heritage Act. Woodchester Villa is open from Canada Day to Labour Day.

Brampton: **Lorne Scots Regimental Museum**
The Armoury, 2 Chapel St., Brampton, ON L6W 2H1
905-451-5724, Fax: 905-454-1533,
goodmanav@sweb.net
Located on 48 John St.

Brantford: **Bell Homestead National Historic Site**
94 Tutela Heights Rd., Brantford, ON N3T 1A1
519-756-6220, Fax: 519-759-5975,
bellhomestead@brantford.ca
www.bellhomestead.ca
Displays at the Bell Homestead National Historic Site depict the 1870 to 1881 household of Alexander Graham Bell, the invention of the telephone, & the origins of Canadian telephone operations.
Brian Wood, Curator
Lorie Steiner, Chair

Brantford: **Brant Museum & Archives**
c/o Brant Historical Society, 57 Charlotte St., Brantford, ON N3T 2W6
519-752-2483, Fax: 519-752-1931,
information@brantmuseums.ca
www.brantmuseum.ca
Operated by the Brant Historical Society, the Brant Museum & Archives collects, preserves, researches, & exhibits items related to the founding, settlement, & diversity of Brant County & the surrounding area. Researchers will discover items such as photographs, diaries, letters, & maps in the archive collection. The museum & archives is open year round.
Stacey McKellar, Curator

Brantford: **Myrtleville House Museum**
34 Myrtleville Dr., Brantford, ON N3V 1C2
519-752-3216, Fax: 519-752-0396,
myrtleville@myrtleville.ca
www.myrtleville.ca
One of the oldest homes in Brant County (1837); the museum also promotes interactive learning and provide hands-on activities to aid students in explore the heritage of the county. Open year-round Monday-Friday 9-4 and Sat/Sun 1-4 in July and August.

Brighton: **Presqu'ile Provincial Park**
RR#4, Brighton, ON K0K 1H0
613-475-2204, Fax: 613-475-4324,
One of Ontario's oldest provincial parks (1922); displays & programs of early history of the area; working lighthouse

Brighton: **Proctor House Museum (SOHO)**
Also known as: **Save Our Heritage Organization**
PO Box 578, 96 Young St., Brighton, ON K0K 1H0
613-475-2144, Fax: 613-475-2144,
proctorhousemuseum@sympatico.ca
www3.sympatico.ca/proctorhousemuseum/
Living museum: 1860s gentleman's home, completely furnished; open daily July & August for tours; or by appt. The Brighton Barn Theatre is housed in the Proctor-Simpson Barn adjacent to the property.
Anna Rittwage, President

Brockville: **Brockville Museum**
5 Henry St., Brockville, ON K6V 6M4
613-342-4397, Fax: 613-342-7345,
info@brockvillemuseum.com
www.brockvillemuseum.com
Founded: 1981 The Brockville Museum is committed to preserving and promoting the history of Brockville through quality exhibits and education programs.
Bonnie Burke, Director, 613-342-4397,
bburke@brockville.com

Bruce Mines: **Bruce Mines Museum**
PO Box 220, 75 Taylor St, Bruce Mines, ON P0R 1C0
705-785-3426, Fax: 705-785-3170,
www.brucemines.ca
Founded: 1961 Situated in a church built in 1894, the Bruce Mines Museum features pioneer items such as an 1876 slot machine, a Victorian doll house, & a Yakaboo canoe.

Burgessville: **Thames Valley Museum School**
PO Box 37, 656 Main St. North, Burgessville, ON N0J 1C0
519-424-9964, Fax: 519-242-9964,
info@museumschool.ca
www.museumschool.ca
1905 Baronial-style two-room schoolhouse; one classroom is restored to reflect the first quarter of the 20th century; the other is a gallery for changing exhibits on educational history; tours, educational programs, archives
Sharon Meek, Curator
Ken Riehl, Chair

Burlington: **Ireland House at Oakridge Farm (Museums)**
2168 Guelph Line, Burlington, ON L7P 5A8
905-332-9888, Fax: 905-332-1714, 800-374-2099
www.museumsofburlington.com
Home of Joseph Ireland, built between 1835 & 1837; open year round
Barbara Teatero

Burlington: **Joseph Brant Museum**
1240 North Shore Blvd. East, Burlington, ON L7S 1C5
905-634-3556, Fax: 905-634-4498, 888-748-5386
www.museumsofburlington.com
Founded: 1942 The museum is a replica of the original 1800 home of Mohawk, Captain Joseph Brant, "Thayendanegea"; exhibits relating to indigeneous culture, with emphasis on the Iroquois; history of Burlington; historical costume exhibit, one of Ontario's finest collection of Victorian clothing & accessories; open year round,
Barbara Teatero, Director of Museums,
teaterob@burlington.ca

Caledonia: **Edinburgh Square Heritage & Cultural Centre**
Also known as: **Edinburgh Square**
PO Box 2056, 80 Caithness St. East, Caledonia, ON N3W 2G6
905-765-3134, Fax: 905-765-3009,
esquare.centre@haldimandcounty.on.ca
Artifacts relating to Town of Haldimand, from pioneer times to 1970s; open year round
Anne Unyi, Curator

Campbellford: **Campbellford-Seymour Heritage Centre**
Campbellford-Seymour Heritage Society, PO Box 1294, 113 Front St. North, Campbellford, ON K0L 1L0
705-653-2634,
csheritage@persona.ca
www.csheritage.org
Founded: 1989 The Campbellford-Seymour Heritage Centre is the home of the Campbellford-Seymour Heritage Society. The Society preserves & communicates the history of Campbellford / Seymour, maintains local archives, & assists with genealogical research.
Anne Linton, Contact

Cannington: **Cannington Historical Museum**
c/o Cannington Historical Society, Cannington Town Hall, PO Box 196, 38 Laidlaw St. South, Cannington, ON L0E 1E0
705-432-3136,
canningtonsecretary@brockhistoricalsocieties.ca
www.brockhistoricalso cieties.ca
Other contact information: E-mail, President:
canningtonpresident@brockhistoricalsocieties.ca
Located in Cannington's MacLeod Park on Peace Street, the Cannington Historical Museum features the following buildings: log homes (circa 1827 & 1857), an 1871 Canadian Northern Railway station, a 1929 Canadian National Railway caboose, the 1934 Derryville (LOL) Hall, & a driving shed. The museum is open from Victoria Day to Labour Day, or by appointment.
Ted Foster, President
Ray Lush, Vice-President
Margaret Crammond, Secretary
Cheryl Dillon, Publicist

Carleton Place: **Victoria School Museum**
267 Edmund St., Carleton Place, ON K7C 3E8
613-253-1395,
Local history of Carleton Place & Beckwith Township

Cayuga: **Haldimand County Museum & Archives**
PO Box 38, 8 Echo St., Cayuga, ON N0A 1E0
905-772-5880, Fax: 905-772-1725,
museum.archives@haldimandcounty.on.ca
tourism.haldimandcounty.on.ca/muse ums/hcmuseum.html
Temporary & permanent exhibits; 1835 log cabin on site; regional & genealogical archives
Jennifer Tigert, Curator

Chapleau: **Chapleau Centennial Museum**
Also known as: **Chapleau Museum & Tourist Information Centre**
PO Box 129, 94 Monk St., Chapleau, ON P0M 1K0
705-864-1122, Fax: 705-864-2138,
salvador@township.chapleau.on.ca
www.chapleau.ca
Founded: 1967 Located in Centennial Park, on Monk St. in Chapleau; tourist information centre; mineral collection, mounted animals, material related to Chapleau & area; archives; educational programming; bilingual services; special needs facilities; picnic area; open May 15 - Oct. 15

Chatham: **Chatham Railroad Museum**
PO Box 434, 2 McLean St., Chatham, ON N7M 5K5
519-352-3097,
CKtourism@chatham-kent.ca
www.chatham-kent.ca
Located in a CN baggage car built in 1955; contains early railroad equipment, several model trains & other memorabilia; open May through Labour Day, with group tours available all year round
Gary Shurgold

Chatham: **Chatham-Kent Museum**
Chatham Cultural Centre, 75 William St. North, Chatham, ON N7M 4L4
519-360-1998, Fax: 519-354-4170,
CKccc@chatham-kent.ca
www.chatham-kent.ca
Local history museum & archives; features a retrospective of Chatham-Kent during first half of 20th century; special exhibitions gallery with changing displays throughout year; open daily
David Benson, Heritage Co-ordinator

***Chatham:* Milner Heritage House**
c/o Chatham-Kent Museum, 75 William St. North, Chatham, ON N7M 4L4
519-360-1998, Fax: 519-354-4170,
ckccc@chatham-kent.ca
www.chatham-kent.ca
Founded: 1943 Museum depicts the turn-of-the-century lifestyle of Robert Milner, a successful, local industrialist and carriage maker; also features award-winning artwork by Robert's wife Emma; second floor features the Rev. Sandys bird collection & the MacPhail exotic animal collection
MS Stephanie Suitor, Curator

***Cheltenham:* The Great War Flying Museum**
Brampton Airport, PO Box 27, 13691 McLaughlin Rd., RR#1, Cheltenham, ON L7C 3L7
905-838-4936,
info@GreatWarFlyingMuseum.com
www.greatwarflyingmuseum.com
Volunteer group builds, maintains & flies WWI replica fighter aircraft; artifacts from WWI

***Cloyne:* Cloyne Pioneer Museum**
***Parent:* The Cloyne & District Historical Society**
PO Box 228, Hwy. 41, Cloyne, ON K0H 1K0
613-336-2203,
pioneer@mazinaw.on.ca
www.mazinaw.on.ca/pioneerclub/
Artifacts from the pioneer days of the area including tools, clothing, kitchen and other households effects, glass bottles, flat irons, a rolling pin made from a block of solid maple, photos and old catalogues; genealogical archive. Located across from the Post Office in Cloyne
Margaret Axford, Co-Chair
Carolyn McCulloch, Co-Chair

***Cobalt:* Cobalt Mining Museum**
***Also known as:* Northern Ontario Mining Museum**
PO Box 215, 24 Silver St., Cobalt, ON P0J 1C0
705-679-8301, Fax: 705-679-1151,
cnomchin@ntl.sympatico.ca
www.museumsnorth.org/cobalt_mining/
Founded: 1953 The museum preserves the world's largest collection of native silver ore, mining & prospecting equipment & artifacts, & fluorescent rock; other displays highlight the early cultural & social life of Cobalt; unique, handcrafted silver jewelry available in the gift shop; underground tours of the Colonial Adit can be arranged. Open all year.
R.M. Holdsworth, Chairman

***Cochrane:* Cochrane Railway & Pioneer Museum**
PO Box 490, 210 Railway St., Cochrane, ON P0L 1C0
705-272-4361, Fax: 705-272-6068,
lise@puc.net
www.town.cochrane.on.ca
Located across from the train station in Cochrane; railway artifacts & memorabilia, photographs, displays
Paul Latondress, Curator

***Coldwater:* Coldwater Canadiana Heritage Museum**
***Also known as:* Woodrow Homestead**
PO Box 125, 1474 Woodrow Rd., Coldwater, ON L0K 1E0
705-835-5032,
dougbi@sympatico.ca
www.coldwaterheritagemuseum.com
1840s log house & other buildings; open May - Oct.
Richard Jolliffe, President

***Collingwood:* The Collingwood Museum**
PO Box 556, 45 St. Paul St., Collingwood, ON L9Y 4B2
705-445-4811, Fax: 705-445-9004,
museum@collingwood.ca
www.collingwood.ca/museum
Located in the "Station"; large collection relating to history of Collingwood & area; exhibits showcasing shipping & shipbuilding & early history; archival materials & special events & activities throughout the year
Anita Miles, Manager

***Comber:* Comber & District Historical Society**
PO Box 158, RR#2, 8840 Hwy. 77, Comber, ON N0P 1J0
519-687-3332,
Pioneer articles & agricultural items; admission by donation; open Thu.-Mon.
Lila McFadden, Sec.-Treas.
Ralph Mellow, President
Kenneth Cranston, Vice-President

***Combermere:* Madonna House Pioneer Museum**
2888 Dafoe Rd., RR#2, Combermere, ON K0J 1L0
613-756-3713, Fax: 613-756-0211,
combermere@madonnahouse.org
www.madonnahouse.org
Founded: 1967 History of early settlers in the area; located in century-old barn
Carolyn Desch, Contact, registrar@madonnahouse.org

***Commanda:* Commanda Heritage Centre**
4077 Hwy. 522, Commanda, ON P0H 1J0
705-729-2113,
commplex@vianet.ca
www.visitamuseum.com
Complete with original shelves, counter & floor from the 1870s; features artifacts from 1870s - 1930s as well as a gift shops which features work from the region; tea room; open daily mid-June - mid-Oct.

***Cornwall:* Cornwall Community Museum**
PO Box 773, 160 Water St. West, Cornwall, ON K6H 5T5
613-936-0842,
ian10@bellnet.ca
Loyalist & local history archives, local domestic manufacturing; open year round, Wed.-Sun.
Ian Bowering, Curator

***Cornwall Island:* Ronathahon:ni Cultural Centre**
RR#3, Cornwall Island, ON K6H 5R7
613-932-9452, Fax: 613-932-0092,
nnate@glen-net.ca
Iroquois, Cree & Ojibwa artifacts

***Cumberland:* Cumberland Heritage Village Museum**
PO Box 159, 2940 Queen St., Cumberland, ON K4C 1E6
613-833-3059, Fax: 613-830-3061,
cumberlandmuseum@ottawa.ca
Representation of a rural village in the Lower Ottawa Valley, with artifacts related to period of 1880-1935; open year round

***Delhi:* Delhi Ontario Tobacco Museum & Heritage Centre**
200 Talbot Rd., Delhi, ON N4B 2A2
519-582-0278, Fax: 519-582-0122,
tobacco.museum@norfolkcounty.on.ca
www.norfolkcounty.on.ca
Tobacco-related machinery; a ginseng exhibit; multicultural exhibits & street scene depicting five historic buildings at turn of the 20th century; a large pavilion complete with barbecues is available in Quance Park nearby
Judy A. Livingstone, Curator/Director
Tanya Zajac, Asst. Curator

***Delhi:* Teeterville Pioneer Museum**
c/o Delhi Ontario Tobacco Museum & Heritage Centre, 200 Talbot Rd., Delhi, ON N4B 2A2
519-582-0278, Fax: 519-582-0122,
teeterville.museum@norfolkcounty.on.ca
Other contact information: Victoria Day - Labour Day: 519/443-4400
Site location: 194 Teeter St., Teeterville ON
Judy A. Livingstone, Curator/Director
Tanya Zajac, Asst. Curator

***Delta:* The Old Stone Mill, National Historic Site (DMS)**
***Also known as:* The Delta Mill Society**
PO Box 172, Delta, ON K0E 1G0
613-928-2584, Fax: 613-928-2584,
info@deltamill.org
www.deltamill.org
Stone mill c. 1810. Part of the Family of National Historic Sites;the oldest surviving automatic stone grist mill in Ontario; showcases milling technology and 1800s industrial heritage; artifacts include buhr millstones, 48 inch Swain turbines, roller mills.
Dr. Paul Fritz, President

***Dresden:* Uncle Tom's Cabin Historic Site (UTCHS)**
***Also known as:* Uncle Tom's Cabin**
29251 Uncle Tom's Rd., Dresden, ON N0P 1M0
519-683-2978, Fax: 519-683-1256,
utchs@heritagetrust.on.ca
www.uncletomscabin.org
Uncle Tom's Cabin educates visitors about fugitive slaves in the Dresden area. The site focuses on the life of the Reverend Josiah Henson, who was a slave who escaped with his family to Upper Canada, via the Underground Railroad. The grounds feature the following attractions: the Josiah Henson Interpretive Centre, the North Star Theatre, the Underground Railroad Freedom Gallery, the Harris House, a smokehouse, a sawmill, the Josiah Henson House, a pioneer church, & the Henson Family Cemetery. Uncle Tom's Cabin Historic Site is open from mid May to the end of October. At other times of the year, groups of twenty or more may make an appointment.
Steven Cook, Curator

***Dryden:* Dryden & District Museum**
15 Van Horne Ave., Dryden, ON P8N 2A5
807-223-4671, Fax: 807-223-7354,
lgardner@dryden.ca
First Nations & pioneer artifacts; minerals; archival material

***Dundas:* Dundas Historical Society Museum**
139 Park St. West, Dundas, ON L9H 1X8
905-627-7412, Fax: 905-627-4872,
mail@dundasmuseum.ca
www.dundasmuseum.ca
Celebrates & preserves the story of the Dundas community; museum features true to life displays, & a diversified collection of exhibits reflecting the varied occupations & activities of those who have contributed to the development of the community
Carolyn Westoby, Curator

***Dunvegan:* The Glengarry Pioneer Museum**
***Also known as:* Dunvegan Museum**
#30, 1645 County Rd., RR#1, Dunvegan, ON K0C 1J0
613-527-5230,
info@glengarrypioneermuseum.ca
www.glengarrypioneermuseum.ca
1840 log inn; miniature cheese factory; 1869 municipal hall; carriage shed & log barn; blacksmith shop
Jennifer Black, Curator

***Ear Falls:* Ear Falls District Museum**
PO Box 309, Ear Falls, ON P0V 1T0
807-222-3624, Fax: 807-222-2384,
eftownship@ear-falls.com
www.ear-falls.com
Dedicated to the history of exploration, transportation, & the settlement of the area

***Egmondville:* The Van Egmond House**
***Also known as:* The Van Egmond Foundation**
PO Box 1033, 80 Kippen Rd., Egmondville, ON N0K 1W0
519-522-0413,
vanegmondfd@tcc.on.ca
www.huroneast.com/images/doorsopen/Egmondville/VanEgmondHouse.pdf
Restored & furnished Georgian county-manor house dating to the mid-19th century with antiques indicitive of the time; founded by Constant Van Egmond.

***Elgin:* Jones Falls Defensible Lockmaster's House & Blacksmith Shop**
PO Box 10, Elgin, ON K0G 1E0
613-359-5377, Fax: 613-359-6042,
Lockmaster's house c. 1841; blacksmith shop produces hardware c. 1843
Sandy Haining, Sector Supervisor

***Elgin:* Kingston Mills Blockhouse**
PO Box 10, Elgin, ON K0G 1E0
613-359-5377, Fax: 613-359-6042, 800-230-0016
1840s animated militia barracks
A.J. \Sandy\"""" Haining, Sector Supervisor

***Elk Lake:* Elk Lake Heritage Museum**
c/o Corporation of Township of James, PO Box 70, Elk Lake, ON P0J 1G0
705-678-2237, Fax: 705-678-2495,
History of area, in particular, mining, lumbering, agriculture
Lionel Venne, Chair

***Elliot Lake:* Elliot Lake Nuclear & Mining Museum**
Lester B. Pearson Centre, Hwy. 108, Elliot Lake, ON P5A 2T1
705-848-2084, Fax: 705-848-0545,
darla.hennessey@city.elliotlake.on.ca
Mining heritage; northern home of the Canadian Mining Hall of Fame; Dr. Franc Joubin Mineral Collection; open Sept. - June, Mon.-Fri.; July - Aug., daily

***Emo:* Rainy River District Women's Institute Museum**
***Also known as:* Emo Women's Institute Museum**
PO Box 511, Emo, ON P0W 1E0
807-482-2007, Fax: 807-482-2556,
Small pioneer museum; open mid May - Oct.; other times by appointment

***Englehart:* Englehart & Area Historical Museum**
PO Box 444, 67 - 6th Ave., Englehart, ON P0J 1H0
705-544-2400, Fax: 705-544-8737,
eahmchin@ntl.sympatico.ca
museumsnorth.org
Exhibits show how settlement along the Temiskaming & Northern Ontario railway created town of Englehart & brought homesteaders to the claybelt's rural communites, 1900-1950; open May 1 - Dec. 1 & exhibition room
Bonnie Rozell-Shortt, Manager, 705-544-2400

***Exeter:* Arkona Lions Museum & Information Centre**
c/o Ausable Bayfield Conservation Authority, 71108 Morrison Line, RR#3, Exeter, ON N0M 1S5
519-828-3071, Fax: 519-235-1963,
info@abca.on.ca
www.abca.on.ca
Arkona Lions Museum & Information Centre features local First Nations artifacts, Devonian era fossils, minerals, & semi-precious stone.
Tom Prout, General Manager, tprout@abca.on.ca

***Fenelon Falls:* Fenelon Falls Museum**
PO Box 179, 50 Oak St., Fenelon Falls, ON K0M 1N0

705-887-1044, Fax: 705-887-1532,
maryboro2003@yahoo.ca
www.maryboro.ca
Open daily June 15 - Labour Day; weekends only May 20-June 15 & Labour Day to Thanksgiving
Ali Scott, Curator

Fergus: **Wellington County Museum & Archives**
RR#1, 0536 County Rd. 18, Fergus, ON N1M 2W3
519-846-0916, Fax: 519-846-9630, 800-663-0750
info@wcm.on.ca
www.wcm.on.ca
Other contact information: Museum: 519-846-0916, ext. 5221; Archives: 519-846-0916, ext. 5225
The Wellington County Museum reflects the history of Wellington County people. The museum is housed in the former House of Industry & Refuge, which was built in 1877. Permanent exhibits include a World War I military exhibit, a pioneer log cabin, a 1920s kitchen, & textiles. The archives feature historical & genealogical records which date back to the first settlement in Wellington County. The Couling Collection consists of architectural information.
Bonnie Callen, Administrator, bonniec@wcm.on.ca
Susan Dunlop, Curator MA, susan@wcm.on.ca
Karen Wagner, Archivist BA, MLS, karen@wcm.on.ca
Patty Whan, Conservator, patty@wcm.on.ca
Libby Walker, Coordinator, Activities, libbyw@wcm.on.ca

Flesherton: **South Grey Museum & Historical Library**
PO Box 299, Flesherton, ON N0C 1E0
519-924-2843, Fax: 519-986-3643,
museum@greyhighlands.ca
www.greyhighlandsmuseum.com
Open Tues. - Sat. end of June - Labour Day, or by appt; Open Thurs. - Sat. Labour Day - June.
Sarah Redmond, Curator

Forest: **Forest-Lambton Museum**
PO Box 707, 59 Broadway St., Forest, ON N0N 1J0
519-786-3239,
www.lambtononline.com/forest_lambton
Local artifacts including doll collection; flax industry; early telephone equipment; Grand Truck Railroad; First Nation's Artifacts; pictures & documents from the 1800s
Sylvia Freeman, Secretary
Ken Kingdon, President

Fort Erie: **Mildred M. Mahoney Silver Jubilee Dolls' House Gallery**
657 Niagara Blvd., Fort Erie, ON L2A 3H9
905-871-5833, Fax: 905-871-2447,
mahoneydollhouse@bellnet.ca
www.mahoneydollhouse.com
Founded: 1983 Collection of miniatures & dollhouses spanning from 1730-1990; housed in historic Bertie Hall which was part of the Underground Railroad
MS Julie Rivet, Assistant Curator

Fort Frances: **Fort Frances Museum & Cultural Centre**
259 Scott St., Fort Frances, ON P9A 1G8
807-274-7891, Fax: 807-274-4103,
phawley@fort-frances.com
www.fort-frances.com/museum
The community museum is housed in an 1898 school house. The exhibits of the Fort Frances Museum & Cultural Centre reflect the development of Fort Frances & the Rainy River District from pre-contact to present day.
Pam Hawley, Curator

Frankville: **Maple Sugar House & Museum**
41 Leacock Rd., RR#1, Frankville, ON K0E 1H0
613-275-2893, Fax: 613-275-1839, 877-440-7887
mail@gibbonsmaple.com
www.gibbonsmaple.com
The House produces & sells maple syrup, maple sugar, maple butter & other maple products. As well, there displays from the past and present of maple syrup making equipment. Tours are offered.

Gananoque: **Gananoque Museum**
PO Box 100, 30 King St. East, Gananoque, ON K7G 2T6
613-382-4024, Fax: 613-382-8587,
Open mid-June - mid-Sept., Mon. - Sun.

Gloucester: **Gloucester Museum**
4550B Bank St., Gloucester, ON K1G 3W6
613-822-2076,
Domestic ware; agricultural implements; Gloucester History Society archives; City of Gloucester archives

Goderich: **Huron County Museum & Historic Gaol**
110 North St., Goderich, ON N7A 2T8
519-524-2686, Fax: 519-524-1922,
mail@huroncountymuseum.on.ca
www.huroncounty.ca/museum
Local history including transportation, military, agriculture & furniture
Claus Breede

Golden Lake: **Golden Lake Algonquin Museum**
PO Box 1657A Mishomis Inamo, Golden Lake, ON K0J 1X0
613-625-2823, Fax: 613-625-2332,
mgr.economicdevelopment@pikwakanagan.ca
Algonquin artifacts; domestic & ornamental artifacts of the early settlers

Gore Bay: **Western Manitoulin Island Historical Society Museum**
PO Box 298, Gore Bay, ON P0P 1H0
705-282-2420,
Canadian 19th century artifacts, including historical & documentary art; open Mar.-Nov.

Gormley: **Whitchurch-Stouffville Museum**
14732 Woodbine Ave., Gormley, ON L0H 1G0
905-727-8954, Fax: 905-727-1282, 888-290-0337
wsmuseum@townofws.com
www.townofws.com/museum
Founded: 1971 The museum is located in the hamlet of Vandorf & includes the Bogarttown Schoolhouse, a restored 1850 log cabin, the Brown House, barn, & the Vandorf Public School; special events & programming, tours, craft workshops, & research material. Open year round.
Stephanie Foley, Curator

Gowganda: **Gowganda & Area Museum**
Lot 12, Third St., Gowganda, ON P0J 1J0
705-624-3171,
Silver mining displays; log cabin; research library & resource centre; open mid-May - mid-Sept.

Grafton: **Barnum House Museum**
PO Box 161, 10568 Country Rd. 2, Grafton, ON K0K 2G0
905-349-2656, Fax: 905-349-3357,
barnum@heritagetrust.on.ca
www.heritagefdn.on.ca
Owned by the Ontario Heritage Trust, Barnum House was built in 1819. The home is an example of Neo-Classical architecture. The decor of Barnum House reflects an Upper Canada home between 1820 & 1840. Barnum House Museum is open from June to Labour Day.
Wayne Kelly, Manager, Public Education & Community Development, 416-314-4913

Grand Bend: **Lambton Heritage Museum**
RR#2, 10035 Museum Rd., Grand Bend, ON N0M 1T0
519-243-2600, Fax: 519-243-2600,
heritage.museum@county-lambton.on.ca
Eight buildings on a 30 acre site; extensive collection of pressed glass & Currier & Ives prints; features history of Sarnia-Lambton area including large collection of agricultural implements

Gravenhurst: **Bethune Memorial House National Historic Site**
235 John St. North, Gravenhurst, ON P1P 1G4
705-687-4261, Fax: 705-687-4935,
ont-bethune@pch.gc.ca
www.pc.gc.ca/bethune
At the Bethune Memorial House National Historic Site, the life & achievements of Dr. Henry Norman Bethune are commemorated. The house is his birthplace. Dr. Bethune is recognized for his time in China, where he served as a surgeon & a teacher. The site is open from June 1st to October 31st. At other times, group tours may be arranged by phone.
Scott Davidson, Site Manager

Gravenhurst: **Muskoka Boat & Heritage Centre**
275 Steamship Bay Rd., Gravenhurst, ON P1P 1Z9
705-687-2115, Fax: 705-687-9408, 866-687-6667
Muskoka Boat & Heritage Centre
www.segwun.com
The Muskoka Boat & Heritage Centre presents the history of boat-building, Muskoka's steamship era, & life on the water in Muskoka. At the site is a large in water collection of antique boats. The RMS Segwun is the oldest operating steamship in North America. The Muskoka Boat & Heritage Centre is open year-round.

Grimsby: **Grimsby Museum**
PO Box 244, 6 Murray St., Grimsby, ON L3M 4G5
905-945-5292, Fax: 905-945-0715,
museum-public@town.grimsby.on.ca
www.town.grimsby.on.ca
Founded: 1984 Owned & operated by the Town of Grimsby, the museum interprets the history of Grimsby from prehistoric times. The Gallery of the Forty explores the settlement of the United Empire Loyalists in 1787. The Grimsby museum provides educational programs, as well as local history & genealogical information. It is open year-round.
Janet Cannon, Curator

Guelph: **Guelph Civic Museum**
6 Dublin St. South, Guelph, ON N1H 4L5
519-836-1221, Fax: 519-836-5280,
museum@guelph.ca
www.guelph.ca/museum
Founded: 1967 The museum is housed in a c. 1850 limestone building and features over 30,000 artifacts and 4,000 photos relating to the istory of Guelph and area; special events and programming for children.
Katherine McCracken, Director,
katherine.mccracken@guelph.ca
Bev Dietrich, Curator, bev.dietrich@guelph.ca

Guelph: **McCrae House**
108 Water St., Guelph, ON N1G 1A6
519-836-1482, Fax: 519-836-5280,
museum@guelph.ca
www.guelph.ca/museum
Founded: 1968 The house, built in 1858, is the 1872 birthplace of John McCrae, author of "In Flanders Fields", and a National Historic Site. Exhibitions interpret McCrae's life and times, and an award-winning historic garden is maintained by volunteers. Activities include garden teas, the Poppy Push, Teddy Bear Picnic and Canada Day celebration.
Katherine McCracken, Director

Haileybury: **Haileybury Heritage Museum**
PO Box 911, 575 Main St., Haileybury, ON P0J 1K0
705-672-1922, Fax: 705-672-2551,
hhmuseum@onlink.net
Haileybury Heritiage Museum is focused on one of Canada's ten worst natural disasters, the Great Fire of 1922 which destroyed 90 percent of the Town of Haileybury & communities in 18 surrounding townships in South Temiskaming; features a restored 1904 Toronto Railway Company streetcar (used as housing after the '22 fire); a 1922 Ruggles Fire Pumper; the tugboat M.V. Beauchene & an Ontario Northlan
Sarah Bowdidge, Curator

Haliburton: **Haliburton Highlands Museum**
PO Box 535, Haliburton, ON K0M 1S0
705-457-2760,
haliburtonmuseum@halhinet.on.ca
www.haliburtonhighlands.com/museum/
Local domestic, lumbering & agricultural history; open year round

Hamilton: **Canadian Football Hall of Fame & Museum**
58 Jackson St. West, Hamilton, ON L8P 1L4
905-528-7566, Fax: 905-528-9781,
info@cfhof.ca; store@cfhof.ca
www.cfhof.ca
Founded: 1962 The Canadian Football Hall of Fame & Museum features exhibits which depict the history of the game at all levels. A special section is dedicated to the Hall of Famers.
Steve Howse, Chair
George Black, Chair, Selection Committee
Mark DeNobile, Executive Director, mark@cfhof.ca
Meghan Sturgeon, Curator, meg@cfhof.ca
Bob Morreale, Treasurer & Office Manager, rob@cfhof.ca

Hamilton: **Dundurn Castle**
610 York Blvd., Hamilton, ON L8R 3H1
905-546-2872, Fax: 905-546-2875,
dundurn@hamilton.ca
www.dundurncastle.com
Restored home of Sir Allan MacNab, one of Canada's first premiers; depiction of mid-19th century life in over 40 rooms; open year round

Hamilton: **Hamilton Children's Museum**
1072 Main St. East, Hamilton, ON L8M 1N6
905-546-4848, Fax: 905-546-4851,
childrensmuseum@hamilton.ca
www.hamilton.ca/CultureandRecreation/Arts_Culture_And_Museums
Founded: 1978 This is an interactive, hands-on learning centre that offers children the opportunity to explore a wide variety of themes from the natural sciences and arts. Closed on Mondays.
MS Karen McCartney, Curator/Site Supervisor, Education, 905-546-2424, X-1886, kmccartn@hamilton.ca

Hamilton: **Hamilton Military Museum / Le musée militaire de Hamilton**
610 York Blvd., Hamilton, ON L8R 3H1
905-546-2872, Fax: 905-546-2875,
dcchin@interlynx.net
Uniforms, weapons & lifestyle from War of 1812, Rebellion of 1837-38, the Victorian era, Boer War, & WWI; open year round

Hamilton: **Hamilton Museum of Steam & Technology**
900 Woodward Ave., Hamilton, ON L8H 7N2
905-546-4797, Fax: 905-546-4798,
steammuseum@hamilton.ca
www.hamilton.ca
The Hamilton Museum of Steam & Technology is housed in a 19th century public works building. The facility is a Civil & Power Engineering Landmark & a National Historic Site. It contains two

steam engines that pumped water to Hamilton more than 140 years ago. The museum is open year-round.

***Hamilton:* Hamilton Psychiatric Hospital Museum**
c/o St. Joseph's Mountain Health Services, PO Box 585, Hamilton, ON L8N 3K7
905-388-2511, Fax: 905-381-5601,
lmuirhea@stjosham.on.ca
www.stjosham.on.ca
With a variety of artifacts and photographs, the museum preserves the history of psychiatric care & treatment in Ontario with an emphasis on events at the Hamilton Psychiatric Hospital & in the regions it serves.
MS Betty Laird, Coordinator, Volunteer Services,
905-522-1155 X-35561

***Hamilton:* Hamilton-Scourge Project**
Dept. of Culture & Recreation, City Hall, 72 Main St. West, Hamilton, ON L8P 3T4
905-546-3967, Fax: 905-546-2338,
Research files on the Hamilton & Scourge, armed merchant schooners from the War of 1812, which capsized & lie in water off Port Dalhousie

***Hamilton:* HMCS Haida National Historic Site of Canada**
658 Catharine St. North (Pier 9), Hamilton, ON L8L 4V7
905-526-0911, Fax: 905-526-9734,
haida.info@pc.gc.ca
www.pc.gc.ca/haida
Commissioned in 1943, Canada's most famous warship, the Tribal class destroyer saw service in WWII & the Korean War

***Hamilton:* Royal Hamilton Light Infantry Heritage Museum**
John Weir Foote VC Armoury, 200 James St. North, Hamilton, ON L8R 2L1
905-528-2945,
www.rhli.ca/museum/
Military artifacts from 1830 to present, with specific reference to the Royal Hamilton Light Infantry; library
Ed Newman, Museum Administrator

***Hamilton:* Whitehern Historic House & Garden**
The McQuesten Residence, 41 Jackson St. West, Hamilton, ON L8P 1L3
905-546-2018, Fax: 905-546-4933,
whitehern@city.hamilton.on.ca
Former home of the McQuesten family from 1852 - 1968; period rooms feature original furnishings
Ken Heaman, Curator

***Hamilton:* Workers Arts & Heritage Centre (WA&HC)**
51 Stuart St., Hamilton, ON L8L 1B5
905-522-3003, Fax: 905-522-5424,
wahc@wahc-museum.ca
www.wahc-museum.ca
Other contact information: Twitter: www.twitter.com/WAHC
Located at Hamilton's former Custom House, which was built in 1860, the Workers Arts & Heritage Centre celebrates the history & culture of all working people in Canada. Exhibits include the labour movement in the Hamilton area, a history of office work, & the history of life on the shop floor, which explores Canada's early industrial days to the rise of automation in the workplace. The museum is open year-round.
Elizabeth McLuhan, Executive Director,
executivedirector@wahc-museum.ca
Fabiola De Vierna, Coordinator, Administration & Finance,
fabiola@wahc-museum.ca
Brian Kelly, Coordinator, Building & Exhibitions,
brian@wahc-museum.ca
Andrew Lochhead, Coordinator, Labour Arts,
andrew@wahc-museum.ca
Ian Walker, Coordinator, Labour Heritage,
ian@wahc-museum.ca

***Harrow:* John R. Park Homestead**
915 County Rd. 50 East, RR#1, Harrow, ON N0R 1G0
519-738-2029, Fax: 519-776-8688, 888-487-4760
jrph@erca.org
www.erca.org
Living history museum; open year round
Janet Cobban, Curator

***Holland Centre:* Comber Pioneer Village**
Rte. 3, Holland Centre, ON N0H 1R0
519-794-3467,
First log school of Holland Township; settler's cabin; log barn; replica of Martins Inn; log smoke house

***Ignace:* Ignace Heritage Centre**
PO Box 480, 36 Main St., Ignace, ON P0T 1T0
807-934-2280, Fax: 807-934-6452,
Local artifacts

***Ingersoll:* Ingersoll Cheese Factory Museum / Musée de la fabrique de fromage d'Ingersoll**
130 Oxford St., Ingersoll, ON N5C 2V5
519-485-0120, Fax: 519-485-3543,
curator@ingersoll.ca
Located in Centennial Park; 6 buildings including cheese factory museum, blacksmith shop; barn; community museum featuring spectacular woodcarved scene "pathway of the giants" & Ingersoll Sports Hall of Fame houses Harold Wilson's Miss Canada IV Speedboat; open daily July - Aug.; open weekends through May & June to Thanksgiving
Shirley Lovell, Curator

***Iron Bridge:* Iron Bridge Historical Museum**
PO Box 460, Iron Bridge, ON P0R 1H0
Pioneer artifacts

***Iroquois:* Carman House Museum**
PO Box 249, Carman Rd., Iroquois, ON K0E 1K0
613-652-4422, Fax: 613-652-4636,
mornet94@mor-net.on.ca
Other contact information: Phone, Summertime: 613-652-4808
Carman House is a United Empire Loyalist home, which was built in 1815. It is a living history museum, which reflects life in 1835. The museum is open from late June to Labour Day.

***Iroquois Falls:* Iroquois Falls Pioneer Museum**
PO Box 448, 245 Devonshire Ave., Iroquois Falls, ON P0K 1E0
705-258-3730, Fax: 705-258-3730,
akw_1594@hotmail.com
Other contact information: Phone, Tours by appointment during the off season: 705-258-3409
Founded: 1970 The Garden Town of the North is home of the Shay Train Engine, the workhorse of the logging industry. The Iroquois Falls Pioneer Museum offers many displays, including the history of a company which became the world's largest producer of pulp & paper, the general store, a telephone exhibit, a hands-on display for children, the 1916 fire, a replica of a tug boat, & the Iroquois Hotel, which was built by the company.
Alexa Wollan, President, Iroquois Falls Historical Society Bd., & Director
Michael Shea, Secretary
Ramona Pepin, Treasurer

***Kakabeka Falls:* Hymers Museum**
RR#1, Kakabeka Falls, ON P0T 1W0
807-577-4787, Fax: 807-577-4459,
lindat@tbaytel.net
Local history
Linda Turk, Contact

***Kapuskasing:* Ron Morel Memorial Museum**
88 Riverside Dr., Kapuskasing, ON P5N 1B3
705-337-4274, Fax: 705-337-1741,
Museum housed in two railway cars & a caboose headed by steam locomotive 5107; changing season exhibits & permanent displays; one railway car is devoted to trains & railway history, with a large working HO-gauge model; also have Heritage Caravan where clay sculptures depict Northern Ontario history; open daily from early June to Labour Day

***Kars:* Swords & Ploughshares Museum**
7500 Reeve Craig Rd. North, RR#1, Kars, ON K0A 2E0
613-489-3447, Fax: 613-489-1166,
swords@calnan.com
www.calnan.com/swords/
Military artifacts, 1914-present; agricultural machinery & implements, 1840-1940; open May - Oct. & by appt.

***Kenora:* Lake of the Woods Museum**
PO Box 497, 300 Main St. South, Kenora, ON P9N 3X5
807-467-2105, Fax: 807-467-2109,
museum@kmts.ca
www.lakeofthewoodsmuseum.ca
Collection of more than 20,000 articles; displays feature native & pioneer artifacts, natural history, minerals, textiles, pictorial & archival material illustrating the history of the Lake of the Woods & surrounding area
Lori Nelson, Director

***Keswick:* Georgina Pioneer Village & Archives**
26557 Civic Centre Rd., RR#2, Keswick, ON L4P 3G1
905-476-4305, Fax: 905-476-7492,
georginapioneervillage@georgina.ca
www.town.georgina.on.ca
Late 19th century historic village; interpreters & demonstrators; special exhibitions, events, tours, workshops & genealogical archives; open June-Sept., Thur.-Sun., 10-5 or by appt.
Phillip Rose-Donahoe, Manager/Curator

***Killarney:* Killarney Centennial Museum**
32 Commissioners St., Killarney, ON P0M 2A0
705-287-2424, Fax: 705-287-2660, 888-597-2721
townkill@vianet.on.ca
www.municipality.killarney.on.ca
Founded: 1967 The museum preserves historical artifacts from the time of the fur trade to the present; collection includes household items, objects from local commercial fishing, logging, mining & tourism industries, & photographs. Located at 29 Commissioners St. in Killarney. Open 6 days per week from late June to early September.
Laurier Low
Rosemarie Roque

***King City:* King Township Museum**
2920 King Rd., King City, ON L7B 1L6
905-833-2331, Fax: 905-833-2331,
kingmuseum@township.king.on.ca

***Kingston:* Bellevue House National Historic Site (BHNHS)**
35 Centre St., Kingston, ON K7L 4E5
613-545-8666, Fax: 613-545-8721,
bellevue.house@pc.gc.ca
www.pc.gc.ca/lhn-nhs/on/bellevue/index_e.asp
Other contact information: TDD: 613-545-8668
Built in the early 1840s, Bellevue House was the home of Sir John A. Macdonald. The site is closed from November to March, but groups may make reservations.

***Kingston:* Canada's Penitentiary Museum (CPM) / Musée du service correctionnel du Canada**
***Also known as:* Canada's Penitentiary Museum/Musée pénitentiaire du Canada**
PO Box 260, 555 King St. West, Kingston, ON K7L 4V8
613-530-3122, Fax: 613-536-4815,
fpm@cogeco.net
www.penitentiarymuseum.ca
To preserve & interpret the past & contemporary experiences of the people & places associated with the history of corrections in Canada; located at 555 King St. West
Dave St. Onge, Curator

***Kingston:* Cataraqui Archaeological Research Foundation/Kingston Archaeological Centre**
611 Princess St., Kingston, ON K7L 1E1
613-542-3483,
carf@carf.info
www.carf.info
Founded: 1986 The Foundation was established to oversee the excavation of Fort Frontenac, and to collect and preserve artifacts from the site. It is now involved in numerous archaeological projects at sites in Eastern Ontario, and operates the Kingston Archaeological Centre; educational programming and research collection. Open Mon to Fri, 9:30-4:00.
Sue Bazely, Executive Director

***Kingston:* Fort Henry**
***Also known as:* The Citadel of Upper Canada**
PO Box 213, Kingston, ON K7L 4V8
613-542-7388, Fax: 613-542-3054, 800-437-2233
john.robertson@forthenry.com, getaway@parks.on.ca
www.forthenry.com
The Citadel of Upper Canada, brought to life by the Fort Henry Guard; restaurant; gift stores; children's muster parades; festivals, events, historic dining
John Robertson, Manager

***Kingston:* City of Kingston Fire Department Museum**
271 Brock St., Kingston, ON K7L 1S5
www.virtualmuseum.ca
Antique firefighting equipment, photographs & models

***Kingston:* International Hockey Hall of Fame & Museum**
PO Box 82, 277 York St., Kingston, ON K7L 4V6
613-544-2355, Fax: 613-544-2844,
info@ihhof.com
www.ihhof.com
Home to 10,000 sq. feet of hockey memories; open mid-June - Labour Day, daily 10-3; off-season group tours by appt.
Larry Paquette, Vice-President
Mark Potter, President

***Kingston:* MacLachlan Woodworking Museum**
2993 Hwy. 2 East, Kingston, ON K7L 4V1
613-542-0543, Fax: 613-547-5968,
mwmuseum@cityofkingston.ca
www.cityofkingston.ca/museum
Founded: 1967 Exhibits include tools & lifestyles of 19th century tradespeople; hands-on workshops, educational programs & demonstrations are offered. The gift shop stocks handmade wooden kitchenware, linen, toys and wooden ornaments.
Annabelle Girard, Program Coordinator
Caroline Petznick, Curator

***Kingston:* Marine Museum of the Great Lakes at Kingston**
55 Ontario St., Kingston, ON K7L 2Y2
613-542-2261, Fax: 613-542-0043,
marmus@marmuseum.ca
www.marmuseum.ca
Founded: 1976 The museum showcases an original pumping station and steam engines built in 1891. Exhibits include the history of boat building, as well as Kingston's maritime history on the Great Lakes. An Eco Gallery focuses on environmental

issues related to the Great Lakes. At dock is the Alexander Henry, a icebreaking ship built in 1959.

***Kingston:* Military Communications & Electronics Museum**
PO Box 17000 Station Forces, 95 Craftsman Blvd., Highway #2, Kingston, ON K7K 7B4
613-541-4675, Fax: 613-540-8111,
staff@c-and-e-museum.org
www.c-and-e-museum.org
Preserves & inteprets the Communications & Electronics Branch military history; provides group & individual tours; responds to research requests & is available to provide expert artifact appraisals; supports community activities with mobile displays & temporary loans of artifacts
Maj. (Ret'd) Mike DeNoble, Director, 613-541-4211, denoble.mp@forces.gc.ca

***Kingston:* Miller Museum of Mineralogy & Geology**
Miller Hall, Queen's University, Kingston, ON K7L 3N6
613-533-6767, Fax: 613-533-6592,
badham@geol.queensu.ca
geol.queensu.ca/museum/
Collection of rocks, minerals & fossils from around the world; education tour programs available by request
Mark Badham, Curator

***Kingston:* Murney Tower Museum**
PO Box 54, Kingston, ON K7L 4V6
613-544-9925,
Tower, built in 1846, now houses military, agricultural, Aboriginal & early settlers' artifacts; open summer

***Kingston:* Pump House Steam Museum**
23 Ontario St., Kingston, ON K7L 2Y2
613-546-4696,
Former pumping station with artifacts relating to steam power; operating steam & pump engines

***Kingston:* The Royal Military College Museum / Le musée du Collège militaire royal du Canada**
***Also known as:* RMC Museum**
PO Box 17000 Forces, Kingston, ON K7K 7B4
613-541-6000, Fax: 613-542-3565,
mckenzie-r@rmc.ca
Housed in the Fort Frederick Martello Tower on the College grounds; holdings relate to the history of the College, the achievements of its ex-cadets & to the history of the Royal Navy Dockyard which once occupied the site; amongst the Museum's most treasured possessions is the superb Douglas Arms Collection; open daily last Sat. in June - Labour Day
Ross McKenzie, Curator
Dr. J.G. Pike, Committee Chair

***Kingsville:* Canadian Transportation Museum & Heritage Village**
6155 Arner Townline, RR#2, Kingsville, ON N9Y 2E5
519-776-6909, Fax: 519-776-8321, 866-776-6909
info@ctmhv.com
www.ctmhv.com
Located on Country Road #23 in Kingsville, Ontario, the Canadian Transportation Museum collects, restores, & exhibits modes of transportation from the mid 1800s to 1992. Examples of displays include horse drawn carts, fire trucks, & Ford Model Ts. The Heritage Village contains buildings, such as a one room schoolhouse, a train station, a log home, & a general store.
Harry Bergman, Chair

***Kingsville:* Jack Miner Museum**
c/o The Jack Miner Foundation, Kingsville, ON N9Y 2E8
Jack Miner memorabilia including wildlife prints, medals, manuscripts & newspaper clippings

***Kirkland Lake:* Museum of Northern History at the Sir Harry Oakes Chateau**
PO Box 1148, 2 Chateau Dr., Kirkland Lake, ON P2N 3M7
705-568-8800, Fax: 705-567-6611,
museum@tkl.ca
www.town.kirklandlake.ca
The Chateau, built by Sir Henry Oakes and has been preserved as a museum exhibit and is also a space to preserve northern history.
Robin Ormerod, Director/Curator
Darren Sutherland, Director, gsutherland@ns.sympatico.ca
Brian Kellock, Director, rbak@gmail.com
Allen Tobey, Director, atobey@eastlink.ca
Gerard MacIsaac, Director, gerard.macisaac@ns.sympatico.ca
Hal Maybe, Director, haroldmaybe@eastlink.ca
Kirk Munro, Director, kmunro@hotmail.com
Robert Mills, Director
Charlie Clarke, Director
Donnie Chaisson, Director
Danny Rankin, Director

***Kitchener:* Doon Heritage Crossroads**
***Also known as:* Doon Pioneer Village**
10 Huron Rd., Kitchener, ON N2P 2R7
519-748-1914, Fax: 519-748-0009,
rtom@region.waterloo.on.ca
www.region.waterloo.on.ca
Other contact information: TTY: 519/748-0537
Turn of the century living history village; open daily May - Dec.
Thomas A. Reitz, Curator/Manager

***Kitchener:* Joseph Schneider Haus Museum**
466 Queen St. South, Kitchener, ON N2G 1W7
519-742-7752, Fax: 519-742-0089,
www.region.waterloo.on.ca
Traces back to the Schneider family, one of the first group of Pennsylvania German Mennonites in the area

***Kitchener:* Woodside National Historic Site of Canada / Lieu historique national de Woodside**
528 Wellington St. North, Kitchener, ON N2H 5L5
519-571-5684, Fax: 519-571-5686, 888-773-8888
ont-woodside@pc.gc.ca
www.pc.gc.ca/lhn-nhs/on/woodside/index.aspx
Woodside National Historic Site was the childhood home of Canada's longest-serving Prime Minister, William Lyon Mackenzie King. Today, the house is restored to the Victorian era of the 1890s. The site is open from mid May to late December. Groups may reserve tours during the off season.
Kim Seward-Hannam, Supt.

***Komoka:* Komoka Railway Museum Inc.**
PO Box 22, 133 Queen St., Komoka, ON N0L 1R0
519-657-1912, Fax: 519-657-6791,
komokarailmuseum@aol.com
www.komokarailmuseum.ca
Restored railroad station; site includes 1913 Shay logging locomotive, 1939 CN baggage car, 1972 caboose & a collection of CN maintenance jiggers

***Lakefield:* Christ Church Community Museum**
c/o St. John the Baptist Anglican Church, PO Box 217, Lakefield, ON K0L 2H0
705-652-8302, Fax: 705-652-8702,
stjohnslakefield@nexicom.net
stjohnslakefield.ca
History of Lakefield, & the Strickland family; The Bill Twist Collection; display of old toys, dolls & doll furniture, cards; open 1:00-4:00 daily

***Lanark:* Lanark & District Museum**
80 George St., Lanark, ON K0G 1K0
613-259-5350,
www.lanarkhighlands.ca/Community/Museums/Lanark.htm
Open weekends, mid-May to mid-Oct.

***Lanark:* Middleville & District Museum**
PO Box 6, Wolf Grove Rd (city rd.16), Lanark, ON K0G 1K0
613-259-5462, Fax: 613-259-2291,
alice006@sympatico.ca
Local pioneer artifacts including items for the maple syrup, cheese & lumbering industries; open May 24-Thanksgiving
Mary Dixon, Chairperson, gdixon@perth.igs.net

***Latchford:* House of Memories**
PO Box 82, Latchford, ON P0J 1N0
705-676-2417,
Local artifacts from 1900-1940; WWI & WWII items; natural history exhibits

***Leamington:* Point Pelee National Park of Canada, Visitor Centre, DeLaurier Historical House, & Trail / Parc national du Canada de la Pointe-Pelée**
407 Monarch Lane, RR#1, Leamington, ON N8H 3V4
519-322-2365, Fax: 519-322-1277, 888-773-8888
pelee.info@pc.gc.ca
www.pc.gc.ca./pelee
Other contact information: TTY: 1-866-787-6221
Located at the southern tip of Canada, Point Pelee National Park features the DeLaurier Historical House. The homestead & barn depict the park's human & cultural heritage. The Visitor Centre houses exhibits, a children's discovery room, & theatre programs about the area's natural & cultural heritage.

***Limehouse:* Canadian Military Studies Museum**
Lot 23, Conc. 6, RR#1, Limehouse, ON L0P 1H0
905-877-6522,
durangedhemi@sympatico.ca
The Canadian Military Studies Museum features artifacts from the mid-17th century, the Boer War, World War I, & World War II, to the Korean & Vietnam Wars.

***Lindsay:* Old Lindsay Jail**
***Parent:* Victoria County Historical Society**
PO Box 187, 50 Victoria Ave. North, Lindsay, ON K9V 4S1
705-324-3404, Fax: 705-324-1805,
info@oldejailmusem.ca
www.oldejailmuseum.com
The Lindsay Jail, built in 1863, was historically known as the County Gaol. The Victoria County Historical Society collects, preserves, & exhibits the history of the County of Victoria.
John Macklem, President

***Little Current:* Centennial Museum of Sheguiandah**
Postal Bag 2000, Little Current, ON P0P 1K0
705-368-2367, Fax: 705-368-0761,
shegmus@vianet.ca
Founded: 1967 pioneer culture & history on Manitoulin Island
Heidi Ferguson, Curator

***London:* Eldon House**
481 Ridout St. North, London, ON N6A 2P8
519-661-0333, Fax: 519-661-2559,
ramurray@museumlondon.ca
www.londonmuseum.on.ca
House of the Harris family from 1834-1959
Brian Meehan, Executive Director

***London:* Fanshawe Pioneer Village (FPV)**
2609 Fanshawe Park Rd. East, London, ON N5X 4A1
519-457-1296, Fax: 519-457-3364,
info@fanshawepioneervillage.ca
www.fanshawepioneervillage.ca
Costumed interpreters demonstrate life in mid-1800s to early 1900s rural Ontario crossroads community
Sheila A. Johnson, Executive Director
Shanna Dunlop, Curator & Head of Operations

***London:* First Hussars: Citizen Soldiers Museum**
399 Ridout St. North, London, ON N6A 2P1
519-471-1538,
www.firsthussars.ca/museum.html
Follows the history of the 1st Hussars from 1856 until today; includes material on the Boer War, the Great War & WWII
Alastair Neely, Curator

***London:* Grosvenor Lodge**
1017 Western Rd., London, ON N6G 1G5
519-645-2845, Fax: 519-645-0981,
hlfgl@golden.net
www.grosvenorlodge.com
1853 estate; operates as London Regional Resource Centre for Heritage & the Environment, administered by the Heritage London Foundation; resources available on heritage & environmental issues; venue for meetings, seminars & social events; library & display areas open to public; open Mon.-Fri. 9-4

***London:* Guy Lombardo Music Centre**
205 Wonderland Rd. South, London, ON N6K 3T3
519-473-9003, Fax: 519-473-9003,
seventyeights@aol.com
Memorabilia relating to bandleader & his band, the Royal Canadians, including original recordings & videotapes; open June-Aug., Wed.-Sun., 11-7; Sept. 12:30-4:30 or by appt.

***London:* London Regional Children's Museum**
21 Wharncliffe Rd. South, London, ON N6J 4G5
519-434-5726, Fax: 519-434-1443,
info@londonchildrensmuseum.ca
www.londonchildrensmuseum.ca
Hands-on, interactive museum; features ten themed galleries, school programs, outreach programs, day camps, workshops, birthday parties & membership programs

***London:* Museum London (LRAHM)**
421 Ridout St. North, London, ON N6A 5H4
519-661-0333, Fax: 519-661-2559,
ramurray@museumlondon.ca
www.londonmuseum.on.ca
Operates: Eldon House, family life, historical & contemporary art & historical artifacts in the London area from 1834 to 1960
Michael Baker, Curator, Regional History
Brian Meehan, Executive Director
Melanie Townsend, Head of Exhibitions

***London:* Museum of Ontario Archaeology & Iroquoian Village Site**
Lawson-Jury Bldg., University of Western Ontario, 1600 Attawandaron Rd., London, ON N6G 3M6
519-473-1360, Fax: 519-473-1363,
museum.of.archaeology@uwo.ca
www.uwo.ca/museum
Archaeological & ethnographical collection; prehistoric archaeological Iroquois village site; museum open year round with reduced hours in fall & winter
Cindy Barrett, Manager
Dr. Robert Pearce, Executive Director

***London:* The Royal Canadian Regiment Museum**
Wolseley Barracks, 701 Oxford St. East, London, ON N5Y 4T7
519-660-5102, Fax: 519-660-5344,
Breede.C@forces.gc.ca

www.theroyalcanadianregiment.ca/thercrmuseum/thercrmuseum.htm
To serve as a training medium to teach regimental history; to preserve regimental history through the collection of documents, pictures, books & artifacts with emphasis on the RCR; to serve as a place of military interest for the public & Canadian Forces personnel; to provide research facilities for the study of Canadian military history as represented by the South-Western Ontario Regiments & the
Claus Breede, Curator
Maj. R.A. Smyth, Director

Lucan: **Donnelly Homestead**
34937 Roman Line, RR#3, Lucan, ON N0M 2J0
519-227-1244,
rsalts@quadro.net
www.quadro.net/~donnelly
Historical on-site tours given on the original Donnelly property by current owner; artifacts & photographs; tours preferably by appt., year round; private residence
Robert Salts, Contact

Madoc: **O'Hara Mill Pioneer Homestead**
PO Box 56, 638 Mill Rd., Madoc, ON K0K 2K0
613-473-2084,
www.ohara-mill.org
Other contact information: Phone, Membership Services: 413-473-1015
Attractions include O'Hara House, a log house, a saw mill, & a one room log schoolhouse. O'Hara House is restored to represent the Victorian era around 1840. The saw mill is a rare working English Gate or Reciprocating Frame saw mill.
Dave Little, Chair, 613-967-2466
Clara Hopkins, Vice-Chair, 613-473-2084
Karen Maguire, Secretary, 613-473-2177
Gayle Ketcheson, Treasurer, 613-473-4680

Magnetawan: **Magnetawan Historical Museum**
PO Box 263, Magnetawan, ON P0A 1P0
705-387-3308,
gomon@vianet.on.ca.
Restored plant & turbine that supplied first electricity for village; log cabin

Manitowaning: **Assiginack Museum & Heritage Park**
PO Box 147, 125 Arthur St., Manitowaning, ON P0P 1N0
705-859-3732, Fax: 705-859-2416,
assigmuse@amtelecom.net
www.manitoulin-island.com/museums/assiginack_complex.htm
The Assiginack Museum & Heritage Park is a community & marine museum. Artifacts are from the mid-1800s to the mid-1900s. Visitors can see a pioneer home & school, a 19th century grist mill, plus the Great Lakes steamship, S.S. Norisle, which was built in 1946. The museum is open from June to October.
Jeanette Allen, Curator, 705-859-3905

Manotick: **Watson's Mill**
Also known as: **Manotick Mill**
PO Box 145, 5525 Dickinson St., Manotick, ON K4M 1A3
613-692-6455, Fax: 613-692-5486, 800-267-3504
watsonsmillmanotick@rogers.com
www.watsonsmill.com
Founded: 1860 19th century working gristmill, built 1860; gift shop; tours; picnic area; live interpretation, gossip tours
Bonnie Gray, President, Board of Directors
Isabelle Geoffrion, Manager, 613-692-6455
Cam Trueman, Interpretation & Education Officer, 613-692-6455

Markham: **Markham Museum & Historic Village**
9350 Hwy. 48, Markham, ON L3P 3J3
905-294-4576, Fax: 905-294-4590,
museuminfo@markham.ca
www.markham.ca/markham/channels/museum/overview.htm
Buildings, vehicles, furnishing & agricultural & industrial equipment that relate to Markham Township's history, from native presence to the 20th century; open year round
George Phillips, Manager

Marten River: **Marten River Provincial Park Logging Museum**
c/o Marten River Provincial Park, Marten River, ON P0H 1T0
705-892-2200,
Artifacts for early logging era in Northern Ontario

Massey: **Massey Area Museum**
160 Sauble St., Massey, ON P0P 1P0
705-865-2266, Fax: 705-865-2266,
info@masseyareamuseum.com
www.masseyareamuseum.com
Founded: 1967 The Massey Area Museum is housed in the original Bretzlaff General Store, which was built in 1909. The museum details logging history, as well as Aboriginal, Fort LaCloche, mining, farming, & early settler history. Model rooms, a chapel, a general store, & Massey's first horse-drawn fire engine are featured at the museum. There is also an historical & genealogical research centre, which includes records of the Township of Sables-Spanish River's ten cemeteries.
Carolyn Hein, Curator

Matheson: **Thelma Miles Historical Museum**
PO Box 601, Matheson, ON P0K 1N0
705-273-2325, Fax: 705-273-1731,
tmhm@ntl.sympatico.ca
History of the communities of Val Gagné, Shillington, Wavel, Ramore, Holtyre & Matheson from 1900-1945
Dianne Bush, Director/Curator

Mattawa: **Mattawa & District Museum**
PO Box 9, 285 First St., Mattawa, ON P0H 1V0
705-744-5495,
mmuseum@vianet.ca
Open daily July - Aug.; weekends in May, June, Sept., Oct.
Bob Einboden, Vice-President
Claudette DesRoches, President of Board

Mattawa: **Voyageur Heritage Centre**
Samuel de Champlain Provincial Park, PO Box 147, Hwy. 17 East, Mattawa, ON P0H 1V0
705-744-2276,
www.ontarioparks.com/english/samu.html
The Voyageur Heritage Centre tells the story of the Mattawa River & the lives of the voyageurs. The centre features one of the largest reproduced birch bark canoes.

Maxville: **Glengarry Sports Hall of Fame**
PO Box 282, Maxville, ON K0C 1T0
613-527-1044,
www.glengarrysports.com

Meaford: **Meaford Museum**
111 Bayfield St., Meaford, ON N4L 1N4
519-538-5974, Fax: 519-538-5974,
meafordmuseum@meaford.ca
www.meafordmuseum.ca
Founded: 1961 The Meaford Museum aims to collect, educate, display, conserve and feature the history of the former Town of Meaford and the surrounding area, from early settlements to the present.
Pam Woolner, Curator

Meldrum Bay: **Mississagi Strait Lighthouse Museum**
General Delivery, Meldrum Bay, ON P0P 1R0
705-282-7258,
Lighthouse built in 1873, includes artifacts related to seafaring & fishing; keeper's house features 19th-century furnishings; open mid-May - Sept.

Meldrum Bay: **The Net Shed Museum**
Water St., Meldrum Bay, ON P0P 1R0
705-283-1818,
jan.island@onlink.net
Open June - Labour Day; artifacts of pioneer fishing, lumbering & farming; display of nursing in WWII
Jan Laurin, Sec.-Treas./Director

Merrickville: **The Blockhouse Museum**
PO Box 294, Merrickville, ON K0G 1N0
613-269-4034,
info@merrickvillehistory.org
www.merrickvillehistory.org
Defence for the Rideau Canal built in 1830 by Lt. Colonel John By
Gillian Hammonds, Manager, The Blockhouse Museum

Midland: **Huronia Museum**
PO Box 638, Midland, ON L4R 4P4
705-526-2844, Fax: 705-527-6622, 800-263-7745
director@huroniamuseum.com
www.huroniamuseum.com;
collections.ic.gc.ca/huronia/huronia.htm
Recreated Huron Village represents one of hundreds that existed in the Georgian Bay area, representing a unique & sophisticated society which lasted nearly 1,000 years; Canada's first recreated Native village; extensive exhibits on regional history, art gallery, archives & Mundys Bay Store; a large selection of native & historical books
Jamie Hunter, Director/Curator

Midland: **Martyrs' Shrine**
PO Box 7, 16163 Hwy. 12 West, Midland, ON L4R 4K6
705-526-3788, Fax: 705-526-1546,
shrine@jesuits.ca
www.martyrs-shrine.com
Founded: 1926 Built in 1926 in tribute to the Jesuit missionaries who laboured among the Huron, 1625-50, and to the eight who were martyred, the interior of this church with its wooden walls and canoe-like ceiling celebrates the melding of historical cultures. Open daily, Victoria Day weekend through Thanksgiving weekend; tours &/or talks given on request.
Rev. Alex F. Kirsten, Director S.J.

Midland: **Sainte-Marie among the Hurons / Sainte-Marie-au-Pays-des-Hurons**
PO Box 160, Hwy. 12 East, Midland, ON L4R 4K8
705-526-7838, Fax: 705-526-9193,
hhp@hhp.on.ca
www.saintemarieamongthehurons.on.ca
Other contact information: TTY: 705-528-7697; E-mail, Friends of Sainte-Marie: friends@csolve.net
During the 17th century, Sainte-Marie served as the fortress & headquarters for the French Jesuit mission to the Huron nation. Based upon archaeological & historical research, Sainte-Marie was recreated on its original site. Special programs & courses are offered about the first European community in Ontario. The site is open from the end of April to the end of October.

Milford: **Mariners Park Museum**
PO Box 12, 2065 County Rd. 13, Milford, ON K0K 2P0
613-476-8392,
marinersmuseum@pecounty.on.ca
pecounty.on.ca/government/rec_parks_culture/rec_culture/museums/index.php
Founded: 1967 Indoor and outdoor exhibits distinguish the site, with displays of various artifacts from marine activity in the area, including treasures from diving expeditions, as well as pieces related to local fishing, ship building, ice harvesting and rum running days. The False Duck Lighthouse has become a memorial to the County's sailors.
MS Jennifer Lyons, Head Curator, Recreation, Parks & Culture, Prince Edward County, 613-476-2148, X-426, Fax: 613-476-9835, museums@pecounty.on.ca

Milton: **Country Heritage Park**
PO Box 38, Milton, ON L9T 2Y3
905-878-8151, Fax: 905-876-4530, 888-307-3276
information@countryheritagepark.com
www.countryheritagepark.com
Display of machinery & tools related to all aspects of agricultural industry in Ontario

Milton: **Halton Region Museum**
5181 Kelso Rd., RR#3 (Kelso Conservation Area), Milton, ON L9T 2X7
905-875-2200, Fax: 905-876-4322, 866-442-5866
museum@halton.ca
www.halton.ca/museum
Founded: 1962 Focusing on Halton's natural & cultural heritage, the main exhibits are located in Alexander Barn and in the Visitor Centre on the main floor. Both Heritage and Environmental Programmes are offered. The Reference Library stores various regional, historical records available for research purposes. Open year round.
MS Nancy Field, Manager, Heritage Services, Halton Region, 905-875-2200, X-22, nancy.field@halton.ca

Milton: **Streetcar & Electric Railway Museum**
c/o Ontario Electric Railway Historical Association Inc., PO Box 578, Milton, ON L9T 5A2
519-856-9802, Fax: 519-856-1399,
streetcar@hcry.org
www.hcry.org
Operating streetcar & electric railway museum
Gord McOuat, Vice-President
J. Borland, President

Minesing: **Simcoe County Museum**
1151 Hwy. 26, Minesing, ON L0L 1Y0
705-728-3721, Fax: 705-728-9130,
museum@simcoe.ca
www.county.simcoe.on.ca
Open daily; 9:00-4:30 Monday to Saturday and 1:00-4:30 Sunday. Admission $6.00 adults, $4.00 seniors/students

Mississauga: **Benares Historic House & Visitor Centre**
1507 Clarkson Rd. North, Mississauga, ON L5J 2W8
905-822-2347, Fax: 905-822-5372,
scott.gillies@city.mississauga.on.ca
www.mississauga.ca/portal/discover/ benareshistorichouse
Founded: 1995 Owned & operated by the City of Mississauga, Community Services Department, the Benares Historic House is a Georgian style home, which was built in 1857. The home has been restored to reflect the early 20th century & displays original artifacts from the Harris family & home. The Benares House is believed to be the inspiration for Mazo de la Roche's Jalna novels.

Mississauga: **Bradley House Museum**
1620 Orr Rd., Mississauga, ON L5J 4T2
905-822-1569, Fax: 905-823-3591,
scott.gillies@mississauga.ca
www.mississauga.ca/portal/discover/bradl eymuseum
The Bradley Museum is owned & operated by the City of Mississauga, Community Services Department. The museum grounds feature an early 19th century home known as The Anchorage, a farmhouse which was built in 1830, & a log cabin.

The farmhouse was owned by the Bradleys, who were a United Empire Loyalist couple. The museum is open year round.

Mississauga: **Lithuanian Museum/Archives of Canada**
2185 Stavebank Rd., Mississauga, ON L5C 1T3
905-566-8755, Fax: 905-275-1336,
litharch@the-wire.com
To collect, display, organize & preserve documents, photographs, fine art, textiles, memorabilia, souvenirs of community events, uniforms, medals, coins, maps, flags, videos, audio tapes & rare books or periodicals which pertain to Lithuania & Lithuanian Canadians; small lending library
Dr. Rasa Mazeika, Director

Mooretown: **Moore Museum**
94 Moore Line, Mooretown, ON N0N 1M0
519-867-2020, Fax: 519-867-2020,
lmason@twp.stclair.on.ca
www.lambtononline.com/moore_museum
Founded: 1975 Open year round; Jan. - Feb. by appt.
Laurie Mason, Curator

Morpeth: **Rondeau Provincial Park Visitor Centre**
RR#1, Morpeth, ON N0P 1X0
519-674-1768, Fax: 519-674-1755,
Herbarium, egg, mammal, insect, archaeological, photographic & bird collection

Morrisburg: **Upper Canada Village**
13740 County Rd. 2, Morrisburg, ON K0C 1X0
613-543-4328, 800-437-2233
www.uppercanadavillage.com
Other contact information: Phone, Village Library Appointments: 613-543-3704
Upper Canada Village features more than forty heritage buildings. The village depicts daily life in the 1860s, through demonstrations, talks, & hands-on activities. The site also has a library & research facility. Upper Canada Village is open from mid May to mid October.

Mount Brydges: **Ska-Nah-Doht Iroquoian Village & Museum**
8449 Irish Dr., RR#1, Mount Brydges, ON N0L 1W0
519-264-2420, Fax: 519-264-1562,
lowerthames@odyssey.on.ca
www.lowerthames-conservation.on.ca/SkaNahDo ht.htm
This recreated Iroquoian village of 1,000 years ago has 18 outdoor exhibits including a palisade with maze & longhouses; museum in resource centre; displays on nature & conservation; trails, wetland boardwalks & picnic areas.There are hands on exhibits and an archaeological collection.
Karen Mattila, Curator

Mount Hope: **Canadian Warplane Heritage Museum (CWH)**
Hamilton Airport, 9280 Airport Rd., Mount Hope, ON L0R 1W0
905-679-4183, Fax: 905-679-4186, 877-347-3359
museum@warplane.com
www.warplane.com
Founded: 1971 The museum is dedicated to the acquisitions & preservation of aircraft flown by Canadians from WWII to the present, & the collection of related aviation artifacts & memorabilia; library & archival resources; meeting room & hangar rental; special events & programming; group tours available. Open daily 9-5, year round.
David G. Rohrer, CEO/Director

Napanee: **Allan Macpherson House**
180 Elizabeth St., Napanee, ON K7R 1B5
613-354-5982, Fax: 613-354-5285,
machouse@kingston.net
www.macphersonhouse.ca
Founded: 1967 1826 mansion of Allan Macpherson, one of Napanee's leading citizens; reflects the taste, public & private activities of an entrepreneurial Scottish immigrant. Open May-Dec. School programs; bridal party rentals; children's summer activity days; annual whiskey tasting.
Sandra Penney, Managing Director

Napanee: **Lennox & Addington County Museum & Archives**
97 Thomas St. East, PO Bag 1000, Napanee, ON K7R 3S9
613-354-3027, Fax: 613-354-1005,
nmuseum@lennox-addington.on.ca
www.lennox-addington.on.ca
Located in former County jail (1864); genealogy & historical research centre, county's origins, Loyalist settlement & development from 1784 to present, displays & extensive archives; open year round
Jane Foster, Manager
Shelley Respondek, Archivist,
archives@lennox-addington.on.ca

Napanee: **Old Hay Bay Church**
c/o 304 Staples Lane, Napanee, ON K7R 3K7
613-373-2877, Fax: 613-373-8816,
www.oldhaybaychurch.org
A National Historic Site, Old Hay Bay Church was erected in 1792. Located at 2365 South Shore Road in Adolphustown, Ontario, the church is the oldest Methodist building in Canada.
Katherine Staples, Contact

Nepean: **Algonquin College Museum**
Applied Museum Studies Program, Algonquin College, 1385 Woodroffe Ave., Nepean, ON K2G 1V8
613-727-4723, Fax: 613-727-7786,
pattilk@algonquincollege.com
Teaching collection
Katherine Pattillo, Coordinator

Nepean: **Nepean Museum Inc.**
Parent: **Nepean Museum Inc.**
16 Rowley Ave., Nepean, ON K2G 1L9
613-723-7936, Fax: 613-723-7936,
reception@nepeanmuseum.ca
www.nepeanmuseum.ca
Founded: 1983 Housed in the first Nepean Library, the museum displays historical objects related to Nepean's past & present. Nepean Museum contains two meeting rooms.
Lindsay MacDonald, Director & Curator,
curator@nepeanmuseum.ca
Kalle Boucher, Manager, Education & Volunteers,
educationservices@nepeanmuseum.ca
Emily Bracewell, Manager, Collections,
collections@nepeanmuseum.ca

New Liskeard: **Little Claybelt Homesteaders Museum**
PO Box 1718, New Liskeard, ON P0J 1P0
705-647-9575,
lchmuse@ntl.sympatico.ca
www.museumsnorth.org/new_liskeard/
Displays of geological origin of Little Claybelt, pioneer activities, historical documents, artifacts & agricultural implements, pioneer family histories
Clair Shepherdson, President

Newmarket: **Elman W. Campbell Museum**
Also known as: **Newmarket Museum**
134 Main St. South, Newmarket, ON L3Y 3Y7
905-953-5314, Fax: 905-898-2083, 877-550-5575
elmanmuseum@rogers.com
www.newmarket.ca
Exhibits trace the development of Newmarket from the time of the first settlers
Elizabeth Sinyard, Curator

Niagara Falls: **Daredevil Gallery**
6170 Fallsview Blvd., Niagara Falls, ON L2G 7T8
905-358-3611, Fax: 905-358-3613, 866-405-4629
info@imaxniagara.com
www.imaxniagara.com/daredevil-gallery
Only collection of original daredevil barrels found in Niagara Falls

Niagara Falls: **Guinness World Records Museum**
4943 Clifton Hill, Niagara Falls, ON L2G 3N5
905-356-2299, Fax: 905-356-8614,
info@guinnessniagarafalls.com
www.guinnessniagarafalls.com
Displays of human achievements; models of the extraordinary; computer databanks & videos; open year round

Niagara Falls: **Laura Secord Homestead**
c/o, PO Box 150, Niagara Falls, ON L2E 6T2
905-262-4851,
Open May-Sept. in Queenston ON

Niagara Falls: **Louis Tussaud's Waxworks**
4983 Clifton Hill, Niagara Falls, ON L2G 3N5
905-374-6601, Fax: 905-374-7345,
www.ripleysniagara.com
Founded: 1953 Museum displays wax models of famous and infamous people, such as artists, musicians, celebrities, politicians and religious & historical figures. Open year round. The museum is located at 5907 Victoria Ave.
MR Tim Parker, Gneral manager Manager,
parker@ripleys.com
André Ross

Niagara Falls: **McFarland House**
c/o Niagara Parks Commission, PO Box 150, Niagara Falls, ON L2E 6T2
905-295-4377, Fax: 905-295-4142, 877-642-7275
www.niagaraparks.com/heritage-trail/mcfarland-house.html
Founded: 1959 Built in 1800 and home to John McFarland and his family for 150 years, the house served as a hospital for both the British & American wounded during the War of 1812. Restored by the Niagara Parks Commission in period style, there are also traditional grounds and the McFarland Tea Garden to enjoy refreshments. Nature trails can be accessed from the park. The house is located at 15927 Niagara Parkway, Niagara-on-the-Lake.
MS April Petrie, Manager, Heritage & Educational Services

Niagara Falls: **Movieland Wax Museum**
4950 Clifton Hill, Niagara Falls, ON L2G 3N4
905-358-3061,
Open year round

Niagara Falls: **Niagara Falls History Museum**
5810 Ferry St., Niagara Falls, ON L2G 1S9
905-358-5082, Fax: 905-358-0920,
llmuseum@niagarafalls.ca
www.niagarafallsmuseum.ca/lundyslanehistoricalmuseum.html
Founded: 1961 The 1874 museum was originally located on Drummond Rd., the site of the Battle of Lundy's Lane, July 25, 1814, but was moved to its present site in 1970. Exhibits include a significant collection of War of 1812 artifacts, as well as historic prints of Niagara Falls. The Museum also houses a variety of artifacts relating to all aspects of the founding and development of the City of Niagara Falls.
MR Gordon West, Board Chairman man
Kathleen Powell, Manager

Niagara Falls: **Old Fort Erie**
PO Box 150, Niagara Parks Commission, 350 Niagara Pkwy., Niagara Falls, ON L2E 6T2
905-356-2241,
Collection of military equipment housed in a reconstructed fort

Niagara Falls: **Ripley's Believe It or Not! Museum**
4960 Clifton Hill, Niagara Falls, ON L2G 3N4
905-356-2238, Fax: 905-374-7345,
www.ripleysniagara.com
Founded: 1963 Ripley's Believe It or Not! in Niagara Falls presents strange & bizarre exhibits. The museum is open year-round.
Tim Parker, General Manager

Niagara Falls: **Willoughby Historical Museum**
9935 Niagara Pkwy., Niagara Falls, ON L2E 6S6
905-295-4036, Fax: 905-295-4036,
whmuseum@niagarafalls.ca
www.niagarafallsmuseum.ca/willoughby.html
The Willoughby Historical Museum collects, preserves, interprets, & displays items related to Ontario's former Township of Willoughby, the Village of Chippawa, & the surrounding region. Examples of artifacts include household objects, school materials, toys, telephones, & a functioning magneto switchboard. The museum is open year-round. Tours & research can be arranged by phoning the museum.

Niagara on the Lake: **Niagara on the Lake Fort George National Historic Site**
Also known as: **Fort George**
Parks Canada, PO Box 787, Niagara on the Lake, ON L0S 1J0
905-468-4257,
Reconstructed fort built in 1799

Niagara on the Lake: **Niagara Apothecary**
PO Box 903, 5 Queen St., Niagara on the Lake, ON L0S 1J0
905-468-3845,
niagaraapothecary@ocpinfo.com
www.niagaraapothecary.ca
The Niagara Apothecary depicts an 1869 pharmacy. Artifacts include the Harvey bottles & jars, which were imported from Britain around 1830, mortars & pestles, a 19th century leech jar, & an early cash register.

Niagara on the Lake: **Niagara Fire Museum**
PO Box 498, Niagara on the Lake, ON L0S 1J0
905-468-7279,
Fire-fighting equipment dating back 140 years

Niagara-on-the-Lake: **Niagara Historical Society & Museum**
Also known as: **Niagara Historical Museum**
PO Box 208, 43 Castlereagh St., Niagara-on-the-Lake, ON L0S 1J0
905-468-3912, Fax: 905-468-1728,
contact@niagarahistorical.museum
www.niagarahistorical.museum
Founded: 1895 Ontario's first purpose-built museum; artifacts from Niagara's social & military history
Clark Bernat, Managing Director
Amy Klassen, Administrator, Niagara Historical Society

Nipigon: **Nipigon Museum**
PO Box 208, Nipigon, ON P0T 2J0
807-887-2727,
Artifacts relating to local lumbering & fur trading; rocks & minerals; bottles

Nipissing: **Nipissing Township Museum**
General Delivery, Nipissing, ON P0H 1W0
705-724-2938, Fax: 705-724-5385,
Housed in a former Anglican church built in late 1800s of logs; displays mostly of tools, clothing & photos pertaining to the families who first settled in the area
Joe Steele, Curator

North Bay: **Callander Bay Heritage Museum**
PO Box 100, 107 Lansdowne St. East, North Bay, ON P0H 1H0
705-752-2282, Fax: 705-752-3116,
museum@callander.ca
www.mycallander.ca/museum
The Callander Bay Heritage Museum was the home & office of Dr. Allan R. Dafoe from 1914 to 1943. Dr. Dafoe was the doctor for the Dionne Quintuplets. The museum contains exhibits about the doctor & the quintuplets. The Alex Dufrense Gallery features the work of local artists. The museum also houses local genealogical sources & historical records for research.
Tom Fletcher, Chair

North Bay: **Dionne Quints Museum**
c/o Chamber of Commerce, PO Box 747, North Bay, ON P1B 8J8
705-472-8480, Fax: 705-472-8027, 888-249-8998
nbcc@northbaychamber.com
www.city.north-bay.on.ca/quints/digitize/dionne .htm
The Quints Museum is a not for profit instution dedicated to Dionne Quintuplets and contains artifacts from the Quint's early day and their growing years; baby buggies, baby dresses, books, newspaper and magazine articles, artisitic reproductions, postcards.
Sharon Berard, Director

North Bay: **North Bay & Area Museum**
100 Main St. East, North Bay, ON P1B 1A8
705-476-2323, Fax: 705-476-9300,
nbamchin@vianet.on.ca
10,000 domestic & business objects related to settling & development of local region; open year round

North Buxton: **Buxton National Historic Site & Museum**
21975 A.D. Shadd Rd., North Buxton, ON N0P 1Y0
519-352-4799, Fax: 519-352-8561,
buxton@ciaccess.com
www.buxtonmuseum.com
Founded: 1967 The site is a memorial to the Elgin Settlement, which was the last stop on the Underground Railroad for many fugitives of the American system of slavery in the pre-Civil War years. The Raleigh (Buxton) Schoolhouse of 1861 & a settlement cabin from 1854 are now part of the museum. The museum preserves the artifacts of the original settlers of the Elgin Settlement & their descendants.
Shannon Prince, Curator

Norwich: **The Norwich & District Museum & Archives**
89 Stover St. North, RR#3, Norwich, ON N0J 1P0
519-863-3101, Fax: 519-863-2343,
norwichdhs@execulink.com
www.ocl.net/projects/norwich_historical/museum/
1889 Quaker Meeting House; archives & genealogical library
Janet Hilliker, Archivist
Kerrie Gill, Curator

Oakville: **Canadian Golf Hall of Fame & Museum (CGHF)**
Glen Abbey Golf Club, 1333 Dorval Dr., Oakville, ON L6J 4Z3
905-849-9700,
cghf@rcga.org
www.rcga.org
Founded: 1971 Located at Glen Abbey, the Canadian Golf Hall of Fame & Museum tells the history of golf in Canada. The Hall of Fame honours amateur & professional golfers & builders of the sport, who have made extraordinary contributions to the game of golf in Canada. The archives & library collects photographs & documents, as well as golf publications about the game, golf courses & golfers. Staff are available to assist with research. The museum also arranges travelling exhibitions. The Canadian Golf Hall of Fame & Museum is open year round.
Karen Hewson, Director, CGHF, & Executive Director, Royal Canadian Golf Association Foundation, 1-800-263-0009, khewson@rcga.org
Meggan Gardner, Curator, mgardner@rcga.org
Jordan Diacur, Museum Assistant, jdiacur@rcga.org

Oakville: **Oakville Museum at Erchless Estate**
8 Navy St., Oakville, ON L6J 2Y5
905-338-4400, Fax: 905-815-5973,
www.oakvillemuseum.com
The Oakville Museum at Erchless Estate features the following historical buildings: Erchless Estate (c. 1858), The Custom House & Toronto Bank (c. 1856), & The Old Post Office (c. 1835). The Thomas Museum is operated by the Oakville Historical Society.
Claire Loughheed, Senior Manager, Culture Services, cloughheed@oakville.ca
Bill Nesbitt, Museum Supervisor, bnesbitt@oakville.ca
Carolyn Cross, Curator, Collections, ccross@oakville.ca
Susan Crane, Officer, Learning & Community Development, scrane@oakville.ca
Julie Hawryszko, Mueum Programmer, Public Programs, jhawryszko@oakville.ca
Preeya Nayee, Mueum Programmer, Education Programs, pnayee@oakville.ca

Odessa: **Historic Babcock Mill**
100 Bridge St., Odessa, ON K0H 2H0
613-386-7351, Fax: 613-386-3833,
clawson@loyalist.ca
Restored, fully operational water-powered 1856 mill
Patrick Beyer, Contact

Ohsweken: **Chiefswood National Historic Site**
Also known as: **Pauline Johnson House**
PO Box 640, Ohsweken, ON N0A 1M0
519-752-5005, Fax: 519-752-9578,
chiefswood@execulink.com
www.chiefswood.com
The site is the location of the Chiefswood Museum, birthplace and childhood home of poet Emily Pauline Johnson (Tekahionwake); educational programming; tours; gift shop; "The Homing Bee" newsletter. Open Tues. through Sunday, 10:00-3:00, May-Oct. Open by appointment Oct.-May.
Paul Whitlow, Curator, Chiefswood Museum

Oil Springs: **Oil Museum of Canada**
PO Box 16, 2423 Kelly Rd., Oil Springs, ON N0N 1P0
519-834-2840, Fax: 519-834-2840,
oil.museum@county-lambton.on.ca
www.lambtononline.com/oil_museum
Situated in Oil Springs, Ontario, The Oil Museum of Canada preserves the site of the first commercial oil well in North America. Visitors learn the story of Canadian oil pioneers, through petroleum industry artifacts, working exhibits, & photographs. Visitors can also see original oil wells, which continue to produce oil.
Connie Bell, Supervisor

Orillia: **Stephen Leacock Museum**
PO Box 625, 50 Museum Dr., Orillia, ON L3V 6K5
705-329-1908, Fax: 705-326-5578,
lmcurator@rogers.com
www.leacockmuseum.com
Fred Addis, Curator

Oshawa: **Canadian Automotive Museum**
99 Simcoe St. South, Oshawa, ON L1G 4G7
905-576-1222, Fax: 905-576-1223,
infoservices@oshawa.ca
www.oshawa.ca
Founded: 1961 The Canadian Automotive Museum depicts the history & future plans of the Canadian automotive industry. More than sixty vehicles, dating from 1898 to 1981 are on display. Items related to the era of the vehicles are also displayed.

Oshawa: **Oshawa Sydenham Museum**
1450 Simcoe St. South, Oshawa, ON L1H 8S8
905-436-7624, Fax: 905-436-7625,
Henry House c1849; Robinson House c1846; Guy House c1835

Oshawa: **Parkwood National Historic Site, The R.S. McLaughlin Estate**
270 Simcoe St. North, Oshawa, ON L1G 4T5
905-433-4311,
info@parkwoodestate.com
www.parkwoodestate.com
Built between 1915 & 1917, Parkwood was the grand estate of R. Samuel McLaughlin, who was the founder of General Motors of Canada. The McLaughlin family lived at the home from 1917 to 1972. Today, it is furnished to reflect the 1920s & 1930s. The National Historic Site is open year-round.

Ottawa: **The Billings Estate National Historical Site / Lieu historique national du domaine Billings**
2100 Cabot St., Ottawa, ON K1H 6K1
613-247-4830, Fax: 613-247-4832,
museums@ottawa.ca
www.ottawa.ca/museums;
www.friendsofbillingsestatemuseum.org
Home & property of Braddish & Lamira Billings, two of Ottawa's earliest settlers, c. 1828; exhibits highlight 5 generations of family & community history
Anik Després, Education Officer
Brahm Lewandowski, Education Officer

Ottawa: **Bytown Museum / Musée Bytown**
PO Box 523 B, Ottawa, ON K1P 5P6
613-234-4570, Fax: 613-234-4846,
program@storm.ca (Appointments)
www.bytownmuseum.com
Bytown Museum is situated in the oldest stone building in Ottawa, which was a treasury & storehouse during the construction of the Rideau Canal. Within the museum, the history of Bytown & the nation's capital is traced. The museum is open from the beginning of April to the end of November, & during March Break. From December to March, the museum is open by appointment only.
Mike Steinhauer, Director, mikesteinhauer@bytownmuseum.ca

Ottawa: **Cameron Highlanders of Ottawa Regimental Museum**
Cartier Sq. Drill Hall, 2 Queen Elizabeth Dr., Ottawa, ON K1A 0K2
www.camerons.ca/Org_Museum.html
The Regimental Museum contains memorabilia of the Cameron Highlanders of Ottawa. It is open one evening each week.

Ottawa: **Canada Agriculture Museum / Musée de l'agriculture du Canada**
Prince of Wales Dr., PO Box 9724 T, Ottawa, ON K1G 5A3
613-991-3044, Fax: 613-993-7923, 866-442-4416
www.agriculture.technomuses.ca
Other contact information: TTY: 613-991-9207; Phone, Media: 613-996-7812
The Canada Agriculture Museum is a demonstration farm & research station, which features animal barns, the Dominion Arboretum, ornamental gardens, & special exhibitions.
David Sutin, Manager, Communications & Marketing, 613-996-7812, dsutin@technomuses.ca

Ottawa: **The Canadian Museum of Scouting**
1345 Baseline Rd., Ottawa, ON K2C 0A7
613-224-5131, Fax: 613-224-3571,
mailbox@scouts.caca
www.scouts.ca
Founded: 1907 Scouting artifacts and historical memorobilia (Canada/UK/World); Open by appointment only
Robert Stewart, Exec. Commissioner & CEO, Scouts Canada
Stephen Kant, Chief Commissioner & Chair of the Board
Gary Boutilier, Director, Financial Services
John Singleton, Vice-President, Finance, Board of Governors
Lisa Nowlan, Director, Communication Services

Ottawa: **Canadian Ski Museum & Canadian Ski Hall of Fame (CSMus) / Musée canadien du ski et Temple de la renommée du ski canad**
#301, 1960 Scott St., Ottawa, ON K1Z 8L8
613-722-3584, Fax: 613-722-2914,
info@skimuseum.ca
www.skimuseum.ca
The Canadian Ski Museum & Canadian Ski Hall of Fame preserves Canadian skiing history & celebrates Canadian skiing & snowboarding traditions & achievements. The Hall of Fame honours Canada's accomplished skiers, snowboarders, coaches, officials, & builders of the sport.
Ivo Krupka, Chair
Walter Boyce, Director, Fundraising
Ron Crook, Director, Communications
Trevor Klotz, Director, Legal
Bruce Meredith, Director & Treasurer
Don Runge, Director, Publications

Ottawa: **The Canadian Wildlife & Wilderness Art Museum (CWWAM) / Musée canadien d'art naturaliste**
PO Box 98 B, Ottawa, ON K1P 6C3
613-237-1581, Fax: 613-237-1581,
cawa@magma.ca
www.magma.ca/cawa
Established by the Canadian Academy of Wilderness Artists (CAWA) "Hall of Fame" Art Foundation; 9,500 artifacts, drawings, prints, lithographs, carvings, sculpture & paintings. Coupled with major Canadian artists from the present and the past: Robert Bateman, Glen Loates, Ely Kish, Neil Blackwell, Norval Morriseau, A.J. Casson, Bernard Loates & many more; are several important American & European artists including Frederic Remington, Charles Marion Russell, Georgia O'Keefe, Eanger Irving Couse, Albert Bierstadt, Manfred Schatz & many more; some pieces are privately held & are on loan
Maria Amati, Executive Director
Gary Slimon, Director

Ottawa: **Governor General's Foot Guards Museum**
Drill Hall, Cartier Sq., Ottawa, ON K1A 0K2
613-990-0620,
elane22@rogers.com
www.ggfg.ottawa.on.ca
Regimental museum; brief history of regiment from 1872 to present by way of artifacts
Martin J. Lane, Curator CD

Ottawa: **Laurier House National Historic Site**
335 Laurier Ave. East, Ottawa, ON K1N 6R4
613-992-8142, Fax: 613-947-4851,
laurier.house@pc.gc.ca
Residence of Sir Wilfrid Laurier & the Right Honourtable William Lyon MacKenzie King, built in 1878

Ottawa: **Mackenzie King Estate / Domaine Mackenzie-King**
National Capital Commission, #202, 40 Elgin St., Ottawa, ON K1P 1C7
819-827-6026, Fax: 819-827-3337, 800-465-1867
dmessier@ncc-ccn.ca
Located in Gatineau Park; open daily from mid-May to the end of Oct.

Denis Messier, Manager

Owen Sound: **Grey Roots: Your Heritage & Visitor Centre**
102599 Grey Rd. 18, RR#4, Owen Sound, ON N4K 5N6
519-376-3690, Fax: 519-376-4654, 877-473-9766
info@greyroots.com
www.greyroots.com
Collects, preserves, restores, documents, interprets & displays the material culture of Grey County & the city of Owen Sound, c. 1815 - present; Grey County's Museum Archives; tourism services, exhibits, research, events

Parry Sound: **West Parry Sound District Museum (WPSDM)**
Also known as: **Museum on Tower Hill**
PO Box 337, 17 George St., Parry Sound, ON P2A 2X4
705-746-5365, Fax: 705-746-8775,
info@wpsdm.com
www.wpsdm.com
Founded: 1983 Situated in Tower Hill Park, the West Parry Sound District Museum displays items related to the First Nations, settlement, logging, shipping, agriculture, recreation, & natural history. The museum is open year-round.
Darcy Yanni, Museum Director, darcy@wpsdm.com
Tanya Bolwerk, Bookkeeper, accounting@wpsdm.com

Pelee Island: **Pelee Island Heritage Centre**
West Dock, Pelee Island, ON N0R 1M0
519-724-2291, Fax: 519-724-2470,
pimuseum@mnsi.net
Rare Flora & fauna exhibits; early navigation displays; local shipwreck information

Pembroke: **Champlain Trail Museum & Pioneer Village**
PO Box 985, 1032 Pembroke St. East, Pembroke, ON K8A 7M5
613-735-0517, Fax: 613-629-5067,
pembrokemuseum@nrtco.net
www.champlaintrailmuseum.com
Economic, political & social history of upper Ottawa Valley & Renfrew County; archival & genealogical material
Tony Cowan, Manager

Penetanguishene: **Discovery Harbour / Havre de la Découverte**
Ministry of Tourism, 93 Jury Dr., Penetanguishene, ON L9M 1G1
705-549-8064, Fax: 705-549-4858, 705-526-7697
hhp@hhp.on.ca
www.discoveryharbour.on.ca
Ontario's leading Marine Heritage Site; orginally built as a military base with its roots tracing back to the War of 1812. Tours, interactive daily activies in the summer. Open weekdays late-May to July 1; open daily July 1 to Labour Day weekend
Jan Gray, General Manager

Penetanguishene: **Penetanguishene Centennial Museum & Archives**
13 Burke St., Penetanguishene, ON L9M 1C1
705-549-2150, Fax: 705-549-7542,
info@pencenmuseum.com
www.pencenmuseum.com
Other contact information: E-mail, Genealogy & History Research Ctr.: genealogy@pencenmuseum.com
Penetanguishene's museum is housed in the former C. Beck Lumber Office & General Store which was built in 1875. The location also features a Genealogy & History Research Center & Archives, which houses the the Georgian Bay Heritage League Collection with more than 500 genealogical files & local history books. Penetanguishene Centennial Museum & Archives is open year-round.
Nicole Jackson, Curator, njackson@pencenmuseum.com
Pam Tessier, Coordinator, Research, ptessier@pencenmuseum.com
Janice Gadsdon, Curatorial Assistant, jgadsdon@pencenmuseum.com

Perth: **Innisville & District Museum**
c/o Willard Shaw, RR#6, Perth, ON K7H 3C8
613-267-6500, Fax: 613-267-2083,
lindav@drummondnorthelmsley.com
Country-style museum
George Jackson

Perth: **The Perth Museum**
Also known as: **Matheson House**
11 Gore St. East, Perth, ON K7H 1H9
613-267-1947, Fax: 613-267-5635,
perthmuseum@town.perth.on.ca
www.perthcanada.com
1840 stone home of Senator Matheson; open year round; National Historic Site; 2 galleries; historic gardens
Karen Rennie, Curator

Petawawa: **Canadian Airborne Forces Museum / Musée des Forces aéroportées canadiennes**
PO Box 9999 Main, 63 Colborne Rd., Petawawa, ON K8H 2X3
613-588-6238,
info@petawawamuseums.com
www.petawawamuseums.com
Other contact information: E-mail, Volunteer Coordinator: volunteers@petawawamuseums.com
The Canadian Airborne Forces Museum preserves & honours the memory of airborne forces which served Canada since World War II. Their history is presented through historical artifacts, dioramas, videos, & a large screen mini-theatre. The museum is a member of the following organizations: the Organization of Military Museums of Canada, the Canadian Museums Association, the Ontario Museums Association, the Ottawa Valley Tourist Association, & the Renfrew County Museums Network. The Canadian Airborne Forces Museum is open year round.
Anne Lindsay, Museologist, Lindsay.A@forces.gc.ca
Ainsley Greenfield, Manager, Collections

Petawawa: **Canadian Forces Base Petawawa Military Museum**
Canadian Forces Base Petawawa, PO Box 9999 Main, 63 Colborne Rd., Petawawa, ON K8H 2X3
613-588-6238,
info@petawawamuseums.com
www.petawawamuseums.com
Other contact information: E-mail, Volunteer Coordinator: volunteers@petawawamuseums.com
The Canadian Forces Base Petawawa Military Museum collects, preserves, & interprets items related to the history of individuals & units of CFB Petawawa since 1905. Museum staff also assist with research requests.
Anne Lindsay, Museologist, Lindsay.A@forces.gc.ca
Ainsley Greenfield, Manager, Collections

Peterborough: **The Canadian Canoe Museum**
910 Monaghan Rd., Peterborough, ON K9J 5K4
705-748-9153, Fax: 705-748-0616, 866-342-2663
inquiries@canoemuseum.net
www.canoemuseum.net
Collection of over 600 canoes & kayaks, plus related artifacts; open year round

Peterborough: **Hope Water-Powered Saw Mill**
Also known as: **Hope Mill**
c/o Otonabee Region Conservation Authority, 250 Milroy Dr., Peterborough, ON K9H 7M9
705-745-5791, Fax: 705-745-7488,
otonabeeca@otonabee.com
www.otonabee.com/orcf/news/events/hope_mill.htm
Built in 1835 by Scottish immigrant Squire William Lang, the Otonabee Conservation Authority purchased the mill from his great grandson in 1966. The saw-powered Hope Mill has been restored to its original charm and is fully functional. Demonstrations and tours are offered. A collection of 19th-century carpentry tools, as well as larger pieces of equipment (lathe, planer, drill-press), are on exhibit. The mill is located at 3414 Hope Mill Rd. on the banks of the Indian River in Lang, ON.
Richard Hunter, CAO
John Williams, Coordinator, Conservation Lands

Peterborough: **Hutchison House Museum**
270 Brock St., Peterborough, ON K9H 2P9
705-743-9710, Fax: 705-740-0395, 866-743-9710
hutchisonhouse@nexicom.net
www.nexicom.net/~history
Living history museum owned & operated by the Peterborough Historical Society open to all interested in the history of Upper Canada in the 1800s
Gale Fewings, Administrator/Curator

Peterborough: **Lang Water Powered Grist Mill**
Also known as: **Lang Mill**
c/o Otonabee Region Conservation Authority, 250 Milroy Dr., Peterborough, ON K9H 7M9
705-745-5791, Fax: 705-745-7488,
otonabeeca@otonabee.com
www.otonabee.com
Fully operational water-powered grist mill located on the west bank of the Indian River at Lang Pioneer Village (Otonabee-South Monaghan Township-County of Peterborough).
John DuChene, CAO
John Williams, Coordinator, Conservation Lands

Peterborough: **Lang Pioneer Village**
470 Water St., Peterborough, ON K9H 3M3
705-295-6694, Fax: 705-295-6644, 866-289-5264
jcorrigan@county.peterborough.on.ca
langpioneervillage.ca
Living history museum from 1800-1900; over 20 restored buildings with costumed interpreters; open Mon.-Fri. May 15-June 30, Sat.-Fri. July 1 to Labour Day; call or see website for hours of operation, admission prices & list of special events
Joe Corrigan, Manager

Peterborough: **Peterborough Museum & Archives**
Ashburnham Memorial Park, PO Box 143, Peterborough, ON K9J 6Y5
705-743-5180, Fax: 705-743-2614,
administration@peterboroughmuseumandarchives.ca
www.peterboroughmuseuman darchives.ca
Other contact information: E-mail, Artifacts: collections@peterboroughmuseumandarchives.ca
The heritage & culture of Peterborough & the surrounding area is preserved & presented at Peterborough Museum & Archives. The Museum houses a variety of artifacts, such as archaeological collections, technological artifacts, & military collections. The Archives holds over 2,000 fonds, including personal letters, maps, photographs, association records, early Peterborough Examiner newspapers, & the early records of Peterborough County Court. The Museum & Archives is open year-round. Appointments are required to visit the Archives (archives@peterboroughmuseumandarchives.ca).
Jon Oldham, Media Contact, joldham@peterborough.ca

Peterborough: **Trent-Severn Waterway National Historic Site of Canada, Lock 21 - Peterborough Lift Lock**
PO Box 567, Peterborough, ON K9J 6Z6
705-750-4900, Fax: 705-742-9644, 888-773-8888
Ont.Trentsevern@pc.gc.ca
www.pc.gc.ca/eng/lhn-nhs/on/trentsevern/visit/v isit6/lock21.aspx
Other contact information: Phone, Group Tours: 705-750-4950; Teletypewriter (TTY): 705-750-4949
Opened in 1904, the Peterborough Lift Lock is the highest hydraulic lift lock in the world. Located next to Lock 21 is the Peterborough Lift Lock Visitor Centre, which contains exhibits & films. The Peterborough Lift Lock Visitor Centre is open during the navigation season.
Peter Frood, Field Unit Superintendent, Parks Canada Central Ontario Field Unit
Sara Atkins, Manager, External Relations & Communications, Parks Canada Central Ontario Field Unit

Petrolia: **Petrolia Discovery**
PO Box 1480, Petrolia, ON N0N 1R0
519-882-0897, Fax: 519-882-4209,
petdisc@xcelco.on.ca
www.petroliadiscovery.com
Petrolia Discovery depicts the history of the pioneer oil men of Lambton County, Ontario. The museum is located at an oilfield which was established in the 1870s. This 19th century oilfield has been restored & is still operational. Petrolia Discovery is open from Victoria Day until Labour Day. School & educational tours may be arranged after the summer season.

Pickering: **Pickering Museum Village**
c/o City of Pickering, One The Esplanade, Pickering, ON L1V 6K7
905-683-8401, Fax: 905-686-4079,
museum@city.pickering.on.ca
www.cityofpickering.com/museum
Located at 2365 Concession Road #6 in Pickering, Ontario, the Pickering Museum Village features fifteen restored heritage buildings, including a schoolhouse, churches, a blacksmith shop, houses, & barns.

Picton: **Macaulay Heritage Park**
Also known as: **Prince Edward County Museum**
PO Box 2150, 35 Church St., Picton, ON K0K 2T0
613-476-3833, Fax: 613-476-9835,
macmuseum@pecounty.on.ca
www.pec.on.ca/macaulay
Founded: 1973 The site encompasses the 1830 Macaulay House, home of the Rev. William Macaulay, carriage house, heritage gardens & former St. Mary Magdalene Church and cemetary; open Tues.-Sun. 1-4:30 from long weekend in May to Thanksgiving; 10-4:30 (July & Aug.)
MS Jennifer Lyons, Head Curator, 613-476-2148, X-426, museums@pecounty.on.ca
Elizabeth Hunter, Museum Manager

Picton: **Rose House Museum**
PO Box 3530, Picton, ON K0K 2T0
613-476-5439,
rosemuseum@pecounty.on.ca
1804 original homestead; home to five generations of the Rose family; living history depicting life in 1800s; guided tours
Susan Rose, Curator

Port Carling: **Muskoka Lakes Museum**
PO Box 432, 1 Joseph St., Port Carling, ON P0B 1J0
705-765-5367, Fax: 705-765-7682,
mlmchin@muskoka.com
www.muskoka.com/tourism/mlm/
Log home from 1875; artifacts of early settlers & lumber industry; displays related to boat building & water transportation; archives of Muskoka region; open May 19 - Thanksgiving
Doug Smith, Director/Curator

Port Colborne: **Port Colborne Historical & Marine Museum**
PO Box 572, 280 King St., Port Colborne, ON L3K 5X8

905-834-7604, Fax: 905-834-6198,
museum@portcolborne.ca
www.portcolborne.ca/page/museum

The Port Colborne Historical & Marine Museum depicts the history of Port Colborne & the Welland Canal. The museum features heritage buildings, such as an 1869 home & carriage house, a log schoolhouse, & an 1850 marine blacksmith shop. A reproduction of the parapet of Port Colborne's Lighthouse contains ship models & marine artifacts. The museum, heritage village, & gift shop are open from May to December.

Stephanie Powell Baswick, Director & Curator
Lynn van Dillen, Assistant Curator, lynnvandillen@portcolborne.ca
Glenn Walker, Technician, Heritage Research, archives@portcolborne.ca

***Port Dover:* Port Dover Harbour Museum**
PO Box 1298, 44 Harbour St., Port Dover, ON N0A 1N0
519-583-2660,
portdover.museum@norfolkcounty.ca
www.norfolkcounty.ca

The Port Dover Harbour Museum tells the story of Port Dover's fishing industry, ship building, Lake Erie shipwrecks, rum running, & other parts of lakeside life. The museum is open year round.

***Port Hope:* Dorothy's House Museum (EDHS)**
***Also known as:* East Durham Historical Society**
PO Box 116, 3632 Ganaraska Rd., Port Hope, ON L1A 3V9
905-797-2247,
info@porthopehistorical.ca
www.porthopehistorical.ca

Artifacts from the Port Hope & Hope Township area; house built around 1869; barn; driveshed; open May - Aug.

Ron Getz, President

***Port Perry:* Scugog Shores Historical Museum**
***Also known as:* Scugog Shores Museum Village & Archives**
16210 Island Rd., Port Perry, ON L9L 1B4
905-985-3589, Fax: 905-985-3492,
cbelfry@scugogshoresmuseum.com
www.scugogshoresmuseum.com

Historic village, comprising a log cabin, Lee House, blacksmith & woodright shops, print shop, school, church, barns, heritage flower, herb & dye plant gardens, & Ojibway Heritage Interpretive Lands; museum archives houses genealogical resources; special events & programming, themed artifact kits for rent, tours, building rentals

Craig Belfry, Manager, Culture & Heritage, Township of Scucog

***Port Rowan:* Backus Heritage Conservation Area & Village (BHCA)**
c/o Long Point Region Conservation Authority, RR#1, Port Rowan, ON N0E 1M0
519-586-2201,
www.lprca.on.ca
Other contact information: Phone, Administration Office: 519-428-4623

Owned & operated by the Long Point Region Conservation Authority, the Backus Heritage Conservation Area features a conservation education centre & a heritage village. The village consists of restored & reconstructed buildings, including the John C. Backhouse Mill, the Teeterville Baptist Church, the Vittoria Carriage Shop, & the Forbes Barn. The history of the Long Point Region Watershed is depicted through exhibits & artifacts.

***Prescott:* Fort Wellington National Historic Site of Canada**
PO Box 479, Prescott, ON K0E 1T0
613-925-2896, Fax: 613-925-1536,
ont-wellington@pc.gc.ca
www.pc.gc.ca/eng/lhn-nhs/on/wellington/ne/ne3.aspx

Built during the War of 1812, Fort Wellington defended the St. Lawrence River shipping route between Kingston & Montréal. It was rebuilt in 1838 to once again defend against possible attack by the United States. Today, the Visitor Centre at the site displays exhibits related to the War of 1812 & the Upper Canada Rebellion. The site is open from Victoria Day weekend to the end of September. During the off-season, groups of ten or more may make an appointment.

***Prescott:* The Forwarders' Museum**
PO Box 2179, 201 Water St., Prescott, ON K0E 1T0
613-925-1861, Fax: 613-925-4381, 800-218-1131
tourism@prescott.ca
www.prescott.ca

Forwarding trade; St Lawrence River & local history; open June-Labour Day

***Red Lake:* Red Lake Regional Heritage Centre**
PO Box 64, 51A Hwy. 105, Red Lake, ON P0V 2M0
807-727-3006, Fax: 807-727-2686,
heritage@redlake.ca
www.redlakemuseum.com

At the Red Lake Regional Heritage Centre, visitors will discover Aboriginal, fur trade, gold mining, & immigration history. The centre also provides information about Woodland Caribou Park. The Red Lake Regional Heritage Centre is open year-round.

Richard Pasloski, Chair
Michele Alderton, Curator
Sara Cuthbertson, Assistant Curator

***Renfrew:* McDougall Mill Museum**
***Also known as:* Renfrew Museum**
PO Box 554, Arthur Ave., Renfrew, ON K7V 4B1
613-432-2129,
museum@renfrewmuseum.ca
www.renfrewmuseum.ca
Other contact information: Tel. (Off-season) 613/432-7015

Founded: 1969 Housed in a stone, 1855 grist mill built on the Bonnechere River by Hudson's Bay Company agent, John Lorne McDougall, the museum displays 3 floors of artifacts, including early appliances from Renfrew's industrial days. There are also exhibits of military articles, Victorian clothing and a wedding dress gallery. The museum is run by the Renfrew And District Historical And Museum Society.

***Richards Landing:* Fort St. Joseph National Historic Site of Canada**
PO Box 220, Richards Landing, ON P0R 1J0
705-246-2664, Fax: 705-246-1796,
fortstjoseph-info@pc.gc.ca
www.pc.gc.ca/lhn-nhs/on/stjoseph/index_e.a sp

Ruins of a fort erected after 1796 to serve as a fur trade centre; artifacts from excavation of site

***Richards Landing:* St. Joseph Island Museum Complex**
***Also known as:* St. Joseph Island Museum Village**
RR#2, Richards Landing, ON P0R 1J0
705-246-2672,

Six artifact buildings represent the pioneer era (1820-1880) & the settlement era after the Homestead Act of 1868; over 6,000 artifacts; farming, lumbering, maple syruping & early navigation displays; 2 schools, a church, a store, a barn, an 1880 log cabin & a general store

Pat Fleming, Curator
Micheline Yandeau, Chair

***Ridgetown:* Ridge House Museum**
PO Box 550, 53 Erie St. South, Ridgetown, ON N0P 2C0
519-674-2223, Fax: 519-674-3747,
ckridgehouse@chatham-kent.on.ca
www.chatham-kent.ca/ridgehouse

Founded: 1975 The Ridge Hose Museum depicts the life of a middle class family In Ridgetown around 1875. Interactive tours & interpretive programs are provided.

Nicole Gignac, Curator

***Ridgeway:* Fort Erie Historical Museum**
c/o Fort Erie Museum Board, PO Box 339, 402 Ridge Rd., Ridgeway, ON L0S 1N0
905-894-5322, Fax: 905-894-6851,
museum@forterie.on.ca
www.museum.forterie.ca/historical.html

Exhibits on archaelogy, genealogy, Fenian Raids, local history & archives; open year-round Sun.-Fri.; daily in July & Aug.

Jane Davies, Curator

***Ridgeway:* Fort Erie Railroad Museum**
Fort Erie Museum Board, PO Box 339, 400 Central Ave., Ridgeway, ON L0S 1N0
905-871-1412, Fax: 905-894-6851,
museum@forterie.on.ca

Located on Central Ave.; includes Steam engine #6218, caboose & 2 train stations; open daily Victoria Day - Labour Day; open weekends until Thanksgiving

Jane Davies, Curator

***Ridgeway:* Ridgeway Battlefield National Historic Site**
c/o Fort Erie Historical Museum, PO Box 339, 402 Ridge Rd., Ridgeway, ON L0S 1N0
905-894-5322, Fax: 905-894-6851,
museum@forterie.on.ca
www.museum.forterie.ca/battlefield.html

The Ridgeway Battlefield national historic site site marks the location where in 1866 Irish-American soldiers, known as Fenians, fought Canadian forces in an attempt to gain Ireland's independence of England. The Fort Erie Museum maintains the original cabin at the battle site, where visitors can see a visual account of the Battle of Ridgeway.

***Rockton:* Westfield Heritage Village (WHV)**
1049 Kirkwall Rd., Rockton, ON L0R 1X0
519-621-8851, Fax: 519-621-6897, 800-883-0104
westfield@speedway.ca
www.westfieldheritage.ca

The Heritage Village presents more than thirty-five historical & reproduction buildings. The site also features Ontario's oldest log cabin & a T.H. & B. steam locomotive.

***Rosemont:* Dufferin County Museum & Archives**
PO Box 120, 936029 Airport Rd., Rosemont, ON L0N 1R0
705-435-1881, Fax: 705-435-9876, 877-941-7787
info@dufferinmuseum.com
www.dufferinmuseum.com

Two log structures; CPR flagging station; historic church; changing exhibits; archives

Wayne Townsend, Director/Curator
Darrell Keenie, General Manager

***St Catharines:* Morningstar Mill (Mountain Mills Museum)**
22 Cliff Rd., St Catharines, ON L2R 3W1
905-688-6050,
info@morningstarmill.ca
www.morningstarmill.ca

Founded: 1962 Museum site is made up of a number of buildings: the water-powered gristmill (built in 1872 & known as Morningstar Mill), the turbine shed, the millers house, the icehouse, sawmill and the barn which houses the blacksmith shop and carpentry shop. School tours are welcome. Admission by donation.

Tom Wilson, St. Catharines, Recreation & Community Services, 905-688-5601 X-3134, Fax: 905-646-9262

***St Catharines:* St. Catharines Museum**
PO Box 3012, 1932 Welland Canals Pkwy., St Catharines, ON L2R 7C2
905-984-8880, Fax: 905-984-6910, 800-355-134
museuminfo@stcatharines.ca
www.stcatharineslock3museum.ca

Founded: 1965 Major collection of artifact, archival & art material related to the history of St. Catharines & the Welland Canal; collections include Girl Guides, Fred Pattison Aviation Collection (BCATP), St. Lawrence Seaway, family papers, marine photographs, Ferranti-Packard & the DeCew Falls Waterworks Collection; guided tours; summer camps, edu-fun camps; guest speakers; tours & special events

Anne Crawford, Administrative Co-ordinator, acrawford@stcatharines.ca

***St. George:* Adelaide Hunter Hoodless Homestead**
PO Box 209, 359 Blue Lake Rd., RR#1, St. George, ON N0E 1N0
519-448-1130, Fax: 519-448-1150,
hoodlesshomestead@gmail.com
www3.sympatico.ca/hoodlesshomestead1/AHH. htm

Birthplace of Adelaide Hunter Hoodless, an educational reformer, one of Canada's early feminists and a co-founder of a number of organizations promoting the cause of women's well-being, including: the Women's Institute, the Victorian Order of Nurses, the YWCA, and the National Council of Women. Hunter Hoodless was instrumental in establishing domestic science on the curriculum of Ontario schools, and wrote the first textbook to be used. Before her untimely death at the age of 53, she was engaged in the cause of promoting technical trades education for women. Her childhood home, built in 1830, is an example of mid-nineteenth century Ontario Neo Gothic style. The homestead property includes picnic facilities and grounds that can be rented for gatherings and other special occasions. Guided tours, and school programs available. Open year round.

***St Jacobs:* The Maple Syrup Museum**
***Also known as:* Maple Syrup Museum of Ontario**
Country Mill, PO Box 701, 1441 King St. North, St Jacobs, ON N0B 2N0
519-664-1232, Fax: 519-669-4259,
www.stjacobs.com

History of maple syrup production; artifacts; photographs

Albert Martin, Contact, 519-669-2423

***St Marys:* Canadian Baseball Hall of Fame & Museum**
PO Box 1838, 140 Queen St., St Marys, ON N4X 1C2
519-284-1838, Fax: 519-284-1234, 877-250-2255
baseball@baseballhalloffame.ca
www.baseballhalloffame.ca

Open May - Thanksgiving; displays include exclusive collection of Ferguson Jenkins memorabilia & artifacts of the Montreal Expos & Toronto Blue Jays

***St Marys:* St Marys Museum**
PO Box 98, 177 Church St. South, St Marys, ON N4X 1A9
519-284-3556, Fax: 519-284-2881,
museum@town.stmarys.on.ca
www.stmarysmuseum.ca

Changing exhibits; seasonal activities; research facilities for genealogy & area history in 1850s limestone house

Mary Smith, Manager
Trisha McKibbin, Curator

***St Thomas:* Elgin County Museum**
450 Sunset Dr., St Thomas, ON N5R 5V1
519-631-1460, Fax: 519-631-9209,
museum@elgin-county.on.ca
www.eglinconnects.ca

Founded: 1957 History of Elgin County; changing exhibits in gallery, workshops & special events

Mike Baker, Curator

***St Thomas:* The Elgin Military Museum**
30 Talbot St., St Thomas, ON N5P 1A3
519-633-7641, Fax: 519-637-0580, emm@exculink.com
Information on veterans from Elgin County; archive collection with military documents & publications

***Sault Ste Marie:* Ermatinger-Clergue National Historic Site**
c/o Historic Sites Board, PO Box 580, Sault Ste Marie, ON P6A 5X6
705-759-5443, Fax: 705-541-7023, old.stone.house@cityssm.on.ca
1814 stone house: features historic crop gardens, recreated rooms, costumed interpreters, hands-on activities; Blockhouse: exhibits & period furnishings; open Mid-Apr. - Nov.
Kathryn Fisher, Curator

***Sault Ste Marie:* St. Mary's River Marine Centre**
***Also known as:* Museum Ship \Norgoma\""""**
PO Box 23099 Mall, Sault Ste Marie, ON P6A 6W6
705-942-2919, Fax: 705-942-2093, marineheritagecentre@shaw.ca
Other contact information: Seasonal Phone: 705/256-7447
An 188-foot passenger/cargo vessel built in 1950; open June - Oct.

***Sault Ste Marie:* Sault Ste Marie Canal National Historic Site of Canada**
1 Canal Dr., Sault Ste Marie, ON P6A 6W4
705-941-6262, Fax: 705-941-6206, info-saultcanal@pc.gc.ca
www.pc.gc.ca/sault
Operates a recreational lock between May & Oct. & offers school programming, guided tours & a large open space for the enjoyment of visitors (boat watching, nature trail, birdwatching, cycling, fishing)
Louise Robillard, Chief, Visitor Activities, louise.robillard@pc.gc.ca

***Sault Ste Marie:* Sault Ste Marie Museum**
690 Queen St. East, Sault Ste Marie, ON P6A 2A4
705-759-7278, Fax: 705-759-3058, heritage@saultmuseum.com
www.saultmuseum.com
Maintained by the Sault St. Marie & 49th Field Regiment R.C.A. Historical Society; the museum collects & preserves artifacts & archival material illustrating the history of Sault Ste Marie & area
Kim Forbes, Curator & Administrator

***Selkirk:* Wilson MacDonald Memorial School Museum**
3513 Rainham Rd., Selkirk, ON N0A 1P0
905-776-3319, Fax: 905-776-0683, wmacdonald.museum@haldimandcounty.on.ca
www.haldimandcounty.on.ca
Wilson MacDonald Memorial School Museum presents the story of poet Wilson Pugsley MacDonald, rural education, & Selkirk, Ontario & its surrounding area. Archival research is available for a fee. The museum is open from mid March to mid December.
Dana B. Stavinga, Curator

***Sharon:* Sharon Temple National Historic Site & Museum**
18974 Leslie St., Sharon, ON L0G 1V0
905-478-2389, info@sharontemple.ca
www.sharontemple.ca
The Sharon Temple National Historic Site features nine historic buildings. The centerpiece of the site is the Temple of the Children of Peace, which was completed in 1832. Sharon Temple is open from mid May to mid October. Group & scholars may make appointments at other times of the year.

***Simcoe:* Eva Brook Donly Museum & Archives**
***Parent:* Norfolk Historical Society**
109 Norfolk St. South, Simcoe, ON N3Y 2W3
519-426-1583, Fax: 519-426-1584, office@norfolklore.com; genealogy@norfolklore.com
www.norfolklore.com
The Museum & Archives feature information about the people, heritage, & history of Norfolk County. Museum artifacts are housed in a two storey brick home which was erected in the 1840s. Archives include family histories, documents, records, & phototgraphs.
Scott Gillies, Curator & Marager, marketing@norfolklore.com
Jo-Anne Barber, President, Norfolk Historical Society

***Sioux Lookout:* Sioux Lookout Museum**
PO Box 1377, Sioux Lookout, ON P8T 1B9
807-737-1562, Fax: 807-737-4624, slrec@slkt.net
First Nations artifacts; pioneer artifacts related to logging, mining, aviation & the Canadian National Railway

***Smiths Falls:* Heritage House Museum / Musée de la maison du patrimoine**
PO Box 695, 11 Old Slys Rd., Smiths Falls, ON K7A 4T6
613-283-8560, Fax: 613-283-4764, heritagehouse@smithsfalls.ca
www.smithsfalls.ca/heritagehouse
Founded: 1981 Built in 1860-1861 by Joshua Bates, the house is located near the Rideau River and displays 7 rooms, including kitchen, parlor and bedroom, all restored to Victorian style. Workshops and programs for children are offered. There is a gift shop. Tours available; open year round.
Carol Miller, Curator

***Smiths Falls:* Industrial Heritage Complex Merrickville Lockstation**
34A Beckwith St. South, Smiths Falls, ON K7A 2A8
613-283-5170,
19th century construction on Rideau Canal, with emphasis on Merrickville; collection includes power generation machinery

***Smiths Falls:* Rideau Canal Museum**
34 Beckwith St. South, Smiths Falls, ON K7A 2B3
613-284-0505,
High-tech displays; artifacts

***Smiths Falls:* Smiths Falls Railway Museum of Eastern Ontario**
PO Box 962, 90 William St. West, Smiths Falls, ON K7A 5A5
613-283-5696, Fax: 613-283-7211, sfrmchin@superaje.com
www.sfrmeo.ca
Railway Museum at the historic CNR station
Robert A. Moore, Vice-President
John Saunders, Treasurer
John Weir, Secretary
George R. Ward, President

***Sombra:* Sombra Museum**
3470 St. Clair Parkway, Sombra, ON N0P 2H0
519-892-3982, Fax: 519-892-3982, www.lambtononline.com/sombra_museum
Local historical artifacts housed in 1881 Victorian frame home; stories of the St. Clair River illustrated through photos & artifacts in 3 rooms; log cabin circa 1830; reference collection & family archives; marine room featuring nautical equipment & photos relating to the St. Clair River & the Great Lakes; special events & programming.
Shelley Lucier, Curator, shelleylucier@hotmail.com

***South Baymouth:* Little Schoolhouse & Museum South Baymouth**
General Delivery, South Baymouth, ON P0P 1Z0
705-859-2344,
Trace the history of Tehkummah Township, one of Ontario's ghost towns, Michael's Bay, and the development of South Baymouth and includes one of the pioneer one room schools. Displays the history of this fishing village through artifacts and pictures.
Bryan Gleason, Contact, 705-859-2344

***South Porcupine:* Timmins Museum: National Exhibition Centre / Musée de Timmins: Centre national d'exposition**
70 Legion Dr., South Porcupine, ON P0N 1H0
705-235-5066, Fax: 705-235-9631, tmnec@city.timmins.on.ca
Preserves, presents & studies the history of the Porcupine Gold Camp, Timmins Ontario

***Southampton:* Bruce County Museum & Cultural Centre**
PO Box 180, 33 Victoria St. North, Southampton, ON N0H 2L0
519-797-2080, Fax: 519-797-2191, 866-318-8889
collections@brucecounty.on.ca
www.brucemuseum.ca
Other contact information: E-mail, Archival Information: archives@brucecounty.on.ca
Permanent galleries at the Bruce County Museum & Cultural Centre include the following: Creation Stories; Our Tropical Past; Geology & The Ice Ages; First People's Gallery; A Time To Remember, featuring military exhibits; Telephone Beginnings, depicting the history of telephone service in Bruce County; Living On The Land, showcasing the area's agricultural history; The Land; Living On The Water, with information about lighthouses, shipbuilding, fishing, & shipwrecks; & Living in Balance, with information about resources & industries.
Barbara Ribey, Director & Curator

***Stittsville:* Goulbourn Museum**
PO Box 621, 2064 Huntley Rd., RR#3, Stittsville, ON K2S 1A7
613-831-2393, goulbmus@rogers.com
www.goulbournmuseum.ca
Collection housed in 1873 Township Hall & 1961 Clerk's Building; displays about a family farms & rural schools; exhibit of military service from 1812 to present; genealogical data & library; open year round

***Stoney Creek:* Battlefield House Museum & Park**
PO Box 66561, 77 King St. West, Stoney Creek, ON L8G 3X9
905-662-8458, Fax: 905-662-0529, battlefield@hamilton.ca
www.battlefieldhouse.ca
The Gage Homestead was built in 1796. During the War of 1812 & the Battle of Stoney Creek, the Gage family fled to the cellar of the home. The Battlefield Monument commemorates the soldiers who died during the battle. Each June, the Battlefield House Museum & Park is the site of a military re-enactment of the Battle of Stoney Creek. The site is open from July 1st to Labour Day.
Susan Ramsay, Curator

***Stoney Creek:* Erland Lee Museum**
***Also known as:* The Women's Institutes Museum**
552 Ridge Rd., Stoney Creek, ON L8J 2Y6
905-662-2691, Fax: 905-662-2045, erlandlee@interlynx.net
www.erlandlee.com
Museum, carriagehoue & gardens; site of the 1897 founding of the Women's Institutes organization; Home of the Stoney Creek family 1790-1970; guided tours, lookout, catering, picnic area & gift shop
Meaghan FitzGibbon, Curator

***Stratford:* Brocksden Country School Museum**
2719 Perth Line 37, RR#1, Stratford, ON N5A 4C7
519-271-0499, Fax: 519-271-1978,
The school which opened in 1853 presents a living history program for classes.
Wilma McCaig, Secretary

***Stratford:* Fryfogel Tavern**
Perth County Historical Foundation, 1931 Line 34, Stratford, ON N0B 2P0

Stagecoach stop & resting place 1844-45; history of Perth County's settlers; open by appt.

***Strathroy:* A.W. Campbell House Museum**
c/o St. Clair Region Conservation Authority, 205 Mill Pond Cres., Strathroy, ON N7G 3P9
519-245-3710, Fax: 519-245-3348, stclair@scrca.on.ca
www.scrca.on.ca
The museum is located in the A.W. Campbell Conservation Area, R.R.#2 Alvinston, ON, off Nauvoo Rd. A typical 1890s southwestern Ontario rural home comprises the museum, and the conservation area also includes a campground and walking trails.
Rick Battson, Director of Communications, rbattson@scrca.on.ca

***Strathroy:* Strathroy Middlesex Museum**
34 Frank St., Strathroy, ON N7G 2R4
519-245-0492, Fax: 519-245-1073, info@strathroymuseum.ca
www.strathroymuseum.ca
Open year round; medical theme room; military display; 1930s electric kitchen; printing shop; archival material

***Sturgeon Falls:* Musée Sturgeon River House Museum**
250 ch Fort Rd., Sturgeon Falls, ON P2B 2N7
705-753-4716, Fax: 705-753-5476, info@sturgeonriverhouse.com
www.sturgeonriverhouse.com
Le musée se trouve sur un site de la Compagnie de la Baie d'Hudson; l'exposition traite de fourrure et les animaux de la région.
Serge Ducharme, Directeur

***Sudbury:* Anderson Farm Museum**
PO Box 6400, Sudbury, ON P3A 3B7
705-692-4448, jim.fortin@city.greatersudbury.on.ca
Open year round

***Sudbury:* Centre franco-ontarien de folklore (CFOF)**
1169, rue Dollard, Sudbury, ON P3A 4G7
705-675-8986, Fax: 705-675-5809, cfof@cfof.on.ca
www.cfof.on.ca
Founded: 1972 A pour mission de mettre en valeur le folklore et le patrimoine franco-ontarien; musée; activités éducatives; bibliothèque; archives; publications; magasin virtuel
Diane Charette-Lavoie, Présidente, Conseil d'administration

***Sudbury:* Copper Cliff Museum**
PO Box 6400 A, Sudbury, ON P3A 3B7
705-692-4448,
Founded: 1901 Located in 1890 log house; contains artifacts pertaining to the lifestyle of residents of a mining community; photographs & documents leading back to establishment of Copper Cliff

***Sutton West:* Eildon Hall Sibbald Memorial Museum**
Sibbald Point Provincial Park, RR#2, Sutton West, ON L0E 1R0

905-722-8061, Fax: 905-722-5416,
Situated by the shore of Lake Simcoe, Eildon Hall was the Sibbald family home

***Thunder Bay:* Centennial Park 1910 Logging Camp and Museum**
Parks Division, Victoria Ville Civic Centre, 111 Syndicate Ave. South, Thunder Bay, ON P7E 6S4
807-625-2351, Fax: 807-625-3528,
www.thunderbay.ca/parks
Full scale replica of a 1910 logging camp re-creates the early history of Northern Ontario's forest industry; park open year round; logging camp and museum open mid-June to Labour Day, 8:00 am.m to 8:00 p.m.; Muskeg Express logging train; Winter sleigh rides; craft shop; picnic area; trails
Bruce Phillips

***Thunder Bay:* Fort William Historical Park (FWHP)**
Vickers Heights PO, Thunder Bay, ON P0T 2Z0
807-577-8461, Fax: 807-473-2327,
info@fwhp.ca
www.fwhp.ca
A living history site that depicts the fur trade activities of the North West Company in the early 1800s; 42 reconstructed buildings on a 225-acre site. Touts that it is the largest Fur Trade Post.
Sergio Buonocore, General Manager, sergio.buonocore@mtr.gov.on.ca

***Thunder Bay:* Northwestern Ontario Sports Hall of Fame**
219 May St. South, Thunder Bay, ON P7E 1B5
807-622-2852, Fax: 807-622-2736,
nwosport@tbaytel.net
www.nwosportshalloffame.com
Founded: 1978 The Hall's mission is to preserve and honour Northwestern Ontario's sports heritage, with displays, photos, archival material, artifacts and other documentation on over 200 athletes; reference library; educational programming. Open all year.
Diane Imrie, Executive Director

***Thunder Bay:* Paipoonge Historical Museum**
RR#6, Thunder Bay, ON P7C 5N5
807-939-1262, Fax: 807-577-3888,
lgarrity@tbaytel.net
Founded: 1952 Reflecting the history of the Municipality of Oliver/Paipoonge & area during the late 1800s & early 1900s. Collection of pioneer material and farm machinery, old school room, kitchen and bedroom displays.
Lois Garrity, Curator & Director

***Thunder Bay:* Thunder Bay Museum**
***Also known as:* Thunder Bay Historical Museum Society**
425 East Donald St., Thunder Bay, ON P7E 5V1
807-623-0801, Fax: 807-622-6880,
info@thunderbaymuseum.com
www.thunderbaymuseum.com
A museum, historical society & archives for Thunder Bay & Northwestern Ontario
Dr. Tory Tronrud, Curator

***Thunder Bay:* Thunder Bay Military Museum**
The Armoury, 317 Park Ave., Thunder Bay, ON P7B 1C7
807-343-5175, Fax: 807-346-4022,
jjyoung@vianet.ca
Georg Hoegel Art Collection - paintings & drawings done by Mr. Hoegel when he was a prisoner of war in Canada from 1941-1946; other military art; tri-service collection, representing all three services, rotated regularly; open 4 afternoons, 2 evenings & by request
Lt.(N) Ken MacAskill, Chair
Lt.Col. John J. Young, Curator

***Tillsonburg:* Annandale National Historic Site**
***Also known as:* Tillsonburg Museum**
30 Tillson Ave., Tillsonburg, ON N4G 2Z8
519-842-2294, Fax: 519-842-9431,
rcorner@tillsonburg.ca
www.tillsonburg.ca
Nationally designated for its Aesthetic *interior, Annandale House is restored to the 1880's period; location of tourist information for Tillsonburg; open year round*
Rita Corner, Curator

***Tobermory:* The Peninsula & St. Edmunds Township Museum**
RR#1, Tobermory, ON N0H 2R0
519-596-2479,

***Toronto:* The Bata Shoe Museum (BSM)**
327 Bloor St. West, Toronto, ON M5S 1W7
416-979-7799, Fax: 416-979-0078,
www.batashoemuseum.ca
Explores footwear in the social & cultural life of humankind from ancient times to present. Exhibits vary but there is a permanant exhibit which includes a pair of Elton John platform shoes and shoes which date back hundreds of years.
Sonja Bata, Chair

***Toronto:* Beth Tzedec Reuben & Helene Dennis Museum**
c/o Beth Tzedec Synagogue, 1700 Bathurst St., Toronto, ON M5P 3K3
416-781-3514, Fax: 416-781-0150,
museum@beth-tzedec.org
www.beth-tzedec.org/museum
Founded: 1965 The museum features a major Judaica collection, including Jewish art & history from ancient times to the present. Appointments may be made for tours.
Dorion Liebgott, Curator

***Toronto:* Black Creek Pioneer Village**
1000 Murray Ross Pkwy., Toronto, ON M3J 2P3
416-736-1733,
bcpvinfo@trca.on.ca
www.blackcreek.ca
Operated by the Toronto & Region Conservation Authority (TRCA), Black Creek Pioneer Village is a living history experience, which spans over 30 acres. It exemplifies a small south central Ontario community between the 1790s & the 1860s. Demonstrations & special activities depict rural life. Black Creek Village also features the historic Black Creek Historic Brewery. The village is open from the beginning of May to the end of December.
Rick Sikorski, Manager, Marketing & Communications, TRCA

***Toronto:* Campbell House**
160 Queen St. West, Toronto, ON M5H 3H3
416-597-0227, Fax: 416-597-0750,
info@campbellhousemuseum.ca
www.campbellhousemuseum.ca
Built in 1822, the Campbell House is the oldest remaining building from the original town of York. The Sir William Campbell Foundation operates the museum. Special programs are available for groups. The Home is open from the beginning of May until Thanksgiving.

***Toronto:* Canada's Sports Hall of Fame (CSHOF) / Panthéon des Sports Canadiens**
Exhibition Place, 115 Prince's Blvd., Toronto, ON M6K 3C3
416-260-6789, Fax: 416-260-9347,
info@cshof.ca; events@cshof.ca
www.cshof.ca
Canada's Sports Hall of Fame tells the stories of Canadian amateur & professional athletes, as well as sport builders, who have made outstanding achievements thoughout sports history.
Janice Smith, Executive Director
Sheryn Posen, Chief Operating Officer
Nick Brentanos, Photo Archivist
Kathy Dostaler, Translator

***Toronto:* Canadian Air & Space Museum (TAM)**
PO Box 1, 65 Carl Hall Rd., Toronto, ON M3K 2E1
416-638-6078, Fax: 416-638-5509,
casm@casmuseum.org
www.casmuseum.org
Aviation industry & history in the Toronto region

***Toronto:* Canadian Broadcasting Corporation Museum & & Graham Spry Theatre**
PO Box 500 A, 250 Front St. West, Toronto, ON M5W 1E6
416-205-5574,
www.cbc.ca/museum
The CBC Museum presents the story of CBC's broadcasting history, since 1936.

***Toronto:* The Canadian Business Hall of Fame / Le Temple de la renommée de l'entreprise canadienne**
#306, 2275 Lakeshore Blvd. West, Toronto, ON M8V 3Y3
416-622-4602, Fax: 416-622-6861,
rmaund@jacan.org
cbhof.org
Located in The Galleria, BCE Place
Ross Maund, President & CEO

***Toronto:* Casa Loma**
1 Austin Terrace, Toronto, ON M5R 1X8
416-923-1171, Fax: 416-923-5734,
info@casaloma.org; kiwanis@casaloma.org
www.casaloma.org
Founded: 1937 Owned by the City of Toronto & operated by The Kiwanis Club of Casa Loma, Casa Loma is the former home of Sir Henry Pellatt, a Canadian financier, industrialist, & military man. The decorated castle contains an 800 foot tunnel, secret passages, towers, & stables. A self-guided audio tour is available in eight languages.
Richard R. Wozenilek, Chair, Board of Trustees of Casa Loma
Lou Seiler, Director, Marketing, lseiler@casaloma.org

***Toronto:* Colborne Lodge**
c/o Museum Services, Metro Hall, 55 John St., 8th Fl., Toronto, ON M5V 3C6
416-392-6916, Fax: 416-392-0375,
clodge@toronto.ca
www.toronto.ca/museums; www.highpark.org/colborne.htm
Site of the 19th century home of High Park founders, John & Jemmina Howard; contains many of their original furnishings, watercolours of early Toronto, & other artifacts; coach house, tomb & restored gardens on the property; special events & programming; party room rentals; located at the south end of High Park, Colborne Lodge Dr., just north of the Queensway. Open year round.
Cheryl Hart, Museum Coordinator

***Toronto:* The Enoch Turner Schoolhouse (1848)**
106 Trinity St., Toronto, ON M5A 3C6
416-863-0010,
aleblanc@enochturnerschoolhouse.ca
www.enochturnerschoolhouse.ca
One of Toronto's oldest institutions & the city's first free school
Andrew LeBlanc, Administrator

***Toronto:* Fort York National Historic Site**
100 Garrison Rd., Toronto, ON M5V 3K9
416-392-6907, Fax: 416-392-6917,
fortyork@toronto.ca
www.toronto.ca/culture/museums/fort-york.htm
Founded: 1934 Built by Lieutenant-Governor John Graves Simcoe as a garrison in 1793, Fort York was purchased by the City of Toronto in 1909 and restored as a museum in 1934. Its fortified walls contain the largest collection of original War of 1812 buildings in Canada. Some of the restored interiors reflect the life of the garrison community, while others serve as exhibit space for artifacts on a military theme. The site offers seasonal guided tours as well as musket, drill, and music demonstrations.
MR David O'Hara, Site Administrator, 416-392-6907, X-222, dohara@toronto.ca

***Toronto:* Gardiner Museum of Ceramic Art**
***Also known as:* Gardiner Museum**
111 Queen's Park, Toronto, ON M5S 2C7
416-586-8080, Fax: 416-586-8085,
mail@gardinermuseum.on.ca
www.gardinermuseum.on.ca
The premier specialized ceramic museum in North America
Alexander Montgomery, Executive Director

***Toronto:* Gibson House Museum**
5176 Yonge St., Toronto, ON M2N 5P6
416-395-7432, Fax: 416-395-7442,
gibsonhouse@toronto.ca
www.toronto.ca/museums
Depicts lives of the Gibson family in 1851 Willowdale
Elizabeth Nelson-Raffaele, Curator

***Toronto:* Mackenzie House**
82 Bond St., Toronto, ON M5B 1X2
416-392-6915, Fax: 416-392-0114,
machouse@toronto.ca
www.toronto.ca/museums
Founded: 1950 The final home of Toronto's first mayor, William Lyon Mackenzie who gained notoriety during the 1837 Upper Canada Rebellion, this 1858 Georgian rowhouse has been refurnished in period style and also showcases a print shop.
MS Janet Schwartz, Site Coordinator

***Toronto:* Montgomery's Inn**
4709 Dundas St. West, Toronto, ON M9A 1A8
416-394-8113, Fax: 416-394-6027,
montinn@toronto.ca
www.montgomerysinn.com
Founded: 1975 Built in 1830, the restored inn reflects life in 1847. Its library holds photographs, artifacts, and archival materials documenting the history of Etobicoke. There is also a tearoom and gift shop.
Mike Lipowski, Curator, 416/394-8112

***Toronto:* Baycrest Heritage Museum**
***Also known as:* The Morris and Sally Justein Heritage Museum**
Baycrest Hospital, 3560 Bathurst St., Main Fl., Toronto, ON M6A 2E1
416-785-2500, Fax: 416-785-2378,
www.baycrest.org
The Morris and Sally Justein Heritage Museum displays Judaica exhibits. The historical & cultural Judaica exhibits & permanent collections are designed for Baycrest Hospital & Home's elderly clients.
Lois Buckstein, Chair

***Toronto:* Museum of Childhood (MOC)**
PO Box 322, c/o 260 Adelaide St. East, Toronto, ON M5A 1N1
416-368-2866, Fax: 416-504-0316,
info@museumofchildhood.ca
www.museumofchildhood.ca

Extensive collection of childhood toys, clothes, furniture, books; opening date before year 2005; educational presentations & traveling exhibits available
Loet Vos, President

***Toronto:* The Queen's Own Rifles of Canada Regimental Museum**
Casa Loma, 1 Austin Terrace, Toronto, ON M5R 1X8
905-407-3675,
Display artifacts pertinent to the history of the regiment from 1860-present

***Toronto:* Queen's York Rangers Regimental Museum**
660 Fleet St., Toronto, ON M5V 1A9
416-203-4200,
Traces the history of the Queen's York Rangers, an active reconnaissance unit of the Army Reserve; displays begin wth the Seven Year's War, through the American Revolution & settlement of Upper Canada & through the campaigns of 19th century & two world wars

***Toronto:* Redpath Sugar Museum**
95 Queen's Quay East, Toronto, ON M5E 1A3
416-933-8341, Fax: 416-366-7550, 800-267-1517
Consumer-Canada@redpathsugar.com
www.redpathsugars.com
Founded: 1979 The Redpath Sugar Museum displays the history of sugar production & refining, models of transportation that bring sugar to the refinery, as well as the story of the Redpath family. The museum offers a program for schools.
Scott Brownrigg, Contact, Media Inquiries, 416-644-4927

***Toronto:* Royal Canadian Military Institute Museum**
426 University Ave., Toronto, ON M5G 1S9
416-597-0286, Fax: 416-597-6919,
info@rcmi.org
www.rcmi.org
Artifacts related to Canadians' participation in the military; library open to researchers & members; open year round
Gregory Loughton, Curator, gregory.loughton@rcmi.org

***Toronto:* The Royal Regiment of Canada Museum**
***Also known as:* The Royals' Museum**
Fort York Armoury, 660 Fleet St., Toronto, ON M5V 1A9
416-755-1727,
rregtc.gmail.com
www.army.dnd.ca/rregtc/coy/museum.html
Founded: 1996 Military artifacts, dating from 1862, of the The Royal Regiment of Canada, & predecessors: the 10th Royal Grenadiers (Toronto Regiment), & the 3rd, 123rd, 124th, 204th & 58th Battalions; archives; school tours by appointment. Located next to the Royals' WO's & Sergeants' Mess on the 2nd floor, at the east end of Fort York Armoury.
Capt. Bruce Barbeau, Curator

***Toronto:* The Salvation Army Museum**
2 Overlea Blvd., Toronto, ON M4H 1P4
416-425-2111,
heritage_centre@can.salvationarmy.org
heritage.salvationarmy.ca
Open to public & gives a pictorial outline of Salvation Army history, particularly as it pertains to Canada & Bermuda, through the use of artifacts, photographs & special techniques; no fee; wheelchair accessible; open Mon.-Fri., closed all statutory holidays
Col. John E. Carew, Director

***Toronto:* Scadding Cabin**
***Parent:* York Pioneeer & Historical Society**
c/o York Pioneers & Historical Society, PO Box 45026, 2482 Yonge St., Toronto, ON M4P 3E3
416-494-0503,
yorkpioneers@gmail.com; information@explace.on.ca
www.yorkpioneers.org; www.explace.on.ca
Built for John Scadding, clerk to Lieutenant-Governor John Graves Simcoe, the cabin is Toronto's oldest dwelling. Located at Exhibition Place, southeast of 25 British Columbia Rd.; wooden house, built in late 1700s, contains furniture which belonged to John Graves Simcoe; open late Aug.-Labour Day (during CNE)

***Toronto:* Scarborough Historical Museum**
1007 Brimley Rd., Toronto, ON M1P 3E8
416-338-8807, Fax: 416-338-8805,
shm@toronto.ca
www.toronto.ca/museums
Includes Cornell House, McCowan Log Cabin & Hough Carriage Works; picnic area; parking
Madeleine Callaghan, Manager/Curator

***Toronto:* Sesquicentennial Museum & Archives**
Toronto District School Board, 155 College St., Toronto, ON M5T 1P6
416-397-3680, Fax: 416-397-3685,
smachin@planeteer.com
Preserves the history of the TDSB & its schools; collects, documents, researches, exhibits, & historical artifacts, fine art, & archival, & published material for its educational community - students, parents, staff & trustees & its citizens
Greg McKinnon, Manager & Board Archivist
David Sowerbatts, Conservator

***Toronto:* Spadina Museum: Historic House & Gardens**
285 Spadina Rd., Toronto, ON M5R 2V5
416-392-6910, Fax: 416-392-0382,
spadina@toronto.ca
www.toronto.ca/culture/museums/spadina.htm
1866 mansion contains four generations of décor, reflecting art movements such as Art Nouveau
Nancy Reynolds, Site Coordinator
Karen Edwards, Curator

***Toronto:* Taras H. Shevchenko Museum**
1614 Bloor St. West, Toronto, ON M6P 1A7
416-534-8662, Fax: 416-535-1063,
shevchenkomuseum@bellnet.ca
www.infoukes.com/shevchenkomuseum
Ethnographic
Wm. Harasym, President

***Toronto:* Textile Museum of Canada**
55 Centre Ave., Toronto, ON M5G 2H5
416-599-5321, Fax: 416-599-2911,
info@textilemuseum.ca
www.textilemuseum.ca
Unique exhibitions & programming; focus on the traditions & aesthetics of historic & contemporary textiles
Patricia Bentley, Sr. Curator

***Toronto:* Todmorden Mills Heritage Museum & Art Centre**
67 Pottery Rd., Toronto, ON M4K 2B8
416-396-2819,
todmorden@toronto.ca
www.toronto.ca/culture/museums/todmorden.htm
Depicts early industry in Toronto; new papermill galleries & theatre feature frequent exhibitions & is available for rental
Ulana Baluk, Administrator

***Toronto:* Toronto Police Museum & Discovery Centre**
40 College St., Toronto, ON M5G 2J3
416-808-7020, Fax: 416-808-7023,
museum@torontopolice.on.ca
www.torontopolice.on.ca
Interactive displays; collection includes uniforms, badges, communication & transportation equipment; high profile crimes; open year round
Norina D'Agostini
Gabi Voigt

***Toronto:* Toronto's First Post Office (TFPO)**
260 Adelaide St. East, Toronto, ON M5A 1N1
416-865-1833, Fax: 416-865-9414,
tfpo@total.net
www.townofyork.com
Canada's only surviving pre-1851 Post Office; restored as a museum & full postal service operation; gift shop
Danielle Pesneau, Curator

***Toronto:* Ukrainian Museum of Canada**
Ukrainian Women's Association of Canada, Ontario Branch, 620 Spadina Ave., Toronto, ON M5S 2H4
416-923-3318, Fax: 416-923-8266,
svi@stvladimir.on.ca
Open Mon.-Fri., Sat.-Sun. by appt. only
Halya Kluchko, Curator

***Toronto:* York Museum**
Centennial Recreation Centre, 2694 Eglinton Ave. West, Toronto, ON M6M 1T9
416-394-2759,
yorkmuseum@toronto.ca
www.toronto.ca/culture/york_museum.htm
York Museum tells the story of the former City of York. Artifacts range from a 3,000 year old stone axe as a reminder of the First Nations history in the area, to a telephone switchboard. Phone 416-338-0492 to arrange a visit.

***Tweed:* Tweed & Area Heritage Centre**
***Also known as:* Houston House 1897**
PO Box 665, 40 Victoria St. North, Tweed, ON K0K 3J0
613-478-3989, Fax: 613-478-6457,
tweedheritageinfo@on.aibn.com
www.ruralroutes.com/tweedheritage
Founded: 1988 An information centre, art gallery, museum, archives & genealogical research centre; local arts & crafts promotional centre
E. Morton, Curator

***Uxbridge:* Thomas Foster Memorial Temple**
PO Box 190, 51 Toronto St. South, Uxbridge, ON L9P 1T1
905-852-9181, Fax: 905-852-9164, 888-559-9022
www.town.uxbridge.on.ca
Built by former mayor of Toronto, Thomas Foster, in 1935/36 as a memorial to his wife, unique in the design of Byzantine architecture; holds tours on the 1st & 2nd Sun., June-Sept.; special concerts throughout the year, with special program in Oct.
Bev Northeast, Contact, bnortheast@powergate.ca

***Uxbridge:* Uxbridge Historical Centre**
***Also known as:* Uxbridge-Scott Museum & Archives**
PO Box 1301, 7239 Conc. 6, Uxbridge, ON L9P 1N5
905-852-5854, Fax: 905-852-5854,
museum@town.uxbridge.on.ca
uxlib.com/museum
Displays of artifacts & photos to help tell the story of the Uxbridge area; special display on The Oak Ridges Moraine; 10 heritage buildings on site; picnic grounds
Allan McGillivray, Curator

***Vernon:* Osgoode Township Historical Society & Museum**
PO Box 74, 7814 Lawrence St., Vernon, ON K0A 3J0
613-821-4062,
oths@magma.ca
www.magma.ca/~oths
The Osgoode Township Historical Society & Museum preserves the development of the Township of Osgoode, situated south of Ottawa, Ontario. Artifacts include indigenous Native & pioneer articles & documents, such as historic furniture & clothing, & agricultural tools & equipment. The Museum is open Tuesdays to Saturdays.
Jenn Hume, Contact

***Wasaga Beach:* Nancy Island Historic Site**
c/o Wasaga Beach Provincial Park, 11 - 22nd St. North, Wasaga Beach, ON L9Z 2V9
705-429-2516, Fax: 705-429-7983,
nancyisland@wasagabeachpark.com
www.wasagabeachpark.com
Remains of the British schooner "Nancy"; replica of Upper Lakes lighthouse; artifacts related to marine aspects of War of 1812

***Waterford:* Spruce Row Museum**
PO Box 457, Waterford, ON N0E 1Y0
519-443-4211, Fax: 519-443-5640,
sprucerow.museum@norfolkcounty.on.ca
www.norfolkcounty.on.ca; www.sprucerowmuseum.ca
History of the Waterford & Townsend area; includes unique collection of agricultural equipment representative of southern Ontario
Jennifer Hunt-Beauchamp, Curator

***Waterloo:* Earth Sciences Museum**
***Also known as:* Biology-Earth Sciences Museum**
Centre for Environmental & Information Technology, University of Waterloo, Waterloo, ON N2L 3G1
519-888-4567, Fax: 519-746-7484,
esmuseum@uwaterloo.ca
www.earth.uwaterloo.ca/outreach/museum
Dinosaurs, gems, minerals & a 60-tonne rock garden
Peter Russell, Director

***Waterloo:* Brubacher House Museum**
c/o University of Waterloo, North Campus, Waterloo, ON N2L 3G6
519-886-3855,
bhouse@watserv1.uwaterloo.ca
www.grebel.uwaterloo.ca/bhouse
Built in 1850, the Brubacher House was later purchased by the University of Waterloo. The home's interior was rebuilt to reflect a Pennsylvania German Mennonite home from the 1850 to 1890 era. Many of the furnishings in the Brubacher House, collected from local Mennonite families, also reflect the time period. Operated by Conrad Grebel University College & the Mennonite Historical Society of Ontario, the House is open from the beginning of May to the end of October.

***Waterloo:* Museum & Archive of Games**
Burt Matthews Hall, University of Waterloo, 200 University Avenue West, Waterloo, ON N2L 3G1
519-888-4424, Fax: 519-886-2440,
musinfo@healthy.uwaterloo.ca
www.gamesmuseum.uwaterloo.ca/
Specializes in the collection, presentation & display of games, both Canadian & international collections; researchers act as a resource for archiving related materials related to games & also provide research facilities & expertise to persons interested in pursuing the study of Games
Prof. Rhonda Ryman, Asst. Curator
Dr. Ronald Johnson, Curator

***Waterloo:* Museum of Visual Science & Optometry**
Optometry Bldg., University of Waterloo, Waterloo, ON N2L 3G1
519-885-1211, Fax: 519-725-0784,
www.optometry.uwaterloo.ca/museum/index.htm
Antique spectacles; eye examining equipment; historical documents & books; open; year round

***Wawa:* Lake Superior Provincial Park Visitor Centre**
PO Box 267, Wawa, ON P0S 1K0

705-856-2284, Fax: 705-856-1333,
www.ontarioparks.com
Open in July & Aug., this interpretive centre includes information on the Lake Superior Provincial Park's natural & cultural features & the area's recreational opportunities

***Welland:* Ball's Falls Centre for Conservation**
c/o Niagara Peninsula Conservation Authority, 250 Thorold Rd. West, 3rd Fl., Welland, ON L3C 3W2
905-788-3135, Fax: 905-788-1121,
www.npca.ca
The Ball's Falls Centre for Conservation offers information about the Niagara Peninsula's history, the natural history of the Twenty Valley & its watershed, & the Niagara Escarpment Biosphere Reserve. Historical homes, a mill, & a church are available for touring.
Christine Hayward, Curator
Diane L. Bois, Administrative Assistant, Operations, dbois@conservation-niagara.on.ca

***Welland:* Welland Historical Museum**
65 Hooker St., Welland, ON L3C 5G9
905-732-2215,
whmchin@niagara.com
History of Welland including the Welland Canal & its industries; open Tue.-Sat.; kids summer camps in July & Aug.; children's museum
Susan Noakes, Curator/Director

***Wellington:* Wellington Heritage Museum**
290 Main St., Wellington, ON K0K 3L0
613-399-5015, Fax: 613-476-9835,
wellmuseum@pecounty.on.ca (May - September)
Other contact information: E-mail, October - April: museums@pecounty.on.ca
The local history collection of the Wellington Heritage Museum is housed within a Quaker Meeting House, which was built in 1885. The museum features a tribute to the Society of Friends, who helped develop the county. A special collection is the Douglas A. Crawford Canning Industry Collection. Wellington Heritage Museum is open from May to mid October.
Jennifer Lyons, Head Curator, 613-476-2148
Janice Hubbs, Site Curator, 613-399-5015

***Westport:* Rideau District Museum**
PO Box 305, Westport, ON K0G 1X0
613-273-2502, Fax: 613-273-3222,
bwlaird@rideau.net
Founded: 1961 Housed in 1850s blacksmith & carriage shop with forges & bellows intact & showing many artifacts from the local district, including a 9-foot tall 19th-century statue of Sally Grant, the Blind Lady of Justice
Wendy Briggs-Jude, Chair, 613-273-5449

***White Lake:* Waba Cottage Museum & Gardens**
PO Box 167, Museum Rd., White Lake, ON K0A 3L0
613-623-4341,
Situated in an 8-acre park amongst heritage buildings, boat launch & flower gardens
B. Stewart, Chair

***Whitney:* Algonquin Visitor Centre & Algonquin Logging Museum**
PO Box 219, Whitney, ON K0J 2M0
613-637-2828, Fax: 613-637-2138,
info@algonquinpark.on.ca
www.algonquinpark.on.ca
Other contact information: Park Information: 705/633-5572
Visitor Centre contains exhibits on the Park's natural & human history, restaurant, & bookstore; wheelchair accessible; Logging Museum presents the history of logging from 1830's to current times; exhibits include a recreated Camboose camp & a steam powered amphibious tug. Visitor Centre open year round. Logging Museum open daily 9:00-5:00 from late June until Thanksgiving.
Rick Stronks, Chief Park Naturalist

***Williamstown:* The Nor'Westers & Loyalist Museum**
PO Box 69, Williamstown, ON K0C 2J0
613-347-3547,
museum@bellnet.ca
Housed in a Georgian-style building; stories of loyalist pioneers & partners of the Northwest Fur Trade Company
Joan P. MacDonald, Chair

***Windsor:* Windsor's Community Museum**
***Also known as:* François Baby House**
254 Pitt St. West, Windsor, ON N9A 5L5
519-253-1812, Fax: 519-253-0919,
wmuseum@city.windsor.on.ca
www.citywindsor.ca
Founded: 1958 The Museum includes the François Baby House on Pitt St. W., and the Duff-Baby Interpretation Centre, located at 221 Mill St.; changing exhibits on the history of the Windsor region; houses over 15,000 artifacts, paintings, drawings, prints and photos, maps, newspapers and books, and a large archival collection. Open year round.
Madelyn Della Valle, Curator

***Windsor:* Ojibway Nature Centre**
5200 Matchette Rd., Windsor, ON N9C 4E8
519-966-5852, Fax: 519-966-9658,
www.ojibway.ca
The Ojibway Nature Centre presents displays about the natural history & ecology of the Ojibway Prairie Complex. Visitors will also discover a live exhibit area, featuring the Eastern Fox Snake & the Eastern Massasauga Rattlesnake. The Centre is staffed by naturalists, who provide lessons & conducted tours. Events & programs are available for all ages.

***Windsor:* Serbian Heritage Museum of Windsor (SHM)**
6770 Tecumseh Rd. East, Windsor, ON N8T 1E6
519-944-4884, Fax: 519-974-3963,
members.tripod.com/swo_heritage/serbian.htm
Founded: 1987 Artifacts & archival material of Serbian people in Windsor dating back to 1920s; tours, educational programming & lectures; gift shop; open year round

***Windsor:* Willistead Manor**
1899 Niagara St., Windsor, ON N8Y 1K3
519-253-2365, Fax: 519-253-5101,
willisteadmanor@city.windsor.on.ca
36-room mansion, built 1904-1906; viewing by appt. Available for special events.

***Wingham:* North Huron District Museum**
PO Box 1522, 273 Josephine St., Wingham, ON N0G 2W0
519-357-1096, Fax: 519-357-1110,
nhdmuseum@wightman.ca
Special events & bi-monthly exhibits featuring the history of North Huron's writers, painters, businesses, farmers & people; Special exhibit & garden dedicated to Alice Munro

***Woodstock:* Woodstock Museum National Historic Site**
Museum Square, 466 Dundas St., Woodstock, ON N4S 1C4
519-537-8411, Fax: 519-537-7235,
museum@city.woodstock.on.ca
www.woodstockmuseum.ca
Other contact information: E-mail, Registrar: apollard@city.woodstock.on.ca
The Woodstock Museum National Historic Site exhibits the local history of Woodstock from 10,000 B.C. to 2001. At the former Town Hall & Market House, which was built in 1853, visitors can see the 1879 Council Chambers & the 1889 Grand Hall. The museum contains a research room, with books & vertical files. It is open to the public by appointment only. School education programs are available, by phoning 519-539-2382, extension 2903, or e-mailing the Education Officer at the following address: kgill@city.woodstock.on.ca. The museum is open year-round.
Karen Houston, Curator, khouston@city.woodstock.on.ca

Prince Edward Island

Provincial Museums

Prince Edward Island Museum & Heritage Foundation / Le Musée et la Fondation du patrimoine de l'Ile-du-Prince-É
2 Kent St., Charlottetown, PE C1A 1M6
902-368-6600, Fax: 902-368-6608,
mhpei@gov.pe.ca
www.peimuseum.com
The organization is the operator of seven provincial museums & heritage sites across Prince Edward Island. Sites include the Elmira Railway Museum, Basin Head Fisheries Museum, Orwell Corner Historic Village & Agricultural Museum, Beaconsfield Historic House, Eptek Art & Culture Centre, The Acadian Museum of Prince Edward Island, & Green Park Shipbuilding Museum & Yeo House. Open year-round are the Beaconsfield Historic House, the Eptek Art & Culture Centre, & the The Acadian Museum of Prince Edward Island. The others are open during the summer months. The Prince Edward Island Museum & Heritage Foundation also has the responsibility for the provincial collection of over 85,000 artifacts.
Dr. David L. Keenlyside, Executive Director, 902-368-6601, Fax: 902-368-6608, dlkeenlyside@gov.pe.ca
Nora Young, Executive Assistant, njyoung@edu.pe.ca

Other Museums in Prince Edward Island

***Alberton:* Alberton Museum**
PO Box 515, Alberton, PE C0B 1B0
902-853-4048, Fax: 902-853-4066,
www.townofalberton.ca/history/museum.htm
Founded: 1964 Genealogy resources on area families; old photo collection; history of the fox industry; Micmac Indian displays; displays of antique furniture, glassware, textiles & toys. Open June - Sept. Located at 457 Church St. in Alberton.
Dr. Allan J. MacRae, Curator

***Belle River PO:* Ripley's Believe It or Not! Museum**
PO Belle River, Belle River PO, PEI C0A 1B0
902-963-2242, Fax: 902-962-2017,
Other contact information: Off season Tel: 902/962-2022
Ripley's presents displays of unual events and things. Located on RR#6 in Cavendish; Robert Ripley's collection of the unusual; open June - Sept.
Tom McMillan

***Charlottetown:* Car Life Museum Inc.**
45 Oak Dr., Charlottetown, PE C1A 6T6
902-892-1754,
Located on Highway 1 in Bonshaw, Prince Edward Island, the Car Life Museum features restored cars which date back to 1898. The museum also houses farm machinery from the early 1800s & the early 1900s. The Car Life Museum is open from June to September.
Doris MacKay, Contact, 902-675-3555

***Charlottetown:* Green Gables House**
2 Palmers Lane, Charlottetown, PE C1A 5V6
902-963-7874,
peinp-pnipe@pc.gc.ca
www.pc.gc.ca/lhn-nhs/pe/greengables/visit/index_E.asp
Dedicated to Anne of Green Gables, a fictional but nonetheless, famous character created by Lucy Maud Montgomery for her book series "Anne of Green Gables". Open May 1 - Oct. 31

***Charlottetown:* Port-la-Joye-Fort Amherst National Historic Site of Canada**
c/o Parks Canada, 2 Palmer's Lane, Charlottetown, PE C1A 5V8
902-566-7626, Fax: 902-566-8295,
information@pc.gc.ca
www.pc.gc.ca/lhn-nhs/pe/amherst/activ.aspx
Visitors to the Port-la-Joye-Fort Amherst National Historic Site of Canada learn the history of the Mi'kmaq of Prince Edward Island. Interpretive services are available in July & August. Guided tours are offered in both English & French. The grounds are open from June to October.

***Charlottetown:* Province House National Historic Site of Canada**
2 Palmer's Lane, Charlottetown, PE C1A 5V6
902-566-7626, Fax: 902-566-8295,
information@pc.gc.ca
www.pc.gc.ca/lhn-nhs/pe/provincehouse/index_e.asp
Includes Confederation Chamber, site of historic discussions regarding union of the BNA colonies; remains of the Legislative Bldg. for PEI; open year round

***Charlottetown:* Spoke Wheel Car Museum**
RR#3, Charlottetown, PE C1A 7J7
Antique automobiles

***Cornwall:* Royal Atlantic Wax Museum**
PO Box 762, Cornwall, PE C0A 1H0
902-963-2350,
119 life-sized wax figures; open daily early June - late Sept.

***Ellerslie:* Ellerslie Shellfish Museum**
Ellerslie, PE C0B 1J0
902-853-2181,
Aquariums of live fish & shellfish; history of oyster cultivation
Joanne Wallace, Director

***Kensington:* Anne of Green Gables Museum at Silver Bush**
PO Box 491, Kensington, PE C0B 1M0
www.annesociety.org/anne/
Artifacts, books & photographs related to the life & times of Lucy Maud Montgomery

***Kensington:* The Keir Memorial Museum**
RR#1, Kensington, PE C0B 1M0
902-836-3054, Fax: 902-836-4801,
ygillespie@auracom.com
Open July - Sept.
Yvonne Gillespie, Treasurer

***Kensington:* Lucy Maud Montgomery Birthplace**
6461 Route 20, Kensington, PE C0B 1M0
902-886-2596,
Open May - Thanksgiving

***Kensington:* Veterans' Memorial Military Museum**
PO Box 182, Kensington, PE C0B 1M0
902-836-3600, Fax: 902-836-7488,
Military memorabilia mostly from WWI & WWII; Boer War items

***Montague:* Garden of the Gulf Museum**
PO Box 1237, 564 Main St., Montague, PE C0A 1R0
902-838-2467,
ggmuseum@eastlink.ca
www.montaguemuseum.com
Other contact information: Off-season Phone: 902/838-2820

Founded: 1958 Early island history; open June - Sept. PEI's oldest Museum.

***Murray Harbour:* Log Cabin Museum**
Route 18 A, Murray Harbour, PE C0A 1V0
902-962-2201,
Local history

***O'Leary:* Prince Edward Island Potato Museum**
PO Box 602, O'Leary, PE C0B 1V0
902-859-2039, 800-565-3457
info@peipotatomuseum.com
www.peipotatomuseum.com
The history of the potato industry is depicted at the Prince Edward Island Potato Museum. Visitors will see a collection of machinery & farm implements related to growing & harvesting potatoes. The museum also includes the Potato Hall of Fame. It is open from mid May to mid October.
Donna Rowley, Manager, 902-853-2312

***Richmond:* The Bottle Houses / Les Maisons de Bouteilles**
PO Box 72, Richmond, PE C0B 2E0
902-854-2987,
www.teleco.org/SitesWebs/bouteilles/index.html
Other contact information: Off season: 902/854-2254
Three fantasy-like buildings made of over 25,000 vari-coloured bottles, creating a symphony of light & colour within; located in Cape Egmont; flower gardens; giftshop; bilingual service
Réjeanne Arsenault, Owner/Operator

***Rustico:* Farmers' Bank of Rustico**
Hunter River, RR#3, Rustico, PE C0A 1N0
902-963-3168,
info@farmersbank.ca
www.farmersbank.ca
Other contact information: (off season): 902/963-2304
Banking artifacts; precursor to the Credit Union movement in North America
J.D. MacDonald, President

***Summerside:* International Fox Museum & Hall of Fame Inc.**
286 Fitzroy St., Summerside, PE C1N 1J2
902-436-2400,
email@address.com
www.isn.net/~cmapei/ifox/
Located at historic Holman Homestead & Gardens; museum tells the story of the PEI silver fox industry heyday between 1894 & WWII

***Tignish:* Tignish Cultural Centre**
PO Box 398, Maple St., Tignish, PE C0B 2B0
902-882-1999, Fax: 902-882-3144,
culturalcentre@tignish.com
www.tignish.com
Local history

***West Point:* West Point Lighthouse**
Lot 8, 364 Cedar Dunes Park Rd., West Point, PE C0B 1V0
902-859-3605, Fax: 902-859-1510, 800-764-6854
westpointlighthouse@gmail.com
www.westpointlighthouse.com
Founded: 1983 The West Point Development Corporation restored the historic West Point Lighthouse, which was built in 1875 & had a keeper until 1963. The lighthouse is one of the tallest on Prince Edward Island. Today, the lighthouse continues to operate as a navigational aid.

Quebec

Provincial Museums

Canadian Centre for Architecture (CCA) / Centre Canadien d'Architecture
1920, rue Baile, Montréal, QC H3H 2S6
514-939-7026, Fax: 514-939-7020,
info@cca.qc.ca; press@cca.qc.ca (Press Relations)
www.cca.qc.ca
Other contact information: Phone, Administration: 514-939-7000; E-mail, Tours: schools@cca.qc.ca
Founded: 1979 The Canadian Centre for Architecture is a museum & an international research centre. The Centre raises awareness of the role of architecture, stimulates design innovation, & promotes scholarly research.
Phyllis Lambert, Founding Director & Chair
Mirko Zardini, Director & Chief Curator
Louise Désy, Curator, Photography
Isabelle Huiban, Head, Media Relations, ihuiban@cca.qc.ca

McCord Museum of Canadian History / Musée McCord d'histoire canadienne
690, rue Sherbrooke ouest, Montréal, QC H3A 1E9
514-398-7100, Fax: 514-398-5045,
info@mccord.mcgill.ca
www.mccord-museum.qc.ca
Founded: 1921 The museum started with the collections of David Ross McCord and a building from McGill University. It conserves a variety of objects reflecting the social history and material culture of Montreal, Quebec and Canada. Exhibits include over 1,440,000 pieces and range from paintings, costumes & decorative arts, to archives of texts and photographs. Open year round with summer/winter hrs.
MS Suzanne Sauvage, President/CEO, suzanne.sauvage@mccord.mcgill.ca
Nicole Vallières, Director Ph.D., Collection, Research & Programmes, nicole.vallières@mccord.mcgill.ca
Philip Leduc, Director, Operations, philip.lLeduc@mccord.mcgill.ca

Musée de l'Amerique française (MAF)
2, côte de la Fabrique, Québec, QC G1R 3V6
418-692-2843, Fax: 418-646-9705, 866-710-8031
mcq@mcq.org
www.mcq.org
Le plus ancien musée au Canada; la collection regroupe des instruments d'enseignement des sciences, monnaies anciennes, médailles, collections de minéralogie, de géologie, de numismatique, de zoologie, de botanique, de fossiles, livres anciens, et de peinture; expositions et activités; centre de référence; boutique; café.
Danielle Poiré, Directrice-générale (intérim)

Musée de la civilisation
CP 155 B, 85, rue Dalhousie, Québec, QC G1K 7A6
418-643-2158, Fax: 418-646-9705, 866-710-8031
mcq@mcq.org
www.mcq.org
Founded: 1988 Le musée est doté de la plus importante collection ethnographique et historique du Québec et se distingue par sa muséologie innovatrice; programmation thématique; activités éducatives et culturelles; ateliers, visites commentées; boutique; café.
Danielle Poiré, Directrice générale (intérim)

Pointe-à-Callière, Montréal Museum of Archaeology & History
Angle de la Commune, 350, place Royale, Montréal, QC H2Y 3Y5
514-872-9150,
info@pacmusee.qc.ca; rhumaines@pacmusee.qc.ca (HR)
www.pacmusee.qc.ca
Other contact information: E-mail, Public Services Department: glemay@pacmusee.qc.ca
Founded: 1992 The Montréal Museum of Archaeology & History is situated on the site where, in 1642, a mass celebrated the founding of Montréal. Pointe-à-Callière was also the location of a home built in 1688 by the third governor of Montréal, Chevalier Louis Hector de Callière. The site features architectural remains, & the museum houses hundreds of artifacts.
Sophie Brochu, President & CEO
Francine Lelièvre, Executive Director
John LeBoutillier, Secretary-Treasurer
Raymond Montpetit, Coordinator, Historical Research

Other Museums in Quebec

***Alma:* L'Odyssée des Bâtisseurs**
1671, av du Pont Nord, Alma, QC G8B 5G2
418-668-2606, Fax: 418-668-5851, 866-668-2606
info@odysseedesbatisseurs.com
www.odysseedesbatisseurs.com
Axé sur l'importance de l'eau au coeur du développement, le parc thématique L'Odyssée des Bâtisseurs vous invite à visiter des expositions vivantes, admirer un panorama naturel et industriel extraordinaire et vivre une expérience multimédia 360 saisissante à l'intérieur d'un ancien château d'eau.
Danielle Larouche, Directrice générale

***Alouette:* Bagotville Air Defence Museum / Musée de la Défense aérienne de Bagotville**
PO Box 567 Main, Alouette, QC G0V 1A0
418-677-7159, Fax: 418-677-4104,
museebagotville@forces.qc.ca
www.bagotville.net
Founded: 1997 Canadian Military Aviation Museum
Claude Chamberland, Director
Captain Mauril Dufort, 3 Wing Heritage Officer

***Angliers:* Site historique T.E Draper/Chantier de Gédéon**
***Parent:* Les Promoteurs d'Angliers inc.**
CP 82, 11, rue du T.E. Draper, Angliers, QC J0Z 1A0
819-949-4431, Fax: 819-949-4431,
tedraper@tlb.sympatico.ca
www3.telebecinternet.com/tedraper
Montez à bord du remorqueur de bois T.E. Draper; visitez le chantier de Gédéon, la reconstitution d'un camp de bûcherons des années 1930-1940.
Cathy Fraser, Contact

***Anse-au-Griffon:* Manoir Leboutillier, lieu historique national du Canada**
578, boul Griffon, Anse-au-Griffon, QC G4X 6A4
418-892-5150, Fax: 418-892-5189,
manoir.leboutillier@globetrotter.net
Built in 1850s by John Le Boutillier; open June - mid-Oct.

***Asbestos:* Musée minéralogique d'Asbestos / Asbestos Mineralogical Museum**
341, boul St-Luc, Asbestos, QC J1T 2W4
819-879-6444,
Minerals from the Jeffrey Mine; local mining history; exploration & survey instruments; workshops for schools; seasonal opening
A.J. Millen, Directeur

***Authier:* École du Rang II d'Authier**
CP 74, 269 Rang II, Authier, QC J0Z 1C0
819-782-3289, 866-336-3289
ecolrgll@tlb.sympatico.ca
pwp.lino.com/ecolrgll
Représente les écoles de rang qui ont meublé le paysage rural du Québec dans les années quarantes
Sasha Lambert, Responsable

***Batiscan:* Vieux presbytère de Batiscan**
340, rue Principale, Batiscan, QC G0X 1A0
418-362-2051, Fax: 418-362-1373,
direction@presbytere-batiscan.com
www.presbytere-batiscan.com
Datant de 1816, propose une reconstitution fidèle de l'intérieur de la maison au milieu du 19e siècle; aperçu du quotidien du curé Fréchette et de sa ménagère Adéline, les deux habitants du presbytère à cette époque; exposition temporaire à chaque année; sentier ornithologique; aire de repos et de pique-nique; boutique souvenir.

***Beauharnois:* Parc archéologique de la Pointe-du-Buisson**
333, rue Émond, Beauharnois, QC J0S 1J0
450-429-7857, Fax: 450-429-5921,
pointe@ville.melocheville.qc.ca
www.pointedubuisson.com/
Archaeology site; prehistoric objects which form a collection that is recognized in the scientific world as one of the most important in the NE of the continent; research, outreach education; over two million objects and fragments of artifacts and ecofacts that mark SW Quebec.
Maurice Binette

***Beaumont:* Moulin de Beaumont**
2, rte du Fleuve, Beaumont, QC G0R 1C0
418-833-1867,
mbeaumont@bellnet.ca
1821 flour mill; open May 15 - June 24, Sept. & Oct., Sat & Sun., Tues. - Fri by appt.; June 24 - Aug., Tues. - Sat.
Gilles Sheedy, Directeur

***Bergeronnes:* Centre Archéo Topo**
498, rue de la Mer, Bergeronnes, QC G0T 1G0
418-232-6286, Fax: 418-232-6695, 866-832-6286
archeo95@bellnet.ca
www.archeotopo.qc.ca
L'histoire de la région de La Haute-Côte-Nord; exposition interactive retrace la vie des tribus amérindiennes dans la région; jeux didactiques; ateliers pour les enfants et les jeunes; excursions; spectacle multimédia; boutique.

***Les Bergeronnes:* Centre d'interprétation et d'observation de Cap-de-Bon-Désir**
13, ch du Cap-de-Bon-Désir, Les Bergeronnes, QC G0T 1G0
418-232-6751, Fax: 418-235-6468, 888-773-8888
parcscanada-que.pc.qc.ca
www.quebecmaritime.ca
Promontoire naturel pour l'observation des mammifères marins; guides-interprètes; salle d'exposition, phare. Ouvert mi-juin-mi-octobre.

***Berthierville:* Chapelle des Cuthbert de Berthier**
461, rue de Bienville, Berthierville, QC J0K 1A0
450-836-7336, Fax: 450-836-8158,
www.patrimoineberthier.org
La plus ancien temple protestant au Québec; expositions, visites commentées; pique-nique sur place; ouverte tous les journs, du juin au fête du Travil, 10h-18h

***Berthierville:* Musée Gilles-Villeneuve**
960, av Gilles-Villeneuve, Berthierville, QC J0K 1A0
450-836-2714, Fax: 450-836-3067, 800-639-0103
museegillesvilleneuve@bellnet.ca
www.museegillesvilleneuve.com
Founded: 1995 Le musée a pour mandat perpétuer le souvenir de Gilles Villeneuve, le grand coureur automobile du F1; voitures, photographies, Galerie M. Trudel.
Alain Bellehumeur, Superviseur

***Bonaventure:* Musée acadien du Québec à Bonaventure**
95, av Port Royal, Bonaventure, QC G0C 1E0

418-534-4000, Fax: 418-534-4105,
reception@museeacadien.com
www.museeacadien.com
Jean-Claude Cyr, Directeur

Boucherville: **Maison Louis-Hippolyte Lafontaine**
314, boul Marie-Victorin, Boucherville, QC J4B 1X1
514-449-8328, Fax: 514-449-4709,

Cascapédia-Saint-Jules: **Musée de la rivière Cascapédia / The Cascapedia River Museum**
275, rte 299, Cascapédia-Saint-Jules, QC G0C 1T0
418-392-5079, Fax: 418-392-5070,
info@cascapedia.org
www.cascapedia.org
Le musée raconte l'histoire de la région autour de la rivière Cascapédia, la pêche au saumon, et le patrimoine gaspésien; boutique.

Causapscal: **Maison Dr. Joseph-Frenette**
3, rue Frenette, Causapscal, QC G0J 1J0
418-756-5999, Fax: 418-756-3344,
www.maisondrjosephfrenette.com
Joseph Frenette exerçait la profession, aujourd'hui disparue, de médecin de campagne. Il consacra sa vie à soigner des malades et des blessés, à faire naître des enfants, à sauver des vies. Tel un livre ouvert, cette exposition fait découvrir son univers familial et professionnel et à comprendre le rôle primordial du médecin de campagne dans l'histoire du Québec.

Causapscal: **Site historique Matamajaw**
53C, rue Saint-Jacques sud, Causapscal, QC G0J 1J0
418-756-5999, Fax: 418-756-3344,
faucuscar@globetrotter.net
www.causapscal.net
Ancien lieu de villégiature de Sir John A. McDonald et de Lord Mount Stephen, le Matamajaw Salmon Club a attiré les membres de la haute société anglaise, américaine et canadienne durant la fin du 19e et au début du 20e siècle. Le Site Matamajaw est le seul ancien établissement privé accessible au public en Amérique du Nord. Ses magnifiques intérieurs et son exposition bilingue témoignent éloquemen

Chambly: **Lieu historique du Fort-Chambly**
2, rue Richelieu, Chambly, QC J3L 2B9
514-658-1585, Fax: 514-658-7216, 888-773-8888
parcscanada-que@pc.gc.ca
www.pc.gc.ca/lhn-nhs/qc/fortchambly
Présente l'histoire et les coutumes de la Nouvelle-France de 1665-1760; expositions; activités.

Chambord: **Village Historique de Val-Jalbert**
95, rue St-Georges, Chambord, QC G0W 1G0
418-275-3132, Fax: 418-275-5875,
valjalbert@valjalbert.com
www.sepaq.com/ct/val/fr/
Partially restored ghost town; created by the 1901 opening of a pulp & paper mill; as the years went by the town flourished & several services & buildings were added including a train station, convent, hotel & general store; on Aug. 13, 1927 the plant shut down forcing workers to leave Val-Jalbert; today it's a rich historical, industrial & religious patrimony; fall height of 72 m, river & canyo
André Turgeon, Directeur

Château-Richer: **Centre d'interpretation de la Côte-de-Beaupré**
CP 40, 7976, av Royale, Château-Richer, QC G0A 1N0
418-824-3677, Fax: 418-824-5907,
info@histoire-cotedebeaupre.org
www.histoire-cotedebeaupre.org
Présente les aspects culturels, géographiques, historiques et patrimoniaux qui témoignent de la beauté de la région; activités pédagogiques complémentaires au programme d'enseignement; ouvert tous les jours, 9h30-16h30
Luc Trépanier, Directeur général

Château-Richer: **Musée de l'Abeille**
Also known as: **Economusée du miel**
8862, boul Sainte-Anne, Château-Richer, QC G0A 1N0
418-824-4411, Fax: 418-824-4422,
info@musee-abeille.com
www.musee-abeille.com
Centre d'interprétation; l'exposition Des Abeilles et Des Hommes; visites guidées; informations sur le miel; boutique.
Redmond Hayes, President

Chicoutimi: **Centre historique des Soeurs de Notre-Dame du Bon-Conseil de Chicoutimi**
700, rue Racine est (porte 688), Chicoutimi, QC G7H 1V2
418-543-4861, Fax: 418-543-7194,
centrehistorique@sndbc.qc.ca
www.sndbc.qc.ca; www.reseaumuseal.com;
www.museevirtuel.ca

Chicoutimi: **La Pulperie de Chicoutimi**
300, rue Dubuc, Chicoutimi, QC G7J 4M1
418-698-3100, Fax: 418-698-3158, 877-998-3100
info@pulperie.com
www.pulperie.com
Collection de plus de 26 000 ojets et oeuvres; maison Arthur-Villeneuve; expositions d'art et d'ethnologie; vestiges restaurés des anciennes installations de la Compagnie de pulpe de Chicoutimi; parc.
Jacques Fortin, Directeur général

Coaticook: **Beaulne Museum / Musée Beaulne**
96, rue Union, Coaticook, QC J1A 1Y9
819-849-6560, Fax: 819-849-9519,
info@museebeaulne.qc.ca
www.museebeaulne.qc.ca
Other contact information: Alternative E-mail:
bonjour@museebeaulne.qc.ca
Founded: 1964 Beaulne Museum depicts the history & achievements of the local Norton family, who were known for manufacturing railway jacks & their philanthropy. The museum is located in Château Arthur Osmore Norton, a Victorian-style mansion which was built in 1912. Beaulne Museum is open year round from Tuesday to Sunday.

Cookshire: **Compton County Historical Museum Society / Societé d'histoire du musée du comté Compton**
PO Box 967, 374 Route 253, Cookshire, QC J0B 1M0
819-875-5256, Fax: 819-875-3182,
mus.eatoncorner@gmail.com
mus.eatoncorner.com
Housed in a former Congregationalist Church built in 1842. Address is 374 Route 253, Eaton Corner, Quebec.
Pat Boychuck, President

Coteau-du-Lac: **Lieu historique national du Canada de Coteau-du-Lac**
Also known as: **Coteau-du-Lac National Historic Site of Canada**
308A, ch du Fleuve, Coteau-du-Lac, QC J0P 1B0
450-763-5631, Fax: 450-763-1654, 888-773-8888
parcscanada-que@pch.gc.ca
www.pc.gc.ca/fra/lhn-nhs/qc/coteaudulac
Exposition et activités: le site stratégique de Coteau-du-Lac, le Blockhaus, coin de famille, circuit nature, jardin archéologique, reconstitution militaire, marché champêtre.

Desbiens: **Centre d'histoire et d'archéologie de la Métabetchouane**
243, rue Hébert, Desbiens, QC G0W 1N0
418-346-5341, Fax: 418-346-5341,
cham@digicom.ca
www.chamans.com
Founded: 1995 Site historique et archéologique; histoire d'il y a 5,000 ans; poste de traite; salle de découverte; animation; exposition thématique; 20 juin - sept. ou par réservation

La Doré: **Le Moulin des Pionniers de La Doré**
4201, rue des Peupliers, La Doré, QC G8J 1E4
418-256-8242, Fax: 418-256-3799, 866-272-2842
info@moulindespionniers.qc.ca
www.moulindespionniers.qc.ca
Moulin à scie à pouvoir hydraulique, toujours à l'oeuvre depuis 1889; Maison de Marie, une des plus anciennes maisons de La Doré, avec un potager et une grange-étable; petite ferme avec des animaux; camp qui abrite un restaurant et un bar; auberge "La Nuit Boréale"; sentiers pédestres; tour d'observation; expositions; programmation.
Guylaine Lapointe, Contact, info@moulindespionniers.qc.ca

Drummondville: **Le Village Québecois d'Antan inc.**
1425, rue Montplaisir, Drummondville, QC J2B 7T5
819-478-1441, Fax: 819-478-8155, 877-710-0267
renseignements@villagequebecois.com
www.villagequebecois.com
Founded: 1977 Reconstitution d'un village canadien-français du siècle dernier (1810-1910)
Pierre Derouin, Directeur général,
pierre@villagequebecois.com
France Lemoine, Trésorière, france@villagequebecois.com
Simon Bourgault, Directeur, Communications,
simon@villagequebecois.com

Duhamel-Ouest: **Lieu historique national du Canada du Fort-Témiscamingue / Fort Témiscamingue National Historic Site of Canada**
834, ch Vieux-Fort, Duhamel-Ouest, QC J9V 1N7
819-629-3222, Fax: 819-629-2977, 888-773-8888
fort.temiscamingue@pc.gc.ca
www.pc.gc.ca/fra/lhn-nhs/qc/temiscamingue
Rappelle la présence millénaire des algonquins et l'histoire de ce poste de traite situé au détroit du Lac Témiscamingue.

Forestville: **Petite Anglicane**
2, 2e rue, Forestville, QC G0T 1E0
418-587-6148,
Archéologie locale, les gardes-feu, les remèdes d'autrefois, la vie domestique, nos pionniers, l'histoire de Forestville en photos; expositions temporaires; visites guidées

Gaspé: **Magasin générale Hyman & Sons et l'entrepôt Parc national du Canada Forillon, 122, boul Gaspé, Gaspé, QC G4X 1A9**
418-368-5505, Fax: 418-368-6837,
parcscanada-que@pc.qc.ca
www.pc.gc.ca/Forillon
Magasin au centre du village, de l'époque 1920, autrefois la propriété de la compagnie de pêche "William Hyman and Sons", au Parc national du Canada Forillon; animation en costumes; programmation; visites guidées.

Gaspé: **Musée de la Gaspésie**
80, boul Gaspé, Gaspé, QC G4X 1A9
418-368-1534, Fax: 418-368-1535,
info@museedelagaspesie.ca
www.museedelagaspesie.ca
Le musée favoriser la connaissance et l'appréciation de l'histoire et du patrimoine gaspésiens; activités de conservation et de recherche; collections y compris les disciplines de l'ethnologie, l'histoire, les beaux-arts, les sciences naturelles, l'archéologie; archives; boutique; programmation.
Sébastien Lévesque, Directeur général,
direction@museedelagaspesie.ca

Gaspé: **Parc national du Canada Forillon / Forillon National Park of Canada**
122 boul Gaspé, Gaspé, QC G4X 1A9
418-368-5505, Fax: 418-368-6837,
parcscanada-quebec@pc.gc.ca
www.pc.gc.ca/forillon

Gatineau: **Musée de l'Auberge Symmes**
Also known as: **Musée d'Aylmer Museum Inc.**
PO Box 311, 1, rue Front, Gatineau, QC J9H 5E6
819-682-0291, Fax: 819-682-6594,
Symmes@ca.inter.net

Godbout: **Musée amérindien et inuit de Godbout**
134, ch Pascal-Comeau, Godbout, QC G0H 1G0
418-568-7306,
Cécile Grenier, Directrice
Claude Grenier, Directeur

Granby: **Centre d'interpretation de la Nature du Lac Boivin**
700, rue Drummond, Granby, QC J2G 8C7
450-375-3861, Fax: 450-375-3736,
marco.lemay@cscantons.qc.ca
www.darwin.cyberscol.qc.ca/centre/cinlb/
Founded: 1980 A pour mission de conserver le territoire, les habitats, la faune et la flore de la région
Mario Fortin, Directeur général

Guérin: **Musée de Guérin**
CP 1110, 913, rue Principale, Guérin, QC J0Z 2E0
819-784-7014, Fax: 819-784-7014,
musee-guerin@sympatico.ca
Le Musée de Guérin offre deux expositions permanentes: "Autour du clocher" et "Le Réveil rural" qui retracent la vie religieuse et agricole des années 1940-50. Situé sur la "Terre de la Fabrique", concédée au début de la paroisse, le site du musée compremd encore un lieu du culte et la ferme de Monsieur le Curé

Havre-Aubert: **Aquarium des Iles-de-la-Madeleine / Island Aquarium**
982 route 199, Havre-Aubert, QC G0B 1J0
418-937-2277, Fax: 418-937-2277,
info@aquariumdesiles.ca
www.ilesdelamadeleine.com/aquarium

Hâvre-Aubert: **Musée de la Mer Inc.**
1023, Rte. 199, Hâvre-Aubert, QC G4T 9C8
418-937-5711, Fax: 418-937-2449,
info@museedelamer-im.com

www.ilesdelamadeleine-guidetouristique.com/Ile-du-Havre/Muse
e-de-la-Mer
L'histoire des Iles-de-la-Madeleine, l'évolution de la navigation, l'histoire de la pêche; collections de roches, de minéraux, de coquillages; photos et objets marins. Ouvert à l'année.
Michelle Joannette, Directrice générale

Inukjuak: **Musée commémoratif et Centre de transmission de la culture Daniel Weetaluktuk / Daniel Weetaluktuk Commemorative Museum & Cultural Transmis**
General Delivery, Inukjuak, QC J0M 1M0
819-254-8919, Fax: 819-254-8148, 866-897-2287
avataq-inukjuak@avataq.qc.ca
www.avataq.qc.ca
Le centre contribue à la protection et à la diffusion de la culture des Inuits d'Inukjuak et du Nunavik; collection de plus de 400 objets anciens et contemporains présentés dans leur contexte

culturel d'origine; oeuvres d'art, vêtements traditionnels, artefacts; exposition permanente; expositions temporaires.
Louis Gagnon, Conservateur, louisgagnon@avataq.qc.ca

***Inverness:* Musée du Bronze d'Inverness**
1760, ch Dublin, Inverness, QC G0S 1K0
418-453-2101, Fax: 418-453-7711,
info@museedubronze.com
www.museedubronze.com
Voué à la recherche, la mise en valeur, la diffusion, la fabrication, l'interprétation et l'éducation relative à l'art du bronze; fonderie; ateliers; visites guidées; jardin; programmation.
Michelle Joannette, Directrice générale

***L'Islet-sur-Mer:* Musée maritime du Québec**
***Also known as:* Musée maritime Bernier**
55, ch des Pionniers est, L'Islet-sur-Mer, QC G0R 2B0
418-247-5001, Fax: 418-247-5002,
info@mmq.qc.ca
www.mmq.qc.ca
Founded: 1968 Le musée a pour mission la sauvegarde, l'étude, et la mise en valeur du patrimoine maritime se rattrachant au fleuve Saint-Laurent, et de la porte des Grands Lacs; la conservation des navires historiques; expositions permanentes: "Gens du pays, gens du fleuve", "Capt. Joseph-Elzéar Bernier", "Ilititaa...Bernier, ses hommes et les Inuits", et "Pirates ou corsaires?"; boutique; visites guidées; accessible aux personnes à mobilité réduite.
Amélia Lemay, Adjointe à la direction

***Kahnawake:* Musée Kateri Tekakwitha**
PO Box 70, Kahnawake, QC J0L 1B0
450-632-6030, Fax: 450-632-6031,
kateritekakwithasanctuary@yahoo.ca
Religious & ethnic artifacts dating back to the 17th century; historical mission buildings (rectory 1717, church 1845) contain Blessed Kateri's tomb (1656-1680) & precious works of art including the Deerfield Bell (17th - 19th cent.); open all year 10-5; Kahnawake is a native Mohawk reservation
Alvaro Salazar, Pastor F.M.M.

***Kamouraska:* Musée régional de Kamouraska**
69, av Morel, Kamouraska, QC G0L 1M0
418-492-9783, Fax: 418-492-3144,
museekam@videotron.ca
www.museekamouraska.com
Founded: 1977 Il assume fidèlement sa mission de protection, conservation et diffusion du riche patrimoine historique et culturel de tout Kamouraska
Yvette Raymond, Directrice générale

***Knowlton:* Brome County Historical Museum (BCHS)**
PO Box 690, 130 Lakeside, Knowlton, QC J0E 1V0
450-243-6782,
bchs@endirect.qc.ca
Managed by the Brome County Historical Society, the Brome County Museum presents the history of Brome County & the surrounding region. The museum's grounds feature an old fire hall from 1904, an academy building from 1854, & the Brome County Court House from 1858-1859. The court house contains the archives of the Brome County Historical Society. The museum is open from mid May to mid September. The archives are open year round.

***Lac-Drolet:* Maison du Granit**
301, rte du Morne, Lac-Drolet, QC G0Y 1C0
819-549-2566,
info@maisondugranit.ca
www.maisondugranit.ca
Founded: 1989 A pour mission de collecter et de diffuser l'histoire de l'industrie du granit et de ses artisans les tailleurs de pierre; exposition permanente; expositions thématiques; visites guidées; jardin panoramique.

***Lachine:* Lieu historique national du Canada du Commerce-de-la-fourrure-à-Lachine / The Fur Trade at Lachine National Historic Site of Canada**
1255, boul St-Joseph, Lachine, QC H8S 2M2
514-637-7433, Fax: 514-637-5325,
parcscanada-que@pc.gc.ca
www.pc.gc.ca/lhn-nhs/qc/lachine.aspx
A bord d'un canot, découvrez le point de départ des grands explorateurs du continent nord-américain; programmes et activités; exposition sur l'apogée du commerce des fourrures; visites thématiques.

***Lachine:* Musée de Lachine**
1, ch du Musée, Lachine, QC H8S 4L9
514-634-3478, Fax: 514-637-6784,
museedelachine@lachine.ca
lachine.ville.montreal.qc.ca/musee
Includes Maison leBer-LeMoyne & the Dépendance, the oldest complete buildings on the Island of Montreal as well as the Benoît-Verdickt Pavillion, a contemporary art exhibition centre; the Pavillion de l'Entrepôt presents multidisciplinary & multicultural exhibitions; educational program available for school-aged visitors as well as others; open Wed. - Sun.; guided tours Thurs. & Fri. by appt.; The
Marc Pitre, Directeur

***Lachine:* Musée des Soeurs de Sainte-Anne**
1300, boul Saint-Joseph, Lachine, QC H8S 2M8
514-637-4616, Fax: 514-637-2746,
msainteanne@ca.inter.net
Musée communautaire de la Congrégation des Soeurs de Sainte-Anne. Le musée a pour mission de faire découvrir la vie des Soeurs de Sainte-Anne marquée par les lieux et les époques où elles ont évolué; open year-round, winter by appt. only
Murielle Gagnon, Responsable du musée

***Lac-Mégantic:* Musée Namesokanjic**
#200, 5527, rue Frontenac, Lac-Mégantic, QC G6B 1H6
819-583-2441, Fax: 819-583-5920,
greffier@ville.lac-megantic.qc.ca
www.lac-megantic.qc.ca
Outils forestiers, objets domestiques, photographies, costumes; programmation et activités.
Jean-François Grandmont, Personne ressource

***Lasalle:* Moulin Fleming**
9675, boul LaSalle, Lasalle, QC H8R 2W8
514-367-6439,
Open May - Sept.

***Laval:* Musée Armand-Frappier, Centre d'interprétation des biosciences / Armand-Frappier Museum**
531, boul des Prairies, Laval, QC H7V 1B7
450-686-5641, Fax: 450-686-5391,
musee-afrappier@iaf.inrs.ca
www.musee-afrappier.qc.ca
Founded: 1992 Le musée offre des activités pour favoriser la compréhension d'enjeux scientifiques reliés à la santé humaine, animale & environnementale; il fait connaître l'oeuvre du Dr Armand Frappier, microbiologiste.
Guylaine Archambault, Directrice générale, guylaine.archambault@iaf.inrs.ca
Caroline Labelle, Agente de réservation, caroline.labelle@iaf.inrs.ca

***Laval:* Musée écologique - (C.J.N.) Vanier**
3995, boul Lévesque Saint-Vincent-de-Paul, Laval, QC H7E 2R3

***Lévis:* Société historique Alphonse-Desjardins (SHAD)**
***Also known as:* Maison Alphonse-Desjardins**
6, rue du Mont-Marie, Lévis, QC G6V 1V9
418-835-2090, Fax: 418-835-9173, 866-835-8444
info@maisonalphonsedesjardins.com
www.desjardins.com
La maison de style néo-gothique fut construite en 1883 pour Alphonse Desjardins, fondateur des caisses populaires. C'est là que Desjardins a conçu son grand projet coopératif et qu'ont débuté, en 1901, les activités de la Caisse populaire de Lévis
Esther Normand, Conservation & Administration Agent

***Lévis:* Musée du College de Lévis**
9, rue Mgr Gosselin, Lévis, QC G6V 5K1
418-837-8600,
Fermé au public, ouvert sur demande
Loic Bernard, Directeur/Conservateur

***Longueuil:* Musée Marie-Rose Durocher**
a/s 80, rue St-Charles est, Longueuil, QC J4H 1A9
450-651-8104, Fax: 450-651-8636,
centremarierose@yahoo.ca
www.snjm.org
Le Centre Marie-Rose est ouvert au public; le musée présente des expositions à caractère religieux et historique de la vie de Marie-Rose Durocher, fondatrice de la Congrégation des Soeurs des Saints Noms de Jésus et de Marie; collection de tableaux et d'artefacts.
Thérèse Laplante, Directrice

***Malartic:* Musée Régional des Mines et des arts de Malartic**
CP 4227, 650, rue de la Paix, Malartic, QC J0Y 1Z0
819-757-4677, Fax: 819-757-4140,
museum@lino.com
Open year round.
Jean Massiscotte, Directeur

***La Malbaie:* Musée de Charlevoix**
10, ch du Hâvre, La Malbaie, QC G5A 2Y8
418-665-4411, Fax: 418-665-4560,
info@museedecharlevoix.qc.ca
museedecharlevoix.qc.ca
Main fields of interest: ethno-history and folk art; textual art; decroative arts; fine arts; history
Patrice Giroux, Directeur général

***Maniwaki:* Le centre d'interprétation de l'historique de la protection de la forêt contre le feu**
8, rue Comeau, Maniwaki, QC J9E 2R8
819-449-7999, Fax: 819-449-5102,
info@ci-chateaulogue.qc.ca
www.ci-chateaulogue.qc.ca
Le Château Logue; centre d'interprétation; expositions y compris l'histoire des grands feux de forêts au Québec, la forêt exploitée, et la forêt protégée; visites et randonnées gratuites; tour d'observation.
François Ledoux, Directeur

***La Martre:* Corporation du Centre d'interprétation archéologique de la Gaspésie**
6, rue des Fermières, La Martre, QC G0E 2H0
418-288-1318,
ci_archeologie_gaspesie@hotmail.com
Interprète sur la préhistoire gaspésienne dont l'accent est mis sur la période paléoindienne récente; exposition et sentier d'interprétation
Carlos Suich, Administrateur

***Mashteuiatsh:* Musée amérindien de Mashteuiatsh**
1787, rue Amishk, Mashteuiatsh, QC G0W 2H0
418-275-4842, Fax: 418-275-7494, 888-875-4042
nadyabegin.adm.museeilnu@cgocable.ca
www.museeilnu.ca
Sauvegarde l'héritage ilnu et permet aux autochtones, la population et les touristes d'en prendre connaissance; expositions permanentes et temporaires; programmes éducatifs.
Bibiane Courtois, Directrice générale

***Matane:* Musée du Vieux-Phare**
968 ave. du Phare ouest, Matane, QC G4W 1V7
418-562-9766, Fax: 418-562-1917,

***Melbourne:* Richmond County Historical Society Museum**
1296 Rte. 243, Melbourne, QC J0B 2B0
819-845-2303, Fax: 819-826-1332,
pages.globetrotter.net/e-dhealy/
To research & preserve historical facts in the Richmond County area; museum refurbished as a typical home of the late 1800s; archives centre

***Métabetchouan-Lac-à-la-Croix:* Centre d'interprétation de l'agriculture et de la ruralité**
281, rue St-Louis, Métabetchouan-Lac-à-la-Croix, QC G8G 2C8
418-349-3633, Fax: 418-349-5013, 877-611-3633
ciar@cgocable.ca
www.ciar-lacalacroix.com
Founded: 1976 Situé au coeur d'une plaine agricole, le CIAR est un site désigné pour découvrir la richesse du patrimoine agricole du Saguenay-Lac-Saint-Jean. A travers l'exposition Gens de la terre, découvrez 150 ans d'histoire, us et coutumes des ancêtres, qui ont bâti le paysage actuel. Labyrinthe dans un Champ de Maïs; ferme pédagogique; camp d'étabissement (1868); programmes éducatifs.
France Lemoine, Directrice générale

***Mont Saint-Hilaire:* Centre de la nature Mont Saint-Hilaire**
422, ch des Moulins, Mont Saint-Hilaire, QC J3G 4S6
450-467-1755, Fax: 450-467-8015,
info@centrenature.qc.ca
www.centrenature.qc.ca
A pour mission d'assurer l'intégrité du patrimoine naturel de la montagne, offrir un contact avec la nature et une gamme d'activités éducatives et culturelles, et promouvoir la conservation des milieux naturels de la région; ouvert 365 jours par année; offre un réseau de 24 km de sentiers, et un trottoir de bois accessible aux personnes à mobilité restreinte
Kees Vanderheyden, Directeur

***Montebello:* Lieu historique national du Canada du Manoir-Papineau / Manoir-Papineau National Historic Site of Canada**
500, rue Notre-Dame, Montebello, QC J0V 1L0
819-423-6965, Fax: 819-423-6455, 888-773-8888
parcscanada-que@pc.gc.ca
www.pc.gc.ca/fra/lhn-nhs/qc/papineau
La maison de la famille Papineau, 1848-1850; plus de 800 objets, meubles, vêtements, oeuvres d'art, livres et documents; fresques de Napoléon Bourassa; Concerts d'Amédée; jardin.

***Montmagny:* Manoir de l'accordéon**
301, boul Taché est, Montmagny, QC G5V 1C5
418-248-7927, Fax: 418-248-1596,
accordeon@montmagny.com
accordeon.montmagny.com
Research centre & collection of accordians

***Montréal:* Atelier d'histoire Hochelaga-Maisonneuve**
2929, av Jeanne-D'Arc, Montréal, QC H1W 3W2
514-899-9979, Fax: 514-259-6466,
atelier.hhm@gmail.com
www.ulaval.ca/vvap/PAGES/pagesprojets/hochelaga.html
Mise en valeur les quatre églises historiques d'Hochelaga-Maisonneuve; expositions en patrimoine; visites guidées d'églises et de bâtiments patrimoniaux à Montréal.

***Montréal:* Basilique Notre-Dame de Montréal**
110, rue Notre-Dame ouest, Montréal, QC H2Y 1T2
514-842-2925, Fax: 514-842-3370,
info@basiliquenddm.org
www.basiliquenddm.org
Construite entre 1824 & 1829, la basilique acceuille des centaines de milliers de visiteurs chaque année; réputée pour la richesse de sa décoration intérieure: les vitraux, les éléments d'architecture, et les oeuvres d'art; visites guidées (individuels/groupes); visites scolaires; services religieux; événements; concerts; location de salles; boutique.
Yoland Tremblay, Directeur général

***Montréal:* Biodôme de Montréal**
4777, av Pierre-De Coubertin, Montréal, QC H1V 1B3
514-868-3000, Fax: 514-868-3065,
biodome@ville.montreal.qc.ca
www2.ville.montreal.qc.ca/biodome/; www.biodome.qc.ca
Le Biodôme recrée des Écosystèmes des Amériques: forêt tropicale, forêt laurentienne, Saint-Laurent marin, monde polaire. Notez que le Biodôme est fermé pour une durée indéterminée en raison d'un conflit de travail à la Ville de Montréal.
Rachel Léger, Directrice

***Montréal:* The Black Watch of Canada (RHR) Regimental Memorial Museum**
2067, rue Bleury, Montréal, QC H3A 2K2
514-496-1686, Fax: 514-496-2758,
info@blackwatchcanada.com
www.blackwatchcanada.com
Uniforms, photographs & artifacts from early 1860s to present; open Tue. evenings, 7-9 pm & by appt.
Bruce D. Bolton, Director
Anne B. Stewart, Curator

***Montréal:* Canadian Jewish Virtual Museum & Archives / Archives et Musée virtuels juifs canadiens**
c/o Canadian Jewish Congress Charities Committee, National Archives, 1590 Docteur Penfield Ave., Montréal, QC H3G 1C5
514-931-7531, Fax: 514-931-0548,
curator@cjvma.org
www.cjvma.org
Founded: 2001 Initiated by Congregation Shaar Hashomayim, Canada's oldest Ashkenazi synagogue, the Canadian Jewish Virtual Museum & Archives is an online museum of Canadian Jewish history. The virtual museum & archives allows users to discover information about Jewish culture & Jewish life in Canada. Categories include museum, vignettes, & archives.
Dr. Norma Joseph, Co-Chair, Site Advisory
Carole Rocklin, Co-Chair, Site Advisory
Janice Rosen, Site Coordinator, Cdn Jewish Congress Charities Committee, National Archives, curator@cjvma.org

***Montréal:* Centre d'exposition de l'Université de Montréal**
Pavillon de la Faculté d'aménagement, CP 6128 Centre-ville, Montréal, QC H3C 3J7
514-343-6111, Fax: 514-343-2183,
www.expo.umontreal.ca
Comment s'y rendre: Pavillon de la faculté de l'Aménagement, 2940, ch d la Côte-Sainte-Catherine, local 0056, Montréal. Centre d'exposition multidisciplinaire. Comprend: collection herbier Marie-Victorin; collection du département d'anthropologie; collection du Laboratoire de recherche sur les musiques du monde; oeuvres d'art; design industriel
Louise Grenier, Directrice, l.grenier@umontreal.ca

***Montréal:* Chapelle Notre-Dame-de-Bon-Secours/Musée Marguerite Bourgeoys**
400, rue Saint-Paul est, Montréal, QC H2Y 1H4
514-282-8670, Fax: 514-282-8672,
info@marguerite-bourgeoys.com
www.marguerite-bourgeoys.com
Chapelle, musée d'histoire, et site archéologique; programmation diversifiée, visites guidées, boutique, location des salles.
Danielle Dubois, Director General

***Montréal:* Écomusée du fier monde**
2050, rue Amherst, Montréal, QC H2L 3L8
514-528-8444, Fax: 514-528-8686,
ecomusee@globetrotter.net
www.ecomusee.qc.ca
Highlights the history of the Centre-Sud heritage since 1980 which is a mircososm of the industrial revoltuion which took place in Canada during the latter half of the 19th century.

***Montréal:* Montréal History Centre / Centre d'histoire de Montréal**
***Also known as:* Fire Station**
335, Place d'Youville, Montréal, QC H2Y 3T1
514-872-3207, Fax: 514-872-9645,
chm@ville.montreal.qc.ca
www2.ville.montreal.qc.ca/chm/engl/centre-doca.shtm
Founded: 1983 This city museum is located in an old firehall. Here Montreal's story is told through exhibits, models, sets, videos and 8,000 photographs from 1642 until today.

***Montréal:* Insectarium de Montréal / Montreal Insectarium**
4581, rue Sherbrooke est, Montréal, QC H1X 2B2
514-872-1400, Fax: 514-872-0662,
insectarium@ville.montreal.qc.ca
www.ville.montreal.qc.ca/insectarium
Largest insectarium in North America; 140,000 scientific specimens collection; 20,000 exhibition collection (including 4,000 on public display); about 100 species of arthropods live collection

***Montréal:* Lieu historique national de Sir George-Etienne Cartier**
***Also known as:* Maison Cartier**
458, Notre-Dame est, Montréal, QC H2Y 1C8
514-283-2282, Fax: 514-283-5560, 888-773-8888
parkscanada-que@pc.qc.ca
Other contact information: TTY 1-866-558-2950
Commemorates the life and accomplishments of Sir George-Étienne Cartier; Cartier family homes; performances and re-enactments that vary depending on season; Open March - December
Thomas Piché, Régisseur

***Montréal:* Maison de la poste/Post Office House**
1250, rue Université, Montréal, QC H3B 3B0
514-846-5401,

***Montréal:* Maison de Mère d'Youville**
138, rue Saint-Pierre, Montréal, QC H2Y 2L7
514-842-9411, Fax: 514-842-7855,
asscong@sgm.qc.ca
www.sgm.qc.ca/sqm
Founded: 1981 Ancien couvent des Soeurs Grises; l'hospice et le couvent restauré en 1981; la chapelle mise en valeur en 1991; les anciens magasins-entrepôts rénovés; par rendez-vous.
Sr. Jacqueline St-Yves

***Montréal:* Maison Saint-Gabriel**
2146, Place Dublin, Montréal, QC H3K 2A2
514-935-8136, Fax: 514-935-5692,
msgrcip@globetrotter.qc.ca
www.maisonsaint-gabriel.qc.ca
Founded: 1966 La Maison est la maison d'accueil des Filles du Roy et pendant 300 ans, la maison de ferme de la Congrégation de Notre-Dame; un exemple de l'architecture du Régime français; expositions qui expliquent le rôle de Marguerite Bourgeoys et la vie à la colonie de l'Ile de Montréal pendant le 17e siècle; jardin; visites guidées.
Madeleine Juneau, Directrice générale

***Montréal:* The Montréal Holocaust Memorial Centre / Le Centre commémoratif de l'Holocauste à Montréal**
Maison Cummings, 5151, ch. de la Côte-Sainte-Catherine, Montréal, QC H3W 1M6
514-345-2605, Fax: 514-344-2651,
info@mhmc.ca
www.mhmc.ca
To collect, research & preserve historical, cultural & ethnographic material related to Jewish communities in Europe & North Africa which fell under Nazi rule
Alice Herscovitch, Executive Director

***Montréal:* Musée de BMO Banque de Montréal / BMO Bank of Montreal Museum**
129, rue St-Jacques, Montréal, QC H2Y 1L6
514-877-6810, Fax: 514-877-7341,
yolaine.toussaint@bmo.com
The office of the Cashier of Canada's oldest banking institution is recreated; open year round (closed on non-banking days); free, self-guided tour
Yolaine Toussaint, Archivist

***Montréal:* Musée de L'Oratoire Saint-Joseph du Mont-Royal / Museum of Saint Joseph Oratory of Mount-Royal**
3800, ch Queen Mary, Montréal, QC H3V 1H6
514-733-8211, Fax: 514-733-9735, 877-672-8647
pelerinage@osj.qc.ca
www.saint-joseph.org
Founded: 1955 Le musée se consacre à l'art chrétien et à l'histoire et le patrimoine québécoise; expositions thématiques. L'Oratoire mise en valeur la vie et l'oeuvre de frère André; visites commentées; boutique; bibliothèque/archives/centre de recherche.
André Bergeron, Directeur

***Montréal:* Musée des Hospitalières de l'Hôtel-Dieu de Montréal**
201, av des Pins ouest, Montréal, QC H2W 1R5
514-849-2919, Fax: 514-849-4199,
museehospitalieres@bellnet.ca
www.museedeshospitalieres.qc.ca
Founded: 1992 Le musée introduit l'histoire des Hospitalières de Saint-Joseph et des Hospitalières de l'Hôtel-Dieu; exposition permanent; programmation et activités; boutique; salles de conférence à louer; 20 000 objets; archives.
Louise Verdant, Directrice générale

***Montréal:* Musée des ondes Émile Berliner**
1050, rue Lacasse, local C-220, Montréal, QC H4C 2Z3
514-932-9663,
info@berliner.montreal.museum
www.berliner.montreal.museum
Founded: 1996 Émile Berliner a inventé le gramophone, le disque horizontal, et la matrice pour imprimer les disques. Le musée possède plus de 30 000 objets et se consacre à l'histoire de l'industrie des ondes; archives; activités.

***Montréal:* Musée du Château Ramezay / Château Ramezay Museum**
280, rue Notre-Dame est, Montréal, QC H2Y 1C5
514-861-3708, Fax: 514-861-8317,
info@chateauramezay.qc.ca
www.chateauramezay.qc.ca
Founded: 1895 Le musée est consacré à la conservation, et la mise en valeur d'une collection axée sur l'histoire de Montréal et du Québec; plus de 25 000 objets, oeuvres d'art, artefacts ethnologiques et archéologiques, objets numismatiques; photographies; meubles; costumes; bibliothèque; jardin; boutique; café.
André J. Delisle, Directeur général/Conservateur

***Montréal:* Musée du Château-Dufresne**
2929, av Jeanne-d'Arc, Montréal, QC H1W 3W2
514-259-9201, Fax: 514-259-6466,
spoirier@chateaudufresne.com
www.chateaudufresne.com
Le Château, construit entre 1915 et 1918 pour servir de résidence aux frères Oscar et Marius Dufresne, met en pratique les principes du style Beaux-Arts. Programmation culturelle; visites guidées; expositions; salles à louer pour réceptions.
MR Paul Labonne, Directeur général, plabonne@chateaudufresne.com

***Montréal:* Musée du Cinéma/Cinémathèque québécoise**
335, boul de la Maisonneuve est, Montréal, QC H2X 1K1
514-842-9763, Fax: 514-842-1816,
info@cinematheque.qc.ca
www.cinematheque.qc.ca
Founded: 1963 La Cinémathèque a le mandat de conserver, documenter et mettre en valeur le patrimoine cinématographique et télévisuel national et international.
Yolande Racine, Directrice générale

***Montréal:* Musée Édouard-Dubeau**
Université de Montréal, #D-129, 2900, rue Édouard-Montpetit, Montréal, QC H3C 3J7
514-343-6750, Fax: 514-343-2233,
rueld@medent.umontreal.ca
History of dentistry in Québec

***Montréal:* Musée Juste pour rire**
2111, boul Saint-Laurent, Montréal, QC H2X 2T5
514-845-4000, Fax: 514-849-5462,
probitaille@hahaha.com
musee.hahaha.com
Founded: 1993 Le musée est consacré à la reconnaissance du rire et de l'humeur comme phénomènes culturels de civilisation; centre d'expositions thématiques; espace multifonctionnel pour des événements publics, corporatifs, ou privés; activités et spectacles pour enfants.
Stéphanie Lirette, Directrice

***Montréal:* Musée Marc-Aurèle Fortin**
118, rue St-Pierre, Montréal, QC H2Y 2L7
514-845-6108, Fax: 514-845-6100,
mafortin@museemafortin.org
www.museemafortin.org
Founded: 1984 L'oeuvre prodigieuse de Marc-Aurèle Fortin, grand peinture québécois.
Jacqueline Sabourin, Directrice

***Montréal:* Le Musée Stewart au Fort de l'Ile Sainte-Hélène / The Stewart Museum at the Fort Ile Sainte-Hélène**
CP 1200 A, Montréal, QC H3C 2Y9
514-861-6701, Fax: 514-284-0123,
info@stewart-museum.org
stewart-museum.org
Fermeture temporaire; l'exposition permanente renouvelée du musée sera accessible au public dès l'automne 2010; activités scolaires et culturelles.
Bruce D. Bolton, Directeur
Guy Vadeboncoeur, Conservateur

***Montréal:* Phonothèque québécoise, Musée du son**
335, boul de Maisonneuve est, Montréal, QC H2X 1K1
514-282-0703, Fax: 514-282-0019,
phono@bellnet.ca
www.phonotheque.org
histoire des archives sonores, de l'industrie du disque, etc. History of sound archives, sound recording and radio industry.

Alcée Penet, Secrétaire de la Phonothèque québécoise

Montréal: **Royal Canadian Ordnance Corps Museum**
Also known as: **RCOC Museum**
Longue-Pointe Garrison, CP 4000 K, 6560, rue Hochlega, Montréal, QC H1N 3R9
514-252-2777,
www.rcocmuseum.com/RCOCMuseum.html
Founded: 1962 An accredited military museum of the Department of National Defence, the Royal Canadian Ordnance Corps Museum depicts the historical mission of the Royal Canadian Ordnance Corps, & other pre-unification support elements of the Canadian Army, the RCAF, & the RCN. These service elements united in 1968 to create the Logistics Branch of the Canadian Forces. The collection of the RCOC Museum is housed in a 1943 building, which originally served as Longue-Pointe Garrison's St-Barbara Catholic & Protestant chapels.
LCol (ret'd) Al Truelove, Director & President, Royal Canadian Ordnance Corps Museum Committee
Andrew Gregory, Curator PhD, agregory17@cogeco.ca
Jacques Monast, Technical Advisor

Montréal: **Redpath Museum**
McGill University, 859, rue Sherbrooke ouest, Montréal, QC H3A 2K6
514-398-4086, Fax: 514-398-3185,
redpath.museum@mcgill.ca
www.mcgill.ca/redpath
Extensive collections in paleontology, mineralogy, zoology & ethnology; family workshop series "Discovery Workshop"
Dr. David M. Green, Director

Montréal: **Univers Maurice Rocket Richard Universe**
2800, rue Viau, Montréal, QC H1V 3J3
514-872-6666, Fax: 514-872-6928,

Mont-Saint-Grégoire: **Centre d'interprétation du milieu écologique du Haut-Richelieu**
16, ch du Sous-Bois, Mont-Saint-Grégoire, QC J3B 6Z5
450-346-0406,
services@cimehautrichelieu.qc.ca
www.cimehautrichelieu.qc.ca
A pour mission la conservation du Mont-Saint-Grégoire, et d'autres sites naturels dans la région du Haut-Richelieu
Renée Gagnon, Directice générale

Mont-Saint-Hilaire: **Maison amérindienne**
510, Montée des Trente, Mont-Saint-Hilaire, QC J3H 2R8
450-464-2500, Fax: 450-464-0071,
info@maisonamerindienne.com
www.maisonamerindienne.com
Founded: 2000 Un lieu d'échanges, de partage et de rapprochement des peuples à travers des activités culturelles (expositions, contes et légendes, conférences), environnementales et gastronomiques; seul site multinations, situé dans une érablière.
André Michel, Fondateur

New Richmond: **Gaspesian British Heritage Village**
351, boul Perron ouest, New Richmond, QC G0C 2B0
418-392-4487, Fax: 418-392-5907,
heritagevillage@globetrotter.net
www.gaspesianvillage.com
British heritage in Gaspé from 1760 to 1900s; June 24th - Aug. 22nd
Mike Geraghty, President

Nicolet: **Musée des religions du monde**
900, boul Louis-Fréchette, Nicolet, QC J3T 1V5
819-293-6148, Fax: 819-293-4161,
musee@museedesreligions.qc.ca
www.museedesreligions.qc.ca
Le musée se consacre à l'histoire des rites religieux du bouddhisme, de l'hindouisme, de l'islam, du judaïsme, et du christianisme; location de salle; boutique; programmation et activités; les installations du musée sont adaptées pour les personnes à mobilité réduite.
Jean-François Royal, Directeur

Nicolet: **Musée historique des Soeurs de l'Assomption de la Sainte Vierge**
Pavillon Leduc, 251, rue St-Jean-Baptiste, Nicolet, QC J3T 1X9
819-293-2011, Fax: 819-293-8315,
musee@sasv.ca
www.musee-soeurs-assomption.net
Founded: 1979 Collection permanente du patrimoine des fondatrices et des fondateurs de la Congrégation; costume religieux; tableaux; meubles; instruments de musique; sculptures; objets liturgiques.
Sr. Gisèle Saint-Louis, Directrice

Notre-Dame-de-l'Ile-Perrot: **Parc historique Pointe-du-Moulin**
2500, boul Don-Quichotte, Notre-Dame-de-l'Ile-Perrot, QC J7V 7P2
514-453-5936, Fax: 514-453-1473,
moulin@netrevolution.com
www.pointedumoulin.com

Notre-Dame-du-Nord: **Centre thématique fossilifère du lac Témiscamingue / Lake Timiskaming Fossil Centre**
CP 296, 5, rue Principale, Notre-Dame-du-Nord, QC J0Z 3B0
819-723-2500, Fax: 819-723-2369,
musee@fossiles.qc.ca
www.fossiles.qc.ca
A pour mission de mettre en valeur la période Orodovicien-Silurien dans la région; recherche; expositions; boutique.
Andrée Nault, Directrice

Nouvelle: **Musée d'histoire naturelle du parc de Miguasha**
231, rte Miguasha ouest, Nouvelle, QC G0C 2E0
418-794-2475, Fax: 418-794-2033,
parc.miguasha@sepaq.com

Odanak: **Musée des Abénakis**
Société historique d'Odanak, 108, Waban-Aki, Odanak, QC J0G 1H0
450-568-2600, Fax: 450-568-5959,
info@museedesabenakis.ca
www.museedesabenakis.ca
Ouvert en 1962 et complètement rénové en 2005, le premier musée amérindien au Québec vous souhaite la bienvenue. Au coeur d'un site historique, un ensemble d'activité est offert pour plaire à toute la famille. Spectacle multimédia, expositions, belvédère, église catholique, chapelle et aire de pique-nique rendront la visite inoubliable.
Michelle Bélanger, Directrice générale

Otterburn Park: **Muséobus - Le Musée des enfants**
760, ch des Patriotes, Otterburn Park, QC J3H 1Z5
450-464-0201, Fax: 450-446-4644,
info@museobus.qc.ca
www.museobus.qc.ca
Musée mobile aménagé dans des autobus scolaires; propose des expositions scientifiques interactives et des sentiers d'interprétation; piste d'hébertisme et aire de pique-nique; programmation; Camp Éco Nature.

Pabos Mills: **Centre d'interprétation du Parc du Bourg de Pabos**
75, rue de la Plage, Pabos Mills, QC G0C 2J0
418-689-6043, Fax: 418-689-4240,
bourg@globetrotter.net
www.lebourgdepabos.com
Promouvoir l'histoire de la seule seigneurie de la Nouvelle-France à exploiter commercialement la pêche; ouvert tous le jours, juin-septembre.

Paspébiac: **Site historique du Banc-de-Pêche-de-Paspébiac**
CP 430, 3e rue, rte du Banc, Paspébiac, QC G0C 2K0
418-752-6229, Fax: 418-752-6408,
shbp@globetrotter.net
www.shbp.ca
Sea heritage & traditional trades; tours; gift shop; restaurant; open June - Oct.

Percé: **Centre d'interprétation du Parc national de l'Ile-Bonaventure et du Rocher-Percé**
4, rue du Quai, Percé, QC G0C 2L0
418-782-2240, Fax: 418-782-2241,
parc.ibrperce@sepaq.com
www.sepaq.com
A pour mission de protéger un refuge d'oiseaux migrateurs, et le patrimoine historique de la région
Rémi Plourde, Directeur

Percé: **Musée Le Chafaud**
145, rte 132, Percé, QC G0C 2L0
418-782-5100, Fax: 418-782-5565,
lebjl@globetrotter.net

Péribonka: **Musée Louis-Hémon**
700, rte Maria-Chapdelaine, Péribonka, QC G0W 2G0
418-374-2177, Fax: 418-374-2516,
museelh@destination.ca
museelh.destination.ca/
Chantale Simard, Directrice

La Pocatière: **Musée François-Pilote**
100, 4e av, La Pocatière, QC G0R 1Z0
418-856-3145, Fax: 418-856-5611,
museefpilote@leadercsa.com
www.leadercsa.com/museefrancoispilote
Founded: 1973 Voir la paroisse rurale d'autrefois sous tous ses aspects, des salles reconstituées d'habitations, de bureaux de professionnels et d'artisans, une collection de sciences naturelles, agriculture et sciences pures, enseignement agricole; expositions; programmes scolaires; rampe d'acces et ascenseur disponible.
Paul-André Leclerc, Directeur général

Pointe-à-la-Croix: **Battle of the Restigouche National Historic Site of Canada**
PO Box 359, rte 132, Pointe-à-la-Croix, QC G0C 1L0
418-788-5676, Fax: 418-788-5895, 888-773-8888
parkscanada-que @pc.gc.ca
www.pc.gc.ca/eng/lhn-nhs/qc/ristigouche/index.aspx
Other contact information: TTY: 1-866-787-6221
Located at the mouth of the Restigouche River, the Battle of the Restigouche National Historic Site is the scene of the last naval battle between France & England for possession of North America in 1760. Visitors to the site can see the vestiges of the vessel, The Machault, as well as several artifacts from the wreck. The national historic site is open daily from June to mid-October.

La Prairie: **Société d'histoire de la Prairie de la Magdeleine**
249, rue Sainte-Marie, La Prairie, QC J5R 1G1
450-659-1393,
histoire@laprairie-shlm.com
Historical society active in the areas of genealogy, historical research & guided tours
René Jolicoeur, Président

Québec: **Centre d'interprétation de Place-Royale**
27, rue Notre-Dame, Québec, QC G1K 4E9
418-646-3167, Fax: 418-646-9705, 866-710-8031
mcqweb@mcq.org
www.mcq.org/fr/cipr/
Founded: 1999 Site historique; le Centre est situé au premier établissement français permanent en Amérique; expositions, visites commentées, animations historiques, espace découverte, activités éducatives, ateliers.

Québec: **Centre d'interprétation du Vieux-Port-de-Québec / Old Port of Québec Interpretation Centre**
CP 2474, 100, Quai Saint-André, Québec, QC G1K 7R3
418-648-3300, Fax: 418-648-3678, 888-773-8888
parkscanada-que@pc.gc.ca
www.pc.gc.ca/vieuxport
Histoire du Vieux-Port-de-Québec au 19e siècle; expositions; ateliers interactifs; présentations audio-visuelles; visites guidées extérieures et intérieures
Nicole Ouellet, Responsable

Québec: **La Citadelle de Québec & Le Musée du Royal 22e Régiment**
La Citadelle, 1, côte de la Citadelle, Québec, QC G1R 4V7
418-694-2815, Fax: 418-694-2853,
information@lacitadelle.qc.ca
www.lacitadelle.qc.ca
Founded: 1980 Située sur le Cap Diamant, La Citadelle est un site du patrimoine mondial de l'UNESCO, et la résidence officielle du Royal 22e Régiment. Le musée offre des visites guidées, activités, et collections d'artefacts militaires (médailles, insignes, uniformes et textiles, armes).
Jocelyne Milot, Directrice

Québec: **Lieu historique national du Canada des Forts-de-Lévis**
Also known as: **Fort Numéro-Un/Fort No.1**
CP 2474 Terminus, 41, ch du Gouvernement, Québec, QC G1K 7R3
418-835-5182, Fax: 418-835-5443, 800-463-6769

Québec: **Lieu historique national du Canada Cartier-Brébeuf / Cartier-Brébeuf National Historic Site of Canada**
CP 10 B, 175, rue de l'Espinay, Québec, QC G1K 7A1
418-648-4038, Fax: 418-948-9181, 888-773-8888
parcscanada-que@pc.gc.ca
www.pc.gc.ca/fra/lhn-nhs/qc/cartierbrebeuf
Commémore l'hivernage de Jacques Cartier et de ses compagnons en 1535-1536, à proximité du village iroquoïen de Stadaconé; activités.
Linda Bernier, Contact

Québec: **Lieu historique national du Canada de la Grosse-Ile-et-le-Mémorial-des-Irlandais / Grosse-Ile & the Irish Memorial National Historic Site of C**
CP 10 B, 2, rue d'Auteuil, Québec, QC G1K 7R3
418-248-8841, Fax: 866-790-8991, 888-773-8888
parcscanada-que@pc.gc.ca
www.pc.gc.ca/fra/lhn-nhs/qc/grosseile
Commémore l'importance de l'immigration au Canada, plus particulièrement via la porte d'entrée de Québec, et les événements tragiques vécus par les immigrants irlandais en ce lieu, notamment l'épidémie de typhus de 1847.

Québec: **Lieu historique national du Canada des Fortifications-de-Québec / Fortifications of Québec National Historic Site of Canada**
CP 10 B, 2, rue d'Auteuil, Québec, QC G1K 7A1
418-648-7016, Fax: 418-648-2506, 888-773-8888
www.pc.gc.ca/fra/lhn-nhs/qc/fortifications
Trésor de l'UNESCO; la Citadelle et ses environs, terrasse Dufferin, Château Frontnac; visites guidées.
Nicole Ouellet, Régisseure

Québec: **Maison Henry-Stuart**
82, Grande Allée ouest, Québec, QC G1R 2G6
418-647-4347, Fax: 418-647-6483, 800-494-4347
cmsq@cmsq.qc.ca
www.cmsq.qc.ca/mhs
Construite en 1849, la maison représente un exemple d'un type d'habitation courant aux 19e siècle à Québec; collection d'objets, meubles; visites thématiques; jardin.

Québec: **Musée Bon-Pasteur**
14, rue Couillard, Québec, QC G1R 3S9
418-694-0243, Fax: 418-694-6233,
info@museebonpasteur.com
www.museebonpasteur.com
Founded: 1992 L'histoire de la Congrégation des Servantes du Coeur Immaculé de Marie (Soeurs du Bon-Pasteur de Québec); condition féminine au XIXe siècle; meubles et peintures d'époque; visites personnalisées en français et en anglais (portugais sur demande)
Claudette Ledet, Directrice

Québec: **Musée de géologie René-Bureau**
Pavillon Adrien Pouliot, Université Laval, Québec, QC G1K 7P4
418-656-2131, Fax: 418-656-7339,
alevesqu@ggl.ulaval.ca
40,000 geological specimens
André Lévesque, Conservateur du musée

Québec: **Musée des Augustines de l'Hôtel-Dieu de Québec**
32, rue Charlevoix, Québec, QC G1R 5C4
418-692-2492, Fax: 418-692-2668,
mahdq@augustines.ca
www.augustines.ca
Founded: 1958 Tableaux canadiens et européens, meubles, vaisselle, broderies, instruments médicaux. Le musée est en réaménagement et est fermée jusqu'en 2011.
S. Nicole Perron, Directrice du Musée AMJ

Québec: **Musée des Ursulines de Québec**
12, rue Donnacona, Québec, QC G1R 3Y7
418-694-0694, Fax: 418-694-2136,
murq@vmuq.com
www.ursulines-uc.com
Le musée met en valeur la collection pédagogique des Ursulines de Québec; documents; instruments de musique; objets scientifiques; spécimens d'histoire naturelle; photographies; broderies; tableaux.
Christine Turgeon, Directrice

Québec: **Musée Naval de Québec / Naval Museum of Québec**
Also known as: **Musée naval Stanislas-Déry**
170, rue Dalhousie, Québec, QC G1K 8M7
418-694-5387, Fax: 418-694-5550,
info@museenavaldequebec.com
www.museenavaldequebec.com
Le musée a pour mission de conserver et communiquer l'histoire navale du Saint-Laurent, et de la Réserve navale du Canada.

Québec: **Parc des Champs-de-Bataille nationaux / National Battlefields Park**
390, av de Bernières, Québec, QC G1R 2L7
418-648-4071, Fax: 418-648-3809,
information@ccbn-nbc.gc.ca
www.ccbn-nbc.gc.ca
Les Plaines d'Abraham; Parc des Braves; Maison de la découverte des plaines d'Abraham; Exposition multimédia Odyssée Canada; Tours Martello; Souper mystère de 1814 à la tour Martello 2; Bus d'Abraham: tour guidé des plaines d'Abraham, Maison patrimoniale Louis S.-St-Laurent, Kiosque Edwin-Bélanger, Jardin Jeanne d'Arc
Michel Leullier, Directeur

Québec: **Site patrimonial du Parc-de-L'Artillerie**
Also known as: **Parc-de-L'Artillerie**
CP 10 B, 2, rue d'Auteuil, Québec, QC G1K 7A1
418-648-7016, Fax: 418-648-2506, 888-773-8888
parcscanada-que@pc.gc.ca
www.pc.gc.ca/fra/lhn-nhs/qc/artiller/index.aspx

Richmond: **Centre d'interprétation de l'ardoise**
5, rue Belmont, Richmond, QC J0B 2H0
819-826-3313, Fax: 819-826-5757,
ardoise@globetrotter.net
www.centreardoise.ca; www.townshipsheritage.com
Founded: 1992 A pour mission de promouvoir le patrimoine de l'ardoise dans la vallée du Saint-Françcois; le centre est logé dans une église presbytérienne construite en 1889, ayant une toiture en ardoise; métiers, techniques et divers usages de cette pierre; histoires de l'industrie sont racontées
Denise Lupien

Rimouski: **Musée régional de Rimouski**
35, rue Saint-Germain ouest, Rimouski, QC G5L 4B4
418-724-2272, Fax: 418-725-4433,
mrdr@globetrotter.net
www.museerimouski.qc.ca
Le musée, qui loge dans la plus ancienne église de pierre de la région, présente des collections thématiques sur l'art contemporain, histoire et sciences; oeuvres et artefacts; guides interprétifs; activités.
Franck Michel, Directeur général

Rimouski: **Site historique maritime de la Pointe-au-Père**
1000, rue du Phare, Rimouski, QC G5M 1L8
418-724-6214, Fax: 418-721-0815,
www.shmp.qc.ca
Founded: 1980 Le musée regroupe les artefacts du navire l'Empress of Ireland, et met en valeur le Phare-de-Pointe-au-Père et le sous-marin ONONDAGA, désarmé par la Défense nationale en 2000.

Rimouski-Est: **Site historique de la Maison Lamontagne**
707, boul du Rivage, Rimouski-Est, QC G5L 1E9
418-722-4038, Fax: 418-722-4038,
maisonlamontagne@globetrotter.net
www.maisonlamontagne.com
Open - 24 juin - 5 sept.
Fanny Côté, Directrice

Rivière-du-Loup: **Musée des bateaux miniatures et de légendes du Bas-Saint-Laurent**
80, boul Cartier, Rivière-du-Loup, QC G5R 2M9
418-868-0800, Fax: 418-856-1815, 866-868-0800
info@museedebateauxminiatures.com
www.museedebateauxminiatures.com
Exposition de 160 bateaux miniatures faits par 20 artistes de la région; boutique souvenir; petite galerie d'art; visites guidées.

Rivière-du-Loup: **Musée du Bas-St-Laurent**
300, rue St-Pierre, Rivière-du-Loup, QC G5R 3V3
418-862-7547, Fax: 418-862-3019,
musee@mbsl.qc.ca
www.mbsl.qc.ca
Founded: 1975 Consacré à la photographie ethnologique, art moderne, et à l'éducation; conservation, recherche, et diffusion; plus de 2 000 objets ethnologiques, et plus de 300 objets d'art; plus de 125 000 photographies anciennes; expositions itinérantes; publication; boutique; location de salles.
Pierre Landry, Directeur général

Rivière-Éternite: **Centre de découverte et de services Le Béluga (secteur Baie Sainte-Marguerite)**
Parc National du Saguenay, 91, rue Notre-Dame, Rivière-Éternite, QC G0V 1P0
418-272-1556, Fax: 418-272-1516, 800-665-6527
parc.saguenay@sepaq.com
www.sepaq.com/pq/sag/fr/interpretation.html
Exposition permanente "Baie comme bélugas"; l'histoire et l'importance de protéger le béluga dans son milieu naturel; activités de découverte.

Rivière-Éternite: **Centre de découverte et de services le Fjord du Saguenay (secteur de la Baie-Éternité)**
Parc National du Saguenay, 91, rue Notre-Dame, Rivière-Éternite, QC G0P 1P0
418-272-1556, Fax: 418-272-3438,
parc.saguenay@sepaq.com
www.sepaq.com/pq/sag/fr/interpretation.html
Découvrez les secrets du fjord; exposition permanente

Rouyn-Noranda: **La Maison Dumulon**
CP 242, 191, av du Lac, Rouyn-Noranda, QC J9X 5C3
819-797-7125, Fax: 819-797-7109,
maison.dumulon@rouyn-noranda.ca
www.maison-dumulon.ca
Founded: 1980 La maison de la famille Dumulon est une reconstitution fidèle du bâtiment d'origine; visites guidées; animation; activités spéciales; location de salles; boutique. L'église orthodoxe russe Saint-Georges est administrée par la Corporation de La maison Dumulon.
Geneviève C. Gauthier, Directrice

Saguenay: **Musée du Fjord**
3346, boul de la Grande-Baie sud, Saguenay, QC G7G 1B2
418-697-5077, Fax: 418-697-5079, 866-697-5077
info@museedufjord.com
www.museedufjord.com
Founded: 1960 Consacré à la préservation et la mise en valeur du patrimoine historique, naturel et artistique du territoire du fjord du Saguenay; exposition permanente; expositions temporaires thématiques; programmation; artefacts historiques; photographies; documents.
Guylaine Simard, Directrice

Saint-André-Avellin: **Musée des Pionniers de Saint-André-Avellin**
20, rue Bourgeois, Saint-André-Avellin, QC J0V 1W0
819-983-2624, Fax: 819-983-3702,
www.petite-nation.qc.ca/patrimoine/musee.html
Relate la vie rurale des 19e et 20e siècles; meubles, objets, outils et machines en expositions; livres du XIXe siècle; photographies.
Raymond Whissell, Sec.-Très.

Saint-André-d'Argenteuil: **Musée régional d'Argenteuil / Caserne-de-Carillon - Lieu historique national du Canada**
44, rte du Long-Sault, Saint-André-d'Argenteuil, QC J0V 1X0
450-537-1893,
info@museearg.com
Historical exhibitions: 8 exhibition rooms
Noreen Lowe, Registrar
Jean-Claude de Guire, Curator

Saint-Constant: **Exporail: Musée ferroviaire canadien / Exporail: Canadian Railway Museum**
110, rue St-Pierre, Saint-Constant, QC J5A 1G7
450-638-1522, Fax: 450-638-1563,
info@exporail.org
www.exporail.org
Canada's largest collection of railway equipment (150 vehicles, a turntable, 2 train stations, a new exhibit pavilion)
Marie-Claude Reid, Director

Sainte-Anne-de-Beaupré: **Musée de Sainte-Anne-de-Beaupré**
9803, boul Sainte-Anne, Sainte-Anne-de-Beaupré, QC G0A 3C0
418-827-6873, Fax: 418-827-6870,
musee@ssadb.qc.ca
www.sanctuairesainteanne.org
Le musée retrace l'histoire d'un pèlerinage et rend hommage à la Vierge Marie; expositions permanentes et temporaires; visites guidées; jardins; magasin du Sanctuaire.

Sainte-Foy: **Maison Hamel-Bruneau**
CP 218, 2608, ch Saint-Louis, Sainte-Foy, QC G1V 1N2
418-641-6280, Fax: 418-654-4151,
patrimoinestefoysillery@ville.quebec.qc.ca
www.ville.quebec.qc.ca; www.paricilavisite.qc.ca
Construit vers 1857; maison historique abrite un centre de diffusion culturelle; programmation thématique variée; concerts; activités; jardins, aire de pique-nique.

Sainte-Foy: **Musée de géologie**
Université Laval, Département de géologie, Pavillon Adrien-Pouliot, Cité Universitaire, Sainte-Foy, QC G1K 7P4
418-656-2131, Fax: 418-656-7339,
alevesqu@ggl.ulaval.ca
André Lévesque, Conservateur

Sainte-Marie: **Maison J.A. Vachon**
383, rue de la Coopérative, Sainte-Marie, QC G6E 3X5
418-387-4052, Fax: 418-387-2454, 866-387-4052
ville.sainte-marie.qc.ca; vachon.com
Canada's largest snack cake factory; open Apr. 1-Oct. 31, Mon.-Fri.; weekends (June 24-Sept. 3)
Bernard Thibault

Saint-Eustache: **Moulin Légaré / Légaré Mill**
232, rue St-Eustache, Saint-Eustache, QC J7R 2L7
450-974-5400, Fax: 450-974-5219,
info@corporationdumoulinlegare.com
www.corporationdumoulinlegare.com
Founded: 1975 This 1762 flour mill has never once stopped working since its completion. The miller produces wheat and buckwheat flour with the original millstones and flour is sold on site. Activities are available for students.
Ms Mélanie Séguin, Director, 450-974-5001 X-5203,
mseguin@corporationdumoulinlegare.com

Saint-Eustache: **Musée de Saint-Eustache et de ses Patriotes**
235, rue Saint-Eustache, Saint-Eustache, QC J7R 2L8
450-974-5170, Fax: 450-974-5174,
musee@ville.saint-eustache.qc.ca
ville.saint-eustache.qc.ca/tourisme2003 /musee_patriotes.htm

Saint-Hyacinthe: **Musée du Centre Élisabeth-Bergeron**
805, av Raymond, Saint-Hyacinthe, QC J2S 5T9
450-773-6067, Fax: 450-773-8044,
ceb@sjsh.org
www.sjsh.org
Présente la vie et l'oeuvre de la fondatrice des Soeurs de Saint-Joseph-de Saint-Hyacinthe; l'histoire d'une communauté de religieuses enseignantes, fondée en terre Maskoutaine; quatre salles d'exposition, visite commentée comprenant une présentation audiovisuelle, un arrêt au tombeau de la vénérable Élisabeth Bergeron ainsi qu'à la chapelle; ouvert tous les jours.

Saint-Hyacinthe: **Musée du séminaire de Saint-Hyacinthe**
650, rue Girouard est, Saint-Hyacinthe, QC J2S 7B7
450-774-0203, Fax: 450-774-7101,
Cash_ntic.qc.ca
Museum of natural sciences, archeology, ethnology, religious heritage & works of art

***Saint-Jean-Port-Joli:* Musée de sculpture sur bois des Anciens Canadiens**
CP 66, 332, av de Gaspé ouest, Saint-Jean-Port-Joli, QC G0R 3G0
418-598-3392, Fax: 418-598-3329,
info@museedesancienscanadiens.com
www.museedesancienscanadiens.com
Collection de plus de 250 sculptures originales, et un vidéo sur la sculpture sur bois et sur neige. Le musée est ouvert du mai jusqu'au novembre.
Camile Michaud
Jean-Guy Desjardins
Denis Michaud

***Saint-Jean-sur-Richelieu:* Musée du Haut-Richelieu**
***Also known as:* Musée d'histoire et de la céramique québécoise**
182, Jacques-Cartier nord, Saint-Jean-sur-Richelieu, QC J3B 7W3
450-347-0649, Fax: 450-347-9994,
info@museeduhaut-richelieu.com
www.museeduhaut-richelieu.com
L'histoire du Haut-Richelieu.

***Saint-Joseph-de-Beauce:* Musée Marius Barbeau**
139, rue Sainte-Christine, Saint-Joseph-de-Beauce, QC G0S 2V0
418-397-4039, Fax: 418-397-6151,
info@museemariusbarbeau.com
www.museemariusbarbeau.com
Le musée a pour mission la conservation, la recherche et la mise en valeur le patrimoine de la Beauce, tant du point de vue historique, ethnologique et artistique.
Lucie Duval, Personne ressource

***Saint-Joseph-de-la-Rive:* Papeterie Saint-Gilles**
***Also known as:* Economusee(R) du papier**
CP 40, 304, rue Félix Antoine-Savard, Saint-Joseph-de-la-Rive, QC G0A 3Y0
418-635-2430, Fax: 418-635-2613, 866-635-2430
papier@papeteriesaintgilles.com
www.papeteriesaintgilles.com
Papier fait à la main, 100% coton, sans acide et chiné de pétales de fleurs de la région, selon des techniques traditionnelles datant du XVIIe siècle

***Saint-Joseph-de-la-Rive:* Musée maritime de Charlevoix**
CP 1, 305, rue de l'Église, Saint-Joseph-de-la-Rive, QC G0A 3Y0
418-635-1131, Fax: 418-635-2600,
expom@charlevoix.net
www.musee-maritime-charlevoix.com
Conserve et communique le patrimoine maritime à travers l'histoire des goélettes qui ont naviguées sur le Saint-Laurent; bâtiment central thématique, scierie, atelier et magasin de l'époque; exposition sur l'astroblème; archives; boutique.

***Saint-Lambert:* Musée du costume et du textile du Québec**
349, Riverside, Saint-Lambert, QC J4P 1A8
450-923-6601, Fax: 450-923-6600,
info@mctq.org
www.mctq.org
Founded: 1979 Le musée se consacre à la recherche, la conservation, l'éducation, et la diffusion; expositions de costume, textiles, et de la fibre; boutique.
Mme Suzanne Chabot, Directrice générale

***Saint-Prime:* Musée du fromage cheddar**
148, av Albert-Perron, Saint-Prime, QC G8J 1L4
418-251-4922, Fax: 418-251-1172, 888-251-4922
cheddar@bellnet.ca
www.museecheddar.org
La vieille Fromagerie Perron est la seule survivante de sa catégorie au Québec. Aujourd'hui transformée en lieu d'interprétation elle vous raconte la fabrication traditionnelle du cheddar; visites guidées; boutique souvenir, vente de fromage; casiers verrouillés pour vélos; ouverte au public juin - sept. et sur réservation pour le reste de l'année.
Mme Diane Hudon, Directrice générale

***Sept-Iles:* Musée Shaputuan / Shaputuan Museum**
290, boul des Montagnais, Sept-Iles, QC G4R 5R2
418-962-4000, Fax: 418-962-3131,
shaputuan@bbsi.net
www.ville.sept-iles.qc.ca
A pour mission de perpétuer la culture des Innus; le musée s'engage a acquérir, étudier et interpréter la culture; expositions; activités.

***Shawinigan:* Cité de l'Énergie**
CP 156, 1000, av Melville, Shawinigan, QC G9N 6T9
819-536-8516, Fax: 819-536-2982, 866-900-2483
infocite@qc.aira.com
www.citedelenergie.com
Centre de sciences, expositions, spectacle multimédia, tour d'observation Hydro-Québec
Robert Trudel

***Shawinigan-Sud:* Église Notre-Dame-de-la-Présentation**
825, av 2e, Shawinigan-Sud, QC G9P 1E1
819-536-3652, Fax: 819-536-4170,
eglisendp@cgocable.ca
www.eglisendp.qc.ca
Lieu historique national du Canada; protection et mise en valeur des oeuvres de Leduc dans l'église
France St-Amant, Coordonnatrice

***Sherbrooke:* Centre d'interprétation de l'histoire de Sherbrooke**
275, rue Dufferin, Sherbrooke, QC J1H 4M5
819-821-5406, Fax: 819-821-5417,
info@societehistoire.com
shs.ville.sherbrooke.qc.ca
Founded: 1992 A pour mission de préserver le patrimoine local, et promouvoir l'histoire de Sherbrooke et les Cantons-de-l'Est
Josée Delage, Directrice

***Sherbrooke:* Musée de la nature et des sciences de Sherbrooke**
225, rue Frontenac, Sherbrooke, QC J1H 1K1
819-564-3200, Fax: 819-564-7388, 877-434-3200
info@naturesciences.qc.ca
www.naturesciences.qc.ca
Situé dans une ancienne usine de textile, le Musée renferme une collection de près de 100 000 objets dont 65 000 en sciences naturelles; expositions; théâtre d'objets intéractifs sur la fonction du cerveau; services d'animation et d'éducation et une salle multifonctionnelle disponible en location.
Mme Marie-Claude Bibeau, Directrice générale

***Sherbrooke:* Musée Régimentaire les Fusiliers de Sherbrooke**
64, rue Belvédère sud, Sherbrooke, QC J1H 4B4
819-564-5940, Fax: 819-564-5641,
fusdesherbrooke@videotron.ca
membres.lycos.fr/fusiliers/
Capt. Beaudoin, Conservatrice

***Sillery:* Villa Bagatelle**
1563 ch St-Louis, Sillery, QC G1S 1G1
418-681-3010, Fax: 418-681-3865,
cataraqui@globetrotter.net
www.museocapitale.qc.ca/050a.htm
Exhibition Centre & garden

***Sorel-Tracy:* Biophare**
6, rue St-Pierre, Sorel-Tracy, QC J3P 3S2
450-780-5740, Fax: 450-780-5734, 877-780-5740
info@biophare.com
www.biophare.com
Founded: 1994 Dédiée à la réserve de la biosphère du lac Saint-Pierre; présente une exposition permanente "l'observatoire du lac Saint-Pierre"; musée, groupes scolaires, boutique, location de salles.
Marc Mineau, Directeur général

***Stanbridge East:* Missisquoi Museum / Musée Missisquoi**
2 River St., Stanbridge East, QC J0J 2H0
450-248-3153, Fax: 450-248-0420,
info@missisquoimuseum.ca
www.museemissisquoi.ca
Founded: 1964 Museum is house in the 1830 three-story, red brick, Cornell Mill. Exhibitions include Missisquoi County Archives, and explore the historic development of the county. Other buildings on site are the Walbridge Barn and Hodge's General Store.
Pamela Realffe, Executive Secretary
Heather Darch, Curator
Judy Antle, Archivist

***Stanstead:* Stanstead Historical Society / Société Historique de Stanstead**
***Also known as:* Colby-Curtis Museum**
535, rue Dufferin, Stanstead, QC J0B 3E0
819-876-7322, Fax: 819-876-7936,
info@colbycurtis.ca
www.colbycurtis.ca
Founded: 1929 Operates the Colby Curtis Museum & Carrollcroft Property
Pierre Rastoul, Director/Curator

***St-Denis:* Maison Chapais**
CP 70, 2, rte 132 est, St-Denis, QC G0L 2R0
418-498-2353, Fax: 418-498-4070,
www.maisonchapais.com
Founded: 1990 Monument historique daté de 1834; trois étages et diverses dépendances; réservations préférables pour les groupes; visites guidées de la maison et ses jardins oubliés; galerie-boutique offre cadeaux et souvenirs, livres.
Sylviane Pilote, Directrice générale

***St-Lin-Laurentides:* Lieu historique national du Canada de Sir-Wilfrid-Laurier / Sir Wilfrid Laurier National Historic Site of Canada**
945, 12e av, St-Lin-Laurentides, QC J5M 2W4
450-439-3702, Fax: 450-439-5721, 888-787-8888
parcscanada-que@pc.gc.ca
www.pc.gc.ca/fra/lhn-nhs/qc/wilfridlaurier
Centre d'interprétation; exposition présente la vie et l'oeuvre de Sir Wilfrid Laurier.
Thomas Piché, Régisseur

***St-Paul-de-l'Ile-aux-Noix:* Lieu historique national du Canada du Fort-Lennox / Fort Lennox National Historic Site of Canada**
1 - 61st Ave., St-Paul-de-l'Ile-aux-Noix, QC J0J 1G0
450-291-5700, Fax: 450-291-4389, 888-773-8888
parcscanada-que @pc.gc.ca
www.pc.gc.ca/fra/lhn-nhs/qc/lennox
Visites guidées; activités; caserne, poudrière, corps de garde, et prison; expositions: "Ces messieurs les officiers", et "Le fort Lennox, Oeuvre des ingénieurs royaux".

***Sutton:* Eberdt Museum of Communications**
30A, rue Principale, Sutton, QC J0E 2K0
514-538-2649,
mchs@aide-internet.org
Special collection for TV and radio

***Sutton:* Musée des communications et d'histoire de Sutton**
CP 430, 30A, rue Principale, Sutton, QC J0E 2K0
450-538-3222,
mchs@aide-internet.org
History of communication

***Tadoussac:* La Petite chapelle de Tadoussac**
***Also known as:* La Chapelle des Indiens**
CP 69, rue Bord de l'Eau, Tadoussac, QC G0T 2A0
418-235-4657, Fax: 418-235-4433,
www.tadoussac.com

***Tadoussac:* Centre d'interprétation des mammifères marins**
***Also known as:* CIMM**
108, de la Cale-Sèche, Tadoussac, QC G0T 2A0
418-235-4701, Fax: 418-235-4325,
info@gremm.org
www.gremm.org
Founded: 2005 A pour mission la conservation du milieu marin & la recherche scientifique sur les mammifères marins du Saint-Laurent

***Tadoussac:* La maison des Dunes**
Rte du Moulin Baude, Tadoussac, QC G0T 2A0
418-235-4238, Fax: 418-235-1203,
Maison faisant partie du patrimoine local, transformée en centre d'interprétation; exposition permanente; présentations, par des naturalistes, sur le phénomène des dunes de sable

***Tadoussac:* Poste de Traite Chauvin Trading Post**
157, rue du Bord-de-l'Eau, Tadoussac, QC G0T 2A0
418-235-4657, Fax: 418-235-4433,
tourisme@bellnet.ca
Réplique du premier poste de traite des fourrures du 17e siècle; présente des objets se rapportant à la vie des autochtones et les produits d'échange; dégustation de phoque tous les dimanches
Gaby Villeneuve

***Thetford Mines:* Musée minéralogique et minier de Thetford Mines**
711, boul Frontenac ouest, Thetford Mines, QC G6E 7Y8
418-335-2123, Fax: 418-335-5605,
service.client@museemineralogique.com
www.museemineralogique.com
Founded: 1976 Présente l'histoire géologique, minière & social de la région de L'Amiante; expositions; activités educatives; excursions
François Cinq-Mars, Directeur,
f.cinq-mars@museemineralogique.com

***Trois-Rivières:* Centre d'exposition sur l'industrie des pâtes et papiers**
CP 368, 800, Parc portuaire, Trois-Rivières, QC G9A 5H3
819-372-4633, Fax: 819-374-1900,
ceipp@v3r.net
www.ceipp.net
Le Centre d'exposition s'engage à vous faire découvrir l'histoire de la région papetière du Québec; activités; groupes scolaires et adultes; ouvert tous les jours 10h-18h, du 30 mai au 27 septembre (2009) et sur réservation pour les groupes

***Trois-Rivières:* Lieu historique national du Canada des Forges-du-Saint-Maurice / Forges du Saint-Maurice National Historic Site of Canada**
10 000, boul des Forges, Trois-Rivières, QC G9C 1B1
819-378-5116, Fax: 819-378-0887, 888-773-8888
parcscanada-que@pc.gc.ca
www.pc.gc.ca/fra/lhn-nhs/qc/saintmaurice

A 20 minutes de Trois-Rivières, commémore l'établissement de la première communauté industrielle au Canada; ouvert de mi-mai à mi-oct.; groupes sur réservation.
Josée Grandmont

***Trois-Rivières:* Musée des Ursulines de Trois-Rivières**
734, rue des Ursulines, Trois-Rivières, QC G9A 5B5
819-375-7922, Fax: 819-375-0238,
mutr@cgocable.ca
www.musee-ursulines.qc.ca; www.ursulines-uc.com
Conserve et met en valeur l'histoire des Ursulines dès 1697; expositions thématiques, visites guidées, galerie d'art.
Josée Grandmont

***Trois-Rivières:* Musée militaire de Trois-Rivières**
***Also known as:* Musée du 12e Régiment blindé du Canada**
574, rue St-François-Xavier, Trois-Rivières, QC G9A 1R6
819-371-5290, Fax: 819-371-5292,
museemilitaire@cgocable.ca
www.mediat-muse.qc.ca/web_12e.html; www.12rbc.ca
Musée et manège militaire; exposition retraçant l'histoire du régiment; salles d'armes; collections d'uniformes, pièces d'équipements, armes blanches et armes à feu en usage dans les Forces canadiennes.

***Trois-Rivières:* Musée Pierre Boucher**
Séminaire Saint-Joseph, 858, rue Laviolette, Trois-Rivières, QC G9A 5S3
819-376-4459, Fax: 819-378-0607,
museepierre-boucher@ssj.qc.ca
Musée fondé en 1920 par Mgr Albert Tessier pour protéger et sauvegarder le patrimoine local et régional; art contemporain (québécois et canadien); un programme d'animation adapté pour les groupes scolaires et les groupes d'adultes est centré sur les expositions temporaires, consacrées aux artistes contemporains et aux collections du musée; le musée est ouvert gratuitement du mardi au dimanche
Françoise Chainé, Directrice

***Trois-Rivières:* Musée québécois de culture populaire**
200, rue Laviolette, Trois-Rivières, QC G9A 6L5
819-372-0406, Fax: 819-372-9907,
info@culturepop.qc.ca
www.culturepop.qc.ca
Founded: 2001 Le Musée propose six expositions audacieuses, non conventionnelles et empreintes de plaisir à la manière des Québécois; reliée au Musée, la Vieille prison de Trois-Rivières, offre une visite-expérience, guidée par des ex-détenus.
Benoît Gauthier, Directeur

***Ulverton:* Moulin à laine d'Ulverton / Ulverton Woolen Mills**
210, ch Porter, Ulverton, QC J0B 2B0
819-826-3157, Fax: 819-826-6266,
info@moulin.ca
www.moulin.ca
Founded: 1982 Initie aux méthodes artisanales et industrielles de production et de traitement de la laine

***Valcourt:* Musée J. Armand Bombardier**
1001, av J.A. Bombardier, Valcourt, QC J0E 2L0
450-532-5300, Fax: 450-532-2260,
info@museebombardier.com
www.museebombardier.com
Le musée présente la vie et l'oeuvre de Joseph-Armand Bombardier, mécanicien, inventeur et entrepreneur; retrace l'évolution de l'industrie de la motoneige; expositions; activités.
Louise Lemay, Directrice des communications
Richard Codère, Conservateur

***Val-d'Or:* La Cité de l'Or**
***Parent:* La Corporation du Village minier de Bourlamaque**
CP 212, 90, av Perreault, Val-d'Or, QC J9P 4P3
819-825-7616, Fax: 819-825-9853, 877-582-5367
courrier@citedelor.qc.ca
www.citedelor.com
Site historique du patrimoine minier en Abitibi-Témiscamingue; visites guidées à la seule mine d'or du Québec accessible à 91 mètre sous terre; expositions; boutique; par réservation.
Ghislaine Brousseau, Responsable des réservations

***Valleyfield:* Écomusée des Deux-Rives**
75, rue St-Jean-Baptiste, Valleyfield, QC J6T 1Z6
450-370-4855, Fax: 450-370-4861,
ecomusee@rocler.qc.ca

***Vaudreuil-Dorion:* Musée régional de Vaudreuil-Soulanges (MRVS)**
431, av St-Charles, Vaudreuil-Dorion, QC J7V 2N3
450-455-2092, Fax: 450-455-6782, 877-455-2092
info@mrvs.qc.ca
www.mrvs.qc.ca
Exposition permanente et expositions temporaires; collections spécialisées; ethnologie et histoire; collection beaux-arts; circuits patrimoniaux; centre de documentation en généaologie et histoire régionale; visites guidées, activités, ateliers, programmation; location de salles; boutique; café.
Daniel Bissonnette, Directeur générale

***Victoriaville:* Musée Laurier**
16, rue Laurier ouest, Victoriaville, QC G6P 6P3
819-357-8655, Fax: 819-357-8655,
info@museelaurier.com
museelaurier.com
Founded: 1929 Résidence de Sir Wilfrid Laurier, ancien premier ministre du Canada, et sa femme Lady Laurier, maintenant la propriété de la Société du Musée Laurier; collection d'objets d'art et de meubles, sculpture, et oeuvres en art contemporain.
Richard Pedneault, Directeur/Conservateur

***Windsor:* Parc histoique de la Poudrière de Windsor / Windsor Powder Mill Historical Park**
342, rue St-Georges, Windsor, QC J1S 2Z5
819-845-5284, Fax: 819-845-5615,
poudriere@bellnet.ca
www.lapoudriere.qc.ca
Fondée en 1864, dans la foulée de la guerre de session, la Poudrière de Windsor s'est investie dans la fabrication de poudre noire, un composé essentiel des explosifs. Jusqu'en 1922, la ville de Windsor a vécu au rythme de cette industrie dangereuse. On peut maintenant découvir les secrets, le comment et le pourquoi de cette industrie via une toute nouvelle exposition permanente et la visite guidé
Thomas Dandurand, Directeur général

Saskatchewan

Provincial Museums

Royal Saskatchewan Museum
2445 Albert St., Regina, SK S4P 4W7
306-787-2815, Fax: 306-787-2820,
rsminfo@royalsaskmuseum.ca
www.royalsaskmuseum.ca
Saskatchewan's natural & human history; archaeology; entomology; botany; natural history; paleontology; geology. Life Sciences Gallery; Earth Sciences Gallery; First Nations Gallery; Paleo Pit interactive gallery for children ; Megamunch, a half-size robotic Tyrannosaurus rex. Publication of informational booklets & nature notes, giftshop, research library.
Harold Bryant, Curator, Earth Sciences
David Baron, Director
Keith Roney, Curator, Life Sciences
Margaret Hanna, Curator, Aboriginal History
Ron Tillie, Supervisor, Exhibits
Paula Hill, Public Programs, Education
Ferne Johnston, Administrator

Western Development Museum (WDM)
2935 Melville St., Saskatoon, SK S7J 5A6
306-934-1400, Fax: 306-934-4467, 800-363-6345
info@wdm.ca
www.wdm.ca
The Western Development Museum preserves Saskatchewan's collective heritage, in order to raise awareness of & interest in the cultural & economic development of western Canada. The Curatorial Centre in Saskatoon coordinates services for the museum's branches in Moose Jaw, North Battleford, Saskatoon, & Yorkton. Tours of the Curatorial Centre may be arranged through the education & extension staff.
David Klatt, Executive Director
Cal Glasman, Director, Administration, cglasman@wdm.ca
Ruth Bitner, Curator, Collections, rbitner@wdm.ca
Warren Clubb, Curator, Exhibits, wclubb@wdm.ca
Dianne Craig, Manager, Corporate Development, dcraig@wdm.ca
Terry Thompson, Manager, Facilities, tthompson@wdm.ca
Brian Newman, Coordinator, Exhibits, bnewman@wdm.ca
Leslee Newman, Coordinator, Education & Extension, lnewman@wdm.ca
Jan Olsen, Coordinator, Marketing, jolsen@wdm.ca
Juanelle Finlay, Library Technician, jfinlay@wdm.ca

Other Museums in Saskatchewan

***Abernethy:* Abernethy Nature-Heritage Museum**
PO Box 158, Abernethy, SK S0A 0A0
306-333-2202,
anhm@sasktel.net
www.saskmuseums.org
Heritage & antique artifacts with a core exhibit of more than 300 wildlife specimens mounted by the late Ralph Stueck (1897-1979); video presentation of Stueck's "talking goose" & other folklore; activities/hands-on displays for children; small art gallery; 1930's classroom. Open daily May - Sept. Wheelchair accessible.
Eileen Gaye, President

***Abernethy:* Motherwell Homestead Natural Historic Site**
PO Box 247, Abernethy, SK S0A 0A0
306-333-2116, Fax: 306-333-2210,
motherwell-homestead@pc.gc.ca
www.pc.gc.ca/motherwell
Founded: 1983 The site includes Lanark Place, the farmstead estate of pioneer farmer and politician, W.R. Motherwell, who had a significant influence on the development of scientific agriculture in Western Canada. The homestead depicts the lifestyles, costumes, and architecture of the early 20th century, with costumed guides. Open Victoria Day - Labour Day.
Flo Miller, Site Coordinator, flo.miller@pc.gc.ca

***Alida:* Gervais Wheels Museum**
PO Box 40, Alida, SK S0C 0B0
306-443-2303,
Pioneer artifacts, music boxes, gramophones, North American automobiles

***Arcola:* Arcola Museum**
PO Box 354, Arcola, SK S0C 0G0
306-455-2462,
Open May-Sept.
Margaret Olsen, Contact
Ruth Gardner, Contact

***Assiniboia:* Assiniboia & District Museum**
PO Box 1211, 506 - 3rd Ave. West, Assiniboia, SK S0H 0B0
306-642-5353, Fax: 306-642-4216,
assini.museum@sasktel.net
southcentralmuseums.ca/assiniboia.html
Other contact information: Phone, appointments: 306-642-4790
The Assiniboia & District Museum features vintage cars from 1916 to 1964, a grain elevator, a Pole Shed with agricultural machinery, a school room & a military display. The museum is open seven days a week during July & August, & Monday to Friday from September to June.

***Avonlea:* Avonlea & District Museum - Heritage House**
PO Box 401, Main St., Avonlea, SK S0H 0C0
306-868-2101, Fax: 306-868-2221,
jeankincaid@sasktel.net
Founded: 1980 The Avonlea & District Museum displays artifacts which depict the geological age, plus the history of native people, pioneers, & ranchers in the area. The Truax Anglican Church is situated on the grounds. The museum is open from June to September. At other times of the year, appointments can be arranged.
Jean Kincaid, President

***Battleford:* Fort Battleford National Historic Site of Canada**
PO Box 70, Battleford, SK S0M 0E0
306-937-2621, Fax: 306-937-3370,
battleford.info@pc.gc.ca
www.parkscanada.gc.ca/battleford
Other contact information: TDD: 306/937-3199
NWMP post, c. 1886; open May long weekend - Sept. long weekend
Glenn Ebert, Site Coordinator

***Battleford:* Fred Light Museum**
PO Box 40, Battleford, SK S0M 0E0
306-937-7111, Fax: 306-937-2450,
Pioneer artifacts, gun collection, military artifacts; open May - Sept.
Bernadette Leslie, Supervisor

***Battleford:* Saskatchewan Baseball Hall of Fame & Museum**
PO Box 1388, 292 - 22nd St., Battleford, SK S0M 0E0
306-446-1983, Fax: 306-446-0509,
saskbaseballmuseum@sasktel.net
Founded: 1983 Has over 3,000 artifacts dealing with baseball plus 6,000 items of archival nature such as pictures, books & magazines
Jane Shury, Executive Director

***Beauval:* Frazer's Museum**
PO Box 64, Beauval, SK S0M 0G0

Aboriginal & pioneer artifacts, including articles from Hudson's Bay Company, missionaries & Métis people

***Big River:* Big River Memorial Museum**
PO Box 220, 205 Third Ave. North, Big River, SK S0J 0E0
306-469-2112,
The Big River Memorial Museum contains items from fishing & logging in the area.

***Biggar:* Biggar Museum & Gallery**
PO Box 1598, 105 - 3rd Ave. West, Biggar, SK S0K 0M0
306-948-3451, Fax: 306-948-3478,
biggarmuseum@sasktel.net
www.biggarmuseum.com
Founded: 1972 The museum collects historical artifacts from the settlement of the town of Biggar & the surrounding district. Among it collections are a general store display & a reconstruction of the Biggar train station. Biggar Museum & Gallery is open year round.
Anne Livingston, Executive Director

Biggar: **Homestead Museum**
PO Box 542, Biggar, SK S0K 0M0
306-948-3427,
Prairie pioneer village including sod house, school, church, barn, general store, 1913 house, 1920 house & bunk house & cook car; collection of Historical Character dolls; open daily Victoria Day - Oct.
Roger Martin, Director

Blaine Lake: **Blaine Lake Museum**
PO Box 10, Blaine Lake, SK S0J 0J0
306-497-2531,
The Blaine Lake Museum is situated in the CNR station, which was built in 1912. The museum depicts the local history of the area.

Briercrest: **Briercrest & District Museum**
PO Box 216, Briercrest, SK S0H 0K0
306-799-2103, Fax: 306-799-2115,
The Briercrest & District Museum houses collections from the Briercrest area's earliest settlers & their descendants. Examples of the museum's artifacts include household items & small farm equipment. The museum is open from May to September.

Broadview: **Broadview Historical Museum**
PO Box 556, Broadview, SK S0G 0K0
306-696-3244,
www.broadview.ca/museum
Founded: 1972 Articles related to Broadview's history are collected & displayed. Visitors can see the Highland School, a blacksmith shop, a post office, a sod house, a log home, & a Canadian Pacific Railway station & caboose. Broadview Historical Museum is open from the beginning of June to the end of August.

Bulyea: **Lakeside Museum**
PO Box 101, Bulyea, SK S0G 0L0
306-725-4558,
Native & pioneer artifacts; Boer War, World War I & II exhibits; display of dinosaur bones; open by appointment
Robert Swanston, Director

Cabri: **Cabri & District Museum**
PO Box 230, 202 - 1st St. South, Cabri, SK S0N 0J0
306-587-2339,
Displays include artifacts from World War I & World War II, First Nations, & household & farm items. The museum is open from May to September.

Cadillac: **Cadillac Museum**
PO Box 118, Centre St., Cadillac, SK S0N 0K0
306-785-2128, Fax: 306-785-2042,
Household articles & early 20th century tools; clothing; fire-fighting equipment; quilt exhibit; demonstrations. Open upon request
Luanne Hancock, Contact

Canwood: **Canwood Museum**
PO Box 269, 635 - 3rd Ave. East, Canwood, SK S0J 0K0
Founded: 1971 Canwood Museum is a community museum located in an old schoolhouse. Displays include farm artifacts, clothing, & pictures.

Carlyle: **Rusty Relics Museum Inc.**
PO Box 840, 115 Railway Ave. W., Carlyle, SK S0C 0R0
306-453-2266, Fax: 306-453-2812,
rustyrelicsmuseum@gmail.com
www.virtualmuseum.ca
A museum of pioneer life in Saskatchewan; artifacts relating to Carlyle area displayed in room settings in a 1910 CN railway station; includes a 1943 CPR caboose, a CN Motor car, CN tool shed with railway tools, furnished 1905 one-room country school, agricultural machinery & old church
Wilbert Hume, President

Climax: **Climax Community Museum Inc.**
PO Box 246, Climax, SK S0N 0N0
306-293-2124, Fax: 306-293-2051,
www.virtualmuseum.ca
Pioneer collection - domestic, tools, farm machinery, military, hospital & sports, community archives
Victor Van Allen, President/Curator

Coronach: **Coronach District Museum**
PO Box 449, Coronach, SK S0H 0Z0
306-267-4923,
Features historical displays, records, photos & artifacts representing the lives of pioneers of the area
Judy Greenwood, Chair

Craik: **Prairie Pioneer Museum**
PO Box 157, 541 Parks Rd., Craik, SK S0G 0V0
306-734-2480,
www.craik.ca/pioneer.html
Founded: 1966 The pioneer way of life in Craik & rural Saskatchewan is portrayed at the Prairie Pioneer Museum. Buildings include two rural schools & a heritage house, which was built in 1906. Artifacts, such as household furnishings & medical & veterinary instruments, are on display. The museum is open during the summer, & is accessible year-round by request.
Mary Eva, Contact

Cupar: **Cupar & District Heritage Museum**
PO Box 164, Cupar, SK S0G 0Y0
306-723-4324,
Founded: 1955 Open May - Sept. or by appt.
Wes Bailey, Chair

Cut Knife: **Clayton McLain Memorial Museum**
PO Box 8, 111A Hill Ave., Cut Knife, SK S0M 0N0
306-398-2920, Fax: 306-398-2951,
cmmmcutknife@gmail.com
www.cmmmcutknife.ca; cmmmcutknife.blogspot.com;
www.virtualmuseum.ca
Located in Tomahawk Park; local history, including First Nations artifacts from early life & Battle of Cutknife Hill, and McLain family collection; archives include personal papers, photgraphs, and a complete collection of the local newspaper; educational programming; research services; open June-Sept.

Denare Beach: **Northern Gateway Museum**
PO Box 70, Beaver Dr., Denare Beach, SK S0P 0B0
306-362-2141, Fax: 306-362-2257,
ngmuseum@sasktel.net
Founded: 1957 The Northern Gateway Museum houses artifacts from fur trade excavations, First Nations life, gold rush activities, & mining operations. Archives include architectural records, photographs, & films.

Dinsmore: **Yester-Years Community Museum**
PO Box 216, Dinsmore, SK S0L 0T0
Features the main museum, blacksmith shop, butter & post office buildings; open July & Aug. upon request
Helyn Tryyki, President

Dodsland: **Dodsland Museum**
125, Dodsland, SK S0L 0V0
306-356-2178,
Old grocery store on lower floor represents a village of the past; top floor represents living quarters of the past
Weldon Bacon, Director

Duck Lake: **Duck Lake Regional Interpretive Centre**
PO Box 328, Duck Lake, SK S0K 1J0
306-467-2057, Fax: 306-467-2257, 866-467-2057
duckmuf@sasktel.net
www.dlric.org
Founded: 1959 Frontier of First Nation, Métis & Pioneer Society, 1870-1905; artifact & art galleries, theatre, gift shop, 24m viewing tower, conference facilities
Celine Perillat, Executive Director

Duff: **Duff Community Heritage Museum**
PO Box 57, Duff, SK S0A 0S0
306-728-3275,
www.spreda.sk.ca/community_Duff.htm
Open by appointment only, this tourist attraction has been built out of an old church and features a recreational pioneer-era kitchen and old rural schoolhouse, along with various other historical items and photos from the village's history.

Eastend: **Eastend Museum & Cultural Centre**
PO Box 214, Eastend, SK S0N 0T0
306-295-3564,
Tie Rail Ranch House, blacksmith shop, operating 1903 Cae Steam Engine, 1927 Federal Truck, & a stage coach; LaRose Building contains 1500 items; Open daily May - Labour Day
Shelly Parker, President
Glen Duke, Treasurer
Doreen Stewart, Secretary

Edam: **Harry S. Washbrook Museum**
PO Box 182, Edam, SK S0M 0V0
306-397-2260,
Local pioneer & First Nations artifacts

Elbow: **Elbow Museum & Historical Society**
PO Box 207, Elbow, SK S0H 1J0
306-854-2277, Fax: 306-854-2229,
elbow@sasktel.net
www.elbowsask.com
Housed in an old schoolhouse; sodhouse built in 1965 & July 1999; artifacts represent era of late 1800s & early 1900s
Joan Soggie, Chair

Elrose: **Elrose Heritage Society**
PO Box 556, 4th Ave.E., Elrose, SK S0L 0Z0
306-378-2213,
Directors collect, restore & catalogue artifacts & antiques; museum open Sun., Wed., & Fri. May - Sept.; guided tours conducted; gift shop
Florence Rowley, Secretary
Betty Rudd, President

Esterhazy: **Esterhazy Community Museum**
PO Box 371, Esterhazy, SK S0A 0X0
306-745-2988,
Pioneer artifacts, taxidermy & music rooms, old store, model of potash mine; fashion show; antique doll and toy show

Esterhazy: **Kaposvar Historic Site**
PO Box 13, Esterhazy, SK S0A 0X0
306-745-2715,
1907 church & rectory; Annual Pilgrimage on the fourth Sun. in Aug.
Rose Kacsmar, Secretary

Estevan: **Estevan Art Gallery & Museum**
118 - 4th St., Estevan, SK S4A 0T4
306-634-7644, Fax: 306-634-2490,
eagm@sasktel.net
www.eagm.ca
NWMP Museum, local artifacts; open summer season; plus art with 2 contemporary exhibiting galleries, with travelling exhibitions, giftshop; open year round
Griffith Aaron Baker, Director/Curator

Eston: **Prairie West Historical Centre & Society**
PO Box 910, Eston, SK S0L 1A0
306-962-3772,
Local history museum & art gallery; wildflower garden
Betty James, Programme Coordinator/Curator

Foam Lake: **Foam Lake Museum**
PO Box 1041, 113 Bray Ave., Foam Lake, SK S0A 1A0
306-272-4292,
Local pioneer museum documenting the settlement of the area. Open June 1st - Aug. 31st and by appointment.
Ruth Gushulak, President
Fina Anderson, Secretary

Fort Qu'appelle: **Fort Qu'Appelle Museum**
PO Box 1093, Fort Qu'appelle, SK S0G 1S0
306-332-6033,
valleycalls@sasktel.net
www.fortquappelle.com/history.html
1864 Hudson Bay Co. post; open June-Sept.
J. Norman, Vice-President
L. Anderson, President

Frenchman Butte: **Frenchman Butte Museum**
PO Box 10, Frenchman Butte, SK S0M 0W0
306-344-4478, Fax: 306-344-4566,
info@frenchmanbuttemuseum.ca
www.frenchmanbuttemuseum.ca
Pioneer & CNR artifacts; arrowhead & gun collections, mounted birds

Frobisher: **Frobisher Threshermen's Museum**
PO Box 194, Frobisher, SK S0C 0Y0
306-486-4513,
Steam engines, wooden threshing separators, gas & diesel tractors, ploughshares

Glen Ewen: **Glen Ewen Community Antique Centre**
Glen Ewen, SK S0C 1C0
306-925-2221,
Features a collection of antique cars that includes a 1910 Ford & a 1937 Packard; also showcases guns, dishes & household articles from the early 1900s; open seasonally or by request
Arne Hansen, Director

Glentworth: **Glentworth Museum**
PO Box 174, Glentworth, SK S0H 1V0
306-266-4320,
Local history artifacts

Goodsoil: **Goodsoil Historical Museum**
PO Box 370, Goodsoil, SK S0M 1A0
306-238-4565, Fax: 306-238-4991,
schamber@sasktel.net
www.saskmuseums.org
Founded: 1977 Natural stone school building built in 1945; first teacherage built in 1934 of logs; miniature church with original steeple from church destroyed by tornado; over 2,500 artifacts, many dating from 1800s; old machinery; doll house with hundreds of dolls from around the world. Open June 30 - Aug. 31
Alex Schamber, President, schamber@sasktel.net
Rudy Leiter, Secretary

Gravelbourg: **Gravelbourg & District Museum**
PO Box 862, 300 Main St., Gravelbourg, SK S0H 1X0
306-648-2332,
Open July & Aug.
Louis Stringer, Manager

Grenfell: **Grenfell Museum Assoc.**
PO Box 1156, 711 Wolseley Ave., Grenfell, SK S0G 2B0
306-697-2930, Fax: 306-697-2500,

Restored 1904 Queen Anne turreted house; added attraction is the annex with furniture & tools of bygone days as well as an outstanding military display
Lloyd Arthur, President
Mary Christie, Secretary

Hague: **Saskatchewan River Valley Museum**
PO Box 630, Hague, SK S0K 1X0
306-225-2112, Fax: 306-225-4642,
rivervalleymuseum@sasktel.net
www.saskmuseums.org; www.townofhague.com;
www.virtualmuseum.ca
Approx. 6,000 artifacts, including First Nations & Mennonite; original European house/barn; country school; Mennonite church; horse-drawn farming machinery, blacksmith tools, pre-1950 furniture & appliances; open May long weekend - Thanksgiving
Len Wudrich, Vice-President
Gerry Kuehn, President

Harris: **Harris Museum**
PO Box 131, 204 Railway Ave., Harris, SK S0L 1K0
306-656-2002, Fax: 306-656-2172,
Founded: 1989 The volunteer operated Harris Museum features local history & archives, plus a C.N. Water Tower & a gas engine water pump. The museum is open from May to September, or by appointment.
Harvey Neil, President
RoseAnn Mireau, Past President, 306-656-4449
Betty McFarlane, Contact, 306-656-4725
Dolores Neil, Contact, 306-656-2172

Hazenmore: **Heritage Hazenmore Museum**
PO Box 103, Hazenmore, SK S0N 1C0
306-264-5149,
Local history; open on request

Hodgeville: **Hodgeville Community Museum**
Also known as: **Country Craft Shoppe & Homestead Museum**
PO Box 264, 102 - 1st St. West, Hodgeville, SK S0H 2B0
306-677-2693, Fax: 306-677-2707,
Eight rooms depicting an early homestead; crafts, gifts & tearoom
Linda Straub, President

Hudson Bay: **Hudson Bay Museum**
PO Box 931, Hudson Bay, SK S0E 0Y0
306-865-2170,
Preserving artifacts of the area; open May 15 - Sept. 10
Jean Geddes, President
Emily Lundeen, Secretary

Humboldt: **Humboldt & District Museum & Gallery**
PO Box 2349, Humboldt, SK S0K 2A0
306-682-5226, Fax: 306-682-1430,
humboldt.museum@sasktel.net
www.humboldtmuseum.ca
Focus on the Humboldt Telegraph Station of 1878, as well as the settlement of Humboldt & district, & the spiritual influence of St. Peter's Abbey; housed in a 1912 post office building
J. Hoesgen, Curator

Imperial: **Imperial & District Museum**
PO Box 269, Imperial, SK S0G 2J0
306-963-2280,
Local history; open by appt.
Marilyn Koza, Co-Chair
Fred Grigg, Co-Chair

Imperial: **Nels Berggren Museum**
PO Box 125, Royal St., Imperial, SK S0G 2J0
306-963-2033,
Lamps, clocks, sewing machines, musical instruments, art

Indian Head: **Indian Head Museum**
PO Box 566, Indian Head, SK S0G 2K0
306-695-3800,
1907 two-storey fire hall displaying artifacts of local pioneer days; also 1926 one-room school, 1883 Bell Farm Cottage; replica of 1930s one-bay village garage; farm implements
Arnold Dales, President

Ituna: **Ituna Cultural & Historical Museum**
Old Ituna & District Recreation Centre, 3rd St., Ituna, SK S0A 1N0
306-795-3348,
Local history including Ukrainian & aboriginal artifacts; open July-Aug.

Kamsack: **Kamsack & District Museum**
PO Box 991, Queen Elizabeth Boulevard, Kamsack, SK S0A 1S0
306-542-4415,
Exhibits focus on both First Nations and European history; Housed in a former power plant, the museum contains one of the original diesel engines which generated the town's electricity until 1958; rooms furnished in the style of a typical 1920s pioneer dwelling. Open May - Sept.; car show & shine mid-June
Fr. John Morarity, President
Nick Trofimenkoff, Secretary/Treasurer

Kelliher: **Kelliher & District Heritage Museum Inc.**
PO Box 111, Kelliher, SK S0A 1V0
306-675-2183,
Walter Oleksyn

Kenosee Lake: **Cannington Manor Provincial Park**
PO Box 220, Kenosee Lake, SK S0C 2S0
306-739-5251, Fax: 306-577-2622,
manor.cannington@gov.sk.ca
www.tpcs.gov.sk.ca/CanningtonManor
Other contact information: Phone, Off Season: 306-577-2600
In the late 1800s, partners in the Moose Mountain Trading Company established the village of Cannington Manor. Buildings from this village have been reconstructed or restored for visitors. Buildings at the site include a Land Titles Office, a bachelor's cabin, a Moose Mountain Trading Company store, a carpenter's shop, a blacksmith shop, a flour mill, & the Mitre Hotel. Cannington Manor is open from Victoria Day to Labour Day.

Kerrobert: **Kerrobert & District Museum**
PO Box 463, 15 Saskatchewan Ave., Kerrobert, SK S0L 1R0
306-834-5277,
Replica of the first tent store and pioneer furniture; Open May-Sept.
Mary Andrews, Secretary

Kincaid: **Kincaid Museum**
PO Box 177, Kincaid, SK S0H 2J0
306-264-3910,
Local historical material

Kindersley: **Kindersley & District Plains Museum**
PO Box 599, 903 - 11th Ave. East, Kindersley, SK S0L 1S0
306-463-6620,
Wide collection of early farm machinery and tools, household items, education items and items from school and churches; fire hall and fire truck; miliary display, a general store, post office & print shop; an archaeological display; Open May to mid-Sept.

Kinistino: **Kinistino & District Pioneer Museum Inc.**
PO Box 10, Kinistino, SK S0J 1H0
306-864-2838,
Displays of artifacts from fur trade & pioneer times; oldest purely agricultural settlement in Saskatchewan; open July - Aug. or by appt.
Shelley Holmes, Sec.-Treas.

Kipling: **Kipling & District Historical Society**
PO Box 414, Kipling, SK S0G 2S0
306-736-8254,
e.hamelin@sasktel.net
Elaine Hamelin, Secretary

Kisbey: **Kisbey Museum**
PO Box 5, 291 Ross St., Kisbey, SK S0C 1L0
306-462-2162,
Detailed history & pictures of Kisbey's namesake, R. Claude Kisbey; 1,000+ objects; open Thu. through July & Aug. & by request
Velma Hale, President

Lancer: **Lancer Centennial Museum**
PO Box 3, Lancer, SK S0N 1G0
306-689-2925, Fax: 306-689-2890,
Open June-Sept.
Cliff Murch

Langham: **Langham & District Heritage Village & Museum**
PO Box 516, 302 Railway St., Langham, SK S0K 2L0
306-283-4342, Fax: 306-283-4772,
www.langham.ca
Preserves & exhibits artifacts illustrating the history & culture of Langham & area; special events & programming. Open May long weekend to Sept. 30, Wed. 9-12 & Sat. 9-3, or by appointment.
Doreen Nickel, President

Lanigan: **Lanigan & District Heritage Centre**
Parent: **Lanigan & District Heritage Association**
PO Box 424, Lanigan, SK S0K 2M0
306-365-2569, Fax: 306-365-2960,
lanigan.dist.heritage@sasktel.net
www.sasktelwebsite.nat/ldha/
Founded: 1994 The Lanigan & District Heritage Association's mission is to preserve the Lanigan CPR Station, where the Centre is currently housed; includes a museum, tourism information, agricultural interpretive display, potash exposition, caboose, recreation & coffee area & storage. Located at 75 Railway Ave., Lanigan.
Ruth Wildeman, Secretary
Andrew Cebryk, Chair

Lashburn: **Lashburn Centennial Museum**
PO Box 275, Corner of Main Street and 1st Ave., Lashburn, SK S0M 1H0
306-285-4145,
www.saskmuseums.org/museums/museum_search.php?id=107
Vetern's Gallery with artifacts from the Boer War to Korean War; 1908 Gully School; Artifacts of the Barr Colony settlers; log cabin and blacksmith shop.

Leross: **Kellross Heritage Museum**
PO Box 215, 2nd Ave., Leross, SK S0A 1V0
306-675-6144,
Open by appt. from June 15
Louise Tereposky

Leroy: **Leroy & District Heritage Museum**
PO Box 47, Leroy, SK S0K 2P0
306-286-3288,
Open July & Aug.

Lumsden: **Lumsden Heritage Museum**
c/o Lumsden Historical Society, PO Box 91, 50 Qu'Appelle Dr. West, Lumsden, SK S0G 3C0
306-731-2905,

Luseland: **Luseland & Districts Museum**
Grand Ave., Luseland, SK S0L 2A0
306-372-4692,
valfin@sasktel.net
Open Sat. or by request
Donna Ruhohr, Chair
Isabell Kasas, Vice-Chair

Macklin: **Macklin & District Museum**
Also known as: **Eid House**
PO Box 423, 5002 Herald St., Macklin, SK S0L 2C0
306-753-2610,
town.macklin@sasktel.net
www.macklin.ca/museum.htm
Founded: 1990 Built in 1919 by Frank Shaw, the town's first bank manager, the house later became a hospital during the 1920s. Open Tu, Th, F, summer.

Macrorie: **Macrorie Museum**
PO Box 177, Macrorie, SK S0L 2E0
306-243-4327, Fax: 306-243-4507,
Consists of 3 sites: an old post office, insurance office, & living quarters which depict the local farming area; an old brick school, heritage site; a caboose & jigger; open Mon. in July & Aug. 2-4, or by appt.
Geraldine Torvik, Treasurer
Lynne Cooper, President
Jean Delparte, Secretary

Maidstone: **Maidstone & District Historical & Cultural Society**
PO Box 250, Maidstone, SK S0M 1M0
306-893-2890,
May - Sept.
Bill McGilvery, President

Main Centre: **Main Centre Heritage Museum**
PO Box 42, Main Centre, SK S0H 2V0
306-784-2953,
Local history & early pioneering artifacts; school & church history; Herbert Ferry Crossing display; open by appt. May - Sept.
Iris Siemens, Secretary
Dora Wall, Chair

Maple Creek: **Fort Walsh National Historic Site**
PO Box 278, Maple Creek, SK S0N 1N0
306-662-2645, Fax: 306-662-2711,
fort.walsh@pc.gc.ca
www.pc.gc.ca/lhn-nhs/sk/walsh/index_e.asp
Other contact information: TTY: 306/662-3124
NWMP fort & Cypress Hills Massacre site; open mid May - last weekend in Sept.
David Rohatensky, Site Manager

Maple Creek: **Jasper Cultural & Historical Centre**
PO Box 1504, Maple Creek, SK S0N 1N0
306-662-2434, Fax: 306-662-4359,
admin@jaspercentre.ca
www.jaspercentre.ca/0000pg.asp/ID/3344/SID/120
Open Mon.-Fri. in winter; daily in summer
Sally Douglas, Manager

Maple Creek: **Southwest Saskatchewan Oldtimers Museum**
PO Box 1540, 218 Jasper St., Maple Creek, SK S0N 1N0
306-662-2474,
oldtimers@sasktel.net
Ranching, First Nations, NWMP, firearms; open May 20 to Sept. 30

Maryfield: **Maryfield Museum**
PO Box 262, Maryfield, SK S0G 3K0
306-646-2201,

Clocks, tools, record players, telephones

***McCord:* McCord & District Museum**
PO Box 82, McCord, SK S0H 2T0
306-478-2522,
ba.wilson@xplornet.com
www.southcentralmuseums.ca/mccord.html
Founded: 1973 Museum is housed in a 1928 CPR railway station and exibits includehistorical items from households and businesses in the area. Of note is an actual caboose on tracks beside the museum. A companion museum is the 1913 church at the opposite end of the street which displays religious articles from various churches in the region.

***Meadow Lake:* Meadow Lake Museum**
PO Box 610, 120 - 1st St. East, Meadow Lake, SK S9X 1Y5
306-236-3622, Fax: 306-236-4299,
meadowlake_townml@sasktel.net
www.meadowlake.ca
Exhibits are related to pioneers, farming, lumbering, & birds. The museum is open from Victoria Day to Labour Day.
Cecil Midgett, Contact

***Melfort:* Melfort & District Museum**
PO Box 3222, 401 Melfort St. West, Melfort, SK S0E 1A0
306-752-5870, Fax: 306-752-5556,
melfort.museum@sasktel.net
www.cityofmelfort.ca
Founded: 1971 Community museum, archives, pioneer village; agricultural machinery displays; located adjacent to the Melfort fairgrounds.
Gailmarie Anderson, Curator

***Melville:* Melville Heritage Museum Inc.**
PO Box 2528, Melville, SK S0A 2P0
306-728-2070, Fax: 306-728-2070,
Regional museum, located in the former Luther Academy (1913-1926); artifacts & histories of local, provincial & national interest; includes chapel, library, Grand Trunk Pacific/CNR & Military; over 100 original B & W framed photographs depict Melville's first quarter century; gift shop; murals; limited wheelchair access
Marj Redenbach, Curator

***Melville:* Melville Railway Museum**
PO Box 1240, Melville, SK S0A 2P0
306-728-6840, Fax: 306-728-5911,
city.clrk@city.melville.sk.ca
www.city.melville.sk.ca/siteengine/activep age.asp?PageID=188
Former CNR steam locomotive #5114; a J-4-5 class 4-6-2 built in 1919; also former Grand Trunk Pacific station from Duff, Saskatchewan containing artifacts including exhibits of communications equipment, from telegraphs, and telephones. There are also records from the Grand Trunk Railway and CNR, including employee records
MR Michael Hotsko, City Manager, mhotsko@melville.ca

***Middle Lake:* Middle Lake Museum**
PO Box 157, Middle Lake, SK S0K 2X0

***Milden:* Milden Community Museum**
PO Box 218, Milden, SK S0L 2L0
306-935-2199,
A community museum holding local artifacts including those of an old-time school, hospital & bedroom
Margaret Herd, Secretary
Brenda Latsay, President

***Moose Jaw:* Moose Jaw Museum & Art Gallery**
Crescent Park, Moose Jaw, SK S6H 0X6
306-692-4471, Fax: 306-694-8016,
mjamchin@sasktel.net
www.mjmag.ca
Founded: 1966 The building houses art, history & science exhibits, with a wide range of human history artifacts with strong representation of First Nations beadwork, women's clothing, and clothing-related artifacts from 1880 onward. There is a gift shop. The Learning Centre offers programs for school children and art classes for all ages. Open year round; admission by donation.
Heather Smith, Curator

***Moose Jaw:* Western Development Museum**
***Also known as:* Moose Jaw Western Development Museum**
50 Diefenbaker Dr., Moose Jaw, SK S6J 1L9
306-693-5989, Fax: 306-691-0511,
moosejaw@wdm.ca
www.wdm.ca
Moose Jaw is one of four exhibit branches of Saskatchewan's Western Development Museum. The other branches are located in North Battleford, Saskatoon, & Yorkton. The Moose Jaw Western Development Museum displays the history of transportation, from the canoe to the railway. The museum also features the Snowbirds Gallery, which presents Canadian military aerobatic flight history.
Katherine Fitton, Manager, Moose Jaw, kfitton@wdm.ca
David Samson, Museum Technician, dsamson@wdm.ca
Jackie Hall, Officer, Programs & Education, jhall@wdm.ca
Shirley Stenko, Officer, Visitor Services, sstenko@wdm.ca

***Moose Jaw:* Sukanen Ship Pioneer Village & Museum of Saskatchewan**
PO Box 2071, Moose Jaw, SK S6H 7T2
306-693-7315,
pmjohnson@Sasktel.net
www.sukanenmuseum.ca
38 acres of land; pioneer village of 20 buildings; antique farm with machinery; 100 collector tractors; 40 cars & trucks
Abe Giesbretch, Secretary
R. Jones, President

***Moosomin:* Jamieson Museum**
PO Box 236, 306 Gertie St., Moosomin, SK S0G 3N0
306-435-3156,
Pre-1900 house, church, military collection; open May - Oct.

***Morse:* Morse Museum & Cultural Centre**
PO Box 308, Morse, SK S0H 3C0
306-629-3230, Fax: 306-629-3230,
morsemuseum@sasktel.net
former school, built in 1912; open year round

***Mossbank:* Mossbank & District Museum Inc.**
PO Box 278, Mossbank, SK S0H 3G0
306-354-2889,
A community history museum dedicated to the history of No. 2 Bombing & Gunnery School which was located three miles east of Mossbank during WWII; blacksmith shop & blacksmith's house are now classified as provincial heritage property
Roy Tollefson, President

***Naicam:* Naicam Museum**
PO Box 238, Naicam, SK S0K 2Z0
306-874-2280, Fax: 306-874-5444,
www.townofnaicam.ca/museum.htm
History & archives of Naicam & District in Heritage building (pioneer school)
Ruby J. Lindsay, Secretary
Joan Gerguson, Chair
Doris Poole, Director

***Nipawin:* Nipawin & District Living Forestry Museum**
PO Box 1917, Hwy. 35 West, Nipawin, SK S0E 1E0
306-862-9299,
Situated on 14 acres; open May - Aug.
James Grandfield

***Nokomis:* Nokomis District Museum & Heritage Co-op**
PO Box 417, Nokomis, SK S0G 3R0
306-528-2979,
Displays & artifacts of early days & local history; open June 1 - Labour Day daily 10-5
Karen Lee, Director

***North Battleford:* Western Development Museum**
***Also known as:* North Battleford Western Development Museum**
PO Box 183, North Battleford, SK S9A 2Y1
306-445-8033, Fax: 306-445-7211,
nbattleford@wdm.ca
www.wdm.ca
North Battleford is one of four exhibit branches of Saskatchewan's Western Development Museum. The other branches are located in Moose Jaw, Saskatoon, & Yorkton. The North Battleford Western Development Museum provides visitors with the opportunity to explore a Heritage Farm & Village. Sights include a Wheat Pool grain elevator, a 1910 Case 110 tractor, A Co-op store, homes, & churches.
Wayne Fennig, Manager, North Battleford, wfennig@wdm.ca
Joyce Smith, Manager, Operations, jsmith@wdm.ca
Cheryl Stewart, Coordinator, Education & Volunteers, cstewart@wdm.ca
Daniel Stewart, Museum Technician, dstewart@wdm.ca

***Outlook:* Outlook & District Heritage Museum & Gallery**
PO Box 1095, 100 Railway Ave., Outlook, SK S0L 2N0
306-867-8285,
outlookmuseum@sasktel.net
Located in a former railway station, the Outlook & District Heritage Museum & Gallery is open from June to August. Exhibits include a caboose & an old jail cell. The Museum also keeps copies of the local newspaper, entitled "The Outlook", dating back to 1910.

***Oxbow:* Ralph Allen Memorial Museum**
PO Box 361, Oxbow, SK S0C 2B0
306-483-5082,
mbartolf@sasktel.net
Open May - Sept.
Michael Bartolf, 2nd Vice-President
Otto Neuman, President

***Paynton:* Bresaylor Heritage Museum**
PO Box 33, Main St., Paynton, SK S0M 2J0
306-895-4813,
The Bresaylor Heritage Museum collects artifacts from the Bresaylor & Paynton area. Items date back to 1882, when the earliest residents settled in Bresaylor. The museum is open in July & August, & at other times of the year by appointment.

***Pelly:* Fort Pelly Livingston Museum**
PO Box 24, 306- 1st Ave. S, Pelly, SK S0A 2Z0
306-595-2030,
www.pelly.ca/museum.html
Brian Clough

***Plenty:* Plenty & District Museum**
PO Box 99, Main St., Plenty, SK S0L 2R0
306-932-4727,
Situated in a 1911 building, which once served as Plenty's post office & hardware store, the Plenty & District Museum depicts pioneer life in the community & surrounding area. Farming equipment is featured in a separate building.

***Porcupine Plain:* Porcupine Plain & District Museum**
PO Box 171, Elm St., Porcupine Plain, SK S0E 1H0
306-278-2317, Fax: 306-278-2073,
www.porcupineplain.com
Other contact information: Phone, Appointments: 306-278-2834; 306-278-2073
Founded: 1968 The Porcupine Plain & District Museum features local pioneer artifacts, such as antique machinery & clothing. The museum also houses a bird displat, with birds from the Porcupine Plain & Somme area. The soldier settlement consists of a log home, a schoolhouse, & a church. The Porcupine Plain & District Museum is open from the beginning of July to the Labour Day weekend in September. At other times, tours may be arranged.

***Prairie River:* Prairie River Museum**
***Also known as:* Prairie River Heritage Society**
PO Box 9, Prairie River, SK S0E 1J0
306-889-4248,
prhs.fl.waskowic@sasktel.net
Railway, agriculture, lumbering, trapping, First Nations artifacts

***Prelate:* St. Angela's Museum & Archives**
PO Box 220, Prelate, SK S0N 2B0
306-673-2200, Fax: 306-673-2635,
To preserve valuable history of pioneer Saskatchewan & of the pioneer Ursulines of St. Angela's Convent Academy at Prelate Saskatchewan; collection tells story of Ursuline life & apostolate that were used in chapel, classroom & other departments
Sister Hermana Blatz, Director

***Prince Albert:* Diefenbaker House**
246 19th Street W., Prince Albert, SK S6V 8A9
306-764-2992,
historypa@citypa.com
historypa.com
Residence of John G. Diefenbaker immediately prior to his becoming Prime Minister of Canada; museum furnished as it was in Mr. Diefenbaker's day & also includes phtographic displays of his life & associations in Prince Albert
James Benson, Manager

***Prince Albert:* Evolution of Education Museum**
10 River St. East, Prince Albert, SK S6V 8A9
306-764-2992,
historypa@citypa.com
historypa.com
Founded: 1963 Housed in the original Claytonville one-room rural school & features a class-room setting, plus displays of many early educational materials & artefacts
James Benson, Manager

***Prince Albert:* Prince Albert Historical Museum**
10 River St. East, Prince Albert, SK S6V 8A9
306-764-2992,
historypa@citypa.com
historypa.com
History, life-styles & people of Prince Albert & area; souvenir shop & tea room
James Benson, Manager

***Prince Albert:* Rotary Museum of Police & Corrections**
c/o Prince Albert Historical Society, 10 River St. East, Prince Albert, SK S6V 8A9
306-764-2992,
historypa@citypa.com
historypa.com
Housed in the guardhouse of the Prince Albert division of the NorthWest Mounted Police & Royal Northwest Mounted police; features artifacts, equipment & uniforms from the RCMP, Prince Albert City Police, the Provincial Correctional Service & the Correctional Service of Canada, as well as from the Saskatchewan Provincial Police
James Benson, Manager

***Raymore:* Raymore Pioneer Museum Inc.**
PO Box 453, Raymore, SK S0A 3J0
306-476-2180, Fax: 306-746-4314,

Collection of local pioneer artifacts
Wayne Focht, Sec.-Treas.

***Regina:* Alex Youck School Museum**
1600 - 4th Ave., Regina, SK S4R 8C8
306-352-8200,
Open by appt. only
Alex Youck, Director

***Regina:* Cumberland House Provincial Historic Park**
#530, 3211 Albert St., Regina, SK S4S 5W6
306-787-9572, Fax: 306-787-7000, 800-205-7070
inquiry@serm.gov.sk.ca

***Regina:* Government House Museum & Heritage Property (GH)**
4607 Dewdney Ave., Regina, SK S4T 1B7
306-787-0846, Fax: 306-787-5714,
ckuyek@gr.gov.sk.ca
www.gr.gov.sk.ca/govhouse
Former residence of the Lieutenant Governor of the Northwest Territories & the Province of Saskatchewan
Charlotte Kuyek, Community Relations Co-ordinator

***Regina:* Regina Plains Museum**
1835 Scarth St., 2nd Fl., Regina, SK S4P 2G9
306-780-9435, Fax: 306-565-2979,
rp.museum@sasktel.net
www.reginaplainsmuseum.com
Founded: 1960 Regina Plains Museum is the civic history museum of the city. It is open year-round.
Christa Donaldson, Executive Director
Jan Morier, Coordinator, Communications

***Regina:* Saskatchewan Military Museum**
The Armouries, 1600 Elphinstone St., Regina, SK S4T 3N1
306-585-3771,
www.saskmuseums.org
Collects & preserves Saskatchewan's military history from 1885 to the present; artifacts, uniforms, badges & medals, vehicles, ammunition; photos, archival material & paintings
Maj. (Ret'd) C. Keith Inches, Curator,
keithinches@sasktel.net

***Regina:* Saskatchewan Pharmacy Museum**
***Parent:* Saskatchewan Pharmacy Museum Society**
#700, 4010 Pasqua St., Regina, SK S4S 6S4
306-584-2292, Fax: 306-584-9695,
saskpharm@sk.sympatico.ca
www.skpharmacists.ca
Collection & preservation of pharmacy artifacts, documentation of pharmacy history
Bill Paterson, President

***Regina:* Saskatchewan Sports Hall of Fame & Museum**
2205 Victoria Ave., Regina, SK S4P 0S4
306-780-9232, Fax: 306-780-9427,
sshfm@sasktel.net
www.sshfm.com
Founded: 1966 3,000 sq. ft. of exhibit space celebrating the sport heritage of Saskatchewan; open year round with extended summer hours
Sheila Kelly, Executive Director

***Riverhurst:* F.T. Hill Museum**
PO Box 201, Riverhurst, SK S0H 3P0
306-353-2112, Fax: 306-353-2220,
Gun collection, aboriginal artifacts, pioneer items; open June 15 - Aug. 31 & by appt.
Betty Peterson

***Rocanville:* Rocanville & District Museum**
PO Box 490, Rocanville, SK S0A 3L0
306-645-2113, Fax: 306-645-2087,
roc.cap@sasktel.net
Other contact information: Phone, Appointments: 306-645-2164
Located at the corner of Qu'appelle Avenue & St. Albert Street, the Rocanville & District Museum showcases a CPR station, a church, a schoolhouse, a blacksmith shop, & a Masonic Lodge. The museum is open during July & August, & by appointment at other times of the year.

***La Ronge:* Mistasinihk Place Interpretive Centre**
c/o Saskatchewan Culture, Youth & Recreation, PO Box 5000, La Ronge, SK S0J 1L0
306-425-4350, Fax: 306-425-4336,
Aboriginal artifacts, artwork by northern artists, displays about northern industries & activites

***Rose Valley:* Rose Valley & District Heritage Museum**
PO Box 248, Rose Valley, SK S0E 1M0
306-322-4545, Fax: 306-322-5822,
jrustad@sask.tel.net
Museum with artifacts from area 1900 to present; open July & Aug., Mon.- Fri.; off season viewing available by request
Judy Rustad, President, 306/322-4474
Irene Martinson, Sec.-Treas., 306/322-4642

***Rosetown:* Rosetown & District Museum**
PO Box 37, Rosetown, SK S0L 2V0
306-882-3106,
Natural history specimens, photographs, handicrafts

***Rosthern:* Mennonite Heritage Museum**
PO Box 116, Rosthern, SK S0K 3R0
306-232-4415,
Museum housed in school, artifacts from 1800 to present, collection of World Wheat champion; open May to Sept.

***Rouleau:* Rouleau & District Museum**
PO Box 132, Rouleau, SK S0G 4H0
306-776-2363,
www.virtualmuseum.ca
A rural town street setting with houses, barn, blacksmith shop, school & other buildings; archives; special events, such as the annual threshing bee in Aug., & other programming. Open by appt., May - Sept.
Gareth Argue, President

***St Brieux:* Musée St. Brieux Museum**
CP 224, 300 Barbier Dr., St Brieux, SK S0K 3V0
306-275-2123,
Documentation au sujet de la vie des pionniers, de leurs origines, des missions environnantes et de l'église catholique pré-Vatican II; des tournées en français ou en anglais sont offertes
Chantel Schur, Curator

***St Victor:* McGillis House**
St Victor, SK S0H 3T0
306-642-3171,
www.willowbunch.ca
Located in St. Victor's regional park, McGillis House was built in 1890. Artifacts in the home include Métis items, kerosene lanterns, early saddles & bridles, & a feathered buffalo skull.

***St Walburg:* St. Walburg & District Museum**
PO Box 87, St Walburg, SK S0M 2T0
306-248-3631,
Local exhibits from pioneer days to 1945

***Saskatoon:* Diefenbaker Canada Centre**
University of Saskatchewan, 101 Diefenbaker Pl., Saskatoon, SK S7N 5B8
306-966-8384, Fax: 306-966-6207,
dief.centre@usask.ca
artsandscience.usask.ca/diefenbaker
The Diefenbaker Canada Centre includes a museum, archives, & research centre. The centre houses artifacts, such as a personal library, papers, & memorabilia, that were bequeathed to the University of Saskatchewan by former prime minister of Canada, John G. Diefenbaker. The archives features collections of press clippings, photographs, & documents related to Diefenbaker's life & Canadian history.
Teresa Carlson, Acting Director, 306-966-8383,
teresa.carlson@usask.ca
Trent Evanisky, Coordinator, Special Exhibits, 306-966-8386
Rob Paul, Coordinator, Archives, 306-966-8387,
rob.paul@usask.ca

***Saskatoon:* Fort Carlton Provincial Historic Park**
#102, 112 Research Dr., Saskatoon, SK S7K 2H6
306-467-5205, Fax: 306-933-5215,
fortcarlton@gov.sk.ca
www.saskparks.net
Located 26 km. west of Duck Lake on Hwy. 212; a reconstructed Hudson's Bay Company fur trade post; open May - Sept.
Janice Crawford, Contact

***Saskatoon:* Meewasin Valley Authority (MVA)**
402 - 3rd Ave. South, Saskatoon, SK S7K 3G5
306-665-6888, Fax: 306-665-6117,
meewasin@meewasin.com
www.meewasin.com
Founded: 1979 Conservation agency for the South Saskatchewan River
Susan Lamb, CEO, 306-665-6887

***Saskatoon:* Museum of Antiquities**
#116, College Bldg., University of Saskatchewan, 107 Administration Pl., Saskatoon, SK S7N 5A2
306-966-7818, Fax: 306-966-1954,
museum_antiquities.usask.ca
www.usask.ca/antiquities/
Founded: 1974 A collection of Near Eastern, Egyptian, Greek, Roman & Medieval sculpture in full scale replica as well as original works & coinage
Tracene Harvey, Acting Director

***Saskatoon:* Natural Sciences Museum**
Dept. of Biology & Geological Sciences, University of Saskatchewan, 112 Science Pl., Saskatoon, SK S7N 5E2
306-966-4399, Fax: 306-966-4461,
peta.bonhams@usask.ca
www.usask.ca
Designed to show evolution through time beginning with marine invertebrates & ending with evolution of animals; displays of living plants & animals correspond to fossils & create an integrated learning experience; free self-guided tours year-round; brochures downloaded from website
Dr. P. Bonham-Smith, Head, Biology,
peta.bonhams@usask.ca
Dr. B. Pratt, Geology, brian.pratt@usask.ca

***Saskatoon:* Western Development Museum**
***Also known as:* Saskatoon Western Development Museum**
2610 Lorne Ave. South, Saskatoon, SK S7J 0S6
306-931-1910, Fax: 306-934-0525,
saskatoon@wdm.ca
www.wdm.ca
Saskatoon is one of four exhibit branches of Saskatchewan's Western Development Museum. The other branches are located in Moose Jaw, North Battleford, & Yorkton. The Saskatoon Western Development Museum presents a 1910 Boomtown. Visitors can explore more than thirty buildings, including a blacksmith shop & a general store. The museum is also home to the Saskatchewan Agricultural Hall of Fame.
Tom Waiser, Manager, Saskatoon, twaiser@wdm.ca
Corinne Daelick, Coordinator, Education & Volunteers,
cdaelick@wdm.ca
Julie Jackson, Museum Technician, jjackson@wdm.ca

***Saskatoon:* Ukrainian Museum of Canada (UMC)**
910 Spadina Cres. East, Saskatoon, SK S7K 3H5
306-244-3800, Fax: 306-652-7620,
ukrmuse@sasktel.net
www.umc.sk.ca
The Ukrainian Museum preserves & encourages Ukrainian folk arts in Canada. The permanent gallery tells the story of Ukrainian immigration to Canada with displays of folk arts, including costumes, embroideries, weaving, ceramics, & Easter eggs. The museum's collection of textiles is one of the largest of its kind in North America.
Janet C.P. Danyliuk, Director

***Saskatoon:* Wanuskewin Heritage Park**
Penner Rd., RR#4, Saskatoon, SK S7K 3J7
306-931-6767, Fax: 306-931-4522, 877-547-6546
wanuskewin@wanuskewin.com
www.wanuskewin.com
Founded: 1992 The Wanuskewin Heritage Park represents the life of the Northern Plains First Nations people. Visitors will find tipi rings, bison kill sites, a medicine wheel, & pottery fragments. The 116 hectare park operates under the leadership & guidance of First Nations people. It is open year-round.

***Sceptre:* Great Sandhills Museum**
PO Box 29, Sceptre, SK S0N 2H0
306-623-4345, Fax: 306-623-4612,
gshs@sasktel.net
www.greatsandhillsmuseum.com
Dedicated to collect, portray & preserve the heritage of the "Great Sandhills" District in SW Saskatchewan through natural history specimens
Gertrude Hale, President

***Scout Lake:* St. Mary's Historical Society of Maxstone**
PO Box 33, Scout Lake, SK S0H 3V0
306-642-3150,
lornesfarm@sasktel.net
Heritage site includes old church (1917) & graveyard, oldschool; open year round, by appt. only
Lorne Kwasnicki, Director

***Shaunavon:* Grand Coteau Heritage & Cultural Centre**
PO Box 966, Centre St., Shaunavon, SK S0N 2M0
306-297-3882, Fax: 306-297-3668,
gchcc@sasktel.net
www.shaunavonmuseum.ca
Natural history museum, heritage museum, art gallery, public library; open year round
Ingrid Cazakoff, Director

***Shell Lake:* Shell Lake Museum**
c/o Shell Lake Village Office, PO Box 280, Shell Lake, SK S0J 2G0
306-427-2272,
The Shell Lake Museum is located in the historic station house. The site also features a log house. It is open on weekends during the summer.

***Sintaluta:* Sintaluta Community Museum**
PO Box 186, Sintaluta, SK S0G 4N0
306-727-4421,
Pioneer & regional artifacts, farm implements housed in former bank, Anglican Church & cottage, c. 1899 & 1907

***Spalding:* Reynold Rapp Museum**
PO Box 308, Spalding, SK S0K 4C0
306-872-2276, Fax: 306-287-4030,
Housed in Reynold Rapp M.P.'s family home
Blanche Franko, President

Garth Ulrich, Secretary

Spy Hill: **Wolverine Hobby & Historical Society Inc.**
PO Box 268, Spy Hill, SK S0A 3W0
306-534-2200,
Three buildings, former country school, former retail outlet & Lutheran church; touring/visiting on request
Glenn Walz, President

Star City: **Star City Heritage Museum**
PO Box 38, 217 - 5th St., Star City, SK S0E 1P0
306-863-2309,
Star City's Heritage Museum presents World War I & World War II memorabilia, personal & household items, & farm equipment. The museum is open from June to August & by appointment during the off season.

Stoughton: **Stoughton & District Museum**
PO Box 492, 327 Main St., Stoughton, SK S0G 4T0
306-457-2413, Fax: 306-457-3162,
stoughtontown@sasktel.net
Pioneer items; open June to Sept.
Betty Wright, Contact

Strasbourg: **Strasbourg & District Museum**
PO Box 369, Strasbourg, SK S0G 4V0
306-725-3293,
Pioneer & First Nations artifacts, mounted animals & birds

Sturgis: **Sturgis Station House Museum**
PO Box 255, 306 Railway Ave. SE, Sturgis, SK S0A 4A0
306-548-2108, Fax: 306-548-2089,
Aboriginal & early settlers artifacts; open June to Aug.

Unity: **Unity & District Heritage Museum**
Unity Regional Park, General Delivery, Unity, SK S0K 4L0
306-228-4464, Fax: 306-228-2149,
www.townofunity.com/recreation/museum.php
The Unity & District Heritage Museum includes the following attractions: a 1909 CP Rail Station, the 1908 St. Thomas Anglican Church, the 1926 St.zwarthmore United Church, restored schools, an original home of Unity, a blacksmith shop, & a harness shop. The museum is open from mid May to October.

Val Marie: **Perrault's Museum**
PO Box 216, Val Marie, SK S0N 2T0
306-298-2241,
Extensive collection on Will James, artist & author of westerns in the 30s; buffalo collection as the last buffalo hunt & hunter in Canada was in Val Marie; approx. 40 oil paintings of sceneries of the Grasslands National Park by Lise Perrault
Lise Perrault, Directrice

Vanguard: **Vanguard Centennial Museum**
General Delivery, Vanguard, SK S0N 2V0
306-582-2244,
vanguard@chinook.lib.sk.ca
Pioneer articles
Iris Minifie, Curator, 306/582-6010, harry.minifie@sasktel.net

Verigin: **National Doukhobour Heritage Village**
PO Box 99, Verigin, SK S0A 4H0
306-542-4441, Fax: 306-542-2017,
Doukhobour artifacts, photos, handicrafts, clothing, hand tools; barns, a blacksmith shop & agricultural equipment; model of early Doukhobour village
Philip Perepelkin, Manager

Verwood: **Verwood Community Museum**
PO Box 213, Verwood, SK S0H 4G0
306-642-5767,
Pioneer articles housed in former church built in 1916

Wadena: **Wadena & District Museum & Gallery**
PO Box 1208, Wadena, SK S0A 4J0
306-338-3454, Fax: 306-338-3804,
wadena.museum@sasktel.net
Early settlers; 1904 CNR station house; 1907 Sunderland School No.1; blacksmith shop; furnishings; artifacts; open June - Aug., Tue.-Sun.
Barb Peace

Wakaw: **Batoche National Historic Site of Canada (BNHS)**
PO Box 1040, RR#1, Wakaw, SK S0K 4P0
306-423-6227, Fax: 306-423-5400,
batoche@pc.gc.ca
www.pc.gc.ca/eng/lhn-nhs/sk/batoche/index.aspx
Other contact information: TTD: 306-423-5540
The Batoche National Historic Site of Canada, on the banks of the South Saskatchewan River, is the scene of the last battlefield in the Northwest Rebellion of 1885. The site displays the remains & several restored buildings of the village of Batoche. The life of the Métis at Batoche between 1860 & 1900 is depicted. The site is open from May to September.

Wakaw: **Diefenbaker Law Office**
PO Box 760, Wakaw, SK S0K 4P0
306-233-5157,
Replica of the former prime minister's law office, located in Wakaw from 1918-1925

Wakaw: **Wakaw Heritage Society Museum**
PO Box 475, 300 1st St.S., Wakaw, SK S0K 4P0
306-233-4257,
Collections associated with pioneer life

Waskesiu Lake: **Prince Albert National Park of Canada Northern Prairies Field Unit, PO Box 100, Waskesiu Lake, SK S0J 2Y0**
306-663-4522,
panp.info@pc.gc.ca
www.pc.gc.ca/eng/pn-np/sk/princealbert/index.aspx
Protecting part of the boreal forest, Prince Albert National Park features the cabin of conservationist Grey Owl, a white pelican nesting colony, & a free-ranging herd of plains bison. Visitors to the park can participate in interpretive programs & special events. The park is open year-round, & the Interpretive Centre is open from the end of June to September.
Alan Fehr, Field Unit Superintendent, Northern Prairies

Wawota: **Wawota & District Museum**
PO Box 179, 101 Main St., Wawota, SK S0G 5A0
306-739-2110,
www.wawota.com/museum.htm
Founded: 1980 The Wawota & District Museum consists of the following buildings: the main building which was built in the early 1900s & used as a municipal office, a 1909 fire hall, the Bethany Schoolhouse, & a farm equipment shed. The museum is open during July & August, & by appointment at other times.

Weekes: **Dunwell & Community Museum**
PO Box 120, Weekes, SK S0E 1V0
306-278-2906,
Restored CNR station, pioneer artifacts & Ukrainian clothes

Weyburn: **Soo Line Historical Museum**
PO Box 1016, 411 Industrial Lane, Weyburn, SK S4H 2L2
306-842-2922, Fax: 306-842-2922,
slhm@sasktel.net
www.silver.sasktelwebsite.net
Largest private collection of silver in the world; collection of artifacts that were used by Weyburn & District pioneers
Jacquie Mallory, Curator

Weyburn: **Turner Curling Museum**
PO Box 370, 157 3rd St. NE, Weyburn, SK S4H 2K6
306-848-3218, Fax: 306-842-2001,
wneiszner@weyburn.ca
www.weyburn.ca
The museum was established by the late Don Turner & his wife Elva Turner; collection includes curling stones, brooms, clothing, pins, crests & books from around the world; tours available; open by appointment.
Elva Turner, Contact

White Fox: **White Fox Museum**
PO Box 68, White Fox, SK S0J 3B0
306-276-2106,
Trapper's cabin, tool & harness shop, pioneer items

Whitewood: **Whitewood Historical Museum**
PO Box 752, 607 North Railway, Whitewood, SK S0G 5C0
306-735-4388,
Pioneer school room & home, military display, Hungarian, French, Finnish & Swedish collections; open July - Aug.

Wilcox: **Athol Murray College of Notre Dame Archives & Museum**
Archives / Museum Bldg., Athol Murray College of Notre Dame Campus, PO Box 100, Wilcox, SK S0G 5E0
306-732-2080, Fax: 306-732-2008,
nd.archives@notredame.sk.ca
www.notredame.sk.ca
The Athol Murray College of Notre Dame Archives & Museum collects & preserves items that tell the story of Père Athol Murray & the history of the Athol Murray College of Notre Dame. The archives & museum features Père Athol Murray's collection of Rare Books, the Rex Beach Repository, the Parthenon Frieze, the Nicholas de Grandmaison Art Portrait collection, sculptures, & stained glass windows. The archives & museum is open seven days a week in July & August, & Monday to Friday from September to June.
Terry McGarry, Curator

Wilkie: **Wilkie & District Museum**
PO Box 26, Wilkie, SK S0K 4W0
306-843-2717,
love@sk.sympatico.ca
Open summer; by appt. the rest of the year
Frances Love, Sec.-Treas.

Willow Bunch: **Willow Bunch Museum**
Parent: **Willow Bunch Museum & Heritage Society**
PO Box 157, 16 Édouard Beaupré St., Willow Bunch, SK S0H 4K0
306-473-2806, Fax: 306-473-2789,
www.willowbunch.ca
Other contact information: Phone, Mid Sept. - Mid May: 306-473-2762 or 306-473-2279
Founded: 1972 The Willow Bunch Museum is located in a Convent school which was built in 1914 by the Sisters of the Cross. One attraction is the display about Edouard Beaupré, an eight foot, three inch tall circus performer who was born in Willow Bunch in 1881. The museum is open from mid May to mid September. Tours may be arranged during the off-season.
Doris O'Reilly, Director

Wolseley: **Wolseley & District Museum**
PO Box 218, Wolseley, SK S0G 5H0
306-698-2360, Fax: 306-698-2360,
Local history of the Wolseley including decorative arts, furnishings, household objects, and maps.
Robert Campbell, Contact

Wood Mountain: **Wood Mountain Rodeo Ranch Museum**
PO Box 53, Wood Mountain, SK S0H 4L0
306-266-4953,
www.woodmountain.ca/RodRanc.html
Other contact information: Phone, Tour Bookings: 306-266-2000
Located in the Wood Mountain Regional Park, Wood Mountain Rodeo Ranch Museum offers a glimpse into the life of ranchers & cowboys who arrived in the area in the 1880s. Exhibits include the history of the Wood Mountain Stampede, which is the oldest continuous rodeo in Canada. An extensive archival collection is also housed at the museum. The museum is open from May to September.
Lois Todd, Museum Contact

Wynyard: **Wynyard & District Museum**
PO Box 743, Wynyard, SK S0A 4T0

CPR hand car, household accesories, farm implements, WWI materials

Yorkton: **Western Development Museum**
Also known as: **Yorkton Western Development Museum**
PO Box 98, Hwy. 16 West, Yorkton, SK S3N 2V6
306-783-8361, Fax: 306-782-1027,
yorkton@wdm.ca
www.wdm.ca
Yorkton is one of four exhibit branches of Saskatchewan's Western Development Museum. The other branches are located in Moose Jaw, North Battleford, & Saskatoon. The Yorkton Western Development Museum presents the times when immigrants settled in western Canada, including the English, Ukrainians, Doukhobors, Germans, Swedes, & Icelanders.
Susan Mandziuk, Manager, Yorkton, smandziuk@wdm.ca
Carla Madsen, Programmer, Education & Special Events, cmadsen@wdm.ca
Phil Lane, Supervisor, Building, plane@wdm.ca

Yukon Territory

Territorial Museums

MacBride Museum
1124 First Ave., Whitehorse, YT Y1A 1A4
867-667-2709, Fax: 867-633-6607,
info@macbridemuseum.com
www.macbridemuseum.com
Founded: 1951 The Yukon Historical Society acquired the unoccupied Government Telegraph Office built in 1900, and in the 1960s opened it to the public as a museum to house the growing collection of cultural & natural history: Yukon heritage from pre-history to present. Exhibits include archeological & paleontological specimens; ethnographic artifacts, historic artifacts, photographs & archival materials; large industrial & transportation artifacts. Also there are outdoor displays, two heritage buildings.
MS Patricia Cunning, Executive Director, MacBride Museum Society, pcunning@macbridemuseum.com
Patricia Cunning, Executive Director

Other Museums in Yukon Territory

Burwash Landing: **Kluane Museum of Natural History**
PO Box 45, Historic Mile 1093, Alaska Hwy., Burwash Landing, YT Y0B 1V0
867-841-5561, Fax: 867-841-5605,
klvanemus@yknet.yk.ca
Workclass wildlife display, native handicrafts; open Victoria Day - Labour Day

Dawson City: **Dawson City Museum**
PO Box 303, Dawson City, YT Y0B 1G0
867-993-5291, Fax: 867-993-5839,
dcmuseum@yknet.yk.ca
users.yknet.yk.ca/dcpages/Museum.html

Three main galleries include objects and photographs which tells of the story of the Klondike era through the Godl Rush; native history; open mid-May to mid- Sept.; other times by appt.
Cheryl Thompson, Director/Administrator
Julia D. Pike, Director/Curator

***Dawson City:* Klondike National Historic Sites**
PO Box 390, Dawson City, YT Y0B 1G0
867-993-5462, Fax: 867-993-7203, dawson.info@pc.gc.ca
www.pch.gc.ca
Historic buildings; artifacts; documents; related to Klondike history, Yukon Consolidated Gold Corp. & the Dawson Daily News
G. MacMillan, Supt.

***Haines Junction:* Kluane National Park**
PO Box 5495, Haines Junction, YT Y0B 1L0
867-634-7250, Fax: 867-634-7208, kluane.info@pc.gc.ca
www.pc.gc.ca/kluane
Natural & cultural history of Kluane National Park & Reserve of Canada; information on park services, hiking & other activities

***Keno City:* Keno City Mining Museum**
PO Box 17, Keno City, YT Y0B 1M0
867-995-2792, Fax: 867-995-3103, www.kenocity.info/museum.htm
Other contact information: Winter phone: 867/995-2411
History of mining of gold & silver in the early 1900s (tools, equipment artifacts); open June-Sept.

***Teslin:* George Johnston Tlingit Indian Museum**
***Also known as:* Teslin Historical & Museum Society**
PO Box 146, Km 1294 Mile 804, Alaska Hwy., Teslin, YT Y0A 1B0
867-390-2550, gjmuseum@hotmail.com
www.gjmuseum.yk.net
Inland Tlingit ethnographic & 20th centrury artifacts; open May 22-Sept. 4

***Whitehorse:* Fort Selkirk**
c/o Tourism & Culture, Cultural Services Branch, PO Box 2703, Whitehorse, YT Y1A 2C6
867-667-5386, Fax: 867-667-8023, 800-661-0408
doug.olynyk@gov.yk.ca
Accessible only by boat or plane; contact Selkirk First Nation, Pelly Crossing, YK Y0B 1P0; 867/537-3331; Fax: 867/537-3902; Attn: Emma Alfred; open mid-May - mid-Sept. URL is a portal to the virtual museum.
Doug Olynyk, Historic Sites Coordinator, Yukon Cultural Services Branch

***Whitehorse:* LePage Park**
c/o Yukon Historical & Museums Association, 3126 Third Ave., Whitehorse, YT Y1A 1E7
867-667-4704, Fax: 867-667-4506, yhma@yknet.yk.ca
heritageyukon.ca/
Walking tours by interpreters in period costume, June - Aug.; open year round
Brent Slobodin, President

***Whitehorse:* Old Log Church Museum**
PO Box 31461, 3rd Ave. & Elliot St., Whitehorse, YT Y1A 6K8
867-668-2555, Fax: 867-667-6258, logchurch@klondiker.com
Open May - Labour Day
Taryn Parker, Curator

***Whitehorse:* Yukon Beringia Interpretive Centre**
PO Box 2703, Mile 914, Alaska Hwy., Whitehorse, YT Y1A 2C6
867-667-8855, Fax: 867-667-8854, beringia@gov.yk.ca
www.beringia.com
Beringia was an ancient place, situated between two continents on the edge of the Arctic. The land connection between Siberia & Alaska was part of the larger area known as Beringia. The land of ice was home to huge mammals, such as woolly mammoths & scimitar cats, & the first people of North America. The Yukon Beringia Interpretive Centre is open from May to September. During the winter, it is open on Sundays, or by appointment.

***Whitehorse:* Yukon Transportation Museum**
30 Electra Cres., Whitehorse, YT Y1A 6E6
867-668-4792, Fax: 867-633-5547, info@goytim.ca
www.yukontransportationmuseum.ca
Transportation displays depicting the first commercial aircraft in the Yukon; construction of the Alaska Highway, the White Pass & Yukon Route Railway. Open daily 10-6, mid-May - end of August.
Casey Mclaughlin, Executive Director/Curator, casey@goytm.ca
Cathy Ritchie, Assistant Director/Curator, cathy@goytm.ca

Observatories

Alberta

***Calgary:* Rothney Astrophysical Observatory (RAO)**
Physics & Astronomy Dept., University of Calgary, Calgary, AB T2N 1N4
403-220-5385, Fax: 403-289-3331, rao@phas.ucalgary.ca
phas.ucalgary.ca/rao
Other contact information: Open House Info: 403/220-7977
The RAO is the University of Calgary's astronomical facility which is home to the following amazing telescopes: the 0.4-m Clarke-Milone Telescope (which is controlable via the internet), the 0.5-m Baker Nunn Telescope (used to search for asteroids), & the 1.8-m A.R. Cross Telescope (one of the 3 largest in Canada). The RAO now boasts a fabulous new Interpretive Centre which is open for drop-in vis
Dr. P. Langill, Director
Dr. R. Plume, Associate Director

***Edmonton:* Devon & Campus Observatories**
Dept. of Physics, University of Alberta, Edmonton, AB T6G 2J1
780-492-5410, Fax: 780-492-0714, Dhube@phys.ualberta.ca
www.phys.ualberta.ca
Consists of a 0.5m-diameter telescope equipped with a prime focus CCD camera; research programs are directed toward stellar photometry & the detection of faint, extended sources such as HII regions & supernova remnants; Campus Observatory has permanently mounted 12 & 14 inch telescopes & an exhibit area; facility used for undergraduate instruction & public observing during academic year
Dr. Douglas P. Hube
Dr. Sharon Morsink, morsink@phys.ualberta.ca

British Columbia

***Kamuela:* Canada-France-Hawaii Telescope**
65-1238 Mamalahoa Hwy., Kamuela, HI 96743 USA
808-885-7944, Fax: 808-885-7288, veillet@cfht.hawaii.edu
www.cfht.hawaii.edu/
The CFH observatory hosts a world-class, 3.6 meter optical/infrared telescope. The observatory is located atop the summit of Mauna Kea, a 4200 meter, dormant volcano located on the island of Hawaii. By appointment only.

***Penticton:* Dominion Radio Astrophysical Observatory**
c/o NRC Herzberg Institute of Astrophysics, PO Box 248, Penticton, BC V2A 6J9
250-493-2277, Fax: 250-493-7767, hia-www@nrc-cnrc.gc.ca
www.nrc-cnrc.gc.ca
Founded: 1960 A world-class radio astronomy facility with several telescopes on site; guided tours Sundays during July and August, 2-5 p.m.; visitor centre open weekdays from Thanksgiving to Easter; open 7 days per week from Easter to Thanksgiving.
Dr. Sean Dougherty, Group Leader Ph.D., sean.dougherty@nrc-cnrc.gc.ca

***Vancouver:* Gordon MacMillan Southam Observatory (GSO)**
1100 Chestnut St., Vancouver, BC V6J 3J9
604-738-7827, Fax: 604-736-5665, info@spacecentre.ca
www.hrmacmillanspacecentre.com/observatory.htm
Part of the Pacific Space Centre
Ms. Donna Livingstone, Executive Director

***Vancouver:* University of British Columbia Observatory**
***Also known as:* Wreck Beach Observatory**
2219 Main Mall, Vancouver, BC V6T 1Z4
604-822-3853, Fax: 604-822-5324, matthews@astro.ubc.ca
www.astro.ubc.ca/
Telescope open for free public viewing on clear Sat. evenings, year round; free tours by appt.
Dr. Jaymie Matthews
Dr. Harvey Richer

***Victoria:* Climenhaga Observatory**
Dept. of Physics & Astronomy, University of Victoria, PO Box 3055 MS-7700, Victoria, BC V8W 3P6
250-721-7750, Fax: 250-721-7715, robb@uvic.ca
www.astro.uvic.ca
Russell Robb

***Victoria:* Dominion Astrophysical Observatory (DAO) / Observatoire fédéral d'astrophysique**
Herzberg Inst. of Astrophysics, National Research Council of Canada, 5071 West Saanich Rd., Victoria, BC V9E 2E7
250-363-0001, Fax: 250-363-0045, hia-www@nrc-cnrc.gc.ca
www.hia-iha.nrc-cnrc.gc.ca
Open year round; see website for hours
James Hesser, Director

Manitoba

***Winnipeg:* The Lockhart Planetarium**
University of Manitoba, 380 University College, 500 Dysart Rd., Winnipeg, MB R3T 2M8
204-474-9785, Fax: 204-261-0021,
www.umanitoba.ca/faculties/science/astronomy/lockhart/lockhart.html
Planetarium theatre; display area; astronomy reference library

***Winnipeg:* Manitoba Planetarium**
190 Rupert Ave., Winnipeg, MB R3B 0N2
204-956-2830, Fax: 204-942-3679, info@manitobamuseum.mb.ca
www.manitobamuseum.mb.ca
A 287 seat space theatre equipped with Zeiss MkV star projector, which is capable of reproducing the night sky as seen from any location on Earth; complimented with advanced video project & multmedia projectors; shows & programs change throughout the year
Javier Schwersensky, Director of Programs
Scott Young, Manager, Planetarium & Science Gallery, Planetary & Science Gallery Programs, scyoung@ManitobaMuseum.mb.ca

Nova Scotia

***Halifax:* Burke-Gaffney Observatory (BGO)**
Loyola Bldg., Saint Mary's University, 923 Robie St., Halifax, NS B3H 3C3
902-420-5633, Fax: 902-420-5141, apwww.stmarys.ca/bgo/
40 cm reflecting telescope; public tours held on the 1st & 3rd Sat. of each month at 7 pm (Nov.-Mar.) or 9 pm (Apr.-Oct.), weather permitting; call 902/496-8257 on Sat. afternoon for the status of that evening's tour; Mon. evenings or daytime groups by arrangement
Dr. G.A. Welch, Director

Ontario

***Hamilton:* W.J. McCallion Planetarium**
Dept. of Physics & Astronomy, McMaster University, 1280 Main St. West, Hamilton, ON L8S 4M1
905-525-9140, Fax: 905-546-1252, planetarium@physics.mcmaster.ca
www.physics.mcmaster.ca/planetarium/

***London:* University of Western Ontario Astronomical Observatory**
***Also known as:* Elginfield Observatory**
Dept. of Physics & Astronomy, University of Western Ontario, 1151 Richmond St., London, ON N6A 3K7
519-661-3283, Fax: 519-661-2033, chair@physics.uwo.ca
phobos.astro.uwo.ca/~dfgray/
David F. Gray, Observatory Director

***London:* Hume Cronyn Memorial Observatory**
Astronomy, University of Western Ontario, London, ON N6A 3K7
519-661-2111, Fax: 519-661-2033, dfgray@uwo.ca
www.astro.uwo.ca/~dfgray/cronyn.html
Built in 1939, observatory houses a 25 cm refactor currently used for teaching & visitor programs
David F. Gray, Observatory Director

***Richmond Hill:* David Dunlap Observatory**
PO Box 360, Richmond Hill, ON L4C 4Y6
905-884-9562, Fax: 905-884-2672, info@astro.utoronto.ca
www.astro.utoronto.ca/DDO/
Wed. mornings: 10 am; Fri. & Sat. evenings Apr.-Oct. by reservation; call the information number or visit the website for the schedule & description of tours
P.G. Martin, Director

***Sudbury:* Doran Planetarium**
Fraser Bldg., Laurentian University, 935 Ramsey Lake Rd., Sudbury, ON P3E 2C6
705-675-1151, Fax: 705-675-4868, plegault@laurentian.ca

www.oldwebsite.laurentian.ca/physics/planetarium/Planetarium.html
Astronomical presentation, show & lecture in both French & English
Paul-Émile Legault, Director

Quebec

Notre-Dame-des-Bois: **Astrolab du Parc du Mont Mégantic**
CP 24, 189, rte du Parc, Notre-Dame-des-Bois, QC J0B 2E0
819-888-2941, Fax: 819-888-2943, 800-665-6527
astronomie@astrolab.qc.ca
www.astrolab.qc.ca
Summer programs

Saskatchewan

Saskatoon: **University of Saskatchewan Observatory**
Dept. of Physics & Engineering Physics, University of Saskatchewan, 116 Science Pl., Saskatoon, SK S7N 5E2
306-966-6429, Fax: 306-966-6400,
physics.usask.ca/observatory/
Open every Saturday evening after dark for public viewing through the telescope
Stan Shadick

National Parks & Outdoor Education Centres

Alberta

Banff: **Banff National Park**
PO Box 900, Banff, AB T1L 1K2
403-762-1550, Fax: 403-762-3380,
banff.vrc@pc.gc.ca
www.pc.gc.ca/pn-np/ab/banff/index_e.asp
In the fall of 1883, three Canadian Pacific Railway construction workers stumbled across a cave containing hot springs on the eastern slopes of Alberta's Rocky Mountains. From that humble beginning was born Banff National Park, Canada's first national park and the world's third. Spanning 6,641 square kilometres (2,564 square miles) of valleys, mountains, glaciers, forests, meadows and rivers, Banff National Park is one of the world's premier destination spots. Hours of Operation: Winter, 9:00-5:00; Spring, 9:00-7:00; Summer, 8:00-8:00; Fall, 9:00-7:00

Fort Saskatchewan: **Elk Island National Park**
Site 4, R.R.#1, Fort Saskatchewan, AB T8L 2N7 Canada
780-922-5790, Fax: 780-992-2983,
elk.island@pc.gc.ca
www.pc.gc.ca/pn-np/ab/elkisland/index_E.asp
Located less than an hour away from Edmonton, Elk Island National Park of Canada protects the wilderness of the aspen parkland, one of the most endangered habitats in Canada. This beautiful oasis is home to herds of free roaming plains bison, wood bison, moose, deer, and elk. Also boasting over 250 species of birds, the park is a bird watcher's paradise. Be it for wildlife viewing, hiking, cross-country skiing, picnicking or overnight camping, there is something for everyone at Elk Island National Park. Hours: Campground Reservations, Administration Building and Wardern Operations Building open year round, 8:00-4:00; Sandy Beach Campground, Golf Course open May-Oct weather permitting; winter campground open Oct-April weather permitting.

Jasper: **Jasper National Park of Canada**
PO Box 10, Jasper, AB T0E 1E0
780-852-6176, Fax: 780-852-6177,
pnj.jnp@pc.gc.ca
www.pc.gc.ca/pn-np/ab/jasper/index_E.asp
Jasper is the largest and most northerly Canadian rocky mountain national park, part of a spectacular World Heritage Site. Comprised of delicate and carefully protected ecosystems, Jasper's scenery is none-the-less rugged and mountainous. In this special corner of Canada you can thrill to the thunder of Sunwapta Falls, enjoy the serene beauty of Mount Edith Cavell, connect with nature along 1,000-plus kilometres of trails, experience Athabasca Glacier up close or just resign yourself to a relaxing soak in Miette Hotsprings. Hours of Operation: Winter 9:00-4:00; Spring 9:00-5:00; Summer 8:30-7:00; Fall 9:00-5:00

Waterton Park: **Waterton Lakes National Park of Canada**
PO Box 200, Waterton Park, AB T0K 2M0
403-859-2224, Fax: 403-859-5152,
waterton.info @pc.gc.ca
www.pc.gc.ca/pn-np/ab/waterton/index_E.asp
Rugged, windswept mountains rise abruptly out of gentle prairie grassland in spectacular Waterton Lakes National Park. Here, several different ecological regions meet and interact in a landscape shaped by wind, fire, flooding, and abundant plants and wildlife. The park helps protect the unique and unusually diverse physical, biological and cultural resources found in the Crown of the Continent: one of the narrowest places in the Rocky Mountains. The highlight of Waterton's sparkling chain of lakes is the international Upper Waterton Lake, the deepest lake in the Canadian Rockies. In 1932, the park was joined with Montana's Glacier National Park to form the Waterton-Glacier International Peace Park - a world first. Hours of Operation: Park Receptionist year round, M-F 8:00-4:00; Campsites and Parkways May-Oct.

British Columbia

Field: **Yoho National Park of Canada**
PO Box 99, Field, BC V0A 1G0
250-343-6783, Fax: 250-343-6012,
yoho.info@pc.gc.ca
www.pc.gc.ca/pn-np/bc/yoho/index_E.asp
Established in 1886, Yoho National Park is one of 41 national parks in Canada. Our nation's parks celebrate and help protect the diversity of Canada's landscapes and the life within. Yoho represents the western slopes of the Rocky Mountains region, and is also a Cree expression of awe and wonder for this place of rock walls, spectacular waterfalls and soaring peaks. In the shadow of the Great Divide, Yoho holds the secrets of ancient ocean life, the power of ice and water, and unique plant and animal communities that continue to evolve today. Hours of Operation: Parklands are open year round; Visitor Centre open in Winter 9:00-4:00, Spring 9:00-5:00, Summer 9:00-7:00, Fall 9:00-5:00; campgrounds open Spring-Fall.

Queen Charlotte: **Gwaii Haanas National Park Reserve and Haida Heritage Site**
PO Box 37, Queen Charlotte, BC V0T 1S0
250-559-8818, Fax: 250-559-8366,
gwaii. haanas@pc.gc.ca
www.pc.gc.ca/pn-np/bc/gwaiihaanas/index_E.asp
Together, the Government of Canada and the Council of the Haida Nation manage the special place called Gwaii Haanas through a unique agreement signed in 1993. The two parties strongly agree on the need to protect Gwaii Haanas, even though the question of ownership is unresolved. Gwaii Haanas embodies the essence of the rugged beauty and rich ecology of the Pacific coast. It is a celebration of more than ten thousand years of Haida connection with the land and sea. For some visitors, this opportunity to witness a living culture, and immerse themselves in nature is a spiritual experience. Hours of Operation: M-F 8:00-12:00, 1:00-4:30.

Radium Hot Springs: **Kootenay National Park of Canada**
PO Box 220, Radium Hot Springs, BC V0A 1M0
250-347-9505, Fax: 250-347-9980,
kootenay.info@pc.gc.ca
www.pc.gc.ca/pn-np/bc/kootenay/index_E.asp
Established in 1920, Kootenay National Park is one of 41 national parks in Canada. Together, they celebrate and protect the diversity of the nation's great landscapes. Kootenay National Park represents the south-western region of the Canadian Rocky Mountains. From glacier-clad peaks along the Continental Divide to semi-arid grasslands of the Rocky Mountain Trench, where cactus grows, this is a park rich in diversity of landscapes and ecology. Hours of Operation: Parklands are open year round. Parks Canada administration office in Radium Hot Springs is open year round, M-F 8:00-12:00, 12:30-4:00.

Revelstoke: **Glacier National Park of Canada**
PO Box 350, Revelstoke, BC V0E 2S0
250-837-7500, Fax: 250-837-7536,
revglacier. reception@pc.gc.ca
www.pc.gc.ca/pn-np/bc/glacier/index_E.asp
Glacier National Park of Canada protects, for all time, a portion of the Columbia Mountains Natural Region, in the interior wet belt of British Columbia. The steep, rugged mountains, warm, moist climate and wide variety of plant and animal life are typical of this natural region. The park protects unique stands of old-growth cedar and hemlock and critical habitat for threatened and endangered wildlife species such as the mountain caribou, mountain goat and grizzly bear. The Rogers Pass National Historic Site is located in Glacier National Park. Rogers Pass was so designated for its importance in the construction and development of the country's first major national transportation route. Hours of Operation: Winter 7:00-5:00; Spring 8:30-4:30; Summer 7:30 am-8:00 pm; Fall (November) M, Th-Su 8:30-4:30.

Revelstoke: **Mount Revelstoke National Park of Canada**
PO Box 350, Revelstoke, BC V0E 2S0
250-837-7500, Fax: 250-837-7536,
revglacier. reception@pc.gc.ca
www.pc.gc.ca/pn-np/bc/revelstoke/index_E.asp
Mount Revelstoke National Park is a place of contrasts. Take a drive along the summit parkway through a variety of geographical zones. From dense old-growth rainforest of giant cedar and pine, travel up through subalpine forest, and finally alpine meadows and tundra. Marvel at the spectacular view of the ice-clad peaks of the Monashee Mountains and, to the east, the Selkirk Mountains. The Giant Cedars hiking trail takes you through a stand of ancient Western Red Cedars, and the Skunk Cabbage trail introduces you to jungle-like wetland, a birder's paradise. Hours of Operation: Welcome Station Kiosk, June-Aug 7:00 am-8:30 pm. Parkway, Spring & Fall 9:00-5:00, Summer 7:00 am-8:30 pm.

Sidney: **Gulf Islands National Park Reserve of Canada**
2220 Harbour Rd., Sidney, BC V8L 2P6
250-654-4000, Fax: 250-654-4014,
gulf.islands@pc.gc.ca
www.pc.gc.ca/pn-np/bc/gulf/index_E.asp
Established in 2003, Gulf Islands National Park Reserve safeguards a portion of British Columbia's beautiful southern Gulf Islands archipelago. These islands are representative of the Strait of Georgia Lowlands, one of the most ecologically at risk natural regions in southern Canada. The first new national park reserve of the twenty-first century includes thirty-five square kilometres of land and intertidal area on fifteen islands, numerous islets and reefs, and approximately twenty-six square kilometres of marine areas. We encourage you to experience this exceptional coastal island landscape and the cultures of the people who live here so that the memories you take home are those that last a lifetime in your heart but leave no lasting trace on park ecosystems. Hours of Operation: Most parklands have full services and charge fees from May-Oct, but parklands are open year round.

Ucluelet: **Pacific Rim National Park Reserve of Canada**
PO Box 280, 2185 Ocean Terrace Rd., Ucluelet, BC V0R 3A0
250-726-7721, Fax: 250-726-4720,
pacrim.info@pc.gc.ca
www.pc.gc.ca/pn-np/bc/pacificrim/index_E.asp
Welcome to Pacific Rim National Park Reserve of Canada. Backed by the Insular Mountains Range of Vancouver Island and facing the open Pacific Ocean, Pacific Rim presents the rich natural and cultural heritage of Canada's west coast. Its cool and wet maritime climate produces an abundance of life in the water and on land. Lush coastal temperate rainforest gives way to bountiful and diverse intertidal and subtidal areas. These natural wonders are interwoven with the long and dynamic history of the Nuu-chah-nulth First Nations and European explorers and settlers. Hours of Operation: year round.

Manitoba

Churchill: **Wapusk National Park of Canada**
PO Box 127, Churchill, MB R0B 0E0
204-675-8863, Fax: 204-675-2026, 888-773-8888
wapusk.np@pc.gc.ca
www.pc.gc.ca/pn-np/mb/wapusk/index_E.asp
Wapusk means "White Bear" in Cree. The park earns its name because it protects one of the world's largest known polar bear maternity denning areas. It represents the Hudson James Lowlands natural region bordering on Hudson Bay. The park lies on the transition between boreal forest and Arctic tundra. The geology, biodiversity, and cultural history of the area all contribute to the unique wilderness character of Wapusk National Park of Canada. Hours of Operation: Access to Wapusk is via authorized commercial tour operators in Churchill. Wapusk National Park has limited visitor capacity at present. Unescorted visits to the park are not recommended.For the most current list of operators, please contact the park office (1-888-773-8888, 1-204-675-8863).

Wasagaming: **Riding Mountain National Park of Canada**
Wasagaming, MB R0J 2H0
204-848-7275, Fax: 204-848-2596,
rmnp.info@pc.gc.ca
www.pc.gc.ca/pn-np/mb/riding/index_E.asp
Situated amidst a sea of agricultural land, Riding Mountain rises dramatically from the prairie landscape. Forming part of the Manitoba Escarpment, this "island" reserve protects a wide variety of wildlife and vegetation areas. The park has numerous hiking trails, and Agassiz Tower overlooks a panoramic view of prairies stretching out to the north. Wasagaming, the park's townsite, offers a full range of visitor services including accommodation, restaurants and shopping. Hours of Operation: Administration Office M-F 8:00-12:00, 12:30-4:00; Visitor Centre, Spring & Fall M-Su 9:30-5:30, Summer 9:30-8:00.

New Brunswick

Alma: **Fundy National Park of Canada**
PO Box 1001, Alma, NB E4H 1B4
506-887-6000, Fax: 506-887-6008,
fundy.info@pc.gc.ca
www.pc.gc.ca/pn-np/nb/fundy/index_E.asp
Fundy National Park of Canada encompasses some of the last remaining wilderness in southern New Brunswick. Here, the conifer dominated Caledonia Highlands roll down to meet the fog-generating Bay of Fundy. The tidal fluctuation of the Bay of Fundy is the highest in the world. Watch fishing boats come and go to the rhythm of the bay. Inland, explore lush forests and deep stream valleys. Hours of Operation: Headquarters Vistory

Reception Centre, Spring & Fall 8:00-4:30; Summer 8:00 am-10:00 pm.

Kouchibouguac National Park: **Kouchibouguac National Park of Canada**
186 Rte. 117, Kouchibouguac National Park, NB E4X 2P1
506-876-2443, Fax: 506-876-4802,
kouch.info@pc.gc.ca
www.pc.gc.ca/eng/pn-np/nb/kouchibouguac/index.aspx
Founded: 1969 Kouchibouguac National Park of Canada is a Canadian Heritage protected area. One of two wilderness Canadian national parks in New Brunswick, Kouchibouguac is a mosaic of bogs, salt marshes, tidal rivers, freshwater systems, sheltered lagoons, abandoned fields, & tall forests, which characterize the Maritime Plain Natural Region. The name Kouchibouguac is of Mi'kmaq origin & means "river of the long tides". This 238 square kilometre national park provides many family activities. There are 60 kilometres of cycling paths for both hikers & cyclists. Canoeing, kayaking, swimming, camping, bird watching, as well as cross country skiing, snowshoeing. & tobogganing in winter, are also available in this area, located on New Brunswick's eastern coast line.

Newfoundland & Labrador

Glovertown: **Terra Nova National Park of Canada**
Glovertown, NL A0G 2L0
709-533-2801, Fax: 709-533-2706,
info.tnnp@pc.gc.ca
www.pc.gc.ca/pn-np/nl/terranova/index_E.asp
Terra Nova National Park of Canada is a place where long fingers of the North Atlantic Ocean touch the island boreal forest of Eastern Newfoundland. Rocky headlands provide shelter from the awesome power of the open ocean. The landscape of the park varies from the rugged cliffs and sheltered inlets of the coastal region to the rolling forested hills, bogs and ponds of the inland. Cultural history abounds in the remnants of sawmills and past human cultures. Hours of Operation: Administration Building, M-F 8:00-4:00; Visitor Centre, Jan 10-May 17 Th-M 9:00-4:00, May 18-June 21 Sa-Su 10:00-5:00, June 22-Sept 2 Sa-Su 9:00-7:00, Sept 3-Oct 8 Th-M 10:00-5:00.

Nain: **Torngat Mountains National Park of Canada**
PO Box 471, 2 Service Rd., Nain, NL A0P 1L0
709-922-1290, Fax: 709-922-1294, 888-922-1290
torngats.info@pc.qc.ca
The Torngat Mountains National Park of Canada is located in northern Labrador and encompasses roughly 10,000 km2. It extends from Saglek Fjord in the south, to the very northern tip of Labrador; and from the provincial boundary with Quebec in the west, to the waters of the Labrador Sea in the east. The national park will protect an area of spectacular Arctic wilderness, with towering mountains, breathtaking fjords, gentle river valleys and rugged coastal landscapes - a wilderness that has been home to the Inuit and their ancestors for thousands of years. Dramatic Nachvak Fjord, which lies near the centre of the park, was formed by a glacier cutting through the Torngat Mountains as it flowed to the sea during the last ice age. Today, the Torngat Mountains include the highest peaks in continental eastern North America, and are dotted by many small glaciers.

Rocky Harbour: **Gros Morne National Park of Canada**
PO Box 130, Rocky Harbour, NL A0K 4N0
709-458-2417, Fax: 709-458-2059,
grosmorne.info @pc.gc.ca
www.pc.gc.ca/pn-np/nl/grosmorne/index_E.asp
Gros Morne National Park of Canada was designated a UNESCO World Heritage Site in 1987. It is an area of great natural beauty with a rich variety of scenery, wildlife, and recreational activities. Visitors can hike through wild, uninhabited mountains and camp by the sea. Boat tours bring visitors under the towering cliffs of a freshwater fjord carved out by glaciers. Waterfalls, marine inlets, sea stacks, sandy beaches, and colourful nearby fishing villages complete the phenomenal natural and cultural surroundings of Gros Morne National Park of Canada. Hours of Operation: Park Headquaters, M-F 8:00-12:00, 1:00-4:30; Visitor Centre, April 30-May 18 M-F 9:00-4:00, May 19-June 22 9:00-5:00, June 23-Sept 3 9:00 am-9:00 pm, Sept 4-Oct 8 9:00-5:00, Oct 9-Oct 26 M-F 9:00-4:00.

Northwest Territories

Fort Smith: **Wood Buffalo National Park of Canada**
149 McDougal Rd., Fort Smith, NT X0E 0P0
867-872-7960, Fax: 867-872-3910, - - 0
wbnp.info@pc.gc.ca
www.pc.gc.ca/buffalo
As part of Canada's system of national parks and national historic sites, Wood Buffalo National Park of Canada is our country's largest national park and one of the largest in the world. It was established in 1922 to protect the last remaining herds of bison in northern Canada. Today, it protects an outstanding and representative example of Canada's Northern Boreal Plains. Hours of Operation: Park is open year round; Fort Smith Visitor Reception Centre open 9:00 AM- noon and 1 PM - 5 PM, Monday to Friday; 1 PM - 5 PM on summer weekends (3rd weekend in May until Labour Day)

Nova Scotia

Ingonish Beach: **Cape Breton Highlands National Park of Canada**
Ingonish Beach, NS B0C 1L0
902-224-2306, Fax: 902-285-2866,
information@pc.gc.ca
www.pc.gc.ca/pn-np/ns/cbreton/index_E.asp
The headlands and cliffs of Cape Breton Highland tower over the rich, natural heritage that is all around. Home to the famous Cabot Trail, the land is blessed with spectacular scenery, abundant wildlife and a human history that stretches back to the last Ice Age. The park offers many accessible treasures and experiences remarkable in their diversity, beauty, and wonder. Hours of Operation: park is open year round; Visitor Centre May 5-June 27 9:00-5:00, June 28-Aug 22 8:00 am-8:00 pm, Aug 23-Sept 26 9:00-6:00, Sept 27-Oct 28 9:00-5:00.

Maitland Bridge: **Kejimkujik National Park and National Historic Site of Canada**
PO Box 236, Maitland Bridge, NS B0T 1B0
902-682-2772, Fax: 902-682-3367,
kejimkujik. info@pc.gc.ca
www.pc.gc.ca/pn-np/ns/kejimkujik/index_E.asp
Kejimkujik, the only inland national park of Canada in the Maritimes, features abundant lakes and rivers ideal for canoeing. The lush woodlands and gently rolling landscapes are home to a variety of wildlife. Visitors will find historic canoe routes, portages and many beautiful hiking trails in the park. Hours of Operation: Visitor Reception Centre, Labour day-Mid June 8:30-4:30, midJune-Labour day 8:30am-9:00 pm; Campground Kiosk Mid June-Labour day 9:00am-9:00 pm.

Nunavut

Fort Simpson: **Nahanni National Park Reserve of Canada**
PO Box 348, Fort Simpson, NWT X0E 0N0
867-695-3151, Fax: 867-695-2446,
nahanni.info@pc.gc.ca
www.pc.gc.ca/pn-np/nt/nahanni/index_E.asp
Nahanni National Park Reserve of Canada protects a portion of the Mackenzie Mountains Natural Region offering the adventurous visitor a wilderness experience. A key feature of the park is the Naha Dehé (South Nahanni River). Four great canyons line this spectacular whitewater river. At Nailicho (Virginia Falls) the river plunges in a thunderous plume. The park's sulphur hotsprings, alpine tundra, mountain ranges, and forests of spruce and aspen are home to many species of birds, fish and mammals. A visitor centre in Fort Simpson features displays on the history, culture and geography of the area. The park was inscribed on UNESCO's World Heritage List in 1978. Hours of Operation: Winter, M-F 8:30-12:00, 1:00-5:00; Summer, daily 8:00-12:00, 1:00-5:00.

Fort Smith: **Wood Buffalo National Park of Canada**
750, Fort Smith, NWT X0E 0P0
867-872-7900, Fax: 867-872-3910,
wbnp.info@pc.gc.ca
www.pc.gc.ca/pn-np/nt/woodbuffalo/index_E.asp
As part of Canada's system of national parks and national historic sites, Wood Buffalo National Park of Canada is our country's largest national park and one of the largest in the world. It was established in 1922 to protect the last remaining herds of bison in northern Canada. Today, it protects an outstanding and representative example of Canada's Northern Boreal Plains. Hours of Operation: Fort Smith Visitor Reception Centre, Oct-Apr M-F 9:00-12:00, 1:00-5:00; May-Sept M-F 9:00-12:00, 1:00-5:00, Sa-Su 1:00-5:00, park is open year round.

Inuvik: **Ivvavik National Park of Canada**
PO Box 1840, Inuvik, NWT X0E 0T0
867-777-8800, Fax: 867-777-8820,
Inuvik.info@pc.gc.ca
www.pc.gc.ca/pn-np/yt/ivvavik/index_E.asp
Ivvavik, meaning 'a place for giving birth, a nursery', in Inuvialuktun, the language of the Inuvialuit, is the first national park in Canada to be created as a result of an aboriginal land claim agreement. The park protects a portion of the calving grounds of the Porcupine caribou herd and represents the Northern Yukon and Mackenzie Delta natural regions. Hours of Operation: Park is open year round, with no available services.

Iqaluit: **Quttinirpaaq National Park of Canada**
PO Box 278, Iqaluit, NU X0A 0H0
867-975-4673, Fax: 867-975-4674,
nunavut.info@pc.gc.ca
www.pc.gc.ca/pn-np/nu/quttinirpaaq/index_E.asp
Welcome ... to the top of the world! During the brief arctic summer on Quttinirpaaq, the sun remains high in the sky bathing the land in continuous daylight. There is no darkness to mark the passage of time telling you when to sleep and when to wake. There are no trees to remind you of lands further south. The scale of the land is both immense and intimate at the same time. Intricate patterns of rock, frost-cracked ground, willows and wildflowers at your feet extend out from where you stand into endless vistas in the clear, dry air. Glaciers on a mountainside 15 km away seem to be details in a landscape within reach. Hours of Operation: Warden station only staffed furing the summer field season. Parks Canada Office in Iqaluit is open M-F 8:30-12:00, 1:00-5:00 year round.

Pangnirtung: **Auyuittuq National Park of Canada**
PO Box 353, Pangnirtung, NU X0A 0R0
867-473-2500, Fax: 867-473-8612,
nunavut.info@pc.gc.ca
www.pc.gc.ca/pn-np/nu/auyuittuq/index_E.asp
Sweeping glaciers and polar sea ice meet jagged granite mountains in Auyuittuq National Park of Canada. Established in 1976, Auyuittuq - an Inuktitut word meaning "land that never melts" - protects 19,089 km 2 of glacier-scoured terrain. Located in the eastern Arctic, on southern Baffin Island, the park includes the highest peaks of the Canadian Shield, the Penny Ice Cap, marine shorelines along coastal fiords, and Akshayuk Pass, a traditional travel corridor used by the Inuit for thousands of years. Whether you wish to climb Auyuittuq's rugged peaks, ski on its pristine icefields, or hike the scenic Akshayuk Pass, this park offers unique opportunities to experience the beauty and majesty of the Arctic. Hours of Operation: Winter M-F 8:30-12:00, 1:00-5:00, Summer hours are posted in June.

Paulatuk: **Tuktut Nogait National Park of Canada**
PO Box 91, Paulatuk, NWT X0E 1N0
867-580-3233, Fax: 867-580-3234,
inuvik.info@pc.gc.ca
www.pc.gc.ca/pn-np/nt/tuktutnogait/index_E.asp
With rolling tundra, wild rivers, precipitous canyons, and a variety of unique wildlife and vegetation, Tuktut Nogait ('young caribou') is one of Canada's undiscovered gems. This remote park is located 170 kilometres north of the arctic circle and is home to the Bluenose West caribou herd, wolves, grizzly bears, muskoxen, arctic char, and a high density of raptors. The wildlife and land have supported aboriginal peoples for thousands of years, from the Copper and Thule cultures to contemporary Inuvialuit. Hours of Operation: open year round.

Pond Inlet: **Sirmilik National Park of Canada**
PO Box 300, Pond Inlet, NU X0A 0S0
867-899-8092, Fax: 867-899-8104,
sirmilik.info@pc.gc.ca
www.pc.gc.ca/sirmilik
Founded: 2001 As part of Canada's national parks system, Sirmilik National Park represents the Northern Eastern Arctic Lowlands Natural Region and portions of the Lancaster Sound Marine Region. The park will comprise four separate land areas. Bylot Island is a spectacular area of rugged mountains, icefields and glaciers, coastal lowlands and seabird colonies. Oliver Sound is a long, narrow fiord with excellent opportunities for boating, hiking and camping. Borden Peninsula is an extensive plateau dissected by broad river valleys. The park features landforms and superb wilderness hiking and camping, and a major seabird colony in the vicinity of Baillarge Bay. Hours of Operation: Administration and Visitor Centre , M-F 8:30-12:00, 1:00-5:00.

Sachs Harbour: **Aulavik National Park of Canada**
PO Box 29, Sachs Harbour, NWT X0E 0Z0
867-690-3904, Fax: 867-690-4808,
Inuvik.info@pc.gc.ca
www.pc.gc.ca/pn-np/nt/aulavik/index_E.asp
Aulavik, meaning "place where people travel" in Inuvialuktun, protects more than 12,000 square kilometres of arctic lowlands on the north end of Banks Island. The park encompasses a variety of landscapes from fertile river valleys to polar deserts, buttes and badlands, rolling hills, and bold seacoasts. At the heart of Aulavik is the Thomsen River, which offers visitors a chance to paddle one of the continent's most northerly navigable waterways. This pristine arctic environment is home to both the endangered Peary caribou and to the highest density of muskoxen in the world. The wildlife and land have supported aboriginal peoples for more than 3,400 years, from Pre-Dorset cultures to contemporary Inuvialuit. Hours of Operation: Open year round.

Ontario

Heron Bay: **Pukaskwa National Park of Canada**
PO Box 212, Heron Bay, ON P0T 1R0
807-229-0801, Fax: 807-229-2097,
ont-pukaskwa @pc.gc.ca
www.pc.gc.ca/pn-np/on/pukaskwa/index_E.asp

Pukaskwa National Park's exceptional beauty is revealed in its vistas of Lake Superior and in the rugged, ancient landscape of the Canadian Shield and northern forest. The spirit of the wilderness envelopes those who explore this special place. The only wilderness national park in Ontario, Pukaskwa protects 1878 square km of an ecosystem that features boreal forest and Lake Superior shoreline. Hours of Operation: Administration Building M-F 8:30-4:30 year round.

***Leamington:* Point Pelee National Park of Canada**
407 Monarch Lane, RR 1, Leamington, ON N8H 3V4
519-322-2365, Fax: 519-322-1277,
pelee.info@pc.gc.ca
www.pc.gc.ca/pn-np/on/pelee/index_E.asp
A lush Carolinian forest oasis at the southern tip of Canada, Point Pelee National Park resounds with migrating song birds in the spring, hums with cicadas in the summer, flutters with Monarch butterflies in the fall and is a peaceful place of reflection in the winter. Located 50 km (30 miles) south-east of Windsor, Ontario, Point Pelee National Park of Canada is one of Canada's smallest national parks, and yet this tiny green oasis attracts approximately 300 000 visitors each year. Our goal is to bring people and the environment together. From picnic areas to the Visitor Centre, to famous vistas like the Tip and the Marsh Boardwalk, all facilities and services are designed to ensure a memorable experience and to preserve the Park's natural environment. Hours of Operation: Oct-March 7:00am-7:00pm; April 6:00am-10:00pm; May 1-May 21 5:00am-10:00pm; May 22-Oct 8 6:00am-10:00pm.

***Mallorytown:* St. Lawrence Islands National Park of Canada**
2 County Road 5, RR 3, Mallorytown, ON K0E 1R0
613-923-5261, Fax: 613-923-1021,
ont-sli@pc.gc.ca
www.pc.gc.ca/pn-np/on/lawren/index_E.asp
Conceived in the 1870s, St. Lawrence Islands is a tiny jewel with a rich and complex natural and human history. The park is located in the heart of the Thousand Islands tourist area. Make St. Lawrence Islands National Park a leisurely and scenic stop on your way through Eastern Ontario. Hours of Operation: Administration Office, M-F 8:00-4:30 year round; Islands, May 18-Oct 8; Mallourytown Landing Visitor Centre, May 18-June 10 & Sept 7-Oct 8, F-Su 10:00-4:00, June 15-Sept 3 Su-Th 10:00-4:00, Fr-Sa 10:00-6:00.

***Midland:* Georgian Bay Islands National Park of Canada**
PO Box 9, 911 Wye Valley Rd., Midland, ON L4R 4K6
705-526-9804, Fax: 705-526-5939,
info.gbi@pc.gc.ca
www.pc.gc.ca/pn-np/on/georg/index_E.asp
Protecting one of Canada's national treasures for your enjoyment: from the Honey Harbour area to Twelve Mile Bay in southern Georgian Bay, you will discover spectacular landscapes, time-worn rock faces, diverse habitats and the rugged beauty of the Canadian Shield. These magnificent islands are accessible by boat only. The largest island, Beausoleil offers island tent camping, overnight and day docking, heritage education programs and hiking trails. Wheelchair accessible sites and reserved campsites are also available at the Cedar Spring campground on Beausoleil Island. Hours of Operation: Parks Canada Welcome Centre, Spring & Fall Sa-Su 9:00-5:00, Summer daily 10:00-6:00.

***Tobermory:* Bruce Peninsula National Park of Canada**
PO Box 189, Tobermory, ON N0H 2R0
519-596-2233, Fax: 519-596-2298,
bruce-fathomfive @pc.gc.ca
www.pc.gc.ca/pn-np/on/bruce/index_E.asp
In the heart of a World Biosphere Reserve, the 'Bruce' is a place of global significance. The massive, rugged cliffs of the park are inhabited by thousand year old cedar trees, overhanging the crystal clear waters of Georgian Bay. The park is comprised of an incredible array of habitats from rare alvars to dense forests and clean lakes. Together these form a greater ecosystem - the largest remaining chunk of natural habitat in southern Ontario. Hours of Operation: Administration Office, M-F 8:00-4:30; Cyprus Lake Campground Office, daily from May-Oct.

Prince Edward Island

***Charlottetown:* Prince Edward Island National Park of Canada**
2 Palmers Lane, Charlottetown, PE C1A 5V6
902-672-6350, Fax: 902-672-6370,
pnipe.peinp@pc.gc.ca
www.pc.gc.ca/pn-np/pe/pei-ipe/index_E.asp
Prince Edward Island National Park of Canada is home to sand dunes, barrier islands and sand pits, beaches, sandstone cliffs, wetlands and forests. These diverse habitats provide a home for a variety of plants and animals, including the endangered Piping Plover. The National Park also features unique cultural resources, notably Green Gables and Dalvay-by-the-Sea National Historic Site. In 1998, six kilometres of the Greenwich Peninsula were added to the Park to protect unique dune formations, rare plants and animals, as well as archaeological findings dating back 10,000 years. Hours of Operation: Greenwich Interpretation Centre, May 20-June 26 & Aug 22-Oct 9 9:00-4:30, June 27-Aug 21 9:00-6:00; Rntrance Kiosks, early June-late August; Cavendish Visitor Centre, late May-mid Oct.

Quebec

***Gaspé:* Forillon National Park of Canada**
122 Gaspé Boulevard, Gaspé, QC G4X 1A9
418-368-5505, Fax: 418-368-6837, 888-773-8888
parkscanada-que @pc.gc.ca
www.pc.gc.ca/pn-np/qc/forillon/index_E.asp
Forillon, a national park created in 1970, is located at the farthest reach of the Gaspé Peninsula. Its majestic landscapes cover a 244 km2 area that is carved out of the sea, cliffs and mountains. Forillon protects a representative sample of the Notre-Dame and Mégantic mountain regions and certain elements of the Gulf of St. Lawrence marine region. The presence of ten different rock formations, colonies of seabirds and enigmatic artic-alpine plants give this park its unique character. Within this seaside park, the Grande-Grave National Heritage Site attests to the way of life of fishing families. Hours of Operation: Park is open all year round, with services mostly offered between June and October.

***Havre-Saint-Pierre:* Mingan Archipelago National Park Reserve of Canada**
1340 de la Digue St., Havre-Saint-Pierre, QC G0G 1P0
418-538-3331, Fax: 418-538-3595,
parkscanada-que @pc.gc.ca
www.pc.gc.ca/pn-np/qc/mingan/index_E.asp
Beyond the 50th parallel, along the North Shore of the Gulf of St. Lawrence, lies a remarkably beautiful scattering of some forty limestone islands and more than 1000 granitic islets and reefs. The territory, the "Mingan Archipelago", became a national park reserve in 1984. This necklace of land carved out of the limestone bedrock is the site of spectacular natural monuments which bear witness to the never-ending wear of the sea and of the centuries. And there is an abundance of life in this strange half-world: plants of variegated hues and shapes, seabirds gathered in colonies, seals, dolphins and whales, swarming the blue vastness in which the islands bathe. Hours of Operation: Havre-Saint-Pierre Reception and Interpretation Center & Longue-Pointe-de-Mingan Reception and Interpretation Centre open June-September.

***Shawinigan:* La Mauricie National Park of Canada**
PO Box 160 Bureau-chef, 702 5th Street, Shawinigan, QC G9N 6T9
819-538-3232, Fax: 819-536-3661,
parkscanada-que @pc.gc.ca
www.pc.gc.ca/pn-np/qc/mauricie/index_E.asp
Covering an area of 536 km2, the park gives off an air of serenity throughout its gently contoured terrain. On this vast plateau of rolling hills intersected by valleys and dotted with myriads of lakes, life moves in perfect unison with nature. Here only the changes of the seasons mark the passage of time, retouching the landscape with subtle strokes and calling visitors with a promise of both activity and relaxation. Since its creation in 1970, the park has safeguarded the continuing integrity of this richly endowed land, protecting it as a representative sample of the southernmost part of the Canadian Shield. Welcome to this haven of peace! La Mauricie National Park, a conservation area that relies on your involvement! Hours of Operation: Reception Centre, May 11-24 & Sept 4-Oct 14 Sa-Th 9:00-4:30, F 9:00 am-10:00 pm, May 25-Sept 3 daily 7:00 am-10:00 pm.

Saskatchewan

***Val Marie:* Grasslands National Park of Canada**
PO Box 150, Val Marie, SK S0N 2T0
306-298-2257, Fax: 306-298-2042,
grasslands.info @pc.gc.ca
www.pc.gc.ca/pn-np/sk/grasslands/index_E.asp
Grasslands is the first national park of Canada to preserve a portion of the mixed prairie grasslands. Eavesdrop on a prairie dog town or learn about how Sitting Bull took refuge here after the battle of the Little Bighorn in 1876. Guided hikes, interpretive trails, bird watching, and nature photography are popular activities in Grasslands. Hours of Operation: Parklands are open year round; Visitor Reception Centre is open daily from mid-May to Labour Day, 8:00-5:00, and from Sept-May, the Centre is open M-F, 8:00-4:30.

***Waskesiu Lake:* Prince Albert National Park of Canada**
PO Box 100, Waskesiu Lake, SK S0J 2Y0
306-663-4522,
panp.info@pc.gc.ca
www.pc.gc.ca/pn-np/sk/princealbert/index_E.asp
Prince Albert National Park protects a slice of the 'boreal' forest. It is also a meeting place or transition zone between the parkland and the northern forest. The park features many outstanding natural wonders and cultural treasures, including the only fully protected white pelican nesting colony in Canada, the isolated, lakeside cabin of conservationist Grey Owl and a free-ranging herd of plains bison. During a visit, enjoy special events and interpretive programs that help you make more connections with the patterns and processes of this ecosystem. The townsite of Waskesiu, located in the park, provides extensive services for visitors. Hours of Operation: Parklands are open year round; Information Centre is open daily 8:00am-8:00 pm from mid-May-early Sept, and on weekends during peak cross country ski season.

Yukon Territory

***Haines Junction:* Kluane National Park and Reserve of Canada**
PO Box 5495, Haines Junction, YT Y0B 1L0
867-634-7250, Fax: 867-634-7208,
kluane.info@pc.gc.ca
www.pc.gc.ca/pn-np/yt/kluane/index_E.asp
A gem in the family of Parks Canada's national treasures, Kluane National Park and Reserve of Canada covers an area of 21,980 square kilometres. It is a land of precipitous, high mountains, immense icefields and lush valleys that yield a diverse array of plant and wildlife species and provides for a host of outdoor activities. Kluane National Park and Reserve is also home to Mount Logan (5959 m/19,545 ft), Canada's highest peak. As part of a larger system of national parks and historic sites found throughout Canada, Kluane National Park and Reserve protects and presents a nationally significant example of Canada's North Coast Mountains natural region and the associated regional cultural heritage. Fostering public understanding, appreciation and enjoyment of Kluane National Park and Reserve while ensuring ecological and commemorative integrity for present and future generations is Parks Canada's goal. Hours of Operation: Visitor Centre, mid-May-mid Sept, daily 9:00-5:00.

***Old Crow:* Vuntut National Park of Canada**
Old Crow, YT Y0B 1N0
867-667-3910, Fax: 867-966-3432,
brenda.frost-charlie @pc.gc.ca
www.pc.gc.ca/pn-np/yt/vuntut/index_E.asp
Vuntut National Park was established in 1995 after extensive negotiations through the Vuntut Gwitchin First Nation's Final Land Claims Agreement between the Vuntut Gwitchin of Old Crow and the Government of Canada and the Yukon. Vuntut, which means "among the lakes" in the Gwitchin language, encompasses 4,345. sq. km of wilderness in the northwestern corner of the Yukon Territory. The park is bounded by the height of land and Ivvavik National Park of the north, the international boundary and the Arctic National Wildlife Refuge to the west, Black Fox Creek to its confluence with the Old Crow River to the east and the Old Crow River to the south. Hours of Operation: Park is open year round, with no services available.

Performing Arts - Dance

International

The Royal Scottish Country Dance Society (RSCDS)
12 Coates Cres., Edinburgh EH3 7AF United Kingdom
Tel: 44-0131-225-3854; *Fax:* 44-0131-225-7783
e-mail: info@rscds.org
URL: www.rscds.org

Elspeth Gray, Secretary

Alberta

Alberta Ballet
Nat Christie Centre, 141 - 18 Ave. SW, Calgary AB T2S 0B8
Tel: 403-245-4222; *Fax:* 403-245-6573
e-mail: info@albertaballet.com
URL: www.albertaballet.com

Kerna St. John, Director, Marketing/Communications
Jean Grand-Maître, Artistic Director
Darryl Lindenbach, Executive Director

Alberta Dance Alliance (ADA)
Percy Page Centre, 11759 Groat Rd., 2nd Fl., Edmonton AB T5M 3K6
Tel: 780-422-8107; *Fax:* 780-422-2663
Toll-Free: 888-422-8107
e-mail: info@abdancealliance.ab.ca
URL: www.abdancealliance.ab.ca

Affiliation(s): Canadian Assembly of Dance; CADA BC, Ontario
Bobbi Westman, Executive Director

Brian Webb Dance Co.
PO Box 53092, Edmonton AB T5N 48A
Tel: 780-452-3282; *Fax:* 780-497-4330
e-mail: webbcdf@shaw.ca
URL: www.bwdc.ca

Brian Webb, Artistic Director

Catalyst Theatre Society of Alberta
8529 Gateway Blvd., Edmonton AB T6E 6P3
Tel: 780-431-1750; *Fax:* 780-433-3060
e-mail: info@catalysttheatre.ca
URL: www.catalysttheatre.ca
Jonathan Christenson, Artistic Director

Decidedly Jazz Danceworks
1514 - 4th St. SW, Calgary AB T2R 0Y4
Tel: 403-245-3533; *Fax:* 403-245-3584
e-mail: djd@decidedlyjazz.com
URL: www.decidedlyjazz.com
Vicki Adams Willis, Artistic Director
Kathi Sundstrom, General Manager

Springboard Dance
205 - 8th Ave. SE, 2nd Fl., Calgary AB T2G 0K9
Tel: 403-265-3230; *Fax:* 403-294-7457
URL: www.springboardperformance.com
Affiliation(s): Alberta Dance Alliance; Canadian Dance Federation; Dance Current
Trina Rasmuson
Shelly Tegnazzini
Nicole Mion

Sun Ergos, A Company of Theatre & Dance
Priddis Greens, 130 Sunset Way, Priddis AB T0L 1W0
Tel: 403-931-1527; *Fax:* 403-931-1534
Toll-Free: 800-743-3351
e-mail: waltermoke@sunergos.com
URL: www.sunergos.com
Affiliation(s): Western Arts Alliance; Arts Northwest; Montana Performing Arts Consortium; Arts MidWest; Arts Touring Alliance of Alberta; BC Touring; Wyoming Arts Alliance
Robert Greenwood, Artistic & Managing Director
Dana Luebke, Artistic & Production Director

Vinok Worldance
PO Box 4867, Edmonton AB T6E 5G7
Tel: 780-454-3739; *Fax:* 780-454-3436
e-mail: vinok@vinok.ca
URL: www.vinok.ca
Doyle Marko, Artistic Director
Leanne Koziak, Executive Director

British Columbia

Ballet British Columbia
677 Davie St., 6th Fl., Vancouver BC V6G 2B6
Tel: 604-732-5003; *Fax:* 604-732-4417
e-mail: info@balletbc.com
URL: www.balletbc.com
Emily Molnar, Interim Artistic Director

Dance Centre
Scotiabank Dance Centre, 677 Davie St., Level 6, Vancouver BC V6B 2G6
Tel: 604-606-6400; *Fax:* 604-606-6401
e-mail: info@thedancecentre.ca
URL: www.thedancecentre.ca
Heather Bray, Marketing Manager
Mirna Zagar, Executive Director

DanceArts Vancouver
Scotiabank Dance Centre, 677 Davie St., 7th Fl., Vancouver BC V6B 2G6
Tel: 604-606-6425; *Fax:* 604-606-6432
e-mail: info@dancearts.bc.ca
Judith Marcuse, Artistic Director

EDAM Performing Arts Society (EDAM)
303 - 8th Ave. East, Vancouver BC V5T 1S1
Tel: 604-876-9559; *Fax:* 604-876-9525
e-mail: info@edamdance.org
URL: www.edamdance.org
Peter Bingham, Artistic Director
Mona Hamill, Administrative Director

Goh Ballet Society
2345 Main St., Vancouver BC V5T 3C9
Tel: 604-872-4014; *Fax:* 604-872-4011
e-mail: admin@gohballet.com
URL: www.gohballet.com
Fei Wong, President
Chan Hon Goh, Artistic Director

Kinesis Dance Society
Scotia Bank Dance Centre, Level 7, 677 Davie St., Vancouver BC V6B 2G6
Tel: 604-684-7844; *Fax:* 604-684-7834
e-mail: info@kinesisdance.org
URL: www.kinesisdance.org
Paras Terezakis, Artistic Director

Lola Dance
#104, 336 - 1st Ave. East, Vancouver BC V5T 4R6
Tel: 604-683-6552; *Fax:* 604-681-1431
e-mail: info@loladance.org
URL: www.loladance.org
Lola MacLaughlin, Artistic Director & Founder

Mascall Dance
1130 Jervis St., Vancouver BC V6E 2C7
Tel: 604-689-9339; *Fax:* 604-689-9399
e-mail: admin@mascalldance.ca
URL: www.mascalldance.ca
Jennifer Mascall, Artistic Director

Vancouver Moving Theatre (VMT)
PO Box 88270, Stn. Chinatown, Vancouver BC V6A 4A4
Tel: 604-628-5672
e-mail: savannahandterry@axion.net
URL: www.vancouvermovingtheatre.com
Savannah Walling, Artistic Director
Terry Hunter, Executive Director

Manitoba

Canadian Square & Round Dance Society (CSRDS)
115 Holly Dr., Oakbank MB R0E 1J2
Tel: 204-444-3115; *Fax:* 204-444-5768
Toll-Free: 866-206-6696
e-mail: info@squaredance.ca
URL: www.csrds.ca
Lorraine Kozera, Secretary
John Kozera, Secretary
Alan Clay, President
Doreen Clay, President

Dance Manitoba Inc.
Pantages Playhouse Theaetre, #204, 180 Market Ave. East, Winnipeg MB R3B 0P7
Tel: 204-989-5260; *Fax:* 204-989-5268
e-mail: info@dancemanitoba.org
URL: www.dancemanitoba.org
Nicole Langevin-Owens, Executive Director

Royal Winnipeg Ballet (RWB)
380 Graham Ave., Winnipeg MB R3C 4K2
Tel: 204-956-0183; *Fax:* 204-943-1994
Toll-Free: 800-667-4792
e-mail: ballet@rwb.org
URL: www.rwb.org
Affiliation(s): Association of Cultural Executives; Canadian Conference of the Arts; Canadian Arts Presenting Association; Council for Business & the Arts in Canada; Dance USA; International Society for the Performing Arts
Arlene Minkhorst, School Director
Charlene Rocke, Chair
André Lewis, Artistic Director

Ruth Cansfield Dance
806 Osborne St., Winnipeg MB R3L 2C7
Tel: 204-284-5810; *Fax:* 204-284-1131
Toll-Free: 866-405-5810
e-mail: info@ruthcansfield.com
URL: www.ruthcansfield.com
Ken Manson, Vice-President
Jon McPhail, Administration Director
Ruth Cansfield, Artistic Director
Ellie Cansfield, President

Winnipeg's Contemporary Dancers
#204, 211 Bannatyne Ave., Winnipeg MB R3B 3P2
Tel: 204-452-0229; *Fax:* 204-287-8618
e-mail: info@winnipegscontemporarydancers.ca
URL: www.winnipegscontemporarydancers.ca
Brian Lott, Artistic Director

New Brunswick

Les Productions DansEncorps Inc.
#12A, 140, rue Botsford, Moncton NB E1C 4X5
Tél: 506-855-0998; *Téléc:* 506-852-3401
Courriel: dencorps@nb.aibn.com
URL: www.dansencorps.ca
Chantal Cadieux, Directrice artistique

Nova Scotia

Dance Nova Scotia
1113 Marginal Rd., Halifax NS B3H 4P7
Tel: 902-422-1749; *Fax:* 902-422-0881
e-mail: office@dancens.ca
URL: www.dancens.ca
Dianne Milligan, Executive Director

Two Planks & a Passion Theatre Association (TP&aP)
PO Box 190, 555 Ross Creek Rd., Canning NS B0P 1H0
Tel: 902-582-3073; *Fax:* 902-582-7943
e-mail: mail@twoplanks.ca
URL: www.twoplanks.ca; www.twoplanksandpassion.blogspot.com
Affiliation(s): Playwrights Union of Canada
Ken Schwartz, Artistic Director

Ontario

Ballet Creole
375 Dovercourt Rd., Toronto ON M6J 3E5
Tel: 416-960-0350; *Fax:* 416-960-2067
e-mail: info@balletcreole.org
URL: www.balletcreole.org
Patrick Parson, Artistic Director

Ballet Jörgen
c/o George Brown College, Casa Loma Campus, Room 126, Building C, 160 Kendal Ave., Toronto ON M5R 1M3
Tel: 416-961-4725; *Fax:* 416-415-2865
e-mail: info@balletjorgen.ca
URL: www.balletjorgen.ca
Affiliation(s): George Brown Dance
Bengt Jörgen, Artistic Director & CEO

Canada Dance Festival Society
PO Box 1376, Stn. B, 53 Elgin St., Ottawa ON K1P 5R4
Tel: 613-947-7000; *Fax:* 613-943-1399
e-mail: cdffdc@nac-cna.ca
URL: www.canadadance.ca
Brian H. Webb, Artistic Director
Pamela Fralick, Chair

Canadian Children's Dance Theatre (CCDT)
509 Parliament St., Toronto ON M4X 1P3
Tel: 416-924-5657; *Fax:* 416-924-4141
e-mail: info@ccdt.org
URL: www.ccdt.org
Elizabeth Varty, Marketing, Development & Arts Educa
Deborah Lundmark, Artistic Director & Resident Choreo
Michael de Coninck Smith, Co-Artistic Director & Production M

Canadian Dance Teachers Association (CDTA) / Association canadienne des professeurs de danse
c/o President, 178 Barrick Rd., Port Colbourne ON L3K 4B4
Tel: 905-834-0077
e-mail: donna.moreau@sympatico.ca
URL: www.cdtanational.ca
Donna Moreau, President

Dance Ontario Association / Association Ontario Danse
Case Goods Bldg. 74, The Distillery District, #304, 55 Mill St., Toronto ON M5A 3C4
Tel: 416-204-1083; *Fax:* 416-204-1085
e-mail: contact@danceontario.ca
URL: www.danceontario.ca
Catherine Carpenko, Chair
Samara Thompson, Vice-Chair
Rosslyn Jacob Edwards, Executive Director
Jennifer Watkins, Secretary
Allison Cummings, Treasurer

Dance Oremus Danse (DOD)
240 Dovercourt Rd., Toronto ON M6J 3E1
Tel: 416-536-9002; *Fax:* 416-536-9002
e-mail: pauljamesdwyer@yahoo.ca
URL: www.danceoremusdanse.org
Paul James Dwyer, Founder/Artistic Director

Dance Umbrella of Ontario (DUO)
#201, 490 Adelaide St. West, Toronto ON M5V 1T2
Tel: 416-504-6429; *Fax:* 416 504 8702
Toll-Free: 800-919-5019
e-mail: duo@danceumbrella.net
URL: www.danceumbrella.net
Affiliation(s): Arts Vote; Dance Ontario
Christine Moynihan, Executive Director

Dancemakers
The Case Goods Warehouse, Bldg. #74, #306, 55 Mill St., Toronto ON M5A 3C4
Tel: 416-367-1800; *Fax:* 416-367-1870
e-mail: info@dancemakers.org
URL: www.dancemakers.org
Michael Trent, Artistic Director
Bradley Kulay, Administrative Manager

Dancer Transition Resource Centre (DTRC) / Centre de ressources et transition pour danseurs (CRTD)
The Lynda Hamilton Centre, #500, 250 The Esplanade, Toronto ON M5A 1J2
Tel: 416-595-5655; *Fax:* 416-595-0009
Toll-Free: 800-667-0851
e-mail: nationaloffice@dtrc.ca
URL: www.dtrc.ca
Affiliation(s): Canadian Dance Alliance; Le Regroupement québécois de la Danse
Amanda Hancox, Executive Director
Garry Neil, Chair

Danny Grossman Dance Company
#202, 157 Carlton St., Toronto ON M5A 2K3
Tel: 416-408-4543; *Fax:* 416-408-2518
e-mail: info@dannygrossman.com
URL: www.dannygrossman.com
Affiliation(s): Dance USA; CAPDO; Dance Ontario
Helen Chapman, Managing Director
Danny Grossman, Artistic Director

FFIDA
Toronto ON
Tel: 416-214-5854
e-mail: info@ffida.org
Michael Menegon, Artistic Director

Fujiwara Dance Inventions
#201, 490 Adelaide St. West, Toronto ON M5V 1T2
Tel: 416-593-4710; *Fax:* 416-504-8702
e-mail: info@fujiwaradance.com
URL: www.fujiwaradance.com
Denise Fujiwara, Artistic Director

Gina Lori Riley Dance Enterprises
401 Sunset Ave., Windsor ON N9B 3P4
Tel: 519-253-3000
e-mail: riley2@uwindsor.ca
URL: www.ginaloririleydanceenterprises.com
Gina Lori Riley, Artistic Director

Le Groupe Dance Lab / Le Groupe lab de danse
#2, 2 Daly St., Ottawa ON K1N 6E2
Tel: 613-235-1492; *Fax:* 613-235-1651
e-mail: info@legroupe.org
URL: www.legroupe.org
Affiliation(s): 10 Gates Dancing Inc.; DanceMakers; Fondation Jean Pierre Perreault
Tony Chong, Associate Artistic Director
Peter Boneham, Artistic Director
Anthony Pan, General Manager

National Ballet of Canada
Walter Carsen Centre, 470 Queens Quay West, Toronto ON M5V 3K4
Tel: 416-345-9686; *Fax:* 416-345-8323
e-mail: info@national.ballet.ca
URL: www.national.ballet.ca
Karen Kain, Artistic Director
Kevin Garland, Executive Director
David Briskin, Music Director/Principal Conductor

Ontario Ballet Theatre
1133 St. Clair Ave. West, Toronto ON M6E 1B1
Tel: 416-656-9568; *Fax:* 416-651-4803
e-mail: tara@ontarioballettheatre.com
URL: www.ontarioballettheatre.com

Ontario Folk Dance Association (OFDA)
35 Touraine Ave., Toronto ON M3H 1R3
e-mail: ontariofolkdancers@gmail.com
URL: www.ofda.ca
Kevin Budd, Vice-President
Beverly Sidney, President

Opéra Atelier (OA)
St. Lawrence Hall, 157 King St. East, 4th Fl., Toronto ON M5C 1G9
Tel: 416-703-3767; *Fax:* 416-703-4895
e-mail: opera.atelier@operaatelier.com
URL: www.operaatelier.com
Jane Hargraft, General Manager

Royal Academy of Dance/Canada
#500, 1200 Sheppard Ave. East, Toronto ON M2K 2S5
Tel: 416-489-2813; *Fax:* 416-489-3222
Toll-Free: 888-709-0895
e-mail: info@radcanada.org
URL: www.radcanada.org
Affiliation(s): Royal Academy of Dance
Jan Garvey, National Administrator

Toronto & District Square & Round Dance Association
8 Seven Oaks Circle, St. Catharines ON L2P 3N6
Tel: 905-641-1872
URL: www3.sympatico.ca/jerry.callen/td/
Affiliation(s): Canadian Square & Round Dance Society
Sharron Hall, Secretary

Toronto Dance Theatre (TDT)
80 Winchester St., Toronto ON M4X 1B2
Tel: 416-967-1365; *Fax:* 416-963-4379
e-mail: info@tdt.org
URL: www.tdt.org
Jay Rankin, Managing Director
Christopher House, Artistic Director

Québec

Ballet Ouest / Ballet West
#218, 269 boul. St. Jean, Pointe-Claire QC H9R 3J1
Tel: 514-783-1245; *Fax:* 514-939-1469
e-mail: centredanse@balletouest.com
URL: www.balletouest.com
Susan Altschul, Company Manager
Marie St-Amour, President
Margaret Mehuys, Artistic Director

bjm danse (BJM)
1210, rue Sherbrooke est, Montréal QC H2L 1L9
Tél: 514-982-6771; *Téléc:* 514-982-9145
Courriel: info@bjmdanse.ca
URL: www.bjmdanse.ca
Louis Robitaille, Directeur artistique
Bernard Lagacé, Directeur général

Le Carré des Lombes
#401, 2022, rue Sherbrooke Est, Montréal QC H2K 1B9
Tél: 514-287-9339; *Téléc:* 514-287-9415
Courriel: info@lecarredeslombes.com
URL: www.lecarredeslombes.com
Suzanne Beaucaire, Coordonatrice Générale

Cercle d'expression artistique Nyata Nyata
4374, boul St-Laurent, 3e étage, Montréal QC H2W 1Z5
Tél: 514-849-9781; *Téléc:* 514-849-7199
Courriel: info@nyata-nyata.org
URL: www.nyata-nyata.org
Zab Maboungou, Directrice artistique

Compagnie de danse Migrations
880, av Pére-Marquette, Québec QC G1S 24A
Tél: 418-684-3132; *Téléc:* 418-684-3134
Courriel: migrations@qc.aira.com
URL: www.migrationsdanse.com
Affiliation(s): Folklore Canada International
Richard Turcotte, Directeur artistique
Blandin Garnier, Adjointe administrative

Compagnie Marie Chouinard
#715, 3981, boul St-Laurent, Montréal QC H2W 1Y5
Tél: 514-843-9036; *Téléc:* 514-843-7616
Courriel: info@mariechouinard.com
URL: www.mariechouinard.com
Marie Chouinard, Directrice artistique
Pierre Des Marais, Directeur général

Danse-Cite inc
#426, 3680, rue Jeanne-Mance, Montréal QC H2X 2K5
Tél: 514-525-3595; *Téléc:* 514-525-3536
Courriel: info@danse-cite.org
URL: www.danse-cite.org
Daniel Soulières, Directeur artistique

Fédération des loisirs-danse du Québec
CP 1000, Succ. M, 4545, av Pierre-de Coubertin, Montréal QC H1V 3R2
Tél: 514-252-3029; *Téléc:* 514-251-8038

Fortier Danse-Création
Succ. C, #301, 2022, rue Sherbrooke Est, Montréal QC H2K 1B9
Tél: 514-529-8158; *Téléc:* 514-529-1222
Courriel: admin@fortier-danse.com
URL: www.fortier-danse.com
Paul-André Fortier, Directeur artistique
Gilles Savary, Directeur général

Les Grands Ballets Canadiens de Montréal (GBCM)
Maison de la Danse, 4816, rue Rivard, Montréal QC H2J 2N6
Tél: 514-849-8681; *Téléc:* 514-849-0098
Courriel: info@grandsballets.com
URL: www.grandsballets.com
Alain Dancyger, Directeur général
Gradimir Pankov, Directeur artistique

La La La Human Steps
#206, 5655, av du Parc, Montréal QC H2V 4H2
Tél: 514-277-9090; *Téléc:* 514-277-0862
Courriel: info@lalalahumansteps.com
URL: www.lalalahumansteps.com
Édouard Lock, Directeur artistique

Louise Bédard Danse
#300, 2022, rue Sherbrooke Est, Montréal QC H2K 1B9
Tél: 514-982-4580; *Téléc:* 514-982-0613
Courriel: infos@lbdanse.org
URL: www.lbdanse.org
Louise Bédard, Directrice artistique

Lucie Grégoire Danse
#405,1030, rue Cherrier, Montréal QC H2L 1H9
Tél: 514-524-7665; *Téléc:* 514-524-7584
Courriel: luciegregoire3@sympatico.ca
URL: www.luciegregoire.ca
Lucie Grégoire, Directrice artistique

Margie Gillis Dance Foundation / Fondation de danse Margie Gillis
3519, rue St-Urbain, Montréal QC H2X 2N6
Tel: 514-845-3115; *Fax:* 514-845-4526
e-mail: info@margiegillis.org
URL: www.margiegillis.org
Margie Gillis, Artistic Director
Manon Laflamme, Administrative Director

Montréal Danse
#109, 372, rue Sainte-Catherine ouest, Montréal QC H3B 1A2
Tél: 514-871-4005; *Téléc:* 514-871-4007
Courriel: info@montrealdanse.com
URL: www.montrealdanse.com
Kathy Casey, Directrice artistique

O Vertigo Danse
175, rue Sainte-Catherine ouest, Montréal QC H1V 1H1
Tél: 514-251-9177; *Téléc:* 514-251-7358
Courriel: info@overtigo.com
URL: www.overtigo.com
Diane Boucher, Directrice générale
Ginette Laurin, Directrice générale

Regroupement québécois de la danse (RQD)
#440, 3680 rue Jeanne-Mance, Montréal QC H2X 2K5
Tél: 514-849-4003; *Téléc:* 514-849-3288
Courriel: info@quebecdanse.org
URL: www.quebecdanse.org
Affiliation(s): Agora de la danse; Regroupement québécois des créateurs professionnels
Anik Bissonette, Présidente

Saskatchewan

Dance Saskatchewan Inc.
PO Box 8789, 205A Pacific Ave., Saskatoon SK S7K 1N9
Tel: 306-931-8480; *Fax:* 306-244-1520
Toll-Free: 800-667-8480
e-mail: dancesask@sasktel.net
URL: www.dancesask.com
Affiliation(s): Canadian Association of Professional Dance Organizations
Linda Coe-Kirkham, Executive Director

Performing Arts - Music

Alberta

Alberta Band Association (ABA)
#206, 10612 - 124 St., Edmonton AB T5M 1S4
Tel: 780-488-2263; *Fax:* 780-488-4132
Toll-Free: 877-687-4239
URL: www.albertabandassociation.com
Neil Corlett, Managing Director

Alberta Choral Federation (ACF)
#103, 10612 - 124 St., Edmonton AB T5N 1S4
Tel: 780-488-7464; *Fax:* 780-488-6403
e-mail: info@albertachoralfederation.ca
URL: www.albertachoralfederation.ca
Ardelle Ries, President
Brendan Lord, Executive Director

Alberta Recording Industries Association (ARIA)
Energy Square, #1205, 10109 - 106 St. NW, Edmonton AB T5J 3L7
Tel: 780-428-3372; *Fax:* 780-426-0188
Toll-Free: 800-465-3117
Affiliation(s): Western Canadian Music Alliance; Factor Caras

Calgary Opera Association
Arrata Opera Centre, 1315 - 7 St. SW, Calgary AB T2R 1A5
Tel: 403-262-7286; *Fax:* 403-263-5428
e-mail: info@calgaryopera.com
URL: www.calgaryopera.com
Affiliation(s): Actors Equity Association
W.R. (Bob) McPhee, General Director

Calgary Philharmonic Society (CPO)
205 - 8 Ave. SE, Calgary AB T2G 0K9
Tel: 403-571-0270; *Fax:* 403-294-7424
e-mail: info@cpo-live.com
URL: www.cpo-live.com
Affiliation(s): American Symphony Orchestra League
Ann Lewis-Luppino, President & CEO

Calgary Youth Orchestra
c/o Mount Royal College Conservatory, 4825 Mount Royal Gate SW, Calgary AB T3E 6K6
Tel: 403-240-5978; *Fax:* 403-240-6594
e-mail: cyo@mtroyal.ca
URL: www.cyo.ab.ca
George Fenwick, Orchestra Manager

Canadian Federation of Music Teachers' Associations (CFMTA) / Fédération canadienne des associations des professeurs de musique
13407, 14A Ave., Surrey AB V4A 7P9
Tel: 604-531-8840; *Fax:* 604-531-8747
e-mail: dbrigs@telus.net
URL: www.cfmta.org
Affiliation(s): International Society of Music Educators' Association
Darlene Brigidear, President

Canadian Society for Traditional Music (CSTM) / Société canadienne pour les traditions musicales (SCTM)
c/o 3-47 Arts Building, University of Alberta, Edmonton AB T6G 2E6
e-mail: cstmsctm@ualberta.ca
URL: www.yorku.ca/cstm
Sherry Johnson, Secretary
Anna Hoefnagels, President
Chris McDonald, Treasurer

Country Music Foundation of Canada Inc.
8607 - 128 Ave., Edmonton AB T5E 0G3
Tel: 780-476-8230; *Fax:* 780-472-2584
William Maxim, Chair

Edmonton Jazz Society (EJS)
11 Tommy Banks Way, Edmonton AB T6E 2M2
Tel: 780-432-0428; *Fax:* 780-433-3773
e-mail: jasiek@yardbirdsuite.com
URL: www.yardbirdsuite.com
Paul Wilde, President

Edmonton Opera Association
Winspear Centre, 9720 - 102 Ave., Edmonton AB T5J 4B2
Tel: 780-424-4040; *Fax:* 780-429-0600
e-mail: edmopera@edmontonopera.com
URL: www.edmontonopera.com
Brian Deedrick, Artistic Director
Mary Phillips-Rickey, General Manager

Edmonton Symphony Orchestra (ESO)
9720 - 102 Ave., Edmonton AB T5J 4B2
Tel: 780-428-1108; *Fax:* 780-425-0167
Toll-Free: 800-563-5081
e-mail: info@winspearcentre.com
URL: www.edmontonsymphony.com
Affiliation(s): International Alliance of Theatrical Stage Employees, Moving Picture Technicians, Artists & Allied Crafts of the US & Canada
Rob McAlear, Artistic Administrator
Annemarie Petrov, Executive Director

Edmonton Youth Orchestra Association (EYO)
PO Box 66041, Stn. Heritage Post Office, Edmonton AB T6J 6T4
Tel: 780-436-7932; *Fax:* 780-436-7932
e-mail: eyo@shaw.ca
URL: www.eyso.com
Michael Massey, Music Director

Festival Chorus of Calgary
EPCOR Centre for Performing Arts, 205 - 8 Ave. SE, Calgary AB T2G 0K9
Tel: 403-294-7400
e-mail: lgneufeld@shaw.ca
URL: www.festivalchorus.ca
Mel Kirby, Artistic Director

Lethbridge Symphony Orchestra
PO Box 1101, Lethbridge AB T1J 4A2
Tel: 403-328-6808; *Fax:* 403-380-4418
e-mail: info@lethbridgesymphony.org
URL: www.lethbridgesymphony.org
Glenn Klassen, Music Director, Artistic, Special P
Dawn Leite, General Manager

Red Deer Symphony Orchestra
Cultural Services Building, PO Box 1116, 3827, 39th St., Red Deer AB T4N 6S5
Tel: 403-340-2948; *Fax:* 403-309-4612
e-mail: reddeersymphony@telus.net
URL: www.rdso.ca
Melody McKnight, Executive Director
Claude Lapalme, Music Director

British Columbia

Delta Youth Orchestra
PO Box 131, Delta BC V4K 3N6
Tel: 604-878-4655; *Fax:* 604-943-9603
e-mail: info@dyo.bc.ca
URL: www.dyo.bc.ca
Stephen Robb, Music Director

Early Music Vancouver (EMV)
1254 - 7 Ave. West, Vancouver BC V6H 1B6
Tel: 604-732-1610; *Fax:* 604-732-1602
e-mail: staff@earlymusic.bc.ca
URL: www.earlymusic.bc.ca
José Verstappen, Executive Director

Fraser Valley Symphony Society
PO Box 122, Abbotsford BC V2S 4N8
Tel: 604-859-3877
e-mail: fvssorchestra@hotmail.com
URL: www.fraservalleysymphony.ca
Lindsay Mellor, Conductor

Friends of Chamber Music
PO Box 38046, Stn. King Edward Mall, Vancouver BC V5Z 4L9
Tel: 604-437-5747; *Fax:* 604-437-4769
e-mail: fcmtickets@yahoo.com
URL: www.friendsofchambermusic.ca
Eric Wilson, Program Chair

Greater Victoria Youth Orchestra (GVYO)
1611 Quadra St., Victoria BC V8W 2L5
Tel: 250-360-1121; *Fax:* 250-381-3573
e-mail: gvyo@telus.net
URL: www.gvyo.org
Affiliation(s): Community Arts Council of Greater Victoria
John Sterk, Q.C., President
Sheila Redhead, Manager

Kamloops Intermediate Orchestra
PO Box 1387, Kamloops BC V2C 6L7
Tel: 250-554-3693
Mark Betuzzi, Music Director

Kamloops Symphony (KSO)
PO Box 57, Kamloops BC V2C 5K3
Tel: 250-372-5000; *Fax:* 250-372-5089
e-mail: info@kamloopssymphony.com
URL: www.kamloopssymphony.com
Bruce Dunn, Music Director

Okanagan Symphony Society
PO Box 20238, #239, 1899 Springfield Road, Kelowna BC V1Y 9H2
Tel: 250-763-7544; *Fax:* 250-763-3553
e-mail: admin@okanagansymphony.com
URL: www.okanagansymphony.com
Rosemary Thomson, Music Director

Pacific Opera Victoria (POV)
#500, 1815 Blanshard St., Victoria BC V8T 5A1
Tel: 250-382-1641; *Fax:* 250-382-4944
e-mail: dshefsiek@pov.bc.ca
URL: www.pov.bc.ca
Timothy Vernon, Artistic Director
David Shefsiek, Executive Director

Prince George Symphony Orchestra Society (PGSO)
2880 - 15 Ave., Prince George BC V2M 1T1
Tel: 250-562-0800; *Fax:* 250-562-0844
e-mail: admin@pgso.com
URL: www.pgso.com
Ruth Langner, General Manager

Richmond Community Orchestra & Chorus
#130, 10691 Shellbridge Way, Richmond BC V6X 2W8
Tel: 604-276-2747; *Fax:* 604-270-3644
e-mail: roca.office@gmail.com
URL: www.roca.ca
Suo Tonch, Administrator

Surrey Symphony Society (SSS)
#181, 6832 King George Hwy., Surrey BC V3W 4Z9
Tel: 604-572-9225
e-mail: inquiries@surreyyouthorchestra.org
URL: www.surreyyouthorchestra.org
Lucille Lewis, Music Director
Carla Birston, Intermediate Strings Conductor
Margaret LaBelle, Business Manager
Rick Dorfer, Junior Strings Conductor

Vancouver Island Symphony
PO Box 661, 150 Commercial St., Nanaimo BC V9R 5L9
Tel: 250-754-0177; *Fax:* 250-754-0165
e-mail: info@vancouverislandsymphony.com
URL: www.viso.bc.ca
Margot Holmes, Executive Director
David W. Covey, President

Vancouver New Music (VNM)
837 Davie St., Vancouver BC V6Z 1B7
Tel: 604-633-0861; *Fax:* 604-633-0871
e-mail: info@newmusic.org
URL: www.newmusic.org
Affiliation(s): Canadian Music Centre
Giorgio Magnanensi, Artistic Director
Nicolas Bragg, President

Vancouver Opera (VOA) / Association de l'opéra de vancouver
835 Cambie St., Vancouver BC V6B 2P4
Tel: 604-682-2871; *Fax:* 604-682-3981
e-mail: tickets@vancouveropera.ca
URL: www.vancouveropera.ca
Affiliation(s): Canadian Actors' Equity Association; IATSE; AFM
James W. Wright, Geneeral Director

Vancouver Philharmonic Orchestra (VPO)
PO Box 27503, Stn. Oakridge, Vancouver BC V5Z 4M4
Tel: 604-878-9989
e-mail: vpo@vcn.bc.ca
URL: www.vanphil.ca
Cathy McCashin, President
Maura Gauditis, Vice-President
Katherine Bailey, Treasurer

Vancouver Symphony Society
601 Smithe St., Vancouver BC V6B 5G1
Tel: 604-684-9100; *Fax:* 604-684-9264
e-mail: customerservice@vancouversymphony.ca
URL: www.vancouversymphony.ca
Jeff Alexander, President & CEO
Mary-Ann Moir, Vice-President, Finance & Administration

Vancouver Youth Symphony Orchestra Society (VYSO)
3214 - 10 Ave. West, Vancouver BC V6K 2L2
Tel: 604-737-0714; *Fax:* 604-737-0739
e-mail: vyso@telus.net
URL: www.vyso.com
Roger Cole, Artistic Director
Holly Littleford, Orchestra Manager

Victoria Symphony
#610, 620 View St., Victoria BC V8W 1J6
Tel: 250-385-9771; *Fax:* 250-385-7767
e-mail: administration@victoriasymphony.ca
URL: www.victoriasymphony.ca
Stephen Smith, Interim Executive Director
Deedrie Ballard, President
Tania Miller, Music Director

Manitoba

Alliance Chorale Manitoba
#212, 340 Provencher Blvd., Winnipeg MB R2H 0G7
Tél: 204-233-7423; *Téléc:* 204-233-3324
Gilles Landry, Contact

Brandon University Orchestra
School of Music, Brandon Univ., Queen Elizabeth II Bldg., 270 - 18th St., Brandon MB R7A 6A9
Tel: 204-728-9631; *Fax:* 204-728-6839
e-mail: music@brandonu.ca
URL: www.brandonu.ca/music/
Mark Rudoff, Director

Canadian Band Association (CBA) / Association canadienne des harmonies
15 Pinecrest Bay, Winnipeg MB R2G 1W2
Tel: 204-663-1226; *Fax:* 204-663-1226
e-mail: cbaband@shaw.ca
URL: cba.usask.ca
Ken Epp, Executive Director

Carl Orff Canada Music for Children (COC)
c/o Joan Linklater, 88 Tunis Bay, Winnipeg MB R3T 2X1
Tel: 204-261-1893
URL: www.orffcanada.ca
Joan Linklater, President

Manitoba Band Association
15 Pinecrest Bay, Winnipeg MB R2G 1W2
Tel: 204-663-1226; *Fax:* 204-663-1226
e-mail: mbband@shaw.ca
URL: www.mbband.org
Wendy McCallum, President

Manitoba Chamber Orchestra (MCO)
Portage Place, 393 Portage Ave., #Y300, Winnipeg MB R3B 3H6
Tel: 204-783-7377; *Fax:* 204-783-7383
e-mail: mco@mts.net
URL: www.manitobachamberorchestra.org
Anne Manson, Music Director
Vicki Young, General Manager

Manitoba Opera Association Inc.
Lower Level, Centennial Concert Hall, #105, 555 Main St., Winnipeg MB R3B 1C3
Tel: 204-942-7479; *Fax:* 204-949-0377
e-mail: mbopera@manitobaopera.mb.ca
URL: www.manitobaopera.mb.ca
Affiliation(s): Opera America; Canadian Actor's Equity; Opera.ca
Peter George, President

Western Canadian Music Alliance (WCMA)
#637, 776 Corydon Ave., Winnipeg MB R3M 0Y1
Tel: 204-943-8485; *Fax:* 204-453-1594
e-mail: info@wcmw.ca
URL: www.wcmw.ca
Affiliation(s): Alberta Recording Industry Association; Saskatchewan Recording Industry Association; Manitoba Audio Recording Industry Association
Bob D'Eith, President

Winnipeg Symphony Orchestra Inc. (WSO)
#101, 555 Main St., Winnipeg MB R3B 1C3
Tel: 204-949-3950; *Fax:* 204-956-4271
e-mail: lmarks@wso.mb.ca
URL: www.wso.mb.ca
Trudy Schroeder, Executive Director
Alexander Mickelthwate, Music Director

New Brunswick

Symphony New Brunswick / Symphonie Nouveau-Brunswick
Brunswick Square, 39 King St., Level III, Saint John NB E2L 4W3
Tel: 506-634-8379; *Fax:* 506-634-0843
e-mail: symphony@nbnet.nb.ca
URL: www.symphonynb.com
Affiliation(s): American Federation of Musicians
Caroline Condon, General Manager

Newfoundland and Labrador

Newfoundland Symphony Orchestra Association (NSO)
Arts & Culture Centre, PO Box 1854, St. John's NL A1C 5P9
Tel: 709-722-4441; *Fax:* 709-753-0561
e-mail: nso.orchestra@nso.nfld.net
URL: www.nso-music.com
Peter Gardner, General & Artistic Director
Alasdair Black, Operations Manager
G.C. (Gerry) Germain, Chair

Newfoundland Symphony Youth Orchestra (NSYO)
PO Box 1854, St. John's NL A1C 5P9
Tel: 709-722-4441; *Fax:* 709-753-0561
Peter Gardner, Director

Nova Scotia

African Nova Scotian Music Association (ANSMA)
PO Box 931, 1149 Main St., Dartmouth NS B2Z 1A8
Tel: 902-404-3036; *Fax:* 902-434-0462
e-mail: ansma@eastlink.ca
URL: www.ansma.com
Louis (Lou) Gannon Jr., President

Association of Canadian Choral Conductors (ACCC) / Association des chefs de choeur canadiens
6303 Duncan St., Halifax NS B3L 1K4
Tel: 902-442-7054; *Fax:* 902-442-7050
e-mail: accc@ca.inter.net
URL: www.choralcanada.org
Affiliation(s): Canadian Conference of the Arts; International Federation for Choral Music
Christina Murray, Executive Director
Bridgid Coult, President

Deep Roots Music Cooperative
PO Box 2360, Wolfville NS B4P 2G9
Tel: 902-542-7668
e-mail: info@deeprootsmusic.ca
URL: www.deeprootsmusic.ca/cooperative
Peter Mowat, Chair

Music Nova Scotia
#302, 5516 Spring Garden Rd., Halifax NS B3J 1G6
Tel: 902-423-6271; *Fax:* 902-423-8841
Toll-Free: 888-343-6426
e-mail: info@musicnovascotia.ca
URL: www.musicnovascotia.ca
Brian Doherty, President
Scott Long, Executive Director

Music NWT
Roman Empire Bldg., 5103 51st St., 2nd Fl., Yellowknife NT X1A 1S8
Tel: 867-873-5577; *Fax:* 867-873-5575
e-mail: info@musicnwt.ca
URL: www.musicnwt.ca

Nova Scotia Band Association
355 Branch St, New Glasgow NS B2H 3A5
Tel: 902-751-5996; *Fax:* 902-755-8490
e-mail: admin@novascotiabandassociation.com
URL: www.novascotiabandassociation.com
Barbara Stetter, President

Nova Scotia Youth Orchestra
6199 Chebucto Rd., Halifax NS B3L 1K7
Tel: 902-423-5984
e-mail: nsyo@ns.sympatico.ca
URL: www.novascotiayouthorchestra.com
Dinuk Wijeratne, Music Director

Scotia Chamber Players
6181 Lady Hammond Rd., Halifax NS B3K 2R9
Tel: 902-429-9467; *Fax:* 902-425-6785
e-mail: admin@scotiafestival.ns.ca
URL: www.scotiafestival.ns.ca
Christopher Wilcox, Managing Director

Symphony Nova Scotia (SNS)
Park Lane Mall, PO Box 218, #301, 5657 Spring Garden Rd., Halifax NS B3J 3R4
Tel: 902-421-1300; *Fax:* 902-422-1209
e-mail: info@symns.cohn.dal.ca
URL: www.symphonynovascotia.ca
Erika Beatty, Chief Executive Officer

Ontario

Alliance for Canadian New Music Projects (ACNMP) / Alliance pour des projets de musique canadienne nouvelle
Canadian Music Centre, 20 St. Joseph St., Toronto ON M4Y 1J9
Tel: 416-963-5937; *Fax:* 416-961-7198
e-mail: acnmp@rogers.com
URL: www.acnmp.ca
Ann La Plante, General Manager
Jill Kelman, President

Bach Elgar Choral Society
86 Homewood St., Hamilton ON L8P 2M4
Tel: 905-527-5995; *Fax:* 905-527-0555
e-mail: bachelgar@bellnet.ca
URL: www.bachelgar.com
Affiliation(s): Ontario Choral Federation; Hamilton & Region Arts Council; Council for Business & the Arts in Canada; Canadian Conference of the Arts

Bluegrass Music Association of Central Canada (BMACC)
c/o Secretary, 339 Wellington St. N, Woodstock ON N4S 6S6
Tel: 519-539-8967
e-mail: weslowe@bmacc.ca
URL: www.bmacc.ca
Denis Chadbourn, President

Brampton Symphony Orchestra
PO Box 93091, Stn. Brampton South, 499 Main St. South, Brampton ON L6Y 4V8
Tel: 905-459-0853
e-mail: info@bramptonsymphony.com
URL: www.bramptonsymphony.com
Michael Todd, President

Brantford Symphony Orchestra Association Inc.
PO Box 24012, 185 King George Rd., Brantford ON N3R 7X3
Tel: 519-759-8781; *Fax:* 519-759-0842
e-mail: administrator@brantfordsymphony.ca
URL: www.brantfordsymphony.com

Canadian Academy of Recording Arts & Sciences (CARAS) / Académie canadienne des arts et des sciences de l'enregistrement (ACASE)
345 Adelaide St. West, 2nd fl., Toronto ON M5V 1J6
Tel: 416-485-3135; *Fax:* 416-485-4978
Toll-Free: 888-440-5866
e-mail: membership@carasonline.ca
URL: www.carasonline.ca
Ed Robinson, Chair, CARAS & MusiCounts
Melanie Berry, President & Chief Executive Officer, CARAS & MusiCounts
Chris Topping, Vice-President, Events & Special Programming
Alex Heming, Senior Coordinator, Marketing & Fulfillment
Meghan McCabe, Senior Coordinator, Communications

Canadian Association for Music Therapy (CAMT) / Association de musicothérapie du Canada (AMC)
#230, 110 Cumberland St., Toronto ON M5R 3V5
Tel: 416-944-0421; *Fax:* 416-944-0431
Toll-Free: 800-996-2268
e-mail: camt@musictherapy.ca
URL: www.musictherapy.ca
Affiliation(s): World Federation of Music Therapy
Guylaine Vaillancourt, President

Canadian Bureau for the Advancement of Music (CBAM)
Exhibition Place, Toronto ON M6K 3C3
Tel: 416-260-6451
e-mail: moreinfo@thecbam.ca
URL: www.thecbam.ca
Nancy Manning, CAO

Canadian Children's Opera Chorus (CCOC)
Opera Centre, #215, 227 Front St. East, Toronto ON M5A 1E8
Tel: 416-366-0467; *Fax:* 416-366-9204
e-mail: info@canadianchildrensopera.com
URL: www.canadianchildrensopera.com
Ken Hall, General Manager
Ann Cooper Gay, Artistic Director

Canadian Country Music Association (CCMA) / Association de la musique country canadienne
30-B Commercial Rd., Toronto ON M4G 1Z4
Tel: 416-947-1331; *Fax:* 416-947-5924
e-mail: country@ccma.org
URL: www.ccma.org
Sheila Hamilton, Executive Director
Heather Ostertag, Chair
Lynne Foster, Sec.-Treas.

Canadian Disc Jockey Association (CDJA)
PO Box 92, Arva ON N0M 1C0
Fax: 519-472-0242
Toll-Free: 877-472-0653
e-mail: pres@cdja.ca
URL: www.cdja.org

Affiliation(s): American DJ Association; National American Mobile Entertainers
Doug Scott, President

Canadian Independent Music Association (CIMA)
30 St. Patrick St., 2nd Fl., Toronto ON M5T 3A3
Tel: 416-485-3152; *Fax:* 416-485-4373
e-mail: cima@cimamusic.ca
URL: www.cimamusic.ca
Duncan McKie, President
Donna Murphy, Research Director
Sharon Hookway, Membership/Communications
Mary Vrantsidis, International Trade Shows

Canadian League of Composers / La Ligue canadienne de compositeurs
c/o Canadian Music Centre, 20 St. Joseph St., Toronto ON M4Y 1J9
Tel: 416-964-1364
Toll-Free: 877-964-1364
e-mail: info@composition.org
URL: www.composition.org
James Rolfe, President, Ontario

Canadian Music Centre (CMC) / Centre de musique canadienne
Chalmers House, 20 St. Joseph St., Toronto ON M4Y 1J9
Tel: 416-961-6601; *Fax:* 416-961-7198
e-mail: info@musiccentre.ca
URL: www.musiccentre.ca; www.centremusique.ca
Affiliation(s): International Association of Music Information Centres; Canadian Music Libraries Association
Allan G. Bell, President
Elisabeth Bihl, Executive Director

Canadian Music Educators' Association (CMEA) / Association canadienne des éducateurs de musique
#A-430A, Wilfrid Laurier University, Waterloo ON N2L 3C5
Tel: 519-884-0710
e-mail: edwin.wasiak@uleth.ca
URL: www.musiceducationonline.org
Affiliation(s): International Society for Music Education
Betty Hanley, Membership
Ed Wasiak, President

Canadian Music Festival Adjudicators' Association (CMFAA)
c/o School of Music, Queen's University, Kingston ON K7L 3N6
Tel: 613-533-6000; *Fax:* 613-533-6808
e-mail: zuki@queensu.ca
URL: www.cmfaa.ca
John Hansen, Vice-President
Ireneus Zuk, President

Canadian Musical Heritage Society (CMHS) / Société pour le patrimoine musical canadien (SPMC)
#15, 120 Walnut Ct., Ottawa ON K1R 7W2
Tel: 613-237-0550
e-mail: enquiries@cliffordfordpublications.ca
Clifford Ford, Executive Secretary

Canadian Opera Company (COC) / Compagnie d'opéra canadienne
145 Queen St. West, Toronto ON M5A 1E8
Tel: 416-363-8231; *Fax:* 416-363-5584
Toll-Free: 800-250-4653
e-mail: info@coc.ca
URL: www.coc.ca
Affiliation(s): The Canadian Opera Foundation; Canadian Opera Volunteer Committee
Alexander Neef, General Director
Robert Lamb, Managing Director

Canadian Recording Industry Association (CRIA) / Association de l'industrie canadienne de l'enregistrement
85 Mowat Ave., Toronto ON M6K 3E3
Tel: 416-967-7272; *Fax:* 416-967-9415
e-mail: info@cria.ca
URL: www.cria.ca
Graham Henderson, President

Canadian University Music Society (CUMS) / Société de musique des universités canadiennes (SMUC)
c/o Secretariat, #202, 10 Morrow Ave., Toronto ON M6R 2J1
Tel: 416-538-1650; *Fax:* 416-489-1713
e-mail: journals@interlog.com
URL: www.cums-smuc.ca/
Affiliation(s): Social Sciences & Humanities Research Council of Canada
Deanna Oye, President

Cathedral Bluffs Symphony Orchestra (CBSO)
PO Box 51074, 18 Eglinton Sq., Toronto ON M1L 2K2
Tel: 416-879-5566
e-mail: info@cathedralbluffs.com
URL: www.cathedralbluffs.com
Norman Reintamm, Artistic Director
Murray Finkelstein, President

Choirs Ontario
A-1442 Bayview Ave., Toronto ON M4G 3A7
Tel: 416-923-1144; *Fax:* 416-929-0415
Toll-Free: 866-935-1144
e-mail: info@choirsontario.org
URL: www.choirsontario.org
Dean Jobin-Bevans, President

Conservatory Canada
#M-2, 130 King St., London ON N6A 1C5
Tel: 519-433-3147; *Fax:* 519-433-7404
Toll-Free: 800-461-5367
e-mail: mail@conservatorycanada.ca
URL: www.conservatorycanada.ca
Warwick Victoria, Executive Director

Counterpoint Community Orchestra
PO Box 41, 552 Church St., Toronto ON M4Y 2E3
Tel: 416-654-9806
e-mail: info@ccorchestra.org
URL: www.ccorchestra.org
Terry Kowalczuk, Music Director

Deep River Symphony Orchestra (DRSO)
PO Box 1496, Deep River ON K0J 1P0
Tel: 613-586-9385
e-mail: symphony@drso.ca
URL: www.drso.ca
Peter Morris, Music Director
Heather Butterworth, Secretary

Edward Johnson Music Foundation (EJMF)
PO Box 1718, 50 Cork St. East, 2nd Floor, Guelph ON N1H 6Z9
Tel: 519-821-7570; *Fax:* 519-821-4403
e-mail: info@edwardjohnsonmusicfoundation.org
URL: www.edwardjohnsonmusicfoundation.org
Rosemary Smith, Executive Director

Etobicoke Philharmonic Orchestra (EPO)
PO Box 66, Stn. D, Etobicoke ON M9A 4X1
Tel: 416-239-5665; *Fax:* 416-239-5665
e-mail: info@eporchestra.ca
URL: www.eporchestra.ca
Tom Fleming, General Manager
Carolyn McGee, Co-President
Pat Butler, Co-President

The Foundation Assisting Canadian Talent on Recordings (FACTOR)
30 Commercial Rd., Toronto ON M5V 1Z4
Tel: 416-696-2215; *Fax:* 416-351-7311
e-mail: general.info@factor.ca
URL: www.factor.ca
Heather Ostertag, C.M., President/CEO
Phil Gumbley, Director of Operations
Julia Train, Communications Manager

Georgian Bay Symphony (GBS)
PO Box 133, 994 - 3rd Ave. East, Owen Sound ON N4K 5P1
Tel: 519-372-0212; *Fax:* 519-372-9023
e-mail: gbs@bmts.com
URL: www.georgianbaysymphony.ca
Affiliation(s): Owen Sound Chamber of Commerce
Richard Nancarrow, President
John Barnum, Music Director

Guild of Canadian Film Composers (GCFC) / Guilde des compositeurs canadiens de musique de film
PO Box 22059, 45 Overlea Blvd., Toronto ON M4H 1N9
Tel: 416-410-5076; *Fax:* 416-410-4516
Toll-Free: 866-657-1117
e-mail: gcfc@gcfc.ca
URL: www.gcfc.ca
Maria Topalovich, Executive Director

Halton Youth Symphony (HYS)
PO Box 494, Oakville ON L6J 5A8
Tel: 905-616-2760
e-mail: manager@haltonyouthsymphony.com
URL: www.haltonyouthsymphony.com

Hamilton Philharmonic Orchestra
#1002, 105 Main St. East, Hamilton ON L8N 1G6
Tel: 905-526-1677; *Fax:* 905-526-0616
e-mail: communications@hpo.org
URL: www.hpo.org
James Sommerville, Music Director
Annelisa Pedersen, Executive Director

Hamilton Philharmonic Youth Orchestra (HPYO)
299 Fennell Ave. West, Hamilton ON L9C 1G3
Tel: 905-573-9094
e-mail: info@hpyo.com
URL: www.hpyo.com
Paul McCulloch, Music Director & Conductor

Hart House Orchestra
University of Toronto, 7 Hart House Circle, Toronto ON M5S 3H3
Tel: 416-978-5362
e-mail: webmaestro@harthouseorchestra.ca
URL: www.harthouseorchestra.ca
Zoe Dille, Programme Advisor

Huronia Symphony Orchestra (HSO)
PO Box 904, Barrie ON L4M 4Y6
Tel: 705-721-4752; *Fax:* 705-737-0679
e-mail: office@huroniasymphony.ca
URL: www.huroniasymphony.ca
David Chambers, President

International Symphony Orchestra of Sarnia, Ontario & Port Huron, Michigan
225 Davis St., Sarnia ON N7T 1B2
Tel: 519-337-7775; *Fax:* 519-337-1822
e-mail: iso@rivernet.net
URL: www.theiso.org
Affiliation(s): American Federation of Symphony Orchestras; Michigan Orchestra Association
Jerome David Summers, Music Director

International Youth Symphony Orchestra
118 North Victoria St., Sarnia ON N7T 5W9
Tel: 519-337-7775; *Fax:* 519-337-1822

Kingston Symphony Association (KSA)
PO Box 1616, #206, 11 Princess St., Kingston ON K7L 5C8
Tel: 613-546-9729; *Fax:* 613-546-8580
e-mail: info@kingstonsymphony.on.ca
URL: www.kingstonsymphony.on.ca
Andrea Haughton, General Manager

Kingston Youth Orchestra
PO Box 1616, #206, 11 Princess St., Kingston ON K7L 5C8
Tel: 613-546-9729; *Fax:* 613-546-8580
Affiliation(s): Kingston Symphony Association

Kitchener-Waterloo Chamber Orchestra (KWCO)
197 Weber St. East, Kitchener ON N2H 1E5
Tel: 519-744-3828; *Fax:* 519-749-0832
e-mail: kwchamberorchestra@gmail.com
URL: www.kwchamberorchestra.ca
Joanna Armbruster, President
Graham Coles, Music Director

Kitchener-Waterloo Symphony Orchestra Association Inc. (KWSOA)
36 King St. West, Kitchener ON N2G 1A3
Tel: 519-745-4711; *Fax:* 519-745-4474
Toll-Free: 888-745-4717
e-mail: info@kwsymphony.on.ca
URL: www.kwsymphony.on.ca
Genevieve Twomey, Executive Director

Kitchener-Waterloo Symphony Youth Orchestra (KWSYO)
36 King St. West, Kitchener ON N2G 1A3
Tel: 519-745-4711
Toll-Free: 888-745-4717
e-mail: info@kwsymphony.on.ca
URL: www.kwsymphony.on.ca
Barbara Kaplanek, Youth Strings Conductor
Julie Baumgartel, Youth Sinfonia Conductor/Director, KWSYO Chamber Music
Paul Pulford, Youth Orchestra Conductor
Peter Maness, Valhalla Brass Conductor

Kiwanis Music Festival Association of Greater Toronto
1422-A Bayview Ave., Toronto ON M4G 3A7
Tel: 416-487-5885; *Fax:* 416-487-5784
e-mail: kiwanismusic@bellnet.ca
URL: kiwanismusictoronto.org/index.html
Pam Allen, General Manager

Korean-Canadian Symphony Orchestra (KGSO)
#203, 703 Bloor St. West, Toronto ON M6G 1L5
Tel: 416-534-3760
e-mail: info@kcso.ca
URL: www.kcso.ca
Myung Sook Kim, President
Richard Lee, Music Director

London Community Orchestra (LCO)
c/o 838 Wellington St. N., London ON N6A 3S7
Tel: 519-433-2074
e-mail: sally.vernon@odyssey.on.ca
URL: www.ontera.net/~lco/
Leonard Ingrao, Music Director
Margaret Whitby, Manager
Ray Thomson, President

London Youth Symphony (LYS)
PO Box 553, Stn. B, London ON N6A 4W8
Tel: 519-686-8070
e-mail: info@londonyouthsymphony.org
URL: www.londonyouthsymphony.org
Len Ingrao, Musical Director
Daina Janitis, Manager

Mariposa Folk Foundation
PO Box 383, Orillia ON L3V 6J8
Tel: 705-326-3655; *Fax:* 705-329-4099
e-mail: info@mariposafolk.com
URL: www.mariposafolk.com
Catherine Brennan, President

Mississauga Youth Orchestra
159 Cavendish Ct., Mississauga ON L6J 5S3
Tel: 905-815-8125; *Fax:* 905-815-8516
e-mail: email@myomusic.ca
URL: www.myomusic.ca
Kathy Grell, Manager

Music for Young Children (MYC) / Musique pour jeunes enfants
39 Leacock Way, Kanata ON K2K 1T1
Tel: 613-592-7565; *Fax:* 613-592-9353
Toll-Free: 800-561-1692
e-mail: myc@myc.com
URL: www.myc.com
Janice Reade, Manager, Public Relations

Music Industries Association of Canada (MIAC) / Association canadienne des industries de la musique
#807, 505 Consumers Rd., Toronto ON M2J 4V8
Tel: 416-490-1871; *Fax:* 416-490-0369
Toll-Free: 877-480-6422
e-mail: info@miac.net
URL: www.miac.net
Affiliation(s): Music Distributors Association - USA; National Association of Music Merchants - USA
Barbara Cole, General Manager

National Arts Centre Orchestra of Canada (NACO) / Orchestre du Centre national des Arts (OCNA)
PO Box 1534, Stn. B, 53 Elgin St., Ottawa ON K1P 5W1
Tel: 613-947-7000
Toll-Free: 866-850-2787
e-mail: info@nac-cna.ca
URL: www.nac-cna.ca
Pinchas Zukerman, Music Director
Alex Gazalé, Production Director
Christopher Deacon, Managing Director

National Shevchenko Musical Ensemble Guild of Canada
626 Bathurst St., Toronto ON M5S 2R1
Tel: 416-533-2725; *Fax:* 416-533-6348
e-mail: info_sme@bellnet.ca
URL: www.shevchenkomusic.com
Ginger Kautto, General Manager

National Youth Orchestra Association of Canada
#500, 59 Adelaide St. East, Toronto ON M5C 1K6
Tel: 416-532-4470; *Fax:* 416-532-6879
Toll-Free: 888-532-4470
e-mail: info@nyoc.org
URL: www.nyoc.org
Barbara Smith, Executive Director

Niagara Youth Orchestra Association
#148, 12 - 111 Fourth Ave., St Catharines ON L2S 3P5
Tel: 905-704-0559; *Fax:* 905-704-0558
e-mail: nyo@vaxxine.com
URL: www.niagarayouthorchestra.ca
Affiliation(s): Niagara Suzuki
Michael Newnham, Music Director

Northumberland Orchestra Society (NOC)
PO Box 1012, Cobourg ON K9A 4W4
Tel: 905-377-1477
e-mail: norchestra@norchestra.org
URL: www.norchestra.org
Michael Newnham, Music Director & Conductor

Oakville Chamber Orchestra
PO Box 76036, 1500 Upper Middle Rd. West, Oakville ON L6M 3H5
Tel: 905-483-6787
e-mail: mail@oakvillechamber.org
URL: www.oakvillechamber.org
Charlotte Meissner, President
Charles Demuynck, Music Director

Oakville Symphony Orchestra (OSO)
#114, 99 Bronte Rd., Oakville ON L6L 3B7
Tel: 905-338-1462; *Fax:* 905-338-7954
e-mail: oakville.symphony@cogeco.ca
URL: www.oakvillesymphony.com
Affiliation(s): Oakville Arts Council
Peggy Steele, General Manager

Ontario Band Association
c/o Membership Co-ordinator, 459 Concord Ave., Toronto ON M6H 2P9
e-mail: membership@onband.ca
URL: www.onband.ca
Sarah Arcand, President
Sommer Buttu, Secretary

Opera Lyra Ottawa
#110, 2 Daly Ave., Ottawa ON K1N 6E2
Tel: 613-233-9200; *Fax:* 613-233-5431
Toll-Free: 877-233-5972
e-mail: marketing@operalyra.com
URL: www.operalyra.ca
Elizabeth Howarth, General Director

Opera Ontario
Opera Hamilton, #905, 105 Main St. East, Hamilton ON L8N 1G6
Tel: 905-527-7627; *Fax:* 905-527-0014
Toll-Free: 800-575-1381
e-mail: info@operaontario.com
URL: www.operaontario.com
Alice Willems, President
David Speers, General Director

Opera.ca
#410, 174 Spadina Ave., Toronto ON M5T 2C2
Tel: 416-591-7222
e-mail: info@opera.ca
URL: www.opera.ca
Christina Loewen, Executive Director
Sandra Cina, Coordinator, Membership & Communications

Orchestra London Canada Inc.
609 Wellington St., London ON N6A 3R6
Tel: 519-679-8558; *Fax:* 519-679-8914
e-mail: rgloor@orchestralondon.ca
URL: www.orchestralondon.ca
Robert Gloor, Executive Director
Brent Kelman, President

Orchestra Toronto (OT)
#402, 131 Beecroft Rd., Toronto ON M2N 6G9
Tel: 416-467-7142
e-mail: otoronto@on.aibn.com
URL: www.orchestratoronto.ca
Judy Mann, Contact
Erroll Gay, Music Director

Orchestras Canada (OC) / Orchestres Canada
230-460 College St., Toronto ON M6G 1A1
Tel: 416-366-8834; *Fax:* 416-366-1780
e-mail: info@oc.ca
URL: orchestrascanada.org
Affiliation(s): American Symphony Orchestra League; International Alliance of Orchestra Associations
Katherine Carleton, Executive Director

Orchestras Mississauga
4141 Living Arts Dr., Mississauga ON L5B 4B8
Tel: 905-615-4405; *Fax:* 905-615-4402
e-mail: symphony.info@livingarts.on.ca
URL: www.mississaugasymphony.ca
Affiliation(s): Mississauga Board of Trade; Orchestras Canada; Mississauga Arts Council
John Barnum, Music Director
Eileen Keown, General Manager

Orillia Youth Symphony Orchestra (OYSO)
168 Parkview Ave., Orillia ON L3V 4M3
Tel: 705-326-7548
URL: www.oyso.ca
Mayumi Kumagai, Music Director

Oshawa-Durham Symphony Orchestra (ODSO)
PO Box 444, Oshawa ON L1H 7L5
Tel: 905-579-6711; *Fax:* 905-987-3083
e-mail: contact@odso.ca
URL: www.odso.ca
John G. Patte, Business Manager
Ronald H. Stead, Chair

Ottawa Symphony Orchestra Inc. (OSO) / Orchestre symphonique d'Ottawa
#250, 2 Daly Ave., Ottawa ON K1N 6E2
Tel: 613-231-7802; *Fax:* 613-231-3610
e-mail: oso@on.aibn.com
URL: www.ottawasymphony.com
David Currie, Music Director

Ottawa Youth Orchestra Academy (OYO) / L'Orchestre des jeunes d'Ottawa
#1, 54 Beech Street, Ottawa ON K1S 3J6
Tel: 613-233-9318; *Fax:* 613-233-5038
e-mail: info@oyoa-aojo.ca
URL: www.oyoa-aojo.ca
John Gomez, Music Director

Pembroke Symphony Orchestra
PO Box 374, Pembroke ON K8A 6X6
Tel: 613-687-2660
e-mail: info@pembrokesymphony.org
URL: pembrokesymphony.org
Angus Armstrong, Concertmaster
Gail Marion, President

Peterborough Symphony Orchestra (PSO)
PO Box 1135, Peterborough ON K9J 7H4
Tel: 705-742-1992; *Fax:* 705-742-2077
Toll-Free: 877-742-1992
e-mail: info@thepso.org
URL: www.thepso.org
Affiliation(s): Peterborough Chamber of Commerce
Michael Newnham, Music Director

The Queen of Puddings Music Theatre Company
The Case Good Warehouse, Bldg. 74, Studio 206, 55 Mill St., Toronto ON M5A 3C4
Tel: 416-203-4149; *Fax:* 416-203-8027
e-mail: queenofpuddings@bellnet.ca
URL: www.queenofpuddingsmusictheatre.com
Dairine Ni Mheadhra, Artistic Director
John Hess, Artistic Director

Quinte Symphony
PO Box 23087, Belleville ON K8P 5J3
Tel: 613-395-3756
e-mail: info@quintesymphony.com
URL: www.quintesymphony.com
Gordon Craig, Music Director
Judith Chalmers, President

Royal Canadian College of Organists (RCCO) / Collège royal canadien des organistes (CRCO)
#202, 204 St. George St., Toronto ON M5R 2N5
Tel: 416-929-6400; *Fax:* 416-929-2265
e-mail: manager@rcco.ca
URL: www.rcco.ca
Valerie Hall, President

Royal Conservatory Orchestra
273 Bloor Street West, Toronto ON M5S 1W2
Tel: 416-408-2824; *Fax:* 416-408-3096
e-mail: glenngouldschool@rcmusic.ca
URL: www.rcmusic.ca
Affiliation(s): The Glenn Gould School
Mervon Mehta, Executive Director

Sault Symphony Association / Orchestre symphonique de Sault Ste-Marie
#2, 121 Brock St., Sault Ste Marie ON P6A 3B6
Tel: 705-945-5337; *Fax:* 705-945-8865
e-mail: symphony@soonet.ca
URL: www.saultsymphony.com
Patti Gardi, General Manager

Scarborough Philharmonic Orchestra
#209, 3007 Kingston Rd., Toronto ON M1M 1P1
Tel: 416-429-0007
e-mail: spo@spo.ca
URL: www.spo.ca

Songwriters Association of Canada (SAC) / Association des auteurs-compositeurs canadiens
129 John St., Toronto ON M5V 2E2
Tel: 416-961-1588; *Fax:* 416-961-2040
Toll-Free: 866-456-7664
e-mail: sacadmin@songwriters.ca
URL: www.songwriters.ca
Don Quarles, Executive Director
Eddie Schwartz, President

Soundstreams Canada
#200, 57 Spadina Ave., Toronto ON M5V 2J2
Tel: 416-504-1282; *Fax:* 416-504-1285
e-mail: info@soundstreams.ca
URL: www.soundstreams.ca
Jennifer Winchester, General Manager

Sudbury Symphony Orchestra Association Inc. (SSO) / Orchestre symphonique de Sudbury inc
#266, 303 York St., Sudbury ON P3E 2A5
Tel: 705-673-1280; *Fax:* 705-673-1434
e-mail: symphon1@bellnet.ca
URL: www.sudburysymphony.com
Victor Sawa, Artistic Director
Marg Barry, Executive Director

Sudbury Youth Orchestra Inc.
PO Box 2241, Stn. A, Sudbury ON P3A 4S1
Tel: 705-566-8101
e-mail: info@sudburyyouthorchestra.ca
URL: www.sudburyyouthorchestra.ca
Jamie Arrowsmith, Music Director
Mary Salem Charette, Director

Symphony Hamilton
PO Box 89007, 991 King St. West, Hamilton ON L8S 4R5
Tel: 905-526-6690
e-mail: info@symphonyhamilton.ca
URL: www.symphonyhamilton.ca
Affiliation(s): Hamilton & Region Arts Council
James R. McKay, Music Director & Conductor
Brenda Sandberg, General Manager
Sydney Hassel, President

Tafelmusik Baroque Orchestra & Chamber Choir
PO Box 14, 427 Bloor St. West, Toronto ON M5S 1X7
Tel: 416-964-9562; *Fax:* 416-964-2782
e-mail: info@tafelmusik.org
URL: www.tafelmusik.org
Tricia Baldwin, Managing Director
Tricia Baldwin, Managing Director

Tapestry New Opera Works
The Cannery, Studio 316, #58, 55 Mill St., Toronto ON M5A 3C4
Tel: 416-537-6066; *Fax:* 416-537-7841
e-mail: information@tapestrynewopera.com
URL: www.tapestrynewopera.com
Wayne Strongman, Artistic Director

Thunder Bay Symphony Orchestra Association (TBSO)
PO Box 29192, Thunder Bay ON P7B 6P9
Tel: 807-345-4331; *Fax:* 807-622-1927
e-mail: info@tbso.ca
URL: www.tbso.ca
Elizabeth Poulin, President
Leanne Atkinson, General Manager
Geoffrey Moull, Music Director

Timmins Symphony Orchestra
PO Box 1365, Timmins ON P4N 7N2
Tel: 705-267-1006; *Fax:* 705-267-1006
e-mail: tsoffice@ntl.sympatico.ca
URL: www.timsym.com

Toronto Chinese Youth Orchestra
21 Holmesdale Dr., Markham ON L6C 1S9
Tel: 905-887-7828
e-mail: tcyo@rogers.com
URL: www.tcyo.ca
Tak-Ng Lai, Music Director

Toronto Downtown Jazz Society
82 Bleecker St., Toronto ON M4X 1L8
Tel: 416-928-2033; *Fax:* 416-928-0533
e-mail: tdjs@tojazz.com
URL: www.torontojazz.com
Patrick Taylor, CEO/Executive Producer
Josh Grossman, Artistic Director

The Toronto Mendelssohn Choir
60 Simcoe St., Toronto ON M5J 2H5
Tel: 416-598-0422; *Fax:* 416-598-2992
e-mail: manager@tmchoir.org
URL: www.tmchoir.org
Cynthia Hawkins, Executive Director

Toronto Philharmonia
#109, 1210 Sheppard Ave. East, Toronto ON M2K 1E3
Tel: 416-499-2204; *Fax:* 416-490-9739
e-mail: office@torontophil.on.ca
URL: www.torontophil.on.ca
Affiliation(s): Ontario Federation of Symphony Orchestras
Kerry Stratton, Music Director

Toronto Philharmonia Youth Orchestra
PO Box 134, Port Hope ON L1W 3W3
Tel: 416-797-2138
Toll-Free: 866-460-5596
e-mail: info@ljyo.ca
URL: www.ljyo.ca
Michael Lyons, Music Director

Toronto Sinfonietta
400 St. Clair Avenue E, Toronto ON M4T 1P5
Tel: 416-410-4379; *Fax:* 416-233-1054
e-mail: info@torontosinfonietta.com
URL: www.torontosinfonietta.com
Krzysztof Liebert, President
Matthew Jaskiewicz, Music Director

Toronto Symphony Orchestra (TSO)
212 King St. West, 6th Fl., Toronto ON M5H 1K5
Tel: 416-593-7769; *Fax:* 416-977-2912
URL: www.tso.ca
Peter Oundjian, Musical Director
Andrew R. Shaw, President/CEO

Toronto Symphony Youth Orchestra (TSYO)
212 King St. West, 6th Fl., Toronto ON M5H 1K5
Tel: 416-593-7769; *Fax:* 416-977-2912
e-mail: cmatt@tso.ca
URL: www.tso.on.ca
Affiliation(s): Toronto Symphony Orchestra
Christy DiFelice, Manager

University of Toronto Symphony Orchestra
Faculty of Music, University of Toronto, 80 Queen's Park Cres., Toronto ON M5S 2C5
Tel: 416-978-3733; *Fax:* 416-946-3353
e-mail: performance.music@utoronto.ca
URL: www.music.utoronto.ca
David Briskin, Conductor

University of Western Ontario Symphony Orchestra (UWOSO)
Faculty of Music, University of Western Ontario, 1151 Richmond St. North, London ON N6A 3K7
Tel: 519-661-2043; *Fax:* 519-661-3531
e-mail: music@uwo.ca
URL: www.music.uwo.ca

Wilfrid Laurier University Symphony Orchestra
Faculty of Music, 75 University Ave. West, Waterloo ON N2L 3C5
Tel: 519-884-0710; *Fax:* 519-747-9129
e-mail: jdupuis@wlu.ca
Paul Pulford, General Manager/Music Director

Windsor Symphony Orchestra (WSO)
487 Ouellette Ave., Windsor ON N9A 4J2
Tel: 519-973-1238; *Fax:* 519-973-0764
Toll-Free: 888-327-8327
e-mail: jgalli@windsorsymphony.com
URL: www.windsorsymphony.com
Affiliation(s): American Symphony Orchestra League
Jeth Mill, Exectuive Director
Rob Gold, Director of Marketing
Sarah Boonstra, Director of Operations

York Symphony Orchestra Inc.
PO Box 355, Richmond Hill ON L4C 4Y6
Tel: 416-410-0860
e-mail: yorksymphonyorchestra@hotmail.com
URL: www.yorksymphony.ca
Affiliation(s): York Symphony Youth Orchestra
Gregory Burton, Music Director

Prince Edward Island

East Coast Music Association (ECMA) / Association de la musique de la côte est
#70, 90 University Ave., Charlottetown PE C1A 4K9
Tel: 902-892-9040; *Fax:* 902-892-9041
e-mail: ecma@ecma.ca
URL: www.ecma.ca
Affiliation(s): Music Industry Associations; Canadian Academy of Recording Arts & Science; FACTOR

Music PEI
#70, 90 University Ave., Charlottetown PE C1A 4K9
Tel: 902-894-6734
e-mail: music@musicpei.com
URL: www.musicpei.com
Shannon Pratt, President
Rob Oakie, Executive Director

Prince Edward Island Symphony Society (PEISO)
PO Box 185, 146 Richmond St., Charlottetown PE C1A 7K4
Tel: 902-892-4333
e-mail: peiso@peisymphony.com
URL: www.peisymphony.com
Annette Campbell, Contact

Québec

Académie de musique du Québec (AMQ)
CP 818, Succ. C, 1231, rue Panet, Montréal QC H2L 4L6
Tél: 514-528-1961; *Téléc:* 514-528-7572
Courriel: prixdeurope@videotron.ca
Jean Marchand, Président

Alliance des chorales du Québec (ACQ)
CP 1000, Succ. M, 4545, av Pierre-de-Coubertin, Montréal QC H1V 3R2
Tél: 514-252-3020; *Téléc:* 514-252-3222
Courriel: information@chorale.qc.ca
URL: www.chorale.qc.ca
Catherine Girard, Directrice générale

Association québécoise de l'industrie du disque, du spectacle et de la vidéo (ADISQ)
6420, rue Saint-Denis, Montréal QC H2S 2R7
Tél: 514-842-5147; *Téléc:* 514-842-7762
Courriel: info@adisq.com
URL: www.adisq.com

Canadian Amateur Musicians (CAMMAC) / Musiciens amateurs du Canada
85 Cammac Rd., Harrington QC J8G 2T2
Tel: 819-687-3938; *Fax:* 819-687-3323
Toll-Free: 888-622-8755
e-mail: national@cammac.ca
URL: www.cammac.ca
Harry Qualman, President
Raymond Vles, Vice-President
Rachel Gagnon, Secretary
Roland Wilk, Treasurer
Radu Kaufman, Executive Director
Patricia Abbott, Artistic Director
Johanne Guérin, Group Coordinator
Solange Marquis, Comptroller

Canadian Music Competitions Inc. / Concours de musique du Canada inc.
#220, 1450, City Councillors, Montréal QC H3A 2E6
Tel: 514-284-5398; *Fax:* 514-284-6828
Toll-Free: 877-879-1959
e-mail: info@cmcnational.com
URL: www.cmcnational.com
Raymonde Boutet, Présidente

Chants Libres, compagnie lyrique de création
#303, 1908, rue Panet, Montréal QC H2L 3A2
Tél: 514-841-2642; *Téléc:* 514-841-2640
Courriel: creation@chantslibres.org
URL: www.chantslibres.org
Pauline Vaillancourt, Directrice générale

Concerts symphoniques de Sherbrooke inc. (CSS) / Sherbrooke Symphony Orchestra
Domain Howard, Pavillon 1, CP 610, 1300, boul de Portland, Sherbrooke QC J1H 5H9
Tél: 819-821-0227; *Téléc:* 819-821-1959
Courriel: oss@abacom.com
URL: www.css-oss.com
Affiliation(s): Conseil Québecois de la Musique
Michel Bédard, Président

Stéphane Laforest, Directeur artistique

Ensemble contemporain de Montréal (ECM+)
3890 rue Clark, Montréal QC H2W 1W6
Tél: 514-524-0173; *Téléc:* 514-524-0179
Courriel: info@ecm.qc.ca
URL: www.ecm.qc.ca
Natalie Watanabe, Directrice générale

Ensemble vocal Ganymède
CP 476, Succ. C, Montréal QC H2L 4K4
Tél: 514-528-6302
Courriel: contacter@evganymede.com
URL: www.evganymede.com
Yvan Sabourin, Directeur

Fédération des harmonies du Québec (FHQ)
CP 1000, Succ. M, 4545, av Pierre-de-Coubertin, Montréal QC H1V 3R2
Tél: 514-252-3026; *Téléc:* 514-251-8038
Courriel: fhq@generation.net
Affiliation(s): Fédération des associations de musiciens éducateurs du Québec

Jeunesses Musicales of Canada (JMC) / Jeunesses musicales du Canada
305, av du Mont-Royal est, Montréal QC H2T 1P8
Tel: 514-845-4108; *Fax:* 514-845-8241
e-mail: info@jeunessesmusicales.com
URL: www.jeunessesmusicales.ca
Jacques Marquis, Executive & Artistic Director

Musicaction
#2, 4385, rue Saint-Hubert, Montréal QC H2J 2X1
Tél: 514-861-8444; *Téléc:* 514-861-4423
Ligne sans frais: 800-861-5561
Courriel: info@musicaction.ca
URL: www.musicaction.ca
Andrée Ménard, Directrice générale

L'Opéra de Montréal (ODM) / Montréal Opera
260, boul de Maisonneuve ouest, Montréal QC H2X 1Y9
Tel: 514-985-2222; *Fax:* 514-985-2219
e-mail: info@operademontreal.com
URL: www.operademontreal.com
Affiliation(s): Professional Opera Companies of Canada; Opera America
Pierre Dufour, General & Production Director
Christine Krebs, Administrative Director
Michel Beulac, Artistic Director
Monique Denis, Donations & Sponsorship Manager
Pierre Vachon, Communications & Marketing Director
Alexandre Taillefer, Chair
Chantal Lambert, Atelier Lyrique Program Director

Opéra de Québec
1220, av Taché, Québec QC G1R 3B4
Tél: 418-529-4142; *Téléc:* 418-529-3735
Courriel: operaqc@mediom.qc.ca
URL: www.operadequebec.qc.ca
Gaston Déry, Président

Orchestre de chambre de Montréal (OCM) / Montréal Chamber Orchestra (MCO)
5476 Côte St-Antoine, Montréal QC H4A 1R2
Tél: 514-871-1224; *Téléc:* 514-871-8967
Courriel: info@mco-ocm.qc.ca
URL: www.mco-ocm.qc.ca
Wanda Kaluzny, Music Director

Orchestre symphonique de Montréal
260, boul de Maisonneuve ouest, 2e étage, Montréal QC H2X 1Y9
Tél: 514-842-3402; *Téléc:* 514-842-0728
URL: www.osm.ca
Madeleine Careau, Chef de la direction
René Mandel, Directeur musical

Orchestre symphonique de Québec
401, av Grande Allée est, Québec QC G1R 2J5
Tél: 418-643-8486; *Téléc:* 418-646-9665
Courriel: billetterie@osq.qc.ca
URL: www.osq.qc.ca
Jean Letarte, Directeur artistique

Orchestre symphonique de Trois-Rivières (OSTR)
CP 1281, Trois-Rivières QC G9A 5K8
Tél: 819-373-5340; *Téléc:* 819-373-6693
Courriel: administration@ostr.ca
URL: www.ostr.ca
Affiliation(s): Guilde des musiciens (AFM)
Thérèse Boutin, Directrice générale
Jacques Lacombe, Directeur artistique
Jean-Marc Vanasse, Président

Orchestre symphonique des jeunes de la Montérégie
31, rue Lorne, Saint-Lambert QC J4P 2G7
Tél: 450-923-3733
Courriel: courrier@aojm.org
URL: www.aojm.org
Jean-Claude Paré, Président

Orchestre symphonique des jeunes de Montréal (OSJM)
CP 83566, Succ. Succursale Garnier, Montréal QC H2J 4E9
Tél: 514-645-0311; *Téléc:* 514-524-9894
Courriel: osjmontreal@gmail.ca
URL: www.osjm.org
Jean-Paul Lejeune, Président

Orchestre symphonique des jeunes du West Island (OSJWI) / West Island Youth Symphony Orchestra (WIYSO)
CP 1028, Succ. Pointe-Claire, Pointe-Claire QC H9S 4H9
Tél: 514-633-1128; *Téléc:* 514-633-1129
Courriel: info@osjwi.qc.ca
URL: www.osjwi.qc.ca
Affiliation(s): Association des orchestres de jeunes du Québec
Isabelle Delage, Présidente

Orchestre symphonique des jeunes Philippe-Filion
2100, boul des Hêtres, Shawinigan QC G9N 8R8
Tél: 819-539-6000; *Téléc:* 819-539-2400
Courriel: morind03@cgocable.ca
Monique Gagnon Carbonneau, Directrice Musicale

Orchestre symphonique du Saguenay-Lac-St-Jean (OSSLSJ)
202, rue Jacques-Cartier est, Chicoutimi QC G7H 6R8
Tél: 418-545-3409; *Téléc:* 418-545-8287
Courriel: info@lorchestre.org
URL: www.lorchestre.org
Jacques Clément, Directeur artisique

Orchestre symphonique régional Abitibi-Témiscamingue
CP 2305, Rouyn-Noranda QC J9X 5A9
Tél: 819-762-0043; *Téléc:* 819-762-0274
Courriel: osr@tlb.sympatico.ca
URL: culture-at.org/osr
Réginald Grenier, Président

Organization of Canadian Symphony Musicians (OCSM) / Organisation des musiciens d'orchestres symphoniques du Canada (OMOSC)
#6, 445, rue Gerard-Morrisset, Québec QC G1S 4V5
Tel: 418-688-0801
URL: www.ocsm-omosc.org
Affiliation(s): Association of Canadian Orchestras; Canadian Conference of the Arts
Francine Schutzman, President
Eline Brock Sanheim, First Vice-President
David Brown, 2nd Vice-President
Robert Fraser, Secretary
Greg Sheldon, Treasurer

Société chorale de Saint-Lambert / St. Lambert Choral Society
CP 36546, Succ. CSP Victoria, Saint-Lambert QC J4P 3S8
URL: www.chorale-stlambert.qc.ca
Nancy Kirkwood, President
David Christiani, Music Director
Kimberley Bartczak, Accompanist

Société Pro Musica Inc. / Pro Musica Society Inc.
3450, rue Saint-Urbain, Montréal QC H2X 2N5
Tél: 514-845-0532; *Téléc:* 514-845-1500
Ligne sans frais: 877-445-0532
Courriel: concerts@promusica.qc.ca
URL: www.promusica.qc.ca
Pierre Rolland, Directeur artistique
Monique Dubé, Directrice générale

Saskatchewan

Barbershop Harmony Society
110, 7th Ave. North, Nashville TN 372033704 USA
Fax: 615-313-7620
Toll-Free: 800-876-7464
e-mail: info@barbershop.org
URL: www.barbershop.org
Ed Watson, CEO

Regina Symphony Orchestra (RSO)
2424 College Ave., Regina SK S4P 1C8
Tel: 306-586-9555; *Fax:* 306-586-2133
Toll-Free: 800-667-8497
e-mail: info@reginasymphony.com
URL: www.reginasymphony.com
Affiliation(s): Saskatchewan Arts Alliance
Victor Sawa, Musical Director
Natasha Bood, Executive Director

Saskatchewan Band Association (SBA)
34 Sunset Dr. North, Yorkton SK S3N 3K9
Tel: 306-783-2263; *Fax:* 306-783-2060
Toll-Free: 877-475-2263
e-mail: sask.band@sasktel.net
URL: www.saskband.org
Adrian Bourgeois, President
Christa MacBride, Vice-President
Chistin Dorgan-Lee, Secretary
Aaron Sikora, Treasurer

Saskatchewan Orchestral Association (SOA)
PO Box 87, Hanley SK S0G 2E0
Tel: 306-544-2230; *Fax:* 306-544-2718
e-mail: soa1@sasktel.net
URL: www.saskorchestras.com
Affiliation(s): SaskCulture
Kathryn Peters, Contact

Saskatoon Symphony Society (SSO)
Standard Life Bldg., #120, 128 Fourth Ave. South, Saskatoon SK S7K 1M8
Tel: 306-665-6414; *Fax:* 306-652-3364
e-mail: saskatoon.symphony@sasktel.net
URL: www.saskatoonsymphony.org
Catherine McKeehan, General Manager

Saskatoon Youth Orchestra
1610 Morgan Ave., Saskatoon SK S7H 2S1
Tel: 306-373-6408; *Fax:* 306-955-6336
e-mail: syo@sasktel.net
URL: toeww.sasktelwebsite.net/SYO.html
Wayne Toews, Music Director

South Saskatchewan Youth Orchestra (SSYO)
101 Leopold Cres., Regina SK S4T 6N5
Tel: 306-586-3007; *Fax:* 306-586-2133
e-mail: ssyo.ca@gmail.com
URL: www.ssyo.ca
Affiliation(s): Regina Symphony Orchestra
Alan Denike, Music Director

Yukon Territory

Jazz Yukon
PO Box 31307, Whitehorse YT Y1A 5P7
Tel: 867-633-3300
e-mail: info@jazzyukon.ca
URL: www.jazzyukon.ca

Performing Arts - Theatre

Alberta

Alberta Playwrights' Network (APN)
2633 Hochwald Ave. SW, Calgary AB T3E 7K2
Tel: 403-269-8564; *Fax:* 403-265-6773
Toll-Free: 800-268-8564
e-mail: admin@albertaplaywrights.com
URL: www.albertaplaywrights.com
Johanne Deleeuw, Executive Director
Brian Dooley, Edmonton Liaison

Evergreen Theatre Society
2633 Hochwald Ave. SW, Calgary AB T3E 7K2
Tel: 403-228-1384; *Fax:* 403-229-1385
Toll-Free: 877-840-9746
e-mail: info@evergreentheatre.com
URL: www.evergreentheatre.com
Lisa Ryan, Director, Residency
Sean Fraser, Executive Director

New West Theatre Society
#111, 210A - 12A St. North, Lethbridge AB T1J 0P5
Tel: 403-381-9378
e-mail: info@newwesttheatre.com
URL: www.newwesttheatre.com
Nicholas Hanson, Artistic Director
Jeremy Mason, General Manager

Theatre Alberta Society
11759 Groat Rd., 3rd Fl., Edmonton AB T5M 3K6
Tel: 780-422-8162; *Fax:* 780-422-2663
Toll-Free: 888-422-8160
e-mail: theatreab@theatrealberta.com
URL: www.theatrealberta.com
Marie Gynane-Willis, Executive Director

Theatre Calgary
220 - 9 Ave. SE, Calgary AB T2G 5C4
Tel: 403-294-7440; *Fax:* 403-294-7493
e-mail: info@theatrecalgary.com
URL: www.theatrecalgary.com
Tom McCabe, President
Dennis Garnhum, Artistic Director

Theatre Network (1975) Society
10708 - 124 St., Edmonton AB T5M 0H1
Tel: 780-453-2440; *Fax:* 780-453-2596
e-mail: info@theartnetwork.ca
URL: www.attheroxy.com
Affiliation(s): Edmonton Arts Council
Jill Roszell, General Manager
Bradley Moss, Artistic Director

British Columbia

Bard on the Beach Theatre Society
#301, 601 Cambie St., Vancouver BC V6B 2P1
Tel: 604-737-0625; *Fax:* 604-737-0425
Toll-Free: 877-739-0559
e-mail: info@bardonthebeach.org
URL: www.bardonthebeach.org
Christopher Gaze, Artistic Director
Robert Barr, Managing Director

British Columbia Drama Association
PO Box 2031, #7, 10 Commercial St., Nanaimo BC V9R 6X6
Tel: 250-591-0018; *Fax:* 250-591-0027
e-mail: info@theatrebc.org
URL: www.theatrebc.org
Affiliation(s): Centre for the Arts Nanaimo
Robb Mowbray, Executive Director
Ray Mordan, President
Ray Mordan, Sec.-Treas.

First Pacific Theatre Society
1440 - 12 Ave. West, Vancouver BC V6H 1M8
Tel: 604-731-5483; *Fax:* 604-733-3880
e-mail: info@pacifictheatre.org
URL: www.pacifictheatre.org
Affiliation(s): Professional Association of Canadian Theatres
Ron Reed, Artistic Director
Alison Chisholm, Theatre Administrator
Frank Nickel, Production Manager
Andrea Loewen, Director, Public Relations
Cindy McPherson, Business Manager

First Vancouver Theatre Space Society (FVTS)
c/o Vancouver Fringe Festival, 1398 Cartwright St., Vancouver BC V6H 3R8
Tel: 604-257-0350; *Fax:* 604-253-1924
e-mail: info@vancouverfringe.com
URL: www.vancouverfringe.com
Eduardo Ottoni, Production Manager
David Jordan, Executive Director

Greater Vancouver Professional Theatre Alliance (GVPTA)
1405 Anderson St., 3rd Fl., Vancouver BC V6H 3R5
Tel: 604-608-6799; *Fax:* 604-608-6923
e-mail: info@gvpta.ca
URL: www.gvpta.ca
Sue Porter, Executive Director

Intrepid Theatre Co. Society
#2, 1609 Blanshard St., Victoria BC V8S 4P6
Tel: 250-383-2663; *Fax:* 250-380-1999
e-mail: info@intrepidtheatre.com
URL: www.intrepidtheatre.com
Affiliation(s): ProArt Alliance of Vancouver, Arts Action BC
Janet Munsil, Producer
Ian Case, General Manager

Playwrights Theatre Centre
#201, 1398 Cartwright St., Vancouver BC V6H 3R8
Tel: 604-685-6228; *Fax:* 604-685-7451
e-mail: plays@playwrightstheatre.com
URL: www.playwrightstheatre.com
Ray Wallis, President
Martin Kinch, Executive Director/Literary Manager
Linda Gorrie, Administrator

Théâtre la Seizième
#266, 1555 - 7e av ouest, Vancouver BC V6J 1S1
Tel: 604-736-2616; *Fax:* 604-736-9151
e-mail: info@seizieme.ca
URL: www.seizieme.ca/
Craig Holzschuh, Directeur général et artistique

Theatre Terrific Society
4397 - 2nd Ave. West, Vancouver BC V6R 1K4
Tel: 604-222-4020; *Fax:* 604-222-4020
e-mail: info@theatreterrific.ca
URL: www.theatreterrific.ca
Affiliation(s): Volunteer Vancouver; Greater Vancouver Professional Theatre Association
Susanna Uchatius, Artistic Director
Nina Hirlaender Hinton, General Manager

The Vancouver Summer Festival Society
#400, 873 Beatty St., Vancouver BC V6B 2M6
Tel: 604-688-1152; *Fax:* 604-688-8441
e-mail: music@festivalvancouver.bc.ca
URL: www.festivalvancouver.bc.ca
George Laverock, Program Director
Morna Edmundson, Administrative Director

Vancouver TheatreSports League (VTSL)
#104, 1177 West Broadway, Vancouver BC V6H 1G3
Tel: 604-738-7013; *Fax:* 604-738-8013
e-mail: info@vtsl.com
URL: www.vtsl.com
Jay Ono, Executive Director

Western Canada Theatre Company Society (WCT)
PO Box 329, Kamloops BC V2C 5K9
Tel: 250-372-3216; *Fax:* 250-374-7099
e-mail: info@westerncanadatheatre.bc.ca
URL: www.westerncanadatheatre.bc.ca
Affiliation(s): Professional Association of Candian Theatres
Lorid Marchand, General Manager

Manitoba

Le Cercle Molière
340, boul Provencher, Saint-Boniface MB R2H 0G7
Tél: 204-233-8053; *Téléc:* 204-233-2373
Courriel: reception@cerclemoliere.com
URL: www.cerclemoliere.com
Roland Mahé, Directeur artistique

Manitoba Association of Playwrights (MAP)
#503, 100 Arthur St., Winnipeg MB R3B 1H3
Tel: 204-942-8941; *Fax:* 204-942-1555
e-mail: mbplay@mts.net
URL: www.mbplays.ca
Rory Runnells, Coordinator

Manitoba Theatre Centre (MTC)
174 Market Ave., Winnipeg MB R3B 0P8
Tel: 204-942-6537; *Fax:* 204-947-3741
Toll-Free: 877-446-4500
e-mail: patronservices@mtc.mb.ca
URL: www.mtc.mb.ca
Steven Schipper, Artistic Director
Zaz Bajon, General Manager

Prairie Theatre Exchange (PTE)
Portage Place, #Y300, 393 Portage Ave., 3rd Fl., Winnipeg MB R3B 3H6
Tel: 204-942-7291; *Fax:* 204-942-1774
e-mail: pte@pte.mb.ca
URL: www.pte.mb.ca
Affiliation(s): Canadian Institute of Theatre Technology
Cherry Karpyshin, General Manager
Wendy Miller, President

New Brunswick

Théâtre l'Escaouette
170, rue Botsford, Moncton NB E1C 4X5
Tél: 506-855-0001; *Téléc:* 506-855-0010
Courriel: escaouet@nbnet.nb.ca

Theatre New Brunswick (TNB)
#31, 55 Whitting Rd., Fredericton NB E3B 5Y5
Tel: 506-460-1381; *Fax:* 506-453-9315
Toll-Free: 800-442-9779
e-mail: general@tnb.nb.ca
URL: www.tnb.nb.ca
Heather VanIderstine, Administrative Assistant

Théâtre populaire d'Acadie (TPA)
#302, 220, boul. St-Pierre ouest, Caraquet NB E1W 1A5
Tél: 506-727-0920; *Téléc:* 506-727-0923
Ligne sans frais: 800-872-0920
Courriel: tpa@pacadie.ca
URL: www.tpacadie.ca
Maurice Arsenault, Directeur artistique et général

Newfoundland and Labrador

Theatre Newfoundland Labrador
PO Box 655, Corner Brook NL A2H 6G1
Tel: 709-639-7238; *Fax:* 709-639-1006
URL: www.theatrenewfoundland.com
Jeff Pitcher, Artistic Director

Nova Scotia

Neptune Theatre Foundation
1593 Argyle St., Halifax NS B3J 2B2
Tel: 902-429-7300; *Fax:* 902-429-1211
Toll-Free: 800-565-7345
e-mail: info@neptunetheatre.com
URL: www.neptunetheatre.com
Doreen E. Malone, General Manager
George Pothitos, Artistic Director

Theatre Nova Scotia (TNS)
1113 Marginal Rd., Halifax NS B3H 4P7
Tel: 902-425-3876; *Fax:* 902-422-0881
e-mail: theatrens@theatrens.ca
URL: www.theatrens.ca
Affiliation(s): Cultural Federation of NS; Professional Association of Canadian Theatres
Sue Leblanc-Crawford, Chair
Christopher Shore, Executive Director

Ontario

The Actors' Fund of Canada / La Caisse des acteurs du Canada inc.
#301, 1000 Yonge St., Toronto ON M4W 2K2
Tel: 416-975-0304; *Fax:* 416-975-0306
Toll-Free: 877-399-8392
e-mail: contact@actorsfund.ca
URL: www.actorsfund.ca
Barry Flatman, President

Association of Summer Theatres 'Round Ontario (ASTRO)
c/o Theatre Ontario, #210, 215 Spadina Ave., Toronto ON M5T 2C7
Tel: 416-408-4556; *Fax:* 416-408-3402
e-mail: tim@theatreontario.org
URL: www.summertheatre.org
Affiliation(s): Theatre Ontario; Professional Association of Canadian Theatres; Canadian Actors' Equity Association; Tourism Federation of Ontario
Steven Thomas, President

Buddies in Bad Times Theatre
12 Alexander St., Toronto ON M4Y 1B4
Tel: 416-975-9130; *Fax:* 416-975-9293
e-mail: chy@artsexy.ca
URL: www.artsexy.ca
Brendan Healy, Artistic Director

Canadian Association for Theatre Research (CATR) / Association canadienne de la recherche théâtrale (ACRT)
#2, 40 River St., Toronto ON M5A 3N9
e-mail: nicholsg@umoncton.ca
URL: www.catr-acrt.ca
Kym Bird, Secretary
Shelley Scott, President
James Dugan, Treasurer

Canadian Institute for Theatre Technology (CITT) / L'Institut Canadien des Technologies Scénographiques (ICTS)
#340, 207 Bank St., Ottawa ON K2P 1N5
Tel: 613-482-1165; *Fax:* 613-482-1212
Toll-Free: 888-271-3383
e-mail: info@citt.org
URL: www.citt.org
Adam Mitchell, President
Monique Corbeil, National Coordinator

The Canadian Stage Company
26 Berkeley St., Toronto ON M5A 2W3
Tel: 416-367-8243; *Fax:* 416-367-1768
e-mail: general@canstage.com
URL: www.canstage.com

Louise Plunkett, Customer Service Manager
Matthew Jocelyn, Artistic & General Director

Canadian Theatre Critics Association (CTCA) / Association des critiques de théâtre du Canada
#724, 2121 Bathurst St., Toronto ON M5N 2P3
Tel: 416-782-0966; *Fax:* 416-782-0366
e-mail: scenechanges@rogers.com
URL: www.canadiantheatrecritics.ca
Affiliation(s): Capital Critics Association; Association québécoise des critiques de théâtre
Jeniva Berger, Founding President
Alvina Ruprecht, Co-President
Don Rubin, Co-President

Compagnie vox théâtre
333 King Edward Ave., Ottawa ON K1N 7M5
Tél: 613-241-1090; *Téléc:* 613-241-0250
Courriel: info@voxtheatre.ca
URL: www.voxtheatre.ca

Gryphon Theatre Foundation
PO Box 454, Barrie ON L4M 4T7
Tel: 705-728-4613; *Fax:* 705-728-4623
e-mail: boxoffice@gryphontheatre.com
URL: www.gryphontheatre.com
Donna Kenwell, Chair

Harbourfront Centre
235 Queens Quay West, Toronto ON M5J 2G8
Tel: 416-973-4600; *Fax:* 416-973-6055
e-mail: info@harbourfrontcentre.com
URL: www.harbourfrontcentre.com
Bruce Hutchinson, Director, Marketing & Media Relations
William J.S. Boyle, CEO
Gregory Burke, Director, The Power Plant
Melanie Fernandez, Director, Community & Education
Tina Rasmussen, Director, Performing Arts
Geoffrey Taylor, Director, Harbourfront Reading Series

Lorraine Kimsa Theatre for Young People (LKTYP)
165 Front St. East, Toronto ON M5A 3Z4
Tel: 416-363-5131; *Fax:* 416-363-5136
e-mail: online@lktyp.ca
URL: www.lktyp.ca
Affiliation(s): Canadian Actor's Equity Association
Allen MacInnis, Artistic Director
Nancy Webster, Managing Director

Native Earth Performing Arts Inc. (NEPA)
Bldg. 74, #300/305, 55 Mill St., Toronto ON M5A 3C4
Tel: 416-531-1402; *Fax:* 416-531-6377
Toll-Free: 877-854-9708
e-mail: office@nativeearth.ca
URL: www.nativeearth.ca
Affiliation(s): Professional Association of Canadian Theatres; Toronto Theatre Alliance
Yvette Nolan, Artistic Director
Donna-Michelle St. Bernard, General Manager

Ontario Puppetry Association
714 Hedgerow Place, London ON K7M 4G9
Tel: 613-389-2996
Toll-Free: 800-379-0446
e-mail: dsmith@kos.net
URL: www.onpuppet.org
Affiliation(s): UNIMA International
Philip Arnold, President
Mike Harding, Vice-President

Playwrights Guild of Canada (PGC)
#210, 215 Spadina Ave., Toronto ON M5T 2C7
Tel: 416-703-0201; *Fax:* 416-703-0059
Toll-Free: 800-561-3318
e-mail: info@playwrightsguild.ca
URL: www.playwrightsguild.ca
Robin Sokoloski, Executive Director

Professional Association of Canadian Theatres (PACT)
#555, 215 Spadina Ave., Toronto ON M5T 2C7
Tel: 416-595-6455; *Fax:* 416-595-6450
Toll-Free: 800-263-7228
e-mail: marlaf@pact.ca
URL: www.pact.ca
Affiliation(s): PACT Communications Centre; Canadian Conference of the Arts
Lucy White, Executive Director
Eric Coates, President
Linda Gorrie, Treasurer

Resurgence Theatre Company (RTC)
211 Main St. South, Newmarket ON L3Y 5Y9
Tel: 905-953-2838; *Fax:* 905-895-0070
e-mail: info@resurgence.on.ca
URL: www.resurgence.on.ca
Affiliation(s): CEA
Anthony Leo, General Manager

Shaw Festival
PO Box 774, 10 Queen's Parade, Niagara-on-the-Lake ON L0S 1J0
Tel: 905-468-2153; *Fax:* 905-468-5438
Toll-Free: 800-657-1106
e-mail: dlg@shawfest.com
URL: www.shawfest.com
Affiliation(s): Canadian Institute for Theatre Technology
Jackie Maxwell, Artistic Director
Colleen Blake, Executive Director

Tarragon Theatre
30 Bridgman Ave, Toronto ON M5R 1X3
Tel: 416-536-5018; *Fax:* 416-533-6372
e-mail: info@tarragontheatre.com
URL: www.tarragontheatre.com
Affiliation(s): Professional Association of Canadian Theatres
Camilla Holland, General Manager
Richard Rose, Artistic Director

Théâtre de la Vieille 17
61A York St., Ottawa ON K1N 5T2
Tél: 613-241-8562; *Téléc:* 613-241-9507
Courriel: info@vieille17.ca
URL: vieille17.ca
Simone Saint-Pierre, Agente des communications et adjoin

Théâtre du Nouvel-Ontario (TNO)
21 Lasalle Blvd., Sudbury ON P3A 6B1
Tél: 705-525-5606; *Téléc:* 705-525-1129
Courriel: tno@letno.ca
URL: www.letno.ca
Geneviève Pineault, Directrice artistique et générale

Théâtre du Trillium
333 King Edward Ave., Ottawa ON K1N 7M5
Tél: 613-789-7643; *Téléc:* 613-789-7641
Courriel: info@theatre-trillium.com
URL: www.theatre-trillium.com/
Natalie Sarafian, Agente des Communications et de la
Sylvie Dufour, Directrice artistique et générale

Théâtre français de Toronto
#501, 2333 Dundas St. West, Toronto ON M6R 3A6
Tél: 416-534-7303; *Téléc:* 416-534-9087
Ligne sans frais: 800-819-4981
Courriel: info@theatrefrancais.com
URL: www.theatrefrancais.com
Ghislain Caron, Directeur administratif
Guy Mignault, Directeur artistique

Théâtre la Catapulte
333 King Edward Ave., Ottawa ON K1N 7M5
Tél: 613-562-0851; *Téléc:* 613-562-0631
Courriel: communications@catapulte.ca
URL: www.catapulte.ca
Joël Beddows, Directeur artistique
Mireille Amyotte, Présidente

Theatre Ontario
#210, 215 Spadina Ave., Toronto ON M5T 2C7
Tel: 416-408-4556; *Fax:* 416-408-3402
e-mail: info@theatreontario.org
URL: www.theatreontario.org
John Goddard, Executive Director

Toronto Alliance for the Performing Arts (TAPA)
#210, 215 Spadina Ave., Toronto ON M5T 2C7
Tel: 416-536-6468; *Fax:* 416-536-3463
Toll-Free: 800-541-0499
e-mail: jacobak@tapa.ca
URL: www.tapa.ca
Affiliation(s): Professional Association of Canadian Theatres (PACT)
Jacoba Knaapen, Executive Director

Prince Edward Island

Theatre PEI
PO Box 1573, Charlottetown PE C1A 7N3
Tel: 902-894-3558; *Fax:* 902-894-3558
e-mail: theatre@isn.net
Affiliation(s): PEI Council of the Arts
Daphne Harker, Administrator
Ron Irving, Artistic Director
Rob MacLean, Associate Artistic Director

Québec

Association québécoise des marionnettistes (AQM)
Centre UNIMA-CANADA (section Québec), CP 7, Succ. de Lorimier, #300, 7755 boul Saint-Laurent, Montréal QC H2H 2N6
Tél: 514-522-1919; *Téléc:* 514-521-3737
Courriel: aqm@aei.ca
URL: www.aqm.ca
Hélène Ducharme, Président

Black Theatre Workshop (BTW)
#432, 3680 Jeanne-Mance, Montréal QC H2X 2K5
Tel: 514-932-1104; *Fax:* 514-932-6311
URL: www.blacktheatreworkshop.ca
Tyrone Benskin, Artistic Director
Jacklin Webb, President

Centre des auteurs dramatiques (CEAD)
#200, 261, rue du Saint-Sacrement, Montréal QC H2Y 3V2
Tél: 514-288-3384; *Téléc:* 514-288-7043
Courriel: cead@cead.qc.ca
URL: www.cead.qc.ca
Marc Drouin, Directeur général
Lise Vaillancourt, Président

Conseil québécois du théâtre (CQT)
#808, 460, rue Ste-Catherine ouest, Montréal QC H3B 1A7
Tél: 514-954-0270; *Téléc:* 514-954-0165
Ligne sans frais: 866-954-0270
Courriel: cqt@cqt.qc.ca
URL: www.cqt.ca
Martine Lévesque, Directrice générale

Fédération québécoise du théâtre amateur (FQTA)
CP 977, 181, boul Bois-Francs sud, Victoriaville QC G6P 8Y1
Tél: 819-752-2501; *Téléc:* 819-758-4466
Courriel: info@fqta.ca
URL: www.fqta.ca
Yoland Roy, Directeur général

Théâtre des épinettes
255, rue Laframboise, Chibougamau QC G8P 2S5
Tél: 418-748-4682
Guy Lalancette

Théâtres associés inc. (TAI)
#405, 1908, rue Panet, Montréal QC H2L 3A2
Tél: 514-842-6361; *Téléc:* 514-842-9730
Courriel: info@theatresassocies.ca
URL: www.theatresassocies.ca
Jacques Vézina, Président
Jacques Cousineau, Secrétaire général

Théâtres unis enfance jeunesse (TUEJ)
CP 627, Succ. Desjardins, Montréal QC H5B 1B7
Tél: 450-446-4863; *Téléc:* 450-467-1982
Courriel: tuej@gelogic.com
URL: www.gelogic.com/tuej
Affiliation(s): Conseil québécois du Théâtre; Academie québécoise du Théâtre; Les Arts et la Ville; Conseil Québécois des ressources humaines en culture; RAPThéâtre
Andrée Garon, Directrice générale
Marc St. Jacques, Président

Saskatchewan

Globe Theatre Society
Globe Theatre, Prince Edward Bldg., 1801 Scarth St., Regina SK S4P 2G9
Tel: 306-525-9553; *Fax:* 306-352-4194
Toll-Free: 866-954-5623
e-mail: onstage@globetheatrelive.com
URL: www.globetheatrelive.com
Affiliation(s): Canadian Actors' Equity
Ruth Smillie, Artistic Director

Saskatchewan Playwrights Centre (SPC)
PO Box 3092, Saskatoon SK S7K 3S9
Tel: 306-665-7707; *Fax:* 306-244-0255
e-mail: sk.playwrights@sasktel.net
URL: www.saskplaywrights.ca
Will Brooks, President

Theatre Saskatchewan
1077 Angus St., Regina SK S4T 1Y4
Tel: 306-352-0797; *Fax:* 306-569-7888
e-mail: info@theatresaskatchewan.com
URL: www.theatresaskatchewan.com

La Troupe du Jour
CP 339, 914 - 20th St. West, Saskatoon SK S7K 3L3
Tél: 306-244-1040; *Téléc:* 306-652-1725
Courriel: communication@latroupedujour.ca
URL: www.latroupedujour.ca
Denis Rouleau, General Manager/Artistic Director

Science Centres

Alberta

***Calgary:* TELUS World of Science - Calgary (TWOSC)**
***Also known as:* Calgary Science Centre**
PO Box 2100 M, #73, 701 - 11 St. SW, Calgary, AB T2P 2M5
403-268-8300, Fax: 403-237-0186,
discover@calgaryscience.ca
www.calgaryscience.ca
Multimedia Discovery Dome presentations & exhibits; open year round
William T. Peters, Executive Director

***Edmonton:* TELUS World of Science - Edmonton**
c/o Edmonton Space & Science Foundation, 11211 - 142 St. NW, Edmonton, AB T5M 4A1
780-451-3344, Fax: 780-455-5882,
info@telusworldofscienceedmonton.com
www.telusworldofscienceedmonton.com
IMAX theatre; planetarium; exhibit galleries; observatory; giftshop; café; Ham Radio Station; science & computer lab
Andrea Kuhlmann, Director, Marketing & Communications
George Smith, President & CEO

British Columbia

***Vancouver:* H.R. MacMillan Space Centre (HRMSC)**
***Also known as:* The Planetarium**
1100 Chestnut St., Vancouver, BC V6J 3J9
604-738-7827, Fax: 604-736-5665,
ddodge@hrmacmillanspacecentre.com
www.hrmacmillanspacecentre.com
Western Canada's premier earth, space science & astronomy attraction & educational resource
Donna Livingstone, Executive Director

***Vancouver:* Science World British Columbia**
1455 Quebec St., Vancouver, BC V6A 3Z7
604-443-7443, Fax: 604-443-7430,
mcotic@scienceworld.ca
www.scienceworld.ca
Hands-on exhibits; demonstrations; Omnimax theatre
Bryan Tisdall, President/CEO

Ontario

Provincial Science Centres

Ontario Science Centre / Centre des sciences de l'Ontario
770 Don Mills Rd., Toronto, ON M3C 1T3
416-696-1000, Fax: 416-696-3124,
www.ontariosciencecentre.ca
Over 800 interactive exhibits on the environment, technology, food, chemistry, communications, sport & space; exhibits, programs, demonstrations, workshops & films for the public; special programs for school groups, children, adults & senior citizens; gift shops & restaurant; Ontario's only OMNIMAX Theatre featuring a 24-metre dome screen with wrap-around sound; open year round
Lesley Lewis, Director General & CEO

***Sudbury:* Science North**
100 Ramsey Lake Rd., Sudbury, ON P3E 5S9
705-522-3701, Fax: 705-522-4954,
www.sciencenorth.ca
Founded: 1984 Science centre, IMAX Theatre, planetarium, living butterfly gallery & special exhibits hall; exhibit design & consulting services.
Jim Marchbank, CEO
Alan Nursall, Science Director

***Toronto:* The Roberta Bondar Earth & Space Centre**
Seneca College, Newnham Campus, 1750 Finch Ave. East, Toronto, ON M2J 2X5
416-491-5050,
stars@senecac.on.ca
60-seat star theatre featuring 2000 visible stars, 5 planets, sun & moon; accessory projectors provide simulations of aurorae, meteor showers, bolides & solar & lunar eclipses

Quebec

Provincial Science Centres

The Montréal Science Centre
King-Edward Pier, Old Port of Montréal, 333 Commune St. West, Montréal, QC H2Y 2E2
514-496-4724, Fax: 514-496-0667, 877-496-4724
www.montrealsciencecentre.com
Visitors acquire an understanding of science & technology & how it affects daily living; three interactive science exhibition halls; IMAX 3D, IMMERSION STUDIOS theatres
Claude Benoit, President & CEO

***Laval:* Cosmodôme - Centre des sciences de l'espace et Camp spatial Canada / Cosmodôme - Space Science Centre & Space Camp**
2150, rte des Laurentides, Laval, QC H7T 2T8
450-978-3600, Fax: 450-978-3624, 800-565-2267
info@cosmodome.org
www.cosmodome.org
Host to the Space Science Centre & to the Space Camp, the Cosmodôme leads its visitors on a journey through the conquest of space.
Nicole Dalpé, Director
Anne-Josée Dionne, Coordinator, Sales & Marketing, marketing@cosmodome.org

***Montréal:* Biosphère**
160, ch Tour-de-L'Isle, Montréal, QC H3G 4G8
514-496-8300, Fax: 514-283-5021,
info.biosphere@ec.gc.ca
www.biosphere.ec.gc.ca
Museum of environment
Susanne Blais, Public Relations

***Montréal:* Planétarium de Montréal / Montréal Planétarium**
1000, rue Saint-Jacques ouest, Montréal, QC H3C 1G7
514-872-4530, Fax: 514-872-8102,
info@planetarium.montreal.qc.ca
www.planetarium.montreal.qc.ca
Multimedia productions about astronomy on a giant hemispheric dome 20 metres across
Pierre Lacombe, Directeur

***Saint-Louis-du-Ha-Ha:* Aster, La Station scientifique du BSL**
59, ch Bellevue, Saint-Louis-du-Ha-Ha, QC G0L 3S0
418-854-2172, Fax: 418-854-1898, 877-775-2172
asterbsl@globetrotter.net
www.asterbsl.ca
Scientific & technical culture; activities include: "Hélios", "Léonard, Ingénieur Créateur" & "Starlab"; educational workshops for schools
Maurice Fallu-Landry, Directeur
Chantale Tardif, Directrice-adjointe

Saskatchewan

***Regina:* Saskatchewan Science Centre**
2903 Powerhouse Dr., Regina, SK S4N 0A1
306-791-7900, Fax: 306-525-0194, 800-667-6300
www.sasksciencecentre.com
Interactive science museum featuring hands-on exhibits, Kramer Imax theatre; open year-round
Scott Langen, Executive Director

Zoos

Alberta

***Calgary:* Bow Habitat Station**
1440 - 17A St. SE, Calgary, AB T2G 4T9
403-297-6561, Fax: 403-297-2839,
bowhabitat.info@gov.ab.ca
www.bowhabitat.gov.ab.ca
Includes: a Visitor Centre, which is an interpretive centre about fresh water, fish, and aquatic habitats; the Sam Livingston Fish Hatchery, a large trout hatchery; and the Pearce Estate Park Interpretive Wetland, a unique collection of constructed wetlands, self-guided trails and interpretive signs.
D. DePape, Superintendent

***Calgary:* Calgary Zoo, Botanical Garden & Prehistoric Park**
1300 Zoo Rd. NE, Calgary, AB T2E 7V6
403-232-9300, Fax: 403-237-7582, 800-588-9993
www.calgaryzoo.org
136 acres + 320 acre off-site breeding & conservation facility; educational programs; gift shop; open year round
Alex Graham, President/CEO

***Calgary:* Inglewood Bird Sanctuary**
PO Box 2100 M, Location 59, 2425 - 9 Ave. SE, Calgary, AB T2P 2M5
403-221-4500, Fax: 403-221-3775,
InglewoodBirdSanctuary@calgary.ca
Offers more than two km. of level trails; more than 250 species of birds & 300 species of plants plus several kinds of mammals have been observed in area; visitor centre; two classrooms where nature-related programs are presented by the Sanctuary's professional naturalists
Did Andrews
Tanya Noseworthy

***Edmonton:* Valley Zoo**
PO Box 2359, Edmonton, AB T5J 2R7
780-496-8787, Fax: 780-944-7529,
attractions@edmonton.ca
www.edmonton.ca/valleyzoo
Features more than 350 endangered & exotic animals; main zoo & children's zoo; minature train, merry-go-round & camel rides available; open daily except Christmas Day
Bryan Monaghan, Director

***Lacombe:* Ellis Bird Farm**
PO Box 5090, Lacombe, AB T4L 1W7
403-346-2211, Fax: 403-346-2211,
myrnap@ellisbirdfarm.ab.ca
www.ellisbirdfarm.ab.ca
Other contact information: summer phone 403/885-4477
Nestboxes; wildlife gardens; tea house; open May - Aug.
Myrna Pearman, Manager

***Patricia:* Dinosaur Provincial Park**
PO Box 60, Patricia, AB T0J 2K0
403-378-4342, Fax: 403-378-4247,
www.dinosaurpark.ca
Some of the most extensive dinosaur fossil fields in the world are found here; the area's badlands & cottonwood river habitat are the other significant features that resulted in the park's designation as a UNESCO World Heritage Site in 1979; also includes the Royal Tyrrell Museum of Palaeontology Field Station, located within the park.

British Columbia

***Aldergrove:* Greater Vancouver Zoo**
5048 - 264th St., Aldergrove, BC V4W 1N7
604-856-6825, Fax: 604-857-9008,
info@gvzoo.com
www.gvzoo.com
Over 960 animals representing 176 species; world's only albino black bear; one of North America's largest grizzly bear habitats.
Malcolm Weatherston, General Manager

***Coombs:* Butterfly World & Gardens**
PO Box 36, 1080 Winchester Rd., Coombs, BC V0R 1M0
250-248-7026, Fax: 250-752-1091,
www.nature-world.com
The Butterfly World & Gardens is a nature park with tropical gardens, orchids, ponds, birds, & butterflies. The park is open from March to October.

***Creston:* Creston Valley Wildlife Management Area (CVWMA)**
PO Box 640, 1874 Wildlife Rd., Creston, BC V0B 1G0
250-402-6900, Fax: 250-402-6910,
askus@crestonwildlife.ca
www.crestonwildlife.ca
17,000-acre wetland habitat. This diverse wildlife resource provides many recreational and educational opportunities. Hiking, cycling, canoeing, picnicking, wildlife viewing, hunting, fishing, and many other outdoor activities can be experienced here. Open May-September.
Marc-André Beaucher, Area Manager
Jim Collins, General Manager

***Duncan:* Cowichan & Chemainus Valleys Ecomuseum**
PO Box 491, Duncan, BC V9L 4T8
250-746-1611,
Located at 160 Jubilee St.

***Kamloops:* British Columbia Wildlife Park**
9077 Dallas Dr., Kamloops, BC V2C 6V1
250-573-3242, Fax: 250-573-2406, 866-872-2066
info@bczoo.org
www.bczoo.org
As a non-profit organization we continually dedicate our efforts to the conservation of BC wildlife through display, interpretation, education, wildlife rehabilitation, endangered species and direct action.
Rob Purdy, General Manager

***Lake Country:* Speedwell Bird Sanctuary**
13724 Lakepine Rd., Lake Country, BC V4V 1A3
250-766-2081, Fax: 250-766-0617,
cabalerro@shaw.ca
Founded: 1985 Breeding facility for amazon parrots, pheasants; botanic garden — trees, shrubs & roses; by appt.
Dan Bruce

***Richmond:* Richmond Nature Park**
11851 Westminster Hwy., Richmond, BC V6X 1B4

604-718-6188, Fax: 604-718-6189,
nature@richmond.ca
www.richmond.ca

Features 5 km. of well-groomed trails through bog & forest; more than 100 species of birds, mammals, reptiles & amphibians may be sighted; seasonal programs & events

Kristine Bauder, Nature Park Coordinator
Petra Murphy, Recreation Facility Clerk
Lori Bartley, Coordinator, School Program

***Vancouver:* Stanley Park Ecology Society**
PO Box 5167, Vancouver, BC V6B 4B2
604-257-6908, Fax: 604-257-8378,
info@stanleyparkecology.ca
www.stanleyparkecology.ca

Encourages stewardship of the natural world through education & action & by fostering awareness; provides public programs for adults & families, school programs, wildlife information & resources promoting coexistence between people & its wild neighbours

Patricia Thomson, Executive Director

***Victoria:* Swan Lake Christmas Hill Nature Sanctuary**
3873 Swan Lake Rd., Victoria, BC V8X 3W1
250-479-0211, Fax: 250-479-0132,
info@swanlake.bc.ca
www.swanlake.bc.ca

Nature education centre; 125 acres including marshy lowlands surrounding Swan Lake and rocky, oak-forested highlands of Christmas Hill.

Terry Morrison, Executive Director

***Victoria:* Victoria Butterfly Gardens**
PO Box 190, 1461 Benvenuto Ave., Victoria, BC V8M 1R3
250-652-3822, Fax: 250-652-4683, 877-722-0272
info@butterflygardens.com
www.butterflygardens.com

Indoor tropical gardens, fish, birds, and butterflies. Open Mar 1-Oct. 31

Manitoba

***Rennie:* Alfred Hole Goose Sanctuary (AHGS)**
***Also known as:* Alf's Hole**
Whiteshell Provincial Park, PO Box 130, Rennie, MB R0E 1R0
204-369-5470, Fax: 204-369-5341,
mschneider@gov.mb.ca
www.manitobaparks.com

Wheelchair accessible Visitor Centre interprets the history of the site as well as the biology of geese; spring, summer & fall program features hands-on activities, guided hikes, school programming & special events

Larry Teetaert, Park Manager
Morgan Schneider, Park Interpreter

***Thompson:* Thompson Zoo**
226 Mystery Lake Rd., Thompson, MB R8N 1S6
204-677-7982, Fax: 204-778-4186,
thompzoo@escape.ca
thompsonzoo.ca

Over 100 animals and birds. The Thompson Zoo is the only northern Wildlife Rehab Cetnre in Manitoba. Open year round.

Erin Wilcox, Director

***Winnipeg:* Assiniboine Park Zoo**
460 Assiniboine Park Dr., Winnipeg, MB R3P 2N7
204-986-2327, Fax: 204-832-5420,
apzoo@winnipeg.ca
www.winnipeg.ca/assiniboinepark

Open daily & currently has 1,700 animals of 300 different species

Douglas Ross, Director

New Brunswick

***Lamèque:* Lamèque Zoo**
Lamèque, NB E0B 1V0
506-344-7214,

***Moncton:* Magnetic Hill Zoo**
c/o City of Moncton, Community Services Dept., 655 Main St., Moncton, NB E1C 1E8
506-877-7718,
info.zoo@moncton.ca
www.moncton.org/zoo/

The Magnetic Hill Zoo is committed to safeguarding animal species and raising public awareness of endangered species. The zoo is designed with the well-being of the animals, as well as the safety of the public, in mind.

Bruce Dougan, Manager

***Saint John:* Cherry Brook Zoo Inc.**
901 Foster Thurston Dr., Saint John, NB E2K 5H9
506-634-1440, Fax: 506-634-0717,
noahsark@rogers.com
www.cherrybrookzoo.com

A non-for profit zoo situated in a 35-acre woodland that is located in the northern section of the city's 2200-acre Rockwood Park. Utilizing the unusual natural terrain of Rockwood Park, the animals are surrounded by a natural setting.

Lynda & Leonard Collrin

Newfoundland & Labrador

***Glovertown:* Terra Nova National Park (TNNP) / Parc national Terra-Nova**
Glovertown, NL A0G 2L0
709-533-2801, Fax: 709-533-2706,
info.tnnp@pc.gc.ca
www.pc.gc.ca/pn-np/nl/terranova/index_E.asp

Represents the unique character of the eastern Newfoundland Atlantic Terrestrial Natural Region; characterized by low relief & a series of rounded hills from sea level to 200 metres; home to 12 of 14 native terrestrial mammals, 8 fish species & more than 200 bird species recorded in the park; artifacts of native & European settlement

***Holyrood:* Salmonier Nature Park**
PO Box 190, Holyrood, NL A0A 2R0
709-229-7888, Fax: 709-229-7078,
brenda.pike@mail.gov.nl.ca
www.env.gov.nl.ca/snp

Open June to Thanksgiving

Tammy Keats, Manager

Nova Scotia

***Shubenacadie:* Provincial Wildlife Park**
PO Box 299, Shubenacadie, NS B0N 2H0
902-758-2040, Fax: 902-758-7011,
wildlifepark@gov.ns.ca
wildlifepark.gov.ns.ca

45 exhibits featuring native & exotic species in natural enclosures along a 2.3 km walking trail; picnic area & playground; open daily May 15-Oct. 15 & weekends only during winter season; fee

Bert J. Vissers, Director

Ontario

***Bowmanville:* Bowmanville Zoological Park**
340 King St. East, Bowmanville, ON L1C 3K5
905-623-5655, Fax: 905-623-0957,
bzpzoo@aol.com
www.bowmanvillezoo.com

Since 1919, Canada's oldest private zoo, featuring Animal Kingdom shows, elephant rides, restaurant & gift shop; CAZA accredited; open May - Sept.

Caroline Yli-Luoma, Vice-President, Sales
Alex Nagy, CEO
Michael Hackenberger, Director

***Cambridge:* African Lion Safari & Game Farm**
RR#1, Cambridge, ON N1R 5S2
519-623-2620, Fax: 519-623-9542, 800-461-9453
admin@lionsafari.com
www.lionsafari.com

African Lion Safari is a Canadian owned family business created in the name of conservation. Our manner of exhibiting animals is completely different from the traditional approach; that is, the visitor is caged in the car, and the animals roam in 2 to 20 hectare (5 to 50 acre) reserves. Our Mission is to provide an entertaining and educational environment in which to display and propagate animals in a safe manner that gives a unique viewing opportunity to all of our visitors. Open May-October.

Mike Takacs, General Manager

***Cambridge:* Wings of Paradise**
2500 Kossuth Rd., Cambridge, ON N3H 4R7
519-653-1234, Fax: 519-650-2582,
info@wingsofparadise.com
www.wingsofparadise.com

Live butterfly conservatory & tropical garden; open daily 10-5

***Earlton:* Temiskaming Wildlife Centre**
***Also known as:* Temiskaming Historical & Zoological Society of Northern Ontario**
PO Box 691, Earlton, ON P0J 1E0
705-563-8300, Fax: 705-563-2200,
info@temiskamingwildlifecentre.org

A wildlife rehabilitation facility that houses & treats local wildlife &, when possible releases them back into the wild; live animal exhibits, guided tours, workshops & special programming to educate visitors about the north & conservation issues; open June-Sept. daily 10-5, Sept.-June call in advance for bookings

Amanda Godden, Wildlife Rehab
Amanda Mongeon, Project Manager

***Kingsville:* Jack Miner's Bird Sanctuary**
PO Box 39, Kingsville, ON N9Y 2E8
519-733-4034, 877-289-8328
info@jackminer.com
www.jackminer.com

Centre for the conservation of migrating Canada geese and wild ducks, originating from the waterfowl refuge management system.Open year-round, free admission; closed Sundays.

***Midland:* Wye Marsh Wildlife Centre**
PO Box 100, 16160 Hwy. 12 E, Midland, ON L4R 4K6
705-526-7809, Fax: 705-526-3294,
info@wyemarsh.com
www.wyemarsh.com

Founded: 1984 Indoor & outdoor natural history exhibits; environmental education & recreation programs; fully accessible nature centre & trails; assistive equipment available

Laurie Schutt, Executive Director

***Morrisburg:* Upper Canada Migratory Bird Sanctuary (UCMBS) / Sanctuaire des oiseaux migrateurs Upper Canada**
Parks of the St. Lawrence, RR#1, Morrisburg, ON K0C 1X0
613-543-3704, Fax: 613-543-2847, 800-437-2233
www.uppercanadabirdsanctuary.com

A natural area with over 8 km. of nature trails, visitor centre & gift shop, campground & group camping area; offers a duck banding program, fall goose feeding program, outdoor education topics & special events such as the Annual Waterfowl Day

Sheila Lefebvre, Bird Sanctuary Programming Officer

***Orono:* Jungle Cat World Inc. (JCW)**
***Also known as:* Orono Exotic Cat World**
3667 Conc. 6, RR#1, Orono, ON L0B 1M0
905-983-5016, Fax: 905-983-9858,
info@junglecatworld.com
www.junglecatworld.com

Jungle Cat World is a wildlife park located on 15 picturesque acres. Though Jungle Cat World is home to a variety of threatened and endangered species such as lemurs, gibbons, cotton-top tamarins and spider monkeys, the park specializes in wild felines. They include the world's largest, the Siberian tiger, to the rarest, the Amur leopard, to some of the smallest like the sand cats from the African deserts.

***St Catharines:* Happy Rolph Bird Sanctuary & Children's Petting Farm**
c/o St Catharines Parks & Recreation Dept., PO Box 3012, St Catharines, ON L2N 2G6
905-937-7210, Fax: 905-646-9262,

A 15-acre municipal park on the shores of Lake Ontario boasts beautiful gardens and pathways, petting farm (open Victoria Day to Thanksgiving weekend), picnic area and playground facilities.

Jim Benson

***Thunder Bay:* Chippewa Wildlife Park**
Victoriaville Civic Centre, 111 Syndicate Ave. South, Thunder Bay, ON P7E 6S4
807-625-2351, Fax: 807-625-3258,
www.thunderbay.ca

The municipally operated zoological park contains bird & mammal species, which are indigenous to northwestern Ontario. The Chippewa Wildlife Park features an elevated walkway (pedestrian boardwalk) for viewing the animals.

Paul Fayrick, Manager, Parks, 807-625-2806,
pfayrick@thunderbay.ca

***Toronto:* High Park Animal Paddocks**
c/o Parks & Recreation, City Hall, 100 Queen St. West, Toronto, ON M5H 2N2
416-392-6599,
www.toronto.ca/parks/highpark.htm

Located on Deer Pen Road, the animal paddocks have always been one of the most popular attractions, dating back to 1890 when deer were kept in High Park. Today, you will find domestic and exotic species including bison, llamas, peacocks, deer, highland cattle and sheep.

Carol Guy, Supervisor

***Toronto:* Kortright Centre for Conservation**
c/o Toronto & Region Conservation, 5 Shoreham Dr., Toronto, ON M3N 1S4
416-661-6600, Fax: 416-661-6898,
info@trca.on.ca
www.kortright.org

Largest environmental education centre in Canada. Located on 325 hectares of pristine woodlands, Kortright Centre combines a natural oasis with some of the most leading edge sustainable education programs and events in Canada.

***Toronto:* Riverdale Farm, Riverdale Park**
c/o Dept. of Parks & Recreation, City Hall, 201 Winchester St., Toronto, ON M4X 1B8
416-392-6794, Fax: 416-392-0329,
farm@toronto.ca
www.friendsofriverdalefarm.com

Riverdale Farm is a Toronto Parks, Forestry and Recreation Division facility located in a park setting in the heart of the downtown community, Cabbagetown. Admission is free. Parking on neighbouring city streets only. Tour the Farm's scenic 7.5 acres along pathways through wooded areas, around ponds, and into butterfly-herb-flower-vegetable gardens.

***Toronto:* Toronto Zoo**
361A Old Finch Ave., Toronto, ON M1B 5K7
416-392-5929, Fax: 416-392-5934,
www.torontozoo.com
The Toronto Zoo is Canada's premier Zoo, known for its interactive education and conservation activities. As a unique wildlife experience, we inspire people to live in ways that promote the well being of the natural world. The Zoo has over 5,000 animals representing over 460 species. Open year round.
Calvin J. White, CEO

Quebec

***Bonaventure:* Bioparc de la Gaspésie**
CP 578, 123, des Vieux Ponts, Bonaventure, QC G0C 1E0
418-534-1997, Fax: 418-534-1998, 866-534-1997
info@bioparc.ca
www.bioparc.ca
Gaspesian wildlife observation centre; through a one mile walk path, visitors discover a collection of fauna & flora indigenous to the region presented in their five respective ecosystems: the Bay, the Lagoon, the River, the Forest & the Tundra
Marie-Josse Bernard, Directrice

***Charlesbourg:* Jardin Zoologique du Québec**
9300, rue de la Faune, Charlesbourg, QC G1G 5H9
418-622-0313, Fax: 418-646-9239, 888-622-0312
spsnq@spsnq.qc.ca
Open year round

***Granby:* Zoo de Granby / Granby Zoo**
525, rue St-Hubert, Granby, QC J2G 5P3
450-372-9113, Fax: 450-372-5531, 877-472-6299
info@zoodegranby.com
www.zoodegranby.com
The Granby Zoological Society is committed to promoting a responsible attitude towards our natural environment by dedicating its efforts to the understanding, appreciation and conservation of living beings and their habitats. Open June - Oct. (Thanksgiving Day).
Joanne Lalumière, Directrice-générale

***Hemmingford:* Parc Safari Africain (Québec) Inc.**
850, route 202, Hemmingford, QC J0L 1H0
450-247-2727, Fax: 450-247-3563, 800-465-8724
info@parcsafari.com
www.parcsafari.com
In the summer, our zoological park transforms into an African landscape thanks to our large group of African animal species. Come and admire a spectacular wildlife including 800 animals from the five continents, many of which you can approach and feed. Observe and pet elephants, rhinos, giraffes, zebras, lions, macaques, chimpanzees, white tigers and many others. ALso includes a water park.

***Sainte-Anne-de-Bellevue:* Ecomuseum / Écomuséum**
21125, ch Sainte-Marie, Sainte-Anne-de-Bellevue, QC H9X 3Y7
514-457-9449, Fax: 514-457-0769,
info@ecomuseum.ca
www.ecomuseum.ca
Open year round; wildlife interpretation centre; animals of the St. Lawrence Valley

***Saint-Eustache:* Ferme de Reptiles Exotarium inc.**
846, ch Fresniere, Saint-Eustache, QC J7R 4K3
450-472-1827,
info@exotarium.net
www.exotarium.net
Rare & endangered reptiles, amphibians & invertebrates
Hervé Maranda, Owner

***Saint-Félicien:* Centre de Conservation de la biodiversité boréale (CCBB) inc.- Zoo Sauvage de Saint-Félicien (CCBB)**
2230, boul du Jardin, Saint-Félicien, QC G8K 2P8
418-679-0543, Fax: 418-679-3647,
ccbb@borealie.org
www.borealie.org
Displays North American wildlife in an innovative context; no cages or bars; open daily May 15 - Oct. 14., 9-5
Dominique Chartier, Directrice générale

***Saint-Félicien:* Zoo sauvage de Saint-Felicien**
2230, boul du Jardin, Saint-Félicien, QC G8K 2P8
418-697-0543, Fax: 418-679-3647, 800-667-5687
CCBB@borealie.org
www.borealie.org
To provide our visitors with a Zoo unlike any other, a Zoo that blends harmoniously into a yet untamed Nature, that offers a dramatic meeting place where Nature and Boreal wildlife come together, and that makes an exceptional contribution to the protection and maintenance of Boreal biodiversity through its educational, scientific and recreational activities.

***Saint-Joachim:* Centre d'interprétation faunique du Cap-Tourmente**
570, ch du Cap-Tourmente, Saint-Joachim, QC G0A 3X0
418-827-4591, Fax: 418-827-6225,
cap.tourmente@ec.gc.ca

Saskatchewan

***Regina:* Wascana Waterfowl Park**
Wascana Centre, PO Box 7111, Lakeshore Dr., Regina, SK S4P 3S7
306-522-3661, Fax: 306-565-2742,
wca@wascana.sk.ca
www.wascanacentre.sk.ca/waterfowlpark.html
The Wascana Waterfowl Park is a 223 hectare thriving marshland within Regina's city limits.
Van Isman, Executive DIrector

SECTION 3
ASSOCIATIONS

Associations in this section are listed alphabetically by subject. Directly following this page is an Entry Index arranged alphabetically by entry name, regardless of subject. Many subjects are also represented in other Sections throughout the book. For example, Section 2: Arts & Culture includes Art Galleries, while this section includes Art Gallery Associations.

Association Name Index

A

B

J

K

L

M

N

O

P

Q

R

T

U

V

W

Y

Z

Accounting

Canadian Academic Accounting Association (CAAA) / Association canadienne des professeurs de comptabilité (ACPC)
3997 Chesswood Dr., Toronto ON M3J 2R8
Tel: 416-486-5361; *Fax:* 416-486-6158
e-mail: admin@caaa.ca
URL: www.caaa.ca
Louise Côté, Présidente
Brenda Blakey, Vice-President
Merridee Bujaki, Vice-President
Jylan Khalil, Treasurer
Gale Evans, Secretary

Canadian Bookkeepers Association
#482, 283 Danforth Ave., Toronto ON M4K 1N2
Fax: 866-804-4617
e-mail: info@canadianbookkeepersassociation.com
URL: www.c-b-a.ca
Norm Eady, President

Canadian Institute of Chartered Accountants (CICA) / Institut canadien des comptables agréés
277 Wellington St. West, Toronto ON M5V 3H2
Tel: 416-977-3222; *Fax:* 416-977-8585
URL: www.cica.ca
Kevin Dancey, FCA, President & Chief Executive Officer
Nigel Byars, CA, Executive Vice-Presidnet
Tim Forristal, CA, Vice-President, Education
Dave Pollard, CA, Vice-President, Knowledge Development
Ron Salole, Vice-President, Standards
Heather Whyte, MBA, APR, Vice-President, Communications & External Relations
Cairine Wilson, MBA, Vice-President, Member Services

Canadian Insurance Accountants Association (CIAA) / Association canadienne des comptables en assurance
c/o Taylor Enterprises Ltd., #310, 2175 Sheppard Ave. East, Toronto ON M2J 1W8
Tel: 416-971-7800; *Fax:* 416-491-1670
e-mail: ciaa@ciaa.org
URL: www.ciaa.org
Catherine Fleming, Executive Assistant

Certified General Accountants Association of Alberta
#100, 325 Manning Rd. NE, Calgary AB T2E 2P5
Tel: 403-299-1300; *Fax:* 403-299-1339
Toll-Free: 800-661-1078
e-mail: questions@cga-alberta.org; studentservices@cga-alberta.org
URL: www.cga-alberta.org
John Carpenter, MBA, FCGA, Chief Executive Officer
Paul V. Ennis, MBA, CGA, Senior Vice-President, Student Services
Larry Presiloski, MBA, FCGA, Senior Vice-President, Corporate Strategy
Theresa Eliuk, Vice-President, Operations
Michelle Everett, Vice-President, Recruitment
Janice Harrington, Vice-President, Communications & Government Relations
Tom Skomorowski, CGA, Vice-President, Education
Breton Thoen, Vice-President, Business Systems
Sandy Umpherville, CGA, Vice-President, Member Services & Regulatory Standards

Certified General Accountants Association of British Columbia
#300, 1867 West Broadway, Vancouver BC V6J 5L4
Tel: 604-732-1211; *Fax:* 604-732-1252
Toll-Free: 800-565-1211
e-mail: info@cga-bc.org
URL: www.cga-bc.org
Social Media: twitter.com/cgabc
John Pankratz, BBA, FCGA, President
Bruce Hurst, CFP, CGA, 1st Vice-President
Bill Caulfield, BA, FCIS, CGA (, Executive Director & Secretary
Stephen Spector, BA (Hons), MA (, Treasurer

Certified General Accountants Association of Canada
#100, 4200 North Fraser Way, Burnaby BC V5J 5K7
Tel: 604-669-3555; *Fax:* 604-689-5845
Toll-Free: 800-663-1529
e-mail: tashlie@cga-canada.org
URL: www.cga-canada.org
Terry LeBlanc, FCGA, Chair
Joyce Evans, FCGA, Vice-Chair
Anthony Ariganello, FCGA, President & Chief Executive Officer
Rock Lefebvre, Vice-President, Research & Standards
Taylore Ashlie, Director, Communications

Certified General Accountants Association of Manitoba
4 Donald St. South, Winnipeg MB R3L 2T7
Tel: 204-477-1256; *Fax:* 204-453-7176
Toll-Free: 800-282-8001
e-mail: info@cga-manitoba.org; memberservices@cga-manitoba.org
URL: www.cga-manitoba.org
Grant B. Christensen, B.A., B.Comm.(H, Chief Executive Officer
Jamie Thomas, B.A., FCGA, President
D. Scott Anderson, FCGA, Director, Member Services & Practice Development
Lynn Bailey, B. Comm. (Hons., Director, Student Services
Nadine Morrill, B.A., C.G.A., Director, Finance & Administration
Kathryn M. Payne, B.Sc., C.G.A., Director, Professional Regulation
Grant Christensen, FCGA, Secretary
Andrea Kinsman, B.A., C.G.A., Treasurer

Certified General Accountants Association of New Brunswick / Association des comptables généraux accrédités du Nouveau-Brunswick
PO Box 1395, #10, 236 St. George St., Moncton NB E1C 8T6
Tel: 506-857-0939; *Fax:* 506-855-0887
Toll-Free: 877-462-4262
e-mail: cganb@cga-nb.org
URL: www.cga-nb.org
Trisha Fournier-Hoyt, CGA, President
Trudy Dryden, FCGA, Executive Director
Jean-Yves Thériault, CGA, Secretary-Treasurer

Certified General Accountants Association of Newfoundland & Labrador (CGA-NL)
#201, 294 Freshwater Rd., St. John's NL A1B 1C1
Tel: 709-579-1863; *Fax:* 709-579-0838
Toll-Free: 800-563-2426
e-mail: office@cganl.org; education@cganl.org
URL: www.cganl.org
Trevor McCormick, CGA, Chair
Tracey Osmond, CGA, Vice-Chair
Michael Duah, CGA, Secretary & Registrar
Kevin Antle, CGA, Treasurer

Certified General Accountants Association of Nova Scotia
#230, 1801 Hollis St., Halifax NS B3J 3N4
Tel: 902-425-4923; *Fax:* 902-425-4983
e-mail: office@cga-ns.org
URL: www.cga-ns.org
Louis Bourque, FCGA, Director, Education
Stana Colovic, Director, Administration & Member Services
Kristin McLellan, Manager, Student Services
Brenda Allison, Registrar

Certified General Accountants Association of Ontario
240 Eglinton Ave. East, Toronto ON M4P 1K8
Tel: 416-322-6520; *Fax:* 416-322-6481
Toll-Free: 800-668-1454
e-mail: info@cga-ontario.org
URL: www.cga-ontario.org
Everett Colby, FCGA, Chair
Frank Mensink, FCGA, Vice-Chair
Doug Brooks, FCGA, Chief Executive Officer
Steve D'Alessandro, CGA, Vice-President, Finance
Kristi Honey, Vice-President, Information Services
Bernie Keim, Vice-President, Member Services & Regulatory Affairs
Lori Keith, Vice-President, Student Services
Delmarie Scherloski, Vice-President, Marketing & Communications
Ted Wigdor, Vice-President, Government & Corporate Affairs
Blake Mercer, CGA, Secretary-Treasurer
Amy Mulhern, Manager, Public Relations

Certified General Accountants Association of Prince Edward Island
PO Box 3, #105, 18 Queen St., Charlottetown PE C1A 4A1
Tel: 902-368-7237; *Fax:* 902-368-3627
e-mail: contact@cga-pei.org
URL: www.cga-pei.org
Jason Macdonald, CGA, President
Phillip A. Rafuse, FCGA, Vice-President
Paula Gallant, BCom, CGA, Secretary
Patricia Robertson, CGA, Treasurer

Certified General Accountants Association of Saskatchewan
#114, 3502 Taylor St. East, Saskatoon SK S7H 5H9
Tel: 306-955-4622; *Fax:* 306-373-9219
Toll-Free: 800-667-4754
e-mail: info@cga-saskatchewan.org; studentservices@cga-manitoba.org
URL: www.cga-saskatchewan.org
Prabha Vaidyanathan, B.A. (Hons.), M, Executive Director
Adam Burke, B.Comm, Manager, Education & Technology
Debbie Rans, Manager, Member Services & Administration
Kayleigh Kazakoff, Coordinator, Technical Services & Administration

Certified General Accountants Association of the Northwest Territories & Nunavut
Graham Bromley Bldg., PO Box 128, 5016 - 50th Ave., 3rd Fl., Yellowknife NT X1A 2N1
Tel: 867-873-5620; *Fax:* 867-873-4469
Toll-Free: 888-633-3221
e-mail: admin@cga-nwt-nu.org
URL: www.cga-nwt-nu.org
Marlene Sutton, Executive Director
Pawan Chugh, CGA, Chair & President
Andy Wong, CGA, Vice-President & Chair, Nominations Committee
Nancy Magrum, CGA, Secretary & Chair, Professional Development Committee
Biswanath Chakrabarty, CGA, Treasurer & Chair, Finance Committee

Certified General Accountants Association of Yukon
PO Box 31536, RPO Main St., Whitehorse YT Y1A 6K8
Tel: 867-668-4461; *Fax:* 867-668-8635
URL: www.cga.org/canada/yukon

CGA Student Services - Maritime Region
Commerce House, PO Box 5100, #403, 236 St. George St., Moncton NB E1C 8R2
Tel: 506-857-0939; *Fax:* 506-855-0887
Toll-Free: 877-855-0887
e-mail: cganb@cga-nb.org
URL: www.cga-nb.org

Chartered Accountants Institute of Bermuda (ICAB)
PO Box 1625, Hamilton HM GX Bermuda
Tel: 441-292-7479; *Fax:* 441-295-3121
e-mail: icab@northrock.bm
URL: www.icab.bm
Annarita G. Marion, President & CEO

CMA Canada / La Société des comptables en management accrédités
#1400, One Robert Speck Pkwy., Mississauga ON L4Z 3M3
Tel: 905-949-4200; *Fax:* 905-949-0888
Toll-Free: 800-263-7622
e-mail: info@cma-canada.org
URL: www.cma-canada.org
Thomas Joy, President & CEO
Suzanne Godbehere, Vice President, Public Affairs

CMA Canada - Alberta
#300, 1210 - 8th St. SW, Calgary AB T2R 1L3
Tel: 403-269-5341; *Fax:* 403-262-5477
Toll-Free: 877-262-2000
e-mail: info@cma-alberta.com
URL: www.cma-alberta.com
Social Media: www.twitter.com/CMAAlberta
David Shaw, President

CMA Canada - British Columbia (CMABC)
Two Bentall Centre, #1055, 555 Burrard St., Box 269, Vancouver BC V7X 1M8
Tel: 604-687-5891; *Fax:* 604-687-6688
Toll-Free: 800-663-9646
e-mail: cmabc@cmabc.com
URL: www.cmabc.com
Colin Bennett, CMA, President & CEO

CMA Canada - Manitoba
#815, 240 Graham Ave., Winnipeg MB R3C 0J7
Tel: 204-943-1538; *Fax:* 204-947-3308
Toll-Free: 800-841-7148
e-mail: cmamb@cma-canada.org
URL: www.cma-manitoba.com
Social Media: www.facebook.com/cmamb
Ron Stoesz, CMA, FCMA, Chief Executive Officer

CMA Canada - Newfoundland & Labrador
PO Box 28090, Stn. Avalon Mall, #104, 31 Peet St., St. John's NL A1B 4J8
Tel: 709-726-3652; *Fax:* 709-726-5513
e-mail: mbradbury@cma-nl.com
URL: www.cma-nl.com
Mark A. Bradbury, CMA, Executive Director

CMA Canada - Northwest Territories & Nunavut
PO Box 512, Yellowknife NT X1A 2N4

Tel: 867-873-2875; Fax: 867-920-2503
e-mail: mdemeule@cma-canada.org
URL: www.cma-nwt.com
Michelle Demeule, CMA, Executive Director

CMA Canada - Nova Scotia, Bermuda & PEI
Sentry Place, #300, 1559 Brunswick St., Halifax NS B3J 2G1
Tel: 902-422-5836; Fax: 902-423-1605
Toll-Free: 800-565-7198
e-mail: nforan@cmans.com
URL: www.cmans.com
Nancy Foran, CMA, Chief Executive Officer

CMA Canada - Ontario
#300, 70 University Ave., Toronto ON M5J 2M4
Tel: 416-977-7741; Fax: 416-977-6079
Toll-Free: 800-387-2991
e-mail: info@cma-ontario.org
URL: www.cma-ontario.org
Merv Hillier, President & CEO

CMA Canada - Québec
715, square Victoria, 3e étage, Montréal QC H2Y 2H7
Tél: 514-849-1155; Téléc: 514-849-9674
Ligne sans frais: 800-263-5390
Courriel: administration@cma-quebec.org
URL: www.cma-quebec.org
François Renauld, CMA, Présiden/Directeur général

CMA Canada - Saskatchewan
#202, 1900 Albert St., Regina SK S4P 4K8
Tel: 306-757-9428; Fax: 306-347-8580
Toll-Free: 800-667-3535
e-mail: sask@cma-canada.org
URL: www.cma-saskatchewan.com
Bob Cochran, CMA, Director of Accreditation
Betty Hoffart, FCMA, CEO

CMA Canada - Yukon
PO Box 31426, Whitehorse YT Y1A 6K8
Tel: 867-668-3388; Fax: 867-668-2402
e-mail: cmayukon@internorth.com
URL: www.cma-canada.org/yukon.asp
Karen Johnson, CMA, Territorial Representative

CMA New Brunswick (CMANB) / La Société des comptables en management du Nouveau-Brunswick
#101, 570 Queen St., Fredericton NB E3B 6Z6
Tel: 506-455-2262; Fax: 506-455-2266
Toll-Free: 877-676-2262
e-mail: cmanb.admin@nb.aibn.com
URL: www.cmanb.com
Shelley Pelkey, FCMA, CEO

Guild of Industrial, Commercial & Institutional Accountants / Guilde des comptables industriels, commerciaux et institutionnels
36 Tandian Ct., Woodbridge ON L4L 8Z9
Tel: 905-264-2713; Fax: 905-264-1043
e-mail: iciaguild@aol.com
URL: www.guildoficia.ca

Institute of Chartered Accountants of Alberta (ICAA)
Manulife Place, #580, 10180 - 101 St., Edmonton AB T5J 4R2
Tel: 780-424-7391; Fax: 780-425-8766
Toll-Free: 800-232-9406
e-mail: info@icaa.ab.ca
URL: www.icaa.ab.ca
Jane Halford, CA, CEO & Executive Director
Peter R. Stephen, FCA, President
Daryl Ritchie, FCA, Vice-President
Brenda McKenzie, Director, Registrations

Institute of Chartered Accountants of British Columbia (ICABC)
One Bentall Centre, #500, 505 Burrard St., Box 22, Vancouver BC V7X 1M4
Tel: 604-681-3264; Fax: 604-681-1523
Toll-Free: 800-663-2677
URL: www.ica.bc.ca
Affiliation(s): All provincial CA institutes in Canada & Bermuda
Sandy Parcher, Manager
Richard Rees, FCA, CEO

Institute of Chartered Accountants of Manitoba (ICAM)
#500, 161 Portage Ave. East, Winnipeg MB R3B 0Y4
Tel: 204-942-8248; Fax: 204-943-7119
Toll-Free: 888-942-8248
e-mail: icam@icam.mb.ca
URL: www.icam.mb.ca
Gary Hannaford, FCA, CEO
Ian R. Seymour, CA, President & Chair
Rick M. MacKay, FCA, Sec.-Treas.

Shirley Sommer, CA, Registrar & Director, Standards Enforcement

Institute of Chartered Accountants of Newfoundland (ICAN)
PO Box 21130, #501, 95 Bonaventure Ave., St. John's NL A1B 2X5
Tel: 709-753-7566; Fax: 709-753-3609
e-mail: tbatstone@icanl.ca
URL: www.icanl.ca
Tashia Batstone, CA, MBA, CEO
Jason Silver, CA, Chair
Scott Shears, CA, Vice-Chair
Dorothy Keating, CA, Sec.-Treas.

Institute of Chartered Accountants of Nova Scotia (ICANS)
#1410, 1791 Barrington St., Halifax NS B3J 3L1
Tel: 902-425-3291; Fax: 902-423-4505
e-mail: icans@icans.ns.ca
URL: www.icans.ns.ca
Michele A. Wood-Tweel, FCA,CFP,TEP, CEO/Executive Director
Kathie Slaunwhite, Office Administrator

Institute of Chartered Accountants of Ontario (ICAO) / Institut des comptables agrées de l'Ontario
69 Bloor St. East, Toronto ON M4W 1B3
Tel: 416-962-1841; Fax: 416-962-8900
Toll-Free: 800-387-0735
e-mail: custserv@icao.on.ca
URL: www.icao.on.ca
Rod N. Barr, FCA, President/CEO
Nora Murrant, FCA, FCBV, Executive Vice President/COO
Tom Warner, B.A., FCIS, PAd, Vice President/Registrar

Institute of Chartered Accountants of Prince Edward Island
PO Box 301, 129 Kent St., Charlottetown PE C1A 7K7
Tel: 902-894-4290; Fax: 902-894-4791
URL: www.icapei.com
Albert M. Ferris, FCA, Executive Director
George Mason, CA, President
Chris Leary, CA, Vice-President
Karen Stanley, CA, Sec.-Treas.

Institute of Chartered Accountants of Saskatchewan
3621 Pasqua St., Regina SK S4S 6W8
Tel: 306-359-1010; Fax: 306-569-8288
Toll-Free: 800-268-3793
e-mail: inst.ca@icas.sk.ca
URL: www.icas.sk.ca
Keri McFadden, CA, CEO

Institute of Chartered Accountants of the Northwest Territories & Nunavut (ICANWT)
c/o Indian & Northern Affairs Canada, PO Box 2433, Yellowknife NT X1A 2P8
Tel: 867-873-3680; Fax: 867-920-4135
URL: www.icanwt.nt.ca
John Laratta, CA, CFE, President

Institute of Chartered Accountants of the Yukon Territory
c/o Institute of Chartered Accountants of British Columbia, Stn. 22, #500, One Bentall Centre, 505 Burrard St., Vancouver BC V7X 1M4
Tel: 604-681-3264; Fax: 604-681-1523
Toll-Free: 800-663-2677
URL: www.icayk.ca
Colleen S. Clark, CA, President

The Institute of Internal Auditors (IIA) / L'Institut des vérificateurs internes
247 Maitland Ave., Altamonte Springs FL 32701-4201 USA
Tel: 407-937-1100; Fax: 407-937-1101
e-mail: custserv@theiia.org
URL: www.theiia.org
David A. Richards, CIA, President

New Brunswick Institute of Chartered Accountants (NBICA) / Institut des comptables agréés du Nouveau-Brunswick
Mercantile Centre, #250, 55 Union St., Saint John NB E2L 2B2
Tel: 506-634-1588; Fax: 506-634-1015
e-mail: nbica@nb.aibn.com
URL: www.nbica.org
Jack Blackier, LLB, CA, Executive Director

Ordre des CGA du Québec
#1800, 500, Place d'Armes, Montréal QC H2Y 2W2
Tél: 514-861-1823; Téléc: 514-861-7661
Ligne sans frais: 800-463-0163
Courriel: ordre@cga-quebec.org
URL: www.cga-quebec.org
Danielle Hébert, FCGA, Présidente
Denis Riendeau, FCGA, 1er Vice-président & Trésorier

L'Ordre des comptables agréés du Québec (OCAQ)
680, rue Sherbrooke ouest, 18e étage, Montréal QC H3A 2S3
Tél: 514-288-3256; Téléc: 514-843-8375
Ligne sans frais: 800-363-4688
Courriel: info@ocaq.qc.ca
URL: www.ocaq.qc.ca
Jean-Pierre Allaire, FCA, Président
Alain Côté, CA, Vice-présidente

Petroleum Accountants Society of Canada (PASC)
PO Box 4520, Stn. C, Calgary AB T2T 5N3
Tel: 403-262-4744; Fax: 403-244-2340
e-mail: info@petroleumaccountants.com
URL: www.petroleumaccountants.com
Matthew Breadner, President
Thomas Latta, Vice President
Gail Quartly, Treasurer

The Society of Professional Accountants of Canada / La Société des comptables professionnels du Canada
#1007, 250 Consumers Rd., Toronto ON M2J 4V6
Tel: 416-350-8145; Fax: 416-350-8146
Toll-Free: 877-515-4447
e-mail: registrar@professionalaccountant.org
URL: www.professionalaccountant.org
William O. Nichols, RPA, President

Addiction

Addictions Foundation of Manitoba (AFM) / Fondation manitobaine de lutte contre les dépendances
1031 Portage Ave., Winnipeg MB R3G 0R8
Tel: 204-944-6236; Fax: 204-786-7768
e-mail: execoff@afm.mb.ca
URL: afm.mb.ca
John Borody, CEO

Adult Children of Alcoholics (ACA)
PO Box 75061, 20 Bloor St. East, Toronto ON M5W 3T3
Tel: 416-631-3614
e-mail: acatoronto@hotmail.com
URL: www.adultchildren.org
Sandra Frattura, Contact

Airspace Action on Smoking & Health
Delta BC V4L 2M4
Tel: 604-943-6789
Toll-Free: 888-245-7722
e-mail: airspace@airspace.bc.ca
URL: airspace.bc.ca
Affiliation(s): Non-Smokers' Rights Association; Canadian Council on Smoking & Health

Al-Anon Family Groups (Canada), Inc. / Groupe familiaux Al-Anon
#245, 9 Antares Dr., Ottawa ON K2E 7V5
Tel: 613-723-8484; Fax: 613-723-0151
Toll-Free: 888-425-2666
e-mail: wso@al-anon.org
URL: www.al-anon.alateen.org
Richard L. Buchanan, CEO

Al-Anon Groupe La Vallée de l'Espoir
CP 21, Chibougamau QC G8P 2K5
Tél: 418-748-3779
URL: www.al-anon-quebec-est.org

Alcoholics Anonymous (GTA Intergroup) (AA)
#202, 234 Eglinton Ave. East, Toronto ON M4P 1K5
Tel: 416-487-5591; Fax: 416-487-5855
URL: www.aatoronto.org
Carole M. Keenan, Executive Director

Alcooliques Anonymes du Québec
3920, rue Rachel est, Montréal QC H1X 1Z3
Tél: 514-376-9230; Téléc: 514-374-2250
Courriel: region87@aa-quebec.org
URL: aa-quebec.org/AA_Quebec/index.htm
Claudette Pichette

Alcooliques Anonymes Groupe La Vallée du Cuivre
CP 21, Chibougamau QC G8P 2K5
Ligne sans frais: 866-376-6279

Canadian Assembly of Narcotics Anonymous (CANA)
PO Box 25073 RPO West Kildonan, Winnipeg MB R2V 4C7
URL: www.canaacna.org

Canadian Centre on Substance Abuse (CCSA) / Centre canadien de lutte contre l'alcoolisme et les toxicomanies (CCLAT)
#300, 75 Albert St., Ottawa ON K1P 5E7
Tel: 613-235-4048; *Fax:* 613-235-8101
Toll-Free: 800-559-4514
e-mail: info@ccsa.ca
URL: www.ccsa.ca
Enid Harrison, Director, Communications & Corporate Services
Michel Perron, CEO
Greg Graves, Senior Analyst, Research & Policy

Centre for Addiction & Mental Health (CAMH) / Centre de toxicomanie et de santé mentale
250 College St., Toronto ON M5T 1R8
Tel: 416-535-8501
Toll-Free: 800-463-6273
e-mail: public_affairs@camh.net
URL: www.camh.net
Affiliation(s): University of Toronto; University of Western Ontario; WHO
Paul Beeston, Chair

Council on Drug Abuse (CODA)
#505, 111 Peter St., Toronto ON M5V 2H1
Tel: 416-763-1491; *Fax:* 416-763-5343
e-mail: info@drugabuse.ca
URL: drugabuse.ca
Roger Gawne, Chair

MADD Canada / Les mères contre l'alcool auvolant
#500, 2010 Winston Park Dr., Oakville ON L6H 5R7
Tel: 905-829-8805
Toll-Free: 800-665-6233
e-mail: info@madd.ca
URL: www.madd.ca
Andrew Murie, CEO
Carolyn Swinson, Chair
Margaret Miller, President

Narcotiques Anonymes
1701, rue St-Luc, Chibougamau QC G8P 2N4
Tél: 418-770-5166

Parent Action on Drugs (PAD)
7 Hawksdale Rd., Toronto ON M3K 1W3
Tel: 416-395-4970; *Fax:* 416-395-4972
Toll-Free: 877-265-9279
e-mail: pad@parentactionondrugs.org
URL: www.parentactionondrugs.org
Diane Buhler, Executive Director
Susan Heim, Chair

Physicians for a Smoke-Free Canada / Médecins pour un Canada sans fumée
1226A Wellington St., Ottawa ON K1Y 3A1
Tel: 613-233-4878; *Fax:* 613-233-7797
e-mail: psc@smoke-free.ca
URL: www.smoke-free.ca
Atul Kapur, President
James Walker, Sec.-Treas.

Responsible Gambling Council (Ontario) (RGC(O)) / Le Conseil ontarien pour le jeu responsable
PO Box 90, #7070, 3080 Yonge St., Toronto ON M4N 3N1
Tel: 416-499-9800; *Fax:* 416-499-8260
Toll-Free: 888-391-1111
e-mail: mail@rgco.org
URL: www.responsiblegambling.org
Jon E. Kelly, PhD, Executive Director

Advertising & Marketing

The Advertising & Design Club of Canada (ADCC)
#205, 344 Bloor St. West, Toronto ON M5S 3A7
Tel: 416-423-4113; *Fax:* 416-423-3362
e-mail: info@theadcc.ca
URL: www.theadcc.ca
Brian Howlett, President
Dawn Wickstrom, Executive Director

Advertising Standards Canada (ASC) / Les normes canadiennes de la publicité
South Tower, #1801, 175 Bloor St. East, Toronto ON M4W 3R8
Tel: 416-961-6311; *Fax:* 416-961-7904
Toll-Free: 888-256-8646
e-mail: info@adstandards.com
URL: www.adstandards.com
Linda J. Nagel, President/CEO

American Marketing Association
#925, 2015, rue Peel, Montréal QC H3A 1T8
Tél: 514-842-5681; *Téléc:* 514-842-8836
Courriel: info@apcm.biz
URL: www.communicationmarketing.org
Mèdia social: www.facebook.com/group.php?gid=2373429565

American Marketing Association
#202, 720 Spadina Ave., Toronto ON M5S 2T9
Tel: 416-944-9529
e-mail: events@ama-toronto.com
URL: www.amatoronto.org
Social Media: www.facebook.com/group.php?gid=30147075783

Association canadienne des annonceurs inc.
#500, 500, rue Sherbrooke ouest, Montréal QC H3A 3C6
Tél: 514-842-6422; *Téléc:* 514-842-6223
Ligne sans frais: 800-883-0422
Courriel: rlund@ACAweb.ca (president)
URL: www.aca-online
Ron Lund, President and CEO

Association des agences de publicité du Québec (AAPQ) / Association of Québec Advertising Agencies
#925, 2015, rue Peel, Montréal QC H3A 1T8
Tél: 514-848-1732; *Téléc:* 514-848-1950
Courriel: aapq@aapq.ca
URL: www.aapq.ca
Yanik Deschênes, Président-directeur général

Association of Canadian Advertisers Inc. (ACA) / Association canadienne des annonceurs
#1103, 95 St. Clair Ave. West, Toronto ON M4V 1N6
Tel: 416-964-3805; *Fax:* 416-964-0771
Toll-Free: 800-565-0109
e-mail: info@aca-online.com
URL: www.aca-online.com
Ronald S. Lund, President & CEO
Dominique De Celles, Chair

Audit Bureau of Circulation (ABC)
Canadian Member Service Office, #850, 151 Bloor St. West, Toronto ON M5S 1S4
Tel: 416-962-5840; *Fax:* 416-962-5844
e-mail: service@accessabc.com
URL: www.accessabc.com
Michael J. Lavery, President & Managing Director

Canadian Advertising Research Foundation (CARF) / Fondation canadienne de recherche en publicité (FCRP)
#1005, 160 Bloor St. East, Toronto ON M4W 1B9
Tel: 416-413-3864; *Fax:* 416-413-3879
e-mail: tkormann@tvb.ca
URL: www.carf.ca
Affiliation(s): Advertising Research Foundation, New York
Melissa Rodway, Contact
Terry Rushbrook, Chairman

Canadian Automatic Merchandising Association (CAMA) / L'Association canadienne d'auto-distribution
Member Services, #100, 2233 Argentia Rd., Mississauga ON L5N 2X7
Fax: 905-826-4873
Toll-Free: 888-849-2262
e-mail: info@vending-cama.com
URL: www.vending-cama.com
Kim Lockie, National President
Amanda Curtis, CAE, Executive Director

Canadian Institute of Marketing / Institut canadien du marketing
205 Miller Dr., Georgetown ON L7G 6G4
Tel: 905-877-5369; *Fax:* 905-877-5369
e-mail: info@cinstmarketing.ca
URL: www.cinstmarketing.ca
Social Media: www.facebook.com/group.php?gid=8099252591
Affiliation(s): Affiliated with 20 other Institutes of Marketing around the world
A. Grant Lee, General Manager
Shiv Seechurn, Vice-President & Registrar
Oswald Emmanuel, Sec.-Treas.

Canadian Marketing Association (CMA) / Association canadienne du marketing (ACM)
#607, 1 Concorde Gate, Toronto ON M3C 3N6
Tel: 416-391-2362; *Fax:* 416-441-4062
e-mail: info@the-cma.org
URL: www.the-cma.org
Affiliation(s): European Direct Marketing Association; Direct Marketing Association - USA
John Gustavson, President & CEO
Wally Hill, Vice President, Public Affairs & Communications

Canadian Media Directors' Council (CMDC)
#1097, 1930 Yonge St., Toronto ON M4S 1Z4
Tel: 416-967-7282
e-mail: bruce.claassen@genesismedia.com
URL: www.cmdc.ca
Affiliation(s): Institute of Communications and Advertising (ICA)
Bruce Claassen, President
Cynthia Fleming, Secretary-Treasurer

Canadian Outdoor Measurement Bureau (COMB)
24 Duncan St., 2nd Fl., Toronto ON M5V 2B8
Tel: 416-968-3823; *Fax:* 416-968-9396
e-mail: hthompson@comb.org
URL: www.comb.org
Hellen Thompson, General Manager

Chartered Institute of Marketing Management of Ontario (CIMMO)
19 Bartley Dr., RR#3, Caledon East ON L0N 1E0
Tel: 905-880-2964
e-mail: goodall@allstream.net
Nigel Goodall, Chair

Conseil des directeurs médias du Québec (CDMQ)
#500, 500, rue Sherbrooke ouest, Montréal QC H3A 3C6
Tél: 514-990-1899
Courriel: info@cdmq.ca
URL: www.cdmq.org/
Affiliation(s): Association canadienne des annonceurs; Association des agences de publicitéu Québec; Canadian Media Directors' Council; Publicité Club de Montréal
François Vary, Pres@'sident

Institute of Communication Agencies (ICA) / Institut des communications et de la publicité (ICP)
#3002, 2300 Yonge St., Toronto ON M4P 1E4
Tel: 416-482-1396; *Fax:* 416-482-1856
Toll-Free: 800-567-7422
e-mail: ica@icacanada.ca
URL: www.ica-ad.com
Jani Yates, President
Gillian Graham, CEO

Marketing Research & Intelligence Association (MRIA) / L'Association de la recherche et de l'intelligence marketing (ARIM)
Bldg. 4, #104, 2600 Skymark Ave., Mississauga ON L4W 5B2
Tel: 905-602-6854; *Fax:* 905-602-6855
Toll-Free: 888-602-6742
e-mail: info@camro.org
URL: www.mria-arim.ca
Brendan Wycks, Executive Director
Barry Watson, President
John Tabone, Sec.-Treas.

National Advertising Benevolent Society (NABS) / Société nationale de bienfaisance en publicité
#903, 45 St. Clair Ave. West, Toronto ON M4V 1K9
Tel: 416-962-0446; *Fax:* 416-962-9149
Toll-Free: 800-661-6227
e-mail: nabs@nabs.org
URL: www.nabs.org
Affiliation(s): Canadian Society of Association Executives
Mike Fenton, President & CEO
Leslie Clare, Executive Director

National Advertising Benevolent Society
PO Box 93571, Vancouver BC V6E 4L7
Tel: 604-688-3087; *Fax:* 604-689-7167
e-mail: nabswest@nabswest.org
URL: www.nabswest.org

National Association of Major Mail Users, Inc. (NAMMU) / Association nationale des grands usagers postaux inc. (ANGUP)
#302, 517 Wellington St. West, Toronto ON M5V 1G1
Tel: 416-977-3703
Toll-Free: 800-453-1308
e-mail: executive@nammu.org
URL: www.nammu.org
Kathleen Rowe, President

Out-of-Home Marketing Association of Canada (OMAC) / Association marketing canadienne de l'affichage (AMCA)
24 Duncan St., 2nd. Fl., Toronto ON M5V 2B8
Tel: 416-968-3435; *Fax:* 416-968-6538
e-mail: rcaron@omaccanada.ca
URL: www.omaccanada.ca
Rosanne Caron, President

Print Measurement Bureau (PMB)
#1101, 77 Bloor St. West, Toronto ON M5S 1M2
Tel: 416-961-3205; *Fax:* 416-961-5052
Toll-Free: 800-762-0899
e-mail: lina@pmb.ca
URL: www.pmb.ca
Hastings Withers, Executive Vice President/Research
Steve Ferley, President
Lina Di Santo, Client Services Manager

Print Production Association (PPA)
PO Box 48027, 1881 Yonge St., Toronto ON M4S 3C0
Tel: 416-410-7841
e-mail: pgonsalves@interbrand.ca
Patricia Gonslaves, Executive Member
Sonya Popovich
Patricia Gonsalves
Mark Greene
Jennifer Whitfield

Promotional Product Professionals of Canada Inc. / Professionnels en produits promotionnels du Canada
#100, Côte-de-Liesse, Saint-Laurent QC H4T 2B5
Tel: 514-489-5359; *Fax:* 514-489-7760
Toll-Free: 866-450-7722
e-mail: info@pppc.ca
URL: www.promocan.com
Affiliation(s): Canadian Professional Sales Association (CPSA); Incentive Marketing Association (IMA); National Advertising Benevolent Society (NABS)
Lise Bujold, CMM, Office Administrator & Director, Events
Susan Beauchamp, Director, Marketing
Chantal Fontaine, PMP, Director, Professional Development & Certification
Carol Phillips, Director, Publications
Debbie Pinkerton, CSP, Manager, National Sales & Membership

Le Publicité Club de Montréal (PCM)
#925, 2015, rue Peel, Montréal QC H3A 1T8
Tél: 514-842-5681; *Téléc:* 514-842-8836
Courriel: info@pcm.qc.ca
URL: www.pcm.qc.ca
Lyse George, Présidente
Roger Sirard, Sec.-trés.

Radio Marketing Bureau (RMB)
#316, 175 Bloor St. East, Toronto ON M4W 3R8
Tel: 416-922-5757; *Fax:* 416-922-6542
Toll-Free: 800-667-2346
e-mail: info@rmb.ca
URL: www.rmb.ca
Gary Belgrave, President

Sign Association of Canada (SAC) / Association canadienne de l'enseigne (ACE)
#1519, 44 Victoria St., Toronto ON M5C 1Y2
Tel: 416-628-6608; *Fax:* 416-628-6607
Toll-Free: 877-470-9787
e-mail: info@sac-ace.ca
URL: www.sac-ace.ca
Bob Bronk, Executive Director
Fred Elkins, President

Trans-Canada Advertising Agency Network (T-CAAN)
#504, 4001 Bayview Ave., Toronto ON M2M 3Z7
Tel: 416-221-6984
e-mail: marketingmonkey@sympatico.ca
URL: www.tcaan.ca
Affiliation(s): Intermarket Agency Network
Alice Zaharchuk, Executive Director
Bill Whitehead, Managing Director

Agriculture & Farming

Agricultural Alliance of New Brunswick (AANB) / Alliance agricole du Nouveau-Brunswick
#303, 259 Brunswick St., Fredericton NB E3B 1G8
Tel: 506-452-8101; *Fax:* 506-452-1085
e-mail: alliance@fermenbfarm.ca
URL: www.fermenbfarm.ca
Nicole Arseneau, Office Manager
Mélanie Godin, Coordinator, Environmental Farm Plan

Agricultural Groups Concerned About Resources & the Environment
Ontario AgriCentre, #106, 100 Stone Rd. West, Guelph ON N1G 5L3
Tel: 519-837-1326; *Fax:* 519-837-3209
e-mail: agcare@agcare.org
URL: www.agcare.org
Affiliation(s): Christian Farmers' Federation of Ontario; Federated Women's Institutes of Ontario; Ontario Beekeepers' Association; Ontario Canola Growers' Association; Ontario Soybean Growers; Ontario Fruit & Vegetable Growers' Association; Ontario Corn Producers' Association; Ontario Wheat Producers' Marketing Board; Ontario Potato Board; Ontario Processing Vegetable Growers; Ontario Bean Producers' Marketing Board; Ontario Seed Growers' Association; Ontario Soil & Crop Improvement Association; Ontario Federation of Agriculture; Flowers Canada (Ontario); Ontario Flue-Cured Tobacco Growers' Marketing Board
Lilian Schaer, Executive Director
Heather Hargrave, Coordinator, Communications

Agricultural Institute of Canada (AIC) / Institut agricole du Canada
#900, 280 Albert St., Ottawa ON K1P 5G8
Tel: 613-232-9459; *Fax:* 613-594-5190
Toll-Free: 888-277-7980
e-mail: office@aic.ca
URL: www.aic.ca
Social Media: www.facebook.com/group.php?gid=14076387524
Affiliation(s): Canadian Agricultural Economics; Canadian Consulting Agrologists' Association; Canadian Society of Agronomy; Canadian Society of Animal Science; Canadian Society for Horticultural Science; Canadian Society of Soil Science; Canadian Society of Agrometeorology; British Columbia Institute of Agrologists; Alberta Institute of Agrologists; Saskatchewan Institute of Agrologists; Manitoba Institute of Agrologists; Ontario Institute of Agrologists; New Brunswick Institute of Agrologists; Nova Scotia Institute of Agrologists; PEI Institute of Agrologists; Newfoundland/Labrador Institute of Agrologists
Graham Gilchrist, President
Susan Simpson, Vice President

Agricultural Institute of Canada Foundation (AICF)
#900, 9 Corvus St., Ottawa ON K2E 7Z4
Tel: 613-232-9459; *Fax:* 613-594-5190
Toll-Free: 888-277-7980
e-mail: office@aic.ca
URL: www.aic.ca
Affiliation(s): Agricultural Institute of Canada
Myles Frosst, CEO
Susan Simpson, MBA, P.Ag., President
Sandy Todd, P.Ag., Treasurer

Agricultural Producers Association of Saskatchewan (APAS)
#100, 2400 College Ave., Regina SK S4P 1C8
Tel: 306-789-7774; *Fax:* 306-789-7779
e-mail: info@apas.ca
URL: www.apas.ca
Nial Kuyek, General Manager

Alberta Association of Agricultural Societies (AAAS)
J.G. O'Donoghue Bldg., #200, 7000 - 113 St., Edmonton AB T6H 5T6
Tel: 780-427-2174; *Fax:* 780-422-7755
e-mail: aaas@gov.ab.ca
URL: www.albertaagsocieties.ca
Tim Carson, Regional Director, Exec. Chair

Alberta Canola Producers Commission (ACPC)
#170, 14315 - 118 Ave., Edmonton AB T5L 4S6
Tel: 780-454-0844; *Fax:* 780-465-5473
Toll-Free: 800-551-6652
e-mail: acpc@canola.ab.ca
URL: www.canola.ab.ca
Affiliation(s): Canadian Canola Growers Association
Ward Toma, General Manager

Alberta Institute of Agrologists
#170, 2257 Premier Way, Sherwood Park AB T8H 2M8
Tel: 780-464-9797; *Fax:* 780-464-1171
e-mail: info@aia.ab.ca
URL: www.aia.ab.ca
Ken Davies, P.Ag., CEO & Registrar
David Lloyd, Chair

Alberta Milk
1303 - 91 St. SW, Edmonton AB T6X 1H1
Tel: 780-453-5942; *Fax:* 780-455-2196
Toll-Free: 877-361-1231
e-mail: cblatz@albertamilk.com
URL: www.albertamilk.com
Affiliation(s): Dairy Farmers of Canada
Bill Feenstra, Chair
Gerald Weiss, Executive Director
Mike Southwood, General Manager
Denise Brattinga, Manager, Finance
Ray Grapentine, Manager, Industry & Member Services
Katherine Loughlin, Manager, Market Development
Gerd Andres, Manager, Policy & Transportation

Animal Nutrition Association of Canada (ANAC) / Association de nutrition animale du Canada
#2, 109 Murray St., Ottawa ON K1N 5M5
Tel: 613-241-6421; *Fax:* 613-241-7970
e-mail: info@anac-anac.ca
URL: www.anac-anac.ca
Affiliation(s): Canola Council of Canada; Canada Grains Council; Canadian Egg Marketing Agency; Canadian Chicken Marketing Agency; Canadian Turkey Marketing Agency
Kathleen Sullivan, General Manager
Gary Golby, Chair

Association des jeunes ruraux du Québec (AJRQ)
65, rang 3 est, Princeville QC G6L 4B9
Tél: 819-364-5606; *Téléc:* 819-364-5006
Courriel: ajrq@ivic.qc.ca
URL: www.ajrq.qc.ca/
Affiliation(s): Conseil des 4-H du Canada
Geneviève Drolet, Présidente
Annie Chabot, Directrice générale

Association québécoise des industries de nutrition animale et céréalière (AQINAC)
CP 175, #200, 4790, rue Martineau, Saint-Hyacinthe QC J2S 7B4
Tél: 450-799-2440; *Téléc:* 450-799-2445
Courriel: info@aqinac.com
URL: www.aqinac.com
Yvan Lacroix, Président-directeur général

Atlantic Dairy Council (ADC)
PO Box 9410, Stn. A, #700, 6009 Quinpool Rd., Halifax NS B3K 5S3
Tel: 902-425-2445; *Fax:* 902-425-2441
e-mail: info@adcrecycles.com
URL: www.adrecycles.com
John K. Sutherland, Executive Secretary

Beef Information Centre (BIC)
Plaza 4, #101, 2000 Argentia Rd., Mississauga ON L5N 1W1
Tel: 905-821-4900; *Fax:* 905-821-4915
e-mail: info@beefinfo.org
URL: www.beefinfo.org

British Columbia Agriculture Council
#230, 32160 South Fraser Way, Abbotsford BC V2T 1W5
Tel: 604-854-4454; *Fax:* 604-854-4485
Toll-Free: 866-522-3477
e-mail: bcac@bcagcouncil.com
URL: www.bcac.bc.ca
Andy Dolberg, Executive Director

British Columbia Dairy Foundation
3236 Beta Ave., Burnaby BC V5G 4K4
Tel: 604-294-3775; *Fax:* 604-294-8199
Toll-Free: 800-242-6455
e-mail: contactus@bcdf.ca
URL: www.bcdairyfoundation.ca
Robin Smith, Executive Director

British Columbia Fruit Growers' Association
1473 Water St., Kelowna BC V1Y 1J6
Tel: 250-762-5226; *Fax:* 250-861-9089
e-mail: info@bcfga.com
URL: www.bcfga.com
Joe Sardinha, President

British Columbia Grape Growers Association (BCGA)
PO Box 2462, Stn. R, Kelowna BC V1X 6A5
Tel: 250-442-8303; *Fax:* 250-442-4076
Toll-Free: 877-762-4652
e-mail: office@grapegrowers.bc.ca
URL: www.grapegrowers.bc.ca
Connie Bielert, Secretary

British Columbia Institute of Agrologists (BCIA)
#205, 733 Johnson St., Victoria BC V8W 3C7
Tel: 250-380-9292; *Fax:* 250-380-9233
Toll-Free: 877-855-9291
e-mail: p.ag@bcia.com
URL: www.bcia.com
Kelly McLaughlin, Financial Officer

Don Rugg, Executive Director

British Columbia Milk Producers Association (BCMPA)
3236 Beta Ave., Burnaby BC V5G 4K4
Tel: 604-294-3737; *Fax:* 604-294-8199
Toll-Free: 877-462-2672
URL: www.bcmilkproducers.ca
Robin Smith, Executive Director

Canada Grains Council
#1215, 220 Portage Ave., Winnipeg MB R3C 0A5
Tel: 204-925-2130; *Fax:* 204-925-2132
e-mail: office@canadagrainscouncil.ca
URL: www.canadagrainscouncil.ca
Richard Wansbutter, Chair

Canadian 4-H Council
1129 Queen's Ave., Brandon MB R7A 1L9
Tel: 204-726-6136; *Fax:* 204-726-6260
e-mail: 4hcouncl@mts.net
URL: www.4h.mb.ca

Canadian 4-H Council
#5, 267 Connell St., Woodstock NB E7M 1L2
Tel: 506-324-6244; *Fax:* 506-325-9266
e-mail: nb4h@nb4h.com
URL: www.nb4h.com

Canadian 4-H Council
PO Box 550, 157 College Rd., Truro NS B2N 5E3
Tel: 902-893-6587; *Fax:* 902-893-2757
e-mail: pickaa@gov.ns.ca
URL: www.gov.ns.ca/agri/4h

Canadian 4-H Council
PO Box 2000, Charlottetown PE C1A 7N8
Tel: 902-368-4833; *Fax:* 902-368-6289
e-mail: pei4h@gov.pe.ca
URL: www.pei4h.pe.ca

Canadian 4-H Council
PO Box 23047, St. John's NL A1B 4J9
Tel: 709-682-1903
e-mail: robynmoss@mail.gov.nf.ca
URL: www.4hnl.ca

Canadian 4-H Council
5653 Hwy. 6, RR#5, Guelph ON N1H 6J2
Tel: 519-824-0101; *Fax:* 519-824-8759
Toll-Free: 877-410-8748
e-mail: inquiries@4-hontario.ca
URL: www.4-hontario.ca

Canadian 4-H Council / Conseil des 4-H du Canada
Central Experimental Farm, #26, 930 Carling Ave., Ottawa ON K1A 0C6
Tel: 613-234-4448; *Fax:* 613-234-1112
URL: www.4-h-canada.ca
Social Media: www.facebook.com/4HCanada; twitter.com/4HCanada
Lyndon Carlson, President
Mike Nowosad, Executive Director
Mike Carroll, Manager, Finance
Ken Lancastle, Manager, Communications & Marketing
Jim Washer, Manager, Programs

Canadian 4-H Council
#1, 904 Maud St., Enderby BC V0E 1V0
Tel: 250-376-0373; *Fax:* 250-554-2723
Toll-Free: 866-776-0373
e-mail: mail@bc4h.bc.ca
URL: www.bc4h.bc.ca

Canadian 4-H Council
Airdrie Office, 97 East Lake Ramp NE, Airdrie AB T4A 0C3
Tel: 403-948-8501; *Fax:* 403-948-2069
e-mail: rob.g.smith@gov.ab.ca
URL: www.4h.ab.ca

Canadian 4-H Council
Rural Service Centre, 3830 Thatcher Ave., Saskatoon SK S7K 2H6
Tel: 306-933-7727; *Fax:* 306-933-7730
e-mail: webmaster@4-h.sk.ca
URL: www.4-h.sk.ca

Canadian Consulting Agrologists Association (CCAA) / Association canadienne des agronomes-conseils
502 - 45 St. West, 2nd Fl., Saskatoon SK S7L 6H2
Tel: 306-933-2974; *Fax:* 306-244-4497
e-mail: info@ccaa.bz
URL: www.ccaa.bz
Adele Buettner, Executive Director
Terry Betker, PAg, CAC, President

Canadian Co-operative Association (CCA) / Association des coopératives du Canada (ACC)
Co-operative House, #400, 275 Bank St., Ottawa ON K2P 2L6
Tel: 613-238-6711
e-mail: info@CoopsCanada.coop
URL: www.coopscanada.coop
Affiliation(s): Conseil canadien de la coopération et de la mutualitéCo-operative Development Initiative (co-managed by CCA and CCCM); Co-operative Development Foundation of Canada (CDF)
Carol Hunter, Executive Director
Jo-Anne Ferguson, Senior Director, International Development
John Anderson, Director, Government Affairs & Public Policy
Norma Jones, Director, Finance & Administration
Donna Balkan, Manager, Communications

Canadian Federation of Agriculture (CFA) / Fédération canadienne de l'agriculture
#1101, 75 Albert St., Ottawa ON K1P 5E7
Tel: 613-236-3633; *Fax:* 613-236-5749
e-mail: info@cfafca.ca
URL: www.cfa-fca.ca
Affiliation(s): BC Agriculture Council; Keystone Agricultural Producers (Manitoba); Ontario Federation of Agriculture; L'Union des producteurs agricoles (Québec); Coopérative fédérée de Québec; NS Federation of Agriculture; PEI Federation of Agriculture; Agriculture Producers Assoc. of New Brunswick; Newfoundland & Labrador Federation of Agriculture; Dairy Farmers of Canada; Canadian Egg Marketing Agency; Chicken Farmers of Canada; Canadian Turkey Marketing Agency; Canadian Broiler Hatching Egg Marketing Agency; Canadian Sugar Beet Producers' Assoc.; Canadian Pork Council; Wild Rose Agricultural Producers
Ron Bonnett, 2nd Vice-President
Bob Friesen, President
Laurent Pellerin, 1st Vice-President

Canadian Feed Information Centre (CFIC)
PO Box 1251, Swift Current SK S9H 3X4
Tel: 306-773-5401; *Fax:* 306-773-3955
e-mail: vknipfel@sasktel.net
J.E. Knipfel, Contact

Canadian Honey Council / Conseil canadien du miel
#236, 234 - 5149 Country Hills Blvd. NW, Calgary AB T3A 5K8
Tel: 403-208-7141; *Fax:* 403-547-4317
e-mail: chc-ccm@honeycouncil.ca
URL: www.honeycouncil.ca
Affiliation(s): Apimondia
Heather Clay, National Coordinator

Canadian Organic Growers Inc. (COG)
323 Chapel St., Ottawa ON K1N 7Z2
Tel: 613-216-0741; *Fax:* 613-236-0743
Toll-Free: 888-375-7383
e-mail: office@cog.ca
URL: www.cog.ca
Affiliation(s): International Federation of Organic Agriculture Movements; Organic Trade Association
Laura Telford, PhD, Executive Director

Canadian Pest Management Association (CPMA) / Association canadienne de la gestion parasitaire (ACGP)
PO Box 1748, Moncton NB E1C 9X5
Fax: 866-957-7378
Toll-Free: 866-630-2762
e-mail: cpma@pestworld.org
URL: www.pestworldcanada.org
Norm Doiron, President

Canadian Plowing Organization
43 Ewen Dr., Uxbridge ON L9P 1L5
Tel: 905-852-6221
e-mail: info@canadianplowing.ca
URL: www.canadianplowing.ca
Affiliation(s): World Ploughing Organization
Robert Timbers, Contact

Canadian Seed Growers' Association (CSGA) / Association canadienne des producteurs de semences
PO Box 8455, #202, 240 Catherine St., Ottawa ON K1G 3T1
Tel: 613-236-0497; *Fax:* 613-563-7855
e-mail: seeds@seedgrowers.ca
URL: www.seedgrowers.ca
Dale Apolphe, Executive Director

Canadian Seed Trade Association (CSTA) / Association canadienne du commerce des semences (ACCS)
#505, 39 Robertson Rd., Ottawa ON K2H 8R2
Tel: 613-829-9527; *Fax:* 613-829-3530
e-mail: csta@cdnseed.org
URL: www.cdnseed.org
W.C. Leask, Executive Vice-President
David Sippell, President

Canadian Society for Bioengineering (CSBE) / Société canadienne de génie agroalimentaire et de bioingénierie (SCGAB)
PO Box 23101, Stn. McGillivray, Winnipeg MB R3T 5S3
Tel: 204-233-1881; *Fax:* 204-231-8282
e-mail: bioeng@shaw.ca
URL: www.bioeng.ca
Affiliation(s): American Society of Agricultural & Biological Engineers
James S. Townsend, Secretary
Stéphane Lemay, President

Canadian Society of Agronomy
S.C. Sheppard, PO Box 637, Pinawa MB R0E 1L0
Tel: 204-753-2747; *Fax:* 204-753-8478
e-mail: sheppards@ecomatters.com
URL: www.agronomycanada.com
Steve Sheppard, Executive Director

Canadian Sphagnum Peat Moss Association (CSPMA) / Association canadienne Tourbe de Sphaigne
#2208, 13 Mission Ave., St Albert AB T8N 1H6
Tel: 780-460-8280; *Fax:* 780-459-0939
Toll-Free: 888-873-7328
e-mail: cspma@peatmoss.com
URL: www.peatmoss.com
Paul Short, President

Canadian Sugar Beet Producers' Association Inc. (CSBPA)
4900 - 50 St., Taber AB T1G 1T3
Tel: 403-223-1110; *Fax:* 403-223-1022
e-mail: sugarmb@telusplanet.net
Affiliation(s): World Association of Beet & Cane Growers
Bruce Webster, General Manager

Canola Council of Canada
#400, 167 Lombard Ave., Winnipeg MB R3B 0T6
Tel: 204-982-2100; *Fax:* 204-942-1841
e-mail: admin@canolacouncil.org
URL: www.canolacouncil.org
JoAnne Bluth, President

Certified Organic Associations of British Columbia (COABC)
#202, 3002 - 32nd Ave., Vernon BC V1T 2L7
Tel: 250-260-4429; *Fax:* 250-260-4436
e-mail: office@certifiedorganic.bc.ca
URL: www.certifiedorganic.bc.ca
Sarah Clark, Administrator
Kristy Wipperman, Office Manager

Christian Farmers Federation of Ontario (CFFO)
7660 Mill Rd., RR#4, Guelph ON N1H 6J1
Tel: 519-837-1620; *Fax:* 519-824-1835
e-mail: cffomail@christianfarmers.org
URL: www.christianfarmers.org
Affiliation(s): AG Care; Christian Farmers Federation of Alberta; Christian Environmental Council; Rural Development Advisory Committee
John Kikkert, President

Conseil des industriels laitiers du Québec inc. (CILQ) / Québec Dairy Council Inc.
#310, 8585, boul St-Laurent, Montréal QC H2P 2M9
Tél: 514-381-5331; *Téléc:* 514-381-6677
Courriel: info@cilq.ca
URL: cilq.ca
Pierre M. Nadeau, Président-directeur général
Charles Langlois, Vice-président, Affaires économiques & Approvisionnement
Yolaine Villeneuve, Coordonnatrice, Finances & développement des affaires

Coopérative fédérée du Québec (CFQ)
#200, 9001, boul de l'Acadie, Montréal QC H4N 3H7
Tél: 514-384-6450; *Téléc:* 514-384-7176
Courriel: information@lacoop.coop
URL: www.coopfed.qc.ca
Denis Richard, Président

CropLife Canada
#627, 21 Four Seasons Pl., Toronto ON M9B 6J8
Tel: 416-622-9771; *Fax:* 416-622-6764
e-mail: timmerk@croplife.ca; siskn@croplife.ca
URL: www.croplife.ca
Kim Trimmer, Contact

Dairy Farmers of Canada (DFC) / Les Producteurs laitiers du Canada (PLC)
21 Florence St., Ottawa ON K2P 0W6
Tel: 613-236-9997; *Fax:* 613-236-0905
URL: www.dairyfarmers.ca
Jacques Laforge, President
Bruce Saunders, 1st Vice-President
Wally Smith, 2nd Vice-President

Dairy Farmers of Nova Scotia (DFNS)
#100, 4060 Hwy. 236, Lower Truro NS B6L 1J9
Tel: 902-893-6455; *Fax:* 902-897-9768
e-mail: hboyd@dfns.ca
URL: www.dfns.ca
Grian Cameron, General Manager
Barron Blois, Chair

Fédération d'agriculture biologique du Québec (FABQ)
#100, 555, boul Roland-Therrien, Longueuil QC J4H 3Y9
Tél: 450-679-0530; *Téléc:* 450-670-4867
Courriel: fabq@upa.qc.ca
URL: www.fabqbio.ca
Gérard Bouchard, Président

Fédération des agricultrices du Québec (FAQ)
555, boul Roland-Therrien, Longueuil QC J4H 4E7
Tél: 450-679-0530; *Téléc:* 450-463-5228
Courriel: info@agricultrices.com
URL: www.agricultrices.com
Carmen Ducharme, Présidente

Fédération des producteurs de bovins du Québec (FPBQ) / Federation of Québec Beef Producers
#305, 555, boul Roland-Therrien, Longueuil QC J4H 4G2
Tél: 450-679-0530; *Téléc:* 450-442-9348
Courriel: fpbq@upa.qc.ca
URL: www.bovin.qc.ca
Affiliation(s): Union des producteurs agricoles
Gaëtan Bélanger, Secrétaire-trésorier

Fédération des producteurs de lait du Québec (FPLQ)
555, boul Roland-Therrien, Longueuil QC J4H 3Y9
Tél: 450-679-0530
Courriel: fplq@upa.qc.ca
URL: www.lait.org
Affiliation(s): Union des producteurs agricoles
Marcel Groleau, Président

Fédération des producteurs de porcs du Québec (FPPQ)
CP 120, 555, boul Roland-Therrien, Longueuil QC J4H 4E9
Tél: 450-679-0540; *Téléc:* 450-679-0102
Ligne sans frais: 800-363-7672
Courriel: fppq@upa.qc.ca
URL: www.leporcduquebec.qc.ca
Affiliation(s): Union des producteurs agricoles du Québec
Bernard Verret, Directeur général

Flax Council of Canada
#465, 167 Lombard Ave., Winnipeg MB R3B 0T6
Tel: 204-982-2115; *Fax:* 204-942-1841
e-mail: flax@flaxcouncil.ca
URL: www.flaxcouncil.ca
M. Barry Hall, President

Horticulture Nova Scotia (HNS)
Kentville Agricultural Centre, 32 Main St., Kentville NS B4N 1J5
Tel: 902-678-9335; *Fax:* 902-678-1280
e-mail: hortns@ns.sympatico.ca
URL: www.hortns.com
Affiliation(s): NS Federation of Agriculture; Canadian Horticultural Council
Donna Crawford, Administrative Coordinator
Lloyd Evans, President

Keystone Agricultural Producers (KAP)
#203, 1700 Ellice Ave., Winnipeg MB R3H 0B1
Tel: 204-697-1140; *Fax:* 204-697-1109
e-mail: kap@kap.mb.ca
URL: www.kap.mb.ca
Yvonne Rideout, General Manager
Ian Wishart, President

Manitoba Institute of Agrologists (MIA)
#201, 38 Dafoe Ave., Winnipeg MB R3T 2N2
Tel: 204-275-3721; *Fax:* 204-474-7521
e-mail: mia@mts.net
URL: www.mia.mb.ca
Jim Weir, Executive Director & Registrar

Mushrooms Canada (CMGA)
7660 Mill Rd., RR#4, Guelph ON N1H 6J1
Tel: 519-829-4125; *Fax:* 519-837-0729
e-mail: info@canadianmushroom.com
URL: www.mushrooms.ca
Affiliation(s): International Society for Mushroom Science (ISMS)
William Stevens, Executive Vice-President
Glenn Martin, President

National Farmers Union (NFU) / Syndicat national des cultivateurs
2717 Wentz Ave., Saskatoon SK S7K 4B6
Tel: 306-652-9465; *Fax:* 306-664-6226
e-mail: nfu@nfu.ca
URL: www.nfu.ca
Affiliation(s): Action Canada Network
Nigel Smith, Youth President
Colleen Ross, Women's President
Stewart Wells, President

New Brunswick Institute of Agrologists (NBIA) / L'Institut des agronomes du Nouveau-Brunswick (IANB)
PO Box 3479, Stn. B, Fredericton NB E3B 5H2
Tel: 506-459-5536; *Fax:* 506-454-7837
e-mail: nbia@nbagrologists.nb.ca
URL: www.nbagrologists.nb.ca
Charles Briggs, President
Duncan Fraser, Secretary
Margaret Mann, Registrar
Rita Rattray, Office Administrator

Newfoundland & Labrador Federation of Agriculture
PO Box 1045, 308 Brookfield Rd., Bldg. 4, Mount Pearl NL A1N 3C9
Tel: 709-747-4874; *Fax:* 709-747-8827
e-mail: info@nlfa.ca
URL: www.nlfa.ca
Paul Connors, Executive Director
Kim O'Rourke, Administrative Assistant

Newfoundland & Labrador Institute of Agrologists (NLIA)
c/o Atlantic Cool Climate Crop Research Centre, PO Box 978, Mount Pearl NL A1N 3C9
Tel: 709-772-4784; *Fax:* 709-772-6064
e-mail: markmacpherson@gov.nl.ca
URL: www.aic.ca/agrology/nlia.cfm
David McKenzie, P.Ag., Registrar
Mark MacPherson, P.Ag, President

Nova Scotia Federation of Agriculture (NSFA)
Covington Place, 332 Willow St., 2nd Fl., Truro NS B2N 5A5
Tel: 902-893-2293; *Fax:* 902-893-7063
e-mail: info@nsfa-fane.ca
URL: www.nsfa-fane.ca
Laurence Nason, CEO
William (Willy) Versteeg, President
Donna Langille, Manager, Operations

Nova Scotia Fruit Growers' Association (NSFGA)
Kentville Agricultural Centre, 32 Main St., Kentville NS B4N 1J5
Tel: 902-678-1093; *Fax:* 902-679-1567
URL: www.nsapples.com
Affiliation(s): Nova Scotia Federation of Agriculture
Brian Boates, President

Nova Scotia Institute of Agrologists (NSIA)
PO Box 550, 35 Tower Rd., Truro NS B2N 5E3
Tel: 902-893-6520; *Fax:* 902-893-6393
e-mail: nsagrologists@eastlink.ca
URL: www.nsagrologists.ca

Ontario Agri Business Association (OABA)
#104, 160 Research Lane, Guelph ON N1G 5B2
Tel: 519-822-3004; *Fax:* 519-822-8862
e-mail: info@oaba.on.ca
URL: www.oaba.on.ca
D.O. Buttenham, CEO
Gwen Paddock, President
Cory McDonald, Vice-President
Dale Cowan, Treasurer

Ontario Beekeepers' Association (OBA)
#476, 8560 Tremaine Road, Milton ON L9T 4Z1
Tel: 905-636-0661; *Fax:* 905-636-0662
e-mail: info@ontariobee.com
URL: www.ontariobee.com
Virginia Steckle, Business Administrator
Brent Halsall, President

Ontario Creamerymen's Association
26 Dominion St., Alliston ON L9R 1L5
Tel: 705-435-6751; *Fax:* 705-435-6797
e-mail: allistoncreamery1@bellnet.ca
Lloyd Kennedy, President

Ontario Dairy Council (ODC)
6533D Mississauga Rd., Mississauga ON L5N 1A6
Tel: 905-542-3620; *Fax:* 905-542-3624
Toll-Free: 866-542-3620
e-mail: info@ontariodairies.ca
URL: www.ontariodairies.ca
Affiliation(s): International Dairy Federation
Tom Kane, President
Christina Lewis, Vice-President

Ontario Federation of Agriculture (OFA)
Ontario AgriCentre, #206, 100 Stone Rd. West, London ON N1G 5L3
Tel: 519-821-8883; *Fax:* 519-821-8810
Toll-Free: 800-668-3276
e-mail: info@ofa.on.ca
URL: www.ofa.on.ca
Affiliation(s): AG Care
Bette Jean Crews, President
Neil Currie, General Manager

Ontario Fruit & Vegetable Growers' Association (OFVGA) / L'Association des fruiticulteurs et des maraîchers de l'Ontario
#105, 355 Elmira Rd. North, Guelph ON N1K 1S5
Tel: 519-763-6160; *Fax:* 519-763-6604
e-mail: info@ofvga.org
URL: www.ofvga.org
Art Smith, CEO

Ontario Institute of Agrologists (OIA)
Ontario AgriCentre, #108, 100 Stone Rd. West, Guelph ON N1G 5L3
Tel: 519-826-4226; *Fax:* 519-826-4228
e-mail: info@oia.on.ca
URL: www.oia.on.ca
Affiliation(s): Certified Crop Advisor Program; Ontario Agricultural Hall of Fame Association; Ontario Agricultural Training Institute; Ontario Farm Animal Council; Western Fair Association
Terry Kingsmill, M.A., P.Ag., Registrar
Bruce Hobin, P.Ag., President
Pat Joannie, Project Manager
Phillis Chang, Ph.D., B.Ed., Director, Finance & Administration

Ontario Maple Syrup Producers' Association (OMSPA)
PO Box 1492, Ridgetown ON N0P 2C0
Tel: 519-674-4000; *Fax:* 519-674-4004
e-mail: ontariomaple@bellnet.ca
URL: www.ontariomaple.com
Sally Huffman Brown, Business Administrator

Ontario Plowmen's Association (OPA)
188 Nicklin Rd., Guelph ON N1H 7L5
Tel: 519-767-2928; *Fax:* 519-767-2101
Toll-Free: 800-661-7569
e-mail: admin@plowingmatch.org
URL: www.plowingmatch.org
Carl Weber, 1st Vice-President
Ralph Millman, 2nd Vice-President
Jerry Smith, General Manager
Graeme Craig, President

Ordre des agronomes du Québec (OAQ)
#810, 1001, rue Sherbrooke est, Montréal QC H2L 1L3
Tél: 514-596-3833; *Téléc:* 514-596-2974
Ligne sans frais: 800-361-3833
Courriel: agronome@oaq.qc.ca
URL: www.oaq.qc.ca
Conrad Bernier, Président

Prince Edward Island Federation of Agriculture (PEIFA)
420 University Ave., Charlottetown PE C1A 7Z5
Tel: 902-368-7289; *Fax:* 902-368-7204
e-mail: ianm@peifa.ca
URL: www.peifa.ca
Ian McIsaac, Executive Director

Prince Edward Island Institute of Agrologists (PEIIA)
PO Box 2712, Charlottetown PE C1A 8C3

Tel: 902-892-1943; Fax: 902-892-0443
e-mail: peiia@pei.sympatico.ca
URL: www.peiia.ca
Brian Beaton, P.Ag., President
Bert Christie, P.Ag., Sec.-Treas.
Claude Gallant, P.Ag., Registrar

Prince Edward Island Vegetable Growers Co-op Association
PO Box 1494, 280 Sherwood Rd., Charlottetown PE C1A 7N1
Tel: 902-892-5361; Fax: 902-566-2383
e-mail: peiveg@eastlink.ca
Don Read, Manager

Québec 4-H
#224, 1040, av Belvédère, Sillery QC G1S 3G3
Tel: 418-529-4705; Fax: 418-529-3021
e-mail: 4h.bc@clubs4h.qc.ca
URL: www.clubs4h.qc.ca
Tammy Oswick-Kearney, Provincial Coordinator

Québec Farmers' Association (QFA)
#255, 555, boul Roland-Therrien, Longueuil QC J4H 4E7
Tel: 450-679-0540; Fax: 450-463-5291
e-mail: qfa@upa.qc.ca
URL: www.quebecfarmers.org
Ivan Hale, Executive Director
Wendy Jones, Director, Operations

Saskatchewan Association of Agricultural Societies & Exhibitions (SAASE)
PO Box 31025, Regina SK S4R 8R6
Tel: 306-565-2121; Fax: 306-565-2079
e-mail: gduck.saase@sasktel.net
URL: www.saase.ca
Affiliation(s): Canadian Association of Fairs & Exhibitions
Glen Duck, Executive Director

Saskatchewan Beekeepers Association (SBA)
PO Box 55, RR#3, Yorkton SK S3N 2X5
Tel: 306-743-5469; Fax: 306-743-5528
e-mail: whowland@accesscomm.ca
URL: www.saskatchewanbeekeepers.ca
Affiliation(s): Canadian Honey Council (CHC)
Calvin Parsons, President
Corey Bacon, Vice-President
Wink Howland, Secetary-Treasurer
Dennis Glennie, Coordinator, SBA Bear Fence Program

Saskatchewan Canola Growers Association (SCGA)
#210, 111 Research Dr., Saskatoon SK S7N 3R2
Tel: 306-668-2380
Toll-Free: 800-690-5788
URL: www.canolagrowers.ca
Affiliation(s): Canola Council of Canada
Wayne Thompson, Executive Director
Stan Jeeves, President
Tyler Markusson, Vice-President
Ed Schafer, Vice-President
Jeff Pylatuik, Secretary

SeCan Association / Association SeCan
#501, 300 March Rd., Kanata ON K2K 2E2
Tel: 613-592-8600; Fax: 613-592-9497
Toll-Free: 800-764-5487
e-mail: seed@secan.com
URL: www.secan.com
Jeff Reid, General Manager

Society of Ontario Nut Growers (SONG)
RR#3, Niagara-on-the-Lake ON L0S 1J0
Tel: 905-935-9773; Fax: 905-935-6887
e-mail: nuttrees@grimonut.com
URL: www.songonline.ca
Affiliation(s): Eastern Chapter Society of Ontario Nut Growers
Ernie Grimo, Treasurer

Union des producteurs agricoles (UPA)
#100, 555, boul. Roland-Therrien, Longueuil QC J4H 3Y9
Tél: 450-679-0530
Courriel: upa@upa.qc.ca
URL: www.upa.qc.ca
Christian Lacasse, Président

Vegetable Growers' Association of Manitoba (VGAM)
PO Box 984, Portage la Prairie MB R1N 3C3
Tel: 204-428-3188; Fax: 204-428-3245
e-mail: vgam@escape.ca
Doug Connery, Chair, Labour

Western Barley Growers Association (WBGA)
Agriculture Centre, 97 East Lake Ramp NE, Airdrie AB T4A 0C3
Tel: 403-912-3998; Fax: 403-948-2069
e-mail: wbga@wbga.org
URL: www.wbga.org
Brian Otto, President
Rick Strankman, Treasurer
Jeff Nielsen, Past President
Doug Robertson, Alberta Vice-President
Art Walde, Saskatchewan Vice-President

Wild Rose Agricultural Producers
#102, 115 Portage Close, Sherwood Park AB T8H 2R5
Tel: 780-416-6530; Fax: 780-416-6531
Toll-Free: 888-616-6530
e-mail: info@wrap.ab.ca
URL: www.wrap.ab.ca
Rod Scarlett, Executive Director

Yukon Agricultural Association
#203, 302 Steele St., Whitehorse YT Y1A 2E5
Tel: 867-668-6864; Fax: 867-393-9566
e-mail: info@yukonag.ca
URL: www.yukonag.ca
Al Falle, President
Rick Tone, Executive Director

AIDS

Action Séro Zéro
CP 246, Succ. C, Montréal QC H2L 4K1
Tél: 514-521-7778; Téléc: 514-521-7665
URL: www.sero-zero.qc.ca
Robert Rousseau, Directeur général

The AIDS Foundation of Canada Inc.
#302, 1224 Hamilton St., Vancouver BC V6B 2S8
Tel: 604-688-7294; Fax: 604-689-4888
Nathan S. Ganapathi, President

AIDS Vancouver (AV)
1107 Seymour St., Vancouver BC V6B 5S8
Tel: 604-893-2201; Fax: 604-893-2211; TTY: 604-893-2215Crisis Hot-Line: 604-687-2437
e-mail: contact@aidsvancouver.org
URL: www.aidsvancouver.org
Social Media: www.facebook.com/group.php?gid=48799305725
David Swan, Executive Director

AIDS Vancouver Island (AVI)
1601 Blanshard St., Victoria BC V8W 2J5
Tel: 250-384-2366; Fax: 250-380-9411
Toll-Free: 800-665-2437Crisis Hot-Line: 250-384-4554
e-mail: info@avi.org
URL: www.avi.org
Social Media: www.facebook.com/group.php?gid=221277862889
Katrina Jensen, Executive Director

Black Coalition for AIDS Prevention
#207, 110 Spadina Ave., Toronto ON M5V 2K4
Tel: 416-977-9955; Fax: 416-977-7664
e-mail: blackcap@black-cap.com
URL: www.black-cap.com
Social Media: www.facebook.com/group.php?gid=10127593377
Shannon Thomas Ryan, Executive Director

Blood Ties Four Directions Centre
4230F - 4th Ave., Whitehorse YT Y1A 1K1
Tel: 867-633-2437; Fax: 867-633-2447
Toll-Free: 877-333-2437
e-mail: bloodties@klondiker.com
URL: www.bloodties.ca

Canadian AIDS Society (CAS) / Société canadienne du sida (SCS)
#800, 190 O'Connor St., Ottawa ON K2P 2R3
Tel: 613-230-3580; Fax: 613-563-4998
Toll-Free: 800-499-1986
e-mail: casinfo@cdnaids.ca
URL: www.cdnaids.ca
Social Media: www.facebook.com/group.php?gid=172950011095
Gerry McConnery, Chair
Jeffrey Keller, Vice-Chair
Monique Doolittle-Romas, Executive Director
Christal Capostinsky, Secretary
Marc Laplerre, Treasurer
Jordan Tarini, Director, Youth
Kim Thomas, Director, Programs

Canadian Foundation for AIDS Research (CANFAR) / Fondation canadienne de recherche sur le SIDA
#901, 165 University Ave., Toronto ON M5H 3B8
Tel: 416-361-6281; Fax: 416-361-5736
Toll-Free: 800-563-2873
e-mail: cure@canfar.com
URL: www.canfar.com
Social Media: www.facebook.com/group.php?gid=147646406275
Elissa Beckett, Executive Director

Canadian HIV/AIDS Legal Network / Réseau juridique canadien VIH/sida
#600, 1240 Bay St., Toronto ON M5R 2A7
Tel: 416-595-1666; Fax: 416-595-0094
e-mail: info@aidslaw.ca
URL: www.aidslaw.ca
Richard Elliott, Executive Director
Richard Pearshouse, Director, Research & Policy

Coalition des organismes communautaires québécois de lutte contre le sida (COCQ-SIDA)
1, rue Sherbrooke est, Montréal QC H2X 3V8
Tél: 514-844-2477; Téléc: 514-844-2498
Courriel: info@cocqsida.com
URL: www.cocqsida.com
Hélène Légaré, Présidente
Ken Monteith, Directeur général

Healing Our Spirit
395 Railway St., Vancouver BC V6A 1A6
Tel: 604-605-8901; Fax: 604-605-8902
Toll-Free: 866-605-8901
e-mail: info@fnes.ca
URL: www.healingourspirit.org
Affiliation(s): Red Road HIV/AIDS Network; BC Aboriginal AIDS Awareness Program; AIDS Vancouver; BC Persons with AIDS
Norma Guerin, Executive Director
Leonard George, President

Maison Plein Coeur
1611, rue Dorion, Montréal QC H2K 4A5
Tél: 514-597-0554; Téléc: 514-597-2788
Courriel: info@maisonpleincoeur.org
URL: www.maisonpleincoeur.org

Toronto PWA Foundation (TPWAF)
399 Church St., 2nd Fl., Toronto ON M5B 2J6
Tel: 416-506-1400; Fax: 416-506-1404
e-mail: info@pwatoronto.org
URL: www.pwatoronto.org
Murray Jose, Executive Director@SUBCHAPTER = Animal Breeding

Appaloosa Horse Club of Canada (ApHCC)
PO Box 940, Claresholm AB T0L 0T0
Tel: 403-625-3326; Fax: 403-625-2274
e-mail: aphcc@appaloosa.ca
URL: www.appaloosa.ca
Rick Miller, President
Karen Bedford, Secretary
Mervin Veinot, Treasurer

Ayrshire Breeders Association of Canada (ABAC) / L'Associaton des éleveurs Ayrshire du Canada
4865, boul Laurier ouest, Saint-Hyacinthe QC J2S 3V4
Tel: 450-778-3535; Fax: 450-778-3531
e-mail: info@ayrshire-canada.com
URL: www.ayrshire-canada.com
Linda Ness, Executive Director
Chad McKell, Registrar

Canadian Angus Association (CAA) / L'Association canadienne Angus
#142, 6715 - 8 St. NE, Calgary AB T2E 7H7
Tel: 403-571-3580; Fax: 403-571-3599
Toll-Free: 888-571-3580
e-mail: tina1@cdnangus.ca; registry@cdnangus.ca; cacp@cdnangus.ca
URL: www.cdnangus.ca
Doug Fee, Chief Executive Officer
Bob Switzer, President
Sharmayne Byrgesen, Registrar

Canadian Arabian Horse Registry
#113, 37 Athabascan Ave., Sherwood Park AB T8A 4H3
Tel: 780-416-4990; Fax: 780-416-4860
e-mail: cahr@cahr.ca
URL: www.cahr.ca
Affiliation(s): Canadian Equestrian Federation
Christine Tribe, Registrar
Marcia Friesen, President
Robert Sproule, Secretary-Treasurer

Canadian Belgian Horse Association
17150, Conc. 10, Schomberg ON L0G 1T0

Tel: 905-939-1186; Fax: 905-939-7547
e-mail: cbha@csolve.net
URL: www.canadianbelgianhorse.com
Barb Meyers, Secretary

Canadian Bison Association (CBA) / Association canadienne du bison
PO Box 3116, #200, 1660 Pasqua St., Regina SK S4P 3G7
Tel: 306-522-4766; Fax: 306-522-4768
URL: www.canadianbison.ca
Affiliation(s): National Bison Association - USA; BC Interior Bison Association; Peace Country Bison Association; Alberta, Saskatchewan, Manitoba, Ontario Bison Association; Québec Bison Union
Gavin Conacher, Executive Director

Canadian Blonde d'Aquitaine Association
c/o Canadian Livestock Records Corp., 2417 Holly Lane, Ottawa ON K1V 0M7
Tel: 613-731-7110; Fax: 613-731-0704
e-mail: cbda@clrc.ca
URL: www.canadianblondeassociation.ca
Myrna Flesch, President

Canadian Brown Swiss & Braunvieh Association / L'association canadienne de la Suisse Brune et de la Braunvieh
RR#5, Hwy. 6 North, Guelph ON N1H 6J2
Tel: 519-821-2811; Fax: 519-763-6582
e-mail: brownswiss@gencor.ca
URL: www.browncow.ca
Ernst Gubelmann, President

Canadian Cattle Breeders' Association (CCBA) / Société des éleveurs de bovins canadiens (SEBC)
4865, boul Laurier ouest, Saint-Hyacinthe QC J2S 3V4
Tel: 450-774-2775; Fax: 450-774-9775
e-mail: info@cqrl.org
URL: www.clrc.ca/canadiancattle.shtml
Michelle Giasson, Sec.-trés.

Canadian Cattlemen's Association (CCA)
#310, 6715 - 8 St. NE, Calgary AB T2E 7H7
Tel: 403-275-8558; Fax: 403-274-5686
e-mail: feedback@cattle.ca
URL: www.cattle.ca
Hugh Lynch-Staunton, President
Brad Wildeman, Vice President
Darcy Davis, Chairman

Canadian Cattlemen's Association
#1207, 350 Sparks St., Ottawa ON K1R 7S8
Tel: 613-233-9375; Fax: 613-233-2860

Canadian Charolais Association (CCA)
2320 - 41 Ave. NE, Calgary AB T2E 6W8
Tel: 403-250-9242; Fax: 403-291-9324
e-mail: cca@charolais.com
URL: www.charolais.com
Neil Gillies, General Manager

Canadian Co-operative Wool Growers Ltd. (CCWG)
PO Box 130, 142 Franktown Rd., Carleton Place ON K7C 3P3
Tel: 613-257-2714; Fax: 613-257-8896
Toll-Free: 800-488-2714
e-mail: ccwghq@wool.ca
URL: www.wool.ca
Eric Bjergso, General Manager

Canadian Cutting Horse Association (CCHA)
RR#3, Innisfail AB T4G 1T8
Tel: 403-227-4444; Fax: 403-227-3030
e-mail: connie@ccha.ca
URL: www.ccha.ca
Les Timmons, President
Jamie Couilliard, Vice-President
Connie Couilliard, National Administrator
Geoff Thomas, Secretary-Treasurer

Canadian Dexter Cattle Association (CDCA) / Société canadienne des bovins Dexter
2417 Holly Lane, Ottawa ON K1V 0M7
Tel: 613-731-7110; Fax: 613-731-0704
e-mail: ron.black@clrc.ca
URL: www.dextercattle.ca
Affiliation(s): Canadian Livestock Records Corporation
Ron Black, Secretary
Glorianne Bjerland, President

Canadian Donkey & Mule Association (CDMA)
PO Box 341, Nanton AB T0L 1R0
Tel: 403-395-2348; Fax: 403-395-2398
e-mail: jutaylor@telusplanet.net
URL: www.donkeyandmule.com
Affiliation(s): American Donkey & Mule Society; British Donkey Breed Society; Breed Societies of Britain, Australia, Sweden, Holland, Germany, New Zealand
Julie Taylor, Secretary

Canadian Fjord Horse Association
PO Box 70, Didsbury AB T0M 0W0
URL: www.cfha.org
Affiliation(s): Canadian Livestock Records Corporation
Burt Shewfelt, President
Dianne Manegre, Secretary-Treasurer
LauraLee Mills, Registrar

Canadian Galloway Association (CGA) / Société canadienne Galloway
c/o CLRC, 2417 Holly Lane, Ottawa ON K1V 0M7
Tel: 613-731-7110; Fax: 613-731-0704
e-mail: galloway@clrc.ca
URL: www.galloway.ca
Brad Card, President
Ron Black, Sec.-Treas.

Canadian Gelbvieh Association (CGA)
#110, 2116 - 27 Ave. NE, Calgary AB T2E 7A6
Tel: 403-250-8640; Fax: 403-291-5624
e-mail: gelbvieh@gelbvieh.ca
URL: www.gelbvieh.ca
Vern Pancoast, President
Wendy Belcher, Secretary Manager

Canadian Goat Society (CGS) / La Société canadienne des éléveurs de chèvres
2417 Holly Lane, Ottawa ON K1V 0M7
Tel: 613-731-9894; Fax: 613-731-0704
e-mail: cangoatsoc@travel-net.com
URL: www.goats.ca
Sharon Hunt, Secretary Manager

Canadian Guernsey Association
5653, Hwy. 6 - RR#5, Guelph ON N1H 6J2
Tel: 519-836-2141; Fax: 519-763-6582
e-mail: info@guernseycanada.ca
URL: www.guernseycanada.ca
Affiliation(s): Canadian Livestock Records Corporation; Joint Classification Board; Agriculture & Agri-Food Canada; Canadian Dairy Network
Vivianne Macdonald, Manager

Canadian Hereford Association (CHA) / Association canadienne Hereford
5160 Skyline Way NE, Calgary AB T2E 6V1
Tel: 403-275-2662; Fax: 403-295-1333
Toll-Free: 888-836-7242
e-mail: herefords@hereford.ca
URL: www.hereford.ca
Affiliation(s): Canadian Cattlemens Association
Gordon Stephenson, General Manager

Canadian Highland Cattle Society (CHCS) / Société canadienne des éleveurs de bovins Highland
Site 3, Box 1, RR#4, Calmar AB T0C OVO
Tel: 780-985-2392; Fax: 780-985-3863
e-mail: highland@chcs.ca
URL: www.chcs.ca
Lesley Jackson, Secretary-Manager

Canadian Icelandic Horse Federation (CIHF)
PO Box 189, Vanscoy SK S0L 3J0
Tel: 306-384-3533
e-mail: lauscher@sprint.ca
URL: www.cihf.ca
Brett Arnason, President
Otmar Fueth, Vice President

Canadian Limousin Association (CLA)
#13, 4101 - 19th St. NE, Calgary AB T2E 7C4
Tel: 403-253-7309; Fax: 403-253-1704
e-mail: limousin@limousin.com
URL: www.limousin.com
Jason Brock, President

Canadian Livestock Records Corporation (CLRC) / Société canadienne d'enregistrement des animaux
2417 Holly Lane, Ottawa ON K1V 0M7
Tel: 613-731-7110; Fax: 613-731-0704
e-mail: clrc@clrc.ca
URL: www.clrc.ca
Ron Black, General Manager

Canadian Maine-Anjou Association (CMAA)
5160 Skyline Way NE, Calgary AB T2E 6V1
Tel: 403-291-7077; Fax: 403-291-0274
e-mail: cmaa@maine-anjou.ca
URL: www.maine-anjou.ca
Stuart Byman, President
Murray Preece, Secretary
Brian Brown, Treasurer

Canadian Milking Shorthorn Society (CMSS)
#202, 8 Speedvale Ave. West, Guelph ON N1H 1J4
Tel: 519-824-2119; Fax: 519-824-2119
e-mail: ryanbarrett@cmss.on.ca
URL: www.cmss.on.ca
Ryan Barrett, Secretary
Diane Naylor, President

Canadian Morgan Horse Association (CMHA) / Association des chevaux Morgan canadien inc.
PO Box 286, Port Perry ON L9L 1A3
Tel: 905-982-0060; Fax: 905-982-0097
e-mail: info@morganhorse.ca
URL: www.morganhorse.ca
Affiliation(s): British Columbia Interior Morgan Horse Club; New Brunswick Morgan Horse Club; Nova Scotia Morgan Horse Club; Ontario Morgan Horse Club; Saskatchewan Morgan Horse Club
Lyle Dietz, President
Andre Laurin, Eastern Vice-President
Bob Watson, Western Vice-President
Charlene Dalen-Brown, Treasurer
Mavis MacDonald, Morgan Registrar

Canadian Murray Grey Association (CMGA)
PO Box 2093, Stettler AB T0C 2L0
Tel: 403-742-3843; Fax: 403-742-3857
e-mail: cmga@electrotel.ca
Barbara Groves, Secretary
Bill Tran, President
Udo Adam, Treasurer

Canadian Palomino Horse Association (CPHA)
c/o Lorraine Holdaway, 631 Hendershott Rd., RR#1, Hannon ON L0R 1P0
Tel: 905-692-4328
e-mail: canadianpalomino@gmail.com
URL: www.clrc.ca/palomino.shtml
Affiliation(s): Canadian Livestock Records Corporation
Lorraine Holdaway, Secretary
Laura Lee Mills, Registrar

Canadian Percheron Association / Association canadienne du cheval Percheron
Tel: 250-379-2855; Fax: 250-379-2213
e-mail: canadapercheron@uniserve.com
URL: www.canadianpercherons.com
David Logies, President
Donna Swanston, Vice-President

Canadian Pork Council (CPC) / Conseil canadien du porc (CCP)
#900, 200 Laurier Ave. West, Ottawa ON K1P 5Z9
Tel: 613-236-9239; Fax: 613-236-6658
e-mail: info@cpc-ccp.com
URL: www.cpc-ccp.com
Jurgen Preugschas, Chair
Martin Rice, Executive Director

Canadian Red Poll Cattle Association / Société Canadienne des Bovins Red Poll
2417 Holly Lane, Ottawa ON K1V 0M7
Tel: 613-731-7110; Fax: 613-731-0704
e-mail: redpoll@clrc.ca
URL: www.clrc.ca/redpoll.shtml
Affiliation(s): Canadian Livestock Records Corporation
Ron Black, Sec.-Treas.

Canadian Sheep Breeders' Association (CSBA) / La société canadienne des éleveurs de moutons
c/o Cathy Gallivan, 1489 Route 560, Deerville NB E7K 1W7
Fax: 506-328-8165
Toll-Free: 866-956-1116
e-mail: office@sheepbreeders.ca
URL: www.sheepbreeders.ca
Murray Emke, President
Cathy Gallivan, Sec.-Treas.

Canadian Sheep Federation / Fédération canadienne du mouton
130 Malcolm Rd., Guelph ON N1K 1B1
Tel: 519-824-6018; Fax: 519-824-9233
Toll-Free: 888-684-7739
e-mail: cansheep@cansheep.ca
URL: www.cansheep.ca
Florence Henning, Chair
André Trépanier, Vice-Chair

Canadian Shorthorn Association
Canada Centre Bldg., Exhibition Park, PO Box 3771, Regina SK S4P 3N8

Tel: 306-757-2212; *Fax:* 306-525-5852
e-mail: info@canadianshorthorn.com
URL: www.canadianshorthorn.com
Belinda Wagner, Sec.-Treas.

Canadian Simmental Association
#13, 4101 - 19 St. NE, Calgary AB T2E 7C4
Tel: 403-250-7979; *Fax:* 403-250-5121
Toll-Free: 866-860-6051
e-mail: cansim@simmental.com
URL: www.simmental.com
Murray Jacobson
Everett Hall, First Vice-President
Rick McIntyre, Second Vice-President
Dale Kelly, General Manager

Canadian Swine Breeders' Association (CSBA) / L'Association canadienne des éleveurs de porcs
Bldg 54, Central Experiemental Farm, 930 Carling Ave., Ottawa ON K1A 0C6
Tel: 613-731-5531; *Fax:* 613-233-8903
e-mail: canswine@canswine.ca
URL: www.canswine.ca
Brian Sullivan, General Manager

Canadian Tarentaise Association (CTA)
PO Box 760, Moosomin SK S0G 3N0
Tel: 306-435-2342; *Fax:* 306-435-2345
Toll-Free: 800-450-4181
e-mail: canadiantarentaise@sasktel.net
URL: www.tarentaise.ca
Affiliation(s): American Tarentaise Association; SOPEXA - Cambery, France
Rosalyn Harris, Secretary
Brent Kennedy, President

Canadian Thoroughbred Horse Society (CTHS) / Société canadienne du cheval Thoroughbred
PO Box 172, Toronto ON M9W 5L1
Tel: 416-675-1370; *Fax:* 416-675-9525
e-mail: cths@idirect.com
URL: www.cthsnational.com
Gordon Wilson, President
Fran Okihiro, National Executive Secretary

Canadian Trakehner Horse Society (CTHS)
PO Box 6009, New Hamburg ON N3A 2K6
Tel: 519-662-3209; *Fax:* 519-662-3209
e-mail: cantrakhsivh@golden.net
URL: www.cantrak.on.ca
Judy Kirkby, President
Ingrid von Hausen, Registrar & Secretary
Laurel Glanfield, Treasurer

Canadian Welsh Black Cattle Society (CWBCS) / Société Canadienne des bovins Welsh Black
c/o Canadian Livestock Records Corporation, 2417 Holly Lane, Ottawa ON K1V 0M7
Tel: 613-731-7110
e-mail: kaiser.randy@gmail.com
URL: www.canadianwelshblack.com
Randy Scott, President
Randy Kaiser, Vice-President
Dale Clark, Secretary-Treasurer

GENCOR
RR#5, Guelph ON N1H 6J2
Tel: 519-821-2150; *Fax:* 519-763-6582
Toll-Free: 888-821-2150
e-mail: boconnor@gencor.ca
URL: www.gencor.ca
Brian O'Connor, General Manager

Holstein Canada
PO Box 610, 20 Corporate Pl., Brantford ON N3T 5R4
Tel: 519-756-8300; *Fax:* 519-756-3502
e-mail: general@holstein.ca
URL: www.holstein.ca
Keith Flaman, Secretary Manager
Germain Lehoux, President

Jersey Canada (JC)
#9, 350 Speedvale Ave. West, Guelph ON N1H 7M7
Tel: 519-821-1020; *Fax:* 519-821-2723
e-mail: info@jerseycanada.com
URL: www.jerseycanada.com
Janna Rémond, President
Dean Sayles, First Vice-President
Larry Sheardown, Second Vice-President
Russell Gammon, Executive Secretary
Jill Dann, Registrar

National Chinchilla Breeders of Canada (NCBC)
RR#2, Norval ON L0P 1K0
e-mail: ncbc@idirect.com
URL: www.chinnet.com/misc/ncbc.html
Affiliation(s): Agriculture Canada; Canadian National Livestock Records
Tom Riedstra, President
Marie Riedstra, Sec.-Treas.

Nova Scotia Mink Breeders' Association
RR#4, Weymouth NS B0W 3T0
Tel: 902-387-5100
e-mail: bradley.nickerson@ns.sympatico.ca
Karen Sabine, Secretary

The Ontario Farm Animal Council (OFAC)
#106, 100 Stone Rd. West, Guelph ON N1G 5L3
Tel: 519-837-1326; *Fax:* 519-837-3209
e-mail: info@ofac.org
URL: www.ofac.org
John Maaskant, Chairman
Crystal Mackay, Executive Director

Salers Association of Canada (SAC) / Association salers du Canada
Stn. 879, #1, 517 - 10th Ave. South, Carstairs AB T0M 0N0
Tel: 403-337-5851; *Fax:* 403-337-3143
e-mail: info@salerscanada.com; salers@telusplanet.net
URL: www.salerscanada.com
Gerald McGee, President
Brian Jones, Treasurer
Adams Kathleen (Kathy), Secretary-Manager & Registrar

Sask Pork
Bay 2, 502 - 45th St. West, Saskatoon SK S7L 6H2
Tel: 306-244-7752; *Fax:* 306-244-1712
Toll-Free: 866-244-7675
e-mail: nketilson@saskpork.com
URL: www.saskpork.com
Neil Ketilson, General Manager

Saskatchewan Stock Growers Association (SSGA)
Main Floor, Canada Centre Building, Evraz Place, PO Box 4752, Regina SK S4P 3Y4
Tel: 306-757-8523; *Fax:* 306-569-8799
e-mail: ssga@sasktel.net; ssga.admin@sasktel.net
URL: www.skstockgrowers.com
Affiliation(s): Saskatchewan Prairie Conservation Action Plan (SK PCAP) Partnership
Chad MacPherson, General Manager
Calvin Knoss, President

Standardbred Canada (SC)
2150 Meadowvale Blvd., Mississauga ON L5N 6R6
Tel: 905-858-3060; *Fax:* 905-858-3111
e-mail: resource@standardbredcanada.ca
URL: www.standardbredcanada.ca
Ted Smith, President/CEO

The Western Stock Growers' Association (WSGA)
Stockmen's Centre, #101, 2116 - 27 Ave. NE, Calgary AB T2E 7A6
Tel: 403-250-9121; *Fax:* 403-250-9122
e-mail: wsga@shaw.com
URL: www.wsga.ca
Verna Mae Gannon, Office Manager

Animals & Animal Science

Alberta Society for the Prevention of Cruelty to Animals
10806 - 124 St., Edmonton AB T5M 0H3
Tel: 780-447-3600; *Fax:* 780-447-4748
Toll-Free: 800-455-9003
e-mail: info@albertaspca.org
URL: www.albertaspca.org
Terra Johnston, Executive Director

Alberta Veterinary Medical Association (AVMA)
Weber Centre, #950, 5555 Calgary Trail NW, Edmonton AB T6H 5P9
Tel: 780-489-5007; *Fax:* 780-484-8311
Toll-Free: 800-404-2862
e-mail: avma@avma.ab.ca
URL: www.avma.ab.ca
Duane Landals, Registrar

Animal Alliance of Canada (AAC) / Alliance animale du Canada
#101, 221 Broadview Ave., Toronto ON M4M 2G3
Tel: 416-462-9541; *Fax:* 416-462-9647
e-mail: info@animalalliance.ca
URL: www.animalalliance.ca
Anne Streeter, Director
George Dupras, Director
Jacqui Barnes, Director
Marie Crawford, Director
Barry Kent MacKay, Director
Liz White, Director

Animal Welfare Foundation of Canada (AWF) / Fondation du bien-être animal du Canada
#343, 300 Earl Grey Dr., Ottawa ON K2T 1C1
e-mail: info@awfc.ca
URL: www.awfc.ca
Affiliation(s): World Society for the Protection of Animals
Ian Duncan, Ph.D, President & Chair
Frances Rodenberg, Honorary Secretary

Atlantic Canadian Anti-Sealing Coalition
e-mail: contact@antisealingcoalition.ca
URL: www.antisealingcoalition.ca

Brandon Humane Society
2200 - 17 St. East, Brandon MB R7A 7M6
Tel: 204-728-1333
e-mail: info@brandonhumanesociety.ca
URL: www.brandonhumanesociety.ca
Rob Lavin, President

British Columbia Society for the Prevention of Cruelty to Animals
1245 East 7th Ave., Vancouver BC V5T 1R1
Tel: 604-681-7271; *Fax:* 604-681-7022
Toll-Free: 800-665-1868
e-mail: info@spca.bc.ca
URL: www.spca.bc.ca
Craig Daniell, CEO & General Manager

British Columbia Veterinary Medical Association (BCVMA)
#107, 828 Harbourside Dr., Vancouver BC V7P 3R9
Tel: 604-929-7090; *Fax:* 604-929-7095
Toll-Free: 800-463-5399
e-mail: info@bcvma.org
URL: www.bcvma.org
Valerie Osborne, Registrar
John Brocklebank, Deputy Registrar

Calgary Humane Society
4455 - 110 Ave. SE, Calgary AB T2C 2T7
Tel: 403-205-4455; *Fax:* 403-723-6050
e-mail: admin@calgaryhumane.ca
URL: www.calgaryhumane.ca
Patricia Cameron, Executive Director

Canadian Animal Health Institute (CAHI) / Institut canadien de la santé animale
#102, 160 Research Lane, Guelph ON N1G 5B2
Tel: 519-763-7777; *Fax:* 519-763-7407
e-mail: cahi@cahi-icsa.ca
URL: www.cahi-icsa.ca
Jean Szkotnicki, President

Canadian Association for Laboratory Animal Science (CALAS)
#640, 144 Front St., Toronto ON M5J 2L7
Tel: 416-593-0268; *Fax:* 416-979-1819
e-mail: office@calas-acsal.org; membership@calas-acsal.org
URL: www.calas-acsal.org
Teresa McKernan, President
Michelle Gillespie, Vice-President
Wendy Ansell, Administrator
Claire Smits, Treasurer, claire.smits@hli.ubc.ca
Khadijah Hewitt, Coordinator, Membership & Registry

Canadian Association of Animal Health Technologists & Technicians (CAAHTT) / Association canadienne des techniciens et technologistes en santé animale (ACTTSA)
PO Box 595, Langham SK S0K 2L0
Tel: 306-329-4956; *Fax:* 306-329-4700
e-mail: info@caahtt-acttsa.ca
URL: www.caahtt-acttsa.ca
Affiliation(s): Canadian Veterinary Medical Association; National Association of Veterinary Technicians in America (NAVTA)
Phyllis Mierau, Executive Director
Lois Ridgway, President

Canadian Association of Professional Pet Dog Trainers (CAPPDT)
PO Box 85, Shelburne ON L0N 1S0
Toll-Free: 877-748-7829
e-mail: info@cappdt.ca
URL: www.cappdt.ca
Pat Renshaw, Membership Secretary

Canadian Association of Zoos & Aquariums (CAZA) / Association des zoos et aquariums du Canada
#400, 280 Metcalfe St., Ottawa ON K2P 1R7
Tel: 613-567-0099; *Fax:* 613-233-5438
e-mail: info@caza.ca
URL: www.caza.ca
Bill Peters, National Director

Canadian Council on Animal Care (CCAC) / Conseil canadien de protection des animaux (CCPA)
#1510, 130 Albert St., Ottawa ON K1P 5G4
Tel: 613-238-4031; *Fax:* 613-238-2837
e-mail: ccac@ccac.ca
URL: www.ccac.ca
Rachelle Fauteux, Office Manager
Clément Gauthier, MD, Ph.D., Executive Director

Canadian Federation of Humane Societies (CFHS) / Fédération des sociétés canadiennes d'assistance aux animaux
#102, 30 Concourse Gate, Ottawa ON K2E 7V7
Tel: 613-224-8072; *Fax:* 613-723-0252
Toll-Free: 888-678-2347
e-mail: info@cfhs.ca
URL: www.cfhs.ca
Affiliation(s): American Humane Association; World Society for the Protection of Animals; Canadian Nature Federation; Delta Society
Steve Carroll, CEO
Christine Chéné, Communications Coordinator
Shelagh MacDonald, Program Director

Canadian Kennel Club (CKC) / Club canin canadien
#400, 200 Ronson Dr., Toronto ON M9W 5Z9
Tel: 416-675-5511; *Fax:* 416-675-6506
Toll-Free: 800-250-8040
e-mail: information@ckc.ca
URL: www.ckc.ca
Dwain McLean, Chair

Canadian Society of Animal Science (CSAS) / Société canadienne de science animale
c/o Agriculture & Agri-Food Canada Research Station, CP 90, #2000, rte 108 est, Sherbrooke QC J1M 1Z3
Tél: 819-565-9171; *Téléc:* 819-564-5507
Courriel: info@aic.ca
URL: www.csas.net
Karen Schwartzkopf-Genswein, PhD, President
Marie-France Palin, Secretary-Treasurer

Canadian Society of Zoologists (CSZ) / Société canadienne de zoologie (SCZ)
c/o Fisheries & Oceans Canada, 531 Brandy Cove Rd., St Andrews NB E5B 2L9
Tel: 506-529-5889; *Fax:* 506-529-5862
e-mail: martelldj@mar.dfo-mpo.gc.ca
URL: www.csz-scz.ca
Affiliation(s): Canadian Council on Animal Care; Canadian Federation of Biological Societies
D. John Martell, Secretary
Patricia Schulte, President

Canadian Veterinary Medical Association (CVMA) / Association canadienne des médecins vétérinaires (ACMV)
339 Booth St., Ottawa ON K1R 7K1
Tel: 613-236-1162; *Fax:* 613-236-9681
e-mail: admin@cvma-acmv.org
URL: www.canadianveterinarians.net
Jost Am Rhyn, Executive Director

Canadians for Ethical Treatment of Food Animals (CETFA)
PO Box 18024, 2225 - 41 Ave. West, Vancouver BC V6M 4L3
e-mail: care@cetfa.com
URL: www.cetfa.com
Patricia Oswald, President

College of Veterinarians of Ontario (CVO)
2106 Gordon St., Guelph ON N1L 1G6
Tel: 519-824-5600; *Fax:* 519-824-6497
Toll-Free: 800-424-2856
e-mail: inquiries@cvo.org
URL: www.cvo.org
Michele Dutnall, President
Susan J. Carlyle, Registrar

East Coast Aquarium Society (ECAS)
c/o 91 Deerbrooke Dr., Dartmouth NS B2V 1X2
URL: www.eastcoastaquariumsociety.ca
Kathryn Purdy, President
Kelly Lively Jones, Director, Membership

Fort McMurray Society for the Prevention of Cruelty to Animals
155 MacAlpine Cres., Fort McMurray AB T9H 4A5
Tel: 780-743-8997; *Fax:* 780-791-3772
e-mail: spca@altech.ab.ca
URL: www.fortmcmurrayspca.com
D. Carmen Cornejo, Manager
Marsha Smart, President

Horse Council British Columbia (HCBC)
27336 Fraser Hwy., Aldergrove BC V4W 3N5
Tel: 604-856-4304; *Fax:* 604-856-4302
Toll-Free: 800-345-8055
e-mail: reception@hcbc.ca; membership@hcbc.ca; education@hcbc.ca
URL: www.hcbc.ca
Lisa Laycock, Executive Director
Sarah Bradley, President
Susan Harrison, Secretary
Gary Patterson, Treasurer

Human-Animal Bond Association of Canada (HABAC) / Association canadienne sur les relations privilégiées liant les humains et les animaux
c/o 5481 Richmond Rd., Ottawa ON K2R 1G4
Tel: 613-591-6228
e-mail: colbourn@rogers.com
URL: www.habac.ca
Joan S. Colbourn, President

Humane Society Yukon
126 Tlingit Rd., Whitehorse YT Y1A 6J2
Tel: 867-633-6019; *Fax:* 867-633-2210
e-mail: shelter@northwestel.net
URL: www.humanesocietyyukon.ca
Corey Roussell, Administrator

Jardin zoologique du Québec (JZQ)
9300, rue de la Faune, Charlesbourg QC G1G 5H9
Tél: 418-622-0312; *Téléc:* 418-646-9239
Courriel: spsnq@spsnq.qc.ca
Jean-Paul Bédard, Directeur

London Humane Society (LHS)
624 Clarke Rd., London ON N5V 3K5
Tel: 519-451-0630; *Fax:* 519-451-8995
e-mail: administration@londonhumane.ca
URL: www.londonhumanesociety.ca
Affiliation(s): OSPCA
Judy Foster, Executive Director

Manitoba Veterinary Medical Association (MVMA)
6014 Roblin Blvd., Winnipeg MB R3R 0H4
Tel: 204-832-1276; *Fax:* 204-832-1382
Toll-Free: 866-338-6862
e-mail: adowd@mvma.ca
URL: www.mvma.ca
Barbara King, Director, Communication & Advocacy

Montréal SPCA
5215, rue Jean-Talon ouest, Montréal QC H4P 1X4
Tél: 514-735-2711; *Téléc:* 514-735-7448
Courriel: admin@spca.com
URL: www.spca.com
Pierre Barnoti, Directeur général

National Retriever Club of Canada
780 East Chestermere Dr., Chestermere AB T1X 1A6
Tel: 403-248-3347
e-mail: secretary@nrcc-canada.com
URL: www.nrcc-canada.com
Gordon Benn, President
Marg Murray, Sec.-Treas.

New Brunswick Society for the Prevention of Cruelty to Animals / Société protectrice des animaux du Nouveau-Brunswick
PO Box 1412, Stn. A, Fredericton NB E3B 5E3
Tel: 506-458-8208; *Fax:* 506-458-8209
URL: www.spca-nb.ca
Brad Horncastle, President

New Brunswick Veterinary Medical Association (NBVMA) / Association des médecins vétérinaires du Nouveau-Brunswick (AMVNB)
1700 Manawagonish Rd., Saint John NB E2M 3Y5
Tel: 506-635-8100
URL: www.nbvma-amvnb.ca
George Whittle, Executive Director

Newfoundland & Labrador Society for the Prevention of Cruelty to Animals
PO Box 1533, RCAF Rd., St. John's NL A1C 5N8
Tel: 709-726-0301; *Fax:* 709-579-8089
e-mail: inquiries@spcashelter.nf.ca
URL: www.spcashelter.nf.ca; www.cfhs.ca

Newfoundland & Labrador Veterinary Medical Association (NLVMA)
PO Box 818, Mount Pearl NL A1N 3C8
Tel: 709-576-2131
e-mail: pubmedcentral@nih.gove
URL: www.pubmedcentral.nih.gov
Martha Sweeting, President
Ellen Melvin, Sec.-Treas.

Nova Scotia Society for the Prevention of Cruelty to Animals
#422, 1600 Bedford Hwy., Bedford NS B4A 1E8
Tel: 902-835-4798; *Fax:* 902-835-7885
Toll-Free: 888-703-7722
e-mail: animals@spcans.ca
URL: www.spcans.ca

Nova Scotia Veterinary Medical Association
15 Cobequid Rd., Lower Sackville NS B4C 2M9
Tel: 902-865-1876; *Fax:* 902-865-2001
e-mail: info@nsvma.ca
URL: www.nsvma.ca
Frank Richardson, Secretary Registrar
Christopher MacDonald, President

Ontario Society for the Prevention of Cruelty to Animals
16586 Woodbine Ave., RR#3, Newmarket ON L3Y 4W1
Tel: 905-898-7122
e-mail: info@ospca.on.ca
URL: www.ospca.on.ca
Social Media: www.facebook.com/group.php?gid=96326261647
Kate MacDonald, CEO
Ward McAlister, Chair

Ontario Veterinary Medical Association (OVMA)
#205, 420 Bronte St. South, Milton ON L9T 0H9
Tel: 905-875-0756; *Fax:* 905-875-0958
Toll-Free: 800-670-1702
e-mail: info@ovma.org
URL: www.ovma.org
Doug Raven, CEO
Melissa Carlaw, Manager, Communications & Public Relations

Ordre des médecins vétérinaires du Québec (OMVQ)
#200, 800, av Ste-Anne, Saint-Hyacinthe QC J2S 5G7
Tél: 450-774-1427; *Téléc:* 450-774-7635
Ligne sans frais: 800-267-1427
Courriel: omvq@omvq.qc.ca
URL: www.omvq.qc.ca
Christiane Gagnon, Présidente
M. Réjean Pedneault, Directeur général/Secrétaire

PIJAC Canada / Conseil consultatif mixte de l'industrie des animaux de compagnie
#102, 2442 St. Joseph Blvd., Ottawa ON K1C 1G1
Tel: 613-834-2111; *Fax:* 613-834-4854
Toll-Free: 800-667-7452
e-mail: information@pijaccanada.com
URL: www.pijaccanada.com
Affiliation(s): PIJAC International
Clarke Cameron, President
Keith Burgess, Vice-President

Prince Edward Island Humane Society (PEIHS)
PO Box 20022, Sherwood PE C1A 9E3
Tel: 902-892-1190; *Fax:* 902-892-3617
e-mail: info@peihumanesociety.com
URL: www.peihumanesociety.com
Norma Guy, President

Prince Edward Island Veterinary Medical Association
Stn. 420 University Ave., Charlottetown PE C1A 7Z5
Tel: 902-628-1318; *Fax:* 902-838-5077
e-mail: admin@peivma.com
URL: www.peivma.com
Marti Hopson, President

Red Deer & District SPCA
PO Box 931, #4505, 77 St., Red Deer AB T4P 2J1
Tel: 403-342-7722; *Fax:* 403-341-3147
e-mail: spca@telusplanet.net
URL: www.reddeerspca.com
Sandi Baker, President

Regina Humane Society Inc.
PO Box 3143, Regina SK S4P 3G7
Tel: 306-543-6363; *Fax:* 306-545-7661*Crisis Hot-Line:* *306-543-6363*

e-mail: rhs.administration@sasktel.net
URL: www.reginahumanesociety.ca
Lisa Koch, Executive Director
Louise Yates, President

Responsible Dog Owners of Canada (RDOC)
160 Oakridge Blvd., Nepean ON K2G 2V2
Tel: 613-228-7764
e-mail: info@responsibledogowners.ca
URL: www.responsibledogowners.ca
Candice O'Connell, Chair

Saskatchewan Society for the Prevention of Cruelty to Animals
PO Box 37, #40, 1736 Quebec Ave., Saskatoon SK S7K 3K1
Tel: 306-382-7722; Fax: 306-384-3425
Toll-Free: 877-382-7722
e-mail: franwach.saskspca@sasktel.net
URL: www.sspca.ca
Frances Wach, Executive Director

Société québécoise pour la défense des animaux (SQDA) / Québec Society for the Defense of Animals (QSDA)
#102, 847, rue Cherrier, Montréal QC H2L 1H6
Tél: 514-524-1970
Courriel: info@sqda.org
URL: www.sqda.org
Affiliation(s): The World Society for the Protection of Animals - England; The Royal Society for the Prevention of Cruelty to Animals - England; The Canadian Federation of Humane Societies; Société nationale pour la défense des animaux - France
Frederick Back, Président

Toronto Humane Society (THS)
11 River St., Toronto ON M5A 4C2
Tel: 416-392-2273; Fax: 416-392-9978
e-mail: info@torontohumanesociety.com
URL: www.torontohumanesociety.com
Social Media: www.facebook.com/group.php?gid=8666187799
Affiliation(s): OSPCA

Toronto Zoo
361A Old Finch Ave., Toronto ON M1B 5K7
Tel: 416-392-5900; Fax: 416-392-5863
e-mail: torontozoo@torontozoo.ca
URL: www.torontozoo.com
Affiliation(s): Canadian Association of Zoos, Parks & Aquariums; American Association of Zoos, Parks & Aquariums; Canadian Centre for Philanthropy
Raymond Cho, Chair
Calvin White, CEO

Western Federation of Individuals & Dog Organizations
8160 Railway Ave., Richmond BC V7C 3K2
Tel: 604-681-1929; Fax: 604-277-4285
Frances Clark, Contact

World Society for the Protection of Animals (WSPA) / Société mondiale pour la protection des animaux
#960, 90 Eglinton Ave. East, Toronto ON M4P 2Y3
Tel: 416-369-0044; Fax: 416-369-0147
Toll-Free: 800-363-9772
e-mail: wspa@wspa.ca
URL: www.wspa.ca
Social Media: www.facebook.com/group.php?gid=143249880633
Michelle Cliffe, Communications Manager

Yukon Schutzhund Association
32 Maple St., Whitehorse YT Y1A 4A8
Tel: 867-668-6118
e-mail: mattson@northwestel.net
URL: www.kaltersberg.com/YSAInformationPage.htm
Randy Mattson, President

ZOOCHECK Canada Inc.
788 1/2 O'Connor Dr., Toronto ON M4B 2S6
Tel: 416-285-1744; Fax: 416-285-4670
e-mail: zoocheck@zoocheck.com
URL: www.zoocheck.com
Lesli Bisgould, Chair
Rob Laidlaw, Executive Director

Zoological Society of Manitoba
54 Zoo Dr., Winnipeg MB R3P 2N8
Tel: 204-982-0660; Fax: 204-982-0673
e-mail: zooquestions@zoosociety.com
URL: www.zoosociety.com
Affiliation(s): American Zoo & Aquarium Association
Julie Eccles, General Manager

Zoological Society of Montréal / Société zoologique de Montréal
#525, 117, rue Ste-Catherine ouest, Montréal QC H3B 1H9
Tel: 514-845-8317
e-mail: contact@zoologicalsocietymtl.org
URL: www.zoologicalsocietymtl.org

Antiques

Antiquarian Booksellers' Association of Canada (ABAC) / Association de la librairie ancienne du Canada (ALAC)
c/o 783 Bank St., Ottawa ON K1S 3V5
e-mail: info@abac.org
URL: www.abac.org
Roger Auger, President
Alexandre Arjomand, Secretary

Antique Automobile Club of America (AACA)
PO Box 417, 501 West Governor Rd., Hershey PA 17033 USA
Tel: 717-534-1910; Fax: 717-534-9101
e-mail: general@aaca.org
URL: www.aaca.org
Michael J. Jones, President
Steven L. Moskowitz, Executive Director

Antique Automobile Club of America
305 Carpathia Rd., Winnipeg MB R3N 1T2
Tel: 204-289-8315

Antique Automobile Club of America
374 Lakeshore Rd., Port Hope ON I1A 1R3
Tel: 905-885-2151
e-mail: peter.elliotinsurance@egale.ca
URL: local.aaca.org/ontario/

Historic Vehicle Society of Ontario (HVSO)
c/o Canadian Transportation Museum & Heritage Village, 6155 Arner Town Line, RR#2, Kingsville ON N9Y 2E4
Tel: 519-776-6909; Fax: 519-776-8321
Toll-Free: 886-776-6909
e-mail: info@ctmhv.com
URL: www.ctmhv.com/The_Museum/members_gallery.htm
Michelle Staley, Curator/Admin. Director

Manitoba Antique Association
PO Box 2881, Stn. M, Winnipeg MB R3C 4B4
e-mail: manitobaantique@gmail.com
URL: www.manitobaantiqueassociation.com
Shawn Holatko, President

Vintage Locomotive Society Inc.
PO Box 33021, RPO Polo Park, Winnipeg MB R3G 3N4
Tel: 204-832-5259; Fax: 866-751-2348
e-mail: info@pdcrailway.com
URL: www.pdcrailway.com
Paul Newsome, General Manager

Archaeology

Archaeological Society of Alberta (ASA)
97 Eton Rd. West, Lethbridge AB T1K 4T9
Tel: 403-381-2655
e-mail: jnermc@telus.net
URL: www.debitage.ca
Jim McMurchy, Executive Sec.-Treas.

Archaeological Society of British Columbia (ASBC)
PO Box 520, Stn. Bentall, Vancouver BC V6C 2N3
Tel: 604-822-2567; Fax: 604-822-6161
e-mail: asbc.president@gmail.com
URL: www.asbc.bc.ca
Affiliation(s): Canadian Archaeological Association
Patricia Ormerod, President

Association des archéologues du Québec (AAQ)
CP 322, Succ. Haute-Ville, Québec QC G1R 4P8
Courriel: info@archeologie.qc.ca
URL: www.archeologie.qc.ca
Richard Fiset, Président

Canadian Archaeological Association (CAA) / Association d'archéologie canadienne
c/o Jack Brink, Royal Alberta Museum, 12845 - 102 Ave., Edmonton AB T5N 0M6
Tel: 780-453-9151
e-mail: president@canadianarchaeology.com
URL: www.canadianarchaeology.com
Jack Brink, President
Eric Damkjar, Vice-President
Jeff Hunston, Secretary-Treasurer

Nova Scotia Archaeology Society (NSAS)
PO Box 36090, Halifax NS B3J 3S9
Tel: 902-446-0473
e-mail: rhjs74@netscape.net (NSAS President)
URL: www.novascotiaarchaeologysociety.com
Robert Shears, President
April MacIntyre, Vice-President
Kimberlee Williams, Secretary
Jeff Turner, Treasurer

The Ontario Archaeological Society Inc.
#102, 1444 Queen St. East, Toronto ON M4L 1E1
Tel: 416-406-5959; Fax: 416-406-5959
Toll-Free: 888-733-0042
e-mail: oasociety@ontarioarchaeology.on.ca
URL: www.ontarioarchaeology.on.ca
Lorie Harris, Executive Director
Jean-Luc Pilon, President
Jim Keron, Sec.-Treas. & Director, Finance

Saskatchewan Archaeological Society (SAS)
#1, 1730 Quebec Ave., Saskatoon SK S7K 1V9
Tel: 306-664-4124; Fax: 306-665-1928
e-mail: saskarchsoc@sasktel.net
URL: www.saskarchsoc.ca
Affiliation(s): Society for American Archaeology; Plains Anthropological Society
Tim Jones, Executive Director
Ken Triol, Business Administrator

Save Ontario Shipwrecks (SOS)
PO Box 2389, Blenheim ON N0P 1A0
Tel: 519-676-4110; Fax: 519-676-7058
URL: www.saveontarioshipwrecks.on.ca
Affiliation(s): Underwater Council
Marg Barker, Sec.-Treas.
Jim Hopkins, President/Board Chair

Underwater Archaeological Society of British Columbia (UASBC)
c/o Vancouver Maritime Museum, 1905 Ogden Ave., Vancouver BC V6J 1A3
Tel: 604-942-9908; Fax: 604-980-0358
e-mail: uasbc@uasbc.com
URL: www.uasbc.com
Jacques Marc, President
David Stone, Executive Director

Architecture

Alberta Association of Architects (AAA)
Duggan House, 10515 Saskatchewan Dr., Edmonton AB T6E 4S1
Tel: 780-432-0224; Fax: 780-439-1431
e-mail: info@aaa.ab.ca
URL: www.aaa.ab.ca
Leonard O. Rodrigues, Registrar
John A. Ennis, M.A., Executive Director

Architects Association of Prince Edward Island (AAPEI)
PO Box 1766, Charlottetown PE C1A 7N4
Tel: 902-566-3699; Fax: 902-566-1235
e-mail: info@aapei.com
URL: www.aapei.com
Heather Mader, President

Architects' Association of New Brunswick (AANB) / Association des architectes du Nouveau-Brunswick
PO Box 5093, Sussex NB E4E 5L2
Tel: 506-433-5811; Fax: 506-432-1122
e-mail: inquiries@aanb.org
URL: www.aanb.org
Malcolm R. Boyd, President
Donald C. Sterritt, Treasurer
Reno Soucy, Registrar

The Architectural Conservancy of Ontario (ACO)
#403, 10 Adelaide St. East, Toronto ON M5C 1J3
Tel: 416-367-8075; Fax: 416-367-8630
Toll-Free: 877-264-8937
e-mail: manager@arconserv.ca
URL: www.arconserv.ca
Affiliation(s): Ontario Heritage Alliance
Lloyd Alter, President

Architectural Institute of British Columbia (AIBC)
#100, 440 Cambie St., Vancouver BC V6B 2N5
Tel: 604-683-8588; Fax: 604-683-8568
Toll-Free: 800-667-0753
e-mail: info@aibc.ca
URL: www.aibc.ca

Affiliation(s): Royal Architectural Institute of Canada
Michael Ernest, Interim Executive Director
Catherine Bolter, Coordinator, Professional Development

Association des Architectes en pratique privée du Québec (AAPPQ) / Association of Architects in Private Practice of Québec
#425, 1980, rue Sherbrooke ouest, Montréal QC H3H 1E8
Tél: 514-937-4140; *Téléc:* 514-937-2329
Courriel: aappq@aappq.qc.ca
URL: www.aappq.qc.ca/
Micheline D'Assylva, Secrétaire administrative
Jacques Belanger, Président

Association of Architectural Technologists of Ontario (AATO)
#207, 1515 Matheson Blvd. East, Mississauga ON L4W 2P5
Tel: 905-238-7594; *Fax:* 905-238-6344
Toll-Free: 866-805-2286
e-mail: aato@bellnet.ca
URL: www.aato.on.ca
Andrew Bennett, President

Canadian Architectural Certification Board (CACB) / Conseil canadien de certification en architecture (CCCA)
#710, 1 Nicholas St., Ottawa ON K1N 7B7
Tel: 613-241-8399; *Fax:* 613-241-7991
e-mail: info@cacb.ca
URL: www.cacb.ca
Gordon Richards, AIBC, MRAIC, President
Myriam Blais, OAQ, Vice-President

Design Exchange (DX)
Toronto Dominion Centre, PO Box 18, 234 Bay St., Toronto ON M5K 1B2
Tel: 416-363-6121; *Fax:* 416-368-0684
e-mail: info@dx.org; membership@dx.org; education@dx.org; media@dx.org
URL: www.dx.org
Catherine Molnar, Coordinator, Professional Programs
Daniela Bryson, Coordinator, Exhibition

Manitoba Association of Architects (MAA)
137 Bannatyne Ave. East, 2nd Fl., Winnipeg MB R3B 0R3
Tel: 204-925-4620; *Fax:* 204-925-4624
e-mail: info@mbarchitects.org
URL: www.mbarchitects.org
Judy Pestrak, Executive Director

Newfoundland Association of Architects
PO Box 5204, Stn. A, St. John's NL A1C 5V5
Tel: 709-726-8550; *Fax:* 709-726-1549
e-mail: naa@warp.nfld.net
URL: www.newfoundlandarchitects.com
Mark Penney, Sec.-Treas.
Greg Snow, President
Lynda Hayward, Administrator

Northwest Territories Association of Architects (NWTAA)
PO Box 1394, Yellowknife NT X1A 2P1
Tel: 867-766-4216; *Fax:* 867-920-2652
e-mail: nwtaa@tamarack.nt.ca
URL: www.nwtaa.ca

Nova Scotia Association of Architects (NSAA)
1359 Barrington St., Halifax NS B3J 1Y9
Tel: 902-423-7607; *Fax:* 902-425-7024
e-mail: info@nsaa.ns.ca
URL: www.nsaa.ns.ca
Diane Scott, Executive Director
Therese LeBlanc, President

Ontario Association of Architects (OAA)
111 Moatfield Dr., Toronto ON M3B 3L6
Tel: 416-449-6898; *Fax:* 416-449-5756
Toll-Free: 800-565-2724
e-mail: oaamail@oaa.on.ca; practiceadvisor@oaa.on.ca
URL: www.oaa.on.ca
Gordon Masters, Director, Operations
David Craddock, President
Sean O'Reilly, Sr. Vice-President & Treasurer

Ordre des architectes du Québec (OAQ)
#100, 1825, boul René-Lévesque ouest, Montréal QC H3H 1R4
Tél: 514-937-6168; *Téléc:* 514-933-0242
Ligne sans frais: 800-599-6168
Courriel: info@oaq.com
URL: www.oaq.com
Affiliation(s): Institut royal d'architecture du Canada
André Bourassa, Président

Royal Architectural Institute of Canada (RAIC) / Institut royal d'architecture du Canada
#330, 55 Murray St., Ottawa ON K1N 5M3
Tel: 613-241-3600; *Fax:* 613-241-5750
e-mail: info@raic.org
URL: www.raic.org
Jon F. Hobbs, Executive Director
Paule Boutin, President

Royal Architectural Institute of Canada
#210, 318 Homer St., Vancouver BC V6B 2V2
Tel: 604-669-9830; *Fax:* 604-669-5513
e-mail: info@raic-syllabus.ca
URL: www.raic-syllabus.ca

Saskatchewan Association of Architects (SAA)
#200, 642 Broadway Ave., Saskatoon SK S7N 1A9
Tel: 306-242-0733; *Fax:* 306-664-2598
URL: www.saskarchitects.com
Patrick Kelly, President
Grant McKercher, 1st Vice-President
Jeff Jurziniec, 2nd Vice-President
John Parry, Executive Director
Reg Squires, Secretary-Treasurer

Society for the Study of Architecture in Canada (SSAC) / Société pour l'étude de l'architecture au Canada (SEAC)
PO Box 2302, Stn. D, Ottawa ON K1P 5W5
e-mail: info@canada-architecture.org
URL: canada-architecture.org
Affiliation(s): Society of Architectural Historians
Pierre du Prey, President
Andrew Waldron, Vice-President
Lucie Morisset, Vice-President

Arts

Alberta Foundation for the Arts (AFA)
10708 - 105 Ave., Edmonton AB T5H 0A1
Tel: 780-427-9968; *Fax:* 780-422-1162
URL: www.affta.ab.ca
Jeffrey Anderson, Executive Director

Alliance for Arts & Culture
#100, 938 Howe St., Vancouver BC V6Z 1N9
Tel: 604-681-3535; *Fax:* 604-681-7848
e-mail: info@allianceforarts.com
URL: www.allianceforarts.com
Amir Ali Alibhai, Executive Director
Minna Schendlinger, President

Assembly of BC Arts Councils
PO Box 92, Stn. A, Nanaimo BC V9R 5G6
Tel: 250-754-3388; *Fax:* 250-754-3390
Toll-Free: 888-315-2288
e-mail: info@assemblybcartscouncils.ca
URL: www.assemblybcartscouncils.ca
Junko Sakamoto, Executive Director

Canadian Artists' Representation (CARFAC) / Le Front des artistes canadiens
#250, 2 Daly Ave., Ottawa ON K1N 6E2
Tel: 613-233-6161; *Fax:* 613-233-6162
Toll-Free: 866-344-6161
e-mail: carfac@carfac.ca
URL: www.carfac.ca
Affiliation(s): Creators Rights Alliance (CRA); Access Copyright
Mario Villeneuve, National President
Deirdre Logue, Vice-President
April Britski, Executive Director
Margaret Ryall, Secretary
Enrique Astorga, Treasurer
Erika Friesen, Coordinator, Membership
Melissa Gruber, Coordinator, Communications

Canadian Arts Presenting Association (CAPACOA) / Association canadienne des organismes artistiques
#200, 17 York St., Ottawa ON K1N 9J6
Tel: 613-562-3515; *Fax:* 613-562-4005
e-mail: mail@capacoa.ca
URL: www.capacoa.ca
Erin Benjamin, Executive Director
Mélanie Bureau, Operations Manager

Canadian Celtic Arts Association
c/o Jean Talman, 91 Stafford St., Toronto ON M6J 3R1
e-mail: jean.talman@utoronto.ca
Jean Talman, President & Membership Secretary
Donald Gillies, Treasurer

Canadian Conference of the Arts (CCA) / Conférence canadienne des arts
#406, 130 Slater St., Ottawa ON K1P 6E2
Tel: 613-238-3561; *Fax:* 613-238-4849
e-mail: info@ccarts.ca
URL: www.ccarts.ca
Alain Pineau, National Director
Alessia Bongiovanni, Executive Assistant

Chorale Les Voix de la Vallée du Cuivre de Chibougamau inc.
CP 128, Chibougamau QC G8P 2K6
Tél: 418-748-7811
Linda Marceau

Conseil des arts et des lettres du Québec
79, boul. René Lévesque est, 3e étage, Québec QC G1R 5N5
Tél: 418-643-1707; *Téléc:* 418-643-4558
Ligne sans frais: 800-897-1707
Courriel: info@calq.gouv.qc.ca
URL: www.calq.gouv.qc.ca
Yvan Gauthier, Président/Directeur général

Council for Business & the Arts in Canada (CBAC) / Conseil pour le monde des affaires et des arts du Canada
#903, 165 University Ave., Toronto ON M5H 3B8
Tel: 416-869-3016; *Fax:* 416-869-0435
e-mail: info@businessforarts.org
URL: www.businessforarts.org
James D. Fleck, Chair
Nichole Anderson, President & CEO

Federation of Canadian Artists (FCA)
1241 Cartwright St., Vancouver BC V6H 4B7
Tel: 604-681-2744; *Fax:* 604-681-2740
e-mail: fcaoffice@artists.ca (Education) fcaadmin@artists.ca (Membership)
URL: www.artists.ca
Tatjana Mirkov-Popovicki, President
Andrew McDermott, 1st Vice-President
Harold Allanson, 2nd Vice-President
Bev Rushworth, Executive Director
Mila Kostic, Director, Gallery
Elaine Chatwin, Secretary
Sandy Kay, Treasurer

Governor General's Performing Arts Awards Foundation (GGPAAF) / Les Prix du Gouverneur Général pour les arts de la scène
#804, 130 Albert St., Ottawa ON K1P 5G4
Tel: 613-241-5297; *Fax:* 613-238-4849
e-mail: nominations@ggpaaf.com
URL: www.bell.ca/ggawards
Deborah Hennig, Executive Director
Peter Herrndorf, President/CEO
Harold Redekopp, Co-Chair
Albert Millaire, Co-Chair

Manitoba Arts Council (MAC) / Conseil des arts du Manitoba (CAM)
#525, 93 Lombard Ave., Winnipeg MB R3B 3B1
Tel: 204-945-2237; *Fax:* 204-945-5925
Toll-Free: 866-994-2787
e-mail: info@artscouncil.mb.ca
URL: www.artscouncil.mb.ca
Douglas Riske, Executive Director

Newfoundland & Labrador Arts Council (NLAC)
PO Box 98, 1 Springdale St., St. John's NL A1C 5H5
Tel: 709-726-2212; *Fax:* 709-726-0619
Toll-Free: 866-726-2212
e-mail: nlacmail@nfld.net
URL: www.nlac.nf.ca
Reg Winsor, Executive Director
John Doyle, Chair

Northwest Territories Arts Council
c/o NWT Education, Culture & Employment, PO Box 1320, Stn. Main, Yellowknife NT X1A 2L9
Tel: 867-920-6370; *Fax:* 867-873-0205
e-mail: Boris_Atamanenko@gov.nt.ca
URL: pwnhc.learnnet.nt.ca/artscouncil/
Boris Atamanenko, Manager, Community Programs

Ontario Arts Council (OAC) / Conseil des arts de l'Ontario
151 Bloor St. West, 5th Fl., Toronto ON M5S 1T6
Tel: 416-961-1660; *Fax:* 416-961-7796
Toll-Free: 800-387-0058
e-mail: info@arts.on.ca
URL: www.arts.on.ca
Social Media: www.facebook.com/group.php?gid=2408704879

John Brotman, Executive Director

Organization of Saskatchewan Arts Councils (OSAC)
1102 - 8th Ave., Regina SK S4R 1C9
Tel: 306-586-1250; *Fax:* 306-586-1550
e-mail: info@osac.sk.ca
URL: www.osac.sk.ca
Affiliation(s): CAPACOA; Arts School Sask; Leavea Legacy Foundation; Saskatchewan Tourism; SPRA
Nancy Martin, Executive Director

Performing Arts NB, Inc. (PANB)
Brunswick Sq., 3rd Level, 39 King St., Saint John NB E2L 4W3
Tel: 506-635-8019; *Fax:* 506-657-7832
e-mail: performingartsnb@nb.aibn.com
URL: performingartsnb.ca
Nancy Schell, Executive Director
Nicole L. Gallant, President

Prince Edward Island Council of the Arts (PEICA)
115 Richmond St., Charlottetown PE C1A 1A7
Tel: 902-368-4410; *Fax:* 902-368-4418
Toll-Free: 888-734-2784
e-mail: info@peica.ca
URL: www.peiartscouncil.com
Social Media: www.facebook.com/group.php?gid=6930656373
Affiliation(s): West Prince Arts Council; East Kings Arts Council; Conseil des arts Evangeline; Southern Kings Arts Council; South Shore Arts Council; Malpak Arts Council
Greg Doran, Chair

SaskCulture Inc.
#600, 2220 - 12 Ave., Regina SK S4P 0M8
Tel: 306-780-9284; *Fax:* 306-780-9252
e-mail: saskculture.info@saskculture.sk.ca
URL: www.saskculture.sk.ca
Affiliation(s): Canadian Society of Association Executives
Rose Gilks, General Manager
Diane Ell, Communications Manager

Scarborough Arts Council (SAC)
1859 Kingston Rd., Toronto ON M1N 1T3
Tel: 416-698-7322; *Fax:* 416-698-7972
e-mail: office@scarborougharts.com
URL: www.scarborougharts.com
Colin Hughes, Chair
Christine Harris, Vice-Chair
Ravinder Shawe, Vice-Chair
Tim Whalley, Executive Director
Carolyn Kim, Secretary
Daniel Broome, Treasurer
Susan Dimitrakopoulos, Coordinator, Office & Membership
Benedict Lopes, Coordinator, Programs

Société de Promotion et de Diffusion des Arts et de la Culture (SPDAC)
CP 653, Succ. C, Montréal QC H2L 4L5
Tél: 514-522-4646
Ligne sans frais: 877-522-4646
Courriel: info@festivaldesarts.org
URL: www.festivaldesarts.org
Stéphane Mabilais, Directeur général

Automotive

Alberta Motor Association (AMA)
PO Box 8180, Stn. South, 10310 - 39A G.A. MacDonald Ave., Edmonton AB T6H 5X9
Tel: 780-430-5555
Toll-Free: 800-642-3810
URL: www.ama.ab.ca/cps/rde/xchg/ama
Affiliation(s): American Automobile Association
Dan VanKeekan, Director, Corporate Communications
Don Smitten, President

Association des propriétaires d'autobus du Québec (APAQ)
#107, 225, boul Charest est, Québec QC G1K 3G9
Tél: 418-522-7131; *Téléc:* 418-522-6455
Courriel: apaq@apaq.qc.ca
URL: www.apaq.qc.ca
Romain Girard, Vice-président exécutif

Association des spécialistes du pneus du Québec inc. (ASPQ) / Québec Tire Specialists Association Inc.
587, ch Rhéaume, Saint-Michel QC J0L 2J0
Courriel: aspq@qc.aira.com
URL: www.aspq.ca/aspq/
Jean Trudel, Président

Atlantic Recreation Vehicle Dealers Association (ARVDA)
PO Box 9410, Stn. A, Halifax NS B3K 5S3
Tel: 902-425-2445; *Fax:* 902-425-2441
e-mail: matthew@hamblys.ca
URL: www.arvda.ca
Wayne Hambly, President

Automobile Journalists Association of Canada (AJAC) / Association des journalistes automobile du Canada
PO Box 398, Stn. Main, Cobourg ON K9A 4L1
Toll-Free: 800-361-1516
e-mail: beth@ajac.ca
URL: www.ajac.ca
Erin Manning

Automobile Protection Association
#1319, 2 Carlton St., Toronto ON M5B 1J3
Tel: 416-204-1444; *Fax:* 416-204-1985
e-mail: apatoronto@apa.ca
URL: www.apa.ca

Automobile Protection Association (APA) / Association pour la protection automobile
292, boul St. Joseph ouest, Montréal QC H2V 2N7
Tel: 514-272-5555; *Fax:* 514-273-0797
e-mail: apamontreal@apa.ca
URL: www.apa.ca
Antoinette Greco, Directrice générale
George Iny, Président

Automotive Industries Association of Canada (AIAC) / Association des industries de l'automobile du Canada
1272 Wellington St. West, Ottawa ON K1Y 3A7
Tel: 613-728-5821; *Fax:* 613-728-6021
Toll-Free: 800-808-2920
e-mail: info.aia@aiacanada.com
URL: www.aiacanada.com
Marc Brazeau, President
Deborah Moynes-Keshen, Vice President

Automotive Parts Manufacturers' Association (APMA)
#801, 10 Four Seasons Pl., Toronto ON M9B 6H7
Tel: 416-620-4220; *Fax:* 416-620-9730
e-mail: info@apma.ca
URL: www.apma.ca
Gerald B. Fedchun, President

Automotive Retailers Association of British Columbia
#1, 8980 Fraserwood Ct., Burnaby BC V5J 5H7
Tel: 604-432-7987; *Fax:* 604-432-1756
e-mail: info@ara.bc.ca
URL: www.ara.bc.ca
Gord Valente, President
H. Dale Finch, Executive Director

BCADA - The New Car Dealers of BC
#70, 10551 Shellbridge Way, Richmond BC V6X 2W9
Tel: 604-214-9964; *Fax:* 604-214-9965
e-mail: info@newcardealers.ca
URL: www.newcardealers.ca
Blair Qualey, President & CEO

British Columbia Automobile Association (BCAA)
4567 Canada Way, Burnaby BC V5G 4T1
Tel: 604-268-5000; *Fax:* 604-268-5560
Toll-Free: 800-663-1956
URL: www.bcaa.com
William G. Bullis, President & CEO
Collin MacKinnon, Sr. Vice-President & CFO
Carolyn Weiler, Corporate Secretary

CAA Manitoba
PO Box 1400, 870 Empress St., Winnipeg MB R3C 2Z3
Tel: 204-262-6161
e-mail: contact@caamanitoba.com
URL: www.caamanitoba.com

CAA-Québec
444, rue Bouvier, Québec QC G2J 1E3
Tél: 418-624-2424; *Téléc:* 418-624-3297
Ligne sans frais: 800-463-7232
Courriel: info@caa-quebec.qc.ca
URL: www.caaquebec.com
Affiliation(s): Alliance internationale du Tourisme; Fédération internationale de l'automobile
Sophie Gagnon, Directrice principale
Philippe St-Pierre, Conseiller en communication

Canadian Automobile Association (CAA) / Association canadienne des automobilistes
National Office, #200, 1145 Hunt Club Rd., Ottawa ON K1V 0Y3
Tel: 613-247-0117; *Fax:* 613-247-0118
e-mail: info@national.caa.ca
URL: www.caa.ca
Affiliation(s): Alliance internationale de tourisme; Fédération internationale de l'automobile; Federacion interamericana de touring y automovil-clubes; Commonwealth Motoring Conference; American Automobile Association
Leanne Maidment, Contact, Public Affairs

Canadian Automobile Association Maritimes
378 Westmorland Rd., Saint John NB E2J 2G4
Tel: 506-634-1400; *Fax:* 506-653-9500

Canadian Automobile Association Niagara
3271 Schmon Pkwy., Thorold ON L2V 4Y6
Tel: 905-984-8585; *Fax:* 905-688-0289
URL: www.caa.niagara.net
Robert J. Spence, President & CEO

Canadian Automobile Association North & East Ontario
c/o Administration Centre, PO Box 8350, Stn. T CSC, Ottawa ON K1G 3T2
Tel: 613-820-1890; *Fax:* 613-820-4646
Toll-Free: 800-267-8713
e-mail: contactcaa@caaneo.on.ca
URL: www.caaneo.ca
Brent Wilson, Chair

Canadian Automobile Association North & East Ontario
PO Box 8350, Stn. T, Ottawa ON K1G 3T2
Tel: 613-820-1890; *Fax:* 613-820-4646
e-mail: contactcaa@caaneo.on.ca
URL: www.caaneo.on.ca

Canadian Automobile Association Saskatchewan
200 Albert St. North, Regina SK S4R 5E2
Tel: 306-791-4314; *Fax:* 306-949-4461
e-mail: caa.admin@caasask.sk.ca
URL: www.caasask.sk.ca
Fred Titanich, President

Canadian Automobile Association South Central Ontario
60 Commerce Valley Dr. East, Thornhill ON L3T 7P9
Tel: 905-771-3000; *Fax:* 905-771-3101
Toll-Free: 866-988-8878
e-mail: info@caasco.ca
URL: www.caasco.ca
Art Leitch, MBA, M.Eng., Ba, Vice Chair

Canadian Automobile Association South Central Ontario
60 Commerce Valley Dr. East, Thornhill ON L3T 7P6
Tel: 905-771-3000; *Fax:* 905-771-3101
Toll-Free: 866-988-8878
e-mail: info@caasco.ca
URL: www.caasco.ca

Canadian Automobile Association Windsor
1215 Ouellette Ave., Windsor ON N8X 1J3
Tel: 519-255-1212; *Fax:* 519-255-7379
e-mail: windsor@caasco.ca
URL: www.central.on.caa.ca

Canadian Automobile Dealers' Association (CADA) / Corporation des associations de détaillants d'automobiles (CADA)
85 Renfrew Dr., Markham ON L3R 0N9
Tel: 905-940-4959; *Fax:* 905-940-6870
Toll-Free: 800-463-5289
e-mail: mail@cada.ca
URL: www.cada.ca
Richard C. Gauthier, President & CEO
Tim Ryan, Director, Industry Relations & General Counsel
Tom Donnelly, Chair

Canadian Automobile Sport Clubs - Ontario Region Inc. (CASC-OR)
703 Petrolia Rd., Toronto ON M3J 2N6
Tel: 416-667-9500; *Fax:* 416-667-9555
Toll-Free: 877-667-9505
e-mail: office@casc.on.ca
URL: www.casc.on.ca
Affiliation(s): ASN Canada FIA
John Adamkowski, Secretary
Scott Ellsworth, President

Canadian Automotive Repair & Service Council
#6, 9120 Leslie St., Richmond Hill ON L4B 3J9
Tel: 905-709-1010; *Fax:* 905-709-1013
e-mail: askus@cars-council.ca
URL: www.cars-council.ca
Affiliation(s): CARS Institute
Jennifer Steeves, Executive Director

Canadian Vehicle Manufacturers' Association (CVMA) / Association canadienne des constructeurs de véhicules
#400, 170 Attwell Dr., Toronto ON M9W 5Z5
Tel: 416-364-9333; *Fax:* 416-367-3221
Toll-Free: 800-758-7122
e-mail: info@cvma.ca
URL: www.cvma.ca
B.A. Gaunt, Chairman
Mark A. Nantais, President

Corporation des concessionnaires d'automobiles du Québec inc. (CCAQ)
#750, 140, Grande-Allée est, Québec QC G1R 5M8
Tél: 418-523-2991; *Téléc:* 418-523-3725
Ligne sans frais: 800-463-5189
Courriel: info@ccaq.com
URL: www.ccaq.com
Jacques Bechard, Président

Japan Automobile Manufacturers Association of Canada
#460, 151 Bloor St. West, Toronto ON M5S 1S4
Tel: 416-968-0150; *Fax:* 416-968-7095
e-mail: jama@jama.ca
URL: www.jama.ca

Manitoba Motor Dealers Association (MMDA)
#230, 530 Century St., Winnipeg MB R3H 0Y4
Tel: 204-985-4200; *Fax:* 204-775-9125
Toll-Free: 800-949-6632
e-mail: info@mmda.mb.ca
URL: www.mmda.mb.ca
Shirley Canty, Executive Director

Motor Dealers' Association of Alberta (MDA)
9249, 48 St., Edmonton AB T6B 2R9
Tel: 780-468-9552; *Fax:* 780-465-6201
e-mail: info@mdaalberta.com
URL: www.mdaalberta.com
Denis Ducharme, President

Nova Scotia Automobile Dealers' Association (NSADA)
PO Box 9410, Stn. A, #700, 6009 Quinpool Rd., Halifax NS B3K 5S3
Tel: 902-425-2445; *Fax:* 902-425-2441
e-mail: info@nsada.ca
URL: www.nsada.ca
John K. Sutherland, Contact

Ontario & Toronto Automobile Dealers' Association (TADA)
85 Renfrew Dr., 2nd Fl., Markham ON L3R 0N9
Tel: 905-940-6232; *Fax:* 905-940-6235
e-mail: doreenr@tada.ca
URL: www.tada.ca
Bob Attrell, President

Prince Edward Island Automobile Dealers Association
PO Box 22004, 6 Jenkins Ave., Charlottetown PE C1A 9J2
Tel: 902-566-3639; *Fax:* 902-368-7116
e-mail: peiada@eastlink.ca
Lisa Doyle-MacBain, Manager

Recreation Vehicle Dealers Association of Alberta
#305, 8657 - 51 Avenue, Edmonton AB T6E 6A8
Tel: 780-455-8562; *Fax:* 780-453-3927
Toll-Free: 888-858-8787
e-mail: rvda@rvda-alberta.org
URL: www.rvda-alberta.org
Dan Merkowsky, Executive Vice-President

Recreation Vehicle Dealers Association of British Columbia (RVDABC)
#201, 17700 - 56th Ave., Surrey BC V3S 1C7
Tel: 604-575-3868; *Fax:* 604-575-3869
e-mail: info@rvda.bc.ca
URL: www.rvda.bc.ca
Joan Jackson, Executive Director

Recreation Vehicle Dealers Association of Canada (RVDA) / Association des commerçants de véhicules recréatifs du Canada
#204, 6411 Buswell St., Richmond BC V6Y 2G5
Tel: 604-718-6325; *Fax:* 604-204-0154
e-mail: info@rvda.ca
URL: www.rvda.ca
Affiliation(s): Recreation Vehicle Dealers Association of America
Eleanore Hamm, Executive Vice-President
Kim Brown, President

Recreation Vehicle Dealers Association of Manitoba
69 Morin Rd., St Francois Xavier MB R4L 1A8
Tel: 204-864-2112; *Fax:* 204-864-2232
e-mail: rvdamb@mts.net
URL: www.manitobarvda.ca
Kim Wozniak, Manager

Recreation Vehicle Dealers Association of Saskatchewan
342 Armstrong Way, Saskatoon SK S7N 3N1
Tel: 306-955-7832; *Fax:* 306-955-7952
e-mail: info@saskatchewanrvda.ca
URL: www.saskatchewanrvda.ca
Sheila Lardner, Manager

Saskatchewan Automobile Dealers Association (SADA)
#212, 1800 - 2nd Ave., Regina SK S4R 8T3
Tel: 306-721-2208; *Fax:* 306-721-1009
e-mail: sbuckle@saskautodealers.com
URL: www.saskautodealers.com
Affiliation(s): Canadian Automobile Dealers Association
Susan Buckle, Executive Director
Paul Savoie, Chair

Tire Dealers Association of Canada (TDAC)
PO Box 516, 34 Edward St., Drayton ON N0G 1P0
Fax: 866-375-6832
Toll-Free: 888-207-9059
Eric Gilbert, President
Bob Bignell, Executive Director

Used Car Dealers Association of Ontario (UCDA)
230 Norseman St., Toronto ON M8X 6A2
Tel: 416-231-2600; *Fax:* 416-232-0775
Toll-Free: 800-268-2598
e-mail: info@ucda.org
URL: www.ucda.org
Affiliation(s): International Auto Theft Investigators; National Independent Automobile Dealers Association
Steve Peck, President

Aviation & Aerospace

Aéro Club des Outardes
1455, de Biencourt, Montréal QC H4E 1T1
Tél: 514-465-7806
Courriel: francisco45@gmail.com
URL: aeroclubdesoutardes.iquebec.com
Jacques Fairpault, Président

Aerospace Industries Association of Canada (AIAC) / Association des industries aérospatiales du Canada
#1200, 60 Queen St., Ottawa ON K1P 5Y7
Tel: 613-232-4297; *Fax:* 613-232-1142
e-mail: info@aiac.ca
URL: www.aiac.ca
Claude Lajeunesse, President/CEO
Paul Kalil, Chair

Air Transport Association of Canada (ATAC) / Association du transport aérien du Canada
#1100, 255 Albert St., Ottawa ON K1P 6A9
Tel: 613-233-7727; *Fax:* 613-230-8648
e-mail: atac@atac.ca
URL: www.atac.ca
Affiliation(s): Aviation Alberta; BC Aviation Council; Canadian Business Aviation Association; Helicopter Association International; National Air Transportation Association; Northern Air Transport Association; Saskatchewan Aviation Council; Federation of Canadian Municipalities; Canadian Owners & Pilots Association; Flight Safety Foundation; Manitoba Aviation Council
Fred Gaspar, Vice-President, Policy & Strategic Planning
Sam Barone, President & CEO

Airport Management Conference of Ontario
10 Geddes Cres., Barrie ON L4N 7B3
Tel: 705-726-2626; *Fax:* 705-739-8520
Toll-Free: 877-636-2626
e-mail: amco@amco.on.ca
URL: www.amco.on.ca
M.Ann McAfee, Web Based Training
Jack Santerre, President

Association québécoise du transport aérien (AQTA)
Aéroport international Jean-Lesage, 600, 6e av de l'Aéroport, Québec QC G2G 2T5
Tél: 418-871-4635; *Téléc:* 418-871-8189
Courriel: aqta@aqta.ca
URL: www.aqta.ca
John McKenna, Président-directeur général

British Columbia Aviation Council (BCAC)
4360 Agar Dr., Richmond BC V7B 1A3
Tel: 604-278-9330; *Fax:* 604-278-8210
e-mail: bcac@telus.net
URL: www.bcaviation.org
Suzanne Calnan, Executive Assistant
R.W. (Rollie) Black, President & CEO

Canadian Aeronautics & Space Institute (CASI) / Institut aéronautique et spatial du Canada
#104, 350 Terry Fox Dr., Ottawa ON K2K 2W5
Tel: 613-591-8787; *Fax:* 613-591-7291
e-mail: casi@casi.ca; membership@casi.ca
URL: www.casi.ca
Affiliation(s): Canadian Air Cushion Technology Society; Canadian Navigation Society; Canadian Remote Sensing Society
Geoff Languedoc, Executive Director
April Duffy, Coordinator, Publications & Information Services
Leanne Cyr, Coordinator, Administration & Membership Services

Canadian Airports Council (CAC) / Conseil des aéroports du Canada
#706, 350 Sparks St., Ottawa ON K1R 7S8
Tel: 613-560-9302; *Fax:* 613-560-6599
e-mail: sharon.redden@cacairports.ca
URL: www.cacairports.ca
Affiliation(s): Air Transport Association of Canada (ATAC); Canadian International Freight Forwarders Association (CIFFA); Canadian Chamber of Commerce; Canadian Tourism Commission; Tourism Industry Association of Canada (TIAC)
Jim Facette, President/CEO
Daniel-Robert Gooch, Director, Communications

Canadian Aviation Historical Society (CAHS)
National Headquarters, PO Box 705, Stn. P, Toronto ON M5S 2Y4
e-mail: cahsnatpres@cahs.ca
URL: www.cahs.com
Timothy Dubé, National President
Bob Baglow, Vice-President
Rachel Heide, Treasurer
Mat Joost, Secretary

Canadian Aviation Maintenance Council (CAMC) / Conseil canadien de l'entretien des aéronefs (CCEA)
#155, 955 Green Valley Cres., Ottawa ON K2C 3V4
Tel: 613-727-8272; *Fax:* 613-727-7018
Toll-Free: 800-448-9715
e-mail: secretariat@camc.ca
URL: www.camc.ca
Raewen Borris, Leader, Communications
Robert Donald, Executive Director

Canadian Federation of AME Associations (CFAMEA)
837 Charlotte St., Fredericton NB E3B 1M7
Tel: 506-452-1809; *Fax:* 506-452-8251
Ben L. McCarty, Chair

Canadian Flight Instructors Association
579 Kingston Rd., Ajax ON L1S 6M1
Tel: 905-683-8986; *Fax:* 905-683-6977
e-mail: bill@jsdavidson.ca
Bill Davidson

Canadian Owners & Pilots Association (COPA)
#207, 75 Albert St., Ottawa ON K1P 5E7
Tel: 613-236-4901; *Fax:* 613-236-8646
e-mail: copa@copanational.org
URL: www.copanational.org
Kevin Psutka, President

Canadian Seaplane Pilots Association (CSPA)
#1001, 75 Albert St., Ottawa ON K1P 5E7
Tel: 613-236-4901; *Fax:* 613-236-8646
Affiliation(s): Seaplane Pilots Association International
Chris Bullerdick, President

International Air Transport Association / Association du transport aérien international
800, Place Victoria, CP 113, Montréal QC H4Z 1M1
Tel: 514-874-0202; *Fax:* 514-874-9632
URL: www.iata.org
Affiliation(s): International Civil Aviation Organization
Giovanni Bisignani, Director General & CEO
Kevin G. Dobby, Corporate Secretary
Mark Hubble, IATA Representative in Canada/Vice-, Marketing & Commercial Services

International Civil Aviation Organization: Legal Affairs & External Relations Bureau
999, rue Université, Montréal QC H3C 5H7
Tel: 514-954-8219; *Fax:* 514-954-6077
e-mail: icaohq@icao.int
URL: www.icao.int
Denys Wibaux, Director
Raymond Benjamin, Secretary General

International Industry Working Group (IIWG)
International Air Transport Association, PO Box 113, 800, Place Victoria, Montréal QC H4Z 1M1
Tel: 514-874-0202; *Fax:* 514-874-9632
e-mail: obrienm@iata.org
URL: www.iata.org
Tony Tyler, Chair
Giovanni Bisignani, Director General & CEO

The Ninety-Nines Inc./International Organization of Women Pilots
4300 Amelia Earhart Rd., Oklahoma City OK 73159 USA
Tel: 405-685-7969; *Fax:* 405-685-7985
Toll-Free: 800-994-1929
e-mail: 99s@ninety-nines.org
URL: www.ninety-nines.org
Margo McCutcheon, Governor, East Canada Section
Wendy Boyes, Governor, West Canada Section
Susan Larson, President

Northern Air Transport Association (NATA)
PO Box 2457, Yellowknife NT X1A 2P8
Tel: 867-920-2985; *Fax:* 867-920-2983
e-mail: nata-yzf@theedge.ca
URL: www.nata-yzf.ca
Don Douglas, Executive Director
Stephen Nourse, President
Teri Arychuk, Secretary-Treasurer

Recreational Aircraft Association (RAA) / Réseau aéronefs amateur
Brampton Airport, RR#1, Cheltenham ON L0P 1C0
Tel: 905-838-1357; *Fax:* 905-838-1359
Toll-Free: 800-387-1028
e-mail: raa@zing-net.ca
URL: www.raa.ca
Affiliation(s): Recreational Aviation Foundation
Gary Wolf, President
Chris Gardiner, Vice-President & Secretary

Ultralight Pilots Association of Canada (UPAC) / Association canadienne des pilotes d'avions ultra-légers
907289 Township Road 12, RR#4, Bright ON N0J 1B0
Tel: 519-684-7628
URL: www.upac.ca
K. Lubitz, President

University of Toronto Institute for Aerospace Studies
Faculty of Applied Science & Engineering, 4925 Dufferin St., Toronto ON M3H 5T6
Tel: 416-667-7700; *Fax:* 416-667-7799
e-mail: info@utias.utoronto.ca
URL: www.utias.utoronto.ca
Affiliation(s): Canadian Aeronautics & Space Institute; Institute for Space & Terrestrial Science; Canadian Space Agency; Intelligent Sensing for Innovative Structures Canada
D.W. Zingg, Director
H.T. Liu, Associate Director
O.L. Gilder, Associate Director

Banking

Canadian Community Reinvestment Coalition (CCRC)
PO Box 821, Stn. B, Ottawa ON K1P 241
Tel: 613-789-5753; *Fax:* 613-241-4758
e-mail: cancrc@web.net
URL: www.canrc.org

Broadcasting

The Alliance for Children & Television (ACT) / Alliance pour l'enfant et la télévision (AET)
#708, 1400, boul René-Lévesque est, Montréal QC H2L 2M2
Tel: 514-597-5417; *Fax:* 514-597-5205
e-mail: alliance@act-aet.tv
URL: www.act-aet.tv
Caroline Fortier, Executive Director

Audio Engineering Society (AES)
AES Toronto Section, PO Box 292, #32E, 223 Pioneer Dr., Kitchner ON N2P 1L9
Tel: 519-894-5308
e-mail: torontoaes@uex.net
URL: www.aes.org
Breen Bob, Chair
Jeffery S. Bamford, Secretary
Syberen Potma, Vice Chair

BBM Canada / Sondages BBM
1500 Don Mills Rd., 3rd Fl., Toronto ON M3B 3L7
Tel: 416-445-9800; *Fax:* 416-445-8644
e-mail: info@bbm.ca
URL: www.bbm.ca
Jim MacLeod, President & CEO
Tom Jenks, Director, Communications

Broadcast Executives Society (BES)
#100-170, 2 Bloor St. West, Toronto ON M4W 3E2
Tel: 416-413-3870; *Fax:* 416-413-3878
e-mail: admin@bes.ca
URL: www.bes.ca
John Tucker, Administrator

Broadcast Research Council of Canada (BRC)
#1005, 160 Bloor St. East, Toronto ON M4W 1B9
Tel: 416-413-3864; *Fax:* 416-413-3879
e-mail: brc@tvb.ca
URL: www.brc.ca
Eva Tolkunow, President

Canadian Association of Broadcasters (CAB) / Association canadienne des radiodiffuseurs (ACR)
PO Box 627, Stn. B, #700, 45 O'Connor St., Ottawa ON K1P 1A4
Tel: 613-233-4035; *Fax:* 613-233-6961
e-mail: cab@cab-acr.ca
URL: www.cab-acr.ca
Pierre-Louis Smith, Vice-President, Radio
Elizabeth Roscoe, Sr. Vice-President, Policy & Public Affairs
Tina Van Dusen, Executive Vice-President & COO
Sylvie Bissonnette, Vice-President/CFO, Finance & Administration
Wayne Charman, Vice-President, Television & Specialty & Pay Services
David Keeble, Sr. Vice-President, Policy & Regulatory Affairs
Sean Kiely, Sr. Vice-President, Marketing & Member Services
Pierre Pontbriand, Vice-President, Communications
Glenn O'Farrell, President & CEO

Canadian Association of Ethnic (Radio) Broadcasters (CAEB) / Association canadienne des radiodiffuseurs ethniques
c/o CHIN Radio, #400, 622 College St., Toronto ON M6G 1B6
Tel: 416-531-9991; *Fax:* 416-531-5274
e-mail: info@chinradio.com
URL: www.chinradio.com
Lenny Lombardi, President

Canadian Satellite Users Association (CSUA)
6835 Century Ave., 2nd Fl., Mississauga ON L5N 2L2
Tel: 905-826-3451; *Fax:* 905-826-4873
e-mail: dbraden@bbandc.com
URL: www.csua.ca

Friends of Canadian Broadcasting (FCB)
#200-238, 131 Bloor St. West, Toronto ON M5S 1R8
Tel: 416-968-7496; *Fax:* 416-968-7406
e-mail: friends@friends.ca
URL: www.friends.ca
Social Media: twitter.com/friendscb
Ian Morrison, Spokesperson

National Campus & Community Radio Association (NCRA) / Association nationale des radio étudiantes et communautaires (ANREC)
#230, 325 Dalhousie, Ottawa ON K1N 7G2
Tel: 613-321-1440; *Fax:* 613-321-1442
e-mail: office@ncra.ca
URL: www.ncra.ca
Affiliation(s): World Association of Community Radio Broadcasters (AMARC); Canadian Radio-Television & Telecommunications Commission (CRTC); Canadian Society of Independent Radio Producers
Kevin Matthews, Executive Director
Erin Flynn, President

Ontario Association of Broadcasters (OAB)
PO Box 54040, 5762, Highway 7 East, Markham ON L3P 7Y4
Tel: 905-554-2730; *Fax:* 905-554-2731
e-mail: memberservices@oab.ca
URL: www.oab.ca
Doug Kirk, President
Valerie Skivington, Administrator

Radio Advisory Board of Canada (RABC) / Conseil consultatif canadien de la radio
#811, 116 Albert St., Ottawa ON K1P 5G3
Tel: 613-230-3261
Toll-Free: 888-902-5768
e-mail: rabc.gm@on.aibn.com
URL: www.rabc.ottawa.on.ca
Roger Poirier, General Manager
Ron Coles, President

Radio Amateurs of Canada Inc. (RAC) / Radio Amateurs du Canada inc.
#217, 720 Belfast Rd., Ottawa ON K1G 0Z5
Tel: 613-244-4367; *Fax:* 613-244-4369
Toll-Free: 877-273-8304
e-mail: rachq@rac.ca
URL: www.rac.ca
Earle Smith, Board Chair
Earle Smith, President

Radio Television News Directors' Association (Canada) (RTNDA) / Association canadienne des directeurs de l'information en radio-télévision
#310, 2175 Sheppard Ave. East, Toronto ON M2J 1W8
Tel: 416-756-2213; *Fax:* 416-491-1670
Toll-Free: 877-257-8632
e-mail: sherryd@taylorenterprises.com
URL: www.rtndacanada.com
Affiliation(s): Radio-Television News Directors Association International
Sherry Denesha, Administrator
Terry Scott, President

Television Bureau of Canada, Inc.
#980, 550, rue Sherbrooke ouest, Montréal QC H3A 1B9
Tel: 514-284-0425; *Fax:* 514-284-0698
e-mail: lgroleau@tvb.ca
URL: www.tvb.ca

Television Bureau of Canada, Inc. (TVB) / Bureau de la télévision du Canada
#1005, 160 Bloor St. East, Toronto ON M4W 1B9
Tel: 416-923-8813; *Fax:* 416-413-3879
Toll-Free: 800-231-0051
e-mail: tvb@tvb.ca
URL: www.tvb.ca
Affiliation(s): Television Bureau of Advertising - New York, USA
Duncan Robertson, Manager, Resource Centre
Theresa Treutler, President & CEO
Rhonda-Lynn Bagnall, Manager, Telecaster Services

Western Association of Broadcast Engineers
#300, 8120 Beddington Blvd. NW, Calgary AB T3K 2A8
Tel: 403-630-4907; *Fax:* 403-295-3135
e-mail: info@wabe.ca
URL: www.wabe.ca
Laverne Siemens, President

Women in Film & Television - Toronto
#601, 110 Eglinton Ave. East, Toronto ON M4P 2Y1
Tel: 416-322-3430; *Fax:* 416-322-3703
e-mail: wift@wift.com
URL: www.wift.com
Affiliation(s): Women in Film Chapters (worldwide)
Susan Ross, Chair
Sadia Zaman, Executive Director

Building & Construction

Aggregate Producers' Association of Ontario (APAO)
#2, 365 Brunel Rd., Mississauga ON L4Z 1Z5
Tel: 905-507-0711; *Fax:* 905-507-0717
e-mail: mmiller@apao.com
URL: www.apao.com
Moreen Miller, President

Alberta Construction Association (ACA)
18012, 107 Ave., Edmonton AB T5S 1M1

Tel: 780-455-1122; *Fax:* 780-451-2152
e-mail: info@abconst.org
URL: www.abconst.org
Ken Gibson, Executive Director

Alberta Ready-Mixed Concrete Association (ARMCA)
9653 - 45 Ave., Edmonton AB T6E 5Z8
Tel: 780-436-5645; *Fax:* 780-436-6503
e-mail: armca@telus.net
URL: www.armca.net
Piero Nanfara, President

Alberta Roadbuilders & Heavy Construction Association (ARHCA)
#201, 9333 - 45 Ave., Edmonton AB T6E 5Z7
Tel: 780-436-9860; *Fax:* 780-436-4910
Toll-Free: 866-436-9860
e-mail: administration@arhca.ab.ca
URL: www.arhca.ab.ca
Affiliation(s): Western Canada Roadbuilders Association; Alberta Construction Safety Association; Roads & Transportation Association Canada
Heidi Harris, Director, Communications
Gene Syvenky, Chief Executive Officer

Alberta Roofing Contractors Association (ARCA)
2380 Pegasus Rd. NE, Calgary AB T2E 8G8
Tel: 403-250-7055; *Fax:* 403-250-1702
Toll-Free: 800-382-8515
e-mail: info@arcaonline.ca
URL: www.arcaonline.ca
Affiliation(s): National Roofing Contractors Association USA
Mike Lloyd, President
Brenwyn Cooley, Executive Manager

Architectural Metal Association
#310, 2175 Sheppard Ave. East, Toronto ON M2J 1W8
Tel: 416-971-7800; *Fax:* 416-971-5411
Don Mockford, Executive Director

Architectural Woodwork Manufacturers Association of British Columbia (AWMA-BC)
#160, 4664 Lougheed Hwy, Burnaby BC V5C 5T5
Tel: 604-298-3555; *Fax:* 604-298-3558
e-mail: awma@awma-bc.ca
URL: www.awma-bc.ca
Frank Beck, President

Architectural Woodwork Manufacturers Association of Canada (AWMAC)
516 - 4 St. West, High River AB T1V 1B6
Tel: 403-652-7685; *Fax:* 403-652-7384
e-mail: info@awmac.com
URL: www.awmac.com
Rick Koehn, Vice-President
Frank VanDonzel, Secretary/Manager
Myron Jonzon, President

Architectural Woodwork Manufacturers Association of Canada - Manitoba
PO Box 737, 290 Burnell St., Winnipeg MB R3V 2L4
Tel: 204-222-9622; *Fax:* 204-928-7459
e-mail: manitoba@awmac.com
URL: www.awmac.com
Harm Hazeu, President
Bill Wagar, Vice-President
Nancy Carpenter, Secretary
Ted Sherritt, Treasurer

Architectural Woodwork Manufacturers Association of Canada - Northern Alberta
15309 - 116 Ave., Edmonton AB T5M 3Z5
Tel: 780-906-9399; *Fax:* 780-455-9545
e-mail: northernalberta@awmac.com
Dean LaTrace, President

Architectural Woodwork Manufacturers Association of Canada - Ontario Chapter (AWMAC-ON)
70 Leek Cres., Richmond Hill ON L4B 1H1
Tel: 416-499-4000; *Fax:* 416-499-8752
e-mail: info@awmacontario.com
URL: www.awmacontario.com
Micah Gingrich, Secretary-Treasurer

Architectural Woodwork Manufacturers Association of Canada - Saskatchewan
PO Box 26032, Stn. Lawson Heights, Saskatoon SK S7K 8C1
Tel: 306-652-2704; *Fax:* 306-664-2552
e-mail: awmac.sask@sasktel.net
Kerry DePape, President

Architectural Woodwork Manufacturers Association of Canada - Southern Alberta
PO Box 40124, Calgary AB T2G 5G5
Tel: 403-264-5979; *Fax:* 403-652-7384
e-mail: southernalberta@awmac.com
URL: www.awmac.com
Wayne Niddrie, Chair
Larry White, Secretary
Darrell Stokes, AWNAC Director

Association de la construction du Québec (ACQ) / Construction Association of Québec
#205, 7400, boul les Galeries d'Anjou, Anjou QC H1M 3M2
Tél: 514-354-0609; *Téléc:* 514-354-8292
Ligne sans frais: 888-868-3424
Courriel: info@prov.acq.org
URL: www.acq.org
Gilbert Grimard, Président
Claude Godbout, Vice-président, Directeur général

Association des constructeurs de routes et grands travaux du Québec (ACRGTQ) / Québec Road Builders & Heavy Construction Association
435, av Grande-Allée est, Québec QC G1R 2J5
Tél: 418-529-2949; *Téléc:* 418-529-5139
Ligne sans frais: 800-463-4672
Courriel: acrgtq@acrgtq.qc.ca
URL: www.acrgtq.qc.ca
Francois Groleau, Président

Association des détaillants de matériaux de construction du Québec (ADMACQ) / The Building Materials Retailers Association of Québec
474, rue Trans-Canada, Longueuil QC J4G 1N8
Tél: 450-646-5842; *Téléc:* 450-646-6171
Ligne sans frais: 877-723-6220
Courriel: information@admacq.qc.ca
URL: www.admacq.qc.ca
Affiliation(s): Conseil québécois du commerce de détail
Richard Darveau, Président-directeur général

Association des entrepreneurs en construction du Québec (AECQ) / Association of Building Contractors of Québec (ABCQ)
#101, 7905, boul Louis-H. Lafontaine, Anjou QC H1K 4E4
Tél: 514-353-5151; *Téléc:* 514-353-6689
Ligne sans frais: 800-361-4304
Courriel: info@aecq.org
URL: www.aecq.org
Affiliation(s): Canadian Construction Association
Pierre Dion, Directeur général

Association des maîtres couvreurs du Québec (AMCQ) / Québec Master Roofers Association
3001, boul Tessier, Laval QC H7S 2M1
Tél: 450-973-2322; *Téléc:* 450-973-2321
Ligne sans frais: 888-973-2322
Courriel: amcq@amcq.qc.ca
URL: www.amcq.qc.ca
Micheline Bonnaud, Directrice générale

Atlantic Building Supply Dealers Association (ABSDA)
70 Englehart St., Dieppe NB E1A 8H3
Tel: 506-858-0700; *Fax:* 506-859-0064
Toll-Free: 800-561-7114
e-mail: absda@nbnet.nb.ca
URL: www.absda.ca
Don Sherwood, President
Pamela Brennan, Chair

Atlantic Provinces Ready-Mixed Concrete Association (APRMCA) / Association des fabricants de béton préparé des provinces atlantiques
30 Damascus Rd., Bedford NS B4A 0C1
Tel: 902-443-4456; *Fax:* 902-429-6696
e-mail: info@atlanticconcrete.ca
URL: www.aprmca.com
Affiliation(s): Canadian Portland Cement Association
Mary Macaulay, Executive Director

British Columbia Construction Association (BCCA)
#210, 174 Wilson St., Victoria BC V9A 7N6
Tel: 250-475-1077; *Fax:* 250-475-1078
e-mail: bcca@bccassn.com
URL: www.bccassn.com
Manley McLachlan, President
Steve Pavelich, Chair

British Columbia Construction Association - North (BCCA-N)
3851 - 18 Ave., Prince George BC V2N 1B1
Tel: 250-563-1744; *Fax:* 250-563-1107
e-mail: constctr@nbcca.bc.ca
URL: www.nbcca.bc.ca
Affiliation(s): British Columbia Construction Association; Canadian Construction Association; Local British Columbia construction associations in Dawson Creek, Bulkley Valley-Lakes District, Fort St. John, Prince George; Terrace-Kitimat; Williams Lake, & Quesnel
Rosalind Thorn, President
Dan Boissevain, Chair
Joe Hart, Secretary
Bradley Stauber, Treasurer

British Columbia Ready-Mixed Concrete Association
26162 - 30A Ave., Aldergrove BC V4W 2W5
Tel: 604-626-4141; *Fax:* 604-626-4143
e-mail: ccampbell@bcrmca.bc.ca
URL: www.bcrmca.bc.ca
Carolyn Campbell, Executive Director

British Columbia Road Builders & Heavy Construction Association (BCRB&HCA)
#307, 8678 Greenall Ave., Burnaby BC V5J 3M6
Tel: 604-436-0220; *Fax:* 604-436-2627
e-mail: info@roadbuilders.bc.ca
URL: www.roadbuilders.bc.ca
Affiliation(s): Western Canada Roadbuilders Association; Canadian Construction Association
Jack W. Davidson, President
Joe Wrobel, Chair
Doug Bjornson, Sec.-Treas.

Building Supply Dealers Association of British Columbia (BSDA-BC)
#2, 19299 - 94th Ave., Surrey BC V4N 4E6
Tel: 604-513-2205; *Fax:* 604-513-2206
Toll-Free: 888-711-5656
e-mail: thomas@bsiabc.ca
URL: www.bsdabc.com
Thomas Foreman, President

Canadian Concrete Masonry Producers Association (CCMPA)
PO Box 54503, 1171 Avenue Rd., Toronto ON M5M 4N5
Tel: 416-495-7497; *Fax:* 416-495-8723
Toll-Free: 888-495-7497
e-mail: information@ccmpa.ca
URL: www.ccmpa.ca
Marina de Souza, Managing Director

Canadian Concrete Pipe Association (CCPA) / Association canadienne des fabricants de tuyaux de béton (ACTB)
205 Miller Dr., Halton Hills ON L7G 6G4
Tel: 905-877-5369; *Fax:* 905-877-5369
e-mail: info@ccpa.com
URL: www.ccpa.com
Social Media:
www.facebook.com/group.php?gid=106265401921
Affiliation(s): Ontario Concrete Pipe Association; Tubecon; American Concrete Pipe Association
John Greer, Chair

Canadian Construction Association (CCA) / Association canadienne de la construction (ACC)
#400, 75 Albert St., Ottawa ON K1P 5E7
Tel: 613-236-9455; *Fax:* 613-236-9526
e-mail: cca@cca-acc.com
URL: www.cca-acc.com
Michael Atkinson, President
Michel Hachey, Director, Communications
Raymond Brunet, Chair

Canadian Masonry Contractors' Association (CMCA)
360 Superior Blvd., Mississauga ON L5T 2N7
Tel: 905-564-6622; *Fax:* 905-564-5744
URL: www.canadamasonrycentre.com/cmca/
Affiliation(s): Ontario Masonry Contractors' Association; Metro Mason Contractors Association; Canada Masonry Centre
John Blair, Executive Director

Canadian Paint & Coatings Association (CPCA) / Association canadienne de l'industrie de la peinture et du revêtement
#1200, 170 Laurier Ave. W, Ottawa ON K1P 5V5
Tel: 613-231-3604; *Fax:* 613-231-4908
e-mail: cpca@cdnpaint.org
URL: www.cdnpaint.org
Jim Quick, President

Canadian Precast / Prestressed Concrete Institute (CPCI) / Institut canadien du béton préfabriqué et précontraint
#100, 196 Bronson Ave., Ottawa ON K1R 6H4
Tel: 613-232-2619; *Fax:* 613-232-5139
Toll-Free: 877-937-2724
e-mail: info@cpci.ca
URL: www.cpci.ca
Brian Hall, President

Canadian Ready-Mixed Concrete Association (CRMCA) / Association canadienne du béton préparé
#3, 365 Brunel Rd., Mississauga ON L4Z 1Z5
Tel: 905-507-1122; *Fax:* 905-890-8122
URL: www.crmca.ca

Canadian Roofing Contractors' Association (CRCA) / Association canadienne des entrepreneurs en couverture (ACEC)
#100, 2430 Don Reid Dr., Ottawa ON K1H 1E1
Tel: 613-232-6724; *Fax:* 613-232-2893
Toll-Free: 800-461-2722
e-mail: crca@on.aibn.com
URL: www.roofingcanada.com
Affiliation(s): Construction Specifications Canada
John E. Hill, Executive Director

Canadian Welding Bureau
CWB Group - Industry Services, 7250 West Credit Ave., Mississauga ON L5N 5N1
Tel: 905-542-1312; *Fax:* 905-542-1318
e-mail: info@cwbgroup.org
URL: www.cwbgroup.org
Doug Luciani, President
Jim MacRae, Registrar

Cement Association of Canada (CAC) / Association canadienne du ciment
#502, 350 Sparks St., Ottawa ON K1R 7S8
Tel: 613-236-9471; *Fax:* 613-563-4498
e-mail: headquarters@cement.ca
URL: www.cement.ca
Pierre Boucher, President & CEO

Construction Association of New Brunswick Inc. (CANB)
59 Avonlea Ct., Fredericton NB E3C 1N8
Tel: 506-459-5770; *Fax:* 506-457-1913
e-mail: canb1@nbnet.nb.ca
URL: www.constructnb.ca
Hilary Howes, Executive Director

Construction Association of Nova Scotia
Parkway Pl., City of Lakes Business Park, #3, 260 Brownlow Ave., Dartmouth NS B3B 1V9
Tel: 902-468-2267; *Fax:* 902-468-2470
e-mail: cans@cans.ns.ca
URL: www.cans.ns.ca
Carol MacCulloch, President
Donna Cruickshank, Office Manager

Construction Association of PEI (CAPEI)
PO Box 728, #226, 40 Enman Cres., Charlottetown PE C1A 7L3
Tel: 902-368-3303; *Fax:* 902-894-9757
e-mail: admin@capei.ca
URL: www.capei.ca
Phillip McInnis, General Manager
Jason Peters, President

Construction Safety Association of Ontario (CSAO)
21 Voyager Ct. South, Toronto ON M9W 5M7
Tel: 416-674-2726; *Fax:* 416-674-8866
Toll-Free: 800-781-2726
e-mail: info@csao.org
URL: www.csao.org
Patricia Dean, Reference Librarian
Donald E. Dickie, Executive Vice-President/General Ma

Construction Specifications Canada (CSC) / Devis de construction Canada
#312, 120 Carlton St., Toronto ON M5A 4K2
Tel: 416-777-2198; *Fax:* 416-777-2197
e-mail: info@csc-dcc.ca
URL: www.csc-dcc.ca
Affiliation(s): Construction Specification Foundation; Construction Specifications Canada/Alberta Section Training Trust Fund; Construction Specifications Institute; Canadian Standards Assoc.; Mechanical Contractors Assoc. of Canada; Ontario Bid Depository Council; Alberta Building Envelope Council; Alberta Roofing Contractor's Assoc.; Canadian Institute of Plumbing & Heating; Assoc. of Professional Engineers of Canada; Royal Architectural Institute of Canada; Canadian Construction Assoc.; Toronto Construction Assoc.; Society of the Plastics Industry of Canada; Thermal Insulation Assoc. of Canada
Michael Schneider, CCCA, RAH, President

Council of Ontario Construction Associations (COCA)
#2001, 180 Dundas St. West, Toronto ON M5G 1Z8
Tel: 416-968-7200; *Fax:* 416-968-0362
e-mail: info@coca.on.ca
URL: www.coca.on.ca
Ian Cunningham, President

Lumber & Building Materials Association of Ontario (LBMAO)
#27, 5155 Spectrum Way, Mississauga ON L4W 5A1
Tel: 905-625-1084; *Fax:* 905-625-3006
Toll-Free: 888-365-2626
e-mail: dwcampbell@lbmao.on.ca
URL: www.lbmao.on.ca
David W. Campbell, President
J.D. VanNoy, Chair
Steve Choquette, Vice-Chair

Manitoba Heavy Construction Association Inc. (MHCA)
1236 Ellice Ave., Winnipeg MB R3G 0E7
Tel: 204-947-1379; *Fax:* 204-943-2279
e-mail: info@mhca.mb.ca
URL: www.mhca.mb.ca
Barry Arnason, Chair
Chris Lorenc, BA, LL.B, President
Henry Borger, Secretary-Treasurer
Stan Kruse, Director, Safety Program
Jaason Rosin, Manager, Communications

Manitoba Ready-Mixed Concrete Association Inc. (MRMCA)
169 Kingston Row, Winnipeg MB R2M 0T1
Tel: 204-667-8539; *Fax:* 204-237-5075
e-mail: info@mrmca.com
URL: www.mrmca.com

Master Insulators' Association of Ontario Inc.
#101, 2600 Skymark Avenue, Bldg. 1, Mississauga ON L4W 5B2
Tel: 905-279-6426; *Fax:* 905-279-6422
e-mail: manager@miaontario.org
URL: www.miaontario.org
Malcolm D. Haylock, Office Manager

Master Painters & Decorators Association (MPDA)
2800 Ingleton Avenue, Burnaby BC V5C 6G7
Tel: 604-298-7578; *Fax:* 604-298-5183
e-mail: info@mpda.net
URL: www.paintinfo.com
Affiliation(s): Master Painters Institute
Barry G. Law, Manager
Greg Boshard, President

Mechanical Contractors Association of Alberta
#204, 2725 - 12 St. NE, Calgary AB T2E 7J2
Tel: 403-250-7237; *Fax:* 403-291-0551
Toll-Free: 800-251-0620
URL: www.mcaalberta.com
Hans Tiedemann, Executive Director

Mechanical Contractors Association of British Columbia (MCABC)
#223, 3989 Henning Dr., Burnaby BC V5C 6N5
Tel: 604-205-5058; *Fax:* 604-205-5075
Toll-Free: 800-663-8473
URL: www.mcabc.org
Dana Taylor, Executive Vice President

Mechanical Contractors Association of Canada (MCAC) / Association des entrepreneurs en mécanique du Canada
#601, 280 Albert St., Ottawa ON K1P 5G8
Tel: 613-232-0492; *Fax:* 613-235-2793
e-mail: mcac@mcac.ca
URL: www.mcac.ca
Affiliation(s): Council of Construction Trade Associations
Richard McKeagan, President & COO

Mechanical Contractors Association of Manitoba (MCAM)
#1, 860 Bradford St., Winnipeg MB R3H 0N5
Tel: 204-774-2404; *Fax:* 204-772-0233
e-mail: mcam@mts.net
URL: www.mca-mb.com
Betty McInerney, Executive Director

Mechanical Contractors Association of New Brunswick / Association des entrepreneurs en mécanique du N.-B.
c/o Moncton Northeast Construction Association, 297 Collishaw St., Moncton NB E1C 9R2
Tel: 506-857-4128; *Fax:* 506-857-8861
e-mail: info@mneca.ca
URL: www.mneca.ca
Affiliation(s): Canadian Construction Association
Bill Dixon, Executive Director

Mechanical Contractors Association of Newfoundland & Labrador
PO Box 745, Mount Pearl NL A1N 2Y2
Tel: 709-747-5577; *Fax:* 709-368-5342
e-mail: ddawe@nfld.net
David Dawe, Executive Director

Mechanical Contractors Association of Nova Scotia
c/o Construction Association of Nova Scotia, #3, 260 Brownlow Ave., Dartmouth NS B3B 1V9
Tel: 902-468-2267; *Fax:* 902-468-2470
e-mail: cans@cans.ns.ca
URL: www.cans.ns.ca
Donna Cruickshank, Manager

Mechanical Contractors Association of Ontario (MCAO)
#103, 10 Director Ct., Woodbridge ON L4L 7E8
Tel: 905-856-0342; *Fax:* 905-856-0385
e-mail: mcao@mcao.org
URL: www.mcao.org
Steve Coleman, Executive Vice-President

Mechanical Contractors Association of Prince Edward Island
c/o Association of Commercial & Industrial Contractors of PEI, PO Box 1685, Charlottetown PE C1A 7N4
Tel: 902-566-3456; *Fax:* 902-368-2754
e-mail: wmm@wmm93.pe.ca
Mary MacDonald

Mechanical Contractors Association of Saskatchewan Inc. (MCAS)
2615B Wentz Ave., Saskatoon SK S7K 5J1
Tel: 306-664-2154; *Fax:* 306-653-7233
e-mail: mca-sask@mca-sask.com
URL: www.mca-sask.com
Judy Nagus, Executive Director

National Building Envelope Council
c/o 5041 Regent St., Burnaby BC V5C 4H4
Tel: 604-473-9587
Dominique Derome, President Elect

National Elevator & Escalator Association (NEEA)
#708, 6299 Airport Rd., Mississauga ON L4V 1N3
Tel: 905-678-9940; *Fax:* 905-677-7634
Andrew Reistetter, Executive Director

New Brunswick Roofing Contractors Association, Inc. (NBRCA) / Association des entrepreneurs en couverture du Nouveau-Brunswick
PO Box 7242, 57 King St., 3rd Fl., Saint John NB E2L 4S6
Tel: 506-652-7003; *Fax:* 506-696-0380
e-mail: info@nbrca.ca
URL: www.nbrca.ca
Ron Hutton, Executive Director
Rob Paterson, President
Robert McGinn, Vice-President
Geoff Munn, Secretary
Serge Robichaud, Treasurer

Newfoundland & Labrador Construction Association (NLCA)
Triman Bldg., PO Box 8008, Stn. A, 78 O'Leary Ave., St. John's NL A1B 3M7
Tel: 709-753-8920; *Fax:* 709-754-3968
e-mail: info@nfld.com
URL: www.nlca.ca
Keith Ryan, Chair
Rhonda Neary, President & Chief Operating Officer
Harry Bartlett, Secretary-Treasurer

Newfoundland & Labrador Road Builders / Heavy Civil Association (NLRB / HCA)
PO Box 23038, St. John's NL A1B 4J9
Tel: 709-364-8811; *Fax:* 709-364-8812
e-mail: nlrbhca@nf.aibn.com; bulletin@nfld.com (Road Builders Bulletin)
URL: www.nfld.net/roadbuilders
Austin Sheppard, Manager, Business
Steve Grainger, President

Brian Johnson, Vice-President
Perry Barrett, Secretary-Treasurer
Perry Barrett, Chair, Sater & Sewer

Northwest Territories Construction Association (NWTCA)
PO Box 2277, 4921 - 49th St., 3rd Fl., Yellowknife NT X1A 2P7
Tel: 867-873-3949; *Fax:* 867-873-8366
e-mail: director@nwtca.ca
URL: www.nwtca.ca
Bob Doherty, President
Niels Konge, Exec. Vice-President
Réjean Jacques, Vice-President, Nunavut
Trina Rentmeister, Sec.-Treas.

Nova Scotia Road Builders Association
#217, 11 Thornhill Dr., Dartmouth NS B3B 1R9
URL: www.nsrba.ca
Grant Feltmate, Executive Director
Ken Thomas, President

Ontario Concrete Pipe Association (OCPA)
5045 South Service Rd., 1st Fl., Burlington ON L7L 5Y7
Tel: 905-631-9696; *Fax:* 905-631-1905
Toll-Free: 800-435-0116
e-mail: info@ocpa.com
URL: www.ocpa.com
Affiliation(s): Municipal Engineers Association; Canadian Concrete Pipe Association; Tubecon; American Concrete Pipe Association; Canadian Portland Cement Association; Water Environment Association of Ontario; Canadian Public Works Association; Ontario Sewer & Watermain Construction Association; Consulting Engineers of Ontario
Drew Black, Vice-President & General Manager
Dave Gajich, Director
John Munro, Director

Ontario General Contractors Association (OGCA)
#703, 6299 Airport Rd., Mississauga ON L4V 1N3
Tel: 905-671-3969; *Fax:* 905-671-8212
e-mail: info@ogca.ca
URL: www.ogca.ca
Affiliation(s): Council of Ontario Construction Associations
Clive Thurston, President
Stephen Bauld, Vice-President

Ontario Industrial Roofing Contractors' Association (OIRCA)
#301, 940 The East Mall, Toronto ON M9B 6J7
Tel: 416-695-4114; *Fax:* 416-695-9920
Toll-Free: 888-336-4722
e-mail: oirca@ontarioroofing.com
URL: www.ontarioroofing.com
Affiliation(s): Construction Safety Association of Ontario
Jim Norman, President
Brian Benham, 1st Vice-President
DaCosta Manuel, Treasurer

Ontario Painting Contractors Association (OPCA)
#305, 211 Consumers Rd., Toronto ON M2J 4G8
Tel: 416-498-1897; *Fax:* 416-498-6757
Toll-Free: 800-461-3630
e-mail: info@ontpca.org
URL: www.ontpca.org
Affiliation(s): Federation of Painting & Decorating Contractors of Toronto; Architectural Painting Specifications Services Ltd.
Andrew Sefton, Executive Director
Gilbert Satov, President

Ontario Pipe Trades Council
930 Sheldon Ct., Burlington ON L7L 5K6
Tel: 905-631-8989; *Fax:* 905-631-9055
e-mail: info@optc.org
URL: www.optc.org
Neil McCormack, Business Manager

Pipe Line Contractors Association of Canada (PLCAC)
#201, 1075 North Service Rd. West, Oakville ON L6M 2G2
Tel: 905-847-9383; *Fax:* 905-847-7824
e-mail: plcac@pipeline.ca
URL: www.pipeline.ca
Barry L. Brown, Executive Director
Sylvia Simmons, Secretary

Prince Edward Island Roadbuilders & Heavy Construction Association
PO Box 1901, Charlottetown PE C1A 7N5
Tel: 902-894-9514; *Fax:* 902-894-9512
e-mail: pei.roadbuilders@pei.sympatico.ca
URL: www3.pei.sympatico.ca/pei.roadbuilders/
Joe Murphy, Manager

Ready Mixed Concrete Association of Ontario (RMCAO)
#3, 365 Brunel Rd., Mississauga ON L4Z 1Z5
Tel: 905-507-1122; *Fax:* 905-890-8122
e-mail: dbiffis@rmcao.org
URL: www.rmcao.org
John D. Hull, President

Road Builders Association of New Brunswick (RBANB)
#5, 59 Avonlea Ct., Fredericton NB E3C 1N8
Tel: 506-454-5079; *Fax:* 506-452-7646
e-mail: rbanb@nb.aibn.com
URL: www.rbanb.com
Kent Duggan, President
Calvin Flight, Vice-President

Roadbuilders & Heavy Construction Association of Saskatchewan
1939 Elphinstone St., Regina SK S4T 3N3
Tel: 306-586-1805; *Fax:* 306-585-3750
e-mail: rb10@sasktel.net
URL: www.rbhca.sk.ca
Affiliation(s): Western Canada Roadbuilders & Heavy Construction Association
Jim Short, Chairman

Roofing Contractors Association of British Columbia (RCABC)
9734 - 201st St., Langley BC V1M 3E8
Tel: 604-882-9734; *Fax:* 604-882-1744
e-mail: roofing@rcabc.org
URL: www.rcabc.org
Affiliation(s): International Federation of Roofing Contractors
Brian Hofler, Executive Vice-President
Ivan Van Spronsen, President
Lyle Nelson, Vice-President
Len Edmondson, Sec.-Treas.

Roofing Contractors Association of Manitoba Inc. (RCAM)
290 Burnell St., Winnipeg MB R3G 2A7
Tel: 204-783-6365; *Fax:* 204-783-6446
e-mail: info@rcam.ca
URL: www.rcam.ca
R.M. Stefanick, Secretary Manager

Roofing Contractors Association of Nova Scotia (RCANS)
PO Box 141, 7 Frederick Ave., Mount Uniacke NS B0N 1Z0
Tel: 902-866-0505; *Fax:* 902-866-0506
Toll-Free: 888-278-0133
e-mail: Contact@rcans.ca
URL: www.rcans.ca
Marg Woodworth, Office Manager
Mike Gilroy, President

Saskatchewan Construction Safety Association Inc. (SCSA)
498 Henderson Dr., Regina SK S4N 6E3
Tel: 306-525-0175; *Fax:* 306-525-1542
Toll-Free: 800-817-2079
e-mail: billj@scsaonline.ca
URL: www.scsaonline.ca
Bill Johnson, Executive Director
Randy Larson, Chair

Saskatchewan Ready-Mixed Concrete Association Inc.
#203, 1801 McKay St., Regina SK S4N 6E7
Tel: 306-757-2788; *Fax:* 306-569-9144
URL: www.srmca.org
Garth Sanders, Executive Director

Sealant & Waterproofing Association (SWA)
70 Leek Cres., Richmond Hill ON L4B 1H1
Tel: 416-499-4000; *Fax:* 416-499-8752
e-mail: info@swao.com
URL: www.swao.com
Andrew Porciello, President
Paul Hanratty, Vice President

Southern Interior Construction Association (SICA)
#104, 151 Commercial Dr., Kelowna BC V1X 7W2
Tel: 250-491-7330; *Fax:* 250-491-3929
e-mail: kelowna@sica.bc.ca
URL: www.sica.bc.ca
Debra Hicks, President

Structural Board Association (SBA) / Association du panneau structural
#27, 25 Valleywood Dr., Markham ON L3R 5L9
Tel: 905-475-1100; *Fax:* 905-475-1101
e-mail: info@osbguide.com
URL: www.osbguide.com
Mark P. Angelini, President/CEO

Terrazzo Tile & Marble Association of Canada (TTMAC) / Association canadienne de terrazzo, tuile et marbre
#8, 163 Buttermill Ave., Concord ON L4K 3X8
Tel: 905-660-9640; *Fax:* 905-660-0513
Toll-Free: 800-201-8599
e-mail: association@ttmac.com
URL: www.ttmac.com
Doug Dickinson, Executive Director
Tony Torriano, President

Toronto Construction Association
70 Leek Cres., Richmond Hill ON L4B 1H1
Tel: 416-499-4000; *Fax:* 416-499-8752
e-mail: bmirsky@tcaconnect.com
URL: www.tcaconnect.com
Affiliation(s): International Council for Building Research Studies & Documentation
Greg Androshko, Chair
Kim F. McKinney, Executive Vice-President
John G. Mollenhauer, President & CEO

Western Canada Roadbuilders Association
1236 Ellice Ave., Winnipeg MB R3G 0E7
Tel: 204-947-1379; *Fax:* 204-943-2279
e-mail: clorenc@mhca.mb.ca
URL: www.wcrhca.org
Affiliation(s): Roads & Transportation Association of Canada
Chris Lorenc, President

Western Retail Lumber Association (WRLA)
Western Retail Lumber Association Inc., #1004, 213 Notre Dame Ave., Winnipeg MB R3B 1N3
Tel: 204-957-1077; *Fax:* 204-947-5195
Toll-Free: 800-661-0253
e-mail: wrla@wrla.org
URL: www.wrla.org
Gary Hamilton, Executive Director
Dwight Dixon, President

Winnipeg Construction Association
290 Burnell St., Winnipeg MB R3G 2A7
Tel: 204-775-8664; *Fax:* 204-783-6446
e-mail: wca@winnipegconstruction.ca
URL: www.winnipegconstruction.ca
John Schubert, President
Ronald Hambley, Executive Vice-President

Business

Association for Corporate Growth, Toronto Chapter (ACG)
#1008, 500 Avenue Rd., Toronto ON M4V 2J6
Tel: 416-868-1881; *Fax:* 416-860-0580
e-mail: acgtoronto@acg.org
URL: www.acg.org/toronto
Sue Anderson, Administrator
Dan Amadori, President

Better Business Bureau of Central & Northern Alberta
Capitol Place, #888, 9707 - 110 St., Edmonton AB T5K 2L9
Tel: 780-482-2341; *Fax:* 780-482-1150
Toll-Free: 800-232-7298
e-mail: info@edmontonbbb.org
URL: www.edmonton.bbb.org
Chris Lawrence, President & CEO

Better Business Bureau of Eastern & Northern Ontario & the Outaouais / Bureau d'éthique commerciale de l'Est et Nord de l'Ontario et l'Outaouais
#505, 700 Industrial Ave., Ottawa ON K1G 0Y9
Tel: 613-237-4856; *Fax:* 613-237-4878
e-mail: info@ottawa.bbb.org
URL: www.ottawa.bbb.org
Diane Iadeluca, Executive Director

Better Business Bureau of Manitoba & Northwest Ontario
1030B Empress St., Winnipeg MB R3G 3H4
Tel: 204-989-9010; *Fax:* 204-989-9016
Toll-Free: 800-385-3074
e-mail: bbbinquiries@mts.net
URL: www.manitoba.bbb.org
Amaro Silva, Manager

Better Business Bureau of Mid-Western Ontario
354 Charles St., Kitchener ON N2G 4L5
Tel: 519-579-3080; *Fax:* 519-570-0072
Toll-Free: 800-459-8875
URL: www.kitchener.bbb.org
Ric Borski, President

Better Business Bureau of Newfoundland
#301, 360 Topsail Rd., St. John's NL A1E 2B6
Tel: 709-364-2222; *Fax:* 709-364-2255
Toll-Free: 877-663-2363
e-mail: info@bbbnl.org
URL: www.nl.bbb.org
Glenn Sullivan, President

Better Business Bureau of Saskatchewan
980 Albert St., Regina SK S4R 7601
Tel: 306-352-7601; *Fax:* 306-565-6236
Toll-Free: 888-352-7601
e-mail: info@bbbsask.com
URL: www.sask.bbb.org
Danny Berehula, Executive Director

Better Business Bureau of Southern Alberta
#350, 7330 Fisher St. SE, Calgary AB T2H 2H8
Tel: 403-531-8784; *Fax:* 403-640-2514
Toll-Free: 800-661-4464
e-mail: info@calgary.bbb.org
URL: www.calgary.bbb.org
Ellen Wright, President

Better Business Bureau of the Maritime Provinces
#805, 1888 Brunswick St., Halifax NS B3J 3J8
Tel: 902-422-6581; *Fax:* 902-429-6457
e-mail: bbbmp@bbbmp.ca
URL: www.maritimeprovinces.bbb.org
Don MacKinnon, President

Better Business Bureau of Vancouver Island
#220, 1178 Cook St., Victoria BC V8V 4A1
Tel: 250-386-6348; *Fax:* 250-386-2367
e-mail: info@bbbvanisland.org
URL: www.vi.bbb.org
Nigel Brown, President
Rosalind Scott, Executive Director

Better Business Bureau of Western Ontario
PO Box 2153, #308, 200 Queens Ave., London ON N6A 4E3
Tel: 519-673-3222; *Fax:* 519-673-5966
Toll-Free: 877-283-9222
e-mail: info@london.bbb.org
URL: www.london.bbb.org
Janet B. Delaney, President

Better Business Bureau of Windsor & Southwestern Ontario
#302, 880 Ouellette Ave., Windsor ON N9A 1C7
Tel: 519-258-7222; *Fax:* 519-258-1198
e-mail: bbb@bbbwindsor.com
URL: www.windsorbbb.com

Better Business Bureau Serving South Central Ontario
100 James St. South, Hamilton ON L8P 2Z2
Tel: 905-526-1111; *Fax:* 905-526-1225
e-mail: info@thebbb.ca, membership@thebbb.ca
URL: www.thebbb.ca

Business Council of British Columbia
#810, 1050 Pender St. West, Vancouver BC V6E 3S7
Tel: 604-684-3384; *Fax:* 604-684-7957
e-mail: info@bcbc.com
URL: www.bcbc.com
Virginia Greene, President/CEO
Jock Finlayson, Executive Vice-President, Policy

Canadian Association of Family Enterprise (CAFE) / Association canadienne des enterprises familiales
#112, 465 Morden Rd., Oakville ON L6K 3W6
Tel: 416-538-9992; *Fax:* 905-337-8260
Toll-Free: 866-849-0099
e-mail: office@cafenational.org
URL: www.cafenational.org
Affiliation(s): Family Enterprise Foundation
Lawrence Barns, National CEO

The Canadian Council for Public-Private Partnerships (CCPPP) / Le Conseil canadien pour les partenariats public-privé
1 First Canadian Place, #1600, 100 King St. West, Toronto ON M5X 1G5
Tel: 416-861-0500; *Fax:* 416-862-7661
e-mail: partners@pppcouncil.ca
URL: www.pppcouncil.ca
Affiliation(s): Federation of Canadian Municipalities; Canadian Water & Wastewater Association
Jane Peatch, Executive Director
Jane Peatch, Executive Director

Canadian Council for Small Business & Entrepreneurship (CCSBE) / Conseil canadien des PME et de l'entrepreneuriat (CCPME)
c/o Centre for Small Business & Entrepreneurship, Acadia University, 38 Crowell Dr., Willet House, Wolfville NS B4P 2R6
Tel: 902-585-1776; *Fax:* 902-585-1057
e-mail: ccsbe.secretariat@acadiau.ca
URL: www.ccsbe.org
Affiliation(s): International Council for Small Business
Jean-Marie Nkongolo-Bakenda, President
Chris Pelham, Secretary

Canadian Council of Better Business Bureaus (CCBBB) / Conseil canadien des bureaux d'éthique commerciale
#800, 2 St. Clair Ave. East, Toronto ON M4T 2T5
Tel: 416-644-4936; *Fax:* 416-644-4945
e-mail: ccbbb@ccbbb.ca
URL: www.ccbbb.ca
Affiliation(s): The Council of Better Business Bureaus, USA
Douglas Simpson, President/CEO

Canadian Council of Chief Executives (CCCE) / Conseil canadien des chefs d'entreprise
#1001, 99 Bank St., Ottawa ON K1P 6B9
Tel: 613-238-3727; *Fax:* 613-236-8679
e-mail: leaders@ceocouncil.ca
URL: www.ceocouncil.ca
Gordon M. Nixon, Chair
John Manley, President & Chief Executive
Ross Laver, Vice-President, Policy & Communications

Canadian Federation of Independent Business (CFIB) / Fédération canadienne de l'entreprise indépendante
#401, 4141 Yonge St., Toronto ON K1P 6L7M2P 2A6
Tel: 416-222-8022; *Fax:* 416-222-6103
e-mail: cfib@cfib
URL: www.cfib-fcei.ca
Catherine Swift, Chair, President, & CEO
Richard Fahey, Senior Vice-President, Strategic Development
Dan Kelly, Senior Vice-President, Legislative Affairs
Brien Gray, Executive Vice-President
Doug Bruce, Director, Research

Canadian Federation of Independent Business
#2420, 630, boul René Levesque ouest, Montréal QC H3B 1S6
Tél: 514-861-3234; *Téléc:* 514-861-1711
Courriel: samque@fcei.ca

Canadian Franchise Association (CFA) / Association canadienne de la franchise
#116, 5399 Eglinton Ave. West, Toronto ON M9C 5K6
Tel: 416-695-2896; *Fax:* 416-695-1950
Toll-Free: 800-665-4232
e-mail: info@cfa.ca
URL: www.cfa.ca
Lorraine McLachlan, President

Canadian Institute of Chartered Business Valuators (CICBV) / L'Institut canadien des experts en évaluation d'entreprises
#710, 277 Wellington St. West, Toronto ON M5V 3H2
Tel: 416-977-1117; *Fax:* 416-977-7066
e-mail: admin@cicbv.ca
URL: www.cicbv.ca
Jeannine Brooks, MBA, CAE, FCGA, President & Chief Executive Officer
Bob Boulton, Director, Professional Affairs
Le Anh Huynh, Coordinator, Programmes
Lauren Kirshner, Coordinator, External Relations
Jennifer Warlow, Coordinator, Communications
Deborah Pelle, Manager, Events
Judith Roth, Manager, Information Technology & Member Services

Canadian International Institute of Applied Negotiation (CIIAN) / L'Institut international canadien de la négociation pratique
1 Nicholas St., Ottawa ON K1N 7B7
Tel: 613-237-9050; *Fax:* 613-237-6952
Toll-Free: 888-244-2637
e-mail: ciian@ciian.org
URL: www.ciian.org
Affiliation(s): Concorde Inc.
Flaurie Storie, Executive Director

Canadian Organization of Small Business Inc. (COSBI)
5405, 129 Ave. NW, Edmonton AB T5A 0A3
Tel: 780-423-2672
Donald Richard Eastcott, Managing Director
Roy E. Shannon, C.A., Chair

Canadian Professional Sales Association (CPSA) / Association canadienne des professionnels de la vente
#800, 310 Front St. West, Toronto ON M5V 3B5
Tel: 416-408-2685; *Fax:* 416-408-2684
Toll-Free: 888-267-2772
e-mail: membership@cpsa.com
URL: www.cpsa.com
Bruce Andrew, Chair
Harvey Copeman, CSP, President/CEO

Canadian Society of Customs Brokers (CSCB) / Société canadienne des courtiers en douane
#320, 55 Murray St., Ottawa ON K1N 5M3
Tel: 613-562-3543; *Fax:* 613-562-3548
e-mail: cscb@cscb.ca
URL: www.cscb.ca
Affiliation(s): International Federation of Customs Brokers Associations
Brian Collins, Director
Michel Vallée, Chair

Canadian Youth Business Foundation (CYBF) / La Fondation canadienne des jeunes entrepreneurs
#1410, 100 Adelaide St. West, Toronto ON M5H 1S3
Tel: 416-408-2923; *Fax:* 416-408-3234
Toll-Free: 866-646-2922
e-mail: info@cybf.ca
URL: www.cybf.ca
Vivian Prokop, CEO
John Risley, O.C., Chair

Conseil du patronat du Québec (CPQ)
#510, 1010, rue Sherbrooke Ouest, Montréal QC H3A 2R7
Tél: 514-288-5161; *Téléc:* 514-288-5165
Ligne sans frais: 877-288-5161
Courriel: info@cpq.qc.ca
URL: www.cpq.qc.ca
Yves-Thomas Dorval, Président

Entrepreneurship Institute of Canada
PO Box 40043, 75 King St. South, Waterloo ON N2J 4V1
Tel: 519-885-1559*Tel:* 1-877-993-9921; *Fax:* 519-885-0990
Toll-Free: 800-665-4497
e-mail: entinst@sympatico.ca
URL: www.entinst.ca

Hong Kong-Canada Business Association (HKCBA) / L'Association commerciale Hong Kong-Canada
#220, 1050 West Pender St., Vancouver BC V6E 3S7
Tel: 604-684-2410; *Fax:* 604-684-6208
e-mail: nationaled@hkcba.com
URL: www.hkcba.com
Affiliation(s): Hong Kong Trade Development Council; Hong Kong Economic & Trade Office, HKSAR Government; Hong Kong Tourism Board; Invest HK; Canadian Chamber of Commerce in Hong Kong
Robert A. Brown, CEO, Special Events
David Pohl, National Chair
Joyce Chung, Executive Director

International Association of Business Communicators / Association internationale de communicateurs professionels
#7, 296 Jarvis St., Toronto ON M5B 2C5
Tel: 416-968-0264; *Fax:* 416-968-6818
e-mail: toronto-info@iabc.com
URL: toronto.iabc.com

Italian Chamber of Commerce of Toronto (ICCT)
1502, 80 Richmond St. West, Toronto ON M5H 2A4
Tel: 416-789-7169; *Fax:* 416-789-7160
e-mail: info.toronto@italchambers.ca
URL: www.italchambers.ca
George Visintin, President
Paolo Palamara, Vice President/Secretary

Kelowna Chamber of Commerce
544 Harvey Ave., Kelowna BC V1Y 6C9
Tel: 250-861-3627; *Fax:* 250-861-3624
e-mail: info@kelownachamber.org
URL: www.kelownachamber.org
Affiliation(s): BC Chamber of Commerce
Norm LeCavalier, President

Lloydminster Chamber of Commerce
4419 - 52 Ave., Lloydminster AB T9V 0Y8
Tel: 780-875-9013; *Fax:* 780-875-0755
e-mail: contact_llc@lloydminsterchamber.com
URL: www.lloydminsterchamber.com
Pat L. Tenney, Executive Director
Peggy Bosch, President

Markham Board of Trade (MBT)
#206, 80F Centurian Dr., Markham ON L3R 8C1
Tel: 905-474-0730; *Fax:* 905-474-0685
e-mail: info@markhamboard.com
URL: www.markhamboard.com
Affiliation(s): Scarborough York Region Chinese Business Association
Richard Cunningham, President/CEO

Meeting Professionals International (MPI)
#1700, 3030 Lyndon B. Johnson Freeway, Dallas TX 75234-2759 USA
Tel: 972-702-3000; *Fax:* 972-702-3070
e-mail: feedback@mpiweb.org
URL: www.mpiweb.org
Larry Luteran, Chair

Meeting Professionals International (MPT)
6519B Mississauga Rd., Mississauga ON L5N 1A6
Tel: 905-286-4807; *Fax:* 905-567-7191
e-mail: mpicanada@mpiweb.org
URL: www.mpiweb.org

Mission Regional Chamber of Commerce
34033 Lougheed Hwy., Mission BC V2V 5X8
Tel: 604-826-6914; *Fax:* 604-826-5916
e-mail: manager@missionchamber.bc.ca
URL: www.missionchamber.bc.ca
Michelle Favero, Manager
Sean Melia, President

Mouvement québécois de la qualité (MQQ)
#1710, 360, rue Saint-Jacques ouest, Montréal QC H2Y 1P5
Tél: 514-874-9933; *Téléc:* 514-866-4600
Courriel: mqq@qualite.qc.ca
URL: www.qualite.qc.ca
Roch Dubé, Président

The National Citizens Coalition / Coalition nationale des citoyens inc.
#501, 27 Queen St. East, Toronto ON M5C 2M6
Tel: 416-869-3838; *Fax:* 416-869-1891
Toll-Free: 888-703-5553
e-mail: ncc@nationalcitizens.ca
URL: www.nationalcitizens.ca
Peter Coleman, President & CEO
Colin T. Brown, Chair

National Quality Institute (NQI) / Institut national de la qualité (INQ)
#307, 2275 Lakeshore West Blvd., Toronto ON M8V 3Y3
Tel: 416-251-7600; *Fax:* 416-251-9131
Toll-Free: 800-263-9648
e-mail: info@nqi.ca
URL: www.nqi.ca
Allan Ebedes, President & CEO

Ontario Public Buyers Association, Inc. (OPBA)
Ridley Square, #361, 111 Fourth Ave., St Catharines ON L2S 3P5
Tel: 905-682-2644; *Fax:* 905-682-9988
e-mail: info@opba.ca
URL: www.opba.ca
Affiliation(s): National Institute of Governmental Purchasing, Inc.; Institute of Purchasing & Supply of Great Britain; International Federation of Purchasing & Materials Management
Lisa Buitenhuis, Secretary
Angela Longreet, Treasurer
Kim Dooling, President
Mark Bolzon, Vice-President

Worldwide Association of Business Coaches
c/o WABC Coaches Inc., PO Box 215, Saanichton BC V8M 2C3
Fax: 250-656-8752
e-mail: info@wabccoaches.com
URL: www.wabccoaches.com
Wendy Johnson, President/CEO

Centraide

Centraide Abitibi Témiscamingue et Nord-du-Québec
1009, 6e rue, Val-d'Or QC J9P 3W4
Tél: 819-825-7139; *Téléc:* 819-825-7155
Courriel: courrier@centraide-atnq.qc.ca
URL: www2.unitedway.ca
Affiliation(s): Chambre de Commerce; Comité prévention des crimes
Huguette Boucher, Directrice générale

Chemical Industry

Canadian Association of Agri-Retailers (CAAR)
#107, 1090 Waverley St., Winnipeg MB R3T 0P4
Tel: 204-989-9300; *Fax:* 204-989-9306
Toll-Free: 800-463-9323
e-mail: info@caar.org
URL: www.caar.org
Ken Clancy, Chair
David MacKay, President & Chief Executive Officer
Bob McNaughton, Vice-President
Delaney Ross, Manager, Membership Relations
Lezlee Oswald, Coordinator, Programs
Andrew Senkiw, Coordinator, Research

Canadian Association of Chemical Distributors (CACD) / Association canadienne des distributeurs de produits chimiques
#301, 627 Lyons Lane, Oakville ON L6J 5Z7
Tel: 905-844-9140; *Fax:* 905-844-5706
e-mail: catherine@cacd.ca; ccampbell@cacd.ca
URL: www.cacd.ca
Cathy Campbell, Managing Director
Rod Paterson, President & Director
Michael Staley, Sec.-Treas.

Canadian Consumer Specialty Products Association (CCSPA)
#800, 130 Albert St., Ottawa ON K1P 5G4
Tel: 613-232-6616; *Fax:* 613-233-6350
e-mail: assoc@ccspa.org
URL: www.ccspa.org
Shannon Coombs, Executive Director
Nancy Hitchins, Director, Administration & Member Services

Canadian Fertilizer Institute (CFI) / Institut canadien des engrais
#802, 350 Sparks St., Ottawa ON K1R 7S8
Tel: 613-230-2600; *Fax:* 613-230-5142
e-mail: fertilizer@cfi.ca
URL: www.cfi.ca
Roger L. Larson, President
Monique MacDonald, Manager, Finance & Corporate Services

Chemical Institute of Canada (CIC) / Institut de chimie du Canada
#550, 130 Slater St., Ottawa ON K1P 6E2
Tel: 613-232-6252; *Fax:* 613-232-5862
Toll-Free: 888-542-2242
e-mail: info@cheminst.ca
URL: www.cheminst.ca
Affiliation(s): Canadian Society for Chemical Engineering; Canadian Society for Chemical Technology; Canadian Society for Chemistry
Roland Andersson, MCIC, Executive Director
Murray Gray, FCIC, Chair

International Plant Nutrition Institute (IPNI)
#550, 3500 Parkway Lane, Norcross GA 30092 USA
Tel: 770-447-0335; *Fax:* 770-448-0439
e-mail: info@ipni.net
URL: www.ppi-ppic.org
Terry L. Roberts, President
Tom Jensen, Northern Great Plains Director, (Saskatchewan)
Tom Bruulsema, N. American-Northeastern Director, (Ontario)

Ordre des chimistes du Québec (OCQ)
#2199, 300 rue Léo-Pariseau, Montréal QC H2X 4B3
Tél: 514-844-3644; *Téléc:* 514-844-9601
Courriel: information@ocq.qc.ca
URL: www.ocq.qc.ca
Martin Turcotte, Vice-président finances et Membre d, Région centre
Guy Collin, Vice-président intermédiaire et Mem, Région de l'est
Luc Séguin, Président du Bureau et du comité ad, Région de l'ouest
Martial Boivin, MBA, Président-directeur général et secr

Society of Chemical Industry - Canadian Section (SCI)
#550, 130 Slater St., Ottawa ON K1P 6E2
e-mail: scicanada@soci.org
URL: www.soci.org
Roger Hayward, Hon. Chair
Rosie Baston, Coorindator

Child & Family Services

Black Family Support Network
719, rue Des Seigneurs, Montréal QC H3J 1Y2
Tel: 514-933-1867; *Fax:* 514-933-1808
e-mail: lbbfs@bell.net
Rosemary Segee, Contact

Elizabeth House / Maison Elizabeth
2131 Marlowe, Montréal QC H4A 3L4
Tel: 514-482-2488; *Fax:* 514-482-9467
e-mail: info@maisonelizabethhouse.com
URL: www.maisonelizabethhouse.com
Linda Schachtler, Contact

Yukon Child Care Association (YCCA)
Whitehorse YT
e-mail: ycca@live.com
URL: www.yukonchildcareassociation.com
Affiliation(s): Canadian Child Care Federation

Childbirth

Alberta Association of Midwives (AAM)
PO Box 11957, #166, 4307-130 Ave. SE, Edmonton AB T2Z 3V8
Tel: 403-660-1696
e-mail: info@albertamidwives.com
URL: www.albertamidwives.com
Affiliation(s): International Confederation of Midwives
Meryl Moulton, R.M., President

Association of Ontario Midwives (AOM) / Association des sages-femmes de l'Ontario
#608, 789 Don Mills, Toronto ON M3C 1T5
Tel: 416-425-9974; *Fax:* 416-425-6905
Toll-Free: 866-418-3773
e-mail: admin@aom.on.ca
URL: www.aom.on.ca
Kelly Stadelbauer, Executive Director

College of Midwives of British Columbia (CMBC)
#210, 1682 West 7th Ave., Vancouver BC V6J 4S6
Tel: 604-742-2230; *Fax:* 604-730-8908
e-mail: information@cmbc.bc.ca
URL: www.cmbc.bc.ca
Jane Kilthei, Registrar & Executive Director

Infant Feeding Action Coalition
6 Trinity Sq., Toronto ON M5G 1B1
Tel: 416-595-9819; *Fax:* 416-591-9355
e-mail: info@infactcanada.ca
URL: www.infactcanada.ca
Elisabeth Sterken, National Director

International Society for the Study of Hypertension in Pregnancy (Canada) Inc. (ISSHP) / Société internationale pour l'étude de l'hypertension en grossesse (Canada) inc.
CHUS, Site Fleurimont, 3001, 12e av nord, Sherbrooke QC J1H 5N4
Tel: 819-346-1110; *Fax:* 819-820-6434
e-mail: jean-marie.moutquin@usherbrooke.ca
Jean-Marie Moutquin, President

La Leche League Canada (LLLC) / Ligue La Leche Canada
PO Box 700, Winchester ON K0C 2K0
Tel: 613-774-4900; *Fax:* 613-774-2798
Toll-Free: 800-665-4324
e-mail: ofm@LLLC.ca
URL: www.lllc.ca
Affiliation(s): La Leche League International
Joan Little, Chair
Fiona Audy, Secretary
Wendy Dale, Treasurer
Sheila Munro, Coordinator, Administration & Donations

Multiple Births Canada (MBC) / Naissances multiples Canada
PO Box 432, Wasaga Beach ON L0L 2P0
Tel: 705-429-0901; *Fax:* 705-429-9809
Toll-Free: 866-228-8824
e-mail: office@multiplebirthscanada.org
URL: www.multiplebirthscanada.org
Gail Moore, Chair
Melanie Dugard, Treasurer

Serena Canada
151 Holland Ave., Ottawa ON K1Y 0Y2
Tel: 613-728-6536
Toll-Free: 888-373-7362

e-mail: serena@on.aibn.com
URL: www.serena.ca
Affiliation(s): International Federation for Family Life Promotion

Children & Youth

Alberta Associations for Bright Children (AABC)
c/o Action for Bright Children Calgary Society, PO Box 36093, Stn. Lakeview, Calgary AB T3E 7C6
Tel: 403-463-9612
URL: www.albertaabc.org

Alberta Child Care Network Association (ACCNA)
#110, 10025 - 106 St., Edmonton AB T5J 1G4
Tel: 780-421-7544; *Fax:* 780-428-0080
Toll-Free: 877-421-9937
e-mail: tbaier.accna@telus.net
URL: www.accna.ca
Tim Baier, Executive Director

Association for Bright Children (Ontario) (ABC) / Société pour enfants doués et surdoués (Ontario)
PO Box 59088, 2238 Dundas St. West, Toronto ON M6R 3B5
Tel: 416-925-6136
e-mail: abcinfo@abcontario.ca
URL: www.abcontario.ca
Christine Thammavongsa, President

Association québécoise des centres de la petite enfance (AQCPE)
#200, 6611, rue Jarry est, Montréal QC H1P 1W5
Tél: 514-326-8008; *Téléc:* 514-326-3322
Ligne sans frais: 888-326-8008
Courriel: info@aqcpe.com
URL: www.aqcpe.com
Affiliation(s): Association des services de garde en milieu scolaire du Québec; Carrefour action municipal et famille; Centrale des syndicats du Québec; Fédération canadienne des services de garde à l'enfance; Fédération des femmes du Québec; Fédération des travailleurs et travailleuses du Québec; Fédération québécoise des organismes communautaires famille; Réseau de la santé et des services sociaux
Jean Robitaille, Directeur général
Violaine Ouellette, Responsable des communications

B'nai Brith Youth Organization Canada (BBYO)
4700 Bathurst St., 2nd Fl., Toronto ON M2R 1W8
Tel: 416-398-2004; *Fax:* 416-398-5780
e-mail: info@bbyo.on.ca
URL: www.bbyo.on.ca
Kevin Goodman, Program Director

Boys & Girls Clubs of Alberta
J. Percy Page Centre, 11759 Groat Rd., Edmonton AB T5M 3K6
Tel: 780-415-1734; *Fax:* 780-415-1737
e-mail: info@bgcalberta.com
URL: www.bgcalberta.com
Social Media: www.facebook.com/group.php?gid=24403790656
Jane Hirst, Regional Executive Director

Boys & Girls Clubs of Canada (BGCC) / Clubs garçons & filles du Canada
#204, 7100 Woodbine Ave., Markham ON L3R 5J2
Tel: 905-477-7272; *Fax:* 905-477-2056
e-mail: info@bgccan.com
URL: www.bgccan.com
Social Media: www.facebook.com/group.php?gid=2233316912
Pam Jolliffe, National Executive Director
Bouchra Sidali, Executive Assistant
Marlene Deboisbriand, Director, Club Services & Development

Boys & Girls Clubs of P.E.I.
PO Box 86, Tyne Valley PE C0B 2C0
Tel: 902-831-3297; *Fax:* 902-831-3466
e-mail: lrobin@pei.sympatico.ca
URL: www.boysandgirlsclubsofpei.org
Lorraine Robinson, Regional Coordinator

Canadian Association for Young Children (CAYC) / Association canadienne pour les jeunes enfants (ACJE)
#302, 1775 West 11th Ave., Vancouver BC V6J 2C1
e-mail: membership@cayc.ca
URL: www.cayc.ca
Deirdre Leighton, President
Laurie Hudyma, Vice-President & Chair, Publications
Kathy Graham, Treasurer

Canadian Child Care Federation (CCCF) / Fédération canadienne des services de garde à l'enfance (FCSGE)
#201, 383 Parkdale Ave., Ottawa ON K1Y 4R4
Tel: 613-729-5289; *Fax:* 613-729-3159
Toll-Free: 800-858-1412
e-mail: info@cccf-fcsge.ca
URL: www.cccf-fcsge.ca

Canadian Young Judaea
788 Marlee Ave., Toronto ON M6B 3K1
Tel: 416-781-5156; *Fax:* 416-787-3100
Toll-Free: 800-804-6661
e-mail: youngjudaea@bellnet.ca
URL: www.youngjudaea.ca
Risa Epstein, National Executive Director

Child Find Alberta (CFA)
3751 - 21 St. NW, Calgary AB T2E 6T5
Tel: 403-270-3463; *Fax:* 403-270-8355
Toll-Free: 800-561-1733
e-mail: childfindalberta@storehouse39.ca
URL: www.childfind.ab.ca
Affiliation(s): Reseau Enfants Retour; AMECO; CMECA
Brad Bostock, Executive Director
Renee Gillespie, Operations Manager

Child Find British Columbia
#208, 2722 Fifth St, Victoria BC V8T 4B2
Tel: 250-382-7311; *Fax:* 250-382-0227
Toll-Free: 888-689-3463
e-mail: childvicbc@shaw.ca
URL: childfindbc.com
Debie Byl, Executive Director

Child Find Canada Inc. (CFC)
PO Box 237, Oakville MB R0H 0Y0
Tel: 204-870-1298
e-mail: childcan@aol.com
URL: www.childfind.ca
Kathryn Anderson, National Co-Ordinator

Child Find Manitoba
#343, 800 Portage Ave., Winnipeg MB R3G 0N4
Tel: 204-945-5735; *Fax:* 204-948-2461
Toll-Free: 800-532-9135
e-mail: childmb@aol.com
URL: www.childfind.mb.ca
Lianna McDonald, Executive Director

Child Find Newfoundland/Labrador
#217, 31 Peet St., St. John's NL A1B 3W8
Tel: 709-738-4400; *Fax:* 709-738-0550
e-mail: childnfld@aol.com
URL: www.childfind.ca
Jeff Sears, President

Child Find Ontario
440A Britannia Rd. East, Mississauga ON L4Z 1X9
Tel: 905-712-3463; *Fax:* 905-712-3462
Toll-Free: 800-543-8477
e-mail: mail@childfindontario.ca
URL: www.ontario.childfind.ca
Trish, Executive Director

Child Find PEI Inc. (CFPEI)
549 North River Rd., Charlottetown PE C1E 1J6
Tel: 902-368-1678; *Fax:* 902-368-1389
Toll-Free: 800-387-7962
e-mail: childpei@aol.com
URL: childfind.ca
Lynn Coyle, President

Child Find Saskatchewan Inc.
#202, 3502 Taylor St. East, Saskatoon SK S7H 5H9
Tel: 306-955-0070; *Fax:* 306-373-1311
Toll-Free: 800-513-3463
e-mail: childsask@aol.com
URL: www.childfind.sk.ca
Affiliation(s): Chamber of Commerce
Phyllis Hallatt, President

Children's Creative Response to Conflict (CCRC)
211 Bronson Ave., Ottawa ON K1R 6H5
Tel: 613-234-9019
e-mail: ccrccanada@gmail.com
URL: www.ccrc-crc.ca

The Children's Wish Foundation of Canada / Fondation canadienne rêves d'enfants
#350, 1101 Kingston Rd., Pickering ON L1V 1B5
Tel: 905-839-8882; *Fax:* 905-839-3745
Toll-Free: 800-700-4437
e-mail: linda.marco@childrenswish.ca
URL: www.childrenswish.ca
Linda Marco, National Manager, Communications & Development

Desta Black Youth Network
The Padua Centre, 1950 rue St.-Antoine Ouest, Montréal QC H3J 1A5
Tel: 514-932-7597; *Fax:* 514-932-9468
e-mail: info@destanetwork.ca
URL: www.destanetwork.ca

Fondation Rêves d'Enfants, div. Nord-du-Québec
423, rue Normand, Chibougamau QC G8P 1A1
Tél: 418-748-3702
Kathy Fortin

Gifted Children's Association of BC (GCABC)
210 West Broadway, 3rd Fl., Vancouver BC V5Y 3W2
Tel: 604-534-6343; *Fax:* 604-534-9143
Toll-Free: 877-707-6111
e-mail: info@gcabc.ca
URL: www.gcabc.ca
Affiliation(s): Coalition for Students with Special Needs
John Kirkness, President
Tasha Carrothers, Secretary

Girl Guides of Canada (GGC) / Guides du Canada
50 Merton St., Toronto ON M4S 1A3
Tel: 416-487-5281; *Fax:* 416-487-5570
URL: www.girlguides.ca
Affiliation(s): World Association of Girl Guides & Girl Scouts
Deborah Del Duca, CEO
Myrtle Corkum, Chief Commissioner

Junior Achievement Canada (JACAN) / Jeunes Entreprises du Canada
#218, 1 Eva Rd., Toronto ON M9C 4Z5
Tel: 416-622-4602; *Fax:* 416-622-6861
Toll-Free: 800-265-0699
e-mail: programs@jacan.org
URL: www.jacan.org
Ross W. Maund, President/CEO
Stephen Ashworth, Vice President, Education
Matthew Sardina, Vice President, Business Development & Marketing
Tim Turnbull, Vice President, Fund Development
Claudia Bishop, CFO

Junior Chamber International Canada / Jeune chambre internationale du Canada
14 Bruce Farm Dr., Toronto ON M2H 1G3
Tel: 416-886-9756; *Fax:* 416-221-9926
Toll-Free: 800-265-0484
e-mail: administration@jcicanada.com
URL: www.jcicanada.com
Affiliation(s): Junior Chamber International
Jean-Simon Deschênes, Chairman of the Board
Leslie Shore, National President

Justice for Children & Youth (JFCY)
#1203, 415 Yonge St., Toronto ON M5B 2E7
Tel: 416-920-1633; *Fax:* 416-920-5855
Toll-Free: 866-999-5329
e-mail: info@jfcy.org
URL: www.jfcy.org
Martha Mackinnon, B.A., B.Ed., M., Executive Director
Jeffery Rosekat, LL.B., President & Chair

Manitoba Child Care Association (MCCA)
2350 McPhillips St., 2nd Fl., Winnipeg MB R2V 4J6
Tel: 204-586-8587; *Fax:* 204-589-5613
Toll-Free: 888-323-4676
e-mail: info@mccahouse.org
URL: www.mccahouse.org
Pat Wege, Executive Director
Michele Henderson, President
Brenda McCarthy, Sec.-Treas.
Karen Gander, Manager, Professional Development

North America Missing Children Association Inc. (NAMCA)
Toll-Free: 800-260-0753
e-mail: namca@nbnet.nb.ca
Affiliation(s): Heidi Search Centre, San Antonio, Texas; Missing Children's Network, Montréal
Patricia Hughes, Executive Director

Ranch Ehrlo Society
PO Box 570, Pilot Butte SK S0G 3Z0
Tel: 306-781-1800; *Fax:* 306-757-0599
e-mail: rescomm@ehrlo.com
URL: www.ehrlo.com
Tim Young, Chair Person

Réseau Enfants Retour Canada / Missing Children's Network Canada
#420, 376, ave Victoria, Montréal QC H3Z 1C3
Tél: 514-843-4333; *Téléc:* 514-843-8211
Ligne sans frais: 888-692-4673
Courriel: info@missingchildren.ca
URL: www.missingchildren.ca
Affiliation(s): Association québécoise Plaidoyer-Victimes; Défense des Droits des Enfants International

Safe Kids Canada / Sécurijeunes Canada
#2105, 180 Dundas St. West, Toronto ON M5G 1Z8
Tel: 416-813-7288; *Fax:* 416-813-4986
Toll-Free: 888-723-3847
e-mail: safekids.web@sickkids.ca
URL: www.safekidscanada.ca
Affiliation(s): The Hospital for Sick Children
Allyson Hewitt, Executive Director

Scouts Canada / Les Scouts du Canada
1345 Baseline Rd., Ottawa ON K2C 0A7
Tel: 613-224-5131; *Fax:* 613-224-3571
Toll-Free: 888-726-8879
e-mail: helpcentre@scouts.ca
URL: www.scouts.ca
Affiliation(s): World Scout Bureau
Barry Hardaker, Executive Director, Field Services
Pierre Laurin, Compliance & Risk Manager
Jennifer Austin, Director, Communications
Gary Boutilier, Director, Finance
Ross Francis, Executive Director, Program
Alan Mimeault, Director, Retail Services
J. Robert Stewart, Executive Commissioner & CEO
Glenn Armstrong, Chief Commissioner & Chair

A World of Dreams Foundation Canada / La Fondation canadienne un monde de rêves
#3575, 6900, boul déCarie, Montréal QC H3A 3L4
Tel: 514-985-3003; *Fax:* 514-985-9280
Toll-Free: 800-567-7254
e-mail: info@awdreams.com
URL: www.awdreams.com
Lora Cianci, Director

Citizenship & Immigration

Canadian Association of Professional Immigration Consultants (CAPIC) / Association Canadienne des Conseillers Professionnels en Immigration (ACCPI)
#602, 245 Fairview Mall Dr., Toronto ON M2J 4T1
Tel: 416-483-7044; *Fax:* 416-483-0884
e-mail: info@capic.ca
URL: capic.ca
Berto Volpentesta, Executive Director
Monica Poon, National Coordinator

Canadian Immigration Historical Society (CIHS)
PO Box 9502, Stn. T, Ottawa ON K1G 3V2
Tel: 613-241-1587
e-mail: cihs@ncf.ca
URL: cihs.ncf.ca
David G. Bullock, Contact

Canadian Ukrainian Immigrant Aid Society (CUIAS)
2383 Bloor St. W., 2nd Fl., Toronto ON M6S 1P9
Tel: 416-767-4595; *Fax:* 416-767-2658
e-mail: cuias@cuias.org
URL: www.cuias.org
Affiliation(s): Ukrainian Canadian Congress
Eugen Duvalko, Executive Director

Centre for Information & Community Services of Ontario (CICS)
c/o Immigrant Resource Centre, 2330 Midland Ave., Toronto ON M1S 5G5
Tel: 416-292-7510; *Fax:* 416-292-7579*Crisis Hot-Line:* 416-292-2832
e-mail: cics@cicscanada.com
URL: www.cicscanada.com
David Pao, President
Moy Wong-Tam, Executive Director
Thomas Li, Secretary

Eritrean Canadian Community Centre of Metropolitan Toronto (ECCC)
579 St. Clair Ave. W, Toronto ON M6C 1A3
Tel: 416-658-8580; *Fax:* 416-658-7442
e-mail: info@eccctoronto.ca
URL: www.eccctoronto.ca

Immigrant Centre Manitoba
100 Adelaide St., Winnipeg MB R3A 0W2
Tel: 204-943-9158; *Fax:* 204-949-0734
e-mail: info@icmanitoba.com
URL: www.international-centre.ca
Affiliation(s): Canadian Council for Refugees
Linda Lalande, Executive Director

Jewish Immigrant Aid Services of Canada (JIAS) / Services canadiens d'assistance aux immigrants juifs
#306, 4580 Dufferin St., Toronto ON M3H 5Y2
Tel: 416-630-9051; *Fax:* 416-630-9029
e-mail: national@jias.org
URL: www.jias.org
Janis Roth, Executive Director

National Organization of Immigrant & Visible Minority Women of Canada (NOIVMWC) / Organisation nationale des femmes immigrantes et des femmes appartenant à une minorité visible du Canada (ONFIFAMVC)
#412, 219 Argyle St., Ottawa ON K2P 2H4
Tel: 613-232-0689; *Fax:* 613-232-0988
e-mail: noivmwc@noivmwc.org
URL: www.noivmwc.org
Eva Pakyam, President

Ontario Council of Agencies Serving Immigrants (OCASI)
#200, 110 Eglinton Ave. West, Toronto ON M4R 1A3
Tel: 416-322-4950; *Fax:* 416-322-8084
e-mail: generalmail@ocasi.org
URL: www.ocasi.org; www.settlement.org
Debbie Douglas, Executive Director
Uzma Shakir, President

Ottawa Community Immigrant Services Organization (OCISO) / Organisme communautaire des services aux immigrants d'Ottawa
959 Wellington St. West, Ottawa ON K1Y 2X5
Tel: 613-725-0202; *Fax:* 613-725-9054
e-mail: info@ociso.org
URL: www.ociso.org
Hamdi Mohamed, Executive Director

Place Benoît Bon Courage Community Centre / Centre Communautaire Bon Courage De Place Benoît
#2, 155 Place Benoît, Ville Saint-Laurent QC H4N 2H4
Tél: 514-744-0897; *Téléc:* 514-744-6205
Dayonn Vann, Contact

Conservation

Nova Scotia Federation of Anglers and Hunters (NSFAH)
PO Box 654, Halifax NS B3J 2T3
Tel: 902-477-8898
e-mail: tonyrodgers@eastlink.ca
URL: www.nsfah.ca
Tony Rodgers, Executive Director

Consumers

Consumers Council of Canada (CCC)
#100, 35 Madison Ave., Toronto ON M5R 2S2
Tel: 416-483-2696; *Fax:* 416-483-4128
e-mail: billhuzar@consumerscouncil.com
URL: www.consumerscouncil.com
Christina Bisanz, Executive Director
Bill Huzar, President

Consumers' Association of Canada (CAC) / Association des consommateurs du Canada
PO Box 9300, 436 Gilmour St., 3rd Fl., Ottawa ON K1G 3T9
Tel: 613-238-2533; *Fax:* 613-238-2538
e-mail: info@consumer.ca
URL: www.consumer.ca
Bruce Cran, President
Mel Fruitman, Vice-President

Copyright

Canadian Artists Representation Copyright Collective Inc.
109A Fourth Ave., Ottawa ON K1S 2L3
Tel: 613-232-3818; *Fax:* 613-232-8384
e-mail: carcc@carcc.ca
URL: www.carcc.ca
Janice Seline, Executive Director

Culture

Albanian-Canadian Community Association
26 Six Point Rd., Etobicoke ON M8Z 2W9
Tel: 416-503-4704; *Fax:* 416-503-4704
e-mail: info@albcan.org
URL: www.albcan.org
Petraq Peci, Chairman

Assemblée communautaire fransaskoise (ACF)
#101 - 2445, 13e ave., Regina SK S4P 0W1
Tél: 306-569-1912; *Téléc:* 306-781-7916
Ligne sans frais: 800-991-1912
Courriel: acf@sasktel.net
URL: www.fransaskois.sk.ca
Michel Dubé, Présidente
Patrice N'Gouandi, Agente aux communications

Assemblée parlementaire de la Francophonie (APF)
Région Amérique, Assemblée nationale, 1020, rue des Parlementaires, 6e étage, Québec QC G1A 1A3
Tél: 418-643-7391; *Téléc:* 418-643-1865
Courriel: alavoie@assnat.qc.ca
URL: www.regionamerique-apf.org
André Lavoie, Secrétaire administrative régionale

Association canadienne-française de l'Alberta (ACFA)
#42, 8697 - 91e rue, Edmonton AB T6C 3N1
Tél: 780-468-7674; *Téléc:* 780-468-1599
Courriel: sfca@virtuelle.ca
URL: francalta.ab.ca
Affiliation(s): Fédération culturelle canadienne-française
Jean Johnson, Président
Joël F. Lavoie, Directeur général

Association canadienne-française de l'Ontario (ACFO)
3349, ch Navan, Gloucester ON K4B 1H9
Tél: 613-841-5525
Courriel: dg@acfo.ca
URL: www.acfo.ca
Jean Poirier, Président

Association franco-yukonnaise (AFY)
302 Strickland St., Whitehorse YT Y1A 2K1
Tél: 867-668-2663; *Téléc:* 867-663-3511
Ligne sans frais: 866-673-7632
Courriel: afy@afy.yk.ca
URL: www.afy.yk.ca
Affiliation(s): Chambre de commerce du Yukon et de Whitehorse
Jeanne Beaudoin, Directrice générale
Sylvie Marcotte, Secrétaire

Association of Canadian Clubs / Association des cercles canadiens
#211, 2415 Holly Lane, Ottawa ON K1V 2P2
Tel: 613-236-8288; *Fax:* 613-236-8299
e-mail: cdnclub@ca.inter.net
URL: www.canadianclub.ca
Lyn Goldman, National President
Christine Merrikin, Executive Secretary
Jim Waters, Regional Director, British Columbia
Marjorie Nickerson, Regional Director, Alberta
Maura Gillis-Cipywnyk, Regional Director, Saskatchewan
Jacqui Blanchard, Regional Director, Manitoba
Allan Mutart, Regional Director, Southern Ontario
Clara Edwardson, Regional Director, Eastern & Northern Ontario
Cynthia Dinsmore, Regional Director, Québec

Canada-Israel Cultural Foundation (CICF) / Fondation culturelle Canada-Israël
4700 Bathurst St., 2nd Fl., Toronto ON M2R 1W8
Tel: 416-932-2260; *Fax:* 416-398-5780
e-mail: cicf@bellnet.ca
Cheryl Wetstein, Executive Director
Ron Bresler, National President

Canadian-Scandinavian Foundation (CSF) / Fondation Canada-Scandinavie
PO Box 135, Stn. B, Montréal QC H3B 3J5
Tel: 514-398-4740; *Fax:* 514-398-7356
e-mail: president@canada-scandinavia.ca
URL: www.canada-scandinavia.ca/
Hans Moller, Interim President

Centre culturel franco-manitobain (CCFM)
340, boul Provencher, Saint Boniface MB R2H 0G7
Tél: 204-233-8972; *Téléc:* 204-233-3324
Courriel: ccfm@ccfm.mb.ca
URL: www.ccfm.mb.ca
Agnès Champagne, Directrice générale

Centre francophone de Toronto (CFT)
20 Lower Spadina Ave., Toronto ON M5V 2Z1
Tél: 416-203-1220; *Téléc:* 416-203-1165
Courriel: contact@centrefranco.org
URL: www.centrefranco.org
Affiliation(s): Assemblée des centres culturels de l'Ontario; Centraide
Jean-Gilles Pelletier, Directrice générale

Chateauguay Valley English-Speaking Peoples' Association (CVESPA)
1493, rte 138, CP 1357, Huntingdon QC J0S 1H0
Tel: 450-264-5386; *Fax:* 450-264-5387
Toll-Free: 800-665-9841
e-mail: neilburdon@sympatico.ca
URL: www.cvespa.org
Alex Ross, President
Neil Burdon, Executive Director

Chinese Canadian Association of Prince Edward Island (CCAPEI)
e-mail: president.ccapei@gmail.com
URL: www.ccapei.org
Zhongyu Zhang, President

Conseil de la vie française en Amérique (CVFA)
#201, 5350, boul Henri-Bourassa, Québec QC G1H 6Y8
Tél: 418-626-5665; *Téléc:* 418-626-5663
Guy Lefebvre, Directeur général
Jean-Louis Desrochers, Président

The Council of Canadians (COC) / Le Conseil des Canadiens
#700, 170 Laurier Ave. West, Ottawa ON K1P 5V5
Tel: 613-233-2773; *Fax:* 613-233-6776
Toll-Free: 800-387-7177
e-mail: inquiries@canadians.org
URL: www.canadians.org
Maude Barlow, National Chairperson
John Urquhart, Executive Director
Brent Patterson, Director, Communications, Campaigns & Communications; Organizing
Marilyn Chute, Director of Development

The Council of Canadians
#700, 207 West Hastings St., Vancouver BC V6B 1H7
Tel: 604-688-8846
Toll-Free: 888-566-3888
e-mail: hgrewal@canadians.org

The Council of Canadians
#210, 116 Spadina Ave., Toronto ON M5V 2K6
Tel: 416-979-5554
Toll-Free: 800-208-7156
e-mail: strew@canadians.org

The Council of Canadians
#34, 9912 - 106 St., Edmonton AB T5K 1C5
Tel: 780-429-4500
Toll-Free: 877-729-4500
e-mail: smuxlow@canadians.org

The Council of Canadians
#211, 2099 Gottigen St., Halifax NS B3K 3B2
Tel: 902-422-7811
Toll-Free: 877-772-7811
e-mail: agiles@canadians.org

Fédération acadienne de la Nouvelle-Écosse (FANE)
La Maison acadienne, 54 Queen St., Dartmouth NS B2Y 1G3
Tél: 902-433-0065; *Téléc:* 902-433-0066
Courriel: fane@federationacadienne.ca
URL: www.federationacadienne.ca
Jean Léger, Directeur général

Fédération culturelle canadienne-française (FCCF)
Place de la Francophonie, #405, 450 Rideau St., Ottawa ON K1N 5Z4
Tél: 613-241-8770; *Téléc:* 613-241-6064
Ligne sans frais: 800-267-2005
Courriel: info@fccf.ca
URL: www.fccf.ca
Éric Dubeau, Directeur général

Fédération de la jeunesse canadienne-française inc. (FJCF)
#403, 450 Rideau St., Ottawa ON K1N 5Z4
Tél: 613-562-4624; *Téléc:* 613-562-3995
Ligne sans frais: 800-267-5173
Courriel: fjcf@fjcf.ca
URL: www.fjcf.ca
Jean-Michel Beaudry, Président

Fédération des communautés francophones et acadienne du Canada (FCFAC)
#300, 450 rue Rideau, Ottawa ON K1N 5Z4
Tél: 613-241-7600; *Téléc:* 613-241-6046
Courriel: info@fcfa.ca
URL: www.fcfa.ca
Marielle Beaulieu, Directrice générale
Lise Routhier-Boudreau, Présidente

Fondation franco-ontarienne (FFO)
#102, 559, av King Edward, Ottawa ON K1N 7N5
Tél: 613-565-4720; *Téléc:* 613-565-8539
Courriel: info@fondationfranco-ontarienne.ca
URL: www.fondationfranco-ontarienne.ca
Solange Fortin, Coordonnatrice générale

Guyana Cultural Association of Montréal (GCAM)
PO Box 29640, Stn. CSP Prom du Parc, St. Hubert QC J3Y 9A9
Tel: 514-676-5771; *Fax:* 514-445-0747
e-mail: gcaminfo@yahoo.com
URL: www.gcaom.org
U. Leebert Sancho, Contact

L'Institut canadien de Québec (ICQ)
350, rue Saint-Joseph est, 4e étage, Québec QC G1K 3B2
Tél: 418-641-6788; *Téléc:* 418-641-6787
Courriel: courrier@institutcanadien.qc.ca
URL: www.icqbdq.qc.ca
Jean Payeur, Directeur général
Gilbert Lacasse, Président
Sylvie Fortin, Secrétaire

The Japan Foundation, Toronto / Kokosai Koryu Kikin Toronto Nihon Bunka Centre
#213, 131 Bloor St. West, Toronto ON M5S 1R1
Tel: 416-966-1600; *Fax:* 416-966-9773
e-mail: info@jftor.org
URL: www.japanfoundationcanada.org
Masayuki Suzuki, Director
Lori Lytle, Program Officer

The Royal Commonwealth Society of Canada (RCS) / La Société royale du Commonwealth du Canada
c/o RCS Ottawa, PO Box 8023, Stn. T, Ottawa ON K1G 3H6
URL: www.rcs.ca
Brian Marley-Clarke, Chair
Ronald Goodall, Vice Chair & Treasurer

St. Vincent and the Grenadines Association of Montreal Inc. (SVGA) / L'Association St.Vincent et Grenadines de Montrèal Inc.
PO Box 396, Stn. Snowdon Station, Montréal QC H3X 3T3
Tel: 514-364-3299
URL: www.svgamontreal.com
Thomas (Tom) Austin, President

Société de développement des entreprises culturelles (SODEC)
#800, 215, rue St-Jacques, Montréal QC H2Y 1M6
Tél: 514-841-2200; *Téléc:* 514-841-8606
Ligne sans frais: 800-363-0401
Courriel: info@sodec.gouv.qc.ca
URL: www.sodec.gouv.qc.ca
Affiliation(s): Ministère de la culture et des communications
Jean G. Chaput, Président et chef de la direction

Société des Acadiens et Acadiennes du Nouveau-Brunswick (SAANB)
#204, 702, rue Principale, Petit-Rocher NB E8J 1V1
Tél: 506-783-4205; *Téléc:* 506-783-0629
Ligne sans frais: 888-722-2343
Courriel: saanb@nb.aibn.com
URL: www.saanb.org
Affiliation(s): Société Nationale de l'Acadie
Marie-Pierre Simard, Présidente
Bruno Godin, Directeur général

Société franco-manitobaine (SFM)
#212, 383 Blvd. Provencher, Winnipeg MB R2H 0G9
Tél: 204-233-4915; *Téléc:* 204-233-1017
Ligne sans frais: 800-665-4443
Courriel: sfm@sfm-mb.ca
URL: www.sfm-mb.ca
Daniel Boucher, Président/Directeur général

Société nationale de l'Acadie (SNA)
415, rue Notre-Dame, Dieppe NB E1A 2A8
Tél: 506-853-0404; *Téléc:* 506-853-0400
Courriel: sna@nbnet.nb.ca
URL: www.snacadie.org
Lucie LeBouthillier, Directrice générale
Martine Aubé, Directrice adjointe

Ted Parisé, Responsable, Communications

Société Saint-Jean-Baptiste de Montréal (SSJBM)
82, rue Sherbrooke ouest, Montréal QC H2X 1X3
Tél: 514-843-8851; *Téléc:* 514-844-6369
Courriel: mbeaulieu@ssjb.com
URL: www.ssjb.com
Jean Dorion, Président général

Townshippers' Association (TA) / Association des Townshippers
#100, 257, rue Queen, Sherbrooke QC J1M 1K7
Tel: 819-566-5717; *Fax:* 819-566-0271
Toll-Free: 866-566-5717
e-mail: ta@townshippers.qc.ca
URL: www.townshippers.qc.ca
Rachel Garber, Executive Director
Michael van Lierop, President

L'Union culturelle des franco-ontariennes (UCFO)
#1, 5330, ch Canotek, Ottawa ON K1J 9C1
Tél: 613-741-1334; *Téléc:* 613-741-8577
Ligne sans frais: 877-520-8226
Courriel: ucfo@on.aibn.com
URL: www.francofemmes.org/ucfo/
Affiliation(s): Fédération nationale des femmes canadiennes françaises; Match International; Réseau national d'action éducation femmes; Regroupement des organismes du patrimoine franco-ontarien; Table féministe francophone de concertation provinciale de l'Ontario; Réseau canadien de développement économique communautaire
Diane Brissette, Présidente provinciale

Dental

Alberta Dental Assistants Association (ADAA)
#166, 14315 - 118 Ave. NW, Edmonton AB T5L 4S6
Tel: 780-486-2526; *Fax:* 780-486-2728
Toll-Free: 800-355-8940
e-mail: contact@abrda.ca
URL: www.abrda.ca
Howards Riddel, Executive Director

Alberta Dental Association & College (ADAC)
#101, 8230 - 105 St., Edmonton AB T6E 5H9
Tel: 780-432-1012; *Fax:* 780-433-4864
Toll-Free: 800-843-3848
e-mail: adaadmin@telusplanet.net
URL: www.abda.ab.ca
G.W. Thompson, Executive Director & Registrar

Association des assistant(e)s dentaires du Québec (CDAA/AADQ)
#203, 6705, Jean-Talon est, Saint Léonard QC H1S 1N2
Tél: 514-722-9900; *Téléc:* 514-340-7514
Courriel: info@cdaa.ca
URL: www.cdaa.ca
Michele Rosko, CDA, BEd., President

Association des chirurgiens dentistes du Québec (ACDQ)
#1425, 425, boul de Maisonneuve ouest, Montréal QC H3A 3G5
Tél: 514-282-1425; *Téléc:* 514-282-0255
Ligne sans frais: 800-361-3794
Courriel: info@acdq.qc.ca
URL: www.acdq.qc.ca
Serge Langlois, Président

Association des denturologistes du Québec (ADQ)
Complexe Raycom, #230, 8150, boul Métropolitain est, Anjour QC H1K 1A1
Tél: 514-252-0270; *Téléc:* 514-252-0392
Ligne sans frais: 800-563-6273
Courriel: denturo@adq-qc.com
URL: www.adq-qc.com

British Columbia Dental Association
#400, 1765 - 8th Ave. West, Vancouver BC V6J 5C6
Tel: 604-736-7202; *Fax:* 604-736-7588
Toll-Free: 888-396-9888
e-mail: post@bcdental.org
URL: www.bcdental.org

Canadian Academy of Endodontics / L'Académie canadienne d'endodontie
c/o Wayne Acheson, #301, 400 St. Mary Ave., Winnipeg MB R3C 4K5
Tel: 306-966-5089; *Fax:* 306-966-5018
e-mail: webmaster@caendo.ca
URL: www.caendo.ca
Affiliation(s): Canadian Dental Association

Wayne Acheson, Executive Secretary
Brian Jafine, President

Canadian Academy of Oral & Maxillofacial Pathology & Oral Medicine (CAOMPOM)
c/o University of Manitoba, Faculty of Dentistry, 780 Bannatyne Ave., Winnipeg MB R3W 0W2
Tel: 204-789-3556; *Fax:* 204-789-3913
Birek Catalena, President

Canadian Association for Dental Research (CADR) / Association canadienne de recherches dentaires (ACRD)
c/o Dr. C. Birek, Faculty of Dentistry, University of Manitoba, 780 Bannatyne Ave., Winnipeg MB R3E 0W2
Tel: 204-789-3256; *Fax:* 204-789-3913
e-mail: birek@ms.umanitoba.ca
URL: www.cadr-acrd.ca
Edward Putnins, President
Michael Greene, President, CADR Student Research Group
Debora Matthews, Vice-President
Catalena Birek, Secretary-Treasurer

Canadian Association of Orthodontists (CAO) / Association canadienne des orthodontists
#310, 2175 Sheppard Ave. East, Toronto ON M2J 1W8
Tel: 416-491-3186; *Fax:* 416-491-1670
Toll-Free: 877-226-8800
e-mail: cao@taylorenterprises.com
URL: www.cao-aco.org
Gordie Organ, President

Canadian Dental Assistants Association (CDAA) / Association canadienne des assistants(es) dentaires
#203, 2255 St. Laurent Blvd., Ottawa ON K1G 4K3
Tel: 613-521-5495; *Fax:* 613-521-5572
Toll-Free: 800-345-5137
e-mail: info@cdaa.ca
URL: www.cdaa.ca
Emily Lindahl, Director, Communications

Canadian Dental Association (CDA) / L'Association dentaire canadienne (ADC)
1815 Alta Vista Dr., Ottawa ON K1G 3Y6
Tel: 613-523-1770; *Fax:* 613-523-7736
e-mail: reception@cda-adc.ca
URL: www.cda-adc.ca
Affiliation(s): FDI World Dental Federation
Deborah Symiest, President
Ronald Smith, Vice President

Canadian Dental Hygienists Association (CDHA) / Association canadienne des hygiènistes dentaires
96 Centrepointe Dr., Ottawa ON K2G 6B1
Tel: 613-224-5515; *Fax:* 613-224-7283
Toll-Free: 800-267-5235
e-mail: info@cdha.ca
URL: www.cdha.ca
Susan A. Ziebarth, Executive Director

Certified Dental Assistants of BC (CDABC)
#103, 3540 West 41st Ave., Vancouver BC V6N 3E6
Tel: 604-714-1766; *Fax:* 604-714-1767
Toll-Free: 800-579-4440
e-mail: info@cdabc.org
URL: www.cdabc.org
Marlene Robinson, Executive Director
Angela Wiebe, President

College of Dental Surgeons of British Columbia (CDSBC)
#500, 1765 West 8th Ave., Vancouver BC V6J 5C6
Tel: 604-736-3621; *Fax:* 604-734-9448
Toll-Free: 800-663-9169
e-mail: postmaster@cdsbc.org
URL: www.cdsbc.org
Peter M. Lobb, President

College of Dental Surgeons of Saskatchewan
#202, 728 Spadina Cres. East, Saskatoon SK S7K 4H7
Tel: 306-244-5072; *Fax:* 306-244-2476
e-mail: cdss@dentalcollege.sk.ca
URL: www.saskdentists.com
Mitch Taillon, President

College of Dental Technologists of Ontario
#300, 2100 Ellesmere Rd., Toronto ON M1H 3B7
Tel: 416-438-5003; *Fax:* 416-438-5004
e-mail: info@cdto.ca
URL: www.cdto.ca
E. Cheung, Registrar

Dental Association of Prince Edward Island (DAPEI)
184 Belvedere Ave., Charlottetown PE C1A 2Z1
Tel: 902-892-4022; *Fax:* 902-892-4470
e-mail: dapei@pei.sympatico.ca
URL: www.dapei.ca
Brian Barrett, Executive Director

Dental Council of Prince Edward Island
184 Belvedere Ave., Charlottetown PE C1A 2Z1
Tel: 902-892-4470; *Fax:* 902-892-4470

Dentistry Canada Fund (DCF) / Fonds dentaire canadien (FDC)
c/o SciCan House, 427 Gilmour St., Ottawa ON K2P 0R5
Tel: 613-236-4763; *Fax:* 613-236-3935
e-mail: information@dcf-fdc.ca
URL: www.dcf-fdc.ca
Affiliation(s): Canadian Dental Association
Bernard Dolansky, President & Chair
Stephanie MacWhirter, Sr. Manager, Development
Donna Bierko, Manager, Operations

Denturist Association of British Columbia
#312C, 9801 King George Hwy., Surrey BC V3T 5H5
Tel: 604-582-6823; *Fax:* 604-582-0317
e-mail: info@denturist.bc.ca
URL: www.denturist.bc.ca
Maria Green, RD, President

Denturist Association of Canada (DAC) / Association des denturologistes du Canada (ADC)
PO Box 45521, 2397 King George Hwy., Surrey BC V4A 9N3
Tel: 604-538-3123; *Fax:* 604-582-0317
Toll-Free: 877-538-3123
e-mail: dacdenturist@telus.net
URL: www.denturist.org
Michael Vout, President
Gerry Hansen, Chief Administrative Officer

Denturist Association of Manitoba
PO Box 70006, #1, 1660 Kenaston Blvd., Winnipeg MB R3P 0X6
Tel: 204-897-1087; *Fax:* 204-488-2872
Toll-Free: 866-897-1087
e-mail: administrator@denturistmb.org
URL: www.denturistmb.org
Paul Hrynchuk, President
Kelli Wagner, Administrator

Denturist Association of Newfoundland & Labrador
9 Bay Bulls Rd., Saint John's NL A1G 1A2
Tel: 709-364-4813; *Fax:* 709-364-4813

Denturist Association of Northwest Territories
PO Box 1506, Yellowknife NT X1A 2P2
Tel: 867-766-3666; *Fax:* 867-669-0103

Denturist Association of Ontario (DAO)
Bldg. B, #203, 6205 Airport Rd., Mississauga ON L4V 1E1
Tel: 905-677-0440; *Fax:* 905-677-5067
Toll-Free: 800-284-7311
e-mail: info@denturist.ca
URL: www.dao.on.ca
Kim Stilwell, Chief Administrative Officer

Denturist Society of Nova Scotia
#5, 141 Commercial St., Glace Bay NS B1A 3B9
Tel: 902-842-1398; *Fax:* 902-849-1496

Denturist Society of Prince Edward Island
Rhyno Denture Clinic, 222 University Avenue, Charlottetown PE C1A 4S7
Tel: 902-892-3253
e-mail: rhynopat@hotmail.com

Manitoba Dental Assistants Association
#17, 595 Clifton Street, Winnipeg MB R3G 2X5
Tel: 204-586-7378; *Fax:* 204-783-9631
e-mail: mdaa@mts.net
URL: www.cdaa.ca/mdaa
Karen Ritchie, President

Manitoba Dental Association (MDA)
#103, 698 Corydon Ave., Winnipeg MB R3M 0X9
Tel: 204-988-5300; *Fax:* 204-988-5310
e-mail: office@manitobadentist.ca
URL: www.manitobadentist.ca
Ross McIntyre, Executive Director
Michael Lasko, Registrar
Patricia Kmet, President
Alexander Mutchmor, Vice-President
Ross McIntyre, Sec.-Treas.

National Dental Examining Board of Canada
#203, 100 Bronson Ave., Ottawa ON K1R 6G8
Tel: 613-236-5912; *Fax:* 613-236-8386
e-mail: director@ndeb.ca
URL: www.ndeb.ca

New Brunswick Dental Assistants Association
PO Box 8997, Shediac NB E4P 8W5
Tel: 506-532-9189; *Fax:* 506-532-9189
Toll-Free: 866-530-9189
Shelley Fletcher, President
Odette Craine, Office Coordinator

New Brunswick Dental Society / Société dentaire du Nouveau-Brunswick
Carleton Place, PO Box 488, Stn. A, #820, 520 King St., Fredericton NB E3B 4Z9
Tel: 506-452-8575; *Fax:* 506-452-1872
e-mail: nbds@nb.aibn.com
URL: www.nbdental.com
Patrick Wilberz, Registrar
Barbara Wishart, Executive Director

New Brunswick Denturists Society / Société des denturologistes du Nouveau-Brunswick
PO Box 5566, 288 West St. Pierre Blvd., Caraquet NB E1W 1B7
Tel: 506-727-7411; *Fax:* 506-727-6728
e-mail: claudetteboudreau@aibn.com
URL: www.nbdenturistsociety.ca
Daniel J. Robichaud, DD, President
Claudette Boudreau, Secretary

Newfoundland & Labrador Dental Association
The Fortis Bldg., #401, 139 Water St., St. John's NL A1C 1B2
Tel: 709-579-2362; *Fax:* 709-579-1250
e-mail: nfdental@nfld.net
URL: www.nlda.net
Anthony Patey, Executive Director

Newfoundland Dental Assistants Association
#274, 38 Pearson St., St. John's NL A1A 3R1
Vera Walsh, President

Newfoundland Dental Board
139 Water St., 6th Fl., St. John's NL A1C 1B2
Tel: 709-579-2391; *Fax:* 709-579-2392
e-mail: nldb@aibn.com
Affiliation(s): National Dental Hygiene Exam Board; National Dental Assistant Exam Board
Paul O'Brien, Sec-Reg.

Northwest Territories & Nunavut Dental Association
PO Box 24, 4916 - 49 St., Yellowknife NT X1A 2N1
Tel: 867-873-6416; *Fax:* 867-920-7798
e-mail: nwtnudentalassoc@theedge.ca
Affiliation(s): Canadian Dental Association

Nova Scotia Dental Assistants' Association (NSDAA)
PO Box 9142, Stn. A, Halifax NS B3K 5M8
Tel: 902-826-1922; *Fax:* 902-820-3015
e-mail: nsdaa@ns.sympatico.ca
URL: www.nsdaa.ca
Sharon Nauss, President
Heather Haskins, Vice-President

Nova Scotia Dental Association (NSDA)
#101, 1559 Brunswick St., Halifax NS B3J 2G1
Tel: 902-420-0088; *Fax:* 902-423-6537
e-mail: nsda@eastlink.ca
URL: www.nsdental.org
D.V. Pamenter, Executive Director

Ontario Dental Assistants Association (ODAA)
869 Dundas St., London ON N5W 2Z8
Tel: 519-679-2566; *Fax:* 519-679-8494
e-mail: odaainfo@ody.ca
URL: www.odnaa.org
Darlene Leiska, President
Suzanne McLachlen, Vice-President
Judy Melville, Executive Director

Ontario Dental Association (ODA)
4 New St., Toronto ON M5R 1P6
Tel: 416-922-3900; *Fax:* 416-922-9005
Toll-Free: 800-387-1393
e-mail: info@oda.on.ca
URL: www.oda.on.ca
Larry Levin, President
Lynn Tomkins, Vice-President

Ordre des dentistes du Québec (ODQ)
625, boul René-Lévesque ouest, 15e étage, Montréal QC H3B 1R2
Tél: 514-875-8511; *Téléc:* 514-393-9248
Ligne sans frais: 800-361-4887
Courriel: dirgen@odq.qc.ca
URL: www.ordredesdentistesduquebec.qc.ca
Affiliation(s): Association dentaire canadienne
Caroline Daoust, Directrice générale et secrétaire

Ordre des denturologistes du Québec (ODQ)
#106, 45, Place Charles Lemoyne, Longueuil QC J4K 5G5
Tél: 450-646-7922; *Téléc:* 450-646-2509
Ligne sans frais: 800-567-2251
Courriel: info@odq.com
URL: www.odq.com
Monique Bouchard, Directrice générale et secrétaire

Prince Edward Island Dental Assistants Association
PO Box 404, Cornwall PE C1A 1H0
Tel: 902-566-9553; *Fax:* 902-367-2207
e-mail: info@peidaa.com
Julie Ready, President

Provincial Dental Board of Nova Scotia
#102, 1559 Brunswick St., Halifax NS B3J 2G1
Tel: 902-420-0083; *Fax:* 902-492-0301
e-mail: admin@pdbns.ca
W.A. MacInnis, DDS, Registrar

Royal College of Dental Surgeons of Ontario
6 Crescent Rd., 5th Fl., Toronto ON M4W 1T1
Tel: 416-961-6555; *Fax:* 416-961-5814
Toll-Free: 800-565-4591
e-mail: info@rcdso.org
URL: www.rcdso.org
Frank Stechey, Chair
Peter Trainor, Vice-President

Royal College of Dentists of Canada (RCDC) / Collège Royal des Chirurgiens Dentistes du Canada
#2003, 180 Dundas St. West, Toronto ON M3G 1Z8
Tel: 416-512-6571
e-mail: office@rcdc.ca
URL: www.rcdc.ca
J. Richard Emery, President
Garnet Packota, Vice-President
Ernest W.N. Lam, Secretary-Treasurer
Patricia A. Main, Registrar
Paul Jackson, Examiner-in-Chief

Saskatchewan Dental Assistants' Association (SDAA)
PO Box 294, 603 - 3rd St., Kenaston SK S0G 2N0
Tel: 306-252-2769; *Fax:* 306-252-2089
e-mail: sdaa@sasktel.net
URL: www.sdaa.sk.ca
Susan Anholt, Executive Director
Calla Effa, President
Robin McKay Ganshorn, Coordinator -, Professional Development

Yukon Denturist Association
#1, 106 Main St., Whitehorse YT Y1A 2A7
Tel: 867-668-6818; *Fax:* 867-668-6811
e-mail: pjallen@northwestel.net
Elsie Bagan, DD, Registrar

Developing Countries

Canadian Consortium for International Social Development (CCISD)
Carleton University, 1719 Dunton Tower, Ottawa ON K1S 5B6
Tel: 613-520-2600; *Fax:* 613-520-2344
e-mail: ccsid@ccs.carleton.ca
URL: www.ccisd.ca
Angela Laird, Contact

Mennonite Central Committee Canada (MCCC)
134 Plaza Dr., Winnipeg MB
Tel: 204-261-6381; *Fax:* 204-269-9875
Toll-Free: 888-622-6337
e-mail: canada@mennonitecc.ca
URL: www.mcc.org/canada

Teamwork Children's Services International
5983 Ladyburn Cres., Mississauga ON L5M 4V9
Tel: 905-542-1047
e-mail: jchacha@teamworkchildrenservices.com
URL: www.teamworkchildrenservices.com
Joel Chacha, Program Director

Disabled Persons

Abilities Foundation of Nova Scotia (AFNS)
3670 Kempt Rd., Halifax NS B3K 4X8
Tel: 902-453-6000; *Fax:* 902-454-6121
e-mail: f.joudrey@abilitiesfoundation.ns.ca
URL: www.abilitiesfoundation.ns.ca
Thomas G. Merriam, President & CEO
Faye Joudrey, Co-ordinator, Community & Client Services

AboutFace
#1003, 123 Edward St., Toronto ON M5G 1E2
Tel: 416-597-2229; *Fax:* 416-597-8494
Toll-Free: 800-665-3223
e-mail: info@aboutfaceinternational.org
URL: www.aboutfaceinternational.org
Anna Pileggi, Executive Director
Sharon Fitzpatrick, Chair

Active Living Alliance for Canadians with a Disability (ALACD) / Alliance de vie active pour les canadiens/canadiennes ayant un handicap
#104, 720 Belfast Rd., Ottawa ON K1G 0Z5
Tel: 613-244-0052; *Fax:* 613-244-4857
Toll-Free: 800-771-0663; *TTY:* 888-771-0663
e-mail: info@ala.ca
URL: www.ala.ca
Affiliation(s): Canadian Amputee Sports Association; Canadian Association for Disabled Skiing; Canadian Association for Health, Physical Education, Recreation & Dance; Canadian Blind Sports Association; Canadian Cerebral Palsy Sports Association; Canadian Deaf Sports Association; Canadian Intramural Recreation Association; Canadian National Institute for the Blind; Canadian Paralympic Committee; Canadian Paraplegic Association; Canadian Parks/Recreation Association; Canadian Red Cross Society; Canadian Special Olympics; Learning Disabilities Association of Canada; National Network for Mental Health
Jane Arkell, Director

Alberta Association for Community Living (AACL)
11724 Kingsway Ave., Edmonton AB T5G 0X5
Tel: 780-451-3055; *Fax:* 780-453-5779
Toll-Free: 800-252-7556
e-mail: mail@aacl.org
URL: www.aacl.org
Affiliation(s): Alberta Community Living Foundation
Bruce Uditsky, CEO
Lori Adamchick, Executive Director
Wendy McDonald, President
Don Anderson, Treasurer

Alberta Association of Rehabilitation Centres (AARC)
#19, 3220 - 5 Ave. NE, Calgary AB T2A 5N1
Tel: 403-250-9495; *Fax:* 403-291-9864
e-mail: acds@acds.ca
URL: www.acds.ca
Ann Nicol, CEO
Bob Greid, President
Winship Bill, Vice-President

Alberta Committee of Citizens with Disabilities (ACCD)
#106, 10423 - 178 St. NW, Edmonton AB T5S 1R5
Tel: 780-488-9088; *Fax:* 780-488-3757
Toll-Free: 800-387-2514; *TTY:* 780-488-9090
e-mail: accd@accd.net
URL: www.accd.net
Affiliation(s): Council of Canadians with Disabilities
Beverley D. Matthiessen, Executive Director

Alberta Easter Seals Society
Baker Centre, #1408, 10025 - 106 St., Edmonton AB T5J 1G4
Tel: 780-429-0137; *Fax:* 780-429-1937
Toll-Free: 877-732-7837; *TTY:* 780-429-2065
e-mail: edmonton@easterseals.ab.ca
URL: www.easterseals.ab.ca
Jodi Zabludowski, Director, Operations
Trish Gooz, Director, Finance & Administration
Susan Law, CEO

ARCH Disability Law Centre
#110, 425 Bloor St. East, Toronto ON M4W 3R5
Tel: 416-482-8255; *Fax:* 416-482-2981
Toll-Free: 866-482-2724; *TTY:* 416-482-1254
e-mail: archlib@lao.on.ca
URL: www.archdisabilitylaw.ca
Ivana Petricone, Executive Director

Association du Québec pour enfants avec problèmes auditifs (AQEPA)
#A446, 3700, rue Berri, Montréal QC H2L 4G9
Tél: 514-842-8706; *Téléc:* 514-842-4006
Ligne sans frais: 877-842-4006
Courriel: aqepa@aqeba.surdite.org
URL: www.aqepa.surdite.org
Daniel Péloquin, Directeur général

Association du Québec pour l'intégration sociale (AQIS) / Québec Association for Community Living
3958, rue Dandurand, Montréal QC H1X 1P7
Tél: 514-725-7245; *Téléc:* 514-725-2796
Ligne sans frais: 866-725-7245
Courriel: direction_generale@aqis-iqdi.qc.ca
URL: www.aqis-iqdi.qc.ca
Diane Milliard, Directrice générale
Marc Babin, Conseiller aux communications

Association for Community Living - Manitoba
#6, 120 Maryland St., Winnipeg MB R3G 1L1
Tel: 204-786-1607; *Fax:* 204-789-9850
e-mail: aclmb@mts.net
URL: www.aclmb.ca
Dale Kendel, Executive Director
Val Surbey, President

Association for the Neurologically Disabled of Canada (AND) / Association canadienne pour les handicapés neurologiques
56 Centre St., Thornhill ON L4J 1E9
Tel: 416-244-1992; *Fax:* 416-244-4099
Toll-Free: 800-561-1497
e-mail: info@and.ca
URL: www.and.ca
Basil Ziv, Executive Director

Association for Vaccine Damaged Children
116 Ashhurst Cres., Brampton ON L6V 3N9
Tel: 905-454-2237
John Unruh, Dr, Director of Rehabilitation

Association québécoise pour le loisir des personnes handicapées (AQLPH)
CP 1000, Succ. M, 4545, av Pierre-de-Coubertin, Montréal QC H1V 3R2
Tél: 514-252-3144; *Téléc:* 514-252-8360
Courriel: info@aqlph.qc.ca
URL: www.aqlph.qc.ca
Guylaine Laforest, Directrice générale

BALANCE
#302, 4920 Dundas St. West, Toronto ON M9A 1B7
Tel: 416-236-1796; *Fax:* 416-236-4280
e-mail: info@balancefba.org
URL: www.balancefba.org
Susan Archibald, Executive Director

The Bob Rumball Centre for the Deaf (BRCD)
2395 Bayview Ave., Toronto ON M2L 1A2
Tel: 416-449-9651; *Fax:* 416-449-8881; *TTY:* 416-449-2728
e-mail: info@bobrumball.org
URL: www.bobrumball.org
Alistair M. Fraser, Chairman
Robert L. Rumball, Interim Executive Director
Karen Chambers, Manager of Finance
Shirley Cassel, Supervisor of Centre Programs

British Columbia Association for Community Living (BCACL)
227 6th St., New Westminster BC V3L 3A5
Tel: 604-777-9100; *Fax:* 604-777-9394
e-mail: info@bcacl.org
URL: www.bcacl.org
Laney Bryenton, Executive Director
Rory Summers, President
Alain LeFebvre, Treasurer

Canadian Abilities Foundation
#401, 340 College St., Toronto ON M5T 3A9
Tel: 416-923-1885; *Fax:* 416-923-9829
e-mail: able@abilities.ca
URL: www.abilities.ca
Raymond D. Cohen, President & Publisher
Gillian Lynne-Davies, Manager, Project Development
Lisa Bendall, Managing Editor

Canadian Association for Community Living (CACL) / Association canadienne pour l'intégration communautaire
Kinsmen Bldg., York University, 4700 Keele St., Toronto ON M3J 1P3

Tel: 416-661-9611; *Fax:* 416-661-5701; *TTY:* 416-661-2023
e-mail: inform@cacl.ca
URL: www.cacl.ca
Affiliation(s): People First of Canada
Michael Bach, Executive Vice-President
Bendina Miller, President
Norm McLeod, Treasurer

Canadian Association of the Deaf (CAD) / Association des sourds du Canada
#203, 251 Bank St., Ottawa ON K2P 1X3
Tel: 613-565-2882; *Fax:* 613-565-1207; *TTY:* 613-565-8882
e-mail: info@cad.ca
URL: www.cad.ca
Social Media: www.facebook.com/group.php?gid=57872523519
Affiliation(s): World Federation of the Deaf; Council of Canadians with Disabilities
Doug Momotiuk, President
James D. Roots, Executive Director

The Canadian Council of the Blind (CCB) / Le Conseil canadien des aveugles
#401, 396 Cooper St., Ottawa ON K2P 2H7
Tel: 613-567-0311; *Fax:* 613-567-2728
Toll-Free: 877-304-0968
e-mail: ccb@ccbnational.net
URL: www.ccbnational.net
Affiliation(s): World Blind Union
Harold Schnellert, National President

Canadian Council on Rehabilitation & Work (CCRW) / Le Conseil canadien de la réadaptation et du travail (CCRT)
#1202, 1 Yonge St., Toronto ON M5E 1E5
Tel: 416-260-3060
Toll-Free: 800-664-0925; *TTY:* 416-260-9223
e-mail: info@ccrw.org
URL: www.ccrw.org
Carole J. Barron, President/CEO
Venatius Babu, Chief Financial Officer
Jacki Challenger, Chair

Canadian Cultural Society of The Deaf, Inc. (CCSD) / Société culturelle canadienne des Sourds
The Stone Distillery, The Distillery Historic District, #101, 55 Mill St., Toronto ON M5A 3C4
Tel: 416-203-1086
e-mail: info@deafculturecentre.ca
URL: www.ccsdeaf.com
Joanne Cripps, Executive Director

Canadian Foundation for Physically Disabled Persons
731 Runnymede Rd., Toronto ON M6N 3V7
Tel: 416-760-7351; *Fax:* 416-760-9405
e-mail: whynot@sympatico.ca
URL: www.cfpdp.com
Vim Kochhar, Chair

Canadian Guide Dogs for the Blind (CGDB)
PO Box 280, 4120 Rideau Valley Dr. North, Manotick ON K4M 1A3
Tel: 613-692-7777; *Fax:* 613-692-0650
e-mail: cgdb@sympatico.ca
URL: www.guidedogs.ca
Jane Thornton, COO

Canadian Hard of Hearing Association (CHHA) / Association des malentendants canadiens (AMEC)
#205, 2415 Holly Lane, Ottawa ON K1V 7P2
Tel: 613-526-1584; *Fax:* 613-526-4718
Toll-Free: 800-263-8068; *TTY:* 613-526-2692
e-mail: chhanational@chha.ca
URL: www.chha.ca
Affiliation(s): Self Help for Hard of Hearing People; VOICE for Hard of Hearing Children
Saralle Lomow, Executive Director
Carole Willans, President
Annie Lee MacDonald, Secretary

Canadian Hearing Society (CHS) / Société canadienne de l'ouïe
271 Spadina Rd., Toronto ON M5R 2V3
Tel: 416-928-2500; *Fax:* 416-928-2525
Toll-Free: 877-347-3427; *TTY:* 877-347-3429
e-mail: info@chs.ca
URL: www.chs.ca
Kelly Duffin, President/CEO
Maribeth Meijer, COO
Katherine Hum-Antonopoulos, Vice-President, Programs & Services
Fred Enzel, Vice-President Finance/CFO
Susan Main, Vice-President, Fundraising & Strategic Communications
Kelly Murray, Vice-President, Marketing & Business Development
Gary Malkowski, Special Advisor to the President, Public Affairs
Donald Prong, Director, Human Resources

The Canadian National Institute for the Blind (INCA)
#750, 2155, rue Guy, Montréal QC H3H 2R9
Tél: 514-934-4622; *Téléc:* 514-934-2131
Ligne sans frais: 800-563-2642
URL: www.cnib.ca

Centre de réadaptation Constance-Lethbridge (CRCL) / Constance Lethbridge Rehabilitation Centre
7005, boul de Maisonneuve ouest, Montréal QC H4B 1T3
Tél: 514-487-1770; *Téléc:* 514-487-0284
Courriel: lharvey@ssss.gouv.qc.ca
URL: www.constance-lethbridge.qc.ca
Affiliation(s): Confédération québécoise des centres d'hébergement et de réadaptation
Ghislaine Prata, Directrice générale

Christian Record Services Inc.
PO Box 31119, #119, 1300 King St. East, Oshawa ON L1H 8N9
Tel: 905-436-6938; *Fax:* 905-436-7102
Toll-Free: 888-899-0006
e-mail: crs-ncb@hotmail.com
URL: www.crsblindservices.ca
Patricia L. Page, Executive Director

CNIB (CNIB) / INCA (INCA)
1929 Bayview Ave., Toronto ON M4G 3E8
Fax: 416-480-7700
Toll-Free: 800-563-2642
e-mail: info@cnib.ca
URL: www.cnib.ca
Affiliation(s): World Blind Union; International Agency for the Prevention of Blindness
Jim Sanders, OC, President
Al Jameson, Chair, National Board of Directors

Community Living Ontario (CLO) / Intégration communautaire Ontario
#403, 240 Duncan Mill Rd., Toronto ON M3B 3S6
Tel: 416-447-4348; *Fax:* 416-447-8974
Toll-Free: 800-278-8025
e-mail: info@communitylivingontario.ca
URL: www.communitylivingontario.ca
Social Media: www.twitter.com/CLOntario
Keith Powell, Executive Director
Dianne Garrels-Munro, President

Council of Canadians with Disabilities (CCD) / Conseil des Canadiens avec déficiences
#926, 294 Portage Ave., Winnipeg MB R3C 0B9
Tel: 204-947-0303; *TTY:* 204-947-4757
e-mail: ccd@ccdonline.ca
URL: www.ccdonline.ca
Affiliation(s): Consumer Organization of Disabled People of Newfoundland & Labrador; PEI Council of the Disabled; Nova Scotia League for Equal Opportunities; PUSH-Ontario; Manitoba League of the Physically Handicapped; Saskatchewan Voice of the Handicapped; Alberta Committee of Disabled Citizens; British Columbia Coalition of the Disabled; Association canadienne des sourds; DAWN Canada; National Network on Mental Health; Thalidomide Victims of Canada; National Education Association of Disabled Students; People First of Canada
Laurie Beachell, National Coordinator

DisAbled Women's Network of Canada
#005, 110, rue Ste. Therese, Montréal QC H2Y 1E6
Tel: 514-396-0009; *Fax:* 514-396-0074
Toll-Free: 866-396-0074
e-mail: hutch@efirehose.net
URL: www.dawncanada.net
Affiliation(s): Council of Canadians with Disabilities
Cathy Marshall, National Coordinator

The Easter Seal Society (Ontario) (TESS) / Société du timbre de Pâques de l'Ontario
#700, One Concorde Gate, Toronto ON M3C 3C6
Tel: 416-421-8377; *Fax:* 416-696-1035
Toll-Free: 800-668-6252
e-mail: info@easterseals.org
URL: www.easterseals.org
Affiliation(s): BC Lions Society for Children with Disabilities; Newfoundland Society for the Physically Disabled; Québec Easter Seal Society; Easter Seal Ability Council - Alberta; Saskatchewan Abilities Council; Society for Manitobans with Disabilities; Rotary Club of Charlottetown; Abilities Foundation of Nova Scotia; CRCD New Brunswick branch; National Easter Seal Society, USA
Carol Lloyd, President & CEO

Easter Seals Canada / Timbres de Pâques Canada
#208, 90 Eglinton Ave. East, Toronto ON M4P 2Y3
Tel: 416-932-8382; *Fax:* 416-932-9844; *TTY:* 416-932-8151
e-mail: info@easterseals.ca
URL: www.easterseals.ca
Jim Biss, Chair
Max Beck, CEO

Easter Seals Newfoundland & Labrador
Southcott Hall, #712, 100 Forest Rd., St. John's NL A1A 1E5
Tel: 709-754-1399; *Fax:* 709-754-1398
Toll-Free: 888-601-6767
e-mail: info@easterseals.nf.ca
URL: www.easterseals.nf.ca
Deirdre Greene, Executive Director/CEO

Independent Living Canada / Vie autonome Canada
#402, 214 Montréal Rd., Ottawa ON K1L 8L8
Tel: 613-563-2581; *Fax:* 613-563-3861; *TTY:* 613-563-4215
e-mail: info@cailc.ca
URL: www.cailc.ca
Kelly J. Nadeau, National Chair
Traci Walters, National Director
Cecilia Carroll, Secretary
Diane Kreuger, Treasurer
Susan Forster, Manager, Services & Accreditation

Kinsmen Foundation of British Columbia & Yukon (KRF)
PO Box 34005, Stn. D, Vancouver BC V6J 4M1
Tel: 604-233-1993; *Fax:* 604-233-1992
Toll-Free: 866-335-1234
e-mail: on-track@shaw.ca
URL: www.kinclubofvancouver.com
Jim Watson, President & CEO

Nanaimo Association for Community Living (NACL)
83 Victoria Cres., Nanaimo BC V9R 5B9
Tel: 250-741-0224; *Fax:* 250-741-0227
e-mail: nacl.office@nanaimoacl.com
URL: www.nanaimoacl.com
Barb Walser, Operations Manager

National Institute of Disability Management & Research (NIDMAR) / Institut national de recherche et de gestion de l'incapacité au travail
#202, 830 Shamrock St., Victoria BC V8X 2V1
Tel: 250-386-4388; *Fax:* 250-386-4398
e-mail: nidmar@nidmar.ca
URL: www.nidmar.ca
Wolfgang Zimmermann, Executive Director

New Brunswick Association for Community Living / Association du Nouveau-Brunswick pour l'intégration communautaire
#209, 440 Wilsey Rd., Fredericton NB E3B 7G5
Tel: 506-453-4400; *Fax:* 506-453-4422
Toll-Free: 866-622-2548
e-mail: nbacl@nbnet.nb.ca
URL: www.nbacl.nb.ca
Tammy Gallant, Director, Finance
Krista Carr, Executive Director

Newfoundland & Labrador Association for Community Living (NLACL)
PO Box 8414, 31 Peet St., St. John's NL A1B 3N7
Tel: 709-722-0790; *Fax:* 709-722-1325
Toll-Free: 800-701-8511
e-mail: nlacl@nf.aibn.com
URL: www.nlacl.ca
Affiliation(s): Canadian Association for Community Living (CACL)
Brianna Hookey, Executive Director
Ray McIsaac, President
Vivienne Kuester, Vice-President
Joey Mackey, Secretary
Richard Chow, Treasurer

Nova Scotia Association for Community Living (NSACL)
#2, 22-24 Dundas St., Dartmouth NS B2Y 4L2
Tel: 902-469-1174; *Fax:* 902-461-0196
e-mail: nsacl@accesswave.ca
Mary Rothman, Executive Director
Roger Isnor, President

Nova Scotia Hearing and Speech Foundation
#5, 1350 Bedford Hwy., Bedford NS B4A 1E1

Tel: 902-423-1947; Fax: 902-423-3765
Toll-Free: 866-278-5678
e-mail: info@hearingandspeech.ca
URL: www.hearingandspeech.ca

Cheryl MacLeod, Office Manager
Phil Otto, Chair

Ontario Federation for Cerebral Palsy (OFCP)
#104, 1630 Lawrence Ave. West, Toronto ON M6A 1C8
Tel: 416-244-9686; Fax: 416-244-6543
Toll-Free: 877-244-9686
e-mail: ofcp@ofcp.on.ca
URL: www.ofcp.on.ca

Clarence Meyers, Executive Director

Ontario March of Dimes (OMOD) / Marche des dix sous de l'Ontario
10 Overlea Blvd., Toronto ON M4H 1A4
Tel: 416-425-3463; Fax: 416-425-1920
Toll-Free: 800-263-3463
e-mail: info@marchofdimes.ca
URL: www.marchofdimes.ca/dimes

Affiliation(s): Polio Canada
Andria Spindel, President & CEO
Jerry Lucas, Vice-President, Programs
Mary Lynne Stewart, Director, Communications & Fund Development

Pamiqsaiji Association for Community Living
PO Box 708, Rankin Inlet NU X0C 0G0
Tel: 867-645-2542; Fax: 867-645-2543
e-mail: pamiqacl@qiniq.com

Yvonne Cooper, Manager

Prince Edward Island Association for Community Living (PEIACL)
161 St. Peters Rd., Charlottetown PE C1A 5P7
Tel: 902-566-4844; Fax: 902-368-8057
e-mail: info@peiacl.ca
URL: www.peiacl.ca

Kenny MacDonald, President
Bridget Cairns, Executive Director

Prince Edward Island Council of the Disabled (PEICOD)
PO Box 2128, #300, 25 University Ave., Charlottetown PE C1A 7N7
Tel: 902-892-9149; Fax: 902-566-1919
e-mail: peicod@peicod.pe.ca
URL: www.peicod.pe.ca

Barry Schmidl, Executive Director

Québec Easter Seal Society / Société des timbres de Pâques du Québec
#810, 1155 University St., Montréal QC H3B 3A7
Tel: 514-866-1969; Fax: 514-866-6124
Toll-Free: 800-263-1969
e-mail: info@easterseal.qc.ca

Robert C. Bédard, Executive Director

R.C.L. (Québec) for the Disabled / R.C.L. (Québec) pour les Handicapés
#410, 1000, rue Saint-Antoine ouest, Montréal QC H3C 3R7
Tel: 514-866-3689; Fax: 514-866-6303
e-mail: rclqc_handicapes@lycos.com

John S. Jamieson, President

The Roeher Institute / L'Institut Roeher
Kinsmen Bldg., York University, 4700 Keele St., Toronto ON M3J 1P3
Tel: 416-661-9611; Fax: 416-661-5701
Toll-Free: 800-856-2207
e-mail: info@roeher.ca
URL: www.roeher.ca

Affiliation(s): International Association for Scientific Study of Intellectual Deficiency; Canadian Association for Community Living
Cameron Crawford, President

Saskatchewan Abilities Council
2310 Louise Ave., Saskatoon SK S7J 2C7
Tel: 306-374-4448; Fax: 306-373-2665
e-mail: provincialservices@abilitiescouncil.sk.ca
URL: www.abilitiescouncil.sk.ca

Ian Wilkinson, Executive Director
Ron Walter, Director, Provincial Services

Saskatchewan Association for Community Living (SACL)
3031 Louise St., Saskatoon SK S7J 3L1
Tel: 306-955-3344
e-mail: sacl@sacl.org
URL: www.sacl.org

Kevin McTavish, Executive Director

Wilda Wallace, President
Gloria Mahussier, Vice-President
Judy Anderson, Treasurer
Becky Machnee, Coordinator, Communications & Fundraising
James Sanheim, Coordinator, Employment Opportunities
Megan Wells, Coordinator, Youth Programs

Silent Voice Canada Inc.
#300, 50 St. Clair Ave. East, Toronto ON M4T 1M9
Tel: 416-463-1104; Fax: 416-778-1876; TTY: 416-463-3928
e-mail: silent.voice@silentvoice.ca
URL: www.silentvoice.ca

Maureen Haan, Executive Director
Norm Forma, President

Société pour les enfants handicapés du Québec (SEHQ) / Québec Society for Disabled Children
2300, boul René-Lévesque ouest, Montréal QC H3H 2R5
Tél: 514-937-6171; Téléc: 514-937-0082
Ligne sans frais: 877-937-6171
Courriel: sehq@enfantshandicapes.com
URL: www.enfantshandicapes.com

Carolle Desjardins, Directrice, Financement
Ronald Davidson, Directeur général
Nicole Amzallag, Assistant to the Director
Chantale Théroux, Director of Services

Society for Manitobans with Disabilities Inc. (SMD)
825 Sherbrook St., Winnipeg MB R3A 1M5
Tel: 204-975-3010; Fax: 204-975-3073
Toll-Free: 866-282-8041; TTY: 204-784-3012
e-mail: info@smd.mb.ca
URL: smd.mb.ca

David L. Steen, Executive Director/President/CEO
Kathryn Tatenaude, Communications Coordinator

The Speech and Stuttering Institute
#2 - 150 Duncan Mill Rd., Toronto ON M3B 3M4
Tel: 416-491-7771; Fax: 416-491-7215
e-mail: sfotcc@speechfoundation.org
URL: www.speechfoundation.org

Margit Pukonen, Program Director
Gail Roberts, Chair

Vision Institute of Canada (VIC)
York Mills Centre, #110, 16 York Mills Rd., Toronto ON M2P 2E5
Tel: 416-224-2273; Fax: 416-224-9234
e-mail: visioninstitute@globalserve.net
URL: visioninstitute.optometry.net

Paul Chris, Executive Director
Catherine Chiarelli, Chief of Clinical Services

Vocational & Rehabilitation Research Institute (VRRI)
3304 - 33 St. NW, Calgary AB T2L 2A6
Tel: 403-284-1121; Fax: 403-284-1146
e-mail: info@vrri.org
URL: www.vrri.org

Affiliation(s): University of Calgary
Leslie Tamagi, Executive Director
Bob Sainsbury, Chair

Yellowknife Association for Community Living
PO Box 981, 4912 - 53 St., Yellowknife NT X1A 2N7
Tel: 867-920-2644; Fax: 867-920-2348
e-mail: info@ykacl.ca
URL: www.ykacl.ca

Jane Whyte, Executive Director
Donna Williston, President
Pam Weeks-Beaton, Vice-President

Yukon Association for Community Living (YACL)
PO Box 31478, Whitehorse YT Y1A 6K8
Tel: 867-667-4606; Fax: 867-668-8169
e-mail: yaclwhse@northwestel.net

Vicki Wilson, Program Coordinator
Lynn Pigage, President

Disarmament

Coalition to Oppose the Arms Trade (COAT)
541 McLeod St., Ottawa ON K1R 5R2
Tel: 613-231-3076
e-mail: overcoat@rogers.com
URL: coat.ncf.ca
Social Media: www.facebook.com/group.php?gid=2337208773

Richard Sanders, Coordinator

Drilling

Alberta Water Well Drilling Association (AWWDA)
PO Box 130, Lougheed AB T0B 2V0
Tel: 780-386-2335; Fax: 780-386-2344
e-mail: awwda@telusplanet.net
URL: www.awwda.com

Brad Meyers, Secretary

Association des enterprises spécialiseés en eau
5930, boul Louis-H. Lafontaine, Anjou QC H1M 1S7
Tél: 514-353-9960; Téléc: 514-353-3393
Ligne sans frais: 800-468-8160
Courriel: contact@aeseq.com
URL: www.aeseq.com

Daniel Schanck, Directeur général

British Columbia Ground Water Association (BCGWA)
c/o Office Of The Secretary, 1708 - 197A St., Langley BC V2Z 1K2
Tel: 604-530-8934; Fax: 604-530-8934
e-mail: secretary@bcgwa.org
URL: www.bcgwa.org

Affiliation(s): Canadian Ground Water Association
Remi Allard, President
Tim Oster, Vice-President
Dave Mellis, Treasurer
Joan Perry, Secretary

Canadian Association of Drilling Engineers (CADE)
#800, 540 - 5 Ave. SW, Calgary AB T2P 0M2
Tel: 403-264-4311; Fax: 403-263-3796
e-mail: info@cade.ca
URL: www.cade.ca

Affiliation(s): Canadian Association of Oilwell Drilling Contractors
Robin Finley, Secretary
Ryan Schoenhals, President

Canadian Association of Oilwell Drilling Contractors (CAODC)
#800, 540 - 5 Ave. SW, Calgary AB T2P 0M2
Tel: 403-264-4311; Fax: 403-263-3796
e-mail: info@caodc.ca
URL: www.caodc.ca

Don Herring, President

Canadian Diamond Drilling Association (CDDA)
City Centre Building, 101 Worthington St. East, North Bay ON P1B 1G5
Tel: 705-476-6992; Fax: 705-476-9494
e-mail: office@cdda.ca
URL: www.canadiandrilling.com

Louise Lowe, Secretary Manager

Canadian Ground Water Association (CGWA) / Association canadienne des eaux souterraines
#100-409, 1600 Bedford Hwy., Bedford NS B4A 1E8
Tel: 902-845-1885; Fax: 902-845-1886
e-mail: info@cgwa.org
URL: www.cgwa.org

Wayne C. MacRae, Executive Officer
Jim Fyfe, President

Manitoba Water Well Association (MWWA)
PO Box 1648, Winnipeg MB R3C 2Z6
Tel: 204-667-6643; Fax: 204-667-6643
e-mail: mwwa@shaw.ca
URL: www.mwwa.ca

Eric Henstridge, President
Ray Ford, Vice-President
Mary Futros, Sec.-Treas.

New Brunswick Ground Water Association
31 Gray Rd., Penobsquis NB E4E 5S7
Tel: 506-433-6767; Fax: 506-432-6888
e-mail: nbgwa@nb.sympatico.ca
URL: www.nbgwa.ca

Terry Burpee, Sec.-Treas.
Roger Roy, President

Newfoundland/Labrador Ground Water Association
PO Box 160, Doyles NL A0N 1J0
Tel: 709-955-2561; Fax: 709-955-3402
e-mail: gwater@nf.sympatico.ca

Francis Gale, Contact

Nova Scotia Ground Water Association (NSGWA)
#417, 3 - 644 Portland St., Dartmouth NS B2W 2M3
Fax: 902-435-0089
Toll-Free: 888-242-4440
e-mail: nsgwa@ns.aliantzinc.ca
URL: www.nsgwa.ca

Paul Verge, President
Noreene McGuire, Sec.-Treas.

Ontario Ground Water Association (OGWA)
48 Front St. East, Strathroy ON N7G 1Y6
Tel: 519-245-7194; *Fax:* 519-245-7196
e-mail: ogwa@bellnet.ca
URL: www.ogwa.ca
Craig Stainton, President
Greg Bullock, Vice-President

Prince Edward Island Ground Water Association
PO Box 857, RR#2, Cornwall PE C0A 1H0
Tel: 902-675-2360; *Fax:* 902-675-2360
Affiliation(s): Canadian Ground Water Association
Watson MacDonald, Contact

Saskatchewan Ground Water Association (SGWA)
PO Box 9434, Saskatoon SK S7K 7E9
Tel: 306-244-7551; *Fax:* 306-343-0001
Kathleen Watson, Contact

Economics

Association des économistes québécois (ASDÉQ)
CP 6128, Succ. Centre-ville, Montréal QC H3C 3J7
Tél: 514-342-7537; *Téléc:* 514-342-3967
Ligne sans frais: 866-342-7537
Courriel: national@asdeq.org
URL: www.asdeq.org
Charles A. Carrier, Directeur général

Association des professionnels en développement économique du Québec (APDEQ) / Economic Development Professionals Association of Québec
CP 297, #203-B, 189, rue Tupper, Magog QC J1X 3W8
Tél: 819-868-9778; *Téléc:* 819-868-9907
Ligne sans frais: 800-361-8470
Courriel: info@apdeq.qc.ca
URL: www.apdeq.qc.ca
Patrice Gagnon, Directeur général

Atlantic Association of Applied Economists (AAAE)
c/o 1583 Hollis St., 5th Fl., Halifax NS B3J 1V4
Tel: 902-420-4601; *Fax:* 902-420-4644
URL: www.chebucto.ns.ca/Commerce/AAAE/
Tara Ainsworth, Sec.-Treas.
David Amirault, President

Atlantic Provinces Economic Council (APEC) / Conseil économique des provinces de l'Atlantique
#500, 5121 Sackville St., Halifax NS B3J 1K1
Tel: 902-422-6516; *Fax:* 902-429-6803
e-mail: info@apec-econ.ca
URL: www.apec-econ.ca
Elizabeth Beale, President & CEO

Canada West Foundation (CWF)
#900, 1202 Centre St. SE, Calgary AB T2G 5A5
Tel: 403-264-9535; *Fax:* 403-269-4776
e-mail: cwf@cwf.ca
URL: www.cwf.ca
Lori Zaremba, Director, Finance & Administration
Roger Gibbins, President & CEO

Canadian Agricultural Economics Society (CAES) / Société canadienne d'agroéconomie (SCAE)
University Of Victoria, PO Box 1700, Stn. CSC, Rm. 360, Business & Economics Bldg., Victoria BC V8W 2Y2
e-mail: caes@aganalysis.com
URL: www.caes.ca
Affiliation(s): Agricultural Institute of Canada
Valerie Johnson, Executive Director

Canadian Association for Business Economics, Inc. (CABE) / Association canadienne de science économique des affaires, inc.
PO Box 828, Stn. B, Ottawa ON K1P 5P9
Tel: 613-238-4831; *Fax:* 613-238-7698
e-mail: info@cabe.ca
URL: www.cabe.ca
Affiliation(s): International Federation of Associations of Business Economists; National Association of Business Economists (Canadian Association for Business Economics's sister organization in the United States)

Canadian Economics Association (CEA) / Association canadienne d'économique
Département des Sciences Économiques, Université du Québec à Montréal, Montréal QC H3C 3P8
Tel: 514-987-3000; *Fax:* 514-987-8494
e-mail: ambler.steven@uqam.ca
URL: www.economics.ca
Aloysius Siow, President
Steve Ambler, Sec.-Treas.

Canadian Law & Economics Association
Faculty of Law, University of Toronto, 78 Queen's Park Cres., Toronto ON M5S 2C5
Tel: 416-978-6767; *Fax:* 416-978-7899
e-mail: kristin.demuth@utoronto.ca
URL: www.canlecon.org
Nadia Gulezko, Contact
Margaret F. Brinig, President

C.D. Howe Institute / Institut C.D. Howe
#300, 67 Yonge St., Toronto ON M5E 1J8
Tel: 416-865-1904; *Fax:* 416-865-1866
e-mail: cdhowe@cdhowe.org
URL: www.cdhowe.org
Finn Poschmann, Vice-President, Research
Kevin Fleming, Editor
William B.P. Robson, President & CEO

Centre interuniversitaire de recherche en économie quantitative (CIREQ)
Pavillon Lionel-Groulx, Université de Montréal, CP 6128, Succ. Centre-Ville, 3150, rue Jean-Brillant, local C-6088, Montréal QC H3C 3J7
Tél: 514-343-6557; *Téléc:* 514-343-5831
Courriel: cireq@umontreal.ca
URL: www.cireq.umontreal.ca
Marie-Christine Thirion, Adjointe administrative

The Conference Board of Canada / Le Conference Board du Canada
255 Smyth Rd., Ottawa ON K1H 8M7
Tel: 613-526-3280; *Fax:* 613-526-4857
Toll-Free: 866-711-2262
e-mail: contactcboc@conferenceboard.ca
URL: www.conferenceboard.ca
Anne Golden, President & CEO
Glen Hodgson, Sr. VP & Chief Economist
Yvette Diepenbrock, Director, Marketing & Communications

Economic Developers Association of Canada (EDAC) / Association canadienne de développement économique
#200, 7 Innovation Dr., Flamborough ON L9H 7H9
Tel: 905-689-8771; *Fax:* 905-689-5925
e-mail: admin@edac.ca
URL: www.edac.ca
Affiliation(s): All Provincial Economic Development Associations; Business Development Bank of Canada; Canadian Business Networks Coalition; European Association of Development Agencies; Federation of Canadian Municipalities; Government of Canada; International Network for Economic Developers; International Economic Development Council; RBC Financial Group; University of Sherbrooke; University of Waterloo
Penny A. Gardiner, Executive Director
Anthony Janes, President
Jay Amer, Secretary
David Paul, Treasurer

Economic Developers Council of Ontario Inc. (EDCO)
PO Box 8030, Cornwall ON K6H 7H9
Tel: 613-931-9827; *Fax:* 613-931-9828
Toll-Free: 877-818-7666
e-mail: edco@sympatico.ca
URL: www.edco.on.ca
Aileen Murray, President
Heather Lalonde, Ec.D., Executive Director

The Fraser Institute
1770 Burrard St., 4th Fl., Vancouver BC V6J 3G7
Tel: 604-688-0221; *Fax:* 604-688-8539
Toll-Free: 800-665-3558
e-mail: info@fraserinstitute.ca
URL: www.fraserinstitute.ca
Social Media: www.twitter.com/FraserInstitute
Affiliation(s): organizations in 57 countries
Sherry Stein, Director, Development
Brett J. Skinner, President
J. Kristin McCahon, Director, Publication Production
Dean Pekley, Director, Communications
Annabel Addington, Director, Administration & Human Resources

The Fraser Institute
#401, 1491 Yonge St., Toronto ON M4T 1Z4
Tel: 416-363-6575; *Fax:* 416-934-1639
e-mail: info@fraserinstitute.ca
URL: www.fraserinstitute.ca

The Fraser Institute
#301, 815 - 1st St. SW, Calgary AB T2P 1N3
Tel: 403-216-7175; *Fax:* 403-234-9010
Toll-Free: 866-716-7175
e-mail: info@fraserinstitute.ca
URL: wwww.fraserinstitute.ca

The North-South Institute (NSI) / L'Institut Nord-Sud
#200, 55 Murray St., Ottawa ON K1N 5M3
Tel: 613-241-3535; *Fax:* 613-241-7435
e-mail: nsi@nsi-ins.ca
URL: www.nsi-ins.ca
Roy Culpeper, President

Public Policy Forum / Forum des politiques publiques
#1405, 130 Albert St., Ottawa ON K1P 5G4
Tel: 613-238-7160; *Fax:* 613-238-7990
e-mail: mail@ppforum.ca
URL: www.ppforum.com
David J. Mitchell, President
Yves Poisson, Vice-President
Ted Williamson, Director, Finance & Administration

Rotman Institute for International Business
University of Toronto, 105 St. George St., Toronto ON M5S 3E6
Tel: 416-978-5781
e-mail: riib@utoronto.ca
URL: www.rotman.utoronto.ca
Affiliation(s): University of Toronto
Wendy Dobson, B.Sc.N., MPA, S, Co-Director
Ignatius J. (Ig) Horstmann, B.A., Ph.D., Co-Director, ihorstmann@rotman.utoronto.ca

Education

Agence universitaire de la Francophonie (AUF)
CP 49714, Succ. Musée, 3034, Boul. Edouard-Montpetit, Montréal QC H3T 1J7
Tél: 514-343-6630; *Téléc:* 514-343-5783
Courriel: recorat@auf.org
URL: www.auf.org
Bernard Cerquiglini, Recteur

Alberta Catholic School Trustees Association
#325, 9940 - 106 St., Edmonton AB T5K 2N2
Tel: 780-484-6209; *Fax:* 780-484-6248
e-mail: admin@acsta.ab.ca
URL: www.acsta.ab.ca
Affiliation(s): Canadian Catholic School Trustees Association
Stefan Michniewski, Executive Director

Alberta Home & School Councils' Association (AHSCA)
#1200, 9925 - 109 St., Edmonton AB T5K 2J8
Tel: 780-454-9867; *Fax:* 780-455-0167
Toll-Free: 800-661-3470
e-mail: parents@albertaschoolcouncils.ca
URL: www.ahsca.ab.ca
Michele Mulder, Executive Director
Marilyn Sheptycki, President
Brad Vonkeman, Vice-President

Alberta School Boards Association (ASBA)
#1200, 9925 - 109 St., Edmonton AB T5K 2J8
Tel: 780-482-7311; *Fax:* 780-482-5659
e-mail: kayers@asba.ab.ca
URL: www.asba.ab.ca
David Anderson, Executive Director
Suzanne Lundrigan, Director, Communications
Heather Welwood, President

Alberta Teachers' Association (ATA)
Barnett House, 11010 - 142 St., Edmonton AB T5N 2R1
Tel: 780-447-9400; *Fax:* 780-455-6481
Toll-Free: 800-232-7208
e-mail: government@teachers.ab.ca
URL: www.teachers.ab.ca
Social Media: www.facebook.com/ABteachers
Gordon Thomas, Executive Secretary

Alliance canadienne des responsables et enseignants en français (langue maternelle)

(ACREF) / Canadian Association for the Teachers of French as a First Language
Place de la Francophonie, Succ. A, #401, 450 rue Reideau, Ottawa ON K1N 5Z4
Tél: 613-744-3192; *Téléc:* 613-744-0154
Courriel: acref@franco.ca
URL: www.franco.ca/acref
Denise Moulun-Pasek, Présidente

Association canadienne d'éducation de langue française (ACELF)
268, rue Marie-de-l'Incarnation, Québec QC G1N 3G4
Tél: 418-681-4661; *Téléc:* 418-681-3389
Courriel: info@acelf.ca
URL: www.acelf.ca
Affiliation(s): UNESCO
Richard Lacombe, Directeur général
Lucie Grégoire, Adjointe administrative

Association canadienne des professeurs d'immersion (ACPI) / Canadian Association of Immersion Teachers (CAIT)
#201, 57 Auriga Dr., Nepean ON K2E 8B2
Tél: 613-228-0333; *Téléc:* 613-727-3831
Courriel: acpi@sevec.ca
URL: acpi.scedu.umontreal.ca
Marie Larivière, Directrice générale

Association des cadres scolaires du Québec
#170, 1195, av Lavigerie, Québec QC G1V 4N3
Tél: 418-654-0014; *Téléc:* 418-654-1719
Courriel: acsq@acsq.qc.ca
URL: www.acsq.qc.ca
Jacques Fortin, Directeur général
Michel Simard, Président
Daniel Trempe, Sec.-Trés.

Association des collèges privés du Québec (ACPQ)
1940, boul Henri-Bourassa est, Montréal QC H2B 1S2
Tél: 514-381-8891; *Téléc:* 514-381-4086
Courriel: acpq@cadre.qc.ca
URL: www.acpq.net
Daniel Delisle, Secrétaire générale
Louise Landry, Responsable, des affaires pédagogiques et de la recherche

Association des directeurs généraux des commissions scolaires du Québec (ADIGECS)
13, rue Saint-Laurent, Longueuil QC J4H 4B7
Tél: 450-670-0730; *Téléc:* 450-670-0902
URL: www.adigecs.qc.ca
Pâquerette Gagnon, Présidente

Association des enseignantes et des enseignants franco-ontariens (AEFO) / Franco-Ontarian Teachers' Association
681 Belfast Rd., Ottawa ON K1G 0Z4
Tél: 613-244-2336; *Téléc:* 613-563-7718
Ligne sans frais: 888-609-7718
Courriel: aefo@aefo.on.ca
URL: www.aefo.on.ca
Affiliation(s): Ontario Teachers' Federation
Laurent Joncas, Directeur général
Marie-Élisabeth Brunet, Reponsable des communications

Association des enseignantes et des enseignants francophones du Nouveau-Brunswick (AEFNB)
CP 712, 650, rue Montgomery, Fredericton NB E3B 5B4
Tél: 506-452-8921; *Téléc:* 506-453-9795
Courriel: aefnb@nbnet.nb.ca
URL: www.aefnb.nb.ca
Monique Caissie, Présidente

Association for Baha'i Studies (ABS) / Association d'études Baha'is
34 Copernicus St., Ottawa ON K1N 7K4
Tel: 613-233-1903; *Fax:* 613-233-3644
e-mail: abs-na@bahai-studies.ca
URL: www.bahai-studies.ca
Martha Schweitz, Chair

Association for Canadian Studies (ACS) / Association d'études canadiennes (AEC)
1822A, rue Sherbooke ouest, Montréal QC H3H 1E4
Tel: 514-925-3094; *Fax:* 514-925-3095
e-mail: general@acs-aec.ca
URL: www.acs-aec.ca
Jack Jedwab, Executive Director
James Ondrick, Director, Programs & Administration

Association francophone internationale des directeurs d'établissements scolaires (AFIDES)
500, boul Crémazie est, Montréal QC H2P 1E7
Tél: 514-383-7335; *Téléc:* 514-384-2139
Ligne sans frais: 877-783-7335
Courriel: afides@afides.org
URL: www.afides.org
Carol Bédard, Présidente

Association francophone pour le savoir (ACFAS)
425, rue de la Gauchetière est, Montréal QC H2L 2M7
Tél: 514-849-0045; *Téléc:* 514-849-5558
Courriel: acfas@acfas.ca
URL: www.acfas.ca
Esther Gaudreault, Directrice générale

Association of Atlantic Universities (AAU) / Association des universités de l'Atlantique
#403, 5657 Spring Garden Rd., Halifax NS B3J 3R4
Tel: 902-425-4230; *Fax:* 902-425-4233
e-mail: info@atlanticuniversities.ca
URL: www.atlanticuniversities.ca
Peter Halpin, Executive Director

Association of British Columbia Teachers of English as an Additional Language (B.C. TEAL)
#206, 640 West Broadway, Vancouver BC V5Z 1G4
Tel: 604-736-6330; *Fax:* 604-736-6306
e-mail: admin@bcteal.org
URL: www.bcteal.org
Affiliation(s): Affiliation of Multicultural Societies & Service Agencies of B.C., TESL Canada, TESOL, and ELSA Net
Alison McBride, Director of Administration

Association of Canadian Community Colleges (ACCC) / Association des collèges communautaires du Canada
#200, 1223 Michael St. North, Ottawa ON K1J 7T2
Tel: 613-746-2222; *Fax:* 613-746-6721
e-mail: info@accc.ca
URL: www.accc.ca
James Knight, President & CEO

Association of Canadian Faculties of Dentistry (ACFD) / Association des facultés dentaires du Canada (AFDC)
#204, 100 Bronson Ave., Ottawa ON K1R 6G8
Tel: 613-237-6505; *Fax:* 613-236-8386
e-mail: director@acfd.ca
URL: www.acfd.ca
John Perry, President

Association of Canadian Universities for Northern Studies (ACUNS) / Association universitaire canadienne d'études nordiques
#405, 17 York St., Ottawa ON K1N 9J6
Tel: 613-562-0515; *Fax:* 613-562-0533
e-mail: office@acuns.ca
URL: www.acuns.ca
Carol Howard Donati, Executive Director
James McDonald, President
Antoni Lewkowicz, Vice-President
Yves Bégin, Sec.-Treas.

Association of Colleges of Applied Arts & Technology of Ontario (ACAATO) / Association des collèges d'arts appliqués et de technologie de l'Ontario
#1010, 655 Bay St., Toronto ON M5G 2K4
Tel: 416-596-0744; *Fax:* 416-596-2364
URL: www.collegesontario.org
Linda Franklin, President & CEO

Association of Deans of Pharmacy of Canada (ADPC) / Association des doyens de pharmacie du Canada (ADPC)
3919 - 13th Ave. West, Vancouver BC V6R 2T1
Tel: 604-222-0221; *Fax:* 604-222-2574
e-mail: fabbott@telus.net
Frank Abbott, Executive Director

Association of Early Childhood Educators, Ontario (AECEO)
#211, 40 Orchard View Blvd., Toronto ON M4R 1B9
Tel: 416-487-3157; *Fax:* 416-487-3758
Toll-Free: 800-463-3391
e-mail: info@aeceo.ca
URL: www.aeceo.ca
Eduarda Sousa, Executive Director

Association of Educational Research Officers of Ontario (AERO) / Association ontarienne des agents de recherche en éducation
c/o York Region District School Board, PO Box 40, 60 Wellington St. West, Aurora ON L4G 3H2
Tel: 905-727-0022; *Fax:* 905-727-6282
URL: www.aero-ontario.org
Affiliation(s): American Educational Research Association
Megan Borner, President

Association of Faculties of Medicine of Canada (AFMC) / L'Association des facultés de médecine du Canada (AFMC)
#800, 265 Carling Ave., Ottawa ON K1S 2E1
Tel: 613-730-0687; *Fax:* 613-730-1196
e-mail: nbusing@afmc.ca
URL: www.afmc.ca
Affiliation(s): Canadian Medical Association; Association of Universities & Colleges of Canada
Nick Busing, President & CEO

Association of Independent Schools & Colleges in Alberta (AISCA)
#201, 11830 - 111 Ave., Edmonton AB T5G 0E1
Tel: 780-469-9868; *Fax:* 780-469-9880
e-mail: office@aisca.ab.ca
URL: www.aisca.ab.ca
Duane Plantinga, Executive Director

Association of Registrars of the Universities & Colleges of Canada (ARUCC) / Association des registraires des universités et collèges du Canada
c/o University of Calgary, 2500 University Dr. NW, Calgary AB T2N 1N4
Tel: 403-220-3832; *Fax:* 403-289-1253
e-mail: sekulic@ucalgary.ca
URL: www.arucc.ca
Mike Sekulic, President

Association of Universities & Colleges of Canada (AUCC) / Association des universités et collèges du Canada
#600, 350 Albert St., Ottawa ON K1R 1B1
Tel: 613-563-1236; *Fax:* 613-563-9745
e-mail: info@aucc.ca
URL: www.aucc.ca
Paul Davidson, President/CEO
Tom Traves, Chair

Association of University Forestry Schools of Canada (AUFSC) / Association des écoles forestières universitaires du Canada
c/o School of Forestry, Lakehead University, 955 Oliver Rd., Thunder Bay ON P7B 5E1
Tel: 807-343-8511
David MacLean, President

Association provinciale des enseignantes et enseignants du Québec (APEQ) / Québec Provincial Association of Teachers (QPAT)
#1, 17035, boul Brunswick, Kirkland QC H9H 5G6
Tél: 514-694-9777; *Téléc:* 514-694-0189
Ligne sans frais: 800-361-9870
Courriel: reception@qpat-apeq.qc.ca
URL: www.qpat-apeq.qc.ca
Alan Lombard, Executive Director

Association québécoise des professeurs de français (AQPF)
#222, 2095, Frank-Carrel, Sainte-Foy QC G1N 4L8
Tél: 418-683-0947; *Téléc:* 418-527-4765
Ligne sans frais: 800-267-0947
Courriel: apqf@bellnet.ca
URL: www.aqpf.qc.ca
Affiliation(s): Fédération internationale des professeurs de français
Érick Falardeau, Présidente, Section de Québec
Réjean Leclair, Président, Section Centre du Québec
Julie Roberge, Président, Section de Montréal
Suzanne Richard, Présidente

Association québécoise des troubles d'apprentissage (AQETA) / Learning Disabilities Association of Québec (LDAQ)
#300, 284, rue Notre-Dame ouest, Montréal QC H2Y 1T7
Tél: 514-847-1324; *Téléc:* 514-281-5187
Courriel: info@aqeta.qc.ca
URL: www.aqeta.qc.ca
Monique Chemorin, Directrice générale
Lise Bastien, Présidente

Association québécoise du personnel de direction des écoles (AQPDE)
#308, 2700, Jean-Perriny, Québec QC G2C 1S9
Tél: 418-845-5088; *Téléc:* 418-845-9699
Courriel: info@aqpde.ca
URL: www.aqpde.ca
Serge Rodrigue, Président

Black Educators Association of Nova Scotia (BEA)
2136 Gottingen St., Halifax NS B3K 3B3
Tel: 902-424-7036; *Fax:* 902-424-0636
Toll-Free: 800-565-3398
e-mail: beaadulted@eastlink.ca
URL: www.thebea.ns.ca

British Columbia Confederation of Parent Advisory Councils (BCCPAC)
#350, 5172 Kingsway, Burnaby BC V5H 2E8
Tel: 604-687-4433; *Fax:* 604-687-4488
Toll-Free: 866-529-4397
e-mail: info@bccpac.bc.ca
URL: www.bccpac.bc.ca
Ann Whiteacre, President
Carla Giles, COO

British Columbia School Trustees Association (BCSTA) / Association des commissaires d'écoles de Colombie-Britannique
1580 West Broadway, 4th Fl., Vancouver BC V6J 5K9
Tel: 604-734-2721; *Fax:* 604-732-4559
e-mail: bcsta@bcsta.org
URL: www.bcsta.org
Stephen Hansen, Executive Director
Connie Denesiuk, President

British Columbia Teachers' Federation (BCTF) / Fédération des enseignants de la Colombie-Britannique
#100, 550 - 6th Ave. West, Vancouver BC V5Z 4P2
Tel: 604-871-2283; *Fax:* 604-871-2293
Toll-Free: 800-663-9163
e-mail: benefits@bctf.ca; rovergaard@bctf.ca (Media Relations)
URL: www.bctf.ca
Irene Lanzinger, President
Susan Lambert, First Vice-President
Jim Iker, Second Vice-President

Canadian Alliance of Student Associations (CASA) / Alliance canadienne des associations étudiantes (ACAE)
PO Box 3408, Stn. D, Ottawa ON K1P 6H8
Tel: 613-236-3457; *Fax:* 613-236-2386
e-mail: casacomm@casa.ca
URL: www.casa.ca
Zach Churchill, National Director
Rick Theis, Government Relations Coordinator
Jillian Flake, Officer, Public Relations & Communications
Lisa Fry, Research & Policy

Canadian Asian Studies Association (CASA) / Association canadienne des études asiatiques (ACEA)
c/o Concordia University, #SB115, 1455, rue de Maisonneuve ouest, Montréal QC H3G 1M8
Tel: 514-848-2280; *Fax:* 514-848-4514
e-mail: casa_acea@bellnet.ca
URL: canadianasianstudies.concordia.ca
Scott Simon, President
Jacques Bertrand, Vice-President
Annamaria Piccioni, Secretariat
Reeta C. Tremblay, Secretariat

Canadian Association for American Studies (CAAS) / Association d'études américaines au Canada
c/o Dana Medoro, Associate Professor, University of Manitoba, 636 Fletcher Argue, Winnipeg MB R3T 5V5
e-mail: webmaster@american-studies.ca
URL: www.american-studies.ca
Social Media: www.facebook.com/group.php?gid=75085833950
Dana Medoro, President
Jason Haslam, Vice-President
Jennifer Harris, Secretary
Percy Walton, Treasurer

Canadian Association for Co-operative Education (CAFCE) / Association canadienne de l'enseignement coopératif
#205, 834 Yonge St., Toronto ON M4W 2H1
Tel: 416-483-3311; *Fax:* 416-483-3365
e-mail: cafce@cafce.ca
URL: www.cafce.ca
Affiliation(s): World Association for Cooperative Education (WACE)
Kevin Rolston, President
Stacey Cool, Secretary
Shane Phillippe, Treasurer

Canadian Association for Graduate Studies (CAGS) / Association canadienne pour les études supérieures (ACES)
#205, 260 Dalhousie St., Ottawa ON K1N 7E4
Tel: 613-562-0949; *Fax:* 613-562-9009
e-mail: cags@uottawa.ca
URL: www.cags.ca
Jean-Pierre Gaboury, Executive Director
Fred Hall, President
Chet Jablonski, Sec.-Treas.

Canadian Association for Pastoral Practice & Education (CAPPE) / Association canadienne pour la pratique et l'éducation pastorales (ACPEP)
660 Francklyn St., Halifax NS B3H 3B5
Tel: 902-820-3085; *Fax:* 902-820-3087
Toll-Free: 866-442-2773
e-mail: office@cappe.org
URL: www.cappe.org
Walton Brian, President
Tony Sedfawi, Executive Director
Dawn Dyer, Secretary
King Harold, Treasurer
Kathy Greig, Office Manager

Canadian Association for Scottish Studies (CASS)
Dept. of History, Centre for Scottish Studies, University of Guelph, 1008 MacKinnon Ext., Guelph ON N1G 2W1
Tel: 519-824-4120; *Fax:* 519-766-9516
e-mail: scottish@uoguelph.ca
URL: www.uoguelph.ca/scottish
Affiliation(s): Scottish Studies Foundation
Graeme Morton, General Editor, IRSS

Canadian Association for Teacher Education (CATE) / Association canadienne pour la formation des enseignants (ACFE)
#204, 260 Dalhousie St., Ottawa ON K1N 7E4
Tel: 613-241-0018; *Fax:* 613-241-0019
URL: www.csse.ca/CATE/home.htm
Affiliation(s): Canadian Association for Research in Early Childhood/Association canadienne pour la recherche préscolaire; Association of Business Teacher Educators of Canada/Association des professeurs en enseignement commercial au Canada
Renate Schulz, Sec.-Treas.

Canadian Association for the Advancement of Netherlandic Studies (CAANS) / Association canadienne pour l'avancement des études néerlandaises (ACAEN)
5291 - 4A Ave., Delta BC V4M 1H4
e-mail: vwermersk@interchange.ubc.ca
URL: www.caans-acaen.ca
Paul de Laat, Sec.-Treas.
Michiel Horn, President

Canadian Association for the Study of Discourse & Writing (CASDW) / Association canadienne de rédactologie (ACR)
c/o W. Brock MacDonald, Woodsworth College, University of Toronto, 119 St. George St., Toronto ON M5S 1A9
e-mail: wb.macdonald@utoronto.ca
URL: cattw-acprts.mcgill.ca
Doreen Starke-Meyerring, President
Anne Parker, Secretary

Canadian Association for University Continuing Education (CAUCE) / Association pour l'éducation permanente dans les universités du Canada (AEPUC)
c/o Centre for Continuing & Distance Education, U. of Saskatchewan, #464, 221 Cumberland Ave. North, Saskatoon SK S7N 1M3
Tel: 306-966-5604; *Fax:* 306-966-5590
e-mail: cauce.secratariat@usask.ca
URL: www.cauce-aepuc.ca
Tracey Taylor-O'Reilly, President

Canadian Association of College & University Student Services (CACUSS) / Association des services aux étudiants des universités et collèges du Canada (ASEUCC)
c/o Events Management Plus Inc., #310, 4 Cataraqui St., Kingston ON K7L 1Z7
Tel: 613-531-9210; *Fax:* 613-531-0626
e-mail: contact@cacuss.ca
URL: www.cacuss.ca
Donna Dennison, Administrative Director
Rob Shea, President
Bernadette Power, Sec.-Treas.

Canadian Association of Foundations of Education (CAFE) / Association canadienne des fondements de l'éducation (ACFE)
Univ. of Manitoba, Faculty Of Education, 256 St John's College, Winnipeg MB R3T 2M5
Tel: 204-474-8741; *Fax:* 204-474-7551
e-mail: mandzukd@ms.umanitoba.ca
URL: www.csse.ca/CAFE/home.htm
Affiliation(s): Canadian Philosophy of Education Society; Canadian History of Education Society; Sociology in Education Network (SOCINET)
David Mandzuk, President

Canadian Association of Geographers (CAG) / Association canadienne des géographes
Department of Geography, McGill University, #425, 805, rue Sherbrooke ouest, Montréal QC H3A 2K6
Tel: 514-398-4946; *Fax:* 514-398-7437
e-mail: cag@geog.mcgill.ca
URL: www.cag-acg.ca
Affiliation(s): Represented on the Canadian Commission for UNESCO, the Social Science Federation of Canada, & the Canadian Committee of the International Geographical Union
Mary-Louise Byrne, Sec.-Treas.
Dan Smith, President

Canadian Association of Independent Schools (CAIS)
12 Bannockburn Ave., Toronto ON M5M 2M8
Tel: 416-780-1779
e-mail: director@cais.ca
URL: www.cais.ca
James Christopher, Executive Director

Canadian Association of Principals (CAP) / Association canadienne des directeurs d'école
#220, 300 Earl Grey Dr., Kanata ON K2T 1C1
Tel: 613-622-0346; *Fax:* 613-622-0258
e-mail: cap@bellnet.ca
URL: www.cdnprincipals.org
Marie Schutt, Executive Assistant

Canadian Association of School Social Workers & Attendance Counsellors (CASSWAC)
c/o Portage la Prairie School Div., 36 - 13th St. NW, Portage la Prairie MB R1N 2T5
Tel: 204-857-7687
e-mail: jmurray@plpsd.mb.ca
URL: www.casswac.ca
June Murray, President
Steve McCann, Past President

Canadian Association of Schools of Nursing (CASN) / Association canadienne des écoles de sciences infirmières (ACESI)
#15, 99 Fifth Ave., Ottawa ON K1S 5K4
Tel: 613-235-3150; *Fax:* 613-235-4476
e-mail: inquire@casn.ca
URL: www.casn.ca
Affiliation(s): Association of Universities and Colleges of Canada (AUCC)
Cynthia Baker, Executive Director

Canadian Association of Schools of Social Work (CASSW) / Association canadienne des écoles de service social (ACESS)
1398 Star Top Rd., Ottawa ON K13 4V7
Tel: 613-792-1953; *Fax:* 613-792-1956
e-mail: cassw@cassw-acess.ca
URL: www.cassw-acess.ca
Sharon Leslie, Office Administrator
Benoît van Caloen, President
Ken Barter, Treasurer

Canadian Association of Second Language Teachers (CASLT) / Association canadienne des professeurs de langues secondes (ACPLS)
#300, 950 Gladstone Ave., Ottawa ON K1Y 3E6
Tel: 613-727-0994; *Fax:* 613-727-3831
Toll-Free: 877-727-0994
e-mail: admin@caslt.org
URL: www.caslt.org
Nicole Thibault, Executive Director
Louise St-Amand, Office & Membership Administrator

Canadian Association of Slavists (CAS) / Association canadienne des slavistes
Alumni Hall, Dept. of Slavic Languages & Literatures, Univ. of Toronto, #403, 121 St. Joseph St., Toronto ON M5S 1J4
Tel: 416-926-1300; *Fax:* 416-333-8243
URL: www.ualberta.ca/~csp/cas/contact.html
Affiliation(s): The Canadian Association for Ukrainian Studies (CAUS)

Maxim Tarnawsky, President
Zinaida Gimpelevich, Sec.-Treas.

Canadian Association of University Business Officers (CAUBO) / Association canadienne du personnel administratif universitaire (ACPAU)
#320, 350 Albert St., Ottawa ON K1R 1B1
Tel: 613-230-6760; *Fax:* 613-563-7739
e-mail: cworkman@caubo.ca
URL: www.caubo.ca
Carole Workman, Executive Director

Canadian Association of University Research Administrators (CAURA) / Association canadienne d'administrateurs de recherche universitaire (ACARU)
#320, 350 Albert St., Ottawa ON K1R 1B1
Tel: 613-563-3961; *Fax:* 613-563-7739
e-mail: admin@caura-acaru.ca
URL: www.caura-acaru.ca
Barbara Crutchley, Vice-President
Sandra Crocker, President

Canadian Association of University Teachers (CAUT) / Association canadienne des professeures et professeurs d'université (ACPPU)
2705 Queensview Dr., Ottawa ON K2B 8K2
Tel: 613-820-2270; *Fax:* 613-820-7244
e-mail: acppu@caut.ca
URL: www.caut.ca
Affiliation(s): Association of Canadian Community Colleges; Association of Universities & Colleges of Canada; Canadian Association for Graduate Studies; Canadian Association of University Business Officers; Canadian Education Association; Canadian Federation for the Humanities and Social Sciences & other discipline-based associations; Canadian Federation of Students; Education International; Network for Education & Academic Rights; Coalition of Contingent Academic Labour
James Turk, Executive Director
Gordon Piché, Associate Executive Director, Administration & Finance
David Robinson, Associate Executive Director, Research & Advocacy
Michael Piva, Assistant Executive Director, Collective Bargaining & Services

Canadian Bureau for International Education (CBIE) / Bureau canadien de l'éducation internationale (BCEI)
#1550, 220 Laurier Ave. West, Ottawa ON K1P 5Z9
Tel: 613-237-4820; *Fax:* 613-237-1073
e-mail: info@cbie.ca
URL: www.cbie.ca
Affiliation(s): UNESCO Canada; National Consortium of Scientific & Educational Societies
Karen McBride, President
Bashir Hassanali, Executive Vice-President

Canadian Catholic School Trustees' Association (CCSTA) / Association canadienne des commissaires d'écoles catholique
Catholic Education Centre, 570 West Hunt Club Rd., Nepean ON K2G 3R4
Tel: 613-224-4455; *Fax:* 613-224-3187
e-mail: ccsta@ottawacatholicschools.ca
URL: www.ccsta.ca
Greg McNally, Executive Director
Regis O'Connor, President
Paula Peroni, Vice-President

Canadian College of Teachers (CCT) / Collège canadien des enseignants et des enseignantes
2490 Don Reid Dr., Ottawa ON K1H 1E1
Tel: 613-558-4705
e-mail: allan@winnipeg.com
URL: www.cct-cce.com
Constance Middleton-Hope, FCCT, Sec.-Treas.
Allan M. Johnson, FCCT, President

Canadian Council for the Advancement of Education Inc. (CCAE) / Le Conseil canadien pour l'avancement de l'éducation
PO Box 41161, Stn. Elmvale, Ottawa ON K1G 5K9
Tel: 613-421-7950; *Fax:* 613-421-7960
e-mail: admin@ccaecanada.org
URL: www.ccaecanada.org
Catherine MacNeill, Executive Director
Ray Satterthwaite, President

Canadian Council of Teachers of English Language Arts (CCTELA)
#10, 730 River Rd., Winnipeg MB R2M 5A4
Tel: 204-255-1676; *Fax:* 204-253-2562
e-mail: cctela@mts.net
URL: www.cctela.ca
Affiliation(s): International Federation of Teachers of English
Linda Ferguson, Executive Director

Canadian Council of University Physical Education & Kinesiology Administrators (CCUPEKA) / Conseil canadien des administrateurs universitaires en éducation physique et kinésiologie (CCAUEPK)
c/o Dr. J. Starkes, Department of Kinesiology, McMaster University, Hamilton ON L8S 4K1
URL: www.ccupeka.ca
Janet Starkes, Coordinator, Accreditation Council

Canadian Education Association (CEA) / Association canadienne d'éducation (ACE)
#300, 317 Adelaide St. West, Toronto ON M5V 1P9
Tel: 416-591-6300; *Fax:* 416-591-5345
e-mail: info@cea-ace.ca
URL: www.cea-ace.ca
Penny Milton, Chief Executive Officer
Carole Olsen, Chair

Canadian Ethnic Studies Association (CESA) / Société canadienne d'études ethniques (SCEE)
Dept. of Geography, Univ. of Winnipeg, 515 Portage Ave., Winnipeg MB R3B 2E9
e-mail: cesa@uwinnipeg.ca
URL: cesa.uwinnipeg.ca
John C Lehr, President
Alexander Freund, Vice-President
Lori Wilkinson, Secretary-Treasurer

Canadian Faculties of Agriculture & Veterinary Medicine (CFAVM) / Facultés d'agriculture et de médecine vétérinaire du Canada
77 Townsend Dr., Nepean ON K2J 2V3
Tel: 613-825-6873
e-mail: dhedley000@sympatico.ca
URL: www.cfavm.ca
Douglas D. Hedley, Executive Director

Canadian Federation for Humanities & Social Sciences (CFHSS) / Fédération canadienne des sciences humaines (FCSH)
#415, 151 Slater St., Ottawa ON K1P 5H3
Tel: 613-238-6112; *Fax:* 613-238-6114
e-mail: fedcan@fedcan.ca
URL: www.fedcan.ca
Jody Ciufo, Executive Director
Noreen Golfman, Dr., President

Canadian Federation of Business School Deans (CFBSD) / Fédération canadienne des doyens des écoles d'administration
3000, ch de la Côte-Sainte-Catherine, Montréal QC H3T 2A7
Tel: 514-340-7116; *Fax:* 514-340-7275
e-mail: info@cfbsd.ca; conferences@cfbsd.ca; surveys@cfbsd.ca
URL: www.cfbsd.ca
Michel Patry, Chair
Bahram Dadgostar, Vice-Chair
Timothy Daniel Daus, Executive Director
Robert Mantha, Secretary-Treasurer

Canadian Federation of Students (CFS) / Fédération canadienne des étudiantes et étudiants (FCEE)
338C Somerset St. West, Ottawa ON K2P 0J9
Tel: 613-232-7394; *Fax:* 613-232-0276
e-mail: web@cfs-fcee.ca
URL: www.cfs-fcee.ca
Katherine Giroux-Bougard, National Chair
Noah Stewart, National Deputy Chair
Dave Molenhuis, National Treasurer
Andrea Balon, Representative, Graduate Students
Roxanne Dubois, Representative, Francophone Students
Sandy Hudson, Representative, Women
Thomas Roussin, Representative, Aboriginal Students
Krishna Saravanamuttu, Representative, Students of Colour

Canadian Federation of University Women (CFUW) / Fédération canadienne des femmes diplômées des universités (FCFDU)
Head Office, #305, 251 Bank St., Ottawa ON K2P 1X3
Tel: 613-234-8252; *Fax:* 613-234-8221
e-mail: cfuwgen@rogers.com
URL: www.cfuw.org
Susan Russell, Executive Director
Samantha Spady, Coordinator, Advocacy & Communications

Canadian Foundation for Economic Education (CFEE) / Fondation d'éducation économique
#201, 110 Eglinton Ave. West, Toronto ON M4R 1A3
Tel: 416-968-2236; *Fax:* 416-968-0488
Toll-Free: 888-570-7610
e-mail: mail@cfee.org
URL: www.cfee.org
Jean Olier Caron, Chair
Lori Cranson, Chair
Steve Petherbridge, Advisor

Canadian Home & School Federation (CHSF) / Fédération canadienne des associations foyer-école (FCAFE)
c/o Fisher Park School, 250 Holland Ave., Ottawa ON K1Y 0Y6
Tel: 613-798-2837; *Fax:* 613-798-2838
e-mail: chsf@bellnet.ca
URL: www.canadianhomeandschool.com
Affiliation(s): Canadian Education Association; Breakfast for Learning; Canadian Teachers Federation; Canadian Association of Principals; Centre for Science in Public Interest; Media Awareness; Council of Ministers of Education Canada
Janet Walsh, President
Judith Cameron, Western Vice-President
Brian Peat, Central Vice-President
Cynthia Richards, Eastern Vice-President
Eva Cameron, Secretary-Treasurer

Canadian Interuniversity Sport (CIS) / Sport interuniversitaire canadien (SIC)
#N205, 801 King Edward, Ottawa ON K1N 6N5
Tel: 613-562-5670; *Fax:* 613-562-5669
e-mail: cisoffice@universitysport.ca
URL: www.cis-sic.ca
Social Media: www.twitter.com/CIS_SIC
Affiliation(s): Atlantic University Sport; Québéc Student Sport Federation; Ontario University Athletics; Canada West Universities Athletic Association
Marg McGregor, CEO

Canadian Network for Innovation in Education (CNIE)
#204, 260 Dalhousie St., Ottawa ON K1N 7E4
Tel: 613-241-0018; *Fax:* 613-241-0019
e-mail: cnie-rcie@cnie-rcie.ca
URL: www.cade-aced.ca
Maureen Baron, President
Anna Sawicki, Sec.-Treas.

Canadian School Boards Association (CSBA) / Association canadienne des commissions/conseils scolaires
PO Box 2095, Stn. D, Ottawa ON K1P 5W3
Tel: 613-235-3724; *Fax:* 613-238-8434
e-mail: admin@cdnsba.org
URL: www.cdnsba.org
Rick Johnson, President

Canadian Society for Education through Art (CSEA) / Société canadienne d'éducation par l'art (SCEA)
Faculty of Education, Department of Curriculum and Instruction, PO Box 3010, Stn. CSC, University of Victoria, Victoria BC V8W 3N4
Tel: 250-721-7896; *Fax:* 250-721-7598
e-mail: info@csea-scea.ca
URL: www.csea-scea.ca
Affiliation(s): British Columbia Art Teachers' Association; Fine Arts Council, Alberta Teachers' Association; Saskatchewan Society for Education through Art; Manitoba Association of Art Educators; Ontario Society for Education through Art; Provincial Association of Art Teachers; Association québécoise des éducateurs spécialisés en arts plastiques; New Brunswick Arts Education Council; Nova Scotia Art Teachers' Association; PEI Art Teachers' Association; Art Council of the Newfoundland Teachers' Association; Canadian Art Gallery Educators
Fiona Blaikie, President, Lakehead University, Orillia Campus

Canadian Society for the Study of Education (CSSE) / Société canadienne pour l'étude de l'éducation (SCEE)
#204, 260 Dalhousie St., Ottawa ON K1N 7E4
Tel: 613-241-0018; *Fax:* 613-241-0019
e-mail: csse-scee@csse.ca
URL: www.csse.ca
Tim Howard, Director of Administration
Rita Irwin, PhD, President

Canadian Society for the Study of Higher Education (CSSHE) / La Société canadienne pour l'étude de l'enseignement supérieur (SCEES)
PO Box 34091, Stn. Fort Richmond, Winnipeg MB R3T 5T5

Tel: 204-474-6404; *Fax:* 204-474-7561
URL: www.ss.ucalgary.ca/csshe/

Stephen Kerr, Treasurer
Ester Enns, President

Canadian Society of Biblical Studies (CSBS) / Société canadienne des études bibliques (SCEB)
c/o Prof. Robert A. Derrenbacker, Jr., Regent College, 5800 University Blvd., Vancouver BC V6T 2E4
e-mail: rderrenbacker@regent-college.edu
URL: www.ccsr.ca/csbs

Terry Donaldson, President
Francis Landy, Vice-President
Robert A. Derrenbacker, Jr., Treasurer & Membership Secretary
Richard S. Ascough, Officer, Communications

Canadian Teachers' Federation (CTF) / Fédération canadienne des enseignantes et des enseignants (FCE)
2490 Don Reid Dr., Ottawa ON K1H 1E1
Tel: 613-232-1505; *Fax:* 613-232-1886
Toll-Free: 866-283-1505
e-mail: info@ctf-fce.ca
URL: www.ctf-fce.ca

Calvin Fraser, Secretary General
Emily Noble, President

Canadian Test Centre Inc. (CTC) / Services d'évaluation pédagogique
#7-8, 85 Citizen Ct., Markham ON L6G 1A8
Tel: 905-513-6636; *Fax:* 905-513-6639
Toll-Free: 800-668-1006
e-mail: info@canadiantestcentre.com
URL: www.canadiantestcentre.com

Ernest W. Cheng, Managing Director

Canadian University & College Conference Organizers Association (CUCCOA) / Association des coordonnateurs de congrès des universités et des collèges du Canada (ACCUCC)
312 Oakwood Ct., Newmarket ON L3Y 3C8
Tel: 905-954-0102; *Fax:* 905-895-1630
e-mail: inquiries@cuccoa.org
URL: www.cuccoa.org

Carol Ford, Manager

Canadian University & College Counselling Association (CUCCA) / Association canadienne de counseling universitaire et collégial
c/o Canadian Association of College & University Student Services, #310, 4 Cataraqui St., Kingston ON K7K 1Z7
Tel: 613-531-9210; *Fax:* 613-531-0626
URL: www.cacuss.ca/en/divisions/CUCCA/overview.htm

David V. Ness, President

Centre d'animation de développement et de recherche en éducation (CADRE)
1940, boul Henri-Bourassa est, Montréal QC H2B 1S2
Tél: 514-381-8891; *Téléc:* 514-381-4086
Ligne sans frais: 888-381-8891
Courriel: info@cadre.qc.ca
URL: www.cadre.qc.ca

Paul Boisvenu, Directeur général

Centre franco-ontarien de ressources pédagogiques (CFORP)
435 Donald St., Ottawa ON K1K 4X5
Tél: 613-747-8000; *Téléc:* 613-747-2808
Ligne sans frais: 877-742-3677
Courriel: cforp@cforp.on.ca
URL: www.cforp.on.ca

Robert Arseneault, Directeur général

The Commonwealth of Learning (COL)
#1200, 1055 Hastings St. West, Vancouver BC V6E 2E9
Tel: 604-775-8200; *Fax:* 604-775-8210
e-mail: info@col.org
URL: www.col.org

Affiliation(s): Commonwealth Educational Media Centre for Asia (CEMCA); Commonwealth Secretariat; Commonwealth Foundation; Commonwealth Connects
John Daniel, President & CEO
Dave Wilson, CAE, Communications Manager

Comparative & International Education Society of Canada (CIESC) / Société canadienne d'éducation comparée et internationale (SCECI)
University of Western Ontario, #2, 1151 Richmond St., London ON N6A 5B8
URL: www.edu.uwo.ca/ciesc/

Affiliation(s): World Congress of Comparative Education Societies

Confederation of Alberta Faculty Associations (CAFA)
Univ. of Alberta, 11043 - 90 Ave., Edmonton AB T6G 2E1
Tel: 780-492-5630; *Fax:* 780-436-0516
e-mail: lori.morinville@ualberta.ca
URL: www.ualberta.ca/~cafa/

John Nicholls, Executive Director
Lori Morinville, Administrative Officer

Confederation of University Faculty Associations of British Columbia (CUFA BC)
#315, 207 West Hastings St., Vancouver BC V6B 1H7
Tel: 604-646-4677; *Fax:* 604-646-4676
e-mail: cufabc@sfu.ca
URL: www.cufa.bc.ca

Robert Clift, Executive Director
Chris Petter, President

Conférence des recteurs et des principaux des universités du Québec (CREPUQ) / Conference of Rectors & Principals of Quebec Universities
c/o Conférence des recteurs et des principaux, #200, 500, rue Sherbrooke ouest, Montréal QC H3A 3C6
Tél: 514-288-8524; *Téléc:* 514-288-0554
Courriel: info@crepuq.qc.ca
URL: www.crepuq.qc.ca

Daniel Zizian, Directeur général

Conference of Independent Schools (Ontario) (CIS)
PO Box 27, Whitby ON L1N 5R7
Tel: 905-665-8622; *Fax:* 905-665-8635
e-mail: admin@cisontario.ca
URL: www.cisontario.ca

Affiliation(s): National Association of Independent Schools
George L. Briggs, B.A., M.Ed., Executive Director

Council of Atlantic Ministers of Education & Training (CAMET) / Conseil atlantique des ministres de l'Éducation et de la Formation (CAMEF)
PO Box 2044, Halifax NS B3J 2Z1
Tel: 902-424-5352; *Fax:* 902-424-8976
e-mail: camet-camef@cap-cpma.ca
URL: www.camet-camef.ca

Rhéal Poirier, Secretary

Council of Canadian Law Deans (CCLD) / Conseil des doyens et des doyennes des facultés de droit du Canada (CDFDC)
57 Louis Pasteur, Ottawa ON K1N 6N5
Tel: 613-824-9233; *Fax:* 613-824-9233
e-mail: brigitteccld@rogers.com
URL: www.ccld-cdfdc.ca

Brigitte Pilon, Executive Director

Council of Catholic School Superintendents of Alberta
e-mail: superintendents@ccssa.ab.ca
URL: www.ccssa.ab.ca

George Zeigner, Executive Director

Council of Ontario Universities (COU) / Conseil des universités de l'Ontario
#1100, 180 Dundas St. West, Toronto ON M5G 1Z8
Tel: 416-979-2165; *Fax:* 416-979-8635
e-mail: cou@cou.on.ca
URL: www.cou.on.ca

Peter George, Chair
Paul C. Genest, President/CEO
John ApSimon, Interim Executive Director
Sharon Berman, Executive Director, Corporate Services
George Granger, Executive Director, Ontario Universities' Application Centre (OUAC)
Jamie Mackay, Vice-President, Policy & Analysis
Barbara Hauser, Secretary to Council & Sr. Advisor

Elementary Teachers' Federation of Ontario (ETFO) / Fédération des enseignantes et des enseignants de l'élémentaire de l'Ontario (FEEO)
#1000, 480 University Ave., Toronto ON M5G 1V2
Tel: 416-962-3836; *Fax:* 416-642-2424
Toll-Free: 888-838-3836
e-mail: glewis@etfo.org
URL: www.etfo.ca

Louise Ewing, Office Manager
Gene Lewis, General Secretary
Ruth Alam, Office Manager
Emily Noble, President

Fédération des cégeps
500, boul Crémazie est, Montréal QC H2P 1E7
Tél: 514-381-8631; *Téléc:* 514-381-2263
Courriel: comm@fedecegeps.qc.ca
URL: www.fedecegeps.qc.ca

Daniel Marcotte, Président
Gaëtan Boucher, Président-directeur général

Fédération des comités de parents du Québec inc. (FCPQ)
2263, boul Louis-XIV, Québec QC G1C 1A4
Tél: 418-667-2432; *Téléc:* 418-667-6713
Ligne sans frais: 800-463-7268
Courriel: courrier@fcpq.qc.ca
URL: www.fcpq.qc.ca

Lise Ouellet, Presidènte

La Fédération des commissions scolaires du Québec (FCSQ)
CP 10490, Succ. Sainte-Foy, 1001, av Bégon, Québec QC G1V 4C7
Tél: 418-651-3220; *Téléc:* 418-651-2574
Courriel: info@fcsq.qc.ca
URL: www.fcsq.qc.ca

Pâquerette Gagnon, Directrice générale
André Caron, Président

Fédération des établissements d'enseignement privés (FEEP)
1940, boul Henri-Bourassa est, Montréal QC H2B 1S2
Tél: 514-381-8891; *Téléc:* 514-381-4086
Ligne sans frais: 888-381-8891
Courriel: info@feep.qc.ca
URL: www.cadre.qc.ca

Paul Boisvenu, Directeur général

Fédération nationale des enseignants et des enseignantes du Québec (FNEEQ) / National Federation of Québec Teachers
1601, av de Lorimier, Montréal QC H2K 4M5
Tél: 514-598-2241; *Téléc:* 514-598-2190
Courriel: fneeq.reception@csn.qc.ca
URL: www.fneeq.qc.ca

Ronald Cameron, Président

Federation of Independent School Associations of BC (FISA)
150 Robson St., Vancouver BC V6B 2A7
Tel: 604-684-6023; *Fax:* 604-684-3163
e-mail: fisabc@telus.net
URL: www.fisabc.ca

Fred Herfst, Executive Director
D. Lauson, President

Federation of Independent Schools in Canada (FISC) / Fédération canadienne des écoles privées (FCEP)
4114 Belanger Dr., Abbotsford BC V3G 1K3
Toll-Free: 888-227-8421
e-mail: fisc@shaw.ca
URL: www.independentschools.ca

Fred Herfst, President

Federation of New Brunswick Faculty Associations (FNBFA) / Fédération des associations de professeures et professeurs d'université du Nouveau-Brunswick (FAPPUNB)
#297, 65 Brunswick St., Fredericton NB E3B 1G5
Tel: 506-458-8977; *Fax:* 506-458-5620
e-mail: fnbfa@nb.aibn.com
URL: www.fnbfa.ca

Gilles Allain, Executive Director
Daniel Bélanger, Sec.-Treas.

Fédération provinciale des comités de parents du Manitoba (FPCP)
1075, promenade Autumnwood, Saint-Boniface MB R2J 1C6
Tél: 204-237-9666; *Téléc:* 204-231-1436
Ligne sans frais: 866-666-8108
Courriel: fpcp@fpcp.mb.ca
URL: www.entreparents.mb.ca

Hélène d'Auteuil, Directrice générale

Fédération québécoise des directeurs et directrices d'établissements d'enseignement (FQDE)
#100, 7855, boul Louis-H-Lafontaine, Anjou QC H1K 4E4
Tél: 514-353-7511; *Téléc:* 514-353-2064
Ligne sans frais: 800-361-4258
Courriel: info@fqde.qc.ca
URL: www.fqde.qc.ca

Marc Brunelle, Secrétaire
Chantal Longpré, Présidente

Fédération québécoise des professeures et professeurs d'université (FQPPU) / Québec Federation of University Professors
#405, 4446, boul St-Laurent, Montréal QC H2W 1Z5
Tél: 514-843-5953; *Téléc:* 514-843-6928
Ligne sans frais: 888-843-5953

Courriel: federation@fqppu.or
URL: www.fqppu.org
Max Roy, Président

Foundation for Educational Exchange Between Canada & the United States of America
#2015, 350 Albert St., Ottawa ON K1R 1A4
Tel: 613-688-5540; *Fax:* 613-237-2029
e-mail: info@fulbright.ca
URL: www.fulbright.ca
Michael K. Hawes, Executive Director
Sandy Hanna, Sr. Program Officer

Halifax Education Foundation
19 Medway Court, Dartmouth NS B2W 4G4
Tel: 902-434-2322; *Fax:* 902-434-2053

Institut de coopération pour l'éducation des adultes (ICEA)
#300, 5225, rue Berri, Montréal QC H2J 2S4
Tél: 514-948-2044; *Téléc:* 514-948-2046
Ligne sans frais: 877-948-2044
Courriel: icea@icea.qc.ca
URL: www.icea.qc.ca
Diane Dupuis, Directrice générale

Learning Disabilities Association of Alberta (LDAA) / Troubles d'apprentissage - Association de l'Alberta
PO Box 29011, Stn. Lendrum, Edmonton AB T6H 5Z6
Tel: 780-448-0360; *Fax:* 780-438-0665
e-mail: info@ldaa.ca
URL: www.ldaa.ca
Kathryn Burke, Executive Director

Learning Disabilities Association of British Columbia (LDAV) / Troubles d'apprentissage - Association de la Colombie-Britannique
3292 East Broadway, Vancouver BC V5M 1Z8
Tel: 604-873-8139; *Fax:* 604-873-8140
e-mail: info@ldav.ca
URL: www.ldav.ca
Diane Sugars, Executive Director

Learning Disabilities Association of Canada (LDAC) / Troubles d'apprentissage - Association canadienne (TAAC)
#616, 250 City Centre Ave., Ottawa ON K1R 6K7
Tel: 613-238-5721; *Fax:* 613-235-5391
Toll-Free: 877-238-5322
e-mail: info@ldac-taac.ca
URL: www.ldac-taac.ca
Judy Kerr, Executive Director
Lynn Green, Chair

Learning Disabilities Association of Manitoba (LDAM) / Troubles d'apprentissage - Association de Manitoba
617 Erin St., Winnipeg MB R3G 2W1
Tel: 204-774-1821; *Fax:* 204-788-4090
e-mail: ldamb@mts.net
URL: www.ldamanitoba.org
Affiliation(s): Learning Disabilities Association of Canada
Marilyn MacKinnon, Executive Director

Learning Disabilities Association of New Brunswick (LDANB) / Troubles d'apprentissage - Association du Nouveau-Brunswick (TA-ANB)
#203, 403 Regent St., Fredericton NB E3B 3X6
Tel: 506-459-7852; *Fax:* 506-455-9300
Toll-Free: 877-544-7852
e-mail: ldanb_taanb@nb.aibn.com
URL: www.nald.ca/ldanb
Partricia Kirby, President
Fabienne McKay, Vice President, Administration

Learning Disabilities Association of Newfoundland & Labrador Inc. (LDANL)
The Board of Trade Bldg., #204, 66 Kenmount Rd., St. John's NL A1B 3V7
Tel: 709-753-1445; *Fax:* 709-753-4747
e-mail: ldanl@nl.rogers.com
URL: www.nald.ca/ldanl
Lynn Green, President
David Earle, Treasurer
Heather Churchill, Coordinator, Projects

Learning Disabilities Association of Nova Scotia (LDANS) / Troubles d'apprentissage - Association de la Nouvelle-Écosse
#601, 46 Portland St., Dartmouth NS B2Y 1H4
Tel: 902-423-2850; *Fax:* 902-423-2834
Toll-Free: 877-238-5322
e-mail: info@ldans.ca
URL: www.ldans.ca
Rachel Perrier, Executive Director
Krista McNamara, Administrative Coordinator

Learning Disabilities Association of Ontario (LDAO) / Troubles d'apprentissage - Association de l'Ontario
Box 39, #1004, 365 Bloor St. East, Toronto ON M4W 3L4
Tel: 416-929-4311; *Fax:* 416-929-3905
Toll-Free: 877-238-5322
e-mail: resource@ldao.ca
URL: www.ldao.ca
Maggie Wygant, Executive Director

Learning Disabilities Association of Prince Edward Island (LADPEI)
#149, 40 Enman Cres., Charlottetown PE C1E 1E6
Tel: 902-894-5032
e-mail: ldapei@eastlink.ca
URL: www.ldapei.ca
Affiliation(s): Learning Disabilities Association of Canada (LDAC)
Lori McCarthy, Executive Director

Learning Disabilities Association of Saskatchewan (LDAS) / Troubles d'apprentissage - Association de la Saskatchewan
3 - 701 2nd Ave. N, Saskatoon SK S7K 2C9
Tel: 306-652-4114; *Fax:* 306-652-3220
e-mail: reception@ldas.org
URL: www.ldas.org
Dale Rempel, Provincial Executive Director

Learning Disabilities Association of The Northwest Territories (LDA-NWT)
PO Box 242, 4901 - 48th St., Yellowknife NT X1A 2N2
Tel: 867-873-6378; *Fax:* 867-873-6378
e-mail: lda-nwt@arcticdata.ca
URL: www.nald.ca/ldanwt.htm

Learning Disabilities Association of Yukon Territory (LDAY)
1154C - 1 Ave., Whitehorse YT Y1A 1A7
Tel: 867-668-5167; *Fax:* 867-668-6504
e-mail: joel.macht@klondiker.com
URL: www.nald.ca/lday.htm
Joel Macht, Executive Director
Anne King, President

Learning Enrichment Foundation (LEF)
116 Industry St., Toronto ON M6M 4L8
Tel: 416-769-0830; *Fax:* 416-769-9912
e-mail: info@lefca.org
URL: www.lefca.org
Fergy Brown, President
Ed Lamoureux, Vice-President
Kathleen Macdonald, Secretary

Manitoba Association of Parent Councils (MAPC)
#1005, 401 York Ave., Winnipeg MB R3C 0P8
Tel: 204-956-1770; *Fax:* 204-948-2855
Toll-Free: 877-290-4702
e-mail: mapc1@mts.net
URL: www.mapc.mb.ca
Naomi Kruse, Administrative Officer

Manitoba Association of School Business Officials (MASBO)
375 Jefferson Avenue, Winnipeg MB R2V 0N3
Tel: 204-254-7570; *Fax:* 204-254-3606
e-mail: masbo@mts.net
URL: www.masbo.ca
Ede Fast, Executive Director

Manitoba Association of School Superintendents (MASS)
375 Jefferson Ave., Winnipeg MB R2V 0N3
Tel: 204-487-7972; *Fax:* 204-487-7974
e-mail: coralie.bryant@7oaks.org
URL: www.mass.mb.ca
Affiliation(s): Canadian Association of School Administrators
Coralie Bryant, Executive Director

Manitoba Association of School Trustees (MAST)
191 Provencher Blvd., Winnipeg MB R2H 0G4
Tel: 204-233-1595; *Fax:* 204-231-1356
Toll-Free: 800-262-8836
URL: www.mast.mb.ca
Carolyn Duhamel, Executive Director
Heather Demetrioff, Associate Director

Manitoba Federation of Independent Schools Inc. (MFIS)
630 Westminster Ave., Winnipeg MB R3C 3S1
Tel: 204-783-4481; *Fax:* 204-774-5534
URL: www.mfis.ca
Susan Eberhard, Executive Director
Joe McLellan, President

Manitoba Teachers' Society (MTS)
McMaster House, 191 Harcourt St., Winnipeg MB R3J 3H2
Tel: 204-888-7961; *Fax:* 204-831-0877
Toll-Free: 800-262-8803
URL: www.mbteach.org
Pat Isaak, President

Mensa Canada Society / La Société Mensa Canada
PO Box 1570, Kingston ON K7L 5C8
Tel: 613-547-0824; *Fax:* 613-531-0626
e-mail: mensa@eventsmgt.com
URL: www.canada.mensa.org

National Christian School Association
PO Box 26005, Saskatoon SK S7K 8C1
Tel: 306-280-9991
e-mail: lbrunelle@aceministries.com
URL: www.aisca.ab.ca/associations.htm
Affiliation(s): Federation of Independent Schools in Canada
Lou Brunelle, President

National Educational Association of Disabled Students (NEADS) / Association nationale des étudiant(e)s handicapé(e)s au niveau postsecondaire
Carleton University, Rm. 426, Unicentre, 1125 Colonel By Dr., Ottawa ON K1S 5B6
Tel: 613-380-8065; *Fax:* 613-369-4391
Toll-Free: 877-670-1256
e-mail: info@neads.ca
URL: www.neads.ca
Affiliation(s): Association québécoise des étudiant(e)s handicapé(e)s au post-secondaire; Council of Canadians with Disabilites
Frank Smith, National Coordinator

New Brunswick Federation of Home & School Associations, Inc. (NBFHSA)
#4, 618 Queen St., Fredericton NB E3B 1C2
Tel: 506-451-6247
e-mail: homeandschool.nb.aibn.com
URL: www.nbhomeandschool.org
Cynthia Richards, President
Vern Garnett, 1st Vice President

New Brunswick Teachers' Federation (Ind.) (NBTF) / Fédération des enseignants du Nouveau-Brunswick (FENB)
PO Box 1535, 650 Montgomery St., Fredericton NB E3B 5G2
Tel: 506-452-8921; *Fax:* 506-453-9795
URL: www.nbta.ca
Bob Fitzpatrick, Executive Director

Newfoundland & Labrador School Boards' Association (NLSBA)
40 Strawberry Marsh Rd., St. John's NL A1B 2V5
Tel: 709-722-7171; *Fax:* 709-722-8214
e-mail: brendapinto@schoolboardsnl.ca
URL: www.schoolboardsnl.ca
Brian Shortall, Executive Director
Brenda Pinto, Executive Assistant
Wayne Noseworthy, Director, Labour Relations

Newfoundland & Labrador Teachers' Association (NLTA) / Association des enseignants de Terre-Neuve
3 Kenmount Rd., St. John's NL A1B 1W1
Tel: 709-726-3223; *Fax:* 709-726-4302
Toll-Free: 800-563-3599
e-mail: mail@nlta.nl.ca
URL: www.nlta.nl.ca
Hancock Hancock, Executive Director
Sean Noah, President
Lily Cole, Vice-President
Jim Fox, Treasurer

Northwest Territories Teachers' Association (NWTTA)
PO Box 2340, 5018 - 48 St., Yellowknife NT X1A 2P7
Tel: 867-873-8501; *Fax:* 867-873-2366
e-mail: nwtta@nwtta.nt.ca
URL: www.nwtta.nt.ca
David Reid, President

Nova Scotia Federation of Home & School Associations (NSFHSA)
3770 Kempt Rd., Halifax NS B3K 4X8
Tel: 902-656-2378; *Fax:* 902-656-2601
Toll-Free: 800-214-8373
e-mail: president@nsfhsa.org
URL: www.nsfhsa.org

Janet Walsh, President

Nova Scotia School Boards Association (NSSBA) / Association des conseils scolaires de la Nouvelle-Écosse
95 Victoria Rd., Dartmouth NS B3A 1V2
Tel: 902-491-2888; *Fax:* 902-429-7405
e-mail: cnass@nssba.ednet.ns.ca
URL: www.nssba.ednet.ns.ca

Ken Meech, Executive Director
Ron Marks, President
Wanda Broome, Treasurer

Nova Scotia Teachers Union (NSTU) / Syndicat des enseignants de la Nouvelle-Écosse
Dr. Tom Parker Bldg., 3106 Joseph Howe Dr., Halifax NS B3L 4L7
Tel: 902-477-5621; *Fax:* 902-477-3517
Toll-Free: 800-565-6788
e-mail: nstu@nstu.ca; library@nstu.ca
URL: www.nstu.ca

Affiliation(s): Canadian Teachers' Federation
Mary-Lou Donnelly, President

Nunavut Teachers Association (NTA)
PO Box 2458, Iqaluit NU X0A 0H0
Tel: 867-979-0750; *Fax:* 867-979-0780
e-mail: piadmin@ntanu.ca
URL: www.ntanu.ca

Robin Langill, President
Emile Hatch, Executive Director

Ontario Alliance of Christian Schools (OACS)
790 Shaver Rd., Ancaster ON L9G 3K9
Tel: 905-648-2100; *Fax:* 905-648-2110
e-mail: oacs@oacs.org
URL: www.oacs.org

Affiliation(s): Christian Schools International; Christian Schools Canada
Adrian Guldemond, B.A., M.A., M.E, Executive Director

Ontario Association of Career Colleges (OACC)
PO Box 340, #2, 155 Lynden Rd., Brantford ON N3T 5N3
Tel: 519-752-2124; *Fax:* 519-752-3649
e-mail: paulkitchin@oacc.on.ca
URL: www.oacc.on.ca

Paul Kitchin, Executive Director
Don Thibert, President
Peter Dykstra, Vice-President & Director, Finance

Ontario Association of Deans of Education (OADE)
#1100, 180 Dundas St. West, Toronto ON M5G 1Z8
Tel: 416-979-2165; *Fax:* 416-979-8635
URL: oade.cou.on.ca

Affiliation(s): Council of Ontario Universities
Josée Martel, Contact

Ontario Association of School Business Officials (OASBO)
#207, 144 Main St. North, Markham ON L3P 5T3
Tel: 905-209-9704; *Fax:* 905-209-9705
e-mail: office@oasbo.org
URL: www.oasbo.org

Bill Blackie, Executive Director

Ontario Catholic School Trustees' Association (OCSTA)
PO Box 2064, #1804, 20 Eglinton Ave. West, Toronto ON M4R 1K8
Tel: 416-932-9460; *Fax:* 416-932-9459
e-mail: ocsta@ocsta.on.ca
URL: www.ocsta.on.ca

Affiliation(s): Canadian Catholic School Trustees Association
John Stunt, Executive Director

Ontario Confederation of University Faculty Associations (OCUFA) / Union des associations des professeurs des universités de l'Ontario
#300, 83 Yonge St., Toronto ON M5C 1S8
Tel: 416-979-2117; *Fax:* 416-593-5607
e-mail: ocufa@ocufa.on.ca
URL: www.ocufa.on.ca

Mark Langer, President
Constance Adamson, Vice-President
Henry Mandelbaum, Executive Director
Mark Rosenfeld, Associate Executive Director, Research & Communications
Glen Copplestone, Treasurer

Ontario Council for University Lifelong Learning
c/o Office of Teaching Support Services, 75 University Ave. West, Waterloo ON N2L 3C5
Tel: 519-661-2111; *Fax:* 519-884-6063
e-mail: cnkelly@uwaterloo.ca
URL: www.ocull.ca

Affiliation(s): Council of Ontario Universities
Cathy Newell Kelly, President

Ontario Council on Graduate Studies (OCGS) / Conseil ontarien des études supérieures
#1100, 180 Dundas St. West, Toronto ON M5G 1Z8
Tel: 416-979-2165; *Fax:* 416-595-7392
e-mail: ocgs@cou.on.ca
URL: ocgs.cou.on.ca/

David Leyton-Brown, Executive Director
Kay Panesar, Contact

Ontario English Catholic Teachers' Association (CLC) (OECTA)
#400, 65 St. Clair Ave. East, Toronto ON M4T 2Y8
Tel: 416-925-2493; *Fax:* 416-925-7764
Toll-Free: 800-268-7230
e-mail: a.oconnor@oecta.on.ca
URL: www.oecta.on.ca

Affiliation(s): Ontario Teachers' Federation
Greg Pollock, General Secretary
Donna Marie Kennedy, President

Ontario Federation of Home & School Associations Inc. (OFHSA)
51 Stuart St., Hamilton ON L8L 1B5
Tel: 905-308-9563; *Fax:* 905-308-7935
e-mail: info@ofhsa.on.ca
URL: www.ofhsa.on.ca

Michele McNabb, President
Lee Gowers, Exec. Vice-President

Ontario Federation of Independent Schools (OFIS)
2199 Regency Terrace, Ottawa ON K2C 1H2
Tel: 613-596-4013; *Fax:* 613-596-4971
e-mail: info@ofis.ca
URL: www.ofis.ca

Elaine Hopkins, Executive Director

Ontario Principals' Council (OPC)
180 Dundas St. West, 25th Fl., Toronto ON M5G 1Z8
Tel: 416-322-6600; *Fax:* 416-322-6618
Toll-Free: 800-701-2362
e-mail: admin@principals.on.ca
URL: www.principals.on.ca

Mike Benson, Executive Director
Lisa Vincent, President

Ontario Public School Boards Association (OPSBA)
439 University Ave., Toronto ON M5G 1Y8
Tel: 416-340-2540; *Fax:* 416-340-7571
e-mail: webmaster@opsba.org
URL: www.opsba.org

Colleen Schenk, President
Gail Anderson, Executive Director
Florenda Tingle, Executive Coordinator

Ontario Secondary School Teachers' Federation (OSSTF) / Fédération des enseignants des écoles secondaires de l'Ontario (FEESO)
60 Mobile Dr., Toronto ON M4A 2P3
Tel: 416-751-8300
Toll-Free: 800-267-7867
URL: www.osstf.on.ca

Ken Coran, President
Paul Elliott, Vice-President
Sandra Sahli, Vice-President
Wendy Bolt, General Secretary
Earl Burt, Treasurer

Ontario Society for Education Through Art (OSEA)
c/o Membership Secretary, 37 Hopewell Ave., Toronto ON M4K 3M8
URL: www.osea.on.ca

Jane Dewar, Vice President
Maira Herenberg, President

Ontario Teachers' Federation (OTF) / Fédération des enseignantes et des enseignants de l'Ontario (FEO)
#200, 1300 Yonge St., Toronto ON M4T 1X3
Tel: 416-966-3424; *Fax:* 416-966-5450
Toll-Free: 800-268-7061
URL: www.otffeo.on.ca

Affiliation(s): Association des enseignantes et des enseignants franco-ontariens; Elementary Teachers' Federation of Ontario; Ontario English Catholic Teachers' Association; Ontario Secondary School Teachers' Federation
Reno Melatti, President
Rhonda Kimberley-Young, Sec.-Treas.

ORT Canada
#208, 5165, rue Sherbrooke ouest, Montréal QC H4A 1T6
Tel: 514-481-2787; *Fax:* 514-481-4119
e-mail: info@ortmontreal.org
URL: www.ortmontreal.org

ORT Canada
#200, 530 Wilson Ave., Toronto ON M3H 5Y9
Tel: 416-787-0339; *Fax:* 416-787-9420
Toll-Free: 866-991-3045
e-mail: info@ort-toronto.org
URL: www.ort-toronto.com

Affiliation(s): World ORT Union
Sandra Chapnik, President
Lindy Meshwork, Executive Director

Parent Co-operative Preschools International (PCPI)
8725 Westport Dr., Niagara Falls ON L2H 0A2
Tel: 905-374-6605; *Fax:* 905-374-0473
URL: preschools.coop

Parents partenaires en éducation (PPE)
#B-150, 2445, boul St-Laurent, Ottawa ON K1G 6C3
Tél: 613-741-8846; *Téléc:* 613-741-7322
Ligne sans frais: 800-342-0663
Courriel: info@reseauppe.ca
URL: www.reseauppe.ca

Geneviève Folliet, Présidente

Prince Edward Island Home & School Federation Inc. (PEIHSF)
PO Box 1012, 40 Enman Cres., Charlottetown PE C1A 7M4
Tel: 902-620-3186; *Fax:* 902-620-3187
Toll-Free: 800-916-0664
e-mail: peihsf@edu.pe.ca
URL: www.edu.pe.ca/peihsf/

Wendy MacDonald, President
Shirley Jay, Executive Director

Prince Edward Island School Trustees Association (PEISTA)
e-mail: trusteespei@yahoo.ca
URL: trusteespei.blogspot.com

Marie Dionne-Sullivan, President

Prince Edward Island Teachers' Federation (PEITF) / Fédération des enseignants de l'Ile-du-Prince-Édouard
PO Box 6000, 24 Glen Stewart Dr., Charlottetown PE C1A 8B4
Tel: 902-569-4157; *Fax:* 902-569-3682
Toll-Free: 800-903-4157
URL: www.peitf.com

Seana Evans-Renaud, President
Myles Ellis, General Secretary

Québec Association for Adult Learning Inc. (QAAL) / Association Québécoise pour l'éducation des adultes
#LB614-3, 1455 Maisonneuve blvd. ouest, Montréal QC H3G 1M8
Tel: 514-848-2424; *Fax:* 514-848-4520
e-mail: qaal@alcor.concordia.ca
URL: doe.concordia.ca/qaal/

Affiliation(s): Concordia University; McGill University
Kelly Howarth, President
Anna-Maria Dumont, Vice President
Mario Pasteris, Treasurer

Québec Association of Independent Schools (QAIS) / Association des écoles privées du Québec
PO Box 398, Stn. Snowdon, Montréal QC H3X 3T6
Tel: 514-483-6111; *Fax:* 514-483-0865
Toll-Free: 866-909-6111
e-mail: qais@qc.aibn.com
URL: www.qais.qc.ca

Elizabeth Therrien-Scanlan, Executive Director

Québec English School Boards Association (QESBA) / Association des commissions scolaires anglophones du Québec (ACSAQ)
#515, 1410, rue Stanley, Montréal QC H3A 1P8
Tel: 514-849-5900; *Fax:* 514-849-9228
Toll-Free: 877-512-7522
e-mail: qesba@qesba.qc.ca
URL: www.qesba.qc.ca

David Birnbaum, Executive Director

Québec Federation of Home & School Associations Inc. (QFHSA) / Fédération des associations foyer-école du Québec Inc.
#560, 3285, boul Cavendish, Montréal QC H4B 2L9
Tel: 514-481-5619; *Fax:* 514-481-5610
Toll-Free: 888-808-5619
e-mail: info@qfhsa.org
URL: www.qfhsa.org
Affiliation(s): Center for Literacy
Debi Brown, President
Beverlee Bishundayal, Secretary

Le Réseau d'enseignement francophone à distance du Canada (REFAD)
CP 47542, Succ. Plateau Mont-Royal, Montréal QC H2H 2S8
Tél: 514-284-9109; *Téléc:* 514-284-9363
Courriel: refad@sympatico.ca
URL: www.refad.ca
Caroll-Ann Keating, Présidente
Alain Langlois, Directeur général

The Retired Teachers of Ontario (RTO) / Les Enseignants et enseignantes retraités de l'Ontario (ERO)
#300, 18 Spadina Rd., Toronto ON M5R 2S7
Tel: 416-962-9463; *Fax:* 416-962-1061
Toll-Free: 800-361-9888
e-mail: info@rto-ero.org
URL: www.rto-ero.org
Howard Braithwaite, Executive Director

Saskatchewan Association for Multicultural Education (SAME)
144 Marsh Cres., Regina SK S4S 5J7
Tel: 306-780-9428
e-mail: same@sasktel.net
URL: www.same.ca
Rhonda Rosenberg, Executive Director

Saskatchewan Association of Historical High Schools (SAHHS)
c/o Luther College High School, 1500 Royal St., Regina SK S4T 6G3
Tel: 306-791-9150; *Fax:* 306-359-6962
URL: www.luthercollege.edu
Berbel Knoll, Principal

Saskatchewan Association of School Councils (SASC)
#243, 221 Cumberland Ave. North, Saskatoon SK S7N 1M3
Tel: 306-955-5723; *Fax:* 306-955-5723
Toll-Free: 877-217-7272
e-mail: sara@suns.ca
URL: www.schoolcouncils.com
Sarah Suns, President
Joy Bastness, Executive Director

Saskatchewan School Boards Association (SSBA)
#400, 2222 - 13th Ave., Regina SK S4P 3M7
Tel: 306-569-0750; *Fax:* 306-352-9633
e-mail: admin@saskschoolboards.ca
URL: www.saskschoolboards.ca
Ernie Cychmistruk, Executive Director
Patti Blackburn, Administrative Officer
Andrea Ashton, Communications Officer
Barry Bashutski, Senior Director, Education Services

Saskatchewan Teachers' Federation (STF) / Fédération des enseignants et des enseignantes de la Saskatchewan
2317 Arlington Ave., Saskatoon SK S7J 2H8
Tel: 306-373-1660; *Fax:* 306-374-1122
Toll-Free: 800-667-7762
e-mail: stf@stf.sk.ca
URL: www.stf.sk.ca
Heather Vermeersch, President
Lyle Vinish, General Secretary

SchoolNet / Rescol canadien
155 Queen St. West, 4th Fl., Ottawa ON K1A 0H5
Tel: 613-993-5452; *Fax:* 613-941-1296
Toll-Free: 800-575-9200
e-mail: schoolnet@ic.gc.ca
URL: www.schoolnet.ca (not working)
Pierre Gendron, Executive Director
David Fransen, General Director

Skills/Compétences Canada
#205, 260, boul Saint Raymond, Gatineau QC J9A 3G7
Tel: 819-771-7545; *Fax:* 819-771-5575
Toll-Free: 877-754-5226
e-mail: skillscanada@skillscanada.com
URL: www.skillscanada.com
Shaun Thorson, Executive Director
Terry Cooke, President
Cynthia Faubert, Communications/Marketing Officer

Society for Educational Visits & Exchanges in Canada (SEVEC) / Société éducative de visites et d'échanges au Canada
300-950 Gladstone Ave., Ottawa ON K1Y 3E6
Tel: 613-727-3832; *Fax:* 613-727-3831
Toll-Free: 800-387-3832
e-mail: info@sevec.ca
URL: www.sevec.ca
Laurie A. Clement, Executive Director
Sandy Dobson, Director, Finance & Administration
Michele Ténière, Director, Marketing & Communications

Society for Educational Visits & Exchanges in Canada
#301, 51, rue des Jardins, Québec QC G1R 4L6
Tél: 418-648-3588; *Téléc:* 418-648-4288
Ligne sans frais: 800-38S-EVEC
Courriel: nbouchar@sevec.ca
URL: www.sevec.ca

Society for Quality Education (SQE)
57 Twyford Rd., Toronto ON M9A 1W5
Tel: 416-231-7247; *Fax:* 416-237-0108
Toll-Free: 888-856-5535
e-mail: info@societyforqualityeducation.org
URL: www.societyforqualityeducation.org
Doretta Wilson, Executive Director
Malkin Dare, President

Society for the Promotion of the Teaching of English as a Second Language in Quebec (SPEAQ) / Société pour la promotion de l'enseignement de l'anglais, langue seconde, au Québec
#309, 7400, boul Saint-Laurent, Montréal QC H2R 2Y1
Tel: 514-271-3700; *Fax:* 514-271-4587
e-mail: speaq@speaq.qc.ca
URL: www.speaq.qc.ca
Affiliation(s): Teachers of English to Speakers of Other Languages, Inc; Canadian Association of Second Language Teachers; Society for Educational Visits & Exchanges in Canada
Micheline Schinck, President
Monique Mainella, Vice President

TESL Canada Federation (TESL Canada)
#408, 4370 Dominion St., Burnaby BC V5G 4L7
Tel: 604-298-0312; *Fax:* 604-298-0372
Toll-Free: 800-393-9199
e-mail: admin@tesl.ca
URL: www.tesl.ca
Affiliation(s): Teachers of English to Speakers of Other Languages (TESOL); Société pour la promotion de l'enseignement de l'anglais (langue seconde) au Québec
Louise Aerts, Executive Director
Jennifer Pearson Terell, President
Sandie Kouritzin, Secretary

United World Colleges
Lester B. Pearson College of the Pacific, 650 Pearson College Dr., Victoria BC V9C 4H7
Tel: 250-391-2411; *Fax:* 250-391-2412
e-mail: admin@pearsoncollege.ca
URL: www.pearsoncollege.ca
David B. Hawley, Director

Yukon Teachers' Association (YTA) / Association des enseignantes et des enseignants du Yukon
2064 - 2 Ave., Whitehorse YT Y1A 1A9
Tel: 867-668-6777; *Fax:* 867-667-4324
e-mail: admin@yta.yk.ca
URL: www.yta.yk.ca
Dennis Rankin, Executive Director
Jim Tredger, President
Katherine Mackwood, Treasurer

Electronics & Electricity

Canadian Electrical Contractors Association (CECA) / Association canadienne des entrepreneurs électriciens (ACEE)
#460, 170 Attwell Dr., Toronto ON M9W 5Z5
Tel: 416-675-3226; *Fax:* 416-675-7736
Toll-Free: 800-387-3226
e-mail: ceca@ceca.org
URL: www.ceca.org/
Rick Brodhurst, President
Garry Fitzpatrick, Treasurer
Eryl M. Roberts, Executive Secretary

Canadian Electrical Manufacturers Representatives Association (CEMRA)
#300, 180 Attwell Dr., Toronto ON M9W 6A9
Tel: 905-602-8877; *Fax:* 416-679-9234
e-mail: info@electrofed.com
URL: www.electrofed.com
Milos Janick, President & CEO

Canadian Electronic & Appliance Service Association (CEASA) / Organisation canadienne de service d'appareils domestiques
#200, 5800 Explorer Dr., Mississauga ON L4W 5K9
Tel: 905-602-8877; *Fax:* 905-602-5686
Toll-Free: 866-602-8877
e-mail: info@electrofed.com
URL: www.electrofed.com/councils/CEASA/
Milos Jancik, President & CEO

Conseil Canadien des Électrotechnologies (CCE) / Canadian Council on Electrotechnologies (CCE)
600, av de la Montagne, Shawinigan QC G9N 7N5
Tél: 819-539-1560; *Téléc:* 819-539-1558
Richard Clayton, President-CCE
Michael P. Dudar, Vice Président-CCE

Consumer Electronics Marketers of Canada: A Division of Electro-Federation Canada (CEMC)
#200, 5800 Explorer Dr., Mississauga ON L4W 5K9
Tel: 905-602-8877; *Fax:* 905-602-5686
URL: www.electrofed.com/councils/CEMC/
Sharon Borda, Manager

Corporation des maîtres électriciens du Québec (CMEQ) / Corporation of Master Electricians of Québec
5925, boul Décarie, Montréal QC H3W 3C9
Tél: 514-738-2184; *Téléc:* 514-738-2192
Ligne sans frais: 800-361-9061
Courriel: webmestre@cmeq.org
URL: www.cmeq.org
Johanne Pulford, Directrice générale

Electrical Contractors Association of Alberta (ECAA)
11235 - 120 St., Edmonton AB T5G 2X9
Tel: 780-451-2412; *Fax:* 780-455-9815
Toll-Free: 800-252-9375
e-mail: ecaa@ecaa.ab.ca
URL: www.ecaa.ab.ca
Sheri McLean, Executive Director

Electrical Contractors Association of BC (ECA-BC)
#201, 3989 Henning Dr., Burnaby BC V5C 6N5
Tel: 604-294-4123; *Fax:* 604-294-4120
e-mail: eca@eca.bc.ca
URL: www.eca.bc.ca
Affiliation(s): National Electrical Contractors Association
Deborah Cahill, Executive Director

Electrical Contractors Association of New Brunswick Inc. (ECANB)
PO Box 322, Fredericton NB E3B 4Y9
Tel: 506-452-7627; *Fax:* 506-452-1786
e-mail: dwe@eca.nb.ca
URL: www.eca.nb.ca
Affiliation(s): Construction Association of New Brunswick Inc.; Canadian Construction Association
David Ellis, Executive Director

Electrical Contractors Association of Ontario (ECAO)
#460, 170 Attwell Dr., Toronto ON M9W 5Z5
Tel: 416-675-3226; *Fax:* 416-675-7736
Toll-Free: 800-387-3226
e-mail: ecao@ecao.org
URL: www.ecao.org
Affiliation(s): 13 Area Electrical Contractors Associations (ECAs); Council of Ontario Construction Associations; Provincial Advisory Committee for the Construction & Maintenance Electrician; Electrical Contractor Registration Agency (ECRA) for Master Electrician & Electrical Contractor Licensing
Fred Black, President
Bill McKee, Treasurer
Eryl M. Roberts, Executive Vice-President, Labour Relations
Lucy Roberts, Contact, Public Relations & Member Services

Electrical Contractors Association of Saskatchewan
Construction house, 1939 Elphinstone St., Regina SK S4T 3N3
Tel: 306-525-0171; *Fax:* 306-347-8595
e-mail: michaelf@scaonline.ca
URL: www.ecas.ca

Affiliation(s): Canadian Electrical Contractors Association; National Electrical Contractors Association; Saskatoon Electrical Contractors Association; Saskatchewan Construction Association; Electrical Contractors Association of BC; Saskatchewan Construction Safety Association; Electrical Contractors Association of Alberta; Electrical Contractors Association of Ontario
Michael Fougere, Executive Director
Rob Istace, President
John Kirby, Treasurer

Electro-Federation Canada Inc. (EFC)
#200, 5800 Explorer Dr., Mississauga ON L4W 5K9
Tel: 905-602-8877; *Fax:* 905-602-5686
Toll-Free: 866-602-8877
e-mail: info@electrofed.com
URL: www.electrofed.com

Milos Jancik, President/CEO
Ken Frankum, Chair
Harald Henze, Treasurer
Larry Moore, Vice-President, Consumer Councils
Joseph Neu, Vice-President, Engineering, Codes & Standards

Institute of Electrical & Electronics Engineers Inc. - Canada
PO Box 63005, Stn. Uuniversity PO, Shoppers Drug Mart #742, 102 Plaza Dr., Dundas ON L9H 4H0
Tel: 905-628-9554; *Fax:* 905-628-9554
e-mail: admin@ieee.ca
URL: www.ieee.ca

Affiliation(s): The Engineering Institute of Canada
Cathie Lowell, IEEE Canada Administrator
Bob Hanna, President
Vijay Sood, Secretary
Rob Anderson, Treasurer

Manitoba Electrical League Inc.
#104, 1780 Wellington Ave., Winnipeg MB R3H 1B3
Tel: 204-783-4125; *Fax:* 204-783-4216
e-mail: office@meleague.net
URL: www.meleague.net

Dave Foreman, General Manager

Ontario Electrical League (OEL)
#300, 180 Attwell Dr., Etobicoke ON M9W 6A9
Tel: 905-238-1382; *Fax:* 905-238-1420
e-mail: communications@oel.org
URL: www.oel.org

Mary Ingram-Haigh, President
Sheila Sage, Manager, Operations
Cynthia Kenth, Contact, Communications

Emergency Response

Canadian Avalanche Association (CAA)
PO Box 2759, 110 MacKenzie Ave., Revelstoke BC V0E 2S0
Tel: 250-837-2435; *Fax:* 250-837-4624
Toll-Free: 800-667-1105
e-mail: info@avalanche.ca
URL: www.avalanche.ca

Affiliation(s): Alpine Club of Canada; Canadian West Ski Areas; Association of Canadian Mountain Guides
Steve Blake, President
John Hetherington, Secretary Treasurer
Clair Israelson, Executive Director

Canadian Fallen Firefighters Foundation / Fondation canadienne des pompiers morts en service
#200, 440 Laurier Ave. W., Ottawa ON K1R 7X6
Tel: 613-786-3024; *Fax:* 613-782-2228
e-mail: info@cfff.ca
URL: www.cfff.ca

Affiliation(s): Canadian Fire Service
Robert Kirkpatrick, President
Douglas Wylie, 1st Vice-President
Mike McKenna, 2nd Vice-President
Doug Lock, Treasurer

The Canadian Red Cross Society (CRCS) / La Société canadienne de la Croix-Rouge
#300, 170 Metcalfe, Ottawa ON K2P 2P2
Tel: 613-740-1900; *Fax:* 613-740-1911
e-mail: feedback@redcross.ca
URL: www.redcross.ca

Affiliation(s): International Committee of the Red Cross; International Federation of Red Cross & Red Crescent Societies (Geneva)
Conrad Sauvé, Secretary General & CEO
Mario Dionne, President
Alan Dean, Vice-President
Edward Tanaka, Vice-President

Civil Air Search & Rescue Association (CASARA)
National Office, PO Box 183, Stn. Westwin, Winnipeg MB R3J 3Y5
e-mail: jkelly@casaranational.ca
URL: www.casara.ca

John Davidson, President
John Kelly, National Administrator
Ted Sherback, Alberta
Chuck Pachal, British Columbia
Dwight Ough, New Brunswick
Brian Bishop, Newfoundland/Labrador
Jim Tennant, NWT
Phil Chatterton, Nova Scotia
Orin Durey, Nunavut
Mike Daniels, Ontario
Doug MacDonald, PEI
Louis Dufresne, Québec
Frank Schuurmans, Saskatchewan
Ian Robertson, Yukon

Corporation des services d'ambulance du Québec
#205, 455, rue Marais, Vanier QC G1M 3A2
Tél: 418-681-4448; *Téléc:* 418-681-4667
URL: www.csaq.org/fr

Affiliation(s): Association des hôpitaux du Québec

Lifesaving Society
PO Box 8065, Stn. A, St. John's NL A1B 3M9
Tel: 709-576-1953; *Fax:* 709-738-1475
e-mail: lifeguard@nl.rogers.com
URL: lifesaving.nl.ca

Lifesaving Society / Société de sauvetage
287 McArthur Ave., Ottawa ON K1L 6P3
Tel: 613-746-5694; *Fax:* 613-746-9929
e-mail: experts@lifesaving.ca
URL: www.lifesaving.ca

Affiliation(s): Canadian Armed Forces; Canadian Parks & Recreation Association; Canadian Red Cross Society; L'Institut Maritime du Québec; Professional Association of Diving Instructors Canada; Royal Canadian Mounted Police; St. John Ambulance; Swimming Canada; YMCA Canada
Alain Rabeau, President
Heather Barnhouse, Corporate Secretary

Lifesaving Society
11759 Groat Rd., Edmonton AB T5M 3K6
Tel: 780-415-1755; *Fax:* 780-427-9334
e-mail: experts@lifesaving.org
URL: www.lifesaving.org

Lifesaving Society
#112, 3989 Henning Dr., Burnaby BC V5C 6N5
Tel: 604-299-5450; *Fax:* 604-299-5795
e-mail: info@lifesaving.bc.ca
URL: www.lifesaving.bc.ca

Lifesaving Society
#504, 138 Portage Ave. East, Winnipeg MB R3C 0A1
Tel: 204-956-2124; *Fax:* 204-944-8546
e-mail: aquatics@lifesaving.mb.ca
URL: www.lifesaving.mb.ca

Lifesaving Society
#205, 440 Wilsey Rd., Fredericton NB E3B 7G5
Tel: 506-455-5762; *Fax:* 506-450-7946
e-mail: lifesave@nb.aibn.com
URL: www.lifesavingnb.ca

Lifesaving Society
5516 Spring Garden Rd., 4th Fl., Halifax NS B3J 1G6
Tel: 902-425-5450; *Fax:* 902-425-5606
e-mail: experts@lifesavingsociety.ns.ca
URL: www.lifesavingsociety.ns.ca

Lifesaving Society
400 Consumers Rd., Toronto ON M2J 1P8
Tel: 416-490-8844; *Fax:* 416-490-8766
e-mail: experts@lifeguarding.com
URL: www.lifesavingsociety.com

Lifesaving Society
PO Box 2411, Charlottetown PE C1A 8C1
Tel: 902-368-7757; *Fax:* 902-368-7757
e-mail: pei.lifesaving@islandtelecom.com

Lifesaving Society
CP 1000, Succ. M, 4545, av Pierre-de-Coubertin, Montréal QC H1V 3R2
Tél: 514-252-3100; *Téléc:* 514-254-6232
Ligne sans frais: 800-265-3093
Courriel: alerte@sauvetage.qc.ca
URL: www.sauvetage.qc.ca

Lifesaving Society
2224 Smith St., Regina SK S4P 2P4
Tel: 306-780-9255; *Fax:* 306-780-9498
e-mail: lifesaving@sasktel.net
URL: www.lifesavingsociety.sk.ca

Occupational First Aid Attendants Association of British Columbia (OFAAA)
#108, 2323 Boundary Rd., Vancouver BC V5M 4V8
Tel: 604-294-0244; *Fax:* 604-294-0289
Toll-Free: 800-667-4566
e-mail: ofaaa@ofaaa.bc.ca
URL: www.ofaaa.bc.ca

Russ Brown, Vice-President
Adrian Metcalf, Treasurer
Irvin Schonbrun, Secretary
Laural Martin, Administrator
Allan Zdunic, President

REACT Canada Inc.
32 The Queensway North, Keswick ON L4P 1E3
Tel: 905-476-5231
e-mail: react@react-canada.org
URL: www.react-canada.org

Affiliation(s): REACT International Inc.; Salvation Army; Red Cross; American Radio Relay League
Ronald W. McCracken, Director

St. John Ambulance / Ambulance Saint-Jean
#400, 1900 City Park Dr., Ottawa ON K1J 1A3
Tel: 613-236-7461; *Fax:* 613-236-2425
e-mail: nhq@sja.ca
URL: www.sja.ca

John Mah, Chancellor
Ian Bennett, CEO
Les Johnson, Director, Client Services
Jennifer Lavoie, Director, Marketing &Communications
Rob Fraser, Director, Business Development

St. John Ambulance
12304 - 118 Ave., Edmonton AB T5L 5G8
Tel: 780-452-6565; *Fax:* 780-452-2835
Toll-Free: 800-665-7114
e-mail: phq@stjohn.ab.ca
URL: www.sja.ca/Alberta

St. John Ambulance
6111 Cambie St., 2nd Fl., Vancouver BC V5Z 3B2
Tel: 604-321-2652; *Fax:* 604-321-5316
Toll-Free: 866-321-2651
e-mail: info@bc.sja.ca
URL: www.sja.ca/BCYukon

St. John Ambulance
535 Doreen St., Winnipeg MB R3G 3H5
Tel: 204-784-7000; *Fax:* 204-786-2295
Toll-Free: 800-471-7771
e-mail: info@mb.sja.ca
URL: www.sja.ca/Manitoba

St. John Ambulance
PO Box 3599, Stn. B, 200 Miles St., Fredericton NB E3A 5J8
Tel: 506-458-9129; *Fax:* 506-452-8699
Toll-Free: 800-563-9998
e-mail: stjohnnb@nbnet.nb.ca
URL: www.sja.ca/NewBrunswick

St. John Ambulance
PO Box 5489, 112 Forest Rd., St. John's NL A1C 5W4
Tel: 709-726-4200; *Fax:* 709-726-4117
Toll-Free: 800-801-0181
e-mail: sja@stjohnambulance.nf.ca
URL: www.sja.ca/NFLD

St. John Ambulance
5023 - 51st St., Yellowknife NT X1A 1S5
Tel: 867-873-5658; *Fax:* 867-920-4458
e-mail: ykadmin@nt.sja.ca
URL: www.sja.ca/NWT

St. John Ambulance
88 Slayter St., Dartmouth NS B3A 2A6
Tel: 902-463-5646; *Fax:* 902-469-9609
Toll-Free: 800-565-5056
e-mail: info@ns.sja.ca
URL: www.sja.ca/NSPEI

St. John Ambulance
#800, 15 Toronto St., Toronto ON M5C 2E3
Tel: 416-923-8411; *Fax:* 416-923-4856
Toll-Free: 800-268-7581
e-mail: info@on.sja.ca
URL: www.sja.ca/Ontario

St. John Ambulance
529, rue Jarry, 4e étage, Montréal QC H2P 1V4
Tél: 514-842-4801; *Téléc:* 514-842-4807
Ligne sans frais: 877-272-7607
Courriel: info@qc.sja.ca
URL: www.sja.ca/Quebec

St. John Ambulance
2625 - 3rd Ave., Regina SK S4T 0C8
Tel: 306-522-7226; *Fax:* 306-525-4177
Toll-Free: 888-273-0003
URL: www.sja.ca/Saskatchewan

St. John Ambulance
5 Corvus Ct., Ottawa ON K2E 7Z4
Tel: 613-722-2002; *Fax:* 613-722-7024
URL: www.sja.ca/Ottawa

St. John Ambulance
128 Copper Rd., #C, Whitehorse YT Y1W 2Z6
Tel: 867-668-5001; *Fax:* 867-668-5050
Toll-Free: 866-321-2651
e-mail: yukon@yt.sja.ca
URL: www.sja.ca/BCYukon

Employment & Human Resources

Association of Canadian Search, Employment & Staffing Services (ACSESS) / Association nationale des entreprises en recrutement et placement de personnel
#100, 2233 Argentia Rd., Mississauga ON L5N 2X7
Tel: 905-826-6869; *Fax:* 905-826-4873
Toll-Free: 888-232-4962
e-mail: acsess@acsess.org
URL: www.acsess.org
Steve Jones, CPC, National President
Amanda Curtis, CAE, Executive Director

Association of Professional Recruiters of Canada
#2210, 1081 Ambleside Dr., Ottawa ON K2B 8C8
Tel: 613-721-5957; *Fax:* 613-721-5850
e-mail: info@workplace.ca
URL: www.workplace.ca/resources/aprc_assoc.html
Nathaly Pinchuk, Executive Director
Brian Pascal, President

Canadian Association of Career Educators & Employers (CACEE) / Association canadienne des spécialistes en emploi et des employeurs (ACSEE)
#202, 720 Spadina Ave., Toronto ON M5S 2T9
Tel: 416-929-5156; *Fax:* 416-929-5256
Toll-Free: 866-922-3303
URL: www.cacee.com
Anne Markey, Executive Director
Janine Clarke, Operations Manager

Canadian Career Information Association (CCIA) / Association canadienne de documentation professionnelle (ACADOP)
205 Humber College Blvd., Toronto ON M9W 5L7
Tel: 416-675-5030
e-mail: karen.fast@humber.ca
URL: www.ccia-acadop.ca
Anna De Grauwe, Chair
Angella Nunes, Treasurer

Canadian Council of Human Resources Associations (CCHRA) / Conseil canadien des associations en ressources humaines (CCARH)
#603, 150 Metcalfe St., Ottawa ON K2P 1P1
Tel: 613-567-2477; *Fax:* 613-567-2478
Toll-Free: 866-560-1288
e-mail: info@cchra-ccarh.ca
URL: www.cchra-ccarh.ca
Merrill Brinton, CHRP, President

Human Resources Professionals Association of Ontario (HRPAO)
#1902, 2 Bloor St. West, Toronto ON M4W 3E2
Tel: 416-923-2324; *Fax:* 416-923-7264
Toll-Free: 800-387-1311
e-mail: info@hrpao.org; boardrelations@hrpao.org
URL: www.hrpao.org
William (Bill) Greenhalgh, CEO
Louise Tagliacozzo, Manager, Board Relations & Administration
Debbie Bennett, Chair

International Association for Human Resource Information Management (IHRIM)
PO Box 1086, Burlington MA 01803 USA
Toll-Free: 800-804-3983
e-mail: information@ihrim.org
URL: www.ihrim.org
Lynne Mealy, President/CEO

International Maritime Organization (IMO) / Organisation maritime internationale
4 Albert Embankment, London SE1 7SR United Kingdom
Tel: 44-20-7735-7611; *Fax:* 44-20-7587-3210
e-mail: info@imo.org
URL: www.imo.org
Lee Adamson, Manager, Public Information
Efthimios E. Mitropoulos, Secretary General

Ordre des conseillers en ressources humaines et en relations industrielles agréés du Québec (ORHRI)
#1400, 1200, av McGill Collège, Montréal QC H3B 2Y5
Tél: 514-879-1636; *Téléc:* 514-879-1722
Courriel: info@rhri.org
URL: www.orhri.org
Florent Francoeur, Executive Director

Energy

Association of Major Power Consumers in Ontario (AMPCO)
Sterling Tower, 372 Bay St., Toronto ON M5H 2W9
Tel: 416-260-0280; *Fax:* 416-260-0442
e-mail: info@ampco.org
URL: www.ampco.org
John Lemay, Chair
Adam White, President
Fareeda Heeralal, Contact

Canadian Coalition for Nuclear Responsibility (CCNR) / Regroupement pour la surveillance du nucléaire (RSN)
PO Box 236, Stn. Snowdon, Montréal QC H3X 3T4
Fax: 514-489-5118
e-mail: ccnr@web.ca
URL: www.ccnr.org
Affiliation(s): Environment Liaison Centre - International; Friends of the Earth - Canada; Canadian Peace Alliance; Abolition 2000
Gordon Edwards, President
Marc Chénier, Sec.-Treas.

Canadian Energy Research Institute (CERI)
#150, 3512 - 33 St. NW, Calgary AB T2L 2A6
Tel: 403-282-1231; *Fax:* 403-284-4181
e-mail: ceri@ceri.ca
URL: www.ceri.ca
Carol Williams, Executive Secretary
Marwan Masri, President/CEO

Canadian Fluid Power Association (CFPA) / Association canadienne d'énergie fluide
#310, 2175 Sheppard Ave. East, Toronto ON M2J 1W8
Tel: 416-499-1416; *Fax:* 416-491-1670
e-mail: info@cfpa.ca
URL: www.cfpa.ca
Carolyne Vigon, Administrator

Canadian Institute of Energy (CIE)
987 Devon Rd., North Vancouver BC V7R 1V8
Tel: 604-904-5777; *Fax:* 604-987-3073
e-mail: info@cienergy.org
URL: www.cienergy.org
Lorelei Hopkins, Administrator

Canadian Nuclear Association (CNA) / Association nucléaire canadienne
#1610, 130 Albert St., Ottawa ON K1P 5G4
Tel: 613-237-4262; *Fax:* 613-237-0989
e-mail: lindsayj@cna.ca
URL: www.cna.ca
Denise Carpenter, President/CEO
Claudia Lemieux, Director, Communications & Media Relations

Canadian Nuclear Society (CNS) / Société nucléaire canadienne (SNC)
#200, 480 University Ave., Toronto ON M5G 1V2
Tel: 416-977-7620; *Fax:* 416-977-8131
e-mail: cns-snc@on.aibn.com
URL: www.cns-snc.ca
Eric Williams, President
P. (Prabhu) Kundurpi, Secretary
J.C. (John) Luxat, Treasurer

Canadian Renewable Fuels Association (CRFA) / Association canadienne des carburants renouvelables
#605, 350 Sparks St., Ottawa ON K1R 7S8
Tel: 613-594-5528; *Fax:* 613-594-3076
URL: www.greenfuels.org
Gordon Quaiattini, President
Deborah Elson, Director, Member Relations & Industry Promotions
Debby Marandola, Director, Operations
Alison Ouellet, Director, Government Affairs

Canadian Solar Industries Association Inc. (CanSIA) / Association des industries solaires du Canada inc.
#208, 2378 Holly Lane, Ottawa ON K1V 7P1
Tel: 613-736-9077; *Fax:* 613-736-8938
Toll-Free: 866-522-6742
e-mail: info@cansia.ca
URL: www.cansia.ca
Elizabeth A. McDonald, Executive Director
Sharon Chester, Office Manager

Canadian Wind Energy Association Inc. (CanWEA) / Association canadienne d'énergie éolienne
#810, 170 Laurier Ave. West, Ottawa ON K1P 5V5
Tel: 613-234-8716; *Fax:* 613-234-5642
Toll-Free: 800-922-6932
e-mail: info@canwea.ca
URL: www.canwea.ca
Social Media: twitter.com/canwindenergy
Robert Hornung, President
Chris Forrest, Vice-President, Communications & Marketing
Sean Whittaker, Vice-President, Policy
Penelope Feather, Director, Finance
Janice Taylor, Director, Conference & Events

Energy Council of Canada / Conseil canadien de l'énergie
#608, 350 Sparks St., Ottawa ON K1R 7S8
Tel: 613-232-8239; *Fax:* 613-232-1079
e-mail: krystal.piamonte@energy.ca
URL: www.energy.ca
Murray J. Stewart, President
Brigitte Svarich, Director, Operations

Energy Probe Research Foundation (EPRF)
225 Brunswick Ave., Toronto ON M5S 2M6
Tel: 416-964-9223; *Fax:* 416-964-8239
e-mail: webadmin@eprf.ca
URL: www.eprf.ca
Affiliation(s): Energy Probe; Probe International; Environment Probe; Consumer Policy Institute; Urban Renaissance Institute; Environmental Bureau of Investigation; Three Gorges Probe; Canadian Environmental News Network
Patricia Adams, President
Lawrence Solomon, Managing Director

Planetary Association for Clean Energy, Inc. (PACE) / Société planétaire pour l'assainissement de l'énergie
#1001, 100 Bronson Ave., Ottawa ON K1R 6G8
Tel: 613-236-6265; *Fax:* 613-235-5876
e-mail: pacenet@canada.com
URL: pacenet.homestead.com
Andrew Michrowski, President

Solar Energy Society of Canada Inc. (SESCI) / Société d'énergie solaire du Canada inc.
406 McLaughlin Hall, Queen's University, Kingston ON K7L 3N6
Tel: 613-533-2657; *Fax:* 613-533-6550
e-mail: info@sesci.ca
URL: www.sesci.ca
Affiliation(s): International Solar Energy Society
Frederic Pouyot, President

Wood Energy Technology Transfer Inc. (WETT)
#7, 296 Jarvis St., Toronto ON M5B 2C5
Tel: 416-968-7718; *Fax:* 416-968-6818
Toll-Free: 888-358-9388
e-mail: WETT@funnel.ca
URL: www.wettinc.ca
Anthony Laycock, Executive Director

Engineering & Technology

American Society of Mechanical Engineers (ASME)
3 Park Ave., New York NY 10016-5990 USA
Tel: 973-882-1170; *Fax:* 973-882-1717
Toll-Free: 800-843-2763
e-mail: infocentral@asme.org
URL: www.asme.org
Virgil R. Carter, Executive Director
Sam Y. Zamrik, President

Applied Science Technologists & Technicians of British Columbia (ASTTBC)
10767 - 148 St., Surrey BC V3R 0S4
Tel: 604-585-2788; *Fax:* 604-585-2790
e-mail: techinfo@asttbc.org
URL: www.asttbc.org
John E. Leech, A.Sc.T., CAE, Executive Director & Registrar

Association des ingénieurs municipaux du Québec (AIMQ) / Association of Québec Municipal Engineers
CP 792, Succ. B, Montréal QC H3B 3K5
Tél: 514-845-5303
Courriel: aimg.rlamarche@videotron.ca
URL: www.aimq.net
Dany Lachance, ing., Président

Association des ingénieurs-conseils du Québec (AICQ) / Consulting Engineers of Québec
#930, 1440, rue Ste-Catherine ouest, Montréal QC H3G 1R8
Tél: 514-871-2229; *Téléc:* 514-871-9903
Courriel: info@aicq.qc.ca
URL: www.aicq.qc.ca

Association of Canadian Engineering Companies (ACEC) / Association des firmes d'ingénierie du Canada
#616, 130 Albert St., Ottawa ON K1P 5G4
Tel: 613-236-0569; *Fax:* 613-236-6193
Toll-Free: 800-565-0569
e-mail: info@acec.ca
URL: www.acec.ca
Jeff Morrison, President/COO

Association of Certified Engineering Technicians & Technologists of Prince Edward Island (ACETTPEI)
PO Box 1436, 92 Queen St., Charlottetown PE C1A 7N1
Tel: 902-892-8324
e-mail: info@acettpei.ca
URL: www.acettpei.ca
Trent Collicutt, CET, President
Alan Robison, CET, Vice-President
Delbert Reeves, CET, Treasurer
Tom MacDonald, CET, Registrar

Association of Engineering Technicians & Technologists of Newfoundland (AETTN)
Donovans Industrial Park, PO Box 790, 22 Sagona Ave., Mount Pearl NL A1N 2Y2
Tel: 709-747-2868; *Fax:* 709-747-2869
Toll-Free: 888-238-8600
e-mail: aettn@nfld.com
URL: www.aettn.com
Ed Duff, President
Linda Hayward, Office Manager

Association of Professional Engineers & Geoscientists of British Columbia (APEGBC)
#200, 4010 Regent St., Burnaby BC V5C 6N2
Tel: 604-430-8035; *Fax:* 604-430-8085
Toll-Free: 888-430-8035
e-mail: apeginfo@apeg.bc.ca
URL: www.apeg.bc.ca
Margaret Li, P.Eng, President
Janet Sinclair, Director, Communications & Engagement
Derek Doyle, P.Eng., Executive Director & Registrar

Association of Professional Engineers & Geoscientists of Manitoba (APEGM)
850A Pembina Hwy., Winnipeg MB R3M 2M7
Tel: 204-474-2736; *Fax:* 204-474-5960
Toll-Free: 866-227-9600
e-mail: apegm@apegm.mb.ca
URL: www.apegm.mb.ca
Grant Koropatnick, P.Eng., Executive Directory & Registrar
Sharon E. Sankar, P.Eng., Director of Admissions

Association of Professional Engineers & Geoscientists of New Brunswick (APEGNB) / Association des ingénieurs et géoscientifiques du Nouveau-Brunswick (AINB)
183 Hanwell Rd., Fredericton NB E3B 2R2
Tel: 506-458-8083; *Fax:* 506-451-9629
e-mail: info@apegnb.com
URL: www.apegnb.com
Andrew McLeod, P.Eng., Executive Director

Association of Professional Engineers & Geoscientists of Saskatchewan (APEGS)
#104, 2255 - 13 Ave., Regina SK S4P 0V6
Tel: 306-525-9547; *Fax:* 306-525-0851
Toll-Free: 800-500-9547
e-mail: apegs@apegs.sk.ca
URL: www.apegs.sk.ca
Dennis Paddock, P.Eng., Executive Director & Registrar
Bob McDonald, P.Eng., LL.B., Director, Membership & Legal Svcs

Association of Professional Engineers of Nova Scotia (APENS)
PO Box 129, 1355 Barrington St., Halifax NS B3J 2M4
Tel: 902-429-2250; *Fax:* 902-423-9769
Toll-Free: 888-802-7367
e-mail: info@apens.ns.ca
URL: www.apens.ns.ca
Len White, P.Eng, MBA, CGA, Executive Director

Association of Professional Engineers of Prince Edward Island (APEPEI)
549 North River Rd., Charlottetown PE C1E 1J6
Tel: 902-566-1268; *Fax:* 902-566-5551
e-mail: apepei@apepei.com
URL: www.apepei.com
Christine MacKinnon, P.Eng., President
Frank D. Parslow, P.Eng., Executive Director/Registrar

Association of Professional Engineers of the Yukon Territory (APEY)
312B Hanson St., Whitehorse YT Y1A 1Y6
Tel: 867-667-6727; *Fax:* 867-668-2142
e-mail: staff@apey.yk.ca
URL: www.apey.yk.ca
Gord Hamilton, President
Richard Trimble, Registrar
Sandy Birrell, P.Eng., Sec.-Treas.

The Association of Professional Engineers, Geologists & Geophysicists of Alberta (APEGGA)
Scotia One, #1500, 10060 Jasper Ave. NW, Edmonton AB T5J 4A2
Tel: 780-426-3990; *Fax:* 780-426-1877
Toll-Free: 800-661-7020
e-mail: email@apegga.org
URL: www.apegga.org
Neil Windsor, P.Eng., Executive Director & Registrar
A.J. Schuld, P.Eng., Deputy Registrar
Len Shrimpton, P.Eng., COO

Association of Professional Engineers, Geologists & Geophysicists of the Northwest Territories & Nunavut (NAPEGG)
#201, 4817 - 49 St., Yellowknife NT X1A 3S7
Tel: 867-920-4055; *Fax:* 867-873-4058
e-mail: napegg@tamarack.nt.ca
URL: www.napegg.nt.ca
Lloyd Henderson, P.Eng., Executive Director
Linda Golding, Deputy Registrar

The Association of Science and Engineering Technology Professionals of Alberta (ASET)
Phipps-McKinnon Building, #1630, 10020 - 101A Ave., Edmonton AB T5J 3G2
Tel: 780-425-0626; *Fax:* 780-424-5053
Toll-Free: 800-272-5619
e-mail: asetadmin@aset.ab.ca
URL: www.aset.ab.ca
Roy Clark, C.E.T., A.Sc.T., President
Kevin Harrison, R.E.T., R.P.T., First Vice President
Dave Merralls, R.E.T., R.P.T., Second Vice President, Communications

Canadian Acoustical Association / Association canadienne d'acoustique
c/o National Research Council of Canada, Institute for Research in Construction, Ottawa ON K1A 0R6
Tel: 613-993-9746; *Fax:* 613-954-1495
e-mail: secretary@caa-aca.ca
URL: www.caa-aca.ca
Christian Giguère, President
Dave Quirt, Executive Secretary

Canadian Advanced Technology Alliance (CATA) / Association canadienne de technologie de pointe
#416, 207 Bank St., Ottawa ON K2P 2N2
Tel: 613-236-6550
e-mail: info@cata.ca; cmalette@cata.ca (Membership)
URL: www.cata.ca
Social Media: www.facebook.com/group.php?gid=5391503953
John Reid, President/CEO
Barry Gander, Executive Vice-President
Charles Duffet, Senior Vice-President & CIO Advisor
Russ Roberts, Senior Vice-President, Tax & Finance
Kevin Wennekes, Vice-President, Research

Canadian Air Cushion Technology Society (CACTS)
#105, 1750 Courtwood Cres., Ottawa ON K2C 2B5
Tel: 613-234-0191; *Fax:* 613-234-9039
e-mail: casi@casi.ca
URL: www.casi.ca
Geoffrey Languedoc, Executive Director
Don Pearsons, President

Canadian Association for Composite Structures & Materials (CACSMA) / Association canadienne pour les structures et matériaux composites (ACSMAC)
c/o J. Denault, Industrial Materials Institute, Ntl. Research Council, Montréal QC H3G 1M6
Tel: 450-641-5105; *Fax:* 450-848-4596
e-mail: Johanne.Denault@imi.cnrc-nrc.gc.ca
URL: www.cacsma.ca
Suong V. Hoa, President
Mehdi Hojjati, Secretary
Johanne Denault, Treasurer

Canadian Council of Technicians & Technologists (CCTT) / Conseil canadien des techniciens et technologues
#295, 1101 Prince Of Wales Dr., Ottawa ON K2C 3W7
Tel: 613-238-8123; *Fax:* 613-238-8822
Toll-Free: 800-891-1140
e-mail: cctadm@cctt.ca
URL: www.cctt.ca
Yaroslaw Zajac, MBA, CAE, Executive Director

Canadian Hydrogen & Fuel Cell Association (CHFCA)
4250 Wesbrook Mall, Vancouver BC V6T 1W5
Tel: 604-822-9178; *Fax:* 604-822-8106
e-mail: info@chfca.ca
URL: www.chfca.ca
John W. Tak, President/CEO
Terry Kimmel, Vice-President

Canadian Remote Sensing Society (CRSS) / Société canadienne de télédétection
1750 Courtlant Cres., Ottawa ON K2C 2B5
Tel: 613-234-0191; *Fax:* 613-234-9039
e-mail: casi@casi.ca
URL: www.casi.ca/canadianremotesensingsociety.aspx
Derek R. Peddle, Chair
Monique Bernier, Vice-Chair
Anne Smith, Secretary-Treasurer

Canadian Society for Civil Engineering (CSCE) / Société canadienne de génie civil
#201, 4920, boul Maisonneuve ouest, Montréal QC H3Z 1N1
Tel: 514-933-2634; *Fax:* 514-933-3504
e-mail: info@csce.ca
URL: www.csce.ca
Peter G. Casquinha, Executive Director

Canadian Society for Engineering Management (CSEM) / Société canadienne de gestion en ingénierie
1295 Hwy. 2 East, Kingston ON K7L 4V1
e-mail: louisem@cogeco.ca
URL: www.csem-scgi.org
John Wood, P.Eng, President
Dominique Janssens, P.Eng, Sec.-Treas.

Canadian Society for Mechanical Engineering (CSME) / Société canadienne de génie mécanique (SCGM)
1295 Hwy. 2 East, Kingston ON K7L 4V1
Tel: 613-547-5989; *Fax:* 613-547-0195
e-mail: csme@cogeco.ca
URL: www.csme-scgm.ca
Rama B. Bhat, Ph.D, FCSME, President

Canadian Technical Asphalt Association (CTAA) / Association technique canadienne du bitume
#300, 895 Fort St., Victoria BC V8W 1H7
Tel: 250-361-9187; *Fax:* 250-361-9187
e-mail: admin@ctaa.ca
URL: www.ctaa.ca
Robert Noble, P.Eng., Sec.-Treas.

Certified Technicians & Technologists Association of Manitoba (CTTAM)
#602, 1661 Portage Ave., Winnipeg MB R3J 3T7
Tel: 204-784-1088; *Fax:* 204-784-1084
e-mail: admin@cttam.com
URL: www.cttam.com
Eileen Ewanchuk, Registrar
Terry Gifford, Executive Director

Community Energy Association
#308, 402 West Pender St., Vancouver BC V6B 1T6

Tel: 604-628-7076; Fax: 778-786-1613
URL: www.communityenergy.bc.ca
Norm Connolly, Executive Director

Consulting Engineers of Alberta (CEA)
Scotia Tw0, #511, 10060 Jasper Ave., Edmonton AB T5J 3R8
Tel: 780-421-1852; Fax: 780-424-5225
e-mail: info@cea.ca
URL: www.cea.ca
Wendy Cooper, Executive Director
Terry Gowing, President

Consulting Engineers of British Columbia (CEBC)
#657, 409 Granville St., Vancouver BC V6C 1T2
Tel: 604-687-2811; Fax: 604-688-7110
e-mail: info@cebc.org
URL: www.cebc.org
Affiliation(s): Association of Consulting Engineers of Canada
Francois Morton, President
Glen Martin, Executive Director

Consulting Engineers of Manitoba Inc. (CEM)
PO Box 1547, Stn. Main, Winnipeg MB R3C 2Z4
Tel: 204-774-5258; Fax: 204-779-0788
e-mail: cemca@shaw.ca
URL: www.cemanitoba.com
Affiliation(s): Association of Professional Engineers of Manitoba; International Federation of Consulting Engineers; Manitoba Association of Architects
Shirley E. Tillett, Executive Director
H. Pankratz, President

Consulting Engineers of New Brunswick (CENB) / Les Ingénieurs-Conseils du Nouveau-Brunswick
183 Hanwell Rd., Fredericton NB E3B 2R2
Tel: 506-470-9211; Fax: 506-451-9629
e-mail: cenbexec@nb.sympatico.ca
URL: www.cenb.nb.ca
Lee MacWilliams, P.Eng, President
John Fudge, P.Eng, Executive Director

Consulting Engineers of Nova Scotia (CENS)
PO Box 613, Stn. M, Halifax NS B3J 2R7
Tel: 902-461-1325; Fax: 902-461-1321
e-mail: cens@eastlink.ca
URL: www.cens.org

Consulting Engineers of Ontario (CEO)
#405, 10 Four Seasons Pl., Toronto ON M9B 6H7
Tel: 416-620-1400; Fax: 416-620-5803
e-mail: staff@ceo.on.ca
URL: www.ceo.on.ca
Saskia Martini-Wong, Manager, Operations & Finance
David Amm, Chair

Consulting Engineers of Saskatchewan (CES)
#12, 2010 - 7 Ave., Regina SK S4R 1C2
Tel: 306-359-3338; Fax: 306-522-5325
e-mail: ces@sasktel.net
URL: www.ces.sk.ca
Val Jakubowski, Executive Director

Consulting Engineers of Yukon (CEY)
c/o EBA Engineering Consultants Ltd., #6, 151 Industrial Rd., Whitehorse YT Y1A 2V3
Tel: 867-668-3068; Fax: 867-668-4349
e-mail: cey@eba.ca
URL: www.cey.ca
Richard Trimble, Executive Director

Continental Automated Buildings Association (CABA) / Association continentale pour l'automatisation des bâtiments
#210, 1173 Cyrville Rd., Ottawa ON K1J 7S6
Tel: 613-686-1814; Fax: 613-744-7833
Toll-Free: 888-798-2222
e-mail: caba@caba.org
URL: www.caba.org
Social Media: twitter.com/caba_news
Martin Cullum, Chair
Ron Zimmer, President/CEO

The Engineering Institute of Canada (EIC) / L'Institut canadien des ingénieurs (ICI)
1295 Hwy. 2 East, Kingston ON K7L 4V1
Tel: 613-547-5989; Fax: 613-547-0195
e-mail: jplant1@cogeco.ca
URL: www.eic-ici.ca
Affiliation(s): Engineers Canada; Association of Canadian Engineering Companies; Canadian Academy of Engineering; International Association for Continuing Education & Training (IACET); Internation Association for Continuing Engineering Education (IACEE)
B. John Plant, Executive Director

Kerry Rowe, President

Engineers Canada / Ingénieurs Canada
#1100, 180 Elgin St., Ottawa ON K2P 2K3
Tel: 613-232-2474; Fax: 613-230-5759
e-mail: info@ccpe.ca
URL: www.ccpe.ca
Affiliation(s): World Federation of Engineering Organizations
Richard Fletcher, President
Chantal Guay, P.Eng., M.Env., CEO

INO / Institut national d'optique
2740, rue Einstein, Sainte-Foy QC G1P 4S4
Tel: 418-657-7006; Fax: 418-657-7009
e-mail: info@ino.ca
URL: www.ino.ca
Jean-Guy Paquet, President & CEO

Institute of Power Engineers (IPE)
PO Box 878, Burlington ON L7R 3Y7
Tel: 905-333-3348; Fax: 905-333-9328
e-mail: ipenat@nipe.ca
URL: www.nipe.ca
Lorne Shewfelt, National President
Jude Rankin, 1st National Vice President
Don Purser, National Secretary

ISIS Canada Research Network (ISIS)
A250 Agricultural & Civil Engineering Bldg., 96 Dafoe Rd., Winnipeg MB R3T 2N2
Tel: 204-474-8506; Fax: 204-474-7519
e-mail: central@isiscanada.com
URL: www.isiscanada.com
Aftab Mufti, P.Eng., Ph.D., President

Municipal Engineers Association (MEA)
#2, 6355 Kennedy Rd., Mississauga ON L5T 2L5
Tel: 905-795-2555; Fax: 905-795-2660
e-mail: info@municipalengineers.on.ca
URL: www.municipalengineers.on.ca
David Shantz, Executive Director
John F. Hammer, President
Gary Carroll, Vice-President
Trevor D. Lewis, Treasurer

NACE International
c/o AMC Atlantic Met Consulting Ltd., #106, 11 Morris Dr., Dartmouth NS B3B 1M2
Tel: 902-405-3600

NACE International
c/o Terasen Gas Inc., 3700 2nd Ave., Burnaby BC V5C 6S4

NACE International
c/o Husky Energy, 707 8th Ave. SW, Calgary AB T2P 3G7
Tel: 403-840-1913

NACE International
c/o Kinectrics Inc., #215, 800 Kipling Ave., Toronto ON M8Z 6C4
Tel: 416-207-6000

NACE International
c/o CSI Coating Systems Inc., 556 Stewart Cres. SW, Edmonton AB T6X 0A8
Tel: 780-955-2856

NACE International
c/o CPI Corrosion Ltd., #300, 1200, boul St-Martin ouest, Laval QC H7S 2E4
Tél: 514-342-2828

NACE International (NACE)
1440 South Creek Dr., Houston TX 77084-4906 USA
Tel: 281-228-6200; Fax: 281-228-6300
Toll-Free: 800-797-6223
e-mail: firstservice@nace.org
URL: www.nace.org
Tony Keane, Executive Director
Jenny Been, Section Secretary/Treasurer, Northern Area
Scott MacIntyre, Area Membership Chairman, Northern Area

NACE International
c/o DCB Services, 814 - 50th St. E, Saskatoon SK S7K 0X6
Tel: 306-931-2820; Fax: 306-931-3344

NACE International
c/o CANMET Materials Technology Laboratory, 568 Booth St., Ottawa ON K1A 0G1
Tel: 613-947-3603

New Brunswick Society of Certified Engineering Technicians & Technologists (NBSCETT) / Société des techniciens et des technologues agréés du génie du Nouveau-Brunswick (STTAGN-B)
#2, 385 Wilsey Rd., Fredericton NB E3B 5N6
Tel: 506-454-6124; Fax: 506-452-7076
Toll-Free: 800-665-8324
e-mail: nbscett@nbscett.nb.ca
URL: www.nbscett.nb.ca
David Sheaves, PTech, President
Jennifer Lawson, Executive Assistant
Edward F. Leslie, CAE, PTech, Executive Director

Ontario Association of Certified Engineering Technicians & Technologists (OACETT)
#404, 10 Four Seasons Pl., Toronto ON M9B 6H7
Tel: 416-621-9621; Fax: 416-621-8694
e-mail: info@oacett.org
URL: www.oacett.org
David J. Thomson, Executive Director
Gene Stodolak, President

Ordre des ingénieurs du Québec (OIQ)
#350, 1100, rue De La Gauchetière ouest, Montréal QC H3B 2S2
Tél: 514-845-6141; Téléc: 514-845-1833
Ligne sans frais: 800-461-6141
Courriel: dirgen@oiq.qc.ca
URL: www.oiq.qc.ca
Affiliation(s): Conseil Interprofessionnel du Québec
Zaki Ghavitian, ing., Président

Ordre des technologues professionnels du Québec (OTPQ)
#720, 1265, rue Berri, Montréal QC H2L 4X4
Tél: 514-845-3247; Téléc: 514-845-3643
Ligne sans frais: 800-561-3459
Courriel: info@otpq.qc.ca
URL: www.otpq.qc.ca
Denis Beauchamp, Directeur général et secrétaire
Alain Bernier, Président

Plant Engineering & Maintenance Association of Canada (PEMAC)
#402, 6 - 2400 Dundas St. West, Mississauga ON L5K 2R8
Tel: 905-823-7255; Fax: 905-823-8001
e-mail: mail@pemac.org
URL: www.pemac.org
Norm Clegg, Executive Director
Brian Malloch, President

Positive Power Co-op (PPC)
#422, 2000 Appleby Line, Burlington ON L7L 7H7
Tel: 519-846-8130
URL: www.positivepowerco-op.com
Stacey Hare, General Manager
Curt Hammond, Chair

Professional Engineers & Geoscientists Newfoundland & Labrador (PEG-NL)
PO Box 21207, St. John's NL A1A 5B2
Tel: 709-753-7714; Fax: 709-753-6131
e-mail: main@pegnl.ca
URL: www.pegnl.ca
Barry J. Thomson, President
K. Sean LaCour, P.Eng., Councilor, Eastern District
Michael W. Greene, P.Eng., Councilor, Labrador District
Carl King, P.Eng., Councilor, Western District
Steve McLean, P.Eng., Executive Director

Professional Engineers Ontario (PEO)
#1000, 25 Sheppard Ave. West, Toronto ON M2N 6S9
Tel: 416-224-1100; Fax: 416-224-8168
Toll-Free: 800-339-3716
e-mail: webmaster@peo.on.ca
URL: www.peo.on.ca
Frank Borsi, B.Comm., CA, Director, Administrative Services
Kim Allen, MBA, P.Eng., CEO & Registrar

Saskatchewan Applied Science Technologists & Technicians (SASTT)
363 Park St., Regina SK S4N 5B2
Tel: 306-721-6633; Fax: 306-721-0112
e-mail: info@sastt.ca
URL: www.sastt.ca
Jaime Briltz, AScT, Executive Director & Registrar
Steve Oszust, CTech, President
Edward Worrall, AScT, 1st Vice-President
Kelly Ljunggren, AScT, 2nd Vice-President

SHAD International
8 Young St. East, Waterloo ON N2J 2L3
Tel: 519-884-8844; Fax: 519-884-8191
e-mail: info@shad.ca
URL: www.shad.ca

Barry Bisson, President

Society of Motion Picture & Television Engineers (SMPTE)
3 Barker Ave, 5th Fl., White Plains NY 10601 USA
Tel: 914-761-1100; *Fax:* 914-761-3115
e-mail: membership@smpte.org
URL: www.smpte.org
Peter Lude, Exec. Vice-President
Pierre Marion, Governor, Canadian Region
Kenneth C. Fuller, President

Society of Motion Picture & Television Engineers
c/o Panasonic Canada Inc., 5770 Ambler Dr., Mississauga ON L4W 2T3

Society of Tribologists & Lubrication Engineers / Société des tribologistes et ingénieurs en lubrification
840 Busse Hwy., Park Ridge IL 60068-2302 USA
Tel: 847-825-5536; *Fax:* 847-825-1456
e-mail: information@stle.org
URL: www.stle.org
Edward P. Salek, Executive Director

Society of Tribologists & Lubrication Engineers
c/o Lubrication Engineers of Canada Ltd., 2200 Bristol Circle, Oakville ON L6H 5R3
Tel: 905-829-3833
e-mail: kimk@lubeng.com

Society of Tribologists & Lubrication Engineers
c/o Suncor Energy Inc., 400 Burlington St. East, Hamilton ON L8L 4H7
Tel: 905-804-4530
e-mail: lbillings@suncor.com

Society of Tribologists & Lubrication Engineers
2310, de la Province, Longueuil QC J4G 1G1
Tél: 450-679-8866; *Téléc:* 450-679-5818

Society of Tribologists & Lubrication Engineers
c/o Fluid Life, 9321 - 48 St., Edmonton AB T6B 2R4
Tel: 780-462-2400; *Fax:* 780-462-2420

Society of Tribologists & Lubrication Engineers
115 Cliveden Ave., Delta BC V3M 6G9
Tel: 604-816-0252; *Fax:* 604-469-5433
URL: www.stle.org

Society of Tribologists & Lubrication Engineers
Univ. of Saskatchewan, Agricultural & Biorex, 57 Campus Dr., Saskatoon SK S7N 5A9
Tel: 306-966-5313; *Fax:* 306-966-5334

Society of Tribologists & Lubrication Engineers
#235, 35 - 2855 Pembina Hwy., Winnipeg MB R3T 2H5
Tel: 204-779-2200

TechNova
#A308, Cambridge 1, 202 Brownlow Ave., Dartmouth NS B3B 1T5
Tel: 902-463-3236; *Fax:* 902-465-7567
Toll-Free: 866-723-8867
e-mail: info@technova.ca
URL: www.technova.ca
Louis LeBel, CET, President

Environmental

Action Nord Terre
535, 4e Rue, Chibougamau QC G8P 1S4
Tél: 418-748-7056
André Naud, Président

Air & Waste Management Association (A&WMA) / Association pour la prévention de la contamination de l'air et du sol
One Gateway Center, 420 Fort Duquesne Blvd., 3rd Fl., Pittsburgh PA 15222-1435 USA
Tel: 412-232-3444; *Fax:* 412-232-3450
Toll-Free: 800-270-3444
e-mail: info@awma.org
URL: www.awma.org
Social Media: www.facebook.com/group.php?gid=33499462923
Affiliation(s): Canadian Prairie & Northern Section (www.cpans.org); Ontario Section (www.awma.on.ca); Québec Section (www.apcas.qc.ca); Ottawa Valley Chapter (www.awma-ovc.ca)
A. Gwen Eklund, President
Mike Kelly, Executive Director & Secretary
Amy Gilligan, Treasurer

Alberta Environmental Network (AEN)
#2, 6328A - 104 St. NW, Edmonton AB T6H 2K9
Tel: 780-439-1916; *Fax:* 780-433-3792
e-mail: aen@web.ca
URL: www.aenweb.ca
Nashina Shariff, Chair

Alberta Fish & Game Association
6924 - 104 St., Edmonton AB T6H 2L7
Tel: 780-437-2342; *Fax:* 780-438-6872
e-mail: office@afga.org
URL: www.afga.org
Maurice Nadeau, President
Martin Sharren, Executive Vice-President

Alberta Water Council
Petroleum Plaza, South Tower, #1400, 9915 - 108 St., Edmonton AB T5K 2G8
Tel: 780-644-7380
URL: www.albertawatercouncil.ca
Gord Edwards, Executive Director

Alberta Wilderness Association (AWA)
455 - 12 St. NW, Calgary AB T2N 1Y9
Tel: 403-283-2025; *Fax:* 403-270-2743
Toll-Free: 866-313-0713
e-mail: awa.info@shawcable.com
URL: albertawilderness.ca
Affiliation(s): Environmental Resource Centre
Christyann Olson, Executive Director

Association for Literature, Environment, and Culture in Canada (ALECC) / Association pour la littérature, l'environnement et la culture au Canada
c/o Department of English, University of Calgary, 2500 University Dr. NW, 11th Fl., Calgary AB T2N 1N4
e-mail: contactus@alecc.ca
URL: www.alecc.ca
Pamela Banting, President

Bedeque Bay Environmental Management Association (BBEMA)
PO Box 8310, Emerald PE C0B 1M0
Tel: 902-886-3211
URL: www.bbema.ca

Big Rideau Lake Association (BRLA)
PO Box 93, Hwy. 15, Portland ON K0G 1V0
Tel: 613-272-3629
e-mail: brla@brla.on.ca
URL: www.brla.on.ca
Peter Copestake, President

BIOQuébec / Québec Bio-Industries Business Network
#300, 381, rue Notre-Dame ouest, Montréal QC H2Y 1V2
Tél: 514-733-8411; *Téléc:* 514-733-8272
Courriel: reception@bioquebec.com
URL: www.bioquebec.com
Bertrand Bolduc, Président
Perry Niro, M.Sc., Directeur général et chef de la dir

British Columbia Environment Industry Association (BCEIA)
#400, 602 West Hastings St., Vancouver BC V6B 1P2
Tel: 604-683-2751; *Fax:* 604-677-5960
e-mail: info@bceia.com
URL: www.bceia.com
Bob Symington, President
Frank Came, Vice-President
Jeff Eltom, Executive Director
Michael Lyons, Secretary-Treasurer

British Columbia Environmental Network (BCEN)
#461, 1755 Robson St., Vancouver BC V6G 3B7
Tel: 604-515-1969
e-mail: editor@ecobc.ca
URL: www.ecobc.org
David Boehm, Treasurer

British Columbia Water & Waste Association (BCWWA)
#221, 8678 Greenall Ave., Burnaby BC V5J 3M6
Tel: 604-433-4389; *Fax:* 604-433-9859
Toll-Free: 877-433-4389
e-mail: contact@bcwwa.org
URL: www.bcwwa.org
Daisy Foster, Chief Executive Officer
David Icharia, Director, Operations
Doug Simons, Manager, Program Development
Sarah Vaughan, Manager, Communications
Monica Han, Coordinator, Member Services
Wendy Szeto, Coordinator, Education & Training

BurlingtonGreen Environmental Association
3281 Myers Lane, Burlington ON L7N 1K6
Tel: 905-466-2171
URL: www.burlingtongreen.org
Social Media: www.facebook.com/burlington.green.environment
Amy Schnurr, Executive Director

Campaign for Nuclear Phaseout (CNP)
#412, 1 Nicholas St., Ottawa ON K1N 7B7
URL: www.cnp.ca
Affiliation(s): Canadian Coalition for Nuclear Responsibility; Concerned Citizens of Renfrew County and Area; Energy Probe; Greenpeace Canada; Sierra Club of Canada

Canadian Arctic Resources Committee
488 Gladstone Ave., Ottawa ON K1N 8V4
Tel: 613-759-4284; *Fax:* 613-237-3845
Toll-Free: 866-949-9006
e-mail: davidg@carc.org
URL: www.carc.org
Chuck Birchall, Chair

Canadian Association for Laboratory Accreditation Inc. (CALA)
#310, 1565 Carling Ave., Ottawa ON K1Z 8R1
Tel: 613-233-5300; *Fax:* 613-233-5501
e-mail: ecummins@cala.ca
URL: www.cala.ca
Charlie Brimley, CEO
Colleen Cotter, Manager, Accreditation
Ned Gravel, Manager, Quality & Training
Ken Middlebrook, Manager, Proficiency Testing
Andrew Morris, Manager, Data & Information

Canadian Association of Recycling Industries (CARI) / Association canadienne des industries du recyclage (ACIR)
#1, 682 Monarch Ave., Ajax ON L1S 4S2
Tel: 905-426-9313; *Fax:* 905-426-9314
URL: www.cari-acir.org
Sheldon Jarcaig, President
Donna Turner, Association Manager

Canadian Association on Water Quality (CAWQ) / Association canadienne sur la qualité de l'eau (ACQE)
PO Box 5050, 867 Lakeshore Rd., Burlington ON L7R 4A6
Tel: 905-336-6291; *Fax:* 905-336-4877
URL: www.cawq.ca
Yves Comeau, President
Janet McAvella, Subscription & Membership

Canadian Centre for Pollution Prevention (C2P2) / Centre canadien pour la prévention de la pollution
#134, 215 Spadina Ave., Toronto ON M5T 2C7
Tel: 905-822-4133; *Fax:* 416-979-3936
Toll-Free: 800-667-9790
e-mail: info@c2p2online.com
URL: www.c2p2online.com
Fred Granek, Chief Operating Officer
Leah Nielsen, Coordinator, Projects
Shari Russell, Coordinator, Projects

Canadian Environment Industry Association (CEIA)
119, Concession 6 Rd., Fisherville ON NOA 1G0
Tel: 416-410-0432; *Fax:* 416-362-5231
URL: www.grn.com/assn/can_envi.html
Christopher Henderson, Chair

Canadian Environmental Certification Approvals Board (CECAB) / Bureau canadien de reconnaissance professionnelle des spécialistes de l'environnement
#200, 308 - 11th Ave. SE, Calgary AB T2G 0Y2
Tel: 403-233-7484; *Fax:* 403-264-6240
e-mail: info@cecab.org
URL: www.cecab.org
Doug Bissett, Chair
Betty-Jo Unis, Registrar

Canadian Environmental Law Association (CELA) / Association canadienne du droit de l'environnement
#301, 130 Spadina Ave., Toronto ON M5V 2L4
Tel: 416-960-2284; *Fax:* 416-960-9392
e-mail: millers@cela.ca
URL: www.cela.ca
Theresa McClenaghan, Executive Director

Canadian Environmental Network (RCEN) / Réseau canadien de l'environnement
39 McArthur Ave., Level 1-1, Ottawa ON K1L 8L7

Tel: 613-728-9810; Fax: 613-728-2963
e-mail: info@cen-rce.org
URL: www.cen-rce.org
Susan Tanner, Executive Director
Emile Massenat, Associate Executive Director
Robert Henri, Communications Coordinator

Canadian Environmental Technology Advancement Corporation - West (CETAC)
Alberta Regional Office, #420, 715 - 5 Ave. SW, Calgary AB T2P 2X6
Tel: 403-777-9595; Fax: 403-777-9599
e-mail: cetac@cetacwest.com
URL: www.cetacwest.com
Margaret Kelly, Vice-President, Alberta
Joe Lukacs, President/CEO

Canadian Institute for Environmental Law & Policy (CIELAP) / Institut canadien du droit et de la politique de l'environnement
#305, 130 Spadina Ave., Toronto ON M5V 2L4
Tel: 416-923-3529; Fax: 416-923-5949
e-mail: cielap@cielap.org
URL: www.cielap.org
Affiliation(s): Canadian Environmental Network; Ontario Environmental Network, Great Lakes United
David Powell, President
Anne Mitchell, Executive Director

Canadian Institute of Resources Law (CIRL) / Institut canadien du droit des ressources
Murray Fraser Hall, University of Calgary, #3353, 2500 University Dr. NW, Calgary AB T2N 1N4
Tel: 403-220-3200; Fax: 403-282-6182
e-mail: cirl@ucalgary.ca
URL: www.cirl.ca
Affiliation(s): International Bar Association, Section on Energy & Resources Law
J. Owen Saunders, Executive Director
Clifford D. Johnson, Q.C., ICD.D, Chair

Canadian Land Reclamation Association (CLRA) / Association canadienne de réhabilitation des sites dégradés (ACRSD)
PO Box 61047, RPO Kensington, Calgary AB T2N 4S6
Tel: 403-289-9435; Fax: 403-289-9435
e-mail: clra@telusplanet.net
URL: www.clra.ca

The Canadian Network for Environmental Education & Communication (EECOM) / Réseau canadien d'éducation et de communication relatives à l'environnement
c/o 336 Rosedale Ave., Winnipeg MB R3L 1L8
e-mail: nswayze@eecom.org
URL: www.eecom.org
Natalie Swayzer, Executive Director
Grant Gardner, Chair
Rick Wishart, Treasurer

Canadian Parks Partnership (CPP) / Partenaires des parcs canadiens
#360, 1414 - 8th St. SW, Calgary AB T2R 1J6
Tel: 613-567-0099
e-mail: nature@canadianparkspartnership.com
Bruce Livingston, Chair

Canadian Peregrine Foundation (CPF)
#214, 1450 O'Connor Dr., Toronto ON M4B 2T8
Tel: 416-481-1233
Toll-Free: 888-709-3944
e-mail: info@peregrine-foundation.ca
URL: www.peregrine-foundation.ca

Canadian Polystyrene Recycling Alliance (CPRA)
260 Peter St., Port Hope ON L1A 3V6
Tel: 905-885-8806; Fax: 905-885-2009

Canadian Society of Environmental Biologists (CSEB) / Société canadienne des biologistes de l'environnement
PO Box 962, Stn. F, Toronto ON M4Y 2N9
e-mail: cseb_on@hotmail.com
URL: www.cseb-scbe.org
Brian Free, President

Canadian Water & Wastewater Association (CWWA) / Association canadienne des eaux potables et usées (ACEPU)
#11, 1010 Polytek Rd., Ottawa ON K1J 9H9
Tel: 613-747-0524; Fax: 613-747-0523
e-mail: tdellison@cwwa.ca
URL: www.cwwa.ca
Schmidt Thomas, P. Eng., President

Canadian Water Resources Association (CWRA) / Association canadienne des ressources hydriques (ACRH)
c/o Membership Office, #900, 280 Albert St., Ottawa ON K1P 5G8
Tel: 613-237-9363; Fax: 613-594-5190
e-mail: services@AIC.ca
URL: www.cwra.org
F.A. (Rick) Ross, Executive Director
Sonya Meek, President
Brenda Toth, Secretary
Ed Dean, Treasurer

Canadian Wildlife Federation (CWF) / Fédération canadienne de la faune
350 Michael Cowpland Dr., Kanata ON K2M 2W1
Tel: 613-599-9594; Fax: 613-599-4428
Toll-Free: 800-563-9453
e-mail: info@cwf-fcf.org
URL: www.cwf-fcf.org
Larry Leigh, President

Carleton Sustainable Campus Network (CSCN)
Carleton University, #326 UC, 1125 Colonel By Dr., Ottawa ON K1S 5B6
Tel: 613-520-2757; Fax: 613-520-3989
e-mail: cscn@carleton.ca
URL: www.carleton.ca/cscn

Carolinian Canada Coalition
Grosvenor Lodge, 1017 Western Rd., London ON N6G 1G5
Tel: 519-433-7077; Fax: 519-913-2449
e-mail: info@carolinian.org
URL: www.carolinian.org
Gordon Nelson, Chair

Citizens for a Safe Environment (CSE)
Tel: 416-461-1092
e-mail: info@csetoronto.org
URL: www.csetoronto.org

Citizens' Clearinghouse on Waste Management (CCWM)
17 Major St., Kitchener ON N2H 4R1
URL: www.citizenswasteinfo.org
John Jackson, Coordinator

Citizens' Environment Watch (CEW)
#204, 147 Spadina Ave., Toronto ON M5V 2L7
Tel: 647-258-3280; Fax: 416-637-2717
e-mail: info@citizensenvironmentwatch.org
URL: www.citizensenvironmentwatch.org
Meredith Cochrane, Executive Director

Citizens' Opposed to Paving the Escarpment (COPE)
PO Box 40548, Stn. Upper Brant, Burlington ON L7P 4W1
e-mail: mail@cope-nomph.org
URL: www.cope-nomph.org
Affiliation(s): Coalition on the Niagara Escarpment; Sierra Club

Clean Nova Scotia (CNS)
126 Portland St., Dartmouth NS B2Y 1H8
Tel: 902-420-3474; Fax: 902-424-5334
Toll-Free: 800-665-5377
e-mail: cns@clean.ns.ca
URL: www.clean.ns.ca
Affiliation(s): Centre for Marine Conservation - Washington DC, USA; Tree Canada Foundation
Judy McMullen, Executive Director

Coalition on the Niagara Escarpment (CONE)
193 James St. South, Hamilton ON L8P 3A8
Tel: 905-529-4955; Fax: 905-529-9503
e-mail: cone@niagaraescarpment.org
URL: www.niagaraescarpment.org
Affiliation(s): The Greenbelt Foundation, Niagara Escarpment Foundation
Robert Patrick, President

The Composting Council of Canada / Conseil canadien du compostage
16 Northumberland St., Toronto ON M6H 1P7
Tel: 416-535-0240; Fax: 416-536-9892
Toll-Free: 877-571-4769
e-mail: ccc@compost.org
URL: www.compost.org
Susan Antler, Executive Director

Conservation Council of New Brunswick (CCNB) / Conseil de la conservation du Nouveau-Brunswick
180 St. John St., Fredericton NB E3B 4A9
Tel: 506-458-8747; Fax: 506-458-1047
e-mail: info@conservationcouncil.ca
URL: www.conservationcouncil.ca
Affiliation(s): Friends of the Earth Canada
Jamie Watson, Executive Director
Stephanie Coburn, President

Conservation Council of Ontario (CCO) / Conseil de conservation de l'Ontario
215 Spadina Ave., Toronto ON M5T 2C7
Tel: 416-533-1635
e-mail: cco@web.ca
URL: www.greenontario.org/cco/index.html
Marcelo Levy, President
Tony Jennings, Vice-President
Leslie Adams, Vice-President
Chris Winter, Executive Director

Conservation Ontario
Box 11, 120 Bayview Pkwy., Newmarket ON L3R 4W3
Tel: 905-895-0716; Fax: 905-895-0751
e-mail: info@conservation-ontario.on.ca
URL: www.conservation-ontario.on.ca
Richard (Dick) Hibma, Chair
Don Pearson, General Manager

Cumulative Environmental Management Association (CEMA)
Morrison Center, #214, 9914 Morrison St., Fort McMurray AB T9H 4A4
Tel: 780-799-3947; Fax: 780-714-3081
e-mail: info@cemaonline.ca
URL: www.cemaonline.ca
Glen Semenchuk, Executive Director

Ducks Unlimited Canada (DUC) / Canards Illimités Canada
PO Box 1160, Stonewall MB R0C 2Z0
Tel: 204-467-3000; Fax: 204-467-9028
Toll-Free: 800-665-3825
e-mail: webfoot@ducks.ca
URL: www.ducks.ca
Affiliation(s): Ducks Unlimited organizations in the U.S. & Mexico
Jeff Nelson, Executive Vice-President
C. Neil Downey, President
Henry R. Murkin, Director, Conservation Programs
Peter D. Carton, Chairman

Earth Day Canada (EDC) / Jour de la terre Canada
#503, 111 Peter St., Toronto ON M5V 2H1
Tel: 416-599-1991; Fax: 416-599-3100
Toll-Free: 888-283-2784
e-mail: info@earthday.ca; donate@earthday.ca; communications@earthday.ca
URL: www.earthday.ca
Affiliation(s): Earth Day Network; 3,500 community-based organizations
Jed Goldberg, President
Keith Treffry, Director, Communications
Paul Bubelis, Chair

Earth Energy Society of Canada (EESC) / Société canadienne de l'énergie du sol
Fax: 613-822-4987
e-mail: info@earthenergy.ca
URL: www.earthenergy.ca

Ecology Action Centre (EAC)
2705 Fern Lane, Halifax NS B3K 4L3
Tel: 902-429-2202; Fax: 902-405-3716
e-mail: info@ecologyaction.ca; getyourlawnoffdrugs@ecologyaction.ca
URL: www.ecologyaction.ca
Maggy Burns, Internal Director & Coordinator, Green Mobility Grants
Mark Butler, Director, Policy

EcoPerth
2196 Old Brooke Rd., RR#2, Maberry ON K0H 2B0
Tel: 613-267-6463; Fax: 613-268-2907
e-mail: info@ecoperth.on.ca
URL: www.ecoperth.on.ca
Bob Argue, Executive Director

Elsa Wild Animal Appeal of Canada
PO Box 45051, 2482 Yonge St., Toronto ON M4P 3E3
Tel: 416-489-8862; Fax: 416-489-4769
e-mail: info@elsacanada.com
URL: www.elsacanada.com
Betty Henderson, President

Enviro-Accès Inc.
Place Andrew-Paton, #150, 85, rue Belvédère nord, Sherbrooke QC J1H 4A7

Tél: 819-823-2230; *Téléc:* 819-823-6632
Courriel: enviro@enviroaccess.ca
URL: www.enviroaccess.ca
Manon Laporte, Présidente-directrice générale

EnviroLink
PO Box 8102, Pittsburgh PA 15217 USA
URL: www.envirolink.org

Environmental Careers Organization of Canada / L'Organisation pour les carrières en environnement du Canada
#200, 308 - 11th Ave. SE, Calgary AB T2G 0Y2
Tel: 403-233-0748; *Fax:* 403-269-9544
e-mail: info@eco.ca; techsupport@eco.ca
URL: www.eco.ca
Jon Ogryzlo, Sec.-Treas.
Grant S. Trump, President/CEO
Michael Kerford, Vice-President
Janelle Thomlinson, Director, Marketing & Communications

The Environmental Coalition of PEI
126 Richmond St., Charlottetown PE C1A 1H9
Tel: 902-566-4696; *Fax:* 902-566-4037
e-mail: energy@ecopei.ca
URL: www.ecopei.ca
Kate McDonald, Energy Coordinator

Environmental Education Association of the Yukon (EEAY)
Whitehorse YT
e-mail: eeyukon@gmail.com
URL: taiga.net/YukonEE

Environmental Health Association of British Columbia (EHABC)
PO Box 30033, Stn. Saanich Centre, Victoria BC V8X 5E1
Tel: 250-658-2027
URL: www.ehabc.org

Environmental Health Association of Ontario (EHAO)
PO Box 33023, Ottawa ON K2C 3Y9
e-mail: office@ehaontario.ca
URL: www.ehaontario.ca

The Environmental Law Centre (Alberta) Society (ELC)
#800, 10025 - 106 Street, Edmonton AB T5J 1G4
Tel: 780-424-5099; *Fax:* 780-424-5133
Toll-Free: 800-661-4238
e-mail: elc@elc.ab.ca
URL: www.elc.ab.ca
Cindy Chiasson, Executive Director

Environmental Managers Association of British Columbia (EMABC)
PO Box 3741, Vancouver BC V6B 3Z8
Tel: 604-998-2226; *Fax:* 604-998-2226
e-mail: info@emaofbc.com
URL: www.emaofbc.com
Patrick Novak, President
Krista Hennebury, Executive Director

Environmental Services Association of Alberta (ESAA)
#102, 2528 Ellwood Dr. SW, Edmonton AB T6X 0A9
Tel: 780-429-6363; *Fax:* 780-429-4249
Toll-Free: 800-661-9278
e-mail: info@esaa.org
URL: www.esaa.org
Craig Robertson, President
Randy Neumann, Secretary
Skip Kerr, Treasurer
Joe Barraclough, Director, Industry & Government Relations
Joe Chowaniec, Director, Program & Event Development

Environmental Services Association of Nova Scotia (ESANS)
Woodside Industrial Park, #211-2, 1 Research Dr., Dartmouth NS B2Y 4M9
Tel: 902-463-3538; *Fax:* 902-466-6889
e-mail: contact@esans.ca
URL: www.esans.ca
Adam Cooney, P.Eng., President

Environmental Youth Alliance (EYA)
PO Box 3601, Stn. Terminal, #517, 119 Pender St. West, Vancouver BC V6B 1S5
Tel: 604-689-4446; *Fax:* 604-689-4242
e-mail: info@eya.ca
URL: www.eya.ca

Environnement jeunesse
454, rue Laurier est, Montréal QC H2J 1E7
Tél: 514-252-3016; *Téléc:* 514-254-5873
Ligne sans frais: 866-377-3016
Courriel: infoenjeu@enjeu.qc.ca
URL: www.enjeu.qc.ca
Affiliation(s): Réseau québécois des groupes écologistes; Association québécoise pour la promotion de l'éducation relative à l'environnement
Jérôme Normand, Directeur général

Evergreen
355 Adelaide St. West, 5th Fl., Toronto ON M5V 1S2
Tel: 416-596-1495; *Fax:* 416-596-1443
Toll-Free: 888-426-3138
e-mail: info@evergreen.ca; donate@evergreen.ca
URL: www.evergreen.ca
Geoff Cape, Executive Director
Matthew Church, Director, Marketing & Communications

FaunENord
313, 3e Rue, 2e étage, Chibougamau QC G8P 1N4
Tél: 418-748-4441; *Téléc:* 418-748-1110
URL: www.faunenord.icr.qc.ca
Justine Desmeules

Fédération des associations pour la protection de l'environnement des lacs inc. (FAPEL)
CP 51128, Succ. Centre, Montréal QC H1N 3T8
Tél: 514-254-5361
Courriel: fapel@fapel.org
URL: fapel.org
Tonny Lesauteur, Directeur général

Fédération québécoise des chasseurs et pêcheurs
#109, 6780, 1re av, Québec QC G1H 2W8
Tél: 418-626-6858; *Téléc:* 418-622-6168
Ligne sans frais: 888-523-2863
Courriel: info@fedecp.qc.ca
URL: www.fqf.qc.ca
Pierre Latraverse, Président

First Nations Environmental Network
PO Box 394, Tofino BC V0R 2Z0
Tel: 250-726-5265; *Fax:* 250-725-2357
e-mail: councilfire@hotmail.com
URL: www.fnen.org
Steve Lawson, Coordinator

Fondation de la faune du Québec (FFQ)
#420, 1175, av Lavigerie, Québec QC G1V 4P1
Tél: 418-644-7926; *Téléc:* 418-643-7655
Ligne sans frais: 877-639-0742
Courriel: ffq@fondationdelafaune.qc.ca
URL: www.fondationdelafaune.qc.ca
André Martin, Président-directeur général

Fort Whyte Centre for Environmental Education
PO Box 124, 1961 McCreary Rd., Winnipeg MB R3P 2K9
Tel: 204-989-8355; *Fax:* 204-895-4700
e-mail: info@fortwhyte.org
URL: www.fortwhyte.org
Bill Elliott, President/CEO

Friends of Red Hill Valley
PO Box 61536, Hamilton ON L8T 5A1
Tel: 905-381-0240; *Fax:* 905-548-6317
e-mail: redhill@hwcn.org
URL: www.hwcn.org/forhv

Friends of the Earth Canada (FoE) / Les Ami(e)s de la Terre Canada
#300, 260 St. Patrick St., Ottawa ON K1N 5K5
Tel: 613-241-0085; *Fax:* 613-241-7998
Toll-Free: 888-385-4444
e-mail: foe@foecanada.org
URL: www.foecanada.org
Affiliation(s): Canadian Environmental Network
Beatrice Olivastri, CEO

Friends of the Greenbelt Foundation
#201, 69 Scollard St., Toronto ON M5R 1G2
Tel: 416-960-0001; *Fax:* 416-960-0030
e-mail: info@greenbelt.ca
URL: www.greenbelt.ca/the-foundation
Burkhard Mausberg, President

Greenpeace Canada
33 Cecil St., Toronto ON M5T 1N1
Tel: 416-597-8408; *Fax:* 416-597-8422
Toll-Free: 800-320-7183
e-mail: members@yto.greenpeace.org
URL: www.greenpeacecanada.org
Bruce Cox, Executive Director
Alex Paterson, Media & Public Relations Officer

Greenspace Alliance of Canada's Capital
PO Box 55085, 240 Sparks St., Ottawa ON K1P 1A1
e-mail: greenspace@greenspace-alliance.ca
URL: www.greenspace-alliance.ca
Cheryl Doran, Chair

Hamilton Industrial Environmental Association (HIEA)
PO Box 35545, Hamilton ON L8H 7S6
Tel: 905-561-4432
e-mail: info@hiea.org
URL: www.hiea.org
Jim Stirling, Chair

Harmony Foundation of Canada / Fondation Harmonie du Canada
PO Box 50022, #15, 1594 Fairfield Rd., Victoria BC V8S 1G1
Tel: 250-380-3001; *Fax:* 250-380-0887
e-mail: harmony@islandnet.com
URL: www.harmonyfdn.ca
Michael Bloomfield, Founder & Executive Director
Robert Bateman, Honorary Chair
Jean-Pierre Soublière, President
Nick Mosky, Secretary
Robert Van Tongerloo, Treasurer

Hope for Wildlife Society
PO Box 1, 5909 Hwy. 207, #14 R.R.#2, Head of Chezzetcook NS B0J 1N0
Tel: 902-452-3339
e-mail: info@hopeforwildlife.net
URL: www.hopeforwildlife.net
Hope Swinimer, CVPM, Founder & Director

Institut de recherche en biologie végétale (IRBV) / Plant Biology Research Institute (PBRI)
4101, rue Sherbrooke est, Montréal QC H1X 2B2
Tél: 514-872-0272; *Téléc:* 514-872-9406
Courriel: irbv@irbv.umontreal.ca
URL: www.irbv.umontreal.ca
André Bouchard, Président

Institute for Sustainable Energy, Economy and Environment Student's Association (ISEEESA)
Scrubfield Hall, #199B, 2500 University Dr., Calgary AB T2N 1N4
e-mail: info@iseeesa.ca
URL: www.iseeesa.ca
Mark Blackwell, President

International Council for the Exploration of the Sea (ICES)
H.C. Andersens Blvd. 44-46, Copenhagen VDK-1553 Denmark
Tel: 45-3338-6700; *Fax:* 45-3393-4215
e-mail: info@ices.dk
URL: www.ices.dk
Gerd Hubold, General Secretary
Sylvain Paradis, ICES Delegate, Canada
Michael M. Sinclair, ICES Delegate, Canada

International Institute for Sustainable Development (IISD) / Institut international du développement durable (IIDD)
161 Portage Ave. East, 6th Fl., Winnipeg MB R3B 0Y4
Tel: 204-958-7700; *Fax:* 204-958-7710
e-mail: info@iisd.ca
URL: www.iisd.org
David Runnalls, President/CEO
William H. Glanville, Vice-President & COO

Jasper Environmental Association (JEA)
PO Box 2198, Jasper AB T0E 1E0
Tel: 780-852-4152; *Fax:* 780-852-4152
e-mail: jea2@telus.net
URL: www.jasperenvironmental.org

Manitoba Eco-Network Inc. (MEN) / Réseau écologique du Manitoba inc.
#3, 303 Portage Ave., Winnipeg MB R3B 2B4
Tel: 204-947-6511; *Fax:* 204-989-8476
e-mail: info@mbeconetwork.org
URL: www.mbeconetwork.org
Anne Lindsey, Executive Director

Manitoba Environment Officers Association Inc. (MEOA)
147 Norcross Cres., Winnipeg MB R3X 1J2
e-mail: meoa@mts.net
URL: www.meoa.ca
Bill Barr, President

Manitoba Environmental Industries Association Inc. (MEIA)
#35, 301 King St., Winnipeg MB R3B 1H4
Tel: 204-783-7090; *Fax:* 204-783-6501
e-mail: admin@meia.mb.ca
URL: www.meia.mb.ca
John Fjeldsted, Executive Director
Paul Deprez, President
Vaughn Bullough, Vice-President & Secretary
Mark Saidi, Treasurer

Manitoba Wildlife Federation (MWF)
70 Stevenson Rd., Winnipeg MB R3H 0W7
Tel: 204-633-5967; *Fax:* 204-632-5200
e-mail: info@mwf.mb.ca
URL: www.mwf.mb.ca
John T. Williams, President

Municipal Waste Association (MWA)
#100, 127 Wyndham St. North, Guelph ON N1H 4E9
Tel: 519 823-1990; *Fax:* 519-823-0084
e-mail: carrie@municipalwaste.ca
URL: www.municipalwaste.ca
Vivian De Giovanni, Executive Director
Sherry Arcaro, Chair

National Energy Conservation Association (NECA) / Association nationale pour la conservation de l'énergie
PO Box 2747, Winnipeg MB R3C 4E7
Tel: 204-956-5888; *Fax:* 204-956-5819
Toll-Free: 866-268-6322
e-mail: neca@neca.ca
URL: www.neca.ca
Laverne Dalgleish, CEO & Sec.-Treas.

The Nature Conservancy of Canada (NCC) / Société canadienne pour la conservation de la nature
#400, 36 Eglinton Ave. West, Toronto ON M4R 1A1
Tel: 416-932-3202; *Fax:* 416-932-3208
Toll-Free: 800-465-0029
e-mail: nature@natureconservancy.ca
URL: www.natureconservancy.ca
Social Media: twitter.com/NatureConsCDA
John Lounds, President

New Brunswick Environment Industry Association (NBEIA) / L'Association des industries de l'environnement du Nouveau-Brunswick (AIENB)
PO Box 637, Stn. A, Fredericton NB E3B 5B3
Tel: 506-455-0212; *Fax:* 506-452-0213
e-mail: nbeia@nbnet.nb.ca
URL: www.nbeia.nb.ca
Pierre Landry, President
Eric Cook, Secretary-Treasurer

New Brunswick Environmental Network (NBEN) / Réseau environnemental du Nouveau-Brunswick (RENB)
167 Creek Rd., Waterford NB E4E 4L7
Tel: 506-433-6101; *Fax:* 506-433-6111
e-mail: nben@nben.ca
URL: www.nben.ca
Mary Ann Coleman, Executive Director

New Brunswick Wildlife Federation (NBWF) / Fédération de la faune du Nouveau-Brunswick
576, rue Principale, St. Leonard NB E7E 2H5
URL: www.nbwildlifefederation.org
Roland Michaud, President
Rod Currie, Secretary

Newfoundland & Labrador Environmental Industry Association (NEIA)
Parsons Bldg., #101, 90 O'Leary Ave., St. John's NL A1B 2C7
Tel: 709-772-3333; *Fax:* 709-772-3213
e-mail: info@neia.org
URL: www.neia.org
Linda Bartlett, Executive Director
Bill Scott, President

Newfoundland & Labrador Wildlife Federation (NWLF)
PO Box 13399, St. John's NL A1E 4S1
Tel: 709-368-6180; *Fax:* 709-739-5454
e-mail: ward.sampson@nf.sympatico.ca
URL: www.nlwf.ca
Affiliation(s): 22 affiliated conservation groups, including the Canadian Wildlife Federation (CWF), & Rod & Gun Clubs from St. John's, Bay Of Islands, Green Bay, Baie d'Espoir, Marystown, South East Placentia, & Grand Falls
Bernie Rumboldt, Contact

North American Recycled Rubber Association (NARRA)
#24, 1621 McEwen Dr., Whitby ON L1N 9A5
Tel: 905-433-7769; *Fax:* 905-433-0905
e-mail: narra@oix.com
URL: www.recycle.net/recycle/assn/narra/
Diane Sarracini, Office Manager

Nova Scotia Environmental Network (NSEN)
55 Willowbend Ct., Halifax NS B3M 3L3
Tel: 902-454-6846; *Fax:* 902-454-6841
e-mail: nsen@cen-rce.org; intern_nsen@cen-rce.org
URL: www.nsen.ca
Affiliation(s): Canadian Environmental Network (CEN)
Tamara Lorincz, Executive Director
Emma Boardman, Secretary & Agent

Nova Scotia Nature Trust (NSNT)
PO Box 2202, 2085 Maitland St., Halifax NS B3J 3C4
Tel: 902-425-5263; *Fax:* 902-429-5263
Toll-Free: 877-434-5263
e-mail: nature@nsnt.ca
URL: www.nsnt.ca
Nil d'Entremont, President
Bonnie Sutherland, Executive Director

Oak Ridges Moraine Foundation (ORMF)
The Gate House, 13990 Dufferin St. North, King City ON L7B 1B3
Tel: 905-833-5733; *Fax:* 905-833-8379
e-mail: support@ormf.com
URL: www.ormf.com
Kim Gavine, Executive Director

Offshore Energy Environmental Research Association (OEER)
Bank of Montreal Building, PO Box 2664, #400, 5151 George St., Halifax NS B3J 3P7
Tel: 902-424-8479; *Fax:* 902-424-0528
Toll-Free: 888-257-8688
e-mail: oeer@offshoreenergyresearch.ca
URL: www.offshoreenergyresearch.ca
Wayne St-Amour, Executive Director

ONEIA - Ontario Environment Industry Association
2395 Speakman Drive, Mississauga ON L5K 1B3
Tel: 416-531-7884; *Fax:* 905-855-0406
e-mail: info@oneia.ca
URL: www.oneia.ca
Affiliation(s): Canadian Standards Association; Cements Association of Canada; Ontario Concrete Pipe Association; Ontario Sewer & Watermain Construtions Association; Ontario Environmental Training Consortium; Ontario Centre for Environmental Technology Advancement
Shai Spetgang, Manager, Membership Recruitment and Sponsor Relations
Alex Gill, Executive Director

Ontario Environment Industry Association (ONEIA)
#218, 330 Adelaide St. West, Toronto ON M5V 1R4
Tel: 416-531-7884
e-mail: info@oneia.ca
URL: www.oneia.ca
Alex Gill, Executive Director

Ontario Environmental Network (OEN)
PO Box 1412, Stn. Main, North Bay ON P1B 8K6
Tel: 705-840-2888; *Fax:* 705-840-5862
e-mail: oen@oen.ca
URL: www.oen.ca
Affiliation(s): Canadian Environmental Network

Ontario Federation of Anglers & Hunters (OFAH)
PO Box 2800, 4601 Gutheir Drive, Peterborough ON K9J 8L5
Tel: 705-748-6324; *Fax:* 705-748-9577
e-mail: ofah@ofah.org
URL: www.ofah.org
John Ford, President
Mike Reader, Executive Director

Ontario Pollution Control Equipment Association (OPCEA)
PO Box 137, Midhurst ON L0L 1X0
Tel: 705-725-0917; *Fax:* 705-725-1068
e-mail: opcea@opcea.com
URL: www.opcea.com
Affiliation(s): Water Environment Association of Ontario
Kelly Manden, Executive Administrator
Brian Allen, President
Wayne Harrison, Vice-President
Heinz Held, Treasurer

Ontario Steelheaders
PO Box 604, Brantford ON N3T 5T3
e-mail: president@ontariosteelheaders.ca
URL: www.ontariosteelheaders.ca

Ontario Streams
50 Bloomington Rd. West, Aurora ON L4G 3G8
Tel: 905-713-7399; *Fax:* 905-713-7361
URL: www.ontariostreams.on.ca
Doug Forder, M.Sc, Field Supervisor

Ontario Waste Management Association (OWMA) / Société ontarienne de gestion des déchets
#3, 2005 Clark Blvd., Brampton ON L6T 5P8
Tel: 905-791-9500; *Fax:* 905-791-9514
e-mail: contact@owma.org
URL: www.owma.org
Rob Cook, President
Michele Goulding, Manager, Finance & Administration

Ottawa Duck Club (ODC)
841 Kingsmere Ave., Ottawa ON K2A 3J8
URL: www.ottawaduckclub.com
Bill Bower, President

Ottawa Riverkeeper
#2, 379 Danforth Ave., Ottawa ON K2A 0E1
Tel: 613-321-1120; *Fax:* 613-822-5258
Toll-Free: 888-953-3737
URL: www.ottawariverkeeper.ca
Meredith Brown, Executive Director

Peace Valley Environment Association (PVEA)
PO Box 6062, Fort St John BC V1J 4H6
e-mail: pvea@shaw.ca
URL: www.peacevalley.ca

The Pembina Institute
#200, 608 - 7th St. SW, Calgary AB T2P 1Z2
Tel: 403-269-3344; *Fax:* 403-269-3377
URL: www.pembina.org
Marlo Raynolds, Executive Director

Pitch-In Canada (PIC) / Passons à l'action Canada
PO Box 45011, Stn. White Rock, White Rock BC V4A 9L1
Fax: 604-535-4653
Toll-Free: 877-474-8244
e-mail: pitch-in@pitch-in.ca
URL: www.pitch-in.ca
Affiliation(s): Clean World International - London, UK
Misha van Veen, Program Manager
Valerie S. Thom, Executive Director

The Pollution Probe Foundation (PPF)
#402, 625 Church St., Toronto ON M4Y 2G1
Tel: 416-926-1907; *Fax:* 416-926-1601
e-mail: pprobe@pollutionprobe.org
URL: www.pollutionprobe.org
Affiliation(s): Clean Air Network; Ontario Clean Air Alliance
Bob Oliver, Executive Director
Patty Chilton, Deputy Executive Director

Prince Edward Island Eco-Net (PEIEN)
126 Richmond St., Charlottetown PE C1A 1H9
Tel: 902-566-4170; *Fax:* 902-566-4037
e-mail: peien@isn.net
URL: www.isn.net/~network
Susan Hawkins, Executive Director

Prince Edward Island Wildlife Federation
#103B, 420 University Ave., Charlottetown PE C1A 7Z5
Tel: 902-892-3332; *Fax:* 902-892-3334
e-mail: peiwfft@pei.aibn.com
Karl McCormack, President

Recycling Council of Alberta (RCA)
PO Box 23, Bluffton AB T0C 0M0
Tel: 403-843-6563; *Fax:* 403-843-4156
e-mail: info@recycle.ab.ca
URL: www.recycle.ab.ca
Philippa Wagner, President
Olena Juzkiw, Secretary
Paula Kuryk, Treasurer

Recycling Council of British Columbia (RCBC)
#10, 119 West Pender St., Vancouver BC V6B 1S5
Tel: 604-683-6009; *Fax:* 604-683-7255
Toll-Free: 800-667-4321
e-mail: rcbc@rcbc.bc.ca
URL: www.rcbc.bc.ca
Brock Macdonald, Executive Director

Recycling Council of Ontario (RCO) / Conseil du recyclage de l'Ontario
#407, 215 Spadina Avenue, Toronto ON M5T 2C7

Tel: 416-657-2797; Fax: 416-960-8053
e-mail: rco@rco.on.ca
URL: www.rco.on.ca
Joanne St. Godard, Executive Director

Réseau environnement
#220, 911, rue Jean Talon est, Montréal QC H2R 1V5
Tél: 514-270-7110; Téléc: 514-270-7154
Courriel: info@reseau-environnement.com
URL: www.reseau-environnement.com
Josée Méthot, Directrice générale

Réseau québécois des groupes écologistes (RQGE)
1557-A, avenue Papineau, Montréal QC H2K 4H7
Tél: 514-392-0096
Courriel: info@rqge.qc.ca
URL: www.rqge.qc.ca
Yvan Croteau, Président

Resource Conservation Manitoba Inc. (RCM)
303 Portage Ave., 3rd Fl., Winnipeg MB R3B 2B4
Tel: 204-925-3777; Fax: 204-942-4207
e-mail: info@resourceconservation.mb.ca
URL: www.resourceconservation.mb.ca

Resource Efficient Agricultural Production (REAP Canada)
Glenaladale House, PO Box 125, 21111, ch Lakeshore, Sainte-Anne-de-Bellevue QC H9X 3V9
Tel: 514-398-7743; Fax: 514-398-7972
e-mail: info@reap-canada.com
URL: www.reap-canada.com
Affiliation(s): Canadian Organic Growers; Ecological Farmers Association of Ontario
Roger Samson, Executive Director

Rideau Environmental Action League (REAL)
PO Box 1061, Smiths Falls ON K7A 5A5
Tel: 613-283-9500; Fax: 613-283-9500
e-mail: info@realaction.ca
URL: www.realaction.ca
Affiliation(s): Green Communities Canada; Ontario Environmental Network
Barb Hicks, President

Rideau Valley Conservation Authority (RVCA)
PO Box 599, 3889 Rideau Valley Dr., Manotick ON K4M 1A5
Tel: 613-692-3571; Fax: 613-692-0831
Toll-Free: 800-267-3504
e-mail: postmaster@rvca.ca
URL: www.rvca.ca
Mary A. Bryden, Chair
Charles Billington, Executive Director

Sackville Rivers Association (SRA)
PO Box 45071, Sackville NS B4E 2Z6
Tel: 902-865-9238
e-mail: sackvillerivers@ns.sympatico.ca
URL: www.sackvillerivers.ns.ca
Walter N. Regan, President

Sarnia-Lambton Environmental Association (SLEA)
1489 London Rd., Sarnia ON N7S 1P6
Tel: 519-332-2010; Fax: 519-332-2015
URL: www.sarniaenvironment.com
Dean Edwardson, General Manager

Saskatchewan Eco-Network (SEN)
#203, 115 - 2 Ave. North, Saskatoon SK S7K 2B1
Tel: 306-652-1275; Fax: 306-665-2128
e-mail: sen@link.ca
URL: www.econet.sk.ca
Affiliation(s): Canadian Environmental Network
Mike Finley, Chair
Lynn Hainsworth, Executive Director
Paddy Tutty, Administrator

Saskatchewan Environmental Industry & Managers' Association (SEIMA)
#113, 2505 - 11th Ave., Regina SK S4P 0K6
Tel: 306-543-1567; Fax: 306-543-1568
e-mail: info@seima.sk.ca
URL: www.seima.sk.ca
Lloyd Saul, President
Greg Kuntz, Vice-President
Kathleen Livingston, Executive Director & COO
Jackie Presnell, Secretary
Fred Antunes, Treasurer
Kevin Marpole, Manager, Environmental Innovations
Robbi Humble, Coordinator, Green Team

Saskatchewan Environmental Society (SES)
PO Box 1372, #203, 115 - 2nd Ave. North, Saskatoon SK S7K 3N9
Tel: 306-665-1915; Fax: 306-665-2128
e-mail: info@environmentalsociety.ca
URL: www.environmentalsociety.ca
Allyson Brady, Executive Director
Peter Prebble, Director, Energy & Water Policy
Jen Antony, Coordinator, Retire Your Ride
Angie Bugg, Coordinator, Energy Conservation
Greg Rooke, Coordinator, Pesticide Reduction
Alina Siegfried, Coordinator, Water Issues

Saskatchewan Soil Conservation Association (SSCA)
PO Box 1360, Indian Head SK S0G 2K0
Tel: 306-695-4233; Fax: 306-695-4236
Toll-Free: 800-213-4287
e-mail: info@ssca.ca
URL: www.ssca.ca
Blair McClinton, P.Ag., Executive Manager
Marilyn Martens, Office Manager

Saskatchewan Waste Reduction Council (SWRC)
#203, 115 - 2 Ave. North, Saskatoon SK S7K 2B1
Tel: 306-931-3242; Fax: 306-665-2128
e-mail: info@saskwastereduction.ca
URL: www.saskwastereduction.ca

Saskatchewan Wildlife Federation (SWF)
9 Lancaster Rd., Moose Jaw SK S6J 1M8
Tel: 306-692-8812; Fax: 306-692-4370
e-mail: sask.wildlife@sasktel.net
URL: www.swf.sk.ca
Ray Wild, President

Sea Shepherd Conservation Society (SSCS)
PO Box 48446, Vancouver BC V7X 1A2
Tel: 604-688-7325
e-mail: canada@seashepherd.org
URL: www.seashepherd.org
Paul Watson, Founder & President

SEEDS Foundation
#400, 144 - 4th Ave. SW., Calgary AB T2P 3N4
Tel: 403-221-0831; Fax: 403-221-0888
Toll-Free: 800-661-8751
e-mail: seeds@telusplanet.net
URL: www.seedsfoundation.ca
Margo Helper, Executive Director

Seventh Generation Community Projects
c/o Trucker House Renewal Centre, #155, 99 Fifth Ave., Ottawa ON K1S 5P5
Tel: 613-446-2117
e-mail: seventhgeneration@tuckerhouse.ca
URL: www.seventhgeneration.ca
Scott McKenzie, Contact

Severn Sound Environmental Association (SSEA)
67 Fourth St., Midland ON L4R 3S9
Tel: 705-527-5166; Fax: 705-527-5167
URL: www.severnsound.ca
Keith Sherman, Executive Director

Sierra Club of British Columbia (SCBC)
#302, 733 Johnson St., Victoria BC V8W 3L7
Tel: 250-386-5255; Fax: 250-386-4453
e-mail: info@sierraclub.bc.ca
URL: www.sierraclub.bc.ca
Social Media:
www.facebook.com/pages/Sierra-Club-BC/136350861428
George Heyman, Executive Director

Sierra Club of Canada (SCC) / Sierre club du Canada
#412 - 1 Nicholas St., Ottawa ON K1N 7B7
Tel: 613-241-4611; Fax: 613-241-2292
Toll-Free: 888-810-4204
e-mail: info@sierraclub.ca
URL: www.sierraclub.ca
Social Media: www.facebook.com/group.php?gid=2232053577
Affiliation(s): Common Front on the World Trade Organization
Stephen Hazell, Executive Director
Susan Paul, National Operations Director
Marilyn McGunigal, Membership Director
Katie Albright, Communications Coordinator

Sierra Club of Canada - Ontario Chapter
#102, 24 Mercer St., Toronto ON M5V 1H3
Tel: 416-960-9606; Fax: 416-960-0020
e-mail: info@sierraclub.on.ca
URL: www.sierraclub.on.ca
Affiliation(s): Sierra Club of Canada; Sierra Club - USA
Dan McDermott, Director

Sierra Club of Canada - Prairie Chapter
6328 - 104 St., Edmonton AB T6H 2K9
Tel: 780-439-1160; Fax: 780-437-3932
e-mail: prairie.chapter@sierraclub.ca
URL: www.sierraclub.ca/prairie/
Lindsay Telfer, Chapter Director

Small Water Users Association of BC
4167 Highway 3A, Nelson BC V1L 6N1
Tel: 250-825-4308
e-mail: smallwaterusers@shaw.ca
URL: www.smallwaterusers.com
Denny Ross-Smith, Executive Director

Society Promoting Environmental Conservation (SPEC)
2150 Maple St., Vancouver BC V6J 3T3
Tel: 604-736-7732; Fax: 604-736-7115
e-mail: admin@spec.bc.ca
URL: www.spec.bc.ca
Joanna Robinson, President
Isle Sarady, Manager, Operations
Catriona Gordon, Coordinator, School Gardens Community
Alicia Embree, Secretary
Jason Fast, Treasurer

Solid Waste Association of North America (SWANA)
PO Box 7219, #700, 1100 Wayne Ave., Silver Spring MD 20907-7219 USA
Tel: 301-467-9262; Fax: 301-589-7068
e-mail: info@swana.org
URL: www.swana.org
Ross Maybee, Contact, Atlantic Canada Chapter
Alan Summers, Contact, B.C./Pacific Chapter
Roland Rusnell, Contact, Northern Lights Chapter
Murray Gale, Contact, Ontario Chapter

Southeast Environmental Association (SEA)
PO Box 1500, 41 Woods Islands Hill, Montague PE C0A 1R0
Tel: 902-838-3351; Fax: 902-838-0610
e-mail: sea@pei.aibn.com
URL: www.seapei.ca
Sarah Jane Bell, Coordinator
Edgar Dewar, Chair

Sustainable Urban Development Association (SUDA)
2637 Council Ring Rd., Mississauga ON L5L 1S6
Tel: 416-400-0553
e-mail: mail@suda.ca
URL: www.suda.ca

TD Friends of the Environment Foundation / Fondation des amis de l'environnement TD
#1100, 45 O'Connor St., Ottawa ON K1P 1A4
Tel: 613-782-1196; Fax: 613-783-6319
Toll-Free: 800-361-5333
e-mail: tdfef@td.com
URL: www.td.com/fef/
Matthew Fortier, Regional Manager, ON North & East, National Programs

Thousand Islands Watershed Land Trust (TIWLT)
19 Reynolds Rd., Landsdowne ON K0E 1L0
URL: www.tiwlt.ca
Dann Michols, President

United Nations Environment Programme (UNEP) / Programme des nations unies pour l'environnement
Regional Office for North America, #506, 900 - 17th St. NW, Washington DC 20006 USA
Tel: 202-785-0465; Fax: 202-785-2096
e-mail: info@rona.unep.org
URL: www.rona.unep.org
Affiliation(s): Canadian Committee for UNEP
Amy Fraenkel, Regional Director
Robin Burgess, Finance/Administration

Water Environment Association of Ontario (WEAO)
PO Box 176, Milton ON L9T 4N9
Tel: 416-410-6933; Fax: 416-410-1626
e-mail: julie.vincent@weao.org
URL: www.weao.org
Affiliation(s): Canadian Water & Wastewater Association
Catherine Jefferson, Executive Director
Julie A. Vincent, Executive Administrator
Peter Takaoka, President
John Presta, Treasurer

Western Canada Water & Wastewater Association (WCWWA)
PO Box 1708, Cochrane AB T4C 1B6
Tel: 403-709-0064; Fax: 403-709-0068
Toll-Free: 877-283-2003
e-mail: member@wcwwa.ca
URL: www.wcwwa.ca

Affiliation(s): Canadian Water & Wastewater Association
Audrey Arisman, Executive Director

Western Canada Wilderness Committee (WCWC)
227 Abbott St., Vancouver BC V6B 2K7
Tel: 604-683-8220; *Fax:* 604-683-8229
Toll-Free: 800-661-9453
e-mail: info@wildernesscommittee.org
URL: www.wildernesscommittee.org
Andrea Reimer, Executive Director
Joe Foy, Director, National Campaign
Gwen Barlee, Director, Policy

Wild Bird Care Centre (WBCC)
PO Box 11159, Nepean ON K2H 7T9
Tel: 613-828-2849
e-mail: mojo@wildbirdcarecentre.org
URL: www.wildbirdcarecentre.org
Kathy Nihei, Founder

Wildlife Habitat Canada (WHC) / Habitat faunique Canada (HFC)
#310, 1740 Courtwood Cres., Ottawa ON K2C 2B5
Tel: 613-722-2090; *Fax:* 613-722-3318
Toll-Free: 800-669-7919
e-mail: reception@whc.org
URL: www.whc.org

Wildlife Preservation Canada (WPC) / Conservation de la faune au Canada
RR#5, 5420 Hwy 6 North, Guelph ON N1H 6J2
Tel: 519-836-9314; *Fax:* 519-836-8840
Toll-Free: 800-956-6608
e-mail: admin@wildlifepreservation.ca
URL: www.wildlifepreservation.ca
Affiliation(s): Wildlife Trust; International Union for Conservation & Nature; Durrell Wildlife Conservation Trust
Elaine Williams, Executive Director
Gerry Kurtz, President
Ellen Reinhart, Member & Donor Relations

Wood Buffalo Environmental Association (WBEA)
#100, 330 Thickwood Blvd., Fort McMurray AB T9K 1Y1
Tel: 780-799-4420
e-mail: info@wbea.org
URL: www.wbea.org
Carna MacEachern, Executive Director
Ann Dort-MacLean, President

World Wildlife Fund - Canada (WWF-Canada) / Fonds mondial pour la nature
#410, 245 Eglinton Ave. East, Toronto ON M4P 3J1
Tel: 416-489-8800; *Fax:* 416-489-3611
Toll-Free: 800-267-2632
e-mail: ca-panda@wwfcanada.org
URL: www.wwf.ca
Affiliation(s): World Wide Fund for Nature (International)
Patricia Koval, Chair
Mike Russill, President & CEO
Arlin Hackman, Vice-President, Conservation
Kim Bilous, Vice-President, Conservation Advancement
Grahame Cliff, Vice-President, Finance
Shawn Mitchell, Vice-President, Communnications & HR
Chris Elliott, Vice-President, Pacific Region
Robert Rangeley, Vice-President, Atlantic Region

Yukon Conservation Society (YCS)
302 Hawkins St., Whitehorse YT Y1A 1X6
Tel: 867-668-5678; *Fax:* 867-668-6637
e-mail: ycs@ycs.yk.ca
URL: www.yukonconservation.org
Karen Baltgailis, Executive Director
Georgia Greetham, Coordinator, Office
Sue Kemmett, Coordinator, Forestry
Anne Middler, Coordinator, Energy
Lewis Rifkind, Coordinator, Mining

Yukon Environmental Network
PO Box 30097, Whitehorse YT Y1A 5M2
Tel: 867-668-5678; *Fax:* 867-668-6637
e-mail: yukonenvironet@gmail.com
Susan Davis, Coordinator

Yukon Fish & Game Association (YFGA)
#1, 4078 - 4th Ave., Whitehorse YT Y1A 1H1
Tel: 867-667-4263; *Fax:* 867-667-4237
e-mail: yfga@klondiker.com
URL: www.yukonfga.ca
Paul Jacobs, President

Equipment & Machinery

Association des Marchands de Machines Aratoires de la province de Québec
7, rue Bernier, Bedford QC J0J 1A0
Tél: 450-248-7946; *Téléc:* 450-248-3264
Courriel: ammaq@ammaq.ca
URL: www.ammaq.ca/
Peter Maurice, Directeur général

Association des propriétaires de machinerie lourde du Québec inc. (APMLQ)
#259, 2750, ch Ste-Foy, Sainte-Foy QC G1V 1V6
Tél: 418-650-1877; *Téléc:* 418-650-3361
Ligne sans frais: 800-268-7318
Courriel: apmlq@videotron.ca
URL: www.apmlq.com/
Affiliation(s): Association des propriétaires de grues du Québec; Regroupement des loueurs de véhicules du Québec
Richard Robitaille, Président

Association of Equipment Manufacturers - Canada (AEM-Canada)
World Exchange Plaza, 111 Albert St., Ottawa ON K1P 1A0
Tel: 613-566-4568; *Fax:* 613-566-2026
URL: www.aem.org/Offices/Canada/index.asp
Howard Mains, Canadian Consultant

Canada East Equipment Dealers' Association (CEEDA)
64 Temperance St., Aurora ON L4G 2P8
Tel: 905-841-6888; *Fax:* 905-841-1214
e-mail: info@orfeda.com
URL: www.orfeda.com
Affiliation(s): North American Equipment Dealers' Association (NAEDA)
Craig Smith, Chair
Keith Stoltz, 1st Vice-Chair
Beverly J. Leavitt, President & CEO
Carol Schoen, Secretary-Treasurer

Canadian Association of Defence & Security Industries (CADSI) / Association des industries canadiennes de défense et de sécurité
#1250, 130 Slater St., Ottawa ON K1P 6E2
Tel: 613-235-5337; *Fax:* 613-235-0784
e-mail: cadsi@defenceandsecurity.ca
URL: www.defenceandsecurity.ca/public/
Tim Page, President
Andrea Walton, Manager

Canadian Association of Equipment Distributors (CAED)
4531 Southclark Pl., Ottawa ON K1T 3V2
Tel: 613-822-8861; *Fax:* 613-822-8862
e-mail: mswan@caed.org
URL: www.caed.org
Affiliation(s): Associated Equipment Distributors (USA)
Mike Christodoulou, Chair
Nancy Ellen Leu, President

Canadian Process Control Association (CPCA)
2100 Banbury Cres., Oakville ON L6H 5P6
Tel: 905-844-6822; *Fax:* 905-901-9913
e-mail: cpca@cpca-assoc.com
URL: www.cpca-assoc.com

Municipal Equipment & Operations Association (Ontario) Inc.
38 Summit Ave., Kitchener ON N2M 4W5
Tel: 519-741-2780; *Fax:* 519-741-2750
e-mail: admin@meoa.org
URL: www.meoa.org
Don Miller, Treasurer
Bill Barr, President

PIMA - Agricultural Manufacturers of Canada
PO Box 636, Regina SK S4P 3A3
Tel: 306-522-2710; *Fax:* 306-781-7293
Toll-Free: 888-999-7462
e-mail: amc@a-m-c.ca
URL: www.pima.ca
Jerry Engel, President

Ethnic Groups

Jamaica Association of Montréal Inc.
4065, Jean-Talon ouest, Montréal QC H4P 1W6
Tel: 514-737-8229; *Fax:* 514-737-4861
e-mail: jamaica_inc@yahoo.ca
URL: www.jam-montreal.com
Noel Alexander, Contact

New Brunswick African Association Inc.
URL: www.nbafricans.com
Donath Mrawira, Ph.D., P.Eng, President

Events

Alberta Music Festival Association
PO Box 416, Blairmore AB T0K 0E0
Tel: 403-562-2434; *Fax:* 403-562-7501
e-mail: president@albertamusicfestival.org
URL: www.albertamusicfestival.org
Paul Bourret, President
Jerry Lonsbury, Provincial Administrator

Associated Manitoba Arts Festivals, Inc. (AMAF)
#202, 1151 Pembina Hwy., Winnipeg MB R3T 2A3
Tel: 204-945-4578; *Fax:* 204-948-2073
e-mail: amaf@mts.net
URL: www.amaf.mb.ca
Cynthia Warkentin, President
Arlene Baschak, Vice-President

Association des professionnels en exposition du Québec (APEQ)
868, rue Brisette, Sainte-Julie QC J3E 2B1
Tél: 514-990-0224; *Téléc:* 450-922-7238
Courriel: info@apeq.org
URL: www.apeq.org
Jacques Perreault, Directeur général

Canadian Association of Exposition Management (CAEM) / Association canadienne des directeurs d'expositions
PO Box 218, #2219, 160 Tycos Dr., Toronto ON M6B 1W8
Tel: 416-787-9377; *Fax:* 416-596-1808
Toll-Free: 866-441-9377
e-mail: info@caem.ca
URL: www.caem.ca
Serge Micheli, CAE, Executive Director
Stephen Dempsey, President
Isabella Wai, 1st Vice-President
Lisa McDonald, 2nd Vice-President
Robert Halasz, Secretary
Gilles Bouchard, Treasurer
Michael Dargavel, CEM, Office Manager

Canadian Association of Fairs & Exhibitions (CAFE) / Association canadienne des foires et expositions
43 Eccles St., Ottawa ON K1R 6S3
Tel: 613-233-0012; *Fax:* 613-233-1154
Toll-Free: 800-663-1714
e-mail: info@canadian-fairs.ca
URL: www.canadian-fairs.ca
Affiliation(s): International Association of Fairs & Exhibitions; Provincial Associations of Agricultural Societies; Outdoor Amusement Business Association; Showmens League of Canada; Canadian 4H Council
Hannah Service, Executive Director
Josh Bueckert, Communications Manager

Carnaval de Québec / Québec Winter Carnival
290, rue Joly, Québec QC G1L 1N8
Tél: 418-626-3716; *Téléc:* 418-626-7252
Ligne sans frais: 866-422-7628
Courriel: comm@carnaval.qc.ca
URL: www.carnaval.qc.ca
André Roy, Président
Jean-François Côté, Directeur général

Exhibition Association of Nova Scotia (EANS)
40 Gateway Rd., Halifax NS B3M 1M9
Tel: 902-443-2039; *Fax:* 902-443-6721
e-mail: glen.jefferson@ns.sympatico.ca
URL: www.eans.ca
Glen E. Jefferson, Executive Director

Federation of Canadian Music Festivals (FCMF) / La Fédération canadienne des festivals de musique
C/O Executive Director, 113 Elm Park Rd., Winnipeg MB R2M 0W3
Tel: 204-231-2401; *Fax:* 204-231-5735
Toll-Free: 800-961-5162
e-mail: fcmf@mts.net
URL: www.fcmf.org
Affiliation(s): Canadian Conference of the Arts; provincial music festival organizations
Cindy Rublee, Executive Director
Dianne Johnstone, President

Federation of Music Festivals of Nova Scotia
82 High St., New Glasgow NS B2H 2W9
Tel: 902-752-9590
e-mail: jessie@novaanalytics.ca
Jessie MacNeil, Provincial Secretary

Festivals & Events Ontario (FEO)
180 Greenwich St., Brantford ON N3S 2X6
Tel: 519-756-3359; *Fax:* 519-756-3231
e-mail: www.festivalsandeventsontario.ca
URL: info@festivalsandeventsontario.ca
Ana Kirkham, Executive Director
Debbie Mann, Membership Development Co-ordinator

Festivals et Événements Québec (FEQ)
CP 1000, Succ. M, 4545, av Pierre-de-Coubertin, Montréal QC H1V 3R2
Tél: 514-252-3037; *Téléc:* 514-254-1617
Ligne sans frais: 800-361-7688
Courriel: info@satqfeq.com
URL: www.festivals.qc.ca/accueil.aspx
Affiliation(s): International Festivals Association
Pierre-Paul Leduc, Directeur
Luc Martineau, Directeur

Greater Vancouver International Film Festival Society (VIFF)
1181 Seymour St., Vancouver BC V6B 3M7
Tel: 604-685-0260; *Fax:* 604-688-8221
e-mail: viff@viff.org
URL: viff.org
Alan Franey, Festival Director

International Special Events Society - Toronto Chapter (ISES)
312 Oakwood Court, Newmarket ON L3Y 3C8
Tel: 905-898-7434; *Fax:* 905-895-1630
Toll-Free: 866-729-4737
e-mail: info@isestoronto.com
URL: www.isestoronto.com
Social Media: www.facebook.com/group.php?gid=7607457535
Carol Ford, Executive Director

New Brunswick Competitive Festival of Music Inc.
PO Box 2022, Saint John NB E2L 3T5
Tel: 506-847-7228
e-mail: info@nbcfm.ca
URL: www.nbcfm.ca
Affiliation(s): New Brunswick Federation of Music Festivals; Canadian Federation of Music Festivals
Elizabeth Collings, Executive Secretary
Chris Titus, President

New Brunswick Federation of Music Festivals Inc. (NBFMF) / La Fédération des festivals de musique du Nouveau-Brunswick inc. (FFMNB)
14640 Rte. 2, Somerville NB E7P 2S4
Tel: 506-375-6752
e-mail: waybar@nbnet.nb.ca
Barbara Long, Secretary

Newfoundland Federation of Music Festivals
c/o 1 Marigold Place, St. John's NL A1E 5N7
Tel: 709-722-9376
URL: www.fcmf.org/province.htm
Joan Woodrow, Provincial Administrator

Ontario Music Festivals Association (OMFA)
c/o Pam Allen, 1422 Bayview Ave., #A, Toronto ON M4G 3A7
Toll-Free: 888-307-6632
e-mail: mail@omfa.info
URL: www.omfa.info
Martha Gregory, President
James Brough, Vice-President
Steven Fielder, Treasurer
Pam Allen, Festival Administrator

Performing Arts BC Festivals Society
C/O Antonia Mahon, Executive Director, Performing Arts BC, PO Box 22042, Penticton BC V2A 8L1
Tel: 250-493-7279; *Fax:* 250-493-7279
e-mail: pafestival@gmail.com
URL: www.performingartsbc.ca
Antonia Mahon, Executive Director

Prince Edward Island Kiwanis Music Festival Association
c/o 227 Keppoch Rd., Stratford PE C1B 2J5
Tel: 902-569-2885; *Fax:* 902-569-2885
e-mail: ddcampbell@eastlink.ca
Affiliation(s): West Prince Music Festival; East Prince Music Festival; Queens County Music Festival; Kings County Music Festival
Diane Campbell, Provincial Administrator

Provincial Exhibition of Manitoba
#3, 1175 - 18 St., Brandon MB R7A 7C5
Tel: 204-726-3590; *Fax:* 204-725-0202
Toll-Free: 877-729-0001
e-mail: info@brandonfairs.com
URL: www.brandonfairs.com
Karen Oliver, General Manager
Jim Ferguson, President

Québec Competitive Festival of Music / Festival de concours du Québec
136 Duke St., Pointe Cliare QC H9R 1X9
Tél: 514-398-4535; *Téléc:* 514-398-8061
Courriel: davidson@music.mcgill.ca
Tom Davidson, Contact

Royal Agricultural Winter Fair Association (RAWF) / Foire agricole royale d'hiver
The Ricoh Coliseum, 100 Princes' Blvd., Toronto ON M6K 3C3
Tel: 416-263-3400; *Fax:* 416-263-3488
e-mail: info@royalfair.org
URL: www.royalfair.org
Bill Duron, CEO

Saskatchewan Music Festival Association Inc.
#2, 62 Westfield Dr., Regina SK S4S 2S4
Tel: 306-757-1722; *Fax:* 306-347-7789
Toll-Free: 888-892-9929
e-mail: sask.music.festival@sasktel.net
URL: www.smfa.ca
Carol Donhauser, Executive Director

Tangofest
c/o #1801, 2350 Dundas St. West, Toronto ON M6P 4B1
Tel: 416-536-8446
e-mail: info@tangofest.ca
URL: www.tangofest.ca
Musharraf Farooqi, Executive Director

Toronto International Film Festival Inc.
#1600, 2 Carlton St., Toronto ON M5B 1J3
Tel: 416-967-7371
Toll-Free: 877-968-3456
e-mail: customerrelations@tiff.net; humanresources@tiff.net
URL: www.tiffg.ca
Paul Atkinson, Chair

Vancouver International Children's Festival
402 - 873 Beatty St., Vancouver BC V6B 2M6
Tel: 604-708-5655; *Fax:* 604-708-5661
e-mail: info@childrensfestival.ca
URL: www.childrensfestival.ca
Ken Daskewech, Chair

Western Association of Exhibition Management (WAEM)
1475 East Georgia St., Vancouver BC V5L 2A9
Tel: 604-205-3955; *Fax:* 604-205-5490
e-mail: info@waem.org
URL: www.waem.org
Affiliation(s): Canadian Association of Exhibition Managers
Nick Szrejter, Secretary

Farming

Friends of the Central Experimental Farm (FCEF)
Building 72, Central Experimental Farm, Ottawa ON K1A 0C6
Tel: 613-230-3276; *Fax:* 613-230-1238
e-mail: info@friendsofthefarm.ca
URL: www.friendsofthefarm.ca
Polly McColl, President

PEI Certified Organic Producers Co-op
PO Box 1776, Charlottetown PE C1A 7N4
Tel: 902-894-9999
URL: www.organicpei.com
Mark Bernard, President

Fashion & Textiles

Alberta Men's Wear Association
PO Box 66037, Stn. Heritage, Edmonton AB T6J 6T4
Tel: 780-455-1881; *Fax:* 780-455-3969
e-mail: amwa@shaw.ca
URL: www.trendsapparel.com
Sue Brochu, Secretary

Allied Beauty Association (ABA)
#26-27, 145 Traders Blvd. East, Mississauga ON L4Z 3L3
Tel: 905-568-0158; *Fax:* 905-568-1581
Toll-Free: 800-268-6644
e-mail: abacan@idirect.com
URL: www.abacanada.com
Marc Speir, Executive Director

Apparel Manufacturers Association of Ontario
#504, 124 O'Connor St., Ottawa ON K1P 5M9
Tel: 613-231-3220; *Fax:* 613-231-2305
URL: www.ontarioapparel.com
Bob Kirke, Executive Director

Canadian Apparel Federation (CAF) / Fédération canadienne du vêtement
#504, 124 O'Connor St., Ottawa ON K1P 5M9
Tel: 613-231-3220; *Fax:* 613-231-2305
e-mail: info@apparel.ca
URL: www.apparel.ca

Canadian Association of Wholesale Sales Representatives (CAWS) / Association canadienne des représentants de ventes en gros
PO Box 54546, 1771 Avenue Rd., Toronto ON M5M 4N5
Tel: 416-782-8961; *Fax:* 416-782-5876
e-mail: caws@bellnet.ca
URL: www.caws.ca
Paul Reynard, Executive Director

Canadian Textile Association (CTA) / La Fédération canadienne du textile
4505 Paddock Trail, Niagara Falls ON L2H 3E6
Tel: 905-371-8985; *Fax:* 905-371-9238
Toll-Free: 877-897-1474
e-mail: info@cdntexassoc.com
URL: www.cdntexassoc.com
John Secondi, President

Canadian Textiles Institute (CTI) / Institut canadien des textiles
#500, 222 Somerset St. West, Ottawa ON K2P 2G3
Tel: 613-232-7195; *Fax:* 613-232-8722
e-mail: cti@textiles.ca
URL: www.textiles.ca
Harvey L. Penner, Chair

Cosmetology Association of Nova Scotia
126 Chain Link Dr., Halifax NS B3S 1A2
Tel: 902-468-6477; *Fax:* 902-468-7147
Toll-Free: 800-765-8757
URL: www.nscosmetology.ca
Dana Sharkey, Office Manager & Administrator
Malcolm Norton, President

Cosmetology Industry Association of British Columbia (CIABC)
899 West 8th Ave., Vancouver BC V5Z 1E3
Tel: 604-871-0222; *Fax:* 604-871-0299
Toll-Free: 800-663-9283
e-mail: info@ciabc.net
URL: www.ciabc.net
Norma Ann Eaton, Chair/CEO

Groupe CTT Group (CTT) / CTT Group Centre for Textile & Geosynthetic Technologies
3000, rue Boullé, Saint-Hyacinthe QC J2S 1H9
Tél: 450-778-1870; *Téléc:* 450-778-3901
Ligne sans frais: 877-288-8398
Courriel: info@gcttg.com
URL: www.groupecttgroup.com; www.gcttg.com
Affiliation(s): Fédération canadienne du textile; Association canadienne des coloristes et chimistes du textile; Société des textiles du Canada; Association des textiles des Cantons de l'Est; Institut canadien du tapis; Institut canadien des textiles; Institut québécois des revêtements de sol; Société des diplômés en textile
Jacek Mlynarek, Ph.D., President/CEO

Institut des manufacturiers du vêtement du Québec (IMVQ) / Apparel Manufacturers Institute of Québec (AMIQ)
#801, 555, rue Chabanel ouest, Montréal QC H2N 2H8
Tél: 514-382-3846; *Téléc:* 514-383-1689
Courriel: info@vetementquebec.com
URL: www.vetementquebec.com
Agar Grinberg, Directrice générale
Jane C. Binder, Administratrice

Luggage, Leathergoods, Handbags & Accessories Association of Canada (LLHA)
PO Box 144, Stn. A, Toronto ON M9C 4V2

Fax: 519-624-6408
Toll-Free: 866-872-2420
e-mail: info@llha.ca
URL: www.llha.ca

Manitoba Fashion Institute (MFI)
c/o Sterling Glove, 165 Selkirk Ave. East, Winnipeg MB R2W 2L3
Tel: 204-586-8189; Fax: 204-582-2992

Men's Clothing Manufacturers Association Inc. (MCMA) / Association des manufacturiers de vêtements pour hommes inc.
#801, 555, rue Chabanel ouest, Montréal QC H2N 2H8
Tel: 514-382-3846; Fax: 514-383-1689
e-mail: david.mcma@macten.net
Affiliation(s): Associated Clothing Manufacturers of the Province of Quebec Inc./Les Manufacturiers associés du vêtement de la Province de Québec inc; Canadian Trimmers Manufacturing Association; Montreal Clothing Contractors Association Inc./L'Association entrepreneurs en confection de Montréal inc; Quebec Council of Odd Pants Employers Inc./Conseil du patronat des fabricants de pantalons du Québec inc; Rainwear & Sportswear Manufacturers Association/L'Association des fabricants de vêtements imperméables et vêtements sports
David Balinsky, Executive Director

Ontario Fashion Exhibitors (OFE)
PO Box 218, #2219, 160 Tycos Dr., Toronto ON M6B 1W8
Tel: 416-596-2401; Fax: 416-596-1808
Toll-Free: 800-765-7508
URL: www.ofeshows.ca
Affiliation(s): Canadian Association of Wholesale Sales Representatives (CAWS)
Les Cappe, President
Jamie Finiffter, Vice-President
Serge Micheli, Executive Director
Gretchen Palmer, Secretary
Stephen Messer, Treasurer
Michael Dargavel, Show Manager

Prairie/Saskatoon Apparel Market
81 Garry St., Winnipeg MB R3C 4J9
Tel: 204-942-2060; Fax: 204-947-0561
Eric Levi, President
Pat Herzog, Market Director

Shoe Manufacturers' Association of Canada (SMAC) / Association des manufacturiers de chaussures du Canada
#203, 90, rue Morgan, Baie d'Urfe QC H9X 3A8
Tel: 514-457-3436; Fax: 514-457-8004
e-mail: hanna@shoecanada.com
George P. Hanna, President

Western Apparel Market
910 Mainland St., Vancouver BC V6B 1A9
Tel: 604-682-5719; Fax: 604-682-3892
e-mail: wambc@telus.net

Western Canada Children's Wear Markets (WCCWM)
#264, 1951 Glen Dr., Vancouver BC V6A 4J6
Tel: 604-681-1719; Fax: 604-681-1730
e-mail: jeffswartz@telus.net
Affiliation(s): WCCM
Jeff Swartz, President

Film & Video

Academy of Canadian Cinema & Television (ACCT) / Académie canadienne du cinéma et de la télévision
172 King St. East, Toronto ON M5A 1J3
Tel: 416-366-2227; Fax: 416-366-8454
Toll-Free: 800-644-5194
e-mail: info@academy.ca
URL: www.academy.ca

Alberta Motion Picture Industries Association (AMPIA)
#318, 8944 - 182 St. NW, Edmonton AB T5T 2E3
Tel: 780-944-0707; Fax: 780-426-3057
Toll-Free: 800-814-7779
e-mail: abrooks@ampia.org
URL: www.ampia.org
Colette Switzer, Office Staff
Alan Brooks, Executive Director

Association des producteurs de films et de télévision du Québec (APFTQ)
Edifice City Centre, #1030, 1450, rue City Councillors, Montréal QC H3A 2E6
Tél: 514-397-8600; Téléc: 514-392-0232
Courriel: info@apftq.qc.ca
URL: www.apftq.qc.ca

Association des réalisateurs et réalisatrices du Québec (ARRQ)
Maison de la Réalisation, 3480, rue St-Denis, Montréal QC H2X 3L3
Tél: 514-842-7373; Téléc: 514-842-6789
Courriel: realiser@arrq.qc.ca
URL: www.arrq.qc.ca
Affiliation(s): Coalition des créateurs et titulaires de droits d'auteur; Association littéraire et artistique internationale
Lise Lachapelle, Directrice générale

Atlantic Filmmakers Cooperative (AFCOOP)
PO Box 2043, Halifax NS B3J 2Z1
Tel: 902-420-4572; Fax: 902-420-4573
e-mail: membership@afcoop.ca
URL: www.afcoop.ca
Affiliation(s): Independent Film & Video Alliance; Academy of Canadian Cinema & TV; Linda Joy Busby Media Arts Foundation; Atlantic Independent Media; Atlantic Film Festival
Walter Forsyth, Executive Director

Canadian Association of Film Distributors & Exporters (CAFDE) / Association canadienne des distributeurs et exportateurs de films (ACDEF)
#1001, 2 Bloor St. West, Toronto ON M4W 3E2
Tel: 416-415-7217; Fax: 416-944-2212
e-mail: teast@cafde.ca
Affiliation(s): Association des producteurs de films et de television du Québec
Ted East, President & CEO

Canadian Film & Television Production Association (CFTPA) / Association canadienne de production de film et télévision
#902, 151 Slater St., Ottawa ON K1P 5H3
Tel: 613-233-1444; Fax: 613-233-0073
Toll-Free: 800-656-7440
e-mail: ottawa@cftpa.ca
URL: www.cftpa.ca
Guy Mayson, President & CEO
Susanne Vaas, Vice-President, Communications

Canadian Film Centre (CFC) / Centre canadien du film
2489 Bayview Ave., Toronto ON M2L 1A8
Tel: 416-445-1446; Fax: 416-445-9481
e-mail: info@cdnfilmcentre.com
URL: www.cfccreates.com

Canadian Film Institute (CFI) / Institut canadien du film (ICF)
#120, 2 Daly Ave., Ottawa ON K1N 6E2
Tel: 613-232-6727; Fax: 613-232-6315
e-mail: info@cfi-ifc.ca
URL: www.cfi-icf.ca
Tom McSorley, Executive Director, Programming

Canadian Filmmakers Distribution Centre (CFMDC)
#119, 401 Richmond St. West, Toronto ON M5V 3A8
Tel: 416-588-0725; Fax: 416-588-7956
e-mail: cfmdc@cfmdc.org
URL: www.cfmdc.org
Lauren Howes, Executive Director

Canadian Motion Picture Distributors Association (CMPDA) / Association canadienne des distributeurs de film
#1603, 22 St. Clair Ave. East, Toronto ON M4T 2S4
Tel: 416-961-1888; Fax: 416-968-1016
e-mail: info@cmpda.ca
URL: www.cmpda.org

Canadian Picture Pioneers (CPP)
#1762, 250 The East Mall, Toronto ON M9B 6L3
Tel: 416-368-1139
e-mail: cdnpicturepioneers@rogers.com
URL: www.canadianpicturepioneers.ca
John Freeborn, Executive Director
Phil May, President
Paul Wroe, Secretary-Treasurer

Canadian Society of Cinematographers (CSC)
#131, 3007 Kingston Rd., Toronto ON M1M 1P1
Tel: 416-266-0591; Fax: 416-266-3996
e-mail: admin@csc.ca; editor@csc.ca (Communications & Publications)
URL: www.csc.ca
Susan Saranchuk, Executive Director

La Cinémathèque québécoise
335, boul de Maisonneuve est, Montréal QC H2X 1K1
Tél: 514-842-9763; Téléc: 514-842-1816
Courriel: info@cinematheque.qc.ca
URL: www.cinematheque.qc.ca
Pierre Jutras, Directeur, Conservation et programmation
Suzanne Hénaut, Présidente
Yolande Racine, Directrice générale

Directors Guild of Canada (DGC) / La Guilde canadienne des réalisateurs
#402, 111 Peter St., Toronto ON M5V 2H1
Tel: 416-482-6640; Fax: 416-482-6639
Toll-Free: 888-972-0098
e-mail: info@dgc.ca
URL: www.dgc.ca
Sturla Gunnarsson, President
Brian Anthony, National Executive Director

The Harold Greenberg Fund
Astral Media, BCE Place, #100, 181 Bay St., Toronto ON M5J 2T3
Tel: 416-956-5431; Fax: 416-363-9005
e-mail: hgfund@tv.astral.com
URL: www.astralmedia.com
John Galway, President

Independent Media Arts Alliance (IMAA) / Alliance des arts médiatiques indépendants (AAMI)
3995, rue Berri, Montréal QC H2L 4H2
Tel: 514-522-8240; Fax: 514-987-1862
e-mail: info@imaa.ca
URL: www.imaa.ca
François-Xavier Tremblay, Interim National Director

The Motion Picture Theatre Associations of Canada (MPTAC) / Les associations des propriétaires des cinémas du Canada
#304, 1240 Bay St., Toronto ON M5R 2A5
Tel: 416-969-7057; Fax: 416-922-5667
e-mail: mptac.ca@ca.inter.net
URL: www.mptac.ca
Adina Lebo, Executive Director

The Moving Pictures Travelling Canadian Film Festival Society
#300, 856 Homer Street, Vancouver BC V6B 2W5
Tel: 604-681-4549; Fax: 604-687-4937
Toll-Free: 877-858-3456
e-mail: info@movingpictures.ca
Sauching Ng, Festival Director

National Screen Institute - Canada (NSI)
#400, 141 Bannatyne Ave., Winnipeg MB R3B 0R3
Tel: 204-956-7800; Fax: 204-956-5811
Toll-Free: 800-952-9307
e-mail: info@nsi-canada.ca
URL: www.nsi-canada.ca
Susan Millican, CEO

North of Superior Film Association (NOSFA)
#352, 1100 Memorial Ave., Thunder Bay ON P7B 4A3
Tel: 807-625-5450
e-mail: info@nosfa.ca
URL: www.nosfa.ca
Marty Mascarin, President
Catherine Powell, Festival Coordinator

Northern Film & Video Industry Association (NFVIA)
PO Box 31340, Whitehorse YT Y1A 5P7
Tel: 867-456-2978
e-mail: info@nfvia.com
URL: www.nfvia.com
Andy Crowther, President

On Screen Manitoba
#100, 62 Albert St., Winnipeg MB R3B 1E9
Tel: 204-927-5898; Fax: 204-943-4007
e-mail: info@onscreenmanitoba.com
URL: www.onscreenmanitoba.com
Tara Walker, Executive Director
Angie Lamirande, Manager, Marketing & Membership

Saskatchewan Motion Picture Association (SMPIA)
#W304, 2440 Broad St., Regina SK S4P 4A1
Tel: 306-525-9899; Fax: 306-569-1818
Toll-Free: 877-247-6742
e-mail: smpia@smpia.sk.ca
URL: www.smpia.sk.ca

Yukon Film Society (YFS)
4137C, 4th Ave., Whitehorse YT Y1A 1H8

Tel: 867-393-3456
e-mail: yukonfilmsociety@yknet.ca
URL: www.yukonfilmsociety.com

Mitch Miyagawa, President
Ross Burnet, General Manager

Finance

L'Alliance des Caisses populaires de l'Ontario limitée (ACPOL)
CP 3500, 1870 Bond St., North Bay ON P1B 4V6
Tél: 705-474-5634; *Téléc:* 705-474-5326
Courriel: support@acpol.com
URL: www.caissealliance.com

Lucie Moncion, Directrice générale

Association de planification fiscale et financière (APFF) / Fiscal & Financial Planning Association
#660, 1100, boul. René-Lévesque ouest, Montréal QC H3B 4N4
Tél: 514-866-2733; *Téléc:* 514-866-0113
Ligne sans frais: 877-866-0113
Courriel: apff@apff.org
URL: www.apff.org

Jean Groleau, Président
Renée Gallant, 1re Vice-présidente/Trésorière

Association des cadres municipaux de Montréal (ACMM)
2e étage, 281, rue St-Paul, Montréal QC H2Y 1H1
Tél: 514-499-1130; *Téléc:* 514-499-1737
Courriel: admin@acmm.qc.ca
URL: www.acmm.qc.ca

René Boucher, Président
Normand Moussette, Directeur général

Association of Canadian Financial Corporations (ACFC) / Association des compagnies financières canadiennes
Sussex Centre, #401, 50 Burnhamthorpe Rd. West, Mississauga ON L5B 3C2
Tel: 905-949-4920; *Fax:* 905-896-9380

Rita Minucci, Corporate Secretary

Association of Canadian Pension Management (ACPM) / Association canadienne des administrateurs de régimes de retraite
#304, 1255 Bay St., Toronto ON M4W 3B8
Tel: 416-964-1260; *Fax:* 416-964-0567
e-mail: info@acpm.com
URL: www.acpm.com

Bryan Hocking, CEO

Canada's Venture Capital & Private Equity Association (CVCA) / Association canadienne du capital de risque et d'investissement (ACCR)
Heritage Bldg., MaRS Centre, #120J, 101 College St., Toronto ON M5G 1L7
Tel: 416-487-0519; *Fax:* 416-487-5899
e-mail: cvca@cvca.ca
URL: www.cvca.ca

Richard M. Rémillard, Executive Director
Rick Nathan, Chair
Gregory Smith, President

Canadian Association of Insolvency & Restructuring Professionals (CAIRP) / Association canadienne des professionnels de l'insolvabilité et de la réorganisation (ACPIR)
277 Wellington St. West, Toronto ON M5V 3H2
Tel: 416-204-3242; *Fax:* 416-204-3410
e-mail: info@cairp.ca
URL: www.cairp.ca

Affiliation(s): The Canadian Institute of Chartered Accountants
Norman H. Kondo, BA, LLB, CIRP (, President
Sheldon Gordon, Communications Manager

Canadian Association of Pension Supervisory Authorities (CAPSA) / Association canadienne des organismes de contrôle des régimes de retraite (ACOR)
c/o CAPSA Secretariat, PO Box 85, 5160 Yonge St., 17th Fl., Toronto ON M2N 6L9
Tel: 416-590-7081; *Fax:* 416-590-7070
e-mail: capsa-acor@fsco.gov.on.ca
URL: www.capsa-acor.org

Mario Marchand, Chair
Philip Howell, Vice-Chair
Mark Prefontaine, Vice-Chair
Christian Nordin, Manager, Policy

Canadian Association of Student Financial Aid Administrators
PO Box 2875, Stony Plain AB T7Z 1Y3
e-mail: gpreston@can-reg.com
URL: www.casfaa.ca

Ken McLellan, Treasurer

Canadian Bankers Association (CBA) / Association des banquiers canadiens
PO Box 348, Stn. Commerce Court West, 199 Bay St., 30th Fl., Toronto ON M5L 1G2
Tel: 416-362-6092; *Fax:* 416-362-7705
Toll-Free: 800-263-0231
e-mail: inform@cba.ca
URL: www.cba.ca

Barbara Stymiest, Chair, Executive Council
Nancy Hughes Anthony, President & Chief Executive Officer
Andrew Addison, Manager, Media Relations

Canadian Finance & Leasing Association (CFLA) / Association canadienne de financement et de location (ACFL)
#301, 15 Toronto St., Toronto ON M5C 2E3
Tel: 416-860-1133; *Fax:* 416-860-1140
Toll-Free: 877-213-7373
e-mail: info@cfla-acfl.ca
URL: www.cfla-acfl.ca

David Powell, President/CEO
Sherry Xinhua Jia-Hatheway, Director, Finance & Administration
Vanessa Foran, CAE, Director, Policy

Canadian Institute of Financial Planning (CIFPs)
#600, 3660 Hurontario St., Mississauga ON L5B 3C4
Tel: 647-723-6450; *Fax:* 647-723-6457
Toll-Free: 866-933-0233
e-mail: cifps@cifps.ca
URL: www.cifps.ca

Keith Costello, President & Chief Executive Officer
Shirley Myers, Vice-President, Member Services & Business Development
Anthony Williams, CFP, Director, Academic Affairs
Andrew Cunningham, Manager, Information Services
Odele Burton, Corporate Secretary

Canadian Investor Relations Institute (CIRI) / Institut canadien de relations avec les investisseurs
#201, 1470 Hurontario St., Mississauga ON L5G 3H4
Tel: 905-274-1639
e-mail: enquiries@ciri.org
URL: www.ciri.org

Tom Enright, President & Chief Executive Officer
Yvette Lokker, Director, Communications & Professional Development
Karen Clutsam, Coordinator, Membership
Jennifer McInnis, Coordinator, Programming
Lisa Williams, Coordinator, Publications
Brenda McCutcheon, Bookkeeper

Canadian Payments Association (CPA) / Association canadienne des paiements (ACP)
180 Elgin St., 12th Fl., Ottawa ON K2P 2K3
Tel: 613-238-4173; *Fax:* 613-233-3385
e-mail: info@cdnpay.ca
URL: www.cdnpay.ca

Janet Cosier, Chair
Ron Morrow, Deputy Chair
Guy Legault, President & Chief Executive Officer

The Canadian Payroll Association (CPA) / L'Association canadienne de la paie (ACP)
#1600, 250 Bloor St. East, Toronto ON M4W 1E6
Tel: 416-487-3380; *Fax:* 416-487-3384
Toll-Free: 800-387-4693
e-mail: infoline@payroll.ca
URL: www.payroll.ca

Patrick Culhane, President & CEO
Wendy McLean, Manager, Marketing & Communications
Wendy Bannon, Atlantic & Ontario Region Contact
Edna Gagné, Québec Region Contact
Kristina Bruce, Pacific Region Contact
Debbie Aldridge, Prairie Region Contact
Deborah Hunt, GTA Region Contact

Canadian Pension & Benefits Institute (CPBI) / Institut canadien de la retraite et des avantages sociaux (ICRA)
CPBI National Office, #305, 465, rue St-Jean, Montréal QC H2Y 2R6
Tel: 514-288-1222; *Fax:* 514-288-1225
e-mail: info@cpbi-icra.ca
URL: www.cpbi-icra.ca

Kevin Press, Chair
Peter Buntain, Vice-Chair & Secretary
Peter Casquinha, Chief Executive Officer
Lena A. Jaoude, Manager, Marketing
Marc Tessier, Manager, Finance
Dominic Tremblay, Manager, Membership Services

The Canadian Securities Institute (CSI) / L'Institut canadien des valeurs mobilières
200 Wellington St., 15th Fl., Toronto ON M5V 3C7
Tel: 416-364-9130; *Fax:* 416-359-0486
Toll-Free: 866-866-2601
e-mail: customer_support@csi.ca
URL: www.csi.ca

Affiliation(s): Investment Dealers Association of Canada; Montreal Exchange; Toronto Stock Exchange; Canadian Venture Exchange
Roberta Wilton, President & CEO

Credit Counselling Canada (CCC) / Conseil de Credit du Canada
Columbia Sky Train Station Bldg., #330, 435 Columbia St., New Westminster BC V3L 5N8
Tel: 604-527-8999; *Fax:* 604-527-8008
Toll-Free: 888-527-8999
URL: www.creditcounsellingcanada.ca

Scott Hannah, Contact

Credit Institute of Canada (CIC) / L'Institut canadien du crédit
#216C, 219 Dufferin St., Toronto ON M6K 3J1
Tel: 416-572-2615; *Fax:* 416-572-2619
Toll-Free: 888-447-3324
e-mail: geninfo@creditedu.org
URL: www.creditedu.org

Peter Finlay, CCP, Chair, President, & Dean
Reggie Delovtich, General Manager & Secretary
Nawshad Khadaroo, CCP, Manager, Operations, Education, & Certification
Mike MacPhee, CGA-ACI, Treasurer
Fern Bellissimo, Coordinator, Membership

Credit Union Central of Canada (CUCC) / La Centrale des caisses de crédit du Canada
Corporate Office, #500, 300 The East Mall, Toronto ON M9B 6B7
Tel: 416-232-1262; *Fax:* 416-232-9196
Toll-Free: 800-649-0222
e-mail: inquiries@cucentral.com; help@cucentral.com
URL: www.cucentral.ca
Social Media: www.facebook.com/group.php?gid=132090159243

Garth Manness, Chair
David Phillips, President & Chief Executive Officer
Cheryl Byrne, Vice-President, Knowledge Services
Stephen Fitzpatrick, Vice-President, Finance & Operations
Brigitte Goulard, Vice-President, Policy
Gary Rogers, Vice-President, Financial Policy

Fédération des caisses populaires acadiennes
Place de l'Acadie, CP 5554, 295, boul St-Pierre ouest, Caraquet NB E1W 1B7
Tél: 506-726-4000; *Téléc:* 506-726-4001
Courriel: info@acadie.net
URL: www.acadie.com

Camille H. Thériault, Président/Directeur général

Fédération des caisses populaires du Manitoba
#200, 605 rue Des Meurons, Winnipeg MB R2H 2R1
Tél: 204-237-8988; *Téléc:* 204-233-6405
Courriel: federation@ciasse.biz
URL: www.caisse.biz

Affiliation(s): Mouvement Desjardins

Financial Executives International Canada (FEIC)
#1201, 170 University Ave., Toronto ON M5H 3B3
Tel: 416-366-3007; *Fax:* 416-366-3008
Toll-Free: 866-677-3007
URL: www.feicanada.org

Karyn Brooks, Chair
Louis Marcotte, Vice-Chair
Michael Conway, National President/Chief Executive
Line Trudeau, Chief Financial Officer & Secretary
Don Comish, Director, Programs
Sydney Freeston, Coordinator, Membership

Financial Planning Standards Council (FPSC)
#902, 375 University Ave., Toronto ON M5G 2J5
Tel: 416-593-8587; *Fax:* 416-593-6903
Toll-Free: 800-305-9886
e-mail: inform@fpsc.ca; communications@fpsc.ca
URL: www.fpsc.ca
Social Media: twitter.com/FPSC_Canada

Affiliation(s): The Financial Advisors Association of Canada; The Canadian Institute of Chartered Accountants; The Canadian

Institute of Financial Planning; Certified General Accountants Association of Canada; Certified Management Accountants of Canada; Credit Union Institute of Canada
Debbie Ammeter, L.L.B., CFP, Chair
James W. Kraft, CA, CFP, CLU, T, Vice-Chair
Cary List, CA, CFP, President & Chief Executive Officer
John Wickett, PhD, Senior Vice-President, Standards & Certification
Stephen Rotstein, B.A. LL.B., General Counsel & Vice-President, Policy & Enforcement
Tamara Smith, MBA, Vice-President, Marketing & Consumer Affairs

Institute of Canadian Bankers (ICB) / Institut des banquiers canadiens
#400, 625, boul René-Lévesque ouest, Montréal QC H3B 1R2
Tel: 514-282-9480; *Fax:* 514-878-4260
Toll-Free: 800-361-7339
e-mail: icb.info@csi.ca
URL: www.csi.ca/icb
Marie Muldowney, Executive Director

Institute of Canadian Bankers
CSI Global Education Inc., 200 Wellington St. West, 15th Floor, Toronto ON M5V 3C7
Tel: 416-364-9130
Toll-Free: 800-361-7339
e-mail: icb.info@csi.ca
URL: www.csi.ca

Investment Counsel Association of Canada (ICAC) / Association des conseillers en gestion de portefeuille du Canada
#1602, 110 Yonge St., Toronto ON M5C 1T4
Tel: 416-504-1118; *Fax:* 416-504-1117
e-mail: icacinfo@investmentcounsel.org
URL: www.investmentcounsel.org
Katie Walmsley, President
Bob Hill, Chair

Investment Funds Institute of Canada (IFIC) / L'Institut des fonds d'investissement du Canada
11 King St. West, 4th Fl., Toronto ON M5H 4C7
Tel: 416-363-2150; *Fax:* 416-861-9937
Toll-Free: 866-347-1961
e-mail: WebAdmin@ific.ca
URL: www.ific.ca
Affiliation(s): The Canadian Institute of Financial Planning
Oliver Murray, Chair
Charles Sims, 1st Vice-Chair
Stéphane Langlois, President

Investment Industry Regulatory Organization of Canada
#2300, 355 - 4th Ave. SW, Calgary AB T2P 0J1
Tel: 403-262-6393; *Fax:* 403-265-4603

Investment Industry Regulatory Organization of Canada (IIROC) / Organisme canadien de réglementation du commerce des valeurs mobilières (OCRCVM)
#1600, 121 King St. West, Toronto ON M5H 3T9
Tel: 416-364-6133; *Fax:* 416-364-0753
e-mail: publicaffairs@iiroc.ca
URL: www.iiroc.ca
Susan Wolburgh Jenah, President/CEO

Investment Industry Regulatory Organization of Canada
Royal Centre, PO Box 11164, #2800, 1055 West Georgia St., Vancouver BC V6E 3R5
Tel: 604-683-6222; *Fax:* 604-683-3491

Investment Industry Regulatory Organization of Canada
#1550, 5, Place Ville-Marie, Montréal QC H3B 2G2
Tél: 514-878-2854; *Téléc:* 514-878-3860

Investment Industry Regulatory Organization of Canada
#900, 145 King St. W., Toronto ON M5H 1J8
Tel: 416-646-7200; *Fax:* 416-646-7265
Toll-Free: 866-214-7200

Investors Association of Canada (IAC)
PO Box 84, #2500, 1 Dundas St. West, Toronto ON M5G 1Z3
e-mail: contact@iac.ca
URL: www.iac.ca
Chuck Chakrapani, Chair

Municipal Finance Officers' Association of Ontario (MFOA)
2169 Queen St. East. 2nd Fl., Toronto ON M4L 1J1
Tel: 416-362-9001; *Fax:* 416-362-9226
e-mail: dan@mfoa.on.ca
URL: www.mfoa.on.ca
Affiliation(s): Association of Municipalities of Ontario (AMO)
Dan Cowin, Executive Director
Nigel White, President
Calvin Barrett, Vice-President
Donna Herridge, Secretary
Ron Kaufman, Treasurer

Mutual Fund Dealers Association of Canada (MFDA) / Association canadienne des courtiers de fonds mutuels
#1000, 121 King St. West, Toronto ON M5H 3T9
Tel: 416-361-6332
Toll-Free: 888-466-6332
e-mail: mfda@mfda.ca
URL: www.mfda.ca
Larry M. Waite, President & CEO
Mark T. Gordon, Executive Vice-President

Ontario Association of Credit Counselling Services (OACCS)
PO Box 189, Grimsby ON L3M 4G3
Tel: 905-945-5644; *Fax:* 905-945-4680
Toll-Free: 888-746-3328
e-mail: oaccs@indebt.org
URL: www.indebt.org

Pension Investment Association of Canada (PIAC) / Association canadienne des gestionnaires de fonds de retraite
39 River St., Toronto ON M5A 3P1
Tel: 416-640-0264; *Fax:* 416-646-9460
e-mail: info@piacweb.org
URL: www.piacweb.org
Peter Waite, CAE, Executive Director

Registered Deposit Brokers Association (RDBA)
#308A, 49 High St., Barrie ON L4N 5J4
Tel: 705-730-7599; *Fax:* 705-730-0477
Toll-Free: 866-261-6263
URL: www.rdba.ca
Vacant, Vice-President
Brenda Molnar, Executive Director
Brian L. Smith, President

Social Investment Organization (SIO)
184 Pearl St., 2nd Fl., Toronto ON M5H 1L5
Tel: 416-461-6042; *Fax:* 416-461-2481
e-mail: info@socialinvestment.ca
URL: www.socialinvestment.ca
Eugene Ellmen, Executive Director
Andrika Boshyk, Assistant Director

Women in Capital Markets (WCM) / Les femmes sur les marchés financiers
#301, 250 Consumers Rd., Toronto ON M2J 4V6
Tel: 416-502-3614; *Fax:* 416-495-8723
e-mail: info@wcm.ca
URL: www.wcm.ca
Caroline Dabau, Chair
Martha Fell, Chief Executive Officer
Cindy Gareau, Executive Director

World Lottery Association (WLA)
Montréal Office, #2000, 500, rue Sherbrooke ouest, Montréal QC H3A 3G6
Tel: 514-282-0273; *Fax:* 514-873-8999
e-mail: lr@world-lotteries.org
URL: www.world-lotteries.org
Lynne Roiter, Head

Fisheries & Fishing Industry

Association québécoise de l'industrie de la pêche (AQIP) / Québec Fish Processor Association
#843, 2600, boul Laurier, Sainte-Foy QC G1V 4W2
Tél: 418-654-1831; *Téléc:* 418-654-1376
Courriel: aqip@quebectel.com
URL: www.quebecweb.com/aqip/

Atlantic Fishing Industry Alliance
38B John St., Yarmouth NS B5A 3H5
Tel: 902-446-4477

Atlantic Salmon Federation (ASF) / Fédération du saumon atlantique
PO Box 5200, St Andrews NB E5B 3S8
Tel: 506-529-1033; *Fax:* 506-529-4438
Toll-Free: 800-565-5666
e-mail: savesalmon@asf.ca
URL: www.asf.ca
Affiliation(s): Federation of Fly Fishers; Theodore Gordon Flyfishers; Trout Unlimited; Canadian Wildlife Federation
Bill Taylor, President & CEO
Sue Ann Scott, Vice President, Communications
Bill Mallory, Vice President & CFO

British Columbia Salmon Farmers Association (BCSFA)
#302, 871 Island Hwy., Campbell River BC V9W 2C2
Tel: 250-286-1636; *Fax:* 250-286-1574
Toll-Free: 800-661-7256
e-mail: info@salmonfarmers.org
URL: www.salmonfarmers.org
Mary Ellen Walling, Executive Director

British Columbia Seafood Alliance (BCSA)
#1100, 1200 West 73rd Ave., Vancouver BC V6P 6G5
Tel: 604-377-9213; *Fax:* 604-683-4510
e-mail: cburridge@telus.net
URL: www.bcseafoodalliance.com
Christina Burridge, Executive Director
Gina Johansen, Safety and Assistance

British Columbia Shellfish Growers Association (BCSGA)
2002 Comox Ave., Unit F, Comox BC V9M 3M6
Tel: 250-890-7561; *Fax:* 250-890-7563
e-mail: roberta@bcsga.ca
URL: www.bcsga.ca
Roberta Stevenson, Executive Director

Canadian Aquaculture Industry Alliance (CAIA) / Alliance de l'industrie canadienne de l'aquiculture
PO Box 81100, Stn. World Exchange Plaza, #705, 116 Albert St., Ottawa ON K1P 1B1
Tel: 613-239-0612; *Fax:* 613-239-0619
e-mail: info@aquaculture.ca
URL: www.aquaculture.ca
Social Media: @CDNaquaculture
Ruth Salmon, Executive Director
Sherry Sadler, Coordinator, Projects

Canadian Centre for Fisheries Innovation (CCFI) / Centre canadien d'innovations des pêches
PO Box 4920, Stn. C, Ridge Rd., St. John's NL A1C 5R3
Tel: 709-778-0517; *Fax:* 709-778-0516
e-mail: ccfi@mi.mun.ca
URL: www.ccfi.ca
Affiliation(s): Memorial University of Newfoundland; Marine Institute
Carey Bonnell, Managing Director
Gabe Gregory, Chair

Canadian Council of Professional Fish Harvesters (CCPFH) / Conseil canadien des pêcheurs professionnels (CCPP)
#712, 1 Nicholas St., Ottawa ON K1N 7B7
Tel: 613-235-3474; *Fax:* 613-231-4313
e-mail: fish@ccpfh-ccpp.org
URL: www.ccpfh-ccpp.org
John Sutcliffe, Executive Director
Earle McCurdy, President
Ronnie Heighton, Vice-President
Daniel Landry, Secretary
O'Neil Cloutier, Treasurer

Environment Resources Managament Association
PO Box 857, Grand Falls-Windsor NL A2A 2P7
Tel: 709-489-7350
URL: www.exploitsriver.ca/association.php

Fisheries Council of Canada (FCC)
#900, 170 Laurier Ave. West, Ottawa ON K1P 5V5
Tel: 613-727-7450; *Fax:* 613-727-7453
e-mail: info@fisheriescouncil.org
URL: www.fisheriescouncil.ca
Affiliation(s): International Coalition of Fisheries Associations
Patrick McGuinness, President

Fisheries Council of Canada - British Columbia Representative
4214 - 199A St., Langley BC V3A 4V6
Tel: 604-530-7258; *Fax:* 604-530-2015
e-mail: gjconsult@telus.net
Garnet Jones, President

Fishermen and Scientists Research Society (FSRS)
PO Box 25125, Halifax NS B3M 4H4
Tel: 902-876-1160; *Fax:* 902-876-1320
URL: www.fsrs.ns.ca
Patricia King, General Manager

Guysborough County Inshore Fishermen's Association (GCIFA)
PO Box 98, 990 Union St., Canso NS B0H 1H0
Tel: 902-366-2266; *Fax:* 902-366-2679
e-mail: gcifa@gcifa.ns.ca
URL: www.gcifa.ns.ca
Eugene O'Leary, President

International Pacific Halibut Commission (IPHC)
PO Box 95009, Seattle WA 98145-2009 USA
Tel: 206-634-1838; *Fax:* 206-632-2983
e-mail: info@iphc.washington.edu
URL: www.iphc.washington.edu
Bruce M. Leaman, Executive Director
Larry Johnson, Canadian Commissioner
Laura Richards, Canadian Commissioner
Gary Robinson, Canadian Commissioner
James Balsiger, US Commissioner
Ralph Hoard, US Commissioner
Phillip Lestenkof, US Commissioner

New Brunswick Salmon Growers Association
PO Box 1054, 107 Mount Pleasent Rd., St.George NB E5C 3S9
Tel: 506-755-3526; *Fax:* 506-755-6237
e-mail: info@nbsga.com
URL: www.nbsga.com
Jamey Smith, Executive Director
Sybil Smith, Director of Operations

North Atlantic Salmon Conservation Organization (NASCO)
11 Rutland Sq., Edinburgh EH1 2AS United Kingdom
Tel: 44-131-228-2551; *Fax:* 44-131-228-4384
e-mail: hq@nasco.int
URL: www.nasco.int
A. Isaksson, President, (NASCO Council, Iceland)
Malcolm Windsor, OBE, Secretary
Peter Hutchinson, Assistant Secretary

North Pacific Anadromous Fish Commission (NPAFC)
#502, 889 West Pender St., Vancouver BC V6C 3B2
Tel: 604-775-5550; *Fax:* 604-775-5577
e-mail: secretariat@npafc.org
URL: www.npafc.org
Vladimir Fedorenko, Executive Director
Suam Kim, President, (Korea)
Guy Beaupré, Canadian Representative

Nova Scotia Salmon Association (NSSA)
PO Box 396, Chester NS B0J 1J0
e-mail: nssalmo@yahoo.ca
URL: www.novascotiasalmon.ns.ca
Carl Purcell, President

Prince Edward Island Fishermen's Association (PEIFA)
#102, 420 University Ave., Charlottetown PE C1A 7Z5
Tel: 902-566-4050; *Fax:* 902-368-3748
e-mail: adminpeifa@pei.eastlink.ca; researchpeifa@pei.eastlink.ca
URL: www.peifa.org
Michael McGeoghegan, President
Ed Frenette, Manager

Prince Edward Island Seafood Processors Association
247 Mason Rd., Stratford PE C1B 2G1
Tel: 902-629-1555; *Fax:* 902-368-8127
e-mail: info@peispa.com
URL: www.peispa.com
Michael A. MacInnis, Executive Director
Eugene Bernard, President

Seafood Producers Association of Nova Scotia
Queen Square, PO Box 991, #1801, 45 Alderney Dr., Dartmouth NS B2Y 3Z6
Tel: 902-463-7790; *Fax:* 902-469-8294
e-mail: spans@ns.sympatico.ca
Roger C. Stirling, President

Food & Beverage Industry

Association des brasseurs du Québec / Québec Brewers Association
Tour Laurentienne, #475, 1981, av McGill College, Montréal QC H3A 2W9
Tél: 514-284-9199; *Téléc:* 514-284-0817
Courriel: asbq@brasseurs.qc.ca
URL: brasseurs.qc.ca
Yvon Millette, Directeur général

Association of Canadian Biscuit Manufacturers (ACBM) / Association canadienne des manufacturiers de biscuits
#301, 885 Don Mills Rd., Toronto ON M3C 1V9
Tel: 416-510-8036; *Fax:* 416-510-8043
e-mail: paigee@fspmc.com
Ileana Lima, Executive Director

Association of Canadian Distillers (ACD) / Association des distillateurs canadiens
#1203, 275 Slater St., Ottawa ON K1P 5H9
Tel: 613-238-8444; *Fax:* 613-238-3411
e-mail: info@acd.ca
URL: www.canadiandistillers.com
Jan H. Westcott, President/CEO
C.J. Hélie, Exec. Vice-President

Atlantic Food & Beverage Processors Association
500 St. George St., Moncton NB E1C 1Y3
Tel: 506-389-7892; *Fax:* 506-854-5850
e-mail: info@atlanticfood.ca
URL: www.atlanticfood.ca
Don Newman, Executive Director

Breakfast Cereal Manufacturers of Canada (BCMC)
#301, 885 Don Mills Rd., Toronto ON M3C 1V9
Tel: 416-510-8036; *Fax:* 416-510-8044
e-mail: ileanal@fcpmc.com
Affiliation(s): Food & Consumer Products Manufacturers of Canada
Kathleen Kennedy, Manager

Brewers Association of Canada / L'Association des brasseurs du Canada
#650, 100 Queen St., Ottawa ON K1P 1J9
Tel: 613-232-9601; *Fax:* 613-232-2283
e-mail: info@brewers.ca
URL: www.brewers.ca
Ian Faris, President & CEO

Brewing & Malting Barley Research Institute (BMBRI) / Institut de recherche - brassage et orge de maltage
#1510, One Lombard Place, Winnipeg MB R3B 0X3
Tel: 204-927-1407; *Fax:* 204-947-5960
e-mail: info@bmbri.ca
URL: www.bmbri.ca
Michael Brophy, President & CEO
R. Chappell, Chair

Canadian Association of Foodservice Professionals (CAFP)
#519, 1543 Bayview Ave., Toronto ON M4G 3B5
Tel: 416-422-3431; *Fax:* 416-421-1598
Toll-Free: 800-675-1189
e-mail: national@cafp.com
URL: www.cafp.com
Peter Lam, CFE, President
Gilles Mallet, CFE, Secretary
David Savage, CFE, Treasurer
Allison Miner, CFE, Contact, National Office

Canadian Association of Sales & Marketing Agencies (CASMA)
#301, 885 Don Mills Rd., Toronto ON M3C 1V9
Tel: 416-385-2322; *Fax:* 416-510-8043
e-mail: btordoff@casmaonline.ca
URL: www.casmaonline.ca
Paul Bourrie, President

Canadian Bottled Water Association (CBWA) / Association canadienne des embouteilleurs d'eau
#337-24, 155 East Beaver Creek Rd., Richmond Hill ON L4B 2N1
Tel: 905-886-6928; *Fax:* 905-886-9531
e-mail: info@cbwa.ca
URL: www.cbwa.ca
Elizabeth Griswold, Executive Director

Canadian College & University Food Service Association (CCUFSA)
National Office, Drew Hall, University of Guelph, Guelph ON N1G 2W1
Tel: 519-824-4120; *Fax:* 519-837-9302
e-mail: boeckner@uoguelph.ca
URL: www.ccufsa.on.ca
David Boeckner, Executive Director

Canadian Council of Grocery Distributors (CCGD) / Conseil canadien de la distribution alimentaire (CCDA)
#402, 6455, rue Jean-Talon est, Montréal QC H1S 3E8
Tel: 514-982-0267; *Fax:* 514-982-0659
Toll-Free: 877-229-0922
URL: www.ccgd.ca
Affiliation(s): Retail Council of Canada
Alex A. Campbell, Chair
Nick Jennery, President/CEO
Bill Sexsmith, Sec.-Treas.

Canadian Federation of Independent Grocers (CFIG) / Fédération canadienne des épiciers indépendants
#902, 2235 Sheppard Ave. East, Toronto ON M2J 5B5
Tel: 416-492-2311; *Fax:* 416-492-2347
Toll-Free: 800-661-2344
e-mail: info@cfig.ca
URL: www.cfig.ca
Francois Bouchard, Chair
John F.T. Scott, President & Chief Executive Officer
Fran Nielsen, Vice-President, Finance & Administratio
Gary Sands, Vice-President
Mark Vickars, Secretary
Brent Battistelli, Treasurer

Canadian Health Food Association (CHFA) / Association canadienne des aliments de santé
#302, 235 Yorkland Blvd., Toronto ON M2J 4Y8
Tel: 416-497-6939; *Fax:* 905-479-3214
Toll-Free: 800-661-4510
e-mail: info@chfa.ca
URL: www.chfa.ca
Terry Johnson

Canadian Meat Council (CMC) / Conseil des viandes du Canada
#305, 955 Green Valley Cres., Ottawa ON K2C 3V4
Tel: 613-729-3911; *Fax:* 613-729-4997
e-mail: info@cmc-cvc.com
URL: www.cmc-cvc.com
James M. Laws, Executive Director

Canadian Meat Science Association (CMSA) / Association scientifique canadienne de la viande (ASCB)
Dept. of Agricultural, Food & Nutritional Science, Univ. of Alberta, #4-10, Agriculture / Forestry Centre, Edmonton AB T6G 2P5
Tel: 780-492-3239; *Fax:* 780-492-4265
e-mail: cindy.rowles@ualberta.ca
URL: cmsa-ascv.ca/default.htm
Frances Nattress, President
Cindy Delaloye, Sec.-Treas.

Canadian National Millers Association (CNMA)
#103, 408 Queen St., Ottawa ON K1R 5A7
Tel: 613-238-2293; *Fax:* 613-235-5866
e-mail: dwiggins@canadianmillers.ca
URL: www.canadianmillers.ca
Gordon Harrison, President
Donna Wiggins, Director, Administration

Canadian Produce Marketing Association (CPMA) / Association canadienne de la distribution de fruits et légumes
162 Cleopatra Dr., Ottawa ON K2G 5X2
Tel: 613-226-4187; *Fax:* 613-226-2984
e-mail: question@cpma.ca
URL: www.cpma.ca
Affiliation(s): Canadian Horticultural Council
Dan Dempster, President

Canadian Snack Food Association (CSFA) / Association canadienne des fabricants des grignotines
#301, 885 Don Mills Rd., Toronto ON M3C 1V9
Tel: 416-510-8036; *Fax:* 416-510-8044
e-mail: ileanal@4reflections.com
Affiliation(s): Canadian Horticultural Council
Ileana Lima, Executive Vice-President

Canadian Sugar Institute (CSI) / Institut canadien du sucre
Water Park Pl., #620, 10 Bay St., Toronto ON M5J 2R8
Tel: 416-368-8091; *Fax:* 416-368-6426
e-mail: info@sugar.ca
URL: www.sugar.ca
Sandra Marsden, President
Jenny Gusba, Director, Nutrition & Scientific Affairs

Canadian Vintners Association (CVA) / L'Association des vignerons du Canada
#200, 440 Laurier Ave. West, Ottawa ON K1R 7X6
Tel: 613-782-2283; *Fax:* 613-782-2239
e-mail: info@canadianvintners.com
URL: www.canadianvintners.com

Affiliation(s): Wine Council of Ontario; British Columbia Wine Institute, Winery Association of Nova Scotia
Paul-André Bosc, President

Coffee Association of Canada (CAC) / Association du café du Canada
#301, 885 Don Mills Rd., Toronto ON M3C 1V9
Tel: 416-510-8032; *Fax:* 416-510-8044
e-mail: info@coffeeassoc.com
URL: www.coffeeassoc.com

Confectionery Manufacturers Association of Canada (CMAC) / Association canadienne des fabricants de confiseries
#301, 885 Don Mills Rd., Toronto ON M3C 1V9
Tel: 416-510-8034; *Fax:* 416-510-8043
e-mail: info@cmaconline.ca
URL: www.confectioncanada.com
John Rowsome, President
Pat Gagne, Executive Assistant

Conseil de la transformation agroalimentaire et des produits de consommation (CTAC) / Council of Food Processing & Consumer Products
#102, 200, rue MacDonald, Saint-Jean-sur-Richelieu QC J3B 8J6
Tél: 450-349-1521; *Téléc:* 450-349-6923
Courriel: info@conseiltac.com
URL: www.conseiltac.com
Jacques Légaré, Président-directeur général

Flavour Manufacturers Association of Canada (FMAC) / Association canadienne de fabricants des arômes
#301, 885 Don Mills Rd., Toronto ON M3C 1V9
Tel: 416-510-8036; *Fax:* 416-510-8044
e-mail: ileanal@fcpmc.com
Ileana Lima, Administrator

Food & Consumer Products of Canada (FCPC) / Produits alimentaires et de consommation du Canada (PACC)
#301, 885 Don Mills Rd., Toronto ON M3C 1V9
Tel: 416-510-8024; *Fax:* 416-510-8043
e-mail: info@fcpc.ca
URL: www.fcpc.ca
Nancy Croitoru, President/CEO
Kathleen Kennedy, Vice-President, Finance & Administration

Food Processors of Canada (FPC) / Fabricants de produits alimentaires du Canada
350 Sparks St., Ottawa ON K1R 7S8
Tel: 613-722-1000; *Fax:* 613-722-1404
e-mail: fpc@foodprocessors.ca; conferences@foodprocessors.ca
URL: www.foodprocessors.ca
Christopher J. Kyte, President
Mel Fruitman, Vice-President

New Brunswick Maple Syrup Association (NBMSA)
#223, 1350 Regent St., Fredericton NB E3C 2G6
Tel: 506-458-8889; *Fax:* 506-454-0652
e-mail: yrp@nb.aibn.com
URL: www.maple.infor.ca
Yvon Poitras, General Manager

Ontario Coffee & Vending Service Association (OCVSA)
#301, 885 Don Mills Rd., Toronto ON M3C 1V9
Tel: 416-510-8032; *Fax:* 416-510-8044
e-mail: info@coffeeassoc.com
URL: www.coffeeassoc.com/ocvsa.htm

Ontario Food Processors Association (OFPA)
7660 Mill Rd., RR#4, Guelph ON N1S 6J1
Tel: 519-767-5599; *Fax:* 519-763-4164
e-mail: ofpa@sentex.net
Jane Graham, Executive Director

Ontario Independent Meat Processors (OIMP)
7660 Mill Rd., Guelph ON N1H 6J1
Tel: 519-763-4558; *Fax:* 519-763-4164
Toll-Free: 800-263-3797
e-mail: info@oimp.ca
URL: www.oimp.ca
Affiliation(s): American Association of Meat Processors, Alliance of Ontario Food Processors
Laurie Nicol, Executive Director
Tony Facciolo, President

Pet Food Association of Canada (PFAC) / Association des fabricants d'aliments pour animaux familiers du Canada
PO Box 35570, 2528 Bayview Ave., Toronto ON M2L 2Y4
Tel: 416-447-9970; *Fax:* 416-443-9137
e-mail: info@pfac.com
URL: www.pfac.com

Refreshments Canada / Association canadienne de l'industrie des boissons gazeuses
#301, 885 Don Mills Rd., Toronto ON M3C 1V9
Tel: 416-362-2424; *Fax:* 416-362-3229
URL: www.refreshments.ca
Anthony Van Heyningen, Acting Executive Director

Tea Association of Canada (TAC) / Association du thé du Canada
#602, 133 Richmond St. West, Toronto ON M5H 2L3
Tel: 416-510-8647; *Fax:* 416-510-8044
e-mail: info@tea.ca
URL: www.tea.ca
Louise Roberge, CAE, President

Wine Council of Ontario
#B205, 110 Hannover Dr., St Catharines ON L2W 1A4
Tel: 905-684-8070; *Fax:* 905-684-2993
e-mail: info@winesofontario.org
URL: www.winesofontario.org
Sherri Haigh, Contact

Yukon Food Processors Association (YFPA)
PO Box 20437, Whitehorse YT Y1A 7A2
Tel: 867-393-3189
URL: processors.yukonfood.com
Michell Spittal, President

Forestry & Forest Products

Alberta Forest Products Association (AFPA)
#500, 10709 Jasper Ave., Edmonton AB T5J 3N3
Tel: 780-452-2841; *Fax:* 780-455-0505
e-mail: info@albertforestproducts.ca
URL: www.albertaforestproducts.ca
Affiliation(s): Alberta Forestry Association; Canadian Lumber Standards; Canadian Wood Council; Forintek Canada; National Lumber Grade Authority
Neil Shelly, Executive Director

Alberta Forestry Association
4331 - 114B St., Edmonton AB T6J 1N8
Tel: 780-432-3683; *Fax:* 780-430-8349
e-mail: jimrmefc@telusplanet.net
Audrey Ruff, Executive Director

Association of British Columbia Forest Professionals (ABCFP)
#1030, 1188 Georgia St. West, Vancouver BC V6E 4A2
Tel: 604-687-8027; *Fax:* 604-687-3264
e-mail: info@abcfp.ca
URL: www.abcfp.ca
Sharon Glover, Executive Director

Association of Registered Professional Foresters of New Brunswick (ARPFNB) / Association des forestiers agréés du Nouveau-Brunswick (AFANB)
#221, 1350 Regent St., Fredericton NB E3C 2G6
Tel: 506-452-6933; *Fax:* 506-450-3128
e-mail: info@arpfnb.ca
URL: www.arpfnb.ca
Affiliation(s): Canadian Federation of Professional Foresters Association (CFPFA)
Jennifer Hacking, RPF, Executive Director
Doug Prosser, RPF, President
John Kershaw, RPF, Vice-President
Edwin Swift, RPF, Secretary-Treasurer

Canadian Forestry Association (CFA) / Association forestière canadienne
#200, 1027 Pembroke St., Pembroke ON K8A 3M4
Tel: 613-732-2917; *Fax:* 613-732-3386
Toll-Free: 866-441-4006
e-mail: cfa@canadianforestry.com
URL: www.canadianforestry.com
Barry Waito, Chair

Canadian Forestry Association of New Brunswick (CFANB) / Association forestière canadienne du Nouveau-Brunswick (AFCNB)
Maritime College of Forest Technology, #248, 1350 Regent St., Fredericton NB E3C 2G6
Tel: 506-452-1339; *Fax:* 506-452-7950
Toll-Free: 866-405-7000
e-mail: info@cfanb.ca
URL: www.cfanb.ca
Valerie Archibald, Associate Director

Canadian Hardwood Plywood & Veneer Association (CHPVA) / Association canadienne du Contreplaqué et de Placages de bois dur (ACCPBD)
47, rue de Richelieu, Chambly QC J3L 2C3
Tel: 514-733-2777; *Fax:* 514-733-2777
e-mail: michel.tremblay2@bellnet.ca
URL: www.chpva.ca
Michel G. Tremblay, Executive vice-president
Céline Brisebois, Coordinator

Canadian Institute of Forestry / Institut forestier du Canada
c/o The Canadian Ecology Centre, PO Box 430, 6905 Hwy. 17 West, Mattawa ON P0H 1V0
Tel: 705-744-1715; *Fax:* 705-744-1716
Toll-Free: 888-747-7577
e-mail: cif@cif-ifc.org
URL: www.cif-ifc.org
John Pineau, Executive Director
Fred Pinto, R.P.F., President

Canadian Lumber Standards Accreditation Board (CLSAB)
#406, 960 Quayside Dr., New Westminster BC V3M 6G2
Tel: 604-524-2338; *Fax:* 604-524-6932
e-mail: info@clsab.ca
URL: www.clsab.ca

Canadian Lumbermen's Association (CLA) / Association canadienne de l'industrie du bois (ACIB)
#200, 30 Concourse Gate, Ottawa ON K2E 7V7
Tel: 613-233-6205; *Fax:* 613-233-1929
e-mail: info@cla-ca.ca
URL: www.canadianlumbermen.com
Jean-François Houde, President & Executive Director

Canadian Pallet Council (CPC) / Conseil des palettes du Canada
239 Division St., Cobourg ON K9A 3P9
Tel: 905-372-1871; *Fax:* 905-373-0230
e-mail: info@cpcpallet.com
URL: www.cpcpallet.com
Belinda Junkin, President/CEO

Canadian Plywood Association
735 - 15 St. West, North Vancouver BC V7M 1T2
Tel: 604-981-4190; *Fax:* 604-985-0342
e-mail: info@canply.org
URL: www.canply.org
Judy White, Office Manager
James F. Shaw, President

Canadian Pulp & Paper Network for Innovation in Education & Research / Réseau canadien de pâtes et papiers pour l'innovation en éducation et en recherche
570, boul St-Jean, Pointe-Claire QC H9R 3J9
Tel: 514-630-4100; *Fax:* 514-630-4107
e-mail: papier@paprican.ca
URL: www.papiernet.ca
J.D. Wright, Interim Chair

Canadian Well Logging Society (CWLS)
Scotia Centre, #2200, 700 - 2nd St. SW, Calgary AB T2P 2W1
Tel: 403-269-9366; *Fax:* 403-269-2787
e-mail: roy_benteau@eogresources.com
URL: www.cwls.org
Gary Drebit, Membership Chair
Roy Benteau, President

Canadian Wood Council (CWC) / Conseil canadien du bois (CCB)
#400, 99 Bank St., Ottawa ON K1P 6B9
Tel: 613-747-5544; *Fax:* 613-747-6264
Toll-Free: 800-463-5091
e-mail: admin@cwc.ca
URL: www.cwc.ca
Pauline Rochefort, President

Canadian Wood Pallet & Container Association (CWPCA) / Association canadienne des manufacturiers de palettes et contenants
PO Box 128, Fenelon Falls ON K0M 1N0
Tel: 705-887-6468; *Fax:* 705-887-1835
Toll-Free: 877-224-3555
e-mail: cwpca@canadianpallets.com
URL: www.canadianpallets.com/home.asp

Affiliation(s): National Wooden Pallet & Container Association; Western Pallet Association
Gordon R. Hughes, Executive General Manager

Canadian Wood Preservers Bureau (WPC) / Préservation du bois Canada
#202, 2141 Thurston Dr., Ottawa ON K1G 6C9
Tel: 613-737-4337; *Fax:* 613-247-0540
e-mail: info@woodpreservation.ca
URL: www.woodpreservation.ca
Henry Walthert, Executive Director

Christmas Tree Farmers Association of Ontario
PO Box 93, Wasaga Beach ON L9Z 1A2
Tel: 705-429-5328; *Fax:* 705-429-6561
e-mail: ctfo@christmastrees.on.ca
URL: www.christmastrees.on.ca

College of Alberta Professional Foresters
#209, 10544 - 106 St., Edmonton AB T5H 2X6
Tel: 780-432-1177; *Fax:* 780-432-7046
e-mail: office@capf.ca
URL: www.capf.ca
Affiliation(s): Alberta Forest Technologists Association; Canadian Institute of Forestry
Ted Gooding, President

Conseil de l'industrie forestière du Québec (CIFQ) / Québec Forestry Industry Council (QFIC)
#200, 1175, av Lavigerie, Sainte-Foy QC G1V 4P1
Tél: 418-657-7916; *Téléc:* 418-657-7971
Courriel: info@cifq.qc.ca
URL: www.cifq.qc.ca
Guy Chevrette, Président-directeur général

Consulting Foresters of British Columbia
PO Box 98, Pender Island BC V0N 2M0
Tel: 250-656-8818
e-mail: info@cfbc.bc.ca
URL: www.cfbc.bc.ca
Robert Schuetz, President
Stan Price, Vice-President

Council of Forest Industries (COFI)
Pender Place I Business Bldg., #1501, 700 Pender St. West, Vancouver BC V6C 1G8
Tel: 604-684-0211; *Fax:* 604-687-4930
e-mail: info@cofi.org
URL: www.cofi.org
John Allan, President/CEO
Paul J. Newman, Market Access & Trade
Anne Mauch, Director, Regulatory Issues
Gary Crooks, Vice-President, Southern Operations
Doug Routledge, Vice-President, Foresty & Northern Operations

La Fédération des producteurs de bois du Québec (FPBQ)
#565, 555, boul Roland-Therrien, Longueuil QC J4H 4E7
Tél: 450-679-0530; *Téléc:* 450-679-4300
Courriel: bois@upa.qc.ca
URL: www.fpbq.qc.ca
Affiliation(s): Union des producteurs agricoles
Jean-Pierre Dansereau, Directeur

Fored BC
#213, 4438 - 10th Ave. West, Vancouver BC V6R 4R8
Tel: 604-737-8555; *Fax:* 604-737-8598
Toll-Free: 888-288-7337
e-mail: info@foredbc.org; education@foredbc.org; admin@foredbc.org
URL: www.landscapesmag.com
Cheryl Ziola, President

Forest Products Association of Canada (FPAC) / Association des produits forestiers du Canada
#410, 99 Bank St., Ottawa ON K1P 6B9
Tel: 613-563-1441; *Fax:* 613-563-4720
e-mail: ottawa@fpac.ca; customercentre@fpac.ca
URL: www.fpac.ca
Avrim Lazar, President/CEO
Jean-Pierre Martel, Sr. Vice-President, Sustainability
Lori Harop, Executive Director, Environmental Reputation Project

Forest Products Association of Nova Scotia (FPANS)
PO Box 696, Truro NS B2N 5E5
Tel: 902-895-1179; *Fax:* 902-893-1197
e-mail: stalbot@fpans.ca
URL: www.fpans.ca
Steve Talbot, Executive Director
Jeff Bishop, Coordinator, Communications

Manitoba Forestry Association Inc.
900 Corydon Ave., Winnipeg MB R3M 0Y4
Tel: 204-453-3182; *Fax:* 204-477-5765
e-mail: mfainc@mts.net
URL: www.mbforestryassoc.ca
Patricia Pohrebnuk, Executive Director
Jennifer Lidgett, President

Maritime Lumber Bureau (MLB) / Bureau de bois de sciage des Maritimes
PO Box 459, Amherst NS B4H 4A1
Tel: 902-667-3889; *Fax:* 902-667-0401
Toll-Free: 800-667-9192
e-mail: mlb@ns.sympatico.ca
URL: www.mlb.ca
Diana L. Blenkhorn, President & CEO

National Aboriginal Forestry Association (NAFA)
#300, 396 Cooper St., Ottawa ON K2P 2H7
Tel: 613-233-5563; *Fax:* 613-233-4329
e-mail: hbombay@nafaforestry.org
URL: www.nafaforestry.org
Harry M. Bombay, Executive Director
Peggy Smith, RPF, Senior Advisor
Janet Pronovost, Office Manager

New Brunswick Forest Products Association Inc. (NBFPA) / L'Association des produits forestiers du Nouveau-Brunswick (APFNB)
Hugh John Flemming Forestry Centre, 1350 Regent St., Fredericton NB E3C 2G6
Tel: 506-452-6930; *Fax:* 506-450-3128
e-mail: info@nbforestry.com
URL: www.nbforestry.com
Mark Arsenault, President and CEO

Newfoundland & Labrador Forest Protection Association
PO Box 728, Mount Pearl NL A1N 2C2
Tel: 709-729-1012; *Fax:* 709-368-2740
e-mail: nlfpa@nfld.com
URL: www.nlfpa.nfol.ca
Doug Rex, Executive Director
William Furey, President

Nova Scotia Forestry Association (NSFA)
PO Box 6901, Port Hawkesbury NS B9A 2W2
Tel: 902-625-2935
e-mail: dwaycott@nsfa.ca
URL: www.nsfa.ca
Debbie Waycott, Executive Director

Ontario Forest Industries Association (OFIA) / l'Industrie forestière de l'Ontario
#950, 20 Toronto St., Toronto ON M5C 2B8
Tel: 416-368-6188; *Fax:* 416-368-5445
e-mail: info@ofia.com
URL: www.ofia.com
Jamie Lim, President/CEO
Mark Holmes, Manager, Public Affairs
Scott Jackson, Manager, Forest Policy

Ontario Forestry Association (OFA) / Association forestière de l'Ontario
#701, 200 Consumers Rd., Toronto ON M2J 4R4
Tel: 416-493-4565; *Fax:* 416-493-4608
Toll-Free: 800-387-0790
e-mail: forestry@oforest.on.ca
URL: www.oforest.on.ca
Carla Grant, Executive Director

Ontario Lumber Manufacturers' Association (OLMA) / Association des manufacturiers de bois de sciage de l'Ontario
PO Box 97530, #1202, 55 York St., Toronto ON M1C 4Z1
Tel: 416-367-9717; *Fax:* 416-367-3415
e-mail: info@olma.ca
URL: www.olma.ca
Affiliation(s): Canadian Lumber Standards Accreditation Board; American Lumber Standards Committee, Inc.
Dale Kaemingh, Chair
Hartley Multamaki, Vice-Chair
David G. Milton, President & Secretary
Hal Brindley, Treasurer
Andre G. Boucher, Chief Grading Inspector

Ontario Professional Foresters Association (OPFA)
PO Box 91523, #201, 5 Wesleyan St., Georgetown ON L7G 2E2
Tel: 905-877-3679; *Fax:* 905-877-6766
e-mail: opfa@opfa.ca
URL: www.opfa.ca
David Milton, President

Carl Corbett, Vice-President

Ontario Urban Forest Council (OUFC)
#23/25, 1523 Warden Ave., Toronto ON M1R 4Z8
Tel: 416-936-6735; *Fax:* 416-291-9584
e-mail: jradec@mountpleasantgroup.com
URL: www.oufc.org
Affiliation(s): Urban Forest Network
Jack Radecki, Executive Director

Ordre des ingénieurs forestiers du Québec (OIFQ)
#110, 2750, rue Einstein, Québec QC G1P 4R1
Tél: 418-650-2411; *Téléc:* 418-650-2168
Courriel: oifq@oifq.com
URL: www.oifq.com
Affiliation(s): Fédération canadienne des associations d'ingénieurs forestiers
Pierre Mathieu, ing.f., Président

Prince Edward Island Forest Improvement Association (PEIFIA)
c/o Richard Gill, RR#5, Mount Stewart PE C0A 1T0
Tel: 902-651-2059

Registered Professional Foresters Association of Nova Scotia (RPFANS)
PO Box 1031, Truro NS B2N 5G9
Tel: 902-893-0099
e-mail: contact@rpfans.ca
URL: www.rpfans.ca
John Ross, President

Regroupement des associations forestières régionales du Québec
#100, 138, rue Wellington nord, Sherbrooke QC J1H 5C5
Tél: 819-562-3388; *Téléc:* 819-562-2433
Courriel: info@afce.qc.ca
URL: www.afvsm.qc.ca/region.htm
Daniel Archambault

Saskatchewan Forestry Association (SFA)
#137, 1061 Central Ave., Prince Albert SK S6V 4V4
Tel: 306-763-2189; *Fax:* 306-764-7463
e-mail: info@whitebirch.ca
URL: www.whitebirch.ca
Affiliation(s): Canadian Forestry Association

Sustainable Forest Management Network (SFMN) / Réseau de la gestion durable des forêts
#3-03 Civil Electrical Bldg., University of Alberta, Edmonton AB T6G 2G7
Tel: 780-492-6659; *Fax:* 780-492-8160
e-mail: info@sfmnetwork.ca
URL: www.sfmnetwork.ca
Dale Bischoff, Network Manager

Wood Preservation Canada / Préservation du bois Canada
#202, 2141 Thurston Dr., Ottawa ON K1G 6C9
Tel: 613-737-4337; *Fax:* 613-247-0540
Toll-Free: 800-463-8733
e-mail: info@woodpreservation.ca
URL: www.woodpreservation.ca
Affiliation(s): Canadian Wood Council
Henry Walthert, Executive Director

Fraternal

Benevolent & Protective Order of Elks of Canada
#100, 2629 - 29 Ave., Regina SK S4S 2N9
Tel: 306-359-9010; *Fax:* 306-565-2860
Toll-Free: 888-843-3557
e-mail: ger@elks-canada.org
URL: www.elks-canada.org
Duane Romuld, Grand Exalted Ruler

Les Chevaliers de Colomb du Québec / Knights of Columbus of Québec
670, av Chambly, Saint-Hyacinthe QC J2S 6V4
Tél: 450-768-0616; *Téléc:* 450-768-1660
Ligne sans frais: 866-893-3681
Courriel: info@chevaliersdecolomb.com
URL: www.chevaliersdecolomb.com

Les Chevaliers de Colomb du Québec, District No 37, Conseil 5198
CP 141, 124, rue des Forces Armées, Chibougamau QC G8P 2L5
Tél: 418-748-2411
URL: www.chevaliersdecolomb.com
Jacques Fortin, Député de district
Reynald Bouchard, Grand Chevalier

Empire Club of Canada
Fairmont Royal York Hotel, 100 Front St. West, Level H, Toronto ON M5J 1E3
Tel: 416-364-2878; *Fax:* 416-364-7271
e-mail: empireclub@bellnet.ca
URL: www.empireclubfoundation.com
Jo-Ann McArthur, President

Foresters
Forester House, 789 Don Mills Rd., Toronto ON M3C 1T9
Tel: 416-429-3000; *Fax:* 416-467-2518
Toll-Free: 800-828-1540
e-mail: service@foresters.com
URL: www.foresters.com
Affiliation(s): Children's Miracle Network; Barnardo's Children's Charity (U.K.)
George Mohacsi, CEO

Grand Orange Lodge of Canada
94 Sheppard Ave. West, Toronto ON M2N 1M5
Tel: 416-223-1690; *Fax:* 416-223-1324
Toll-Free: 800-565-6248
e-mail: secretary@grandorangelodge.ca
URL: www.grandorangelodge.ca
John Chalmers, Grand Secretary

International Association of Rebekah Assemblies
c/o The Sovereign Grand Lodge IOOF, 422 Trade St., Winston-Salem NC 27101 USA
Tel: 336-725-6037; *Fax:* 336-773-1066
Toll-Free: 800-766-1838
e-mail: iarasec@aol.com
URL: www.ioof.org/rebekahs.html

IODE Canada (IODE)
#254, 40 Orchard View Blvd., Toronto ON M4R 1B9
Tel: 416-487-4416; *Fax:* 416-487-4417
Toll-Free: 866-827-7428
e-mail: iodecanada@bellnet.ca
URL: www.iode.ca
Affiliation(s): IODE Bahamas
Chris Bateman, President

Knights Hospitallers, Sovereign Order of St. John of Jerusalem, Knights of Malta, Grand Priory of Canada (OSJ)
Grand Chancery Canada, 52 Kingswood Dr., Bowmanville ON L1E 1Z3
Tel: 905-579-0326; *Fax:* 905-579-3773
Affiliation(s): United Nations - Canada, participant
Joseph Frendo Cumbo, Grand Master
M. Sillato, Secretary General
Violet Sillato, Treasurer General

Knights of Pythias - Domain of British Columbia
#B7, 7155 ETC Hwy., Kamloops BC V2C 4T1
Tel: 250-573-3056
URL: www.members.shaw.ca/veng/
Affiliation(s): Supreme Lodge Knights of Pythias
Edward J. Eagles, Grand Secretary

Ladies' Orange Benevolent Association of Canada
c/o Grand Orange Lodge of Canada, 94 Sheppard Ave. West, Toronto ON M2N 1M5
Fax: 416-223-1324
Toll-Free: 800-565-6248
URL: www.grandorangelodge.ca/loba; www.orangenet.org/loba.htm
Chalmers John, Grand Secretary, Grand Lodge of Canada

Order of Sons of Italy in Canada
5 Barbican Gate, St Catharines ON L2T 3Z6
Tel: 905-227-9236; *Fax:* 905-227-4600
URL: ordersonsofitalycanada.com
Patsy Giammarco, National Administative Secretary
Fernando Forcucci, National President

The Order of United Commercial Travelers of America (UCT)
#300, 901 Centre St. North, Calgary AB T2E 2P6
Tel: 403-277-0745; *Fax:* 403-277-6662
Toll-Free: 800-267-2371
e-mail: lmaxwell@uct.org
URL: www.uct.org
Lindsay Maxwell, Chief Agent

Réseau Hommes Québec (RHQ)
#134, 911, rue Jean-Talon est, Montréal QC H2R 1V5
Tél: 514-276-4545
Ligne sans frais: 877-908-4545
Courriel: info@rhq.ca
URL: www.rhq.ca
Affiliation(s): Réseau Hommes Belgique; Réseau Hommes France; Réseau Hommes Romandie; Réseau Femmes Québec
Guy Corneau, Fondateur

Royal Arch Masons of Canada
361 King St. West, Hamilton ON L8P 1B4
Tel: 905-522-5775; *Fax:* 905-522-5099
e-mail: melduke@netcom.ca
Melvyn J. Duke, Grand Scribe E.

Society of Kabalarians of Canada
5912 Oak St., Vancouver BC V6M 2W2
Tel: 604-263-9551; *Fax:* 604-263-5514
Toll-Free: 866-489-1188
e-mail: info1@kabalarians.com
URL: www.kabalarians.com
Lorenda Bardell, President

Sons of Scotland Benevolent Association
#202, 40 Eglinton Ave. East, Toronto ON M4P 3A2
Tel: 416-482-1250; *Fax:* 416-482-9576
Toll-Free: 800-387-3382
e-mail: info@sonsofscotland.com
URL: www.sonsofscotland.com
Robert Stewart, Executive Director

Yukon Order of Pioneers (YOOP)
Tel: 867-667-2564
e-mail: h_rwilcox@hotmail.com
URL: www.yukon-seniors-and-elders.org/yukonorder.home.htm
Rob Wilcox, President

Funeral Services

Alberta Funeral Service Association (AFSA)
#5, 5431 - 43 St., Calgary AB T2X 3C9
Tel: 403-342-2460; *Fax:* 403-342-2495
Toll-Free: 800-803-8809
e-mail: inquiry@afsa.ca
URL: www.afsa.ab.ca
Affiliation(s): Funeral Service Association of Canada
Deanna Schroeder, Executive Administrator

Cemetery & Crematorium Association of British Columbia (CCABC)
#211, 2187 Oak Bay Ave., Victoria BC V8R 1G1
Tel: 866-587-3213
e-mail: info@ccabc.org
URL: www.ccabc.org
John Chasca, President
Blair Wallin, Vice-President

Corporation des thanatologues du Québec (CTQ)
#115, 4600, boul Henri-Bourassa, Québec QC G1H 3A5
Tél: 418-622-1717; *Téléc:* 418-622-5557
Ligne sans frais: 800-463-4935
Courriel: info@corpothanato.com
URL: www.corpothanato.com
Marc Porier, Président

Funeral & Cremation Services Council of Saskatchewan
3847C Albert St., Regina SK S4S 3R4
Tel: 306-584-1575; *Fax:* 306-584-1576
Toll-Free: 800-892-0116
e-mail: sask.funeral@sasktel.net
URL: www.fcscs.ca
Affiliation(s): Funeral Service Association of Canada
Terry Zip, Chair
R.G. (Bob) Carter, Registrar

Funeral Advisory & Memorial Society (FAMS)
55 St. Phillips Rd., Toronto ON M9P 2N8
Tel: 416-241-6274
e-mail: info@fams.ca
URL: www.fams.ca
Albert Tucker, Chair
Paul Siemens, Vice-Chair & Secretary
Johanna Ntiforo, Office Administrator

Funeral Service Association of British Columbia (FSABC)
#211, 2187 Oak Bay Ave., Victoria BC V8R 1G1
Tel: 250-592-3213; *Fax:* 250-592-4362
Toll-Free: 800-665-3899
e-mail: info@bcfunerals.com
URL: www.bcfunerals.com

Funeral Service Association of Canada (FSAC) / L'Association des services funéraires du Canada
#6, 14845 Yonge St., Suite 192, Aurora ON L4G 6H8
Tel: 905-841-7779
Toll-Free: 866-841-7779
e-mail: info@fsac.ca
URL: www.fsac.ca
Marc Poirier, President
Ric Hamre, Vice-President

Manitoba Funeral Service Association
PO Box 243, Winnipeg MB R3C 2G9
Tel: 204-947-0927; *Fax:* 204-269-7148
e-mail: mfsa@shaw.ca
URL: www.mfsa.mb.ca
Lorrie Waugh, Executive Secretary

Newfoundland & Labrador Funeral Services Association (NLFSA)
PO Box 839, Lewisporte NL A0G 3A0
Tel: 709-535-2827; *Fax:* 709-535-8440
e-mail: contact@nlfuneralboard.ca
URL: www.nlfuneralboard.ca
Affiliation(s): Funeral Service Association of Canada
Milton Peach, President
Wayne Bennett, Vice-President

Ontario Association of Cemetery & Funeral Professionals (OACFP)
PO Box 10173, 27 Legend Ct., Ancaster ON L9K 1P3
Tel: 905-383-6528
Toll-Free: 888-558-3335
e-mail: info@oacfp.com
URL: www.oacfp.com
Jo-Anne Rogerson, Executive Director
Matt Wren, President
Daniel Reid, First Vice-President
Tim Vreman, Sec.-Treas.

Ontario Funeral Service Association (OFSA)
#203, 3425 Harvester Rd., Burlington ON L7N 3N1
Tel: 905-637-3371; *Fax:* 905-637-3583
Toll-Free: 800-268-2727
e-mail: info@ofsa.org
URL: www.ofsa.org
Myles O'Riordan, President
Cathie Turner, Vice-President
Kerri Douglas, Executive Coordinator
Lesley Bingley, Secretary-Treasurer

Prince Edward Island Funeral Directors & Embalmers Association
PO Box 540, Kensington PE C0B 1M0
Tel: 902-836-3313; *Fax:* 902-836-4461
Affiliation(s): Funeral Service Association of Canada
Faye Doucette, President

Fur Trade

Canadian Association for Humane Trapping (CAHT)
PO Box 7115, Stn. Maplehurst, Burlington ON L7T 4J8
Tel: 905-637-9623; *Fax:* 905-637-3912
e-mail: caht1@cogeco.ca
URL: www.caht.ca
Jim Bandow, Executive Director

The Fur Council of Canada (FCC) / Conseil canadien de la fourrure
#1270, 1435, rue Saint-Alexandre, Montréal QC H3A 2G4
Tel: 514-844-1945; *Fax:* 514-844-8593
e-mail: info@furcouncil.com
URL: www.furcouncil.com
Alan Herscovici, Executive Director
Angela Gurley, Secretary
Paula Lishman, President

Fur Institute of Canada (FIC) / Institut de la fourrure du Canada (IFC)
#701, 331 Cooper St., Ottawa ON K2P 0G5
Tel: 613-231-7099; *Fax:* 613-231-7940
e-mail: info@fur.ca
URL: www.fur.ca
Robert B. Cahill, Executive Director
Bruce Williams, Chair
Mary Baskin, Manager, Corporate & Communications

Fur-Bearer Defenders (FBD)
#101, 225 - 17th Ave. East, Vancouver BC V5V 1A6
Tel: 604-435-1850; *Fax:* 604-435-1840
e-mail: fbd@banleghold traps.com
URL: www.banlegholdtraps.com; www.dogcatfur.com
Fannya Eden, Program Coordinator

Furriers Guild of Canada
#211, 4174 Dundas St. West, Toronto ON M8X 1X3
Tel: 416-234-9494; *Fax:* 416-234-2244
e-mail: furriersguildca@ica.net
Lynda Jagros-May, Executive Director
Harry Papadopoulos, President

Galleries & Museums

Alberta Museums Association
Rossdale House, 9829 - 103 St., Edmonton AB T5K 0X9
Tel: 780-424-2626; *Fax:* 780-425-1679
e-mail: info@museums.ab.ca
URL: www.museums.ab.ca
Alexandra Hatcher, Executive Director

Association Museums New Brunswick (AMNB) / Association des musées du Nouveau-Brunswick
668 Brunswick St., Fredericton NB E3B 1H6
Tel: 506-452-2908; *Fax:* 506-459-0481
e-mail: amnb@nb.aibn.com
URL: www.amnb.ca
Affiliation(s): Canadian Heritage Information Network
Barbara McIntyre, President

Association of Manitoba Museums (AMM)
#1040, 555 Main St., Winnipeg MB R3B 1C3
Tel: 204-947-1782; *Fax:* 204-942-3749
Toll-Free: 866-747-9323
e-mail: info@museumsmanitoba.com
URL: www.museumsmanitoba.com
Monique Brandt, Executive Director

Atlantic Provinces Art Gallery Association (APAGA)
c/o MSVU Art Gallery, 166 Bedford Hwy., Halifax NS B3M 2J6
Tel: 902-457-6160; *Fax:* 902-457-2447
e-mail: info@apaga.com
URL: www.apaga.ca
Affiliation(s): Canadian Museums Association
Ingrid Jenkner, Director

British Columbia Museums Association (BCMA)
#204, 26 Bastion Sq., Victoria BC V8W 1H9
Tel: 250-356-5700; *Fax:* 250-387-1251
Toll-Free: 800-663-7867
e-mail: bcma@museumsassn.bc.ca
URL: www.museumsassn.bc.ca
Jim Harding, Executive Director
Shelley Gauthier, Member Services Coordinator

Canadian Federation of Friends of Museums (CFFM) / Fédération canadienne des amis de musées (FCAM)
c/o Art Gallery of Ontario, 317 Dundas St. West, Toronto ON M5T 1G4
Tel: 416-979-6650; *Fax:* 416-979-6674
e-mail: cffm_fcam@ago.net
URL: www.cffm-fcam.ca
Affiliation(s): World Federation of Friends of Museums - Mexico City; Canadian Museums Association
Suzanne Breyfogle, National Director

Canadian Museums Association (CMA) / Association des musées canadiens
#400, 280 Metcalfe St., Ottawa ON K2P 1R7
Tel: 613-567-0099; *Fax:* 613-233-5438
Toll-Free: 888-822-2907
e-mail: info@museums.ca
URL: www.museums.ca
John G. McAvity, Executive Director
Jon Tupper, President
René Binette, Vice-President

Community Museums Association of Prince Edward Island
PO Box 22002, 161 St. Peter's Rd., Charlottetown PE C1A 9J2
Tel: 902-892-8837; *Fax:* 902-892-1459
e-mail: info@museumspei.ca
URL: www.museumspei.ca
Barbara Boys MacCormac, President
Barry King, Ph.D., Executive Director

ICOM Museums Canada / ICOM Musées Canada
#400, 280 Metcalfe St., Ottawa ON K2P 1R7
Tel: 613-567-0099; *Fax:* 613-233-5438
e-mail: icom@museums.ca
Francine Caron, Contact

Museum Association of Newfoundland & Labrador (MANL)
The Colonial Building, PO Box 5785, Military Rd., St. John's NL A1C 5X3
Tel: 709-722-9034; *Fax:* 709-722-9035
e-mail: manl@nf.aibn.com
URL: www.manl.nf.ca
Ken Flynn, Executive Director
Peter Latta, President
Teresita McCarthy, Vice-President
Joan Kane, Secretary
Kathy Elliott, Treasurer

Museums Association of Saskatchewan (MAS)
422 McDonald St., Regina SK S4N 6E1
Tel: 306-780-9279; *Fax:* 306-780-9463
e-mail: mas@saskmuseums.org
URL: www.saskmuseums.org
Brenda Sherring, Executive Director
Royce Pettyjohn, President
Patricia Fiori, Director, Learning
Wendy Fitch, Director, Museum Operation Services

Ontario Association of Art Galleries (OAAG)
#617, 111 Peter St., Toronto ON M5V 2H1
Tel: 416-598-0714; *Fax:* 416-598-4128
e-mail: oaag@oaag.com
URL: www.oaag.org
Demetra Christakos, Executive Director

Ontario Museum Association (OMA) / Association des musées de l'Ontario
George Brown House, 50 Baldwin St., Toronto ON M5T 1L4
Tel: 416-348-8672; *Fax:* 416-348-0438
e-mail: communications@museumsontario.com
URL: www.museumsontario.com
Affiliation(s): Ontario Heritage Alliance
Tammy Adkin, President
Kathleen Powell, Vice-President

Organization of Military Museums of Canada, Inc. (OMMC) / L'Organisation des musées militaires du Canada inc.
PO Box 213, Gatineau QC J9H 5E5
Tel: 819-682-5192; *Fax:* 819-682-8348
e-mail: ommc@storm.ca
URL: www.ommc.ca
Affiliation(s): Department of National Defence/Director of History & Heritage; Friends of the Canadian War Museum; Military Collectors Club of Canada
Don Yaworsky, CD, Executive Director
Marilyn Gurney, President

La Société des musées québécois (SMQ)
CP 8888, Succ. Centre-Ville - UQAM, Montréal QC H3C 3P8
Tél: 514-987-3264; *Téléc:* 514-987-3379
Courriel: info@smq.uqam.ca
URL: www.musees.qc.ca
Michel Perron, Directeur général

Yukon Historical & Museums Association (YHMA)
3126 - 3 Ave., Whitehorse YT Y1A 1E7
Tel: 867-667-4704; *Fax:* 867-667-4506
e-mail: yhma@northwestel.net
URL: heritageyukon.ca
Affiliation(s): Heritage Canada; BC Heritage Trust
Tracey Anderson, Executive Director

Gas & Oil

Canadian Association of Petroleum Producers (CAPP) / Association canadienne des producteurs pétroliers
#2100, 350 - 7 Ave. SW, Calgary AB T2P 3N9
Tel: 403-267-1100; *Fax:* 403-261-4622
e-mail: communication@capp.ca; membership@capp.ca; publications@capp.ca
URL: www.capp.ca
David Collyer, President
Janet Annesley, Vice-President, Communications
Tom Huffaker, Vice-President, Policy & Environment
David Pryce, Vice-President, Operations
Nick Schultz, Vice-President, Pipeline Regulation
Greg Stringham, Vice-President, Oil Sands & Markets

Canadian Energy Pipeline Association (CEPA)
#1860, 205 - 5th Ave. SW, Calgary AB T2P 2V7
Tel: 403-221-8777; *Fax:* 403-221-8760
e-mail: info@cepa.com
URL: www.cepa.com
Brenda Kenny, President
Myra Paul, Administrative Assistant

Canadian Gas Association (CGA) / Association canadienne du gaz
#809, 350 Sparks St., Ottawa ON K1R 7S8
Tel: 613-748-0057; *Fax:* 613-748-9078
e-mail: info@cga.ca
URL: www.cga.ca
Affiliation(s): International Gas Union; Canadian Gas Research Institute
Michael Cleland, President/CEO

Canadian Society of Petroleum Geologists (CSPG)
#600, 640 - 8th Ave. SW, Calgary AB T2P 1G7
Tel: 403-264-5610; *Fax:* 403-264-5898
e-mail: cspg@cspg.org
URL: www.cspg.org
Tim Howard, Business Manager
Lisa Griffith, President

Gas Processing Association Canada (GPAC)
#505, 900 - 6th Avenue SW, Calgary AB T2P 3K2
Tel: 403-705-0223; *Fax:* 403-263-6886
e-mail: info@gpacanada.com
URL: www.gpacanada.com
Affiliation(s): Gas Processors Association (USA)
Richard Bosomworth, President
Joel Hayes, Secretary

Industrial Gas Users Association Inc. (IGUA) / Association des consommateurs industriels de gaz (ACIG)
#1201, 99 Metcalfe St., Ottawa ON K1P 6L7
Tel: 613-236-8021; *Fax:* 613-230-9531
URL: www.igua.ca
Murray Newton, President

NOIA
Atlantic Place, #602, 215 Water St., St. John's NL A1C 6C9
Tel: 709-758-6610; *Fax:* 709-758-6611
URL: www.noianet.com
Robert Cadigan, President & CEO

Offshore/Onshore Technologies Association of Nova Scotia (OTANS)
#400, 1718 Argyle St., Halifax NS B3J 3N6
Tel: 902-425-4774; *Fax:* 902-422-2332
e-mail: otans@otans.com
URL: www.otans.com
Paul McEachern, Managing Director

Ontario Petroleum Institute Inc. (OPI)
#104, 555 Southdale Rd. East, London ON N6E 1A2
Tel: 519-680-1620; *Fax:* 519-680-1621
e-mail: opi@ontpet.com
URL: www.ontpet.com
Bill Fay, President
Joe Van Overberghe, Executive Director
Ray Neal, Treasurer
Scott Tompkins, Secretary
Fran McCallum, Executive Assistant

Petroleum Research Atlantic Canada (PRAC)
1321 Edward St., Halifax NS B3H 3H5
Tel: 902-494-2960; *Fax:* 902-494-2489
e-mail: info@pr-ac.ca
URL: www.pr-ac.ca
David Finn, President

Petroleum Services Association of Canada (PSAC)
#1150, 800 - 6 Ave. SW, Calgary AB T2P 3G3
Tel: 403-264-4195; *Fax:* 403-263-7174
Toll-Free: 800-818-7722
e-mail: info@psac.ca
URL: www.psac.ca
Roger Soucy, CAE, President & CEO

Petroleum Society of CIM
#425, 500 - 5th Ave. SW, Calgary AB T2P 3L5
Tel: 403-237-5112; *Fax:* 403-262-4792
e-mail: info@petsoc.org
URL: www.petsoc.org
Anthony Au, Treasurer

Propane Gas Association of Canada Inc. (PGAC) / Association canadienne du gaz propane inc.
#800, 717 - 7th Ave. SW, Calgary AB T2P 3C4
Tel: 403-543-6500; *Fax:* 403-543-6508
Toll-Free: 877-784-4636
e-mail: info@propanegas.ca
URL: www.propanegas.ca
Affiliation(s): Propane Training Institute, a division of the PGAC; Liquefied Petroleum Gas Emergency Response Corporation, a wholly owned subsidiary of the PGAC
Ann Marie Hann, President
Tracy Walden, Manager, Communications
Bill Egbert, General Manager, Propane Training Institute

Gems & Jewellery

Alberta Federation of Rock Clubs (AFRC)
14827 - 45 Ave., Edmonton AB T6H 5R4

Tel: 780-430-6694
e-mail: paulinez@telus.net
URL: www.afrc.ca
Affiliation(s): Gem & Mineral Federation of Canada
Alice Watts, President
Pauline Zeschuk, Secretary

Canadian Gemmological Association (CGA)
1767 Avenue Rd., Toronto ON M5M 3Y8
Tel: 416-785-0962; Fax: 416-785-9043
Toll-Free: 877-244-3090
e-mail: info@canadiangemmological.com
URL: www.canadiangemmological.com
Affiliation(s): Gemmological Association & Gem Testing Laboratory of Great Britain
Duncan Parker, BA, FGA, FCGmA, President
Brad Wilson, MSc, P.Geo, FCG, Vice-President
Glen King, BA, FLMI, FCGmA, Treasurer

Canadian Institute of Gemmology (CIG) / Institut canadien de gemmologie
c/o School of Jewellery Arts, PO Box 57010, Vancouver BC V5K 5G6
Tel: 604-530-8569
e-mail: wolf@cigem.ca
URL: www.cigem.ca
Wolf Kuehn, Executive Director

Canadian Jewellers Association (CJA)
#600, 27 Queen St. East, Toronto ON M5C 2M6
Tel: 416-368-7616; Fax: 416-368-1986
Toll-Free: 800-580-0942
e-mail: cja@canadianjewellers.com
URL: www.canadianjewellers.com
Ken Mulhall, President & CEO

Corporation des bijoutiers du Québec (CBQ) / Québec Jewellers' Corporation
868, rue Brisette, Sainte-Julie QC J3E 2B1
Tél: 514-485-3333; Téléc: 450-649-8984
Courriel: info@cbq.qc.ca
URL: www.cbq.qc.ca
André Marchand, Président
Lise Petitpas, Directrice générale

Gem & Mineral Federation of Canada (GMFC) / Fédération canadienne des gemmes et des minéraux
PO Box 42015, Stn. North, Winfield BC V4V 1Z8
e-mail: president@gmfc.ca
URL: www.gmfc.ca
Darlene Itcush, President

Jewellers Vigilance Canada Inc. (JVC)
#600, 27 Queen St. East, Toronto ON M5C 2M6
Tel: 416-368-4840; Fax: 416-368-5552
Toll-Free: 800-636-9536
e-mail: info@jewellersvigilance.ca
URL: www.jewellersvigilance.ca
Phyllis Richard, Executive Director

Government & Public Administration

Alberta Association of Municipal Districts & Counties (AAMD&C)
2510 Sparrow Dr., Nisku AB T9E 8N5
Tel: 780-955-3639; Fax: 780-955-3615
e-mail: aamdc@aamdc.com
URL: www.aamdc.com
Gerald Rhodes, Executive Director
Donald Johnson, Director, frank@aamdc.com

Alberta Municipal Clerks Association (AMCA)
c/o City of Spruce Grove, 315 Jespersen Dr., Spruce Grove AB T7X 3E8
Tel: 780-962-7634
e-mail: communications@albertamunicipalclerks.com
URL: www.albertamunicipalclerks.com
Steve Thompson, President

Alberta Rural Municipal Administrators Association
6027 - 4 St. NE, Calgary AB T2K 4Z5
Tel: 403-275-0622; Fax: 403-275-8179
e-mail: d_vschmaltz@shaw.ca
URL: www.armaa.ca
Valerie Schmaltz, Sec.-Treas.
Ross Rawlusyk, President

Alberta Urban Municipalities Association (AUMA)
10507 Saskatchewan Dr. NW, Edmonton AB T6E 4S1
Tel: 780-433-4431; Fax: 780-433-4454
Toll-Free: 800-310-2862
e-mail: main@auma.ca
URL: www.auma.ca
John McGowan, CEO

Association des directeurs généraux des municipalités du Québec
#129, 10, rue Hugues-Pommier, Beauport QC G1E 4T9
Tél: 418-660-7591; Téléc: 418-660-0848
Courriel: adgmq@adgmq.qc.ca
URL: www.adgmq.qc.ca/
Jacques Poulin, Président
Jacques Alain, Directeur Exécutif

Association des directeurs municipaux du Québec (ADMQ)
#500, 580, av Grande-Allée est, Québec QC G1R 2K2
Tél: 418-647-4518; Téléc: 418-647-4115
Courriel: admq@admq.qc.ca
URL: admq.qc.ca/
Sylvie Dubois, Présidente

Association francophone des municipalités du Nouveau-Brunswick inc. (AFMNB)
#322, 702, rue Principale, Petit-Rocher NB E8J 1V1
Tél: 506-542-2622; Téléc: 506-542-2618
Ligne sans frais: 888-236-2622
Courriel: afmnb@afmnb.org
URL: www.afmnb.org
Affiliation(s): Association internationale des maires et responsables des capitales et métropoles partiellement ou entièrement francophones; Fédération canadienne des municipalités; Union des municipalités régionales de comté et des municipalités locales du Québec
Lise Ouellette, Directrice générale
Jean Lanteigne, Président

Association internationale des maires francophones - Bureau à Québec (AIMF)
CP 700, Succ. Haute-Ville, #312, 2, rue des Jardins, Québec QC G1R 4S9
Tél: 418-641-6434; Téléc: 418-641-6318
Jean-Paul L'Allier

Association of Manitoba Municipalities (AMM)
1910 Saskatchewan Ave. West, Portage la Prairie MB R1N 0P1
Tel: 204-857-8666; Fax: 204-856-2370
e-mail: amm@amm.mb.ca
URL: www.amm.mb.ca
Joe Masi, Executive Director
Ron Bell, President

Association of Municipal Administrators of New Brunswick (AMANB) / Association des administrateurs municipaux du Nouveau-Brunswick (AAMNB)
PO Box 30044, Stn. Prospect Plaza RPO, Fredericton NB E3B 0H8
Tel: 506-453-4229; Fax: 506-444-5452
e-mail: amanb@nb.aibn.com
URL: www.amanb-aamnb.ca
Cynthia Geldart, President
Eva Turnbull, Executive Director

Association of Municipal Administrators, Nova Scotia (AMANS)
#1106, 1809 Barrington St., Halifax NS B3J 3K8
Tel: 902-423-2215; Fax: 902-425-5592
e-mail: amans@eastlink.ca
URL: www.amans.ca
Janice Wentzell, Executive Director

Association of Municipal Managers, Clerks & Treasurers of Ontario (AMCTO) / Association des directeurs généraux, secrétaires et trésoriers municipaux de l'Ontario (ASTMO)
#910, 2680 Skymark Ave., Mississauga ON L4W 5L6
Tel: 905-602-4294; Fax: 905-602-4295
e-mail: amcto@amcto.com
URL: www.amcto.com
Affiliation(s): Association of Municipalities of Ontario; International Institute of Municipal Clerks; Municipal Information Systems Association
Andy Koopmans, Executive Director

Association of Municipalities of Ontario (AMO)
#801, 200 University Ave., Toronto ON M5H 3C6
Tel: 416-971-9856; Fax: 416-971-6191
Toll-Free: 877-426-6527
e-mail: amo@amo.on.ca; municom@amo.on.ca; policy@amo.on.ca
URL: www.amo.on.ca
Pat Vanini, Executive Director
Doug Reycraft, President
Jim Wilson, Sec.-Treas.

Association of Yukon Communities (AYC)
#15, 1114 - 1st Ave., Whitehorse YT Y1A 1A3
Tel: 867-668-4388; Fax: 867-668-7574
e-mail: ayc@northwestel.net
URL: www.ayc.yk.ca
Affiliation(s): Federation of Canadian Municipalities
Tom Paterson, Executive Director
Susan Gleason, Office Manager

Association québécoise du loisir municipal (AQLM)
CP 1000, Succ. M, 4545, Pierre-de-Coubertin, Montréal QC H1V 3R2
Tél: 514-252-3142; Téléc: 514-252-3150
Courriel: infoaqlm@loisirmunicipal.qc.ca
URL: www.loisirmunicipal.qc.ca
Normand Caron, Directeur, Communications

Canadian Association of Municipal Administrators (CAMA)
PO Box 128, Stn. A, Fredericton NB E3B 4Y2
Tel: 866-771-2262
Toll-Free: 866-771-2262
e-mail: admin@camacam.ca
URL: www.camacam.ca
Barry Carroll, President
Owen Tobert, First Vice-President

Canadian Council on Social Development (CCSD) / Conseil canadien de développement social (CCDS)
#100, 190 O'Connor St., Ottawa ON K2P 2R3
Tel: 613-236-8977; Fax: 613-236-2750
e-mail: council@ccsd.ca; research@ccsd.ca; media@ccsd.ca; work@ccsd.ca
URL: www.ccsd.ca
Wayne Helgason, Chair
Peggy Taillon, President & Chief Executive Officer
Gail Dugas, Vice-President, Public Affairs & Community Engagement
Penelope Feather, Vice-President, Operations
Katherine Scott, Vice-President, Research
Pat Steenberg, Vice-President, Strategic Partnerships & Alliances

Cities of New Brunswick Association
PO Box 1421, Stn. A, 95 Duffie Dr., Fredericton NB E3B 5E3
Tel: 506-693-0008; Fax: 506-693-0009
e-mail: cnbacnb@nbnet.nb.ca
Sandra Mark, Executive Director

Corporation des officiers municipaux agréés du Québec (COMAQ) / Corporation of Chartered Municipal Officers of Québec
Édifice Lomer-Gouin, #R02, 575, rue Saint-Amable, Québec QC G1R 2G4
Tél: 418-527-1231; Téléc: 418-527-4462
Ligne sans frais: 800-305-1031
Courriel: info@comaq.qc.ca
URL: www.comaq.qc.ca
Erick Parent, Secrétaire général

Council of Maritime Premiers/Council of Atlantic Premiers (CMP/CAP) / Conseil des premiers ministres des Maritimes/Conseil des premiers ministres de l'Alantique
PO Box 2044, #1006, 5161 George St., Halifax NS B3J 2Z1
Tel: 902-424-7590; Fax: 902-424-8976
e-mail: info@cap-cpma.ca
URL: www.cap-cpma.ca
Don Osmond, Secretary

Democracy Watch
PO Box 821, Stn. B, #1210, 1 Nicholas St., Ottawa ON K1P 5P9
Tel: 613-241-5179; Fax: 613-241-4758
e-mail: dwatch@web.net
URL: www.dwatch.ca
Duff Conacher, Coordinator

Federation of Canadian Municipalities (FCM) / Fédération canadienne des municipalités
24 Clarence St., Ottawa ON K1N 5P3
Tel: 613-241-5221; Fax: 613-241-7440
e-mail: federation@fcm.ca
URL: www.fcm.ca
Brock Carlton, CEO
Basil L. Stewart, President

Federation of Northern Ontario Municipalities (FONOM)
PO Box 117, Corbeil ON P0H 1K0

Tel: 705-752-2783; Fax: 705-752-1138
e-mail: fonom.info@sympatico.ca
URL: www.fonom.org
Vonda Croissant, Executive Director
Frank Gillis, President

Federation of Prince Edward Island Municipalities Inc. (FPEIM)
1 Kirkdale Rd., Charlottetown PE C1E 1R3
Tel: 902-566-1493; Fax: 902-566-2880
e-mail: info@fpeim.ca
URL: www.fpeim.ca
Affiliation(s): Association of Municipal Administrators, PEI
John Dewey, Executive Director
Bruce MacDougall, President

Fédération Québécoise des Municipalités (FQM)
#560, 2954, boul Laurier, Sainte-Foy QC G1V 4T2
Tél: 418-651-3343; Téléc: 418-651-1127
Courriel: fqm@fqm.ca
URL: www.fqm.ca
Bernard Généreux, Président

Foreign Service Community Association (FSCA) / Association de la communauté du service extérieur (ACSE)
L.B. Pearson Building, 125 Sussex Dr., Ottawa ON K1A 0G2
Tel: 613-944-5729; Fax: 613-995-9335
e-mail: fsca.acse@international.gc.ca
URL: www.fsca-acse.org
Tova Lynch, Interim President
Mandy Bailey, First Vice-President
Jennifer McCrea-Logie, Secretary
Marlene Lundy, Interim Treasurer

Government Finance Officers Association (GFOA)
#2700, 203 North LaSalle St., Chicago IL 60601-1210 USA
Tel: 312-977-9700; Fax: 312-977-4806
e-mail: inquiry@gfoa.org
URL: www.gfoa.org
Jeffrey Esser, Executive Director & CEO
Kenneth L. Rust, President
John Jurkash, Chief Financial Officer, Financial Administration

Institute of Public Administration of Canada (IPAC) / Institut d'administration publique du Canada (IAPC)
#401, 1075 Bay St., Toronto ON M5S 2B1
Tel: 416-924-8787; Fax: 416-924-4992
URL: www.ipac.ca
Gabriel Sékaly, Executive Director

Institute On Governance (IOG) / Institut sur la gouvernance
122 Clarence St., Ottawa ON K1N 5P6
Tel: 613-562-0090; Fax: 613-562-0097
e-mail: info@iog.ca
URL: www.iog.ca
Maryantonett Flumian, President
Laura Edgar, Vice President
John Graham, Senior Associate
Scott Serson, Chair

Local Government Management Association of British Columbia (LGMA)
Central Bldg., 737 Fort St., 7th Fl., Victoria BC V8W 1J6
Tel: 250-383-7032; Fax: 250-384-4879
e-mail: office@lgma.ca
URL: www.lgma.ca
Tom MacDonald, Executive Director
Elsie Lemke, President
Warren Waycheshen, Sec.-Treas.

Manitoba Municipal Administrators' Association Inc.
533 Buckingham Rd., Winnipeg MB R3R 1B9
Tel: 204-255-4883; Fax: 204-255-2623
e-mail: mmaa@mts.net
URL: www.mmaa.mb.ca
Mel Nott, Executive Director

Municipalities Newfoundland & Labrador
460 Torbay Rd., St. John's NL A1A 5J3
Tel: 709-753-6820; Fax: 709-738-0071
Toll-Free: 800-440-6536
e-mail: mnl@municipalitiesnl.com
URL: www.municipalitiesnl.com
Craig Pollett, Executive Director
Christine Cave, Administrative Officer

National Association of Federal Retirees (FSNA) / L'Association nationale des retraités fédéraux (ANRF)
1052 St. Laurent Blvd., Ottawa ON K1K 3B4
Tel: 613-745-2559; Fax: 613-745-5457
e-mail: info@fsna.com
URL: www.fsna.com
Sylvia Ceacero, Executive Director
Stan Hrabchuk, National President

Northwest Territories Association of Communities (NWTAC)
Finn Hansen Bldg., #200, 5105 - 50th St., Yellowknife NT X1A 1S1
Tel: 867-873-8359; Fax: 867-873-3042
Toll-Free: 866-973-8359
URL: www.nwtac.com
Yvette Gonzalez, CEO

Northwestern Ontario Municipal Association (NOMA)
161 Brock St. East, Thunder Bay ON P7E 4H1
Tel: 807-626-0155; Fax: 807-626-8163
e-mail: ktaniwa@tbaytel.net
URL: www.noma.on.ca
Affiliation(s): Association of Municipalities of Ontario
Ken Taniwa, Executive Director
Anne Krassilowsky, President
Brian Larson, Exec. Vice-President

Ontario Municipal Human Resources Association (OMHRA)
#307, 1235 Fairview St., Burlington ON L7S 2K9
Tel: 905-525-4000; Fax: 905-525-9833
e-mail: admin@omhra.ca
URL: www.omhra.ca
Peggy Mellor, President
Kandy Webb, Vice-President
Christine A. Ball, Executive Officer

Ontario Municipal Management Institute (OMMI)
618 Balmoral Dr., Oshawa ON L1J 3A7
Tel: 905-434-8885; Fax: 905-434-7381
URL: www.ommi.on.ca
Bill McKim, Executive Director
Jackie Russell, Administrator, Training & Accreditation

Organization of Small Urban Municipalities (Ontario) (OSUM)
c/o Association of Municipalities of Ontario, #801, 200 University Ave., Toronto ON M5H 3C6
Tel: 416-971-9856; Fax: 416-971-6191
Toll-Free: 877-426-6527
URL: www.amo.on.ca/AM/Template.cfm?Section=About_Us6
Pat Vanini, Executive Director
Gary McNamara, Chair

The Public Affairs Association of Canada (PAAC) / Association des affaires publiques du Canada
#301, 250 Consumers Rd., Toronto ON M2J 4V6
Tel: 416-367-2223; Fax: 416-495-8723
e-mail: info@publicaffairs.ca
URL: www.publicaffairs.ca
John Capobianco, President
Erika Mozes, Events Chair
Chris May, Sec.-Treas.

Rural Municipal Administrators' Association of Saskatchewan (RMAA)
PO Box 130, Wilcox SK S0G 5E0
Tel: 306-732-2030; Fax: 306-732-4495
e-mail: rmaa@sasktel.net
URL: www.rmaa.ca
Affiliation(s): Saskatchewan Association of Rural Municipalities
Kevin Ritchie, Executive Director
Don McCallum, President
Tim Leurer, Vice-President

Saskatchewan Association of Rural Municipalities (SARM)
2075 Hamilton St., Regina SK S4P 2E1
Tel: 306-757-3577; Fax: 306-565-2141
Toll-Free: 800-667-3604
e-mail: sarm@sarm.ca
URL: www.sarm.ca
Ken Engel, Executive Director
David Marit, President

Saskatchewan Urban Municipalities Association (SUMA)
#200, 2222 - 13th Ave., Regina SK S4P 3M7
Tel: 306-525-3727; Fax: 306-525-4373
e-mail: suma@suma.org
URL: www.suma.org
Laurent Mougeot, Executive Director
Dan McGready, Communications Officer
Shantel Lipp, Manager, Member & Corporate Svcs

Society of Local Government Managers of Alberta
PO Box 308, 4629 - 54 Ave., Bruderheim AB T0B 0S0
Tel: 780-796-3836; Fax: 780-796-2081
e-mail: linda.davies@shaw.ca
URL: www.clgm.net
Linda M. Davies, Executive Director/Registrar

Union des municipalités du Québec (UMQ)
#680, 680, rue Sherbrooke ouest, Montréal QC H3A 2M7
Tél: 514-282-7700; Téléc: 514-282-8893
Courriel: info@umq.qc.ca
URL: www.umq.qc.ca
Affiliation(s): Conseil du patronat du Québec; Fédération canadienne des municipalités
Pierre Prévost, Directeur général par intérim
Robert Coulombe, Président

Union of British Columbia Municipalities
#60, 10551 Shellbridge Way, Richmond BC V6X 2W9
Tel: 604-270-8226; Fax: 604-270-9116
e-mail: ubcm@civicnet.bc.ca
URL: www.civicnet.bc.ca
Richard Taylor, Executive Director
Brenda Binnie, President

Union of Municipalities of New Brunswick (UMNB) / Union des municipalités du Nouveau-Brunswick
#4, 79 Main St., Rexton NB E4W 1Z9
Tel: 506-523-4522; Fax: 506-523-4523
e-mail: umnb@nb.aibn.com
Raymond Murphy, Executive Director

Union of Nova Scotia Municipalities (UNSM)
#1106, 1809 Barrington St., Halifax NS B3J 3K8
Tel: 902-423-8331; Fax: 902-425-5592
e-mail: mainunsm@eastlink.ca
URL: www.unsm.ca
Kenneth Simpson, Executive Director
Judy Webber, Event Planner/Financal Officer

Urban Municipal Administrators' Association of Saskatchewan (UMAAS)
PO Box 603, Hudson Bay SK S0E 0Y0
Tel: 306-865-2825; Fax: 306-865-2800
e-mail: umaas@sasktel.net
URL: www.umaas.ca
Richard Dolezsar, Executive Director

Health & Medical

Acoustic Neuroma Association of Canada (ANAC) / Association pour les neurinomes acoustiques du Canada
#163, 171A Rink St., Peterborough ON K0J 2J6
Tel: 705-750-1550
Toll-Free: 800-561-2622
e-mail: info@anac.ca
URL: www.anac.ca

Acupuncture Foundation of Canada Institute (AFCI) / Institut de la fondation d'acupuncture du Canada
#204, 2131 Lawrence Ave. East, Toronto ON M1R 5G4
Tel: 416-752-3988; Fax: 416-752-4398
e-mail: info@afcinstitute.com
URL: www.afcinstitute.com
Affiliation(s): World Federation of Acupuncture Societies; Pan Pacific Medical Acupuncture Forum
Cheryll A. Kwok, Executive Director
Linda Rapson, MD, Executive President

African Medical & Research Foundation Canada (AMREF Canada)
#407, 489 College St., Toronto ON M5G 1A5
Tel: 416-961-6981; Fax: 416-961-6984
e-mail: info@amrefcanada.org
URL: www.amrefcanada.org
Affiliation(s): African Medical & Research Foundations Nairobi; Canadian Centre for Philanthropy; Ontario Council for International Cooperation; Canadian Council for International Cooperation; Canadian Society of International Health

Alberta Association of Naturopathic Practitioners (AANP)
PO Box 21142, 665 - 8th St. SW, Calgary AB T2P 4H5
Tel: 403-266-2446
e-mail: aanb_ab@telusplanet.net
URL: www.naturopathic-alberta.com
Alissa Gaul, ND, President

Alberta Association of Optometrists (AAO)
#100, 8407 Argyll Road, Edmonton AB T6C 4B2

Tel: 780-451-6824; *Fax:* 780-452-9918
Toll-Free: 800-272-8843
e-mail: alberta.association@optometrists.ab.ca
URL: www.optometrists.ab.ca
Brian Wik, Executive Director

Alberta Heritage Foundation for Medical Research (AHFMR)
#1500, 10104 - 103 Ave., Edmonton AB T5J 4A7
Tel: 780-423-5727; *Fax:* 780-429-3509
Toll-Free: 877-423-5727
e-mail: info@ahfmr.ab.ca
URL: www.ahfmr.ab.ca
Jacques Magnan, Interim President & CEO
Kathleen Thurber, Director, Communications & Education

Alberta Lung Association (ALA)
PO Box 4500, Stn. South, #208, 17420 Stony Plain Rd., Edmonton AB T5E 6K2
Tel: 780-488-7195; *Fax:* 780-488-6819
Toll-Free: 888-566-5864
e-mail: info@ab.lung.ca
URL: www.ab.lung.ca
Tony Hudson, President

Alberta Lung Association
PO Box 2866, Yellowknife NT X1A 2R2
Tel: 867-669-0921
Toll-Free: 888-566-5864
e-mail: info@ab.lung.ca
URL: www.ab.lung.ca

Alberta Medical Association
12230 - 106 Ave. NW, Edmonton AB T5N 3Z1
Tel: 780-482-2626; *Fax:* 780-482-5445
Toll-Free: 800-272-9680
e-mail: amamail@albertadoctors.org
URL: www.albertadoctors.org/home
Darryl D. LaBuick, President Elect
Michael A. Gormley, Executive Director
G.N. (Gerry) Kiefer, President

Alberta Public Health Association (APHA)
c/o ACICR, 4075 RTF, 8308 - 114th St., Edmonton AB T6G 2E1
Tel: 780-492-6014; *Fax:* 780-492-7154
e-mail: info@apha.ab.ca
URL: www.apha.ab.ca
Kim Raine, President
Sharon Yanicki, Executive Director

Allergy Asthma Information Association (AAIA) / Allergie Asthme association d'information
Vaughan Professional Centre, #1 - 111 Zenway Blvd., Vaughan ON L4H 3H9
Tel: 905-265-3322; *Fax:* 905-850-2070
Toll-Free: 800-611-7011
e-mail: admin@aaia.ca
URL: www.aaia.ca
Affiliation(s): Canadian Society of Allergy & Immunology
Mary Allen, CEO

ALS Society of Canada (ALS) / La Société canadienne de la SLA (SLA)
#300, 265 Yorkland Blvd., Toronto ON M2J 1S5
Tel: 416-497-2267; *Fax:* 416-497-1256
Toll-Free: 800-267-4257
e-mail: alscanada@als.ca
URL: www.als.ca
Social Media: www.facebook.com/group.php?gid=7533609459
Affiliation(s): Health Charities Council of Canada
David Cameron, CAE, President & CEO
Claudia Daniel, Development Coordinator

Alzheimer Manitoba
#10, 120 Donald St., Winnipeg MB R3C 4G2
Tel: 204-943-6622; *Fax:* 204-942-5408
Toll-Free: 800-378-6699
e-mail: alzmb@alzheimer.mb.ca
URL: www.alzheimer.mb.ca
Sylvia Rothney, Executive Director

Alzheimer Society Canada (ASC) / Société Alzheimer Canada
#1200, 20 Eglinton Ave. West, Toronto ON M4R 1K8
Tel: 416-488-8772; *Fax:* 416-488-3778
Toll-Free: 800-616-8816
e-mail: info@alzheimer.ca
URL: www.alzheimer.ca
Social Media: www.facebook.com/group.php?gid=31592784821
Affiliation(s): HealthPartners
Ray Congdon, President

Alzheimer Society of Alberta & Northwest Territories
10531 Kingsway Ave., Edmonton AB T5H 4K1
Tel: 780-488-2266; *Fax:* 780-488-3055
Toll-Free: 866-950-5465
e-mail: info@alzheimer.ab.ca
URL: www.alzheimer.ab.ca
Affiliation(s): Canadian Association on Gerontology; Alberta Association on Gerontology; Canadian Centre for Philanthropy
Bill Gaudette, Chief Executive Officer
Tash Taylor, Provincial Director, Community Relations

Alzheimer Society of BC
#300, 828 West 8th Ave., Vancouver BC V5Z 1E2
Tel: 604-681-6530; *Fax:* 604-669-6907
Toll-Free: 800-667-3742
e-mail: info@alzheimerbc.org
URL: www.alzheimerbc.org
Rosemary Rawnsley, Executive Director

Alzheimer Society of New Brunswick / Société alzheimer du nouveau brunswick
33 Main St., Fredericton NB E3A 1B7
Tel: 506-459-4280; *Fax:* 506-452-0313
Toll-Free: 800-664-8411
e-mail: info@alzheimernb.ca
URL: www.alzheimernb.ca
Gloria McIlveen, Executive Director

Alzheimer Society of Newfoundland & Labrador
PO Box 37013, 687 Water St., St. John's NL A1E 1C2
Tel: 709-576-0608; *Fax:* 709-576-0798
Toll-Free: 877-776-0608
e-mail: alzheimersociety@nf.aibn.com
URL: www.alzheimernl.org
Christine Caravan, Director

Alzheimer Society of Nova Scotia
#300, 6009 Quinpool Rd., Halifax NS B3K 5J7
Tel: 902-422-7961; *Fax:* 902-422-7971
Toll-Free: 800-611-6345
e-mail: info@alzheimer.ns.ca
URL: www.alzheimer.ns.ca
Menna MacIsaac, Executive Director

Alzheimer Society of PEI
166 Fitzroy St., Charlottetown PE C1A 1S1
Tel: 902-628-2257; *Fax:* 902-368-2715
Toll-Free: 866-628-2257
e-mail: society@alzpei.ca
URL: www.alzpei.ca
Colleen Laybolt, Executive Administrator

Alzheimer Society Of Saskatchewan Inc. (ASOS)
#301, 2550 - 12 Ave., Regina SK S4P 3X1
Tel: 306-949-4141; *Fax:* 306-949-3069
Toll-Free: 800-263-3367
e-mail: info@alzheimer.sk.ca
URL: www.alzheimer.sk.ca
Joanne Bracken, Executive Director
Kathleen Defoe, Coordinator, Finance & Administration

Alzheimer Society Ontario / Société Alzheimer Ontario
#202, 1200 Bay St., Toronto ON M5R 2A5
Tel: 416-967-5900; *Fax:* 416-967-3826
Toll-Free: 800-879-4226
e-mail: staff@alzheimeront.org
URL: www.alzheimerontario.org
Social Media: www.facebook.com/group.php?gid=45861243971
Nancy MacArthur, President

Aplastic Anemia & Myelodysplasia Association of Canada (AAMAC)
#321, 11181 Yonge St., Richmond Hill ON L4S 1L2
Tel: 905-780-0698; *Fax:* 905-780-1648
Toll-Free: 888-840-0039
e-mail: info@aamac.ca
URL: www.aamac.ca
Affiliation(s): Network of Rare Blood Disorders
Gord Sanford, President
Joyce Burnett, Secretary
Sylvia Scow, Coordinator, British Columbia
Chris Meyer, Coordinator, Ontario

The Arthritis Society (TAS) / La Société de l'arthrite
#1700, 393 University Ave., Toronto ON M5G 1E6
Tel: 416-979-7228; *Fax:* 416-979-8366
Toll-Free: 800-321-1433
e-mail: info@arthritis.ca
URL: www.arthritis.ca
Affiliation(s): The Bone & Joint Decade
Steven McNair, President/CEO

Lysianne Buie, Senior Director, Marketing, Communications & Direct Response

Association canadienne des ataxies familiales (ACAF) / Canadian Association of Friedreich's Ataxia
#110, 3800, rue Radisson, Montréal QC H1M 1X6
Tél: 514-321-8684; *Téléc:* 514-899-9158
Courriel: ataxie@lacaf.org
URL: www.lacaf.org
Kilda Gosselin, Directrice générale

Association d'orthopédie du Québec
CP 216, #3000, 2, Complexe Desjardins, Montréal QC H5B 1G8
Tél: 514-844-0803; *Téléc:* 514-844-6786
Courriel: aoq@fmsq.org
URL: www.orthoquebec.ca/
Jacques Desnoyers, Président

Association d'oto-rhino-laryngologie et de chirurgie cervico-faciale du Québec
#3000, 2, Complexe Desjardins, Montréal QC H5B 1G8
Tél: 514-350-5125; *Téléc:* 514-350-5165
Courriel: assorl@fmsq.org
URL: www.orlquebec.org
Pascal Desrochers, Secrétaire
Raynald Ferland, Président

L'Association de spina-bifida et d'hydrocéphalie du Québec (ASBHQ)
#542, 3333, ch. Queen-Mary, Montréal QC H3V 1A2
Tél: 514-340-9019; *Téléc:* 514-340-9109
Ligne sans frais: 800-567-1788
Courriel: info@spina.qc.ca
URL: www.spina.qc.ca
Affiliation(s): Institut de réadaptation en déficience physique de Québec; Hôpital Shriners, Centre de réadaptation Constance-Lethbridge, Centre de réadaptation en déficience physique Chaudière-Appalaches
Marc Picard, Président

Association des Allergologues et Immunologues du Québec
CP 216, Succ. Desjardins, #3000, 2, Complexe Desjardins, Montréal QC H5B 1G8
Tél: 514-350-5101; *Téléc:* 514-350-5146
Courriel: jdelisle@fmsq.org
URL: www.allerg.qc.ca
Normand Dubé, Président

Association des cardiologues du Québec
#3000, 2, Complexe Desjardins, Montréal QC H5B 1G8
Tél: 514-350-5106; *Téléc:* 514-350-5156
Courriel: acq@fmsq.org
Gaëtan Houde, Président
Louise Girard, Directrice

Association des chiropraticiens du Québec
7960, boul Métropolitain est, Anjou QC H1K 1A1
Tél: 514-355-0557; *Téléc:* 514-355-0070
Ligne sans frais: 866-292-4476
Courriel: acq@chiropratique.com
URL: www.chiropratique.com
Richard Giguère, Président

Association des chirurgiens cardio-vasculaires et thoraciques du Québec / Association of Cardiovascular & Thoracic Surgeons of Québec
Hôpital Général Juif, Bureau A-520, 3755 Chemin de la Côte Ste-Catherine, Montréal QC H3T 1E2
Tél: 514-340-8222; *Téléc:* 514-340-7561
Yves Langlois, Président
Suzan Allard, Secrétariat

Association des chirurgiens généraux du Québec / Québec Association of General Surgeons
#3000, 2, Complexe Desjardins, Montréal QC H5B 1G8
Tél: 514-350-5107; *Téléc:* 514-350-5157
URL: www.chirurgiequebec.ca

Association des conseils des médecins, dentistes et pharmaciens du Québec (ACMDP) / Association of Councils of Physicians, Dentists & Pharmacists of Québec
#212, 560, boul Henri-Bourassa ouest, Montréal QC H3L 1P4
Tél: 514-858-5885; *Téléc:* 514-858-6767
Courriel: acmdp@acmdp.qc.ca
URL: www.acmdp.qc.ca
Dominique Derome, Directrice générale
Nicole Durand, Adjointe administrative

Association des dermatologistes du Québec (ADQ) / Association of Dermatologists of Québec
#3000, 2, Complexe Desjardins, Montréal QC H5B 1G8
Tél: 514-350-5111; *Téléc:* 514-350-5161
Courriel: dermato@fmsq.org
URL: www.adq.org
Affiliation(s): Fédération des médecins spécialistes du Québec
Chantal Bolduc, Présidente
Julie Powell, MD, Vice-président
Deana Funard, MD, Secrétaire
Francine Labelle, MD, Directrice, Administration

Association des gastro-entérologues du Québec
CP 216, 2, Complexe Desjardins, Montréal QC H5B 1G8
Tél: 514-350-5112; *Téléc:* 514-350-5146
URL: www.ageq.qc.ca

Association des médecins biochimistes du Québec
#3000, 2, Complexe Desjardins, Montréal QC H5B 1G8
Tél: 514-350-5105; *Téléc:* 514-350-5151
Courriel: ambq@fmsq.org
URL: www.ambq.med.usherbrooke.ca
Elaine Letendre, Présidente

Association des médecins de langue française du Canada (AMLFC)
8355, boul Saint-Laurent, Montréal QC H2P 2Z6
Tél: 514-388-2228; *Téléc:* 514-388-5335
Ligne sans frais: 800-387-2228
Courriel: info@amlfc.org
URL: www.amlfc.org
Jacques Étienne des Marchais, Président

Association des médecins endocrinologues du Québec
#3000, 2, Complexe Desjardins, Montréal QC H5B 1G8
Tél: 514-350-5135; *Téléc:* 514-350-5049
Courriel: ameq@fmsq.org
URL: www.ameq.qc.ca/
Jean-Hugues Brossard, Président

Association des médecins généticiens du Québec
#300, 2, Complexe Desjardins, Montréal QC H5B 1G8
Tél: 514-350-5141; *Téléc:* 514-350-5151
Courriel: mfcaron@fmsq.org
Emmanuelle Lemyre, Présidente
Sandrine Guillot, Directrice

Association des médecins gériatres du Québec
CP 216, Succ. Desjardins, #3000, 2, Complexe Desjardins, Montréal QC H5B 1G8
Tél: 514-350-5145; *Téléc:* 514-350-5151
Courriel: amgq@fmsq.org; clavoie@fmsq.org
URL: www.fmsq.org/amgq
Maurice St-Laurent, Président

Association des médecins hématologistes-oncologistes du Québec (AMHOQ)
#3000, 2, Complexe Desjardins, Montréal QC H5B 1G8
Tél: 514-350-5121; *Téléc:* 514-350-5126
Ligne sans frais: 800-561-0703
Courriel: amhoq@fmsq.org
Daniel Bélanger, Président

Association des médecins microbiologistes infectiologues du Québec
#3000, 2, Complexe Desjardins, Montréal QC H5B 1G8
Tél: 514-350-5104; *Téléc:* 514-350-5144
Courriel: info@ammiq.org
URL: www.ammiq.org
Charlotte Lavoie, Directeur

Association des médecins ophtalmologistes du Québec (AMOQ)
CP 216, 2, Complexe Desjardins, Montréal QC H5B 1G8
Tél: 514-350-5124; *Téléc:* 514-350-5174
Courriel: amoq@fmsq.org
URL: www.amoq.org
Denis Tardif, MD, Sec.-Tres.
Jean-Daniel Arbour, MD, Président

Association des médecins rhumatologues du Québec
#3000, 2, Complexe Desjardins, Montréal QC H5B 1G8
Tél: 514-350-5136; *Téléc:* 514-350-5152
Courriel: amrq@fmsq.org
URL: www.fmsq.org7
François Couture, Président

Association des médecins spécialistes en médecine nucléaire du Québec (AMSMNQ)
#3000, 2, Complexe Desjardins, Montréal QC H5B 1G8
Tél: 514-350-5133; *Téléc:* 514-350-5151
Ligne sans frais: 800-561-0703
Courriel: amsmnq@fmsq.org
URL: www.medecinenucleaire.com/
François Lamoureux, Président
Jean Guimond, Vice-président

Association des médecins spécialistes en santé communautaire du Québec (AMSSCQ)
#3000, 2, Complexe Desjardins, Montréal QC H5B 1G8
Tél: 514-350-5138; *Téléc:* 514-350-5151
Courriel: amsscq@fmsq.org
URL: www.amsscq.org
Jacques Ringuet, Président
Marc Rhainds, Vice-président

Association des néphrologues du Québec
#3000, 2, Complexe Desjardins, Montréal QC H5B 1G8
Tél: 514-350-5134; *Téléc:* 514-350-5151
Courriel: mfcaron@fmsq.org
Robert Charbonneau, Président
Marie-France Caron, Directrice

Association des neurochirurgiens du Québec
#3000, 2, Complexe Desjardins, Montréal QC H5B 1G8
Tél: 514-350-5120; *Téléc:* 514-350-5151
Courriel: ancq@fmsq.org
URL: www.ancq.net
Léo Cantin, Président
Raymonde Dionne, Directrice
Jean-François Turcotte, Secrétaire

Association des neurologues du Québec
#3000, 2, Complexe Desjardins, Montréal QC H5B 1G8
Tél: 514-350-5122; *Téléc:* 514-350-5172
Courriel: anq@fmsq.org
URL: www.anq.qc.ca
Ginette Guilbeault, Directrice
Martin Veilleux, Président
Marc Girard, Secrétaire

Association des obstétriciens et gynécologues du Québec (AOGQ)
#3000, 2, Complexe Desjardins, Montréal QC H5B 1G8
Tél: 514-849-4969; *Téléc:* 514-849-5011
Courriel: info@gynecoquebec.com
URL: www.gynecoquebec.com
Affiliation(s): Fédération des médecins spécialistes du Québec
Francine Charlebois, CAÉ, Directrice administrative

Association des optométristes du Québec (AOQ) / Québec Optometric Association
#740, 1265, rue Berri, Montréal QC H2L 4X4
Tél: 514-288-6272; *Téléc:* 514-288-7071
Courriel: aoq@aoqnet.qc.ca
URL: www.aoqnet.qc.ca
Francois Charbonneau, Directeur général
Steven Carrier, Président

Association des pathologistes du Québec
CP 216, #3000, 2, Complexe Desjardins, Montréal QC H5B 1G8
Tél: 514-350-5102; *Téléc:* 514-350-5152
Ligne sans frais: 800-561-0703
Courriel: info@apq.qc.ca
URL: www.apq.qc.ca/index.asp
Nancy Fortin, Directrice

Association des pédiatres du Québec
#3000, 2, Complexe Desjardins, Montréal QC H5B 1G8
Tél: 514-350-5127; *Téléc:* 514-350-5177
Courriel: pediatrie@fmsq.org
URL: www.fmsq.org
Thérése Côté-Boileau, Présidente

Association des pharmaciens des établissements de santé du Québec (APES)
#320, 4050, rue Molson, Montréal QC H1Y 3N1
Tél: 514-286-0776; *Téléc:* 514-286-1081
Courriel: info@apesquebec.org
URL: www.apesquebec.org
Linda Vaillant, Directrice générale
France Boucher, Directrice générale adjointe

Association des physiatres du Québec
#3000, 2, Complexe Desjardins, Montréal QC H5B 1G8
Tél: 514-350-5119; *Téléc:* 514-350-5181
Courriel: apq@fmsq.org
René Parent, Secrétaire-trésorier
Marcel Morand, Président

Association des pneumologues de la province de Québec
#3000, 2, Complexe Desjardins, Montréal QC H5B 1G8
Tél: 514-350-5117; *Téléc:* 514-350-5153
Courriel: appq@fmsq.org
URL: www.pneumologue.ca
Simon Mathieu, Secrétaire-trésorier
Robert Boileau, Président

Association des radiologistes du Québec
CP 216, Complexe Desjardins, Montréal QC H5B 1G8
Tél: 514-350-5129; *Téléc:* 514-350-5179
Courriel: bureau@arq.qc.ca
URL: www.arq.qc.ca
Gaetan Barrette, Président

Association des radio-oncologues du Québec
#3000, 2, Complexe Desjardins, Montréal QC H5B 1G8
Tél: 514-350-5130; *Téléc:* 514-350-5152
Courriel: aroq@fmsq.org
URL: www.aroq.ca
Francis Méthot, Président

Association des sexologues du Québec (ASQ)
#404, 7400, boul Saint-Laurent, Montréal QC H2R 2V1
Tél: 514-270-9289; *Téléc:* 514-270-6351
Courriel: info@associationdessexologues.com
URL: www.associationdessexologues.com
Renée Pichette, Directrice générale par interim
Normande Couture, Présidente

Association des spécialistes en chirurgie plastique et esthétique du Québec (ASCPEQ)
CP 216, Succ. Desjardins, 2, Complexe Desjardins, Montréal QC H5B 1G8
Tél: 514-350-5109; *Téléc:* 514-350-5246
URL: www.ascpeq.org
André Chollet, Président

Association des spécialistes en médecine d'urgence du Québec
#3000, 2, Complexe Desjardins, Montréal QC H5B 1G8
Tél: 514-350-5115; *Téléc:* 514-350-5116
Courriel: asmuq@fmsq.org
URL: www.asmuq.org/
Stephen Rosenthal, Président

Association des spécialistes en médecine interne du Québec
#3000, 2, Complexe Desjardins, Montréal QC H5B 1G8
Tél: 514-350-5118; *Téléc:* 514-350-5168
Courriel: med.interne@fmsq.org
Marc Giasson, Président

Association des urologues du Québec (AUQ) / Quebec Urological Association (QUA)
#3000, 2, Complexe Desjardins, Montréal QC H5B 1G8
Tél: 514-350-5131; *Téléc:* 514-350-5181
Courriel: auq@fmsq.org
URL: www.auq.org
Lorne Aaron, Président
Liliane Verret, Secrétariat

Association diabète Québec (ADQ) / Québec Diabetes Association
#300, 8550, boul Pie-IX, Montréal QC H1Z 4G2
Tél: 514-259-3422; *Téléc:* 514-259-9286
Ligne sans frais: 800-361-3504
Courriel: info@diabete.qc.ca
URL: www.diabete.qc.ca
Serge Langlois, Président-directeur général

Association médicale du Québec (AMQ) / Québec Medical Association (QMA)
#3200, 380, rue Saint-Antoine ouest, Montréal QC H2Y 3X7
Tel: 514-866-0660; *Fax:* 514-866-0670
Toll-Free: 800-363-3932
e-mail: admin@amq.ca
URL: www.amq.ca
Claudette Duclos, CEO

Association of Local Public Health Agencies (ALPHA)
#1306, 2 Carlton St., Toronto ON M5G 1T6
Tel: 416-595-0006; *Fax:* 416-595-0030
e-mail: info@alphaweb.org
URL: www.alphaweb.org
Affiliation(s): ANDSOOHA - Public Health Nursing Management; Association of Ontario Public Health Business Administrators; Association of Public Health Epidemiologists in Ontario; Association of Supervisors of Public Health Inspectors of Ontario; Health Promotion Ontario; Ontario Association of Public Health Dentistry; Ontario Society of Nutrition Professionals in Public Health
Linda Stewart, Executive Director
Gordon Fleming, Manager, Public Health Issues

Tannisha Lambert, Manager, Administrative & Association Services

Association of Medical Microbiology & Infectious Disease Canada (AMMI Canada) / Fondation canadienne des maladies infectieuses (FCMI)
#101, 298 Elgin St., Ottawa ON K2P 1M3
Tel: 613-260-3233; *Fax:* 613-260-3235
e-mail: info@ammi.ca; communications@ammi.ca; manager@ammi.ca
URL: www.ammi.ca
Richard M. McCoy, CAE, Executive Director
Michel Laverdière, MD, FRCPC, President
Joanne Langley, MD, FRCPC, Secretary
Baldwin Toye, Treasurer

Association pour la santé publique du Québec (ASPQ) / Québec Public Health Association
#200, 4126, rue St-Denis, Montréal QC H2W 2M5
Tél: 514-528-5811; *Téléc:* 514-528-5590
Courriel: info@aspq.org
URL: www.aspq.org
Lucie Granger, Directrice Générale
Martine Deschênes, Adjointe administrative

Association pulmonaire du Québec / Québec Lung Association
#222, 855, rue Sainte-Catherine est, Montréal QC H2L 4N4
Tél: 514-287-7400; *Téléc:* 514-287-1978
Ligne sans frais: 800-295-8111
Courriel: info@pq.poumon.ca
URL: www.pq.poumon.ca
Louis P. Brisson, Directeur général

Association québécoise de l'épilepsie
#111, 1015, côte du Beaver Hall, Montréal QC H2Z 1S1
Tél: 514-875-5595; *Téléc:* 514-875-0077
Courriel: aqe@cam.org
URL: www.cam.org/~aqe/
France Picard, Directrice générale

Association québécoise de la fibrose kystique (AQFK) / Québec Cystic Fibrosis Association
#510, 425, rue Viger ouest, Montréal QC H2Z 1X2
Tél: 514-877-6161; *Téléc:* 514-877-6116
Ligne sans frais: 800-363-7711
Courriel: tvudo@aqfk.qc.ca
URL: www.aqfk.qc.ca
Andrée Bélanger, Directrice générale

Asthma Society of Canada (ASC) / Société canadienne de l'asthme
#2306, 4680 Yonge St., Toronto ON M2N 6K1
Tel: 416-787-4050; *Fax:* 416-787-5807
Toll-Free: 866-787-4050
e-mail: info@asthma.ca
URL: www.asthma.ca
Affiliation(s): Family Physicians Asthma Group of Canada; Health Canada Laboratory Centre for Disease Control's National Asthma Control Task Force
Christine Hampson, President & Chief Executive Officer
Jim Martin, Director, Fund Raising
Oxana Latycheva, PhD, CAE, Vice President, Asthma Control Pro.

Autism Ontario
#004, 1179A King St. West, Toronto ON M6K 3C5
Tel: 416-246-9592; *Fax:* 416-246-9417
URL: www.autismontario.com
Marg Spuelstra, Executive Director

Autism Society Alberta (ASA)
#101, 11720 Kingsway Ave., Edmonton AB T5G 0X5
Tel: 780-453-3971; *Fax:* 780-447-4948
e-mail: autism@austismedmonton.org
URL: www.autismedmonton.org
Affiliation(s): Edmonton Autism Society; Autism Calgary Association; Autism Society Central Alberta
Karen Phillips, Director
Jean Ashmore, Secretary

Autism Society Canada (ASC) / Société canadienne d'autisme
PO Box 22017, 1670 Heron Rd., Ottawa ON K1V 0C2
Tel: 613-789-8943; *Fax:* 613-789-6985
e-mail: info@autismsocietycanada.ca
URL: www.autismsocietycanada.ca
Kathleen Provost, Executive Director
Lynn Andrews, Information Services Coordinator

Autism Society Manitoba
825 Sherbrook St., 2nd Fl., Winnipeg MB R3A 1M5
Tel: 204-783-9563; *Fax:* 204-975-3012
Toll-Free: 800-225-9108
e-mail: info@smd.mb.ca
URL: www.smd.mb.ca
Shannon Roberts, President

Autism Society New Brunswick
PO Box 1493, Stn. A, Fredericton NB E3B 5G2
Tel: 506-372-9011; *Fax:* 506-372-9011
Toll-Free: 888-773-1916
e-mail: autism_nb@yahoo.com
URL: www.autismnb.org/
Darlene Puglsey, Contact

Autism Society Newfoundland & Labrador (ASNL)
PO Box 14078, 70 Clinch Cres., St. John's NL A1B 4G8
Tel: 709-722-2803; *Fax:* 709-722-4926
e-mail: info@autisms.nf.net
URL: www.autism.nf.net
Trish Williams, Executive Director
Christopher Dedde, Program Coordinator

Autism Society of British Columbia
#301, 3701 East Hastings St., Burnaby BC V5C 2H6
Tel: 604-434-0880; *Fax:* 604-434-0801
Toll-Free: 888-437-0880
e-mail: info@autismbc.ca
URL: www.autismbc.ca
Michael Lewis, President

Autism Society of Nova Scotia (ASNS)
PO Box 195, Dartmouth NS B2Y 3Y3
Tel: 902-429-5529
e-mail: autismns@ns.aliantzinc.ca
URL: www.autismsocietynovascotia.ca
Affiliation(s): Society for Treatment of Autism
Dana Shaw, Executive Director
Tracey Avery, Chair

Autism Society PEI
Vernon Bridge, RR#1, Avondale PE C0A 2E0
Tel: 902-651-2661; *Fax:* 902-962-3332
e-mail: douse@isn.net
URL: ca.geocities.com/peiautism/
Victor Douse, President

Autism Treatment Services of Canada (ATSC) / Association canadienne pour l'obtention des services aux personnes autistiques
404 - 94 Ave. SE, Calgary AB T2J 0E8
Tel: 403-253-6961; *Fax:* 403-253-6974
Toll-Free: 888-301-2872
e-mail: atsc@autism.ca
URL: www.autism.ca
Dave Mikkelsen, CAE, Executive Director
Joe Fardell, Chair

Blood Pressure Canada
c/o Centre of Activity & Aging, #208A, 1490 Richmond St. North, London ON N6G 2M3
Tel: 519-661-1610; *Fax:* 519-661-1635
URL: www.hypertension.ca/bpc

Blood Pressure Canada
c/o Centre of Activity & Aging, #208A, 1490 Richmond St. North, London ON N6G 2M3
Tel: 519-661-1610; *Fax:* 519-661-1635
e-mail: hyperten@ucalgary.ca
URL: www.hypertension.ca/bpc
Norman Campbell, President
Selina Omar Allu, National Coordinator
Mark Makowsky, Secretary
Ross Feldman, Treasurer

Breast Cancer Action (BCA) / Sensibilisation au cancer du sein
Riverside Mall, 739A Ridgewood Ave., Ottawa ON K1V 6M8
Tel: 613-736-5921; *Fax:* 613-736-8422
e-mail: info@bcaott.ca
URL: www.bcaott.ca
Diane Ryan, President

Breast Cancer Society of Canada / Société du cancer du sein du Canada
118 Victoria St. N., Sarnia ON N7T 5W9
Tel: 519-336-0746; *Fax:* 519-336-5725
Toll-Free: 800-567-8767
e-mail: bcsc@bcsc.ca
URL: www.bcsc.ca
Sherry Johnston, Executive Director

The British Columbia Association of Optometrists (BCAO)
#502, 1755 West Broadway, Vancouver BC V6J 4S5
Tel: 604-737-9907; *Fax:* 604-737-9967
Toll-Free: 888-393-2226
e-mail: info@optometrists.bc.ca
URL: www.optometrists.bc.ca
Cheryl Williams, CEO
Antoinette Dumalo, President

British Columbia Cancer Foundation (BCCF)
#200, 601 Broadway St. West, Vancouver BC V5Z 4C2
Tel: 604-877-6040; *Fax:* 604-877-6161
Toll-Free: 888-906-2873
e-mail: info@bccancer.bc.ca
URL: www.bccancer.bc.ca
Affiliation(s): British Columbia Cancer Research Centre; British Columbia Cancer Agency
Mary McNeil, President & CEO

British Columbia Centre for Ability Association (BCCFA)
2805 Kingsway, Vancouver BC V5R 5H9
Tel: 604-451-5511; *Fax:* 604-451-5651
e-mail: home@centreforability.bc.ca
URL: www.centreforability.bc.ca
Angela Kwok, Executive Director

British Columbia Chiropractic Association (BCCA)
#125, 3751 Shell Rd., Richmond BC V6X 2W2
Tel: 604-270-1332; *Fax:* 604-278-0093
Toll-Free: 866-256-1474
e-mail: info@bcchiro.com
URL: www.bcchiro.com
D. Nixdorf, Executive Director

British Columbia Lung Association (BCLA)
2675 Oak St., Vancouver BC V6H 2K2
Tel: 604-731-5864; *Fax:* 604-731-5810
Toll-Free: 800-665-5864
e-mail: info@bc.lung.ca
URL: www.bc.lung.ca
Affiliation(s): The Canadian Thoracic Society; The Canadian Respiratory Health Professionals
Scott McDonald, Executive Director

British Columbia Lupus Society (BCLS)
#200, 1645 - 7 Ave. West, Vancouver BC V6J 1S4
Tel: 604-714-5564
Toll-Free: 866-585-8787
e-mail: info@bclupus.org
URL: www.bclupus.org
Michael Hinman, President

British Columbia Medical Association (BCMA)
#115, 1665 West Broadway, Vancouver BC V6J 5A4
Tel: 604-736-5551; *Fax:* 604-736-4566
Toll-Free: 800-665-2262
e-mail: communications@bcma.bc.ca
URL: www.bcma.org
Brian Brodie, President

British Columbia Naturopathic Association (BCNA)
2238 Pine St., Vancouver BC V6J 5G4
Tel: 604-736-6646; *Fax:* 604-736-6048
Toll-Free: 800-277-1128
e-mail: bcna@bcna.ca
URL: www.bcna.ca
Affiliation(s): Canadian Association of Naturopathic Doctors
Christoph Kind, President
Deborah Phair, Vice-President
Tonia Mitchell, Treasurer

British Columbia Transplant Society (BCTS)
555 West 12th Ave., 3rd Fl., Vancouver BC V5Z 3X7
Tel: 604-877-2240; *Fax:* 604-877-2111
Toll-Free: 800-663-6189
e-mail: BCTS_Webmaster@bcts.hnet.bc.ca
URL: www.transplant.bc.ca
Affiliation(s): University of British Columbia
Jonathan Guss, CEO
Darrel Weinkauf, Chief Operations Officier

Canada Health Infoway / Inforoute Santé du Canada
#1200, 1000, rue Sherbrooke ouest, Montréal QC H3A 3G4
Tel: 514-868-0550; *Fax:* 514-868-1120
Toll-Free: 866-868-0550
e-mail: info@infoway-inforoute.ca
URL: www.infoway-inforoute.ca
Richard C. Alvarez, President & CEO

Canadian Agency for Drugs & Technologies in Health (CADTH) / Agence canadienne des médicaments et des technologies de la santé (ACMTS)
#600, 865 Carling Ave., Ottawa ON K1S 5S8

Tel: 613-226-2553; *Fax:* 613-226-5392
e-mail: info@cadth.ca; publications@cadth.ca
URL: www.cadth.ca

Jill M. Sanders, President & CEO

Canadian Alliance of Physiotherapy Regulators / Alliance canadienne des organismes de réglementation de la physiothérapie
#501, 1243 Islington Ave., Toronto ON M8X 1Y9
Tel: 416-234-8800; *Fax:* 416-234-8820
e-mail: email@alliancept.org
URL: www.alliancept.org

Joseph Vibert, CEO

Canadian Anesthesiologists' Society (CAS) / Société canadienne des anesthésiologistes (SCA)
#208, One Eglinton Ave. East, Toronto ON M4P 3A1
Tel: 416-480-0602; *Fax:* 416-480-0320
e-mail: anesthesia@cas.ca; adminservices@cas.ca
URL: www.cas.ca

Affiliation(s): Canadian Anesthesia Research Foundation (CARF); CAS International Education Foundation (CAS IEF)
Pierre Fiset, President
Richard Chisholm, Vice-President
S. Stanley Mandarich, Executive Director
Patricia Houston, Secretary
Susan O'Leary, Treasurer

Canadian Association for Clinical Microbiology & Infectious Diseases (CACMID) / Association canadienne de microbiologie clinique et des maladies contagieuses
c/o Dr. A. Petrich, St. Luke's Wing, St. Joseph's Healthcare, #424L, 50 Charlton Ave. East, Hamilton ON L8N 4A6
Tel: 905-522-1155; *Fax:* 905-521-6083
URL: www.cacmid.ca

Karam Ramotar, President
Greg Tyrrell, Vice-President
Astrid Petrich, Secretary-Treasurer

Canadian Association for Health Services & Policy Research (CAHSPR) / Association canadienne pour la recherche sur les services et les politiques de la santé (ACRSPS)
292 Somerset St. West, Ottawa ON K2P 0J6
Tel: 613-235-7180; *Fax:* 613-235-5451
e-mail: cahspr@cahspr.ca
URL: www.cahspr.ca

Kevin Barclay, Executive Director
Renaldo Battista, President
Marcel Saulnier, Secretary
Eric Latimer, Treasurer

Canadian Association of Cardio-Pulmonary Technologists (CACPT)
PO Box 848, Stn. A, Toronto ON M5W 1G3
e-mail: contactus@cacpt.ca
URL: www.cacpt.ca

Affiliation(s): Canadian Cardiovascular Society; Canadian Cardiovascular Congress
David Hu, Head, Pulmonary
Mike Stevenson, Head, Cardiac

Canadian Association of Centres for the Management of Hereditary Metabolic Diseases
820 Sherbrook St., #FE229, Winnipeg MB R3A 1R9
Tel: 204-787-2711; *Fax:* 204-787-1419
e-mail: cgreenberg@hsc.mb.ca
URL: www.garrod.ca

Cheryl R. Greenberg, Sec.-Treas.

Canadian Association of Child Neurology (CACN) / L'Association canadienne de neurologie pédiatrique (ACNP)
Secretariat, PO Box 5456, Stn. A, #709, 7015 Macleod Trail, Calgary AB T2H 1X8
Tel: 403-229-9544; *Fax:* 403-229-1661
e-mail: brains@ccns.org
URL: www.ccns.org

Affiliation(s): Amyotrophic Lateral Sclerosis Research Foundation; Canadian Brain Tumour Consortium; Canadian Epilepsy Consortium; Canadian Headache Society; Canadian League Against Epilepsy; Canadian Movement Disorders Group; Canadian Network of MS Clinics; Canadian Neurocritical Care Group; Canadian Stroke Consortium; Consortium of Canadian Centres for Clinical Cognitive Research
Joseph Dooley, President
Jerome Yager, Sec.-Treas.
Sally Gregg, Managing Director

Canadian Association of Emergency Physicians (CAEP) / Association canadienne des médecins d'urgence (ACMU)
#104, 1785 Alta Vista Dr., Ottawa ON K1G 3Y6
Tel: 613-523-3343; *Fax:* 613-523-0190
Toll-Free: 800-463-1158
e-mail: admin@caep.ca; board@caep.ca; committees@caep.ca
URL: www.caep.ca

Valoree McKay, Chief Executive Officer
Chris Evans, MD, President
Mark Reardon, MD, FRCPC, Treasurer
Vera Klein, Manager, CME
Nadine Lunt, Manager, Communications & Marketing

Canadian Association of Gastroenterology / Association canadienne de gastroentérologie
2902 South Sheridan Way, Oakville ON L6J 7L6
Tel: 905-829-2504; *Fax:* 905-829-0242
Toll-Free: 888-780-0007
e-mail: cagoffice@cag-acg.org
URL: www.cag-acg.org

Affiliation(s): Canadian Medical Association; World Organization of Gastroenterology
William Paterson, President

Canadian Association of General Surgeons (CAGS) / Association canadienne des chirurgiens généraux (ACCG)
774 Echo Dr., Ottawa ON K1S 5N8
Tel: 613-730-6280; *Fax:* 613-730-1116
e-mail: cags@rcpsc.edu
URL: www.cags-accg.ca

Affiliation(s): Canadian Medical Association; Royal College of Physicians & Surgeons of Canada
Jasmin Lidington, Executive Director

Canadian Association of Medical Biochemists (CAMB) / Association des médecins biochimistes du Canada (AMBC)
774 Echo Dr., Ottawa ON K1S 5N8
Tel: 613-730-8177; *Fax:* 613-730-1116
Toll-Free: 800-668-3740
e-mail: camb@rcpsc.edu
URL: www.camb-ambc.ca

Danièle Saintonge, Association Manager

Canadian Association of Medical Oncologists (CAMO) / Association canadienne des oncologues médicaux (ACOM)
c/o CAMO Secretariat Office, 774 Echo Dr., Ottawa ON K1S 5N8
Tel: 613-730-6284; *Fax:* 613-730-1116
e-mail: camo@rcpsc.edu
URL: www.cos.ca/camo/default.asp

Charles Butts, President
Kara Laing, Secretary-Treasurer

Canadian Association of Medical Radiation Technologists (CAMRT) / Association canadienne des technologues en radiation médicale (ACTRM)
#1000, 85 Albert St., Ottawa ON K1P 6A4
Tel: 613-234-0012; *Fax:* 613-234-1097
Toll-Free: 800-463-9729
e-mail: lgoulet@camrt.ca
URL: www.camrt.ca

Fiona Mitchell, President
Charles Jr. Shields, Chief Executive Officer
Fran Lapenna, Registrar

The Canadian Association of Naturopathic Doctors (CAND) / Association canadienne des docteurs en naturopathie
1255 Sheppard Ave. East, Toronto ON M2K 1E2
Tel: 416-496-8633; *Fax:* 416-496-8634
Toll-Free: 800-551-4381
e-mail: info@cand.ca
URL: www.cand.ca

Shawn O'Reilly, Executive Director
Alex McKenna, Marketing Director

Canadian Association of Neuropathologists (CANP) / Association canadienne de neuropathologistes
Ottawa Hospital, Dept. of Pathology, Civic Campus, 1053 Carling Ave., Ottawa ON K1Y 4E9
Tel: 613-798-5555; *Fax:* 613-761-4846
URL: canp.medical.org

Affiliation(s): International Society of Neuropathology
John Woulfe, Secretary-Treasurer
S. Nag, President

Canadian Association of Occupational Therapists (CAOT) / Association canadienne des ergothérapeutes (ACE)
CTTC Bldg., #3400, 1125 Colonel By Dr., Ottawa ON K1S 5R1
Tel: 613-523-2268; *Fax:* 613-523-2552
Toll-Free: 800-434-2268
e-mail: insurance@caot.ca
URL: www.caot.ca

Claudia von Zweck, Executive Director
Susan Forwell, President
Maureen Coulthard, Sec.-Treas.

Canadian Association of Optometrists (CAO) / Association canadienne des optométristes
234 Argyle Ave., Ottawa ON K2P 1B9
Tel: 613-235-7924; *Fax:* 613-235-2025
Toll-Free: 888-263-4676
e-mail: info@opto.ca
URL: www.opto.ca

Affiliation(s): Eye Health Council of Canada
Kirsten North, President
Glenn Campbell, Executive Director
Catherine Heinmiller, National Coordinator, Children's Vision Initiative & Member Programs
Paul Geneau, Secretary-Treasurer
Leslie Laskarin, Director, Communications

Canadian Association of Oral & Maxillofacial Surgeons (CAOMS) / Association canadienne de spécialistes en chirurgie buccale et maxillo-faciale (ACSCBMF)
#25, 174 Colonnade Rd., Ottawa ON K2E 7J5
Tel: 613-721-1816; *Fax:* 613-721-3581
Toll-Free: 888-369-5641
e-mail: caoms@caoms.com
URL: www.caoms.com

Affiliation(s): Canadian Dental Association

Canadian Association of Paediatric Surgeons (CAPS) / Association de la chirurgie infantile canadienne
c/o Children's Hospital Of Eastern Ontario, 401 Smyth Rd., Ottawa ON K1H 8L1
Tel: 613-737-7600; *Fax:* 613-738-4849
e-mail: bass.caps@gmail.com
URL: www.caps.ca

Juan Bass, Secretary Treasurer

Canadian Association of Pathologists (CAP) / Association canadienne des pathologistes
774 Echo Dr., Ottawa ON K1S 5N8
Tel: 613-730-6230; *Fax:* 613-730-1116
Toll-Free: 800-668-3740
e-mail: cap@rcpsc.edu
URL: www.cap.medical.org

Jagdish Butany, President

Canadian Association of Physical Medicine & Rehabilitation (CAPM&R) / Association canadienne de médecine physique et de réadaptation
774 Echo Dr., Ottawa ON K1S 5N8
Tel: 613-730-6245; *Fax:* 613-730-1116
e-mail: capmr@rcpsc.edu
URL: www.capmr.ca

Patrick Potter, Chair

Canadian Association of Prosthetics & Orthotics (CAPO) / Association canadienne en prothèses et orthèses
#605, 294 Portage Ave., Winnipeg MB R3C 0B9
Tel: 204-949-4970; *Fax:* 204-947-3627
e-mail: capo@mts.net
URL: www.pando.ca

Affiliation(s): Canadian Board for Certification of Prosthetists & Orthotists
Kathy Kostycz, Manager

Canadian Association of Radiologists (CAR) / L'Association canadienne des radiologistes
#310, 377 Dalhousie St., Ottawa ON K1N 9N8
Tel: 613-860-3111; *Fax:* 613-860-3112
e-mail: info@car.ca
URL: www.car.ca

Affiliation(s): Canadian Medical Association
Adele Fifield, CEO

Canadian Association of Speech-Language Pathologists & Audiologists (CASLPA) / Association canadienne des orthophonistes et audiologistes
#1000, 1 Nicholas St., Ottawa ON K1N 7B7
Tel: 613-567-9968; *Fax:* 613-567-2859
Toll-Free: 800-259-8519

e-mail: caslpa@caslpa.ca
URL: www.caslpa.ca
Affiliation(s): International Association of Logopedics & Phoniatrics
Ondina Love, Executive Director
Linda Walsh, President
Sharon Fotheringham, Manager, Speech-Language Pathology & Standards
Chantal Kealey, Manager, Audiology & Supportive Personnel

Canadian Association of Thoracic Surgeons
c/o Dept. of Surgery, Univ. of BC, 910 - 10th Ave. West, Vancouver BC V5Z 4E3
e-mail: joanne.clifton@vch.ca
URL: www.canats.org
Joanne Clifton, Secretariat

Canadian Association of Transplantation
10207 - 107 St., Fort Saskatchewan AB T8L 2H9
Toll-Free: 800-263-2833
e-mail: transplantcanada@yahoo.ca
URL: www.transplant.ca
Ingrid Larsen, President

Canadian Athletic Therapists Association (CATA) / Association canadienne des thérapeutes du sport
#402, 1040 - 7th Ave. SW, Calgary AB T2P 3G9
Tel: 403-509-2282; *Fax:* 403-509-2280
e-mail: info@athletictherapy.org
URL: www.athletictherapy.org
Grant Slessor, Executive Director

Canadian Blood Services (CBS) / Société canadienne du sang
1800 Alta Vista Dr., Ottawa ON K1G 4J5
Tel: 613-739-2300; *Fax:* 613-731-1411
Toll-Free: 888-236-6283
e-mail: feedback@blood.ca; fundraising@blood.ca
URL: www.bloodservices.ca
Graham D. Sher, Chief Executive Officer
Verna M. Skanes, Ph.D, Chair
Ian Mumford, Chief Operating Officer

Canadian Brain Tumour Tissue Bank
#301, 620 Colborne St.,, London ON N6B 3R9
Tel: 519-642-7755; *Fax:* 519-642-7192
Toll-Free: 800-265-5106
e-mail: braintumor@braintumor.ca
URL: www.braintumor.ca
Affiliation(s): The Brain Tumour Foundation of Canada
D. Ramsay, Director

Canadian Cancer Society (CCS) / Société canadienne du cancer
National Office, #200, 10 Alcorn Ave., Toronto ON M4V 3B1
Tel: 416-961-7223; *Fax:* 416-961-4189
Toll-Free: 888-939-3333
e-mail: ccs@cancer.ca; info@cis.cancer.ca
URL: www.cancer.ca
Social Media: www.facebook.com/CanadianCancerSociety
Affiliation(s): National Cancer Institute of Canada
Barbara Whylie, Chief Executive Officer
James Simon, President
Monique Porlier, Chief Financial Officer

Canadian Cancer Society Research Institute
#200, 10 Alcorn Ave., Toronto ON M4V 3B1
Tel: 416-961-7223; *Fax:* 416-961-4189
e-mail: ccsri@cancer.ca; research@cancer.ca; agiorgi@cancer.ca (Media)
URL: www.cancer.ca/research
Michael Wosnick, Scientific Director
Christine Williams, Director, Research
Cecilia Pangilinan, Senior Program Administrator, Programs & Awards
Joanne Reynolds, Administrator, Research
Lori Moser, Project Manager, Prevention Initiative

Canadian Cardiovascular Society (CCS) / Société canadienne de cardiologie
#1403, 222 Queen St., Ottawa ON K1P 5V9
Tel: 613-569-3407; *Fax:* 613-569-6574
Toll-Free: 877-569-3407
e-mail: info@ccs.ca
URL: www.ccs.ca
Affiliation(s): Canadian Society of Clinical Perfusionists; Canadian Society of Cardiology Technologists; Canadian Association of Cardiopulmonary Technologists; Canadian Medical Association; Royal College of Physicians & Surgeons of Canada; Canadian Council of Cardiovascular Nursing
Anne Ferguson, Executive Director

Canadian Celiac Association (CCA) / L'Association canadienne de la maladie coeliaque
#204, 5170 Dixie Rd., Mississauga ON L4W 1E3
Tel: 905-507-6208; *Fax:* 905-507-4673
Toll-Free: 800-363-7296
e-mail: info@celiac.ca
URL: www.celiac.ca
Jim McCarthy, Executive Director
Janet Dalziel, President
Robert Beddie, Treasurer

Canadian Chiropractic Association (CCA) / Association chiropratique canadienne (ACC)
#600, 30 St. Patrick St., Toronto ON M5T 3A3
Tel: 416-585-7902; *Fax:* 416-585-2970
Toll-Free: 877-222-9303
URL: www.chiropracticcanada.ca
Affiliation(s): Canadian Chiropractic Examining Board; Canadian Federation of Chiropractic Regulatory & Educational Accrediting Boards; Canadian Chiropractic Historical Associationl; Canadian Memorial Chiropractic College; Université du Québec á Trois-Rivières Programme de Doctorat en Chiropratique; Canadian Chiropractic Protective Association; Canadian Chiropractic Research Foundation; World Federation of Chiropractic
Richard Valade, Chair
Eleanor White, President
H. James Duncan, Executive Director
Allan Gotlib, DC, Director, Research
Maureen McCandless, Director, Communications
John Tucker, PhD, Director, Government & Inter-professional Relations
Jeffrey M. Warren, Secretary-Treasurer

Canadian Coalition for Immunization Awareness & Promotion (CCIAP) / La Coalition canadienne pour la sensibilisation et la promotion de la vaccination (CCSPV)
c/o Canadian Public Health Association, #400, 1565 Carling Ave., Ottawa ON K1Z 8R1
Tel: 613-725-3769; *Fax:* 613-725-9826
e-mail: immunize@cpha.ca
URL: www.immunize.cpha.ca
Ian Gemmill, Co-Chair
David Allison, Co-Chair

Canadian College of Health Service Executives (CCHSE) / Collège canadien des directeurs de services de santé
292 Somerset St. West, Ottawa ON K2P 0J6
Tel: 613-235-7218; *Fax:* 613-235-5451
Toll-Free: 800-363-9056
e-mail: cchse@cchse.org
URL: www.cchse.org
Ray J. Racette, CHE, President/CEO

Canadian College of Medical Geneticists (CCMG) / Collège canadien de généticiens médicaux
774 Echo Dr., Ottawa ON K1S 5N8
Tel: 613-730-6250; *Fax:* 613-730-1116
e-mail: ccmg@rcpsc.edu
URL: www.ccmg.medical.org
Affiliation(s): Canadian Association of Genetic Counsellors (CAGC)
Albert Chudley, President
Gail Graham, Treasurer

Canadian Council of Food & Nutrition (CCFN) / Conseil canadien des aliments et de la nutrition
2810 Matheson Blvd. East, 1st Fl., Mississauga ON L4W 4X7
Tel: 905-625-5746; *Fax:* 905-265-9372
e-mail: info@ccfn.ca
URL: www.ccfn.ca
Francey Pillo-Blocka, President & CEO

Canadian Critical Care Society (CCCS) / Société canadienne de soins intensifs
c/o Toronto General Hospital, 10 Eaton North, Room 220, 200 Elizabeth St., Toronto ON M5G 2C4
Tel: 416-340-4800; *Fax:* 416-340-4211
e-mail: info@canadiancriticalcare.org
URL: www.canadiancriticalcare.org
Affiliation(s): Canadian Medical Association; World Federation of Societies of Intensive & Critical Care Medicine
Deborah Wilson, Secretary

Canadian Cystic Fibrosis Foundation (CCFF) / Fondation canadienne de la fibrose kystique (FCFK)
#601, 2221 Yonge St., Toronto ON M4S 2B4
Tel: 416-485-9149; *Fax:* 416-485-0960
Toll-Free: 800-378-2233
e-mail: info@cysticfibrosis.ca
URL: www.cysticfibrosis.ca; www.fibrosekystique.ca
Affiliation(s): Cystic Fibrosis Worldwide
Julie Cookson, COO & Director, Development
June Pierotti, Director, Communications
Cheryl Woods, Director, Volunteer & Personnel
Cathleen Morrison, CEO

Canadian Deafblind & Rubella Association (CDBRA) / Association canadienne de la surdicécité et de la rubéole
2652 Morien Hwy., Port Morien NS B1B 1C6
Tel: 902-737-1453; *Fax:* 902-737-1095
Toll-Free: 866-229-5832
e-mail: cdbra@seaside.ns.ca
URL: www.cdbra.ca
Stan Munro, Administrative Coordinator
A.P. Peterson, President

Canadian Dermatology Association (CDA) / Association canadienne de dermatologie (ACD)
#425, 1385 Bank St., Ottawa ON K1H 8N4
Tel: 613-738-1748; *Fax:* 613-738-4695
Toll-Free: 800-267-3376
e-mail: contact.cda@dermatology.ca
URL: www.dermatology.ca
Affiliation(s): Canadian Medical Association; American Academy of Dermatology
John Toole, President
Karen Edstrom, Secretary
Brian Kunimoto, Treasurer

Canadian Diabetes Association (CDA) / Association canadienne du diabète
#1400, 522 University Ave, Toronto ON M5G 2R5
Tel: 416-363-0177; *Fax:* 416-408-7117
Toll-Free: 800-226-8464
e-mail: info@diabetes.ca
URL: www.diabetes.ca
Social Media: www.facebook.com/group.php?gid=129834841137
Affiliation(s): Association du diabète du Québec
Garth Herbert, Chair

Canadian Down Syndrome Society (CDSS) / Société canadienne du syndrome de Down
811 - 14 St. NW, Calgary AB T2N 2A4
Tel: 403-270-8500; *Fax:* 403-270-8291
Toll-Free: 800-883-5608
e-mail: info@cdss.ca
URL: www.cdss.ca
Elizabeth Dolman, Executive Director

Canadian Dyslexia Association (CDA) / Association canadienne de la dyslexie
207 Bayswater Ave., Ottawa ON K1Y 2G5
Tel: 613-722-2699; *Fax:* 613-722-4799
e-mail: info@dyslexiaassociation.ca
URL: www.dyslexiaassociation.ca
Affiliation(s): Canadian Dyslexia Centre, Heritage Academy

Canadian Epilepsy Alliance (CAE) / L'Alliance canadienne de l'épilepsie (ACE)
#224, 510 King St. East, Toronto ON M5C 1E5
Tel: 416-964-9095; *Fax:* 416-964-2492
URL: www.epilepsymatters.com
Catherine Sauerwein, President

Canadian Foundation for the Study of Infant Deaths (CFSID) / Fondation canadienne pour l'étude de la mortalité infantile
#403, 60 James St., St. Catharines ON L2R 7E7
Tel: 905-688-8884; *Fax:* 905-688-3300
Toll-Free: 800-363-7437
e-mail: sidsinfo@sidscanada.org
URL: www.sidscanada.org
Affiliation(s): SIDS International
Andrea Clement-Christie, Chair

Canadian Health Coalition (CHC) / Coalition canadienne de la santé
2841 Riverside Dr., Ottawa ON K1V 8X7
Tel: 613-521-3400; *Fax:* 613-521-9638
e-mail: info@medicare.ca
URL: www.healthcoalition.ca
Kathleen Connors, Chair

Canadian Hematology Society (CHS) / Société canadienne d'hématologie
#199, 435 St. Laurent Blvd., Ottawa ON K1K 2Z8
Tel: 613-748-9613; *Fax:* 613-748-6392
e-mail: cag@ca.inter.net
URL: www.canadianhematologysociety.org

Canadian Hemochromatosis Society (CHS) / Société canadienne de l'hémochromatose
#272, 7000 Minoru Blvd., Richmond BC V6Y 3Z5
Tel: 604-279-7135; *Fax:* 604-279-7138
Toll-Free: 877-223-4766
e-mail: office@toomuchiron.ca
URL: www.toomuchiron.ca
Affiliation(s): Haemochromatosis Society of Great Britain; Haemochromatosis Society of Southern Africa; American Hemochromatosis Society Inc.; Association hémochromatose France; Haemochromatosis Society Australia; Iron Disorders Institute of America
Elizabeth Minish, National President
Ross Gilley, National Vice-President

Canadian Hemophilia Society (CHS) / Société canadienne de l'hémophilie
#400, 1255 rue University, Montréal QC H3B 3B6
Tel: 514-848-0503; *Fax:* 514-848-9661
Toll-Free: 800-668-2686
e-mail: chs@hemophilia.ca
URL: www.hemophilia.ca
Affiliation(s): World Federation of Hemophilia
David Page, National Executive Director
Hélène Bourgaize, National Director, Volunteer Development & Human Resources
Deborah Franz Currie, National Director, Resource Development

Canadian Hospice Palliative Care Association (CHPCA) / Association canadienne de soins palliatifs (ACSP)
Annex B, Saint-Vincent Hospital, 60 Cambridge St. North, Ottawa ON K1R 7A5
Tel: 613-241-3663; *Fax:* 613-241-3986
Toll-Free: 800-668-2785
e-mail: info@chpca.net
URL: www.chpca.net
Sharon Baxter, Executive Director
Larry Librach, President
Andrea Taylor, Sec.-Treas.

Canadian Hypertension Society (CHS) / Société canadienne d'hypertension artérielle
Botterell Hall, 5th Fl., Queen's University, Kingston ON K7L 3N6
Tel: 613-533-3299; *Fax:* 613-533-6927
e-mail: info@hypertension.ca
URL: www.hypertension.ca
Affiliation(s): Canadian Society for Clinical Investigation; Canadian Coalition for Prevention & Control of Blood Pressure; Canadian Cardiovascular Society
Mansoor Husain, President
J. Geoffrey Pickering, Sec.-Treas.

Canadian Institute of Child Health (CICH) / Institut canadien de la santé infantile
#300, 384 Bank St., Ottawa ON K2P 1Y4
Tel: 613-230-8838; *Fax:* 613-230-6654
e-mail: cich@cich.ca
URL: www.cich.ca
Affiliation(s): Canadian Children's Environmental Health Network; Key Institution of Childwatch International; International Network for Child Health, Environment & Safety; WHO/European Environment Agency Working Group on the Environment & Children's Health

Canadian Institute of Public Health Inspectors (CIPHI) / Institut Canadien des inspecteurs en santé publique (ICISP)
#720, 999 West Broadway Ave., Vancouver BC V5Z 1K5
Tel: 604-739-8180; *Fax:* 604-738-4080
Toll-Free: 888-245-8180
e-mail: questions@ciphi.ca; office@ciphi.ca
URL: www.ciphi.ca
Affiliation(s): National Environmental Health Association (NEHA)
Adam Grant, National President

Canadian Liver Foundation (CLF) / Fondation canadienne du foie (FCF)
#1500, 2235 Sheppard Ave. East, Toronto ON M2J 5B5
Tel: 416-491-3353; *Fax:* 416-491-4952
Toll-Free: 800-563-5483
e-mail: clf@liver.ca
URL: www.liver.ca
Kevork Peltekian, M.D., FRCPC, Chair
Paul Derksen, CA, Sec.-Treas.

Canadian Lung Association (CLA) / Association pulmonaire du Canada
#300, 1750 Courtwood Cres., Ottawa ON K2C 2B5
Tel: 613-569-6411; *Fax:* 613-569-8860
Toll-Free: 888-566-5864
e-mail: info@lung.ca
URL: www.lung.ca
Affiliation(s): Canadian Nurses' Respiratory Society; Canadian Thoracic Society; Canadian Physiotherapy Cardio-Respiratory Society
Keith Murray, Chair
Heather Borquez, President/CEO

Canadian Marfan Association / Association du syndrome de Marfan
PO Box 42257, Stn. Centre Plaza, 128 Queen St. S, Mississauga ON L5M 4Z0
Tel: 905-826-3223; *Fax:* 905-826-2125
Toll-Free: 866-722-1722
e-mail: info@marfan.ca
URL: www.marfan.ca
Shirley Otway, Contact, Southern Alberta
Roy Braunberger, Contact, Lacombe, Alberta
Lisa McDonald, Contact, British Columbia
Jan Landsiedel, Contact, Manitoba & N.W. Ontario
Robert French, Contact, Newfoundland
Michelle Reid, Contact, Nova Scotia
Michael Stern, Contact, Montréal
Arleta Taylor, Contact, Saskatchewan
Eva Theofilopoulos, Executive Manager, GTA Chapter

Canadian Massage Therapist Alliance (CMTA) / Alliance canadienne de massothérapeutes
c/o Massage Therapists' Association of British Columbia, #180, 1200 - 73rd Ave., Vancouver BC V6P 6G5
Tel: 604-873-4467; *Fax:* 604-873-6211
e-mail: locke@massagetherapy.bc.ca
URL: www.cmta.ca
Brenda Locke, Executive Director

Canadian Medical Association (CMA) / Association médicale canadienne (AMC)
1867 Alta Vista Dr., Ottawa ON K1G 5W8
Tel: 613-731-8610; *Fax:* 613-236-8864
Toll-Free: 888-855-2555
e-mail: cmamsc@cma.ca
URL: www.cma.ca
Affiliation(s): Assn. of Cdn. Medical Colleges; Cdn. Anesthesiologists' Soc.; Cdn. Assn. of Medical Biochemists; Cdn. Assn. of Physicians with Disabilities; Cdn. Assn. of Physicians for the Environment; Cdn. Assn. of Radiation Oncologists; Cdn. Fedn. of Medical Students; Cdn. Infectious Disease Soc.; Cdn. Neurological/Neurosurgical/Clinical Neurophysiologists Societies; Cdn. Ophthalmological Soc.; Cdn. Orthopaedic Assn.; Cdn. Paediatric Soc.; Cdn. Psychiatric Assn; Cdn. Rheumatology Assn.; Cdn. Soc. of Addiction Medicine; Cdn. Soc. of Internal Medicine; Cdn. Soc. of Nuclear Medicine; Cdn. Soc. of Otolaryngoly
William Tholl, Secretary General

The Canadian Medical Protective Association / Association canadienne de protection médicale
PO Box 8225, Stn. T, 875 Carling Ave., Ottawa ON K1G 3H7
Tel: 613-725-2000; *Fax:* 613-725-1300
Toll-Free: 800-267-6522
e-mail: mediainquiries@cmpa.org
URL: www.cmpa-acpm.ca
John E. Gray, MD, CCFP, FCFP, Executive Director & CEO
William S. Tucker, President
Michael R. Lawrence, MB, BS, 1st Vice-President
Lawrence E. Groves, MD, MCFP, 2nd Vice-President

Canadian MedicAlert Foundation / Fondation canadienne MedicAlert
#800, 2005 Sheppard Ave. East, Toronto ON M2J 5B4
Tel: 416-696-0267; *Fax:* 416-696-0156
Toll-Free: 800-668-1507
e-mail: medinfo@medicalert.ca
URL: www.medicalert.ca
Affiliation(s): MedicAlert Foundation International

Canadian Memorial Chiropractic College (CMCC)
6100 Leslie St., Toronto ON M2H 3J1
Tel: 416-482-2340; *Fax:* 416-646-1114
Toll-Free: 800-463-2923
e-mail: communications@cmcc.ca
URL: www.cmcc.ca
Ron Brady, Chair of the Board
J.A. Moss, President

Canadian Natural Health Association (CNHA)
#105, 5 Wakunda Pl., Toronto ON M4A 1A2
Tel: 416-686-7056
Toll-Free: 866-686-7056
e-mail: mark.ansara@3web.net
Mark Ansara, Executive Director

Canadian Network of Toxicology Centres (CNTC) / Réseau canadien des centres de toxicologie
Bovey Bldg., 2nd Fl., Gordon St., Guelph ON N1G 2W1
Tel: 519-824-4120; *Fax:* 519-837-3861
e-mail: dwarner@uoguelph.ca
URL: www.uoguelph.ca/cntc/
Affiliation(s): Metals in the Environment Research Network
Len Ritter, Executive Director
Donna Warner, Program Coordinator

Canadian Neurological Sciences Federation (CCNS) / Fédération des sciences neurologiques du Canada
#709, 7015 Macleod Trail SW, Calgary AB T2H 2K6
Tel: 403-229-9544; *Fax:* 403-229-1661
e-mail: info@cnsfederation.org
URL: www.cnsfederation.org
Affiliation(s): Amyotrophic Lateral Sclerosis Research Foundation; Canadian Brain Tumour Consortium; Canadian Neuromuscular Group; Canadian Headache Society; Canadian League Against Epilepsy; Canadian Movement Disorders Group; Canadian Network of Multiple Sclerosis Clinics; Canadian Neurocritical Care Society; Canadian Stroke Consortium; Consortium of Canadian Centres for Clinical Cognitive Research
Andrew Kirk, President

Canadian Neurological Society (CNS) / Société canadienne de neurologie
#709, 7015 Macleod Trail SW, Calgary AB T2H 2K1
Tel: 403-229-9544; *Fax:* 403-229-1661
e-mail: brains@ccns.org
URL: www.cnsfederation.org/
Sally Gregg, Managing Director
Richard Desbiens, Sec.-Treas.
Andrew Kirk, President

Canadian Occupational Therapy Foundation (COTF) / La Fondation canadienne d'ergothérapie (FCE)
CTTC Bldg., #3401, 1125 Colonel By Dr., Ottawa ON K1S 5R1
Tel: 613-523-2268; *Fax:* 613-523-2552
Toll-Free: 800-434-2268
e-mail: skamble@cotfcanada.org
URL: www.cotfcanada.org
Sangita Kamblé, CAE, Executive Director
Sandra Wittenberg, Executive Assistant

Canadian Oncology Societies
c/o 82-84 Barrie St., Kingston ON K7L 3N6
Tel: 613-533-6000; *Fax:* 613-533-2941
e-mail: bvancersluis@ctg.queensu.ca
URL: www.cos.ca
Jean Maroun, Chair of COS Committee
Belinda Vandersluis, COS Website Coordinator

Canadian Ophthalmological Society (COS) / Société canadienne d'opthalmologie (SCO)
#610, 1525 Carling Ave., Ottawa ON K1Z 8R9
Tel: 613-729-6779; *Fax:* 613-729-7209
e-mail: cos@eyesite.ca
URL: www.eyesite.ca
Affiliation(s): Canadian Medical Association; Concilium Ophthalmological Universale
Jennifer Brunet-Colvey, Chief Executive Officer

Canadian Organization for Rare Disorders (CORD)
#600, 151 Bloor St. West, Toronto ON M5S 1S4
Tel: 416-969-7464
Toll-Free: 877-302-7273
e-mail: office@cord.ca
URL: www.cord.ca
Durhane Wong-Rieger, President
Ed Koning, Vice-President
John Adams, Treasurer

Canadian Orthopaedic Association (COA) / Association canadienne d'orthopédie
#360, 4150, rue Ste-Catherine ouest, Montréal QC H3Z 2Y5
Tel: 514-874-9003; *Fax:* 514-874-0464
e-mail: cynthia@canorth.org
URL: www.coa-aco.org
Douglas C. Thomson, CEO

Canadian Orthopaedic Foundation (COF) / Fondation orthopédique du Canada (FOC)
PO Box 7029, Innisfil ON L9S 1A8
Tel: 416-410-2341
Toll-Free: 800-461-3639
e-mail: mailbox@canorth.org
URL: www.canorth.org
Affiliation(s): World Orthopaedic Concern; Canadian Medical Association
Patti Watkins, Administration Coordinator
Angelique Berg, President & CEO

Canadian Orthoptic Council / Conseil canadien d'orthoptique
CHUL, 2705 Boul, Laurier, Ste. Foy QC G1V 4G2
Fax: 418-654-2188
e-mail: info@orthopticscanada.org
URL: www.orthopticscanada.org
Affiliation(s): Canadian Medical Association; Canadian Ophthalmological Society
Louis-Etienne Marcoux, Sec.-Treas.

Canadian Paediatric Society (CPS) / Société canadienne de pédiatrie
2305 St. Laurent Blvd., Ottawa ON K1G 4J8
Tel: 613-526-9397; *Fax:* 613-526-3332
e-mail: info@cps.ca
URL: www.cps.ca
Kenneth J. Henderson, MD, President
Marie Adèle Davis, Executive Director
Elizabeth Moreau, Director, Communications & Public Education

Canadian Pain Society / Société canadienne pour le traitement de la douleur
1143 Wentworth St. West, Oshawa ON L1J 8P7
Tel: 905-404-9545; *Fax:* 905-404-3727
e-mail: ellen@canadianpainsociety.ca
URL: www.canadianpainsociety.ca
Affiliation(s): International Association for the Study of Pain; Canadian Pain Foundation
Ellen Maracle-Benton, Office Manager

Canadian Paraplegic Association (CPA) / Association canadienne des paraplégiques
#230, 1101 Prince of Wales Dr., Ottawa ON K2C 3W7
Tel: 613-723-1033; *Fax:* 613-723-1060
Toll-Free: 800-720-4933
e-mail: info@canparaplegic.org; cpanational@canparaplegic.org
URL: www.canparaplegic.org
David Hinton, Executive Director & Manager, International Projects
Bruce Drewett, President
Jeffrey Moore, Treasurer

Canadian Pediatric Foundation (CPF) / La fondation canadienne de pédiatrie
2305 St. Laurent Blvd., Ottawa ON K1G 4J8
Tel: 613-526-9397; *Fax:* 613-526-3332
e-mail: cpf@cps.ca
URL: www.cps.ca
Marie Adèle Davis, Executive Director

Canadian Physiotherapy Association (CPA) / L'Association canadienne de physiothérapie
#410, 2345 Yonge St., Toronto ON M4P 2E5
Tel: 416-932-1888; *Fax:* 416-932-9708
Toll-Free: 800-387-8679
e-mail: information@physiotherapy.ca
URL: www.physiotherapy.ca
Affiliation(s): World Confederation for Physical Therapy; Alliance of Physiotherapy Regulatory Boards of Canada; Canadian University Physiotherapy Academic Council; Health Action Lobby (HEAL); Physiotherapy Foundation of Canada; Accreditation Council for Canadian Physiotherapy Academic Programs
Michel Landry, President

Canadian Podiatric Medical Association (CPMA) / Association médicale podiatrique canadienne
#2063, 61 Broadway Blvd., Sherwood Park AB T8H 2C1
Toll-Free: 888-220-3338
e-mail: askus@podiatrycanada.org
URL: www.podiatrycanada.org
Affiliation(s): Canadian Podiatric Education Foundation (CPEF)
Mario Turanovic, President

Canadian Porphyria Foundation Inc. (CPF) / La Fondation canadienne de la porphyrie
PO Box 1206, Neepawa MB R0J 1H0
Tel: 204-476-2800; *Fax:* 204-476-2800
Toll-Free: 866-476-2801
e-mail: porphyria@cpf-inc.ca
URL: www.cpf-inc.ca
Lois J. Aitken, President/Executive Director

Canadian Post-MD Education Registry (CAPER) / Système informatisé sur les stagiaires post-MD en formation clinique
#800, 265 Carling Ave., Ottawa ON K1S 2E1
Tel: 613-730-1204; *Fax:* 613-730-1196
e-mail: caper@afmc.ca
URL: www.caper.ca
Affiliation(s): Association of Faculties of Medicine of Canada
Yannick Fortin, Project Manager
Hélène LeBlanc, Executive Assistant

Canadian Public Health Association (CPHA) / Association canadienne de santé publique (ACSP)
#400, 1565 Carling Ave., Ottawa ON K1Z 8R1
Tel: 613-725-3769; *Fax:* 613-725-9826
e-mail: info@cpha.ca
URL: www.cpha.ca
Social Media: www.facebook.com/group.php?gid=159289860285?ref
Affiliation(s): World Health Organization; World Federation of Public Health Associations
Cordell Neudorf, BSc, MD, MHSc,, Chair
Debra Lynkowski, Chief Executive Officer

Canadian Public Health Association - NB/PEI Branch
#34, 2865 Rothesay Rd., Rothesay NB E3B 4P2
Tel: 506-847-0311; *Fax:* 506-847-0311
Cristin Muecke, President
Ann Harling, Secretary-Treasurer

Canadian Public Health Association - NWT/Nunavut Branch
PO Box 1000, Stn. 1000, Iqaluit NU X0A 0H0
Tel: 867-975-5774; *Fax:* 867-975-5755
e-mail: isobol@gov.nu.ca
Isaac Sobol, President

Canadian Rheumatology Association (CRA) / Société canadienne de rhumatologie
912 Tegal Pl., Newmarket ON L3X 1L3
Tel: 905-952-0698; *Fax:* 905-952-0708
e-mail: cra@rogers.com
URL: www.rheum.ca; www.rhumato.ca
Affiliation(s): Canadian Medical Association, Royal College of Physicians & Surgeons of Canada
Gunnar Kraag, President
Jamie Henderson, Sec.-Treas.

Canadian Sickle Cell Society / La société de l'anémie falciforme du Canada
#33, 6999, Côte des Neiges, Montréal QC H3S 2B8
Tel: 514-735-5100; *Fax:* 514-735-5109
e-mail: cslaf@total.net
Rosetta Cadogan, Regional Director

Canadian Society for Clinical Investigation (CSCI) / Société canadienne de recherches cliniques (SCRC)
774 Echo Dr., Ottawa ON K1S 5N8
Tel: 613-730-6240; *Fax:* 613-730-1116
e-mail: csci@rcpsc.edu
URL: www.csci-scrc.org
Jonathan Angel, President

Canadian Society for International Health (CSIH) / Société canadienne de la santé internationale
#1105, 1 Nicholas St., Ottawa ON K1N 7B7
Tel: 613-241-5785; *Fax:* 613-241-3845
e-mail: csih@csih.org
URL: www.csih.org
Janet Hatcher-Roberts, Executive Director

Canadian Society for Medical Laboratory Science (CSMLS) / Société canadienne de science de laboratoire médical
PO Box 2830, Stn. LCD 1, 33 Wellington Ave. N, Hamilton ON L8N 3N8
Tel: 905-528-8642; *Fax:* 905-528-4968
URL: www.csmls.org
Affiliation(s): International Association of Medical Laboratory Technologists; Intersociety Council of Laboratory Medicine; Conjoint Council on Accreditation of Allied Programs in Health Care
Kurt H. Davis, CAE, Executive Director

Canadian Society for Surgical Oncology (CSSO) / Société canadienne d'oncologie chirurgicale
c/o J. Hanes, Surgical Oncology, Princess Margaret Hospital, #3-130, 610 University Ave., Toronto ON M5G 2M9
Tel: 416-946-6583; *Fax:* 416-946-6590
e-mail: jane.hanes@uhn.on.ca
URL: www.cos.ca/csso
Affiliation(s): Royal College of Physicians & Surgeons of Canada (RCPSC)
Jane Hanes, CSSO Coordinator
Richard Nason, President
Carmen Giacomantonio, Secretary-Treasurer

Canadian Society for the History of Medicine (CSHM) / Société canadienne d'histoire de la médecine (SCHM)
c/o McMaster Univ., History of Medicine, #3NIO Health Sciences Ctr, Hamilton ON L8N 3Z5
Tel: 905-525-9140; *Fax:* 905-522-9509
URL: www.cshm-schm.ca
Patricia Prestwich, President
C. Peter Warren, Vice-President
Peter Twohig, Secretary-Treasurer

Canadian Society for Transfusion Medicine (CSTM) / Société canadienne de médecine transfusionnelle
774 Echo Dr., Ottawa ON K1S 5N8
Tel: 613-260-6198; *Fax:* 613-730-1116
e-mail: office@transfusion.ca
URL: www.transfusion.ca
Lois Shepherd, MD, President

Canadian Society for Vascular Surgery / Société canadienne de chirurgie vasculaire
c/o Medical Office Bldg., Regina General Hospital, 1440 - 14th Ave., 3rd Fl., Regina SK S4P 0W5
Tel: 416-480-4734; *Fax:* 416-680-5586
URL: csvs.vascularweb.org
Don McCarville, Secretary

Canadian Society of Allergy & Clinical Immunology (CSACI) / Société canadienne d'allergie et d'immunologie clinique
774 Echo Dr., Ottawa ON K1S 5N8
Tel: 613-730-6272; *Fax:* 613-730-1116
e-mail: csaci@rcpsc.edu
URL: www.csaci.ca
Charles Frankish, President
Richard Warrington, Vice-President
Stuart Carr, Secretary-Treasurer

Canadian Society of Cardiac Surgeons / Société des chirurgiens cardiaques
Christopher Feindel, President
Roy Masters, Secretary-Treasurer

Canadian Society of Clinical Neurophysiologists (CSCN) / Société canadienne de neurophysiologistes cliniques
PO Box 5456, Stn. A, #709, 7015 Macleod Trail SW, Calgary AB T2H 1X8
Tel: 403-229-9544; *Fax:* 403-229-1661
e-mail: brains@ccns.org
URL: www.ccns.org
Affiliation(s): Cdn. Brain Tumour Consortium; Cdn. Epilepsy Consortium; Cdn. Stroke Consortium; Cdn. League Against Epilepsy; Cdn. Headache Society; Cdn. Movement Disorders Group; Cdn. Network of MS Clinics; Cdn. Neurocritical Care Group; Amyotrophic Lateral Sclerosis Research Foundation; Consortium of Canadian Centres for Clinical Cognitive Research; Associate Societies: Assn. of Electromyography Technologists of Canada; Canadian Assn. of Electroneurophysiology Technologists; Canadian Assn. of Neuroscience; Canadian Assn. of Neuroscience Nurses; Canadian Assn. of Physical Medicine & Rehabilitation

Canadian Society of Cytology (CSC) / Société canadienne de cytologie
c/o Dr. Dirk van Niekirk, BC Cancer Agency, 600 West 10th Ave., Vancouver BC V5Z 4E6
e-mail: dvanniek@bccancer.bc.ca
URL: www.cap.medical.org/cytology.htm
Linda Kapusta, Chair
Michele Weir, Vice-Chair
Dirk van Niekerk, Treasurer

Canadian Society of Diagnostic Medical Sonographers (CSDMS)
PO Box 1220, Kemptville ON K0G 1J0
Tel: 613-258-0855; *Fax:* 613-258-0899
Toll-Free: 888-273-6746
e-mail: info@csdms.com
URL: www.csdms.com
Kathleen Foran, Executive Director

Canadian Society of Endocrinology & Metabolism (CSEM) / Société canadienne d'endocrinologie et métabolisme
c/o Lady David Institute, 3755, ch Côte St-Catherine, Montréal QC H3T 1E2
Tel: 514-340-6260
e-mail: contactus@endo-metab.ca
URL: www.mcgill.ca/csem/
Affiliation(s): Canadian Society of Clinical Investigation
Robert Josse, President
Ivy Fettes, Sec.-Treas.

Canadian Society of Gastroenterology Nurses & Associates (CSGNA)
27 Nicholson Dr., Lakeside NS B3T 1B3
Fax: 902-473-4406
e-mail: ednalang@hotmail.com
URL: www.csgna.com

Affiliation(s): Canadian Nurses Association
Karen Moricz, Executive Assistant
Debra Taggart, President

Canadian Society of Internal Medicine (CSIM) / Société canadienne de médecine interne
774 Echo Dr., Ottawa ON K1S 5N8
Tel: 613-730-6244; *Fax:* 613-730-1116
URL: www.csimonline.com
Affiliation(s): Canadian Medical Association
Bert Govig, President

The Canadian Society of Intestinal Research
855 - 12th Ave., Vancouver BC V5Z 1M9
Tel: 604-875-4875; *Fax:* 604-875-4429
Toll-Free: 866-600-4875
e-mail: info@badgut.com
URL: www.badgut.com
Gail Attara, Executive Director
Kwynn Vodnak, Associate Director

Canadian Society of Nephrology (CSN) / Société canadienne de néphrologie (SCN)
c/o Patient Research Centre, Health Sciences Centre, 300 Prince Philip Dr., St. John's NL A1B 3V6
Tel: 709-777-8073; *Fax:* 709-777-6995
e-mail: bbarrett@mun.ca
URL: www.csnscn.ca
Affiliation(s): Royal College of Physicians & Surgeons of Canada
Brendan Barrett, President
Amit Garg, Sec.-Treas.

Canadian Society of Nuclear Medicine (CSNM) / La Société canadienne de médecine nucléaire (SCMN)
774 Echo Dr., Ottawa ON K1S 5N8
Tel: 613-730-6254; *Fax:* 613-730-1116
e-mail: csnm@rcpsc.edu
URL: www.csnm-scmn.ca
Affiliation(s): Canadian Medical Association; Society of Nuclear Medicine - USA; Canadian Association of Radiation Protection

Canadian Society of Nutrition Management / Société canadienne de gestion de la nutrition
#300, 1370 Don Mills Rd., Toronto ON M3B 3N7
Fax: 416-441-0591
Toll-Free: 866-355-2766
e-mail: csnm@csnm.ca
URL: www.csnm.ca
Pat Sylvain, President Elect
Heather Truber, President

Canadian Society of Orthopaedic Technologists (CSOT) / Société canadienne des technologistes en orthopédie
#715A, 18 Wynford Dr., Toronto ON M3C 3S2
Tel: 416-445-4516
e-mail: csot@look.ca
URL: www.pappin.com/csot
Pamela Smith, Registrar/Office Manager

Canadian Society of Otolaryngology - Head & Neck Surgery (CSO-HNS) / Société canadienne d'otolaryngologie et de chirurgie cervico-faciale
221 Millford Cres., Elora ON N0B 1S0
Tel: 519-846-0630; *Fax:* 519-846-9529
Toll-Free: 800-655-9533
e-mail: cso.hns@sympatico.ca
URL: www.entcanada.org
Affiliation(s): International Federation of Oto-Rhino-Laryngological Societies; Canadian Medical Association; Canadian Deaf & Hard of Hearing Forum
Robert Burke, Secretary
Martin Corsten, Treasurer
Dominique Dorion, President

Canadian Society of Plastic Surgeons (CSPS) / Société canadienne des chirurgiens plasticiens
#4, 1469, boul St-Joseph est, Montréal QC H2K 1M6
Tel: 514-843-5415; *Fax:* 514-843-7005
Toll-Free: 800-665-5415
e-mail: csps_sccp@bellnet.ca
URL: www.plasticsurgery.ca
Affiliation(s): Canadian Medical Association
Karyn Wagner, Executive Director
Gordon Wilkes, President
Achilleas Thoma, Vice-President

Canadian Society of Respiratory Therapists (CSRT) / La Société canadienne des thérapeutes respiratoires (SCTR)
#102, 1785 Alta Vista Dr., Ottawa ON K1G 3Y6
Tel: 613-731-3164; *Fax:* 613-521-4314
Toll-Free: 800-267-3422
e-mail: info@csrt.com
URL: www.csrt.com
Christiane Ménard, Executive Director

Canadian Spinal Research Organization (CSRO)
#2, 120 Newkirk Rd., Richmond Hill ON L4C 9S7
Tel: 905-508-4000; *Fax:* 905-508-4002
Toll-Free: 800-361-4004
e-mail: csro@globalserve.net
URL: www.csro.com
Wayne Archibald, Director, Research
Barry Munro, President

Canadian Sport Massage Therapists Association (CSMTA) / Association canadienne des massothérapeutes du sport
#306, 50 Eccleston Dr., Toronto ON M4A 1K8
Tel: 416-285-1745; *Fax:* 416-285-1914
e-mail: natoffice@csmta.ca
URL: www.csmta.ca
Affiliation(s): Canadian Olympic Committee; Expert Provider Group
Trish Scheidel, President
Joanne Baker, National Office Coordinator
Aurel Hamran, President, Alberta Chapter
Kim Mark-Goldsworthy, President, BC Chapter
Johanna Thackwray, President, Ontario Chapter
Al Bodnarchuk, President, Saskatchewan Chapter

Canadian Thoracic Society (CTS) / Société canadienne de thoracologie (SCT)
c/o Suzanne Desmarais, CTS Program Manager, #300, 1750 Courtwood Cres., Ottawa ON K2C 2B5
Tel: 613-569-6411; *Fax:* 613-569-8860
Toll-Free: 888-566-5864
e-mail: info@lung.ca, ctsinfo@lung.ca
URL: www.lung.ca/cts
Affiliation(s): American Thoracic Society; American College of Chest Physicians; Royal College of Physicians & Surgeons of Canada; Canadian Medical Association; European Respiratory Society
Janet Sutherland, Director

Canadian Transplant Association (CTA) / Association canadienne des greffes
11230 - 72 Ave., Edmonton AB T6G 0B5
Tel: 416-782-8892
Toll-Free: 877-779-5991
e-mail: davidsmith@txworks.ca
URL: www.organ-donation-works.org
Dave Smith, President

Canadian Urological Association (CUA) / Association des urologues du Canada
#1155, 1155, rue University, Montréal QC H3B 3A7
Tel: 514-395-0376; *Fax:* 514-875-0205
e-mail: cua@cua.org
URL: www.cua.org
Affiliation(s): Canadian Medical Association
Richard Bolton, Executive Secretary
Isabel Kolodny, Membership

Canadians for Health Research (CHR) / Les Canadiens pour la recherche médicale
PO Box 126, Westmount QC H3Z 2T1
Tel: 514-398-7478; *Fax:* 514-398-8361
e-mail: info@chrcrm.org
URL: www.chrcrm.org

CancerCare Manitoba (CCMB)
675 McDermot Ave., Winnipeg MB R3E 0V9
Tel: 204-787-2197
Toll-Free: 866-561-1026
e-mail: donate@cancercare.mb.ca
URL: www.cancercare.mb.ca
Annitta L. Stenning, Executive Director
Sandra Tym, Director, Finance & Administration
Roberta Koscielny, Director, Communications & Public Affairs

Catholic Health Association of British Columbia (CHABC)
9387 Holmes St., Burnaby BC V3N 4C3
Tel: 604-524-3427; *Fax:* 604-524-3428
e-mail: smhouse@shawlink.ca
URL: chabc.bc.ca
Affiliation(s): Euthanasia Prevention Coalition; Canadian Association of Parish Nurse Ministries
Dianne Doyle, President

Catholic Health Association of Canada (CHAC) / Association catholique canadienne de la santé (ACCS)
1247 Kilborn Pl., Ottawa ON K1H 6K9
Tel: 613-731-7148; *Fax:* 613-731-7797
e-mail: info@chac.ca
URL: www.chac.ca
Dianne Doyle, Chair
Gerard Lewis, President/CEO
Joan Lawrence, Administrator & Coordinator, Member Services

Catholic Health Association of Manitoba (CHAM) / Association catholique manitobaine de la santé (ACMS)
SBGH Education Bldg., #N5067, 409 Taché Ave., Winnipeg MB R2H 2A6
Tel: 204-235-3136; *Fax:* 204-235-3811
e-mail: executivedirector@cham.mb.ca
URL: www.cham.mb.ca
Affiliation(s): Bishops of Manitoba; Diocese of Churchill-Hudson Bay, Northwest Territories
Wilmar Chopyk, Executive Director
Daniel Lussier, Chair
Julie Turenne-Maynard, Vice-Chair
Charles Gagné, Secretary-Treasurer

Catholic Health Association of Saskatchewan (CHAS)
1702 - 20 St. West, Saskatoon SK S7M 0Z9
Tel: 306-655-5330; *Fax:* 306-655-5333
e-mail: cath.health@sasktel.net
URL: www.chassk.ca
Edwin Hoffart, President
Bert Yakichuk, Vice-President
Fenton Yeo, Secretary-Treasurer

Catholic Health Corporation of Ontario (CHCO)
PO Box 1879, 712 College Ave. West, Guelph ON N1H 7A1
Tel: 519-767-5600; *Fax:* 519-767-5602
e-mail: chco@chco.ca
URL: www.chco.ca
Don McDermott, President
Sarah Quackenbush, Vice-President

Childhood Cancer Foundation Candlelighters Canada (CCCFC) / Fondation pour le Cancer chez l'enfant
#405, 1300 Yonge St., Toronto ON M4T 1X3
Tel: 416-489-6440; *Fax:* 416-489-9812
Toll-Free: 800-363-1062
e-mail: info@childhoodcancer.ca
URL: www.childhoodcancer.ca/
Glenn Fraser, Vice-Chair
David Stones, President/CEO
Victor S. Blanchette, Director
Janet Rieksts-Alderman, Director
John B. Sandusky, Director
Dan Mornar, Director
Brent Akeson, Director
Ian Young, Chair
Jody L. Saunders, Secretary
Claude Francoeur, Treasurer

Chiropractic Awareness Council (CAC)
595 Woolwich St., Guelph ON N1H 3Y5
Tel: 519-822-1879; *Fax:* 519-822-1239
Toll-Free: 877-997-9927
e-mail: totalhealth@chiropracticawarenesscouncil.org
URL: www.chiropracticawarenesscouncil.org
Steven Silk, Chair

Christian Health Association of Alberta (CHAA)
132 Warwick Rd., Edmonton AB T5X 4P8
Tel: 780-488-8074; *Fax:* 780-475-7968
e-mail: chaaa@compusmart.ab.ca
URL: www.chaaa.ab.ca
Glyn J. Smith, Administrator

Chronic Pain Association of Canada (CPAC)
PO Box 66017, Stn. Heritage, #130, 2323 - 111 St., Edmonton AB T6J 6T4
Tel: 780-482-6727; *Fax:* 780-433-3128
e-mail: cpac@chronicpaincanada.com
URL: www.chronicpaincanada.com
Barry Ulmer, Executive Director
Heather Divine, President

Collège des médecins du Québec (CMQ)
2170, boul René-Lévesque ouest, Montréal QC H3H 2T8
Tél: 514-933-4441; *Téléc:* 514-933-3112
Ligne sans frais: 888-633-3246
Courriel: info@cmq.org
URL: www.collegedesmedecins.qc.ca
Affiliation(s): Federation of Medical Licensing Authorities of Canada
Yves Lamontagne, Président-directeur général

College of Chiropractors of Alberta (CCOA)
Manulife Place, 11203 - 70 St. NW, Edmonton AB T5B 1T1
Tel: 780-420-0932; *Fax:* 780-425-6583
e-mail: office@albertachiro.com
URL: www.albertachiro.com
Deb Manz, Chief Executive Officer

College of Dieticians of Ontario (CDO) / L'Ordre des diététistes de l'Ontario
PO Box 30, #1810, 5775 Yonge St., Toronto ON M2M 4J1
Tel: 416-598-1725; *Fax:* 416-598-0274
Toll-Free: 800-668-4990
e-mail: information@cdo.on.ca
URL: www.cdo.on.ca
Mary Lou Gignac, Registrar

College of Dietitians of Alberta
#540, 10707 - 100 Ave., Edmonton AB T5J 3M1
Tel: 780-448-0059; *Fax:* 780-489-7759
e-mail: office@collegeofdietitians.ab.ca
URL: www.collegeofdietitians.ab.ca
Lynda Heyworth, Registrar

College of Dietitians of British Columbia (CDBC)
#103, 1765 West 8th Ave., Vancouver BC V6J 5C6
Tel: 604-736-2016; *Fax:* 604-736-2018
Toll-Free: 877-736-2016
e-mail: info@collegeofdietitiansbc.org
URL: www.collegeofdietitiansbc.org
Fern Hubbard, Registrar

College of Dietitians of Manitoba
#36, 1313 Border St., Winnipeg MB R3H 0X4
Tel: 204-694-0532; *Fax:* 204-889-1755
e-mail: office.cdm@mts.net
URL: www.manitobadietitians.ca
Michelle Hagglund, RD, Registrar

College of Family Physicians of Canada (CFPC) / Collège des médecins de famille du Canada
2630 Skymark Ave., Mississauga ON L4W 5A4
Tel: 905-629-0900; *Fax:* 905-629-0893
Toll-Free: 800-387-6197
e-mail: info@cfpc.ca
URL: www.cfpc.ca
Calvin Gutkin, Executive Director
Ruth Wilson, President

College of Family Physicians of Canada (BCCFP)
#350, 1665 West Broadway, Vancouver BC V6J 1X1
Tel: 604-736-1877; *Fax:* 604-736-4675
e-mail: office@bccfp.bc.ca
URL: www.bccfp.bc.ca

College of Family Physicians of Canada
Centre 170, 370, 10403 - 172 St., Edmonton AB T5S 1K9
Tel: 780-488-2395; *Fax:* 780-488-2396
e-mail: info@acfp.ca
URL: www.acfp.ca

College of Family Physicians of Canada
PO Box 7111, Saskatoon SK S7K 4J1
Tel: 306-665-7714; *Fax:* 306-665-7714
e-mail: scfp@shaw.ca
URL: www.ocfp.on.ca/English/regional/saskatchewan

College of Family Physicians of Canada
#240, 1695 Henderson Hwy., Winnipeg MB R2G 1P1
Tel: 204-668-3667; *Fax:* 204-668-3663
e-mail: spatek@mcfp.mb.ca
URL: www.mcfp.mb.ca

College of Family Physicians of Canada
340 Richmond St. West, Toronto ON M5V 1X2
Tel: 905-867-9646; *Fax:* 905-867-9990
Toll-Free: 800-670-6237
e-mail: ocfp@cfpc.ca
URL: www.ocfp.on.ca

College of Family Physicians of Canada
#202, 3210, av Jacques-Bureau, Laval QC H7P 0A9
Tél: 450-973-2228; *Téléc:* 450-973-4329
Ligne sans frais: 800-481-5962
Courriel: cqmf@bellnet.ca
URL: www.cqmf.qc.ca

College of Family Physicians of Canada
614 Dysart St., Dieppe NB E1A 4T9
Tel: 506-852-1086; *Fax:* 506-855-7134
e-mail: nbcfp@nb.sympatico.ca
URL: www.ocfp.on.ca/English/regional/new brunswick

College of Family Physicians of Canada
Sunnyside Mall, #302, 1595 Bedford Hwy., Bedford NS B4A 3Y4
Tel: 902-499-0303; *Fax:* 902-457-2584
e-mail: administrator@nsfamdocs.com
URL: www.nsfamdocs.com

College of Family Physicians of Canada
RR#4, Kensington PE C0B 1M0
Tel: 902-836-4638; *Fax:* 902-836-3291
e-mail: cfpc.pei@pei.sympatico.ca

College of Family Physicians of Canada
c/o Health Sciences Centre, #2420, 300 Prince Philip Dr., St. John's NL A1B 3V6
Tel: 709-744-3434; *Fax:* 709-777-7913
e-mail: cfpc@nf.aibn.com
URL: www.ocfp.on.ca/English/regional/newfoundland

College of Physicians & Surgeons of Alberta (CPSA)
Telus Plaza South, #2700, 10020 - 100 St. NW, Edmonton AB T5J 0N3
Tel: 780-423-4764; *Fax:* 780-420-0651
Toll-Free: 800-561-3899
e-mail: info@cpsa.ab.ca
URL: www.cpsa.ab.ca
Trevor Theman, Registrar

College of Physicians & Surgeons of British Columbia (CPSBC)
#400, 858 Beatty St., Vancouver BC V6B 1C1
Tel: 604-733-7758; *Fax:* 604-733-3503
Toll-Free: 800-461-3008
URL: www.cpsbc.ca
E.J. Phillips, Deputy Registrar

College of Physicians & Surgeons of Manitoba (CPSM)
#1000, 1661 Portage Ave., Winnipeg MB R3J 3T7
Tel: 204-774-4344; *Fax:* 204-774-0750
Toll-Free: 877-774-4344
e-mail: cpsm@cpsm.mb.ca
URL: www.cpsm.mb.ca
William Pope, Registrar

College of Physicians & Surgeons of New Brunswick / Collège des médecins et chirurgiens du Nouveau-Brunswick
#300, One Hampton Rd., Rothesay NB E2E 5K8
Tel: 506-849-5050; *Fax:* 506-849-5069
Toll-Free: 800-667-4641
e-mail: info@cpsnb.org
URL: www.cpsnb.org
Ed Schollenberg, MD, LLB, FRCPC, Registrar

College of Physicians & Surgeons of Newfoundland & Labrador
#603, 139 Water St., St. John's NL A1C 1B2
Tel: 709-726-8546; *Fax:* 709-726-4725
e-mail: cpsnl@cpsnl.ca
URL: www.cpsnl.ca
Robert W. Young, MD, FRCPC, Registrar
William Moulton, MD, Chair

College of Physicians & Surgeons of Nova Scotia (CPSNS)
#5005, 7071 Bayers Rd., Halifax NS B3L 2C2
Tel: 902-422-5823; *Fax:* 902-422-5035
Toll-Free: 877-282-7767
e-mail: mmchugh@cpsns.ns.ca
URL: www.cpsns.ns.ca
Cameron D. Little, CEO & Registrar
Pat Pettit, Director, Administration

College of Physicians & Surgeons of Ontario (CPSO)
80 College St., Toronto ON M5G 2E2
Tel: 416-967-2603; *Fax:* 416-961-3330
Toll-Free: 800-268-7096
e-mail: feedback@cpso.on.ca
URL: www.cpso.on.ca
Rocco Gerace, Registrar
Rayudu Koka, President

College of Physicians & Surgeons of Prince Edward Island
199 Grafton St., Charlottetown PE C1A 1L2
Tel: 902-566-3861; *Fax:* 902-566-3861
e-mail: mmacdonald@collegeofphysicians.pe.ca
URL: www.cpspei.ca
Cyril Moyse, Registrar
Melissa MacDonald, Office Secretary
Roland Chiasson, MD, President

College of Physicians & Surgeons of Saskatchewan (CPSS)
#500, 321A - 21st St. East, Saskatoon SK S7K 0C1
Tel: 306-244-7355; *Fax:* 306-244-0090
e-mail: cpss@quadrant.net
URL: www.quadrant.net/cpss/
J. Wolan, Director, Communications & Education
B. Salte, Associate Registrar
K. Shaw, Deputy Registrar
D.A. Kendel, M.D., Registrar

Community & Hospital Infection Control Association Canada / Association pour la prévention des infections à l'hôpital et dans la communauté - Canada
PO Box 46125, RPO Westdale, Winnipeg MB R3R 3S3
Tel: 204-897-5990; *Fax:* 204-895-9595
Toll-Free: 866-999-7111
e-mail: chicacda@mts.net
URL: www.chica.org
Marion Yetman, President

Consumer Health Organization of Canada (CHOC)
#1901, 355 St. Clair Ave. West, Toronto ON M5P 1N5
Tel: 416-924-9800; *Fax:* 416-924-6404
e-mail: info@consumerhealth.org
URL: www.consumerhealth.org
Affiliation(s): National Health Federation in US

Crohn's & Colitis Foundation of Canada (CCFC) / Fondation canadienne des maladies inflammatoires de l'intestin
#600, 60 St. Clair Ave. East, Toronto ON M4T 1N5
Tel: 416-920-5035; *Fax:* 416-929-0364
Toll-Free: 800-387-1479
e-mail: ccfc@ccfc.ca
URL: www.ccfc.ca; www.thegutsygeneration.ca
Kevin W. Glasgow, MD, CEO
George Tolomiczenko, Executive Director
Victoria Prince, National President

DES Action Canada
#107, 5890 Monkland Ave., Montréal QC H4A 1G2
Tel: 514-482-3204
Toll-Free: 800-482-1337
e-mail: desact@web.net
URL: www.web.net/~desact
Affiliation(s): DES Action Australia; DES Action Britain; DES Action New Zealand; DES Action The Netherlands; DES Action USA; DES Action Ireland; Info DES France; DES Action Belgium
Harriet Simand, President

Dietitians of Canada (DC) / Les diététistes du Canada
#604, 480 University Ave., Toronto ON M5G 1V2
Tel: 416-596-0857; *Fax:* 416-596-0603
e-mail: centralinfo@dietitians.ca
URL: www.dietitians.ca
Marsha Sharp, CEO

Doctors Manitoba
20 Desjardins Dr., Winnipeg MB R3X 0E8
Tel: 204-985-5888; *Fax:* 204-985-5844
Toll-Free: 888-322-4242
URL: www.docsmb.org
Debbie Bride, Communications Officer
John A. Laplume, CEO

Doctors Nova Scotia
25 Spectacle Lake Dr., Dartmouth NS B3B 1X7
Tel: 902-468-1866; *Fax:* 902-468-6578
e-mail: webmaster@doctorsns.com
URL: www.doctorsns.com
Don Wescott, President
Doug Clarke, CEO

Dystonia Medical Research Foundation Canada / Fondation de recherches médicales sur la dystonie
#106, 8 King St. East, Toronto ON M5C 1B5
Tel: 416-488-6974; *Fax:* 416-488-5878
Toll-Free: 800-361-8061
e-mail: info@dystoniacanada.org
URL: www.dystonia-foundation.org
Sarah Smith, National Director

Epilepsy Canada (EC) / Épilepsie Canada
#336, 2255B Queen St. East, Toronto ON M4E 1G3
Fax: 905-764-1231
Toll-Free: 877-734-0873
e-mail: epilepsy@epilepsy.ca
URL: www.epilepsy.ca
Donald F. Weaver, National President

Epilepsy Manitoba / Épilepsie Manitoba
#301, 309 Hargrave St., Winnipeg MB R3B 2J8
Tel: 204-783-0466; *Fax:* 204-784-9689
Toll-Free: 866-374-5377
e-mail: pthomson@mb.imag.net
URL: www.manitobaepilepsy.org
Darryl Dacombe, President
Phyllis Thomson, Executive Director
Tom Hansen, Vice-President
Diane Wall, Treasurer
Frances Held, Secretary

Epilepsy Ontario / Épilepsie Ontario
#308, 1 Promenade Circle, Thornhill ON L4J 4P8
Tel: 905-764-5099; *Fax:* 905-764-1231
Toll-Free: 800-463-1119
e-mail: info@epilepsyontario.org
URL: epilepsyontario.org
Affiliation(s): Canadian Epilepsy Alliance; Epilepsy Canada
Dianna Findlay, Provincial Executive Director

Eye Bank of BC (EBBC)
Eye Care Centre, 2550 Willow St., Vancouver BC V5Z 3N9
Tel: 604-875-4567; *Fax:* 604-875-5316
Toll-Free: 800-667-2060
e-mail: eyebankofbc@vch.ca
URL: www.eyebankofbc.ca
Affiliation(s): Canadian National Institute for the Blind; Eye Bank Association of America; Canadian Ophthalmological Society
Linda Dempster, Manager
M. McCarthy, Medical Director

Eye Bank of Canada - Ontario Division
One Spadina Cres., Toronto ON M5S 2J5
Tel: 416-497-8735; *Fax:* 416-978-1522
e-mail: eye.bank@utoronto.ca
URL: eyebank.med.utoronto.ca
Affiliation(s): Canadian National Institute for the Blind; University of Toronto
Fides Coloma, Manager

Fédération des médecins omnipraticiens du Québec (FMOQ) / Québec Federation of General Practitioners
#1000, 1440, rue Ste-Catherine ouest, Montréal QC H3G 1R8
Tél: 514-878-1911; *Téléc:* 514-878-4455
Ligne sans frais: 800-361-8499
Courriel: info@fmoq.org
URL: www.fmoq.org
Louis Godin, Président-directeur général

Fédération des médecins spécialistes du Québec (FMSQ) / Federation of Medical Specialists of Québec
CP 216, Succ. Desjardins, #3000, 2, Complexe Desjardins, Montréal QC H5B 1G8
Tél: 514-350-5000; *Téléc:* 514-350-5100
Ligne sans frais: 800-561-0703
Courriel: president@fmsq.org
URL: www.fmsq.org
Gaétan Barrette, Président

Federation of Canadian Naturists (FCN)
PO Box 186, Stn. D, Toronto ON M9A 4X2
Tel: 416-410-6833; *Fax:* 416-410-6833
Toll-Free: 888-512-6833
e-mail: information@fcn.ca
URL: www.fcn.ca
Affiliation(s): International Naturist Federation
Stéphane Deschênes, President

Federation of Regulatory Authorities of Canada (FMRAC) / Fédération des ordres des médecins du Canada
#103, 2283 St. Laurent Blvd., Ottawa ON K1G 5A2
Tel: 613-738-0372; *Fax:* 613-738-9169
e-mail: info@fmrac.ca
URL: www.fmrac.ca
B. Ward, President

Fédération québécoise de l'autisme et des autres troubles envahissants du développement (FQATED) / Québec Federation for Autism & Other Pervasive Developmental Disorders
#104, 65, rue de Castelnau ouest, Montréal QC H2R 2W3
Tél: 514-270-7386; *Téléc:* 514-270-9261
Ligne sans frais: 888-830-2833
Courriel: secretariatfqa@contact.net
URL: www.autisme.qc.ca
Jo-Ann Lauzon, Directrice générale

Fédération québécoise des massothérapeutes (FQM)
1265, av Mont-Royal est, Montréal QC H2J 1Y4
Tél: 514-597-0505; *Téléc:* 514-597-0141
Ligne sans frais: 800-363-9609
Courriel: administration@fqm.qc.ca
URL: www.fqm.qc.ca
Sylvie Bédard, Directrice générale

Fédération québécoise des sociétés Alzheimer (FQSA) / Federation of Québec Alzheimer Societies
#211, 5165, rue Sherbrooke ouest, Montréal QC H4A 1T6
Tél: 514-369-7891; *Téléc:* 514-369-7900
Ligne sans frais: 888-636-6473
Courriel: info@alzheimerquebec.ca
URL: www.alzheimerquebec.ca
Nathalie Ross, Directrice générale

A fleur de sein & Objectif Santé Mammaire
CP 518, 492, 2e Rue, Chibougamau QC G8P 2X9
Tél: 418-748-7914; *Téléc:* 418-748-4422
Courriel: afleurdesein@tlb.sympatico.ca
URL: www.cbcn.ca/afleurdesein/
Affiliation(s): Réseau québécoise pour la santé du sein
Marie Lefrançois, Présidente, · fleur de sein
Nicole Pagé, Coordonnatrice, Objectif Santé Mammaire

La Fondation canadienne du rein, section Chibougamau
CP 462, Chibougamau QC G8P 2Y8
Tél: 418-748-4730
Hélène Ross-Arseneault

Fondation de la banque d'yeux du Québec inc. / Québec Eye Bank Foundation
5415, boul de l'Assomption, Montréal QC H1T 2M4
Tél: 514-252-3886; *Téléc:* 514-252-3821
Courriel: fondby@ssss.gouv.qc.ca
Daniel Michaluk, Coordonnatrice administrative

Fondation des maladies du coeur du Québec (FMCQ) / Heart & Stroke Foundation of Québec
#500, 1434, rue Sainte-Catherine ouest, Montréal QC H3G 1R4
Tél: 514-871-1551; *Téléc:* 514-871-9385
Ligne sans frais: 800-567-8563
URL: www.fmcoeur.qc.ca
Jean Nöel, Président et chef de la direction
Claude Sabourin, Président du conseil

Fondation québécoise du cancer
2075, rue de Champlain, Montréal QC H2L 2T1
Tél: 514-527-2194; *Téléc:* 514-527-1943
Ligne sans frais: 800-363-0063
Courriel: cancerquebec.mtl@fqc.qc.ca
URL: www.fqc.qc.ca
Pierre Audet-Lapointe, MD, Président-fondateur

The Foundation Fighting Blindness (FFB)
890 Yonge St., 12th Fl., Toronto ON M4W 3P4
Tel: 416-360-4200; *Fax:* 416-360-0060
Toll-Free: 800-461-3331
e-mail: info@ffb.ca
URL: www.ffb.ca
Affiliation(s): US RP Foundation
Donna Green, President
Ron Lalonde, Vice-President
Rahn Dodick, Treasurer
Andrew Burke, Secretary

Health Action Network Society (HANS)
#202, 5262 Rumble St., Burnaby BC V5J 2B6
Tel: 604-435-0512; *Fax:* 604-435-1561
e-mail: info@hans.org; membership@hans.org; events@hans.org
URL: www.hans.org
Lorna Hancock, Director

Health Association of African Canadians (HAAC)
1149 Main St., Dartmouth NS B2Z 1A8
Tel: 902-405-4222
e-mail: haac@chebucto.ns.ca
URL: www.haac.ca
Phyllis Marsh-Jarvis, President

Health Care Public Relations Association of Canada (HCPRA) / Association des relations publiques des organismes de la santé, Canada (ARPOS)
PO Box 36029, 1106 Wellington St., Ottawa ON K1Y 4V3
Tel: 613-729-2102; *Fax:* 613-729-7708
e-mail: info@hcpra.org
URL: www.hcpra.org
Affiliation(s): Association for Healthcare Philanthropy
Jane Petricic, National Coordinator
Pat Stephens, HCPRA President

Health Sciences Centre Foundation (HSCF)
Thorlakson Building, 820 Sherbrook St., #MS1, Winnipeg MB R3A 1R9
Tel: 204-787-2022; *Fax:* 204-787-2804
Toll-Free: 800-679-8493
e-mail: hsc_foundation@hsc.mb.ca
URL: www.hscfoundation.mb.ca
Affiliation(s): Health Sciences Centre; Foundations for Health; Breakthrough!
F.L. (Lynn) Bishop, Chair
Dawne Smithson, CFRE, Vice-President/COO

Heart & Stroke Foundation of Alberta, NWT & Nunavut (HSFA)
#200, 119 - 14 St. NW, Calgary AB T2N 1Z6
Tel: 403-264-5549; *Fax:* 403-237-0803
URL: www.hsf.ab.ca
Diana Kreczy, CEO

Heart & Stroke Foundation of British Columbia & Yukon (HSFBCY)
1212 West Broadway, Vancouver BC V6H 3V2
Tel: 604-736-4404; *Fax:* 604-736-8732
Toll-Free: 888-473-4636
e-mail: info@hsf.bc.ca
URL: www.heartandstroke.bc.ca
Bobbe Wood, CEO

Heart & Stroke Foundation of Canada (HSFC) / Fondation des maladies du coeur du Canada
#1402, 222 Queen St., Ottawa ON K1P 5V9
Tel: 613-569-4361; *Fax:* 613-569-3278
URL: www.heartandstroke.ca
Affiliation(s): International Society & Federation of Cardiology; Canadian Coalition for High Blood Pressure Prevention & Control
Sally Brown, MHSc., CEO
Robert Brools, Chair

Heart & Stroke Foundation of Manitoba (HSFM)
The Heart & Stroke Bldg., 6 Donald St., Winnipeg MB R3L 0K6
Tel: 204-949-2000; *Fax:* 204-957-1365
URL: www.heartandstroke.mb.ca
Debbie Brown, CEO

Heart & Stroke Foundation of New Brunswick / Fondation des maladies du coeur du Nouveau-Brunswick
#606, 133 Prince William St., Saint John NB E2L 2B5
Tel: 506-634-1620; *Fax:* 506-648-0098
Toll-Free: 800-663-3600
e-mail: heart.stroke@hsf.nb.ca
URL: www.heartandstroke.nb.ca
Daniel Connolly, CEO

Heart & Stroke Foundation of Newfoundland & Labrador
PO Box 5819, Stn. C, 1037 Topsail Rd., St. John's NL A1C 5X3
Tel: 709-753-8521; *Fax:* 709-753-3117
URL: www.heartandstroke.nf.ca
Steve Browne, CEO

Heart & Stroke Foundation of Nova Scotia (HSFNS)
5161 George St., 7th Fl., Halifax NS B3J 1M7
Tel: 902-423-7530; *Fax:* 902-492-1464
Toll-Free: 800-423-4432
e-mail: contactus@heartandstroke.ns.ca
URL: www.heartandstroke.ns.ca
Jane Farquharson, CEO
Ian McDonald, Chair

Heart & Stroke Foundation of Ontario (HSFO)
PO Box 2414, #1300, 2300 Yonge St., Toronto ON M4P 1E4
Tel: 416-489-7111; *Fax:* 416-489-7111
Toll-Free: 888-473-4636
URL: www.heartandstroke.on.ca
Rocco Rossi, CEO

Heart & Stroke Foundation of Prince Edward Island Inc.
PO Box 279, 180 Kent St., Charlottetown PE C1A 7K4
Tel: 902-892-7441; *Fax:* 902-368-7068
Toll-Free: 888-473-4636
e-mail: info@hsfpei.ca
URL: www.heartandstroke.pe.ca
Charlotte Comrie, CEO & Executive Director
Wilma Hambly, Chair
Joan Sinclair, Director, Development

Susan Taylor-McConnell, Coordinator, Health Promotion
Sue Platts, Coordinator, School Programs & Events
Cathy Sinclair, Coordinator, Stroke Strategy

Heart & Stroke Foundation of Saskatchewan (HSFS) / Fondation des maladies du coeur de la Saskatchewan
279 - 3 Ave. North, Saskatoon SK S7K 2H8
Tel: 306-244-2124; *Fax:* 306-664-4016
Toll-Free: 888-473-4636
e-mail: heart.stroke@hsf.sk.ca
URL: www.heartandstroke.sk.ca
Diane Waterer, CEO
Nikki Gerrard, President

Hepatitis Outreach Society
Halifax Shopping Centre, PO Box 29120, 2973 Oxford St., Halifax NS B3J 4T8
Tel: 902-420-1767; *Fax:* 902-463-6725
Toll-Free: 800-521-0572
e-mail: info@hepatitisoutreach.com
URL: www.hepatitisoutreach.com
Angus Campbell, Contact

Huntington Society of Canada / Société Huntington du Canada
#400, 151 Frederick St., Kitchener ON N2H 2M2
Tel: 519-749-7063; *Fax:* 519-749-8965
Toll-Free: 800-998-7398
e-mail: info@huntingtonsociety.ca
URL: www.huntingtonsociety.org
Don Lamont, Executive Director & CEO
John Stainsby, Chair
Leslie M. Giroday, Secretary
Anne Brace, Treasurer

Huntington Society of Québec (HSQ) / Société Huntington du Québec (SHQ)
2300, boul René-Lévesque ouest, Montréal QC H3H 2R5
Tel: 514-282-4272; *Fax:* 514-937-0082
e-mail: shq@total.net
URL: www.hsc-ca.org

International Association for Medical Assistance to Travellers
#1, 1287 St. Clair Ave. West, Toronto ON M6E 1B8
Tel: 416-652-0137

International Association for Medical Assistance to Travellers (IAMAT)
2162 Gordon St., Guelph ON N1L 1G6
Tel: 519-836-0102; *Fax:* 519-836-3412
e-mail: info@iamat.org
URL: www.iamat.org
Mike Marcolongo, B.A., Director

Juvenile Diabetes Research Foundation Canada (JDRF)
#311, 7100 Woodbine Ave., Markham ON L3R 5J2
Tel: 905-944-8700; *Fax:* 905-944-0800
Toll-Free: 877-287-3533
e-mail: general@jdrf.ca; communications@jdrf.ca
URL: www.jdrf.ca
Andrew McKee, President/CEO
Aubrey Baillie, Chair
David Kozloff, Secretary
Alex Davidson, Treasurer

The Kidney Foundation of Canada (KFOC) / La Fondation canadienne du rein
#300, 5165, rue Sherbrooke ouest, Montréal QC H4A 1T6
Tel: 514-369-4806; *Fax:* 514-369-2472
Toll-Free: 800-361-7494
e-mail: webmaster@kidney.ca
URL: www.kidney.ca
Marlene Shoucair, Director, National Communications
Peter Davis, National President
Gavin Turley, National Executive Director

L.E. Society of Saskatchewan (LESS)
c/o Royal University Hospital, PO Box 88, 103 Hospital Dr., Saskatoon SK S7N 0W0
Tel: 306-781-6123
Toll-Free: 877-566-6123
e-mail: less@sasklupus.com
URL: www.sasklupus.com
Lloyd Driedger, President

Leprosy Mission Canada / La Mission évangélique contre la lèpre (Canada)
#100, 100 Mural St., Richmond Hill ON L4B 1J3
Tel: 905-886-2885
e-mail: info@leprosy.ca
URL: www.leprosy.ca
Affiliation(s): The Leprosy Mission International
Peter Derrick, Executive Director

The Leukemia & Lymphoma Society of Canada (LLSC) / Société de leucémie et lymphome du Canada
#804, 2 Lansing Square, Toronto ON M2J 4P8
Tel: 416-661-9541; *Fax:* 416-661-7799
Toll-Free: 877-668-8326
e-mail: PutnsR@lls.org
URL: www.lls.org/canada
Affiliation(s): Canadian Centre for Philanthropy
Bob Rae, OC, PC, QC, National Spokesperson
Rudy Putns, CEO

The Lung Association of Nova Scotia (LANS)
17 Alma Cres., Halifax NS B3N 3E6
Tel: 902-443-8141; *Fax:* 902-445-2573
Toll-Free: 888-566-5864
e-mail: info@ns.lung.ca
URL: www.ns.lung.ca
Louis Brill, President & CEO
Linda Gregory, Chairman

Lung Association of Saskatchewan
1231 - 8 St. East, Saskatoon SK S7H 0S5
Tel: 306-343-9511; *Fax:* 306-343-7007
Toll-Free: 888-566-5864
e-mail: info@sk.lung.ca
URL: www.sk.lung.ca
Frank Scott, Chair
Helen Cotton, Vice-Chair
Brian Graham, President & Chief Executive Officer
Jan Haffner, BPT, C.R.E, Vice-President, Health Initiatives
Sharon Kremeniuk, BA, Vice-President, Development
Leah Sullivan, BComm, CMA, Vice-President, Finance & Operations
Paul Van Loon, MSc, Vice-President, Health Education
Pat Smith, Treasurer

Lupus Canada
#211, 590 Alden Rd., Markham ON L3R 8N2
Tel: 905-513-0004; *Fax:* 905-513-9516
Toll-Free: 800-661-1468
e-mail: lupuscanada@bellnet.ca
URL: www.lupuscanada.org
Catherine Madden, Executive Director
Judi Farrell, Chief Operating Officer
Mae Boa, President
Kendra MacDonald, Treasurer

Lupus Foundation of Ontario (LFO)
PO Box 687, 294 Ridge Rd. North, Ridgeway ON L0S 1N0
Tel: 905-894-4611; *Fax:* 905-894-4616
Toll-Free: 800-368-8377
e-mail: lupusont@vaxxine.com
URL: www.vaxxine.com/lupus
Patricia Leece, President

Lupus New Brunswick
c/o N. Votour, #23A, 13 Ivan Ct., Moncton NB E1C 8T3
Tel: 506-384-6227
Toll-Free: 877-303-8080
e-mail: lupus@fundy.net
URL: www.sjfn.nb.ca/community_hall/L/lupu3203.html

Lupus Newfoundland & Labrador
PO Box 8121, Stn. A, Kenmount Rd., St. John's NL A1B 3M9
Tel: 709-368-8130
e-mail: lupusnfld@nl.rogers.com
URL: www.envision.ca/webs/lupusnfldlab
Dale Williams, President

Lupus Ontario (OLA)
#230, 2900 John St., Markham ON L3R 5G3
Tel: 905-415-1099; *Fax:* 905-415-9874
Toll-Free: 877-240-1099
e-mail: admin@lupusontario.org; lupusontario@bellnet.ca
URL: www.lupusontario.org
Julia Kane, President
Tina Sarta, Vice-President
Sharon Coslett, Secretary
Emily Leung, Treasurer

Lupus PEI
PO Box 23002, Charlottetown PE C1E 1Z6
Tel: 902-892-3875; *Fax:* 902-626-3585
Toll-Free: 800-661-1468
e-mail: bargri@pei.sympatico.ca
URL: www.lupuscanada.org

Lupus Society of Alberta (LESA)
#200, 1301 - 8 St. SW, Calgary AB T2R 1B7
Tel: 403-228-7956; *Fax:* 403-228-7853
Toll-Free: 888-242-9182
e-mail: lsaservices@shaw.ca
URL: www.lupus.ab.ca
Rosemary E. Church, Executive Director
Marleery E. Winston, President

Lupus Society of Manitoba Inc.
#105, 386 Broadway Ave., Winnipeg MB R3C 3R6
Tel: 204-942-6825; *Fax:* 204-942-4894
Toll-Free: 888-942-6825
e-mail: lupus@mts.net
Darlene Garner, President

Lupus Society of Nova Scotia
PO Box 38038, Dartmouth NS B3B 1X2
Tel: 902-425-0358; *Fax:* 902-798-0772
Toll-Free: 800-394-0125
e-mail: lubpussocietyns@ns.sympatico.ca
URL: www.lupuscanada.org

Manitoba Association of Optometrists (MAO)
#200B, 392 Academy Rd., Winnipeg MB R3N 0B8
Tel: 204-943-9811; *Fax:* 204-943-1208
e-mail: mao@optometrists.mb.ca
URL: www.optometrists.mb.ca
Lorne Ryall, Registrar

Manitoba Chiropractors' Association (MCA)
#610, 1445 Portage Ave., Winnipeg MB R3G 3P4
Tel: 204-942-3000; *Fax:* 204-942-3010
e-mail: info@mbchiro.org
URL: www.mbchiro.org
John Toth, DC, President
Sony Canteenwala, DC, Vice-President
Pamela Wylie, Executive Director
Ernie Miron, DC, Registrar

The Manitoba Lung Association
629 McDermot Ave., 2nd Fl., Winnipeg MB R3A 1P6
Tel: 204-774-5501; *Fax:* 204-772-5083
Toll-Free: 888-566-5864
e-mail: info@mb.lung.ca
URL: www.mb.lung.ca
Margaret Bernhardt-Lowdon, Executive Director

Manitoba Medical Service Foundation Inc. (MMSF)
599 Empress St., Winnipeg MB R3G 3P3
Tel. 204-788-6801; *Fax:* 204-774-1761
e-mail: info@mmsf.ca
URL: www.mmsf.ca
Affiliation(s): Manitoba Blue Cross
John McKenzie, Executive Director
Allen Rouse, Chair

Manitoba Naturopathic Association (MNA)
PO Box 2339, Stn. Main, #2, 161 Stafford St., Winnipeg MB R3C 4A6
Tel: 204-947-0381; *Fax:* 204-452-7044
Christopher Turner, N.D., Contact

Manitoba Paraplegia Foundation Inc.
825 Sherbrook St., Winnipeg MB R3A 1M5
Tel: 204-786-4753; *Fax:* 204-786-1140
e-mail: winnipeg@canparaplegic.org
URL: www.cpamanitoba.ca/mpf
Doug Finkbeiner, QC, President

Manitoba Public Health Association (MPHA)
c/o Klinic Community Health Centre, 870 Portage Ave., Winnipeg MB R3G 0P1
e-mail: manitobapha@mts.net
URL: www.manitobapha.ca
Barb Wasilewski, President

Medical Council of Canada (MCC) / Le Conseil médical du Canada
PO Box 8234, Stn. T, #100, 2283 St. Laurent Blvd., Ottawa ON K1G 3H7
Tel: 613-521-6012; *Fax:* 613-521-9509
e-mail: MCC_Admin@mcc.ca
URL: www.mcc.ca
Ian Bowmer, Executive Director

Medical Devices Canada
#900, 405 The West Mall, Toronto ON M9C 5J1
Tel: 416-620-1915; *Fax:* 416-620-1595
Toll-Free: 866-586-3332
e-mail: info@medec.org
URL: www.medec.org
James Wilson, Chair
Stephen Dibert, President & CEO

Medical Society of Prince Edward Island (MSPEI)
2 Myrtle St., Stratford PE C1B 2W2
Tel: 902-368-7303; *Fax:* 902-566-3934
Toll-Free: 888-368-7303
URL: www.mspei.org
Kathy Maher, Communications Director
Sandy Irwin, Executive Director

The Michener Institute for Applied Health Sciences
222 St. Patrick St., Toronto ON M5T 1V4
Tel: 416-596-3101; *Fax:* 416-596-3180
Toll-Free: 800-387-9066
e-mail: info@michener.ca
URL: www.michener.on.ca
Affiliation(s): 170 hospitals, labs, & clinics across Canada
Cathy Fooks, Chair
Paul Gamble, Secretary/President & CEO

Multiple Sclerosis Society of Canada (MS) / Société canadienne de la sclérose en plaques
#700, 175 Bloor St. East, Toronto ON M4W 3R8
Tel: 416-922-6065; *Fax:* 416-922-7538
Toll-Free: 800-268-7582
e-mail: info@mssociety.ca
URL: www.mssociety.ca
Affiliation(s): Canadian Medical Association
Lou J. Maroun, Chair
Deanna Groetzinger, Vice-President, Communications
Alistair M. Fraser, President

Muscular Dystrophy Association of Canada (MDAC) / Association canadienne de la dystrophie musculaire (ACDM)
#900, 2345 Yonge St., Toronto ON M4P 2E5
Tel: 416-488-0030; *Fax:* 416-488-7523
Toll-Free: 866-687-2538
e-mail: info@muscle.ca
URL: www.muscle.ca
Michel Chalifoux, Chair
Catherine Sherrard, CEO

Myasthenia Gravis Association of British Columbia (MGABC)
2805 Kingsway Ave., Vancouver BC V5R 5H9
Tel: 604-451-5511; *Fax:* 604-451-5651
e-mail: mgabc@centreforability.bc.ca
URL: www.myastheniagravis.ca
Brenda Kelsey, President
Judy Bonny, Vice-President/Treasurer

National Eating Disorder Information Centre (NEDIC)
ES 7-421, 200 Elizabeth St., Toronto ON M5G 2C4
Tel: 416-340-4156; *Fax:* 416-340-4736
Toll-Free: 866-633-4220
e-mail: nedic@uhn.on.ca
URL: www.nedic.ca
Merryl Bear, Director

National ME/FM Action Network / Réseau national d'action EM/FM encéphalomyélite myalgique/fibromyalgie
512, 33 Banner Rd., Nepean ON K2H 8V7
Tel: 613-829-6667; *Fax:* 613-829-8518
e-mail: ag922@ncf.ca
URL: www.mefmaction.net
Affiliation(s): Volunteer Ottawa; Volunteer Canada
Lydia E. Neilson, CEO

New Brunswick Association of Dietitians (NBAD) / Association des diététistes du Nouveau-Brunswick (ADNB)
#101, 333 Champlain St., Dieppe NB E1A 1P2
Tel: 506-856-6881; *Fax:* 506-856-6855
e-mail: registrar@adnb-nbad.com; info@adnb-nbad.com
URL: www.adnb-nbad.com
Maryse Vautour, Registrar

New Brunswick Association of Naturopathic Doctors
2278 King George Hwy., Miramichi NB E1V 6N6
Tel: 506-773-3700; *Fax:* 506-773-3704
URL: www.nband.ca
Crystal Charest, Contact

New Brunswick Association of Optometrists (NBAO) / Association des optométristes du Nouveau-Brunswick
#1, 490 Gibson St., Fredericton NB E3A 4E9
Tel: 506-458-8759; *Fax:* 506-450-1271
e-mail: nbao@nbnet.nb.ca
URL: www.nbao.ca
Joan Hicks, President

New Brunswick Catholic Health Association (NBCHA)
1773 Water St., Miramichi NB E1N 1B2
Tel: 506-778-5302; *Fax:* 506-778-5303
e-mail: nbcha@nb.aibn.com
URL: www.chanb.com/chanb/
Robert Stewart, Executive Director

New Brunswick Chiropractors' Association (NBCA) / Association des chiropraticiens du Nouveau-Brunswick
#200, 125 Whiting Rd., Fredericton NB E3B 5Y5
Tel: 506-445-6800; *Fax:* 506-457-1114
e-mail: comments@nbchiropractic.ca
URL: www.nbchiropractic.ca
Mohamed El-Bayoumi, President

New Brunswick Lung Association / Association pulmonaire du Nouveau-Brunswick
Victoria Health Centre, 65 Brunswick St., Fredericton NB E3B 1G5
Tel: 506-455-8961; *Fax:* 506-462-0939
Toll-Free: 800-565-5864
e-mail: nblung@nbnet.nb.ca
URL: www.nb.lung.ca
Ken Maybee, President & CEO

New Brunswick Medical Society (NBMS) / Société médicale du Nouveau-Brunswick
176 York St., Fredericton NB E3B 3N7
Tel: 506-458-8860; *Fax:* 506-458-9853
e-mail: nbms@nbnet.nb.ca
URL: www.nbms.nb.ca
Rose Anne Goodine, President

Newfoundland & Labrador Association of Optometrists (NLAO)
PO Box 8042, Stn. C, St. John's NL A1B 3M7
Tel: 709-739-8284; *Fax:* 709-739-8378
e-mail: nlao@nl.rogers.com
URL: www.nao.opto.ca
Grace Hwang, President

Newfoundland & Labrador Chiropractic Association
25 Allandale Rd., Upper Level, St. John's NL A1B 2Z6
Tel: 709-739-7762; *Fax:* 709-739-7703
e-mail: nlca@nf.aibn.com
URL: www.nlchiropractic.ca
Debbie Brake-Patten, Communications
Keith Cassell, President

Newfoundland & Labrador College of Dietitians (NLCD)
PO Box 1756, Stn. C, St. John's NL A1C 5P5
Tel: 709-753-4040
Toll-Free: 877-753-4040
URL: www.nlcd.ca; www.dietitians.ca

Newfoundland & Labrador Lung Association (NLLA)
Cornell Bldg, PO Box 13457, Stn. A, 15 Pippy Place, 2nd Fl., St. John's NL A1B 4B8
Tel: 709-726-4664; *Fax:* 709-726-2550
Toll-Free: 888-566-5864
e-mail: info@nf.lung.ca
URL: www.nf.lung.ca
Paul Thomey, Executive Director

Newfoundland & Labrador Medical Association (NLMA)
164 MacDonald Dr., St. John's NL A1A 4B3
Tel: 709-726-7424; *Fax:* 709-726-7525
Toll-Free: 800-563-2003
e-mail: nlma@nlma.nf.ca
URL: www.nlma.nf.ca
Lynn Barter, Director, Communications & Public Affairs
Robert Ritter, Executive Director

Newfoundland & Labrador Public Health Association (NLPHA)
PO Box 8172, St. John's NL A1B 3M9
Fay Matthews, President
Elizabeth Wright, Secretary
Pat Murray, Treasurer

Northwest Territories Medical Association (NWTMA)
PO Box 1732, Yellowknife NT X1A 2P3
Tel: 867-920-4575; *Fax:* 867-920-4575
e-mail: nwtmedassoc@ssimicro.com
URL: www.nwtma.ca
Anna Reid, President
Marlena Guzowski, Executive Director

Nova Scotia Association of Naturopathic Doctors
#16, 3514 Joseph Howe Dr., Halifax NS B3L 4H7
Tel: 902-431-8001; *Fax:* 902-542-4554
URL: www.nsand.ca
Sarah Baille, ND, Co-President
Jyl Bishop Veale, ND, Co-President

Nova Scotia Association of Optometrists (NSAO)
PO Box 9410, Stn. A, #700, 6009 Quinpool Rd., Halifax NS B3K 5S3
Tel: 902-435-2845; *Fax:* 902-425-2441
e-mail: nsao@accesswave.ca
URL: www.nsoptometrists.ca
Sheldon Pothier, Registrar

Nova Scotia College of Chiropractors (NSCC)
PO Box 9410, Stn. A, 6009 Quinpool Road, Halifax NS B3K 5S3
Tel: 902-425-2445; *Fax:* 902-425-2441
e-mail: inquiries@chiropractors.ns.ca
URL: www.chiropractors.ns.ca
Lisa Richard, Registrar

Nova Scotia Dietetic Association (NSDA)
#212, 1496 Bedford Hwy., Bedford NS B4A 1E5
Tel: 902-835-0253; *Fax:* 902-835-0523
e-mail: info@nsdassoc.ca
URL: www.nsdassoc.ca
Jennifer Hutchinson, President

Occupational & Environmental Medical Association of Canada (OEMAC) / Association canadienne de la médecine du travail et de l'environnement (ACMTE)
#1430, 1101 Upper Middle Rd. East, Oakville ON L6H 5Z9
Tel: 905-849-9925; *Fax:* 905-338-8523
e-mail: oemac@oemac.org
URL: www.oemac.org
Affiliation(s): Canadian Medical Association; Canadian Board of Occupational Medicine; Royal College of Physicians & Surgeons of Canada
Howard Hamer, President

Ontario Association of Naturopathic Doctors (OAND)
#603, 789 Don Mills Rd., Toronto ON M3C 1T5
Tel: 416-233-2001; *Fax:* 416-233-2924
Toll-Free: 877-628-7284
e-mail: info@oand.org
URL: www.oand.org
Affiliation(s): Canadian Association of Naturopathic Doctors
Alison Dantas, CEO
Shelley Burns, Chair
Darlene Ahenakew, Secretary
Stephen Jones, ND, Treasurer

Ontario Association of Optometrists (OAO)
Plaza 3, #300, 2000 Argentia Rd., Mississauga ON L5N 1V9
Tel: 905-826-3522
Toll-Free: 800-540-3837
e-mail: wbishop@optom.on.ca
URL: www.optom.on.ca
William Ulakovic, President

Ontario Chiropractic Association (OCA) / Association chiropratique de l'Ontario
#30, 5160 Explorer Dr., Mississauga ON L4W 4T7
Tel: 905-629-8211; *Fax:* 905-629-8214
Toll-Free: 877-327-2273
e-mail: lirwin@chiropractic.on.ca
URL: www.chiropractic.on.ca
Marny Hamilton, Director, Operations
Robert Haig, Executive Director

Ontario Lung Association (OLA)
573 King St. East, Toronto ON M5A 4L3
Tel: 416-864-9911; *Fax:* 416-864-9916
Toll-Free: 800-972-2636
e-mail: olalung@on.lung.ca
URL: www.on.lung.ca
Affiliation(s): Ontario Thoracic Society; Ontario Respiratory Care Society
George Habib, President & CEO
Jane Wallingford, Chair

Ontario Medical Association (OMA)
#200, 525 University Ave., Toronto ON M5G 2K7
Tel: 416-599-2580; *Fax:* 416-599-1951
Toll-Free: 800-268-7215
URL: www.oma.org
Jonathan Guss, CEO
Darrel Weinkauf, COO

Ontario Public Health Association (OPHA) / Association pour la santé publique de l'Ontario
Lawrence Square, #310, 700 Lawrence Ave. West, Toronto ON M6B 3B4
Tel: 416-367-3313; *Fax:* 416-367-2844
Toll-Free: 800-267-6817
e-mail: info@opha.on.ca
URL: www.opha.on.ca
Affiliation(s): Canadian Public Health Association
Carol Timmings, President
Liz Haugh, Vice-President

Opticians Association of Canada (OAC)
#2706, 83 Garry St., Winnipeg MB R3C 4J9
Tel: 204-982-6060; *Fax:* 204-947-2519
Toll-Free: 800-842-3155
e-mail: canada@opticians.ca
URL: www.opticians.ca
Lorne Kashin, President

Ordre des ergothérapeutes du Québec (OEQ)
#920, 2021, av Union, Montréal QC H3A 2S9
Tél: 514-844-5778; *Téléc:* 514-844-0478
Ligne sans frais: 800-265-5778
Courriel: ergo@oeq.org
URL: www.oeq.org
Lucie Ouellet, Responsable, Communications
Christiane L. Charbonneau, Directrice générale et secrétaire

Ordre des orthophonistes et audiologistes du Québec (OOAQ)
#601, 235, boul René-Levesque est, Montréal QC H2X 1N8
Tél: 514-282-9123; *Téléc:* 514-282-9541
Ligne sans frais: 888-232-9123
Courriel: info@ooaq.qc.ca
URL: www.ooaq.qc.ca
Marie-Pierre Caouette, Présidente

Ordre professionnel des diététistes du Québec (OPDQ)
#1220, 2155, rue Guy, Montréal QC H3H 2R9
Tél: 514-393-3733; *Téléc:* 514-393-3582
Ligne sans frais: 888-393-8528
Courriel: opdq@opdq.org
URL: www.opdq.org
Annie Chapados, Directrice générale et secrétaire

Ordre professionnel des physiothérapeutes du Québec (OPPQ)
#1000, 7151, Jean Talon est, Anjou QC H1M 3N8
Tél: 514-351-2770; *Téléc:* 514-351-2658
Ligne sans frais: 800-361-2001
Courriel: physio@oppq.qc.ca
URL: www.oppq.qc.ca
Lucie Forget, Présidente/directrice générale

Organ Donors Canada / Donneurs d'organes du Canada
5326 Ada Blvd. NW, Edmonton AB T5W 4N7
Tel: 780-474-9363
Mae Cox, Executive Director

Osteoporosis Canada / Ostéoporose Canada
#301, 1090 Don Mills Rd., Toronto ON M3C 3R6
Tel: 416-696-2663; *Fax:* 416-696-2673
Toll-Free: 800-463-6842
e-mail: info@osteoporosis.ca
URL: www.osteoporosis.ca
Julie M. Foley, President & CEO
Diane Thériault, M.D., Chair
Fred Goddard, B.S.c., CGA, CF, Treasurer

Ovarian Cancer Canada (OCC) / Cancer de l'ovaire Canada (COC)
#101, 145 Front St. East, Toronto ON M5A 1E3
Tel: 416-962-2700; *Fax:* 416-962-2701
Toll-Free: 877-413-7970
e-mail: info@ovariancanada.org
URL: www.ovariancanada.org
Elisabeth Ross, Executive Director
Moira Lambertus, Information Coordinator

Parkinson Society - Maritime Region
#830, 5991 Spring Garden Rd., Halifax NS B3H 1Y6
Tel: 902-422-3656; *Fax:* 902-422-3797
Toll-Free: 800-663-2468
e-mail: info@parkinsonmaritimes.ca
URL: www.parkinsonmaritimes.ca
Mary Hatcher, Executive Director

Parkinson Society British Columbia (PSBC)
#600, 890 West Pender St., Vancouver BC V6C 1J9
Tel: 604-662-3240; *Fax:* 604-687-1327
Toll-Free: 800-668-3330
e-mail: info@parkinson.bc.ca
URL: www.parkinson.bc.ca
Diane Robinson, Executive Director

Parkinson Society Canada / Société Parkinson Canada
#316, 4211 Yonge St., Toronto ON M2P 2A9
Tel: 416-227-9700; *Fax:* 416-227-9600
Toll-Free: 800-565-3000
e-mail: general.info@parkinson.ca
URL: www.parkinson.ca
Joyce Gordon, President & CEO

Parkinson Society Canada - Central & Northern Ontario Region
#321, 4211 Yonge St., Toronto ON M2P 2A9
Tel: 416-227-1200; *Fax:* 416-227-1520
Toll-Free: 800-565-3000
e-mail: info.cno@parkinson.ca
URL: www.cno.parkinson.ca
Debbie Davis, CEO

Parkinson Society Canada - Manitoba Region
7 - 414 Westmount Dr., Winnipeg MB R2J 1P2
Tel: 204-786-2637; *Fax:* 204-786-2327
Toll-Free: 866-999-5558
e-mail: laura.asher@parkinson.ca
URL: www.parkinson.ca
Howard Koks, Executive Director

Parkinson Society Canada - Southwestern Ontario Region
Meadowbrook Business Park, #117, 4500 Blaikie Rd., London ON N6L 1G5
Tel: 519-652-9437; *Fax:* 519-652-9267
Toll-Free: 888-851-7376
e-mail: info@parkinsonsociety.ca
URL: www.parkinsonsociety.ca
Carolyn Conners, CEO

Parkinson Society Newfoundland & Labrador
#305, 136 Crosbie Rd., St. John's NL A1B 3K3
Tel: 709-574-4428; *Fax:* 709-754-5868
Toll-Free: 800-567-7020
e-mail: parkinson@nf.aibn.com
Patricia Morrissey, Executive Director

Parkinson Society of Canada - Toronto Chapter
#321, 4211 Yonge St., Toronto ON M2P 2A9
Tel: 416-227-1200; *Fax:* 416-227-1520
Toll-Free: 800-565-3000
e-mail: communications@parkinson.ca
URL: www.parkinson.ca
Debbie Davis, CEO (Central & Northern Ontario)
Sarah Rooje, CNO Admin./Client Services

Parkinson Society of Ottawa
1053 Carling Ave., Ottawa ON K1Y 4E9
Tel: 613-722-9238; *Fax:* 613-722-3241
e-mail: psoc@lri.ca
URL: www.parkinsons.ca
Affiliation(s): Parkinson Foundation of Canada
Dennise Taylor-Gilhen, Executive Director

The Parkinson's Society of Southern Alberta (PSSA)
#102, 5636 Burbank Cres. SE, Calgary AB T2H 1Z6
Tel: 403-243-9901; *Fax:* 403-243-8283
Toll-Free: 800-561-1911
e-mail: pssa@parkinsons-society.org
URL: www.parkinsons-society.org
John Petryshen, CEO

Post-Polio Awareness & Support Society of BC (PPASS/BC)
#2, 2630 Ross Lane, Victoria BC V8T 5L5
Tel: 250-477-8244; *Fax:* 250-477-8287
e-mail: ppass@pacificcoast.net
URL: www.ppass.bc.ca
Joan Toone, President

Post-Polio Network Manitoba Inc. (PPN-MB)
#204, 825 Sherbrook Street, Winnipeg MB R3A 1M5
Tel: 204-975-3037; *Fax:* 204-975-3027
URL: www.smd.mb.ca/post_polio_network_manitoba_inc.aspx
Affiliation(s): Polio Canada; SMD - Fostering Growth & Clearinghouse of Self-Help Organizations
Charlene Craig, President
Dolores Horobetz, Treasurer
Clare Simpson, Secretary

Prince Edward Island Association of Optometrists (PEIAO)
PO Box 1812, Charlottetown PE C1A 7N5
Tel: 902-626-3937; *Fax:* 902-626-3973
e-mail: info@peioptometrists.ca
URL: www.peioptometrists.ca
Susan Judson, President
Catherine Arsenault, Vice-President
Murray Rusk, Secretary
J.E. Hickey, Treasurer

Prince Edward Island Chiropractic Association (PEICA)
228 Grafton St., Charlottetown PE C1A 1L5
Tel: 902-894-4400; *Fax:* 902-894-3762
e-mail: chiro.whitty@pei.aibn.com
David Whitty, President
Darren MacLean, Registrar

Prince Edward Island Dietetic Association
153 Spring St., Summerside PE C1N 3G2
Tel: 902-436-2438
e-mail: peidrb@pei.sympatico.ca
Katherine Schaefer, Registrar

Prince Edward Island Lung Association
#2, 1 Rochford St., Charlottetown PE C1A 9L2
Tel: 902-892-5957; *Fax:* 902-566-9901
Toll-Free: 888-566-5864
e-mail: info@pei.lung.ca
URL: www.pei.lung.ca
Affiliation(s): Canadian Thoracic Society; Canadian Nurses Respiratory Society; Canadian Physio-Cardio Respiratory Society; Respiratory Therapy Society
Joanne Ings, Executive Director

Psoriasis Society of Canada / Société psoriasis du Canada
National Office, PO Box 25015, Halifax NS B3M 4H4
Tel: 902-443-8680; *Fax:* 902-443-2073
Toll-Free: 800-656-4494
URL: www.psoriasissociety.org
Affiliation(s): International Federation of Psoriasis Associations
Judy Misner, President
Charmaine Fader, Vice-President
Diana Stevens, Secretary
Diane Drake, Director

Public Health Association of British Columbia (PHABC)
#219, 2187 Oak Bay Ave., Vancouver BC V8R 1G1
Tel: 250-595-8422; *Fax:* 250-595-8622
e-mail: admin@phabc.org
URL: www.phabc.org
Shannon Turner, President

Public Health Association of Nova Scotia (PHANS)
PO Box 33074, Halifax NS B3L 4T6
Tel: 902-477-2960; *Fax:* 902-477-4584
e-mail: phans@cpha.ca
URL: www.phans.ca
Marie McCully Collier, President

Québec Black Medical Association
#101, Sherbrooke St. W, Montréal QC H3H 1E4
Tel: 514-937-8432; *Fax:* 514-933-5929
E.C. Tucker, Contact

The Royal College of Physicians & Surgeons of Canada (RCPSC) / Le Collège royal des médecins et chirurgiens du Canada (CRMCC)
774 Echo Dr., Ottawa ON K1S 5N8
Tel: 613-730-8177; *Fax:* 613-730-8830
Toll-Free: 800-668-3740
e-mail: info@royalcollege.ca
URL: rcpsc.medical.org
Affiliation(s): Canadian Medical Association; College of Family Physicians of Canada; Association of Canadian Medical Colleges; National Specialty Societies; Federation of Medical Licensing Authorities of Canada
Andrew Padmos, BA, MD, FRCPC, CEO
Danielle Fréchette, MPA, Director, Health Policy & Governance Support
Karen McCarthy, APR, Director, Communications & External Relations
Tim Julien, CA, CAE, CFO

Saint Elizabeth Health Care (SEHC) / Les soins de santé Sainte-Elizabeth
#300, 90 Allstate Pkwy., Markham ON L3R 6H3
Tel: 905-940-9655; *Fax:* 905-940-9934
e-mail: communications@saintelizabeth.com;

foundation@saintelizabeth.com
URL: www.saintelizabeth.com
Affiliation(s): Canadian Council on Health Services Accreditation
Shirlee M. Sharkey, President & CEO
Michael Decter, Chair
Daniele Bertrand, Vice-Chair & Treasurer
Ruth Corbin, Secretary

Saskatchewan Association of Naturopathic Practitioners (SANP)
1814 Lorne Ave., Saskatoon SK S7H 1Y4
Tel: 306-955-2633; *Fax:* 306-955-2638
e-mail: naturdoctor@sasktel.net
URL: www.sanp.ca
Leshia Ferguson, President
Kent Bailey, Vice-President
Tanya Gokavi, Secretary
Jacqui Fleury, Treasurer
Vanessa DiCicco, Registrar
Julie Zepp Rutledge, Liaison, Government, Media, & Public

Saskatchewan Association of Optometrists (SAO)
#108, 2366 Ave. C North, Saskatoon SK S7L 5X5
Tel: 306-652-2069; *Fax:* 306-652-2642
Toll-Free: 877-660-3937
e-mail: sao@sasktel.net
URL: www.optometrists.sk.ca
Sheila Spence, Executive Director
Janann Blackburn, Coordinator, Vision Care Program

Saskatchewan Dietitians Association (SDA)
PO Box 3894, #17, 2010 - 7th Ave., Regina SK S4R 1C2
Tel: 306-359-3040; *Fax:* 306-359-3046
e-mail: registrar@saskdietitians.org
URL: www.saskdietitians.org
Affiliation(s): Network of Interprofessional Regulatory Organizations; Alliance of Dietetic Regulatory Bodies
Victoria Jurgens, President
Lana Moore, Registrar

Saskatchewan Families for Effective Autism Treatment (SASKFEAT)
PO Box 2150, Tisdale SK S0E 1T0
Tel: 306-862-4768
e-mail: saskfeat@hotmail.com
URL: www.saskfeat.com
Affiliation(s): Autism Society Canada
Tim Verklan, President
Carolyn Forsey, Vice-President
Ron Luciw, Secretary
Brad Hayes, Treasurer

Saskatchewan Medical Association (SMA)
#402, 321A - 21st St. East, Saskatoon SK S7K 0C1
Tel: 306-244-2196; *Fax:* 306-653-1631
Toll-Free: 800-667-3781
e-mail: sma@sma.sk.ca
URL: www.sma.sk.ca
George Miller
Martin Vogel, Executive Director
Ed Hobday, Administrative Director
Phillip Fourie, Treasurer

Saskatchewan Parkinson's Disease Foundation (SPDF)
Royal University Hospital, PO Box 102, 103 Hospital Dr., Saskatoon SK S7N 0W8
Tel: 306-966-1348; *Fax:* 306-966-8030
e-mail: spdf@sasktel.net
URL: www.parkinson.ca/en/9.5.saskatchewan%20L1.html
Linda Beatty, Contact

Saskatchewan Public Health Association Inc.
PO Box 845, Regina SK S4P 3B1
e-mail: terry.gibson@saskatoonhealthregion.ca
Saqib Shahab, President

Société canadienne de la sclérose en plaques (Division du Québec) (SCSP) / Multiple Sclerosis Society of Canada (Québec Division)
Tour Est, #1010, 550, rue Sherbrooke ouest, Montréal QC H3A 1E7
Tél: 514-849-7591; *Téléc:* 514-849-8914
Ligne sans frais: 800-268-7582
Courriel: info.qc@scleroseenplaques.ca
URL: www.scleroseenplaques.ca/qc
Affiliation(s): Fédération internationale de la sclérose en plaques
François Coupal, Chair

Société Parkinson du Québec / Parkinson Society Québec
#1470, 550 rue Sherbrooke ouest, Montréal QC H3A 1B9
Tél: 514-861-4422; *Téléc:* 514-861-4510
Ligne sans frais: 800-720-1307
Courriel: infos@parkinsonquebec.ca
URL: www.parkinsonquebec.ca
Nathalie Ross, Directrice générale

Society of Obstetricians & Gynaecologists of Canada (SOGC) / Société des obstétriciens et gynécologues du Canada
780 Echo Dr., Ottawa ON K1S 5R7
Tel: 613-730-4192; *Fax:* 613-730-4314
Toll-Free: 800-561-2416
e-mail: helpdesk@sogc.com
URL: www.sogc.org
Michel Fortier, MD, President
André Lalonde, Executive Vice-President
Vyta Senikas, Associate Executive Vice President
Linda Desjardins, Director, Finance & Information Technology
Natalie Wright, Director, Communications Division
Mark Heywood, MD, Treasurer

Society of Rural Physicians of Canada (SRPC) / Société de la médecine rurale du Canada
PO Box 893, 269 Main St., Shawville QC J0X 2Y0
Tel: 819-647-7054; *Fax:* 819-647-2485
Toll-Free: 877-276-1949
e-mail: admin@srpc.ca
URL: www.srpc.ca
Affiliation(s): Canadian Medical Association; World Organization of Rural Doctors
Karl Stobbe, President
Lee Teperman, Administrative Officer

Spina Bifida & Hydrocephalus Association of Canada (SBHAC) / Association de spina-bifida et d'hydrocephalie du Canada
#428, 167 Lombard Ave., Winnipeg MB R3B 0V3
Tel: 204-925-3650; *Fax:* 204-925-3654
Toll-Free: 800-565-9488
e-mail: info@sbhac.ca
URL: www.sbhac.ca
Affiliation(s): International Federation for Hydrocephalus & Spina Bifida
Jody Stadnyk, Executive Director
Lorelei Fletcher, President

The Terry Fox Foundation / La Fondation Terry Fox
#303, 46165 Yale Rd., Chilliwack BC V2P 2P2
Tel: 604-701-0246; *Fax:* 604-701-0247
Toll-Free: 888-836-9786
e-mail: national@terryfoxrun.org
URL: www.terryfoxrun.org
Darrell Fox, National Director
Judith Fox-Alder, International Director

Thalidomide Victims Association of Canada (TVAC) / Association canadienne des victimes de la thalidomide (ACVT)
Centre commercial Joseph Renaud, #211, 6830, boul Joseph Renaud, Montréal QC H1K 3V4
Tel: 514-355-0811; *Fax:* 514-355-0860
e-mail: mercedes.acvt@sympatico.ca
URL: www.thalidomide.ca
Affiliation(s): Council of Canadians with Disabilities; Canadian Centre for Philanthropy
Mercedes Benegbi, Executive Director

Thyroid Foundation of Canada / La Fondation canadienne de la Thyroïde
#304, 797 Princess St., Kingston ON K7L 1G1
Tel: 613-544-8364; *Fax:* 613-544-9731
Toll-Free: 800-267-8822
URL: www.thyroid.ca
Katherine Keen, National Office Coordinator

Toronto Children's Care Inc. (TCC)
26 Gerrard St. East, Toronto ON M5B 1G3
Tel: 416-977-0458; *Fax:* 416-977-8807
e-mail: info@rmhtoronto.org
URL: www.rmhtoronto.org
Jane Marco, Executive Director
John Davis, President

Tourette Syndrome Foundation of Canada (TSFC) / La Fondation canadienne du syndrome de Tourette
#206, 194 Jarvis St., Toronto ON M5B 2B7
Tel: 416-861-8398; *Fax:* 416-861-2472
Toll-Free: 800-361-3120
e-mail: tsfc@tourette.ca
URL: www.tourette.ca
Affiliation(s): Health Charities Council of Canada
Rosie Wartecker, Executive Director
Lorne Perrin, President
Ray Robertson, Secretary
Sybil Berenstein, Treasurer

Trillium Gift of Life Network
#900, 522 University Ave., Toronto ON M5G 1W7
Tel: 416-363-4001; *Fax:* 416-363-4002
Toll-Free: 800-263-2833
e-mail: info@giftoflife.on.ca
URL: www.giftoflife.on.ca
Frank Markel, PhD, President & CEO

Turner's Syndrome Society (TSS) / Société du syndrome de Turner
323 Chapel St., Ottawa ON K1N 7Z2
Tel: 613-321-2267; *Fax:* 613-321-2268
Toll-Free: 800-465-6744
e-mail: tssincan@web.net
URL: www.turnersyndrome.ca

United Ostomy Association of Canada Inc. (UOAC)
PO Box 825, 50 Charles St. East, Toronto ON M4Y 2N7
Tel: 416-595-5452; *Fax:* 416-595-9924
Toll-Free: 888-969-9698
e-mail: info@ostomycanada.ca
URL: www.ostomycanada.ca
Affiliation(s): United Ostomy Association - USA
Doug Graham, President

Vocational Rehabilitation Association of Canada (VRA Canada)
#310, 310 Cataraqui St., Kingston ON K7K 1Z7
Tel: 613-507-5530; *Fax:* 888-441-8002
Toll-Free: 888-876-9992
e-mail: info@vracanada.com
URL: www.vracanada.com
Affiliation(s): Canadian Association for Vocational Evaluation & Work Adjustment
Garry Derenoski, National President
Kathy Regan, Executive Director

Yukon Lung Association
PO Box 33122, Whitehorse YT Y1A 5Y5
Tel: 867-638-6974
Toll-Free: 800-665-5864

Yukon Medical Association
5 Hospital Rd., Whitehorse YT Y1A 3H7
Tel: 867-393-8949; *Fax:* 867-393-8869
e-mail: yma@yukondoctors.ca
URL: www.yukondoctors.ca
Affiliation(s): British Columbia Medical Association
Rao Tadepalli, President
Stephanie Buchanan, Vice-President
Isabelle Gagnon, Secretary-Treasurer

Yukon Public Health Association (YPHA)
Tel: 867-393-8784
Ron Pearson, Contact
Val Pike, President

Heating, Air Conditioning, Plumbing

Canadian Institute of Plumbing & Heating (CIPH) / Institut canadien de plomberie et de chauffage
#330, 295 The West Mall, Toronto ON M9C 4Z4
Tel: 416-695-0447; *Fax:* 416-695-0450
Toll-Free: 800-639-2474
e-mail: rcp@ciph.com
URL: www.ciph.com
Ralph Suppa, President & General Manager
Kevin Wong, Membership Contact

Heating, Refrigeration & Air Conditioning Contractors Association Atlantic
Tel: 902-425-0475
John Sutherland, Contact
Dallas McDonald, Contact

Heating, Refrigeration & Air Conditioning Institute of Canada (HRAI) / Institut canadien du chauffage, de la climatisation et de la réfrigération (ICCCR)
Bldg. 1, #201, 2800 Skymark Ave., Mississauga ON L4W 5A6
Tel: 905-602-4700; *Fax:* 905-602-1197
Toll-Free: 800-267-2231
e-mail: hraimail@hrai.ca
URL: www.hrai.ca
Warren J. Heeley, President
Martin Luymes, Vice-President
Andrew Hall, Director, Energy Conservation/Demand Management Programs
Joanne Spurrell, Director, Education & Market Development

Heather Grimoldby-Campbell, Manager, Administration & Wholesalers Division
Daisy Del Prado, Communications Coordinator

Ontario Plumbing Inspectors Association (OPIA)
129 Dumble Ave., Peterborough ON K9H 5A9
Tel: 705-742-7777; *Fax:* 705-742-5218
e-mail: sgould@city.peterborough.on.ca
URL: www.opia.info
Affiliation(s): Ontario Ministry of Municipal Affairs, Building Branch
Dan Devlin, President
Walter Falcomer, Vice-President

Ontario Refrigeration & Air Conditioning Contractors Association (ORAC)
#43, 6770 Davand Dr., Mississauga ON L5T 2G3
Tel: 905-670-0010; *Fax:* 905-670-0474
e-mail: info@orac.ca
URL: www.orac.ca
David Irwin, President
Grant Sheahan, Vice-President
Dave Honsberger, Managing Director
Ted Martin, Treasurer

Refrigeration Service Engineers Society (Canada) (RSES Canada)
PO Box 3, Stn. B, Toronto ON M9W 5K9
Tel: 905-842-9199
Toll-Free: 877-955-6255
URL: www.rsescanada.com
David Chafe, President
Nick Reggi, CMS, Secretary

Thermal Environmental Comfort Association (TECA)
PO Box 73105, Stn. Evergreen RO, Surrey BC V3R 0J2
Tel: 604-594-5956; *Fax:* 604-594-5091
Toll-Free: 888-577-3818
e-mail: training@teca.ca
URL: www.teca.ca
Terry Regier, President

History, Heritage, Genealogy

Alberta Family History Society (AFHS)
712 - 16 Ave. NW, Calgary AB T2M 0J8
Tel: 403-214-1447
e-mail: afhs@afhs.ab.ca
URL: www.afhs.ab.ca
Affiliation(s): Federation of Family History Societies (England)
Irene Oickle, Membership
Kay Clarke, President

Alberta Historical Resources Foundation (AHRF)
8820 - 112 St., Edmonton AB T6G 2P8
Tel: 780-431-2300; *Fax:* 780-427-5598
URL: culture.alberta.ca/ahrf/default.aspx
David Link, Director

Alberta Pioneer Railway Association
PO Box 70014, Stn. Londonderry, Edmonton AB T5C 3R6
Tel: 780-472-6229; *Fax:* 780-968-0167
e-mail: hdixon@incentre.net
URL: www.railwaymuseum.ab.ca
Affiliation(s): Heritage Canada
Herb Dixon, Contact

Association québécoise d'interprétation du patrimoine (AQIP)
CP 48048, Québec QC G1R 5R5
Tél: 418-525-0888
Courriel: aqip@aqip.ca
URL: www.aqip.ca
René Charest, Président

British Columbia Genealogical Society (BCGS)
PO Box 88054, Stn. Lansdowne Mall, Richmond BC V6X 3T6
Tel: 604-502-9119; *Fax:* 604-502-9119
e-mail: bcgs@bcgs.ca
URL: www.bcgs.ca
Affiliation(s): Richmond Heritage
Jean List, President
Kenneth Livingstone, Corresponding Secretary

British Columbia Historical Federation (BCHF)
PO Box 5254, Stn. B, Victoria BC V8R 6N4
Tel: 604-277-2627; *Fax:* 604-277-2657
e-mail: info@bchistory.ca
URL: www.bchistory.ca
P.E. Roy, President
Pamela Welwood, Secretary

British Columbia Railway Historical Association (BCRHA)
1148 Balmoral Rd., Victoria BC V8T 1B1
Tel: 250-383-7063
e-mail: bcrha@shaw.ca
URL: www.trainweb.org/bcrha
Paul J. Smith, President

Bus History Association, Inc. (BHA)
965 McEwan, Windsor ON N9B 2G1
Tel: 519-977-0664
URL: www.bus-history.org

Canada's National History Society (CNHS) / Société d'histoire nationale du Canada
#478, 167 Lombard Ave., Winnipeg MB R3B 0T6
Tel: 204-988-9300; *Fax:* 204-988-9309
Toll-Free: 800-816-6777
e-mail: memberservices@historysociety.ca
URL: www.historysociety.ca
Deborah Morrison, President & CEO

Canadian Association for Conservation (CAC) / Association canadienne pour la conservation et la restauration (ACCR)
PO Box 87028, 332 Bank St., Ottawa ON K2P 1X0
Tel: 613-231-3977; *Fax:* 613-231-4406
e-mail: coordinator@cac-accr.com
URL: www.cac-accr.ca
Affiliation(s): International Institute for Conservation of Historic & Artistic Works
Dee Stubbs-Lee, President
James Hay, Vice-President

Canadian Association of Professional Heritage Consultants (CAPHC) / Association canadienne d'experts-conseils en patrimoine (ACECP)
George Brown House, #211, 50 Baldwin St., Toronto ON M5T 1L4
Tel: 416-515-7450; *Fax:* 416-515-0961
e-mail: admin@caphc.ca
URL: www.caphc.ca
Affiliation(s): ICOMOS International (International Council on Monuments & Sites); ICOMOS Canada - English-Speaking Committee
Ken Hoyle, President
David Waverman, Vice-President
Peter Stewart, Treasurer

Canadian Catholic Historical Association - English Section (CCHA) / Société canadienne d'histoire de l'église catholique - Section anglaise
c/o St. Michael's College, 81 St. Mary St., Toronto ON M5S 1J4
Tel: 905-893-9754; *Fax:* 416-934-3444
e-mail: revedjackman@rogers.com
URL: www.umanitoba.ca/colleges/st_pauls/ccha/ccha.html
Edward Jackman, Secretary General

Canadian Heritage Information Network (CHIN) / Réseau canadien d'information sur le patrimoine (RCIP)
#2F1, 15 rue Eddy, Gatineau QC K1A 0M5
Tel: 819-994-1200; *Fax:* 819-994-9555
Toll-Free: 800-520-2446
e-mail: service@chin.gc.ca
URL: www.chin.gc.ca; www.virtualmuseum.ca
Gabrielle Blais, Director General
Paul Lima, Senior Policy Advisor
Louise Filiatrault, Director
Nancy Larivière, Assistant to the Director

Canadian Historical Association (CHA) / Société historique du Canada (SHC)
395 Wellington St., Ottawa ON K1A 0N4
Tel: 613-233-7885; *Fax:* 613-567-3110
e-mail: cha-shc@lac-bac.gc.ca
URL: www.cha-shc.ca
Craig Heron, President
Joanne Mineault, Administrative Assistant

Canadian Oral History Association (COHA) / Société canadienne d'histoire orale (SCHO)
PO Box 2064, Stn. D, Ottawa ON K1P 5W3
Tel: 613-996-0879; *Fax:* 613-995-6575
e-mail: cforcier-holloway@archives.ca
URL: www.ncf.carleton.ca/oral-history
Alphine Jefferson, President
Ken Clavette, Contact

Canadian Railroad Historical Association (CRHA) / Association canadienne d'histoire ferroviaire
110, rue St-Pierre, Saint-Constant QC J5A 1G7
Tel: 450-632-2410; *Fax:* 450-638-1563
e-mail: info@exporail.org
URL: www.exporail.org

Canadian Society for the Study of Names (CSSN) / Société canadienne d'onomastique (SCO)
c/o GNBC Secretariat, Centre for Topographic Information, #634, 615 Booth St., Ottawa ON K1A 0E9
Tel: 613-992-3892; *Fax:* 613-943-8282; *TTY:* 613-996-4397
e-mail: geonames@NRCan.gc.ca
URL: geonames.rncan.gc.ca/info/cssn_e.php
Wolfgang Ahrens, President
Léo LaBrie, Sec.-Treas.

Canadian Society of Church History (CSCH) / Société canadienne d'histoire de l'Église
c/o Robynne R. Healey, Dept. of History, Trinity Western University, 7600 Glover Rd., Langley BC V2Y 1Y1
e-mail: robynne.healey@twu.ca
URL: www.augustana.ab.ca/csch/
Todd Webb, President
Marguerite Van Die, Vice-President & Program Chair
Robynne Rogers Healey, Administrative Secretary
John H. Young, Treasurer

Canadian Society of Mayflower Descendants
e-mail: deb121clarke@rogers.com
URL: www.rootsweb.com/~canms/canada.html
Affiliation(s): General Society of Mayflower Descendants - USA
Joyce Cutler, Governor

Canadian Warplane Heritage (CWH)
9280 Airport Rd., Mount Hope ON L0R 1W0
Tel: 905-679-4183; *Fax:* 905-679-4186
Toll-Free: 877-347-3359
e-mail: museum@warplane.com
URL: www.warplane.com
Pamela Rickards, Deputy Director
Robin Hill, Manager, Marketing

Canadiana.org
#468, 395 Wellington St., Ottawa ON K1A 0N4
Tel: 613-235-2628; *Fax:* 613-235-9752
e-mail: info@canadiana.org
URL: www.canadiana.org/eco.php?doc=cihm
John Teskey, President

Conseil des monuments et sites du Québec (CMSQ)
82, Grande-Allée ouest, Québec QC G1R 2G6
Tél: 418-647-4347; *Téléc:* 418-647-6483
Ligne sans frais: 800-494-4347
Courriel: cmsq@cmsq.qc.ca
URL: www.cmsq.qc.ca
Louise Mercier, Présidente

The CRB Foundation (CRBF) / La Fondation CRB
1170, rue Peel, 8e étage, Montréal QC H3B 4P2
Tel: 514-878-5250; *Fax:* 514-878-5299
Charles R. Bronfman, Chair
Johanne McDonald, Director of Operations

Family History Society of Newfoundland & Labrador
Waterford Valley Plaza, 657 Topsail Rd., St. John's NL A1E 2E3
Tel: 709-754-9525; *Fax:* 709-754-6430
e-mail: fhs@fhsnl.ca
URL: www.fhsnl.ca

Fédération des sociétés d'histoire du Québec
CP 1000, Succ. M, 4545, av Pierre-De Coubertin, Montréal QC H1V 3R2
Tél: 514-252-3031; *Téléc:* 514-251-8038
Ligne sans frais: 866-691-7207
Courriel: fshq@histoirequebec.qc.ca
URL: www.histoirequebec.qc.ca
Richard M. Bégin, Président

Federation of Nova Scotian Heritage (FNSH)
1113 Marginal Rd., Halifax NS B3H 4P7
Tel: 902-423-4677; *Fax:* 902-422-0881
Toll-Free: 800-355-6873
e-mail: fnsh@hfx.andara.com
Affiliation(s): Heritage Canada; Canadian Museums Association; Association for State & Local History
Anita Price, Executive Director

Fédération québécoise des sociétés de généalogie (FQSG)
CP 9454, Succ. Sainte-Foy, Québec QC G1V 4B8
Tél: 418-653-3940; *Téléc:* 418-653-3940
Courriel: federationgenealogie@bellnet.ca
URL: www.federationgenealogie.qc.ca
Denis Racine, Président

Genealogical Association of Nova Scotia (GANS) / Association généalogique de la Nouvelle-Écosse
#222, 3045 Robie St., Halifax NS B3K 4P6
Tel: 902-454-0322
e-mail: gans@chebucto.ns.ca
URL: www.chebucto.ns.ca/Recreation/GANS
Affiliation(s): Genealogical Institute of the Maritimes; Council of Nova Scotia Archives
Allan Marble, President

Genealogical Institute of The Maritimes (GIM) / Institut généalogique des Provinces Maritimes
PO Box 36022, 5675 Spring Garden Rd., Halifax NS B3J 1G0
e-mail: don.clark@ns.sympatico.ca
URL: nsgna.ednet.ns.ca/gim/
Allen Marble, President
Robert Pierce, Registrar

Halifax Citadel Regimental Association (HCRA)
PO Box 9080, Stn. A, Halifax NS B3M 5K7
Tel: 902-426-1990
e-mail: info@regimental.com
URL: www.regimental.com
Brian Andrecyk, President
Roderick MacLean, Administrative Officer

Heritage Canada Foundation (HCF) / Fondation Héritage Canada
5 Blackburn Ave., Ottawa ON K1N 8A2
Tel: 613-237-1066; *Fax:* 613-237-5987
e-mail: heritagecanada@heritagecanada.org
URL: www.heritagecanada.org
Affiliation(s): Canadian Heritage Network
Carolyn Quinn, Director, Communications
Natalie Bull, Executive Director

L'Héritage canadien du Québec (HCQ) / The Canadian Heritage of Québec (CHQ)
1181, rue de la Montagne, Montréal QC H3G 1Z2
Tél: 514-393-1417; *Téléc:* 514-393-9444
Courriel: chq@total.net
URL: www.hcq-chq.org/french/
John Molson, Président

Heritage Foundation of Newfoundland & Labrador
PO Box 5171, 1 Springdale St., St. John's NL A1C 5V5
Tel: 709-739-1892; *Fax:* 709-739-5413
Toll-Free: 888-739-1892
e-mail: info@heritagefoundation.ca
URL: www.heritagefoundation.ca
George Chalker, Executive Director
Robert Parsons, Chairperson

Heritage Society of British Columbia
914 Garthland Pl. West, Victoria BC V9A 4J5
Tel: 250-384-4840
e-mail: hsbc@islandnet.com
URL: www.heritagebc.ca
Affiliation(s): Heritage Canada
Rick Goodacre, Executive Director
Jonathan Yardley, President
Leslie Gilbert, Sec.-Treas.

Historic Sites Association of Newfoundland & Labrador (HSANL)
PO Box 5542, St. John's NL A1C 5W4
Tel: 709-753-9262; *Fax:* 709-753-0879
Toll-Free: 877-753-9262
e-mail: info@historicsites.ca
URL: www.historicsites.ca
Affiliation(s): Parks Canada; Museum Association of Newfoundland & Labrador; Canadian Museum Association
Catherine Dempsey, Executive Director

Historic Theatres' Trust (HTT) / Société des salles historiques
PO Box 539, Stn. Westmount, Montréal QC H3Y 3H9
Tel: 514-933-8077
e-mail: theatres1@sympatico.ca
Claude Fortin, Sec.-Treas.
Dane Lanken, Vice-President
Janet MacKinnon, President

Historical Society of Alberta (HSA)
PO Box 4035, Stn. C, #622, 304 - 8th Ave. SW, Calgary AB T2P 1C5
Tel: 403-261-3662; *Fax:* 403-269-6029
e-mail: info@albertahistory.org
URL: www.albertahistory.org
Affiliation(s): Heritage Canada; Alberta Heritage Council
William Baergen, President

Huguenot Society of Canada / Société Huguenote du Canada
#105 - 4936 Yonge St., Toronto ON M2N 6S3
Affiliation(s): Ontario Historical Society
Peter Dupuy, President

ICOMOS Canada
PO Box 737, Stn. B, Ottawa ON K1P 5P8
Tel: 613-749-0971
e-mail: canada@icomos.org
URL: www.canada.icomos.org
Affiliation(s): UNESCO; International Centre for the Study of the Preservation & Restoration of Cultural Property (ICCROM)
Michel Bonnette, President
Alain Dejeans, Vice-président, Comité francophone
John Ward, Vice President, English Speaking Committee

J. Douglas Ferguson Historical Research Foundation
PO Box 5079, Shediac NB E4P 8T8
Tel: 506-532-6025; *Fax:* 506-532-6025
e-mail: gbel@nb.sympatico.ca
URL: www.canadian-numismatic.org/
Robert J. Graham, Secretary
Geoffrey G. Bell, Chair
Len Buth, Treasurer

Jewish Genealogical Society of Canada (JGSC)
PO Box 91006, 2901 Bayview Ave., Toronto ON M2K 2Y6
e-mail: info@jgstoronto.ca
URL: www.jgstoronto.ca
Shelley Stillman, President
Lucy Sadowski, Secretary
Steve Gora, Treasurer

Literary & Historical Society of Québec (LHSQ) / Société littéraire et historique de Québec
44, chaussée des Écossais, Québec QC G1R 4H3
Tel: 418-694-9147; *Fax:* 418-694-0754
e-mail: info@morrin.org
URL: www.morrin.org
Simon Auclair, Library Manager

Manitoba Genealogical Society Inc. (MGS)
1045 St. James St., #E, Winnipeg MB R3H 1B1
Tel: 204-783-9139; *Fax:* 204-783-0190
e-mail: contact@mbgenealogy.com
URL: www.mbgenealogy.com
Mary Bole, Library Chair

Manitoba Historical Society (MHS)
61 Carlton St., Winnipeg MB R3C 1N7
Tel: 204-947-0559; *Fax:* 204-943-1093
e-mail: info@mhs.mb.ca; questions@mhs.mb.ca; journal@mhs.mb.ca
URL: www.mhs.mb.ca
Harry W. Duckworth, President
Linda Neyedly, Director, Dalnavert
Victor Sawelo, Manager, Ross House

Monarchist League of Canada (MLC) / Ligue Monarchiste du Canada
Tel: 905-912-0916
e-mail: chairman@monarchist.ca
URL: www.monarchist.ca
Affiliation(s): Canadian Royal Heritage Trust
Nathan Tidridge, Education Co-ordinator
Gavin Guthrie, Vice-Chairman
Robert Finch, Chairman

New Brunswick Genealogical Society Inc. (NBGS, Inc.) / Société Généalogique du Nouveau-Brunswick Inc.
PO Box 3235, Stn. B, Fredericton NB E3A 5G9
e-mail: sbalch@nbnet.nb.ca
URL: www.nbgs.ca
George Sabean, President
David Fraser, Treasurer
Michelle Falkjar, Secretary, Membership

New Brunswick Historical Society
Loyalist House, 120 Union St., Saint John NB E2L 1A3
Tel: 506-652-3590
URL: www.loyalisthouse.com
Erma Hadzic, Secretary
George F. Teed, Treasurer
David Goss, Vice-President
Kathy Wilson, President

New Westminster Hyack Festival Association
204, 6th St., New Westminster BC V3L 3A1
Tel: 604-522-6894; *Fax:* 604-522-6094
e-mail: info@hyack.bc.ca
URL: www.hyack.bc.ca
Melanie Vogel, Executive Director

Newfoundland Historical Society (NHS)
Office: #15, 90 Military Rd., PO Box 23154 Churchill Sq., St. John's NL A1B 4J9
Tel: 709-722-3191; *Fax:* 709-729-7989
e-mail: nhs@nf.aibn.com
URL: www.infonet.st-johns.nf.ca/providers/nfldhist
Melanie Martin, President

Ontario Black History Society (OBHS) / Société historique des Noirs de l'Ontario
Ontario Heritage Centre, #402, 10 Adelaide St. East, Toronto ON M5C 1J3
Tel: 416-867-9420; *Fax:* 416-867-8691
e-mail: admin@blackhistorysociety.ca
URL: www.blackhistorysociety.ca
Affiliation(s): Ontario Historical Society
Rosemary J. Sadlier, President

Ontario Electric Railway Historical Association
PO Box 578, 13629 Guelph Line Rd., Milton ON L9T 5A2
Tel: 519-856-9802; *Fax:* 519-856-1399
e-mail: streetcar@hcry.org
URL: www.hcry.org
Affiliation(s): Association of Railway Museums; Ontario Museum Association; Canadian Museums Association
J. Borland, President
Ian Campbell, Vice-President

Ontario Genealogical Society (OGS) / Société de généalogie de l'Ontario
#102, 40 Orchard View Blvd., Toronto ON M4R 1B9
Tel: 416-489-0734; *Fax:* 416-489-9803
e-mail: provoffice@ogs.on.ca
URL: www.ogs.on.ca
Affiliation(s): Ontario Heritage Alliance
Don Hinchley, President
Nancy Trimble, Vice-President

Ontario Historical Society (OHS) / La Société historique de l'Ontario
34 Parkview Ave., Toronto ON M2N 3Y2
Tel: 416-226-9011; *Fax:* 416-226-2740
e-mail: ohs@ontariohistoricalsociety.ca
URL: www.ontariohistoricalsociety.ca
Robert Leverty, Executive Director

Pier 21
1055 Marginal Rd., Halifax NS B3H 4P6
Tel: 902-425-7770; *Fax:* 902-423-4045
e-mail: info@pier21.ca
URL: www.pier21.ca
Affiliation(s): Parks Canada
Robert Moody, CEO

Postal History Society of Canada (PHSC)
PO Box 82055, 1400 - 12th Ave. SW, Calgary AB T3C 3W5
URL: www.postalhistorycanada.org
Affiliation(s): American Philatelic Society; British North America Philatelic Society
Stephane Cloutier, Contact

Prince Edward Island Genealogical Society Inc. (PEIGS)
PO Box 2744, Charlottetown PE C1A 8C4
e-mail: peigs_queries@yahoo.ca
URL: www.islandregister.com/peigs.html
Affiliation(s): Genealogy Institute of the Maritimes

Prince Edward Island Museum & Heritage Foundation (PEIMHF) / Le Musée et la fondation du patrimoine de l'Ile-du-Prince-Édouard
2 Kent St., Charlottetown PE C1A 1M6
Tel: 902-368-6600; *Fax:* 902-368-6608
e-mail: mhpei@gov.pe.ca
URL: www.peimuseum.com

Québec Family History Society (QFHS) / Société de l'histoire des familles du Québec
PO Box 1026, Pointe-Claire QC H9S 4H9
Tel: 514-695-1502; *Fax:* 514-695-3508
e-mail: admin@qfhs.ca
URL: www.qfhs.ca
Affiliation(s): International Federation of Family History Societies
Gary Schroder, President

Regroupement des organismes du patrimoine franco-ontarien (ROPFO)
CP 74205, #B151, 2445, boul. Saint-Laurent, Ottawa ON K1G 6C3

Tél: 613-567-6363; *Téléc:* 613-567-6563
Courriel: info@ropfo.ca
URL: www.ropfo.ca
Linda Lauzon, Directrice générale

Richard III Society of Canada
175 Logan Ave, Toronto ON M4M 2N2
Tel: 416-486-0031
e-mail: richardiii@cogeco.ca
URL: home.cogeco.ca/~richardiii/
Noreen Armstrong, Secretary

Royal Heraldry Society of Canada / Société royale héraldique du Canada
PO Box 8128, Stn. T, Ottawa ON K1G 3H9
Tel: 613-998-1976; *Fax:* - - 0
e-mail: secretary@heraldry.ca
URL: www.heraldry.ca
Affiliation(s): Commonwealth Heraldry Board
Allan Bird, President
Kevin Greaves, Vice-President

The Royal Nova Scotia Historical Society (RNSHS)
PO Box 2622, Halifax NS B3J 3P7
e-mail: david.sutherland@dal.ca
URL: nsgna.ednet.ns.ca/rnshs
Affiliation(s): Genealogical Association of Nova Scotia
David Sutherland, President

Saskatchewan Architectural Heritage Society (SAHS)
#214, 1808 Smith St., Regina SK S4P 2N4
Tel: 306-359-0933; *Fax:* 306-359-3899
e-mail: sahs@sasktel.net
URL: www.sahsonline.ca

Saskatchewan Cultural Exchange Society (SCES)
2431 - 8 Ave., Regina SK S4R 5J7
Tel: 306-780-9494; *Fax:* 306-780-9487
e-mail: sces@sasktel.net
URL: www.sces.ca
Affiliation(s): Tourism Saskatchewan; Canadian Tourism Human Resource Council; Saskatchewan Fiddle Association
Andrew Gilbert, Business Officer
Margaret Fry, CEO
John Yewman, Chair

Saskatchewan Genealogical Society (SGS)
PO Box 1894, #110, 1514 - 11th Ave., Regina SK S4P 3E1
Tel: 306-780-9207; *Fax:* 306-780-3615
e-mail: saskgenealogy@sasktel.net
URL: www.saskgenealogy.com
Celeste Rider, Provincial Librarian

Société canadienne d'histoire de l'Église Catholique - Section française (SCHEC) / Canadian Catholic Historical Association - French Section
SCHEC, Université du Québec à Trois-Rivières, 3351, boul des Forges, Trois-Rivières QC G9A 5H7
Tél: 819-376-5011; *Téléc:* 819-376-5179
URL: www.cieq.ca/schec
René Hardy, Président

Société d'histoire régionale de Chibougamau
646, 3e Rue, Chibougamau QC G8P 1P1
Tél: 418-748-3124
Christian Claveau, Président

Société franco-ontarienne d'histoire et de généalogie (SFOHG)
#B151, 2445 boul St-Laurent, Ottawa ON K1G 6C3
Tél: 613-729-5769; *Téléc:* 613-729-2209
Ligne sans frais: 866-307-9995
Courriel: sfohg@francogenealogie.com
URL: www.sfohg.ca
Linda Lauzon, Directrice générale
Michel Duquet, Chargé de projets
Richard St-Georges, Président
Juliette Denis, Vice-présidente

Société généalogique canadienne-française (SGCF)
3440, rue Davidson, Montréal QC H1W 2Z5
Tél: 514-527-1010; *Téléc:* 514-527-0265
Courriel: info@sgcf.com
URL: www.sgcf.com
Gisèle Monarque, Présidente

La Société historique de Québec
1070, De La Chevrotière, Québec QC G1R 3J4
Tél: 418-692-0556; *Téléc:* 418-692-0614
Courriel: shq1@bellnet.ca
URL: www.societehistoriquedequebec.qc.ca
Jean Dorval, Président
Jean-François Caron, Trésorier

Doris Drolet, Secrétaire

United Empire Loyalists' Association of Canada (UELAC)
Dominion Office, The George Brown House, #202, 50 Baldwin St., Toronto ON M5T 1L4
Tel: 416-591-1783; *Fax:* 416-591-7506
e-mail: uela@becon.org
URL: www.uelac.org
Fredrick H. Hayward, UE, President
Carl Stymiest, UE, Sr. Vice-President

West Coast Railway Association (WCRA)
PO Box 2790, Vancouver BC V6B 3X2
Tel: 604-524-1011; *Fax:* 604-876-4104
Toll-Free: 800-722-1233
e-mail: info@wcra.org
URL: www.wcra.org
Don Evans, Executive Director

Homosexuality

Alliance des gais et lesbiennes Laval-Laurentides (AGLLL Inc.)
CP 98030, 95, boul Labelle, Sainte-Thérèse QC J7E 5R4
Courriel: aglll@hotmail.com
URL: www.algi.qc.ca/asso/aglll/

AlterHéros
CP 476, Succ. C, Montréal QC H2L 4K4
Tél: 514-846-1398
Courriel: info@alterheros.com
URL: www.alterheros.com
Marc-Olivier Ouellet, Fondateur

Amazones des grands espaces
Montréal QC
Tél: 514-525-3663
Courriel: info@plein-air-amazones.org
URL: www.plein-air-amazones.org

ARC: Aînés et retraités de la communauté
Montréal QC
Tél: 514-529-7471
Courriel: arcmontreal@hotmail.com
URL: www.algi.qc.ca/asso/retraitesgais

Archives gais du Québec
#202, 4067, boul St-Laurent, Montréal QC H2W 1Y7
Tél: 514-287-9987
URL: www.agq.qc.ca
Ian Blair, Président

Association des Gais et Lesbiennes du Bas-St-Laurent
Courriel: info_aglbsl@yahoo.ca
URL: www.algi.qc.ca/asso/aglbsl/

Association des lesbiennes et des gais sur Internet (ALGI)
CP 476, Succ. C, Montréal QC H2L 4K4
Tél: 514-528-8424; *Téléc:* 514-528-9708
Courriel: info@algi.qc.ca
URL: www.algi.qc.ca

Association des pères gais de Montréal inc. (APGM) / Gay Fathers of Montréal Inc.
4245, rue Laval, Montréal QC H2W 2J6
Tél: 514-528-8424; *Téléc:* 514-528-9708
Courriel: peresgais@yahoo.ca
URL: www.algi.qc.ca/asso/apgm/

Bi Unité Montréal (BUM)
CP 476, Succ. C, Montréal QC H2L 4K4
Courriel: webmaster@biunitemontreal.org
URL: www.algi.qc.ca/asso/bum/

Les Bolides
Montréal QC
Courriel: info@lesbolides.org
URL: www.lesbolides.org
Fernand

Canadian Lesbian & Gay Archives (CLGA)
PO Box 699, Stn. F, 34 Isabella St., Toronto ON M4Y 1N1
Tel: 416-777-2755
e-mail: queeries@clga.ca
URL: www.clga.ca
Affiliation(s): Association of Canadian Archivists; Ontario Association of Archives
Martin Lanigan, President

Centre communautaire des gais et lesbiennes de Montréal
CP 476, Succ. C, Montréal QC H2L 4K4
Tél: 514-528-8424; *Téléc:* 514-528-9708
Courriel: info@ccglm.org
URL: www.ccglm.org

Centre d'orientation sexuelle de l'université McGill (COSUM) / McGill University Sexual Identity Centre (MUSIC)
Dép. de psychiatrie, Hôpital général de Montréal, #A2-160, 1650, av Cedar, Montréal QC H3G 1A4
Tél: 514-934-1934; *Téléc:* 514-934-8471
Courriel: music-cosum@mcgill.ca
URL: www.mcgill.ca/cosum; www.algi.qc.ca/asso/cosum
Karine J. Igartua, MDCM, FRCPC, CM, Psychiatre

Centre de solidarité lesbienne
#301, 4126, rue St-Denis, Montréal QC H2W 2M5
Tél: 514-526-2452; *Téléc:* 514-526-3570
Courriel: info@solidaritelesbienne.qc.ca
URL: www.solidaritelesbienne.qc.ca

Coalition des familles homoparentales
Montréal QC
Tél: 514-846-1543
Courriel: info@familleshomoparentales.org
URL: www.familleshomoparentales.org
Mona Greenbaum, Directrice

Coalition for Lesbian & Gay Rights in Ontario (CLGRO) / Coalition pour les droits des lesbiennes et personnes gaies en Ontario
PO Box 822, Stn. A, Toronto ON M5W 1G3
Tel: 416-405-8253
e-mail: query@clgro.org
URL: www.clgro.org
Affiliation(s): International Lesbian & Gay Association

Comité des gais et lesbiennes du conseil central du Montréal métropolitain (CSN) (CGLCCMM-CSN)
Montréal QC
Tél: 514-598-2012
URL: www.algi.qc.ca/asso/cglccmm
Jacques Tricot

Community One Foundation
PO Box 760, Stn. F, Toronto ON M4Y 2N6
Tel: 416-920-5422
e-mail: info@communityone.ca
URL: www.communityone.ca
Philip Wong, Executive Director
Lenore MacAdam, Board Co-Chair
Larry Hughsam, Board Co-Chair/Treasurer

Conseil québécois des gais et lesbiennes du Québec (CQGL)
CP 182, Succ. C, Montréal QC H2L 4K1
Tél: 514-759-6844
Courriel: info@cqgl.ca
URL: www.cqgl.ca
Steve Foster, Président

Council on Homosexuality & Religion (CHR) / Conseil de l'homosexualité et la religion
PO Box 1912, Winnipeg MB R3C 3R2
Tel: 204-772-8215; *Fax:* 204-478-1160
Toll-Free: 888-399-0005
e-mail: cvogel@mts.net
Chris Vogel, Sec.-Treas.
A.E. Millward, President

Dignity Canada Dignité
PO Box 2102, Stn. D, Ottawa ON K1P 5W3
Tel: 613-746-7279
e-mail: info@dignitycanada.org
URL: www.dignitycanada.org
Dennis Benoit, President
Frank Testin, Sec.-Treas.

Egale Canada
#430, 1 Nicholas St., Ottawa ON K1N 7B7
Tel: 613-230-1043; *Fax:* 613-230-9395
Toll-Free: 888-204-7777
e-mail: egale.canada@egale.ca
URL: www.egale.ca

Fondation Mario-Racine / Mario Racine Foundation
2075, rue Plessis, Local 110, Montréal QC H2L 2Y4
Tél: 514-528-5940
Courriel: info@fondation-mario-racine.qc.ca
URL: www.fondation-mario-racine.qc.ca
Michel Durocher, MBA, Président

Gai-Côte-Sud
#100, 708, 4e Av, La Pocatière QC G0R 1Z0
Courriel: gaicotesud@hotmail.com
URL: www.algi.qc.ca/asso/gcs/
Magella Dionne, Président

GRIS-Centre-du-Québec
Tél: 819-477-3953
Courriel: risennev@cgocable.ca
Richard Senneville, Président

Groupe de discussion au masculin (GDM)
CP 476, Succ. C, Montréal QC H2L 4K4
Tél: 514-528-8424
Courriel: gdminfo@gmail.com
URL: www.gai-gdm.org

Groupe de recherche et d'intervention sociale (GRIS-Montréal)
CP 476, Succ. C, Montréal QC H2L 4K4
Tél: 514-590-0016; *Téléc:* 514-590-0764
Courriel: info@gris.ca
URL: www.gris.ca
Robert Pilon, Président

Groupe gai de l'Outaouais
Gatineau QC
Tél: 819-776-2727
Courriel: marlan@videotron.ca
URL: www.algi.qc.ca/asso/gdhgfo/

Groupe gai de l'Université Laval
Pavillon Mauice-Pollack, 2305, rue de l'Université, Québec QC G1V 0A6
Tél: 418-656-2131
Courriel: ggul@public.ulaval.ca
URL: www.algi.qc.ca/asso/ggul/

Groupe régional d'intervention social - Québec (GRIS-Québec)
363, rue de la Couronne, local 202, Québec QC G1K 6E9
Tél: 418-523-5572; *Téléc:* 418-523-9758
Courriel: gris@grisquebec.org
URL: www.grisquebec.org
Guy Lefebvre, Coordonnateur

Hors sentiers
5828, rue de Normanville, Montréal QC H2S 2B4
Tél: 450-963-9710
Courriel: hors_sentiers@yahoo.ca
URL: www.algi.qc.ca/asso/horssentiers/

Jeunesse Lambda
a/s Centre communautaire des gais et lesbiennes de Montréal, 2075, rue Plessis, 3e étage, Montréal QC H2L 2Y4
Tél: 514-528-7535
Courriel: info@jeunesselambda.org
URL: www.algi.qc.ca/asso/jlambda/
Gabriel Boisvert, Président

Projet 10 / Project 10
#218, 2000, Northcliffe, Montréal QC H4A 3K5
Tél: 514-989-4585; *Téléc:* 514-989-0001
Courriel: questions@p10.qc.ca
URL: www.p10.qc.ca; www.myspace.com/p10montreal
Carly Boyce, Co-coordinatrice
Shauna Thomas, Co-coordinatrice

Réseau des lesbiennes du Québec (RLQ) / Québec Lesbian Network
#110, 2075, rue Plessis, Montréal QC H2L 2Y4
Tél: 514-528-8424
Courriel: rlqln.info@gmail.com
URL: rlq-qln.algi.qc.ca
Diane Heffernan, Coordonnatrice

TimeOut / TempsLibre
PO Box 1087, Stn. B, Ottawa ON K1P 5R1
e-mail: timeout@gayottawa.com
URL: www.gayottawa.com

La Trame
CP 845, Succ. Desjardins, Montréal QC H5B 1B9
Tél: 514-374-0227
Courriel: la.trame@hotmail.com
URL: www.latrame.blogspot.com
Mireille Robillard, Contact

Horticulture & Gardening

Les Amis du Jardin botanique de Montréal / Friends of the Montréal Botanical Garden
#A-206, 4101, rue Sherbrooke est, Montréal QC H1X 2B2
Tél: 514-872-1493; *Téléc:* 514-872-3765
URL: www.amisjardin.qc.ca
Michèle-E. Hogue, Directrice générale
Paule Lamontagne, Présidente

British Columbia Landscape & Nursery Association (BCLNA)
#102, 5783 - 176A St., Surrey BC V3S 6S6
Tel: 604-574-7772; *Fax:* 604-574-7773
Toll-Free: 800-421-7963
e-mail: info@bclna.com
URL: www.bclna.com
Werner Knittel, Executive Director

Canadian Horticultural Council (CHC) / Conseil canadien de l'horticulture
9 Corvus Ct., Ottawa ON K2E 7Z4
Tel: 613-226-4880; *Fax:* 613-226-4497
e-mail: webmaster@hortcouncil.ca
URL: www.hortcouncil.ca
Anne Fowlie, Executive Vice-President

Canadian Iris Society (CIS)
c/o Ed Jowett, 1960 Sideroad 15, RR#2, Tottenham ON L0G 1W0
Tel: 905-936-9941
e-mail: cdn-iris@rogers.com
URL: www.cdn-iris.ca
Ed Jowett, President
Ann Granatier, Secretary

Canadian Nursery Landscape Association (CNLA)
7856 Fifth Line South, Milton ON L9T 2X8
Tel: 905-875-1399; *Fax:* 905-875-1840
Toll-Free: 888-446-3499
e-mail: info@canadanursery.com
URL: www.canadanursery.com
Affiliation(s): Flowers Canada; Canadian Ornamental Plant Foundation; Associated Landscape Contractors of America; International Garden Centres Association; North American Plant Protection Organization; American Nursery & Landscape Association; International Ornamental Growers Association; Canadian Plant Protection Advisory Committee; Canadian Horticultural Council
Michael Murray, President

Canadian Ornamental Plant Foundation (COPF) / Fondation canadienne des plantes ornementales
5A - #218, 975 McKeown Ave., North Bay ON P1B 9P2
Tel: 705-495-2563; *Fax:* 705-495-1449
Toll-Free: 800-265-1629
e-mail: info@copf.org
URL: www.copf.org
Peggy Walsh Craig, Managing Director

Canadian Rose Society (CRS)
c/o #504, 334 Queen Mary Rd., Kingston ON K7M 7E7
e-mail: info@canadianrosesociety.org
URL: www.canadianrosesociety.org
Affiliation(s): World Federation of Rose Societies
Ralph Bullough, President
Marie Farnady, Membership Sec.-Treas.

Canadian Society for Horticultural Science (CSHS) / Société canadienne de science horticole
#1112, 141 Laurier Ave. West, Ottawa ON K1P 5J3
Tel: 613-232-9459; *Fax:* 613-594-5190
e-mail: services@aic.ca
URL: www.cshs.ca
David Percival, President
Denis Charlebois, Vice-President
Samir Debnath, Secretary-Treasurer

City Farmer - Canada's Office of Urban Agriculture
c/o City Farmer- Canada's Office Of Urban Agriculture, PO Box 74567, Stn. Kitslano, Vancouver BC V6K 4P4
Tel: 604-685-5832
e-mail: cityfarm@interchange.ubc.ca
URL: www.cityfarmer.org
Michael Levenston, Executive Director

Fédération des sociétés d'horticulture et d'écologie du Québec (FSHÉQ)
CP 1000, Succ. M, 4545, av Pierre-de-Coubertin, Montréal QC H1V 3R2
Tél: 514-252-3010; *Téléc:* 514-251-8038
Courriel: fsheq@fsheq.com
URL: www.fsheq.com
Thérèse Tourigny, Directrice générale

Fédération interdisciplinaire de l'horticulture ornementale du Québec (FIHOQ)
#300E, 3230, rue Sicotte ouest, Saint-Hyacinthe QC J2S 7B3
Tél: 450-774-2228; *Téléc:* 450-774-3556
Courriel: fihoq@fihoq.qc.ca
URL: www.fihoq.qc.ca
Affiliation(s): Association internationale des producteurs en horticulture; Conseil canadien de l'horticulture; Conseil québécois de l'horticulture
Luce Daigneault, Directrice générale
Jean Grégoire, Président

Flowers Canada (FC) / Fleurs Canada
Retail & Distribution Sector, #305, 99 Fifth Ave., Ottawa ON K1S 5P5
Fax: 866-671-8091
Toll-Free: 800-447-5147
e-mail: flowers@flowerscanada.org
URL: www.flowerscanada.org
Arman Patel, Executive Director

Landscape Alberta Nursery Trades Association (LANTA)
#200, 10331 - 178 St., Edmonton AB T5S 1R5
Tel: 780-489-1991; *Fax:* 780-444-2152
Toll-Free: 800-378-3198
e-mail: info@landscape-alberta.com
URL: www.landscape-alberta.com
Affiliation(s): Saskatchewan Nursery Landscape Association
Nigel Bowles, Executive Director

Landscape New Brunswick Horticultural Trades Association (LNBHTA)
PO Box 742, Saint John NB E2L 4B3
Fax: 506-633-1621
Toll-Free: 866-752-6862
e-mail: nbhta@nbnet.nb.ca
URL: www.nbhta.ca
John Evans, President

Landscape Newfoundland & Labrador (LNL)
PO Box 21328, St. John's NL A1A 5G6
Tel: 709-726-5651; *Fax:* 709-726-8441
e-mail: axisconsulting@nl.rogers.com
URL: www.landscapenf.org
Pamela Pippy, Executive Secretary

Landscape Nova Scotia
Executive Plus Business Centre, #44, 201 Brownlow Ave., Dartmouth NS B3B 1W2
Tel: 902-463-0519; *Fax:* 902-463-6308
Toll-Free: 877-567-4769
e-mail: info@landscapenovascotia.ca
URL: www.landscapenovascotia.ca
Scott Mosher, President

Landscape Ontario Horticultural Trades Association (LOHTA)
7856 Fifth Line South, RR#4, Milton ON L9T 2X8
Tel: 905-875-1805; *Fax:* 905-875-3942
Toll-Free: 800-265-5656
URL: www.horttrades.com
Affiliation(s): Horticultural Human Resource Council
Tony DiGiovanni, Executive Director

North American Native Plant Society (NANPS)
PO Box 84, Stn. D, Toronto ON M9A 4X1
Tel: 416-631-4438
e-mail: nanps@nanps.org
URL: www.nanps.org
Ruth Zaugg, Secretary

Ontario Horticultural Association (OHA)
312 Simcoe St., Tilsonburg ON N4G 2J6
Tel: 519-842-9829; *Fax:* 519-648-9716
e-mail: president@gardenontario.org
URL: www.gardenontario.org
Jim Mabee, President

PEI Horticultural Association
404 Mount Edward Rd, Charlottetown PE C1E 2A1
Tel: 902-566-2733; *Fax:* 902-566-5637
e-mail: peihort@pei.aibn.com

Rhododendron Society of Canada (RSC)
RR#2, St George Brant ON N0E 1N0
Tel: 519-448-1537
H.G. Hedges, Contact

Royal Botanical Gardens (RBG) / Les jardins botaniques royaux
680 Plains Rd. West, Hamilton ON L7T 4H4
Tel: 905-527-1158; *Fax:* 905-577-0375
Toll-Free: 800-694-4769
e-mail: info@rbg.ca
URL: www.rbg.ca
Mark C. Runciman, Executive Director

Saskatchewan Nursery Landscape Association (SNLA)
c/o Landscape Alberta Nursery Trades Association, 10215 - 176 St., Edmonton AB T5S 1M1
Tel: 780-489-1991; *Fax:* 780-444-2152
Toll-Free: 800-378-3198
URL: www.snla.ca

Seeds of Diversity Canada (SoDC) / Semences du patrimoine Canada
PO Box 36, Stn. Q, Toronto ON M4T 2L7
Toll-Free: 866-509-7333
e-mail: mail@seeds.ca
URL: www.seeds.ca
Affiliation(s): Rare Breeds Canada; Canadian Organic Growers
Bob Wildfong, Executive Director
Judy Newman, Office Manager
Valérie Girard, Communication Coordinator

Société d'Horticulture et d'Écologie de Prévost
CP 611, Prévost QC J0R 1T0
Tél: 450-224-9252
Affiliation(s): Fédération des Sociétés d'horticulture et d'écologie du Québec
Florence Frigon, Présidente
Marie-Ange Fréchette, Présidente

Hospitals

Accreditation Canada / Agrément Canada
#100, 1730 St. Laurent Blvd., Ottawa ON K1G 5L1
Tel: 613-738-3800; *Fax:* 613-738-7755
Toll-Free: 800-814-7769
e-mail: LearnMore@accreditation.ca; Communications@accreditation.ca
URL: www.accreditation.ca
Wendy Nicklin, President & Chief Exectuive Officer
Gilles Lanteigne, Executive Vice-President & COO
Donna Anderson, Vice-President, Strategic Communications & External Relations
Danielle Dorschner, Director, National Services

Alberta Long Term Care Association (ALTCA)
Centre 104, #509, 5241 Calgary Trail South, Edmonton AB T6H 5G8
Tel: 780-435-0699; *Fax:* 780-436-9785
Toll-Free: 888-212-4581
e-mail: info@ab-cca.ca
URL: www.longtermcare.ab.ca
Dianne Nielsen, Executive Director

Association des établissements privés conventionnés - santé services sociaux (AEPC)
#200, 204, rue Notre-Dame ouest, Montréal QC H2Y 1T3
Tél: 514-499-3630; *Téléc:* 514-873-7063
Courriel: info@aepc.qc.ca
URL: www.aepc.qc.ca
André Côté, Vice-président exécutif

Association of Canadian Academic Healthcare Organizations (ACAHO)
780 Echo Dr., Ottawa ON K1S 5R7
Tel: 613-730-5818; *Fax:* 613-730-4314
e-mail: brimacombe@acaho.org
URL: www.acaho.org
Affiliation(s): Association of Canadian Medical Colleges
Glenn Brimacombe, CEO

Association of Ontario Health Centres (AOHC) / Association des centres de santé de l'Ontario (ACSO)
#500, 907 Lawrence Ave. West, Toronto ON M6A 3B6
Tel: 416-236-2539; *Fax:* 416-236-0431
e-mail: mail@aohc.org
URL: www.aohc.org
Affiliation(s): Healthy Communities; Ontario Rural Council; Health Determinants Partnership; Canadian Health Network
Adrianna Tetley, Executive Director
Cory LeBlanc, Office Manager

Association québécoise d'établissements de santé et de services sociaux (AQESSS) (AQESS) / Québec Hospital Association
#400, 505, boul de Maisonneuve ouest, Montréal QC H3A 3C2
Tél: 514-842-4861; *Téléc:* 514-282-4271
Ligne sans frais: 800-361-4661
URL: www.aqesss.qc.ca
Lise Denis, Directrice générale

Auxiliaires bénévoles de l'Hôpital de Chibougamau
51, 3e Rue, Chibougamau QC G8P 1N1
Tél: 418-748-2676

Canadian Association of Healthcare Auxiliaries (CAHA) / L'association des auxiliaires bénévoles des soins de santé du Canada
c/o Canadian Healthcare Assn., #100, 17 York St., Ottawa ON K1N 9J6
Tel: 613-236-9364; *Fax:* 613-236-9350
e-mail: caha.office@rogers.com
URL: www.caha.freeservers.com
Joyce Nash, President

Canadian Association of Paediatric Health Centres (CAPHC) / Association canadienne des centres de santé pédiatriques
c/o Canadian Association of Paediatric Health Centres, #104, 2141 Thurston Dr., Ottawa ON K1G 6C9
Tel: 613-738-4164; *Fax:* 613-738-3247
e-mail: eoorbine@caphc.org
URL: www.caphc.org
Elaine Orrbine, CEO

Canadian Healthcare Association (CHA) / Association canadienne des soins de santé
#100, 17 York St., Ottawa ON K1N 9J6
Tel: 613-241-8005; *Fax:* 613-241-5055
e-mail: info@cha.ca
URL: www.cha.ca
Affiliation(s): American Hospital Association; Canadian Council on Health Services Accreditation
Pamela C. Fralick, President/CEO
Teresa Neuman, Communications Specialist

Canadian Home Care Association (CHCA) / Association canadienne de soins et services à domicile
#401, 17 York St., Ottawa ON K1N 9J6
Tel: 613-569-1585; *Fax:* 613-569-1604
URL: www.cdnhomecare.ca
Alice Mah Wren, President

Continuing Care Association of Nova Scotia (CCANS)
Tower I, #215A, 7001 Mumford Rd., Halifax NS B3L 4N9
Tel: 902-956-0090; *Fax:* 902-453-2967
e-mail: ccans@eastlink.ca
URL: www.nsnet.org/ccans/
Debra Leigh, COO

Health Association of PEI (HAPEI)
10 Pownal St., Charlottetown PE C1A 3V6
Tel: 902-368-3901; *Fax:* 902-368-3231
e-mail: emholmes@ihis.org
URL: www.cha.ca/members.htm#Health_Association_of_PEI_(HAPEI) _

Health Employers Association of British Columbia (HEABC)
#200, 1333 West Broadway, Vancouver BC V6H 4C6
Tel: 604-736-5909; *Fax:* 604-736-2715
e-mail: contact@heabc.bc.ca
URL: www.heabc.bc.ca
Lee Doney, CEO

Hospital Auxiliaries Association of Ontario (HAAO)
#2800, 200 Front St. West, Toronto ON M5V 3L1
Tel: 416-205-1407; *Fax:* 416-205-1337
Toll-Free: 800-598-8002
e-mail: ebarbeau@haao.com
URL: www.haao.com
Joan Babij, President
Joan Farlinger, Vice-President
Janet Simms-Baldwin, Secretary
Margaret Anne Robertson, Treasurer

New Brunswick Association of Healthcare Auxiliaries
220 Driftwood Loop, Fredericton NB E3B 7P2
Tel: 506-452-5432
e-mail: r3jbooker@health.nb.ca
R. John Booker, President

New Brunswick Association of Nursing Homes, Inc. (NBANH) / Association des foyers de soins du Nouveau-Brunswick, inc. (AFSNB)
#302, 1113 Regent St., Fredericton NB E3B 3Z2
Tel: 506-460-6262; *Fax:* 506-460-6253
URL: www.nbanh.com
Éric Mourant, Executive Director
Pat Diotte, President
Paul Thomas, Treasurer

New Brunswick Healthcare Association (NBHA) / L'Association des soins de santé du Nouveau-Brunswick (ASSNB)
861 Woodstock Rd., Fredericton NB E3B 7R7
Tel: 506-451-0750; *Fax:* 506-451-0760
e-mail: nbha@nbhealthcare.com
URL: www.nbhealthcare.com
Robert Simpson, CEO
Norah Wilson, Executive Secretary

Newfoundland & Labrador Health Boards Association (NLHBA)
2nd Fl. Beothuck Bldg., 20 Crosbie Pl., St. John's NL A1B 3Y8
Tel: 709-364-7701; *Fax:* 709-364-6460
e-mail: nlhba@nlhba.nf.ca
URL: www.nlhba.nl.ca
John F. Peddle, Executive Director
Cindy Parsons, Secretary

Northwest Territories Health Care Association (NWTHCA)
c/o Hay River Community Health Board, 3 Gaetz Dr., Hay River NT X0E 0R0
Tel: 867-874-7110; *Fax:* 867-874-7109
Wes Drodge, NWT Representative

Nova Scotia Association of Health Organizations (NSAHO)
Bedford Professional Centre, 2 Dartmouth Rd., Halifax NS B4A 2K7
Tel: 902-832-8500; *Fax:* 902-832-8505
e-mail: sandi@nsaho.ns.ca
URL: www.nsaho.ns.ca
Mary Lee, President/CEO

Ontario Association of Medical Laboratories (OAML)
#710, 5160 Yonge St., Toronto ON M2N 6L9
Tel: 416-250-8555; *Fax:* 416-250-8464
e-mail: oaml@oaml.com
URL: www.oaml.com

Ontario Association of Non-Profit Homes & Services for Seniors (OANHSS)
#700, 7050 Weston Rd., Woodbridge ON L4L 8G7
Tel: 905-851-8821; *Fax:* 905-851-0744
e-mail: drubin@oanhss.org
URL: www.oanhss.org
Donna A. Rubin, CEO
Sheldon Wolfson, Board Chair

Ontario Hospital Association (OHA)
#2800, 200 Front St. West, Toronto ON M5V 3L1
Tel: 416-205-1300; *Fax:* 416-205-1301
Toll-Free: 800-598-8002
e-mail: info@oha.com
URL: www.oha.com
Kevin P.D. Smith, Chair
Tom Closson, President & Chief Executive Officer
Warren DiClemente, Chief Operating Officer & VP, Educational Services
Julie Giraldi, Chief Human Resources & Officer, Information Technology
Doug Miller, Chief Financial Officer
Paul Davies, Treasurer

Ontario Long Term Care Association (OLTCA)
345 Renfrew Dr., 3rd Fl., Markham ON L3R 9S9
Tel: 905-470-8995; *Fax:* 905-470-9595
e-mail: Info@oltca.com
URL: www.oltca.com
Janet Lambert, Executive Director
David Cutler, President

The Regional Health Authorities of Manitoba (RHAM)
#2, 203 Duffield St., Winnipeg MB R3J 0H6
Tel: 204-833-1721; *Fax:* 204-940-2042
e-mail: mebbitt@rham.mb.ca
URL: www.rham.mb.ca
Tom Kapac, Program Manager

Saskatchewan Association of Health Organizations (SAHO)
#600, 2002 Victoria Ave., Regina SK S4P 0R7
Tel: 306-347-5500; *Fax:* 306-525-1960
e-mail: info@saho.org
URL: www.saho.org
Susan Antosh, President/CEO
Alex Taylor, Chair

Housing

Association of Condominium Managers of Ontario (ACMO)
#100, 2233 Argentia Rd., Mississauga ON L5N 2X7
Tel: 905-826-6890; *Fax:* 905-826-4873
Toll-Free: 800-265-3263
e-mail: rcm@acmo.org
URL: www.acmo.org

Chris Antipas, R.C.M., President
Amanda Curtis, CAE, Executive Director

Association provinciale des constructeurs d'habitations Québec (APCHQ) / Provincial Home Builders Association of Québec
5930, boul Louis-H. Lafontaine, Anjou QC H1M 1S7
Tél: 514-353-9960; *Téléc:* 514-353-4825
Ligne sans frais: 800-468-8160
URL: www.apchq.com

Canadian Association of Home & Property Inspectors (CAHPI) / Association canadienne des inspecteurs de biens immobiliers
PO Box 13715, Ottawa ON K2K 1X6
Tel: 613-839-5344; *Fax:* 613-839-2554
Toll-Free: 888-748-2244
e-mail: info@cahpi.ca
URL: www.cahpi.ca

Affiliation(s): American Association of Home Inspectors (ASHI)
Bill Sutherland, President
Sharry Featherston, Administrator/Registrar
Blaine Swan, Treasurer

Canadian Condominium Institute (CCI)
#310, 2175 Sheppard Ave. East, Toronto ON M2J 1W8
Tel: 416-491-6216; *Fax:* 416-491-1670
e-mail: cci.national@taylorenterprises.com
URL: www.cci.ca

Peter Leong, Chair
Diane Gaunt, National Executive Director
John Peart, President

Canadian Federation of Apartment Associations (CFAA) / Fédération canadienne des Associations de propriétaires immobiliers
#640, 1600 Carling Ave., Ottawa ON K1Z 1G3
Tel: 613-235-0101; *Fax:* 613-238-0101
e-mail: admin@cfaa-fcapi.org
URL: www.cfaa-fcapi.org

John Dickie, President
David Benes, Administrator

Canadian Home Builders' Association (CHBA) / Association canadienne des constructeurs d'habitations
#500, 150 Laurier Ave. West, Ottawa ON K1P 5J4
Tel: 613-230-3060; *Fax:* 613-232-8214
e-mail: chba@chba.ca
URL: www.chba.ca

Gary Friend, President
John Kenward, Chief Operating Officer

Canadian Housing & Renewal Association (CHRA) / Association canadienne d'habitation et de rénovation urbaine (ACHRU)
#310, 130 Slater St., Ottawa ON K1P 6E2
Tel: 613-594-3007; *Fax:* 613-594-9596
e-mail: info@chra-achru.ca
URL: www.chra-achru.ca

Sharon Chisholm, Executive Director

Canadian Manufactured Housing Institute (CMHI)
#500, 150 Laurier Ave. West, Ottawa ON K1P 5J4
Tel: 613-563-3520; *Fax:* 613-232-8600
e-mail: cmhi@cmhi.ca
URL: www.cmhi.ca

Confederation of Resident & Ratepayer Associations (CORRA)
31 Dalton Rd., Toronto ON M5R 2Y8
Tel: 416-962-2786; *Fax:* 416-964-8837
e-mail: valladp@echo-on.net

David Vallance, Chair

Cooperative Housing Association of Newfoundland & Labrador
PO Box 453, #206, 75 Barbour Dr., Mount Pearl NL A1N 2C4
Tel: 709-747-5615; *Fax:* 709-747-5606
e-mail: chanal@nl.rogers.com
URL: chanal.no-ip.org

Bill Vardy, President

Cooperative Housing Federation of British Columbia (CHF BC)
#200, 5550 Fraser St., Vancouver BC V5W 2Z4
Tel: 604-879-5111; *Fax:* 604-879-4611
Toll-Free: 866-879-5111
e-mail: info@chf.bc.ca
URL: www.chf.bc.ca

Thom Armstrong, Executive Director

Cooperative Housing Federation of Canada (CHF Canada) / Fédération de l'habitation coopérative du Canada (FHCC)
#311, 225 Metcalfe St., Ottawa ON K2P 1P9
Tel: 613-230-2201; *Fax:* 613-230-2231
Toll-Free: 800-465-2752
e-mail: info@chfcanada.coop
URL: www.chfc.ca

Nicholas Gazzard, Executive Director
David Granovsky, Coordinator, National Government Relations

Cooperative Housing Federation of Canada
#313, 720 Spadina Ave., Toronto ON M5S 2T9
Tel: 416-366-1711; *Fax:* 416-366-3876
Toll-Free: 800-268-2537
e-mail: info @ chfcanada.coop
URL: www.chfcanada.coop/eng/pages2007/onthome.asp?Checked=1,2
Publications: Newsbriefs, Ontario Edition , Bulletin for Ontario-program Co-ops , SHRA Details

Cooperative Housing Federation of Canada (CHFNS)
#201, 1099 Marginal Rd., Halifax NS B3H 4P7
Tel: 902-423-7119; *Fax:* 902-423-7058
Toll-Free: 866-213-2667

Cooperative Housing Federation of Canada
#192, 162-2025 Corydon Ave., Winnipeg MB R3P 0N5
Tel: 204-947-5411; *Fax:* 204-947-5412
Toll-Free: 888-591-3301
URL: www.chfcanada.coop/eng/pages2007/chfc_6.asp
Publications: Newsbriefs, Manitoba Edition

Federation of Metro Toronto Tenants' Associations (FMTA)
#500, 27 Carlton St., Toronto ON M5B 1L2
Tel: 416-646-1772; *Fax:* 416-921-4177*Crisis Hot-Line:* 416-921-9494
e-mail: hotline@torontotenants.org; membership@torontotenants.org
URL: www.torontotenants.org

Ontario Association of Property Standards Officers Inc.
#1000, 1 Municipal Drive, Aurora ON L4G 6J1
URL: www.oapso.org

Garry Anderson, President

Ontario Non-Profit Housing Association (ONPHA)
#400, 489 College St., Toronto ON M6G 1A5
Tel: 416-927-9144; *Fax:* 416-927-8401
Toll-Free: 800-297-6660
e-mail: mail@onpha.org; communications@onpha.org; municipal@onpha.org
URL: www.onpha.on.ca

Keith Ward, President
Sharad Kerur, Executive Director
Jo Ferris-Davies, Director, Member Development & Education
Alice Radley, Treasurer
Diana Summers, Manager, Policy, Research, & Government Relations
Rhona Duncan, Coordinator, Communications & Marketing

ShareOwner Education Inc.
#806, 4 King St. West, Toronto ON M5H 1B6
Tel: 416-595-9600; *Fax:* 416-595-0400
Toll-Free: 800-268-6881
e-mail: customercare@shareowner.com
URL: www.shareowner.com

John Bart, Chief Mentor

Human Rights & Civil Liberties

Alberta Civil Liberties Research Centre (ACLRC)
c/o Faculty of Law, University of Calgary, 2500 University Dr. NW, Calgary AB T2N 1N4
Tel: 403-220-2505; *Fax:* 403-284-0945
e-mail: aclrc@ucalgary.ca
URL: www.aclrc.com

Affiliation(s): University of Calgary
Linda McKay-Panos, Executive Director

Amnesty International, Canadian Section (AICS(ES))
312 Laurier Ave. East, Ottawa ON K1N 1H9
Tel: 613-744-7667; *Fax:* 613-746-2411
Toll-Free: 800-266-3789
e-mail: info@amnesty.ca
URL: www.amnesty.ca

Affiliation(s): Formal relations with the United Nations Economic & Social Council (ECOSOC), UNESCO, the Council of Europe; the Organization of American States, the Organization of African Unity & the Inter-Parliamentary Union
Robert Goodfellow, Executive Director

Amnesty International, Canadian Section
1992 Yonge St., 3rd Fl., Toronto ON M4S 1Z7
Tel: 416-363-9933; *Fax:* 416-363-3103
e-mail: toronto@amnesty.ca
URL: www.amnesty.ca

Amnesty International, Canadian Section
#430, 319 West Pender St., Vancouver BC V6B 1T4
Tel: 604-294-5160; *Fax:* 604-294-5130
e-mail: pro@amnesty.ca

Amnistie internationale, Section canadienne (Francophone) / Amnesty International, Canadian Section (Francophone)
6250, boul Monk, Montréal QC H4E 3H7
Tél: 514-766-9766; *Téléc:* 514-766-2088
Ligne sans frais: 800-565-9766
Courriel: info@amnistie.ca
URL: www.amnistie.ca

Black Coalition of Québec / La Ligue des Noirs du Québec
5201, boul Decarie, Montréal QC H3W 3C2
Tel: 514-489-3830; *Fax:* 514-489-2843
e-mail: info@liguedesnoirs.org
URL: www.liguedesnoirs.org

Dan Philip, Founding Director

British Columbia Civil Liberties Association (BCCLA)
#550, 1188 West Georgia St., Vancouver BC V6E 4A2
Tel: 604-687-2919; *Fax:* 604-687-3045
e-mail: info@bccla.org
URL: www.bccla.org

Murray Mollard, Executive Director
Michael Vonn, Policy Director

Canada Tibet Committee (CTC)
#2250, 300 Léo-Pariseau, Montréal QC H2X 4B3
Tel: 514-487-0665
e-mail: ctcoffice@tibet.ca
URL: www.tibet.ca

The Canadian Centre/International P.E.N. (PEN)
#301, 24 Ryerson Ave., Toronto ON M5T 2P3
Tel: 416-703-8448; *Fax:* 416-703-3870
e-mail: info@pencanada.ca
URL: www.pencanada.ca

Ellen Seligman, President
Isobel Harry, Executive Director
Kendra Ward, Office Manager

Canadian Civil Liberties Association (CCLA) / Association canadienne des libertés civiles
#506, 360 Bloor St. West, Toronto ON M5S 1X1
Tel: 416-363-0321; *Fax:* 416-861-1291
e-mail: mail@ccla.org
URL: www.ccla.org

Nathalie Des Rosiers, General Counsel
Marsha Hanen, President

Canadian Tribute to Human Rights (CTHR) / Monument canadien pour les droits de la personne (MCDP)
#170, 99 - 5th Ave., Ottawa ON K1P 5P5
Tel: 613-828-5492; *Fax:* 613-828-3647
e-mail: info@cthr-mcdp.com
URL: www.cthr-mcdp.com

Andrew Fenus, Vice-President
George Wilkes, Sec.-Treas.
Teena Hendelman, President

Citizens for Public Justice (CPJ)
#501, 309 Cooper St., Ottawa ON K2P 0G5
Fax: 613-232-1275
Toll-Free: 800-667-8046
e-mail: cpj@cpj.ca
URL: www.cpj.ca

Joe Gunn, Executive Director

CPJ Corp. (CPJ)
#501, 309 Cooper St., Ottawa ON K2P 0G5

Fax: 613-232-1275
Toll-Free: 800-867-8046
e-mail: cpj@cpj.ca
URL: www.cpj.ca
Joe Gunn, Executive Director

Equitas - International Centre for Human Rights Education / Equitas - Centre international d'éducation aux droits humains
#1100, 666, rue Sherbrooke ouest, Montréal QC H3A 1E7
Tel: 514-954-0382; Fax: 514-954-0659
e-mail: info@equitas.org
URL: www.equitas.org
Rob Yalden, President
Ian Hamilton, Executive Director

Human Rights Institute of Canada (HRIC) / Institut canadien des droits humains
#905, 280 Albert St., Ottawa ON K1P 5G8
Tel: 613-232-2920; Fax: 613-232-3735
e-mail: hric@humanrightsinstitute.com
URL: www.humanrightsinstitute.com
Marguerite E. Ritchie, President

International Centre for Human Rights & Democratic Development (ICHRDD) / Centre international des droits de la personne et du développement démocratique
#1100, 1001, boul de Maisonneuve est, Montréal QC H2L 4P9
Tel: 514-283-6073; Fax: 514-283-3792
e-mail: dd-rd@dd-rd.ca
URL: www.dd-rd.ca
Affiliation(s): Consultative status with United Nations Economic & Social Council; observer status with the World Intellectual Property Organization & the African Commission on Human & Peoples' Rights; Organization of American States; consultative status with United Nations (CONGO)
Rémy M. Beauregard, President

League for Human Rights of B'nai Brith Canada / Ligue des droits de la personne de B'nai Brith Canada
15 Hove St., Toronto ON M3H 4Y8
Tel: 416-633-6224; Fax: 416-630-2159
Toll-Free: 800-892-2624
e-mail: league@bnaibrith.ca
URL: www.bnaibrith.ca/league/league.htm
Affiliation(s): Anti-Defamation League
Frank Dimant, CEO

Macedonian Human Rights Movement of Canada (MHRMC) / Mouvement canadien de défense des droits de la personne dans la communauté macédonienne
#434, 157 Adelaide St., Toronto ON M5H 4E7
Tel: 416-850-7125; Fax: 416-850-7127
e-mail: info@mhrmi.org
URL: www.mhrmi.org
Andy Plukov, Treasurer
Luby Vidinovski, Vice-President
Bill Nicholov, President
Mark Opashinov, Secretary

Minority Rights Association of Greater Châteauguay
#310, 155 boul. St.-Jean Baptiste, Châteauguay QC J6K 3B1
Tel: 450-699-5910
Margaret Wilheim, Contact

Industry

Canadian Mechanical Contracting Education Foundation (CMCEF)
#601, 280 Albert St., Ottawa ON K1P 5G8
Tel: 613-232-5169; Fax: 613-235-2793
e-mail: cmef@cmcef.org
URL: www.cmcef.org
Tania Johnston, Executive Director

Information Technology

Association for Image & Information Management International - 1st Canadian Chapter (AIIM Canada)
c/o Teranet Inc., #600, 1 Adelaide St. East, Toronto ON M5C 2V9
e-mail: winnie.tsang@teranet.ca
URL: www.aiim.org/chapters/firstcanadian
Affiliation(s): Association for Information & Image Management
Winnie Tsang, President
Darin Davis, Secretary

Association of Professional Computer Consultants - Canada (APCC)
#400, 2323 Yonge St., Toronto ON M4P 2C9
Tel: 416-545-5275
Toll-Free: 800-487-2722
e-mail: info@apcconline.com
URL: www.apcconline.com

Canadian Association of Internet Providers (CAIP) / Association canadienne des fournisseurs internet (ACFI)
#416, 207 Bank St., Ottawa ON K2P 2N2
Tel: 613-236-6550; Fax: 613-236-8189
e-mail: info@cata.ca
URL: www.caip.ca
Tom Copeland, Chair

Canadian Association of SAS Users (CASU) / Association canadienne des utilisateurs SAS (ACUS)
#500, 280 King St. East, Toronto ON M5A 1K7
Tel: 416-363-4424; Fax: 416-363-5399
Carl Farrell, President

Canadian Community of Computer Educators (CCCE)
15 Lone Oak Ave., Brampton ON L6S 5V4
e-mail: info@ccce.on.ca
URL: www.ccce.on.ca

Canadian Image Processing & Pattern Recognition Society (CIPPRS) / Association canadienne de traitement d'images et de reconnaissance des formes (ACTIRF)
Dept. of Computer Sciences, Univ. of Western Ontario, Middlesex College 383, London ON N6A 5B7
Tel: 519-661-2111; Fax: 519-661-3515
e-mail: barron@csd.uwo.ca
URL: www.cipprs.org
Affiliation(s): Canadian Information Processing Society
John Barron

Canadian Information Processing Society (CIPS) / L'Association canadienne de l'informatique (ACI)
#801, 5090 Explorer Dr., Mississauga ON L4W 4T9
Tel: 905-602-1370; Fax: 905-602-7884
Toll-Free: 877-275-2477
e-mail: info@cips.ca
URL: www.cips.ca
Social Media: www.facebook.com/group.php?gid=2459351719
Affiliation(s): British Computer Society; Australian Computer Society; Association for Computing Machinery
Mary Jean Kucerak, CAE, Executive Director

CANARIE
#500, 45 O'Connor St., Ottawa ON K1P 1A4
Tel: 613-943-5454; Fax: 613-943-5443
e-mail: info@canarie.ca
URL: www.canarie.ca
Guy Bujold, President & CEO

Centre international pour le développement de l'inforoute en français (CIDIF)
165, Blvd. Hébert, Edmundston NB E3V 2S8
Tél: 506-737-5280; Téléc: 506-737-5281
Courriel: info@cidif.org
URL: www.cidif.org
Roger Gervais, Directeur général

Chinese Canadian Information Processing Professionals (CIPro)
PO Box 316, 7305 Woodbine Ave., Markham ON L3R 3V7
e-mail: info@cipro.ca
URL: www.cipro.ca
Scaven Liow, President

COACH - Canada's Health Informatics Association (COACH)
#301, 250 Consumers Rd., Toronto ON M2J 4V6
Tel: 416-494-9324; Fax: 416-495-8723
Toll-Free: 888-253-8554
e-mail: info@coachorg.com
URL: www.coachorg.com
Renee Levine, Executive Director

Communications & Information Technology Ontario (CITO)
#200, 2625 Queensview Dr., Ottawa ON K2B 8K2
Tel: 613-726-3420; Fax: 613-726-3424
Toll-Free: 566-759-6014
Don Wilford, Managing Director, Centre of Excellence for Photonics

Electronic Frontier Canada Inc. (EFC) / Frontière électronique du Canada
20 Richmond Ave., Kitchener ON N2G 1Y9
Tel: 905-525-9140; Fax: 905-546-9995
e-mail: damien@efc.ca
URL: www.efc.ca
Affiliation(s): The Electronic Frontier Foundation, San Francisco
Jeffrey Shallit, Vice-President/Treasurer
Richard Rosenberg, Vice-President
David Jones, President

GS1 Canada
#800, 1500 Don Mills Rd., Toronto ON M3B 3L1
Tel: 416-510-8039; Fax: 416-510-1916
Toll-Free: 800-567-7084
e-mail: info@gs1ca.org
URL: www.gs1ca.org
N. Arthur Smith, President/CEO

Information & Communications Technology Council of Canada (ICTC) / Conseil des technologies de l'information et des communications du Canada (CTIC)
#300, 116 Lisgar St., Ottawa ON K2P 0C2
Tel: 613-237-8551; Fax: 613-230-3490
e-mail: info@ictc-ctic.ca
URL: www.ictc-ctic.ca
Faye West, Chair

Information Resource Management Association of Canada (IRMAC)
PO Box 5639, Stn. A, Toronto ON M5W 1N8
Tel: 403-329-2672; Fax: 403-329-2038
e-mail: info@irmac.ca
URL: www.irmac.ca
Affiliation(s): DAMA International; British Columbia Data Management Association
Mark O'Gorman, President
Robert Hickman, Vice-President
Aliza Schneid, Secretary
Joanne Scher, Treasurer

Information Technology Association of Canada (ITAC) / Association canadienne de la technologie de l'information
#801, 5090 Explorer Dr., Mississauga ON L4W 4T9
Tel: 905-602-8345; Fax: 905-602-8346
e-mail: info@itac.ca
URL: www.itac.ca
Alberta Fraccaro, Accounting Coordinator
Bill Munson, Vice President
Brendan Seaton, President, ITAC Health
Carlo Viola, Director, Finance

Information Technology Industry Alliance of Nova Scotia (ITANS)
PO Box 9410, Stn. A, Halifax NS B3K 5S3
Tel: 902-423-5332; Fax: 902-484-5094
e-mail: info@itans.ns.ca
URL: www.itans.ns.ca
Affiliation(s): Information Technology Association of Canada
Michael McConnell, CEO

The Instrumentation, Systems & Automation Society of America (ISA)
PO Box 12277, 67 Alexander Dr., Research Triangle Park NC 27709 USA
Tel: 919-549-8411; Fax: 919-549-8288
e-mail: info@isa.org
URL: www.isa.org
Affiliation(s): American Association for the Advancement of Science; American Institute of Physics; International Measurement Confederation; National Institute for Certification in Engineering Technologies; National Inventors Hall of Fame; American National Standards Institute; American Society of Mechanical Engineers; Fluid Controls Institute; Institute of Electrical & Electronic Engineers
Patrick Gouhin, Executive Director

National Capital FreeNet (NCF) / Libertel de la Capitale Nationale
Trailhead Building, #302, 1960 Scott St., Ottawa ON K1Z 8L8
Tel: 613-520-9001; Fax: 613-520-3524
e-mail: ncf@ncf.ca
URL: www.ncf.ca

Newfoundland & Labrador Association of Technology Companies (NLATC)
#5, 391 Empire Ave., St. John's NL A1E 1W6
Tel: 709-772-8324; Fax: 709-757-6284
e-mail: info@nati.net
URL: www.nati.net

Affiliation(s): Canadian Advanced Technology Association; Information Technology Association of Canada
Paul Dubé, Chief Executive Officer

reBOOT Canada
#110, 136 Geary Ave., Toronto ON M6H 4H1
Tel: 416-534-6017; *Fax:* 416-534-6083
e-mail: rose@rebootcanada.ca
URL: www.rebootcanada.ca
Nicholas Brinckman, Executive Director

Insurance Industry

Advocis
#209, 390 Queens Quay West, Toronto ON M5V 3A2
Tel: 416-444-5251; *Fax:* 416-444-8031
Toll-Free: 800-563-5822
e-mail: info@advocis.ca
URL: www.advocis.ca
Kristan Birchard, Chair
Greg Pollock, President & CEO

Canadian Association of Blue Cross Plans (CABCP) / Association Canadienne des Croix Bleue (ACCB)
Stn. 2000, Toronto ON M9C 5P1
Toll-Free: 888-261-4033
URL: www.bluecross.ca
Affiliation(s): Blue Cross (USA); Blue Shield (USA); International Federation of Health Funds

Canadian Association of Mutual Insurance Companies (CAMIC) / Association canadienne des compagnies d'assurance mutuelles (ACCAM)
#205, 311 McArthur Ave., Ottawa ON K1L 6P1
Tel: 613-789-6851; *Fax:* 613-789-7665
e-mail: nlafreniere@camic.ca
URL: www.camic.ca
Normand Lafrenière, B.A., M.P.A., President

Canadian Board of Marine Underwriters (CBMU)
#100, 2233 Argentia Rd., Mississauga ON L5N 2X7
Tel: 905-826-4768; *Fax:* 905-826-4873
e-mail: info@cbmu.com
URL: www.cbmu.com
Amanda Curtis, CAE, Executive Director

Canadian Independent Adjusters' Association (CIAA) / Association canadienne des experts indépendants (ACEI)
Centennial Centre, #100, 5401 Eglinton Ave. West, Toronto ON M9C 5K6
Tel: 416-621-6222; *Fax:* 416-621-7776
Toll-Free: 877-255-5589
e-mail: info@ciaa-adjusters.ca
URL: www.ciaa-adjusters.ca
Patricia M. Battle, Executive Director
Patti M. Kernaghan, FCIP, CRM, President
Mary Charman, CIP, 1st Vice-President
Greg G. Merrithew, CIP, FIFAA, 2nd Vice-President
Marie C. Gallagher, FCIP, CRM, Secretary
Randy P. LaBrash, CIP, CFE, CFEI, Treasurer, Randy.Labrash@crawco.ca

Canadian Institute of Actuaries (CIA) / Institut canadien des actuaires (ICA)
#800, 150 Metcalfe St., Ottawa ON K2P 1P1
Tel: 613-236-8196; *Fax:* 613-233-4552
e-mail: secretariat@actuaries.ca
URL: www.actuaries.ca
Daniel Lapointe, Executive Director
Lynn Blackburn, Director, Volunteer & Member Services
Les Dandridge, Director, Communications
Jacques Leduc, Director, Operations, Finance, & Administration

Canadian Life & Health Insurance Association Inc. (CLHIA) / Association canadienne des compagnies d'assurances de personnes inc.
#1700, 1 Queen St. East, Toronto ON M5C 2X9
Tel: 416-777-2221; *Fax:* 416-777-1895
Toll-Free: 800-268-8099
e-mail: info@clhia.ca
URL: www.clhia.ca
Pierre-Yves Julien, Chair

Canadian Life & Health Insurance Association Inc.
#630, 1001, boul de Maisonneuve ouest, Montréal QC H3A 3C8
Tel: 514-845-9004; *Fax:* 514-845-6182

Canadian Life & Health Insurance Association Inc.
#400, 46 Elgin St., Ottawa ON K1P 5K6
Tel: 613-230-0031; *Fax:* 613-230-0297

Centre for Study of Insurance Operations (CSIO) / Centre d'étude de la pratique d'assurance (CEPA)
#500, 110 Yonge St., Toronto ON M5C 1T4
Tel: 416-360-1773; *Fax:* 416-364-1482
Toll-Free: 800-463-2746
e-mail: helpdesk@csio.com
URL: www.csio.com
Robert Fitzgerald, Chair
Steven Kaukinen, President
Francine Davis, Manager, EDI & Forms Standards
Sebastian Penalosa, Manager, Network & Membership Services
Connie Strange, Manager, XML Standards

Chambre de l'assurance de dommages (CHAD)
#1200, 999, boul de Maisonneuve ouest, Montréal QC H3A 3L4
Tél: 514-842-2591; *Téléc:* 514-842-3138
Ligne sans frais: 800-361-7288
Courriel: info@chad.qc.ca
URL: www.chad.qc.ca
Bernard Drouin, Vice-président
Serge Lyras, Président

Facility Association
PO Box 121, #2400, 777 Bay St., Toronto ON M5G 2C8
Tel: 416-863-1750; *Fax:* 416-868-0894
Toll-Free: 800-268-9572
e-mail: mail@facilityassociation.com
URL: www.facilityassociation.com
David J. Simpson, President & CEO

Financial Services Commission of Ontario (FSCO) / Commission des services financiers de l'Ontario (CSFO)
PO Box 85, 5160 Yonge St., 17th Fl., Toronto ON M2N 6L9
Tel: 416-250-7250; *Fax:* 416-590-7070
Toll-Free: 800-668-0128
e-mail: contactcentre@fsco.gov.on.ca
URL: www.fsco.gov.on.ca
John Solursh, Chair

GAMA International Canada / GAMA International du Canada
#209, 390 Queens Quay West, Toronto ON M4V 3A2
Tel: 416-444-5252; *Fax:* 416-444-8031
Toll-Free: 800-563-5822
e-mail: info@gamacanada.com
URL: www.gamacanada.com
Greg D. Powell, President

Groupement des assureurs automobiles (GAA)
Tour de la Bourse, CP 336, #2410, 800 Place-Victoria, Montréal QC H3A 3C6
Tél: 514-288-4321
Ligne sans frais: 877-288-4321
Courriel: cinfo@gaa.qc.ca
URL: www.gaa.qc.ca
Brigitte Corbeil, Directeur général

L'Institut d'assurance de dommages du Québec (IADQ)
#2230, 1200, av McGill College, Montréal QC H3B 4G7
Tél: 514-393-8156; *Téléc:* 514-393-9222
Courriel: iadqmontreal@iadq.qc.ca
URL: www.iadq.qc.ca
Lucien Bergeron, B.A., FPAA, Directeur général et secrétaire

Insurance Brokers Association of Alberta (IBAA)
3010 Calgary Trail, Edmonton AB T6J 6V4
Tel: 780-424-3320; *Fax:* 780-424-7418
Toll-Free: 800-318-0197
e-mail: ibaa@ibaa.ca; education@ibaa.ca; convention@ibaa.ca
URL: www.ibaa.ca
Ginny Bannerman, Chief Executive Officer
Karen Dyberg, President
Dean Bailey, Vice-President

Insurance Brokers Association of British Columbia (IBABC)
#1300, 1095 West Pender St., Vancouver BC V6E 2M6
Tel: 604-606-8000; *Fax:* 604-683-7831
URL: www.ibabc.org
Charles (Chuck) Byrne, CIP, Executive Director
Trudy Lancelyn, Deputy Executive Director

Insurance Brokers Association of Manitoba (IBAM)
#205, 530 Kenaston Blvd., Winnipeg MB R3N 1Z4
Tel: 204-488-1857; *Fax:* 204-489-0316
Toll-Free: 800-204-5649
e-mail: info@ibam.mb.ca
URL: www.ibam.mb.ca
Wade Garriock, President

Insurance Brokers Association of New Brunswick (IBANB) / Association des courtiers d'assurances du Nouveau-Brunswick
PO Box 1523, #201, 590 Brunswick St., Fredericton NB E3B 5G2
Tel: 506-450-2898; *Fax:* 506-450-1494
e-mail: ibanb@nbinsurancebrokers.ca
URL: www.ibanb.org
Georges Leger, President
Linda M. Dawe, FIIC, CAIB, CEO

Insurance Brokers Association of Newfoundland (IBAN)
Chimo Bldg., 151 Crosbie Rd., 3rd Floor, St. John's NL A1B 4B4
Tel: 709-726-4450; *Fax:* 709-754-4399
e-mail: iban@nfld.net
URL: www.iban.ca
Mary Geralyn Rahal, Office Administrator

Insurance Brokers Association of Nova Scotia (IBANS)
380 Bedford Hwy, Halifax NS B3M 2L4
Tel: 902-876-0526; *Fax:* 902-876-0527
e-mail: info@ibans.com
URL: www.ibans.com
Stephen Greene, Executive Director

Insurance Brokers Association of Ontario (IBAO)
#700, 1 Eglinton Ave. East, Toronto ON M4P 3A1
Tel: 416-488-7422; *Fax:* 416-488-7526
Toll-Free: 800-268-8845
e-mail: contact@ibao.com
URL: www.ibao.org
Randy Carroll, CEO
Bryan Yetman, CIP, CRM, President
Peter Blodgett, CIP, Chair

Insurance Brokers Association of Prince Edward Island
c/o Hyndman & Co. Limited, PO Box 790, 57 Queen St., Charlottetown PE C1A 4A5
Tel: 902-566-4244; *Fax:* 902-566-5990
e-mail: hyndmaninsurance@anchorgroup.com
Helen Hyndman, Contact

Insurance Brokers Association of Saskatchewan (IBAS)
#310, 2631 - 28 Ave., Regina SK S4S 6X3
Tel: 306-525-5900; *Fax:* 306-569-3018
e-mail: IBASinfo@ibas.sk.ca
URL: www.ibas.sk.ca
Ernie Gaschler, Executive Director

Insurance Bureau of Canada
#1100, 2235 Sheppard Ave. East, Atria II, Toronto ON M2J 5B5
Tel: 416-445-5912; *Fax:* 416-449-9357
Toll-Free: 800-761-6703

Insurance Bureau of Canada (IBC) / Bureau d'assurance du Canada
#2400, 777 Bay St., Toronto ON M5G 2C8
Tel: 416-362-2031; *Fax:* 416-644-4961
Toll-Free: 800-387-2880
URL: www.ibc.ca
Don Forgeron, Vice-President, Ontario

Insurance Bureau of Canada
Tour de la Bourse, CP 336, #2410, 800, Place-Victoria, Montréal QC H4Z 0A2
Tél: 514-288-1563; *Téléc:* 514-288-0753
Ligne sans frais: 877-288-4321

Insurance Bureau of Canada
#1706, 1969 Upper Water St., Halifax NS B3J 3R7
Tel: 902-429-2730; *Fax:* 902-420-0157
Toll-Free: 800-565-7189

Insurance Bureau of Canada
#401, 10722 - 103 Ave., Edmonton AB T5J 5G6
Tel: 780-423-2212; *Fax:* 780-423-4796
Toll-Free: 800-377-6378

Insurance Bureau of Canada
#1010, 510 Burrard St., Vancouver BC V6C 3A8
Tel: 604-684-3635; *Fax:* 604-684-6235
Toll-Free: 877-772-3777

Insurance Bureau of Canada
#808, 155 Queen St., Ottawa ON K1P 6L1
Tel: 613-236-5043; *Fax:* 613-236-5208

Insurance Institute of British Columbia (IIBC)
#1110, 800 West Pender St., Vancouver BC V6C 2V6
Tel: 604-681-5491; *Fax:* 604-681-5479
Toll-Free: 888-681-5491
e-mail: IIBCmail@insuranceinstitute.ca
URL: www.iibc.org
Danielle Bolduc, BComm, CIP, General Manager
Shaun Sinclair, MBA, FCIP, CRM, President
Pierre Chavigny, CIP, CRM, Sec.-Treas.

Insurance Institute of Canada (IIC) / Institut d'assurance du Canada (IAC)
18 King St. East, 6th Fl., Toronto ON M5C 1C4
Tel: 416-362-8586; *Fax:* 416-362-4239
Toll-Free: 866-362-8585
e-mail: IICmail@insuranceinstitute.ca
URL: www.insuranceinstitute.ca
Affiliation(s): Insurance Institute of America; Chartered Insurance Institute; Australian Insurance Institute; Insurance Institute of India; Insurance Institute of Malaysia
Peter G. Hohman, MBA, FCIP, ICD., President & CEO

Insurance Institute of Manitoba (IIM)
#533, 167 Lombard Ave., Winnipeg MB R3B 0V3
Tel: 204-956-1702; *Fax:* 204-956-0758
e-mail: iimmail@insuranceinstitute.ca
URL: www.insuranceinstitute.ca
Ted Teterenko, President
Jennifer Tougas, CIP, Manager

Insurance Institute of New Brunswick (IINB)
25 Hedgewood Dr., Moncton NB E1E 2W4
Tel: 506-386-5896; *Fax:* 506-386-1130
e-mail: IINBmail@insuranceinstitute.ca
URL: www.insuranceinstitute.ca
Monique LeBlanc, Manager
Darrel Coates, CIP, President

Insurance Institute of Newfoundland & Labrador Inc. (IINL)
Chimo Bldg., 151 Crosbie Rd., St. John's NL A1B 4B4
Tel: 709-754-4398; *Fax:* 709-754-4399
e-mail: IINLmail@insuranceinstitute.ca
URL: www.insuranceinstitute.ca
Lorrie Nightingale, CIP, CAIB, Manager

Insurance Institute of Northern Alberta (IINA)
202 Solar Court, 10350 - 124 St., Edmonton AB T5N 3V9
Tel: 780-424-1268; *Fax:* 780-420-1940
e-mail: IINAmail@insuranceinstitute.ca
URL: www.insuranceinstitute.ca
Affiliation(s): CIP Society of Canada
Wanda Wylie, Manager

Insurance Institute of Nova Scotia (IINS)
#503, 73 Tacoma Dr., Dartmouth NS B2W 3Y6
Tel: 902-433-0070; *Fax:* 902-433-0072
e-mail: IINSmail@insuranceinstitute.ca
URL: www.insuranceinstitute.ca
Sandra Reinders, FCIP, CAIB, President
Susanne Paulsen, FCIP, Treasurer
Jenny Renyo, Manager

Insurance Institute of Ontario (IIO)
18 King St. East, 16th Fl., Toronto ON M5C 1C4
Tel: 416-362-8586; *Fax:* 416-362-8081
e-mail: agervasio@insuranceinstitute.ca
URL: www.insuranceinstitute.ca
André Fredette, FCIP, President
Paul Martin, CIP, Sr. Vice-President
Linda Wahrer, FCIP, Secretary
Randy Bushey, AIIC, Treasurer
Peter Hohman, MBA, FCIP, ICD., Manager

Insurance Institute of Prince Edward Island (IIPEI)
PO Box 811, 51 University Ave., Charlottetown PE C1A 4K8
Tel: 902-892-1692; *Fax:* 902-368-7305
e-mail: IIPEImail@insuranceinstitute.ca
URL: www.insuranceinstitute.ca
Monique LeBlanc, Manager

Insurance Institute of Saskatchewan (IIS)
#310, 2631 - 28 Ave., Regina SK S4S 6X3
Tel: 306-525-9799; *Fax:* 306-569-3018
e-mail: IISmail@insuranceinstitute.ca
URL: www.insuranceinstitute.ca
Jennifer Meshka, CIP, President
Lisa Todd, FCIP, CRM, Secretary
Joanne Duke, Manager

Insurance Institute of Southern Alberta (IISA)
#1110, 833 - 4 Ave. SW, Calgary AB T2P 3T5
Tel: 403-266-3427; *Fax:* 403-269-3199
e-mail: IISAmail@insuranceinstitute.ca
URL: www.insuranceinstitute.ca
Caroline Logan, B.Comm., Manager

LOMA Canada
675 Cochrane Dr., East Tower, 6th Floor, Markham ON L3R 0B8
Tel: 905-530-2302; *Fax:* 905-530-2001
e-mail: lomacanada@loma.org
URL: www.lomacanada.org
Brent Lemanski, Resident Director, Canada

Marine Insurance Association of British Columbia (MIABC)
c/o Coast Underwriters Ltd., #1610, 200 Granville St., Vancouver BC V6C 1S4
Tel: 604-629-3820; *Fax:* 604-629-8561
URL: www.m-i-a-b-c.org

Nuclear Insurance Association of Canada (NIAC) / Association canadienne d'assurance nucléaire
c/o CGI, 150 Commerce Valley Dr. West, Lock Box 200, Markham ON L3T 7Z3
Tel: 905-695-6657; *Fax:* 905-771-5312
Colleen P. DeMerchant, FCIP, CRM, Assistant Manager

Ontario Insurance Adjusters Association (OIAA)
29 De Jong Dr., Mississauga ON L5M 1B9
Tel: 905-542-0576; *Fax:* 905-542-1301
Toll-Free: 888-259-1555
e-mail: manager@oiaa.com
URL: www.oiaa.com
Norman McGlashan, President

Ontario Mutual Insurance Association (OMIA)
PO Box 3187, 350 Pinebush Rd., Cambridge ON N3H 4S6
Tel: 519-622-9220; *Fax:* 519-622-9227
e-mail: information@omia.com
URL: www.omia.com
Affiliation(s): Canadian Association of Mutual Insurance Companies

Regroupement des cabinets de courtage d'assurance du Québec (RCCAQ) / Insurance Brokers Association of Québec - Assembly
#139, 955, rue D'Assigny, Longueuil QC J4K 5C3
Tél: 450-674-6258; *Téléc:* 450-674-3609
Ligne sans frais: 800-516-6258
Courriel: info@rccaq.com
URL: www.rccaq.com
Mario Lanouette, Président
Johanne Lamanque, Directrice générale

Reinsurance Research Council (RRC) / Conseil de recherche en réassurance (CRR)
#7, 296 Jarvis St., Toronto ON M5B 2C5
Tel: 416-968-0183; *Fax:* 416-968-6818
e-mail: mail@rrccanada.org
URL: www.rrccanada.org
Anthony Laycock, General Manager

Risk & Insurance Management Society Inc. (RIMS)
c/o Bonnie Wasser, 42 Arlstan Dr., Toronto ON M3H 4V9
Tel: 416-638-1645
e-mail: bwasser@sympatico.ca
URL: www.rimscanada.ca
Affiliation(s): International Federation of Risk & Insurance Management Associations
Bonnie Wasser, Canadian Consultant
Kim Hunton, Chair, RIMS Canada Council
Sue Mepham, Secretary, RIMS Canada Council
Charles Parker, Treasurer, RIMS Canada Council

Saskatchewan Municipal Hail Insurance Association (SMHI)
2100 Cornwall St., Regina SK S4P 2K7
Tel: 306-569-1852; *Fax:* 306-522-3717
Toll-Free: 877-414-7644
e-mail: smhi@smhi.ca
URL: www.smhi.ca
Murray Otterson, CEO
Rodney Schoettler, COO

Society of Public Insurance Administrators of Ontario (SPIAO)
c/o The Municipality Of Clarington, 40 Temperance St., Bowmanville ON L1C 3A6
e-mail: info@spiao.ca
URL: www.spiao.ca
Nancy Taylor, Treasurer

Chambre de la sécurité financière (CSF)
300, rue Léo-Pariseau, 26e étage, Montréal QC H3A 3C6
Tél: 514-282-5777; *Téléc:* 514-282-2225
Ligne sans frais: 800-361-9989
Courriel: renseignements@chambresf.com
URL: www.chambresf.com
Luc Labelle, Président

Underwriters' Laboratories of Canada (ULC) / Laboratoires des assureurs du Canada
7 Underwriters Rd., Toronto ON M1R 3B4
Tel: 416-757-3611; *Fax:* 416-757-8727
Toll-Free: 866-937-3852
e-mail: ulcinfo@ulc.ca
URL: www.ulc.ca
Affiliation(s): Underwriters Laboratories Inc., Northbrook IL
John Roberts, President

Interior Design

Associated Designers of Canada (ADC)
#201, 192 Spadina Ave., Toronto ON M5T 2C2
Tel: 416-410-4209; *Fax:* 416-703-6601
Toll-Free: 800-361-2721
e-mail: adc@designers.ca
URL: www.designers.ca
Jackie McAlpine, Contact

Association des designers industriels du Québec (ADIQ)
CP 182, Succ. Rosemont, Montréal QC H1X 3B7
Tél: 514-287-6531; *Téléc:* 514-278-3049
Courriel: info@adiq.ca (Noémi Marquis)
URL: www.adiq.ca
Mario Gagnon, Président
Assam Michel Daoud, Vice-président

Association of Canadian Industrial Designers (ACID) / Association des designers industriels du Canada
157 Adelaide St. West, Toronto ON M5H 4E7
e-mail: info@designcanada.org
URL: www.designcanada.org
Affiliation(s): International Council of Societies of Industrial Design - Helsinki, Finland

Association of Interior Designers of Nova Scotia (IDNS)
PO Box 2042, Halifax NS B3J 3B4
Tel: 902-425-4367
e-mail: info@idns.ca
URL: www.idns.ca
Karen Deveau, President

Association of Registered Interior Designers of New Brunswick (ARIDNB) / Association des designers d'intérieur immatriculés du Nouveau-Brunswick (ADIINB)
PO Box 1541, Fredericton NB E3B 5G2
Tel: 506-459-3014
e-mail: info@aridnb.ca
URL: www.aridnb.ca
Daphne Rae, President
Louise Duguay, Vice-President
Sara Dunton, Treasurer & Registrar
Lyn Van Tassel, Secretary

Association of Registered Interior Designers of Ontario (ARIDO)
#220, 6 Adelaide St. East, Toronto ON M5C 1H6
Tel: 416-921-2127; *Fax:* 416-921-3660
Toll-Free: 800-334-1180
e-mail: adminoffice@arido.ca
URL: www.arido.ca
Affiliation(s): Interior Designers Educators Council; National Council for Interior Design Education; American Society of Interior Designers; Foundation for Interior Design Education; International Federation of Interior Designers
Susan Wiggins, Executive Director

Association professionnelle des designers d'intérieur du Québec (APDIQ)
#306, 19, Cours Le Royer Ouest, Montréal QC H2Y 1W4
Tél: 514-284-6263; *Téléc:* 514-284-6112
Ligne sans frais: 888-247-2790
Courriel: apdiq@videotron.ca
URL: www.apdiq.com
André Lapointe, Président

British Columbia Industrial Designer Association (BCID)
PO Box 33943, Vancouver BC V6J 4L7
Tel: 604-608-3204; *Fax:* 604-608-3204
e-mail: info@bcid.com
URL: www.bcid.com

Interior Designers Association of Saskatchewan (IDAS)
PO Box 32005, Stn. Erindale, Saskatoon SK S7S 1N8
Tel: 306-343-3311; *Fax:* 306-249-3011
e-mail: char.vaughn@sasktel.net
URL: www.idas.ca
Charlene Vaughn, President

Interior Designers Institute of British Columbia (IDIBC)
#400, 601 West Broadway, Vancouver BC V5Z 4C2
Tel: 604-298-5211; *Fax:* 604-421-5211
e-mail: info@idibc.org
URL: www.idibc.org
Affiliation(s): Design Resource Association
Robert Ledingham, RID/IDC, President
Paul Zanette, RID/IDC, Vice President, National

Interior Designers of Canada (IDC) / Designers d'intérieur du Canada
#220, 6 Adelaide St. East, Toronto ON M5C 1H6
Tel: 416-594-9310; *Fax:* 416-921-3660
e-mail: info@interiordesigncanada.org
URL: www.interiordesigncanada.org
Linda Makins, President

Professional Interior Designers Institute of Manitoba
137 Bannatyne Ave. East, 2nd Fl., Winnipeg MB R3B 0R3
Tel: 204-925-4625; *Fax:* 204-925-4624
e-mail: pidim@shaw.ca
URL: www.pidim.ca

Registered Interior Designers of Alberta
PO Box 21171, Edmonton AB T6R 2V4
Tel: 780-413-0013; *Fax:* 780-413-0076
e-mail: infol@interiordesignalberta.com
URL: www.interiordesignalberta.com
Michele Gunn, IDA, LID, IDC, President
Jill Lane, Association Manager

International Cooperation/International Relations

AFS Interculture Canada (AFSIC)
1425, boul René-Lévesque ouest, Montréal QC H3G 1T7
Tel: 514-288-3282; *Fax:* 514-843-9119
Toll-Free: 800-361-7248
e-mail: info-canada@afs.org
URL: www.afscanada.org
Social Media: www.facebook.com/group.php?gid=20406511761
Affiliation(s): United Nations
Robert Deslandes, President
Bernard Roy, Executive Director

Aga Khan Foundation Canada
The Delegation of the Ismaili Imamat, 199 Sussex Dr., Ottawa ON K1N 1K6
Tel: 613-237-2532; *Fax:* 613-567-2532
Toll-Free: 800-267-2532
e-mail: info@akfc.ca
URL: www.akfc.ca
Khalil Z. Shariff, CEO

Atlantic Council of Canada (ACC) / Conseil atlantique du Canada (CAC)
Stn. 701, 165 University Ave., Toronto ON M5H 3B8
Tel: 416-979-1875; *Fax:* 416-979-0825
e-mail: info@atlantic-council.ca
URL: www.atlantic-council.ca
Affiliation(s): NATO; Atlantic Treaty Association - Paris, France
Julie Lindhout, President
Goran S. Pesic, Executive Director

Canada World Youth (CWY) / Jeunesse Canada Monde (JCM)
2330, rue Notre-Dame ouest, 3e étage, Montréal QC H3J 1N4
Tel: 514-931-3526; *Fax:* 514-939-2621
Toll-Free: 800-605-3526
e-mail: recruitment@cwy-jcm.org
URL: www.canadaworldyouth.org
Social Media: www.facebook.com/group.php?gid=6244934985
Affiliation(s): World Assembly of Youth
Sean Riley, Chair
Iris Almeida-Côté, President/CEO

Canada World Youth
#205, 10816A - 82nd Ave., Edmonton AB T6E 2B3
Tel: 780-432-1877; *Fax:* 780-433-4489
e-mail: west-ouest@cwy-jcm.org

Canada World Youth
#404, 317 Adelaide St. West, Toronto ON M5V 1P9
Tel: 416-596-9702; *Fax:* 416-596-9642
Toll-Free: 888-421-9761
e-mail: gl@cwy-jcm.org

Canada World Youth
#303, 2360, rue Notre-Dame ouest, Montréal QC H3J 1N4
Tel: 514-931-3933; *Fax:* 514-935-4580
e-mail: est-east@cwy-jcm.org

Canadian Association for Latin American & Caribbean Studies (CALACS) / Association canadienne des études latino-américaines et caraïbes (ACELAC)
CCASLS SB-115, Corcordia Univ., 1455 de Maisonneuve ouest, Montréal QC H3G 1M8
Tel: 514-848-2280; *Fax:* 514-848-4514
e-mail: calacs_acelac@bellnet.ca
URL: calacs.concordia.ca
Annamaria Piccioni, Executive Director
Stuart McCook, President

Canadian Association for the Study of International Development (CASID) / L'Association canadienne d'études du développement international (ACEDI)
c/o The North-South Institute, #200, 55 Murray St., Ottawa ON K1N 5M3
Tel: 613-241-3535; *Fax:* 613-241-7435
e-mail: casid@nsi-ins.ca
URL: www.casid-acedi.ca
Diane Pichette, Secretary

Canadian Commission for UNESCO / Commission canadienne pour l'UNESCO
PO Box 1047, 350 Albert St., Ottawa ON K1P 5V8
Tel: 613-566-4414; *Fax:* 613-566-4405
Toll-Free: 800-263-5588
e-mail: info@unesco.ca
URL: www.unesco.ca
Affiliation(s): Network of 180 national commissions for UNESCO
David A. Walden, Secretary-General

Canadian Council for International Co-operation (CCIC) / Conseil canadien pour la coopération internationale
#300, 1 Nicholas St., Ottawa ON K1N 7B7
Tel: 613-241-7007; *Fax:* 613-241-5302
e-mail: info@ccic.ca
URL: www.ccic.ca
Gerry Barr, President/CEO

Canadian Foundation for the Americas (FOCAL) / Fondation canadienne pour les Amériques
#720, 1 Nicholas St., Ottawa ON K1N 7B7
Tel: 613-562-0005; *Fax:* 613-562-2525
e-mail: focal@focal.ca
URL: www.focal.ca
Carlo Dade, Executive Director
Madeleine Bélanger, Director, Communications

Canadian Friends of Burma (CFOB) / Les Amis canadiens de la Birmanie
#206, 145 Spruce St., Ottawa ON K1R 6P1
Tel: 613-237-8056; *Fax:* 613-563-0017
e-mail: cfob@cfob.org
URL: www.cfob.org
Affiliation(s): World University Service of Canada; Canadian Asia Pacific Working Group; Peacefund Canada; Canadian Peacebuilding Coordinating Committee
Tin Maung Htoo, Executive Director

Canadian Friends of Ukraine (CFU)
South Bldg., 620 Spadina Ave., 2nd Fl., Toronto ON M5S 2H4
Tel: 416-964-6644; *Fax:* 416-964-6085
e-mail: canfun@interlog.com
URL: www.canadianfriendsofukraine.com
Margareta Shpir, President
John Pidkowich, Vice-President
Lisa Shymko, Executive Director
Walentina Rodak, Treasurer
John Kuzyk, Chair, Canada-Ukraine Library Centres

Canadian Institute for Conflict Resolution (CICR) / Institut canadien pour la résolution des conflits
c/c St. Paul University, 223 Main St., Ottawa ON K1S 1C4
Tel: 613-235-5800; *Fax:* 613-235-5801
Toll-Free: 866-684-2427
e-mail: info@cicr-icrc.ca
URL: www.cicr-icrc.ca
Brian Strom, Executive Director

Canadian Institute of Cultural Affairs / Institut canadien des affaires culturelles
655 Queen St. East, Toronto ON M4M 1G4
Tel: 416-691-2316; *Fax:* 416-691-2491
Toll-Free: 877-691-1422
e-mail: ica@icacan.ca
URL: www.icacan.ca
Affiliation(s): Part of a network of nationally autonomous ICAs in 32 countries; through ICA International in Brussels, ICA Canada has consultative status with the UN, UNICEF, the World Health Organization & the Food & Agricultural Organization
Fred Simon, Executive Director

Canadian International Council (CIC) / Conseil international du Canada
PO Box 210, 45 Willcocks St., Toronto ON M5S 1C7
Tel: 416-977-9000; *Fax:* 416-946-7319
Toll-Free: 800-668-2442
e-mail: mailbox@canadianinternationalcouncil.org
URL: www.canadianinternationalcouncil.org
Douglas Goold, President
Jim Balsillie, Chair

Canadian Peace Alliance (CPA) / Alliance canadienne pour la paix
#13, 427 Bloor St. West, Toronto ON M5S 1X7
Tel: 416-588-5555; *Fax:* 416-588-5556
e-mail: cpa@web.ca
URL: www.acp-cpa.ca
Affiliation(s): Canadian Network to Abolish Nuclear Weapons; International Peace Bureau
Sid Lacombe, Coordinator

Canadian Physicians for Aid & Relief (CPAR)
1425 Bloor St. West, Toronto ON M6P 3L6
Tel: 416-369-0865; *Fax:* 416-369-0294
Toll-Free: 800-263-2727
e-mail: info@cpar.ca
URL: www.cpar.ca
Social Media: twitter.com/cpar
Affiliation(s): Canadian Environmental Network; Canadian Centre for Philanthropy
Diane Lacaille, Chair
Joe Chouinard, Treasurer
Kevin O'Brien, Executive Director

CARE Canada
#200, 9 Gurdwara Rd., Ottawa ON K2E 7X6
Tel: 613-228-5600; *Fax:* 613-226-5777
Toll-Free: 800-267-5232
e-mail: info@care.ca
URL: www.care.ca
Paul Drager, Chair
L. Denis Desautels, Executive Director

Carrefour de solidarité internationale inc.
165, rue Moore, Sherbrooke QC J1H 1B8
Tél: 819-566-8595; *Téléc:* 819-566-8076
Courriel: info@csisher.com
URL: www.csisher.com
Marco Labrie, Directeur général

Centre canadien d'étude et de coopération internationale (CECI) / Canadian Centre for International Studies & Cooperation
3000, rue Omer-Lavallée, Montréal QC H1Y 3R8
Tél: 514-875-9911; *Téléc:* 514-875-6469
Ligne sans frais: 877-875-2324
Courriel: info@ceci.ca
URL: www.ceci.ca
Pierre Bélanger, Chair

CHF
323 Chapel St., Ottawa ON K1N 7Z2
Tel: 613-237-0180; *Fax:* 613-237-5969
Toll-Free: 866-242-4243
e-mail: info@chf-partners.ca
URL: www.chf-partners.ca
Deborah Turnbull, Chair
Tony Breuer, Secretary

Child Haven International / Accueil international pour l'enfance
RR#1, 19014 - 7th Conc., Maxville ON K0C 1T0
Tel: 613-527-2829; *Fax:* 613-527-1118
e-mail: fred@childhaven.ca
URL: www.childhaven.ca
Affiliation(s): Child Haven International - USA, India, Nepal
Fred Cappuccino, Director
Bonnie Cappuccino, Director

Children's International Summer Villages (Canada) Inc. (CISV) / Villages internationaux d'enfants
PO Box 1384, Stn. B, Ottawa ON K1P 5R4
Tel: 613-230-2949
e-mail: canada@cisv.org
URL: www.cisv.ca
Coreen Blackburn, National Secretary

Christian Blind Mission International (CBMI)
PO Box 800, 3844 Stoufville Rd., Stouffville ON L4A 7Z9
Tel: 905-640-6464; *Fax:* 905-640-4332
Toll-Free: 800-567-2264
e-mail: cbmi@cbmcanada.org
URL: www.cbmi-can.org
Ed Epp, Executive Director

CNEC - Partners International
#56, 8500 Torbram Rd., Brampton ON L6T 5C6
Tel: 905-458-1202; *Fax:* 905-458-4339
Toll-Free: 800-883-7697
e-mail: info@partnersinternational.ca
URL: www.partnersinternational.ca
Harry Doxsee, P. Eng., Chair

CODE
321 Chapel St., Ottawa ON K1N 7Z2
Tel: 613-232-3569; *Fax:* 613-232-7435
Toll-Free: 800-661-2633
e-mail: codehq@codecan.org
URL: www.codecan.org
Affiliation(s): International Book Bank; CODE Europe; CODE Inc.; CODE Foundation
Scott Walter, Executive Director

CoDevelopment Canada (CODEV)
#101, 2747 East Hastings St., Vancouver BC V5K 1Z8
Tel: 604-708-1495; *Fax:* 604-708-1497
e-mail: codev@codev.org
URL: www.codev.org
Rhonda Spence, President

Compassion Canada
PO Box 5591, London ON N6A 5G8
Tel: 519-668-0224; *Fax:* 519-685-1107
Toll-Free: 800-563-5437
e-mail: info@compassion.ca
URL: www.compassion.ca
Barry Slauenwhite, President

Conseil canadien de la coopération (CCC)
#201, 450 Rideau St., Ottawa ON K1N 5Z4
Tél: 613-789-5492; *Téléc:* 613-789-0743
Courriel: info@ccc.coop
URL: www.ccc.coop
Affiliation(s): Alliance coopérative internationale
Brigitte Gagné, Directrice générale

Conseil de coopération de l'Ontario (CCO)
#201, 435, boul St-Laurent, Ottawa ON K1K 2Z8
Tél: 613-745-8619; *Téléc:* 613-745-4649
Ligne sans frais: 866-290-1168
Courriel: info@cco.coop
URL: cco.coop
Affiliation(s): Association canadienne française de l'Ontario
Gilles Levasseur, Président

Conseil québécois de la coopération et de la mutualité (CCQ)
#204, 5955, rue Saint-Laurent, Lévis QC G6V 3P5
Tél: 418-835-3710; *Téléc:* 418-835-6322
Courriel: info@coopquebec.coop
URL: www.coopquebec.qc.ca
Affiliation(s): Conseil canadien de la coopération; Alliance coopérative internationale
Hélène Simard, Présidente

CUSO-VSO
#516, 1657 Barrington St., Halifax NS B3J 2A1
Tel: 902-892-2610; *Fax:* 902-423-9736
e-mail: atlanticconnect@cuso.ca

CUSO-VSO
233 - 10 St. NW, Calgary AB T2N 1V5
Tel: 403-283-2871; *Fax:* 403-283-2275
e-mail: westconnect@cuso.ca

CUSO-VSO
1657, boul St-Joseph est, Montréal QC H2J 1N1
Tel: 514-528-8465; *Fax:* 514-528-1750
e-mail: quebecconnect@cuso.ca, francoconnect@cuso.ca

CUSO-VSO
#200, 44 Eccles St., Ottawa ON K1R 6S4
Tel: 613-829-7445; *Fax:* 613-829-7996
Toll-Free: 888-434-2876
e-mail: questions@cuso-vso.org
URL: www.cuso-vso.org
Jean-Marc Magin, Executive Director
Carole Trépanier, Manager, Communications & Donor Relations

CUSO-VSO
#619, 2 Carlton St., Toronto ON M5B 1J3
Tel: 416-596-2266; *Fax:* 416-596-9874
e-mail: outreach@cuso.ca

CUSO-VSO
Dominion Building, #802, 207 West Hastings St., Vancouver BC V6B 1H7
Tel: 604-683-2099; *Fax:* 604-683-8536
e-mail: cuso.bc@cuso.ca

Forum for International Trade Training (FITT) / Forum pour la formation en commerce international
#300, 116 Lisgar St., Ottawa ON K2P 0C2
Tel: 613-230-3553; *Fax:* 613-230-6808
Toll-Free: 800-561-3488
e-mail: info@fitt.ca
URL: www.fitt.ca
Affiliation(s): Founding Partners: Canadian Manufacturers & Exporters Association; Canadian Chamber of Commerce; Rounding Partners: Canadian Association of Importers & Exporters; Canadian Professional Logistics Institute; World Trade Centres of Canada; Industry Canada; DFAIT; HRDC; Canadian Professional Sales Association; Canadian Federation of Labour
Caroline Tompkins, CAE, President

Group of 78 / Groupe des 78
#206, 145 Spruce St., Ottawa ON K1R 6P1
Tel: 613-230-0860; *Fax:* 613-563-0017
e-mail: group78@web.net
URL: www.group78.org
Peggy Mason, Chair

HOPE International Development Agency
214 - 6 St., New Westminster BC V3L 3A2
Tel: 604-525-5481; *Fax:* 604-525-3471
Toll-Free: 866-525-4673
e-mail: hope@hope-international.com
URL: www.hope-international.com
David S. McKenzie, Executive Director
Aklilu Mulat, COO
John King, Director of Development

Horizons of Friendship (HOF)
PO Box 402, Stn. Main, 50 Covert St., Cobourg ON K9A 4L1
Tel: 905-372-5483; *Fax:* 905-372-7095
Toll-Free: 888-729-9928
e-mail: info@horizons.ca
URL: www.horizons.ca
Affiliation(s): Americas Policy Group
Patricia Rebolledo, Executive Director

Inter Pares / Among Equals
221 Laurier Ave. East, Ottawa ON K1N 6P1
Tel: 613-563-4801; *Fax:* 613-594-4704
Toll-Free: 866-563-4801
e-mail: info@interpares.ca
URL: www.interpares.ca
Molly Kane, Executive Director

International Relief Agency Inc. (IRA)
#84, 95 Wood St., Toronto ON M4Y 2Z3
Tel: 416-928-0901
e-mail: ira@ica.net
Affiliation(s): Best of 7 Continents Inc.; International Hippocrates Foundation; Council of Nations
Adam A. Budzanowski, Director General
Olivia Aquino, Chair
Eileen Brown, Office Manager

Mahatma Gandhi Canadian Foundation for World Peace
PO Box 60002, RPO University of Alberta, Edmonton AB T6G 2S4
Tel: 780-492-5504; *Fax:* 780-492-0113
e-mail: yhong@ualberta.ca
URL: www.gandhi.ca
Prem Kalia, Chair

Manitoba Council for International Cooperation (MCIC) / Conseil du Manitoba pour la coopération internationale
#302, 280 Smith St., Winnipeg MB R3C 1K2
Tel: 204-987-6420; *Fax:* 204-956-0031
e-mail: info@mcic.ca; mcic@web.ca
URL: www.mcic.ca

The Marquis Project, Inc.
912 Rosser Ave., Brandon MB R7A 0L4
Tel: 204-727-5675; *Fax:* 204-727-5683
e-mail: marquisp@mts.net
URL: www.marquisproject.com
Affiliation(s): Canadian Council for International Cooperation; Manitoba Council for International Cooperation; Partnership Africa-Canada; Canadian Peace Alliance; Manitoba Eco-Network
Lynn Slobogian, Executive Director

Ontario Council for International Cooperation (OCIC) / Conseil de l'Ontario pour la coopération internationale
#405, 344 Bloor St. West, Toronto ON M6S 5A2
Tel: 416-972-6303; *Fax:* 416-972-6996
e-mail: info@ocic.on.ca
URL: www.ocic.on.ca

Operation Eyesight Universal
4 Parkdale Cres. NW, Calgary AB T2N 3T8
Tel: 403-283-6323*Tel:* 1-800-585-0265 USA; *Fax:* 403-270-1899
e-mail: info@operationeyesight.ca
URL: www.operationeyesight.ca
Affiliation(s): International Agency for the Prevention of Blindness; L.V. Prasad Eye Institute; Vision 2020
Pat Ferguson, President & CEO

Operation Eyesight Universal
#2, 252 East 1st St., North Vancouver BC V7L 1B3
Tel: 604-988-3484; *Fax:* 604-988-1445
e-mail: vancouver@operationeyesight.ca

Operation Eyesight Universal
#208, 2100 Ellesmere Rd., Toronto ON M1H 3B7
Tel: 416-438-7280; *Fax:* 416-438-6132
e-mail: toronto@operationeyesight.ca

Oxfam Canada
#400, 250 City Centre Ave., Ottawa ON K1R 6K7
Tel: 613-237-5236; *Fax:* 613-237-0524
Toll-Free: 800-466-9326
e-mail: info@oxfam.ca; donor_relations@oxfam.ca
URL: www.oxfam.ca
Affiliation(s): Oxfam International
Robert Fox, Executive Director
Kelly Bruton, Chair
Don MacMillan, Treasurer

Peace Brigades International (Canada) (PBI)
#206, 145 Spruce St., Ottawa ON M5V 1Z7
Tel: 613-237-6968; *Fax:* - - 0
URL: www.pbicanada.org/home
Affiliation(s): Canadian Peace Alliance
Christine Jones, National Coordinator

Physicians for Global Survival (Canada) (PGS) / Médecins pour la survie mondiale (Canada)
#208, 145 Spruce St., Ottawa ON K1R 6P1
Tel: 613-233-1982; *Fax:* 613-233-9028
e-mail: pgsadmin@web.ca
URL: www.pgs.ca
Affiliation(s): International Physicians for the Prevention of Nuclear War (IPPNW)
Nancy Covington, President

Project Peacemakers
745 Westminster Ave., Winnipeg MB R3G 1A5
Tel: 204-775-8178; *Fax:* 204-784-1339
e-mail: info@projectpeacemakers.org
URL: www.projectpeacemakers.org
Affiliation(s): Canadian Centre for Arms Control & Disarmament; Manitoba Environmental Network; Project Ploughshares; Mennonite Central Committee; Peace Alliance Winnipeg

Project Ploughshares
57 Erb St. West, Waterloo ON N2L 6C2
Tel: 519-888-6541; *Fax:* 519-888-0018
e-mail: plough@ploughshares.ca
URL: www.ploughshares.ca
Affiliation(s): Canadian Council of Churches; Conrad Grebel College
John Siebert, Executive Director

Saskatchewan Council for International Co-operation (SCIC) / Conseil de la Saskatchewan pour la co-opération internationale
2138 McIntyre St., Regina SK S4P 2R7
Tel: 306-757-4669; *Fax:* 306-757-3226
e-mail: scic@web.net
URL: www.earthbeat.sk.ca

Save a Family Plan (SAFP)
PO Box 3622, London ON N6A 4L4

Tel: 519-672-1115; Fax: 519-672-6379
e-mail: safpinfo@safp.org
URL: www.safp.org
Lesley Porter, Executive Director
Lois Côté, President

Save the Children - Canada (SCC) / Aide à l'enfance - Canada
#300, 4141 Yonge St., Toronto ON M2P 2A8
Tel: 416-221-5501; Fax: 416-221-8214
Toll-Free: 800-668-5036
e-mail: sccan@savethechildren.ca
URL: www.savethechildren.ca
Affiliation(s): International Save the Children Alliance
David Morley, President/CEO

Science for Peace (SfP) / Science et paix
c/o University College, #306A, 15 King's College Circle, Toronto ON M5S 3H7
Tel: 416-978-3606; Fax: 416-978-3606
e-mail: sfp@physics.utoronto.ca
URL: www.scienceforpeace.ca
Judith Deutsch, President
Margrit Eichler, Secretary
Chandler Davis, Treasurer

United Nations Association in Canada (UNAC) / Association canadienne pour les Nations-Unies (ACNU)
#300, 309 Cooper St., Ottawa ON K2P 0G5
Tel: 613-232-5751; Fax: 613-563-2455
e-mail: info@unac.org
URL: www.unac.org
Affiliation(s): World Federation of United Nations Associations
Kathryn White, Executive Director

United Nations Association in Canada
c/o Univ. of Winnipeg Library, 515 Portage Ave., Winnipeg MB R3B 2E9
Tel: 204-586-0173; Fax: 204-783-8910
e-mail: unacwinnipeg@gmail.com
URL: www.unacwinnipeg.ca

United Nations Association in Canada
2305-867 Hamilton St., Vancouver BC V6B 6B7
Tel: 604-732-0448; Fax: 604-736-8963
e-mail: unacvancouver@gmail.com

United Nations Association in Canada
a/s #J-4350, Université du Québec à Montréal, CP 8888, Succ. Centre-Ville, Montréal QC H3C 3P8
Tél: 514-987-8743; Téléc: 514-987-0249
Courriel: acnu@uqam.ca
URL: www.acnugrandmontreal.org

United Nations Association in Canada
C/O Institut Québécois des Hautes Études Internationales (IQHEI), CP Pavillon Charles-de-Koninck, local 5458, Université Laval, Québec QC G1K 7P4
Courriel: infos@acnu-quebec.org
URL: www.acnu-quebec.org

United Nations Association in Canada
PO Box 26008, 2345 Yonge St., Toronto ON M4P 3E0
Tel: 416-467-4672
e-mail: info@to.unac.org
URL: www.to.unac.org

United Nations Association in Canada
c/o Nora Curry, 950 Foulbay Rd., Victoria BC V8S 4H8
Tel: 250-360-0284
e-mail: noracurry@hotmail.com

United Nations Association in Canada
a/s UQAC, Département des sciences humaines, 555, boul de l'Université, Chicoutimi QC G7H 2B1
Tél: 418-545-5011; Téléc: 418-545-5012
Courriel: jules_dufour@uqac.uquebec.ca
URL: acnu-slsj.uqac.ca

United Nations Association in Canada
c/o C. Mensah, Grant MacEwan College, 10700 - 104 Ave., Edmonton AB T5J 4S2
Tel: 780-432-6531; Fax: 780-497-5308
e-mail: info@edmonton.unac.org
URL: www.edmonton.unac.org

United Nations Association in Canada
25 Lynndale Dr., Dundas ON L9H 3L4
Toll-Free: 866-436-8622
e-mail: info@hamilton.unac.org
URL: www.hamilton.unac.org

United Nations Association in Canada
PO Box 760, Grand Forks BC V0H 1H0
Tel: 250-442-8252; Fax: 250-442-3433
e-mail: tdrop@web.ca

United Nations Association in Canada
#300, 309 Cooper St., Ottawa ON K2P 0G5
Tel: 613-232-5751; Fax: 613-563-2455
e-mail: info@ncrb.unac.org
URL: www.ncrb.unac.org

United Nations Association in Canada
221 Charles St., Belleville ON K8N 3M3
Tel: 613-966-3928; Fax: 613-966-3928
e-mail: globalperspectives@cogeco.ca

United Nations Association in Canada
50 Carlisle Dr., Paradise NL A1L 1E7
e-mail: lesleyherridge@esdnl.ca

United Nations Association in Canada
PO Box 6593, Stn. D, Calgary AB T2Z 2M3
e-mail: unac.calgary@gmail.com
URL: www.calgary.unac.org

World Federalist Movement - Canada (WFMC)
#207, 145 Spruce St., Ottawa ON K1R 6P1
Tel: 613-232-0647; Fax: 613-563-0017
e-mail: wfcnat@web.ca
URL: www.worldfederalistscanada.org
Affiliation(s): World Federalist Movement
Warren Allmand, PC, OC, QC, President
Fergus Watt, Executive Director
Simon Rosenblum, Chair

World University Service of Canada (WUSC) / Entraide universitaire mondiale du Canada (EUMC)
1404 Scott St., Ottawa ON K1Y 2N2
Tel: 613-798-7477; Fax: 613-798-0990
Toll-Free: 800-267-8699
e-mail: wusc@wusc.ca
URL: www.wusc.ca
Affiliation(s): Canadian Council for International Cooperation
Paul Davidson, Executive Director
Ravi Gupta, Associate Executive Director

World Vision Canada (WVC) / Vision Mondiale
1 World Dr., Mississauga ON L5T 2Y4
Tel: 905-565-6100; Fax: 905-696-2162
Toll-Free: 866-595-5550
e-mail: info@worldvision.ca
URL: www.worldvision.ca
Affiliation(s): Evangelical Fellowship of Canada
Dave Toycen, President & CEO

Labour Relations

ADR Institute of Canada
PO Box 22015, Stn. Wildwood, Saskatoon SK S4H 5P1
Tel: 306-262-0261; Fax: 306-477-0761
Toll-Free: 866-596-7275
e-mail: adrsask@yahoo.ca
URL: www.adrsaskatchewan.ca

ADR Institute of Canada (ADRIC) / Institut d'arbitrage et de médiation du Canada
#405, 234 Eglinton Ave. East, Toronto ON M4P 1K5
Tel: 416-487-4733; Fax: 416-487-4429
Toll-Free: 877-475-4353
e-mail: admin@adrcanada.ca
URL: www.adrcanada.ca
Mary Anne Harnick, Executive Director

ADR Institute of Canada (AAMS)
Lethbridge Bldg., #605, 10707 - 100th Ave., Edmonton AB T5J 3M1
Tel: 780-433-4881; Fax: 780-433-9024
Toll-Free: 800-232-7214
e-mail: aams@aams.ab.ca
URL: www.aams.ab.ca

ADR Institute of Canada
PO Box 123, Halifax NS B3J 2M4
Tel: 902-435-3084; Fax: 902-435-3084
e-mail: admin@adratlantic.ca
URL: www.adratlantic.ca

ADR Institute of Canada
#203, 1530 - 6th St., Tsawwassen BC V4L 2A8
Tel: 604-736-6614; Fax: 604-736-6611
Toll-Free: 877-332-2264
e-mail: info@bcami.com
URL: www.bcami.com

ADR Institute of Canada
#405, 234 Eglinton Ave. East, Toronto ON M4P 1K5
Tel: 416-487-4447; Fax: 416-487-4429
e-mail: admin@adrontario.ca
URL: www.adrontario.ca

ADR Institute of Canada
PO Box 436, Stn. Corydon, Winnipeg MB R3M 3V3
Tel: 204-783-0529; Fax: 204-897-7191
e-mail: info@amim.mb.ca
URL: www.amim.mb.ca

Association canadienne des relations industrielles (ACRI) / Canadian Industrial Relations Association
Département des relations industrielles, Université Laval, Pavillon J.-A.-deSève, Sainte-Foy QC G1K 7P4
Tél: 418-656-2468; Téléc: 418-656-3175
Courriel: acri-cira@rlt.ulaval.ca
URL: www.cira-acri.ca
Affiliation(s): International Industrial Relations Association; Industrial Relations Research Association; La Fédération canadienne des sciences sociales
Guy Bellemare, Président
Jean-Noël Grenier, Sec.-trés.

Association of Workers' Compensation Boards of Canada (AWCBC) / Association des commissions des accidents du travail du Canada
6551B Mississauga Rd., Mississauga ON L5N 1A6
Tel: 905-542-3633; Fax: 905-542-0039
e-mail: contact@awcbc.org
URL: www.awcbc.org
Brenda Croucher, Executive Director

Canadian Association of Administrators of Labour Legislation (CAALL) / Association canadienne des administrateurs de la législation ouvrière (ACALO)
CAALL Secretariat, Phase II, Place du Portage, 165, rue Hôtel-de-Ville, 8e étage, Gatineau QC K1A 0J2
Tel: 819-953-0969; Fax: 819-953-9779
e-mail: CAALL-secretariat@hrsdc-rhdsc.gc.ca
URL: www.caall-acalo.org/home_e.shtml
Margaret MacDonald, President
Debra Young, Secretary
Sandy Jones, Acting Manager, Intergovernmental Relations & Social Dialogue
Nina Chretien, Officer, Research & Project, Intergovernmental Relations & Social Dialogue

Canadian Association of Labour Media (CALM) / Association canadienne de la presse syndicale (ACPS)
76 Westmount Ave., Toronto ON M6H 3K1
Tel: 416-656-2256; Fax: 416-656-7649
Toll-Free: 888-290-2256
e-mail: editor@calm.ca
URL: www.calm.ca
Affiliation(s): Canadian Labour Congress
Pat Van Horne, President
Mikael Swayze, Secretary-Treasurer
Rosemarie Bahr, CALM Editor

Canadian Committee on Labour History (CCLH) / Comité canadien sur l'histoire du travail
c/o Canadian Committee on Labour History, Athabasca University, #1200, 10011 - 109 St., Edmonton AB T5J 3S8
e-mail: cclh@athabascau.ca
URL: www.cclh.ca
Affiliation(s): International Association of Labour History Institutions; Canadian Historical Association; Conference of Historical Journals; Council of Editors of Learned Journals
G.S. Kealey, Treasurer

Canadian Injured Workers Alliance (CIWA) / L'Alliance canadienne des victimes d'accidents et de maladies du travail (ACVAMT)
PO Box 10098, 1201 Jasper Dr., Thunder Bay ON P7B 6T6
Tel: 807-345-3429; Fax: 807-344-8683
Toll-Free: 877-787-7010
e-mail: ciwa@vianet.ca
URL: www.ciwa.ca
Phil Brake, National Coordinator

Cape Breton Injured Workers Association (CBIWA)
714 Alexandra St., Sydney NS B1S 2H4
Tel: 902-539-4650; Fax: 902-539-4171
e-mail: cbiaw@ns.aliantzinc.ca
URL: www.cbiwa.com

Centre canadien d'arbitrage commercial (CCAC) / Canadian Commercial Arbitration Centre (CCAC)
#06, 215, rue Caron, Québec QC G1K 5V6

Tél: 418-649-1374; *Téléc:* 418-649-0845
Ligne sans frais: 877-909-3794
Courriel: info@ccac-adr.org
URL: www.ccac-adr.org
Nabil N. Antaki, Président et fondateur

Construction Labour Relations - An Alberta Association (CLRA)
#207, 2725 - 12 St. NE, Calgary AB T2E 7J2
Tel: 403-250-7390; *Fax:* 403-250-5516
Toll-Free: 800-308-9466
URL: www.clra.org
R. Neil Tidsbury, President

Construction Labour Relations Association of British Columbia
PO Box 820, 97 - 6 St., New Westminster BC V3L 4Z8
Tel: 604-524-4911; *Fax:* 604-524-3925
e-mail: wendym@clra-bc.com
URL: www.clra-bc.com
Clyde Scollan, President
Wendy Mazur, Office Manager

Construction Labour Relations Association of Newfoundland & Labrador Inc. (CLRA)
Ultramar Bldg., Main Floor, PO Box 8144, Stn. A, 39 Pippy Pl., St. John's NL A1B 3M9
Tel: 709-753-5770; *Fax:* 709-753-5771
e-mail: nchaplin@clra.nf.net
Neil Chaplin, President

Institut de médiation et d'arbitrage du Québec (IMAQ)
CP 874, Succ. B, Montréal QC H3B 3k5
Tél: 514-282-3327; *Téléc:* 514-282-2214
Courriel: info@imaq.org
URL: www.imaq.org
Serge Pisapia, Président
Thierry Bériault, Vice-président

Inter-American Commercial Arbitration Commission (IACAC)
OAS Administrative Bldg., Rm. 211, 19th & Constitution Ave. NW, Washington DC 20006 USA
Tel: 202-458-3249; *Fax:* 202-458-3293
e-mail: sice@sice.oas.org
Julio Gonzales Soria, President
Guillermo Fernandez de Soto, Director General

Inter-American Commercial Arbitration Commission
Canadian Arbitration Centre & Amicable Composition Centre, Inc., PO Box 450, Stn. A, Faculty of Law, Civil Law Section, Univ. of Ottawa, Ottawa ON K1N 6N5
Tel: 613-232-1476; *Fax:* 613-564-9800

Provincial Building & Construction Trades Council of Ontario
35 International Blvd., Toronto ON M9W 6H3
Tel: 416-679-8887; *Fax:* 416-679-8882
e-mail: info@ontariobuildingtrades.com
URL: www.ontariobuildingtrades.com
Affiliation(s): International Foundation of Employee Benefit Plans - Building Trades Department
Richard Baxter, President
Patrick J. Dillon, Business Manager & Sec.-Treas.

Pulp & Paper Employee Relations Forum
6035 - 237 A Place, Langley BC V2Z 1A7
Tel: 604-532-0642; *Fax:* 604-532-0639
e-mail: smaclean@paperforum.com
URL: paperforum.com
D. Scott MacLean, Executive Director

Union of Injured Workers of Ontario, Inc.
2888 Dufferin St., Toronto ON M6B 3S6
Tel: 416-785-8787; *Fax:* 416-785-6390
e-mail: uiw@web.net
Affiliation(s): Ontario Network of Injured Workers Groups
Philip Biggin, Executive Director

Western Employers Labour Relations Association
#203, 27126 Fraser Hwy., Langley BC V4W 3P6
Tel: 604-857-5540; *Fax:* 604-857-5547
e-mail: westernemployers@welra.com
URL: www.welra.com
Jim Galbraith, Senior Consultant

World at Work
PO Box 4520, Stn. A, Toronto ON M5W 4M4
Toll-Free: 877-951-9191
e-mail: customerrelations@worldatwork.com
URL: www.worldatwork.org
Anne Ruddy, Executive Director

Labour Unions

Agriculture Union
#1000, 233 Gilmour St., Ottawa ON K2P 0P2
Tel: 613-560-4306; *Fax:* 613-235-0517
URL: www.agrunion.com
Bob Kingston, National President

Air Canada Pilots Association (ACPA) / L'Association des pilotes d'Air Canada
#205, 6299 Airport Rd., Mississauga ON L4V 1N3
Tel: 905-678-9008; *Fax:* 905-678-9016
Toll-Free: 800-634-0944
e-mail: info@acpa.ca
URL: acpa.ca
Affiliation(s): Association of Star Alliance Pilots
Andy Wilson, President
Ron Pellatt, Secretary-Treasurer
Paul Strachan, Chair, Master Executive Council

Air Line Pilots Association, International - Canada (ALPA)
#1301, 155 Queen St., Ottawa ON K1P 6L1
Tel: 613-569-5668; *Fax:* 613-569-5681
URL: www.alpa.org
Social Media:
www.facebook.com/pages/We-Are-ALPA/200676905671
Affiliation(s): International Federation of Air Line Pilots' Associations; Canadian Labour Congress
John Prater, President
W. Randolph Helling, Sec.-Treas.

Alberta Federation of Labour (AFL) / Fédération du travail de l'Alberta
10802 - 172 St., Edmonton AB T5S 2T3
Tel: 780-483-3021; *Fax:* 780-484-5928
Toll-Free: 800-661-3995
e-mail: afl@afl.org
URL: www.afl.org
Gil McGowan, President
Nancy Furlong, Secretary-Treasurer

Alberta Union of Provincial Employees / Syndicat de la fonction publique de l'Alberta
10451 - 170 St., Edmonton AB T5P 4S7
Tel: 780-930-3300; *Fax:* 780-930-3392
Toll-Free: 800-232-7284
URL: www.aupe.org
Carl Soderstrom, Director, Labour Relations
Ron Hodgins, Executive Director

Alliance des professeures et professeurs de Montréal (APPM)
8225, boul Saint-Laurent, Montréal QC H2P 2M1
Tél: 514-384-5756; *Téléc:* 514-383-4880
Courriel: presidence@alliancedesprofs.qc.ca
URL: www.alliancedesprofs.qc.ca
Salvadora Garcia, Directrice générale

Alliance du personnel professionnel et technique de la santé et des services sociaux (APTS)
#1050, 1111 rue Saint-Charles Ouest, Longueuil QC J4K 5G4
Tél: 450-670-2411; *Téléc:* 450-679-0107
Ligne sans frais: 866-521-2411
Courriel: info@aptsq.com
URL: www.aptsq.com
Dominique Verreault, Présidente
Thérèse Sainte-Marie, Directrice administrative

Alliance of Canadian Cinema, Television & Radio Artists (ACTRA) / Alliance des artistes canadiens du cinéma, de la télévision et de la radio
#300, 625 Church St., Toronto ON M4Y 2G1
Tel: 416-489-1311; *Fax:* 416-489-8076
Toll-Free: 800-387-3516
e-mail: national@actra.ca
URL: www.actra.ca
Social Media: twitter.com/ACTRAnat
Affiliation(s): Canadian Labour Congress
Raymond Guardia, Regional Executive Director
Ferne Downey, National President
Anna Falsetta, National Director, Finance & Administration

Amalgamated Transit Union (AFL-CIO/CLC) / Syndicat uni du transport (FAT-COI/CTC)
5025 Wisconsin Ave. NW, Washington DC 20016 USA
Tel: 202-537-1645; *Fax:* 202-244-7824
URL: www.atu.org
Oscar Owens, Sec.-Treas.
Warren S. George, President

Amalgamated Transit Union (AFL-CIO/CLC)
#210, 61 International Blvd., Rexdale ON M9W 6K4
Tel: 416-679-8846; *Fax:* 416-679-9195
e-mail: director@atucanada.ca
URL: www.atucanada.ca

American Federation of Musicians of the United States & Canada (AFL-CIO/CLC) (AFM) / Fédération des musiciens des États-Unis et du Canada (FAT-COI/CTC)
#600, 1501 Broadway, New York NY 10036 United States
Tel: 212-869-1330; *Fax:* 212-764-6134
URL: www.afm.org
Thomas F. Lee, President

American Federation of Musicians of the United States & Canada (AFL-CIO/CLC)
#1010, 75 The Donway West, Toronto ON M3C 2E9
Tel: 416-391-5161; *Fax:* 416-391-5165
Toll-Free: 800-463-6333
e-mail: afmcan@afm.org
URL: www.afm.org

Association canadienne des métiers de la truelle, section locale 100 (CTC) / Trowel Trades Canadian Association, Local 100 (CLC)
a/s FTQ-Construction, #2900, 565, rue Crémazie est, Montréal QC H2M 2V6
Tél: 514-381-7300; *Téléc:* 514-381-5173
Ligne sans frais: 877-666-4060
URL: www.ftqconstruction.org
Yves Mercure, Président

Association nationale des peintres et métiers connexes, section locale 99 (CTC) (ANPMC) / National Association of Painters & Allied Trades, Local 99 (CLC)
#200, 5275, rue Jean-Talon est, Saint-Léonard QC H1S 1L2
Tél: 514-593-5413; *Téléc:* 514-727-8331
Ligne sans frais: 877-593-5413
Courriel: info@local99.org
URL: local99.org/index.asp
Affiliation(s): Fédération des travailleuses et travailleurs du Québec - Construction
Georges Lannéval, Directeur général

Association of Allied Health Professionals: Newfoundland & Labrador (Ind.) (AAHP) / Association des professionnels unis de la santé: Terre-Neuve et Labrador (ind.)
6 Mount Carson Ave., Mount Pearl NL A1N 3W9
Tel: 709-722-3353; *Fax:* 709-722-0987
Toll-Free: 800-728-2247
e-mail: info@aahp.nf.ca
URL: www.aahp.nf.ca
Patti O'Keefe, President

Association of Canadian Film Craftspeople
Local 2020 Communications, Energy & Paperworkers Union of Canada, #108, 3993 Henning Dr., Burnaby BC V5C 6P7
Tel: 604-299-2232; *Fax:* 604-299-2243
e-mail: info@acfcwest.com
URL: www.acfcwest.com
Wendy Subity, President
Richard Chilton, Ssecretary/Treasurer
Greg Chambers, Business Manager

Association of Canadian Financial Officers (ACFO) / Association canadienne des agents financiers
#400, 2725 Queensview Dr., Ottawa ON K2B 0A1
Tel: 613-728-0695; *Fax:* 613-761-9568
Toll-Free: 877-728-0695
e-mail: general@acfo-acaf.com
URL: www.acfo-acaf.com
Milt Isaacs, CMA, President & Chair
Robert Loiselle, CGA, Executive Vice-President
Raoul Andersen, MBA, Vice-President
Tony Bourque, CGA, Vice-President
Karen Hall, CGA, Vice-President
Nicole Bishop-Tempke, CGA, Vice-President
John Leduc, CGA, MBA, Vice-President
Daniel J. Larose, Executive Director

Association of New Brunswick Professional Educators (ANBPE) / Association des éducateurs professionnels du Nouveau-Brunswick
c/o Wayne Milner, Counselling Services, NBCC Moncton, #1101A, 1234 Mountain Rd., Moncton NB E1C 8H9
Wayne Milner, BA, B.Ed, M.Ed., President & Director

Association professionnelle des ingénieurs du gouvernement du Québec (ind.) (APIGQ) /

Association of Professional Engineers of the Government of Québec (Ind.)
Complexe Iberville, #600, 2954, boul Laurier, Sainte-Foy QC G1V 4T2
Tél: 418-683-3633; *Téléc:* 418-683-6878
Courriel: lepont@apigq.qc.ca
URL: www.apigq.qc.ca
Michel Gagnon, ing., Président

Association professionnelle des inhalothérapeutes du Québec (ind.) / Professional Association of Inhalation Therapists of Québec (Ind.)
#201, 4101, rue Molson, Montréal QC H1Y 3L1
Tél: 514-251-8050; *Téléc:* 514-259-8084
Ligne sans frais: 800-361-3498
Courriel: accueil@apiq.ca
URL: www.apiq.ca

Association professionnelle des technologistes médicaux du Québec (ind.) / Québec Professional Association of Medical Technologists (Ind.)
1595, rue St-Hubert, 3e étage, Montréal QC H2L 3Z2
Tél: 514-524-3734; *Téléc:* 514-524-7863
Ligne sans frais: 800-361-4306
Courriel: info@aptmq.qc.ca
Francine Genest, Présidente

Atlantic Communication & Technical Workers' Union (Ind.) (AC&TWU) / Syndicat des travailleurs en communication et des techniciens de l'Atlantique (ind.)
#7, 50 Akerley Blvd., Dartmouth NS B3B 1R8
Tel: 902-453-2058; *Fax:* 902-422-4647
Toll-Free: 800-565-2289
Bruce W. Lambert, Business Manager & Financial Secret

Atlantic Federation of Musicians (AFM)
221 Herring Cove Rd., Halifax NS B3P 1L3
Tel: 902-479-3200; *Fax:* 902-479-1312
Toll-Free: 866-240-4809
e-mail: afm571@eastlink.ca
URL: www.afm571.ca
Affiliation(s): American Federation of Musicians of the United States & Canada
Kenneth R. MacKay, President

Bakery, Confectionery, Tobacco Workers & Grain Millers International Union (AFL-CIO/CLC) (BCTGM)
#9, 380 Adelaide St. North, London ON N6B 3P6
Tel: 519-432-2024; *Fax:* 519-432-2153
e-mail: bctgm154@execulink.com
URL: www.bctgm.org
David D. Durkee, International Sec.-Treas./Director
Frank Hurt, International President

Bakery, Confectionery, Tobacco Workers & Grain Millers International Union (AFL-CIO/CLC)
3329, rue Ontario est, Montréal QC H1W 1P8
Tel: 514-527-9371; *Fax:* 514-527-8105

Bricklayers, Masons Independent Union of Canada (CLC) / Syndicat indépendant des briqueteurs et des maçons du Canada (CTC)
#200, 1263 Wilson Ave., Toronto ON M3M 3G3
Tel: 416-241-1183; *Fax:* 416-241-9845
Giuseppe Bellotto, President
John Meiorin, Secretary

British Columbia Carpenters Union (BCPCC)
#305, 2806 Kingsway, Vancouver BC V5R 5T5
Tel: 604-437-0471; *Fax:* 604-437-1110
e-mail: info@bccarpentersunion.com
URL: www.bccarpentersunion.com
Jan Noster, President
Pat Haggarty, Sec.-Treas.

British Columbia Federation of Labour (BCFL) / Fédération du travail de la Colombie-Britannique
#200, 5118 Joyce St., Vancouver BC V5R 4H1
Tel: 604-430-1421; *Fax:* 604-430-5917
e-mail: bcfed@bcfed.com
URL: www.bcfed.com
Affiliation(s): Canadian Centre for Policy Alternatives; Canadian Association of Labour Media
Jim Sinclair, CAW/UFAWU, President
Angela Schira, Sec.-Treas.

British Columbia Ferry & Marine Workers' Union (CLC) (BCFMWU) / Syndicat des travailleurs marins et de bacs de la Colombie-Britannique (CTC)
1511 Stewart Ave., Nanaimo BC V9S 4E3
Tel: 250-716-3454; *Fax:* 250-716-3455
Toll-Free: 800-663-7009
e-mail: mailroom@bcfmwu.com
URL: www.bcfmwu.com
Affiliation(s): BC Federation of Labour; National Union of Public & General Employees (NUPGE)
Kelly Carson, Sec.-Treas.
Richard Goode, President

British Columbia Government & Service Employees' Union (BCGEU) / Syndicat des fonctionnaires provinciaux et de service de la Colombie-Britannique
4911 Canada Way, Burnaby BC V5G 3W3
Tel: 604-291-9611; *Fax:* 604-291-6030
Toll-Free: 800-663-1674
URL: www.bcgeu.ca
Affiliation(s): BC Federation of Labour; Canadian Labour Congress
Judi Filion, Treasurer
Darryl Walker, President

Brotherhood of Maintenance of Way Employees (AFL-CIO/CLC)
#1, 2775 Lancaster Rd., Ottawa ON K1B 4V8
Tel: 613-731-7356; *Fax:* 613-733-3158
e-mail: bmwe@interlog.com

Canada Employment & Immigration Union (CEIU) / Syndicat de l'emploi et de l'immigration du Canada (SEIC)
#1004, 233 Gilmour St., Ottawa ON K2P 0P2
Tel: 613-236-9634; *Fax:* 613-236-7871
e-mail: courchs@ceiu-seic.ca
URL: www.ceiu-seic.ca
Jeannette Meunier-McKay, National President
Steve McCuaig, National Executive Vice-President

Canadian Actors' Equity Association (CLC) (CAEA)
#505, 321 Water St., Vancouver BC V6B 1B8
Tel: 604-682-6173; *Fax:* 604-682-6174
URL: www.caea.com
Ian Ross McDonald, Business Representative

Canadian Actors' Equity Association (CLC) (CAEA)
44 Victoria St., 12th Fl., Toronto ON M5C 3C4
Tel: 416-867-9165; *Fax:* 416-867-9246
e-mail: info@caea.com; membership@caea.com; reception@caea.com
URL: www.caea.com
Arden R. Ryshpan, Executive Director
Allan Teichman, President
Lynn McQueen, Director, Communications

Canadian Association of Professional Employees (CAPE)
World Exchange Plaza, 100 Queen St., 4th Fl., Ottawa ON K1P 1J9
Tel: 613-236-9181; *Fax:* 613-236-6017
Toll-Free: 800-265-9181
e-mail: general@acep-cape.ca
URL: www.acep-cape.ca
Affiliation(s): International Labour Organization
Claude Poirier, President

Canadian Federal Pilots Association (CFPA) / Association des pilotes fédéraux du Canada (APFC)
#509, 350 Sparks St., Ottawa ON K1R 7S8
Tel: 613-230-5476; *Fax:* 613-230-2668
e-mail: cfpa@cfpa-apfc.ca
URL: www.cfpa-apfc.ca
Greg Holbrook, Chair
Denis Brunelle, Vice-Chair
Greg McConnell, Sec.-Treas.

Canadian Federation of Nurses Unions (CFNU) / La Fédération canadienne des syndicats d'infirmières/infirmiers
2841 Riverside Dr., Ottawa ON K1V 8X7
Tel: 613-526-4661; *Fax:* 613-526-1023
Toll-Free: 800-321-9821
e-mail: cfnu@nursesunions.ca
URL: www.nursesunions.ca
Linda Silas, President

Canadian Football League Players' Association (CFLPA) / Association des joueurs de la ligue de football canadienne
#207, 603 Argus Rd., Oakville ON L6J 6G6
Tel: 905-844-7852; *Fax:* 905-844-5127
Toll-Free: 800-616-6865
e-mail: admin@cflpa.com
URL: www.cflpa.com
Stu Laird, President
Mike O'Shea, 1st Vice-President
Jay McNeil, 2nd Vice-President
Sean Fleming, Member-at-Large
Edward Molstad, Legal Counsel
Fred James, Benefits Chairman
Deanne Mitchell, Executive Assistant

Canadian Iron, Steel & Industrial Workers' Union (Ind.)
17 East Broadway, Vancouver BC V5T 1V4
Tel: 604-681-6002; *Fax:* 604-873-9112

Canadian Labour Congress
#201, 5118 Joyce St., Vancouver BC V5R 4H1
Tel: 604-430-6766; *Fax:* 604-430-6762
e-mail: pacific@clc-ctc.ca
URL: www.canadianlabour.ca/pacific-region

Canadian Labour Congress
1888 Angus St., Regina SK S4T 1Z4
Tel: 306-525-6137; *Fax:* 306-525-9514
e-mail: prairie@clc-ctc.ca
URL: www.canadianlabour.ca/prairie-region

Canadian Labour Congress
#305, 15 Gervais Dr., Toronto ON M3C 1Y8
Tel: 416-441-3710; *Fax:* 416-441-4073
e-mail: ontario@clc-ctc.ca
URL: www.canadianlabour.ca/ontario-region

Canadian Labour Congress
2282 Mountain Rd., Moncton NB E1G 1B4
Tel: 506-858-9350; *Fax:* 506-858-9571
e-mail: atlantic@clc-ctc.ca

Canadian Labour Congress (CLC) / Congrès du travail du Canada (CTC)
2841 Riverside Dr., Ottawa ON K1V 8X7
Tel: 613-521-3400; *Fax:* 613-521-4655
e-mail: communications@clc-ctc.ca
URL: www.clc-ctc.ca
Barbara Byers, Executive Vice President
Kenneth V. Georgetti, President
Marie Clarke Walker, Executive Vice President
Karl Flecker, Director, Anti-Racism & Human Rights
Jean Wolff, Director, Communications
Hassan Yussuff, Sec.-Treas.
Penni Richmond, Director, Womens' & Human Rights
Stephen Benedict, Director, International
Cindy Wiggins, Director, Education & Labour College
Andrew Jackson, Director, Social & Economic Policy

Canadian Marine Officers' Union (AFL-CIO/CLC) / Syndicat canadien des officiers de la marine marchande (FAT-COI/CTC)
17 Front St. North, Thorold ON L2V 1X3
Tel: 905-227-6226; *Fax:* 905-227-9164
e-mail: cmou@cogeco.net
URL: www.cmou.ca
Richard Vezina, President

Canadian Marine Pilots' Association (CLC) / Association des pilotes de la marine canadienne (CTC)
1150 Morrison Dr., Ottawa ON K2H 8S9
Tel: 613-829-9531; *Fax:* 613-596-6079
Larry Dempsey, Sec.-Treas.
Michel Pouliot, President

Canadian Media Guild (CMG) / La Guilde canadienne des médias
#810, 310 Front St. West, Toronto ON M5V 3B5
Tel: 416-591-5333; *Fax:* 416-591-7278
Toll-Free: 800-465-4149
e-mail: info@cmg.ca
URL: www.cmg.ca
Affiliation(s): CWA/SCA Canada
Lise Lareau, President
Scott Edmonds, Vice-President
Rick Basarke, Secretary-Treasurer
Karen Wirsig, Coordinator, Communications

Canadian Merchant Service Guild (CLC) (CMSG) / Guilde de la marine marchande du Canada (CTC) (GMMC)
#150, 1150 Morrison Dr., Ottawa ON K2H 8S9
Tel: 613-829-9531; *Fax:* 613-596-6079
e-mail: cmsgott@on.aibn.com
URL: www.cmsg-gmmc.ca
Lawrence Dempsey, National President
Mark Boucher, National Sec.-Treas.

Canadian Merchant Service Guild (CLC)
#10B, 3107, Ave des Hôtels, Québec QC G1W 4W5
Tel: 418-650-6471; *Fax:* 418-650-1484
e-mail: quebec@cmsg-gmmc.ca
URL: www.cmsg-gmmc.ca

Canadian Merchant Service Guild (CLC)
#310, 218 Blue Mountain St., Coquitlam BC V3K 4H2
Tel: 602-939-8990; *Fax:* 602-939-8950
e-mail: cmsgwb@cmsg.org
URL: www.cmsg-gmmc.ca

Canadian National Federation of Independent Unions (CNFIU) / Fédération canadienne nationale des syndicats indépendants (FCNSI)
#200, 526 Winona Rd. North, Stoney Creek ON L8E 5E9
Tel: 905-735-0531; *Fax:* 905-643-8319
Toll-Free: 800-638-9438
e-mail: info@cnfiu.com
URL: www.cnfiu.com
Affiliation(s): Division of Laborers' International Union of North America
Ann Waller, President
Brenda Lowes, Sec.-Treas.

Canadian Office & Professional Employees Union (COPE)
4595 Canada Way, 2nd Fl., Burnaby BC V5G 1J9
Tel: 604-299-0378; *Fax:* 604-299-8211
Toll-Free: 800-665-6838
URL: www.cope378.ca
Affiliation(s): B.C. Federation of Labour, Canadian Labour Congress
Andy Ross, President
Lori Mayhew, Secretary-Treasurer
David Black, Vice President

Canadian Postmasters & Assistants Association (CPAA) / Association canadienne des maîtres de poste et adjoints (ACMPA)
281 Queen Mary St., Ottawa ON K1K 1X1
Tel: 613-745-2095; *Fax:* 613-745-5559
e-mail: mail@cpaa-acmpa.ca
URL: www.cpaa-acmpa.ca
Affiliation(s): Canadian Labour Congress
Leslie A. Schous, National President
Pierre Charbonneau, National Vice-President
Shirley L. Dressler, National Sec.-Treas.
Pat E. Fagan, National Vice-President

Canadian Telephone Employees' Association (Ind.) / Association canadienne des employés de téléphone (ind.)
PO Box 103, #1903, 777 Bay St., Toronto ON M5G 2C8
Tel: 416-977-2251; *Fax:* 416-977-9738
Toll-Free: 800-595-2696
Brenda Knight, President

Canadian Union of Postal Workers (CUPW) / Syndicat des travailleurs et travailleuses des postes (STTP)
377 Bank St., Ottawa ON K2P 1Y3
Tel: 613-236-7238; *Fax:* 613-563-7861
URL: www.cupw-sttp.org
Denis Lemelin, National President
George Kuehnbaum, National Sec.-Treas.

Canadian Union of Public Employees (CUPE) / Syndicat canadien de la fonction publique (SCFP)
1375 St. Laurent Blvd., Ottawa ON K1G 0Z7
Tel: 613-237-1590; *Fax:* 613-237-5508
e-mail: lleclair@cupe.ca
URL: www.cupe.ca
Affiliation(s): Canadian Labour Congress
Claude Généreux, National Sec.-Treas.
Paul Moist, National President

Canadian Union of Public Employees (CUPE)
1375 St. Laurent, Ottawa ON K1G 0Z7
Tel: 613-237-1590; *Fax:* 613-237-5508
URL: www.cupe.ca

Canadian Union of Public Employees
#500, 4940 Canada Way, Burnaby BC V5G 4T3
Tel: 604-291-1940; *Fax:* 604-291-1194
URL: www.cupe.bc.ca

Canadian Union of Public Employees
25 Belfield Rd., Etobicoke ON M9W 1E8
Tel: 416-798-3399; *Fax:* 416-674-6824
URL: acc.cupe.ca

Canadian Union of Public Employees
Starlite Bldg., #308, 7071 Bayers Rd., Halifax NS B3L 2C2
Tel: 902-455-4180; *Fax:* 902-455-5915
URL: www.novascotia.cupe.ca
Publications: CUPE Nova Scotia Bulletin

Centrale des syndicats démocratiques (CSD)
#300, 801, 4e rue, Québec QC G1J 2T7
Tél: 418-529-2956; *Téléc:* 418-529-6323
Courriel: info@csd.qc.ca
URL: www.csd.qc.ca
Affiliation(s): Fédération démocratique de la métallurgie, des mines et des produits chimiques; Fédération des syndicats du textile et du vêtement inc.

Centrale des syndicats du Québec (CSQ)
9405, rue Sherbrooke est, Montréal QC H1L 6P3
Tél: 514-356-8888; *Téléc:* 514-356-9999
Courriel: communications.montreal@csq.qc.net
URL: csq.qc.net
Affiliation(s): Internationale de l'Éducation; Confédération des éducateurs d'Amérique
Gabriel Marchand, Directeur général
Réjean Parent, Président

CEP Local 2003
#105, 2065 Dundas St. East, Mississauga ON L4X 2W1
Tel: 905-238-0877; *Fax:* 905-238-9567
Toll-Free: 800-263-0855
e-mail: cuoe@cuoe.org
URL: www.ceplocal2003.org
Affiliation(s): Canadian Labour Congress
Paul Sauve, National President
George Reid, National Vice-President
Kenneth B. Spiece, National Treasurer
Larry Lynch, National Recording Secretary

Christian Labour Association of Canada (Ind.) (CLAC) / Association chrétienne du travail du Canada (ind.)
2335 Argentia Rd., Mississauga ON L5N 5N3
Tel: 905-812-2855; *Fax:* 905-812-5556
Toll-Free: 800-268-5281
e-mail: headoffice@clac.ca
URL: www.clac.ca
Dick Heinen, Executive Director

Communications, Energy & Paperworkers Union of Canada (CEP) / Syndicat canadien des communications, de l'énergie et du papier (SCEP)
301 Laurier Ave. West, Ottawa ON K1P 6M6
Tel: 613-230-5200; *Fax:* 613-230-5801
Toll-Free: 877-230-5201
e-mail: info@cep.ca
URL: www.cep.ca
Affiliation(s): Canadian Labour Congress
Gaétan Ménard, Sec.-Treas.
Dave Coles, President

Compensation Employees' Union (Ind.) (CEU) / Syndicat des employés d'indemnisation (ind.)
#200, 8120 Granville Ave., Richmond BC V6Y 1P3
Tel: 604-278-4050; *Fax:* 604-278-5002
URL: www.ceu.bc.ca
Sandra Wright, President
Carol Velon, Secretary

Confédération des syndicats nationaux (CSN) / Confederation of National Trade Unions
1601, av De Lorimier, Montréal QC H2K 4M5
Tél: 514-598-2121; *Téléc:* 514-598-2052
Courriel: csncommunications@csn.qc.ca
URL: www.csn.qc.ca
Affiliation(s): Confédération internationale des syndicats libres
Pierre Patry, Trésorier
Claudette Carbonneau, Présidente
Lise Poulin, Secrétaire générale

Congress of Union Retirees Canada (CURC) / Association des syndicalistes retraités du Canada (ASRC)
2841 Riverside Dr., Ottawa ON K1V 8X7
Tel: 613-526-7422; *Fax:* 613-521-4655
e-mail: curc@clc-ctc.ca
URL: curc.clc-ctc.ca
Affiliation(s): Canadian Labour Congress
Pat Kerwin, President
Len Hope, First Vice-President
Doug MacPherson, Second Vice-President
Bob McGarry, Secretary
Betty Ann Bushell, Treasurer

Customs Excise Union Douanes Accise (CEUDA)
1741 Woodward Dr., Ottawa ON K2C 0P9
Tel: 613-723-8008; *Fax:* 613-723-7895
e-mail: web@ceuda.ca; magazine@ceuda.ca
URL: www.ceuda.psac.com
Affiliation(s): Canadian Professional Police Association (CPPA); Child Find Canada; Mother Against Drunk Driving (MADD Canada); Canadian Federation of Students (CFS); Canadian American Border Trade Alliance (CABTA); Canadian Labour Congress (CLC); Canadian Manufacturers and Exporters (CME); Fédération des travailleurs et travailleuses du Québec; Federation of Canadian Municipalities (FCM); Labour College of Canada; National Treasury Employees Union (NTEU), U.S.; Public Service Alliance of Canada (PSAC)
Ron Moran, National President
Michelle Tranchemontagne, Legal Counsel & Director, Office
Jonathan Choquette, Officer, Communications & Political Coordination

Employees' Association, St. Mary's of the Lake Hospital (CNFIU) / Association des employés, l'Hôpital Saint Mary's of the Lake (FCNSI)
PO Box 207, Kingston ON K7L 4V8
Tel: 613-544-5220

Fédération autonome du collégial (ind.) (FAC) / Autonomous Federation of Collegial Staff (Ind.)
#400, 1259, rue Berri, Montréal QC H2L 4C7
Tél: 514-848-9977; *Téléc:* 514-848-0166
Ligne sans frais: 800-701-1369
Courriel: fac@lafac.qc.ca
URL: www.lafac.qc.ca
Alain Dion, Président

Fédération CSN - Construction (CSN) / CNTU Federation - Construction (CNTU)
2100B, boul de Maisonneuve est, 4e étage, Montréal QC H2K 4S1
Tél: 514-598-2421; *Téléc:* 514-598-2425
Courriel: sec-montreal@csnconstruction.qc.ca
URL: www.csnconstruction.qc.ca
Alain Mailhot, Président
François Trépanier, Secrétaire général
Yves Coté, Coordonateur

Fédération de la métallurgie (CSN) / Federation of Metal Trades (CNTU)
#204, 2100, boul de Maisonneuve est, Montréal QC H2K 4S1
Tél: 514-529-4937; *Téléc:* 514-529-4935
Courriel: metallurgie@csn.qc.ca
URL: www.metallurgie.csn.qc.ca
Alain Lampron, Président
Jean-Pierre Tremblay, Secrétaire
Yvan Gamelin, Trésorier

Fédération de la santé et des services sociaux
1601, av de Lorimier, Montréal QC H2K 4M5
Tél: 514-598-2210; *Téléc:* 514-598-2223
Courriel: fsss@fsss.qc.ca
URL: www.fsss.qc.ca
Francine Lévesque, Présidente
Denyse Paradis, Secrétaire-trésorière

Fédération des employées et employés de services publics inc. (CSN) (FEESP) / Federation of Public Service Employees Inc. (CNTU)
1601, av de Lorimier, Montréal QC H2K 4M5
Tél: 514-598-2231
Courriel: feesp.courrier@csn.qc.ca
URL: www.feesp.csn.qc.ca
Affiliation(s): Confédération des syndicats nationaux
Danielle Beaulieu, Présidente

Fédération des enseignants de cégeps
9405, rue Sherbrooke est, Montréal QC H1L 6P3
Tél: 514-356-8888; *Téléc:* 514-354-8535
Courriel: fec@csq.qc.net
URL: www.fec.csq.qc.net

Fédération des intervenantes en petite enfance du Québec
9405, rue Sherbrooke est, Montréal QC H1L 6P3
Tél: 514-356-8888; *Téléc:* 514-356-9999
Ligne sans frais: 800-465-0897
Courriel: fipeq@csq.qc.net
URL: www.petitmonde.com
Sylvie Tonnelier, Présidente

Fédération des médecins résidents du Québec inc. (ind.) (FMRQ) / Québec Federation of Residents (Ind.)
#510, 630, rue Sherbrooke ouest, Montréal QC H3A 1E4

Tél: 514-282-0256; *Téléc:* 514-282-0471
Ligne sans frais: 800-465-0215
Courriel: fmrq@fmrq.qc.ca
URL: www.fmrq.qc.ca

Jean Gouin, Executive Director
Patrick Labelle, Administrative Director

Fédération des policiers et policières municipaux du Québec (ind.) (FPMQ) / Québec Federation of Policemen (Ind.)
7955, boul Louis-Hippolyte-La Fontaine, Anjou QC H1K 4E4
Tél: 514-356-3321; *Téléc:* 514-356-1158
Ligne sans frais: 800-361-0321
Courriel: info@fpmq.org
URL: www.fpmq.org

Denis Côté, Président

Fédération des professionnèles (FPCSN) / Quebec Federation of Managers & Professional Salaried Workers (CNTU)
1601, av de Lorimier, Montréal QC H2K 4M5
Tél: 514-598-2143; *Téléc:* 514-598-2491
Ligne sans frais: 888-633-2143
Courriel: fp@csn.qc.ca
URL: www.fpcsn.qc.ca

Michel Tremblay, Président
Lucie Dufour, Secrétaire générale

Fédération des professionnelles et professionnels de l'éducation du Québec (FPPE) / Québec Federation of Professional Employees in Education
9405, rue Sherbrooke est, Montréal QC H1L 6P3
Tél: 514-356-0505; *Téléc:* 514-356-1324
Courriel: infos@fppe.qc.ca
URL: www.fppe.qc.ca

Jean Falardeau, Président
Johanne Pomerleau, Vice-présidente
Patrice Lemay, Vice-président, Affaires administratives

Fédération des Syndicats de l'Enseignement (FSE)
CP 100, 320, rue Saint-Joseph est, Québec QC G1K 9E7
Tél: 418-649-8888; *Téléc:* 418-649-1914
Courriel: fse@csq.qc.net
URL: www.fse.qc.net

Jean Guy Baril, Directeur général

Fédération des syndicats de professionnelles et professionnels de la santé et des services sociaux (FPSSS) / Federation of Health & Social Services Professionals
9405, rue Sherbrooke est, Montréal QC H1L 6P3
Téléc: 514-356-9999
Courriel: fsppsss@csq.qc.net

René Beauséjour, Président

Fédération des travailleurs et travailleuses du Québec (FTQ) / Québec Federation of Labour
#12100, 565, boul Crémazie est, Montréal QC H2M 2W3
Tél: 514-383-8000; *Téléc:* 514-383-8038
Courriel: ftq@ftq.qc.ca
URL: www.ftq.qc.ca

Michel Arsenault, Président
René Roy, Secrétaire général

Fédération des travailleurs et travailleuses du Québec - Construction
#2900, 565, boul Crémazie est, Montréal QC H2M 2V6
Tél: 514-381-7300; *Téléc:* 514-381-5173
Ligne sans frais: 877-666-4060
URL: www.ftqconstruction.org

Affiliation(s): Fraternité inter-provinciale des ouvriers en électricitéFraternité provinciale des ouvriers en électricitéFraternité nationale des charpentiers-menuisiers; Union des opérateurs de machinerie lourde; Assn. des manoeuvres interprovinciaux; Assn. nationale des travailleurs en réfrigération, climatisation & protection-incendie; Assn. canadienne des métiers de la truelle; Union nationale des poseurs de systèmes intérieurs & revêtements souples; Assn. nationale des ferblantiers & couvreurs; Assn. nationale des peintres & métiers connexes; Fraternité internationale des peintres & métiers connexes
Richard Goyette, Directeur général

Fédération des travailleuses et travailleurs du papier et de la forêt (CSN) (FTPF) / Federation of Paper & Forest Workers (CNTU)
155, boul Charest est, Québec QC G1K 3G6
Tél: 418-647-5775; *Téléc:* 418-647-5884
Courriel: direction.ftpf@videotron.net
URL: www.ftpf.csn.qc.ca

Affiliation(s): Fédération internationale des syndicats des travailleurs de la chimie, de l'énergie, des mines et des industries diverses (ICEM)
Sylvain Parent, Président
Guy Normandin, Secrétaire-trésorier

Fédération du personnel de l'enseignement privé (FPEP)
9405, rue Sherbrooke est, Montréal QC H1L 6P3
Tél: 514-356-8888; *Téléc:* 514-356-1866
Courriel: fpep@csq.qc.net
URL: www.fpep.csq.qc.net

Francine Lamoureux, Présidente

Fédération du personnel de la santé et des services sociaux (CEQ)
9405, rue Sherbrooke est, Montréal QC H1L 6P3
Tel: 514-356-8888; *Fax:* 514-356-2845
URL: www.csq.qc.net/index.cfm/2,0,1676,9703,2298,0,html

Pierre Boily, Président

Fédération du personnel de soutien scolaire (CSQ) (FPSS) / Federation of Support Staff
9405, rue Sherbrooke est, 4e étage, Montréal QC H1L 6P3
Tél: 514-356-8888; *Téléc:* 514-493-3697
Courriel: webfpss@csq.qc.net
URL: www.fpss.csq.qc.net

Diane Cinq-Mars, Présidente

Fédération du personnel du loisir, de la culture et du communautaire (CEQ) (FPLCC)
9405, rue Sherbrooke est, Montréal QC H1L 6P3
Tél: 514-356-8888; *Téléc:* 514-356-9999
Courriel: fplcc@csq.qc.net
URL: www.csq.qc.net/fede/fplcc.htm

Jacques Legault, Président

Fédération du personnel professionnel des collèges (FPPC)
9405, rue Sherbrooke est, Montréal QC H1L 6P3
Tél: 514-356-8888; *Téléc:* 514-356-3377
Courriel: fppc@csq.qc.net
URL: www.fppc.csq.qc.net

Bernard Bérubé, Président

Fédération du personnel professionnel des universités et de la recherche (FPPU)
CP 500, Trois-Rivières QC G9A 5H7
Tél: 819-376-5043; *Téléc:* 819-376-5234
Courriel: fppu@uqtr.ca
URL: www.fppu.qc.ca

Bernard Gaucher, Président

Fédération indépendante des syndicats autonomes (FISA) / Independent Federation of Autonomous Unions
#201, 1778, boul Wilfrid-Hamel, Québec QC G1N 3Y8
Tél: 418-529-4571; *Téléc:* 418-529-4695
Ligne sans frais: 800-407-3472
Courriel: info@fisa.ca
URL: www.fisa.ca

Jean Gagnon, Président

Fédération nationale des communications (CSN) (FNC) / National Federation of Communication Workers (CNTU)
1601, av de Lorimier, Montréal QC H2K 4M5
Tél: 514-598-2132; *Téléc:* 514-598-2431
Courriel: fnc@fncom.org
URL: www.fncom.org

Chantale Larouche, Présidente

Fraternité interprovinciale des ouvriers en électricité (CTC) (FIPOE) / Interprovincial Brotherhood of Electrical Workers (CLC)
#11100, 565, boul Crémazie est, Montréal QC H2M 2W2
Tél: 514-385-3476; *Téléc:* 514-385-9298
Courriel: fratip@fipoe.org
URL: www.fipoe.org

Gérald Castilloux, Président
Jean Lavallée, Directeur général

Fraternité nationale des forestiers et travailleurs d'usine (CTC) / National Brotherhood of Foresters & Industrial Workers (CLC)
Locale 299, #101, 2, boul Desaulniers, Saint-Lambert QC J4P 1L2
Tél: 450-465-2218; *Téléc:* 450-465-1301
Ligne sans frais: 800-317-1818
Courriel: fnftu@qc.aira.com
URL: www.scep299.ca

Affiliation(s): Fédération des travailleurs et travailleuses de Québec
Sylvie Labelle, Adjointe au président
Yves Guérette, Président

Government Services Union (GSU) / Syndicat des services gouvernementaux
#100, 1770 Woodward Dr., Ottawa ON K2C 0P8
Tel: 613-226-5983; *Fax:* 613-226-8241
e-mail: gsu-ssg@psac.com
URL: www.gsu-ssg.ca

Mark Brunell, President

Grain Services Union (CLC) (GSU) / Syndicat des services du grain (CTC)
2334 McIntyre St., Regina SK S4P 2S2
Tel: 306-522-6686; *Fax:* 306-565-3430
Toll-Free: 866-522-6686
e-mail: gsu.regina@sasktel.net
URL: www.gsu.ca

Affiliation(s): Interntaionl Longshore and Warehouse Union
Carolyn Illerbrun, President
Hugh J. Wagner, Secretary/Manager

Health Sciences Association of Alberta (HSAA) / Association des sciences de la santé de l'Alberta (ind.)
10212 - 112 St., Edmonton AB T5K 1M4
Tel: 780-488-0168; *Fax:* 780-488-0534
Toll-Free: 800-252-7904
URL: www.hsaa.ca

Elisabeth Ballermann, President
Patricia Heffel, Director, Administrative Services
Lynette McAvoy, Director, Labour Relations

Health Sciences Association of Saskatchewan (HSAS) / Association des sciences de la santé de la Saskatchewan (ind.)
#42, 1736 Quebec Ave., Saskatoon SK S7K 1V9
Tel: 306-955-3399; *Fax:* 306-955-3396
Toll-Free: 888-565-3399
e-mail: hsasstoon@sasktel.net; hsasregina@sasktel.net
URL: www.hsa-sk.com

Bill Craik, Executive Director
Chris Driol, President
Cathy Dickson, Vice-President
Mary Spurr, Secretary
Karen Wasylenko, Treasurer

Hospital Employees' Union (HEU) / Syndicat des employés d'hôpitaux
5000 North Fraser Way, Burnaby BC V5J 5M3
Tel: 604-438-5000; *Fax:* 604-739-1510
Toll-Free: 800-663-5813
e-mail: heu@heu.org
URL: www.heu.org

Affiliation(s): Labour Councils
Ken Robinson, President
Judy Darcy, Secretary & Business Manager

International Alliance of Theatrical Stage Employees, Moving Picture Technicians, Artists & Allied Crafts of the U.S., Its Territories & Canada (IATSE)
1430 Broadway, 20th Fl., New York NY 10018 USA
Tel: 212-730-1770; *Fax:* 212-921-7699
e-mail: webmaster@iatse-intl.org
URL: www.iatse-intl.org

Matthew D. Loeb, International President
John M. Lewis, Director, Canadian Affairs

International Alliance of Theatrical Stage Employees, Moving Picture Technicians, Artists & Allied Crafts of the U.S., Its Territories & Canada (IATSE)
511 Adelaide St. W., Toronto ON M5V 1T4
Tel: 416-364-5565; *Fax:* 416-364-5987
e-mail: iatse58@iatse58.org
URL: www.iatse58.org

International Association of Bridge, Structural, Ornamental & Reinforcing Iron Workers (AFL-CIO) / Association internationale des travailleurs de ponts, de fer structural et ornemental (FAT-COI)
#400, 1750 New York Ave. NW, Washington DC 20006 USA
Tel: 202-383-4800; *Fax:* 202-638-4856
URL: www.ironworkers.org

Joseph J. Hunt, President
Fred Marr, Director, Canadian Operations

International Association of Fire Fighters (AFL-CIO/CLC) (IAFF) / Association internationale des pompiers (FAT-COI/CTC)
1750 New York Ave. NW, Washington DC 20006 USA
Tel: 202-737-8484; *Fax:* 202-737-8418
URL: www.iaff.org

Harold A. Schaitberger, General President

International Association of Fire Fighters (AFL-CIO/CLC)
#403, 350 Sparks St., Ottawa ON K1R 7S8
Tel: 613-567-8988; *Fax:* 613-567-8986
URL: www.iaff.org/canada

International Association of Machinists & Aerospace Workers (AFL-CIO/CLC) / Association internationale des machinistes et des travailleurs de l'aérospatiale (FAT-COI/CTC)
Machinists Bldg., 9000 Machinists Pl., Upper Marlboro MD 20772 USA
Tel: 301-967-4500
e-mail: websteward@goiam.org
URL: www.iamaw.org
R. Thomas Buffenbarger, President

International Association of Machinists & Aerospace Workers (AFL-CIO/CLC) (IAMAW-AIMTA) / L'Association internationale des machinistes et des travailleurs et travailleuses de l'aérospatiale
#707, 15 Gervais Dr., Toronto ON M3C 1Y8
Tel: 416-386-1789; *Fax:* 416-386-0210
e-mail: info@iamaw.ca
URL: www.iamaw.ca

International Brotherhood of Boilermakers, Iron Ship Builders, Blacksmiths, Forgers & Helpers (AFL-CIO)
#206, 17205 - 106A Ave., Edmonton AB T5S 1M7
Tel: 780-483-0823; *Fax:* 780-489-3043

International Brotherhood of Boilermakers, Iron Ship Builders, Blacksmiths, Forgers & Helpers (AFL-CIO) (IBB) / Fraternité internationale des chaudronniers, constructeurs de navires en fer, forgerons, forgeurs et aides (FAT-COI)
New Brotherhood Bldg., #570, 753 State Ave., Kansas City MO 66101 USA
Tel: 913-371-2640; *Fax:* 913-281-8101
URL: www.boilermakers.org
Newton B. Jones, International President
Joseph Maloney, International Vice President, Western Canada
Edward Power, International Vice President, Eastern Canada

International Brotherhood of Boilermakers, Iron Ship Builders, Blacksmiths, Forgers & Helpers (AFL-CIO)
#139, 1216 Sandcove Rd., Saint John NB E2M 5V8
Tel: 506-634-8203; *Fax:* 506-634-0307

International Brotherhood of Electrical Workers (AFL-CIO/CFL) (IBEW) / Fraternité internationale des ouvriers en électricité (FAT-COI/FCT)
900 Seventh St. NW, Washington DC 20001 USA
Tel: 202-833-7000; *Fax:* 202-728-7676
URL: www.ibew.org
Lindell K. Lee, International Secretary-Treasurer
Edwin d. Hill, International President

International Brotherhood of Electrical Workers (AFL-CIO/CLC) (IBEW)
#300, 1450 Meyerside Dr., Mississauga ON L5T 2N5
Tel: 905-564-5441; *Fax:* 905-564-8114
e-mail: ivpd_01@ibew.org
URL: www.ibew1st.org

International Federation of Professional & Technical Engineers (AFL-CIO/CLC) (IFPTE) / Fédération internationale des ingénieurs et techniciens (FAT-COI/CTC)
#701, 501 3rd St. NW, Washington DC 20001 USA
Tel: 202-239-4880
URL: www.ifpte.org
Affiliation(s): AFL-CIO; Canadian Labour Congress; IMF; UNI; PSI
Gregory J. Junemann, President

International Federation of Professional & Technical Engineers (AFL-CIO/CLC)
#300, 425 Bloor St. East, Toronto ON M4W 3R5
Tel: 416-979-2709; *Fax:* 416-979-5794
Toll-Free: 866-288-1788
e-mail: society@society.on.ca
URL: www.thesociety.ca

International Longshore & Warehouse Union (CLC) / Syndicat international des débardeurs et magasiniers (CTC)
1188 Franklin St., 4th Fl., San Francisco CA 94109 USA
Tel: 415-775-0533; *Fax:* 415-775-1302
e-mail: info@ilwu.org
URL: www.ilwu.org
James Spinosa, President

International Longshore & Warehouse Union (CLC) (ILWU Canada)
#180, 111 Victoria Ave., Vancouver BC V5L 4C4
Tel: 604-254-8141; *Fax:* 604-254-8183
e-mail: officers@ilwu.ca
URL: www.ilwu.ca
Affiliation(s): Retail Wholesale Union of BC; Retail Wholesale Department Store Union of SK; Grain Services Union of SK

International Longshoremen's Association (AFL-CIO/CLC) (ILA) / Association internationale des débardeurs (FAT-COI/CTC)
#930, 17 Battery Pl., New York NY 10004 USA
Tel: 212-425-1200; *Fax:* 212-425-2928
e-mail: jmcnamara@ilaunion.org
URL: ilaunion.org
Richard P. Hughes, President
Robert E. Gleason, Sec.-Treas.

International Longshoremen's Association (AFL-CIO/CLC)
15070, rue Notre-Dame est, Montréal QC H1A 1W6
Tel: 514-644-0509

International Union of Bricklayers & Allied Craftworkers (AFL-CIO/CFL) (BAC Canada)
496 Argyle St., Saint John NB E2M 3B1
Tel: 613-233-7920
Toll-Free: 877-276-7771
URL: www.bacweb.org/aboutus/canada.htm

International Union of Bricklayers & Allied Craftworkers (AFL-CIO/CFL) (BAC) / Union internationale des briqueteurs et métiers connexes (FAT-COI/FCT)
620 F St. NW, Washington DC 20004 USA
Tel: 202-783-3788
Toll-Free: 888-880-8222
e-mail: askbac@bacweb.org
URL: www.bacweb.org
John J. Flynn, President

International Union of Elevator Constructors (AFL-CIO/CFL) (IUEC) / Union internationale des constructeurs d'ascenseurs (FAT-COI/FCT)
7154 Columbia Gateway Dr., Columbia MD 21046 USA
Tel: 410-953-6150; *Fax:* 410-953-6169
e-mail: contact@iuec.org
URL: www.iuec.org
Kevin P. Stringer, General Sec.-Treas.
Dana A. Brigham, General President

International Union of Elevator Constructors (AFL-CIO/CFL) (IUEC)
400 Westney Rd. South, Ajax ON L1S 6M6
Tel: 905-754-2424; *Fax:* 905-686-7355
URL: www.iuec50.org

International Union of Operating Engineers (AFL-CIO/CFL) / Union internationale des opérateurs de machines lourdes (FAT-COI/FCT)
1125 - 17 St. NW, Washington DC 20036 USA
Tel: 202-429-9100; *Fax:* 202-778-2613
URL: www.iuoe.org
Vincent J. Giblin, President

International Union of Operating Engineers (AFL-CIO/CFL)
Mount James Square, $401, 1030 Upper James St., Hamilton ON L9C 6X6
Tel: 905-527-5250; *Fax:* 905-527-6336
e-mail: iuoe772hamilton@mountaincable.net
URL: www.iuoe772.org

International Union of Painters & Allied Trades (AFL-CIO/CFL) / Syndicat international des peintres et métiers connexes (FAT-COI/FCT)
1750 New York Ave. NW, Washington DC 20006 USA
Tel: 202-637-0700
e-mail: mail@iupat.org
URL: www.iupat.org
James A. Williams, President

International Union of Painters & Allied Trades (AFL-CIO/CFL)
7621 Kingsway, Burnaby BC V3N 3C7
Tel: 604-524-8334; *Fax:* 604-524-8011
Toll-Free: 800-866-1527
URL: www.dc38.ca

International Union, United Automobile, Aerospace & Agricultural Implement Workers of America, Local 251 (CLC) / Syndicat international des travailleurs unis de l'automobile, de l'aérospatiale et de l'outillage agricole d'Amérique (C
8000 East Jefferson Ave., Detroit MI 48214 USA
Tel: 313-926-5000
URL: www.uaw.org
Elizabeth Bunn, Sec.-Treas.
Ron Gettelfinger, President

International Union, United Automobile, Aerospace & Agricultural Implement Workers of America (CLC)
88 Elm Dr. South, Wallacebury ON N8A 5E7
Tel: 519-627-1629; *Fax:* 519-627-2055
Toll-Free: 800-646-5437
e-mail: local251@uaw.ca
URL: www.uaw251.ca

Laborers' International Union of North America (AFL-CIO/CLC) (LiUNA) / Union internationale des journaliers d'Amérique (FAT-COI/CTC)
905 - 16 St. NW, Washington DC 20006 USA
Tel: 202-737-8320; *Fax:* 202-737-2754
e-mail: communications@liuna.org
URL: www.liuna.org
Affiliation(s): American Federation of Labour & Congress of Industrial Organizations; Canadian Labour Congress
Armand Sabitoni, General Sec.-Treas.
Terence M. O'Sullivan, President

Laborers' International Union of North America (AFL-CIO/CLC)
44 Hughson St. South, Hamilton ON L8N 2A7
Tel: 905-522-7177; *Fax:* 905-522-9310
URL: www.liuna.ca; www.liuna.org/about/regions.html

Major League Baseball Players' Association (Ind.) / Association des joueurs de la Ligue majeure de baseball (ind.)
12 East 49th St., 24th Fl., New York NY 10017 USA
Tel: 212-826-0808; *Fax:* 212-752-4378
e-mail: feedback@mlbpa.org
URL: www.majorleaguebaseball.com/
Donald M. Fehr, Executive Director
Gene Orza, Chief Operating Officer

Management & Professional Employees Society of BC Hydro (Ind.) (MAPES) / Société des employés professionnels et administratifs (ind.)
12388 - 88 Ave., Surrey BC V3W 7R7
Tel: 604-590-7454; *Fax:* 604-597-6656
e-mail: john.vandermaar@powertech.bc.ca
Livio Gambone, President

Manitoba Association of Health Care Professionals (MAHCP) / Association des professionnels de la santé du Manitoba
#101, 1500 Notre Dame Ave., Winnipeg MB R3E 0P9
Tel: 204-772-0425; *Fax:* 204-775-6829
Toll-Free: 800-315-3331
e-mail: info@mahcp.ca
URL: www.mahcp.com
Wendy Despins, President

Manitoba Federation of Labour / Fédération du travail du Manitoba
#303, 275 Broadway, Winnipeg MB R3C 4M6
Tel: 204-947-1400; *Fax:* 204-943-4276
URL: www.mfl.mb.ca
Darlene Dziewit, President

Maritime Fishermen's Union (CLC) (MFU) / Union des pêcheurs des Maritimes (CTC) (UPM)
408 Main St., Shediac NB E4P 2G1
Tel: 506-532-2485; *Fax:* 506-532-2487
e-mail: shediac@mfu-upm.com
URL: www.mfu-upm.com
Christian Brun, Executive Secretary

Mechanical Service Contractors of Canada (MSCC)
#601, 280 Albert St., Ottawa ON K1P 5G8
Tel: 613-232-0017; *Fax:* 613-235-2793
e-mail: daryl@mcac.ca
URL: www.servicecontractor.ca
Daryl Sharkey, Chief Operating Officer

National Automobile, Aerospace, Transportation & General Workers Union of Canada (CLC) (CAW-Canada) / Syndicat national de l'automobile, de l'aérospatiale, du transport et des autres travailleurs et travailleuses du Canada
205 Placer Ct., Toronto ON M2H 3H9
Tel: 416-497-4110; *Fax:* 416-495-6559
e-mail: caw@caw.ca
URL: www.caw.ca

Basil "Buzz" Hargrove, National President
Jim O'Neil, National Sec.-Treas.
Luc Desnoyers, Québec Director

Native Brotherhood of British Columbia (NBBC) / Fraternité des Indiens de la Colombie-Britannique
#710, 100 Park Royal South, Vancouver BC V7T 1A2
Tel: 604-913-3372; *Fax:* 604-913-3374
e-mail: nbbc@nativevoice.bc.ca
URL: www.nativevoice.bc.ca

Natural Resources Union (NRU)
#600, 233 Gilmour St., Ottawa ON K2P 0P2
Tel: 613-560-4378; *Fax:* 613-233-7012
e-mail: info@nru-srn.com
URL: www.nru-srn.com
Claudia Thompson, National President

New Brunswick Federation of Labour (NBFL) / Fédération des travailleurs et travailleuses du Nouveau-Brunswick
#208, 96 Norwood Ave., Moncton NB E1C 6L9
Tel: 506-857-2125; *Fax:* 506-383-1597
e-mail: nbfl@nbnet.nb.ca
URL: www.nbfl-fttnb.ca
Michel Boudreau, President

Newfoundland & Labrador Association of Public & Private Employees (NAPE)
PO Box 8100, 330 Portugal Cove Pl., St. John's NL A1B 3M9
Tel: 709-754-0700; *Fax:* 709-754-0726
Toll-Free: 800-563-4442
e-mail: inquiries@nape.nf.ca
URL: www.nape.nf.ca
Affiliation(s): Newfoundland & Labrador Federation of Labour
Bert Blundon, Sec.-Treas.
Carol Furlong, President
Arlene Sedlickas, Vice President

Newfoundland & Labrador Federation of Labour (NLFL) / Fédération du travail de Terre-Neuve et du Labrador
NAPE Bldg., PO Box 8597, Stn. A, 330 Portugal Cove Pl., 2nd Fl., St. John's NL A1B 3P2
Tel: 709-754-1660; *Fax:* 709-754-1220
e-mail: fed@nlfl.nf.ca
URL: www.nlfl.nf.ca
Lana Payne, President
Linda Rideout, Executive Secretary

Northern Territories Federation of Labour / Fédération du travail des Territoires du Nord
PO Box 2787, Yellowknife NT X1A 2R1
Tel: 867-873-3695; *Fax:* 867-873-6979
e-mail: ntfl@yk.com
URL: www.ntfl.yk.com
Mary Lou Cherwaty, President

Nova Scotia Federation of Labour / Fédération du travail de la Nouvelle-Écosse
#225, 3700 Kempt Rd., Halifax NS B3K 4X8
Tel: 902-454-6735; *Fax:* 902-454-7671
e-mail: info@nsfl.ns.ca
URL: www.nsfl.ns.ca
Rick Clarke, President
Ivy Shaw, Sec.-Treas.

Nova Scotia Government & General Employees Union (NSGEU) / Syndicat de la fonction publique de la Nouvelle-Écosse
100 Eileen Stubbs Ave., Dartmouth NS B3B 1Y6
Tel: 902-424-4063; *Fax:* 902-424-2111
Toll-Free: 877-556-7438
e-mail: inquiry@nsgeu.ns.ca
URL: www.nsgeu.ns.ca
Affiliation(s): Canadian Labour Congress; Nova Scotia Federation of Labour; National Union of Public & General Employees
Joan Jessome, President

Nova Scotia Union of Public & Private Employees (CCU) (NSUPE) / Syndicat des employés du secteur public de la Nouvelle-Écosse (CCU)
6309 Chebucto Rd., Halifax NS B3L 1K9
Tel: 902-422-9495; *Fax:* 902-429-7655
e-mail: nsupe@ns.sympatico.ca
URL: www.nsupe.ca
Affiliation(s): Confederation of Canadian Unions; Atlantic Council of the Confederation of Canadian Unions
John Hanrahan, President
Nancy Travis, Vice-President

Nunavut Employees Union (NEU)
PO Box 869, Iqaluit NU X0A 0H0
Tel: 867-979-4209; *Fax:* 867-979-4522
Toll-Free: 877-243-4424
e-mail: info@neu.ca
URL: www.neu.ca
Doug Workman, President
Susan Gardener, Director of Finance and Admin.

Office & Professional Employees International Union (AFL-CIO/CLC) / Union internationale des employés professionnels et de bureau (FAT-COI/CTC)
1660 L St. NW, Washington DC 20036 USA
Tel: 202-393-4464
e-mail: opeiu@opeiu.org
URL: www.opeiu.org
Michael Goodwin, President

Ontario Federation of Labour (OFL) / Fédération du travail de l'Ontario
#202, 15 Gervais Dr., Toronto ON M3C 1Y8
Tel: 416-441-2731; *Fax:* 416-441-0722
Toll-Free: 800-668-9138; *TTY:* 416-443-6305
e-mail: info@ofl.ca
URL: www.ofl.ca
Flora Clegg, President
Judy Chow, Sec.-Treas.

Ontario Professional Fire Fighters Association (OPFFA) / Association des pompiers professionnels de l'Ontario (ind.)
292 Plains Rd. East, Burlington ON L7T 2C6
Tel: 905-681-7111; *Fax:* 905-681-1489
URL: www.opffa.org
Affiliation(s): International Association of Fire Fighters
Fred LeBlanc, President
Mark McKinnon, Executive Vice-President
Barry Quinn, Secretary-Treasurer
Jeff Braun-Jackson, Office Manager & Researcher

Ontario Public Service Employees Union (OPSEU) / Syndicat des employées et employés de la fonction publique de l'Ontario
100 Lesmill Rd., Toronto ON M3B 3P8
Tel: 416-443-8888; *Fax:* 416-443-9670
Toll-Free: 800-268-7376
e-mail: opseu@opseu.org
URL: www.opseu.org
Affiliation(s): Canadian Labour Council; Ontario Federation of Labour
Smokey Thomas, President

Operative Plasterers' & Cement Masons' International Association of the US & Canada (AFL-CIO/CFL) - Canadian Office
Varette Bldg., #1902, 130 Albert St., Ottawa ON K1P 5G4
Tel: 613-236-0653; *Fax:* 613-230-5138
e-mail: cdnoffice@buildingtrades.ca
URL: www.buildingtrades.ca
Robert Blakely, Director, Canadian Affairs

Prince Edward Island Federation of Labour / Fédération du travail de l'Ile-du-Prince-Édouard
22 Enman Cres., Charlottetown PE C1A 1E6
Tel: 902-368-3068; *Fax:* 902-368-3192
e-mail: peifed@pei.aibn.com
URL: www.peifl.ca
Carl Pursey, President

Prince Edward Island Union of Public Sector Employees / Syndicat de la fonction publique de l'Ile-du-Prince-Édouard
PO Box 1116, 4 Enman Cres. South, Charlottetown PE C1A 7M8
Tel: 902-892-5335; *Fax:* 902-569-8186
Toll-Free: 800-897-8773
e-mail: peiupse@peiupse.ca
URL: www.peiupse.ca
Shelly Ward, President

Professional Association of Foreign Service Officers (Ind.) (PAFSO) / L'Association professionnelle des agents du service extérieur (ind.) (APASE)
#412, 47 Clarence St., Ottawa ON K1N 9K1
Tel: 613-241-1391; *Fax:* 613-241-5911
e-mail: info@pafso.com
URL: www.pafso.com
Ron Cochrane, Executive Director

Professional Association of Internes & Residents of Newfoundland (PAIRN) / Association professionnelle des internes et résidents de Terre-Neuve
c/o Student Affairs, Health Sciences Complex, Memorial University, #2867, 300 Prince Philip Dr., St. John's NL A1B 3V6
Tel: 709-777-7118; *Fax:* 709-777-6968
e-mail: pairn@mun.ca
URL: www.pairn.nl.ca
Affiliation(s): Canadian Association of Internes & Residents; Newfoundland & Labrador Medical Association; Canadian Medical Association
Chris Smith, President
Pamela Hebbard, Vice-President
Deanna Murphy, Secretary
Sohaib Al-Asaaed, Treasurer

Professional Association of Interns & Residents of Saskatchewan (PAIRS) / Association professionnelle des internes et résidents de la Saskatchewan (ind.)
C Wing, Royal University Hospital, PO Box 23, #5687, 103 Hospital Dr., 5th Fl., Saskatoon SK S7N 0W8
Tel: 306-655-2134; *Fax:* 306-655-2134
e-mail: pairs.sk@usask.ca
URL: www.usask.ca/pairs
Affiliation(s): Canadian Association of Internes & Residents
Gavin Beck, President
Sue Sidhu, Vice-President
Nove Kalia, Secretary-Treasurer
Joan Cheyne, Executive Director

Professional Association of Residents & Interns of Manitoba (PARIM) / Association professionnelle des résidents et internes du Manitoba
#AD107, 720 McDermot Ave., Winnipeg MB R3E 0T3
Tel: 204-787-3673; *Fax:* 204-787-2692
e-mail: parim@mts.net
URL: www.parim.org
Affiliation(s): Canadian Association of Internes & Residents
Marc Fournier, Co-President
Paul Wawryko, Co-President
Jay Hingwala, Vice-President, Internal Affairs & Finance
Fatemeh Kojori, Vice-President, Social & Well-being
Kanwal Kumar, Vice-President, Communications

Professional Association of Residents in the Maritime Provinces (PARI-MP) / Association professionnelle des résidents des provinces maritimes
Halifax Professional Centre, #460, 5991 Spring Garden Rd., Halifax NS B3H 1Y6
Tel: 902-404-3595; *Fax:* 902-404-3599
Toll-Free: 877-972-7467
e-mail: sandi@parimp.ca
URL: www.parimp.ca
Affiliation(s): Canadian Association of Internes & Residents
Laine Green, President
Matt Smith, Vice-President
Bryan Chung, Secretary
Kerri Purdy, Treasurer
Sandi Carew Flemming, Executive Director
Leanne Bryan, Coordinator, Benefits & Events

Professional Association of Residents of Alberta (PARA) / Association professionnelle des résidents de l'Alberta
Garneau Professional Center, #340, 11044 - 82 Ave., Edmonton AB T6G OJ2
Tel: 780-432-1749; *Fax:* 780-432-1778
e-mail: para-ab@shawbiz.ca
URL: www.para-ab.ca
Affiliation(s): Canadian Association of Internes & Residents
Michelle Carle, President
Henry Conter, Vice-President, Internal Affairs
Kenman Gan, Vice-President, Operations & Finance
Jillian Schwartz, Vice-President, External Affairs
Sarah Thomas, Executive Director
Tana Findlay, Executive Director, Operations

Professional Association of Residents of British Columbia (PAR-BC) / Association professionnelle des résidents de la Colombie-Britannique
#2010, 401 West Georgia St., Vancouver BC V6B 5A1
Tel: 604-876-7636; *Fax:* 604-876-7690
Toll-Free: 888-877-2722
e-mail: par@par-bc.org
URL: www.par-bc.org
Affiliation(s): Canadian Association of Internes & Residents
Mark Masterson, President
Sam Gharbi, Vice-President
Sana Ahmed, Director, Communications
May Tee, Director, Finance

Professional Employees Association (Ind.) (PEA) / Association des employés professionnels (ind.)
#201, 1001 Wharf St., Victoria BC V8W 1T6
Tel: 250-385-8791; *Fax:* 250-385-6629
e-mail: jjensen@pea.org
URL: www.pea.org
Jodi Jensen, Executive Director

Professional Employees Association (Ind.)
Station Tower, #1410, 13401 - 108 Ave., Surrey BC V3T 5T3
Tel: 604-581-6662; *Fax:* 604-581-6609
Toll-Free: 800-323-0488

Professional Engineers & Architects of the Ontario Public Service (Ind.) / Ingénieurs et architectes de la fonction publique de l'Ontario (ind.)
#206, 3199 Bathurst St., Toronto ON M6A 2B2
Tel: 416-784-1284; *Fax:* 416-784-1366
e-mail: pego@pego.on.ca
URL: www.pego.on.ca
Ian Cameron, President

The Professional Institute of the Public Service of Canada
#610, 1718 Argyle St., Halifax NS B3J 3N6
Tel: 902-420-1519; *Fax:* 902-422-8516
Toll-Free: 800-565-0727

The Professional Institute of the Public Service of Canada
#2015, 401 West Georgia St., Vancouver BC V6B 5A1
Tel: 604-688-8238; *Fax:* 604-688-8290
Toll-Free: 800-663-0485

The Professional Institute of the Public Service of Canada
#1700, 10020 - 101A Ave., Edmonton AB T5J 3G2
Tel: 780-428-1347; *Fax:* 780-426-5962
Toll-Free: 800-661-3939

The Professional Institute of the Public Service of Canada
#701, 110 Yonge St. East, Toronto ON M5C 1T4
Tel: 416-487-1114; *Fax:* 416-487-7268
Toll-Free: 800-668-3943

The Professional Institute of the Public Service of Canada
#2330, 1000, rue Sherbrooke ouest, Montréal QC H3A 3G4
Tél: 514-288-3545; *Téléc:* 514-288-0494
Ligne sans frais: 800-363-0622

The Professional Institute of the Public Service of Canada
#700, 125 Garry St., Winnipeg MB R3C 3P2
Tel: 204-942-1304; *Fax:* 204-942-4348
Toll-Free: 800-665-0094

The Professional Institute of the Public Service of Canada (PIPSC) / Institut professionnel de la fonction publique du Canada
250 Tremblay Rd., Ottawa ON K1G 3J8
Tel: 613-228-6310; *Fax:* 613-228-9048
Toll-Free: 800-267-0446
URL: www.pipsc.ca
Michèle Demers, President
Edward Gillis, Executive Secretary

Public Service Alliance of Canada (CLC) (PSAC) / Alliance de la Fonction publique du Canada (CTC) (AFPC)
233 Gilmour St., Ottawa ON K2P 0P1
Tel: 613-560-4200; *Fax:* 613-567-0385
Toll-Free: 888-604-7722
URL: www.psac.com
Affiliation(s): Public Services International
John Gordon, National President
Jeannie Baldwin, Regional Executive Vice-President, Atlantic
Kay Sinclair, Regional Executive Vice-President, B.C.
Robyn Benson, Regional Executive Vice-President, Prairies
Patty Ducharme, National Vice-President
Gerry Halabecki, Regional Executive Vice-President, Ontario
Jérôme Turcq, Vice-président exécutif régional, Québec
Jean-François Des Lauriers, Regional Executive Vice-President, North
Maria Fitzpatrick, Regional Executive Vice-President, National Capital Region

Pulp, Paper & Woodworkers of Canada (CCU) (PPWC)
#201, 1184 - 6 Ave. West, Vancouver BC V6H 1A4
Tel: 604-731-1909; *Fax:* 604-731-6448
e-mail: louise@web.net
URL: www.ppwc.ca
Affiliation(s): Confederation of Canadian Unions
Jim King, President

Research Council Employees' Association (Ind.) (RCEA) / Association des employés du conseil de recherches (ind.) (AECR)
PO Box 8256, Ottawa ON K1G 3H7
Tel: 613-746-9341; *Fax:* 613-745-7868
e-mail: office@rcea.ca
URL: www.rcea.ca
Serge Croteau, President

Royal Newfoundland Constabulary Association (RNCA) / Fraternité des policiers de la gendarmerie royale de Terre-Neuve
125 East White Hills Rd., St. John's NL A1A 5R7
Tel: 709-739-5946; *Fax:* 709-739-6276
e-mail: office@rnca.ca
URL: www.rnca.ca
Tim Buckle, President

Saskatchewan Government & General Employees' Union (SGEU) / Syndicat de la fonction publique de la Saskatchewan
1440 Broadway Ave., Regina SK S4P 1E2
Tel: 306-522-8571; *Fax:* 306-352-1969
Toll-Free: 800-667-5221
URL: www.sgeu.org
Bob Bymoen, President

Saskatchewan Joint Board, Retail, Wholesale & Department Store Union (CLC) / Conseil mixte du syndicat des employés de gros, de détail et de magasins à rayons de la Saskatchewan (CTC)
1233 Winnipeg St., Regina SK S4R 1K1
Tel: 306-569-9311; *Fax:* 306-569-9521
Toll-Free: 877-747-9378
e-mail: rwdsu.regina@sasktel.net
URL: www.rwdsu.sk.ca
Chris Banting, Secretary Treasurer

Schneider Employees' Association (Ind.) / Association des employés de Schneider (ind.)
321 Courtland Ave. East, Kitchener ON N2G 3X8
Tel: 519-741-5000; *Fax:* 519-744-5099
e-mail: sea321@execulink.com
Dennis Lesperance, National President

Seafarers' International Union of Canada (AFL-CIO/CLC) / Syndicat international des marins canadiens (FAT-COI/CTC)
1333, rue Saint-Jacques, Montréal QC H3C 4K2
Tel: 514-931-7859; *Fax:* 514-931-3667
Affiliation(s): Seafarers' International Union of North America (AFL-CIO); International Transport Workers' Federation

Service Employees International Union (AFL-CIO/CLC) / Union internationale des employés des services (FAT-COI/CTC)
1800 Massachusetts Ave. NW, Washington DC 20036 USA
Tel: 202-730-7000; *Fax:* 202-898-3402
Toll-Free: 800-424-8592
URL: www.seiu.org
Andrew L. Stern, International President

Service Employees International Union (AFL-CIO/CLC)
#810, 75 The Donway West, Toronto ON M3C 2E9
Tel: 416-447-2311; *Fax:* 416-447-2428
URL: www.seiu.ca

Sheet Metal Workers' International Association (AFL-CIO/CFL) / Association internationale des travailleurs du métal en feuilles (FAT-COI/FCT)
1750 New York Ave. NW, Washington DC 20006 USA
Tel: 202-783-5880
e-mail: info@smwia.org
URL: www.smwia.org
Mike Sullivan, General President

Sheet Metal Workers' International Association (AFL-CIO/CFL)
190 Thames Rd. East, Exeter ON N0M 1S3
Tel: 519-235-3766; *Fax:* 519-235-3765
e-mail: smwia@on.aibn.com

Shipyard General Workers' Federation of British Columbia (CLC) / Fédération des ouvriers des chantiers navals de la Colombie-Britannique (CTC)
#130, 111 Victoria Dr., Vancouver BC V5L 4C4
Tel: 604-254-8204; *Fax:* 604-254-7447
e-mail: office@bcshipyardworkers.com
URL: www.bcshipyardworkers.com
Affiliation(s): Machinists, Fitters & Helpers Industrial Union #3, Marine Workers & Boilerworkers' Industrial Union #1, Shipwrights, Joiners & Caulkers' Industrial Union #9
George MacPherson, President
Quentin Del Vecchio, General Secretary

Société des Auteurs de Radio, Télévision et Cinéma (SARTEC) / Society of Writers in Radio, Television & Cinema
1229, rue Panet, Montréal QC H2L 2Y6
Tél: 514-526-9196; *Téléc:* 514-526-4124
Courriel: information@sartec.qc.ca
URL: www.sartec.qc.ca
Affiliation(s): International Affiliation of Writers Guilds (IAWG)
Yves Légaré, Directeur général
Marc Grégoire, Président

Société des technologues en nutrition (STN)
895, boul. Charest ouest, Québec QC G1N 2C9
Tél: 418-990-0309
Courriel: stn@stnq.ca
URL: www.stnq.ca
Affiliation(s): Centrale des professionelles et professionels de la santé (CPS)

The Society of Energy Professionals
#300, 425 Bloor St. East., Toronto ON M4W 3R4
Tel: 416-979-2709; *Fax:* 416-979-5794
Toll-Free: 866-288-1788
e-mail: society@society.on.ca
URL: www.thesociety.ca
Affiliation(s): Canadian Court of Utility Professionals & Associated Societies (CCUPAS)
Rodney Sheppard, President

Society of Professional Engineers & Associates / Société des ingénieurs professionnels et associés
2275 Speakman Dr., Mississauga ON L5K 1B1
Tel: 905-823-3606; *Fax:* 905-823-9602
e-mail: spea@outer-net.com
URL: www.spea.ca
Ritu Luther, Office Administrator

Space Systems Engineers & Scientists Association (SSESA) / Association des ingénieurs et des scientifiques des systèmes spatiaux (AISSS)
1073, rue Saint-Denis, Montréal QC H2X 3J3
Tel: 514-844-1347; *Fax:* 514-844-8037
e-mail: lauzon.d@ems-t.ca
URL: www.aisss-ssesa.org
Dominick Lauzon, President

Syndicat de la fonction publique du Québec inc. (ind.) (SFPQ) / Québec Government Employees' Union (Ind.)
5100, boul des Gradins, Québec QC G2J 1N4
Tél: 418-623-2424; *Téléc:* 418-623-6109
Courriel: communication@sfpq.qc.ca
URL: www.sfpq.qc.ca
Lucie Martineau, Présidente général

Syndicat de professionnelles et professionnels du gouvernement du Québec (SPGQ) / Union of Professional Employees of the Québec Government
7, rue Vallière, Québec QC G1K 6S9
Tél: 418-692-0022; *Téléc:* 418-692-1338
Ligne sans frais: 800-463-5079
Courriel: courrier@spgq.qc.ca
URL: www.spgq.qc.ca
Gilles Dussault, Président
Michael Isaacs, Secrétaire

Syndicat des agents de la paix en services correctionnels du Québec (ind.) (SAPSCQ) / Union of Prison Guards of Québec (Ind.)
4906, boul Gouin est, Montréal QC H1G 1A4
Tél: 514-328-7774; *Téléc:* 514-328-0889
Ligne sans frais: 800-361-3559
Courriel: s.lemaire@sapscq.com
URL: www.sapscq.com
Stéphane Lemaire, Président national
Arthur Kassombola, Vice-président
Sylvain Maltais, Secrétaire général

Syndicat des agents de maîtrise de TELUS (ind.) (SAMT) / TELUS Professional Employees Union (Ind.) (TPEU)
#605, 2, St-Germain est, Rimouski QC G5L 8T7
Tél: 418-722-6144; *Téléc:* 418-724-0765
Courriel: samt2@globetrotter.net

Harold Morrissey, Président
Lynda Fortin, Secrétaire

Syndicat des employé(e)s de magasins et de bureau de la Société des alcools du Québec (ind.) / Québec Liquor Board Store & Office Employees Union (Ind.)
1065, rue St-Denis, Montréal QC H2X 3J3
Tél: 514-849-7754; *Téléc:* 514-849-7914
Ligne sans frais: 800-361-8427
Courriel: info@semb-saq.com
URL: www.semb-saq.com/index.html
Éric Brunet, Président

Syndicat des employés en radio-télédiffusion de Télé-Québec (CSQ) / Télé-Québec Television Broadcast Employees' Union
1000, rue Fullum, Montréal QC H2K 3L7
Tél: 514-529-2805; *Téléc:* 514-873-0826
Courriel: sert@colba.net
URL: sert.csq.qc.net/
Philippe Ouimet, Président

Syndicat des intervenants professionnels de la santé du Québec (SIPSQ)
#850, 1001, rue Sherbrooke est, Montréal QC H2L 1L3
Tél: 514-521-4469; *Téléc:* 514-521-0086
Ligne sans frais: 866-480-0086
Courriel: infocps@cpsq.qc.ca
Affiliation(s): Centrale des professionnels de la Santé
Maria Piazza, Présidente

Syndicat des physiothérapeutes et des thérapeutes en réadaptation physique du Québec (SPTRPQ)
#850, 1001, rue Sherbrooke est, Montréal QC H2L 1L3
Tél: 514-521-4469; *Téléc:* 514-521-0086
Pauline Caux, Présidente

Syndicat des pompiers et pompières du Québec (CTC) (SPQ) / Québec Union of Firefighters (CLC)
#3900, 565, boul Crémazie est, Montréal QC H2M 2V6
Tél: 514-383-4698; *Téléc:* 514-383-6782
Ligne sans frais: 800-461-4698
Courriel: spq@spq-ftq.com
URL: www.spq-ftq.com
Affiliation(s): FTQ
Gilles Raymond, Président

Syndicat des professeures et professeurs de l'Université de Sherbrooke (SPPUS)
2500, boul Université, Sherbrooke QC J1K 2R1
Tél: 819-821-7656; *Téléc:* 819-821-7995
Courriel: sppus@usherbrooke.ca
URL: www.usherbrooke.ca/sppus
Affiliation(s): Fédération québécoise des professeures et professeurs du Québec
Bernard Héraud, Secrétaire général

Syndicat des professeurs de l'État du Québec (ind.) (SPEQ) / Union of Professors for the Government of Québec (Ind.)
#1003, 2120, rue Sherbrooke est, Montréal QC H2K 1C3
Tél: 514-525-7979; *Téléc:* 514-525-4655
Ligne sans frais: 877-525-7979
Courriel: luc.perron@speq.org
URL: www.speq.org/
Luc Perron, Président

Syndicat des professionnels et des techniciens de la santé du Québec (SPTSQ) / Québec Union of Health Professionals & Technicians
#850, 1001, rue Sherbrooke est, Montréal QC H2L 1L3
Tél: 514-521-4469; *Téléc:* 514-521-0086
Affiliation(s): Centrale des professionnelles et professionnels de la santé
Carolle Dubé, Présidente

Syndicat des technicien(ne)s et artisan(e)s du réseau français de Radio-Canada (ind.) (STARF) / CBC French Network Technicians' Union (Ind.)
1250, rue de la Visitation, 1e étage, Montréal QC H2L 3B4
Tél: 514-524-1100; *Téléc:* 514-524-6023
Ligne sans frais: 888-838-1100
Courriel: secretariat@starf.qc.ca
URL: www.starf.qc.ca
François Lewis, Président
Benoît Celestino, Secrétaire-trésorier

Syndicat des technologues en radiologie du Québec (ind.) (STRQ) / Union of Radiology Technicians of Québec
#850, 1001, rue Sherbrooke est, Montréal QC H2L 1L3
Tél: 514-521-4469; *Téléc:* 514-521-0086
Robert Carrier, Président

Syndicat des travailleurs de la construction du Québec (CSD)
#300, 801, 4e rue, Québec QC G1J 2T7
Tél: 418-522-3918; *Téléc:* 418-529-6323
URL: www.csdconstruction.qc.ca
Affiliation(s): Centrale des syndicats démocratiques
Michel Fournier, Président
Pierre Ross, Vice-président
François Duval, Secrétaire

Syndicat du personnel technique et professionnel de la Société des alcools du Québec (ind.) (SPTPSAQ) / Québec Liquor Board's Union of Technical & Professional Employees (Ind.)
905, rue de Lorimier, Montréal QC H2K 3V9
Tél: 514-873-5878; *Téléc:* 514-873-5896
Courriel: sptp@bellnet.ca
Yves St-Georges, Président

Syndicat général du cinéma et de la télévision - Section Office national du film (ind.) (SGCT)
#25A, 2340, ch Lucerne, Mont-Royal QC H3R 2J8
Tél: 514-344-9399; *Téléc:* 514-344-9509

Syndicat interprovincial des ferblantiers et couvreurs, la section locale 2016 à la FTQ-Construction
#400, 8550, boul Pie IX, Montréal QC H1Z 4G2
Tél: 514-374-1515; *Téléc:* 514-374-2282
Ligne sans frais: 866-374-1515
Courriel: administration@ftq2016.org
URL: www.ftq2016.org
Affiliation(s): Fédération des travailleurs et travailleuses du Québec - Construction
Dorima Aubut, Directeur provincial

Syndicat professionnel des diététistes et nutritionnistes du Québec (SPDNQ) / Québec Professional Union of Dieticians (Ind.)
2665, rue Beaubien est, Montréal QC H1Y 1G8
Tél: 514-725-5535; *Téléc:* 514-725-4433
Courriel: executif@spdnq.qc.ca
URL: www.spdnq.qc.ca
Claudette Péloquin-Antoun, Présidente

Syndicat professionnel des ingénieurs d'Hydro-Québec (ind.) (SPIHQ) / Hydro-Québec Professional Engineers Union (Ind.)
#1400, rue University, Montréal QC H3B 3X1
Tél: 514-845-4239; *Téléc:* 514-845-0082
Ligne sans frais: 800-567-1260
Courriel: spihq@spihq.qc.ca
URL: www.spihq.qc.ca
Ramzi Chahine, Président
Michel Touchette, Secrétaire

Syndicat professionnel des médecins du gouvernement du Québec (ind.) (SPMGQ) / Professional Union of Government of Québec Physicians (Ind.)
1390, rue du Père-Jamet, Sainte-Foy QC G1W 3G5
Tél: 418-266-4670; *Téléc:* 418-266-4672
Courriel: christine.gagne@csst.qc.ca
Christine Gagné, Présidente

Syndicat québécois de la construction (SQC) / North Shore Construction Inc. (Ind.)
2121, av Sainte-Anne, Saint-Hyacinthe QC J2S 5H5
Tél: 450-773-8833; *Téléc:* 450-773-2232
Ligne sans frais: 888-773-8834
Courriel: info@sqc.ca
URL: www.sqc.ca
Sylvain Gendron, Président

Teaching Support Staff Union (TSSU)
Simon Fraser University, AQ 5129/5130, 8888 University Dr., Burnaby BC V5A 1S6
Tel: 604-291-4735; *Fax:* 604-291-5369
e-mail: tssu@tssu.ca
URL: www.tssu.ca
Social Media: www.twitter.com/TSSU
Affiliation(s): Vancouver & District Labour Council
Scott Drake, Organizer

Teamsters Canada (CLC)
#804, 2540, boul Daniel Johnson, Laval QC H7T 2S3
Tél: 450-682-5521; *Téléc:* 450-681-2244
Ligne sans frais: 866-888-6466
Courriel: info@teamsters-canada.org
URL: www.teamsters.ca
Mèdia social: www.facebook.com/group.php?gid=5512214518
Affiliation(s): International Brotherhood of Teamsters
Robert Bouvier, Président
Tom Fraser, Vice-président
Don McGill, Vice-président

Teamsters Canada (CLC)
Airway Centre, Phase 1, #252, 5945 Airport Rd., 2nd Fl., Mississauga ON L4V 1R9
Tel: 905-678-6652; *Fax:* 905-678-6178
URL: www.teamsters.ca

Teamsters Canada (CLC)
#204, 1867 West Broadway, Vancouver BC V6J 4W1
Tel: 604-736-3517; *Fax:* 604-736-3518
e-mail: mjcteamsters@shawcable.com

Teamsters Canada Rail Conference (TCRC) / Conference ferroviaire de Teamsters Canada (CFTC)
#1710, 130 Albert St., Ottawa ON K1P 5G4
Tel: 613-235-1828; *Fax:* 613-235-1069
e-mail: info@teamstersrail.ca
URL: www.teamstersrail.ca
Dan Shewchuk, President

Telecommunications Employees Association of Manitoba (Ind.) (TEAM) / Association des employés en télécommunications du Manitoba (ind.)
#200, 1 Wesley Ave., Winnipeg MB R2H 1K1
Tel: 204-984-9470; *Fax:* 204-231-2809
Toll-Free: 877-984-9470
e-mail: team@teamunion.mb.ca
URL: www.teamunion.mb.ca
Misty Hughes-Newman, President

Telecommunications Workers' Union (CLC) (TWU) / Syndicat des travailleurs en télécommunications (CTC) (STT)
5261 Lane St., Burnaby BC V5H 4A6
Tel: 604-437-8601; *Fax:* 604-435-7760
Toll-Free: 888-986-3971
e-mail: twu@twu-stt.ca
URL: www.twu-stt.ca
Affiliation(s): BC Federation of Labour; Canadian Labour Congress; National Alliance of Communication Unions; Alberta Federation of Labour; Union Network International
John Carpenter, Vice-President
Betty Carrasco, Vice-President
George Doubt, President
Sherryl Anderson, Sec.-Treas.

Union canadienne des travailleurs en communication (ind.) / Canadian Union of Communication Workers (Ind.)
502, 90e av, Lasalle QC H8R 2Z7
Tél: 514-595-9095; *Téléc:* 514-595-8911
Courriel: uctcpresident@bellnet.ca
URL: www.unionuctc.com
Pierre Lebrun, Président

Union des artistes (UDA) / Artists' Union
#400, 1441, boul. René-Lévesque ouest, Montréal QC H3G 1T7
Tél: 514-288-6682; *Téléc:* 514-285-6789
Courriel: info@uniondesartistes.com
URL: www.uniondesartistes.com
Raymond Legault, Président
François Ferland, Directeur général

Union of Canadian Transportation Employees (UCTE) / Union canadienne des employés des transports (UCET)
#702, 233 Gilmour St., Ottawa ON K2P 0P2
Tel: 613-238-4003; *Fax:* 613-236-0379
e-mail: ucte_webmaster@psac.com
URL: www.ucte.com
Michael Wing, National President

Union of National Defence Employees (UNDE) / Union des employés de la Défense nationale (UEDN)
#700, 116 Albert St., Ottawa ON K1P 5G3
Tel: 613-594-4505; *Fax:* 613-594-8233
Toll-Free: 866-594-4505
URL: www.unde-uedn.com
John MacLennan, National President

Union of Northern Workers / Syndicat des travailleurs du Nord
#200, 5112 - 52 St., Yellowknife NT X1A 3Z5
Tel: 867-873-5668; *Fax:* 867-920-4448
Toll-Free: 877-906-4447
URL: www.unw.ca
Todd Parsons, President

Union of Postal Communications Employees (UPCE) / Syndicat des employés des postes et des communications (SEPC)
#701, 233 Gilmour St., Ottawa ON K2P 0P2
Tel: 613-560-4342; *Fax:* 613-594-3849
e-mail: sepc-upce@psac.com
URL: www.upce.ca
Richard L. Des Lauriers, National President

Union of Solicitor General Employees (USGE) / Syndicat des employés du Solliciteur général (SESG)
#603, 233 Gilmour St., Ottawa ON K2P 0P2
Tel: 613-232-4821; *Fax:* 613-232-3311
e-mail: info@usge-sesg.com
URL: www.usge-sesg.com
Mireille Laniel, Operations Manager

Union of Taxation Employees (UTE) / Syndicat des employé(e)s de l'impôt (SEI)
#602, 233 Gilmour St., Ottawa ON K2P 0P2
Tel: 613-235-6704; *Fax:* 613-234-7290
URL: www.ute-sei.org
Betty Bannon, National President

Union of Veterans' Affairs Employees (UVAE) / Syndicat des employé(e)s des affaires des anciens combattants (SEAC)
#703, 233 Gilmour St., Ottawa ON K2P 0P2
Tel: 613-560-5460; *Fax:* 613-237-8282
e-mail: thauvey@psac.com
URL: uvae-seac.ca
Yvan Thauvette, National President

UNITE HERE Canada
460 Richmond St. West, 2nd Fl., Toronto ON M5V 1Y1
Tel: 416-510-0887; *Fax:* 416-510-0891
Toll-Free: 800-268-4046
e-mail: info@unitehere.ca
URL: www.unitehere.ca
Alexandra Dagg, National Co-Director
Nick Worhaug, National Co-Director

United Association of Journeymen & Apprentices of the Plumbing & Pipe Fitting Industry of the U.S. & Canada (AFL-CIO/CFL) / Association unie des compagnons & apprentis de l'industrie de la plomberie & de la tuyauterie des Etats-Unis & du Canada
3 Park Place, Annapolis MD 21401 USA
Tel: 410-269-2000; *Fax:* 410-267-0262
URL: ua.org
William P. Hite, General President
Patrick R. Perno, General Sec.-Treas.
Stephen F. Kelly, Assistant General President

United Association of Journeymen & Apprentices of the Plumbing & Pipe Fitting Industry of the U.S. & Canada (AFL-CIO/CFL)
#600, 225 Metcalfe St., Ottawa ON K2P 1P9
Tel: 613-565-1100; *Fax:* 613-562-1200
e-mail: uacanada@on.aibn.com

United Brotherhood of Carpenters & Joiners of America (AFL-CIO/CLC) / Fraternité unie des charpentiers et menuisiers d'Amérique (FAT-COI/CTC)
101 Constitution Ave. NW, Washington DC 20001 USA
Tel: 202-546-6206; *Fax:* 202-543-5724
URL: www.carpenters.org
Douglas J. McCarron, General President

United Brotherhood of Carpenters & Joiners of America (AFL-CIO/CLC)
#807, 5799 Yonge St., Toronto ON M2M 3V3
Tel: 416-225-8885; *Fax:* 416-225-5390
Toll-Free: 800-268-2951
Affiliation(s): Canadian Labour Congress

United Food & Commercial Workers Canada (UFCW CANADA)
#300, 61 International Blvd., Toronto ON M9W 6K4
Tel: 416-675-1104; *Fax:* 416-675-6919
e-mail: ufcw@ufcw.ca
URL: www.ufcw.ca
Wayne Hanley, National President

United Food & Commercial Workers' International Union (UFCW) / Union internationale des travailleurs et travailleuses unis de l'alimentation et du commerce
1775 K St. NW, Washington DC 20006 USA
Tel: 202-223-3111; *Fax:* 202-466-1562
e-mail: ufcw@ufcw.org
URL: www.ufcw.org
Social Media: www.facebook.com/group.php?gid=19812849944
Joseph T. Hansen, International President
Anthony M. Perrone, International Sec.-Treas.

United Mine Workers of America (CLC)
33 Gallant St., Glace Bay NS B1A 1T2
Tel: 902-849-8692
e-mail: umwa@ns.sympatico.ca
URL: www.umwa.org

United Mine Workers of America (CLC) / Mineurs unis d'Amérique (CTC)
8315 Lee Hwy., Fairfax VA 22031 USA
Tel: 703-208-7200
URL: www.umwa.org
Cecil Roberts, President

United Mine Workers of America (CLC)
33 Gallant St., Glace Bay NS B1A 1T2
Tel: 902-849-8692
e-mail: umwa@ns.sympatico.ca
URL: www.umwa.org

United Steelworkers of America (AFL-CIO/CLC)
234 Eglinton Ave. East, 8th Fl., Toronto ON M4P 1K7
Tel: 416-487-1571; *Fax:* 416-482-5548
e-mail: uswa@uswa.ca
URL: www.uswa.ca
Affiliation(s): IMF International Metalworkers' Federation; American Federation of Labour

United Steelworkers of America (AFL-CIO/CLC) / Métallurgistes unis d'Amérique (FAT-COI/CTC)
5 Gateway Center, Pittsburgh PA 15222 USA
Tel: 412-562-2400
e-mail: webmaster@uswa.org
URL: www.uswa.org
Leo W. Gerard, International President

United Transportation Union (AFL-CIO/CLC) - Canada
71 Bank St., 7th Fl., Ottawa ON K1P 5N2
Tel: 613-747-7979; *Fax:* 613-747-2815

Yukon Employees Union (YEU) / Syndicat des employés du Yukon
#201, 2285 Second Ave., Whitehorse YT Y1A 1C9
Tel: 867-667-2331; *Fax:* 867-667-6521
e-mail: admint@yeu.ca
URL: www.yeu.ca
Laurie Butterworth, President
Denise L. Norman, Executive Director

Yukon Federation of Labour (YFL) / Fédération du travail du Yukon
#102, 106 Strickland St., Whitehorse YT Y1A 2J5
Tel: 867-667-6676; *Fax:* 867-633-5558
e-mail: yfl@yukonfed.com
URL: www.yukonfed.com
Doug Rody, Director, Policy & Legislative Affairs

Landscape Architecture

Alberta Association of Landscape Architects (AALA)
PO Box 21052, Edmonton AB T6R 2V4
Tel: 780-435-9902; *Fax:* 780-413-0076
e-mail: aala@aala.ab.ca
URL: www.aala.ab.ca
Jill Lane, Manager
Jill Lane, Office Administrator
Michelle Lefebre, Secretary

Association des architectes paysagistes du Québec (AAPQ)
4655, De Lorimier, Montréal QC H2H 2B4
Tél: 514-990-7731; *Téléc:* 877-990-7731
Courriel: info@aapq.org
URL: www.aapq.org
Affiliation(s): Association des Architectes Paysagistes du Canada
Marie-Claude Robert, Directrice générale

Atlantic Provinces Association of Landscape Architects (APALA)
PO Box 653, Stn. Halifax CRO, Halifax NS B3J 2Z1
e-mail: info@apala.ca
URL: www.apala.ca
Edward Versteeg, Sec.-Treas.
Gordon Smith, President

British Columbia Society of Landscape Architects (BCSLA)
#110, 355 Burrard St., Vancouver BC V6C 2G8
Tel: 604-682-5610; *Fax:* 604-681-3394
e-mail: admin@bcsla.org
URL: www.bcsla.org
Pawel Gradowski, President

Canadian Society of Landscape Architects (CSLA) / Association des architectes paysagistes du Canada (AAPC)
PO Box 13594, Ottawa ON K2K 1X6
Tel: 866-781-9799; *Fax:* 866-871-1419
e-mail: info@csla.ca
URL: www.csla.ca
Affiliation(s): International Federation of Landscape Architects; Landscape Alliance
Paulette Vinette, Executive Director

Manitoba Association of Landscape Architects (MALA)
131 Callum Cres., Winnipeg MB R2G 2C7
Tel: 204-663-4863; *Fax:* 204-668-5662
e-mail: malaoffice@shaw.ca
URL: www.mala.net
Valerie Lindberg, Executive Director

Newfoundland & Labrador Association of Landscape Architects (NLALA)
PO Box 5262, Stn. C, St. John's NL A1C 5W1
Tel: 709-579-5855; *Fax:* 709-579-5844
e-mail: info@tract.nf.net
URL: www.nlala.com

Northwest Territories Association of Landscape Architects (NWTALA)
PO Box 1394, Yellowknife NT X1A 2P1
Tel: 867-920-2986; *Fax:* 867-920-2986
e-mail: atborow@internorth.com
Affiliation(s): Canadian Society of Landscape Architects (CSLA)

Ontario Association of Landscape Architects (OALA)
#407, 3 Church St., Toronto ON M5E 1M2
Tel: 416-231-4181; *Fax:* 416-231-2679
e-mail: oala@oala.ca
URL: www.oala.ca
Affiliation(s): American Society of Landscape Architects
Sarah Holland, Executive Director
Arnis Budrevics, President

Saskatchewan Association of Landscape Architects (SALA)
#200, 642 Broadway Ave., Saskatoon SK S7N 1A9
URL: www.sala.sk.ca
Arnold Thiessen, President
Ray Foret, Treasurer

Language, Linguistics, Literature

ABC CANADA Literacy Foundation / Fondation pour l'alphabétisation ABC CANADA
#235, 4211 Yonge St., Toronto ON M4P 2A9
Tel: 416-218-0010; *Fax:* 416-218-0457
Toll-Free: 800-303-1004
e-mail: info@abc-canada.org
URL: www.abc-canada.org
Margaret Eaton, President
Kathy St. John, Director, Development

Association canadienne de traductologie (ACT) / Canadian Association for Translation Studies (CATS)
a/s École de traduction et d'interprétation, Université d'Ottawa, 70, av Laurier est, Ottawa ON K1N 6N5
URL: www.uottawa.ca/associations/act-cats/
Georges Bastin, Président
Denise Nevo, Vice-présidente

Association of Canadian Corporations in Translation & Interpretation (ACCTI) / Association canadienne de compagnies de traductions et d'interpretation
#306, 421 Bloor St. East, Toronto ON M4W 3T1
Tel: 416-975-5000; *Fax:* 416-975-0505
e-mail: english_info@accti.org; info_francais@accti.org
URL: www.accti.org
Paul Penzo, President
Maryse M. Benhoff, Vice-President

Association of Translators & Interpreters of Alberta (ATIA) / Association des traducteurs et interprètes de l'Alberta
PO Box 546, Stn. Main, Edmonton AB T5J 2K8
Tel: 780-434-8384
URL: www.atia.ab.ca
Regina Landeck, President

Association of Translators & Interpreters of Manitoba (ATIM) / Association des traducteurs et des interprètes du Manitoba
PO Box 83, 200, av de la Cathédrale, Winnipeg MB R2H 0H7
Tel: 204-797-3247
e-mail: info@atim.mb.ca
URL: www.atim.mb.ca
Carmen Roberge, President
Carmen Roberge, President

Association of Translators & Interpreters of Nova Scotia (ATINE) / Association des traducteurs et interprètes de la nouvelle-écosse
PO Box 372, Halifax NS B3J 2P8
Tel: 902-443-0350
e-mail: info@atins.org
URL: www.atins.org
Affiliation(s): Fédération internationale des traducteurs (FIT)
Hélène Lemay, President

Association of Translators & Interpreters of Ontario (ATIO) / Association des traducteurs et interprètes de l'Ontario
#1202, 1 Nicholas St., Ottawa ON K1N 7B7
Tel: 613-241-2846; *Fax:* 613-241-4098
Toll-Free: 800-234-5030
e-mail: info@atio.on.ca
URL: www.atio.on.ca
Catherine Bertholet, Executive Director
Nancy McInnis, President

Association of Translators & Interpreters of Saskatchewan (ATIS) / Association des traducteurs et interprètes de la Saskatchewan
2341 Broad St., Regina SK S4P 1Y9
Tel: 306-522-2847
URL: www.atis-sk.ca
Affiliation(s): Canadian Translators & Interpreters Council, Regional Center for North America (USA, Canada, Mexico); Fédération internationale des traducteurs
Elisabet Ráfouls-Sagués, President
Brigitte Haguès, Vice-President

Association of Visual Language Interpreters of Canada (AVLIC) / Association des interprètes en langage visuel du Canada
PO Box 56025, Valley Centre RPO, Langley BC V3A 8B3
Tel: 604-308-0197; *Fax:* 604-530-0867
e-mail: avlic@avlic.ca
URL: www.avlic.ca
Colleen Friel, President
Chris Racine, Secretary
Suzane Giroux, Treasurer
Barb Mykle-Hotzon, Administrative Manager

The Brontë Society - Canada
142 Glenforest Rd., Toronto ON M4N 1Z9
Tel: 416-488-0888
e-mail: judith_watkins@rogers.com
Judith Watkins, Canadian Representative

Canadian Association for Commonwealth Literature & Language Studies (CACLALS) / Association canadienne pour l'étude des langues et de la littérature du Commonwealth
c/o Surrey Campus, Kwantlen University College, 12666 - 72 Ave., Surrey BC V3W 2M8
Tel: 604-599-2187; *Fax:* 604-599-2068
e-mail: sukeshi_kamra@carleton.ca; aclals@aclals.org
URL: www.aclals.org
Affiliation(s): Association for Commonwealth Literature & Language Studies (ACLALS)
Ranjini Mendis, Chair
Julie McGonegal, Sec.-Treas.

Canadian Comparative Literature Association (CCLA) / Association canadienne de littérature comparée (ACLC)
c/o English Dept., University of Northern British Columbia, 3333 University Way, Prince George BC V2N 4Z9
URL: quarles.unbc.ca/ccla/
Stan Beeler, Dr., Treasurer
Angela Esterhammer, President

Canadian Linguistic Association (CLA) / Association canadienne de linguistique (ACL)
c/o University of Toronto Press, Journals Division, 5201 Dufferin Ave., Toronto ON M3H 5T8
Tel: 416-667-7810; *Fax:* 416-667-7881
e-mail: daniel.hall@utoronto.ca
URL: www.chass.utoronto.ca/~cla-acl/
Affiliation(s): International Permanent Committee of Linguists
Yves Roberge, President

Canadian Literary & Artistic Association / Association littéraire et artistique canadienne inc.
PO Box 83641, Stn. Garnier, Montréal QC H2J 4E9
Tel: 514-993-1556; *Fax:* 514-525-1553
e-mail: alaican@aei.ca
URL: www.alai.ca/index-a.php
Jean-Philippe Mikus, President

Canadian Parents for French (CPF)
#310, 176 Gloucester St., Ottawa ON K2P 0A6
Tel: 613-235-1481; *Fax:* 613-230-5940
e-mail: cpf@cpf.ca
URL: www.cpf.ca
David M. Brennick, National President
James Shea, Executive Director
Nicole Chatelain, Communications Officer

Canadian Translators, Terminologists & Interpreters Council (CTTIC) / Conseil des traducteurs, terminologues et interprètes du Canada (CTTIC)
#1202, One Nicholas St., Ottawa ON K1N 7B7
Tel: 613-562-0379; *Fax:* 613-241-4098
e-mail: info@cttic.org
URL: www.cttic.org
Roxanne Lepage, Administrative Director
Michel Parent, President

Centre interdisciplinaire de recherches sur les activités langagières (CIRAL)
Pavillon Charles-de-Koninck, Université Laval, #2260-A, Faculté des lettres, Québec QC G1V 0A6
Tél: 418-656-3040; *Téléc:* 418-656-7144
Courriel: ciral@ciral.ulaval.ca
URL: www.ciral.ulaval.ca
Johanna-Pascale Roy, Directrice

Corporation des traducteurs, traductrices, terminologues et interprètes du Nouveau-Brunswick (CTINB) / Corporation of Translators, Terminologists & Interpreters of New Brunswick
CP 427, Fredericton NB E3B 4Z9
Tél: 506-458-1519
Courriel: ctinb@nbnet.nb.ca
URL: www.ctinb.nb.ca
Affiliation(s): Fédération internationale des traducteurs
Faith Cormier, Présidente

Esperanto Association of Canada (KEA) / Association canadienne d'esperanto
6358-A, rue de Bordeaux, Montréal QC H2G 2R8
URL: www.esperanto.ca/en/kea
Affiliation(s): Universal Esperanto Association - Rotterdam
Normand Fleury, President

Fédération canadienne pour l'alphabétisation en français (FCAF)
#205, 235 Montréal Rd., 2nd Fl., Ottawa ON K1L 6C7
Tél: 613-749-5333; *Téléc:* 613-749-2252
Ligne sans frais: 888-906-5666
Courriel: info@fcaf.net
URL: www.fcaf.net
Suzanne Benoit, Présidente, Ontario
Luce Lapierre, Directrice générale
Jean-Denis Julien, Vice-président, Québec

Internatial Unio For Kanadio (sic) (IUK)
92 Glenholm Av., Toronto ON M6H 3B1
Jonathan Keitz, Prezzident

Jane Austen Society of North America (JASNA)
#105, 195 Wynford Dr., Toronto ON M3C 3P3
Tel: 416-425-2195
Toll-Free: 800-836-3911
e-mail: info@jasna.org
URL: www.jasna.org
Nancy Stokes, Canadian Membership Secretary

L. M. Montgomery Institute (LMMI)
University of Prince Edward Island, 550 University Ave., Charlottetown PE C1A 4P3
Tel: 902-628-4346; *Fax:* 902-628-4345
e-mail: lmmi@upei.ca
URL: www.lmmontgomery.ca
Mark Leggott, Chair

Literary Translators' Association of Canada (LTAC) / Association des traducteurs et traductrices littéraires du Canada (ATTLC)
Concordia University LB 631, 1455, boul de Maisonneuve ouest, Montréal QC H3G 1M8
Tel: 514-848-2424; *Fax:* 514-848-4514
e-mail: info@attlc-ltac.org
URL: www.attlc-ltac.org
Margarita Feliciano, President

Movement for Canadian Literacy (MCL) / Rassemblement canadien pour l'alphabétisation (RCA)
#300, 180 Metcalfe St., Ottawa ON K2P 1P5
Tel: 613-563-2464; *Fax:* 613-563-2504
e-mail: mcl@literacy.ca
URL: www.literacy.ca
Melody Paruboczy, Executive Director

National Adult Literacy Database (NALD) / Base de données en alphabétisation des adultes (BDAA)
Sterling House, 767 Brunswick St., Fredericton NB E3B 1H8
Tel: 506-457-6900; *Fax:* 506-457-6910
Toll-Free: 800-720-6253
e-mail: contactnald@nald.ca
URL: www.nald.ca
Katherine d'Entremont, Executive Director

Ordre des traducteurs, terminologues et interprètes agréés du Québec (OTTIAQ)
#1108, 2021, rue Union, Montréal QC H3A 2S9
Tél: 514-845-4411; *Téléc:* 514-845-9903
Ligne sans frais: 800-265-4815
Courriel: info@ottiaq.org
URL: www.ottiaq.org
Claude Laurent, Directeur général

Quebec English Literacy Alliance (QELA)
PO Box 3542, Knowlton QC J0E 1V0
Tel: 450-242-2360; *Fax:* 450-242-2543
Toll-Free: 866-242-7352
e-mail: qelamail@gmail.com
URL: www.qela.qc.ca
Louise Quinn, Executive Director

Saskatchewan Elocution & Debate Association (SEDA) / Association d'élocution et des débats de la Saskatchewan
1860 Lorne St., Regina SK S4P 2L7
Tel: 306-780-9243; *Fax:* 306-781-6021
e-mail: info@saskdebate.com
URL: www.saskdebate.com
Affiliation(s): Canadian Student Debating Federation
Lorelie DeRoose, Executive Director

Saskatchewan Organization for Heritage Languages Inc. (SOHL)
2144 Cornwall St., Regina SK S4P 2K7
Tel: 306-780-9275; *Fax:* 306-780-9407
e-mail: sohl@sasktel.net
URL: www.heritagelanguages.sk.ca
Affiliation(s): SaskCulture
Tamara Ruzic, Executive Director

Société québécoise d'espéranto (SQE) / Québec Esperanto Society (QES)
6358A, rue de Bordeaux, Montréal QC H2G 2R8
Courriel: informo@esperanto.qc.ca
URL: www.esperanto.qc.ca
Affiliation(s): Universala Esperanto-Asocio
Boris-Antoine Legault, Président
Sylvain Auclair, Trésurer
Jérôme-Frédéric Bouchard, Secretaire

Society of Translators & Interpreters of British Columbia (STIBC)
#511, 850 West Hastings St., Box 33, Vancouver BC V6C 1E1
Tel: 604-684-2940; *Fax:* 604-684-2947
e-mail: stibc@stibc.org
URL: www.stibc.org
Terry J. Clark, Executive Director
Evelyna Radoslavova, President

Sweetgrass First Nations Language Council
PO Box 1506, 184 Mohawk St., Brantford ON N3T 5V6
Tel: 519-759-2650; *Fax:* 519-759-8912
e-mail: amos@woodland-centre.on.ca
URL: www.woodland-centre.on.ca
Amos Key, Director

Universala Esperanto Asocio
PO Box 2159, Sidney BC V8L 3S6
e-mail: esperanto@shaw.ca
URL: www.uea.org
Olga du Temple, Canadian Representative

World Literacy of Canada (WLC) / Alphabétisation mondiale Canada
#236, 401 Richmond St. West, Toronto ON M5V 3A8
Tel: 416-977-0008; *Fax:* 416-977-1112
e-mail: info@worldlit.ca
URL: www.worldlit.ca
Sandra Onufryk, President
Marguerite Pigott, Vice-President
Jamie Zeppa, Secretary
Mamta Mishra, Executive Director

Law

The Advocates' Society
#1700, 480 University Ave., Toronto ON M5G 1V2
Tel: 416-597-0243; *Fax:* 416-597-1588
e-mail: mail@advocates.ca
URL: www.advocates.ca
Alexandra Chyczij, Executive Director
Sonia Holiad, Director, Communications & Events

Alberta Civil Trial Lawyers' Association (ACTLA)
#550, 10055 - 106 St., Edmonton AB T5J 2Y2
Tel: 780-429-1133; *Fax:* 780-429-1199
Toll-Free: 800-665-7248
e-mail: admin@actla.com
URL: www.actla.com
Affiliation(s): Association of Trial Lawyers of America
Lyn Bromilow, Executive Director
James D. Cuming, President

Alberta Federation of Police Associations (AFPA)
Energy Square, #100, 7024 - 101 Ave., Edmonton AB T6A 0H7
Fax: 403-795-7173
e-mail: information@albertapolice.ca
URL: www.albertapolice.ca
Bob Walsh, President

Alberta Government Civil Lawyers Association (AGCLA)
Bowker Building, Civil Law Division, Alberta Justice, 9833 - 109 St., 5th Fl., Edmonton AB T5K 2E8
Tel: 780-422-0500; *Fax:* 780-425-0307

Alberta Law Foundation (ALF)
#300, 407 - 8 Ave. SW, Calgary AB T2P 1E5
Tel: 403-264-4701; *Fax:* 403-294-9238
e-mail: contact@albertalawfoundation.org
URL: www.albertalawfoundation.org
Affiliation(s): Association of Canadian Law Foundations
David Aucoin, Executive Director
Diana M. Porter, Administrative Assistant

Association des juristes d'expression française de l'Ontario (AJEFO)
#201, 214 ch Montréal, Ottawa ON K1L 8L8
Tél: 613-842-7462; *Téléc:* 613-842-8389
Courriel: bureau@ajefo.ca
URL: www.ajefo.ca
Sean McGee, Président
Sonia Ouellet, Directrice générale

Association des juristes d'expression française de la Saskatchewan (AJEFS) / French Jurists Association of Saskatchewan
#120, 3850, rue Hillsdale, Regina SK S4S 7J5
Tél: 306-924-8543; *Téléc:* 306-781-7916
Ligne sans frais: 800-579-2507
Courriel: ajefs@sasktel.net
URL: www.ajefs.ca
Neil Turcotte, Président

Association des policières et policiers provinciaux du Québec (ind.) (APPQ) / Québec Provincial Police Association (Ind.)
1981, rue Léonard-De Vinci, Sainte-Julie QC J3E 1Y9
Tél: 450-922-5414; *Téléc:* 450-922-5417
Courriel: dagenais@appq-sq.qc.ca
URL: www.appq-sq.qc.ca
Jean-Guy Dagenais, Président
Jocelyn Boucher, Vice-président, Ressources humaines
Luc Fournier, Vice-président, Finances
Jacques Painchaud, Vice-président, Discipline et déontologie
Pierre Veilleux, Vice-président, Griefs et formation
Daniel Rolland, Vice-président, Ress. matérielles et santé et sécurité du travail

Association of Black Lawyers & Notaries
#10, 10, rue Notre-Dame est, Montréal QC H2Y 1B7
Tel: 514-878-9112
Sharon Sandiford, Contact

Association of Canadian Court Administrators (ACCA) / Association des administrateurs judiciaires du Canada
#518B, 45 Main St. East, Hamilton ON L8P 1H4
Tel: 905-645-5333; *Fax:* 905-645-5375
URL: www.acca-aajc.ca
Debbie Baker, President
Christine Mosher, Secretary
Anne Roland, Treasurer
Linda Bogard, Vice-President

Association of Legal Court Interpreters & Translators (ALCIT) / Association des traducteurs et interprètes judiciares (ATIJ)
483, rue Saint-Antoine est, Montréal QC H2Y 1A5
Tel: 514-845-3113; *Fax:* 514-845-3006
e-mail: admin@atij.ca
URL: www.atij.ca; www.alcit.ca
Henri Keleny, President

Atlantic Association of Chiefs of Police
c/o Fredericton Police Force, 311 Queen St., Fredericton NB E3B 1B1
Tel: 506-460-2300; *Fax:* 506-460-2316
e-mail: mac.carlise@city.fredericton.nb.ca

Barreau de Montréal / Bar of Montréal
Palais de Justice, #980, 1, rue Notre Dame est, Montréal QC H2Y 1B6
Tél: 514-866-9392; *Téléc:* 514-866-1488
Courriel: info@barreaudemontreal.qc.ca
URL: www.barreaudemontreal.qc.ca
Doris Larrivée, Directrice générale
Stephen G. Schenke, Bâtonnier

British Columbia Federation of Police Officers (Ind.)
PO Box 42601, #105, 1005 Columbia St., New Westminster BC V3M 6H5
Tel: 604-650-1510; *Fax:* 604-850-1303
URL: www.bcfedpolice.com
Daryl Tottenhan, Director

Canadian Association of Black Lawyers (CABL) / L'Association des Avocats Noirs du Canada
#300, 20 Toronto St., Toronto ON M5C 2B8
URL: www.cabl.ca
Frank Walwyn

Canadian Association of Chiefs of Police (CACP) / Association canadienne des chefs de police (ACCP)
582 Somerset St. West, Ottawa ON K1R 5K2
Tel: 613-233-1106; *Fax:* 613-233-6960
e-mail: cacp@cacp.ca
URL: www.cacp.ca
Magda Mitilineos, Office Manager
Jack Ewatski, President
Peter Cuthbert, Executive Director

Canadian Association of Legal Translators / Association canadienne des juristes-traducteurs
PO Box 919, Stn. B, Ottawa ON K1P 5P9
Claire Vallée, President

Canadian Association of Police Boards (CAPB) / Association canadienne des commissions de police
PO Box 4670, Stn. E, Ottawa ON K1S 5H8
Tel: 819-682-1440; *Fax:* 819-682-4569
e-mail: jlanzon.capb.ca
URL: www.capb.ca
Jennifer Lanzon, Executive Director

Canadian Association of Provincial Court Judges (CAPCJ) / L'Association canadienne des juges de cours provinciales
c/o Provincial Court of Newfoundland, PO Box 68, Stn. Atlantic Place, 215 Water St., St. John's NL A1C 6C9
Fax: 709-729-6272
e-mail: gbrown@judicom.gc.ca
URL: www.judges-juges.ca/en/index.htm
Gregory O. Brown, Contact

Canadian Bar Association (CBA) / Association du barreau canadien
#500, 865 Carling Ave., Ottawa ON K1S 5S8
Tel: 613-237-2925; *Fax:* 613-237-0185
Toll-Free: 800-267-8860
e-mail: info@cba.org
URL: www.cba.org
Affiliation(s): Canadian Association of Law Teachers; Canadian Law Information Council; Commonwealth Bar Association; Inter-American Bar Association; International Bar Association; Union internationale des avocats
John D.V. Hoyles, CEO
Bernard Amyot, President

The Canadian Corporate Counsel Association (CCCA) / L'Association canadienne des conseillers juridiques d'entreprises
#410, 20 Toronto St., Toronto ON M5C 2B8
Tel: 416-869-0522; *Fax:* 416-869-0946
e-mail: ccca@ccca-cba.org
URL: www.cancorpcounsel.org
Derek Edward Patterson, President
Kari F. Horn, Treasurer

Canadian Council on International Law (CCIL) / Conseil canadien de droit international (CCDI)
275 Bay St., Ottawa ON K1R 5Z5
Tel: 613-235-0442; *Fax:* 613-232-8228
e-mail: info@ccil-ccdi.ca
URL: www.ccil-ccdi.ca
Affiliation(s): Société québécoise de droit international; American Society of International Law; Japanese Association of International Law
Mark Jewett, President
Elizabeth Macaulay, Manager

Canadian Criminal Justice Association (CCJA) / Association canadienne de justice pénale (ACJP)
#308, 1750 Courtwood Cres., Ottawa ON K2C 2B5
Tel: 613-725-3715; *Fax:* 613-725-3720
e-mail: ccja@bellnet.ca
URL: www.ccja-acjp.ca
Affiliation(s): Alberta Criminal Justice Association; British Columbia Criminal Justice Association; Manitoba Criminal Justice Association; New Brunswick Criminal Justice Association; Newfoundland & Labrador Criminology & Corrections Association; Nova Scotia Criminology & Corrections Association; Ontario Association of Corrections & Criminology; Saskatchewan Criminal Justice Association; Société de criminologie du Québec
Irving Kulik, Executive Director

Canadian Institute for the Administration of Justice (CIAJ) / Institut canadien d'administration de la justice (ICAJ)
Faculté de droit, Univ. de Montréal, PO Box 6128, Stn. Centre-Ville, #3421, 3101 Chemin de la Tour, Montréal QC H3C 3J7
Tel: 514-343-6157; *Fax:* 514-343-6296
e-mail: ciaj@ciaj-icaj.ca
URL: www.ciaj-icaj.ca
Christine Huglo Robertson, Executive Director

Canadian Law & Society Association (CLSA) / Association canadienne de droit et société (ACDS)
c/o Journals Division, University of Toronto Press, 5201 Dufferin St., Toronto ON M3H 5T8
Tel: 416-667-7810; *Fax:* 416-667-7881
Toll-Free: 800-221-9985
URL: www.acds-clsa.org

Canadian Maritime Law Association / Association canadienne de droit maritime
#4600, 800, place Victoria, Montréal QC H4Z 1H6
Tel: 514-849-4161; *Fax:* 514-849-4167
e-mail: cmla@cmla.org
URL: www.cmla.org
Alfred H.E. Popp, QC, Sec.-Treas.
Michael J. Bird, President
John G. O'Connor, Vice-President, Québec
M. Robert Jetté, QC, Vice-President, East

Canadian Petroleum Law Foundation
PO Box 4143, Stn. C, Calgary AB T2T 5M9
Tel: 403-237-2423
e-mail: lara.h.pella@esso.ca
URL: www.cplf.org
Ben Rogers, President
Miles Pittman, Treasurer

Canadian Police Association (CPPA) / L'Association canadienne des policiers (ACPP)
#100, 141 Catherine St., Ottawa ON K2P 1C3
Tel: 613-231-4168; *Fax:* 613-231-3254
e-mail: cpa-acp@cpa-acp.ca
URL: www.cpa-acp.ca
Charles Momy, President
Tom Stamatakis, Vice-President

Chambre des notaires du Québec
#600, 1801, av McGill College, Montréal QC H3B 3L2
Tél: 514-879-1793; *Téléc:* 514-879-1923
Ligne sans frais: 800-668-2473
Courriel: information@cdnq.org
URL: www.cdnq.org
Affiliation(s): Fédération des professions juridiques
Pierre Cléroux, Directeur général

Church Council on Justice & Corrections (CCJC) / Conseil des églises pour la justice et la criminologie
507 Bank St., 2nd Fl., Ottawa ON K2P 1Z5
Tel: 613-563-1688; *Fax:* 613-237-6129
e-mail: info@ccjc.ca
URL: www.ccjc.ca
Affiliation(s): The Network - Interaction for Conflict Resolution
Lorraine Berzins, Communication Chair of Justice

Community Legal Education Association (Manitoba) Inc. (CLEA) / Association d'éducation juridique communautaire (Manitoba) inc.
#205, 414 Graham Ave., Winnipeg MB R3C 0L8
Tel: 204-943-2382; *Fax:* 204-943-3600
e-mail: info@communitylegal.mb.ca
URL: www.communitylegal.mb.ca
Mary Troszko, Executive Director
Heather Dixon, President

Community Legal Education Ontario (CLEO)
#600, 119 Spadina Ave., Toronto ON M5V 2L1
Tel: 416-408-4420; *Fax:* 416-408-4424
e-mail: cleo@cleo.on.ca
URL: www.cleo.on.ca; www.cleonet.ca

Community Legal Information Association of Prince Edward Island (CLIA)
Sullivan Bldg., 1st Fl., PO Box 1207, Charlottetown PE C1A 7M8
Tel: 902-892-0853; *Fax:* 902-368-4096
Toll-Free: 800-240-9798
e-mail: clia@cliapei.ca
URL: www.cliapei.ca

Congress of Black Lawyers and Jurists of Québec
#500, 445, boul St-Laurent, Montréal QC H2Y 3T8
Tel: 514-954-3471; *Fax:* 514-954-3451

Continuing Legal Education Society of BC
#300, 845 Cambie St., Vancouver BC V6B 5T2
Tel: 604-669-3544; *Fax:* 604-669-9260
Toll-Free: 800-663-0437
e-mail: custserv@cle.bc.ca
URL: www.cle.bc.ca

Criminal Lawyers' Association (CLA)
#7, 296 Jarvis St., Toronto ON M5B 2C5
Tel: 416-214-9875; *Fax:* 416-968-6818
e-mail: anthony@criminallawyers.ca
URL: www.criminallawyers.ca
Affiliation(s): US National Association of Criminal Defence Lawyers; The Canadian Counsel of Criminal Defence Lawyers (CCCDL); The County & District Law President's Association (CDLPA)
Anthony Laycock, Executive Director
Frank Addario, President

Federation of Law Reform Agencies of Canada
c/o Manitoba Law Reform Commission, 405 Broadway, 12th Fl., Winnipeg MB R3C 3L6
Tel: 604-822-0142; *Fax:* 604-822-0144
Jeffrey A. Schnoor, President

Federation of Law Societies of Canada (FLSC) / Fédération des ordres professionnels de juristes du Canada
World Exchange Plaza, #1810, 45 O'Connor St., Ottawa ON K1P 1A4
Tel: 613-236-7272; *Fax:* 613-236-7233
e-mail: info@flsc.ca
URL: www.flsc.ca
Affiliation(s): International Bar Association; Union Internationale des Avocats
John Campion, President
Ian Donaldson, Q.C., Vice-President
Ronald J. MacDonald, Q.C., Vice-President
Bob Linney, Director, Communications

Fondation du barreau du Québec
Maison du Barreau, #404, 445, boul Saint-Laurent, Montréal QC H2Y 3T8
Tél: 514-954-3400; *Téléc:* 514-954-3449
Ligne sans frais: 800-361-8495
Courriel: fondation@barreau.qc.ca
URL: www.barreau.qc.ca
Alain Létourneau, Président

Foundation for Legal Research / La foundation pour la recherche juridique
c/o Law Foundation Of British Columbia, #1340, 605 Robsen Street, Vancouver BC V6B 5J3
Toll-Free: 800-267-8860
URL: www.cba.org
John R.R. Jennings, Chair
Francois Letourneaux, Secretary
Stephen Bresolin, Treasurer

Institute of Law Clerks of Ontario (ILCO)
#502, 20 Adelaide St. East, Toronto ON M5C 2T6
Tel: 416-214-6252; *Fax:* 416-214-6255
e-mail: receiption@ilco.on.ca
URL: www.ilco.on.ca
Lisa Matchim, President
Debra A. Bell, Secretary-Treasurer

International Centre for Criminal Law Reform & Criminal Justice Policy (ICCLR)
1822 East Mall, Vancouver BC V6T 1Z1
Tel: 604-822-9875; *Fax:* 604-822-9317
e-mail: icclr@law.ubc.ca
URL: www.icclr.law.ubc.ca
Affiliation(s): UN Crime Prevention & Criminal Justice Programme
Kathleen Macdonald, Executive Director

International Commission of Jurists (Canadian Section) (ICJ) / La Commission internationale de juristes (section canadienne) (CIJ)
#500, 865 Carling Ave., Ottawa ON K1S 5S8
Tel: 613-237-2925; *Fax:* 613-237-0185
e-mail: patw@cba.org
URL: www.icjcanada.org
Paul D.K. Fraser, Q.C., President
Pat Whiting, Executive Director

Law Foundation of British Columbia
#1340, 605 Robson St., Vancouver BC V6B 5J3
Tel: 604-688-2337; *Fax:* 604-688-4586
e-mail: lfbc@tlfbc.org
URL: www.lawfoundationbc.org
Wayne Robertson, Executive Director
Dev Dley, Chair
Jo-Anne Kaulius, Director, Finance

Law Foundation of Newfoundland & Labrador
Murray Premises, 2nd Fl., PO Box 5907, #49, 55 Elizabeth Ave., St. John's NL A1C 5X4
Tel: 709-754-4424; *Fax:* 709-754-4320
URL: www.atyp.com/lawfoundationnl/

Law Foundation of Nova Scotia
PO Box 325, Halifax NS B3J 2N7
Tel: 902-422-8335; *Fax:* 902-492-0424
e-mail: nslawfd@nslawfd.ca
URL: www.nslawfd.ca
Kerry L. Oliver, Executive Director

Law Foundation of Ontario / La fondation du droit de l'Ontario
PO Box 19, #3002, 20 Queen St. West, Toronto ON M5H 3R3
Tel: 416-598-1550; *Fax:* 416-598-1526
e-mail: general@lawfoundation.on.org
URL: www.lawfoundation-on.org
Mark J. Sandler, Chair
Elizabeth Goldberg, Chief Executive Officer

Law Foundation of Prince Edward Island
49 Water St., Charlottetown PE C1A 7K2
Tel: 902-566-1666
Affiliation(s): Association of Canadian Law Foundations
M. Jane Ralling, Chair

Law Foundation of Saskatchewan
#200, 2208 Scarth St., Regina SK S4P 2J6
Tel: 306-352-1121; *Fax:* 306-522-6222
e-mail: lfsk@virtusgroup.ca
URL: www.lawfoundation.sk.ca
Robert Arscott, F.C.A., Secretary
Karen Prisciak, Q.C., Chair
J. Gordon Wicijowski, LL.D., F.C.A., Treasurer

Law Society of Alberta (LSA)
#500, 919 - 11 Ave. SW, Calgary AB T2R 1P3
Tel: 403-229-4700; *Fax:* 403-228-1728
Toll-Free: 800-661-9003
e-mail: comdir@lawsocietyalberta.com
URL: www.lawsocietyalberta.com
Affiliation(s): Federation of Law Societies of Canada
Don Thompson, Executive Director
Eileen Dooley, Communications Director
Perry Mack, Q.C., President

Law Society of British Columbia
845 Cambie St., 8th Fl., Vancouver BC V6B 4Z9
Tel: 604-669-2533; *Fax:* 604-669-5232
e-mail: communications@lsbc.org
URL: www.lawsociety.bc.ca
Affiliation(s): Federation of Law Societies of Canada
Timothy E. McGee, CEO & Executive Director
Gordon Turriff, QC, President

Law Society of Manitoba (LSM) / La Société du Barreau du Manitoba
219 Kennedy St., Winnipeg MB R3C 1S8
Tel: 204-942-5571; *Fax:* 204-956-0624
e-mail: admin@lawsociety.mb.ca
URL: www.lawsociety.mb.ca
Allan Fineblit, CEO
Douglas A. Bedford, President
Grant Mitchell, Q.C., Vice-President

Law Society of New Brunswick / Barreau du Nouveau-Brunswick
#206, 1133 Regent St., Fredericton NB E3B 3Z2
Tel: 506-458-8540; *Fax:* 506-451-1421
e-mail: general@lawsociety-barreau.nb.ca
URL: www.lawsociety-barreau.nb.ca
Affiliation(s): Federation of Law Societies of Canada
Marc L. Richard, Q.C., Executive Director
David R. Ames, Q.C., President

Law Society of Newfoundland & Labrador
PO Box 1028, St. John's NL A1C 5M3
Tel: 709-722-4740; *Fax:* 709-722-8902
e-mail: CLE@lawsociety.nf.ca
URL: www.lawsociety.nf.ca
Affiliation(s): Federation of Law Societies of Canada
Peter G. Ringrose, Executive Director

Law Society of Nunavut (LSNU)
PO Box 149, Iqaluit NU X0A 0H0
Tel: 867-979-2330; *Fax:* 867-979-2333
e-mail: lawsociety@qiniq.com
URL: www.lawsociety.nu.ca
Craig Goebel, CEO

Law Society of Prince Edward Island
PO Box 128, 49 Water St., Charlottetown PE C1A 7K2
Tel: 902-566-1666; *Fax:* 902-368-7557
e-mail: lawsociety@lspei.pe.ca
URL: lawsociety@lspei.pe.ca
Affiliation(s): Federation of Law Societies of Canada
Susan M. Robinson, Sec.-Treas.

Law Society of Saskatchewan
#1100, 2002 Victoria Ave., Regina SK S4P 0R7
Tel: 306-569-8242; *Fax:* 306-352-2989
e-mail: reception@lawsociety.sk.ca
URL: www.lawsociety.sk.ca
Affiliation(s): Federation of Law Societies of Canada
A. Kirsten Logan, Q.C., Secretary & Co-Director, Administration
Allan T. Snell, Q.C., General Counsel & Co-Director, Administration

Law Society of the Northwest Territories / Le Barreau des Territoires du Nord-Ouest
PO Box 1298, 5004 - 50 Ave., Main Fl., Yellowknife NT X1A 2N9
Tel: 867-873-3828; *Fax:* 867-873-6344
e-mail: lsnt@theedge.ca or lawsocnt@lawsociety.nt.ca
URL: www.lawsociety.nt.ca
Affiliation(s): Federation of Law Societies of Canada
Linda Whitford, Executive Director

Law Society of Upper Canada / Barreau du Haut-Canada
Osgoode Hall, 130 Queen St. West, Toronto ON M5H 2N6
Tel: 416-947-3300; *Fax:* 416-947-3924
Toll-Free: 800-668-7380
e-mail: lawsociety@lsuc.on.ca
URL: www.lsuc.on.ca
Affiliation(s): Federation of Law Societies of Canada
Malcolm L. Heins, CEO
Diana Miles, Director, Professional Development & Competence

Law Society of Yukon (LSY)
#202, 302 Steele St., Whitehorse YT Y1A 2C5
Tel: 867-668-4231; *Fax:* 867-667-7556
e-mail: info@lawsocietyyukon.com
URL: www.lawsocietyyukon.com
Affiliation(s): Federation of Law Societies of Canada

Lynn Daffe, Executive Secretary

Legal Education Society of Alberta (LESA)
#2610, 10104 - 103 Ave., Edmonton AB T5J 0H8
Tel: 780-420-1987; *Fax:* 780-425-0885
Toll-Free: 800-282-3900
e-mail: lesa@lesa.org
URL: www.lesa.org
Paul Wood, Executive Director & Director, Canadian Centre for Professional Legal Education (CPLED) Alberta
Alan D. Fielding, Q.C., Chair
Thomas Achymichuk, Sec.-Treas.

Legal Information Society of Nova Scotia (LISNS)
5523B Young St., Halifax NS B3K 1Z7
Tel: 902-454-2198; *Fax:* 902-455-3105
Toll-Free: 800-665-9779
e-mail: lisns@legalinfo.org
URL: www.legalinfo.org

The Manitoba Law Foundation / La Fondation manitobaine du droit
412 McDermot Ave., Winnipeg MB R3C 0A9
e-mail: bpalace@gatewest.net
Barbara Palace, Executive Director

Municipal Law Enforcement Officers' Association (Ontario) Inc.
c/o City Of Barrie, PO Box 400, Barrie ON L4M 4T5
Tel: 705-739-4241; *Fax:* 705-739-4279
e-mail: mleo@mleoa.ca
URL: www.mleoa.ca
Brenda Russell, President

New Brunswick Law Foundation / Fondation pour l'avancement du droit au Nouveau-Brunswick
#206, 1133 Regent St., Fredericton NB E3B 3Z2
Tel: 506-458-8540; *Fax:* 506-451-1421
e-mail: general@lawsociety-barreau.nb.ca
URL: www.lawsociety.nb.ca
David R. Ames, President

New Brunswick Police Association / Association policière du Nouveau-Brunswick
284 Main St., Sackville NB E4L 3H5
Tel: 506-536-3445; *Fax:* 506-536-2745
Toll-Free: 800-561-4422
e-mail: www.policenb.ca
Dean Secord, President

Northwest Territories Association of Provincial Court Judges
c/o Territorial Court of Northwest Territories, PO Box 550, 4093 - 49th St., Yellowknife NT X1A 2N4
Tel: 867-873-7604; *Fax:* 867-873-0203
Affiliation(s): Canadian Association of Provincial Court Judges
Robert Gorin, Northwest Territories Director, Canadian Association of Provincial Court Judges

Northwest Territories Law Foundation
PO Box 2594, 5212 - 55th St., Yellowknife NT X1A 2P9
Tel: 867-873-8275; *Fax:* 867-873-6383
e-mail: action@theedge.ca
URL: www.lawsociety.nt.ca/NWTLawFoundation/tabid/212/Default.aspx
Wendy Carter, Executive Manager
Glenn Tait, Chair
Gerard Phillips, Vice-Chair

Nova Scotia Barristers' Society (NSBS)
#1101, 1645 Granville St., Halifax NS B3J 1X3
Tel: 902-422-1491; *Fax:* 902-429-4869
e-mail: info@nsbs.org
URL: www.nsbs.org
Affiliation(s): Canadian Lawyers' Insurance Association; Federation of Law Societies; Law Foundation of Nova Scotia; Law Reform Commission of Nova Scotia; Lawyers' Insurance Association of Nova Scotia; Nova Scotia Legal Aid Commission; Canadian Bar Association
Darrel I. Pink, Executive Director
Joel E. Pink, Q.C., President
Jacqueline L. Mullenger, Director, Admissions & Professional Development
Victoria Rees, Director, Professional Responsibility

Ontario Association of Corrections & Criminology
PO Box 949, Stn. K, Toronto ON M4P 2V3
Tel: 416-304-1974; *Fax:* 416-304-1977
e-mail: info@oacconline.org
URL: www.oacconline.org
Affiliation(s): Canadian Criminal Justice Association
Frances McKeague, President

Ontario Association of Police Services Boards (OAPSB)
10 Peel Centre Dr., Brampton ON L6T 4B9
Tel: 905-458-1488; *Fax:* 905-458-2260
Toll-Free: 800-831-7727
e-mail: admin@oapsb.ca
URL: www.oapsb.ca
Christina Bisanz, Consulting Executive Coordinator
Mary Smiley, President

Ontario Crown Attorneys Association (OCAA)
PO Box 30, #1015, 180 Dundas St. West, Toronto ON M5G 1Z8
Tel: 416-977-4517; *Fax:* 416-977-1460
e-mail: reception@ocaa.ca
URL: www.ocaa.ca
William K. Lightfoot, President

People's Law School
#150, 900 Howe St., Vancouver BC V6Z 2M4
Tel: 604-331-5400; *Fax:* 604-331-5401
e-mail: staff@publiclegaled.bc.ca
URL: www.publiclegaled.bc.ca

Police Association of Nova Scotia (PANS) / Association des policiers de la Nouvelle-Écosse
#22, 1000 Windmill Rd., Dartmouth NS B3B 1L7
Tel: 902-468-7555; *Fax:* 902-468-2202
Joseph W. Ross, Executive Director

Police Association of Ontario (PAO) / Association des policiers de l'Ontario
#1-3, 6730 Davand Dr., Mississauga ON L5T 2K8
Tel: 905-670-9770; *Fax:* 905-670-9755
e-mail: pao@pao.on.ca
URL: www.pao.on.ca
Ronald Middel, CAO
Larry Molyneaux, President

Probation Officers Association of Ontario (POAO)
#6245, 2100 Bloor St. West, Toronto ON M6S 5A5
Tel: 905-329-3219
URL: www.poao.org
Catherine Hutchison, President
Donald Larman, Vice-President

Provincial Judges Association of Manitoba
Provincial Court, PO Box 34, 59 Elizabeth Dr., Thompson MB R8N 1X4
Tel: 204-677-6773; *Fax:* 204-677-6584
Brian Colli, President

The Public Interest Advocacy Centre (PIAC) / Centre pour la défense de l'intérêt public
#1204, One Nicholas St., Ottawa ON K1N 7B7
Tel: 613-562-4002
e-mail: piac@piac.ca
URL: www.piac.ca
Michael Janigan, Executive Director

Public Legal Education Association of Saskatchewan, Inc. (PLEA Sask.)
#300, 201 - 21st East, Saskatoon SK S7K 0B8
Tel: 306-653-1868; *Fax:* 306-653-1869
e-mail: plea@plea.org
URL: www.plea.org
Joel Janow, Executive Director
Doug Surtees, President

Public Legal Information Association of Newfoundland (PLIAN)
Fortis Bldg., #227, 31 Peet St., St. John's NL A1B 3W8
Tel: 709-722-2643; *Fax:* 709-722-0054
Toll-Free: 888-660-7788
e-mail: info@publiclegalinfo.com
URL: www.publiclegalinfo.com
Susan M. Doyle, Executive Director

Saskatchewan Federation of Police Officers (SFPO)
26 Chase Cres., Regina SK S4R 7Y4
Tel: 306-539-0960
URL: www.saskpolice.com
Bernie Eiswirth, Executive Officer
Haye Dave, President

Société de criminologie du Québec (SCQ)
#201, 2000, boul Saint-Joseph est, Montréal QC H2H 1E4
Tél: 514-529-4391; *Téléc:* 514-529-6936
Courriel: crimino@societecrimino.qc.ca
URL: www.societecrimino.qc.ca
Affiliation(s): Canadian Criminal Justice Association
Caroline Savard, Directrice générale

The Society of Notaries Public of British Columbia
PO Box 44, #1220, 625 Howe St., Vancouver BC V6C 2T6
Tel: 604-681-4516; *Fax:* 604-681-7258
Toll-Free: 800-663-0343
e-mail: society@notaries.bc.ca
URL: www.notaries.bc.ca
Val Wilson, Editor-In-Chief
Susan Davis, President
John Eastwood, First Vice President

Toronto Lawyers Association
361 University Ave., Toronto ON M5G 1T3
Tel: 416-327-5700; *Fax:* 416-947-9148
e-mail: info@tlaonline.ca
URL: www.tlaonline.ca
Anne Matthewman, Executive Director

Yukon Law Foundation
PO Box 31789, Whitehorse YT Y1A 6L3
Tel: 867-667-7500; *Fax:* 867-393-3904
e-mail: execdir@yukonlawfoundation.com
URL: www.yukonlawfoundation.com
Deana Lemke, Executive Director
Malcolm Campbell, Chair

Yukon Public Legal Education Association (YPLEA)
PO Box 2799, Yukon College, Whitehorse YT Y1A 5K4
Tel: 867-668-5297; *Fax:* 867-668-5541
Toll-Free: 866-667-4305
e-mail: yplea@yukoncollege.yk.ca
URL: www.yplea.com
Robert Pritchard, Contact

Libraries & Archives

Administrators of Small Public Libraries of Ontario (ASPLO)
c/o Brant County Public Library, 12 William St., Paris ON N3L 1K7
Tel: 519-442-2433; *Fax:* 519-442-7582
e-mail: gay.kozakselby@county.brant.on.ca

Alberta Association of College Librarians (AACL)
c/o Red Deer College, PO Box 5005, 56 Ave. & 32 St., Red Deer AB T4N 5H5
Tel: 403-342-3306
e-mail: alice.mcnair@rdc.ab.ca
URL: www.aacl.engineseven.com
Geoff Owens, Chair
Lillian Li, Sec.-Treas.
Karin Hering, Director-at-Large

Alberta Association of Library Technicians (AALT)
PO Box 700, Edmonton AB T5J 2L4
Toll-Free: 866-350-2258
e-mail: marketing@aalt.org; membership@aalt.org; journal@aalt.org
URL: www.aalt.org
Social Media: www.facebook.com/group.php?gid=96867929556
Kim Martin, President
Melanie Belliveau, Director, Marketing
Sarah Stephens, Director, Membership
Lilla Lesko, Treasurer

Alberta Library Trustees Association (ALTA)
#6-24, 7 Sir Winston Churchill Sq., Edmonton AB T5J 2V5
Tel: 780-481-1725; *Fax:* 780-572-4447
e-mail: admin@librarytrustees.ab.ca; president@librarytrustees.ab.ca
URL: www.librarytrustees.ab.ca
Social Media: www.facebook.com/group.php?gid=89423578711
Karen Lynch, President
Doug Cooper, Vice-President
Martin Shields, Secretary-Treasurer

Archives Association of British Columbia (AABC)
#249, 34A-2755 Lougheed Hwy., Port Coquitlam BC V3B 5Y9
e-mail: aabc@aabc.bc.ca
URL: www.aabc.bc.ca
Lara Wilson, President
Lisa Glandt, Secretary
Sharon Walz, Treasurer

Archives Association of Ontario (AAO) / L'Association des archives de l'Ontario
#202, 10 Morrow Ave., Toronto ON M6R 2J1
Tel: 416-538-1650; *Fax:* 416-489-1713
e-mail: aao@aao.fis.utoronto.ca
URL: aao.fis.utoronto.ca
Affiliation(s): Ontario Heritage Foundation
Heather McCafferty-Leger, President
Marianne Henskens, Executive Director

Mary Gladwin, Secretary

Archives Council of Prince Edward Island
Public Archives, George Coles Bldg., PO Box 1000, Charlottetown PE C1A 7M4
Tel: 902-368-4290; *Fax:* 902-368-6327
e-mail: acpei@gov.pe.ca
URL: www.archives.pe.ca
Fred Horne, President

Archives Society of Alberta (ASA)
PO Box 4067, Stn. South Edmonton, Edmonton AB T6E 4S8
Tel: 780-424-2697; *Fax:* 780-425-1679
e-mail: jahsena@shaw.ca
URL: www.archivesalberta.org
Debby Shoctor, President

Art Libraries Society of North America (ARLIS/NA)
Technical Enterprises, Inc., 7044 S. 13th St., Oak Creek WI 53154 USA
Tel: 414-768-8000; *Fax:* 414-768-8001
Toll-Free: 800-817-0621
e-mail: info@arlisna.org
URL: www.arlisna.org
Elizabeth Clarke, Executive Director
Amy Lucker, President
Marilyn Russell, Vice-President
Edward (Ted) Goodman, Treasurer

Association des archivistes du Québec (AAQ)
CP 9768, Succ. Sainte-Foy, Québec QC G1V 4C3
Tél: 418-652-2357; *Téléc:* 418-646-0868
Courriel: infoaaq@archivistes.qc.ca
URL: www.archivistes.qc.ca
Andrée Gingras, Directrice générale

Association des bibliothécaires du Québec (ABQ) / Québec Library Association (QLA)
CP 1095, Pointe-Claire QC H9S 4H9
Tél: 514-697-0146; *Téléc:* 514-697-0146
Courriel: abqla@abqla.qc.ca
URL: www.abqla.qc.ca
Mèdia social: www.facebook.com/group.php?gid=52867661827
Susan Perles, Présidente

Association des bibliothécaires professionnel(le)s du Nouveau-Brunswick (ABPNB) / Association of Professional Librarians of New Brunswick (APLNB)
CP 423, Succ. A, Fredericton NB E3B 4Z9
Tél: 506-458-7058; *Téléc:* 506-453-4831
Courriel: info@abpnb-aplnb.ca
URL: www.abpnb-aplnb.ca
Victoria Volkanova, Présidente
Hector Alvarez, Secrétaire
Robin Sexton-Mayes, Trésorier

Association des bibliothèques de droit de Montréal (ABDM) / Montréal Association of Law Libraries (MALL)
Tour de la Bourse, CP 482, 800, Square Victoria, Montréal QC H4Z 1J7
Tél: 514-875-4100; *Téléc:* 514-875-6246
Courriel: ftrudeau@pouliotmercure.com
URL: www.abdm-mall.org
François Trudeau, Président

Association des bibliothèques publiques de l'Estrie (ABIPE)
5086, rue Frontenac, Lac-Mégantic QC G6B 1H3
Tél: 819-845-7115; *Téléc:* 819-845-5516
Courriel: mpmorin@abacom.com
URL: www.bpq-estrie.qc.ca
Marie-Pascale Morin, Présidente
Karine Corbeil, Vice-présidente

Association for Manitoba Archives (AMA)
PO Box 26005, Stn. Maryland, Winnipeg MB R3G 3R3
Tel: 204-942-3491; *Fax:* 204-942-3492
e-mail: ama1@mts.net
URL: www.mbarchives.mb.ca
Affiliation(s): Association of Canadian Archivists
Diane Haglund, Program Coordinator

Association of Canadian Archivists (ACA)
PO Box 2596, Stn. D, Ottawa ON K1P 5W6
Tel: 613-234-6977; *Fax:* 613-234-8500
e-mail: aca@archivists.ca
URL: www.archivists.ca
Affiliation(s): Bureau of Canadian Archivists
Duncan Grant, Executive Director
Scott Goodine, President
Heather Home, Sec.-Treas.

Association of Canadian Map Libraries & Archives (ACMLA) / Association des cartothèques et archives cartographiques du Canada (ACACC)
c/o Legal Deposit, Maps, Published Heritage, Library & Archives Canada, 550, boul de la Cité, Gatineau ON K1N ON4
e-mail: membership@acmla.org; president@acmla.org; secretary@acmla.org
URL: www.acmla.org
Andrew Nicholson, President
Dan Duda, First Vice-President
Wenonah Van Heyst, Second Vice-President
Susan McKee, Secretary
Susan Greaves, Treasurer

Association of Newfoundland & Labrador Archives (ANLA)
PO Box 23155, RPO Churchill Sq., St. John's NL A1B 4J9
Tel: 709-726-2867; *Fax:* 709-729-7989
e-mail: anla@nf.aibn.com
URL: www.anla.nf.ca
Stephanie Harlick, President

Association of Parliamentary Libraries in Canada (APLIC) / Association des bibliothéques parlementaires au Canada (ABPAC)
c/o Melissa Bennett, Librarian, Saskatchewan Legislative Library, #234, 2405 Legislative Dr., Regina SK S4S 0B3
e-mail: mbennett@legassembly.sk.ca (President)
URL: www.aplic-abpac.ca
Melissa Bennett, President

Association pour l'avancement des sciences et des techniques de la documentation (ASTED)
#202, 3414, av du Parc, Montréal QC H2X 2H5
Tél: 514-281-5012; *Téléc:* 514-281-8219
Courriel: info@asted.org
URL: www.asted.org
Affiliation(s): Fédération internationale des bibliothécaires (IFLA)
Julie LaRocque, Secétariat
Francis Farley-Chevrier, Directeur général

Atlantic Provinces Library Association (APLA)
c/o School of Information Management, Kenneth C. Rowe Management Bldg., 6100 University Ave., Halifax NS B3H 3J5
e-mail: mccay@dal.ca (Secretary)
URL: www.apla.ca
Social Media: www.facebook.com/group.php?gid=10792140537
Sarah Gladwell, President
Jocelyne Thompson, Vice-President
Ann Smith, Vice-President, Membership
Lori McCay-Peet, Secretary
Bill Slauenwhite, Treasurer

Bibliographical Society of Canada (BSC) / Société bibliographique du Canada (SBC)
PO Box 575, Stn. P, Toronto ON M5S 2T1
e-mail: gretagolick@rogers.com
URL: www.library.utoronto.ca/bsc
David McKnight, President
Greta Golick, Secretary

Les bibliothèques publiques des régions de Québec et Chaudière-Appalaches
4705, rue de la Promenade-des-Soeurs, Cap-Rouge QC G1Y 2W2
Tél: 418-641-6143; *Téléc:* 418-650-7795
Courriel: info@bibliotheques.qc.ca
URL: www.bibliotheques.qc.ca
Suzanne Rochefort, Présidente

Les bibliothèques publiques du Québec (BPQ)
7855, av San-Francisco, Brossard QC J4X 2A4
Tél: 514-886-7779; *Téléc:* 450-923-7042
Courriel: lucie.lachapelle@bibliothequespubliquesduquebec.ca
URL: http://bibliothequespubliquesduquebec.ca
Suzanne Payette, Présidente
Lachapelle Lucie, Directrice générale

British Columbia Courthouse Library Society
800 Smithe St., Vancouver BC V6Z 2E1
Tel: 604-660-2910; *Fax:* 604-660-9418
Toll-Free: 800-665-2570
e-mail: bccls@bccls.bc.ca
URL: www.bccls.bc.ca
Johanne Blenkin, Executive Director

British Columbia Library Association (BCLA)
#150, 900 Howe St., Vancouver BC V6Z 2M4
Tel: 604-683-5354; *Fax:* 604-609-0707
Toll-Free: 888-683-5354
e-mail: office@bcla.bc.ca
URL: www.bcla.bc.ca
Alane Wilson, Executive Director
Marjorie Mitchell, President
Christopher Kevlahan, Vice-President
Adrienne Wass, Second Vice-President
Chris Middlemass, Treasurer
Allie Douglas, Office Manager

British Columbia Library Trustees' Association (BCLTA)
PO Box 4334, Stn. Terminal, Vancouver BC V6B 3Z7
Tel: 604-913-1424; *Fax:* 604-913-1413
e-mail: admin@bclta.org
URL: www.bclta.org
Affiliation(s): British Columbia Library Association
Andy Ackerman, President
Ivan Idzan, Vice-President
Philip Mantler, Secretary-Treasurer

Canadian Association for Information Science (CAIS) / Association canadienne des sciences de l'information (ACSI)
c/o CAIS President, Faculty of Information & Media Studies, #240E, North Campus Bldg., University of Western Ontario, London ON N6A 5B7
Tel: 519-661-2111
e-mail: leckie@uwo.ca
URL: www.cais-acsi.ca

Canadian Association for School Libraries (CASL)
c/o Canadian Library Association, 328 Frank St., Ottawa ON K2P 0X8
Tel: 613-232-9625; *Fax:* 613-563-9895
e-mail: info@cla.ca; membership@cla.ca; cpd@cla.ca (Continuing Education)
URL: www.cla.ca/AM/Template.cfm?Section=CASL2
Linda Shantz-Keresztes, President
Diana Gauthier, Secretary-Treasurer
Derrick Grose, Editor, School Libraries in Canada: A Journal of the CASL
Victoria Pennell, Editor, Impact

Canadian Association of Children's Librarians (CACL)
c/o Canadian Library Association, 328 Frank St., Ottawa ON K2P 0X8
Tel: 613-232-9625
URL: www.cla.ca/AM/Template.cfm?Section=CAPL2
Lita Barrie, President
Ann Foster, Secretary-Treasurer

Canadian Association of College & University Libraries (CACUL)
c/o Canadian Library Association, 328 Frank St., Ottawa ON K2P 0X8
Tel: 613-232-9625; *Fax:* 613-563-9895
e-mail: info@cla.ca; membership@cla.ca; cpd@cla.ca (Continuing Education)
URL: www.cla.ca/AM/Template.cfm?Section=CACUL
Affiliation(s): Association of College and Research Libraries (ACRL)
Pam Ryan, President
Gillian Byrne, Vice-President & Director, Membership
Wendy Rodgers, Director, Awards
Carol Shepstone, Director, Grants
Christine E. Sammon, Secretary-Treasurer

Canadian Association of Family Resource Programs / Association canadienne des programmes de ressources pour la famille (PRF Canada)
#707, 331 Cooper St., Ottawa ON K2P 0G5
Tel: 613-237-7667; *Fax:* 613-237-8515
Toll-Free: 866-637-7226
e-mail: info@frp.ca
URL: www.frp.ca
Janice MacAulay, Executive Director
Crystal Elliott, President
Natalie Chapman, Vice-President
Trish Plant, Secretary
Stéphane Rivest, Treasurer
Jill Heckman, Director, Operations

Canadian Association of Law Libraries (CALL) / Association canadienne des bibliothèques de droit (ACBD)
PO Box 1570, #310, 4 Cataraqui St., Kingston ON K7L 5C8
Tel: 613-531-9338; *Fax:* 613-531-0626
e-mail: office@callacbd.ca
URL: www.callacbd.ca
Elizabeth Hooper, CAE, National Officer
Rosalie Fox, BA, MLS, President
Cyndi Murphy, Vice-President

Ann Marie Melvie, Secretary
Sandra Wilkins, Treasurer

Canadian Association of Music Libraries, Archives & Documentation Centres (CAML) / Association canadienne des bibliothèques, archives et centres de documentation musicaux inc. (ACBM)
c/o Music Section, Library & Archives Canada, 395 Wellington St., Ottawa ON K1A 0N4
e-mail: kirsten.walsh@ubc.ca (President); sacassin@yorku.ca (Webmaster)
URL: www.yorku.ca/caml
Affiliation(s): Canadian University Music Society (CUMS); International Association of Music Libaries (IAML); Library & Archives Canada
Kirsten Walsh, President
Rob van der Bliek, Treasurer
Laura Snyder, Secretary
Kyla Jemison, Membership Secretary
Stacy Allison-Cassin, Officer, Communications

Canadian Association of Public Libraries (CAPL)
c/o Canadian Library Association, 328 Frank St., Ottawa ON K2P 0X8
Tel: 613-232-9625; *Fax:* 613-563-9895
e-mail: info@cla.ca
URL: www.cla.ca/AM/Template.cfm?Section=CAPL2
Social Media: www.facebook.com/group.php?gid=7514940812
Andre Gagnon, President
Nancy Mackenzie, Vice-President
Maureen Sawa, Secretary-Treasurer

Canadian Association of Research Libraries (CARL) / Association des bibliothèques de recherche du Canada (ABRC)
Morisset Library, University of Ottawa, #239, 65 University St., Ottawa ON K1N 9A5
Tel: 613-562-5385; *Fax:* 613-562-5297
e-mail: carladm@uottawa.ca
URL: www.carl-abrc.ca
Ernie Ingles, President
Brent Roe, Executive Director
Diego Argáez, Officer, Research
Katherine McColgan, Coordinator, Programs

Canadian Association of Special Libraries & Information Services (CASLIS)
c/o Canadian Library Association, 328 Frank St., Ottawa ON K2P 0X8
Tel: 613-232-9625; *Fax:* 613-563-9895
e-mail: info@cla.ca; membership@cla.ca; cpd@cla.ca (Continuing Education)
URL: www.cla.ca/caslis
Social Media: www.facebook.com/group.php?gid=27554915813
Affiliation(s): Canadian Region of ARMA International
Robyn Stockand, President
Juanita Richardson, Vice-President
Melissa Fraser, Secretary
Laura Lemmens, Treasurer

Canadian Council of Archives (CCA) / Conseil canadien des archives
#501, 130 Albert St., Ottawa ON K1P 5G4
Tel: 613-565-1222; *Fax:* 613-565-5445
Toll-Free: 866-254-1403
e-mail: cca@archivescanada.ca
URL: www.cdncouncilarchives.ca
Ian Forsyth, CAE, Chairperson
Leslie Latta-Guthrie, Vice-Chair

Canadian Health Information Management Association (CHIMA)
#1404, 148 Fullarton St., London ON N6A 5P3
Tel: 519-438-6700; *Fax:* 519-438-7001
Toll-Free: 877-332-4462
e-mail: gail.crook@echima.ca
URL: www.echima.ca
Affiliation(s): International Federation of Health Records Organizations
Gail Crook, CEO & Registrar

Canadian Health Libraries Association (CHLA) / Association des bibliothèques de la santé du Canada (ABSC)
39 River St., Toronto ON M5A 3P1
Tel: 416-646-1600; *Fax:* 416-646-9460
e-mail: info@chla-absc.ca; pr@chla-absc.ca (Public Relations)
URL: www.chla-absc.ca
Orvie Dingwall, President
Miriam Ticoll, Vice-President
Lindsay Glynn, Director, Continuing Education
Rebecca Raworth, Director, Public Relations

Canadian Library Association (CLA) / Association canadienne des bibliothèques (ACB)
328 Frank St., Ottawa ON K2P 0X8
Tel: 613-232-9625; *Fax:* 613-563-9895
e-mail: info@cla.ca; membership@cla.ca; publishing@cla.ca; orders@cla.ca
URL: www.cla.ca
Social Media: www.facebook.com/group.php?gid=2229890224
Affiliation(s): Canadian Association of Public Libraries; Canadian Association of College & University Libraries; Canadian Library Trustees Association; Canadian Association for School Libraries; Canadian Association of Special Libraries & Information Services
Keith Walker, President
Kelly Moore, Executive Director
Wendy Walton, Officer, Conference & Professional Development
Judy Green, Manager, Marketing & Communications
Rizwan Choudhary, Manager, Web & IT Infrastructure
Ingrid Langhammer, Treasurer

Canadian Library Trustees Association (CLTA)
c/o Canadian Library Association, 328 Frank St., Ottawa ON K2P 0X8
Tel: 613-232-9625; *Fax:* 613-563-9895
e-mail: info@cla.ca; membership@cla.ca; cpd@cla.ca (Continuing Education)
URL: www.cla.ca/AM/Template.cfm?Section=CLTA
Jan Harder, President
Betty Thomas, Vice-President
Elaine Kivisto, Secretary-Treasurer

Canadian Urban Libraries Council (CULC)
c/o Brampton Public Library, 65 Queen St. East, Brampton ON L6W 3L6
Tel: 905-793-4636; *Fax:* 905-453-0810
e-mail: info@culc.ca
URL: www.culc.ca
Betty Ferreira, Executive Director

Church Library Association of Ontario (CLAO)
c/o Margaret Godefroy, CLAO Membership Secretary, #603, 155 Navy St., Oakville ON L6J 2Z7
Tel: 905-845-0222
e-mail: agodefroy@cogeco.ca (Membership Secretary)
URL: www.churchlibraries.ca
Social Media: www.facebook.com/group.php?gid=117754255215
Arthur McClelland, President
Thelma Campbell, Secretary
Margaret Godefroy, Membership Secretary
Jo-Anne Vandermey, Treasurer
Jane Rocoski, Coordinator, Resources

Corporation des bibliothécaires professionnels du Québec (CBPQ) / Corporation of Professional Librarians of Québec
#103, 353, rue St. Nicolas, Montréal QC H2Y 2P1
Tél: 514-845-3327; *Téléc:* 514-845-1618
Courriel: info@cbpq.qc.ca
URL: www.cbpq.qc.ca
Régine Horinstein, Directrice générale
Guylaine Beaudry, Présidente

Council of Archives New Brunswick (CANB) / Conseil des archives du Nouveau-Brunswick
PO Box 1204, Stn. A, 23 Dineen Dr., Fredericton NB E3B 5C8
Tel: 506-453-4327; *Fax:* 506-453-3288
e-mail: archives.advisor@gnb.ca
URL: www.canbarchives.ca/canb
Anne LeClair, Archives Advisor

Council of Nova Scotia Archives (CNSA)
6016 University Ave., Halifax NS B3H 1W4
Tel: 902-424-7093; *Fax:* 902-424-0628
e-mail: advisor@councilofnsarchives.ca
URL: www.councilofnsarchives.ca
Karen White, Advisor, Archives

Council of Prairie & Pacific University Libraries (COPPUL)
2005 Sooke Rd., Victoria BC V9B 5Y4
Tel: 250-391-2554; *Fax:* 250-391-2556
e-mail: coppul@royalroads.ca
URL: www.coppul.ca
Sandy Slade, Executive Director

Federal Libraries Coordination Secretariat
chives Canada, 395 Wellington St., Ottawa ON K1A 0N4
Tel: 819-934-7427; *Fax:* 819-934-7534
e-mail: FLCS-SCBGF@lac-bac.gc.ca
URL: www.collectionscanada.ca/cfl-cbgf
Fabio Onesi, Director
Katherine Miller-Gatenby, Manager
Deane Zeeman, Coordinator, Federal Libraries Consortium

Golden Horseshoe Health Libraries Association
c/o St. Joseph's Centre for Mountalin Health Services, PO Box 585, 100 West 5th St., Hamilton ON L8N 3K7
Tel: 905-522-1155
e-mail: devries@mcmaster.ca
URL: www.chla-absc.ca/chapter/ghhla/index.html
Anne Devries, President

Halifax Library Association
c/o 5940 South St., Halifax NS B3H 1S6
URL: www.smu.ca/administration/archives/hla
Social Media: www.facebook.com/group.php?gid=20160077946
Collette Saunders, President

Health Libraries Association of British Columbia (HLABC)
c/o Devon Greyson, UBC Centre for Health Services & Policy Research, #201, 2206 East Mall, Vancouver BC V6T 1Z3
Tel: 604-822-7353; *Fax:* 604-822-5690
e-mail: devon-at-chspr.ubc.ca (President)
URL: www.hlabc.bc.ca
Social Media: www.facebook.com/group.php?gid=2347253553
Devon Greyson, President
Brooke Ballantyne-Scott, Vice-President
Elisheba Muturi, Secretary
Anne Allgaier, Treasurer & Contact, Membership

Indexing Society of Canada / Société canadienne d'indexation
PO Box 664, Stn. P, Toronto ON M5S 2Y4
URL: www.indexers.ca
Affiliation(s): Society of Indexers; American Society of Indexers; Australian Society of Indexers
Mary Newberry, Co-President
Vivien Cartmell, Co-President/Prairies & N. Cda Rep
Audrey McClellan, Membership Secretary
Gillian Watts, Treasurer
Elspeth Richmond, Co-Representative, British Columbia
Marie Gabe, Representative, Central Canada
Ruth Pincoe, International Liaison

Library Association of Alberta (LAA)
80 Baker Cres. NW, Calgary AB T2L 1R4
Tel: 403-284-5818; *Fax:* 403-282-6646
Toll-Free: 877-522-5550
e-mail: info@laa.ca; info@albertalibraryconference.com
URL: www.laa.ca
Mary Jane Bilsland, President
Pat Sandercock, First Vice-President
Linda Williams, 2nd Vice-President
Julia Reinhart, Treasurer

Library Boards Association of Nova Scotia (LBANS)
c/o Gary Archibald, Secretary, PO Box 2680, RR#2, Yarmouth NS B5A 4A6
Tel: 902-742-4195
e-mail: archibaldg@eastlink.ca
URL: www.standupforlibraries.ca
Mary MacLellan, President
Shirley McNamara, Vice-President
Gary Archibald, Secretary
Marie Hogan Loker, Treasurer

London Area Health Libraries Association (LAHLA)
c/o South Huron Hospital, Shared Library Services, 24 Huron St. West, Exeter ON N0M 1S2
Tel: 519-235-5168; *Fax:* 519-235-4476
e-mail: linda.wilcox@shha.on.ca
Linda Wilcox, President

Manitoba Association of Health Information Providers (MAHIP)
c/o Christine Shaw-Diagle, 2340 Pembina Hwy., Winnipeg MB R3T 2E8
Tel: 204-477-3284; *Fax:* 204-269-7936
e-mail: diana_stojanovic-lewis@umanitoba.ca
URL: www.chla-absc.ca/chapter/mahip/index.html
Diana Stojanovic-Lewis, President

Manitoba Association of Library Technicians (MALT)
PO Box 1872, Winnipeg MB R3C 4R1
e-mail: malt_info@yahoo.com
URL: www.malt.mb.ca
Social Media: www.facebook.com/group.php?gid=47603963419
Catherine Taylor, President
Elizabeth Stregger, Vice-President
Jonine Bergen, Secretary & Coordinator, Communications
Alyssa Campbell, Treasurer
Jodi Turner, Coordinator, Membership

Manitoba Library Association (MLA)
#606, 100 Arthur St., Winnipeg MB R3B 1H3
Tel: 204-943-4567; *Fax:* 866-202-4567
e-mail: manitobalibrary@gmail.com
URL: www.mla.mb.ca
Social Media: www.facebook.com/group.php?gid=6003904478
Sherri Vokey, President
Emma Hill Kepron, Vice-President
Rebecca Schramm, Secretary
Kristen Kruse, Treasurer
Lesley Mackie, Director, Membership

Manitoba School Library Association (MSLA)
c/o Sherry Gibson, Wayoata School, 605 Wayoata St., Winnipeg MB R2C 1J8
URL: www.manitobaschoollibraries.com
Jo-Anne Gibson, President
Rhonda Morrissette, Webmaster

Maritimes Health Libraries Association (MHLA) / Association des bibliothèques de la santé des Maritimes (ABSM)
c/o W.K. Kellogg Health Sciences Library, Tupper Medical Building, PO Box 2100, 5850 College St., Halifax NS B3H 1X5
Tel: 902-494-2483
URL: www.chla-absc.ca/mhla/
Shelley McKibbon, President

New Brunswick Library Trustees' Association (NBLTA) / Association des commissaires de bibliothèque du Nouveau-Brunswick, inc.
c/o Doug Goss, 209 Saunders Rd., McAdam NB E6J 1M3
e-mail: gossdj@nbed.nb.ca
Doug Goss, Chair

Newfoundland & Labrador Health Libraries Association (NLHLA)
c/o Health Sciences Library, Memorial Univ. of Newfoundland, St. John's NL A1B 3V6
Tel: 709-737-6676; *Fax:* 709-737-6866
e-mail: lbarnett@mun.ca
URL: www.infonet.st-johns.nf.ca/nlhla/
Affiliation(s): Canadian Health Libraries Association
Linda Barnett, Secretary
Alison Reid, President

Northern Alberta Health Libraries Association
c/o Library, Institute of Health Economics, #1200, 10405 Jasper Ave., Edmonton AB T5J 3N4
Tel: 780-448-4881
e-mail: nahla@nahla.ca
URL: www.nahla.ca
Liz Dennett, President

Northern Lights Health Library Association
c/o Sault Area Hospital, 969 Queen Street East, Sault Ste Marie ON P6A 2C4
Tel: 705-759-3434; *Fax:* 705-759-3847
e-mail: aslettk@sah.on.ca
Kim Aslett, President

Northwest Territories Archives Council (NWTAC)
c/o Northwest Territories Archives, Gov't of Northwest Territories, PO Box 1320, Yellowknife NT X1A 2L9
Tel: 867-873-7698; *Fax:* 867-873-0205
e-mail: peter_harding@gov.nt.ca
URL: www.pwnhc.ca/nwtac/
Karen Ashbury, President

Northwestern Ontario Health Libraries Association (NOHLA)
c/o S. Regalado, Librarian, SJCG Library Svs., St. Joseph's Care Group, PO Box 2930, 580 Algoma St. North, Thunder Bay ON P7B 5G4
Tel: 807-343-4362; *Fax:* 807-343-4306
e-mail: regalads@tbh.net; cmackenzie@hscn.on.ca
Sophie M. Regalado, MISt, MA, Chair

Nova Scotia Government Libraries Council (NSGLC)
c/o Dept. of Justice Library
Tel: 902-424-7699; *Fax:* 902-424-0510
e-mail: lamietm@gov.ns.ca
URL: nsglc.ednet.ns.ca
Ruth Hart, Chair
Natalie MacPherson, Secretary
Anne Van Iderstine, Treasurer

Nova Scotia Library Association (NSLA)
c/o Kelli WooShue, Spring Garden Memorial Public Library, 5381 Spring Garden Rd., Halifax NS B3J 1E9
Tel: 902-490-5710
e-mail: wooshuk@halifax.ca; nslanewsletter@gmail.com (Newsletter)
URL: www.nsla.ns.ca
Lynn Lavoie, President
Denise Corey, Secretary
Carin Cress, Treasurer
Mary Landry, Convenor, Continuing Education
Rachel Crosby, Contact, Membership
Lori Noseworthy, Contact, Newsletter

Ontario Association of Library Technicians (OALT) / Association des bibliotechniciens de l'Ontario (ABO)
Abbey Market, PO Box 76010, 1500 Upper Middle Rd. West, Oakville ON L6M 3H5
e-mail: info@oaltabo.on.ca
URL: www.oaltabo.on.ca
Kathryn Suffoletta, President
Shannon Matthews, Treasurer
Donna Brown, Coordinator, External Communications
Lisa Eschli, Coordinator, Internal Communications
Amy Dwyer, Coordinator, Membership
Maria Ripley, Coordinator, Chapters
Kathi Vandenheuvel, Archivist

Ontario College & University Library Association (OCULA)
135 Fennell Ave. W., Hamilton ON L9C 1E9
Tel: 905-575-1212; *Fax:* 416-941-9581
e-mail: info@accessola.com
URL: www.accessola.com
Affiliation(s): Ontario Library Association
Nathalie Soini, Vice-President
Cynthia Williamson, President

Ontario Council of University Libraries (OCUL)
c/o Library, University of Toronto, 130 St. George Street, Toronto ON M5S 1A5
Tel: 416-978-4211; *Fax:* 416-978-6755
URL: www.ocul.on.ca
Faye Abrams, Projects Officer

Ontario Library & Information Technology Association (OLITA)
c/o OLA, 100 Lombard, Toronto ON M5C 1M3
Tel: 416-363-3380; *Fax:* 416-941-9581
e-mail: info@accessola.com
URL: www.accessola.com/olita/
Michael Vandenburg, President

Ontario Library Association (OLA)
#201, 50 Wellington St. East, Toronto ON M5E 1C8
Tel: 416-363-3388; *Fax:* 416-941-9581
Toll-Free: 866-873-9867
e-mail: info@accessola.com
URL: www.accessola.com
Social Media: www.facebook.com/group.php?gid=2233680329
Affiliation(s): Ontario College & University Library Association; Ontario Library & Information Technology Association; Ontario Library Boards' Association; Ontario Public Library Association; Ontario School Library Association; L'Association des bibliothécaires francophones de l'Ontario
Shelagh Paterson, Executive Director
Mary Ann Mavrinac, President
Paul Takala, Treasurer
Helios He, Manager, Operations

Ontario Library Boards' Association (OLBA)
c/o Ontario Library Association, #201, 50 Wellington St. East, Toronto ON M5E 1C8
Tel: 416-363-3388; *Fax:* 416-941-9581
Toll-Free: 866-873-9867
e-mail: info@accessola.com; membership@accessola.com
URL: www.accessola.com/olba
Affiliation(s): Ontario Library Association
Jane Hilton, President
Joyce Cunningham, Vice-President

Ontario Public Library Association (OPLA)
#201, 50 Wellington St. East, Toronto ON M5E 1C8
Tel: 416-363-3388; *Fax:* 416-941-9581
Toll-Free: 866-873-9867
e-mail: info@accessola.com
URL: www.accessola.com/opla/bins/index.asp
Jill Nicholoson, President
Tammy Robinson, Vice-President
Aegard Joanna, Secretary
Laura Carter, Treasurer

Ontario School Library Association (OSLA)
c/o Ontario Library Association, #201, 50 Wellington St. East, Toronto ON M5E 1C8
Tel: 416-363-3388; *Fax:* 416-941-9581
Toll-Free: 866-873-9867
URL: www.accessola.com/osla
Ruth Hall, President
Beth McEwen, Secretary-Treasurer

Ottawa Valley Health Libraries Association (OVHLA) / Association des bibliothèques de santé de la Vallée d'Outaouais
c/o The Ottawa Hospital, 1053 Carling Ave., Ottawa ON K1Y 4E9
Tel: 613-798-5555; *Fax:* 613-761-5292
e-mail: mquirie@ottawahospital.on.ca
URL: www.ovhla.on.ca
Margaret Quirie, President
Debbie Ayotte, Secretary

Prince Edward Island Professional Librarians Association (PEIPLA)
c/o Robertson Library Reference Dept., 550 University Ave., Charlottetown PE C1A 4P3
Tel: 902-566-9558; *Fax:* 902-566-9552
Brenda Brady, Contact

Regroupement des bibliothèques publiques de l'Abitibi-Témiscamingue (RBPAT)
201, ave. Dallaire, Rouyn-Noranda QC J9X 4T5
Tél: 819-762-4305; *Téléc:* 819-762-5903
Courriel: info@crsbpat.qc.ca
URL: www.biblrn.qc.ca/rbpat/

Regroupement des bibliothèques publiques de la Côte-Nord
Bibliothèque centrale de prêt de la Côte-Nord, 59, rue Napoléon, Sept-Iles QC G4R 5C5
Tél: 418-962-1020
Courriel: info@rbpcn.com
Yvon Grondin, Président

Regroupement Les bibliothèques publiques du Saguenay-Lac-Saint-Jean (RABLES)
100, rue Price ouest, Alma QC G8B 4S1
Tél: 418-662-6425; *Téléc:* 418-662-7593
Ligne sans frais: 800-563-6425
Courriel: sbolduc@reseaubiblioslsj.qc.ca
URL: catweb.crsbpslsj.biblio.qc.ca
Sophie Bolduc, Directrice générale (par intérim)

Réseau des archives du Québec (RAQ)
a/s Archives nationales du Québec à Montréal, 535 av Viger est, local 5.27.1, Montréal QC H2L 2P3
Tél: 514-864-9213
Courriel: raq@bellnet.ca
URL: www.raq.qc.ca
Danielle Aubin, Présidente
Bernard Savoie, Secrétaire

Saskatchewan Association of Library Technicians, Inc. (SALT)
PO Box 24019, Saskatoon SK S7K 8B4
Fax: 306-543-4487
e-mail: salt@lib.sk.ca
URL: www.lib.sk.ca/salt
Dorothy Richard, President
Carole-Anne Wilson-Hough, Secretary

Saskatchewan Council for Archives & Archivists (SCAA)
#202, 2080 Broad St., Regina SK S4P 1Y3
Tel: 306-780-9414
e-mail: scaa@sasktel.net
URL: www.scaa.sk.ca
Carey Isaak, Executive Director & Advisor, Archives
Tim Hutchinson, President
May Chan, Treasurer

Saskatchewan Health Libraries Association (SHLA)
c/o Regina-Qu'Appelle Health Region, Health Sciences Library, 1440 - 14th Ave., Regina SK S4P 0W5
Tel: 306-766-3833; *Fax:* 306-766-3839
e-mail: kelly.mcivor@usask.ca
URL: www.lib.sk.ca/shla/
Kelly McIvor, President

Saskatchewan Library Association (SLA)
#15, 2010 - 7th Ave., Regina SK S4R 1C2
Tel: 306-780-9413; *Fax:* 306-780-9447
e-mail: slaexdir@sasktel.net; slaprograms@sasktel.net
URL: www.saskla.ca
Social Media: www.facebook.com/group.php?gid=106445391816
Jeff Mason, President
Caroline Selinger, Executive Director

Kirsten Hansen, Program Administrator
Brett Waytuck, Treasurer

Saskatchewan Library Trustees Association (SLTA)
c/o Wendy Thienes, PO Box 573, Shaunavon SK S0N 2M0
Tel: 306-297-6368; *Fax:* 306-297-3668
e-mail: wendy.thienes@gmail.com
URL: www.libraries.gov.sk.ca/slta
Wendy Thienes, Executive Director
Bev Dubois, President
Dennis Taylor, Vice-President
Kae Campbell, Treasurer

Southern Alberta Health Libraries Association (SAHLA)
c/o Health Sciences Library, University of Calgary, 3330 University Dr. NW, Calgary AB T2N 4N1
Tel: 403-220-6858; *Fax:* 403-282-7992
e-mail: sahla@sahla.org
URL: www.sahla.org
Taryn Lenders, President

Southwestern Ontario Health Library Information Network
c/o Hotel Dieu Grace Hospital Medical Library, 1030 Ouellette Ave., Windsor ON N9A 1E1
Tel: 519-973-4411
e-mail: linda.wilcox@shha.on.ca
URL: www.chla-absc.ca/sohlin
Linda Wilcox, President

Special Libraries Association (SLA)
331 South Patrick St., Alexandria VA 22314-3501 USA
Tel: 703-647-4900; *Fax:* 703-647-4901
e-mail: cschatz@sla.org (Public Relations); membership@sla.org
URL: www.sla.org
Janice R. Lachance, Chief Executive Officer
Linda Broussard, Chief Community Officer
Quan O. Logan, Chief Technology Officer
Doug Newcomb, Chief Policy Officer

Toronto Health Libraries Association (THLA)
PO Box 94056, 3409 Yonge St., Toronto ON M4N 2L0
Tel: 416-485-0377; *Fax:* 416-485-6877
e-mail: president@thla.ca
URL: www.thla.ca
Affiliation(s): Ontario Hospital Libraries Association
Weina Wang, President

Yukon Council of Archives (YCA)
PO Box 31089, Whitehorse YT Y1A 5P7
Tel: 867-667-5321; *Fax:* 867-393-6253
e-mail: yukoncouncilofarchives@yahoo.ca
URL: www.yukoncouncilofarchives.ca
Clara Rutherford, President
Vanessa Thorson, Vice-President

Yukon Teacher-Librarians' Association (YTLA)
2064 - 2nd Ave., Whitehorse YT Y1A 1A9
Tel: 867-668-6777; *Fax:* 867-667-4324
e-mail: admin@yta.yk.ca
URL: www.yta.yk.ca
Affiliation(s): Association of Teacher Librarians in Canada; Canadian School Library Association
Sandra Henderson, President

Literacy

Regroupement de Bouches à Oreilles (RBO)
265, rue Lanctôt, Chibougamau QC G8P 1C1
Tél: 418-748-2239; *Téléc:* 418-748-2735
URL: www.abc02.org/chibougamau/
Céline Laliberté, Coordonnatrice

Literary Arts

L'arc-en-ciel littéraire
CP 180, Succ. C, Montréal QC H2L 4K1
Courriel: arcenciellitteraire@yahoo.ca
URL: arcenciellitteraire.site.voila.fr
Réjean Roy, Président fondateur

Long-Term Care

New Brunswick Special Care Home Association Inc.
c/o Seely Lodge Inc., 2443 Westfield Rd., Saint John NB E2M 6L4
Tel: 506-738-8514; *Fax:* 506-738-0892
e-mail: janseely@rogers.com
URL: www.nbscha.com
Jan Seely, President

Management & Administration

Administrative Sciences Association of Canada (ASAC) / Association des sciences administratives du Canada
c/o Sobey School of Business, Saint Mary's University, Halifax NS B3H 3C3
Tel: 902-496-8139
e-mail: jean.mills@smu.ca
URL: www.asac.ca
Jean Helms Mills, ASAC Bulletin Editor
Diane Miller, President

Alberta Institute Purchasing Management Association of Canada (AIPMAC)
Centre 104, #612, 5241 Calgary Trail, Edmonton AB T6H 5G8
Tel: 780-944-0355; *Fax:* 780-944-0356
Toll-Free: 866-610-4089
e-mail: info@aipmac.ab.ca
URL: www.aipmac.ab.ca
Jacki Richards, Chief Operating Officer
Jean Loitz, President
Bernie Dauvin, Treasurer

ARMA Canada (ARMA)
PO Box 6000, Fredericton NB E3B 5H1
Tel: 506-453-5618; *Fax:* 506-462-2046
e-mail: bernita.cogswell@gnb.ca
URL: www.armacanada.org
Social Media: www.facebook.com/group.php?gid=14876329775
Bernita Cogswell, Canadian Regional Manager
Fred Wideman, Sec.-Treas.

Association des MBA du Québec (AMBAQ)
#900, 500, rue Sherbrooke ouest, Montréal QC H3A 3C6
Tél: 514-282-3810; *Téléc:* 514-844-7556
Courriel: mba@affaires.com
URL: www.ambaq.com
Jean-Guy Renaud, Directeur général

Association of Administrative Assistants (AAA) / Association des adjoints administratifs
c/o 11110 - 108 St., Edmonton AB T5G 2T2
Tel: 780-423-2929; *Fax:* 780-407-3340
e-mail: info@aaa.ca
URL: www.aaa.ca
Doris Kurtz, QAA, Director

Association of Cultural Executives (ACE) / Association des cadres d'institutions culturelles (ACIC)
c/o Centre for Cultural Management, #HH142, University of Waterloo, Waterloo ON N2L 3G1
Tel: 519-888-4567; *Fax:* 519-746-3956
e-mail: ccm@watarts.uwaterloo.ca
URL: www.arts.uwaterloo.ca/ccm/ace/
Jeremy Morgan, President

Association of Fundraising Professionals (AFP)
#412, 260 King St. East, Toronto ON M5A 4L5
Tel: 416-941-9212; *Fax:* 416-941-9013
Toll-Free: 800-796-7373
e-mail: info@afptoronto.org
URL: www.afptoronto.org
Cynthia Quigley, Manager, Administration

Association of Professional Executives of the Public Service of Canada (APEX) / L'Association professionnelle des cadres de la fonction publique du Canada
#508, 75 Albert St., Ottawa ON K1P 5E7
Tel: 613-995-6252; *Fax:* 613-943-8919
e-mail: info@apex.gc.ca
URL: www.apex.gc.ca
Denise Amyot, President
Hanny Toxopeus, Chief Executive Officer

British Columbia Institute of the Purchasing Management Association of Canada
#200, 435 Columbia St., New Westminster BC V3L 5N8
Tel: 604-540-4494; *Fax:* 604-540-4023
Toll-Free: 800-411-7622
e-mail: admin@bci-pmac.bc.ca
URL: www.bci-pmac.bc.ca
Chris Dodds, President

Canadian Association of Management Consultants (CMC - Canada) / Association canadienne des conseillers en management
#815, 4 King St. West, Toronto ON M5H 1B6
Tel: 416-860-1515; *Fax:* 416-860-1535
Toll-Free: 800-268-1148
e-mail: consulting@cmc-canada.ca
URL: www.cmc-canada.ca
Todd Williams, Chair
Mauro Meneghetti, Vice Chair
Glenn Yonemitsu, Chief Executive Officer
Rainer Beltzner, Treasurer
Mary Blair, Managing Director
Suzie Fernandes, Director, Membership & Certification
Lora Rossi, Director, Stakeholder Relations

Canadian Association of School Administrators (CASA) / Association canadienne des administrateurs et des administratrices scolaires (ACAS)
1123 Glenashton Dr., Oakville ON L6H 5M1
Tel: 905-845-2345; *Fax:* 905-845-2044
e-mail: leslea@opsoa.org
URL: www.casa-acas.ca
Affiliation(s): College of Alberta School Superintendents; Manitoba Association of School Superintendents; Ontario Catholic Supervisory Officers' Association; Ontario Public Supervisory Officials' Association; Association of Administrators of English Schools of Québec; Association of Nova Scotia Educational Administrators; School Administrators of Prince Edward Island; Newfoundland & Labrador Association of Superintendents of Education; Association of Directors General of English School Boards of Québec; New Brunswick School Superintendents Association
Frank Kelly, Executive Director
Leslea Wylie, Administrative Assistant

Canadian Executive Service Organization (CESO) / Service d'assistance canadienne aux organismes (SACO)
PO Box 328, #700, 700 Bay St., Toronto ON M5G 1Z6
Tel: 416-961-2376; *Fax:* 416-961-1096
Toll-Free: 800-268-9052
e-mail: toronto@ceso-saco.com
URL: www.ceso-saco.com
Dorothy Nyambi, Vice President, International Services
Paul van der Wel, President & CEO
Bob Dickson, Vice President, National Services

Canadian Institute of Certified Administrative Managers (CICAM)
#800, 2 St. Clair Ave. East, Toronto ON M4T 2T5
Tel: 416-921-7962; *Fax:* 416-921-3959
Toll-Free: 800-233-5864
e-mail: mailbox@cicam.org
URL: www.cicam.org
Phil Russo
Sal Mian, President

Canadian Institute of Management (CIM) / Institut canadien de gestion
National Office, 15 Collier St., Lower Level, Barrie ON L4M 1G5
Tel: 705-725-8926; *Fax:* 705-725-8196
Toll-Free: 800-387-5774
e-mail: office@cim.ca
URL: www.cim.ca
Deb Johnstone, C.I.M., ATM-S,, President
Paul Markle, C.I.M., P. Mgr, National Secretary
Mardi Stevenson, C.I.M., P.Mgr., National Treasurer
Paul Walsh, National Academic Dean

Canadian Management Centre
150 York St., 5th Fl., Toronto ON M5H 3S5
Fax: 416-313-4985
Toll-Free: 877-262-2519
e-mail: cmcinfo@cmctraining.org
URL: www.cmctraining.org
Affiliation(s): American Management Association International
John Eckmire, Vice President, Development
Greg Breen, Vice President, Corporate Learning Solutions
Bruce Peer, President & Managing Director
Andre Proulx, Director, Marketing

Canadian Public Relations Society (CPRS) / La Société canadienne des relations publiques
#346, 4195 Dundas St. West, Toronto ON M8X 1Y4
Tel: 416-239-7034; *Fax:* 416-239-1076
e-mail: admin@cprs.ca
URL: www.cprs.ca
Social Media: twitter.com/CPRSNational
Terry Flynn, APR, FCPRS, President

Pierrette Leonard, APR, FSCRP, Vice-President & Secretary
Anita Wasiuta, APR, Vice-President & Treasurer
Karen Dalton, APR, Executive Director

Canadian Society of Association Executives (CSAE) / Société canadienne des directeurs d'association (SCDA)
#1100, 10 King St. East, Toronto ON M5C 1C3
Tel: 416-363-3555; *Fax:* 416-363-3630
Toll-Free: 800-461-3608
e-mail: csae@csae.com
URL: www.csae.com
Affiliation(s): European Society of Association Executives; American Society of Association Executives
Michael Anderson, President & CEO

Canadian Society of Corporate Secretaries (CSCS)
#255, 55 St. Clair Ave. West, Toronto ON M4V 2Y7
Tel: 416-921-5449; *Fax:* 416-967-6320
Toll-Free: 800-774-2850
e-mail: info@cscs.org
URL: www.cscs.org
Pamela Smith, Administrative Director
Lynn Beauregard, President

Canadian Society of Physician Executives (CSPE) / Société canadienne des médecins gestionnaires
PO Box 59005, 1559 Alta Vista Dr., Ottawa ON K1G 5T7
Tel: 613-731-9331; *Fax:* 613-731-1779
e-mail: carol.rochefort@cma.ca
URL: www.cspexecs.com
Affiliation(s): Canadian Medical Association
Carol Rochefort, Director

Confédération nationale des cadres du Québec (CNCQ)
a/s Association des cadres des collèges du Québec, 2430, ch Ste-Foy, Sainte-Foy QC G1V 1TZ
Tél: 418-877-1500; *Téléc:* 418-877-4469
Courriel: info@cncq.qc.ca
URL: www.cncq.qc.ca/
Affiliation(s): Confédération internationale des cadres
Gilles Lachance, Président

Corporation des approvisionneurs du Québec (CAQ)
Complexe Tassé, #302, 895, boul Séminaire nord, Saint-Jean-sur-Richelieu QC J3A 1J2
Tél: 450-357-0033; *Téléc:* 450-357-0044
Ligne sans frais: 800-977-1877
Courriel: info@caq.qc.ca
URL: www.caq.qc.ca
Jean-Pierre Ménard, a.p.a., Président

Couchiching Institute on Public Affairs (CIPA)
#301, 250 Consumers Rd., Toronto ON M2J 4V6
Tel: 416-642-6374; *Fax:* 416-495-8723
Toll-Free: 866-647-6374
e-mail: couch@couch.ca
URL: www.couch.ca
Gwen Burrows, President
Ruth Abrahamson, Executive Director

Fédération des secrétaires professionnelles du Québec (FSPQ)
#300-11, 1173, boul Charest ouest, Québec QC G1N 2C9
Tél: 418-527-5041
Courriel: info@fspq.qc.ca
URL: www.fspq.qc.ca
Line Ross, Présidente

Institute of Certified Management Consultants of Alberta (ICMCA)
PO Box 761, Stn. M, Calgary AB T2P 2J3
Toll-Free: 800-268-1148
e-mail: dwartman@icmca.ca
URL: www.camc.com/index.cfm?PID=12769&PIDLIST=12769; www.icmca.ca
Jennifer Jennax, CMC, President
Christopher Lavin, CMC, Vice-President
Russell Mascarenhas, CMC, Sec-Treas.
David Wartman, CMC, Registrar

Institute of Certified Management Consultants of Atlantic Canada (ICMCAC)
PO Box 1440, Sackville NB E0A 3C0
Tel: 902-491-4483; *Fax:* 902-429-5237
Toll-Free: 800-565-5314
e-mail: holser@camc-consult.org
Steven Parker, CMC, President

Institute of Certified Management Consultants of British Columbia (CMC-BC)
c/o CAMC, #815, 4 King St. West, Toronto ON M5H 1B6
Tel: 416-860-1515; *Fax:* 416-860-1535
Toll-Free: 800-268-1148
e-mail: consulting@camc.com; cmc-bc@shaw.ca
URL: www.camc.com/index.cfm?PID=12770&PIDLIST=12770
Simon Wong, CMC, President
Mary Colak, CMC, Vice-President
Ken Lee, CMC, Treasurer

Institute of Certified Management Consultants of Manitoba (ICMCM) / Institut manitobain des conseillers en administration agréés
PO Box 40, Niverville MB R0A 1E0
Tel: 204-388-5340
e-mail: consulting@camc.com
URL: www.camc.com
Lisa Elliott, CMC, President

Institute of Certified Management Consultants of Saskatchewan
c/o Koenig & Associates H.R. Services Inc., 402 Queen St., Saskatoon SK S7K 0M3
e-mail: info@koenig.ca
URL: www.koenig.ca
Peggie Koenig, B.Comm., MBA, C, Registrar

Institute of Chartered Secretaries & Administrators - Canadian Division (ICSA Canada) / Institut des secrétaires et administrateurs agréés au Canada
#310, 2175 Sheppard Ave. E., Toronto ON M2J 1W8
Tel: 416-944-9727; *Fax:* 416-491-1670
Toll-Free: 800-501-3440
e-mail: info@icsacanada.org
URL: www.icsacanada.org
Affiliation(s): International Institute of Chartered Secretaries & Administrators
Grace Woo, Director of Operations

Institute of Corporate Directors (ICD) / Institut des administrateurs de sociétés
#602, 40 University Ave., Toronto ON M5J 1T1
Tel: 416-593-7741; *Fax:* 416-593-0630
e-mail: admin@icd.ca
URL: www.icd.ca
Affiliation(s): Institute of Directors
Beverly Topping, President & CEO
Vicki Jordan, Vice President, Marketing & Membership Services

Institute of Professional Management (IPM)
#2210, 1081 Ambleside Dr., Ottawa ON K2B 8C8
Tel: 613-721-5957; *Fax:* 613-721-5850
e-mail: info@workplace.ca
URL: www.workplace.ca
Affiliation(s): Association of Professional Recruiters of Canada; Canadian Management Professional Association
Nathaly Pinchuk, Executive Director
Brian Pascal, President

International Personnel Management Association - Canada (IPMA-Canada)
National Office, #74, 21 Midland Cres., Ottawa ON K2H 8P6
Tel: 613-226-2297; *Fax:* 613-226-2298
Toll-Free: 866-226-5002
e-mail: info@ipma-aigp.ca
URL: www.ipma-aigp.ca
Affiliation(s): IPMA-HR
Carol Hopkins, Executive Director
Sharalyn Young, IPMA-CP, President
Heather Bowser, IPMA-CP, Director, Communications & Marketing

Manitoba Institute of the Purchasing Management Association of Canada
#200, 5 Donald St., Winnipeg MB R3L 2T4
Tel: 204-231-0965; *Fax:* 204-233-1250
Toll-Free: 877-231-0965
e-mail: mbpmac@mts.net
URL: www.mipmac.com
Jamie Bednarz, Executive Director

New Brunswick Institute of the Purchasing Management Association of Canada
PO Box 8977, Shediac NB E4P 8W5
Tel: 506-533-9418; *Fax:* 506-532-3630
e-mail: bernioff@nb.sympatico.ca
URL: www.pmacnb.com
Bernice Leger, Administrative Assistant

Newfoundland Institute of the Purchasing Management Association of Canada
PO Box 29011, Stn. Torbay Road, St. John's NL A1A 5B5
Tel: 709-778-4033; *Fax:* 709-724-5625
e-mail: info@pmacnl.org
URL: www.pmacnl.org
Nancy Harte, Seminar Contact

Northwest Territories Institute of the Purchasing Management Association of Canada
PO Box 2736, Yellowknife NT X1A 3T1
Tel: 867-880-2169; *Fax:* 867-880-4603
e-mail: derrick.w.chatman@bhpbilliton.com
URL: www.theedge.ca/pmacnwt
Derrick Chatman, President

Nova Scotia Institute of the Purchasing Management Association of Canada
PO Box 21, Stn. CRO, Halifax NS B3J 2L4
Tel: 902-425-4029; *Fax:* 902-431-7220
e-mail: info@nsipmac.com
URL: www.nsipmac.com
Colleen Millen, Seminar Contact

Ontario Institute of the Purchasing Management Association of Canada
PO Box 64, #2704, 1 Dundas St. West, Toronto ON M5G 1Z3
Tel: 416-977-7566; *Fax:* 416-977-4135
Toll-Free: 877-SCM-NYOU
e-mail: info@ontarioinstitute.com
URL: www.ontarioinstitute.com
Chie Shin Fraser, Executive Director

Ordre des administrateurs agréés du Québec (OAAQ)
#100, 910, rue Sherbrooke ouest, Montréal QC H3A 1G3
Tél: 514-499-0880; *Téléc:* 514-499-0892
Ligne sans frais: 800-465-0880
Courriel: info@adma.qc.ca
URL: www.adma.qc.ca
Denise Brosseau, Directrice générale et Secrétaire

Purchasing Management Association of Canada (PMAC) / Association canadienne de gestion des achats (ACGA)
PO Box 112, #2701, 777 Bay St., Toronto ON M5G 2C8
Tel: 416-977-7111; *Fax:* 416-977-8886
Toll-Free: 888-799-0877
e-mail: info@pmac.ca
URL: www.pmac.ca
Affiliation(s): Canadian Purchasing Research Foundation
Robert W. Dye, President/COO
Sharon Ferriss, Director
LouAnn Birkett, Board Chair

Saskatchewan Institute of the Purchasing Management Association of Canada (SIPMAC)
#221A, 3521 - 8th Street E, Saskatoon SK S7H 0W5
Tel: 306-653-8899; *Fax:* 306-653-8870
Toll-Free: 866-665-6167
e-mail: sipmac@sasktel.net
URL: www.si.pmac.ca
Nicole Burgess, Executive Director

Société québécoise des professionnels en relations publiques
#200, 4316, boul St-Laurent, Montréal QC H2W 1Z3
Tél: 514-845-4441; *Téléc:* 514-842-4886
Courriel: info@srq.qc.ca
URL: www.sqprp.ca

Strategic Leadership Forum, The Toronto Society for Strategic Management (SLF)
PO Box 98150, 970 Queens Street East, Toronto ON M4M 1J0
Tel: 416-481-7228; *Fax:* 416-489-3304
e-mail: slf-toronto@rogers.com
URL: www.slftoronto.com
Thomas G. Carter, President
Margo Street, Executive Director

Manufacturing & Industry

American Foundry Society
#23, 174 Martindale Rd., St Catharines ON L2S 3Z9
Tel: 905-688-9655
URL: www.afsontario.com

American Foundry Society
460 Sinclair St., Winnipeg MB R2X 1Y1
Tel: 204-586-6563

American Foundry Society
c/o Inproheat Industries Ltd., 680 Raymur Ave., Vancouver BC V6A 2R1
Tel: 604-254-0461; *Fax:* 604-254-6377
URL: www.afsbc.ca

APICS Association for Operations Management
#300, 1370 Don Mills Rd., Toronto ON M3B 3N7
Tel: 416-366-5388; *Fax:* 416-381-4054
e-mail: info@apics.ca
URL: www.apics.ca
Shari Bricks, Executive Director

Association de la recherche industrielle du Québec (ADRIQ)
#901, 1155, rue University, Montréal QC H3B 3A7
Tél: 514-337-3001; *Téléc:* 514-337-2229
Courriel: adriq@adriq.com
URL: www.adriq.com
Claude Demers, Président

Association of Independent Corrugated Converters
PO Box 73063, Stn. White Shields, 2300 Lawrence Ave. E., Toronto ON M1P 4Z5
Tel: 905-727-9405; *Fax:* 905-727-1061
e-mail: info@aicc11.com
URL: www.aiccbox.org

British Columbia Paint Manufacturers' Association (BCPMA)
c/o Cloverdale Paint Inc., 6950 King George Hwy., Surrey BC V3W 4Z1
Tel: 604-596-6261; *Fax:* 604-597-2677
URL: www.bcpma.bc.ca
Ed Linton, President
Ron Vanderdrift, Vice-President
Deryk Pawsey, Secretary
Yvon Poitras, Treasurer

Canadian Appliance Manufacturers Association (CAMA)
c/o Electro-Federation Canada, #200, 5800 Explorer Dr., Mississauga ON L4W 5K9
Tel: 905-602-8877; *Fax:* 905-602-5686
Toll-Free: 866-602-8877
e-mail: info@electrofed.com
URL: www.electrofed.com/councils/CAMA/
Sharon Borda, Manager, CAMA
Larry Moore, Vice-President, Consumer Councils

Canadian Association of Mould Makers (CAMM)
c/o St. Clair College (FCEM), PO Box 16, 2000 Talbot Rd. West, Windsor ON N9A 6S4
Tel: 519-255-7863; *Fax:* 519-255-9446
e-mail: info@camm.ca
URL: www.camm.ca
Affiliation(s): Canadian Tooling & Machining Association
Dan Moynahan, President
Giancarlo DiMaio, Treasurer
Diane Deslippe, Manager, Office

Canadian Brush Manufacturers Association (CBMA) / Association canadienne des fabricants de brosses
#310, 2175 Sheppard Ave. East, Toronto ON M2J 1W8
Tel: 416-971-7800; *Fax:* 416-491-1670
e-mail: cbma@cbma.org
URL: www.cbma.org
Catherine Fleming, Contact, Administration

Canadian Carpet Institute / Institut canadien du tapis
1064 Carboro Rd., Ottawa ON K1K 1H8
Tel: 819-684-8444; *Fax:* 819-684-5444
e-mail: info@canadiancarpet.org
URL: www.canadiancarpet.org
Affiliation(s): World Carpet & Rug Council
Alexandre Lacroix, President

Canadian Cosmetic, Toiletry & Fragrance Association (CCTFA) / Association canadienne des cosmétiques, produit de toilette et parfums
#102, 420 Britannia Rd. East, Mississauga ON L4Z 3L5
Tel: 905-890-5161; *Fax:* 905-890-2607
e-mail: cctfa@cctfa.ca
URL: www.cctfa.ca
Myles Robinson, Chair

Canadian Council of Furniture Manufacturers (CCFM) / Conseil canadien des fabricants de meubles
c/o Accro Furniture Industries, 305 McKay Ave., Winnipeg MB R2G 0N5
Tel: 204-654-1114; *Fax:* 204-654-2792
e-mail: info@accro-acmechrome.com
Terry J. Clark, President

Canadian Hardware & Housewares Manufacturers' Association (CHHMA) / Association canadienne des fabricants de produits de quincaillerie et d'articles ménagers
#101, 1335 Morningside Ave., Toronto ON M1B 5M4
Tel: 416-282-0022; *Fax:* 416-282-0027
e-mail: chhma@chhma.ca
URL: www.chhma.ca
Vaughn Crofford, President
Maureen Hizaka, Director of Operations

Canadian Innovation Centre (CIC)
c/o Waterloo Research & Technology Park, #15, 295 Hagey Blvd., Waterloo ON N2L 6R5
Tel: 519-885-5870; *Fax:* 519-513-2421
Toll-Free: 800-265-4559
e-mail: info@innovationcentre.ca
URL: www.innovationcentre.ca
Ted Cross, Chair & CEO

Canadian Kitchen Cabinet Association (CKCA) / Association canadienne de fabricants d'armoires de cuisine (ACAC)
130 Albert St., Ottawa ON K1P 5G4
Tel: 613-567-9171; *Fax:* 613-567-4664
e-mail: info@ckca.ca
URL: www.ckca.ca
Caroline Castrucci, President
Melissa Lemay, Association Affaris Officer

Canadian Laboratory Suppliers Association (CLSA) / Association canadienne de fournisseurs de laboratoire
#131, 525 Highland Rd. West, Kitchener ON N3M 5P4
Tel: 519-579-7598; *Fax:* 519-579-8134
e-mail: jhowes@clsassoc.com
URL: www.clsassoc.com
Wayne England, President

Canadian Manufacturers & Exporters (CME) / Manufacturiers et Exportateurs Canada
#1500, 1 Nicholas St., Ottawa ON K1N 7B7
Tel: 613-238-8888; *Fax:* 613-563-9218
e-mail: national@cme-mec.ca
URL: www.cme-mec.ca
Jayson Myers, President
Jeff Brownlee, Vice-President, Communications

Canadian Manufacturers & Exporters
#1931, 10060 Jasper Ave., Edmonton AB T5J 3R8
Tel: 780-426-6622; *Fax:* 780-426-1509
e-mail: ab.team@cme-mec.ca

Canadian Manufacturers & Exporters
#540, 688 West Hastings St., Vancouver BC V6B 1P1
Tel: 604-713-7800; *Fax:* 604-713-7801
Toll-Free: 866-713-7802
e-mail: bc.reception@cme-mec.ca

Canadian Manufacturers & Exporters
110 Lowson Cres., Winnipeg MB R3P 2H8
Tel: 204-949-1454; *Fax:* 204-943-3476
e-mail: mb.reception@cme-mec.ca

Canadian Manufacturers & Exporters
PO Box 7129, #12, 567 Coverdale Rd., Riverview NB E1B 4T8
Tel: 506-861-9071; *Fax:* 506-857-3059
e-mail: nb@cme-mec.ca

Canadian Manufacturers & Exporters
Parsons Bldg., 90 O'Leary Ave., 1st Fl., St. John's NL A1B 2C7
Tel: 709-772-3682; *Fax:* 709-772-3213
Toll-Free: 888-772-3682

Canadian Manufacturers & Exporters
#200, 6725 Airport Rd., Mississauga ON L4V 1V2
Tel: 905-672-3466; *Fax:* 905-672-1764
Toll-Free: 800-268-9684
e-mail: ian.howcroft@cme-mec.ca

Canadian Manufacturers & Exporters
#210, 2000, rue Peel, Montréal QC H3A 2W5
Tél: 514-866-7774; *Téléc:* 514-866-9447
Ligne sans frais: 800-363-0226
Courriel: info@meq.ca

Canadian Manufacturers & Exporters
Collins' Bank Building, 1869 Upper Water St., 3rd Fl., Halifax NS B3J 1S9
Tel: 902-422-4477; *Fax:* 902-422-9563
e-mail: jacqui.squires@cme-mec.ca

Canadian Plastics Industry Association (CPIA) / Association canadienne de l'industrie des plastiques
#712, 5915 Airport Rd., Mississauga ON L4V 1T1
Tel: 905-678-7748; *Fax:* 905-678-0774
e-mail: national@cpia.ca
URL: www.cpia.ca
Serge Lavoie, President & CEO
Judy Mark, Executive Vice President

Canadian Sanitation Supply Association (CSSA) / Association canadienne des fournisseurs de produits sanitaires
PO Box 10009, 910 Dundas St. West, Whitby ON L1P 1P7
Tel: 905-665-8001; *Fax:* 905-430-6418
Toll-Free: 866-684-8273
e-mail: info@cssa.com
URL: www.cssa.com
Kim Murtha, President
Kerry Nevatte, Vice-President
Mike Nosko, Interim Executive Director

Canadian Tooling & Machining Association (CTMA)
#3, 140 McGovern Dr., Cambridge ON N3H 4R7
Tel: 519-653-7265; *Fax:* 519-653-6764
Toll-Free: 888-437-3661
e-mail: info@ctma.com
URL: www.ctma.com
Affiliation(s): Auto Parts; Canadian Foundry Association; Canadian Plastics Institute; GTMA England; PMPTB - Ohio, USA; SPI - Toronto; CAMM - Windsor
Les Payne, Executive Director

Canadian Toy Association / Canadian Toy & Hobby Fair (CTA) / L'Association canadienne du Jouet
#212, 7777 Keele St., Concord ON L4K 1Y7
Tel: 905-660-5690; *Fax:* 905-660-6103
e-mail: info@cdntoyassn.com
URL: www.cdntoyassn.com
Sheila Edmondson, Executive Director

Canadian Urethane Manufacturers Association (CUMA)
151 Briarcliffe Cres., Waterloo ON N2L 5T6
Tel: 519-884-2855; *Fax:* 519-884-0653
URL: www.cumahome.org
Scott Woodworth, President
Noel Campbell, Manager

Canadian Window & Door Manufacturers Association (CWDMA) / Association canadienne des manufacturiers de portes et fenêtres (ACMPF)
#1208, 130 Albert St., Ottawa ON K1P 5G4
Tel: 613-235-5511; *Fax:* 613-235-4664
e-mail: info@cwdma.ca
URL: www.cwdma.ca
Henry Banman, President
Tony Hall, Treasurer

Door & Hardware Institute in Canada
#310, 2175 Sheppard Ave. East, Toronto ON M2J 1W8
Tel: 416-492-6502; *Fax:* 416-491-1670
e-mail: dhicanada@dhi.org
URL: www.dhicanada.ca
Malcolm B. Eyre, President
Carolyne Vigon, Administrator

National Floor Covering Association (NFCA) / Association nationale des revêtements de sol
987 Clarkson Rd. South, Mississauga ON L5J 2V8
Tel: 905-822-2280; *Fax:* 905-822-2494
URL: www.nfcaonline.ca

Organization of CANDU Industries (OCI) / Association des industries CANDU
#102, 345 Kingston Rd., Pickering ON L1V 1A1
Tel: 905-509-0073
e-mail: mrwash@eagle.ca
URL: www.oci-aic.org
Affiliation(s): Atomic Energy of Canada
Martyn Wash, President
Lois Marsh, Administrator

Paint & Decorating Retailers Association Canada (PDRA)
403 Axminister Dr., Fenton MO 63026-2941 USA
Tel: 636-326-2636; *Fax:* 636-326-1823
Toll-Free: 800-737-0107
e-mail: info@pdra.org
URL: www.pdra.org
Affiliation(s): National Decorating Products Association
Robert Mueller, President
Dan Simon, Exec. Vice-President

The Rubber Association of Canada (RAC) / Association canadienne de l'industrie du caoutchouc
Plaza 4, #250, 2000 Argentia Rd., Mississauga ON L5N 1W1
Tel: 905-814-1714; *Fax:* 905-814-1085
e-mail: info@rubberassociation.ca
URL: www.rubberassociation.ca
Glenn Maidment, President
Ralph Warner, Director, Operations
Gilles Paquette, Communications Manager

Saskatchewan Trade & Export Partnership Inc. (STEP)
PO Box 1787, #320, 1801 Hamilton St., Regina SK S4P 3C6
Tel: 306-787-9210; *Fax:* 306-787-6666
Toll-Free: 877-313-7244
e-mail: inquire@sasktrade.com
URL: www.sasktrade.com
Lionel LaBelle, President & CEO
Nicole Grande, Administrative Coordinator
Heather Swan, Manager, Corporate Services
Janice Lawless, Membership Coordinator
Stephanie Pappas, Technology & Communications
Brad Michnik, Executive Director, Trade Development

Marine Trades

Association of Canadian Port Authorities (ACPA)
#1502, 85 Albert St., Ottawa ON K1P 6A4
Tel: 613-232-2036; *Fax:* 613-232-9554
e-mail: leroux@acpa-ports.net
URL: www.acpa-ports.net
Affiliation(s): American Association of Port Authorities
Gary Leroux, Executive Director

British Columbia Marine Trades Association (BCMTA)
#300, 1275 West 6th Ave., Vancouver BC V6H 1A6
Tel: 604-683-5191; *Fax:* 604-893-8808
e-mail: mta@bcmta.com
URL: www.bcmta.com
Alan Stovell, President

British Columbia Maritime Employers Association (BCMEA)
#500, 349 Railway St., Vancouver BC V6A 1A4
Tel: 604-688-1155; *Fax:* 604-684-2397
URL: www.bcmea.com
Onkar Athwal, Vice-President, Human Resources
Frank A. Pasacreta, President & CEO
Grant Melos, Executive Vice-President & COO
Terry Duggan, Vice-President, Finance

Canadian Centre for Marine Communications (CCMC)
PO Box 8454, 155 Ridge Rd., St. John's NL A1B 3N9
Tel: 709-579-4872; *Fax:* 709-579-0495
e-mail: ccmc@ccmc.nf.ca
URL: www.ccmc.nf.ca
Ronald V. Newhook, President & CEO
Randy Gillespie, Vice-President
Clayton S. Burry, Director, Industry Development

Canadian Navigation Society (CNS)
#105, 1750 Courtwood Cres., Ottawa ON K2C 2B5
Tel: 613-234-0191; *Fax:* 613-234-9039
e-mail: casi@casi.ca
URL: www.casi.ca
Affiliation(s): Canadian Aeronautics & Space Institute
Susan Skone, Society Chair

Chamber of Maritime Commerce (CMC) / Chambre du commerce maritime (CCM)
#700, 350 Sparks St., Ottawa ON K1R 7S8
Tel: 613-233-8779; *Fax:* 613-233-3743
e-mail: email@cmc-ccm.com
URL: www.cmc-ccm.com
Linda Jeannotte, Administrative Assistant
Ray Johnston, President

The Great Lakes Marine Heritage Foundation
55 Ontario St., Kingston ON K7L 2Y2
Tel: 613-542-2261; *Fax:* 613-542-0043
e-mail: marmus@marmuseum.ca
URL: www.marmuseum.ca
Mark Siemons, Chair

National Marine Manufacturers Association (NMMA)
#5100, 200 E. Randolph Dr., Chicago IL 60601 USA
Tel: 312-946-6200
URL: www.nmma.org
Affiliation(s): National Association of Boat Manufacturers; National Association of Marine Products & Services; Association of Marine Engine Manufacturers
Thomas Dammrich, President
Linda Waddell, Vice President, Northern Shows

National Marine Manufacturers Association Canada (NMMA)
#8, 14 McEwan Dr., Bolton ON L7E 1H1
Tel: 905-951-0009; *Fax:* 905-951-0018
e-mail: sanghel@nmma.org
URL: www.cmma.ca
Rick Layzell, Chair

Shipbuilding Association of Canada / Association de la construction navale du Canada
#1502, 222 Queen St., Ottawa ON K1P 5V9
Tel: 613-232-7127; *Fax:* 613-238-5519
e-mail: pcairns@cfncon.com
URL: www.shipbuilding.ca
Peter Cairns, President
David Reid, Chair

Mental Health

Association des médecins-psychiatres du Québec (AMPQ) / Québec Psychiatrists' Association
CP 216, Succ. Desjardins, 2, complexe Desjardins, Tour de l'Est, 30e étage, Montréal QC H5B 1G8
Tél: 514-350-5128; *Téléc:* 514-350-5198
Courriel: sbresse@fmsq.org; ampq@fmsq.org
URL: www.ampq.org
Diane Guay, Directrice, Administration
Brian Bexton, Président
Gérard Cournoyer, Secrétaire

Canadian Art Therapy Association (CATA) / L'association canadienne d'art thérapie
26 Earl Grey Rd., Toronto ON M4J 3L2
URL: www.catainfo.ca
Nick Zwaagstra, President
Lori Boyko, Registrar
Marie Alexander, Chair, Ethics
Olena Darewych, Chair, Membership

Canadian Association for Suicide Prevention (CASP) / L'Association canadienne pour la prévention du suicide (ACPS)
870 Portage Ave., Winnipeg MB R3G 0P1
Tel: 204-784-4073; *Fax:* 204-772-7998
e-mail: casp@casp-acps.ca; admin@casp-acps.ca
URL: www.casp-acps.ca
Marion Cooper, President
Joan Seabrook, Vice-President
Tim Wall, Executive Director
Yvonne Bergmans, Secretary
Ian Ross, Treasurer

Canadian Centre for Stress & Well-Being
#1801, 1 Yonge St., Toronto ON M5E 1W7
Tel: 416-363-6204; *Fax:* 416-658-9536
e-mail: smcen@yahoo.com
Lucille Peszat, Executive Director

Canadian Group Psychotherapy Association (CGPA)
Tel: 416-736-5225; *Fax:* 416-736-5782
e-mail: tsimonik@rogers.com
URL: www.cgpa.ca
Terry Simonik, RN, MEd, FCGPA, President
Linda McFadyen, Secretary
Alina Isaac, Treasurer

Canadian Institute of Stress
PO Box 665, Stn. U, Toronto ON M8Z 5Y9
e-mail: info@stresscanada.org
URL: www.stresscanada.org
Richard Earle, Director

Canadian Mental Health Association (CMHA) / Association canadienne pour la santé mentale
Phenix Professional Building, #303, 595 Montreal Rd., Ottawa ON K1K 4L2
Tel: 613-745-7750; *Fax:* 613-745-5522
e-mail: info@cmha.ca
URL: www.cmha.ca
Affiliation(s): Canadian Alliance on Mental Illness & Mental Health; Canadian Health Network
Taylor Alexander, CEO
Judith Watson, President
David Alge, Controller

Canadian Psychiatric Association (CPA) / Association des psychiatres du Canada
#701, 141 Laurier Ave. West, Ottawa ON K1P 5J3
Tel: 613-234-2815; *Fax:* 613-234-9857
Toll-Free: 800-267-1555
e-mail: cpa@cpa-apc.org
URL: www.cpa-apc.org
Affiliation(s): Canadian Medical Association; World Psychiatric Association
Ted Callanan, Sec.-Treas.
Alex Saunders, CEO

Canadian Psychiatric Research Foundation (CPRF) / Fondation canadienne de recherche en psychiatrie (FCRP)
#200, 133 Richmond St., Toronto ON M5H 2L3
Tel: 416-351-7757; *Fax:* 416-351-7765
Toll-Free: 800-915-2773
e-mail: admin@cprf.ca
URL: www.cprf.ca
Jean Milligan, Executive Director
Andrea Swinton, Director, Fund Development & Marketing

Canadian Psychoanalytic Society (CPS) / Société canadienne de psychanalyse (SCP)
7000, ch Côte-des-Neiges, Montréal QC H3S 2C1
Tel: 514-738-6105; *Fax:* 514-738-6393
e-mail: psyanal@qc.aira.com
URL: www.psychoanalysis.ca
Affiliation(s): International Psychoanalytic Association
David Schaffelburg, President

Canadian Psychological Association (CPA) / Société canadienne de psychologie
#702, 141 Laurier Ave. West, Ottawa ON K1P 5J3
Tel: 613-237-2144; *Fax:* 613-237-1674
Toll-Free: 888-472-0657
e-mail: cpa@cpa.ca
URL: www.cpa.ca
Affiliation(s): Canadian Register of Health Service Providers in Psychology; Council of Provincial Associations of Psychologists; International Union of Psychological Science; Canadian Federation for the Humanities & Social Sciences
Karen R. Cohen, Acting Executive Director
Daniel Berman, Manager, Communications & Membership Services
Thomas Hadjistavropoulos, President

Centre de ressources et d'intervention pour hommes abusés sexuellement dans leur enfance (CRIPHASE) / Resource and Intervention Center for Men Sexually Abused during their Childhood
#100, 8105, rue de Gaspé, Montréal QC H2P 2J9
Tél: 514-529-5567; *Téléc:* 514-529-0571
Courriel: info@criphase.org
URL: www.criphase.org
Benoit St-Jean, Directeur général

Child & Parent Resource Institute (CPRI)
600 Sanatorium Rd., London ON N6H 3W7
Tel: 519-858-2774; *Fax:* 519-858-3913
URL: www.cpri.thehealthline.ca
Anne Stark, Administrator

Children's Mental Health Ontario (CMHO) / Santé Mentale pour Enfants Ontario (SMEO)
#309, 40 St. Clair Ave. East, Toronto ON M4T 1M9
Tel: 416-921-2109; *Fax:* 416-921-7600
Toll-Free: 888-234-7054
e-mail: info@cmho.org
URL: www.kidsmentalhealth.ca
Gordon Floyd, Executive Director & CEO

Fédération des familles et amis de la personne atteinte de maladie mentale (FFAPAMM) / Federation of Families & Friends of Persons with a Mental Illness
#203, 1990, rue Jean-Talon nord, Sainte-Foy QC G1N 4K8
Tél: 418-687-0474; *Téléc:* 418-687-0123
Ligne sans frais: 800-323-0474
Courriel: info@ffapamm.qc.ca
URL: www.ffapamm.qc.ca
Hélène Fradet, Directrice générale

International Schizophrenia Foundation
16 Florence Ave., Toronto ON M2N 1E9
Tel: 416-733-2117; *Fax:* 416-733-2352
e-mail: centre@orthomed.org
URL: www.orthomed.org
Steven Carter, Executive Director

Mood Disorders Association of Ontario (MDAO)
#602, 36 Eglinton Avenue, Toronto ON M4R 1A1

Tel: 416-486-8046; *Fax:* 416-486-8127
Toll-Free: 888-486-8236
e-mail: info@mooddisorders.on.ca
URL: www.mooddisorders.on.ca
Karen Liberman, Executive Director

Mood Disorders Society of Canada (MDSC) / La Société pour les troubles de l'humeur du Canada
#736, 3-304 Stone Rd. West, Guelph ON N1G 4W4
Tel: 519-824-5565; *Fax:* 519-824-9569
e-mail: info@mooddisorderscanada.ca
URL: www.mooddisorderscanada.ca
Phil Upshall, National Executive Director
John Starzynski, President

Ontario Psychological Association (OPA)
#221, 730 Yonge St., Toronto ON M4Y 2B7
Tel: 416-961-5552
Toll-Free: 800-268-0069
e-mail: info@psych.on.ca; opa@psych.on.ca
URL: www.psych.on.ca
Mary Broga, President
Ruth Berman, Ph.D, C.Psych, Executive Director
Connie Kushnir, Financial Officer
Carla Mardonet, Administrative Officer
Anna DiDonato, Coordinator, Membership Services
Jenna Barclay, Secretary, Referral Service

L'Ordre des psychologues du Québec (OPQ)
#510, 1100, av Beaumont, Montréal QC H3P 3H5
Tél: 514-738-1881; *Téléc:* 514-738-8838
Ligne sans frais: 800-363-2644
URL: www.ordrepsy.qc.ca
Affiliation(s): American Psychological Association
Rose-Marie Charest, Présidente

The Organization for Bipolar Affective Disorders Society (OBAD)
1019 - 7th Ave. SW, Calgary AB T2P 1A8
Tel: 403-263-7408
Toll-Free: 866-263-7408
e-mail: obad@obad.ca
URL: www.obad.ca
Kaj Korvela, Executive Director

Saskatchewan Psychiatric Association
c/o Dhanapal Natarajan, Regina Qu'Appelle Health Region, 2180 - 23rd Ave., Regina SK S4S 0A5
e-mail: kidsdoctor@accesscomm.ca
Affiliation(s): Canadian Psychiatric Association
Dhanapal Natarajan, Provincial Director

Schizophrenia Society of Canada (SSC) / Société canadienne de schizophrénie
#100, 4 Fort St., Winnipeg MB R3C 1C4
Tel: 204-786-1616; *Fax:* 204-783-4898
Toll-Free: 800-263-5545
e-mail: info@schizophrenia.ca
URL: www.schizophrenia.ca
Jim Adamson, President
Chris Summerville, D. Min; CPRP, Chief Executive Officer
Catherine Willinsky, Manager, National Programs & Projects

Survivors of Suicide Support Program
10 Trinity Sq., Toronto ON M5G 1B1
Tel: 416-595-1716
e-mail: karen@torontodistresscentre.com
Karen Lefotsky, Contact

Mentally Challenged Persons

Autism Resolution Ontario
Tel: 416-352-8813
e-mail: info@autismresolutionontario.com
URL: www.autismresolutionontario.com
Sharon Aschaiek, Founder

Military & Veterans

Air Cadet League of Canada / Ligue des cadets de l'air du Canada
66 Lisgar St., Ottawa ON K2P 0C1
Tel: 613-991-4349; *Fax:* 613-991-4347
Toll-Free: 877-422-6359
e-mail: webadmin@aircadetleague.com
URL: www.aircadetleague.com
Social Media: www.facebook.com/group.php?gid=19248248746
Craig Hawkins, President

Air Force Association of Canada (AFAC) / L'Association des forces aériennes du Canada
PO Box 2460, Stn. D, Ottawa ON K1P 5W6
Tel: 613-232-2303; *Fax:* 613-232-2156
Toll-Free: 866-351-2322
e-mail: director@airforce.ca
URL: www.airforce.ca
Affiliation(s): Air Force Association of United States; Royal Air Forces Association
Dean Black, Executive Director
John Melbourne, National President

The Army Cadet League of Canada (ACLC) / Ligue des cadets de l'armée du Canada
66 Lisgar St., Ottawa ON K2P 0C1
Tel: 613-991-4348; *Fax:* 613-990-8701
Toll-Free: 877-276-9223
e-mail: national@armycadetleague.ca
URL: www.armycadetleague.ca
Affiliation(s): Army Cadet Force Association, UK; Deutscher-Bundeswehr-Verband
Terrence Whitty, Executive Director

Army, Navy & Air Force Veterans in Canada (ANAVETS) / Les Anciens combattants de l'armée, de la marine et des forces aériennes au Canada
#2, 6 Beechwood Ave., Vanier ON K1L 8B4
Tel: 613-744-0222; *Fax:* 613-744-0208
e-mail: anavets@storm.ca
URL: www.anavets.ca
Lorne McCartney, Sec.-Treas.

Canadian Association of Veterans in United Nations Peacekeeping
PO Box 46026, 2339 Ogilvie Rd., Gloucester ON K1J 9M7
e-mail: griffisgrove@xcountry.tv
URL: www.cavunp.org
Ronald R. Griffis, National President
J. Robert O'Brien, CD, Chair
Paul Greensides, CD, National Secretary-Treasurer

Canadian Battlefields Foundation
c/o Canadian War Museum, 1 Vimy Pl., Ottawa ON K1R 1C2
Tel: 613-731-7767
e-mail: gruchy@canadianbattlefieldsfoundation.ca
URL: www.canadianbattlefieldsfoundation.ca
H.G. Needham, CD (Ret'd), Treasurer
Charles Belzile, CMM, CM, CD, President
Antonio Lamer, CP, CC, CD, Honorary Patron

Canadian Corps Association
201 Niagara St., Toronto ON M5V 1C9
Tel: 416-504-6694
E.V. Heesaker, President
Shirley Wood Heesaker, Dominion Secretary

The Canadian Corps of Commissionaires / Le Corps Canadien des Commissionnaires
#201, 100 Gloucester St., Ottawa ON K2P 0A4
Tel: 613-688-0710; *Fax:* 613-688-0719
Toll-Free: 888-688-0715
e-mail: info@commissionaires.ca
URL: www.commissionaires.ca
Gerald Moodie, CEO
André Dorval, CD, Executive Secretary

Canadian Merchant Navy Veterans Association Inc. (CMNVA) / L'Association des Anciens Combattants de la marine marchande canadienne Inc.
PO Box 496, Annapolis Royal NS B0S 1A0
e-mail: sailorjail@ns.sympatico.ca
URL: www3.ns.sympatico.ca/sailorjail/
Cyril E. Caines, Contact

Canadian Peacekeeping Veterans Association (CPVA)
PO Box 905, Kingston ON K7L 4X8
Tel: 506-627-6437
e-mail: info@cpva.ca
URL: www.cpva.ca
Ray Kokkonen, CD, President

Commission canadienne d'histoire militaire (CCHM) / Canadian Commission of Military History (CCMH)
Quartier général de la Défense nationale, 101 Colonel By Dr., Ottawa ON K1A 0K2
Téléc: 613-990-8579
Affiliation(s): Commission internationale d'histoire militaire
R. Legault, Président, Direction - Histoire et patrimoine (DHP)

Commonwealth War Graves Commission - Canadian Agency (CWGC) / Commission des sépultures de guerre du Commonwealth
#1707, 66 Slater St., Ottawa ON K1A 0P4
Tel: 613-992-3224; *Fax:* 613-995-0431
e-mail: cwgc-canada@vac-acc.gc.ca
URL: www.cwgc.org
Affiliation(s): Commonwealth War Graves Commission
Bradley N. Hall, Secretary General

Conference of Defence Associations (CDA) / Conférence des associations de la défense
#400B, 222 Somerset St. West, Ottawa ON K2P 2G3
Tel: 613-236-1252; *Fax:* 613-236-8191
e-mail: cda@cda-cdai.ca
URL: cda-cdai.ca
Affiliation(s): Conference of Defence Associations Institute
Gord Metcalfe, (Ret'd), Executive Secretary
Alain Pellerin, OMM, CD (Ret'd), Executive Director

Defence Research & Education Centre (DREC)
#46Z, 1652 Whitesails Dr., RR#1, Bowen Island BC V0N 1G0
e-mail: ian@web.net
URL: www.vana.ca
Affiliation(s): Veterans Against Nuclear Arms
Kell Antoft, Administrator

Federation of Military & United Services Institutes of Canada (FMUSIC) / Fédération des instituts militaires et des instituts des services unis du Canada (FIMIC)
PO Box 1700, Stn. Forces, Kingston ON K7K 7B4
A. Cooper, Executive Vice-Chair

Jewish War Veterans of Canada / Les Anciens Combattants Juifs du Canada
#353, 1111 Finch Ave., Toronto ON M3J 2E5
Tel: 905-669-5989; *Fax:* 416-736-6744
e-mail: drlevy@rogers.com
URL: www.cjwv.org
Affiliation(s): Centre for Jewish Studies, York University
Lou VanDelman, Executive Director
Joseph Levy, Director, Research

Korea Veterans Association of Canada Inc. (KVA) / Association canadienne des vétérans de la Corée (ACVC)
#21, 160 Conway Dr., London ON N6E 3M6
Tel: 519-668-5999
e-mail: rochonp@execulink.com
URL: www.kvacanada.com
Terry Wickens, CD, President
Gordon J.H. Strathy, National Secretary
Doug Finney, National Treasurer

Military Collectors Club of Canada (MCC of Canada)
c/o John Zabarylo, Secretary-treasurer, PO Box 64009, 525 London St., Winnipeg MB R2K 3Y4
Tel: 204-669-0871
e-mail: militarycollectorsclubofcanada@yahoo.ca
URL: www.mccofc.org
John Zabarylo, Sec.-Treas.

National Council of Veteran Associations (NCVA)
c/o The War Amps Of Canada, 2827 Riverside Dr., Ottawa ON K1V 0C4
Tel: 613-731-3821; *Fax:* 613-731-3234
Toll-Free: 800-465-2677
e-mail: communications@waramps.ca
URL: www.waramps.ca/cliff/ncva.html
H. Clifford Chadderton, Chair

The Naval Officers' Association of Canada (NOAC) / L'Association des officiers de la marine du Canada
12 Zokol Crescent, Kanata ON K2K 2K5
Tel: 613-270-9597
e-mail: noacexdir@msn.com
URL: www.noac-national.ca/noac
Ray Zuliani, President
Richard Archer, Executive Director

Navy League of Canada / Ligue navale du Canada
66 Lisgar St., Ottawa ON K2P 0C1
Tel: 613-302-1744; *Fax:* 613-990-8701
Toll-Free: 800-375-6289
e-mail: national@navyleague.ca
URL: www.navyleague.ca
Social Media: twitter.com/NavyLeagueCA
Affiliation(s): Conference of Defence Associates
Douglas J. Thomas, National Executive Director
Jerrod Riley, National Deputy Director

New Brunswick Signallers Association (NB Sigs)
c/o Fred LeBlanc, 17 Dewitt Acres, Fredericton NB E3A 6S3
Tel: 506-472-3215
e-mail: fredleb@nbnet.nb.ca
URL: www.nbsigs.ca
Claude Jodouin, President

Princess Patricia's Canadian Light Infantry Association
Canadian Forces Base Edmonton, PO Box 10500, Stn. Forces, Edmonton AB T5J 4J5
Tel: 780-973-4011; *Fax:* 780-973-1613
e-mail: scott.br@forces.gc.ca
URL: assoc.ppcli.com
Bert Scott, National President

Royal Canadian Air Force Benevolent Fund (RCAF BF) / Caisse de bienfaisance de l'Aviation royale du Canada
Legion House, #202, 359 Kent St., Ottawa ON K2P 0R6
Tel: 613-992-6082; *Fax:* 613-992-3426
e-mail: rcafbf@magma.ca
Marion Blair, Secretary-Manager

The Royal Canadian Legion (RCL) / La Légion royale canadienne
Dominion Command, 86 Aird Place, Ottawa ON K2L 0A1
Tel: 613-591-3335; *Fax:* 613-591-9335
e-mail: info@legion.ca
URL: www.legion.ca
Affiliation(s): Royal Commonwealth Ex-Services League
Pat Varga, Dominion 1st Vice President
R. Duane Daly, OSTJ, MSM, CD,, Dominion Secretary
Michael Cook, Dominion Treasurer
Wilf Edmond, Dominion President

The Royal Canadian Legion
2020 - 15th St. NW, Calgary AB T2M 3N8
Tel: 403-284-1161; *Fax:* 403-284-9899
e-mail: commandsecretary@abnwtlegion.com
URL: www.abnwtlegion.com

The Royal Canadian Legion
#152, 5489 Byrne Rd., Burnaby BC V5J 3J1
Tel: 604-736-8166; *Fax:* 604-736-1635
Toll-Free: 888-261-2211
e-mail: jhenderson@bcyuk.legion.ca
URL: www.bcyuk.legion.ca

The Royal Canadian Legion
563 St. Mary's Rd., Winnipeg MB R2M 3L6
Tel: 204-233-3405; *Fax:* 204-237-1775
e-mail: mblegion@mts.net
URL: www.manitobanwontariocommand.ca

The Royal Canadian Legion
490 Douglas Ave., Saint John NB E2K 1E7
Tel: 506-634-8850; *Fax:* 506-633-4836
e-mail: legion@nbnet.nb.ca
URL: www.nb.legion.ca

The Royal Canadian Legion
PO Box 5745, St. John's NL A1C 5X3
Tel: 709-753-6666; *Fax:* 709-753-5514
e-mail: emcasey@nfld.net
URL: www1.nfld.net/rclnfprovcom/

The Royal Canadian Legion
Burnside Business Park, 61 Gloria McCluskey Ave., Dartmouth NS B3B 2Z3
Tel: 902-429-4090; *Fax:* 902-429-7481
e-mail: info@ns.legion.ca
URL: www.ns.legion.ca

The Royal Canadian Legion
89 Industrial Pkwy. North, Aurora ON L4G 4C4
Tel: 905-841-7999; *Fax:* 905-841-9992
e-mail: info@on.legion.ca
URL: www.on.legion.ca

The Royal Canadian Legion
PO Box 20132, 47 Kensington Rd., Charlottetown PE C1A 9E3
Tel: 902-892-2161; *Fax:* 902-368-8853
e-mail: royalcanadianlegion@pei.aibn.com
URL: www.peilegion.com

The Royal Canadian Legion
#410, 1000, rue Saint-Antoine ouest, Montréal QC H3C 3R7
Tél: 514-866-7491; *Téléc:* 514-866-6303
Ligne sans frais: 877-401-7111
Courriel: rclegionrc@videotron.ca
URL: www.qc.legion.ca

The Royal Canadian Legion
3079 - 5th Ave., Regina SK S4T 0L6
Tel: 306-525-8739; *Fax:* 306-525-5023
e-mail: murrayc.legion@sasktel.net

Royal Canadian Military Institute (RCMI)
426 University Ave., Toronto ON M5G 1S9
Tel: 416-597-0286; *Fax:* 416-597-6919
Toll-Free: 800-585-1072
e-mail: info@rcmi.org
URL: www.rcmi.org
Brian S. MacDonald, Acting Executive Director

Royal Canadian Mounted Police Veterans' Association / Gendarmarie royale du Canada association des ancien
295 Coventry Rd., Ottawa ON K1A 0R2
Tel: 613-993-8633; *Fax:* 613-993-4353
Toll-Free: 877-251-1771
e-mail: rcmp.vets@rcmp-grc.gc.ca
URL: www.rcmp.ca/vets/vets_e.htm

Royal Canadian Naval Benevolent Fund (RCNBF)
PO Box 505, Stn. B, Ottawa ON K1P 5P6
Tel: 613-996-5087; *Fax:* 613-236-8830
Toll-Free: 888-557-8777
e-mail: rcnbf@sympatico.ca
URL: www.rcnbf.ca
L.F. Harrison, Sec.-Treas.

Ste. Anne's Association of War Veterans Inc. / Association Ste-Anne des anciens combattants inc.
305, boul des Anciens Combattants, Sainte-Anne-de-Bellevue QC H9X 1Y9
Tel: 514-457-3440; *Fax:* 514-457-8412
Toll-Free: 800-361-9287
e-mail: steanne@vac-acc.gc.ca
Ivette Glimont, Secretary

Mines & Mineral Resources

Association de l'exploration minière de Québec (AEMQ)
#203, 132, avenue du Lac, Rouyn-Noranda QC J9X 4N5
Tél: 819-762-1599; *Téléc:* 819-762-1522
Courriel: aemq@aemq.org
URL: www.aemq.org
Jean-Pierre Thomassin, Directeur général
Julie Charette, Ajointe administrative

Association for Mineral Exploration British Columbia (AMEBC)
#800, 889 Pender St. West, Vancouver BC V6C 3B2
Tel: 604-689-5271; *Fax:* 604-681-2363
e-mail: info@amebc.ca
URL: www.amebc.ca
Affiliation(s): Mining Association of Canada; Mining Association of BC
Dan Jepsen, President & CEO

Association minière du Québec (AMQ) / Québec Mining Association
Place de la Cité - Tour Belle Cour, #720, 2590, boul Laurier, Québec QC G1V 4M6
Tél: 418-657-2016; *Téléc:* 418-657-2154
Courriel: mines@amq-inc.com
URL: www.amq-inc.com
Carole Côté, Directrice, Administration
Yves Harvey, Président

Association of Applied Geochemists (AEG)
PO Box 26099, 72 Robertson Rd., Nepean ON K2H 9R0
Tel: 613-828-0199; *Fax:* 613-828-9288
e-mail: office@appliedgeochemists.org
URL: www.appliedgeochemists.org
David R. Cohen, President
Betty Arseneault, Business Manager

Canadian Copper & Brass Development Association
#415, 49 The Donway West, Toronto ON M3C 3M9
Tel: 416-391-5599; *Fax:* 416-391-3823
Toll-Free: 877-640-0946
e-mail: coppercanada@onramp.ca
URL: www.coppercanada.ca
Affiliation(s): International Copper Association
Stephen A.W. Knapp, Executive Director

Canadian Institute of Mining, Metallurgy & Petroleum (CIM) / Institut canadien des mines, de la métallurgie et du pétrole
#855, 3400, boul de Maisonneuve ouest, Montréal QC H3Z 3B8
Tel: 514-939-2710; *Fax:* 514-939-2714
e-mail: cim@cim.org
URL: www.cim.org
Jean Vavrek, Executive Director
James L. Popowich, President

Canadian Mineral Analysts (CMA) / Analystes des minéraux canadiens
444 Harold Ave. West, Winnipeg MB R2C 2E2
Tel: 204-224-1443
e-mail: jgregorchuk@shaw.ca
URL: www.canadianmineralanalysts.com
John Gregorchuk, Managing Secretary
Sean Murry, Treasurer
Eric Arseneault, Executive Secretary

Chamber of Mineral Resources of Nova Scotia (CMRNS)
PO Box 2171, Windsor NS B0N 2T0
Tel: 902-798-0187; *Fax:* 902-798-2141
e-mail: terry.daniels@ns.sympatico.ca
Affiliation(s): Mining Association of Canada
Terry Daniels, Managing Director

Chamber of Mines of Eastern British Columbia
215 Hall St., Nelson BC V1L 5X4
Tel: 250-352-5242; *Fax:* 250-352-7227
e-mail: chamberofminesebc@netidea.com
URL: www.cmebc.com
Dennis Llewellyn, Chamber Manager
Jack Denny, President

Chrysotile Institute
#1640, 1200, av McGill College, Montréal QC H3B 4G7
Tel: 514-877-9797; *Fax:* 514-877-9717
e-mail: info@chrysotile.com
URL: www.chrysotile.com/
Denis Hamel, Director General

Coal Association of Canada
#150, 205 - 9th Ave. SE, Calgary AB T2G 0R3
Tel: 403-262-1544; *Fax:* 403-265-7604
Toll-Free: 800-910-2625
e-mail: info@coal.ca
URL: www.coal.ca
Allen Wright, President & CEO

East Kootenay Chamber of Mines
#201, 12 - 11th Avenue South, Cranbrook BC V1C 2P1
Tel: 250-489-2255; *Fax:* 250-426-8755
URL: www.ekcm.org/chamber2
Ross Stanfield, President

Mineralogical Association of Canada (MAC) / Association minéralogique du Canada
490, rue de la Couronne, Québec QC G1K 9A9
Tel: 418-653-0333; *Fax:* 418-653-0777
e-mail: office@mineralogicalassociation.ca
URL: www.mineralogicalassociation.ca
Kurt Kyser, President
Peter C. Burns, Vice-President
David A. Fowle, Secretary
Martine M. Savard, Treasurer

Mining Association of British Columbia (MABC)
#900, 808 West Hastings St., Vancouver BC V6C 2X4
Tel: 604-681-4321; *Fax:* 604-681-5305
e-mail: mabcinfo@mining.bc.ca
URL: www.mining.bc.ca
Michael McPhie, President/CEO
Byng Giraud, Vice-President, Policy & Communications
Nicole Bourgouin, Secretary

Mining Association of Canada (MAC) / Association minière du Canada
#1105, 350 Sparks St., Ottawa ON K1R 7S8
Tel: 613-233-9391; *Fax:* 613-233-8897
e-mail: info@mining.ca
URL: www.mining.ca
Gordon R. Peeling, President & CEO
Marilyn Fortin, Office Manager & Member Services
Monique Laflèche, Executive Assistant

Mining Association of Manitoba Inc. (MAMI)
#700, 305 Broadway Ave., Winnipeg MB R3C 3J7
Tel: 204-989-1890
e-mail: pmarsden@mines.ca
URL: www.mines.ca
Ed Huebert, Executive Vice President

Mining Society of Nova Scotia
88 Leeside Dr., Sydney NS B1R 1S6
Tel: 902-567-2147
e-mail: florence@ns.sympatico.ca

Affiliation(s): Canadian Institute of Mining, Metallurgy & Petroleum
Howard Donohoe, President

New Brunswick Mining Association / L'Association minière du Nouveau-Brunswick
#420, 1133 St. George Blvd., Moncton NB E1E 4E1
Tel: 506-857-3056; *Fax:* 506-857-3059
Blaine Lewis, Manager

NWT & Nunavut Chamber of Mines
PO Box 2818, Yellowknife NT X1A 2R1
Tel: 867-873-5281; *Fax:* 867-920-2145
e-mail: nwtmines@ssimicro.com
URL: www.miningnorth.com
Affiliation(s): Mining Association of Canada; Canadian Institute of Mining, Metallurgy & Petroleum
Mike Vaydik, General Manager

Ontario Mining Association (OMA)
#520, 5775 Yonge St., Toronto ON M2M 4J1
Tel: 416-364-9301; *Fax:* 416-364-5986
e-mail: pmcbride@oma.on.ca
URL: www.oma.on.ca
Chris Hodgson, President

Prospectors & Developers Association of Canada (PDAC) / Association canadienne des prospecteurs & entrepreneurs
#900, 34 King St. East, Toronto ON M5C 2X8
Tel: 416-362-1969; *Fax:* 416-362-0101
e-mail: info@pdac.ca
URL: www.pdac.ca
Anthony Andrews, Executive Director
Patricia Dillon, President
Saley E. Lawton, Secretary
Dean Braunsteiner, Treasurer

Saskatchewan Mining Association (SMA)
#1500, 2002 Victoria Ave., Regina SK S4P 0R7
Tel: 306-757-9505; *Fax:* 306-569-1085
e-mail: saskmining@sasktel.net
URL: www.saskmining.ca
Kelvin Dereski, President
Pamela Schwann, Executive Director
David Neuburger, 1st Vice-President
Stewart Brown, 2nd Vice-President
Tracey Irwin, Manager, Communications & Membership

Yukon Chamber of Mines (YCM)
3151B - 3rd Ave., Whitehorse YT Y1A 1G1
Tel: 867-667-2090; *Fax:* 867-668-7127
e-mail: info@ycmines.ca
URL: www.ycmines.ca
Affiliation(s): Mining Association of Canada
Joanne Rice, Executive Officer
Carl Schulze, President

Yukon Mine Training Association (YMTA)
#120, 205 Black St., Whitehorse YT Y1A 2M8
Tel: 867-633-6463; *Fax:* 867-633-2605
e-mail: info@ymta.org
URL: www.yukonminetraining.com
Al Doherty, Chair
Tracy Thomas, Executive Director

Yukon Prospectors' Association (YPA)
3151B - 3rd Ave., Whitehorse YT Y1A 1G1
URL: north-land.com/ypa
Jim McFaull, President

Multiculturalism

Affiliation of Multicultural Societies & Service Agencies of BC (AMSSA)
#205, 2929 Commercial Dr., Vancouver BC V5N 4C8
Tel: 604-718-2777; *Fax:* 604-298-0747
Toll-Free: 888-355-5560
e-mail: amssa@amssa.org
URL: www.amssa.org
Affiliation(s): Canadian Council for Refugees
Tim Welsh, Program Director
Lynn Moran, Executive Director

Armenian National Federation of Canada (ANF) / Fédération national arménienne du Canada
3401, rue Olivar-Asselin, Montréal QC H4J 1L5
Tel: 514-334-1299; *Fax:* 514-334-6853
e-mail: a_babikian@hotmail.com
Affiliation(s): Armenian National Committee of Canada
Aris Babikian, President

Australia-New Zealand Association (ANZA)
3 - 8 Ave. West, Vancouver BC V5Y 1M8
Tel: 604-876-7128
e-mail: info@anzaclub.org
URL: www.anzaclub.org
Chari Keet, Manager

B'nai Brith Canada (BBC)
15 Hove St., Toronto ON M3H 4Y8
Tel: 416-633-6224; *Fax:* 416-630-2159
e-mail: bnb@bnaibrith.ca
URL: www.bnaibrith.ca
Affiliation(s): B'nai Brith International
Frank Dimant, Executive Vice President
Joe Bogoroch, President
Joyce Aster, Ontario Regional Director

B'nai Brith Canada
#202, 7155 Côte St. Luc, Montréal QC H4V 1J2
Tel: 514-733-5377; *Fax:* 514-342-9632
e-mail: infoquebec@bnaibrith.ca
URL: www.bnaibrith.ca/quebec

B'nai Brith Canada
#C403, 123 Doncaster St., Winnipeg MB R3N 2B2
Tel: 204-487-9623; *Fax:* 204-487-9648
e-mail: wbb@bnaibrith.ca
URL: www.bnaibrith.ca

B'nai Brith Canada
PO Box 67306, Stn. Hawkstone R.P.O., Edmonton AB T6M 0J5
Tel: 780-483-6939
e-mail: bnaibrith.westcan@shaw.ca
URL: www.bnaibrith.ca

B'nai Brith Canada
#1, 7330 Goreway Dr., Mississauga ON L4T 4J2
Tel: 905-678-9691
URL: www.bnaibrith.ca

B'nai Brith Canada Institute for International Affairs
15 Hove St., Toronto ON M3H 4Y8
Tel: 416-633-6224; *Fax:* 416-630-2159
e-mail: institute@bnaibrith.ca
URL: www.bnaibrith.ca/institute.html
Frank Dimant, CEO
Ruth Klein, National Director

Baltic Federation in Canada
1590 Stewart Cres., Milton ON L9T 6P9
Tel: 905-693-8780
URL: www.balticfederation.ca
Peter Meiklejohn, President

Belgo-Canadian Association (BCA)
121 Chillery Ave., Toronto ON M1K 4T5
Tel: 416-261-4603
URL: www.belgo-canadian.com

Black Cultural Society for Nova Scotia
1149 Main St., Dartmouth NS B2Z 1A8
Tel: 902-434-6223; *Fax:* 902-434-2306
Toll-Free: 800-465-0767
e-mail: contact@bccns.com
URL: www.bccns.com
Henry V. Bishop, Director & Chief Curator
Leslie Oliver, President

Canadian Arab Federation (CAF) / La Fédération Canado-Arabe
1057 McNicoll Ave., Toronto ON M1W 3W6
Tel: 416-493-8635; *Fax:* 416-493-9239
Toll-Free: 866-886-4675
e-mail: info@caf.ca
URL: www.caf.ca
Mohamed Boudjenane, Executive Director
Sara Amash, Manager, Projects
Nora Abdulkarim, Coordinator, Job Search Workshop Program

The Canadian Doukhobor Society (CDS)
#27, Comp 4, R.R.#1, South Slocan BC V0G 2G0
Tel: 250-428-9634; *Fax:* 250-428-3519
e-mail: awishlow@kootenay.com
Marion Verigin, Secretary
Anne Stormes, Treasurer
Alex Wishlow, Chair

Canadian Ethnocultural Council (CEC) / Conseil ethnoculturel du Canada
#400, 176 Gloucester St., Ottawa ON K2P 0A6
Tel: 613-230-3867; *Fax:* 613-230-8051
e-mail: cec@web.net
URL: www.ethnocultural.ca
Peter Ferreira, President
Emmanuel J. Dick, Director

Canadian Institute for Jewish Research (CIJR) / Institut canadien de recherche sur le Judaïsme
PO Box 175, Stn. H, Montréal QC H3G 2K7
Tel: 514-486-5544; *Fax:* 514-486-8284
e-mail: cijr@isranet.org
URL: www.isranet.org
Paula Driedger, Programs and Information Officer

Canadian Jewish Congress (CJC) / Congrès juif canadien
#650, 100 Sparks St., Ottawa ON K1P 5B7
Tel: 613-233-8703; *Fax:* 613-233-8748
e-mail: canadianjewishcongress@cjc.ca
URL: www.cjc.ca
Affiliation(s): World Jewish Congress; Conference on Jewish Material Claims Against Germany, Inc.; Memorial Foundation for Jewish Culture
Bernie M. Farber, CEO
Joshua Rotblatt, Director, Operations
Benjamin Shinewald, National Executive Director

Canadian Jewish Congress
#801, 1166 Alberni St., Vancouver BC V6E 3Z3
Tel: 604-622-4240; *Fax:* 604-622-4244
e-mail: cjcpr@cjc.ca

Canadian Jewish Congress
1607 - 90 Ave. SW, Calgary AB T2V 4V7
Tel: 403-444-3152; *Fax:* 403-253-7915
e-mail: dpowers@cjcc.ca
URL: www.jewishcalgary.org

Canadian Jewish Congress
7200 - 156 St., Edmonton AB T5R 1X3
Tel: 780-487-5120; *Fax:* 780-481-1854
e-mail: edjfed@attcanada.ca
URL: www.jewishedmonton.org

Canadian Jewish Congress
#300C, 123 Doncaster St., Winnipeg MB R3N 2B2
Tel: 204-477-7423; *Fax:* 204-477-7405
e-mail: bfreedman@jewishwinnipeg.org
URL: www.jewishwinnipeg.org

Canadian Jewish Congress
21 Nadolny Sachs Private, Ottawa ON K2A 1R9
Tel: 613-798-4696; *Fax:* 613-789-4695
e-mail: vaad@jccottawa.com

Canadian Jewish Congress
4600 Bathurst St., Toronto ON M2R 3V2
Tel: 416-635-2883; *Fax:* 416-635-1408
e-mail: bfarber@on.cjc.ca

Canadian Jewish Congress
#508, 5670 Spring Garden Rd., Halifax NS B3J 1H6
Tel: 902-422-7491; *Fax:* 902-425-3722
e-mail: jgoldberg@theajc.ns.ca

Canadian Jewish Congress
c/o Congregation Agudas Israel, 715 McKinnon Ave., Saskatoon SK S7H 2G2
Tel: 306-343-7023; *Fax:* 306-343-1244
e-mail: ajavivi@shaw.ca

Canadian Jewish Congress
c/o Beth Jacob Synagogue, 4715 McTavish St., Regina SK S4S 6H2
Tel: 306-569-8166; *Fax:* 306-569-8166

Canadian Jewish Congress
1, carré Cummings, Montréal QC H3W 1M6
Tel: 514-345-6411; *Fax:* 514-345-6412
e-mail: cjc-quebec@cjc.ca

Canadian Latvian Business & Professional Association (CLBPA)
123 Overland Dr., Toronto ON M3C 2C7
Tel: 416-444-5201; *Fax:* 416-444-5208
e-mail: alex@budrevics.com
Alexander Budrevics, President

Canadian Polish Congress (CPC) / Congrès canadien polonais
288 Roncesvalles Ave., Toronto ON M6R 2M4
Tel: 416-532-2876; *Fax:* 416-532-5730
e-mail: kongres@kpk.org
URL: www.kpk.org
Affiliation(s): Polonia of the Free World; Canadian Polish Research Institute; Adam Mickiewicz Foundation; Polish Combattants Association; Polish National Union
Wladyslaw Lizon, President

Jaroslaw Nowinka, Vice-President

Canadian Slovak League
Central Assembly, 221 Arlington Ave., Ottawa ON K1S 5B6
George Frajkor, Acting President

Canadian Tibetan Association of Ontario
#201, 160 Springhurst Ave., Toronto ON M6K 1C2
Tel: 416-410-5606; *Fax:* 416-410-5606
e-mail: info@ctao.org
URL: www.ctao.org
Thupten Wangyal, President

Canadian Zionist Federation (CZF) / La fédération sioniste canadienne
#206, 1, carré Cummings, Montréal QC H3W 1M6
Tel: 514-739-7300; *Fax:* 514-739-9412
e-mail: czfnational@fedcjamtl.org
URL: www.doingzionism.org/federations/fed_home.asp?fed=czf
Affiliation(s): World Zionist Organization; Jewish Agency
Florence Simon, National Executive Director
Norman Stern, President
Shya Finestone, CA, Treasurer
Norma Rubin, Secretary

Canadian-Croatian Congress / Kanadsko-Hrvatski Kongres
3550 Commercial St., Vancouver BC V5A 4E9
Tel: 604-871-7190; *Fax:* 604-879-2256
URL: www.canada.crocc.org
Affiliation(s): Croatian World Congress
Ivan Curman, President

Caribbean Cultural Committee
Caribana House, 138 Hamilton St., Toronto ON M4M 2E1
Tel: 416-466-0321; *Fax:* 416-466-4913
Toll-Free: 800-768-5442
e-mail: caribana@rogers.com
URL: www.caribana.com
Elsworth James, Chair, Public Relations
Joanna Parris, Office Manager

Chinese Canadian National Council (CCNC) / Conseil national des canadiens chinois
#507, 302 Spadina Ave., Toronto ON M5T 2E7
Tel: 416-977-9871; *Fax:* 416-977-1630
e-mail: national@ccnc.ca
URL: www.ccnc.ca
Affiliation(s): Canadian Council for Refugees; Coalition for a Just Immigration Refugee Policy
Victor Wong, Executive Director

Clans & Scottish Societies of Canada (CASSOC)
#78, 24 Fundy Bay Blvd., Newmarket ON L3Y 6T6
Tel: 905-898-6381; *Fax:* 905-773-0991
Toll-Free: 800-593-0518
e-mail: editor@cassoc.ca
URL: www.cassoc.ca
Ian A. Munro, Chair

Cypriot Federation of Canada / Fédération chypriote du Canada
6 Thorncliff Park Dr., Toronto ON M4H 1H1
Tel: 416-696-7400; *Fax:* 416-696-9465
e-mail: cypriotfederation@rogers.com
Kyriacos Elles, President

Czech & Slovak Association of Canada
PO Box 564, 3044 Bloor St. West, Toronto ON M8X 2Y8
Tel: 416-925-2241; *Fax:* 416-925-1940
e-mail: ustredi@cssk.ca
URL: www.cssk.ca
Milos Suchma, President
Radmila Locher, Contact

Federation of Canada-China Friendship Associations
#705, 175 Laurier, Gatineau QC J8X 4G3
Tel: 819-777-8434
e-mail: lolan.merklinger@sympatico.ca
URL: www.fccfa.ca
Lolan Wang Merklinger, President

Federation of Canadian Turkish Associations (FCTA)
#15, 1170 Sheppard Ave. W, Toronto ON M3K 2A3
Tel: 647-230-9397
e-mail: info@canturkfed.net
URL: www.canturkfed.net
Mehmet Bor, Chair
Celal Ucar, Secretary
Hussein Nurgel, Treasurer

Federation of Chinese Canadian Professionals (Ontario) (FCCP)
Coral Place, 55 Glenn Hawthorne Blvd., Mississauga ON L5R 3S6
Tel: 905-890-3235; *Fax:* 905-568-5293
e-mail: webmaster@fccpontario.com
URL: www.fccpontario.com
Dennis Woo, President

Federation of Chinese Canadian Professionals (Québec) (FCCP Québec) / Fédération des professionnels chinois canadiens (Québec)
PO Box 1004, Stn. B, Montréal QC H3B 3K5
Tel: 514-747-2488
e-mail: htan222@yahoo.ca
URL: www.fccp.ca
Howard Tan, President
John Chen, Vice-President
Renee Chin, Treasurer

Federation of Danish Associations in Canada / Fédération des associations danoises du Canada
679 Eastvale Ct., Gloucester ON K1J 6Z7
URL: home.ca.inter.net/~robuch/dan-fed.htm
Rolf Buschardt Christensen, National President
Ole D. Larsen, National Vice-President
Ella Wolder, National Secretary
Annie Kruus, National Treasurer

Federation of Korean Canadian Associations
1133 Leslie St., Toronto ON M3L 2J6
Tel: 416-383-0777; *Fax:* 416-383-1113
e-mail: koreancanadian@canada.org
URL: www.koreancanadian.org

Federation of Scottish Clans in Nova Scotia (FSCNS)
PO Box 477, Lower Sackville NS B4C 3K3
e-mail: info@scotsns.ca
URL: www.scotsns.ca
Thomas (Tom) E.S. Wallace, President
Frank L. Logan, 1st Vice-President
Carol Terry, Secretary
Jean Watson, Treasurer

Finnish Canadian Cultural Federation / Fédération culturelle finno-canadienne
128 Quartz Ave., Timmins ON P4N 4L6
e-mail: margaretk@personainternet.com
URL: www.finnishcanadian.com
Affiliation(s): Finland Society, R.Y.; Finn Fest USA, Inc.
Margaret Kangas, Treasurer

Finnish Organization of Canada
PO Box 65070, Toronto ON M4K 3Z2
Tel: 416-651-0317; *Fax:* 416-651-0236
e-mail: eajokinen@sympatico.ca
Elsie Jokinen, President

German-Canadian Congress (GCC) / Congrès germano-canadien
#58, 81 Garry St., Winnipeg MB R3C 4J9
Tel: 204-989-8300; *Fax:* 204-989-8304
e-mail: gccmb@hotmail.com
URL: gccongressmb.tripod.com
Helmut Hesse, President

Goethe-Institut (Montréal)
418, rue Sherbrooke est, Montréal QC H2L 1J6
Tel: 514-499-0159; *Fax:* 514-499-0905
e-mail: info@montreal.goethe.org
URL: www.goethe.de/montreal
Manfred Stoffl, Directeur

Goethe-Institut (Toronto)
PO Box 136, #201, 100 University Ave., Toronto ON M5J 1V6
Tel: 416-593-5257; *Fax:* 416-593-5145
e-mail: info@toronto.goethe.org
URL: www.goethe.de/toronto
Sonja Griegoschewski, Director
Beate Biczo, Administrator

Greater Vancouver Japanese Canadian Citizens' Association
Nikkei Heritage Centre, #200, 6688 Southoaks Cres., Burnaby BC V5E 4M7
Tel: 604-777-5222; *Fax:* 604-777-5223
e-mail: gvjcca@shaw.ca
Ron Nishimura, President

Hellenic Canadian Congress / Congrès hellénique du Québec
846 Pape Ave., 2nd Fl., Toronto ON M4K 3T6
Tel: 416-461-0824; *Fax:* 416-463-9514
Jimmy Sidiropoulos, President

Holocaust Centre of Toronto
Lipa Green Bldg., 4600 Bathurst St., 4th Fl., Toronto ON M2R 3V2
Tel: 416-635-2883; *Fax:* 416-635-0925
e-mail: info@ujafed.org
URL: www.jewishtoronto.net
Adam Fuerstenberg, Director

Hungarian Canadian Cultural Centre
840 St. Clair Ave. West, Toronto ON M6C 1C1
Tel: 416-654-4926; *Fax:* 416-654-4927
e-mail: office@hccc.org
URL: www.hccc.org
Gabor Vaski, President

Icelandic National League of North America (INL/NA)
#103, 94 - 1st Ave., Gimli MB R0C 1B1
Tel: 204-642-5897; *Fax:* 204-642-9382
e-mail: inl@mts.net
URL: www.inlofna.org
Garry Oddleifson, President
Rosa Johnston, Executive Secretary

Irish Canadian Cultural Association of New Brunswick (ICCA NB)
c/o 189 Carlisle Rd., Douglas NB E3A 7M8
e-mail: info@newirelandnb.ca
URL: www.newirelandnb.ca
Pat Murphy, President

Islamic Foundation of Toronto
441 Nugget Ave., Toronto ON M1S 5E1
Tel: 416-321-0909; *Fax:* 416-321-1995
e-mail: info@islamicfoundation.ca
URL: www.islamicfoundation.ca
Shakil Akhter, Administrator
Zaib Mirza, Social Services Coordinator

Islamic Information Foundation (IIF)
8 Laurel Lane, Halifax NS B3M 2P6
Tel: 902-445-2494; *Fax:* 902-445-2494
Jamal Badawi, Chairperson

Italian Cultural Institute / Istituto Italiano di Cultura
496 Huron St., Toronto ON M5R 2R3
Tel: 416-921-3802; *Fax:* 416-962-2503
URL: www.iictoronto.esteri.it
Martin Stiglio, Director

Jamaican Canadian Association (JCA)
995 Arrow Rd., Toronto ON M9M 2Z5
Tel: 416-746-5772; *Fax:* 416-746-7035
e-mail: info@jcassoc.com
URL: www.jcassoc.org
Audrey Campbell, President

Japanese Canadian Association of Yukon (JCAY)
531 Grove St., Whitehorse YT Y1A 5J9
Tel: 867-393-2588
Fumi Torigai, Contact

Kashmiri Canadian Council (KCC)
#44516, 2376 Eglinton Ave. East, Toronto ON M1K 5K3
Tel: 416-282-6933; *Fax:* 416-282-7488
e-mail: kcc@kashmiri-cc.ca
URL: www.kashmiri-cc.ca

Latvian National Federation in Canada / Fédération nationale lettone au Canada
4 Credit Union Dr., Toronto ON M4A 2N8
Tel: 416-755-2353; *Fax:* 416-755-1244
e-mail: inak@inak.org
URL: www.lnak.org
Alexander Budrevics, President

League of Ukrainian Canadians
83-85 Christie St., Toronto ON M6G 3B1
Tel: 416-516-8223; *Fax:* 416-516-4033
Toll-Free: 866-714-4132
e-mail: luc@lucorg.com
URL: www.lucorg.com
Affiliation(s): Ukrainian Canadian Congress
Volodymyr Paslavskyi, Executive Director

The Lithuanian Canadian Community / La Communauté lithuanienne du Canada
1 Resurrection Rd., Toronto ON M9A 5G1
Tel: 416-533-3292; *Fax:* 416-533-2282
e-mail: info@klb.org
URL: www.klb.org
Joana Kuras-Lasys, President

Lithuanian Canadian R.C. Cultural Society
2185 Stavebank Rd., Mississauga ON L5C 1T3
Tel: 905-275-4672; *Fax:* 905-290-9802
e-mail: tevzib@pathcom.com
P. Gaida, Msgr., Editor in Chief
Joana Kuras, President

Maltese-Canadian Society of Toronto, Inc. (MCST)
255 Medland St., Toronto ON M6P 2N6
Tel: 416-767-3645; *Fax:* 416-767-5707
e-mail: mcst@intiss.com
URL: www.intiss.com/mcst
Affiliation(s): Maltese-Canadian Federation Inc.
J. Zammit, Contact
C. Grixti, Contact
R. Cumbo, Contact

Manitoba Multicultural Resources Centre Inc. (MMRC)
#101, 1555 St. James St., Winnipeg MB R3H 1B5
Tel: 204-831-6672
Affiliation(s): Coalition for Human Equity

Mizrachi Organization of Canada
296 Wilson Ave., Toronto ON M3H 1S8
Tel: 416-630-9266; *Fax:* 416-630-2305
e-mail: mizrachi@rogers.com
URL: www.mizrachi.ca
Jack Kahn, National President

Multicultural Association of Northwestern Ontario (MANWO)
711 Victoria Ave. East, Thunder Bay ON P7C 5X9
Tel: 807-622-4666; *Fax:* 807-622-7271
e-mail: manwoyc@tbaytel.net
Moffat S. Makuto, Executive Director

Multicultural Association of Nova Scotia (MANS) / Association multiculturelle de la Nouvelle-Écosse
1113 Marginal Rd., Halifax NS B3H 4P7
Tel: 902-423-6534; *Fax:* 902-422-0881
e-mail: admin@mans.ns.ca; communications@mans.ns.ca
URL: www.mans.ns.ca
Ifty Illyas, Executive Director
Mukhtyar Tomar, President
Mike Fitzgerald, Vice-President
Tahira Ahmed, Secretary
Faddoul Faddoul, Treasurer

Multicultural History Society of Ontario (MHSO)
c/o Oral History Museum, #307, 901 Lawrence Ave. West, Toronto ON M5S 1C3
Tel: 416-979-2973; *Fax:* 416-979-7947
e-mail: mhso.mail@utoronto.ca
URL: www.mhso.ca
Jennifer Harrington, Contact, Oral History Museum

Muslim Association of Canada (MAC)
#332, 1568 Merivale Rd., Ottawa ON K2G 5Y7
Tel: 613-321-5000; *Fax:* 613-321-5001
e-mail: mac@macnet.ca
URL: www.macnet.ca

Muslim Education & Welfare Foundation of Canada (MEWFC)
2580 McGill St., Vancouver BC V5K 1H1
Tel: 604-255-9941; *Fax:* 604-255-9941
Nazih Hammad, Librarian, Jannat Bibi Library

Muslim World League
#220, 2550 Argentia Rd., Mississauga ON L5N 5R1
Tel: 905-542-1050; *Fax:* 905-542-1054
e-mail: mwl@mwlcanada.org
URL: www.mwlcanada.org
Mohamad Khatib, Director

National Association of Canadians of Origin in India (NACOI) / Association nationale des Canadiens d'origine indienne
PO Box 2308, Stn. D, Ottawa ON K1P 5W5
e-mail: dbdavis@web.net
URL: www.web.net/~dbdavis
Baljinder Gill, President

National Association of Japanese Canadians (NAJC)
#1, 222 Osborne St., Winnipeg MB R3L 1Z3
Tel: 204-943-2910; *Fax:* 204-947-3145
e-mail: national@najc.ca
URL: www.najc.ca
Affiliation(s): Canadian Ethnocultural Council; Canadian Council for Refugees; National Capital Alliance on Race Relations
Terumi Kuwada, President

National Congress of Italian Canadians (NCIC) / Congrès national des italo-canadiens
PO Box 8144, Stn. Terminal, Ottawa ON K1G 3H6
URL: www.ncf.ca/italcongress/

National Council of Trinidad & Tobago Organizations in Canada (NCTTOC)
#1, 66 Oakmeadow Blvd., Toronto ON M1E 4G5
Tel: 416-283-9672; *Fax:* 416-283-9672
e-mail: manniedick@hotmail.com
Affiliation(s): National Visible Minority Council on Labour Force Development
Emmanuel J. Dick, President

National Federation of Pakistani Canadians Inc. (NFPC)
#1100, 251 Laurier Ave. W, Ottawa ON K1P 5J6
Tel: 613-741-8881; *Fax:* 613-745-4696
e-mail: tanveer_ottawa@hotmail.com
Tanveer Ahmed, President
Naki Chaudhary, Treasurer

New Brunswick Multicultural Council (NBMC) / Conseil multiculturel du Nouveau-Brunswick (CMNB)
#301, 390 King St., Fredericton NB E3B 1E3
Tel: 506-453-1091; *Fax:* 506-474-8095
e-mail: nbmc@nb-mc.ca
URL: www.nb-mc.ca
Affiliation(s): Canadian Federation of Multicultural Councils
George Maicher, President

Pacific Peoples Partnership (PPP)
#407, 620 View St., Victoria BC V8W 1J6
Tel: 250-381-4131; *Fax:* 250-388-5258
e-mail: info@pacificpeoplespartnership.org
URL: www.pacificpeoplespartnership.org
Affiliation(s): Nuclear Free & Independent Pacific Movement
Glenn Raynor, Executive Director

Polish Alliance of Canada
1015 Barton St. East, Hamilton ON L8L 3C8
Tel: 905-545-0799
Stanislaw Glogowski, President

Serbian National Shield Society of Canada
#303, 1900 Sheppard Ave. East, Toronto ON M2J 4T4
Tel: 416-496-7881; *Fax:* 416-493-0335
e-mail: diddra@sympatico.ca
Bora Dragasevich, President

UIA Federations Canada
#315, 4600 Bathurst St., Toronto ON M2R 3V3
Tel: 416-636-7655; *Fax:* 416-636-9897
e-mail: info@uiafed.org
URL: www.jewishcanada.org
Steven Ain, Executive Vice-President

UJA Federation of Greater Toronto
4600 Bathurst St., Toronto ON M2R 3V2
Tel: 416-635-2883; *Fax:* 416-635-9565
e-mail: info@ujafed.org
URL: www.jewishtoronto.net
Affiliation(s): Toronto Jewish Library; Board of Jewish Education; Committee for Yiddish; Holocaust Centre of Greater Toronto; Jewish Information Service of Greater Toronto; Ontario Jewish Archives; Bathurst JCC & Miles Nadal JCC; Jewish Family & Child Service; Hillel of Greater Toronto; Bernard Betel Centre for Creative Living; Jewish Immigrant Aid Services Toronto; Jewish Vocational Services Toronto, Jewish Russian Community Centre
Ted Sokolsky, President & CEO
David Engel, Chair

Ukrainian Canadian Congress (UCC) / Congrès des ukrainiens canadiens
#647, 167 Lombard Ave., Winnipeg MB R3B 0V3
Tel: 204-942-4627; *Fax:* 204-947-3882
Toll-Free: 866-942-4627
e-mail: ucc@ucc.ca
URL: www.ucc.ca
Affiliation(s): Ukrainian Catholic Brotherhood; Ukrainian Self-Reliance Association (Orthodox); Ukrainian National Federation; League of Ukrainian Canadians; Ukrainian Canadian Professional & Business Federation
Paul Grod, President

Ukrainian Canadian Research & Documentation Centre (UCRDC) / Centre canadien-ukrainien de recherches et de documentation
#200, 620 Spadina Ave., Toronto ON M5S 2H4
Tel: 416-966-1819; *Fax:* 416-966-1820
e-mail: info@ucrdc.org
URL: www.ucrdc.org
Affiliation(s): St. Vladimir Institute
Wsevolod Isajiw, Chair

Urban Alliance on Race Relations (UARR)
#507, 302 Spadina Ave., Toronto ON M5T 2E7
Tel: 416-703-6607; *Fax:* 416-703-4415
e-mail: info@urbanalliance.ca
URL: www.urbanalliance.ca
Sri-Guggan Sri-Skanda Rajah, President
Yumei Lin, Administrative Assistant

Vietnamese Canadian Federation / Fédération vietnamienne du Canada
249 Rochester St., Ottawa ON K1R 7M9
Tel: 613-230-8282; *Fax:* 613-230-8281
e-mail: vietfederation@yahoo.ca
URL: www.vietfederation.ca
Affiliation(s): Canadian Ethnocultural Council
Diep Trinh, Executive Director
Ut V. Ngo, President
Duc Q. Duong, Treasurer

Museums

Museum London
421 Ridout St. North, London ON N6A 5H4
Tel: 519-661-0333; *Fax:* 519-661-2559
e-mail: info@museumlondon.ca
URL: www.museumlondon.ca
Brian Meehan, Executive Director

Native Peoples

Aboriginal Friendship Centres of Saskatchewan
1615, 29th St., Saskatoon SK S7L 0N6
Tel: 306-955-0762; *Fax:* 306-955-0972
e-mail: afcs.pa@sasktel.net
URL: www.afcs.ca
Lennard Young, Provincial Director
Glen Lafleur, President

Aboriginal Nurses Association of Canada (ANAC) / Association des infirmières et infirmiers autochtones du Canada
#502, 56 Sparks St., Ottawa ON K1P 5A9
Tel: 613-724-4677; *Fax:* 613-724-4718
Toll-Free: 866-724-3049
e-mail: info@anac.on.ca
URL: www.anac.on.ca
Social Media: www.facebook.com/group.php?gid=8896466083
Affiliation(s): Health Canada; Canadian Nurses Association
Brenda Thomas, Executive Director
Rosella Kinoshameg, President
Evelyna Voyageur, Vice-President
Elaine Innes, Sec.-Treas.

Aboriginal Women's Association of PEI
PO Box 145, Lennox Island PE C0B 1P0
Tel: 902-831-3059; *Fax:* 902-831-3468
e-mail: awapei@pei.aibn.com
Marilyn Sark

Alberta Aboriginal Women's Society
PO Box 5168, Stn. Main, Peace River AB T8S 1R8
Tel: 780-624-3416; *Fax:* 780-624-3409
e-mail: aaws@telusplanet.net
Ruth Kidder, President

Alberta Native Friendship Centres Association (ANFCA)
10336 - 121 St., Edmonton AB T5N 1K8
Tel: 780-423-3138; *Fax:* 780-425-6277
e-mail: info@anfca.com
URL: www.anfca.com
Trudy Krysta, Treasurer
Jim Short, President

Alliance autochtone du Québec inc. / Native Alliance of Québec Inc.
21, rue Brodeur, Hull QC J8Y 2P6
Tél: 819-770-7763; *Téléc:* 819-770-6070
Courriel: info@aaqnaq.com
URL: www.aaqnaq.com
Carl Dubé, Grand Chief

Assembly of First Nations (AFN) / Assemblée des Premières Nations (APN)
Trebla Building, 473 Albert St., Ottawa ON K1R 5B4
Tel: 613-241-6789; *Fax:* 613-241-5808
Toll-Free: 866-869-6789

e-mail: imcleod@afn.ca
URL: www.afn.ca

Shawn Atleo, National Chief

Assembly of Manitoba Chiefs
#200, 260 St. Mary Ave., Winnipeg MB R3C 0M6
Tel: 204-956-0610; *Fax:* 204-956-2109
Toll-Free: 888-324-5483
e-mail: assembly@manitobachiefs.com
URL: www.manitobachiefs.com/

Affiliation(s): Assembly of First Nations
Irene Linklater, Executive Director

Association for Native Development in the Performing & Visual Arts (ANDPVA)
#171, 601 Christie St., Toronto ON M6G 4C7
Tel: 416-535-4567; *Fax:* 416-535-9331
e-mail: info@andpva.com
URL: www.andpva.com

Harmony Rice, President

Association of Iroquois & Allied Indians
387 Princess Ave., London ON N6B 2A7
Tel: 519-434-2761; *Fax:* 519-679-1653
e-mail: general@aiai.on.ca
URL: www.aiai.on.ca

Randall Phillips, Grand Chief

British Columbia Association of Aboriginal Friendship Centres (BCAAFC)
#200, 506 Fort St., Victoria BC V8W 1E6
Tel: 250-388-5522; *Fax:* 250-388-5502
e-mail: admin@bcaafc.com
URL: www.bcaafc.com

Paul Lacerte, Executive Director
Grace Nielsen, President
Wayne Jack, Secretary
Debbie Williams, Treasurer

British Columbia Native Women's Society
4213 Alexis Park Dr., Vernon BC V1T 7T8
Tel: 250-542-5029
e-mail: mbono@sd22.bc.ca
URL: www.bcnativewomen.com

Mollie Bono

Canadian Aboriginal & Minority Supplier Council (CAMSC)
95 Berkeley St., Toronto ON M5A 2W8
Tel: 416-941-0004; *Fax:* 416-941-9282
e-mail: info@camsc.ca
URL: www.camsc.ca

Doug Lord, Chair

Canadian Association for the Study of Indigenous Education (CASIE) / Association canadienne pour l'etude de l'education des autochtones (ACÉFÉ)
c/o Canadian Society for the Study of Education, #204, 260 Dalhousie St., Ottawa ON K1N 7E4

Canadian Council for Aboriginal Business (CCAB) / Conseil canadien pour le commerce autochtone
#204, 250 The Esplanade, Toronto ON M5A 1J2
Tel: 416-961-8663; *Fax:* 416-961-3995
e-mail: info@caab.com
URL: www.ccab.com

Canadian Native Friendship Centre (CNFC)
11205 - 101 St. NW, Edmonton AB T5G 2A4
Tel: 780-479-1999; *Fax:* 780-479-0043
e-mail: cnfc@shawbiz.ca
URL: www.cnfc.ca

Barb Maytwayashing, Management Director

Centre indien cri de Chibougamau
95, rue Jaculet, Chibougamau QC G8P 2G1
Tél: 418-748-7667

Jo-Ann Toulouse, Directice générale

Chiefs of Ontario
#804, 111 Peter St., Toronto ON M5V 2H1
Tel: 416-597-1266; *Fax:* 416-597-8365
Toll-Free: 877-517-6527
e-mail: margarert@coo.org
URL: www.chiefs-of-ontario.org

Affiliation(s): Assembly of First Nations
Lori Jacobs, Executive Director

Confederacy of Mainland Mi'kmaq (CMM)
PO Box 1590, 57 Martin Cresc., Truro NS B2N 6N7
Tel: 902-895-6385; *Fax:* 902-893-1520
Toll-Free: 877-892-2424
URL: www.cmmns.com

Donald M. Julien, Executive Director

Congress of Aboriginal Peoples (CAP) / Congrès des Peuples Autochtones
867 St. Laurent Blvd., Ottawa ON K1K 3B1
Tel: 613-747-6022; *Fax:* 613-747-8834
e-mail: info@abo-peoples.org
URL: www.abo-peoples.org

Al Fleming, Senior Communications Advisor
Libby Williams, Director of Operations

Council of Yukon First Nations (CYFN)
11 Nisutlin Dr., Whitehorse YT Y1A 3S4
Tel: 867-393-9200
URL: www.cyfn.ca

Andy Carvill, Grand Chief

Federation of Newfoundland Indians
CIBC Bldg., PO Box 956, #7, 9 Main St., 3rd Fl., Corner Brook NL A2H 6J3
Tel: 709-634-0996; *Fax:* 709-634-3477
Toll-Free: 800-563-2549
e-mail: adminasst@fni.nf.ca
URL: www.fni.nf.ca

Brendan Sheppard, President

Federation of Saskatchewan Indian Nations
Asimakaniseekan Askiy Reserve, #100, 103A Packham Ave., Saskatoon SK S7N 4K4
Tel: 306-665-1215; *Fax:* 306-244-4413
URL: www.fsin.com

Lawrence Joseph, Contact

Femmes autochtones du Québec inc. (FAQ) / Québec Native Women's Association Inc.
CP 1989, Kahnawake QC J0L 1B0
Tél: 450-632-0088; *Téléc:* 450-632-9280
Ligne sans frais: 800-363-0322
Courriel: info@faq-qnw.org
URL: www.faq-qnw.org

Carole Bussière, Executive Director

First Nations Confederacy of Cultural Education Centres
#302, 666 Kirkwood Ave., Ottawa ON K1Z 5X9
Tel: 613-728-5999; *Fax:* 613-728-2247
e-mail: info@fnccec.com; cecp@fnccec.com
URL: www.fnccec.com

Claudette Commanda, National Coordinator
Keith Matthew, President
Tiffany Sark-Carr, Vice-President
Dorothy Myo, Sec.-Treas.

Grand Council of the Crees / Grand Conseil des Cris
2, rue Lakeshore, Némiscau QC J0Y 3B0
Tel: 819-673-2600; *Fax:* 819-673-2606
e-mail: cra@lino.ca
URL: www.gcc.ca

Bill Namagoose, Executive Director

Indian Council of First Nations of Manitoba, Inc. (ICFNM)
PO Box 10299, Opaskwayak MB R0B 2J0
Tel: 204-623-7227; *Fax:* 204-623-4041
e-mail: jhead@mts.net

Andrew Kirkness, Grand Chief

Indigenous Bar Association
#9, 9785 - 152B St., Surrey BC V3R 9W2
Tel: 604-951-8807; *Fax:* 604-951-8806
e-mail: glangan@indigenousbar.ca
URL: www.indigenousbar.ca

Germaine Langan, Administrative Support

Inuit Art Foundation (IAF) / Fondation d'art Inuit
2081 Merivale Rd., Ottawa ON K2G 1G9
Tel: 613-224-8189
e-mail: iaf@inuitart.org; projects@inuitart.org
URL: www.inuitart.org

Marybelle Mitchell, Executive Director

Inuit Tapiriit Kanatami
#1101, 75 Albert St., Ottawa ON K1P 5E7
Tel: 613-238-8181; *Fax:* 613-234-1991
Toll-Free: 866-262-8181
e-mail: info@itk.ca
URL: www.itk.ca

Mary May Simon, President
Jim Moore, Executive Director
Stephen Hendrie, Communications Director

Labrador Inuit Association
PO Box 70, 12 Sandbanks Rd., Nain NL A0P 1L0
Tel: 709-922-2942; *Fax:* 709-922-2931
e-mail: nainreception@nunatsiavut.com
URL: www.nunatsiavut.com

Affiliation(s): Labrador Inuit Development Corporation; Torngasok Culture Centre; Labrador Inuit Health Commission
William Andersen III, President

Labrador Native Women's Association
PO Box 542, Stn. B, Happy Valley-Goose Bay NL A0P 1S0
Tel: 709-896-5071; *Fax:* 709-896-5071
e-mail: mnha@nf.aibn.com

Makivik Corporation / Société Makivik
PO Box 179, Kuujjuaq QC J0M 1C0
Tel: 819-964-2925; *Fax:* 819-964-2613
Toll-Free: 877-625-4825
e-mail: info@makivik.org
URL: www.makivik.org

Pita Aatami, President
Anthony Ittoshat, Treasurer
George Berthe, Corporate Secretary

Manitoba Association of Friendship Centres (MAC)
#200, 388 Donald St., Winnipeg MB R3B 2J4
Tel: 204-942-6299; *Fax:* 204-942-6308
e-mail: info@mac.mb.ca
URL: www.mac.mb.ca

Sheena Reed, President
Ella Mayer, Provincial Coordinator

Manitoba Indian Cultural Education Centre (MICEC)
119 Sutherland Ave., Winnipeg MB R2W 3C9
Tel: 204-942-0228; *Fax:* 204-947-6564
e-mail: micec@shawcable.com
URL: www.micec.com

Dennis Daniels, Executive Director

Manitoba Métis Federation / Fédération des Métis du Manitoba
Head Office, #300, 150 Henry Ave., Winnipeg MB R3B 0J7
Tel: 204-586-8474; *Fax:* 204-947-1816
e-mail: mmf@mmf.mb.ca
URL: www.mmf.mb.ca

Affiliation(s): Métis National Council
David Chartrand, President

Maritime Aboriginal Peoples Council (MAPC)
172 Truro Heights Rd., Truto NS B6L 1X1
Tel: 902-895-2982; *Fax:* 902-895-3844

Métis Nation - Saskatchewan
406 Jessop Ave., Saskatoon SK S7N 2S5
Tel: 306-343-8285; *Fax:* 306-343-0171
Toll-Free: 888-343-6667
e-mail: reception@mnsask.ca
URL: www.mn-s.ca

Affiliation(s): Métis National Council; Métis Women of Saskatchewan; Métis Nation of Saskatchewan Youth Council
Robert G. Doucette, President, Provincial Métis Council

Métis Nation Northwest Territories
PO Box 1375, 5125 - 50 St., Yellowknife NT X1A 2P1
Tel: 867-873-3505; *Fax:* 867-873-3395
e-mail: metisnwt@internorth.com

Gary Bohnet, President

Métis Nation of Alberta
Delia Gray Bldg., #100, 41738 Kingsway Ave., Edmonton AB T5G 0X5
Tel: 780-455-2200; *Fax:* 780-452-8948
Toll-Free: 800-252-7553
e-mail: apoitras@metis.org
URL: www.albertametis.ca

Affiliation(s): Métis Urban Housing; Métis Child & Family Services; Métis Development Inc.
Audrey Poitras, President

Métis Nation of Ontario
#3, 500 Old St. Patrick St., Ottawa ON K1N 9G4
Tel: 613-798-1488; *Fax:* 613-722-4225
Toll-Free: 800-263-4889
e-mail: ottawareception@metisnation.org
URL: www.metisnation.org

Affiliation(s): Métis National Council
Gary Lipinski, President

Métis National Council (MNC) / Ralliement national des Métis
#201, 350 Sparks St., Ottawa ON K1R 7S8
Tel: 613-232-3216; *Fax:* 613-232-4262
Toll-Free: 800-928-6330
e-mail: info@metisnation.ca
URL: www.metisnation.ca

Clément Chartier, President

Métis National Council of Women (MNCW) / Conseil national des femmes métisses, inc. (CNFM)
PO Box 293, Woodlawn ON K0A 3M0
Tel: 613-567-4287; *Fax:* 613-567-9644
Toll-Free: 888-867-2635
e-mail: info@metiswomen.ca
URL: www.metiswomen.ca
Sheila D. Genaille, LL.D. honoris c, President

Métis Provincial Council of British Columbia
#905, 1130 West Pender St., Vancouver BC V6E 4A4
Tel: 604-801-5853; *Fax:* 604-801-5097
Toll-Free: 800-940-1150
e-mail: traceyt@mnbc.ca
URL: www.mpcbc.bc.ca
Affiliation(s): Métis National Council
Bruce Dumont, President

Métis Settlements General Council
#200, 10335 - 172 St., Edmonton AB T5S 1K9
Tel: 780-822-4096; *Fax:* 780-489-9558
Toll-Free: 888-213-4400
e-mail: reception@msgc.ca
URL: www.msgc.ca
Gerald Cunningham, President

Mi'Kmaq Association for Cultural Studies (MACS)
47 Maillard St., Membertou NS B1S 2P5
Tel: 902-567-1752; *Fax:* 902-567-0776
e-mail: macs@mikmaq-assoc.ca
URL: www.mikmaq-assoc.ca

Mi'kmaq Native Friendship Centre
2158 Gottingen St., Halifax NS B3K 3B4
Tel: 902-420-1576; *Fax:* 902-423-6130
e-mail: micmacfriendshipcentre@msn.com
URL: www.micmaccentre.ca
Gordon V. King, Executive Director

Mother of Red Nation's Women's Council of Manitoba
141 Bannatyne Ave., 3rd Fl., Winnipeg MB R3B 0R3
Tel: 204-942-6676; *Fax:* 204-942-7639
e-mail: morn@morn.ca
URL: morn.cimnet.ca

National Aboriginal Achievement Foundation
#759, 2160 Fourth Line Rd., Oshweken ON N0A 1M0
Tel: 416-926-0775; *Fax:* 416-926-7554
Toll-Free: 800-329-9780
e-mail: info@naaf.ca
URL: www.naaf.ca
Roberta Jamieson, CEO
John Kim Bell, Founder

National Aboriginal Circle Against Family Violence
Kahnawake Business Complex, PO Box 2169, Kahnawake QC J0L 1B0
Tel: 450-638-2968; *Fax:* 450-638-9415
URL: www.nacafv.ca
Brenda Combs, Chair

National Association of Friendship Centres (NAFC) / Association nationale des centres d'amitié
275 MacLaren St., Ottawa ON K2P 0L9
Tel: 613-563-4844; *Fax:* 613-594-3428
e-mail: nafcgen@nafc.ca
URL: www.nafc-aboriginal.com
Peter Dinsdale, Executive Director

Native Addictions Council of Manitoba (NACM)
160 Salter St., Winnipeg MB R2W 4K1
Tel: 204-586-8395; *Fax:* 204-589-3921
e-mail: nacm@escape.ca
URL: www.mts.net/~nacm/
Elizabeth Fontaine, Supervisor/Rehab
Bertha Fontaine, Executive Director

Native Council of Nova Scotia (NCNS)
129 Truro Heights Rd., Truro NS B6L 1X2
Tel: 902-895-1523; *Fax:* 902-895-0024
Toll-Free: 800-565-4372
e-mail: info@ncns.ca
URL: www.ncns.ca
Grace Conrad, Chief & President
Theresa Hare, Finance

Native Council of Prince Edward Island
6 F.J. McAuley Ct., Charlottetown PE C1A 9M7
Tel: 902-892-5314; *Fax:* 902-368-7464
e-mail: admin@ncpei.com
URL: www.ncpei.com/
Nora Richard, Vice-President
Jamie Gallant, President

Native Counselling Services of Alberta (NCSA)
10975 - 124 St., Edmonton AB T5M 0H9
Tel: 780-451-4002; *Fax:* 780-428-0187
URL: www.ncsa.ca
Allen Benson, CEO

Native Friendship Centre of Montréal Inc. (NFCM) / Centre d'amitié autochtone de Montréal Inc.
2001, boul St-Laurent, Montréal QC H2X 2T3
Tel: 514-499-1854; *Fax:* 514-499-9436
e-mail: info@nfcm.org
URL: www.nfcm.org
Leandro Tolentino, Interim Executive Director

Native Investment & Trade Association (NITA)
6520 Salish Dr., Vancouver BC V6N 2C7
Tel: 604-275-6670; *Fax:* 604-275-0307
Toll-Free: 800-337-7743
e-mail: nita@express.ca
URL: www.native-invest-trade.com
Calvin Helin, President

Native Women's Association of Canada (NWAC) / L'Association des femmes autochtones du Canada (AFAC)
Six Nations of the Grand River, PO Box 331, 1721 Chiefswood Rd., Ohsweken ON N0A 1M0
Tel: 519-445-0990; *Fax:* 519-445-0924
URL: www.nwac-hq.org
Karen Green, CEO

New Brunswick Aboriginal Peoples Council (NBAPC)
320 St. Mary's St., Fredericton NB E3A 2S4
Tel: 506-458-8422; *Fax:* 506-451-6130
URL: www.nbapc.org
Bruce Harquail, Interim Chief & President

New Brunswick Aboriginal Women's Council
120 Paul St., Fredericton NB E3A 2V8
Tel: 506-458-1114; *Fax:* 506-451-9386
e-mail: nbawci@nb.aibn.com

Newfoundland Native Women's Association
General Delivery, Benoits Cove NL A0L 1A0
Tel: 709-789-3430; *Fax:* 709-789-2207
e-mail: nf.nativewomen@nf.aibn.com

Northwest Territories Council of Friendship Centres
c/o Soaring Eagle Friendship Centre, #2, 8 Gagnier St., Hay River NT X0E 1G1
Tel: 867-874-2792; *Fax:* 867-874-2894

Nova Scotia Native Women's Society
PO Box 805, Truro NS B2N 5E8
Tel: 902-893-7402; *Fax:* 902-897-7162
e-mail: gracefrancis@eastlink.ca

Ontario Coalition of Aboriginal Peoples (OCAP)
PO Box 189, Wabigoon ON P0V 2W0
Tel: 807-938-1321
URL: www.o-cap.ca
Affiliation(s): 23 organizations
Elmer St. Pierre, Vice Chief
Brad Maggrah, President
Ronald Swain, Chair

Ontario Federation of Indian Friendship Centres (OFIFC)
219 Front St. East, Toronto ON M5A 1E8
Tel: 416-956-7575; *Fax:* 416-956-7577
Toll-Free: 800-772-9291
e-mail: ofifc@ofifc.org; oahai@ofifc.org (health advocacy initiative)
URL: www.ofifc.org
Sylvia Maracle, Executive Director
Celeste Hayward, Director, Programme
Juliette Nicolet, Director, Policy
Meri Saunders, Director, Finance

Ontario Native Women's Association (ONWA)
212 Miles St. East, Thunder Bay ON P7C 1J6
Tel: 807-623-3442; *Fax:* 807-623-1104
Toll-Free: 800-667-0816
URL: www.nwac-hq.org
Marianne Borg, Executive Director

Quaker Aboriginal Affairs Committee (QAAC)
60 Lowther Ave., Toronto ON M5R 1C7
Tel: 416-920-5213; *Fax:* 416-920-5214
e-mail: qaac@quaker.ca
URL: cfsc.quaker.ca/pages/contact_abor.html
Affiliation(s): Aboriginal Rights Coalition
Jennifer Preston Howe, Program Coordinator

Regroupement des centres d'amitié autochtone du Québec (RCAAQ)
#250, 225, rue Max-Gros-Louis, Wendake QC G0A 4V0
Tél: 418-842-6354; *Téléc:* 418-842-9795
Ligne sans frais: 877-842-6354
Courriel: infos@rcaaq.info
URL: www.rcaaq.info
Josée Goulet, Directrice générale

Saskatchewan Aboriginal Women's Circle Corporation
PO Box 1174, #17, 5th Ave. North, Yorkton SK S3N 2X3
Tel: 306-783-1228; *Fax:* 306-783-1080
e-mail: sawcc.admin@sasktel.net

Society of Yukon Artists of Native Ancestry (SYANA)
#205, 302 Steele St., Whitehorse YT Y1A 2C5
Tel: 867-668-2695
Linda Polyck, Contact

2-Spirited People of the First Nations (TPFN)
#202, 593 Yonge St., Toronto ON M4Y 1Z4
Tel: 416-944-9300; *Fax:* 416-944-8381
e-mail: info@2spirits.com
URL: www.2spirits.com
Art Zoccole, Executive Director

Union of British Columbia Indian Chiefs
#500, 342 Water St., Vancouver BC V6B 1B6
Tel: 604-684-0231; *Fax:* 604-684-5726
e-mail: ubcic@ubcic.bc.ca
URL: www.ubcic.bc.ca
Stewart Phillip, President

Union of Nova Scotia Indians (UNSI)
PO Box 961, 47 Maillard St., Membertou NS B1S 2P5
Tel: 902-539-4107; *Fax:* 902-564-2137
e-mail: rec@unsi.ns.ca
URL: www.unsi.ns.ca
Joe B. Marshall, Executive Director

Union of Ontario Indians (UOI)
Nipissing First Nation, PO Box 711, North Bay ON P1B 8J8
Tel: 705-497-9127; *Fax:* 705-497-9135
Toll-Free: 877-702-5200
e-mail: recnip@anishinabek.ca
URL: www.anishinabek.ca
John Beaucage, Grand Council Chief

United Native Nations Society
#341, 1979 Marine Dr., Nnorth Vancouver BC V7G 3G2
Tel: 604-688-1821; *Fax:* 604-980-0324
Toll-Free: 800-555-9756
e-mail: unn@unns.bc.ca
URL: www.unns.bc.ca
George Holem, President
Lillian George, Vice-President

Woodland Cultural Centre (WCC)
PO Box 1506, 184 Mohawk St., Brantford ON N3T 5V6
Tel: 519-759-2650; *Fax:* 519-759-8912
e-mail: woodlandcentre@execulink.com
URL: www.woodland-centre.on.ca
Amos Key Jr., Executive Director

Yukon Aboriginal Women's Council
#102, 307 Jarvis St., Whitehorse YT Y1A 2H3
Tel: 867-667-6162; *Fax:* 867-668-7539
Toll-Free: 866-667-6162
e-mail: yawc@northwestel.net
Louise Bouvier, President

Naturalists

Avicultural Advancement Council of Canada (AACC)
PO Box 123, Chemainus BC V0R 1K0
Tel: 250-246-4803; *Fax:* 250-246-4912
e-mail: exec@aacc.ca
URL: www.aacc.ca
Affiliation(s): American Singer Canary Club of Canada; Assoc. des amateurs d'oiseaux de la Mauricie; Assoc. des éleveurs d'oiseaux de Montréal; BC Avicultural Society; BC Exotic Bird Society; Budgerigar & Foreign Bird Society; Cage Bird Society of Hamilton; Calgary Canary Club; Canadian Dove Assoc.; Canadian Gloster Club; Cowichan Valley & Upper Island Cage Bird Club; Durham Avicultural Society; Edmonton Avicultural Association; Essex-Kent Cage Bird Society; Feather Fanciers Club; Golden Triangle Parrot Club; Kamloops Aviculturalist Society; London & District Cage Bird Society; Manitoba Canary & Finch Club
Dunstan H. Browne, President

Mark S. Curtis, Executive Director
Chris Holoboff, Vice-President

British Columbia Nature (Federation of BC Naturalists) (FBCN)
c/o Parks Heritage Centre, 1620 Mount Seymour Rd., North Vancouver BC V7G 2R9
Tel: 604-985-3057
e-mail: manager@bcnature.ca
URL: www.bcnature.ca
Bev Ramey, President
Elisa Kreller, Treasurer
Maria Hamann, Office Manager

British Columbia Waterfowl Society
5191 Robertson Rd., RR#1, Delta BC V4K 3N2
Tel: 604-946-6980; *Fax:* 604-946-6980
URL: www.reifelbirdsanctuary.com
Kathleen Fry, Acting Manager
Jack Bates, President

Federation of Alberta Naturalists (FAN)
11759 Groat Rd., Edmonton AB T5M 3K6
Tel: 780-427-8124; *Fax:* 780-422-2663
e-mail: info@fanweb.ca
URL: www.fanweb.ca

Jack Miner Migratory Bird Foundation, Inc.
PO Box 39, Kingsville ON N9Y 2E8
Tel: 519-733-4034
Toll-Free: 877-289-8328
e-mail: info@jackminer.com
URL: www.jackminer.com
Kirk W. Miner, Executive Director

Manitoba Naturalists Society (MNS)
#401, 63 Albert St., Winnipeg MB R3B 1G4
Tel: 204-943-9029
e-mail: mns1@mts.net
URL: www.manitobanature.ca
Les McCann, President
Frank Machovec, Exec. Vice-President
Helen Leeds, Secretary
Sean Worden, Treasurer

Natural History Society of Newfoundland & Labrador
c/o The Osprey, PO Box 1013, Stn. C, St. John's NL A1C 5M3
Tel: 709-754-0455
e-mail: nhs@nhs.nf.ca
URL: www.nhs.nf.ca
Allan Stein, Acting Vice-President
Don Steele, Secretary

Nature Canada / Canada Nature
#900, 85 Albert St., Ottawa ON K1P 6A4
Tel: 613-562-3447; *Fax:* 613-562-3371
Toll-Free: 800-267-4088
e-mail: info@naturecanada.ca
URL: www.naturecanada.ca
Affiliation(s): International Union for the Conservation of Nature; Committee on the Status of Endangered Wildlife in Canada; BirdLife International
Ruth Catana, Acting President
Richard Yank, Chair

Nature NB
#110, 924 Prospect St., Fredericton NB E3B 2T9
Tel: 506-459-4209; *Fax:* 506-459-4209
e-mail: nbfn@nb.aibn.com
URL: www.naturenb.ca
Vanessa Roy-McDougall, Executive Director

Nature Nova Scotia (Federation of Nova Scotia Naturalists)
c/o Nova Scotia Museum of Natural History, 1747 Summer St., Halifax NS B3H 3A6
e-mail: naturens@chebucto.ns.ca
URL: www.naturens.ca; www.chebucto.ns.ca/Environment/FNSN/
Affiliation(s): Nature Canada (formerly the Canadian Nature Federation)
Larry Bogan, President
Sue Abbot, Vice-President
Doug Linzey, Secretary
Jean Gibson, Treasurer

Nature Québec
#207, 870, av de Salaberry, Québec QC G1R 2T9
Tél: 418-648-2104; *Téléc:* 418-648-0991
Courriel: conservons@naturequebec.org
URL: www.naturequebec.org
Christian Simard, Directeur général

Nature Saskatchewan
#206, 1860 Lorne St., Regina SK S4P 2L7
Tel: 306-780-9273; *Fax:* 306-780-9263
Toll-Free: 800-667-4668
e-mail: info@naturesask.ca
URL: www.naturesask.ca
Gary Seib, General Manager
Karen McIver, Manager, Conservation & Education
Margaret Skeel, Manager, Natural Heritage & Contact, Living by Water & Last Mountain Bird Observatory Education Progra
Carolyn Gaudet, Coordinator, Habitat Stewardship
Andrea Kotylak, Coordinator, Habitat Stewardship (Operation Burrowing Owl)
Deanna Trowsdale-Mutafov, Coordinator, Saskatchewan PlantWatch
Sarah Vinge, Coordinator, Habitat Stewardship (Rare Plant Rescue)

Ontario Nature
#201, 366 Adelaide St. West, Toronto ON M5V 1R9
Tel: 416-444-8419; *Fax:* 416-444-9866
Toll-Free: 800-440-2366
e-mail: info@ontarionature.org
URL: www.ontarionature.org
Affiliation(s): Coalition on the Niagara Escarpment; Conservation Council of Ontario; Great Lakes United; International Union for Conservation of Nature & Natural Resources; International Committee for Bird Preservation
Peter Gilchrist, President
Caroline Schultz, Executive Director

Society of Canadian Ornithologists (SCO) / Société des ornithologistes du Canada (SOC)
a/s Thérèse Beaudet, SCO Membership Secretary, 1281, ch des Lièges, St-Jean de l'Ile d'Orléans QC G0A 3W0
e-mail: beaudet.lamothe@sympatico.ca
URL: www.sco-soc.ca
Erica Nol, President
Joe Nocera, Vice-President
Thérèse Beaudet, M.Sc., M.A.P, Membership Secretary
Pierre Lamothe, Treasurer

Nursing

Academy of Canadian Executive Nurses (ACEN)
c/o Association Strategy Group, #1, 136 Lewis St., Ottawa ON K2P 0S7
Tel: 613-235-3033; *Fax:* 613-233-6158
e-mail: info@acen.ca
URL: www.acen.ca
Noreen Linton, President
Marcia James, Admininistrative Coordinator

Association of Registered Nurses of Newfoundland & Labrador (ARNNL)
55 Military Rd., St. John's NL A1C 2C5
Tel: 709-753-6040; *Fax:* 709-753-4940
Toll-Free: 800-563-3200
e-mail: info@arnnl.nf.ca
URL: www.arnnl.nf.ca
Patricia Pilgrim, President
Jeanette Andrews, Executive Director

Association of Registered Nurses of Prince Edward Island (ARNPEI)
53 Grafton St., Charlottetown PE C1A 1K8
Tel: 902-368-3764; *Fax:* 902-628-1430
e-mail: info@arnpei.ca
URL: www.arnpei.ca
Paul Boudreau, Coordinator, Regulatory Services
Becky Gosbee, Executive Director

British Columbia Nurses' Union (BCNU) / Syndicat des infirmières de la Colombie-Britannique
4060 Regent St., Burnaby BC V5C 6P5
Tel: 604-433-2268; *Fax:* 604-433-7945
Toll-Free: 800-663-9991
e-mail: contactbcnu@bcnu.org
URL: www.bcnu.org
Melanie Leckovic, Vice-President
Debra McPherson, President

Canadian Association for Nursing Research (CANR) / Association canadienne pour la recherche infirmière
c/o P. Petrucka, College of Nursing, University of Saskatchewan, 107 Wiggins Rd., Saskatoon SK S7N 5E5
Tel: 306-337-2228; *Fax:* 306-966-6221
e-mail: pammla.petrucka@usask.ca
URL: www.canr.ca
Pamela Hawranik, RN,PhD
Pammla Petrucka, Secretary
Riek van den Berg, Treasurer

Canadian Association for the History of Nursing (CAHN) / Association canadienne pour l'histoire du nursing
723 Colborne St., New Westminster BC V3L 5V6
URL: www.cahn-achn.ca
Affiliation(s): Canadian Nurses Association
Geertje Boschma, President
Sandra Bassendowski, Secretary
Carol Helmstadter, Treasurer

Canadian Association of Burn Nurses (CABN) / Association canadienne des infirmières et infirmiers en soins aux brûlés
c/o Shannon Bonn, IWK Health Centre, PO Box 9700, 5850-5980 University Ave., Halifax NS B3K 6R8
e-mail: shannon.bonn@iwk.nshealth.ca
URL: www.cabn.ca
Affiliation(s): Canadian Nurses Association
Shannon Bonn, President
Amelia Potter, Vice-President
Judy Sleith, Treasurer

Canadian Association of Critical Care Nurses (CACCN) / Association canadienne des infirmières et infirmiers en soins de phase aiguë
PO Box 25322, London ON N6A 1X6
Tel: 519-649-5284; *Fax:* 519-649-1458
Toll-Free: 866-477-9077
e-mail: caccn@caccn.ca
URL: www.caccn.ca
Cecilia St. George-Hyslop, President
Kate Mahon, Vice-President, Publications & Research
Pamela Cybulski, Secretary & Contact, Membership
Joanne Baird, Treasurer
Tricia Bray, Director, Awards & Corporate Sponsorship
Christine R. Halfkenny-Zellas, CIM, National Administrator

Canadian Association of Nephrology Nurses & Technologists (CANNT) / Association canadienne des infirmières et infirmiers et technologues de néphrologie (ACITN)
#322, 336 Yonge St., Barrie ON L4N 4C8
Tel: 705-720-2819; *Fax:* 705-720-1451
Toll-Free: 877-720-2819
e-mail: cannt@cannt.ca
URL: www.cannt.ca
Affiliation(s): Kidney Foundation of Canada; Canadian Nurses Association
Alison Thomas, President
Susan Placko, Treasurer & Coordinator, Website

Canadian Association of Neuroscience Nurses (CANN) / Association canadienne des infirmiers et infirmières en sciences neurologiques (ACIISN)
6357 Lumberman Way, Ottawa ON K1C 1V6
e-mail: canninfo@cann.ca; cjnn@cann.ca (Journal)
URL: www.cann.ca
Affiliation(s): Canadian Nurses Association; Canadian Congress of Neurological Sciences; Canadian Brain & Nerve Health Coalition (CBANHC); Canadian Council on Donation and Transplantation (CCDT); National Stroke Leadership Group; Canadian Association of Brain Tumor Coalition (CABTO); Think First
Karen Waterhouse, President
Sandra Berube, President
Mark Bonin, Treasurer
Jeanne Evans, Chair, Membership

Canadian Association of Nurses in AIDS Care (CANAC) / Association canadienne des infirmières et infirmiers en sidologie
PO Box 93, Pontypool ON L0A 1K0
e-mail: info@canac.org
URL: www.canac.org
Affiliation(s): Canadian Nurses Association
Jennifer Shaw, Executive Assistant

Canadian Association of Nurses in Oncology (CANO) / Association canadienne des infirmières en oncologie (ACIO)
#201, 375 West 5th Ave., Vancouver BC V5Y 1J6
Tel: 604-874-4322; *Fax:* 604-874-4378
e-mail: cano@malachite-mgmt.com
URL: www.cano-acio.ca
Affiliation(s): Canadian Nurses Association; International Society of Cancer Nurses; Canadian Oncology Societies
Kim Chapman, President
Jeanne Robertson, Treasurer

Canadian Association of Pediatric Nurses (CAPN) / Association canadienne des infirmières et infirmiers en pédiatrie (ACIIP)
c/o The Hospital for Sick Children, Room 7763, 555 University Ave., Toronto ON M5G 1X8
Tel: 416-813-6998; *Fax:* 416-813-8082
e-mail: karen.breen-reid@sickkids.ca
Barbara Bearivage, Sec.-Treas.
Karen Breen-Reid, Interim President

Canadian Council of Cardiovascular Nurses (CCCN) / Conseil canadien des infirmières et infirmiers en nursing cardiovasculaire (CCINC)
#1402, 222 Queen St., Ottawa ON K1P 5V9
Tel: 613-569-4361; *Fax:* 613-569-3278
e-mail: info@cccn.ca
URL: www.cccn.ca
Affiliation(s): Heart & Stroke Foundation of Canada; Canadian Coalition for High Blood Pressure Prevention & Control; Canadian Cardiovascular Society
Wes Clark, Executive Director
June MacDonald, President
Faye Lazar, Sec.-Treas.

Canadian Council of Practical Nurse Regulators (CCPNR)
c/o College Of LPN's of Alberta (CLPNA), #13163, 143 St., Edmonton AB T5L 4S8
Tel: 780-484-8886; *Fax:* 780-484-9069
e-mail: chair@ccpnr.ca
URL: www.ccpnr.ca
Linda Stranger, RN, MSA, Chair

Canadian Federation of Mental Health Nurses (CFMHN) / Fédération canadienne des infirmières et infirmiers en santé mentale
#109, 1 Concorde Gate, Toronto ON M3C 3N6
Tel: 416-426-7029; *Fax:* 416-426-7280
e-mail: info@cfmhn.ca
URL: www.cfmhn.ca
Affiliation(s): Canadian Nurses Association
Chris Davis, President

Canadian Gerontological Nursing Association (CGNA) / Association canadienne des infirmières et infirmiers en gérontologie
c/o Membership, #370, 101-1001 West Broadway, Vancouver BC V6H 4E4
e-mail: cgna@cgna.net
URL: www.cgna.net
Affiliation(s): Canadian Nurses Association
Beverly Laurila, RN, BN, MSA, GN, President

Canadian Holistic Nurses Association (CHNA) / Association canadienne des infirmières en soins holistiques
c/o Marie Knapp, RR#7, Owen Sound ON N4K 6V5
Tel: 519-371-1255
e-mail: info@chna.ca
URL: www.chna.ca
Affiliation(s): Canadian Nurses Association
Marie Knapp, President
Michele Bourgeois, Secretary

Canadian Nurses Association (CNA) / Association des infirmières et infirmiers du Canada
50 Driveway, Ottawa ON K2P 1E2
Tel: 613-237-2133; *Fax:* 613-237-3520
Toll-Free: 800-361-8404
e-mail: info@cna-aiic.ca; executiveoffice@cna-aiic.ca; media@cna-aiic.ca
URL: www.cna-aiic.ca
Rachel Bard, CEO
Kaaren Neufeld, RN, MN, President

Canadian Nurses Foundation (CNF) / Fondation des infirmières et infirmiers du Canada
50 Driveway, Ottawa ON K2P 1E2
Tel: 613-237-2133; *Fax:* 613-237-3520
Toll-Free: 800-361-8404
e-mail: info@cnf-fiic.ca
URL: www.cnf-fiic.ca
Hélène Sabourin, Executive Director
Jonelle Istead, Director, Fundraising

Canadian Nurses Protective Society (CNPS) / Société de protection des infirmières et infirmiers du Canada (SPIIC)
50 Driveway, Ottawa ON K2P 1E2
Tel: 613-237-2092; *Fax:* 613-237-6300
Toll-Free: 800-267-3390
e-mail: info@cnps.ca
URL: www.cnps.ca
Affiliation(s): College & Association of Registered Nurses of Alberta; Saskatchewan Registered Nurses' Association; College of Registered Nurses of Manitoba; Registered Nurses' Association of Ontario; Nurses Association of New Brunswick; College of Registered Nurses of Nova Scotia; Association of Registered Nurses of Prince Edward Island; Association of Registered Nurses of Newfoundland & Labrador; Registered Nurses Association of the Northwest Territories & Nunavut; Yukon Registered Nurses Association

Canadian Occupational Health Nurses Association (COHNA) / Association canadienne des infirmières et infirmiers en santé du travail (ACIIST)
c/o Health Canada, #412, 101 - 22nd St. E, Saskatoon SK S7K 0E1
e-mail: valerie_adrian@hc-sc.gc.ca
URL: www.cohna-aciist.ca
Affiliation(s): Canadian Nurses Association
Valerie Adrian, President
Marg Creen, Secretary/Treasurer
Ellen Coe, Vice President

Canadian Orthopaedic Nurses Association (CONA) / Association canadienne des infirmières et infirmiers en orthopédie
2890 Gosnell Rd., Kelowna BC V1Y 3K2
e-mail: judy.macaulay@ubc.ca
URL: www.cona-nurse.org
Affiliation(s): Canadian Nurses Association
Marian Chalifoux, President

Canadian Vascular Access Association (CVAA) / Association canadienne d'Accès Vasculaire
PO Box 66572, 685 McCowan Rd., Toronto ON M1J 3N8
Tel: 416-696-7761; *Fax:* 416-696-8437
URL: www.cvaa.info
Michele Bellows, Vice-President & Secretary
Diane Sharp, RN, CVAA(c), President

The College & Association of Registered Nurses of Alberta (CARNA)
11620 - 168 St., Edmonton AB T5M 4A6
Tel: 780-451-0043; *Fax:* 780-452-3276
Toll-Free: 800-252-9392
e-mail: carna@nurses.ab.ca
URL: www.nurses.ab.ca
Joan Petruk, President

College of Licensed Practical Nurses of Alberta (CLPNA)
13163 - 146 St., Edmonton AB T5L 4S8
Tel: 780-484-8886; *Fax:* 780-484-9069
Toll-Free: 800-661-5877
e-mail: info@clpna.com
URL: www.clpna.com
Linda L. Stanger, Executive Director/Registrar

College of Licensed Practical Nurses of BC (CLPNBC)
#260, 3480 Gilmore Way, Burnaby BC V5G 4Y1
Tel: 604-660-5750; *Fax:* 604-660-2899
Toll-Free: 888-440-6900
e-mail: info@clpnbc.org
URL: www.clpnbc.org
Gordon MacDonald, Executive Director-Registrar

College of Licensed Practical Nurses of Manitoba (CLPNM)
463 St. Anne's Rd., Winnipeg MB R2M 3C9
Tel: 204-663-1212; *Fax:* 204-663-1207
Toll-Free: 877-663-1212
e-mail: info@clpnm.ca
URL: www.clpnm.ca
Verna Holgate, Executive Director

College of Licensed Practical Nurses of Nova Scotia (CLPNNS)
Cogswell Tower, #1212, 2000 Barrington St., Halifax NS B3J 3K1
Tel: 902-423-8517; *Fax:* 902-425-6811
e-mail: info@clpnns.ca
URL: www.clpnns.ca
Ann Mann, Executive Director/Registrar

College of Nurses of Ontario (CNO) / Ordre des infirmières et infirmiers de l'Ontario
101 Davenport Rd., Toronto ON M5R 3P1
Tel: 416-928-0900; *Fax:* 416-928-6507
Toll-Free: 800-387-5526
e-mail: cno@cnomail.org
URL: www.cno.org
Anne Coghlan, Executive Director

College of Registered Nurses of British Columbia (CRNBC)
2855 Arbutus St., Vancouver BC V6J 3Y8
Tel: 604-736-7331; *Fax:* 604-738-2272
Toll-Free: 800-565-6505
e-mail: info@crnbc.bc.ca
URL: www.crnbc.bc.ca
L. Gray, Director, Practice Support
Val Cartmel, President
Laurel Brunke, Executive Director

College of Registered Nurses of Manitoba (CRNM)
890 Pembina Hwy., Winnipeg MB R3M 2M8
Tel: 204-774-3477; *Fax:* 204-775-6052
Toll-Free: 800-665-2027
e-mail: info@crnm.mb.ca
URL: www.crnm.mb.ca
Kathy Doerksen, RN, President
Susan D. Neilson, Executive Director
Glenn Hildebrand, Director, Communications, Member & Government Relations

College of Registered Nurses of Nova Scotia (CRNNS)
#4005, 7071 Bayers Rd., Halifax NS B3L 2C2
Tel: 902-491-9744; *Fax:* 902-491-9510
Toll-Free: 800-565-9744
e-mail: info@crnns.ca
URL: www.crnns.ca
Linda Hamilton, Executive Director

College of Registered Psychiatric Nurses of Alberta
#201, 9711 - 45 Ave., Edmonton AB T6E 5V8
Tel: 780-434-7666; *Fax:* 780-436-4165
Toll-Free: 877-234-7666
e-mail: crpna@crpna.ab.ca
URL: www.crpna.ab.ca
Pamela Gulay, President

College of Registered Psychiatric Nurses of British Columbia
#307, 2502 St. Johns St., Port Moody BC V3H 2B4
Tel: 604-931-5200; *Fax:* 604-931-5277
Toll-Free: 800-565-2505
e-mail: donna_higenbottam@crpnbc.ca
URL: www.crpnbc.ca
Dorothy Jennings, Chair
Donna Higenbottom, Executive Director & Registrar

College of Registered Psychiatric Nurses of Manitoba (CRPNM)
1854 Portage Ave., Winnipeg MB R3J 0G9
Tel: 204-888-4841; *Fax:* 204-888-8638
e-mail: crpnm@crpnm.mb.ca
URL: www.crpnm.mb.ca
Annette D. Osted, Executive Director

Community Health Nurses of Canada (CHNC) / Infirmières et infirmiers en santé communautaire au Canada
182 Clendenan Ave., Toronto ON M6P 2X2
Tel: 647-239-9554; *Fax:* 416-426-7280
e-mail: info@chnc.ca
URL: www.chnc.ca
Affiliation(s): Registered Nurses Association Community Health Nurses Initiatives Group
Kate Thompson, BScN, MSc, CCHN, President
Evelyn Butler, RN, BN, MPA, Administrative Manager
Ruth Schofield, RN, MSc(T), Secretary
Anne Clarotto, RN, BN, MHS, Treasurer
Yvette Laforet-Fliesser, RN, BScN, MScN,, Officer, Communications

Council for Licensed Practical Nurses Newfoundland & Labrador
9 Paton St., St. John's NL A1B 4S8
Tel: 709-579-3843; *Fax:* 709-579-8268
Toll-Free: 888-579-2576
e-mail: info@clpnnl.ca
URL: www.clpnnl.ca
Paul D. Fisher, LPN, Executive Director/Register

Fédération des infirmières et infirmiers du Québec
#300, 1260, boul Lebourgneuf, Québec QC G2K 2G2
Tél: 418-626-2226; *Téléc:* 418-626-2111
Ligne sans frais: 800-463-6770

Fédération des infirmières et infirmiers du Québec
#106, 170, av Principale, Rouyn-Noranda QC J9X 4P7
Tél: 819-797-1748; *Téléc:* 819-797-1937
Ligne sans frais: 800-567-6564

Fédération des infirmières et infirmiers du Québec
#206, 2630, rue King ouest, Sherbrooke QC J1J 2H1
Tél: 819-346-4914; *Téléc:* 819-563-9825
Ligne sans frais: 800-567-2776

Fédération des infirmières et infirmiers du Québec
#219, 84, rue St-Germain est, Rimouski QC G5L 7K1
Tél: 418-723-2251; *Téléc:* 418-723-7928
Ligne sans frais: 800-463-0628

Fédération des infirmières et infirmiers du Québec
#2, 3803, boul Royal, Shawinigan QC G9N 8L6
Tél: 819-539-6463; *Téléc:* 819-539-5111
Ligne sans frais: 800-567-8607

Fédération des infirmières et infirmiers du Québec
#230, 370, boul Gréber, Gatineau QC J8T 5R6
Tél: 819-568-4243; *Téléc:* 819-568-0493
Ligne sans frais: 800-567-9651

Fédération des infirmières et infirmiers du Québec
451, rue Racine est, Chicoutimi QC G7H 1T5
Tél: 418-690-2252; *Téléc:* 418-690-3216
Ligne sans frais: 800-567-8105

Fédération interprofessionnelle de la santé du Québec (FIQ)
1234, av Papineau, Montréal QC H2K 0A4
Tél: 514-987-1141; *Téléc:* 514-987-7273
Ligne sans frais: 800-363-6541
Courriel: info@fiqsante.qc.ca
URL: www.fiqsante.qc.ca
Brigitte Fauteux, Secrétaire
Lina Bonamie, Présidente

Gerontological Nursing Association of Ontario (GNA)
PO Box 368, Stn. K, Toronto ON M4P 2G7
e-mail: info@gnaontario.org
URL: www.gnaontario.org
Affiliation(s): Registered Nurses Association of Ontario; Canadian Gerontological Nursing Association
Mary Bawden, President
Patricia Bassa, Treasurer

Licensed Practical Nurses Association & Regulatory Board of PEI
PO Box 20058, 161 St. Peter's Rd., Charlottetown PE C1A 9E1
Tel: 902-566-1512; *Fax:* 902-892-6315
e-mail: info@lpna.ca
URL: www.lpna.ca
Genevieve Poole, Registrar

Manitoba Nurses' Union (MNU) / Syndicat des infirmières du Manitoba
#301, 275 Broadway, Winnipeg MB R3C 4M6
Tel: 204-942-1320; *Fax:* 204-942-0958
Toll-Free: 800-665-0043
URL: www.nursesunion.mb.ca
Maureen Hancharyk, President
Sandi Mowat, Vice-President
Fernand Beasse, Sec.-Treas.
Marilyn Kenny, Director, Operations
Irene Giesbrecht, Director, Negotiations

National Emergency Nurses Affiliation (NENA) / Affiliation des infirmières et infirmiers d'urgence
112 Old River Rd., RR#2, Mallorytown ON K0E 1R0
URL: www.nena.ca
Affiliation(s): Canadian Nurses Association
Landon James, President

New Brunswick Nurses Union (NBNU) / Syndicat des infirmières et infirmiers du Nouveau-Brunswick (SIINB)
103 Woodside Lane, Fredericton NB E3C 2R9
Tel: 506-453-0820; *Fax:* 506-453-0828
Toll-Free: 800-442-4914
URL: www.nbnu-siinb.nb.ca
David Brown, Executive Director
Marilyn Quinn, President

Newfoundland & Labrador Nurses' Union (NLNU) / Syndicat des infirmières de Terre-Neuve et du Labrador
PO Box 416, Stn. C, 229 Major's Path, St. John's NL A1C 5J9
Tel: 709-753-9961; *Fax:* 709-753-1210
Toll-Free: 800-563-5100
e-mail: nlnu@nlnu.nf.net
URL: www.nlnu.nf.ca
John Vivian, Executive Director
Colleen O'Leary, Communications Specialist

Nova Scotia Nurses' Union (NSNU)
30 Frazee Ave., Dartmouth NS B3B 1X4
Tel: 902-469-1474; *Fax:* 902-466-6935
Toll-Free: 800-469-1474
URL: www.nsnu.ns.ca
Affiliation(s): Canadian Nurses Association; Canadian Labour Congress; Canadian Federation of Nurses Unions
Jean Candy, Executive Director
Janet Hazelton, President

Nurses Association of New Brunswick (NANB) / Association des infirmières et infirmiers du Nouveau-Brunswick (AIINB)
165 Regent St., Fredericton NB E3B 7B4
Tel: 506-458-8731; *Fax:* 506-459-2838
Toll-Free: 800-442-4417
e-mail: aiinb@aiinb.nb.ca; nanb@nanb.nb.ca
URL: www.aiinb.nb.ca; www.nanb.nb.ca
Monique Cormier-Daigle, President

Ontario Nurses' Association (ONA) / Association des infirmières et infirmiers de l'Ontario
#400, 85 Grenville St., Toronto ON M5S 3A2
Tel: 416-964-8833; *Fax:* 416-964-8864
Toll-Free: 800-387-5580
e-mail: onamail@ona.org
URL: www.ona.org
Lesley M. Bell, RN, CEO
Linda Haslam-Stroud, President

Operating Room Nurses Association of Canada (ORNAC) / Association des infirmières et infirmiers de salles d'opération du Canada
Tel: 604-466-7965
e-mail: info@ornac.ca
URL: www.ornac.ca
Bonnie McLeod, President
Alaine Young, Treasurer

Ordre des infirmières et infirmiers auxiliaires du Québec (OIIAQ)
531, rue Sherbrooke est, Montréal QC H2L 1K2
Tél: 514-282-9511; *Téléc:* 514-282-0631
Ligne sans frais: 800-283-9511
Courriel: service.communications@oiiaq.org
URL: www.oiiaq.org
Jacques Gaulin, Président du comité

Ordre des infirmières et infirmiers du Québec (OIIQ)
4200, boul Dorchester ouest, Westmount QC H3Z 1V4
Tél: 514-935-2501; *Téléc:* 514-935-1799
Ligne sans frais: 800-363-6048
Courriel: inf@oiiq.org
URL: www.oiiq.org
Gyslaine Desrosiers, Présidente
Carole Mercier, Secrétaire générale
Johanne Messier, Directrice, Services administratifs

Practical Nurses Canada
#255, 55 St. Clair Ave. West, Toronto ON M1E 4X9
Tel: 416-922-5968; *Fax:* 416-967-6320
Toll-Free: 866-454-5968
e-mail: info@pncanada.ca
URL: www.pncanada.ca
Linda Gould, President
Barbara Boudreau, Vice-President
Sue O'Hare, Treasurer

Practical Nurses Federation of Ontario (PFNO)
Building 4, #200, 5025 Orbitor Dr., Mississauga ON L4W 4Y5
Tel: 905-602-6705; *Fax:* 905-602-4666

Prince Edward Island Nurses' Union (PEINU) / Syndicat des infirmières de l'Île-du-Prince-Édouard
326 Patterson Dr., Charlottetown PE C1A 8K4
Tel: 902-892-7152; *Fax:* 902-368-2974
Toll-Free: 866-368-2974
e-mail: office@peinu.com
URL: www.peinu.com
Affiliation(s): Canadian Federation of Nurses Unions; Canadian Labour Congress
Barbara Brookins, President

Registered Nurses Association of Ontario (RNAO) / L'Association des infirmières et infirmiers autorisés de l'Ontario
158 Pearl St., Toronto ON M5H 1L3
Tel: 416-599-1925; *Fax:* 416-599-1926
Toll-Free: 800-268-7199
e-mail: info@rnao.org
URL: www.rnao.org
Social Media: www.facebook.com/group.php?gid=30442334943
Wendy Fucile, President
Doris Grinspun, Executive Director

The Registered Nurses Association of the Northwest Territories & Nunavut (RNANT/NU)
PO Box 2757, Yellowknife NT X1A 2R1
Tel: 867-873-2745; *Fax:* 867-873-2336
e-mail: admin@rnantnu.ca
URL: www.rnantnu.ca
Barb Round, Executive Director/Registrar/PR Cou

Registered Practical Nurses Association of Ontario (RPNAO)
Bldg. 4, #200, 5025 Orbitor Dr., Mississauga ON L4W 4Y5
Tel: 905-602-4664; *Fax:* 905-602-4666
e-mail: info@rpnao.org
URL: www.rpnao.org
Dianne Martin, CAE, Executive Director
Monica Seawright, President
Ann Marie Hann, Secretary

Registered Psychiatric Nurses Association of Saskatchewan (RPNAS)
2055 Lorne St., Regina SK S4P 2M4
Tel: 306-586-4617; *Fax:* 306-586-6000
e-mail: rpnas@rpnas.com
URL: www.rpnas.com
Mary K. Renwick, President
Robert Allen, Executive Director

Saskatchewan Association of Licensed Practical Nurses (SALPN)
#100, 2216 Lorne St., Regina SK S4P 2M7
Tel: 306-525-1436; *Fax:* 306-347-7784
Toll-Free: 888-257-2576
e-mail: lpnadmin@salpn.com (general); praccon@salpn.com (practice)
URL: www.salpn.com
Colin Hein, Executive Director
Kim Kehrig, LPN, President
Cara Brewster, LPN, Registrar
Bonnie Downes, Assistant Registrar
Della Bartzen, LPN, Investigator

Saskatchewan Registered Nurses' Association (SRNA)
2066 Retallack St., Regina SK S4T 7X5
Tel: 306-359-4200; *Fax:* 306-525-0849
Toll-Free: 800-667-9945
e-mail: info@srna.org; SRNAnewsbulletin@srna.org; register@srna.org
URL: www.srna.org
David Kline, RN, President
Karen Eisler, RN, Executive Director

Saskatchewan Union of Nurses (SUN) / Syndicat des infirmières de la Saskatchewan
2330 - 2 Ave., Regina SK S4R 1A6
Tel: 306-525-1666; *Fax:* 306-522-4612
Toll-Free: 800-667-7060
e-mail: sunregina@sasktel.net
URL: www.sun-nurses.sk.ca
Affiliation(s): Saskatchewan Federation of Labour; Canadian Labour Congress; Canadian Federation of Nurses Unions
Rosalee Longmoore, President

Union of Psychiatric Nurses / Syndicat des infirmières psychiatriques
#200, 508 Clarke Rd., Coquitlam BC V3J 3X2
Tel: 604-931-2471; *Fax:* 604-931-1070
Toll-Free: 877-931-2471
e-mail: dmclaren@telus.net
URL: www.upnbc.org
Affiliation(s): BC Government Employees Union; BC Federation of Labour
Sherry Moller, President
Philip Oosterman, Director, Operations & Membership Services

Union québécoise des infirmières et infirmiers (UQII) / Québec Union of Nurses
9405, rue Sherbrooke est, Montréal QC H1L 6P3
Tél: 514-356-8888; *Téléc:* 514-356-9999
Courriel: uqii@csq.qc.net
Affiliation(s): Centrale des syndicats du Québec (CSQ)
Monique Bélanger, Présidente

United Nurses of Alberta (UNA) / Infirmières unies de l'Alberta
Park Plaza, 10611 - 98 Ave., 9th Fl., Edmonton AB T5K 2P7
Tel: 780-425-1025; *Fax:* 780-426-2093
Toll-Free: 800-252-9394
e-mail: provincialoffice@una.ab.ca
URL: www.una.ab.ca
Social Media: twitter.com/unitednurses

Heather Smith, President

Victorian Order of Nurses for Canada (VON Canada) / Infirmières de l'Ordre de Victoria du Canada
110 Argyle Ave., Ottawa ON K2P 1B4
Tel: 613-233-5694; *Fax:* 613-230-4376
Toll-Free: 888-866-2273
e-mail: national@von.ca
URL: www.von.ca
Judith Shamian, President & CEO
Diane McLeod, Executive Vice President

Yukon Registered Nurses Association (YRNA)
#204, 4133 - 4th Ave., Whitehorse YT Y1A 1H8
Tel: 867-667-4062; *Fax:* 867-668-5123
e-mail: yrna@yknet.ca
URL: www.yrna.ca
Patricia McGarr, RN, Executive Director
Peggy Heynen, RN, President

Packaging

North American Packaging Association - Canada
#400, 701 Evans Ave., Toronto ON M9C 1A3
Tel: 416-626-7056; *Fax:* 416-626-7054
e-mail: info@paperbox.org
URL: www.paperbox.org
Anne Adams, Office Manager

Packaging Association of Canada (PAC) / Association canadienne de l'emballage
#E420, 2255 Sheppard Ave. East, Toronto ON M2J 4Y1
Tel: 416-490-7860; *Fax:* 416-490-7844
e-mail: info@pac.ca
URL: www.pac.ca
James D. Downham, President/CEO
Colin Turner, Communications Director

Paper Packaging Canada
#400, 701 Evans Ave., Toronto ON M9C 1A3
Tel: 416-626-0350; *Fax:* 416-626-7054
e-mail: info@paperpackaging.ca
URL: www.cccassociation.com
John Mullinder, President & CEO

Patents & Copyright

Access Copyright
#800, One Yonge St., Toronto ON M5E 1E5
Tel: 416-868-1620; *Fax:* 416-868-1621
Toll-Free: 800-893-5777
e-mail: info@accesscopyright.ca
URL: www.accesscopyright.ca
Affiliation(s): International Federation of Reproduction Rights Organization
Maureen Cavan, Executive Director
Suzanne Dugard, Communications Manager
Brian O'Donnell, Director, Business Development
Roanie Levy, Director, Legal & External Affairs

Canadian Copyright Institute (CCI)
#107, 192 Spadina Ave., Toronto ON M5T 2C2
Tel: 416-975-1756; *Fax:* 416-975-1839
e-mail: info@thecci.ca
URL: www.canadiancopyrightinstitute.ca
Affiliation(s): Book & Periodical Council
Grace Westcott, Executive Secretary
Anne McClelland, Administrator

Canadian Musical Reproduction Rights Agency (CMRRA) / Agence canadienne des droits de production musicaux limitée
#320, 56 Wellesley St. West, Toronto ON M5S 2S3
Tel: 416-926-1966; *Fax:* 416-926-7521
e-mail: inquiries@cmrra.ca
URL: www.cmrra.ca
David A. Basskin, President
Fred Merritt, Vice-President, Finance & Administration

Copyright Collective of Canada (CCC) / Société de perception de droit d'auteur du Canada (SPDAC)
#1603, 22 St. Clair Ave. East, Toronto ON M4T 2S3
Tel: 416-961-1888; *Fax:* 416-968-1016
e-mail: speacock@ccofcan.org
Susan Peacock, Vice-President

Intellectual Property Institute of Canada (IPIC) / Institut de la Propriété Intellectuelle du Canada (IPIC)
#606, 60 Queen St., Ottawa ON K1P 5Y7
Tel: 613-234-0516; *Fax:* 613-234-0671
e-mail: info@ipic.ca
URL: www.ipic.ca
Affiliation(s): Industry Canada

Society of Composers, Authors & Music Publishers of Canada (SOCAN) / Société canadienne des auteurs, compositeurs et éditeurs de musique
41 Valleybrook Dr., Toronto ON M3B 2S6
Tel: 416-445-8700; *Fax:* 416-445-7108
Toll-Free: 800-557-6226
e-mail: socan@socan.ca
URL: www.socan.ca
Joel M. Grad, CFO/Executive Vice-President
Jeff King, Vice-President, Licensing and General Management
C. Paul Spurgeon, Vice-President, Legal Services & General Counsel
Marion Wilson, Vice-President, Information Technology
Randy Wark, Vice-President, Human Resources
France Lafleur, Vice-President, Member Operations
David Wood, Vice-President, Finance
André LeBel, CEO

Performing Arts - Dance

Alberta Ballet
Nat Christie Centre, 141 - 18 Ave. SW, Calgary AB T2S 0B8
Tel: 403-245-4222; *Fax:* 403-245-6573
e-mail: info@albertaballet.com
URL: www.albertaballet.com
Kerna St. John, Director, Marketing/Communications
Jean Grand-Maître, Artistic Director
Darryl Lindenbach, Executive Director

Alberta Dance Alliance (ADA)
Percy Page Centre, 11759 Groat Rd., 2nd Fl., Edmonton AB T5M 3K6
Tel: 780-422-8107; *Fax:* 780-422-2663
Toll-Free: 888-422-8107
e-mail: info@abdancealliance.ab.ca
URL: www.abdancealliance.ab.ca
Affiliation(s): Canadian Assembly of Dance; CADA BC, Ontario
Bobbi Westman, Executive Director

Ballet British Columbia
677 Davie St., 6th Fl., Vancouver BC V6G 2B6
Tel: 604-732-5003; *Fax:* 604-732-4417
e-mail: info@balletbc.com
URL: www.balletbc.com
Emily Molnar, Interim Artistic Director

Ballet Creole
375 Dovercourt Rd., Toronto ON M6J 3E5
Tel: 416-960-0350; *Fax:* 416-960-2067
e-mail: info@balletcreole.org
URL: www.balletcreole.org
Patrick Parson, Artistic Director

Ballet Jörgen
c/o George Brown College, Casa Loma Campus, Room 126, Building C, 160 Kendal Ave., Toronto ON M5R 1M3
Tel: 416-961-4725; *Fax:* 416-415-2865
e-mail: info@balletjorgen.ca
URL: www.balletjorgen.ca
Affiliation(s): George Brown Dance
Bengt Jörgen, Artistic Director & CEO

Ballet Ouest / Ballet West
#218, 269 boul. St. Jean, Pointe-Claire QC H9R 3J1
Tel: 514-783-1245; *Fax:* 514-939-1469
e-mail: centredanse@balletouest.com
URL: www.balletouest.com
Susan Altschul, Company Manager
Marie St-Amour, President
Margaret Mehuys, Artistic Director

BJM DANSE (BJM)
1210, rue Sherbrooke est, Montréal QC H2L 1L9
Tél: 514-982-6771; *Téléc:* 514-982-9145
Courriel: info@bjmdanse.ca
URL: www.bjmdanse.ca
Mèdia social: www.facebook.com/group.php?gid=4068138492
Louis Robitaille, Directeur artistique
Bernard Lagacé, Directeur général

Brian Webb Dance Co.
PO Box 53092, Edmonton AB T5N 48A
Tel: 780-452-3282; *Fax:* 780-497-4330
e-mail: webbcdf@shaw.ca
URL: www.bwdc.ca
Brian Webb, Artistic Director

Canada Dance Festival Society
PO Box 1376, Stn. B, 53 Elgin St., Ottawa ON K1P 5R4
Tel: 613-947-7000; *Fax:* 613-943-1399
e-mail: cdffdc@nac-cna.ca
URL: www.canadadance.ca
Social Media: www.facebook.com/group.php?gid=13144509823
Brian H. Webb, Artistic Director
Pamela Fralick, Chair

Canadian Alliance of Dance Artists (CADA ON) / Alliance canadiennes des artistes de danse
c/o Centre Of Social Innovation, #400, 215 Spadina Ave., Toronto ON M5T 2C7
Tel: 416-657-2276; *Fax:* 416-644-0116
e-mail: onchapter@cadadance.org
URL: www.cadadance.org
Affiliation(s): Canadian Alliance of Dance Artists, British Columbia Chapter
Nova Bhattacharya, Co-Chair
Lucy Rupert, Co-Chair
Elizabeth Chitty, Executive Director
Ariel Lin, Coordinator, Membership Services

Canadian Alliance of Dance Artists (CADA BC)
c/o Scotiabank Dance Centre, 677 Davie St., 7th Fl., Vancouver BC V6B 2G6
Tel: 604-606-6414
e-mail: bcchapter@cadadance.org
URL: www.cadadance.org
Caroline Liffmann, Chair
Josh Martin, Vice-Chair
Roxoliana Prus, Secretary
Julie Lebel, Treasurer
Caroline Farquhar, Chapter Administrator

Canadian Children's Dance Theatre (CCDT)
509 Parliament St., Toronto ON M4X 1P3
Tel: 416-924-5657; *Fax:* 416-924-4141
e-mail: info@ccdt.org
URL: www.ccdt.org
Elizabeth Varty, Marketing, Development & Arts Educa
Deborah Lundmark, Artistic Director & Resident Choreo
Michael de Coninck Smith, Co-Artistic Director & Production M

Canadian Dance Teachers Association (CDTA) / Association canadienne des professeurs de danse
c/o President, 178 Barrick Rd., Port Colbourne ON L3K 4B4
Tel: 905-834-0077
e-mail: donna.moreau@sympatico.ca
URL: www.cdtanational.ca
Donna Moreau, President

Canadian Square & Round Dance Society (CSRDS)
115 Holly Dr., Oakbank MB R0E 1J2
Tel: 204-444-3115; *Fax:* 204-444-5768
Toll-Free: 866-206-6696
e-mail: info@squaredance.ca
URL: www.csrds.ca
Lorraine Kozera, Secretary
John Kozera, Secretary
Alan Clay, President
Doreen Clay, President

Le Carré des Lombes
#401, 2022, rue Sherbrooke Est, Montréal QC H2K 1B9
Tél: 514-287-9339; *Téléc:* 514-287-9415
Courriel: info@lecarredeslombes.com
URL: www.lecarredeslombes.com
Mèdia social: www.facebook.com/pages/Le-Carre-des-Lombes/161816823394
Suzanne Beaucaire, Coordonatrice Générale

Catalyst Theatre Society of Alberta
8529 Gateway Blvd., Edmonton AB T6E 6P3
Tel: 780-431-1750; *Fax:* 780-433-3060
e-mail: info@catalysttheatre.ca
URL: www.catalysttheatre.ca
Jonathan Christenson, Artistic Director

Cercle d'expression artistique Nyata Nyata
4374, boul St-Laurent, 3e étage, Montréal QC H2W 1Z5
Tél: 514-849-9781; *Téléc:* 514-849-7199
Courriel: info@nyata-nyata.org
URL: www.nyata-nyata.org
Zab Maboungou, Directrice artistique

Compagnie de danse Migrations
880, av Pére-Marquette, Québec QC G1S 24A
Tél: 418-684-3132; *Téléc:* 418-684-3134
Courriel: migrations@qc.aira.com
URL: www.migrationsdanse.com
Affiliation(s): Folklore Canada International
Richard Turcotte, Directeur artistique

Blandin Garnier, Adjointe administrative

Compagnie Marie Chouinard
#715, 3981, boul St-Laurent, Montréal QC H2W 1Y5
Tél: 514-843-9036; *Téléc:* 514-843-7616
Courriel: info@mariechouinard.com
URL: www.mariechouinard.com
Mèdia social:
www.facebook.com/pages/Compagnie-Marie-Chouinard/90299878696
Marie Chouinard, Directrice artistique
Pierre Des Marais, Directeur général

Dance Centre
Scotiabank Dance Centre, 677 Davie St., Level 6, Vancouver BC V6B 2G6
Tel: 604-606-6400; *Fax:* 604-606-6401
e-mail: info@thedancecentre.ca
URL: www.thedancecentre.ca
Heather Bray, Marketing Manager
Mirna Zagar, Executive Director

Dance Manitoba Inc.
Pantages Playhouse Theatre, #204, 180 Market Ave. East, Winnipeg MB R3B 0P7
Tel: 204-989-5260; *Fax:* 204-989-5268
e-mail: info@dancemanitoba.org
URL: www.dancemanitoba.org
Nicole Langevin-Owens, Executive Director

Dance Nova Scotia
1113 Marginal Rd., Halifax NS B3H 4P7
Tel: 902-422-1749; *Fax:* 902-422-0881
e-mail: office@dancens.ca
URL: www.dancens.ca
Dianne Milligan, Executive Director

Dance Ontario Association / Association Ontario Danse
Case Goods Bldg. 74, The Distillery District, #304, 55 Mill St., Toronto ON M5A 3C4
Tel: 416-204-1083; *Fax:* 416-204-1085
e-mail: contact@danceontario.ca
URL: www.danceontario.ca
Catherine Carpenko, Chair
Samara Thompson, Vice-Chair
Rosslyn Jacob Edwards, Executive Director
Jennifer Watkins, Secretary
Allison Cummings, Treasurer

Dance Oremus Danse (DOD)
240 Dovercourt Rd., Toronto ON M6J 3E1
Tel: 416-536-9002; *Fax:* 416-536-9002
e-mail: pauljamesdwyer@yahoo.ca
URL: www.danceoremusdanse.org
Paul James Dwyer, Founder/Artistic Director

Dance Saskatchewan Inc.
PO Box 8789, 205A Pacific Ave., Saskatoon SK S7K 1N9
Tel: 306-931-8480; *Fax:* 306-244-1520
Toll-Free: 800-667-8480
e-mail: dancesask@sasktel.net
URL: www.dancesask.com
Affiliation(s): Canadian Association of Professional Dance Organizations
Linda Coe-Kirkham, Executive Director

Dance Umbrella of Ontario (DUO)
#201, 490 Adelaide St. West, Toronto ON M5V 1T2
Tel: 416-504-6429; *Fax:* 416-504-8702
Toll-Free: 800-919-5019
e-mail: duo@danceumbrella.net
URL: www.danceumbrella.net
Affiliation(s): Arts Vote; Dance Ontario
Christine Moynihan, Executive Director

DanceArts Vancouver
Scotiabank Dance Centre, 677 Davie St., 7th Fl., Vancouver BC V6B 2G6
Tel: 604-606-6425; *Fax:* 604-606-6432
e-mail: info@dancearts.bc.ca
Judith Marcuse, Artistic Director

Dancemakers
The Case Goods Warehouse, Bldg. #74, #306, 55 Mill St., Toronto ON M5A 3C4
Tel: 416-367-1800; *Fax:* 416-367-1870
e-mail: info@dancemakers.org
URL: www.dancemakers.org
Michael Trent, Artistic Director
Bradley Kulay, Administrative Manager

Dancer Transition Resource Centre (DTRC) / Centre de ressources et transition pour danseurs (CRTD)
The Lynda Hamilton Centre, #500, 250 The Esplanade, Toronto ON M5A 1J2
Tel: 416-595-5655; *Fax:* 416-595-0009
Toll-Free: 800-667-0851
e-mail: nationaloffice@dtrc.ca
URL: www.dtrc.ca
Affiliation(s): Canadian Dance Alliance; Le Regroupement québécois de la Danse
Amanda Hancox, Executive Director
Garry Neil, Chair

Danny Grossman Dance Company
#202, 157 Carlton St., Toronto ON M5A 2K3
Tel: 416-408-4543; *Fax:* 416-408-2518
e-mail: info@dannygrossman.com
URL: www.dannygrossman.com
Affiliation(s): Dance USA; CAPDO; Dance Ontario
Helen Chapman, Managing Director
Danny Grossman, Artistic Director

Danse-Cite inc
#426, 3680, rue Jeanne-Mance, Montréal QC H2X 2K5
Tél: 514-525-3595; *Téléc:* 514-525-3536
Courriel: info@danse-cite.org
URL: www.danse-cite.org
Daniel Soulières, Directeur artistique

Decidedly Jazz Danceworks
1514 - 4th St. SW, Calgary AB T2R 0Y4
Tel: 403-245-3533; *Fax:* 403-245-3584
e-mail: djd@decidedlyjazz.com
URL: www.decidedlyjazz.com
Vicki Adams Willis, Artistic Director
Kathi Sundstrom, General Manager

EDAM Performing Arts Society (EDAM)
303 - 8th Ave. East, Vancouver BC V5T 1S1
Tel: 604-876-9559; *Fax:* 604-876-9525
e-mail: info@edamdance.org
URL: www.edamdance.org
Peter Bingham, Artistic Director
Mona Hamill, Administrative Director

Fédération des loisirs-danse du Québec
CP 1000, Succ. M, 4545, av Pierre-de Coubertin, Montréal QC H1V 3R2
Tél: 514-252-3029; *Téléc:* 514-251-8038

Fringe Festival of Independent Dance Artists (FFIDA)
Toronto ON
Tel: 416-214-5854
e-mail: info@ffida.org
Michael Menegon, Artistic Director

Fortier Danse-Création
Succ. C, #301, 2022, rue Sherbrooke Est, Montréal QC H2K 1B9
Tél: 514-529-8158; *Téléc:* 514-529-1222
Courriel: admin@fortier-danse.com
URL: www.fortier-danse.com
Mèdia social: www.facebook.com/profile.php?id=1331329089
Paul-André Fortier, Directeur artistique
Gilles Savary, Directeur général

Fujiwara Dance Inventions
#201, 490 Adelaide St. West, Toronto ON M5V 1T2
Tel: 416-593-4710; *Fax:* 416-504-8702
e-mail: info@fujiwaradance.com
URL: www.fujiwaradance.com
Denise Fujiwara, Artistic Director

Gina Lori Riley Dance Enterprises
401 Sunset Ave., Windsor ON N9B 3P4
Tel: 519-253-3000
e-mail: riley2@uwindsor.ca
URL: www.ginaloririleydanceenterprises.com
Gina Lori Riley, Artistic Director

Goh Ballet Society
2345 Main St., Vancouver BC V5T 3C9
Tel: 604-872-4014; *Fax:* 604-872-4011
e-mail: admin@gohballet.com
URL: www.gohballet.com
Social Media: www.twitter.com/GohBallet
Fei Wong, President
Chan Hon Goh, Artistic Director

Les Grands Ballets Canadiens de Montréal (GBCM)
Maison de la Danse, 4816, rue Rivard, Montréal QC H2J 2N6
Tél: 514-849-8681; *Téléc:* 514-849-0098
Courriel: info@grandsballets.com
URL: www.grandsballets.com
Alain Dancyger, Directeur général
Gradimir Pankov, Directeur artistique

Le Groupe Dance Lab / Le Groupe lab de danse
#2, 2 Daly St., Ottawa ON K1N 6E2
Tel: 613-235-1492; *Fax:* 613-235-1651
e-mail: info@legroupe.org
URL: www.legroupe.org
Social Media: www.facebook.com/group.php?gid=21206927029
Affiliation(s): 10 Gates Dancing Inc.; DanceMakers; Fondation Jean Pierre Perreaut
Tony Chong, Associate Artistic Director
Peter Boneham, Artistic Director
Anthony Pan, General Manager

Kinesis Dance Society
Scotia Bank Dance Centre, Level 7, 677 Davie St., Vancouver BC V6B 2G6
Tel: 604-684-7844; *Fax:* 604-684-7834
e-mail: info@kinesisdance.org
URL: www.kinesisdance.org
Paras Terezakis, Artistic Director

La La La Human Steps
#206, 5655, av du Parc, Montréal QC H2V 4H2
Tél: 514-277-9090; *Téléc:* 514-277-0862
Courriel: info@lalalahumansteps.com
URL: www.lalalahumansteps.com
Mèdia social:
www.facebook.com/pages/LA-LA-LA-HUMAN-STEPS/54786888171
Édouard Lock, Directeur artistique

Lola Dance
#104, 336 - 1st Ave. East, Vancouver BC V5T 4R6
Tel: 604-683-6552; *Fax:* 604-681-1431
e-mail: info@loladance.org
URL: www.loladance.org
Lola MacLaughlin, Artistic Director & Founder

Louise Bédard Danse
#300, 2022, rue Sherbrooke Est, Montréal QC H2K 1B9
Tél: 514-982-4580; *Téléc:* 514-982-0613
Courriel: infos@lbdanse.org
URL: www.lbdanse.org
Mèdia social: www.facebook.com/lbdanse; www.twitter.com/lbdanse
Louise Bédard, Directrice artistique

Lucie Grégoire Danse
#405,1030, rue Cherrier, Montréal QC H2L 1H9
Tél: 514-524-7665; *Téléc:* 514-524-7584
Courriel: luciegregoire3@sympatico.ca
URL: www.luciegregoire.ca
Lucie Grégoire, Directrice artistique

Margie Gillis Dance Foundation / Fondation de danse Margie Gillis
3519, rue St-Urbain, Montréal QC H2X 2N6
Tel: 514-845-3115; *Fax:* 514-845-4526
e-mail: info@margiegillis.org
URL: www.margiegillis.org
Social Media:
www.facebook.com/pages/Margie-Gillis/63111821500
Margie Gillis, Artistic Director
Manon Laflamme, Administrative Director

Mascall Dance
1130 Jervis St., Vancouver BC V6E 2C7
Tel: 604-689-9339; *Fax:* 604-689-9399
e-mail: admin@mascalldance.ca
URL: www.mascalldance.ca
Jennifer Mascall, Artistic Director

Montréal Danse
#109, 372, rue Sainte-Catherine ouest, Montréal QC H3B 1A2
Tél: 514-871-4005; *Téléc:* 514-871-4007
Courriel: info@montrealdanse.com
URL: www.montrealdanse.com
Mèdia social:
www.facebook.com/pages/Montreal-Danse/100944976616149
Kathy Casey, Directrice artistique

National Ballet of Canada
Walter Carsen Centre, 470 Queens Quay West, Toronto ON M5V 3K4
Tel: 416-345-9686; *Fax:* 416-345-8323
e-mail: info@national.ballet.ca
URL: www.national.ballet.ca
Karen Kain, Artistic Director
Kevin Garland, Executive Director

David Briskin, Music Director/Principal Conductor

O Vertigo Danse
175, rue Sainte-Catherine ouest, Montréal QC H1V 1H1
Tél: 514-251-9177; *Téléc:* 514-251-7358
Courriel: info@overtigo.com
URL: www.overtigo.com
Diane Boucher, Directrice générale
Ginette Laurin, Directrice générale

Ontario Ballet Theatre
1133 St. Clair Ave. West, Toronto ON M6E 1B1
Tel: 416-656-9568; *Fax:* 416-651-4803
e-mail: tara@ontarioballettheatre.com
URL: www.ontarioballettheatre.com

Ontario Folk Dance Association (OFDA)
35 Touraine Ave., Toronto ON M3H 1R3
e-mail: ontariofolkdancers@gmail.com
URL: www.ofda.ca
Kevin Budd, Vice-President
Beverly Sidney, President

Opéra Atelier (OA)
St. Lawrence Hall, 157 King St. East, 4th Fl., Toronto ON M5C 1G9
Tel: 416-703-3767; *Fax:* 416-703-4895
e-mail: opera.atelier@operaatelier.com
URL: www.operaatelier.com
Jane Hargraft, General Manager

Les Productions DansEncorps Inc.
#12A, 140, rue Botsford, Moncton NB E1C 4X5
Tél: 506-855-0998; *Téléc:* 506-852-3401
Courriel: dencorps@nb.aibn.com
URL: www.dansencorps.ca
Chantal Cadieux, Directrice artistique

Regroupement québécois de la danse (RQD)
#440, 3680 rue Jeanne-Mance, Montréal QC H2X 2K5
Tél: 514-849-4003; *Téléc:* 514-849-3288
Courriel: info@quebecdanse.org
URL: www.quebecdanse.org
Affiliation(s): Agora de la danse; Regroupement québécois des créateurs professionnels
Anik Bissonette, Présidente

Royal Academy of Dance/Canada
#500, 1200 Sheppard Ave. East, Toronto ON M2K 2S5
Tel: 416-489-2813; *Fax:* 416-489-3222
Toll-Free: 888-709-0895
e-mail: info@radcanada.org
URL: www.radcanada.org
Affiliation(s): Royal Academy of Dance
Jan Garvey, National Administrator

The Royal Scottish Country Dance Society (RSCDS)
12 Coates Cres., Edinburgh EH3 7AF United Kingdom
Tel: 44-0131-225-3854; *Fax:* 44-0131-225-7783
e-mail: info@rscds.org
URL: www.rscds.org
Elspeth Gray, Secretary

Royal Winnipeg Ballet (RWB)
380 Graham Ave., Winnipeg MB R3C 4K2
Tel: 204-956-0183; *Fax:* 204-943-1994
Toll-Free: 800-667-4792
e-mail: ballet@rwb.org
URL: www.rwb.org
Affiliation(s): Association of Cultural Executives; Canadian Conference of the Arts; Canadian Arts Presenting Association; Council for Business & the Arts in Canada; Dance USA; International Society for the Performing Arts
Arlene Minkhorst, School Director
Charlene Rocke, Chair
André Lewis, Artistic Director

Ruth Cansfield Dance
806 Osborne St., Winnipeg MB R3L 2C7
Tel: 204-284-5810; *Fax:* 204-284-1131
Toll-Free: 866-405-5810
e-mail: info@ruthcansfield.com
URL: www.ruthcansfield.com
Ken Manson, Vice-President
Jon McPhail, Administration Director
Ruth Cansfield, Artistic Director
Ellie Cansfield, President

Springboard Dance
205 - 8th Ave. SE, 2nd Fl., Calgary AB T2G 0K9
Tel: 403-265-3230; *Fax:* 403-294-7457
URL: www.springboardperformance.com
Social Media: www.facebook.com/group.php?gid=87776623119
Affiliation(s): Alberta Dance Alliance; Canadian Dance Federation; Dance Current
Trina Rasmuson
Shelly Tegnazzini
Nicole Mion

Sun Ergos, A Company of Theatre & Dance
Priddis Greens, 130 Sunset Way, Priddis AB T0L 1W0
Tel: 403-931-1527; *Fax:* 403-931-1534
Toll-Free: 800-743-3351
e-mail: waltermoke@sunergos.com
URL: www.sunergos.com
Social Media: www.facebook.com/pages/SunErgos/189482516084
Affiliation(s): Western Arts Alliance; Arts Northwest; Montana Performing Arts Consortium; Arts MidWest; Arts Touring Alliance of Alberta; BC Touring; Wyoming Arts Alliance
Robert Greenwood, Artistic & Managing Director
Dana Luebke, Artistic & Production Director

Toronto & District Square & Round Dance Association
8 Seven Oaks Circle, St. Catharines ON L2P 3N6
Tel: 905-641-1872
URL: www3.sympatico.ca/jerry.callen/td/
Affiliation(s): Canadian Square & Round Dance Society
Sharron Hall, Secretary

Toronto Dance Theatre (TDT)
80 Winchester St., Toronto ON M4X 1B2
Tel: 416-967-1365; *Fax:* 416-963-4379
e-mail: info@tdt.org
URL: www.tdt.org
Jay Rankin, Managing Director
Christopher House, Artistic Director

Two Planks & a Passion Theatre Association (TP&aP)
PO Box 190, 555 Ross Creek Rd., Canning NS B0P 1H0
Tel: 902-582-3073; *Fax:* 902-582-7943
e-mail: mail@twoplanks.ca
URL: www.twoplanks.ca; www.twoplanksandpassion.blogspot.com
Social Media: www.facebook.com/group.php?gid=2337674729
Affiliation(s): Playwrights Union of Canada
Ken Schwartz, Artistic Director

Vancouver Moving Theatre (VMT)
PO Box 88270, Stn. Chinatown, Vancouver BC V6A 4A4
Tel: 604-628-5672
e-mail: savannahandterry@axion.net
URL: www.vancouvermovingtheatre.com
Savannah Walling, Artistic Director
Terry Hunter, Executive Director

Vinok Worldance
PO Box 4867, Edmonton AB T6E 5G7
Tel: 780-454-3739; *Fax:* 780-454-3436
e-mail: vinok@vinok.ca
URL: www.vinok.ca
Doyle Marko, Artistic Director
Leanne Koziak, Executive Director

Winnipeg's Contemporary Dancers
#204, 211 Bannatyne Ave., Winnipeg MB R3B 3P2
Tel: 204-452-0229; *Fax:* 204-287-8618
e-mail: info@winnipegscontemporarydancers.ca
URL: www.winnipegscontemporarydancers.ca
Brian Lott, Artistic Director

Performing Arts - Music

Académie de musique du Québec (AMQ)
CP 818, Succ. C, 1231, rue Panet, Montréal QC H2L 4L6
Tél: 514-528-1961; *Téléc:* 514-528-7572
Courriel: prixdeurope@videotron.ca
Jean Marchand, Président

African Nova Scotian Music Association (ANSMA)
PO Box 931, 1149 Main St., Dartmouth NS B2Z 1A8
Tel: 902-404-3036; *Fax:* 902-434-0462
e-mail: ansma@eastlink.ca
URL: www.ansma.com
Louis (Lou) Gannon Jr., President

Alberta Band Association (ABA)
#206, 10612 - 124 St., Edmonton AB T5M 1S4
Tel: 780-488-2263; *Fax:* 780-488-4132
Toll-Free: 877-687-4239
URL: www.albertabandassociation.com
Neil Corlett, Managing Director

Alberta Choral Federation (ACF)
#103, 10612 - 124 St., Edmonton AB T5N 1S4
Tel: 780-488-7464; *Fax:* 780-488-6403
e-mail: info@albertachoralfederation.ca
URL: www.albertachoralfederation.ca
Ardelle Ries, President
Brendan Lord, Executive Director

Alberta Recording Industries Association (ARIA)
Energy Square, #1205, 10109 - 106 St. NW, Edmonton AB T5J 3L7
Tel: 780-428-3372; *Fax:* 780-426-0188
Toll-Free: 800-465-3117
Affiliation(s): Western Canadian Music Alliance; Factor Caras

Alliance Chorale Manitoba
#212, 340 Provencher Blvd., Winnipeg MB R2H 0G7
Tél: 204-233-7423; *Téléc:* 204-233-3324
Gilles Landry, Contact

Alliance des chorales du Québec (ACQ)
CP 1000, Succ. M, 4545, av Pierre-de-Coubertin, Montréal QC H1V 3R2
Tél: 514-252-3020; *Téléc:* 514-252-3222
Courriel: information@chorale.qc.ca
URL: www.chorale.qc.ca
Catherine Girard, Directrice générale

Alliance for Canadian New Music Projects (ACNMP) / Alliance pour des projets de musique canadienne nouvelle
Canadian Music Centre, 20 St. Joseph St., Toronto ON M4Y 1J9
Tel: 416-963-5937; *Fax:* 416-961-7198
e-mail: acnmp@rogers.com
URL: www.acnmp.ca
Ann La Plante, General Manager
Jill Kelman, President

Association of Canadian Choral Conductors (ACCC) / Association des chefs de choeur canadiens
6303 Duncan St., Halifax NS B3L 1K4
Tel: 902-442-7054; *Fax:* 902-442-7050
e-mail: accc@ca.inter.net
URL: www.choralcanada.org
Affiliation(s): Canadian Conference of the Arts; International Federation for Choral Music
Christina Murray, Executive Director
Bridgid Coult, President

Association québécoise de l'industrie du disque, du spectacle et de la vidéo (ADISQ)
6420, rue Saint-Denis, Montréal QC H2S 2R7
Tél: 514-842-5147; *Téléc:* 514-842-7762
Courriel: info@adisq.com
URL: www.adisq.com

Bach Elgar Choral Society
86 Homewood St., Hamilton ON L8P 2M4
Tel: 905-527-5995; *Fax:* 905-527-0555
e-mail: bachelgar@bellnet.ca
URL: www.bachelgar.com
Affiliation(s): Ontario Choral Federation; Hamilton & Region Arts Council; Council for Business & the Arts in Canada; Canadian Conference of the Arts

Bluegrass Music Association of Central Canada (BMACC)
c/o Secretary, 339 Wellington St. N, Woodstock ON N4S 6S6
Tel: 519-539-8967
e-mail: weslowe@bmacc.ca
URL: www.bmacc.ca
Denis Chadbourn, President

Brampton Symphony Orchestra
PO Box 93091, Stn. Brampton South, 499 Main St. South, Brampton ON L6Y 4V8
Tel: 905-459-0853
e-mail: info@bramptonsymphony.com
URL: www.bramptonsymphony.com
Michael Todd, President

Brandon University Orchestra
School of Music, Brandon Univ., Queen Elizabeth II Bldg., 270 - 18th St., Brandon MB R7A 6A9
Tel: 204-728-9631; *Fax:* 204-728-6839
e-mail: music@brandonu.ca
URL: www.brandonu.ca/music/
Social Media: www.facebook.com/group.php?gid=31991706716
Mark Rudoff, Director

Brantford Symphony Orchestra Association Inc.
PO Box 24012, 185 King George Rd., Brantford ON N3R 7X3

Tel: 519-759-8781; Fax: 519-759-0842
e-mail: administrator@brantfordsymphony.ca
URL: www.brantfordsymphony.com

Calgary Opera Association
Arrata Opera Centre, 1315 - 7 St. SW, Calgary AB T2R 1A5
Tel: 403-262-7286; Fax: 403-263-5428
e-mail: info@calgaryopera.com
URL: www.calgaryopera.com
Social Media:
www.facebook.com/pages/Calgary-Opera/18782898651
Affiliation(s): Actors Equity Association
W.R. (Bob) McPhee, General Director

Calgary Philharmonic Society (CPO)
205 - 8 Ave. SE, Calgary AB T2G 0K9
Tel: 403-571-0270; Fax: 403-294-7424
e-mail: info@cpo-live.com
URL: www.cpo-live.com
Social Media: www.twitter.com/calgaryphil
Affiliation(s): American Symphony Orchestra League
Ann Lewis-Luppino, President & CEO

Calgary Youth Orchestra
c/o Mount Royal College Conservatory, 4825 Mount Royal Gate SW, Calgary AB T3E 6K6
Tel: 403-240-5978; Fax: 403-240-6594
e-mail: cyo@mtroyal.ca
URL: www.cyo.ab.ca
George Fenwick, Orchestra Manager

Canadian Academy of Recording Arts & Sciences (CARAS) / Académie canadienne des arts et des sciences de l'enregistrement (ACASE)
345 Adelaide St. West, 2nd fl., Toronto ON M5V 1J6
Tel: 416-485-3135; Fax: 416-485-4978
Toll-Free: 888-440-5866
e-mail: membership@carasonline.ca
URL: www.carasonline.ca
Ed Robinson, Chair, CARAS & MusiCounts
Melanie Berry, President & Chief Executive Officer, CARAS & MusiCounts
Chris Topping, Vice-President, Events & Special Programming
Alex Heming, Senior Coordinator, Marketing & Fulfillment
Meghan McCabe, Senior Coordinator, Communications

Canadian Amateur Musicians (CAMMAC) / Musiciens amateurs du Canada
85 Cammac Rd., Harrington QC J8G 2T2
Tel: 819-687-3938; Fax: 819-687-3323
Toll-Free: 888-622-8755
e-mail: national@cammac.ca
URL: www.cammac.ca
Harry Qualman, President
Raymond Vles, Vice-President
Rachel Gagnon, Secretary
Roland Wilk, Treasurer
Radu Kaufman, Executive Director
Patricia Abbott, Artistic Director
Johanne Guérin, Group Coordinator
Solange Marquis, Comptroller

Canadian Association for Music Therapy (CAMT) / Association de musicothérapie du Canada (AMC)
#230, 110 Cumberland St., Toronto ON M5R 3V5
Tel: 416-944-0421; Fax: 416-944-0431
Toll-Free: 800-996-2268
e-mail: camt@musictherapy.ca
URL: www.musictherapy.ca
Affiliation(s): World Federation of Music Therapy
Guylaine Vaillancourt, President

Canadian Band Association (CBA) / Association canadienne des harmonies
15 Pinecrest Bay, Winnipeg MB R2G 1W2
Tel: 204-663-1226; Fax: 204-663-1226
e-mail: cbaband@shaw.ca
URL: cba.usask.ca
Ken Epp, Executive Director

Canadian Bureau for the Advancement of Music (CBAM)
Exhibition Place, Toronto ON M6K 3C3
Tel: 416-260-6451
e-mail: moreinfo@thecbam.ca
URL: www.thecbam.ca
Nancy Manning, CAO

Canadian Children's Opera Chorus (CCOC)
Opera Centre, #215, 227 Front St. East, Toronto ON M5A 1E8
Tel: 416-366-0467; Fax: 416-366-9204
e-mail: info@canadianchildrensopera.com
URL: www.canadianchildrensopera.com
Ken Hall, General Manager
Ann Cooper Gay, Artistic Director

Canadian Country Music Association (CCMA) / Association de la musique country canadienne
30-B Commercial Rd., Toronto ON M4G 1Z4
Tel: 416-947-1331; Fax: 416-947-5924
e-mail: country@ccma.org
URL: www.ccma.org
Sheila Hamilton, Executive Director
Heather Ostertag, Chair
Lynne Foster, Sec.-Treas.

Canadian Disc Jockey Association (CDJA)
PO Box 92, Arva ON N0M 1C0
Fax: 519-472-0242
Toll-Free: 877-472-0653
e-mail: pres@cdja.ca
URL: www.cdja.org
Affiliation(s): American DJ Association; National American Mobile Entertainers
Doug Scott, President

Canadian Federation of Music Teachers' Associations (CFMTA) / Fédération canadienne des associations des professeurs de musique
13407, 14A Ave., Surrey AB V4A 7P9
Tel: 604-531-8840; Fax: 604-531-8747
e-mail: dbrigs@telus.net
URL: www.cfmta.org
Affiliation(s): International Society of Music Educators' Association
Darlene Brigidear, President

Canadian Independent Music Association (CIMA)
30 St. Patrick St., 2nd Fl., Toronto ON M5T 3A3
Tel: 416-485-3152; Fax: 416-485-4373
e-mail: cima@cimamusic.ca
URL: www.cimamusic.ca
Duncan McKie, President
Donna Murphy, Research Director
Sharon Hookway, Membership/Communications
Mary Vrantsidis, International Trade Shows

Canadian League of Composers / La Ligue canadienne de compositeurs
c/o Canadian Music Centre, 20 St. Joseph St., Toronto ON M4Y 1J9
Tel: 416-964-1364
Toll-Free: 877-964-1364
e-mail: info@composition.org
URL: www.composition.org
James Rolfe, President, Ontario

Canadian Music Centre (CMC) / Centre de musique canadienne
Chalmers House, 20 St. Joseph St., Toronto ON M4Y 1J9
Tel: 416-961-6601; Fax: 416-961-7198
e-mail: info@musiccentre.ca
URL: www.musiccentre.ca; www.centremusique.ca
Affiliation(s): International Association of Music Information Centres; Canadian Music Libraries Association
Allan G. Bell, President
Elisabeth Bihl, Executive Director

Canadian Music Centre (CMC)
Chalmers House, 20 St. Joseph St., Toronto ON M4Y 1J9
Tél: 416-961-6601; Téléc: 416-961-7198
Courriel: info@musiccentre.ca
URL: www.centremusique.ca

Canadian Music Centre
Chalmers House, 20 St. Joseph St., Toronto ON M4Y 1J9
Tel: 416-961-6601; Fax: 416-961-7198
e-mail: ontario@musiccentre.ca

Canadian Music Centre
837 Davie St., Vancouver BC V6Z 1B7
Tel: 604-734-4622; Fax: 604-734-4627
e-mail: bcregion@musiccentre.ca

Canadian Music Centre
Canadian Music Centre, Atlantic Region, 134 Main St., Sackville NB E4L 1A6
Tel: 506-536-4263
e-mail: atlantic@musiccentre.ca
URL: www.musiccentre.ca/atl.cfm

Canadian Music Centre
Viotel Archer Library, #911, 2500 University Dr. NW, Calgary AB T2N 1N4
Tel: 403-220-7403; Fax: 403-289-4877
e-mail: prairie@musiccentre.ca
URL: www.musiccentre.ca/pra.cfm

Canadian Music Competitions Inc. / Concours de musique du Canada inc.
#220, 1450, City Councillors, Montréal QC H3A 2E6
Tel: 514-284-5398; Fax: 514-284-6828
Toll-Free: 877-879-1959
e-mail: info@cmcnational.com
URL: www.cmcnational.com
Raymonde Boutet, Présidente

Canadian Music Educators' Association (CMEA) / Association canadienne des éducateurs de musique
#A-430A, Wilfrid Laurier University, Waterloo ON N2L 3C5
Tel: 519-884-0710
e-mail: edwin.wasiak@uleth.ca
URL: www.musiceducationonline.org
Affiliation(s): International Society for Music Education
Betty Hanley, Membership
Ed Wasiak, President

Canadian Music Festival Adjudicators' Association (CMFAA)
c/o School of Music, Queen's University, Kingston ON K7L 3N6
Tel: 613-533-6000; Fax: 613-533-6808
e-mail: zuki@queensu.ca
URL: www.cmfaa.ca
John Hansen, Vice-President
Ireneus Zuk, President

Canadian Musical Heritage Society (CMHS) / Société pour le patrimoine musical canadien (SPMC)
#15, 120 Walnut Ct., Ottawa ON K1R 7W2
Tel: 613-237-0550
e-mail: enquiries@cliffordfordpublications.ca
Clifford Ford, Executive Secretary

Canadian Opera Company (COC) / Compagnie d'opéra canadienne
145 Queen St. West, Toronto ON M5A 1E8
Tel: 416-363-8231; Fax: 416-363-5584
Toll-Free: 800-250-4653
e-mail: info@coc.ca
URL: www.coc.ca
Affiliation(s): The Canadian Opera Foundation; Canadian Opera Volunteer Committee
Alexander Neef, General Director
Robert Lamb, Managing Director

Canadian Recording Industry Association (CRIA) / Association de l'industrie canadienne de l'enregistrement
85 Mowat Ave., Toronto ON M6K 3E3
Tel: 416-967-7272; Fax: 416-967-9415
e-mail: info@cria.ca
URL: www.cria.ca
Graham Henderson, President

Canadian Society for Traditional Music (CSTM) / Société canadienne pour les traditions musicales (SCTM)
c/o 3-47 Arts Building, University of Alberta, Edmonton AB T6G 2E6
e-mail: cstmsctm@ualberta.ca
URL: www.yorku.ca/cstm
Sherry Johnson, Secretary
Anna Hoefnagels, President
Chris McDonald, Treasurer

Canadian University Music Society (CUMS) / Société de musique des universités canadiennes (SMUC)
c/o Secretariat, #202, 10 Morrow Ave., Toronto ON M6R 2J1
Tel: 416-538-1650; Fax: 416-489-1713
e-mail: journals@interlog.com
URL: www.cums-smuc.ca/
Affiliation(s): Social Sciences & Humanities Research Council of Canada
Deanna Oye, President

Carl Orff Canada Music for Children (COC)
c/o Joan Linklater, 88 Tunis Bay, Winnipeg MB R3T 2X1
Tel: 204-261-1893
URL: www.orffcanada.ca
Joan Linklater, President

Cathedral Bluffs Symphony Orchestra (CBSO)
PO Box 51074, 18 Eglinton Sq., Toronto ON M1L 2K2
Tel: 416-879-5566
e-mail: info@cathedralbluffs.com
URL: www.cathedralbluffs.com
Norman Reintamm, Artistic Director
Murray Finkelstein, President

Chants Libres, compagnie lyrique de création
#303, 1908, rue Panet, Montréal QC H2L 3A2
Tél: 514-841-2642; *Téléc:* 514-841-2640
Courriel: creation@chantslibres.org
URL: www.chantslibres.org
Pauline Vaillancourt, Directrice générale

Choirs Ontario
A-1442 Bayview Ave., Toronto ON M4G 3A7
Tel: 416-923-1144; *Fax:* 416-929-0415
Toll-Free: 866-935-1144
e-mail: info@choirsontario.org
URL: www.choirsontario.org
Dean Jobin-Bevans, President

Concerts symphoniques de Sherbrooke inc. (CSS) / Sherbrooke Symphony Orchestra
Domain Howard, Pavillon 1, CP 610, 1300, boul de Portland, Sherbrooke QC J1H 5H9
Tél: 819-821-0227; *Téléc:* 819-821-1959
Courriel: oss@abacom.com
URL: www.css-oss.com
Affiliation(s): Conseil Québecois de la Musique
Michel Bédard, Président
Stéphane Laforest, Directeur artistique

Conservatory Canada
#M-2, 130 King St., London ON N6A 1C5
Tel: 519-433-3147; *Fax:* 519-433-7404
Toll-Free: 800-461-5367
e-mail: mail@conservatorycanada.ca
URL: www.conservatorycanada.ca
Warwick Victoria, Executive Director

Counterpoint Community Orchestra
PO Box 41, 552 Church St., Toronto ON M4Y 2E3
Tel: 416-654-9806
e-mail: info@ccorchestra.org
URL: www.ccorchestra.org
Terry Kowalczuk, Music Director

Country Music Foundation of Canada Inc.
8607 - 128 Ave., Edmonton AB T5E 0G3
Tel: 780-476-8230; *Fax:* 780-472-2584
William Maxim, Chair

Deep River Symphony Orchestra (DRSO)
PO Box 1496, Deep River ON K0J 1P0
Tel: 613-586-9385
e-mail: symphony@drso.ca
URL: www.drso.ca
Peter Morris, Music Director
Heather Butterworth, Secretary

Deep Roots Music Cooperative
PO Box 2360, Wolfville NS B4P 2G9
Tel: 902-542-7668
e-mail: info@deeprootsmusic.ca
URL: www.deeprootsmusic.ca/cooperative
Peter Mowat, Chair

Delta Youth Orchestra
PO Box 131, Delta BC V4K 3N6
Tel: 604-878-4655; *Fax:* 604-943-9603
e-mail: info@dyo.bc.ca
URL: www.dyo.bc.ca
Stephen Robb, Music Director

Early Music Vancouver (EMV)
1254 - 7 Ave. West, Vancouver BC V6H 1B6
Tel: 604-732-1610; *Fax:* 604-732-1602
e-mail: staff@earlymusic.bc.ca
URL: www.earlymusic.bc.ca
Social Media: www.facebook.com/earlymusicvancouver
José Verstappen, Executive Director

East Coast Music Association (ECMA) / Association de la musique de la côte est
#70, 90 University Ave., Charlottetown PE C1A 4K9
Tel: 902-892-9040; *Fax:* 902-892-9041
e-mail: ecma@ecma.ca
URL: www.ecma.ca
Affiliation(s): Music Industry Associations; Canadian Academy of Recording Arts & Science; FACTOR

Edmonton Jazz Society (EJS)
11 Tommy Banks Way, Edmonton AB T6E 2M2
Tel: 780-432-0428; *Fax:* 780-433-3773
e-mail: jasiek@yardbirdsuite.com
URL: www.yardbirdsuite.com
Social Media: www.facebook.com/YardbirdSuite
Paul Wilde, President

Edmonton Opera Association
Winspear Centre, 9720 - 102 Ave., Edmonton AB T5J 4B2
Tel: 780-424-4040; *Fax:* 780-429-0600
e-mail: edmopera@edmontonopera.com
URL: www.edmontonopera.com
Brian Deedrick, Artistic Director
Mary Phillips-Rickey, General Manager

Edmonton Symphony Orchestra (ESO)
9720 - 102 Ave., Edmonton AB T5J 4B2
Tel: 780-428-1108; *Fax:* 780-425-0167
Toll-Free: 800-563-5081
e-mail: info@winspearcentre.com
URL: www.edmontonsymphony.com
Social Media: www.facebook.com/edmontonsymphony
Affiliation(s): International Alliance of Theatrical Stage Employees, Moving Picture Technicians, Artists & Allied Crafts of the US & Canada
Rob McAlear, Artistic Administrator
Annemarie Petrov, Executive Director

Edmonton Youth Orchestra Association (EYO)
PO Box 66041, Stn. Heritage Post Office, Edmonton AB T6J 6T4
Tel: 780-436-7932; *Fax:* 780-436-7932
e-mail: eyo@shaw.ca
URL: www.eyso.com
Michael Massey, Music Director

Edward Johnson Music Foundation (EJMF)
PO Box 1718, 50 Cork St. East, 2nd Floor, Guelph ON N1H 6Z9
Tel: 519-821-7570; *Fax:* 519-821-4403
e-mail: info@edwardjohnsonmusicfoundation.org
URL: www.edwardjohnsonmusicfoundation.org
Rosemary Smith, Executive Director

Ensemble contemporain de Montréal (ECM+)
3890 rue Clark, Montréal QC H2W 1W6
Tél: 514-524-0173; *Téléc:* 514-524-0179
Courriel: info@ecm.qc.ca
URL: www.ecm.qc.ca
Natalie Watanabe, Directrice générale

Ensemble vocal Ganymède
CP 476, Succ. C, Montréal QC H2L 4K4
Tél: 514-528-6302
Courriel: contacter@evganymede.com
URL: www.evganymede.com
Yvan Sabourin, Directeur

Etobicoke Philharmonic Orchestra (EPO)
PO Box 66, Stn. D, Etobicoke ON M9A 4X1
Tel: 416-239-5665; *Fax:* 416-239-5665
e-mail: info@eporchestra.ca
URL: www.eporchestra.ca
Tom Fleming, General Manager
Carolyn McGee, Co-President
Pat Butler, Co-President

Fédération des harmonies et des orchestres symphonies du Québec (FHOSQ)
CP 1000, Succ. M, 4545, av Pierre-de-Coubertin, Montréal QC H1V 3R2
Tél: 514-252-3026; *Téléc:* 514-252-3115
Courriel: info@fhosq.org
URL: www.fhosq.org
Affiliation(s): Fédération des associations de musiciens éducateurs du Québec

Festival Chorus of Calgary
EPCOR Centre for Performing Arts, 205 - 8 Ave. SE, Calgary AB T2G 0K9
Tel: 403-294-7400
e-mail: lgneufeld@shaw.ca
URL: www.festivalchorus.ca
Mel Kirby, Artistic Director

The Foundation Assisting Canadian Talent on Recordings (FACTOR)
30 Commercial Rd., Toronto ON M5V 1Z4
Tel: 416-696-2215; *Fax:* 416-351-7311
e-mail: general.info@factor.ca
URL: www.factor.ca
Heather Ostertag, C.M., President/CEO
Phil Gumbley, Director of Operations
Julia Train, Communications Manager

Fraser Valley Symphony Society
PO Box 122, Abbotsford BC V2S 4N8
Tel: 604-859-3877
e-mail: fvssorchestra@hotmail.com
URL: www.fraservalleysymphony.ca
Lindsay Mellor, Conductor

Friends of Chamber Music
PO Box 38046, Stn. King Edward Mall, Vancouver BC V5Z 4L9
Tel: 604-437-5747; *Fax:* 604-437-4769
e-mail: fcmtickets@yahoo.com
URL: www.friendsofchambermusic.ca
Eric Wilson, Program Chair

Georgian Bay Symphony (GBS)
PO Box 133, 994 - 3rd Ave. East, Owen Sound ON N4K 5P1
Tel: 519-372-0212; *Fax:* 519-372-9023
e-mail: gbs@bmts.com
URL: www.georgianbaysymphony.ca
Social Media: www.facebook.com/pages/Georgian-Bay-Symphony/41551049364
Affiliation(s): Owen Sound Chamber of Commerce
Richard Nancarrow, President
John Barnum, Music Director

Greater Victoria Youth Orchestra (GVYO)
1611 Quadra St., Victoria BC V8W 2L5
Tel: 250-360-1121; *Fax:* 250-381-3573
e-mail: gvyo@telus.net
URL: www.gvyo.org
Affiliation(s): Community Arts Council of Greater Victoria
John Sterk, Q.C., President
Sheila Redhead, Manager

Guild of Canadian Film Composers (GCFC) / Guilde des compositeurs canadiens de musique de film
PO Box 22059, 45 Overlea Blvd., Toronto ON M4H 1N9
Tel: 416-410-5076; *Fax:* 416-410-4516
Toll-Free: 866-657-1117
e-mail: gcfc@gcfc.ca
URL: www.gcfc.ca
Maria Topalovich, Executive Director

Halton Youth Symphony (HYS)
PO Box 494, Oakville ON L6J 5A8
Tel: 905-616-2760
e-mail: manager@haltonyouthsymphony.com
URL: www.haltonyouthsymphony.com

Hamilton Philharmonic Orchestra
#1002, 105 Main St. East, Hamilton ON L8N 1G6
Tel: 905-526-1677; *Fax:* 905-526-0616
e-mail: communications@hpo.org
URL: www.hpo.org
James Sommerville, Music Director
Annelisa Pedersen, Executive Director

Hamilton Philharmonic Youth Orchestra (HPYO)
299 Fennell Ave. West, Hamilton ON L9C 1G3
Tel: 905-573-9094
e-mail: info@hpyo.com
URL: www.hpyo.com
Paul McCulloch, Music Director & Conductor

Hart House Orchestra
University of Toronto, 7 Hart House Circle, Toronto ON M5S 3H3
Tel: 416-978-5362
e-mail: webmaestro@harthouseorchestra.ca
URL: www.harthouseorchestra.ca
Zoe Dille, Programme Advisor

Huronia Symphony Orchestra (HSO)
PO Box 904, Barrie ON L4M 4Y6
Tel: 705-721-4752; *Fax:* 705-737-0679
e-mail: office@huroniasymphony.ca
URL: www.huroniasymphony.ca
David Chambers, President

International Symphony Orchestra of Sarnia, Ontario & Port Huron, Michigan
225 Davis St., Sarnia ON N7T 1B2
Tel: 519-337-7775; *Fax:* 519-337-1822
e-mail: iso@rivernet.net
URL: www.theiso.org
Affiliation(s): American Federation of Symphony Orchestras; Michigan Orchestra Association
Jerome David Summers, Music Director

International Youth Symphony Orchestra
118 North Victoria St., Sarnia ON N7T 5W9
Tel: 519-337-7775; *Fax:* 519-337-1822

Jazz Yukon
PO Box 31307, Whitehorse YT Y1A 5P7
Tel: 867-633-3300
e-mail: info@jazzyukon.ca
URL: www.jazzyukon.ca

Jeunesses Musicales of Canada (JMC) / Jeunesses musicales du Canada
305, av du Mont-Royal est, Montréal QC H2T 1P8
Tel: 514-845-4108; *Fax:* 514-845-8241
e-mail: info@jeunessesmusicales.com
URL: www.jeunessesmusicales.ca
Jacques Marquis, Executive & Artistic Director

Kamloops Intermediate Orchestra
PO Box 1387, Kamloops BC V2C 6L7
Tel: 250-554-3693
Mark Betuzzi, Music Director

Kamloops Symphony (KSO)
PO Box 57, Kamloops BC V2C 5K3
Tel: 250-372-5000; *Fax:* 250-372-5089
e-mail: info@kamloopssymphony.com
URL: www.kamloopssymphony.com
Bruce Dunn, Music Director

Kingston Symphony Association (KSA)
PO Box 1616, #206, 11 Princess St., Kingston ON K7L 5C8
Tel: 613-546-9729; *Fax:* 613-546-8580
e-mail: info@kingstonsymphony.on.ca
URL: www.kingstonsymphony.on.ca
Andrea Haughton, General Manager

Kingston Youth Orchestra
PO Box 1616, #206, 11 Princess St., Kingston ON K7L 5C8
Tel: 613-546-9729; *Fax:* 613-546-8580
Affiliation(s): Kingston Symphony Association

Kitchener-Waterloo Chamber Orchestra (KWCO)
197 Weber St. East, Kitchener ON N2H 1E5
Tel: 519-744-3828; *Fax:* 519-749-0832
e-mail: kwchamberorchestra@gmail.com
URL: www.kwchamberorchestra.ca
Joanna Armbruster, President
Graham Coles, Music Director

Kitchener-Waterloo Symphony Orchestra Association Inc. (KWSOA)
36 King St. West, Kitchener ON N2G 1A3
Tel: 519-745-4711; *Fax:* 519-745-4474
Toll-Free: 888-745-4717
e-mail: info@kwsymphony.on.ca
URL: www.kwsymphony.on.ca
Genevieve Twomey, Executive Director

Kitchener-Waterloo Symphony Youth Orchestra (KWSYO)
36 King St. West, Kitchener ON N2G 1A3
Tel: 519-745-4711
Toll-Free: 888-745-4717
e-mail: info@kwsymphony.on.ca
URL: www.kwsymphony.on.ca
Social Media: www.facebook.com/group.php?gid=2208830153
Barbara Kaplanek, Youth Strings Conductor
Julie Baumgartel, Youth Sinfonia Conductor/Director, KWSYO Chamber Music
Paul Pulford, Youth Orchestra Conductor
Peter Maness, Valhalla Brass Conductor

Kiwanis Music Festival Association of Greater Toronto
1422-A Bayview Ave., Toronto ON M4G 3A7
Tel: 416-487-5885; *Fax:* 416-487-5784
e-mail: kiwanismusic@bellnet.ca
URL: kiwanismusictoronto.org/index.html
Pam Allen, General Manager

Korean-Canadian Symphony Orchestra (KGSO)
#203, 703 Bloor St. West, Toronto ON M6G 1L5
Tel: 416-534-3760
e-mail: info@kcso.ca
URL: www.kcso.ca
Myung Sook Kim, President
Richard Lee, Music Director

Lethbridge Symphony Orchestra
PO Box 1101, Lethbridge AB T1J 4A2
Tel: 403-328-6808; *Fax:* 403-380-4418
e-mail: info@lethbridgesymphony.org
URL: www.lethbridgesymphony.org
Glenn Klassen, Music Director, Artistic, Special P
Dawn Leite, General Manager

London Community Orchestra (LCO)
c/o 838 Wellington St. N., London ON N6A 3S7
Tel: 519-433-2074
e-mail: sally.vernon@odyssey.on.ca
URL: www.ontera.net/~lco/
Leonard Ingrao, Music Director
Margaret Whitby, Manager
Ray Thomson, President

London Youth Symphony (LYS)
PO Box 553, Stn. B, London ON N6A 4W8
Tel: 519-686-8070
e-mail: info@londonyouthsymphony.org
URL: www.londonyouthsymphony.org
Len Ingrao, Musical Director
Daina Janitis, Manager

Manitoba Band Association
15 Pinecrest Bay, Winnipeg MB R2G 1W2
Tel: 204-663-1226; *Fax:* 204-663-1226
e-mail: mbband@shaw.ca
URL: www.mbband.org
Wendy McCallum, President

Manitoba Chamber Orchestra (MCO)
Portage Place, 393 Portage Ave., #Y300, Winnipeg MB R3B 3H6
Tel: 204-783-7377; *Fax:* 204-783-7383
e-mail: mco@mts.net
URL: www.manitobachamberorchestra.org
Anne Manson, Music Director
Vicki Young, General Manager

Manitoba Opera Association Inc.
Lower Level, Centennial Concert Hall, #105, 555 Main St., Winnipeg MB R3B 1C3
Tel: 204-942-7479; *Fax:* 204-949-0377
e-mail: mbopera@manitobaopera.mb.ca
URL: www.manitobaopera.mb.ca
Social Media: www.twitter.com/ManitobaOpera
Affiliation(s): Opera America; Canadian Actor's Equity; Opera.ca
Peter George, President

Mariposa Folk Foundation
PO Box 383, Orillia ON L3V 6J8
Tel: 705-326-3655; *Fax:* 705-329-4099
e-mail: info@mariposafolk.com
URL: www.mariposafolk.com
Catherine Brennan, President

Mississauga Youth Orchestra
159 Cavendish Ct., Mississauga ON L6J 5S3
Tel: 905-815-8125; *Fax:* 905-815-8516
e-mail: email@myomusic.ca
URL: www.myomusic.ca
Kathy Grell, Manager

Music for Young Children (MYC) / Musique pour jeunes enfants
39 Leacock Way, Kanata ON K2K 1T1
Tel: 613-592-7565; *Fax:* 613-592-9353
Toll-Free: 800-561-1692
e-mail: myc@myc.com
URL: www.myc.com
Janice Reade, Manager, Public Relations

Music Industries Association of Canada (MIAC) / Association canadienne des industries de la musique
#807, 505 Consumers Rd., Toronto ON M2J 4V8
Tel: 416-490-1871; *Fax:* 416-490-0369
Toll-Free: 877-480-6422
e-mail: info@miac.net
URL: www.miac.net
Affiliation(s): Music Distributors Association - USA; National Association of Music Merchants - USA
Barbara Cole, General Manager

Music Nova Scotia
#302, 5516 Spring Garden Rd., Halifax NS B3J 1G6
Tel: 902-423-6271; *Fax:* 902-423-8841
Toll-Free: 888-343-6426
e-mail: info@musicnovascotia.ca
URL: www.musicnovascotia.ca
Brian Doherty, President
Scott Long, Executive Director

Music NWT
Roman Empire Bldg., 5103 51st St., 2nd Fl., Yellowknife NT X1A 1S8
Tel: 867-873-5577; *Fax:* 867-873-5575
e-mail: info@musicnwt.ca
URL: www.musicnwt.ca

Music PEI
#70, 90 University Ave., Charlottetown PE C1A 4K9
Tel: 902-894-6734
e-mail: music@musicpei.com
URL: www.musicpei.com
Shannon Pratt, President
Rob Oakie, Executive Director

Musicaction
#2, 4385, rue Saint-Hubert, Montréal QC H2J 2X1
Tél: 514-861-8444; *Téléc:* 514-861-4423
Ligne sans frais: 800-861-5561
Courriel: info@musicaction.ca
URL: www.musicaction.ca
Andrée Ménard, Directrice générale

National Arts Centre Orchestra of Canada (NACO) / Orchestre du Centre national des Arts (OCNA)
PO Box 1534, Stn. B, 53 Elgin St., Ottawa ON K1P 5W1
Tel: 613-947-7000
Toll-Free: 866-850-2787
e-mail: info@nac-cna.ca
URL: www.nac-cna.ca
Social Media: www.facebook.com/CanadasNAC; www.twitter.com/canadasnac
Pinchas Zukerman, Music Director
Alex Gazalé, Production Director
Christopher Deacon, Managing Director

National Shevchenko Musical Ensemble Guild of Canada
626 Bathurst St., Toronto ON M5S 2R1
Tel: 416-533-2725; *Fax:* 416-533-6348
e-mail: info_sme@bellnet.ca
URL: www.shevchenkomusic.com
Ginger Kautto, General Manager

National Youth Orchestra Association of Canada
#500, 59 Adelaide St. East, Toronto ON M5C 1K6
Tel: 416-532-4470; *Fax:* 416-532-6879
Toll-Free: 888-532-4470
e-mail: info@nyoc.org
URL: www.nyoc.org
Social Media: www.twitter.com/nyoc_onjc
Barbara Smith, Executive Director

Newfoundland Symphony Orchestra Association (NSO)
Arts & Culture Centre, PO Box 1854, St. John's NL A1C 5P9
Tel: 709-722-4441; *Fax:* 709-753-0561
e-mail: nso.orchestra@nso.nfld.net
URL: www.nso-music.com
Peter Gardner, General & Artistic Director
Alasdair Black, Operations Manager
G.C. (Gerry) Germain, Chair

Newfoundland Symphony Youth Orchestra (NSYO)
PO Box 1854, St. John's NL A1C 5P9
Tel: 709-722-4441; *Fax:* 709-753-0561
Peter Gardner, Director

Niagara Youth Orchestra Association
#148, 12 - 111 Fourth Ave., St Catharines ON L2S 3P5
Tel: 905-704-0559; *Fax:* 905-704-0558
e-mail: nyo@vaxxine.com
URL: www.niagarayouthorchestra.ca
Affiliation(s): Niagara Suzuki
Michael Newnham, Music Director

Northumberland Orchestra Society (NOC)
PO Box 1012, Cobourg ON K9A 4W4
Tel: 905-377-1477
e-mail: norchestra@norchestra.org
URL: www.norchestra.org
Michael Newnham, Music Director & Conductor

Nova Scotia Band Association
355 Branch St, New Glasgow NS B2H 3A5
Tel: 902-751-5996; *Fax:* 902-755-8490
e-mail: admin@novascotiabandassociation.com
URL: www.novascotiabandassociation.com
Barbara Stetter, President

Nova Scotia Youth Orchestra
6199 Chebucto Rd., Halifax NS B3L 1K7
Tel: 902-423-5984
e-mail: nsyo@ns.sympatico.ca
URL: www.novascotiayouthorchestra.com
Dinuk Wijeratne, Music Director

Oakville Chamber Orchestra
PO Box 76036, 1500 Upper Middle Rd. West, Oakville ON L6M 3H5
Tel: 905-483-6787
e-mail: mail@oakvillechamber.org
URL: www.oakvillechamber.org
Charlotte Meissner, President
Charles Demuynck, Music Director

Oakville Symphony Orchestra (OSO)
#114, 99 Bronte Rd., Oakville ON L6L 3B7

Tel: 905-338-1462; *Fax:* 905-338-7954
e-mail: oakville.symphony@cogeco.ca
URL: www.oakvillesymphony.com
Affiliation(s): Oakville Arts Council
Peggy Steele, General Manager

Okanagan Symphony Society
PO Box 20238, #239, 1899 Springfield Road, Kelowna BC V1Y 9H2
Tel: 250-763-7544; *Fax:* 250-763-3553
e-mail: admin@okanagansymphony.com
URL: www.okanagansymphony.com
Rosemary Thomson, Music Director

Ontario Band Association
c/o Membership Co-ordinator, 459 Concord Ave., Toronto ON M6H 2P9
e-mail: membership@onband.ca
URL: www.onband.ca
Sarah Arcand, President
Sommer Buttu, Secretary

L'Opéra de Montréal (ODM) / Montréal Opera
260, boul de Maisonneuve ouest, Montréal QC H2X 1Y9
Tel: 514-985-2222; *Fax:* 514-985-2219
e-mail: info@operademontreal.com
URL: www.operademontreal.com
Social Media:
www.facebook.com/pages/Opera-de-Montreal/23275515418
Affiliation(s): Professional Opera Companies of Canada; Opera America
Pierre Dufour, General & Production Director
Christine Krebs, Administrative Director
Michel Beulac, Artistic Director
Monique Denis, Donations & Sponsorship Manager
Pierre Vachon, Communications & Marketing Director
Alexandre Taillefer, Chair
Chantal Lambert, Atelier Lyrique Program Director

Opéra de Québec
1220, av Taché, Québec QC G1R 3B4
Tél: 418-529-4142; *Téléc:* 418-529-3735
Courriel: operaqc@mediom.qc.ca
URL: www.operadequebec.qc.ca
Gaston Déry, Président

Opera Lyra Ottawa
#110, 2 Daly Ave., Ottawa ON K1N 6E2
Tel: 613-233-9200; *Fax:* 613-233-5431
Toll-Free: 877-233-5972
e-mail: marketing@operalyra.com
URL: www.operalyra.ca
Elizabeth Howarth, General Director

Opera Ontario
Opera Hamilton, #905, 105 Main St. East, Hamilton ON L8N 1G6
Tel: 905-527-7627; *Fax:* 905-527-0014
Toll-Free: 800-575-1381
e-mail: info@operaontario.com
URL: www.operaontario.com
Alice Willems, President
David Speers, General Director

Opera.ca
#410, 174 Spadina Ave., Toronto ON M5T 2C2
Tel: 416-591-7222
e-mail: info@opera.ca
URL: www.opera.ca
Christina Loewen, Executive Director
Sandra Cina, Coordinator, Membership & Communications

Orchestra London Canada Inc.
609 Wellington St., London ON N6A 3R6
Tel: 519-679-8558; *Fax:* 519-679-8914
e-mail: rgloor@orchestralondon.ca
URL: www.orchestralondon.ca
Robert Gloor, Executive Director
Brent Kelman, President

Orchestra Toronto (OT)
#402, 131 Beecroft Rd., Toronto ON M2N 6G9
Tel: 416-467-7142
e-mail: otoronto@on.aibn.com
URL: www.orchestratoronto.ca
Social Media:
www.facebook.com/pages/Orchestra-Toronto/172229189138
Judy Mann, Contact
Erroll Gay, Music Director

Orchestras Canada (OC) / Orchestres Canada
230-460 College St., Toronto ON M6G 1A1
Tel: 416-366-8834; *Fax:* 416-366-1780
e-mail: info@oc.ca
URL: orchestrascanada.org
Social Media: www.facebook.com/orchestrascanada?ref=ts
Affiliation(s): American Symphony Orchestra League; International Alliance of Orchestra Associations
Katherine Carleton, Executive Director

Orchestras Mississauga
4141 Living Arts Dr., Mississauga ON L5B 4B8
Tel: 905-615-4405; *Fax:* 905-615-4402
e-mail: symphony.info@livingarts.on.ca
URL: www.mississaugasymphony.ca
Social Media:
www.facebook.com/group.php?v=wall&gid=14456410182
Affiliation(s): Mississauga Board of Trade; Orchestras Canada; Mississauga Arts Council
John Barnum, Music Director
Eileen Keown, General Manager

Orchestre de chambre de Montréal (OCM) / Montréal Chamber Orchestra (MCO)
5476 Côte St-Antoine, Montréal QC H4A 1R2
Tél: 514-871-1224; *Téléc:* 514-871-8967
Courriel: info@mco-ocm.qc.ca
URL: www.mco-ocm.qc.ca
Wanda Kaluzny, Music Director

Orchestre symphonique de Montréal
260, boul de Maisonneuve ouest, 2e étage, Montréal QC H2X 1Y9
Tél: 514-842-3402; *Téléc:* 514-842-0728
URL: www.osm.ca
Mèdia social: www.twitter.com/OSM_official
Madeleine Careau, Chef de la direction
René Mandel, Directeur musical

Orchestre symphonique de Québec
401, av Grande Allée est, Québec QC G1R 2J5
Tél: 418-643-8486; *Téléc:* 418-646-9665
Courriel: billetterie@osq.qc.ca
URL: www.osq.qc.ca
Jean Letarte, Directeur artistique

Orchestre symphonique de Trois-Rivières (OSTR)
CP 1281, Trois-Rivières QC G9A 5K8
Tél: 819-373-5340; *Téléc:* 819-373-6693
Courriel: administration@ostr.ca
URL: www.ostr.ca
Affiliation(s): Guilde des musiciens (AFM)
Thérèse Boutin, Directrice générale
Jacques Lacombe, Directeur artistique
Jean-Marc Vanasse, Président

Orchestre symphonique des jeunes de la Montérégie
31, rue Lorne, Saint-Lambert QC J4P 2G7
Tél: 450-923-3733
Courriel: courrier@aojm.org
URL: www.aojm.org
Jean-Claude Paré, Président

Orchestre symphonique des jeunes de Montréal (OSJM)
CP 83566, Succ. Succursale Garnier, Montréal QC H2J 4E9
Tél: 514-645-0311; *Téléc:* 514-524-9894
Courriel: osjmontreal@gmail.ca
URL: www.osjm.org
Jean-Paul Lejeune, Président

Orchestre symphonique des jeunes du West Island (OSJWI) / West Island Youth Symphony Orchestra (WIYSO)
CP 1028, Succ. Pointe-Claire, Pointe-Claire QC H9S 4H9
Tél: 514-633-1128; *Téléc:* 514-633-1129
Courriel: info@osjwi.qc.ca
URL: www.osjwi.qc.ca
Affiliation(s): Association des orchestres de jeunes du Québec
Isabelle Delage, Présidente

Orchestre symphonique des jeunes Philippe-Filion
2100, boul des Hêtres, Shawinigan QC G9N 8R8
Tél: 819-539-6000; *Téléc:* 819-539-2400
Courriel: morind03@cgocable.ca
Monique Gagnon Carbonneau, Directrice Musicale

Orchestre symphonique du Saguenay-Lac-St-Jean (OSSLSJ)
202, rue Jacques-Cartier est, Chicoutimi QC G7H 6R8
Tél: 418-545-3409; *Téléc:* 418-545-8287
Courriel: info@lorchestre.org
URL: www.lorchestre.org
Jacques Clément, Directeur artisique

Orchestre symphonique régional Abitibi-Témiscamingue
CP 2305, Rouyn-Noranda QC J9X 5A9
Tél: 819-762-0043; *Téléc:* 819-762-0274
Courriel: osr@tlb.sympatico.ca
URL: culture-at.org/osr
Mèdia social: www.facebook.com/group.php?gid=359183264101
Réginald Grenier, Président

Organization of Canadian Symphony Musicians (OCSM) / Organisation des musiciens d'orchestres symphoniques du Canada (OMOSC)
#6, 445, rue Gerard-Morrisset, Québec QC G1S 4V5
Tel: 418-688-0801
URL: www.ocsm-omosc.org
Affiliation(s): Association of Canadian Orchestras; Canadian Conference of the Arts
Francine Schutzman, President
Eline Brock Sanheim, First Vice-President
David Brown, 2nd Vice-President
Robert Fraser, Secretary
Greg Sheldon, Treasurer

Orillia Youth Symphony Orchestra (OYSO)
168 Parkview Ave., Orillia ON L3V 4M3
Tel: 705-326-7548
URL: www.oyso.ca
Mayumi Kumagai, Music Director

Oshawa-Durham Symphony Orchestra (ODSO)
PO Box 444, Oshawa ON L1H 7L5
Tel: 905-579-6711; *Fax:* 905-987-3083
e-mail: contact@odso.ca
URL: www.odso.ca
John G. Patte, Business Manager
Ronald H. Stead, Chair

Ottawa Symphony Orchestra Inc. (OSO) / Orchestre symphonique d'Ottawa
#250, 2 Daly Ave., Ottawa ON K1N 6E2
Tel: 613-231-7802; *Fax:* 613-231-3610
e-mail: oso@on.aibn.com
URL: www.ottawasymphony.com
David Currie, Music Director

Ottawa Youth Orchestra Academy (OYO) / L'Orchestre des jeunes d'Ottawa
#1, 54 Beech Street, Ottawa ON K1S 3J6
Tel: 613-233-9318; *Fax:* 613-233-5038
e-mail: info@oyoa-aojo.ca
URL: www.oyoa-aojo.ca
John Gomez, Music Director

Pacific Opera Victoria (POV)
#500, 1815 Blanshard St., Victoria BC V8T 5A1
Tel: 250-382-1641; *Fax:* 250-382-4944
e-mail: dshefsiek@pov.bc.ca
URL: www.pov.bc.ca
Timothy Vernon, Artistic Director
David Shefsiek, Executive Director

Pembroke Symphony Orchestra
PO Box 374, Pembroke ON K8A 6X6
Tel: 613-687-2660
e-mail: info@pembrokesymphony.org
URL: pembrokesymphony.org
Angus Armstrong, Concertmaster
Gail Marion, President

Peterborough Symphony Orchestra (PSO)
PO Box 1135, Peterborough ON K9J 7H4
Tel: 705-742-1992; *Fax:* 705-742-2077
Toll-Free: 877-742-1992
e-mail: info@thepso.org
URL: www.thepso.org
Affiliation(s): Peterborough Chamber of Commerce
Michael Newnham, Music Director

Prince Edward Island Symphony Society (PEISO)
PO Box 185, 146 Richmond St., Charlottetown PE C1A 7K4
Tel: 902-892-4333
e-mail: peiso@peisymphony.com
URL: www.peisymphony.com
Annette Campbell, Contact

Prince George Symphony Orchestra Society (PGSO)
2880 - 15 Ave., Prince George BC V2M 1T1
Tel: 250-562-0800; *Fax:* 250-562-0844
e-mail: admin@pgso.com
URL: www.pgso.com
Ruth Langner, General Manager

The Queen of Puddings Music Theatre Company
The Case Good Warehouse, Bldg. 74, Studio 206, 55 Mill St., Toronto ON M5A 3C4
Tel: 416-203-4149; *Fax:* 416-203-8027
e-mail: queenofpuddings@bellnet.ca
URL: www.queenofpuddingsmusictheatre.com
Dairine Ni Mheadhra, Artistic Director
John Hess, Artistic Director

Quinte Symphony
PO Box 23087, Belleville ON K8P 5J3
Tel: 613-395-3756
e-mail: info@quintesymphony.com
URL: www.quintesymphony.com
Gordon Craig, Music Director
Judith Chalmers, President

Red Deer Symphony Orchestra
Cultural Services Building, PO Box 1116, 3827, 39th St., Red Deer AB T4N 6S5
Tel: 403-340-2948; *Fax:* 403-309-4612
e-mail: reddeersymphony@telus.net
URL: www.rdso.ca
Melody McKnight, Executive Director
Claude Lapalme, Music Director

Regina Symphony Orchestra (RSO)
2424 College Ave., Regina SK S4P 1C8
Tel: 306-586-9555; *Fax:* 306-586-2133
Toll-Free: 800-667-8497
e-mail: info@reginasymphony.com
URL: www.reginasymphony.com
Affiliation(s): Saskatchewan Arts Alliance
Victor Sawa, Musical Director
Natasha Bood, Executive Director

Richmond Community Orchestra & Chorus
#130, 10691 Shellbridge Way, Richmond BC V6X 2W8
Tel: 604-276-2747; *Fax:* 604-270-3644
e-mail: roca.office@gmail.com
URL: www.roca.ca
Sue Tench, Administrator

Royal Canadian College of Organists (RCCO) / Collège royal canadien des organistes (CRCO)
#202, 204 St. George St., Toronto ON M5R 2N5
Tel: 416-929-6400; *Fax:* 416-929-2265
e-mail: manager@rcco.ca
URL: www.rcco.ca
Valerie Hall, President

Royal Conservatory Orchestra
273 Bloor Street West, Toronto ON M5S 1W2
Tel: 416-408-2824; *Fax:* 416-408-3096
e-mail: glenngouldschool@rcmusic.ca
URL: www.rcmusic.ca
Social Media: www.twitter.com/the_rcm
Affiliation(s): The Glenn Gould School
Mervon Mehta, Executive Director

Saskatchewan Band Association (SBA)
34 Sunset Dr. North, Yorkton SK S3N 3K9
Tel: 306-783-2263; *Fax:* 306-783-2060
Toll-Free: 877-475-2263
e-mail: sask.band@sasktel.net
URL: www.saskband.org
Adrian Bourgeois, President
Christa MacBride, Vice-President
Chistin Dorgan-Lee, Secretary
Aaron Sikora, Treasurer

Saskatchewan Orchestral Association (SOA)
PO Box 87, Hanley SK S0G 2E0
Tel: 306-544-2230; *Fax:* 306-544-2718
e-mail: soa1@sasktel.net
URL: www.saskorchestras.com
Affiliation(s): SaskCulture
Kathryn Peters, Contact

Saskatoon Symphony Society (SSO)
Standard Life Bldg., #120, 128 Fourth Ave. South, Saskatoon SK S7K 1M8
Tel: 306-665-6414; *Fax:* 306-652-3364
e-mail: saskatoon.symphony@sasktel.net
URL: www.saskatoonsymphony.org
Catherine McKeehan, General Manager

Saskatoon Youth Orchestra
1610 Morgan Ave., Saskatoon SK S7H 2S1
Tel: 306-373-6408; *Fax:* 306-955-6336
e-mail: syo@sasktel.net
URL: toeww.sasktelwebsite.net/SYO.html
Wayne Toews, Music Director

Sault Symphony Association / Orchestre symphonique de Sault Ste-Marie
#2, 121 Brock St., Sault Ste Marie ON P6A 3B6
Tel: 705-945-5337; *Fax:* 705-945-8865
e-mail: symphony@soonet.ca
URL: www.saultsymphony.com
Patti Gardi, General Manager

Scarborough Philharmonic Orchestra
#209, 3007 Kingston Rd., Toronto ON M1M 1P1
Tel: 416-429-0007
e-mail: spo@spo.ca
URL: www.spo.ca

Scotia Chamber Players
6181 Lady Hammond Rd., Halifax NS B3K 2R9
Tel: 902-429-9467; *Fax:* 902-425-6785
e-mail: admin@scotiafestival.ns.ca
URL: www.scotiafestival.ns.ca
Christopher Wilcox, Managing Director

Société chorale de Saint-Lambert / St. Lambert Choral Society
CP 36546, Succ. CSP Victoria, Saint-Lambert QC J4P 3S8
URL: www.chorale-stlambert.qc.ca
Nancy Kirkwood, President
David Christiani, Music Director
Kimberley Bartczak, Accompanist

Société Pro Musica Inc. / Pro Musica Society Inc.
3450, rue Saint-Urbain, Montréal QC H2X 2N5
Tél: 514-845-0532; *Téléc:* 514-845-1500
Ligne sans frais: 877-445-0532
Courriel: concerts@promusica.qc.ca
URL: www.promusica.qc.ca
Pierre Rolland, Directeur artistique
Monique Dubé, Directrice générale

Songwriters Association of Canada (SAC) / Association des auteurs-compositeurs canadiens
129 John St., Toronto ON M5V 2E2
Tel: 416-961-1588; *Fax:* 416-961-2040
Toll-Free: 866-456-7664
e-mail: sacadmin@songwriters.ca
URL: www.songwriters.ca
Don Quarles, Executive Director
Eddie Schwartz, President

Soundstreams Canada
#200, 57 Spadina Ave., Toronto ON M5V 2J2
Tel: 416-504-1282; *Fax:* 416-504-1285
e-mail: info@soundstreams.ca
URL: www.soundstreams.ca
Jennifer Winchester, General Manager

South Saskatchewan Youth Orchestra (SSYO)
101 Leopold Cres., Regina SK S4T 6N5
Tel: 306-586-3007; *Fax:* 306-586-2133
e-mail: ssyo.ca@gmail.com
URL: www.ssyo.ca
Affiliation(s): Regina Symphony Orchestra
Alan Denike, Music Director

Sudbury Symphony Orchestra Association Inc. (SSO) / Orchestre symphonique de Sudbury inc
#266, 303 York St., Sudbury ON P3E 2A5
Tel: 705-673-1280; *Fax:* 705-673-1434
e-mail: symphon1@bellnet.ca
URL: www.sudburysymphony.com
Victor Sawa, Artistic Director
Marg Barry, Executive Director

Sudbury Youth Orchestra Inc.
PO Box 2241, Stn. A, Sudbury ON P3A 4S1
Tel: 705-566-8101
e-mail: info@sudburyyouthorchestra.ca
URL: www.sudburyyouthorchestra.ca
Jamie Arrowsmith, Music Director
Mary Salem Charette, Director

Surrey Symphony Society (SSS)
#181, 6832 King George Hwy., Surrey BC V3W 4Z9
Tel: 604-572-9225
e-mail: inquiries@surreyyouthorchestra.org
URL: www.surreyyouthorchestra.org
Lucille Lewis, Music Director
Carla Birston, Intermediate Strings Conductor
Margaret LaBelle, Business Manager
Rick Dorfer, Junior Strings Conductor

Symphony Hamilton
PO Box 89007, 991 King St. West, Hamilton ON L8S 4R5
Tel: 905-526-6690
e-mail: info@symphonyhamilton.ca
URL: www.symphonyhamilton.ca
Affiliation(s): Hamilton & Region Arts Council
James R. McKay, Music Director & Conductor
Brenda Sandberg, General Manager
Sydney Hassel, President

Symphony New Brunswick / Symphonie Nouveau-Brunswick
Brunswick Square, 39 King St., Level III, Saint John NB E2L 4W3
Tel: 506-634-8379; *Fax:* 506-634-0843
e-mail: symphony@nbnet.nb.ca
URL: www.symphonynb.com
Affiliation(s): American Federation of Musicians
Caroline Condon, General Manager

Symphony Nova Scotia (SNS)
Park Lane Mall, PO Box 218, #301, 5657 Spring Garden Rd., Halifax NS B3J 3R4
Tel: 902-421-1300; *Fax:* 902-422-1209
e-mail: info@symns.cohn.dal.ca
URL: www.symphonynovascotia.ca
Erika Beatty, Chief Executive Officer

Tafelmusik Baroque Orchestra & Chamber Choir
PO Box 14, 427 Bloor St. West, Toronto ON M5S 1X7
Tel: 416-964-9562; *Fax:* 416-964-2782
e-mail: info@tafelmusik.org
URL: www.tafelmusik.org
Tricia Baldwin, Managing Director
Tricia Baldwin, Managing Director

Tapestry New Opera Works
The Cannery, Studio 316, #58, 55 Mill St., Toronto ON M5A 3C4
Tel: 416-537-6066; *Fax:* 416-537-7841
e-mail: information@tapestrynewopera.com
URL: www.tapestrynewopera.com
Wayne Strongman, Artistic Director

Thunder Bay Symphony Orchestra Association (TBSO)
PO Box 29192, Thunder Bay ON P7B 6P9
Tel: 807-345-4331; *Fax:* 807-622-1927
e-mail: info@tbso.ca
URL: www.tbso.ca
Elizabeth Poulin, President
Leanne Atkinson, General Manager
Geoffrey Moull, Music Director

Timmins Symphony Orchestra
PO Box 1365, Timmins ON P4N 7N2
Tel: 705-267-1006; *Fax:* 705-267-1006
e-mail: tsoffice@ntl.sympatico.ca
URL: www.timsym.com

Toronto Chinese Youth Orchestra
21 Holmesdale Dr., Markham ON L6C 1S9
Tel: 905-887-7828
e-mail: tcyo@rogers.com
URL: www.tcyo.ca
Tak-Ng Lai, Music Director

Toronto Downtown Jazz Society
82 Bleecker St., Toronto ON M4X 1L8
Tel: 416-928-2033; *Fax:* 416-928-0533
e-mail: tdjs@tojazz.com
URL: www.torontojazz.com
Social Media: www.facebook.com/group.php?gid=8698568268
Patrick Taylor, CEO/Executive Producer
Josh Grossman, Artistic Director

The Toronto Mendelssohn Choir
60 Simcoe St., Toronto ON M5J 2H5
Tel: 416-598-0422; *Fax:* 416-598-2992
e-mail: manager@tmchoir.org
URL: www.tmchoir.org
Cynthia Hawkins, Executive Director

Toronto Philharmonia
#109, 1210 Sheppard Ave. East, Toronto ON M2K 1E3
Tel: 416-499-2204; *Fax:* 416-490-9739
e-mail: office@torontophil.on.ca
URL: www.torontophil.on.ca
Affiliation(s): Ontario Federation of Symphony Orchestras
Kerry Stratton, Music Director

Toronto Philharmonia Youth Orchestra
PO Box 134, Port Hope ON L1W 3W3
Tel: 416-797-2138
Toll-Free: 866-460-5596

e-mail: info@ljyo.ca
URL: www.ljyo.ca
Michael Lyons, Music Director

Toronto Sinfonietta
400 St. Clair Avenue E, Toronto ON M4T 1P5
Tel: 416-410-4379; *Fax:* 416-233-1054
e-mail: info@torontosinfonietta.com
URL: www.torontosinfonietta.com
Krzysztof Liebert, President
Matthew Jaskiewicz, Music Director

Toronto Symphony Orchestra (TSO)
212 King St. West, 6th Fl., Toronto ON M5H 1K5
Tel: 416-593-7769; *Fax:* 416-977-2912
URL: www.tso.ca
Social Media: www.facebook.com/group.php?gid=52219459772
Peter Oundjian, Musical Director
Andrew R. Shaw, President/CEO

Toronto Symphony Youth Orchestra (TSYO)
212 King St. West, 6th Fl., Toronto ON M5H 1K5
Tel: 416-593-7769; *Fax:* 416-977-2912
e-mail: cmatt@tso.ca
URL: www.tso.on.ca
Affiliation(s): Toronto Symphony Orchestra
Christy DiFelice, Manager

University of Toronto Symphony Orchestra
Faculty of Music, University of Toronto, 80 Queen's Park Cres., Toronto ON M5S 2C5
Tel: 416-978-3733; *Fax:* 416-946-3353
e-mail: performance.music@utoronto.ca
URL: www.music.utoronto.ca
David Briskin, Conductor

University of Western Ontario Symphony Orchestra (UWOSO)
Faculty of Music, University of Western Ontario, 1151 Richmond St. North, London ON N6A 3K7
Tel: 519-661-2043; *Fax:* 519-661-3531
e-mail: music@uwo.ca
URL: www.music.uwo.ca

Vancouver Island Symphony
PO Box 661, 150 Commercial St., Nanaimo BC V9R 5L9
Tel: 250-754-0177; *Fax:* 250-754-0165
e-mail: info@vancouverislandsymphony.com
URL: www.viso.bc.ca
Margot Holmes, Executive Director
David W. Covey, President

Vancouver New Music (VNM)
837 Davie St., Vancouver BC V6Z 1B7
Tel: 604-633-0861; *Fax:* 604-633-0871
e-mail: info@newmusic.org
URL: www.newmusic.org
Affiliation(s): Canadian Music Centre
Giorgio Magnanensi, Artistic Director
Nicolas Bragg, President

Vancouver Opera (VOA) / Association de l'opéra de vancouver
835 Cambie St., Vancouver BC V6B 2P4
Tel: 604-682-2871; *Fax:* 604-682-3981
e-mail: tickets@vancouveropera.ca
URL: www.vancouveropera.ca
Social Media: www.facebook.com/vancouveropera
Affiliation(s): Canadian Actors' Equity Association; IATSE; AFM
James W. Wright, Geneeral Director

Vancouver Philharmonic Orchestra (VPO)
PO Box 27503, Stn. Oakridge, Vancouver BC V5Z 4M4
Tel: 604-878-9989
e-mail: vpo@vcn.bc.ca
URL: www.vanphil.ca
Cathy McCashin, President
Maura Gauditis, Vice-President
Katherine Bailey, Treasurer

Vancouver Symphony Society
601 Smithe St., Vancouver BC V6B 5G1
Tel: 604-684-9100; *Fax:* 604-684-9264
e-mail: customerservice@vancouversymphony.ca
URL: www.vancouversymphony.ca
Jeff Alexander, President & CEO
Mary-Ann Moir, Vice-President, Finance & Administration

Vancouver Youth Symphony Orchestra Society (VYSO)
3214 - 10 Ave. West, Vancouver BC V6K 2L2
Tel: 604-737-0714; *Fax:* 604-737-0739
e-mail: vyso@telus.net
URL: www.vyso.com
Roger Cole, Artistic Director
Holly Littleford, Orchestra Manager

Victoria Symphony
#610, 620 View St., Victoria BC V8W 1J6
Tel: 250-385-9771; *Fax:* 250-385-7767
e-mail: administration@victoriasymphony.ca
URL: www.victoriasymphony.ca
Stephen Smith, Interim Executive Director
Deedrie Ballard, President
Tania Miller, Music Director

Western Canadian Music Alliance (WCMA)
#637, 776 Corydon Ave., Winnipeg MB R3M 0Y1
Tel: 204-943-8485; *Fax:* 204-453-1594
e-mail: info@wcmw.ca
URL: www.wcmw.ca
Affiliation(s): Alberta Recording Industry Association; Saskatchewan Recording Industry Association; Manitoba Audio Recording Industry Association
Bob D'Eith, President

Wilfrid Laurier University Symphony Orchestra
Faculty of Music, 75 University Ave. West, Waterloo ON N2L 3C5
Tel: 519-884-0710; *Fax:* 519-747-9129
e-mail: jdupuis@wlu.ca
Paul Pulford, General Manager/Music Director

Windsor Symphony Orchestra (WSO)
487 Ouellette Ave., Windsor ON N9A 4J2
Tel: 519-973-1238; *Fax:* 519-973-0764
Toll-Free: 888-327-8327
e-mail: jgalli@windsorsymphony.com
URL: www.windsorsymphony.com
Affiliation(s): American Symphony Orchestra League
Jeth Mill, Exectuive Director
Rob Gold, Director of Marketing
Sarah Boonstra, Director of Operations

Winnipeg Symphony Orchestra Inc. (WSO)
#101, 555 Main St., Winnipeg MB R3B 1C3
Tel: 204-949-3950; *Fax:* 204-956-4271
e-mail: lmarks@wso.mb.ca
URL: www.wso.mb.ca
Trudy Schroeder, Executive Director
Alexander Mickelthwate, Music Director

York Symphony Orchestra Inc.
PO Box 355, Richmond Hill ON L4C 4Y6
Tel: 416-410-0860
e-mail: yorksymphonyorchestra@hotmail.com
URL: www.yorksymphony.ca
Affiliation(s): York Symphony Youth Orchestra
Gregory Burton, Music Director

Performing Arts - Theatre

The Actors' Fund of Canada / La Caisse des acteurs du Canada inc.
#301, 1000 Yonge St., Toronto ON M4W 2K2
Tel: 416-975-0304; *Fax:* 416-975-0306
Toll-Free: 877-399-8392
e-mail: contact@actorsfund.ca
URL: www.actorsfund.ca
Barry Flatman, President

Alberta Playwrights' Network (APN)
2633 Hochwald Ave. SW, Calgary AB T3E 7K2
Tel: 403-269-8564; *Fax:* 403-265-6773
Toll-Free: 800-268-8564
e-mail: admin@albertaplaywrights.com
URL: www.albertaplaywrights.com
Johanne Deleeuw, Executive Director
Brian Dooley, Edmonton Liaison

Association of Summer Theatres 'Round Ontario (ASTRO)
c/o Theatre Ontario, #210, 215 Spadina Ave., Toronto ON M5T 2C7
Tel: 416-408-4556; *Fax:* 416-408-3402
e-mail: tim@theatreontario.org
URL: www.summertheatre.org
Affiliation(s): Theatre Ontario; Professional Association of Canadian Theatres; Canadian Actors' Equity Association; Tourism Federation of Ontario
Steven Thomas, President

Association québécoise des marionnettistes (AQM)
Centre UNIMA-CANADA (section Québec), CP 7, Succ. de Lorimier, #300, 7755 boul Saint-Laurent, Montréal QC H2H 2N6
Tél: 514-522-1919; *Téléc:* 514-521-3737
Courriel: aqm@aei.ca
URL: www.aqm.ca
Hélène Ducharme, Président

Bard on the Beach Theatre Society
#301, 601 Cambie St., Vancouver BC V6B 2P1
Tel: 604-737-0625; *Fax:* 604-737-0425
Toll-Free: 877-739-0559
e-mail: info@bardonthebeach.org
URL: www.bardonthebeach.org
Social Media: www.facebook.com/bardonthebeach
Christopher Gaze, Artistic Director
Robert Barr, Managing Director

Black Theatre Workshop (BTW)
#432, 3680 Jeanne-Mance, Montréal QC H2X 2K5
Tel: 514-932-1104; *Fax:* 514-932-6311
URL: www.blacktheatreworkshop.ca
Tyrone Benskin, Artistic Director
Jacklin Webb, President

British Columbia Drama Association
PO Box 2031, #7, 10 Commercial St., Nanaimo BC V9R 6X6
Tel: 250-591-0018; *Fax:* 250-591-0027
e-mail: info@theatrebc.org
URL: www.theatrebc.org
Affiliation(s): Centre for the Arts Nanaimo
Robb Mowbray, Executive Director
Ray Mordan, President
Ray Mordan, Sec.-Treas.

Buddies in Bad Times Theatre
12 Alexander St., Toronto ON M4Y 1B4
Tel: 416-975-9130; *Fax:* 416-975-9293
e-mail: chy@artsexy.ca
URL: www.artsexy.ca
Brendan Healy, Artistic Director

Canadian Association for Theatre Research (CATR) / Association canadienne de la recherche théâtrale (ACRT)
#2, 40 River St., Toronto ON M5A 3N9
e-mail: nicholsg@umoncton.ca
URL: www.catr-acrt.ca
Kym Bird, Secretary
Shelley Scott, President
James Dugan, Treasurer

Canadian Institute for Theatre Technology (CITT) / L'Institut Canadien des Technologies Scénographiques (ICTS)
#340, 207 Bank St., Ottawa ON K2P 1N5
Tel: 613-482-1165; *Fax:* 613-482-1212
Toll-Free: 888-271-3383
e-mail: info@citt.org
URL: www.citt.org
Adam Mitchell, President
Monique Corbeil, National Coordinator

The Canadian Stage Company
26 Berkeley St., Toronto ON M5A 2W3
Tel: 416-367-8243; *Fax:* 416-367-1768
e-mail: general@canstage.com
URL: www.canstage.com
Louise Plunkett, Customer Service Manager
Matthew Jocelyn, Artistic & General Director

Canadian Theatre Critics Association (CTCA) / Association des critiques de théâtre du Canada
#724, 2121 Bathurst St., Toronto ON M5N 2P3
Tel: 416-782-0966; *Fax:* 416-782-0366
e-mail: scenechanges@rogers.com
URL: www.canadiantheatrecritics.ca
Affiliation(s): Capital Critics Association; Association québécoise des critiques de théâtre
Jeniva Berger, Founding President
Alvina Ruprecht, Co-President
Don Rubin, Co-President

Centre des auteurs dramatiques (CEAD)
#200, 261, rue du Saint-Sacrement, Montréal QC H2Y 3V2
Tél: 514-288-3384; *Téléc:* 514-288-7043
Courriel: cead@cead.qc.ca
URL: www.cead.qc.ca
Marc Drouin, Directeur général
Lise Vaillancourt, Président

Le Cercle Molière
340, boul Provencher, Saint-Boniface MB R2H 0G7
Tél: 204-233-8053; *Téléc:* 204-233-2373
Courriel: reception@cerclemoliere.com
URL: www.cerclemoliere.com
Roland Mahé, Directeur artistique

Compagnie vox théâtre
333 King Edward Ave., Ottawa ON K1N 7M5
Tél: 613-241-1090; *Téléc:* 613-241-0250
Courriel: info@voxtheatre.ca
URL: www.voxtheatre.ca

Conseil québécois du théâtre (CQT)
#808, 460, rue Ste-Catherine ouest, Montréal QC H3B 1A7
Tél: 514-954-0270; *Téléc:* 514-954-0165
Ligne sans frais: 866-954-0270
Courriel: cqt@cqt.qc.ca
URL: www.cqt.ca
Martine Lévesque, Directrice générale

Evergreen Theatre Society
2633 Hochwald Ave. SW, Calgary AB T3E 7K2
Tel: 403-228-1384; *Fax:* 403-229-1385
Toll-Free: 877-840-9746
e-mail: info@evergreentheatre.com
URL: www.evergreentheatre.com
Social Media:
www.facebook.com/group.php?gid=102554315596
Lisa Ryan, Director, Residency
Sean Fraser, Executive Director

Fédération québécoise du théâtre amateur (FQTA)
CP 211, Succ. Saint-Élie-d'Orford, sherbrooke QC J1R 1A1
Tél: 819-752-2501; *Téléc:* 819-758-4466
Ligne sans frais: 877-752-2501
Courriel: info@fqta.ca
URL: www.fqta.ca
Yoland Roy, Directeur général

First Pacific Theatre Society
1440 - 12 Ave. West, Vancouver BC V6H 1M8
Tel: 604-731-5483; *Fax:* 604-733-3880
e-mail: info@pacifictheatre.org
URL: www.pacifictheatre.org
Affiliation(s): Professional Association of Canadian Theatres
Ron Reed, Artistic Director
Alison Chisholm, Theatre Administrator
Frank Nickel, Production Manager
Andrea Loewen, Director, Public Relations
Cindy McPherson, Business Manager

First Vancouver Theatre Space Society (FVTS)
c/o Vancouver Fringe Festival, 1398 Cartwright St., Vancouver BC V6H 3R8
Tel: 604-257-0350; *Fax:* 604-253-1924
e-mail: info@vancouverfringe.com
URL: www.vancouverfringe.com
Eduardo Ottoni, Production Manager
David Jordan, Executive Director

Globe Theatre Society
Globe Theatre, Prince Edward Bldg., 1801 Scarth St., Regina SK S4P 2G9
Tel: 306-525-9553; *Fax:* 306-352-4194
Toll-Free: 866-954-5623
e-mail: onstage@globetheatrelive.com
URL: www.globetheatrelive.com
Affiliation(s): Canadian Actors' Equity
Ruth Smillie, Artistic Director

Greater Vancouver Professional Theatre Alliance (GVPTA)
1405 Anderson St., 3rd Fl., Vancouver BC V6H 3R5
Tel: 604-608-6799; *Fax:* 604-608-6923
e-mail: info@gvpta.ca
URL: www.gvpta.ca
Sue Porter, Executive Director

Gryphon Theatre Foundation
PO Box 454, Barrie ON L4M 4T7
Tel: 705-728-4613; *Fax:* 705-728-4623
e-mail: boxoffice@gryphontheatre.com
URL: www.gryphontheatre.com
Social Media: www.facebook.com/group.php?gid=34543726924
Donna Kenwell, Chair

Harbourfront Centre
235 Queens Quay West, Toronto ON M5J 2G8
Tel: 416-973-4600; *Fax:* 416-973-6055
e-mail: info@harbourfrontcentre.com
URL: www.harbourfrontcentre.com
Bruce Hutchinson, Director, Marketing & Media Relations
William J.S. Boyle, CEO
Gregory Burke, Director, The Power Plant
Melanie Fernandez, Director, Community & Education
Tina Rasmussen, Director, Performing Arts
Geoffrey Taylor, Director, Harbourfront Reading Series

Intrepid Theatre Co. Society
#2, 1609 Blanshard St., Victoria BC V8S 4P6
Tel: 250-383-2663; *Fax:* 250-380-1999
e-mail: info@intrepidtheatre.com
URL: www.intrepidtheatre.com
Affiliation(s): ProArt Alliance of Vancouver, Arts Action BC
Janet Munsil, Producer
Ian Case, General Manager

Lorraine Kimsa Theatre for Young People (LKTYP)
165 Front St. East, Toronto ON M5A 3Z4
Tel: 416-363-5131; *Fax:* 416-363-5136
e-mail: online@lktyp.ca
URL: www.lktyp.ca
Affiliation(s): Canadian Actor's Equity Association
Allen MacInnis, Artistic Director
Nancy Webster, Managing Director

Manitoba Association of Playwrights (MAP)
#503, 100 Arthur St., Winnipeg MB R3B 1H3
Tel: 204-942-8941; *Fax:* 204-942-1555
e-mail: mbplay@mts.net
URL: www.mbplays.ca
Social Media: www.facebook.com/group.php?gid=5729134541
Rory Runnells, Coordinator

Manitoba Theatre Centre (MTC)
174 Market Ave., Winnipeg MB R3B 0P8
Tel: 204-942-6537; *Fax:* 204-947-3741
Toll-Free: 877-446-4500
e-mail: patronservices@mtc.mb.ca
URL: www.mtc.mb.ca
Steven Schipper, Artistic Director
Zaz Bajon, General Manager

Native Earth Performing Arts Inc. (NEPA)
Bldg. 74, #300/305, 55 Mill St., Toronto ON M5A 3C4
Tel: 416-531-1402; *Fax:* 416-531-6377
Toll-Free: 877-854-9708
e-mail: office@nativeearth.ca
URL: www.nativeearth.ca
Affiliation(s): Professional Association of Canadian Theatres; Toronto Theatre Alliance
Yvette Nolan, Artistic Director
Donna-Michelle St. Bernard, General Manager

Neptune Theatre Foundation
1593 Argyle St., Halifax NS B3J 2B2
Tel: 902-429-7300; *Fax:* 902-429-1211
Toll-Free: 800-565-7345
e-mail: info@neptunetheatre.com
URL: www.neptunetheatre.com
Social Media: www.facebook.com/neptunetheatre
Doreen E. Malone, General Manager
George Pothitos, Artistic Director

New West Theatre Society
#111, 210A - 12A St. North, Lethbridge AB T1J 0P5
Tel: 403-381-9378
e-mail: info@newwesttheatre.com
URL: www.newwesttheatre.com
Nicholas Hanson, Artistic Director
Jeremy Mason, General Manager

Ontario Puppetry Association
714 Hedgerow Place, London ON K7M 4G9
Tel: 613-389-2996
Toll-Free: 800-379-0446
e-mail: dsmith@kos.net
URL: www.onpuppet.org
Social Media: www.facebook.com/group.php?gid=7360606673
Affiliation(s): UNIMA International
Philip Arnold, President
Mike Harding, Vice-President

Playwrights Guild of Canada (PGC)
#210, 215 Spadina Ave., Toronto ON M5T 2C7
Tel: 416-703-0201; *Fax:* 416-703-0059
Toll-Free: 800-561-3318
e-mail: info@playwrightsguild.ca
URL: www.playwrightsguild.ca
Robin Sokoloski, Executive Director

Playwrights Theatre Centre
#201, 1398 Cartwright St., Vancouver BC V6H 3R8
Tel: 604-685-6228; *Fax:* 604-685-7451
e-mail: plays@playwrightstheatre.com
URL: www.playwrightstheatre.com
Ray Wallis, President
Martin Kinch, Executive Director/Literary Manager
Linda Gorrie, Administrator

Prairie Theatre Exchange (PTE)
Portage Place, #Y300, 393 Portage Ave., 3rd Fl., Winnipeg MB R3B 3H6
Tel: 204-942-7291; *Fax:* 204-942-1774
e-mail: pte@pte.mb.ca
URL: www.pte.mb.ca
Affiliation(s): Canadian Institute of Theatre Technology
Cherry Karpyshin, General Manager
Wendy Miller, President

Professional Association of Canadian Theatres (PACT)
#555, 215 Spadina Ave., Toronto ON M5T 2C7
Tel: 416-595-6455; *Fax:* 416-595-6450
Toll-Free: 800-263-7228
e-mail: marlaf@pact.ca
URL: www.pact.ca
Social Media:
www.facebook.com/group.php?gid=189415132023
Affiliation(s): PACT Communications Centre; Canadian Conference of the Arts
Lucy White, Executive Director
Eric Coates, President
Linda Gorrie, Treasurer

Resurgence Theatre Company (RTC)
211 Main St. South, Newmarket ON L3Y 5Y9
Tel: 905-953-2838; *Fax:* 905-895-0070
e-mail: info@resurgence.on.ca
URL: www.resurgence.on.ca
Social Media: www.facebook.com/group.php?gid=2388084182
Affiliation(s): CEA
Anthony Leo, General Manager

Saskatchewan Playwrights Centre (SPC)
PO Box 3092, Saskatoon SK S7K 3S9
Tel: 306-665-7707; *Fax:* 306-244-0255
e-mail: sk.playwrights@sasktel.net
URL: www.saskplaywrights.ca
Will Brooks, President

Shaw Festival
PO Box 774, 10 Queen's Parade, Niagara-on-the-Lake ON L0S 1J0
Tel: 905-468-2153; *Fax:* 905-468-5438
Toll-Free: 800-657-1106
e-mail: dlg@shawfest.com
URL: www.shawfest.com
Affiliation(s): Canadian Institute for Theatre Technology
Jackie Maxwell, Artistic Director
Colleen Blake, Executive Director

Tarragon Theatre
30 Bridgman Ave, Toronto ON M5R 1X3
Tel: 416-536-5018; *Fax:* 416-533-6372
e-mail: info@tarragontheatre.com
URL: www.tarragontheatre.com
Social Media:
www.facebook.com/pages/Tarragon-Theatre/77224001635
Affiliation(s): Professional Association of Canadian Theatres
Camilla Holland, General Manager
Richard Rose, Artistic Director

Theatre Alberta Society
11759 Groat Rd., 3rd Fl., Edmonton AB T5M 3K6
Tel: 780-422-8162; *Fax:* 780-422-2663
Toll-Free: 888-422-8160
e-mail: theatreab@theatrealberta.com
URL: www.theatrealberta.com
Marie Gynane-Willis, Executive Director

Theatre Calgary
220 - 9 Ave. SE, Calgary AB T2G 5C4
Tel: 403-294-7440; *Fax:* 403-294-7493
e-mail: info@theatrecalgary.com
URL: www.theatrecalgary.com
Tom McCabe, President
Dennis Garnhum, Artistic Director

Théâtre de la Vieille 17
61A York St., Ottawa ON K1N 5T2
Tél: 613-241-8562; *Téléc:* 613-241-9507
Courriel: info@vieille17.ca
URL: vieille17.ca
Simone Saint-Pierre, Agente des communications et adjoin

Théâtre des épinettes
255, rue Laframboise, Chibougamau QC G8P 2S5
Tél: 418-748-4682
Guy Lalancette

Théâtre du Nouvel-Ontario (TNO)
21 Lasalle Blvd., Sudbury ON P3A 6B1
Tél: 705-525-5606; *Téléc:* 705-525-1129
Courriel: tno@letno.ca
URL: www.letno.ca
Geneviève Pineault, Directrice artistique et générale

Théâtre du Trillium
333 King Edward Ave., Ottawa ON K1N 7M5
Tél: 613-789-7643; *Téléc:* 613-789-7641
Courriel: info@theatre-trillium.com
URL: www.theatre-trillium.com/
Natalie Sarafian, Agente des Communications et de la
Sylvie Dufour, Directrice artistique et générale

Théâtre français de Toronto
#501, 2333 Dundas St. West, Toronto ON M6R 3A6
Tél: 416-534-7303; *Téléc:* 416-534-9087
Ligne sans frais: 800-819-4981
Courriel: info@theatrefrancais.com
URL: www.theatrefrancais.com
Ghislain Caron, Directeur administratif
Guy Mignault, Directeur artistique

Théâtre l'Escaouette
170, rue Botsford, Moncton NB E1C 4X5
Tél: 506-855-0001; *Téléc:* 506-855-0010
Courriel: escaouet@nbnet.nb.ca

Théâtre la Catapulte
333 King Edward Ave., Ottawa ON K1N 7M5
Tél: 613-562-0851; *Téléc:* 613-562-0631
Courriel: communications@catapulte.ca
URL: www.catapulte.ca
Joël Beddows, Directeur artistique
Mireille Amyotte, Présidente

Théâtre la Seizième
#266, 1555 - 7e av ouest, Vancouver BC V6J 1S1
Tel: 604-736-2616; *Fax:* 604-736-9151
e-mail: info@seizieme.ca
URL: www.seizieme.ca/
Social Media: www.facebook.com/group.php?gid=7629935063
Craig Holzschuh, Directeur général et artistique

Theatre Network (1975) Society
10708 - 124 St., Edmonton AB T5M 0H1
Tel: 780-453-2440; *Fax:* 780-453-2596
e-mail: info@theartnetwork.ca
URL: www.attheroxy.com
Affiliation(s): Edmonton Arts Council
Jill Roszell, General Manager
Bradley Moss, Artistic Director

Theatre New Brunswick (TNB)
#31, 55 Whitting Rd., Fredericton NB E3B 5Y5
Tel: 506-460-1381; *Fax:* 506-453-9315
Toll-Free: 800-442-9779
e-mail: general@tnb.nb.ca
URL: www.tnb.nb.ca
Heather VanIderstine, Administrative Assistant

Theatre Newfoundland Labrador
PO Box 655, Corner Brook NL A2H 6G1
Tel: 709-639-7238; *Fax:* 709-639-1006
URL: www.theatrenewfoundland.com
Jeff Pitcher, Artistic Director

Theatre Nova Scotia (TNS)
1113 Marginal Rd., Halifax NS B3H 4P7
Tel: 902-425-3876; *Fax:* 902-422-0881
e-mail: theatrens@theatrens.ca
URL: www.theatrens.ca
Affiliation(s): Cultural Federation of NS; Professional Association of Canadian Theatres
Sue Leblanc-Crawford, Chair
Christopher Shore, Executive Director

Theatre Ontario
#210, 215 Spadina Ave., Toronto ON M5T 2C7
Tel: 416-408-4556; *Fax:* 416-408-3402
e-mail: info@theatreontario.org
URL: www.theatreontario.org
John Goddard, Executive Director

Theatre PEI
PO Box 1573, Charlottetown PE C1A 7N3
Tel: 902-894-3558; *Fax:* 902-894-3558
e-mail: theatre@isn.net
Affiliation(s): PEI Council of the Arts
Daphne Harker, Administrator
Ron Irving, Artistic Director
Rob MacLean, Associate Artistic Director

Théâtre populaire d'Acadie (TPA)
#302, 220, boul. St-Pierre ouest, Caraquet NB E1W 1A5
Tél: 506-727-0920; *Téléc:* 506-727-0923
Ligne sans frais: 800-872-0920
Courriel: tpa@pacadie.ca
URL: www.tpacadie.ca
Maurice Arsenault, Directeur artistique et général

Theatre Saskatchewan
1077 Angus St., Regina SK S4T 1Y4
Tel: 306-352-0797; *Fax:* 306-569-7888
e-mail: info@theatresaskatchewan.com
URL: www.theatresaskatchewan.com

Theatre Terrific Society
4397 - 2nd Ave. West, Vancouver BC V6R 1K4
Tel: 604-222-4020; *Fax:* 604-222-4020
e-mail: info@theatreterrific.ca
URL: www.theatreterrific.ca
Social Media: www.facebook.com/group.php?gid=2394111093
Affiliation(s): Volunteer Vancouver; Greater Vancouver Professional Theatre Association
Susanna Uchatius, Artistic Director
Nina Hirlaender Hinton, General Manager

Théâtres associés inc. (TAI)
#405, 1908, rue Panet, Montréal QC H2L 3A2
Tél: 514-842-6361; *Téléc:* 514-842-9730
Courriel: info@theatresassocies.ca
URL: www.theatresassocies.ca
Jacques Vézina, Président
Jacques Cousineau, Secrétaire général

Théâtres unis enfance jeunesse (TUEJ)
CP 627, Succ. Desjardins, Montréal QC H5B 1B7
Tél: 450-446-4863; *Téléc:* 450-467-1982
Courriel: tuej@gelogic.com
URL: www.gelogic.com/tuej
Affiliation(s): Conseil québécois du Théâtre; Academie québécoise du Théâtre; Les Arts et la Ville; Conseil Québécois des ressources humaines en culture; RAPThéâtre
Andrée Garon, Directrice générale
Marc St. Jacques, Président

Toronto Alliance for the Performing Arts (TAPA)
#210, 215 Spadina Ave., Toronto ON M5T 2C7
Tel: 416-536-6468; *Fax:* 416-536-3463
Toll-Free: 800-541-0499
e-mail: jacobak@tapa.ca
URL: www.tapa.ca
Affiliation(s): Professional Association of Canadian Theatres (PACT)
Jacoba Knaapen, Executive Director

La Troupe du Jour
CP 339, 914 - 20th St. West, Saskatoon SK S7K 3L3
Tél: 306-244-1040; *Téléc:* 306-652-1725
Courriel: communication@latroupedujour.ca
URL: www.latroupedujour.ca
Denis Rouleau, General Manager/Artistic Director

The Vancouver Summer Festival Society
#400, 873 Beatty St., Vancouver BC V6B 2M6
Tel: 604-688-1152; *Fax:* 604-688-8441
e-mail: music@festivalvancouver.bc.ca
URL: www.festivalvancouver.bc.ca
George Laverock, Program Director
Morna Edmundson, Administrative Director

Vancouver TheatreSports League (VTSL)
#104, 1177 West Broadway, Vancouver BC V6H 1G3
Tel: 604-738-7013; *Fax:* 604-738-8013
e-mail: info@vtsl.com
URL: www.vtsl.com
Social Media: www.twitter.com/VanTheatreSport
Jay Ono, Executive Director

Western Canada Theatre Company Society (WCT)
PO Box 329, Kamloops BC V2C 5K9
Tel: 250-372-3216; *Fax:* 250-374-7099
e-mail: info@westerncanadatheatre.bc.ca
URL: www.westerncanadatheatre.bc.ca
Affiliation(s): Professional Association of Candian Theatres
Lorid Marchand, General Manager

Pharmaceutical

Alberta College of Pharmacists (ACP)
#1200, 10303 Jasper Ave., Edmonton AB T5J 3N6
Tel: 780-990-0321; *Fax:* 780-990-0328
Toll-Free: 877-227-3838
e-mail: acpinfo@pharmacists.ab.ca
URL: www.pharmacists.ab.ca
Greg Eberhart, CAE, Registrar

Association of Faculties of Pharmacy of Canada (AFPC) / Association des facultés de pharmacie du Canada
3919 - 13th Ave. West, Vancouver BC V6R 2T1
Tel: 604-222-0221; *Fax:* 604-222-2574
e-mail: fabbott@telus.net
URL: www.afpc.info
Affiliation(s): Canadian Pharmacists Association
Frank Abbott, Executive Director

Association professionnelle des pharmaciens salariés du Québec (APPSQ)
3560, rue la Verendrye, Sherbrooke QC J1L 1Z6
Tél: 819-563-6464; *Téléc:* 819-563-6464
Courriel: appsq@hotmail.com
Denis Godin, Président

Association québécoise des pharmaciens propriétaires (AQPP) / Québec Association of Pharmacy Owners
4378, av Pierre-de Coubertin, Montréal QC H1V 1A6
Tél: 514-254-0676; *Téléc:* 514-254-1288
Ligne sans frais: 800-361-7765
Courriel: info@aqpp.qc.ca
URL: www.aqpp.qc.ca
Normand Cadieux, Directeur général

British Columbia Pharmacy Association (BCPhA)
#1530, 1200 West 73rd Ave., Vancouver BC V6P 6G5
Tel: 604-261-2092; *Fax:* 604-261-2097
Toll-Free: 800-663-2840
URL: www.bcpharmacy.ca
Marnie Mitchell, CEO
Linda Lytle, President

Canada's Research-Based Pharmaceutical Companies (Rx&D) / Les companies de recherche pharmaceutique du Canada
#1220, 55 Metcalfe St., Ottawa ON K1P 6L5
Tel: 613-236-0455; *Fax:* 613-236-6861
e-mail: info@canadapharma.org
URL: www.canadapharma.org
Russell Williams, President
Paul Lucas, Chair

Canadian Association for Pharmacy Distribution Management (CAPDM) / Association canadienne de la gestion de l'approvisionnement pharmaceutique (ACGAP)
#301A, 3800 Steeles Ave. West, Woodbridge ON L4L 4G9
Tel: 905-265-1706; *Fax:* 905-265-9372
e-mail: david@capdm.ca
URL: www.capdm.ca
David W. Johnston, President/CEO
Derek Desrosiers, Chair

Canadian Association of Pharmacy Students & Interns (CAPSI) / Association canadienne des étudiants et internes en pharmacie (ACEIP)
PO Box 68552, 360A Bloor St. West, Toronto ON M5S 1X0
e-mail: president@capsi.ca
URL: www.capsi.ca
Affiliation(s): International Pharmacy Student Foundation; Canadian Pharmaceutical Association; Academy of Students; Canadian Society of Hospital Pharmacists
Brad Elliott, President

Canadian Association of Pharmacy Technicians (CAPT)
#164, 9-6975 Meadowvale Town Centre Circle, Mississauga ON L5N 2V7
Tel: 416-410-1142
e-mail: info@capt.ca
URL: www.capt.ca
Tim Fleming, President/CEO
Cathy Schuster, Director, Promotions & Public Relations

The Canadian Council for Accreditation of Pharmacy Programs (CCAPP) / Le Conseil canadien de l'agrément des programmes de pharmacie
#200, 1765 West 8th Ave., Vancouver BC V6J 5C6
Tel: 604-676-4230; *Fax:* 604-676-4231
URL: www.ccapp-accredit.ca
David Hill, Executive Director

The Canadian Council on Continuing Education in Pharmacy (CCCEP) / Le conseil canadien de l'éducation permanente en pharmacie
#102, 4010 Pasqua St., Regina SK S4S 7B9
Tel: 306-545-7790; *Fax:* 306-545-7795
e-mail: info@cccep.ca; admin.assistant@cccep.ca
URL: www.cccep.ca
Arthur Whetstone, Executive Director
Anick Minville, President
Bev Zwicker, Vice-President

Canadian Foundation for Pharmacy (CFP) / Fondation canadienne pour la pharmacie
5809 Fieldon Rd., Mississauga ON L5M 5K1
Tel: 905-997-3238; *Fax:* 905-997-4264
e-mail: dacorn@cfpnet.ca
URL: www.cfpnet.ca
Affiliation(s): Canadian Phamacists Association
Fred Smith, President
Dayle Acorn, Executive Director

Canadian Generic Pharmaceutical Association (CGPA) / L'Association canadienne du médicament générique (ACMG)
#409, 4120 Yonge St., Toronto ON M2P 2B8
Tel: 416-223-2333; *Fax:* 416-223-2425
e-mail: info@canadiangenerics.ca
URL: www.canadiangenerics.ca
Jeff Connell, Director, Public Affairs

Canadian Pharmacists Association (CPhA) / Association des pharmaciens du Canada
1785 Alta Vista Dr., Ottawa ON K1G 3Y6
Tel: 613-523-7877; *Fax:* 613-523-0445
Toll-Free: 800-917-9489
e-mail: cpha@pharmacists.ca; members@pharmacists.ca
URL: www.pharmacists.ca
Affiliation(s): Commonwealth Pharmaceutical Association; Fédération internationale pharmaceutique
Jeff Poston, Executive Director
Paul Kuras, President

Canadian Society of Hospital Pharmacists (CSHP) / Société canadienne des pharmaciens d'hôpitaux
#3, 30 Concourse Gate, Ottawa ON K2E 7V7
Tel: 613-736-9733; *Fax:* 613-736-5660
e-mail: info@cshp.ca
URL: www.cshp.ca
Myrella Roy, Executive Director
Jason Howorko, President

College of Pharmacists of British Columbia
#200, 1765 - 8 Ave. West, Vancouver BC V6J 5C6
Tel: 604-733-2440; *Fax:* 604-733-2493
Toll-Free: 800-663-1940
e-mail: info@bcpharmacist.org
URL: www.bcpharmacists.org
Marshall Moleschi, Registrar
Ashifa Keshavji, Director, Professional Development

Council for Continuing Pharmaceutical Education (CCPE) / Conseil de formation pharmaceutique continue (CFPC)
3489, rue Ashby, Saint-Laurent QC H4R 2K3
Tel: 514-333-8362; *Fax:* 514-333-1119
Toll-Free: 888-333-8362
e-mail: info@ccpe-cfpc.com
URL: www.ccpe-cfpc.com
Michelle Austin, Coordinator, Corporate Customers

Manitoba Pharmaceutical Association
187 St. Mary's Rd., Winnipeg MB R2H 1J2
Tel: 204-233-1411; *Fax:* 204-237-3468
e-mail: info@mpha.mb.ca
URL: www.napra.org/provinces/manitoba/
Gary Cavanagh, President

Manitoba Society of Pharmacists Inc. (MSP)
#202, 90 Garry St., Winnipeg MB R3C 4H1
Tel: 204-956-6680; *Fax:* 204-956-6686
Toll-Free: 800-677-7170
e-mail: info@msp.mb.ca
URL: www.msp.mb.ca
Scott Ransome, Executive Director
Mel Baxter, President
Elmer Kuber, Vice-President
Michelle Glass, Secretary-Treasurer

National Association of Pharmacy Regulatory Authorities (NAPRA) / Association nationale des organismes de réglementation de la pharmacie
#750, 220 Laurier Ave. West, Ottawa ON K1P 5Z9
Tel: 613-569-9658; *Fax:* 613-569-9659
e-mail: info@napra.ca
URL: www.napra.ca
Carole Bouchard, Executive Director

NDMAC, Advancing Canadian Self-Care
#406, 1111 Prince of Wales Dr., Ottawa ON K2C 3T2
Tel: 613-723-0777; *Fax:* 613-723-0779
e-mail: ndmac@ndmac.ca
URL: www.ndmac.ca
David S. Skinner, President
Mary McEwen, Director, Communications & Member Services

New Brunswick Pharmaceutical Society (NBPhS) / Ordre des pharmaciens du N.-B.
373B Urquhart Ave., Moncton NB E1H 2R4
Tel: 506-857-8957; *Fax:* 506-857-8838
e-mail: info@nbpharmacists.ca
Bill Veniot, Registrar
Jacqueline A. Cormier, Office Manager

New Brunswick Pharmacists' Association Inc. (NBPA) / Association des pharmaciens du Nouveau-Brunswick inc. (APNB)
#410, 212 Queen St., Fredericton NB E3B 1A8
Tel: 506-459-6008; *Fax:* 506-453-0736
URL: www.nbpharma.ca
Paul Blanchard, Executive Director

Nova Scotia College of Pharmacists (NSCP)
1464 Dresden Row, Halifax NS B3J 3T5
Tel: 902-422-8528; *Fax:* 902-422-0885
e-mail: info@nspharmacists.ca
URL: www.nspharmacists.ca
Susan Wedlake, Registrar
Sujay Khiroya, President
Thomas Mahaffey, Sec.-Treas.

Ontario College of Pharmacists (OCP)
483 Huron St., Toronto ON M5R 2R4
Tel: 416-962-4861; *Fax:* 416-847-8200
Toll-Free: 800-220-1921
e-mail: ocpclientservices@ocpinfo.com
URL: www.ocpinfo.com
Stephen Clement, President & Chair
Bonnie Hauser, Vice-President

Ontario Pharmacists' Association (OPA)
#800, 375 University Ave., Toronto ON M5G 2J5
Tel: 416-441-0788; *Fax:* 416-441-0791
Toll-Free: 877-341-0788
e-mail: mail@opatoday.com
URL: www.opatoday.com
Dean Miller, CEO
Ken Burns, Chair

Ordre des pharmaciens du Québec (OPQ)
#301, 266, rue Notre Dame ouest, Montréal QC H2Y 1T6
Tél: 514-284-9588; *Téléc:* 514-284-3420
Ligne sans frais: 800-363-0324
Courriel: ordrepharm@opq.org
URL: www.opq.org
Diane Lamarre, Présidente

Pharmacy Association of Nova Scotia (PANS)
1470 Dresden Row, Halifax NS B3J 3T5
Tel: 902-422-9583; *Fax:* 902-422-2619
e-mail: pans@pans.ns.ca
URL: www.pans.ns.ca
Susan MacDonnell, President

The Pharmacy Examining Board of Canada (PEBC) / Le Bureau des examinateurs en pharmacie du Canada (BEPC)
717 Chursh St., Toronto ON M4W 2M4
Tel: 416-979-2431; *Fax:* 416-599-9244
e-mail: pebcinfo@pebc.ca
URL: www.pebc.ca
Darcy McLurg, President
Peter Gdyczynski, Vice-President

Prince Edward Island Pharmacy Board
PO Box 89, Trans Canada Hwy., Crapaud PE C0A 1J0
Tel: 902-658-2780; *Fax:* 902-658-2198
e-mail: peipharm@pei.aibn.com
Affiliation(s): National Association of Boards of Pharmacy
Neila I. Auld, Registrar

Saskatchewan College of Pharmacists (SCP)
#700, 4010 Pasqua St., Regina SK S4S 7B9
Tel: 306-584-2292; *Fax:* 306-584-9695
e-mail: info@saskpharm.ca
URL: www.napra.ca/pages/Saskatchewan
Affiliation(s): Canadian Council on Continuing Education; Council of Pharmacy Registrars of Canada; National Association of Pharmacy Regulatory Authorities
Randy Wiser, President
Joan Bobyn, Vice-President
Ray Joubert, Registrar

Photography

Alberta Professional Photographers Association (APPA)
9404 - 129A Ave., Edmonton AB T5E 0N7
Tel: 780-483-4275; *Fax:* 780-472-7720
e-mail: es@ppoc-alberta.ca
URL: www.ppoc-alberta.ca
Ian Grant, President

Canadian Association for Photographic Art (CAPA) / L'Association canadienne d'art photographique
PO Box 357, Logan Lake BC V0K 1W0
Tel: 604-824-9490; *Fax:* 604-824-9496
e-mail: capa@capacanada.ca
URL: www.capacanada.ca
Affiliation(s): Fédération internationale de l'art photographique
Jacques S. Mailloux, President

Canadian Association of Photographers & Illustrators in Communications (CAPIC) / Association canadienne de photographes et illustrateurs de publicité
Case Goods Bldg. 74, #302, 55 Mill St., Toronto ON M5A 3C4
Tel: 416-462-3677; *Fax:* 416-462-9570
Toll-Free: 888-252-2742
e-mail: info@capic.org; administrator@capic.org
URL: www.capic.org
Social Media: www.facebook.com/group.php?gid=33315648062
Affiliation(s): American Society of Media Photographers (ASMP)
John Harquail, Managing Director
Ewan Nicholson, President
Brian Summers, Treasurer

Canadian Imaging Trade Association (CITA) / Association canadienne de l'industrie de l'imagerie
PO Box 71058, 570 Mulock Dr., Newmarket ON L3X 1Y8
Tel: 416-226-2750; *Fax:* 416-226-3347
e-mail: cita2@sympatico.ca
URL: www.citacanada.ca
Dori Gospodaric, General Manager

Corporation des maîtres photographes du Québec inc. (CMPQ) / Québec Corporation of Master Photographers Inc.
358, rue Brock, Drummondville QC J2B 1C8
Tél: 514-990-7313; *Téléc:* 819-663-7850
Courriel: information@cmpq.qc.ca
URL: www.cmpq.qc.ca
Lorraine Lacroix, Contact
Daniel Osborne, Président

Paved Arts New Media Inc.
424 - 20th St. West, Saskatoon SK S7M 0X4
Tel: 306-652-5502
URL: www.pavedarts.ca
Laura Margita, Executive Director
David LaRiviere, Artistic Director

Photo Marketing Association International - Canada (PMAI)
PO Box 81191, Ancaster ON L9G 4X2
Tel: 905-304-8800; *Fax:* 905-304-7700
Toll-Free: 800-461-4350
e-mail: bmoggach@pmai.org
URL: www.pmai.org/international/canada/canada_default.htm
Don Spring Jr., President

Photographic Historical Society of Canada (PHSC)
PO Box 239, 6021 Yonge St., Toronto ON M2M 3W2
Tel: 416-691-1555; *Fax:* 416-693-0018
e-mail: info@phsc.ca
URL: www.phsc.ca
Clint Hyrorijiw, President

Professional Photographers Association of British Columbia (PPABC)
PO Box 1329, Aldergrove BC V4W 2V1
Tel: 604-857-1569; *Fax:* 604-857-1570
Toll-Free: 877-857-1569
e-mail: sandyg@uniserve.com
URL: www.ppabc.com
Affiliation(s): Professional Photographers of America
Sandy Dunn, CAE, Executive Secretary

Professional Photographers Association of Canada - Atlantic / Atlantique (PPAC Atlantic)
136 Russell Lake Dr., Dartmouth NS B2W 6J5
Tel: 902-462-1502; *Fax:* 902-468-7818
e-mail: beth@tenwoldephoto.com
URL: www.mppaphoto.com
Affiliation(s): The Professional Photographers of Canada
Sib Pye, CPA, President
Peter Tenwolde, Treasurer
Beth Tenwolde, Executive Secretary

Professional Photographers of Canada 1970 Incorporated (PPOC) / Photographes Professionnels du Canada
209 Light St., Woodstock ON N4S 6H6
Tel: 519-537-2555; *Fax:* 519-537-5573
Toll-Free: 888-643-7762
URL: www.ppoc.ca
Affiliation(s): Professional Photographers Association of British Columbia (PPABC); Professional Photographers of Canada Alberta (PPOC-AB); Professional Photographers of Saskatchewan (PPOC-SK); Professional Photographers of Canada Manitoba (PPOC-MB); Professional Photographers of Ontario (PPO); Corporation des Maîtres Photographes du Québec (CMPQ); Professional Photographers of Canada Atlantic (PPOC-Atlantic); Professional Government Military Photographers of Canada (PGMPC)
Tanya Thompson, Executive Director
Chris Stambaugh, MPA, President
Brian Boyle, MPA, SPA, FPPO, Vice-President
John Beesley, MPA, Corporate Secretary
Cam Colclough, MPA,SPA, Corporate Treasurer

Professional Photographers of Ontario Inc. (PPO)
209 Light St., Woodstock ON N4S 6H6
Tel: 519-536-7714
Toll-Free: 888-368-6776
URL: www.ppontario.ca
Eileen K. Gilbert, Executive Director

Saskatchewan Professional Photographers Association Inc.
2057 Athol St., Regina SK S4T 3E6
Tel: 306-757-1470
Toll-Free: 888-643-7762
e-mail: admin@sppa.org
URL: www.sppa.org
Affiliation(s): Professional Photographers of Canada
Larry Raynard, President
Tanya Thompson, Administrative Coordinator

Planning & Development

Alberta Association, Canadian Institute of Planners (AACIP)
PO Box 596, Edmonton AB T5J 2K8
Tel: 780-435-8716; *Fax:* 780-452-7718
Toll-Free: 888-286-8716
e-mail: aacip@aacip.com
URL: www.aacip.com
Gary Buchanan, President

Association of Professional Community Planners of Saskatchewan
3803 Lakeview Ave., Regina SK S4S 1H3
e-mail: president@apcps.ca
URL: www.apcps.ca
Jim Walters, President
Marilyn Steranka, Executive Director

Atlantic Planners Institute (API) / Institut des Urbanistes de l'atlantique (IVA)
57 Parkside Dr., Charlottetown PE C1E 1N1
Tel: 902-892-3684
Toll-Free: 800-207-2138
e-mail: krlewis@pei.eastlink.ca
URL: www.atlanticplanners.org
Affiliation(s): Canadian Institute of Planners
Kingsley Lewis

Canadian Association of Certified Planning Technicians (CACPT)
PO Box 3844, Stn. C, Hamilton ON L8H 7R6
Tel: 905-578-4681; *Fax:* 905-578-9581
e-mail: director@cacpt.org
URL: www.cacpt.org
Diane LeBreton, CPT, BES, Executive Director
Julie Owens, President
Norman Pearson, PhD, CPT, MCIP, Registrar

Canadian Institute of Planners (CIP) / Institut canadien des urbanistes (ICU)
#1112, 141 Laurier Ave. West, Ottawa ON K1P 5J3
Tel: 613-237-7526; *Fax:* 613-237-7045
Toll-Free: 800-207-2138
e-mail: general@cip-icu.ca
URL: www.cip-icu.ca
Affiliation(s): Alberta Association, Canadian Institute of Planners; Association of Professional Community Planners of Saskatchewan; Atlantic Planners Institute; Manitoba Professional Planners Institute; Ontario Professional Planners Institute; Ordre des urbanistes du Québec; Planning Institute of British Columbia
Marni Cappe, MCIP, RPP, President
William Budd, MCIP, RPP, Vice-President

Intergovernmental Committee on Urban & Regional Research (ICURR) / Comité intergouvernemental de recherches urbaines et régionales (CIRUR)
#206, 40 Wynford Dr., Toronto ON M3C 1J5
Tel: 416-973-5629; *Fax:* 416-973-1375
URL: www.muniscope.ca
Richard Copeland, Executive Director

Manitoba Professional Planners Institute (MPPI)
137 Bannatyne Ave., 2nd Fl., Winnipeg MB R3B 0R3
Tel: 204-943-3637; *Fax:* 204-925-4624
e-mail: mjohnson@mts.net
URL: www.mppi.mb.ca
Affiliation(s): Canadian Institute of Planners (CIP)
Valdene Buckley, President

Ontario Professional Planners Institute (OPPI) / Institut des planificateurs professionnels de l'Ontario
#201, 234 Eglinton Ave. East, Toronto ON M4P 1K5
Tel: 416-483-1873; *Fax:* 416-483-7830
Toll-Free: 800-668-1448
e-mail: info@ontarioplanners.on.ca
URL: www.ontarioplanners.on.ca
Affiliation(s): Canadian Institute of Planners (CIP)
Sue Cumming, President
Mary Ann Rangam, Executive Director
Robert Fraser, Manager, Finance & Administration
Loretta Ryan, Manager, Policy & Communications
Ron Keeble, Registrar

Ordre des urbanistes du Québec (OUQ)
#410, 85, rue St-Paul ouest, Montréal QC H2Y 3V4
Tél: 514-849-1177; *Téléc:* 514-849-7176
Courriel: info@ouq.qc.ca
URL: www.ouq.qc.ca
Claude Beaulac, Directeur général
Odette Michaud, Directrice, gestion administrative

Planning Institute of British Columbia (PIBC)
#110, 355 Burrard St., Vancouver BC V6C 2G8
Tel: 604-696-5031; *Fax:* 604-696-5032
Toll-Free: 866-696-5032
e-mail: info@pibc.bc.ca
URL: www.pibc.bc.ca
Hazel Christy, President
Gary Holisko, Secretary

Urban Development Institute of Canada (UDI) / Institut de développement urbain du Canada
200-602 West Hastings St., Vancouver BC V6B 1P2
Tel: 604-669-9585; *Fax:* 604-689-8691
e-mail: info@udi.org
URL: www.udi.bc.ca
Maureen Enser, Executive Director
Jeff Fisher, Deputy Executive Director

Police

Ontario Association of Chiefs of Police (OACP)
#605, 40 College St., Toronto ON M5G 2J3
Tel: 416-926-0424; *Fax:* 416-926-0436
Toll-Free: 800-816-1767
e-mail: oacpadmin@oacp.ca
URL: www.oacp.on.ca
Ron Bain, Executive Director

Politics

Alberta Greens
PO Box 61251, Stn. Brentwood, Calgary AB T2L 2K6
Tel: 403-282-4788; *Fax:* 403-289-6658
e-mail: secretary@albertagreens.ca
URL: albertagreens.ca
Affiliation(s): Green Alternatives Institute of Alberta
David Crowe, Treasurer/Chief Financial Officer
Grant Neufeld, President
George Read, Leader

Alberta Liberal Party
10247 - 124 St., Edmonton AB T5N 1P8
Tel: 780-414-1124; *Fax:* 780-414-1125
Toll-Free: 800-661-9201
e-mail: office@albertaliberal.com
URL: www.albertaliberal.com
David Swann, Leader

Tony Sansotta, President
Corey Hogan, Executive Director

Bloc québécois (BQ)
3750, boul Crémazie est, 4e étage, Montréal QC H2A 1B4
Tél: 514-526-3000; *Téléc:* 514-526-2868
URL: www.blocquebecois.org
Gilles Duceppe, Chef

Canadian Political Science Association (CPSA) / Association canadienne de science politique (ACSP)
#204, 260 Dalhousie St., Ottawa ON K1N 7E4
Tel: 613-562-1202; *Fax:* 613-241-0019
e-mail: cpsa@csse.ca
URL: www.cpsa-acsp.ca
Michelle Hopkins, Administrator
Richard Johnston, President

Christian Heritage Party of Canada (CHP) / Parti de l'héritage du Canada
PO Box 4958, Stn. E, Ottawa ON K1S 5J1
Tel: 819-281-6686; *Fax:* 819-281-7174
Toll-Free: 888-868-3247
e-mail: nationaloffice@chp.ca
URL: www.chp.ca
Affiliation(s): CHP New Zealand; Christian Heritage International Political Society
Jim Hnatiuk, National Leader
Tom Kroesbergen, Interim President

Communist Party of Canada (CPC) / Parti Communiste du Canada
290A Danforth Ave., Toronto ON M4K 1N6
Tel: 416-469-2446; *Fax:* 416-469-4063
e-mail: info@cpc-pcc.ca
URL: www.communist-party.ca
Miguel Figueroa, Organizer/Spokesperson

Communist Party of Canada (Marxist-Leninist) (CPC(ML)) / Parti communiste du Canada (marxiste-léniniste)
National Headquarters, 1876, rue Amherst, Montréal QC H2L 3L7
Tel: 514-522-1373; *Fax:* 514-522-5872
Toll-Free: 800-263-4203
e-mail: office@cpcml.ca
URL: www.cpcml.ca

Conservative Party of Canada / Parti conservateur du Canada
#1204, 130 Albert St., Ottawa ON K1P 5G4
Tel: 613-755-2000; *Fax:* 613-755-2001
Toll-Free: 866-808-8407
URL: www.conservative.ca
Social Media: www.facebook.com/pmharper; www.twitter.com/PMHarper
Stephen Harper, PC, MP, Leader

Green Party of British Columbia (GPBC)
Dominion Bldg., PO Box 2827, Stn. Terminal, #610, 207 West Hastings St., Vancouver BC V6B 3X2
Tel: 604-687-1199; *Fax:* 604-909-4722
Toll-Free: 888-473-3686
e-mail: info@greenparty.bc.ca
URL: www.greenparty.bc.ca
Walter Meyer zu Erpen, Party Chair
Jane Sterk, Leader
Peter McKiernan, Treasurer & Financial Agent

Green Party of Canada (GPC) / Parti vert du Canada
PO Box 997, Stn. B, #204, 396 Cooper St., Ottawa ON K1P 5R1
Tel: 613-562-4916; *Fax:* 613-482-4632
Toll-Free: 888-868-3447
e-mail: info@greenparty.ca
URL: www.greenparty.ca
Social Media: www.twitter.com/canadiangreens
Elizabeth May, Leader
Maureen Murphy, Executive Director

Green Party of Canada in New Brunswick
Tel: 902-621-0719
Sharon Labchuk, Organizer
Erik Millet, Representative

The Green Party of Manitoba
PO Box 26023, Stn. Maryland, Winnipeg MB R3C 3R3
Tel: 204-488-2831; *Fax:* 204-992-2712
Toll-Free: 866-742-4292
e-mail: info@greenparty.mb.ca
URL: www.greenparty.mb.ca
James Beddome, President

The Green Party of Ontario (GPO) / Parti Vert d'Ontario
PO Box 1132, Stn. F, Toronto ON M4Y 2T8
Tel: 416-977-7476; *Fax:* 416-977-5476
Toll-Free: 888-647-3366
e-mail: admin@gpo.ca
URL: www.gpo.ca
Mike Schreiner, Leader
Becky Smit, Executive Director

International Political Science Association (IPSA) / Association internationale de science politique (AISP)
#331, 1590, av Docteur-Penfield, Montréal QC H3G 1C5
Tel: 514-848-8717; *Fax:* 514-848-4095
e-mail: info@ipsa.ca
URL: www.ipsa.ca
Guy Lachapelle, Secretary General
Mathieu St-Laurent, Coordinator, Membership & External Relations

The Liberal Party of Canada (LPC) / Le Parti Libéral du Canada (PLC)
#400, 81 Metcalfe St., Ottawa ON K1P 6M8
Tel: 613-237-0740; *Fax:* 613-235-7208
e-mail: info@liberal.ca
URL: www.liberal.ca
Social Media: www.facebook.com/LiberalCA; www.twitter.com/Liberal_party
Affiliation(s): Liberal International
Michael Ignatieff, Leader
Alfred Apps, National President
Rocco Rossi, National Director
Stephen Kukucha, National Vice-President, English
Brigitte Garceau, National Vice-President, French

The Liberal Party of Canada (British Columbia) (LPC(BC)) / Parti libéral du Canada (Colombie-Britannique)
#460, 580 Hornby St., Vancouver BC V6C 3B6
Tel: 604-664-3777; *Fax:* 604-874-8966
Toll-Free: 888-411-6511
e-mail: info@lpcbc.com
URL: www.lpcbc.com; www.teambc.ca
Diane Rabbani, Executive Director

The Liberal Party of Canada (Manitoba) / Parti libéral au Manitoba
635 Broadway, Winnipeg MB R3C 0X1
Tel: 204-988-9540; *Fax:* 204-988-9549
e-mail: lpcmb@liberalpartyofcanada-mb.ca
URL: www.liberalpartyofcanada-mb.ca
Sharon MacArthur, President

Liberal Party of Canada (Ontario) (LPC(O)) / Parti libéral du Canada (Ontario)
#205, 10 St. Mary St., Toronto ON M4Y 1P9
Tel: 416-921-2844; *Fax:* 416-921-3880
Toll-Free: 800-361-3881
e-mail: admin@lpco.ca
URL: www.lpco.ca
Mike Crawley, President
Judi Longfield, Executive Director

The Liberal Party of Canada in Alberta (LPC(A))
Guardian Bldg., #50, 10240 - 124 St. NW, Edmonton AB T5N 3W6
Tel: 780-424-1984; *Fax:* 780-424-1966
Toll-Free: 800-879-8294
e-mail: office@liberalalberta.ca
URL: www.liberalalberta.ca
Carole Halko, Administrator

Liberal Party of Newfoundland & Labrador / Parti libéral de Terre-Neuve et du Labrador
Beothuk Bldg., #205, 20 Crosbie Place, St. John's NL A1B 3Y8
Tel: 709-754-1813; *Fax:* 709-754-0820
Toll-Free: 866-726-7116
e-mail: libcan@nf.aibn.com
URL: www.nlliberals.ca.perfectdaycanada.com
Social Media: www.twitter.com/nlliberals
Yvonne Jones, Leader
Judy Morrow, President

Liberal Party of Nova Scotia
PO Box 723, #304, 1660 Hollis St., Halifax NS B3J 2T3
Tel: 902-429-1993; *Fax:* 902-423-1624; *TTY:* 902-429-1772
e-mail: office@liberal.ns.ca
URL: www.liberal.ns.ca
Social Media: www.twitter.com/StephenMcNeil
Stephen McNeil, Leader
Derek M. Wells, President

Liberal Party of Prince Edward Island / Parti libéral de l'Ile du Prince Édouard
PO Box 2559, #205, 129 Kent St., Charlottetown PE C1A 8C2
Tel: 902-368-3449; *Fax:* 902-368-3687
Toll-Free: 877-740-3449
e-mail: office@liberal.pe.ca
URL: www.liberal.pe.ca
Social Media: www.facebook.com/group.php?gid=38261891616
Barrie Harris, President

The Libertarian Party of Canada
2938E More Cres., Regina SK S4V 0T7
Tel: 416-443-5423
e-mail: info@libertarian.ca
URL: www.libertarian.ca
Dennis Young, Leader

New Brunswick Liberal Association
715 Brunswick St., Fredericton NB E3B 1H8
Tel: 506-453-3950; *Fax:* 506-453-2476
Toll-Free: 800-453-2476
e-mail: info@liberal.ca
URL: www.nbliberal.ca
Léopold Mallet, Executive Director

New Democratic Party (NDP) / Nouveau Parti Démocratique
Federal Office, #300, 279 Laurier West, Ottawa ON K1P 5J9
Tel: 613-236-3613; *Fax:* 613-230-9950
Toll-Free: 866-525-2555; *TTY:* 866-776-7742
e-mail: jack@fed.ndp.ca
URL: www.ndp.ca
Social Media: www.facebook.com/JackLayton; twitter.com/jacklayton
Jack Layton, Leader
Adam Giambrone, Federal President

Nunavut Liberal Party
PO Box 1059, Iqaluit NU X0A 0H0
Tel: 867-979-1488; *Fax:* 867-979-1478
Alain Carrière, Riding President
Willie Adams, Provinvial Senator (Nunavut)

Parti communiste du Québec
CP 482, Succ. Place d'Armes, Montréal QC H2Y 3H3
Tél: 514-528-6142
Courriel: info@pcq.qc.ca
URL: www.pcq.qc.ca
Affiliation(s): Solidarité populaire Québec; Ligue des droits et libertés
André Parizeau, Party Leader

Parti libéral du Québec (PLQ) / Québec Liberal Party (QLP)
#422, 110, Boul Cremazie West, Montréal QC H2P 1B9
Tél: 514-381-8888; *Téléc:* 514-381-1515
Ligne sans frais: 800-361-8839
Courriel: reception@lpcq.ca
URL: www.qc.liberal.ca
Jean Charest, Chef du Parti
Françoise Patry, Présidente

Parti québécois (PQ)
#150, 1200 ave. Papineau, Montréal QC H2K 4R5
Tél: 514-526-0020; *Téléc:* 514-526-0272
Ligne sans frais: 800-363-9531
Courriel: info@pq.org
URL: www.pq.org
Mèdia social: www.facebook.com/group.php?gid=9067252699
Pauline Marois, Chef du Parti Québécois
Jonathan Valois, Président

Parti Vert du Québec (PVQ) / Green Party of Québec
#220, 10000 rue Lajeunesse, Montréal QC H3L 2E1
Tél: 514-303-7750
Ligne sans frais: 888-998-8378
Courriel: info@partivertquebec.org
URL: www.partivertquebec.org
Guy Rainville, Chef

Saskatchewan Liberal Association / Association libérale de la Saskatchewan
845 McDonald St., Regina SK S4N 2X5
Tel: 306-522-8507; *Fax:* 306-569-9271
e-mail: saskliberal@accesscomm.ca
URL: www.saskliberal.ca
Frank Proto, President

Socialist Party of Canada (SPC) / Parti Socialiste du Canada
PO Box 4280, Victoria BC V8X 3X8
e-mail: spc@iname.com
URL: www.worldsocialism.org/canada/
Affiliation(s): World Socialist Movement
John Ayers, Contact

Western Arctic Liberal Party
PO Box 965, Yellowknife NT XIA 2N7
Tel: 867-445-2377; *Fax:* 867-766-4915
e-mail: lroeland@iandd.ca
Lana Roeland, President

Yukon Liberal Party
PO Box 183, #108 Elliot St., Whitehorse YT Y1A 2C6
Tel: 867-667-4748; *Fax:* 867-667-4720
e-mail: info@ylp.ca
URL: www.ylp.ca
Kirk Cameron, President

Poultry & Eggs

Alberta Egg Producers' Board (AEPB)
#101, 90 Freeport Blvd., NE, Calgary AB T3J 5J9
Tel: 403-250-1197; *Fax:* 403-291-9216
Toll-Free: 877-302-2344
e-mail: info@eggs.ab.ca
URL: www.eggs.ab.ca
Affiliation(s): Alberta Agriculture; Alberta SPCA; Canadian Egg Marketing Agency; Canadian Food Inspection Agency
Steve Howe, Chair

Atlantic Provinces Hatchery Federation
PO Box 550, Truro NS B2N 5E3
Tel: 902-893-6532; *Fax:* 902-893-6035
e-mail: aoderkirk@gov.ns.ca
Alex Oderkirk, Sec.-Treas.

British Columbia Broiler Hatching Egg Producers' Association (BCBHEC)
#180, 32160 South Fraser Way, Abbotsford BC V2T 1W5
Tel: 604-850-1854; *Fax:* 604-850-1683
e-mail: info@bcbhec.com
URL: www.bcbhec.com
Affiliation(s): BC Broiler Hatching Egg Commission
Brian Ens, President
Peter Van Hemert, Vice-Chair
Dave Cherniwchan, General Manager

Canadian Broiler Hatching Egg Marketing Agency (CBHEMA) / Office canadien de commercialisation des oeufs d'incubation de poulet à chair (OCCOIPC)
#1101, 75 Albert St., Ottawa ON K1P 5E7
Tel: 613-232-3023; *Fax:* 613-232-5241
e-mail: info@chep-poic.ca
URL: www.chep-poic.ca
Gyslain Loyer, Chair
Errol Halkai, General Manager

Canadian Turkey Marketing Agency (CTMA) / Office canadien de commercialisation du dindon
Bldg. One, #202, 7145 West Credit Ave., Mississauga ON L5N 6J7
Tel: 905-812-3140; *Fax:* 905-812-9326
e-mail: ctma@canadianturkey.ca
URL: www.canadianturkey.ca
Affiliation(s): Further Poultry Processors Association of Canada; Canadian Poultry & Egg Processors Council
Philip J. Boyd, Executive Director

Chicken Farmers of Canada (CFC) / Les Producteurs de poulet du Canada
#1007, 350 Sparks St., Ottawa ON K1R 7S8
Tel: 613-241-2800; *Fax:* 613-241-5999
e-mail: cfc@chicken.ca
URL: www.chicken.ca
David Fuller, Chair

Éleveurs de volailles du Québec
#250, 555, boul Roland-Therrien, Longueuil QC J4H 4G1
Tél: 450-679-0530; *Téléc:* 450-679-5375
Courriel: evq@upa.qc.ca
URL: www.volaillesduquebec.qc.ca
Martin Dufresne, Président

Fédération des producteurs d'oeufs de consommation du Québec (FPOCQ)
#320, 555, boul Roland-Therrien, Longueuil QC J4H 4E7
Tél: 450-679-0530; *Téléc:* 450-679-0855
Courriel: info@oeuf.ca
URL: www.oeuf.ca
Serge Lefebvre, Président

Printing Industry & Graphic Arts

British Columbia Printing & Imaging Association (BCPIA)
PO Box 75218, Stn. WRPO, White Rock BC V4B 5L4
Tel: 604-542-0902; *Fax:* 604-538-8581
e-mail: mknoch@bcpia.org
URL: www.bcpia.org
Affiliation(s): Printing Industries of America
Marilynn Knoch, Executive Director

Canadian Printing Industries Association (CPIA) / Association canadienne de l'imprimerie (ACI)
#1110, 151 Slater St., Ottawa ON K1P 5H3
Tel: 613-236-7208; *Fax:* 613-232-1334
e-mail: info@cpia-aci.ca
URL: www.cpia-aci.ca
Affiliation(s): Graphic Arts Technical Foundation; Printing Industries of America
Bob Elliott, CAE, President
Cheri Nixon, Senior Exec. Assistant

Canadian Printing Ink Manufacturers Association (CPIMA)
52 Palmer Rd., Grimsby ON L3M 5L4
Tel: 905-309-5883; *Fax:* 905-309-5838
e-mail: cpima@sympatico.ca
URL: www.cpima.org
Affiliation(s): Society of British Ink Manufacturers; National Association of Printing Ink Manufacturers
Shiona Finlayson, President

New Brunswick Printing Industries Association (NBPIA) / Association des industries d'imprimierie du Nouveau-Brunswick (AIINB)
c/o Quebecor World Atlantic, PO Box 6250, Stn. A, Saint John NB E2L 4S3
Tel: 506-633-3600; *Fax:* 506-633-3607
e-mail: laureen.douglas@quebecorworld.com
Jacques Bourgeois, President
Stuart Taylor, Sec.-Treas.

Ontario Printing & Imaging Association (OPIA)
#14, 2601 Matheson Blvd. East, Mississauga ON L4W 5A8
Tel: 905-602-4441; *Fax:* 905-602-9798
e-mail: info@opia.on.ca
URL: www.opia.on.ca
Affiliation(s): Canadian Printing Industries Association (CPIA); Printing Industries of America (PIA); Graphic Arts Technical Foundation (GATF)
Mike McInnes, Chair
Kim Stewart, Vice-Chair
Tracey Preston, President
Ryan Anderson, Treasurer

Printing & Graphics Industries Association of Alberta (PGIA)
PO Box 61229 RPO Kensington, Calgary AB T2N 4S6
Tel: 403-281-1421; *Fax:* 403-225-1421
e-mail: info@pgia.ca
URL: www.pgia.ca
Caron Evans, Association Manager
Dean McElhinney, President

Printing Equipment & Supply Dealers' Association of Canada (PESDA)
PO Box 135, Ridgeville ON L0S 1M0
Fax: 905-892-4303
Toll-Free: 888-359-4784
e-mail: info@pesda.com
URL: www.pesda.com
Evan Cambray, President
Evan Cambray, President

Saskatchewan Graphic Arts Industries Association (SGAIA)
PO Box 7152, Saskatoon SK S7K 4J1
Tel: 306-373-3202; *Fax:* 306-373-3246
e-mail: sgaia@sasktel.net
URL: www.sgaia.org
Affiliation(s): Canadian Printing Industries Association; Printing Industries of America; Graphic Arts Technical Foundation
Daryl Schaffer, President
Don Breher, Executive Director
Daryl Breckner, Secretary-Treasurer

Society of Graphic Designers of Canada (GDC) / Société des designers graphiques du Canada
Arts Court, 2 Daly Ave., Ottawa ON K1N 6E2
Tel: 613-567-5400; *Fax:* 613-564-4428
Toll-Free: 877-496-4453
e-mail: info@gdc.net
URL: www.gdc.net
Social Media: twitter.com/gdcntl
Affiliation(s): International Council of Graphic Design Associations
Roderick CJ Roodenburg, MGDC, President
Melanie MacDonald, Administrative Director

Prisoners & Ex-Offenders

Canadian Association of Elizabeth Fry Societies (CAEFS) / Association canadienne des sociétés Elizabeth Fry (ACSEF)
#701, 151 Slater St., Ottawa ON K1P 5H3
Tel: 613-238-2422; *Fax:* 613-232-7130
e-mail: caefs@web.net
URL: www.elizabethfry.ca
Affiliation(s): Canadian Association of Sexual Assault Centres; Congress of Black Women; National Anti-Poverty Organization; Equality for Gays & Lesbians Everywhere; National Associations Active in Criminal Justice; National Action Committee on the Status of Women; National Association of Women & the Law; National Organization of Immigrant & Visible Minority Women of Canada; National Voluntary Organizations; Native Women's Association of Canada; Pauktuutit, the Inuit Women's Association; Women's Legal Education & Action Fund; National Council of Women of Canada; United Way National Agencies Committee
Kim Pate, Executive Director
Ailsa Watkinson, President

Canadian Coalition Against the Death Penalty (CCADP) / Coalition canadien contre la peine de mort
80 Lillington Ave., Toronto ON M1N 3K7
Tel: 416-693-9112; *Fax:* 416-693-9112
e-mail: info@ccadp.org
URL: www.ccadp.org
Tracy Lamourie, Director & Founder
Dave Parkinson, Director & Founder

The John Howard Society of Canada / Société John Howard du Canada
809 Blackburn Mews, Kingston ON K7P 2N6
Tel: 613-384-6272; *Fax:* 613-384-1847
e-mail: national@johnhoward.ca
URL: www.johnhoward.ca
Craig Jones, Ph.D, Executive Director
Gordon Cook, President

Operation Springboard
#800, 2 Carlton St., Toronto ON M5B 1J3
Tel: 416-977-0089; *Fax:* 416-977-2840
e-mail: tterranova@operationspringboard.on.ca
URL: www.operationspringboard.on.ca
Margaret Stanowski, Executive Director
Liz Conrad, Director of Programs

Quaker Committee on Jails & Justice (QCJJ)
32959 Third Ave., Mission BC V2V 1N5
Tel: 604-832-0954
e-mail: qcjj@quaker.ca
URL: cfsc.quaker.ca/pages/contact_jails.html
Affiliation(s): Alternatives to Violence Project - Canada
Meredith Egan, Program Associate

St. Leonard's Society of Canada (SLSC) / Société St-Léonard du Canada
Bronson Centre, #208, 211 Bronson Ave., Ottawa ON K1R 6H5
Tel: 613-233-5170; *Fax:* 613-233-5122
Toll-Free: 888-560-9760
URL: www.stleonards.ca
Affiliation(s): Volunteer Ottawa; Imagine Canada; Canada Helps.org
Elizabeth White, Executive Director

Seventh Step Society of Canada
PO Box 85040, Stn. Albert Park, Calgary AB T2A 7R7
Tel: 403-995-4029
e-mail: seventh@7thstep.ca
URL: www.7thstep.ca
Patrick Graham, Executive Director

Public Utilities

Canadian Association of Members of Public Utility Tribunals (CAMPUT) / Association canadienne des membres des tribunaux d'utilité publique
#646, 200 North Service Rd. West, Oakville ON L6M 2Y1
Tel: 905-827-5139; *Fax:* 905-827-3260
e-mail: info@camput.org
URL: www.camput.org
Terry Rochefort, Executive Director
Peter Gurnham, QC, Chair
Alison Rhodes, Secretary-Treasurer

Canadian Public Works Association (CPWA) / Association Canadienne des Travaux Publics
#191, 253 College St., Toronto ON M5T 1R5
Tel: 202-408-9541; *Fax:* 202-408-9542
e-mail: cpwa@cpwa.net
URL: www.cpwa.net
W. Gary Losier, P.Eng, President

Electrical & Utilities Safety Association of Ontario (EUSA)
#400, 5110 Creekbank Rd., Mississauga ON L4W 0A1
Tel: 905-625-0100; *Fax:* 905-625-8998
Toll-Free: 800-263-5024
e-mail: info@eusa.on.ca
URL: www.eusa.on.ca
Ted Vandevis, CET, MBA, CUSA, President/CEO & Sec.-Treas.
B.A. (Brian) Weber, Chair

Electricity Distributors Association (EDA)
#1100, 3700 Steeles Ave. West, Vaughan ON L4L 8K8
Tel: 905-265-5300; *Fax:* 905-265-5301
Toll-Free: 800-668-9979
e-mail: email@eda-on.ca
URL: www.eda-on.ca
Mara Ostby, Director, Administration
Tanya Fobear, Coordinator, Communications & Member Relations
Charlie Macaluso, President & CEO

Ontario Municipal Water Association (OMWA)
c/o Doug Parker, 43 Chelsea Cres., Belleville ON K8N 4Z5
Tel: 613-966-1100; *Fax:* 613-966-3024
Toll-Free: 888-231-1115
e-mail: dparker@omwa.org
URL: www.omwa.org
Affiliation(s): Ontario Water Works Association (a section of the American Water Works Association)
Peter Veltheer, President
Douglas Parker, Executive Director

Utility Contractors' Association of Ontario Inc. (UCA)
#201, 1075 North Service Rd. West, Oakville ON L6M 2G2
Tel: 905-847-7305; *Fax:* 905-847-7824
e-mail: info@pipeline.ca
URL: www.uca.on.ca
Barry L. Brown, General Manager

Publishing

Alberta Weekly Newspapers Association (AWNA)
Terrace Plaza, #800, 4445 Calgary Trail South, Edmonton AB T6H 5R7
Tel: 780-434-8746; *Fax:* 780-438-8356
Toll-Free: 800-282-6903
e-mail: info@awna.com
URL: www.awna.com
Dennis Merrell, CAE, Executive Director
George Brown, President

Alcuin Society
PO Box 3216, Vancouver BC V6B 3X8
e-mail: info@alcuinsociety.com
URL: www.alcuinsociety.com
Howard Greaves, Chair

Association des libraires du Québec (ALQ)
#580, 1001, boul de Maisonneuve est, Montréal QC H2L 4P9
Tél: 514-526-3349; *Téléc:* 514-526-3340
Courriel: info@alq.qc.ca
URL: www.alq.qc.ca

Association for the Export of Canadian Books (AECB) / Association pour l'exportation du livre canadien
#504, One Nicholas St., Ottawa ON K1N 7B7
Tel: 613-562-2324; *Fax:* 613-562-2329
e-mail: aecb@aecb.org
URL: www.aecb.org
Affiliation(s): Association of Canadian Publishers; Canadian Publishers Council; Association of Canadian University Presses; Association nationale des éditeurs de livres
François Charette, Executive Director
Daniel Bilodeau, Financial Officer & Office Manager
Philip Cercone, Chair

Association nationale des éditeurs de livres (ANEL)
2514, boul Rosemont, Montréal QC H1Y 1K4
Tél: 514-273-8130; *Téléc:* 514-273-9657
Ligne sans frais: 866-900-2635
Courriel: info@anel.qc.ca
URL: www.anel.qc.ca
Pierre Le François, Directeur général

Association of Book Publishers of British Columbia (ABPBC)
#600, 402 West Pender St., Vancouver BC V6B 1T6
Tel: 604-684-0228; *Fax:* 604-684-5788
e-mail: e.admin@books.bc.ca
URL: www.books.bc.ca
Affiliation(s): Association of Canadian Publishers
Margaret Reynolds, Executive Director
Andrew Wooldridge, President

Association of Canadian Publishers (ACP) / Association des éditeurs canadiens
#306, 174 Spadina Ave., Toronto ON M5T 2C2
Tel: 416-487-6116; *Fax:* 416-487-8815
e-mail: admin@canbook.org
URL: www.publishers.ca
Affiliation(s): Association of Book Publishers of British Columbia; Book Publishers Association of Alberta; Saskatchewan Publishers Group; Association of Manitoba Book Publishers; Ontario Publishers Group; Association des editeurs anglophones du Québec; Atlantic Publishers Association; The Literary Press Group of Canada
Carolyn Wood, Executive Director

Association of Canadian University Presses (ACUP) / Association des presses universitaires canadiennes (APUC)
#700, 10 St. Mary St., Toronto ON M4Y 2W8
Tel: 416-978-2239; *Fax:* 416-978-4738
e-mail: clarose@utpress.utoronto.ca
Bill Harnum, President

Association of English Language Publishers of Québec (AELAQ) / Association des éditeurs de langue anglaise du Québec
#3, 1200, av Atwater, Montréal QC H3Z 1X4
Tel: 514-932-5633; *Fax:* 514-932-5456
e-mail: info@aelaq.org
URL: www.aelaq.org
Aparna Sanyal, Executive Director

Association of Manitoba Book Publishers (AMBP)
#404, 100 Arthur St., Winnipeg MB R3B 1H3
Tel: 204-947-3335; *Fax:* 204-956-4689
e-mail: ambp@mts.net
URL: www.bookpublishers.mb.ca
Michelle Peters, Executive Director

Association québécoise des salons du livre (AQSL)
CP 353, Rimouski QC G5L 7C3
Téléc: 418-725-4543
Ligne sans frais: 888-542-2075
Courriel: info@aqsl.ca
URL: www.aqsl.org
Robin Doucet, Directeur

Atlantic Community Newspapers Association (ACNA)
#216, 7075 Bayers Rd., Halifax NS B3L 2C2
Tel: 902-832-4480; *Fax:* 902-832-4484
Toll-Free: 877-842-4480
e-mail: mail@acna.com
URL: www.acna.com
Shawn Woodford, President

Atlantic Publishers Marketing Association (APMA)
1484 Carlton St., Halifax NS B3H 3B7
Tel: 902-420-0711; *Fax:* 902-423-4302
e-mail: apma.admin@atlanticpublishers.ca
URL: www.atlanticpublishers.ca
Peggy Walt, Executive Director

Book & Periodical Council (BPC)
#107, 192 Spadina Ave., Toronto ON M5T 2C2
Tel: 416-975-9366; *Fax:* 416-975-1839
e-mail: info@thebpc.ca
URL: www.bookandperiodicalcouncil.ca
Anne McClelland, Executive Director

Book Promoters Association of Canada (BPAC)
Hudson Bay Postal Outlet, "The Wicket", PO Box 75115, 20 Bloor St. East, Toronto ON M4W 3T3
Tel: 905-430-5134
e-mail: bookpromoters@gmail.com
URL: bookpromotersassociationofcanada.blogspot.com
David Leonard, President
Selina Rajani, Director, West Coast
Miranda Snyder, Membership Director
Nadia de Freitas, Network News Managing Editor
Doug Blair, Treasurer

Book Publishers Association of Alberta (BPAA)
10523 - 100 Ave., Edmonton AB T5J 0A8
Tel: 780-424-5060; *Fax:* 780-424-7943
e-mail: info@bookpublishers.ab.ca
URL: www.bookpublishers.ab.ca
Affiliation(s): Publishers Association of the West
Katherine Shute, Executive Director

British Columbia & Yukon Community Newspapers Association (BCYCNA)
#122, 1020 Mainland St., Vancouver BC V6B 2T4
Tel: 604-669-9222; *Fax:* 604-684-4713
Toll-Free: 866-669-9222
e-mail: info@bccommunitynews.com
URL: www.bccommunitynews.com
Sylvia Myles, Accounting Manager
George Affleck, General Manager

Canadian Book Manufacturers' Association (CBMA)
#906, 75 Albert St., Ottawa ON K1P 5E7
Tel: 613-236-7208; *Fax:* 613-236-8169
e-mail: neilfitz@istar.ca
Affiliation(s): Book Manufacturers' Institute Inc.
Jeff Wilkins, Chair

Canadian Bookbinders & Book Artists Guild (CBBAG) / Guilde canadienne des relieurs et des artisans du livre
#112, 60 Atlantic Ave., Toronto ON M6K 1X9
Tel: 416-581-1071; *Fax:* 416-581-1053
e-mail: cbbag@cbbag.ca
URL: www.cbbag.ca
Social Media: www.facebook.com/group.php?gid=77394956232
Affiliation(s): Ontario Crafts Council
Scott Duncan, President

Canadian Booksellers Association (CBA)
#700, 789 Don Mills Rd., Toronto ON M3C 1T5
Tel: 416-467-7883; *Fax:* 416-467-7886
Toll-Free: 866-788-0790
e-mail: enquiries@cbabook.org
URL: www.cbabook.org
Susan Dayus, Executive Director
Paul McNally, President
Steve Budnarchuk, Vice-President
Tim Pearce, Treasurer

The Canadian Children's Book Centre (CCBC)
#101, 40 Orchard View Blvd., Toronto ON M4R 1B9
Tel: 416-975-0010; *Fax:* 416-975-8970
e-mail: info@bookcentre.ca
URL: www.bookcentre.ca
Affiliation(s): Book & Periodical Council; Book Promoters Association of Canada; Canadian Booksellers Association; Canadian Coalition of School Libraries
Charlotte Teeple, Executive Director

Canadian Circulations Audit Board Inc. (CCAB) / Office canadien de vérification de la diffusion
Div. of BPA International, #800, 1 Concorde Gate, Toronto ON M3C 3N6
Tel: 416-487-2418; *Fax:* 416-487-6405
URL: www.bpaww.com
Richard Matte, General Manager

Canadian Community Newspapers Association (CCNA)
#200, 890 Yonge St., Toronto ON M4W 3P4
Tel: 416-482-1090; *Fax:* 416-482-1908
Toll-Free: 877-305-2262
e-mail: info@ccna.ca
URL: www.communitynews.ca
John Hinds, Chief Executive Officer

Canadian Newspaper Association (CNA) / Association canadienne des journaux (ACJ)
#200, 890 Yonge St., Toronto ON M4W 3P4
Tel: 416-923-3567; *Fax:* 416-923-7206
e-mail: info@cna-acj.ca
URL: www.cna-acj.ca
Affiliation(s): Newspaper Association of America
Anne Kothawala, President/CEO
Alan Allnutt, Chair
Blair Mackenzie, Treasurer

The Canadian Press (CP) / La presse canadienne
36 King St. East, Toronto ON M5C 2L9
Tel: 416-364-0321; *Fax:* 416-364-0207
e-mail: sales@thecanadianpress.com
URL: www.thecanadianpress.com
Social Media: twitter.com/CdnPress_News
Eric Morrison, President
Scott White, Editor-in-Chief

The Canadian Press
#504, 10109 - 106 St. NW, Edmonton AB T5J 3L7
Tel: 780-428-6107; *Fax:* 780-428-0663
URL: www.thecanadianpress.com

The Canadian Press
#250, 840 Howe St., Vancouver BC V6Z 2L2
Tel: 604-687-1662; *Fax:* 604-687-5040
URL: www.thecanadianpress.com

The Canadian Press
#101, 386 Broadway Ave., Winnipeg MB R3C 3R6
Tel: 204-988-1780; *Fax:* 204-942-4788
URL: www.thecanadianpress.com

The Canadian Press
PO Box 37, Stn. M, #701, 1888 Brunswick St., Halifax NS B3J 2L4
Tel: 902-422-8496; *Fax:* 902-425-2675
URL: www.thecanadianpress.com

The Canadian Press
PO Box 595, Stn. B, #800, 165 Sparks St., Ottawa ON K1P 5P7
Tel: 613-236-4122; *Fax:* 613-238-4452
URL: www.thecanadianpress.com

The Canadian Press
#100, 215, rue St-Jacques, Montréal QC H2Y 1M6
Tél: 514-849-3212; *Téléc:* 514-282-6915
URL: www.thecanadianpress.com

The Canadian Press
#2.43, 1050, des Parlementaires, Québec QC G1R 5J1
Tel: 418-646-5377; *Fax:* 418-523-9686
URL: www.thecanadianpress.com

The Canadian Press
PO Box 5951, #901, 139 Water St., St. John's NL A1C 5X4
Tel: 709-576-0687; *Fax:* 709-576-0049
URL: www.thecanadianpress.com

The Canadian Press
#335, Press Gallery, Legislative Bldg., Regina SK S4S 0B3
Tel: 306-585-1011; *Fax:* 306-585-1027
URL: www.thecanadianpress.com

The Canadian Press
#700, 100 - 4th Ave. SW, Calgary AB T2P 3N2
Tel: 403-233-7004; *Fax:* 403-262-7520
URL: www.thecanadianpress.com

The Canadian Press
#350, Press Gallery, Legislative Building, Victoria BC V8V 1X4
Tel: 250-384-4912; *Fax:* 250-356-9597
URL: www.thecanadianpress.com

The Canadian Press
c/o Press Gallery, Box 6000, New Brunswick Legislature, Queen St., Fredericton NB E3B 5H1
Tel: 506-458-5785; *Fax:* 506-457-9708
URL: www.thecanadianpress.com

The Canadian Press
National Press Bldg., #1128, 529 - 14th St. NW, Washington DC 20045 USA
Tel: 202-638-3367; *Fax:* 202-638-3369
URL: www.thecanadianpress.com

Canadian Publishers' Council (CPC)
#203, 250 Merton St., Toronto ON M4S 1B1
Tel: 416-322-7011; *Fax:* 416-322-6999
e-mail: bpellas@pubcouncil.ca
URL: www.pubcouncil.ca
Affiliation(s): International Publishers Association
Jacqueline Hushion, Executive Director
Colleen O'Neill, Executive Director, Trade (Consumer) & Higher Education Publishers' Groups

Canadian Telebook Agency
#401, 110 Eglinton Ave. West, Toronto ON M4R 1A3
Tel: 416-545-1595; *Fax:* 416-545-1590
e-mail: admin@cta.geis.com
Affiliation(s): Book & Periodical Council
Elizabeth Bryant, Executive Director

Canadian University Press (CUP) / Presse universitaire canadienne
#503, 920 Yonge St., Toronto ON M4W 3C7
Tel: 416-962-2287
Toll-Free: 866-250-5595
e-mail: president@cup.ca
URL: www.cup.ca
Bryna Wolfe-Wylie, National Bureau Chief
Amanda McCuaig, President

CMC Circulation Management Association / Association canadienne des chefs de tirage
CMC, c/o TAMi, Jackson Place, #6, 50 Main St. East, Beeton ON L0G 1A0
Tel: 905-729-1046; *Fax:* 905-729-0227
URL: www.circ.org
Affiliation(s): Newspaper Association of America
Camile Diodati, President
Colleen Burton, Contact

Connexions Information Sharing Services
#305, 489 College St., Toronto ON M6G 1A5
Tel: 416-964-1511
URL: www.connexions.org
Ulli Diemer, Coordinator

Conseil de presse du Québec (CPQ) / Québec Press Council
#208C, 1000, rue Fullum, Montréal QC H2K 3L7
Tél: 514-529-2818; *Téléc:* 514-873-4434
Courriel: info@conseildepresse.qc.ca
URL: www.conseildepresse.qc.ca
Robert Maltais, Secrétaire général

Hebdos Québec
538, Place Saint-Henri, Montréal QC H4C 2R9
Tél: 514-861-2088; *Téléc:* 514-861-1966
Ligne sans frais: 866-861-2088
Courriel: communications@hebdos.com
URL: www.hebdos.com
Affiliation(s): Publicité Club de Montréal; Société des relationnistes du Québec; Société canadienne des directeurs d'associations
Paul Brisson, Directeur général

International Board on Books for Young People - Canadian Section (IBBY - Canada) / Union internationale pour les livres de jeunesse
c/o Canadian Children's Book Centre, #101, 40 Orchard View Blvd., Toronto ON M4R 1B9
Tel: 416-975-0010; *Fax:* 416-975-8970
e-mail: info@ibby-canada.org
URL: www.ibby-canada.org
Brenda Halliday, President
Randi Robin, Secretary, Membership

The Literary Press Group of Canada (LPG)
#501, 192 Spadina Ave., Toronto ON M5T 2C2
Tel: 416-483-1321; *Fax:* 416-483-2510
e-mail: info@lpg.ca
URL: www.lpg.ca
Affiliation(s): Association of Canadian Publishers
Ronda Kellington, Executive Director
Petra Morin, Sales & Marketing Manager

Magazines Canada
#700, 425 Adelaide St. West, Toronto ON M5V 3C1
Tel: 416-504-0274; *Fax:* 416-504-0437
e-mail: info@magazinescanada.ca
URL: www.magazinescanada.ca; www.cmpa.ca
Mark Jamison, CEO
Gary Garland, Executive Director, Advertising Services
Jim Everson, Executive Director, Public Affairs

Manitoba Community Newspapers Association (MCNA)
#600, 275 Portage Ave., Winnipeg MB R3B 2B3
Tel: 204-947-1691; *Fax:* 204-947-1919
Toll-Free: 800-782-0051
e-mail: tanis@mcna.com; kimb@mcna.com
URL: www.mcna.com
Affiliation(s): Canadian Community Newspapers Association (CCNA); Atlantic Community Newspapers Association

Manitoba Press Council Inc.
#101, 2033 Portage Ave., Winnipeg MB R3J 0K8
Tel: 204-888-5189; *Fax:* 204-831-6359
e-mail: query@mbpress.org
URL: www.mbpress.org
John Cochrane, Chair
Diane Cullen, Executive Secretary-Treasurer

National Magazine Awards Foundation (NMAF) / Fondation nationale des prix du magazine canadien
#700, 425 Adelaide St. West, Toronto ON M5V 3C1
Tel: 416-422-1358; *Fax:* 416-504-0437
e-mail: staff@magazine-awards.com
URL: www.magazine-awards.com
Social Media: twitter.com/natmagawards
Patrick Walsh, President

Ontario Community Newspapers Association (OCNA)
#103, 3050 Harvester Rd., Burlington ON L7N 3J1
Tel: 905-639-8720; *Fax:* 905-639-6962
URL: www.ocna.org
Abbas Homayed, President

Ontario Press Council / Conseil de presse de l'Ontario
#1706, 2 Carlton St., Toronto ON M5B 1J3
Tel: 416-340-1981; *Fax:* 416-340-8724
e-mail: info@ontpress.com
URL: www.ontpress.com
Mel Sufrin, Executive Secretary
Robert Elgie, Chair

Periodical Marketers of Canada (PMC)
South Tower, #1007, 175 Bloor St. East, Toronto ON M4W 3R8
Tel: 416-968-7311; *Fax:* 416-968-6281
Ray Argyle, Executive Director

Québec Community Newspaper Association (QCNA) / Association des journaux régionaux du Québec (AJRQ)
#5, 400, boul Grand, L'Ile-Perrot QC J7V 4X2
Tel: 514-453-6300; *Fax:* 514-453-6330
e-mail: info@qcna.qc.ca
URL: www.qcna.org
Affiliation(s): Conseil du presse du Québec
Greg Duncan, Executive Director

Saskatchewan Publishers Group (SPG)
2405 - 11th Ave., Regina SK S4P 0K4
Tel: 306-780-9808; *Fax:* 306-780-9810
e-mail: spg@saskpublishers.sk.ca
URL: www.saskpublishers.sk.ca
Affiliation(s): Association of Canadian Publishers
Brenda Niskala, Co-Executive Director
Jillian Bell, Co-Executive Director

Saskatchewan Weekly Newspapers Association (SWNA)
#14, 401 - 45th St. West, Saskatoon SK S7L 5Z9
Tel: 306-382-9683; *Fax:* 306-382-9421
Toll-Free: 800-661-7962
e-mail: info@swna.com
URL: www.swna.com
Steven Nixon, Executive Director
Louise Simpson, Treasurer & Office Manager
Julie Schau, Officer, Communications

Société de développement des périodiques culturels québécois (SODEP)
#716, 460, rue Ste-Catherine ouest, Montréal QC H3B 1A7
Tél: 514-397-8669; *Téléc:* 514-397-6887
Courriel: info@sodep.qc.ca
URL: www.sodep.qc.ca
Francine Bergeron, Directrice générale
Yves Beauregard, Président

Toronto Press Club (TPC)
PO Box 262, Stn. Commerce Court South, Toronto ON M4L 1E8
Tel: 416-363-0651; *Fax:* 416-363-9717
URL: www.torontopressclub.net
Bill Somerville, President

Radio Broadcasting

Halifax Amateur Radio Club (HARC)
PO Box 663, Halifax NS B3J 2T3
Tel: 902-490-6421
URL: www.halifax-arc.org
Murray MacDonald, President

Real Estate

Alberta Association of the Appraisal Institute of Canada (AA-AIC)
#245, 495 - 36 St. NE, Calgary AB T2A 6K3
Tel: 403-207-7892; *Fax:* 403-207-7857
e-mail: info@appraisal.ab.ca
URL: www.appraisal.ab.ca
Ken Morris, AACI, President
Suzanne E. Teal, Executive Director

Alberta Building Officials Association
PO Box 4766, Edmonton AB T6E 5G6
e-mail: dlmartin@st-albert.net
URL: www.aboa.ab.ca
Darryl Poburan, President
Dave Venhuis, Secretary

Alberta Real Estate Association (AREA)
#300, 4954 Richard Rd. SW, Calgary AB T3E 6L1
Tel: 403-228-6845; *Fax:* 403-228-4360
Toll-Free: 800-661-0231
e-mail: info@abrea.ab.ca
URL: www.abrea.ab.ca

Annapolis Valley Real Estate Board
PO Box 117, 2110 Hwy. 1, Auburn NS B0P 1A0
Tel: 902-847-9336; *Fax:* 902-847-9869
Cathy Simpson, Executive Officer

Appraisal Institute of Canada (AIC) / Institut canadien des évaluateurs
#403, 200 Catherine St., Ottawa ON K2P 2K9
Tel: 613-234-6533; *Fax:* 613-234-7197
e-mail: info@aicanada.ca
URL: www.aicanada.ca
Social Media: twitter.com/AIC_Canada
Georges Lozano, MPA, CEO
Joanne Charlebois, Director, Marketing & Communications

Association des courtiers et agents immobiliers du Québec (ACAIQ) / Québec Real Estate Association
#300, 6300, rue Auteuil, Brossard QC J4Z 3P2
Tél: 450-676-4800; *Téléc:* 450-676-7801
Ligne sans frais: 800-440-5110
Courriel: info@acaiq.com
URL: www.acaiq.com
Robert Nadeau, Président et chef de la direction

Association des propriétaires du Québec inc. (APQ) / Quebec Landlords Association (QLA)
8350, boul St-Laurent, Montréal QC H2P 2M3
Tél: 514-382-9670; *Téléc:* 514-382-9676
Ligne sans frais: 888-382-9670
Courriel: info@apq.org
URL: www.apq.org

L'Association du Québec de l'Institut canadien des évaluateurs (AQICE) / Québec Association of the Appraisal Institute of Canada
587, ch Rhéaume, Saint-Michel QC J0L 2J0
Tél: 450-454-0377; *Téléc:* 450-454-1166
Ligne sans frais: 877-454-0377
Courriel: aqice@qc.aira.com
URL: www.aqice.ca
Ginette St-Jean, Executive Director

Association of Battlefords Realtors
PO Box 611, North Battleford SK S9A 2Y7
Tel: 306-445-6300; *Fax:* 306-445-9020
e-mail: bfords.realestate@sasktel.net
Rick Cann, Executive Officer

Association of Regina Realtors Inc.
1854 McIntyre St., Regina SK S4P 2P9
Tel: 306-791-2700; *Fax:* 306-781-7940
e-mail: arr@reginarealtors.com
URL: www.reginarealtors.com
Rick Roland, President

Association of Saskatchewan Realtors (ASR)
2811 Estey Dr., Saskatoon SK S7J 2V8
Tel: 306-373-3350; *Fax:* 306-373-5377
Toll-Free: 877-306-7732
e-mail: info@saskatchewanrealestate.com
URL: www.saskatchewanrealestate.com
Bill Madder, Executive Vice President
Patty Kalytuk, Director, Communication & Administration
Arvid Kuhnle, Director, Professional Development
Linda Minor, Member Services Coordinator

Bancroft District Real Estate Board
PO Box 1522, Bancroft ON K0L 1C0
Tel: 613-332-3842
e-mail: bdreb@bancroftrealestate.on.ca
URL: www.bancroftrealestate.on.ca
Dana Yonemitsu, Executive Officer

Barrie & District Real Estate Board Inc.
30 Mary St., Barrie ON L4N 1S8
Tel: 705-739-4650; *Fax:* 705-721-9101
e-mail: info@barrie.mls.ca
URL: www.barrie.mls.ca
Frances Clarke, Executive Officer

Brampton Real Estate Board
#10, 35 Van Kirk Dr., Brampton ON L7A 1A5
Tel: 905-791-9913; *Fax:* 905-791-9430
e-mail: info@breb.org
URL: www.breb.org
Lynn M. Martin, Executive Officier

Brandon Real Estate Board (BREB)
907 Princess Ave., Brandon MB R7A 6E3
Tel: 204-727-4672; *Fax:* 204-727-8331
e-mail: info@breb.mb.ca
URL: www.breb.mb.ca

Brantford Regional Real Estate Association Inc.
106 George St., Brantford ON N3T 2Y4
Tel: 519-753-0308
e-mail: brantfordreb@rogers.com
URL: www.mls.ca/boards/brantford/

British Columbia Association of the Appraisal Institute of Canada (BCAAIC)
#845, 1200 West 73rd Ave., Vancouver BC V6P 6G5
Tel: 604-266-8287; *Fax:* 604-266-3034
Toll-Free: 888-707-8287
e-mail: info@appraisal.bc.ca
URL: www.appraisal.bc.ca
Dan Wilson, AACI, P.App., President
Janice P. O'Brien, CAE, Executive Director

British Columbia Northern Real Estate Board
2609 Queensway, Prince George BC V2L 1N3
Tel: 250-563-1236; *Fax:* 250-563-3637
e-mail: inquiries@bcnreb.bc.ca
URL: boards.mls.ca/bcnreb/
Dorothy Friesen, President

British Columbia Real Estate Association (BCREA)
#1420, 701 Georgia St. W., Vancouver BC V7Y 1C6
Tel: 604-683-7702; *Fax:* 604-683-8601
e-mail: bcrea@bcrea.bc.ca
URL: www.bcrea.bc.ca
Affiliation(s): National Association of Realtors - USA
Robert Laing, CEO
Melinda Entwistle, COO
Norma Miller, Director, Communications
June Piry, Director, Education
Scott Veitch, President
John Tillie, Vice President

Brooks Real Estate Board
PO Box 997, Brooks AB T1R 1B8
Tel: 403-362-4643; *Fax:* 403-362-3276
e-mail: brecoop@telusplanet.net
Carol Breakell, Executive Officer
Creitia Morishita, President

Building Owners & Managers Association - Canada
#850, 36 Toronto St., Toronto ON M5C 2C5
Tel: 416-214-1912; *Fax:* 416-360-3838
e-mail: info@bomacanada.ca
URL: www.bomacanada.ca
Affiliation(s): BOMA International.
Deb Cross, CAE, Executive Vice-President
Diana Osler-Zortega, President

Calgary Real Estate Board Cooperative Limited (CREB)
300 Manning Rd. NE, Calgary AB T2E 8K4
Tel: 403-263-0530; *Fax:* 403-218-3688
e-mail: ron.esch@creb.ca
URL: www.creb.com
Ron Esch, Exec. Vice-President

Canadian Institute of Professional Home Inspectors Inc.
#720, 999 West Broadway, Vancouver BC V5Z 1K5
Tel: 604-732-0617
e-mail: info@edwitzke.com
URL: www.edwitzke.com
Ed R.R. Witzke, BA, B.Arch., A., President

The Canadian Real Estate Association (CREA) / Association canadienne de l'immeuble
200 Catherine St., 6th Fl., Ottawa ON K2P 2K9
Tel: 613-237-7111; *Fax:* 613-234-2567
Toll-Free: 800-842-2732
e-mail: info@crea.ca
URL: www.crea.ca
Affiliation(s): National Association of Realtors; International Real Estate Federation; International Consortium Real Estate Associations
Pierre J. Beauchamp, FRI (E), CEO
Calvin Lindberg, President
Georges Pahud, Vice-President

Cariboo Real Estate Association
2609 Queensway, Prince George BC V2L 1N3
Tel: 250-563-1236; *Fax:* 250-563-3637
John Castle, Chair

Chambre immobilière Centre du Québec Inc.
139C, rue Hériot, Drummondville QC J2C 2B1
Tél: 819-477-1033; *Téléc:* 819-474-7913
Courriel: chambre@cgocable.ca
Johanna Paquette, Secrétaire exécutive

Chambre immobilière de l'Abitibi-Témiscamingue Inc. (CIAT)
#203, 33, av Horne, Rouyn-Noranda QC J9X 4S1
Tél: 819-762-1777; *Téléc:* 819-762-4030
Courriel: ciat@cablevision.qc.ca
URL: www.ciat.qc.ca
Raynald Rail, Président
Gilles Langlais, Directeur général

Chambre immobilière de l'Estrie inc.
19, rue King Ouest, Sherbrooke QC J1H 1N4
Tél: 819-566-7616; *Téléc:* 819-566-7688
Courriel: info@mon-toit.net
URL: www.mon-toit.net
Johanne Beaudoin, Secrétaire exécutive

Chambre immobilière de l'Outaouais
106, boul Sacré-Coeur, Gatineau QC J8X 1E1
Tél: 819-771-5221; *Téléc:* 819-771-8715
Courriel: info@avecunagent.com
URL: www.avecunagent.com
Chantal Legault, Directrice générale

Chambre immobilière de la Haute Yamaska Inc. (CIHY) / Haute Yamaska Real Estate Board
#104, 96, rue Principale, Granby QC J2G 2T4
Tél: 450-378-6702; *Téléc:* 450-375-5268
Courriel: cihy@sympatico.ca

Chambre immobilière de la Mauricie Inc. / Trois-Rivières Real Estate Board
#102, 1640 - 6e rue, Trois-Rivières QC G8Y 5B8
Tél: 819-379-9081; *Téléc:* 819-379-9262
Courriel: cimauricie@cgocable.ca
URL: www.cimauricie.com
Lise Girardeau, Adjointe exécutive

Chambre immobilière de Lanaudière Inc.
765, boul Manseau, Joliette QC J6E 3E8
Tél: 450-759-8511; *Téléc:* 450-759-6557
URL: www.immobilierlanaudiere.com
Élise Roch, Directrice générale

Chambre immobilière de Québec
990, av Holland, Québec QC G1S 3T1
Tél: 418-688-3362; *Téléc:* 418-688-3577
Ligne sans frais: 866-688-3362
Courriel: info@ciq.qc.ca
URL: www.fciq.ca
Gina Gaudreault, Directrice générale

Chambre immobilière de Saint-Hyacinthe Inc.
CP 667, Saint-Hyacinthe QC J2S 7P5
Tél: 450-799-2210; *Téléc:* 450-799-2210
Courriel: chimmob@ntic.qc.ca

Chambre immobilière des Laurentides (CIL)
570, boul. des Laurentides, Piedmont QC J0R 1K0
Tél: 450-240-0006; *Téléc:* 450-240-0096
Courriel: optionlaurentides@cgocable.ca
URL: www.chambreimmobilieredeslaurentides.ca
Francine Soucy, Présidente
Rose Girard, Directrice générale

Chambre immobilière du Grand Montréal / Greater Montréal Real Estate Board
600, ch du Golf, Ile-des-Soeurs QC H3E 1A8
Tél: 514-762-2440; *Téléc:* 514-762-1490
Ligne sans frais: 888-762-2440
Courriel: cigm@cigm.qc.ca
URL: www.cigm.qc.ca
Michel Beauséjour, Directeur général

Chambre immobilière du Saguenay-Lac St-Jean Inc. (CISL)
#140, 2655, boul du Royaume, Jonquière QC G7S 4S9
Tél: 418-548-8808; *Téléc:* 418-548-2588
Courriel: chambre@immobiliersaguenay.com
URL: www.immobiliersaguenay.com
Ginette Gaudreault, Directrice générale

Chatham-Kent Real Estate Board
PO Box 384, Chatham ON N7M 5K5
Tel: 519-352-4351; *Fax:* 519-351-1498
e-mail: ckreb@mnsi.net
URL: www.boards.mls.ca/chatham
Dorothy Ritchie, Executive Officer

Chilliwack & District Real Estate Board
#1, 8433 Harvard Pl., Chilliwack BC V2P 7Z5
Tel: 604-792-0912; *Fax:* 604-792-6795
e-mail: cadreb@telus.net
URL: cadreb.com
Sharon J. Labiuk, Executive Officer

Cobourg-Port Hope District Real Estate Board
#23, 1011 Eligin St. West, Cobourg ON K9A 5J4
Tel: 905-372-8630; *Fax:* 905-372-1443
e-mail: districtrealestate@bellnet.ca
URL: boards.mls.ca/cobourg/

Cornwall & District Real Estate Board
407B Pitt St., Cornwall ON K6J 3R3
Tel: 613-932-6457; *Fax:* 613-932-1687
e-mail: cdreb@cogeco.net
URL: www.homesacrosscanada.com/cwon.html

Durham Region Real Estate Board (DRREB)
#14, 50 Richmond St. East, Oshawa ON L1G 7C7
Tel: 905-723-8184; *Fax:* 905-723-7531
e-mail: drar@durhamrealestate.org
URL: www.durhamrealestate.org
B. Cail Maclean, Executive Officer

Edmonton Real Estate Board Co-operative Listing Bureau Ltd.
14220 - 112 Ave., Edmonton AB T5M 2T8
Tel: 780-451-6666; *Fax:* 780-452-1135
e-mail: connection@ereb.com
URL: www.ereb.com
Marc Perras, President
Ron Hutchinson, CAE, Executive Vice-President

Estevan Real Estate Board
PO Box 445, Estevan SK S4A 2A4
Tel: 306-634-7885; *Fax:* 306-634-8610
e-mail: jjb.law@sasktel.net
URL: boards.mls.ca/estevan/
D. Dickin, Executive Officer

Fédération des Chambres immobilières du Québec (FCIQ)
600, ch du Golf, Verdun QC H3E 1A8
Tél: 514-762-0212; *Téléc:* 514-762-0365
Courriel: fciq@fciq.ca
URL: www.fciq.ca
Larry Kenline, Président

Fort McMurray Real Estate Board Co-operative Limited
9909 Sutherland St., Fort McMurray AB T9H 1V3
Tel: 780-791-1124; *Fax:* 780-743-4724
e-mail: moskalykc@shaw.ca
Greg Walsh, President
Chris Moskalyk, Executive Officer

Fraser Valley Real Estate Board
PO Box 99, 15463 - 104 Ave., Surrey BC V3T 4W4
Tel: 604-930-7600; *Fax:* 604-588-0325
Toll-Free: 800-906-0258
e-mail: mls@fvreb.bc.ca
URL: www.fvreb.bc.ca
Paul Penner, President

Georgian Triangle Real Estate Board
54 Third St., Collingwood ON L9Y 1K3
Tel: 705-445-7295; *Fax:* 705-445-7253
e-mail: realestate@gtreb.com
URL: www.gtreb.com

Greater Moncton Real Estate Board Inc.
541 St. George Blvd., Moncton NB E1E 2B6
Tel: 506-857-8200; *Fax:* 506-857-1760
e-mail: mls@nbnet.nb.ca
URL: www.monctonrealestateboard.com
Faye Andersen, Executive Officer
Stephen McWilliam, President

Guelph & District Real Estate Board
400 Woolwich St., Guelph ON N1H 3X1
Tel: 519-824-7270; *Fax:* 519-824-6730
URL: www.gdreb.ca

Hamilton-Burlington & District Real Estate Board (HBDREB)
505 York Blvd., Hamilton ON L8R 3K4
Tel: 905-529-8101; *Fax:* 905-529-4349
e-mail: info@rahb.ca
URL: www.rahb.ca
Ross Godsoe, Executive Officer

Highland Real Estate Board
c/o The Prudential Highland Properties, #104, 219 Main St., Antigonish NS B2G 2C1
Tel: 902-863-1878; *Fax:* 902-863-1933
Valerie Chugg, President

Huron Perth Real Estate Board
#6, 55 Lorne Ave. East, Stratford ON N5A 6S4
Tel: 519-271-6870; *Fax:* 519-271-3040
e-mail: gwen@on.aibn.com
URL: boards.mls.ca/huron/
Gwen Kirkpatrick, Executive Officer

Institute of Municipal Assessors
#206, 10720 Yonge St., Richmond Hill ON L4C 3C9
Tel: 905-884-1959; *Fax:* 905-884-9263
e-mail: info@assessorsinstitute.ca
URL: www.assessorsinstitute.ca
Karen Russell, MIMA, President
Frank Martini, MIMA, 1st Vice President

Kamloops & District Real Estate Association (KADREA)
#101, 418 St. Paul St., Kamloops BC V2C 2J6
Tel: 250-372-9411; *Fax:* 250-828-1986
e-mail: cboer@kadrea.com
URL: www.boards.mls.ca/kamloops
Cathy Boer, Executive Director
Craig McIntyre, President

Kawartha Lakes Real Estate Association
31 Kent St. East, Lindsay ON K9V 2C3
Tel: 705-324-4515; *Fax:* 705-324-3916
e-mail: sschell@kawarthalakes-mls.ca
URL: www.kawarthalakes-mls.ca
Susan Schell, Executive Officer
Peter Witt, President

Kingston & Area Real Estate Association
720 Arlington Park Pl., Kingston ON K7M 8H9
Tel: 613-384-0880; *Fax:* 613-384-0863
e-mail: info@karea.ca
URL: www.karea.ca
Susan Swann, Executive Officer

Kootenay Real Estate Board (KREB)
#208, 402 Baker St., Nelson BC V1L 4H8
Tel: 250-352-5477; *Fax:* 250-352-7184
e-mail: kreb@telus.net
URL: www.kreb.ca
Ian Mason, Executive Officer
Bill Biagioni, President

Lethbridge Real Estate Board (LRED)
522 - 6 St. South, Lethbridge AB T1J 2E2
Tel: 403-328-8838; *Fax:* 403-328-8906
e-mail: lreb@telus.net
URL: boards.mls.ca/Lethbridge/
Brent Black, President
Margaret Van, Executive Officer

Lloydminster Real Estate Board
#203, 5009 - 48 St., Lloydminster AB T9V 0H7
Tel: 780-875-6939; *Fax:* 780-875-5560
e-mail: lloydreb@telus.net
Eileen Rohs, Executive Officer
Scott Musgrave, President

London & St. Thomas Real Estate Board
342 Commissioners Rd. West, London ON N6J 1Y3
Tel: 519-641-1400; *Fax:* 519-641-4613
e-mail: mls@lstreb.com
URL: www.lstreb.com
Greg Harris, President

Manitoba Association of the Appraisal Institute of Canada (MB AIC)
#193, 162 - 2025 Corydon Ave., Winnipeg MB R3P 0N5
Tel: 204-934-1177; *Fax:* 204-947-1332
e-mail: mbaic@mts.net
URL: www.aimanitoba.ca
Lynne Smith Dark, Executive Director
Brett Ferguson, AACI, P.App., President

Manitoba Building Officials Association
PO Box 2063, Winnipeg MB R3C 3R4
Tel: 204-832-1512; *Fax:* 204-897-8094
e-mail: info@mboa.mb.ca
URL: www.mboa.mb.ca
John Barnes, President

Manitoba Real Estate Association (MREA)
1240 Portage Ave., 2nd Fl., Winnipeg MB R3G 0T6
Tel: 204-772-0405; *Fax:* 204-775-3781
Toll-Free: 800-267-6019
e-mail: cduheme@mrea.mb.ca; rfinch@mrea.mb.ca (education)
URL: www.realestatemanitoba.com
Brian M. Collie, Executive Director

Medicine Hat Real Estate Board Co-operative Ltd.
403 - 4 St. SE, Medicine Hat AB T1A 0K5
Tel: 403-526-2879; *Fax:* 403-526-0307
e-mail: mhreb@telus.net
URL: boards.mls.ca/medicinehat/
Dennis Schlenker, President
Brian Patterson, Executive Officer

Melfort Real Estate Board
c/o Royal Lepage Hodgins Realty, PO Box 3070, Melfort SK S0E 1A0
Tel: 306-752-5751; *Fax:* 306-752-5754
e-mail: derwooddodds@royallepage.ca
Derwood Dodds, President

Midland-Penetang District Real Estate Board Inc.
PO Box 805, 578 King St., Midland ON L4R 4P4
Tel: 705-526-8706; *Fax:* 705-526-0701
e-mail: info@midland-penetang-mls.ca

Mississauga Real Estate Board
#29, 3355 The Collegeway, Mississauga ON L5L 5T3
Tel: 905-608-6732; *Fax:* 905-608-9988
e-mail: administration@mreb.ca
URL: www.mreb.ca
Judith Juelsberg, Administrator
Tom Lebour, President
Sophia Tang, President Elect

Moose Jaw Real Estate Board
79 Hochelaga St. West, Moose Jaw SK S6H 2E9
Tel: 306-693-9544; *Fax:* 306-692-4463
e-mail: mjreb@sasktel.net
Trudy Rees, Executive Officer

Muskoka & Haliburton Association of Realtors
18 Chaffey St., Huntsville ON P1H 1K7
Tel: 705-788-1504; *Fax:* 705-788-2040
e-mail: mhar@vianet.on.ca
URL: boards.mls.ca/muskoka/
Susan Glassford, Executive Officer

New Brunswick Association of Real Estate Appraisers (NBAREA) / Association des évaluateurs immobiliers du Nouveau-Brunswick (AEIN-B)
#204, 403 Regent St., Fredericton NB E3B 3X6
Tel: 506-450-2016; *Fax:* 506-450-3010
e-mail: nbarea@nb.aibn.com
URL: www.nbarea.org
Jennifer Nemeth, Executive Director

New Brunswick Building Officials Association (NBBOA) / L'Association des officiels de la construction du Nouveau-Brunswick
PO Box 3193, Stn. B, Fredericton NB E3A 5G9
Tel: 506-658-2911; *Fax:* 506-632-6199
e-mail: secretary@nbboa.ca
URL: www.nbboa.ca
Bill Edwards, President
David Somerville, Secretary

New Brunswick Real Estate Association (NBREA) / Association des agents des immeubles du Nouveau-Brunswick
#1, 22 Durelle St., Fredericton NB E3C 1N8
Tel: 506-459-8055; *Fax:* 506-459-8057
URL: www.nbrea.nb.ca
Jamie Ryan, Executive Director/CEO

Newfoundland & Labrador Association of Realtors
28 Logy Bay Rd., St. John's NL A1A 1J4
Tel: 709-726-5110
URL: boards.mls.ca/nl/index.htm

Newfoundland & Labrador Association of the Appraisal Institute of Canada
PO Box 1571, Stn. C, St. John's NL A1C 5P3
Tel: 709-753-7644; *Fax:* 709-753-7627
e-mail: naaic@nf.aibn.com
Sherry House, Executive Director
Neil Tedstone, AACI,P.App, President

Niagara Association of REALTORS (NAR)
116 Niagara St., St Catharines ON L2R 4L4
Tel: 905-684-9459; *Fax:* 905-687-7010
e-mail: admin@mls-niagara.com
URL: www.mls-niagara.com
Lynda Kitchen, Executive Officer

North Bay Real Estate Board
926 Castle St., North Bay ON P1B 4A8
Tel: 705-472-6812; *Fax:* 705-472-0529
e-mail: nbreb@nbreb.com
URL: www.nbreb.com
Don Young, President
Nona Patterson, President Elect

Northern Lights Real Estate Board
1101 - 103 Ave., Dawson Creek BC V1G 2G8
Tel: 250-782-4876; *Fax:* 250-782-8574
e-mail: nlreb@shawcable.com
Al Mattishaw, President
Marie Chilton, Executive Officer

Northern New Brunswick Real Estate Board Inc.
PO Box 185, #5, 360 Parkside Dr., Bathurst NB E2A 3Z2
Tel: 506-548-3045; *Fax:* 506-548-4002
e-mail: nnbreb@nb.sympatico.ca
URL: boards.mls.ca/n-newbrunswick/index.htm
Carmelle F. Mallet, Executive Officer

Nova Scotia Association of REALTORS (NSAR)
#100, 7 Scarfe Ct., Dartmouth NS B3B 1W4
Tel: 902-468-2515; *Fax:* 902-468-2533
Toll-Free: 800-344-2001
e-mail: info@nsar.ns.ca
URL: www.nsar-mls.ca
Arnold G. Jones, Executive Officer

Nova Scotia Real Estate Appraisers Association (NSREAA)
#602, 5670 Spring Garden Rd., Halifax NS B3J 1H6
Tel: 902-422-4077; *Fax:* 902-422-3717
e-mail: nsreaa@nsappraisal.ns.ca
URL: www.nsappraisal.ns.ca
Alfred Mullally, AACI, President
Davida Mackay, CPS, Executive Director & Registrar
Richard Colbourne, AACI, Vice President

The Oakville, Milton & District Real Estate Board
125 Navy St., Oakville ON L6J 2Z5
Tel: 905-844-6491; *Fax:* 905-844-6699
e-mail: info@omdreb.on.ca
URL: www.omdreb.on.ca

Okanagan Mainline Real Estate Board (OMREB)
#112, 140 Commercial Dr., Kelowna BC V1X 7X6
Tel: 250-491-4560; *Fax:* 250-491-4580
e-mail: admin@omreb.com
URL: www.omreb.com
Janice Myers, Executive Director

Ontario Association of the Appraisal Institute of Canada (OA-AIC)
#108, 16 Four Seasons Place, Toronto ON M9B 6E5
Tel: 416-695-9333; *Fax:* 416-695-9321
Toll-Free: 800-771-8087
e-mail: info@oaaic.on.ca
URL: www.oaaic.on.ca
Signe Holstein, CAE, Executive Director
Dave Cunningham, CRA, President

Ontario Building Officials Association Inc. (OBOA) / Association de l'Ontario des officers en bâtiment inc.
#8, 200 Marycroft Ave., Woodbridge ON L4L 5X4
Tel: 905-264-1662; *Fax:* 905-264-8696
e-mail: admin@oboa.on.ca
URL: www.oboa.on.ca
Dean Findlay, Vice-President
Lynn C. Balfour, President
Ken Andrus, Sec.-Treas.

Ontario Real Estate Association (OREA)
99 Duncan Mill Rd., Toronto ON M3B 1Z2
Tel: 416-445-9910; *Fax:* 416-445-2644
Toll-Free: 800-265-6732

e-mail: info@orea.com
URL: www.orea.com

Edward Barisa, CEO
Gerry Weir, President
Bob McLean, Director, Communication
Bill Shepherd, Executive Director, OREA Centre for Leadership Development

Orangeville & District Real Estate Board
228 Broadway Ave., Orangeville ON L9W 1K5
Tel: 519-941-4547; *Fax:* 519-941-8482
e-mail: odreb@bellnet.ca

Orillia & District Real Estate Board
PO Box 551, Orillia ON L3V 6K2
Tel: 705-325-9958; *Fax:* 705-325-0605
e-mail: dottie@orilliarealestateboard.ca
URL: www.mls.ca/boards/orillia

Parry Sound Real Estate Board
47A James St., Parry Sound ON P2A 1T6
Tel: 705-746-4020; *Fax:* 705-746-2955
e-mail: psreb@vianet.on.ca
URL: www.parrysoundrealestateboard.ca

Peterborough & the Kawarthas Association of Realtors Inc. (PKAR)
PO Box 1330, 273 Charlotte St., Peterborough ON K9J 7H5
Tel: 705-745-5724; *Fax:* 705-745-9377
e-mail: info@peterbororealestate.com
URL: www.peterbororealestate.com

Carolyn J. Mills, Executive Officer

Portage La Prairie Real Estate Board
39 Royla Rd. North, Portage la Prairie MB R1N 1T9
Tel: 204-857-4111
e-mail: preb@escape.ca

Powell River Sunshine Coast Real Estate Board
PO Box 307, 4699 Marine Avenue, Powell River BC V8A 5C2
Tel: 604-485-6944; *Fax:* 604-485-6944
e-mail: prscreb@shaw.ca

Geri Powell, Board Administrator

Prince Albert Real Estate Board
218B South Industrial Dr., Prince Albert SK S6V 7L8
Tel: 306-764-8755; *Fax:* 306-763-0555
e-mail: pareb@sasktel.net
URL: www.mls.ca/boards/princealbert/

Charlene Welch-Leachman, Executive Officer

Prince Edward Island Association of the Appraisal Institute of Canada
PO Box 1796, Charlottetown PE C1A 7N4
Tel: 902-368-3355; *Fax:* 902-368-3582
e-mail: peiaic@xplornet.com

Scott Wilson, AACI, P.App., President
Suzanne Pater, Executive Director

Prince Edward Island Real Estate Association
75 St. Peter's Rd., Charlottetown PE C1A 5N7
Tel: 902-368-8451; *Fax:* 902-894-9487
e-mail: office@peirea.com
URL: www.peirea.com

Danny Moase, President
Fred Ripley, First Vice-President, Education
Ron MacLean, Second Vice-President, Finance
Dorothy Smith, Executive Officer

Quinte & District Real Estate Board
PO Box 128, 51 Cannifton Rd. North, Cannifton ON K0K 1K0
Tel: 613-969-7873; *Fax:* 613-962-1851
e-mail: quintemls@connect.reach.net
URL: www.quinte-mls.com

Real Estate Board of Cambridge
75 Ainslie St. North, Cambridge ON N1R 3J7
Tel: 519-623-3660; *Fax:* 519-623-8253
e-mail: office@realestateboardcambridge.com
URL: www.realestateboardcambridge.com

Real Estate Board of Greater Vancouver
2433 Spruce St., Vancouver BC V6H 4C8
Tel: 604-730-3000; *Fax:* 604-730-3100
URL: www.rebgv.org

Robert K. Wallace, CEO

Real Estate Board of Ottawa-Carleton / Chambre d'immeuble d'Ottawa-Carleton
1826 Woodward Dr., Ottawa ON K2C 0P7
Tel: 613-225-2240; *Fax:* 613-225-6420
e-mail: orebadmin@ottawarealestate.org
URL: www.ottawarealestate.org

Real Estate Board of the Fredericton Area Inc. (FREB)
544 Brunswick St., Fredericton NB E3B 1H5
Tel: 506-458-8163; *Fax:* 506-459-8922
e-mail: freb01@nb.sympatico.ca
URL: www.frederictonrealestateboard.com

Affiliation(s): Mortgage Lenders Association
Edie Whitman, Executive Officer

Real Estate Institute of Canada (REIC) / Institut canadien de l'immeuble (ICI)
#208, 5407 Eglinton Ave. West, Toronto ON M9C 5K6
Tel: 416-695-9000; *Fax:* 416-695-7230
Toll-Free: 800-542-7342
e-mail: infocentral@reic.com
URL: www.reic.ca

Maura McLaren, Executive Director
Elaine Leibner, Associate Director, Education
Lee Arbon, Manager, Marketing & Communications

Real Property Association of Canada
#1410, One University Ave., Toronto ON M5J 2P1
Tel: 416-642-2700; *Fax:* 416-642-2727
e-mail: info@realpac.ca
URL: www.realpac.ca

S. Michael Brooks, Executive Director
Robert S. Campanelli, Manager, Marketing & Member Services

REALTORS Association of Grey Bruce Owen Sound (RAGBOS)
517 - 10 St., Hanover ON N4N 1R4
Tel: 519-364-3827; *Fax:* 519-364-6800
e-mail: info@ragbos.com
URL: www.realtorsgreybruceowensound.com

Anne Schneider, Executive Officer

Red Deer & District Real Estate Board Co-op Ltd.
4922 - 45 St., Red Deer AB T4N 1K6
Tel: 403-343-0881; *Fax:* 403-347-9080
e-mail: office@rdreb.ca
URL: www.rdreb.ca

Nancy A. MacKie, Executive Officer
Todd Reid, President

Renfrew County Real Estate Board
197 Pembroke St. East, Pembroke ON K8A 3J6
Tel: 613-735-5840; *Fax:* 613-735-0405
e-mail: orebadmin@ottawarealestate.org

Ann Anderson, Executive Officer

Rideau-St. Lawrence Real Estate Board
#12, 1275 Kensington Pkwy., Brockville ON K6V 6C3
Tel: 613-342-3103; *Fax:* 613-342-1637
e-mail: rideau@bellnet.ca
URL: boards.mls.ca/rideau/

Saint John Real Estate Board Inc.
Hilyard Place, #120, 600 Main St., Saint John NB E2K 1J5
Tel: 506-634-8772; *Fax:* 506-634-8775
e-mail: sjreb@nbnet.nb.ca
URL: www.mls.ca/boards/saintjohn/

Linda Rector, Executive Officer

Sarnia-Lambton Real Estate Board (SLREB)
555 Exmouth St., Sarnia ON N7T 5P6
Tel: 519-336-6871; *Fax:* 519-344-1928
e-mail: dburke@rivernet.net
URL: mlssarnia.com

Dave Burke, Executive Director

Saskatchewan Association of the Appraisal Institute of Canada
3803 Lakeview Ave., Regina SK S4S 1H3
Tel: 306-352-4195; *Fax:* 306-352-6913
e-mail: skaic@sasktel.net
URL: www.skaic.org

Dave R. Gabruch, President
Marilyn Sterdnica, Executive Director

Saskatchewan Building Officials Association Inc. (SBOA)
PO Box 460, North Battleford SK S9A 2Y6
Tel: 306-445-1733; *Fax:* 306-445-1739
e-mail: membership@sboa.sk.ca; conference@sboa.sk.ca
URL: www.sboa.sk.ca

Dan Knutson, President
LeRoy Evenson, Secretary-Treasurer

Saskatoon Real Estate Board (SREB)
1149 - 8 St. East., Saskatoon SK S7H 0S3
Tel: 306-244-4453; *Fax:* 306-343-1420
e-mail: info@sreb.com
URL: www.sreb.com

Harry H. Janzen, CAE, Executive Officer

Sault Ste Marie Real Estate Board (SSMREB)
#477, 206 Queen St. East, Sault Ste Marie ON P6A 1Z5
Tel: 705-949-4560; *Fax:* 705-949-5935
e-mail: rebpictures@vianet.ca
URL: www.saultstemarierealestate.ca

Claudia Devoe, President

Simcoe & District Real Estate Board
191 Queensway West, Simcoe ON N3Y 2M8
Tel: 519-426-4454; *Fax:* 519-426-9330
e-mail: realsim@kwic.com
URL: www.sdreb.com

Mike Brown, President

South Okanagan Real Estate Board (SOREB)
365 Van Horne Street, Penticton BC V2A 8S4
Tel: 250-492-0626; *Fax:* 250-493-0832
e-mail: soreb@vip.net
URL: www.soreb.org

Louise Baier, Executive Officer

Sudbury Real Estate Board
190 Elm St., Sudbury ON P3C 1V3
Tel: 705-673-3388; *Fax:* 705-673-3197
e-mail: sreb@vianet.on.ca
URL: www.sudburyrealestateboard.on.ca

Myra Lahti, Executive Officer

Swift Current Real Estate Association
#211, 12 Cheadle St. West, Swift Current SK S9H 0A9
Tel: 306-773-4326; *Fax:* 306-773-3917
e-mail: screa@sasktel.net

Nancy Hunter, President

Thompson Real Estate Board
55 Selkirk, Thompson MB R8N 0M5
Tel: 204-778-6303; *Fax:* 204-778-5652
e-mail: brealt@norcom.mb.ca

Wayne Grier, President

Thunder Bay Real Estate Board
1135 Barton St., Thunder Bay ON P7B 5N3
Tel: 807-623-8422; *Fax:* 807-623-0375
e-mail: info@thunderbay-MLS.on.ca
URL: www.thunderbay-mls.on.ca

Erin Nadon, Executive Officer

Tillsonburg District Real Estate Board
PO Box 35, 1 Library Lane, Tillsonburg ON N4G 4H3
Tel: 519-842-9361; *Fax:* 519-688-6850
e-mail: tburgreb@bellnet.ca
URL: www.tburgreb.ca

Linda Coldham, President

Timmins Real Estate Board
225 Algonquin Blvd. E, Timmins ON P4N 1B4
Tel: 705-268-5451; *Fax:* 705-264-6420
e-mail: treb@ntl.sympatico.ca

Anne Marie Vaillancourt, Executive Officer

Toronto Real Estate Board (TREB)
1400 Don Mills Rd., Toronto ON M3B 3N1
Tel: 416-443-8100; *Fax:* 416-443-0797
URL: www.torontorealestateboard.com

William E. Johnston, President
Stuart Braund, Director

Valley Real Estate Board Inc. / Association Immobilière de la Vallée Ltée
PO Box 192, 72 Daigle St., Edmundston NB E3V 1M1
Tel: 506-737-8083; *Fax:* 506-737-8145
e-mail: valleyboard@nb.aibn.com

Lyne LeBel, Executive Officer

Vancouver Island Real Estate Board (VIREB)
6374 Metral Dr., Nanaimo BC V9T 2L8
Tel: 250-390-4212; *Fax:* 250-390-5014
e-mail: bbenoit@vireb.com
URL: www.vireb.com

Subhadra Ghose, President
Ray Francis, Vice-President
Bill Benoit, CAE, Executive Officer

Victoria Real Estate Board (VREB)
3035 Nanaimo St., Victoria BC V8T 4W2
Tel: 250-385-7766; *Fax:* 250-385-8773
e-mail: vreb@vreb.org
URL: www.vreb.org

Glenn Terrell, Executive Officer
Tony Joe, President

West Central Alberta Real Estate Board
162 Athabasca Ave., Hinton AB T7V 2A5

Tel: 780-865-7511; Fax: 780-865-7517
e-mail: wcareb@shaw.ca
Sandy Atfield, Executive Officer
Marcel Dery, President

Weyburn Real Estate Board
110 Souris Ave., Weyburn SK S4H 2Z8
Tel: 306-848-1000; Fax: 306-842-3989
e-mail: remax.weyburn@sasktel.net
Shelly Baudria, Vice-President
Lyle Leonard, President

Windsor-Essex County Real Estate Board
3020 Deziel Dr., Windsor ON N8W 5H8
Tel: 519-966-6432; Fax: 519-966-4469
e-mail: info@windsorrealestate.com
URL: www.windsorrealestate.com
Krista Del Gatto, Executive Officer

Winnipeg Real Estate Board (WREB)
1240 Portage Ave., Winnipeg MB R3G 0T6
Tel: 204-786-8854; Fax: 204-784-2343
e-mail: jwood@winnipegrealtors.ca
URL: www.winnipegrealtors.ca
Affiliation(s): Winnipeg Chamber of Commerce
Peter Squire, Contact

Woodstock-Ingersoll & District Real Estate Board
#6, 65 Springbank Ave., Woodstock ON N4S 8V8
Tel: 519-539-3616; Fax: 519-539-1975
e-mail: widreb@bellnet.ca
URL: boards.mls.ca/woodstock
Carol Smith-Gee, Executive Officer

Yellowknife Real Estate Board
#201, 5204 - 50 Ave., Yellowknife NT X1A 1E2
Tel: 867-920-4624; Fax: 867-873-6387
e-mail: officecomp@ssimicro.com
URL: boards.mls.ca/yellowknife
Nicole Chernish, Secretary/Treasurer & Executive Off

York Region Real Estate Board (YRREB)
28 Main St. North, Newmarket ON L3Y 3Z7
Tel: 905-895-7624; Fax: 905-895-9216
Susanne Miller, President

Yorkton Real Estate Association Inc. (YREA)
#040, 41 Broadway West, Yorkton SK S3N 0L6
Tel: 306-783-3067; Fax: 306-782-3231
e-mail: yrea@sasktel.net
Judy Pfeifer, Executive Officer
Ron Skinner, President

Yukon Real Estate Association
49 Waterfront Pl., Whitehorse YT Y1A 6V1
Tel: 867-633-4290; Fax: 867-667-2299
e-mail: colleen@yrea.ca; president@yrea.ca
URL: www.yrea.yk.ca

Recreation, Hobbies & Games

Alberta Camping Association (ACA)
Percy Page Centre, 11759 Groat Rd., Edmonton AB T5M 3K6
Tel: 780-427-6605; Fax: 780-427-6695
e-mail: info@albertacamping.com
URL: www.albertacamping.com
Laureen Wray, President
Scott Lister, Treasurer

Alberta Recreation & Parks Association (ARPA)
11759 Groat Rd., Edmonton AB T5M 3K6
Tel: 780-415-1745; Fax: 780-451-7915
Toll-Free: 877-544-1747
e-mail: arpa@arpaonline.ca
URL: www.arpaonline.ca
Rick Curtis, Executive Director
Shelley Shea, President
Terry Welsh, Secretary
Judi Frank, Treasurer

Alberta Snowmobile Association (ASA)
11759 Groat Rd., Edmonton AB T5M 3K6
Tel: 780-427-2695; Fax: 780-415-1779
e-mail: info@altasnowmobile.ab.ca
URL: www.altasnowmobile.ab.ca
Affiliation(s): Canadian Council of Snowmobile Organizations
Louise A. Sherren, Executive Director

Alberta Sport Parachuting Association (ASPA)
#63, 2505 - 42 St., Edmonton AB T6L 7G8
e-mail: admin@aspa.ca
URL: www.aspa.ca
Phil Perry, President

Alberta Sprint Racing Canoe Association
11759 Groat Rd., Edmonton AB T5M 3K6
Tel: 780-203-3987
e-mail: arsca@shaw.ca
URL: www.albertasprintcanoe.com
Rick Hill, President

Alberta Whitewater Association (AWA)
Percy Page Centre, 11759 Groat Rd., Edmonton AB T5M 3K6
Tel: 780-427-6717; Fax: 780-427-0524
e-mail: kayakawa@telusplanet.net
URL: www.albertawhitewater.ca
Affiliation(s): Canadian Recreational Canoe Association
Sue Azofeifa, President

All Terrain Vehicle Association of Nova Scotia (ATVANS)
PO Box 46020, Stn. Novalea, Halifax NS B3K 5V8
Tel: 902-241-3200
Toll-Free: 877-288-4244
e-mail: admin@atvans.org
URL: www.atvans.org
Mike Marriott, President
Ray Gouthro, Executive Director

Association canadienne de saut de barils inc. / Canadian Barrel Jumping Association Inc.
1465, Place Louis-Fréchette, Saint-Bruno QC J3V 2T8
Tél: 450-653-9460
Gilles Leclerc, Président

Association des camps du Québec inc. (ACQ) / Québec Camping Association
CP 1000, Succ. M, 4545, av Pierre-de-Coubertin, Montréal QC H1V 3R2
Tél: 514-252-3113; Téléc: 514-252-1650
Ligne sans frais: 800-361-3586
Courriel: info@camps.qc.ca
URL: www.camps.qc.ca
Affiliation(s): Regroupement loisir Québec; Association des camps du Canada
Louis Jean, Directeur général
François Vézina, Président

Association of Canadian Mountain Guides (ACMG) / Association des guides de montagne canadiens
PO Box 8341, Canmore AB T1W 2V1
Tel: 403-678-2885; Fax: 403-609-0070
e-mail: acmg@acmg.ca
URL: www.acmg.ca
Peter Tucker, Executive Director
Scott Davis, President

Association québécoise de canoë-kayak de vitesse (AQCKV)
CP 1000, Succ. M, 4545, av Pierre-de Coubertin, Montréal QC H1V 3R2
Tél: 514-252-3086; Téléc: 514-252-3094
Courriel: directeur.technique@aqckv.qc.ca
URL: www.aqckv.qc.ca
Luc Therrien, Président

British Columbia Camping Association
c/o Sasamat Outdoor Centre, 3302 Senkler Rd., Belcarra BC V3H 4S3
Tel: 604-931-6449; Fax: 604-939-8522
e-mail: info@bccamping.org
URL: www.bccamping.org
Hart Banack, President

British Columbia Fishing Resorts & Outfitters Association (BCFROA)
PO Box 3301, Kamloops BC V2C 6B9
Tel: 250-374-6836; Fax: 250-374-6640
Toll-Free: 800-374-6836
e-mail: bcfroa@bcfroa.ca
URL: www.bcfroa.ca
Jan Lingford, Executive Director

British Columbia Hang Gliding/Paragliding Association (BCHPA)
PO Box 41, Heffley Creek BC V0E 1Z0
Tel: 250-767-6717
e-mail: confusedone@uniserve.ca
URL: www.bchpa.org
Mike Miller, President

British Columbia Recreation & Parks Association (BCRPA)
#101, 4664 Lougheed Hwy., Burnaby BC V5C 5T5
Tel: 604-629-0965; Fax: 604-629-2651
Toll-Free: 866-929-0965
e-mail: bcrpa@bcrpa.bc.ca
URL: www.bcrpa.bc.ca
Sharon Meredith, Operations Manager
Suzanne Allard Strutt, CEO

British Columbia Sailing Association
#223, 3820 Cessna Dr., Richmond BC V7B 0A2
Tel: 604-333-3628; Fax: 604-333-3626
e-mail: crew@bcsailing.bc.ca
URL: www.bcsailing.bc.ca
Affiliation(s): Canadian Yachting Association; International Sailing Federation; Sport BC
Tine Moberg-Parker, Executive Director

British Columbia Snowmobile Federation (BCSF)
Stn. 400, 2439 Poulton Ave., Houston BC V0Y 1Z0
Tel: 250-845-7705; Fax: 250-845-7715
Toll-Free: 877-537-8716
e-mail: office@bcsf.org
URL: www.bcsf.org
Affiliation(s): International Snowmobile Council; Canadian Council of Snowmobile Organizations
Les Auston, Executive Director

The Bruce Trail Association (BTA)
PO Box 857, Hamilton ON L8N 3N9
Tel: 905-529-6821; Fax: 905-529-6823
Toll-Free: 800-665-4453
e-mail: info@brucetrail.org
URL: www.brucetrail.org
Affiliation(s): Ontario Trails Council; Coalition on the Niagara Escarpment; Federation of Ontario Naturalists; Hike Ontario
Beth K□mmling, Executive Director

Campground Owners Association of Nova Scotia (COANS)
c/o Arm of Gold Campground, 24 Church Rd., Little Bras d'Or, Cape Breton NS B1Y 2Y2
Tel: 902-736-6671
e-mail: info@campingnovascotia.com
URL: www.campingnovascotia.com
John Brennick, President
Chris Miller, Vice-President

Canadian Aerophilatelic Society (CAS) / La société canadienne d'aérophilatélie (SCA)
203A Woodfield Dr., Nepean ON K2G 4P2
URL: www.aerophilately.ca
Chris Hargreaves, President
Neil Hunter, Vice-President
Brian Wolfenden, Secretary-Treasurer

The Canadian Association of Fitness Professionals / Association canadienne des professionnels en conditionnement physique
#110, 255 Consumers Rd., Toronto ON M2J 1R4
Tel: 416-493-3515; Fax: 416-493-1756
Toll-Free: 800-667-5622
e-mail: info@canfitpro.com
URL: www.canfitpro.com
Social Media: www.facebook.com/group.php?gid=2524100816
Maureen Hagan, Executive Director
Kathy Ash, Contact, Administration

Canadian Association of Numismatic Dealers (CAND) / Association canadienne des marchands numismatiques
PO Box 10272, Stn. Winona, Stoney Creek ON L8E 5R1
Tel: 905-643-4988; Fax: 905-643-6329
e-mail: info@cand.org
URL: www.cand.org
Richard Simpson, President
Jo-Anne Simpson, Executive Secretary

Canadian Association of Wooden Money Collectors (CAWMC)
c/o Norm Belsten, 86 Hamilton Dr., Newmarket ON L3Y 3E8
e-mail: nbelsten@sympatico.ca
Norm Belsten, Contact

Canadian Baton Twirling Federation (CBTF) / Fédération baton canadienne
35 Traynor Bay, Winnipeg MB R2M 4H7
Tel: 204-257-2206; Fax: 204-257-2206
e-mail: info_cbtf@canada.com
URL: www.cbtf.ca
Gail Ashcroft, President
Loranne Meek, First Vice-President

Canadian Boating Federation / Fédération nautique du Canada
410, rue Victoria, Valleyfield QC J6K 4M3

Tel: 450-377-4122; *Fax:* 450-377-5282
e-mail: cbfnc@bellnet.ca
URL: www.cbfnc.ca

Lise Haineault, President
Derek Anderson, Vice-President, Racing
Pierre Foucher, Vice-President, Public Relations
Scott Toole, Vice-President, Outboard
Natalie Bourdeau, Secretary
Denise Mack, Treasurer

Canadian BodyBuilding Federation (CBBF) / Fédération canadienne de culturisme

e-mail: info@cbbf.ca
URL: www.cbbf.ca

Affiliation(s): International Federation for Body Building & Fitness (IFBB); British Columbia Amateur BodyBuilding Association; Alberta BodyBuilding Association; Saskatchewan Amateur BodyBuilders Association (SABBA); Manitoba Amateur BodyBuilding Association; Ontario Physique Association (OPA); FCPAQ (Quebec); New Brunswick Physique & Figure Association; Nova Scotia Amateur BodyBuilders Association; Newfoundland & Labrador Amateur BodyBuilding Association
Mark Smishek, President
Karen MacLean, Vice-President
John MacLellan, Secretary-Treasurer

Canadian Bridge Federation (CFB) / La Fédération canadienne incorporée de bridge
2719 East Jolly Pl., Regina SK S4V 0X8

Tel: 306-761-1677; *Fax:* 306-789-4919
e-mail: can.bridge.fed@sasktel.net
URL: www.cbf.ca

Affiliation(s): American Contract Bridge League
Janice Anderson, Executive Assitant
Mike Hartop, President

Canadian Camping Association (CCA) / Association des camps du Canada (ACC)
2494, rte 125 sud, St-Donat QC J0T 2C0

Tel: 819-424-2662; *Fax:* 819-424-2662
Toll-Free: 877-427-6958
e-mail: info@ccamping.org
URL: www.ccamping.org

Jeff Bradshaw, President

Canadian Casting Federation
c/o Toronto Sportsmen's Association, 17 Mill St., Toronto ON M2P 1B3

Tel: 416-487-4477; *Fax:* 416-487-4478
URL: www.torontosportsmens.ca/Casting.html

Canadian Correspondence Chess Association (CCCA) / L'Association canadienne des échecs par correspondance (ACEC)
#4, 1669 Country Rd., L'Orignal QC K0B 1K0

Tel: 613-632-3166
e-mail: ccca@cogeco.ca
URL: correspondencechess.com/ccca/index.htm

Manny Migicovsky, President

Canadian Council of Snowmobile Organizations (CCSO) / Conseil canadien des organismes de motoneige (CCOM)
PO Box 21059, Thunder Bay ON P7A 8A7

Tel: 807-345-5299
e-mail: ccso.ccom@tbaytel.net
URL: www.ccso-ccom.ca

Kevin Sweetland, President
Patrick McGrath, 1st Vice-President, Communications
Brenda R. Welsh, Secretary-Treasurer
Craig Giles, National Coordinator, Safety

Canadian Fitness & Lifestyle Research Institute (CFLRI) / Institut canadien de la recherche sur la condition physique et le mode de vie
#201, 185 Somerset St. West, Ottawa ON K2P 0J2

Tel: 613-233-5528; *Fax:* 613-233-5536
e-mail: info@cflri.ca
URL: www.cflri.ca

Lawrence Brawley, Chair
Cora Lynn Craig, President & Chief Scientist

Canadian Flag Association (CFA) / Association canadienne de vexillologie (ACV)
50 Heathfield Dr., Toronto ON M1M 3B1

Tel: 416-267-9618; *Fax:* 416-267-9618
e-mail: kevin.harrington@sympatico.ca
URL: www.crwflags.com/fotw/flags/vex-cfa.html

Kevin Harrington, President

Canadian International DX Club (CIDX)
PO Box 67063, Stn. Lemoyne, Saint-Lambert QC J4R 2T8

e-mail: cidxclub@yahoo.com
URL: www.anarc.org/cidx

Sheldon Harvey, President

Canadian Motorcycle Association (CMA) / Association motocycliste canadienne
PO Box 448, Hamilton ON L8L 8C4

Tel: 905-522-5705; *Fax:* 905-522-5716
e-mail: registration@canmocycle.ca
URL: www.canmocycle.ca

Affiliation(s): Fédération internationale motocycliste; Canadian Olympic Association; North American Motorcycle Union
Marilyn Bastedo, General Manager
Joseph Godsall, President

Canadian Numismatic Association (CNA) / Association canadienne de numismatique
#432, 5694 Hwy. 7 East, Markham ON L3P 1B4

Tel: 647-401-4014; *Fax:* 905-472-9645
e-mail: cnainfo@rogers.com
URL: www.nunet.ca

Michael Walsh, President
Daniel Gosling, F.C.N.A., Librarian

Canadian Orienteering Federation (COF) / Fédération canadienne de course d'orientation
1239 Colgrove Ave. NE, Calgary AB T2C 5C3

Tel: 403-283-0807; *Fax:* 403-451-1681
e-mail: info@orienteering.ca
URL: www.orienteering.ca

Social Media: www.facebook.com/group.php?gid=64406548384
Affiliation(s): International Orienteering Federation
Charlotte MacNaughton, President

Canadian Paper Money Society (CPMS)
Attn: Dick Dunn, PO Box 562, Pickering ON L1V 2R7

Tel: 905-509-1146
e-mail: cpms@idirect.com
URL: www.nunetcan.net/cpms.htm

Dick Dunn, Sec.-Treas.

Canadian Parks & Recreation Association (CPRA) / Association canadienne des parcs et loisirs
#404, 2197 Riverside Dr., Ottawa ON K1H 7X3

Tel: 613-523-5315; *Fax:* 613-523-1182
e-mail: cpra@cpra.ca
URL: www.cpra.ca

Sharon Jollimore, Director, National Initiatives & Alliances
Tanara Pickard, Director, Corporate Development & Member Services
Kathleen Luten, Office Manager

Canadian Parks & Wilderness Society (CPAWS) / Société pour la nature et les parcs du Canada (SNAP)
#506, 250 City Centre Ave., Ottawa ON K1R 6K7

Tel: 613-569-7226; *Fax:* 613-569-7098
Toll-Free: 800-333-9453
e-mail: info@cpaws.org
URL: www.cpaws.org

Chris Henschel, National Manager, Domestic & International Affairs
Sabine Jessen, National Manager, Oceans & Great Freshwater Lakes Program
Chris Miller, National Manager, Wilderness Conservation & Climate Change
Aran O'Carroll, LLB, National Manager, Legislative & Regulatory Affairs

Canadian Power & Sail Squadrons (Canadian Headquarters) (CPS) / Escadrilles canadiennes de plaisance (ECP)
26 Golden Gate Ct., Toronto ON M1P 3A5

Tel: 416-293-2438; *Fax:* 416-293-2445
Toll-Free: 888-277-2628
e-mail: hgg@cps-ecp.ca
URL: www.cps-ecp.ca

Alain Brière, Executive Director
John Gullick, Manager, Government & Special Programs

Canadian Racing Pigeon Union Inc.
#C, 261 Tillson Ave., Tillsonburg ON N4G 5X2

Tel: 519-842-9771; *Fax:* 519-842-8809
Toll-Free: 866-652-5704
e-mail: crpu@execulink.com
URL: www.canadianracingpigeonunion.com

Affiliation(s): Fédération colombophile internationale
Nick Oud, President
Monica Collins, Sec.-Treas.

Canadian Sport Parachuting Association (CSPA) / Association canadienne du parachutisme sportif (ACPS)
300 Forced Rd., Russell ON K4R 1A1

Tel: 613-445-1881; *Fax:* 613-445-2698
e-mail: office@cspa.ca
URL: www.cspa.ca

Judy Donnelly, Executive Secretary
Tim Grech, President

Canadian Stamp Dealers' Association (CSDA) / Association canadienne des négociants en timbres-poste (ACNTP)
PO Box 81, Stn. Lambeth, London ON N6P 1P9

e-mail: director@csdaonline.com
URL: www.csdaonline.com

John Sheffield, Executive Director
Rick Day, President
Lyse Rousseau, Vice-President
John Beddows, Secretary
Isidore Baum, Treasurer

Canadian Table Soccer Federation
8311, rue Ouimet, Brossard QC J4Y 3B3

Tel: 514-668-2326
e-mail: secretary@canadafoos.com
URL: www.canadafoos.com

Eric Dunn, President
Adam Imanpoor, Secretary

Canadian Table Tennis Association (CTTA) / Association canadienne de tennis de table
#400, 2211 Riverside Dr., Ottawa ON K1H 7X5

Tel: 613-733-6272; *Fax:* 613-733-7279
e-mail: ctta@ctta.ca
URL: www.ctta.ca

Affiliation(s): Sports Council of Canada
Manali Haridas, Office Administrator
Tony Kiesenhofer, Director General

Canadian Toy Collectors' Society Inc. (CTCS)
#245, 91 Rylander Blvd., Unit 7, Toronto ON M1B 5M5

e-mail: ctcsweb@hotmail.com
URL: www.ctcs.org

Affiliation(s): Dufferin County Museum & Archives
Ron Blair, President

Canadian Trapshooting Association (CTA)
RR#1, Penhold AB T0M 1R0

Tel: 403-886-2600; *Fax:* 403-886-2600

Bob Brown, President

Canadian Yachting Association (CYA) / Association canadienne de yachting
Portsmith Olympic Harbour, 53 Yonge St., Kingston ON K7M 6G4

Tel: 613-545-3044; *Fax:* 613-545-3045
Toll-Free: 877-416-4720
e-mail: sailcanada@sailing.ca
URL: www.sailing.ca

Affiliation(s): International Sailing Federation; International Sailing Schools Association
Gerry Giffin, President

Canoe Kayak New Brunswick
PO Box 263, Moncton NB E1C 8K9

Toll-Free: 800-363-6060
e-mail: president@canoenb.org
URL: www.canoekayaknb.org

Evan Young, President

Canoe Kayak Nova Scotia (CKNS)
5516 Spring Garden Rd., 4th Fl., Halifax NS B3J 1G6

Tel: 902-425-5454; *Fax:* 902-425-5606
e-mail: canoens@sportnovascotia.ca
URL: www.ckns.ca

Ike Whitehead, Administrator

Canoe Kayak Saskatchewan (CKS)
1870 Lorne St., Regina SK S4P 2L7

Tel: 306-729-4220; *Fax:* 306-729-4216
e-mail: cks@accesscomm.ca
URL: www.saskcanoe.ca

Jan Hanson, Executive Director
Fiona Vincent, President
Jeanette Hamilton, Treasurer

Canoe Newfoundland & Labrador
PO Box 23072, Stn. Churchill Sq., Saint John's NL A1B 4J9

Tel: 709-364-1601; *Fax:* 709-368-8357
e-mail: tumblehomecanoeclub@hotmail.com
URL: www.canoenfld.ca

Frank Galway, President

Canoe Ontario
c/o OCSRA, 570 Blenheim Cres., Oakville ON L6J 6P6
Tel: 905-337-8314
e-mail: jorlando1@cogeco.ca
URL: www.canoeontario.ca
Affiliation(s): Ontario Canoe Sprint Racing Affiliation; Ontario Marathon Canoe Racing Association; Whitewater Ontario
John Orlando, Treasurer

CanoeKayak BC
20585 - 124A Ave., Maple Ridge BC V2X 0M6
Tel: 604-465-5268; *Fax:* 604-460-0587
e-mail: info@canoekayakbc.ca
URL: www.canoekayakbc.ca
Mary Jane Abbot, Executive Director

CanoeKayak Canada (CKC)
#705, 2197 Riverside Dr., Ottawa ON K1H 7X3
Tel: 613-260-1818; *Fax:* 613-260-5137
e-mail: christine@canoekayak.ca
URL: www.canoekayak.ca
Anne Merklinger, Director General
Christine Lafontaine, Administrative Coordinator

CanoeKayak Canada - Atlantic Division
c/o Sport NS, 5516 Spring Garden Rd., 4th Fl., Halifax NS B3J 3G6
Tel: 902-425-5450; *Fax:* 902-425-5606
e-mail: ccaatlantic@sportnovascotia.ca
URL: www.ccaatlantic.ca
Liz Orton, Program Coordinator

Charlottetown Duplicate Bridge Club
500 Queen St., Charlottetown PE C1A 8K9
Tel: 902-894-3067

Chess Federation of Canada / Fédération canadienne des échecs
#E1, 2212 Gladwin Cres., Ottawa ON K1B 5N1
Tel: 613-733-2844; *Fax:* 613-733-5209
Toll-Free: 800-563-4476
e-mail: info@chess.ca
URL: www.chess.ca
Affiliation(s): Fédération internationale des échecs
Peter Palsson, President

Citizens for Safe Cycling (CfSC)
PO Box 248, Stn. B, Ottawa ON K1P 6C4
Tel: 613-722-4454; *Fax:* 613-722-4454
e-mail: info@safecycling.ca
URL: www.safecycling.ca
Zlatko Krstulich, President

Classical & Medieval Numismatic Society (CMNS)
PO Box 956, Stn. B, Toronto ON M2K 2T6
Tel: 416-490-8659; *Fax:* 416-490-6452
e-mail: billmcdo@idirect.com
URL: www.cmns.ca
W.H. McDonald, Executive Sec.-Treas.

Climb Yukon Association
e-mail: climbyukon@gmail.com
URL: www.climbyukon.net
Ryan Agar, President

Dominion of Canada Rifle Association (DCRA) / L'Association de tir dominion du canada
45 Shirley Blvd., Ottawa ON K2K 2W6
Tel: 613-829-8281; *Fax:* 613-829-0099
e-mail: office@dcra.ca
URL: www.dcra.ca
Jim Thompson, Executive Director
Stan E. Frost, Executive Vice-President
T.F. deFaye, President

Fédération des clubs de motoneigistes du Québec (FCMQ)
CP 1000, Succ. M, 4545, av Pierre-de Coubertin, Montréal QC H1V 3R2
Tél: 514-252-3076; *Téléc:* 514-254-2066
Courriel: info@fcmq.qc.ca
URL: www.fcmq.qc.ca
Mario Côté, Président

Federation of Mountain Clubs of British Columbia
PO Box 19673, 130 West Broadway, Vancouver BC V5T 4E7
Tel: 604-873-6096; *Fax:* 604-873-6086
e-mail: fmcbc@mountainclubs.bc.ca
URL: www.mountainclubs.bc.ca
Patrick R. Harrison, President
Ron Ford, Registrar
Brian Jones, Manager
Peter Rothermel, Vice-President

Federation of Ontario Cottagers' Associations (FOCA)
#201, 159 King St., Peterborough ON K9J 2R8
Tel: 705-749-3622; *Fax:* 705-749-6522
e-mail: info@foca.on.ca
URL: www.foca.on.ca
Terry Rees, Executive Director
Lara Griffin, Contact, Membership
Tracy Logan, Contact, Programs

Fédération québécoise de camping et de caravaning inc. (FQCC)
CP 100, 1560, rue Eiffel, Boucherville QC J4B 5Y1
Tél: 450-650-3722; *Téléc:* 450-650-3721
Ligne sans frais: 877-650-3722
Courriel: info@fqcc.ca
URL: www.fqcc.ca
Louise Saindon, Présidente
Claude Cournoyer, Trésorier

Fédération québécoise de canoë-kayak d'eau vive
CP 1000, Succ. M, 4545, av Pierre-de-Coubertin, Montréal QC H1V 3R2
Tél: 514-252-3099; *Téléc:* 514-252-3094
Courriel: fqckev@kayak.qc.ca
URL: www.kayak.qc.ca
Patrick Lévesque, Coordonnateur

Fédération québécoise de la marche
CP 1000, Succ. M, 4545, av Pierre-de Coubertin, Montréal QC H1V 3R2
Tél: 514-252-3157; *Téléc:* 514-252-5137
Ligne sans frais: 866-252-2065
Courriel: infomarche@fqmarche.qc.ca
URL: www.fqmarche.qc.ca

Fédération québécoise des échecs (FQE) / Québec Chess Federation
CP 1000, Succ. M, Montréal QC H1V 3R2
Tél: 514-252-3034; *Téléc:* 514-251-8038
Courriel: info@fqechecs.qc.ca
URL: www.fqechecs.qc.ca
Daniel Rousseau, Président

Fédération québécoise des jeux récréatifs (FQJR)
CP 1000, Succ. M, 4545, av Pierre-de Coubertin, Montréal QC H1V 3R2
Tél: 514-252-3032
Courriel: jeuxrecr@fqjr.qc.ca
URL: www.fqjr.qc.ca
André Leclerc, Directeur général

Fédération québécoise du canot et du kayak (FQCK)
CP 1000, Succ. M, 4545, av Pierre-de Coubertin, Montréal QC H1V 3R2
Tél: 514-252-3001; *Téléc:* 514-252-3091
Courriel: info@canot-kayak.qc.ca
URL: www.canot-kayak.qc.ca
Pierre Trudel, Directeur général

Guide Outfitters Association of British Columbia (GOABC)
PO Box 94675, Richmond BC V6Y 4A4
Tel: 604-278-2688; *Fax:* 604-278-3440
e-mail: info@goabc.org
URL: www.goabc.org
Affiliation(s): Council of Tourism Associations of British Columbia
Dale Drown, General Manager

Halifax North West Trails Association (HNWTA)
c/o 27 Warwick Lane, Halifax NS B3M 4J3
Tel: 902-443-5051
e-mail: info@halifaxnorthwesttrails.ca
URL: www.halifaxnorthwesttrails.ca
Todd Beal, Chair

Hang Gliding & Paragliding Association of Atlantic Canada (HPAAC)
General Delivery, Diligent River NS B0M 1H0
Tel: 902-254-2972
e-mail: jnewman@eastlink.ca
URL: www.hpaac.ca
Affiliation(s): Hang Gliding & Paragliding Association of Canada
Judith Newman, Contact

Hang Gliding & Paragliding Association of Canada (HPAC) / Association canadienne de vol libre (ACVL)
5 Millennium Dr., Stratford PE C1B 2H2
Fax: 902-367-3358
Toll-Free: 877-370-2078
e-mail: admin@hpac.ca
URL: www.hpac.ca
Domagoj Juretic, President

Sam Jeyes, Business Manager

Hike Ontario
#400, 165 Dundas St. West, Mississauga ON L5B 2N6
Tel: 905-277-4453
Toll-Free: 800-894-7249
e-mail: info@hikeontario.com
URL: www.hikeontario.com
Affiliation(s): Ontario Trails Council (OTC); Hike Canada En Marche
Terri Leroux, President
Henry Graupner, Secretary
Ron Knight, Treasurer

Ikaluktutiak Paddling Association
PO Box 125, Cambridge Bay NU X0B 0C0
Tel: 867-983-2068
e-mail: ipanorth69@gmail.com
Rob Harmer, President

International Computer Games Association (ICGA)
c/o David N.L. Levy, 34 Courthope Rd., Hampstead, London NW3 2LD England
e-mail: info@icga.org; board@icga.org; journal@icga.org
David N.L. Levy, President
Yngvi Björnsson, Vice-President
Hiroyuki Iida, Secretary-Treasurer

Manitoba Camping Association (MCA)
#302, 960 Portage Ave., Winnipeg MB R3G 0R4
Tel: 204-784-1134; *Fax:* 204-784-4177
e-mail: info@mbcamping.ca; sunshinefund@mbcamping.ca
URL: www.mbcamping.ca
Bryan Ezako, Executive Director
Laura-Ann Peterson, Coordinator, General Office Administration & Sunshine Fund Program

Manitoba Paddling Association Inc. (MPA)
200 Main St., Winnipeg MB R3C 4M2
Tel: 204-925-5678; *Fax:* 204-925-5703
e-mail: mpa@sport.mb.ca; dragonboat@sport.mb.ca
URL: www.mpa.mb.ca
Jeff Dzikowicz, Executive Director
Robin McClure, President
Marcia Hrechkosy, Secretary
Bob Hunter, Treasurer

Manitoba Recreational Canoeing Association (MRCA)
PO Box 2663, Winnipeg MB R3C 4B3
Tel: 204-338-6722
URL: www.paddle.mb.ca
Affiliation(s): Manitoba Paddling Association
Cameron White, President

Manitoba Sport Parachute Association (MSPA)
#309, 200 Main St., Winnipeg MB R3C 4M2
Tel: 204-925-5682; *Fax:* 204-925-5703
e-mail: president@mspa.mb.ca
URL: www.mspa.mb.ca
Jill Forbes, President

Model Aeronautics Association of Canada Inc. (MAAC) / Modélistes Aéronautiques Associés du Canada
#9, 5100 South Service Rd., Burlington ON L7L 6A5
Tel: 905-632-9808; *Fax:* 905-632-3304
e-mail: maachq@on.aibn.com
URL: www.maac.ca
Affiliation(s): Aero Club of Canada; Fédération aeronautique internationale
Richard Lyle Barlow, President

National Association of Watch & Clock Collectors (NAWCC)
514 Poplar St., Columbia PA 17512 USA
Tel: 717-684-8261; *Fax:* 717-684-0878
URL: www.nawcc.org
J. Steven Humphrey, Executive Director
Chuck Auman, Controller

National Association of Watch & Clock Collectors
1673, St-Jean-Baptiste, Nicolet QC J3T 1G8
e-mail: denis.h@sogetel.net

National Association of Watch & Clock Collectors
16 Brian Cres., Nepean ON K2H 6X3
e-mail: 111ovwcc@gmail.com
URL: www.ottawaclocksandwatches.ca

National Association of Watch & Clock Collectors
9952 Powell Rd., Port Franks ON N0M 2L0
e-mail: ckoolen@htl.net

National Association of Watch & Clock Collectors
846-5300 #3 Rd., Richmond BC V6X 2X9
Tel: 604-278-1631
e-mail: ron.theclockgallery@shaw.ca
URL: community.nawcc.org/NAWCC/Chapter121/Home/Default.aspx

National Association of Watch & Clock Collectors
6 Canova Rd. SW, Calgary AB T2W 2G3
URL: www.nawcc.org

National Association of Watch & Clock Collectors
PO Box 5, Beamsville ON L0R 1B0
e-mail: wmj.keel@sympatico.ca
URL: www.nawcc.org/

National Association of Watch & Clock Collectors
31 Purcell's Cove Rd., Halifax NS B3N 1R3
e-mail: blackmagik@ns.sympatico.ca
URL: www.nawcc.org

National Association of Watch & Clock Collectors
305 Victoria St., Kingston ON K7L 3Z2
e-mail: wayne.precoor@durham.on.ca
URL: www.nawcc.org

National Association of Watch & Clock Collectors
6545, 44e av, Montréal QC H1T 2N9
e-mail: denis.h@sogetel.net
URL: www.nawcc.org

National Darts Federation of Canada (NDFC) / Fédération nationale de dards du Canada
2417, rue Montante, Ascot QC J1H 6M3
Tel: 819-823-1392; *Fax:* 819-821-3539
e-mail: secretary@ndfc.ca
URL: www.ndfc.ca
Affiliation(s): World Darts Federation
Bill Hatter, President
Mary Dezan, General Secretary

National Firearms Association (NFA)
PO Box 52183, Edmonton AB T6G 2T5
Tel: 780-439-1394; *Fax:* 780-439-4091
e-mail: info@nfa.ca
URL: www.nfa.ca

New Brunswick Competitive Canoe Association
c/o Sport New Brunswick, 181 Kennebecasis River Rd., Hampton NB E5N 6L1
e-mail: nbcca_m@hotmail.com
J. Timothy Flood, President

Newfoundland & Labrador Camping Association
PO Box 50846, SS#3, St. John's NL A1B 4M2
Tel: 709-576-6198; *Fax:* 709-576-8146
e-mail: malcolmcturner@gmail.com
Malcolm C. Turner

Newfoundland & Labrador Paddling Association (NLPA)
103« Forest Rd., St. John's NL A1A 1E4
Affiliation(s): Kayak Newfoundland & Labrador; Tumblehome Recreational Canoe Club
Allan Goodridge, President
Brian Hemeon, Vice-President, Canoeing
Darren MacDonald, Vice-President, Kayaking
Neil Burgess, Secretary
Alex Mcgruer, Treasurer

Northwest Territories Recreation & Parks Association
PO Box 841, Yellowknife NT X1A 2N6
Tel: 867-873-5340; *Fax:* 867-669-6791
URL: www.nwtrpa.org
Affiliation(s): Sport North
Wendy Lahey, Executive Director
Ruth Rolfe, President

Nova Scotia Trails Federation (NSTF)
5516 Spring Garden Rd., 4th Fl., Halifax NS B3J 1G6
Tel: 902-425-5450; *Fax:* 902-425-5606
e-mail: nstrails@sportnovascotia.ca
URL: www.novascotiatrails.com
Social Media: www.twitter.com/NSTrails
Ted Scrutton, President

Ontario Camps Association (OCA)
#403, 250 Merton St., Toronto ON M4S 1B1
Tel: 416-485-0425; *Fax:* 416-485-0422
e-mail: info@ontariocamps.ca
URL: www.ontariocamps.ca
Rick Howard, President
Aruna Ogale, Executive Director

Ontario Federation of Snowmobile Clubs (OFSC)
#9, 501 Welham Rd., Barrie ON L4N 8Z6
Tel: 705-739-7669; *Fax:* 705-739-5005
URL: www.ofsc.on.ca

Ontario Marine Operators Association (OMOA)
15 Laurier Rd., Penetanguishene ON L9M 1G8
Tel: 705-549-1667; *Fax:* 705-549-1670
Toll-Free: 888-547-6662
e-mail: omoa@marinasontario.com
URL: www.marinasontario.com
Dick Peever, President
Graham Lacey, Vice-President
Al Donaldson, Executive Director
Ed Leeman, Secretary
Bob Eaton, Director, Environmental Services

Ontario Numismatic Association (ONA)
PO Box 40033, Stn. Waterloo Square, Waterloo ON N2J 4V1
Tel: 519-745-3104
e-mail: robb4359@hotmail.com
URL: www.nunetcan.net/ona.htm
Tom Rogers, President
Paul Petch, First Vice-President

Ontario Parks Association (OPA)
7956 - 5 Line South, Milton ON L9T 2X8
Tel: 905-864-6182; *Fax:* 905-864-6184
Toll-Free: 866-560-7783
e-mail: opa@opassoc.on.ca
URL: www.opassoc.on.ca
Affiliation(s): International Society of Aboriculture Ontario; Landscape Ontario; Ontario Association of Landscape Architects; Ontario Environment Network; Ontario Trails Council; Sports Turf Association; Parks & Recreation Ontario; Ontario Recreation Facilities Association
Eric Trogdon, Executive Director
Maureen Sinclair, President
Bill Harding, Vice-President

Ontario Recreation Facilities Association Inc. (ORFA)
#102, 1 Concorde Gate, Toronto ON M3C 3N6
Tel: 416-426-7062; *Fax:* 416-426-7385
Toll-Free: 800-661-6732
e-mail: info@orfa.com; admin@orfa.com
URL: www.orfa.com
Rob Lilbourne, President & Chair
John Milton, Chief Administrative Officer
Remo Petrongolo, Director, Business Development
Terry Piche, RRFA, CIT, Director, Technical
Hubie Basilio, Coordinator, Public Relations & Communications
Rebecca Russell, Facilities Librarian

Ontario Recreational Canoeing and Kayaking Association (ORCKA)
#411, 1185 Eglinton Ave. East, Toronto ON M3C 3C6
Tel: 416-426-7016; *Fax:* 416-426-7363
e-mail: info@orca.on.ca
URL: www.orca.on.ca
Gordon Haggert, President

Ontario Research Council on Leisure (ORCOL) / Conseil Ontarien de Recherche en Loisir
c/o Recreation & Leisure Studies, Faculty of Applied Health Sciences, University of Waterloo, Waterloo ON N2L 3G1
e-mail: smale@healthy.uwaterloo.ca
URL: www.orcol.uwaterloo.ca
Bryan Smale, President
Don Reid, Treasurer

Ontario Sport Fishing Guides' Association (OSGA)
PO Box 39, Cedar Springs ON N0P 1E0
Tel: 519-676-7421
e-mail: fish@mnsi.net
URL: www.ontariofishcharters.ca
Adam Godfrey, Secretary, fish@mnsi.net

Ontario Trails Council
#130, 556 O'Connor Dr., Kingston ON K7P 1N3
Tel: 613-389-7678; *Fax:* 613-389-6329
Toll-Free: 877-668-7245
e-mail: admin@ontariotrails.on.ca
URL: www.ontariotrails.on.ca
Affiliation(s): Bruce Trail Association; Canadian Motorcycling Association; Guelph Trail Club; Hike Ontario; Kawartha Rail-Trail; Ontario Federation of Snowmobile Clubs; Ontario Cycling Association; Ontario Competitive Trail Riders Association; Ontario Working Dog Association; Parry Sound Rail Line Task Force; Rideau Trail Association; Northland Associates; Ontario Trail Riders Association; Rails to Trails Conservancy - USA; Credit Valley Conservation Authority; Georgian Cycle & Ski Trail Association; Grand Valley Trail Association; Southeastern Ontario Rails to Tracks
Jack deWit, President

Ontario Vintage Radio Association (OVRA)
197 Humberside Ave., Toronto ON M6P 1K7
Tel: 416-769-9627
URL: www.ovra.ca
Ted Catton, President

Orienteering Association of British Columbia (OABC)
4337 San Cristo Pl., Victoria BC V8N 5G5
URL: www.orienteeringbc.ca
Affiliation(s): Canadian Orienteering Federation (COF); Coaching Association of Canada
John Rance, President
Alex Kerr, Secretary

Outdoor Recreation Council of British Columbia (ORC)
#334, 1367 West Broadway, Vancouver BC V6H 4A9
Tel: 604-737-3058; *Fax:* 604-737-3666
e-mail: orc@intergate.ca
URL: www.orcbc.ca
Affiliation(s): Environmental Fund of BC
Gordon F. Weetman, Chair
Jeremy McCall, Secretary/Treasurer

Outward Bound Canada
996 Chetwynd Rd., RR #2, Burks Falls ON P0A 1C0
Fax: 705-382-5959
Toll-Free: 888-688-9273
URL: www.outwardbound.ca
Dave Wolfenden, Executive Director

Paddle Canada (PC) / Pagaie Canada
PO Box 20069, Stn. RPO Taylor-Kidd, Kingston ON K7P 2T6
Tel: 613-547-3196; *Fax:* 613-547-4880
Toll-Free: 888-252-6292
e-mail: info@paddlingcanada.com
URL: www.paddlingcanada.com
Affiliation(s): Active Living Alliance for Canadians with a Disability; Canadian Heritage Rivers System; Girl Guides of Canada
Sue J. Hopson, Business Manager

Parks & Recreation Ontario (PRO) / Parcs et loisirs de l'Ontario
#302, 1 Concorde Gate, Toronto ON M3C 3N6
Tel: 416-426-7142; *Fax:* 416-426-7371
e-mail: pro@prontario.org
URL: www.prontario.org
Larry Ketcheson, CEO

Prince Edward Island Canoe Kayak Association
RR#4, Alliston, Montague PE C0A 1R0
Tel: 902-962-3883; *Fax:* 902-962-3883
e-mail: justin.heidi@windsinc.com
URL: www.windsinc.com/canoekayak/canoekayak.htm
Justin Richard Batten, President

Prince Edward Island Recreational Canoeing Association
PO Box 5604, RR#5, Charlottetown PE C1A 7J8
Tel: 902-368-6355; *Fax:* 902-368-6186
Shawn Shea, Chair

Prince Edward Island Underwater Council
c/o Sport PEI, 3 Queen St., Charlottetown PE C1A 7K7
Tel: 902-368-4110
e-mail: a.cannon@pei.sympatico.ca

Recreation and Parks Association of the Yukon (RPAY)
4061, 4th Ave., Whitehorse YT Y1A 1H1
Tel: 867-668-3010; *Fax:* 867-668-2455
e-mail: rpay@klondiker.com
URL: www.rpay.org
Ian Spencer, President
Anne Morgan, Executive Director

Recreation Facilities Association of British Columbia (RFABC)
PO Box 320, #110, 174 Wilson St., Victoria BC V9A 7N7
Fax: 604-414-0068
Toll-Free: 877-285-3421
e-mail: info@rfabc.com
URL: www.rfabc.com
Lori Blackman, President
Karin Carlson, Chair, Marketing
Garry Rushton, Chair, Membership
Shallon Touet, Chair, Education

Recreation New Brunswick
#34, 55 Whiting Road, Fredericton NB E3B 5Y5
Tel: 506-459-1929; *Fax:* 506-450-6066
e-mail: info@recreationnb.ca
URL: www.recreationnb.ca
Jamie Shanks, Executive Director

Recreation Newfoundland & Labrador
Bldg. 810, Pleasantville, PO Box 8700, Stn. A, St. John's NL A1B 4J6
Tel: 709-729-3892; *Fax:* 709-729-3814
URL: www.recreationnl.com
Affiliation(s): Provincial/Territorial parks & recreation associations
Wanda Wight, President
Gary Milley, Executive Director

Recreation Nova Scotia (RNS)
#309, 5516 Spring Garden Rd., Halifax NS B3J 1G6
Tel: 902-425-1128; *Fax:* 902-422-8201
e-mail: info@recreationns.ns.ca
URL: www.recreationns.ns.ca
Dawn Stegan, Executive Director
Dianne Paquet, President Elect
Dawn Stegen, Executive Director

Recreational Canoeing Association BC (RCABC)
1755 East 7th Ave., Vancouver BC V5N 1S1
Tel: 604-253-5410; *Fax:* 604-253-5490
e-mail: sec@bccanoe.com
URL: www.bccanoe.com
Alan Thomson, President
Jean Chandler, Secretary

Roller Sports Canada / Sports à roulettes du Canada
c/o Roller Sports Manitoba, #312, 200 Main St., Winnipeg MB R3C 4M2
Tel: 204-925-5699; *Fax:* 204-925-5703
e-mail: rollersportsmb@shawbiz.ca
URL: www.rollersport.mb.ca

The Royal Philatelic Society of Canada (RPSC) / La Société royale de philatélie du Canada (SRPC)
PO Box 929, Stn. Q, Toronto ON M4T 2P1
Tel: 416-921-2077; *Fax:* 416-921-1282
Toll-Free: 888-285-4143
e-mail: info@rpsc.org
URL: www.rpsc.org
George Pepall, FRPSC, President
Peter Butler, Executive Director

S.A.L.T.S. Sail & Life Training Society (SALTS)
PO Box 5014, Stn. B, Victoria BC V8R 6N3
Tel: 250-383-6811; *Fax:* 250-383-7781
e-mail: info@saltsociety.com
URL: www.saltsociety.ca
Loren Hagerty, Executive Director

Saskatchewan Association of Recreation Professionals (SARP)
2205 Victoria Ave., Regina SK S4P 0S4
Tel: 306-780-9267; *Fax:* 306-525-4009
Toll-Free: 800-667-7780
e-mail: sarp.sk@sasktel.net
URL: www.sarp-online.ca
Warren Poncsak, Executive Director
Chantelle Erdman, Chantelle

Saskatchewan Camping Association (SCA)
PO Box 8862, 390 Castle Road, Saskatoon SK S4S 6A4
Tel: 306-586-4026; *Fax:* 306-790-8634
e-mail: info@saskcamping.ca
URL: www.saskcamping.ca
Donna Wilkinson, Executive Director

Saskatchewan Parks & Recreation Association (SPRA)
#100, 1445 Park St., Regina SK S4N 4C5
Tel: 306-780-9231; *Fax:* 306-780-9257
Toll-Free: 800-563-2555
e-mail: office@spra.sk.ca
URL: www.spra.sk.ca
Norm Campbell, Chief Executive Officer
Randy Durovick, Manager, Facilities & Membership Services
Norm Campbell, CEO

Saskatchewan Snowmobile Association Inc. (SSA)
PO Box 533, 221 Centre St., Regina Beach SK S0G 4C0
Tel: 306-729-3500; *Fax:* 306-729-3505
Toll-Free: 800-499-7533
e-mail: sasksnow@sasktel.net
URL: www.sasksnowmobiling.sk.ca
Barry Bradshaw, Chair
George Belchamber, Co-Chair

Shooting Federation of Canada (SFC) / Fédération de tir du Canada (FTC)
45 Shirley Blvd., Nepean ON K2K 2W6
Tel: 613-727-7483; *Fax:* 613-727-7487
e-mail: info@sfc-ftc.ca
URL: www.sfc-ftc.ca
Affiliation(s): Canadian Shooting Sports Association
Reg Potter, President

Snowmobilers Association of Nova Scotia (SANS)
5516 Spring Garden Rd., 4th Fl., Halifax NS B3J 3G6
Tel: 902-425-5450; *Fax:* 902-425-5606
e-mail: info@snowmobilersNS.com
URL: www.snowmobilersns.com
John Cameron, General Manager

Snowmobilers of Manitoba Inc.
2121 Henderson Hwy., Winnipeg MB R2G 1P8
Tel: 204-940-7533; *Fax:* 204-940-7531
e-mail: info@snoman.mb.ca
URL: www.snoman.mb.ca
Affiliation(s): Canadian Council of Snowmobile Organizations
Duncan Stokes, Executive Director

Soaring Association of Canada (SAC) / Association canadienne de vol à voile (ACVV)
#107, 1025 Richmond Rd., Ottawa ON K2B 8G8
Tel: 613-829-0536; *Fax:* 613-829-9497
e-mail: sac@sac.ca
URL: www.sac.ca
Affiliation(s): Aero Club of Canada; International Gliding Commission of the Fédération Aéronautique Internationale
John Toles, President
James F. McCollum, Executive Director

Sport Parachute Association of Saskatchewan
PO Box 37056, Regina SK S4S 7K3
Tel: 306-934-8528
URL: www.skydive.sk.ca
Craig Skihar, President
Burk Reiman, Vice-President

Taoist Tai Chi Society of Canada
134 Darcy St., Toronto ON M5T 1K3
Tel: 416-656-2110; *Fax:* 416-654-3937
e-mail: headoffice@taoist.org
URL: www.taoist.org

Trail Riders of the Canadian Rockies
PO Box 6742, Stn. D, Calgary AB T2P 2E6
Tel: 403-652-8672; *Fax:* 403-261-2813
e-mail: admin@trail-rides.ca
URL: www.trail-rides.ca
Terry Stowell, Executive Director
Penny Egeland, Secretary

Trans Canada Trail Foundation (TCTF) / Fondation du sentier transcanadian
43, av Westminster nord, Montréal QC H4X 1Y8
Tel: 514-485-3959; *Fax:* 514-485-4541
Toll-Free: 800-465-3636
e-mail: info@tctrail.ca
URL: www.tctrail.ca
Deborah Apps, President & CEO

Tunnelling Association of Canada (TAC) / Association canadienne des tunnels
c/o Earthtech, 105 Commerce Valley Dr. West, 7th Fl., Markham ON L3T 7W3
Tel: 905-886-7022
e-mail: info@tunnelcanada.ca
URL: www.tunnelcanada.ca
Derek Zoldy, Treasurer
Garry Stevenson, President

Velo Halifax Bicycle Club
PO Box 125, Dartmouth NS B2Y 3Y2
URL: www.velohalifax.ca
Walton Watt, Registrar

Whitewater Kayaking Association of British Columbia (WKABC)
PO Box 91549, Stn. West Vancouver, Vancouver BC V7V 3P2
Tel: 604-515-6376
e-mail: admin@whitewater.org
URL: www.whitewater.org
Affiliation(s): Outdoor Recreation Council of BC
Don Butler, President

Whitewater Ontario
411 Carnegie Beach Rd., Port Perry ON L9L 1B6
Tel: 905-985-4585; *Fax:* 905-985-5256
Toll-Free: 888-322-2849
e-mail: info@whitewaterontario.ca
URL: www.whitewaterontario.ca
Claudia Kerkoff, Vice-President

Wilderness Canoe Association (WCA)
PO Box 91068, 2901 Bayview Ave., Toronto ON M2K 2Y6
Tel: 416-223-4646
e-mail: info@wildernesscanoe.ca
URL: www.wildernesscanoe.ca
Aleks Gusev, Chair

YMCA Canada
42 Charles St. East, 6th Fl., Toronto ON M4Y 1T4
Tel: 416-967-9622; *Fax:* 416-967-9618
URL: www.ymca.ca
Affiliation(s): Canadian Centre for Philanthropy; Canadian Child Care Federation; Canadian Coalition for the Rights of Children; Canadian Council for International Cooperation; Canadian Council on Children & Youth; Canadian Recreational Canoeing Association; Coalition on National Voluntary Organizations; Conference Board of Canada; Huronia Tourism Association; National Fitness Leadership Advisory Committee; National Life Guard Service; National Voluntary Health Agencies; National Youth Serving Agencies; Partnership Africa Canada; Resorts Ontario; Royal Life Saving Society; Voluntary Sector Round Table
Janet Emmett, Interim CEO
Marty Reynolds, Chair

Yukon Canoe & Kayak Club
PO Box 40080, 3 Sitka Cres., Whitehorse YT Y1A 6M6
Tel: 867-456-4827
e-mail: current@yckc.ca
URL: www.yckc.ca
Eyvi Smith, President

Yukon Outdoors Club
4061, 4th Ave., Whitehorse YT Y1A 1H1
e-mail: yukonoutdoorsclub@gmail.com
URL: www.yukonoutdoorsclub.ca
Tony Gonda, President

YWCA Canada / Association des jeunes femmes chrétiennes du Canada
#422, 75 Sherbourne St., Toronto ON M5A 2P9
Tel: 416-962-8881; *Fax:* 416-962-8084
e-mail: national@ywcacanada.ca
URL: www.ywcacanada.ca
Affiliation(s): Selective: Canadian Policy Research Network; National Council of Women; National Youth Serving Organizations; Women's Future Fund; Canadian Centre for Philanthropy; National Action Committee on the Status of Women
Elizabeth Bourns, President
Michelle Bullas, Vice President

Recycling

New Brunswick Solid Waste Association (NBSWA) / l'Association des déchets solides du Nouveau-Brunswick (ADSNB)
32 Wedgewood Dr., Rothesay NB E2E 3P7
Tel: 506-849-4218; *Fax:* 506-847-1369
Toll-Free: 877-777-4218
e-mail: nbswa@nbnet.nb.ca
URL: www.recyclenb.ca
Don Shea, Executive Director

Reproductive Issues

Birthright / Accueil Grossesse
777 Coxwell Ave., Toronto ON M4C 3C6
Tel: 416-469-1111; *Fax:* 416-469-1772
Toll-Free: 800-550-4900
e-mail: info@birthright.org
URL: www.birthright.org
Louise R. Summerhill, Co-President & Founder
Mary Berney, Co-President

Canadian Federation for Sexual Health (CFSH) / Fédération canadienne pour la santé sexuelle
#430, One Nicholas St., Ottawa ON K1N 7B7
Tel: 613-241-4474; *Fax:* 613-241-7550
Toll-Free: 888-270-7444
e-mail: admin@cfsh.ca
URL: www.cfsh.ca
Jolanta Scott-Parker, Executive Director

Canadian Fertility & Andrology Society (CFAS) / Société canadienne de fertilité et d'andrologie
#1107, 1255 University, Montréal QC H3B 3W7

Tel: 514-524-9009; Fax: 514-524-2163
e-mail: info@cfas.ca
URL: www.cfas.ca

Benjamin Tsang, Ph.D., President

Canadians for Choice (CFC) / Canadien(ne)s pour la liberté de choix
PO Box 539, Stn. B, Ottawa ON K1N 7E4
Tel: 613-789-9958; Fax: 613-789-9960
Toll-Free: 888-642-2725
e-mail: info@canadiansforchoice.ca
URL: www.canadiansforchoice.ca

Norman Barwin, President
Barbara Legowski, Vice-President
Patricia LaRue, Executive Director

Childbirth By Choice Trust / Choisir de donner naissance
#502, 344 Bloor St. West, Toronto ON M5S 3A7
Tel: 416-961-7812
e-mail: info@cbctrust.com
URL: www.cbctrust.com

Jane Koster, Administrator

Fédération du Québec pour le planning des naissances (FQPN)
#405, 110, rue Ste-Thérèse, Montréal QC H2Y 1E6
Tél: 514-866-3721; Téléc: 514-866-1100
Courriel: info@fqpn.qc.ca
URL: www.fqpn.qc.ca

Natalie Parent, Coordonnatrice

Infertility Awareness Association of Canada (IAAC) / Association canadienne de sensibilisation à l'infertilité (ACSI)
#342, 2100, av Marlowe, Montréal QC H4A 3L5
Tel: 514-484-2891; Fax: 514-484-0454
Toll-Free: 800-263-2929
e-mail: info@iaac.ca
URL: www.iaac.ca

Affiliation(s): Canadian Fertility & Andrology Society; Society of Obstetricians & Gynaecologists of Canada
Jocelyn Smith, President

League for Life in Manitoba / Ligue pour la vie au Manitoba
Winnipeg MB
Tel: 204-233-8047; Fax: 204-233-0523
e-mail: l4l@mts.net
URL: www.leagueforlife.mb.ca

Marie-Jo Laroche, Executive Director

Natural Family Planning Association
#205, 3050 Yonge St., Toronto ON M4N 2K4
Tel: 416-481-5465
e-mail: nfptoronto@primus.ca
URL: www.naturalfamilyplanning.ca

Merrilyn Currie, Executive Director

Ontario Coalition for Abortion Clinics (OCAC)
PO Box 495, Stn. P, 427 Bloor St. West, Toronto ON M5S 2Z1
Tel: 416-969-8463; Fax: 416-789-0762
e-mail: ocac@sympatico.ca

Carolyn Egan, Coordinating Committee Member

Options for Sexual Health (OPT)
3550 East Hastings St., Vancouver BC V5K 2A7
Tel: 604-731-4252; Fax: 604-731-4698
Toll-Free: 800-739-7367
e-mail: admin@optbc.org
URL: www.optionsforsexualhealth.org

Affiliation(s): International Planned Parenthood Federation
Greg Smith, Executive Director
Saira Hansen, Coordinator, Education

Planned Parenthood - Newfoundland & Labrador Sexual Health Centre (NLSHC)
203 Merrymeeting Rd., St. John's NL A1C 2W6
Tel: 709-579-1009; Fax: 709-726-2308
Toll-Free: 877-666-9847
e-mail: info@nlsexualhealthcentre.org
URL: www.nlsexualhealthcentre.org

Costa Kasimos, Executive Director
Rolanda Ryan, President
Andrea Murphy, Secretary
Maureen O'Keefe, Treasurer

Planned Parenthood Alberta (PPA)
#1010, 1202 Centre St. SE, Calgary AB T2G 5A5
Tel: 403-283-8591; Fax: 403-283-8563
e-mail: info@sexualhealthaccess.org
URL: www.plannedparenthoodalta.com

Affiliation(s): Calgary Birth Control Association; Planned Parenthood Association of Edmonton; Planned Parenthood Alberta - Banff Sexual Health Clinic
Laura Wershler, Executive Director

Planned Parenthood Saskatoon Centre (PPSC)
#314, 220 - 3rd Ave. South, Saskatoon SK S7K 1M1
Tel: 306-244-7989; Fax: 306-652-4034
e-mail: info@sexualhealthcentresaskatoon.ca
URL: www.sexualhealthcentresaskatoon.ca

Pro-Life BC (PLBC)
#112, 32868 Ventura Avenue, Abbotsford BC V2S 6J3
Tel: 604-853-3425; Fax: 604-853-3413
Toll-Free: 877-774-4625
e-mail: life@prolifebc.ca
URL: www.prolifebc.ca

Yvonne Douma, Executive Director
Michelle Doherty, President
Monique Van Berkel, Assistant to Executive Director

Right to Life Association of Newfoundland & Labrador
PO Box 5427, St. John's NL A1C 5W2
Tel: 709-579-1500; Fax: 709-579-3818
e-mail: nffriendsforlife@nl.rogers.com
URL: home.thezone.net/~nfrtla/

Right to Life Association of Toronto
Stn. 67073, 2300 Yonge St., Toronto ON M4P 3C8
Tel: 416-483-7869; Fax: 416-483-7052
e-mail: righttolife@on.aibn.com
URL: www.rtl-toronto.org

Affiliation(s): Life Canada

Sexuality Education Resource Centre Manitoba (SERC)
555 Broadway, 2nd Fl., Winnipeg MB R3C 0W4
Tel: 204-982-7800; Fax: 204-982-7819
Toll-Free: 800-432-1957
e-mail: info@serc.mb.ca
URL: www.serc.mb.ca

Affiliation(s): Planned Parenthood Federation of Canada; International Planned Parenthood Federation
Lori Johnson, Executive Director

World Organization Ovulation Method Billings Inc.
1506 Dansey Ave., Coquitlam BC V3K 3J1
Tel: 604-936-4472; Fax: 604-936-5690
e-mail: info@woomb.ca
URL: www.woomb.ca

Affiliation(s): WOOMB International - Australia
Lou Specken, President

Research & Scholarship

Advanced Foods & Materials Network / Réseau des aliments et des matériaux d'avant-garde
#215, 150 Research Lane, Guelph ON N1G 4T2
Tel: 519-822-6253; Fax: 519-824-8453
URL: www.afmnet.ca

Ron Woznow, Executive Director
Rickey Yada, Ph.D., Scientific Director

Allergy, Genes & Environment Network
Michael DeGroote Centre for Learning & Discovery, McMaster Univ., #3120, 1200 Main St. West, Hamilton ON L8N 3Z5
Tel: 905-525-9140; Fax: 905-524-0611
e-mail: info@allergen-nce.ca
URL: www.allergen-nce.ca

Diana Royce, Managing Director & COO

AquaNet - Network in Aquaculture
Ocean Sciences Centre, Memorial University of Newfoundland, St. John's NL A1C 5S7
Tel: 709-737-3245; Fax: 709-737-3500
e-mail: info@aquanet.ca
URL: www.aquanet.ca

Scott McKinley, Executive Scientific Director

ArcticNet Inc.
Pavillon Alexandre-Vachon, Université Laval, #4081, 1045, av de la Médecine, Québec QC G1V 0A6
Tel: 418-656-5830; Fax: 418-656-2334
e-mail: arcticnet@arcticnet.ulaval.ca
URL: www.arcticnet-ulaval.ca

Martin Fortier, Executive Director
Louis Fortier, Scientific Director
Réal Choquette, Administrative Director
Jean-Luc Bernier, Officer, Communications
Keith Levesque, Coordinator, Ship-based Research
Josée Michaud, Coordinator, Data

AUTO21 - The Automobile of the 21st Century
754 California Ave., Windsor ON N9B 2Z2
Tel: 519-253-3000; Fax: 519-971-3626
e-mail: info@auto21.ca
URL: www.auto21.ca

Sandra Bortolotti, Operations Manager
Stephanie Campeau, Communications Manager

Canadian Arthritis Network (CAN) / Le Réseau canadien de l'arthrite
#1002, 522 University Ave., Toronto ON M5T 1W7
Tel: 416-586-4770; Fax: 416-586-8395
e-mail: can@arthritisnetwork.ca
URL: www.arthritisnetwork.ca

Affiliation(s): The Arthritis Society; Canadian Institute of Health Research Institute of Musculoskeletal Health & Arthritis
Robin Armstrong, Chair
John Riley, MHA, Managing Director
Claire Bombardier, MD, FRCPC, Co-Scientific Director
Monique Gignac, PhD, Co-Scientific Director
Brian Bobechko, Director, Research & Development
Stacey Johnson, MSc, Director, Communications
Joanner Wright, Manager, Training & International Programs

Canadian Association for Research in Nondestructive Evaluation (CARNDE) / Association canadienne de recherches en évaluation non-destructive (ACREND)
75, boul de Montagne, Boucherville QC J4B 6Y4
Tel: 450-641-5252; Fax: 450-641-5106
e-mail: jean.bussiere@nrc.ca
URL: www.nrc.ca

Jean Bussière, Research Editor

Canadian Carbonization Research Association (CCRA)
PO Box 2460, Burlington ON L8N 3J5
Tel: 905-548-4796
URL: www.cancarb.ca

Ted Todoschuk, Chairman
G.A. Chapman, Treasurer

Canadian Centre for Policy Alternatives (CCPA) / Centre canadien de politique alternative
#410, 75 Albert St., Ottawa ON K1P 5E7
Tel: 613-563-1341; Fax: 613-233-1458
e-mail: ccpa@policyalternatives.ca
URL: www.policyalternatives.ca

Bruce Campbell, Executive Director
Diane Touchette, Director, Operations

Canadian Centre for Policy Alternatives
#1400, 207 West Hastings St., Vancouver BC V6B 1H7
Tel: 604-801-5121; Fax: 604-801-5122
e-mail: info@bcpolicyalternatives.org
URL: www.policyalternatives.ca/bc_office_of_the_ccpa/index.cfm

Canadian Centre for Policy Alternatives
#309, 323 Portage Ave., Winnipeg MB R3B 2C1
Tel: 204-927-3200; Fax: 204-927-3201
e-mail: ccpamb@policyalternatives.ca
URL: www.policyalternatives.ca/index.cfm?act=main&call=DEFBBA2D

Canadian Committee of Byzantinists
Talbot College, Univ. of Western Ontario, London ON N6A 3K7
Tel: 519-661-3045; Fax: 519-850-2388
e-mail: splinter@uwo.ca

A.R. Littlewood, Contact

Canadian Federation for Robotics
c/o Precarn Inc., #510, 1525 Carling Ave., Ottawa ON K1Z 8R9
Tel: 613-727-9576; Fax: 613-727-5672
e-mail: johnston@precarn.ca
URL: www.precarn.ca

Affiliation(s): PRECARN; IRIS
Paul Johnston, President

Canadian Genetic Diseases Network (CGDN) / Réseau canadien sur les maladies génétiques (RCMG)
#201, 2150 Western Pkwy., Vancouver BC V6T 1Z4
Tel: 604-221-7300; Fax: 604-221-0778
e-mail: info@cgdn.ca
URL: www.cgdn.ca

Rob Abbott, CEO

Canadian Institute for Advanced Research (CIFAR) / Institut canadien de recherches avancées (ICRA)
#1400, 180 Dundas St. West, Toronto ON M5G 1Z8
Tel: 416-971-4251; *Fax:* 416-971-6169
e-mail: info@cifar.ca
URL: www.ciar.ca
Richard W. Ivey, Chair
Chaviva Hosek, President/CEO

Canadian Institute for Mediterranean Studies / Institut canadien d'études méditerranéennes
c/o Carr Hall, University of Toronto, 100 St. Joseph St., Toronto ON M5S 1J4
e-mail: scarci@chass.utoronto.ca
URL: www.utoronto.ca/cims/
Affiliation(s): Canadian Institute in Egypt; Canadian Archaeological Institute at Athens; Canadian Academic Centre in Italy
Alex Gropper, President

Canadian Institute for Photonics Innovations (CIPI)
Université Laval, Pavillion d'optique-photonique, #2111, 2375 rue de la Terrasse, Québec QC G1V 0A6
Tel: 418-656-3013; *Fax:* 418-656-2995
e-mail: cipi@cipi.ulaval.ca
URL: www.cipi.ulaval.ca
Robert Corriveau, President

Canadian Institute of Strategic Studies (CISS) / Institut canadien d'études stratégiques
#702, 165 University Ave., Toronto ON M5H 3B8
Tel: 416-322-8128; *Fax:* 416-322-8129
Toll-Free: 800-831-5695
e-mail: info@ciss.ca
URL: www.ciss.ca
Alex Morrison, President

Canadian Institute of Ukrainian Studies (CIUS) / Institut canadien d'études ukrainiennes
#4-50, Athabasca Hall, Univ. of Alberta, Edmonton AB T6G 2E8
Tel: 780-492-2972; *Fax:* 780-492-4967
e-mail: cius@ualberta.ca
URL: www.cius.ca
Zenon E. Kohut, Ph.D., Director

Canadian Language & Literacy Research Network
Elborn College, University of Western Ontario, 1201 Western Rd., London ON N6G 1H1
Tel: 519-661-3619; *Fax:* 519-661-4223
e-mail: info@cllrnet.ca
URL: www.cllrnet.ca
Donald G. Jamieson, CEO/Scientific Director

Canadian Mathematical Society (CMS) / Société mathématique du Canada
#105, 1785 Alta Vista Dr., Ottawa ON K1G 3Y6
Tel: 613-733-2662; *Fax:* 613-733-8994
e-mail: office@cms.math.ca
URL: www.cms.math.ca
Johan Rudnick, Executive Director

Canadian Mining Industry Research Organization (CAMIRO)
935 Ramsey Lake Rd., Sudbury ON P3E 2C6
Tel: 705-673-6595; *Fax:* 705-671-6606
e-mail: info@camiro.org
URL: www.camiro.org
Larry Urbanoski, Director, Research, Metallurgical Division
Tom Lane, Director, Research Development, Exploration Division
Charles Graham, Contact, Mining Division

Canadian Nautical Research Society (CNRS) / Société canadienne pour la recherche nautique
PO Box 511, Kingston ON K7L 4W5
URL: www.cnrs-scrn.org
Affiliation(s): International Commission for Maritime History
Richard H. Gimblett, President

Canadian Network for Vaccines & Immunotherapeutics
#790, 5160, boul Décarie, Montréal QC H3X 2H9
Tel: 514-343-6111; *Fax:* 514-343-7854
e-mail: michel.klein@canvac.ca
URL: www.canvac.ca
Michel Klein, Executive Director

Canadian Numismatic Research Society (CNRS)
PO Box 1351, Victoria BC V8W 2W7
Fax: 250-598-5539
e-mail: ragreene@telus.net
URL: www.nunetcan.net/cnrs/cnrs.htm
Ronald Greene, Secretary

Canadian Operational Research Society (CORS) / Société canadienne de recherche opérationelle (SCRO)
PO Box 2225, Stn. D, Ottawa ON K1P 5W4
e-mail: cors@uwindsor.ca
URL: www.cors.ca
Vinh Quan, President
Corinne MacDonald, Secretary

Canadian Philosophical Association (CPA) / Association canadienne de philosophie
C/O University of Ottawa, #241, 70 Laurier Ave. East, Ottawa ON K1N 6N5
Tel: 613-562-5367; *Fax:* 613-562-5370
e-mail: acpa@uottawa.ca
URL: www.acpcpa.ca
Affiliation(s): Fédération internationale des sociétés de philosophie
Jocelyne Couture, President

Canadian Quaternary Association / Association canadienne pour l'étude du Quaternaire
Dept. of Geography, Univ. of Regina, Regina SK S4S 0A2
Tel: 306-585-4030; *Fax:* 306-585-4815
e-mail: sauchyn@uregina.ca
URL: www.mun.ca/canqua
Martin Batterson, Sec.-Treas.
Dave Sauchyn, President

Canadian Research Institute for the Advancement of Women (CRIAW) / Institut canadien de recherches sur les femmes (ICREF)
#408, 151 Slater St., Ottawa ON K1P 5H3
Tel: 613-563-0681; *Fax:* 613-563-0682
e-mail: info@criaw-icref.ca
URL: www.criaw-icref.ca
Jane Robinson, President

Canadian Society for Aesthetics (CSA) / Société canadienne d'ésthetique (SCE)
c/o Dawson College, 4729, av de Maisonneuve, Westmount QC H3Z 1M3
e-mail: info@csa-sce.ca
URL: www.csa-sce.ca
Adrienne Dangeriuk Chaplin, Anglophone President
Syliane Charles, Francophone President
Victor Y. Haines, Secretary

Canadian Society for Eighteenth-Century Studies (CSECS) / Société canadienne d'étude du dix-huitième siècle (SCEDS)
c/o CSECS Secretary, Department of English, University of Victoria, PO Box 3070, Stn. CSC, Victoria BC V8W 3W1
e-mail: gdfulton@uvic.ca
URL: c18.net/scedhs-csecs/
Affiliation(s): International Society for Eighteenth-Century Studies
Betty A. Schellenberg, President
Gordon Fulton, Secretary
Gefen Bar-On, Treasurer

The Canadian Society for Mesopotamian Studies (CSMS) / La Société canadienne des études mésopotamiennes
c/o Dept. of Near & Middle Eastern Civilizations, 4 Bancroft Ave., 4th Fl., Toronto ON M5S 1C1
Tel: 416-978-4531; *Fax:* 416-978-3305
e-mail: gframe@chass.utoronto.ca
Affiliation(s): Canadian Mediterranean Institute; Royal Inscriptions of Mesopotamia Project
N.J. Johnson, Administrator
G. Frame, President
R. Thomas, Sec.-Treas.

Canadian Society for the Study of Religion (CSSR) / Société canadienne pour l'étude de la religion (SCER)
c/o Dr. Mark D. Chapman, #100, 30 Carrier Dr., Toronto ON M9W 5T7
e-mail: mchapman@alumni.uwaterloo.ca
URL: www.ccsr.ca/cssr
Affiliation(s): Canadian Federation for the Humanities & Social Sciences (CFHSS)
Michel Desjardins, President
Mark Chapman, Membership Secretary
Richard Mann, Treasurer

Canadian Society of Patristic Studies (CSPS) / Association canadienne des études patristiques
c/o Membership, 45 Inkerman Dr., Charlottetown PE C1A 2P4
e-mail: lturcesc@alcor.concordia.ca
URL: www.ccsr.ca/csps
Affiliation(s): Canadian Corporation for the Study of Religion
Steven Muir, Treasurer
Lucien Turcescu, President
Lorraine Buck, Secretary

Canadian Sociological Association (CSA)
#SB-323, 1455, boul de Maisonneuve ouest, Montréal QC H3G 1M8
Tel: 514-848-8780; *Fax:* 514-848-8780
e-mail: info@csaa.ca
URL: www.csaa.ca
Gilles Laflamme, Directeur

Canadian Stroke Network (CSN) / Réseau canadien contre les accidents cérébrovasculaires
#301, 600 Peter Morand Cres., Ottawa ON K1G 5Z3
Tel: 613-562-5696; *Fax:* 613-521-9215
e-mail: info@canadianstrokenetwork.ca
URL: www.canadianstrokenetwork.ca
Michael Cloutier, Chair
Antoine Hakim, MD, CEO & Scientific Director
Katie Lafferty, Executive Director
Mike Sharma, Deputy Director

Canadian Technion Society
#206, 970 Lawrence Ave. West, Toronto ON M6A 3B6
Tel: 416-789-4545; *Fax:* 416-789-0255
Toll-Free: 800-935-8864
e-mail: info@cdntech.org
URL: www.cdntech.org
Harold Goldberg, National President
Cheryl Koperwas, National Executive Director
Natana Shek Dor, National Vice-President, Fundraising & Development

Canadian Theosophical Society Inc. / Association théosophique canadienne inc.
27 Northmount Cr. NW, Calgary AB T2K 2V6
Tel: 403-275-7817
e-mail: office@theosophical.ca
URL: www.theosophical.ca
Affiliation(s): 70 other countries
Lorraine Christensen, President

Canadian Water Network (CWN) / Réseau canadien de l'eau
University of Waterloo, 200 University Ave. West, Waterloo ON N2L 3G1
Tel: 519-888-4567; *Fax:* 519-883-7574
e-mail: info@cwn-rce.ca
URL: www.cwn-rce.ca
Bernadette Conant, Director of Programs
Mark Servos, Scientific Director
David Cotter, Director of Communications

The Cancer Research Society (CRS) / La Société de recherche sur le cancer
#402, 625, av Président-Kennedy, Montréal QC H3A 3S5
Tel: 514-861-9227; *Fax:* 514-861-9220
Toll-Free: 866-343-2262
e-mail: src@src-crs.ca
URL: www.cancer-research-society.ca
Mario Chevrette, President
Marie-Claude Lafleur, National Director, Public Affairs & Communications

Centre for Research on Latin America & The Caribbean (CERLAC)
8th Fl., York Research Tower, 4700 Keele St., Toronto ON M3J 1P3
Tel: 416-736-5237; *Fax:* 416-736-5688
e-mail: cerlac@yorku.ca
URL: www.yorku.ca/cerlac
Affiliation(s): Canadian Association for Latin American & Caribbean Studies; Development Education Centre; OXFAM-Canada; Centre for Spanish Speaking People; CCIC; AFG: KAIROS
Eduardo Canel, Director

Classical Association of Canada (CAC) / Société canadienne des études classiques (SCEC)
Dept. of History, York University; 2178 Vari Hall, 4700 Keele Street, Toronto ON M3J 1P3
Tel: 416-736-2100
URL: www.cac-scec.ca
Affiliation(s): Canadian Federation for Humanities & Social Sciences
John Serrati, Secretary
Jonathan Edmundson, President
Annabel Robinson, Treasurer

Commission canadienne pour la théorie des machines et des mécanismes (CCToMM) / Canadian Committee for the Theory of Machines & Mechanisms
Faculté d'ingénierie, Univ. de Moncton, Moncton NB E1A 3E9
URL: me.queensu.ca/people/notash/CCToMM/
Roger Boudreau, Secrétaire général

Forest Engineering Research Institute of Canada, A Division of FPInnovations (FERIC) / Institut canadien de recherches en génie forestier
580, boul Saint-Jean, Pointe-Claire QC H9R 3J9
Tel: 514-694-1140; *Fax:* 514-694-4351
e-mail: admin@fpinnovations.ca
URL: www.feric.ca

Geomatics for Informed Decisions Network
#3732, Pavillon Casault, Université Laval, Québec QC G1V 0A6
Tel: 418-656-7758; *Fax:* 418-656-2611
e-mail: info@geoide.ulaval.ca
URL: www.geoide.ulaval.ca
Réal Choquette, Network Manager
Mark Zacharias, Executive Director

Great Lakes Institute for Environmental Research (GLIER)
University of Windsor, 401 Sunset Ave., Windsor ON N9B 3P4
Tel: 519-253-3000; *Fax:* 519-971-3616
e-mail: glier@uwindsor.ca
URL: cronus.uwindsor.ca/glier
Brian Fryer, Contact

Humanist Association of Canada (HAC) / Association humaniste du Canada
401B Weber St. North, Waterloo ON N2J 3J2
Fax: 613-739-5969
Toll-Free: 877-486-2671
e-mail: hac_memberships@yahoo.ca
URL: www.humanistcanada.com
Affiliation(s): International Humanist & Ethical Union (UK)
Dorothy Hays, President

Innovation Management Association of Canada (IMAC) / Association canadienne de la gestion de l'innovation (ACGI)
c/o CATAAlliance, #416, 207 Bank St., Ottawa ON K2P 2N2
Tel: 613-236-6550; *Fax:* 613-236-8189
e-mail: info@cata.ca
URL: www.cata.ca/imac/
Cathi Malette, Membership Coordinator

Institute for Research on Public Policy / Institut de recherche en politiques publiques
#200, 1470, rue Peel, Montréal QC H3A 1T1
Tel: 514-985-2461; *Fax:* 514-985-2559
e-mail: irpp@irpp.org
URL: www.irpp.org
Mel Cappe, President

Institute for Robotics & Intelligent Systems (IRIS) / Institut de robotique et d'intelligence des systèmes
Precarn Incorporated, #510, 1525 Carling Ave., Ottawa ON K1Z 8R9
Tel: 613-727-9576; *Fax:* 613-727-5672
e-mail: info@precarn.ca
URL: www.precarn.ca
Affiliation(s): Precarn Incorporated
Henri Rothschild, B.Sc., M.Sc., P, President & CEO, Precarn Incorporated
Rick Schwartzburg, Senior Manager, Academic Partnerships
Derek Best, Director, Research Programs

Institute for Stuttering Treatment & Research (ISTAR)
College Plaza, #1500, 8215 - 112 St., Edmonton AB T6G 2C8
Tel: 780-492-2619; *Fax:* 780-492-8457
e-mail: istar@ualberta.ca
URL: www.istar.ualberta.ca
Affiliation(s): The University of Alberta; Alberta Stutterers Association; Speech & Hearing Association of Alberta; Canadian Association of Speech & Language Pathology & Audiology; American Speech & Hearing Association; Canadian Association of People who Stutter

Institute of Urban Studies (IUS)
University of Winnipeg, #103, 520 Portage Ave., Winnipeg MB R3C 0G2
Tel: 204-982-1140; *Fax:* 204-943-4695
e-mail: ius@uwinnipeg.ca
URL: ius.uwinnipeg.ca
Jino Distasio, Director

International Council for Canadian Studies (ICCS) / Conseil international d'études canadiennes (CIEC)
#303, 250 City Centre Ave., Ottawa ON K1R 6K7
Tel: 613-789-7834; *Fax:* 613-789-7830
e-mail: lise.nichol@iccs-ciec.ca
URL: www.iccs-ciec.ca
Affiliation(s): Assn. for Cdn. Studies in the US; Assn. for Cdn. Studies; British Assn. of Cdn. Studies; Assn. française d'études canadiennes; Associazione Italiana di Studi Canadesi; Japanese Assn. for Cdn. Studies; Gesellschaft für Kanada-Studien; Assn. for Cdn. Studies in Australia & New Zealand; Assn. of Cdn. Studies in Ireland; Nordic Assn. for Cdn. Studies; Assn. for Cdn. Studies in China; Assn. for Cdn. Studies in The Netherlands; Indian Assn. for Cdn. Studies; Israel Assn. for Cdn. Studies; Asociacion Espanola de Estudios Canadienses; Russian Assn. for Cdn. Studies; Associacao Brasileira de Estudios
Guy Leclair, Co-Director
Lise Nichol, Administrative Coordinator

International Council for Central & East European Studies (Canada) (ICCEES) / Conseil international d'études de l'Europe centrale et orientale (Canada)
Intl. Studies Program, Glendon College, York University, 2275 Bayview Ave., Toronto ON M4N 3M6
Tel: 416-736-2100; *Fax:* 416-487-6852
e-mail: stankosk@glendon.yorku.ca
URL: www.rusin.fi/ICCEES
Affiliation(s): American Assoc. for the Advancement of Slavic Studies; Assoc. hellénique d'études Slaves; Associazione Italiana degli Slavisti; Australasian Assoc. for the Study of the Socialist Countries; Australia & New Zealand Slavists' Association; British Association for Soviet, Slavonic & East European Studies; Canadian Association of Slavists; Centre Belge D'Études Slaves; Deutsche Gesellschaft für Osteuropakunde; Dutch Slavists' Assoc.; Finnish Institute for Russian & East European Studies; Institut d'études slaves; Irish Slavists' Association; Israeli Association of Slavic & East European Studies

International Geographical Union - Canadian Committee
Simon Fraser Univ., Dept. of Geography, 8888 University Dr., Burnaby BC V5A 1S6
Tel: 604-291-3321; *Fax:* 604-291-5841
e-mail: agill@sfu.ca
URL: www.igu-net.org/uk/what_is_igu/nationalcommittees.html
Alison Gill

International Society for Research in Palmistry Inc. / Société internationale de recherches en chirologie inc.
351, av Victoria, Westmount QC H3Z 2N1
Tel: 514-488-2292; *Fax:* 514-488-3822
URL: www.palmistry.com

Lakehead Social History Institute (LSHI)
c/o Lakehead University, 955 Oliver Rd., Thunder Bay ON P7B 5E1
Tel: 807-767-0934; *Fax:* 807-767-0934
e-mail: epp@swedesincanada.ca
URL: www.swedesincanada.ca
Ernie Epp, Chief Officer
Donald W. Sjöberg, Chief Officer

Mathematics of Information Technology & Complex Systems (MITACS)
Technology Enterprise Facility, University of British Columbia, #301, 6190 Agronomy Rd., Vancouver BC V6T 1Z3
Tel: 604-822-9189; *Fax:* 604-822-3689
e-mail: mitacs@mitacs.ca
URL: www.mitacs.math.ca
Arvind Gupta, CEO & Scientific Director

The M.S.I. Foundation
#12230, 106 Avenue NW, Edmonton AB T5N 3Z1
Tel: 780-421-7532; *Fax:* 780-425-4467
e-mail: info@msifoundation.ca
URL: www.msifoundation.ca
M. Yates, Associate Secretary
L.H. Le Riche, Chairperson

Ontario Centres of Excellence - Centre for Earth & Environmental Technologies (OCE-ETech)
#200, 156 Front St. West, Toronto ON M5J 2L6
Tel: 416-861-1092; *Fax:* 416-971-7164
Toll-Free: 866-759-6014
URL: www.oce-ontario.org
Mark Romoff, President & CEO
Tanya Dunn, Manager, Office of President

Ontario Public Interest Research Group (OPIRG) / Groupe de recherche d'intérêt public de l'Ontario
North Borden Building, #101, 563 Spadina Ave., Toronto ON M5S 2J7
Tel: 416-978-7770; *Fax:* 416-971-2292
e-mail: opirg.toronto@utoronto.ca
URL: www.opirguoft.org
Azada Rahi, Director

Pearson Peacekeeping Centre (PPC) / Centre pour le maintien de la paix Pearson
HCI Bldg., #5110, 1125 Colonel By Dr., Ottawa ON K1S 5B6
Tel: 613-520-5617; *Fax:* 613-520-3787
e-mail: info@peaceoperations.org
URL: www.peaceoperations.org
Suzanne Monaghan, President

Pulp & Paper Research Institute of Canada (PAPRICAN) / Institut canadien de recherches sur les pâtes et papiers
570, boul Saint-Jean, Pointe-Claire QC H9R 3J9
Tel: 514-630-4101; *Fax:* 514-630-4134
e-mail: info@paprican.ca
URL: www.paprican.ca
David McDonald, Vice-President, Research & Education

Pulp & Paper Technical Association of Canada (PAPTAC) / Association technique des pâtes et papiers du Canada
#1070, 740, rue Notre-Dame ouest, Montréal QC H3C 3X6
Tel: 514-392-0265; *Fax:* 514-392-0369
e-mail: ccrotogino@paptac.ca
URL: www.paptac.ca
Robert Wood, Executive Director
Marie Dumontier, Chair

The Royal Canadian Geographical Society (RCGS) / La Société géographique royale du Canada
39 McArthur Ave., Ottawa ON K1L 8L7
Tel: 613-745-4629; *Fax:* 613-744-0947
Toll-Free: 800-267-0824
e-mail: rcgs@rcgs.org
URL: www.rcgs.org
Louise Maffett, Executive Director
Gisèle Jacob, President

Royal Canadian Institute (RCI)
#H7D, 700 University Ave., Toronto ON M5G 1X6
Tel: 416-977-2983; *Fax:* 416-962-7314
e-mail: royalcanadianinstitute@sympatico.ca
URL: www.royalcanadianinstitute.org
Roy Pearson, President
John A.G. Grant, Treasurer

The Royal Society for the Encouragement of Arts, Manufactures & Commerce (RSA)
8 John Adam St., London WC2N 6EZ United Kingdom
Tel: 44-020-7930-5115; *Fax:* 44-020-7839-5805
e-mail: general@rsa.org.uk
URL: www.rsa.org.uk
Social Media: www.facebook.com/theRSAorg; www.twitter.com/theRSAorg
Matthew Taylor, Chief Executive
Philip Duke of Edinburgh, KG, KT, President

The Royal Society for the Encouragement of Arts, Manufactures & Commerce
1146 Studley Ave., Halifax NS B3H 3R7

The Royal Society of Canada (RSC) / La Société royale du Canada
170 Waller St., Ottawa ON K1N 9B9
Tel: 613-991-6990; *Fax:* 613-991-6996
e-mail: theacademies@rsc.ca
URL: www.rsc.ca
Darren Gilmour, Executive Director

Society for the Study of Egyptian Antiquities (SSEA) / Société pour l'Étude de l'Égypte Ancienne
PO Box 578, Stn. P, Toronto ON M5S 2T1
Tel: 416-906-0180; *Fax:* 416-978-3305
e-mail: info@thessea.org
URL: www.thessea.org
Affiliation(s): Canadian Institute in Egypt; Canadian Mediterranean Institute
Lyn Green, President
Jean McGrady, Secretary

Stem Cell Network (SCN) / Réseau de cellules souches
#501 Smyth Rd., Room CCW-6293, Ottawa ON K1H 8L6

Tel: 613-739-6675
e-mail: info@stemcellnetwork.ca
URL: www.stemcellnetwork.ca
Lisa Willemse, Director of Communications
Drew Lyall, Executive Director

Traffic Injury Research Foundation (TIRF) / Fondation de recherches sur les blessures de la route
#200, 171 Nepean St., Ottawa ON K2P 0B4
Tel: 613-238-5235; *Fax:* 613-238-5292
Toll-Free: 877-238-5235
e-mail: deanm@trafficinjuryresearch.com
URL: www.trafficinjuryresearch.com
Robyn D. Robertson, President & CEO
Dean Morin, Manager, Marketing & Communications

Restaurants & Food Services

Association des fournisseurs d'hôtels et restaurants inc. (AFHR) / Hotel & Restaurant Suppliers Association Inc. (HRSA)
#230, 9300, boul Henri-Bourassa ouest, Saint-Laurent QC H4S 1L5
Tel: 514-334-5161; *Fax:* 514-334-1279
Toll-Free: 888-766-0601
e-mail: info@afhr.com
URL: www.afhr.com
Victor Francoeur, President & CEO
Isabelle Julien, Operation Manager
Hughes Moisan, Vice-President, Business Development

Association des restaurateurs du Québec (ARQ) / Québec Restaurant Association
7085, rue Beaubien est, Montréal QC H1M 2Y2
Tél: 514-527-9801; *Téléc:* 514-527-3066
Ligne sans frais: 800-463-4237
Courriel: arqc@arqc.qc.ca
URL: www.restaurateurs.ca/
Bernard Fortin, Président directeur général

British Columbia Restaurant & Foodservices Association (BCRFA)
439 Helmcken St., Vancouver BC V6B 2E6
Tel: 604-669-2239; *Fax:* 604-669-6175
Toll-Free: 800-663-4482
e-mail: info@bcrfa.com
URL: www.bcrfa.com
Ian Tostenson, President & CEO

Canadian Culinary Federation (CCFCC) / Fédération Culinaire Canadienne
c/o Roy Butterworth, 30 Hamilton Ct., Riverview NB E1B 3C3
e-mail: admin@ccfcc.ca
URL: www.ccfcc.ca
Bruno Marti, Chair
Judson Simpson, President
Roy Butterworth, National Administrator
Simon Smotkowicz, National Secretary
Don Dubay, National Treasurer

Canadian Restaurant & Foodservices Association (CRFA) / Association canadienne des restaurateurs et des services alimentaires
316 Bloor St. West, Toronto ON M5S 1W5
Tel: 416-923-8416; *Fax:* 416-923-1450
Toll-Free: 800-387-5649
e-mail: sjones@crfa.ca
URL: www.crfa.ca
Garth Whyte, President/CEO
David Harris, Sr. Exec. Vice-President

Canadian Restaurant & Foodservices Association
#201, 5121 Sackville St., Halifax NS B3J 1K1
Tel: 902-425-0061; *Fax:* 902-422-1161
Toll-Free: 877-755-1938
e-mail: luc@crfa.ca
URL: www.crfa.ca

Canadian Restaurant & Foodservices Association
PO Box 12125, #2410, 555 West Hastings St., Vancouver BC V6B 4N6
Tel: 604-685-9655; *Fax:* 604-685-9633
Toll-Free: 866-300-7675

Manitoba Restaurant & Food Services Association (MRFA)
103-D Scurfield Blvd., Winnipeg MB R3Y 1M6
Tel: 204-783-9955; *Fax:* 204-783-9909
Toll-Free: 877-296-2909
e-mail: info@mrfa.mb.ca
URL: www.mrfa.mb.ca
Scott Jocelyn, Executive Director

Société des chefs, cuisiniers et pâtissiers du Québec (SCCPQ)
7534, rue Fabre, Montréal QC H2E 2B5
Courriel: mtcgreen@hotmail.com
URL: www.sccpq.ca
Thomas Green, Président de chapitre
Patrick Gerome, Secrétaire

Retail Trade

Association des détaillants en alimentation du Québec (ADA) / Québec Food Retailers' Association
#1100, 300 rue Léo-Pariseau, Montréal QC H2X 4C1
Tél: 514-982-0104; *Téléc:* 514-849-3021
Ligne sans frais: 800-363-3923
Courriel: info@adaq.qc.ca
URL: www.adaq.qc.ca
Florent Gravel, Président-directeur général

Association nationale des distributeurs aux petites surfaces alimentaires (ANDPSA) / National Convenience Stores Distributors Association (NACDA)
#410, 1695, boul Laval, Laval QC H7S 2M2
Tel: 450-967-3858; *Fax:* 450-967-8839
Toll-Free: 800-686-2823
e-mail: nacda@nacda.ca
URL: www.nacda.ca
Marc Fortin, Président

Canadian Association of Chain Drug Stores (CACDS) / Association canadienne des chaînes de pharmacies
#301, 45 Sheppard Ave. East, Toronto ON M2N 5W9
Tel: 416-226-9100; *Fax:* 416-226-9185
e-mail: cacds@cacds.com
URL: www.cacds.com
Nadine Saby, President/CEO
Russell Cohen, Chair
Reza Farmand, Treasurer
Nancy Bagworth, Director, Communications

Canadian Gift & Tableware Association (CGTA) / Association canadienne de cadeaux et d'accessoires de table
42 Voyager Ct. South, Toronto ON M9W 5M7
Tel: 416-679-0170; *Fax:* 416-679-0175
Toll-Free: 800-611-6100
e-mail: info@cgta.org
URL: www.cgta.org

Canadian Sporting Goods Association (CSGA) / Association canadienne d'articles de sport (ACAS)
#420, 300, rue du Saint-Sacrement, Montréal QC H2Y 1X4
Tel: 514-393-1132; *Fax:* 514-393-9513
Toll-Free: 888-393-3002
e-mail: csga@csga.ca
URL: www.csga.ca
Affiliation(s): World Federation of the Sporting Goods Industry
Gord Cundell, President
Andy Stevens, Chair

Conseil québécois du commerce de détail (CQCD) / Retail Council of Québec
#910, 630, rue Sherbrooke ouest, Montréal QC H3A 1E4
Tél: 514-842-6681; *Téléc:* 514-842-7627
Ligne sans frais: 800-364-6766
Courriel: cqcd@cqcd.org
URL: www.cqcd.org
Gaston Lafleur, Président-directeur général

Direct Sellers Association of Canada / Association de ventes directes du Canada
#250, 180 Attwell Dr., Toronto ON M9W 6A9
Tel: 416-679-8555; *Fax:* 416-679-1568
e-mail: info@dsa.ca
URL: www.dsa.ca
Ross Creber, President & Secretary

Gift Packaging & Greeting Card Association of Canada (GPGCA) / Association canadienne du papier cadeau et de la carte de voeux
1407 Military Trail, Westhill ON M1C 1A7
Tel: 416-281-8147; *Fax:* 416-286-4868
e-mail: greetingcardoffice@rogers.com
Affiliation(s): World Alliance of Greeting Card Associations
Jim Driscoll, Chairman
Clancy Delbarre, Executive Director
Jerry Seligman, Vice-Chairman

Pool & Hot Tub Council of Canada
#10B, 242 Applewood Cres., Vaughan ON L4K 4E5
Tel: 905-761-7920; *Fax:* 905-761-8837
Toll-Free: 800-879-7066
e-mail: aspect@poolcouncil.ca
URL: www.poolcouncil.ca
Terry Coulter, Managing Director

Retail Council of Canada (RCC) / Conseil canadien du commerce de détail
#800, 1255 Bay St., Toronto ON M5R 2A9
Tel: 416-922-6678; *Fax:* 416-922-8011
Toll-Free: 888-373-8245
e-mail: mboydbonsu@retailcouncil.org
URL: www.retailcouncil.org
Affiliation(s): Canadian Health Food Association; Footwear Council of Canada; Le Conseil quebeçois du commerce de rétail; Retail Merchants' Association of Alberta; Retail Merchants' Association of Manitoba
Diane J. Brisebois, CAE, President/CEO
Bill Yetman, COO
Ruth Thorkelson, Senior Vice-President, Public Affairs
Terrance Oakey, Vice-President, Federal Government Relations

Retail Merchants' Association of BC (RMABC)
1758 - 8 Ave. West, Vancouver BC V6J 1V6
Tel: 604-736-0368; *Fax:* 604-736-3154
Toll-Free: 800-663-5135
e-mail: inquiry@retailbc.org
URL: www.retailbc.org
Mark Startup, CAE, President & CEO

Retirees

McMaster University Retirees Association (MURA)
c/o McMaster University, Gilmour Hall, #B108, 1280 Main St. W, Hamilton ON L8S 4L8
Tel: 905-525-9140
e-mail: mura@mcmaster.ca
URL: mura.mcmaster.ca

Safety & Accident Prevention

Alberta Safety Council
4831 - 93 Ave. NW, Edmonton AB T6B 3A2
Tel: 780-462-7300; *Fax:* 780-462-7318
Toll-Free: 800-301-6407
URL: www.safetycouncil.ab.ca
Affiliation(s): Canada Safety Council; National Safety Council
Karen Bruce, Executive Director

Association de santé et sécurité des industries de la forêt du Québec inc. (ASSIFQ) / Québec Logging Health & Safety Association Inc.
Place Iberville II, #210, 1175, av Lavigerie, Sainte-Foy QC G1V 4P1
Tél: 418-657-2267; *Téléc:* 418-651-4622
Courriel: info@assppq.qc.ca
URL: www.assifq.org
Affiliation(s): Association canadienne des producteurs de pâtes et papiers; Association des industries de la forêt du Québec ltée; Canadian Safety Council; Conseil du patronat du Québec; Canadian Society of Safety Engineering
Hervé Deschênes, Président et directeur général
Suzanne Lavoie, Secrétaire

Association de santé et sécurité des pâtes et papiers du Québec inc. (ASSPPQ) / Québec Pulp & Paper Health & Safety Association Inc.
#210, 1175, av Lavigerie, Sainte-Foy QC G1V 4P1
Tél: 418-657-2267; *Téléc:* 418-651-4622
Courriel: info@assppq.qc.ca
URL: www.assppq.org
Affiliation(s): Association canadienne des producteurs de pâtes et papiers; Canadian Safety Council; Conseil du Patronat de Québec; Canadian Society of Safety Engineering
Hervé Deschênes, Président et directeur général

Association des chefs en sécurité incendie du Québec (ACSIQ) / Québec Fire Chief Association
CP 88, Beloeil QC J3G 4S8
Tél: 450-464-6413; *Téléc:* 450-467-6297
Courriel: administration@acsiq.qc.ca
URL: www.acsiq.qc.ca
Michel Morin, Directeur général

Association paritaire pour la santé et la sécurité du travail - Administration provinciale
#10, 1220, boul Lebourgneuf, Québec QC G2K 2G4
Tél: 418-624-4801; *Téléc:* 418-624-4858
Courriel: apssap@apssap.qc.ca
URL: www.apssap.qc.ca
Colette Trudel, Directrice générale

Association paritaire pour la santé et la sécurité du travail - Affaires municipales (APSAM)
#710, 715, carré Victoria, Montréal QC H2Y 2H7
Tél: 514-849-8373; *Téléc:* 514-849-8873
Ligne sans frais: 800-465-1754
Courriel: info@apsam.com
URL: www.apsam.com
Alain Langlois, Directeur général

Association paritaire pour la santé et la sécurité du travail - Affaires sociales
#950, 5100, rue Sherbrooke est, Montréal QC H1V 3R9
Tél: 514-253-6871; *Téléc:* 514-253-1443
Ligne sans frais: 800-361-4528
Courriel: info@asstsas.qc.ca
URL: www.asstsas.qc.ca
Diane Parent, Directrice générale

Association paritaire pour la santé et la sécurité du travail - Habillement
#301, 2271, boul Fernand-Lafontaine, Longueuil QC J4G 2R7
Tél: 450-651-4348; *Téléc:* 450-442-2332
Courriel: info@aspme.org
URL: www.asp-habillement.org/
Alain Plourde, Directeur général

Association paritaire pour la santé et la sécurité du travail - Imprimerie et activités connexes
#450, 7450, boul Galeries d'Anjou, Anjou QC H1M 3M3
Tél: 514-355-8282; *Téléc:* 514-355-6818
URL: www.aspimprimerie.qc.ca
Marie Ménard, Directrice générale

Association paritaire pour la santé et la sécurité du travail - Mines et services miniers (APSM)
#570, 979, av de Bourgogne, Sainte-Foy QC G1W 2L4
Tél: 418-653-1933; *Téléc:* 418-653-7726
Courriel: info@apsam.com
URL: www.apsam.com
Pierre Lapointe, Directeur général

Association paritaire pour la santé et la sécurité du travail - Produits en métal et électriques
#301, 2271, boul Fernand-Lafontaine, Longueuil QC J4G 2R7
Tél: 450-442-7763; *Téléc:* 450-442-2332
Courriel: jarsenault@aspme.org
URL: www.aspme.org
Jocelyne Arsenault, Conseillère en gestion
Éric Bélanger, Conseiller technique

Association paritaire pour la santé et la sécurité du travail - Services automobiles
#150, 8, rue de la Place-Du-Commerce, Brossard QC J4W 3H2
Tél: 450-672-9330; *Téléc:* 450-672-4835
Ligne sans frais: 800-363-2344
Courriel: info@autoprevention.qc.ca
URL: www.autoprevention.qc.ca
Jean-Guy Trottier, Directeur général

Association québécoise des pompiers volontaires et permanents
#460, 9401, Côte des Saints, Mirabel QC J7N 2X4
Tél: 514-990-1338
Mèdia social: www.facebook.com/group.php?gid=27982231370
Eric Lacasse, Président

Association sectorielle - Fabrication d'équipement de transport et de machines (ASFETM) / Sectorial Association - Transportation Equipment & Machinery Manufacturing (SATEMM)
#202, 3565, rue Jarry est, Montréal QC H1Z 4K6
Tél: 514-729-6961; *Téléc:* 514-729-8628
Ligne sans frais: 888-527-3386
Courriel: info@asfetm.com
URL: www.asfetm.com
Arnold Dugas, Directeur général
Suzanne Ready, Chargée de l'information

Association Sectorielle Transport Entreposage (ASTE)
#301, 6455, boul Jean-Talon est, Montréal QC H1S 3E8
Tél: 514-955-0454; *Téléc:* 514-955-0449
Ligne sans frais: 800-361-8906
Courriel: info@aste.qc.ca
URL: www.aste.qc.ca
Alain Lajoie, Directeur général

Board of Canadian Registered Safety Professionals (BCRSP) / Conseil canadien des professionnels en securité agréés
6519B Mississauga Rd., Mississauga ON L5N 1A6
Tel: 905-567-7198; *Fax:* 905-567-7191
Toll-Free: 888-279-2777
e-mail: bcrsp@sympatico.ca
URL: www.bcrsp.ca
Edward J. Miller, Chair
Peter Fletcher, Executive Director

British Columbia Safety Council (BCSC)
#2225, 21331 Gordon Way, Richmond BC V6W 1J9
Tel: 604-214-7433; *Fax:* 604-214-7434
e-mail: bcsc@safetycouncil.bc.ca
URL: www.safetycouncil.bc.ca
Affiliation(s): Canada Safety Council; National Safety Council
Bryan Lowes, Executive Director

Canada Safety Council (CSC) / Conseil canadien de la sécurité (CCS)
1020 Thomas Spratt Pl., Ottawa ON K1G 5L5
Tel: 613-739-1535; *Fax:* 613-739-1566
e-mail: canadasafetycouncil@safety-council.org
URL: www.safety-council.org
Jack Smith, President
Raynard Marchand, General Manager, Programs

Canadian Association of Fire Chiefs (CAFC) / Association canadienne des chefs de pompiers (ACCP)
#702, 280 Albert St., Ottawa ON K1P 5G8
Tel: 613-270-9138; *Fax:* 613-233-9138
e-mail: info@cafc.ca
URL: www.cafc.ca
Affiliation(s): International Association of Fire Chiefs
Vicky Roper, Office Administrator
Patrick R. Burke, President

Canadian Association of Road Safety Professionals (CARSP) / Association canadienne des professionnels de la sécurité routière (ACPSER)
c/o Joseph Chan, Transportation Centre, University of Saskatchewan, 57 Campus Dr., Saskatoon SK S7N 5A9
Tel: 306-966-7010; *Fax:* 306-966-7014
e-mail: askcarsp@magma.ca
URL: www.carsp.ca
Joseph Chan, Membership Sec. and Treasurer
Paul Boase, President

Canadian Automatic Sprinkler Association (CASA)
#302, 335 Renfrew Dr., Markham ON L3R 9S9
Tel: 905-477-2270; *Fax:* 905-477-3611
e-mail: info@casa-firesprinkler.org
URL: www.casa-firesprinkler.org
John Galt, President

Canadian Centre for Occupational Health & Safety (CCOHS) / Centre canadien d'hygiène et de sécurité au travail (CCHST)
135 Hunter St. East, Hamilton ON L8N 1M5
Tel: 905-572-2981; *Fax:* 905-572-2206
Toll-Free: 800-668-4284
e-mail: clientservices@ccohs.ca
URL: www.ccohs.ca
Bonnie Easterbrook, Secretary/Treasurer
S. Len Hong, President/CEO

Canadian Fire Safety Association (CFSA)
#310, 2175 Sheppard Ave. East, Toronto ON M2J 1W8
Tel: 416-492-9417; *Fax:* 416-491-1670
e-mail: cfsa@taylorenterprises.com
URL: www.canadianfiresafety.com
Leo Grellette, President

Canadian Radiation Protection Association (CRPA) / Association canadienne de radioprotection (ACRP)
PO Box 83, Carleton Place ON K7C 3P3
Tel: 613-253-3779; *Fax:* 888-551-0712
e-mail: secretariat2007@crpa-acrp.ca
URL: www.crpa-acrp.ca
Affiliation(s): International Radiation Protection Association (IRPA).
Gary Wilson, President
Wayne Tiefenbach, Treasurer

Canadian Security Association (CANASA) / L'Association canadienne de la sécurité
#100, 610 Alden Rd., Markham ON L3R 9Z1
Tel: 905-513-0622; *Fax:* 905-513-0624
Toll-Free: 800-538-9919
e-mail: staff@canasa.org
URL: www.canasa.org
Social Media: twitter.com/CANASA_News
JF Champagne, Executive Director

Canadian Society of Air Safety Investigators (CSASI)
139 West 13th Ave., Vancouver BC V5Y 1V8
e-mail: avsafe@rogers.com
Affiliation(s): International Society of Air Safety Investigators
Barbara M. Dunn, President
Barry Wiszniowski, Vice-President
Elaine Parker, Secretary-Treasurer

Canadian Society of Safety Engineering, Inc. (CSSE) / Société canadienne de la santé et de la sécurité, inc.
39 River St., Toronto ON M5A 3P1
Tel: 416-646-1600; *Fax:* 416-646-9460
e-mail: wglover@associationsfirst.com
URL: www.csse.org
Affiliation(s): American Society of Safety Engineers
Wayne Glover, CAE, Executive Director
Eldeen Pozniak, President

Centre patronal de santé et sécurité du travail du Québec (CPSSTQ) / Employers Center for Occupational Health & Safety of Quebec
#1000, 500, rue Sherbrooke ouest, Montréal QC H3A 3C6
Tél: 514-842-8401; *Téléc:* 514-842-9375
Courriel: reception@centrepatronalsst.qc.ca
URL: www.centrepatronalsst.qc.ca
Germaine Archambault, Président
Denise Turenne, pdg, Présidente-directrice générale

Council of Canadian Fire Marshals & Fire Commissioners (CCFMFC) / Conseil canadien des directeurs provinciaux et des commissaires des incendies
c/o 491 McLeod Hill Rd., Fredericton NB E3A 6H6
Tel: 506-453-1208; *Fax:* 506-457-0793
e-mail: philippag@rogers.com
URL: www.ccfmfc.ca
Eugene Marotta, P. Eng., President
Benoit Laroche, Vice-President
Philippa Gourley, Sec.-Treas.

Council of Private Investigators - Ontario (CPIO)
#200, 148 York Street, London ON N6A 1A9
Tel: 416-955-9450
e-mail: director@cpi-ontario.com
URL: www.cpi-ontario.com
Bill Joynt, President
Charlie Robb, Administration Manager

Farm Safety Association Inc. (FSA)
#101, 75 Farquhar St., Guelph ON N1H 3N4
Tel: 519-823-5600; *Fax:* 519-823-8880
Toll-Free: 800-361-8855
e-mail: info@farmsafety.ca
URL: www.fsai.on.ca
Dean Anderson, President/CEO
Michele Brown, Director, Finance & Corporate Services
Jean-Guy Seguin, Chair

Federal Association of Security Officials (FASO) / Association fédérale des représentants de la sécurité
PO Box 2384, Stn. D, Ottawa ON K1P 5W5
Tel: 613-990-2615; *Fax:* 613-990-8297
Toll-Free: 888-330-3276
e-mail: info@faso-afrs.ca
URL: www.faso-afrs.ca
Claude J.G. Levesque, President

Fire Prevention Canada (FPC)
PO Box 47037, Ottawa ON K1B 5P9
Tel: 613-749-3844; *Fax:* 613-749-0109
Toll-Free: 877-906-6651
e-mail: info@fiprecan.ca
URL: www.fiprecan.ca
E. David Hodgins, President

Industrial Accident Prevention Association (IAPA) / Association pour la prévention des accidents industriels - Ontario
Centre for Health & Safety Innovation, #300, 5110 Creekbank Rd., Mississauga ON L4W 0A1

Tel: 905-614-4272; *Fax:* 905-614-1414
Toll-Free: 800-406-4272
e-mail: communications@iapa.ca
URL: www.iapa.ca
Affiliation(s): Amalgamated Industry Groups - Ceramics & Stone Accident Prevention Association; Chemical Industries Accident Prevention Association; Food Products Accident Prevention Association; Grain, Feed & Fertilizer Accident Prevention Association; Leather, Rubber & Tanners Accident Prevention Association; Metal Trades Accident Prevention Association; Printing Trades Accident Prevention Association; Textile & Allied Industries Accident Prevention Association; Woodworkers' Accident Prevention Association; High Tech; Offices & Related Services
Maureen C. Shaw, President/CEO
J.P. (Jeffrey) Mitchell, Chair
Tom Howe, Sec.-Treas.

Industrial Accident Victims Group of Ontario (IAVGO)
#203, 489 College St., Toronto ON M6G 1A5
Tel: 416-924-6477
Toll-Free: 877-230-6311
URL: www.iavgo.org
Mary DiNucci, Coordinator

Institut de recherche Robert-Sauvé en santé et en sécurité du travail (IRSST) / Robert Sauvé Occupational Health & Safety Research Institute
505, boul de Maisonneuve ouest, 15e étage, Montréal QC H3A 3C2
Tél: 514-288-1551; *Téléc:* 514-288-7636
Courriel: communications@irsst.qc.ca
URL: www.irsst.qc.ca
Affiliation(s): International Occupational Safety & Health Information Centre
Marie Larue, Présidente/Directrice générale

New Brunswick Safety Council Inc. (NBSC) / Conseil de sécurité du Nouveau-Brunswick inc.
#204, 440 Wilsey Rd., Fredericton NB E3B 7G5
Tel: 506-458-8034; *Fax:* 506-444-0177
Toll-Free: 877-762-7233
e-mail: info@nbsafety.com
URL: www.nbsafety.com
Affiliation(s): Canada Safety Council
Ronald J. Carr, President & CEO
Bill Walker, Director of Operations

Newfoundland & Labrador Safety Council
Regatta Plaza II, #84, 86 Elizabeth Ave., 2nd Fl., St. John's NL A1A 1W7
Tel: 709-754-0210; *Fax:* 709-754-0010
e-mail: info@safetycouncil.net
Affiliation(s): Canada Safety Council

Nova Scotia Safety Council
Vantage Point 3, #3F, 110 Chain Lake Dr., Halifax NS B3S 1A9
Tel: 902-454-9621; *Fax:* 902-454-6027
URL: www.nssafety.ns.ca
Affiliation(s): Canada Safety Council
Jackie Norman, Executive Director

Ontario Association of Fire Chiefs (OAFC)
#206, 335 Bayly St. West, Ajax ON L1S 6M2
Tel: 905-426-9865; *Fax:* 905-426-3032
Toll-Free: 800-774-6651
e-mail: administration@oafc.on.ca
URL: www.oafc.on.ca
Barry Malmsten, Executive Director
Richard Boyes, President
Kevin Foster, Treasurer

Ontario Industrial Fire Protection Association (OIFPA)
193 James St. South, Hamilton ON L8P 3A8
Tel: 905-527-0700; *Fax:* 905-527-6254
e-mail: oifpa@interlynx.net
URL: www.oifpa.org
Roy Graham, President
Jim Belrose, Vice-President
Todd Wilson, 2nd Vice-President
George Fawcett, Treasurer

Ontario Safety League (OSL) / Ligue de sécurité de l'Ontario
Bldg. 11, #100, 5045 Orbitor Dr., Mississauga ON L4W 4Y4
Tel: 905-625-0556; *Fax:* 905-625-0677
e-mail: info@osl.org
URL: www.osl.org
Affiliation(s): Canada Safety Council; Provincial Safety Leagues/Councils

Brian J. Patterson, President & General Manager

Opération Nez rouge / Operation Red Nose
Maison Couillard, Université Laval, 2539, rue Marie-Fitzbach, Québec QC G1V 0A6
Tél: 418-653-1492; *Téléc:* 418-653-3315
Ligne sans frais: 800-463-7222
URL: www.operationnezrouge.com
Étienne Talbot, Directeur général

Préventex - Association paritaire du textile
#203, 2035, av Victoria, Saint-Lambert QC J4S 1H1
Tél: 450-671-6925; *Téléc:* 450-671-9267
Courriel: info@preventex.qc.ca
URL: www.preventex.qc.ca
Michel Rouleau, Directeur général

Radiation Safety Institute of Canada / Institut de radioprotection du Canada
#607, 1120 Finch Ave. West, Toronto ON M3J 3H7
Tel: 416-650-9090; *Fax:* 416-650-9920
Toll-Free: 800-263-5803
e-mail: info@radiationsafety.ca
URL: www.radiationsafety.ca
Fergal Nolan, President/CEO
R. Moridi, Vice-President, Chief Scientist

Radiation Safety Institute of Canada
#102, 110 Research Dr., Saskatoon SK S7N 3R3
Tel: 306-975-0566; *Fax:* 306-975-0494

Safe Communities Foundation (SCF)
#201, 64 Charles St. East, Toronto ON M4Y 1T1
Tel: 416-964-0008; *Fax:* 416-964-0089
e-mail: info@safecommunities.ca
URL: www.safecommunities.ca
Affiliation(s): Health & safety workplace associations including: the Ontario Service Safety Alliance, Industrial Accident Prevention Association, Transportation Health & Safety Association of Ontario; Construction Safety Association of Ontario, provincial ministries of labour, provincial workers insurance organizations & others; Alberta Centre for Injury Control & Research; Alberta Workers Compensation Board; Canadian Centre for Occupational Health & Safety; St. John Ambulance; Canadian Red Cross; YMCA/YWCA; Safe Kids Canada; SmartRisk; Think First; Canada Safety Council; Nova Scotia Safety Council
Paul Kells, Founder & President
Jocelyne Achat, Vice-Chair

Safety Services Manitoba (SSM)
#3, 1680 Notre Dame Ave., Winnipeg MB R3H 1H6
Tel: 204-949-1085; *Fax:* 204-949-2897
Toll-Free: 800-661-3321
e-mail: registrar@safetyservicesmanitoba.ca
URL: www.safetyservicesmanitoba.ca
Mike Waite, Executive Director

Saskatchewan Safety Council
445 Hoffer Dr., Regina SK S4N 6E2
Tel: 306-757-3197; *Fax:* 306-569-1907
e-mail: info@sasksafety.org
URL: www.sasksafety.org
Harley P. Toupin, Executive Director
Dianne Wolbaum, Director, Operations

Transportation Health & Safety Association of Ontario (THSAO)
#101, 555 Dixon Rd., Toronto ON M9W 1H8
Tel: 416-242-4771; *Fax:* 416-242-4714
Toll-Free: 800-263-5016
e-mail: info@thsao.on.ca
URL: www.thsao.on.ca
Michael J. Burke, President/CEO
John Bond, COO
Alex Vasilescu, Administrator

Scholarly

Canadian Association for the Study of Humanities and the Environment
c/o Institute for Governance Studies, Simon Fraser University, Burnaby BC V5A 1S6
Tel: 778-782-4293; *Fax:* 778-782-4786
e-mail: igs@sfu.ca
URL: www.sfu.ca/igs/cashe.html
Rebecca Raglon, Secretary

Scientific

Alberta Society of Professional Biologists (ASPB)
PO Box 21104, Edmonton AB T6R 2V4
Tel: 780-434-5765; *Fax:* 780-413-0076
e-mail: pbiol@aspb.ab.ca
URL: www.aspb.ab.ca
Robin Leech, Executive Director
Carol Engstrom, President
Gary Ash, Treasurer

Arctic Institute of North America (AINA)
University of Calgary, 2500 University Dr. NW, Calgary AB T2N 1N4
Tel: 403-220-7515; *Fax:* 403-282-4609
e-mail: arctic@ucalgary.ca
URL: www.arctic.ucalgary.ca
Affiliation(s): The University of Alaska
Michel Scott, Board Chair
Benoît Beauchamp, Executive Director

Association des microbiologistes du Québec (AMQ)
5094A, av Charlemagne, Montréal QC H1X 3P3
Tél: 514-728-1087; *Téléc:* 514-374-3988
Courriel: amq@microbiologistes.ca
URL: www.cooptel.qc.ca/~amqweb/
Christian Beaulac, Président

Association of Canadian Ergonomists (ACE) / L'Association canadienne d'ergonomie
#1003, 105-150 Crowfoot Cres. NW, Calgary AB T3G 3T2
Tel: 403-219-4001; *Fax:* 403-451-1503
Toll-Free: 888-432-2223
e-mail: info@ace-ergocanada.ca
URL: www.ace-ergocanada.ca
Margo Fraser, Executive Director
Brenda Mallat, President

Association of Professional Biologists of British Columbia (APBBC)
#205, 733 Johnson St., Victoria BC V8W 3C7
Tel: 250-383-3306; *Fax:* 250-383-2400
e-mail: apbbc@apbbc.bc.ca
URL: www.apbbc.bc.ca
Affiliation(s): BC Institute of Agrologists; Canadian Society of Professional Biologists; Professional Pest Management Association of BC; Association of BC Forestry Professionals; Alberta Society of Professional Biologists; Association des biologistes du Québec; Association of Professional Engineers & Geoscientists; Applied Science Technologists & Technicians of BC
Gerry Leering, President
Linda Stordeur, R.P.Bio., Registrar
Linda Michaluk, R.P.Bio., Executive Director

Atlantic Provinces Council on the Sciences (APCS) / Conseil des provinces atlantiques pour les sciences (CPAS)
1390 Le Marchant St., Halifax NS B3H 3P9
Tel: 902-494-3421; *Fax:* 902-494-6643
e-mail: apics@dal.ca
URL: www.apics.dal.ca
Lois Whitehead, Executive Director

Biophysical Society of Canada (BSC) / La société de biophysique du Canada
a/s Dept. de chimie-biologie, Univ. du Québec à Trois-Rivières, CP 500, Trois-Rivières QC G9A 5H7
Tel: 819-376-5011; *Fax:* 819-376-5057
e-mail: fragata@uqtr.ca
URL: www.uqtr.ca/sbc/
Mario Julio Fragata, Secretary

BIOTECanada
#420, 130 Albert St., Ottawa ON K1P 5G4
Tel: 613-230-5585; *Fax:* 613-563-8850
e-mail: info@biotech.ca
URL: www.biotech.ca
Peter Brenders, President & CEO

Canadian Association for Anatomy, Neurobiology & Cell Biology (CAANCB) / Association canadienne d'anatomie, de neurobiologie et de biologie cellulaire (ACANBC)
Dept. of Anatomy & Cell Biology, Queens University, Kingston ON K7L 3N6
Tel: 613-533-2864; *Fax:* 613-533-2566
URL: caancb.blogspot.com/
Bernie Juurlink, President, Department of Saskatchewan, University of Saskatchewan

Canadian Association of Palynologists (CAP) / Association canadienne des palynologues
c/o Parks Canada, Western Canada Services Ctr., #300, 300 West Georgia St., Vancouver BC V6B 6B4
URL: www.scirpus.ca/cap/cap.shtml
Affiliation(s): International Federation of Palynological Societies
Marlow G. Pellatt, Sec.-Treas.
Catharine H. Yansa, President

Canadian Association of Physicists (CAP) / Association canadienne des physiciens et physiciennes (ACP)
MacDonald Bldg., #112, 150 Louis Pasteur Priv., Ottawa ON K1N 6N5
Tel: 613-562-5614; *Fax:* 613-562-5615
e-mail: cap@uottawa.ca
URL: www.cap.ca
Affiliation(s): Chemical Institute of Canada; Canadian Organization of Medical Physicists; American Physical Society; Institute of Physics; Mexican Physical Society; Brazilian Physical Society
Francine M. Ford, Executive Director

Canadian Astronomical Society (CASCA) / Société canadienne d'astronomie
Business Office, Dept. of Physics, Queens Univ., Kingston ON K7L 3N6
Tel: 613-533-6439; *Fax:* 613-533-6463
e-mail: casca@astro.queensu.ca
URL: www.casca.ca
Paul Hickson, President

Canadian Botanical Association (CBA) / Association botanique du Canada (ABC)
PO Box 160, Aberdeen SK S0K 0A0
Tel: 902-424-3564; *Fax:* 902-424-0560
e-mail: daya@alcor.concordia.ca
URL: www.cba-abc.ca
Affiliation(s): Botanical Society of America
Christian Lacroix, President
Marian Munro, Secretary
Santokh Singh, Vice-President
Hugues Massicotte, Treasurer

Canadian College of Physicists in Medicine (CCPM) / Collège canadien des physiciens en médecine
PO Box 72024, Kanata North RPO, Kanata ON K2K 2P4
Tel: 613-599-1948; *Fax:* 613-599-1949
URL: www.ccpm.ca
Affiliation(s): Canadian Organization of Medical Physicists (COMP)
Nancy Barrett, Executive Director
Wayne A. Beckham, PhD, FCCPM, MAC, CCPM Registrar
Rasika Rajapakshe, Ph.D., FCCPM, Chair, Accreditation Committee on Physics of Mammography

Canadian Federation of Biological Societies (CFBS) / Fédération canadienne des sociétés de biologie (FCSB)
#305, 1750 Courtwood Cres., Ottawa ON K2C 2B5
Tel: 613-225-8889; *Fax:* 613-225-9621
URL: www.cfbs.org
Gabrielle Adams, Ph.D., Executive Director & Consultant, Science Policy
Bruce Sells, PhD, FRS(C), Executive Director Emeritus
Peter Fischer, President
Ken Fisher, Honourary Secretary
Ric Devon, Honourary Treasurer

Canadian Federation of Earth Sciences (CFES) / Fédération canadienne des sciences de la Terre
c/o Managing Director, 210 Main St., Wolfville NS B4P 1C4
Tel: 902-542-6125
e-mail: cfes@magma.ca
URL: www.geoscience.ca
Bill Mercer, President

Canadian Hydrographic Association (CHA) / Association canadienne d'hydrographie
867 Lakeshore Rd., Burlington ON L7R 4A6
Tel: 905-336-4501
URL: www.hydrography.ca
Affiliation(s): Canadian Institute of Geomatics (formal affiliation); The Hydrographic Society (informal affiliation)
George McFarlane, National President
Scott Youngblut, National Treasurer
Terese Herron, National Secretary

Canadian Institute of Food Science & Technology (CIFST) / Institut canadien de science et technologie alimentaires (ICSTA)
#1311, 3-1750 The Queensway, Toronto ON M9C 5H5
Tel: 905-271-8338; *Fax:* 905-271-8344
e-mail: cifst@cifst.ca
URL: www.cifst.ca
Carol Ann Burell, CAE, Executive Director

Canadian Medical & Biological Engineering Society Inc. (CMBES) / Société canadienne de génie biomédical inc. (SCGB)
1485 Laperrière Ave., Ottawa ON K1Z 7S8
Tel: 613-728-1759
e-mail: secretariat@cmbes.ca
URL: www.cmbes.ca
Affiliation(s): International Federation for Medical & Biological Engineering
Donald Russell, President
Martin Poulin, Treasurer

Canadian Meteorological & Oceanographic Society (CMOS) / Société canadienne de météorologie et d'océanographie (SCMO)
PO Box 3211, Stn. D, Ottawa ON K1P 6H7
Tel: 613-990-0300; *Fax:* 613-990-1617
e-mail: communications@cmos.ca; accounts@cmos.ca; publications@cmos.ca
URL: www.cmos.ca
Ian D. Rutherford, PhD, Executive Director
Crawford Bill, President
Bourque Sheila, Director, Education & Outreach
Qing Liao, Manager, Office

Canadian Physiological Society (CPS) / Société canadienne de physiologie
c/o CFBS, #305, 1750 Courtwood Cres., Ottawa ON K2C 2B5
Tel: 613-225-8889; *Fax:* 613-225-9621
e-mail: c.elainechapman@umontreal.ca
URL: www.physiol.ca
Affiliation(s): International Union of Physiological Sciences; Canadian Journal of Physiology & Pharmacology
Steven Barnes, President
C. Elaine Chapman, Secretary

Canadian Phytopathological Society (CPS) / Société Canadienne de Phytopathologie (SCP)
c/o Crop Protection & Food Research Ctr Agriculture & Agri-Food Canada, 1391 Sandford St., London ON N5V 4T3
e-mail: connk@agr.gc.ca
URL: www.cps-scp.ca
Kenneth Conn, Contact

Canadian Science & Technology Historical Association (CSTHA) / Association pour l'histoire de la science et de la technologie au Canada (AHSTC)
PO Box 9724, Stn. T, Ottawa ON K1G 3H9
e-mail: secretary@cstha-ahstc.ca
URL: www.cstha-ahstc.ca
Suzanne Beauvais, Secretary
Bertrum H. MacDonald, President

Canadian Society for Analytical Sciences & Spectroscopy
PO Box 46122, 2339 Ogilvie Rd., Ottawa ON K1J 9M7
Fax: 204-954-5984
URL: www.csass.org
Affiliation(s): Society for Applied Spectroscopy - USA; Colloquium Spectroscopicum Internationale; Chemical Institute of Canada; Canadian Society of Forensic Science
Teresa Switzer, President
Doug Goltz, Treasurer

Canadian Society for the History & Philosophy of Science (CSHPS) / Société Canadienne d'Histoire et Philosophie des Sciences (SCHPS)
Dept. of History & Classics, University of Alberta, Edmonton AB T6G 2H4
Tel: 416-736-2100
e-mail: aede@ualberta.ca
URL: www.yorku.ca/cshps1/
Affiliation(s): International Union for History & Philosophy of Science
Gordon McOuat, President (2005-2008)
Andrew Ede, Sec.-Treas.

The Canadian Society for the Weizmann Institute of Science (CSWIS)
4700 Bathurst St., 2nd Fl., Toronto ON M2R 1W8
Tel: 416-733-9220; *Fax:* 416-733-9430
Toll-Free: 800-387-3894
e-mail: weizmann@ca.inter.net
URL: www.weizmann.ac.il; www.weizmann.ca
Sheri Federman, Director, Programs & Operations
Michael E. Meyer, National Executive Vice-President

The Canadian Society of Biochemistry, Molecular & Cellular Biology / Société canadienne de biochimie et de biologie moléculaire et cellulaire
c/o Department of Biochemistry, University of Toronto, Medical Sciences Bldg., 1 King's College Circle, Toronto ON M5S 1A8
Tel: 416-978-0774
e-mail: rob.reedijk@utoronto.ca
URL: www.csbmcb.ca
Rob Reedijk, Contact
Laura Frost, President

Canadian Society of Exploration Geophysicists (CSEG)
#600, 640 - 8th Ave. SW, Calgary AB T2P 1G7
Tel: 403-262-0015; *Fax:* 403-262-7383
e-mail: csegoffice@shaw.ca
URL: www.cseg.ca
Affiliation(s): Society of Exploration Geophysicists - USA; European Association of Geoscientists & Engineers - Netherlands
Jim Racette, Managing Director

Canadian Society of Forensic Science (CSFS)
PO Box 37040, 3332 McCarthy Rd., Ottawa ON K1V 0W0
e-mail: csfs@bellnet.ca
URL: www.csfs.ca
G. Anderson, President
G. Verret, Secretary
D. Camellato, Treasurer

Canadian Society of Microbiologists (CSM) / Société canadienne des microbiologistes
CSM-SCM Secretariat, #305, 1750 Courtwood Cres., Ottawa ON K2C 2B5
Tel: 613-225-8889; *Fax:* 613-225-9621
e-mail: info@csm-scm.org
URL: www.csm-scm.org
Affiliation(s): Youth Science Foundation; International Union of Microbiological Societies
Colin R. Bell, President
Louise M. Nelson, Secretary-Treasurer

Canadian Society of Pharmacology & Therapeutics (CSPT) / Société de pharmacologie du Canada
Dept. of Physiology & Pharmacology, Univ. of Western Ontario, M216 Medical Services Bldg., London ON N6A 5C1
Tel: 519-661-3312
URL: www.pharmacologycanada.org
Gaebel Kathryn, Executive Administrator
Richard Kim, President
Fiona Parkinson, Vice-President
Cindy Woodland, Secretary-Treasurer

Canadian Society of Plant Physiologists (CSPP) / Société canadienne de physiologie végétale (SCPV)
c/o Dr. Harold Weger, Department of Biology, University of Regina, 3737 Wascana Pkwy., Regina SK S4S 0A2
e-mail: treasurer@cspp-scpvca.ca
URL: www.cspp-scpv.ca
Priti Krishna, Senior Director
Peter Pauls, President
Line Lapointe, Secretary
Harold G. Weger, Treasurer

Canadian Society of Soil Science (CSSS) / Société canadienne de la science du sol
Business Office, PO Box 637, Pinawa MB R0E 1L0
Tel: 204-753-2747; *Fax:* 204-753-8478
e-mail: sheppards@ecomatters.com
URL: www.csss.ca
Affiliation(s): International Union of Soil Science
Gordon Price, President
Barbara Cade-Menun, Secretary
Paul Bullock, Treasurer

Canadian Space Society (CSS) / La société canadienne de l'espace
Parc Downsview Park, 65 Carl Hall Rd., Toronto ON M3K 2E1
URL: www.css.ca
Kevin Shortt, President
Vivian Lee, Coordinator, Membership

Citizen Scientists
c/o Rouge Valley Conservation Centre, 1749 Meadowvale Rd., Toronto ON M1B 5W8
e-mail: info@citizenscientists.ca
URL: www.citizenscientists.ca
Social Media: www.facebook.com/group.php?gid=2259994028

Club d'astronomie Quasar de Chibougamau
783, 6e Rue, Chibougamau QC G8P 2W4

Tél: 418-748-4642
URL: www.faaq.org/clubs/quasar/
Pierre Bureau, Président

Genetics Society of Canada (GSC) / Société de génétique du Canada
c/o The Snider's Web, 59 Aulac Rd., Aulac NB E4L 2V6
Tel: 506-536-1768; *Fax:* 902-484-5694
e-mail: gsc@thesnidersweb.com
URL: life.biology.mcmaster.ca/GSC/
Affiliation(s): Canadian Federation of Biological Sciences; International Genetics Federation
Paul Lasko, President
Elizabeth Stendel, Contact

Geological Association of Canada (GAC) / Association géologique du Canada (AGC)
Department of Earth Sciences, Memorial University of Newfoundland, #ER4063, Alexander Murray Bldg., St. John's NL A1B 3X5
Tel: 709-737-7660; *Fax:* 709-737-2532
e-mail: gac@mun.ca
URL: www.gac.ca
Affiliation(s): Canadian Society of Petroleum Geologists; Toronto Geological Discussion Group; Atlantic Geoscience Society; Canadian Quaternary Association; Canadian Geophysical Union
Carolyn Anglin, President
Robert Marquis, Sec.-Treas.

Innovation and Technology Association of Prince Edward Island (ITAP)
PO Box 241, Charlottetown PE C1A 7K4
Tel: 902-894-4827; *Fax:* 902-894-4867
e-mail: itap@itap.ca
URL: www.itap.ca
Kelly Dawson, President

Institute of Textile Science (ITS) / Institut des sciences textiles
c/o Jerry Bauerle, BodyCote Ortech Inc., 2395 Speakman Dr., Mississauga ON L5K 1B3
Tel: 905-822-4111; *Fax:* 905-823-1446
e-mail: info@textilescience.ca
URL: www.textilescience.ca
Kasper Van Veen, President

International Association of Hydrogeologists - Canadian National Chapter (IAH-CNC)
c/o WESA, 3108 Carp Rd., Carp ON K0A 1L0
Tel: 613-839-3053
URL: www.iah.ca
Affiliation(s): International Union of Geological Congresses
Nell van Walsum, Secretary

International Association of Science & Technology for Development (IASTED)
Bldg B6, #101, 2509 Dieppe Ave. SW, Calgary AB T3E 7J9
Tel: 403-288-1195; *Fax:* 403-247-6851
e-mail: calgary@iasted.com
URL: www.iasted.org

International Oceans Institute of Canada (IOIC)
c/o Dalhousie Univ., 1226 LeMarchant St., Halifax NS B3H 3P7
Tel: 902-494-6918; *Fax:* 902-494-1334
e-mail: ioi@dal.ca
URL: internationaloceaninstitute.dal.ca
Affiliation(s): International Oceans Institute; Atlantic Coastal Zone Information Steering Committee

Life Science Association of Manitoba (LSAM)
1000 Waverley St., Winnipeg MB R3T 0P3
Tel: 204-272-5095; *Fax:* 204-272-2961
e-mail: info@lsam.ca
URL: www.lsam.ca
Affiliation(s): BIOTECanada; BioTalent Canada; Life Sciences British Columbia; BioAlberta; Ag-West Biotech Inc.; Ontario Agri-Food Technologies; MaRS; Ottawa Life Sciences Council; Toronto Biotechnology Initiative; TechAlliance; The Golden Horseshoe Biosciences Network; York Biotech; BioQuebec; BioAtlantech; BioNova; PEI BioAlliance; Newfoundland & Labrador Assn of Technology Industries
Dawson Reimer, President

Microscopical Society of Canada (MSC) / Société de Microscopie du Canada
c/o Occupational & Environmental Health Laboratory, McMaster Univ., #3H50, 1200 Main St. West, Hamilton ON L8N 3Z5
Tel: 905-525-9140; *Fax:* 905-528-8860
e-mail: clarkn@mcmaster.ca
URL: msc.rsvs.ulaval.ca
Craig Bennett, President
Nancy Clark, Treasurer
Frances Leggett, Executive Secretary

North Pacific Marine Science Organization (PICES)
c/o Institute of Ocean Sciences, PO Box 6000, Sidney BC V8L 4B2
Tel: 250-363-6366; *Fax:* 250-363-6827
e-mail: secretariat@pices.int
URL: www.pices.int
Alexander Bychkov, Executive Secretary

Nova Scotian Institute of Science (NSIS)
Science Services, Killam Library, Dalhousie Univ., 6225 University Ave., Halifax NS B3H 4H8
Tel: 902-494-3621; *Fax:* 902-494-2062
e-mail: nsis@chebucto.ns.ca
URL: www.chebucto.ns.ca/Science/NSIS
David Richardson, President
Ron MacKay, Vice-President
Linda Marks, Secretary
Elaine McCullogh, Treasurer

Ontario Kinesiology Association (OKA)
6519B Mississauga Rd., Mississauga ON L5N 1A6
Tel: 905-567-7194; *Fax:* 905-567-7191
e-mail: info@oka.on.ca
URL: www.oka.on.ca
Francis Puchalski, President

Royal Astronomical Society of Canada (RASC) / Société royale d'astronomie du Canada
136 Dupont St., Toronto ON M5R 1V2
Tel: 416-924-7973; *Fax:* 416-924-2911
Toll-Free: 888-924-7272
e-mail: nationaloffice@rasc.ca
URL: www.rasc.ca
Dave Lane, President
Jo Taylor, Executive Secretary

Science Alberta Foundation
#260, 3512 - 33 St. NW, Calgary AB T2L 2A6
Tel: 403-220-0077; *Fax:* 403-284-4132
e-mail: info@sciencealberta.org
URL: www.sciencealberta.org
Arlene Ponting, CEO
Jill Maryniuk, Manager, Marketing & Communications

Society of Toxicology of Canada (STC) / Société de toxicologie du Canada
PO Box 55094, Montréal QC H3G 2W5
Tel: 514-697-9219; *Fax:* 514-697-9309
e-mail: stcsecretariat@mcgill.ca
URL: www.stcweb.ca
Affiliation(s): Canadian Federation of Biological Societies; International Union of Toxicology
Genevieve Bondy, President
Elise Boivin-Ford, Executive Secretary

Southern Ontario Seismic Network (SOSN)
c/o University of Western Ontario, London ON N6A 5B7
Tel: 519-661-3605; *Fax:* 519-661-3198
URL: www.gp.uwo.ca
R.F. Mereu, Administrator

Statistical Society of Canada (SSC) / Société statistique du Canada
#105, 1785 Alta Vista Dr., Ottawa ON K1G 3Y6
Tel: 613-733-2662; *Fax:* 613-733-1386
e-mail: info@ssc.ca; admin@ssc.ca
URL: www.ssc.ca
Román Viveros-Aguilera, President
Edward Chen, Treasurer
Paul Cabilio, Executive Secretary

Youth Science Foundation Canada (YSF) / Fondation sciences jeunesse Canada (FSJ)
PO Box 523, Stn. R, Toronto ON M4G 4E1
Tel: 416-341-0040; *Fax:* 416-341-0040
Toll-Free: 866-341-0040
e-mail: info@ysf-fsj.ca
URL: www.ysf-fsj.ca
Reni Barlow, Executive Director
Lorne Heslop, Chair
Thomas C. Lee, Sec.-Treas.

Search & Rescue

New Brunswick Ground Search and Rescue Association (NBGSARA)
c/o President
Tel: 506-850-3461; *Fax:* 506-462-2105
URL: www.nbgsara.nb.ca
Joseph LaBelle, President

Senior Citizens

Active Living Coalition for Older Adults (ALCOA) / Coalition d'une vie active pour les ainé(e)s
PO Box 143, Shelburne ON L0N 1S0
Tel: 519-925-1676; *Fax:* 905-925-3955
Toll-Free: 800-549-9799
e-mail: alcoa@ca.inter.net
URL: www.alcoa.ca
Don Fletcher, Chair
Patricia Clark, Executive Director

Advocacy Centre for the Elderly (ACE)
#701, 2 Carlton St., Toronto ON M5B 1J3
Tel: 416-598-2656; *Fax:* 416-598-7924
URL: www.advocacycentreelderly.org
Paula Psyllakis, Chair
Judith Wahl, Executive Director

Alberta Council on Aging
#210, 14964 - 121A Ave., Edmonton AB T5V 1A3
Tel: 780-423-7781; *Fax:* 780-425-9246
Toll-Free: 888-423-9666
e-mail: info@acaging.ca
URL: www.acaging.ca
Gary Pool, President
Paul Lemay, Vice-President

Alberta Provincial Pensioners & Senior Citizens Organization (APSCO)
#334, 1237 - 4 Ave. South, Lethbridge AB T1J 0P9
Tel: 403-327-3264
e-mail: gwaldern@uleth.ca
Violet Segouin, Treasurer
Betty Waldern, President

Alberta Senior Citizens Sport & Recreation Association (ASCSRA)
#101, 525 - 11 Ave. SW, Calgary AB T2R 0C9
Tel: 403-297-2703; *Fax:* 403-297-6669
e-mail: ascsra@telus.net
URL: www.alberta55plus.ca
Affiliation(s): Alberta Sport, Recreation, Parks & Wildlife Foundation

Association des personnes en perte d'autonomie de Chibougamau inc. & Jardin des aînés
101, av du Parc, Chibougamau QC G8P 3A5
Tél: 418-748-4411
Chantal Lessard, Directrice générale

Canadian Association on Gerontology (CAG) / Association canadienne de gérontologie
#106, 222 College St, Toronto ON M5T 3J1
Tel: 613-271-1083; *Fax:* 613-599-7027
e-mail: cagacg@igs.net
URL: www.cagacg.ca
Sandra Nirst, President

Canadian Pensioners Concerned Inc. (CPC) / Retraités canadiens en action (RCA)
6 Trinity Sq., Toronto ON M5G 1B1
Tel: 416-368-5222; *Fax:* 416-368-0443
Toll-Free: 888-822-6750
e-mail: info@canpension.ca
URL: www.canpension.ca
Sylvia Hall, Chair

CARP Canada's Association for the Fifty-Plus (CARP)
#1304, 27 Queen St. East, Toronto ON M5C 2M6
Tel: 416-363-8748; *Fax:* 416-363-8747
Toll-Free: 800-363-9736
e-mail: carp@50plus.com
URL: www.carp.ca
Lillian Morgenthau, President & Co-Founder
Moses Znaimer, Executive Director

Club de l'âge d'or Les intrépides de Chibougamau
126, rue des Forces-Armées, Chibougamau QC G8P 3A1
Tél: 418-748-7541
Henriette Roy, Présidente

Council for Black Aging
3007 Delisle, Montréal QC H4C 1M8
Tel: 514-935-4951; *Fax:* 514-935-8466
Elisee Faure, Contact

Elder Active Recreation Association (ERA)
4061, 4th Ave., Whitehorse YT Y1A 1H1

Tel: 867-633-5010
URL: www.yukon-seniors-and-elders.org/era.home.htm
Bill Simpson, President

FADOQ - Mouvement des aînés du Québec / Québec Federation of Senior Citizens
CP 1000, Succ. M, 4545, av Pierre-de Couberin, Montréal QC H1V 3R2
Tél: 514-252-3017; *Téléc:* 514-252-3154
Ligne sans frais: 800-828-3344
Courriel: info@fadoq.ca
URL: www.fadoq.ca
Affiliation(s): Association québécoise de gérontologie; Conseil canadien de développement social; Réseau canadien des aînés (One Voice); l'Assemblée des aîné(e)s francophones du Canada
Ernest Boyer, Président

Fédération des aînées et aînés francophones du Canada (FAAFC)
#300, 450 rue Rideau, Ottawa ON K1N 5Z4
Tél: 613-564-0212; *Téléc:* 613-564-0212
Courriel: info@faafc.ca
URL: www.faafc.ca/fr
Roger Doiron, Président
Jean-Luc Racine, Directeur général
Michel Vézina, Premier vice-président, Saskatchewan
André Faubert, Deuxième vice-présidente, Québec
Richard Martin, Trésorier, Terre-Neuve & Labrador
Mélina Gallant, Secrétaire, Ile-du-Prince-Édouard
Marie-Christine Aubrey, Administratrice, Territoire du Nord-Ouest
Louis Bernardin, Administrateur, Manitoba
Roland Gallant, Administrateur, Nouveau-Brunswick
Charles Gaudet, Administrateur, Nouvelle-Écosse
Claire Grisé, Administratrice, Colombie-Britannique
Germaine Lehodey, Administratrice, Alberta
Francine Poirier, Administratrice, Ontario
Roxanne Thibaudeau, Administratrice, Yukon

Help the Aged (Canada) (HTA) / Aide aux aînés (Canada)
#205, 1300 Carling Ave., Ottawa ON K1Z 7L2
Tel: 613-232-0727; *Fax:* 613-232-7625
Toll-Free: 800-648-1111
e-mail: info@helptheaged.ca; adoptagran@helptheaged.ca
URL: www.helptheaged.ca; www.aideauxainescanada.ca
Affiliation(s): HelpAge International
Pierre Barbeau, Executive Director
Jacqueline A. Bannister, Chair
Pierrette Leonard, Vice-Chair
Peter Hamilton, Secretary
Jacqueline Hallé, Treasurer

Manitoba Association on Gerontology (MAG)
884 William Ave., Winnipeg MB R3E 0Z6
Tel: 204-783-8389
Pamela Hawranik, President

Manitoba Society of Seniors (MSOS)
#202, 323 Portage Ave., Winnipeg MB R3B 2C1
Tel: 204-942-3147; *Fax:* 204-943-1290
Toll-Free: 800-561-6767
e-mail: membership@msos.mb.ca
URL: www.msos.mb.ca
Kimberly Weihs, Executive Director
Harry Paine, President

National Pensioners & Senior Citizens Federation (NPSCF) / Fédération nationale des retraités et citoyens âgés
c/o Fern Haight, PO Box 393, Hanley SK S0G 2E0
Tel: 306-544-2737; *Fax:* 306-544-2757
e-mail: fern.h@sasktel.net
URL: www.npscf.org
Affiliation(s): International Senior Citizens Association
Art Kube, President
Fern Haight, Secretary

New Brunswick Senior Citizens Federation Inc. (NBSCF) / Fédération des citoyens aînés du Nouveau-Brunswick inc. (FCANB)
36 Albert St., Moncton NB E1C 1W1
Tel: 506-857-8242; *Fax:* 506-857-0315
Toll-Free: 800-453-4333
e-mail: horizons@nbnet.nb.ca
URL: www.nbscf.ca
Isabelle Thériault-Arseneault, Administration Officer

Older Adult Centres' Association of Ontario (OACAO) / Association des centres pour aînés de l'Ontario
43 North Riverdale Dr., Inglewood ON L7C 3K3
Tel: 905-838-0240; *Fax:* 905-838-1053
Toll-Free: 866-835-7693
e-mail: lbloom@oacao.org
URL: www.oacao.org
Lawrie Bloom, Executive Director
Ellen Hope, President
Marilyn Latham, Treasurer
Debra Prescott, Secretary

Ontario Coalition of Senior Citizens' Organizations (OCSCO) / Coalition des organismes d'aînés et d'aînées de l'Ontario (COAAO)
#207, 660 Briar Hill Ave., Toronto ON M6B 4B7
Tel: 416-785-8570; *Fax:* 416-785-7361
Toll-Free: 800-265-0779
e-mail: ocsco@web.net
URL: www.ocsco.ca
Morris Jesion, Executive Director
Lisa Hems, Program Coordinator

Prince Edward Island Senior Citizens Federation Inc. (PEISCF)
40 Enman Cres., Charlottetown PE C1E 1E6
Tel: 902-368-9008; *Fax:* 902-368-9006
Toll-Free: 877-368-9008
e-mail: peiscf@pei.aibn.com
URL: sites.townsquare.ca/PEISeniorsFed/index.cfm
Irene Larkin, Executive Director

Routes to Learning Canada (RLC)
4 Cataraqui St., Kingston ON K7K 1Z7
Fax: 613-530-2096
Toll-Free: 866-745-1690
e-mail: information@routestolearning.ca
URL: www.routestolearning.ca
Victoria Pearson, President/CEO

SAGE - Seniors Association of Greater Edmonton
15 Sir Winston Churchill Sq., Edmonton AB T5J 2E5
Tel: 780-423-5510; *Fax:* 780-426-5175
e-mail: info@mysage.ca
URL: www.mysage.ca
Bill McDonald, President
Ivett Campos, Office Services Coordinator

United Senior Citizens of Ontario Inc. (USCO)
3033 Lakeshore Blvd. West, Toronto ON M8V 1K5
Tel: 416-252-2021; *Fax:* 416-252-5770
Toll-Free: 888-320-2222
e-mail: office@uscont.ca
URL: www.uscont.ca
Ken Cunningham, President

Service Clubs

Association des Grands Frères/Grandes Soeurs du Québec (GFGS) / Big Brothers/Big Sisters of Québec
#206, 4030, rue St-Ambroise, Montréal QC H4C 2C7
Tél: 514-286-9531; *Téléc:* 514-286-1131
Ligne sans frais: 888-286-9531
Courriel: info@gfgsq.ca
URL: www.gfgs.qc.ca
Gérard Vallée, Président

Big Brothers Big Sisters of Canada (BBBSC) / Les Grands Frères Grandes Soeurs du Canada
#113E, 3228 South Service Rd., Burlington ON L7N 3H8
Tel: 905-639-0461; *Fax:* 905-639-0124
Toll-Free: 800-263-9133
URL: www.bbbsc.ca
Bruce MacDonald, President
Renée Hébert, Regional Director, Atlantic
Rob Lweis, Regional Director, Western
Joelle Lewis, Regional Director, Ontario

British Columbia Lions Society for Children with Disabilities (BCLS)
3981 Oak St., Vancouver BC V6H 4H5
Tel: 604-873-1865; *Fax:* 604-873-0166
Toll-Free: 800-818-4483
e-mail: info@lionsbc.ca
URL: www.lionsbc.ca
Affiliation(s): Custom Service Transit Society; Easter Seal House Society; 24 HR Relay Society
Stephen J. Miller, President
Surinder Gahir, Chair
Beth McInnis, Financial Advisor

Canadian Federation of Junior Leagues / Fédération canadienne des jeunes ligues
4 Steeplehill Cres., Carlisle ON L0R 1H3
Tel: 905-659-9339
e-mail: info@cfjl.org
URL: www.cfjl.org
Deborah Maw, National Coordinator

Canadian Progress Club / Club progrès du Canada
#143, 75 Lavinia St., New Glasgow NS B2H 1N5
Fax: 888-337-9826
Toll-Free: 877-944-4726
e-mail: info@progressclub.ca
URL: www.progressclub.ca
Sharon Ward, National President
Carmel Kinder, National Club Administrator

Club Kiwanis Chibougamau
CP 61, Chibougamau QC G8P 2K5
Tél: 418-748-2231
Roy Lavoie, Président

Club Lions de Chibougamau
CP 11, Chibougamau QC G8P 2K5
Courriel: lionschibougamau@hotmail.com
URL: lionschibougamau.icr.qc.ca
Robin Pearson

Club Optimiste Chibougamau
1614, rue St-Jacques, Chibougamau QC G8P 2L7
Tél: 418-748-7272
Sylvie Cayouette, Présidente

Club Optimiste de Rivière-du-Loup inc.
CP 1344, Rivière-du-Loup QC G5R 4L9
Tél: 418-862-8454; *Téléc:* 418-862-3366
Courriel: service@optimiste.org
URL: www.optimiste.org
Denise Desbiens, Présidente

Kin Canada
PO Box KIN, 1920 Hal Rogers Dr., Cambridge ON N3H 5C6
Tel: 519-653-1920; *Fax:* 519-650-1091
Toll-Free: 800-742-5546
e-mail: kinhq@kincanada.ca
URL: www.kincanada.ca
Ric McDonald, Executive Director
Sean Thompson, President

Kiwanis International/Eastern Canada & the Caribbean District
PO Box 26040, 260 St. Paul Ave., Brantford ON N3R 7X4
Tel: 519-304-0745; *Fax:* 519-756-3183
Toll-Free: 888-921-9054
e-mail: district@kiwanisecc.org
URL: www.kiwanisecc.org
Jacqueline Ashcroft, District Administrative Secretary
Ted Sievert, Sec.-Treas.

Kiwanis International/Western Canada District
c/o 14622, 95 Ave., Edmonton AB T5N 0B3
Tel: 780-452-9735; *Fax:* 780-452-9735
URL: www.kiwaniswesterncanada.org
Walter P. Voth, Sec.-Treas.
Dick Southworth, Governor
Lori Beneteau, Governor Elect

Last Post Fund
Veteran Affairs Divison- High Commission of Canada, MacDonald House, 1 Grosvenor Sq., London W1X 0AB United Kingdom
Tel: 44(0)20-7258-6339; *Fax:* 44(0)20-7258-6645
e-mail: suzanne.happe@dfait-maeci.gc.ca
URL: www.lastpostfund.ca

Last Post Fund
Building B, #202, 580 Main St., Saint John NB E2K 1J5
Tel: 506-658-9707; *Fax:* 506-658-9623
Toll-Free: 800-561-0505
e-mail: lpfnbpei@nbnet.nb.ca
URL: www.lastpostfund.ca

Last Post Fund (LPF) / Fonds du Souvenir
#401, 505, boul René-Lévesque ouest, Montréal QC H2Z 1Y7
Tel: 514-866-2727; *Fax:* 514-866-2147
Toll-Free: 800-465-7113
e-mail: lpfnoqc@lastpostfund.ca
URL: www.lastpostfund.ca
Alexander Bialosh, Executive Director
Louis Cuppens, National President
Evelyn Kelly, Vice President (West)
René Pothier, Vice President (East)

Last Post Fund
#905, 55 St. Clair Ave. East, Toronto ON M4T 1M2
Tel: 416-923-1608; *Fax:* 416-923-3695
Toll-Free: 800-563-2508

e-mail: lpfon@bellnet.ca
URL: www.lastpostfund.ca

Last Post Fund
#402, 505, boul. René-Lévesque ouest, Montréal QC H2Z 1Y7
Tél: 514-866-2888; Téléc: 514-866-1471
Ligne sans frais: 800-866-5229
Courriel: lpfqc@lastpostfund.ca
URL: www.lastpostfund.ca

Last Post Fund
51 St. Anne's Rd., Winnipeg MB R2M 1Y4
Tel: 204-233-3073; Fax: 204-237-1169
Toll-Free: 888-233-3073
e-mail: lastpostfund@mts.net
URL: www.lastpostfund.ca

Last Post Fund
Federal Building, #403, 101 - 22 St. East, Saskatoon SK S7K 0E1
Tel: 306-975-6045; Fax: 306-975-6678
Toll-Free: 800-667-3668
e-mail: lastpost@sasktel.net
URL: www.lastpostfund.ca

Last Post Fund
Canada Place, #1130, 9700 Jasper Ave., Edmonton AB T5J 4C3
Tel: 780-495-3766; Fax: 780-495-6960
Toll-Free: 888-495-3766
e-mail: lpfab@telusplanet.net
URL: www.lastpostfund.ca

Last Post Fund
#203, 7337 - 137th St., Surrey BC V3W 1A4
Tel: 604-572-3242; Fax: 604-572-3306
Toll-Free: 800-268-0248
e-mail: lastpost@telus.net
URL: www.lastpostfund.ca

Last Post Fund
Prudential Bldg., 49 Elizabeth Ave., St. John's NL A1A 1W9
Tel: 709-579-4288; Fax: 709-579-0966
Toll-Free: 888-579-4288
e-mail: lfpn@nf.aibn.com
URL: www.lastpostfund.ca

Last Post Fund
Chebucto Place, #200A, 7105 Chebucto Rd., Halifax NS B3L 4W8
Tel: 902-455-5283; Fax: 902-455-4058
Toll-Free: 800-565-4777
e-mail: lpfnsb@eastlink.ca
URL: www.lastpostfund.ca

Soroptimist Foundation of Canada
c/o #104, 13311 Yonge Street, Richmond Hill ON L4E 3L6
e-mail: corinne@cmrlaw.ca
URL: www.soroptimistfoundation.ca
Affiliation(s): Soroptimist International of the Americas
Connie Rivers, Chair

Variety - The Children's Charity (Ontario)
3701 Danforth Ave., Toronto ON M1N 2G2
Tel: 416-367-2828; Fax: 416-367-0028
e-mail: info@varietyontario.ca
URL: www.varietyontario.ca
Affiliation(s): Variety Village; Variety Ability Systems Inc.
Maureen Burgess, Executive Director

Variety - The Children's Charity of BC
4300 Still Creek Dr., Burnaby BC V5C 6C6
Tel: 604-320-0505; Fax: 604-320-0535
Toll-Free: 800-381-2040
e-mail: info@variety.bc.ca
URL: www.variety.bc.ca
Barbara Hislop, Executive Director

Variety - The Children's Charity of Manitoba, Tent 58 Inc.
#2 - 1313 Border St., Winnipeg MB R3H 0X4
Tel: 204-982-1058; Fax: 204-475-3198
e-mail: office@varietymanitoba.com
URL: www.varietymanitoba.com
Wayne Rogers, Executive Director

Variety Club of Northern Alberta, Tent 63
#1205 Energy Square, 10109 - 106th St., Edmonton AB T5J 3L7
Tel: 780-448-9544; Fax: 780-448-9289
Sue McEachern, Executive Director

Variety Club of Southern Alberta
#201 - 1740B, 11A St. NE, Calgary AB T2E 6M6
Tel: 403-228-6168; Fax: 403-245-9282
e-mail: info@varietyalberta.ca
URL: www.varietyclub61.ab.ca
Affiliation(s): Variety Children's Lifeline
Audrey Garratt, Chief
Graham Kuntz, Executive Director

Social Clubs

Brunch-rencontre pour personnes seules
#102, 161, rue du Parc, Chibougamau QC G8P 2H3
Tél: 418-748-4951
Réjeanne Lalancette

Canadian Black Community Association
#30, 6999, Côte-des-Neiges, Montréal QC H3S 2B6
Tel: 514-737-8321; Fax: 514-737-6893
Michael Gittens, Contact

Social Response/Social Services

Agincourt Community Services Association (ACSA)
#100, 4155 Sheppart Ave. East, Toronto ON M1S 1T4
Tel: 416-321-6912; Fax: 416-321-6922
e-mail: info@agincourtcommunityservices.com
URL: www.agincourtcommunityservices.com
Gael Gilbert, Executive Director
Paul Rook, Chair

Alberta Association of Marriage & Family Therapy (AAMFT)
420 Norway Cres., Sherwood Park AB T8A 5Z4
Tel: 780-410-0579; Fax: 780-434-7511
Toll-Free: 877-435-5070
e-mail: jkholman@telus.net
URL: www.aamft.ab.ca
Affiliation(s): American Association for Marriage & Family Therapy
Jane Holman, Adminstrative Assistant

Alberta Association of Services for Children & Families (AASCF)
Bonnie Doon Mall, #945, 10020 - 101A Ave., Edmonton AB T6C 4E3
Tel: 780-428-3660; Fax: 780-428-3844
e-mail: aascf@aascf.com
URL: www.aascf.com
Patty Kilgallon, President

Alberta Block Parent Association
#1501, 820 - 5nd Ave. SW, Calgary AB T2P 0N4
Tel: 403-262-2864; Fax: 403-262-5221
Toll-Free: 866-586-7666
e-mail: albertabpa@shaw.ca
URL: www.albertablockparent.ca/

Alberta College of Social Workers (ACSW) / Association des travailleurs sociaux de l'Alberta
#550, 10707 - 100 Ave., Edmonton AB T5J 3M1
Tel: 780-421-1167; Fax: 780-421-1168
Toll-Free: 800-661-3089
e-mail: acsw@acsw.ab.ca
URL: www.acsw.ab.ca
Affiliation(s): International Federation of Social Workers
Rod Adachi, Executive Director/Registrar
Alison MacDonald, Associate Registrar & Director, Complaints

Applegrove Community Complex
60 Woodfield Rd., Toronto ON M4L 2W6
Tel: 416-461-8143
e-mail: applegrove@applegrovecc.ca
URL: www.applegrovecc.ca
Susan Fletcher, Executive Director
Pierre Trudel, Chair

Association des services de réhabilitation sociale du Québec inc. (ASRSQ) / Association of Social Rehabilitation Agencies of Québec Inc.
2000, boul St-Joseph est, Montréal QC H2H 1E4
Tél: 514-521-3733; Téléc: 514-521-3753
Courriel: webmaster@asrsq.ca
URL: www.asrsq.ca
Josée Rioux, Présidente

The Association of Social Workers of Northern Canada (ASWNC) / L'Association des travailleurs sociaux du Nord canadien (ATSNC)
PO Box 2963, Yellowknife NT X1A 2R2
Tel: 867-699-7964
e-mail: gerled@socialworknorth.com
URL: www.socialworknorth.com
Dana Jennejohn, President

Association québécoise des personnes de petite taille (AQPPT) / Association of Little People of Quebec
#205, 2177, rue Masson, Montréal QC H2H 1B1
Tél: 514-521-9671; Téléc: 514-521-3369
Courriel: info@aqppt.org
URL: www.aqppt.org
Louiselle St-Pierre, Directrice générale

Association québécoise Plaidoyer-Victimes (AQPV)
#201, 4305, rue l'Iberville, Montréal QC H2H 2L5
Tél: 514-526-9037; Téléc: 514-526-9951
Courriel: aqpv@aqpv.ca
URL: www.aqpv.ca

Battlefords United Way Inc.
PO Box 904, #93, 891 - 99th St., North Battleford SK S9A 2Z3
Tel: 306-445-1717; Fax: 306-445-1720
e-mail: office@battlefords.unitedway.ca
URL: www.battlefords.unitedway.ca
Treena Rathwell, Executive Director
Michael Brokop, Treasurer

Bereaved Families of Ontario (BFO)
PO Box 10015, Stn. Watline, Mississauga ON L4Z 4G5
Tel: 416-440-0290; Fax: 416-440-0304
Toll-Free: 800-236-6364
e-mail: info@bereavedfamilies.net
URL: www.bereavedfamilies.net
Jeff Thorsteinson, Treasurer

Birchmount Bluffs Neighbourhood Centre (BBNC)
93 Birchmount Rd., Toronto ON M1N 3J7
Tel: 416-396-4310; Fax: 416-396-4314
e-mail: info@bbnc.ca
URL: www.bbnc.ca
Enrique Robert, Executive Director

Block Parent Program of Canada Inc. (BPPCI) / Programme Parents-Secours du Canada inc.
50 Dunlop St. East, Lower Level, Barrie ON L4N 6S7
Tel: 705-792-4245; Fax: 705-792-4245
Toll-Free: 800-663-1134
e-mail: info@blockparent.ca
URL: www.blockparent.ca
Donna Ducey, Newfoundland Contact
Linda Patterson, President

Block Watch Society of British Columbia (BCBPS)
#275, 6450 Roberts St., Burnaby BC V5G 4E1
Tel: 604-418-3827; Fax: 604-299-2503
Toll-Free: 877-602-3358
e-mail: blockwatch@blockwatch.com
URL: www.blockwatch.com
Gerrie Wise, President
Colleen Staresina, Vice-President
Michelle Wulff, Secretary
Betty Gilbert, Treasurer

Brant United Way (BUW)
30 Brant Ave., Brantford ON N3T 3C6
Tel: 519-752-7848; Fax: 519-752-7913
e-mail: info@brantunitedway.org
URL: www.brantunitedway.org
Dianne Austin, Executive Director

British Columbia Association of Social Workers (BCASW) / Association des travailleurs sociaux de la Colombie-Britannique
402 - 1755 West Broadway, Vancouver BC V6J 4S5
Tel: 604-730-9111; Fax: 604-730-9112
Toll-Free: 800-665-4747
e-mail: bcasw@bcasw.org
URL: www.bcasw.org
Affiliation(s): End Legislated Poverty; End the Arms Race Coalition; BC Human Rights Coalition
Linda Korbin, MSW, RSW, Executive Director

British Columbia Council for Families (BCCF)
#204, 2590 Granville St., Vancouver BC V6H 3H1
Tel: 604-660-0675; Fax: 604-732-4813
Toll-Free: 800-663-5638
e-mail: bccf@bccf.bc.ca
URL: www.bccf.bc.ca
Sylvia Tremblay, President
Glenn Hope, Executive Director

British Columbia Federation of Foster Parent Associations (BCFFPA)
#207, 22561 Dewdney Trunk Rd., Maple Ridge BC V2X 3K1
Tel: 604-466-7487; Fax: 604-466-7490
Toll-Free: 800-663-9999

e-mail: bcffpa@istar.ca
URL: www.bcfosterparents.ca
Sheila Davis, Secretary
Melanie Filiatrault, President

Campbell River & District United Way
PO Box 135, Campbell River BC V9W 5A7
Tel: 250-702-2911
Brad Bayly, Community Development Coordinator

Canada Without Poverty / Canada Sans Pauvreté
#1210, 1 Nicholas St., Ottawa ON K1N 7B7
Tel: 613-789-0096; *Fax:* 613-244-5777
Toll-Free: 800-810-1076
URL: www.cwp-csp.ca
Affiliation(s): Citizens for Public Justice; Public Interest Law Centre; Amnesty International Canada; Assembly of First Nations; Canadian Association of Social Workers; Canadian Co-operative Assocation; Canadian Council on Social Development; Canadian Labour Congress & a number of labour unions/organizations
Rob Rainer, Executive Director
Kelly Law, Associate Director

Canadian Association for the Prevention of Discrimination & Harassment in Higher Education (CAPDHHE) / Association canadienne pour la prévention de la discrimination et ou harcèlement en milieu d'enseignement supérieur (ACPDHMES)
c/o University of British Columbia, Vancouver BC V6T 1Z2
Tel: 604-822-4859; *Fax:* 604-822-3260
e-mail: amlong@equity.ubc.ca
URL: www.capdhhe.org
Anne-Marie Long, President

Canadian Association of Sexual Assault Centres (CASAC) / Association canadienne des centres contre les agressions à caractère sexuel (ACCCACS)
77 East 20th Ave., Vancouver BC V5V 1L7
Tel: 604-876-2622; *Fax:* 604-876-8450
e-mail: casac01@shaw.ca
URL: www.casac.ca

Canadian Association of Social Workers (CASW) / Association canadienne des travailleurs sociaux (ACTS)
#402, 383 Parkdale Ave., Ottawa ON K1Y 4R4
Tel: 613-729-6668; *Fax:* 613-729-9608
e-mail: casw@casw-acts.ca
URL: www.casw-acts.ca
Affiliation(s): International Federation of Social Workers
Eugenia Repetur Moreno, Executive Director

Canadian Career Development Foundation (CCDF) / Fondation canadienne pour le développement de carrière (FCDC)
#202, 119 Ross Ave., Ottawa ON K1Y 0N6
Tel: 613-729-6164; *Fax:* 613-729-3515
Toll-Free: 877-729-6164
e-mail: information@ccdf.ca
URL: www.ccdf.ca
Affiliation(s): International Association for Educational & Vocational Guidance
Lynne Bezanson, Executive Director
Sareena Hopkins, Co-Executive Director

Canadian Centre for Victims of Torture (CCVT)
194 Jarvis St., 2nd Fl., Toronto ON M5B 2B7
Tel: 416-363-1066; *Fax:* 416-363-2122
e-mail: mabai@ccvt.org
URL: www.ccvt.org
Mulugeta Abai, Executive Director

Canadian Council for Refugees (CCR) / Conseil canadien pour les réfugiés
#302, 6839, rue Drolet, Montréal QC H2S 2T1
Tel: 514-277-7223; *Fax:* 514-277-1447
e-mail: info@ccrweb.ca
URL: www.ccrweb.ca
Liz McWeeny, President
Janet Dench, Executive Director

Canadian Counselling Association (CCA) / Association canadienne de counseling (ACC)
#600, 16 Concourse Gate, Ottawa ON K2E 7S8
Tel: 613-237-1099; *Fax:* 613-237-9786
Toll-Free: 877-765-5565
e-mail: info@ccacc.ca
URL: www.ccacc.ca
Barbara MacCallum, Executive Director
Ron Lehr, President

Canadian Crossroads International
#131, 1657 Barrington St., Halifax NS B3J 2A1
Tel: 902-422-2933; *Fax:* 902-423-0579
e-mail: atlantic@cciorg.ca
URL: www.cciorg.ca

Canadian Crossroads International
2000, boul Saint-Joseph est, Montréal QC H2H 1E4
Tél: 514-528-5363; *Téléc:* 514-528-5367
Courriel: www.cciorg.ca/quebec/

Canadian Crossroads International
#103, 119 West Pender St., Vancouver BC V6B 1S5
Tel: 604-734-4677; *Fax:* 604-734-4675
e-mail: west@cciorg.ca
URL: www.cciorg.ca/west/

Canadian Crossroads International (CCI) / Carrefour canadien international
#201, 49 Bathurst St., Toronto ON M5V 2P2
Tel: 416-967-1611; *Fax:* 416-967-9078
Toll-Free: 877-967-1611
e-mail: info@cciorg.ca
URL: www.cciorg.ca
Karen Takacs, Executive Director

Canadian Crossroads International
#500, 317 Adelaide St. West, Toronto ON M5V 1P9
Tel: 416-967-1611; *Fax:* 416-967-9078
e-mail: ontario@cciorg.ca

Canadian Feed The Children (CFTC)
174 Bartley Dr., Toronto ON M4A 1E1
Tel: 416-757-1220; *Fax:* 416-757-3318
Toll-Free: 800-387-1221
e-mail: contact@canadianfeedthechildren.ca
URL: www.canadianfeedthechildren.ca
Jim Dahl, Executive Director

Canadian Grandparents' Rights Association (CGRA)
#207, 14980 - 104 Ave., Surrey BC V3R 1M9
Tel: 604-585-8242; *Fax:* 604-585-8241
Toll-Free: 866-585-8242
e-mail: cgra222@vcn.bc.ca
URL: www.vcn.bc.ca/cgra222/
Nancy Wooldridge, National President
Florence Knight, National Director

Canadian Social Work Foundation (CSWF) / Fondation canadienne du service social
PO Box 64177, 1620 Scott St., Ottawa ON K1Y 4V2
Tel: 613-729-6668; *Fax:* 613-729-9608
e-mail: casw@casw-acts.ca
URL: www.casw-acts.ca
Ellen Oliver, President

Canadian Society for the Prevention of Cruelty to Children (CSPCC)
PO Box 700, 362 Midland Ave., Midland ON L4R 4P4
Tel: 705-526-5647; *Fax:* 705-526-0214
e-mail: cspcc@bellnet.ca
URL: www.empathicparenting.org
Affiliation(s): EPOCH Worldwide; The Infant-Parent Institute, USA; Attachmente Parenting International; Center for Parent Education, USA
E.T. Barker, MD, President

Canadian Urban Institute (CUI)
PO Box 612, #402, 555 Richmond St. West, Toronto ON M5V 3B1
Tel: 416-365-0816; *Fax:* 416-365-0650
e-mail: cui@canurb.com
URL: www.canurb.com
Glen Murray, President & CEO

Canadians Addressing Sexual Exploitation (CASE) / Canadiens opposés à l'exploitation sexuelle (COES)
85 Ellesmere Rd., PO Box 62569, Stn. Parkway, 85 Ellesmere Rd., Toronto ON M1R 5G8
Tel: 416-412-6065; *Fax:* 416-412-1321
e-mail: case@4case.ca
URL: www.4case.ca
Dolina Smith, President

Canadians Concerned About Violence in Entertainment (C-CAVE)
167 Glen Rd., Toronto ON M4W 2W8
Tel: 416-961-0853; *Fax:* 416-929-2720
e-mail: info@c-cave.com
URL: www.c-cave.com
Affiliation(s): Coalition for Responsible Television (CRTV)
Rose Anne Dyson, EdD, Chairperson

Carrefour communautaire de Chibougamau
CP 163, 512, rte 167, Chibougamau QC G8P 2K6
Tél: 418-748-7266
Brigitte Rosa, Coordonnatrice
Huguette Fradet, Présidente

Castlegar United Way
1995 - 6 Ave., Castlegar BC V1N 4B7
Tel: 250-365-7331; *Fax:* 250-365-5778
e-mail: office@castlegar.unitedway.ca
URL: www.castlegar.unitedway.ca
Steve Martin, President

Catholic Charities of The Archdiocese of Toronto
#400, 1155 Yonge St., Toronto ON M4T 1W2
Tel: 416-934-3401; *Fax:* 416-934-3402
e-mail: info@catholiccharitiestor.org
URL: www.catholiccharitiestor.org
Affiliation(s): Catholic Family Services of Toronto & 26 member agencies
Maryann Burton, Association Administrator

Centraide Bas St-Laurent
#303, 1555, boul. Jacques Cartier, Mont-Joli QC G5H 2W1
Tél: 418-775-5555; *Téléc:* 418-775-5525
Courriel: direction@centraidebsl.org
URL: www.centraidebsl.org
Michel Daigle, Directeur général

Centraide Centre du Québec
#200, 154, rue Dunkin, Drummondville QC J2B 5V1
Tél: 819-477-0505; *Téléc:* 819-477-6719
Courriel: bureau@centraide-cdq.ca
URL: www.centraide-cdq.ca
Annie Jean, Directrice générale

Centraide du Grand Montréal / Centraide of Greater Montréal
493, rue Sherbrooke ouest, Montréal QC H3A 1B6
Tél: 514-288-1261; *Téléc:* 514-350-7282
Courriel: communications@centraide-mtl.org
URL: centraide-mtl.org
Michèle Thibodeau-DeGuire, Présidente et Directrice générale

Centraide Duplessis
#217, 456, rue Arnaud, Sept-Iles QC G4R 3B1
Tel: 418-962-2011; *Fax:* 418-968-4694
e-mail: administration@centraideduplessis.org
Denis Miousse, Directeur général

Centraide Estrie
1150, rue Belvédère sud, Sherbrooke QC J1H 4C7
Tél: 819-569-9281; *Téléc:* 819-569-5195
Courriel: centraide_estrie@qc.aibn.com, bureau@estrie.centraide.ca
URL: www.estrie.centraide.ca
Claude Forgues, Directeur général

Centraide Gaspésie Iles-de-la-Madeleine
#E216, 230, rte du Parc, Sainte-Anne-des-Monts QC G4V 2C4
Tél: 418-763-2171; *Téléc:* 418-763-7677
Courriel: centraidegim@globetrotter.net
URL: www.gim.centraide.ca
Yvon Lemieux, Directeur général

Centraide Gatineau-Labelle-Hautes-Laurentides
671, rue de la Madone, Mont-Laurier QC J9L 1T2
Tél: 819-623-4090; *Téléc:* 819-623-7646
Courriel: bureau@glhl.centraide.ca
URL: www.gatineaulabellehlaurentides.centraide.ca
Annie Lajoie, Directrice générale

Centraide Haute-Côte-Nord/Manicouagan
#301, 858, rue de Puyjalon, Baie-Comeau QC G5C 1N1
Tél: 418-589-5567; *Téléc:* 418-295-2567
Courriel: info@centraidehcnmanicouagan.ca
URL: www.centraidehcnmanicouagan.ca
Christine Brisson, Directrice générale

Centraide KRTB-Côte-du-Sud
100, 4e av, La Pocatière QC G0R 1Z0
Tél: 418-856-5105; *Téléc:* 418-856-4385
Courriel: centraideportage@bellnet.ca
URL: centraidekrtbcotedusud.org
Sylvain Roy, Directeur général

Centraide Lanaudière
1446, rue de Lanaudière, Joliette QC J6E 3P2
Tél: 450-752-1999; *Téléc:* 450-752-2603
Courriel: cent.lanaudiere@qc.aira.com
URL: www.joliette.centraide.ca
Louise Guilbault, Directrice générale

Centraide Laurentides
CP 335, 281, rue Brière, Saint-Jérôme QC J7Z 5T9
Tél: 450-436-1584; *Téléc:* 450-436-3025
Courriel: bureau@laurentides.centraide.ca
URL: www.centraidelaurentides.org
Suzanne M. Piché, Directrice générale
Monique Richer, Présidente
Violette Gingras, Directrice de communications

Centraide Mauricie
880, Place Boland, Trois-Rivières QC G8Z 4H2
Tél: 819-374-6207; *Téléc:* 819-374-6857
Courriel: centraide.mauricie@bellnet.ca
URL: www.centraidemauricie.ca
Lise Beaulieu, Directrice générale

Centraide Outaouais
74, boul. Montclair, Hull QC J8Y 2E7
Tél: 819-771-7751; *Téléc:* 819-771-0301
Courriel: information@centraide-outaouais.qc.ca
URL: www.centraide-outaouais.qc.ca
Guylaine Beaulieu, Directrice générale

Centraide Québec
#101, 3100, av Bourg-Royal, Québec QC G1C 5S7
Tél: 418-660-2100; *Téléc:* 418-660-2111
Courriel: centraide@centraide-quebec.com
URL: www.centraide-quebec.com
Pierre Métivier, Président/Directeur général

Centraide Richelieu-Yamaska
320, ave. de la Concorde nord, Saint-Hyacinthe QC J2S 4N7
Tél: 450-773-6679; *Téléc:* 450-773-4734
Courriel: bureau@centraidery.org
URL: www.richelieuyamaska.centraide.ca
Manon Bouthot, Directrice générale

Centraide Saguenay-Lac St-Jean
#107, 475, boul. Talbot, Chicoutimi QC G7H 4A3
Tél: 418-543-3131; *Téléc:* 418-543-0665
Courriel: centraideslsj@bellnet.ca
URL: www.centraidesaglac.ca
Martin St-Pierre, Directeur général

Centraide sud-ouest du Québec
#200, 100, rue Ste-Cécile, Salaberry-de-Valleyfield QC J6T 1M1
Tél: 450-371-2061; *Téléc:* 450-377-2309
Courriel: centraid@rocler.qc.ca
URL: www.centraidesudouest.org
Steve Hickey, Directeur général

Centre for Suicide Prevention
#320, 1202 Centre St. SE, Calgary AB T2G 5A5
Tel: 403-245-3900; *Fax:* 403-245-0299
e-mail: csp@suicideinfo.ca
URL: www.suicideinfo.ca
Affiliation(s): Canadian Mental Health Association - Alberta Division
Diane Yackel, Executive Director

The Child Abuse Survivor Monument Project (CASMP)
274 Rhodes Ave., Toronto ON M4L 3A3
Tel: 416-469-4764; *Fax:* 416-963-8892
e-mail: mci@irvingstudios.com
URL: www.childabusemonument.org
Affiliation(s): Children's Aid Foundation
Michael C. Irving, Artistic Director

Child Care Advocacy Association of Canada (CCAAC) / Association canadienne pour la promotion des services de garde à l'enfance (ACPSGE)
#714, 151 Slater St., Ottawa ON K1N 7Z2
Tel: 613-594-3196; *Fax:* 613-594-9375
e-mail: info@ccaac.ca
URL: www.ccaac.ca
Affiliation(s): Canadian Labour Congress; Public Service Alliance; Canadian Union of Public Employees
Emily King, Project Director, Women's equality in Child Care Policy

Child Welfare League of Canada (CWLC) / Ligue pour le bien-être de l'enfance du Canada (LBEC)
226 Argyle Ave., Ottawa ON K2P 1B9
Tel: 613-235-4412; *Fax:* 613-235-7616
e-mail: info@cwlc.ca
URL: www.cwlc.ca
Affiliation(s): Child Welfare League of America
Peter M. Dudding, M.M., M.S.W., R, Executive Director

Christie-Ossington Neighbourhood Centre (CONC)
854 Bloor St. West, Toronto ON M6G 1M2
Tel: 416-534-8941; *Fax:* 416-534-8704
URL: www.conccommunity.org
Lynn Daly, Executive Director
Danny Anckle, Chair

Community Action Resource Centre (CARC)
1652 Keele St., Toronto ON M6M 3W3
Tel: 416-652-2273; *Fax:* 416-652-8992
e-mail: info@communityarc.ca
URL: www.communityarc.ca

Community Social Planning Council of Toronto (CSPC)
#1001, 2 Carlton St., Toronto ON M5B 1J3
Tel: 416-351-0095; *Fax:* 416-351-0107
e-mail: cspc@cspc.toronto.on.ca
URL: www.socialplanningtoronto.org
John Campey, Executive Director
Maria Serrano, Director of Operations

Comox Valley United Way
PO Box 3097, Courtenay BC V9N 5N3
Tel: 250-338-1151; *Fax:* 250-897-1099
June Munro, Executive Director

Confédération des organismes familiaux du Québec inc. (COFAQ)
#205, 4360 rue D'Iberville, Montréal QC H2H 2L8
Tél: 514-521-4777; *Téléc:* 514-521-6272
Courriel: famille@cofaq.qc.ca
URL: www.cofaq.qc.ca
Affiliation(s): Service à la famille - Canada
Sylvie Dumouchel, Directrice générale

Cooper Institute / L'Institut Cooper
81 Prince St., Charlottetown PE C1A 4R3
Tel: 902-894-4573; *Fax:* 902-368-7180
URL: www.cooperinstitute.ca
Joe Byrne, President

COSTI
Education Centre, 1710 Dufferin St., Toronto ON M6E 3P2
Tel: 416-658-1600; *Fax:* 416-658-8537
e-mail: info@costi.org
URL: www.costi.org
Panfilo Corvetti, President

Cowichan United Way
102-435 Trunk Road, Duncan BC V9L 2P5
Tel: 250-748-1312; *Fax:* 250-748-7652
e-mail: office@cowichan.unitedway.ca
URL: www.cowichan.unitedway.ca
Jackie Scott, Secretary
Carol Stenberg, Executive Secretary

Deep River District United Way
PO Box 188, Deep River ON K0J 1P0
Tel: 613-584-3985
e-mail: office@deepriver.unitedway.ca
URL: www.deepriver.unitedway.ca
Bob French, President
Nancy Bourgoin, Treasurer
Sue Deon, Secretary

Delta Family Resource Centre
Jane & Sheppard Mall, #14, 2721 Jane St., Toronto ON M3L 1S3
Tel: 416-747-1172; *Fax:* 416-747-7415
e-mail: contactus@dfrc.ca
URL: www.dfrc.ca
Rosalyn Miller, Executive Director

Distress Centres Ontario (DCO)
#475A, 700 Lawrence Ave. West, Toronto ON M6A 3B4
Tel: 416-486-2242; *Fax:* 416-486-8405
e-mail: info@dcontario.org
URL: www.dcontario.org
Danielle Lin, DCO Treasurer

Doorsteps Neighbourhood Services
PO Box 95, #211, 1700 Wilson Ave., North York ON M3L 1B2
Tel: 416-243-5480; *Fax:* 416-243-7406
e-mail: mbeckford@doorsteps.ca
URL: www.doorsteps.ca
Morris Beckford, Executive Director

Dying with Dignity (DWD) / Mourir dans la dignité
#802, 55 Eglinton Ave. East, Toronto ON M4P 1G8
Tel: 416-486-3998; *Fax:* 416-486-5562
Toll-Free: 800-495-6156
e-mail: info@dyingwithdignity.ca
URL: www.dyingwithdignity.ca
Affiliation(s): World Federation of Right to Die Societies
Donald Babey, President

Edmonton Social Planning Council (ESPC)
#37, 9912 - 106 St., Edmonton AB T5K 1C6
Tel: 780-423-2031; *Fax:* 780-425-6244
e-mail: info@edmontonsocialplanning.ca
URL: www.edmontonsocialplanning.ca
Susan Morrissey, Executive Director
Douglas Meggison, President

Education Wife Assault (EWA)
PO Box 7, #220, 215 Spadina Ave., Toronto ON M5T 2C7
Tel: 416-968-3422; *Fax:* 416-968-2026; *TTY:* 416-968-7335
e-mail: info@womanabuseprevention.com
URL: www.springtideresources.org
Affiliation(s): The National Action Committee on the Status of Women; Ontario Association of Interval & Transition Houses; Woman Abuse Council of Toronto
Marsha Sfeir, Executive Director

Elgin-St.Thomas United Way Services
300 South Edgeware Rd., St Thomas ON N5P 4L1
Tel: 519-631-3171; *Fax:* 519-631-9253
e-mail: office@stthomasunitedway.ca
URL: www.stthomasunitedway.ca
Sharon Lechner, CEO

Eston United Way
PO Box 23, Eston SK S0L 1A0
Tel: 306-962-3612
Brenda Myer, President

Family & Community Support Services Association of Alberta (FCSSAA)
Belmead Professional Bldg., #106, 8944 - 182 St., Edmonton AB T5T 2E3
Tel: 780-415-4791; *Fax:* 780-415-4793
e-mail: fcssaa@telus.net
URL: www.fcssaa.ab.ca
Sharlyn White, Executive Director
Mary Ann Eckstrom, President
Anita Polturak, Coordinator, Member Services

Family Mediation Canada (FMC) / Médiation Familiale Canada
#180, 55 Northfield Dr. East, Waterloo ON N2K 3T6
Tel: 519-585-3118; *Fax:* 416-849-0643
Toll-Free: 877-362-2005
e-mail: fmc@fmc.ca; carrie@fmc.ca
URL: www.fmc.ca
Linda Bonnell, President
Bev Porter, Secretary
Betty Ife, Treasurer

Family Mediation Canada
c/o Appropriate Resolutions
Tel: 250-380-8389
e-mail: fmc@fmc.ca
URL: www.fmc.ca

Family Mediation Canada
#1650, 246 Stewart Green SW, Calgary AB T3H 3C8
Tel: 403-233-0143
Toll-Free: 877-233-0143
e-mail: info@afms.ca
URL: www.afms.ca

Family Mediation Canada
PO Box 3765, Regina SK S4P 3N8
Tel: 306-565-3939; *Fax:* 306-586-6711
Toll-Free: 866-565-3938
e-mail: admin@conflictresolutionsk.ca
URL: www.mediationsaskatchewan.ca

Family Mediation Canada
PO Box 2369, Winnipeg MB R3C 4A6
Tel: 204-989-5330; *Fax:* 204-694-7555
e-mail: info@fmm.winnipeg.mb.ca
URL: www.fmm.winnipeg.mb.ca

Family Mediation Canada (OAFM)
PO Box 433, Carleton Place ON K7C 3P5
Fax: 866-352-1579
Toll-Free: 800-989-3025
e-mail: oafm@oafm.on.ca
URL: www.oafm.on.ca

Family Mediation Canada
#546, 7400, boul. Saint-Laurent, Montréal QC H2R 2Y1
Tél: 514-990-4011; *Téléc:* 514-270-4155
Ligne sans frais: 800-667-7559
Courriel: info@mediationquebec.ca
URL: www.mediationquebec.ca

Family Mediation Canada / Médiation Familiale Nouveau-Brunswick
c/o Art Gallant, 110 Charlotte St., Saint John NB E2L 2J3
Tel: 506-658-2783

Family Mediation Canada (FMNS)
2830 Agricola St., Halifax NS B3K 4E4
Tel: 902-420-3450; *Fax:* 902-420-2873
e-mail: karen.hudson@nslegalaid.ca
URL: nsfamilymediation.ca

Family Mediation Canada

Family Mediation Canada
c/o Unified Family Court, 21 Kings Bridge Rd., St. John's NL A1C 3K4
Tel: 709-729-2258; *Fax:* 709-729-0784

Family Mediation Canada
PO Box 1806, Yellowknife NT X1A 2P4
Tel: 403-873-4283

Family Mediation Canada
PO Box 31102, 211 Main St., Whitehorse YT Y1A 5P7
Tel: 867-667-7910; *Fax:* 867-667-7910
e-mail: mediationyukon@gmail.com
URL: mediationyukon.com

Family Service Association of Toronto (FSA)
355 Church St., Toronto ON M5B 1Z8
Tel: 416-595-9618; *Fax:* 416-595-0242
e-mail: sau@fsatoronto.com
URL: www.fsatoronto.com
Affiliation(s): Family Service Canada
Peter Crosby, Division Director

Family Service Canada (FSC) / Services à la famille - Canada
c/o 312 Parkdale Ave., Ottawa ON K1Y 4X45
Tel: 613-722-9006; *Fax:* 613-722-8610
Toll-Free: 800-668-7808
e-mail: info@familyservicecanada.org
URL: www.familyservicecanada.org
Margaret Fietz, President & CEO
Judi Varga-Toth, National Programs Manager
Sylvie M. Charron, Executive Assistant

Fédération des associations de familles monoparentales et recomposées du Québec (FAFMRQ) / Federation of Single-Parent Family Associations of Québec
584, rue Guizot Est, Montréal QC H2P 1N3
Tél: 514-729-6666; *Téléc:* 514-729-6746
Courriel: fafmrq.info@videotron.ca
URL: www.fafmrq.org
Sylvie Lévesque, Directrice générale

Fédération des centres d'action bénévole du Québec (FCABQ)
1557, av Papineau, Montréal QC H2K 4H7
Tél: 514-843-6312; *Téléc:* 514-843-6485
Ligne sans frais: 800-715-7515
Courriel: info@fcabq.org
URL: www.fcabq.org
Affiliation(s): International Association for Volunteer Effort
Pierre Riley, Directeur général

Flemingdon Neighbourhood Services
#104, 10 Gateway Blvd., Toronto ON M3C 3A1
Tel: 416-424-2900; *Fax:* 416-424-3455
e-mail: info@fnservices.org
URL: www.fnservices.org
John Carey, Executive Director

Food Banks Canada / Banques alimentaires Canada
#303, 2968 Dundas St. West, Toronto ON M6P 1Y8
Tel: 416-203-9241; *Fax:* 416-203-9244
e-mail: info@cafb-acba.ca
URL: www.foodbankscanada.ca
Katharine Schmidt, Executive Director
Ron L'Esperance, Chair
Robin Garrett, Vice-Chair
Riki Turofsky, Secretary
Brian Meagher, Treasurer
Marzena Gersho, Director, National Partnerships & Programs
Shawn Pegg, Senior Manager, Policy & Research

Fred Victor Centre
59 Adelaide St. East, Toronto ON M5C 1K6
Tel: 416-364-8228; *Fax:* 416-364-4728
URL: www.fredvictor.org
Mark Aston, Executive Director

Frontiers Foundation (FF/OB) / Fondation Frontière
419 Coxwell Ave., Toronto ON M4L 3B9
Tel: 416-690-3930; *Fax:* 416-690-3934
Toll-Free: 800-668-4130
e-mail: marcoguzman@frontiersfoundation.ca
URL: www.frontiersfoundation.ca
Social Media: www.facebook.com/pages/Frontiers-Foundation/66661443145
Affiliation(s): Native Council of Canada
Marco A. Guzman, Executive Director
Lawrence Gladue, President

Good Jobs Coalition
#407, Gervais Dr., Toronto ON M3C 1Y8
Tel: 416-441-3663
e-mail: info@goodjobscoalition.ca
URL: www.goodjobscoalition.ca

Goodwill Industries of Alberta
8761 - 51 Ave., Edmonton AB T6E 5H1
Tel: 780-944-1414; *Fax:* 780-463-7396
e-mail: goodwill@goodwill.ab.ca
URL: www.goodwill.ab.ca
Social Media: www.twitter.com/goodwillab
Affiliation(s): United Way of the Capital Region
Wendy Doughty, Chair
Heather Rennebohm, President & CEO

Goodwill Industries of Toronto
#1400, 365 Bloor St. East, Toronto ON M4W 3L4
Tel: 416-362-4711; *Fax:* 416-362-0720; *TTY:* 416-815-4791
e-mail: info@goodwill.on.ca
URL: www.goodwill.on.ca
Myna Kota, Manager, External Relations

GRAND Society
c/o #509, 14 Spadina Rd., Toronto ON M5R 3M4
Tel: 416-513-9404
Joan Brooks, President/Chair
L. Watson, Vice-President

Grande Prairie & Region United Way
#213, 11330 - 106 St., Grande Prairie AB T8V 7X9
Tel: 780-532-1105; *Fax:* 780-532-3532
e-mail: info@gpunitedway.org
URL: www.gpunitedway.org
Gladys Blackmore, President/Executive Director

Groupe d'entraide des personnes séparées/divorcées
#106, 161, av du Parc, Chibougamau QC G8P 2H3
Tél: 418-748-2777
Rita Tremblay

Huron United Way
PO Box 211, #207, 35A East St., Goderich ON N7A 3Z2
Tel: 519-524-7900; *Fax:* 519-524-1121
e-mail: huronunitedway@tcc.on.ca
URL: www.huronunitedway.ca
Jerry McDonnell, Chair

Imagine Canada
#600, 2 Carlton St., Toronto ON M5B 1J3
Tel: 416-597-2293; *Fax:* 416-597-2294
Toll-Free: 800-263-1178
e-mail: info@imaginecanada.ca
URL: www.imaginecanada.ca
Marcel Lauzière, President/CEO

InformOntario (IO)
3010 Forest Glade Dr., Windsor ON N8R 1L5
e-mail: info@informontario.on.ca
URL: www.informontario.on.ca
Pamela Hillier, President
Trudy Beaulne, Vice-President

International Social Service Canada (ISSC) / Service Social International Canada (SSIC)
#506, 1580 Merivale Rd., Ottawa ON K2G 4B5
Tel: 613-236-6161; *Fax:* 613-233-7306
e-mail: issc@issc-ssic.ca
URL: www.issc-ssic.ca
Affiliation(s): International Social Service - Geneva, Switzerland
Richard Chamney, President

Kids First Parent Association of Canada
3916 32nd St. NW, Edmonton AB T6T 1J9
Tel: 604-291-0088
e-mail: info@kidsfirstcanada.org
URL: www.kidsfirstcanada.org
Helen Ward, President

Kids Help Phone (KHP) / Jeunesse j'écoute
#300, 439 University Ave., Toronto ON M5G 1Y8
Tel: 416-586-5437; *Fax:* 416-586-0651
Toll-Free: 800-668-6868
e-mail: info@kidshelp.sympatico.ca
URL: www.kidshelpphone.ca
F.T. (Tom) McAllister, President/CEO
Jerry Patava, Chair
Steven G. Golick, Secretary & Legal Counsel
Kerry Arbour, Treasurer

Lakeland United Way
PO Box 8369, #204, 1301 - 8th Ave., Cold Lake AB T9M 1N3
Tel: 780-826-0045; *Fax:* 780-639-2699
e-mail: luw2699@telus.net
URL: www.lakelandunitedway.com
Ajaz Quraishi, President

Lawyers for Social Responsibility (LSR) / Avocats en faveur d'une conscience sociale (AFCS)
c/o 5120 Carney Rd. NW, Calgary AB T2L 1G2
Tel: 403-282-8260
e-mail: bevdelong@shaw.ca
URL: www.peacelawyers.ca
Affiliation(s): International Association of Lawyers Against Nuclear Arms; Mines Action Canada; Canadian Network to Abolish Nuclear Weapons
Beverley Delong, President

Lloydminster & District United Way
4419 - 52nd Ave., Lloydminster AB T9V 0Y8
Tel: 780-875-3743; *Fax:* 780-875-3793
e-mail: luw@telusplanet.net
URL: www.lloydminster.unitedway.ca
Eric Rounce, President

Manitoba Association of Social Workers (MASW) / Association des travailleurs sociaux du Manitoba
#101, 2033 Portage Ave., Winnipeg MB R3J 0K6
Tel: 204-888-9477; *Fax:* 204-831-6359
URL: www.maswmirsw.ca
Affiliation(s): Manitoba Institute of Registered Social Workers (MIRSW)

Manitoba Association of Women's Shelters (MAWS)
c/o Genesis House, PO Box 389, Winkler MB R6W 4A6
Tel: 204-325-9957; *Fax:* 204-325-5889*Crisis Hot-Line:* 877-977-0007
URL: www.maws.mb.ca
Angela Braun, MAWS Chair

Manitoba Block Parent Program
466 Gertrude Ave., Winnipeg MB R3L 0M8
Tel: 204-284-7562
e-mail: winnipegblockparents@hotmail.com
URL: www.winnipegblockparents.mb.ca

Manitoba Institute of Registered Social Workers (MIRSW)
#101, 2033 Portage Ave., Winnipeg MB R3J 0K6
Tel: 204-888-9477; *Fax:* 204-831-6359
e-mail: masw@mts.net
URL: www.maswmirsw.ca
Miriam Browne, Executive Director

La Mine d'Or, entreprise d'insertion sociale
449, 3e Rue, Chibougamau QC G8P 1N6
Tél: 418-748-4183; *Téléc:* 418-748-2837
Courriel: informations@laminedor.org
URL: www.laminedor.org
Suzan Amyot, Présidente

Mouvement ATD Quart Monde Canada / ATD Fourth World Movement Canada
6747, rue Drolet, Montréal QC H2S 2T1
Tél: 514-279-0468; *Téléc:* 514-279-7759
URL: www.atdquartmonde.ca
Affiliation(s): Mouvement international ATD Quart-Monde (France)
Monique Morval, Présidente

Neepawa & District United Way
PO Box 1545, Neepawa MB R0J 1H0
Tel: 204-476-2829
Angela Pearen-Burnside, President

Nelson & District United Way
PO Box 89, Nelson BC V1L 5P7
Tel: 250-352-6012
e-mail: united_way@netidea.com
URL: www.uw.kics.bc.ca
Carol-Joy Kaill, President

New Brunswick Association of Food Banks
c/o Grand Falls Regional Food Bank Inc., 363 Portage Rd., Grand Falls NB E3Z 1M2

Tel: 506-473-2001; *Fax:* 506-473-6883
Max Oates, Provincial Coordinator

New Brunswick Association of Social Workers (NBASW) / Association des travailleurs sociaux du Nouveau-Brunswick
PO Box 1533, Stn. A, Fredericton NB E3B 5G2
Tel: 506-459-5595; *Fax:* 506-457-1421
e-mail: nbasw@nbasw-atsnb.ca
URL: www.nbasw-atsnb.ca

New Brunswick Block Parent Association (NBBPAI)
#47, 100 Howe Ct., Oromocto NB E2V 2R3
Tel: 506-446-5992; *Fax:* 506-446-5992
Toll-Free: 800-665-4900
e-mail: nbbpai@nbnet.nb.ca
URL: www.nb-blockparent.com
Linda Patterson, President

Newfoundland & Labrador Association of Social Workers (NLASW) / Association des travailleurs sociaux de Terre-Neuve et Labrador
PO Box 39039, St. John's NL A1E 5Y7
Tel: 709-753-0200; *Fax:* 709-753-0120
e-mail: info@nlasw.ca
URL: www.nlasw.ca
Lisa Crockwell, Executive Director

Non-Smokers' Rights Association (NSRA) / Association pour les droits des non-fumeurs
#221, 720 Spadina Ave., Toronto ON M5S 2T9
Tel: 416-928-2900; *Fax:* 416-928-1860
e-mail: toronto@nsra-adnf.ca
URL: www.nsra-adnf.ca
Affiliation(s): Smoking & Health Action Foundation (SHAF)
Garfield Mahood, Executive Director
Lorraine Fry, General Manager

North of 60 Degrees Block Parent Program
PO Box 112, Yellowknife NT X1A 2N1
Tel: 867-873-5735; *Fax:* 867-669-0761
e-mail: rpower@internorth.com
Affiliation(s): Crime Prevention Program; Neighbourhood Watch

Northumberland United Way
#203, 1005 Elgin St. West, Cobourg ON K9A 5J4
Tel: 905-372-6955; *Fax:* 905-372-4417
e-mail: office@northumberland.unitedway.ca
URL: www.northumberland.unitedway.ca
Lynda Kay, Executive Director
Cathy Cavanagh, Manager, Finance & Operations

Nova Scotia Association of Social Workers (NSASW) / Association des travailleurs sociaux de la Nouvelle-Écosse
Plaza 1881, #106, 1891 Brunswick St., Halifax NS B3J 2G8
Tel: 902-429-7799; *Fax:* 902-429-7650
e-mail: nsasw@nsasw.org
URL: www.nsasw.org
Affiliation(s): Canadian Association of Social Workers
Robert R. Shepherd, MSW, RSW, Executive Director

Nova Scotia Block Parent Advisory Board
Tel: 902-883-7148
e-mail: info@novascotiablockparent.com
URL: www.novascotiablockparent.com
Jean Hiltz, Chairman

One Parent Families Association of Canada / Association des familles uniparentales du Canada
PO Box 111, Pickering ON L1V 2R2
Tel: 905-831-7098; *Fax:* 905-831-2580
Toll-Free: 877-773-7714
e-mail: opfa222@aol.com
URL: www.opfa.net
R. Bounds, President

Ontario Association for Marriage & Family Therapy (OAMFT)
PO Box 693, Tottenham ON L0G 1W0
Tel: 905-936-3338; *Fax:* 905-267-2638
Toll-Free: 800-267-2638
e-mail: admin@oamft.on.ca
URL: www.oamft.on.ca
Annette Dekker, President Elect
Pam Santon, President

Ontario Association of Children's Aid Societies (OACAS) / Association ontarienne des sociétés de l'aide à l'enfance
75 Front St. East, 2nd Fl., Toronto ON M5E 1V9
Tel: 416-987-7725; *Fax:* 416-366-8317
e-mail: info@oacas.org
URL: www.oacas.org
Jeanette Lewis, Executive Director
Dennis Nolan, President

Ontario Association of Interval & Transition Houses (OAITH)
#1404, 2 Carleton St., Toronto ON M5B 1J3
Tel: 416-977-6619
e-mail: president@oaith.ca
URL: www.oaith.ca
Cindy Cowan, Chair of the Board

Ontario Association of Social Workers (OASW) / Association des travailleuses et travailleurs sociaux de l'Ontario (ATTSO)
410 Jarvis St., Toronto ON M4Y 2G6
Tel: 416-923-4848; *Fax:* 416-923-5279
e-mail: info@oasw.org
URL: www.oasw.org; www.findasocialworker.ca; www.socialworkjobs.ca

Ontario Block Parent Program Inc. (OBPPI)
902 Maitland St., London ON N5Y 2X1
Tel: 519-438-2016
Toll-Free: 800-563-2771
e-mail: mrooke902@rogers.com
URL: www.blockparent.on.ca
Marg Rooke, Chair

Ontario Coalition for Better Child Care (OCBCC)
#206, 489 College St., Toronto ON M6G 1A5
Tel: 416-538-0628; *Fax:* 416-538-6737
Toll-Free: 800-594-7514
e-mail: info@childcareontario.org
URL: www.childcareontario.org
Affiliation(s): Canadian Child Care Advocacy Association
Shellie Bird, President
Carrol Anne Sceviour, Vice-President
Jenny Robinson, Executive Director

Ontario Coalition of Rape Crisis Centres (OCRCC) / Coalition des centres anti-viol de l'Ontario
c/o TRCC, PO Box 6597, Stn. A, Toronto ON M5W 1X4
Tel: 416-597-1171; *Fax:* 416-597-9648
e-mail: ocrcc_pres@hotmail.com
URL: www.ocrcc.ca
Marilyn Oladimeji, Contact

Ontario Community Support Association (OCSA) / Association ontarienne de soutien communautaire
#104, 970 Lawrence Ave. West, Toronto ON M6A 3B6
Tel: 416-256-3010; *Fax:* 416-256-3021
Toll-Free: 800-267-6272
e-mail: ocsainfo@ocsa.on.ca
URL: www.ocsa.on.ca
Susan Thorning, Acting CEO

Ontario Municipal Social Services Association (OMSSA) / Association des services sociaux des municipalités de l'Ontario
#100, 5720 Timberlea Blvd., Mississauga ON L4W 4W2
Tel: 905-629-3115; *Fax:* 905-629-1633
e-mail: info@omssa.com
URL: www.omssa.com
Kira Heineck, Executive Director
Brenda Patterson, President
Patti Moore, Vice-President
David Rennie, Secretary-Treasurer

The Ontario Trillium Foundation / La Fondation Trillium de l'Ontario
45 Charles St. East, 5th Fl., Toronto ON M4Y 1S2
Tel: 416-963-4927; *Fax:* 416-963-8781
Toll-Free: 800-263-2887; *TTY:* 416-963-7905
e-mail: trillium@trilliumfoundation.org
URL: www.trilliumfoundation.org
L. Robin Cardozo, CEO

Ordre professionnel des travailleurs sociaux du Québec (OPTSQ)
#520, 255, boul. Crémazie est, Montréal QC H2M 1M2
Tél: 514-731-3925; *Téléc:* 514-731-6785
Ligne sans frais: 888-731-9420
Courriel: info.general@optsq.org
URL: www.optsq.org
Affiliation(s): Conseil interprofessionnel du Québec
Claude Leblond, Président

Parcelles de tendresse
CP 582, Chibougamau QC G8P 2Y8
Tél: 418-748-3644
Pierette Boulay

Parent Finders of Canada
19 English Bluff Rd., Delta BC V4M 2M4
Tel: 604-948-1069; *Fax:* 604-948-2036
URL: www.parentfinders.org
Affiliation(s): American Adoption Congress; International Soundex Reunion Register
Joan E. Vanstone, National Director

Parent Support Services Society of BC (PSSS)
#201, 1155 West Pender St., Vancouver BC V6E 2P4
Tel: 604-669-1616; *Fax:* 604-669-1636
Toll-Free: 800-665-6880
e-mail: office@parentsupportbc.ca
URL: www.parentsupportbc.ca
Barry J. Corrin, Executive Director

Parents-secours du Québec inc. (PSQI)
#203, 17, rue Fusey, Trois-Rivières QC G8T 2T3
Ligne sans frais: 800-588-8173
Courriel: info@parentssecours.ca
URL: www.parentssecours.ca

People, Words & Change (PWC) / Monde des mots
Heartwood House, 153 Chapel St., Ottawa ON K1N 1H5
Tel: 613-234-2494; *Fax:* 613-234-4223
e-mail: info@pwc-ottawa.ca
URL: www.nald.ca/pwc
Kae McColl, Coordinator

Petites-Mains
7595 St.-Laurent Boul., Montréal QC H2R 1W9
Tél: 514-738-8989; *Téléc:* 514-738-6193
Courriel: info@petitesmains.com
URL: www.petitesmains.com
Nahid Aboumansour, Contact

PFLAG Canada Inc.
PO Box 29211, 1633 Mountain Rd., Moncton NB E1G 4R3
Tel: 506-869-8191; *Fax:* 506-387-8349
Toll-Free: 888-530-6777
e-mail: pflagcanada@nb.aibn.com
URL: www.pflagcanada.ca
Cherie MacLeod, Executive Director
Gemma Schlamp-Hickey, President
Ray Lam, Vice-President
Ryan Walkinshaw, Treasurer

Plan Canada
#1001, 95 St. Clair Ave. West, Toronto ON M4V 3B5
Tel: 416-920-1654; *Fax:* 416-920-9942
Toll-Free: 800-387-1418
e-mail: info@plancanada.ca
URL: plancanada.ca
Social Media: www.facebook.com/PlanCanada
Rosemary McCarney, President & CEO

Porcupine United Way
PO Box 984, #312, 60 Wilson Ave., Timmins ON P4N 7H6
Tel: 705-268-9696; *Fax:* 705-268-9700
e-mail: puw@ntl.sympatico.ca
URL: porcupineunitedway.com
Jean Warren, Executive Director

Portage Plains United Way
224 Saskatchewan Ave. East, Portage la Prairie MB R1N 0K9
Tel: 204-857-4440; *Fax:* 204-239-1740
e-mail: ppuw@mts.net
URL: www.portageplainsuw.ca
Darrell Lee, President
Tara Pettinger, Executive Director

Powell River & District United Way
PO Box 379, Powell River BC V8A 5C2
Tel: 604-485-2791
e-mail: bennobabe@shaw.ca
URL: www.unitedwayofpowellriver.ca
Pat Hull, President

Prince Edward Island Association of Social Workers / Association des travailleurs sociaux de l'Ile-du-Prince-Édouard
81 Prince St., Charlottetown PE C1A 4R3
Tel: 902-368-7337; *Fax:* 902-368-7080
e-mail: vrc@eastlink.cat
Kelly MacWilliams, President

Prince Edward Island Block Parent Advisory Board
RR#3 Middleton, Summerside PE C1N 4J9
Tel: 902-887-2480; *Fax:* 902-887-2874
e-mail: kjoffer@eastlink.ca
URL: www.blockparent.ca

Prince George United Way
1600 - 3rd Avenue, Prince George BC V2L 3G6
Tel: 250-561-1040; *Fax:* 250-562-8102
e-mail: trevorw@pguw.bc.ca
URL: www.pguw.bc.ca
Trevor Williams, Executive Director
Scotty Raitt, President

Project Genesis
4735 Côte-Ste.-Catherine, Montréal QC H3W 1M1
Tel: 514-738-2036; *Fax:* 514-738-6385
Michael Chervin, Contact

Québec Association of Marriage & Family Therapy (QAMFT) / Association québécoise pour la thérapie conjugale et familiale
#300, 360 Victoria Avenue, Westmount QC H3H 2N4
Tel: 514-315-6111
e-mail: info@qamft.org
URL: www.qamft.org
Andrew Sofin, President

Reena
927 Clark Ave. West, Thornhill ON L4J 8G6
Tel: 905-889-6484; *Fax:* 905-889-3827
Toll-Free: 877-324-4114
e-mail: info@reena.org
URL: www.reena.org
Affiliation(s): Jewish Federation of Greater Toronto
Minnie Ross, Manager, Media & Communications
Sandy Keshen, Executive Director

Regroupement des Auberges du Coeur
#32, 2000, boul Saint-Joseph est, Montréal QC H2H 1E4
Tél: 514-523-8559; *Téléc:* 514-523-5148
Courriel: regroupement@aubergesducoeur.com
URL: www.aubergesducoeur.com
Pierre Audette, Directeur général

The Right to Die Society of Canada (RTDSC) / Société Canadienne pour le Droit de Mourir (SCDM)
145 Macdonell Ave., Toronto ON M6R 2A4
Tel: 416-535-0690
Toll-Free: 866-535-0690
e-mail: contact-rtd@righttodie.ca
URL: www.righttodie.ca
Ruth von Fuchs, President & Secretary

Ronald McDonald House Charities of Canada (RMHC) / Oeuvres pour enfants Ronald McDonald du Canada
McDonald's Place, Toronto ON M3C 3L4
Tel: 416-443-1000; *Fax:* 416-446-3762
Toll-Free: 800-387-8808
URL: www.rmhc.ca
Barbara Ann Thompson, Sr. Executive Director
Shelagh Barrett, Grant Manager
Maijia Zeibots, Director

Samaritan's Purse Canada
20 Hopewell Way NE, Calgary AB T3J 5H5
Tel: 403-250-6565; *Fax:* 403-250-6567
Toll-Free: 800-663-6500
e-mail: canada@samaritan.org
URL: www.samaritanspurse.ca
Affiliation(s): Samaritan's Purse USA
Jeff Adams, Communications Director
Franklin Graham, President & CEO
Sean P. Campbell, Executive Director

Saskatchewan Association of Social Workers (SASW) / Association des travailleurs sociaux de la Saskatchewan
2110 Lorne St., Regina SK S4P 2M5
Tel: 306-545-1922; *Fax:* 306-545-1895
Toll-Free: 877-517-7279
e-mail: sasw@accesscomm.ca
URL: www.sasw.ca

Secours aux lépreux (Canada) inc. (SLC) / Leprosy Relief (Canada) Inc.
#305, 1805, rue Sauvé ouest, Montréal QC H4N 3H4
Tél: 514-744-3199; *Téléc:* 514-744-9095
Ligne sans frais: 866-744-3199
Courriel: info@slc-lr.ca
URL: www.slc-lr.ca
Maryse Legault, Executive Director

Sex Information & Education Council of Canada (SIECCAN) / Conseil d'information et éducation sexuelles du Canada
850 Coxwell Ave., Toronto ON M4C 5R1
Tel: 416-466-5304; *Fax:* 416-778-0785
e-mail: sieccan@web.ca
URL: www.sieccan.org
Michael Barrett, Executive Director
Stephen Holzapfel, M.D., Chair
Alexander McKay, Ph.D., Research Coordinator

ShareLife
1155 Yonge St., Toronto ON M4T 1W2
Tel: 416-934-3400; *Fax:* 416-934-3412
Toll-Free: 800-263-2595
e-mail: slife@archtoronto.org
URL: www.sharelife.org
Affiliation(s): Canadian Centre for Philanthropy
Arthur Peters, Executive Director
Bill Steinburg, Communications Manager

Social Planning & Research Council of BC (SPARC)
4445 Norfolk St., Burnaby BC V5G 0A7
Tel: 604-718-7733; *Fax:* 604-736-8697
e-mail: info@sparc.bc.ca
URL: www.sparc.bc.ca
Social Media: www.twitter.com/SPARC_BC
Clement Woo, Executive Director
Daniel Hill, President

Social Planning Council of Ottawa-Carleton / Conseil de planification sociale d'Ottawa-Carleton
#501, 280 Metcalfe St., Ottawa ON K2P 1R7
Tel: 613-236-9300; *Fax:* 613-236-7060
e-mail: office@spcottawa.on.ca
URL: www.spcottawa.on.ca
Affiliation(s): District Health Council; Ontario Social Development Council
Diane Urquhart, Executive Director

Social Planning Council of Winnipeg
412 McDermot Ave., Winnipeg MB R3A 0A9
Tel: 204-943-2561; *Fax:* 204-942-3221
e-mail: info@spcw.mb.ca
URL: www.spcw.mb.ca
Social Media: www.facebook.com/group.php?gid=54256670713
Wayne Helgason, Executive Director

Society of Transition Houses - BC & Yukon
#325, 119 West Pender St., Vancouver BC V6B 1S5
Tel: 604-669-6943; *Fax:* 604-682-6962
Toll-Free: 800-661-1040
e-mail: admin@bcysth.ca
URL: www.bcysth.ca
Shabna Ali, Executive Director

SOS Children's Villages Canada / SOS Villages d'Enfants Canada
#200, 244 Rideau St., Ottawa ON K1N 5Y3
Tel: 613-232-3309; *Fax:* 613-232-6764
Toll-Free: 800-767-5111
e-mail: info@soschildrensvillages.ca
URL: www.soschildrensvillages.ca
Affiliation(s): SOS-Kinderdorf International
Boyd McBride, National Director

Streetkids' Foundation (SKF)
First Global Place, #201, 7 Concorde Pl., Toronto ON M3C 3N4
Tel: 416-391-1801; *Fax:* 416-391-2616
Affiliation(s): Beat the Street; Trickle Up
J.H. Vowles, President
Robert Atkinson, Treasurer

Swift Current United Way
PO Box 485, #203B Professional Bldg. - 12 Cheadle St. West, Swift Current SK S9H 0A9
Tel: 306-773-4828; *Fax:* 306-773-4870
e-mail: unitedway@sasktel.net
Jennifer Olfert, Executive Director

Thompson Crisis Centre
PO Box 1226, Thompson MB R8N 1P1
Tel: 204-677-9668; *Fax:* 204-677-9042
Toll-Free: 800-442-0613

Thompson, Nicola, Cariboo United Way
#203, 239 Victoria St., Kamloops BC V2C 2A1
Tel: 250-372-9933; *Fax:* 250-372-5926
e-mail: office@unitedwaytnc.ca
URL: www.unitedwaytnc.ca
Brenda Aynsley, Executive Director

Toronto Community Foundation (TCF)
#1603, 2 Bloor St. West, Toronto ON M4W 3H1
Tel: 416-921-2035; *Fax:* 416-921-1026
e-mail: info@tcf.ca
URL: www.tcf.ca
Rahul K. Bhardwaj, President & CEO
Rosalyn Morrison, VP, Community Initiatives
Carole Boivin, VP, Communications & Marketing, Communications
Anne Brayley, VP, Professional Advisory Services
Susan Hartnett, VP, Finance

211 Toronto
c/o Findhelp Information Services, #125, 543 Richmond St. W., Toronto ON M5V 1Y6
Tel: 416-392-4605; *Fax:* 416-392-4404
URL: www.211toronto.ca
Affiliation(s): United Way of Greater Toronto
Janice Hayes, Executive Director
Bruce Reynolds, President

United Generations Ontario (UGO) / Générations Unies Ontario
1185 Eglinton Ave. East, Toronto ON M3C 3C6
Tel: 416-426-7115; *Fax:* 416-426-7421
e-mail: info@unitedgenerations.ca
URL: www.unitedgenerations.ca
Affiliation(s): Ontario Gerontological Association; Older Adults Association of Ontario; BC Council for Families; Canadian Health Network
Russ De Cou, Executive Director
Richard Cox, Chief Operating Officer

United Way Central & Northern Vancouver Island
3156 Barons Rd., Nanaimo BC V9T 4B5
Tel: 250-729-7400; *Fax:* 250-729-8084
e-mail: info@uwcnvi.ca
URL: www.uwcnvi.ca
Lynne Brown, COO

United Way Community Services of Guelph & Wellington
85 Westmount Rd., Guelph ON N1H 5J2
Tel: 519-821-0571; *Fax:* 519-821-7847
e-mail: info@unitedwayguelph.com
URL: www.unitedwayguelph.com
Steve Allen, President
Ken Dardano, Executive Director

United Way for the City of Kawartha Lakes (UWVC)
50 Mary St. West, Lindsay ON K9V 2N6
Tel: 705-878-5081; *Fax:* 705-878-0475
e-mail: office@ckl.unitedway.ca
URL: www.ckl.unitedway.ca
Penny Barton Dyke, Executive Director

United Way of Ajax-Pickering-Uxbridge
#303, 230 Westney Rd. West, Ajax ON L1S 7J5
Tel: 905-686-0606; *Fax:* 905-686-0609
e-mail: office@uwayapu.org
URL: www.uwayapu.org
Edna Klazek, Executive Director

United Way of Brandon & District Inc.
Scotia Towers, 201-1011 Rosser Ave., Brandon MB R7A 0L5
Tel: 204-571-8929; *Fax:* 204-727-8939
e-mail: office@brandonuw.ca
URL: www.brandonuw.ca
Debbie Arsenault, CEO

United Way of Burlington & Greater Hamilton
177 Rebecca St., Hamilton ON L8R 1B9
Tel: 905-527-4543; *Fax:* 905-527-5152
e-mail: uway@uwaybh.ca
URL: www.uwaybh.ca
Len Lifchus, CEO

United Way of Calgary & Area
#600, 1202 Centre St. SE, Calgary AB T2G 5A5
Tel: 403-231-6265; *Fax:* 403-355-3135
e-mail: uway@calgaryunitedway.org
URL: www.calgaryunitedway.org
Linda Hohol, Chair
Ruth Ramsden-Wood, President

United Way of Cambridge & North Dumfries
150 Main St., Cambridge ON N1R 6P9
Tel: 519-621-1030; *Fax:* 519-621-6220
e-mail: ron@uwcambridge.on.ca
URL: www.uwcambridge.on.ca
Heidi Duarte, Manager, Development & Marketing
Brad Park, Director, Development
Ron Dowhaniuk, Executive Director

United Way of Canada - Centraide Canada
#404, 56 Sparks St., Ottawa ON K1P 5A9
Tel: 613-236-7041; *Fax:* 613-236-3087
Toll-Free: 800-267-8221

e-mail: info@unitedway.ca
URL: www.unitedway.ca; www.centraide.ca
Affiliation(s): United Way International
Patricia McDermott, Chair
Al Hatton, President/CEO

United Way of Cape Breton
Cabot House, PO Box 1929, 500 Kings Rd., 2nd Fl., Sydney NS B1P 6W4
Tel: 902-562-5226; *Fax:* 902-562-5721
e-mail: unitedway@ns.aliantzinc.ca
URL: www.sydney.unitedway.ca
Allister Taylor, Executive Director

United Way of Central Alberta
4811 - 48th St., Red Deer AB T4N 1S6
Tel: 403-343-3900; *Fax:* 403-309-3820
e-mail: info@caunitedway.ca
URL: www.caunitedway.ca
Heather Gardiner, CEO

United Way of Chatham-Kent County
PO Box 606, 425 McNaughton Avenue West, Chatham ON N7M 5K8
Tel: 519-354-0430; *Fax:* 519-354-9511
e-mail: united.way@united-kent.on.ca
URL: unitedway.chatham-kent.on.ca
Karen S. Kirkwood-Whyte, Executive Director
Patrick Weaver, President

United Way of Cranbrook & Kimberley
PO Box 657, 930 Baker St., Cranbrook BC V1C 4J2
Tel: 250-426-8833; *Fax:* 250-426-5455
e-mail: cranunitedway@shaw.ca; office@cranbrook.unitedway.ca
URL: www.cranbrook.unitedway.ca
Donna Brady, Executive Director

United Way of Cumberland County
PO Box 535, 43 Prince Arthur St., Amherst NS B4H 4A1
Tel: 902-667-2203; *Fax:* 902-667-3819
e-mail: unitedway.cumberland@ns.aliantzinc.ca
Jeff Brennan, Chair
Cathy Skinner, Executive Director

United Way of Elrose & District Corp.
PO Box 123, Elrose SK S0L 0Z0
Tel: 306-378-2532
Jack Elliott, Chair

United Way of Estevan
PO Box 611, Estevan SK S4A 2A5
Tel: 306-634-7348; *Fax:* 306-634-2197
e-mail: secretary@unitedwayofestevan.com
James Lainton, Chair

United Way of Fort McMurray
#207, 9912A Franklin Ave., Fort McMurray AB T9H 2K5
Tel: 780-791-0077; *Fax:* 780-791-0088
e-mail: office@fortmcmurray.unitedway.ca
URL: www.fortmcmurray.unitedway.ca/
Diane Shannon, Executive Director

United Way of Greater Moncton & Southeastern NB Region Inc. / Centraide de la région du Grand Moncton et du Sud-Est du NB Inc.
PO Box 768, 123 Halifax St., Moncton NB E1C 8M9
Tel: 506-858-8600; *Fax:* 506-858-0584
e-mail: office@moncton.unitedway.ca
URL: www.gmsenbunitedway.ca
Social Media: www.facebook.com/group.php?gid=76467525679
Debbie McInnis, Executive Director

United Way of Greater Saint John Inc.
61 Union St., 2nd Fl., Saint John NB E2L 1A2
Tel: 506-658-1212; *Fax:* 506-633-7724
e-mail: office@saintjohn.unitedway.ca
URL: www.saintjohn.unitedway.ca
Elizabeth Jadoo, Executive Director

United Way of Greater Simcoe County
#100, 136 Bayfield St., Barrie ON L4M 3B1
Tel: 705-726-2301; *Fax:* 705-726-4897
e-mail: info@unitedwaysimcoecounty.on.ca
URL: www.unitedwaysimcoecounty.on.ca
Seija Suutari, CEO
Bethany Obermayer, Director, Finance & Administration

United Way of Haldimand-Norfolk
PO Box 472, #3, 39 Kent St. North, Simcoe ON N3Y 3L5
Tel: 519-426-5660; *Fax:* 519-426-0017
Toll-Free: 866-792-7394
e-mail: uw@unitedwayhn.on.ca
URL: www.unitedwayhn.on.ca
Evelyn Nobbs, Executive Director
Mark Liota, President

United Way of Halifax Region
Royal Bank Bldg., 46 Portland St., 7th Fl.., Halifax NS B2Y 1H4
Tel: 902-422-1501; *Fax:* 902-423-6837
e-mail: info@unitedwayhalifax.ca
URL: www.unitedwayhalifax.ca
Catherine J. Woodman, President/CEO

United Way of Halton Hills
PO Box 286, Georgetown ON L7G 4Y5
Tel: 905-877-3066; *Fax:* 905-877-3067
e-mail: office@haltonhills.unitedway.ca
URL: www.haltonhills.unitedway.ca
Janet Foster, Executive Director

United Way of Kingston, Frontenac, Lennox & Addington
417 Bagot St., Kingston ON K7K 3C1
Tel: 613-542-2674; *Fax:* 613-542-1379
e-mail: uway@unitedwaykfla.ca
URL: www.unitedwaykfla.ca
Bhavana Varma, President
Clara Lambert, Director, Finance
Maura Doyle, Campaign Manager

United Way of Kitchener-Waterloo & Area
20 Erb St. West, 11th Fl., Waterloo ON N2L 1T2
Tel: 519-888-6100; *Fax:* 519-888-7737
e-mail: info@united-way-kw.org
URL: www.uwaykw.org
Dave Fitzpatrick, Board Chair
Jan Varner, CEO

United Way of Lanark County
15 Bates Dr., Carleton Place ON K7C 4J8
Tel: 613-253-9074; *Fax:* 613-235-9075
e-mail: unitedway@trytel.com
URL: www.lanarkunitedway.com
Sarah Bridson, Executive Director

United Way of Leeds & Grenville
PO Box 576, 42 George St., Brockville ON K6V 5V7
Tel: 613-342-8889; *Fax:* 613-342-8850
e-mail: unitedway@ripnet.com
URL: www.uwlg.org
Judi Baril, Executive Director

United Way of Lethbridge & South Western Alberta
1277 - 3 Ave. South, Lethbridge AB T1J 0K3
Tel: 403-327-1700; *Fax:* 403-317-7940
e-mail: uwaysw@telusplanet.net
URL: www.lethbridgeunitedway.ca

United Way of London & Middlesex
409 King St., London ON N6B 1S5
Tel: 519-438-1721; *Fax:* 519-438-9938
e-mail: uwl@uwlondon.on.ca
URL: www.uwlondon.on.ca
Andrew Lockie, CEO

United Way of Milton
PO Box 212, 1 Chris Hadfield Way, Milton ON L9T 4N9
Tel: 905-875-2550; *Fax:* 905-875-2402
e-mail: office@milton.unitedway.ca
URL: www.miltonunitedway.ca
Anne Eadie, Executive Director

United Way of Morden & District Inc.
114 Nelson St., Morden MB R6M 1S2
Tel: 204-822-6992
e-mail: mordendistrictuw@gmail.com
Cindy Kolwalski, Chair

United Way of Niagara Falls & Greater Fort Erie
MacBain Community Ctr., 7150 Montrose Rd., Niagara Falls ON L2H 3N3
Tel: 905-354-9342; *Fax:* 905-354-2717
e-mail: unitedway@mail.caninet.com
URL: www.unitedwayniagara.org
Carol Stewart-Kirkby, Executive Director

United Way of North Okanagan Columbia Shuswap
3107 - 32 Ave., Vernon BC V1T 2M2
Tel: 250-549-1346; *Fax:* 250-549-1357
e-mail: office@vernon.unitedway.ca
URL: www.vernon.unitedway.ca
Linda Yule, Executive Director

United Way of Oakville (UWO)
#200, 466 Speers Rd., Oakville ON L6K 3W9
Tel: 905-845-5571; *Fax:* 905-845-0166
e-mail: info@uwoakville.org
URL: www.uwoakville.org
Barbara Burton, CEO
Gordon Ross, Chair

United Way of Oshawa-Whitby-Clarington-Brock & Scugog
345 Simcoe St. South, Oshawa ON L1H 4J2
Tel: 905-436-7377; *Fax:* 905-436-6414
e-mail: mail@unitedwayowc.com
URL: www.unitedwayowc.com
Cindy J. Murray, Executive Director
Robert Howard, Campaign Director

United Way of Oxford
#2, 65 Springbank Ave. North, Woodstock ON N4S 8V8
Tel: 519-539-3851; *Fax:* 519-539-3209
Toll-Free: 877-280-1391
e-mail: info@unitedwayoxford.ca
URL: www.unitedwayoxford.ca
Kelly Gilson, Executive Director

United Way of Peel Region
#300, 5170 Dixie Rd., Mississauga ON L4W 1E3
Tel: 905-602-3650; *Fax:* 905-602-3651; *TTY:* 905-602-3653
e-mail: jpereira@unitedwaypeel.org
URL: www.unitedwaypeel.org
Social Media: twitter.com/Unitedwaypeel
Shelley White, Executive Director
Shirley Crocker, Director, Finance & Administration
Ted Fauteux, Director, Resource Development
Liz Leake, Director, Communications & Marketing
Anita Stellinga, Director, Community Investment

United Way of Perth County
32 Erie St., Stratford ON N5A 2M4
Tel: 519-271-7730; *Fax:* 519-273-9350
Toll-Free: 877-818-8867
e-mail: info@unitedwayperth.on.ca
URL: www.unitedwayperth.on.ca
Affiliation(s): Perth County Community Development Council; Local Voices
Ellen Balmain, Executive Director
Shelley Groenestege, President

United Way of Peterborough & District
277 Stewart St., Peterborough ON K9J 3M8
Tel: 705-742-8839; *Fax:* 705-742-9186
e-mail: office@uwpeterborough.ca
URL: www.uwpeterborough.ca
Len Lifchus, Executive Director

United Way of Pictou County
Victoria Plaza, PO Box 75, #1, 342 Stewart St., New Glasgow NS B2H 5E1
Tel: 902-755-1754; *Fax:* 902-755-0853
e-mail: info@pictoucountyunitedway.ca
URL: www.pictoucountyunitedway.ca
Social Media: www.facebook.com/group.php?gid=81512980650
Dodie Goodwin, Executive Director

United Way of Prince Edward Island / Centraide PEI
PO Box 247, 180 Kent St., Charlottetown PE C1A 7K4
Tel: 902-894-8202; *Fax:* 902-894-9643
Toll-Free: 877-902-4438
e-mail: inquiries@peiunitedway.com
URL: www.peiunitedway.com
Clair F. Smith, Executive Director
Paul Chaulk, President

United Way of Quinte
Sears Unity Place, PO Box 815, 249 William St., Belleville ON K8N 5B5
Tel: 613-962-9531; *Fax:* 613-962-4165
e-mail: office@belleville.unitedway.ca
URL: www.unitedwayofquinte.ca
Social Media: www.facebook.com/group.php?gid=75482448853
Julia Gosson, Executive Director

United Way of Regina
1440 Scarth St., Regina SK S4R 2E9
Tel: 306-757-5671; *Fax:* 306-522-7199
e-mail: office@unitedwayregina.ca
URL: www.unitedwayregina.ca
Joanne Grant, CEO
Tracey Mann, Vice-President, Community Impact & Investments
Kristin Gushuliak, Campaign Manager

United Way of St Catharines & District
#3, 80 King St., Ground Fl., St Catharines ON L2R 7G1
Tel: 905-688-5050; *Fax:* 905-688-2997
e-mail: office@stcatharines.unitedway.ca
URL: www.unitedwaysc.ca

Frances Hallworth, Executive Director

United Way of Sarnia-Lambton
PO Box 548, 420 East St. North, Sarnia ON N7T 6Y5
Tel: 519-336-5452; *Fax:* 519-383-6032
e-mail: info@theunitedway.on.ca
URL: www.theunitedway.on.ca
Dave Brown, Executive Director
Paddy Roach, Manager, Resource Development
Pamela Bodkin, Director, Community Investment & Finance

United Way of Saskatoon & Area
100, 506 - 25 St. East, Saskatoon SK S7K 4A7
Tel: 306-975-7700; *Fax:* 306-244-0583
e-mail: office@unitedwaysaskatoon.ca
URL: www.unitedwaysaskatoon.ca
Sheri Benson, Executive Director

United Way of Sault Ste Marie
7A Oxford Street, Sault Ste Marie ON P6B 1R7
Tel: 705-256-7476; *Fax:* 705-759-5899
e-mail: uwssm@ssmunitedway.ca
URL: www.saultstemarie.unitedway.ca
Affiliation(s): United Way of Ontario; Regional Professional Advisory Council
Gary Vipond, Executive Director

United Way of Slave Lake Society
PO Box 1985, Slave Lake AB T0G 2A0
Tel: 780-849-3820

United Way of South Eastern Alberta
PO Box 783, Stn. M, #101, 928 Allowance Ave., Medicine Hat AB T1A 7G7
Tel: 403-526-5544; *Fax:* 403-526-5244
e-mail: utdway@telus.net
URL: www.utdway.ca
Cam Jacques, President of the Board
Holly Beauchamp-Stadnicki, Director, Fund Development

United Way of South Georgian Bay
PO Box 284, #9, 275 First St., Collingwood ON L9Y 3Z5
Tel: 705-444-1141; *Fax:* 705-444-0981
e-mail: dkunitedwaysgb@gmail.com
URL: www.unitedwaysgb.ca
Debbie Kesheshian, Executive Director

United Way of Stormont, Dundas & Glengarry / Centraide de Stormont, Dundas & Glengarry
331 Water St. East, Cornwall ON K6H 1A5
Tel: 613-932-2051; *Fax:* 613-932-7534
e-mail: info@unitedwaysdg.com
URL: www.unitedwaysdg.com
Claudette Blanchard, Campaign Clerk
Kevin Wilson, President
Karen Turchetto, Executive Director

United Way of the Alberta Capital Region
15132 Stony Plain Rd., Edmonton AB T5P 3Y3
Tel: 780-990-1000; *Fax:* 780-990-0203
e-mail: united@myunitedway.ca
URL: www.unitedthisistheway.ca
Dale Mulek, Chair
Robert Ascah, Vice-President, Government Relations, Research & Analysis
Anne Smith, Secretary/Treasurer

United Way of the Central Okanagan & South Okanagan/Similkameen
249 Lawrence Ave., Kelowna BC V1Y 6L2
Tel: 250-860-2356; *Fax:* 250-868-3206
Toll-Free: 888-636-2356
e-mail: office@kelowna.unitedway.ca
URL: www.kelownaunitedway.com
Harry Grossmith, CEO
Judy Doucette, Office Manager

United Way of the Fraser Valley (UWFV)
#201, 31667 South Fraser Way, Abbotsford BC V2T 1T8
Fax: 604-852-2316
Toll-Free: 888-251-7777
e-mail: wayne@uwfv.bc.ca
URL: www.uwfv.bc.ca
Wayne Green, Executive Director

United Way of the Lower Mainland
4543 Canada Way, Burnaby BC V5G 4T4
Tel: 604-294-8929
e-mail: info@uwlm.ca
URL: www.uwlm.ca
Michael McKnight, President & CEO

United Way of Thompson Inc.
PO Box 202, Thompson MB R8N 1N1
Tel: 204-778-5564; *Fax:* 204-778-5564
e-mail: uway@mts.net
Bobbie Montean, Executive Director

United Way of Trail
792 Rossland Avenue, Trail BC V1R 3T3
Tel: 250-364-0999; *Fax:* 250-364-1564
e-mail: unitedw@telus.net
Trish Milne, Executive Director

United Way of Windsor-Essex County
#A1, 300 Giles Blvd. East, Windsor ON N9A 4C4
Tel: 519-258-0000; *Fax:* 519-258-2346
e-mail: united@weareunited.com
URL: www.weareunited.com
Sheila Wisdom, Executive Director

United Way of Winnipeg / Winnipeg Centraide
5 Donald St., 3rd Fl., Winnipeg MB R3L 2T4
Tel: 204-477-5360; *Fax:* 204-453-6198
e-mail: uway@unitedwaywinnipeg.mb.ca
URL: www.unitedwaywinnipeg.mb.ca
Susan Lewis, President

United Way of York Region (UWYR)
#200, 80F Centurian Dr., Markham ON L3R 8C1
Tel: 905-474-9974; *Fax:* 905-474-0051
Toll-Free: 877-241-4516
e-mail: vnorman@uwyr.on.ca
URL: www.uwyr.on.ca
Daniele Zanotti, CEO

United Way South Niagara (UWSN) / Centraide de Niagara Sud
Seaway Mall, 800 Niagara St., Welland ON L3C 5Z4
Tel: 905-735-0490; *Fax:* 905-735-5432
e-mail: office@southniagara.unitedway.ca
URL: www.unitedway.websweet.ca
Bill Auchterlonie, Executive Director

United Way Toronto
26 Wellington St. East, 2nd Fl., Toronto ON M5E 1W9
Tel: 416-777-2001; *Fax:* 416-777-0962; *TTY:* 416-359-2083
URL: www.unitedwaytoronto.com; www.uwgt.org
Social Media: www.facebook.com/group.php?gid=108587420188
Frances Lankin, President & CEO
Alnasir Samji, Chair

United Way/Centraide (Central NB) Inc.
#400, 1133 Regent St., Fredericton NB E3B 3Z2
Tel: 506-459-7773; *Fax:* 506-451-1104
e-mail: unitedwy@nbnet.nb.ca
URL: www.unitedwaycentral.com
Frank Russell, Executive Director

United Way/Centraide of the Upper Ottawa Valley Inc.
PO Box 727, 214 Church St., Pembroke ON K8A 6X9
Tel: 613-735-0436; *Fax:* 613-735-8362
Toll-Free: 888-592-2213
e-mail: unitedw@nrtco.net; office@pembroke.unitedway.ca
URL: www.pembroke.unitedway.ca
Affiliation(s): Arnprior Community Council; Upper Ottawa Valley Chamber of Commerce; Pembroke Downtown Development Commission
Etienne Lantos, Chair
Sheila Bucholtz, Executive Director

United Way/Centraide Ottawa (UW/CO)
363 Coventry Rd., Ottawa ON K1K 2C5
Tel: 613-228-6700; *Fax:* 613-228-6730
e-mail: info@unitedwayottawa.ca
URL: www.unitedwayottawa.ca
Social Media: www.facebook.com/group.php?gid=35673670196
Michael Allen, President/CEO

United Way/Centraide Sudbury & District
#E-6, 105 Elm Street, Sudbury ON P3C 1T3
Tel: 705-560-3330; *Fax:* 705-560-3337
e-mail: office@sudbury.unitedway.ca
URL: www.unitedwaysudbury.com
Vicky Lafond, Executive Director

Vanier Institute of The Family (VIF) / Institut Vanier de la famille
94 Centrepointe Dr., Ottawa ON K2G 6B1
Tel: 613-228-8500; *Fax:* 613-228-8007
Toll-Free: 800-331-4937
e-mail: webmaster@vifamily.ca
URL: www.vifamily.ca
Clarence Lochhead, Executive Director
Verna Bruce, President

Victims of Violence Canadian Centre for Missing Children (VOV)
211 Pretoria Ave., Ottawa ON K1S 1X1
Tel: 613-233-0052; *Fax:* 613-233-2712
Toll-Free: 888-606-0000
e-mail: vofv@victimsofviolence.on.ca
URL: www.victimsofviolence.on.ca
Affiliation(s): National Organization for Victim Assistance - Washington DC; RCMP Missing Children's Registry
Gary Rosenfeldt, Executive Director

Volunteer Canada / Bénévoles Canada
353 Dalhousie St., Ottawa ON K1N 7G1
Tel: 613-231-4371; *Fax:* 613-231-6725
Toll-Free: 800-670-0401
e-mail: info@volunteer.ca
URL: www.volunteer.ca
Ruth MacKenzie, President

Volunteer Grandparents (VIP)
#203, 2101 Holdom Ave., Burnaby BC V5B 0A4
Tel: 604-736-8271; *Fax:* 604-294-6814
e-mail: info@volunteergrandparents.ca
URL: www.volunteergrandparents.ca
Affiliation(s): Volunteer Burnaby
Stephen Sjoberg, President

The War Amputations of Canada / Les Amputés de guerre du Canada
2827 Riverside Dr., Ottawa ON K1V 0C4
Tel: 613-731-3821; *Fax:* 613-731-3234
Toll-Free: 800-465-2677
e-mail: communications@waramps.ca
URL: www.waramps.ca
H. Clifford Chadderton, CEO
Laurie Rasberry, National President
Claire Roy, Director of Administration

Weyburn & District United Way
PO Box 608, Weyburn SK S4H 2K7
Tel: 306-842-7880
e-mail: weyburn.unitedway@accesscomm.ca
URL: www.weyburnunitedway.com
Gary Erickson, President

Winkler & District United Way
PO Box 1528, Winkler MB R6W 4B4
Tel: 204-829-3843
e-mail: ron@wiband.ca
Karen Schellenberg, President

Yorkton & District United Way Inc.
PO Box 44, Yorkton SK S3N 2V6
Tel: 306-783-2582; *Fax:* 306-783-2502
e-mail: bandgofyorkton@sasktel.net
Brian Pohorelic, Chair
Lisa Washington, Secretary

Sports

Abbotsford Female Hockey Association (AFHA)
2167 Essex Dr., Abbotsford BC V2S 7R8
e-mail: info@abbotsfordfemalehockey.com
URL: www.abbotsfordfemalehockey.com
Jerry Ward, President

Alberta 5 Pin Bowlers' Association (A5-PBA)
432 - 14 St. South, Lethbridge AB T1J 2X7
Tel: 403-320-2695; *Fax:* 403-320-2676
Toll-Free: 800-762-3075
e-mail: a5pba@telusplanet.net
URL: www.alberta5pin.com
Annette Bruneau, President

Alberta Amateur Speed Skating Association (AASSA)
2500 University Dr. NW, Calgary AB T2N 1N4
Tel: 403-220-7911; *Fax:* 403-220-9226
e-mail: info@albertaspeedskating.ca
URL: www.albertaspeedskating.ca
Wendy Walker, Office Administrator

Alberta Bicycle Association (ABA)
Percy Page Centre, 11759 Groat Rd., Edmonton AB T5M 3K6
Tel: 780-427-6352; *Fax:* 780-427-6438
Toll-Free: 877-646-2453
e-mail: office@albertabicycle.ab.ca
URL: www.albertabicycle.ab.ca
Kipp Kaufmann, Executive Director

Alberta Bobsleigh Association
Bob Niven Training Centre, #205, 88 Canada Olympic Rd. SW, Calgary AB T3B 5R5

Tel: 403-297-2721; *Fax:* 403-286-7213
e-mail: slide@albertabobsleigh.com
URL: www.albertabobsleigh.com
Devin Findlay, Technical Director

Alberta Broomball Association
Percy Page Centre, 11759 Groat Rd., Edmonton AB T5M 3K6
Tel: 780-459-7668; *Fax:* 780-460-0527
e-mail: neigel@telus.net
Greg Mastervick, President

Alberta Curling Federation (ACF)
11759 Groat Rd., Edmonton AB T5M 3K6
Tel: 780-643-0809; *Fax:* 780-427-8103
e-mail: jim@albertacurling.ab.ca
URL: www.albertacurling.ab.ca
J.W. (Jim) Pringle, Executive Director
Kathy Odegard, Office Manager

Alberta Deaf Sports Association (ADSA)
11404 - 142 St., Edmonton AB T5M 1V1
e-mail: adsa@shaw.ca
URL: adsa.deafalberta.org
Arista Haas, President
Ryan Bercier, Vice-President
Brenda Hillcox, Secretary

Alberta Diving
426 Reeves Cres., Edmonton AB T6R 2A4
Tel: 780-988-5571; *Fax:* 780-988-7753
URL: www.albertadiving.ca
Cindy Casper, President
Susan Zwaenepoel, Vice-President
Barb Bush, Executive Director
Jim MacDonald, Secretary
Curtis Yano, Treasurer

Alberta Equestrian Federation (AEF)
#100, 251 Midpark Blvd. SE, Calgary AB T2X 1S3
Tel: 403-253-4411; *Fax:* 403-252-5260
Toll-Free: 877-463-6233
e-mail: execdir@albertaequestrian.com
URL: www.albertaequestrian.com
Sonia Meyer, Executive Director

Alberta Golf Association (AGA)
#22, 11410 - 27 St. SE, Calgary AB T2Z 3R6
Tel: 403-236-4616; *Fax:* 403-236-2915
Toll-Free: 888-414-4849
e-mail: info@albertagolf.org
URL: www.albertagolf.org
Brent Ellenton, Executive Director

Alberta Luge Association (ALA)
Rm 201, BNTC, 88 Canada Olympic Rd. SW, Calgary AB T3B 5R5
Tel: 403-202-6570; *Fax:* 403-247-5497
e-mail: admin@albertaluge.com
URL: www.albertaluge.com
Affiliation(s): Canadian Luge Association
Darryl Gunn, President

Alberta Northern Lights Wheelchair Basketball Society
6788 - 99th St., Edmonton AB T6E 5B8
Tel: 780-433-4310; *Fax:* 780-431-1764
Toll-Free: 800-465-2992
e-mail: info@albertanorthernlights.com
URL: www.albertanorthernlights.com

Alberta Rugby Football Union
Percy Page Centre, 11759 Groat Rd., Edmonton AB T5M 3K6
Tel: 780-415-1773; *Fax:* 780-422-5558
Toll-Free: 866-784-2922
e-mail: rugbyab@telus.net
URL: www.rugbyalberta.com
Bert Radford, President

Alberta Schools' Athletic Association (ASAA)
Percy Page Centre, 11759 Groat Rd., Edmonton AB T5M 3K6
Tel: 780-427-8182; *Fax:* 780-415-1833
e-mail: info@asaa.ca
URL: www.asaa.ca
Affiliation(s): National Federation of State High School Associations
John F. Paton, Executive Director
Dave M. Jones, President

Alberta Soaring Council
PO Box 13, Black Diamond AB T0L 0H0
Tel: 403-933-4968
e-mail: asc@platinum.ca
URL: www.soaring.ab.ca
Phil Stade, Executive Director

Alberta Soccer Association
Commonwealth Stadium, 1100 Stadium Rd., Edmonton AB T5H 4E2
Tel: 780-474-2200; *Fax:* 780-474-6300
Toll-Free: 866-250-2200
URL: www.albertasoccer.com
Ron Axelson, Executive Director

Alberta Sports & Recreation Association for the Blind (ASRAB)
#007, 15 Colonel Baker Pl. NE, Calgary AB T2E 4Z3
Tel: 403-262-5332; *Fax:* 403-265-7221
Toll-Free: 888-882-7722
e-mail: marilyn@asrab.ab.ca
URL: www.asrab.ab.ca
Marilyn McIntosh, Executive Director
Peter Wettlaufer, President

Alberta Tennis Association (ATA)
11759 Groat Rd., Edmonton AB T5M 3K6
Tel: 780-415-1661; *Fax:* 780-415-1693
e-mail: info@tennisalberta.com
URL: www.tennisalberta.com
Darryl Szafranski, Chief Executive Officer
Eva Wolicki, Technical Director

Alberta Volleyball Association (AVA)
Percy Page Centre, 11759 Groat Rd., Edmonton AB T5M 3K6
Tel: 780-415-1703; *Fax:* 780-415-1700
e-mail: info@albertavolleyball.com
URL: www.albertavolleyball.com
Affiliation(s): Federation of Outdoor Volleyball Associations
Terry Gagnon, Executive Director
Gail Senkiw, Office Manager

Alberta Water Polo Association (AWPA)
PO Box 54, 2225 Macleod Trail South, Edmonton AB T2G 5B6
Tel: 403-475-6747; *Fax:* 403-475-6748
e-mail: office@albertawaterpolo.ca
URL: www.albertawaterpolo.ca
Mike Erickson, President

Alpine Canada ALPIN
#153, 401 - 9th Ave. SW, Calgary AB T2P 3C5
Tel: 403-777-3200; *Fax:* 403-777-3213
e-mail: info@canski.org
URL: www.canski.org
Gary Allan, President
Jennifer Duggan, Manager, National Services

The Alpine Club of Canada (ACC) / Club alpin du Canada
PO Box 8040, Indian Flats Rd., Canmore AB T1W 2T8
Tel: 403-678-3200; *Fax:* 403-678-3224
e-mail: info@alpineclubofcanada.ca
URL: www.alpineclubofcanada.ca
Affiliation(s): International Union of Alpinist Associations
Lawrence White, Executive Director
Peter Muir, President

American & Canadian Underwater Certification Inc.
379 West St., Brantford ON N3R 3V9
Tel: 519-750-5767; *Fax:* 519-750-5769
e-mail: acuchq@acuc.ca
URL: www.acuc.es/
Affiliation(s): World Diving Federation; Undersea Hyperbaric Medical Society
Nancy Hilton, Office Manager
R.W. Cronkwright, President
Marg Cronkwright, Vice-President

Aquatic Federation of Canada / Fédération canadienne des sports aquatiques
4 Calgary St., St. John's NL A1A 3W2
Tel: 709-753-2398; *Fax:* 709-753-2398
e-mail: whogan@nl.rogers.com
URL: www.swimming.ca/AFC.aspx
Affiliation(s): Synchro Canada; Canadian Amateur Diving Association Inc.; Water Polo Canada; Swimming Canada
Bill Hogan, President

Arctic Winter Games International Committee (AWGIC)
#400, 5201 - 50 Ave., Yellowknife NT X1A 3S9
Tel: 867-873-7245; *Fax:* 867-920-6467
URL: www.awg.ca
Lloyd Bentz, Secretary
Gerry Thick, President
Wendell Shiffler, Vice-President
Ian D. Legaree, Technical Director

Association chasse & pêche de Chibougamau
CP 171, Chibougamau QC G8P 2K6
Tél: 418-748-2021
Courriel: info@acpcchibougamau.com
URL: www.acpcchibougamau.com
Serge Picard, Président

Association des plongeurs de Chibougamau
535, 4e Rue, Chibougamau QC G8P 1S4
Tél: 418-748-7056
André Naud

Association sportive des aveugles du Québec inc.
CP 1000, Succ. M, 4545, av Pierre-de Coubertin, Montréal QC H1V 3R2
Tél: 514-252-3178; *Téléc:* 514-254-1303
URL: www.sportsaveugles.qc.ca
Robert Deschênes, Président

Association sportive des sourds du Québec inc. (ASSQ)
CP 1000, Succ. M, 4545, av Pierre-de Coubertin, Montréal QC H1V 3R2
Tél: 514-252-3069; *Téléc:* 514-252-3049
Courriel: info@assq.org
URL: www.assq.org
Gérard Labrecque, Président

Athabasca Landing Pool Association (ALPA)
4705 - 48th Ave., Athabasca AB T9S 1R3
Tel: 780-675-5656; *Fax:* 780-675-4700
e-mail: athpool@telusplanet.net
Jaymie Mullin, Manager
Alan Fisher, President

Athletics Canada / Athlétisme Canada
#B1-110, 2445 St-Laurent Blvd, Ottawa ON K1G 6C3
Tel: 613-260-5580; *Fax:* 613-260-0341
e-mail: athcan@athletics.ca
URL: www.athletics.ca
Social Media: twitter.com/athleticscanada
Affiliation(s): International Amateur Athletic Federation
Joanne Mortimore, CEO

Atlantic Canada Trail Riding Association
Sylvia Gillies, #344 Route 875, Belleisle Creek NB E5P 1C8
Roy Drinnan, Chair

Badminton Alberta
c/o Alberta Badminton Centre, 60 Patterson Blvd SW, Calgary AB T3H 2E1
Tel: 403-297-2722; *Fax:* 403-297-2706
Toll-Free: 888-397-2722
e-mail: info@badmintonalberta.ca
URL: www.badmintonalberta.ca
Jeff Bell, Executive Director

Badminton Alberta
c/o Alberta Badminton Centre, 60 Patterson Blvd. SW, Calgary AB T3H 2E1
Tel: 403-297-2722; *Fax:* 403-297-2706
Toll-Free: 888-397-2722
e-mail: info@badmintonalberta.ca

Badminton BC
#252, 3820 Cessna Dr., Richmond BC V7B 0A2
Tel: 604-333-3595; *Fax:* 604-333-3594
Toll-Free: 800-483-2473
e-mail: info@badmintonbc.com
URL: www.badmintonbc.com
Brock Turner, Executive Director
Ken Thiesen, Operations & Programs Manager

Badminton Canada
#99, 2201 Riverside Dr., Ottawa ON K1H 8K9
Tel: 613-569-2424; *Fax:* 613-569-3232
e-mail: badminton@badminton.ca
URL: www.badminton.ca
Affiliation(s): International Badminton Federation
Sonia Blanchard, Office Administrator
Kyle Hunter, Executive Director

Badminton New Nouveau Brunswick
PO Box 355, Stn. Main, Bathurst NB E2A 3Z3
Tel: 506-783-4654
e-mail: badminton@bnnb.ca
URL: www.bnnb.ca
Bernard Duguay, Administration
Diane MacLeod, President

Badminton Newfoundland & Labrador Inc.
PO Box 21248, #213, 810 East White Hills Rd., St. John's NL A1A 5B2
Tel: 709-576-7606; *Fax:* 709-576-7493
e-mail: badminton@sportnf.com
URL: www.badmintonnl.ca/

Janice Reid-Boland, Executive Director
Mike Alexander, President

Badminton Québec
4940, rue Hochelaga est, Montréal QC H1V 1E7
Tél: 514-252-3066; *Téléc:* 514-252-3175
Courriel: badmintonquebec@videotron.ca
URL: www.badmintonquebec.com
Maryse Bellavance, Directrice générale

Baseball Alberta (BA)
Percy Page Centre, 11759 Groat Rd., Edmonton AB T5M 3K6
Tel: 780-427-8943; *Fax:* 780-427-9032
e-mail: bradwolansky@baseballalberta.com
URL: www.baseballalberta.com
Affiliation(s): Alberta Amateur Baseball Council

Baseball BC
#310, 15225 - 104th Ave., Surrey BC V3R 6Y8
Tel: 604-586-3310; *Fax:* 604-586-3311
e-mail: info@baseball.bc.ca
URL: www.baseball.bc.ca

Baseball Canada / Fédération canadienne de baseball amateur
2212 Gladwin Cres., #A7, Ottawa ON K1B 5N1
Tel: 613-748-5606; *Fax:* 613-748-5767
e-mail: info@baseball.ca
URL: www.baseball.ca
Affiliation(s): Canadian Olympic Association
Jim Baba, Director General
Ray Carter, President

Baseball New Brunswick (BNB) / Baseball Nouveau-Brunswick
#13, 900 Hanwell Rd., Fredericton NB E3B 6A2
Tel: 506-451-1329; *Fax:* 506-451-1325
e-mail: baseballnb2003@nb.aibn.com
URL: www.baseballnb.ca
Affiliation(s): Sport New Brunswick; Baseball Atlantic

Baseball Nova Scotia (BNS)
5516 Spring Garden Rd., 4th Fl., Halifax NS B3J 1J
Tel: 902-425-5450; *Fax:* 902-425-5606
URL: www.baseballnovascotia.com
Brad Lawlor, Executive Director

Baseball Ontario
#3, 131 Sheldon Dr., Cambridge ON N1R 6S2
Tel: 519-740-3900; *Fax:* 519-740-6311
e-mail: baseball@baseballontario.com
URL: www.baseballontario.com
Affiliation(s): Little League Ontario
Mary-Ann Smith, Administrative Director

Basketball Alberta
Percy Page Centre, 11759 Groat Rd., Edmonton AB T5M 3K6
Tel: 780-427-9044; *Fax:* 780-427-9124
e-mail: bballab@basketballalbert.ab.ca
URL: www.basketballalberta.ca
Bob Mitchell, President
Brian Anstice, Vice President

Basketball BC
#310, 7155 Kingsway, Burnaby BC V5E 2V1
Tel: 604-718-7852; *Fax:* 604-525-7762
e-mail: hoopsbc@basketball.bc.ca
URL: www.basketball.bc.ca
Michael Hind, Executive Director

Basketball Manitoba
200 Main St., Winnipeg MB R3C 4M2
Tel: 204-925-5775; *Fax:* 204-925-5929
Toll-Free: 800-282-8069
e-mail: info@basketball.mb.ca
URL: www.basketball.mb.ca
Adam Wedlake, Executive Director

Basketball New Brunswick (BNB) / Basketball Nouveau-Brunswick
#13, 900 Hanwell Rd., Fredericton NB E2E 6A2
Tel: 506-849-4667; *Fax:* 506-451-1325
e-mail: info@basketball.nb.ca
URL: www.basketball.nb.ca
Affiliation(s): New Brunswick Association of Approved Basketball Officials; New Brunswick Interscholastic Athletic Association
Marg Jones, Executive Director
Chuck Beyea, President

Basketball Nova Scotia
5516 Spring Garden Rd., 4th Fl., Halifax NS B3J 1G6
Tel: 902-425-5450; *Fax:* 902-425-5606
e-mail: bnsadmin@basketball.ns.ca
URL: www.basketball.ns.ca
Affiliation(s): Sport Nova Scotia
Donnie Ehler, Executive Director
Mike Brien, President

Basketball NWT
e-mail: info@bnwt.ca
URL: www.bnwt.ca

Basketball PEI
PO Box 302, 40 Enman Cres., Charlottetown PE C1A 7K7
Tel: 902-368-4208; *Fax:* 902-368-4208
Toll-Free: 800-247-6712
e-mail: info@basketballpei.ca
URL: www.basketballpei.ca
Stephen Marchbank, Executive Director

Basketball Saskatchewan Inc. (BSI)
2205 Victoria Ave., Regina SK S4P 0S4
Tel: 306-780-9264; *Fax:* 306-525-4009
e-mail: mbarr@basketballsask.com
URL: www.basketballsask.com
Affiliation(s): Sask Sport
Marg Barr, Executive Director

Basketball Yukon
4061, 4th Ave., Whitehorse YT Y1A 1H1
Tel: 867-668-3802
e-mail: bballyukon@klondiker.com
URL: www.basketballyukon.ca
Affiliation(s): Sport Yukon, Canada Basketball
Tim Brady, President
Linda Sutherland, Administrative Assistant

Biathlon Alberta
818 - 16 Ave. NW, Calgary AB T2M 0K1
Tel: 403-297-2719; *Fax:* 403-297-2702
e-mail: info@biathlon.ca
URL: www.biathlon.ca
Alan Ball, Sport Development

Biathlon Canada
#111, 2197 Riverside Dr., Ottawa ON K1H 7X3
Tel: 613-748-5608; *Fax:* 613-748-5762
e-mail: jthomson@biathloncanada.ca
URL: www.biathloncanada.ca
Affiliation(s): International Biathlon Union; Canadian Olympic Committee
Joanne Thomson, Executive Director
Chris Lindsay, Coordinator, Technical Programs

Biathlon Yukon
PO Box 31673, Whitehorse YT Y1A 6L3
URL: www.sportyukon.com/membership/?member=11
Keith Clarke, President
Katrina Brogden, Secretary

Bicycle Newfoundland & Labrador
PO Box 2127, Stn. C, St. John's NL A1C 5R6
Tel: 709-753-5788; *Fax:* 709-753-3301
e-mail: bnl@bnl.nf.ca
URL: www.bnl.nf.ca/
Leon Organ, President

Bicycle Nova Scotia (BNS)
5516 Spring Garden Rd., 4th Fl., Halifax NS B3J 1G6
Tel: 902-425-5454; *Fax:* 902-425-5606
e-mail: staff@bicycle.ns.ca
URL: www.bicycle.ns.ca
Simon Myatt, President

Bicycle Trade Association of Canada (BTAC) / Association canadienne de l'industrie du vélo (ACIV)
17 Main St. North, Newmarket ON L3Y 3Z6
Tel: 905-853-5031; *Fax:* 905-853-7632
Toll-Free: 866-528-2822
e-mail: info@btac.org
URL: www.btac.org
Janet O'Connell, Executive Director

Blind Sports Nova Scotia
c/o CNIB, 6136 Almon St., Halifax NS B3K 1T8
Tel: 902-453-1480; *Fax:* 902-454-6570
e-mail: blindsports@yahoo.ca
URL: www.blindsportnovascotia.ca
Yvon Clement, President

Bobsleigh Canada Skeleton
140 Canada Olympic Rd. SW, Calgary AB T3B 5R5
Tel: 403-247-5950; *Fax:* 403-247-5951
e-mail: ddreher@bobsleigh.ca
URL: www.bobsleigh.ca/
Affiliation(s): Fédération internationale de bobsleigh et de tobogganing
Shane Pearsall, Managing Director

Bowling Federation of Canada / Fédération des quilles du Canada
c/o Administrator, #206, 720 Belfast Rd., Ottawa ON K1G 0Z5
Tel: 613-744-5090; *Fax:* 613-744-2217
e-mail: info@canadabowls.ca
URL: www.canadabowls.ca
Affiliation(s): Bowling Proprietors Association of Canada; Canadian 5-pin Bowlers Association; Canadian Tenpin Federation.
Sheila Carr, Interim Administrator

Bowling Federation of Saskatchewan
#101, 1805 - 8th Ave., Regina SK S4R 1E8
Tel: 306-780-9412; *Fax:* 306-780-9455
e-mail: bowling@sasktel.net
URL: saskbowl.com
Rhonda Sereda, Executive Director

Bowling Proprietors' Association of BC
#209, 332 Columbia St., New Westminster BC V3L 1A6
Tel: 604-522-2990; *Fax:* 604-522-2055
e-mail: bowl4fun@bowlbc.com
URL: www.bowlbc.com
Sheilagh Meyers, Executive Director

Bowling Proprietors' Association of Canada (BPAC)
#10A, 250 Shields Ct., Markham ON L3R 9W7
Tel: 905-479-1560; *Fax:* 905-479-8613
e-mail: bowling@bpac.ca
URL: www.bpac.ca
Paul Oliveira, Executive Director
Claude Rhéaume, President

Bowling Proprietors' Association of Ontario (BPAO)
#202, 500 Alden Road, Markham ON L3R 5H5
Tel: 905-940-8200
e-mail: bpao@bpao.ca
URL: www.bpao.ca
Affiliation(s): Bowling Proprietors' Association of Canada
Walter J. Valentan, Secretary
Don Gorman, President/Chair
Margaret Gorman, Administrative Assistant

Bowls BC (BBC)
#148, 5525 West Blvd., Vancouver BC V6M 3W6
URL: www.bowlsbc.ca
Affiliation(s): World Bowls Board; World Indoor Bowls Board
Keith Terlson, President
Pat Cutt, Vice-President
Marjorie Mitchell, Treasurer
Juanita Tucker, Secretary

Bowls Canada Boulingrin (BCB)
#207, 720 Belfast Rd., Ottawa ON K1G 0Z5
Tel: 613-244-0021; *Fax:* 613-244-0041
Toll-Free: 800-567-2695
e-mail: office@bowlscanada.com
URL: www.bowlscanada.com
Affiliation(s): Commonwealth Games Association of Canada
Kevin Penny, Executive Director

Bowls Manitoba
200 Main St., Winnipeg MB R3C 4M2
Tel: 204-925-5694; *Fax:* 204-925-5703
e-mail: bowls@shawbiz.ca
URL: www.bowls.mb.ca
Cathy Derewianchuk, Executive Director

Bowls Saskatchewan Inc.
#102, 1860 Lorne St., Regina SK S4P 2L7
Tel: 306-780-9426; *Fax:* 306-781-6021
e-mail: bowlsask@sasktel.net
URL: www.bowls.sk.ca
Karen Swanson, Executive Director
Jean Roney, President

Boxing Alberta
Percy Page Centre, 11759 Groat Rd., Edmonton AB T5M 3K6
Tel: 780-427-6515; *Fax:* 780-427-1205
e-mail: dbelair@telus.net
URL: www.boxingalberta.com
Tom Daly, President
Dennis Belair, Executive Director

Boxing BC Association
250 Willingdon Ave., Burnaby BC V5C 5E9
Tel: 604-291-7921; *Fax:* 604-291-7927
e-mail: boxingbc@telus.net
URL: www.boxing.bc.ca
Affiliation(s): Canadian Amateur Boxing Association
Scotty Jackson, President

Boxing Ontario
#207, 1185 Eglinton Ave. East, Toronto ON M3C 3C6
Tel: 416-426-7250; *Fax:* 416-426-7367
e-mail: info@boxingontario.com
URL: www.boxingontario.com
Doug Hannum, Executive Director

Boxing Saskatchewan
PO Box 4711, Regina SK S4P 3Y3
Tel: 306-525-6678; *Fax:* 306-569-3454
e-mail: skboxing@accesscomm.ca
URL: www.saskboxing.com
Affiliation(s): Canadian Amateur Boxing Association
Graham Craig, Executive Director

British Columbia Amateur Hockey Association (BCAHA) / Association de hockey amateur de la Colombie-Britannique
6671 Oldfield Rd., Saanichton BC V8M 2A1
Tel: 250-652-2978; *Fax:* 250-652-4536
e-mail: info@bchockey.net
URL: www.bchockey.net
Barry Petrachenko, Executive Director
Ed Mayert, President

British Columbia Ball Hockey Association (BCBHA)
1302 Cliveden Ave., Delta BC V3M 6G4
Tel: 604-812-6720; *Fax:* 604-588-7760
URL: www.bcbha.com
Affiliation(s): Canadian Ball Hockey Association
Wade Traversy, President
Kris Little, Vice-President
Rob Moxness, Secretary
Roger Sidhu, Treasurer

British Columbia Blind Sports & Recreation Association (BCBSRA)
#330, 5055 Joyce St., Vancouver BC V5R 6B2
Tel: 604-325-8638; *Fax:* 604-325-1638
e-mail: info@bcblindsports.bc.ca
URL: www.bcblindsports.bc.ca
Affiliation(s): International Blind Sports Association; BC Sport & Fitness Council for the Disabled
Brian Cowie, President
Tami Grenon, Vice President

British Columbia Broomball Society
Rick Przybysz, 5356 Lochside Dr., Victoria BC V8Y 2G7
Tel: 250-658-4406
e-mail: president@broomballbc.com
URL: www.broomballbc.com
Rick Przybysz, President

British Columbia Competitive Trail Riders Association (BCCTRA)
c/o 2980 Giovando Road, Nanaimo BC V9X 1K5
Tel: 250-245-4405
e-mail: nicole.vaugeois@viu.ca
URL: www.bcctra.ca
Nicole Vagueois, Sec.-Treas.

British Columbia Deaf Sports Federation (BCDSF)
#254, 3820 Cessna Dr., Richmond BC V7B 0A2
Fax: 604-738-7175; *TTY:* 604-333-3606
e-mail: bcdeafsports@telus.net
URL: www.bcdeafsports.bc.ca
Affiliation(s): BC Sport & Fitness Council for the Disabled
Roger Chan, President
Mandy Harker, Media/Programming

British Columbia Diving
2630 Dogwood Dr., Surrey BC V4A 3K5
Tel: 604-541-9332; *Fax:* 604-541-9303
e-mail: info@bcdiving.ca
URL: www.bcdiving.ca
Bev Boys, Executive Director
Joyne MacDonald, Manager, Operations

British Columbia Golf Association (BCGA)
#2105, 21000 Westminster Hwy., Richmond BC V6V 2S9
Tel: 604-279-2580; *Fax:* 604-207-9535
Toll-Free: 888-833-2242
e-mail: info@bcga.org
URL: www.bcga.org
Affiliation(s): Canadian Golf Foundation; Professional Golf Association of BC; Canadian Ladies Golf Association of BC; Golf Course Superintendents Association of BC; International Association of Golf Administrators; National Golf Foundation; Pacific Coast Golf Association; Pacific Northwest Golf Association
George Faithfull, President
Kris Jonasson, Executive Director

British Columbia Ringette Association (BCRA) / Association de ringuette de Colombie-Britannique
#319, 789 West Pender Street, Vancouver BC V6C 1H2
Fax: 604-629-0876
URL: www.bcringette.org
Glen Ritchie, President
Donna Mihalcheon, Vice President

British Columbia Rugby Union
#203, 210 West Broadway, Vancouver BC V5Y 3W2
Tel: 604-737-3065; *Fax:* 604-737-3916
e-mail: bcrugby@telus.net
URL: www.bcrugby.com
Louise Wheeler, Manager, Member Services
Jeff Sauvé, CEO

British Columbia School Sports (BCSS)
#100, 4585 Canada Way, Burnaby BC V5G 4L6
Tel: 604-737-3066; *Fax:* 604-737-9844
e-mail: info@bcschoolsports.ca
URL: www.bcschoolsports.ca
Affiliation(s): USA National Federation of State High Schools
Sue Keenan, Executive Director
Raj Puri, President

British Columbia Soccer Association
#510, 375 Water St., Vancouver BC V6B 5C6
Tel: 604-299-6401; *Fax:* 604-299-9610
e-mail: bcsoccer@gmail.com
URL: www.bcsoccer.net
Bjorn Osieck, Executive Director

British Columbia Speed Skating Association
33844 King Rd., Abbotsford BC V2S 7M8
Tel: 604-557-4020; *Fax:* 604-853-4629
e-mail: speedskating@ucfv.ca
URL: www.speed-skating.bc.ca/
Lorna Holbech, Office Administrator

British Columbia Water Polo Association (BCWPA)
#227, 3820 Cessna Dr., Richmond BC V7B 0A2
Tel: 604-333-3480; *Fax:* 604-333-3450
e-mail: bcwaterpolo@telus.net
URL: www.bcwaterpolo.com
Dave Soul, Executive Director

British Columbia Wrestling Association (BCWA)
#208, 1367 West Broadway, Vancouver BC V6H 4A9
Tel: 604-737-3092; *Fax:* 604-737-6043
e-mail: info@bcwrestling.com
URL: www.bcwrestling.com
Affiliation(s): BC School Sports
MaryAnn DeCorby, Executive Director

Broomball Newfoundland & Labrador
734 Birch St., Labrador City NL A2V 1C8
Tel: 709-944-5780; *Fax:* 709-944-5780
e-mail: clarkep@nf.sympatico.ca
Harold Clarke, President

Calgary Boxing & Wrestling Commission (CBWC)
PO Box 2100, Stn. M #63, Calgary AB T2P 2M5
Tel: 403-268-5367
e-mail: cscchair@tooks.net
Candy S. Schacter, Chair

Canada Basketball
#11, 1 Westside Dr., Toronto ON M9C 1B2
Tel: 416-614-8037; *Fax:* 416-614-9570
e-mail: info@basketball.ca
URL: www.basketball.ca
Affiliation(s): 10 provincial + 2 territorial associations; Canadian Interuniversity Athletic Union; Canadian Colleges Athletic Association; Canadian School Sports Federation; Toronto Raptors; Canadian Wheelchair Basketball Association; Canadian Association of Basketball Officials; National Association of Basketball Coaches of Canada; Women's Basketball Coaches Association
Wayne Parrish, Executive Director & CEO

Canada Games Council (CGC) / Conseil des jeux du Canada
#701, 2197 Riverside Dr., Ottawa ON K1H 7X3
Tel: 613-526-2320; *Fax:* 613-526-4068
e-mail: canada.games@canadagames.ca
URL: www.canadagames.ca
Sue Hylland, President/CEO
Kelly Dearborn, Director of Sport and Games

Canada's Sports Hall of Fame / Temple de la renommée des sports du Canada
Exhibition Place, 115 Princes' Blvd., Toronto ON M6K 3C3
Tel: 416-260-6789; *Fax:* 416-260-9347
e-mail: info@cshof.ca
URL: www.cshof.ca
Sheryn Posen, COO
J. Trevor Eyton, Chair

Canadian 5 Pin Bowlers' Association (C5PBA) / Association canadienne des cinq quilles (AC5Q)
#206, 720 Belfast Rd., Ottawa ON K1G 0Z5
Tel: 613-744-5090; *Fax:* 613-744-2217
e-mail: c5pba@c5pba.ca
URL: www.c5pba.ca
Affiliation(s): Bowling Federation of Canada
Sheila Carr, Executive Director
Mel Osmond, President
Don MacIver, Corporate Sec.-Treas.

Canadian Academy of Sport Medicine (CASM) / Académie canadienne de médecine du sport (ACMS)
#4, 5330 Canotek Rd., Ottawa ON K1J 9C1
Tel: 613-748-5851; *Fax:* 613-748-5792
Toll-Free: 877-585-2394
e-mail: bfalardeau@casm-acms.org
URL: www.casm-acms.org
Affiliation(s): World Federation of Sport Medicine
Dawn Haworth, Executive Director

Canadian Adult Recreational Hockey Association (CARHA)
#610, 1420 Blair Pl., Ottawa ON K1J 9L8
Tel: 613-244-1989; *Fax:* 613-244-0451
Toll-Free: 800-267-1854
e-mail: hockey@carhahockey.ca
URL: www.carhahockey.ca
Mike Peski, President

Canadian Amateur Boxing Association (CABA) / Association canadienne de boxe amateur (ACBA)
888 Belfast Rd., Ottawa ON K1G 0Z6
Tel: 613-238-7700; *Fax:* 613-238-1600
e-mail: caba@boxing.ca
URL: www.boxing.ca
Affiliation(s): International Amateur Boxing Association
Robert G. Crête, Executive Director
Daniel Trépanier, Coordinator, Technical
Michelle Ethier, Registrar & Accountant

Canadian Amateur Wrestling Association (CAWA) / Association canadienne de lutte amateur
#7, 5370 Canotek Rd., Gloucester ON K1J 9E6
Tel: 613-748-5686; *Fax:* 613-748-5756
e-mail: info@wrestling.ca
URL: www.wrestling.ca
Tamara Medwidsky, Executive Director
Doug Cox, President
Clint Kingsbury, Manager, Domestic Development
Dave Mair, Manager, High Performance
Dave McKay, National Coach, Senior Men
Leigh Vierling, National Coach, Senior Women

Canadian Amputee Sports Association (CASA) / Association canadienne des sports pour amputés
1399 Weslemkoon Lake Rd., Gilmour ON K0L 1W0
Tel: 613-474-1397
e-mail: bobfox1@hotmail.com
URL: www.canadianamputeesports.ca
Affiliation(s): Canadian Paralympic Committee; Hockey Canada
Robert Fox, President

Canadian Aquafitness Leaders Alliance Inc. (CALA)
125 Lilian Dr., Toronto ON M1R 3W6
Tel: 416-751-9823; *Fax:* 416-755-1832
Toll-Free: 888-751-9823
e-mail: cala@interlog.com
URL: www.calainc.org
Affiliation(s): CanFitPro; BCRPA; Ontario Fitness Council; Go50 (UK); AGEconcern (UK); LEAD (Ger.); Univ. of Stellenbosch (SA); H2Oz (Aus.)
Charlene Kopansky, President

Canadian Association for Disabled Skiing (CADS) / Association canadienne pour les skieurs handicapés (ACSH)
91 Nelson St., Barrie ON L4M 4K4
Tel: 705-725-4845; *Fax:* 705-725-4804
e-mail: michelle.bavington@sympatico.ca
URL: www.disabledskiing.ca
David O'Brien, Executive Director
Al Matile, President
Helen Grimm, Secretary
Jeff Laidlaw, Treasurer

Canadian Association for Disabled Skiing - Alberta (CADS - Alberta)
11759 Groat Rd., Edmonton AB T5M 3K6
Tel: 780-427-8104; *Fax:* 780-427-0524
e-mail: info@cadsalberta.ca
URL: www.cadsalberta.ca
Peter Quaiattini, President
Allyson Szafranski, Executive Coordinator

Canadian Association for Disabled Skiing - Newfoundland & Labrador Division
6 Albany Pl., St. John's NL A1E 1Y2
Tel: 709-753-3625; *Fax:* 709-777-4884
e-mail: margaret.tibbo@easternhealth.ca
Marg Tibbo, Secretary

Canadian Association for Disabled Skiing Nova Scotia
c/o Alpine Ski Nova Scotia, 5516 Spring Garden Rd., Halifax NS B3J 1G6
Tel: 902-425-5450; *Fax:* 902-425-5606
e-mail: alpinens@sportnovascotia.ca
Lorraine Burch

Canadian Association of Nordic Ski Instructors (CANSI)
Secrétariat, CANSI National Office, 8 Douglas Rd., Chelsea QC J9B 1K4
Tel: 819-360-6700; *Fax:* 819-827-1800
e-mail: office@cansi.ca; membership@cansi.ca; communications@cansi.ca
URL: www.cansi.ca
Paul Graner, President
Keith Payne, First Vice-President
Henry Madsen, Secretary-Treasurer

Canadian Association of Snowboard Instructors (CASI) / Association canadienne des moniteurs de surf des neiges (ACMS)
#220, 4900, Jean-Talon ouest, Montréal QC H4P 1W9
Tel: 514-748-2648; *Fax:* 514-748-2476
Toll-Free: 800-811-6428
e-mail: national@casi-acms.com
URL: www.casi-acms.com
Affiliation(s): Canadian Ski Instructors Alliance; Canadian Snowboard Federation
Dan Genge, Executive Director

Canadian Ball Hockey Association / Association canadienne de hockey-balle
#5, 56 Pennsylvania Ave, Concord ON L4K 3V9
Tel: 905-832-6200; *Fax:* 905-856-1331
e-mail: info@cbha.com
URL: www.cbha.com
Social Media: www.facebook.com/group.php?gid=20107004444
Domenic de Gironimo, President

Canadian Blind Sports Association Inc. / Association canadienne des sports pour aveugles inc.
#325, 5055 Joyce St., Vancouver BC V5R 6B2
Tel: 604-419-0480; *Fax:* 604-419-0481
Toll-Free: 866-604-0480
e-mail: jane@canadianblindsports.ca
URL: www.canadianblindsports.ca
Affiliation(s): International Blind Sports Association; Canadian Paralympic Committee; Active Living Alliance
Jane D. Blaine, Executive Director

Canadian Broomball Federation / Fédération canadienne de ballon sur glace
#302, 200 Main St., Winnipeg MB R3C 4M2
Tel: 204-925-5656; *Fax:* 204-925-5703
e-mail: cbfbroomball@shaw.ca
URL: www.broomball.ca

Canadian Centre for Ethics in Sport (CCES) / Centre canadien pour l'éthique dans le sport
#350, 955 Green Valley Cr., Ottawa ON K2C 3V4
Tel: 613-521-3340; *Fax:* 613-521-3134
e-mail: info@cces.ca
URL: www.cces.ca
Affiliation(s): True Sport Foundation
Roger Jackson, Chair
Paul Melia, CEO

Canadian Cerebral Palsy Sports Association (CCPSA) / Association canadienne de sport pour paralytiques cérébraux (ACPSA)
PO Box 41009, 1910 St. Laurent Blvd., Ottawa ON K1G 5K9
Tel: 613-748-1430; *Fax:* 613-748-1355
Toll-Free: 866-247-9934
e-mail: ccpsa@bellnet.ca
URL: www.ccpsa.ca
Affiliation(s): Canadian Paralympic Committee; Cerebral Palsy International Sport & Recreation Association
Sandy Hermiston, President

Canadian Colleges Athletic Association / Association canadienne du sport collégial
c/o St. Lawrence College, 2 Belmont St., Cornwall ON K6H 4Z1
Tel: 613-937-1508; *Fax:* 613-937-1530
e-mail: sandra@ccaa.ca
URL: www.ccaa.ca
Affiliation(s): Atlantic Colleges Athletic Association; Fédération québécoise du sport étudiant; Ontario Colleges Athletic Association; Alberta Colleges Athletic Conference; British Columbia Colleges Athletic Association
Sandra Murray-MacDonell, Executive Director

Canadian Curling Association (CCA) / Association canadienne de curling
1660 Vimont Ct., Cumberland ON K4A 4J4
Tel: 613-834-2076; *Fax:* 613-834-0716
Toll-Free: 800-550-2875
e-mail: cca@curling.ca
URL: www.curling.ca
Affiliation(s): World Curling Federation
Greg Stremlaw, CEO

Canadian Cycling Association (CCA) / Association cycliste canadienne
#203, 2197 Riverside Dr., Ottawa ON K1H 7X3
Tel: 613-248-1353; *Fax:* 613-248-9311
e-mail: general@canadian-cycling.com
URL: www.canadian-cycling.com/
Lorraine Lafrenière, CEO

Canadian Deaf Ice Hockey Federation (CDIHF)
c/o C. Cooper, #137, 201 Queen Victoria Dr., Hamilton ON L8W 1W7
e-mail: cdihf@rogers.com
URL: www.cdihf.deafhockey.com
Social Media: www.facebook.com/group.php?gid=152070790142
Affiliation(s): Canadian Hockey Association; Ontario Deaf Sports Association, Inc.; Canadian Deaf Sports Association
Danny Daniels, President
Eugene Franciosi, Vice-President
Brenda Stanley, Secretary
Raymond Patterson, Treasurer

Canadian Deaf Sports Association (CDSA) / Association des sports des sourds du Canada (ASSC)
#202A, 10217 boul Pie IX, Montréal-Nord QC H1H 3Z5
Tel: 514-321-4520; *Fax:* 514-321-2937
Toll-Free: 800-855-0511
e-mail: office@assc-cdsa.com
URL: www.assc-cdsa.com
Affiliation(s): International Committee of Sports for the Deaf
Kimberley D. Rizzi, Executive Director
Bradford Bentley, External Relations Director
Greg Desrosiers, President

Canadian Fencing Federation (CFF) / Fédération canadienne d'escrime
10 Masterson Dr., St. Catharines ON L2T 3P1
Tel: 647-476-2401; *Fax:* 647-476-2402
e-mail: cff@fencing.ca
URL: www.fencing.ca
Affiliation(s): Fédération internationale d'escrime
Stephen Symons, President
Ron Dewar, Vice-President

Canadian Football League (CFL) / Ligue canadienne de football (LCF)
50 Wellington St. East, 3rd Fl., Toronto ON M5E 1C8
Tel: 416-322-9650; *Fax:* 416-322-9651
e-mail: info@cfl.ca
URL: www.cfl.ca
Social Media: www.facebook.com/CFL
Brent Scrimshaw, Chief Marketing Officer
Michael Copeland, Chief Operating Officer
Mark Cohon, Commissioner
Alexis Redmond, Director, Communications

Canadian Freestyle Ski Association / Association canadienne de ski acrobatique
808 Pacific St., Vancouver BC V6Z 1C2
Tel: 604-714-2233; *Fax:* 604-714-2232
e-mail: info@freestyleski.com
URL: www.freestyleski.ca
Affiliation(s): Canadian Ski & Snowboard Association
Peter Judge, CEO

Canadian Golf Industry Association / Association canadienne de l'industrie du golf
7 Aspendale Dr., Toronto ON M1P 4J5
Tel: 416-289-1305; *Fax:* 416-289-1412
e-mail: cgiacgi@bellnet.ca
Chuck Fitzpatrick, Executive Director

Canadian Golf Superintendents Association (CGSA) / Association canadienne des surintendants de golf
#205, 5520 Explorer Dr., Mississauga ON L4W 5L1
Tel: 905-602-8873; *Fax:* 905-602-1958
Toll-Free: 800-387-1056
e-mail: cgsa@golfsupers.com
URL: www.golfsupers.com
Kenneth S. Cousineau, CAE, Executive Director
Bob Burrows, President
Patrick Moir, Vice-President
Greg Holden, Secretary-Treasurer

Canadian Handball Association (CHA) / Fédération de balle au mur du Canada
30 Melwood Ave., Halifax NS B3N 1E3
Tel: 902-477-2902; *Fax:* 902-431-3145
e-mail: handball@cdnhandball.ca
URL: www.cdnhandball.ca
Brian Goto, President
Mike Wilson, Treasurer

Canadian Jiu-jitsu Association Inc. / Association canadienne du jiu-jitsu inc.
c/o Pro Spar Martial Arts Centre, #10, 4 Alliance Blvd., Barrie ON L4M 5J1
Tel: 705-725-9186
Toll-Free: 800-352-1338
e-mail: info@canadianjiujitsu.com
URL: www.canadianjiujitsu.com
Affiliation(s): World Council of Jiu-Jitsu Organizations
Gary Pilon, Vice-President/Treas.
Terry Yanke, President

Canadian Kendo Federation (CKF) / Fédération canadienne de kendo
8013 Hunter St., Burnaby BC V5A 2B8
Tel: 604-420-0438; *Fax:* 604-420-1971
e-mail: hokusa@kendo-canada.com
URL: www.kendo-canada.com
Hiro Okusa, President
Yoshiaki Taguchi, Vice-President
Christian d'Orangeville, 2nd Vice-President
Kim Taylor, Secretary
John Maisonneuve, Treasurer

Canadian Lacrosse Association (CLA) / Association canadienne de crosse (ACC)
#B4, 2211 Riverside Dr., Ottawa ON K1H 7X5
Tel: 613-260-2028; *Fax:* 613-260-2029
e-mail: info@lacrosse.ca
URL: www.lacrosse.ca
Social Media: www.twitter.com/LacrosseCanada
Affiliation(s): International Lacrosse Federation; International Federation of Women's Lacrosse Associations; Fédération internationale d'Inter-crosse; Canadian Lacrosse Foundation; Sport Canada; Coaching Association of Canada
David Miriguay, CLA General Manager

Canadian Luge Association / Association canadienne de luge
88 Canada Olympic Rd. SW, Calgary AB T3B 5R5
Tel: 403-202-6581; *Fax:* 403-247-8820
e-mail: tfarstad@coda.ca
URL: www.luge.ca
Tim Farstad, Executive Director

Canadian Masters Athletic Association (CMAA)
426 Valermo Dr., Toronto ON M8W 2L9
Tel: 416-252-7047
e-mail: masters@sympatico.ca
URL: www.canadianmastersathletics.com
Brian Keaveney, President
Joan Christiensen, Membership

Canadian Masters Cross-Country Ski Association (CMCSA) / Association canadienne des maîtres en ski de fond
2 MacNeil Crescent, Stephenville NL A2N 3E3
Tel: 709-643-3259
e-mail: bruce.legrow@nf.sympatico.ca
URL: www.canadian-masters-xc-ski.ca/en_index.htm
Affiliation(s): World Masters Cross-Country Ski Association; Cross-Country Canada
Bruce Legrow, National Director

Canadian Modern Pentathlon Association (CAMPA) / Association canadienne du pentathlon moderne
70 Como Gardens, Hudson QC J0P 1H0
Tel: 450-458-7974; *Fax:* 450-458-1746
e-mail: president@pentathloncanada.ca
URL: www.pentathloncanada.ca
Affiliation(s): Union internationale de pentathlon moderne et biathlon
Angela Ives, President

Canadian Olympic Committee
#900, 21 St. Clair Ave. East, Toronto ON M4T 1L9
Tel: 416-962-0262; *Fax:* 416-967-4902
URL: www.olympic.ca

Canadian Olympic Committee (COC) / Comité olympique canadien
#900, 21 St Clair Ave. East, Toronto ON M4T 1L9
Tel: 416-962-0262; *Fax:* 416-967-4902
URL: www.olympic.ca
Chris Rudge, CEO

Canadian Olympic Committee
85 Albert St. 14th Fl., Ottawa ON K1P 6A4
Tel: 613-244-2020; *Fax:* 613-244-0169

Canadian Olympic Committee
#300, 2070, rue Peel, Montréal QC H3A 1W6
Tel: 514-861-3371; *Fax:* 514-861-2896
URL: www.olympic.ca

Canadian Paralympic Committee (CPC) / Comité paralympique canadien
#1401, 85 Albert St., Ottawa ON K1P 6A4
Tel: 613-569-4333; *Fax:* 613-569-2777
e-mail: reachus@paralympic.ca
URL: www.paralympic.ca
Affiliation(s): International Paralympic Committee
Brian MacPherson, Director General
Manali Haridas, Coordinator, Office and Leadership

Canadian Polo Association (CPA)
#301, 250 Consumers Rd., Toronto ON M2J 4V6
Tel: 416-494-0724; *Fax:* 416-495-8723
Toll-Free: 888-494-0724
e-mail: info@polocanada.ca
URL: www.polocanada.ca
Affiliation(s): Canadian Amateur Athletic Association (RCAAA); Federation of International Polo (FIP); Equine Canada; Ontario Equestrian Federation (OEF); International Olympic Committee (IOC)
Justin R. Fogarty, President
Don. B. Pennycook, Vice-President
Wayne Venhuizen, Secretary
Dave Offen, Treasurer

Canadian Pony Club (CPC)
PO Box 127, Baldur MB R0K 0B0
Tel: 204-535-2368; *Fax:* 204-535-2289
Toll-Free: 888-286-7669
e-mail: info@canadianponyclub.org
URL: www.canadianponyclub.org
Affiliation(s): Ontario Equestrian Federation
Karol Shipley, National Chair
Val Crowe, Administrator

Canadian Powerlifting Organization (CPO)
PO Box 51180 RPO Beddington, Calgary AB T3K EV9
Fax: 403-698-2434
e-mail: powerlifting@gmail.com; info@wpc-canada.com
URL: www.worldpowerlifting.com/cpo

Canadian Powerlifting Union (CPU)
#17, 1063 Coteau St. W, Moose Jaw SK S6H 5G3
Tel: 306-694-6116; *Fax:* 306-693-3301
e-mail: jbutt@sasktel.net
URL: www.powerlifting.ca
Affiliation(s): International Powerlifting Federation
Jeff Butt, President

Canadian Professional Golfers' Association (CPGA) / Association canadienne des golfeurs professionnels
13450 Dublin Line, RR#1, Acton ON L7J 2W7
Tel: 519-853-5450; *Fax:* 519-853-5449
Toll-Free: 800-782-5764
e-mail: cpga@cpga.com
URL: www.cpga.com
Gary Bernard, Interim Executive Director

Canadian Racquetball Association (CRA) / Association canadienne de racquetball
25 Golflinks Dr., Ottawa ON K2J 4Y1
Tel: 613-692-5394
e-mail: emlane@rogers.com
URL: www.racquetball.ca
Affiliation(s): Canadian Sport Council; Canadian Olympic Association; Coaching Association of Canada
Usher Barnoff, President

Canadian Rhythmic Sportive Gymnastic Federation (CRSGF) / Fédération canadienne de gymnastique rythmique sportive
c/o 2288 Covington Place, Victoria BC V8N 5N6
Tel: 250-472-3322; *Fax:* 250-472-2659
e-mail: dfrattaroli@shaw.ca
Danielle Frattaroli, GCG-RG Program Coordinator

Canadian Ski Coaches Federation (CSCF) / Fédération des entraîneurs de ski du Canada
#220, 4900 Jean Talon ouest, Montréal QC H4P 1W9
Tel: 514-748-2648; *Fax:* 514-748-2476
Toll-Free: 800-811-6428
e-mail: national@snowpro.com
URL: www.snowpro.com/csia/e
Michel Lamothe, Chief Executive Officer

Canadian Ski Council (CSC) / Conseil canadien du ski
21 Fourth St. East, Collingwood ON L9Y 1T2
Tel: 705-445-9140; *Fax:* 705-445-0525
e-mail: info@skicanada.org
URL: www.skicanada.org
Affiliation(s): Canadian Association for Disabled Skiing; Canadian Association of Nordic Ski Instructors; Canadian Ski Area Operators' Association; Canadian Ski Association; Canadian Ski Instructors' Alliance; Canadian Ski Coaches Federation; Canadian Ski Patrol System; Canadian Association of Snowboard Instructors; National Snow Industries Association
Colin S. Chedore, President

Canadian Ski Instructors' Alliance (CSIA) / Alliance des moniteurs de ski du Canada
#220, 4900, Jean Talon ouest, Montréal QC H4P 1W9
Tel: 514-748-2648; *Fax:* 514-748-2476
Toll-Free: 800-811-6428
e-mail: national@snowpro.com
URL: www.snowpro.com/csia/e
Affiliation(s): International Ski Instructors Association
Martin Jean, National Program Director
Michel Lamothe, CEO

Canadian Ski Marathon (CSM) / Marathon canadien de ski
#200, 81 Jean-Prolux, Gatineau QC J8Z 1W2
Tel: 819-770-6556; *Fax:* 819-770-7428
Toll-Free: 877-770-6556
e-mail: ski@csm-mcs.com
URL: www.csm-mcs.com
Affiliation(s): Tourisme Outaouais; Tourisme Laurentides
Gregory Koegl, President

Canadian Ski Patrol System (CSPS) / Patrouille canadienne de ski (OPCS)
4531 Southclark Pl., Ottawa ON K1T 3V2
Tel: 613-822-2245; *Fax:* 613-822-1088
Toll-Free: 900-565-2777
e-mail: info@skipatrol.ca
URL: www.csps.ca
John Leu, Executive Director
Brian Low, Chair
Bill Powell, Corporate Secretary

Canadian Snowsports Association (CSA) / L'Association canadienne des sports d'hiver (ACSH)
#202, 1451 West Broadway, Vancouver BC V6H 1H6
Tel: 604-734-6800; *Fax:* 604-669-7954
e-mail: lillianalderton@hotmail.com
URL: www.canadaskiandsnowboard.net
Chris Robinson, President
David Pym, Managing Director

Canadian Soccer Association (CSA) / Association canadienne de soccer
237 Metcalfe St., Ottawa ON K2P 1R2
Tel: 613-237-7678; *Fax:* 613-237-1516
e-mail: info@soccercan.ca
URL: www.canadasoccer.com
Affiliation(s); Féderation Internationale de Football Association, FIFA; Football Confederation; Canadian Olympic Association
Dominic Maestracci, President
Richard Scott, Director, Communications

Canadian Society for Exercise Physiology (CSEP) / Société canadienne de physiologie de l'exercice (SCPE)
#202, 185 Somerset St. West, Ottawa ON K2P 0J2
Tel: 613-234-3755; *Fax:* 613-234-3565
Toll-Free: 877-651-3755
e-mail: info@csep.ca
URL: www.csep.ca
Affiliation(s): Active Living Coalition for Older Adults; Canadian Federation of Biological Societies; Canadian Fitness & Lifestyle Research Institute; Canadian Association of Cardiac Rehabilitation; American College of Sports Medicine; Public Health Agency of Canada - Physical Activity Unit; Canadian Ethnocultural Council; Active Living Alliance for Canadians with a Disability; Coalition for Active Living
Phillip Gardiner, Executive Director
Mary Duggan, Manager, Administration
Brian MacIntosh, President
Panagiota Klentrou, Treasurer

Canadian Society for Psychomotor Learning & Sport Psychology (CSPLSP) / Société canadienne d'apprentissage psychomoteur et de psychologie du sport (SCAPPS)
c/o College of Kinesiology, University of Saskatchewan, Saskatoon SK S7N 5B2
e-mail: webmaster@scapps.org
URL: www.scapps.org
Affiliation(s): International Society of Sport Psychology
Lybbert Larry, President
Gordon Binstead, Sec.-Treas.

Canadian Sport Horse Association (CSHA)
PO Box 970, 7904 Franktown Rd., Richmond ON K0A 2Z0
Tel: 613-686-6161; *Fax:* 613-686-6170
e-mail: csha@canadian-sport-horse.org
URL: www.canadian-sport-horse.org
Paul Morgan, President
David Lancaster, Treasuerer

Canadian Team Handball Federation (CTHF) / Fédération canadienne de handball olympique (FCHO)
453, rue Jacob-Nicol, Sherbrooke QC J1J 4E5
Tel: 819-563-7937; *Fax:* 819-563-5352
e-mail: f.lebeau@videotron.ca
URL: www.handballcanada.ca
Affiliation(s): International Handball Federation; Pan American Team Handball Federation; Commonwealth Handball Federation
François LeBeau, COO
Ward Hrabi, President

Canadian Tenpin Federation, Inc. (CTF) / Fédération canadienne des dix-quilles, inc.
916 3 Ave. N., Lethbridge AB T1H 0H3
Tel: 403-381-2830; *Fax:* 403-381-6247
URL: www.gotenpinbowling.ca
Affiliation(s): Fédération internationale des quilleurs
Stan May, Executive Director

Canadian Therapeutic Riding Association / Association canadienne d'équitation thérapeutique
#11, 5420 Hwy. 6 North, RR#5, Guelph ON N1H 6J2
Tel: 519-767-0700; *Fax:* 519-767-0435
e-mail: ctra@golden.net
URL: www.cantra.ca
Lisa Burd, President
Donna Naylor, Executive Director

Canadian University Football Coaches Association (CUFCA)
c/o Huskies Football, St. Mary's University, Halifax NS B3H 3C3
Tel: 902-420-5550
Affiliation(s): Canadian Interuniversity Athletic Union
Blake Nill, President

Canadian Wheelchair Basketball Association (CWBA) / Association canadienne de basketball en fauteuil roulant (ACBFR)
#B2, 2211 Riverside Dr., Ottawa ON K1H 7X5
Tel: 613-260-1296; *Fax:* 613-260-1456
Toll-Free: 877-843-2922
e-mail: info@wheelchairbasketball.ca
URL: www.wheelchairbasketball.ca
Affiliation(s): Canada Basketball
Wendy Gittens, Executive Director
Steven Bach, President

Canadian Wheelchair Sports Association (CWSA) / Association canadienne des sports en fauteuil roulant (ACSFR)
#108, 2255 St. Laurent Blvd., Ottawa ON K1G 4K3
Tel: 613-523-0004; *Fax:* 613-523-0149
e-mail: info@cwsa.ca
URL: www.cwsa.ca
Affiliation(s): International Stoke Mandeville Wheelchair Sports Federation
Cathy Cadieux, Executive Director
Donald Royer, President

Cape Breton County Minor Hockey Association (CBCMHA)
PO Box 6003, 95 Keltic Dr., Coxheath NS B1S 3V9
Tel: 902-562-1767; *Fax:* 902-562-1833
e-mail: info@cbchma.org
URL: www.cbcmha.ca

Centre de plein air du Mont Chalco
CP 55, Chibougamau QC G8P 2K5
Tél: 418-748-7162
Serge Boutin, Directeur des opérations

Cerebral Palsy Sports Association of British Columbia (CPSABC)
6235A - 136th St., Surrey BC V3X 1H3
Tel: 604-599-5240; *Fax:* 604-599-5241
Toll-Free: 877-711-3111
e-mail: sportinfo@telus.net
URL: www.cpsports.com
Affiliation(s): Sport BC
Terri Moore, Executive Director

Charlottetown Minor Baseball Association
c/o 42 Trafalgar St., Charlottetown PE C1A 3Z1
Tel: 902-628-4028
e-mail: daleclair@pei.eastlink.ca
David LeClair, President

City of Edmonton Combative Sports Commission
PO Box 82079, Stn. Yellowbird, Edmonton AB T6J 7E6
Tel: 780-915-3239
e-mail: ozmyndak@telusplanet.net
Affiliation(s): Association of Boxing Commissions
Orest Zmyndak, Executive Director

Club 'Les Pongistes d'Ungava'
109, rue Obalski, Chibougamau QC G8P 2E8
Tél: 418-748-4903
Lynn Labbé

Club d'auto-neige Chibougamau inc.
CP 43, Chibougamau QC G8P 2K5
Tél: 418-748-3065
Mario Simard

Club de boxe Chibougamau
224, rue Mgr Houe, Chibougamau QC G8P 2Y5
Tél: 418-748-2592
David Pelletier, Président

Club de football Troilus de Chibougamau-Chapais
CP 622, Chibougamau QC G8P 2Y8
Tél: 418-748-3554
URL: footballchibougamau.com
Serge Bouchard, Président

Club de golf de Chibougamau inc.
CP 81, Chibougamau QC G8P 2K5
Tél: 418-748-3249
Richard Simard

Club de karaté Shotokan
417, rue Demers, Chibougamau QC G8P 1E8
Tél: 418-748-3639
France Bélanger, Présidente

Club de nage synchronisée Synchrogamau de Chibougamau
CP 181, Chibougamau QC G8P 2K6
Tél: 418-748-3198
Maureen Tanguay

Club de natation Natchib inc.
CP 213, Chibougamau QC G8P 2K7
Tél: 418-748-3214
Denise Caron

Club de patinage artistique Les lames givrées inc.
CP 453, Chibougamau QC G8P 2X9
Tél: 418-748-2339
Joline Bélanger

Club nautique de Chibougamau inc.
CP 395, Chibougamau QC G8P 2X8
Tél: 418-748-6628
Marcel Steinmetzer

Club Vélogamik
CP 594, Chibougamau QC G8P 2Y8
Tél: 418-748-6406
Fabien Laprise, Président

Coaches Association of British Columbia (CABC)
#200, 3820 Cessna Drive, Richmond BC V7B 0A2
Tel: 604-333-3600; *Fax:* 604-333-3450
e-mail: info@coaches.bc.ca
URL: www.coaches.bc.ca
Gordon May, CAE, Executive Director

Coaches Association of PEI (CAPEI)
PO Box 302, Charlottetown PE C1A 7K7
Tel: 902-569-0583; *Fax:* 902-368-4548
Toll-Free: 800-247-6712
e-mail: cgcrozier@sportpei.pe.ca
URL: www.coachespei.ca
Cheryl G. Crozier, Executive Director

Coaching Association of Canada (CAC) / Association canadienne des entraîneurs
#300, 141 Laurier Ave. West, Ottawa ON K1P 5J3
Tel: 613-235-5000; *Fax:* 613-235-9500
e-mail: coach@coach.ca
URL: www.coach.ca
Affiliation(s): Professional Arm: Canadian Professional Coaches Association
John Bales, CEO
Gaëtan Robitaille, COO

Commission de Ski pour Personnes Handicapées du Québec (CSPHQ)
165 Place Lilas, Pincourt QC J7V 5B6
Tél: 514-425-8894; *Téléc:* 514-425-8894
Courriel: hwohler@yahoo.com
Henry Wohler, President

The Commonwealth Games Association of Canada Inc. (CGAC) / Association canadienne des jeux du Commonwealth inc.
#120, 2255 St. Laurent Blvd., Ottawa ON K1G 4K3
Tel: 613-244-6868; *Fax:* 613-244-6826
e-mail: info@commonwealthgames.ca
URL: www.commonwealthgames.ca
Affiliation(s): Commonwealth Games Federation - London, England
Kelly Laframboise, Administrative Coordinator
Thomas Jones, CEO

Cricket Canada
Sport Alliance Centre, #306, 1185 Eglinton Ave. East, Toronto ON M3C 3C3
Tel: 416-426-7209
e-mail: canada@cricamericas.com
URL: www.canadiancricket.org
Affiliation(s): International Cricket Council; Kanga Ball Canada
Banwarilal (Ben) Sennik, President
Calvin Clarke, General Secretary

Cross Country Canada (CCC) / Ski de fond Canada (SFC)
c/o Bill Warren Training Centre, #100, 1995 Olympic Way, Canmore AB T1W 2T6
Tel: 403-678-6791; *Fax:* 403-678-3644
Toll-Free: 877-609-3215
e-mail: info@cccski.com
URL: www.cccski.com
Affiliation(s): Canadian Ski & Snowboard Association
Jim McCarthy, President
Davin MacIntosh, Executive Director
Cathy Sturgeon, Director, Administration & Communication

Curl BC
#320, 1367 West Broadway, Vancouver BC V6H 4A9
Tel: 604-737-3040; *Fax:* 604-737-1476
Toll-Free: 800-667-2875
e-mail: curling@curlbc.ca
URL: www.curlbc.ca
Scott Braley, Executive Director & CEO
Terry Vandale, President

Curling Chibougamau
733, boul Campbell, Chibougamau QC G8P 1L2
Tél: 418-748-2671
Serge Boutin, Directeur

Curling Québec
CP 1000, Succ. M, 4545, av Pierre-de Coubertin, Montréal QC H1V 3R2
Tél: 514-252-3088; *Téléc:* 514-252-3342
Ligne sans frais: 888-292-2875
Courriel: info@curling-quebec.qc.ca
URL: www.curling-quebec.qc.ca
Marco Berthelot, Directeur général

Cycling Association of the Yukon
4061, 4th Avenue, Whitehorse YT Y1A 1H1
Tel: 867-668-4990; *Fax:* 867-668-8212
e-mail: sue.richards@gov.yk.ca
Sue Richards, President

Cycling British Columbia (CBC)
#201, 210 West Broadway, Vancouver BC V5Y 3W2
Tel: 604-737-3034; *Fax:* 604-737-3141
e-mail: assist@cycling.bc.ca
URL: www.cycling.bc.ca
Ryan Keith, Chief Executive Officer

Cycling PEI (CPEI)
Sport PEI, PO Box 302, 40 Enman Cresent, Charlottetown PE C1A 7K7
Tel: 902-368-4985; *Fax:* 902-368-4548
e-mail: mconnolly@sportpei.pe.ca
URL: www.cpei.ca
Mike Connolly, Executive Director

Disabled Skiers Association of BC (DSABC)
#220, 3820 Cessna Dr., Richmond BC V7B 0A2
Tel: 604-333-3630; *Fax:* 604-333-3450
e-mail: disabledskiers@telus.net
URL: www.disabledskiingbc.com
Brian Forrester, Executive Director
Kevin ter Kuile, President

Distance Riders of Manitoba (DRM)
PO Box 36, RR#2, Dugald MB R0E 0K0
Tel: 204-444-2314
e-mail: maura.leahy@mts.net
URL: www.kucera.mb.ca/drma/
Affiliation(s): American Endurance Ride Conference
Maura Leahy, Membership Director

Dive Ontario
#207, 1185 Eglinton Ave. East, Toronto ON M3C 3C6
Tel: 416-426-7040; *Fax:* 416-426-7367
e-mail: info@diveontario.com
URL: www.diveontario.com
Bev Lauder, Executive Director

Diving Plongeon Canada (DPC) / Association canadienne du plongeon amateur Inc.
#703, 2197 Riverside Dr., Ottawa ON K1H 7X3
Tel: 613-736-5238; *Fax:* 613-736-0409
e-mail: cada@diving.ca
URL: www.diving.ca
Affiliation(s): Aquatics Federation of Canada; Swimming Natation Canada; Synchronized Swimming; Water Polo Canada
Penny Joyce, Chief Operating Officer
Mitch Geller, Chief Technical Officer
Nancy Brawley, Director, National Team
Kathy Seaman, President

Dr. James Naismith Basketball Foundation / La fondation de basketball Dr James Naismith
PO Box 1030, 14 Bridge St., Almonte ON K0A 1A0
Tel: 613-256-0492; *Fax:* 613-256-7883
e-mail: naismith@trytel.com
Affiliation(s): Basketball Canada
John Gosset, Executive Director
Allen G. Rae, President

Drive Canada
PO Box 2062, Vancouver BC V6B 3S3
Tel: 604-875-1905; *Fax:* 604-857-9582
e-mail: drivecanada@shaw.ca
URL: www.drivecanada.org
Affiliation(s): American Driving Society
Simon Rosenman, President

Edmonton Bicycle & Touring Club (EBTC)
PO Box 52017, Stn. Garneau, Edmonton AB T6G 2T5
Tel: 780-424-2453
URL: www.bikeclub.ca
Affiliation(s): Alberta Bicycle Association

Endurance Riders Association of British Columbia (ERABC)
c/o 1624 Duncan Dr., Delta BC V4L 1S2
Affiliation(s): Canadian Long Distance Riding Association
Terre O'Brennan

Endurance Riders of Alberta (ERA)
c/o President, PO Box 418, Seba Beach AB T0E 2B0
Tel: 780-797-5404
URL: www.enduranceridersofalberta.com
Affiliation(s): Canadian Long Distance Riding Association
Carol Wadey, Treasurer
Owen Fulcher, President

Equestrian Association for the Disabled
8360 Leeming Rd., RR#3, Mount Hope ON L0R 1W0
Tel: 905-679-8323; *Fax:* 905-679-1705
URL: www.tead.on.ca
Jim Sykes, Chair & President
Patrick Warner, Vice-President
Hilary Webb, Executive Director
Gord Hyland, Treasurer
Trish Brakewell, Coordinator
Pat Bullock, Instructor, Riding

Equine Canada (EC) / Canada Hippique
#100, 2685 Queensview Dr., Ottawa ON K2B 8K2
Tel: 613-248-3433; *Fax:* 613-248-3484
Toll-Free: 866-282-8395
e-mail: inquiries@equinecanada.ca
URL: www.equestrian.ca
Affiliation(s): Provincial Partners: Horse Council of B.C., Alberta Equestrian Federation, Saskatchewan Horse Federation, Manitoba Horse Council, Ontario Equestrian Federation, Fédération Équestre du Quebec, New Brunswick Equestrian Association, PEI Horse Council, Nova Scotia Equestrian Federation, Newfoundland Equestrian Association, Canadian Pony Club
Akaash Maharaj, CEO

Fédération de basketball du Québec (FBBQ) / Québec Basketball Federation
CP 1000, Succ. M, 4545, av Pierre-De Coubertin, Montréal QC H1V 3R2
Tél: 514-252-3057; *Téléc:* 514-252-3357
Ligne sans frais: 866-557-3057
Courriel: basket@basketball.qc.ca
URL: www.basketball.qc.ca
Daniel Méthot, Directeur général

Fédération de patinage artistique du Québec (FPAQ)
CP 1000, Succ. M, 4545, av Pierre-de-Coubertin, Montréal QC H1V 3R2
Tél: 514-252-3073; *Téléc:* 514-252-3170
Courriel: patinage@patinage.qc.ca
URL: www.patinage.qc.ca
Josée Beauséjour, Directeur exécutif

Fédération de Patinage de Vitesse du Québec
930, av Roland Beaudin, Sainte-Foy QC G1V 4H8
Tél: 418-651-1973; *Téléc:* 418-651-1977
Courriel: fpvq@fpvq.org
URL: www.fpvq.org
Hélène Savard, Adjointe administrative

Fédération de pétanque du Québec
CP 1000, Succ. M, 4545, av Pierre-de Coubertin, Montréal QC H1V 3R2
Tél: 514-252-3077
Courriel: petanque@loisirquebec.qc.ca
URL: www.petanque.qc.ca
Denise Coutu, Secrétaire administrative

Fédération de rugby du Québec (FRQ) / Quebec Rugby Union
CP 1000, Succ. M, 4545, av Pierre-de Coubertin, Montréal QC H1V 3R2
Tél: 514-252-3189; *Téléc:* 514-252-3159
Courriel: rugbyquebec@rugbyquebec.qc.ca
URL: www.rugbyquebec.qc.ca
Nicholas Clapinson, Directeur

Fédération de soccer du Québec
955, av Bois-de-Boulogne, Laval QC H7N 4G1
Tél: 450-975-3355; *Téléc:* 450-975-1001
Courriel: courriel@federation-soccer.qc.ca
URL: www.federation-soccer.qc.ca
Brigitte Frot, Directrice générale

Fédération de volleyball du Québec (FVBQ)
CP 1000, Succ. M, 4545, av Pierre-de Coubertin, Montréal QC H1V 3R2
Tél: 514-252-3065; *Téléc:* 514-252-3176
Courriel: info-fvbq@volleyball.qc.ca
URL: www.volleyball.qc.ca
Affiliation(s): Sports Québec; Regroupement loisirs Québec
Alain D'Amboise, Directeur général
Charles H. Cardinal, Président

Fédération du baseball amateur du Québec
CP 1000, Succ. M, 4545, av Pierre-de Coubertin, Montréal QC H1V 3R2
Tél: 514-252-3075; *Téléc:* 514-252-3134
Courriel: info@baseballquebec.qc.ca
URL: www.baseballquebec.qc.ca

Fédération du plongeon amateur du Québec (FPAQ)
CP 1000, Succ. M, 4545, av Pierre-de-Coubertin, Montréal QC H1V 3R2
Tél: 514-252-3096; *Téléc:* 514-252-3094
Courriel: fpaq@plongeon.qc.ca
URL: www.plongeon.qc.ca
Isabelle Cloutier, Directrice exécutive

Fédération équestre du Québec inc. (FEQ)
CP 1000, Succ. M, 4545, av Pierre-de Coubertin, Montréal QC H1V 3R2
Tél: 514-252-3053; *Téléc:* 514-252-3165
Courriel: infocheval@feq.qc.ca
URL: www.feq.qc.ca
Richard Mongeau, Directeur général

Fédération internationale de bobsleigh et de tobogganing
Via Piranesi, 44/B, Milan 120137 Italy
Tél: 39-02-757-3319; *Téléc:* 39-02-757-3384
Courriel: egarde@tin.it
URL: www.fibt.com
Affiliation(s): Canadian Amateur Bobsleigh & Tobogganing Association
Robert H. Storey, Président
Ermanno Gardella, Secrétaire général

Fédération Internationale de Luge de Course (FIL) / International Luge Federation
Rathausplatz 9, Berchtesgaden 83471 Germany
Tél: 49-86-526-6960; *Téléc:* 49-86-526-6969
Courriel: office@fil-luge.org
URL: www.fil-luge.org
Affiliation(s): Canadian Luge Association
Josef Fendt, Président
Svein Romstad, Secrétaire général

Federation of Broomball Associations of Ontario
515 Gascon St., Russell ON K4R 1C6
Tel: 613-445-0904; *Fax:* 613-445-9844
e-mail: gerry.wever@ontariobroomball.ca
URL: www.ontariobroomball.ca
Gerry Wever, President

Federation of Canadian Archers Inc. (FCA) / Fédération canadienne des archers inc.
#108, 2255 St. Laurent Blvd., Ottawa ON K1G 4K3
Tel: 613-260-2113; *Fax:* 613-260-2114
e-mail: information@fca.ca
URL: www.fca.ca
Kathleen Millar, Executive Director
Roger Murray, President

Fédération québécoise de ballon sur glace
CP 1000, Succ. M, 4545, av Pierre-de Coubertin, Montréal QC H1V 3R2
Tél: 514-252-3078; *Téléc:* 514-252-3051
Courriel: info@fqbg.net
URL: www.fqbg.net
Richard Mimeau, Président

Fédération québécoise de boxe olympique (FQBO)
CP 1000, Succ. M, 4545, av Pierre-de Coubertin, Montréal QC H1V 3R2
Tél: 514-252-3047; *Téléc:* 514-254-2144
Ligne sans frais: 866-241-3779
Courriel: info@fqbo.qc.ca
URL: www.fqbo.qc.ca
Kenneth Piché, Directeur général
Victoria Sullivan-Smith, Adjointe administrative

Fédération québécoise des activités subaquatiques (FQAS)
CP 1000, Succ. M, 4545, av Pierre-de Coubertin, Montréal QC H1V 3R2
Tél: 514-252-3009; *Téléc:* 514-254-1363
Ligne sans frais: 866-391-8835
Courriel: info@fqas.qc.ca
URL: www.fqas.qc.ca
Affiliation(s): Confédération mondiale des activités subaquatiques
Jean-Sébastien Naud, Directeur général

Fédération québécoise des sports cyclistes (FQSC) / Québec Cycling Sports Federation
4545, av Pierre-de-Coubertin, Montréal QC H1V 3R2
Tél: 514-252-3071; *Téléc:* 514-252-3165
Courriel: reception@fqsc.net
URL: www.fqsc.net
Affiliation(s): Association cycliste canadienne; Union cycliste internationale; Sports-Québec; Regroupement loisir Québec
Simon Thériault, Directeur technique
Louis Barbeau, Directeur général
André Michaud, Président

Fédération québécoise du sport étudiant (FQSE)
CP 1000, Succ. M, 4545, av Pierre-De Coubertin, Montréal QC H1V 3R2
Tél: 514-252-3300; *Téléc:* 514-254-3292
URL: www.fqse.qc.ca; www.sportetudiant.com
Yves Paquette, Président

Fédération sportive de ringuette du Québec
CP 1000, Succ. M, 4545, av Pierre-de-Coubertin, Montréal QC H1V 3R2
Tél: 514-252-3085; *Téléc:* 514-254-1069
Courriel: ringuette@ringuette-quebec.qc.ca
URL: www.ringuette-quebec.qc.ca
Florent Gravel, Président

Field Hockey Canada (FHC) / Hockey sur gazon Canada
#240, 1101 Prince of Wales Dr., Ottawa ON K2C 3W7
Tel: 613-521-8774; *Fax:* 613-521-0261
e-mail: fhc@fieldhockey.ca
URL: www.fieldhockey.ca
Social Media: www.facebook.com/group.php?gid=151599479507
Mary Cicinelli, President
Suzzanne Nicholson, Executive Director
Ian Clark, Administrative Coordinator

Football Canada
#100, 2255 St. Laurent Blvd., Ottawa ON K1G 4K3
Tel: 613-564-0003; *Fax:* 613-564-6309
e-mail: info@footballcanada.com
URL: footballcanada.com
Richard Munro, CEO
Bob Swan, Technical Consultant
Cara Lynch, Manager, Non-Contact Programs
Josh Sacobie, Technical Coordinator
Christine Piché, Administrative Coordinator

Football PEI
40 Enman Crescent, Charlottetown PE C1E 1E6
Tel: 902-368-4262; *Fax:* 902-368-4548
e-mail: admin@footballcanada.com
URL: www.footballpei.com
Glen Flood, Executive Director
Carl Adams, President

Golf Association of Ontario (GAO)
PO Box 970, Uxbridge ON L9P 1N3
Tel: 905-852-1101; *Fax:* 905-852-8893
Toll-Free: 800-668-2949
e-mail: administration@gao.ca
URL: www.gao.ca
Social Media: twitter.com/GAOGolf
Stephen James, President
David Mills, Executive Director

Golf Manitoba Inc.
200 Main St., Winnipeg MB R3C 4M2
Tel: 204-925-5730; *Fax:* 204-925-5731
e-mail: golfmb@golfmanitoba.mb.ca
URL: golfmanitoba.mb.ca
Dave Comaskey, Executive Director

Golf Newfoundland & Labrador (GNL)
77 Morgan Dr., Gander NL A1V 2K3
Tel: 709-722-2470; *Fax:* 709-722-8104
e-mail: golf@hnl.ca
URL: www.golfnewfoundland.ca
Greg Hillier, President

Golf Québec
#110, 415, rue Bourke, Dorval QC H9S 3W9
Tél: 514-633-1088; *Téléc:* 514-633-1074
Courriel: golfquebec@golfquebec.org
URL: www.golfquebec.org
Diane Dunlop-Hébert, President
Jean-Pierre Beaulieu, Directeur général

Gymnastics Canada Gymnastique (GCG)
#120, 1900 City Park Dr., Ottawa ON K1J 1A3
Tel: 613-748-5637; *Fax:* 613-748-5691
e-mail: info@gymcan.org
URL: www.gymcan.org
Affiliation(s): Fédération internationale de gymnastique
Jean-Paul Caron, President & CEO

Halifax County United Soccer Club
#7, 102 Chain Lake Dr., Halifax NS B3S 1A7
Tel: 902-876-8784; *Fax:* 902-446-3620
e-mail: info@hcusoccer.ca
URL: www.hcusoccer.ca
Mike Maddalena, President
Laura Yost, Administrator

Halifax Sport and Social Club (HSSC)
PO Box 8821, Halifax NS B3K 5M5
Tel: 902-431-8326
e-mail: info@halifaxsport.ca
URL: www.halifaxsport.ca
Lael Morgan, General Manager

Hockey Alberta / Hockey l'Alberta
#1, 7875 - 48 Ave., Red Deer AB T4P 2K1
Tel: 403-342-6777; *Fax:* 403-346-4277
e-mail: operations@hockeyalberta.ca
URL: www.hockey-alberta.ca
Social Media: www.facebook.com/group.php?gid=43831380491
Rob Litwinski, General Manager
Brad Robbins, Senior Manager, Operations & Member Services
Tim Leer, Senior Manager, Hockey Development

Hockey Canada
#N204, 801 King Edward Ave., Ottawa ON K1N 6N5
Tel: 613-562-5677; *Fax:* 613-562-5676
Toll-Free: 800-667-2242
e-mail: nsouliere@hockeycanada.ca
URL: www.hockeycanada.ca
Social Media: www.facebook.com/HockeyCanada
Affiliation(s): International Ice Hockey Federation
Bob Nicholson, President
Al Morris, Chairman

Hockey Manitoba
#217, 200 Main St., Winnipeg MB R3C 4M2
Tel: 204-925-5755; *Fax:* 204-925-5761
e-mail: info@hockeymanitoba.mb.ca
URL: www.hockeymanitoba.mb.ca
Affiliation(s): Hockey Canada
Peter Woods, Executive Director
Brian Franklin, President
Bernie Reichardt, Director, Hockey Development

Hockey New Brunswick (HNB) / Hockey Nouveau-Brunswick
PO Box 456, 861 Woodstock Rd., Fredericton NB E3B 4Z9
Tel: 506-453-0089; *Fax:* 506-453-0868
URL: www.hnb.ca
Brian Whitehead, Executive Director
Tom Donovan, President
Pat MacFadzen, Director, Administration

Hockey Newfoundland & Labrador (NLHA) / Association de hockey de Terre-Neuve et Labrador
PO Box 176, 13B High St., Grand Falls-Windsor NL A2A 2J4
Tel: 709-489-5512; *Fax:* 709-489-2273
e-mail: office@hockeynl.ca
URL: www.hockeynl.ca
Craig Tulk, Executive Director
Tamar Hobbs, Administrative Assistant

Hockey North
47 Pine Cres., Hay River NT X0E 0R5
Tel: 867-874-6903; *Fax:* 867-874-4603
Cheryl Carriere, Executive Director

Hockey Northwestern Ontario (HNO)
#100, 216 Red River Rd., Thunder Bay ON P7B 1A6
Tel: 807-623-1542; *Fax:* 807-623-0037
John Pucci, General Manager
Ron MacKinnon, Development Coorindator

Hockey Nova Scotia
#200, 6300 Lady Hammond Rd., Halifax NS B3K 2R6
Tel: 902-454-9400; *Fax:* 902-454-3883
URL: www.hockeynovascotia.ca
Social Media: www.facebook.com/group.php?gid=2222858784
Darren Cossar, Executive Director

Hockey Québec (FQHG)
CP 1000, Succ. M, 4545, av Pierre-de-Coubertin, Montréal QC H1V 3R2
Tél: 514-252-3079; *Téléc:* 514-252-3158
Courriel: info@hockey.qc.ca
URL: www.hockey.qc.ca
Mèdia social: www.facebook.com/group.php?gid=66611750398
Sylvain B. Lalonde, Directeur général
Claude Allain, Président

Horse Trials New Brunswick
c/o Donna Lee Cole, 7515 Rte.102, Browns Flat NB E5M 2N8
Tel: 506-468-2098
URL: www.htnb.org
Affiliation(s): Horse Trials Canada
Donna Lee Cole, President
Louise McSheffrey, Secretary

Horse Trials Nova Scotia (HTNS)
60 Rockwell Drive, Mount Uniacke NS B0N 1Z0
Tel: 902-866-3889
URL: www.htns.org
Affiliation(s): Horse Trials Canada; Nova Scotia Equestrian Federation
Kim Elliott-Foster, President

International Badminton Federation (IBF)
Stadium Badminton Kuala Lumpur, Batu 3 «, Jalan Cheras, Kuala Lumpur 56000 Malaysia
Tel: 603-9283 7155; *Fax:* 603-9284 71553
e-mail: bwf@internationalbadminton.org
URL: www.internationalbadminton.org
Kang Young Joong, President

International Curling Information Network Group (ICING)
73 Appleford Rd., Hamilton ON L9C 6B5
Tel: 905-389-7781
e-mail: psmith@icing.org
URL: www.icing.org
Peter M. Smith, Contact

International Masterathlete Federation (IMAF)
PO Box 185, Richmond Hill ON L4B 4R5
Tel: 905-473-9714; *Fax:* 905-473-9715
Toll-Free: 888-883-3315
Liz Roach, President
Iain Douglas, Vice-President

Island Horse Council (IHC)
PO Box 1887, Charlottetown PE C1A 7N5
e-mail: islandhorsecouncil@yahoo.ca
URL: www.islandhorsecouncil.ca
Affiliation(s): Equine Canada
Ken Smith, Chair
Bobbi Jo Duffy, Treasurer

Japan Karate Association of Yukon
4061, 4th Ave., Whitehorse YT Y1A 1H1
Tel: 867-334-9009
URL: www.sportyukon.com/membership/?member=80
Mike Tribes, President

Jeux Olympiques Spéciaux du Québec Inc. (JOSQ) / Québec Special Olympics
5311, de Maisonneuve ouest, Montréal QC H7A 1Z5
Tél: 514-843-8778; *Téléc:* 514-843-8223
Courriel: info@josq.qc.ca
URL: www.specialolympicsquebec.qc.ca
Pierre Langlois, Directeur général

Jockey Club of Canada / Jockey Club du Canada
PO Box 66, Stn. B, Toronto ON M9W 5K9
Tel: 416-675-7756; *Fax:* 416-675-6378
e-mail: jockeyclub@bellnet.ca
URL: www.jockeyclubcanada.com
Richard Bonnycastle, Steward
Bridget Bimm, Executive Director

Judo Canada
#212, 1725 St. Laurent, Ottawa ON K1G 3V4
Tel: 613-738-1200; *Fax:* 613-738-1299
e-mail: info@judocanada.org
URL: www.judocanada.org
Affiliation(s): International Judo Federation
Andrzej Sadej, Director General
Phil Moreau, Administrative Coordinator

Judo-Québec inc
CP 1000, Succ. M, 4545, av Pierre-de-Coubertin, Montréal QC H1V 3R2
Tél: 514-252-3040; *Téléc:* 514-254-5184
Courriel: info@judo-quebec.qc.ca
URL: www.judo-quebec.qc.ca
Affiliation(s): Fédération internationale de Judo; Union panaméricaine du Judo
Daniel De Angelis, Président
Patrick Esparbès, Directeur général
Patrick Vesin, Coordonnateur technique

Karate Ontario
#160, 2 County Ct. Blvd., Brampton ON L6W 4V1
Tel: 905-455-2170
e-mail: info@karateontario.org
URL: www.karateontario.org
Affiliation(s): World Karate Federation; Sport Alliance of Ontario; Coaches Association of Ontario
Joshua Drury, Secretary

Lawn Bowls Association of Alberta
Percy Page Centre, 11759 Groat Rd., 3rd Fl., Edmonton AB T5M 3K6
Tel: 780-427-8119; *Fax:* 780-422-2663
e-mail: lawnbowl@telusplanet.net
URL: www.bowls.ab.ca
Neil Douglas, Treasurer
Betty Mertens, Secretary

Ligue de dards Ungava
712, 6e Rue ouest, Chibougamau QC G8P 2V1
Tél: 418-748-6732
Claire Patoine

Little League Canada / Petite ligue Canada
235 Dale Ave., Ottawa ON K1G 0H6
Tel: 613-731-3301; *Fax:* 613-731-2829
e-mail: canada@littleleague.org
URL: www.littleleague.ca
Roy Bergerman, President & Chair
Marthe Dubroy, Secretary
Bruce Campbell, Treasurer

Lloydminster & District Fish & Game Association
PO Box 116, Lloydminster AB T9V 0X9
Tel: 780-875-3641
e-mail: admin@lloydfishandgame.org
URL: www.lloydfishandgame.org
Affiliation(s): Saskatchewan Wildlife Federation; Alberta Fish & Game Association
Gerry Russell, President

Lutte NB Wrestling
e-mail: gdouc5110@rogers.com
URL: www.luttenbwrestling.ca
Greg Doucette, Vice-President, Administration
Don Ryan, President

Manitoba Amateur Boxing Association
#302, 200 Main St., Winnipeg MB R3C 4M2
Tel: 204-925-5658
Rosemary Broadbent

Manitoba Amateur Broomball Association (MABA)
#305, 200 Main St., Winnipeg MB R3C 4M2
Tel: 204-925-5668; *Fax:* 204-925-5703
Toll-Free: 866-792-7666
e-mail: info@mbbroomball.com
URL: www.mbbroomball.com
Alan Park, President
Scott Marohn, Vice President

Manitoba Badminton Association
200 Main St., Winnipeg MB R3C 4M2
Tel: 204-925-5679; *Fax:* 204-925-5703
Toll-Free: 888-243-0890
e-mail: badminton@shawbiz.ca
URL: www.badminton.mb.ca
Ron Waterman, President
Connie Blamie, Executive Director

Manitoba Ball Hockey Association
200 Main St., Winnipeg MB R3C 4M2
Tel: 204-925-5602
e-mail: mbha1@hotmail.com
URL: www.manitobaballhockey.com
Social Media: www.facebook.com/group.php?gid=50027852199
Jeff Dzikowcz, President

Manitoba Baseball Association
200 Main St., Winnipeg MB R3C 4M2
Tel: 204-925-5763; *Fax:* 204-925-5928
e-mail: info.baseball@sport.mb.ca
URL: www.baseballmanitoba.ca
Morgan de Pe¤a, Executive Director

Manitoba Blind Sport Association
#311, 200 Main St., Winnipeg MB R3C 4M2
Tel: 204-925-5694; *Fax:* 204-925-5703
e-mail: blindsport@shawbiz.ca
URL: www.blindsport.mb.ca
Cathy Drewianchuk, Executive Director

Manitoba Boxing Commission
#420, 213 Notre Dame Ave., Winnipeg MB R3B 1N3
Tel: 204-945-8954; *Fax:* 204-945-1675
e-mail: mansport@sport.mb.ca
Henry Janzen, Chair
Dan Vandal, Contact

Manitoba Curling Association (MCA)
#208, 200 Main St., Winnipeg MB R3C 4M2
Tel: 204-925-5723; *Fax:* 204-925-5720
Toll-Free: 800-706-1486
e-mail: mca@curlmanitoba.org
URL: www.curlmanitoba.org
Affiliation(s): Canadian Curling Association
Ian Staniloff, Executive Director
Kyla Denisuik, Event/Media Coordinator
Dale Brooks, President

Manitoba Diving Association
Sport Manitoba Building, 200 Main St., Winnipeg MB R3C 1A8
Tel: 204-925-5654; *Fax:* 204-925-5703
e-mail: headcoach@panamdiving.com
URL: www.manitobadiving.com
Jim Lambie, Head Coach

Manitoba Five Pin Bowling Federation, Inc.
#219, 200 Main Street, Winnipeg MB R3C 4M2
Tel: 204-925-5766; *Fax:* 204-925-5767
Toll-Free: 800-282-8069
URL: www.mfpbf.org
Deanne Zilinsky, Executive Director

Manitoba Freestyle Wrestling Association
200 Main St., Winnipeg MB R3C 4M2
Tel: 204-925-5670; *Fax:* 204-925-5703
e-mail: mbfreewr@mb.sympatico.ca
Nat Brigante, Executive Director/Coach

Manitoba High Schools Athletic Association (MHSAA)
#405, 200 Main St., Winnipeg MB R3C 4M2
Tel: 204-925-5640; *Fax:* 204-925-5624
e-mail: info@mhsaa.ca
URL: www.mhsaa.mb.ca
Morris Glimcher, Executive Director
Don Hurton, President

Manitoba Horse Council Inc.
#207, 200 Main St., Winnipeg MB R3C 4M2
Tel: 204-925-5718; *Fax:* 204-925-5792
e-mail: admin@manitobahorsecouncil.ca
URL: www.manitobahorsecouncil.ca
Dave Myers, President
Sheilagh Antoniuk, Executive Director

Manitoba Ringette Association (MRA) / Association de ringuette du Manitoba
Sport Manitoba, #309, 200 Main St., Winnipeg MB R3C 4M2
Tel: 204-925-5710; *Fax:* 204-925-5925
e-mail: ringette@sport.mb.ca
URL: www.manitobaringette.ca
Affiliation(s): Sport Manitoba
Cheryl Adlard, Executive Director
Melanie Perkins, Technical Director

Manitoba Soaring Council
200 Main St., Winnipeg MB R3C 4M2
Tel: 204-925-5682; *Fax:* 204-925-5703
URL: www.wgc.mb.ca/msc/Manitoba_Soaring_Council_Home_Page.htm

Manitoba Speed Skating Association
200 Main St., Winnipeg MB R3C 4M2
Tel: 204-925-5657; *Fax:* 204-925-5703
Toll-Free: 888-628-9921
e-mail: mssa@shawbiz.ca
URL: www.mbspeedskating.org
Nicolle Masken, Office Administrator

Manitoba Trail Riding Club Inc.
838 Alfred Ave., Winnipeg MB R2X 0T6
e-mail: Kelli.Hayhurst@pwgsc.gc.ca
URL: www.mbtrailridingclub.ca
Affiliation(s): Canadian Long Distance Riding Association
Kelli Hayhurst, President
Mary Anne Kirk, Treasurer

Manitoba Underwater Council (MUC)
PO Box 711, Winnipeg MB R3C 2K3
Tel: 204-632-8508
e-mail: info@manunderwater.com
URL: www.manunderwater.com

Manitoba Volleyball Association (MVA)
200 Main St., Winnipeg MB R3C 4M2
Tel: 204-925-5783; *Fax:* 204-925-5786
e-mail: mbvolley@sport.mb.ca
URL: www.manitobavolleyball.com
Affiliation(s): Volleyball Canada
Greg Jarvis, Executive Director
Leanne Leskiw, President
Pat Alexander, Vice-President & Treasurer
Colin Glass, Secretary

Minor Hockey Alliance of Ontario
71 Albert St., Stratford ON N5A 3K2
Tel: 519-273-7209; *Fax:* 519-273-2114
e-mail: alliance@alliancehockey.com
URL: www.alliancehockey.com
Tony Martindale, Executive Director

National Snow Industries Association (NSIA) / Association nationale des industries de la neige
#810, 245, av Victoria, Montréal QC H3Z 2M6
Tel: 514-939-7370; *Fax:* 514-939-7371
Toll-Free: 800-263-6742
e-mail: central.station@nsia.ca
URL: www.nsia.ca
Anna Di Meglio, President
Nicole Garand, Administration & Customer Service

National Youth Bowling Council
#10A, 250 Shields Ct., Markham ON L3R 9W7
Tel: 905-479-1560; *Fax:* 905-479-8613
e-mail: bpac@bpac.ca
URL: www.bpac.ca/YBC.html
Paul Oliveira, Executive Director

New Brunswick Ball Hockey Association (NBBHA)
16 Reflection Lane, Quispamsis NB E2E 6E7
Tel: 506-333-7772; *Fax:* 506-847-8585
e-mail: sheila@committedtoyourgoals.com
Sheila Elliott, Contact

New Brunswick Broomball Association
c/o Daniel Savoie
Tel: 506-381-0919
Daniel Savoie, Contact

New Brunswick Candlepin Bowlers Association
PO Box 4315, 11 Sawyer Rd., Woodstock NB E7M 6B7
Tel: 506-328-8418
Bill Hamilton, Contact

New Brunswick Curling Association (NBCA) / Association de Curling du Nouveau-Brunswick (ACNB)
PO Box 812, Moncton NB E1C 8N6
Tel: 506-854-9143; *Fax:* 506-388-5708
Toll-Free: 800-592-2875
e-mail: nbca@nb.sympatico.ca
URL: www.nbcurling.nb.ca
Affiliation(s): Curl Atlantic
Tradina Meadows-Forgeron, Executive Director
Jerry McCann, President
Catherine MacLean, Treasurer

New Brunswick Equestrian Association (NBEA)
c/o Sport NB, #13, 900 Hanwell Rd., Fredericton NB E3B 6A3
Tel: 506-454-2353; *Fax:* 506-454-2363
e-mail: generalinfo@equestrian.nb.ca
URL: www.equestrian.nb.ca
Jeremy Hoyt, President
Jennifer Everett, Secretary

New Brunswick Golf Association (NBGA) / Association de golf du nouveau brunswick
PO Box 1555, Stn. A, Fredericton NB E3B 1G2
Tel: 506-451-1324; *Fax:* 506-451-1348
e-mail: nbgolf@nbnet.nb.ca
URL: www.nbga.nb.ca
Pierre Arsenault, Executive Director

New Brunswick Lawn Bowling Association
929A Cloverdale Rd., Riverview NB E1B 5E6
e-mail: rkhm118@aol.com
Dugald Richford, Executive Secretary

New Brunswick Sailing Association (NBSA)
c/o Executive Director, 105 Bird Ave., Fredericton NB E2A 2H8
Tel: 506-472-2117
URL: www.nbsailing.nb.ca
Sharon Mills, Executive Director

New Brunswick Speed Skating Association
246 St. Pierre East Blvd., Caraquet NB E1E 1B1
Tel: 506-727-6334; *Fax:* 506-727-6334
e-mail: speedskates@nb.aibn.com
URL: www.homestead.com/ssnb
Chantal Brideau, Office Administrator

Newfoundland & Labrador Amateur Wrestling Association (NLAWA)
1 Wade's Ln., Flatrock NL A1K 1C3
Fax: 709-643-5103
e-mail: contact@nlawa.com
URL: www.nlawa.com
Randy Ralph, President

Newfoundland & Labrador Ball Hockey Association (NLBHA)
PO Box 2579, Stn. C, St. John's NL A1C 6K1
Tel: 709-729-0689
e-mail: paulbarron@gov.nl.ca
Paul Barron, President

Newfoundland & Labrador Basketball Association
PO Box 21029, St. John's NL A1A 5B2
Tel: 709-576-0247; *Fax:* 709-576-8787
e-mail: nlba@sportnf.com
URL: www.nlba.nf.ca
Bill Murphy, Executive Director
Roger Head, Secretary-Treasurer
Bas Kavanagh, President

Newfoundland & Labrador Curling Association
c/o Bob Osborne, 54 Hoyles Ave., St. John's NL A1B 1E3
Tel: 709-738-3640
URL: www.curlingnl.ca
Bob Osborne, President
Roy Hodder, Vice-President
Baxter House, Secretary
Carl C. Loughlin, Treasurer
Jean Blackie, Coordinator, Technical
Len Kostaszek, Coordinator, Tournament

Newfoundland & Labrador Soccer Association
PO Box 21029, St. John's NL A1A 5B2
Tel: 709-576-0601; *Fax:* 709-576-0588
e-mail: nlsa@sportnl.ca
URL: www.nlsa.ca
Doug Redmond, President
Dragan Mirkovic, Technical Director

Newfoundland & Labrador Volleyball Association (NLVA)
PO Box 21248, St. John's NL A1A 5B2
Tel: 709-576-0817; *Fax:* 709-576-7493
e-mail: nlvaruss@sportnl.ca
URL: www.nlva.net
Russell Jackson, Executive Director
Eric Hiscock, President
Mike Murrran, Elite Development Chair

Newfoundland Baseball
83 Ashford Dr., Mount Pearl NL A1N 3N7
Tel: 709-368-2819; *Fax:* 709-368-6080
e-mail: nlbaseball@nl.rogers.com
URL: www.sport.ca/nlbaseball
John Janes, President

Newfoundland Equestrian Association (NEA)
PO Box 372, Stn. C, St. John's NL A1C 5J9
URL: www.horsenewfoundland.com
Katrina Butler, President
Sheila Anstey, Vice-President & Director, Competitions
Katie Murray, Secretary
Cathy Favre, Treasurer

Newfoundland Speed Skating Association
75 Carter Ave., Corner Brook NL A2H 2P9
Tel: 709-637-8215
e-mail: vic.simmons@aliant.ca
Vic Simmons, Office Coordinator

North American Riding for the Handicapped Association (NARHA)
PO Box 33150, Denver CO 80233 USA
Tel: 303-452-1212; *Fax:* 303-252-4610
Toll-Free: 800-369-7433
e-mail: narha@narha.org
URL: www.narha.org
Carol Nickell, CEO

Northern Alberta Curling Association (NACA)
#110, 9440 - 49 St., Edmonton AB T6B 2M9
Tel: 780-440-4270; *Fax:* 780-463-4519
e-mail: naca@planet.eon.net
URL: northernalbertacurling.com
Marylynn Morris, Executive Director

Northern Ontario Curling Association
PO Box 940, Unit #4, 214 Main St. West, Atikokan ON P0T 1C0

Tel: 807-597-8730; Fax: 807-597-4241
Toll-Free: 888-597-8730
e-mail: info@curlnoca.ca
URL: www.curlnoca.ca
Leslie Kerr, Executive Director
Al Gemmell, President

Northern Ontario Hockey Association (NOHA)
108 Lakeshore Dr., North Bay ON P1A 2A8
Tel: 705-474-8851; Fax: 705-474-6019
e-mail: noha@noha.on.ca
URL: www.noha.on.ca
Affiliation(s): Ontario Hockey Federation
Chris May, Executive Director
Bryce Kulik, President

Northwest Territories 5 Pin Bowlers' Association (NWT5PBA)
PO Box 2643, Yellowknife NT X1A 2P9
Tel: 867-873-8189; Fax: 867-873-8237
e-mail: gary@nwt5pba.ca
URL: www.nwt5pba.ca
Gary Black, President

Northwest Territories Broomball Association
Stn. 529 Range Lake Road, Yellowknife NT X1A 3Y1
e-mail: nwtbroomball@yahoo.ca
URL: www.nwtbroomball.com
Jan Vallillee, President

Northwest Territories Curling Association
c/o PO Box 11089, Yellowknife NT X1A 3X7
e-mail: nwtca@auroranet.nt.ca
URL: www.curlingnwt.ssimicro.com
Jennifer Keith, Secretary

Northwest Territories Ringette / Association de ringuette des Territoires Nord-Ouest
#2, 496 Range Lake Road, Yellowknife NT X1A 3R5
Tel: 867-920-7419; Fax: 867-920-2843
e-mail: nwt_ringette@yahoo.com
Affiliation(s): Ringette Alberta
Miles Harris, President

Northwest Territories Soccer Association (NWTSA)
PO Box 11089, Yellowknife NT X1A 3X7
Tel: 867-669-8326; Fax: 867-669-8327
Toll-Free: 800-661-0797
URL: www.nwtkicks.ca
Affiliation(s): Sport North Federation
Melanie Kornacki, Sport Consultant
Ryan Fequet, President

Northwest Territories Volleyball Association (NWTVA)
Tel: 867-920-2712
e-mail: terrel_hobbs@nwtvolleyball.ca
URL: www.nwtvolleyball.ca
Terrell Hobbs, President & Regl Official Chair
Micher Haener, Vice-President
Ryan Nichols, Secretary
Kim Weir, Treasurer

Northwestern Ontario Curling Association (NWOCA)
433 Catherine St., Thunder Bay ON P7E 1K9
Tel: 807-622-8254; Fax: 807-626-9622
URL: www.norontcurl.tripod.com
Colleen Syrja, Sec.-Treas.
Don R. MacLeod, President

Northwestern Québec Curling Association (NWQCA) / Association de curling du Nord-Ouest québécois
281, 3e rue est, Amos QC J9T 2A7
Tel: 819-732-2089; Fax: 819-732-1617
Claude Noel, Secretary

Nova Scotia Badminton Association
5516 Spring Garden Road, Halifax NS B3J 1G6
Tel: 902-425-5450; Fax: 902-425-5606
e-mail: nsbadminton@sportnovascotia.ca
URL: www.nsba.ca
Jennifer Petrie, Executive Director
Linda Pride, President

Nova Scotia Ball Hockey Association
100 Auburn Drive, Dartmouth NS B2W 3S6
Tel: 902-462-5433; Fax: 902-477-0243
Affiliation(s): Canadian Ball Hockey Association; Sport Nova Scotia
Bill Davidson, Contact

Nova Scotia Boxing Authority (NSBA)
c/o Amanda Noonan, PO Box 864, 5516 Spring Garden Rd., 2nd Fl., Halifax NS B3J 2V2
Tel: 902-457-0413; Fax: 902-484-6937
e-mail: anoonan@micco.ca
Michael MacDonald, Chairman
Hubert Earle, Director, Combat Sports

Nova Scotia Broomball Association (NSBA)
c/o Rob McKellar, PO Box 3010, Stn. South, Halifax NS
Tel: 902-548-2600

Nova Scotia Curling Association (NSCA)
5516 Spring Garden Rd., 4th Fl., Halifax NS B3J 1G6
Tel: 902-421-2875; Fax: 902-425-5606
e-mail: nsca@sportnovascotia.ca
URL: www.nscurl.com
Affiliation(s): Canadian Curling Association
Jeremiah Anderson, Executive Director
Shirley Osborne, President

Nova Scotia Distance Riding Association (NSDRA)
RR#3, Site 802, Newport NS B0N 2A0
Affiliation(s): Canadian Long Distance Riding Association

Nova Scotia Equestrian Federation
5516 Spring Garden Rd., 4th Fl., Halifax NS B3J 1G6
Tel: 902-425-5450; Fax: 902-425-5606
e-mail: nsef@sportnovascotia.ca
URL: www.horsenovascotia.ca
Heather Myrer, Executive Director

Nova Scotia Golf Association (NSGA)
#4, 24 Simmonds Dr., Dartmouth NS B3B 1R3
Tel: 902-468-8844; Fax: 902-484-5327
e-mail: adminexec@ns.aliantzinc.ca
URL: www.nsga.ns.ca
David Campbell, Executive Director
Shelley Pineault, Executive Assistant

Nova Scotia Powerlifting Association
Sydney NS B1P 3W7
Tel: 902-567-0893
e-mail: president@nspowerlifting.org
URL: www.nspowerlifting.org
Cliff Samms, Vice-President
John Fraser, President

Nova Scotia Rugby Football Union
5516 Spring Garden Rd., Halifax NS B3J 1G6
Tel: 902-425-5450; Fax: 902-425-5606
e-mail: rugby@sportnovascotia.ca
URL: www.rugbyns.ns.ca
Affiliation(s): International Rugby Board
Marty Williams, CEO

Nova Scotia School Athletic Federation
PO Box 3010, Stn. South, 5516 Spring Garden Rd., Halifax NS B3J 3G6
Tel: 902-425-8662; Fax: 902-425-5606
e-mail: dweston@sportnovascotia.ca (D.Weston Secretary)
URL: nssaf.ednet.ns.ca
Tom Fahie, Executive Director
Dianne Weston, Secretary

Nova Scotia Speed Skating Association
10 Thistle Dr., North Sydney NS B2A 3R1
Tel: 902-794-8954
e-mail: laurolea@ns.sympatico.ca
Judith Brown, President

Nova Scotia Table Tennis Association (NSTTA)
9 Londra Ct., Dartmouth NS B2W 5A5
Tel: 902-406-6286
URL: www.freewebs.com/nstta
Erica Ans, President

Nova Scotia Tennis Association
5516 Spring Garden Rd., Halifax NS B3J 1G6
Tel: 902-425-5450; Fax: 902-425-5606
e-mail: tennisns@sportnovascotia.ca
URL: www.tennisnovascotia.ca
Roger Keating, Executive Director

Nunavut Speed Skating Association
PO Box 761, Iqaluit NU X0A 0H0
Tel: 867-979-1226; Fax: 867-975-3384
e-mail: jtmaurice@northwestel.net
John Maurice, Branch President

NWT Badminton Association
4407 School Draw Ave., Yellowknife NT X1A 2K2
Tel: 867-669-2606
e-mail: jimu@ssimicro.com
URL: www.nwtbadminton.yk.com
Jim Umpherson, President

NWT Speed Skating Association
PO Box 2664, Yellowknife NT X1A 2P9
e-mail: pamela@ssimicro.com
URL: www.nwtspeedskating.ca
Pam Dunbar, President

Ontario 5 Pin Bowlers' Association (O5PBA)
#302, 3 Concorde Gate, Toronto ON M3C 3N7
Tel: 416-426-7167; Fax: 416-426-7364
e-mail: o5pba@o5pba.ca
URL: www.o5pba.ca
Rhonda Gifford, Program Coordinator
Harold Stoddart, Technical Director
Al Hong, Executive Director

Ontario Amateur Wrestling Association (OAWA)
#213, 3 Concorde Gate, Toronto ON M3C 3N7
Tel: 416-426-7274; Fax: 416-426-7343
e-mail: admin@oawa.ca
URL: www.oawa.ca
Affiliation(s): International Amateur Wrestling Association; Canadian Amateur Wrestling Association
Tim MaGarrey, Provincial Director

Ontario Badminton Association (OBA)
#209, 3 Concorde Gate, Toronto ON M3C 3N7
Tel: 416-426-7192; Fax: 416-426-7346
e-mail: info@ontariobadminton.on.ca
URL: www.ontariobadminton.on.ca
Affiliation(s): Badminton Canada; Badminton World Federation
Val Butler, Executive Director

Ontario Ball Hockey Association (OBHA)
#5, 56 Pennsylvania Ave., Concord ON L4K 3V9
Tel: 905-738-3320; Fax: 905-738-3321
URL: www.ontarioballhockey.ca
Social Media: www.facebook.com/group.php?gid=2374843443
Affiliation(s): Canadian Ball Hockey Association; International Street & Ball Hockey Association; Sport Canada; Canadian Hockey Association
Mauro Cugini, Executive Director

Ontario Basketball
#311, 3 Concorde Gate, Toronto ON M3C 3N7
Tel: 416-426-7200; Fax: 416-426-7360
e-mail: info@basketball.on.ca
URL: www.basketball.on.ca
Affiliation(s): Provincial Sports Organizations Council; Canada Basketball; Toronto Raptors Basketball Club; NBA Canada; Coaches Association of Ontario; Canadian Sports Centre; and other provincial basketball organizations
Michele O'Keefe, Executive Director
Ken Urbach, President
Greg Verner, Vice President

Ontario Blind Sport Association (OBSA)
#102, 1185 Eglinton Ave. East, Toronto ON M3C 3C6
Tel: 416-426-7191; Fax: 416-426-7361
e-mail: mary@blindsports.on.ca
URL: www.blindsports.on.ca
Shirley Shelby, President

Ontario Competitive Trail Riding Association Inc. (OCTRA)
R.R.#4, Tottenham ON L0G 1W0
Tel: 905-936-3362
e-mail: webmaster@octra.on.ca
URL: www.octra.on.ca
Affiliation(s): Horse Ontario; Ontario Equestrian Federation
Mark Ford, President
Joe Mezenberg, Vice-President
Marg Murray, Secretary
Kelly Corbyn, Treasurer

Ontario Curling Association (OCA)
Office Mall 2, #2B, 1400 Bayly St., Pickering ON L1W 3R2
Tel: 905-831-1757; Fax: 905-831-1083
Toll-Free: 877-668-2875
e-mail: doug@ontcurl.com
URL: www.ontcurl.com
Affiliation(s): Curl Ontario
Doug Bakes, General Manager

Ontario Cycling Association (OCA) / Association cycliste ontarienne
#307, 3 Concorde Gate, Toronto ON M3C 3N7
Tel: 416-426-7416; Fax: 416-426-7349
e-mail: info@ontariocycling.org; ocamagazine@ontariocycling.org
URL: www.ontariocycling.org
Affiliation(s): Canadian Cycling Association
Duncan Vipond, President
Malcolm Eade, Vice-President, Administration & Finance

Glenn Meeuwisse, Vice-President, High Performance
Matthias Schmidt, Vice-President, Development
Jim Crosscombe, Executive Director
Denise Kelly, Director, Provincial Coaching
Chris Baskys, Coordinator, Membership
Nicky Pearson, Coordinator, BMX Growth & Development

Ontario Deaf Sports Association
219 Carlton St., Toronto ON M5A 2L2
Tel: 416-413-0299
e-mail: office@ontariodeafsports.on.ca
URL: www.ontariodeafsports.on.ca
Rohan Smith, President

Ontario Equestrian Federation (OEF)
#203, 9120 Leslie St., Richmond Hill ON L4B 3J9
Tel: 905-709-6545; *Fax:* 905-709-1867
Toll-Free: 877-441-7112
e-mail: horse@horse.on.ca
URL: www.horse.on.ca
Affiliation(s): Equine Guelph; Ontario Trails Council; Ontario Federation of Agriculture
Deborah Thompson, Executive Director
Gary Yaghdjian, President
Kathy Fremes, Secretary

Ontario Federation of School Athletic Associations (OFSAA) / Fédération des associations du sport scolaire de l'Ontario
#204, 3 Concorde Gate, Toronto ON M3C 3N7
Tel: 416-426-7391; *Fax:* 416-426-7317
e-mail: lindsey@ofsaa.on.ca (Newsletter)
URL: www.ofsaa.on.ca
Social Media: www.facebook.com/group.php?gid=57198022397
Martin Ritsma, President
Lynn Kelman, Vice-President
Doug Gellatly, Executive Director
Lindsey Evanoff, Coordinator, Marketing & Communications

Ontario Hockey Federation (OHF)
Sport Alliance of Ontario Bldg., #212, 3 Concorde Gate, Toronto ON M3C 3N7
Tel: 416-426-7249; *Fax:* 416-426-7347
e-mail: info@ohf.on.ca
URL: www.ohf.on.ca
Affiliation(s): Minor Hockey Alliance of Ontario; Greater Toronto Hockey League; Northern Ontario Hockey Association; Ontario Minor Hockey Association; Ontario Hockey Association; Ontario Hockey League; Ontario Women's Hockey Association
Joe Drago, Executive Director
Bill Bowman, 1st Vice-President
Frank Pindar, 2nd Vice-President
Phil McKee, Executive Director
Wayne Tod, Secretary-Treasurer
Ryan Berg, Coordinator, Hockey Development
Cheryl Boston, Coordinator, Communications, Marketing, & Events

Ontario Horse Trials Canada (OHTC)
#186, 3-304 Stone Rd. West, Guelph ON N1G 4W4
e-mail: Roseanne.Corbett@gmail.com
URL: www.horsetrials.on.ca
Robin Winn, President
Vickie Witherspoon, Secretary

Ontario Lawn Bowls Association
c/o Elaine Stevenson, 23018 Lakeridge Rd., RR#2, Sunderland ON L0C 1H0
Tel: 705-228-8058
e-mail: olba@olba.ca
URL: www.olba.ca
Arja Nesbitt, President
Elaine Houtby, Vice-President
Alan Dean, 2nd Vice-President
Bob O'Neil, Executive Director
Edith Pedden, Secretary
Richard Peart, Treasurer

Ontario Minor Hockey Association (OMHA)
#3, 25 Brodie Dr., Richmond Hill ON L4B 3K7
Tel: 905-780-6642; *Fax:* 905-780-0344
e-mail: omha@omha.net
URL: www.omha.net
Social Media: twitter.com/HometownHockey
Affiliation(s): Ontario Hockey Federation
Marg Ensoll, President
Richard Ropchan, Executive Director
Kevin Boston, Director, Marketing & Events
Ian Taylor, Director, Development
Bill Rowney, Treasurer
Mark Dickie, Manager, Communications & IT

Ontario Ringette Association (ORA) / Association de ringuette de l'Ontario
#207, 3 Concorde Gate, Toronto ON M3C 3N7
Tel: 416-426-7204; *Fax:* 416-426-7359
e-mail: info@ontario-ringette.com
URL: www.ontario-ringette.com
Ellorie Hanson, President
Mike Beaton, Executive Director

Ontario Rugby Union (ORU)
#702A, 1185 Eglinton Ave. East, Toronto ON M3C 3C6
Tel: 416-426-7050; *Fax:* 416-426-7369
e-mail: rugbyregistration@osrc.com
URL: www.rugbyontario.com
Affiliation(s): Canadian Rugby Union
Allen Piggott, Executive Director

Ontario Soaring Association
10 Courtwood Pl., Toronto ON M2K 1Z9
Tel: 416-223-6487
Walter Chmela, Contact

Ontario Soccer Association (OSA)
7601 Martin Grove Rd., Vaughan ON L4L 9E4
Tel: 905-264-9390; *Fax:* 905-264-9445
e-mail: TheOSA@soccer.on.ca
URL: www.soccer.on.ca
Colin Linford, President
Dan Tomlinson, Secretary
Brian Avey, Executive Director

Ontario Speed Skating Association (OSSA)
Memorial Hall, PO Box 1179, 2 Queen St., 2nd Fl., Lakefield ON K0L 2H0
Tel: 705-652-0653; *Fax:* 705-652-1227
e-mail: jdeschenes@speedskatingontario.org
URL: www.speedskatingontario.org
Jackie Deschenes, Executive Director
Bill Allen, Director of Sport

Ontario Tennis Association (OTA)
#200, 1 Shoreham Dr., Toronto ON M3N 3A7
Tel: 416-514-1100; *Fax:* 416-514-1112
Toll-Free: 800-387-5066
e-mail: ota@tennisontario.com
URL: www.tennisontario.com
Michel Lecavalier, President
Jim Boyce, Executive Director
Simon Bartram, Vice-President
Scott Fraser, Vice-President, Finance & Administration
Glenna Poick, Vice-President, Marketing & Communications
Liz Wood, Vice-President, Membership & Regional Development

Ontario Trail Riders Association (OTRA)
PO Box 3038, Elmvale ON L0L 1P0
URL: www.otra.ca
Affiliation(s): Ontario Trails Council; Ontario Equestrian Federation
Janice Clegg, President

Ontario Underwater Council (OUC)
#104, 1185 Eglinton Ave. East, Toronto ON M3C 3C6
Tel: 416-426-7033; *Fax:* 416-426-7280
e-mail: ouc@underwatercouncil.com
URL: www.underwatercouncil.com
Raimund Krob, President

Ontario Volleyball Association (OVA)
#304, 3 Concorde Gate, Toronto ON M3C 3N7
Tel: 416-426-7316; *Fax:* 416-426-7109
Toll-Free: 800-563-5938
e-mail: ova@ontariovolleyball.org
URL: www.ontariovolleyball.org
Social Media: twitter.com/ova_updates
Kristine Drakich, President
Orest Stanko, Executive Director
Jason Trepanier, Technical Director

Ontario Water Polo Association (OWPA) / L'Association de water polo d'Ontario
#206, 3 Concorde Gate, Toronto ON M3C 3N7
Tel: 416-426-7028; *Fax:* 416-426-7356
e-mail: info@ontariowaterpolo.ca
URL: www.ontariowaterpolo.ca
Ross McDonald, Technical Director

Ontario Women's Hockey Association (OWHA) / Association de hockey féminin de l'Ontario
#3, 5155 Spectrum Way, Mississauga ON L4W 5A1
Tel: 905-282-9980; *Fax:* 905-282-9982
e-mail: info@owha.on.ca
URL: owha.on.ca
Fran Rider, President

Ottawa District Minor Hockey Association (ODMHA)
#300, 1247 Kilborn Place, Ottawa ON K1H 6K9
Tel: 613-224-3589; *Fax:* 613-224-4625
URL: www.odmha.on.ca
Social Media: www.facebook.com/group.php?gid=2228819818
Mike Depratto, President

Ottawa Valley Curling Association (OVCA)
PO Box 40129, Ottawa ON K1V 0W8
Tel: 613-521-5822; *Fax:* 613-521-5344
Toll-Free: 800-385-6621
e-mail: events@ovca.com
URL: www.ovca.com
Affiliation(s): Curling Quebec
Perry Anderson, President
Lily Ooi, Coordinator, Events

Paralympic Sports Association (Alberta) (PSA)
10024 - 79 Ave., Edmonton AB T6E 1R5
Tel: 780-439-8687; *Fax:* 780-432-0486
e-mail: info@parasports.net
URL: www.parasports.net
Affiliation(s): Wheelchair Sports Alberta
Kim McDonald, Executive Director

Paralympics Ontario
1185 Eglinton Ave. East, Toronto ON M3C 3C6
Tel: 416-426-7187; *Fax:* 416-426-7361
Toll-Free: 800-265-1539
e-mail: info@paralympicsontario.ca
URL: www.paralympicsontario.ca
Affiliation(s): Ontario Amputee & Les Autres Sports Association; Ontario Blind Sports Association; Ontario Cerebral Palsy Sports Association; Ontario Wheelchair Sports Association
Cathy Vincelli, Executive Director

Paralympics PEI
c/o Royalty Center House Of Sport, PO Box 841, 40 Enman Cres., Charlottetown PE C1A 7L9
Tel: 902-368-4540; *Fax:* 902-368-4548
e-mail: info@website.paralympicspei.pe.ca
URL: www.paralympicspei.pe.ca
Tracy Stevenson, Executive Director

Patrouille de ski St-Jean
651, 6e Rue ouest, Chibougamau QC G8P 2T8
Tél: 418-748-6914
Patrice Bolduc

Peace Curling Association (PCA)
PO Box 265, Grande Prairie AB T8V 3A4
Tel: 780-532-4782; *Fax:* 780-538-2485
Toll-Free: 800-567-0171
e-mail: peaccurl@telusplanet.net
URL: www.peacecurl.org
Elaine Muceniek, President

Pemberton Soaring Centre
Pemberton BC V0N 2L1
Tel: 604-894-5727; *Fax:* 604-894-5776
Toll-Free: 800-831-2611
e-mail: info@pembertonsoaring.com
URL: www.pembertonsoaring.com
Rudy Rozsypalek

Physical & Health Education Canada / Éducation physique et santé Canada
#301, 2197 Riverside Dr., Ottawa ON K1H 7X3
Tel: 613-523-1348; *Fax:* 613-523-1206
Toll-Free: 800-663-8708
e-mail: info@phecanada.ca
URL: www.phecanada.ca
Mark Jones, President
Andrea Grantham, Executive Director
Sharon May, Director, Programs

Prince Edward Island Alpine Ski Association
PO Box 2026, Charlottetown PE CIA 7N7
Tel: 902-368-4110; *Fax:* 902-368-4548
Toll-Free: 800-247-6712
e-mail: sports@sportpei.pe.ca
URL: www.sportpei.pe.ca
Fred Horrelt, President

Prince Edward Island Amateur Baseball Association
PO Box 302, Charlottetown PE C1A 7K7
Tel: 902-368-4208; *Fax:* 902-368-4548
Toll-Free: 800-235-5687
e-mail: kmcintosh@sportpei.pe.ca
URL: www.baseballpei.ca
Kelsey McIntosh, Executive Director

Prince Edward Island Amateur Boxing Association
2595 Horne Cross Rd., Wilsloe PE C1E 1Z3

Tel: 902-394-1574; *Fax:* 902-628-3865
Holly Morrison, President

Prince Edward Island Badminton Association
c/o Sport PEI, PO Box 302, Charlottetown PE C1A 7K7
Tel: 902-368-4262; *Fax:* 902-368-4548
Dawna Woodside, President

Prince Edward Island Curling Association (PEICA)
PO Box 302, 40 Enman Cres., Charlottetown PE C1A 7K7
Tel: 902-368-4986; *Fax:* 902-368-4548
e-mail: glucas@sportpei.pe.ca
URL: www.peicurling.com
Affiliation(s): Sports PEI, Curl Atlantic
Ray McCourt, President

Prince Edward Island Five Pin Bowlers Association Inc.
c/o Sport PEI, PO Box 302, Charlottetown PE C1A 7K7
Tel: 902-368-4110; *Fax:* 902-368-4548
Toll-Free: 800-247-6712
e-mail: sports@sportpei.pe.ca
URL: www.pei5pba.com
Sue MacPherson, President

Prince Edward Island Golf Association
PO Box 51, Charlottetown PE C1A 7K2
Tel: 902-393-3293; *Fax:* 902-628-2260
e-mail: peiga@peiga.ca
URL: www.peiga.ca
Don Chandler, Executive Director
Jean Kelly, President

Prince Edward Island Hockey Association / Association de hockey de l'Ile-du-Prince-Edouard
40 Enman Cres., Charlottetown PE C1A 7K7
Tel: 902-368-4334; *Fax:* 902-368-4337
e-mail: peiha@pei.sympatico.ca
Mike Whelan, Secretary/Manager

Prince Edward Island Hockey Referees Association
c/o Hockey PEI, 40 Enman Cres., Charlottetown PE C1A 7K7
Tel: 902-367-8373
e-mail: troyhowatt@eastlink.ca
URL: www.peihra.com
Troy Howatt, Chair

Prince Edward Island Lawn Bowling Association
Sport PEI, PO Box 302, Charlottetown PE C1A 7K7
e-mail: sharonrenner@eastlink.ca
Sharon Renner, President

Prince Edward Island Roadrunners Club
40 Villa Ave., Charlottetown PE C1A 2B1
e-mail: runners@peiroadrunners.ca
URL: www.peiroadrunners.ca
Kim Bailey, President

Prince Edward Island Sailing Association (PEISA)
PO Box 6708, York Point PE C0A 1H0
URL: www.peisailing.com
Ellen McPhail, Executive Director

Prince Edward Island School Athletic Association (PEISAA)
PEISAA, 109 Water St., Summerside PE C1N 1A8
Tel: 902-888-8037; *Fax:* 902-569-7530
URL: www.edu.pe.ca/peisaa
Garth Turtle, Executive Director
Lona Ryan, Game Reporting
Gerald MacCormack, Sec.-Treas.

Prince Edward Island Soccer Association (PEISA)
House of Sports, Holland College Royalty Centre, PO Box 1863, Charlottetown PE C1A 7N5
Tel: 902-368-6251; *Fax:* 902-569-7693
e-mail: admin@peisoccer.com
URL: www.peisoccer.com
Dianne Bishop, Executive Administrator
Colleen Arsenault, Treasurer
Gerald MacDonald, President

Prince Edward Island Speed Skating Association
PO Box 383, Charlottetown PE C1A 7K7
Tel: 902-569-3701; *Fax:* 902-368-7347
e-mail: speedskate@hotmail.com
URL: www.isn.net/speedskating/contacts.html
Fred Foster, Executive Director (Sport PEI)
Glenn Holmes, President

Prince Edward Island Tennis Association
PO Box 302, 40 Enman Cres., Charlottetown PE C1A 7K7
Tel: 902-368-4208; *Fax:* 902-368-4548
e-mail: brianhall@peitennis.ca
URL: www.peitennis.ca
Fred Foster, Executive Director
Brian Hall, Contact

Prince Edward Island Track & Field Association
c/o Sport PEI, 3 Queen St., Charlottetown PE C1A 7K7
Tel: 902-368-4110

Prince Edward Island Water Ski Association
c/o Regional President, 8 Falconwood Rd., Charlottetown PE C1A 6B5
Tel: 902-894-5740
Stuart Smith, President

Provincial Water Polo Association (PWPA)
c/o Sport Nova Scotia, 5516 Spring Garden Rd., Halifax NS B3J 1G6
e-mail: lavoie.ghg@forces.gc.ca
URL: www.hfxh2o.ca
Guy Lavoie, Contact

Québec Ball Hockey Association
#203, 5960 Jean-Talon E, St. Leonard QC H1S 1M2
Tel: 514-251-9346; *Fax:* 514-251-8285
e-mail: info@ballhockeynews.ca
URL: www.ballhockeynews.ca
Tony Iannitto

Québec Lawn Bowling Federation / Fédération de Boulingrin du Québec
c/o #662 Oak Ave., Saint-Lambert QC J4P 2R6
URL: www.qlbf.org
Shirley Ahern, Contact

Rhythmic Gymnastics Alberta (RGA)
c/o Percy Page Centre, 11759 Groat Rd., 3rd Fl., Edmonton AB T5M 3K6
Tel: 780-427-8152; *Fax:* 780-427-8153
Toll-Free: 800-881-2504
e-mail: rga@rgalberta.com
URL: www.rgalberta.com
Joan Jack, President
Odette Lindstrom, Treasurer
Helen Marchak, Vice-President

Rhythmic Gymnastics Manitoba Inc. (RGM)
Sport Manitoba Bldg., 200 Main St., Winnipeg MB R3C 4M2
e-mail: rhythmic@sport.mb.ca
URL: www.rgmanitoba.com
Affiliation(s): Sport Manitoba; Rhythmic Gymnastics Canada; Gymnastics Canada; International Gymnastics Federation; Canadian Sport Centre - Manitoba; Coaching Manitoba; Gymnastics Manitoba
Zlatica Stauder, Executive Director
Raymond Chu, President
Susan Yurkiw, Vice-President

Ringette Association of Saskatchewan (RAS) / Association de ringuette de Saskatchewan
#204, 1860 Lorne St., Regina SK S4P 2L7
Tel: 306-780-9432; *Fax:* 306-780-9460
e-mail: executivedirector@ringettesask.com
URL: www.ringettesask.com
Darrell Liebrecht, President
Crystal Gellner, Executive Director

Ringette Canada (RC) / Ringuette Canada
#201, 5510 Canotek Rd., Ottawa ON K1J 9J4
Tel: 613-748-5655; *Fax:* 613-748-5860
e-mail: ringette@ringette.ca
URL: www.ringette.ca
Jim Dawson, President
David Patterson, Executive Director

Ringette New Brunswick (RNB) / Ringuette Nouveau-Brunswick
c/o Marise Aufrey, Administrative Assistant, 940 Centrale St., Memramcook NB E4K 3T4
Tel: 506-758-2546
e-mail: MariseA@rrsb.nb.ca
URL: www.sport.nb.ca/ringette/
Ron Richard, President
Hélène L. Beaulieu, Q.C., Vice-President

Ringette Nova Scotia
5516 Spring Garden Rd., 4th Fl., Halifax NS B3J 1G6
Tel: 902-425-5450; *Fax:* 902-425-5606
e-mail: ringette@sportnovascotia.ca
URL: www.ringette.ns.ca
Lindsay Bennett, Executive Director
Dennis Barnhart, President

Rowing Canada Aviron (RCA) / Association canadienne d'aviron amateur
100 - 4636 Elk Lake Dr., Victoria BC V8Z 5M1
Fax: 250-361-4211
Toll-Free: 877-722-4769
e-mail: rca@rowingcanada.org
URL: www.rowingcanada.org
Affiliation(s): Fédération Internationale des Sociétés d'Aviron; Canadian Olympic Association
Donna Atkinson, Executive Director

Royal Canadian Golf Association (RCGA) / Association royale de golf du Canada
Golf House, #1, 1333 Dorval Dr., Oakville ON L6M 4X7
Tel: 905-849-9700; *Fax:* 905-845-7040
e-mail: cboag@rcga.org
URL: www.rcga.org
Social Media: www.facebook.com/group.php?gid=61328126412
Affiliation(s): World Amateur Golf Council
Scott Simmons, Executive Director
Peter Beresford, COO
Rick Desrochers, Senior Director, Corporate Planning

Royal Canadian Golf Association Foundation
#1, 1333 Dorval Dr., Oakville ON L6M 4X7
Tel: 905-849-9700; *Fax:* 905-845-7040
Toll-Free: 800-263-0009
e-mail: khewson@rcga.org
URL: www.rcga.org
Karen Hewson, Executive Director

Sarnia Highland Games
PO Box 713, 137 Davis St., Sarnia ON N7S 7J7
Tel: 519-336-5054; *Fax:* 519-336-5564
Toll-Free: 888-772-8170
e-mail: highland@rivernet.net
URL: www.sarniahighlandgames.com
Shirley Kelly, Director
John W. Stewart, Chair

Sask Sport Inc.
1870 Lorne St., Regina SK S4P 2L7
Tel: 306-780-9300; *Fax:* 306-781-6021
e-mail: sasksport@sasksport.sk.ca
URL: www.sasksport.sk.ca
Don MacAulay, President

Saskatchewan 5 Pin Bowlers' Association
#100, 1805 - 8th Ave., Regina SK S4R 1E8
Tel: 306-780-9412; *Fax:* 306-780-9455
e-mail: bowling@sasktel.net
URL: saskbowl.com
Affiliation(s): Bowling Federation of Saskatchewan
Rhonda Sereda, Executive Director

Saskatchewan Amateur Speed Skating Association (SASSA)
2205 Victoria Ave., Regina SK S4P 0S4
Tel: 306-780-9400; *Fax:* 306-525-4009
e-mail: sassa@sasktel.net
URL: www.saskspeedskating.ca
Affiliation(s): Sask Sport Inc.
Shawn MacLennan, Executive Director

Saskatchewan Amateur Wrestling Association (SAWA)
510 Cynthia St., Saskatoon SK S7L 7K7
Tel: 306-975-0822; *Fax:* 306-242-8007
e-mail: sk.wrestling@shaw.ca
URL: www.saskwrestling.com
Anna-Beth Zulkowkey, Executive Director

Saskatchewan Badminton Association (SBA)
3615 Pasqua St., Regina SK S4S 6W8
Tel: 306-780-9368; *Fax:* 306-780-9369
e-mail: saskbadminton@sasktel.net
URL: www.saskbadminton.ca
Frank Gaudet, Executive Director

Saskatchewan Baseball Association (SBA)
1870 Lorne St., Regina SK S4P 2L7
Tel: 306-780-9237; *Fax:* 306-352-3669
e-mail: mramage@sasktel.net
URL: www.saskbaseball.ca
Mike Ramage, Executive Director

Saskatchewan Blind Sports Association Inc.
510 Cynthia St., Saskatoon SK S7L 7K7
Tel: 306-975-0888; *Fax:* 306-242-8007
Toll-Free: 877-772-7798
e-mail: sbsa.sk@shaw.ca
URL: www.saskblindsports.ca
Darren Newberry, Executive Director
Terry Parsons, President

Saskatchewan Broomball Association (SBA)
2205 Victoria Ave., Regina SK S4P 0S4
Tel: 306-780-9215; *Fax:* 306-525-4009
e-mail: saskbroomball@sasktel.net
URL: www.saskbroomball.ca
Greg Perreaux, Executive Director

Saskatchewan Curling Association (SCA)
613 Park St., Regina SK S4N 5N1
Tel: 306-780-9202; *Fax:* 306-780-9404
Toll-Free: 877-722-2875
e-mail: saskcurling@sasktel.net
URL: www.saskcurl.com/sca/scahome.htm
Del Jones, President

Saskatchewan Cycling Association
2205 Victoria Ave., Regina SK S4P 0S4
Tel: 306-780-9299; *Fax:* 306-525-4009
e-mail: cycling@accesscomm.ca
URL: www.saskcycling.ca
Wayne Walker, President

Saskatchewan Deaf Sports Association
511 Main St. East, Saskatoon SK S7N 0C2
Tel: 306-787-3432; *Fax:* 306-924-1421
Toll-Free: 800-855-0511
e-mail: lbirley@cableregina.com
Affiliation(s): Regina Deaf Athletic Club; Saskatoon Deaf Athletic Club
Kenneth Dittrick, President

Saskatchewan Diving
1870 Lorne St., Regina SK S4P 2L7
Tel: 306-780-9405; *Fax:* 306-781-6021
e-mail: skdiving@accesscomm.ca
URL: www.saskdiving.ca
Karen Swanson, Provincial Administrator
Carol Lunn, President

Saskatchewan Golf Association
510 Cynthia St., Saskatoon SK S7L 7K7
Tel: 306-975-0850; *Fax:* 306-975-0840
e-mail: info@saskgolf.ca
URL: www.saskgolf.ca
Daniel Rauckman, Executive Director

Saskatchewan Hockey Association (SHA) / Association de hockey de la Saskatchewan
#2, 575 Park St., Regina SK S4N 5B2
Tel: 306-789-5101; *Fax:* 306-789-6112
URL: www.sha.sk.ca
Greg Camp, President
Kelly McClintock, General Manager

Saskatchewan Horse Federation (SHF)
2205 Victoria Ave., Regina SK S4P 0S4
Tel: 306-780-9244; *Fax:* 306-525-4009
e-mail: sk.horse@sasktel.net
URL: www.saskhorse.ca
Affiliation(s): Sask Sport; Western College Veterinary Medicine; SK Agriculture & Food (SAF)
Mae Smith, Executive Director

Saskatchewan Long Riders
C/O Diane Trundle, Stn. 429, Balgonie SK S0G 0E0
Tel: 306-978-1225; *Fax:* 306-230-1224
e-mail: bsutherland@shaw.ca
URL: www.sasklongriders.com
Affiliation(s): Canadian Long Distance Riding Association
Rachel Croskery, President

Saskatchewan Rugby Union (SRU)
510 Cynthia St., Saskatoon SK S7L 7K7
Tel: 306-975-0895; *Fax:* 306-242-8007
e-mail: sru@sasktel.net
URL: www.saskrugby.com

Saskatchewan Ski Association - Skiing for Disabled (SASKI)
17 Clark Cres., Saskatoon SK S7H 3L8
Tel: 306-374-7745; *Fax:* 306-955-5979
e-mail: sask.ski@sasktel.net
URL: www.saski.ca
Alana Ottenbreit, Executive Director
Pat Prokopchuk, Contact, Skiing for Disabled
Doug Sylvester, Contact, Biathlon

Saskatchewan Soccer Association Inc. (SSA)
1870 Lorne St., Regina SK S4P 2L7
Tel: 306-780-9225; *Fax:* 306-780-9480
e-mail: coo@sasksoccer.com
URL: www.sasksoccer.com
Boyd Clark, Executive Director

Saskatchewan Volleyball Association
1758 McAra St., Regina SK S4N 6L4
Tel: 306-780-9250; *Fax:* 306-780-9288
Toll-Free: 800-321-1685
e-mail: officemanager@saskvolleyball.ca
URL: www.saskvolleyball.ca
Dalene Phillips, President
Sandra Sandbeck, Program Coordinator
Dennis Pomeroy, Executive Director

School Sports Newfoundland & Labrador (SSNL)
PO Box 8700, Bldg. 810, Pleasantville NL A1B 4J6
Tel: 709-729-2795; *Fax:* 709-729-2705
e-mail: ssnl@sportnl.ca
URL: www.schoolsportsnl.ca
Karen Richard, Executive Director

Skate Canada / Patinage Canada
865 Shefford Rd., Ottawa ON K1J 1H9
Tel: 613-747-1007; *Fax:* 613-748-5718
Toll-Free: 888-747-2372
e-mail: skatecanada@skatecanada.ca
URL: www.skatecanada.ca
Social Media: www.facebook.com/group.php?gid=129815677038
William Thompson, CEO
Brenda Gorman, Chief Communications Officer
Benoît Lavoie, Chair

Snowboard Yukon
72 Teslin Rd., Whitehorse YT Y1A 3M6
Tel: 867-456-2174
e-mail: info@snowboardyukon.com
URL: www.snowboardyukon.com
Affiliation(s): Canadian Snowboard Federation
Chris McNutt, President

Soccer New Brunswick
#2, 125 Russ Howard Dr., Moncton NB E1C 0L7
Tel: 506-382-7529; *Fax:* 506-382-5621
e-mail: office@soccernb.org
URL: www.soccernb.org
Social Media: www.facebook.com/group.php?gid=183461681180
Jeff Salvis, Executive Director

Soccer Nova Scotia
210 Thomas Raddall Dr., Halifax NS B3S 1K3
Tel: 902-445-0265; *Fax:* 902-445-0258
e-mail: soccerns@ns.sympatico.ca
URL: www.soccerns.ns.ca
George Athanasiou, Executive Director

Softball Canada
#212, 223 Colonnade Rd., Ottawa ON K1H 7X3
Tel: 613-523-3386; *Fax:* 613-523-5761
e-mail: info@softball.ca
URL: www.softball.ca
Social Media: www.facebook.com/pages/Softball-Canada/203017655217
Hugh Mitchener, CEO
Kevin Quinn, President

Southern Alberta Curling Association (SACA)
#720, 3 St. NW, Calgary AB T2N 1N9
Tel: 403-246-9300; *Fax:* 403-246-9349
e-mail: curling@saca.ca
URL: www.saca.ca
Brent Syme, General Manager

Special Olympics Alberta (SOA)
Percy Page Centre, 11759 Groat Rd., Edmonton AB T5M 3K6
Tel: 780-415-0719; *Fax:* 780-422-2663
Toll-Free: 800-444-2883
e-mail: info@specialolympics.ab.ca
URL: www.specialolympics.ab.ca
Carmen Wyton, President & CEO

Special Olympics BC (SOBC)
#210, 3701 East Hastings St., Burnaby BC V5C 2H6
Tel: 604-737-3078; *Fax:* 604-737-3080
Toll-Free: 888-854-2276
e-mail: info@specialolympics.bc.ca
URL: www.specialolympics.bc.ca
Affiliation(s): Special Olympics Canada; Special Olympics International
Dan Howe, President & CEO
Betty J. Simpson, Office Administrator

Special Olympics Canada (SOC) / Jeux olympiques spéciaux
#700, 60 St. Clair Ave. East, Toronto ON M4T 1N5
Tel: 416-927-9050; *Fax:* 416-927-8475
e-mail: info@specialolympics.ca
URL: www.specialolympics.ca
Affiliation(s): Special Olympics International
Deborah Bright, President & CEO
Frank Selke, Executive Vice-President
Susana Petti, Director, Marketing & Public Relations
Edgar Vardy, Director, Finance & Operations

Special Olympics Manitoba (SOM)
#402, 200 Main Street, Winnipeg MB R3C 4M2
Tel: 204-925-5628; *Fax:* 204-925-5624
e-mail: som@specialolympics.mb.ca
URL: www.specialolympics.mb.ca
Simon Mundey, President & CEO

Special Olympics New Brunswick
#107, 146 Main St., Fredericton NB E3A 1C8
Tel: 506-459-3999; *Fax:* 506-451-1325
Toll-Free: 888-362-5926
e-mail: info@sonb.ca
URL: nb.specialolympics.ca
Joseph Trevors, Executive Director

Special Olympics Newfoundland & Labrador
#426, 354 Water St., St. John's NL A1C 1C4
Tel: 709-738-1923; *Fax:* 709-738-0119
Toll-Free: 877-738-1913
e-mail: sonl@sonl.ca
URL: www.sonl.ca
Ken Marshall, Chair

Special Olympics Northwest Territories
PO Box 1691, Yellowknife NT X1A 2N1
Tel: 867-873-6906; *Fax:* 867-669-0225
e-mail: braden@internorth.com
URL: www.sonwt.ca
Valery Braden, President

Special Olympics Nova Scotia (SONS)
PO Box 3010, #305, 5516 Spring Garden Rd., Halifax NS B3J 1G6
Tel: 902-429-2266; *Fax:* 902-425-5606
Toll-Free: 866-299-2019
e-mail: greekmr@sportnovascotia.ca
URL: www.sons.ca
Mike Greek, President/CEO

Special Olympics Ontario (SOO)
#300, 18 Wynford Dr., Toronto ON M3C 3S2
Tel: 416-447-8326; *Fax:* 416-447-6336
Toll-Free: 888-333-5515
URL: www.osoinc.com
Glenn MacDonell, President & CEO

Special Olympics Prince Edward Island (SOPEI)
PO Box 822, #240, 40 Enman Cres., Charlottetown PE C1A 7L9
Tel: 902-368-8919; *Fax:* 902-892-4553
Toll-Free: 800-287-1196
e-mail: sopei@sopei.com
URL: www.sopei.com
Valerie Downe, President

Special Olympics Saskatchewan
353 Broad St., Regina SK S4R 1X2
Tel: 306-780-9247; *Fax:* 306-780-9441
Toll-Free: 888-307-6226
e-mail: sos@specialolympics.sk.ca
URL: www.specialolympics.sk.ca
Howard Schweitzer, CEO

Special Olympics Yukon (SOY) / Les Jeux Olympiques Spéciaux du Yukon
4061 - 4 Ave., Whitehorse YT Y1A 1H1
Tel: 867-668-6511; *Fax:* 867-667-4237
e-mail: specialolympics@sportyukon.com
Affiliation(s): Special Olympics International
Serge Michaud, Executive Director
James Tucker, President

Speed Skating Canada (SSC) / Patinage de vitesse Canada
#402, 2781 Lancaster Rd., Ottawa ON K1B 1A7
Tel: 613-260-3669; *Fax:* 613-260-3660
e-mail: ssc@speedskating.ca
URL: www.speedskating.ca
Affiliation(s): International Skating Union
Jean R. Dupré, Director General
Brian Rahill, Director of Sport
Mylène Croteau, Manager of Communications

Sport Alliance of Ontario
3 Concorde Gate, Toronto ON M3C 3N7

Tel: 416-426-7000; *Fax:* 416-426-7381
e-mail: jjoseph@sportalliance.com
URL: www.sportalliance.com

Jim Bradley, CEO
Larry Rudner, Interim CFO

Sport BC
#260, 3820 Cessna Dr., Richmond BC V7B 0A2
Tel: 604-333-3400; *Fax:* 604-333-3401
e-mail: info@sport.bc.ca
URL: www.sport.bc.ca
Social Media: www.facebook.com/pages/Sport-BC/86675020979
Paul Varian, President/CEO

Sport Manitoba
200 Main St., Winnipeg MB R3C 4M2
Tel: 204-925-5600; *Fax:* 204-925-5916
Toll-Free: 866-774-2220
e-mail: info@sport.mb.ca
URL: www.sportmanitoba.ca
Jeff Hnatiuk, President/CEO
Tara Skibo, Communications/Public Relations

Sport New Brunswick / Sport Nouveau-Brunswick
#13, 900 Hanwell Rd., Fredericton NB E3B 6A2
Tel: 506-451-1320; *Fax:* 506-451-1325
e-mail: director@sportnb.com
URL: www.sportnb.com
Jason Dickson, Executive Director

Sport Newfoundland & Labrador
PO Box 8700, St. John's NL A1B 4J6
Tel: 709-576-4932; *Fax:* 709-576-7493
e-mail: sportnl@sportnl.ca
URL: www.sportnl.ca
Troy Croft, Executive Director

Sport North Federation
Don Cooper Building, PO Box 11089, 4908-49 St., Yellowknife NT X1A 3X7
Tel: 867-669-8326; *Fax:* 867-669-8327
Toll-Free: 800-661-0797
URL: www.sportnorth.com
Doug Rentmeister, Executive Director

Sport Nova Scotia (SNS)
PO Box 3010, Stn. South, 5516 Spring Garden Rd., Halifax NS B3J 1G6
Tel: 902-425-5450; *Fax:* 902-425-5606
e-mail: sportns@sportnovascotia.ca
URL: www.sportnovascotia.ca
Jamie Ferguson, CEO

Sport PEI Inc.
PO Box 302, Charlottetown PE C1A 7K7
Tel: 902-368-4110; *Fax:* 902-368-4548
Toll-Free: 800-247-6712
e-mail: sports@sportpei.pe.ca
URL: www.sportpei.pe.ca
Lyall Huggan, Special Projects
Gemma Koughan, Executive Director
Wendy Reid, President
Nick Murray, Communications
Lisa MacKay, Finance & Administration

Sport Physiotherapy Canada (SPC)
#416, 11411A Carling Ave., Ottawa ON K1Z 1A7
Tel: 613-748-5794; *Fax:* 613-748-5792
e-mail: info@sportphysio.ca
URL: www.sportphysio.ca

Sport Yukon
4061 - 4 Ave., Whitehorse YT Y1A 1H1
Tel: 867-668-4236; *Fax:* 867-667-4237
e-mail: news@sportyukon.com
URL: www.sportyukon.com
George Arcand, President

Sports-Québec
CP 1000, Succ. M, 4545, av Pierre-De Coubertin, Montréal QC H1V 3R2
Tél: 514-252-3114; *Téléc:* 514-254-9621
Courriel: sports@sportsquebec.com
URL: www.sportsquebec.com
André-François Lafond, Directeur général

Squash Canada
#401, 2197 Riverside Dr., Ottawa ON K1H 7X3
Tel: 613-731-7385; *Fax:* 613-731-6291
e-mail: squash.canada@squash.ca
URL: www.squash.ca
Linda MacPhail, Executive Director
Robert Wyma, President

STARS Sports Association
PO Box 15, Okotoks AB T1S 1A4
Tel: 403-938-3475; *Fax:* 403-938-3625
e-mail: info@starsvolleyball.ca; info@starsbasketball.com

Summerside & Area Minor Hockey Association (SAMHA)
PO Box 1454, Summerside PE C1N 4K4
e-mail: info@summersideminorhockey.com
URL: www.summersideminorhockey.com
Bruce Cameron, President

Swim Yukon
4061, 4th Ave., Whitehorse YT Y1A 1H1
URL: www.swimyukon.ca
Affiliation(s): Swim BC; Swimming Canada
Ron Sumanik, President

Swimming/Natation Canada
#700, 2197 Riverside Dr., Ottawa ON K1H 7X3
Tel: 613-260-1348; *Fax:* 613-260-0804
e-mail: natloffice@swimming.ca
URL: www.swimming.ca
Social Media: www.facebook.com/group.php?gid=56320144853
Affiliation(s): Aquatic Federation of Canada
Pierre Lafontaine, CEO/National Coach
Mark Hahto, COO
Larry Clough, CFO
Martin Richard, Communications Director

Synchro Canada / Association canadienne de nage synchronisée amateur
#200, 1010 Polytek St., Unit 14, Gloucester ON K1J 9H9
Tel: 613-748-5674; *Fax:* 613-748-5724
e-mail: catherine@synchro.ca
URL: www.synchro.ca
Catherine Gosselin-Després, Chief Operations Officer
Diane Oligny, Chief Technical Officer

Synchro Yukon Association
4061, 4th Ave., Whitehorse YT Y1A 1H1
Tel: 867-668-7441
e-mail: specialk@northwestel.net
URL: www.sportyukon.com/membership/?member=34
Sandra Duncan, President

Table Tennis Yukon
4061, 4th Ave, Whitehorse YT Y1A 1H1
Tel: 867-668-3358
e-mail: stockdale@yknet.ca
URL: www.sportyukon.com/membership/?member=72
David Stockdale, President

Temiskaming & Northern Ontario Curling Association
c/o Stephen Chenier, PO Box 735, Englehart ON P0J 1H0
Tel: 705-647-2589; *Fax:* 705-544-8525
e-mail: jcdhh@ntl.sympatico.ca
URL: www.tnoca.curlingclub.ca
Stephen Chenier, Secretary/Treasurer

Tennis BC
#204, 210 West Broadway, Vancouver BC V5Y 3W2
Tel: 604-737-3086; *Fax:* 604-737-3124
e-mail: tbc@tennisbc.org
URL: tennisbc.org
Ryan Clark, Chief Executive Officer

Tennis Canada
Rexall Centre, #100, 1 Shoreham Dr., Toronto ON M3N 3A6
Tel: 416-665-9777; *Fax:* 416-665-9017
Toll-Free: 877-283-6647
e-mail: info@tenniscanada.com
URL: www.tenniscanada.com
Michael S. Downey, President & CEO
Tony Eames, Chair

Tennis Manitoba
#303, 200 Main St., Winnipeg MB R3C 4M2
Tel: 204-925-5660; *Fax:* 204-925-5703
e-mail: tennismb@shawbiz.ca
URL: www.tennismanitoba.com
Rick Bochinski, Executive Director
Brigitte Epp, Administrative Assistant

Tennis New Brunswick
PO Box 604, Fredericton NB E3B 5A6
Tel: 506-444-0885
e-mail: tnb@tennisnb.net
URL: www.tennisnb.net

Tennis Newfoundland & Labrador
Bldg. 810, PO Box 8700, Stn. Pleasantville, St. John's NL A1B 4J6
Tel: 709-765-0426; *Fax:* 709-722-1670
e-mail: tennis@sportnl.ca
URL: www.tennisnl.ca
Ryan Maarschalk, Technical Director

Tennis Northwest Territories
PO Box 671, Yellowknife NT X1A 2N5
Tel: 867-873-2018
e-mail: eastarm@ssimicro.com
URL: www.tennisnwt.ca
Fran Hurcomb, President

Tennis Québec (TQ)
285, rue Faillon ouest, Montréal QC H2R 2W1
Tél: 514-270-6060; *Téléc:* 514-270-2700
Courriel: courrier@tennis.qc.ca
URL: www.tennis.qc.ca
Jean François Manibal, Directeur général
Réjean Genois, Président

Tennis Saskatchewan
2205 Victoria Ave., Regina SK S4P 0S4
Tel: 306-780-9410; *Fax:* 306-525-4009
e-mail: tennissask@sasktel.net
URL: www.tennissask.com
Affiliation(s): Sask Sport Incorporated
Rory Park, Executive Director

Tennis Yukon Association
4 Kluhini Cres., Whitehorse YT Y1A 3P3
Tel: 867-393-2621; *Fax:* 867-393-2621
e-mail: tennisyukon@mac.com
URL: www.tennisyukon.com
Stacy Lewis, President

Toronto Bicycling Network
PO Box 279, #200, 131 Bloor St. West, Toronto ON M5S 1R8
Tel: 416-760-4191
e-mail: info@tbn.ca
URL: www.tbn.ca
Brian Mclean, President

Toronto Cycling Committee (TCC)
850 Coxwell Ave., 2nd Fl., Toronto ON M4C 5R1
Tel: 416-392-7592
e-mail: btww@toronto.ca
URL: www.toronto.ca/cycling
Adrian A. Heaps, Chair

Trail Riding Alberta Conference (TRAC)
738 Wheeler Road, Edmonton AB T6M 2E8
Tel: 403-486-0957
e-mail: shanharms@shaw.ca
URL: www.trailriding.ab.ca
Affiliation(s): Canadian Long Distance Riding Association
Brent Seufert, President

Triathlon Canada
#106, 3 Concorde Gate, Toronto ON M3C 3N7
Tel: 416-426-7180; *Fax:* 416-426-7294
e-mail: info@triathloncanada.com
URL: www.triathloncanada.com
Alan Trivett, Executive Director

Vélo New Brunswick
536 McAllister Rd., Riverview NB E1B 4G1
Tel: 506-474-0214
e-mail: christine.martin@velo.nb.ca
URL: www.velo.nb.ca
Affiliation(s): Sport New Brunswick
Kelly Murray, President
Michelle Chase, Vice-President
Sheila Colbourne, Executive Director

Vélo Québec
1251, rue Rachel est, Montréal QC H2J 2J9
Tél: 514-521-8356; *Téléc:* 514-521-5711
Ligne sans frais: 800-567-8356
Courriel: velo_quebec@velo.qc.ca
URL: www.velo.qc.ca
Jean-François Pronovost, Directeur général

Volleyball BC
Harry Jerome Sports Centre, 7564 Barnet Hwy., Burnaby BC V5A 1E7
Tel: 604-291-2007; *Fax:* 604-291-2602
e-mail: contact@volleyballbc.ca
URL: www.volleyballbc.ca
Tom Caverly, Executive Director

Volleyball Canada (VC)
#202, 5510 Canotek Rd., Gloucester ON K1J 9J5

Tel: 613-748-5681; Fax: 613-748-5727
e-mail: info@volleyball.ca
URL: www.volleyball.ca
Affiliation(s): International Volleyball Federation; Canadian Olympic Association; Coaching Association of Canada
John-Paul Cody-Cox, Executive General
Hugh Wong, President

Volleyball New Brunswick
#13, 900 Hanwell Rd., Fredericton NB E3B 6A3
Tel: 506-451-1346; Fax: 506-451-1325
e-mail: vnb@nb.aibn.com
URL: www.vnb.nb.ca
James Cress, Executive Director
John Richard, President

Volleyball Nova Scotia
5516 Spring Garden Rd., 4th Floor, Halifax NS B3J 1G6
Tel: 902-425-5450; Fax: 902-425-5606
e-mail: vns@sportnovascotia.ca
URL: www.volleyballnovascotia.ca
Liam Blanchard, Executive Director
Steve Stuart, Treasurer
Eugene Tan, President

Volleyball Prince Edward Island
PO Box 302, Charlottetown PE C1N 7K7
Tel: 902-569-0583; Fax: 902-368-4548
Toll-Free: 800-247-6712
e-mail: cgcrozier@sportpei.pe.ca
URL: www.volleyballpei.com
Affiliation(s): Sport PEI
Cheryl Crozier, Executive Director
Krista Walsh, President
Harvey Mazerolle, Vice-President

Volleyball Yukon
4061 - 4th Ave., Whitehorse YT Y1A 1H1
Tel: 867-334-4592; Fax: 867-667-4237
e-mail: bunpalamar@whtvcable.com
URL: www.volleyballyukon.com
Tara Wardle, President
Bunne Palamar, Executive Director

Water Polo Canada (WPC)
#12, 1010 Polytek St., Gloucester ON K1G 9H9
Tel: 613-748-5682; Fax: 613-748-5777
e-mail: dvilleneuve@waterpolo.ca
URL: www.waterpolo.ca
Affiliation(s): Aquatic Federation of Canada
Debbie Villeneuve, Manager of Administration

Water Polo Saskatchewan Inc.
1860 Lorne St., Regina SK S4P 2L7
Tel: 306-780-9260; Fax: 306-780-9467
e-mail: admin@wpsask.ca
URL: www.wpsask.ca
Jymmi Kaye-Demchuk, Executive Director

Water Ski & Wakeboard Canada / Ski nautique et planche Canada
#210, 223 Colonnade Rd. South, Ottawa ON K2E 7K3
Tel: 613-526-0685; Fax: 613-526-4380
e-mail: wswc@waterski-wakeboard.ca
URL: www.waterski-wakeboard.ca
Glenn Bowie, President
Dan Wolfenden, Executive Director

Whitehorse Cross Country Ski Club
#200, 1 Sumanik Dr., Whitehorse YT Y1A 6J6
Tel: 867-668-4477
e-mail: info@xcskiwhitehorse.ca
URL: www.xcskiwhitehorse.ca
Mike Gladish, Manager
Tom Ullyett, President

Whitehorse Minor Hockey Association
4061, 4th Ave., Whitehorse YT Y1A 1H1
Tel: 867-393-4698
URL: www.whitehorseminorhockey.ca
John Grant, President

Whitehorse Minor Soccer Association (WMS)
4061, 4th Ave., Whitehorse YT Y1A 1H1
Tel: 867-667-2445
e-mail: wms@sportyukon.com
URL: www.yukonsoccer.yk.ca/minor
Gerald Haase, President

Wild Rose Ball Hockey Association
7604 - 182 St., Edmonton AB T5T 1Y9
Tel: 780-970-0637; Fax: 780-484-9957
e-mail: info@wrbha.com
URL: www.wrbha.com
Craig Thiessen, Contact

World Curling Federation (WCF)
74 Tay St., Perth PH2 8N Scotland
Tel: 44-173-845-1630; Fax: 44-173-845-1641
e-mail: wcf@dial.pipex.com
URL: www.worldcurling.net
Lester Harrison, President
Kate Caithness, Vice-President
Mike Thomson, Secretary General

Wrestling Nova Scotia
General Delivery, Bear River NS B0S 1B0
Tel: 902-857-1761
e-mail: wrestlingns@canada.com
URL: www.wrestlingnovascotia.ca
Peter Coulthard, President
Scott Aldridge, Vice-President
Debbie MacDonald, Sec.-Treas.

Yukon Aboriginal Sport Circle (YASC)
4061, 4th Ave., Whitehorse YT Y1A 1H1
Tel: 867-668-2840; Fax: 867-667-4237
e-mail: aboriginalsport@sportyukon.com
URL: www.yasc.ca
Greg Edgelow, Executive Director
Brian MacDonald, President

Yukon Amateur Hockey Association
4061, 4th Ave., Whitehorse YT Y1A 1H1
Tel: 867-393-4501
e-mail: yaha@sportyukon.com
URL: www.yukonhockey.ca
Walter Brennan, President

Yukon Badminton Association
4061 - 4th Ave., Whitehorse YT Y1A 1H1
Tel: 867-668-4821
e-mail: bluestone@northwestel.net
Michael Muller, President
Randy Carlson, Vice-President

Yukon Broomball League
4061, 4th Ave., Whitehorse YT Y1A 1H1
Tel: 867-668-3589
e-mail: biz@yukonbroomball.com
URL: www.yukonbroomball.com
Allan Milford, President

Yukon Curling Association (YCA)
4061 - 4th Ave., Whitehorse YT Y1A 1H1
Tel: 867-668-7121; Fax: 867-667-4237
e-mail: yca@sportyukon.com
URL: yukoncurling.inthehack.com
Affiliation(s): Watson Lake Curling Club; Mayo Curling Club
Gord Zealand, President

Yukon Freestyle Ski Association
4061, 4th Ave., Whitehorse YT Y1A 1H1
Tel: 867-633-5615; Fax: 867-393-8779
URL: www.sportyukon.com/membership/?member=71
Laura Wilson, Registrar

Yukon Golf Association
4061, 4th Ave., Whitehorse YT Y1A 1H1
Tel: 867-633-3364
e-mail: zealandg@northwestel.net
URL: www.sportyukon.com/membership/?member=57
Gordon Zealand, President

Yukon Horse and Rider Association (YHRA)
PO Box 31482, Whitehorse YT Y1A 6K8
Tel: 867-456-2030
e-mail: info@yhra.ca
URL: www.yhra.ca
Paul Choquette, President

Yukon Indian Hockey Association (YIHA)
PO Box 31769, Whitehorse YT Y1A 6L3
Tel: 867-456-7294; Fax: 867-456-7290
e-mail: info@yiha.ca
URL: www.yiha.ca
Social Media: www.facebook.com/group.php?gid=169614299786
Karee Vallevand, President

Yukon Schools' Athletic Association (YSAA)
c/o Porter Creek Secondary School, 1405 Hickory St., Whitehorse YT V1A 4M4
e-mail: paul.macdonald@yesnet.yk.ca
URL: www.yesnet.yk.ca/ysaa/ysaainside.html
Paul MacDonald, President

Yukon Shooting Federation
4061, 4th Ave., Whitehorse YT Y1A 1H1
Tel: 867-668-6776
URL: www.sportyukon.com/membership/?member=64
Jim Sias, President

Yukon Soccer Association
4061 - 4th Ave., Whitehorse YT Y1A 1H1
Tel: 867-633-4625; Fax: 867-667-4237
e-mail: yukonsoccer@sportyukon.com
URL: www.yukonsoccer.yk.ca
Kim King, Administrator

Yukon Speed Skating Association
11 Buttercup Pl., Whitehorse YT Y1A 5V1
Tel: 867-668-4591; Fax: 867-393-8101
Bruce Henry, Branch President

Yukon Underwater Diving Association (YUDA)
e-mail: alyon@yukon.net
URL: www.yukonweb.com/community/yuda/
Allyn Lyon, President

Yukon Weightlifting Association
4061, 4th Ave., Whitehorse YT Y1A 1H1
URL: www.sportyukon.com/membership/?member=79
Moira Lassen, President

Standards & Testing

Cable Television Standards Foundation / Fondation des normes de télévision par câble
#515, 350 Albert St., Ottawa ON K1P 5G4
Tel: 613-230-5442; Fax: 613-230-5679
Affiliation(s): Canadian Cable Television Association
Claudette Cardinal, Chair

Canadian Educational Standards Institute (CESI) / Institut canadien des normes d'enseignement
PO Box 3013, 2 Ridley Rd., St. Catharines ON L2R 7C3
Tel: 905-684-5658; Fax: 905-684-5057
e-mail: execdir@cesi.edu
URL: www.cesi.edu
Anne-Marie Kee, Executive Director

Canadian Evaluation Society (CES) / Société canadienne d'évaluation
1485 Laperriere Ave., Ottawa ON K1Z 7S8
Tel: 613-725-2526; Fax: 613-729-6206
e-mail: secretariat@evaluationcanada.ca
URL: www.evaluationcanada.ca
Affiliation(s): American Evaluation Society; Australasian Evaluation Society
François Dumaine, President

Canadian General Standards Board (CGSB) / Office des normes générales du Canada (ONGC)
CGSB, #6B1, Place Du Portage III, Gatineau QC K1A 1G6
Tel: 819-956-0425; Fax: 819-956-1634
Toll-Free: 800-665-2472
e-mail: ncr.cgsb-ongc@pwgsc.gc.ca
URL: www.ongc-cgsb.gc.ca
Affiliation(s): Standards Council of Canada; National Standards Authority of Ireland; Standards & Industrial Research Institute of Malaysia; Business & Institutional Furniture Manufacturers' Association; American Society for Testing & Materials; Canadian Centre for Occupational Health & Safety; Information Handling Services; Canadian International Development Agency; Canadian Society for Nondestructive Testing, Inc.; Techstreet; Provincial Territorial Committee on Building Standards; Canadian Council of Fire Marshals & Fire Commissioners
Terrence Davies, Acting Director

Canadian Institute for NDE
135 Fennell Ave. West, Hamilton ON L8N 3T2
Tel: 905-387-1655; Fax: 905-574-6080
Toll-Free: 800-964-9488
e-mail: info@cinde.ca
URL: www.cinde.ca
Doug Marshall, Managing Director

Canadian Metric Association (CMA) / Association métrique canadienne
PO Box 35, Fonthill ON L0S 1E0
Tel: 905-892-3800
e-mail: albertjmettler@gmail.com
Affiliation(s): US Metric Association
Albert J. Mettler, Secretary
John Douglas Bailes, President

CSA International
13799 Commerce Pkwy., Richmond BC V6V 2N9
Tel: 604-273-4581; Fax: 604-244-6600
e-mail: terry.nagy@csa-international.org

CSA International
865, rue Ellingham, Pointe-Claire QC H9R 5E8
Tel: 514-694-8110; *Fax:* 514-694-5001
e-mail: alain.ste-marie@csa-international.org

CSA International
1707 - 94 St., Edmonton AB T6N 1E6
Tel: 780-450-2111; *Fax:* 780-461-5322
e-mail: patricia.pasemko@csa-international.org

CSA International
178 Rexdale Blvd., Toronto ON M9W 1R3
Tel: 416-747-4000; *Fax:* 416-747-4149
Toll-Free: 866-797-4272
e-mail: certinfo@csa-international.org
URL: www.csa-international.org
Randall W. Luecke, President, CSA International
Robert J. Falconi, VP, Gen. Counsel & Corp. Secretary, CSA Group
Robert M. Griffin, President & CEO, CSA Group
Pat Keindel, Vice President, Business Development, CSA Group

CSA International
5060 Spectrum Way, Mississauga ON L4W 5N6
Toll-Free: 800-463-6727

Steel & Metal Industries

Canadian Die Casters Association (CDCA) / Association canadienne des mouleurs sous pression
#3, 247 Barr St., Renfrew ON K7V 1J6
Fax: 613-432-6840
Toll-Free: 866-809-7032
e-mail: info@diecasters.ca
URL: www.diecasters.ca
Bonnie James, Executive Director
Murray Abramovitch, President
Yahia Reguieg, Vice-President
Danny Di Liello, Treasurer

Canadian Foundry Association (CFA) / Association des fonderies canadiennes
#1500, 1 Nicholas St., Ottawa ON K1N 7B7
Tel: 613-789-4894; *Fax:* 613-789-5957
e-mail: judy@foundryassociation.ca
URL: www.foundryassociation.ca
Judith Arbour, CAE, Executive Director
Brad Wannamaker, President

Canadian Institute of Steel Construction (CISC) / Institut canadien de la construction en acier (ICCA)
#200, 3760 - 14th Ave., Markham ON L3R 3T7
Tel: 905-946-0864; *Fax:* 905-946-8574
e-mail: info@cisc-icca.ca
URL: www.cisc-icca.ca
Affiliation(s): Canadian Steel Construction Council; Steel Structures Education Foundation
E. Whalen, President

Canadian Sheet Steel Building Institute (CSSBI) / Institut canadien de la tôle d'acier pour le bâtiment (ICTAB)
#2A, 652 Bishop St. North, Cambridge ON N3H 4V6
Tel: 519-650-1285; *Fax:* 519-650-8081
e-mail: info@cssbi.ca
URL: www.cssbi.ca

Canadian Steel Construction Council (CSCC) / Conseil canadien de la construction en acier
#300, 201 Consumers Rd., Toronto ON M2J 4G8
Tel: 416-491-9898; *Fax:* 416-491-6461
e-mail: hakrentz@telus.net
Affiliation(s): Canadian Institute of Steel Construction; Steel Structures Education Foundation
Hugh A. Krentz, Chairman

Canadian Steel Producers Association (CSPA) / Association canadienne des producteurs d'acier (ACPA)
#906, 350 Sparks St., Ottawa ON K1R 7S8
Tel: 613-238-6049; *Fax:* 613-238-1832
e-mail: info@canadiansteel.ca
URL: www.canadiansteel.ca
Ron Watkins, President

Canadian Steel Trade & Employment Congress
#501, 234 Eglinton Ave. East, Toronto ON M4P 1K7
Tel: 416-480-1797; *Fax:* 416-480-2986
e-mail: general@cstec.ca
URL: www.cstec.ca
Robert Jones, Executive Director

Corrugated Steel Pipe Institute (CSPI) / Institut pour tuyaux de tôle ondulée
#2A, 652 Bishop St. North, Cambridge ON N3H 4V6
Tel: 519-650-8080; *Fax:* 519-650-8081
e-mail: info@cspi.ca
URL: www.cspi.ca
David J. Penny, Marketing Manager

Nickel Institute
#1801, 55 University Ave., Toronto ON M5J 2H7
Tel: 416-591-7999; *Fax:* 416-591-7987
e-mail: ni_toronto@nickelinstitute.org
URL: www.nickelinstitute.org
Peter Johnston, Chairman
Stephen Barnett, President

Ontario Sheet Metal & Air Handling Group (OSM)
#26, 30 Wertheim Ct., Richmond Hill ON L4B 1B9
Tel: 905-886-9627; *Fax:* 905-886-9959
e-mail: shtmetal@bellnet.ca
URL: www.ontsm.org
Wayne Peterson, Executive Director
Harry Vogt, President

Reinforcing Steel Institute of Canada (RSIC) / Institut d'acier d'armature du Canada
70 Leek Cres., Richmond Hill ON L4B 1H1
Tel: 416-499-4000; *Fax:* 416-499-8752
Wendy R. May, Administrator

Surveying & Mapping

Alberta Land Surveyors' Association (ALSA)
#1000, 10020 - 101A Ave., Edmonton AB T5J 3G2
Tel: 780-429-8805; *Fax:* 780-429-3374
Toll-Free: 800-665-2572
e-mail: info@alsa.ab.ca
URL: www.alsa.ab.ca
Brian Munday, Executive Director
David McWilliam, Registrar
Donald R. George, President
David R. McWilliam, Sec.-Treas.

Association of British Columbia Land Surveyors (ABCLS)
#301, 2400 Bevan Ave., Sidney BC V8L 1W1
Tel: 250-655-7222; *Fax:* 250-655-7223
e-mail: office@abcls.ca
URL: www.bclandsurveyors.bc.ca
Janice Henshaw, Executive Director
Chuck Salmon, Secretary & Registrar
Richard Wey, Foundation Chair

Association of Canada Lands Surveyors / Association des arpenteurs des terres du Canada
100E, 900 Dynes Rd., Ottawa ON K2C 3L6
Tel: 613-723-9200; *Fax:* 613-723-5558
e-mail: admin@acls-aatc.ca
URL: www.acls-aatc.ca
Jean-Claude Tétreault, Executive Director

Association of Manitoba Land Surveyors
#202, 83 Garry St., Winnipeg MB R3C 4J9
Tel: 204-943-6972; *Fax:* 204-957-7602
e-mail: amls@mts.net
URL: www.amls.ca
Affiliation(s): Canadian Institute of Surveying & Mapping; Western Canadian Board of Examiners for Land Surveyors
A.W. Phillips, President

Association of New Brunswick Land Surveyors (ANBLS) / Association des arpenteurs-géomètres du Nouveau-Brunswick (AA-GN-B)
#408, 212, rue Queen, Fredericton NB E3B 1A8
Tel: 506-458-8266; *Fax:* 506-458-8267
e-mail: anbls@nbnet.nb.ca
URL: www.anbls.nb.ca

Association of Newfoundland Land Surveyors
#204, 62-64 Pippy Pl., St. John's NL A1B 4H7
Tel: 709-722-2031; *Fax:* 709-722-4104
e-mail: anls@nf.aibn.com
URL: www.surveyors.nf.ca
Wilfred Thorne, President
Gary Hughes, Vice-President
Dominic Howard, Secretary-Treasurer

Association of Nova Scotia Land Surveyors (ANSLS)
325A Prince Albert Rd., Dartmouth NS B2Y 1N5
Tel: 902-469-7962; *Fax:* 902-469-7963
e-mail: ansls@accesswave.ca
URL: www.ansls.ca
Fred Hutchinson, Executive Director

Association of Ontario Land Economists
PO Box 97510, 364 Old Kingston Rd., Toronto ON M1C 4Z1
Tel: 416-283-0440; *Fax:* 416-283-1399
URL: aole.org
Valdemar Nickel, President

Association of Ontario Land Surveyors (AOLS)
1043 McNicoll Ave., Toronto ON M1W 3W6
Tel: 416-491-9020; *Fax:* 416-491-2576
Toll-Free: 800-268-0718
e-mail: admin@aols.org
URL: www.aols.org
S. James Statham, Executive Director & Treasurer
John G. Boyd, President

Association of Prince Edward Island Land Surveyors (APEILS)
PO Box 20100, 8 Park Rd., Kensington PE C0B 1M0
Tel: 902-836-3823; *Fax:* 902-836-3823
James Clow, Sec.-Treas.

Canadian Cartographic Association (CCA) / Association canadienne de cartographie
c/o Department of Geography, University of Victoria, PO Box 3050, Stn. CSC, Victoria BC V8W 3P5
e-mail: awood@mun.ca
URL: www.cca-acc.org
Affiliation(s): International Cartographic Association
Alberta Auringer Wood, Secretary
Paul Heersink, Treasurer

Canadian Council of Land Surveyors (CCLS) / Conseil Canadien des arpenteurs-géomètres
#100E, 900 Dynes Rd., Ottawa ON K2C 3N6
Tel: 613-226-5110; *Fax:* 613-723-5558
Toll-Free: 800-241-7200
e-mail: admin@ccls-ccag.ca
URL: www.ccls-ccag.ca
Denis Blais, President
Sarah J. Cornett, B.Sc., OLS, OLI, Executive Director

Canadian Geophysical Union (CGU) / Union géophysique canadienne (UGC)
c/o Dept. of Geology & Geophysics, University of Calgary, ES #278, 2500 University Dr. NW, Calgary AB T2N 1N4
Tel: 403-220-2794; *Fax:* 403-284-0074
e-mail: cgu@ucalgary.ca
URL: www.cgu-ugc.ca
Gary Jarvis, President
Jim Craven, Treasurer
Masaki Hayashi, Secretary

Canadian Institute of Quantity Surveyors (CIQS)
#19, 90 Nolan Ct., Markham ON L3R 4L9
Tel: 905-477-0008; *Fax:* 905-477-6774
Toll-Free: 866-345-1168
e-mail: info@ciqs.org
URL: www.ciqs.org
Lois Metcalfe, Executive Director
Ian Duncan, President

Geomatics Industry Association of Canada (GIAC) / Association canadienne des entreprises de géomatique
Covent Glen, PO Box 62009, 6491 Jeanne D'Arc Blvd., Ottawa ON K1C 2S0
Fax: 613-851-1256
e-mail: dhtessier@giac.ca
URL: www.giac.ca
Dave Gariepy, Chairman

Ordre des arpenteurs-géomètres du Québec (OAGQ) / Québec Land Surveyors Association
#350, 2954, boul Laurier, Sainte-Foy QC G1V 4T2
Tél: 418-656-0730; *Téléc:* 418-656-6352
Courriel: oagq@oagq.qc.ca
URL: www.oagq.qc.ca
Affiliation(s): Fédération des arpenteurs-géomètres du Québec

Saskatchewan Land Surveyors' Association (SLSA)
#230, 408 Broad St., Regina SK S4R 1X3
Tel: 306-352-8999; *Fax:* 306-352-8366
e-mail: info@slsa.sk.ca
URL: www.slsa.sk.ca
D.L. Gurnsey, SLS, P. Surv.,, President
A. Carl Shiels, M. Sc., P. Eng., Executive Director & Registrar
Ron J. Eichel, Vice-President

Taxation

Association of Municipal Tax Collectors of Ontario
#119, 14845 - 6 Yonge St., Aurora ON L4G 6H8
Tel: 905-725-0019
e-mail: amtco@sympatico.ca
URL: www.amtco.on.ca
Chris Heersink, President

Canadian Property Tax Association, Inc. (CPTA) / Association canadienne de taxe foncière, inc
#225, 6 Lansing Sq., Toronto ON M2J 1T5
Tel: 416-493-3276; *Fax:* 416-493-3905
e-mail: cpta@on.aibn.com
URL: www.cpta.org
Gerry I.G. Divaris, President
James D. Fraser, Executive Vice-President
Grace L. Marsh, Vice-President, Administration
J. Bradford Nixon, Vice-President, Communication
Viviane Marcotte, Managing Director

Canadian Tax Foundation (CTF) / L'Association canadienne d'études fiscales (ACEF)
#1200, 595 Bay St., Toronto ON M5G 2N5
Tel: 416-599-0283; *Fax:* 416-599-9283
Toll-Free: 877-733-0283
e-mail: lchapman@ctf.ca
URL: www.ctf.ca
Charles J.R. Taylor, CA, Chair
Scott Wilkie, Vice-Chair
Larry Chapman, FCA, Director & Chief Executive Officer
Jane Meagher, Director, Québec Office
Debbie Selley, CGA, Treasurer
Judy Singh, Librarian

Canadian Taxpayers Federation (CTF)
#105, 438 Victoria Ave. East, Regina SK S4N 0N7
Tel: 306-352-7199; *Fax:* 306-352-7203
e-mail: admin@taxpayer.com
URL: www.taxpayer.com
Social Media: www.facebook.com/group.php?gid=6095483909
Michael Binnion, Chair
Troy Lanigan, President & Chief Executive Officer
Derek Fildebrandt, Director, National Research
Lee Harding, Director, New Development
Melanie Harvie, Manager, Finance
Shannon Morrison, Manager, Administration

Canadian Taxpayers Federation - Alberta (CTF)
#202, 10621 - 100th Ave., Edmonton AB T5J 0B3
Tel: 800-661-0187; *Fax:* 877-482-1744
e-mail: ab.director@taxpayer.com
URL: www.taxpayer.com
Social Media: twitter.com/scotthennig
Scott Hennig, Director, Alberta

Canadian Taxpayers Federation - British Columbia (CTF)
PO Box 20539, Stn. Howe St. RPO, Vancouver BC V6Z 2N8
Tel: 800-699-2282; *Fax:* 604-608-6773
e-mail: bc.director@taxpayer.com
URL: www.taxpayer.com
Maureen Bader, Director, British Columbia

Canadian Taxpayers Federation - Ontario (CTF)
Varette Bldg., #512, 130 Albert St., Ottawa ON K1P 5G4
Tel: 800-265-0442; *Fax:* 613-234-7748
e-mail: federal.director@taxpayer.com
URL: www.taxpayer.com
Social Media: twitter.com/KevinGaudet
Kevin Gaudet, Director, Federal & Ontario

Canadian Taxpayers Federation - Saskatchewan & Manitoba (CTF)
#212, 428 Portage Ave., Winnipeg MB R3C 0E2
Tel: 204-982-2150; *Fax:* 204-982-2154
Toll-Free: 800-772-9955
e-mail: ccraig@taxpayer.com
URL: www.taxpayer.com
Social Media: twitter.com/colincraig1
Colin Craig, Director, Prairies

Teaching

Québec Board of Black Educators (QBBE)
#310, Cavendish Blvd., Montréal QC H4B 2M5
Tel: 514-481-9400; *Fax:* 514-481-0611
e-mail: qbbe@videotron.ca
URL: www.qbbe.org
Phylicia Burke, Contact
Clarence Bayne, President

Telecommunications

Bell Aliant Pioneers
PO Box 1430, Saint John NB E2L 4K2
Toll-Free: 800-565-1436
e-mail: candace.salkey@aliant.ca
Candace Salkey, Manager

Canadian Association of Telecom Dealers (CATD)
39 Parisian Rd., Brampton ON L6P 2T2
Tel: 416-273-8797

Canadian Call Management Association (CAM-X)
#10, 24 Olive St., Grimsby ON L3M 2B6
Tel: 905-309-0224; *Fax:* 905-309-0225
Toll-Free: 800-896-1054
e-mail: info@camx.ca
URL: www.camx.ca
Linda Osip, Executive Director

Canadian Independent Telephone Association (CITA) / Association canadienne du téléphone indépendant
1402 Queen St. West, Alton ON L7K 0C3
Tel: 519-940-0460; *Fax:* 519-940-1137
e-mail: mhtaylor@allstream.net
URL: www.cita.ca
Margi Taylor, General Manager/Administrator
Rob Figliuzzi, Director

Canadian Internet Registration Authority (CIRA)
#110, 350 Sparks St., Ottawa ON K1R 7S8
Tel: 613-237-5335; *Fax:* 800-285-0517
Toll-Free: 800-285-0517
e-mail: Through website.
URL: www.circ.ca
Maureen Cubberley, Chair

Canadian Telecommunications Consultants Association (CTCA)
#179, 160-2 County Court Blvd., Brampton ON L6J 4V1
Tel: 416-233-7946; *Fax:* 905-451-9410
Toll-Free: 800-463-2569
e-mail: admin@ctca.ca; membership@ctca.ca
URL: www.ctca.ca
Jeanne Eddington, President
David Whyte, Vice-President & Sec.-Treas.

Canadian Wireless Telecommunications Association (CWTA) / Association canadienne des télécommunications sans fil (ACTS)
#1110, 130 Albert St., Ottawa ON K1P 5G4
Tel: 613-233-4888; *Fax:* 613-233-2032
e-mail: info@cwta.ca
URL: www.cwta.ca

Frequency Co-ordination System Association (FCSA) / Association pour la coordination des fréquences
#700, 1 Nicholas St., Ottawa ON K1N 7B7
Tel: 613-241-3080; *Fax:* 613-241-9632
e-mail: amoreno.fcsa@sympatico.ca
URL: www.fcsa.ca
A. Moreno, General Manager/Sec.-Treas.

Halifax Regional CAP Association (HRCAP)
c/o 1673 Barrington St., 2nd Fl., Halifax NS B3J 1Z9
Tel: 902-482-4729; *Fax:* 902-482-5014
e-mail: admin@hrca.ns.ca
URL: www.halifaxcap.ca
Social Media: www.twitter.com/hrcap
Ryan Deschamps, Chair

Ontario Pioneers
21 Meadowland Dr., Brampton ON L6W 2R5
Tel: 905-451-5607; *Fax:* 905-453-3996
e-mail: she.rob@sympatico.ca
Sheila O'Donoghue, Manager

SaskTel Pioneers
2121 Saskatchewan Dr., 12th Fl., Regina SK S4P 3Y2
Tel: 306-777-2515
Toll-Free: 866-944-4442
e-mail: sasktel.pioneers@sasktel.sk.ca
URL: www.sasktelpioneers.com
Darrell Liebrecht, Manager

Telecommunities Canada Inc.
c/o President, #220, 4252 Commerce Circle, Victoria BC V8Z 4M2
Tel: 250-479-2851; *Fax:* 250-727-6418
e-mail: shearman@victoria.tc.ca
URL: www.tc.ca
Gareth Shearman, President

TelecomPioneers
950 - 15th St., 12th Fl., Denver CO 80202 USA
Tel: 303-571-1200; *Fax:* 303-572-0520
Toll-Free: 800-872-5995
e-mail: info@pioneersvolunteer.org
URL: www.telecompioneers.org
Marty Lee, President

TelecomPioneers of Alberta
9 Munro Cresc., Red Deer AB T4N 0H8
Tel: 403-343-1201
e-mail: chap46@telus.net
Ken Davies, Manager

TelecomPioneers of Canada
PO Box 880, 1505 Barrington St., Halifax NS B3J 2W3
Fax: 902-484-5189
Toll-Free: 888-994-3232
URL: www.telecompioneers.ca

Tenants & Landlords

Action Dignité de Saint-Léonard
9089A, boul Viau, Saint-Léonard QC H1R 2V6
Tél: 514-251-2874; *Téléc:* 514-251-2874
Courriel: actdigsl@cooptel.qc.ca

Association des locataires de l'×le-des-Soeurs (ALIS/NITA) / Nuns' Island Tenants Association
CP 63008, 40, Place du Commerce, Verdun QC H3E 1V6
Tél: 514-667-0914; *Téléc:* 514-995-2773
Courriel: alis_nita@yahoo.com

Comité d'action des citoyennes et citoyens de Verdun
3972, rue de Verdun, Verdun QC H4G 1K9
Tél: 514-769-2228; *Téléc:* 514-769-0825
Courriel: cacv@videotron.ca
URL: www.cacv-verdun.org
Chantal Lamarre, Directrice

Comité d'action Parc Extension (CAPE)
#9, 419, St-Roch, Montréal QC H3N 1R8
Tél: 514-278-6028; *Téléc:* 514-278-0900
Courriel: cape@cooptel.qc.ca
URL: www.comitelogement.org

Comité des citoyens et citoyennes du quartier Saint-Sauveur
301, rue Carillon, Québec QC G1K 5B3
Tél: 418-529-6158
Courriel: cccqss@bellnet.ca
URL: www.cccqss.org

Comité logement de Lacine-Lasalle
426, rue St-Jacques, Lachine QC H8R 1E8
Tél: 514-544-4294; *Téléc:* 514-366-0505
Courriel: logement.lachine-lasalle@videotron.ca

Comité logement du Plateau Mont-Royal
4450, St-Hubert, local 328, Montréal QC H2J 2W9
Tél: 514-527-3495; *Téléc:* 514-527-6653
Courriel: clplateau@yahoo.ca

Comité logement Rosemont
5350, rue Lafond, local R-145, Montréal QC H1X 2X2
Tél: 514-597-2581; *Téléc:* 514-524-9813
Courriel: info@comitelogement.org
URL: www.comitelogement.org
Martine Poitras, Coordonnatrice

Conseil communautaire Notre-Dame-de-Grâce / Notre-Dame-de-Grâce Community Council
5964, av Notre-Dame-de-Grâce, Montréal QC H4A 1N1
Tél: 514-484-1471; *Téléc:* 514-484-1687
Courriel: ndgcc@ndg.ca
URL: www.ndg.ca
Gillian Keefe, Directrice

POPIR-Comité logement (St-Henri, Petite Bourgogne, Ville Émard, Côte St-Paul)
4017, rue Notre-Dame ouest, Montréal QC H4C 1R3
Tél: 514-935-4649; *Téléc:* 514-935-4067
Courriel: popir@videotron.ca

Tourism & Travel

Alberta Hotel & Lodging Association
#401, 5241 Calgary Trail South, Edmonton AB T6H 5G8

Tel: 780-436-6112; *Fax:* 780-436-5404
Toll-Free: 888-436-6112
e-mail: info@ahla.ca
URL: www.ahla.ca
Dave Kaiser, President & CEO

Algoma Kinniwabi Travel Association (AKTA)
#204, 485 Queen St. East, Sault Ste Marie ON P6A 1Z9
Tel: 705-254-4293; *Fax:* 705-254-4892
Toll-Free: 800-263-2546
e-mail: info@algomacountry.com
URL: www.algomacountry.com
Lori Johnson, President

Almaguin-Nipissing Travel Association
PO Box 351, 1375 Seymour St., North Bay ON P1B 8H5
Tel: 705-474-6634; *Fax:* 705-474-9271
Toll-Free: 800-387-0516
e-mail: info@ontariosnearnorth.on.ca
URL: www.ontariosnearnorth.on.ca

Association des hôteliers du Québec (AHQ) / Québec Hoteliers' Association
#1004, 425, boul De Maisonneuve ouest, Montréal QC H3A 3G5
Tél: 514-448-6215; *Téléc:* 514-849-1157
Ligne sans frais: 877-769-9776
Courriel: info@hoteliersquebec.org
URL: www.hoteliersquebec.org
Micheline de Gongre, Présidente-directrice générale

Association moto-tourisme Chibougamau
CP 580, Chibougamau QC G8P 2Y8
Tél: 418-745-3765
Jean-Paul Mercier

Association of Canadian Travel Agencies (ACTA) / Association canadienne des agences de voyages
#328, 2560 Matheson Blvd. East, Mississauga ON L4W 4Y9
Tel: 905-282-9294; *Fax:* 905-282-9826
Toll-Free: 866-725-2282
e-mail: actacan@acta.travel
URL: www.acta.ca
Affiliation(s): Universal Federation of Travel Agency Associations
Heather Craig-Peddie, Director, Operations
David McCaig, President/COO

Association of Canadian Travel Agencies - Atlantic (ACTA)
PO Box 21007, Quispamsis NB E2E 4Z4
Tel: 506-847-4030; *Fax:* 506-847-4048
Toll-Free: 866-725-2282
e-mail: actaatlantic@acta.travel
URL: www.acta.ca
Lorie Cohen Hackett, Regional Manager

Association of Canadian Travel Agents - Alberta/NWT
PO Box 73034, 6290, 199 St., Edmonton AB T5T 3X1
Tel: 780-756-6606; *Fax:* 780-756-6639
Toll-Free: 800-667-8314
e-mail: cgannon@acta.ca
Allan Ronneseth, Regional, Chair
Colleen Gannon, Regional Manager

Association of Canadian Travel Agents - British Columbia/Yukon
#213, 5760 Minoru Blvd., Richmond BC V6X 2A9
Tel: 604-231-0544; *Fax:* 604-231-6020
e-mail: actabcyu@telus.net
David McCaig, Regional Manager

Association of Canadian Travel Agents - Manitoba
#700, 177 Lombard Ave., Winnipeg MB R3B 0W5
Tel: 204-831-0831; *Fax:* 204-925-8000
e-mail: smmorris@mts.net
Shelley Morris, Regional Manager

Association of Canadian Travel Agents - Ontario
#328, 2560 Matheson Blvd. East, Mississauga ON L4W 4Y5
Tel: 905-282-9294; *Fax:* 905-282-9826
Toll-Free: 888-257-2282
e-mail: actaon@on.aibn.com
URL: www.acta.ca
Heather Craig-Peddie, Director of Operations
Mike Foster, Regional Chair

Association of Canadian Travel Agents - Québec / Association des agents de voyages du Québec
#401, 152, rue Notre-Dame est, Montréal QC H2Y 3P6
Tél: 514-397-9977; *Téléc:* 514-397-1581
Courriel: actaquebec@acta.travel
Henri Castillo, Directeur général

Association touristique des Laurentides (ATL) / Laurentian Tourist Association
14 142, rue de la Chapelle, Mirabel QC J7J 2C8
Tél: 450-436-8532
Ligne sans frais: 800-561-6673
Courriel: info-tourisme@laurentides.com
URL: www.laurentides.com

Association touristique régionale de Charlevoix
495, boul de Comporté, La Malbaie QC G5A 3G3
Tél: 418-665-4454; *Téléc:* 418-665-3811
Ligne sans frais: 800-667-2276
Courriel: info@tourisme-charlevoix.com
URL: www.tourisme-charlevoix.com/fr/accueil/index.asp

Association touristique régionale de Duplessis (ATRD)
312, av Brochu, Sept-Iles QC G4R 2W6
Tél: 418-962-0808; *Téléc:* 418-962-6518
Ligne sans frais: 888-463-0808
Courriel: info@tourismeduplessis.com
URL: www.tourismeduplessis.com
Marie-Soleil Vigneault, Directrice générale
Danys Jomphe, Président

Association touristique régionale du Saguenay-Lac-Saint-Jean
#100, 412, boul. Saguenay Est, Chicoutimi QC G7H 7Y8
Tél: 418-543-9778; *Téléc:* 418-543-1805
Ligne sans frais: 800-463-9651
Courriel: info@tourismesaglac.net
URL: www.saguenaylacsaintjean.net
Carol Martel, Directeur général
Robert Bilodeau, Président

Association touristique régionale Manicouagan
#304, 337, boul LaSalle, Baie-Comeau QC G4Z 2Z1
Tél: 418-294-2876; *Téléc:* 418-294-2345
Ligne sans frais: 888-463-5319
Courriel: atrmanic@globetrotter.net
URL: www.tourismemanicouagan.com/fr/
Denis Cardinal, Directeur général

Associations touristiques régionales associées du Québec (ATRAQ) / Québec Regional Tourist Associations Inc.
#330, 1575, boul de l'Avenir, Laval QC H7S 2N5
Tél: 450-686-8358; *Téléc:* 450-686-9630
Ligne sans frais: 877-686-8358
Courriel: information@atrassociees.com
URL: www.atrassociees.com
Louis Rome, Directeur général

British Columbia Lodging & Campgrounds Association (BCLCA)
#209, 3003 St. John's St., Port Moody BC V3H 2C4
Tel: 604-945-7676; *Fax:* 604-945-7606
Toll-Free: 888-923-4678
e-mail: info@bclca.com
URL: www.bclca.com
Joss Penny, Executive Director

Cambridge Tourism
750 Hespeler Rd., Cambridge ON N3H 5L8
Tel: 519-622-2336; *Fax:* 519-622-0662
Toll-Free: 800-749-7560
e-mail: visit@cambridgetourism.com
URL: www.cambridgetourism.com
Affiliation(s): Ontario Motor Coach Association; Grand River County; Tourism Toronto; Southern Ontario Travel Organization; Canadian Society of Associations Executives
Anita Tomins, Director of Tourism

Camping Québec
#700, 2001, rue de la Metropole, Longueuil QC J4G 1S9
Tél: 450-651-7396; *Téléc:* 450-651-7397
Ligne sans frais: 800-363-0457
URL: www.destinationcamping.ca
Maryse Catellier, Vice-président exécutif

Canadian Hotel Marketing & Sales Executives (CHMSE)
26 Avonhurst Rd., Toronto ON M9A 2G8
Tel: 416-252-9800; *Fax:* 416-252-7071
e-mail: info@chmse.com
URL: www.chmse.com
Shelley Macdonald, Executive Director
Julie Wiggins, Vice-President
Susan Aguilo, Vice-President
Monika Nowak, Vice-President
Linda Stott, President

Canadian Institute of Travel Counsellors (CITC) / Institut canadien des conseillers en voyages
#406, 505 Consumers Rd., Toronto ON M2J 4V8
Tel: 416-484-4450; *Fax:* 416-484-4140
Toll-Free: 800-589-5776
e-mail: info@citc.ca
URL: www.citc.ca
Steve Gillick, President/COO

Canadian Recreational Vehicle Association (CRVA) / Association canadienne du véhicule récréatif
#310, 2175 Sheppard Ave. East, Toronto ON M2J 1W8
Tel: 416-971-7800; *Fax:* 416-491-1670
e-mail: crva@crva.ca
URL: www.crva.ca
Don Mockford, Executive Vice-President

Canadian Resort Development Association (CRDA)
#807, 1240 Bay St., Toronto ON M5R 2A7
Tel: 416-960-4930; *Fax:* 416-923-8348
Toll-Free: 800-646-9205
e-mail: crda@istar.ca
URL: www.crda.com
Affiliation(s): American Resort & Residential Development Association; Global Alliance for Timeshare Excellence - Washington DC
Gloria A. Collinson, Director/President

Canadian Tourism Research Institute
255 Smyth Rd., Ottawa ON K1H 8M7
Tel: 613-526-3280; *Fax:* 613-526-4857
Toll-Free: 866-711-2262
e-mail: ctri@conferenceboard.ca
URL: www.conferenceboard.ca/ctri/
Harry French, Director

Cariboo Chilcotin Coast Tourism Association
118A North 1 Ave., Williams Lake BC V2G 1Y8
Tel: 250-392-2226; *Fax:* 250-392-2838
Toll-Free: 800-663-5885
e-mail: info@landwithoutlimits.com
URL: www.landwithoutlimits.com
Affiliation(s): Council of Regional Tourist Associations; Cariboo Chilcotin Guide Outfitters Association; Guest Ranch Association of BC
Kim Burgoyne, Executive Director
Shawna Ludwig, Financial Comptroller

Central Nova Tourist Association (CNTA)
PO Box 1761, 574 Prince St., Truro NS B2N 5Z5
Tel: 902-893-8782; *Fax:* 902-893-2269
Toll-Free: 800-895-1177
e-mail: info@centralnovascotia.com
URL: www.centralnovascotia.com
Joyce Mingo, Executive Director

Convention & Visitors Bureau of Windsor, Essex County & Pelee Island
City Centre, #103, 333 Riverside Dr. West, Windsor ON N9A 5K4
Tel: 519-255-6530; *Fax:* 519-255-6192
Toll-Free: 800-265-3633
e-mail: cvb@city.windsor.on.ca
URL: www.visitwindsor.com
Gordon Orr, Managing Director

Cornwall & Seaway Valley Tourism
11 Water St. West, Cornwall ON K6J 1A1
Tel: 613-938-4748; *Fax:* 613-938-4751
Toll-Free: 800-937-4748
e-mail: info@cornwalltourism.com
URL: www.cornwalltourism.com
Michael Lalonde, Executive Manager

Council of Tourism Associations of British Columbia (COTA)
#1208, 409 Granville St., Vancouver BC V6C 1T2
Tel: 604-685-5956; *Fax:* 604-685-5915
e-mail: cotabc@telus.net
URL: www.cotabc.com
Jim Storie, Chair
Stephen Regan, President/CEO
Peter Larose, Director, Policy & Planning

Destination Winnipeg Inc. (DW)
#300, 259 Portage Ave., Winnipeg MB R3B 2A9
Tel: 204-943-1970; *Fax:* 204-942-4043
Toll-Free: 800-665-0204
e-mail: wpginfo@destinationwinnipeg.ca
URL: www.destinationwinnipeg.ca
Nick Logan, Chair
Stuart Duncan, President

Evangeline Trail Tourism Association (ETTA)
5518 Prospect Road, New Minas NS B4N 3K8
Tel: 902-861-1645
Beth Caldwell, Executive Director

Fondation Tourisme Jeunesse
3514, ave. Lacombe, Montréal QC H3T 1M1
Tél: 514-252-3208; *Téléc:* 514-252-3024
Courriel: fondationtourismejeunesse@gmail.com
URL: www.tourismejeunesse.org
Affiliation(s): Fédération internationale des auberges de jeunesse; Regroupement loisir Québec; Bureau canadien de l'éducation internationale; Bureau international du tourisme social
Veronica Gomez, Directrice générale

Fredericton Visitor & Convention Bureau (TIANB) / Services aux visiteurs et congrès de Fredericton
PO Box 130, Fredericton NB E3B 4Y7
Tel: 506-460-2041; *Fax:* 506-460-2474
Toll-Free: 888-888-4768
e-mail: tourism@fredericton.ca
URL: www.tianb.com
Affiliation(s): Canadian Association of Visitor & Convention Bureaux
Nancy Lockerbie, Tourism Manager
Angela Watson, Tourism Coordinator
Rebecca Wilson, Administration Officer
Mary Ellen Hudson, Tourism Coordinator
David Seabrook, Tourism Coordinator/Acting Manager
Laura Chase, Promotions Officer

The Georgian Triangle Tourist Association & Tourist Information Centre
30 Mountain Rd., Collingwood ON L9Y 5H7
Tel: 705-445-7722
Toll-Free: 888-227-8667
e-mail: info@georgiantriangle.com
URL: www.georgiantriangle.com
Social Media: www.facebook.com/group.php?gid=99129054579
Nancy Kindler, Executive Director

Halifax Tourism, Culture & Heritage
PO Box 1749, Halifax NS B3J 3A5
Tel: 902-490-5948; *Fax:* 902-490-5950
e-mail: ivc@region.halifax.ns.ca
URL: www.halifaxinfo.com
Lewis M. Rogers, Director

HomeLink International Home Exchange (HLCA)
1707 Platt Cres., North Vancouver BC V7J 1X9
Tel: 604-987-3262
e-mail: info@homelink.ca
URL: www.homelink.ca
Jack Graber, Director

Hospitality Newfoundland & Labrador (HNL)
ICON Bldg., 187 Kenmonunt Rd., 2nd Fl., St. John's NL A1B 3P9
Tel: 709-722-2000; *Fax:* 709-722-8104
Toll-Free: 800-563-0700
e-mail: hnl@hnl.ca
URL: www.hnl.ca
Carol-Ann Gilliard, Chief Executive Officer

Hostelling International - Canada (HI-C)
#400, 205 Catherine St., Ottawa ON K2P 1C3
Tel: 613-237-7884; *Fax:* 613-237-7868
e-mail: info@hostellingintl.ca
URL: www.hostellingintl.ca
Affiliation(s): International Youth Hostel Federation
Joël Marier, National Executive Director

Hotel Association of Canada Inc. (HAC) / Association des hôtels du Canada
#1206, 130 Albert St., Ottawa ON K1P 5G4
Tel: 613-237-7149; *Fax:* 613-237-8928
e-mail: info@hotelassociation.ca
URL: www.hotelassociation.ca
Affiliation(s): American Hotel & Lodging Association; International Hotel & Restaurant Association; Canadian Tourism Commission; Tourism Industry Association of Canada; Meeting Planners International
Andrea Myers, Director, Marketing & Member Services
Anthony P. Pollard, President
Walter Willett, Director, Business Development

Hotel Association of Nova Scotia
PO Box 473, Stn. M, Halifax NS B3J 2P8
Tel: 902-425-4890
URL: www.novascotiahotels.ca
Jeff Ransome, President

Hotel Association of Prince Edward Island
c/o 129 Queen St., Charlottetown PE C1A 4B3
Tel: 902-368-3688; *Fax:* 902-368-3108
Elaine Thompson, President

Huronia Tourism Association (HTA)
1110 Hwy. 26, Midhurst ON L0L 1X0
Tel: 705-726-9300; *Fax:* 705-726-3991
Toll-Free: 866-893-9300
e-mail: info@county.simcoe.on.ca
URL: www.county.simcoe.on.ca
Rose Cambourne, Administrator

Institut de tourisme et d'hôtellerie du Québec (ITHQ)
3535, rue Saint-Denis, Montréal QC H2X 3P1
Tél: 514-282-5108; *Téléc:* 514-873-4529
Ligne sans frais: 800-361-5111
Courriel: webmestre@ithq.qc.ca
URL: www.ithq.qc.ca
Lucille Daoust, Directrice générale
Robert Gagnon, Président

Klondike Visitors Association (KVA)
PO Box 389, Dawson YT Y0B 1G0
Tel: 867-993-5575; *Fax:* 867-993-6415
e-mail: kva@dawson.net
URL: www.dawsoncity.ca
Valerie Anderson, Executive Director

Kootenay Rockies Tourism
PO Box 10, 1905 Warren Ave., Kimberley BC V1A 2Y5
Tel: 250-427-4838; *Fax:* 250-427-3344
Toll-Free: 800-661-6603
e-mail: info@kootenayrockies.com
URL: www.kootenayrockies.com
Chris Dadson, President

Muskoka Tourism
1342 Hwy. 11 North, RR#2, Kilworthy ON P0E 1G0
Tel: 705-689-0660; *Fax:* 705-689-9118
Toll-Free: 800-267-9700
e-mail: info@muskokatourism.ca
URL: www.discovermuskoka.ca

Niagara Falls Tourism
5400 Robinson St, Niagara Falls ON L2G 2A6
Tel: 905-356-6061; *Fax:* 905-356-5567
Toll-Free: 800-563-2557
e-mail: office@niagarafallstourism.com
URL: www.niagarafallstourism.com

North of Superior Tourism Association (NOSTA)
PO Box 5, RR#1, Nipigon ON P0T 2J0
Tel: 807-887-3333; *Fax:* 807-887-3030
Toll-Free: 800-265-3951
e-mail: info@nosta.on.ca
URL: www.nosta.on.ca
Bruce Fallen, Managing Director

Northern British Columbia Tourism Association (NBCTA)
PO Box 2373, 1274 - 5th Ave., Prince George BC V2N 2S6
Tel: 250-561-0432; *Fax:* 250-561-0450
Toll-Free: 800-663-8843
e-mail: info@nbctourism.com
URL: www.nbctourism.com
Anthony Everett, CEO

Northern Frontier Visitors Association
#4, 4807 - 49 St., Yellowknife NT X1A 3T5
Tel: 867-873-4262; *Fax:* 867-873-3654
Toll-Free: 877-881-4262
e-mail: office@northernfrontier.com
URL: www.northernfrontier.com
Denie Olmstead, Executive Director

Northern Rockies Alaska Highway Tourism Association (NRAHTA)
PO Box 6850, Stn. Main, #300, 9523 - 100 St., Fort St John BC V1J 4J3
Tel: 250-785-2544; *Fax:* 250-785-4424
Toll-Free: 888-785-2544
e-mail: info@hellonorth.com
URL: www.hellonorth.com
Affiliation(s): Tourism BC
April Moi, Executive Director

Northwest Ontario Sunset Country Travel Association
PO Box 647W, Kenora ON P9N 3X6
Tel: 807-468-5853; *Fax:* 807-468-5484
Toll-Free: 800-665-7567
e-mail: info@ontariossunsetcountry.ca
URL: www.ontariossunsetcountry.ca
Gerry Cariou, Executive Director

Northwest Territories Tourism (NWTT)
PO Box 610, Yellowknife NT X1A 2N5
Tel: 867-873-5007*Tel:* 1-867-873-7200; *Fax:* 867-873-4059
Toll-Free: 800-661-0788
e-mail: info@spectacularnwt.com; communications@spectacularnwt.com
URL: www.spectacularnwt.com
Affiliation(s): Canadian Tourism Commission (CTC); Yukon Travel; Nunavut Tourism; Travel Alberta; Tourism BC
Gerard (Gerry) LePrieur, Executive Director

Nunavut Tourism
PO Box 1450, Iqaluit NU X0A 0H0
Tel: 867-979-6551; *Fax:* 867-979-1261
Toll-Free: 866-686-2888
e-mail: info@nunavuttourism.com
URL: www.nunavuttourism.com
Affiliation(s): Team Canada
Bill Lyall, Chair
Paul Lewis, CEO
Betty Ann Eaton, Vice-Chair

NWC, the Business Travellers' Association (NWC)
PO Box 336, 28 Queen Elizabeth Way, Winnipeg MB R3C 2H6
Tel: 204-284-8900; *Fax:* 204-284-8909
Toll-Free: 800-665-6928
e-mail: nwcta@nwcta.com
URL: www.nwcta.com
Affiliation(s): Maritime Commercial Travellers Association
Diane McDonald, Membership Services Coordinator

Office du tourisme et des congrès de Québec (OTCQ) / Québec City & Area Tourism & Convention Board
399, rue St-Joseph est, Québec QC G1K 8E2
Tél: 418-641-6654; *Téléc:* 418-641-6578
Ligne sans frais: 877-783-1608
Courriel: danielle.doyon@quebecregion.com
URL: www.quebecregion.com
Pierre Labrie, Directeur général
Daniel Gagnon, Directeur, Communication et publicité
Gilles Proulx, Directeur, Administration, accueil et services aux membres
Hélène Pomerleau, Directrice, Promotion, ventes et services

Ontario Accommodation Association (OAA)
#2, 347 Pido Rd., RR#6, Peterborough ON K9J 6X7
Tel: 705-745-4982; *Fax:* 705-745-4983
Toll-Free: 800-461-1972
e-mail: info@ontarioaccommodation.com
URL: www.ontarioaccommodation.com
Affiliation(s): Tourism Industry Association of Canada; Tourism Federation of Ontario
Bruce M. Gravel, President

Ontario East Tourism Association (OETA)
PO Box 730, #200, 104 St. Lawrence Street, Merrickville ON K0G 1N0
Tel: 613-269-4113; *Fax:* 613-659-4306
Toll-Free: 800-567-3278
e-mail: info@realontario.ca
URL: www.realontario.ca
Rose Bertoia, Executive Director
John Bonser, President

Ontario Private Campground Association (OPCA)
#8, 220 Royal Crest Ct., Markham ON L3R 9Y2
Tel: 905-947-9500; *Fax:* 905-947-9501
Toll-Free: 877-672-2226
e-mail: opca@campingontario.ca
URL: www.campingontario.ca
Affiliation(s): Campgrounds Campings Canada; Go RVing Canada
Beth Potter, Executive Director

Ontario Restaurant, Hotel & Motel Association (ORHMA)
#8-201, 2600 Skymark Ave., Mississauga ON L4W 5B2
Tel: 905-361-0268; *Fax:* 905-361-0288
Toll-Free: 800-668-8906
e-mail: info@orhma.com
URL: www.orhma.com
David Blades, Chair
Tony Elenis, President & CEO
Al Richards, Secretary-Treasurer
Michelle Saunders, Manager, Government Relations
Alice Tjan, Manager, Membership Services

Ontario's Wilderness Region
PO Box 920, 76 McIntyre Rd., Schumacher ON P0N 1G0

Tel: 705-360-1989; Fax: 705-268-5526
Toll-Free: 800-461-3766
e-mail: info@ontarioswildernessregion.com
URL: www.ontarioswildernessregion.com
Jennifer Rowe, Executive Director
Sean Mackey, President

Ottawa Tourism / Tourisme Ottawa
#1800, 130 Albert St., Ottawa ON K1P 5G4
Tel: 613-237-5150; Fax: 613-237-7339
Toll-Free: 800-363-4465
e-mail: info@ottawatourism.ca
URL: www.ottawatourism.ca
Noel Buckley, President & CEO

Ottawa Valley Tourist Association (OVTA)
c/o Ottawa Valley Tourist Association, 9 International Dr., Pembroke ON K8A 6W5
Tel: 613-732-4364; Fax: 613-735-2492
Toll-Free: 800-757-6580
e-mail: adventureplayground@ottawavalley.org
URL: www.ottawavalley.org
Mitchell Wilkie, Manager
Charlotte Gebhart, President

Peterborough & the Kawarthas Tourism
175 George St. North, Peterborough ON K9J 3G6
Tel: 705-742-2201; Fax: 705-742-2494
Toll-Free: 800-461-6424
e-mail: info@thekawarthas.net
URL: www.thekawarthas.net

Pictou County Tourist Association
PO Box 1839, 40 Water St., Pictou NS B0K 1H0
Tel: 902-485-6151; Fax: 902-485-4415
Toll-Free: 877-816-2326
e-mail: admin@tourismpictoucounty.com
URL: www.tourismpictoucounty.com

Rainbow Country Travel Association (RCTA)
2726 Whippoorwill Ave., Sudbury ON P3G 1E9
Tel: 705-522-0104; Fax: 705-522-3132
Toll-Free: 800-465-6655
e-mail: rainbow@vianet.on.ca
URL: www.rainbowcountry.com
Erin Downey, Executive Director

Resorts Ontario
29 Albert St. North, Orillia ON L3V 5J9
Tel: 705-325-9115; Fax: 705-325-7999
Toll-Free: 800-363-7227
e-mail: escapes@resorts-ontario.com
URL: www.resorts-ontario.com

Saskatchewan Hotel & Hospitality Association (SHHA)
#302, 2080 Broad St., Regina SK S4P 1Y3
Tel: 306-522-1664; Fax: 306-525-1944
Toll-Free: 800-667-1118
e-mail: lorane.has@sasktel.net
URL: www.hotelsofsask.com
Bill Nelson, Executive Director

Stratford Tourism Alliance
47 Downie St., Stratford ON N5A 1W7
Tel: 519-271-5140; Fax: 519-273-1818
Toll-Free: 800-561-7926
e-mail: info@welcometostratford.com
URL: www.welcometostratford.com
Affiliation(s): National Tour Association; Ontario Motor Coach Association
Eugene Zakreski, Executive Director
Christina Phillips, Membership &Advertising Coordinator
Cathy Rehberg, Marketing Coordinator

Sudbury Visitor & Convention Services
PO Box 5000, Stn. A, 200 Brady St., Sudbury ON P3A 5P3
Tel: 705-674-4455; Fax: 705-671-6767
Toll-Free: 877-304-8222
e-mail: renee.germain@sudbury.ca
URL: www.grandsudbury.ca
Renee Germain, Coordinator

Thompson Okanagan Tourism Association (TOTA)
2280-D Leckie Rd., Kelowna BC V1X 6G6
Tel: 250-860-5999; Fax: 250-860-9993
Toll-Free: 800-567-2275
e-mail: info@totabc.com
URL: www.totabc.com
Deanna Rainey, CEO
Carolyn Carr, Director of Marketing

Tourism Brantford
399 Wayne Gretzky Pkwy., Brantford ON N3R 8B4
Tel: 519-751-9900; Fax: 519-751-2617
Toll-Free: 800-265-6299
e-mail: tourism@brantford.ca
URL: www.visitbrantford.ca
Susan Sager, Manager, Tourism & Marketing

Tourism Burlington
414 Locust St., Burlington ON L7S 1T7
Tel: 905-634-5594; Fax: 905-634-7220
Toll-Free: 877-499-9989
e-mail: info@tourismburlington.com
URL: www.tourismburlington.com
Pam Belgrade, Executive Director

Tourism Calgary
#200, 238 - 11 Ave. SE, Calgary AB T2G 0X8
Tel: 403-263-8510; Fax: 403-262-3809
Toll-Free: 800-661-1678
URL: www.tourismcalgary.com
Aldon Wells, Acting CEO

Tourism Cape Breton
PO Box 1448, Sydney NS B1P 6R7
Tel: 902-563-4636; Fax: 902-564-5422
Toll-Free: 800-565-0000
e-mail: info@cbisland.com
URL: www.cbisland.com
Sandra MacDonald, General Manager

Tourism Hamilton
34 James St. South, Hamilton ON L8P 2X8
Tel: 905-546-2666; Fax: 905-546-2667
Toll-Free: 800-263-8590
e-mail: tourism@hamilton.ca
URL: www.tourismhamilton.com
David Adames, Executive Director

Tourism Industry Association of Canada (TIAC) / Association de l'industrie touristique du Canada (AITC)
#803, 130 Albert St., Ottawa ON K1P 5G4
Tel: 613-238-3883; Fax: 613-238-3878
e-mail: swong@tiac.travel
URL: www.tiac-aitc.ca
Randall Williams, President/CEO
Ken Lambert, Chair
Christopher Jones, Vice President, Public Affairs

Tourism Industry Association of New Brunswick Inc. (TIANB) / Association de l'industrie touristique du Nouveau-Brunswick inc.
PO Box 23001, #440, 500 Beaverbrook Ct., Fredericton NB E3B 7B3
Tel: 506-458-5646; Fax: 506-459-3634
Toll-Free: 800-668-5313
e-mail: info@tianb.com
URL: www.tianb.com
Joanne Bérubé-Gagné, President

Tourism Industry Association of Nova Scotia (TIANS)
2089 Maitland St., Halifax NS B3K 2Z8
Tel: 902-423-4480; Fax: 902-422-0184
Toll-Free: 800-948-4267
e-mail: information_central@tians.org
URL: www.tians.org
Affiliation(s): Innkeepers Guild of Nova Scotia; Adventure Tourism Association of Nova Scotia; Campground Owners Association of Nova Scotia; Metropolitan Area Tourism Association; Nova Scotia Bed & Breakfast Association
Darlene Grant Fiander, President
Danny Morton, Chair
Bill Walsh, Sec.-Treas.

Tourism Industry Association of PEI (TIAPEI)
PO Box 2050, 25 Queen St., 3rd Fl., Charlottetown PE C1A 7N7
Tel: 902-566-5008; Fax: 902-368-3605
Toll-Free: 866-566-5008
e-mail: tiapei@tiapei.pe.ca
URL: www.tiapei.pe.ca
Thom MacMillan, President

Tourism Industry Association of the Yukon
#3, 1109 - 1st Ave., Whitehorse YT Y1A 5G4
Tel: 867-668-3331; Fax: 867-667-7379
e-mail: tiayukon@klondiker.com
URL: www.tiayukon.com
Patti Balsillie, CEO

Tourism London
696 Wellington Rd. South, London ON N6C 4R2
Tel: 519-661-5000; Fax: 519-661-6160
Toll-Free: 800-265-2602
e-mail: tourism@londontourism.ca
URL: www.londontourism.ca
John Winston, General Manager

Tourism Regina Convention & Visitor Bureau
PO Box 3355, Hwy. 1 East, Regina SK S4P 3H1
Tel: 306-789-5099; Fax: 306-789-3171
Toll-Free: 800-661-5099
URL: www.tourismregina.com
Loni Kaufmann, Executive Director
Alison Fraser, Dir., Sales, Conventions & Events
Cindy Wright, Membership Services Manager

Tourism Saint John / Bureau de tourisme et de congrés de Saint John
PO Box 1971, 15 Market Sq., 11th Fl., Saint John NB E2L 4L1
Tel: 506-658-2990; Fax: 506-632-6118
Toll-Free: 866-463-8639
e-mail: visitsj@saintjohn.ca
URL: www.tourismsaintjohn.com; www.venuesaintjohn.com
Margaret Totten, Manager

Tourism Sarnia Lambton (TSL)
556 North Christina St., Sarnia ON N7T 5W6
Tel: 519-336-3232; Fax: 519-336-3278
Toll-Free: 800-265-0316
e-mail: info@tourismsarnialambton.com
URL: www.tourismsarnialambton.com
Leona Allen, Office Administrator
John Dickson, General Manager/Executive Director

Tourism Saskatoon
#101, 202 Fourth Avenue North, Saskatoon SK S7K 0K1
Tel: 306-242-1206; Fax: 306-242-1955
Toll-Free: 800-567-2444
e-mail: info@tourismsaskatoon.com
URL: www.tourismsaskatoon.com
Affiliation(s): Tourism Saskatchewan
Todd Brandt, CEO

Tourism Thunder Bay
500 Donald St. East, Thunder Bay ON P7E 5V3
Tel: 807-625-2149; Fax: 807-623-5468
Toll-Free: 800-667-8386
e-mail: visit@thunderbay.com
URL: www.visitthunderbay.com
Paul Pepe, Tourism Manager
Rose Marie Tarnowski, Coord., Convention & Visitor Svcs.

Tourism Toronto (TCVA)
Queen's Quay Terminal at Harbourfront, PO Box 126, 207 Queen's Quay West, Toronto ON M5J 1A7
Tel: 416-203-2600; Fax: 416-203-6753
Toll-Free: 800-499-2514
e-mail: toronto@torcvb.com
URL: www.torontotourism.com
Social Media: www.facebook.com/visittoronto
Affiliation(s): International Association of Convention & Visitor Bureaux; Toronto Board of Trade; American Society of Association Executives
David Whitaker, President/CEO
Andrew Weir, Vice-President, Communications

Tourism Vancouver/Greater Vancouver Convention & Visitors Bureau
#210, 200 Burrard St., Vancouver BC V6C 3L6
Tel: 604-682-2222; Fax: 604-682-1717
URL: www.tourismvancouver.com
Social Media: www.facebook.com/insidevancouver
Affiliation(s): Canadian Association of Convention & Visitors Bureaus
Rick Antonson, President/CEO
Paul Vallee, Exec. Vice-President
Ted Lee, CFO

Tourism Victoria/Greater Victoria Visitors & Convention Bureau
Administration Office, 31 Bastion Sq., 4th Fl., Victoria BC V8W 1J1
Tel: 250-414-6999; Fax: 250-361-9733
Toll-Free: 800-663-3883
e-mail: info@tourismvictoria.com
URL: www.tourismvictoria.com
Robert Gialloreto, CEO
Helen Welch, Vice-President, Marketing

Tourisme Abitibi-Témiscamingue
#100, 155 av Dallaire, Rouyn-Noranda QC J9X 4T3
Tél: 819-762-8181; Téléc: 819-762-5212
Ligne sans frais: 800-808-0706
Courriel: info@tourisme-abitibi-temiscamingue.org
URL: www.abitibi-temiscamingue-tourism.org
Randa Napky, Directeur général
Jocelyn Carrier, Présidente

Tourisme Baie-James (TBJ) / James Bay Tourism
CP 134, 1252, rte 167 sud, Chibougamau QC G8P 2K6
Tél: 418-748-8140; *Téléc:* 418-748-8150
Ligne sans frais: 888-748-8140
Courriel: info@tourismebaiejames.com
URL: www.tourismebaiejames.com
Christian Claveau, Président

Tourisme Bas-Saint-Laurent
148, rue Fraser, Rivière-du-Loup QC G5R 1C8
Tél: 418-867-1272; *Téléc:* 418-867-3245
Ligne sans frais: 800-563-5268
Courriel: atrbsl@qc.aira.com
URL: www.tourismebas-st-laurent.com
Pierre Laplante, Directeur général
Gaston Gendreau, Président

Tourisme Cantons-de-l'Est
20, rue Don-Bosco sud, Sherbrooke QC J1L 1W4
Tél: 819-820-2020; *Téléc:* 819-566-4445
Ligne sans frais: 800-355-5755
URL: www.cantonsdelest.com
Affiliation(s): Tourisme Québec
Alain Larouche, Directeur général
Francine Patenaude, Directrice, Marketing & développement

Tourisme Centre-du-Québec
20, boul Carignan ouest, Princeville QC G6L 4M4
Tél: 819-364-7177; *Téléc:* 819-364-2120
Ligne sans frais: 888-816-4007
Courriel: gturcotte@tcdq.com
URL: www.tourismecentreduquebec.com
Guylaine Turcotte, Adjointe administrative

Tourisme Chaudière-Appalaches (ATCA)
800, autoroute Jean-Lesage, Saint-Nicolas QC G7A 1E3
Tél: 418-831-4411; *Téléc:* 418-831-8442
Ligne sans frais: 888-831-4411
Courriel: info@chaudiereappalaches.com
URL: www.chaudiereappalaches.com
Richard Moreau, Director général

Tourisme Gaspésie
357, route de la Mer, Sainte-Flavie QC G0J 2L0
Tél: 418-775-2223; *Téléc:* 418-775-2234
Ligne sans frais: 800-463-0323
Courriel: info@tourisme-gaspesie.com
URL: www.tourisme-gaspesie.com
Sylvain Tanguay, Directeur général
Joëlle Ross, Directrice adjointe

Tourisme Iles de la Madeleine
128, ch Principal, Cap-aux-Meules QC G4T 1C5
Tél: 418-986-2245; *Téléc:* 418-986-2327
Ligne sans frais: 877-624-4437
Courriel: info@tourismeilesdelamadeleine.com
URL: www.tourismeilesdelamadeleine.com/magdalen-islands/index.cfm
Nancy Vézina, Directrice générale par intérim

Tourisme Lanaudière
3568, rue Church, Rawdon QC J0K 1S0
Tél: 450-834-2535; *Téléc:* 450-834-8100
Ligne sans frais: 800-363-2788
Courriel: info@lanaudiere.ca
URL: www.lanaudiere.ca/fr/
Évangéline Richard, Présidente

Tourisme Laval
2900, boul Saint-Martin ouest, Laval QC H7T 2J2
Tél: 450-682-5522; *Téléc:* 450-682-7304
Ligne sans frais: 877-465-2825
Courriel: info@tourismelaval.com
URL: www.tourismelaval.com
Andrée Courteau, Directeur général
Jean-Louis Bédard, Président

Tourisme Mauricie
795, 5e Rue, Local 102, Shawinigan QC G9N 1G2
Tél: 819-536-3334; *Téléc:* 819-536-3373
Ligne sans frais: 800-567-7603
Courriel: info@tourismemauricie.com
URL: www.tourismemauricie.com
M. André Nollet, Genreal Manager

Tourisme Montérégie
2001, Boul. De Rome, 3e étage, Brossard QC J4W 3K5
Tél: 450- 46-6466; *Téléc:* 450-466-6668
Ligne sans frais: 866-469-0069
Courriel: info@tourisme-monteregie.qc.ca
URL: www.tourisme-monteregie.qc.ca
Eric Fournier, Directeur général
Claude Marchesseault, Président

Tourisme Montréal/Office des congrès et du tourisme du Grand Montréal / Greater Montréal Convention & Tourism Bureau
CP 979, 1001 Square, Dorchester St., Montréal QC H3C 2W3
Tél: 514-873-2015; *Téléc:* 514-844-0541
Ligne sans frais: 877-266-5687
Courriel: howell.gail@tourisme-montreal.org
URL: www.tourism-montreal.org; www.tourisme-montreal.org
Affiliation(s): Canadian Society of Association Executives
François Goulet, Vice-président exécutif

Tourisme Outaouais
103, rue Laurier, Gatineau QC J8X 3V8
Tél: 819-778-2222; *Téléc:* 819-778-7758
Ligne sans frais: 800-265-7822
Courriel: info@tourisme-outaouais.ca
URL: www.tourisme-outaouais.ca
Louise Boudrias, Présidente
Gilles Picard, Directeur général

Travellers' Aid Society of Toronto (TAS)
#B19-23, Union Station, 65 Front St. West, Toronto ON M5J 1E6
Tel: 416-366-7788; *Fax:* 416-366-0829
e-mail: exec.director@travellersaid.ca
URL: www.travellersaid.ca
Affiliation(s): Travellers Aid International
I.A.J. Sloan, President

Vancouver Coast & Mountains Tourism Region
#600, 210 West Broadway St., Vancouver BC V5Y 3W2
Tel: 604-638-6927; *Fax:* 604-739-0153
Toll-Free: 800-667-3306
e-mail: info@vcmbc.com
URL: www.vcmbc.com
Social Media: www.twitter.com/vcmbc
Kevan Ridgway, Executive Director
Doleen Dean, Coordinator

Wilderness Tourism Association of the Yukon (WTAY)
#4, 1114 First Ave., Whitehorse YT Y1A 1A3
Tel: 867-668-3369; *Fax:* 867-668-3370
URL: www.wtay.com
Affiliation(s): Yukon Wild
Neil Hartling, President

Trade

Asia Pacific Foundation of Canada (APFC) / Fondation Asie Pacifique du Canada
#220, 890 West Pender St., Vancouver BC V6C 1J9
Tel: 604-684-5986; *Fax:* 604-681-1370
e-mail: info@asiapacific.ca
URL: www.asiapacific.ca
Yuen Pau Woo, President & Co-CEO
Paul Evans, Co-CEO & Chair
Melinda Czerwinski, Coordinator, Communications

Association of International Automobile Manufacturers of Canada (AIAMC) / Association des fabricants internationaux d'automobiles du Canada
PO Box 5, #1804, 2 Bloor St. W, Toronto ON M4W 3E2
Tel: 416-595-8251; *Fax:* 416-595-2864
e-mail: auto@aiamc.com
URL: www.aiamc.com
David C. Adams, President

British Canadian Chamber of Trade & Commerce
PO Box 1358, Stn. K, Toronto ON M4P 3J4
Tel: 416-502-0847; *Fax:* 416-502-9319
e-mail: central@bcctc.ca
URL: www.bcctc.ca
Ann Mulvale, Executive Director, Central
Liam J. Hopkins, Executive Director, Western
Philip Gorlick, Executive Director, Eastern

Canada Beef Export Federation
#235, 6715 - 8th St. NE, Calgary AB T2E 7H7
Tel: 403-274-0005; *Fax:* 403-274-7275
e-mail: canada@cbef.com
URL: www.cbef.com
Ted Haney, President
Gib Drury, Chairman

Canada China Business Council (CCBC) / Conseil commercial Canada Chine
#407, 100 Adelaide St. West, Toronto ON M5H 1S3
Tel: 416-954-3800; *Fax:* 416-954-3806
e-mail: ccbc@ccbc.com
URL: www.ccbc.com
Eumie Leung, Director of Operations
Sarah Kutulakos, Executive Director

Canada China Business Council (CCBC)
SFU at Harbour Centre, #2600, 515 West Hastings St., Vancouver BC V6B 5K3
Tel: 604-291-5190; *Fax:* 604-291-5039
e-mail: ccbcvan@ccbc.com
URL: www.ccbc.com

Canadian Association of Footwear Importers Inc. (CAFI)
c/o Canadian Association of Importers & Exporters, PO Box 60, #1618, 438 University Ave., Toronto ON M5G 2K8
Tel: 416-595-5333; *Fax:* 416-595-8226
e-mail: info@iecanada.com
URL: www.importers.ca/about_us/cafi.html
Melissa McCormack, Director, Communications

The Canadian Association of Importers & Exporters / Association canadienne des importateurs & exportateurs
#300, 160 Eglinton Ave. East, Toronto ON M4P 3B5
Tel: 416-595-5333; *Fax:* 416-595-8226
e-mail: info@iecanada.com
URL: www.importers.ca
Affiliation(s): National Trade Committees - Association of International Automobile Manufacturers of Canada; Canadian Meat Importers Committee; Canadian Association of Footwear Importers, Inc., Customs & Legislation Committee; Electronics Import Committee; International Cheese Council of Canada
Mary Anderson, MBA, President
Linda M. Bott, CMA, Vice-President, Finance & Administration
Carol Osmond, Vice-President, Policy
Andrea MacDonald, Communications Consultant

Canadian Association of Regulated Importers (CARI) / Association canadienne des importateurs règlementés
#203, 2525 St. Laurent Blvd., Ottawa ON K1H 8P5
Tel: 613-738-1729; *Fax:* 613-733-9501
e-mail: devalk@magma.ca
URL: www.cariimport.org
Robert De Valk, Executive Secretary

Canadian Council for the Americas (CCA) / Conseil Canadien pour les Amériques
#2300, 1066 West Hastings St., Vancouver BC V6E 3X2
Tel: 778-388-5206; *Fax:* 604-806-6112
e-mail: info@cca-bc.com
URL: www.cca-bc.com
Leon Teicher, Secretary
André Nudelman, Chair

Canadian Courier & Logistics Association (CCLA)
#7-266, 91 Rylander Blvd., Toronto ON M1B 5M5
Tel: 905-837-1302; *Fax:* 905-837-1758
Toll-Free: 877-766-6604
e-mail: info@canadiancourier.org
URL: www.canadiancourier.org
Affiliation(s): Ontario Trucking Association; Canadian Trucking Alliance
David Turnbull, President & CEO

Canadian Meat Importers & Exporters Committee (CMIC) / Comité canadien des importeurs de viande
#300, 160 Eglinton Ave. East, Toronto ON M4P 3B5
Tel: 416-595-5333; *Fax:* 416-595-8226
e-mail: info@iecanada.com
URL: www.caie.ca/about_us/cmiec.html
Amesika Baeta, Contact

Citizens Concerned About Free Trade (CCAFT)
PO Box 1983, Saskatoon SK S7K 3S5
Tel: 306-664-8443; *Fax:* 306-244-3790
Toll-Free: 877-937-8263
e-mail: davidorchard@sasktel.net
URL: www.davidorchard.com

Electronics Import Committee (EIC)
PO Box 60, #1618, 438 University Ave., Toronto ON M5G 2K8
Tel: 416-595-5333; *Fax:* 416-595-8226
e-mail: jbescec@iecanada.com
John Bescec, Vice-President, International Trade & Government Relations

Groupe export agroalimentaire Québec - Canada (GEAQC) / Agri-Food Export Group Québec - Canada
668, montée Montarville, Saint-Bruno QC J3V 6B1
Tél: 450-461-6266; *Téléc:* 450-461-6255
Ligne sans frais: 800-563-9767
Courriel: info@groupexport.ca
URL: www.clubexport.ca

André A. Coutu, Président-directeur général

Hong Kong Trade Development Council
Hong Kong Trade Centre, 1st Fl., 9 Temperance St., Toronto ON M5H 1Y6
Tel: 416-366-3594; *Fax:* 416-366-1569
e-mail: toronto.office@tdc.org.hk

Hong Kong Trade Development Council
Office Tower, Convention Plaza, 1 Harbour Rd., 38th Fl., Wanchai Hong Kong
Tel: 852-1830-668; *Fax:* 852-2824-0249
e-mail: hktdc@tdc.org.hk
URL: www.tdctrade.com

International Cheese Council of Canada (ICCC)
c/o CAIE, #300, 160 Eglinton Ave. East, Toronto ON M4P 3B5
Tel: 416-595-5333; *Fax:* 416-595-8226
e-mail: info@iecanada.com
URL: www.caie.ca
Amesika Baeta, Committee Director
Jane Carter, Administrative Assistant

Ontario Association of Trading Houses (OATH)
PO Box 43086, 4841 Yonge St., Toronto ON M2N 6N1
Tel: 416-223-2028; *Fax:* 416-223-5707
e-mail: info@oath.on.ca
URL: www.oath.on.ca
Karel Urban, President
David Archer, Vice-President
Saeed Omar, Vice-President
Louis Papp, Vice-President

The Parliamentary Centre / Le Centre parlementaire
#802, 255 Albert St., Ottawa ON K1P 6A9
Tel: 613-237-0143; *Fax:* 613-235-8237
e-mail: parlcent@parl.gc.ca
URL: www.parlcent.ca
Amelita Armit, President/CEO

Trade Facilitation Office Canada (TFOC) / Bureau de promotion du commerce Canada
#300, 56 Sparks St., Ottawa ON K1P 5A9
Tel: 613-233-3925; *Fax:* 613-233-7860
Toll-Free: 800-267-9674
e-mail: info@tfocanada.ca
URL: www.tfocanada.ca
Dwayne Wright, Executive Director

World Trade Centre Montréal (WTCM)
#6000, 380, rue St-Antoine ouest, Montréal QC H2Y 3X7
Tél: 514-871-4002; *Téléc:* 514-849-3813
Ligne sans frais: 877-590-4040
Courriel: wtcmontreal@ccmm.qc.ca
URL: www.wtcmontreal.com
Affiliation(s): Chambre de commerce du Montréal Metropolitain
Isabelle Hudon, President/CEO
Elliot Lifson, Chair

Transportation & Shipping

Alberta Construction Trucking Association (ACTA)
PO Box 4520, Stn. C, Calgary AB T2T 5N3
Tel: 403-244-4487; *Fax:* 403-244-2340

Alberta Motor Transport Association (AMTA)
3660 Blackfoot Trail SE, Calgary AB T2G 4E6
Tel: 403-243-4161; *Fax:* 403-243-4610
Toll-Free: 800-267-1003
e-mail: amtamsc@amta.ca
URL: www.amta.ca
Mayne Root, Executive Director
Richard Warnock, President

Association du camionnage du Québec inc. (ACQ) / Québec Trucking Association Inc.
#200, 6450, rue Notre Dame ouest, Montréal QC H4C 1C4
Tél: 514-932-0377; *Téléc:* 514-932-1358
Ligne sans frais: 800-361-5813
Courriel: info@carrefour-acq.org
URL: www.carrefour-acq.org
Affiliation(s): Union Internationale des Transports Routiers - Genève; American Trucking Association - Washington, DC
Éric Gignac, Président du conseil
Michel Robert, 1er vice-président du conseil
René Rouillard, Secrétaire du conseil
Bernard Boutin, Trésorier du conseil
Jean-Claude Fortin, Vice-President
Yves Marchand, Vice-President

Association du transport écolier du Québec (ATEQ)
#300, 5300, boul des Galeries, Québec QC G2K 2A2
Tél: 418-622-6544; *Téléc:* 418-622-6595
Ligne sans frais: 877-622-6544
Courriel: courrier@ateq.qc.ca
URL: www.ateq.qc.ca
Gaston Lemay, Président

Association du transport urbain du Québec (ATUQ)
#8090, 800, rue de la Gauchetière, Montréal QC H5A 1J6
Tél: 514-280-4640; *Téléc:* 514-280-7053
Courriel: info@atuq.com
URL: www.atuq.com
Jean-Jacques Beldié, Président
Monique Léveillé, Secrétaire générale
Roxane Fafard, Responsable, Communications et relations publiques
Martine Diotte, Responsable, Bureau d'études et de recherche

Association nationale des camionneurs artisans inc. (ANCAI)
#235, 670, rue Bouvier, Québec QC G2J 1A7
Tél: 418-623-7923; *Téléc:* 418-623-0448
Courriel: infos@ancai.com
URL: www.ancai.com
Clément Bélanger, Président
Gaétan Légaré, Directeur général
Ghislain Bernier, Directeur du bureau juridique
Sylvain Lacombe, Conseiller juridique

Association québécoise du transport et des routes inc. (AQTR)
#200, 1255, rue University, Montréal QC H3B 3B2
Tél: 514-523-6444; *Téléc:* 514-523-2666
Courriel: info@aqtr.qc.ca
URL: www.aqtr.qc.ca
Marc Blanchet, Président
Louis D'Amour, Vice-President
Dominique Lacoste, Directrice générale
Jean Mastropietro, Secrétaire-trésorier

Atlantic Provinces Trucking Association (APTA)
#400, 725 Champlain St., Dieppe NB E1A 1P6
Tel: 506-855-2782; *Fax:* 506-853-7424
Toll-Free: 866-866-1679
e-mail: apta@apta.ca
URL: www.apta.ca
Ralph Boyd, President
Peter Nelson, Executive Director
Georgia Smallwood, Marketing/Membership Services
Chris McKee, Managing Editor- Atlantic Trucking
Shane Esson, Chairperson

British Columbia Supercargoes' Association
#206, 3711 Delbrook Ave., North Vancouver BC V7N 3Z4
Tel: 604-878-1258; *Fax:* 604-904-6545
e-mail: admin@supercargoes.bc.ca; president@supercargoes.bc.ca
URL: www.supercargoes.bc.ca
Terry Stuart, President
David Hood, Director
Magnus Fjortoft, Director

British Columbia Trucking Association (BCTA)
#100, 20111 - 93A Ave., Langley BC V1M 4A9
Tel: 604-888-5319; *Fax:* 604-888-2941
Toll-Free: 800-565-2282
e-mail: bcta@bctrucking.com
URL: www.bctrucking.com
Paul Landry, President & CEO
Michele Nicol, Director, Business Operations
Louise Yako, Vice President, Policy, Communications & Partnerships

Bytown Railway Society (BRS)
PO Box 47076, Ottawa ON K1B 5P9
Tel: 613-745-1201; *Fax:* 613-745-1201
e-mail: info@bytownrailwaysociety.ca
URL: www.bytownrailwaysociety.ca
David Stremes, President
Leslie Goodwin, Treasurer
Paul Bown, Vice-President

Canadian Association of Movers (CAM) / Association canadienne des déménageurs (ACD)
#525, 2085 Hurontario St., Mississauga ON L5A 4G1
Tel: 905-848-6579; *Fax:* 905-848-8499
Toll-Free: 866-860-0065
e-mail: admin@mover.net
URL: www.mover.net
Affiliation(s): American Moving & Storage Association

Canadian Association of Railway Suppliers / Association canadienne des fournisseurs de chemins de fer
#901, 99 Bank St., Ottawa ON K1P 6B9
Tel: 613-237-3888; *Fax:* 613-237-4888
e-mail: info@railwaysuppliers.ca
URL: www.railwaysuppliers.ca
Jay Nordenstrom, Executive Director

Canadian Bus Association (CBA) / Association canadienne de l'autobus
c/o #2001, 45 O'Connor St., Ottawa ON K1P 1A4
Tel: 613-238-1800; *Fax:* 613-241-4936
e-mail: mresnick@rothwellgroup.ca

Canadian Business Aviation Association (CBAA) / Association canadienne de l'aviation d'affaires (ACAA)
#430, 55 Metcalfe St., Ottawa ON K1P 6L5
Tel: 613-236-5611; *Fax:* 613-236-2361
e-mail: info@cbaa.ca
URL: www.cbaa.ca
Affiliation(s): National Business Aviation Association; International Business Aviation Council; European Business Aircraft Association
Rich Gage, President & CEO
Bill Boucher, Vice President
Terry Stonebridge, Executive Assistant/Office Admin.
Peter Saunders, Manager POC Program
Doug Ware, Chairman

Canadian Council of Motor Transport Administrators (CCMTA) / Conseil canadien des administrateurs en transport motorisé (CCATM)
2323 St. Laurent Blvd., Ottawa ON K1G 4J8
Tel: 613-736-1003; *Fax:* 613-736-1395
e-mail: ccmta-secretariat@ccmta.ca
URL: www.ccmta.ca
Carolyn Burggraaf, President
Sherry Wolf, Vice-President

Canadian Ferry Operators Association (CFOA) / Association canadienne des opérateurs de traversiers
c/o Anthonie A. de Hoog, CFOA Executive Director, 21 Meredith Dr., Sussex Corner NB E4E 2T8
Tel: 506-433-4810; *Fax:* 506-432-9505
e-mail: adehoog@cfoa.ca
URL: www.cfoa.ca
Anthonie A. de Hoog, Executive Director
David Miller, President

Canadian Heartland Training Railway
PO Box 1174, Camrose AB T4V 1X2
Tel: 780-679-4008; *Fax:* 780-672-4032
URL: www.chtr.ca
Joe Bracken, President

Canadian Industrial Transportation Association (CITA) / Association canadienne de transport industriel (ACTI)
#405, 580 Terry Fox Dr., Ottawa ON K2L 4C2
Tel: 613-599-3283; *Fax:* 613-599-1295
e-mail: info@cita-acti.ca
URL: www.cita-acti.ca
Bob Ballantyne, P.Eng, President
Denise Fata, Manager, Marketing and Events
Cindy Hick, Vice-President

Canadian Institute of Traffic & Transportation (CITT) / Institut canadien du trafic et du transport
#400, 10 King St. East, Toronto ON M5C 1C3
Tel: 416-363-5696; *Fax:* 416-363-5698
e-mail: info@citt.ca
URL: www.citt.ca
Social Media: www.facebook.com/group.php?gid=148552441716
Patrick K. Bohan, Chair
Catherine Viglas, CAE, President
Chrissy Aitchison, Marketing Manager
Jennifer Barry, Membership/Events Coordinator
Maria Murjani, Customer Service Representative
Sue MacMillan, Program Manager

Canadian International Freight Forwarders Association, Inc. (CIFFA) / Association des transitaires internationaux canadiens, inc. (ATIC)
#480, 170 Attwell Dr., Toronto ON M9W 5Z5
Tel: 416-234-5100; *Fax:* 416-234-5152
Toll-Free: 866-282-4332
e-mail: ciffa@ciffa.com
URL: www.ciffa.com

Affiliation(s): International Federation of Freight Forwarders Associations
Marc D. Bibeau, President
Donna Letterio, First Vice-President
Mark Soubry, Second Vice-President
Paul Glionna, Third Vice-President
H. Ruth Snowden, Executive Director
Gary Vince, Treasurer
Paul Lobas, Secretary

Canadian National Railways Police Association (Ind.) (CNRPA) / Association des policiers des chemins de fer nationaux du Canada (ind.)
6479 Miller's Grove, Mississauga ON L5N 3E5
Tel: 905-824-0856; *Fax:* 905-824-4584
e-mail: fjmorgan@ica.net
URL: www.cnrpa.ca
Frank Morgan, National President

Canadian Northern Society (CNoS)
PO Box 1174, Camrose AB T4V 1X2
Tel: 780-672-3099
e-mail: canadiannorthern@telus.net
URL: www.canadiannorthern.ca
Leslie S. Kozma, President
Lorrie R. Tiegs, Vice-President
Shawn I. Smith, Treasurer

Canadian Parking Association (CPA)
#350, 2255 St. Laurent Blvd., Ottawa ON K1G 4K3
Tel: 613-727-0700; *Fax:* 613-727-3183
e-mail: info@canadianparking.ca
URL: www.canadianparking.ca
Carole Whitehorne, Executive Director

Canadian Ports Clearance Association
#500, 101 Syndicate Ave. North, Thunder Bay ON P7C 3V4
Tel: 807-623-8491; *Fax:* 807-623-2676

Canadian Professional Logistics Institute / Institut canadien des professionnels de la logistique
#200, 160 John St., Toronto ON M5V 2E5
Tel: 416-363-3005; *Fax:* 416-363-5598
Toll-Free: 877-363-3005
e-mail: loginfo@loginstitute.ca
URL: www.loginstitute.ca
Affiliation(s): Canadian Institute of Traffic & Transportation; Canadian International Freight Forwarders Association
Victor S. Deyglio, President
Jim Davidson, P.Log Chair
Ruth Snowden, Managing Director
Karyn Ferguson, P.Log., Program Director
Jackie Denholm, Finance/Administrator
Giselle Carasco, P.Log., Program Administrator
Karyn Milne, Communications/Member Services
Robyn Short, Office Coordinator

Canadian Shipowners Association (CSA) / Association des armateurs canadiens (AAC)
#705, 350 Sparks St., Ottawa ON K1R 7S8
Tel: 613-232-3539; *Fax:* 613-232-6211
e-mail: csa@shipowners.ca
URL: www.shipowners.ca
Bruce Bowie, President
Silvie Dagenais, Sec.-Treas.
Michel Drolet, Vice-President, Operations
Shane Foreman, Policy/Research Manager

Canadian Transport Lawyers Association
c/o S.S.T. Thibault, Heenan Blaikie LLP, #600, 900, rue René-Lévesque ouest, Québec QC G1R 2B5
URL: www.ctla.ca
Geoffrey L. Spencer, President
Louis A. Amato-Gauci, Vice-President & Secretary
Douglas I. Evanchuk, Treasurer
Stephanie S.T. Thibault, Director, Communications

Canadian Transport Workers Union (Ind.) (CTWU) / Syndicat canadien des travailleurs du transport (ind.)
c/o Local #213, 73 Misty St., Kitchener ON N2B 3V6
Tel: 519-896-2671
Don White, President

Canadian Transportation Equipment Association (CTEA) / Association d'équipement de transport du canada (AETC)
#3B, 16 Barrie Blvd., St Thomas ON N5P 4B9
Tel: 519-631-0414; *Fax:* 519-631-1333
e-mail: transportation@ctea.on.ca
URL: www.ctea.ca
Don Moore, P.Eng., Executive Director
Butch Medemblik, P. Eng., President
Stan Delaney, Administrator, Communications

Canadian Transportation Research Forum (CTRF) / Groupe de recherches sur les transports au Canada
PO Box 23033, Woodstock ON N4T 1R0
Tel: 519-421-9701; *Fax:* 519-421-9319
e-mail: feedback@ctrf.ca, cawoudsma@ctrf.ca
URL: www.ctrf.ca
Doug Johnson, President
Carole Ann Woudsma, Secretary
Malcolm Cairns, Executive Vice-President
Mark Hemmes, Vice-President External
Gerry Kolaitis, VP Finance/Treasurer
Vijay Gill, Vice-President Program/Publications
Linda McAusland, Vice-President Meetings
Gordon E. Tufts, P.Eng, VP Organization/Development

Canadian Trucking Alliance (CTA) / L'Alliance canadienne du camionnage (ACC)
324 Somerset St. West, Ottawa ON K2P 0J9
Tel: 613-236-9426; *Fax:* 866-823-4076
e-mail: info@cantruck.ca
URL: www.cantruck.com
Dietmar Krause, Chairperson
Paul Landry, President/CEO
Louise Yako, Director Policy/Communications
Michele Nicol, Director Business Programs
Sandra Stashuk, Member Services Coordinator
Susan Van Egdom, Accounting Coordinator

Canadian Trucking Human Resources Council (CTHRC) / Conseil canadien des ressources humaines en camionnage
#203, 720 Belfast Rd., Ottawa ON K1G 0Z5
Tel: 613-244-4800; *Fax:* 613-244-4535
e-mail: info@cthrc.com
URL: www.cthrc.com
Affiliation(s): CCA Truck Driver Training Ltd.; Capilano Truck Driver Training Institute; JVI Provincial Transportation & Safety Academy; Mountain Transport Institute Ltd.; Red Deer College; SK Driver Training Ltd.; Wheels On Ltd. / Training & Driver Training

Canadian Urban Transit Association (CUTA) / Association canadienne du transport urbain (ACTU)
#1401, 55 York St., Toronto ON M5J 1R7
Tel: 416-365-9800; *Fax:* 416-365-1295
e-mail: transit@cutaactu.ca
URL: www.cutaactu.ca
Michael W. Roschlau, Ph.D., President/CEO
Charles Stolte, Chair

Canadian Urban Transit Association
1500 St. Laurent Blvd., Ottawa ON K1G 0Z8
Tel: 613-842-3616

Canadians for Responsible & Safe Highways (CRASH)
PO Box 1042, Stn. B, Ottawa ON K1P 5R1
Tel: 613-860-0529; *Fax:* 613-567-6204
Toll-Free: 800-530-9945
e-mail: crash@web.net
URL: www.web.net/~crash/about.html
Harry Gow, President

Carefree Society Transportation Service
2832 Queensway St., Prince George BC V2L 4M5
Tel: 250-562-1394; *Fax:* 250-562-1393
e-mail: carefree_society@telus.net
Affiliation(s): BC Transit
Cathy Hickman, Executive Director
Lynnelle Sutherland, President

Central British Columbia Railway & Forest Industry Museum Society
850 River Rd., Prince George BC V2L 5S8
Tel: 250-563-7351; *Fax:* 250-563-3697
e-mail: trains@pgrfm.bc.ca
URL: www.pgrfm.bc.ca
Laura Williams, General Manager

Chartered Institute of Logistics & Transport (CILT)
Earlstrees Court, Earlstrees Rd., Corbyn NN17 4Ax United Kingdom
Tel: 44-0-1536-740-100; *Fax:* 44-0-1536-740-101
e-mail: enquiry@ciltuk.org.uk
URL: www.cilt-international.com
Affiliation(s): Integrated in UK with Institute of Logistics UK section now titled Institute of Logistics & Transport
Bernard Auton, Director General

Chartered Institute of Logistics and Transport in North America (CILT) / Institut agréé de la logistique et des transports Amérique du Nord
#900, 275 Slater St., Ottawa ON K1P 5H9
Tel: 613-688-1438; *Fax:* 613-688-0966
e-mail: ghonima@ciltna.com
URL: www.ciltna.com
Gilles Legault, FCILT, Chair
Hazem Ghonima, FCILT, CEO
Donald McKnight, FCILT Executive Director
Sam Barone, FCILT Treasurer
Mike Paré, FCILT Secretary

Chatham Railroad Museum Society
PO Box 434, 2 McLean Street, Chatham ON N7M 5K5
Tel: 519-352-3097

Club de trafic de Québec
CP 72, Saint-Jean-Chrysostome QC G6Z 2L3
Tél: 418-654-5446; *Téléc:* 418-619-1044
Courriel: jcoulombe@videotron.ca
URL: www.clubtraficqc.org
Allain Gagnon, Président
Julie Coulombe, Secrétaire-trésorière

The Company of Master Mariners of Canada
c/o Tom Kearsey, 5 Averill St., Dartmouth NS B3A 2H1
e-mail: postmaser@mastermariners-capital.ca
URL: www.mastermariners.ca
Affiliation(s): Master Mariner organizations in the UK, USA, South Africa, Australia & NZ
Jim Valvesbert, National Master
Ratch Wallace, Secretary
John McCann, Deputy Master
Andy Whitelaw, Treasurer

Dewdney-Alouette Railway Society (DARS)
22520 - 116 Ave., Maple Ridge BC V2X 0S4
Tel: 604-463-5311
e-mail: ras1@uniserve.com
Affiliation(s): National Model Railway Association; Pacific Northwest Region 7th Division Society; BC Heritage Society; Maple Ridge Historical Society; Maple Ridge Museum
Dick Sutcliff, Contact

Edmonton Radial Railway Society
PO Box 45040, Stn. Lansdowne, Edmonton AB T6H 5Y1
Tel: 780-437-7721; *Fax:* 780-457-9315
e-mail: info@edmonton-radial-railway.ab.ca
URL: www.edmonton-radial-railway.ab.ca
Affiliation(s): Association of Railway Museums; Alberta Museums Association
Harvey Bradley, President
David Higgins, Treasurer

Electric Vehicle Council of Ottawa Inc. (EVCO)
PO Box 4044, Stn. E, Ottawa ON K1S 5B1
e-mail: info@evco.ca
URL: www.evco.ca

Electric Vehicle Society of Canada (EVS)
21 Burritt Rd., Toronto ON M1R 3S5
Tel: 416-755-4324; *Fax:* 416-755-4324
e-mail: info@evsociety.ca
URL: www.evsociety.ca
Howard W. Hutt, President
Steven Lam, Treasurer

Freight Carriers Association of Canada (FCA)
#3-4, 427 Garrison Rd., Fort Erie ON L2A 6E6
Tel: 905-994-0560; *Fax:* 905-994-0117
Toll-Free: 800-559-7421
e-mail: info@fca-natc.org
URL: www.fca-natc.org
Affiliation(s): North American Transportation Council
David J. Sirgey, President
Ken Leising, Manager Rate Research/Development
Diane Sheppard, Accountant
Jon Ainsworth, Senior Analyst/Programmer
Mary Anne Vehrs, Sales/Marketing

Hope Air / Vols d'espoir
Procter & Gamble Bldg., #703, 4711 Yonge St., Toronto ON M2N 6K8
Tel: 416-222-6335; *Fax:* 416-222-6930
Toll-Free: 877-346-4673
e-mail: mail@hopeair.org
URL: www.hopeair.org
Doug Keller-Hobson, Executive Director
Wayne Twaits, Chair
Robert Reeves, Vice-Chair

Huntsville & Lake of Bays Railway Society
26 Centre St. North, Huntsville ON P1H 1X4

Tel: 705-635-2227; *Fax:* 705-635-2227
e-mail: nicholls@vianet.ca
URL: www.portageflyer.org

Affiliation(s): Muskoka Heritage Place
Russell A.F. Nicholls, President

Industrial Truck Association (ITA)
#460, 1750 K St. NW, Washington DC 20006 USA
Tel: 202-296-9880; *Fax:* 202-296-9884
URL: www.indtrk.org

William Montwieler, Manager

INFORM Inc.
5 Hanover Square, 19th Floor, New York NY 10004 USA
Tel: 212-361-2400; *Fax:* 212-361-2412
e-mail: inform@informinc.org
URL: www.informinc.org

Virginia Ramsey, President
Julia J. Mair, Director, Foundation & Corporate Relations
Sophie Cardona, Manager, Communications & Operations

Intermodal Association of North America (IANA)
#1100, 11785 Beltsville Dr., Calverton MD 20705 USA
Tel: 301-982-3400; *Fax:* 301-982-4815
e-mail: iana@intermodal.org
URL: www.intermodal.org

Joanne F. Casey, President/CEO
Greg P. Stefflre, Chair

International Association of Ports & Harbours (IAPH)
7F South Tower, New Pier Takeshiba, 1-16-1 Kaigan, Minato-Ku, Tokyo 105-0022 Japan
Tel: 81-3-5403-2770; *Fax:* 81-3-5403-7651
e-mail: info@iaphworldports.org
URL: www.iaphworldports.org

Affiliation(s): International Maritime Organization; United Nations Conference on Trade & Development; United Nations Economic & Social Council; Permanent International Association of Navigation Congresses; International Cargo Handling Coordination Association; International Maritime Pilots Association; International Association of Independent Tanker Owners; Baltic & International Martime Council
Satoshi Inoue, Secretary General
H. Thomas Kornegay, Executive Director

Locomotive & Railway Historical Society of Western Canada
#4104, 2120 Southland Dr. SW, Calgary AB T2V 4W3
Tel: 403-265-9229; *Fax:* 403-261-1057
e-mail: laniganj@telus.net

James E. Lanigan, President

Manitoba Trucking Association
25 Bunting St., Winnipeg MB R2X 2P5
Tel: 204-632-6600; *Fax:* 204-694-7134
e-mail: info@trucking.mb.ca
URL: www.trucking.mb.ca

Affiliation(s): Canadian Trucking Alliance; Canadian Council of Motor Transport Administrators; Canadian Trucking Human Resource Council; Winnipeg Chamber of Commerce; Manitoba Chamber of Commerce; Infrastructure Council of Manitoba; Employers' Task Force on Workers' Compensation; Manitoba Employers' Council
Earl Coleman, President
Susan Snyder, 1st Vice President
Tom Payne, Jr., 2nd Vice President
Bob Dolyniuk, General Manager
Susan Green, Coordinator, Program & Member Services

Motorcycle & Moped Industry Council (MMIC) / Le Conseil de l'industrie de la motocyclette et du cyclomoteur (CIMC)
#100, 716 Gordon Baker Rd., Toronto ON M2H 3B4
Tel: 416-491-4449; *Fax:* 416-493-1985
Toll-Free: 877-470-6642
e-mail: info@mmic.ca
URL: www.mmic.ca

Collin Richard, Contact
Dalton Burger, Government Relations
Li Liu, Coordinator Technical Standards/Tra
Tim Stover, Manager Shows/Member Services
Mary Anne Morrison, Statistics

National Association of Railroad Passengers (NARP)
#308, 900 - 2 St. NE, Washington DC 20002-3557 USA
Tel: 202-408-8362; *Fax:* 202-408-8287
e-mail: narp@narprail.org
URL: www.narprail.org

Affiliation(s): Transport 2000 Ltd.
Ross Capon, President

National Transportation Brokers Association
PO Box 238, Markham ON L3P 3J7
Tel: 416-798-7211
e-mail: info@ntba-brokers.com
URL: www.ntba-brokers.com

New Brunswick Potato Shippers Association
8824 Route 2, Grand-Sault/Grand Falls NB E3Z 1P8
Tel: 506-473-5520; *Fax:* 506-473-6701
e-mail: tatered@nbnet.nb.ca

Ed Kavanaugh, President

North America Railway Hall of Fame
RPO Centre, PO Box 20040, St Thomas ON N5P 4H4
Tel: 519-633-2535; *Fax:* 519-633-3087
e-mail: info@narhf.org
URL: www.narhf.org

Paul Corriveau, President

Northwestern Ontario Air Carriers Association (NOACA)
PO Box 4075, 143 Cedar Point Dr., Sioux Lookout ON P8T 1J9
Tel: 807-737-7470; *Fax:* 807-583-2812

Jennifer Chwastyk, Vice-Chair

Ontario Community Transit Association (OCTA)
#306, 4141 Yonge St., Toronto ON M2P 2A8
Tel: 416-229-6222; *Fax:* 416-229-6281
URL: www.octa.on.ca

Kelly Paleczny, Chair
Ted Galinis, Vice-Chair
Norman Cheesman, Chief Executive Officer
Pat Delmore, Secretary
Chris Prentice, Treasurer

Ontario Good Roads Association (OGRA)
#2, 6355 Kennedy Rd., Mississauga ON L5T 2L5
Tel: 905-795-2555; *Fax:* 905-795-2660
e-mail: info@ogra.org
URL: www.ogra.org

Joseph W. Tiernay, Executive Director
Brian Anderson, Coordinator, Infrastructure Services
Colette Caruso, Coordinator, Communications & Marketing
Cherry-Lyn Sales, Coordinator, Training Services

Ontario Milk Transport Association (OMTA)
#301, 660 Speedvale Ave. West, Guelph ON N1K 1E5
John Johnston, General Manager

Ontario Traffic Conference (OTC)
#2, 6355 Kennedy Rd., Mississauga ON L5T 2L5
Tel: 647-346-4050; *Fax:* 647-346-4060
e-mail: info@otc.org
URL: www.otc.org
Social Media: twitter.com/ontariotraffic

Marco D'Angelo, Executive Director
Ron Hamilton, President
Keith Haines, Vice-President
Mike Pelzowski, Secretary/Treasurer
Heide Schlegl, Director Engineering
Robyn Zutis, Director of Education
Kimberly Rossi, Director Marketing

Ontario Trucking Association (OTA)
555 Dixon Rd., Toronto ON M9W 1H8
Tel: 416-249-7401; *Fax:* 416-245-6152
e-mail: info@ontruck.org
URL: www.ontruck.org

Jackie Dobrowolski, Office Manager
David H. Bradley, President
Mark Seymour, Chairman
Stephen Laskowski, Vice-President
Barrie Montague, Senior Policy Advisor
Doug Switzer, Manager Government Relations
Rebecka Torn, Manager Communications
Rolf VanderZwaag, Manager Maintenance/Tech. Issues

Ontario Trucking Association Education Foundation Inc.
555 Dixon Rd., Toronto ON M9W 1H8
Tel: 416-249-7401; *Fax:* 416-245-6152
e-mail: education.foundation@ontruck.org

Operation Lifesaver (OL) / Opération Gareautrain
#1401, 99 Bank St., Ottawa ON K1P 6B9
Tel: 613-564-8100; *Fax:* 613-567-6726
e-mail: admin@operationlifesaver.ca
URL: www.operationlifesaver.ca

Dan Di Tota, National Director

Pharmaceutical & Personal Care Logistics Association (PPCLA) / Association de logistique des soins personnels et pharmaceutiques
PO Box 40598, Stn. Six Points Plaza, Toronto ON M9B 6K8
Tel: 416-232-6817; *Fax:* 416-232-6818
Toll-Free: 866-293-1238
e-mail: ppcla@ppcla.org
URL: www.ppcla.org

Scott Gibson, Executive Director

Private Motor Truck Council of Canada (PMTC) / Association canadienne du camionnage d'entreprise (ACCE)
#11, 1155 North Service Rd. West, Oakville ON L6M 3E3
Tel: 905-827-0587; *Fax:* 905-827-8212
Toll-Free: 877-501-7682
e-mail: info@pmtc.ca
URL: www.pmtc.ca

Affiliation(s): National Private Truck Council
Bruce J. Richards, President
Richard Lalonde, Chair
Raymond Anctil, Quebec Director

The Railway Association of Canada (RAC) / L'Association des chemins de fer du Canada (ACFC)
#901, 99 Bank St., Ottawa ON K1P 6B9
Tel: 613-567-8591; *Fax:* 613-567-6726
e-mail: rac@railcan.ca
URL: www.railcan.ca

Affiliation(s): Association of American Railroads
Cliff Mackay, President & CEO
Bruce Burrows, Vice-President, Public & Corporate Affairs

Saskatchewan Trucking Association (STA)
1335 Wallace St., Regina SK S4N 3Z5
Tel: 306-955-7833; *Fax:* 306-569-1008
Toll-Free: 800-563-7623
e-mail: sta@sasktrucking.com
URL: www.sasktrucking.com

Denis Prudhomme, President
Glen Ertell, First Vice-President
Quint Stacey, Second VP
Russ Turgeon, Treasurer

The Shipping Federation of Canada / La Fédération maritime du Canada
#326, 300, rue St-Sacrement, Montréal QC H2Y 1X4
Tel: 514-849-2325; *Fax:* 514-849-8774
Toll-Free: 877-534-7367
e-mail: info@shipfed.ca
URL: www.shipfed.ca

Karen Kancens, Director of Communications
Michael H. Broad, President
David Cardin, Chairman
Ivan A. Lantz, Director Marine Operations
James Moram, Director Marine Administration
Anne Legars, Director Policy/Public Affairs
Caroline Gravel, Director Environmental Affairs
Mario Minotti, Director Finance/Administration

Société des traversiers du Québec (STQ)
250, rue Saint-Paul, Québec QC G1K 9K9
Tél: 418-643-2019; *Téléc:* 418-643-7308
Ligne sans frais: 877-787-7483
Courriel: stq@traversiers.gouv.qc.ca
URL: www.traversiers.gouv.qc.ca

Georges Farrah, Président/directeur général

Sydney & Louisburg Railway Historical Society / Le Musée de chemin de fer de Sydney à Louisburg
7330 Main St., Louisbourg NS B1C 1P5
William Bussey, President

Toronto Transportation Society (TTS)
PO Box 5187, Stn. A, Toronto ON M5W 1N5
e-mail: ttswebmaster@torontotransportationsociety.org
URL: www.torontotransportationsociety.org

Kevin Nichol, President

Transport Action Canada
Bronson Centre, PO Box 858, Stn. B, #303, 211 Bronson Ave., Ottawa ON K1P 5P9
Tel: 613-594-3290; *Fax:* 613-594-3271
e-mail: info@transport-action.ca
URL: www.transport-action.ca

Affiliation(s): Transport 2000 International
David Jeanes, President
Justin Bur, VP East
Peter Lacey, VP West
Tony Turrittin, Secretary
Klaus Beltzner, Treasurer
Bert Titcomb, Manager

Transportation Association of Canada (TAC) / Association des transports du Canada (ATC)
2323 St. Laurent Blvd., Ottawa ON K1G 4J8
Tel: 613-736-1350; *Fax:* 613-736-1395
e-mail: secretariat@tac-atc.ca
URL: www.tac-atc.ca
Michel Gravel, CAE, Executive Director
Guylaine Brousseau, Manager, Finance & Administration
Sarah Wells, Director, Technical Programs
Deb Cross, Director, Communications & Member Services
John Law, President
Joseph K. Lam, Vice-President
Alex Turnbull, Treasurer

Truck Training Schools Association of Ontario Inc. (TTSAO)
Fax: 519-858-0920
Toll-Free: 866-475-9436
e-mail: training@ttsao.com
URL: www.ttsao.com
Affiliation(s): Ontario Trucking Association; Ministry of Education, Ministry of Transportation
Gus Rahim, President

Truckers Association of Nova Scotia
PO Box 1527, 184 Arthur St., Truro NS B2N 5V2
Tel: 902-895-7447; *Fax:* 902-897-0487
Toll-Free: 800-232-6631
e-mail: contact@tans.ca
URL: www.tans.ca
Dave Roberts, Contact

Upper Canada Railway Society
PO Box 122, Stn. A, Toronto ON M5W 1A2
Tel: 416-921-4023
e-mail: ucrs@btinternet.com
Scott Haskill, President

The Van Horne Institute for International Transportation & Regulatory Affairs
#620 Earth Sciences Bldg., 2500 University Dr. NW, Calgary AB T2N 1N4
Tel: 403-220-8455; *Fax:* 403-282-4663
e-mail: vanhorne@ucalgary.ca
URL: www.vanhorne.info/
Affiliation(s): University of Calgary; University of Alberta; Southern Alberta Institute of Technology
Peter C. Wallis, President & CEO
Sarah Ingram, Programs Manager
Carla Frede, Webmaster
Mel Belich, Chairman

Western Transportation Advisory Council (WESTAC)
#1140, 800 Pender St. West, Vancouver BC V6C 2V6
Tel: 604-687-8691; *Fax:* 604-687-8751
e-mail: infoservices@westac.com
URL: www.westac.com
Lisa Baratta, Director, Strategy
Ruth Sol, President
Marcella Szel, Chairman (Executive Committee)
Lois Jackson, Chairman of the Board

Universities

African Students Association of Concordia (ASAC)
Concordia Hall Building, Concordia University, #1031-7, 1455 boul. de Maisonneuve Ouest, Montréal QC H4A 1M8
Tel: 514-848-2424
e-mail: asacextcomm@gmail.com
URL: asac.concordia.ca
Yves F. Nimbona, President

Visual Art, Crafts, Folk Arts

AICA Canada Inc.
172 Roselawn Ave., Toronto ON M4R 1E6
URL: www.artfocus.com/aicacanada.com/index.html
Affiliation(s): UNESCO

Alberta Craft Council (ACC)
10186 - 106 St., Edmonton AB T5J 1H4
Tel: 780-488-6611; *Fax:* 780-488-8855
Toll-Free: 800-362-7238
e-mail: acc@albertacraft.ab.ca
URL: www.albertacraft.ab.ca
Tom McFall, Executive Director
James Lavoie, Chair

Art Dealers Association of Canada Inc. (ADAC) / Association des marchands d'art du Canada
#501, 111 Peter St., Toronto ON M5V 2H1
Tel: 416-934-1583; *Fax:* 416-934-1584
Toll-Free: 866-435-2322
e-mail: info@ad-ac.ca
URL: www.ad-ac.ca
Affiliation(s): AGAC; CMA
Nicole Plaskett-Kennedy, Manager
Jane Corkin, President

Artists in Stained Glass (AISG)
RR#3, Scotch Line West, Minden ON K0M 2K0
e-mail: amazing@halhinet.on.ca
URL: www.aisg.on.ca
Affiliation(s): Ontario Crafts Council
Julia Williamson, Treasurer
Robert Brown, President

Association des collections d'entreprises / Corporate Art Collectors Association
Secrétariat: Banque Nationale du Canada, 600, rue de la Gauchetière ouest, 8e étage, Montréal QC H3C 4L2
Tél: 514-394-8533; *Téléc:* 514-394-6258
Ligne sans frais: 800-361-6266
Courriel: joann.kane@bnc.ca
JoAnn Kane, Présidente et secrétaire
Louis Pelletier, Vice-président
François Rochon, Trèsorier
Anne-Claude Bacon, Administratrice

The Canadian Art Foundation
#320, 215 Spadina Ave., Toronto ON M5T 2C7
Tel: 416-368-8854; *Fax:* 416-368-6135
Toll-Free: 800-222-4762
e-mail: info@canadianart.ca
URL: www.canadianart.ca
Ann Webb, Executive Director
Sara Graham, Development & Administrative Coord
Melony Ward, Publisher, Canadian Art
Richard Rhodes, Editor, Canadian Art

Canadian Association of Professional Conservators (CAPC) / Association canadienne des restaurateurs professionnels (ACRP)
c/o Canadian Museums Association, #400, 280 Metcalfe St., Ottawa ON K2P 1R7
Fax: 613-233-5438
e-mail: swarren@technomuses.ca (Applications)
URL: www.capc-acrp.ca
Affiliation(s): Canadian Association for the Conservation of Cultural Property (CAC)
Greg Hill, President
Diana Komejan, Vice-President
Anne Maheux, Treasurer

Canadian Craft & Hobby Association (CCHA)
55 Macewan Park Rd. NW, Calgary AB T3K 3G1
Tel: 403-770-1023; *Fax:* 403-668-9166
e-mail: ccha@cdncraft.org
URL: www.cdncraft.org
Alan Robinson, Manager

Canadian Crafts Federation (CCF) / Fédération canadienne des métiers d'art (FCMA)
PO Box 6000, 457 Queen St., Fredericton NB E3B 5H1
Tel: 506-444-3315; *Fax:* 506-457-7352
e-mail: info@canadiancraftsfederation.ca
URL: www.canadiancraftsfederation.ca
Affiliation(s): World Crafts Council
Yvan Gauthier, President

Canadian Guild of Crafts / Guilde canadienne des métiers d'art
1460, rue Sherbrooke ouest, Suite B, Montréal QC H3G 1K4
Tel: 514-849-6091; *Fax:* 514-849-7351
Toll-Free: 866-477-6091
e-mail: info@canadianguild.com
URL: www.canadianguildofcrafts.com
Diane Labelle, Managing Director

Canadian Quilters Association (CQA) / Association canadienne de la courtepointe (ACC)
c/o 6 Spruce St., Pasadena NL A0L 1K0
Tel: 709-686-5882; *Fax:* 709-686-5883
Toll-Free: 877-672-8777
e-mail: administration@canadianquilter.com
URL: www.canadianquilter.com
Johanna Alford, President
Vivian Kapusta, Secretary/Publicist

Canadian Society of Painters in Water Colour (CSPWC) / Société canadienne de peintres en aquarelle (SCPA)
#102, 258 Wallace Ave., Toronto ON M6P 3M9
Tel: 416-533-5100
e-mail: info@cspwc.com
URL: www.cspwc.com
Affiliation(s): John B. Aird Gallery

Conseil des arts de Montréal (CAM)
1210, rue Sherbrooke Est, Montréal QC H2L 1L9
Tél: 514-280-3580; *Téléc:* 514-280-3784
Courriel: info-cam@cum.qc.ca
URL: www.artsmontreal.org
Mèdia social: www.twitter.com/ConseilArtsMtl
Danielle Sauvage, directrice générale et sec. conseil
Line Lampron, secrétaire de direction

Conseil des arts textiles du Québec (CATQ)
811A, rue Ontario est, Montréal QC H2L 2T2
Tél: 514-524-6645
Ligne sans frais: 800-524-6645
Courriel: info@catq.qc.ca
URL: www.catq.qc.ca
Isabel Moreau, Coordanatrice Administrative

Conseil des métiers d'art du Québec (ind.) (CMA) / Québec Crafts Council (Ind.)
#400, 350, rue St-Paul est, Montréal QC H2Y 1H2
Tél: 514-861-2787; *Téléc:* 514-861-9191
Courriel: cmaq@metiers-d-art.qc.ca
URL: www.metiers-d-art.qc.ca
Serge Demers, Directeur général

Craft Council of Newfoundland & Labrador
Devon House, 59 Duckworth St., St. John's NL A1C 1E6
Tel: 709-753-2749; *Fax:* 709-753-2766
e-mail: info@craftcouncil.nf.ca
URL: www.craftcouncil.nf.ca
Affiliation(s): Canadian Crafts Federation
Anne Manuel, Executive Director

Crafts Association of British Columbia (CABC) / Conseil de l'artisanat de la Colombie-Britannique
Granville Island, 1386 Cartwright St., Vancouver BC V6H 3R8
Tel: 604-687-6511; *Fax:* 604-687-6711
Toll-Free: 888-687-6511
e-mail: info@cabc.net
URL: www.cabc.net
Yvonne Chui, Executive Director

Embroiderers' Association of Canada, Inc. (EAC)
477 Gordon Ave., Peterborough ON K9J 6G7
Tel: 705-743-6635
e-mail: president@eac.ca
URL: www.eac.ca
Leslie Burrows, President
Marie Cron, Secretary

Folklore Canada International (FCI)
2040, rue Alexadre-De-Sève, Montréal QC H2L 2W4
Tel: 514-524-8552; *Fax:* 514-524-0262
e-mail: patrimoine@qc.aira.com
URL: www.folklore-canada.org
Guy Landry, Director General

Manitoba Crafts Council (MCC)
c/o Arts & Cultural Industries Assn of Manitoba, #501, 62 Albert St., Winnipeg MB R3B 1E9
Tel: 204-927-2787
e-mail: mcc@mts.net
URL: www.manitobacrafts.ca
Judy Jennings, President
Donna L. Turner, Executive Director

The Metal Arts Guild of Canada (MAGC)
88 Elm Grove Ave., Toronto ON M6K 2J3
Tel: 416-252-6242
e-mail: maguild@interlog.com
URL: www.metalartsguild.ca
Social Media: www.twitter.com/MAGcanada
Affiliation(s): Ontario Crafts Council
Sarah Dougal-Hamel, President
Kathryn Dieroff, Treasurer

New Brunswick Crafts Council / Conseil d'artisanat du Nouveau-Brunswick
PO Box 1231, Fredericton NB E3B 5C8
Tel: 506-450-8989; *Fax:* 506-457-6010
e-mail: nbcrafts@nb.aibn.com
URL: www.nbcraftscouncil.com
Linda Brine, President

Kitty Bourne, Administrator

Nova Scotia Designer Crafts Council (NSDCC)
1113 Marginal Rd., Halifax NS B3H 4P7
Tel: 902-423-3837; *Fax:* 902-422-0881
e-mail: office@nsdcc.ns.ca
URL: www.nsdcc.ns.ca
Alison Cude, Chair

Ontario Crafts Council (OCC)
990 Queen St. West, Toronto ON M6J 1H1
Tel: 416-925-4222; *Fax:* 416-925-4223
e-mail: info@craft.on.ca
URL: www.craft.on.ca
Emma Quin, Executive Director

Prince Edward Island Crafts Council (PEICC)
PO Box 20071, Stn. Sherwood, Charlottetown PE C1A PE3
Tel: 902-892-5152; *Fax:* 902-628-8740
e-mail: info@peicraftscouncil.com
URL: www.peicraftscouncil.com
Darrin White, President
Barb Boss, Executive Director

Royal Canadian Academy of Arts (RCA) / Académie royale des arts du Canada
#375, 401 Richmond St. West, Toronto ON M5V 3A8
Tel: 416-408-2718; *Fax:* 416-408-2286
e-mail: rcaarts@interlog.com
URL: www.rca-arc.ca
Affiliation(s): National Gallery of Canada (founded by RCA in 1880); Royal Academy, England
Jeffrey Spalding, President

Saskatchewan Craft Council (SCC)
813 Broadway Ave., Saskatoon SK S7N 1B5
Tel: 306-653-3616; *Fax:* 306-244-2711
Toll-Free: 866-653-3616
e-mail: saskcraftcouncil@sasktel.net
URL: www.saskcraftcouncil.org
Affiliation(s): Canadian Crafts Federation
Ken Wilkinson, Chair
Mark Stobbe, Executive Director

Sculptors' Society of Canada (SSC) / Société des sculpteurs du Canada
c/o J.M. Young, #204, 60 Atlantic Ave., Toronto ON M6K 1X9
Tel: 416-533-0126
e-mail: gallery@cansculpt.org
URL: www.cansculpt.org
Judi M. Young, President

Society of Canadian Artists (SCA) / Société des artistes canadiens (SAC)
Lawrence Plaza, PO Box 54029, 500 Lawrence Ave. West, Toronto ON M6A 3B7
Tel: 416-584-9823
e-mail: info@societyofcanadianartists.com
URL: www.societyofcanadianartists.com
Dorothy Chisholm, Vice-President, Finance

Visual Arts Nova Scotia (VANS)
1113 Marginal Rd., Halifax NS B3H 4P7
Tel: 902-423-4694; *Fax:* 902-422-0881
Toll-Free: 866-225-8267
e-mail: vans@visualarts.ns.ca
URL: vans.ednet.ns.ca
Affiliation(s): Nova Scotia College of Art & Design; Visual Arts of Ontario; Canadian Conference of the Arts
Briony Carros, Executive Director

Visual Arts Ontario (VAO)
PO Box 1159, Stn. TDC, 77 King St. West, Toronto ON M5K 1P2
Tel: 416-591-8883; *Fax:* 416-591-2432
e-mail: info@vao.org
URL: www.vao.org
Hennie L. Wolff, Executive Director

Wildlife

Club d'ornithologie de Mirabel (COMIR)
CP 3418, 9009, Rte Arthur-Sauvé, Mirabel QC J7N 2T8
Tél: 450-258-4924
Courriel: info@comirabel.org
URL: comirabel.org
Affiliation(s): Regroupement QuébecOiseaux
Normande Lapensée, Présidente
Denis Lauzon, Vice-président

Spruce City Wildlife Association (SCWA)
Stn. 1384 River Rd., Prince George BC V2L 5S8
Tel: 250-563-5437; *Fax:* 250-563-5438
e-mail: info@scwa.bc.ca
URL: www.scwa.bc.ca
Denise Collett, President/Treasurer

Women

Alberta Women's Institutes (AWI)
5405 - 36 Ave., Wetaskiwin AB T9A 3C7
Tel: 780-312-2440; *Fax:* 780-312-2482
e-mail: altawi@telusplanet.net
Affiliation(s): Associated Country Women of the World
Fern Killeen, Executive Director

Alliance des femmes de la francophonie canadienne (AFFC)
Place de la francophonie, #302, 450, rue Rideau, Ottawa ON K1N 5Z4
Tél: 613-241-3500; *Téléc:* 613-241-6679
Ligne sans frais: 866-535-9422
Courriel: info@affc.ca
URL: www.affc.ca
Affiliation(s): Fédération des communautés francophones et acadienne du Canada
Nicole Pépin, Directrice générale

Association féminine d'éducation et d'action sociale (AFEAS) / Feminine Association for Education & Social Action
5999, rue de Marseille, Montréal QC H1N 1K6
Tél: 514-251-1636; *Téléc:* 514-251-9023
Courriel: info@afeas.qc.ca
URL: www.afeas.qc.ca
Affiliation(s): Union mondiale des organisations féminines catholiques (UMOFC)

Association féminine d'éducation et d'action sociale - Chibougamau
CP 293, Chibougamau QC G8P 2K7
Tél: 418-748-2031
Martine Savard

Association Marie-Reine de Chibougamau
CP 295, Chibougamau QC G8P 2K7
Tél: 418-748-4289
Fernande Fiset

Association of Canadian Women Composers (ACWC) / L'Association des femmes compositeurs canadiennes (AFCC)
20 St. Joseph St., Toronto ON M4Y 1J9
Tel: 416-239-5195
e-mail: webmaster@acwc.ca
URL: www.acwc.ca
Affiliation(s): Fondezione Adkins Chiti: Donne in Musica, Italy; Women in Music Foundation

British Columbia Women's Institutes (BCWI)
#203B, 750 Cottonwood Ave., Kamloops BC V2B 3X2
Tel.: 250-554-5406; *Fax:* 250-554-5406
e-mail: info@bcwi.org
URL: www.bcwi.org
Affiliation(s): BC Federation of Agriculture
Elsie Karl, Vice-President
Joan Holthe, President

Canadian Association for the Advancement of Women & Sport & Physical Activity (CAAWS) / Association canadienne pour l'avancement des femmes du sport et de l'activité physique (ACAFS)
#202N, 801 King Edward Ave., Ottawa ON K1N 6N5
Tel: 613-562-5667; *Fax:* 613-562-5668
e-mail: caaws@caaws.ca
URL: www.caaws.ca
Karin Lofstrom, Executive Director
Sydney Millar, Manager, National Program
Stéphanie Legault, Manager, Marketing & Projects
Jessica Lowe, Administrator & Office Coordinator

Canadian Association of Women Executives & Entrepreneurs (CAWEE) / Association canadienne des femmes cadres et entrepreneurs
#202, 720 Spadina Ave., Toronto ON M5S 2T9
Tel: 416-756-0000; *Fax:* 416-862-0315
e-mail: contact@cawee.net
URL: www.cawee.net
Beth Parker, President

Canadian Federation of Business & Professional Women's Clubs (CFBPWC) / Fédération canadienne des clubs des femmes de carrières commerciales et professionnelles (FCCFCCP)
85 Brydges, Moncton NB E1C 2E9
Tel: 506-877-2343; *Fax:* 506-877-1912
e-mail: bpw@bpwcanada.com
URL: www.bpwcanada.com
Sue Calhoun, President
Doris Hall, 1st Vice President

Canadian Hadassah WIZO
#900, 1310, av Greene, Montréal QC H3Z 2B8
Tel: 514-937-9431; *Fax:* 514-933-6483
e-mail: info@chw.ca
URL: www.chw.ca
Affiliation(s): Canadian Jewish Congress; Canadian Zionist Federation; National Council of Women of Canada; United Nations Association; Women's International Zionist Organization; Hadassah International
Sandy Martin, National President
Freda Ginsberg, National Executive Vice-President

Canadian Women in Communications (CWC) / Association canadienne des femmes en communication (AFC)
#804, 67 Yonge St., Toronto ON M5E 1J8
Tel: 416-363-1880; *Fax:* 416-363-1882
Toll-Free: 800-361-2978
e-mail: cwcafc@cwc-afc.com
URL: www.cwc-afc.com
Nicole Lang, Chair, Calgary Chapter
Lisa Woznica, Co-Chair, GTA Chapter
Angela J. Wheldon, Co-Chair, NCR Chapter
Judith Campbell, Vice-President
Diane Johnson, Chair, BC Chapter
Sue Timanson, Chair, Edmonton Chapter
Claire A. Cockell, Co-Chair, GTA Chapter
Marye Menaard-Bos, Co-Chair, NCR Chapter
Christianne Vaillancourt, Chair, NB Chapter
Loraine Dumas, Chair, Québec
Nathalie Noël, Chair, SW Ontario Chapter
Stephanie MacKendrick, President
Robin Hildebrandt, Chair, Manitoba Chapter

Canadian Women's Foundation (CWF) / Fondation canadienne des femmes
#504, 133 Richmond St. West, Toronto ON M5H 2L3
Tel: 416-365-1444; *Fax:* 416-365-1745
Toll-Free: 866-293-4483
e-mail: info@canadianwomen.org
URL: www.cdnwomen.org
Beverley Wybrow, President & CEO

Caribbean Pioneer Women of Canada
PO Box 51, Stn. Snowdon, Montréal QC H3X 3T3
Tel: 514-488-3716
e-mail: jntsmith@yahoo.com
Janet Smith, Contact

Centre Afrique au Féminin
419, rue St-Roch, Montréal QC H3N 1K2
Tél: 514-272-3274; *Téléc:* 514-272-8617
URL: www.familis.org
Valerie Balton

Centre de Femmes Les Elles du Nord
#2, 570, 3e Rue, Chibougamau QC G8P 1N9
Tél: 418-748-7171
Ghyslaine Bergeron, Présidente
Linda Boulanger, Coordonnatrice

Cercle des Fermières - Chibougamau
CP 123, Chibougamau QC G8P 2K6
Tél: 418-748-2126
URL: www.cfq.qc.ca
Keri Dallaire

Comité condition féminine Baie-James
#203, 552, 3e Rue, Chibougamau QC G8P 1N9
Tél: 418-748-4408; *Téléc:* 418-748-2486
Courriel: ccfbj@tlb.sympatico.ca
URL: ccfbj.com
Mamon Fortier, Présidente

Coverdale Centre for Women Inc.
10 Culloden Court, Saint John NB E2L 3B9
Tel: 506-634-1649; *Fax:* 506-634-1647
e-mail: coverdalesj@yahoo.ca
Lynda Hanson, Acting Executive Director

Les EssentiElles
Centre de la francophonie, 302, rue Strickland, Whitehorse YT Y1A 2K1

Tél: 867-668-2636; *Téléc:* 867-668-3511
Courriel: elles@yknet.ca
URL: www.lesessentielles.org
Julie Ménard, Coordonnatrice

Federated Women's Institutes of Canada (FWIC) / Fédération des instituts féminins du Canada
PO Box 209, 359 Blue Lake Rd., St George ON N0E 1N0
Tel: 519-448-3873; *Fax:* 519-448-3506
e-mail: fwic@bellnet.ca
URL: www.nald.ca/fwic.htm
Barbara Sheardown, Executive Director
Sheila Needham, President

Federated Women's Institutes of Ontario (FWIO)
7382 Wellington Rd. 30, RR#5, Guelph ON N1H 6J2
Tel: 519-836-3078; *Fax:* 519-836-9456
e-mail: lynnr@fwio.on.ca
URL: www.fwio.on.ca
Lynn Ruigrok, Executive Director

Fédération des femmes du Québec (FFQ)
#309, 110, rue St-Thérèse, Montréal QC H2Y 1E6
Tél: 514-876-0166; *Téléc:* 514-876-0162
Courriel: info@ffq.qc.ca
URL: www.ffq.qc.ca
Alexa Conradi, Présidente
Nancy Burrows, Coordonnatrice

Federation of Medical Women of Canada (FMWC) / Fédération des femmes médecins du Canada
780 Echo Dr., Ottawa ON K1S 5R7
Tel: 613-569-5881; *Fax:* 613-569-4432
Toll-Free: 877-771-3777
e-mail: fmwcmain@fmwc.ca
URL: www.fmwc.ca
Affiliation(s): Canadian Medical Association; Medical Women's International Association
Kathleen Gartke, President

Halifax Women's Network
PO Box 48030, Bedford NS B4A 3Z2
e-mail: info@halifaxwomensnetwork.com
URL: www.halifaxwomensnetwork.com
Lee Ross, President

Immigrant Women Services Ottawa (IWSO) / Services pour femmes immigrantes d'Ottawa
#400, 219 Argyle Ave., Ottawa ON K2P 2H4
Tel: 613-729-3145; *Fax:* 613-729-9308
e-mail: infomail@immigrantwomenservices.com
URL: www.immigrantwomenservices.com

Interval House
#200, 131 Bloor St., Toronto ON M5S 1R8
Tel: 416-924-1411; *Fax:* 416-928-9020
e-mail: info@intervalhouse.ca
URL: www.intervalhouse.ca

Jewish Women International of Canada (JWIC)
#210, 638A Sheppard Ave. West, Toronto ON M3H 2S1
Tel: 416-630-9313; *Fax:* 416-630-9319
Toll-Free: 866-333-5942
e-mail: jwic@jwicanada.com
URL: www.jwicanada.com
Affiliation(s): Jewish Women International
Jill Lieberman, President
Penny Krowitz, CAE, Executive Director

Korean Canadian Women's Association (KCWA)
27 Madison Ave., Toronto ON M5R 2S2
Tel: 416-340-1234; *Fax:* 416-340-8114
e-mail: kcwa@kcwa.net
URL: www.kcwa.net

Manitoba Women's Institutes (MWI)
1129 Queens Ave., Brandon MB R7A 1L9
Tel: 204-945-8976; *Fax:* 204-328-5294
e-mail: mbwi@mts.net
URL: www.gov.mb.ca/agriculture/organizations/wi/
Affiliation(s): Associated Country Women of the World; Consumers Association of Canada (Manitoba); Manitoba Agricultural Hall of Fame; Agriculture in the Classroom - Manitoba; Keystone Agricultural Producers
Shirley Bell, Executive Administrator

MATCH International Centre / Centre international Match
#201, 15 Grenfell Cres., Nepean ON K2G 0G3
Tel: 613-238-1312; *Fax:* 613-238-6867
Toll-Free: 888-414-8717
e-mail: info@matchinternational.org
URL: www.matchinternational.org
Darlene MacLeod, Accounting Officer
Madonna Larbi, Executive Director

Mouvement des Femmes Chrétiennes
3013, ch des Trois-Cantons, Nicholas Denys NB E3K 3C1
Tél: 506-783-4745; *Téléc:* 506-783-4745
Courriel: secretariat@mfcnational.net
URL: www.mfcnational.net

Na'amat Canada Inc.
National Office, #6, 7005 Kildare Rd., Montréal QC H4W 1C1
Tel: 514-488-0792; *Fax:* 514-487-6727
Toll-Free: 888-278-0792
e-mail: naamat@total.net
URL: www.naamat.com
Affiliation(s): Canadian Jewish Congress; National Action Committee on the Status of Women
Rivka Shaffir, National President

National Action Committee on the Status of Women (NAC) / Comité canadien d'action sur le statut de la femme (CCA)
#203, 234 Eglinton Ave. East, Toronto ON M4P 1K5
Tel: 416-932-1718; *Fax:* 416-932-0646
e-mail: nac@web.ca
URL: www.nac-cca.ca
Sandra Carnegie Douglas, Executive Coordinator
Denise Andrea Campbell, President

National Association of Women & the Law (NAWL) / Association nationale de la femme et du droit (ANFD)
#305, 251 Bank St., Ottawa ON K1Y 4T3
Tel: 613-241-7570; *Fax:* 613-241-4657
e-mail: info@nawl.ca
URL: www.nawl.ca
Louise Aucoin, Coordinator
Alana Patterson, Coordinator, National Steering Committee
Bonnie Diamond, Executive Director

National Council of Jewish Women of Canada
#118, 1588 Main St., Winnipeg MB R2V 1Y3
Tel: 204-339-9700; *Fax:* 204-334-3779
e-mail: info@ncjwc.org
URL: www.ncjwc.org
Affiliation(s): International Council of Jewish Women

The National Council of Women of Canada (NCWC) / Le Conseil national des femmes du Canada
#205, 251 Bank St., Ottawa ON K2P 1X3
Tel: 613-232-5025; *Fax:* 613-232-8419
Toll-Free: 877-319-0993
e-mail: ncwc@magma.ca
URL: www.ncwc.ca
Karen Dempsey, President
Catherine Tillsley, Executive Director

Native Women's Association of the N.W.T.
PO Box 2321, 5017 49th St., Yellowknife NT
Tel: 867-873-5509; *Fax:* 867-873-3152
URL: www.nativewomens.com
Affiliation(s): Yellowknife Victim Services
Nancy Peel, Executive Director

New Brunswick Women's Institute (NBWI)
Victoria Health Centre, #279, 65 Brunswick St., Fredericton NB E3B 1G5
Tel: 506-454-0798; *Fax:* 506-451-8949
e-mail: nbwi@nb.aibn.com
URL: www.nbwi.ca
Affiliation(s): Associated Country Women of the World
Debbie Johnson, Administrative Officer
Glenna Geer, President

Newfoundland & Labrador Women's Institutes
PO Box 1854, St. John's NL A1C 5P9
Tel: 709-753-8780; *Fax:* 709-753-8780
e-mail: nlwi@nfld.com
URL: www.nlwi.ca
Barbara Taylor, President

NSERC/Petro-Canada Chair for Women in Science & Engineering
c/o Faculty of Engineering & Applied Sciences, Memorial University, St. John's NL A1B 3X5
Tel: 709-737-7960; *Fax:* 709-737-7658
e-mail: cwse@morgan.ucs.mun.ca
URL: www.mun.ca/cwse/
Carolyn J. Emerson, Chair, Atlantic Region

The Older Women's Network (OWN) / Réseau des femmes aînées
115 The Esplanade, Toronto ON M5E 1Y7
Tel: 416-214-1518; *Fax:* 416-214-1541
e-mail: info@olderwomensnetwork.org
URL: www.olderwomensnetwork.org
Affiliation(s): One Voice; National Association of Women & the Law; Women's Legal Education & Action Fund
Janice Tait, Chair
Andrea Brigneti, Provincial Coordinator

Prince Edward Island Business Women's Association (PEIBWA)
161 St. Peter's Rd., Charlottetown PE C1A 5P7
Tel: 902-892-6040; *Fax:* 902-892-6050
Toll-Free: 866-892-6040
e-mail: office@peibwa.org
URL: www.peibwa.org
Michelle Ryder-MacEwen, President

Prince Edward Island Women's Institute
PO Box 2000, 40 Enman Cres., Charlottetown PE C1A 7N8
Tel: 902-368-4860; *Fax:* 902-368-4439
e-mail: wi@gov.pe.ca
Karen Craig, Contact

Québec Women's Institutes (QWI)
Macdonald Campus, McGill University, Raymond Bldg., PO Box 58, 21111, ch Lakeshore, Montréal QC H9X 3V9
Tel: 514-398-7844; *Fax:* 514-398-7972
e-mail: lhoy@sympatico.ca
Affiliation(s): Associated Country Women of the World
Ina Kingour, Honorary President
Linda Hoy, Executive Secretary

Réseau des femmes d'affaires du Québec inc. (RFAQ)
#100, 10794, rue Lajeunesse, Montréal QC H3L 2E8
Tél: 514-521-2441; *Téléc:* 514-521-1410
Ligne sans frais: 800-332-2683
Courriel: info@rfaq.ca
URL: www.rfaq.ca
Nicole Beaudoin, Présidente/Directrice générale

Réseau Femmes Québec (RFQ)
#134, 911, rue Jean-Talon est, Montréal QC H2R 1V5
Tél: 514-484-2375
Courriel: reseau.femmes.quebec@gmail.com
URL: www.reseau-femmes-quebec.qc.ca
Affiliation(s): Réseau Hommes Québec
Nadia Nadège, Présidente

Réseau national d'action-éducation des femmes (RNAEF)
#302, 450, rue Rideau, Ottawa ON K1N 5Z4
Tél: 613-241-3500; *Téléc:* 613-241-6679
Courriel: affc@franco.ca
URL: www.affc.ca/rnaef

Saskatchewan Women's Institutes (SWI)
117 Science Pl., Rm. 10.2, Kirk Hall, Saskatoon SK S7N 5C8
Tel: 306-272-4191
e-mail: sask.wi@usask.ca
Affiliation(s): Saskatchewan Council of Women; Saskatchewan Safety Council; Saskatchewan Federation of Agriculture; Saskatchewan Farm Vacation Association; Saskatchewan Action Committee, Status of Women; Saskatchewan Agricultural Hall of Fame; Saskatchewan Committee on Rural Area Development

Society for Canadian Women in Science & Technology (SCWIST) / Société des canadiennes dans la science et la technologie
#471, 411 Dunsmuir St., Vancouver BC V6B 1X4
Tel: 604-893-8657; *Fax:* 604-893-8692
e-mail: scwist@sfu.ca
URL: www.harbour.sfu.ca/scwist/
Affiliation(s): BC Ministry of Advanced Education, Training & Technology; Industry, Science & Technology Canada; BC Ministry of Education; Canada Employment & Immigration Council; Secretary of State Canada, Women's Program; University of BC, Faculty of Science; Simon Fraser University; BC Institute of Technology; Capilano College; Vancouver School Board; Knowledge Network; Vancouver Foundation; Immigrant Women in Science Program; Douglas College
Elana Brief, President

South Asian Women's Centre (SAWC)
8163 Main St., Vancouver BC V5X 3L2
Tel: 604-325-6637; *Fax:* 604-325-4462
e-mail: sawc@asia.com
URL: www.sawc.8m.com

Transition House Association of Nova Scotia (THANS)
#319, 1657 Barrington St., Halifax NS B3J 2A1

Tel: 902-429-7287; *Fax:* 902-429-0561
e-mail: coordinator@thans.ca
URL: www.thans.ca
Pamela Harrison, Provincial Coordinator

Western Businesswomen's Association (WBA)
#302, 1107 Homer St., Vancouver BC V6B 2Y1
Tel: 604-688-0951; *Fax:* 604-681-4545
Teena Keizer, Administrator

Women Business Owners of Manitoba (WBOM)
PO Box 2748, Winnipeg MB R3C 4B3
Tel: 204-775-7981; *Fax:* 204-897-8094
e-mail: info@wbom.ca
URL: www.wbom.ca
Yvonne Thompson, President
Christine Dubyts, Vice-President
Charlene Hiebert, Treasurer

Women Entrepreneurs of Canada (WEC) / Les Femmes chefs d'entreprises du Canada
Toronto Chapter & Head Office, 202, 720 Spadina Ave., Toronto ON M5S 2T9
Tel: 416-921-5150; *Fax:* 416-929-5256
Toll-Free: 866-207-4439
e-mail: wec@wec.ca
URL: www.wec.ca
Social Media: www.facebook.com/group.php?gid=5398494151
Carissa Reiniger, President

Women on the Rise
5775 rue Saint-Jacques, Montréal QC H4A 2E8
Tel: 514-485-7418; *Fax:* 514-485-7418
e-mail: womenontherise@bellnet.cs
Grace Campbell, Director

Women's Art Association of Canada (WAAC)
23 Prince Arthur Ave., Toronto ON M5R 1B2
Tel: 416-922-2060; *Fax:* 416-922-4657
e-mail: womensart@bellnet.ca
URL: www.womensartofcanada.ca
Karin Ungar, President

Women's Art Resource Centre (WARC)
#122, 401 Richmond St. West, Toronto ON M5V 3A8
Tel: 416-977-0097; *Fax:* 416-977-7425
e-mail: warc@warc.net
URL: www.warc.net

Women's Centre of Montreal / Centre des femmes de Montréal
3585, rue Saint-Urbain, Montréal QC H2X 2N6
Tél: 514-842-1066; *Téléc:* 514-842-6376
Courriel: cfmwcm@centredesfemmesdemtl.org
URL: www.centredesfemmesdemtl.org
Johanne Bélisle, Directrice générale

Women's Counselling & Referral & Education Centre (WCREC)
#303B, 489 College St., Toronto ON M6G 1A5
Tel: 416-534-7501
e-mail: generalmail@wcrec.org; phoneline@wcrec.org; resources@wcrec.org
URL: www.wcrec.org

Women's Healthy Environments Network
#400, 215 Spadina Ave., Toronto ON M5T 2C7
Tel: 416-928-0880; *Fax:* 416-644-0116
e-mail: office@womenshealthyenvironments.ca
URL: www.womenshealthyenvironments.ca
Affiliation(s): National Action Committee on the Status of Women

Women's Institutes of Nova Scotia (WINS)
NSAC, PO Box 550, 35 Rock Garden Rd., Truro NS B2N 5E3
Tel: 902-893-6520; *Fax:* 902-893-6393
e-mail: wins@gov.ns.ca
URL: www.gov.ns.ca/agri/wi/
Affiliation(s): Associated Country Women of the World
Lauren Seaton, President

Women's Inter-Church Council of Canada (WICC) / Conseil oecuménique des chrétiennes du Canada
47 Queen's Park Cres. East, Toronto ON M5S 2C3
Tel: 416-929-5184; *Fax:* 416-929-4064
e-mail: wicc@wicc.org
URL: www.wicc.org
Janet Anstead, President

Women's International League for Peace & Freedom (WILPF)
#901, 6659 Southoak Cres., Burnaby BC V5E 4M9
Tel: 604-517-0581
e-mail: joangord@shaw.ca
URL: www.wilpf.int.ch/world/canada.htm
Ellen Woodsworth, President
Bruna Nota, Vice-President

Women's Legal Education & Action Fund (LEAF) / Fonds d'action et d'éducation juridiques pour les femmes (FAEJ)
#703, 60 St. Clair Ave. East, Toronto ON M4T 1N5
Tel: 416-595-7170; *Fax:* 416-595-7191
Toll-Free: 888-824-5323
e-mail: info@leaf.ca
URL: www.leaf.ca

Women's Network PEI
PO Box 233, 40 Enman Cres., Charlottetown PE C1A 7K4
Tel: 902-368-5040; *Fax:* 902-368-5039
Toll-Free: 888-362-7373
e-mail: wnpei@wnpei.org
URL: www.wnpei.org
Michelle MacCallum, Executive Director

Writers & Editors

Association de la presse francophone (APF) / Association of Francophone Newspapers
267 Dalhousie St., Ottawa ON K1N 7E3
Tél: 613-241-1017; *Téléc:* 613-241-6313
Courriel: apf@apf.ca
URL: www.apf.ca
Gilles Haché, Président
Francis Potié, Directeur

Canadian Association of Journalists (CAJ) / L'Association canadienne des journalistes
c/o Algonquin College, #B224, 1385 Woodroffe Ave., Ottawa ON K2G 1V8
Tel: 613-526-8061; *Fax:* 613-521-3904
e-mail: caj@caj.ca
URL: www.caj.ca
John Dickins, Executive Director
Mary Agnes Welch, President

Canadian Authors Association (CAA)
PO Box 419, 320 South Shores Rd., Campbellford ON K0L 1L0
Tel: 705-653-0323; *Fax:* 705-653-0593
Toll-Free: 866-216-6222
e-mail: admin@canauthors.org
URL: www.canauthors.org
Alec McEachern, National Director
Joan Eyolfson Cadham, President
Deborah Ranchuk, Sec.-Treas.

Canadian Ethnic Media Association (CEMA)
24 Tarlton Rd., Toronto ON M5P 2M4
Tel: 416-260-3625; *Fax:* 416-260-3810
e-mail: madeline.ziniak@rci.rogers.com
URL: www.canadianethnicmedia.com
Ace Alvarez, President
Madaine Ziniak, Chair
Doreen Vanini, Secretary
Irene Chu, Treasurer

Canadian Farm Writers' Federation (CFWF)
PO Box 250, Ormstown QC J0S 1K0
Fax: 450-829-2226
Toll-Free: 877-782-6456
e-mail: hugh@quanglo.ca
URL: www.cfwf.ca
Affiliation(s): International Federation of Agricultural Journalist (IFAJ); British Columbia Farm Writers' Association (BCFWA); Alberta Farm Writers' Association (AFWA); Saskatchewan Farm Writers' Association (SFWA); Manitoba Farm Writers' & Broadcasters' Association; Eastern Canada Farm Writers' Association (ECFWA)
John Greig, President
Myrna Stark Leader, Vice-President
Hugh Maynard, Secretary-Treasurer

Canadian Journalism Foundation (CJF) / La Fondation pour le journalisme canadien
117 Peter St., 3rd Fl., Toronto ON M5V 2G9
Tel: 416-955-0394; *Fax:* 416-955-0395
e-mail: info@cijf-fjc.ca
URL: www.cjf-fjc.ca
Jody Jacobson, Executive Director
Heather McCall, Program Manager

Canadian Science Writers' Association (CSWA) / Association canadienne des rédacteurs scientifiques
PO Box 75, Stn. A, Toronto ON M5W 1A2
Toll-Free: 800-796-8595
e-mail: office@sciencewriters.ca
URL: www.sciencewriters.ca
Kristina Bergen, Executive Director
Tim Lougheed, President

Canadian Society of Children's Authors, Illustrators & Performers (CANSCAIP) / La société canadienne des auteurs, illustrateurs et artistes pour enfants
#104, 40 Orchard View Blvd., Toronto ON M4R 1B9
Tel: 416-515-1559
e-mail: office@canscaip.org
URL: www.canscaip.org
Deb Loughead, President

The Crime Writers of Canada (CWC)
PO Box 113, 3007 Kingston Rd., Toronto ON M1M 1P1
Tel: 416-597-9938
e-mail: info@crimewriterscanada.com
URL: www.crimewriterscanada.com
Cheryl Freedman, Sec.-Treas.

Editors' Association of Canada (EAC) / Association canadienne des réviseurs (ACR)
#502, 27 Carlton St., Toronto ON M5B 1L2
Tel: 416-975-1379; *Fax:* 416-975-1637
Toll-Free: 866-226-3348
e-mail: info@editors.ca; webmaster@editors.ca
URL: www.editors.ca; www.reviseurs.ca
Affiliation(s): Canadian Conference of the Arts
Marta Horban, Executive Director
Moira White, President
Julia Cochrane, Secretary
Greg Ioannou, Treasurer

Federation of British Columbia Writers (FBCW)
PO Box 3887, Stn. Terminal, Vancouver BC V6B 2Z3
Tel: 604-683-2057; *Fax:* 604-608-5522
e-mail: bcwriters@shaw.ca
URL: www.bcwriters.com
Fernanda Viveiros, Executive Director

Fédération québécoise du loisir littéraire (FQLL)
CP 1000, Succ. M, 4545, av Pierre-de Coubertin, Montréal QC H1V 3R2
Tél: 514-252-3033; *Téléc:* 514-251-8038
Ligne sans frais: 866-533-3755
Courriel: info@litteraire.ca
URL: www.litteraire.ca
Christine Dumas, Directrice générale
Élizabeth Filion, Présidente

The League of Canadian Poets (LCP)
#608, 920 Yonge St., Toronto ON M4W 3C7
Tel: 416-504-1657; *Fax:* 416-504-0096
e-mail: info@poets.ca
URL: www.poets.ca
Affiliation(s): Book & Periodical Council
Joanna Poblocka, Executive Director

Manitoba Writers' Guild Inc. (MWG)
#206, 100 Arthur St., Winnipeg MB R3B 1H3
Tel: 204-942-6134; *Fax:* 204-942-5754
Toll-Free: 888-637-5802
URL: www.mbwriter.mb.ca
Robyn Maharaj, Executive Director
John Toone, President
Dorryce Smelts, Secretary
Michael Van Rooy, Treasurer

The Ontario Poetry Society (TOPS)
c/o I.B. Iskov, 31 Marisa Ct., Thornhill ON L4J 6H9
Tel: 905-738-0309
e-mail: ibiskov_tops2000@yahoo.ca
URL: www.theontariopoetrysociety.ca
Kate Marshall Flaherty, Secretary
Shirley A. McCormick, President
Debbie Okun Hill, Vice-President
Bunny Iskov, Treasurer

Professional Writers Association of Canada (PWAC)
#123, 215 Spadina Ave., Toronto ON M5T 2C7
Tel: 416-504-1645; *Fax:* 416-913-2327
e-mail: info@pwac.ca
URL: www.pwac.ca
Carolyn Gibson, President
Clare Leporati, Membership Coordinator

Québec Writers' Federation (QWF) / Fédération des Écrivaines et Écrivains du Québec
#3, 1200, av Atwater, Montréal QC H3Z 1X4
Tel: 514-933-0878; *Fax:* 514-933-0878
e-mail: info@qwf.org
URL: www.qwf.org

Lori Schubert, Executive Director
Peter Dubé, Secretary

Saskatchewan Writers Guild (SWG)
PO Box 3986, Regina SK S4P 3R9
Tel: 306-757-6310; *Fax:* 306-565-8554
Toll-Free: 800-667-6788
e-mail: swg@sasktel.net
URL: www.skwriter.com
Susan Hogarth, Executive Director
Laura Malhiot, Administrative Assistant

Société des écrivains canadiens (SEC)
#105, 870, av Salaberry, Montréal QC H3A 1H9
Tél: 514-843-5876; *Téléc:* 514-843-5876
URL: www.culture-quebec.qc.ca/sec/
Georges Hélal, Président général
Louis Lasnier, Secrétaire général

Société professionnelle des auteurs et des compositeurs du Québec (SPACQ)
#115, 4030, rue St-Ambroise, Montréal QC H4C 2C7
Tél: 514-845-3739; *Téléc:* 514-845-1903
Ligne sans frais: 866-445-3739
Courriel: info@spacq.qc.ca
URL: www.spacq.qc.ca
Jean-Christian Céré, MBA, Directeur général
Nancy Hamelin, Adjointe comptable
Suzan Thibault, Administratrice de contrats
Mario Chenart, Président

Society of American Travel Writers - Canadian Chapter (SATW)
24 Louisa St., Toronto ON M8V 2K6
Tel: 416-521-7462; *Fax:* 416-521-7467
e-mail: bea@bcpictures.com
URL: www.satw.ca
Jane Stokes, Chair

Union des écrivaines et écrivains québécois (UNEQ)
La Maison des écrivains, 3492, av Laval, Montréal QC H2X 3C8
Tél: 514-849-8540; *Téléc:* 514-849-6239
Ligne sans frais: 888-849-8540
Courriel: ecrivez@uneq.qc.ca
URL: www.uneq.qc.ca
Stanley Péan, Président
Pierre Lavoie, Directeur général

Writers Association for Resourceful Minds (WARM)
614, rue Martel, Longueuil QC J4J 1C5
Tel: 450-651-7044
e-mail: warmwriters@yahoo.com
URL: geocities.com/warmwriters
Jeanette Paul, President
Alex MacLeod, Vice-President
Harry Ghosh, Treasurer

Writers Guild of Alberta (WGA)
Percy Page Centre, 11759 Groat Rd., Edmonton AB T5M 3K6
Tel: 780-422-8174; *Fax:* 780-422-2663
Toll-Free: 800-665-5354
e-mail: mail@writersguild.ab.ca
URL: www.writersguild.ab.ca
Affiliation(s): Manitoba Writers' Guild; Federation of BC Writers; Saskatchewan Writers' Guild; Writers' Union of Canada; Newfoundland & Labrador Guilds; Periodical Writers' Association of Canada; League of Canadian Poets
Carol Holmes, Executive Director
Blaine Newton, President
Audrey Seehagen, Vice-President

Writers Guild of Canada (WGC)
#401, 366 Adelaide St. West, Toronto ON M5V 1R9
Tel: 416-979-7907; *Fax:* 416-979-9273
Toll-Free: 800-567-9974
e-mail: info@wgc.ca
URL: www.wgc.ca
Affiliation(s): Coalition of Canadian Audio-Visual Unions
Maureen Parker, Executive Director

Writers' Alliance of Newfoundland & Labrador (WANL)
PO Box 2681, Stn. C, #102, 155 Water St., St. John's NL A1C 6K1
Tel: 709-739-5215; *Fax:* 709-739-5931
e-mail: wanl@nfld.com
URL: www.writersalliance.nf.ca
Social Media: www.twitter.com/WANL
Théa Morash, Executive Director

Writers' Federation of New Brunswick (WFNB)
PO Box 37, Stn. A, Fredericton NB E3B 4Y2
Tel: 506-459-7228; *Fax:* 506-459-7228
e-mail: wfnb@nb.aibn.com
URL: www.umce.ca/wfnb
Grace Morris, Secretary
Marilyn Lerch, President
Laurie Glenn Norris, Treasurer
Lee Thompson, Executive Director

Writers' Federation of Nova Scotia (WFNS)
1113 Marginal Rd., Halifax NS B3H 4P7
Tel: 902-423-8116; *Fax:* 902-422-0881
e-mail: talk@writers.ns.ca
URL: www.writers.ns.ca
Affiliation(s): Cultural Federation of Nova Scotia; Writers' Trust; Access Copyright; Canadian Children's Book Centre; International Board on Books for Youth
Jane Buss, Executive Director
Susan Mersereau, Program Officer

The Writers' Trust of Canada
#200, 90 Richmond St. East, Toronto ON M5C 1P1
Tel: 416-504-8222; *Fax:* 416-504-9090
e-mail: info@writerstrust.com
URL: www.writerstrust.com
Laurence C. Murray, Chair
Don Oravec, Executive Director
Amanda Hopkins, Program Coordinator

The Writers' Union of Canada (TWUC)
#200, 90 Richmond St. East, Toronto ON M5C 1P1
Tel: 416-703-8982; *Fax:* 416-504-9090
e-mail: info@writersunion.ca
URL: www.writersunion.ca
Affiliation(s): Canadian Copyright Licensing Agency; Canadian Conference of the Arts; Cultural Human Resources Council
Erna Paris, Chair
Deborah Windsor, Executive Director

Youth

Black Community Resource Centre (BCRC)
#497, 6767, ch de la Côte-des-Neiges, Montréal QC H3S 2T6
Tel: 514-342-2247; *Fax:* 514-342-2283
e-mail: bcrc@qc.aira.com
URL: www.bcrcmontreal.com/bcrc/; www.blackyouthproject.org/bcrc/

Centre Afrika
1644, rue St-Hubert, Montréal QC H2L 3Z3
Tél: 514-843-4019
Courriel: centreafrika@centreafrika.com
URL: www.centreafrika.com
Jean-François Bégin

Club Richelieu Boréal de Chibougamau
CP 522, Chibougamau QC G8P 2X9
Tél: 418-748-3008
URL: portail.richelieu.org
Josée Bélanger

Force Jeunesse
#322, 1000, rue Saint-Antoine ouest, Montréal QC H3C 3R7
Tél: 514-384-8666; *Téléc:* 514-384-6442
Courriel: info@forcejeunesse.qc.ca
URL: www.forcejeunesse.qc.ca
Jonathan Plamondon, Président

Head and Hands / A deux mains
5833, rue Sherbrooke ouest, Montréal QC H4A 1X4
Tel: 514-481-0277; *Fax:* 514-481-2336
e-mail: info@headandhands.ca
URL: www.headandhands.ca
Marlo Turner-Ritchie, Contact

Jeunes en partage
Succ. 204, 2e Avenue, Chibougamau QC G8P 2Z5
Tél: 418-748-2935
Dany Larouche

Richelieu International (RI)
#25, 1010 rue Polytek, Ottawa ON K1J 9J1
Tél: 613-742-6911; *Téléc:* 613-742-6916
Ligne sans frais: 800-267-6525
Courriel: international@richelieu.org
URL: www.richelieu.org
Laurier Thériault, Directeur général
Denis Daigle, Directeur administratif

SECTION 4
BROADCASTING

The listings in this section are arranged by Province, then City within Province, except the Major Broadcasting Companies, which are arranged alphabetically by company name.

Major Broadcasting Companies

1330 CJYM / CFYM 1210
208 Highway 4 North, Rosetown, SK SOL 2VO
306-882-2686, Fax: 306-882-3037, 866-463-2692
www.cjym.com

Arctic Radio
316 Green Street, Flin Flon, MB R8A 0H2
204-687-3469,
cfar@arcticradio.ca
www.arcticradio.ca
Operates 3 AM Radio stations in Northern Manitoba.
Maureen Kozar, Manager, mkozar@arcticradio.ca

Astral Media Inc.
PO Box 2700, 1800, av McGill College, Montréal, QC H3A 3J6
514-939-5000, Fax: 514-939-1515,
www.astral.com
Canada's largest broadcaster of English-and French-language pay and specialty television services and is currently involved, on its own or with partners, in 20 television services. Astral Media and its television networks also play a vital role as the largest private sector investor in Canadian feature films. Astral Media owns 82 radio stations. Astral Media employs more than 8,000 people at its facilities in Montréal, Toronto, and a number of cities throughout Québec and the Atlantic provinces
André Bureau, Chairman of the Board
Ian Greenberg, President/CEO
Sidney Greenberg, Vice-President

Astral Media Radio
1717, boul. René-Lévesque Est, Montréal, QB H2L 4T9
514-529-3229, Fax: 614-529-9308,
www.astralmediaradio.com
Owns 29 radio stations, including 21 French-language FM stations in Québec
Ian Greenberg, President/CEO
André Bureau, Chairman of the Board
Sidney Greenberg, Vice-President

Astral Media Radio Atlantic
206 Rockwood Avenue, Fredericton, NB E3B 2M2
506-455-1069, Fax: 506-452-2345,
www.astralmedia.com
Owns 8 radio stations located in Fredericton, Bathurst, Woodstock and Grand Falls in New Brunswick, and Truro, Nova Scotia. These stations are focused on serving the local communities in which they are based.
André Bureau, Chairman of the Board
Ian Greenberg, President/CEO

Atlantic Television Network / ATV
2885 Robie St., Halifax, NS B3K 5Z4
902-453-4000, Fax: 902-454-3302,
admin@atlantistv.eu
atlantictv.net
Social Media: twitter.com/AtlantisATV
The ATV (Atlantic Television Network) launched September 13, 1972. It is an online television network providing 24/7 output

Bayshore Broadcasting Corporation
270 Ninth Street East, Owen Sound, ON N4K 5P5
519-376-2030, Fax: 519-371-4242,
bayshore@radioowensound.com
www.radioowensound.com
Bayshore Broadcasting Corporation is an independent broadcaster. It operates six radio stations in Grey, Bruce, Simcoe, & Huron counties in southern Ontario. The following stations are operated by Bayshore Broadcasting: 560 CFOS, Mix 106 (CIXK-FM), Country 93 (CKYC-FM), 98 the Beach (CFPS-FM), 97.7 the Beach (CHGB-FM), & 104.9 the Beach (CHWC-FM). Sunshine 89 (89.1 FM) was established in 2009.
Doug Caldwell, President

Blackburn Radio Inc.
#204, 700 Richmond St., London, ON N6A 5C7
519-679-8680, Fax: 519-679-5321,
info@630cfco.com
www.blackburnradio.com
Social Media: twitter.com/BLACKBURNRADIO
Blackburn Radio is an AM-FM radio broadcaster which operates stations in Chatham, Leamington, London, Sarnia, Windsor, and Wingham. Facebook link is:
www.facebook.com/pages/Country-929-FM630-AM-CFCO/2065 97195084
Richard Costley-White, President/CEO
Ron Dann, General Manager, Sarnia, rdann@blackburnradio.com

Camosun College - Village 900
3100 Foul Bay Road, Victoria, BC V8P 5J2
250-370-3658, Fax: 250-370-3679,
feedback@village900.ca
www.village900.ca
Village 900 is a non-profit campus/instructional radio station located at Camosun College in Victoria, British Columbia.
Colin Easton, President Board of Directors
Kim O'Hare, VP Board of Directors

Canadian Broadcasting Corporation - Canadian Broadcasting Centre Société Radio-Canada
PO Box 500 A, 250 Front St. West, Toronto, ON M5W 1E6
416-205-3311, 866-306-4636
cbcinput@cbc.ca
www.cbc.ca
Other information: TDD: 416/205-6688
The CBC is a Canadian crown corporation & serves as Canada's national public radio & television broadcaster; in French, the CBC is called la Société Radio-Canada (SRC), & the corporation also operates Radio Canada International (RCI); offers programming in English, French & 8 Aboriginal languages on radio, & in 9 languages on RCI; provides regional & local television programming in both official languages; broadcasts locally produced programs in English & native languages for people living in the far north; primarily funded by federal statutory grants.
Timothy W. Casgrain, Chair, Board of Directors

Canadian Broadcasting Corporation - Head Office / CBC Société Radio-Canada
PO Box 3220 C, 181 Queen St., Ottawa, ON K1Y 1E4
613-288-6000,
liaison@cbc.ca
www.cbc.radio-canada.ca
Social Media: www.facebook.com/CBCRadioCanada
CBC/Radio-Canada is Canada's national public broadcaster and one of its largest cultural institutions. With 28 services offered on radio, television, the Internet, satellite radio, digital audio, as well as through its record and music distribution service and wireless WAP and SMS messaging services, CBC/Radio-Canada is available how, where, and when Canadians want it.
Timothy W. Casgrain, Chair, Board of Directors
Hubert T. Lacroix, President/CEO, CBC/Radio-Canada

Canwest Global Communications Corp.
CanWest Global Pl., 201 Portage Ave., 31st Fl., Winnipeg, MB R3B 3L7
204-956-2025, Fax: 204-947-9841,
www.canwestglobal.com
CanWest Global Communications Corp. is Canada's leading international media company. The Company's diversified holdings include CanWest MediaWorks, which in turn owns Global Television, a coast-to-coast Canadian broadcasting network that reaches more than 94% of English - speaking Canada; CH, a second station group that broadcasts in Montreal, Hamilton and Victoria; eight specialty channels that offer niche programming including Prime TV; radio stations in Winnipeg, Kitchener, and Halifax in 2006, and the National Post newspaper
Derek H. Burney, Chairman
Leonard Asper, President/CEO
David A. Asper, Exec. Vice-President

Cariboo Central Interior Radio Inc.
1940 Third Ave., Prince George, BC V2M 1G7
250-564-2524, Fax: 250-564-6611
Operates AM & FM radio stations in British Columbia
Terry Shepherd, President & Managing Director

Cariboo Central Interior Radio Inc.
150 West Columbia Street, PO Box 1370, Vanderhoof, BC V0J 3A0
250-567-4914, Fax: 250-567-4982,
ciradio@hwy16.com
Owns and operates several radio stations serving the British Columbia Interior.

Cégep De Rimouski
60, rue de lévêché Quest, Rimouski, QC G5L 4H6
418-723-1880, Fax: 418-724-4961,
infoscol@cegep-rimouski.qc.ca
www.cegep-rimouski.qc.ca

CHUM Radio Kingston
#10, 993 Princess St., Kingston, ON K7L 1H3
613-544-1380, Fax: 613-546-9751,
www.chumkingston.com
Operates 3 radio stations in the Kingston area: 103.7 BOB FM, 98.3 FLY FM, and 98.9 The Drive.
Greg Hinton, Vice President/General Manager, greg.hinton@chumkingston.com
Brian Johnston, Sales Manager, brian.johnston@chumkingston.com
Jennifer Yascheshyn, Program Director, jennifer.yascheshyn@chumkingston.com

CJMR
284 Church Street, Oakville, ON L6J 7N2
905-845-2821, Fax: 905-842-1250,
contact@cjmr1320.ca
www.cjmr.ca
An ethnic radio station serving the Greater Toronto Area in 15 different languages.

CKMW Radio Ltd.
5302 Dundas Street West, Brampton, ON M9B 1B2
416-213-1035, Fax: 416-233-8617,
www.am530.ca
Provides programming in more than a dozen languages

CKPR Inc.
87 Hill Street North, Thunder Bay, ON P7A 5V6
807-346-2600, Fax: 807-345-9923,
radio@ckpr.com
www.ckpr.com
A community radio station serving Thunder Bay, Ontario.

CKUA Radio Network
10526 Jasper Ave., Edmonton, AB T5J 1Z7
403-428-7595, Fax: 403-428-7624, 800-494-2582
radio@ckua.org
www.ckua.com
The CKUA Radio Network was founded in 1927 on the University of Alberta campus in Edmonton. CKUA is Canada's first educational broadcaster and Canada's first public broadcaster. CKUA's radio signal is carried province-wide on AM and FM through a network of 17 transmitters, strategically located throughout Alberta. CKUA also broadcasts in western Canada on select satellite providers and around the world through ckua.com. Recognized as the voice of Alberta artists, musicians and cultural enthusiasts
Ken Regan, General Manager
Wanda Bornn, Sales Manager

Coast Radio
909 Ironwood Street, Campbell River, BC V9W 3E5
250-287-7106, Fax: 250-287-7170,
coastradio@coastradio.com
www.coastradio.com

COGECO inc.
#100, 612 rue Saint-Jacques, Montréal, QC H3C 5R1
514-390-6035, Fax: 514-390-0773,
www.cogeco.ca
COGECO is a diversified telecommunication company which strives to meet the communication needs of consumers and advertisers through broadcasting, in Québec and cable distribution in Canada and Portugal. Second largest cable system operator in Ontario, Québec and Portugal, in terms of the number of basic cable service customers served. COGECO is the controlling shareholder of the TQS network serving Québec's major markets in the French language through the operation of nine television stations
Louis Audet, President/CEO
Pierre Gagné, Vice-President/CFO, Finances

Concordia University
1455 de Maisonneuve Boulevard W, Montreal, QC H3G 1M8
514-848-2424,
www.concordia.ca
Operates CJLO, a not-for-profit instructional radio station operating out of the Loyola Campus of Concordia University.

Corus Entertainment Inc.
BCE Place, #1630, 181 Bay St., Toronto, ON M5J 2T3
416-642-3770, Fax: 416-642-3779,
www.corusent.com
Corus Entertainment is one of Canada's most successful integrated media and entertainment companies. Television services include: YTV, Treehouse, W Network, CMT, The Documentary Channel, SCREAM, Discovery Kids, Telelatino and TELETOON (50%); Western Canada's exclusive pay-TV movie service on six thematic channels under the Movie Central brand; three local over-the-air television stations; Corus Custom Networks advertising services for television and Max Trax, a residential subscription digital music service. They also operate 52 radio stations throughout Canada
John Cassaday, CEO
John Hayes, President, Corus Radio

CPAM Radio Union.com Inc.
3733, Jarry Est, 2e Étage, Montreal, QC H1Z 2G1

** For details on this company see listing in Major Broadcasting Companies section; † French language station*

514-287-1288, Fax: 514-287-3299,
info@cpam-radiounion.com
www.cpam-radiounion.com
Station de radio AM ethnique de langue française à Montréal, CPAM offre une programmation axée sur les besoins et la culture des communautés ethnoculturelles francophones d'origine haïtienne, latino-américaine et africaine de la région métropolitaine de Montréal

CTVglobemedia Inc.
299 Queen St. West, Toronto, ON M5V 2Z5
416-384-8000,
ctvglobemediacommunications@ctvglobemedia.com
www.ctvglobemedia.com
CTVglobemedia, Canada's largest private broadcaster, offers a wide range of news, sports, information, and entertainment programming, via radio and television; CTVglobemedia's main broadcast media asset is CTV Television Inc.; it also owns CHUM, now called CTV Limited, and operates Toronto radio stations CP24 Radio 1050 (formerly 1050 CHUM), and CHUM-FM; the CHUM Radio Network is a subsidiary of CTVglobemedia, as is The Globe and Mail newspaper.
Ivan Fecan, President/CEO

Dauphin Broadcasting Co. Ltd.
27-3 Avenue NE, Dauphin, MB R7N 0Y5
204-638-3230, Fax: 204-638-8257,
730ckdm@mb.sympatico.ca
730ckdm.com
Operates 730 CKDM, a community radio station serving Dauphin, Manitoba for over 50 years.
Rene Maillard, President

Diffusion Laval inc.
2040, Autoroute Laval, Laval, QC H7S 2M9
450-680-1570, Fax: 450-680-1598,
info@laval1570am.com
www.boomer1570.ca
CFAV/Radio Boomer 1570 AM; Laval 1570 AM (septembre, 2010).
Michel Mathieu, Président/Directeur général

Fairchild Radio
135 East Beaver Creek Road, Unit 7-8, Richmond Hill, ON L4B 1E2
905-763-3350, Fax: 905-889-9828,
operation@am1430.com
www.fairchildradio.com
Chinese Canadian multicultural radio network with stations in Toronto, Vancouver, and Calgary. Provides program schedules and internet simulcasting
Thomas Fung, Chairman

Fairchild Television Ltd. / FTV
Aberdeen Centre, #3300, 4151 Hazelbridge Way, Vancouver, BC V6X 4J7
604-295-1313, Fax: 604-295-1300,
info@fairchildtv.com
www.fairchildtv.com
Provides programming mainly in Cantonese and Mandarin, broadcast through cable and satellite across Canada and part of the U.S.
Joe Chan, President

Fawcett Broadcasting Ltd.
PO Box 777, Fort Frances, ON P9A 3N1
807-274-7580, Fax: 807-274-8746
Operates AM & FM radio stations in north-western Ontario
Lois Fawcett, President

Golden West Broadcasting Ltd.
#201, 125 Centre Ave., Altona, MB R0G 0B0
204-324-6464, Fax: 204-324-8918,
www.gwm.ca
Headquartered in Altona, Manitoba. Golden West has 28 radio stations scattered across Manitoba, Saskatchewan, and Alberta
Elmer Hildebrand, President & CEO
David Wiebe, General Manager

Groupe Radio Antenne 6
568, boul St-Joseph, Roberval, QC G8H 2K6
418-275-1831
Operates 5 stations in Lac-Saint-Jean region; also has a presence in Abitibi, Outaouais, and Montreal
Marc-André Levesque, President

Groupe TVA inc.
1600, boul de Maisonneuve est, Montréal, QC H2L 4P6
514-526-9251, Fax: 514-598-0673,
www.tva.canoe.com
Groupe TVA fondée en 1960 sous le nom de Corporation Télé-Métropole inc., est une entreprise de communication intégrée active dans les secteurs de la diffusion, de la production de produits audiovisuels, de la publication de magazines, de l'édition ainsi que de la distribution de films.
Pierre Dion, Président/Chef de la direction
Yves Beaupré, Vice-président, Exploitation

Harvard Broadcasting Inc.
2060 Halifax St., Regina, SK S4P 1T7
306-546-6200, Fax: 306-781-7338,
rpettigrew@harvardbroadcasting.com
www.harvardbroadcasting.com
Harvard Broadcasting came into being in 1977, when The Hill Companies purchased CKCK-TV, the Regina-based CTV affiliate station. In 1981, Harvard expanded into radio with the purchase of CKRM and CFMQ, also both local stations. Today, Harvard Broadcasting Inc. includes 620 CKRM, Lite 92 FM, and 104.9 The Wolf in Regina and CFEX-FM, X92.9, in Calgary and CFVR-FM in Fort McMurray
Bruce Cowie, Vice-President

Hector Broadcasting Co. Ltd.
84 Provost Street, PO Box 519, New Glasgow, NS B2H 5E7
902-752-4200, Fax: 902-755-2468,
ckec@ckec.com
www.ckec.com
Operates 1320 CKEC, a community radio station serving Pictou County, NS

Hildebrand Group
366 - 3rd Ave. S, Saskatoon, SK S7K 1M5
306-244-1975, Fax: 306-665-5501,
cjww.radio@sasktel.net
www.cjwwradio.com
Operates 600 CJWW out of Saskatoon.
Vic Dubois, General Manager
Ken McFarlane, General Sales Manager
Myles Myrol, Retail Sales Manager

Inuit Broadcasting Corporation / IBC
#301, 331 Cooper St., Ottawa, ON K2P 0G5
613-235-1892, Fax: 613-230-8824,
www.inuitbroadcasting.ca
The Inuit Broadcasting Corporation provides a window to the Arctic by producing television programming by Inuit, for Inuit. IBC has 5 production centres scattered across Nunavut, with 34 Inuit staff at every level of the production chain, from director of network programming to technical producer to administrative assistant. IBC is a founding member of Television Northern Canada and the Aboriginal Peoples Television Network
Debbie Brisebois, Executive Director

Island Radio Ltd.
4550 Willingdon Rd., Nanaimo, BC V9T 2H3
250-758-1131, Fax: 250-758-4644,
info@islandradio.bc.ca
www.islandradio.bc.ca
Island Radio consists of six radio stations on Vancouver Island, British Columbia
Paul Larsen, President

James Bay Broadcasting Corp. Inc.
PO Box 400, Moosonee, ON P0L 1Y0
705-336-2466, Fax: 705-336-2186
Operates CHMO, a community radio station that serves Moosonee and Moose Factory, Ontario.

The Jim Pattison Broadcast Group
460 Pemberton Terrace, Kamloops, BC V2C 1T5
250-372-3322, Fax: 250-374-0445,
info@jpbroadcast.com
www.jpbroadcast.com
The Jim Pattison Broadcast Group is Canada's largest private western-based broadcasting company
Rick Arnish, President
Joel Simmons, Technical Director
Bruce Davis, VP Sales

Klondike Broadcasting Ltd.
203-4103 4th Avenue, Whitehorse, YK Y1A 1H6
867-668-6100, Fax: 867-668-4209,
ckrwcopy@ckrw.com
www.ckrw.com
Operates CKRW-FM in Whitehorse, YK.
Jennifer Johnstone, General Manager, ckrwcopy@ckrw.com
Eva Birdman, Sales & Ad Copy, marketing@ckrw.com

Learning Skills Television of Alberta
Also known as: ACCESS - The Education Station
3720 - 76 Ave., Edmonton, AB T6B 2N9
780-440-7777, Fax: 780-440-8899, 888-440-4640
access@incentre.net
www.accesslearning.com
Television broadcasting and multimedia learning company based in Edmonton, AB. Established in 1994 to privatize Alberta's provincial educational television service. LTA is the designated educational broadcasting Authority for Alberta as defined in the Broadcasting Act
Ron Keast, President
Peter Palframan, Vice-President, Finance & Administration

Lethbridge Community College
Student Service Centre, 3000 College Drive South, Lethbridge, AB T1K 1L6
403-329-7237, Fax: 403-320-1461
Operates CRLC The Kodiak, a college radio station.

Mainstream Broadcasting Corporation
#100-1200 West 73rd Avenue, Vancouver, BC V6P 6G5
604-263-1320, Fax: 604-261-0310,
www.am1320.com
Mainstream Broadcasting Corporation is a British Columbia media company owned and operated by local Vancouver resident and businessman, James Ho. In 1993, OCV programming was incorporated into the multicultural AM radio station of CHMB AM 1320, serving the needs of Vancouver's multicultural community.
James Ho, President
Teresa Wat, CEO/COO
George Feng, VP Business Development

Maritime Broadcasting System
5121 Sackville St., Halifax, NS B3J 1K1
902-425-1225, Fax: 902-423-2093,
mail@mbsradio.com
www.mbsradio.com
Originally established in 1969 as Eastern Broadcasting Limited, MBS Radio is a 100% maritime owned, private broadcasting company, with 25 radio stations and 410 employees serving communities in the three Maritime Provinces of Nova Scotia, New Brunswick and Prince Edward Island
Merv Russell, President

MCTV-TV
699 Frood Rd., Sudbury, ON P3C 5A3
705-674-8301, Fax: 705-671-2789
Scott Lund, Vice-President

Merritt Broadcasting
#201, 2196 Quilchena Avenue, PO Box 1630, Merritt, BC V1K 1B8
250-378-4288, Fax: 250-378-6979,
news@cjnl.com
Devoted to local community service

NewCap Inc.
745 Windmill Rd., Dartmouth, NS B3B 1C2
902-468-7557, Fax: 902-468-7558,
ncc@ncc.ca
www.ncc.ca
NewCap is one of Canada's leading radio broadcasters with 76 licences across Canada
Robert G. Steele, President & CEO
David J. Murray, COO
Scott Weatherby, CFO & Corporate Secretary

Newcap Radio
745 Windmill Road, Dartmouth, NS B3B 1C2
902-468-7557, Fax: 902-468-7558,
ncc@newcapradio.com
www.ncc.ca.ca
Newcap Radio is one of Canada's leading radio broadcasters with 76 licences across Canada. The Company reaches millions of listeners each week through a variety of formats and is a recognized industry leader in radio programming, sales and networking.
Harry R Steele, Chairman
Robert G Steele, President/CEO
David J Murray, COO

Newfoundland Broadcasting Co. Ltd.
PO Box 2020, 446 Logy Bay Rd., St. John's, NL A1C 5S2
709-722-5015, Fax: 709-726-5017,
ntv@ntv.ca
www.ntv.ca
Reaches 8 million households across Canada via digital cable & satellite

Okalakatiget Society
PO Box 160, Nain, NL A0P 1L0
709-922-2955, Fax: 709-922-2293,
okradio@oksociety.com
www.oksociety.com
The OKalaKatiget Society was incorporated in 1982. Stationed in Nain, Labrador the Society provides a regional, native communication service for the people on the North Coast and the Lake Melville region of Labrador. People have come to rely on the Society for information and entertainment via radio and

** For details on this company see listing in Major Broadcasting Companies section; † French language station*

television. Their mandate is to preserve and promote the language and culture of the Inuit within the region
Fran Williams, Exec. Director

Radio Canada International
1400, boul René-Lévesque est, Montréal, QC H2L 2M2
514-597-7500, Fax: 514-597-6607,
www.rcinet.ca
Social Media: www.facebook.com/CBCRadioCanada
Radio Canada International has been broadcasting around the World since 1945, with live radio in English, French, Spanish, Portuguese, Arabic, Mandarin, and Russian. RCI's mandate is to increase awareness of Canadian values, as well as its social, economic and cultural activities to specific geographic areas as determined in consultation with the government of Canada. RCI also has the complementary mandate of addressing these same topics to new immigrants to Canada.
Jean Larin, Executive Director

RAWLCO Radio Ltd.
715 Saskatchewan Cres. West, Saskatoon, SK S7M 5V7
306-934-2222, Fax: 306-477-0002
Rawlco Radio Ltd. is a Saskatchewan company with radio stations in Saskatoon, Regina, Prince Albert, North Battleford, and Meadow Lake. Operates 12 radio stations
Michael Zaplitny, Vice-President

Red River College
2055 Notre Dame Avenue, Winnipeg, MB R3H 0J9
204-632-3960,
www.rrc.mb.ca
Home of 92.9 KICK-FM, a non-profit instructional radio station based at Red River College in Winnipeg, Manitoba.

RNC MEDIA
#1523, 1, Place Ville Marie, Montréal, QC H3B 2B5
514-866-8686, Fax: 514-866-8056,
www.rncmedia.ca
Radiodiffusion (Planète Radio, Radio X); télédiffusion (TVA Gatineau-Ottawa et Abitibi-Témiscamingue; TQS Gatineau-Ottawa et Abitibi-Témiscamingue; SRC Abitibi-Témiscamingue); programmation de haute qualité et services de publicité.
Raynald Brière, Président/Chef de la direction, rbriere@rncmedia.ca
Pierre R. Brosseau, Président exécutif du conseil, pbrosseau@rncmedia.ca

Rogers Broadcasting Ltd.
777 Jarvis St., Toronto, ON M4Y 3B7
416-935-8200, Fax: 416-935-8202
Rogers Broadcasting has 46 AM and FM radio stations across Canada. Television properties include Toronto multicultural television broadcasters OMNI.1 (CFMT) and OMNI.2, televised and electronic shopping service, The Shopping Channel, Rogers Sportsnet and manages two digital television services
Anthony P. Viner, President/CEO
Chuck McCoy, Exec. Vice-President, Programming

SCN
#E-313, 2440 Broad St., Regina, SK S4P 0A5
306-787-0490, Fax: 306-787-0496, 800-667-5055
inquiries@scn.ca
www.scn.ca
SCN operates as an agency of the Government of Saskatchewan, in accordance with The Communications Network Corporation Act (1989). The Minister of Culture Youth and Recreation serves as the Minister Responsible for SCN
Jim Johns, Manager, Information Systems
David Stanchuk, Manager, Technology
Ken Alecxe, President & CEO
Richard Gustin, Executive Director, Programming
Twyla MacDougall, Executive Director, Finance & Human Resources & Strategic Plannin
Maureen MacDonald, Manager, Communications

Seneca College
1750 Finch Avenue East, Toronto, ON M2J 2X5
604-263-1320, Fax: 604-261-0310,
www.senecac.on.ca
Home of Radio CS, a not-for-profit instructional radio station.
Dr. Rick Miner, President
Jean Anne McLeod BA, Chair of the Board of Governors

Shaw Communications Inc.
Also known as: Shaw Cable
#900, 630 - 3rd Ave. SW, Calgary, AB T2P 4L4
403-750-4500, Fax: 403-750-4501, 888-750-7429
www.shaw.ca
Shaw Communications Inc. is a diversified communications company whose core business is providing broadband cable television, high-speed Internet, digital phone, telecommunications services, and satellite direct-to-home services to more than 3 million customers throughout Canada
J.R. Shaw, Executive Chair
Peter Bissonnette, President & CEO

Société Radio-Canada
Canadian Broadcasting Corporation
1400, boul René-Lévesque est, Montréal, QC H2L 2M2
514-597-6000, Fax: 514-597-5545, 866-306-4636
auditoire@radio-canada.ca
www.radio-canada.ca
Social Media: www.facebook.com/CBCRadioCanada
Radio-Canada est le radiodiffuseur public national du Canada et l'une des plus grandes institutions culturelles du pays. Avec ses 28 services offerts sur des plateformes comme la radio, la télévision, Internet, la radio par satellite, l'audio numérique, sans compter son service de distribution de disques et de musique et ses services de messagerie sans fil WAP et SMS, CBC/Radio-Canada est maintenant accessible aux Canadiens à leur convenance.
Hubert T. Lacroix, Président/Chef de la direction, CBC/Radio-Canada

Standard Broadcasting Corp. Ltd.
2 St. Clair Ave. West, 2nd Fl., Toronto, ON M4V 1L6
416-960-9911, Fax: 416-323-6828,
www.standardradio.com
Launched in 1927; 51 stations provide music and information to 29 markets across Canada
Gary Slaight, President/CEO
Ian Lurie, Vice-President/CFO
Bill Herz, Vice-President, Sales
Dave Simon, Vice-President, Engineering

Standard Radio Office
2 St. Clair Avenue West, 2nd Floor, Toronto, ON M4V 1L6
416-960-9911, Fax: 416-323-6828,
www.standardradio.com
Standard Radio is the largest privately owned broadcast company in Canada
Gary Slaight, President/CEO
Ian Lurie, VP/CFO
Dave Simon, VP Engineering

Steele Communications
PO Box 8-590, 391 Kenmount Rd., St. Johns, NL A1B 3P5
709-726-5590, Fax: 709-726-4633,
www.vocm.com
Steele Communications is the broadcast leader in Newfoundland and Labrador, with a network of 26 radio licenses across the province. Providing both AM and FM networks in a variety of formats, delivering to listeners, consistent quality programming with a local focus
Greg Hinton, VP/General Manager

Taqramiut Nipingat Inc. / TNI
Also known as: Voice of the North
#200, 1985 - 55 Ave., Dorval, QC H9P 1G9
514-683-2330, Fax: 514-683-1078,
tnigeneral@taqramiut.qc.ca
www.taqramiut.qc.ca
Taqramiut Nipingat Inc. is a non-profit organization incorporated on September 8, 1975 under Part II of the Canada Business Corporation Act. Offers video production and a variety of broadband telecommunications services to institutional and individual clients on a profit generating basis. TNI's 15 hours of weekly radio programs are broadcast via the Northern Service of the Canadian Broadcast Corporation
George Kakayuk, President
Sammy Duncan, Vice-President

Télé Inter-Rives ltée
Inter-Riverbank Television
15, rue de la Chute, Rivière-du-Loup, QC G5R 5B7
418-867-8080, Fax: 418-867-4710
Tele Inter-Rives Ltd. dirige 4 stations de télévision régionales dans l'est du Québec; CKRT-TV (SRC), CIMT-TV, CHAU (TVA), et CFTF (V).

Télé-Québec
Also known as: Société de télédiffusion du Québec
1000, rue Fullum, Montréal, QC H2K 3L7
514-521-2424, Fax: 514-873-2601,
info@telequebec.tv
www.telequebec.qc.ca
La Société a pour objet d'exploiter une entreprise de télédiffusion éducative et culturelle afin d'assurer, par tout mode de diffusion, l'accessibilité de ses produits au public.
Télé-Québec est une société publique de production et de diffusion, desservant plus de 92 % de la population québécoise à travers son réseau riche de 17 émetteurs, alimenté par un lien satellite portant sa programmation de Montréal.
Michèle Fortin, Présidente/Directrice générale

TQS inc.
#100, 612, rue St-Jacques, Montréal, QC H3C 5R1
514-390-6035, Fax: 514-390-0773,
tvpublic@tqs.ca
www.tqs.ca
Established in September 1986; covers all Quebec regions
René Guimond, President/CEO
Monique Lacharité, Exec. Vice-President, Finance & Administration

TVOntario / OECA
Also known as: Ontario Educational Communications Authority
PO Box 200 Q, 2180 Yonge St., Toronto, ON M4T 2T1
416-484-2600, Fax: 416-484-6285, 800-613-0513
asktvo@tvontario.org
www.tvontario.org
In 1970, TVOntario was established as the Ontario Educational Communications Authority (OECA) by the government of Ontario, for the purpose of using technology to support the province's education priorities. TVO, TVOntario's English-language service, is Canada's oldest educational broadcaster, and is available to over 98% of Ontario homes. TVO provides educational programming and online resources that enhance and extend learning at home and in the classroom, as well as promoting Ontario's rich cultural identity
Lisa de Wilde, CEO

VOWR
PO Box 7430, Patrick St., St. Johns, NF A1E 3Y5
709-579-9233,
vowr@vowr.org
www.vowr.org
Radio station VOWR broadcasts from studios located in Wesley United Church in St. John's, Newfoundland, Canada. The station's first broadcast occurred on July 24, 1924
JG Joyce, Founder of VOWR

Wawatay Native Communications Society
PO Box 1180, Sioux Lookout, ON P8T 1B7
807-737-2951, Fax: 807-737-3224, 800-243-9059
christinec@wawatay.on.ca
www.wawatay.on.ca
Wawatay Native Communications Society is a self-governing, independent community-driven entrepreneurial native organization dedicated to using appropriate technologies to meet the communication needs of people of Aboriginal ancestry in Northern Ontario
Christine Chisel, Executive Director

AM Radio Stations

Alberta

***Athabasca:* CKBA** (Freq: 850)
Owned by: **NewCap Inc.**
#2, 4907 - 51 St., Athabasca, AB T9S 1E7
780-675-5301, Fax: 780-675-4938,
jpeckham@ab.ncc.ca
Mark Maheau, Vice-President

***Banff:* CJMT** (Freq: 1340)
Owned by: **CHMN-FM**
Banff, AB

***Blairmore:* CJEV** (Freq: 1340)
Owned by: **NewCap Inc.**
PO Box 840, 13213 - 20 Ave., Blairmore, AB T0K 2E2
403-562-2806, Fax: 403-562-8114

***Brooks:* CIBQ** (Freq: 1340)
Owned by: **NewCap Inc.**
PO Box 180, #8, 403 - 2nd Ave. West, Brooks, AB T1R 0S3
403-362-3418, Fax: 403-362-8168
John Petrie, Station Manager

***Calgary:* CBR** (Freq: 1010)
Owned by: **Canadian Broadcasting Corporation**
PO Box 2640 D, 1724 Westmount Blvd. NW, Calgary, AB T2P 2M7
403-521-6000,
www.calgary.cbc.ca

***Calgary:* CFAC** (Freq: 960)
Owned by: **Rogers Broadcasting Ltd.**
2723 - 37 Ave. NE, Calgary, AB T1Y 5R8

* For details on this company see listing in Major Broadcasting Companies section; † French language station

403-246-9696,
www.fan960.com

Kelly Kirch, Program Director

Calgary: **CFFR** (Freq: 660)
Owned by: **Rogers Broadcasting Ltd.**
2723 - 37 Ave. NE, Calgary, AB T1Y 5R8
403-291-0000, Fax: 403-291-4368,
www.660news.com

Calgary: **CHQR** (Freq: 770)
Owned by: **Corus Entertainment Inc.**
#105, 630 - 3 Ave. SW, Calgary, AB T2P 4L4
403-716-6500, Fax: 403-716-2111, 800-563-7770
www.am770chqr.com

John Vos, Program Director

Calgary: **CKMX** (Freq: 1060)
Owned by: **Standard Radio Office**
1110 Centre St. NE, 3rd Fl., Calgary, AB T2E 2R2
403-240-5800, Fax: 403-240-5801,
www.classiccountryam1060.com

Camrose: **CFCW** (Freq: 790)
Owned by: **CFCW**
Camrose, AB

Drumheller: **CKDQ** (Freq: 910)
Owned by: **NewCap Inc.**
PO Box 1480, 515 Hwy. 10 East, Drumheller, AB T0J 0Y0
403-823-3384, Fax: 403-823-7241,
ckdq@ab.ncc.ca

Hugh MacDonald, General Manager

Edmonton: **AM 930 The Light** (Freq: 930)
5316 Calgary Trail, Edmonton, AB T6H 4J8
780-466-4930, Fax: 780-469-5335,
www.cjca.ca/cms

Malcolm Hunt, Program Director
Carlo Bruno, Business Manager

Edmonton: **CBX** (Freq: 740)
Owned by: **Canadian Broadcasting Corporation**
#123, Edmonton City Centre, Edmonton, AB T5J 2Y8
780-468-7500,
www.cbc.ca/edmonton

Edmonton: **CFCW** (Freq: 790)
Owned by: **NewCap Inc.**
#600, 5241 Calgary Trail NW, Edmonton, AB T6H 5G8
780-468-3939, Fax: 780-435-0844,
www.cfcw.com

Edmonton: **CFRN** (Freq: 1260)
Owned by: **Standard Radio Office**
#100, 18520 Stony Plain Rd., Edmonton, AB T5S 2E2
780-486-2800, Fax: 780-489-6927,
team1260@cfrn.com
www.cfrn.com

Edmonton: **CHED** (Freq: 630)
Owned by: **Corus Entertainment Inc.**
5204 - 84 St., Edmonton, AB T6E 5N8
780-440-6300, Fax: 780-469-5937,
info@630ched.com
www.630ched.com

†***Edmonton:*** **CHFA** (Freq: 680)
Owned by: **Canadian Broadcasting Corporation**
CP 555, 123, 10062 - 102 Ave., Edmonton, AB T5J 2P4
780-468-7800, Fax: 780-468-7812,
lecarnet@radio-canada.ca

François Pageau, Chef, Émissions radio & télévision françaises (AB)

Edmonton: **CHQT** (Freq: 880)
Owned by: **Corus Entertainment Inc.**
5204 - 84 St., Edmonton, AB T6E 5N8
780-424-8800, Fax: 780-469-5937,
www.cool880.com

Edson: **CJYR** (Freq: 970)
Owned by: **NewCap Inc.**
PO Box 7800, 4813 - 4th Ave., Edson, AB T7E 1V8
780-723-4461, Fax: 780-723-3765

High Prairie: **CKVH** (Freq: 1020)
Owned by: **NewCap Inc.**
PO Box 2219, High Prairie, AB T0G 1E0
780-523-5111, Fax: 780-523-3360,
ckvh@ab.ncc.ca

High River: **CHRB** (Freq: 1140)
Owned by: **Golden West Broadcasting Ltd.**
11 - 5th Ave. SE, High River, AB T1V 1G2
403-652-2472, Fax: 403-652-7861, 866-652-2472
am1140@am1140.com
www.am1140radio.com

J. Young, Station Manager

Lethbridge: **CLCC**
Owned by: **Lethbridge College***
Student Service Centre, 3000 College Dr. South, Lethbridge, AB T1K 1L6
403-329-7237, Fax: 403-320-1461

Medicine Hat: **CHAT** (Freq: 1270)
Owned by: **The Jim Pattison Broadcast Group**
PO Box 1270, Medicine Hat, AB T1A 7H5
403-548-8282, Fax: 403-548-8270,
www.1270chat.com

Dwaine Dietrich, General Manager

Peace River: **CKYL** (Freq: 610)
PO Box 300, Peace River, AB T8S 1T5
780-624-2535, Fax: 780-624-5424,
www.ylcountry.com

Terry Babiy, General Manager

St Paul: **CHLW** (Freq: 1310)
#201, 4341 - 50 Ave., St Paul, AB T0A 3A3
780-645-4425, Fax: 780-645-2383,
dwhite@newcap.ca
www.angelfire.com/ca/chlw

Danny White, Station Manager

Stettler: **CKSQ** (Freq: 1400)
Owned by: **NewCap Inc.**
PO Box 2050, 4812A - 50th St., Stettler, AB T0C 2L0
403-742-2930, Fax: 403-742-0660

Wainwright: **CKKY** (Freq: 830)
Owned by: **NewCap Inc.**
1037 - 2nd Ave.. 2nd Fl., Wainwright, AB T9W 1K7
780-842-4311, Fax: 780-842-4636

Ron Prochner, Station Manager

Westlock: **CFOK** (Freq: 1370)
Owned by: **NewCap Inc.**
#17, 10030 - 106 St., Westlock, AB T7P 2K4
780-349-4421, Fax: 780-349-6259,
wbetts@newcap.ca

Wray Betts, Station Manager

Wetaskiwin: **CKJR** (Freq: 1440)
Owned by: **NewCap Inc.**
5214A - 50 Ave., Wetaskiwin, AB T9A 0S8
780-352-0144, Fax: 780-352-5656,
www.catcountry.ca

British Columbia

100 Mile House: **CKBX** (Freq: 840)
Owned by: **Cariboo Central Interior Radio Inc.**
260 - 3rd St., 100 Mile House, BC V0K 2E0
250-395-3848, Fax: 250-395-4147,
trard@vistaradio.ca
www.thewolfonline.ca

Tracey Gard, Director

Burns Lake: **CFLD** (Freq: 760)
Owned by: **Vista Broadcast Group**
PO Box 600, Burns Lake, BC V0J 1E0
250-692-3414

Bill Waugh

Campbell River: **CFWB** (Freq: 1490)
Owned by: **Coast Radio***
909 Ironwood St., Campbell River, BC V9W 3E5
250-287-7106, Fax: 250-287-7170,
coastradio@coastradio.com
www.coastradio.com

N.E. Browne, President
Greg Phelps, Operations Manager

Creston: **CFKC** (Freq: 1340)
Owned by: **Standard Radio Office**
PO Box 310, 1013 Canyon St., Creston, BC V0B 1G0
250-428-5312, Fax: 250-428-5015,
kbs@sri.ca
www.kbsradio.ca

Dawson Creek: **CJDC** (Freq: 890)
Owned by: **Standard Radio Office**
901 - 102 Ave., Dawson Creek, BC V1G 2B6
250-782-3341, Fax: 250-782-3154,
peacereception@sri.ca
www.cjdcam.com

Tracy Gard

Golden: **CKGR** (Freq: 1400)
Owned by: **Standard Radio Office**
PO Box 1403, 825 - 10th Ave. South, Golden, BC V0A 1H0
250-344-7177, Fax: 250-344-8138,
myezrock.com

Harvey Davidson, President

Granisle: **CHLD** (Freq: 1480)
Owned by: **Vista Broadcast Group**
Granisle, BC

Invermere: **CKIR** (Freq: 870)
742 - 13th St., Invermere, BC V0A 1K4
250-342-4434

Kamloops: **CHNL** (Freq: 610)
611 Lansdowne St., Kamloops, BC V2C 1Y6
250-372-2292, Fax: 250-372-2293,
info@radionl.com
www.radionl.com

Robbie Dunn, General Manager, rdunn@radionl.com
Jim Reynolds, Manager, Operations, programming@radionl.com
Peter Angle, Manager, Sales, advertising@radionl.com

Kelowna: **CKFR** (Freq: 1150)
Owned by: **Standard Radio Office**
#300, 435 Bernard Ave., Kelowna, BC V1Y 6N8
250-860-8600, Fax: 250-880-8856

Paul Mann, General Manager

Kelowna: **CKOV** (Freq: 630)
Owned by: **The Jim Pattison Broadcast Group**
3805 Lakeshore Rd., Kelowna, BC V1W 3K6
250-762-3331, Fax: 250-762-2141, 888-763-4212
info@ckov63.com
www.ckov63.com

Rick Arnish, President
Bruce Davis, General Manager & VP

Merritt: **CJNL** (Freq: 1230)
Owned by: **Merritt Broadcasting***
PO Box 1630, #201, 2196 Quilchena Ave., Merritt, BC V1K 1B8
250-378-4288, Fax: 250-378-6979,
news@cjnl.com

Oliver: **CJOR-1** (Freq: 1490)
Owned by: **CJOR**
Oliver, BC

Osoyoos: **CIOR** (Freq: 1400)
PO Box 539, Osoyoos, BC V0H 1V0
250-295-6991, Fax: 250-495-7228,
Osr@tvcablelan.com

Hawse Ross, General Manager

Penticton: **CJOR** (Freq: 1240)
33 Carmi Ave., Penticton, BC V2A 3G4
250-492-2800, Fax: 250-493-0370

Penticton: **CKOR** (Freq: 800)
Owned by: **Standard Radio Office**
33 Carmi Ave., Penticton, BC V2A 3G4
250-492-2800, Fax: 250-493-0370

Port Hardy: **CFNI** (Freq: 1240)
Owned by: **Coast Radio***
Magic 1240, PO Box 1240, 5050 Beaver Harbour Rd., Port Hardy, BC V0N 2P0
250-949-6500, Fax: 250-949-6580,
cfni@cablerocket.com
www.coastradio.com

N.E. Browne, President
Greg Phelps, Operations Manager

Prince Rupert: **CFPR** (Freq: 860)
Owned by: **Canadian Broadcasting Corporation**
#1, 222 - 3 Ave. West, Prince Rupert, BC V8J 1L1

** For details on this company see listing in Major Broadcasting Companies section; † French language station*

250-624-2161, Fax: 250-627-8594,
daybreaknorth@cbc.ca
www.cbc.ca/bc

Laura Chapin, Sr. Announcer/Operator

***Quesnel:* CKCQ**
#502, 410 Kinchant St., Quesnel, BC V2J 7K5
250-992-7046, Fax: 250-992-2354,
www.vistaradio.ca

Brian Edwards, President

***Revelstoke:* CKCR** (Freq: 1340)
Owned by: **Standard Radio Office**
PO Box 1420, Revelstoke, BC V0E 2F0
250-837-2149, Fax: 250-837-5577,
www.revelstoke.myezrock.com

***Richmond:* CISL** (Freq: 650)
Owned by: **Standard Radio Office**
#20, 11151 Horseshoe Way, Richmond, BC V7A 4S5
604-272-6500, Fax. 604-272-0917,
oldies@650cisl.com
www.650cisl.com

Gary Slaight, President

***Richmond:* CJVB** (Freq: 1470; Fairchild Radio Group)
Owned by: **Fairchild Radio**
#2090, 4151 Hazelbridge Way, Richmond, BC V6X 4J7
604-295-1234, Fax: 604-295-1201,
general@am1470.com
www.am1470.com

George Lee, Sr. Vice-President & General Manage

***Smithers:* CFBV** (Freq: 870)
PO Box 335, Smithers, BC V0J 2N0
250-847-2277, Fax: 250-847-9411,
thepeak@bulkley.net

Gareth Reid, General & Sales Manager

***Summerland:* CHOR** (Freq: 1450)
Owned by: **Standard Radio Office**
PO Box 1170, #200, 901 Main St., Summerland, BC V0H 1Z0
250-494-0333, Fax: 250-493-0370

***Terrace:* CFTK** (Freq: 590)
Owned by: **Standard Radio Office**
4625 Lazelle Ave., Terrace, BC V8G 1S4
250-638-6316, Fax: 250-638-6320,
www.standardradio.com

Bryan Edwards, President
Tim MacLean, Vice-President

***Vancouver:* CBU** (Freq: 690)
Owned by: **Canadian Broadcasting Corporation**
PO Box 4600, 775 Cambie St., Vancouver, BC V6B 4A2
604-662-6920, Fax: 604-662-6088,
www.cbc.ca/bc

***Vancouver:* CFTE** (Freq: 1410)
Owned by: **Rogers Broadcasting Ltd.**
#300, 380 West 2nd Ave., Vancouver, BC V5Y 1C8
604-871-9000, Fax: 604-871-2901,
www.teamradio.ca

James Stuart, Vice President/General Manager, CHUM Radio Vancouver

***Vancouver:* CHMB** (Freq: 1320)
Owned by: **Mainstream Broadcasting Corp.**
#100, 1200 West 73 Ave., Vancouver, BC V6P 6G7
604-263-1320, Fax: 604-263-0320,
info@am1320.com
www.am1320.com

Wayne Lee, General Manager

***Vancouver:* CHMJ** (Freq: 730)
Owned by: **Corus Entertainment Inc.**
#2000, 700 West Georgia St., Vancouver, BC V7Y 1K9
604-681-7511, Fax: 604-331-2722,
www.am730traffic.com

***Vancouver:* CISL** (Freq: 650)
Owned by: **CISL**
Vancouver, BC

***Vancouver:* CKBD** (Freq: 600)
Owned by: **The Jim Pattison Broadcast Group**
#300, 1401 - 8th Ave. West, Vancouver, BC V6H 1C9
604-731-6111, Fax: 604-731-0493,
600am@600am.com
www.600am.com

***Vancouver:* CKNW** (Freq: 980)
Owned by: **Corus Entertainment Inc.**
#2000, 700 West Georgia St., Vancouver, BC V7Y 1K9
604-331-2711, Fax: 604-331-2722,
info@cknw.com
www.cknw.com

J.J. Johnston, General Manager

***Vancouver:* CKST** (Freq: 1040)
Owned by: **Rogers Broadcasting Ltd.**
#300, 380 West 2nd Ave., Vancouver, BC V5Y 1C8
604-871-9000, Fax: 604-871-2901,
www.teamradio.ca

James Stuart, Vice President/General Manager, CHUM Radio Vancouver

***Vancouver:* CKWX** (Freq: 1130)
Owned by: **Rogers Broadcasting Ltd.**
2440 Ash St., Vancouver, BC V5Z 4J6
604-873-2599, Fax: 604-873-0877,
news1130@news1130.rogers.com
www.news1130.com

***Vanderhoof:* CIVH** (Freq: 1340)
Owned by: **Central Interior Radio Inc.***
PO Box 1370, 150 West Columbia St., Vanderhoof, BC V0J 3A0
250-567-4914, Fax: 250-567-4982,
ciradio@hwy16.com

Tom Bulmer, Station Manager

***Victoria:* C-FAX** (Freq: 1070)
1420 Broad St., Victoria, BC V8W 2B1
250-386-1070, Fax: 250-920-4603,
cfax.reception@chumradio.com
www.cfax1070.com

Adam Salvisburg, Production Manager
Alan Brown, Senior Account Manager

***Victoria:* CKMO** (Freq: 900)
Owned by: **Camosun College**
3100 Foul Bay Rd., Victoria, BC V8P 5J2
250-370-3658, Fax: 250-370-3679,
feedback@village900.ca
www.village900.ca

Doug Ozeroff, General Manager

***White Rock:* KARI** (Freq: 550)
PO Box 75150, White Rock, BC V4B 5L3
604-536-7733,
info@kari55.com
www.kari55.com

***Williams Lake:* CKWL** (Freq: 570)
Owned by: **Cariboo Central Interior Radio Inc.**
83 South First Ave., Williams Lake, BC V2G 1H4
250-392-6551, Fax: 250-392-4142,
tgard@vistaradio.ca
www.thewolfonline.ca

Tracey Gard, Manager, 250-392-6551 ex

Manitoba

***Altona:* CFAM** (Freq: 950)
Owned by: **Golden West Broadcasting Ltd.**
PO Box 950, 125 Centre Ave. East, Altona, MB R0G 0B0
204-324-6464, Fax: 204-324-8918,
arlindueck@goldenwestradio.com

Elmer Hildebrand, President & CEO

***Boissevain:* CJRB** (Freq: 1220)
Owned by: **Golden West Broadcasting Ltd.**
Boissevain, MB
Elmer Hildebrand, President & CEO

***Brandon:* CKLQ** (Freq: 880)
624 - 14 St. East, Brandon, MB R7A 7E1
204-725-0515, Fax: 204-726-1270,
qcountry@cklq.mb.ca
www.cklq.mb.ca

David Baxter, President
Don Kille, General Manager

***Dauphin:* CKDM**
Owned by: **Dauphin Broadcasting Co. Ltd.**
27 - 3rd Ave., Dauphin, MB R7N 0Y5
204-638-3230, Fax: 204-638-8257, 866-997-2536
730ckdm@mts.net
www.730ckdm.com

Allan Truman, General Manager

***Flin Flon:* CFAR** (Freq: 590)
Owned by: **Arctic Radio (1982) Ltd.**
316 Green St., Flin Flon, MB R8A 0H2
204-687-3469, Fax: 204-687-6786,
cfar@arcticradio.ca
www.arcticradio.ca

Maureen Kozar, Office Manager
Tom O'Brien

***Portage la Prairie:* CFRY** (Freq: 920)
Owned by: **Golden West Broadcasting Ltd.**
PO Box 920, 350 River Rd., Portage la Prairie, MB R1N 0N6
204-239-5111, Fax: 204-857-3456,
info@goldenwestradio.com
www.cfryradio.ca

***Steinbach:* CHSM** (Freq: 1250)
Owned by: **Golden West Broadcasting Ltd.**
#105, 32 Brandt St., Steinbach, MB R5G 2J7
204-326-3737, Fax: 204-326-2299,
info@goldenwestradio.com
www.am1250online.com

***The Pas:* CJAR** (Freq: 1240)
Owned by: **Arctic Radio (1982) Ltd.**
PO Box 2980, 130 - 3rd St. West, The Pas, MB R9A 1R7
204-623-5307, Fax: 204-623-5337,
cjar@arcticradio.ca
www.arcticradio.ca

***Thompson:* CHTM** (Freq: 610)
Owned by: **Arctic Radio (1982) Ltd.**
103 Cree Rd., Thompson, MB R8N 0B9
204-778-7361, Fax: 204-778-5252,
chtm@arcticradio.ca
www.arcticradio.ca

Tom O'Brien

***Winkler:* CKMW** (Freq: 1570)
Owned by: **Golden West Broadcasting Ltd.**
PO Box 399, #201, 295 Main St., Winkler, MB R6W 4A6
204-325-7602, Fax: 204-325-2206,
info@goldenwestradio.com
www.ckmwradio.com

Elmer Hildebrand

***Winnipeg:* CBW** (Freq: 990)
Owned by: **Canadian Broadcasting Corporation**
PO Box 160, 541 Portage Ave., Winnipeg, MB R3C 2H1
204-788-3222, Fax: 204-788-3227

John Bertrand, Regional Director

***Winnipeg:* CFRW** (Freq: 1290)
Owned by: **Rogers Broadcasting Ltd.**
1445 Pembina Hwy., Winnipeg, MB R3T 5C2
204-477-5120, Fax: 204-453-0815,
info@cfrw.ca
www.cfrw.ca

Chris Brooke, Program Director
Lorne Anderson, Technical Director

***Winnipeg:* CHFC** (Freq: 1230)
Owned by: **Canadian Broadcasting Corporation**
c/o CBC Winnipeg, PO Box 160, 541 Portage Ave., Winnipeg, MB R3C 2H1
204-788-3222, Fax: 204-788-3225

John Bertrand, General Manager

***Winnipeg:* CJOB** (Freq: 680)
Owned by: **Corus Entertainment Inc.**
930 Portage Ave., Winnipeg, MB R3G 0P8
204-786-2471, Fax: 204-783-4512,
www.cjob.com

***Winnipeg:* CKJS** (Freq: 810)
Owned by: **NewCap Inc.**
520 Corydon Ave., Winnipeg, MB R3L 0P1
204-477-1221, Fax: 204-453-8244,
info@ckjs.com
www.ckjs.com

Tony Carta, President, carta@ckjs.com

†*Winnipeg:* CKSB (Freq: 1050)
Owned by: **Canadian Broadcasting Corporation**
607, rue Langevin, Winnipeg, MB R2H 2W2

** For details on this company see listing in Major Broadcasting Companies section; † French language station*

204-788-3236, Fax: 204-788-3245,
rene_fontaine@radio-canada.ca
www.radio-canada.ca/regions/manitoba
Gilles Fréchette, Chef des Émissions

***Winnipeg:* CMOR**
Owned by: **Red River College***
#CM20, 2055 Notre Dame Ave., Winnipeg, MB R3H 0J9
204-632-2475, Fax: 204-632-7896,
cmor@rrc.mb.ca
www.rrcsa.com/index.php?content=cmor
Guy Lissier, Advertising Director

New Brunswick

***Campbellton:* CKNB** (Freq: 950)
Owned by: **Maritime Broadcasting System**
100 Water St., Campbellton, NB E3N 3G7
506-753-4415, Fax: 506-789-9505,
cknb@nb.sympatico.ca
www.mbsradio.com/www/cknb/index.html
Claude Arseneault, Manager
Mark Firth, Program Director

†*Caraquet:* CJVA (Freq: 810)
Owned by: **CKLE-FM**
Caraquet, NB

***Fredericton:* CBZ** (Freq: 970)
Owned by: **Canadian Broadcasting Corporation**
PO Box 2200 A, 1160 Regent St., Fredericton, NB E3B 5G4
506-451-4000,
www.cbc.ca/nb
Susan Mitton, Regional Director - Radio

***Fredericton:* CKHJ** (Freq: 1260)
Owned by: **Astral Media Radio Atlantic**
206 Rookwood Ave., Fredericton, NB E3B 2M2
506-454-2444, Fax: 506-452-4345
Bob Coy, President

***Moncton:* CBA** (Freq: 1070)
Owned by: **Canadian Broadcasting Corporation**
PO Box 950, 250 University Ave., Moncton, NB E1C 8N8
506-853-6666, Fax: 506-853-6400,
www.cbc.ca/nb
Social Media: twitter.com/cbcnb
Dan Goodyear, Executive Producer, CBC, New Brunsw
Mary-Pat Schutta, Program Manager, CBC, New Brunswick
John Channing, Sales Manager, CBC, New Brunswick

***Saint John:* CFBC**
Owned by: **Maritime Broadcasting System**
226 Union St., Saint John, NB E2L 1B1
506-658-5100, Fax: 506-658-5116,
mail@mbsradio.com
www.mbsradio.com

***Sussex:* CJCW** (Freq: 590)
Owned by: **Maritime Broadcasting System**
PO Box 5900, Sussex, NB E4E 5M2
506-432-2529, Fax: 506-433-4900,
cjcw@nbnet.nb.ca
Roger White

Newfoundland & Labrador

***Carbonear:* CHVO** (Freq: 560)
1 CHVO Dr., Carbonear, NL A1Y 1A2
709-596-1560, Fax: 709-596-8626, 800-595-1560
www.vocm.com
Aiden Hibbs, Manager

***Corner Brook:* CBY** (Freq: 990)
Owned by: **Canadian Broadcasting Corporation**
PO Box 610, 162 Premier Dr., Corner Brook, NL A2H 6G1
709-637-1151, Fax: 709-634-8506,
www.cbc.ca/nl

***Corner Brook:* CFCB** (Freq: 570)
Owned by: **NewCap Inc.**
PO Box 570, 345 O'Connell Dr., Corner Brook, NL A2H 6H5
709-634-4570, Fax: 709-634-4081,
cfcb@vocm.com
Daryl Stevens, Operation Manager
Darlene Myers, Sales Manager
Mike Murphy, General Manager

***Corner Brook:* CFLW** (Freq: 1340)
Owned by: **Steele Communications**
PO Box 570, 345 O'Connel Dr., Corner Brook, NL A2H 6H5
709-282-3601

***Gander:* CBG-AM** (Freq: 1400)
Owned by: **Canadian Broadcasting Corporation**
PO Box 369, Gander, NL A1V 1W7
709-256-4311, Fax: 709-651-2021, 800-563-7933
www.cbc.ca/nl; www.cbc.ca/radio
Social Media: www.facebook.com/radiocbc;
www.twitter.com/cbcradio
Other information: Phone, Transmission Information:
1-888-353-7006; TTY: 1-866-220-6045
Maureen Anonsen, Manager, Partnership & Communications
Debbie Hynes, Senior Officer, Communications, 709-576-5150
Wayne Tilley, Manager, Accounts, 709-576-5019

***Gander:* CKGA** (Freq: 650)
Owned by: **NewCap Inc.**
PO Box 650, Gander, NL A1V 1X2
709-651-3650, Fax: 709-651-2542,
ckga.newsroom@nf.sympatico.ca

***Grand Falls-Windsor:* CBT-AM** (Freq: 540)
Owned by: **Canadian Broadcasting Corporation**
PO Box 218, 2 Harris Ave., Grand Falls-Windsor, NL A2A 2Y2
709-489-2102, Fax: 709-489-1055, 800-563-7933
www.cbc.ca/nl; www.cbc.ca/radio
Social Media: www.facebook.com/radiocbc;
www.twitter.com/cbcradio
Other information: Phone, Transmission Information:
1-888-353-7006
Denise Wilson, Managing Director, Newfoundland & Labrador
Kathy Porter, Executive Producer, English Radio
Debbie Hynes, Senior Officer, Communications, 709-576-5150

***Grand Falls-Windsor:* CKCM** (Freq: 620)
Owned by: **NewCap Inc.**
PO Box 620, 35A Grenfell Heights, Grand Falls-Windsor, NL A2A 2K2
709-489-2192, Fax: 709-489-8626,
ckcm@vocm.com
John Steele
John Murphy

***Grand Falls-Windsor:* CKIM** (Freq: 1240)
VOCM Radio Newfoundland Ltd., PO Box 620, 35 Grenfell Heights, Grand Falls-Windsor, NL A2A 2K2
709-489-2192, Fax: 709-489-8626

***Happy Valley-Goose Bay:* CFLN** (Freq: 1230)
Owned by: **NewCap Inc.**
PO Box 160 C, 176 Hamilton River Rd., Happy Valley-Goose Bay, NL A0P 1C0
709-896-2968, Fax: 709-896-8708

***Marystown:* CHCM** (Freq: 740)
Owned by: **NewCap Inc.**
PO Box 560, Ville Marie Dr., Marystown, NL A0E 2M0
709-279-2560, Fax: 709-279-3538
Russell Murphy, General Manager

***Mount Pearl:* VOAR** (Freq: 1210)
1041 Topsail Rd., Mount Pearl, NL A1N 5E9
709-745-8627, Fax: 709-745-1600, 800-563-1991
voar@voar.org
www.voar.org
Sherry Griffin, Station Manager

***Port au Choix:* CFNW** (Freq: 790)
Owned by: **CFCB**
Port au Choix, NL

***St. John's:* CBN-AM** (Freq: 640)
Owned by: **Canadian Broadcasting Corporation**
PO Box 12010 A, St. John's, NL A1B 3T8
709-576-5000, Fax: 709-576-5234, 800-563-7933
www.cbc.ca/nl; www.cbc.ca/radio
Social Media: www.facebook.com/radiocbc;
www.twitter.com/cbcradio
Other information: Phone, CBC Radio One Newsroom:
709-576-5225
Denise Wilson, Managing Director, Newfoundland & Labrador
Kathy Porter, Executive Producer, English Radio
Maureen Anonsen, Manager, Partnership & Communications, 709-576-5013
Debbie Hynes, Senior Officer, Communications, 709-576-5150

***St. John's:* CJYQ** (Freq: 930)
Owned by: **NewCap Inc.**
PO Box 8590 A, 391 Kenmount Rd., St. John's, NL A1B 3P5
709-726-5590, Fax: 709-726-4633,
www.radionewfoundland.net
John Murphy, General Manager
Bob Templeton, President
Hilary Montbourquette, Operations Manager

***St. John's:* CKVO** (Freq: 710)
Owned by: **NewCap Inc.**
VOCM(AM), PO Box 8590 A, 391 Kenmount Rd., St. John's, NL A1B 3P5
709-466-2710, Fax: 709-726-8626,
feedback@vocm.com
www.vocm.com
John Murphy, General Manager

***St. John's:* VOCM** (Freq: 590)
Owned by: **NewCap Inc.**
PO Box 8590, 391 Kenmount Rd., St. John's, NL A1B 3P5
709-726-5590, Fax: 709-726-4633,
feedback@vocm.com
www.vocm.com

***St. Johns':* VOWR** (Freq: 800)
Owned by: **VOWR Radio Board**
PO Box 7430, Patrick St., St. Johns', NL A1E 3Y5
709-579-9233, Fax: 709-579-9232,
vowr@vowr.org
www.vowr.org
Marvin Barnes, Chair
John Tessier, Station Manager
Brian Wentzell, Treasurer

***Stephenville:* CFGN** (Freq: 1230)
Owned by: **NewCap Inc.**
60 West St., Stephenville, NL A2N 1C6
709-643-2191, Fax: 709-643-5025,
cfsx@vocm.com

***Stephenville:* CFSX** (Freq: 870)
Owned by: **NewCap Inc.**
60 West St., Stephenville, NL A2N 1C6
709-643-2191, Fax: 709-643-5025,
cfsx@vocm.com
Gerry Murphy, Manager

Northwest Territories

***Inuvik:* CFCT** (Freq: 600)
Owned by: **Canadian Broadcasting Corporation**
Radio Station CHAK, Bag 8, Bag # 8, Inuvik, NT X0E 0T0
867-777-7600, Fax: 867-777-7640
Peter Skinner, General Manager

***Inuvik:* CHAK** (Freq: 860)
Owned by: **Canadian Broadcasting Corporation**
155 MacKenzie Rd., Bag Service No. 8, Inuvik, NT X0E 0T0
867-920-5400, Fax: 867-777-7640,
www.cbc.ca/north

***Yellowknife:* CFYK** (Freq: 1340)
Owned by: **Canadian Broadcasting Corporation**
PO Box 160, 5002 Forest Dr., Yellowknife, NT X1A 2N2
867-920-5400, Fax: 867-920-5440,
www.cbc.ca/north

Nova Scotia

***Amherst:* CKDH** (Freq: 900)
Owned by: **Maritime Broadcasting System**
32 Church St., Amherst, NS B4H 4B8
902-667-3875, Fax: 902-667-4490,
ckdh@ckdh.net
www.ckdh.net
Gary Crowell, General Manager

***Digby:* CKDY** (Freq: 1420)
Owned by: **Maritime Broadcasting System**
53 Sydney St., Digby, NS

** For details on this company see listing in Major Broadcasting Companies section; † French language station*

902-245-2111, Fax: 902-245-9720,
avr@avrnetwork.com
www.avrnetwork.com

Halifax: **CFDR** (Freq: 780)
Owned by: **NewCap Inc.**
PO Box 9316 A, Halifax, NS B3K 6B2
902-453-2530, Fax: 902-453-3132,
www.780kixx.ca
Ted Hyland, General Manager

Halifax: **CFSM** (Freq: 550)
Student Union Bldg., 5th Fl., St. Mary's University, Halifax, NS B3H 3C3
902-496-8776, Fax: 902-425-4636,
cfsm@squid.stmarys.ca
Kevin Smith, Station Manager
Mark Lee, Program Director

Halifax: **CJCH** (Freq: 920)
Owned by: **Rogers Broadcasting Ltd.**
PO Box 9316, RPO, CSC, Halifax, NS B3K 6A7
902-453-2524, Fax: 902-453-3132
Scott Bodnarchuck, General Manager

Middleton: **CKAD** (Freq: 1350)
Owned by: **Maritime Broadcasting System**
PO Box 550, 10 Bridge St., Middleton, NS B0S 1P0
902-825-3429, Fax: 902-825-6009,
avr@avrnetwork.com
www.avrnetwork.com
Dianne Best, General Manager

New Glasgow: **CKEC** (Freq: 1320)
Owned by: **Hector Broadcasting Co. Ltd.***
PO Box 519, 84 Provost St., New Glasgow, NS B2H 5E7
902-752-4200, Fax: 902-755-2468,
ckec@ckec.com
www.ckec.com
Michael Freeman, Vice-President
D.B. Freeman, CEO

Sydney: **CBI**
Owned by: **Canadian Broadcasting Corporation**
285 Alexandra St., Sydney, NS B1S 2E8
902-539-5050, Fax: 902-563-1562,
www.cbc.ca
Andrew Cochran, Managing Director for the Maritimes

Sydney: **CHER** (Freq: 950)
Owned by: **Maritime Broadcasting System**
318 Charlotte St., Sydney, NS B1P 1C8
902-564-5596, Fax: 902-562-1873,
www.capebretonradio.com

Sydney: **CJCB** (Freq: 1270)
Owned by: **Maritime Broadcasting System**
318 Charlotte St., Sydney, NS B1P 1C8
902-564-5596, Fax: 902-564-1873,
www.cjcbradio.com

Windsor: **CFAB** (Freq: 1450)
Owned by: **Maritime Broadcasting System**
169A Water St., Windsor, NS B0N 2T0
902-798-2111, Fax: 902-798-8140,
avr@avrnetwork.com
www.avrnetwork.com

Nunavut

Iqaluit: **CFFB** (Freq: 1230)
Owned by: **Canadian Broadcasting Corporation**
PO Box 490, Iqaluit, NU X0A 0H0
867-979-6100, Fax: 867-979-6147,
patrick_nagle@cbc.ca
cbc.ca/north
Patrick Nagle, Area Manager

Ontario

Atikokan: **CKDR-6** (Freq: 1240)
Owned by: **CKDR-FM**
Atikokan, ON

Belleville: **CJBQ** (Freq: 800)
PO Box 488, 10 Front St. South, Belleville, ON K8N 5B2
613-969-5555, Fax: 613-969-8122,
info@cjbq.com
www.cjbq.com
Bill Morton

Brampton: **CIAO** (Freq: 530)
Owned by: **CKMW Radio Ltd.***
5302 Dundas St. West, Brampton, ON M9B 1B2
416-213-1035, Fax: 416-233-8617,
www.am530.ca
Bill Evanov, President

Brantford: **CKPC** (Freq: 1380)
571 West St., Brantford, ON N3T 5P8
519-759-1000, Fax: 519-753-1470,
am1380@ckpc.on.ca
www.ckpc.on.ca
Richard Buchanan, President/General Manager

Chatham: **CFCO** (Freq: 630)
Owned by: **Blackburn Radio Inc.**
PO Box 100, 117 Kell Dr. South, Chatham, ON N7M 5K1
519-352-3000, Fax: 519-354-2880,
info@630cfco.com
www.630cfco.com

Cobourg: **CHUC** (Freq: 1450)
PO Box 520, Cobourg, ON K9A 4L3
905-372-5401, Fax: 905-372-6280,
chuc@chuc1450.com
www.chuc1450.com
Don Conway, President

Cornwall: **CJUL** (Freq: 1220)
Owned by: **Corus Entertainment Inc.**
709 Cotton Mill St., Cornwall, ON K6H 7K7
613-932-5180, Fax: 613-938-0355, 888-678-8122
www.am1220.ca
Scott Armstrong, General Manager, scott@seawayvalley.com

Ear Falls: **CKDR-4** (Freq: 1450)
Owned by: **CKDR-FM**
Ear Falls, ON

Guelph: **CJOY** (Freq: 1460)
Owned by: **Corus Entertainment Inc.**
75 Speedvale Ave. East, Guelph, ON N1E 6M3
519-824-7000, Fax: 519-824-4118,
cjoy@cjoy.com
www.cjoy.com

Hamilton: **CHAM** (Freq: 820)
Owned by: **Standard Radio Office**
#401, 883 Upper Wentworth St., Hamilton, ON L9A 4Y6
905-574-1150, Fax: 905-575-6429, 866-559-7677
www.820cham.com
Tom Cooke, Vice-President & General Manager

Hamilton: **CHML** (Freq: 900)
Owned by: **Corus Entertainment Inc.**
#900, 875 Main St. West, Hamilton, ON L8S 4R1
905-521-9900, Fax: 905-521-2306,
www.900chml.com

Hamilton: **CKOC** (Freq: 1150)
Owned by: **Standard Radio Office**
#401, 883 Upper Wentworth St., Hamilton, ON L9A 4Y6
905-574-1150, Fax: 905-575-6429,
ckoc@oldies1150.com
www.oldies1150.com
Tom Cooke, Manager

Hudson: **CKDR-3** (Freq: 1450)
Owned by: **CKDR-FM**
Hudson, ON

Ignace: **CKDR-1** (Freq: 1340)
Owned by: **CKDR-FM**
Ignace, ON

Kingston: **CKLC** (Freq: 1380)
Owned by: **CTVglobemedia Inc./CHUM Radio Kingston**
PO Box 1380, #10, 993 Princess St., Kingston, ON K7L 1H3
613-544-1380, Fax: 613-546-9751,
gperrin@chumkingston.com
Gary Perrin, General Manager

Kitchener: **CKGL** (Freq: 570)
Owned by: **Rogers Broadcasting Ltd.**
305 King St. West, 11th Fl., Kitchener, ON N2G 4E4
519-743-2611, Fax: 519-743-7510,
news570@rogers.com
www.570news.com

Kitchener: **CKKW** (Freq: 1090)
Owned by: **CKKW**
Kitchener, ON

London: **CFPL** (Freq: 980)
Owned by: **Corus Entertainment Inc.**
380 Wellington St., London, ON N6A 5B5
519-931-6000, Fax: 519-679-1967,
www.am980.ca
Dave Farough, General Manager

London: **CJBK** (Freq: 1290)
Owned by: **Standard Radio Office**
743 Wellington Rd. South, London, ON N6C 4R5
519-686-2525, Fax: 519-686-9067,
www.cjbk.com
Braden Doerr, President & General Manager, bdoerr@sri.ca

London: **CKSL** (Freq: 1410)
Owned by: **Standard Radio Office**
743 Wellington St. South, London, ON N6C 4R5
519-686-2525, Fax: 519-686-3658,
www.oldies1410.com
Braden Doerr, General Manager

Moosonee: **CHMO** (Freq: 1450)
Owned by: **James Bay Broadcasting Corp. Inc.***
PO Box 400, 38 First St., Moosonee, ON P0L 1Y0
705-336-2466, Fax: 705-336-2186
John Kirk, President

North Bay: **CKAT** (Freq: 600)
Owned by: **Rogers Broadcasting Ltd.**
PO Box 3000, 743 Main St. East, North Bay, ON P1B 8K8
705-474-2000, Fax: 705-474-7761
Peter McKeown, General Manager

Oakville: **CJMR** (Freq: 1320)
Owned by: **CJMR 1320 Radio Ltd.***
284 Church St., Oakville, ON L6J 7N2
905-271-1320, Fax: 905-842-1250,
hmcdonald@whiteoaksgroup.ca
Harry H. McDonald, Vice-President & General Manager

Oakville: **CJYE** (Freq: 1250)
Broadcast Centre, 284 Church St., Oakville, ON L6J 7N2
905-845-2821, Fax: 905-842-1250,
contact@joy1250.ca
www.joy1250.ca
Harry H. McDonald, General Manager
Michael H. Caine, President

Ottawa: **CBOF-1** (Freq: 990)
Owned by: **Canadian Broadcasting Corporation**
PO Box 3220 C, 250 Lanark Ave., Ottawa, ON K1Y 1E4
613-724-1200, Fax: 613-562-8447,
commho@ottawa.cbc.ca
www.cbc.ca
Denis Simard, General Manager

Ottawa: **CFGO** (Freq: 1200)
Owned by: **Rogers Broadcasting Ltd.**
87 George St., Ottawa, ON K1N 9H7
613-750-1200, Fax: 613-739-4040,
dmitchell@team1200.com
www.team1200.com
Dianne Wilson

Ottawa: **CFRA** (Freq: 580)
Owned by: **Rogers Broadcasting Ltd.**
87 George St., Ottawa, ON K1N 9H7
613-789-2486, Fax: 613-523-6423,
www.cfra.com

Ottawa: **CIWW** (Freq: 1310)
Owned by: **Rogers Broadcasting Ltd.**
2001 Thurston Dr., Ottawa, ON K1G 6C9
613-736-2001, Fax: 613-736-2002,
www.oldies1310.com
Scott Parsons, General Manager

Owen Sound: **CFOS** (Freq: 560)
Owned by: **Bayshore Broadcasting Corporation**
PO Box 280, 270 - 9th St. East, Owen Sound, ON N4K 5P5

** For details on this company see listing in Major Broadcasting Companies section; † French language station*

519-376-2030, Fax: 519-371-4242,
bayshore@bayshorebroadcasting.ca
www.bayshorebroadcasting.ca

Ross Kentner, General Manager,
rkentner@bayshorebroadcasting.ca
Kevin Brown, General Sales Manager,
kbrown@bayshorebroadcasting.ca
Rob Brignell, Director, Marketing & Business Development,
rbrignell@bayshorebroadcasting.ca

***Peterborough:* CKPT** (Freq: 99.7)
Owned by: **Rogers Broadcasting Ltd.**
PO Box 177, 59 George St. North, Peterborough, ON K9J 6Y8
705-742-8844, Fax: 705-742-1417,
energy997@chumradio.com
www.energy997.ca

Steve Fawcett, General Manager

***Peterborough:* CKRU** (Freq: 980)
Owned by: **Corus Entertainment Inc.**
151 King St., Peterborough, ON K9J 2R8
705-748-6101, Fax: 705-742-7708,
www.980kruz.ca

***Red Lake:* CKDR-5** (Freq: 1340)
Owned by: **CKDR-FM**
Red Lake, ON

***Richmond Hill:* CHKT** (Freq: 1430)
Owned by: **Fairchild Radio**
#7-8, 135 East Beaver Creek Rd., Richmond Hill, ON L4B 1E2
905-763-3360, Fax: 905-889-9828,
www.fairchildradio.com

Cyril Lai, General Manager

***Sarnia:* CHOK** (Freq: 1070)
Owned by: **Blackburn Radio Inc.**
1415 London Rd., Sarnia, ON N7S 1P6
519-542-5500, Fax: 519-542-1520,
www.chok.com

***Sioux Lookout:* CKDR-2** (Freq: 1400)
Owned by: **CKDR-FM**
Sioux Lookout, ON

***St Catharines:* CHSC** (Freq: 1220)
36 Queenston St., St Catharines, ON L2R 2Y9
905-682-6691, Fax: 905-682-9434,
info@1220chsc.ca
www.1220chsc.ca

***St Catharines:* CKTB** (Freq: 610)
Owned by: **Standard Radio Office**
12 Yates St., St Catharines, ON L2R 6Z4
905-684-1176, Fax: 905-684-4800,
newsroom@610cktb.com
www.610cktb.com

Clyde Ross, clyder@610cktb.com

***Stratford:* CJCS** (Freq: 1240)
376 Romeo St. South, Stratford, ON N5A 4T9
519-271-2450, Fax: 519-271-3102,
info@cjcsradio.com
www.cjcsradio.com

Steve Rae, President

***Sudbury:* CIGM** (Freq: 790)
Owned by: **Rogers Broadcasting Ltd.**
880 Lasalle Blvd., Sudbury, ON P3A 1X5
705-566-4480, Fax: 705-560-7232,
www.790cigm.com

Claude Beaudoin, President
Jim Hamm, General Manager

***Thunder Bay:* CKPR** (Freq: 580)
87 Hill St. North, Thunder Bay, ON P7A 5V6
807-346-2600, Fax: 807-345-9923,
radio@ckpr.com
www.ckpr.com

***Tillsonburg:* CKOT** (Freq: 1510)
PO Box 10, 77 Broadway St., Tillsonburg, ON N4G 4H3
519-842-4281, Fax: 519-842-4284,
jlamers@country1510.com

John D. Lamers, President & General Manager

***Toronto:* AM 740**
#205, 550 Queen St. East, Toronto, ON M5A 1V2
416-544-0740, Fax: 905-842-1250,
www.am740.ca

Social Media:
www.facebook.com/pages/AM740-Zoomer-Radio/114114771541

George Grant, President/CEO, ggrant@classical963fm.com
Gene Stevens, Director, Programming & Operations,
gstevens@am740radio.ca
Christopher Randall, Director, Promotions,
christopher@mzmedia.com
Steven J. Shiaman, Director, Retail Sales,
sshiaman@am740radio.ca

***Toronto:* CFMJ** (Freq: 640)
Owned by: **Corus Entertainment Inc.**
#1600, 1 Dundas St. West, Toronto, ON M5G 1Z3
416-221-6400, Fax: 416-847-3300,
www.640toronto.com

***Toronto:* CFRB** (Freq: 1010)
Owned by: **Standard Broadcasting Corp. Ltd.**
2 St. Clair Ave. West, 2nd Fl., Toronto, ON M4V 1L6
416-924-5711, Fax: 416-872-8683,
gm@cfrb.com
cfrb.com

Pat Holiday, Vice-President & General Manager

***Toronto:* CFTR** (Freq: 680)
Owned by: **Rogers Broadcasting Ltd.**
777 Jarvis St., Toronto, ON M4Y 3B7
416-935-8468, Fax: 416-935-8480,
680info@680news.com
www.680news.com

John Hinnen, Vice-President, Radio News Programming
Derek Berghuis, General Manager

***Toronto:* CHIN** (Freq: 1540)
622 College St., Toronto, ON M6G 1B6
416-531-9991, Fax: 416-531-5274,
info@chinradio.com
www.chinradio.com

Leonard Lombardi, President

***Toronto:* CHWO** (Freq: 740)
PO Box 740 A, Toronto, ON M5W 4K6
416-544-0740, Fax: 905-842-1250,
general@am740radio.ca
www.am740.ca

†*Toronto:* CJBC (Freq: 860)
Owned by: **Canadian Broadcasting Corporation**
CP 500 A, 205 Wellington St. West, Toronto, ON M5W 1E6
416-205-2522, Fax: 416-205-5622

***Toronto:* CJCL** (Freq: 590)
Owned by: **Rogers Broadcasting Ltd.**
The Fan, 777 Jarvis St., Toronto, ON M4Y 3B7
416-935-0590, Fax: 416-413-4116,
contact@fan590.com
www.fan590.com

Nelson Millmen, Station Manager

***Toronto:* CP24 Radio 1050** (Freq: 1050)
Owned by: **Rogers Broadcasting Ltd.**
299 Queen St. West, Toronto, ON M5V 2Z5
416-384-2700,
now@cp24.com
www.cp24.com

Robert McLaughlin, Vice President/General Manager, CP24

***Toronto:* CRSC**
Owned by: **Seneca College**
1750 Finch Ave. East, Toronto, ON M2J 2X5
416-491-5050, Fax: 416-756-2765

***Toronto:* CSCA**
Owned by: **Seneca College**
#2051, 70 The Pond Rd., Toronto, ON M3J 3M6
416-491-5050, Fax: 416-739-1856,
scainfo@senecac.on.ca
scainfo@senecac.on.ca

***Waterloo:* CKKW** (Freq: 1090)
Owned by: **Rogers Broadcasting Ltd.**
#207, 255 King St. North, Waterloo, ON N2J 4V2
519-884-4470, Fax: 519-884-6482,
www.oldies1090.com

†*Windsor:* CBEF (Freq: 540)
Owned by: **Canadian Broadcasting Corporation**
825 Riverside Dr. West, Windsor, ON N9A 5K9
519-255-3411, 800-551-2985
auditoire@radio-canada.ca; liaison@radio-canada.ca
www.radio-canada.ca/radio

***Windsor:* CKLW** (Freq: 800)
Owned by: **Rogers Broadcasting Ltd.**
1640 Ouellette Ave., Windsor, ON N8X 1L1
519-258-8888, Fax: 519-258-0182,
www.am800cklw.com

Eric Proksch, Vice President/General Manager

***Windsor:* CKWW** (Freq: 580)
Owned by: **Rogers Broadcasting Ltd.**
1640 Ouellette Ave., Windsor, ON N8X 1L1
519-258-8888, Fax: 519-258-0182,
info@am580radio.com
www.am580radio.com

Eric Proksch, Vice President/General Manager

***Wingham:* CKNX** (Freq: 920)
Owned by: **Blackburn Radio Inc.**
215 Carling Terrace, Wingham, ON N0G 2W0
519-357-1310, Fax: 519-357-1897,
info@am920.ca
www.am920.ca

Prince Edward Island

***Charlottetown:* CFCY** (Freq: 630)
Owned by: **Maritime Broadcasting System**
5 Prince St., Charlottetown, PE C1A 4P4
902-892-1066, Fax: 902-566-1338,
www.cfcy.pe.ca

Québec

†*Alma:* CFGT (Freq: 1270)
Owned by: **Groupe Radio Antenne 6**
#200, 460, rue Sacré-Coeur ouest, Alma, QC G8B 1L9
418-662-6673, Fax: 418-662-6070

Marc-André Levesque

***Baie-Comeau:* CFRP** (Freq: 620)
907, rue de Puyjalon, Baie-Comeau, QC G5C 1N3
418-589-3771, Fax: 418-589-9086,
www.chlc.com

Mike Minville, directeur de la programmation,
programmes971-1005@globetrotter.net

†*Chibougamau:* CJMD (Freq: 1240)
Owned by: **Groupe Radio Antenne 6**
539, 3e rue, Chibougamau, QC G8P 1N8
418-275-1831, Fax: 418-275-2475

Marc-André Levesque

†*Chicoutimi:* CKRS (Freq: 590)
Owned by: **Corus Entertainment Inc.**
CP 1090, 121, rue Racine est, Chicoutimi, QC G7H 5G4
418-545-2577, Fax: 418-545-9186,
auditoire@ckrs.ca
www.ckrs.ca

Michel Gagnon

†*Gaspé:* CHGM (Freq: 1150)
Owned by: **CHNC**
Gaspé, QC

†*Gatineau:* CJRC (Freq: 1150)
Owned by: **Corus Entertainment Inc.**
150, rue Edmonton, Gatineau, QC J8Y 3S6
819-561-8801, Fax: 819-561-3333,
www.cjrc1150.com

Richard Lachance

†*La Tuque:* CFLM (Freq: 1240)
CP 850, 529, rue St-Louis, La Tuque, QC G9X 3P6
819-523-4575, Fax: 819-676-8000

***Laval:* CFAV** (Freq: 1570)
Owned by: **Diffusion Laval Inc**
2040, autoroute Laval, Laval, QC H7S 2M9
450-680-1570, Fax: 450-680-1570,
radio@boomer1570.ca.ca
www.boomer1570.ca

Claire Bellefeville, General Manager

***Montréal:* CFMB** (Freq: 1280)
35, rue York, Montréal, QC H3Z 2Z5

** For details on this company see listing in Major Broadcasting Companies section; † French language station*

514-483-2362, Fax: 514-483-1362, admin@cfmb.ca
www.cfmb.ca
Anne-Marie Stanczykowski, Vice-President
Andrew Mielewczyk

Montréal: CINF (Freq: 690)
Owned by: **Corus Entertainment Inc.**
#1100, 800 rue de Gauchetière Ouest, Montréal, QC H5A 1M1
514-787-0690, Fax: 514-849-0733,
www.info690.com
Maurice Tietolman

Montréal: CINW (Freq: 940)
Owned by: **Corus Entertainment Inc.**
#333, 215, rue St-Jacques, Montréal, QC H2Y 1M6
514-849-0940, Fax: 519-849-0733,
www.940news.com

Montréal: CJAD (Freq: 800)
Owned by: **Standard Radio Office**
1411, rue du Fort, Montréal, QC H3H 2R1
514-989-2523, Fax: 514-989-3847,
www.cjad.com
Rob Braide, Vice-President & General Manager

Montréal: CJLO
Owned by: **Concordia University***
#CC-430, 7141, rue Sherbrooke ouest, Montréal, QC H4B 1R6
514-848-8663, Fax: 514-848-7450,
manager@cjlo.com
www.cjlo.com

Montréal: CJWI (Freq: 1610)
Owned by: **CPAM Radio Union.com Inc***
3733 Jarry Est, 2e étage, Montréal, QC H1Z 2G1
514-287-1288, Fax: 514-287-3299,
info@cpam-radiounion.com
www.cpam-radiounion.com
Jean-Ernest Pierre

†Montréal: CKAC (Freq: 730)
#1100, 800, rue de la Gauchetière Ouest, Montréal, QC H5A 1M1
514-787-0730, Fax: 514-787-7943,
www.ckac.com
Sylvain Chamberland, Vice-président exécutif-Directeur g

Montréal: CKGM (Freq: 990)
Owned by: **Rogers Broadcasting Ltd.**
#300, 1310, av Greene, Montréal, QC H3Z 2B5
514-931-4487, Fax: 514-931-4079,
writetous@team990.com
www.team990.com
Jim Waters, President, CHUM Limited

†New Carlisle: CHNC (Freq: 610)
153, boul Gérard-D.-Levesque, New Carlisle, QC G0C 1Z0
418-752-2215, Fax: 418-752-6939,
radiochnc@globetrotter.net
www.radiochnc.com
Francis Rémillard, General Manager, francis@radiochnc.com
Brigitte Paquet, Sales Director, brigitte@radiochnc.com

†Québec: CHRC (Freq: 800)
2136, ch Sainte-Foy, Québec, QC G1V 1R8
418-688-8080, Fax: 418-682-8429,
www.chrc.com

†Rimouski: CJBR (Freq: 900)
Owned by: **Canadian Broadcasting Corporation**
273, rue St-Jean Baptiste ouest, Rimouski, QC G5L 4J8
418-723-2217, Fax: 418-723-6126,
www.radio-canada.ca

†Rimouski: Radio étudiante CAJT
Owned by: **CEGEP de Rimouski***
Cégep de Rimouski, 60, rue de l'Évêché ouest, Rimouski, QC G5L 4H6
418-723-1880, Fax: 418-724-4961, 800-463-0617
radio.cajt@mail.com; infoscol@cegep-rimouski.qc.ca
www.cegep-rimouski.qc.ca
Philippe Daigle, Contact

†Roberval: CFED (Freq: 1340)
Owned by: **Groupe Radio Antenne 6**
568, boul St-Joseph, Roberval, QC G8H 2K6
418-275-1831, Fax: 418-275-2475
Marc-André Levesque

Saint-Constant: CJMS (Freq: 1040)
143, rue St-Pierre, Saint-Constant, QC J5A 2G9
514-990-2567, Fax: 450-632-1052,
cjms1040@citenet.net
www.cjms.ca
Jean-François Dubois

Shawinigan: CKSM (Freq: 1220)
Owned by: **Astral Media Inc.**
6183, boul Royal, Shawinigan, QC G9N 8P3
819-539-4899

†Sherbrooke: CHLT (Freq: 630)
Owned by: **Astral Media Inc.**
4020, boul de Portland, Sherbrooke, QC J1L 2V6
819-563-6363, Fax: 819-566-4222, 800-842-2458
www.chlt630.com

†Trois-Rivières: CHLN (Freq: 550)
Owned by: **Astral Media Inc.**
#1200, 1500, rue Royale, Trois-Rivières, QC G9A 4J4
819-376-3556, Fax: 819-374-3222,
nouvelles@chln550.com
www.chln550.com

Saskatchewan

Estevan: CJSL (Freq: 1280)
Owned by: **Golden West Broadcasting Ltd.**
#200, 1236 - 5th St., Estevan, SK S4A 0Z6
306-634-1280, Fax: 306-634-6364,
info@goldenwestradio.com
Laverne Pappel, Station Manager

†Gravelbourg: CBKF-1
Owned by: **Canadian Broadcasting Corporation (CBC)**
Gravelbourg, SK

Kindersley: CFYM (Freq: 1210)
Owned by: **CJYM**
Kindersley, SK

Melfort: CKJH (Freq: 750)
Radio CJVR Ltd., PO Box 750, 611 Main St. North, Melfort, SK S0E 1A0
306-752-2587, Fax: 306-752-5932, 800-668-2587
sales@cjvr.com
www.ck750.com
Ken Singer, Vice President

Moose Jaw: CHAB (Freq: 800)
Owned by: **Golden West Broadcasting Ltd.**
1704 Main St. North, Moose Jaw, SK S6J 1L4
306-694-0800, Fax: 306-692-8880,
www.chabradio.com

North Battleford: CJNB (Freq: 1050)
PO Box 1460, 1711 - 100th St., North Battleford, SK S9A 2Z5
306-445-2477, Fax: 306-445-4599,
cjnb@rawlco.com
David Dekker

Prince Albert: CKBI (Freq: 900)
Owned by: **RAWLCO Radio Ltd.**
PO Box 900, 1316 Central Ave., Prince Albert, SK S6V 7R4
306-763-7421, Fax: 306-764-1850, 800-667-9000
900ckbi@rawlco.com
www.900ckbi.com
Jim Scarrow, General Manager/Vice-President

Regina: CBK-FM (Freq: 96.9)
Owned by: **Canadian Broadcasting Corporation**
PO Box 540 Main, 2440 Broad St., Regina, SK S4P 4A1
306-347-9540,
www.cbc.ca/sask; www.cbc.ca/radio2
Social Media: www.facebook.com/cbcsask;
www.twitter.com/cbcradio2
Other information: Phone, Regina Radio: 306-347-9692; Twitter:
www.twitter.com/cbcsask
Lenora Sturge, Coordinator, Program Marketing, 306-347-9714
Justin Anders, Regional Web Developer, 306-788-3285

Regina: CJME (Freq: 980)
Owned by: **RAWLCO Radio Ltd.**
#210, 2401 Saskatchewan Dr., Regina, SK S4P 4H8
306-525-0000, Fax: 306-347-8557,
www.cjme.com

Regina: CKRM (Freq: 620)
Owned by: **Harvard Broadcasting Inc.**
1900 Rose St., Regina, SK S4P 0A9
306-546-6200, Fax: 306-781-7338, 866-767-0620
www.620ckrm.com
Michael Olstrom

Rosetown: CJYM (Freq: 1330)
Owned by: **Dace Broadcasting Corp.***
PO Box 490, Rosetown, SK S0L 2V0
306-882-2686, Fax: 306-882-3037,
www.cjym.com
D.W. (Wax) Williams, President
Dennis Dyck, Vice-President/General Manager

†Saskatoon: CBKF-2
Owned by: **Canadian Broadcasting Corporation**
144 - 2nd Ave., Saskatoon, SK S7K 1K5
306-956-7400, Fax: 306-956-7476
David Kyle, General Manager

Saskatoon: CJWW (Freq: 600)
366 - 3 Ave. South, Saskatoon, SK S7K 1M5
306-244-1975, Fax: 306-665-5501,
cjwwradio@sasktel.net
www.cjwwradio.com
Vic Dubois, General Manager

Saskatoon: CKOM (Freq: 650)
Owned by: **RAWLCO Radio Ltd.**
715 Saskatchewan Cres. West, Saskatoon, SK S7M 5V7
306-934-2222, Fax: 306-477-0002,
www.ckom.com
Ted Farr

Shaunavon: CJSN (Freq: 1490)
Owned by: **Golden West Broadcasting Ltd.**
PO Box 1176, 410 Centre St., Shaunavon, SK S0N 2M0
306-297-2671, Fax: 306-297-3051,
info@goldenwestradio.com
www.cjsn1490.ca

Swift Current: CKSW (Freq: 570)
Owned by: **Golden West Broadcasting Ltd.**
134 Central Ave. North, Swift Current, SK S9H 0L1
306-773-4605, Fax: 306-773-6390, 800-821-8073
cmr@goldenwestradio.com
www.ckswradio.ca
Deborah Gager, General Manager & Sales

Weyburn: CFSL (Freq: 1190)
Owned by: **Golden West Broadcasting Ltd.**
PO Box 340, 305 Souris Ave., Weyburn, SK S4H 2K2
306-848-1190, Fax: 306-842-2720,
info@goldenwestradio.com
Laverne Pappel, Station Manager

Yorkton: CJGX (Freq: 940)
120 Smith St. East, Yorkton, SK S3N 3V3
306-782-2256, Fax: 306-783-4994,
country@gx94radio.com
www.gx94radio.com
Lyle Walsh, President
Lyle Walsh, General Manager

Yukon Territory

Whitehorse: CFWH (Freq: 570)
Owned by: **Canadian Broadcasting Corporation**
3103 - 3rd Ave., Whitehorse, YT Y1A 2A2
867-668-8400,
cbcnorth@cbc.ca
www.cbc.ca/north
Doug Caldwell, Area Manager
Mike Linder, Sr. News Editor

Whitehorse: CKRW (Freq: 610)
Owned by: **Klondike Broadcasting Co.Ltd.**
#203, 4103 - 4th Ave., Whitehorse, YT Y1A 1H6
867-668-6100, Fax: 867-668-4209,
ckrwcopy@ckrw.com
www.ckrw.com
Jennifer Jonstone, General Manager

** For details on this company see listing in Major Broadcasting Companies section; † French language station*

FM Radio Stations

Alberta

***Blairmore:* CJPR-FM** (Freq: 94.9)
Owned by: **NewCap Inc.**
PO Box 840, Blairmore, AB T0K 0E0
403-562-2806, Fax: 403-562-8114

***Calgary:* CBR-FM** (Freq: 102.1)
Owned by: **Canadian Broadcasting Corporation**
PO Box 2640, 1724 Westmount Blvd. NW, Calgary, AB T2P 2M7
403-521-6000,
www.cbc.ca/calgary
Helen Henderson, Deputy Regional Director of Radion

***Calgary:* CFGQ-FM** (Freq: 107.3)
Owned by: **Corus Entertainment Inc.**
#105, 630 - 3 Ave. SW, Calgary, AB T2P 4L4
403-716-6500, Fax: 403-716-2111,
www.q107fm.ca
Garth Ross, Music Director

***Calgary:* CHFM-FM** (Freq: 95.9)
Owned by: **Rogers Broadcasting Ltd.**
#240, 2723 - 37 Ave. NE, Calgary, AB T1Y 5R8
403-246-9696, Fax: 403-246-4126,
www.lite96.ca

***Calgary:* CHKF-FM** (Freq: 94.7)
Owned by: **Fairchild Radio**
#109, 2723 - 37 Ave. NE, Calgary, AB T1Y 5R8
403-717-1940, Fax: 403-717-1945,
general@fm947.com
www.fm947.com

***Calgary:* CIBK-FM** (Freq: 98.5)
Owned by: **Standard Radio Office**
1110 Centre St. NE, Calgary, AB T2E 2R2
403-240-5800, Fax: 403-240-5801,
feedback@vibe985.com
www.vibe985.com
Tom Peacock, General Manager

***Calgary:* CIQX-FM** (Freq: 103.1)
Owned by: **NewCap Inc.**
#100, 1110 Centre St. NE, Calgary, AB T2E 2R2
403-271-6366, Fax: 403-278-6772,
feedback@california103.com
www.california103.com
Stephen Peck, General Manager

***Calgary:* CJAY-FM** (Freq: 92.1)
Owned by: **Standard Radio Office**
1110 Centre St. North, Calgary, AB T2E 2R2
403-240-5850, Fax: 403-240-5801,
info@cjay92.com
www.cjay92.com
Tom Peacock, General Manager

***Calgary:* CJSI-FM** (Freq: 88.9)
4510 Macleod Trail South, Calgary, AB T2G 0A4
403-276-1111, Fax: 403-276-1114,
www.cjsi.ca

***Calgary:* CJSW-FM** (Freq: 90.9)
#127, MacEwan Hall, University of Calgary, Calgary, AB T2N 1N4
403-220-3902, Fax: 403-289-8212,
cjswfm@ucalgary.ca
www.cjsw.com
Chad Saunders, Station Manager

***Calgary:* CKIS-FM** (Freq: 96.9)
Owned by: **Rogers Broadcasting Ltd.**
2723 - 37 Ave. NE, Calgary, AB T1Y 5R8
403-250-9797, Fax: 403-291-4368,
www.jackfm.ca

***Calgary:* CKRY-FM** (Freq: 105.1)
Owned by: **Corus Entertainment Inc.**
#105, 630 - 3rd Ave. SW, Calgary, AB T2P 4L4
403-716-6500, Fax: 403-716-2111,
www.country105.com
Garry McKenzie, General Manager

***Calgary:* CMRC-FM** (Freq: 107.5)
4825 Richard Rd. SW, Calgary, AB T3E 6K6
403-440-6119, Fax: 403-440-6563,
www.cmrcradio.ca
Jillian Hunter, Station Manager

***Camrose:* CLCR-FM**
4901 - 46 Ave., Camrose, AB T4V 2R3
780-679-1541, Fax: 780-672-5252,
aucsa@augustana.ca
www.augustana.ab.ca/sa
Matthew Gusul, Station Manager

***Canmore:* CHMN-FM** (Freq: 106.5)
Owned by: **Rogers Broadcasting Ltd.**
749 Railway Ave., Canmore, AB T1W 1P2
403-678-2222, Fax: 403-678-6844

***Cold Lake:* CJXK-FM** (Freq: 95.3)
Owned by: **NewCap Inc.**
5414 - 55 St., Cold Lake, AB T9M 1R5
780-594-2459, Fax: 780-594-3001
Roger Thorpe

***Drayton Valley:* CIBW-FM** (Freq: 92.9)
Owned by: **The Jim Pattison Broadcast Group**
PO Box 929, 5164 - 52 Ave., Drayton Valley, AB T7A 1V3
780-542-9290, Fax: 780-542-9319, 888-884-2448
bwc929@telus.net
Trevor Grinde

***Edmonton:* CBX-FM** (Freq: 90.9)
Owned by: **Canadian Broadcasting Corporation**
Edmonton, AB

***Edmonton:* CFBR-FM** (Freq: 100.3)
Owned by: **Standard Radio Office**
#100, 18520 Stony Plain Rd., Edmonton, AB T5S 2E2
780-486-2800, Fax: 780-489-6927,
www.thebearrocks.com
M. Forbes, General Manager, forbes@worldgate.com

***Edmonton:* CFMG-FM** (Freq: 104.9)
Owned by: **Standard Radio Office**
#100, 18520 Stony Plain Rd., Edmonton, AB T5S 2E2
780-435-1049, Fax: 780-489-6927,
cfmg@sri.ca
www.ezrock1049.com
Marty Forbes, Vice-President & General Manager

***Edmonton:* CFWE-FM** (Freq: 89.9)
13245 - 146th St., Edmonton, AB T5L 4S8
780-447-2393, Fax: 780-454-2820,
cfwe@ammsa.com
www.ammsa.com/cfwe
Bert Crowfoot, General Manager

***Edmonton:* CHBN-FM** (Freq: 91.7)
Owned by: **Rogers Broadcasting Ltd.**
10212 Jasper Ave., Edmonton, AB T5J 5A3
780-424-2222, Fax: 780-401-1600,
www.thebounce.ca
Gisele Sowa, General Manager

***Edmonton:* CIRK-FM** (Freq: 97.3)
Owned by: **NewCap Inc.**
2394 West Edmonton Mall, #8882, 170 St., Edmonton, AB T5T 4M2
780-437-4996, Fax: 780-435-0844,
www.k-rock973.com
Randy Lemay, General Manager

***Edmonton:* CISN-FM** (Freq: 103.9)
Owned by: **Corus Entertainment Inc.**
5204 - 84 St., Edmonton, AB T6E 5N8
780-428-1104, Fax: 780-469-5937,
info@cisnfm.com
www.cisnfm.com
Doug Rutherford, General Manager

***Edmonton:* CJRY-FM** (Freq: 105.9)
5316 Calgary Trail, Edmonton, AB T6H 4J8
780-466-4930, Fax: 780-469-5335,
www.shinefm.com
Malcolm Hunt, Program Director
Carlo Bruno, Business Manager

***Edmonton:* CJSR-FM** (Freq: 88.5)
#0-09 Students Union Bldg., University of Alberta, Edmonton, AB T6G 2J7
780-492-2477, Fax: 780-492-3121,
www.cjsr.com
Charlotte Bourne, Administration Manager

***Edmonton:* CKER-FM** (Freq: 101.7)
5915 Gateway Blvd., Edmonton, AB T6H 2H3
780-702-1188, Fax: 780-437-5129,
cker@cker.ca
www.cker.ca
Roger Charest, President

***Edmonton:* CKNG-FM** (Freq: 92.5)
Owned by: **Corus Entertainment Inc.**
5204 - 84 St., Edmonton, AB T6E 5N8
780-440-6300, Fax: 780-469-5937,
info@joefm.ca
www.joefm.ca

***Edmonton:* CKRA-FM** (Freq: 96.3)
Owned by: **NewCap Inc.**
4752 - 99 St., Edmonton, AB T6E 5H5
780-437-4996, Fax: 780-436-5719,
www.96x.ca
Al Anderson, General Manager

***Edmonton:* CKUA-FM** (Freq: 94.9)
10526 Jasper Ave., 4th Fl., Edmonton, AB T5J 1Z7
780-428-7595, Fax: 780-428-7624,
radio@ckua.org
www.ckua.com

***†Falher:* CKRP-FM** (Freq: 95.7; 102.9; 90.3)
CP 718, Falher, AB T0H 1M0
780-837-2346, Fax: 780-837-2092,
akrpfm@yahoo.ca
Éric Charron
Julie Cadieux

***Fort McMurray:* CJOK-FM** (Freq: 93.3)
9912 Franklin Ave., Fort McMurray, AB T9H 2K5
780-743-2246, Fax: 780-791-7250,
info@cjok.fm
mymcmurray.com
Craig Picton, Program Director
Jim Schneider, Sales Manager
Kelly Boyd, General Manager

***Fort McMurray:* CKYX-FM** (Freq: 97.9)
9912 Franklin Ave., Fort McMurray, AB T9H 2K5
780-743-2246, Fax: 780-791-7250,
info@kyx98.fm
mymcmurray.com
Craig Picton, Program Director
Jim Schneider, Sales Manager
Kelly Boyd, General Manager

***Fort Vermilion:* CIAM-FM** (Freq: 92.7; 104.3; 95.5; 94.1; 102.9)
PO Box 609, 4709 River Rd., Fort Vermilion, AB T0H 1N0
780-927-2426, Fax: 780-927-2427, 866-927-2426
ciam@telus.net
www.ciamradio.com
Michael Sandstrom, General Manager

***Fox Creek:* CFFC-FM** (Freq: 92.1)
Owned by: **CKYL**
Fox Creek, AB

***Grande Prairie:* CFGP-FM** (Freq: 97.7)
#200, 9835 - 101 Ave., Grande Prairie, AB T8V 5V4
780-539-9700, Fax: 780-532-1600,
comments@sunfm.com
www.sunfm.com
Tom Bedore, General Manager

***Grande Prairie:* CJXX-FM** (Freq: 93.1)
Owned by: **The Jim Pattison Broadcast Group**
Big Country 93.1 FM, #202, 9817 - 101 Ave., Grande Prairie, AB T8V 0X6
780-532-0840, Fax: 780-538-1266,
general@bigcountryxx.com
www.bigcountryxx.com
Barbara Baxter

***High Level:* CKHL-FM** (Freq: 102.1)
PO Box 3759, High Level, AB T0H 1Z0
780-926-4531, Fax: 780-926-4564,
www.ylcountry.com
Terry Babiy, General Manager, tbabiy@ylcountry.com

***High River:* CFXL-FM** (Freq: 100.9)
Owned by: **Golden West Broadcasting Ltd.**
11 - 5th Ave. SE., High River, AB T1V 1G2
403-995-9611, Fax: 403-938-0732,
info@goldenwestradio.com
www.theeagle1009.com

** For details on this company see listing in Major Broadcasting Companies section; † French language station*

***Hinton:* CFXH-FM**
Owned by: **NewCap Inc.**
#102, 506 Carmichael Dr., Hinton, AB T7V 1S8
780-865-8804, Fax: 780-865-7792,
feedback@fox-radio.ca
www.thefoxradio.ca
Dave Schuk, Division General Manager

***La Crete:* CKLA-FM** (Freq: 92.1)
Owned by: **CKYL**
La Crete, AB

***Lethbridge:* CFRV-FM** (Freq: 107.7)
Owned by: **Rogers Broadcasting Ltd.**
PO Box 820, 1015 - 3rd Ave. South, Lethbridge, AB T1J 0J3
403-328-1077, Fax: 403-380-1539,
www.1077theriver.ca
Terry Voth, General Manager

***Lethbridge:* CHLB-FM** (Freq: 95.5)
Owned by: **The Jim Pattison Broadcast Group**
401 Mayor Magrath Dr. South, Lethbridge, AB T1J 3L8
403-329-0995, Fax: 403-329-0195,
gm@country95.fm
www.country95.fm
Rob Bye, General Manager

***Lethbridge:* CJBZ-FM** (Freq: 93.3)
Owned by: **The Jim Pattison Broadcast Group**
401 Mayor Magrath Dr. South, Lethbridge, AB T1J 3L8
403-394-9300, Fax: 403-329-0195,
rbye@country95.fm
www.b93.fm
Rob Bye, General Manager

***Lethbridge:* CJRX-FM** (Freq: 106.7)
Owned by: **Rogers Broadcasting Ltd.**
PO Box 820, 1015 - 3rd Ave. South, Lethbridge, AB T1J 3Z9
403-320-1220, Fax: 403-380-1539,
www.rock106.ca
Terry Voth, General Manager, Tvoth2@rci.rogers.com

***Lethbridge:* CJTS-FM** (Freq: 97.1)
508B - 5th Ave. South, Lethbridge, AB T1J 0T9
403-394-0971, Fax: 403-394-0938,
97@spiritfm.ca
www.spiritfm.ca
Terry Fleming, General Manager

***Lloydminster:* CKLM-FM** (Freq: 106.1; 99.7)
Atrium Center, PO Box 21, Lloydminster, AB T9V 0K2
780-875-5400, Fax: 780-875-4628,
admin@borderrock.com
www.borderrock.com
Stew Dent, General Manager

***Lloydminster:* CKSA-FM** (Freq: 95.9)
Owned by: **NewCap Inc.**
5026 - 50 St., Lloydminster, AB T9V 1P3
780-875-3321, Fax: 780-875-4704,
Lloyd@newcap.ca
www.959lloydfm.com
Ken Ruptash, General Manager

***Nordegg:* CHBW-FM-1** (Freq: 93.9)
Owned by: **CIBW-FM**
Nordegg, AB

***Peace River:* CKKX-FM** (Freq: 106.1)
PO Box 300, 9807 - 100 Ave., Peace River, AB T8S 1T5
780-624-2535, Fax: 780-624-5424,
www.kix106.net

***Red Deer:* CFDV-FM** (Freq: 106.7)
Owned by: **The Jim Pattison Broadcast Group**
2840 Bremner Ave., Red Deer, AB T4R 1M9
403-343-7105, Fax: 403-343-2573,
news@big105.fm
www.1067thedrive.fm
Paul Mason, General Manager

***Red Deer:* CHUB-FM** (Freq: 105.5)
Owned by: **The Jim Pattison Broadcast Group**
2840 Bremner Ave., Red Deer, AB T4R 1M9
403-343-7105, Fax: 403-343-2573,
news@big105.fm
www.big105.fm
Paul Mason, General Manager

***Red Deer:* CIZZ-FM** (Freq: 98.9)
Owned by: **Corus Entertainment Inc.**
PO Bag 5339, Red Deer, AB T4N 6W1
403-343-1303, Fax: 403-346-1230,
zed99@newcap.ca
www.zedfm.com
R.C. (Ron) Thompson, General Manager
John Hayes, President

***Red Deer:* CKGY-FM** (Freq: 95.5)
Owned by: **Corus Entertainment Inc.**
PO Bag 5339, Red Deer, AB T4N 6W1
403-348-0955, Fax: 403-346-1230,
kgbirthdays@newcap.ca
www.ckgy.com
R.C. (Ron) Thompson, General Manager
John Hayes, President

***Redcliffe:* CFMY-FM** (Freq: 96.1)
Owned by: **The Jim Pattison Broadcast Group**
PO Box 1270, 10 Boundary Rd., Redcliffe, AB T0J 2P0
403-548-8282, Fax: 403-548-8270,
my96fm@jpbg.com
www.my96fm.com
Dwaine Dietrich, General Manager

***Rocky Mountain House:* CHBW-FM** (Freq: 94.5)
Owned by: **CIBW-FM**
Rocky Mountain House, AB

***Siksika:* CHDH-FM** (Freq: 97.7)
PO Box 1490, Siksika, AB T0J 3W0
403-734-5339, Fax: 403-734-5497,
siksikamedia@siksikanation.com

***Slave Lake:* CKWA-FM** (Freq: 92.7)
Owned by: **NewCap Inc.**
PO Box 2470, #207, 201 Main St. NE, Slave Lake, AB T0G 2A0
780-849-2577, Fax: 780-849-4833

***Wainwright:* CKWY-FM** (Freq: 93.7)
Owned by: **NewCap Inc.**
#2, 1037 - 2nd Ave., Wainwright, AB T9W 1K7
780-842-4311, Fax: 780-842-4636,
www.waynefm.com

***Wetaskiwin:* CIHS-FM** (Freq: 93.5)
5206 - 50th Ave., Wetaskiwin, AB T9A 0S8
780-352-2508, Fax: 780-352-2502,
mail@cihsfm.com
www.cihsfm.com
Tony Greengrass, General Manager
Paula Osha, Station Manager

British Columbia

***100 Mile House:* CFFM-FM-2** (Freq: 99.7)
Owned by: **CFFM-FM**
100 Mile House, BC

***Abbotsford:* CKQC-FM** (Freq: 107.1)
#318, 31935 South Fraser Way, Abbotsford, BC V2T 5N7
604-853-4756, Fax: 604-853-1071,
country1071.com
Ken Geiger, General Manager

***Burnaby:* CFML-FM** (Freq: 107.9 FM)
Bldg. SE-10, 3700 Willingdon Ave., Burnaby, BC V5G 3H2
604-432-8510, Fax: 604-432-1792,
allofus@radiocfml.com
www.radiocfml.com; www.evolution1079.com
Brian Antonson

***Burnaby:* CJSF-FM** (Freq: 90.1)
TC216, Simon Fraser University, Burnaby, BC V5A 1S6
604-291-3727, Fax: 604-291-3695,
cjsfmgr@sfu.ca
www.cjsf.ca
Magnus Thyrold, Station Manager
Elvira Balakshin, Program Coordinator

***Castlegar:* CKGF-FM-2** (Freq: 96.7)
525 - 11th Ave., Castlegar, BC V1N 1J6
250-365-7600, Fax: 250-365-8480
Dennis Gerein, General Manager

***Castlegar:* CKQR-FM** (Freq: 99.3)
525 - 11 Ave., Castlegar, BC V1N 1J6
250-365-7600, Fax: 250-365-8480, 800-665-1178
dgilmore@bkradio.com
www.bkradio.com
Dennis Gerein, General Manager

***Chetwynd:* CHAD-FM** (Freq: 104.1)
PO Box 214, Chetwynd, BC V0C 1J0
250-784-1880, Fax: 250-782-7566,
info@chetchad.com
www.chetchad.com
Leo Sabulsky, General Manager

***Chetwynd:* CHET-FM** (Freq: 94.5)
PO Box 214, #102, 4612 North Access Rd., Chetwynd, BC V0C 1J0
250-788-9452, Fax: 250-788-9402,
info@peacefm.ca
www.peacefm.ca
Leo Sabulsky, General Manager

***Chilliwack:* CKSR-FM** (Freq: 98.3)
Owned by: **Rogers Broadcasting Ltd.**
#309, 46167 Yale Rd., Chilliwack, BC V2P 2N2
604-795-5711, Fax: 604-702-3212,
www.starfm.com
Ken Geiger, General Manager

***Courtenay:* CKLR-FM** (Freq: 97.3)
Owned by: **Island Radio Ltd.**
801B - 29th St., Courtenay, BC V9N 7Z5
250-703-2200, Fax: 250-703-9611,
info@973theeagle.com
www.973theeagle.com
Steve Power, Program Director

***Cranbrook:* CHBZ-FM** (Freq: 104.7)
Owned by: **The Jim Pattison Broadcast Group**
19 - 9 Ave. South, Cranbrook, BC V1C 2L9
250-426-2224, Fax: 250-426-5520,
info@b104.ca
www.b104.ca

***Cranbrook:* CHDR-FM** (Freq: 102.9)
Owned by: **The Jim Pattison Broadcast Group**
19 - 9 Ave. South, Cranbrook, BC V1C 2L9
250-426-2224, Fax: 250-426-5520,
info@thedrivefm.ca
www.thedrivefm.ca

***Cranbrook:* CJDR-FM** (Freq: 99.1)
19 - 9th Ave. South, Cranbrook, BC V1C 2L9
250-426-2224,
info@thedrivefm.ca
www.thedrivefm.ca
Rene Ross, General Manager

***Crawford Bay:* CBTE-FM** (Freq: 89.9)
Owned by: **Canadian Broadcasting Corporation**
Crawford Bay, BC
866-306-4636
www.cbc.ca/bc; www.cbc.ca/radio
Social Media: www.facebook.com/radiocbc;
www.twitter.com/cbcradio

***Duncan:* CJSU-FM** (Freq: 89.7)
130 Trans Canada Hwy., Duncan, BC V9L 2P7
250-746-0897, Fax: 250-748-1517,
onair@897sunfm.com
www.897sunfm.com

***Egmont:* CIEG-FM** (Freq: 104.7)
Owned by: **CISQ-FM**
Egmont, BC

***Fort Nelson:* CKRX-FM** (Freq: 102.3)
Owned by: **CKNL-FM**
Fort Nelson, BC

***Fort St John:* CHRX-FM** (Freq: 98.5)
Owned by: **Standard Radio Office**
10532 Alaska Rd., Fort St John, BC V1J 1B3
250-785-6634, Fax: 250-785-4544,
energyfmrequest@sri.ca
Tracey Gard

***Fort St John:* CKFU-FM** (Freq: 100.1)
10423 - 101 Ave., Fort St John, BC V1J 2B7
250-787-7100, Fax: 250-263-9749,
reception@moosefm.ca
www.moosefm.ca
Russ Beerling, General Manager

** For details on this company see listing in Major Broadcasting Companies section; † French language station*

Fort St John: **CKNL-FM** (Freq: 101.5)
Owned by: **Standard Radio Office**
10532 Alaska Rd., Fort St John, BC V1J 1B3
250-785-6634, Fax: 250-785-4544,
peacereception@sri.ca
Tracy Gard, General Manager & General Sales Man

Gold River: **CJGR-FM** (Freq: 101.1)
Owned by: **CFWB**
Gold River, BC

Grand Forks: **CKGF-FM** (Freq: 96.7)
7474 - 19th St., Grand Forks, BC V0H 1H0
250-442-5844, Fax: 250-442-3340,
www.bkradio.com

Kamloops: **CFBX-FM** (Freq: 92.5)
900 McGill Rd., House 8, Kamloops, BC V2C 5N3
250-377-3988, Fax: 250-372-5055,
radio@tru.ca
www.theX.ca
Brant Zwicker, Station Manager

Kamloops: **CIFM-FM** (Freq: 98.3)
Owned by: **The Jim Pattison Broadcast Group**
460 Pemberton Terrace, Kamloops, BC V2C 1T5
250-372-3322, Fax: 250-374-0445,
info@98.3cifm.com
www.98.3cifm.com
Rick Arnish, President & General Manager

Kamloops: **CKBZ-FM** (Freq: 100.1)
Owned by: **The Jim Pattison Broadcast Group**
460 Pemberton Terrace, Kamloops, BC V2C 1T5
250-372-3322, Fax: 250-374-0445,
info@b100.ca
www.b100.ca
Rick Arnish, President

Kamloops: **CKRV-FM** (Freq: 97.5)
611 Lansdowne St., Kamloops, BC V2C 1Y6
250-372-2197, Fax: 250-372-2293,
river@ckrv.com
www.ckrv.com
Robbie Dunn

Kelowna: **Astral Media Radio G.P.** (Freq: 99.9 Sun FM/CHSU-FM; 101.5 Silk FM/CILK-FM; AM 1150/CKFR-AM)
Owned by: **Standard Radio Office**
435 Bernard Ave., Kelowna, BC V1Y 6N8
250-860-8600, Fax: 250-860-8856,
info@thesun.net; info@silk.fm; info@am1150.ca
www.thesun.net; www.silk.fm; www.am1150.ca

Kelowna: **CBTK-FM** (Freq: 88.9)
Owned by: **Canadian Broadcasting Corporation**
Kelowna, BC
866-306-4636
www.cbc.ca/bc; www.cbc.ca/radio
Social Media: www.facebook.com/radiocbc;
www.twitter.com/cbcradio
Jennifer Smith, Director, Sales & Marketing, Western Canada, 604-662-6616

Kelowna: **CILK-FM** (Freq: 101.5)
1598 Pandosy St., Kelowna, BC V1Y 1P4
250-860-1010, Fax: 250-860-0505,
info@silk.fm
www.silk.fm

Kelowna: **CKLZ-FM** (Freq: 104.7)
Owned by: **The Jim Pattison Broadcast Group**
3805 Lakeshore Rd., Kelowna, BC V1W 3K6
250-763-1047, Fax: 250-762-2141,
info@power104.fm
www.power104.fm

Kootenay: **CJLY-FM** (Freq: 93.5; 96.5)
PO Box 767, Kootenay, BC V1L 5R4
250-352-9600, Fax: 250-352-9663,
www.kootenaycoopradio.com

Lillooet: **CHLS-FM** (Freq: 100.5)
PO Box 2124, Lillooet, BC V0K 1V0
250-256-2457, Fax: 250-256-7405,
vivianbj@telus.net
www.lss.sd74.bc.ca/chls
Tom Willey, Station Manager

Mackenzie: **CHMM-FM** (Freq: 103.5)
PO Box 547, 86 Centennial Ave., Mackenzie, BC V0J 2C0
250-997-6277, Fax: 250-997-6222,
jd@chmm.ca
www.chmm.ca
J. D. MacKenzie, Station Manager

Nanaimo: **CHLY-FM** (Freq: 101.7)
The Radio Malaspina Society, #2, 34 Victoria Rd., Nanaimo, BC V9R 5B8
250-716-3410, Fax: 250-716-1082,
music@chly.ca
www.chly.ca
James Booker, Station Manager

Nanaimo: **CHWF-FM** (Freq: 106.9)
Owned by: **Island Radio Ltd.**
4550 Wellington Rd., Nanaimo, BC V9T 2H3
250-758-1131, Fax: 250-758-4644,
info@1069thewolf.com
www.1069thewolf.com
Rob Bye, General Manager

Nanaimo: **CKWV-FM** (Freq: 102.3)
Owned by: **Island Radio Ltd.**
4550 Wellington Rd., Nanaimo, BC V9T 2H3
250-758-1131, Fax: 250-758-4644,
info@1023thewave.com
www.1023thewave.com
Rob Bye, General Manager

Nelson: **CKKC-FM** (Freq: 106.9)
513C Front St., Nelson, BC V1L 4B4
250-368-5510, Fax: 250-368-8471,
kbs@sri.ca
www.kbsradio.ca

Parksville: **CHPQ-FM** (Freq: 99.9)
Owned by: **Island Radio Ltd.**
PO Box 1370, 141 Memorial Ave., Parksville, BC V9P 2H3
250-248-4211, Fax: 250-248-4210,
info@theloungefm.com
www.islandradio.bc.ca
Paul Larsen, President

Parksville: **CIBH-FM** (Freq: 88.5)
Owned by: **Island Radio Ltd.**
141 Memorial Ave., Parksville, BC V9P 2H3
250-248-4211, Fax: 250-248-4210,
info@885thebeach.com
885thebeach.com
Paul Larsen, President & General Manager

Parksville: **CKWV-FM-1** (Freq: 102.3)
Owned by: **CKWV-FM**
Parksville, BC

Pender Harbour: **CIPN-FM** (Freq: 104.7)
Owned by: **CISQ-FM**
Pender Harbour, BC

Penticton: **CIGV-FM** (Freq: 100.7)
125 Nanaimo Ave. West, Penticton, BC V2A 1N2
250-493-6767, Fax: 250-493-0098, 888-493-6767
info@giantfm.ca
www.giantfm.ca
James Robinson, General Manager

Penticton: **CJMG-FM** (Freq: 97.1)
Owned by: **Standard Radio Office**
33 Carmi Ave., Penticton, BC V2A 3G4
250-492-2800, Fax: 250-493-0370,
www.thesun.net

Port Alberni: **CJAV-FM** (Freq: 93.3)
Owned by: **Island Radio Ltd.**
3296 - 3rd Ave., Port Alberni, BC V9Y 4E1
250-723-2455, Fax: 250-723-0797,
info@933thepeak.com
www.933thepeak.com
Bye Rob, General Manager

Port Alice: **CFPA-FM** (Freq: 100.3)
Owned by: **CFNI**
Port Alice, BC

Powell River: **CJMP-FM** (Freq: 90.1)
4476 Marine Ave., Powell River, BC V8A 2K2
604-485-2688, Fax: 604-485-2683,
modelcommunity@prcn.org
Geraldine Braak, General Manager

Prince George: **CBYG-FM** (Freq: 91.5)
Owned by: **Canadian Broadcasting Corporation**
#1, 890 Victoria St., Prince George, BC V2L 5P1
250-562-6701, Fax: 250-562-4777,
daybreaknorth@cbc.ca
www.cbc.ca/bc

Prince George: **CFUR-FM** (Freq: 88.7)
3333 University Way, Prince George, BC V2N 4Z9
250-960-7664, Fax: 250-960-5995,
info@cfur.ca
www.cfur.ca
Christopher Earl, Station Manager

Prince George: **CIRX-FM** (Freq: 94.3)
1940 - 3 Ave., Prince George, BC V2M 1G7
250-564-2524, Fax: 250-562-6611,
onair@94xfm.com
www.94xfm.com
Terry Shepherd, President & General Manager

Prince George: **CJCI-FM** (Freq: 97.3)
1940 - 3 Ave., Prince George, BC V2M 1G7
250-564-2524, Fax: 250-562-6611,
thewolf@97fm.ca
www.97fm.ca

Prince George: **CKDV-FM** (Freq: 99.3)
Owned by: **The Jim Pattison Broadcast Group**
1810 - 3rd Ave., 2nd Fl., Prince George, BC V2M 1G4
250-564-8861, Fax: 250-562-8768,
ckpgmail@ckpg.bc.ca
www.993thedrive.com
Ken Kilcullen, General Manager

Prince George: **CKKN-FM** (Freq: 101.3)
Owned by: **The Jim Pattison Broadcast Group**
1810 3rd Ave., 2nd Fl., Prince George, BC V2M 1G4
250-564-8861, Fax: 250-562-8768,
ckpgmail@ckpg.bc.ca
www.1013hitsfm.com

Prince Rupert: **CJFW-FM** (Freq: 103.1)
Owned by: **Standard Radio Office**
#212, 215 Cow Bay Rd., Prince Rupert, BC V8J 1A2
250-624-9111, Fax: 250-624-3100,
www.cjfw.ca
Bryan Edwards, President

Quesnel: **CFFM-FM-2** (Freq: 94.9)
Owned by: **CFFM-FM**
Quesnel, BC

Richmond: **CHKG-FM** (Freq: 96.1)
Owned by: **Fairchild Radio**
2090 Aberdeen Centre, 4151 Hazelbridge Way, Richmond, BC V6X 4J7
604-708-1234, Fax: 604-708-1201,
general@fm961.com
www.fm961.com
George Lee, Sr. Vice-President & General Manage

Richmond: **CKZZ-FM** (Freq: 95.3)
Owned by: **Standard Radio Office**
#20, #20, 11151 Horseshoe Way, Richmond, BC V7A 4S5
604-241-0953, Fax: 604-272-0917,
info@z95.com
www.z95.com

Salmon Arm: **CKXR-FM** (Freq: 91.5)
Owned by: **Standard Radio Office**
PO Box 69, 360 Ross St. NE, Salmon Arm, BC V1E 4N2
250-832-2161, Fax: 250-832-2240,
www.myezrock.com
Claude Beaudoin

Sechelt: **CKKS-FM** (Freq: 104.7)
Owned by: **CISQ-FM**
Sechelt, BC

Squamish: **CISC-FM**
Owned by: **Rogers Broadcasting Ltd.**
#202, 40147 Glenalder Place, Squamish, BC V8B 0G2
604-892-1021, Fax: 604-892-6383,
mountainfm@mountainfm.com
www.mountainfm.com
Joe Polito, Manager

** For details on this company see listing in Major Broadcasting Companies section; † French language station*

***Squamish:* CISP-FM**
Owned by: **Rogers Broadcasting Ltd.**
#202, 40147 Glenalder Place, Squamish, BC V8B 0G2
604-892-1021, Fax: 604-892-6383, 888-429-2724
mountainfm@mountainfm.com
www.mountainfm.com
Gary Miles, President
Joe Polito, Manager

***Squamish:* CISQ-FM**
Owned by: **Rogers Broadcasting Ltd.**
#202, 40147 Glenalder Place, Squamish, BC V8B 0G2
604-892-1021, Fax: 604-892-6383, 888-429-2724
moutainfm@mountainfm.com
www.mountainfm.com
Joe Polito, Manager

***Terrace:* CFNR-FM** (Freq: 92.1)
4562B Queensway Dr., Terrace, BC V8G 3X6
250-638-8137, Fax: 250-638-8027,
cfnr.mailbag@monarch.net
www.mycfnr.com

***Terrace:* CKTK-FM** (Freq: 1230)
Owned by: **Standard Radio Office**
4625 Lazelle Ave., Terrace, BC V8G 1S4
250-635-6316, Fax: 250-638-6320
Doug Anderson, Station Manager

***Trail:* CJAT-FM** (Freq: 95.7)
Owned by: **Standard Radio Office**
1560 Second Ave., Trail, BC V1R 1M4
250-368-5510, Fax: 250-368-8471,
kbs@sri.ca
www.kbsradio.ca
Karl Johnston, General Manager

***Trail:* CKZX-FM** (Freq: 93.5)
Owned by: **Standard Radio Office**
1560 - 2nd Ave., Trail, BC V1R 1M4
250-368-5510, Fax: 250-368-8471,
www.trail.kbsradio.ca
Lee Sterry, Operations Manager

†*Vancouver:* CBUF-FM (Freq: 97.7)
Owned by: **Canadian Broadcasting Corporation**
CP 4600, 700 Hamilton St., Vancouver, BC V6B 4A2
604-662-6000,
www.radio-canada.ca/regions/colombie-britannique

***Vancouver:* CBU-FM** (Freq: 105.7)
Owned by: **Canadian Broadcasting Corporation**
Vancouver, BC

***Vancouver:* CBUX-FM** (Freq: 90.9)
Owned by: **Canadian Broadcasting Corporation**
PO Box 4600, 775 Cambie St., Vancouver, BC V6B 4A2
604-662-6000, Fax: 604-662-6335,
www.radio-canada.ca/c-b

***Vancouver:* CFBT-FM** (Freq: 94.5)
#300, 380 West 2nd Ave., Vancouver, BC V5Y 1C8
604-871-9000, Fax: 604-871-2901,
www.thebeat.com

***Vancouver:* CFMI-FM** (Freq: 101.1)
Owned by: **Corus Entertainment Inc.**
#2000, 700 West Georgia St., Vancouver, BC V7Y 1K9
604-331-2808, Fax: 604-331-2722,
rock101@rock101.com
www.rock101.com
Lou Del Gobbo, General Manager

***Vancouver:* CFOX-FM** (Freq: 99.3)
Owned by: **Corus Entertainment Inc.**
#2000, 700 West Georgia St., Vancouver, BC V7Y 1K9
604-684-7221, Fax: 604-331-2722,
www.cfox.com

***Vancouver:* CFRO-FM** (Freq: 102.7)
#110, 360 Columbia St., Vancouver, BC V6A 4J1
604-684-8494,
www.coopradio.org
McNabb Robin, Membership & Outreach Coordinator

***Vancouver:* CHQM-FM** (Freq: 103.5)
Owned by: **Rogers Broadcasting Ltd.**
#300, 380 West 2nd Ave., Vancouver, BC V5Y 1C8
604-871-9000, Fax: 604-871-2901,
www.qmfm.com
Mel Kemmis, Program Director

***Vancouver:* CITR-FM** (Freq: 101.9)
#233, 6138 Sub Blvd., Vancouver, BC V6T 1Z1
604-882-1242, Fax: 604-882-9364,
citrmgr@ams.ubc.ca
www.citr.ca
Linda Scholten, Station Manager

***Vancouver:* CJJR-FM** (Freq: 93.7)
Owned by: **The Jim Pattison Broadcast Group**
#300, 1401 - 8th Ave. West, Vancouver, BC V6H 1C9
604-731-7772, Fax: 604-731-0493,
cjjr@jfrm.com
www.jrfm.com

***Vancouver:* CKCL-FM** (Freq: 107.5)
Owned by: **Rogers Broadcasting Ltd.**
2440 Ash St., Vancouver, BC V5Z 4J6
604-877-6357,
www.1049clearfm.com
David Carsen, General Manager

***Vancouver:* CKLG-FM** (Freq: 96.9)
Owned by: **Rogers Broadcasting Ltd.**
2440 Ash St., Vancouver, BC V5Z 4J6
604-872-2557, Fax: 604-877-4494,
www.jackfm.com
Wolfgang von Petrie

***Vancouver:* CKZZ-FM** (Freq: 95.3)
Owned by: **CKZZ-FM**
Vancouver, BC

***Vanderhoof:* CIRX-FM-1** (Freq: 95.9)
Owned by: **CIRX-FM**
Vanderhoof, BC

***Vernon:* CICF-FM** (Freq: 105.7)
2800 - 31 St., Vernon, BC V1T 5H4
250-545-9222, Fax: 250-542-2083,
vernonmail@sri.ca
www.thesun.net

***Vernon:* CKIZ-FM** (Freq: 107.5)
Owned by: **Rogers Broadcasting Ltd.**
3313 - 32 Ave., Vernon, BC V1T 2E1
250-545-2141, Fax: 250-545-9008,
www.1075kiss.com
Patrick Nicol, General Manager

***Victoria:* CBCV-FM** (Freq: 90.5)
Owned by: **Canadian Broadcasting Corporation**
1025 Pandora Ave., Victoria, BC V8V 3P6
250-360-2227, Fax: 250-360-2600, 866-306-4636
victoria@radio.cbc.ca
www.cbc.ca/bc; www.cbc.ca/radio
Social Media: www.facebook.com/radiocbc;
www.twitter.com/cbcradio
Other information: TTY: 1-866-220-6045
Jennifer Smith, Director, Sales & Marketing, Western Canda, 604-662-6616

***Victoria:* CFUV-FM** (Freq: 101.9)
PO Box 3035, Victoria, BC V8W 3P3
250-721-8702, Fax: 250—,
director@uvic.ca
cfuv.uvic.ca

***Victoria:* CHBE-FM** (Freq: 107.3)
Owned by: **CTVglobemedia Inc.**
1420 Broad St., Victoria, BC V8W 2B1
250-382-1073,
www.1073kool.fm
Robin Haggar, Program Director

***Victoria:* CHTT-FM** (Freq: 103.1)
Owned by: **Rogers Broadcasting Ltd.**
817 Fort St., Victoria, BC V8W 1H6
250-382-0900, Fax: 250-382-4358,
www.1031jackfm.com

***Victoria:* CIOC-FM** (Freq: 98.5)
Owned by: **Rogers Broadcasting Ltd.**
817 Fort St., Victoria, BC V8W 1H6
250-382-0900, Fax: 250-382-4358,
www.ocean985.com

***Victoria:* CJZN-FM** (Freq: 91.3)
2750 Quadra St., Top Floor, Victoria, BC V8T 4E8
250-475-6611, Fax: 250-475-3299,
modernrock@thezone.fm
www.thezone.fm
Dan McAllister, General Manager

***Victoria:* CKKQ-FM** (Freq: 100.3)
2750 Quadra St., 3rd Fl., Victoria, BC V8T 4E8
250-475-0100, Fax: 250-475-3299,
thecrew@theq.fm
www.theq.fm
Stu Morton, President/General Manager

***Whistler:* CISW-FM** (Freq: 102.1)
PO Box 1239, 4335 Blackcomb Way, Whistler, BC V0N 1B4
604-938-0002, Fax: 604-938-0015

***Williams Lake:* CFFM-FM** (Freq: 97.5)
83 South First Ave., Williams Lake, BC V2G 1H4
250-392-6551, Fax: 250-392-4142,
www.cffmthemax.com
Tracey Gard, Manager, 250-392-6551 ex, tgard@vistaradio.ca

Manitoba

***Brandon:* CINC-FM** (Freq: 91.5)
Owned by: **CINC-FM**
Brandon, MB

***Brandon:* CJJJ-FM** (Freq: 106.5)
Assiniboine Community College, #223, 1430 Victoria Ave. East, Brandon, MB R7A 2A9
204-725-8700, Fax: 204-726-7014,
www.assiniboine.net
Bob Crighton, Station Manager

***Brandon:* CKLF-FM** (Freq: 94.7)
624 - 14 St. East, Brandon, MB R7A 7E1
204-726-8888, Fax: 204-726-1270,
tyler@starfmradio.com
www.starfmradio.com
David Baxter, President
Don Kille, General Manager

***Brandon:* CKXA-FM** (Freq: 101.1)
Owned by: **Standard Radio Office**
2940 Victoria Ave., Brandon, MB R7B 3Y3
204-728-1150, Fax: 204-725-3794,
staylor@hotqx.com
www.1011thefarm.com
Taylor Sharon, General Manager

***Brandon:* CKX-FM** (Freq: 96.1)
Owned by: **Standard Radio Office**
2940 Victoria Ave., Brandon, MB R7B 3Y3
204-728-1150, Fax: 204-725-3794,
kx96@kx96online.com
www.kx96online.com
Alan Cruise, CEO & President

***Cross Lake:* CFNC-FM** (Freq: 1490)
PO Box 129, Cross Lake, MB R0B 0J0
204-676-2331, Fax: 204-676-2911
Joyce Halcrow, Station Manager

***Portage la Prairie:* CFRY-FM** (Freq: 93.1)
Owned by: **CFRY**
Portage la Prairie, MB

***Pukatawagan:* CFPX-FM** (Freq: 98.3)
Pukatawagan, MB R0B 1G0
204-553-2155, Fax: 204-553-2158
John Colomb, General Manager

***St. Boniface:* CKXL-FM** (Freq: 91.1)
340 Provencher Blvd., St. Boniface, MB R2H 0G7
204-233-4243, Fax: 204-233-3646,
info@envol91.mb.ca
www.envol91.mb.ca

***Steinbach:* CILT-FM** (Freq: 96.7)
Owned by: **Golden West Broadcasting Ltd.**
#105, 32 Brandt St., Steinbach, MB R5G 2J7
204-326-3737, Fax: 204-326-2299,
info@goldenwestradio.com
www.lite967online.com

***The Pas:* CINC-FM** (Freq: 92.7)
Owned by: **CINC-FM**
The Pas, MB

** For details on this company see listing in Major Broadcasting Companies section; † French language station*

***Thompson:* CBWK-FM** (Freq: 100.9)
Owned by: **Canadian Broadcasting Corporation**
7 Selkirk Ave., Thompson, MB R8N 0M4
204-677-1680,
north@cbc.ca
www.cbc.ca/northcountry

***Thompson:* CINC-FM** (Freq: 96.3)
Owned by: **CINC-FM**
Thompson, MB

***Winkler:* CJEL-FM** (Freq: 93.5)
Owned by: **Golden West Broadcasting Ltd.**
PO Box 399, Winkler, MB R6W 4A6
204-325-7602, Fax: 204-325-2206,
info@goldenwestradio.com
www.eagle935fm.com

***Winnipeg:* CBW-FM** (Freq: 98.3)
Owned by: **Canadian Broadcasting Corporation**
541 Portage Ave., Winnipeg, MB R3C 2G1
204-788-3222,
www.cbc.ca/manitoba

***Winnipeg:* CFEQ-FM** (Freq: 107.1)
738 Osborne St., Winnipeg, MB R3L 2C2
204-944-8961, Fax: 204-772-5854,
www.freq107.com
Tom Hiebert, General Manager

***Winnipeg:* CFQX-FM** (Freq: 104.4)
177 Lombard Ave., 3rd Fl., Winnipeg, MB R3B 0W5
204-944-1031, Fax: 204-943-7687,
www.qx104fm.com
Lee Sterry, General Manager

***Winnipeg:* CFWM-FM** (Freq: 99.9)
Owned by: **Rogers Broadcasting Ltd.**
1445 Pembina Hwy., Winnipeg, MB R3T 5C2
204-477-5120, Fax: 204-453-0815,
bob@999bobfm.com
www.999bobfm.com
Chris Stevens, Vice President/General Manager

***Winnipeg:* CHIQ-FM** (Freq: 94.3)
Owned by: **Rogers Broadcasting Ltd.**
1445 Pembina Hwy., Winnipeg, MB R3T 5C2
204-477-5120, Fax: 204-453-0815,
www.curve943.com

***Winnipeg:* CHNR-FM** (Freq: 100.7)
3586 Portage Ave., Winnipeg, MB R3K 0Z8
204-889-2586, Fax: 204-831-1512,
chnr@shawbiz.ca

***Winnipeg:* CHVN-FM** (Freq: 95.1)
Owned by: **Golden West Broadcasting Ltd.**
PO Box 1812, 1111 Chevrier Blvd., Winnipeg, MB R3C 3R1
204-452-9602, Fax: 204-478-6735,
chvn@chvnradio.com
www.chvnradio.com
Wade Kehler, General Manager

***Winnipeg:* CICY-FM** (Freq: 105.5)
1507 Inkster Blvd., Winnipeg, MB R2X 1R2
204-772-8255, Fax: 204-779-5628,
info@ncifm.com
www.ncifm.com
Hoa Bui, Broadcast Technical Manager

***Winnipeg:* CINC-FM** (Freq: 105.5 fm)
1507 Inkster Blvd., Winnipeg, MB R2X 1R2
204-772-8255, Fax: 204-779-5628,
info@ncifm.com
www.ncifm.com
David McLeod, General Manager
Marshall Lank, Director, Sales & Marketing

***Winnipeg:* CITI-FM** (Freq: 92.1)
Owned by: **Rogers Broadcasting Ltd.**
#4, 166 Osborne St., Winnipeg, MB R3L 1Y8
204-788-3400, Fax: 204-788-3401,
www.92citi.ca

***Winnipeg:* CJKR-FM** (Freq: 97.5)
Owned by: **Corus Entertainment Inc.**
930 Portage Ave., Winnipeg, MB R3G 0P8
204-786-2471, Fax: 204-780-9750,
www.power97.com

Garth Buchko, General Manager

***Winnipeg:* CJUM-FM** (Freq: 101.5)
#308, University Centre, Winnipeg, MB R3T 2N2
204-474-7027, Fax: 204-269-1299,
cjum@cjum.com
www.umfm.com
Jared McKetiak, Station Manager
Jared McKetiak, Program Director

***Winnipeg:* CJZZ-FM** (Freq: 99.1)
Canwest Global Pl., 201 Portage Ave., 30th Fl., Winnipeg, MB R3B 3K6
204-253-2665, Fax: 204-926-1674,
www.cooljazz.ca

***Winnipeg:* CKIC-FM** (Freq: 92.9)
W106, 160 Princess St., Winnipeg, MB R3B 1K9
204-949-8473, Fax: 204-949-0057,
www.kick.fm
Rick Everett, Station Manager

***Winnipeg:* CKMM-FM** (Freq: 103.1)
177 Lombard Ave., 3rd Fl., Winnipeg, MB R3B 0W5
204-944-1031, Fax: 204-943-7687,
www.hot103live.com
Russ Tyson, Vice-President, Programming & Operations

***Winnipeg:* CKUW-FM** (Freq: 95.9)
University of Winnipeg, #4CM11, 515 Portage, Winnipeg, MB R3B 2E9
204-786-9782, Fax: 204-783-7080,
ckuw@uwinnipeg.ca
www.ckuw.ca
Rob Schmidt, Station Manager

***Winnipeg:* CKY-FM** (Freq: 102.3)
Owned by: **Rogers Broadcasting Ltd.**
#4, 166 Osborne St., Winnipeg, MB R3L 1Y8
204-780-3400, Fax: 204-788-3401,
www.102clearfm.com
Geoff Poulton, General Manager

New Brunswick

***†Balmoral:* CIMS-FM** (Freq: 103.9)
CP 2561, 1991, av des Pionniers, Balmoral, NB E8E 2W7
506-826-1040, Fax: 506-826-2400,
cim.traffic@restigouche.net
www.cimsfm.ca
Annie L. Levesque, General Manager

***Bathurst:* CKBC-FM** (Freq: 104.9)
Owned by: **Astral Media Radio Atlantic**
176 Main St., Bathurst, NB E2A 1A4
506-547-1360, Fax: 506-547-1367,
maxfm@radioatl.ca
Jamie Robichaud

***Bathurst:* CKLE-FM** (Freq: 92.9)
195 Main St., Bathurst, NB E2A 3Z1
506-546-4600, Fax: 506-546-6611,
superstation@ckle.fm
www.ckle.fm

***†Edmundston:* CFAI-FM** (Freq: 101.1; 105.1)
165, boul Hebert, 6e étage, Edmundston, NB E3V 2S8
506-737-5060, Fax: 506-737-5084,
cfai@101rock105.com
www.101rock105.com
Serge Parent, Dir de la Station

***†Edmundston:* CJEM-FM** (Freq: 92.7)
174, rue de l'Église, Edmundston, NB E3V 1K2
506-735-3351, Fax: 506-739-5803,
cjem@nbnet.nb.ca

***Edmundston:* CKMV-FM** (Freq: 95.1)
174 Church St., Edmundston, NB E3V 1K2
506-735-3351, Fax: 506-739-5803,
cjem@nbnet.nb.ca
Murillo Soucy, General Manager

***Fredericton:* CBZF-FM** (Freq: 99.5)
Owned by: **Canadian Broadcasting Corporation**
PO Box 2200, 1160 Regent St., Fredericton, NB E3B 5G4
506-451-4000, Fax: 506-451-4170,
www.cbc.ca/nb

***Fredericton:* CFXY-FM** (Freq: 105.3)
Owned by: **Astral Media Radio Atlantic**
206 Rookwood Ave., Fredericton, NB E3B 2M2
506-454-2444, Fax: 506-452-2345,
www.foxrocks.ca
John Eddy, Exec. Vice-President

***Fredericton:* CHSR-FM** (Freq: 97.9)
PO Box 4400, Fredericton, NB E3B 5A3
506-453-4985,
chsr@unb.ca
www.unb.ca/chsr
Tristis Ward, Station Manager
Alan Wong, Program Director

***Fredericton:* CIBX-FM** (Freq: 106.9)
Owned by: **Astral Media Radio Atlantic**
206 Rookwood Ave., Fredericton, NB E3B 2M2
506-455-1069, Fax: 506-452-2345,
www.capitalfm.ca
Pat Brennan, General Manager

***Fredericton:* CIXN-FM** (Freq: 96.5)
#10, 1010 Hanwell Rd., Fredericton, NB E3B 6A4
506-454-9600, Fax: 506-454-0991,
welcome@joyfm.ca
www.joyfm.ca
Garth McCrea, General Manager

***Fredericton:* CJPN-FM** (Freq: 90.5)
715, rue Priestman, Fredericton, NB E3B 5W7
506-454-2576, Fax: 506-453-3958,
cjpn@nbnet.nb.ca
www.cjpn.ca

***Fredericton:* CKTP-FM** (Freq: 95.7)
PO Box R13, 150 Cliffe St., Fredericton, NB E3A 0A1
506-459-4487, Fax: 506-459-4404,
info@cktpradio.com
www.cktpradio.com
Timothy Paul, General Manager

***Grand Falls:* CIKX-FM** (Freq: 93.5)
Owned by: **Astral Media Radio Atlantic**
399 Broadway Blvd., Grand Falls, NB E3Z 2K5
506-473-9393, Fax: 506-473-3893,
grdprod@radioatl.ca
Pat Brennan, General Manager
Rick McGuire, Program Director
Jacques LaFrance, Sales Manager

***Kedgwick:* CFJU-FM**
PO Box 1043, Kedgwick, NB E8B 1Z9
506-235-9000, Fax: 506-235-9001,
cfjufm@rogers.com
Lucille Thériault, General Manager

***Miramichi:* CFAN-FM** (Freq: 99.3)
Owned by: **Maritime Broadcasting System**
396 Pleasant St., Miramichi, NB E1V 1X5
506-622-3311, Fax: 506-627-0335,
cfan@nb.sympatico.ca
www.993theriver.com

***†Moncton:* CBAF-FM**
Owned by: **Canadian Broadcasting Corporation**
250, av Université, Moncton, NB E1C 5K3
506-853-6666, Fax: 506-853-8000, 800-561-7010
www.radio-canada.ca/regions/acadie

***†Moncton:* CBAL-FM** (Freq: 98.3; 95.3; 101.9; 98.9)
Owned by: **Canadian Broadcasting Corporation**
CP 950, 250, av Université, Moncton, NB E1C 8N8
506-853-6666, Fax: 506-853-6739, 800-561-7010
www.radio-canada.ca/radio
Susan Mitton, Regional Director-Radio

***Moncton:* CFQM-FM** (Freq: 103.9)
Owned by: **Maritime Broadcasting System**
1000 St. George Blvd., Moncton, NB E1E 4M7
506-858-1220, Fax: 506-858-1209,
magic104@radiomoncton.com
www.radiomoncton.com

***†Moncton:* CHOY-FM** (Freq: 99.9)
Owned by: **Maritime Broadcasting System**
1000, boul St-George, Moncton, NB E1E 4M7

** For details on this company see listing in Major Broadcasting Companies section; † French language station*

506-858-1220, Fax: 506-858-1209,
choix@radiomoncton.com
www.radiomoncton.com

Moncton: **CITA-FM** (Freq: 105.9)
3170 Mountain Rd., Moncton, NB E1G 2W8
506-384-1059, Fax: 506-854-8609,
www.citafm.com

Moncton: **CJMO-FM** (Freq: 103.1)
Owned by: **NewCap Inc.**
27 Arsenault Ct., Moncton, NB E1E 4J8
506-858-5525, Fax: 506-858-5539,
c103@c103.com
www.c103.com
Dave Ostler, Sales Manager
Andrew Stewart, Program Director
Hilary Montbourquette, General Manager

Moncton: **CJXL-FM** (Freq: 96.9)
27 Arsenault Ct., Moncton, NB E1E 4J8
506-858-5525, Fax: 506-858-5539,
xl96@xl96.com
www.xl96.com
Hilary Montbourquette, General Manager

Moncton: **CKCW-FM** (Freq: 94.5)
Owned by: **Maritime Broadcasting System**
1000 St. George Blvd., Moncton, NB E1E 4M7
506-858-1220, Fax: 506-858-1209,
www.radiomoncton.com
Dan Barton, General Manager

Moncton: **CKOE-FM** (Freq: 107.3)
3030 Mountain Rd., Moncton, NB E1G 2W8
506-388-6212, Fax: 506-383-9699,
info@ckoefm.com
www.ckoefm.com
Kurk Parks, Station Manager

†Moncton: **CKUM-FM** (Freq: 93.5)
Université de Moncton, Centre étudiant, 2e étage, Moncton, NB E1A 3E9
506-858-3750, Fax: 506-858-4524,
radioj@radioj935.com
www.radioj935.com
Michèle Routier, Directrice

Pokemouche: **CKRO-FM** (Freq: 97.1)
142 Rte 113, Pokemouche, NB E8P 1K7
506-336-9706, Fax: 506-336-9058,
radio@ckro.ca
www.ckro.ca
Donald Noel, Dir de la Station

Sackville: **CHMA-FM** (Freq: 106.9)
#303, Student Union Bldg., Mount Allison University, #303, 152A Main St., Sackville, NB E4L 1B4
506-364-2221,
chma@mta.ca
www.mta.ca/chma

Saint John: **CBD-FM** (Freq: 91.3)
Owned by: **Canadian Broadcasting Corporation**
PO Box 2358, 560 Main St., Saint John, NB E2L 3V6
506-632-7750, Fax: 506-632-7761, 866-306-4636
www.cbc.ca/nb; www.cbc.ca/radio
Social Media: www.facebook.com/radiocbc;
www.twitter.com/cbcradio
Other information: TTY: 1-866-220-6045
Andrew Cochran, Managing Director, Maritimes
Dan Goodyear, Executive Producer, News, New Brunswick
Deborah Irvine, Executive Producer, Radio Saint John
Janet Irwin, Senior Regional Manager, News & Current Affairs
Nadine Antle, Regional Manager, Partnerships, Communications, Brand, & Promot, 506-451-4054
John Channing, Manager, Sales
Mary-Pat Schutta, Manager, Programs
Lori Wheeler, Senior Officer, Communications, 506-451-4080

Saint John: **CFMH-FM** (Freq: 92.5)
Student Services, PO Box 5050, Saint John, NB E2L 4L5
506-648-5667, Fax: 506-648-5541,
cfmh@unbsj.ca
www.unbsj.ca/cfmh
Linda Pelletier, Station Manager

Saint John: **CHSJ-FM** (Freq: 94.1)
PO Box 2000, Saint John, NB E2L 3T4
506-633-3323, Fax: 506-644-3485,
mail@country94.ca
www.country94.ca
Jim MacMullin, General Manager

Saint John: **CHWV-FM** (Freq: 97.3)
PO Box 2000, Saint John, NB E2L 3T4
506-633-3323, Fax: 506-644-3485,
mail@thewave.ca
www.thewave.ca
Jim MacMillin, Genera; Manager

Saint John: **CINB-FM** (Freq: 96.1)
PO Box 96, Saint John, NB E2L 3X1
506-657-9600, Fax: 506-657-7664,
www.newsongfm.com
Don Mabee, Station Manager

Saint John: **CIOK-FM**
Owned by: **Maritime Broadcasting System**
226 Union St., Saint John, NB E2L 1B1
506-658-5100, Fax: 506-658-5116,
mailbag@k100.ca
www.k100.ca

Saint John: **CJEF-FM** (Freq: 103.5)
#3E, 28 King St., Saint John, NB E2L 1G3
506-657-1035, Fax: 506-642-7408,
onair@thepirate.ca
www.thepirate.ca
Gary Stackhouse, General Manager
Geoffrey Rnett, CEO

Saint John: **CJYC-FM**
Owned by: **Maritime Broadcasting System**
226 Union St., Saint John, NB E2L 1B1
506-658-5100, Fax: 506-658-5116,
mailbag@989bigjohnfm.com
www.989bigjohnfm.com

Shediac: **CJSE-FM** (Freq: 89.5, 101.7, 107.5)
96, rue Providence, Shediac, NB E4P 2E9
506-532-0080, Fax: 506-532-0120, 800-604-0080
cjse@cjse.ca
www.cjse.ca
Gilles Arsenault

St Stephen: **CHDT-FM** (Freq: 98.1)
112 Milltown Blvd., St Stephen, NB E3L 1G6
506-466-1000,
mail@thetide.ca
www.thetide.ca
Jim MacMillin, General Manager

St Stephen: **WQDY-FM** (Freq: 92.7)
PO Box 305, St Stephen, NB E3L 2X2
506-465-0989, Fax: 207-454-3062, 888-855-2992
wqdy@wqdy.fm
www.wqdy.fm
Bill McVicar

Woodstock: **CJCJ-FM** (Freq: 104.1)
Owned by: **Astral Media Radio Atlantic**
#1, 131 Queen St., Woodstock, NB E7M 2M8
506-325-3030, Fax: 506-325-3031
Pat Brennan, General Manager
Rick McGuire, Program Director
Bev Whiteway, Sales Manager

Newfoundland & Labrador

Corner Brook: **CFLC-FM** (Freq: 97.9)
Owned by: **NewCap Inc.**
PO Box 570, Corner Brook, NL A2H 6H5
709-634-3111, Fax: 709-634-4081
Michael Murphy, Station Manager

Corner Brook: **CKXX-FM** (Freq: 103.9)
Owned by: **NewCap Inc.**
PO Box 570, 345 O'Connell Dr., Corner Brook, NL A2H 6H5
709-634-4570, Fax: 709-634-4081,
www.k-rock1039.com
Mike Murphy, General Manager

Deer Lake: **CFDL-FM** (Freq: 97.9)
Owned by: **CFCB**
Deer Lake, NL

Gander: **CKXD-FM** (Freq: 98.7)
Owned by: **NewCap Inc.**
PO Box 650, Gander, NL A1V 1X2
709-651-3650, Fax: 709-651-2542
John Murphy, General Manager

Grand Falls-Windsor: **CKXG-FM** (Freq: 102.3; 101.3)
Owned by: **NewCap Inc.**
35A Grenfell Heights, Grand Falls-Windsor, NL A2A 2K2
709-489-2192, Fax: 709-489-8626,
ckxg@vocm.com
www.k-rock975.com

Happy Valley-Goose Bay: **CFGB-FM** (Freq: 89.5)
Owned by: **Canadian Broadcasting Corporation**
PO Box 1029 C, Happy Valley-Goose Bay, NL A0P 1C0
709-896-2911, Fax: 709-896-8900,
www.cbc.ca/nl

Labrador City: **CBDQ-FM** (Freq: 96.3)
Owned by: **Canadian Broadcasting Corporation**
PO Box 576, Labrador City, NL A2V 2L3
709-944-3616, Fax: 709-944-5472, 800-563-7933
www.cbc.ca/nl; www.cbc.ca/radio
Social Media: www.facebook.com/radiocbc;
www.twitter.com/cbcradio
Other information: Phone, Transmission Information: 1-888-353-7006; TTY: 1-866-220-6045
Denise Wilson, Managing Director, Newfoundland & Labrador
Kathy Porter, Executive Producer, English Radio
Maureen Anonsen, Manager, Partnership & Communications, 709-576-5013
Wayne Tilley, Account Manager, 709-576-5019
Debbie Hynes, Senior Officer, Communications, 709-576-5150

Labrador City: **CJRM-FM** (Freq: 97.3)
PO Box 453, 308, rue Hudson, Labrador City, NL A2V 2K7
709-944-7600, Fax: 709-944-5125,
cjrm@hotmail.com

St Andrews: **CFCV-FM** (Freq: 97.7)
Owned by: **CFSX**
St Andrews, NL

St Anthony: **CFNN-FM** (Freq: 97.9)
Owned by: **CFCB**
St Anthony, NL

St. John's: **CBN-FM** (Freq: 106.9)
Owned by: **Canadian Broadcasting Corporation**
PO Box 12010 A, St. John's, NL A1B 3T8
709-576-5000, 800-563-7933
www.cbc.ca/nl; www.cbc.ca/radio2
Social Media: www.facebook.com/CBC.Radio2.Official?ref=nf
Other information: Phone, Transmission: 888-353-7006; Twitter:
www.twitter.com/cbcradio2
Denise Wilson, Managing Director, Newfoundland & Labrador
Kathy Porter, Executive Producer, English Radio
Maureen Anonsen, Manager, Partnership & Communications, 709-576-5013
Wayne Tilley, Manager, Accounts, 709-576-5019
Debbie Hynes, Senior Officer, Communications, 709-576-5150

St. John's: **CFOZ-FM** (Freq: 100.3)
Owned by: **Newfoundland Broadcasting Co. Ltd.***
PO Box 2020, 446 Logy Bay Rd., St. John's, NL A1C 5S2
709-726-2922, Fax: 709-726-3300,
www.ozfm.com
Brian O'Connell, Station Manager

St. John's: **CHMR-FM** (Freq: 93.5)
PO Box A-119, Memorial University, St. John's, NL A1C 5S7
709-737-4777, Fax: 709-737-7688,
chmr@mun.ca
www.mun.ca/chmr
Kathy Rowe, Station Manager

St. John's: **CHOS-FM** (Freq: 95.9)
Owned by: **Newfoundland Broadcasting Co. Ltd.***
PO Box 2020, 446 Logy Bay Rd., St. John's, NL A1C 5S2
709-726-2922, Fax: 709-726-3300,
www.ozfm.com
Brian O'Connell, Station Manager

St. John's: **CHOZ-FM** (Freq: 94.7)
Owned by: **Newfoundland Broadcasting Co. Ltd.***
PO Box 2020, 446 Logy Bay Rd., St. John's, NL A1C 5S2

** For details on this company see listing in Major Broadcasting Companies section; † French language station*

709-726-2922, Fax: 709-726-3300,
requests@ozfm.com
www.ozfm.com

Doug Neal, General Manager

***St. John's:* CIOS-FM** (Freq: 98.5)
Owned by: **Newfoundland Broadcasting Co. Ltd.***
PO Box 2020, 446 Logy Bay Rd., St. John's, NL A1C 5S2
709-726-2922, Fax: 709-726-3300,
www.ozfm.com

Brian O'Connell, Station Manager

***St. John's:* CIOZ-FM** (Freq: 96.3)
Owned by: **Newfoundland Broadcasting Co. Ltd.***
PO Box 2020, 446 Logy Bay Rd., St. John's, NL A1C 5S2
709-726-2922, Fax: 709-726-3300,
www.ozfm.com

***St. John's:* CJKK-FM** (Freq: 105.3)
Owned by: **Newfoundland Broadcasting Co. Ltd.***
CHOZ-FM, 446 Logy Bay Rd., St. John's, NL A1C 5R6
709-726-2922, Fax: 709-726-3300

Brian O'Connell, Station Manager

***St. John's:* CJOZ-FM** (Freq: 92.1)
Owned by: **Newfoundland Broadcasting Co. Ltd.***
PO Box 2020, 466 Logy Bay Rd., St. John's, NL A1C 5S2
709-726-2922, Fax: 709-726-3300,
www.ozfm.com

Brian O'Connell, Station Manager

***St. John's:* CKIX-FM** (Freq: 99.1)
Owned by: **NewCap Inc.**
PO Box 8590, 391 Kenmount Rd., St. John's, NL A1B 3P5
709-726-5590, Fax: 709-726-4633,
www.991hitsfm.com

Hilary Montbourquette, Operations Manager
Bob Templeton, President
John Murphy, General Manager

***St. John's:* CKOZ-FM** (Freq: 92.3)
Owned by: **Newfoundland Broadcasting Co. Ltd.***
CHOZ-FM, PO Box 2020, 446 Logy Bay Rd., St. John's, NL A1C 5S2
709-726-2922, Fax: 709-726-3300,
www.ozfm.com

Biran O'Connell, Station Manager

***St. John's:* CKSJ-FM** (Freq: 101.1)
PO Box 28106, 48 Kenmount Rd., St. John's, NL A1B 4J8
709-754-6748, Fax: 709-754-6749,
onair@coast1011.com
www.coast1011.com

***St. John's:* CKSS-FM** (Freq: 96.9)
Owned by: **Newfoundland Broadcasting Co. Ltd.***
PO Box 202, 446 Logy Bay Rd., St. John's, NL A1C 5S2
709-726-2922, Fax: 709-726-3300,
www.ozfm.com

Brian O'Connell, Station Manager

***St. John's:* VOCM-FM** (Freq: 97.5)
Owned by: **NewCap Inc.**
PO Box 8590 A, 391 Kenmount Rd., St. John's, NL A1B 3P5
709-726-5590, Fax: 709-726-4633,
feedback@vocm.com
www.k-rock975.com

Northwest Territories

***Hay River:* CKHR-FM** (Freq: 107.3)
PO Box 4394, Hay River, NT X0E 1G3
403-874-2547, Fax: 403-874-2547,
ckhr@northwestel.nt

†*Yellowknife:* CIVR-FM (Freq: 103.5)
CP 1586, 5106-48th St., Yellowknife, NT X1A 2P2
867-766-3308, Fax: 867-766-3314,
civr@franco-nord.com
www.radiotaiga.ca

Sylvie Boisclair, General Manager

***Yellowknife:* CJCD-FM** (Freq: 100.1)
PO Box 218, Yellowknife, NT X1A 2N2
867-920-2523, Fax: 867-920-4033,
info@cjcd.ca
www.cjcd.ca

Eileen Dent
Charles Dent

***Yellowknife:* CKLB-FM** (Freq: 101.9)
4 Lessard Dr., Yellowknife, NT X1A 2G5
867-920-2277, Fax: 867-920-4205,
www.ncsnwt.com

Elizabeth Biscaye, Executive Director
Chris Rodgers, TV Manager

Nova Scotia

***Antigonish:* CFXU-FM** (Freq: 92.5)
PO Box 948, St. Francis Xavier University, Antigonish, NS B2G 2X1
902-867-3941, Fax: 902-867-5138,
thefox@stfx.ca
radiocfxu.ca

Caitlin Can Horne, Internal Station Manager

***Antigonish:* CJFX-FM** (Freq: 98.9)
PO Box 5800, Antigonish, NS B2G 2R9
902-863-4580, Fax: 902-863-6300,
cjfx@cjfx.ca
989xfm.supremeserver11.com

David MacLean, General Manager

***Bridgewater:* CKBW-FM** (Freq: 98.1)
215 Dominion St., Bridgewater, NS B4V 2G8
902-543-2401, Fax: 902-543-1208,
ckbw@ckbw.com
www.ckbw.com

Michael Prud'homme, General Manager

***Bridgewater:* CKBW-FM-2** (Freq: 93.1)
215 Dominion St., Bridgewater, NS B4V 2G8
902-543-2401, Fax: 902-543-1208,
ckbw@ckbw.com
www.ckbw.com

John Wiles, General Manager

†*Cheticamp:* CKJM-FM (Freq: 106.1)
CP 699, Cheticamp, NS B0E 1H0
902-224-1242, Fax: 902-224-1770,
info@ckjm.ca
www.ckjm.ca

Auguste LeFort, Station Manager

***Digby:* CJLS-FM-2** (Freq: 93.5)
Owned by: **CJLS-FM**
Digby, NS

***Digby:* CKDY-FM-1** (Freq: 103.3)
Owned by: **CKDY**
Digby, NS

***Eastern Passage:* CFEP-FM** (Freq: 94.7)
PO Box 196, Eastern Passage, NS B3G 1M5
902-469-9231, Fax: 902-469-0966,
seasidefm@ns.sympatico.ca
www.seasidefm.com

Wayne Harrett, General Manager

***Eskasoni:* CICU-FM** (Freq: 94.1)
PO Box 7100, 130 Anslum Rd., Eskasoni, NS B1W 1A1
902-379-2955, Fax: 902-379-2966

***Halifax:* C100-FM** (Freq: 100.1)
PO Box 9316 A, 2900 Agricola St., Halifax, NS B3K 6B2
902-453-2524, Fax: 902-453-3132,
chris.duggan@chumradio.com
www.c100fm.com

Trent McGrath, General Manager, trent.mcgrath@chumradio.com
Chris Duggan, Program Manager, chris.duggan@chumradio.com

†*Halifax:* CBAX-FM (Freq: 91.5)
CP 3000, Halifax, NS B3J 3E9
902-420-8311, 866-306-4636
www.radio-canada.ca

Andrew Cochran, Managing Director, Maritimes
Nadine Antle, Regional Manager, Partnerships, Communications, Brand, & Promot, 506-451-4054
John Channing, Manager, Nova Scotia Sales & Marketing
Kathy Large, Manager, Nova Scotia Programs
Chantal Bernard, Senior Officer, Communications, 902-420-4306

***Halifax:* CBHA-FM** (Freq: 90.5)
Owned by: **Canadian Broadcasting Corporation**
PO Box 3000, Halifax, NS B3J 3E9
902-420-8311, Fax: 902-420-4357, 866-306-4636
www.cbc.ca/ns; www.cbc.ca/radio
Social Media: www.facebook.com/radiocbc; www.twitter.com/cbcradio
Other information: Phone, CBC Radio One Newsroom, Halifax: 902-420-4350

Andrew Cochran, Managing Director, Maritimes
Janet Irwin, Senior Manager, News & Current Affairs
John Channing, Manager, Sales, Nova Scotia
Kathy Large, Manager, Programs
Chantal Bernard, Senior Officer, Communications, 902-420-4306

***Halifax:* CBH-FM** (Freq: 102.7)
Owned by: **Canadian Broadcasting Corporation**
PO Box 3000, Halifax, NS B3J 3E9
902-420-8311, 866-306-4636
www.cbc.ca/ns; www.cbc.ca/radio2
Social Media: www.facebook.com/CBC.Radio2.Official?ref=nf
Other information: Twitter: www.twitter.com/cbcradio2

Andrew Cochran, Managing Director, Maritimes
Nancy Waugh, Executive Producer, Nova Scotia News
Chantal Bernard, Senior Officer, Communications, 902-420-4306

***Halifax:* CFRQ-FM** (Freq: 104.3)
Owned by: **NewCap Inc.**
PO Box 9316 A, Halifax, NS B3K 6B2
902-453-4004, Fax: 902-453-3132,
www.q104.ca

Ted Hyland, General Manager

***Halifax:* CHFX-FM**
Owned by: **Maritime Broadcasting System**
5121 Sackville St., 3rd Fl., Halifax, NS B3J 1K1
902-422-1651, Fax: 902-422-5330,
chfx@mbsradio.com
www.fx1019.ca

Robert Pace, Chairman
Ian Kent, General Sales Manager, ian.kent@mbsradio.com

***Halifax:* CHNS-FM** (Freq: 89.9)
Owned by: **Maritime Broadcasting System**
5121 Sackville St., 3 Fl., Halifax, NS B3J 1K1
902-425-1225, Fax: 902-425-5330,
www.chnsradio.com

***Halifax:* CKDU-FM** (Freq: 88.1)
Student Union Bldg., 6136 University Ave., Halifax, NS B3H 4J2
902-494-6479, Fax: 902-494-1110,
info@ckdu.ca
www.ckdu.ca

Michael Wile, Chair
Fiona York, Station Manager

***Halifax:* CKUL-FM** (Freq: 96.5)
Owned by: **NewCap Inc.**
2900 Agricola St., Halifax, NS B3K 6A7
902-453-4004, Fax: 902-453-3120,
www.planetkool.ca

Ted Hyland, General Manager

***Inverness:* CJFX-FM** (Freq: 102.5)
Owned by: **CJFX-FM**
Inverness, NS

***Kentville:* CKEN-FM** (Freq: 97.7)
Owned by: **Maritime Broadcasting System**
PO Box 310, 29 Oakdene Ave., Kentville, NS B4N 1H5
902-678-2111, Fax: 902-678-9894,
avr@avrnetwork.com
www.avrnetwork.com

***Kentville:* CKWM-FM** (Freq: 94.9)
Owned by: **Maritime Broadcasting System**
PO Box 310, 29 Oakdene Ave., Kentville, NS
902-678-2111, Fax: 902-678-9894,
avr@avrnetwork.com
www.magic949.ca

Dianne Best, General Manager

***Membertou:* CJIJ-FM** (Freq: 99.9)
PO Box 99, 49 Tupsi Dr., Membertou, NS B1S 3K6
902-562-0009, Fax: 902-539-6645,
c99fm@hotmail.com
c99fm@homestead.com

Peter Christmas, Jr, General Manager

** For details on this company see listing in Major Broadcasting Companies section; † French language station*

***Port Hawkesbury:* 101.5 The Hawk (CIGO-FM)** (Freq: 101.5)
#201, 609 Church St., Port Hawkesbury, NS B9A 2X4
902-625-1220, Fax: 902-625-2664,
bob@1015thehawk.com
www.1015thehawk.com
Bob MacEachern, President & General Manager
Brenda MacEachern

***Saulnierville:* CIFA-FM** (Freq: 104.1)
PO Box 8, Saulnierville, NS B0W 2Z0
902-769-2432, Fax: 902-769-3101,
info@cifafm.ca
www.cifa.com
Darlene Comeau, General Manager

***Shelburne:* CJLS-FM-1** (Freq: 96.3)
Owned by: **CJLS-FM**
Shelburne, NS

***†Sydney:* CBI-FM**
Owned by: **Canadian Broadcasting Corporation**
Sydney, NS

***Sydney:* CKPE-FM** (Freq: 94.9)
Owned by: **Maritime Broadcasting System**
318 Charlotte St., Sydney, NS B1P 1C8
902-564-5596, Fax: 902-564-1873,
mail@capebretonradio.com
www.capebretonradio.com

***Truro:* CKTO-FM**
Owned by: **Astral Media Radio Atlantic**
187 Industrial Ave., Truro, NS B2N 6V3
902-893-6060, Fax: 902-893-7771, 877-891-6060
www.bigdog1009.ca
Mike Worsley, Sales Manager, mworsley@radioatl.ca

***Truro:* CKTY-FM**
Owned by: **Astral Media Radio Atlantic**
187 Industrial Ave., Truro, NS B2N 6V3
902-893-6060, Fax: 902-893-7771, 877-891-6060
www.catcountry995.ca
Mike Worsley, Sales Manager, mworsley@radioatl.ca

***Yarmouth:* CJLS-FM** (Freq: 95.5)
#201, 328 Main St., Yarmouth, NS B5A 1E4
902-742-7175, Fax: 902-742-3143,
cjls@cjls.com
www.cjls.com
Ray Zinck, President

Nunavut

***Baker Lake:* CKQN-FM** (Freq: 99.3)
Owned by: **Canadian Broadcasting Corporation**
PO Box 13, Baker Lake, NU X0C 0A0
867-793-2962, Fax: 867-793-2509

***†Iqaluit:* CFRT-FM** (Freq: 107.3)
CP 880, Iqaluit, NU X0A 0H0
867-979-4606, Fax: 867-979-0800,
cfrt@nunafranc.ca
www.franconunavut.ca
Daniel Cuerrier, General Manager

***Iqaluit:* CKIQ-FM** (Freq: 99.9)
PO Box 417, Iqaluit, NU X0A 0H0
867-975-2547, Fax: 867-975-2598,
99.9@ckiq.ca
www.ckiq.cq
Glenn Craig, Station Manager

***Rankin Inlet:* CBQR-FM** (Freq: 105.1)
Owned by: **Canadian Broadcasting Corporation**
PO Box 130, Rankin Inlet, NU X0C 0G0
867-645-2885, Fax: 867-645-2820,
www.cbc.ca/north

Ontario

***Aylmer:* CHPD-FM** (Freq: 107.7)
16 Talbot St., Aylmer, ON N5H 1H4
519-773-8555, Fax: 519-773-8606,
radio@mccayl.org
H.G. (Hein) Rempel, Manager

***Bala:* CFWP-FM** (Freq: 98.3)
PO Box 711, 2350 Muskoka Rd. 38, Bala, ON P0C 1A0
705-762-1274, Fax: 705-762-2045,
hawk98@wahta.com
www.wahta.com/hawkradio
Carl White, Station Manager

***Bancroft:* CHMS-FM** (Freq: 97.7)
PO Box 1240, Bancroft, ON K0L 1C0
613-332-1423, Fax: 613-332-0841,
moose977@hbgradio.com
www.moosefm.com

***Barrie:* CFJB-FM** (Freq: 95.7)
#205, 400 Bayfield St., Barrie, ON L4M 5A1
705-725-7304, Fax: 705-721-7842,
www.rock95.com

***Barrie:* CHAY-FM** (Freq: 93.1)
Owned by: **Corus Entertainment Inc.**
PO Box 937, 1125 Bayfield St. North, Barrie, ON L4M 4Y6
705-737-3511, Fax: 705-737-0603,
promo@thenewchay.com
www.thenewchay.com
Other information: Newsroom Phone: 705/726-1597; Fax: 705/722-5631
J. Kim Noel, General Manager

***Barrie:* CJLF-FM** (Freq: 100.3)
#111, 115 Bell Farm Rd., Barrie, ON L4M 5G1
705-735-3370, Fax: 705-735-3301,
www.lifeonline.fm
Scott Jackson, Station Manager, scott@lifeonline.fm
Simon Slessor, Director
Janice Baird, CFO

***Barrie:* CKMB-FM** (Freq: 107.5)
#205, 400 Bayfield St., Barrie, ON L4M 5A1
705-725-7304, Fax: 705-721-7842,
www.1075koolfm.com
Doug Bingley, General Manager

***Belleville:* CHCQ-FM** (Freq: 100.1)
354 Pinnacle St., Belleville, ON K8N 3B4
613-966-0955, Fax: 613-967-2565,
www.cool100.fm

***Belleville:* CIGL-FM** (Freq: 97.1)
PO Box 488, 10 Front St. South, Belleville, ON K8N 5B2
613-969-5555, Fax: 613-969-8122,
www.mix97.com

***Belleville:* CJLX-FM** (Freq: 91.3)
PO Box 4200, Belleville, ON K8N 5B9
613-969-0923, Fax: 613-966-1993,
contact@91x.fm; sales@91x.fm; music@91x.fm
www.91x.fm
Other information: Phone, Newsroom: 613-966-6797; Fax, News: 613-969-9382
Greg Schatzmann, General Manager

***Belleville:* CJOJ-FM** (Freq: 95.5)
354 Pinnacle St., Belleville, ON K8N 3B4
613-966-0955, Fax: 613-967-2565,
www.classichits955.fm
John Sherratt, President

***Bracebridge:* CFBG-FM** (Freq: 99.5)
#50, 2 Balls Dr., Bracebridge, ON P1L 1T1
705-645-2218, Fax: 705-645-6957,
moose995@hbgradio.com
www.moosefm.com

***Brantford:* CFWC-FM** (Freq: 93.9)
271 Greenwich St., Brantford, ON N3S 2X9
519-759-2339, Fax: 519-753-1157,
info@power93.ca
www.power93.ca
Vicki Schleifer, Station Manager

***Brantford:* CKPC-FM** (Freq: 92.1)
571 West St., Brantford, ON N3T 5P8
519-759-1000, Fax: 519-753-1470,
ops@ckpc.on.ca
www.ckpc.on.ca
Richard Buchanan, President/General Manager

***Brockville:* CFJR-FM** (Freq: 104.9)
Owned by: **Rogers Broadcasting Ltd.**
PO Box 666, 601 Stewart Blvd., Brockville, ON K6V 5V9
613-345-1666, Fax: 613-342-2438,
www.1049jrfm.com
Greg Hinton, Vice President/General Manager

***Brockville:* CJPT-FM** (Freq: 103.7)
Owned by: **Rogers Broadcasting Ltd.**
PO Box 666, 601 Stewart Blvd., Brockville, ON K6V 5V9
613-345-1666, Fax: 613-342-2438,
www.bob.fm
Greg Hinton, Vice President/General Manager

***Cambridge:* CJDV-FM** (Freq: 107.5)
Owned by: **Corus Entertainment Inc.**
#100, 1315 Bishop St. North, Cambridge, ON N1R 6Z2
519-621-7510, Fax: 519-621-0165,
www.davefm.com

***Campbellford:* CKOL-FM** (Freq: 93.7)
PO Box 551, 15 Raglan St. South, Campbellford, ON K0L 1L0
705-653-1089,
ckol-radio@excite.com
Dave Lockwood, General Manager

***Chatham:* CFCO-FM** (Freq: 92.9)
Owned by: **CFCO**
Chatham, ON

***Chatham:* CKSY-FM** (Freq: 94.3)
Owned by: **Blackburn Radio Inc.**
PO Box 100, 117 Keil Dr., Chatham, ON N7M 5K1
519-354-2200, Fax: 519-354-2880,
info@cksyfm.com
www.cksyfm.com

***Chatham:* CKUE-FM** (Freq: 95.1)
Owned by: **Blackburn Radio Inc.**
PO Box 100, 117 Keil Dr., Chatham, ON N7M 5K1
519-354-2200, Fax: 519-354-2880,
info@therock951.com
www.therock951.com
Carl Veroba

***Cobourg:* CKSG-FM** (Freq: 93.3)
PO Box 520, Cobourg, ON K9A 4L3
905-372-5401, Fax: 905-372-6280, 866-782-7933
info@star933.com
www.star933.com
Don Conway, President

***Cochrane:* CHPB-FM** (Freq: 98.1)
PO Box 855, 135 - 3rd St., Cochrane, ON P0L 1C0
705-267-6467, Fax: 705-267-6467,
moose981@hbgradio.com
www.moosefm.com

***Cochrane:* CJWL-FM** (Freq: 101.1)
PO Box 855, 153 - 3rd St., Cochrane, ON P1L 1C1
705-272-6467, Fax: 705-272-6467,
moose981@hbgradio.com
www.moosefm.com/cjwl/index.php

***Collingwood:* CKCB-FM** (Freq: 95.1)
Owned by: **Corus Entertainment Inc.**
1400 Hwy. 26 East, Collingwood, ON L9Y 4W2
705-446-9510, Fax: 705-444-6776,
www.thepeakfm.com
John Eaton, General Manager

***Cornwall:* CFLG-FM** (Freq: 104.5)
Owned by: **Corus Entertainment Inc.**
PO Box 969, 237 Water St. East, Cornwall, ON K6H 5V1
613-932-5180, Fax: 613-938-0355,
variety104@seawayvalley.com
www.seawayvalley.com
Paul Vincent, General Manager

***†Cornwall:* CHOD-FM** (Freq: 92.1)
#202, 1111 Montreal Rd., Cornwall, ON K6H 1E1
613-936-2463, Fax: 613-936-2568,
chodfm@chodfm.ca
www.chod.on.ca
François Cotê

***Cornwall:* CJSS-FM** (Freq: 101.9)
Owned by: **Corus Entertainment Inc.**
PO Box 969, 709 Cotton Mill St., Cornwall, ON K6H 7K7
613-932-5180, Fax: 613-938-0355, 888-678-8122
www.seawayvalley.com
Tim Wieczorek, General Manager

***Cornwall:* CKON-FM** (Freq: 97.3)
PO Box 1496, Cornwall, ON K6H 5V5
613-575-2100, Fax: 613-575-2566,
ckon@ckon.com
www.cnwl.igs.net/~ckon/

** For details on this company see listing in Major Broadcasting Companies section; † French language station*

***Dryden:* CJIV-FM** (Freq: 97.3)
PO Box 112, Dryden, ON P8N 2Y7
807-937-9731, Fax: 807-937-6490,
cjiv@canada.com
www.cjjv973.net

***Dryden:* CKDR-FM** (Freq: 92.7)
Owned by: **Northwoods Broadcasting Ltd.**
PO Box 580, 122 King St., Dryden, ON P8N 2Z3
807-223-2355, Fax: 807-223-5090,
mail@ckdr.net
www.ckdr.net

***Elliot Lake:* CKNR-FM**
144 Ontario Ave., Elliot Lake, ON P5A 1Y3
705-848-3608, Fax: 705-848-1378, 800-565-7359
moose941@moosefm.com
www.moosefm.com/cknr
Erika MacLellan, Operations Manager/Sales Executive,
emaclellan@moosefm.com
Bob Alexander, Promotions Director/Host,
balexander@moosefm.com

***Englehart:* CJBB-FM** (Freq: 103.1)
50 Third St., Englehart, ON P0J 1H0
705-544-1121, Fax: 705-544-2286,
cjbb@ntl.sympatico.ca
Rick Stow, Station Manager

***Fort Frances:* CFOB-FM** (Freq: 93.1)
Owned by: **Northwoods Broadcasting Ltd.**
242 Scott St., Fort Frances, ON P9A 1G7
807-274-5341, Fax: 807-274-2033
Hugh Syrja

***Guelph:* CFRU-FM** (Freq: 93.3)
University Centre, Level 2, University of Guelph, Guelph, ON N1G 2W1
519-824-4120, Fax: 519-763-9603,
info@cfru.ca
www.cfru.ca
Lori Guest, Music Programming Coordinator
Ignace Ntirushwamaboko, Spoken Word Coordinator
John Leacock, Music Coordinator/Advertising Coord
Richard Watson, Promotions Coordinator
Kim Iezzi, Operations Coordinator

***Guelph:* CIMJ-FM** (Freq: 106.1)
Owned by: **Corus Entertainment Inc.**
75 Speedvale Ave. East, Guelph, ON N1E 6M3
519-824-7000, Fax: 519-824-4118,
magic@magic106.com
www.magic106.com

***Haliburton:* CKHA-FM** (Freq: 100.9)
PO Box 1125, Haliburton, ON K0M 1S0
705-457-9603, Fax: 705-457-9522,
info@canoefm1009.com
www.canoefm.com
Dave Sovereign, Station Manager

***Hamilton:* CFMU-FM** (Freq: 93.3)
#B119, McMaster University Student Centre, Hamilton, ON L8S 4S4
905-525-9140, Fax: 905-529-3208,
bhandari@msu.mcmaster.can.ca
cfmu.mcmaster.ca
Sandeepa Bhandari, Station Manager

***Hamilton:* CING-FM** (Freq: 107.9)
Owned by: **Corus Entertainment Inc.**
875 Main St. West, Hamilton, ON L8S 4R1
905-521-9900, Fax: 902-540-2453,
www.country953.com

***Hamilton:* CIOI-FM** (Freq: 101.5)
PO Box 2034, 135 Fennell Ave., Hamilton, ON L8N 3T2
905-575-2175, Fax: 905-575-2385,
les.palango@mohawkcollege.ca
www.mohawkcollege.ca/msa/cioi
Les Palango, Station Manager
Jamie Smith, Program & Music Director
Jeff Cudahy, Chief Engineer

***Hamilton:* CIWV-FM** (Freq: 94.7)
589 Upper Wellington, Hamilton, ON L9A 3P8
905-388-8911, Fax: 905-388-7947, 866-388-8911
www.wave947.fm
Douglas E. Kirk, President

***Hamilton:* CJXY-FM** (Freq: 107.9)
Owned by: **Corus Entertainment Inc.**
#900, 875 Main St. West, Hamilton, ON L8S 4R1
905-521-0953, Fax: 905-521-2306,
www.y108.ca

***Hamilton:* CKLH-FM** (Freq: 102.9)
Owned by: **Standard Radio Office**
#401, 883 Upper Wentworth St., Hamilton, ON L9A 4Y6
905-574-1150, Fax: 905-574-6429,
info@k-litefm.com
www.k-lite.com
David Jones, Program Director
Tom Cooke, General Manager
Robyn Foley, News Director

***Hanover:* CFBW-FM** (Freq: 91.3 FM; Radio Station)
267 - 10th St., Hanover, ON N4N 1P1
519-364-0200, Fax: 519-364-5175,
bluewaterradio@on.aibn.com
www.bluewaterradio.ca
Andrew McBride, Station Manager, 519-370-9090

***†Hawkesbury:* CHPR-FM** (Freq: 102.1)
Owned by: **Radio Nord Communications Inc.**
#37, 115 Main St., Hawkesbury, ON K6A 1A1
613-632-1000, Fax: 514-632-1110,
infocouleurfm@radionord.com

***†Hearst:* CINN-FM** (Freq: 91.1)
CP 2648, 1004, rue Prince, Hearst, ON P0L 1N0
705-372-1011, Fax: 705-362-7411, 866-362-5168
cinnfm@cinnfm.com
www.cinnfm.com
Gaetane Morrissette

***Huntsville:* CFBK-FM** (Freq: 105.5)
#2, 15 Main St. East, Huntsville, ON P1H 2C6
705-789-4461, Fax: 705-789-1269,
105.5@morefm.ca
L. Byers, President/Owner

***Kapuskasing:* CKAP-FM** (Freq: 100.9)
Moose FM, #2A, 22 Queen St., Kapuskasing, ON P5N 1G8
705-335-2379, Fax: 705-337-6391, 866-505-2379
moose1009@hbgradio.com
hbgradio.com
Christopher Grossman, President

***†Kapuskasing:* CKGN-FM** (Freq: 89.7 FM Kapuskasing et 94.7 FM Smooth Rock Falls)
77, ch Brunelle nord, Kapuskasing, ON P5N 2M1
705-335-5915, Fax: 705-335-3508, 800-385-2741
ckgn-fm@nt.net
www.ckgn.ca
Claude Chabot, Directeur général, claudechabot@ckgn.ca

***Kenora:* CJRL 89.5 Mix FM**
Owned by: **Northwoods Broadcasting Ltd.**
128 Main St. South, Kenora, ON P9N 1S9
807-468-3181, Fax: 807-468-4188,
cjrl@cjrl.ca
www.cjrl.ca/89fm

***Kenora:* CJRL-FM** (Freq: 89.5)
Owned by: **Northwoods Broadcasting Ltd.**
128 Main St. South, Kenora, ON P9N 1S9
807-468-3181, Fax: 807-468-4188,
carolyn@89.5mix.fm
Henry Syrja, Manager

***Killaloe:* CHCR-FM** (Freq: 102.9; 104.5)
PO Box 195, 7A Lake St., 2nd Fl., Killaloe, ON K0J 2A0
613-757-0657, Fax: 613-757-0818,
stationmanager@chcr.org
www.chcr.org
Ambrose Mullin, Station Manager

***Kingston:* CBBK-FM** (Freq: 92.9)
Owned by: **Canadian Broadcasting Corporation**
Kingston, ON
866-306-4636
www.cbc.ca/radio2
Social Media: www.facebook.com/CBC.Radio2.Official?ref=nf
Other information: Twitter: www.twitter.com/cbcradio2

***Kingston:* CFFX** (Freq: 104.3)
Owned by: **Corus Entertainment Inc.**
170 Queen St., Kingston, ON K7K 1B2
613-544-2340, Fax: 613-544-5508,
www.lite1043.ca
Mike Ferguson, General Manager
Brad Gibb, Program Director

***Kingston:* CFLY-FM** (Freq: 98.3)
Owned by: **Rogers Broadcasting Ltd.**
#10, 993 Princess St., Kingston, ON K7L 1H3
613-544-1380, Fax: 613-546-9751,
flyfm@flyfmkingston.com
flyfmkingston.com
Greg Hinton, Vice President/General Manager

***Kingston:* CFMK-FM** (Freq: 96.3)
Owned by: **Corus Entertainment Inc.**
170 Queen St., Kingston, ON K7K 1B2
613-544-2340, Fax: 613-544-5508,
www.fm96.ca
Mike Ferguson, General Manager
Brad Gibb, Program Director

***Kingston:* CFRC-FM** (Freq: 101.9)
Carruthers Hall, Kingston, ON K7L 3N6
613-533-2121, Fax: 613-533-6049,
cfrc@ams.queensu.ca
www.cfrc.ca
Maureen Plunkett, Station Manager

***Kingston:* CIKR-FM** (Freq: 105.7)
#301, 863 Princess St., Kingston, ON K7L 5N4
613-549-1057, Fax: 613-549-5302,
feedback@krock1057.ca
www.krock1057.ca

***Kingston:* CKVI-FM** (Freq: 91.9)
#119, 235 Frontenac St., Kingston, ON K7L 3S7
613-544-7864, Fax: 613-544-8795,
ckvi@limestone.ca
www.thecave.ca
Max Lienhard, Station Manager

***Kirkland Lake:* CJKL-FM** (Freq: 101.5)
PO Box 430, 5 Kirkland St., Kirkland Lake, ON P2N 3J4
705-567-3366, Fax: 705-567-6101,
cjkl@cjklfm.com
cjklfm.com
Rob Connelly, President

***Kitchener:* CFCA-FM** (Freq: 105.3)
Owned by: **CFCA-FM**
Kitchener, ON

***Kitchener:* CHYM-FM** (Freq: 96.7)
Owned by: **Rogers Broadcasting Ltd.**
305 King St. West, Kitchener, ON N2G 4E4
519-743-2611, Fax: 519-743-7510,
www.chymfm.com

***Kitchener:* CJIQ-FM** (Freq: 88.3)
299 Doon Valley Dr., Kitchener, ON N2G 4M4
519-748-5220, Fax: 519-748-5971,
cjiqinfo@cjiq.fm
www.cjiq.fm
Paul Scott, Manager, Sales & Marketing
Mark Burley, Station Manager

***Kitchener:* CJTW-FM** (Freq: 94.3)
PO Box 1433 C, 207, 659 King St. East, Kitchener, ON N2G 4H6
519-575-9090, Fax: 519-575-9119, 877-741-9430
info@faithfm.org
www.faithfm.org
Dave MacDonald, General Manager

***Leamington:* CHYR-FM** (Freq: 96.7)
Owned by: **Blackburn Radio Inc.**
100 Talbot St. East, Leamington, ON N8H 1L3
519-326-6171, Fax: 519-322-1110,
96.7@chyr.com
www.chyr.com

***Lindsay:* CKLY-FM** (Freq: 91.9)
Owned by: **Rogers Broadcasting Ltd.**
249 Kent St. West, Lindsay, ON K9V 2Z3
705-324-9103, Fax: 705-324-4149,
www.919bobfm.com
Steve Fawcett, General Manager

***Little Current:* CFRM-FM** (Freq: 101.1)
PO Box 871, 10 Campbell St. East, Little Current, ON P0P 1K0
705-368-1419, Fax: 705-368-1080,
radio@manitoulin.net
www.101rocks.com

** For details on this company see listing in Major Broadcasting Companies section; † French language station*

Rick Nelson, Station Manager

London: **CBBL-FM** (Freq: 100.5)
Owned by: **Canadian Broadcasting Corporation**
#4, 208 Piccadilly St., London, ON N6A 1S1
866-306-4636
www.cbc.ca/radio2
Social Media: www.facebook.com/CBC.Radio2.Official?ref=nf
Other information: Twitter: www.twitter.com/cbcradio2

London: **CBCL-FM** (Freq: 93.5)
Owned by: **Canadian Broadcasting Corporation**
#4, 208 Piccadilly St., London, ON N6A 1S1
519-667-1990, 866-306-4636
www.cbc.ca/radio
Social Media: www.facebook.com/radiocbc; www.twitter.com/cbcradio
Other information: TTY: 1-866-220-6045

London: **CFHK-FM** (Freq: 103.1)
Owned by: **Corus Entertainment Inc.**
#222, 380 Wellington Rd., London, ON N6A 5B5
519-931-6000, Fax: 519-679-1967,
www.energy103.ca

London: **CFPL-FM** (Freq: 95.9)
Owned by: **Corus Entertainment Inc.**
#222, 380 Wellington St., London, ON N6A 5B5
519-931-6000, Fax: 519-679-1967,
www.fm96.com
Rick Moss

London: **CHJX-FM** (Freq: 105.9)
Sound of Faith Broadcasting Inc., 100 Fullarton St., London, ON N6A 1K1
519-679-9882, Fax: 519-679-2459,
info@gracefm.ca
www.gracefm.ca
Doug Chaplin, Station Manager

London: **CHRW-FM** (Freq: 94.9)
#250, UCC Bldg., London, ON N6A 3K7
519-661-3601, Fax: 519-661-3372,
chrwgm@uwo.ca
www.chrwradio.com
Grant Stein, Station Manager
Zoltan Haraszthy, Program Director
James McMillan, News & Sports Director

London: **CHST-FM** (Freq: 102.3)
Owned by: **Rogers Broadcasting Ltd.**
1 Communications Rd., London, ON N6J 4Z1
519-690-0102, Fax: 519-686-5942,
www.1023bob.com
Don Mumford, General Manager, don.mumford@chumradio.com
Ann LaRocque, Sales Manager, ann.larocque@chumradio.com
Janice Pearce, Business Manager, janice.pearce@chumradio.com
Montea Sherritt, Traffic Manager, montea.sherritt@chumradio.com

London: **CIQM-FM** (Freq: 97.5)
Owned by: **Standard Radio Office**
743 Wellington Rd. South, London, ON N6C 4R5
519-686-2525, Fax: 519-686-3658,
www.q975.com
Braden Doerr, General Manager

London: **CIXX-FM** (Freq: 106.9)
Fanshawe College, 1460 Oxford St. East, London, ON N5V 1W2
519-453-2810, Fax: 519-452-4152,
www.6xnews.com
Bob Collins, Contact

London: **CJBX-FM** (Freq: 92.7)
Owned by: **Standard Radio Office**
743 Wellington Rd. South, London, ON N6C 4R5
519-685-2525, Fax: 519-686-3658,
bx93@bx93.com
www.bx93.com
Braden Doerr, General Manager

Marathon: **CFNO-FM** (Freq: 93.1; 100.7)
PO Box 1000, 93 Evergreen Dr., Marathon, ON P0T 2E0
807-229-1010, Fax: 807-229-1686,
www.cfno.fm
S. Spencer Bell, President

Midland: **CICZ-FM** (Freq: 104.1)
PO Box 609, 355 Cranston Cres., Midland, ON L4R 4L3
705-526-2268, Fax: 705-526-3060,
www.kicxfm.com

Mississauga: **CFRE-FM**
#115, 3359 Mississauga Rd., Mississauga, ON L5L 1C6
905-820-1640, Fax: 905-569-4714,
www.cfreradio.com

New Liskeard: **CJTT-FM** (Freq: 104.5)
PO Box 1058, 55 Whitewood Ave., New Liskeard, ON P0J 1P0
705-647-7334, Fax: 705-647-8660,
cjtt@cjttfm.com
www.cjttfm.com
Other information: Phone, News & Sports: 705-647-7171; Phone, Studio: 705-647-6565

Niagara Falls: **CFLZ-FM** (Freq: 105.1)
PO Box 710, 4668 St. Clair Ave., Niagara Falls, ON L2E 6X7
905-356-6710, Fax: 905-356-0644,
www.river.fm
Elizabeth Lewis, General Manager

Niagara Falls: **CKEY-FM** (Freq: 101.1)
PO Box 710, 4668 St. Claire Ave., Niagara Falls, ON L2E 6X7
905-356-6710, Fax: 905-356-0696,
www.wild101.com
Dave Universal, Program Director, daveuniv@niagara.com

North Bay: **CHUR-FM** (Freq: 100.5)
Owned by: **Rogers Broadcasting Ltd.**
PO Box 3000, 743 Main St. East, North Bay, ON P1B 8K8
705-479-2000, Fax: 705-474-7761,
www.ezrocknorthbay.com
Andy Wilson, Program Director

North Bay: **CKFX-FM** (Freq: 101.9)
Owned by: **Rogers Broadcasting Ltd.**
743 Main St. East, North Bay, ON P1B 1C2
705-474-2000, Fax: 705-474-7761,
thefox@foxradio.ca
www.foxradio.ca
Mitch Belanger, Program Director
Mike Belanger, Program Director

North Bay: **CRFM-FM** (Freq: 89.9)
Canadore College, PO Box 5001, 100 College Dr., North Bay, ON P1B 8K9
705-474-7600, Fax: 705-474-2384,
info@thepanther.ca
www.ThePanther.ca

Oakville: **CORS-FM**
Sheridan College, 1430 Trafalgar Rd., Oakville, ON L6H 2L1
905-845-9430, Fax: 905-815-4043

Ohsweken: **CKRZ-FM** (Freq: 100.3)
PO Box 189, Ohsweken, ON N0A 1M0
519-445-4140, Fax: 519-445-0177,
ckrzinfo@ckrz.com
www.ckrz.com
Sandra Muse, Station Manager

Orillia: **CICX-FM** (Freq: 105.9)
Owned by: **Rogers Broadcasting Ltd.**
PO Box 550, 7 Progress Dr., Orillia, ON L3V 6K2
705-326-3511, Fax: 705-326-1816,
www.1059jackfm.com

Oshawa: **CJKX-FM** (Freq: 95.9; 89.9)
#207, 1200 Airport Blvd., Oshawa, ON L1J 8P5
905-428-9600, Fax: 905-571-1150,
kx96@kx96.fm
www.kx96.fm
Steve Kassay, Operations Manager

Oshawa: **CKDO-FM** (Freq: 107.7; 1350; 96.0)
#207, 1200 Airport Blvd., Oshawa, ON L1J 8P5
905-571-0949, Fax: 905-571-1150,
bfisher@accel.net
www.kx96.fm
Steve Kassay, Operations Manager

Oshawa: **CKGE-FM** (Freq: 94.9)
#207, 1200 Airport Blvd., Oshawa, ON L1J 8P5
905-571-0949, Fax: 905-579-1150, 866-799-7625
steve@therock.fm
www.therock.fm
Steve Kassav, Operations Manager
Stephen A. Kassay, Vice-President, Operations

Ottawa: **CBO-FM** (Freq: 91.5)
Owned by: **Canadian Broadcasting Corporation**
PO Box 3220 C, 181 Queen St., Ottawa, ON K1Y 1E4
613-288-6000,
www.cbc.ca/ottawa
Laurence Wall, Producer
Tom New, Communications Officer

Ottawa: **CBOQ-FM** (Freq: 103.3)
Owned by: **Canadian Broadcasting Corporation**
Ottawa, ON

Ottawa: **CBOX-FM** (Freq: 102.5)
Owned by: **Canadian Broadcasting Corporation**
PO Box 3220 C, 181 Queen St., Ottawa, ON K1Y 1E4
613-288-6000,
www.radio-canada.ca/regions/ontario

Ottawa: **CHEZ-FM** (Freq: 106.1)
Owned by: **Rogers Broadcasting Ltd.**
2001 Thurston Dr., Ottawa, ON K1G 6C9
613-736-2001, Fax: 613-736-2002,
www.chez106.com

Ottawa: **CHRI-FM** (Freq: 99.1)
#3, 1010 Thomas Spratt Pl., Ottawa, ON K1G 5L5
613-247-1440, Fax: 613-247-7128, 866-924-7436
chri@chri.ca
www.chri.ca
Bill Stevens, General Manager
Robert Du Broy, Director & General Manager

Ottawa: **CHUO-FM** (Freq: 89.1)
#0038, 65 University Pvt., Ottawa, ON K1N 9A5
613-562-5965,
info@chuo.fm
www.chuo.fm
Chris Jack, Interim Station Manager

Ottawa: **CIHT-FM** (Freq: 89.9)
Owned by: **NewCap Inc.**
1500 Merivale Rd., Ottawa, ON K2E 6Z5
613-723-8990, Fax: 613-723-7016,
www.hot899.com

Ottawa: **CISS-FM** (Freq: 105.3)
Owned by: **Rogers Broadcasting Ltd.**
2001 Thurston Dr., Ottawa, ON K1G 6C9
613-736-2001, Fax: 613-736-2002,
www.1053kissfm.com
Danny Kingsbury, Station Manager/Program Director

Ottawa: **CJLL-FM** (Freq: 97.9)
#100, 30 Murray St., Ottawa, ON K1N 5M4
613-244-0979, Fax: 613-244-3858,
chinottawa@chinradio.com
www.chinradio.com
Ed Ylanen, General Manager

Ottawa: **CJMJ-FM** (Freq: 100.3)
Owned by: **Rogers Broadcasting Ltd.**
87 George St., Ottawa, ON K1N 9H7
613-789-2486, Fax: 613-750-0100,
www.majic100.fm
Al Smith, Program Director

Ottawa: **CKBY-FM** (Freq: 101.1)
Owned by: **Rogers Broadcasting Ltd.**
2001 Thurston Dr., Ottawa, ON K1G 6C9
613-736-2001, Fax: 613-736-2002,
www.y101.fm
Al Campagnola, General Manager, acampagn@rci.rogers.com

Ottawa: **CKCU-FM** (Freq: 93.1)
#517, University Centre, Carleton University, 1125 Colonel By Dr., Ottawa, ON K1S 5B6
613-520-2898,
info@ckcufm.com
www.ckcufm.com
Barry Rueger, Station Manager

Ottawa: **CKDJ-FM** (Freq: 107.9)
Algonquin College, 1385 Woodroffe Ave., Ottawa, ON K2G 1V8
613-727-4723, Fax: 613-727-7689,
crockfd@algonquincollege.com
www.ckdj.net
Kyra Kratzmann, Station Manager

** For details on this company see listing in Major Broadcasting Companies section; † French language station*

***Ottawa:* CKKL-FM** (Freq: 93.9)
Owned by: **Rogers Broadcasting Ltd.**
87 George St., Ottawa, ON K1N 9H7
613-789-2486, Fax: 613-739-5626,
www.939bobfm.com
Al Smith, Program Director

***Ottawa:* CKQB-FM** (Freq: 106.9)
Owned by: **Standard Radio Office**
1504 Merivale Rd., Ottawa, ON K2E 6Z5
613-225-1069, Fax: 613-226-3381, 800-754-1069
bearinfo@thebear.fm
www.thebear.fm
Gord Taylor, Program Director
Kath Thompson, Music, Director
Scott Broderick, General Sales Manager
Rebecca Crow, Promotion Director
Eric Stafford, General Manager

***Owen Sound:* CIXK-FM** (Freq: 106.5)
Owned by: **Bayshore Broadcasting Corporation**
PO Box 280, 270 - 9 St. East, Owen Sound, ON N4K 5P5
519-376-2030, Fax: 519-371-4242,
bayshore@radioowensound.com
www.radioowensound.com
Ross Kentner, General Manager, rkentner@bayshorebroadcasting.ca
Kevin Brown, General Sales Manager, kbrown@bayshorebroadcasting.ca
Rob Brignell, Director, Marketing & Business Development, rbrignell@bayshorebroadcasting.ca

***Owen Sound:* CKYC-FM** (Freq: 93.7)
Owned by: **Bayshore Broadcasting Corporation**
PO Box 280, 270 - 9 St. East, Owen Sound, ON N4K 5P5
519-376-2030, Fax: 519-371-4242,
bayshore@radioowensound.com
www.radioowensound.com
Ross Kentner, General Manager, rkentner@bayshorebroadcasting.ca
Kevin Brown, General Sales Manager, kbrown@bayshorebroadcasting.ca
Rob Brignell, Director, Marketing & Development, rbrignell@bayshorebroadcasting.ca

***Parry Sound:* CKLP-FM** (Freq: 103.3)
#301, 60 James St., Parry Sound, ON P2A 1T5
705-746-2163, Fax: 705-746-4292,
moose1033@hbgradio.com
www.hbgradio.com
Kimberley Ward-Grossman, Vice-President
Dave Keeble, Operations Manager
Christopher Grossman, President

***Pembroke:* CHVR-FM** (Freq: 96.7)
Owned by: **Standard Radio Office**
595 Pembroke St. East, Pembroke, ON K8A 3L7
613-735-9670, Fax: 613-735-7748,
star96@sri.ca
www.star96.ca
Al Kennedy

†*Penetanguishene:* CFRH-FM (Freq: 88.1)
CP 5099, 63, rue Main, Penetanguishene, ON L9M 2G3
705-549-3116, Fax: 705-549-6463,
cfrh@lacle.ca
www.cfrh.ca
Peter Hominuk, General Manager

***Peterborough:* CFFF-FM** (Freq: 92.7)
Trent University, 715 George St. North, Peterborough, ON K9H 3T2
705-741-4011, Fax: 705—,
trentradio@trentradio.ca
www.trentradio.ca

***Peterborough:* CKQM-FM** (Freq: 105.1)
Country 105, PO Box 177, 59 George St. North, Peterborough, ON K9J 6Y8
705-742-8844, Fax: 705-742-1417,
country@chumradio.com
www.country105.fm
Steve Fawcett, General Manager
Brian Young, Program Director

***Peterborough:* CKWF-FM** (Freq: 101.5)
Owned by: **Corus Entertainment Inc.**
159 King St., Peterborough, ON K9J 2R8
705-748-6101, Fax: 705-742-7708,
info@thewolf.ca
www.thewolf.ca
Kathleen McNair, General Manager

***Port Elgin:* CFPS-FM** (Freq: 97.9)
Owned by: **Bayshore Broadcasting Corporation**
382 Goderich St., Port Elgin, ON N0H 2C1
519-832-9800, Fax: 519-832-9808, 877-652-9800
bayshore@radioowensound.com
www.radioowensound.com
Lois Reid, Business, Manager
Rob Brignell, Station Manager
Deb Shaw, Sales Manager
Don Vail, Promotion Director

***Sarnia:* CBEG-FM** (Freq: 90.3)
Owned by: **Canadian Broadcasting Corporation**
Sarnia, ON
866-306-4636
www.cbc.ca/windsor; www.cbc.ca/radio
Social Media: www.facebook.com/radiocbc;
www.twitter.com/cbcradio
Other information: TTY: 1-866-220-6045
Sandra Porteous, Managing Editor, Radio & Television, 519-255-3563
David Daigneault, Executive Producer, Radio & Television, 519-255-3410

***Sarnia:* CFGX-FM** (Freq: 99.9)
Owned by: **Blackburn Radio Inc.**
1415 London Rd., Sarnia, ON N7S 1P6
519-542-5500, Fax: 519-542-1520,
www.foxfm.com

***Sarnia:* CHKS-FM** (Freq: 106.3)
Owned by: **Blackburn Radio Inc.**
1415 London Rd., Sarnia, ON N7S 1P6
519-542-5500, Fax: 519-542-1520,
rock@k106fm.com
www.k106fm.com

***Sault Ste Marie:* CHAS-FM** (Freq: 100.5)
Owned by: **Rogers Broadcasting Ltd.**
642 Great Northern Rd., Sault Ste Marie, ON P6B 4Z9
705-759-9200, Fax: 705-946-3575,
www.ezrocksoo.com
Scott Sexsmith, General Manager, scott.sexsmith@ssmradio.rogers.com

***Sault Ste Marie:* CJQM-FM** (Freq: 104.3)
Owned by: **Rogers Broadcasting Ltd.**
642 Great Northern Rd., Sault Ste Marie, ON P6B 4Z9
705-759-9200, Fax: 705-946-3575,
www.qcountry.ca
Scott Sexsmith, General Manager, scott.sexsmith@ssmradio.rogers.com

***Simcoe:* CHCD-FM** (Freq: 98.9)
PO Box 98, 55 Park Rd., Simcoe, ON N3Y 4K8
519-426-7700, Fax: 519-426-8574,
www.cd989.com
Jim MacLeod, President

***Sioux Lookout:* CKWT-FM** (Freq: 89.1)
PO Box 1180, 16 - 5 Ave., Sioux Lookout, ON P8T 1B7
807-737-2951, Fax: 807-737-3224,
www.wrn.wawatay.on.ca

***Smiths Falls:* CJET-FM** (Freq: 92.3)
Owned by: **Rogers Broadcasting Ltd.**
PO Box 630, Smiths Falls, ON K7A 4T4
613-283-4630, Fax: 613-283-7243,
www.923jackfm.com

***St Catharines:* CFBU-FM** (Freq: 103.7)
500 Glenridge Ave., St Catharines, ON L2S 3A1
905-688-2644,
pd@cfbu.ca
www.cfbu.ca
Russell Gragg, Station Manager

***St Catharines:* CHRE-FM** (Freq: 105.7)
Owned by: **Standard Radio Office**
PO Box 610, 12 Yates St., St Catharines, ON L2R 6Z4
905-688-1057, Fax: 905-684-4800,
sgibbons@sri.ca
www.1057ezrock.com
Madelyn Hamilton, General Manager

***St Catharines:* CHTZ-FM** (Freq: 97.7)
Owned by: **Standard Radio Office**
PO Box 977, 12 Yates St., St Catharines, ON L2R 6Z4
905-684-0977, Fax: 905-684-4800,
www.htzfm.com
Bruce Gilbert, Program Director, pd@htzfm.com

***Stratford:* CHGK-FM** (Freq: 107.7)
376 Romeo St. South, Stratford, ON N5A 4T9
519-271-2450, Fax: 519-271-3102,
info@1077mixfm.com
www.1077mixfm.com
Steve Rae, General Manager

***Sturgeon Falls:* CFSF-FM** (Freq: 99.3)
#7, 12006 Hwy. 17, Sturgeon Falls, ON P2B 3K8
705-753-6776, Fax: 705-753-6776,
joco@bellnet.ca
www.joco.ca
Joseph Cormier, General Manager

***Sudbury:* CBBS-FM** (Freq: 90.1)
Owned by: **Canadian Broadcasting Corporation**
15 MacKenzie St., Sudbury, ON P3C 4Y1
705-688-3200, Fax: 705-688-3220, 866-306-4636
www.cbc.ca/sudbury; www.cbc.ca/radio2
Social Media: www.facebook.com/CBC.Radio2.Official?ref=nf
Other information: Twitter: www.twitter.com/cbcradio2
Fiona Christensen, Managing Editor, Sudbury, 705-688-3232

†*Sudbury:* CBBX-FM (Freq: 90.9)
Owned by: **Canadian Broadcasting Corporation**
15 Mackenzie St., Sudbury, ON P3C 4Y1
705-688-3200, 866-306-4636
www.cbc.ca/sudbury; www.radio-canada.ca
Fiona Christensen, Managing Editor, Sudbury, 705-688-3232

***Sudbury:* CBCS-FM** (Freq: 99.9)
Owned by: **Canadian Broadcasting Corporation**
15 MacKenzie St., Sudbury, ON P3C 4Y1
705-688-3200, 866-306-4636
www.cbc.ca/sudbury; www.cbc.ca/radio
Social Media: www.facebook.com/radiocbc;
www.twitter.com/cbcradio
Other information: Phone, Sudbury News: 705-688-3240;
Toll-Free: 1-800-461-1138
Fiona Christensen, Managing Editor, 705-688-3232

†*Sudbury:* CBON-FM (Freq: 98.1)
Owned by: **Canadian Broadcasting Corporation**
15 MacKenzie St., Sudbury, ON P3C 4Y1
705-688-3200,
www.radio-canada.ca/regions/ontario

***Sudbury:* CHNO-FM** (Freq: 103.9)
493B Barrydowne Rd., Sudbury, ON P3A 3T4
705-560-8323, Fax: 705-560-7765,
z103@z103fm.com
www.z103fm.com
Christopher Grossman

†*Sudbury:* CHYC-FM (Freq: 98.9)
493B Barrydowne Rd., Sudbury, ON P3A 3T4
705-560-8323, Fax: 705-560-2492,
chycfm@chycfm.com
www.chycfm.com
Christopher Grossman

***Sudbury:* CJMX-FM** (Freq: 105.3)
Owned by: **Rogers Broadcasting Ltd.**
880 Lasalle Blvd., Sudbury, ON P3A 1X5
705-566-4480, Fax: 705-560-7232,
www.ezrocksudbury.com
Gary Miles, CEO
Rick Doughty, General Manager

***Sudbury:* CJRQ-FM** (Freq: 92.7)
Owned by: **Rogers Broadcasting Ltd.**
880 Lasalle Blvd., Sudbury, ON P3A 1X5
705-566-4480, Fax: 705-560-7232,
www.q92rocks.com
Gary Miles, President
Rick Doughty, General Manager

***Sudbury:* CJTK-FM** (Freq: 95.5)
417 Notre Dame Ave., Sudbury, ON P3C 5K6

** For details on this company see listing in Major Broadcasting Companies section; † French language station*

705-674-2585, Fax: 705-688-1081,
mail@cjtk.com
www.cjtk.com

Curtis L. Belcher, General Manager

***Sudbury:* CKLU-FM** (Freq: 96.7)
935 Ramsey Rd., Sudbury, ON P3E 2C6
705-673-6538, Fax: 705-675-4878,
info@cklu.ca
www.cklu.ca

Sheila Bianconi, News Director
Carl Jorgensen, Operations Director
Tara Lévesque, Music Director

***Thunder Bay:* CBQ-FM** (Freq: 101.7)
Owned by: **Canadian Broadcasting Corporation**
213 Miles St. East, Thunder Bay, ON P7C 1J5
807-625-5000, Fax: 807-625-5035,
www.cbc.ca/thunderbay

***Thunder Bay:* CBQT-FM** (Freq: 88.3)
Owned by: **Canadian Broadcasting Corporation**
213 Miles St. East, Thunder Bay, ON P7C 1J5
807-625-5000, Fax: 807-625-5035,
www.cbc.ca/thunderbay/

***Thunder Bay:* CBQX-FM** (Freq: 98.7)
Owned by: **Canadian Broadcasting Corporation**
213 Miles St. East, Thunder Bay, ON P7C 1J5
807-625-5002, Fax: 807-625-5035,
www.cbc.radio-canada.ca

Tom Grand, General Manager

***Thunder Bay:* CFQK-FM** (Freq: 103.5; 104.5)
87 North Hill St., Thunder Bay, ON P7A 5V6
807-346-2600, Fax: 807-345-9923,
www.hotfm.ca

***Thunder Bay:* CJOA-FM** (Freq: 95.1)
#42, 63 Carrie St., Thunder Bay, ON
807-344-9525, Fax: 807-344-9525,
info@cjoa.org
www.cjoa.org

Bonnie Gauthier, Music Director

***Thunder Bay:* CJSD-FM** (Freq: 94.3)
87 Hill St. North, Thunder Bay, ON P7A 5V6
807-346-2600, Fax: 807-345-9923,
rock@rock94.com
www.rock94.com

Brad Hilgers, Program Director

***Thunder Bay:* CJUK-FM** (Freq: 99.9)
Owned by: **NewCap Inc.**
#200, 180 Park Ave., Thunder Bay, ON P7B 6J4
807-345-9999, Fax: 807-346-5000,
admin@magic999.fm
www.magic999.fm

Dennis Landriault, General Manager

***Thunder Bay:* CKTG-FM** (Freq: 105.3)
Owned by: **NewCap Inc.**
#200, 180 Park Ave., Thunder Bay, ON P7B 6J4
807-344-2000, Fax: 807-346-5000,
www.thegiant.fm

Darlene Palmer, General Manager

***Tillsonburg:* CKOT-FM** (Freq: 101.3)
PO Box 10, 77 Broadway St., Tillsonburg, ON N4G 4H3
519-842-4281, Fax: 519-842-4284,
jlamers@easy101.com

John Lamars, President & General Manager

***Timmins:* CHIM-FM** (Freq: 102.3)
226 Delnite Rd., Timmins, ON P4N 7C2
705-264-2150,
chimfm@vianet.ca
www.chimfm.com

Roger de Brabant

***Timmins:* CHMT-FM** (Freq: 93.1)
49 Cedar St. South, Timmins, ON P4N 2G5
705-267-6070, Fax: 705-267-6095,
moose931@hbgradio.com
www.moosefm.com

, General Manager, blecour@moosefm.com

***Timmins:* CHOH-FM** (Freq: 92.9)
#103, 32 Mountjoy St. North, Timmins, ON P4N 4V6
705-267-6070, Fax: 705-267-6095,
moose931@hbgradio.com
www.moosefm.com

Christopher Grossman, President

***Timmins:* CHYK-FM** (Freq: 104.1)
#103, 32 Mountjoy St. North, Timmins, ON P4N 4V6
705-267-6070, Fax: 705-267-6095,
chykfm@hbgroup.com
www.chykfm.com

***Timmins:* CJQQ-FM** (Freq: 92.1)
Owned by: **Rogers Broadcasting Ltd.**
260 - 2nd Ave., Timmins, ON P4N 8A4
705-264-2351, Fax: 705-264-2984,
www.q92timmins.com

***Timmins:* CKGB-FM** (Freq: 99.3)
Owned by: **Rogers Broadcasting Ltd.**
260 - 2nd Ave., Timmins, ON P4N 8A4
705-264-2351, Fax: 705-264-2984,
www.ezrocktimmins.com

Art Pultz, Operations Manager

***Toronto:* CBLA-FM** (Freq: 99.1)
Owned by: **Canadian Broadcasting Corporation**
PO Box 500, 205 Wellington St. West, Toronto, ON M5W 1E6
416-205-3311, Fax: 416-205-6336, 866-306-4636
www.cbc.ca/toronto; www.cbc.ca/radio
Social Media: www.facebook.com/radiocbc;
www.twitter.com/cbcradio
Other information: Phone, Radio Newsroom: 416-205-5808;
TTY: 1-866-220-6045

Susan Marjetti, Managing Director, 416-205-5791
Don Ioi, Team Manager, Toronto Sales, 416-205-2732

***Toronto:* CBL-FM** (Freq: 94.1)
Owned by: **Canadian Broadcasting Corporation**
PO Box 500 A, 205 Wellington St. West, Toronto, ON M5W 3G7
416-205-3311, 866-306-4636
www.cbc.ca/toronto; www.cbc.ca/radio2
Social Media: www.facebook.com/cbcsask;
www.twitter.com/cbcradio2

Susan Marjetti, Managing Director, 416-205-5791
Don Ioi, Team Manager, Toronto Sales

***Toronto:* CFIE-FM** (Freq: 106.5)
#323, 366 Adelaide St. East, Toronto, ON M5A 3X9
416-703-1287, Fax: 416-703-4328,
www.aboriginalradio.com

***Toronto:* CFMX-FM** (Freq: 96.3; 103.1)
#205, 550 Queen St. East, Toronto, ON M5A 1V2
416-367-5353, Fax: 416-367-1742,
info@classical963fm.com
www.classical963fm.com

John van Driel, General Manager/CEO

***Toronto:* CFNY-FM** (Freq: 102.1)
Owned by: **Corus Entertainment Inc.**
#1600, 1 Dundas St. West, Toronto, ON M5G 1Z3
416-408-3343, Fax: 416-847-3333,
info@edge.ca
www.edge.ca

***Toronto:* CFXJ-FM** (Freq: 93.5)
#400, 211 Yonge St., Toronto, ON M5B 1M4
416-214-5000, Fax: 416-214-0660,
info@flow935.com
www.flow935.com

***Toronto:* CHFI-FM** (Freq: 98.1)
Owned by: **Rogers Broadcasting Ltd.**
777 Jarvis St., Toronto, ON M4Y 3B7
416-935-8298, Fax: 416-935-8288,
www.chfi.com

Chuck McCoy, Toronto Market Manager
Paul Fisher, Vice-President & General Manager

***Toronto:* CHIN-FM** (Freq: 100.7)
622 College St., Toronto, ON M6G 1B6
416-531-9991, Fax: 416-531-5274,
info@chinradio.com
www.chinradio.com

Leonard Lombardi, President

***Toronto:* CHKT-FM** (Freq: 88.9)
Owned by: **CHKT**
Toronto, ON

***Toronto:* CHRY-FM** (Freq: 105.5)
York University, Student Centre, #413, 4700 Keele St., Toronto, ON M3J 1P3
416-736-5293, Fax: 416-650-8052,
chry@yorku.ca
www.yorku.ca/chry

***Toronto:* CHUM-FM** (Freq: 104.5)
Owned by: **Rogers Broadcasting Ltd.**
250 Richmond St. West, Toronto, ON M5V 1W4
416-925-6666, Fax: 416-926-4026,
www.chumfm.com

David Corey, Program Director/Vice President, Programming/CTVglobmedia Inc., CHUM Radio Div
Chris Gordon, President, CTVglobemedia Inc., CHUM Radio Division

***Toronto:* CIDC-FM** (Freq: 103.5)
5302 Dundas St. West, Toronto, ON M9B 1B2
416-213-1035, Fax: 416-233-8617,
info@z1035.com
www.z1035.com

***Toronto:* CILQ-FM** (Freq: 107.1)
Owned by: **Corus Entertainment Inc.**
#1600, 1 Dundas St. West, Toronto, ON M5G 1Z3
416-221-0107, Fax: 416-847-3300,
www.q107.com

J. Hayes, President

***Toronto:* CIRV-FM** (Freq: 88.9)
1087 Dundas St. West, Toronto, ON M6J 1W9
416-537-1088, Fax: 416-537-2463,
info@cirvfm.com
www.cirvfm.com

Alberto Elmir, Station Manager

***Toronto:* CIUT-FM** (Freq: 89.5)
91 St. George St., Toronto, ON M5S 2E8
416-978-0909, Fax: 416-946-7004,
www.ciut.fm

***Toronto:* CJAQ-FM** (Freq: 92.5)
Owned by: **Rogers Broadcasting Ltd.**
777 Jarvis St., Toronto, ON M4Y 3B7
416-935-8392, Fax: 416-935-8410,
www.925jackfm.com

Steve Kennedy, General Manager

***Toronto:* CJBC-FM** (Freq: 90.3)
Owned by: **Canadian Broadcasting Corporation**
PO Box 500 A, Toronto, ON M5W 1E6
416-205-3311,
www.radio-canada.ca/regions/ontario

***Toronto:* CJEZ-FM** (Freq: 97.3)
Owned by: **Standard Radio Office**
2 St. Clair Ave. West, 2nd Fl., Toronto, ON M4V 1L6
416-482-0973, Fax: 416-486-5696,
www.ezrock.com

Mario Cecchini, Executive Vice-President

***Toronto:* CJRT-FM** (Freq: 91.1)
#100, 4 Pardee Ave., Toronto, ON M6K 3H5
416-595-0404, Fax: 416-595-9413, 888-595-0404
info@jazz.fm
www.jazz.fm

Bernard Webber, Chair
Ross Porter, President & CEO

***Toronto:* CKDX-FM** (Freq: 88.5)
5302 Dundas St. West, Toronto, ON M9B 1B2
416-213-1035, Fax: 416-233-8617,
info@foxy885.com
www.foxy885.com

***Toronto:* CKHC-FM** (Freq: 96.9)
205 Humber College Blvd., Toronto, ON M9W 5L7
416-675-6622, Fax: 416-675-9730,
radiohumber@humber.ca
radio.humberc.on.ca

***Toronto:* CKLN-FM** (Freq: 88.1)
55 Gould St., Toronto, ON M5B 1E9
416-979-5251, Fax: 416-595-0226,
ckln@ckln.fm
www.ckln.fm

David Barnard, Chair

***Toronto:* CSCR-FM** (Freq: 90.3)
1265 Military Trail, Toronto, ON M1C 1A4

** For details on this company see listing in Major Broadcasting Companies section; † French language station*

416-287-7051,
info@fustionradio.ca
www.fusionradio.ca

Liam Michell, Station Manager

***Toronto:* Virgin Radio 999 FM** (Freq: 99.9)
2 St. Clair Ave. West, Toronto, ON M4V 1L6
416-922-9999, Fax: 416-872-8683,
info@virginradio.com
www.virginradio999.com

***Trenton:* CJTN-FM** (Freq: 107.1)
31 Quinte St., Trenton, ON K8V 3S7
613-771-1071,
www.lite107.ca

***Waterloo:* CFCA-FM** (Freq: 105.3)
Owned by: **Rogers Broadcasting Ltd.**
#207, 255 King St. North, Waterloo, ON N2J 4V2
519-884-4470, Fax: 519-884-6482,
www.koolfm.com

Paul Cugliari, Vice President/General Manager

***Waterloo:* CIKZ-FM** (Freq: 106.7)
#C2, 490 Dutton Dr., Waterloo, ON N2L 6H7
519-746-3331, Fax: 519-746-3364,
www.kicx106.com

***Waterloo:* CKMS-FM** (Freq: 100.3)
University of Waterloo, Bauer Warehouse, 200 University Ave. West, Waterloo, ON N2L 3G1
519-886-2567, Fax: 519-884-3530,
ckmsfm@web.ca
ckmsfm.uwaterloo.ca

Heather Majaury, Station Manager

***Waterloo:* CKWR-FM** (Freq: 98.5)
375 University Ave. East, Waterloo, ON N2K 3M7
519-886-9870, Fax: 519-886-0090,
general@ckwr.com
www.ckwr.com

***Wawa:* CJWA-FM** (Freq: 107.1)
PO Box 1447, 57 Broadway Ave., Wawa, ON P0S 1K0
705-856-4555, Fax: 705-856-1520

***Welland:* CHOW-FM** (Freq: 91.7)
860 Forks Rd. West, Welland, ON L3B 5R6
905-732-4433, Fax: 905-732-4780, 877-342-5917
country@spirit917fm.com

Pat St John, President

***Welland:* CRNC-FM** (Freq: 90.1)
300 Woodlawn Rd., Welland, ON L3C 7L3
905-735-2211, Fax: 905-736-6002,
www.broadcasting.niagarac.on.ca

***Wiarton:* CHFN-FM** (Freq: 100.1)
RR#5, Wiarton, ON N0H 2T0
519-534-1003, Fax: 519-534-0063,
chfn@bellnet.ca
www.georgeloney.com

Jessica Nadjiwon, Station Manager

***Windsor:* CBE-FM** (Freq: 89.9)
Owned by: **Canadian Broadcasting Corporation**
825 Riverside Dr. West, Windsor, ON N9A 5K9
519-255-3411, 866-306-4636
www.cbc.ca/windsor; www.cbc.ca/radio2
Social Media: www.facebook.com/cbcsask;
www.twitter.com/cbcradio2
Other information: Phone, Newsroom: 519-255-3456

Sandra Porteous, Managing Editor, Radio & Television, 519-255-3563
David Daigneault, Executive Producer, Radio & Television, 519-255-3410
Nancy Lauzon, Manager, Windsor Accounts, 519-255-3510

***Windsor:* CIDR-FM** (Freq: 93.9)
Owned by: **Rogers Broadcasting Ltd.**
1640 Ouellette Ave., Windsor, ON N8X 1L1
519-258-8888, Fax: 519-258-0182,
www.939theriverradio.com

Eric Proksch, Vice President/General Manager

***Windsor:* CIMX-FM** (Freq: 88.7)
Owned by: **Rogers Broadcasting Ltd.**
1640 Ouellette Ave., Windsor, ON N8X 1L1
519-258-8888, Fax: 519-258-0182,
www.89xradio.com
Social Media: www.facebook.com/89XFANS

Eric Proksch, Vice President/General Manager

***Windsor:* CJAM-FM** (Freq: 91.5)
401 Sunset Ave., Windsor, ON N9B 3P4
519-971-3606, Fax: 519-971-3605,
statcjam@uwindsor.ca
www.cjam.ca

Christien Gagnier

***Wingham:* CKNX-FM** (Freq: 101.7)
Owned by: **Blackburn Radio Inc.**
215 Carling Terrace, Wingham, ON N0G 2W0
519-357-1310, Fax: 519-357-1897,
info@1017theone.ca
www.1017theone.ca

***Woodstock:* CJFH-FM** (Freq: 94.3)
535 Mill St., Woodstock, ON N4S 7V6
519-539-2304, Fax: 519-539-2100,
info@hopefm.ca
www.hopefm.ca

Gary Hill, General Manager

***Woodstock:* CKDK-FM** (Freq: 103.9)
Owned by: **Corus Entertainment Inc.**
290 Dundas St., Woodstock, ON N4S 1B7
519-539-1040, Fax: 519-539-7479,
www.thehawk.ca

Dean Sinclair, General Manager

Prince Edward Island

***Charlottetown:* CBCT-FM** (Freq: 96.1)
Owned by: **Canadian Broadcasting Corporation**
PO Box 2230, 430 University Ave., Charlottetown, PE C1A 8B9
902-629-6400, Fax: 902-629-6518, 866-306-4636
www.cbc.ca/pei; www.cbc.ca/radio
Social Media: www.facebook.com/radiocbc;
www.twitter.com/cbcradio
Other information: Phone, News: 902-629-6402; TTY: 1-866-220-6045

Andrew Cochran, Managing Director, Maritimes
Donna Allen, Executive Producer, Prince Edward Island News
Janet Irwin, Senior Regional Manager, News & Current Affairs
Lenny Jackson, Station Manager, Prince Edward Island
Nadine Antle, Regional Manager, Partnerships, Communications, Brand, & Promot, 506-451-4054
John Channing, Manager, Sales
Heather McGrath, Senior Officer, Communications, 902-629-6416

***Charlottetown:* CHLQ-FM** (Freq: 93.1)
Owned by: **Maritime Broadcasting System**
5 Prince St., Charlottetown, PE C1A 4P4
902-892-1066, Fax: 902-566-1338,
requests@magic93.pe.ca
www.magic93.pe.ca

***Charlottetown:* CHTN-FM** (Freq: 100.3)
Owned by: **NewCap Inc.**
90 University Ave., Charlottetown, PE C1A 4K9
902-569-1003, Fax: 902-569-8693,
www.ocean1003.com

***Summerside:* CJRW-FM** (Freq: 102.1)
Owned by: **Maritime Broadcasting System**
763 Water St. East, Summerside, PE C1N 4J3
902-436-2201, Fax: 902-436-8573,
c102@c102.com
www.c102.com

Paul M. Schurman

Québec

†*Alma:* CKYK-FM (Freq: 95.7)
#200, 460, Sacré-Coeur ouest, Alma, QC G8B 1L9
418-662-6888,
www.kykfm.com

Marc-André Levesque, Président

†*Amqui:* CFVM-FM (Freq: 99.9)
Owned by: **Astral Media Inc.**
111, rue de l'Hopital, Amqui, QC G5J 2K1
418-629-2025, Fax: 418-629-2599,
nouvelle999@boomfm.astral.com
www.boomfm.com

†*Asbestos:* CJAN-FM (Freq: 99.3)
#301, 185, rue du Roi, Asbestos, QC J1T 1S4
819-879-5439, Fax: 819-879-7922,
info@fm993.ca
fm993.ca

***Baie-Comeau:* CBMI-FM** (Freq: 93.7)
Owned by: **Canadian Broadcasting Corporation**
Baie-Comeau, QC
866-306-4636
www.cbc.ca/montreal; www.cbc.ca/radio
Social Media: www.facebook.com/radiocbc;
www.twitter.com/cbcradio
Other information: TTY: 1-866-220-6045

†*Baie-Comeau:* CBSI-FM-24 (Freq: 106.1)
Owned by: **Canadian Broadcasting Corporation**
Baie-Comeau, QC
866-954-1341
auditoire.quebec@radio-canada.ca
www.radio-canada.ca/regions/quebec

***Baie-Comeau:* CHLC-FM** (Freq: 97.1)
907, rue de Puyjalon, Baie-Comeau, QC G5C 1N3
418-589-3771, Fax: 418-589-9086,
programmes971-1005@globetrotter.net
www.chlc.com

Georges Daviault, Directeur Général

***Baie-Saint-Paul:* CHOX-1** (Freq: 94.1)
Owned by: **CHOX-FM**
Baie-Saint-Paul, QC

†*Cap-aux-Meules:* CFIM-FM (Freq: 92.7)
CP 8192, Cap-aux-Meules, QC G4T 1R3
418-986-5233, Fax: 418-986-5319,
www.cfim.ca

Gisele Deraspe, Directrice générale

†*Carleton:* CIEU-FM (Freq: 94.9; 106.1)
1645, boul Perron est, Carleton, QC G0C 1J0
418-364-7094, Fax: 418-364-3150,
cieufm@cieufm.com
www.cieufm.com

***Charlesbourg:* CIMI-FM** (Freq: 103.7)
#103, 4500, boul Henri-Bourassa, Charlesbourg, QC G1H 3A5
418-624-0700, Fax: 418-623-2538,
www.cimifm.com

***Châteauguay:* CHAI-FM** (Freq: 101.9)
25, boul St-Francis, Châteauguay, QC J6J 1Y2
450-698-3131, Fax: 450-698-3339,
chai@videotron.ca
chaifm.iquebec.com

Sylvain Poirier

†*Chicoutimi:* CBJ-FM (Freq: 93.7FM)
Owned by: **Canadian Broadcasting Corporation**
500, rue des Sagueneens, Chicoutimi, QC G7H 6N4
418-696-6600, Fax: 418-696-6689,
www.radio-canada.ca/regions/saguenay-lac

†*Chicoutimi:* CBJX-FM
Owned by: **Canadian Broadcasting Corporation**
500, rue des Saguenéens, Chicoutimi, QC G7H 6N4
418-696-6600, Fax: 418-696-6689,
www.radio-canada.ca/regions/saguenay-lac

***Chicoutimi:* CFIX-FM** (Freq: 96.9)
Owned by: **Astral Media Inc.**
267, rue Racine est, Chicoutimi, QC G7H 5K3
418-543-9797, Fax: 418-543-7968,
www.rockdetente.com

†*Chicoutimi:* CJAB-FM (Freq: 94.5)
Owned by: **Astral Media Inc.**
CP 1506, 267, rue Racine est, Chicoutimi, QC G7H 5K3
418-545-9450, Fax: 418-543-7968,
www.radioenergie.com

Richard Turcotte

†*Dégelis:* CFVD-FM (Freq: 95.5)
654, 6e rue est, Dégelis, QC G5T 1Y1
418-853-3370, Fax: 418-853-3321,
CFVD@FM95.ca

Gilles Caron

** For details on this company see listing in Major Broadcasting Companies section; † French language station*

†*Dolbeau-Mistassini:* CHVD-FM (Freq: 100.3)
Owned by: **Groupe Radio Antenne 6**
1975, boul Wallberg, Dolbeau-Mistassini, QC G8L 1J5
418-276-3333, Fax: 418-276-6755,
chvd@antenne6.com
Marc-André Levesque, Président

***Donnacona:* CKNU-FM** (Freq: 100.9)
Owned by: **Radio Nord Communications Inc.**
274, rue Notre-Dame, Donnacona, QC G6M 1G7
418-285-2568, Fax: 418-263-0286,
www.tagradio.fm

†*Drummondville:* CHRD-FM (Freq: 105.3)
Owned by: **Astral Media Inc.**
2070, St-Georges, Drummondville, QC J2C 5G6
819-475-1480, Fax: 819-747-6610,
receptionchrd@boomfm.com
www.boomfm.com
Joël Rioux, Directeur général

†*Drummondville:* CJDM-FM (Freq: 92.1)
Owned by: **Astral Media Inc.**
2070 rue St-Georges, Drummondville, QC J2C 5G6
819-474-1892, Fax: 819-474-6610,
nouvelles@cjdm.fm
www.radioenergie.com
Pierre Gaudreau

***Fermont:* CBMR-FM** (Freq: 105.1)
Owned by: **Canadian Broadcasting Corporation**
Fermont, QC
866-306-4636
www.cbc.ca/montreal; www.cbc.ca/radio
Social Media: www.facebook.com/radiocbc;
www.twitter.com/cbcradio
Other information: TTY: 1-866-220-6045

†*Fermont:* CFMF-FM (Freq: 103.1)
CP 280, 20, Place Daviault, Fermont, QC G0G 1J0
418-287-5147, Fax: 418-287-5776,
administration@diffusionfermont.ca

†*Fort-Coulonge:* CHIP-FM (Freq: 101.7)
CP 820, 138, rue Principale, Fort-Coulonge, QC J0X 1V0
819-683-3155, Fax: 819-683-3211, 888-775-3155
radiopontiac@chipfm.com
www.chipfm.com
Frank Doyle

***Gaspé:* CJRE-FM** (Freq: 97.9)
162, rue Jacques Cartier, Gaspé, QC G4X 1M9
418-368-3511, Fax: 418-368-1663, 866-360-3511
accueil@radiogaspesie.ca
www.radiogaspesie.ca
Jacques Chartier, General Manager

†*Gaspé:* CJRG-FM (Freq: 94.5)
162, rue Jacques Cartier, Gaspé, QC G4X 1M9
418-368-3511, Fax: 418-368-1663, 866-360-3511
accueil@radiogaspesie.ca
www.radiogaspesie.ca

†*Gatineau:* CHLX-FM (Freq: 97.1)
Owned by: **Radio Nord Communications Inc.**
171A, rue Jean-Proulx, Gatineau, QC J8Z 1W5
819-770-9710, Fax: 819-770-9740,
monchoix@radionord.com
www.radionord.com

†*Gatineau:* CIMF-FM (Freq: 94.9)
Owned by: **Astral Media Inc.**
15, rue Taschereau, Gatineau, QC J8Y 2V6
819-770-2463, Fax: 819-770-9338,
www.rockdetente.com

***Harrington Harbour:* CFTH-FM**
PO Box 88, Harrington Harbour, QC G0G 1N0
418-795-3344, Fax: 418-795-3200,
cfthh1@globetrotter.net
Kate Nadeau, Director
Nancy Bobbitt, Animator
Monica Anderson, Animator
Lois Jones, Secretary

***Harrington Harbour:* CFTH-FM-2**
PO Box 88, Harrington Harbour, QC G0G 1N0
418-795-3349, Fax: 418-795-3200,
cfthhl@globetrotter.net
Kate Nadeau, Director
Monica Anderson, Animator, 418-795-3344
Nancy Anderson, Animator, 418-795-3344, cfthonair@live.ca
Lois Jones, Animator & Secretary, 418-795-3344

†*Havre-Saint-Pierre:* CBSI-FM-7 (Freq: 92.5)
Owned by: **Canadian Broadcasting Corporation**
Havre-Saint-Pierre, QC
866-954-1341
auditoire.quebec@radio-canada.ca
www.radio-canada.ca/regions/quebec

***Hâvre-Saint-Pierre:* CILE-FM** (Freq: 95.1)
992, rue du Bouleau, Hâvre-Saint-Pierre, QC G0G 1P0
418-538-2453, Fax: 418-538-3870,
cilemf@globetrotter.net
www.cilemf.com

***Hull:* CKTF-FM** (Freq: 104.1)
Owned by: **Astral Media Inc.**
15, rue Taschereau, Hull, QC J8Y 2V6
819-243-5555, Fax: 819-243-6816,
www.radioenergie.com

†*Joliette:* CJLM-FM (Freq: 103.5)
540, rue Thomas, Joliette, QC J6E 3R4
450-756-1035, Fax: 450-756-8097,
radio@m1035fm.com
www.m1035fm.com
Normand Masse

†*Jonquière:* CKAJ-FM (Freq: 92.5)
CP 872, 3791, rue de la Fabrique, 4e étage, Jonquière, QC G7X 7W5
418-546-2525, Fax: 418-546-2528,
www.ckaj.org

***Kahnawake:* CKRK-FM** (Freq: 103.7)
PO Box 1050, Kahnawake, QC J0L 1B0
450-638-1313, Fax: 450-638-4009,
programming@k103radio.com
www.k103radio.com

***Kuujjuaq:* CKUJ-FM** (Freq: 97.3)
PO Box 1082, Kuujjuaq, QC J0M 1C0
819-964-2921, Fax: 819-964-2229

***L'Annonciation:* CFLO-FM** (Freq: 101.9)
Owned by: **CFLO-FM**
L'Annonciation, QC

†*La Pocatière:* CHOX-FM (Freq: 97.5)
#50, 601, 1ère av, La Pocatière, QC G0R 1Z0
418-856-1310, Fax: 418-856-3747,
chox@chox97.com
www.chox97.com

***Lac-Etchemin:* CFIN-FM** (Freq: 100.5)
#11, 201, rue Claude-Bilodeau, Lac-Etchemin, QC G0R 1S0
418-625-3737, Fax: 418-625-3730,
cfinfm@sogetel.net
www.cfin-fm.com
Jacques Thériault

†*Lac-Mégantic:* CFJO-FM (Freq: 101.7)
Owned by: **CFJO-FM**
Lac-Mégantic, QC

†*Lac-Mégantic:* CJIT-FM (Freq: 106.7)
4766, rue Laval, Lac-Mégantic, QC G6B 1C7
819-583-0663, Fax: 819-583-0665,
radiocjit@bellnet.ca
www.cjitfm.com
Ritha Breton

***Lac-Simon:* CHUT-FM** (Freq: 95.3)
1016, rue Wabanonik, Lac-Simon, QC J0Y 3M0
819-736-4501, Fax: 819-736-2333
Alain Flamand, General Manager

***Lachute:* CJLA-FM** (Freq: 104.9)
Owned by: **Radio Nord Communications Inc.**
11, rue Argenteuil, Lachute, QC J8H 1X8
450-562-8862, Fax: 450-562-1902,
infocouleur@radionord.com
www.radionord.com

†*Laval:* CFGL-FM (Freq: 105.7)
#100, 2830, boul St-Martin est, Laval, QC H7E 5A1
450-664-4647, Fax: 450-664-4138,
www.rythmefm.com
Jacques Boiteau, General Manager

***Lennoxville:* CJMQ-FM** (Freq: 88.9)
PO Box 2135, Lennoxville, QC J1M 1Z7
819-822-9600,
cjmq@ubishops.ca
www.cjmq.fm
David Teasdale

***Les Escoumins:* CHME-FM** (Freq: 94.9)
34, rue de la Reserve, Les Escoumins, QC G0T 1K0
418-233-2700, Fax: 418-233-3326,
chme@B2B2C.ca
Gilles Labelle

***Listuguj:* CFIC-FM** (Freq: 105.1)
PO Box 304, 44A Riverside ouest, Listuguj, QC
418-788-5166, Fax: 418-788-3524,
www.105hotcountry.com
Chris Dedam, General Manager

***Longueuil:* CHAA-FM** (Freq: 103.3)
91, rue St-Jean, Longueuil, QC G0T 1K0
450-646-6800, Fax: 450-646-7378,
general admin@fm1033.ca
www.fm1033.ca
Eric Tetreault

†*Lourdes-de-Blanc-Sablon:* CFBS-FM (Freq: 89.9)
CP 8, Lourdes-de-Blanc-Sablon, QC G0G 1W0
418-461-2445, Fax: 418-461-2425,
cfbsradio@gmailcom
www.cfbsradio.com
Patrick Beurbe, Station Manager
Dominque Jones, Music Director
Vicki Driscoll, President

†*Maniwaki:* CFOR-FM
139, rue Principal sud, Maniwaki, QC J9E 1Z8
819-441-0993, Fax: 819-441-3488,
cfor993@b2b2c.ca
www.cforfm.com
Laure Voilquin, Directrice commerciale, laure@cforfm.com

†*Maniwaki:* CHGA-FM (Freq: 97.3)
163, rue Laurier, Maniwaki, QC J9E 2K6
819-449-5590, Fax: 819-449-7331,
chga@bellnet.ca
www.chga.qc.ca

***Maniwaki:* CKWE-FM** (Freq: 103.9)
PO Box 309, Maniwaki, QC J9E 3C9
819-449-5170, Fax: 819-449-5097,
anita.tenasco@kza.qc.ca
Anita Penasco, General Manager

***Maria:* CHRG-FM** (Freq: 101.7)
PO Box 118, 120 School St., Maria, QC G0C 1Y0
418-759-5424, Fax: 418-759-5424,
radio@globetrotter.net
Douglas Martin, General Manager

†*Mashteuiatsh:* CHUK-FM (Freq: 107.3)
1491, rue Ouiatchouan, Mashteuiatsh, QC G0W 2H0
418-275-4684, Fax: 418-275-7964,
chuk@chukfm.ca
www.chukfm.ca
Marc Gill, General Manager

***Matagami:* CHEF-FM** (Freq: 99.9)
PO Box 39, 110, boul Matagami, Matagami, QC J0Y 2A0
819-739-9990, Fax: 819-739-6003
Marie-Eve C. Gallant, General Manager

†*Matane:* CBGA-FM (Freq: 102.1)
Owned by: **Canadian Broadcasting Corporation**
Matane, QC
514-597-6000, Fax: 514-597-5545, 800-306-4636
auditoire@radio-canada.ca
www.radio-canada.ca/radio

†*Matane:* CHOE-FM (Freq: 95.3)
800, av du Phare ouest, Matane, QC G4W 1V7
418-562-8181, Fax: 418-562-0778,
choefm@globetrotter.net
www.choefm.com
Kenneth Gagné Jr.

†*Matane:* CHRM-FM (Freq: 105.3)
800, av du Phare ouest, Matane, QC G4W 1V7
418-562-4141, Fax: 418-562-0778
Kenneth Gagné Jr.

** For details on this company see listing in Major Broadcasting Companies section; † French language station*

***Mont-Laurier:* CFLO-FM** (Freq: 104.7)
332, rue de la Madone, Mont-Laurier, QC J9L 1R9
819-623-6610, Fax: 819-623-7406,
cflofm@cflo.ca
www.cflo.ca
Alain Desjardins

***†Montmagny:* CFEL-FM** (Freq: 102.1)
Owned by: **Corus Entertainment Inc.**
191, ch des Poirier, Montmagny, QC G5V 4L2
418-248-1122, Fax: 418-248-1951,
cfel@globetrotter.net
www.cfelfm.com

***†Montréal:* CBF-FM** (Freq: 95.1)
Owned by: **Canadian Broadcasting Corporation**
CP 6000 Centre-ville, 1400, boul René-Lévesque est, Montréal, QC H3C 3A8
514-597-6000, 866-306-4636
auditoire@radio-canada.ca; liaison@radio-canada.ca
www.radio-canada.ca/radio
Other information: TDD: 514-597-6013
Pia Marquard, Managing Director, Radio & Television, Québec
Sally Caudwell, Executive Producer, Montréal News, 514-597-4089, Fax: 514-597-4511
Kenny King, Senior Manager, CBC Media Sales & Marketing
Helen Evans, Program Manager, Radio Current Affairs

***†Montréal:* CBFX-FM** (Freq: 100.7)
Owned by: **Canadian Broadcasting Corporation**
CP 6000 Centre-ville, 1400, boul René-Lévesque est, Montréal, QC H3C 3A8
514-597-6000, Fax: 514-597-5545, 866-306-4636
auditoire@radio-canada.ca
www.radio-canada.ca/espace_musique
Pia Marquard, Managing Director, Radio & Television, Québec Region
Hugh Brodie, Manager, Partnerships & Communications, Québec, 514-597-5813
Helen Evans, Program Manager, Radio Current Affairs

***Montréal:* CBJE-FM**
Owned by: **Canadian Broadcasting Corporation**
PO Box 6000, 1400, boul René Lévesque est, Montréal, QC H3C 3A8
514-597-4444, Fax: 514-597-4416,
info@radio.cbc.ca
www.cbc.ca/radio
Patricia Pleszczynska, General Manager

***Montréal:* CBME-FM** (Freq: 88.5)
Owned by: **Canadian Broadcasting Corporation**
PO Box 6000, Montréal, QC H3C 3A8
514-597-6000, Fax: 514-597-6510,
www.cbc.ca/radio
Social Media: www.facebook.com/radiocbc;
www.twitter.com/cbcradio
Other information: Phone, CBC Radio One Newsroom: 514-597-6300; TTY: 1-866-220-6045
Pia Marquard, Managing Director, Radio & Television, Québec Region
Sally Caudwell, Executive Producer, News, Montréal, 514-597-4089, Fax: 514-597-4511
Mary-Jo Barr, News Director, English Services
Kenny King, Senior Manager, CBC Media Sales & Marketing
Hugh Brodie, Manager, Partnership & Communications, Québec, 514-597-5813
Helen Evans, Program Manager, Radio Current Affairs
Carolyn Warren, Regional Manager, Cultural Programming, Integrated Content

***Montréal:* CBM-FM** (Freq: 93.5)
Owned by: **Canadian Broadcasting Corporation**
Maison Radio-Canada, PO Box 6000 Centre-ville, 1400, boul René-Lévesque est, Montréal, QC H3C 3A8
514-597-6000, Fax: 514-597-5545, 866-306-4636
auditoire@radio-canada.ca
www.cbc.ca/montreal; www.cbc.ca/radio2
Social Media: www.facebook.com/CBC.Radio2.Official?ref=nf
Other information: Twitter: www.twitter.com/cbcradio2
Pia Marquard, Managing Director, Radio & Television, Québec Region
Kenny King, Senior Manager, CBC Media Sales & Marketing
Hugh Brodie, Manager, Partnership & Communications, Québec
Helen Evans, Program Manager, Radio Current Affairs

***Montréal:* CFQR-FM** (Freq: 92.5)
Owned by: **Corus Entertainment Inc.**
#100, 800, rue de la Gauchetière ouest, Montréal, QC H5A 1K6
514-767-9250, Fax: 514-766-9569,
reception@q92fm.com
www.q92fm.com

***Montréal:* CHOM-FM** (Freq: 97.7)
Owned by: **Standard Radio Office**
1411, rue Fort, 3e étage, Montréal, QC H3H 2R1
514-937-2466, Fax: 514-846-4741,
www.chom.com

***†Montréal:* CIBL-FM** (Freq: 101.5)
1691, boul Pie-IX, 2e étage, Montréal, QC H1V 2C3
514-526-2581, Fax: 514-526-3583,
info@cibl.cam.org
www.cibl.cam.org
Pierre Paquette, Président

***Montréal:* CINQ-FM** (Freq: 102.3)
5212, boul St-Laurent, 2e étage, Montréal, QC H2T 1S1
514-495-2597, Fax: 514-495-2429,
cinqfm@radiocentreville.com
www.radiocentreville.com
Magalie Pare

***Montréal:* CIRA-FM** (Freq: 91.3)
#199, 4020, St-Ambroise, Montréal, QC H4C 2C7
514-382-3913, Fax: 514-858-0965,
cira@radiovm.com
www.radiovm.com
Jean-Guy Roy, Dir de la Station

***Montréal:* CISM-FM** (Freq: 89.3)
#C-1509, 2332, Edouard-Montpetit, Montréal, QC H3C 3J7
514-343-7511, Fax: 514-343-2418,
cism@cam.org
www.cismfm.qc.ca
Dave Ouellet

***Montréal:* CITE-FM** (Freq: 107.3)
Owned by: **Astral Media Inc.**
1717, boul René-Lévesque est, Montréal, QC H2L 4T9
514-529-3293, Fax: 514-288-1073,
www.rockdetente.com
Sylvain Langlois, Vice-President & General Manager

***Montréal:* CJFM-FM** (Freq: 95.9)
Owned by: **Standard Radio Office**
1411, rue du Fort, Montréal, QC H3H 2R1
514-989-2536, Fax: 514-989-2554,
www.themix.com
Gary Slaight, President
Rob Braide, Vice-President

***Montréal:* CJPX-FM** (Freq: 99.5)
Isle Notre-Dame, Parc Jean-Drapeau, Montréal, QC H3C 1A9
514-871-0995, Fax: 514-871-0990,
www.cjpx.ca
Francois Pare

***Montréal:* CKDG-FM** (Freq: 105.1)
5899, av du Parc, Montréal, QC H2V 4H4
514-273-2481, Fax: 514-273-3707,
info@ckdgfm.ca
www.ckdgfm.ca
Marie Griffiths, Station Manager

***Montréal:* CKLX-FM** (Freq: 91.9)
Owned by: **Radio Nord Communications Inc.**
#250, 200, av Laurier ouest, Montréal, QC H2T 2N8
514-871-0919, Fax: 514-871-8884,
www.coleurjazz.com
Guy Banville

***†Montréal:* CKMF-FM** (Freq: 94.3)
Owned by: **Astral Media Inc.**
#050, 1717, boul René-Lévesque est, Montréal, QC H2L 4T9
514-529-3229, Fax: 514-529-9308,
www.radioenergie.com

***†Montréal:* CKOI-FM** (Freq: 96.9)
Owned by: **Corus Entertainment Inc.**
#1100, 800, rue de la Gauchetière ouest, Montréal, QC H5A 1K6
514-766-2311, Fax: 514-766-2474,
information@ckoi.com
www.ckoi.com

***Montréal:* CKUT-FM** (Freq: 90.3)
3647, rue University, Montréal, QC H3A 2B3
514-398-6787, Fax: 514-398-8261,
sales@ckut.ca
www.ckut.ca

***†Natashquan:* CKNA-FM** (Freq: 104.1)
CP 9, 29, ch d'en Haut, Natashquan, QC G0G 2E0
418-726-3284, Fax: 418-726-3367,
ckna@globetrotter.net
pages.globetrotter.net/ckna

***Pikogan:* CKAG-FM** (Freq: 100.1)
45 rue Migwan, Pikogan, QC J9T 3A3
819-727-3237, Fax: 819-732-1569,
ckagfm@cableamos.com

***†Pohenegamook:* CFVD-FM-2** (Freq: 92.1)
Owned by: **CFVD-FM**
Pohenegamook, QC

***†Port-Cartier:* CIPC-FM**
52, rue Elie-Rochefort, Port-Cartier, QC G5B 1N2
418-766-6868, Fax: 418-766-6870,
cipc991@globetrotter.net; 991@live.ca
www.laradioactive.com
Yvan Beaulieu, Directeur général, direction991@globetrotter.net
Mathieu Pineau, Directeur, Programmation, dirprog991@globetrotter.net

***Port-Menier:* CJBE-FM** (Freq: 90.1)
PO Box 15, Port-Menier, QC G0G 2Y0
418-535-0292, Fax: 418-535-0292
Denis Tremblay, Dir de la Station

***Québec:* CBVE-FM** (Freq: 104.7)
Owned by: **Canadian Broadcasting Corporation**
888, rue Saint-Jean, Québec, QC G1R 5H6
418-691-3613, Fax: 418-691-3610
Claude Saindon, General Manager

***Québec:* CBVE-FM** (Freq: 104.7)
Owned by: **Canadian Broadcasting Corporation**
PO Box 18800, 888, rue Saint-Jean, Québec, QC G1K 9L4
418-691-3613, Fax: 418-691-3610

***†Québec:* CBV-FM** (Freq: 106.3)
Owned by: **Canadian Broadcasting Corporation**
CP 18800, 888, rue St-Jean, Québec, QC G1K 9L4
418-654-1341, Fax: 418-656-8842,
cbvt@radio-canada.ca
www.radio-canada.ca/regions
Louise Cordeau, Directrice de Radio-Canada, Québec

***Québec:* CBV-FM** (Freq: 106.3)
Owned by: **Canadian Broadcasting Corporation**
PO Box 18800, 888, rue Saint-Jean, Québec, QC G1K 9L4
418-691-3620, Fax: 418-691-3620,
www.radio-canada.ca/regions
Susan Campbell, General Manager

***Québec:* CBVX-FM** (Freq: 95.3)
Owned by: **Canadian Broadcasting Corporation**
PO Box 18800, 888, rue Saint-Jean, Québec, QC G1K 9L4
418-691-3620, Fax: 418-691-3610,
www.radio-canada.ca/regions/

***†Québec:* CHIK-FM** (Freq: 98.9)
Owned by: **Astral Media Inc.**
900, rue d'Youville, 1er étage, Québec, QC G1R 3P7
418-687-9900, Fax: 418-687-3106,
www.radioenergie.com

***Québec:* CION-FM** (Freq: 90.9; 102.5; 106.7)
3196, ch Sainte-Foy, Québec, QC G1X 1R4
418-659-9090, Fax: 418-650-3306, 800-447-2466
cionfm@radiogalilee.qc.ca
Denis Veilleux

***†Québec:* CITF-FM** (Freq: 107.5)
Owned by: **Astral Media Inc.**
900, rue d'Youville, 1er étage, Québec, QC G1R 3P7
418-527-3232, Fax: 418-687-3106,
www.rockdetente.com

** For details on this company see listing in Major Broadcasting Companies section; † French language station*

***Québec:* CJEC-FM** (Freq: 91.9)
1305, ch Ste-Foy, 4e étage, Québec, QC G1S 4Y5
418-688-0919, Fax: 418-527-0919,
www.rythmefm.com
Jean-Paul Lemire, General Manager

†*Québec:* CJMF-FM (Freq: 93.3)
1305, ch Ste-Foy, 4e étage, Québec, QC G1S 4Y5
418-687-9330, Fax: 418-687-0211,
commentaire@le933.com
www.le933.com
Jean-Paul Lemire

†*Québec:* CKIA-FM (Freq: 88.3)
600, côte d'Abraham, Québec, QC G1R 1A1
418-529-9026, Fax: 418-529-4156,
ckiafm@meduse.org
www.ckiafm.org
Andrée Pomerleau

†*Québec:* CKRL-FM (Freq: 89.1)
405, 3e av, Québec, QC G1L 2W2
418-640-2575, Fax: 418-640-1588,
programmation@ckrl.qc.ca
www.ckrl.qc.ca
Jean-Pierre Bédard

†*Radisson:* CIAU-FM (Freq: 103.1)
CP 285, 143, rue Jolliet, Radisson, QC J0Y 2X0
819-638-7033, Fax: 819-638-7033,
ciaufm@lino.com
www.ciaufm.com
Martin Beaucage, Station Manger

***Restigouche:* CHRQ-FM** (Freq: 106.9)
PO Box 180, 116 Riverside Dr., Restigouche, QC G0C 2R0
418-788-2449, Fax: 418-788-2653,
chrq1069@globetrotter.net
Sandra Bulmer, Station Manager

†*Rimouski:* CBRX-FM (Freq: 101.5)
Owned by: **Canadian Broadcasting Corporation**
Rimouski, QC
866-954-1341
auditoire.quebec@radio-canada.ca
www.radio-canada.ca/espace_musique;
www.radio-canada.ca/regions/quebec

†*Rimouski:* CIKI-FM (Freq: 98.7)
Owned by: **Astral Media Inc.**
CP 3875, 875, boul St-Germain ouest, Rimouski, QC G5L 7P3
418-724-9870, Fax: 418-722-7508,
www.radioenergie.com

†*Rimouski:* CJBR-FM (Freq: 101.5)
Owned by: **Canadian Broadcasting Corporation**
Rimouski, QC

†*Rimouski:* CJOI-FM (Freq: 102.9)
Owned by: **Astral Media Inc.**
CP 3875, 875, boul St-Germain ouest, Rimouski, QC G5L 7P3
418-723-2323, Fax: 418-722-7508,
www.rockdetente.com

***Rimouski:* CKMN-FM** (Freq: 96.5)
323, Montée industrielle, Rimouski, QC G5M 1A7
418-722-2566, Fax: 418-724-7815,
ckmn-fm@cgocable.ca
www.ckmn.ca
Vic Talbot

†*Rivière-du-Loup:* CIBM-FM (Freq: 107.1)
64, rue Hôtel-de-Ville, Rivière-du-Loup, QC G5R 1L5
418-867-1071, Fax: 418-867-4940,
ventes@cibm107.com
cibm107.com

†*Rivière-du-Loup:* CIEL-FM (Freq: 103.7)
64, rue Hôtel-de-Ville, Rivière-du-Loup, QC G5R 1L5
418-862-8241, Fax: 418-867-4940,
info@ciel103.com
www.cibm107.com
Guy Simard

†*Roberval:* CHRL-FM (Freq: 99.5)
Owned by: **Groupe Radio Antenne 6**
568, boul St-Joseph, Roberval, QC G8H 2K6
418-275-1831, Fax: 418-275-2475
M. Levesque, General Manager

***Rouyn-Noranda:* CHIC-FM** (Freq: 88.7)
PO Box 2185, 120, 9e Rue, Rouyn-Noranda, QC J9X 5A6
819-797-4242, Fax: 819-797-3803
Jocelyn Côté, General Manager, ccechic@cablevision.qc.ca

†*Rouyn-Noranda:* CHLM-FM (Freq: 90.7)
70, av Principal, Rouyn-Noranda, QC J9X 4P2
819-762-8155, Fax: 819-762-1279,
www.radio-canada.ca/regions/abitibi

†*Rouyn-Noranda:* CHOA-FM (Freq: 96.5)
Owned by: **Radio Nord Communications Inc.**
380, av Murdoch, Rouyn-Noranda, QC J9X 1G5
819-762-0741, Fax: 819-762-6331,
www.couleurfm.cam

***Rouyn-Noranda:* CJMM-FM** (Freq: 99.1)
Owned by: **Astral Media Inc.**
33B, rue Gamble ouest, Rouyn-Noranda, QC J9X 2R3
819-797-2566, Fax: 819-797-1664,
www.radioenergie.com

***Saint-Gabriel-de-Brandon:* CFNJ-FM** (Freq: 99.1)
Owned by: **Radio Nord Communications Inc.**
245, rue Beauvilliers, Saint-Gabriel-de-Brandon, QC J0K 2N0
450-835-3437, Fax: 450-835-3581,
www.cfnj.qc.ca
Denis Roch

†*Saint-Hilarion:* CIHO-FM (Freq: 96.3)
315, ch Cartier nord, Saint-Hilarion, QC G0A 3V0
418-457-3333, Fax: 418-457-3518,
ciho@charlevoix.net
www.cihofm.com

†*Saint-Hyacinthe:* CFEI-FM (Freq: 106.5)
Owned by: **Astral Media Inc.**
2596, boul Casavant ouest, Saint-Hyacinthe, QC J2S 7R8
450-774-6486, Fax: 450-774-7785,
www.boomfm.com

***Saint-Jean-Port-Joli:* CHOX-4** (Freq: 100.1)
Owned by: **CHOX-FM**
Saint-Jean-Port-Joli, QC

†*Saint-Jean-sur-Richelieu:* CFZZ-FM (Freq: 104.1)
Owned by: **Astral Media Inc.**
104, rue Richelieu, Saint-Jean-sur-Richelieu, QC J3B 6X3
450-346-0104, Fax: 450-348-2274,
www.boomfm.com
Pierre De Mondehare, Directeur Général par intérim

†*Saint-Jérôme:* CIME-FM (Freq: 101.3; 103.9)
Owned by: **Corus Entertainment Inc.**
120, de la Gare, Saint-Jérôme, QC J7Z 2C2
450-431-2463, Fax: 450-456-5975,
www.cime.fm

***Saint-Pamphile:* CHOX-2** (Freq: 101.1)
Owned by: **CHOX-FM**
Saint-Pamphile, QC

***Saint-Pamphile:* CJDS-FM** (Freq: 94.7)
PO Box 550, 109, rue de l'église, Saint-Pamphile, QC G0R 3X0
418-356-1303, Fax: 418-356-2586,
cjdsradio@globetrotter.net
Jean-Claude Dignard, General Manager

***Saint-Régis:* CKON-FM** (Freq: 97.3)
Owned by: **CKON-FM**
Saint-Régis, QC

***Saint-Rémi:* CHOC-FM** (Freq: 104.9)
107, Chevrefils, Saint-Rémi, QC J0L 2L0
450-454-5500, Fax: 450-454-9435,
webchoc.fr.fm

†*Sainte-Anne-des-Monts:* CJMC-FM (Freq: 100.3)
170, boul Ste-Anne est, Sainte-Anne-des-Monts, QC G4V 1N1
418-763-5522, Fax: 418-763-7211

†*Sainte-Foy:* CFOM-FM (Freq: 102.9)
Owned by: **Astral Media Inc.**
2136, ch Sainte-Foy, 3e étage, Sainte-Foy, QC G1V 1R8
418-694-1029, Fax: 418-682-8430,
mharvey@cfom1029.com
www.cfom1029.com
Pierre DeMondehare, General Manager

***Sainte-Foy:* CHYZ-FM** (Freq: 94.3)
#023, Pavillon Pollack, Universitaire Laval, Sainte-Foy, QC G1K 7P4
418-656-2131, Fax: 450-656-3660,
chyz@public.ulaval.ca
www.chyz.qc.ca
Jean-Philippe Lessard, General Manager

***Salaberry-de-Valleyfield:* CKOD-FM** (Freq: 103.1)
249, rue Victoria, Salaberry-de-Valleyfield, QC J6T 1A9
450-373-0103, Fax: 450-373-4297,
fm103@ckod.qc.ca
www.ckod.qc.ca
Robert Brunet, Directeur Général

†*Senneterre:* CIBO-FM (Freq: 100.5)
CP 1150, 121, 1re rue Est, Senneterre, QC J0Y 2M0
819-737-2222, Fax: 819-737-8599,
cibo.fm@moncourrier.com
Guy Bilodeau, General Manager

†*Sept-Iles:* CBSI-FM (Freq: 98.1)
Owned by: **Canadian Broadcasting Corporation**
Sept-Iles, QC
866-954-1341
auditoire.quebec@radio-canada.ca
www.radio-canada.ca/regions/quebec

***Sept-Iles:* CKAU-FM** (Freq: 90.1; 104.5)
PO Box 338, Sept-Iles, QC G4R 4K6
418-927-2476, Fax: 418-927-2800,
ckau@chau.com
www.ckau.com
Yves Rock, General Manager

†*Sept-Iles:* CKCN-FM (Freq: 94.1)
437, av Arnaud, Sept-Iles, QC G4R 3B3
418-962-3838, Fax: 418-968-6662,
ckcn@globetrotter.net
www.quebec.fm/ckcn
Dominique Marquis, Directrice
Caroline Michaud, Directeur des programmes

***Sherbrooke:* CFAK-FM** (Freq: 88.3)
2500, boul de Université, Sherbrooke, QC J1K 2R1
819-821-8000, Fax: 819-821-7930,
info@cfak.qc.ca
www.cfak.qc.ca
Steve Bazinet, General Manager

†*Sherbrooke:* CFLX-FM (Freq: 95.5)
67, rue Wellington Nord, Sherbrooke, QC J1H 5A9
819-566-2787, Fax: 819-566-7331,
cflx@cflx.qc.ca
www.cflx.qc.ca
Jose Deschenes

†*Sherbrooke:* CIMO-FM (Freq: 106.1)
Owned by: **Astral Media Inc.**
#200, 1845, rue King ouest, Sherbrooke, QC J1J 2E4
819-347-1414, Fax: 819-347-1061,
www.radioenergie.com

†*Sherbrooke:* CITE-FM-1 (Freq: 102.7)
Owned by: **Astral Media Inc.**
#200, 1845, rue King ouest, Sherbrooke, QC J1L 2E4
819-566-6655, Fax: 819-566-1011,
www.rockdetente.com

†*Sillery:* CHOI-FM (Freq: 98.1)
#300, 1134, ch St-Louis, Sillery, QC G1S 1E5
418-687-9810, Fax: 418-682-8427,
www.choiradiox.com
Patrice Demers

†*Sorel-Tracy:* CJSO-FM (Freq: 101.7)
52, rue du Roi, Sorel-Tracy, QC J3P 4M7
450-743-2772, Fax: 450-743-0293, 888-489-1017
cjso@cjso.qc.ca
www.cjso.qc.ca

†*Squatec:* CFVD-FM-3 (Freq: 92.1)
Owned by: **CFVD-FM**
Squatec, QC

***St. Augustine:* CJAS-FM** (Freq: 93.5)
PO Box 100, St. Augustine, QC G0G 2R0
418-947-2239, Fax: 418-947-2664,
sajcr@globetrotter.net
cjasradio.pic30.com

** For details on this company see listing in Major Broadcasting Companies section; † French language station*

Laurette Gallibois, General Manager

†*St-Georges-de-Beauce:* CHJM-FM (Freq: 99.7)
CP 100, 11760, 3e av, St-Georges-de-Beauce, QC G5Y 5C4
418-227-0997, Fax: 418-228-0096,
adminrb@cgocable.ca
www.mix997.com

†*St-Georges-de-Beauce:* CKRB-FM (Freq: 103.3)
CP 100, 11760, 3e av, St-Georges-de-Beauce, QC G5Y 5C4
418-228-1460, Fax: 418-228-0096,
admnrb@cgocable.ca
www.coolfm.biz

†*Ste-Marie-de-Beauce:* CHEQ-FM (Freq: 101.3)
#101, 1068, boul Vachon Nord, Ste-Marie-de-Beauce, QC G6E 1M6
418-387-1013, Fax: 418-387-3757, 877-387-1013
info@cheqfm.qc.ca
www.cheqfm.qc.ca
Mario Paquin, Directeur général

†*Témiscaming:* CKVM-FM-1 (Freq: 92.1)
Owned by: **CKVM-FM**
Témiscaming, QC

†*Thetford Mines:* CFJO-FM (Freq: 97.3)
CP 69, 327, rue Labbé, Thetford Mines, QC G6G 5S3
418-338-1009, Fax: 418-338-0386,
info@O973.com
www.o973.com
Annie Labbé, Directrice générale

†*Thetford Mines:* CKLD-FM (Freq: 105.5)
327, rue Labbé, Thetford Mines, QC G6G 1Z2
418-335-7533, Fax: 418-335-9009,
info@passionrock.com
www.passionrock.com

***Trois-Rivières:* CFOU-FM** (Freq: 89.1)
3351, boul des Forges, Trois-Rivières, QC G9A 5H7
819-697-2368, Fax: 819-697-3888,
cfou@uqtr.uquebec.ca
www.cfoufm.com
Eric Leclair, General Manager

†*Trois-Rivières:* CHEY-FM (Freq: 94.7)
Owned by: **Astral Media Inc.**
#260, 1500, boul Royale, Trois-Rivières, QC G9A 6J4
819-376-0947, Fax: 819-378-1360,
chey2@rock-detente.com
www.rockdetente.com

†*Trois-Rivières:* CIGB-FM (Freq: 102.3)
Owned by: **Astral Media Inc.**
#260, 1500, rue Royal, Trois-Rivières, QC G9A 6J4
819-378-1023, Fax: 819-378-1360,
www.radioenergie.com

†*Val-d'Or:* CHGO-FM (Freq: 104.3)
Owned by: **Radio Nord Communications Inc.**
1729, 3e av, Val-d'Or, QC J9P 1W3
819-825-0010, Fax: 819-825-7313,
www.gofm.net
André Houle, General Manager

†*Val-d'Or:* CHGO-FM (Freq: 104.3; 95.7)
Owned by: **Radio Nord Communications Inc.**
1729, 3e av, Val-d'Or, QC J9P 1W3
819-825-9994, Fax: 819-825-7313,
www.gofm.net

***Val-d'Or:* CJMV-FM** (Freq: 102.7)
Owned by: **Astral Media Inc.**
173, rue Perreault, Val-d'Or, QC J9P 2H3
819-825-2568, Fax: 819-825-2840,
www.radioenergie.com
Marlene Trottier, General Manager

†*Verdun:* CHMP-FM (Freq: 98.5)
Owned by: **Corus Entertainment Inc.**
211, av Gordon, Verdun, QC H4G 2R2
514-767-2435, Fax: 514-761-0985, 866-790-9850
www.985fm.ca
Jacques Papin, Directeur général
Yves Delisle, Directeur adjoint, émissions

†*Victoriaville:* CFDA-FM (Freq: 101.9)
55, rue St-Jean Baptiste, Victoriaville, QC G6P 6T3
819-752-5545, Fax: 819-752-7552,
info@passionrock.com
www.passionrock.com

†*Victoriaville:* CFJO-FM (Freq: 97.3; 101.7)
CP 490, 55, rue St-Jean-Baptiste, Victoriaville, QC G6P 6T3
819-752-2785, Fax: 819-752-3182,
info@o973.com
www.o973.com
Annie Labbé, Diectrice Général

†*Ville-Marie:* CKVM-FM (Freq: 93.1)
62, rue Ste-Anne, Ville-Marie, QC J9V 2B7
819-629-2710, Fax: 819-622-0716,
ckvm@ckvm.qc.ca
Martin Héroux, Directeur-général

***Windsor:* CIAX-FM** (Freq: 98.3)
49 Sixth Ave., Windsor, QC J1S 1T2
819-845-5900, Fax: 819-845-2692,
unite@qc.aira.ca
Patrick Levesque, General Manager

Saskatchewan

***Cumberland House:* CJCF-FM** (Freq: 89.9)
PO Box 100, Cumberland House, SK S0E 0S0
306-888-2176, Fax: 306-888-4444
Rachel Fiddler, General Manager

***Hudson Bay:* CFMQ-FM** (Freq: 98.1)
PO Box 1272, Hudson Bay, SK S0E 0Y0
306-865-3065, Fax: 306-865-2227,
cfmq@sasktel.net
www.townofhudsonbay.com
Dan Brann, General Manager

***Kenosee Lake:* CIDD-FM** (Freq: 97.7)
PO Box 121, Kenosee Lake, SK A0C 2S0
306-577-2450
Lana Littlechief, General Manager

***La Ronge:* CBKA-FM**
Owned by: **Canadian Broadcasting Corporation**
PO Box 959, La Ronge, SK S0J 1L0
306-425-3324,
www.cbc.ca/sk

***La Ronge:* CJLR-FM** (Freq: 89.9)
PO Box 1529, 712 Finlayson St., La Ronge, SK S0J 1L0
306-425-4003, Fax: 306-425-3123,
mbcradio@mbcradio.com
www.mbcradio.com

***Meadow Lake:* CFDM-FM** (Freq: 105.7)
PO Box 8168, Meadow Lake, SK S9X 1T8
306-236-1445, Fax: 306-236-2821,
cfdm.radio@sasktel.net
Ben Lachance, Station Manager

***Meadow Lake:* CJNS-FM** (Freq: 102.3)
PO Box 1660, 225 Centre St., Meadow Lake, SK S9X 1Z2
306-236-6494, Fax: 306-236-6141

***Melfort:* CJVR-FM** (Freq: 105.1)
PO Box 750, 611 Main St. North, Melfort, SK S0E 1A0
306-752-2587, Fax: 306-752-5932, 800-668-2587
sales@cjvr.com
www.cjvr.com
Kevin Gemmel, Station Manager

***Moose Jaw:* CILG-FM** (Freq: 100.7)
Owned by: **CHAB**
Moose Jaw, SK

***Nipawin:* CJNE-FM** (Freq: 94.7)
PO Box 220, Nipawin, SK S0E 1E0
306-862-9478, Fax: 306-862-2334,
pro.cjne@sasktel.net
www.cjnefm.com
Norman Rudock, General Manager

†*North Battleford:* CBKF-FM-5
Owned by: **Canadian Broadcasting Corporation**
North Battleford, SK

***North Battleford:* CJCQ-FM** (Freq: 98.1)
Owned by: **CJNB**
North Battleford, SK

***Pinehouse Lake:* CFNK-FM** (Freq: 89.9)
PO Box 370, Pinehouse Lake, SK S0J 2B0
306-884-2011, Fax: 306-884-2365, 306-884-2016
cfnkradio@sasktel.net
www.cfnk.radiok.sympatico.ca
Jamie Iron, General Manager

***Prince Albert:* CFMM-FM** (Freq: 99.1)
PO Box 900, 1316 Central Ave., Prince Albert, SK S6V 7R4
306-763-7421, Fax: 306-764-1850,
power99fm@rawlco.com
www.power99fm.com
Garth Kalin, Operations Manager

***Prince Albert:* CHQX-FM** (Freq: 101.5)
PO Box 900, 1316 Central Ave., Prince Albert, SK S6V 7R4
306-763-7421, Fax: 306-764-1850,
mix101@rawlco.com
www.mix101fm.com

†*Regina:* CBKF-FM
Owned by: **Canadian Broadcasting Corporation**
CP 540, 2440 Broad St., Regina, SK S4P 4A1
306-347-9540, Fax: 306-347-9414, 800-413-2253
webmestre@radio-canada.ca
www.radio-canada.ca/saskatchewan
René Fontaine, Directeur des services français dan, 204-788-3236, rene.fontaine@radio-canada.ca

***Regina:* CBK-FM**
Owned by: **Canadian Broadcasting Corporation**
2440 Broad St., Regina, SK S4P 4A1
306-347-9540,
www.cbc.ca/sask
David Kyle, News Director

***Regina:* CFWF-FM** (Freq: 104.9)
Owned by: **Harvard Broadcasting Inc.**
1900 Rose St., Regina, SK S4P 0A9
306-546-6200, Fax: 306-781-7338,
hurricane@thewolfrocks.com
www.thewolfrocks.com
Michael Olstrom

***Regina:* CHMX-FM** (Freq: 92.1)
Owned by: **Harvard Broadcasting Inc.**
1900 Rose St., Regina, SK S4P 0A9
306-936-0092, Fax: 306-546-6200,
dholien@lite92fm.com
www.lite92fm.com
Michael Olstrom

***Regina:* CIZL-FM** (Freq: 98.9)
Owned by: **RAWLCO Radio Ltd.**
#210, 2401 Saskatchewan Dr., Regina, SK S4P 4H8
306-525-0000, Fax: 306-347-8557,
www.z99.com
Tom Newton, Program Director

***Regina:* CJTR-FM** (Freq: 91.3)
PO Box 334 Main, Regina, SK S4P 3A1
306-525-7274, Fax: 306-525-9741,
radius@cjtr.ca
www.cjtr.ca
Keith Colhoun

***Regina:* CKCK-FM** (Freq: 94.5)
Owned by: **RAWLCO Radio Ltd.**
#210, 2401 Saskatchewan Dr., Regina, SK S4P 4H8
306-525-0000, Fax: 306-547-8557,
www.jackfmregina.com

***Saskatoon:* CFCR-FM** (Freq: 90.5)
PO Box 7544, Saskatoon, SK S7K 4L4
306-664-6678,
cfcr@cfcr.ca
www.cfcr.ca
Ron Spizziri

***Saskatoon:* CFMC-FM** (Freq: 95.1)
715 Saskatchewan Cres. West, Saskatoon, SK S7M 5V7
306-934-2222, Fax: 306-477-0002,
www.c95.com
Jamie Wall, General Manager

***Saskatoon:* CJDJ-FM** (Freq: 102.1)
715 Saskatchewan Cres. West, Saskatoon, SK S7M 5V7
306-934-2222, Fax: 306-477-0002,
www.rock102rocks.com
Jamie Wall, General Manager

** For details on this company see listing in Major Broadcasting Companies section; † French language station*

Saskatoon: **CJMK-FM** (Freq: 98.3)
366 - 3rd Ave. South, Saskatoon, SK S7K 1M5
306-244-1975, Fax: 306-665-8484,
magic@magic983.fm
www.magic983.fm

Saskatoon: **CKBL-FM** (Freq: 92.9)
366 - 3rd Ave. South, Saskatoon, SK S7K 1M5
306-244-1975, Fax: 306-665-8484,
thebull@929thebullrocks.com
www.929thebullrocks.com
Vic Dubois, President & General Manager

Swift Current: **CIMG-FM** (Freq: 94.1)
Owned by: **Golden West Broadcasting Ltd.**
134 Central Ave. North, Swift Current, SK S9H 0L1
306-773-4605, Fax: 306-773-6390, 800-821-8073
eaglecontrol@goldenwestradio.com
www.eagle94.com
Deborah Gauger, Station General Manager & Sales

Tagish: **CFET-FM** (Freq: 106.7)
Mile 234, Tagish, SK Y0B 1T0
867-399-3012, Fax: 867-668-2633,
info@cfetradio.ca
www.cfetradio.ca
Robert G. Hopkins, General Manager

Waskesiu: **CJVR-FM** (Freq: 106.3)
Owned by: **CJVR-FM**
Waskesiu, SK

Whitehorse: **CIAY-FM** (Freq: 100.7)
91806 Alaska Hwy., Whitehorse, SK Y1A 5B7
867-393-2429, Fax: 867-393-2439,
info@ciay.ca
www.ciay.ca
Rod Carby, Station Manager

Wynyard: **CJVR-FM** (Freq: 100.3)
Owned by: **CJVR-FM**
Wynyard, SK

Yorkton: **CFGW-FM** (Freq: 94.1)
Owned by: **CJGX**
Yorkton, SK

†Zenon Park: **CBKF-FM-3**
Owned by: **Canadian Broadcasting Corporation**
Zenon Park, SK

Yukon Territory

Whitehorse: **CHON-FM** (Freq: 98.1; 90.5)
4230A - 4 Ave., Whitehorse, YT Y1A 1K1
867-668-6629, Fax: 867-668-6612,
nnby@nnby.net
www.nnby.net

Television Stations

Alberta

Ashmont: **CFRN-TV-4**(Channel: 12)
Owned by: **CTVglobemedia Inc.**
Ashmont, AB

Athabasca: **CBXT-TV-1**(Channel: 8)
Owned by: **CBXT-TV**
Athabasca, AB

Athabasca: **CFRN-TV**(Channel: 13)
Owned by: **CTVglobemedia Inc.**
Athabasca, AB

Banff: **CBRT-TV-1**(Channel: 5 (VHF))
Owned by: **Canadian Broadcasting Corporation (CBC)**
Banff, AB
866-306-4636
www.cbc.ca/calgary; www.cbc.ca/television
Social Media: www.twitter.com/cbccalgary
Other information: TTY: 1-866-220-6045

Banff: **CFCN-TV-2**(Channel: 7)
Owned by: **CTVglobemedia Inc.**
Banff, AB

Bassano: **CFCN-TV-7**(Channel: 10)
Owned by: **CTVglobemedia Inc.**
Bassano, AB

Battle River: **CBXAT-TV-6**(Channel: 9)
Owned by: **CBXT-TV**
Battle River, AB

Beaverlodge: **CBXT-TV**(Channel: 4)
Owned by: **Canadian Broadcasting Corporation**
Beaverlodge, AB

Bellevue: **CBRT-TV-10**(Channel: 57 (UHF))
Owned by: **Canadian Broadcasting Corporation (CBC)**
Bellevue, AB
866-306-4636
www.cbc.ca/calgary; www.cbc.ca/television
Social Media: www.twitter.com/cbccalgary
Other information: TTY: 1-866-220-6045

Bonnyville: **CITL-TV4**(Channel: 7)
Owned by: **CITL-TV**
Bonnyville, AB

Bonnyville: **CKSA-TV**(Channel: 9)
Owned by: **CKSA-TV**
Bonnyville, AB

Brooks: **CFCN-TV-3**(Channel: 9)
Owned by: **CTVglobemedia Inc.**
Brooks, AB

Burmis: **CBRT-TV-8**(Channel: 47 (UHF))
Owned by: **Canadian Broadcasting Corporation (CBC)**
Burmis, AB
866-306-4636
www.cbc.ca/calgary; www.cbc.ca/television
Social Media: www.twitter.com/cbccalgary
Other information: TTY: 1-866-220-6045

Burmis: **CFCN-TV-4**(Channel: 5)
Owned by: **CTVglobemedia Inc.**
Burmis, AB

Calgary: **CBRT-TV**(Channel: 9 (VHF))
Owned by: **Canadian Broadcasting Corporation**
PO Box 2640, 1724 Westmount Blvd. NW, Calgary, AB T2P 2M7
403-521-6000, Fax: 403-521-6079, 866-306-4636
www.cbc.ca/calgary; www.cbc.ca/television
Social Media: www.twitter.com/cbccalgary
Other information: Phone, TV Newsroom: 403-521-6055; TTY: 1-866-220-6045
Diane Humber, Director, Calgary Centre, 403-521-6252
Dave Budge, Director, News, 403-521-6016
Helen Henderson, Director, Programs, 403-521-6221
Jim Haskins, Manager, Calgary Sales Team, 403-521-6184
Shawna Kelly, Manager, Communications, 403-521-6207
Del Simon, Senior Officer, Communications, 403-521-6008

Calgary: **CFCN-TV**(Channel: 3)
Owned by: **CTVglobemedia Inc.**
80 Patina Rise SW, Calgary, AB T3H 2W4
403-240-5600, Fax: 403-240-8879,
calgarynews@ctv.ca
www.cfcn.ca
Patricia McDougall, Vice-President & General Manager, pmcdougall@ctv.ca

Calgary: **CICT-TV**(Channel: 7)
Owned by: **Canwest Global Communications Corp.**
222 - 23 St. NE, Calgary, AB T2E 7N2
403-235-7777, Fax: 403-248-0252,
www.globaltv.com/calgary

Calgary: **CKAL-TV**(Channel: 5)
Owned by: **Rogers Broadcasting Ltd.**
535 - 7th Ave. SW, Calgary, AB T2P 0Y4
403-508-2222, Fax: 403-508-2224,
calgaryfeedback@a-channel.com
www.a-channel.com

Cardston: **CBRT-TV-12**(Channel: 6 (VHF))
Owned by: **Canadian Broadcasting Corporation (CBC)**
Cardston, AB
866-306-4636
www.cbc.ca/calgary; www.cbc.ca/television
Social Media: www.twitter.com/cbccalgary
Other information: TTY: 1-866-220-6045

Chateh: **CBXAT-TV-7**(Channel: 5)
Owned by: **CBXT-TV**
Chateh, AB

Coleman: **CBRT-TV-11**(Channel: 17 (UHF))
Owned by: **Canadian Broadcasting Corporation (CBC)**
Coleman, AB
866-306-4636
www.cbc.ca/calgary; www.cbc.ca/television
Social Media: www.twitter.com/cbccalgary
Other information: TTY: 1-866-220-6045

Coutts: **CBRT-TV-16**(Channel: 4 (VHF))
Owned by: **Canadian Broadcasting Corporation (CBC)**
Coutts, AB
866-306-4636
www.cbc.ca/calgary; www.cbc.ca/television
Social Media: www.twitter.com/cbccalgary
Other information: TTY: 1-866-220-6045

Cowley: **CBRT-TV-15**(Channel: 27 (UHF))
Owned by: **Canadian Broadcasting Corporation (CBC)**
Cowley, AB
866-306-4636
www.cbc.ca/calgary; www.cbc.ca/television
Social Media: www.twitter.com/cbccalgary
Other information: TTY: 1-866-220-6045

Drumheller: **CBRT-TV-2**(Channel: 6 (VHF))
Owned by: **Canadian Broadcasting Corporation (CBC)**
Drumheller, AB
866-306-4636
www.cbc.ca/calgary; www.cbc.ca/television
Social Media: www.twitter.com/cbccalgary
Other information: TTY: 1-866-220-6045

Drumheller: **CFCN-TV-6**(Channel: 10)
Owned by: **CTVglobemedia Inc.**
Drumheller, AB

†Edmonton: **CBXFT-TV**(Channel: 11)
Owned by: **Canadian Broadcasting Corporation**
Edmonton City Centre, CP 555, #123, 10062 - 102 Ave., Edmonton, AB T5J 2Y8
780-468-7500, Fax: 780-468-7779,
tjalberta@edmonton.radio-canada.ca
www.radio-canada.ca/regions/alberta/

Edmonton: **CBXT-TV**(Channel: 5)
Owned by: **Canadian Broadcasting Corporation**
123 Edmonton City Centre, PO Box 555, 10062 - 102nd Ave., Edmonton, AB T5J 2P4
780-468-7500, Fax: 780-468-7897,
kelly_walter@cbc.ca
www.cbc.ca/edmonton
Kelly Walter, Regional Sales Manager

Edmonton: **CFRN-TV**(Channel: 3)
Owned by: **CTVglobemedia Inc.**
18520 Stony Plain Rd., Edmonton, AB T5S 1A8
780-483-3311, Fax: 780-484-4426,
www.cfrntv.ca
Lloyd Lewis, General Manager & Vice-President

Edmonton: **CITV-TV**(Channel: 13)
Owned by: **Canwest Global Communications Corp.**
5325 Allard Way, Edmonton, AB T6H 5B8
780-436-1250, Fax: 780-989-4686,
globalnews.ed@globaltv.com
Tim Spelliscy, General Manager

** For details on this company see listing in Major Broadcasting Companies section; † French language station*

***Edmonton:* CKEM-TV**(Channel: 51)
Owned by: **Rogers Broadcasting Ltd.**
10212 Jasper Ave., Edmonton, AB T5J 5A3
780-424-2222, Fax: 780-424-0357,
newsnow@chumtv.com
www.a-channel.com
Jim Haskins, General Manager

***Etzikom:* CHAT-TV-5**(Channel: 12)
Owned by: **CHAT-TV**
Etzikom, AB

***Exshaw:* CBRT-TV-17**(Channel: 34 (UHF))
Owned by: **Canadian Broadcasting Corporation (CBC)**
Exshaw, AB
866-306-4636
www.cbc.ca/calgary; www.cbc.ca/television
Social Media: www.twitter.com/cbccalgary
Other information: TTY: 1-866-220-6045

***Exshaw:* CBRT-TV-3**(Channel: 6 (VHF))
Owned by: **Canadian Broadcasting Corporation (CBC)**
Exshaw, AB
866-306-4636
www.cbc.ca/calgary; www.cbc.ca/television
Social Media: www.twitter.com/cbccalgary
Other information: TTY: 1-866-220-6045

***Fort McMurray:* CBXT-TV-6**(Channel: 12)
Owned by: **CBXT-TV**
Fort McMurray, AB

***Fort Vermilion:* CBXAT-TV-5**(Channel: 11)
Owned by: **CBXT-TV**
Fort Vermilion, AB

***Fox Creek:* CBXT-TV-7**(Channel: 5)
Owned by: **CBXT-TV**
Fox Creek, AB

***Fox Lake:* CBXAT-TV-10**(Channel: 9)
Owned by: **CBXT-TV**
Fox Lake, AB

***Grande Prairie:* CBXAT-TV**(Channel: 10)
Owned by: **CBXT-TV**
Grande Prairie, AB

***Grande Prairie:* CFRN-TV-1**(Channel: 13)
Owned by: **CTVglobemedia Inc.**
Grande Prairie, AB

***Hand Hills:* CFCN-TV-1**(Channel: 12)
Owned by: **CTVglobemedia Inc.**
Hand Hills, AB

***Harvie Heights:* CBRT-TV-13**(Channel: 22 (UHF))
Owned by: **Canadian Broadcasting Corporation (CBC)**
Harvie Heights, AB
866-306-4636
www.cbc.ca/calgary; www.cbc.ca/television
Social Media: www.twitter.com/cbccalgary
Other information: TTY: 1-866-220-6045

***High Level:* CBXAT-TV-4**(Channel: 8)
Owned by: **CBXT-TV**
High Level, AB

***High Prairie:* CBXAT-TV-2**(Channel: 2)
Owned by: **CBXT-TV**
High Prairie, AB

***High Prairie:* CFRN-TV**(Channel: 18)
High Prairie, AB

***Hinton:* CBXT-TV-3**(Channel: 8)
Owned by: **CBXT-TV**
Hinton, AB

***Jasper:* CBXT-TV-4**(Channel: 5)
Owned by: **CBXT-TV**
Jasper, AB

***Jasper:* CFRN-TV**(Channel: 11)
Owned by: **CTVglobemedia Inc.**
Jasper, AB

***Jean Cote:* CBXAT-TV-13**(Channel: 31)
Owned by: **CBXT-TV**
Jean Cote, AB

***Jean D'Or:* CBXAT-TV-9**(Channel: 13)
Owned by: **CBXT-TV**
Jean D'Or, AB

***Lac La Biche:* CBXT-TV-5**(Channel: 10)
Owned by: **CBXT-TV**
Lac La Biche, AB

***Lac La Biche:* CFRN-TV-5**(Channel: 2)
Owned by: **CTVglobemedia Inc.**
Lac La Biche, AB

***Lake Louise:* CBRT-TV-4**(Channel: 12 (VHF))
Owned by: **Canadian Broadcasting Corporation (CBC)**
Lake Louise, AB
866-306-4636
www.cbc.ca/calgary; www.cbc.ca/television
Social Media: www.twitter.com/cbccalgary
Other information: TTY: 1-866-220-6045

***Lake Louise:* CFLL-TV-1**(Channel: 6)
Owned by: **CTVglobemedia Inc.**
Lake Louise, AB

***Lethbridge:* CBRT-TV-6**(Channel: 10)
Owned by: **Canadian Broadcasting Corporation (CBC)**
Lethbridge, AB
866-306-4636
www.cbc.ca/calgary; www.cbc.ca/television
Social Media: www.twitter.com/cbccalgary
Other information: TTY: 1-866-220-6045

***Lethbridge:* CFCN-TV**(Channel: 13)
Owned by: **CTVglobemedia Inc.**
640-13 Street North, Lethbridge, AB T1H 2S8
403-329-3644,
cfcnlethbridge@ctv.ca
www.cfcn.ca

***Lethbridge:* CFCN-TV-5**(Channel: 13)
Owned by: **CTVglobemedia Inc.**
640 - 13 St. North, Lethbridge, AB T1H 2S8
403-329-3644, Fax: 403-317-2420,
cfcnlethbridge@ctv.ca
www.cfcn.ca
Dave Lelek, General & Sales Manager
Terry Vogt, News Director
Dale Munro, Chief Engineer & Operations Manager

***Lethbridge:* CISA-TV**(Channel: 7)
Owned by: **Canwest Global Communications Corp.**
1401 - 28 St. North, Lethbridge, AB T1H 6H9
403-327-1521, Fax: 403-320-2620,
www.canada.com/lethbridge
Peter Deys, General Manager

***Lethbridge:* CJIL-TV (The Miracle Channel)**(Channel: 17)
PO Box 1566, 450-31 St. N., Lethbridge, AB T1H 3Z3
403-380-3399, Fax: 403-380-3322,
mail@miraclechannel.ca
www.miraclechannel.ca

***Lethbridge:* CKAL-TV**(Channel: 6)
Owned by: **CKAL-TV**
Lethbridge, AB

***Lloydminster:* CITL-TV (Newcap TV)**(Channel: 4)
Owned by: **NewCap Inc.**
5026 - 50th St., Lloydminster, AB T9V 1P3
780-875-3321, Fax: 780-875-4704,
tvnews@newcap.ca
www.newcaptv.com
Mike Keller, General Manager, mkeller@newcap.ca

***Lloydminster:* CKSA-TV**(Channel: 2)
Owned by: **NewCap Inc.**
5026 - 50 St., Lloydminster, AB T9V 1P3
780-875-3321, Fax: 780-875-4704,
tvnews@newcap.ca
www.newcap.ca
Mike Keller

***Lougheed:* CFRN-TV-7**(Channel: 7)
Owned by: **CTVglobemedia Inc.**
Lougheed, AB

***Manning:* CBXAT-TV-3**(Channel: 12)
Owned by: **CBXT-TV**
Manning, AB

***Marten Mtn./Slave Lake:* CBXAT-TV-11**(Channel: 11)
Owned by: **CBXT-TV**
Marten Mtn./Slave Lake, AB

***Medicine Hat:* CFCN-TV-8**(Channel: 8)
Owned by: **CTVglobemedia Inc.**
Medicine Hat, AB

***Oyen:* CFON-TV-1**(Channel: 2)
Owned by: **CTVglobemedia Inc.**
Oyen, AB

***Oyen:* CHAT-TV-4**(Channel: 4, 6)
Owned by: **CHAT-TV**
Oyen, AB

***Peace River:* CBXAT-TV-1**(Channel: 7)
Owned by: **CBXT-TV**
Peace River, AB

***Peace River:* CFRN-TV-2**(Channel: 3)
Owned by: **CTVglobemedia Inc.**
Peace River, AB

***Pincher Creek:* CBRT-TV-9**(Channel: 15 (UHF))
Owned by: **Canadian Broadcasting Corporation (CBC)**
Pincher Creek, AB
866-306-4636
www.cbc.ca/calgary; www.cbc.ca/television
Social Media: www.twitter.com/cbccalgary
Other information: TTY: 1-866-220-6045

***Pincher Creek:* CHPC-TV-2**(Channel: 11)
Owned by: **CTVglobemedia Inc.**
Pincher Creek, AB

***Provost:* CITL-TV2**(Channel: 5)
Owned by: **CITL-TV**
Provost, AB

***Provost:* CKSA-TV**(Channel: 12)
Owned by: **CKSA-TV**
Provost, AB

***Rainbow Lake:* CBXAT-TV-8**(Channel: 11)
Owned by: **CBXT-TV**
Rainbow Lake, AB

***Red Deer:* CFRN-TV-6**(Channel: 8)
Owned by: **CTVglobemedia Inc.**
Red Deer, AB

***Red Deer:* CHCA-TV**(Channel: 6)
2840 Bremner Ave., Red Deer, AB T4R 1M9
403-346-2573, Fax: 403-346-9980,
info@chtv.ca
www.canada.com/chtv/reddeer
Stan Schmidt, Station Manager
Bob Bourns, Operations Manager

***Red Deer:* CKEM-TV**(Channel: 8)
Owned by: **CKEM-TV**
Red Deer, AB

***Redcliff:* CHAT-TV**(Channel: 6)
Owned by: **The Jim Pattison Broadcast Group**
10 Boundary Rd. S.E., Redcliff, AB T0J 2P0
403-548-8008, Fax: 403-548-6766,
info@chattv6-3.com
www.chattv6-3.com
Dwaine Dietrich, General Manager

***Rocky Mountain House:* CFMH-TV-2**(Channel: 12)
Owned by: **CTVglobemedia Inc.**
Rocky Mountain House, AB

***Rosemary:* CBRT-TV-5**(Channel: 11 (VHF))
Owned by: **Canadian Broadcasting Corporation (CBC)**
Rosemary, AB
866-306-4636
www.cbc.ca/calgary; www.cbc.ca/television

** For details on this company see listing in Major Broadcasting Companies section; † French language station*

Social Media: www.twitter.com/cbccalgary
Other information: TTY: 1-866-220-6045

Slave Lake: **CKHP-TV-1**(Channel: 4)
Owned by: **CTVglobemedia Inc.**
Slave Lake, AB

Sundre: **CFCN-TV**(Channel: 7)
Owned by: **CTVglobemedia Inc.**
Sundre, AB

Wabasca: **CBXAT-TV-12**(Channel: 7)
Owned by: **CBXT-TV**
Wabasca, AB

Wainwright: **CITL-TV1**(Channel: 6)
Owned by: **CITL-TV**
Wainwright, AB

Wainwright: **CKSA-TV**(Channel: 8)
Owned by: **CKSA-TV**
Wainwright, AB

Waterton Park: **CBRT-TV-7**(Channel: 4 (VHF))
Owned by: **Canadian Broadcasting Corporation (CBC)**
Waterton Park, AB

866-306-4636
www.cbc.ca/calgary; www.cbc.ca/television
Social Media: www.twitter.com/cbccalgary
Other information: TTY: 1-866-220-6045

Waterton Park: **CJWP-TV-2**(Channel: 6)
Owned by: **CTVglobemedia Inc.**
Waterton Park, AB

Whitecourt: **CBXT-TV-2**(Channel: 9)
Owned by: **CBXT-TV**
Whitecourt, AB

Whitecourt: **CFRN-TV-3**(Channel: 12)
Owned by: **CTVglobemedia Inc.**
Whitecourt, AB

British Columbia

100 Mile House: **CFJC-TV-6**(Channel: 5)
Owned by: **CFJC-TV**
100 Mile House, BC

100 Mile House: **CHAN-TV**(Channel: 3)
Owned by: **CHAN-TV**
100 Mile House, BC

16 Mile House: **CHCS-TV-1**(Channel: 7)
Owned by: **CHAN-TV**
16 Mile House, BC

Alert Bay: **CBUT-TV-16**(Channel: 11)
Owned by: **CBUT-TV**
Alert Bay, BC

Alexis Creek: **CHIL-TV-1**(Channel: 8)
Owned by: **CFJC-TV**
Alexis Creek, BC

Alexis Creek: **CIAC-TV**(Channel: 11)
Owned by: **CHAN-TV**
Alexis Creek, BC

Alice Arm: **CFTK-TV**(Channel: 7)
Owned by: **CFTK-TV**
Alice Arm, BC

Anahim Lake: **CIAL-TV-1**(Channel: 5)
Owned by: **CHAN-TV**
Anahim Lake, BC

Ashcroft: **CHAC-TV-2**(Channel: 2)
Owned by: **CHAN-TV**
Ashcroft, BC

Ashcroft: **CJAC-TV-2**(Channel: 5)
Owned by: **CFJC-TV**
Ashcroft, BC

Avola: **CFJC-TV**(Channel: 11)
Owned by: **CFJC**
Avola, BC

Avola: **CJVO-TV**(Channel: 13)
Owned by: **CHAN-TV**
Avola, BC

Barkerville: **CKPG-TV**(Channel: 9)
Owned by: **CKPG-TV**
Barkerville, BC

Barriere: **CKTV-TV-1**(Channel: 12)
Owned by: **CFJC-TV**
Barriere, BC

Barriere: **CKTV-TV-2**(Channel: 7)
Owned by: **CHAN-TV**
Barriere, BC

Beaton: **CHBC-TV**(Channel: 8)
Owned by: **CHBC-TV**
Beaton, BC

Bella Bella: **CBUT-TV**(Channel: 13)
Owned by: **CBUT-TV**
Bella Bella, BC

Bella Bella: **CFTK-TV**(Channel: 9)
Owned by: **CFTK-TV**
Bella Bella, BC

Bella Coola: **CFTK-TV**(Channel: 7)
Owned by: **CFTK-TV**
Bella Coola, BC

Blue River: **CFJC-TV**(Channel: 3)
Owned by: **CFJC**
Blue River, BC

Blue River: **CHAN-TV**(Channel: 13)
Owned by: **CHAN-TV**
Blue River, BC

Bonnington: **CBUDT-TV**(Channel: 13)
Owned by: **CBUT-TV**
Bonnington, BC

Boston Bar: **CFJC-TV-1**(Channel: 5)
Owned by: **CFJC-TV**
Boston Bar, BC

Boston Bar: **CHAN-TV**(Channel: 3)
Owned by: **CHAN-TV**
Boston Bar, BC

Bowen Island: **CBUT-TV-4**(Channel: 13)
Owned by: **CBUT-TV**
Bowen Island, BC

Bowen Island: **CHAN-TV-2**(Channel: 3)
Owned by: **CHAN-TV**
Bowen Island, BC

Brackendale: **CBUT-TV-34**(Channel: 35)
Owned by: **CBUT-TV**
Brackendale, BC

Brackendale: **CHAN-TV-5**(Channel: 9)
Owned by: **CHAN-TV**
Brackendale, BC

Bullhead Mountain: **CJDC-TV-2**(Channel: 8)
Owned by: **CJDC-TV**
Bullhead Mountain, BC

Burns Lake: **CKHS-TV**(Channel: 13)
Owned by: **CHAN-TV**
Burns Lake, BC

Cache Creek: **CHAC-TV-1**(Channel: 12)
Owned by: **CHAN-TV**
Cache Creek, BC

Cache Creek: **CJAC-TV-1**(Channel: 10)
Owned by: **CFJC-TV**
Cache Creek, BC

Campbell River: **CBUT-TV-8**(Channel: 3, 82)
Owned by: **CBUT-TV**
Campbell River, BC

866-220-6045

Canal Flats: **CBUBT-TV-1**(Channel: 12)
Owned by: **CBUT-TV**
Canal Flats, BC

Canoe: **CHBC-TV-8**(Channel: 6)
Owned by: **CHBC-TV**
Canoe, BC

Castlegar: **CBUAT-TV-2**(Channel: 3)
Owned by: **CBUT-TV**
Castlegar, BC

Castlegar: **CKTN-TV-1**(Channel: 5)
Owned by: **CHAN-TV**
Castlegar, BC

Cawston: **CHBC-TV**(Channel: 3)
Owned by: **CHBC-TV**
Cawston, BC

Celista: **CHBC-TV-6**(Channel: 3)
Owned by: **CHBC-TV**
Celista, BC

Chase: **CFJC-TV-8**(Channel: 11)
Owned by: **CFJC-TV**
Chase, BC

Chase: **CHSH-TV-1**(Channel: 7)
Owned by: **CHAN-TV**
Chase, BC

Chase: **CHSH-TV-2**(Channel: 13)
Owned by: **CHAN-TV**
Chase, BC

Cherryville: **CJCC-TV**(Channel: 13)
Owned by: **CHAN-TV**
Cherryville, BC

Cherryville: **CJWR-TV-1**(Channel: 10)
Owned by: **CHBC-TV**
Cherryville, BC

Chilliwack: **CBUT-TV-2**(Channel: 3)
Owned by: **CBUT-TV**
Chilliwack, BC

Chilliwack: **CHAN-TV-1**(Channel: 11)
Owned by: **CHAN-TV**
Chilliwack, BC

Christina Lake: **CBUAT-TV-7**(Channel: 13)
Owned by: **CBUT-TV**
Christina Lake, BC

Clearwater: **CHCW-TV-1**(Channel: 2)
Owned by: **CFJC-TV**
Clearwater, BC

Clearwater: **CHCW-TV-2**(Channel: 10)
Owned by: **CHAN-TV**
Clearwater, BC

Clinton: **CFJC-TV-4**(Channel: 9)
Owned by: **CFJC-TV**
Clinton, BC

Clinton: **CHTS-TV-1**(Channel: 13)
Owned by: **CHAN-TV**
Clinton, BC

Coal Harbour: **CBUT-TV-20**(Channel: 8)
Owned by: **CBUT-TV**
Coal Harbour, BC

Coal Harbour: **CHAN-TV**(Channel: 10)
Owned by: **CHAN-TV**
Coal Harbour, BC

Columbia Valley: **CFCN-TV**(Channel: 6)
Owned by: **CTVglobemedia Inc.**
Columbia Valley, BC

Courtenay: **CBUT-TV-1**(Channel: 9)
Owned by: **CBUT-TV**
Courtenay, BC

Courtenay: **CHAN-TV-4**(Channel: 13)
Owned by: **CHAN-TV**
Courtenay, BC

** For details on this company see listing in Major Broadcasting Companies section; † French language station*

Courtenay: **CHEK-TV-5**(Channel: 13)
Owned by: **CHEK-TV**
Courtenay, BC

Cranbrook: **CBUBT-TV-7**(Channel: 65)
Owned by: **CBUT-TV**
Cranbrook, BC

Crawford Bay: **CBUCT-TV-1**(Channel: 5)
Owned by: **CBUT-TV**
Crawford Bay, BC

Crescent Valley: **CBUCT-TV-4**(Channel: 33)
Owned by: **CBUT-TV**
Crescent Valley, BC

Creston: **CBUCT-TV-2**(Channel: 3)
Owned by: **CBUT-TV**
Creston, BC

Creston: **CKTN-TV-4**(Channel: 12)
Owned by: **CHAN-TV**
Creston, BC

Dawson Creek: **CJDC-TV**(Channel: 5)
Owned by: **Standard Radio Office**
901 - 102 Ave., Dawson Creek, BC V1G 2B6
250-782-3341, Fax: 250-782-3154, 800-663-6634
traffic@cjdcam.com
Tracey Gard, General Manager

Donald Station: **CBUBT-TV-4**(Channel: 3)
Owned by: **CBUT-TV**
Donald Station, BC

Downie: **CHBC-TV**(Channel: 9)
Owned by: **CHBC-TV**
Downie, BC

Elks Falls Lookout: **CHAN-TV**(Channel: 49)
Owned by: **CHAN-TV**
Elks Falls Lookout, BC

Endako: **CKPG-TV**(Channel: 6)
Owned by: **CKPG-TV**
Endako, BC

Enderby: **CFEN-TV-1**(Channel: 4)
Owned by: **CHBC-TV**
Enderby, BC

Enderby: **CFEN-TV-2**(Channel: 11)
Owned by: **CHAN-TV**
Enderby, BC

Erie: **CBUAT-TV-4**(Channel: 13)
Owned by: **CBUT-TV**
Erie, BC

Falkland: **CFAW-TV**(Channel: 12)
Owned by: **CHAN-TV**
Falkland, BC

Falkland: **CFWS-TV-1**(Channel: 10)
Owned by: **CHBC-TV**
Falkland, BC

Fernie: **CBUBT-TV-9**(Channel: 8)
Owned by: **CBUT-TV**
Fernie, BC

Field: **CBUBT-TV-13**(Channel: 11)
Owned by: **CBUT-TV**
Field, BC

Fort Nelson: **CBUGT-TV**(Channel: 8)
Owned by: **CBUT-TV**
Fort Nelson, BC

Fort St James: **CFFS-TV**(Channel: 10, 3)
Owned by: **CHAN-TV**
Fort St James, BC

Fountain: **CFDF-TV-1**(Channel: 5)
Owned by: **CHAN-TV**
Fountain, BC

Fraser Lake: **CFFL-TV-1**(Channel: 9)
Owned by: **CHAN-TV**
Fraser Lake, BC

Fraser Lake: **CFFL-TV-2**(Channel: 6)
Owned by: **CKPG-TV**
Fraser Lake, BC

Fruitvale/Montrose: **CBUAT-TV-3**(Channel: 9)
Owned by: **CBUT-TV**
Fruitvale/Montrose, BC

Glacier: **CHBC-TV**(Channel: 13)
Owned by: **CHBC-TV**
Glacier, BC

Glacier Camp: **CHAN-TV**(Channel: 11)
Owned by: **CHAN-TV**
Glacier Camp, BC

Gold Bridge: **CJGB-TV-1**(Channel: 6)
Owned by: **CHAN-TV**
Gold Bridge, BC

Gold River: **CBUT-TV-12**(Channel: 7)
Owned by: **CBUT-TV**
Gold River, BC

Gold River: **CHAN-TV**(Channel: 2)
Owned by: **CHAN-TV**
Gold River, BC

Golden: **CBUBT-TV-2**(Channel: 13)
Owned by: **CBUT-TV**
Golden, BC

Grand Forks: **CBUT-TV-37**(Channel: 5)
Owned by: **CBUT-TV**
Grand Forks, BC

Grand Forks: **CKSR-TV-1**(Channel: 7)
Owned by: **CHAN-TV**
Grand Forks, BC

Granisle: **CFTK-TV**(Channel: 6)
Owned by: **CFTK-TV**
Granisle, BC

Granisle: **CIGR-TV-1**(Channel: 7)
Owned by: **CHAN-TV**
Granisle, BC

Greenwood: **CBUT-TV-31**(Channel: 13)
Owned by: **CBUT-TV**
Greenwood, BC

Grinrod: **CHBC-TV**(Channel: 72)
Owned by: **CHBC-TV**
Grinrod, BC

Hagensborg: **CBUIT-TV-4**(Channel: 11)
Owned by: **CBUT-TV**
Hagensborg, BC

Hagensborg: **CFTK-TV**(Channel: 9)
Owned by: **CFTK-TV**
Hagensborg, BC

Harrison Hot Springs: **CBUT-TV-23**(Channel: 13)
Owned by: **CBUT-TV**
Harrison Hot Springs, BC

Hazelton: **CFTK-TV**(Channel: 9)
Owned by: **CFTK-TV**
Hazelton, BC

Hendrix Lake: **CIHL-TV**(Channel: 12)
Owned by: **CHAN-TV**
Hendrix Lake, BC

Hixon: **CKPG-TV-1**(Channel: 10)
Owned by: **CKPG-TV**
Hixon, BC

Holberg: **CBUT-TV-21**(Channel: 2)
Owned by: **CBUT-TV**
Holberg, BC

Holberg: **CHAN-TV**(Channel: 4, 8)
Owned by: **CHAN-TV**
Holberg, BC

Hope: **CBUT-TV-6**(Channel: 9)
Owned by: **CBUT-TV**
Hope, BC

Houston: **CFHO-TV**(Channel: 8)
Owned by: **CHAN-TV**
Houston, BC

Hudson's Hope: **CJDC**(Channel: 11)
Owned by: **CJDC-TV**
Hudson's Hope, BC

Invermere: **CBUBT-TV-3**(Channel: 2)
Owned by: **CBUT-TV**
Invermere, BC

Jubilee Mountain: **CFCN-TV**(Channel: 8)
Owned by: **CTVglobemedia Inc.**
Jubilee Mountain, BC

Juskatla: **CFTK-TV**(Channel: 2)
Owned by: **CFTK-TV**
Juskatla, BC

Kamloops: **CFJC-TV**(Channel: 4)
Owned by: **The Jim Pattison Broadcast Group**
460 Pemberton Terrace, Kamloops, BC V2C 1T5
250-372-3322, Fax: 250-374-0445,
info@cfjctv.com
www.cfjctv.com
Rick Arnish, President & General Manager

Kamloops: **CHKM-TV**(Channel: 6)
Owned by: **CHAN-TV**
Kamloops, BC

Kelowna: **CHBC-TV**(Channel: 2)
Owned by: **Canwest Global Communications Corp.**
342 Leon Ave., Kelowna, BC V1Y 6J2
250-762-4535, Fax: 250-868-0662, 888-762-4535
comments@chbc.com
www.chbc.com

Kelowna: **CHKL-TV**(Channel: 5)
Owned by: **CHAN-TV**
Kelowna, BC

Keremeos: **CHBC-TV**(Channel: 4)
Owned by: **CHBC-TV**
Keremeos, BC

Kildala: **CFTK-TV**(Channel: 5)
Owned by: **CFTK-TV**
Kildala, BC

King Island: **CBUT-TV**(Channel: 9)
Owned by: **CBUT-TV**
King Island, BC

Kitwanga: **CFTK-TV**(Channel: 13)
Owned by: **CFTK-TV**
Kitwanga, BC

Kokish: **CHAN-TV**(Channel: 9)
Owned by: **CHAN-TV**
Kokish, BC

Kootenay Lake: **CHAN-TV**(Channel: 10)
Owned by: **CHAN-TV**
Kootenay Lake, BC

Lillooet: **CFDF-TV-2**(Channel: 13)
Owned by: **CHAN-TV**
Lillooet, BC

Lillooet: **CFMZ-TV-1**(Channel: 2)
Owned by: **CFJC-TV**
Lillooet, BC

Little Fort: **CKTV-TV-1**(Channel: 12)
Owned by: **CFJC-TV**
Little Fort, BC

Logan Lake: **CFJC-TV**(Channel: 11)
Owned by: **CFJC-TV**
Logan Lake, BC

Logan Lake: **CHLK-TV-2**(Channel: 13)
Owned by: **CHAN-TV**
Logan Lake, BC

Loos: **CBUHT-TV-2**(Channel: 6)
Owned by: **CBUT-TV**
Loos, BC

** For details on this company see listing in Major Broadcasting Companies section; † French language station*

Lumby: **CHBC-TV**(Channel: 4)
Owned by: **CHBC-TV**
Lumby, BC

Lumby: **CHID-TV-2**(Channel: 9)
Owned by: **CHAN-TV**
Lumby, BC

Lytton: **CHWS-TV-1**(Channel: 11)
Owned by: **CFJC-TV**
Lytton, BC

Lytton: **CILY-TV-2**(Channel: 8)
Owned by: **CHAN-TV**
Lytton, BC

Mabel Lake: **CHPL-TV-1**(Channel: 13)
Owned by: **CHAN-TV**
Mabel Lake, BC

Mabel Lake: **CHPP-TV-1**(Channel: 8)
Owned by: **CHBC-TV**
Mabel Lake, BC

Mackenzie: **CIMK-TV-1**(Channel: 9)
Owned by: **CHAN-TV**
Mackenzie, BC

Mackenzie: **CKPG-TV-4**(Channel: 6)
Owned by: **CKPG-TV**
Mackenzie, BC

Malakwa: **CFFI-TV-1**(Channel: 4)
Owned by: **CHBC-TV**
Malakwa, BC

Malakwa: **CFFI-TV-2**(Channel: 11)
Owned by: **CHAN-TV**
Malakwa, BC

Masset: **CHMH-TV-1**(Channel: 8)
Owned by: **CFTK-TV**
Masset, BC

McBride: **CBUHT-TV-3**(Channel: 2)
Owned by: **CBUT-TV**
McBride, BC

McBride: **CHAN-TV**(Channel: 12)
Owned by: **CHAN-TV**
McBride, BC

Merritt: **CFJC-TV-3**(Channel: 8)
Owned by: **CFJC-TV**
Merritt, BC

Mica Creek: **CHAN-TV**(Channel: 7, 4)
Owned by: **CHAN-TV**
Mica Creek, BC

Mica Creek: **CHBC-TV**(Channel: 5)
Owned by: **CHBC-TV**
Mica Creek, BC

Midway: **CBUT-TV-32**(Channel: 7)
Owned by: **CBUT-TV**
Midway, BC

Midway: **CHAN-TV**(Channel: 3)
Owned by: **CHAN-TV**
Midway, BC

Minto: **CFMT-TV-3**(Channel: 3)
Owned by: **CFJC-TV**
Minto, BC

Monte Lake: **CFJC-TV**(Channel: 8)
Owned by: **CFJC**
Monte Lake, BC

Mount Hamilton: **CFHM-TV-1**(Channel: 7)
Owned by: **CFJC-TV**
Mount Hamilton, BC

Mount Hamilton: **CHAN-TV**(Channel: 9)
Owned by: **CHAN-TV**
Mount Hamilton, BC

Mount McDonald: **CBUT-TV-27**(Channel: 59)
Owned by: **CBUT-TV**
Mount McDonald, BC

Mount Wells: **CFTK-TV**(Channel: 12)
Owned by: **CFTK-TV**
Mount Wells, BC

Moyie: **CBUBT-TV-14**(Channel: 6)
Owned by: **CBUT-TV**
Moyie, BC

Nakusp: **CJNP-TV-1**(Channel: 2)
Owned by: **CHBC-TV**
Nakusp, BC

Nakusp: **CJNP-TV-3**(Channel: 7)
Owned by: **CHAN-TV**
Nakusp, BC

Nass Valley: **CFTK-TV**(Channel: 7)
Owned by: **CFTK-TV**
Nass Valley, BC

Natal: **CBUBT-TV-10**(Channel: 11)
Owned by: **CBUT-TV**
Natal, BC

Nelson: **CBUCT-TV**(Channel: 9)
Owned by: **CBUT-TV**
Nelson, BC

Nelson: **CKTN-TV-3**(Channel: 3)
Owned by: **CHAN-TV**
Nelson, BC

New Denver: **CBUCT-TV-6**(Channel: 17)
Owned by: **CBUT-TV**
New Denver, BC

New Denver: **CHJV-TV**(Channel: 13)
Owned by: **CHAN-TV**
New Denver, BC

Newcastle Ridge: **CFKB-TV-1**(Channel: 7)
Owned by: **CHEK-TV**
Newcastle Ridge, BC

Newcastle Ridge: **CHAN-TV**(Channel: 7)
Owned by: **CHAN-TV**
Newcastle Ridge, BC

Nicola Valley: **CFJC-TV-12**(Channel: 10)
Owned by: **CFJC-TV**
Nicola Valley, BC

Nimpkish: **CBUT-TV**(Channel: 9)
Owned by: **CBUT-TV**
Nimpkish, BC

Nimpkish: **CHAN-TV**(Channel: 6)
Owned by: **CHAN-TV**
Nimpkish, BC

Noranda Mines: **CFJC-TV**(Channel: 7)
Owned by: **CFJC-TV**
Noranda Mines, BC

North Forks: **CHAN-TV**(Channel: 7)
Owned by: **CHAN-TV**
North Forks, BC

Ocean Falls: **CBUT-TV**(Channel: 11)
Owned by: **CBUT-TV**
Ocean Falls, BC

Ocean Falls: **CFTK-TV**(Channel: 2)
Owned by: **CFTK-TV**
Ocean Falls, BC

Olalla: **CHBC-TV**(Channel: 11)
Owned by: **CHBC-TV**
Olalla, BC

Olalla: **CHKC-TV-5**(Channel: 11)
Owned by: **CHAN-TV**
Olalla, BC

Oliver: **CHAN-TV**(Channel: 3)
Owned by: **CHAN-TV**
Oliver, BC

Oliver: **CHBC-TV-3**(Channel: 8)
Owned by: **CHBC-TV**
Oliver, BC

Ottertail: **CBUT-TV**(Channel: 53)
Owned by: **CBUT-TV**
Ottertail, BC

Palliser: **CBUT-TV**(Channel: 40)
Owned by: **CBUT-TV**
Palliser, BC

Peachland: **CHPT-TV-1**(Channel: 4)
Owned by: **CHBC-TV**
Peachland, BC

Peachland: **CIPL-TV**(Channel: 9)
Owned by: **CHAN-TV**
Peachland, BC

Pemberton: **CBUPT-TV**(Channel: 4)
Owned by: **CBUT-TV**
Pemberton, BC

Penticton: **CHBC-TV-1**(Channel: 13)
Owned by: **CHBC-TV**
Penticton, BC

Penticton: **CHKL-TV-1**(Channel: 10)
Owned by: **CHAN-TV**
Penticton, BC

Phoenix: **CBUT-TV-30**(Channel: 15)
Owned by: **CBUT-TV**
Phoenix, BC

Pine Valley: **CFJC-TV**(Channel: 2)
Owned by: **CFJC**
Pine Valley, BC

Port Alberni: **CBUT-TV-3**(Channel: 4)
Owned by: **CBUT-TV**
Port Alberni, BC

Port Alberni: **CHEK-TV-3**(Channel: 11)
Owned by: **CHEK-TV**
Port Alberni, BC

Port Alice: **CBUT-TV-17**(Channel: 10)
Owned by: **CBUT-TV**
Port Alice, BC

Port Alice: **CHAN-TV**(Channel: 2, 7)
Owned by: **CHAN-TV**
Port Alice, BC

Port Hardy: **CBUT-TV-19**(Channel: 6)
Owned by: **CBUT-TV**
Port Hardy, BC

Port Hardy: **CHAN-TV**(Channel: 3)
Owned by: **CHAN-TV**
Port Hardy, BC

Port McNeill: **CBUT-TV-18**(Channel: 2)
Owned by: **CBUT-TV**
Port McNeill, BC

Port Renfrew: **CJTV-TV-1**(Channel: 11)
Owned by: **CHAN-TV**
Port Renfrew, BC

Prince George: **CIFG-TV**(Channel: 12)
Owned by: **CHAN-TV**
Prince George, BC

Prince George: **CKPG-TV**(Channel: 2)
Owned by: **The Jim Pattison Broadcast Group**
1220 - 6th Ave., Prince George, BC V2L 3M8
250-564-8861, Fax: 250-562-7681,
ckpgmail@ckpg.bc.ca
www.993thedrive.com
Ken Kilcullen, kkilcullen@ckpg.bc.ca

Prince Rupert: **CFTK-TV**(Channel: 3)
Owned by: **Standard Broadcasting Corp. Ltd.**
#212, 215 Cow Bay Rd., Prince Rupert, BC V8J 1A2
250-624-9111, Fax: 250-624-3100,
smenhinick@srt.ca
Brian Langston, General Manager

Prince Rupert: **CFTK-TV-1**(Channel: 6)
Owned by: **CFTK-TV**
Prince Rupert, BC

** For details on this company see listing in Major Broadcasting Companies section; † French language station*

Princeton: **CHBC-TV**(Channel: 5)
Owned by: **CHBC-TV**
Princeton, BC

Princeton: **CHNJ-TV-1**(Channel: 11)
Owned by: **CHAN-TV**
Princeton, BC

Pritchard: **CFJC-TV-19**(Channel: 5)
Owned by: **CFJC-TV**
Pritchard, BC

Pritchard: **CHKM-TV-1**(Channel: 9)
Owned by: **CHAN-TV**
Pritchard, BC

Puntzi: **CHAN-TV**(Channel: 2)
Owned by: **CHAN-TV**
Puntzi, BC

Purden: **CBUHT-TV-1**(Channel: 10)
Owned by: **CBUT-TV**
Purden, BC

Queen Charlotte: **CFTK-TV**(Channel: 4)
Owned by: **CFTK-TV**
Queen Charlotte, BC

Quesnel: **CFJC-TV-11**(Channel: 7)
Owned by: **CFJC-TV**
Quesnel, BC

Quesnel: **CITM-TV-2**(Channel: 8)
Owned by: **CHAN-TV**
Quesnel, BC

Quesnel: **CKPG-TV-5**(Channel: 13)
Owned by: **CKPG-TV**
Quesnel, BC

Radium Hot Springs: **CBUBT-TV-5**(Channel: 77)
Owned by: **CBUT-TV**
Radium Hot Springs, BC

Revelstoke: **CHRP-TV-1**(Channel: 7)
Owned by: **CHBC-TV**
Revelstoke, BC

Revelstoke: **CHRP-TV-2**(Channel: 2)
Owned by: **CHAN-TV**
Revelstoke, BC

Rim Rock: **CFJC-TV**(Channel: 9)
Owned by: **CFJC**
Rim Rock, BC

Rimrock: **CKRR-TV-1**(Channel: 9)
Owned by: **CFJC-TV**
Rimrock, BC

Rimrock: **CKRR-TV-2**(Channel: 11)
Owned by: **CHAN-TV**
Rimrock, BC

River Jordan: **CBUT-TV**(Channel: 9)
Owned by: **CBUT-TV**
River Jordan, BC

River Jordan: **CHEK-TV**(Channel: 11)
Owned by: **CHEK-TV**
River Jordan, BC

Rock Creek: **CBUT-TV-33**(Channel: 33)
Owned by: **CBUT-TV**
Rock Creek, BC

Rock Creek: **CHAN-TV**(Channel: 3)
Owned by: **CHAN-TV**
Rock Creek, BC

Ruby Creek: **CBUT-TV-26**(Channel: 25)
Owned by: **CBUT-TV**
Ruby Creek, BC

Salmo: **CBUAT-TV-5**(Channel: 10)
Owned by: **CBUT-TV**
Salmo, BC

Salmon Arm: **CFSA-TV-1**(Channel: 13)
Owned by: **CHAN-TV**
Salmon Arm, BC

Salmon Arm: **CHBC-TV-4**(Channel: 9)
Owned by: **CHBC-TV**
Salmon Arm, BC

Santa Rosa: **CKSR-TV**(Channel: 83)
Owned by: **CHAN-TV**
Santa Rosa, BC

Savona: **CFSC-TV-1**(Channel: 8)
Owned by: **CFJC-TV**
Savona, BC

Savona: **CFSC-TV-2**(Channel: 13)
Owned by: **CHAN-TV**
Savona, BC

Sawmill: **CBUT-TV**(Channel: 7)
Owned by: **CBUT-TV**
Sawmill, BC

Sayward: **CBUT-TV-10**(Channel: 4)
Owned by: **CBUT-TV**
Sayward, BC

Shalalth: **CJBT-TV-1**(Channel: 5)
Owned by: **CFJC-TV**
Shalalth, BC

Shalalth: **CJBT-TV-2**(Channel: 11)
Owned by: **CHAN-TV**
Shalalth, BC

Shoulder Mtn.: **CFTK-TV**(Channel: 9)
Owned by: **CFTK-TV**
Shoulder Mtn., BC

Skaha Lake: **CHBC-TV-7**(Channel: 7)
Owned by: **CHBC-TV**
Skaha Lake, BC

Slocan: **CBUCT-TV-5**(Channel: 39)
Owned by: **CBUT-TV**
Slocan, BC

Smithers: **CFHO-TV-1**(Channel: 13)
Owned by: **CHAN-TV**
Smithers, BC

Smithers: **CFTK-TV**(Channel: 5)
Owned by: **CFTK-TV**
Smithers, BC

www.cftktv.com

Soda Creek: **CKSC-TV-1**(Channel: 4)
Owned by: **CFJC-TV**
Soda Creek, BC

Soda Creek: **CKSC-TV-2**(Channel: 2)
Owned by: **CHAN-TV**
Soda Creek, BC

Sointula: **CHAN-TV**(Channel: 5)
Owned by: **CHAN-TV**
Sointula, BC

Sooke: **CBUT-TV-28**(Channel: 3)
Owned by: **CBUT-TV**
Sooke, BC

Sooke: **CHEK-TV**(Channel: 13)
Owned by: **CHEK-TV**
Sooke, BC

Spences Bridge: **CJNA-TV-1**(Channel: 3)
Owned by: **CFJC-TV**
Spences Bridge, BC

Spences Bridge: **CJNA-TV-2**(Channel: 7)
Owned by: **CHAN-TV**
Spences Bridge, BC

Spillimacheen: **CBUBT-TV-6**(Channel: 69)
Owned by: **CBUT-TV**
Spillimacheen, BC

Squamish: **CBUT-TV-5**(Channel: 11)
Owned by: **CBUT-TV**
Squamish, BC

Squamish: **CHAN-TV-3**(Channel: 7)
Owned by: **CHAN-TV**
Squamish, BC

Stewart: **CFTK-TV**(Channel: 11)
Owned by: **CFTK-TV**
Stewart, BC

Surrey: **CHNU-TV**(Channel: 10)
Owned by: **Rogers Broadcasting Ltd.**
PO Box 100, 5668 192 St. Ste. 204, Surrey, BC V3S 2V7
604-576-6880, Fax: 604-576-6895,
info@nowtv.ca
www.nowtv.ca

Terry Mahoney, Station Manager

Tabor Mountain: **CBUHT-TV**(Channel: 78)
Owned by: **CBUT-TV**
Tabor Mountain, BC

Taghum: **CKTN-TV-2**(Channel: 23)
Owned by: **CHAN-TV**
Taghum, BC

Tahsis: **CBUT-TV-14**(Channel: 9)
Owned by: **CBUT-TV**
Tahsis, BC

Tasu: **CFTK-TV**(Channel: 11)
Owned by: **CKPG-TV**
Tasu, BC

Tatla Lake: **CIAL-TV-2**(Channel: 9)
Owned by: **CHAN-TV**
Tatla Lake, BC

Telkwa: **CFTK-TV-2**(Channel: 7)
Owned by: **CFTK-TV**
Telkwa, BC

Tête Jaune: **CBUHT-TV-4**(Channel: 10)
Owned by: **CBUT-TV**
Tête Jaune, BC

Tofino: **CBUT-TV-22**(Channel: 10)
Owned by: **CBUT-TV**
Tofino, BC

Topley Landing: **CHAN-TV**(Channel: 8)
Owned by: **CHAN-TV**
Topley Landing, BC

Trail: **CBUAT-TV-6**(Channel: 11)
Owned by: **CBUT-TV**
Trail, BC

Trail: **CKTN-TV**(Channel: 8)
Owned by: **CHAN-TV**
Trail, BC

Ucluelet: **CBUT-FM-7**(Channel: 7)
Owned by: **CBUT-TV**
Ucluelet, BC

Ucluelet: **CKUP-TV-1**(Channel: 6)
Owned by: **CHAN-TV**
Ucluelet, BC

Valemount: **CBUHT-TV-5**(Channel: 6)
Owned by: **CBUT-TV**
Valemount, BC

Valemount: **CFJC-TV**(Channel: 8)
Owned by: **CFJC**
Valemount, BC

Valemount: **CHAN-TV**(Channel: 4)
Owned by: **CHAN-TV**
Valemount, BC

†***Vancouver:*** **CBUFT-TV**(Channel: 26)
Owned by: **Canadian Broadcasting Corporation**
CP 4600, 700 Hamilton St., Vancouver, BC V6B 4A2
604-662-6000, Fax: 604-662-6161

Michèle Smolkin

Vancouver: **CBUT-TV**(Channel: 2)
Owned by: **Canadian Broadcasting Corporation**
PO Box 4600, 700 Hamilton St., Vancouver, BC V6B 4A2

** For details on this company see listing in Major Broadcasting Companies section; † French language station*

604-662-6000, Fax: 604-662-6414,
canadanow@vancouver.cbc.ca
www.vancouver.cbc.ca

Vancouver: **CHAN-TV**(Channel: 8)
Owned by: **Canwest Global Communications Corp.**
7850 Enterprise St., Vancouver, BC V6B 4A3
604-444-9500, Fax: 604-444-9555,
globalbc.news@globaltv.ca
www.canada.com/vancouver
Roy Gardner

Vancouver: **CIVT-TV**(Channel: 32)
Owned by: **CTVglobemedia Inc.**
#300, 750 Burrard St., Vancouver, BC V6Z 1X5
604-608-2868, Fax: 604-609-5799,
bccomments@ctv.ca
www.ctv9.ca
Jim Rusnak, Vice-President & General Manager

Vancouver: **CKVU-TV**(Channel: 10)
Owned by: **Rogers Broadcasting Ltd.**
180 West 2nd St., Vancouver, BC V5Y 3T9
604-876-1344, Fax: 604-874-8225, 888-336-9978
contactjuliac@citytv.com
vancouver.citytv.com
Brad Phillips

Vancouver: **KVOS-TV**(Channel: 12)
#320, 1385 West 8 Ave., Vancouver, BC V6H 3V9
604-681-1212, Fax: 604-736-4510,
www.kvos.com
David Reid, President

Vanderhoof: **CKIN-TV-1**(Channel: 8)
Owned by: **CHAN-TV**
Vanderhoof, BC

Vavenby: **CKVA-TV-1**(Channel: 8)
Owned by: **CHAN-TV**
Vavenby, BC

Vernon: **CHBC-TV-2**(Channel: 7)
Owned by: **CHBC-TV**
Vernon, BC

Vernon: **CHKL-TV-2**(Channel: 12)
Owned by: **CHAN-TV**
Vernon, BC

Victoria: **CHEK-TV**(Channel: 6)
Owned by: **Canwest Global Communications Corp.**
780 Kings Rd., Victoria, BC V8T 5A2
250-383-2435, Fax: 250-384-7766,
ch@chtv.ca
http://www.canada.com/chtv/vancouverisland/
Ron Eberle, General Manager

Victoria: **CIVI-TV**(Channel: 17, 53)
Owned by: **Rogers Broadcasting Ltd.**
1420 Broad St., Victoria, BC V8W 2B1
250-381-2484, Fax: 250-381-2485, 866-242-2484
islandcontactus@achannel.ca
www.achannel.ca/victoria
Richard Gray, Station Manager

Wells: **CKPG-TV**(Channel: 9)
Owned by: **CKPG-TV**
Wells, BC

Wells/Barkerville: **CKWB-TV**(Channel: 11)
Owned by: **CHAN-TV**
Wells/Barkerville, BC

Westwold: **CHBC-TV**(Channel: 12)
Owned by: **CHBC-TV**
Westwold, BC

Whistler: **CBUWT-TV**(Channel: 13)
Owned by: **CBUT-TV**
Whistler, BC

Williams Lake: **CFJC-TV-5**(Channel: 8)
Owned by: **CFJC-TV**
Williams Lake, BC

Williams Lake: **CITM-TV-1**(Channel: 13)
Owned by: **CHAN-TV**
Williams Lake, BC

Winlaw: **CBUCT-TV-3**(Channel: 12)
Owned by: **CBUT-TV**
Winlaw, BC

Wokas Lake: **CBUT-TV**(Channel: 60)
Owned by: **CBUT-TV**
Wokas Lake, BC

Wokas Lake: **CHAN-TV**(Channel: 11)
Owned by: **CHAN-TV**
Wokas Lake, BC

Woos Camp: **CBUT-TV**(Channel: 12)
Owned by: **CBUT-TV**
Woos Camp, BC

Manitoba

Baldy Mountain: **CBWT-TV**(Channel: 8)
Owned by: **CBWT-TV**
Baldy Mountain, MB

Brandon: **CKX-TV**(Channel: 5)
Owned by: **Rogers Broadcasting Ltd.**
2940 Victoria Ave., Brandon, MB R7B 3Y3
204-728-1150, Fax: 204-727-2505,
feedbackbrandon@chumtv.com
www.ckxtv.com
Alan Cruise

Brandon: **CKYB-TV**(Channel: 4)
Owned by: **CTVglobemedia Inc.**
Brandon, MB

Cross Lake: **CBWNT-TV**(Channel: 12)
Owned by: **CBWT-TV**
Cross Lake, MB

Dauphin: **CKYD-TV**(Channel: 12)
Owned by: **CTVglobemedia Inc.**
Dauphin, MB

Easterville: **CBWHT-TV-2**(Channel: 11)
Owned by: **CBWT-TV**
Easterville, MB

Fairford: **CBWGT-TV-2**(Channel: 7)
Owned by: **CBWT-TV**
Fairford, MB

Fisher Branch: **CBWGT-TV**(Channel: 10)
Owned by: **CBWT-TV**
Fisher Branch, MB

Fisher Branch: **CKYA-TV**(Channel: 8)
Owned by: **CTVglobemedia Inc.**
Fisher Branch, MB

Flin Flon: **CBWBT-TV**(Channel: 10)
Owned by: **CBWT-TV**
Flin Flon, MB

Flin Flon: **CKYF-TV**(Channel: 13)
Owned by: **CTVglobemedia Inc.**
Flin Flon, MB

Gillam: **CBWLT-TV**(Channel: 8)
Owned by: **CBWT-TV**
Gillam, MB

Gods Lake Narrows: **CBWXT-TV**(Channel: 13)
Owned by: **CBWT-TV**
Gods Lake Narrows, MB

Grand Rapids: **CBWHT-TV**(Channel: 8)
Owned by: **CBWT-TV**
Grand Rapids, MB

Jackhead: **CBWGT-TV-1**(Channel: 5)
Owned by: **CBWT-TV**
Jackhead, MB

Lac du Bonnet: **CBWT-TV-2**(Channel: 4)
Owned by: **CBWT-TV**
Lac du Bonnet, MB

Leaf Rapids: **CBWQT-TV**(Channel: 13)
Owned by: **CBWT-TV**
Leaf Rapids, MB

Lynn Lake: **CBWRT-TV**(Channel: 6)
Owned by: **CBWT-TV**
Lynn Lake, MB

Mafeking: **CBWYT-TV**(Channel: 2)
Owned by: **CBWT-TV**
Mafeking, MB

Manigotagan: **CBWGT-TV-3**(Channel: 22)
Owned by: **CBWT-TV**
Manigotagan, MB

McCreary: **CKX-TV-3**(Channel: 11)
Owned by: **CKX-TV**
McCreary, MB

McCusker Lake: **CBWUT-TV**(Channel: 10)
Owned by: **CBWT-TV**
McCusker Lake, MB

Melita: **CKX-TV-2**(Channel: 5)
Owned by: **CKX-TV**
Melita, MB

Moose Lake: **CBWIT-TV-1**(Channel: 10)
Owned by: **CBWT-TV**
Moose Lake, MB

Nelson House: **CBWPT-TV**(Channel: 11)
Owned by: **CBWT-TV**
Nelson House, MB

Norway House: **CBWOT-TV**(Channel: 9)
Owned by: **CBWT-TV**
Norway House, MB

Oxford House: **CBWVT-TV**(Channel: 8)
Owned by: **CBWT-TV**
Oxford House, MB

Portage la Prairie: **CHMI-TV**(Channel: 13)
Owned by: **Rogers Broadcasting Ltd.**
PO Box 13000, 350 River Rd., Portage la Prairie, MB R1N 3V3
204-239-1113, Fax: 204-956-0252,
www.a-channel.com
Drew Craig

Pukatawagan: **CBWBT-TV-1**(Channel: 11)
Owned by: **CBWT-TV**
Pukatawagan, MB

Snow Lake: **CBWKT-TV**(Channel: 8)
Owned by: **CBWT-TV**
Snow Lake, MB

Snow Lake: **CKYS-TV**(Channel: 11)
Owned by: **CTVglobemedia Inc.**
Snow Lake, MB

The Pas: **CBWT-TV**(Channel: 7)
Owned by: **CBWT-TV**
The Pas, MB

The Pas: **CKYP-TV**(Channel: 12)
Owned by: **CTVglobemedia Inc.**
The Pas, MB

Thompson: **CBWT-TV**(Channel: 8)
Owned by: **CBWT-TV**
Thompson, MB

Thompson: **CKYT-TV**(Channel: 9)
Owned by: **CTVglobemedia Inc.**
Thompson, MB

Waasagomach: **CBWT-TV**(Channel: 9)
Owned by: **CBWT-TV**
Waasagomach, MB

Wabowden: **CBWMT-TV**(Channel: 10)
Owned by: **CBWT-TV**
Wabowden, MB

Westman: **CKND-TV**(Channel: 2)
Owned by: **CKND-TV**
Westman, MB

** For details on this company see listing in Major Broadcasting Companies section; † French language station*

†*Winnipeg:* **CBWFT-TV**(Channel: 3)
Owned by: **Canadian Broadcasting Corporation**
CP 160 Main, 541 Portage Ave., Winnipeg, MB R3C 2H1
204-788-3141, Fax: 204-788-3639

Winnipeg: **CBWT-TV**(Channel: 6)
Owned by: **Canadian Broadcasting Corporation**
PO Box 160, 541 Portage Ave., Winnipeg, MB R3C 2H1
204-788-3222, Fax: 204-788-3167
John Bertrand, Regional Director
Dave White, TV Operation Manager

Winnipeg: **CHMI-TV**(Channel: 13)
8 Fork Markets Rd., Winnipeg, MB R3C 4Y3
204-947-9613, Fax: 204-956-0811,
a-channel.com

Winnipeg: **CKND-TV**(Channel: 2)
Owned by: **Canwest Global Communications Corp.**
603 St. Mary's Rd., Winnipeg, MB R2M 3L8
204-233-3304, Fax: 204-233-5615,
newsroom@globaltv.ca
http://globalwinnipeg.com
Tim Schellenberg

Winnipeg: **CKY-TV**(Channel: 5)
Owned by: **CTVglobemedia Inc.**
400-345 Graham Ave., Winnipeg, MB R3C 5S6
204-788-3300, Fax: 204-788-3399,
winnipegnews@ctv.ca
www.cky.com
Hanson Bill, Vice-President & General Manager, whanson@ctv.ca
Tara Vosbourgh, Human Resources Manager, tvosbourgh@ctv.ca

New Brunswick

Bathurst: **CKAM-TV**(Channel: 12)
Owned by: **CKCW-TV**
Bathurst, NB

Blackville: **CKAM-TV-3**(Channel: 9)
Owned by: **CKCW-TV**
Blackville, NB

Boiestown: **CKLT-TV-2**(Channel: 7)
Owned by: **CTVglobemedia Inc.**
Boiestown, NB

Campbellton: **CKCD-TV**(Channel: 7)
Owned by: **CKCW-TV**
Campbellton, NB

Chatham: **CKAM-TV-2**(Channel: 10)
Owned by: **CKCW-TV**
Chatham, NB

Doaktown: **CKAM-TV-4**(Channel: 10)
Owned by: **CKCW-TV**
Doaktown, NB

†*Edmundston:* **CIMT-TV**(Channel: 4)
Owned by: **CIMT-TV**
Edmundston, NB E3V 1H3
506-737-9810

Fredericton: **CBAT-TV**(Channel: 4 (antenna): 3 (cable))
Owned by: **Canadian Broadcasting Corporation**
PO Box 2200, 1160 Regent St., Fredericton, NB E3B 5G4
506-451-4000, 866-306-4636
www.cbc.ca/nb; www.cbc.ca/television
Other information: Phone, CBC News: 506-451-4044; Fax: 506-451-4170
Andrew Cochran, Managing Director, Maritimes
Janet Irwin, Senior Regional Manager, News & Current Affairs
Nadine Antle, Regional Manager, Partnerships, Communications, Brand, & Promot, 506-451-4054
John Channing, Manager, New Brunswick Sales
Mary-Pat Schutta, Manager, New Brunswick Programs
Lori Wheeler, Senior Officer, Communications, 506-451-4080

Fredericton: **CIHF-TV**(Channel: 11)
Owned by: **CIHF-TV**
Fredericton, NB

†*Kedgwick:* **CBAFT-TV-9**(Channel: 44)
Owned by: **CBAFT-TV/Canadian Broadcasting Corporation**
Kedgwick, NB

†*Kedgwick:* **CHAU-TV**(Channel: 3)
Owned by: **CHAU-TV**
Kedgwick, NB

Miramichi: **CIHF-TV**(Channel: 40)
Owned by: **CIHF-TV**
Miramichi, NB

†*Moncton:* **CBAFT-TV**
Owned by: **Canadian Broadcasting Corporation**
250, av Université, Moncton, NB E1C 5K3
506-853-6666, Fax: 506-867-8031, 800-561-7010
www.radio-canada.ca/regions/acadie
Social Media: www.facebook.com/CBCRadioCanada
Louise Imbeault, Director & Station Manager

†*Moncton:* **CBAFT-TV-1 - Fredericton/Saint-Jean**
Owned by: **CBAFT-TV/Canadian Broadcasting Corporation**
a/s CBAFT-TV, 250, av Université, Moncton, NB E1C 5K3
800-561-7010
www.radio-canada.ca/regions/acadie
Social Media: www.facebook.com/CBCRadioCanada

†*Moncton:* **CBAFT-TV-10 - Fredericton**
Owned by: **CBAFT-TV/Canadian Broadcasting Corporation**
a/s CBAFT-TV, 250, av Université, Moncton, NB E1C 5K3
800-561-7010
www.radio-canada.ca/regions/acadie
Social Media: www.facebook.com/CBCRadioCanada

†*Moncton:* **CBAFT-TV-2 - Edmundston**
Owned by: **CBAFT-TV/Canadian Broadcasting Corporation**
a/s CBAFT-TV, 250, av Université, Moncton, NB E1C 5K3
800-561-7010
www.radio-canada.ca/regions/acadie
Social Media: www.facebook.com/CBCRadioCanada

†*Moncton:* **CBAFT-TV-4 - Grand Falls**
Owned by: **CBAFT-TV/Canadian Broadcasting Corporation**
a/s CBAFT-TV, 250, av Université, Moncton, NB E1C 5K3
800-561-7010
www.radio-canada.ca/regions/acadie
Social Media: www.facebook.com/CBCRadioCanada

†*Moncton:* **CBAFT-TV-5 - Charlottetown**
Owned by: **CBAFT-TV/Canadian Broadcasting Corporation**
a/s CBAFT-TV, 250, av Université, Moncton, NB E1C 5K3
800-561-7010
www.radio-canada.ca/regions/acadie
Social Media: www.facebook.com/CBCRadioCanada

†*Moncton:* **CBHFT-TV - Halifax**
Owned by: **CBAFT-TV/Canadian Broadcasting Corporation**
a/s CBAFT-TV, 250, av Université, Moncton, NB E1C 5K3
800-561-7010
www.radio-canada.ca/regions/acadie
Social Media: www.facebook.com/CBCRadioCanada

†*Moncton:* **CBHFT-TV-1 - Yarmouth**
Owned by: **CBAFT-TV/Canadian Broadcasting Corporation**
a/s CBAFT-TV, 250, av Université, Moncton, NB E1C 5K3
800-561-7010
www.radio-canada.ca/regions/acadie
Social Media: www.facebook.com/CBCRadioCanada

†*Moncton:* **CBHFT-TV-2 - Mulgrave**
Owned by: **CBAFT-TV/Canadian Broadcasting Corporation**
a/s CBAFT-TV, 250, av Université, Moncton, NB E1C 5K3
800-561-7010
www.radio-canada.ca/regions/acadie
Social Media: www.facebook.com/CBCRadioCanada

†*Moncton:* **CBHFT-TV-3 - Sydney**
Owned by: **CBAFT-TV/Canadian Broadcasting Corporation**
a/s CBAFT-TV, 250, av Université, Moncton, NB E1C 5K3
800-561-7010
www.radio-canada.ca/regions/acadie
Social Media: www.facebook.com/CBCRadioCanada

†*Moncton:* **CBHFT-TV-4 - Chéticamp**
Owned by: **CBAFT-TV/Canadian Broadcasting Corporation**
a/s CBAFT-TV, 250, av Université, Moncton, NB E1C 5K3
800-561-7010
www.radio-canada.ca/regios/acadie
Social Media: www.facebook.com/CBCRadioCanada

†*Moncton:* **CBHFT-TV-5 - Middleton**
Owned by: **CBAFT-TV/Canadian Broadcasting Corporation**
a/s CBAFT-TV, 250, av Université, Moncton, NB E1C 5K3
800-561-7010
www.radio-canada.ca/regions/acadie
Social Media: www.facebook.com/CBCRadioCanada

†*Moncton:* **CBHFT-TV-6 - Digby**
Owned by: **CBAFT-TV/Canadian Broadcasting Corporation**
a/s CBAFT-TV, 250, av Université, Moncton, NB E1C 5K3
800-561-7010
www.radio-canada.ca/regions/acadie
Social Media: www.facebook.com/CBCRadioCanada

†*Moncton:* **CBHFT-TV-7 - New Glasgow**
Owned by: **CBAFT-TV/Canadian Broadcasting Corporation**
a/s CBAFT-TV, 250, av Université, Moncton, NB E1C 5K3
800-561-7010
www.radio-canada.ca/regions/acadie
Social Media: www.facebook.com/CBCRadioCanada

Moncton: **CIHF-TV-3**(Channel: 27)
Owned by: **CIHF-TV**
Moncton, NB

Moncton: **CKCW-TV**(Channel: 2)
Owned by: **CTVglobemedia Inc.**
191 Halifax St., Moncton, NB E1C 9R7
506-857-2600, Fax: 506-857-2617,
www.ctv.ca
Mike Elgie, General Manager

Newcastle: **CKAM-TV-1**(Channel: 10)
Owned by: **CKCW-TV**
Newcastle, NB

Saint John: **CIHF-TV-2**(Channel: 12)
Owned by: **CIHF-TV**
Saint John, NB

Saint John: **CKLT-TV**(Channel: 9)
Owned by: **CTVglobemedia Inc.**
#420, 75 Prince William St., Saint John, NB E2L 2B2
506-658-1010, Fax: 506-658-1208,
cklt@ctv.ca
www.atv.ca

†*Saint-Quentin:* **CBAFT-TV-8**(Channel: 21)
Owned by: **CBAFT-TV/Canadian Broadcasting Corporation**
Saint-Quentin, NB

†*Saint-Quentin:* **CHAU-TV**(Channel: 31)
Owned by: **CHAU-TV**
Saint-Quentin, NB

St Stephen: **CIHF-TV**(Channel: 21)
Owned by: **CIHF-TV**
St Stephen, NB

Tignish: **CKCW-TV-2**(Channel: 5)
Owned by: **CKCW-TV**
Tignish, NB

Woodstock: **CIHF-TV**(Channel: 38)
Owned by: **CIHF-TV**
Woodstock, NB

Woodstock: **CKLT-TV-1**(Channel: 3)
Owned by: **CTVglobemedia Inc.**
Woodstock, NB

** For details on this company see listing in Major Broadcasting Companies section; † French language station*

Newfoundland & Labrador

Baie Verte: **CBNAT-TV-1**(Channel: 3, 12)
Owned by: **CBNT-TV**
Baie Verte, NL

Bay Bulls: **CJON-TV**(Channel: 10)
Owned by: **CJON-TV**
Bay Bulls, NL

Bonavista: **CJWB-TV**(Channel: 10)
Owned by: **CJON-TV**
Bonavista, NL

Brents Cove: **CBNAT-TV-18**(Channel: 10)
Owned by: **CBNT-TV**
Brents Cove, NL

Buchans: **CBNAT-TV-2**(Channel: 13)
Owned by: **CBNT-TV**
Buchans, NL

Cape Broyle: **CJBL-TV-13**(Channel: 13)
Owned by: **CJON-TV**
Cape Broyle, NL

Cartwright: **CBNT-TV-21**(Channel: 9)
Owned by: **CBNT-TV**
Cartwright, NL

Centreville-Wareham-Trinity: **CBNT-TV-16**(Channel: 2)
Owned by: **CBNT-TV**
Centreville-Wareham-Trinity, NL

Clarenville: **CBNT-TV-10**(Channel: 7)
Owned by: **CBNT-TV**
Clarenville, NL

Clarenville: **CJCN-TV-10**(Channel: 10)
Owned by: **CJON-TV**
Clarenville, NL

Coachmans Cove: **CBNAT-TV-16**(Channel: 8)
Owned by: **CBNT-TV**
Coachmans Cove, NL

Conche: **CBNAT-TV-8**(Channel: 13)
Owned by: **CBNT-TV**
Conche, NL

Corner Brook: **CBYT-TV**(Channel: 5)
Owned by: **Canadian Broadcasting Corporation**
PO Box 610, 162 Premier Dr., Corner Brook, NL A2H 6G1
709-634-3141, Fax: 709-634-8506, 866-220-6045
www.stjohns.cbc.ca

Corner Brook: **CJWN-TV**(Channel: 10)
Owned by: **CJON-TV**
Corner Brook, NL

Deer Lake: **CJLW-TV-7**(Channel: 7)
Owned by: **CJON-TV**
Deer Lake, NL

Elliston: **CBNT-TV-7**(Channel: 4)
Owned by: **CBNT-TV**
Elliston, NL

Fermeuse: **CBNT-TV-5**(Channel: 11)
Owned by: **CBNT-TV**
Fermeuse, NL

Fermeuse: **CJFR-TV-12**(Channel: 12)
Owned by: **CJON-TV**
Fermeuse, NL

Ferryland: **CBNT-TV-38**(Channel: 4)
Owned by: **CBNT-TV**
Ferryland, NL

Fleur de Lys: **CBNAT-TV-20**(Channel: 5)
Owned by: **CBNT-TV**
Fleur de Lys, NL

Fogo Island: **CBNAT-TV-6**(Channel: 2)
Owned by: **CBNT-TV**
Fogo Island, NL

Fortune: **CBNT-TV-33**(Channel: 9)
Owned by: **CBNT-TV**
Fortune, NL

Fox Harbour PB: **CBNAT-TV-10**(Channel: 7)
Owned by: **CBNT-TV**
Fox Harbour PB, NL

Freshwater PB: **CJAP-TV**(Channel: 3)
Owned by: **CJON-TV**
Freshwater PB, NL

Glovertown: **CBNT-TV-13**(Channel: 3)
Owned by: **CBNT-TV**
Glovertown, NL

Grand Bank: **CJOX-TV**(Channel: 2)
Owned by: **CJON-TV**
Grand Bank, NL

Grand Falls-Windsor: **CJCN-TV**(Channel: 4)
Owned by: **CJON-TV**
Grand Falls-Windsor, NL

Hampden: **CBNAT-TV-23**(Channel: 13)
Owned by: **CBNT-TV**
Hampden, NL

Harbour Breton: **CBNT-TV-22**(Channel: 13)
Owned by: **CBNT-TV**
Harbour Breton, NL

Harbour Mille: **CBNT-TV-29**(Channel: 13)
Owned by: **CBNT-TV**
Harbour Mille, NL

Harbour Round: **CBNAT-TV-19**(Channel: 12)
Owned by: **CBNT-TV**
Harbour Round, NL

Hermitage: **CBNT-TV-24**(Channel: 4)
Owned by: **CBNT-TV**
Hermitage, NL

Hickman's Harbour: **CBNT-TV-18**(Channel: 4)
Owned by: **CBNT-TV**
Hickman's Harbour, NL

La Scie: **CBNAT-TV-21**(Channel: 9)
Owned by: **CBNT-TV**
La Scie, NL

Lamaline: **CBNT-TV-35**(Channel: 18 UHF)
Owned by: **CBNT-TV**
Lamaline, NL

Lawn: **CBNT-TV-36**(Channel: 6)
Owned by: **CBNT-TV**
Lawn, NL

Lawn: **CJLN-TV**(Channel: 10)
Owned by: **CJON-TV**
Lawn, NL

Lord's Cove: **CBNT-TV-34**(Channel: 9)
Owned by: **CBNT-TV**
Lord's Cove, NL

Lumsden: **CBNT-TV-20**(Channel: 12)
Owned by: **CBNT-TV**
Lumsden, NL

Marystown: **CBNT-TV-3**(Channel: 5)
Owned by: **CBNT-TV**
Marystown, NL

Marystown: **CJMA-TV-11**(Channel: 11)
Owned by: **CJON-TV**
Marystown, NL

Millertown: **CBNAT-TV-5**(Channel: 9)
Owned by: **CBNT-TV**
Millertown, NL

Mings Bight: **CBNAT-TV-14**(Channel: 10)
Owned by: **CBNT-TV**
Mings Bight, NL

Musgrave Harbour: **CBNAT-TV-11**(Channel: 9)
Owned by: **CBNT-TV**
Musgrave Harbour, NL

Musgravetown: **CBNT-TV-17**(Channel: 9)
Owned by: **CBNT-TV**
Musgravetown, NL

North West Brook: **CBNT-TV-11**(Channel: 4)
Owned by: **CBNT-TV**
North West Brook, NL

Pacquet: **CBNAT-TV-17**(Channel: 6)
Owned by: **CBNT-TV**
Pacquet, NL

Petty Harbour: **CBNT-TV-37**(Channel: 13)
Owned by: **CBNT-TV**
Petty Harbour, NL

Placentia: **CBNT-TV-2**(Channel: 12)
Owned by: **CBNT-TV**
Placentia, NL

Port Blandford: **CBNT-TV-32**(Channel: 2)
Owned by: **CBNT-TV**
Port Blandford, NL

Port Hope Simpson: **CBNAT-TV-12**(Channel: 12)
Owned by: **CBNT-TV**
Port Hope Simpson, NL

Port Rexton: **CBNT-TV-1**(Channel: 13)
Owned by: **CBNT-TV**
Port Rexton, NL

Ramea: **CBNT-TV-25**(Channel: 13)
Owned by: **CBNT-TV**
Ramea, NL

Random Island: **CBNT-TV-19**(Channel: 43 UHF)
Owned by: **CBNT-TV**
Random Island, NL

Red Rock: **CJRF-TV-11**(Channel: 11)
Owned by: **CJON-TV**
Red Rock, NL

Roddickton: **CBNAT-TV-22**(Channel: 11)
Owned by: **CBNT-TV**
Roddickton, NL

Seal Cove: **CBNAT-TV-15**(Channel: 7)
Owned by: **CBNT-TV**
Seal Cove, NL

Springdale: **CBNAT-TV-13**(Channel: 13)
Owned by: **CBNT-TV**
Springdale, NL

St Alban's: **CBNT-TV-4**(Channel: 9)
Owned by: **CBNT-TV**
St Alban's, NL

St Albans: **CJST-TV-13**(Channel: 13)
Owned by: **CJON-TV**
St Albans, NL

St Anthony: **CBNAT-TV-4**(Channel: 6)
Owned by: **CBNT-TV**
St Anthony, NL

St Bernard's: **CBNT-TV-30**(Channel: 6)
Owned by: **CBNT-TV**
St Bernard's, NL

St Mary's: **CBNT-TV-6**(Channel: 10)
Owned by: **CBNT-TV**
St Mary's, NL

St Vincent's: **CBNT-TV-26**(Channel: 7)
Owned by: **CBNT-TV**
St Vincent's, NL

St. John's: **CBNT-TV**(Channel: 8)
Owned by: **Canadian Broadcasting Corporation**
PO Box 12010 A, 95 University Ave., St. John's, NL A1B 3T8
709-576-5000,
www.cbc.ca/nl
Social Media: www.facebook.com/cbcnl; twitter.com/cbcnl
Maureen Anonsen, Manager, Partnership & Communicatio, 709-576-5013
Debbie Hynes, Senior Communications Officer, CBC, 709-576-5050

** For details on this company see listing in Major Broadcasting Companies section; † French language station*

St. John's: **CJON-TV**(Channel: 6)
Owned by: **Newfoundland Broadcasting Co. Ltd.***
PO Box 2020, 499 Logy Bay Rd., St. John's, NL A1C 5S2
709-722-5015, Fax: 709-722-0023,
ntv@ntv.ca
www.ntv.ca

G. Scott Stirling, President
Douglas W. Neal, General Manager
Keith Soper, Sales Manager

St. Lawrence: **CBNT-TV-28**(Channel: 12)
Owned by: **CBNT-TV**
St. Lawrence, NL

Swift Current: **CBNT-TV-31**(Channel: 5)
Owned by: **CBNT-TV**
Swift Current, NL

Swift Current: **CJSC-TV-10**(Channel: 10)
Owned by: **CJON-TV**
Swift Current, NL

Tors Cove: **CJON-TV-5**(Channel: 2)
Owned by: **CJON-TV**
Tors Cove, NL

Trepassey: **CJTP-TV-10**(Channel: 10)
Owned by: **CJON-TV**
Trepassey, NL

Wesleyville: **CBNT-TV-9**(Channel: 5)
Owned by: **CBNT-TV**
Wesleyville, NL

Northwest Territories

Yellowknife: **CFYK-TV**(Channel: 8)
Owned by: **Canadian Broadcasting Corporation**
PO Box 160, 5129 49th St., Yellowknife, NT X1A 1P8
867-669-3500, Fax: 867-920-5489, 866-306-4636
www.north.cbc.ca

Nova Scotia

Annapolis Valley: **CJCH-TV-1**(Channel: 10)
Owned by: **CTVglobemedia Inc.**
Annapolis Valley, NS

Antigonish: **CIHF-TV**(Channel: 21)
Owned by: **CIHF-TV**
Antigonish, NS

Antigonish: **CJCB-TV-2**(Channel: 9)
Owned by: **CTVglobemedia Inc.**
Antigonish, NS

Bay St. Lawrence: **CBIT-TV-17**(Channel: 13)
Owned by: **Canadian Broadcasting Corporation**
Bay St. Lawrence, NS

Bay St. Lawrence: **CJCB-TV-5**(Channel: 7)
Owned by: **CTVglobemedia Inc.**
Bay St. Lawrence, NS

Bridgetown: **CJCH-TV-4**(Channel: 13)
Owned by: **CTVglobemedia Inc.**
Bridgetown, NS

Bridgewater: **CIHF-TV-6**(Channel: 9)
Owned by: **CIHF-TV**
Bridgewater, NS

Cheticamp: **CBIT-TV-2**(Channel: 2)
Owned by: **Canadian Broadcasting Corporation**
Cheticamp, NS

Dartmouth: **CIHF-TV**(Channel: 8)
Owned by: **Canwest Global Communications Corp.**
14 Akerley Blvd., Dartmouth, NS B3B 1J3
902-481-7400, Fax: 902-468-2154
Barry Saunders, General Manager

Digby: **CBHT**(Channel: 52)
Owned by: **CBHT-TV**
Digby, NS

Dingwall: **CBIT-TV-16**(Channel: 12)
Owned by: **Canadian Broadcasting Corporation**
Dingwall, NS

Dingwall: **CJCB-TV-3**(Channel: 9)
Owned by: **CTVglobemedia Inc.**
Dingwall, NS

Halifax: **CBHT-TV**(Channel: 3)
Owned by: **Canadian Broadcasting Corporation**
PO Box 3000, 1840 Bell Rd., Halifax, NS B3J 3E9
902-420-8311, 866-306-4636
www.cbc.ca/ns
Social Media: twitter.com/cbcns

Andrew Cochran, Managing Director for the Maritimes
Kathy Large, Program Manager, CBC, Nova Scotia
Chantal Bernard, Senior Communications Officer, 902-420-4306

Halifax: **CIHF-TV**(Channel: 8)
Owned by: **CIHF-TV**
Halifax, NS

Halifax: **CJCH-TV**(Channel: 9)
Owned by: **CTVglobemedia Inc.**
PO Box 1653, 2885 Robie St., Halifax, NS B3K 5Z4
902-453-4000, Fax: 902-454-3302
Michael Elgie, General Manager

Ingonish: **CBIT-TV-15**(Channel: 2)
Owned by: **Canadian Broadcasting Corporation**
Ingonish, NS

Inverness: **CJCB-TV-1**(Channel: 6)
Owned by: **CTVglobemedia Inc.**
Inverness, NS

Liverpool: **CBHT-TV-1**
Owned by: **CBHT-TV**
Liverpool, NS

Mabou: **CBIT-TV-4**(Channel: 10)
Owned by: **Canadian Broadcasting Corporation**
Mabou, NS

Margaree: **CBIT-TV-5**(Channel: 8)
Owned by: **Canadian Broadcasting Corporation**
Margaree, NS

Marinette: **CJCH-TV-8**(Channel: 23)
Owned by: **CTVglobemedia Inc.**
Marinette, NS

Middleton: **CBHT-TV-6**(Channel: 8)
Owned by: **CBHT-TV**
Middleton, NS

Mulgrave: **CBHT-TV-11**(Channel: 12)
Owned by: **Canadian Broadcasting Corporation**
Mulgrave, NS

Mulgrave: **CIHF-TV**(Channel: 28)
Owned by: **CIHF-TV**
Mulgrave, NS

New Glasgow: **CBHT-TV-5**(Channel: 4)
Owned by: **CBHT-TV**
New Glasgow, NS

New Glasgow: **CIHF-TV**(Channel: 34)
Owned by: **CIHF-TV**
New Glasgow, NS

New Glasgow: **CJCB-TV-4**(Channel: 2)
Owned by: **CTVglobemedia Inc.**
New Glasgow, NS

North East Margaree: **CBIT-TV-6**(Channel: 13)
Owned by: **Canadian Broadcasting Corporation**
North East Margaree, NS

Pleasant Bay: **CBIT-TV-3**(Channel: 8)
Owned by: **Canadian Broadcasting Corporation**
Pleasant Bay, NS

Sheet Harbour: **CBHT-TV-4**(Channel: 11)
Owned by: **CBHT-TV**
Sheet Harbour, NS

Sheet Harbour: **CJCH-TV-5**(Channel: 2)
Owned by: **CTVglobemedia Inc.**
Sheet Harbour, NS

Shelburne: **CBHT-TV-2**(Channel: 7)
Owned by: **CBHT-TV**
Shelburne, NS

Shelburne: **CIHF-TV**(Channel: 10)
Owned by: **CIHF-TV**
Shelburne, NS

Sherbrooke: **CBHT-TV-16**(Channel: 4)
Owned by: **Canadian Broadcasting Corporation**
Sherbrooke, NS

Sunnybrae: **CBHT-TV-17**(Channel: 6)
Owned by: **Canadian Broadcasting Corporation**
Sunnybrae, NS

Sydney: **CBIT-TV**(Channel: 5)
Owned by: **Canadian Broadcasting Corporation**
285 Alexandra St., Sydney, NS B1S 2E8
902-539-5050, Fax: 902-563-4170,
www.cbc.ca/ns

Sydney: **CIHF-TV**(Channel: 11)
Owned by: **CIHF-TV**
Sydney, NS

Sydney: **CJCB-TV**(Channel: 4)
Owned by: **CTVglobemedia Inc.**
PO Box 469, 1283 George St., Sydney, NS B1P 1N7
902-562-5511, Fax: 902-562-9714,
cjcb@ctv.ca
www.ctv.ca

Glenn McLanders, 902-562-5511

Truro: **CBHT-TV-8**(Channel: 55)
Owned by: **CBHT-TV**
Truro, NS

Truro: **CIHF-TV**(Channel: 18)
Owned by: **CIHF-TV**
Truro, NS

Truro: **CJCH-TV-2**(Channel: 12)
Owned by: **CTVglobemedia Inc.**
Truro, NS

Wolfville: **CIHF-TV**(Channel: 20)
Owned by: **CIHF-TV**
Wolfville, NS

Yarmouth: **CBHT-TV-3**(Channel: 11)
Owned by: **CBHT-TV**
Yarmouth, NS

Yarmouth: **CIHF-TV**(Channel: 45)
Owned by: **CIHF-TV**
Yarmouth, NS

Yarmouth: **CJCH-TV-7**(Channel: 40)
Owned by: **CTVglobemedia Inc.**
Yarmouth, NS

Ontario

Atikokan: **CBWCT-TV-1**(Channel: 7)
Owned by: **CBWT-TV**
Atikokan, ON

Barrie: **CKVR-TV**
Owned by: **Rogers Broadcasting Ltd.**
33 Beacon Rd., Barrie, ON L4M 4T9

** For details on this company see listing in Major Broadcasting Companies section; † French language station*

705-734-3300, Fax: 705-733-0302, 800-461-5820
inbox@atv.ca
www.atv.ca
Peggy Hebden, Station Manager, peggy.hebden@atv.ca

Belleville: **CJOH-TV**(Channel: 6)
Owned by: **CTVglobemedia Inc.**
Belleville, ON

Big Trout Lake: **CBWT-TV-1**(Channel: 13)
Owned by: **CBWT-TV**
Big Trout Lake, ON

†Chapeau: **CBOFT-TV**(Channel: 11)
Owned by: **CBOFT-TV**
Chapeau, ON

Chapleau: **CITO-TV-4**(Channel: 9)
Owned by: **CTVglobemedia Inc.**
Chapleau, ON

Chatham: **CKCO-TV**(Channel: 42)
Owned by: **CTVglobemedia Inc.**
Chatham, ON

Cornwall: **CJOH-TV**(Channel: 8)
Owned by: **CTVglobemedia Inc.**
Cornwall, ON

Deseronto: **CJOH-TV**(Channel: 6)
Owned by: **CTVglobemedia Inc.**
Deseronto, ON

Dryden: **CBWDT-TV**(Channel: 8)
Owned by: **CBWT-TV**
Dryden, ON

Ear Falls: **CBWJT-TV**(Channel: 13)
Owned by: **CBWT-TV**
Ear Falls, ON

Elliot Lake: **CICI-TV-1**(Channel: 3)
Owned by: **CTVglobemedia Inc.**
Elliot Lake, ON

Fort Frances: **CBWCT-TV**(Channel: 5)
Owned by: **CBWT-TV**
Fort Frances, ON

Hamilton: **CHCH-TV**(Channel: 11)
Owned by: **Canwest Global Communications Corp.**
PO Box 2230 A, 163 Jackson St. West, Hamilton, ON L8N 3A6
905-522-1101, Fax: 905-523-8011,
www.canada.com/hamilton

Hearst: **CITO-TV-3**(Channel: 4)
Owned by: **CTVglobemedia Inc.**
Hearst, ON

Ignace: **CBWDT-TV-2**(Channel: 13)
Owned by: **CBWT-TV**
Ignace, ON

Kapuskasing: **CFCL-TV-3**(Channel: 2)
Owned by: **CFCL-TV**
Kapuskasing, ON

Kapuskasing: **CITO-TV-1**(Channel: 10)
Owned by: **CTVglobemedia Inc.**
Kapuskasing, ON

Kearns: **CFCL-TV-2**(Channel: 2)
Owned by: **CFCL-TV**
Kearns, ON

Kearns: **CITO-TV-2**(Channel: 11)
Owned by: **CTVglobemedia Inc.**
Kearns, ON

Keewatin: **CJBN-TV**(Channel: 13)
102 - 10th St., Keewatin, ON P0X 1C0
807-547-2853, Fax: 807-547-2348,
cjbn@norcomcable.ca
http://www.gokenora.com/cjbn/index.shtml
Warren Ritchie, General Manager, warren.ritchie.sjrb.ca
Darryl Michaluk, Station Manager, darryl.michaluk@sjrb.ca

Kenora: **CBWT-TV-7**(Channel: 8)
Owned by: **CBWT-TV**
Kenora, ON

Kingston: **CJOH-TV**(Channel: 6)
Owned by: **CTVglobemedia Inc.**
Kingston, ON

Kingston: **CKWS-TV**(Channel: 11)
Owned by: **Corus Entertainment Inc.**
170 Queen St., Kingston, ON K7K 1B2
613-544-2340, Fax: 613-544-5508,
newswatch@corusent.com (News room)
www.ckwstv.com
Other information: Phone, News Department: 613-542-9232;
Fax, Sales Dept.: 613-544-3587
Mike Ferguson, General Manager
Jay Westman, News Director

Kitchener: **CBLN-TV-1**(Channel: 56 (antenna))
Owned by: **Canadian Broadcasting Corporation (CBC)**
Kitchener, ON
866-306-4636
www.cbc.ca/television
Other information: TTY: 1-866-220-6045

Kitchener: **CKCO-TV**(Channel: 13)
Owned by: **CTVglobemedia Inc.**
PO Box 91026 C, 864 King St. West, Kitchener, ON N2G 4E9
519-578-1313, Fax: 519-743-0730,
viewermail@southwesternontario.ctv.ca
www.southwesternontario.ctv.ca/
Watson Dennis, VP,GM, dwatson@ctv.ca

London: **CBLN-TV**(Channel: 40 (antenna))
Owned by: **Canadian Broadcasting Corporation (CBC)**
London, ON
866-306-4636
www.cbc.ca/television
Other information: TTY: 1-866-220-6045

London: **CFPL-TV (A-Channel-London)**(Channel: 10)
Owned by: **Rogers Broadcasting Ltd.**
PO Box 5810, 1 Communications Rd., London, ON N6A 6E9
519-686-8810, Fax: 519-668-3288, 800-403-7912
newsnow@thenewpl.com
www.achannel.ca/london
Greg Mudry

London: **CKCO-TV**(Channel: 13)
Owned by: **CTVglobemedia Inc.**
London, ON

North Bay: **CKNY-TV (CTV North Bay)**(Channel: 10)
Owned by: **CTVglobemedia Inc.**
245 Oak St. East, North Bay, ON P1B 8P8
705-476-3111, Fax: 705-495-4474,
www.ctv.ca
Scott Lund, General Manager

Oshawa: **CHEX-TV**(Channel: 22)
Owned by: **Corus Entertainment Inc.**
#7, 500 Wentworth St. East, Oshawa, ON L1H 3V9
905-434-2421, Fax: 905-432-2315,
www.chextv.com

Osnaburgh: **CBWDT-TV-4**(Channel: 13)
Owned by: **CBWT-TV**
Osnaburgh, ON

†Ottawa: **CBOFT-TV**(Channel: 9)
Owned by: **Canadian Broadcasting Corporation**
CP 3220 C, Ottawa, ON K1Y 1E4
613-724-1200, Fax: 613-724-5233,
standard@radio-canada.ca
www.radio-canada.ca/ottawa/

Ottawa: **CBOT-TV**(Channel: 4)
Owned by: **Canadian Broadcasting Corporation**
PO Box 3220 C, Ottawa, ON K1Y 1E4
613-724-1200, Fax: 613-724-5512,
www.ottawa.cbc.ca

Ottawa: **CHOT-TV**(Channel: 40)
Owned by: **CHOT-TV**
Ottawa, ON

Ottawa: **CHRO-TV**(Channel: 6)
Owned by: **Rogers Broadcasting Ltd.**
87 George St., Ottawa, ON K1N 9H7
613-789-0606, Fax: 613-789-6590,
ottawa.promotions@Achannel.ca
www.Achannel.ca
Don Mumford, Station Manager

Ottawa: **CTV Ottawa**(Channel: 13)
Owned by: **CTVglobemedia Inc.**
1500 Merivale Rd., Ottawa, ON K2E 6Z5
613-224-1313, Fax: 613-274-4215,
ctvottawa.ctv.ca
www.ottawa.ctv.ca
Louis Douville, Vice-President/General Manager

Owen Sound: **CKCO-TV**(Channel: 2)
Owned by: **CTVglobemedia Inc.**
Owen Sound, ON

Pembroke: **CHRO-TV (A-Channel Ottawa)**(Channel: 6)
Owned by: **CHRO-TV**
PO Box 1010, 611 TV Tower Rd., Pembroke, ON K8A 6Y6
613-735-1036, Fax: 613-735-4374,
www.achannel.ca/ottawa
Mike Keller, General Manager
Richard Gray, News Director

Peterborough: **CHEX-TV**(Channel: 12)
Owned by: **Corus Entertainment Inc.**
743 Monaghan Rd., Peterborough, ON K9J 5K2
705-742-0451, Fax: 705-742-7274,
viewermail@chextv.com
www.chextv.com
Ron Johnston, General Manager

Pickle Lake: **CBWDT-TV-5**(Channel: 9)
Owned by: **CBWT-TV**
Pickle Lake, ON

Pikangikum: **CBWDT-TV-6**(Channel: 7)
Owned by: **CBWT-TV**
Pikangikum, ON

Red Lake: **CBWET-TV**(Channel: 10)
Owned by: **CBWT-TV**
Red Lake, ON

Sandy Lake: **CBWDT-TV-7**(Channel: 10)
Owned by: **CBWT-TV**
Sandy Lake, ON

Sarnia: **CBLN-TV-2**(Channel: 34 (antenna))
Owned by: **Canadian Broadcasting Corporation (CBC)**
Sarnia, ON
866-306-4636
www.cbc.ca/television
Other information: TTY: 1-866-220-6045

Sarnia: **CKCO-TV**(Channel: 42)
Owned by: **CTVglobemedia Inc.**
Sarnia, ON

Sault Ste Marie: **CHBX-TV**(Channel: 2)
Owned by: **CTVglobemedia Inc.**
PO Box 370, 119 East St., Sault Ste Marie, ON P6A 5M2
705-759-8232, Fax: 705-759-7783,
mctvnews@ctv.ca
www.ctv.ca/servlet/ArticleNews/show/CTVShows/1065552962668_60956580

Savant Lake: **CBWDT-TV-3**(Channel: 8)
Owned by: **CBWT-TV**
Savant Lake, ON

Sioux Lookout: **CBWDT-TV-1**(Channel: 12)
Owned by: **CBWT-TV**
Sioux Lookout, ON

Sioux Narrows: **CBWAT-TV-1**(Channel: 4)
Owned by: **CBWT-TV**
Sioux Narrows, ON

Sudbury: **CICI-TV**(Channel: 5)
Owned by: **CTVglobemedia Inc.**
699 Frood Rd., Sudbury, ON P3C 5A3
705-674-8301, Fax: 705-674-2789

** For details on this company see listing in Major Broadcasting Companies section; † French language station*

Thunder Bay: **CHFD-TV**(Channel: 4)
87 North Hill St., Thunder Bay, ON P7A 5V6
807-346-2600, Fax: 807-345-9923,
tbt@tbtv.com
www.tbtv.com

Thunder Bay: **CKPR-TV**(Channel: 2)
87 North Hill St., Thunder Bay, ON P7A 5V6
807-346-2600, Fax: 807-345-9923,
tbt@tbtv.com
www.tbtv.com
H.F. Dougall, President

Timmins: **CITO-TV**(Channel: 3)
Owned by: **CTVglobemedia Inc.**
PO Box 620, Timmins, ON P4N 7G3
705-264-4211, Fax: 705-264-3266,
www.ctv.ca
Scott Lund

†Toronto: **CBLFT-TV**(Channel: 25 (UHF); 24 (UHF))
Owned by: **Canadian Broadcasting Corporation**
Société Radio-Canada, CP 500, 205 Wellington St. West, Toronto, ON M5V 3G7
416-205-2887, Fax: 416-205-2500, 800-551-2985
auditoire@radio-canada.ca
www.radio-canada.ca/regions/ontario
Social Media: www.twitter.com/RC_TV
Other information: Phone, Television Newsroom: 416-205-2500

Toronto: **CBLT-TV**(Channel: 5 (antenna); 6 (cable))
Owned by: **Canadian Broadcasting Corporation**
PO Box 500, 205 Wellington St. West, Toronto, ON M5W 1E6
416-205-3311, Fax: 416-205-2500, 866-306-4636
www.cbc.ca/toronto; www.cbc.ca/television
Other information: Phone, Television Newsroom: 416-205-2500
Susan Marjetti, Managing Director, 416-205-5791
Don Ioi, Team Manager, Toronto Sales, 416-205-2732

Toronto: **CFMT-TV**(Channel: 47)
Owned by: **Rogers Broadcasting Ltd.**
545 Lakeshore Blvd. West, Toronto, ON M5V 1A3
416-260-0047, Fax: 416-260-3621, 888-260-0047
info@omni1.ca
www.omnitv.ca
Leslie A. Sole, Exec. Vice-President
Madeline Ziniak, Vice-President & Exec. Producer
Jim Nelles, Vice-President, Marketing
Kelly Colasanti, Vice-President, Operations
Anthony P. Viner, President

Toronto: **CFTO-TV**(Channel: 9)
Owned by: **CTVglobemedia Inc.**
9 Channel Nine Ct., Toronto, ON M1S 4B5
416-332-7100, Fax: 416-299-2273,
cftonews@ctv.ca
www.ctv.ca

Toronto: **CHLF-TV**(Channel: 13)
PO Box 200 Q, 2180 Yonge St., Toronto, ON M4T 2T1
416-484-2636, 800-387-8435
tfodiffusion@tfo.org
www.tfo.org
Louise Jourdain

Toronto: **CICA-TV (TVO)**(Channel: 19)
PO Box 200 Q, 2180 Yonge St., Toronto, ON M4T 2T1
416-484-2600, Fax: 416-484-2725,
askTVO@tvontario.org
www.tvo.org

Toronto: **CIII-TV**(Channel: 41)
Owned by: **Canwest Global Communications Corp.**
81 Barber Greene Rd., Toronto, ON M3C 2A2
416-406-5311, Fax: 416-446-5543, 800-387-8001
globalnews.tor@globaltv.com
http://www.canada.com/globaltv/ontario/

Toronto: **CITY-TV**(Channel: 57)
Owned by: **Rogers Broadcasting Ltd.**
299 Queen St. West, Toronto, ON M5V 2Z5
416-591-5757, Fax: 416-593-6397,
news@citynews.ca
www.citytv.com

Toronto: **CJMT-TV**(Channel: 44, 14)
Owned by: **Rogers Broadcasting Ltd.**
545 Lakeshore Blvd. West, Toronto, ON M5V 1A3
416-260-0060, Fax: 416-260-3621, 888-260-0047
info@omni2.ca
www.omnitv.ca

Toronto: **CKXT-TV**(Channel: 52, 15)
Owned by: **Groupe TVA**
25 Ontario St., Toronto, ON M5A 4L6
416-601-0010, Fax: 416-601-0004,
sendit@canoelive.ca
www.toronto1.tv, http://suntv.canoe.ca

Wawa: **CHBX-TV-1**(Channel: 7)
Owned by: **CTVglobemedia Inc.**
Wawa, ON

Windsor: **CBET-TV**(Channel: 9)
Owned by: **Canadian Broadcasting Corporation**
825 Riverside Dr. West, Windsor, ON N9A 5K9
519-255-3411, 866-306-4636
www.cbc.ca/windsor
Other information: Phone, Windsor Newsroom: 519-255-3456
Sandra Porteous, Managing Edior, Radio & Television, 519-255-3563
David Daigneault, Executive Producer, Radio & Television, 519-255-3410
Nancy Lauzon, Manager, Windsor Accounts, 519-255-3510

Windsor: **CHWI-TV**(Channel: 16)
Owned by: **Rogers Broadcasting Ltd.**
75 Riverside Drive East, Windsor, ON N9A 7C4
519-977-7432, Fax: 519-977-0564,
http://www.windsorbusiness.com/Radio_&_TV_Stations/CHWI-TV-553-1-0-0.html
Greg Mudry

Windsor: **CKCO-TV**(Channel: 42)
Owned by: **CTVglobemedia Inc.**
Windsor, ON

Wingham: **CBLN-TV-4**(Channel: 45 (antenna))
Owned by: **Canadian Broadcasting Corporation (CBC)**
Wingham, ON
866-306-4636
www.cbc.ca/television
Other information: TTY: 1-866-220-6045

Wingham: **CKNX-TV**(Channel: 8)
Owned by: **Rogers Broadcasting Ltd.**
215 Carling Terrace, Wingham, ON N0G 2W0
519-357-4438, Fax: 519-357-4398,
info@1017theone.ca
www.fm102.ca
Greg Mudry, Vice-President & General Manager

Prince Edward Island

Charlottetown: **CBCT-TV**(Channel: 13 (antenna))
Owned by: **Canadian Broadcasting Corporation**
PO Box 2230, 430 University Ave., Charlottetown, PE C1A 8B9
902-629-6400, 866-306-4636
www.cbc.ca/pei; www.cbc.ca/television
Other information: Phone, CBC News Compass: 902-629-6403; Toll-Free: 1-800-671-2228
Andrew Cochran, Managing Director, Maritimes
Donna Allen, Executive Producer, News, Prince Edward Island
Janet Irwin, Senior Regional Manager, News & Current Affairs
Nadine Antle, Regional Manager, Partnerships, Communications, Brand, & Promot, 506-451-4054
Lenny Jackson, Station Manager, Prince Edward Island
John Channing, Manager, Sales
Heather McGrath, Senior Officer, Communications, 902-629-6416

Charlottetown: **CIHF-TV**(Channel: 42)
Owned by: **CIHF-TV**
Charlottetown, PE

Charlottetown: **CKCW-TV-1**(Channel: 8)
Owned by: **CKCW-TV**
Charlottetown, PE

†St Edward: **CBAFT-TV-6**(Channel: 9)
Owned by: **CBAFT-TV/Canadian Broadcasting Corporation**
St Edward, PE

Québec

Alma: **CBJET-TV-1**(Channel: 32)
Owned by: **Canadian Broadcasting Corporation (CBC)**
Alma, QC

†Anse-à-Valleau: **CHAU-TV**(Channel: 12)
Owned by: **CHAU-TV**
Anse-à-Valleau, QC

Baie-Comeau: **CBMIT-TV**(Channel: 28 (UHF))
Owned by: **Canadian Broadcasting Corporation (CBC)**
Baie-Comeau, QC
866-306-4636
www.cbc.ca/television
Other information: TTY: 1-866-220-6045

†Carleton: **CHAU-TV**(Channel: 5)
Owned by: **Télé Inter-Rives ltée***
349, boul Perron, Carleton, QC G0C 1J0
418-364-3344, Fax: 418-364-7168,
info@chautva.com
www.chautva.com
Thibault Octave, Directeur de l'information, othibault@chautva.com
Arseneault Chantale, Journaliste, carseneault@chautva.com

†Carleton: **CIVK-TV**(Channel: 15)
Owned by: **CIVM-TV**
Carleton, QC

†Chandler: **CHAU-TV**(Channel: 6)
Owned by: **CHAU-TV**
Chandler, QC

†Chapais: **CBFAT-TV-1**(Channel: 12)
Owned by: **CBFT-TV**
Chapais, QC
514-597-6000, Fax: 514-597-5545, 866-306-4636
auditoire@radio-canada.ca
www.radio-canada.ca/television
Social Media: www.twitter.com/RC_TV

†Chibougamau: **CBFAT-TV**(Channel: 5)
Owned by: **CBFT-TV**
Chibougamau, QC
514-597-6000, Fax: 514-597-5545, 866-306-4636
auditoire@radio-canada.ca
www.radio-canada.ca/television
Social Media: www.twitter.com/RC_TV

Chibougamau: **CBMCT-TV**(Channel: 4)
Owned by: **Canadian Broadcasting Corporation (CBC)**
Chibougamau, QC
866-306-4636
www.cbc.ca/television
Other information: TTY: 1-866-220-6045

Chicoutimi: **CBJET-TV**(Channel: 58)
Owned by: **Canadian Broadcasting Corporation (CBC)**
Chicoutimi, QC

†Chicoutimi: **TVA - CJPM**(Channel: 6)
Owned by: **Groupe TVA**
CP 600, 1, rue Mont Ste-Claire, Chicoutimi, QC G7H 5G3
418-549-2576, Fax: 418-545-1130, 800-267-2576
cjpm@saglac.qc.ca
www.reseau.tva.ca
Roger Jobin, General & Sales Manager

†Cloridorme: **CHAU-TV**(Channel: 11)
Owned by: **CHAU-TV**
Cloridorme, QC

†Gaspé: **CHAU-TV**(Channel: 7)
Owned by: **CHAU-TV**
Gaspé, QC

Harrington-Harbour: **CBMUT-TV**(Channel: 13 (VHF))
Owned by: **Canadian Broadcasting Corporation**
Harrington-Harbour, QC
866-306-4636
www.cbc.ca/television
Other information: TTY: 1-866-220-6045

** For details on this company see listing in Major Broadcasting Companies section; † French language station*

Hull: **CBOT-TV**(Channel: 4)
Owned by: **CBOT-TV**
Hull, QC

†*Hull:* **CFGS-TV**(Channel: 34)
Owned by: **Radio Nord Communications Inc.**
171A, rue Jean-Proulx, Hull, QC J8Z 1W5
819-770-1040, Fax: 819-770-0272
Robert H. Parent

†*Hull:* **CHOT-TV**(Channel: 40)
Owned by: **Radio Nord Communications Inc.**
171, rue Jean-Proulx, Hull, QC J8Z 1W5
819-770-1040, Fax: 819-770-1490,
chot@radionord.com
www.radionord.com
Robert H. Parent

Hull: **CIVO-TV**(Channel: 30)
Owned by: **CIVM-TV**
Hull, QC

†*Jonquière:* **CFRS-TV**(Channel: 4)
Owned by: **TQS inc.**
2303, rue Sir Wilfrid Laurier, Jonquière, QC G7X 5Z2
418-542-4551, Fax: 418-542-7217,
cgotv-saglar@cgotv.ca
www.tqs.ca
Martin Gagnon, General Manager

†*Jonquière:* **CIVO-TV**
Owned by: **CIVM-TV**
Jonquière, QC

†*Jonquière:* **CIVV-TV**(Channel: 8)
Owned by: **Télé-Québec**
CP 23041, Jonquière, QC G7X 9Z8
418-695-8152, Fax: 418-695-8155,
lgagnon@telequebec.qc.ca
telequebec.tv
Laval Gagnon

†*Jonquière:* **CKTV-TV**(Channel: 12)
Owned by: **TQS inc.**
2303, rue Sir Wilfrid Laurier, Jonquière, QC G7X 5Z2
418-542-4551, Fax: 418-542-7217,
cgotv-saglac@cgotv.ca
www.tqs.ca

†*Kuujjuarapik:* **CBFK-TV**(Channel: 9)
Owned by: **Canadian Broadcasting Corporation (CBC)**
Kuujjuarapik, QC
514-597-6000, Fax: 514-597-5545, 866-306-4636
auditoire@radio-canada.ca
www.radio-canada.ca/television
Social Media: www.twitter.com/RC_TV

La Tabatière: **CBMLT-TV**(Channel: 10)
Owned by: **Canadian Broadcasting Corporation (CBC)**
La Tabatière, QC
866-306-4636
www.cbc.ca/television
Other information: TTY: 1-866-220-6045

La Tuque: **CBMET-TV**(Channel: 9)
Owned by: **Canadian Broadcasting Corporation (CBC)**
La Tuque, QC
866-306-4636
www.cbc.ca/television
Other information: TTY: 1-866-220-6045

†*La Tuque:* **CBVT-TV**(Channel: 3)
Owned by: **Canadian Broadcasting Corporation**
La Tuque, QC

†*Lac-Mégantic:* **CBVT-TV**(Channel: 2)
Owned by: **Canadian Broadcasting Corporation**
Lac-Mégantic, QC

†*Matane:* **CIVF-TV**(Channel: 12)
Owned by: **CIVM-TV**
Matane, QC

†*Montréal:* **CBFT-TV**(Channel: 2 (VHF); 19 (UHF))
Owned by: **Canadian Broadcasting Corporation**
Maison de Radio-Canada, CP 6000 Centre-ville, 1400, boul René-Lévesque est, Montréal, QC H3C 3A8
514-597-6000, Fax: 514-597-5545, 866-306-4636
auditoire@radio-canada.ca
www.radio-canada.ca/television
Social Media: www.twitter.com/RC_TV
Other information: Phone, Montréal TV Newsroom: 514-597-6371; Fax: 514-597-6354
Pia Marquard, Managing Director, Radio & Television, Québec Region
Sally Caudwell, Executive Producer, Montréal News, 514-597-4089, Fax: 514-597-4511

Montréal: **CBMT-TV**(Channel: 6 (VHF); 20 (UHF))
Owned by: **Canadian Broadcasting Corporation**
PO Box 6000, Montréal, QC H3C 3A8
514-597-6000, Fax: 514-597-6354,
www.cbc.ca/montreal; www.cbc.ca/television
Other information: Phone, CBC Montréal TV Newsroom: 514-597-6371
Pia Marquard, Managing Director, Radio & Television, Québec Region
Sally Caudwell, Executive Producer, News, Montréal, 514-597-4089, Fax: 514-597-4511
Mary-Jo Barr, News Director, English Services
Laura Tarulli, Senior Manager, Production & Resources
Carolyn Warren, Regional Manager, Cultural Programming & Integrated Content
Hugh Brodie, Manager, Partnership & Communications, Québec, 514-597-5813

Montréal: **CFCF-TV**(Channel: 12)
Owned by: **CTVglobemedia Inc.**
1205, ave. Papineau, Montréal, QC H2K 4R2
514-273-6311, Fax: 514-276-9399,
montrealnews@ctv.ca, mpiperni@ctv.ca
www.cfcf.ca
Donald M. Bastien, Senior Vice President and General M

†*Montréal:* **CFJP-TV**(Channel: 35)
Owned by: **TQS inc.**
#100, 612, rue St-Jacques, Montréal, QC H3C 5R1
514-390-6035, Fax: 514-390-6070,
www.tqs.ca
René Guimond, Président et chef de la direction

†*Montréal:* **CFTM-TV**(Channel: 10)
Owned by: **Groupe TVA**
1600 Est, boul de Maisonneuve, Montréal, QC H2L 4P2
514-526-9251, Fax: 514-598-6078,
relations.auditoire@tva.ca
www.tva.ca, http://tva.canoe.com

†*Montréal:* **CIVM-TV**(Channel: 17)
Owned by: **Télé-Québec**
1000, rue Fullum, Montréal, QC H2K 3L7
514-521-2424, Fax: 514-873-2601, 800-361-4362
info@telequebec.tv
www.telequebec.tv
Claude Dufault, Directeur de la commandite et des v, cdufault@telequebec.tv
Desroches Gérard, Représentant, gdesroche@telequebec.tv

Montréal: **CJNT-TV**(Channel: 62, 14)
Owned by: **Canwest Global Communications Corp.**
1600, boul de Maisonneuve est, 9e étage, Montréal, QC H2L 4P2
514-522-4150, Fax: 514-522-9579,
info@chmontreal.com
www.canada.com/chtv/montreal

Montreal: **CKMI-TV (Global Quebec)**(Channel: 5)
Owned by: **Canwest Global Communications Corp.**
1600 de Maisonneuve E., Montreal, QC H2L 4P2
514-521-4923, Fax: 514-590-4060,
quebecprog@globaltv.ca, globalnews.que@globaltv.co
www.canada.com/globaltv/quebec/
Maureen Rogers, General Manager
Karen MacDonald, Station Manager

Murdochville: **CBMMT-TV**(Channel: 21 (UHF))
Owned by: **Canadian Broadcasting Corporation (CBC)**
Murdochville, QC
866-306-4636
www.cbc.ca/television
Other information: TTY: 1-866-220-6045

†*Notre-Dame-du-Laus:* **CBOFT-TV-3**(Channel: 10)
Owned by: **CBFT-TV**
Notre-Dame-du-Laus, QC

†*Percé:* **CHAU-TV**(Channel: 13)
Owned by: **CHAU-TV**
Percé, QC

†*Plessisville:* **CKYQ-FM**(Channel: 95.7)
1646, av St-Laurent, Plessisville, QC G6L 2Y6
819-362-3737, Fax: 819-362-3414,
studio@kyqfm.com
www.kyqfm.com

Pointe-au-Père: **CFER-TV**(Channel: 5, 11)
Owned by: **Groupe TVA**
465, boul Ste-Anne, Pointe-au-Père, QC G5M 1G1
418-722-6011, Fax: 418-724-7810,
nouvelles@cfer.tva.ca
cfer.tva.ca

†*Port-Daniel:* **CHAU-TV**(Channel: 10)
Owned by: **CHAU-TV**
Port-Daniel, QC

†*Québec:* **CBVT-TV**(Channel: 11)
Owned by: **Canadian Broadcasting Corporation**
CP 18800, 888, rue Saint-Jean, Québec, QC G1K 9L4
418-654-1341,
www.radio-canada.ca/regions/quebec

†*Québec:* **CFAP-TV**(Channel: 2)
Owned by: **TQS inc.**
330, rue Saint-Vallier est, bureau 025, Québec, QC G1K 9C5
418-624-2222, Fax: 418-624-8930,
regiecentraleQC@tqs.ca, tvpublic@tqs.ca
www.tqs.ca/quebec/

†*Québec:* **CFER-TV-2**(Channel: 5)
Owned by: **CFER-TV**
Québec, QC

†*Québec:* **CIVQ-TV**(Channel: 15)
Owned by: **CIVM-TV**
Québec, QC

†*Rapides-des-Joachims:* **CBOFT-TV-2**(Channel: 31)
Owned by: **CBOFT-TV**
Rapides-des-Joachims, QC

†*Rimouski:* **CFER-TV**(Channel: 11)
Owned by: **CFER-TV**
Rimouski, QC

†*Rimouski:* **CIVB-TV**(Channel: 8)
Owned by: **Télé-Québec**
79, rue de l'Évêché est, Rimouski, QC G5L 1X7
418-727-3743, Fax: 418-727-3814,
bureau.rimouski@telequebec.tv
www.telequebec.tv
Diane Dube

Rivière-Saint-Paul: **CBMPT-TV**(Channel: 11)
Owned by: **Canadian Broadcasting Corporation (CBC)**
Rivière-Saint-Paul, QC
866-306-4636
www.cbc.ca/television
Other information: TTY: 1-866-220-6045

†*Rivière-au-Rénard:* **CHAU-TV**(Channel: 4)
Owned by: **CHAU-TV**
Rivière-au-Rénard, QC

†*Rivière-du-Loup:* **CFTF-TV**(Channel: 29)
103, rue des Équipements, Rivière-du-Loup, QC G5R 5W7
418-862-2909, Fax: 418-867-4710,
typublic@tqs.ca
www.tqs.ca
Nancy Fortin, Production Director
Marc Simard, Président
Ginette Dumont, Administrative Secretary
Stéphane Grégoire, Vice-President, Finances
Michel Bélanger, Vice-President, Operations

** For details on this company see listing in Major Broadcasting Companies section; † French language station*

†Rivière-du-Loup: **CIMT-TV**(Channel: 9)
Owned by: **Télé Inter-Rives ltée***
15, rue de la Chute, Rivière-du-Loup, QC G5R 5B7
418-867-1341, Fax: 418-867-4710
Marc Simard, President
Ginette Dumont, Administrative Secretary
Germain Gélinas, Vice-President, Operations
Stéphane Grégoire, Vice-President, Finances

†Rivière-du-Loup: **CKRT-TV**(Channel: 7)
Owned by: **Canadian Broadcasting Corporation**
15, rue de la Chute, Rivière-du-Loup, QC G5R 5B7
418-867-8080, Fax: 418-867-4710, ckrt@icrdl.net
Marc Simard, President
Ginette Dumont, Administrative Secretary
Germain Gélinas, Vice-President, Operations
Stéphane Grégoire, Vice-President, Finances

†Rouyn-Noranda: **CFEM-TV**(Channel: 13)
Owned by: **Radio Nord Communications Inc.**
380, av Murdoch, Rouyn-Noranda, QC J9X 1G5
819-762-0744, Fax: 819-762-2280, abrosseau@radionord.com
www.radionord.com
Ghislain Beaulieu

†Rouyn-Noranda: **CIVA-TV**(Channel: 8)
Owned by: **CIVM-TV**
Rouyn-Noranda, QC

†Rouyn-Noranda: **CKRN-TV**(Channel: 4)
Owned by: **Radio Nord Communications Inc.**
380, av Murdoch, Rouyn-Noranda, QC J9X 1G5
819-762-0744, Fax: 819-762-2280, www.radionord.com
Ghislain Beaulieu

†Saguenay: **TVA - CJPM**(Channel: 6)
Owned by: **TVA - CJPM**
Saguenay, QC

Saint-Augustin: **CBMXT-TV**(Channel: 7)
Owned by: **Canadian Broadcasting Corporation (CBC)**
Saint-Augustin, QC
866-306-4636
www.cbc.ca/television
Other information: TTY: 1-866-220-6045

†Sainte-Foy: **CFCM-TV**(Channel: 4)
Owned by: **Groupe TVA**
CP 2026, 1000, av Myrand, Sainte-Foy, QC G1V 2W3
418-688-9330, Fax: 418-681-4239, 800-463-5608
administration@tele-4.tva.ca
www.tva.ca
Richard Renaud, Vice-President, Regional Stations &

†Sainte-Marguerite-Marie: **CHAU-TV**(Channel: 3)
Owned by: **CHAU-TV**
Sainte-Marguerite-Marie, QC

†Sept-Iles: **CBST-TV**(Channel: 3)
Owned by: **CBVT-TV**
Sept-Iles, QC

†Sept-Iles: **CIVG-TV**(Channel: 9)
Owned by: **CIVM-TV**
Sept-Iles, QC

Sherbrooke: **CBMT-TV-3**(Channel: 50 (UHF))
Owned by: **Canadian Broadcasting Corporation (CBC)**
Sherbrooke, QC
866-306-4636
www.cbc.ca/television
Other information: TTY: 1-866-220-6045

Sherbrooke: **CFKS-TV**(Channel: 30)
Owned by: **TQS inc.**
3720, boul Industriel, Sherbrooke, QC J1L 1Z9
819-565-9999, Fax: 819-565-3787, typublic@tqs.ca
www.tqs.ca

†Sherbrooke: **CHLT-TV**(Channel: 7)
Owned by: **Groupe TVA**
3330, rue King ouest, Sherbrooke, QC J1L 1C9
819-565-7777, Fax: 819-565-4650, http://tva.canoe.com/stations/chlt/

†Sherbrooke: **CIVS-TV**(Channel: 24)
Owned by: **CIVM-TV**
Sherbrooke, QC

†Sherbrooke: **CKSH-TV**(Channel: 9)
Owned by: **TQS inc.**
3720, boul Industriel, Sherbrooke, QC J1L 1Z9
819-565-9999, Fax: 819-822-4205

†St-Fabien-de-Panet: **CBVT-TV**(Channel: 13)
Owned by: **Canadian Broadcasting Corporation**
St-Fabien-de-Panet, QC

†St-Georges: **CBVT-TV**(Channel: 6)
Owned by: **Canadian Broadcasting Corporation**
St-Georges, QC

Thetford Mines: **CBMT-TV-4**(Channel: 32 (UHF))
Owned by: **Canadian Broadcasting Corporation (CBC)**
Thetford Mines, QC
866-306-4636
www.cbc.ca/television
Other information: TTY: 1-866-220-6045

†Tracadie: **CHAU-TV**(Channel: 9)
Owned by: **CHAU-TV**
Tracadie, QC

Trois-Rivières: **CBMT-TV-1**(Channel: 28 (UHF))
Owned by: **Canadian Broadcasting Corporation (CBC)**
Trois-Rivières, QC
866-306-4636
www.cbc.ca/television
Other information: TTY: 1-866-220-6045

†Trois-Rivières: **CFKM-TV**(Channel: 16)
Owned by: **TQS inc.**
4141, boul St-Jean, Trois-Rivières, QC G9B 2M8
819-377-6053, Fax: 819-377-5442, 800-424-1441
www.cgotv.ca
Michel Cloutier, General Manager

Trois-Rivières: **CFKM-TV**(Channel: 29)
Owned by: **CFKM-TV**
Trois-Rivières, QC

†Trois-Rivières: **CHEM-TV**(Channel: 8)
Owned by: **Groupe TVA**
3625, boul Chanoine-Moreau, Trois-Rivières, QC G8Y 5N6
819-376-8880, Fax: 819-376-2906, tva.canoe.com/stations/chem

†Trois-Rivières: **CIVC-TV**(Channel: 45)
Trois-Rivières, QC

†Val-d'Or: **CFVS-TV**(Channel: 20)
Owned by: **Radio Nord Communications Inc.**
1729, 3e av, Val-d'Or, QC J9P 1W3
819-762-0741, Fax: 819-762-2466
Frantz Boivin

Vieux-Fort: **CBMVT-TV**(Channel: 13)
Owned by: **Canadian Broadcasting Corporation (CBC)**
Vieux-Fort, QC
866-306-4636
www.cbc.ca/television
Other information: TTY: 1-866-220-6045

Saskatchewan

Beauval: **CBKBT-TV**(Channel: 7)
Owned by: **CBKST-TV; Canadian Broadcasting Corporation**
Beauval, SK

Big River: **CIPA-TV-3**(Channel: 7)
Owned by: **CTVglobemedia Inc.**
Big River, SK

Big River: **CKBI-TV-5**(Channel: 9)
Owned by: **CKBI-TV**
Big River, SK

Buffalo Narrows: **CBKDT-TV**(Channel: 11)
Owned by: **CBKST-TV; Canadian Broadcasting Corporation**
Buffalo Narrows, SK

Carlyle Lake: **CIEW-TV**(Channel: 7)
Owned by: **CTVglobemedia Inc.**
Carlyle Lake, SK

Colgate: **CKCK-TV-1**(Channel: 12)
Owned by: **CTVglobemedia Inc.**
Colgate, SK

Cumberland House: **CBWIT-TV**(Channel: 9)
Owned by: **CBWT-TV**
Cumberland House, SK

Elrose: **CKEL-TV-1**(Channel: 7)
Owned by: **CJFB-TV**
Elrose, SK

Fort Qu'Appelle: **CBKT-TV-3**(Channel: 4)
Owned by: **CBKT-TV**
Fort Qu'Appelle, SK

Fort Qu'appelle: **CKTV-TV**(Channel: 7)
Owned by: **CTVglobemedia Inc.**
Fort Qu'appelle, SK

Golden Prairie: **CKMC-TV-1**(Channel: 10)
Owned by: **CTVglobemedia Inc.**
Golden Prairie, SK

Greenwater Lake: **CKBI-TV-3**(Channel: 4)
Owned by: **CKBI-TV**
Greenwater Lake, SK

Hudson Bay: **CICC-TV-3**(Channel: 11)
Owned by: **CTVglobemedia Inc.**
Hudson Bay, SK

Humboldt: **CIWH-TV-1**(Channel: 32)
Owned by: **CTVglobemedia Inc.**
Humboldt, SK

Ile-a-la-Crosse: **CBKCT-TV**(Channel: 9)
Owned by: **CBKST-TV; Canadian Broadcasting Corporation**
Ile-a-la-Crosse, SK

Indian Lake: **CBWT-TV**(Channel: 10)
Owned by: **CBWT-TV**
Indian Lake, SK

Island Falls: **CBWBT-TV-2**(Channel: 7)
Owned by: **CBWT-TV**
Island Falls, SK

La Loche: **CBKDT-TV-2**(Channel: 13)
Owned by: **CBKST-TV; Canadian Broadcasting Corporation**
La Loche, SK

La Ronge: **CBKST-TV-2**(Channel: 12)
Owned by: **CBKST-TV; Canadian Broadcasting Corporation**
La Ronge, SK

Leoville: **CBKST-TV-3**(Channel: 12)
Owned by: **CBKST-TV; Canadian Broadcasting Corporation**
Leoville, SK

Maple Creek: **CHAT-TV-2**(Channel: 4)
Owned by: **CHAT-TV**
Maple Creek, SK

Meadow Lake: **CITL-TV3**(Channel: 3)
Owned by: **CITL-TV**
Meadow Lake, SK

Meadow Lake: **CKSA-TV**(Channel: 8)
Owned by: **CKSA-TV**
Meadow Lake, SK

** For details on this company see listing in Major Broadcasting Companies section; † French language station*

Melfort: **CKBQ-TV**(Channel: 2)
Owned by: **CTVglobemedia Inc.**
Melfort, SK

Montreal Lake: **CBKST-TV-5**(Channel: 11)
Owned by: **CBKST-TV; Canadian Broadcasting Corporation**
Montreal Lake, SK

Moose Jaw: **CBKT-TV-1**(Channel: 4)
Owned by: **CBKT-TV**
Moose Jaw, SK

Moose Jaw: **CKMJ-TV**(Channel: 7)
Owned by: **CTVglobemedia Inc.**
Moose Jaw, SK

Nipawin: **CKBQ-TV-1**(Channel: 12)
Owned by: **CTVglobemedia Inc.**
Nipawin, SK

Norquay: **CICC-TV-2**(Channel: 7)
Owned by: **CTVglobemedia Inc.**
Norquay, SK

North Battleford: **CFQC-TV-2**(Channel: 6)
Owned by: **CTVglobemedia Inc.**
North Battleford, SK

North Battleford: **CKBI-TV-2**(Channel: 7)
Owned by: **CKBI-TV**
North Battleford, SK

Palmbere Lake: **CBKDT-TV-1**(Channel: 8)
Owned by: **CBKST-TV; Canadian Broadcasting Corporation**
Palmbere Lake, SK

Pelican Narrows: **CBWBT-TV-3**(Channel: 5)
Owned by: **CBWT-TV**
Pelican Narrows, SK

Pinehouse Lake: **CBKST-TV-6**(Channel: 10)
Owned by: **CBKST-TV; Canadian Broadcasting Corporation**
Pinehouse Lake, SK

Prince Albert: **CIPA-TV**(Channel: 9)
Owned by: **CTVglobemedia Inc.**
22 - 10 St. West, Prince Albert, SK S6V 3A5
306-922-6066, Fax: 306-763-3041

Prince Albert: **CKBI-TV**(Channel: 5)
Owned by: **Canadian Broadcasting Corporation**
22 - 10 St. West, Prince Albert, SK S6V 3A5
306-922-6066, Fax: 306-763-3041

†Regina: **CBKFT-TV**(Channel: 13)
Owned by: **Canadian Broadcasting Corporation**
CP 540, 2440 Broad St., Regina, SK S4P 4A1
306-347-9540,
rene_fountaine@radio-canada.ca
www.radio-canada.ca/regions/saskatchewan
Fontaine René, 204-788-3236, rene_fountaine@radio-canada.ca

Regina: **CBKT-TV**(Channel: 9)
Owned by: **Canadian Broadcasting Corporation**
PO Box 540, 2440 Broad St., Regina, SK S4P 4A1
306-347-9540, Fax: 306-347-9635,
audienceinfo@regina.cbc.ca
www.sask.cbc.ca
Social Media: www.facebook.com/cbcsask; twitter.com/cbcsask
Lenora Sturge, Program Marketing Co-ordinator, 306-347-9714

Regina: **CFRE-TV**(Channel: 5)
Owned by: **Canwest Global Communications Corp.**
370 Hoffer Dr., Regina, SK S4N 7A4
306-775-4000, Fax: 306-721-4817,
www.canada.com

Regina: **CKCK-TV**(Channel: 2)
Owned by: **CTVglobemedia Inc.**
PO Box 2000, Regina, SK S4P 3E5
306-569-2000, Fax: 306-522-0090,
ckck@ctv.ca
www.ctv.ca
Dennis Dunlop, Vice-President, General Manager, Ge, CTV Saskatchewan

Saskatoon: **CBKST-TV**(Channel: 11)
Owned by: **Canadian Broadcasting Corporation**
144 - 2nd Ave. South, Saskatoon, SK S7K 1K5
306-956-7430, Fax: 306-975-7488,
www.cbc.ca/sask
Social Media: www.facebook.com/cbcsask; twitter.com/cbcsask

Saskatoon: **CFSK-TV**(Channel: 4)
Owned by: **Canwest Global Communications Corp.**
218 Robin Cres., Saskatoon, SK S7L 7C3
306-665-6969, Fax: 306-665-6069,
globalnews.sask@globaltv.com
www.canada.com/saskatoon
Wayne Rorke, Station Manager, wrorke@globaltv.com
Lisa Ford, News Director, lford@globaltv.com

Saskatoon: **CTV Television Inc.**(Channel: 8)
Owned by: **CTVglobemedia Inc.**
216 - 1 Ave. North, Saskatoon, SK S7K 3W3
306-665-8600, Fax: 306-665-0450,
www.ctv.ca
Dennis Dunlop, General Manager

Southend: **CBKST-TV-8**(Channel: 13)
Owned by: **CBKST-TV; Canadian Broadcasting Corporation**
Southend, SK

Spiritwood: **CIPA-TV-1**(Channel: 10)
Owned by: **CTVglobemedia Inc.**
Spiritwood, SK

Spiritwood: **CKBI-TV-6**(Channel: 2)
Owned by: **CKBI-TV**
Spiritwood, SK

Stanley Mission: **CBKST-TV-4**(Channel: 8)
Owned by: **CBKST-TV; Canadian Broadcasting Corporation**
Stanley Mission, SK

Stranraer: **CBKST-TV-1**(Channel: 9)
Owned by: **CBKST-TV; Canadian Broadcasting Corporation**
Stranraer, SK

Stranraer: **CFQC-TV-1**(Channel: 3)
Owned by: **CTVglobemedia Inc.**
Stranraer, SK

Swift Current: **CBKT-TV-4**(Channel: 5)
Owned by: **CBKT-TV**
Swift Current, SK

Swift Current: **CKMC-TV**(Channel: 12)
Owned by: **CTVglobemedia Inc.**
Swift Current, SK

Tisdale: **CKBI-TV-6**(Channel: 13)
Owned by: **CKBI-TV**
Tisdale, SK

Warmley: **CFSS-TV**(Channel: 3)
Warmley, SK

Willow Bunch: **CBKT-TV-2**(Channel: 10)
Owned by: **CBKT-TV**
Willow Bunch, SK

Willow Bunch: **CKCK-TV-2**(Channel: 6)
Owned by: **CTVglobemedia Inc.**
Willow Bunch, SK

Wynyard: **CHSS-TV**(Channel: 6)
Owned by: **CTVglobemedia Inc.**
Wynyard, SK

Wynyard: **CIWH-TV**(Channel: 12)
Owned by: **CTVglobemedia Inc.**
Wynyard, SK

Yorkton: **CTV Television Inc.**(Channel: 10, 5)
Owned by: **CTVglobemedia Inc.**
95 East Broadway, Yorkton, SK S3N 0L1
306-786-8400, Fax: 306-782-7212,
cciccnews@ctv.ca
www.ctv.ca
Dennis dunlop, General Manager

Cable Companies

Alberta

Calgary: **Shaw Cable**
PO Box 90 J, 2001 - 27 Ave. NE, Calgary, AB T2A 6T9
403-716-6070, Fax: 403-291-0880,
www.shaw.ca
John Mlazgar, Manager, Regional System

Calgary: **Shaw Communications Inc.**
#900, 630 - 3rd Ave. SW, Calgary, AB T2P 4L4
403-750-4500, Fax: 403-750-4501, 888-750-7429
www.shaw.ca
Jim Shaw, CEO

Camrose: **Cable TV of Camrose**
4910 - 46 St., Camrose, AB T4V 1H1
780-672-8839, Fax: 780-672-8830,
www.cable-lynx.net

Edmonton: **Persona Communications**
3552 - 78th Ave., Edmonton, AB T6B 2X9
780-440-2525, Fax: 780-440-2828,
www.personainc.ca

Edmonton: **Regional Cablesytems - Western Division**
PO Box 4005, 3552 - 78th Ave., Edmonton, AB T6E 4S8
780-440-2525, Fax: 780-440-2828
Jeff Bertram, Director, Sales & Marketing
Rick Miciak, Director, Finance
Dave Paquet, Director, Technical Services
Fred Hockerong, Vice-President & General Manager

Edmonton: **Shaw Cablesystems G.P.**
10450 - 178 St. NW, Edmonton, AB T5S 1S2
780-665-9977, Fax: 780-490-3411

Fort McMurray: **Shaw Cablesystems G.P.**
#200, 208 Beaconhill Dr., Fort McMurray, AB T9H 2R1
780-714-3717, Fax: 780-790-1193

Galahad: **Galahad Cablevision Society**
PO Box 31, Galahad, AB T0B 1R0
780-583-3989, Fax: 780-583-3787

Gift Lake: **Gift Lake Metis Settlement**
General Delivery, Gift Lake, AB T0G 1B0
403-767-3894, Fax: 403—

Grimshaw: **High Level Cable**
PO Box 8, Grimshaw, AB T0H 1W0
780-332-1780

Hanna: **Prairie Cable TV Ltd.**
PO Box 520, Hanna, AB T0J 1P0
403-854-4659, Fax: 403-854-4917

High Prairie: **KBS TV**
PO Box 29, 5319 - 48th St., High Prairie, AB T0G 1E0
780-523-3223, Fax: 780-523-3411

Lethbridge: **Shaw Cablesystems G.P.**
1232 - 3 Ave. South, Lethbridge, AB T1J 0J9
403-380-7352, Fax: 403-320-1675

Medicine Hat: **Monarch Cablesystems Ltd.**
361 - 1 St. SE, Medicine Hat, AB T1A 0A5
403-526-4529, Fax: 403-504-8135, 800-442-8664
info@monarchcable.net
www.monarch.net
Chad Cunningham, Sales & Marketing Manager

Oyen: **Oyen Cable**
PO Box 95, Oyen, AB T0J 2J0
403-664-3811, Fax: 403-664-3811,
aberg@telusplanet.net; es1016@telusplanet.net
Art Berg, Owner/Operator

Rainbow Lake: **Rainbow Lake Cable TV**
PO Box 149, Rainbow Lake, AB T0H 2Y0
780-956-3934, Fax: 780-956-3570,
rainbowlake@telusplanet.net
www.rainbowlake.ca

Red Deer: **Shaw Cablesystems**
4761 - 62 St., Red Deer, AB T4N 2R4

** For details on this company see listing in Major Broadcasting Companies section; † French language station*

403-340-6400, Fax: 403-340-6414, 888-270-2433
katie.wood@sjrb.ca
www.shaw.ca

Peter Bissonnette, President

***Slave Lake:* Cable TV Slave Ltd**
PO Box 1008, 800 Main St. North, Slave Lake, AB T0G 2A0
403-849-5188, Fax: 403-849-6809,
cable-lynx.net

***Veteran:* Veteran Television Society**
PO Box 428, Veteran, AB T0C 2S0
403-575-3892, Fax: 403-575-3938

British Columbia

***100 Mile House:* Williams Communications**
PO Box 927, 100 Mile House, BC V0K 2E0
250-395-3333, Fax: 250-397-2297

***Abbotsford:* Shaw Cablesystems**
PO Box 2125 Clearbrook, 31450 Marshall Rd., Abbotsford, BC V2T 3X8
604-856-5721, Fax: 604-850-2517

***Ashcroft:* Copper Valley Cablevision Ltd.**
PO Box 1120, 312 - 4th St., Ashcroft, BC V0K 1A0
250-453-2616, Fax: 250-453-9960,
www.coppervalley.ca

***Brackendale:* Britannia Cablevision**
PO Box 461, Brackendale, BC V0N 1H0
604-898-9767

G.C. Pickard

***Campbell River:* Campbell River TV Association**
500 Robron Rd., Campbell River, BC V9W 5Z2
250-923-8899, Fax: 250-923-7796,
jim.forsyth@crtv.net
www.crtv.net

Jim Forsyth, General Manager

***Campbell River:* Sayward Valley Communications Ltd.**
#112, 1720 - 14th Ave., Campbell River, BC V9W 8B9
250-287-4199, Fax: 250-287-8840,
cs@saywardvalley.net
saywardvalley.net

***Castlegar:* Shaw Cablesystems**
1951 Columbia Ave., Castlegar, BC V2N 2W8
250-365-3122, Fax: 250-365-2676

***Chilliwack:* Shaw Cablesystems**
9275 Nowell St., Chilliwack, BC V2P 7G7
604-793-9944, Fax: 604-792-0966

***Courtenay:* Shaw Cablesystems**
1591 McPhee Ave., Courtenay, BC V9N 3A6
604-334-0888, Fax: 604-334-3640

***Cranbrook:* Shaw Cablesystems G.P.**
720 Kootenay St. North, Cranbrook, BC V1C 3V2
250-342-9415, Fax: 250-417-3890

***Dawson Creek:* Shaw Cable**
#204, 9817 - 100 Ave., Dawson Creek, BC V1J 1Y4
250-782-6669

***Delta:* Delta Cable**
5381 Ladner Trunk Rd., Delta, BC V4K 1W7
604-946-1144, Fax: 604-946-5627,
admin@deltacable.com
www.deltacable.com

***Duncan:* Shaw Cable**
35 Queens Rd., Duncan, BC V9L 2W1
250-782-9113, Fax: —0

***Fernie:* Monarch Cable**
PO Box 1769, 691 - 9 Ave., Fernie, BC V0B 1M0
250-423-3334, Fax: 250-423-3855

***Fort Nelson:* Northwestel Cable**
PO Box 1949, 5404 - 50th Ave., Fort Nelson, BC V0C 1R0
250-774-3021, Fax: 250-774-3020, 800-661-0834
cable@theedge.ca
www.tvnwt.com

***Grand Forks:* Sunshine Communications**
PO Box 2618, 7474 - 19 St., Grand Forks, BC V0H 1H0
250-442-5844, Fax: 250-442-2665,
www.sunshinecable.com

***Hope:* Hope Cable Television**
PO Box 489, 360 Wallace St., Hope, BC V0X 1L0
604-869-2616, Fax: 604-869-9393, 800-663-5038
www.rainbowcountry.bc.ca/archive/hopecable/

***Kaslo:* Kaslo Cable Ltd.**
PO Box 637, Kaslo, BC V0G 1M0
250-353-2547, Fax: 250-353-2547

***Kelowna:* Shaw Cablesystems G.P.**
2350 Hunter Rd., Kelowna, BC V1X 7H6
250-712-2307, Fax: 250-712-2310

***Lindell Beach:* Lindell Beach Residents Association**
1946 Vera Rd., Lindell Beach, BC V2R 4X1
604-858-4643, Fax: 604-858-4670

W. Woodall, TV Committee

***Logan Lake:* Logan Lake TV Society**
PO Box 56, Logan Lake, BC V0K 1W0
250-523-9339, Fax: 250-523-9339,
ve7ffk@mail.ocis.net

Dean Neighbour, Vice President

***Lower Post:* Daulu Dena Council**
PO Box 10, Lower Post, BC V0C 1W0
250-779-3161, Fax: 250-779-3371

Roma Walker, Executive Director

***Masset:* Masset Haida Television Society**
PO Box 602, 1356 Main St., Masset, BC V0T 1M0
250-626-3994, Fax: 250-626-3941,
cs@mhtv.ca
www.mhtv.ca

Alfred Brockley, President
Gerald Jennings, Vice-President

***Merritt:* Shaw Cablesystems (BC) Ltd.**
PO Box 908, 2 Thorpe Ave., Merritt, BC V1K 1B8
250-378-4919

***Nanaimo:* Shaw Cable**
4316 Boban Dr., Nanaimo, BC V8A 2N5
250-760-1966, Fax: 250-760-1991

***Nanaimo:* Shaw Cablesystems (BC) Ltd.**
4316 Boban Dr., Nanaimo, BC V9T 6A7
250-760-1999, Fax: 250-760-1998,

***Oliver:* Persona Communications Inc.**
PO Box 790, 9502 - 348th Ave., Oliver, BC V0H 1T0
250-498-3630, Fax: 250-498-8810, 866-737-7662
www.personainc.ca

***Penticton:* Shaw Cable**
1372 Fairview Rd., Penticton, BC V2A 5Z8
250-492-5832, Fax: 250-492-3445

***Port Alberni:* Shaw Cable**
4278 - 8 Ave., Port Alberni, BC V9Y 7S8
250-723-6295, Fax: 250-723-4024

***Port Hardy:* Keta Cable**
PO Box 63, 7020 Market St., Port Hardy, BC V0N 2P0
250-949-6109, Fax: 250-949-6566,
ketacable@cablerocket.com
www.ketacable.com

***Port Simpson:* Rose Island Ventures Inc.**
PO Box 992, Port Simpson, BC V0V 1H0
250-625-3352, Fax: 250-625-3246

***Prince George:* Shaw Cablesystems G.P.**
2519 Queensway St., Prince George, BC V2L 1N1
250-562-1345, Fax: 250-614-7340

***Quesnel:* Shaw Cablesystems (BC) Ltd.**
156 Front St., Quesnel, BC V2J 2K1
250-992-7811

***Revelstoke:* Revelstoke Cable TV**
PO Box 651, 416 - 2nd St. West, Revelstoke, BC V0E 2S0
250-837-5246, Fax: 250-837-2900,
rctv@rctvonline.net
www.rctvonline.net

Don Gillespie

***Riondel:* Riondel Community Cable & Video Society**
PO Box 59, Riondel, BC V0B 2B0
250-225-3433, Fax: 250-225-3433,
www.bluebell.ca

W. Nelson, President

***Salmo:* Salmo Cabled Programmes Limited**
PO Box 402, Salmo, BC V0G 1Z0
250-357-9553, Fax: 250-357-9553

L.R. Street

***Salmon Arm:* Mascon Communications Corp.**
PO Box 3386, 4901 Auto Rd. SE, Salmon Arm, BC V1E 4S2
250-832-6000, Fax: 250-832-5575,
mascon@mascon.bc.ca
www.mascon.bc.ca

***Salmon Arm:* Sun Country Cablevision Ltd.**
PO Box 1360, 10 Harbourfront Dr. NE, Salmon Arm, BC V1E 4P5
250-832-9711, Fax: 250-832-2146,
info@sunwave.net
www.sunwave.net

***Salt Spring Island:* Saltspring Cablevision (1981) Ltd.**
PO Box 300, PO Ganges, Salt Spring Island, BC V8K 2V9
250-537-5550, Fax: 250-537-5550

Linda Phillips
Geoff Phillips

***Valemount:* Valemount Entertainment Society/CHVC-TV Community Television**
PO Box 922, Valemount, BC V0E 2Z0
250-566-8288, Fax: 250-566-4645,
tv@vctv.ca
www.vctv.ca

Andru McCracken, Station Manager
Barb Riswok, Vice-President
Penni Osadchuk, Station Manager

***Vananda:* Texada Community TV Association**
PO Box 158, Vananda, BC V0N 3K0
604-486-7640, Fax: 604—

Jack Cawthorpe

***Vancouver:* Okanagan Skeena Group Ltd.**
1130 West Pender St., Vancouver, BC V6E 4A4
604-685-1160, Fax: 604-684-3537

H. McKinnon, President

***Vernon:* Shaw Cable**
2924 - 28 Ave., Vernon, BC V1T 8W6
250-542-4007, Fax: 250-542-2928

Rennie Sirianni

***Victoria:* Shaw Cablesystems G.P.**
861 Cloverdale Ave., Victoria, BC V8X 4S7
250-475-5655, Fax: 250-475-7289,
eservice_victoria@sjrb.ca
www.shaw.ca

***Waglisla:* Heiltsuk Cablevision Co. Ltd.**
PO Box 880, Waglisla, BC V0T 1Z0
250-957-2381, Fax: 250-957-2544

***Whistler:* Whistler Cable Television Ltd.**
PO Box 630, #214, 4368 Main St., Whistler, BC V0N 1B4
604-932-1111, Fax: 604-932-1852,
info@whistlercable.com
www.whistlercable.com

R.J. Saperstein

***Williams Lake:* Shaw Cablesystems (BC) Ltd.**
1290 Borland Rd., Williams Lake, BC V2G 3Y1
250-392-3911, Fax: 250-392-8915

***Winfield:* Wood Lake Cable**
9570 Bottom Wood Lake Rd., Winfield, BC V4V 1S7
250-766-3123, Fax: 250-766-3946, 800-561-3699
info@wlcweb.com
www.woodlakecable.bc.ca

Darren Muloin, General Manager

Manitoba

***Brandon:* Westman Communications Group**
1906 Park Ave., Brandon, MB R7B 0R9
204-725-4300, Fax: 204-726-0853,
info@westmancom.com
www.westmancom.com

David Baxter, President/CEO, Marketing & Sales
Leo Boixain, Director, Technical Operations
David Baxter, President & CEO

***La Riviere:* La Riviere TV Club Inc.**
PO Box 132, La Riviere, MB R0G 1A0
204-242-2189, Fax: 204—

Michael Currie

** For details on this company see listing in Major Broadcasting Companies section; † French language station*

Thompson: **Shaw Cable**
50 Selkirk Ave., Thompson, MB R8N 0M7
204-778-8949, Fax: 204-677-9953,
shawcable11@yahoo.ca
www,shaw.ca

New Brunswick

Bathurst: **Rogers Cable**
PO Box 880, Bathurst, NB E2A 4H7
506-549-8877, Fax: 506-549-6609

Fredericton: **Rogers Cable**
377 York St., Fredericton, NB E3B 3P6
506-462-3642, Fax: 506-452-2846,
sdelong@rci.rogers.com
www.rogerstelevision.com

Miramichi: **Rogers Cable**
454 King George Hwy., Miramichi, NB E1V 1M1
506-778-3009, Fax: 506-778-3035,
www.rogerstelevision.com

Moncton: **Rogers Cable**
70 Assomption Blvd., Moncton, NB E1C 1A1
506-388-8405, Fax: 506-388-8622,
scott.jackson@rci.rogers.com
www.rogerstelevision.com
Serge Parent, Station Manager

Saint John: **Rogers Cable**
60 Waterloo St., Saint John, NB E2L 3P3
www.rogerstelevision.com
James A. MacMurray, Chair
C. William Stanley, President & CEO

Newfoundland & Labrador

Burgeo: **Burgeo Broadcasting System**
147 Reach Rd., Burgeo, NL A0M 1A0
709-886-2935, Fax: 709-886-1243,
www.bbsict.com/bbs/bbs.html
Claude Strickland, Operations Manager, claude@bbsict.ca
Marie Rose, Program Director

Churchill Falls: **Churchill Falls Satellite TV Association**
PO Box 252, Churchill Falls, NL A0R 1A0
709-925-3740, Fax: 709-925-8220,
ehillier@cancom.net
Ted Hillier, President

Glovertown: **Glovertown Cable TV Ltd.**
PO Box 131, Glovertown, NL A0G 2L0
709-533-2377, Fax: 709-533-2702

Happy Valley-Goose Bay: **CFS Cable**
PO Box 148 A, Happy Valley-Goose Bay, NL A0P 1S0
709-896-6900, Fax: 709-896-6948
Reg Wells, Chair
Jean Noseworthy, Office Manager

Labrador City: **Community Recreation Rebroadcasting Service Association/CRRS TV**
208 Amherst Ave., Labrador City, NL A2V 2Y5
709-944-7676, Fax: 709-944-7675,
info@crrstv.net
www.crrstv.net

Lewisporte: **Phoenix Cable TV**
PO Box 939, 139 Main St., Lewisporte, NL A0G 3A0
709-535-6771, Fax: 709-535-0417

Musgravetown: **BMC Cablevision Co. Ltd.**
PO Box 16, Musgravetown, NL A0C 1Z0
709-467-5306, Fax: 709-467-2489

Ramea: **Ramea Broadcasting Co.**
PO Box 23, Ramea, NL A0M 1N0
709-625-2618, Fax: 709-625-2048,
samuel.fiander@nf.sympatico.ca
Samuel Fiander

Reefs Harbour: **Clearview Cable Ltd.**
PO Box 10, Reefs Harbour, NL A0K 4L0
709-847-7441, Fax: 709-847-7100,
clearview.harold@nf.sympatico.ca
Harold G. Tucker, President/Manager

St. John's: **Persona Communications Inc.**
PO Box 12155 A, 17 Duffy Place, St. John's, NL A1B 4L5
709-754-3775, Fax: 709-754-3883,
www.personainc.ca
Dean MacDonald, EO
Brendan Paddick, President & COO

Northwest Territories

Deline: **Great Bear Co-operative**
PO Box 159, Deline, NT X0E 0G0
867-589-3361, Fax: 867-589-4517

Fort McPherson: **Tetlit Service Co-operative**
PO Box 27, Fort McPherson, NT X0E 0J0
867-952-2417, Fax: 867-952-2606

Fort Simpson: **HR Thomson**
PO Box 313, Fort Simpson, NT X0E 0N0
867-695-3107, Fax: 867-695-2144,
fortsim@cancom.net
Ivan Simons, Contact

Fort Smith: **Gardtal Holdings Ltd.**
PO Box 478, Fort Smith, NT X0E 0P0
867-872-3456, Fax: 867-872-5630,
gardtal@northwestel.net
www.gardtal.com
Chad Dubanow, 867/872-0080

Yellowknife: **Northwestel Cable Inc.**
PO Box 1469, 5120 - 49th St., Yellowknife, NT X1A 2P1
867-669-5469, Fax: 867-920-2331, 800-661-0834

Nova Scotia

Canning: **Cross Country TV Ltd.**
PO Box 310, Canning, NS B0P 1H0
902-678-2395, Fax: 902-678-2455,
wireless@xcountry.tv
www.xcountry.tv

Cheticamp: **Acadien Communications Ltd.**
PO Box 648, Cheticamp, NS B0E 1H0
902-224-2226, Fax: 902-224-3000,
www.aclnet.ca/home/default.asp

Digby: **Eastlink Cable**
PO Box 1090, 88 Warwick St., Digby, NS B0V 1A0
902-245-2519, Fax: 902-245-6511

Halifax: **EastLink**
PO Box 8660 A, Halifax, NS B3K 5M3
902-453-2800, Fax: 902-446-4171, 888-345-1111
www.eastlink.ca
Lee Bragg
Dan McKeen

Liverpool: **Eastlink Cable**
PO Box 449, 4130 Highway #3, Liverpool, NS B0T 1K0
902-356-3588, Fax: 902-354-2246,
www.eastlink.ca

Lower Sackville: **Eastlink Cable**
367 Sackville Dr., Lower Sackville, NS B4C 2R7
902-446-3588, Fax: 902-453-5714,
www.eastlink.ca

New Minas: **Eastlink Television**
PO Box 4000, 1001 How Ave., New Minas, NS B4N 4S8
902-681-0300, Fax: 902-681-6470,
www.eastlink.ca

Port Hawkesbury: **Rush Communications**
PO Box 790, 23 Paint St., Port Hawkesbury, NS B0E 2V0
902-625-3320, Fax: 902-625-0064, 888-769-2316
info@rushcomm.ca
www.rushcomm.ca

Reserve: **Seaside Communications**
PO Box 4558, 1318 Grand Lake Rd., Reserve, NS B1E 1L2
902-539-6250, Fax: 902-539-2597, 866-872-2253
www.seaside.ns.ca
Roland McCaffrey, General Manager, rmccaffrey@seaside.ns.ca

Shelburne: **Seabreeze Cablevision Ltd.**
PO Box 1090, 25B King St., Shelburne, NS B0T 1W0
902-875-1267, Fax: 902-875-4219,
www.eastlink.ca

Sydney: **Eastlink**
61 Melody Lane, Sydney, NS B1P 3K4
902-539-9611, Fax: 902-564-5428,
www.eastlink.ca
Paul Power, Contact

Truro: **Eastlink**
69 Walker St., Truro, NS B2N 4A8
902-843-3588, Fax: 902-843-3067,
www.eastlink.ca

Nunavut

Arctic Bay: **Taqqut Co-operative**
General Delivery, Arctic Bay, NU X0A 0A0
867-439-9934, Fax: 867-439-8765,
info@arcticco-op.com
inuit.pail.ca/taqqut-co-op.htm

Arviat: **Padlei Co-operative Association**
PO Box 90, Arviat, NU X0C 0E0
867-857-2933, Fax: 867-857-2762,
info@arcticco-op.com
arcticco-op.com/co-op_location.html

Baker Lake: **Sanavik Co-op**
PO Box 69, Baker Lake, NU X0C 0A0
867-793-2912, Fax: 867-793-2594,
info@arcticco-op.com
www.arcticco-op.com/acl-keewatin-baker-lake.htm

Cambridge Bay: **Ikaluktutiak Cooperative Limited**
PO Box 38, Cambridge Bay, NU X0B 0C0
867-983-2201, Fax: 867-983-2085,
info@arcticco-op.com
www.arcticco-op.com/acl-kitikmeot-cambridge-bay.htm

Cape Dorset: **Kingait Cablevision**
PO Box 209, Cape Dorset, NU X0A 0C0
867-897-8080, Fax: 867-897-8410,
mikeperry@qiniq.com
capedorset.qiniq.com
Mike Perry, Contact

Chesterfield Inlet: **Pitsiulak Co-operative**
PO Box 500, General Delivery, Chesterfield Inlet, NU X0C 0B0
867-898-9975, Fax: 867-898-9056,
info@arcticco-op.com
www.arcticco-op.com/acl-keewatin-chesterfield-inlet .htm

Coral Harbour: **Katudgevik Cooperative**
PO Box 201, Coral Harbour, NU X0C 0C0
867-925-9969, Fax: 867-925-8308,
info@arcticco-op.com
www.arcticco-op.com/acl-keewatin-coral-habour.htm

Gjoa Haven: **Kekertak Co-operative**
PO Box 120, General Delivery, Gjoa Haven, NU X0E 1J0
867-360-7271, Fax: 867-360-6018

Iqaluit: **Eastern Arctic TV Ltd.**
PO Box 730, Iqaluit, NU X0A 0H0
867-979-6707, Fax: 867-979-2535

Kugluktuk: **Kugluktuk Co-operative**
PO Box 279, Kugluktuk, NU X0E 0E0
867-982-4231, Fax: 867-982-3070,
info@arcticco-op.com
www.arcticco-op.com/acl-kitikmeot-kugluktuk.htm

Qikiqtarjuaq: **Tulugaq Co-Op**
PO Box 8, Qikiqtarjuaq, NU X0A 0B0
867-927-8061, Fax: 867-927-8044,
info@arcticco-op.com
www.arcticco-op.com/acl-baffin-region-qikiqtarjuaq. htm

Rankin Inlet: **Kissarvik Co-Op**
PO Box 40, Rankin Inlet, NU X0C 0G0
867-645-2801, Fax: 867-645-2280,
info@arcticco-op.com
www.arcticco-op.com/acl-keewatin-rankin-inlet.htm

Repulse Bay: **Naujat Co-operative**
General Delivery, Repulse Bay, NU X0C 0H0
867-462-9943, Fax: 867-462-4152,
info@arcticco-op.com
www.arcticco-op.com/acl-keewatin-repulse-bay.htm

Whale Cove: **Issatik Eskimo Co-op Ltd.**
PO Box 60, Whale Cove, NU X0C 0J0
867-896-9956, Fax: 867-896-9087,
info@arcticco-op.com
www.arcticco-op.com/acl-keewatin-whale-cove.htm

Ontario

Aurora: **Aurora Cable Internet**
350 Industrial Pkwy. South, Aurora, ON L4G 3H3

** For details on this company see listing in Major Broadcasting Companies section; † French language station*

905-727-1981, Fax: 905-727-7407,
info.aci@rci.rogers.com
www.aci.on.ca

***Barrie:* Rogers Cable**
PO Box 8500, 1 Sperling Dr., Barrie, ON L4M 6B8
705-737-4660, Fax: 705-737-0778, 800-461-4349
www.rogers.com

***Beardmore:* Beardmore Television**
PO Box 102, Beardmore, ON P0T 1G0
807-875-2096

***Belleville:* Cablevue (Quinte) Ltd.**
PO Box 149, 10 Front St. South, Belleville, ON K8N 4Z9
613-966-3226, Fax: 613-966-5329

***Brampton:* Rogers Community 10**
13 Hansen Rd. South, Brampton, ON L6W 3H6
905-457-3270, Fax: 905-456-1067

***Brockville:* COGECO Cable Canada LP**
PO Box 806, #13A, 333 California Ave., Brockville, ON K6V 5V5
613-342-7414, Fax: 613-342-6521,
ron.harrison@cogeco.com

***Burlington:* COGECO Cable Canada LP**
950 Syscon Rd., Burlington, ON L7R 4S1
905-333-5343, Fax: 905-332-8426, 800-267-9000
www.cogeco.com
Louis Audet, President & Chief Executive Officer
Louise St-Pierre, Vice-President, Customer Services & Ontario Operations
Maureen Tilson Dyment, Senior Director, Programming & Communications
Glenda Lloyd, Manager, Communications, Glenda.Lloyd@cogeco.com

***Chapleau:* Superior TV System**
PO Box 669, 31 Birch St., Chapleau, ON P0M 1K0
705-864-1462, Fax: 705-864-1341,
supertv@vianet.ca
Sandra Roposo, Manager

***Chatham:* COGECO Cable Canada LP**
491 Richmond St., Chatham, ON N7M 1R2
519-352-8810, Fax: 519-352-8274,
www.tvcogeco.com
Peter Martin, Manager, Programming & Community Relations

***Clifford:* Maitland Cable TV**
PO Box 70, 100 Elora St. North, Clifford, ON N0G 1M0
519-327-8012, Fax: 519-327-8010,
mcatv@wightman.ca
www.wightman.ca

***Collingwood:* Rogers Cablesystems**
4 Sandford Fleming Dr., Collingwood, ON L9Y 4V9
705-445-3400, Fax: 705-445-9949
David R. Scott, System Manager

***Cornwall:* COGECO Cable Canada LP**
517 Pitt St., Cornwall, ON K6J 3R4
613-937-2507, Fax: 613-932-3176,
viewer@cogeco.ca

***Dryden:* Shaw Cable**
75 Queen St., Dryden, ON P8N 1A1
807-223-5525, Fax: 807-223-4445

***Dublin:* Mitchell-Seaforth Cable TV Ltd.**
123 Ontario St., Dublin, ON N0K 1E0
519-345-2341, Fax: 519-345-2873, 800-360-1556
cabletv@ezlink.ca
www.ezlink.ca

***Eganville:* Bonnechere Cable Co. Ltd.**
PO Box 209, 179 Bonnechere St. East, Eganville, ON K0J 1T0
613-628-2727, Fax: 613-628-9258
William A. MacPhee, President

***Fenelon Falls:* Cable Cable Inc.**
16 Cable Rd., Fenelon Falls, ON K0M 1M0
705-887-6433, Fax: 705-887-2580,
www.cablecable.net
Tony Fiorini, President

***Fergus:* COGECO Cable Canada LP**
475 St. Patrick St. West, Fergus, ON N1M 1M2
519-843-3700, Fax: 519—,
www.tvcogeco.com

***Fort Frances:* Shaw Cable**
1037 First St. East, Fort Frances, ON P9A 1L8
807-274-5522, Fax: 807-274-0603

***Geraldton:* Astrocom Cablevision Inc.**
PO Box 910, 109 Greer Ave. West, Geraldton, ON P0T 1M0
807-854-1569, Fax: 807-854-2169,
jim@astrocom-on.com
www.astrocom-on.com
John S. Emmans, President

***Goderich:* EastLink TV**
PO Box 305, 141 Huckins St., Goderich, ON N7A 4C6
519-482-9233, Fax: 519-482-7098, 888-345-1111
cable@cabletv.on.ca
www.cabletv.on.ca

***Gore Bay:* Gore Bay Community TV**
PO Box 371, Gore Bay, ON P0P 1H0
705-282-1595, Fax: 705-282-1595

***Gravenhurst:* COGECO Cable Canada LP**
205 Jones Rd., Gravenhurst, ON P1P 1M8
705-687-8818, Fax: 705-687-4789,
www.tvcogeco.com

***Guelph:* Rogers Cablesystems**
130 Silvercreek Pkwy., Guelph, ON N1H 7Y5
519-824-1900, Fax: 519-824-4210, 888-894-1172
rogerstvweb@rogers.com
www.rogerstelevision.com
Jeremy Clark, Regional Station Manager
Al Haggith, Manager, Network Operations
Gregory K. Grimes, Station Manager

***Hamilton:* Mountain Cablevision Ltd.**
141 Hester St., Hamilton, ON L9A 2N9
905-389-1347, Fax: 905-574-6330,
info@mountaincable.net
www.mountaincable.net
John King

***Hamilton:* Source Cable Ltd.**
1074 Upper Wellington St., Hamilton, ON L9A 3S6
905-574-6465, Fax: 905-574-4909,
info@sourcecable.ca
www.sourcecable.ca

***Hamilton:* TV Hamilton**
150 Dundurn St. South, Hamilton, ON L8P 4K3
905-523-1414, Fax: 905-523-8141,
events@cable14.com
www.cable14.com
Brent Rickert, General Manager

***Hanover:* Saugeen Telecable Ltd.**
111 - 7th Ave., Hanover, ON N4N 2G8
519-364-2131, Fax: 519-364-4380

***Hawkesbury:* COGECO Cable Canada LP - Hawkesbury Office**
1444 Aberdeen St., Hawkesbury, ON K6A 1K7
Fax: 613-632-8531,
ronald.handfield@cogeco.com
www.cogeco.ca
Louis Audet, CEO

***Huntsville:* COGECO Cable Canada LP**
20 West St. South, Huntsville, ON P1H 1P2
705-789-9801, Fax: 705-789-2331,
www.tvcogeco.com
Michael Bradley, General Manager
Norm Bradley, President

***Keewatin:* Norcom Telecommunications Ltd.**
102 - 10th St., Keewatin, ON P0X 1C0
807-547-2853, Fax: 807-547-2236,
info@norcomcable.ca
www.norcomcable.ca

***Kincardine:* Kincardine Cable TV Ltd.**
223 Bruce Ave., Kincardine, ON N2Z 2P2
519-396-8880, Fax: 519-396-2599,
kctv@tnt21.com
www.tnt21.com

***Kingston:* COGECO Cable Systems Inc.**
PO Box 5500 Main, 170 Colborne St., Kingston, ON K7L 5M7
613-544-6311, Fax: 613-545-0169,
cogeco.13@cogeco.com
www.cogeco.ca

***Kitchener:* Rogers Cable**
85 Grand Crest Pl., Kitchener, ON N2G 4A8
519-893-2101, Fax: 519-893-5861,

***London:* Rogers Cable**
800 York St., London, ON N6A 5B1
519-672-0030, Fax: 519-672-0199

***Longlac:* Longlac Indian Reserve**
PO Box 609, Longlac, ON P0T 2A0
807-876-2292, Fax: 807-876-2757

***Madoc:* Hastings Cable Vision Ltd.**
31 Durham St. South, Madoc, ON K0K 2K0
613-473-2839, Fax: 613-473-4853

***Markdale:* Markdale Cable TV**
20 Eliza St., Markdale, ON N0C 1H0
519-986-2262, Fax: 519-986-2612,
marcable@cablerocket.com
www.markdalecabletv.com
Dave Armstrong, President

***Milton:* TVCogeco**
500 Laurier Ave., Milton, ON L9T 4R3
905-878-9306, Fax: 905-878-7927,
sandy.french@cogeco.com
www.cogeco.ca
Mike Hancock, Producer
Sandy French, Producer

***Mississauga:* Rogers Cablesystems**
3573 Wolfedale Rd., Mississauga, ON L5C 3T6
905-897-3906, Fax: 905-273-9661

***Moose Factory:* Mocreebec Development Corporation Ltd.**
PO Box 4, Moose Factory, ON P0L 1W0
705-658-4769, Fax: 705-658-4487

***Newmarket:* Rogers Cable Inc.**
395A Mulock Dr., Newmarket, ON L3Y 8P3
905-896-7199, Fax: 905-898-7577

***Niagara Falls:* COGECO Cable Solutions**
7170 McLeod Rd., Niagara Falls, ON L2G 3H2
905-374-2248, Fax: 905-374-2398, 800-706-4221
www.cogeco.com

***North Bay:* COGECO Cable Canada LP**
PO Box 3170 Main, 240 Fee St., North Bay, ON P1B 8S4
705-472-9868, Fax: 705-472-7854,
www.tvcogeco.com
Melanie Miller, Production Supervisor

***Norwich:* Nor-Del Cablevision Ltd.**
PO Box 340, Norwich, ON N0J 1P0
519-879-6527, Fax: 519-879-6387, 800-563-1954
nordel@nor-del.com
www.nor-del.com
Glenn I. Baxter, President

***Oshawa:* Rogers Cable**
301 Marwood Dr., Oshawa, ON L1H 1J4
905-436-4141, Fax: 905-579-5559, 800-738-7893
durham@rci.rogers.com
www.rogerstelevision.com
Steve Simic, Station Manager

***Ottawa:* Rogers Cable**
475 Richmond Rd., Ottawa, ON K2A 3Y8
613-728-2222, Fax: 613-728-9793,
ottawa22@rci.rogers.com
www.rogerstelevision.com

***Pembroke:* COGECO Cable Solutions**
185 Lake St., Pembroke, ON K8A 5M1
613-735-1228, Fax: 613-735-6177,
www.cogeco.ca

***Port Perry:* Compton Cable TV Ltd.**
PO Box 73 Main, Port Perry, ON L9L 1A2
905-985-8171, Fax: 905-985-0010,
community10@compton.net
www.compton.net

***Richmond Hill:* Rogers Cable**
244 Newkirk Rd., Richmond Hill, ON L4C 3S5
905-884-8111, Fax: 905-884-8151

***Sault Ste Marie:* Shaw Cablesystems G.P**
23 Manitou Dr., Sault Ste Marie, ON P6B 6GN
705-946-2234, Fax: 705-946-4773,
www.shaw.ca
Kevin Boll, Technical Manager

** For details on this company see listing in Major Broadcasting Companies section; † French language station*

Schreiber: **Shaw Cablesystems**
224 Park St., Schreiber, ON P0T 2S0
807-824-2619, Fax: 807—

Sudbury: **Persona Communications**
PO Box 4500, #15, 500 Barrydowne Rd., Sudbury, ON P3A 5W1
705-560-1560, Fax: 705-560-8385,
www.personainc.ca
Brendon Paddick, President & General Manager
Irv Whipple, Director, Engineering

Thunder Bay: **Fibre-Tel Enterprises**
1043 Gorham St., Thunder Bay, ON P7B 4A5
807-622-0100, Fax: 807-626-8282

Thunder Bay: **Shaw Cablesystems**
1635 Paquette Rd., Thunder Bay, ON P7G 2J2
807-766-7025, Fax: 807-766-7022, 888-472-2222

Toronto: **Rogers Cable**
855 York Mills Rd., Toronto, ON M3B 1Z1
416-446-6500, Fax: 416-446-6658

Val Gagne: **Val Gagne Communications Association**
PO Box 1, Val Gagne, ON P0K 1W0
705-232-6952, Fax: 705-232-6303,
vgca@ntl.sympatico.ca
Marcel R. Fortier, President/General Manager

Westport: **North Leeds Cablecom Inc.**
PO Box 252, 1234 - 8th Concession, Westport, ON K0G 1X0
613-273-7000, Fax: 613-273-2323,
cable@rideau.net
www.brockville.com

Windsor: **COGECO Cable Canada LP**
2525 Dougall Ave., Windsor, ON N8X 5A7
519-972-6677, Fax: 519-972-6688,
windsorcable11@wincom.net
www.cogeco.ca
Robert Scussolin, Programming and Community Relations

Woodstock: **Rogers Cable**
PO Box 1208, 21 Ridgeway Circle, Woodstock, ON N4S 8P6
519-539-8103, Fax: 519-539-7731, 866-384-4422
joe.brown@rci.rogers.com
www.rogerstelevision.com

Prince Edward Island

Summerside: **Eastlink**
PO Box 4 Main, Summerside, PE C1N 4P6
902-436-2249, Fax: 902-436-5799

Québec

†*Albanel:* **Télé-câble Albanel inc.**
227, rue Principale, Albanel, QC G8M 3K3
418-279-5940, Fax: 418-279-3113,
info@tcalbanel.com
www.tcalbanel.com
Fernand Plourde, Fondateur

†*Betsiamites:* **Télécâble Pessamit**
18, rue Messek, Betsiamites, QC G0H 1B0
418-567-8863, Fax: 418-567-8868,
www.pessamit.ca

†*Brossard:* **Cablevision SDM-TRP inc.**
8285, boul Pelletier, Brossard, QC J4X 1P6
450-671-4251, Fax: 450-923-1873, 800-465-9215
www.totalsat.qc.ca

†*Chicoutimi:* **Cablo-Saguenay**
70 Pric Rue Ouest, Chicoutimi, QC G7J 1G7
418-696-1581, Fax: 418-543-7995

†*Chisasibi:* **Ginwat Cable Television Inc.**
CP 420, Chisasibi, QC J0M 1E0
819-855-2191, Fax: 819-855-3186

Drummondville: **COGECO Cable Canada LP**
1970, boul Lemire, Drummondville, QC J2B 6X5
819-477-3978, Fax: 819-474-5313,
tvcogeco.drummondville@cgocable.ca
www.cogeco.ca
Reno Longpré, Contact

†*Eaton:* **Transvision inc.**
2080, rue Spring, Eaton, QC J1M 2A2
819-346-0760, Fax: 819-346-5790

†*Fermont:* **Coopérative de la télévision communautaire de Fermont**
CP 1379, 20, place Daviault, Fermont, QC G0G 1J0
418-287-5443, Fax: 418-287-5776

†*Grande-Rivière-Ouest:* **Briand et Moreau Câble inc.**
CP 63, 205 B, rue du Parc, Grande-Rivière-Ouest, QC G0C 1W0
418-385-2680, Fax: 418-385-3705,
bmcable@bmcable.ca
www.bmcable.ca

†*Havre-Saint-Pierre:* **R&T Communautaire Hâvre-St-Pierre**
992, rue du Bouleau, Havre-Saint-Pierre, QC G0G 1P0
418-538-2451, Fax: 418-538-3870,
info@cilemf.com
www.cilemf.com

†*La Malbaie:* **Coopérative de câblodistribution de St-Fidèle**
8, ch St-Paul, La Malbaie, QC G5A 2G6
418-434-2486, Fax: 418-434-1076,
marcel.couturier@sympatico.ca
Marcel Couturier, Secrétaire

†*Labelle:* **Télécâble Nordique inc.**
CP 630, 128, boul Curé-Labelle, Labelle, QC J0T 1H0
819-686-2662, 800-293-8093

†*Lennoxville:* **Transvision Réseau**
#105, 175 Queen St., Lennoxville, QC J1M 1K1
819-563-1001, Fax: 819-563-3116, 877-946-3116
www.transvision.net

†*Lourdes-de-Blanc-Sablon:* **Coopérative de câblodistribution de Brest**
1147, boul Dr.-Camille-Marcoux, Lourdes-de-Blanc-Sablon, QC G0G 1W0
418-461-2003, Fax: 418-461-2070,

†*Magog:* **Cable Axion inc.**
250, ch de l'Axion, Magog, QC J1X 6J2
819-843-0611, Fax: 819-868-4249, 866-552-9466
info@axion.ca
www.axion.ca
Paul Girard, Président

†*Magog:* **COGECO Cable Canada LP**
15, rue St-Patrice ouest, Magog, QC J1X 1V8
819-843-3370, Fax: 819-843-0698,
tvcogeco.magog@cgocable.ca
www.cogeco.ca

†*Marsoui:* **GD Télévision Enrg.**
CP 118, Marsoui, QC G0E 1S0
418-288-5591, Fax: 418-288-1391,
ghisde@globetrotter.net

†*Matagami:* **Cablevision Matagami**
3, rue Vanier, Matagami, QC J0Y 2A0
819-739-2148, Fax: 819-739-2612

†*Matane:* **Tele-Cable Multi-Vision inc.**
655, ch de la Greve, Matane, QC G4W 7A1
418-562-1950
Raymond Vachon, Contact

†*Montréal:* **Cable VDN Inc.**
#206, 2600, rue Ontario est, Montréal, QC H2K 4K4
514-522-1590, Fax: 514-522-1568,
info@vdn.ca
web.vdn.ca

†*Montréal:* **COGECO Cable Canada LP**
#915, 5 Place Ville-Marie, Montréal, QC H3B 2G2
514-874-2600, Fax: 514-874-2625,
www.cogeco.ca

†*Montréal:* **Vidéotron ltée**
612, rue St-Jacques, Montréal, QC H3C 4M8
514-281-1711,
www.quebecor.com
Robert Dépatie, Président/Chef de la direction

†*Percé:* **Télédistribution de la Gaspésie**
CP 234, 155, Place du Quai, Percé, QC G0C 2L0
418-782-5355, Fax: 418-782-5407,
TDG01@bmcable.ca
www.bmcable.ca

†*Québec:* **Coopérative de câblodistribution de l'arrière-pays**
20860, boul Henri-Bourassa, Québec, QC G2N 1P7
418-849-7125, Fax: 418-849-7128,
info@ccapcable.com
www.ccapcable.com
Jacques Perron, Directeur général
Stephane Arseneau, Directeur, Service à la clientèle

†*Rimouski:* **COGECO Cable Canada LP**
384, av de la Cathédrale, Rimouski, QC G5L 5L1
418-724-6058, Fax: 418-724-7167,
tvcogecorimouski@cogeco.com
www.cogeco.com

†*Rivière-Saint-Jean:* **Télévision communautaire Rivière-St-Jean inc.**
376, St-Jean/Poste Restante, Rivière-Saint-Jean, QC G0G 2N0
418-949-2340
Jacques Lévesque, Président

Rivière-du-Loup: **Le Cable de Rivière-du-Loup ltée**
279A, rue Lafontaine, CP 1390, Rivière-du-Loup, QC G5R 4L9
418-867-1479, Fax: 418-867-2829,
rivieredulop@canalvox.com
Pierre Simon, Président

†*Saint-Gabriel-de-Valcarti:* **Valcartier Cable**
1743, boul Valcartier, Saint-Gabriel-de-Valcarti, QC G0A 4S0
418-844-3666, Fax: 418-844-3030,
mbaker@munsgdv.ca
www.saint-gabriel-de-valcartier.ca

†*Saint-Jean-des-Piles:* **Gagnon et Fils Electronique Inc.**
1470, rue Principale, Saint-Jean-des-Piles, QC G0X 2V0
819-538-8508, Fax: 819—

†*Saint-Just-de-Bretenières:* **Coopérative de câblodistribution de Saint-Just-de-Bretenières**
11, rue du Couvent, Saint-Just-de-Bretenières, QC G0R 3H0
418-244-3560, Fax: 418-244-3560,
cablo-st-just@globetrotter.net
Réjean Poulin, Président

†*Saint-Pamphile:* **Guy Chouinard Cable TV**
CP 216, 9, rue de L'Église, Saint-Pamphile, QC G0R 3X0
418-356-5276, Fax: 418-356-5276

Sainte-Adèle: **COGECO Cable Canada LP**
PO Box 1375, 605, Pierre-Péladeau, Sainte-Adèle, QC J8B 1Z3
450-229-7668, Fax: 450-229-7910,
tvcogeco.laurentides@cgocable.ca
www.cogeco.ca
Guy Goyer, Contact

†*Sainte-Jeanne-d'Arc:* **Cable FB**
480, rue Principale, Sainte-Jeanne-d'Arc, QC G0W 1E0
418-276-5309, Fax: 418-276-1891
G. Gauthier

†*Sainte-Thècle:* **Télécâble Groleau inc.**
CP 22, 120, route 352, Sainte-Thècle, QC G0X 3G0
418-289-2871, Fax: 418-289-3871,
grolo@globetrotter.net
Aurel Groleau, Contact

Sanikiluaq: **Mitiq Co-operative**
General Delivery, Sanikiluaq, QC X0A 0W0
867-266-8860, Fax: 867-266-8844,
info@arcticco-op.com
www.arcticco-op.com/acl-baffin-region-sanikiluaq.ht m

Sept-Iles: **COGECO Cable Canada LP**
410, rue Evangeline, Sept-Iles, QC G4R 2N5
418-962-3508, Fax: 418-962-3531

Shannon: **Shannon Vision inc.**
50, rue St. Patrick, Shannon, QC G0A 4N0
418-844-3849, Fax: 418-844-0347

Shawinigan: **COGECO Cable Canada LP**
1222, 47e rue, Shawinigan, QC G9N 5B4
819-539-9501, Fax: 819-539-6789,
www.cogeco.ca

Sillery: **Genex Communications Inc.**
#300, 1134, Grande-Allée, Sillery, QC G1S 1E5
418-687-9810, Fax: 418-682-8427,
patrice.demers@genexcommunications.com
www.choiradiox.com
Patrice Demers

** For details on this company see listing in Major Broadcasting Companies section; † French language station*

***St-Georges-de-Beauce:* COGECO Cable Canada LP**
11197 - 2e av, St-Georges-de-Beauce, QC G5Y 1V9
418-228-9828, Fax: 418-228-3015,
tvcogeco.beauce@cgocable.ca
www.cogeco.ca

†*St-Zacharie:* Cablovision ACL Enr
515, 9e Avenue, St-Zacharie, QC G0M 2C0
418-593-5262, Fax: 418-593-3260

†*Ste-Catherine-de-la-Jacques-Cartier:* Coopérative de câblodistribution Ste-Catherine-Fossambault
130, rue Désiré-Juneau,
Ste-Catherine-de-la-Jacques-Cartier, QC G3N 2X3
418-875-1118, Fax: 418-875-1971,
gestion@coopcscf.com
www.coopcscf.com

†*Thetford Mines:* COGECO Cable Canada LP
39 - 10e Rue Sud, Thetford Mines, QC G6G 7X6
418-338-2079, Fax: 418-335-9125,
tvcogeco.thetford@cgocable.ca
www.cogeco.ca

***Trois-Rivières:* COGECO Câble Québec inc.**
1630 - 6e rue, Trois-Rivières, QC G8Y 5B8
819-693-8353, Fax: 819-379-2232,
www.cgocable.ca
Jean-Guy Proulx, Contact

†*Val-D'Or:* Cablevision du Nord de Québec inc.
45, boul de Hôtel de Ville, Val-D'Or, QC J9P 2M5
819-825-5133, 800-567-6353
www.cablevision.qc.ca
Bernard Gauthier, Président

†*Warwick:* Cablovision Warwick inc.
CP 999, 14, boul Beaumier, Warwick, QC J0A 1M0
819-358-5858, Fax: 819-358-5592,
service@cablovision.com
www.cablovision.com

†*Waswanipi:* Waswanipi Cable TV
20 Poplar St., Waswanipi, QC J0Y 3C0
819-753-2557, Fax: 819-753-2555

Saskatchewan

***Arcola:* Town of Arcola**
PO Box 359, Arcola, SK S0C 0G0
306-455-2212, Fax: 306-455-2445,
arcadmin@sasktel.net
www.creda.sk.ca/arcola/

***Birch Hills:* Northern Native Public Broadcasting Inc.**
PO Box 204, Birch Hills, SK S0J 0G0
306-749-2578, Fax: 306—

***Craik:* Craik Cablevision**
PO Box 60, Craik, SK S0G 0V0
306-734-2250, Fax: 306-734-2688,
town.craik@sasktel.net
www.craik.ca
Rod Haugerud, Mayor
Jason Kemp

***Esterhazy:* Leaf Cable Inc.**
PO Box 1540, Esterhazy, SK S0A 0X0
306-745-3592, Fax: 306-745-3597, 866-484-0344
Mark Larsen, President
Glenda Colbourne, Manager

***Ile-a-la-Crosse:* Ile a la Crosse Communications Society Inc.**
PO Box 480, Ile-a-la-Crosse, SK S0M 1C0
306-833-2173, Fax: 306-833-2042,
ilexcomm@sk.sympatico.ca
Mike Bouvier, Manager

***Imperial:* Imperial Cable System**
PO Box 90, Imperial, SK S0G 2J0
306-963-2220, Fax: 306-963-2445,
town.imperial@sasktel.net

***Kinistino:* Kinistino Cable TV**
PO Box 10, Kinistino, SK S0J 1H0
306-864-2461, Fax: 306-864-2880,
townofkinistino@sasktel.net
Leonard Margolis
Shirley Jackson

***La Ronge:* Cable Ronge Inc.**
PO Box 1397, La Ronge, SK S0J 1L0
306-425-2276, Fax: 306-425-2042,
marley@cableronge.sk.ca
www.cableronge.sk.ca
Marilyn Chernoff, General Manager

***Limerick:* Village of Limerick**
PO Box 129, Limerick, SK S0H 2P0
306-263-2020, Fax: 306-263-2013
Tammy Franks, Administrator

***Moose Jaw:* Shaw Cable**
201 Manitoba St. East, Moose Jaw, SK S6H 0A4
306-693-8585, Fax: 306-692-4859

***Moose Jaw:* Shaw Cable Moose Jaw.**
201 Manitoba St. East, Moose Jaw, SK S6H 0A4
306-693-8585, Fax: 306-692-4859
Bob Anderson, Regional Manager
Jim Shaw Jr., Chief Officer

***North Battleford:* Access Communications Co-operative Ltd.**
1192 - 99 St., North Battleford, SK S9A 0P3
306-445-4045, Fax: 306-445-0755, 866-363-2225
help@accesscomm.ca
www.accesscomm.ca
Jim Deane, President/CEO
Trevor Derksen, Vice-President, Marketing & Sales
Carmela Haines, Vice-President, Finance & Administr

***Ponteix:* Ponteix T.V. Club**
PO Box 684, Ponteix, SK S0N 1Z0
306-625-3884, Fax: 306-625-3204
Dennis Ward

***Prince Albert:* Shaw Cable Prince Albert**
2990 - 2nd Ave. West, Prince Albert, SK S6V 7E9
306-922-0202, Fax: 306-922-7122

***Regina:* Access Communications Co-operative Ltd.**
2250 Park St., Regina, SK S4N 7K7
306-569-3510, Fax: 306-565-5395, 866-363-2225
help@accesscomm.ca
www.accesscomm.ca
Jim Deane, President & CEO
Trevor Derksen, Vice-President, Marketing & Sales
Carmela Haines, Vice-President, Finance & Administr

***Rouleau:* Rouleau Cable TV Association Inc.**
PO Box 250, Rouleau, SK S0G 4H0
306-776-2270, Fax: 306-776-2482

***Saskatoon:* Askivision Systems Inc.**
826 - 57th St. East, Saskatoon, SK S7K 5Z1
519-686-0909, Fax: 519-686-1916, 800-819-9718
cs@aski.ca
www.aski.ca
Don Wolhberg, President
Michelle Kimmett, General Manager

***Saskatoon:* Shaw Cable**
2326 Hanselman Ave., Saskatoon, SK S7L 5Z3
306-664-2121, Fax: 306-244-0105

***Southey:* Southey Cable**
PO Box 248, Southey, SK S0G 4P0
306-726-2202, Fax: 306-726-2916,
www.southey.ca
C. Flaman

***Swift Current:* Shaw Cable**
15 Dufferin St. West, Swift Current, SK S9H 5A1
306-773-7218, Fax: 306-773-6421

***Weyburn:* Access Communications Co-operative Ltd.**
120 - 10th Ave., Weyburn, SK S4H 1G9
306-842-0320, Fax: 306-842-3465, 866-363-2225
help@accesscomm.ca
www.accesscomm.ca
Jim Deane, President & CEO
Jim Deane, President & CEO
Carmela Haines, Vice-President, Finance & Administr

***Yorkton:* Image Wireless Communications - a division of YOURLINK Inc.**
PO Box 20051, 552 D Broadway Ave. East, Yorkton, SK S3N 4A9
306-782-4388, Fax: 306-786-7686, 888-462-4388
talk2us@imagewireless.ca
www.imagewireless.ca

***Young:* Village of Young**
PO Box 359, Young, SK S0K 4Y0
306-259-2242, Fax: 306-259-2247,
villageofyoung2@sasktel.net
Robert Speiser, Mayor

Yukon Territory

***Dawson City:* Dawson City Cable**
PO Box 308, Dawson City, YT Y0B 1G0
867-993-7400, Fax: 867-993-7434,
cityofdawson@yknet.ca

***Whitehorse:* Northern Television Systems Ltd.**
#203, 4103 - 4th Ave., Whitehorse, YT Y1A 1H6
867-393-2225, Fax: 867-393-2224,
info@whtvcable.com
www.whtvcable.com

Specialty Broadcasters

Alberta

***Calgary:* Max Trax**
#501, 630 - 3 Ave. SW, Calgary, AB T2P 4L4
403-444-4233, Fax: 403-444-4240,
www.corusmaxtrax.com

***Edmonton:* CourtTV Canada**
10212 Jasper Ave., Edmonton, AB T5J 5A3
780-440-7777, Fax: 780-440-8899,
info@courttvcanada.ca
www.courttvcanada.ca

***Edmonton:* Movie Central**
#200, 5324 Calgary Trail, Edmonton, AB T6H 4J8
780-430-2800, Fax: 780-437-3188,
web.moviecentral@corusent.com
www.moviecentral.ca

British Columbia

***Burnaby:* Knowledge Network**
4355 Mathissi Pl., Burnaby, BC V5G 4S8
604-431-3222, Fax: 604-431-3387, 877-456-6988
knonline@knowledgenetwork.ca
www.knowledgenetwork.ca
Wayne Robert, General Manager

***Richmond:* Talentvision TV**
3300-4151 Hazelbridge Way, Richmond, BC V6X 4J7
604-295-1328, Fax: 604-295-1300,
info@fairchildtv.com
www.talentvisiontv.com
Joseph Chan

Manitoba

***Winnipeg:* Aboriginal Peoples Television Network**
339 Portage Ave., Winnipeg, MB R3B 2C3
204-947-9331, Fax: 204-947-9307, 888-330-2786
info@aptn.ca
www.aptn.ca
Social Media: www.facebook.com/pages/APTN/88781789916
Jean LaRose, CEO
Peter Strutt, Director, Programming
Vera Houle, Director, News & Current Affairs
Ken Earl, Director, Human Resources
Wayne McKenzie, Director, Operations
Sky Bridges, Director, Marketing
Jamie Veilleux, CFO

***Winnipeg:* CoolTV**
#2100, One Lombard Pl., Winnipeg, MB R3B 0X3
Fax: 204-926-4853, 866-729-7140
contactus@globaltv.ca
www.canada.com/topics/entertainment/tvchannels/coo ltv

***Winnipeg:* Dejaview**
#2100, One Lombard Pl., Winnipeg, MB R3B 0X3
Fax: 204-926-4653, 866-729-7140
contactus@globaltv.ca
www.canada.com/topics/entertainment/tvchannels/dej aview

***Winnipeg:* Fox Sports World Canada**
#2100, One Lombard Pl., Winnipeg, MB R3B 0X3
Fax: 204-926-4853, 866-729-7140
contactus@globaltv.com
www.canada.com/topics/entertaintment/tvchannels/f oxsports/

***Winnipeg:* Lonestar**
#2100, One Lombard Pl., Winnipeg, MB R3B 0X3

** For details on this company see listing in Major Broadcasting Companies section; † French language station*

Fax: 204-926-4853, 866-729-7140
contactus@globaltv.ca
www.canada.com/topics/entertainment/tvchannels/lon estar

***Winnipeg:* MenTV**
#2100, One Lombard Pl., Winnipeg, MB R3B 0X3
Fax: 204-926-4853, 866-729-7140
contactus@globaltv.com
www.canada.com/topics/entertainment/tvchannels/me ntv

***Winnipeg:* Mystery**
#2100, One Lombard Pl., Winnipeg, MB R3B 0X3
Fax: 204-926-4853, 866-729-7140
contactus@globaltv.com
www.canada.com/topics/entertainment/tvchannels/my stery

***Winnipeg:* Xtreme Sports**
#2100, One Lombard Pl., Winnipeg, MB R3C 0X3
Fax: 204-926-4853, 866-729-7140
contacus@globaltv.ca
www.canada.com/topics/entertainment/tvchannels/xtre mesports

Nova Scotia

***Halifax:* Independent Film Channel Canada**
#103, 1649 Brunswick St., Halifax, NS B3J 2G3
902-423-2662, Fax: 902-423-7862,
viewercomments-hfx@ifctv.ca
www.ifctv.ca
John Gill, Sr. Vice-President, Drama
Emily Morgan, Vice-President, Programming, Showcase Action, Showcase Diva

Nunavut

***Yellowknife:* CBC North**
CBC Mackenzie, PO Box 160, 5002 Forrest Dr., Yellowknife, NWT X1A 2N2
867-920-5400, 866-306-4636
www.cbc.ca/north
Social Media:
www.facebook.com/group.php?gid=481521000412
Sue Glowach, Senior Officer, Communications, 867-669-3531, Fax: 867-669-3573
Donna Lee, Contact, CBC North News, 867-920-5448

Ontario

***Burlington:* CTS - Crossroads TV System**
1295 North Service Rd., Burlington, ON L7R 4X5
905-331-7333, Fax: 905-331-7222,
cts@ctstv.com
www.ctstv.com
Dick Gray, President
Lorne Freed, Director, Programming & Operations

***King City:* TrackPower**
765 - 15th Sideroad, King City, ON L7B 1K5
905-773-1987, Fax: 905-773-1241,
info@trackpower.com
www.trackpower.com

***Mississauga:* BITE Television**
2196 Dunwin Dr., Mississauga, ON L5L 1C7
905-828-2483, Fax: 905-828-7660,
info@bite.ca
www.bitetv.ca
Jeffrey Elliot, Co-CEO/Manager, Marketing & Sales
Raja Khanna, Co-CEO, Finance
Simon Foster, Director, Sales, 905-828-2483, X, simon@glassbox.tv
Sharon Stevens, Director, Programming, 905-828-2483, X, sharon@glassbox.tv

***Mississauga:* Shaw Broadcast Services**
2055 Flavelle Blvd., Mississauga, ON L5K 1Z8
905-403-2020, Fax: 905-403-2022, 800-268-2943
www.shawbroadcast.com

***Mississauga:* The Shopping Channel**
59 Ambassador Dr., Mississauga, ON L5T 2P9
905-362-2020,
www.theshoppingchannel.com

***Newmarket:* Asian Television Network**
130 Pony Dr., Newmarket, ON L3Y 7B6
905-836-6460, Fax: 905-853-5212,
atn@asiantelevision.com
www.asiantelevision.com
Shan Chandrasekar, President/CEO/Founder
Shan Chandrasekar, President/CEO/Founder
Jaya Chandrasekar, Executive Vice-President/Vice-Presi
Prakash Naidoo, Vice-President, Operations/General

***North York:* Telelatino Network Inc.**
5125 Steeles Ave. West, North York, ON M9L 1R5
416-744-8200, Fax: 416-744-0966, 800-551-8401
info@tlntv.com
www.tlntv.com
Aldo DiFelice, President

***Oakville:* The Weather Network**
2655 Bristol Circle, Oakville, ON L6H 7W1
905-829-1159, Fax: 905-829-5800,
www.theweathernetwork.com
Pierre L. Morrissette

***Ottawa:* CPAC**
PO Box 81099, Ottawa, ON K1P 1B1
613-567-2722, Fax: 613-567-2741, 877-287-2722
comments@cpac.ca
www.cpac.ca

***Ottawa:* Galaxie**
PO Box 3220 C, Ottawa, ON K1Y 1E4
613-288-6308, Fax: 613-288-6205, 877-425-2943
information@galaxie.ca
www.galaxie.ca

***Ottawa:* The Green Channel**
342 MacLaren St., Ottawa, ON K2P 0M6
613-238-4580, Fax: 613-238-5642,
info@wetv.com
www.wetv.com

***Toronto:* Animal Planet**
9 Channel Nine Ct., Toronto, ON M1S 4B5
416-332-5000, Fax: 416-332-4230,
comments@animalplanet.ca
www.animalplanet.ca
Social Media: twitter.com/animalplanetca

***Toronto:* BBC Canada**
#200, 121 Bloor St. East, Toronto, ON M4W 3M5
416-967-3249, Fax: 416-967-0044, 866-813-3222
www.bbccanada.com

***Toronto:* BBC Kids**
#200, 121 Bloor St. East, Toronto, ON M4W 3M5
416-967-3250, 866-322-2543
www.bbckids.ca

***Toronto:* The Biography Channel**
545 Lakeshore Blvd. West, Toronto, ON M5V 1A3
416-260-0033, Fax: 416-260-3810, 866-260-0033
info@thebiographychannel.ca
www.thebiographychannel.ca
Malcolm Dunlop, Vice-President, Marketing & Programming
Andrea Gagliardi, Director, Consumer Marketing & Public Relations

***Toronto:* BookTelevision**
299 Queen St. West, Toronto, ON M5V 2Z5
416-591-7400, Fax: 416-591-5117,
info@booktelevision.com
www.booktelevision.com
Catherine McCutcheon, Director, Specialty Sales, CTVglobe, sales@ctv.ca

***Toronto:* BPM: TV**
105 Gordon Baker Rd., 8th Fl., Toronto, ON M2H 3P8
416-756-2404, Fax: 416-756-5526,
info@stornoway.com
www.stornoway.com
Martha Fusca, President/CEO, mfusca@stornoway.com
David Vowell, Director, Marketing, dvowell@stornoway.com
Cindy Boyd, Operations Manager, cboyd@stornoway.com

***Toronto:* Bravo! The New Style Arts Channel**
299 Queen St. West, Toronto, ON M5V 2Z5
416-591-5757, Fax: 416-591-7482,
bravomail@bravo.ca
www.bravo.ca

***Toronto:* Canadian Learning Television**
CHUM Ltd., 299 Queen St. West, Toronto, ON M5V 2Z5
416-591-7400, Fax: 416-591-5117,
info@clt.ca
www.clt.ca
Ron Keast, President & CEO
Peter Palframan, Vice-President, Finance & Operations
Ross Mayot, Vice-President, Development

***Toronto:* CBC News Network**
PO Box 500 A, Toronto, ON M5W 1E6
866-306-4636
www.cbc.ca/news;
www.cbc.ca/programguide/daily/today/cbc_news_network
Social Media: www.facebook.com/newscbc;
www.twitter.com/cbcnews
Other information: TTY: 1-866-220-6045
Roger Ramalsingh, Affiliate Relations Officer

***Toronto:* The Christian Channel**
#230, 171 East Liberty St., Toronto, ON M6K 3P6
416-368-3194, Fax: 416-368-9774,
info@christianchannel.ca
www.christianchannel.ca
Mark Prasuhn, President & General Manager

***Toronto:* The Comedy Network**
9 Channel Nine Ct., Toronto, ON M1S 4B5
416-332-5300, Fax: 416-332-5301,
mail@thecomedynetwork.ca
www.thecomedynetwork.ca
Ed Robinson, President & General Manager

***Toronto:* Country Canada**
PO Box 500 A, Toronto, ON M5W 1E6
866-306-4636
cbccountrycanada.ca

***Toronto:* Country Music Television**
#18, 64 Jefferson Ave., Toronto, ON M6K 3H4
416-534-1191, Fax: 416-530-5206,
www.cmtcanada.com
John P. Wright

***Toronto:* CP24**
299 Queen St. West, Toronto, ON M5V 2Z5
416-591-5757, Fax: 416-593-6397,
now@cp24.com
www.cp24.com

***Toronto:* CTV News Channel**
Owned by: **CTVglobemedia Inc.**
9 Channel Nine Ct., Toronto, ON M1S 4B5
416-384-5000,
ctvcommunications@ctv.ca
www.ctv.ca/newschannel/

***Toronto:* The Discovery Channel**
PO Box 1200, 9 Channel Nine Ct., Toronto, ON M1S 5R6
416-332-5000,
comments@discovery.ca
discoverychannel.ca

***Toronto:* Discovery Civilization**
PO Box 1200, 9 Channel Nine Ct., Toronto, ON M1S 4R6
416-332-5000, Fax: 416-332-4245,
comments@discoverycivilization.ca
discoverycivilization.ca

***Toronto:* Discovery Health Channel**
#200, 121 Bloor St. East, Toronto, ON M4W 3M5
416-967-3248, 866-967-3248
www.discoveryhealth.ca

***Toronto:* Discovery Kids Canada**
#18, 64 Jefferson St., Toronto, ON M6K 3H4
416-534-1191, Fax: 416-588-6987,
www.discoverykids.ca

***Toronto:* Distribution Access**
#702, 27 Queen St. East, Toronto, ON M5C 2M6
416-363-6765, Fax: 416-363-7834,
ontariosales@distributionaccess.com
www.distributionaccess.com/new/main. cfm
Doug Connolly, President/COO, doug.connolly@distributionaccess.com
Peter Palframan, CEO/Secretary-Treasurer

***Toronto:* documentary**
PO Box 500 A, Toronto, ON M6W 1E6
866-306-4636
www.cbc.ca/documentarychannel/
Michael Burns, Director of Programming

***Toronto:* Drive-In Classics**
299 Queen St. West, Toronto, ON M5V 2Z5
416-591-7400,
driveinclassics@driveinclassics.ca
www.driveinclassics.ca

***Toronto:* ESPN Classic Canada**
9 Channel Nine Ct., Toronto, ON M1S 4B5
416-332-5000, Fax: 416-332-7657,
www.tsn.ca/classic

** For details on this company see listing in Major Broadcasting Companies section; † French language station*

Toronto: The Family Channel Inc.
BCE Place, PO Box 787, 181 Bay St., Toronto, ON M5J 2T3
416-956-2030, Fax: 416-956-2035, 800-893-4862
info@family.ca
www.family.ca
Joe Tedesco, Vice-President & General Manager

Toronto: Fashion TV
299 Queen St. West, Toronto, ON M5V 2Z5
416-591-5757, Fax: 416-591-3545,
fashion@citytv.com
www.fashiontelevision.com

Toronto: Fine Living
#200, 121 Bloor St. East, Toronto, ON M4W 3M5
416-967-3260, Fax: 416-960-0971,
feedback@fineliving.ca
www.fineliving.ca

Toronto: Food Network Canada
121 Bloor St. East, Toronto, ON M4W 3M5
416-967-1174,
foodtv.ca

Toronto: G4techTV
545 Lakeshore Blvd. West, Toronto, ON M5V 1A3
416-260-0047, Fax: 416-260-3810, 866-260-0055
info@g4techtv.ca
www.g4techtv.ca
Andrea Gagliardi, Director, Consumer Marketing & Public Relations
Malcolm Dunlop, Vice-President, Marketing & Programming

Toronto: HGTV Canada
#200, 121 Bloor St. East, Toronto, ON M4W 3M5
416-967-3246, Fax: 416-967-0971,
feedback@hgtv.ca
www.hgtv.ca

Toronto: History Television Inc.
#200, 121 Bloor St. East, Toronto, ON M4W 3M5
416-967-3252, Fax: 416-960-0971,
feedback@historytelevision.ca
www.historytelevision.ca
Phyllis Yaffe, President/CEO
Bill Dawson, Senior Vice-President

Toronto: Home & Garden Television
#200, 121 Bloor St. East, Toronto, ON M4W 3M5
416-967-0022, Fax: 416-960-0971,
feedback@hgtv.ca
hgtv.ca

Toronto: HPItv
PO Box 156, 555 Rexdale Blvd., Toronto, ON M9W 5L2
416-675-3993,
www.horseplayerinteractive.com

Toronto: HPItv Canada
PO Box 156, 555 Rexdale Blcd., Toronto, ON M9W 5L2
416-675-3993, Fax: 416-213-2138,
www.horseplayerinteractive.com

Toronto: HPItv International
PO Box 156, 555 Rexdale Blvd., Toronto, ON M9W 5L2
416-675-3993, Fax: 416-213-2138,
www.horseplayerinteractive.com

Toronto: HPItv Odds
PO Box 156, 555 Rexdale Blvd., Toronto, ON M9W 5L2
416-675-3993,
www.horseplayerinteractive.com

Toronto: HPItv West
PO Box 156, 555 Rexdale Blvd., Toronto, ON M9W 5L2
416-675-3993, Fax: 416-213-2138,
www.horseplayerinteractive.com

Toronto: Ichannel
Stornoway Communications, 115 Gordon Baker Rd., 8th Fl., Toronto, ON M2G 3R6
416-756-2404, Fax: 416-756-5526,
comments@ichannel.ca
www.ichannel.ca

Toronto: Leafs TV
307 Lakeshore Blvd. East, Toronto, ON M5A 1C1
416-815-2400, Fax: 416-681-9181,
www.mapleleafs.com

Toronto: Movieola - The Short Film Channel
2844 Dundas St. West, Toronto, ON M6P 1Y7
416-492-1595, Fax: 416-492-9539,
info@movieola.ca
www.movieola.ca

Toronto: MOVIEPIX
PO Box 787, #100, 181 Bay St., Toronto, ON M5J 2T3
416-956-2010, Fax: 416-956-2018,
www.moviepix.ca
Karen Spierkel, Vice-President, Communications
Lisa de Wilde, President & CEO

Toronto: MTV Canada
888 Yonge St., Toronto, ON M4W 2J2
416-355-3888, Fax: 416-355-3993,
info@mtvcanada.ca
www.mtvcanada.ca

Toronto: MuchLOUD
299 Queen St. West, Toronto, ON M5V 2Z5
416-591-7400, Fax: 416-591-0080,
muchloud@muchmusic.com
www.muchloud.com

Toronto: MuchMore Music
299 Queen St. West, Toronto, ON M5V 2Z5
416-591-5757,
muchmoremail@muchmusic.com
www.muchmoremusic.com

Toronto: MuchMoreRetro
299 Queen St. West, Toronto, ON M5V 2Z5
416-591-5757, Fax: 416-591-0080,
request@muchmoreretro.com
www.muchmoreretro.com

Toronto: MuchMusic Network
299 Queen St. West, Toronto, ON M5V 2Z5
416-591-5757,
muchmail@muchmusic.com
www.muchmusic.com
Denise Donlon, Vice-President/General Manager

Toronto: MuchVibe
299 Queen St. West, Toronto, ON M5V 2Z5
416-591-5757,
muchvibe@muchmusic.com
www.muchvibe.ca

Toronto: National Geographic Channel
#200, 121 Bloor St. East, Toronto, ON M4W 3M5
416-967-3251, 866-967-3251
www.nationalgeographic.ca

Toronto: NHL Network
9 Channel Nine Ct., Toronto, ON M1S 4B5
416-332-5000, Fax: 416-324-675,
audiencerelations@tsn.ca
www.tsn.ca/nhl_network/

Toronto: Odyssey
#300, 437 Danforth Ave., Toronto, ON M4K 1P1
416-462-1200, Fax: 416-462-1818,
info@odysseytv.ca
www.odysseytv.ca
Peter Maniatakos

Toronto: One: the Body, Mind & Spirit Channel
Liberty Market Bldg., #230, 171 East Liberty St., Toronto, ON M6K 3P6
416-595-6465, Fax: 416-368-9774, 877-872-7480
www.onebodymindspirit.com
Bill Roberts, Chair/CEO
Mark Prasuhn, General Manager/COO

Toronto: Ontario Legislature Broadcast & Recording Service
Legislative Bldg., Queen's Park, Toronto, ON M7A 1A2
416-325-7900, Fax: 416-325-7916,
www.ontla.on.ca
Bill Somerville

Toronto: Outdoor Life Network Canada
9 Channel Nine Ct., Toronto, ON M1S 4B5
416-332-7660, Fax: 416-332-5861,
olncanada@ctv.ca
www.tsn.ca/oln

Toronto: OUTtv
#200, 491 Church St., Toronto, ON M4Y 2C6
416-979-2900, Fax: 416-979-1300,
inquiries@pridevision.com
www.outtv.ca

Toronto: The Pet Network
115 Gordon Baker Rd., 8th Fl., Toronto, ON M2H 3R6
416-756-2404, Fax: 416-756-5526,
www.mypetnetwork.tv

Toronto: Pridevision TV
200, 491 Church St., Toronto, ON M4Y 2C6
416-979-2900, Fax: 416-979-1300,
inquiries@pridevisiontv.com
www.pridevisiontv.com

Toronto: Raptors NBA TV
307 Lakeshore Blvd. East, Toronto, ON M5A 1C1
416-815-2400, Fax: 416-681-9181,
www.raptors.com

Toronto: Razer
299 Queen St. West, Toronto, ON M5V 2Z5
www.razer.ca

Toronto: Report on Business Television
720 King St. West, 10th Fl., Toronto, ON M5V 2T3
416-957-8100, Fax: 416-657-8181,
robtv.com

Toronto: responseTV
#2020, 3266 Yonge St., Toronto, ON M4N 3P6
416-737-0457, Fax: 416-488-0796,
info@responsetv.ca
www.responsetv.ca
Beverly Milligan, President/CEO
Peter Greensmith, COO
Christie Christelis, Chief Technology Officer

Toronto: The Score Television Network
PO Box 10, #435, 370 King St. West, Toronto, ON M5V 1J9
416-977-6787, Fax: 416-977-0238,
www.thescore.ca

Toronto: Scream
#18, 64 Jefferson St., Toronto, ON M6K 3H4
416-534-1191,
scream@corusent.com
www.screamtelevision.ca

Toronto: SexTV
299 Queen St. West, Toronto, ON M5V 2Z5
416-591-5757,
sextvchannel@chum.com
www.sextelevision.net

Toronto: SHOPTV Canada
1 Yonge St., 9th Fl., Toronto, ON M5E 1E6
416-869-4700, Fax: 416-869-4566,
info@tmgtv.ca
www.shoptvcanada.com
Don Shafer, Vice-President & General Manager

Toronto: Showcase
#200, 121 Bloor St. East, Toronto, ON M4W 3M5
416-967-3253, Fax: 416-960-0971,
feedback@showcase.ca
www.showcase.ca

Toronto: Showcase Action
#200, 121 Bloor St. East, Toronto, ON M4W 3M5
416-967-3254, Fax: 416-967-0044,
feedback@showcase.ca
www.showcase.ca/action

Toronto: Showcase Diva
121 Bloor St. East, Toronto, ON M4S 3M5
416-967-3255, Fax: 416-967-0044,
feedback@showcase.ca
www.showcase.ca/diva

Toronto: Silver Screen Classics
PO Box 6143 A, Toronto, ON M5W 1P6
416-492-1595, Fax: 416-492-9539,
info@silverscreenclassics.ca
www.silverscreenclassics.com

Toronto: Slice
#200, 121 Bloor St. East, Toronto, ON M4W 3M5
416-967-0022, Fax: 416-960-0971, 886-457-4433
www.slice.ca

Toronto: Space - The Imagination Station
299 Queen St. West, Toronto, ON M5V 2Z5
416-591-5757, Fax: 416-591-6619,
space@spacecast.com
www.spacecast.com

** For details on this company see listing in Major Broadcasting Companies section; † French language station*

Toronto: **Sports Net**
9 Channel Nine Ct., Toronto, ON M1S 4B5
Fax: 416-332-5724,
feedback@sportsnet.rogers.ca
www.sportsnet.ca

Toronto: **The Sports Network**
9 Channel Nine Ct., Toronto, ON M1S 4B5
416-332-5000,
www.tsn.ca

Toronto: **Star! The Entertainment Information Station**
299 Queen St. West, Toronto, ON M5V 2Z5
416-591-5290, Fax: 416-591-3514,
info@star-tv.com
www.star-tv.com
Marcia Martin
James Wood

Toronto: **Talk TV**
9 Channel Nine Ct., Toronto, ON M1S 4B5
416-332-6049, Fax: 416-332-6041,
www.talktv.ca
Ed Robinson, General Manager

Toronto: **TELETOON Canada Inc.**
BCE Place, PO Box 787, 181 Bay St., Toronto, ON M5J 2T3
416-956-2060, Fax: 416-956-2070,
www.teletoon.com
Len Cochrane
Darrell Atherley
Leslie Krueger
Carole Bonneau
Trent Locke

†*Toronto:* **TFO**
CP 200 Q, 2180, rue Yonge, Toronto, ON M4T 2T1
416-484-2636, Fax: 416-484-2705, 800-463-6886
asktvo@tvo.org
www.tfo.org

Toronto: **TMN The Movie Network**
BCE Place, PO Box 787, #100, 181 Bay St., Toronto, ON M5M 3G5
416-956-2010, Fax: 416-956-2018,
www.themovienetwork.ca

Toronto: **Travel + Escape**
Owned by: **CTVglobemedia Inc.**
299 Queen St. West, Toronto, ON M5V 2Z5
416-384-5000, Fax: 416-384-4375,
insidetravel@ctv.ca
www.travelandescape.ca

Toronto: **Treehouse TV**
#18, 64 Jefferson Ave., Toronto, ON M6K 3H3
416-534-1191,
www.treehousetv.com

Toronto: **TVtropolis**
#1700, 250 Yonge St., Toronto, ON M5B 2L7
416-383-2300, Fax: 416-593-9844,
viewerinquiries@TVtropolis.com
www.canada.com/tvtropolis/index.html

Toronto: **Viewer's Choice Canada**
BCE Place, PO Box 787, #100, 181 Bay St., Toronto, ON M5J 2T3
416-565-2010, Fax: 416-565-2018,
www.viewerschoice.ca

Toronto: **Vision TV**
Liberty Market Bldg., #230, 171 East Liberty St., Toronto, ON M6K 8P6
416-368-3194, Fax: 416-368-9774, 888-321-2567
visiontv@visiontv.ca
www.visiontv.ca
Bill Roberts, President & CEO

Toronto: **W Network**
#18, 64 Jefferson Ave., Toronto, ON M6K 3H4
416-543-1191,
comments@wnetwork.com
www.wnetwork.com
John Cassidy, President & CEO

Toronto: **YTV Canada Inc.**
#18, 64 Jefferson Ave., Toronto, ON M6K 3H3
416-534-1191, Fax: 416-534-4398,
info@ytv.ca
www.ytv.com
Paul Robertson, President

Québec

†*Longueuil:* **Canal Evasion**
992, rue Joliette, Longueuil, QC J4K 4V9
450-677-0054, Fax: 450-677-9964,
info@canalevasion.com
www.canalevasion.com
Christine Hill, Directrice générale
Chantal Fortier, Directrice de la programmation
Michel Chamberland, Président et chef de la direction

†*Montréal:* **ARGENT**
1600, boul de Maisonneuve est, Montréal, QC H2L 4P2
514-526-9251, Fax: 514-598-6075,
www.argent.canoe.com; tva.canoe.ca
Yves Daoust, Directeur général

†*Montréal:* **ARTV**
#A 53-1, 1400, boul René-Lévesque est, Montréal, QC H2L 2M2
514-597-3636, Fax: 514-597-3633, 800-363-3307
www.artv.ca
Social Media: www.facebook.com/artv.ca
Marie Côté, Directrice générale

†*Montréal:* **Canal D**
#700, 2100, rue Sainte-Catherine ouest, Montréal, QC H3H 2T3
514-983-3330, Fax: 514-939-3151,
info@chaines.astral.com
www.canald.com
Sylvain Beauregard, Director, Communications
Jean-Pierre Laurendeau, Vice-President, Programming
Judith Brosseau, Sr. Vice-President, Programming & Communications

Montréal: **Canal Indigo**
#900, 2100, rue Sainte-Catherine ouest, Montréal, QC H3H 2T3
514-939-5090, Fax: 514-939-5098,
info@canalindigo.com
www.canalindigo.com
Johanne Saint-Laurent, Vice-président et Directeur général, Astral Télé Reseaux

†*Montréal:* **Le Canal Nouvelles TVA (LCN)**
1600, boul de Maisonneuve est, Montréal, QC H2L 4P2
514-526-9251, Fax: 514-598-6071,
lcn@tva.ca
www.lcn.canoe.com
Martin Cloutier, Dir.-gén., LCN et Argent

†*Montréal:* **Canal Savoir**
Canal Savoir, CP 8888 Centre-ville, Montréal, QC H3C 3P8
514-987-6633, Fax: 514-987-4337, 888-640-2626
info@canal.qc.ca
www.canal.qc.ca
Sylvie Godbout, General Director

†*Montréal:* **Canal Vie**
#700, 2100, rue Ste-Catherine ouest, Montréal, QC H3H 2T3
514-938-3330, Fax: 514-939-3151,
auditoire@canalvie.com
www.canalvie.com
Véronique Lussier, Director, Communications
Lyne Denault, Vice-President, Programming
Marie Collin, Sr. Vice-President, Programming & Communications

†*Montréal:* **Les Chaines Télé Astral**
#1600, 1800, av McGill College, Montréal, QC H3A 3J6
514-939-3150, Fax: 514-939-3151,
www.astral.com
Nathalie Roy, Relationniste, Canal Vie/Historia, nroy@chaines.astral.com
Christine Marceau, Relationniste, Canal D/Séries+, cmarceau@chaines.astral.com
Ian Greenberg, Président/Chef de la direction, Astral Media inc.
André Bureau, Président du Conseil, Astral Media inc.

†*Montréal:* **Historia**
2100, rue Sainte-Catherine ouest, bureau 1000, Montréal, QC H3H 2T3
514-939-5000, Fax: 514-939-1515,
info@chaines.astral.com
www.astralmedia.com
Judith Brosseau, Sr. Vice-President, Programming & Communications
Fabrice Brasier, Vice-President, Programming
Sophie Dufort, Director, Communications

†*Montréal:* **MétéoMédia**
#251, 1755, boul René-Lévesque est, Montréal, QC H2K 4P6
514-597-0232, Fax: 514-597-1591,
www.meteomedia.com

Montréal: **MusiMax**
355, rue Ste-Catherine ouest, Montréal, QC H3B 1A5
514-284-7587, Fax: 514-284-1889,
auditoire@musimax.com
www.musimax.com

†*Montréal:* **MusiquePlus**
355, rue Ste-Catherine ouest, Montréal, QC H3B 1A5
514-284-7587, Fax: 514-284-1889,
www.musiqueplus.com; www.musimax.com; www.astral.com
Ian Greenberg, Président/Chef de la direction, Astral Media inc.

†*Montréal:* **Quebecor Media inc.**
612, rue St-Jacques, Montréal, QC H3C 4M8
514-877-9777, Fax: 514-877-9757,
www.quebecor.com
Pierre Karl Péladeau, Président/Chef de la direction

†*Montréal:* **RDI - Le réseau de l'information**
CP 6000 Centre-Ville, 1400, boul René-Lévesque est, Montréal, QC H3C 3A8
514-597-6000,
rdi@montreal.radio-canada.ca
radio-canada.com/nouvelles
Martin Cloutier, Director
Gilles Desjardins, Director, Business Development

†*Montréal:* **Le Reseau de l'information (RDI)**
CP 6000 Centre-Ville, Montréal, QC H3C 3A8
514-597-6000,
rdi@radio-canada.ca
www.radio-canada.ca/nouvelles

Montréal: **Le Réseau des Sports**
#300, 1755, boul René-Lévesque est, Montréal, QC H2K 4P6
514-599-2244, Fax: 514-599-2299, 888-737-6363
info@rds.ca
www.rds.ca
Gerry Frappier, President & General Manager

†*Montréal:* **Séries+**
#1600, 1800, av McGill College, Montréal, QC H3A 3J6
514-939-3150, Fax: 514-939-3151,
info@chaines.astral.com
www.astral.com
Ian Greenberg, Président/Chef de la direction, Astral Media inc.
André Bureau, Président du Conseil, Astral Media inc.

Montréal: **Super Écran**
#1000, 2100, rue Sainte-Catherine ouest, Montréal, QC H3H 2T3
514-939-5090, Fax: 514-939-5098,
www.superecran.com
Pierre Roy, Président et chef de la direction

†*Montréal:* **TATV**
Bureau 260, 1200, rue Papineau, Montréal, QC H2K 4R5
Fax: 514-526-1354, 866-877-1110
support@tc.astral.com
www.ta.tv

†*Montréal:* **TV5 Québec Canada**
#101, 1755, boul René-Lévesque est, Montréal, QC H2K 4P6
514-522-5322, Fax: 514-522-6572, 877-522-6660
info@tv5.ca
www.tv5.ca
Suzanne Gouin, Présidente/Directrice générale

Montréal: **Vrak.TV**
2100, rue Ste-Catherine ouest, Montréal, QC H3H 2T3
514-939-3150, Fax: 514-539-3151,
www.vrak.tv
Véronique Lussier, Director, Communications
Marie Collin, Sr. Vice-President, Programming & Communications
Denis Dubois, Vice-President, Programming

†*Montréal:* **Ztélé**
a/s Astral Media, #1600, 1800, av McGill College, Montréal, QC H3A 3J6
514-939-3150, Fax: 514-939-3151,
info@chaines.astral.com
www.ztele.com; www.astral.com
Social Media: www.facebook.com/ztele
Ian Greenberg, Président/Chef de la direction, Astral Media inc.
André Bureau, Président du conseil, Astral Media inc.
Sidney Greenberg, Vice-Président, Astral Media inc.

** For details on this company see listing in Major Broadcasting Companies section; † French language station*

†*Québec:* Assemblée nationale du Québec - Canal de l'Assemblée
Édifice Pamphile-Le May, #211, Direction de la diffusion des débats, Québec, QC G1A 1A3
418-643-4272, Fax: 418-646-8498,
diffusion.debats@assnat.qc.ca
www.assnat.qc.ca
Martin-Philippe Côté, Directeur

** For details on this company see listing in Major Broadcasting Companies section; † French language station*

SECTION 5
BUSINESS & FINANCE

The listings in this section are arranged alphabetically unless otherwise indicated below.

Accounting Firms

Firms are organized by Major Accounting Firms, which are listed alphabetically by the name of the accounting firm; the remaining firms are arranged by provinces, subdivided by cities. Where senior accountants are indicated, they may include Chartered Accountants, Certified General Accountants and Certified Management Accountants.

BDO Dunwoody LLP
#600, 36 Toronto St.
Toronto, ON M5C 2C5

416-865-0111
Fax: 416-367-3912
national@bdo.ca
www.bdo.ca

Ownership: Private
Year Founded: 1921
Number of Employees: 1,965
Revenues: $100-500 million
Profile: Canada's sixth-largest accounting firm concentrates on the special needs of independent business & community-based organizations. The firm provides a full range of comprehensive business advisory services.
Directors:
Dianne McMullen, Chair, Policy Board
Walter Flasza, Member, Policy Board
Kenneth Grower, Member, Policy Board
Anne McArel, Member, Policy Board
Kurt Oelschlagel, Member, Policy Board
Executives:
Keith Farlinger, CEO
R.J. Berry, COO
Offices:
Abbotsford
#100, 2890 Garden St.
Abbotsford, BC V2T 4W7 Canada
604-853-6677
Fax: 604-853-4876
abbotsford@bdo.ca
Ben Baartman, Partner

Donald Gillialand, Partner
Alexandria
55 Anik St.
Alexandria, ON K0C 1A0 Canada
613-525-1585
Fax: 613-525-1436
alexandria@bdo.ca
Pierre Vaillancourt, Partner
Alfred
PO Box 539
497 St-Philippe St.
Alfred, ON K0B 1A0 Canada
613-679-1332
Fax: 613-679-1801
alfred@bdo.ca
Alliston
#13, 169 Dufferin St. South
Alliston, ON L9R 1E6 Canada
705-435-5585
Fax: 705-435-5587
alliston@bdo.ca
Doug Holmes, Partner
Altona
26 Centre Ave. East
Altona, MB R0G 0B0 Canada
204-324-8653
Fax: 204-324-1629
altona@bdo.ca
Robert Martins, Partner
Barrie
#300, 300 Lakeshore Dr.
Barrie, ON L4N 0B4 Canada
705-726-6331
Fax: 705-722-6588
barrie@bdo.ca
Joe Hilton, Manager
Boissevain
372 South Railway St.
Boissevain, MB R0K 0E0 Canada
204-534-6935
boissevain@bdo.ca
Tony DeVligere, Partner & Trustee
Bracebridge
#239, 1 Manitoba St.
Bracebridge, ON P1L 1S2 Canada
705-645-5215
Fax: 705-645-8125
bracebridge@bdo.ca
Murray Maw, Managing Partner
Brandon
117 - 10th St.
Brandon, MB R7A 4E7 Canada
204-727-0671
Fax: 204-726-4580
brandon@bdo.ca
Tony DeVliegere, Partner & Trustee
Brantford
#110B, 325 West St.
Brantford, ON N3R 3V6 Canada
519-759-8320
Fax: 519-759-8421
brantford@bdo.ca
Bill H. Kavelman, Partner
Calgary
#1900, 801 - 6 Ave. SW
Calgary, AB T2P 3W2 Canada
403-266-5608
Fax: 403-233-7833
calgary@bdo.ca
Richard Edwards, Partner/Sr. Vice-President
Cambridge
764 King St. East
Cambridge, ON N3H 3N9
519-653-7126
Fax: 519-653-8218
cambridge@bdo.ca
Don Laird, Chartered Accountant
Cardston
259 Main St.
Cardston, AB T0K OKO Canada
403-653-4137
cardson@bdo.ca
Charlottetown
PO Box 2158
91 Water St.
Charlottetown, PE C1A 8B9 Canada
902-892-5365
Fax: 902-892-0383
Chatham
375 St. Clair St.
Chatham, ON N7L 3K3 Canada
519-354-1560
Fax: 519-354-9346
chatham@bdo.ca
Rick Elliott, Partner
Cobourg
PO Box 627
204 Division St.
Cobourg, ON K9A 4L3 Canada
905-372-6863
Fax: 905-372-6650
cobourg@bdo.ca
Michael Machon, Partner
Collingwood
#202, 186 Hurontario St.
Collingwood, ON L9Y 3Z5 Canada
705-445-4421
Fax: 705-445-6691
collingwood@bdo.ca
Pierre Vaillancourt, Partner
Cornwall
PO Box 644
113 Second St. East
Cornwall, ON K6H 5T3 Canada
613-932-8691
Fax: 613-932-7591
cornwall@bdo.ca
Pierre Vaillencourt, Partner
Cranbrook
#200, 35 - 10 Ave. South
Cranbrook, BC V1C 2M9 Canada
250-426-4285
Fax: 250-426-8886
cranbrook@bdo.ca
Harley Lee, Partner; 250-426-4285
Dryden
37 King St.
Dryden, ON P8N 3G3 Canada
807-223-5321
Fax: 807-223-2978
dryden@bdo.ca
Doug Hannah, Partner
Edmonton
First Edmonton Pl.
#1000, 10665 Jasper Ave. NW
Edmonton, AB T5J 3S9 Canada
780-423-4353
Fax: 780-424-2110
edmonton@bdo.ca
Orest Bilous, Partner
Embrun
PO Box 128
991 Limoges Rd.
Embrun, ON K0A 1W0 Canada
613-443-5201
Fax: 613-443-2538
embrun@bdo.ca
Pierre Bourgon, Partner
Essex
180 Talbot St. South
Essex, ON N8M 1B6 Canada
519-776-6488
Fax: 519-776-6090
essex@bdo.ca
Mike McCreight, Partner
Fort Frances
375 Scott St.
Fort Frances, ON P9A 1H1 Canada
807-274-9848
Fax: 807-274-5142
fortfrances@bdo.ca
Marie Allan, Partner
Golden
PO Box 1709
#205, 421 - 9th Ave. North
Golden, BC V0A 1H0 Canada
250-344-5845
Fax: 250-344-7131
golden@bdo.ca
John Wilkey, Partner
Grande Prairie
Grande Prairie Place
9909 - 102 St., 5th Fl.
Grande Prairie, AB T8V 2V4 Canada
780-539-7075
Fax: 780-538-1890
grandeprairie@bdo.ca
Don Blonke, Partner
Guelph
#201, 660 Speedvale Ave. West
Guelph, ON N1K 1E5 Canada
519-824-5410
Fax: 519-824-5497
877-236-4835
Dan Cremasco, Partner
Hamilton
#2, 505 York Blvd.
Hamilton, ON L8R 3K4 Canada
905-525-6800
Fax: 905-525-6566
888-236-2383
hamilton@bdo.ca
Rino H. Bellavia, Partner
Hanover
485 - 10th St.
Hanover, ON N4N 1R2 Canada
519-364-3790
Fax: 519-364-5334
hanover@bdo.ca
John Hunt, Partner
Huntsville
PO Box 5484
2 Elm St.
Huntsville, ON P1H 2K8 Canada
705-789-4469
Fax: 705-789-1079
huntsville@bdo.ca
Bill McDonnell
Kamloops
#300, 272 Victoria St.
Kamloops, BC V2C 1Z6 Canada
250-372-9505
Fax: 250-374-6323
kamloops@bdo.ca
Bill Callandar, Partner
Kelowna
Landmark Technology Centre
#300, 1632 Dickson Ave.
Kelowna, BC V1Y 7T2 Canada
250-763-6700
Fax: 250-763-4457
kelowna@bdo.ca
Kevin Berry, Partner
Kenora
#300, 301 First Ave. South
Kenora, ON P9N 4E9 Canada
807-468-5531
Fax: 807-468-9774
kenora@bdo.ca
Jim Corbett, Partner
Kincardine
970 Queen St.
Kincardine, ON N2Z 2Y2 Canada
519-396-3425
Fax: 519-396-9829
kincardine@bdo.ca
Steven Watson, Partner

Kitchener
#401, 305 King St. West
Kitchener, ON N2G 1B9 Canada
519-576-5220
Fax: 519-576-5471
kitchenerwaterloo@bdo.ca
Dean Elliott, Partner
Langley
#220, 19916 - 64th Ave.
Langley, BC V2Y 1A2 Canada
604-534-8691
Fax: 604-534-8900
langley@bdo.ca
Ken Baker, Partner
Lethbridge
Southland Terrace
#200, 220 - 3rd Ave. South
Lethbridge, AB T1J 0G9 Canada
403-328-5292
Fax: 403-328-9534
lethbridge@bdo.ca
Jim Berezan, Partner
Lindsay
PO Box 358
165 Kent St. West
Lindsay, ON K9V 4S3 Canada
705-324-3579
Fax: 705-324-0774
lindsay@bdo.ca
Paul Allen, Partner
London
Station Park
#201, 252 Pall Mall St.
London, ON N6A 5P6 Canada
519-672-8940
Fax: 519-672-5562
london@bdo.ca
Ed Ramsay, Partner
MacGregor
78 Hampton St.
MacGregor, MB R0H 0R0 Canada
204-685-2323
Fax: 204-685-2341
macgregor@bdo.ca
Bernard Lapchuk, Partner
Manitou
330 Main St.
Manitou, MB R0G 1G0 Canada
204-242-2637
manitou@bdo.ca
Ron Westfall, Partner
Markham
#400, 60 Columbia Way
Markham, ON L3R 0C9 Canada
905-946-1066
Fax: 905-946-9524
markham@bdo.ca
Mohammad Ashraf, Partner
Minnedosa
39 Main St. South
Minnedosa, MB R0J 1E0 Canada
204-867-2957
minnedosa@bdo.ca
Jeanne Mills, Partner
Mississauga
4255 Sherwoodtowne Blvd.
Mississauga, ON L4Z 1Y5 Canada
905-270-7700
Fax: 905-671-7915
mississauga@bdo.ca
Glenn Agro, Partner
Mitchell
PO Box 792
11 Victoria St.
Mitchell, ON N0K 1N0 Canada
519-348-8412
Fax: 519-348-4300
mitchell@bdo.ca
Coralee J. Foster, Partner
Montréal
Westmount Premier
#600, 4150, rue Ste-Catherine ouest
Montréal, QC H3Z 2Y5 Canada
514-931-0841
Fax: 514-931-9491
montreal@bdo.ca
Pierre Lussier, Regional Managing Partner
Morden
133 - 7th St.
Morden, MB R6M 1S3 Canada
204-822-5486
Fax: 204-822-4828
morden@bdo.ca
Sam Andrew, Partner
Mount Forest
PO Box 418
191 Main St. South
Mount Forest, ON N0G 2L0 Canada
519-323-2351
Fax: 519-323-3661
mountforest@bco.ca
Kevin Drier, Partner
Nakusp
PO Box 1078
220 Broadway St.
Nakusp, BC V0G 1R0 Canada
250-265-4750
Fax: 250-837-7170
nakusp@bdo.ca
Ken Davidson, Partner
Newmarket
Gates of York Plaza
#2, 17310 Yonge St.
Newmarket, ON L3Y 7R8 Canada
905-898-1221
Fax: 905-898-0028
866-275-8836
newmarket@bdo.ca
Michael Jones, Partner
North Bay
PO Box 20001
142 Main St. West
North Bay, ON P1B 9N1 Canada
705-495-2000
Fax: 705-495-2001
800-461-6324
northbay@bdo.ca
Jack Campbell, Partner
Oakville
151 Randall St.
Oakville, ON L6J 1P5 Canada
905-844-3206
Fax: 905-844-7513
oakville@bdo.ca
Jim Booth, Partner
Orangeville
77 Broadway Ave., 2nd Fl.
Orangeville, ON L9W 1K1 Canada
519-941-0681
Fax: 519-941-8272
orangeville@bdo.ca
James Blackwell, Partner
Orillia
PO Box 670
19 Front St. North
Orillia, ON L3V 6K5 Canada
705-325-1386
Fax: 705-325-6649
orillia@bdo.ca
Ross Mitchell, Regional Managing Partner
Oshawa
Oshawa Executive Centre
#502, 419 King St. West
Oshawa, ON L1J 2K5 Canada
905-576-3430
Fax: 905-436-9138
oshawa@bdo.ca
Nigel Allen, Partner
Ottawa
#204, 260 Centrum Blvd
Ottawa, ON K1E 3P4 Canada
613-837-3300
Fax: 613-837-7733
800-754-1579
ottawa@bdo.ca
Daniel Suprenant, Partner
Owen Sound
PO Box 397
1717 - 2nd Ave. East
Owen Sound, ON N4K 5P7 Canada
519-376-6110
Fax: 519-376-4741
owensound@bdo.ca
Steve Lowe, Partner
Penticton
#102, 100 Front St.
Penticton, BC V2A 1H1 Canada
250-492-6020
Fax: 250-492-8110
penticton@bdo.ca
Michael Bovin, Partner
Peterborough
PO Box 1018
#202, 201 George St. North
Peterborough, ON K9J 7A5 Canada
705-742-4271
Fax: 705-742-3420
888-369-6600
peterborough@bdo.ca
Bill Gordanier, Partner
Petrolia
PO Box 869
4495 Petrolia Line
Petrolia, ON N0N 1R0 Canada
519-882-3333
Fax: 519-882-2703
petrolia@bdo.ca
Doug Johnston, Partner
Picture Butte
339 Highway Ave.
Picture Butte, AB T0K 1V0 Canada
403-732-4469
Fax: 403-732-5701
picturebutte@bdo.ca
Phillip Wever, Sr. Manager
Port Elgin
PO Box 1390
625 Mill St.
Port Elgin, ON N0H 2C0 Canada
519-832-2049
Fax: 519-832-5659
portelgin@bdo.ca
Mike Bolton, Partner
Portage La Prairie
480 Saskatchewan Ave. West
Portage La Prairie, MB R1N 0M4 Canada
204-857-2856
Fax: 204-239-1664
portagelaprairie@bdo.ca
Red Deer
4719 - 48 Ave., 3rd Fl.
Red Deer, AB T4N 3T1 Canada
403-346-1566
Fax: 403-343-3070
reddeer@bdo.ca
James Scott, Partner
Red Lake
PO Box 234
207 Discovery Centre
Red Lake, ON P0V 2M0 Canada
807-727-3227
Fax: 807-727-1172
redlake@bdo.ca
Revelstoke
PO Box 2100
#202, 103 - 1st St. East
Revelstoke, BC V0E 2S0 Canada
250-837-5225
Fax: 250-837-7170
revelstoke@bdo.ca
Ken Davidson, Partner
Ridgetown
211 Main St. East
Ridgetown, ON N0P 2C0 Canada
519-674-5418
Fax: 519-674-5410
ridgetown@bdo.ca
Rick Elliott, Partner
Rockland
#5, 2784 Laurier St.
Rockland, ON K4K 1A2 Canada
613-446-6497
Fax: 613-446-7117
rockland@bdo.ca
Judith Gratton, Partner
St Pierre Jolys
Place Lavergne
#6, 467, rue Sabourin
St Pierre Jolys, MB R0A 1V0 Canada
204-433-7508
Fax: 204-433-7181
saintpierrejolys@bdo.ca
Mona Marcotte, Partner
Salmon Arm
#201, 571 - 6th St. NE
Salmon Arm, BC V1E 1R6 Canada
250-832-7171
Fax: 250-832-2429
salmonarm@bdo.ca
Doug Adams, Partner
Sarnia
PO Box 730
250 Christina St. North
Sarnia, ON N7T 7V3 Canada
519-336-9900
Fax: 519-332-4828
sarnia@bdo.ca
Don Dafoe, Partner

Sault Ste Marie
PO Box 1109
747 Queen St. East
Sault Ste Marie, ON P6A 5N7 Canada
705-945-0990
Fax: 705-942-7979
ssm@bdo.ca
Thom Ambeault, Partner
Selkirk
378 Main St.
Selkirk, MB R1A 1T8 Canada
204-482-5626
Fax: 204-482-4969
selkirk@bdo.ca
Bill Findlater, Partner
Sicamous
PO Box 392
314 Finlayson St.
Sicamous, BC V0E 2V0 Canada
250-836-4493
Fax: 250-837-7170
sicamous@bdo.ca
Ken Davidson, Partner
Sioux Lookout
61 King St.
Sioux Lookout, ON P8T 1A5 Canada
807-737-1500
Fax: 807-737-4443
siouxlookout@bdo.ca
Slave Lake
PO Box 297
#303, Lakeland Centre
Slave Lake, AB T0G 2A0 Canada
780-849-3622
Fax: 780-849-3625
slavelake@bdo.ca
Ray McComb, Partner
Sorrento
PO Box 59
#2, 1266 Trans Canada Hwy.
Sorrento, BC V0E 2W0 Canada
250-675-3288
Fax: 250-832-2429
sorrento@bdo.ca
Squamish
PO Box 168
38143 - 2nd Ave.
Squamish, BC V0N 3G0 Canada
604-892-9424
Fax: 604-892-9356
squamish@bdo.ca
Theresa Walterhouse, Partner
St-Claude
76 First St.
St-Claude, MB R0G 1Z0 Canada
204-379-2332
800-268-3337
stclaude@bdo.ca
Henri Magne, Partner
Stratford
134 Waterloo St. South
Stratford, ON N5A 6S8 Canada
519-271-2491
Fax: 519-271-4013
stratford@bdo.ca
Montagu J. Smith, Managing Partner
Strathroy
28636 Centre Rd., RR#5
Strathroy, ON N7G 3H6 Canada
519-245-1913
Fax: 519-245-5987
strathroy@bdo.ca
Garry Harris, Partner
Sudbury
#202, 888 Regent St.
Sudbury, ON P3E 6C6 Canada
705-671-3336
Fax: 705-671-9552
877-820-0404
sudbury@bdo.ca
Ted Hargreaves, Partner
Summerland
c/o Bell Jacoe & Co.
13211 North Victoria Rd.
Summerland, BC V0H 1Z0 Canada
250-494-9255
Fax: 250-494-9755
summerland@bdo.ca
David Braumberger, Partner
Surrey
#200, 15225 - 104 Ave.
Surrey, BC V3R 6Y8 Canada
604-584-2121
Fax: 604-584-3823
surrey@bdo.ca
Larry C. Mueller, Partner
Thunder Bay
1095 Barton St.
Thunder Bay, ON P7B 5N3 Canada
807-625-4444
Fax: 807-623-8460
thunderbay@bdo.ca
John Aikin, Partner
Tiverton
84 Main St.
Tiverton, ON N0G 2T0 Canada
519-368-5331
tiverton@bdo.ca
Toronto
Royal Bank Plaza, 33rd Fl.
PO Box 32
Toronto, ON M5J 2J8 Canada
416-865-0200
Fax: 416-865-0887
toronto@bdo.ca
Keith Farlinger, Regional Managing Partner
Treherne
274 Railway Ave.
Treherne, MB R0G 2V0 Canada
204-723-2454
treherne@bdo.ca
Allan Nichol, Partner
Uxbridge
#1, 1 Brock St. East
Uxbridge, ON L9P 1P6 Canada
905-852-9714
Fax: 905-852-9898
uxbridge@bdo.ca
Randy Hickey, Partner
Vancouver
#600, 925 West Georgia St.
Vancouver, BC V6L 3L2 Canada
604-688-5421
Fax: 604-688-5132
vancouver@bdo.ca
Bill Cox, Partner
Vernon
3201 - 30th Ave.
Vernon, BC V1T 2C6 Canada
250-545-2136
Fax: 250-545-3364
vernon@bdo.ca
Brian Cockburn, Partner
Virden
PO Box 1900
255 Wellington St. West
Virden, MB R0M 2C0 Canada
204-748-1200
Fax: 204-748-1976
virden@bdo.ca
Bob Lawrence, Partner
Vulcan
112 - 3 Ave. North
Vulcan, AB T0L 2B0 Canada
403-485-2923
Fax: 403-485-6098
vulcan@bdo.ca
Walkerton
PO Box 760
121 Jackson St.
Walkerton, ON N0G 2V0 Canada
519-881-1211
Fax: 519-881-3530
walkerton@bdo.ca
Gary Munroe, Partner
Welland
37 Dorothy St.
Welland, ON L3B 3V6 Canada
905-735-6433
Fax: 905-735-6514
welland@bdo.ca
Dale Hajdu, Partner
Whistler
#104, 1080 Millar Creek Rd.
Whistler, BC V0N 1B1 Canada
604-932-3799
Fax: 604-932-3764
whistler@bdo.ca
Theresa Walterhouse, Partner
Whitehorse
#201, 3059 - 3rd Ave.
Whitehorse, YT Y1A 1E2 Canada
867-667-7907
Fax: 867-668-3087
whitehorse@bdo.ca
Ben Baartman, Partner
Wiarton
PO Box 249
663 Berford St.
Wiarton, ON N0H 2T0 Canada
519-534-1520
Fax: 519-534-3454
wiarton@bdo.ca
Forbes Simon, Partner
Windsor
3630 Rhodes Dr.
Windsor, ON N8W 5A4 Canada
519-944-6900
Fax: 519-944-6116
windsor@bdo.ca
Ted Herbert, Partner
Wingham
PO Box 1420
152 Josephine St.
Wingham, ON N0G 2W0 Canada
519-357-3231
Fax: 519-357-3230
wingham@bdo.ca
Allan Reed, Partner
Winkler
#2, 583 Main St.
Winkler, MB R6W 1A4 Canada
204-325-4787
Fax: 204-325-8040
winkler@bdo.ca
Frank Wiebe, Partner
Winnipeg
Wawanesa Bldg.
#700, 200 Graham Ave.
Winnipeg, MB R3C 4L5 Canada
204-956-7200
Fax: 204-926-7201
winnipeg@bdo.ca
David Anderson, Partner
Woodstock
PO Box 757
94 Graham St.
Woodstock, ON N4S 8A2 Canada
519-539-2081
Fax: 519-539-2571
woodstock@bdo.ca
Dwayne De Vries, Partner

Deloitte & Touche LLP

PO Box 8
#1200, 2 Queen St. East
Toronto, ON M5C 3G7

416-874-3874
Fax: 416-874-3888
www.deloitte.ca

Ownership: Private partnership; Deloitte in Canada is a member firm of Deloitte Touche Tohmatsu.
Year Founded: 1861
Number of Employees: 5,568
Revenues: $500m-1 billion
Profile: Deloitte & Touche LLP is one of Canada's leading firms, providing a range of auditing, tax, financial advisory, & consulting services. Deloitte's offices in Québec operate under the corporate name Samson Bélair/Deloitte & Touche.
Partners:
John Bowey, Chair
Alan MacGibbon, Managing Partner & CEO
Branches:
Alma
Complexe Jacques Gagnon
#110, 100, rue St-Joseph sud
Alma, QC G8B 7A6 Canada
418-669-6969
Fax: 418-668-2966
Amos
#200, 101, av 1re est
Amos, QC J9T 1H4 Canada
819-732-8273
Fax: 819-732-9143
Baie-Comeau
1191, boul Laflèche, 2e étage
Baie-Comeau, QC G5C 1E1 Canada
418-589-5761
Fax: 418-589-5764

Burlington
#202, 1005 Skyview Dr.
Burlington, ON L7P 5B1 Canada
905-315-6770
Fax: 905-315-6700
866-836-6770
Calgary

Scotia Centre
#3000, 700 - 2nd St. SW
Calgary, AB T2P 0S7 Canada
403-267-1700
Fax: 403-264-2871
Chicoutimi
#400, 901, boul Talbot
Chicoutimi, QC G7H 0A1 Canada
418-549-6650
Fax: 418-549-4694
Dolbeau-Mistassini
110, 8e av
Dolbeau-Mistassini, QC G8L 1Y9 Canada
418-276-0133
Fax: 418-276-8559
Edmonton
Manulife Place
#2000, 10180 - 101st St.
Edmonton, AB T5J 4E4 Canada
780-421-3611
Fax: 780-421-3782
Farnham
149, rue Desjardins est
Farnham, QC J2N 2W6 Canada
450-293-5327
Fax: 450-293-2817
Granby
PO Box 356
74, rue Court
Granby, QC J2G 4Y5 Canada
450-372-3347
Fax: 450-372-8643
Grand-Mère
PO Box 280
1671, 6e av
Grand-Mère, QC G9T 5K8 Canada
819-538-1721
Fax: 819-538-1882
Halifax
Purdy's Wharf Tower II
#1500, 1569 Upper Water St.
Halifax, NS B3J 3R7 Canada
902-422-8541
Fax: 902-423-5820
Hawkesbury
300, rue McGill
Hawkesbury, ON K6A 1P8 Canada
613-632-4178
Fax: 613-632-7703
Jonquière
Complexe A E Fortin
2266, boul René Lévesque
Jonquière, QC G7S 6C5 Canada
418-542-9523
Fax: 418-542-8814
Kitchener
4210 King St. East
Kitchener, ON N2P 2G5 Canada
519-650-7600
Fax: 519-650-7601
La Baie
365, rue Victoria
La Baie, QC G7B 3M5 Canada
418-544-7313
Fax: 418-544-0275
La Sarre
226, 2e rue est
La Sarre, QC J9Z 2G9 Canada
819-339-5764
Fax: 819-333-2517
Langley
#225, 20316 - 56th Ave.
Langley, BC V3A 3Y7 Canada
604-534-7477
Fax: 604-534-4220
Laval
Les Tours Triomphe
#300, 2450, boul Daniel-Johnson
Laval, QC H7T 2S3 Canada
514-978-3500
Fax: 514-382-4984
London
One London Place
255 Queen's Ave., 7th Fl.
London, ON N6A 5R8 Canada
519-679-1880
Fax: 519-640-4625
Longueuil
Tour Est
#550, 1111, rue St-Charles ouest
Longueuil, QC J4K 5G4 Canada
450-670-4270
Fax: 450-670-6420
Magog
#203, 101, rue du Moulin
Magog, QC J1X 4A1 Canada
819-843-6596
Fax: 819-843-6931
Markham
#400, 15 Allstate Pkwy.
Markham, ON L3R 5B4 Canada
905-948-6200
Fax: 905-948-6250

Matane
750, rue de Phare ouest
Matane, QC G42 3N2 Canada
418-566-2637
Fax: 418-566-2830
Mississauga - Britannia Rd. East
#132, 425 Britannia Rd. East
Mississauga, ON L4Z 3E7 Canada
416-601-6150
Fax: 416-601-6151
Mississauga - City Centre Dr.
#1100, 1 City Centre Dr.
Mississauga, ON L5B 1M2 Canada
905-601-6150
Fax: 905-803-5101
Montréal
#3000, 1, Place Ville-Marie
Montréal, QC H3B 4T9 Canada
514-393-7115
Fax: 514-390-4100
Ottawa
#800, 100 Queen St.
Ottawa, ON K1P 5T8 Canada
613-236-2442
Fax: 613-236-2195
Prince Albert
#5, 77 - 15 St. East
Prince Albert, SK S6V 1E9 Canada
306-763-7411
Fax: 306-763-0191
Prince George
#500, 299 Victoria St.
Prince George, BC V2L 5B8 Canada
250-564-1111
Fax: 250-562-4950
Québec
#400, 925, ch Saint-Louis
Québec, QC G1S 4Z4 Canada
418-624-3333
Fax: 418-624-0414
Regina
Bank of Montreal Bldg.
#900, 2103 - 11th Ave.
Regina, SK S4P 3Z8 Canada
306-525-1600
Fax: 306-525-2244
Rimouski
287, rue Pierre-Saindon
Rimouski, QC G5L 8V5 Canada
418-724-4136
Fax: 418-724-3807
Roberval
713, boul St-Joseph
Roberval, QC G8H 2L3 Canada
418-275-2111
Fax: 418-275-6398
Rouyn-Noranda
155, av Dallaire
Rouyn-Noranda, QC J9X 4T3 Canada
819-762-5764
Fax: 819-797-1471
Saint John
Brunswick House
PO Box 6549
44 Chipman Hill, 7th Fl.
Saint John, NB E2L 4R9 Canada
506-632-1080
Fax: 506-632-1210
St Catharines
25 Corporate Park Dr., 3rd Fl.
St Catharines, ON L2S 3W2 Canada
905-323-6000
Fax: 905-323-6001
Saint-Hyacinthe
2200, av Léon-Pratte
Saint-Hyacinthe, QC J2S 4B6 Canada
450-774-4000
Fax: 450-774-1709
St. John's
Fort William Bldg.
10 Factory Lane
St. John's, NL A1C 6H5 Canada
709-576-8480
Fax: 709-576-8460
Saskatoon
PCS Tower
#300, 122 - 1st Ave.
Saskatoon, SK S7K 7E5 Canada
306-343-4400
Fax: 306-343-4480
Sept-Iles
#200, 421, av Arnaud
Sept-Iles, QC G4R 3B3 Canada
418-962-2513
Fax: 418-968-6422
Sherbrooke
#300, 2727, rue King ouest
Sherbrooke, QC J1L 1C2 Canada
819-823-1616
Fax: 819-564-8078
St-Félicien
1133, rue Notre-Dame
St-Félicien, QC G8K 1Z7 Canada
418-679-4711
Fax: 418-679-8723

Toronto - Bay St.
BCE Place, Bay Wellington Tower
#1400, 181 Bay St.
Toronto, ON M5J 2V1 Canada
416-601-6150
Fax: 416-601-6151
Toronto - King St.
#300, 121 King St.
Toronto, ON M5H 3T9 Canada
416-601-6150
Fax: 416-601-5901
Toronto - Wellington St. West
30 Wellington St. West
Toronto, ON M5L 1B1 Canada
416-601-6150
Fax: 416-601-5901
Toronto - Yonge St.
North York City Centre
#1700, 5140 Yonge St.
Toronto, ON M2N 6L7 Canada
416-601-6150
Fax: 416-229-2524
Trois-Pistoles
546a Jean Rioux
Trois-Pistoles, QC G0L 4K0 Canada
418-851-2232
Fax: 418-851-4244
Trois-Rivières
PO Box 1600
1500, rue Royale
Trois-Rivières, QC G9A 5L9 Canada
819-691-1212
Fax: 819-691-1127
Val-d'Or
#240, 450 - 3e av
Val-d'Or, QC J9P 1S2 Canada
819-825-4101
Fax: 819-825-1155
Vancouver
4 Bentall Centre
#2800, 1055 Dunsmuir St.
Vancouver, BC V7X 1P4 Canada
604-669-4466
Fax: 604-685-0395
Windsor
#200, 150 Ouellette Place
Windsor, ON N8Y 1L9 Canada
519-967-0388
Fax: 519-967-0324
Winnipeg
#2300, 360 Main St.
Winnipeg, MB R3C 3Z3 Canada
204-942-0051
Fax: 204-947-9390

Ernst & Young LLP

Ernst & Young Tower, Toronto-Dominion Centre
PO Box 251
222 Bay St.
Toronto, ON M5K 1J7

416-864-1234
Fax: 416-864-1174
www.ey.com

Ownership: Private
Year Founded: 1864
Number of Employees: 2,907
Profile: The following services are offered: assurance & advisory business services; corporate finance; tax; & other

services. It is affiliated with Ernst & Young Orenda Corporate Finance/EGAN LLP.
Executives:
Louis P. Pagnutti, Chair/CEO
Irene David, Contact
Guy Fréchette, Contact
Murray McDonald, Contact
Fiona Macfarlane, Contact
Paul Roberts, Contact
Affiliated Companies:
Ernst & Young Orenda Corporate Finance
Offices:
Calgary
Ernst & Young Tower
1000, 440 2nd Ave. SW
Calgary, AB T2P 5E9 Canada
403-290-4100
Fax: 403-290-4265
Dieppe
11 Englehart St.
Dieppe, NB E1A 7Y7 Canada
506-853-3097
Fax: 506-859-7190

Note: The Dieppe office of the firm LeBlanc Nadeau Bujold merged with Ernst & Young in Sept., 2009.
Edmonton - Scotia Place
Scotia Place, 1801 Scotia 2
10060 Jasper Ave.
Edmonton, AB T5J 3R9 Canada
780-423-5811
Fax: 780-428-8977

Edmonton - Stony Plain Rd.
300, 12220 Stony Plain Rd.
Edmonton, AB T5N 3Y4 Canada
780-482-2349
Fax: 780-452-9060
Halifax
1959 Upper Water St., 13th Fl
Halifax, NS B3J 2Z1 Canada
902-420-1080
Fax: 902-420-0503
Kitchener
515 Riverbend Dr.
Kitchener, ON N2K 3S3 Canada
519-744-1171
Fax: 519-744-9604
London
One London Place, #1800
255 Queens Ave.
London, ON N6A 5S7 Canada
519-672-6100
Fax: 519-438-5785
Montréal
#1900, 800, boul René-Lévesque O
Montréal, QC H3B 1X9 Canada
514-875-6060
Fax: 514-879-2600
Ottawa
#1600, 100 Queen St.
Ottawa, ON K1P 1K1 Canada
613-232-1511
Fax: 613-232-5324
Québec
#1200, 150, boul René-Lévesque
Québec, QC G1R 6C6 Canada
418-524-5151
Fax: 418-524-0061
Saint John
#1209, 1 Germain St.
Saint John, NB E2L 4V1 Canada
506-634-7000
Fax: 506-634-2129
St. John's
The Fortis Building
139 Water St., 7th Fl
St. John's, NL A1C 1B2 Canada
709-726-2840
Fax: 709-726-0345
Thornhill
#600, 175 Commerce Valley Dr. West
Thornhill, ON L3T 7P6 Canada
905-731-1500
Fax: 905-882-3050
Vancouver
Pacific Centre
700 West Georgia St.
Vancouver, BC V7Y 1C7 Canada
604-891-8200
Fax: 604-643-5422
Winnipeg
Commodity Exchange Tower, #2700
360 Main St.
Winnipeg, MB R3C 4G9 Canada
204-947-6519
Fax: 204-956-0138

Evancic Perrault Robertson

PO Box 21148, Maple Ridge Square Stn. Maple Ridge Square
Maple Ridge, BC V2X 17P
604-476-2009
Fax: 604-467-1219
eprnat@epr.ca
www.epr.ca

Ownership: Private
Year Founded: 1979
Profile: Evancic Perrault Robertson is a firm of Certified General Accountants, with member offices across the country. EPR has an international reach, through its affiliations with NACPAF (a US-based national association of CPA firms) & with Morison International (a UK-based global accountancy & law office network). The firm offers an integrated approach to auditing, accounting, taxation, & management consulting.
Executives:
Paul Walker, Chair
Camille Belliveau, Exec. Director
Verle Spindor, National Administrator
Branches:
Abbotsford
#201, 2669 Langdon St.
Abbotsford, BC V2T 3L3 Canada
604-853-1538
Fax: 604-853-7178
eprabby@mindlink.net
Bathurst
1935, av St. Peter
Bathurst, NB E2A 7J5 Canada
506-548-1984
Fax: 506-548-0904
eprbath@eprbathurst.ca
Bradford
PO Box 753
27 John St. West
Bradford, ON L3Z 2B3 Canada
905-778-8964
Fax: 905-775-9550
800-246-5591
bbcm@bellnet.ca
Michael Falcone
Calgary
#110, 7330 Fisher St. SE
Calgary, AB T2H 2H8 Canada
403-278-5800
Fax: 403-253-9479
general@eprcal.com
Chatham
40 Centre Sq.
Centre St.
Chatham, ON N7M 5W3 Canada
519-436-0556
Fax: 519-436-1291
rieger@ciaccess.com
Lance Rieger, Partner
Coquitlam
566 Lougheed Hwy., 2nd Fl.
Coquitlam, BC V3K 3S3 Canada
604-936-4377
Fax: 604-936-8376
eprcoq@eprcoq.com
www.eprcoq.com
Fort Erie
PO Box 277
#8, 450 Garrison Road
Fort Erie, ON L2A 1N2 Canada
905-871-6620
Fax: 905-871-2544
eprfeo@eprnia.ca
Fredericton
#205, 206 Rookwood Ave.
Fredericton, NB E3B 2M2 Canada
506-458-8620
Fax: 506-450-8286
eprfred@nbnet.nb.ca
Grande Prairie
#215, 10006 - 101st Ave.
Grande Prairie, AB T8V 0Y1 Canada
780-539-3400
Fax: 780-538-1544
epgrand@telusplanet.net
Hamilton
176 Rymal Rd. East
Hamilton, ON L9B 1C2 Canada
905-388-7453
Fax: 905-388-7397
eprhamilton@iprimus.ca
Langley
20688 - 56 Ave.
Langley, BC V3A 3Z1 Canada
604-534-1441
Fax: 604-534-1491
pwalker@eprcga.com
www.eprcga.com
Paul Walker, Partner
London
#804, 150 Dufferin Ave.
London, ON N6A 5N6 Canada
519-434-5847
Fax: 519-645-0727
Maple Ridge
22377 Dewdney Trunk Rd.
Maple Ridge, BC V2X 3J4 Canada
604-467-5561
Fax: 604-467-1219
eprmr@eprcga.com
www.eprcga.com
Miramichi
Waterfront Place
1773 Water St.
Miramichi, NB E1N 1B2 Canada
506-773-6990
Fax: 506-773-3197
eprmira@nbnet.nb.ca
Moncton
84 Brandon St.
Moncton, NB E1C 7E9 Canada
506-857-3893
Fax: 506-859-4148
Niagara Falls
#7, 3930 Montrose Rd.
Niagara Falls, ON L2H 3C9 Canada
905-358-5729
Fax: 905-358-7188
eprnfo@eprnia.ca
North Vancouver
#102, 1975 Lonsdale Ave.
North Vancouver, BC V7M 2K3 Canada
604-987-8101
Fax: 604-987-1794
cga@eprnv.ca
Saint-Hyacinthe
#200, 450 ave St-Joseph
Saint-Hyacinthe, QC J2S 8K5 Canada
450-774-7165
Fax: 450-774-1589
eprsthyacinthe@cgaquebec.com
Rene Benoit, Partner; rene.benoit@eprquebec.com
St. John's
74 O'Leary Ave.
St. John's, NL A1B 2C7 Canada
709-726-0000
Fax: 709-726-2200
eprstjohns@hotmail.com
Saskatoon
259 Robin Cres.
Saskatoon, SK S7L 6M8 Canada
306-934-3944
Fax: 306-934-3409
eprstoon@sasktel.net
Slave Lake
405 - 6th Ave. SW
Slave Lake, AB T0G 2A4 Canada
780-849-4949
Fax: 780-849-3401
eprslave@telusplanet.net
St-Jérôme
34, rue de Martigny ouest
Saint-Jérome, QC J7Y 2E9 Canada
450-569-2641
Fax: 450-569-2647
François Marchand, Partner; francois.marchand@eprquebec.com
Stonewall
Westside Plaza Mall
PO Box 1038
333 Main St.
Stonewall, MB R0C 2Z0 Canada
204-467-5566
Fax: 204-467-9133
eprstonewall@shawcable.com
Ryan Smith, Partner; rsmith.sprstonewall@shawcable.com
Terrebonne
3300, boul des Entreprises
Terrebonne, QC J6X 4J8 Canada
450-477-0377
Fax: 450-477-4023

Tilbury
40 Queen Sq.
Tilbury, ON N0P 2L0 Canada
519-682-2300
Fax: 519-682-0705
reiger@ciaccess.com
White Rock
#104, 1656 Martin Dr.
White Rock, BC V4A 5E7 Canada
604-536-7778
Fax: 604-536-7745
Glenn Parks, Partner; gparks@eprcga.com
Winnipeg
#1010, 1661 Portage Ave.
Winnipeg, MB R3J 3T7 Canada
204-954-9690
Fax: 204-786-1003
bemond@mts.net

Grant Thornton LLP
50 Bay St., 12th Fl.
Toronto, ON M5J 2Z8

416-366-4420
Fax: 416-360-4944
800-366-0100
national@grantthornton.ca
www.grantthornton.ca

Ownership: Private
Year Founded: 1939
Number of Employees: 1,172
Revenues: $100-500 million
Executives:
Phil Noble, CEO & Exec. Partner
John Garritsen, Partner, Administration; jgarritsen@grantthornton.ca
John Holdstock, Partner, Client & Services; jholdstock@grantthornton.ca
Dave Peneycad, Chief Operating Officer
Bill Brushett, Partner, Client Services
Sharon Healy, Director, Human Resources; shealy@grantthornton.ca
Anita Ferrari, Regional Managing Partner; aferrari@grantthornton.ca
Kevin Ladner, Regional Managing Partner; kladner@grantthornton.ca
Rick Mudie, Regional Managing Partner; rmudie@grantthornton.ca
Branches:
Antigonish
PO Box 1480
257 Main St.
Antigonish, NS B2G 2L7 Canada
902-863-4587
Fax: 902-863-0917
B.M. Cullen, Partner
Barrie
#201, 85 Bayfield St.
Barrie, ON L4M 3A7 Canada
705-730-6574
Fax: 705-730-6575
R.D. Woodman, Partner
Bathurst
Harbourview Pl.
PO Box 220
#500, 275 Main St.
Bathurst, NB E2A 3Z2 Canada
506-546-6616
Fax: 506-548-5622
Bridgewater
PO Box 220
197 Dufferin St.
Bridgewater, NS B4V 2W8 Canada
902-543-8115
Fax: 902-543-7707
R.W. Oakley, Partner
Calgary
#1000, 112 - 4th Ave. SW
Calgary, AB T3P 0H3 Canada
403-260-2500
Fax: 403-260-2571
G.G. McFarlane, Partner
Charlottetown
PO Box 187
#501, 199 Grafton St.
Charlottetown, PE C1A 7K4 Canada
902-892-6547
Fax: 902-566-5358
J.K. Ladner, Partner
Corner Brook
PO Box 356
#49, 51 Park St.
Corner Brook, NL A2H 6E3 Canada
709-634-4382
Fax: 709-634-9158
R.G. Flynn, Partner
Digby
Basin Place
PO Box 848
68 Water St.
Digby, NS B0V 1A0 Canada
902-245-2553
Fax: 902-245-6161
Digby@GrantThornton.ca
M. Rutherford, Partner
Edmonton
Scotia Place 2
#1401, 10060 Jasper Ave. NW
Edmonton, AB T5J 3R8 Canada
780-422-7114
Fax: 780-426-3208
G.G. McFarlane, Partner; 403-260-2500
Fredericton
PO Box 1054
#400, 570 Queen St.
Fredericton, NB E3B 5C2 Canada
506-458-8200
Fax: 506-453-7029
Bruce Lewis, Partner
Grand Falls - Windsor
PO Box 83
9 High St.
Grand Falls-Windsor, NL A2A 2J3 Canada
709-489-6622
Fax: 709-489-6625
K. Simms, Principal
Halifax
Cogswell Tower
#1100, 2000 Barrington St.
Halifax, NS B3J 3K1 Canada
902-421-1734
Fax: 902-420-1068
Michele Williams, Partner
Hamilton
Standard Life Centre
#1040, 120 King St. West
Hamilton, ON L8P 4V2 Canada
905-525-1930
Fax: 905-527-4413
D.A. MacLean, Partner
Kelowna
#200, 1633 Ellis St.
Kelowna, BC V1Y 2A8 Canada
250-712-6800
Fax: 250-661-3416
J.P. Mills, Partner
Kentville
PO Box 68
15 Webster St.
Kentville, NS B4N 3V9 Canada
902-678-7307
Fax: 902-679-1870
G.B. Caldwell, Partner
Langley
#320, 8700 - 200th St.
Langley, BC V2Y 0G4 Canada
604-532-3761
Fax: 604-532-8130
T.G. Davies, Partner
London
#406, 140 Fullarton St.
London, ON N6A 5P2 Canada
519-672-2930
Fax: 519-672-6455
P.R. Coleman, Partner
Markham
#200, 15 Allstate Pkwy.
Markham, ON L3R 5B4 Canada
905-475-1100
Fax: 905-475-8906
A.R. Byrne, Partner
Marystown
PO Box 518
2 Queen St.
Marystown, NL A0E 2M0 Canada
709-279-2300
Fax: 709-279-2340
Marystown@GrantThornton.ca
Miramichi
135 Henry St.
Miramichi, NB E1V 2N5 Canada
506-622-0637
Fax: 506-622-5174
H.K. Raper, Partner
Mississauga
#401, 350 Burnhamthorpe Rd. West
Mississauga, ON L5R 3J1 Canada
905-804-0905
Fax: 905-804-0509
G.R. Popp, Partner
Moncton
PO Box 1005
#500, 633 Main St.
Moncton, NB E1C 8P2 Canada
506-857-0100
Fax: 506-857-0105
Jean Marc Delaney, Partner
Montague
PO Box 70
1 Bailey Dr.
Montague, PE C0A 1R0 Canada
902-838-4121
Fax: 902-838-4802
C. Chapman, Partner
New Glasgow
PO Box 427
610 East River Rd.
New Glasgow, NS B2H 5E5 Canada
902-752-8393
Fax: 902-752-4009
B.L. Wilson, Partner
New Liskeard
PO Box 2170
17 Wellington St.
New Liskeard, ON P0J 1P0 Canada
705-647-8100
Fax: 705-647-7026
R.R. Hacquard, Partner
New Westminster
628 - 6th Ave., 6th Fl.
New Westminster, BC V3M 6Z1 Canada
604-521-3761
Fax: 604-521-8170
R.W. Mudie, Partner
North Bay
#200, 222 McIntyre St. West
North Bay, ON P1B 2Y8 Canada
705-472-6500
Fax: 705-472-7760
G.G. Weckwerth, Partner
Orillia
#300, 6 West St. North
Orillia, ON L3V 5B8 Canada
705-326-7605
Fax: 705-326-0837
R.D. Woodman, Partner
Port Colborne
PO Box 336
222 Catharine St, #B
Port Colborne, ON L3K 5W1 Canada
905-834-3651
Fax: 905-834-5095
J. Brennan, Principal
Saint John
Brunswick House
44 Chipman Hill, 4th Fl.
Saint John, NB E2L 2A9 Canada
506-634-2900
Fax: 506-634-4569
G. Dewar, Partner
St. John's
PO Box 8037
187 Kenmount Rd.
St. John's, NL A1B 3P9 Canada
709-722-5960
Fax: 709-722-7892
Jeff Pardy, Partner
Sault Ste Marie
421 Bay St., 5th Fl.
Sault Ste Marie, ON P6A 1X3 Canada
705-945-9700
Fax: 705-945-9705
B.C. Magill, Partner
Summerside
Royal Bank Bldg.
PO Box 1660
220 Water St.
Summerside, PE C1N 2V5 Canada
902-436-9155
Fax: 902-436-6913
L.B. Murray, Partner
Sydney
George Place
#200, 500 George St.
Sydney, NS B1P 1K6 Canada
902-562-5581
Fax: 902-562-0073
J. MacNeil, Partner

Thunder Bay
#300, 979 Alloy Dr.
Thunder Bay, ON P7B 5Z8 Canada
807-345-6571
Fax: 807-345-0032
D. Vanderwey, Partner
Truro
PO Box 725
#400, 35 Commercial St.
Truro, NS B2N 5E8 Canada
902-893-1150
Fax: 902-893-9757
G.D. Hutchings, Partner
Vancouver
#1600, 333 Seymour St.
Vancouver, BC V6B 0A4 Canada
604-687-2711
Fax: 604-685-6569
Vancouver@GrantThornton.ca
P.B. Noble, Partner
Victoria
888 Fort St., 3rd Fl.
Victoria, BC V8W 1H8 Canada
250-383-4191
Fax: 250-381-4623
S. Mehinagic, Partner
Wetaskiwin
5108 - 51st Ave.
Wetaskiwin, AB T9A 0V2 Canada
780-352-1679
Fax: 780-352-2451
T.R. Bolivar, Partner
Winnipeg
94 Commerce Drive
Winnipeg, MB R3P 0Z3 Canada
204-944-0100
Fax: 204-957-5442
D.H. Anthony, Partner
Yarmouth
PO Box 297
328 Main St.
Yarmouth, NS B5A 4B2 Canada
902-742-7842
Fax: 902-742-0224
M. Rutherford, Partner

KPMG

Commerce Court West
PO Box 31, Commerce Court Stn. Commerce Court
199 Bay St.
Toronto, ON M5L 1B2

416-777-8500
Fax: 416-777-8818
webmaster@kpmg.ca
www.kpmg.ca

Ownership: Private
Year Founded: 1860
Number of Employees: 4,500
Assets: $500m-1 billion
Revenues: $500m-1 billion
Executives:
Bill Thomas, Chief Executive Officer
John Herhalt, Managing Partner, Advisory Services
Greg Wiebe, Managing Partner, Tax
Peter Doyle, Managing Partner, Audit
Jean-Pierre Desrosiers, Managing Partner, Markets
Mary Lou Hamher, CFO
Mario Paron, Chief HR Officer
Vancouver - Burnaby
#2400, 4720 Kingsway
Burnaby, BC V5H 4N2
Branches:
Abbotsford
32575 Simon Ave.
Abbotsford, BC V2T 4W6 Canada
604-854-2200
Fax: 604-853-2756
Calgary
Bow Valley Square II
#2700, 205 - 5th Ave. SW
Calgary, AB T2P 4B9 Canada
403-691-8000
Fax: 403-691-8008
Jason Brown, Partner, Audit

Curtis Lester, Partner, Tax
Chilliwack
#200, 9123 Mary St.
Chilliwack, BC V2P 4H7 Canada
604-793-4700
Fax: 604-793-4747
Edmonton
Commerce Pl.
10125 - 102 St.
Edmonton, AB T5J 3V8 Canada
780-429-7300
Fax: 780-429-7379
Robert Borrelli, Partner, Audit
Fredericton
Frederick Sq., TD Tower
#700, 77 Westmorland St.
Fredericton, NB E3B 6Z3 Canada
506-452-8000
Fax: 506-450-0072
Todd MacIntosh, Partner, Tax
Halifax
Purdy's Wharf, Tower One
#1500, 1959 Upper Water St.
Halifax, NS B3J 3N2 Canada
902-429-6000
Fax: 902-423-1307
Gregory Simpson, Partner, Tax
Hamilton
Commerce Place
#700, 21 King St. West
Hamilton, ON L8P 4W7 Canada
905-523-8200
Fax: 905-523-2222
Kamloops
#200, 206 Seymour St.
Kamloops, BC V2C 6P5 Canada
250-372-5581
Fax: 250-828-2928
Kelowna
#300, 1674 Bertram St.
Kelowna, BC V1Y 9G4 Canada
250-763-5522
Fax: 250-763-0044
Kingston
#400, 863 Princess St.
Kingston, ON K7L 5N4 Canada
613-549-1550
Fax: 613-549-6349
Lethbridge
Lethbridge Centre Tower
#500, 400 - 4th Ave. South
Lethbridge, AB T1J 4E1 Canada
403-380-5700
Fax: 403-380-5760
London
#1400, 140 Fullarton St.
London, ON N6A 5P2 Canada
519-672-4880
Fax: 519-672-5684
Moncton
Place Marvin's
One Factory Lane
Moncton, NB E1C 9M3 Canada
506-856-4400
Fax: 506-856-4499
Montréal
#1500, 600 boul de Maisonneuve Ouest
Montréal, QC H3A 0A3 Canada
514-840-2100
Fax: 514-840-2187
Philippe Grubert, Partner, Audit

Brian Mustard, Partner, Tax
North Bay
PO Box 990
#300, 925 Stockdale Rd.
North Bay, ON P1B 8K3 Canada
705-472-5110
Fax: 705-472-1249

Ottawa
World Exchange Plaza
#2000, 160 Elgin Street
Ottawa, ON K2P 2P8 Canada
613-212-5764
Fax: 613-212-2896
Andrew Newman, Partner, Audit
Prince George
#400, 177 Victoria St.
Prince George, BC V2L 5R8 Canada
250-563-7151
Fax: 250-563-5693
Regina
McCallum Hill Centre, Tower II
1881 Scarth St., 20th Fl.
Regina, SK S4P 4K9 Canada
306-791-1200
Fax: 306-757-4703
Saint John
Harbour Bldg.
PO Box 2388
#306, 133 Prince William St.
Saint John, NB E2L 3V6 Canada
506-634-1000
Fax: 506-633-8828
St Catharines
#901, One Saint-Paul St.
St Catharines, ON L2R 7L2 Canada
905-685-4811
Fax: 905-682-2008
Saskatoon
#600, 128 - 4th Ave. South
Saskatoon, SK S7K 1M8 Canada
306-934-6200
Fax: 306-934-6233
Sault Ste Marie
#200, 111 Elgin St.
Sault Ste Marie, ON P6A 6L6 Canada
705-949-5811
Fax: 705-949-0911
Sudbury
Claridge Executive Centre
144 Pine St.
Sudbury, ON P3C 1X3 Canada
705-675-8500
Fax: 705-675-7586
Laurie Bissonette, Partner, Audit
Toronto
Yonge Corporate Centre
#200, 4100 Yonge St.
Toronto, ON M2P 2H3 Canada
416-228-7000
Fax: 416-228-7123
Vancouver
Pacific Centre
PO Box 10426
777 Dunsmuir St.
Vancouver, BC V7Y 1K3 Canada
604-691-3000
Fax: 604-691-3031
Jim Bennett, Partner, Audit

Carlo De Mello, Partner, Audit
Vernon
Credit Union Bldg.
3205 - 32 St., 3rd Fl.
Vernon, BC V1T 9A2 Canada
250-503-5300
Fax: 250-545-6440
Waterloo
Marsland Centre
115 King St. South
Waterloo, ON N2J 5A3 Canada
519-747-8800
Fax: 519-747-8811
Shelley Wickenheiser, Partner, Tax
Windsor
Greenwood Centre
#618, 3200 Deziel Dr.
Windsor, ON N8W 5K8 Canada
519-251-3500
Fax: 519-251-3530
Winnipeg
#2000, One Lombard Place
Winnipeg, MB R3B 0X3 Canada
204-957-1770
Fax: 204-957-0808

MacKay LLP

#1100, 1177 West Hastings St.
Vancouver, BC V6E 4T5

604-687-4511
Fax: 780-425-8780
800-351-0426
Other Contact Information: Fax: 604/687-5805
HughLivingstone@Van.MacKayLLP.ca
www.mackayllp.ca

Ownership: Private
Year Founded: 1969
Number of Employees: 220
Profile: Services provided include bookkeeping, audit & accounting, taxation, corporate financing, executive financial planning, microcomputer support, management consulting, business investigation, valuation & litigation support, solvency & restructuring, & international affiliations.
Branches:
Calgary - 7 Avenue
Iveagh House
#1700, 717 - 7 Ave. SW
Calgary, AB T2P 0Z3 Canada
403-294-9292
Fax: 403-294-9262
Calgary@Cal.MacKay.ca

Calgary - Macleod Trail
Southcentre Executive Tower
#400, 11012 MacLeod Trail SE
Calgary, AB T2J 6A5 Canada
403-640-2227
Fax: 403-640-2505
calgary@cal.mackay.ca
Christine Heemskerk, General Manager
Edmonton
Highfield Place
#705, 10010 - 106th St.
Edmonton, AB T5J 3L8 Canada
780-420-0626
Fax: 780-425-8780
800-622-5293
edmonton@edm.mackay.ca
Don Smith, General Manager

Donald J. Smith

Bob McAneeley

Brent Penner
Kelowna
#500, 1620 Dickson Ave.
Kelowna, BC V1Y 9Y2 Canada
250-763-5021
Fax: 250-763-3600
866-763-5021
kelowna@kel.mackay.ca
Don Turri, General Manager

Don Turri

Ken Laloge

Chris White

Dan Basso

Angela C. Bailey
Surrey
#112, 7565 - 132nd St.
Surrey, BC V3W 1K5 Canada
604-591-6181
Fax: 604-591-5676
surrey@van.mackay.ca
Keith Gagnon, Manager

Jack Arnold

Bill Gill

Keith Gagnon
Whitehorse
#200, 303 Strickland St.
Whitehorse, YT Y1A 2J8 Canada
867-667-7651
Fax: 867-668-3797
markp@mackayandpartners.ca
Blaine Anderson

Norman McIntyre

Mark Pike
Yellowknife
PO Box 727
#301, 5120 - 49th St
Yellowknife, NT X1A 1P8 Canada
867-920-4404
Fax: 867-920-4135
866-920-4404
yellowknife@yel.mackay.ca
John Laratta

Gillian Lee

Meyers Norris Penny (MNP)
715 - 5th Ave. SW, 7th Fl.
Calgary, AB T2P 2X6

403-444-0150
Fax: 403-444-0199
www.mnp.ca

Year Founded: 1945
Number of Employees: 1300
Revenues: $100-500 million
Profile: MNP is a leading Western Canadian chartered accountancy & business advisory firm. In addition to traditional accounting services like taxation & assurance, MNP offers business services including corporate financing, human resource consulting, business & strategic planning, succession planning, valuations support, information technology consulting, self-employment training, & agricultural advisory services.
Executives:
Daryl Ritchie, FCA, CEO; daryl.ritchie@mnp.ca
Kelly Bernakevitch, FCA, Exec. Vice-President, Operations; kelly.bernakevitch@mnp.ca
Ted Poppitt, CA, Exec. Vice-President, Practice Development; ted.poppitt@mnp.ca
Laurel Wood, CMC, Exec. Vice-President, Advisory Services; laurel.wood@mnp.ca
Steve Kerr, CMA, CFO; steve.kerr@mnp.ca
Randy Mowat, Vice-President, Marketing; randy.mowat@mnp.ca
Phil O'Brien-Moran, Vice-President, Technology; phil.obrienmoran@mnp.ca
Bob Twerdun, CA, Vice-President, Human Capital; bob.twerdun@mnp.ca
Charmaine Toms, General Counsel; charmaine.toms@mnp.ca
Affiliated Companies:
Tamarack Capital Advisors Inc.
Offices:
Abbotsford
#300, 2975 Gladwin Rd.
Abbotsford, BC V2T 5T4 Canada
604-853-9471
Fax: 604-850-3672
Darrell P. Tracey, Contact; darrell.tracey@mnp.ca
Airdrie
#110A, 400 Main St. NE
Airdrie, AB T4B 2N1 Canada
403-912-6235
Fax: 403-912-6332
Sandra Steele, CA; sandra.steele@mnp.ca

Rhonda Stewart Tarney; rhonda.stewarttarney@mnp.ca
Brandon
1401 Princess Ave.
Brandon, MB R7A 7L7 Canada
204-727-0661
Fax: 204-726-1543
800-446-0890
Jeff Cristall; jeff.cristall@mnp.ca
Brooks
PO Box 1210
247 - 1st St. West
Brooks, AB T1R 1C1 Canada
403-362-8909
Fax: 403-362-6869
877-500-5696
Randy Dykin
Burnaby
Metrotower II
#900, 4720 Kingsway
Burnaby, BC V5H 4N2 Canada
604-435-4317
Fax: 604-435-4319
Rita Kilkenny; rita.kilkenny@mnp.ca
Calgary - Bantrel
#900, 700 6th Ave. SW
Calgary, AB T2P 0T8 Canada
403-263-3385
Fax: 403-648-4115
Kelly Brook, Contact; kelly.brook@mnp.ca
Calgary - North
#210, 5010 - 4th St. NE
Calgary, AB T2K 5X8 Canada
403-275-8457
Fax: 403-275-8416
Don Isaman; don.isaman@mnp.ca
Calgary Downtown - MNP Place
#300, 622 - 5th Ave. SW
Calgary, AB T2P 0M6 Canada
403-263-3385
Fax: 403-269-8450
Durell Wiley; durell.wiley@mnp.ca
Cambridge
#600, 73 Water St. N.
Cambridge, ON N1R 7L6 Canada
519-623-3820
Fax: 519-623-3144
Rhonda Lovell, CA; rhonda.lovell@mnp.ca
Campbell River
#201, 990 Cedar St.
Campbell River, BC V9W 7Z8 Canada
250-287-2131
Fax: 250-287-2134
800-450-9977
Chilliwack
#1, 45780 Yale Rd.
Chilliwack, BC V2P 2N4 Canada
604-792-1915
Fax: 604-795-6526
800-444-4070
Darrell P. Tracey; darrell.tracey@mnp.ca
Courtenay
467 Cumberland Rd.
Courtenay, BC V9N 2C5 Canada
250-338-5464
Fax: 250-338-0609
800-445-9988
Ben Vanderhorst
Dauphin
PO Box 6000
32 - 2nd Ave. SW
Dauphin, MB R7N 2V5 Canada
204-638-6767
Fax: 204-638-8634
877-500-0790

Gerry Musey; gerry.musey@mnp.ca
Deloraine
PO Box 528
130 Broadway St. North
Deloraine, MB R0M 0M0 Canada
204-747-2842
Fax: 204-747-2956
Julee Galvin, CA; julee.galvin@mnp.ca
Drumheller
PO Box 789
365 - 2nd St. East
Drumheller, AB T0J 0Y0 Canada
403-823-7800
Fax: 403-823-8914
877-932-3387
Jeff Hall; jeffhall@mnp.ca
Duncan
372 Coronation Ave.
Duncan, BC V9L 2T3 Canada
250-748-3761
Fax: 250-746-1712
Gordon John, CA; gordon.john@mnp.ca
Edmonton - City Centre
#400, 10104 - 103 Ave. NW
Edmonton, AB T5J 0H8 Canada
780-451-4406
Fax: 780-454-1908
Gordon Reid; gordon.reid@mnp.ca
Edmonton - South
#201, 9426 - 51 Ave. NW
Edmonton, AB T6E 5A6 Canada
780-462-8626
Fax: 780-462-8643
Murray Gray; murray.gray@mnp.ca
Estevan
#100, 1219 - 5th St.
Estevan, SK S4A 0Z5 Canada
306-634-2603
Fax: 306-634-8708
Brian Drayton; brian.drayton@mnp.ca
Fort McMurray
9707 Main St.
Fort McMurray, AB T9H 1T5 Canada
780-791-9000
Fax: 780-791-9047
Pat Olivier; pat.olivier@mnp.ca
Fort St. John
#2, 10611 - 102nd St.
Fort St. John, BC V1J 5L3 Canada
250-785-8166
Fax: 250-785-5660
Marvin Beaumont; marvin.beaumont@mnp.ca
Grande Prairie
214 Place
PO Box 43
9909 - 102 St.
Grande Prairie, AB T8V 2V4 Canada
780-831-1700
Fax: 780-539-9600
888-831-2870
Bridget Henniger; bridget.henniger@mnp.ca
Hope
PO Box 1689
100-E Fort St.
Hope, BC V0X 1L0 Canada
604-869-9599
Fax: 604-869-3044
800-969-6060
Keith Britz, Contact; keith.britz@mnp.ca
Humboldt
PO Box 2590
701 - 9th St.
Humboldt, SK S0K 2A0 Canada
306-682-2673
Fax: 306-682-5910
877-500-0789
Larry Rode; larry.rode@mnp.ca
Kelowna
600 - 1628 Dickson Ave.
Kelowna, BC V1Y 9X1 Canada
250-763-8919
Fax: 250-763-1121
John Orisko; john.orisko@mnp.ca
Kenora
315 Main St. South
Kenora, ON P9N 1T4 Canada

807-468-3338
Fax: 807-468-1418
Joseph Fregeau; jfregeau@fregeauandtompkin.ca
Killarney
501 Broadway Ave.
Killarney, MB R0K 1G0 Canada
204-523-4633
Fax: 204-523-4538
877-500-0760
Carla Beaudry; carla.beaudry@mnp.ca
Lacombe
#5, 5265 - 45th St.
Lacombe, AB T4L 2A2 Canada
403-782-7790
Fax: 403-782-7703

Gerald Wasylyshen; gerald.wasylyshen@mnp.ca
Leduc
#200, 5019 - 49th Ave.
Leduc, AB T9E 6T5 Canada
780-986-2626
Fax: 780-986-2621
Deborah A. Sarnecki; deborah.sarnecki@mnp.ca
Lethbridge
3425 - 2nd Ave. South
Lethbridge, AB T1J 4V1 Canada
403-329-1552
Fax: 403-329-1540
Gordon Tait; gord.tait@mnp.ca
Lloydminster
2905 - 50 Ave.
Lloydminster, SK S9V 0N7 Canada
306-825-9855
Fax: 306-825-9640
Ralph Cormack; ralph.cormack@mnp.ca
Maple Ridge
#201 - 11939 224th St.
Maple Ridge, BC V2X 6B2 Canada
604-463-8831
Fax: 604-463-0401
Tere Stykalo; tere.stykalo@mnp.ca
Medicine Hat
PO Box 580
666 - 4 St. SE
Medicine Hat, AB T1A 7G5 Canada
403-527-4441
Fax: 403-526-6218
877-500-0786
Michael Keck, Managing Partner; michael.keck@mnp.ca
Melfort
PO Box 2020
601 Main St.
Melfort, SK S0E 1A0 Canada
306-752-5800
Fax: 306-752-5933
877-500-0787
John Harder; john.harder@mnp.ca
Moosomin
PO Box 670
715 Main St.
Moosomin, SK S0G 3N0 Canada
306-435-3347
Fax: 306-435-2494
877-500-0784
Layne McFarlane; layne.mcfarlane@mnp.ca
Nanaimo
PO Box 514
96 Wallace St.
Nanaimo, BC V9R 5L5 Canada
250-753-8251
Fax: 250-754-3999
877-340-3330
Lucie Gosselin; lucie.gosselin@mnp.ca
Neepawa
PO Box 760
251 Davidson St.
Neepawa, MB R0J 1H0 Canada
204-476-2326
Fax: 204-476-3663
877-500-0795
Marvin Beaumont; marvin.beaumont@mnp.ca
Peace River
PO Box 6030
10012 - 101st St.
Peace River, AB T8S 1S1 Canada
780-624-3252
Fax: 780-624-8758
Bill Hirtle, CA; william.hirtle@mnp.ca
Port Moody
#601 - 205 Newport Dr.
Port Moody, BC V3H 5C9 Canada
604-949-2088
Fax: 604-949-0509

Harry Gross; harry.gross@mnp.ca
Portage La Prairie
780 Saskatchewan Ave. West
Portage La Prairie, MB R1N 0M7 Canada
204-239-6117
Fax: 204-857-3972
Jerry Lupkowski; jerry.lupkowski@mnp.ca
Prince Albert
25 - 11th St. East
Prince Albert, SK S6V 0Z8 Canada
306-764-6873
Fax: 306-763-0766
Garth Busch; garth.busch@mnp.ca
Red Deer
4922 - 53 St.
Red Deer, AB T4N 2E9 Canada
403-346-8878
Fax: 403-341-5599
877-500-0779
Tim Dekker; tim.dekker@mnp.ca
Red Lake
179 Howey St.
Red Lake, ON P0V 2M0 Canada
807-727-1114

Gary Porter; gary.porter@mnp.ca
Regina
Royal Bank Bldg.
#900, 2010 - 11th Ave.
Regina, SK S4P 0J3 Canada
306-790-7900
Fax: 306-790-7990
877-500-0780
Don Stewart; don.stewart@mnp.ca
Richmond Hill
#4, 10 West Pearce
Richmond Hill, ON L4B 1B6 Canada
905-763-2436
Fax: 905-709-9952
Kris Holbeck; kris.holbeck@mnp.ca
Rimbey
PO Box 317
4714 - 50th Ave.
Rimbey, AB T0C 2J0 Canada
403-843-4666
Fax: 403-843-4616
Chris Simpson; chris.simpson@mnp.ca
Rocky Mountain House
PO Box 2138
5004 - 50th St.
Rocky Mountain House, AB T4T 1B6 Canada
403-845-2422
Fax: 403-845-3794
Gary Porter; gary.porter@mnp.ca
Saskatoon
800 - 119 4th Ave. South
Saskatoon, SK S7K 5X2 Canada
306-665-6766
Fax: 306-665-9910
877-500-0778
David Kunaman; david.kunaman@mnp.ca
Steinbach
#100 - 250 Main St.
Steinbach, MB R5G 1Y8 Canada
204-326-9816
Fax: 204-326-9586
Alyson Kennedy; alyson.kennedy@mnp.ca
Surrey
#316, 5455 - 152 St.
Surrey, BC V3S 5A5 Canada
604-574-7211
Fax: 778-571-3549
Rick Bisson; rick.bisson@mnp.ca
Swift Current
50 - 1st Ave. NE
Swift Current, SK S9H 4W4 Canada
306-773-8375
Fax: 306-773-7735
877-500-0762
Al Lightfoot; al.lightfoot@mnp.ca
Thunder Bay
#210, 1205 Amber Dr.
Thunder Bay, ON P7B 6M4 Canada
807-623-2141
Fax: 807-622-1282
Ed Stromsmoe; ed.stromsmoe@mnp.ca
Toronto
#1100, 2 Bloor St. E.
Toronto, ON M4W 1A8 Canada
416-596-1711
Fax: 416-596-7894
Don Hornford; don.hornford@mnp.ca
Vancouver

PO Box 49148
#2300, 1055 Dunsmuir St.
Vancouver, BC V1T 1J1 Canada
604-685-8408
Fax: 604-685-8594
Ronald Anderson; ronald.anderson@mnp.ca
Vernon
#100, 2903 - 35th Ave.
Vernon, BC V1T 2S7 Canada
778-475-5678
Fax: 778-475-5618
Tom Plishka; tom.plishka@mnp.ca
Virden
PO Box 670
233 Queen St. West
Virden, MB R0M 2C0 Canada
204-748-1340
Fax: 204-748-3294
Tom Kirkup; tom.kirkup@mnp.ca
Waterloo
554 Weber St. N.
Waterloo, ON N2L 5C6 Canada
519-725-7700
Fax: 519-725-7708
Heather Farfard; heather.farfard@mnp.ca
Weyburn
#301 - 117 3rd St. NE
Weyburn, SK S4H 0W3 Canada
306-842-8915
Fax: 306-842-1966

Sean Wallace, CA, CFP; sean.wallace@mnp.ca
Winnipeg
#2500, 201 Portage Ave.
Winnipeg, MB R3B 3K6 Canada
204-775-4531
Fax: 204-783-8329
Dena Weiss; dena.weiss@mnp.ca
Winnipeg - Polo Park
#301, 1661 Portage Ave.
Winnipeg, MB R3J 3T7 Canada
204-336-6167
Fax: 204-772-9687
877-500-0795
Wayne McWhirter; wayne.mcwhirter@mnp.ca

Welch LLP
151 Slater St., 12th Fl.
Ottawa, ON K1P 5H3

613-236-9191
Fax: 613-236-8258
www.welchllp.com

Former Name: Welch & Company LLP
Ownership: Private
Year Founded: 1918
Number of Employees: 200
Profile: The firm serves business, government, & not-for-profit clients. Taxation, accounting, auditing, personal financial planning, & wealth management services are provided.
Executives:
Michel Bossé, CA, Principal, Ottawa; mbosse@welchllp.com
Micheal Burch, CA, CFP, Managing Partner, Ottawa; mburch@welchllp.com
Don Timmins, CA, Partner, Ottawa; dtimmins@welchllp.com
Branches:
Belleville
525 Dundas St. East
Belleville, ON K8N 1G4 Canada
613-966-2844
Fax: 613-966-2206
Glenn Collins, CA, Partner; gcollins@welch.on.ca
Campbellford
PO Box 1209
57 Bridge St. East
Campbellford, ON K0L 1L0 Canada
705-653-3194
Fax: 705-653-1703
Marie Northey, CA, Partner; mnorthey@welch.on.ca
Cornwall
36 Second St. East
Cornwall, ON K6H 1Y3 Canada
613-932-4953
Fax: 613-932-1731
Ron Mulligan, CA, Partner; rmulligan@welchllp.com
Gatineau
#201, 975, boul St-Joseph
Gatineau, QC J8Z 1W8 Canada
819-771-7381
Fax: 819-771-3089
Guy Coté, CA, Partner; gcote@levesquemarchand.ca
Napanee
36 Bridge St. East
Napanee, ON K7R 1J8 Canada

613-354-2169
Fax: 613-354-2160
Dan Atkinson, FCA, Partner; datkinson@welch.on.ca
Pembroke
PO Box 757
270 Lake St.
Pembroke, ON K8A 6X9 Canada
613-735-1021
Fax: 613-735-2071
Hal Ward, CA, Partner; hward@welchllp.com
Picton
290 Main St.
Picton, ON K0K 2T0 Canada
613-476-3283
Fax: 613-476-1627
Charles Thompson, CA, Partner; cthompson@welch.on.ca
Renfrew
101 Raglan St. North
Renfrew, ON K7V 1N7 Canada
613-432-8399
Fax: 613-432-9154
Dan Amyotte, CA, Partner; damyotte@welchllp.com
Trenton
#4, 290 Dundas St. West
Trenton, ON K8V 3S1 Canada
613-392-1287
Fax: 613-392-5456
John Bailey, CA, Partner; jbailey@welch.on.ca
Tweed
PO Box 807
63 Victoria St. North
Tweed, ON K0K 3J0 Canada
613-478-5051
Fax: 613-478-3069
Marie Northey, CA, Partner; mnorthey@welch.on.ca

Accounting Firms by Province

Alberta

Banff:Collins Barrow Chartered Accountants - Banff
Cascade Plaza
PO Box 1000
#370, 317 Banff Ave.
Banff, AB T1L 1H4
403-762-8383
Fax: 403-762-8384
cbbanff@cbrockies.com
www.cbrockies.com

Banff:Kenway Mack Slusarchuk Stewart Bow Valley LLP Chartered Accountants
PO Box 930
201 Bear St.
Banff, AB T1L 1A9
403-762-2271
Fax: 403-762-8817
info@kmss.ca
www.kmss.ca

Calgary:Alger & Associates Inc.
#400, 602 - 11th Ave. SW
Calgary, AB T2R 1J8
403-298-5800
Fax: 403-296-2988
310-8888
www.alger.ca

Calgary: Bernard Martens Professional Corp.
38 West Springs Gate SW
Calgary, AB T3H 4P5
403-255-1262
Fax: 403-640-4652
b.martens@home.com

Calgary:Buchanan Barry LLP
#800, 840 - 6th Ave. SW
Calgary, AB T2P 3E5
403-262-2116
Fax: 403-265-0845
mailbox@buchananbarry.ca
www.buchananbarry.ca

Calgary:Catalyst Chartered Accountants & Consultants
#250, 200 Quarry Park Blvd. SE
Calgary, AB T2C 5E3
403-296-0082
Fax: 403-296-0088
inquire@catalystsolutions.ca
www.catalystsolutions.ca

Calgary: Chartered Accountants For You, LLP
5917 - 1A St. SW
Calgary, AB T2H 0G4
403-209-2248
Fax: 403-539-2248
calgaryhelp@ca4u.ca
www.ca4u.ca

Calgary: CompassTAX Chartered Accountants
Dorchester Square
#600, 1333 - 8th St. SW
Calgary, AB T2R 1M6
403-531-2200
Fax: 403-263-1826
866-531-2281
www.compasstax.ca

Calgary:Daunheimer Lynch Anderson LLP
6620 Crowchild Trail SW
Calgary, AB T3E 5R8
403-217-5925
Fax: 403-217-5934
888-452-5925
www.dlallp.com

Calgary:Dick Cook Whyte Schulli Chartered Accountants
#555, 999 - 8th St. SW
Calgary, AB T3K 2L2
403-245-1717
Fax: 403-244-9306

Calgary: D.W. Robart Professional Corporation
#1480, 540 - 5th Ave. SW
Calgary, AB T2P 0M2
403-266-2611
Fax: 403-265-8626
don@robart.ca

Calgary:Flood & Associates Consulting Ltd.
#410, 840 - 6 Ave. SW
Calgary, AB T2P 3E5
403-263-1523
Fax: 403-263-1524
flood_co@telusplanet.net

Calgary: Garrett Gray Chartered Accountants
Parkside Place
#920, 602 - 12 Ave. SW
Calgary, AB T2R 1J3
403-806-2850
Fax: 403-806-2854
info@garrettgray.com
www.garrettgray.com

Calgary:Hamilton & Rosenthal Chartered Accountants
1034 - 8th Ave. SW
Calgary, AB T2P 1J2
403-266-2175
Fax: 403-514-2211
www.hamrose.com

Calgary: Kenway Mack Slusarchuk Stewart LLP
#220, 333 - 11 Ave. SW
Calgary, AB T2R 1L9
403-233-7750
Fax: 403-266-5267
info@kmss.ca
www.kmss.ca

Calgary:Kirk Wormley Chartered Accountant
#806, 7015 Macleod Trail SW
Calgary, AB T2H 2K6
403-266-5607
Fax: 403-201-0248
kirkwormley@shaw.ca
www.kirkwormley.ca

Calgary:Lalani & Co.
#101, 4707 - 1 St. SW
Calgary, AB T2G 0A1
403-693-3310
Fax: 403-214-7869

Calgary: Laurie Mounteer Professional Corp.
560 Parkridge Dr. SE
Calgary, AB T2J 4Z3
403-249-9944
laurie@mounteer.ca
www.expatax.ca

Calgary:Lo Porter Hétu
#601, 2535 - 3 Ave. SE
Calgary, AB T2A 7W5
403-283-1088
Fax: 403-283-1044
calgary@porterhetu.com
www.porterhetu.com

Calgary: McKinnon & Co., Chartered Accountants
740, 10655 Southport Rd. SW
Calgary, AB T2W 4Y1
403-262-9260

Calgary: Mitchell Kelly Jones & Associates Inc.
#1070, 340 - 12 Ave. SW
Calgary, AB T2R 1L5
403-265-8545
Fax: 403-265-8554

Calgary:PricewaterhouseCoopers LLP, Canada - Calgary
Petro-Canada Centre
#3100, 111 - 5th Ave. SW
Calgary, AB T2P 5L3
403-509-7500
Fax: 403-781-1825
www.pwc.com/ca

Calgary:The Matthews Group
#201, 1508 - 8th St. SW
Calgary, AB T2R 1R6
403-229-0066
Fax: 403-229-2817
matthewsgrp@telus.net
www.matthewsgrp.com

Calgary:Vertefeuille Rempel Chartered Accountants
#401, 304 - 8 Ave. SW
Calgary, AB T2P 1C2
403-294-0733
Fax: 403-294-0734
877-794-0733
www.vertrempel.com

Canmore:Collins Barrow Chartered Accountants - Canmore
#1, 714 - 10th St.
Canmore, AB T1W 2A6
403-678-4444
Fax: 403-678-5163
cbcanmore@cbrockies.com
www.cbrockies.com

Cochrane:W. Callaway Professional Corporation
PO Box 61
Site 5, RR#1
Cochrane, AB T4C 1A1
403-932-5433
Fax: 403-932-5577
bill@wcallaway.com
www.wcallaway.com

Drayton Valley:Collins Barrow Chartered Accountants - Drayton Valley
PO Box 6927
5204 - 52nd Ave.
Drayton Valley, AB T7A 1S3
780-542-4468
Fax: 780-542-5275
888-542-4468
draytonvalley@collinsbarrow.com

Edmonton:Bernhard Brinkmann Chartered Accountant
PO Box 82090, Yellowbird Stn. Yellowbird
#200, 3205 - 97 St. NW
Edmonton, AB T6N 1B7
780-434-2756
Fax: 780-463-7605
bhbrinkmann@brinkmann.ca
www.brinkmann.ca

Edmonton:Collins Barrow Chartered Accountants - Edmonton
Commerce Place
#2380, 10155 - 102 St. NW
Edmonton, AB T5J 4G8
780-428-1522
Fax: 780-425-8189
edmonton@collinsbarrow.com

Edmonton:DFK Canada Inc.
1923 - 151 Ave.
Edmonton, AB T5Y 1W1
780-472-4334
Fax: 780-472-4334
exec@dfk.ca
www.dfk.ca

Edmonton:**Givens LLP, Edmonton**
#201, West Chambers - 12220 Stony Plain Rd.
Edmonton, AB T5N 3Y4
780-482-7337
Fax: 780-482-7423
edmonton@porterhetu.com
www.porterhetu.com

Edmonton:**Hawkings Epp Dumont Chartered Accountants**
Mayfield Square I
10476 Mayfield Rd.
Edmonton, AB T5P 4P4
780-489-9606
Fax: 780-484-9689
www.hawkings.com

Edmonton:**King & Company**
#1201, Energy Sq.
10109 - 106 St.
Edmonton, AB T5J 3L7
780-423-2437
Fax: 780-426-5861

Edmonton:**Koehli Wickenberg Chartered Accountants**
#105, 4990 - 92nd Ave.
Edmonton, AB T6B 2V4
780-466-6204
Fax: 780-466-6262

Edmonton: **Liu Raymond C S Chartered Accountant**
#410, 10665 Jasper Ave.
Edmonton, AB T5J 3S9
780-429-1047

Edmonton:**PricewaterhouseCoopers LLP, Canada - Edmonton**
Toronto-Dominion Tower, Edmonton City Centre
#1501, 10088 - 102 Ave. NW
Edmonton, AB T5J 3N5
780-441-6700
Fax: 780-441-6776
www.pwc.com/ca

Edmonton:**Romanovsky & Associates, Chartered Accountants**
10260 - 112 St.
Edmonton, AB T5K 1M4
780-447-5830
Fax: 780-451-6291
800-861-5830
www.romanovsky.com

Edmonton:**SVS Group LLP**
#100, 17010 - 103 Ave.
Edmonton, AB T5S 1K7
780-486-3357
Fax: 780-486-3320
dvisser@svsgroup.ca
www.svsgroup.ca

Edmonton:**Watson Aberant Chartered Accountants (L.L.P.)**
4212 - 98th St.
Edmonton, AB T6E 6A1
780-438-5969
Fax: 780-437-3918
info@watsonaberant.com

Fort Saskatchewan:**Givens LLP, Fort Saskatchewan**
9928 - 99 Ave.
Fort Saskatchewan, AB T8L 4G8
780-998-2110
Fax: 780-998-0276
fortsask@porterhetu.com
www.porterhetu.com

High River:**Muth & Company**
PO Box 5039
19 - 3 Ave. SE
High River, AB T1V 1M3
403-652-4272
Fax: 403-652-2339
highriver@porterhetu.com
www.porterhetu.com

Lacombe: **Cookson Kooyman Chartered Accountants**
#220, 5001 - 52nd St.
Lacombe, AB T4L 2A6
403-782-3361
Fax: 403-782-3070
lacombe@ckca.net

Leduc: **Luchak Wright Wnuk Chartered Accountants**
4716 - 51 Ave.
Leduc, AB T9E 6Y8
780-986-8383
Fax: 780-986-4499
888-986-8383
lww@lwwca.com
www.lwwca.com

Lethbridge:**John Van Dyk, Professional Corporation**
#801B, 3 Ave. South
Lethbridge, AB T1J 2B9
403-317-4500
Fax: 403-317-4501
justin.vandyk@telus.net

Lethbridge:**Young Parkyn McNab LLP (YPM)**
#100, 530 - 8 St. South
Lethbridge, AB T1J 2J8
403-382-6800
Fax: 403-327-8990
800-665-5034
www.ypm.ca

Red Deer:**Collins Barrow Chartered Accountants - Red Deer**
#300, 5010 - 43 St.
Red Deer, AB T4N 6H2
403-342-5541
Fax: 403-347-3766
reddeer@collinsbarrow.com
www.collinsbarrowreddeer.ab.ca

Slave Lake:**Nash & Company**
PO Box 129
Slave Lake, AB T0G 2A0
780-849-3977
Fax: 780-849-3244
slavelake@porterhetu.com
www.porterhetu.com

St Paul:**Desjardins & Company**
PO Box 1600
4440 - 50 Ave.
St Paul, AB T0A 3A0
780-645-5516
Fax: 780-645-6010
office@desjardins-co.com
www.desjardins-co.com

Stettler:**Gitzel Krejci Dand Peterson**
PO Box 460
4912 - 51 St.
Stettler, AB T0C 2L0
403-742-4431
Fax: 403-742-1266
877-742-4431
gkdpca@gkdpca.com
www.gkdpca.com

Sundre: **Valerie L. Burrell Chartered Accountant**
#201, 101 - 6 St. SW
Sundre, AB T0M 1X0
403-638-3116
Fax: 403-638-9166
valb@telusplanet.net
www.sundre-cornerbrook.com/Accountant/

Vegreville:**Wilde and Company**
PO Box 70
4902 - 50th St.
Vegreville, AB T9C 1R1
780-632-3673
Fax: 780-632-6133
800-808-0998
office@wildeandco.com
www.wildeandco.com

Wainright:**Hall & Company**
291 - 10th St.
Wainright, AB T9W 1N7
780-842-6106
Fax: 780-842-5540
888-842-6106
barry@hallco.ca
www.hallco.ca

British Columbia

Abbotsford:**McDonald & Co.**
#301, 2955 Gladwin Rd.
Abbotsford, BC V2T 5T4
604-853-5225

Burnaby:**Barkman & Tanaka**
Lougheed Plaza
#225, 9600 Cameron St.
Burnaby, BC V3J 7N3
604-421-2591
Fax: 604-421-1171

Burnaby: **Kanester Johal Chartered Accountants**
#208, 3993 Henning Dr.
Burnaby, BC V5C 6P7
604-451-8300
Fax: 604-451-8301
info@kjca.com
www.kjca.com

Burnaby:**Kemp Harvey Goodison Inc.**
#210, 6400 Roberts St.
Burnaby, BC V5G 4C9
604-291-1470
Fax: 604-291-0264
Burnaby@khgcga.com
www.khgcga.com

Burns Lake:**M. McPhail & Associates Inc.**
PO Box 597
Burns Lake, BC V0J 1E0
250-692-7595
Fax: 250-692-3872
mcphail@mcphailcga.com
www.mcphailcga.com

Campbell River:**Chase Sekulich Chartered Accountants**
#101, 400 Tenth Ave.
Campbell River, BC V9W 4E3
250-287-8331
Fax: 250-287-7224
866-317-8331
office@chasesekulich.com
www.chasesekulich.com; www.bcdebtsolutions.com

Campbell River:**Eidsvik & Co.**
#303, 1100 Island Hwy.
Campbell River, BC V9W 8C6
250-286-6629
Fax: 250-286-6779

Castlegar:**Craig Gutwald Inc.**
880 Waterloo Rd.
Castlegar, BC V1N 4K8
250-365-0434
Fax: 250-365-0469
www.gutwald.ca

Duncan:**Atchison Palmer Leslie Chartered Accountants**
#301, 394 Duncan St.
Duncan, BC V9L 3W4
250-748-1426
Fax: 250-748-9724
www.aplaccountants.com

Grand Forks:**Kemp Harvey Burch Kientz Inc.**
PO Box 2020
619 Central Ave.
Grand Forks, BC V0H 1H0
250-442-2121
Fax: 250-442-5825
GrandForks@khgcga.com
www.khgcga.com

Kelowna:**Chun & Company**
#202, 3320 Richter St.
Kelowna, BC V1W 4V5
250-860-8687
Fax: 250-860-8413
www.chun.ca

Kelowna:**Wahl & Associates**
#103, 1441 Ellis St.
Kelowna, BC V1Y 2A3
250-762-3362
Fax: 250-762-3409
info@wahlcga.com
www.wahlcga.com

Madeira Park:**Bonnie Murray Inc.**
PO Box 70
Madeira Park, BC V0N 2H0
604-883-2857
Fax: 604-883-2861

***Maple Ridge:*Choquette & Company Accounting Group**
10662 - 240A St.
Maple Ridge, BC V2W 2B1
604-463-8202
Fax: 604-463-8210
800-667-9254
Other Contact Information: Skype: 604-463-8202
info@choquetteco.com
www.choquetteco.com

***Nanaimo:*Church Pickard & Co.**
#301, 17 Church St.
Nanaimo, BC V9R 5H5
250-754-6396
Fax: 250-754-8177
866-754-6396
mail@churchpickard.com
www.churchpickard.com

***Nanaimo:*Gary Ruffle Ltd.**
5107 Somerset Dr., #C
Nanaimo, BC V9T 2K5
250-758-5557
Fax: 250-758-5720
garyruffleltd@shaw.ca
www.garyruffleltd.com

***Nanaimo:*Robert F. Fischer & Company Inc., C.G.A.**
#13, 327 Prideaux St.
Nanaimo, BC V9R 2N4
250-753-7287
Fax: 250-753-7453

***Nelson:* Carmichael, Toews, Irving Inc.**
247 Baker St.
Nelson, BC V1L 4H4
250-354-4451
Fax: 250-354-4427
admin@cti-cga.com
www.cti-cga.com

***New Denver:*Mark Adams Ltd.**
316 6th Ave.
New Denver, BC V0G 1S0
250-358-2411

***North Vancouver:*C. Topley & Company Ltd.**
#200, 260 West Esplanade
North Vancouver, BC V7M 3G7
604-987-8688
Fax: 604-904-8628
877-363-3437

***North Vancouver:*Gray & Associates**
#201, 1075 West 1st St.
North Vancouver, BC V7P 3T4
604-990-0550
Fax: 604-990-0509
800-990-0550
info@grayandassociates.ca
grayandassociates.ca

***North Vancouver:* J. Casperson & Associates Ltd.**
221 Rondoval Cres.
North Vancouver, BC V7N 2W6
604-983-2113
Fax: 604-983-2114
jindra@jcasperson.com
jcaspersonassociatesltd.supersites.ca

***North Vancouver:* MacDonald Tash & Associates**
#120, 889 Harbourside Dr.
North Vancouver, BC V7P 3S1
604-987-2300
Fax: 604-987-2888
taxmatters@taxmatters.ca
www.taxmatters.ca

***North Vancouver:* Misam Canada Consulting Ltd.**
#107, 998 Harbourside Dr.
North Vancouver, BC V7P 3T2
604-984-3309
Fax: 604-984-3308
info@misamcanada.com
www.misamcanada.com

***Oliver:*Kemp Harvey Casorso Inc.**
PO Box 1478
34864 - 97th St.
Oliver, BC V0H 1T0
250-498-4977
Fax: 250-498-4330
Oliver@khgcga.com
www.khgcga.com

***Osoyoos:*Kemp Harvey Kemp - Osoyoos**
8901 Main St.
Osoyoos, BC V0H 1V0
250-495-3223
Fax: 250-495-3559
888-9850-5595
Osoyoos@khgcga.com
www.khgcga.com

***Osoyoos:*White Kennedy, Chartered Accountants - Osoyoos**
PO Box 260
#204, 8309 Main St.
Osoyoos, BC V0H 1V0
250-495-2688
Fax: 250-495-3525
osoyoos@whitekennedy.com
www.whitekennedy.com

***Penticton:* Harvey Lister & Webb Incorporated**
502 Ellis St.
Penticton, BC V2A 4M3
250-492-8821
Fax: 250-492-8288
info@harveylisterwebb.com
www.harveylisterwebb.com

***Penticton:*Kemp Harvey Kemp - Penticton**
445 Ellis St.
Penticton, BC V2A 4M1
250-492-8800
Fax: 250-492-6921
Penticton@khgcga.com
www.khgcga.com

***Penticton:*White Kennedy, Chartered Accountants - Penticton**
#201, 99 Padmore Ave. East
Penticton, BC V2A 7H7
250-493-0600
Fax: 250-493-4709
penticton@whitekennedy.com
www.whitekennedy.com

***Port Coquitlam:* Kemp Harvey de Roca Chan Inc.**
#2300, 2850 Shaughnessy St.
Port Coquitlam, BC V3C 6K5
604-552-4388
Fax: 604-552-7709
poco@khgcga.com
www.khgcga.com

***Port Moody:*Gregory & Associates**
#402, 130 Brew St.
Port Moody, BC V3H 0E3
604-939-2929
Fax: 604-936-4002
info@gregorywhittle.ca
www.gregorywhittle.ca

***Prince George:*Terlesky Braithwaite Janzen, Certified General Accountants**
#300, 180 Victoria St.
Prince George, BC V2L 2J2
250-564-2014
Fax: 250-564-5613
888-564-2014
tbjpg@tbjcga.com
www.tbjcga.com

***Richmond:*Bruce Dunn & Company Inc., Chartered Accountants**
#200, 5760 Minoru Blvd.
Richmond, BC V6X 2A9
604-241-8824
Fax: 604-241-8800
info@brucedunn.ca
www.brucedunn.ca

***Richmond:*Greig Sheppard Ltd.**
5090 - 8171 Ackroyd Rd.
Richmond, BC V6X 3K1
604-270-7601
Fax: 604-270-3314
cga@greigsheppard.com
www.greigsheppard.com

***Richmond:*Jerry's Accounting Ltd.**
#530, 130 - 8191 Westminster Hwy.
Richmond, BC V6X 1A7
604-273-7789
Fax: 604-273-9449
jerryky@shaw.ca
www.jerryaccounting.com

***Richmond:*Sunny Sun & Associates Inc.**
#708, 6081 No. 3 Rd.
Richmond, BC V6Y 2B2
604-270-4610
Fax: 604-270-4618
info@sunnycga.com
www.sunnycga.com

***Squamish:*McMillan Thorn, Certified General Accountants - Squamish**
PO Box 2120
38013 - 3rd Ave.
Squamish, BC V0N 3G0
604-892-5281
Fax: 604-892-5276
squamish@mcmillanthorn.com
www.mcmillanthorn.com

***Surrey:*Heming, Wyborn & Grewal**
#200, 17618 - 58 Ave.
Surrey, BC V3S 1L3
604-576-9121
Fax: 604-576-2890
hwgca@hwgca.com
www.hwgca.com

***Surrey:*Luckett Wenman & Associates**
#204, 10252 - 135th St.
Surrey, BC V3T 4C2
604-584-3566
Fax: 604-584-0629
866-584-3566
contact@luckettwenman.com
www.luckettwenman.com

***Surrey:*PricewaterhouseCoopers LLP, Canada - Surrey**
10190 - 152A St., 3rd Fl.
Surrey, BC V3R 1J7
604-806-7000
Fax: 604-806-7806
www.pwc.com/ca

***Surrey:*Sharma & Associates**
#205, 8388 - 128th St.
Surrey, BC V3W 4G2
604-597-5612
Fax: 604-590-5808
satish@sharmacga.com; hari@sharmacga.com
www.sharmacga.com

***Surrey:* Sunny Sun & Associates Inc. - Surrey**
#200, 10193 - 152A St.
Surrey, BC V3R 4H6
604-270-4613
Fax: 604-270-4618
info@sunnycga.com
www.sunnycga.com

***Surrey:*Van Wensem, Eakins & George**
17678 - 58A Ave.
Surrey, BC V3S 8V7
604-576-9242
Fax: 604-576-9258
info@vweg-cga.com
www.vweg-cga.com

***Terrace:*Demers & Associates**
#201, 4716 Lazelle Ave.
Terrace, BC V8G 1T2
250-638-8705
Fax: 250-638-0600
info@demerscga.com
www.demerscga.com

***Vancouver:*Bing C. Wong & Associates Ltd.**
124 East Pender St., 3rd Fl.
Vancouver, BC V6A 1T3
604-682-7561
Fax: 604-682-7665

***Vancouver:*Blair Crosson Voyer Chartered Accountants**
Commerce Pl.
#1650, 400, Burrard St.
Vancouver, BC V6C 3A6
604-684-3371
Fax: 604-684-9832
bcv@taxsolve.com

***Vancouver:*Campbell, Saunders Ltd.**
#1000, 570 Granville St.
Vancouver, BC V6C 3P1

604-915-5550
Fax: 604-915-5560
info@csvan.com
www.csvan.com

***Vancouver:*Cawley & Associates**
1622 - 7th Ave. West, 3rd Fl.
Vancouver, BC V6J 1S5
604-731-1191
Fax: 604-731-3511
bcawley@cawley.ca
www.cawley.ca

***Vancouver:*Collins Barrow Chartered Accountants - Vancouver**
Burrard Bldg.
#800, 1030 West Georgia St.
Vancouver, BC V6E 3B9
604-685-0564
Fax: 604-685-2050
vancouver@collinsbarrow.com

***Vancouver:*D&H Group**
1333 West Broadway St., 10th Fl.
Vancouver, BC V6H 4C1
604-731-5881
Fax: 604-731-9923
info@dhgroup.ca
www.dhgroup.ca

***Vancouver:*David Lin, Certified General Accountant**
5728 East Blvd.
Vancouver, BC V6M 4M4
604-267-0381
dlin@telus.net
www3.telus.net/davidlin

***Vancouver:*Davidson & Co.**
Stock Exchange Tower
PO Box 10372
#1200, 609 Granville St.
Vancouver, BC V7Y 1G6
604-687-0947
Fax: 604-687-6172
davidson@davidson-co.com
www.davidson-co.com

***Vancouver:*Equity Business Services Inc.**
#200, 1892 West Broadway
Vancouver, BC V6J 1Y9
604-874-9080
Fax: 604-874-9080
ehoy@equityinc.ca
www.equityinc.ca

***Vancouver:*Galloway Botteselle & Company**
Maple Place Professional Centre
#300, 2000 West 12th Ave.
Vancouver, BC V6J 2G2
604-736-6581
Fax: 604-736-0152
vancouver@porterhetu.com
www.porterhetu.com

***Vancouver:*Greenberg Associates**
North Office Tower, Oakridge Centre
#489, 650 West 41st Ave.
Vancouver, BC V5Z 2M9
604-264-5170
Fax: 604-264-5101
general@cga-gb.com
www.cga-gb.com

***Vancouver:* Lam Lo Nishio Chartered Accountants**
659-G Moberly Rd.
Vancouver, BC V5Z 4B2
604-872-8883
Fax: 604-872-8889
info@lamlonishio.ca
www.lamlonishio.ca

***Vancouver:*Lancaster & David, Chartered Accountants**
PO Box 10122, Pacific Centre Stn. Pacific Centre
#510, 701 West Georgia St.
Vancouver, BC V7Y 1C6
604-717-5526
Fax: 604-717-5560
admin@lancasteranddavid.ca
www.lancasteranddavid.ca

***Vancouver:*Manning Elliott**
1050 West Pender, 11th Fl.
Vancouver, BC V6J 3S7
604-714-3600
Fax: 604-714-3669
info@manningelliott.com
www.manningelliott.com

***Vancouver:*N.I. Cameron Inc.**
#303, 475 Howe St.
Vancouver, BC V6C 2B3
604-669-9631
Fax: 604-669-1848
info@nicameroninc.com
www.nicameroninc.com

***Vancouver:*PricewaterhouseCoopers LLP, Canada - Vancouver**
PricewaterhouseCoopers Place
250 Howe St., 7th Fl.
Vancouver, BC V6C 3S7
604-806-7000
Fax: 604-806-7806
www.pwc.com/ca

***Vancouver:* Quantum Accounting Services Inc.**
#205, 873 Beatty St.
Vancouver, BC V6B 2M6
604-662-8985
Fax: 604-662-8986
www.qas.bc.ca

***Vancouver:* Rolfe, Benson Chartered Accountants**
#1400, 900 West Hastings St.
Vancouver, BC V6C 1E3
604-684-1101
Fax: 604-684-7937
admin@rolfebenson.com
www.rolfebenson.com

***Vancouver:*Smythe Ratcliffe Chartered Accountants**
#700, 355 Burrard St.
Vancouver, BC V6C 2G8
604-687-1231
Fax: 604-688-4675
reception@smytheratcliffe.com
www.smytheratcliffe.com

***Vancouver:*Stan W. Lee**
North Tower
#628, 650 West 41st Ave.
Vancouver, BC V5Z 2M9
604-291-6016
Fax: 604-291-2018
stan@stanwleeca.com
www.stanwleeca.com

***Vancouver:*Strategex Group**
#210, 1075 West Georgia St.
Vancouver, BC V6E 3C9
604-688-2355
Fax: 604-688-2315
www.strategexgroup.ca

***Vancouver:*Watson Dauphinee & Masuch Chartered Accountants**
#420, 1501 West Broadway Ave.
Vancouver, BC V6J 4Z6
604-734-3247
Fax: 604-734-4802
info@wdmca.com
www.wdmca.com

***Vernon:*Clark Robinson**
3109 - 32nd Ave.
Vernon, BC V1T 2M2
250-545-7264
Fax: 250-542-5116
info@clarkrobinson.com
www.clarkrobinson.com

***Vernon:*Kemp Harvey Laidman-Betts Inc.**
#204, 3334 - 30th Ave.
Vernon, BC V1T 2C8
250-545-1544
Fax: 250-260-3641
877-547-1544
Vernon@khgcga.com
www.khgcga.com

***Vernon:*Willis Associates**
#100, 2903 - 35th Ave.
Vernon, BC V1T 2S7
250-549-2922
Fax: 250-542-8300
888-333-2922
www.willisassociates.ca

***Victoria:*Burkett & Abercrombie Chartered Accountants**
#200, 3561 Shelbourne St.
Victoria, BC V8P 4G8
250-370-9718
Fax: 250-370-9179
accountants@burkett.ca
www.burkett.ca

***Victoria:*Feil & Co.**
1580 Cook St.
Victoria, BC V8T 3N8
250-382-6177
Fax: 250-385-0154
email@feilnco.com
www.feilnco.com

***Victoria:*Ian B. Lawson & Co. Inc.**
Shamrock Professional Centre
#201, 830 Shamrock St.
Victoria, BC V8X 2V1
250-475-0222
Fax: 250-475-0229
victoria@porterhetu.com
www.porterhetu.com; www.iblawson.shawbiz.ca

***Westbank:*White Kennedy, Chartered Accountants - Westbank**
#1, 2429 Dobbin Rd.
Westbank, BC V4T 2L4
250-768-3400
Fax: 240-768-3445
westbank@whitekennedy.com
www.whitekennedy.com

***Whistler:*Gershon & Company**
#207A, 4368 Main St.
Whistler, BC V0N 1B0
604-938-1892
Fax: 604-938-1870
www.gershonandco.com

***Whistler:* Gordon J. Wiber & Associates Inc.**
#22, 1212 Alpha Lake Rd.
Whistler, BC V0N 1B2
604-935-1114
Fax: 604-935-1154
www.whistlerca.com

***Whistler:*J. Casperson & Associates Ltd. - Whistler**
2509 Whistler Road
Whistler, BC V7X 1B0
604-932-2450
jindra@jcasperson.com
jcaspersonassociatesltd.supersites.ca

***Whistler:*McMillan Thorn, Certified General Accountants - Whistler**
#204, 1085 Millar Creek Rd.
Whistler, BC V0N 1B1
604-938-1544
Fax: 604-938-1577
mail@mcmillanthorn.com
www.mcmillanthorn.com

Manitoba

***Carman:*Nakonechny & Power Chartered Accountants Ltd.**
PO Box 880
31 Main St. South
Carman, MB R0G 0J0
204-745-2061
Fax: 204-745-6322
www.nakandpow.com

***Souris:*Karen G. Duthie, CGA**
PO Box 927
Souris, MB R0K 2C0
204-483-3903
Fax: 204-483-2489
kduthie@porterhetu.com
www.porterhetu.com

***Swan River:*Pacak Kowal Hardie & Company, Chartered Accountants**
PO Box 1660
#100, 4th Avenue North
Swan River, MB R0L 1Z0
204-734-9331
Fax: 204-734-4785
800-743-8447
pkhl@pkhl.ca
www.pacakkowalhardie.com

***Swan River:*Reimer & Company Inc.**
PO Box 146
359 Kelsey Trail
Swan River, MB R0L 1Z0
204-734-2599
Fax: 204-734-3184
info@reimerco.ca
www.reimerco.ca

***Thompson:*Kendall Wall Pandya, Chartered Accountants**
118 Cree Rd.
Thompson, MB R8N 0C1
204-778-7312
Fax: 204-778-7919

***Winnipeg:*A.L. Schellenberg, Chartered Accountant**
474 Panet Rd.
Winnipeg, MB R2C 3B9
204-669-5143
Fax: 204-669-5145
leon@mts.net

***Winnipeg:*BCCA LLP Chartered Accountants**
#1505, 444 St. Mary Ave.
Winnipeg, MB R3C 3T1
204-957-7000
Fax: 204-949-1191
mail@bccallp.com
www.bccallp.com

***Winnipeg:*Booke & Partners**
#500, 5 Donald St.
Winnipeg, MB R3L 2T4
204-284-7060
Fax: 204-284-7105
booke@bookeandpartners.ca
www.bookeandpartners.ca

***Winnipeg:*Chochinov Porter Hétu**
#1250, 363 Broadway Ave.
Winnipeg, MB R3C 3N9
204-956-1685
Fax: 204-957-7694
schochinov@porterhetu.com
www.porterhetu.com

***Winnipeg:*Collins Barrow Chartered Accountants - Winnipeg**
Century Plaza
#401, 1 Wesley Ave.
Winnipeg, MB R3C 4C6
204-942-0221
Fax: 204-944-8371
winnipeg@collinsbarrow.com

***Winnipeg:* Craig & Ross Chartered Accountants**
#1515, 1 Lombard Place
Winnipeg, MB R3B 0X3
204-956-9400
Fax: 204-956-9424
info@craigross.com
www.craigross.com

***Winnipeg:*Craig R. Burgess, CGA**
383 McMillan Ave.
Winnipeg, MB R3L 0N3
204-334-8972
Fax: 204-334-8448
cburgess@porterhetu.com
www.porterhetu.com

***Winnipeg:*Gaudette Elvers LLP**
738 Osborne St.
Winnipeg, MB R3L 2C2
204-489-2781
Fax: 204-452-5956
gelvers@porterhetu.com; egaudette@porterhetu.com
www.porterhetu.com

***Winnipeg:*Knowles Warkentin & Bridges, Chartered Accountants**
#800, 125 Garry St.
Winnipeg, MB R3C 3P2
204-982-3878
Fax: 204-982-3888
connor@kwb.ca
www.kwb.ca

***Winnipeg:*Lazer Grant LLP Chartered Accountants & Business Advisors**
#300, 309 McDermot Ave.
Winnipeg, MB R3A 1T3
204-942-0300
Fax: 204-957-5611
800-220-0005
LazerGrant@lazergrant.ca
www.lazergrant.ca

***Winnipeg:*M Group Chartered Accountants**
710 Corydon Ave.
Winnipeg, MB R3M 0X9
204-992-7200
Fax: 204-992-7208
info@mgroup.ca
www.mgroup.ca

***Winnipeg:* Magnus & Buffie Chartered Accountants**
#1810, 444 St. Mary Ave.
Winnipeg, MB R3C 3T1
204-942-4441
Fax: 204-944-0400

***Winnipeg:*PKBW Group, Chartered Accountants & Business Advisors Inc.**
219 Fort St.
Winnipeg, MB R3C 1E2
204-942-0861
Fax: 204-947-6834
senez@pkbwgroup.ca
www.pkbwgroup.ca

***Winnipeg:*Pope & Brookes, DFK LLP, Chartered Accountants**
#300, 530 Kenaston Blvd.
Winnipeg, MB R3N 1Z4
204-487-7957
Fax: 204-487-1243
advice@pb-dfk.com
www.pb-dfk.com

***Winnipeg:*PPW Chartered Accountants LLP**
#209, 1661 Portage Ave.
Winnipeg, MB R3J 3T7
204-772-4936
Fax: 204-774-4462
solutions@ppw.ca
www.ppw.ca

***Winnipeg:*PricewaterhouseCoopers LLP, Canada - Winnipeg**
Richardson Bldg.
#2300, 1 Lombard Pl.
Winnipeg, MB R3B 0X6
204-926-2400
Fax: 204-994-1020
www.pwc.com/ca

***Winnipeg:*RDK Chartered Accountant Ltd.**
5 Whitkirk Place
Winnipeg, MB R3R 2A2
204-885-5280
Fax: 204-831-6670
admin@rdkcharteredaccountant.com
www.rdkcharteredaccountant.com

***Winnipeg:*Scarrow & Donald LLP**
#100, 5 Donald St.
Winnipeg, MB R3L 2T4
204-982-9800
Fax: 204-474-2886
sd@scarrowdonald.mb.ca
www.scarrowdonald.mb.ca

***Winnipeg:*The Exchange Chartered Accountants LLP**
#100, 123 Bannatyne Ave.
Winnipeg, MB R3B 0R3
204-943-4584
Fax: 204-957-5195
info@exg.ca
www.exg.ca

New Brunswick

***Campbellton:*Allen, Paquet & Arseneau LLP**
PO Box 519
207 Roseberry St.
Campbellton, NB E3N 3G9
506-789-0820
Fax: 506-759-7514
apada@apa-ca.com
www.apa-ca.com

***Edmundston:* LeBlanc Nadeau Bujold - Edmundston**
25 Carrier St.
Edmundston, NB E3V 4A3
506-735-1820
Fax: 506-735-1821
edmundston@lnb.ca
www.lnb.ca

***Florenceville:*McCain & Company Chartered Accountants**
PO Box 437
393 Main St.
Florenceville, NB E7L 1Y9
506-392-5517
Fax: 506-392-5341
fhmccain@mccainandco.com
www.mccainandco.com

***Fredericton:*Bringloe Feeney**
#401, 212 Queen St.
Fredericton, NB E3B 1A8
506-458-8326
Fax: 506-458-9293

***Fredericton:*Bringloe Feeney LLP**
#401, 212 Queen St.
Fredericton, NB E3B 1A8
506-458-8326
Fax: 506-458-9293
shawn.bringloe@bringloefeeney.ca

***Fredericton:*Thornton VanTassel Chartered Accountants - Fredericton**
514 Queen St.
Fredericton, NB E3B 1B9
506-451-9261
Fax: 506-459-7595
edwin.corey@thorntonvantassel.com
www.thorntonvantassel.com

***Grand Falls:*LeBlanc Nadeau Bujold - Grand Falls**
796, boul Éverard H. Daigle
Grand Falls, NB E3Z 3C8
506-473-4240
Fax: 506-473-9450
grand-falls@lnb.ca
www.lnb.ca

***Grand Falls:*Thornton VanTassel Chartered Accountants - Grand Falls**
#201, 218 Broadway Blvd.
Grand Falls, NB E3Z 2J9
506-473-5068
Fax: 506-473-7077
joe.mcphail@thorntonvantassel.com
www.thorntonvantassel.com

***Moncton:*Boudreau Porter Hétu**
66 Donald Ave.
Moncton, NB E1A 3B1
506-857-0262
Fax: 506-857-0232
eboudreau@porterhetu.com
www.porterhetu.com

***Moncton:*PricewaterhouseCoopers LLP, Canada - Moncton**
#100, 1199 Main St.
Moncton, NB E1C 0L9
506-859-8822
Fax: 506-859-8829
www.pwc.com/ca

***Perth-Andover:*Thornton VanTassel Chartered Accountants - Perth-Andover**
#2, 15 Station St.
Perth-Andover, NB E7H 4Y2
506-273-2276
Fax: 506-273-2033
jim.vantassel@thorntonvantassel.com
www.thorntonvantassel.com

***Plaster Rock:*Thornton VanTassel Chartered Accountants - Plaster Rock**
240A Main St.
Plaster Rock, NB E7G 2E1
506-356-2641
Fax: 506-356-8493
theresa.wark@thorntonvantassel.com
www.thorntonvantassel.com

***Riverview:*Stevenson & Partners LLP**
567 Coverdale Rd.
Riverview, NB E1B 3K7
506-387-4044
Fax: 506-387-7270
sp@parternsnb.com
www.acgca.ca

*Rothesay:*Steeves Porter Hétu
Professional Centre
PO Box 4591
9 Scott Ave.
Rothesay, NB E2E 5X3
506-847-7471
Fax: 506-847-3151
dsteeves@porterhetu.com
www.porterhetu.com

*Saint John:*Beers Neal LLP
#301, 53 King St.
Saint John, NB E2L 1G5
506-632-9020
Fax: 506-632-9030
www.acgca.ca

*Saint John:*Curry & Betts
Admiral Beatty Building
PO Box 6789, A Stn. A
72 Charlotte St., 1st Fl.
Saint John, NB E2L 4S2
506-635-8181
Fax: 506-633-5943
888-635-8181
curbetts@nbnet.nb.ca
www.curry-betts.ca

*Saint John:*PricewaterhouseCoopers LLP, Canada - Saint John
Brunswick House
PO Box 789
#300, 44 Chipman Hill
Saint John, NB E2L 4B9
506-632-1810
Fax: 506-632-8997
www.pwc.com/ca

*Saint John:*Ralph H. Green & Associates
#200, 53 King St.
Saint John, NB E2L 1G5
506-632-3000
Fax: 506-632-1007
igreen@rhgreenassociates.ca
www.rhgreenassociates.ca

*St. Stephen:*L K Toombs Chartered Accountants
#207, 73 Milltown Blvd.
St. Stephen, NB E3L 1G5
506-466-3291
Fax: 506-466-9825
lktpc@nb.aibn.com
www.acgca.ca

*Sussex:*Turnbull and Kindred
PO Box 4608
44 Moffett Ave.
Sussex, NB E4E 5L8
506-433-4202
aturnbull@porterhetu.com; jkindred@porterhetu.com
www.porterhetu.com

Newfoundland & Labrador

*Corner Brook:*J. Pike & Company Ltd.
A98-98 Broadway
Corner Brook, NL A2H 4C8
709-639-7774
Fax: 709-639-7775

*Creston:*Jody Murphy, Chartered Accountant
PO Box 508
437 Creston Blvd.
Creston, NL A0E 1K0
709-279-1888
Fax: 709-279-1895
jmurphyca@nf.sympatico.ca

*Gander:*Walters Hoffe
30 Roe Ave.
Gander, NL A1V 1X5
709-651-4100

*Mount Pearl:*Feltham Attwood
#202, 39 Commonwealth Ave.
Mount Pearl, NL A1N 1W7
709-364-7300
Fax: 709-364-7731
debra@feltham-attwood.ca
www.porterhetu.com

*St. John's:*Belanger Clarke Follett & McGettigan
53 Bond St.
St. John's, NL A1C 1S9
709-579-2161
Fax: 709-738-2391

*St. John's:*PricewaterhouseCoopers LLP, Canada - St. John's
Atlantic Place
#802, 215 Water St.
St. John's, NL A1C 6C9
709-722-3883
Fax: 709-722-5874
www.pwc.com/ca

Northwest Territories

*Yellowknife:*Avery Cooper & Co.
Laurentian Building
PO Box 1620
4918, 50th St.
Yellowknife, NT X1A 2P2
867-873-3441
Fax: 867-873-2353
800-661-0787
avery@averyco.nt.ca
www.averyco.nt.ca

Nova Scotia

*Amherst:*sj mcisaac Chartered Accountants
PO Box 217
Amherst, NS B4H 3Z2
902-661-1027
Fax: 902-667-0884
877-282-6632
contact@sjmcisaac.ca
www.sjmcisaac.ca

*Bedford:*David B. Etter
117 Brentwood Dr.
Bedford, NS B4A 3S3
902-456-1031
Fax: 902-835-5431
detter@porterhetu.com
www.porterhetu.com

*Bedford:*WBLI Chartered Accountants
26 Union St.
Bedford, NS B4A 2B5
902-835-7333
Fax: 902-835-5297
www.wbli.ca

*Bridgewater:*Belliveau Veinotte Inc.
PO Box 29
11 Dominion St.
Bridgewater, NS B4V 2W6
902-543-4278
Fax: 902-543-1818
office@bvca.ca
www.acgca.ca

*Cheticamp:*Harold Patrick Aucoin CGA, Inc.
15262 Cabot Trail
Cheticamp, NS B0E 1H0
902-224-3748
Fax: 902-224-2092
haroldaucoin@haroldaucoincga.ca
www.haroldaucoincga.ca; www.porterhetu.com

*Dartmouth:*Hunter Tellier Belgrave Adamson
Cambridge 1
#200, 202 Brownlow Ave.
Dartmouth, NS B3B 1T5
902-468-1949
Fax: 902-468-4865
service@achba.ca

*Dartmouth:*Jean-Marc Chassé Inc.
#44, 201 Browlow Ave.
Dartmouth, NS B3B 1W2
902-468-0282
Fax: 902-468-6150
jmchasse@porterhetu.com
www.porterhetu.com

*Dartmouth:*McNeil Porter Hétu
344 Prince Albert Rd.
Dartmouth, NS B2Y 1N6
902-464-9300
Fax: 902-464-7246
dmcneil@porterhetu.com
www.porterhetu.com

*Halifax:*Dockrill Horwich Rossiter
#440, 36 Solutions Dr.
Halifax, NS B3S 1N2
902-835-0232
Fax: 902-835-0060
www.acgca.ca

*Halifax:*Lyle Tilley Davidson
#720, 1718 Argyle St.
Halifax, NS B3J 3N6
902-423-7225
Fax: 902-422-3649
info@ltdca.com; ward@ltdca.com
www.ltdca.com

*Halifax:*PricewaterhouseCoopers LLP, Canada - Halifax
#400, 1601 Lower Water St.
Halifax, NS B3J 3P6
903-491-7400
Fax: 903-422-1166
www.pwc.com/ca

*New Glasgow:*Williams MacDonald Inc.
400 East River Rd.
New Glasgow, NS B2H 3P7
902-752-0463
Fax: 902-755-2823
www.acgca.ca

Sydney: MGM & Associates Chartered Accountants
PO Box 1
Sydney, NS B1P 6G9
902-539-3900
Fax: 902-564-6062
mail@mgm.ca
www.mgm.ca

*Sydney:*PricewaterhouseCoopers LLP, Canada - Sydney
#220, 500 Grange St.
Sydney, NS B1P 1K6
902-564-0802
Fax: 902-564-1470
www.pwc.com/ca

*Truro:*PricewaterhouseCoopers LLP, Canada - Truro
PO Box 632, Prince Stn. Prince
710 Prince St.
Truro, NS B2N 5E5
902-895-1641
Fax: 902-893-0460
www.pwc.com/ca

*Wolfville:*Bishop & Company Chartered Accountants Inc.
189 Dykeland St.
Wolfville, NS B4P 1A3
902-542-7665
Fax: 902-542-4554
rbishop@bcica.ca

Ontario

*Ajax:*Thomas and Chase
#211, 50 Commercial Ave.
Ajax, ON L1S 2H5
905-686-2407
Fax: 905-686-2276
thomaschase@on.aibn.com
www.thomasandchase.com; www.porterhetu.com

Ajax: ToniolоPetersTurnerMoore LLP
#6, 676 Monarch Ave.
Ajax, ON L1S 4S2
905-427-6768
Fax: 905-427-1505
details@ptmcga.com
www.tptmcga.com

*Almonte:*Colby McGeachy PC
PO Box 970
258 Greystone Cres.
Almonte, ON K0A 1A0
613-259-2878
Fax: 613-256-7569
866-259-2878
ecolby@porterhetu.com
www.porterhetu.com

*Ancaster:*Brownlow & Associates
259 Wilson St. East
Ancaster, ON L9G 2B8

905-648-0404
Fax: 905-648-0403
888-648-0404
info@brownlowcas.com
www.brownlowcas.com

***Arnprior:*Dave H. Laventure Professional Corporation**
106 McGonigal St. West, #B
Arnprior, ON K7S 1M4
613-623-3181
Fax: 613-623-4299
dhlaventurecga@dhlaventurecga.com
www.porterhetu.com

***Aylmer:*Den Harder McNames Button CGA**
174 Sydenham St. East
Aylmer, ON N5H 1L7
519-773-5348
Fax: 519-773-7409
cbutton@epraylmer.com

***Bancroft:*Dale Rose, CGA and Peter Stone, CA**
PO Box 1209
294 Hastings St. North
Bancroft, ON K0L 1C0
613-332-0834
Fax: 613-332-4154
800-333-0834
drose@porterhetu.com; pstone@porterhetu.com
www.porterhetu.com

***Barrie:*Alan Martin Associates - Barrie**
72 Ross St.
Barrie, ON L4N 1G3
705-727-0407
Fax: 705-727-7677

***Barrie:* KoutroulakisTurnerMoore LLP**
204 Dunlop St. West
Barrie, ON L4N 1B3
705-722-5519
Fax: 705-722-7840
pkoutroulakis@turnermoore.com
www.turnermoore.com

***Barrie:*Powell, Jones**
121 Anne St. South
Barrie, ON L4N 7B6
705-728-7461
Fax: 705-728-8317
info@powelljones.ca
www.powelljones.ca

***Belleville:*Soden & Co.**
25 Campbell St.
Belleville, ON K8N 1S6
613-968-3495
Fax: 613-968-7359

***Belleville:*Wilkinson & Company LLP**
PO Box 757
139 Front St.
Belleville, ON K8N 5B5
613-966-5105
Fax: 613-962-7072
888-728-3890
bellevil@wilkinson.net
www.wilkinson.net

***Bobcaygeon:*Collins Barrow Chartered Accountants - Bobcaygeon**
PO Box 10
21 King St. West
Bobcaygeon, ON K0M 1A0
705-738-4166
Fax: 705-738-5787
bobcaygn@collinsbarrow.com

***Bobcaygeon:* TeeuwenTurnerMoore LLP**
PO Box 1065
3401 County Rd. 36
Bobcaygeon, ON
705-738-1581
Fax: 705-738-0031
lteeuwen@turnermoore.com
www.turnermoore.com

***Bradford:* FalconeTurnerMoore LLP**
PO Box 753
27 John St. West
Bradford, ON L3Z 2B3
905-778-8964
Fax: 905-775-9550
800-246-5591
mfalcone@turnermoore.com
www.turnermoore.com

***Brampton:*Buttar & Associates Inc.**
Jaipur Chrysler Centre
#1, 470 Chrysler Dr.
Brampton, ON L6S 0C1
905-866-6543
Fax: 905-866-6566
delta@buttarbuttar.com
www.buttar.ca

***Brampton:*Kenneth Bell CA Business Advisory Group**
#34, 18 Regan Rd.
Brampton, ON L7A 1C2
905-453-0844
Fax: 905-453-1530
www.kenbell.ca

***Brampton:*SMCA Professional Corporation**
#201, 197 County Court Blvd.
Brampton, ON L6W 4P6
905-451-4034
Fax: 905-451-7158
888-524-4844
carrollm@smca.ca
www.smca.ca

***Brantford:* Millard, Rouse & Rosebrugh LLP**
PO Box 367
96 Nelson St.
Brantford, ON N3T 5N3
519-759-3511
Fax: 519-759-7961
csmith@millards.com
www.millards.com

***Brantford:*Susan L. Rice**
#15, 340 Henry St.
Brantford, ON N3S 7V9
519-752-8290
Fax: 519-752-9784
srice@obwr.ca

***Brockville:*G.A. Porter, CA**
21 Ormond St.
Brockville, ON K6V 2K2
613-865-9664
gporter@porterhetu.com
www.porterhetu.com

***Brockville:* George Caners Chartered Accountant**
#210, 9 Broad St.
Brockville, ON K6V 6Z4
613-342-1555
Fax: 613-342-2845
888-829-9952
www.caners.com

***Burlington:*Bateman MacKay**
PO Box 5015
4200 South Service Rd.
Burlington, ON L7R 3Y8
905-632-6400
Fax: 905-639-2285
866-787-1117
Other Contact Information: Toronto Phone: 416-360-6400
info@batemanmackay.com
www.batemanmackay.com

***Burlington:*Durward Jones Barkwell & Company LLP**
#103, 3430 South Service Rd.
Burlington, ON L7N 3T9
905-681-6900
Fax: 905-681-6874
866-407-5318
burl@djb.com
www.djb.com

***Burlington:*Prapavessis Jasek**
3410 South Service Rd., Lower Fl.
Burlington, ON L7N 3T2
905-634-8999
Fax: 905-634-5057
jim@pj.on.ca
www.pj.on.ca

***Burlington:*Scott & Pichelli Ltd.**
#109, 3600 Billings Ct.
Burlington, ON L7N 3N6
905-632-5853
Fax: 905-632-6113
www.bankruptcy-trustees.ca/

***Burlington:*Steven J. Obranovich**
650 Plains Rd. East
Burlington, ON L7T 2E9
905-632-8400
Fax: 905-632-9505
sobranovich@obwr.ca

***Burlington:*Stevenson & Lehocki**
310 Plains Rd. East
Burlington, ON L7T 4J2
905-632-0640
Fax: 905-632-0645
joe@stevensonlehocki.com
www.stevensonlehocki.com

***Burlington:*Wade & Partners LLP, Chartered Accountants**
#102, 5096 South Service Rd.
Burlington, ON L7L 5H4
905-333-9888
Fax: 905-333-9583
ca@wadegroup.ca
www.wadegroup.ca

***Cambridge:*Collins Barrow Chartered Accountants - Cambridge**
#600, 73 Water St. North
Cambridge, ON N1R 7L6
519-623-3820
Fax: 519-622-3144
cbcambridge@collinsbarrow.com

***Cambridge:*Graham Mathew & Partners LLP**
PO Box 880
150 Pinebush Rd.
Cambridge, ON N1R 5X9
519-623-1870
Fax: 519-623-9490
admin@gmpca.com
www.gmpca.com

***Carleton Place:*Collins Barrow Chartered Accountants - Carleton Place**
143-A Bridge St.
Carleton Place, ON K7C 2V6
613-253-0014
Fax: 613-253-0129
carletonplace@collinsbarrow.com

***Chatham:*Collins Barrow Chartered Accountants - Chatham**
62 Keil Dr. South
Chatham, ON N7M 3G8
519-351-2024
Fax: 519-351-8831
chatham@collinsbarrow.com

***Chatham:*Gilhula & Grant**
PO Box 488
141 Grand Ave. East
Chatham, ON N7L 1W1
519-352-3470
Fax: 519-352-7344
gilgrant@ciaccess.com

***Chelmsford:*Collins Barrow Chartered Accountants - Chelmsford**
PO Box 673
48 Main St. East
Chelmsford, ON P0M 1L0
705-855-9024
Fax: 705-855-3693
chelmsford@collinsbarrow.com

***Churchill:* MayerhoferTurnerMoore LLP**
1027 Sloan Circle Dr.
Churchill, ON L0L 1K0
705-456-8069
Fax: 705-456-8071
wmayerhofer@turnermoore.com
www.turnermoore.com

***Concord:* Burghout Viola, Chartered Accountants**
#105, 7941 Jane St.
Concord, ON L4K 4L6
905-738-6402
Fax: 905-738-1805
john@burghoutviola.com
www.burghoutviola.com

***Concord:*Miller, Saperia & Company**
#418, 1600 Steeles Ave. West
Concord, ON L4K 4M2
905-660-6840
Fax: 905-660-6729

Concord: **Starkman Salsberg & Feldberg**
#316, 1600 Steeles Ave. West
Concord, ON L4K 4M2
905-669-9900
Fax: 905-669-9901

Elginburg: **Randy E. Brown CGA**
2908 Leeman Rd.
Elginburg, ON K0H 1M0
613-542-0151
Fax: 613-549-1427
rbrown@porterhetu.com

Elmvale: **Alan Martin Associates**
42 Queen St.
Elmvale, ON L0L 1P0
705-322-2440
Fax: 705-322-1462

Elora: **Collins Barrow Chartered Accountants - Elora**
PO Box 580
342, Gerrie Rd.
Elora, ON N0B 1S0
519-846-5315
Fax: 519-846-9120
info@collinsbarrow.com

Exeter: **Collins Barrow Chartered Accountants - Exeter**
PO Box 2405
412 Main St.
Exeter, ON N0M 1S7
519-235-0345
Fax: 519-235-3235
exeter@collinsbarrow.com

Fort Erie: **Durward Jones Barkwell & Company, Fort Erie**
#15, 1264 Garrison Rd.
Fort Erie, ON L2A 1P1
905-871-3565
Fax: 905-871-9232
866-720-2194
forterie@djb.com
www.djb.com

Fredericton: **Nicholson & Beaumont Chartered Accountants**
328 King St.
Fredericton, ON E3B 5C2
506-458-9815
Fax: 506-459-7575
jbeaumont@porterhetu.com
www.porterhetu.com

Gravenhurst: **C.R. Barclay, CA, CMA, MBA**
10 Woods Hollow
Gravenhurst, ON P1P 1Y7
705-684-8115
Fax: 705-684-8227
877-644-4838
cbarclay1@cogeco.ca

Grimsby: **Durward Jones Barkwell & Company, Grimsby**
PO Box 261
8 Christie St.
Grimsby, ON L3M 4G5
905-945-5439
Fax: 905-945-1103
866-830-7531
grimsby@djb.com
www.djb.com

Grimsby: **Southcott Davoli Professional Corporation**
PO Box 68
76 Main St. West
Grimsby, ON L3M 4G1
905-945-4942
Fax: 905-945-0306
contactus@southdav.com

Guelph: **Bairstow, Smart & Smith LLP**
100 Gordon St.
Guelph, ON N1H 4H6
519-822-7670
Fax: 519-822-6997
bss@bssllp.ca
www.bssllp.ca

Guelph: **Embree & Co. LLP**
#8, 350 Speedvale Ave. West
Guelph, ON N1H 7M7
519-821-1555
Fax: 519-821-6168
866-531-1555
www.embreelp.ca

Guelph: **Robinson, Lott & Brohman LLP**
15 Lewis Rd.
Guelph, ON N1H 1E9
519-822-9933
Fax: 519-822-9212
866-822-9992
guelph_inquiries@rlb.ca
www.rlb.ca

Guelph: **Weiler & Company**
#3, 512 Woolwich St.
Guelph, ON N1H 3X7
519-837-3111
Fax: 519-837-1049
888-239-3111
weiler@weiler.ca
www.weiler.ca

Halton Hills: **BrightTurnerMoore LLP**
305 Mountainview Rd. South
Halton Hills, ON L7G 4K1
905-702-1730
Fax: 905-702-1731
pbright@turnermoore.com
www.turnermoore.com

Hamilton: **BC&C Professional Corporation**
20 Jackson St. West
Hamilton, ON L8P 1L2
905-570-1370
Fax: 905-570-1212
fred@bccpc.ca
www.bccpc.ca

Hamilton: **Durward Jones Barkwell & Company, Hamilton**
Standard Life Bldg.
#780, 120 King St. West
Hamilton, ON L8P 4V2
905-525-9520
Fax: 905-522-3113
866-358-8240
hamilton@djb.com
www.djb.com

Hamilton: **Galano, Enzo & Associates**
#400, 20 Hughson St. South
Hamilton, ON L8N 2A1
905-528-0144
Fax: 905-528-0144
enzo@netinc.ca

Hamilton: **Herpers Chagani Gowling Inc.**
#300, 4 Hughson St. South
Hamilton, ON L8N 3Z1
905-529-3328
Fax: 905-529-3980
310-3328
www.bankruptcyanswers.com

Hamilton: **MacGillivray Partners, LLP**
33 Main St. East
Hamilton, ON L8N 4K5
905-523-7732
Fax: 905-572-9333
hamilton@macgillivray.com
www.macgillivray.com

Hamilton: **PricewaterhouseCoopers LLP, Canada - Hamilton**
21 King St. West, Main Fl.
Hamilton, ON L8P 4W7
905-777-7000
Fax: 905-777-7060
www.pwc.com/ca

Hamilton: **Taylor Leibow LLP, Accountants & Advisors**
#700, 105 Main St. East
Hamilton, ON L8N 1G6
905-523-0000
Fax: 905-523-4681
888-287-2525
info@taylorleibow.com
www.taylorleibow.com

Hamilton: **ThomsonTurnerMoore LLP**
645 Upper James St.
Hamilton, ON L9C 2Y9
905-388-7229
Fax: 905-388-3134
jrthomson@turnermoore.com
www.thomsonturnermoore.ca

Hearst: **Collins Barrow Chartered Accountants - Hearst**
PO Box 637
1021 George St.
Hearst, ON P0L 1N0
705-362-4261
Fax: 705-362-4641
hearst@collinsbarrow.com

Jackson's Point: **Duncan Goodwin, CGA**
#4, 915 Lake Dr.
Jackson's Point, ON L0E 1L0
905-722-8587
Fax: 904-722-6519
dgoodwin@porterhetu.com
www.porterhetu.com

Kapuskasing: **Collins Barrow Chartered Accountants - Kapuskasing**
2 Ash St.
Kapuskasing, ON P5N 3H4
705-337-6411
Fax: 705-335-6563
kapuskasing@collinsbarrow.com

Kelowna: **Kemp Harvey Hunt Ward Inc.**
#101, 1593 Sutherland Ave.
Kelowna, ON V1Y 5Y7
250-763-8029
Fax: 250-763-5155
Kelowna@khgcga.com
www.khgcga.com

Kenora: **Claudette M. Edie, CGA**
685 Lakeview Dr.
Kenora, ON P9N 3P6
807-468-8899
Fax: 807-468-6800
cedie@porterhetu.com
www.porterhetu.com

Kingston: **Collins Barrow Chartered Accountants - Kingston**
#301, 1471 Counter St.
Kingston, ON K7M 8S8
613-544-2903
Fax: 613-544-6151
kingston@collinsbarrow.com

Kingston: **Davies & Wyngaarden Chartered Accountants**
Clock Tower Plaza
819 Norwest Rd.
Kingston, ON K7P 2N4
613-389-8177
Fax: 613-389-7789
888-715-3555
acctg@dwca.com
www.dwca.com

Kingston: **GibsonTurnerMoore LLP**
4 Cataraqui St.
Kingston, ON K7K 1Z7
613-547-5099
Fax: 613-547-5102
sgibson@turnermoore.com
www.turnermoore.com

Kitchener: **Clarke Starke & Diegel (CSD)**
#202, 871 Victoria St. North
Kitchener, ON N2B 3S4
519-579-5520
Fax: 519-570-3611
www.csdca.com

Kitchener: **YNC LLP**
650 Riverbend Dr., Suite A1
Kitchener, ON N2K 3S2
519-772-0125
Fax: 519-772-0428
info@yncllp.ca
www.youngandcompany.ca

Leamington: **Collins Barrow Leamington LLP**
92 Talbot St. East
Leamington, ON N8H 1L3
519-326-2666
Fax: 519-326-7008
leamington@collinsbarrow.com
www.collinsbarrow.com

*Lindsay:*Collins Barrow Chartered Accountants - Lindsay
237 Kent St. West
Lindsay, ON K9V 2Z3
705-324-5031
Fax: 705-328-3121
lindsay@collinsbarrow.com

*London:*Collins Barrow Chartered Accountants - London
PO Box 5005
#700, 495 Richmond St.
London, ON N6A 5G4
519-679-8550
Fax: 519-679-1812
london@collinsbarrow.com

*London:*Davis Martindale LLP
373 Commissioners Rd. West
London, ON N6J 1Y4
519-673-3141
Fax: 519-645-1646
info@davismartindale.com
www.davismartindale.com

London: GiannoulisTurnerMoore LLP
266 Oxford St. East
London, ON N6A 1V1
519-439-4440
Fax: 519-439-3888
jgiannoulis@turnermoore.com
www.turnermoore.com

*London:*MacNeill Edmundson
82 Wellington St.
London, ON N6B 2K3
519-660-6060
Fax: 519-672-6416
info@meb.on.ca
www.meb.on.ca

London: Michael A. King, Chartered Accountant
#502, 383 Richmond St.
London, ON N6A 3C4
519-679-8391
Fax: 519-679-1446
mike@michaelkingca.ca
www.michaelkingca.ca

*London:*Neal, Pallett & Townsend LLP Chartered Accountants
#300, 633 Colborne St.
London, ON N6B 2V3
519-432-5534
Fax: 519-432-6544
www.nptca.com

*London:*PricewaterhouseCoopers LLP, Canada - London
#300, 465 Richmond St.
London, ON N6A 5P4
519-640-8000
Fax: 519-640-8015
www.pwc.com/ca

*London:*SummersTurnerMoore LLP
857 Consortium Ct.
London, ON N6E 2S8
519-686-4114
Fax: 519-686-4884
csummers@turnermoore.com
www.turnermoore.com

*Manotick:*Collins Barrow Chartered Accountants - Manotick
PO Box 291
1136 Clapp Lane
Manotick, ON K4M 1A3
613-692-2553
Fax: 613-692-2995
manotick@collinsbarrow.com
www.collinsbarrowottawa.com

*Manotick:*Newton & Co.
PO Box 978
5494 Manotick Main St.
Manotick, ON K4M 1A8
613-236-2939
Fax: 613-692-2874
www.newtonco.com

Markham: Kestenberg, Rabinowicz & Partners
2797 John St.
Markham, ON L3R 2Y8
905-946-1300
Fax: 905-946-9797
rrabinowicz@krp.ca
www.krp.ca

Markham: Sheldon & Brates Tax Consultants Ltd.
#220, 60 Renfrew Dr.
Markham, ON L3R 0E1
905-475-5400
Fax: 905-475-4246
sheldonbrates.com

*Milton:*Mercer & Mercer
245 Commercial St.
Milton, ON L9T 2J3
905-876-1144
Fax: 905-876-4209
mail@mercerandmercer.com
www.mercerandmercer.com

*Mississauga:*Bimal Shah
#14, 5484 Tomken Rd.
Mississauga, ON L4W 2Z6
905-629-2653
Fax: 905-629-8701
info@shah-cga.com
www.shah-cga.com

*Mississauga:*Bolton & Dignan, Chartered Accountants
6509 Mississauga Rd., Unit D
Mississauga, ON L5N 1A6
905-858-5006

*Mississauga:*Clarkson Rouble LLP
5190 Shuttle Dr.
Mississauga, ON L4W 4J8
905-629-4047
Fax: 905-629-3070
office@crllp.ca
clarksonrouble.on.ca/

*Mississauga:*Clewes & Associates Life Insurance Consultancy Inc.
#803, 251 Queen St. South
Mississauga, ON L5M 1L7
416-493-5586
Fax: 416-493-5061
clewesb@sympatico.ca
www.clewesconsult.com

Mississauga: D'AnnaTurnerMoore LLP
#3A, 3045 Southcreek Rd.
Mississauga, ON L4X 2X6
416-410-4118
Fax: 416-352-7600
info@DannaTurnerMoore.com
www.dannaturnermoore.com

*Mississauga:*H&A Forensic Accounting
#400, 2680 Matheson Blvd. East
Mississauga, ON L4W 0A5
416-233-5577
Fax: 416-233-5578
www.haforensics.com

*Mississauga:*Kutum & Associates
#A1, 5659 McAdam Rd.
Mississauga, ON L4Z 1N9
905-276-1154
Fax: 905-276-2003
info@kutum.com
www.kutum.com

*Mississauga:*Laurel L. Stultz
#211, 1425 Dundas St. East
Mississauga, ON L4X 2W4
905-602-0001
Other Contact Information: Cell: 416-996-3919
info@certifiedgeneralaccountant.ca
www.certifiedgeneralaccountant.ca

*Mississauga:*Lemoine Hyland Group LLP
#207, 2085 Hurontario St.
Mississauga, ON L5A 4G1
905-275-7794
Fax: 905-275-5677
877-544-7687
rlemoine@lhgroup.com
lhgroup.com

*Mississauga:*MDP Chartered Accountants (MDP LLP)
#200, 4230 Sherwoodtowne Blvd.
Mississauga, ON L4Z 2G6
905-279-7500
Fax: 905-279-9300
mdp@mdp.on.ca
www.mdp.on.ca

*Mississauga:*PricewaterhouseCoopers LLP, Canada - Mississauga
Mississauga Executive Centre
#1100, 1 Robert Speck Pkwy.
Mississauga, ON L4Z 3M3
905-949-7400
Fax: 905-949-7415
www.pwc.com/ca

*Mississauga:*Sidler & Company LLP
#204/205, 6465 Millcreek Dr.
Mississauga, ON L5N 5R3
905-821-9215
Fax: 905-821-8212
info@sidler.ca
www.sidler.ca

*Montréal:*PricewaterhouseCoopers LLP, Canada - Montréal
1250, boul René-Lévesque ouest
Montréal, ON H3B 2G4
514-205-5000
Fax: 514-938-5709
www.pwc.com/ca

*Nepean:*Jack R. Bowerman, CA - Professional Corporation
#10, 28 Concourse Gate
Nepean, ON K2E 7T7
613-723-8202
Fax: 613-723-1216
800-282-1879
info@jrbowerman.com
www.jrbowerman.com

*Niagara Falls:*Durward Jones Barkwell & Company, Niagara Falls
PO Box 873
#1, 6100 Thorold Stone Rd.
Niagara Falls, ON L2E 6V6
905-357-5711
Fax: 905-357-7932
866-223-8459
nfalls@djb.com
www.djb.com

Niagara Falls: WhiteHillTurnerMoore LLP
#10, 3483 Portage Rd.
Niagara Falls, ON L2J 2K5
905-358-1652
Fax: 905-358-8759
dwhite@turnermoore.com; jhill@turnermoore.com
www.turnermoore.com

*North Bay:*Collins Barrow Chartered Accountants - North Bay
630 Cassells St.
North Bay, ON P1B 4A2
705-494-9336
Fax: 705-494-8783
northbay@collinsbarrow.com
www.collinsbarrowsudburynipissing.com

*Orangeville:*Collins Barrow Chartered Accountants - Orangeville
Mono Plaza
RR#4, 633419 Hwy. 10
Orangeville, ON L9W 2Z1
519-941-5526
Fax: 519-941-8721
orangeville@collinsbarrow.com

*Orleans:*Andrews & Company, Chartered Accountants
540 Lacolle Way
Orleans, ON K4A 0N9
613-837-8282
Fax: 613-837-7482
website@andrews.ca
www.andrews.ca; www.porterhetu.com

*Orleans:*EthierTurnerMoore LLP
352 Timbertrain Terrace
Orleans, ON K4A 5A6
613-837-7829
Fax: 613-834-4741
methier@turnermoore.com
www.turnermoore.com

***Orleans:*Pyndus & Associates Ltd.**
1813 Woodhaven Heights
Orleans, ON K1E 2W3
613-834-5054
Fax: 613-837-1591
pyndus.associates@sympatico.ca
www3.sympatico.ca/cpyndus/

***Ottawa:*Charles Ghadban Accounting**
544 Bronson Ave.
Ottawa, ON K1R 6J9
613-234-7856
info@ghadbanaccounting.com
www.ghadbanaccounting.com

***Ottawa:*Collins Barrow Chartered Accountants - Ottawa**
#400, 301 Moodie Dr.
Ottawa, ON K2H 9C4
613-820-8010
Fax: 613-820-0465
ottawa@collinsbarrow.com
www.collinsbarrowottawa.com

***Ottawa:*David Ingram & Associates**
329 Waverly St.
Ottawa, ON K2P 0V9
613-234-8023
Fax: 613-234-8925
info@accessfp.com

***Ottawa:* Gary G. Timmons, Chartered Accountant**
#105, 2442 St. Joseph Blvd.
Ottawa, ON K1C 1G1
613-830-0200
Fax: 613-830-8824
gtimmons@gtimmons.com
www.gtimmons.com

***Ottawa:* Ginsberg Gluzman Fage & Levitz, LLP**
287 Richmond Rd.
Ottawa, ON K1Z 6X4
613-728-5831
Fax: 613-728-8085
info@ggfl.ca
www.ggfl.ca

***Ottawa:* Hartel Financial Management Corporation**
540 Lacolle Way
Ottawa, ON K4A 0N9
613-837-8282
Fax: 613-837-7482
jleblanc@hartel.ca; brighten@hartel.ca
www.hartel.ca; www.porterhetu.com

***Ottawa:*Logan Katz LLP**
#105, 6 Gurdwara Rd.
Ottawa, ON K2E 8A3
613-228-8282
Fax: 613-228-8284
office@logankatz.com
www.logankatz.com

***Ottawa:*McLarty & Co.**
#110, 495 Richmond Rd.
Ottawa, ON K2A 4B2
613-726-1010
Fax: 613-726-9009
www.mclartyco.ca

***Ottawa:*Newton & Co.**
#1205, 150 Isabella St.
Ottawa, ON K1S 1V7
613-236-2939
Fax: 613-236-1220
nco@newtonco.com
www.newtonco.com

***Ottawa:*Newton & Co., Ottawa**
#1205, 150 Isabella St.
Ottawa, ON K1S 1V7
613-236-2939
Fax: 613-236-1220
www.newtonco.com

***Ottawa:*PricewaterhouseCoopers LLP, Canada - Ottawa**
#800, 99 Bank St.
Ottawa, ON K1P 1E4
613-237-3702
Fax: 613-237-3963
www.pwc.com/ca

***Ottawa:*Robertson Sharpe & Associates**
#2, 200 Colonnade Rd.
Ottawa, ON K2E 7M1
613-727-3845
Fax: 613-727-7075
info@robertson-sharpe.com
www.robertson-sharpe.com

***Ottawa:*Rosalind Schlessinger Certified General Accountant**
332 Gilmour St.
Ottawa, ON K2P 0R3
613-235-1807
Fax: 613-235-2253

***Ottawa:*Scott Rankin & Gardiner Chartered Accountants**
#207, 2650 Queensview Dr.
Ottawa, ON K2B 8H6
613-596-2767
Fax: 613-596-2775

***Ottawa:*Surgeson Carson Associates Inc.**
#8, 99 Fifth Ave.
Ottawa, ON K1S 5K4
613-567-6434
Fax: 613-567-0752
questions@surgesoncarson.com
www.surgesoncarson.com

***Ottawa:*Swindells & Company**
#101, 1700 Woodward Dr.
Ottawa, ON K2C 3R8
613-230-1010
Fax: 613-230-1957
www.swindellsandwheatley.com

***Ottawa:*Thomas R. West CGA Professional Corporation**
21 Perrin Ave.
Ottawa, ON K2J 2Y1
613-825-8871
Fax: 613-825-4089
Tom@Thomasrwestcga.com
www.thomasrwestcga.com

***Owen Sound:*Gaviller & Company LLP**
PO Box 460
#201, 945 - 3rd Ave. East
Owen Sound, ON N4K 5P7
519-376-5850
Fax: 519-376-5532
800-567-7234
www.gaviller.com

***Penetanguishene:*Alan Martin Associates - Penetanguishene**
75 Main St.
Penetanguishene, ON L9M 1S8
705-549-3146
Fax: 705-549-5736

***Peterborough:*Collins Barrow Chartered Accountants - Peterborough**
418 Sheridan St.
Peterborough, ON K9H 3J9
705-742-3418
Fax: 705-742-9775
peterborough@collinsbarrow.com

***Peterborough:*Jon S. Thornton, Chartered Accountant**
PO Box 2402
294 Rink St.
Peterborough, ON K9J 7Y8
705-742-2308
Fax: 705-748-4824
jon@thorntonca.com
www.thorntonca.com

***Peterborough:* WrightlyTurnerMoore LLP**
#203, 311 George St. North
Peterborough, ON K9J 3H3
705-745-8643
Fax: 705-745-6358
robin@rewcga.com
www.rewcga.com

***Richmond Hill:*MDS LLP**
#4, 30 Wertheim Ct.
Richmond Hill, ON L4B 1B9
905-881-2244
Fax: 905-881-8006
reception@mdsllp.com
www.mdsllp.com

***Richmond Hill:*Truster Zweig LLP**
#200, 66 West Beaver Creek Rd.
Richmond Hill, ON L4B 1G5
416-222-5555
Fax: 905-707-1322
tzcas@trusterzweig.com
www.trusterzweig.ca

***Richmond Hill:*Willington Martin Professional Corporation**
#510. 100 York Blvd.
Richmond Hill, ON L4B 1J8
905-770-3532
Fax: 905-770-4128
jwillington@porterhetu.com; tmartin@porterhetu.com
www.porterhetu.com; www.inbalance.org

***Ridgetown:*UreTurnerMoore LLP**
23 Cecil St.
Ridgetown, ON N0P 2C0
519-674-5551
Fax: 519-674-0983
aure@turnermoore.com

***Sarnia:*Collins Barrow Chartered Accountants - Sarnia**
1350 L'Heritage Dr.
Sarnia, ON N7S 6H8
519-542-7725
Fax: 519-542-8321
sarnia@collinsbarrow.com

***Sarnia:*Hazlitt Steeves Harris LLP**
301 Front St. North
Sarnia, ON N7T 5S6
519-336-6133
Fax: 519-336-9995
www.hshca.com

***Sarnia:*TurnerMoore Group (TMG)**
PO Box 212
866 Confederation St.
Sarnia, ON N7T 7H9
519-344-1271
Fax: 519-344-1268
bmoore@turnermoore.com
www.turnermoore.com

***St Catharines:*Durward Jones Barkwell & Company, St. Catharines**
PO Box 505
69 Ontario St.
St Catharines, ON L2R 6V9
905-684-9221
Fax: 905-684-0566
866-219-9431
stcath@djb.com
www.djb.com

***St Catharines:*Finucci Watters LLP**
58 St. Paul St. West
St Catharines, ON L2S 2C5
905-682-2406
Fax: 905-682-1466
rwatters@porterhetu.com; afinucci@porterhetu.com
www.porterhetu.com

***St Catharines:* O'BrienTurnerMoore LLP**
266 Welland Ave.
St Catharines, ON L2R 2P8
905-682-8299
Fax: 905-687-9741
877-682-8299
tobrien@turnermoore.com
www.turnermoore.com

***St Thomas:*Kee, Perry & Lassam**
15 Barrie Blvd.
St Thomas, ON N5P 4B9
519-631-6360
Fax: 519-631-2198
info@kpl-accountants.ca
www.kpl-accountants.ca

***Stoney Creek:*Durward Jones Barkwell & Company, Stoney Creek**
PO Box 56062
#7C, 45 Goderich Rd.
Stoney Creek, ON L8G 5C9
905-561-2992
Fax: 905-561-7152
866-897-2965
screek@djb.com
www.djb.com

***Stouffville:*Joe Nemni Financial Services**
33 Katherine Cres.
Stouffville, ON L4A 1K4
905-640-0065
jnemni@sympatico.ca
www.joenemni.com

***Stratford:*Collins Barrow Chartered Accountants - Stratford**
413 Hibernia St.
Stratford, ON N5A 5W2
519-272-0000
Fax: 519-272-0030
stratford@collinsbarrow.com

***Sturgeon Falls:*Collins Barrow Chartered Accountants - Sturgeon Falls**
#7, 12006 Hwy. 17 East
Sturgeon Falls, ON P2B 3K8
705-753-1830
Fax: 705-753-2496
sturgeonfalls@collinsbarrow.com
www.collinsbarrowsudburynipissing.com

***Sudbury:*Collins Barrow Chartered Accountants - Sudbury**
1174 St. Jerome St.
Sudbury, ON P3A 2V9
705-560-5592
Fax: 705-560-8832
sudbury@collinsbarrow.com
www.collinsbarrowsudburynipissing.com

***Thornhill:*Brockman & Partners Forensic Accountants Inc.**
10 Maxwell Ct.
Thornhill, ON L4J 6Y3
905-764-3851
Fax: 905-764-3537
jay.brockman@brockmanandpartners.ca
www.brockmanandpartners.ca

***Thornhill:*Harendorf, Lebane, Moss LLP**
#200, 8500 Leslie St.
Thornhill, ON L3T 7M8
905-886-8812
Fax: 905-886-6034
888-337-9222
hsm@hsmllpcas.com
www.hsmca.ca

***Thornhill:* Herb Kokotow, Chartered Accountant**
3 German Mills Rd.
Thornhill, ON L3T 4H4
905-764-6175
kokotow6175@rogers.com
www.charteredaccountantontario.ca

***Thornhill:*Ralph Lando Orvitz**
#300, 8500 Leslie St.
Thornhill, ON L3T 7M8
905-889-1549
Fax: 905-889-2054
Ralph@ralphlandoorvitz.ca
www.ralphlandoorvitz.ca

***Thunder Bay:*Fukushima Enstrom LLP**
577 Eleventh Ave.
Thunder Bay, ON P7B 2R5
807-345-1393
Fax: 807-345-4630
mail@fe-llp.com

***Toronto:*Albert L. Stal**
#301, 1370 Don Mills Rd.
Toronto, ON M3B 3N7
416-449-0130
Fax: 416-444-7363
albertstal@bondexec.com

***Toronto:*Bass & Murphy Chartered Accountants LLP**
885 Progress Ave., #LPH1
Toronto, ON M1H 3G3
416-431-3030
Fax: 416-431-3340
tom@bassmurphy.com
www.bassmurphy.com

***Toronto:*Beallor & Partners LLP**
28 Overlea Blvd.
Toronto, ON M4H 1B6
416-423-0707
Fax: 416-423-7000
service@beallor.com
www.beallor.com

***Toronto:*Bennett Gold LLP, Chartered Accountants**
#900, 150 Ferrand Dr.
Toronto, ON M3C 3E5
416-449-2249
Fax: 416-449-4133
rygold@bennettgold.ca
www.bennettgold.ca

***Toronto:*Brief Rotfarb Wynberg Cappe**
#402, 3854 Bathurst St.
Toronto, ON M3H 3N2
416-635-9080
Fax: 416-635-0462
lcappe@brwc.com
www.brwc.com

***Toronto:* Cadesky & Associates LLP - King St.**
Toronto-Dominion Centre, Royal Trust Tower
PO Box 93
#2401, 77 King St. West
Toronto, ON M5K 1G8
416-594-9500
Fax: 416-594-9501
taxpros@cadesky.com
www.cadesky.com

***Toronto:*Cadesky & Associates LLP - Sheppard Ave. East**
Atria III
#1001, 2225 Sheppard Ave. East
Toronto, ON M2J 5C2
416-498-9500
Fax: 416-498-9501
taxpros@cadesky.com
www.cadesky.com

***Toronto:* Canham Rogers Chartered Accountants**
#500, 2 Lansing Sq.
Toronto, ON M2J 4P8
416-494-8000
Fax: 416-494-8032
Info@CanhamRogers.com
www.canhamrogers.com

***Toronto:* Chaplin & Co. Chartered Accountants**
#710, 1110 Finch Ave. West
Toronto, ON M3J 2T2
416-667-7060
Fax: 416-663-3746
ca@chaplinco.com
www.chaplinco.com

***Toronto:* ChiShenTurnerMoore LLP**
#408, 515 Consumers Rd.
Toronto, ON M2J 4Z2
416-410-0400
Fax: 416-756-0388
jchi@turnermoore.com; hshen@turnermoore.com
www.turnermoore.com

***Toronto:*Cholkan & Stepczuk LLP**
#300, 1 Eva Rd.
Toronto, ON M9C 4Z5
416-695-9500
Fax: 416-695-3837
800-3639500
info@c-s.ca
www.cholkan.com

***Toronto:*Cole & Partners**
#2000, 80 Richmond St. West
Toronto, ON M5H 2A4
416-364-9700
Fax: 416-364-9707
www.coleandpartners.com

***Toronto:*Collins Barrow Toronto LLP**
#1900, 390 Bay St.
Toronto, ON M5H 2Y2
416-361-1622
Fax: 416-480-2646
www.collinsbarrowtoronto.com

***Toronto:*Cooper & Company Ltd.**
#108, 1120 Finch Ave. West
Toronto, ON M3J 3H7
416-665-3383
Fax: 416-665-0897
info@cooperco.ca
www.cooperco.ca

***Toronto:*Cunningham LLP**
#810, 2001 Sheppard Ave. East
Toronto, ON M2J 4Z8
416-496-1051
Fax: 416-496-1546
800-461-4618
info@cunninghamca.com
www.cunninghamca.com

***Toronto:*Duffy, Allain & Rutten LLP**
908 The East Mall
Toronto, ON M9B 6K2
416-620-7740

***Toronto:*Emondson Ball Davies LLP, Chartered Accountants**
#501, 10 Milner Business Ct.
Toronto, ON M1B 3C6
416-293-5560
Fax: 416-293-5377
www.ebdcas.com

***Toronto:*Finucci Watters LLP (Toronto)**
#802, 390 Bay St.
Toronto, ON M5H 2Y2
647-259-1766
Fax: 647-259-1776
afinucci@porterhetu.com
www.porterhetu.com

***Toronto:*Galloway Consulting Group Inc.**
#703, 1200 Eglinton Ave. East
Toronto, ON M3C 1H9
416-803-5638
Fax: 416-449-7342
info@gallowayconsulting.ca
www.gallowayconsulting.ca

***Toronto:*Gardner Zuk Dessen, Chartered Accountants**
#205, 265 Rimrock Rd.
Toronto, ON M3J 3C6
416-631-9800
Fax: 416-631-9183
info@gzd.ca
www.gzd.ca

***Toronto:*Hilborn Ellis Grant LLP**
PO Box 49
#3100, 401 Bay St.
Toronto, ON M5H 2Y4
416-364-1359
Fax: 416-364-9503
www.heg.ca

***Toronto:*Kelly Porter Hétu**
475 Queen St. East
Toronto, ON M5A 1T9
416-955-0060
Fax: 416-955-0061
jkelly@porterhetu.com
www.porterhetu.com

***Toronto:*Kenneth Michalak**
1576 Bloor St. West
Toronto, ON M6P 1A4
416-588-2808
Fax: 416-588-3634
866-258-4788
info@kjmcga.coma
www.kjmcga.com

***Toronto:*Klingbaum Barkin LLP**
The Madison Centre
#1906, 4950 Yonge St.
Toronto, ON M2N 6K1
416-512-1221
Fax: 416-512-1284
mk@klingbaumbarkin.com
www.klingbaumbarkin.com

***Toronto:*Koster, Spinks & Koster LLP (KSK)**
4 Glengrove Ave. West
Toronto, ON M4R 1N4
416-489-8100
Fax: 416-489-9194
info@ksk.ca
www.ksk.ca

***Toronto:*Kwan Chan Law Chartered Accountants Professional Corporation**
#910, 4950 Yonge St.
Toronto, ON M2N 6K1
416-226-6862

***Toronto:*M. Schwab Accounting Services Ltd.**
#606, 94 Cumberland St.
Toronto, ON M5R 1A3

416-324-9933
Fax: 416-324-8733

Toronto: **McGovern, Hurley, Cunningham LLP**
#300, 2005 Sheppard Ave. East
Toronto, ON M2J 5B4

416-496-1234
Fax: 416-496-0125
info@mhc-ca.com
www.mhc-ca.com

Toronto: **Mehl & Reynolds LLP**
#200, 1 Yorkdale Rd.
Toronto, ON M6A 3A1

416-787-0681
Fax: 416-787-7630
webhome.idirect.com/~gmr

Toronto: **Michael Argue, Chartered Accountant, Professional Corporation**
#206, 1210 Sheppard Ave. East
Toronto, ON M2K 1E3

416-490-8544
Fax: 416-490-8096
michaelargue@bellnet.ca
www.argueca.com

Toronto: **Michael I. Atlas, Chartered Accountant**
#2500, 120 Adelaide St. West
Toronto, ON M5H 1T1

416-860-9175
Fax: 416-860-9189
matlas@taxca.com
www.taxca.com

Toronto: **Mintz & Partners LLP**
#200, 1 Concorde Gate
Toronto, ON M3C 4G4

416-391-2900
Fax: 416-391-2748
info@mintzca.com
www.mintzca.com

Toronto: **Nevcon Accounting Services**
PO Box 43541
1531 Bayview Ave.
Toronto, ON M4G 4G8

416-487-7996
Fax: 416-946-1098
888-463-8366
info@nevcon.com
www.nevcon.com

Toronto: **PKF Hill LLP**
#200, 41 Valleybrook Dr.
Toronto, ON M3B 2S6

416-449-9171
Fax: 416-449-7401
info@pkfhill.com
www.pkfhill.com

Toronto: **PricewaterhouseCoopers LLP, Canada**
Royal Trust Tower, Toronto-Dominion Centre
PO Box 82
Toronto, ON M5K 1G8

416-863-1133
Fax: 416-365-8178
www.pwc.com/ca

Toronto: **PricewaterhouseCoopers LLP, Canada - Toronto - King St. West**
145 King St. West
Toronto, ON M5H 1V8

416-869-1130
Fax: 416-863-0926
www.pwc.com/ca

Toronto: **PricewaterhouseCoopers LLP, Canada - Toronto - Yonge St.**
North American Life Bldg.
#1900, 5700 Yonge St.
Toronto, ON M2M 4K7

416-218-1500
Fax: 416-218-1499
www.pwc.com/ca

Toronto: **Renée S. Karn, CGA**
86 Acton Ave.
Toronto, ON M3H 4H1

416-499-0012
Fax: 416-499-0194
rkarn@porterhetu.com
www.porterhetu.com

Toronto: **Rich Rotstein LLP**
South Tower
#303, 175 Bloor St. East
Toronto, ON M4W 3R8

416-863-1400
Fax: 416-863-4881
lsr@richrotstein.com; lwr@richrotstein.com
www.richrotstein.com

Toronto: **Rosen & Associates Limited**
PO Box 101
#2200, 121 King St. West
Toronto, ON M5H 3T9

416-363-4515
Fax: 416-363-4849
l.gallant@rosen-associates.com
www.rosen-associates.com

Toronto: **Rosenberg Smith & Partners LLP**
#200, 2000 Steeles Ave. West
Toronto, ON L4K 3E9

416-798-4997
Fax: 905-660-3064
rsp@rsp.ca
www.rsp.ca

Toronto: **Rosenthal Consulting Group**
13 Balmoral Ave.
Toronto, ON M4V 1J5

416-617-9966
Fax: 416-964-2371
hsrosenthal@alumni.uwaterloo.ca

Toronto: **Rumanek & Company Ltd.**
#714, 1280 Finch Ave. West
Toronto, ON M3J 3K6

416-665-8326
Fax: 416-665-7634
info@trustee-in-bankruptcy.com
www.rumanek.com; www.trustee-in-bankruptcy.com

Toronto: **SBLR LLP Chartered Accountants**
#300, 2345 Yonge St.
Toronto, ON M4P 2E5

416-488-2345
Fax: 416-488-3765
www.sblr.ca

Toronto: **Segal & Partners Inc.**
#500, 2005 Sheppard Ave. East
Toronto, ON M2J 5B4

416-391-1460
Fax: 416-391-2285
800-206-7307
info@segalpartners.com
www.segalbankruptcy.com

Toronto: **Serbinski Partners PC**
183 Sheppard Ave. West
Toronto, ON M2N 1M9

416-733-0300
Fax: 416-352-6004
888-878-2937
mtscpa@serbinski.com
www.serbinski.com

Toronto: **SF Partnership, LLP**
The Madison Centre
#400, 4950 Yonge St.
Toronto, ON M2N 6K1

416-250-1212
Fax: 416-250-1225
general@sfgroup.ca
www.sfgroup.ca

Toronto: **Sloan Partners LLP**
#6, 4646 Dufferin St.
Toronto, ON M3H 5S4

416-665-7735
Fax: 416-649-7725
info@sloangroup.ca
www.sloangroup.ca

Toronto: **Soberman LLP Chartered Accountants**
#1100, 2 St. Clair Ave. East
Toronto, ON M4T 2T5

416-964-7633
Fax: 416-964-6454
info@soberman.com
www.soberman.com

Toronto: **Sone & Rovet**
#406, 1200 Sheppard Ave. East
Toronto, ON M2K 2S5

416-498-7200
Fax: 416-498-6877
www.sonerovet.com

Toronto: **Spergel Inc.**
#200, 505 Consumers Rd.
Toronto, ON M2J 4V8

416-497-1660
Fax: 416-494-7199
800-563-8251
aspergel@trustee.com
www.trustee.com

Toronto: **Stewart & Kett Financial Advisors Inc.**
#911, 123 Front St. West
Toronto, ON M5J 2M2

416-362-6322
Fax: 416-362-6302
www.stewartkett.com

Toronto: **The Clarke Henning Group**
#801, 10 Bay St.
Toronto, ON M5J 2R8

416-364-4421
Fax: 416-367-8032
888-422-1241
ch@clarkehenning.com
www.clarkehenning.com

Toronto: **Tomlin Associates**
#445, 700 Lawrence Ave. West
Toronto, ON M6A 3B4

416-488-6969
Fax: 416-783-9117
Other Contact Information: Cell: 416-302-8169
larry.tomlin@gmail.com
www.tomlin.ca

Toronto: **V.B. Sharma Professional Corporation, Chartered Accountants**
#200, 3390 Midland Ave.
Toronto, ON M1V 5K3

416-292-4431
Fax: 416-292-7247
vbsharma@vbsharma.ca
www.vbsharma.ca

Toronto: **Zeifman & Company**
201 Bridgeland Ave.
Toronto, ON M6A 1Y7

416-256-4000
Fax: 416-256-4001
info@zeifman.ca
www.zeifman.ca

Toronto: **Zwaig Consulting Inc.**
#801, 20 Adelaide St. East
Toronto, ON M5X 2T6

416-863-0140
Fax: 416-863-0428
zwaigm@zwaig.com
www.zwaig.com

Trenton: **Wilkinson & Company LLP**
PO Box 400
71 Dundas St. West
Trenton, ON K8V 5R6

613-392-2592
Fax: 613-392-8512
888-713-7283
trenton@wilkinson.net
www.wilkinson.net

Vaughan: **Collins Barrow Chartered Accountants - Vaughan**
#600, 3300 Hwy. 7 West
Vaughan, ON L4K 4M3

416-213-2600
Fax: 905-669-8705
info@collinsbarrowvaughan.com

Vaughan: **Domenic Galati CGA**
#510, 3100 Steeles Ave. West
Vaughan, ON L4K 3R1

416-745-0245
dgalati@porterhetu.com
www.porterhetu.com

Vaughan: **PellegrinoTurnerMoore LLP**
#35, 100 Bass Pro Mills Dr.
Vaughan, ON L4K 5X1

905-761-8080
Fax: 905-761-8190
robert@pellegrinogroup.ca
www.pellegrinogroup.ca

***Wallaceburg:*TurnerMoore LLP**
233 Nelson St.
Wallaceburg, ON N8A 4G5
519-627-9971
Fax: 519-627-0400
peturner@turnermoore.com
www.turnermoore.com

***Waterloo:*Collins Barrow Chartered Accountants - Waterloo**
554 Weber St. North
Waterloo, ON N2L 5C6
519-725-7700
Fax: 519-725-7708
cbwaterloo@collinsbarrow.com

***Waterloo:*Collins Barrow Chartered Accountants - Waterloo National Office**
554 Weber St. North
Waterloo, ON N2L 5C6
519-725-7700
Fax: 519-725-7708
cbwaterloo@collinsbarrow.com
www.collinsbarrows.com

***Waterloo:*PricewaterhouseCoopers LLP, Canada - Waterloo**
#201, 95 King St. South
Waterloo, ON N2J 5A2
519-570-5700
Fax: 519-570-5730
www.pwc.com/ca

***Waterloo:* Transport Financial Services Ltd.**
105 Bauer Pl.
Waterloo, ON N2L 6B5
519-886-8070
Fax: 519-886-5214
800-461-5970
www.tfsgroup.com/tfs

***Welland:*Durward Jones Barkwell & Company, Welland**
PO Box 9
171 Division St.
Welland, ON L3B 5N9
905-735-2140
Fax: 905-735-4706
866-552-0997
welland@djb.com
www.djb.com

***Welland:*Lifestyle Financial Planning & Management Services Ltd.**
190 Division St.
Welland, ON L3B 4A2
905-732-1640
Fax: 905-732-1397
stalosi@lifestylefinancial.com
www.lifestylefinancial.com

***Windsor:* BellemoreTurnerMoore LLP**
#6, 242 Lauzon Rd.
Windsor, ON N8S 3L6
519-944-4777
Fax: 519-944-4011
dbellemore@turnermoore.com
www.turnermoore.com

***Windsor:*BoggsTurnerMoore LLP**
711 Kennedy Dr. West
Windsor, ON N9G 1S8
519-972-3030
Fax: 519-972-4904
gboggs@turnermoore.com
www.turnermoore.com

***Windsor:*Collins Barrow Windsor LLP**
3260 Devon Dr.
Windsor, ON N8X 4L4
519-258-5800
Fax: 519-256-6152
windsor@collinsbarrow.com
www.collinsbarrow.com

***Windsor:*Hyatt Lassaline LLP**
#203, 2510 Ouellette Ave.
Windsor, ON N8X 1L4
519-966-4626
Fax: 519-966-9206
www.hyattlassaline.com

***Windsor:*PricewaterhouseCoopers LLP, Canada - Windsor**
245 Ouellette Ave., 3rd Fl.
Windsor, ON N9A 7J4
519-985-8900
Fax: 519-258-5457
www.pwc.com/ca

***Windsor:*Roth Mosey & Partners LLP**
#300, 3100 Temple Dr.
Windsor, ON N8W 5J6
519-977-6410
Fax: 519-977-7083
info@roth-mosey.com
www.roth-mosey.com

***Woodbridge:* NandanCharkoTurnerMoore LLP**
#9, 70 Silton Rd.
Woodbridge, ON L4L 8B9
905-265-8400
rnandan@turnermoore.com
www.turnermoore.com

***Woodbridge:*Rashid & Quinney Chartered Accountants**
#401, 216 Chrislea Rd.
Woodbridge, ON L4L 8S5
905-856-2677
Fax: 905-856-2679
rick@randg.ca

***Woodstock:*Thornton VanTassel Chartered Accountants - Woodstock**
318 Connell St.
Woodstock, ON E7M 6B7
506-324-8040
Fax: 506-325-2262
stephen.thornton@thorntonvantassel.com
www.thorntonvantassel.com

Prince Edward Island

***Charlottetown:*Beaton Fitzpatrick Murray**
PO Box 2158
#200, 155 Belevedere Ave.
Charlottetown, PE C1A 8B9
902-892-5365
Fax: 902-892-0383
bfm@bfm.pe.ca
www.bfm.pe.ca

***Summerside:*Peter M. Baglole, Chartered Accountant**
PO Box 1373
#7, 293 Water St.
Summerside, PE C1N 4K2
902-436-1663
Fax: 902-436-1604
peter@baglole.ca
www.baglole.ca

***Summerside:* Schurman Sudsbury & Associates Ltd.**
189 Water St.
Summerside, PE C1N 1B2
902-436-2171
Fax: 902-436-0960
schurman-sudsbury@isn.net

Quebec

***Anjou:* Brunet, Roy, Dubé, Comptables agrées**
#1200, 7100 rue Jean-Talon
Anjou, QC H1M 3S3
514-255-1001

***Blainville:* Lévesque CA, Comptables agréés**
#204, 10, boul de la Seigneurie Est
Blainville, QC J7C 3V5
450-437-8969
Fax: 450-437-8996
infos@levesqueca.com
www.levesqueca.com

***Drummondville:*Samson Bélair/Deloitte & Touche s.e.n.c.r.l.**
212, rue Heriot
Drummondville, QC J2C 1J8
819-477-6311
Fax: 819-477-9572
www.deloitte.com

***Joliette:* Martin, Boulard & Associés, sencrl**
#200, 37, Place Bourget sud
Joliette, QC J6E 5G1
450-759-2825
Fax: 450-752-1235
jvarin@mba.qc.ca

***Lacine:*Martin & Cie**
1100, rue Notre-Dame
Lacine, QC H8S 2C4
514-637-7887
Fax: 514-637-3566
l.martin@martin-cie.com
www.martin-cie.com

***Longueuil:*Dubé & Tétreault, Comptables agréés, S.E.N.C.**
#200, 3065, chemin de Chambly
Longueuil, QC J4L 1N3
450-442-0944
Fax: 450-442-2166
richard@dube-tetreault.com
www.dube-tetreault.com

***Montréal:*A. Bertucci, Chartered Accountant**
1445, rue Lambert Closse
Montréal, QC H3H 1Z5
514-932-3229
Fax: 514-932-4634
abertucci@abertucci.com
www.abertucci.com

***Montréal:*Accountatax Inc.**
147 Spring Garden Rd.
Montréal, QC H9B 2T7
514-685-7394
Fax: 514-685-7411
877-685-7394
www.accountatax.ca

***Montréal:*Aubry, Hijazi, CA - s.e.n.c.r.l.**
#215, 1331, ave. Green
Montréal, QC H3Z 2A5
514-935-7787
Fax: 514-935-5865

***Montréal:*Beauchemin Trépanier Comptables agréés inc.**
#1102, 4200, boul. St-Laurent
Montréal, QC H2W 2R2
514-847-0182
Fax: 514-849-9082
bt@btca.qc.ca
www.btca.qc.ca

***Montréal:*Bessner Gallay Kreisman**
#600, 340, rue Ste-Catherine Ouest
Montréal, QC H3Z 2Y5
514-908-3600
Fax: 514-908-3630
admin@bgk.com
www.bgsk.com

***Montréal:*Fine et associés/ Fine & Associates**
5101, rue Buchan
Montréal, QC H4P 1S4
514-731-0761
Fax: 514-731-4639

***Montréal:*Gestion Tellier St-Germain**
PO Box 324, P.A.T. Stn. P.A.T.
11536 Lagauchetière
Montréal, QC H1B 5J5
514-640-8922
Fax: 514-640-4801
ghislaine@gestionrg.qc.ca
www.gestionrg.qc.ca

***Montréal:*Goldsmith Hersh s.e.n.c.r.l.**
#200, 1411, rue Fort
Montréal, QC H3H 2N6
514-933-8611
Fax: 514-933-1142
info@ghmca.com
www.gmhca.com

***Montréal:*H&A eDiscovery**
#401, 360, rue Notre Dame ouest
Montréal, QC H2Y 1T9
514-844-5577
Fax: 514-844-1088
www.haediscovery.com; www.haforensics.com

***Montréal:*Info Comptabilité Plus**
#201, 2035, Côte de Liesse
Montréal, QC H4N 2M5
514-337-2677
Fax: 514-337-1594
info@infocplus.com
www.infocplus.com

***Montréal:*J. Kromida, Chartered Accountant**
750, av Sainte-Croix
Montréal, QC H4L 3Y2
514-747-3413
Fax: 514-747-0799
jamesk@kromida.com
www.kromida.com

***Montréal:* Jacques Davis Lefaivre & Associés**
#1900, 1080, côte du Beaver Hall
Montréal, QC H2Z 1S8
514-878-2600
Fax: 514-878-2600
800-363-6800
jdl@jdl.ca

***Montréal:*JDM Consultation Inc.**
#203, 759, Victoria Sq.
Montréal, QC H2Y 2J7
514-844-4536
Fax: 514-849-8647
jimmy@menegakis.ca
www.menegakis.ca

***Montréal:*Jean J. Drouin, CGA**
#201, 6455, rue Christophe-Colomb
Montréal, QC H2S 2G5
514-274-6831
Fax: 514-274-8128
info@drouin-cga.com

***Montréal:*Le Groupe Belzile Tremblay**
2675, rue Masson
Montréal, QC H1Y 1W3
514-384-3620
Fax: 514-384-3710
bt@belziletremblay.ca
www.belziletremblay.ca

***Montréal:*Leclerc Forensic Accountants - Montréal**
#2821, 1, Place Ville-Marie
Montréal, QC H3B 4R4
514-798-5874
Fax: 514-788-4837
www.leclerc-ifa.com

***Montréal:*Martel Desjardins**
Édifice de la Banque Nationale de Paris
#1440, 1981, av McGill College
Montréal, QC H3A 2Y1
514-849-2793
Fax: 514-849-7104
md@marteldesjardins.com
www.marteldesjardins.com

***Montréal:*Mazars Harel Drouin**
#1200, 215, rue Saint-Jacques
Montréal, QC H2Y 1M6
514-845-9253
Fax: 514-845-3859
www.mazars.ca

***Montréal:*MCA Consulting Group**
5240-B, rue Saint Denis
Montréal, QC H2J 2M2
514-277-8081
Fax: 514-276-9150
info@groupemca.com
www.groupemca.com

***Montréal:*Padgett Business Services**
88, boul Brunswick
Montréal, QC H9B 2C5
514-684-8086
Fax: 514-684-0884
www.padgettwestisland.com

***Montréal:* Perreault, Wolman, Grzywacz & Co.**
#814, 5250, rue Ferrier
Montréal, QC H4P 2N7
514-731-7987
Fax: 514-731-8782
www.pwgca.com

***Montréal:*Petrie Raymond Inc.**
#1000, 255, boul Crémazie est
Montréal, QC H2M 1M2
514-342-4740
Fax: 514-737-4049
info@petrieraymond.qc.ca
www.petrieraymond.qc.ca/

***Montréal:*Porter Hétu International**
5800, av. Monkland, 2ième étage
Montréal, QC H4A 1G1
514-369-7529
Fax: 514-482-0036
www.porterhetu.com

***Montréal:*PSB Boisjoli**
#400, 3333 boul Graham
Montréal, QC H3R 3L5
514-341-5511
Fax: 514-342-0589
www.psb.ca

***Montréal:*RSM Richter**
#1820, 2, Place Alexis Nihon
Montréal, QC H3Z 3C2
514-934-3400
Fax: 514-934-3408
mtlinfo@rsmrichter.com
www.richter.ca

***Montréal:*Ruby Stein Wagner S.E.N.C. Chartered Accountants**
Place du Parc
#1900, 300, rue Léo-Pariseau
Montréal, QC H2X 4B5
514-842-3911
Fax: 514-849-3447
866-842-3911
info@rswca.com
www.rswca.com

***Montréal:*Schlesinger Newman Goldman**
#1100, 625, boul René-Lévesque ouest
Montréal, QC H3B 1R2
514-866-8553
Fax: 514-866-8469
info@sng.ca
www.sng.ca

***Montréal:*Schwartz Levitsky Feldman LLP (SLF)**
1980, rue Sherbrooke ouest, 10e étage
Montréal, QC H3H 1E8
514-937-6392
Fax: 514-933-9710
www.slf.ca

***Montréal:*Stamos Porter Hétu**
800, av Ste. Croix
Montréal, QC H4L 3Y2
514-744-1100
Fax: 514-744-2200
jstamos@porterhetu.com
www.porterhetu.com

***Montréal:* Victor & Gold Chartered Accountants**
#400, 759 Victoria Sq.
Montréal, QC H2Y 2J7
514-282-1836
Fax: 514-282-6640
www.victorgold.com

***Montréal:*WAKED**
#2825, 500, Place d'Armes
Montréal, QC H2Y 2W2
514-875-6400
Fax: 514-861-6301
info@wakedcma.com
www.wakedcma.com

***Québec:*Bergeron Lavigne SENC**
1780, Damiron
Québec, QC G2E 5S8
418-877-8705
Fax: 418-877-0057
michelbergeronca@videotron.ca
www.guideformationquickbooks.com

***Québec:*Blouin, Julien, Potvin Comptables agréés, S.E.N.C.**
#300, 2795, boul Laurier
Québec, QC G1V 4M7
418-651-0405
Fax: 418-651-0285
groupe@boulinjulienpotvin.qc.ca

***Québec:* Brassard Carrier, Comptables Agréés**
#200, 1651, chemin Ste-Foy
Québec, QC G1S 2P1
418-682-2929
Fax: 418-682-0282
info@groupebca.com
www.groupebca.com

***Québec:* Cauchon Turcotte Thériault Latouche**
Place Iberville Un
#310, 1195, av Lavigerie
Québec, QC G1V 4N3
418-658-8808
Fax: 418-658-3136
equipe@cttlca.com
www.cttlca.com

***Québec:*Choquette Corriveau, Chartered Accountants**
Place Iberville I
#300, 1195, av Lavigerie
Québec, QC G1V 4N3
418-658-5555
Fax: 418-658-1010
courrier@choquettecorriveau.com
choquettecorriveau.com

***Québec:* Dallaire Forest Kirouac S.E.N.C.R.L.**
#580, 1175, av Lavigerie
Québec, QC G1V 4P1
418-650-2266
Fax: 418-650-2529
877-650-2266
comptable@dfk.qc.ca
www.dfk.qc.ca

***Québec:*Gagnon, Moisan, Comptables agréés**
#227, 945, av Newton
Québec, QC G1P 4M3
418-871-6262
Fax: 418-871-9526
www.fortune1000.ca/gagnon-moisan/

***Québec:*Gariépy, Gravel, Larouche comptables agréés S.E.N.C.**
601, av du Cénacle
Québec, QC G1E 6W4
418-666-3704
Fax: 418-666-6913
www.gglca.qc.ca

***Québec:* Laberge Lafleur Brown S.E.N.C.R.L.**
Place de la Cité
#1060, 2590, boul Laurier
Québec, QC G1V 4M6
418-659-7265
Fax: 418-659-5937
www.llbca.com

***Québec:* Leclerc Forensic Accountants - Québec**
#360, 580, Grande-Allée est
Québec, QC G1R 2K2
418-780-5874
Fax: 418-780-3191
www.leclerc-ifa.com

***Québec:*Legaré Porter Hétu**
#201, 3181 ch Ste-Foy
Québec, QC G1X 1R3
418-780-1333
Fax: 418-780-1339
miclegar@porterhetu.com
www.porterhetu.com

***Québec:* Malenfant Dallaire Comptables Agréés**
Place de la Cité
#872, 2600, boul Laurier
Québec, QC G1V 4W2
418-654-0636
Fax: 418-654-0639
maldal@malenfantdallaire.com
www.malenfantdallaire.com

***Québec:*PricewaterhouseCoopers LLP, Canada - Québec**
Place de la Cité, Tour Cominar
#1700, 2640, boul Laurier
Québec, QC G1V 5C2
418-522-7001
Fax: 418-522-5663
www.pwc.com/ca

***Québec:*Roy, Labrecque, Busque, Comptables Agréés**
#160, 5055, boul Hamel ouest
Québec, QC G2E 2G6
418-871-0013
Fax: 418-871-0162

rlb@roylabrecquebusque.com
www.roylabrecquebusque.com

***Québec:* Signature comptable Mc Nicoll CA inc.**
#210, 1220, boul Lebourgneuf
Québec, QC G2K 2G4
418-622-6666
Fax: 418-622-3904
mcnicollp@signaturecomptable.ca
www.signaturecomptable.ca

***Saint-Hubert:*Hébert, Turgeon, CGA Inc.**
7695, ch de Chambly
Saint-Hubert, QC J3Y 5K2
450-676-0624
Fax: 450-676-7677
info@htcga.qc.ca
www.htcga.qc.ca

***Saint-Rémi:* Lefaivre Labrèche Gagné, sencrl**
151, rue Perras
Saint-Rémi, QC J0L 2L0
450-454-3974
Fax: 450-454-7320
info@lefaivre-labreche.com
www.le-lab-ca.qc.ca

***Shawville:*Smith Porter Hétu**
PO Box 896
389, rue Main
Shawville, QC J0X 2Y0
819-647-2403
Fax: 819-647-3103
pbsmith@porterhetu.com
www.porterhetu.com; www.thetaxsmith.com

***St-Laurent:*Porter Hétu International (Québec) inc.**
790, boul Marcel-Laurin
St-Laurent, QC H4M 2M6
514-744-1500
Fax: 514-744-6441
mplaliberte@porterhetu.com; esauve@porterhetu.com
www.porterhetu.com

***Ste-Thérèse:*Marcil Girard Porter Hétu International**
8, rue St-Charles
Ste-Thérèse, QC J7E 2A2
450-430-7526
Fax: 450-430-6809
guylaine@porterhetu.com
www.porterhetu.com

Saskatchewan

***Esterhazy:*Skilnick Miller Moar Grodecki & Kreklewich, Chartered Accountants - Esterhazy**
Bank of Montreal Bldg.
420 Main St.
Esterhazy, SK S0A 1X0
306-745-6611
Fax: 306-745-2899
kenmoar@sasktel.net
www.skilnick.ca

***Melville:*Skilnick Miller Moar Grodecki & Kreklewich, Chartered Accountants**
PO Box 1660
#155, 3rd Ave. East
Melville, SK S0A 2P0
306-728-4525
Fax: 306-728-2599
melvilleoffice@skilnick.ca
www.skilnick.ca

***Saskatoon:*Byron J. Reynolds, Chartered Accountant**
PO Box 32029, Erindale Stn. Erindale
Saskatoon, SK S7S 1N8
306-384-1130
Fax: 306-373-6431
br@byronjreynolds.ca
www.byronjreynolds.ca

***Saskatoon:*Hergott Duval Stack LLP**
Saskatoon Square
#1200, 410 - 22nd St. East
Saskatoon, SK S7K 5T6
306-934-8000
Fax: 306-653-5859
www.hergott.com

***Saskatoon:*Hounjet Tastad Harpham**
1633A Quebec Ave.
Saskatoon, SK S7K 1V6
306-653-5100
Fax: 306-653-5141
www.hth-accountants.ca

***Saskatoon:*Lizée Gauthier Certified General Accountants**
473 - 2nd Ave. North
Saskatoon, SK S7K 2C1
306-653-4444
Fax: 306-665-5662
lizee@sasktel.net

***Saskatoon:*PricewaterhouseCoopers LLP, Canada - Saskatoon**
#200, 123 - 2nd Ave. South
Saskatoon, SK S7K 7E6
306-668-5900
Fax: 306-652-1315
www.pwc.com/ca

Domestic Banks: Schedule I

See Index for Bank of Canada, and the Federal Business Development Bank, which are Crown Corporations, listed in the Government Section. Chartered banks in Canada are incorporated by letters patent. They are governed by the Bank Act, which establishes the legislative framework for Canada's banking system. The Bank Act provides for the incorporation of banks. The Office of the Superintendent of Financial Institutions Canada regulates and supervises the Canadian financial system.

Domestic banks are federally regulated Canadian banks. The subsidiaries of foreign banks are federally regulated foreign banks. Both domestic and foreign banks have the same powers, restrictions and obligations under the Bank Act.

Foreign bank representative offices are established by foreign banks in Canada. They act as a liaison between the foreign bank and its clients in Canada. These offices generally promote the services of the foreign bank, and do not accept deposits in Canada.

Foreign bank branches are federally regulated. They are permitted to establish specialized, commercially- focused branches in Canada, in accordance with the Bank Act. Full service branches generally are not permitted to accept deposits of less than $150,000.

ATB Financial exemplifies a savings bank in Canada. In Alberta, ATB Financial operates under the authority of the Alberta Treasury Branches Act Chapter A-37.9, 1997 and Treasury Branches Regulation 187/97.

Banks are listed alphabetically under Domestic Banks, Foreign Banks, and Savings Banks.

Alterna Bank
400 Albert St., 3rd Fl.
Ottawa, ON K1R 5B2
613-560-0120
Fax: 613-560-0177
866-560-0120
questions@alterna.ca
www.alterna.ca

Former Name: CS Alterna Bank
Ownership: Wholly-owned subsidiary of Alterna Savings & Credit Union Limited.
Year Founded: 2000

The Bank of Nova Scotia (BNS)/ La Banque de Nouvelle-Écosse
Scotia Plaza
44 King St. West
Toronto, ON M5H 1H1
416-866-6161
Fax: 416-866-3750
Other Contact Information: Telex: WUI6719400
email@scotiabank.com
www.scotiabank.com

Also Known As: Scotiabank
Ownership: Public
Year Founded: 1832
Number of Employees: 42,046

Bank West
PO Box 5328
#1010, 24th St. SE
High River, AB T1V 1A7
403-652-2107
Fax: 403-652-2237
888-440-2265
info@bankwest.ca
www.bankwest.ca

Ownership: Owned by Western Financial Group
Year Founded: 2002
Number of Employees: 15
Assets: $50-100 million
Revenues: Under $1 million

BCP Bank Canada
1106 Dundas St. West
Toronto, ON M6J 1X2
416-588-8597
Fax: 416-588-8564

Former Name: SottoBank Canada; Sottomayor Bank Canada
Ownership: Part of BMO Financial Group.
Year Founded: 1990

BMO Financial Group (BMO)
119, rue St-Jacques ouest
Montréal, QC H2Y 1L6
514-877-7373
Fax: 514-877-7399
877-225-5266
Other Contact Information: 1-877-225-5266 (French); 1-800-665-8800 (Cantonese & Mandarin); 1-866 889-0889 (TTY service); mosaik@bmo.com (Credit cards) feedback@bmo.com; remarque@bmo.com (French); mutualfunds@bmo.com
www.bmo.com

Former Name: Bank of Montréal
Ownership: Public
Year Founded: 1817
Number of Employees: 37,000+
Assets: $416,000,000,000 Year End: 20081031

Bridgewater Bank
Also listed under: *Financing & Loan Companies*
#150, 926 - 5th Ave. SW
Calgary, AB T2P 0N7
403-232-6556
Fax: 403-233-2609
888-837-2326
www.bridgewaterfinancial.ca

Former Name: Bridgewater Financial Services Ltd.
Ownership: Private. Wholly owned subsidiary of Alberta Motor Association.
Year Founded: 1997
Number of Employees: 170

Canadian Imperial Bank of Commerce (CIBC)/ Banque Canadienne Impériale de Commerce
Commerce Court
PO Box 1, Stn Commerce Court
Toronto, ON M5L 1A2
416-980-2211
Fax: 416-218-9440
800-465-2422
Other Contact Information: 1-800-465-2255 (Customer Care); 1-800-465-4653 (Credit Cards); 1-888-264-6843 (Mortgages); 416-980-4523 (Corporate Communications & Public Affairs)
customer.care@cibc.com; investorrelations@cibc.com
www.cibc.com

Ownership: Public
Year Founded: 1858
Number of Employees: 40,000
Assets: 3,700,000,000 Year End: 20081031

Canadian Tire Financial Services Ltd. (CTAL)
Also listed under: *Financial Planning & Investment Management Companies*
PO Box 3000
Welland, ON L3B 5S5
866-681-2837
www.ctfs.com

Ownership: Wholly-owned subsidiary of Canadian Tire Corporation Limited
Year Founded: 1966
Number of Employees: 1,300

Canadian Western Bank (CWB)/ Banque Canadienne de l'Ouest
#3000, 10303 Jasper Ave.
Edmonton, AB T5J 3X6
780-423-8888
Fax: 780-423-8897
comments@cwbank.com
www.cwbank.com

Also Known As: Canada's Western Bank
Ownership: Widely held Canadian corporation
Year Founded: 1984
Number of Employees: 1,000

Citizens Bank of Canada
#401, 815 West Hastings St.
Vancouver, BC V6C 1B4
604-682-7171
Fax: 604-708-7790
888-708-7800

service@citizensbank.ca
www.citizensbank.ca
Ownership: Subsidiary of Vancouver City Savings Credit Union
Year Founded: 1997
Number of Employees: 120

Dundee Bank of Canada (DBC)
1 Adelaide St. East, 20th Fl.
Toronto, ON M5C 2V9

Fax: 416-849-1700
866-884-3434
support@dbc.ca
www.dbc.ca
Former Name: Dundee Wealth Bank
Ownership: Member of Dundee Financial Group (DFG), a division of Dundee Wealth Management Inc.
Year Founded: 2006

First Nations Bank of Canada
224 - 4th Ave. South
Saskatoon, SK S7K 5M5

306-931-2409
Fax: 306-955-6811
888-454-3622
service@firstnationsbank.com
www.firstnationsbank.com
Ownership: Private
Year Founded: 1996
Number of Employees: 05
Assets: $100-500 million
Revenues: $5-10 million

General Bank of Canada(GBC)
c/o LeMarchand Mansion
#006, 11523 - 100 Ave.
Edmonton, AB T5K 0J8

780-443-5626
Fax: 780-443-5628
877-443-5620
info@generalbank.ca
www.generalbank.ca
Ownership: Parent company is Firstcan Management Inc.
Year Founded: 2005

Laurentian Bank of Canada/ Banque Laurentienne du Canada
1981, av McGill College
Montréal, QC H3A 3K3

877-522-3863
Other Contact Information: 1-866-262-2231 (TTY service); 514-284-4500, ext. 7511 or 8143 (Invesrtors & analysts); 514-284-4500, ext. 7511 (Media)
www.laurentianbank.ca
Ownership: Public
Year Founded: 1846
Number of Employees: 3,393
Assets: $19,000,000,000+ Year End: 20081031
Revenues: $630,500,500 Year End: 20081031

Manulife Bank of Canada
PO Box 1602, Waterloo Stn. Waterloo
#500MA, 500 King St. North
Waterloo, ON N2J 4C6

519-747-7000
877-765-2265
manulife_bank@manulife.com
www.manulifebank.ca
Ownership: Private. Wholly-owned subsidiary of Manulife Financial.
Year Founded: 1993
Number of Employees: 200+
Assets: $1-10 billion

National Bank of Canada (NBC)/ Banque Nationale du Canada(BNC)
National Bank Tower
600, rue de La Gauchetière ouest
Montréal, QC H3B 4L2

514-394-6081
Fax: 514-394-8434
www.nbc.ca
Former Name: The Provincial Bank of Canada; The Mercantile Bank of Canada
Ownership: Public
Year Founded: 1859
Number of Employees: 14,484

National Bank of Greece (Canada)/ Banque Nationale de Grèce (Canada)
1170, place du Frère André
Montréal, QC H3B 3C6

514-954-1522
Fax: 514-954-1224
800-954-1005
www.nbgbank.com
Ownership: Foreign
Year Founded: 1971
Number of Employees: 255

Pacific & Western Bank of Canada
#2002, 140 Fullarton St.
London, ON N6A 5P2

519-645-1919
Fax: 519-645-2060
866-979-1919
www.pwbank.com
Ownership: Parent company is Pacific & Western Credit Corp., a public company.
Year Founded: 1979
Number of Employees: 61
Assets: $1-10 billion
Revenues: $5-10 million

President's Choice Bank
439 King St. West, 5th Fl.
Toronto, ON M5V 1K4

416-204-2600
888-723-8881
www.banking.pcfinancial.ca

Royal Bank of Canada (RBC)
200 Bay St.
Toronto, ON M5J 2S5

416-974-5151
Fax: 416-955-7800
www.rbc.com
Also Known As: RBC Financial Group
Year Founded: 1869
Number of Employees: 65,045

Sears Bank Canada
222 Jarvis St.
Toronto, ON M5B 2B8

416-941-3606
Fax: 416-941-2325
800-265-3675
scb@sears.ca
www.sears.ca
Ownership: Wholly owned subsidiary of Sears Canada Inc.

The Toronto-Dominion Bank
TD Centre
PO Box 1
Toronto, ON M5K 1A2

416-982-8222
866-222-3456
www.td.com
Also Known As: TD Bank; TD Canada Trust
Ownership: Public
Year Founded: 1855
Number of Employees: 51,163

Ubiquity Bank of Canada
***Also listed under:** Financing & Loan Companies*
#303, 32071 South Fraser Way
Abbotsford, BC V2T 1W3

888-881-0188
contact@ubiquitybank.ca
www.ubiquitybank.ca
Ownership: Private.
Year Founded: 2004
Assets: $100-500 million
Revenues: Under $1 million

Foreign Banks: Schedule II

Amex Bank of Canada
***Also listed under:** Credit Card Companies*
101 McNabb St.
Markham, ON L3R 4H8

905-474-0870
800-668-2639
Other Contact Information: Toll-Free TTY/TDD: 1-866-549-6426; Local TTY/TDD: 905-940-7702
www.americanexpress.com/canada
Ownership: Wholly-owned subsidiary of American Express Travel Related Services Company, Inc., New York, USA.
Year Founded: 1853
Number of Employees: 3,700

Bank of China (Canada)
The Exchange Tower
PO Box 356
#2730, 130 King St. West
Toronto, ON M5X 1E1

416-362-2991
Fax: 416-362-3047
Ownership: Wholly owned subsidiary of the Bank of China Limited, Beijing, China.
Year Founded: 1992
Number of Employees: 85
Assets: $100-500 million
Revenues: $10-50 million

The Bank of East Asia (Canada)
East Asia Centre
#102-103, 350 Hwy. 7 East
Richmond Hill, ON L4B 3N2

905-882-8182
Fax: 905-882-5220
Other Contact Information: (852) 3608 0200 (Phone, Overseas Branch Operations & Development Department in Hong Kong)
info@hkbea.com, OsEnquiry@hkbea.com
ca.hkbea.com
Ownership: Private. Member of The Bank of East Asia Group, Hong Kong.
Year Founded: 1991

Bank of Tokyo-Mitsubishi UFJ (Canada)
#1700, South Tower, Royal Bank Plaza
PO Box 42
Toronto, ON M5J 2J1

416-865-0220
Fax: 416-865-0196
www.bk.mufg.jp/english
Ownership: Foreign. Part of The Bank of Tokyo-Mitsubishi UFJ, Ltd., Tokyo,Japan.
Year Founded: 1996

BNP Paribas (Canada)
1981, av McGill College
Montréal, QC H3A 2W8

514-285-6000
Fax: 514-285-6278
bnpp.canada@americas.bnpparibas.com
www.bnpparibas.ca
Former Name: Banque Nationale de Paris (Canada)
Ownership: Foreign. Wholly owned subsidiary of BNP Paribas, Paris, France
Year Founded: 1961
Number of Employees: 240
Assets: $1-10 billion

Citibank Canada
Citigroup Place
#1700, 123 Front St. West
Toronto, ON M5J 2M3

416-947-5500
Fax: 416-947-5387
www.citibank.com/canada
Ownership: Wholly owned indirect subsidiary of Citibank, N.A.
Year Founded: 1982
Number of Employees: 5,000+

CTC Bank of Canada (CTCB)
1518 West Broadway
Vancouver, BC V6J 1W8

604-683-3882
Fax: 604-683-3723
service@ctcbank.com
www.ctcbank.com
Ownership: Private. Part of Chinatrust Commercial Bank.

Habib Canadian Bank
#1B, 918 Dundas St. East
Mississauga, ON L4Y 4H9

905-276-5300
Fax: 905-276-5400
info@habibcanadian.com
www.habibcanadian.com
Ownership: Private. Foreign. Wholly owned by Habib Bank of AG Zurich, Switzerland.
Year Founded: 1967
Assets: $50-100 million
Revenues: $1-5 million

HSBC Bank Canada
#300, 885 West Georgia St.
Vancouver, BC V6C 3E9

604-525-4722
Fax: 604-641-1849
888-310-4722
info@hsbc.ca
www.hsbc.ca
Ownership: Subsidiary of HSBC Holdings plc, London, UK.
Year Founded: 1981
Number of Employees: 7,500

ICICI Bank Canada
PO Box 396
Toronto, ON M3C 2S7

888-424-2422

customercare.ca@icicibank.com
www.icicibank.ca
Ownership: Wholly-owned subsidiary of ICICI Bank Limited, Mumbai, India.

ING Bank of Canada
111 Gordon Baker Rd.
Toronto, ON M2H 3R1

416-758-5344
Fax: 416-756-2422
800-464-3473
Other Contact Information: 1-866-464-3473 (Toll Free, French service)
clientservices@ingdirect.ca
www.ingdirect.ca
Also Known As: ING DIRECT
Ownership: Wholly owned subsidiary of ING Group, Netherlands
Year Founded: 1997
Number of Employees: 850+
Assets: $10-100 billion

J.P. Morgan Bank Canada
South Tower, Royal Bank Plaza
PO Box 80
#1800, 200 Bay St.
Toronto, ON M5J 2J2

416-981-9200
Fax: 416-981-9133
www.jpmorgan.com

Korea Exchange Bank of Canada (KEBOC)
Madison Centre
#103, 4950 Yonge St.
Toronto, ON M2N 6K1

416-222-5200
Fax: 416-222-5822
www.kebcanada.com
Year Founded: 1981
Number of Employees: 90

MBNA Canada Bank
1600 James Naismith Dr.
Ottawa, ON K1B 5N8

613-907-4800
Fax: 613-907-3501
800-404-1319
Other Contact Information: 1-877-862-7759 (Toll Free for card applications); 1-800-872-5758 (TTY/TTD)
www.mbna.com/canada
Ownership: Private. MBNA Corporation, Wilmington, Delaware, USA.
Year Founded: 1997

Mega International Commercial Bank (Canada)
Madison Centre
#1002, 4950 Yonge St.
Toronto, ON M2N 6K1

416-947-2800
Fax: 416-947-9964
megato@ipoline.com
www.megabank.com.tw
Former Name: International Commercial Bank of Cathay (Canada)
Ownership: Wholly-owned subsidiary of Mega International Commercial Bank Co., Ltd., Taipei City, Taiwan.

Mizuho Corporate Bank (Canada) (MHCB)
PO Box 29
#1102, 100 Yonge St.
Toronto, ON M5C 2W1

416-874-0222
Fax: 416-367-3452
800-668-5917
www.mizuhocbk.co.jp/english
Former Name: Mizuho Bank (Canada)
Ownership: Foreign. Part of Mizuho Corporate Bank, Ltd., Tokyo, Japan.
Year Founded: 2000

Société Générale (Canada)
#1800, 1501, av McGill College
Montréal, QC H3A 3M8

514-841-6000
Fax: 514-841-6250
www.socgen.com
Ownership: Wholly-owned subsidiary of Société Générale Group, Paris, France.
Year Founded: 1974

State Bank of India (Canada)
#1600, Royal Bank Plaza, North Tower
PO Box 81, Royal Bank Stn. Royal Bank
200 Bay St.
Toronto, ON M5J 2J2

416-865-0414
Fax: 416-865-1735
800-668-8947
sbican@sbicanada.com
www.sbicanada.com
Ownership: Subsidiary of State Bank of India
Year Founded: 1982
Number of Employees: 45
Assets: $100-500 million
Revenues: $1-5 million

Sumitomo Mitsui Banking Corporation of Canada
#1400, Ernst & Young Tower
PO Box 172, TD Centre Stn. TD Centre
Toronto, ON M5K 1H6

416-368-4766
Fax: 416-367-3565
www.smbc.co.jp/aboutus/english
Former Name: Sakura Bank (Canada); The Sumitomo Bank of Canada
Ownership: Private. Foreign. Wholly owned subsidiary of Sumitomo Mitsui Banking Corporation, Tokyo, Japan.
Year Founded: 2001
Number of Employees: 32

UBS Bank (Canada)
Also listed under: *Financial Planning & Investment Management Companies; Investment Management*
#800, 154 University Ave.
Toronto, ON M5H 3Z4

416-343-1800
Fax: 416-343-1900
800-268-9709
www.ubs.com/canada
Also Known As: UBS Canada
Ownership: Foreign. Public.
Year Founded: 1856
Number of Employees: 70,000
Assets: $100 billion +
Revenues: $10-100 billion

Foreign Banks: Schedule III

ABN AMRO Bank N.V., Canada Branch
Toronto-Dominion Centre
PO Box 114, T-D Centre Stn. T-D Centre
#1500, 79 Wellington St. West, 15th Fl.
Toronto, ON M5K 1G8

416-367-0850
Fax: 416-367-7937
Other Contact Information: canada.jobs@abnamro.com (Employment Enquiries); 416-367-7943 (Business & Commercial Fax); 416-367-7937 (Corporate & Institutional Fax)
canada.branch@abnamro.com
www.abnamro.ca
Ownership: Branch of ABN AMRO Bank N.V.
Year Founded: 1824

Bank of America, National Association
#2500, 200 Front St. West
Toronto, ON M5V 3L2

416-349-4100
Fax: 416-349-4278
800-387-1729
www.bankofamerica.com

Capital One Bank (Canada Branch)
Also listed under: *Credit Card Companies*
#1300, 5650 Yonge St.
Toronto, ON M2M 4G3

Fax: 416-228-5113
800-481-3239
Other Contact Information: Customer Relations Address: PO Box 503, Stn. D, Toronto, ON M1R 5L1; Payment Address: PO Box 521, Stn. D, Toronto, ON M1R 5S4
ombudsman@capitalone.com
www.capitalone.ca
Ownership: Foreign. Part of Capital One Services, Inc., McLean, VA, USA.

Comerica Bank
South Tower, Royal Bank Plaza
PO Box 61
#2210, 200 Bay St.
Toronto, ON M5J 2J2

416-646-4797
Fax: 416-367-6435
www.comerica.com
Ownership: Foreign. Branch of Comerica Bank, Detroit, Michigan, USA.

Credit Suisse Securities (Canada), Inc.
PO Box 301, First Canadian Pl. Stn. First Canadian Pl.
#3000, 1 First Canadian Pl.
Toronto, ON M5X 1C9

416-352-4500
Fax: 416-352-4680
www.csfb.com
Ownership: Part of Credit Suisse Group, Zurich, Switzerland.

Deutsche Bank AG
Commerce Court West
PO Box 263
#4700, 199 Bay St.
Toronto, ON M5L 1E9

416-682-8000
Fax: 416-682-8383
deutsche.bank@db.com
www.db.com
Ownership: Foreign. Branch of Deutsche Bank AG, Frankfurt, Germany.

Dexia Crédit Local S.A. Canada
PO Box 201
#1620, 800, du carré Victoria
Montréal, QC H4A 1E3

514-868-1200
webmaster@dexia.com
www.dexia.com
Ownership: Branch of Dexia Crédit Local, Paris, France.

Fifth Third Bank
20 Bay St., 12th Fl.
Toronto, ON M5J 2N8

416-216-4638
www.53.com
Ownership: Foreign. Branch of Fifth Third Bank, Cincinnati, Ohio, USA

First Commercial Bank
#100, 5611 Cooney Rd.
Richmond, BC V6X 3J6

604-207-9600
Fax: 604-207-9638
www.firstbank.com
Ownership: Foreign. Branch of First Commercial Bank, Taiwan.

HSBC Bank USA, National Association
70 York St., 4th Fl.
Toronto, ON M5J 1S9

416-868-8000
www.us.hsbc.com, www.hsbc.ca

JPMorgan Chase Bank, National Association
South Tower, Royal Bank Plaza
PO Box 80
#1800, 200 Bay St.
Toronto, ON M5J 2J2

416-981-9200
Fax: 416-981-9175
888-430-9844
www.jpmorganchase.com
Former Name: The Chase Manhattan Bank; Morgan Guaranty Trust Co. of New York; Sears Bank Canada
Ownership: Branch of J.P. Morgan Chase & Co. Inc., Chicago, IL, USA.

Maple Bank GmbH
c/o Maple Financial Group Inc., Maritime Life Tower, TD Centre
PO Box 328
#3500, 79 Wellington St. West
Toronto, ON M5K 1K7

416-350-8200
Fax: 416-350-8226
info@maplefinancial.com
www.maplebank.com; www.maplefinancial.com
Former Name: First Marathon Bank GmbH
Ownership: Subsidiary of Maple Financial Group Inc.

Mellon Bank, N.A., Canada Branch
PO Box 16
#1710, 95 Wellington St. West
Toronto, ON M5J 2N7

416-860-0777
www.mellon.com
Ownership: Foreign. Branch of Mellon Financial Corp., Pittsburgh, PA, USA.
Year Founded: 1983

National City Bank - Canada Branch
The Exchange Tower
PO Box 462
#2140, 130 King St. West
Toronto, ON M5X 1E4

416-361-1744
Fax: 416-361-0085
www.nationalcity.com
Ownership: owned by National City Bank, Cleveland, Ohio
Year Founded: 1845
Number of Employees: 5

Ohio Savings Bank, Canadian Branch
Centre Tower, Clarica Centre
#3110, 3300 Bloor St. West
Toronto, ON M8X 2X3
800-696-2222
www.ohiosavings.com
Ownership: Foreign. Branch of Ohio Savings Bank, Cleveland, OH, USA.

Rabobank Nederland
Royal Trust Tower
#4520, 77 King St. West
Toronto, ON M5K 1E7
416-941-9777
Fax: 416-941-9750
www.rabobank.com
Former Name: Rabobank Canada
Ownership: Cooperative. Foreign. Branch of Rabobank Nederland, Netherlands
Year Founded: 2001
Number of Employees: 14
Assets: $1-10 billion

State Street Bank & Trust Company - Canada
Also listed under: Trust Companies
#1100, 30 Adelaide St. East
Toronto, ON M5C 3G6
416-362-1100
Fax: 416-956-2525
888-287-8639
www.statestreet.com
Former Name: State Street Trust Company Canada
Ownership: State Street Corporation
Year Founded: 1990
Number of Employees: 700

Union Bank of California, N.A.
#730, 440 - 2 Ave. SW
Calgary, AB T2P 5E9
403-264-2700
Fax: 403-264-2770
www.uboc.com
Ownership: Parent Union BanCal Corporation
Year Founded: 1864

United Overseas Bank Limited (UOB)
Vancouver Centre
PO Box 11616
#1680, 650 West Georgia St.
Vancouver, BC V6B 4N9
604-662-7055
Fax: 604-662-3356
UOB.Vancouver@uobgroup.com
www.uobgroup.com
Ownership: Foreign. Branch of United Overseas Bank Limited, Singapore.
Year Founded: 1987

U.S. Bank National Association - Canada Branch
Adelaide Centre
#2300, 120 Adelaide St. West
Toronto, ON M5H 1T1
877-332-7461
www.usbankcanada.com
Ownership: Part of U.S. Bank, Minneapolis, MN, USA.

WestLB AG
North Tower, Royal Bank Plaza
PO Box 41
#2301, 200 Bay St.
Toronto, ON M5J 2J1
416-216-5000
Fax: 416-216-5020
info@westlb.de
www.westlb.com
Ownership: Foreign. Branch of WestLB AG, Düsseldorf, Germany.

Foreign Banks Representative Offices

Allied Irish Banks, p.l.c. (AIB)
20 Bay St., 12th Fl.
Toronto, ON M5J 2N8
www.aib.ie
Ownership: Foreign. Office of Allied Irish Banks p.l.c., Dublin, Ireland.

American Express Bank Ltd.
#1350, 1090 West Georgia St.
Vancouver, BC V6E 3V7
Ownership: Foreign. Office of American Express Bank, New York, NY, USA.

Banco Comercial dos Açores
836 Dundas St. West
Toronto, ON M6J 1V5
416-603-0802
Fax: 416-603-8892
www.bca.pt

Banco Espirito Santo e Comercial de Lisboa, SA
860C College St.
Toronto, ON M6H 1A2
416-530-1700
www.bes.pt
Ownership: Private

Banco Santander Totta, SA
1110 Dundas St. West
Toronto, ON M6J 1X2
416-538-7111
www.santandertotta.pt

Bank Hapoalim B.M.
#2105, 4950 Yonge St.
Toronto, ON M2N 6K1
416-398-4250
Fax: 416-398-4246
www.bankhapoalim.com

Bank Leumi Le-Israel, B.M.
#400, 1 carré Westmount
Montréal, QC H3Z 2P9
514-931-4457
Fax: 514-931-5240
bllmtl@sprint.ca
english.leumi.co.il
Ownership: Office of Bank Leumi Le-Israel, B.M., Tel Aviv, Israel.
Year Founded: 1902
Assets: $10-100 billion
Revenues: $100-500 million

Bank of Cyprus, Canada Representative Office
#302, 658 Danforth Ave.
Toronto, ON M4J 5B9
416-461-5570
Fax: 416-461-6062
888-529-2265
info@bankofcyprus.ca
www.bankofcyprus.ca
Ownership: Office of the Bank of Cyprus Group, Cyprus.
Year Founded: 1997

Bank of Ireland Asset Management (U.S.) Limited
#2460, 1800, av McGill College
Montréal, QC H3A 3J6
514-849-6868
Fax: 514-849-8118
canada@biam.boi.ie
www.biam.ie
Year Founded: 1987

Bank of Valletta p.l.c., Canada Representative Office
West Tower
#625, 3300 Bloor St. West, 6th Fl.
Toronto, ON M8X 2X2
416-234-2265
Fax: 416-234-2281
800-567-2265
bovcanada@bov.com
www.bov.com

Bank Vontobel AG
#1760, 999 West Hastings St.
Vancouver, BC V6C 2W2
604-688-1122
Fax: 604-688-1123
www.vontobel.com
Ownership: Office of Bank Vontobel AG, Zürich, Switzerland.

Banque Centrale Populaire du Maroc
#1514, 1010 rue Sherbrooke ouest
Montréal, QC H3A 2R7
514-281-1855
Fax: 514-281-1974
gbpmaroc@qc.aira.com
www.bp.co.ma

Baring Asset Management Inc.
TD Canada Trust Tower, Brookfield Place
161 Bay St., 27th Fl.
Toronto, ON M5J 2S1
416-572-2400
Fax: 416-572-4100
william.tsotsos@barings.com
www.baring-asset-can.com
Ownership: Private
Year Founded: 1977

Bayerische Landesbank
#2060, 1501, av McGill College
Montréal, QC H3A 3M8
514-985-0047
Fax: 514-985-3459
info.montreal@bayernlb.com
www.bayernlb.de
Ownership: Foreign. Part of Bayerische Landesbank (BayernLB), Munich, Germany.

Calxa Economica Montepio Gual
1286 Dundas St. West
Toronto, ON M6J 1X7
416-588-7776
Fax: 416-588-0030
mg503@montepio.pt
www.montepio.pt

Calyon
#1900, 2000, av McGill College
Montréal, QC
Ownership: Office of Credit Agricole Group, Paris, France.
Year Founded: 2004

Centurion Bank of Punjab, Ltd.
#337, 1515 Britannia Rd. East
Mississauga, ON L4W 4K1
905-696-0943
Fax: 905-696-0976
nri.services@centurionbop.co.in
www.centurionbop.co.in
Ownership: Office of Centurion Bank of Punjab, India.

Crédit Libanais S.A.L. Representative Office (Canada)
Place du Canada
#1325, 1010, rue de la Gauchetière ouest
Montréal, QC H3B 2N2
514-866-6688
Fax: 514-866-6220
800-864-5512
info@creditlibanais.com
www.creditlibanais.com
Ownership: Office of Credit Libanais S.A.L., Beirut, Lebanon.

Cyprus Popular Bank Ltd.
484 Danforth Ave., 2nd Fl.
Toronto, ON M4K 1P6
416-466-8180
Fax: 416-466-9609
877-524-5422
laiki.toronto@laiki.com, laikiebank@laiki.com
www.laiki.com
Also Known As: Laiki Bank
Ownership: Office of Laiki Group, Cyprus.

Glitnir banki hf
#810, 1718 Argyle St.
Halifax, NS B3J 3N6
902-429-3113
Fax: 902-422-0288
glitnir@glitnir.is
www.glitnir.is
Ownership: Office of Glitnir, Iceland.
Year Founded: 2006

Jamaica National Overseas (Canada) Ltd.
1672 Eglinton Ave. West
Toronto, ON M6E 2H2
416-784-2075
Fax: 416-784-2076
800-462-9003
info@jnocanada.com, rosbourne@jnocanada.com, sstamp@jnocanada.com
www.jnbs.com
Ownership: Office of Jamaica National Building Society, Kingston Jamaica.

Japan Bank for International Cooperation - Toronto Liaison Office (JBIC)
Exchange Tower
PO Box 493, 2 First Canadian Pl. Stn. 2 First Canadian Pl.

#3660, 130 King St. West
Toronto, ON M5X 1E5

416-865-1700
Fax: 416-865-0124
www.jbic.go.jp

Ownership: Office of Japan Bank for International Cooperation, Tokyo, Japan.

JCB International (Canada) Ltd.
Also listed under: *Credit Card Companies*
#510, 1030 West Georgia St.
Vancouver, BC V6E 2Y3

604-689-8110
Fax: 604-689-8101
www.jcbinternational.com

Ownership: Office of JCB International Co., Ltd., Tokyo, Japan
Year Founded: 1961

JS Trasta komercbanka
#800, St. Clair Ave. East
Toronto, ON M4T 2T5

416-644-4941
Fax: 416-644-4946
canada@tkb.lv, info@tkb.lv
www.tkb.lv

Ownership: Office of JS Trasta komercbanka, Riga, Latvia.

Landsbanki Islands hf
George Mitchell House
5112 Prince St.
Halifax, NS B3J 1L3

902-576-3100
info@landsbanki.is
www.landsbanki.is

Ownership: Office of Landsbanki Islands hf, Reykjavik, Iceland.

Lebanese Canadian Bank, s.a.l.
#1508, 1, Place Ville-Marie
Montréal, QC H3B 2B5

514-871-3999
Fax: 514-871-2079
Other Contact Information: Alternative Phone Numbers: 514-871-1905; 514-871-1913; 514-871-1926
www.lebcanbank.com

National Bank of Pakistan
#210, 175 Commerce Valley Dr. West
Thornhill, ON L3T 7P6

905-707-0244
Fax: 905-707-1040
chiefrep@nbpcanada.com, enquiries@nationalbank.com.pk
www.nbp.com.pk

Ownership: Office of National Bank of Pakistan, Karachi, Pakistan.

Schroder Investment Management North America Limited - Canadian Representative Office
Also listed under: *Financial Planning & Investment Management Companies*
Canada Trust Tower, BCE Place
#4720, 161 Bay St.
Toronto, ON M5J 2S1

416-360-1200
Fax: 416-360-1202
www.schroders.com/ca

Former Name: Schroder Investment Management Canada Limited
Ownership: Office of Schroders plc, London, UK.

Stanford International Bank Ltd. (SIBL)
#3010, 1800, av McGill College
Montréal, QC H3A 3J6

514-985-3600
SIBprivate@stanfordeagle.com
www.stanfordinternational.com

Ownership: Office of Stanford International Bank Ltd., St. Johns, Antigua, West Indies.
Year Founded: 2004

UBS AG
PO Box 3
#650, 999 West Hastings St.
Vancouver, BC V6C 2W2

604-691-8061
Fax: 604-691-8098
www.ubs.com

Ownership: Office of UBS AG, Zürich, Switzerland.

Victoria Mutual Building Society - Canadian Representative Office (VMBS)
3117A Dufferin St.
Toronto, ON M6A 2S9

416-652-8652
Fax: 416-652-5266
800-465-6500
manager@vmbs.com
www.vmbs.com

Ownership: Office of Victoria Mutual Building Society, Kingston, Jamaica.

Westdeutsche Landesbank Girozentrale
North Tower, Royal Bank Plaza
PO Box 41
#2301, 200 Bay St.
Toronto, ON M5J 2J1

416-216-5000
Fax: 416-216-5020
info@westlb.de
www.westlb.de

Also Known As: WestLB
Ownership: Office of Westdeutsche Landesbank Girozentrale, Düsseldorf, Germany

Savings Banks

ATB Financial
ATB Place
9888 Jasper Ave. NW
Edmonton, AB T5J 1P1

780-408-7000
Fax: 780-422-4178
800-332-8383
atbinfo@atb.com
www.atb.com

Former Name: Alberta Treasury Branches
Ownership: Crown. 100% owned by the Provincial Government of Alberta
Year Founded: 1938
Number of Employees: 4,100

Boards of Trade & Chambers of Commerce

This section of the Almanac is organized in 3 subchapters: International Chambers & Business Councils, which are listed alphabetically, Provincial Boards of Trade & Chambers of Commerce, which are also listed in alphabetical, and other chambers which are listed in alphabetical order by provinces.

International Chambers & Business Councils

British Canadian Chamber of Trade & Commerce
PO Box 1358, Stn. K, Toronto ON M4P 3J4
Tel: 416-502-0847; *Fax:* 416-502-9319
e-mail: central@bcctc.ca
URL: www.bcctc.ca

Ann Mulvale, Executive Director, Central
Liam J. Hopkins, Executive Director, Western
Philip Gorlick, Executive Director, Eastern

Canada China Business Council (CCBC) / Conseil commercial Canada Chine
#407, 100 Adelaide St. West, Toronto ON M5H 1S3
Tel: 416-954-3800; *Fax:* 416-954-3806
e-mail: ccbc@ccbc.com
URL: www.ccbc.com

Eumie Leung, Director of Operations
Sarah Kutulakos, Executive Director

Canada Czech Republic Chamber of Commerce (CNACC)
PO Box 163, Stn. A, Toronto ON M9C 4V3
Tel: 416-559-2868; *Fax:* 289-232-1352
e-mail: admin@ccrcc.net
URL: www.ccrcc.net

Miroslav Princ, MBA, Chamber President

Canada-Arab Business Council (CABC) / Conseil de commerce canado-arabe (CCCA)
#600, 357 Bay St., Toronto ON M5M 2T7
Tel: 416-362-0050; *Fax:* 416-362-7633
e-mail: info@canada-arabbusiness.org
URL: www.canada-arabbusiness.org

Affiliation(s): Canadian Chamber of Commerce
Dwain Lingenfelter, Chairman/CEO

Canada-Finland Chamber of Commerce
c/o Finnish Credit Union, 191 Eglinton Ave. East, Toronto ON M4P 1K1
Tel: 416-486-1533; *Fax:* 416-486-1592
e-mail: info@canadafinlandcc.com
URL: www.canadafinlandcc.com

Canada-India Business Council (C-IBC) / Conseil de commerce Canada-Inde
#804, 1 St. Clair Ave. East, Toronto ON M4T 2V7
Tel: 416-214-5947; *Fax:* 416-214-9081
e-mail: info@canada-indiabusiness.ca
URL: www.canada-indiabusiness.ca

Kam Rathie, Executive Director
Sylvia Betan Court, Office Manager

Canada-Indonesia Business Council
PO Box 11-C, #110, 260 Adelaide St. East, Toronto ON M5A 1N1
Tel: 416-366-8490; *Fax:* 416-947-1534

Peter J. Dawes, Chair

Canada-Poland Chamber of Commerce of Toronto
77 Stoneham Rd., Toronto ON M9C 4Y7
Tel: 416-621-2032; *Fax:* 416-621-2472
e-mail: info@canada-poland.com
URL: www.canada-poland.com

Wojciech Sniegowski, President

Canadian Armenian Business Council Inc. (CABC) / Conseil commercial canadien-arménien inc.
#302-2, 1805, rué Sauve ouest, Montréal QC H4N 3B8
Tel: 514-333-7655; *Fax:* 514-333-7280
e-mail: info@cabc.ca
URL: www.cabc.ca

Canadian Council for the Americas (BCCC)
#300, 160 Eglington Ave. E., Toronto ON M5G 2K8
Tel: 416-364-3555; *Fax:* 416-595-8226
e-mail: cca@iecanada.com
URL: www.ccacanada.com

Mary Anderson, President

Canadian Council for the Americas (CCA) / Conseil Canadien pour les Amériques
#2300, 1066 West Hastings St., Vancouver BC V6E 3X2
Tel: 778-388-5206; *Fax:* 604-806-6112
e-mail: info@cca-bc.com
URL: www.cca-bc.com

Leon Teicher, Secretary
André Nudelman, Chair

Canadian German Chamber of Industry & Commerce Inc. / Deutsch-Kanadische Industrie- und Handelskammer
#1500, 480 University Ave., Toronto ON M5G 1V2
Tel: 416-598-3355; *Fax:* 416-598-1840
e-mail: info@germanchamber.ca
URL: www.germanchamber.ca

Canadian-Croatian Chamber of Commerce
630 The East Mall, Toronto ON M9B 4B1
Tel: 416-641-2829; *Fax:* 416-641-2700
e-mail: contactus@croat.ca
URL: www.croat.ca

Joh Marion, President

Chambre de commerce Canada-Pologne
PO Box 326, Stn. Ahuntsic, Montréal QC H3L 3N8
Tel: 514-278-7617; *Fax:* 514-384-6936
e-mail: info@chambrecp.ca
URL: www.chambrecp.ca

Catherine Zemelka, Executive Director

Chambre de commerce Canado-Tunisienne (CCCT) / Tunisian Canadian Chamber of Commerce
#806, 276, rue St-Jacques, Montréal QC H2Y 1N3
Tél: 514-847-1281; *Téléc:* 514-849-4910
Courriel: info@cccantun.ca
URL: www.cccantun.ca

Abdeljelil Ouanès, Président

Chambre de commerce française au canada (CCFC) / French Chamber of Commerce
#202, 1819, boul René-Lévesque ouest, Montréal QC H3H 2P5
Tél: 514-281-1246; *Téléc:* 514-289-9594
Courriel: acceuil@ccfcmtl.ca
URL: www.ccife.org/canada/montreal

Florent Belleste, Directeur

Danish Canadian Chamber of Commerce
#2110, 2 Bloor St. West, Toronto ON M4W 3E2
Tel: 416-923-1811; *Fax:* 416-962-3668
e-mail: info@dccc.ca
URL: www.dccc.ca

Anders Fisker, Chair
Knud Westergaard, Executive Director

Indo-Canada Chamber of Commerce (ICCC) / Chambre de commerce Indo-Canada
#900, 45 Sheppard Ave. East, Toronto ON M2N 5W9
Tel: 416-224-0090; *Fax:* 416-224-0089
Toll-Free: 866-873-4222
e-mail: iccc@iccc.org
URL: www.iccc.org

Asha Luthra, President
Neena Gupta, Vice-President & Corp. Secretary

International Chamber of Commerce (ICC) / Chambre de Commerce Internationale
38, cours Albert 1er, Paris 75008 France
Tel: 33-149-53-28-28; *Fax:* 33-149-53-28-59
e-mail: icc@iccwbo.org
URL: www.iccwbo.org
Affiliation(s): United Nations; World Trade Organization
Guy Sebban, Secretary General
Marcus Wallenberg, Chair

Ireland-Canada Chamber of Commerce (ICCC)
121 Decarie Circle, Toronto ON M9B 3J6
Tel: 416-622-7773; *Fax:* 416-621-3433
e-mail: main@iccctto.com
URL: www.iccctto.com
Michael Power, President

Italian Chamber of Commerce of Toronto (ICCT)
1502, 80 Richmond St. West, Toronto ON M5H 2A4
Tel: 416-789-7169; *Fax:* 416-789-7160
e-mail: info.toronto@italchambers.ca
URL: www.italchambers.ca
George Visintin, President
Paolo Palamara, Vice President/Secretary

Southeast Asia-Canada Business Council
5294 Imperial St., Burnaby BC V5J 1E4
Tel: 604-439-0779; *Fax:* 604-439-0284
e-mail: info@asean-canadatrade.org
URL: www.asean-canadatrade.org

The Swedish-Canadian Chamber of Commerce (SCCC)
#2120, 2 Bloor St. West, Toronto ON M4W 3E2
Tel: 416-925-8661; *Fax:* 416-929-8639
e-mail: mglindmark@sccc.ca
URL: www.sccc.ca
Monika G. Lindmark, Executive Director

Swiss Canadian Chamber of Commerce (Montréal) Inc. / Chambre de commerce Canado-Suisse (Montréal) Inc.
1572 Dr. Penfield Ave., Montréal QC H3G 1C4
Tel: 514-937-5822; *Fax:* 514-693-1032
e-mail: info@cccsmtl.com
URL: www.cccsmtl.com
Jacques Thevenoz, President

World Chambers Federation (WCF)
38 cours Albert 1er, Paris 75008 France
Tel: 33-149-532-944; *Fax:* 33-149-533-079
e-mail: wcf@iccwbo.org
URL: www.iccwbo.org; www.worldchambersfederation.org
Affiliation(s): Specialized div. of International Chamber of Commerce
François-Gabriel Ceyrac, Director

Chambers of Mines

Alberta Chamber of Resources
#1940, 10180 - 101 St., Edmonton AB T5J 3S4
Tel: 780-420-1030; *Fax:* 780-425-4623
e-mail: acr-mail@acr-alberta.com
URL: www.acr-alberta.com
Roger Thomas, President

Chamber of Mineral Resources of Nova Scotia (CMRNS)
PO Box 2171, Windsor NS B0N 2T0
Tel: 902-798-0187; *Fax:* 902-798-2141
e-mail: terry.daniels@ns.sympatico.ca
Affiliation(s): Mining Association of Canada
Terry Daniels, Managing Director

Chamber of Mines of Eastern British Columbia
215 Hall St., Nelson BC V1L 5X4
Tel: 250-352-5242; *Fax:* 250-352-7227
e-mail: chamberofminesebc@netidea.com
URL: www.cmebc.com
Dennis Llewellyn, Chamber Manager
Jack Denny, President

East Kootenay Chamber of Mines
#201, 12 - 11th Avenue South, Cranbrook BC V1C 2P1
Tel: 250-489-2255; *Fax:* 250-426-8755
URL: www.ekcm.org/chamber2
Ross Stanfield, President

NWT & Nunavut Chamber of Mines
PO Box 2818, Yellowknife NT X1A 2R1
Tel: 867-873-5281; *Fax:* 867-920-2145
e-mail: nwtmines@ssimicro.com
URL: www.miningnorth.com
Affiliation(s): Mining Association of Canada; Canadian Institute of Mining, Metallurgy & Petroleum
Mike Vaydik, General Manager

Yukon Chamber of Mines (YCM)
3151B - 3rd Ave., Whitehorse YT Y1A 1G1
Tel: 867-667-2090; *Fax:* 867-668-7127
e-mail: info@ycmines.ca
URL: www.ycmines.ca
Affiliation(s): Mining Association of Canada
Joanne Rice, Executive Officer
Carl Schulze, President

Provincial & Territorial Boards of Trade & Chambers of Commerce

Alberta Chambers of Commerce (ACC)
#1808, 10025 - 102A Ave., Edmonton AB T5J 2Z2
Tel: 780-425-4180; *Fax:* 780-429-1061
Toll-Free: 800-272-8854
e-mail: info@abchamber.ca
URL: www.abchamber.ca
Affiliation(s): Canadian Chamber of Commerce
Ken Kobly, President & CEO
Don Oszli, Chair

British Columbia Chamber of Commerce
#1201, 750 West Pender St., Vancouver BC V6C 2T8
Tel: 604-683-0700; *Fax:* 604-683-0416
e-mail: bccc@bcchamber.org
URL: www.bcchamber.org
John Winter, President & CEO

Creston Chamber of Commerce
PO Box 268, 1607 Canyon St., Creston BC V0B 1G0
Tel: 250-428-4342; *Fax:* 250-428-9411
Toll-Free: 866-528-4342
e-mail: crestonchamber@kootenay.com
URL: www.crestonbc.com/chamber
Murray Oswald, President

Fédération des chambres de commerce du Québec
555, boul. René-Lévesque ouest, 19e étage, Montréal QC H2Z 1B1
Tél: 514-844-9571; *Téléc:* 514-844-0226
Ligne sans frais: 800-361-5019
Courriel: info@fccq.ca
URL: www.fccq.ca
Françoise Bertand, Présidente-directrice générale

The Manitoba Chambers of Commerce
227 Portage Ave., Winnipeg MB R3B 2A6
Tel: 204-948-0100; *Fax:* 204-948-0110
Toll-Free: 877-444-5222
e-mail: mbchamber@mbchamber.mb.ca
URL: www.mbchamber.mb.ca
Ken Wilk, Chairman

New Brunswick Chamber of Commerce (NBCC)
#21, 236 St. George St., Moncton NB E1C 1W1
Tel: 506-854-9920; *Fax:* 506-854-8910
e-mail: pierrev@nb.aibn.com
Pierre Michaud, Contact

Newfoundland & Labrador Chamber of Commerce
PO Box 352, 109 Trans Canada Hwy., Gander NL A1V 1W7
Tel: 709-651-6522; *Fax:* 709-256-5808
e-mail: nlcc@nf.aibn.com
URL: www.nlchamber.ca
Maureen O'Reilly, Executive Director

Northwest Territories Chamber of Commerce
NWT Commerce Place, #13, 4910 - 50th Ave., Yellowknife NT X1A 3S5
Tel: 867-920-9505; *Fax:* 867-873-4174
e-mail: admin@nwtchamber.com
URL: www.nwtchamber.com
Robin Wotherspoon, Executive Director
Don Yamkowy, President
Ann Marie Tout, Vice-President
Doreen Farrants, Secretary
Steve Meister, Treasurer

Nova Scotia Chambers of Commerce
605 Prince Street, Truro NS B2N 5B6
Tel: 902-895-6329; *Fax:* 902-897-6641
e-mail: info@nschamber.ca
URL: www.nschamber.ca
Dan Fougere, President

Ontario Chamber of Commerce (OCC)
#505, 180 Dundas St. West, Toronto ON M5G 1Z8
Tel: 416-482-5222; *Fax:* 416-482-5879
e-mail: info@occ.on.ca
URL: www.occ.on.ca
Shayne Smith, Chair

Ontario Gay & Lesbian Chamber of Commerce
39 River St., Toronto ON M5A 3P1
Tel: 416-646-1600
e-mail: info@oglcc.com
URL: www.oglcc.com
John Kenyon, President

Prince Edward Island Chamber of Commerce
c/o Drake Truck Bodies, Riverview Crescent, RR#1, Vernon Bridge PE C0A 2E0
Tel: 902-651-2782; *Fax:* 902-652-2786
Allison Drake, President

Saskatchewan Chamber of Commerce
Chateau Tower, #1630, 1920 Broad St., Regina SK S4P 3V2
Tel: 306-352-2671; *Fax:* 306-781-7084
e-mail: info@saskchamber.com
URL: www.saskchamber.com
Mary Ann McFayden, Executive Director
Dale Lemke, President

Swiss Canadian Chamber of Commerce (Ontario) Inc. (SCCC)
756 Royal York Rd., Toronto ON M8Y 2T6
Tel: 416-236-0039; *Fax:* 416-236-3634
e-mail: sccc@swissbiz.ca
URL: www.swissbiz.ca
Ernst Notz, President
Patricia Keller Schläpfer, Executive Assistant

Yukon Chamber of Commerce (YCC)
#101, 307 Jarvis St., Whitehorse YT Y1A 2H3
Tel: 867-667-2000; *Fax:* 867-667-2001
Toll-Free: 800-661-0543
e-mail: president@yukonchamber.com
URL: www.yukonchamber.com
Dave Austin, President & CEO

Alberta

Airdrie Chamber of Commerce
PO Box 3661, Airdrie AB T4B 2B8
Tel: 403-948-4412; *Fax:* 403-948-3141
e-mail: info@airdriechamber.ab.ca
URL: www.airdriechamber.ab.ca
Lynda Barker, Treasurer
Mike Brandrick, President

Alberta Beach & District Chamber of Commerce
PO Box 280, Alberta Beach AB T0E 0A0
Tel: 780-924-3889; *Fax:* 780-924-3425
e-mail: gwte@telusplanet.net
Phyllis Stark, President

Alix Chamber of Commerce
PO Box 145, Alix AB T0C 0B0
Tel: 403-747-2405; *Fax:* 403-747-2403
e-mail: cpete@oanet.com
URL: www.villageofalix.ca
Clarence Verveda, President

Athabasca & District Chamber of Commerce (ADCofC)
PO Box 3074, Athabasca AB T9S 2B9
Tel: 780-213-4600
Affiliation(s): Canadian Chambers of Commerce
Joanne Peckham, President
Michael Neville, Secretary

Barrhead Chamber of Commerce
PO Box 4524, Barrhead AB T7N 1A4
Tel: 403-674-2338; *Fax:* 403-674-5648
e-mail: info@barrheadchamber.ca
URL: www.barrheadchamber.ca
Darren Strawson, President

Bashaw Chamber of Commerce
PO Box 645, Bashaw AB T0B 0H0
e-mail: bashawcc@gmail.com
URL: www.townofbashaw.com/chamber
Peter Graham, President

Bassano & District Chamber of Commerce
PO Box 849, General Delivery, Bassano AB T0J 0B0
Tel: 403-641-3014
Tammie Rothnie, Secretary

Beaverlodge Chamber of Commerce
PO Box 303, Beaverlodge AB T0H 0C0
Tel: 780-354-8785; *Fax:* 780-354-2107
e-mail: olsom@telusplanet.net
Judy Olson, Treasurer
Keith Tourand, President

Beiseker & District Chamber of Commerce
PO Box 277, Beiseker AB T0M 0G0
Tel: 403-947-2356; *Fax:* 403-947-3227
Al Henuset, Contact

Blackfalds Chamber of Commerce
PO Box 249, Blackfalds AB T0M 0J0
Tel: 403-885-2386; *Fax:* 403-885-2386
Curtis Pedde, President

Bluffton Chamber of Commerce
PO Box 38, RR#2, Bluffton AB T0C 0M0
Tel: 403-843-6514; *Fax:* 403-843-3506
e-mail: lawman@telusplanet.net
Lawrence Wright, President

Bonnyville & District Chamber of Commerce
PO Box 6054, Hwy. 28 West, Bonnyville AB T9N 2G7
Tel: 780-826-3252; *Fax:* 780-826-4525
e-mail: manager@bonnyvillechamber.ab.ca
URL: www.bonnyvillechamber.com
Lorne Ringuette, President
Al Arbour, Vice President

Bow Island/Burdett District Chamber of Commerce
PO Box 1001, 502 Centre St., Bow Island AB T0K 0G0
Tel: 403-545-5134; *Fax:* 403-542-2449
e-mail: info@bowislandchamber.com
URL: www.bowislandchamber.com/
Nan Maclean, Co Chair
Dale Meier
Ron Thomson, Vice President
Nan Maclean, President

Boyle & District Chamber of Commerce
PO Box 496, Boyle AB T0A 0M0
Tel: 780-689-4646; *Fax:* 780-689-2250
Monica Hill, President

Bragg Creek Chamber of Commerce
PO Box 216, Bragg Creek AB T0L 0K0
Tel: 403-949-0004; *Fax:* 403-949-2748
e-mail: office@braggcreekchamber.ca
URL: www.braggcreekchamber.ca
Shannon Duncan, Secretary
Chris Tucker, President

Breton & District Chamber of Commerce
PO Box 364, Breton AB T0C 0P0
Tel: 780-696-2557; *Fax:* 780-696-2572
Glory Tornack, President

Brooks & District Chamber of Commerce
PO Box 400, #6, 403 - 2 Ave. West, Brooks AB T1R 1B4
Tel: 403-362-7641; *Fax:* 403-362-6893
e-mail: manager@brookschamber.ab.ca
URL: www.brookschamber.ab.ca
Gillenne Bégin, Manager
George Newton, President

Calgary Chamber of Commerce
100 - 6 Ave. SW, Calgary AB T2P 0P5
Tel: 403-750-0400; *Fax:* 403-266-3413
e-mail: chinfo@calgarychamber.com
URL: www.calgarychamber.com
Elizabeth Leitch, Manager, Communications
Heather M. Douglas, President & CEO

Camrose Chamber of Commerce
5402 - 48 Ave., Camrose AB T4V 0J7
Tel: 780-672-4217; *Fax:* 780-672-1059
e-mail: camcham@telusplanet.net
URL: www.camrosechamber.ca
Sharon Anderson, Executive Director
Diane Hutchinson, President

Cardston & District Chamber of Commerce
PO Box 1212, 490 Main St., Cardston AB T0K 0K0
Tel: 403-795-1032
e-mail: Info@CardstonChamber.com
URL: www.cardstonchamber.com/
Marian Carlson, Economic Development Officer
Zenith Gaynor, President

Caroline & District Chamber of Commerce
PO Box 90, Caroline AB T0M 0M0
Tel: 403-722-4066; *Fax:* 403-722-4002
e-mail: ccoc@telus.net
URL: www.carolinechamber.ca
Deana Knight, Manager
Reg Dean, President

Carstairs Chamber of Commerce
PO Box 370, Carstairs AB T0M 0N0
Tel: 403-337-3341
URL: www.town.carstairs.ab.ca/chamber.html
Dennis Schmick, President
Karen Kneeland, Vice-President

Claresholm & District Chamber of Commerce
PO Box 1092, Claresholm AB T0L 0T0
Tel: 403-625-4229
e-mail: info@claresholchamber.com
URL: www.claresholmchamber.com
Russell Sawatsky, President

Coaldale & District Chamber of Commerce
PO Box 1117, 1401 - 20 Ave., Coaldale AB T1M 1M9
Tel: 403-345-2358; *Fax:* 403-345-2339
e-mail: info@coaldalechamber.com
URL: www.coaldalechamber.com
Elizabeth McLachlan, Executive Director
Leonard Fast, President

Cochrane & District Chamber of Commerce
#5, 205 - 1st St. East, Cochrane AB T4C 1X6
Tel: 403-932-6810; *Fax:* 403-932-6824
e-mail: c.business@cochranechamber.ca
URL: www.cochranechamber.ca
Dawn Martin, Coordinator
Adamo Cocuzzoli, President

Cold Lake Regional Chamber of Commerce
PO Box 454, Cold Lake AB T9M 1P1
Tel: 780-594-4747; *Fax:* 780-594-3711
e-mail: clrcc@incentre.net
URL: www.coldlakechamber.ca
Rob Brassard, President
Sherri Bohme, Executive Director

Consort Chamber of Commerce
PO Box 490, 4901 - 50 Ave., Consort AB T0C 1B0
Tel: 403-577-3623; *Fax:* 403-577-2024
e-mail: webmaster@village.consort.ab.ca
URL: www.village.consort.ab.ca/ChamberofCommerce.htm
Peter G. Ringrose, Executive Director

Coronation Chamber of Commerce
PO Box 960, Coronation AB T0C 1C0
Tel: 403-578-4220; *Fax:* 403-578-3020
Jackie Morettin, President

Cremona Water Valley & District Chamber of Commerce
PO Box 356, 106 Railway Ave. West, Cremona AB T0M 0R0
Tel: 403-335-8398; *Fax:* 403-637-7022
e-mail: vhoogenboom@aol.com
URL: www.cremonawatervalley.com
Gabriel Grenier, President

La Crete & Area Chamber of Commerce
PO Box 1088, La Crete AB T0H 2H0
Tel: 780-928-2278; *Fax:* 780-928-2234
e-mail: office@lacretechamber.com
URL: www.lacretechamber.com
Barbara Peters, Office Manager
Larry Buhler, President

Crossfield Chamber of Commerce
PO Box 1490, Crossfield AB T0M 0S0
e-mail: crossfieldchamber@shaw.ca
URL: www.crossfieldchamber.com

Crowsnest Pass Chamber of Commerce
PO Box 706, Blairmore AB T0K 0E0
Tel: 403-562-7108; *Fax:* 403-562-7493
Toll-Free: 888-562-7108
e-mail: cncpchamber@telus.net
URL: www.crowsnest-pass.com
Affiliation(s): Alberta Chamber of Commerce
Jenine Trotz, Secretary/Treasurer
Lowry Toombs, President

Delburne & District Chamber of Commerce
PO Box 254, Delburne AB T0M 0V0
Tel: 403-749-2808; *Fax:* 403-749-2800
e-mail: delburne@telusplanet.net
URL: www.delburne.ca
Brenda Smith, President

Devon & District Chamber of Commerce
35 Athabasca Ave., Devon AB T9G 1G5
Tel: 780-987-5177; *Fax:* 780-987-5135
e-mail: devoncc@telus.net
Gerry Daniel, Administrator
Wade Kosiorek, Contact

Diamond Valley Chamber of Commerce
PO Box 61, Turner Valley AB T0L 2A0
Tel: 403-652-3700; *Fax:* 866-855-2065
e-mail: info@diamondvalleychamber.com
URL: www.diamondvalleychamber.com
R. Williamson, President

Didsbury Chamber of Commerce
PO Box 981, 1811 - 20 St., Didsbury AB T0M 0W0
Tel: 403-335-3265; *Fax:* 403-335-3265
e-mail: info@didsburychamber.ca
URL: www.didsburychamber.ca
Joelle Fournier, Office Manager
Margo Ward, President

Drayton Valley & District Chamber of Commerce (DVDCC)
PO Box 5318, Drayton Valley AB T7A 1R5
Tel: 780-542-7578; *Fax:* 780-542-9211
e-mail: chambrdv@telusplanet.net
URL: www.dvchamber.com
Tom Campbell, President

Drumheller & District Chamber of Commerce (DDCC)
PO Box 999, 60 First Ave. West, Drumheller AB T0J 0Y0
Tel: 403-823-8100; *Fax:* 403-823-4469
e-mail: info@drumhellerchamber.com
URL: www.drumhellerchamber.com
Cindy Clark, President
Heather Bitz, General Manager

Eckville & District Chamber of Commerce
PO Box 609, Eckville AB T0M 0X0
Tel: 403-746-2353; *Fax:* 403-746-3470
e-mail: eckville@telusplanet.net
URL: www.eckvillechamber.com
Mitch Krescy, President

Edgerton & District Chamber of Commerce
PO Box 303, Edgerton AB T0B 1K0
Tel: 780-755-3947
Kim Kimball, President

Edmonton Chamber of Commerce
World Trade Centre, Sun Life Place, #700, 9990 Jasper Ave., Edmonton AB T5J 1P7
Tel: 780-426-4620; *Fax:* 780-424-7946
e-mail: info@edmontonchamber.com
URL: www.edmontonchamber.com
Kimberly Nishikaze, Contact, Communications
Martin Salloum, President/CEO

Edson & District Chamber of Commerce
5433 - 3rd Ave., Edson AB T7E 1L5
Tel: 780-723-4918; *Fax:* 780-723-5545
e-mail: info@edsonchamber.com
URL: www.edsonchamber.com
Nicole Bethge, President
Heather Kelly, Manager

Elk Point Chamber of Commerce
PO Box 639, Elk Point AB T0A 1A0
Tel: 780-724-4087; *Fax:* 780-724-4087
e-mail: vbooker@stpaul.greatwest.ca
Vicki Booker, Secretary

Evansburg & Entwistle Chamber of Commerce
PO Box 598, Evansburg AB T0E 0T0
Tel: 780-727-4035; *Fax:* 780-727-4035
e-mail: info@partnersonthepembina.com
URL: www.partnersonthepembina.com
Maxine Lappe, President

Fairview & District Chamber of Commerce
PO Box 1034, Fairview AB T0H 1L0
Tel: 780-835-5999; *Fax:* 780-835-5991
e-mail: executivedirector@fairviewchamber.com
URL: www.fairviewchamber.com
Winita Mitchell, President
Kathryn Currie, Executive Director
Jasmine Adams, Contact

Falher Chamber of Commerce
PO Box 814, Falher AB T0H 1M0
Tel: 780-925-2708; *Fax:* 780-837-2647
e-mail: patrysha@incredibleimpressions.com
Affiliation(s): Falher & Area Economic Development & Tourism
Sarah Williams, President
Aline Desaulniers, Treasurer

Foremost & District Chamber of Commerce
PO Box 272, Foremost AB T0K 0X0
Tel: 403-867-3077; *Fax:* 403-867-3579
e-mail: cofc4mst@la.shockware.com
URL: www.foremostalberta.com
Lorne Buis, President

Fort Macleod & District Chamber of Commerce
PO Box 178, Fort MacLeod AB T0L 0Z0
Tel: 403-553-3355
e-mail: EDO@FortMacleod.com
URL: www.fortmacleod.com/business/chamber_commerce.cfm
Emily McTighe, President

Fort McMurray Chamber of Commerce
#304, 9612 Franklin Ave., Fort McMurray AB T9H 2J9
Tel: 780-743-3100; *Fax:* 780-790-9757
e-mail: fmcoc@telus.net
URL: www.fortmcmurraychamber.ca
Jack Bonville, President
Diane Slater, Executive Director

Fort Saskatchewan Chamber of Commerce
PO Box 3072, 10030 - 99 Ave., Fort Saskatchewan AB T8L 2T1
Tel: 780-998-4355; *Fax:* 780-998-1515
e-mail: chamber@fortsaskchamber.com
URL: www.fortsaskchamber.com
Affiliation(s): Alberta Chamber of Commerce; Canadian Chamber of Commerce
Michelle Gamache, President
Janine Brisebois, Executive Director

Fort Vermilion & Area Board of Trade
PO Box 456, Fort Vermilion AB T0H 1N0
Tel: 780-927-3505
Frank Rosenberger, President

Fox Creek Chamber of Commerce
PO Box 774, Fox Creek AB T0H 1P0
Tel: 780-622-2670; *Fax:* 780-622-2677
e-mail: fcchamb@telus.net
Bernie Hornby, President
Barb Souter, Treasurer
Rose Hearn, Secretary

Glendon & District Chamber
PO Box 300, Glendon AB T0A 1P0
Tel: 780-635-2557
Ron Mack, President

Grande Cache Chamber of Commerce
PO Box 1342, Grande Cache AB T0E 0Y0
Tel: 780-827-3790; *Fax:* 780-827-5698
Affiliation(s): Alberta Chamber of Commerce; Canadian Chamber of Commerce
Jean Bourdua, President

Grande Prairie & District Chamber of Commerce
#217, 11330 - 106 St., Grande Prairie AB T8V 7X9
Tel: 780-532-5340; *Fax:* 780-532-2926
e-mail: info@gpchamber.com
URL: www.grandeprairiechamber.com
Karen Kluyt, Office Manager
Dan Pearcy, CEO

Grimshaw Chamber of Commerce
PO Box 919, Grimshaw AB T0H 1W0
Tel: 780-332-4370; *Fax:* 780-332-4375
e-mail: blossomb@telus.net
Theresa Bruce, President
Jenny Borys, Secretary

Hanna & District Chamber of Commerce
PO Box 2248, Hanna AB T0J 1P0
Tel: 403-854-4004; *Fax:* 403-854-4060
e-mail: hannachamber@telus.net
URL: www.aroundhanna.com/hannachamberofcommerce
Barb Larson, Chamber Manager

Hardisty & District Chamber of Commerce
PO Box 628, Hardisty AB T0B 1V0
Tel: 780-888-3836
e-mail: ernie.ziegler@midfieldsupply.com
Rob Rondeau, President

High Level & District Chamber of Commerce
10803 - 96 St., High Level AB T0H 1Z0
Tel: 780-926-2470; *Fax:* 780-926-4017
e-mail: hlchambr@incentre.net
URL: www.highlevelchamber.com
Sylvia Kennedy, President
Daina French, Administrative contact

High River & District Chamber of Commerce
PO Box 5244, 149B Macleod Trail SW, High River AB T1V 1M4
Tel: 403-652-3336; *Fax:* 403-652-7660
e-mail: hrdcc@telus.net
URL: www.highriverchamber.com
Clair Noad, President
Lynette McCracken, Executive Director

Hinton & District Chamber of Commerce
309 Gregg Ave., Hinton AB T7V 2A7
Tel: 780-865-2777; *Fax:* 780-865-1062
Toll-Free: 877-446-8666
e-mail: hintoncc@telus.net
URL: www.hintonchamber.com
Janice Calihoo, Vice-President
Risa Croken, Office Manager

Hythe & District Chamber of Commerce
PO Box 404, Hythe AB T0C 2C0
Tel: 780-356-2168; *Fax:* 780-356-2009
e-mail: chamber@hythe.ca
URL: www.hythe.ca/chamber.html
Steve Greene, Chair

Innisfail & District Chamber of Commerce
5031, 40th St., Innisfail AB T4G 1H8
Tel: 403-227-1177; *Fax:* 403-227-6749
e-mail: ichamber@telusplanet.net
URL: www.innisfailchamber.ca
Jean Barclay, President
Donna Arnold, Secretary

Irma & District Chamber of Commerce
PO Box 284, Irma AB T0B 2H0
Tel: 780-754-3996
e-mail: cwilli@telusplanet.net
Claudia Williams, President

Jasper Park Chamber of Commerce
PO Box 98, 632 Connaught Dr., Jasper AB T0B 1E0
Tel: 780-852-3858; *Fax:* 780-852-4932
Toll-Free: 800-473-8135
e-mail: info@jaspercanadianrockies.com
URL: www.jaspercanadianrockies.com
George Andrew, President
Krista Rodger, General Manager

Kainai Chamber of Commerce
PO Box 350, Stand Off AB T0L 1Y0
Tel: 403-737-8207
e-mail: chamber@bloodtribe.org
Tony Manyfingers, President
Donald Cotton, Manager

Killam & District Chamber of Commerce
PO Box 272, Killam AB T0B 2L0
Tel: 780-385-3644
Jerry Gordon, President

Lac La Biche & District Chamber of Commerce
PO Box 804, 10307, 100 St., Lac La Biche AB T0A 2C0
Tel: 780-623-2818; *Fax:* 780-623-7217
e-mail: llbcofc@telusplanet.net
URL: www.llbchamber.ca
Affiliation(s): Alberta Chamber of Commerce
Elaine Poulin, Executive Director
Bill Abougoush, President

Lacombe & District Chamber of Commerce
6005 - 50 Ave., Lacombe AB T4L 1K7
Tel: 403-782-4300; *Fax:* 403-782-4302
e-mail: info@lacombechamber.ca
URL: www.lacombechamber.ca
Faye Chomoway, Chamber Manager

Leduc & District Chamber of Commerce
6420 - 50 St., Leduc AB T9E 7K9
Tel: 780-986-5454; *Fax:* 780-986-8108
e-mail: info@leduc-chamber.com
URL: www.leduc-chamber.com
Carroll Hales, Secretary
Iris Yanish, Manager
Donna Tona, President

Legal & District Chamber of Commerce
PO Box 338, General Delivery, Legal AB T0G 1L0
Tel: 780-456-3424
URL: www.legalchamberofcommerce.com
Affiliation(s): Greater Edmonton Regional Chambers of Commerce
Frank Klassen, President
Carol Tremblay, Secretary

Lethbridge Chamber of Commerce
#200, 529 - 6 St. South, Lethbridge AB T1J 2E1
Tel: 403-327-1586; *Fax:* 403-327-1001
e-mail: office@lethbridgechamber.com
URL: www.lethbridgechamber.com
Jody Nilsson, General Manager
Paul G. Pharo, President

Lloydminster Chamber of Commerce
4419 - 52 Ave., Lloydminster AB T9V 0Y8
Tel: 780-875-9013; *Fax:* 780-875-0755
e-mail: contact_llc@lloydminsterchamber.com
URL: www.lloydminsterchamber.com
Pat L. Tenney, Executive Director
Peggy Bosch, President

Mallaig Chamber of Commerce
PO Box 144, Mallaig AB T0A 2K0
Tel: 780-635-3849
Tammy Bodnar, President

Mannville & District Chamber of Commerce
PO Box 54, Mannville AB T0B 2W0
Tel: 780-763-3795
Shirley J. Wosnik, President

Marwayne & District Chamber of Commerce
PO Box 183, Marwayne AB T0B 2X0
Tel: 780-847-3962; *Fax:* 780-847-3324
e-mail: vilmar@telusplanet.net
URL: www.village.marwayne.ab.ca
Sharon Kneen, President

Mayerthorpe & District Chamber of Commerce
PO Box 1279, Mayerthorpe AB T0E 1N0
Tel: 780-786-2444
Arnold Lotholz, Treasurer
Cynthia Eichhorn, President

McLennan Chamber of Commerce
PO Box 90, McLennan AB T0H 2L0
Tel: 780-324-3894; *Fax:* 780-324-3932
Bruce Brulotte, President
Sandra Thrall, Secretary

Medicine Hat & District Chamber of Commerce
413 - 6th Ave. SE, Medicine Hat AB T1A 2S7
Tel: 403-527-5214; *Fax:* 403-527-5182
e-mail: info@medicinehatchamber.com
URL: www.medicinehatchamber.com
Affiliation(s): Alberta Chamber of Commerce; Canadian Chamber of Commerce
Mary Lou Hansen, Executive Director
Jason Melhoff, Chair

Millet & District Chamber of Commerce
PO Box 389, Millet AB T0C 1Z0
Tel: 780-387-4534
e-mail: milletchamber@canada.com
Debbie Swanson, President

Morinville & District Chamber of Commerce
PO Box 3130, Morinville AB T8R 1S1
Tel: 780-939-9462; *Fax:* 780-939-3087
e-mail: chamber@town.morinville.ab.ca
URL: www.morinvillechamber.com
Sheldon Fingler, President

Nanton & District Chamber of Commerce
PO Box 711, Nanton AB T0L 1R0
Tel: 403-646-2029
e-mail: president@nantonchamber.com
URL: www.nantonchamber.com
Jason Calvert, Acting President

Okotoks & District Chamber of Commerce
PO Box 1053, 14 McRae Street, Okotoks AB T1S 1B1
Tel: 403-938-2848; *Fax:* 403-938-6649
e-mail: okotokschamber@telus.net
URL: www.okotokschamber.ca
Cathy Huth, President
Tanya McAvena, Executive Director

Olds & District Chamber of Commerce
PO Box 4210, Olds AB T4H 1P8
Tel: 403-556-7070; *Fax:* 403-556-1515
e-mail: oldscham@telusplanet.net
URL: www.oldsalberta.com
Debbie Packer, President
Barb Babiak, Executive Director
Paul Hildebrand, Vice-President

Onoway & District Chamber of Commerce
PO Box 723, Onoway AB T0E 1V0
Tel: 780-967-4754
e-mail: tbulletin@icrossroads.com
Lyle Robinson, President

Oyen & District Chamber of Commerce
PO Box 718, Oyen AB T0J 2J0
Tel: 403-664-0406
e-mail: oyenecho@telusplanet.net
Francis MacQuarrie, President

Picture Butte & District Chamber of Commerce
PO Box 540, Picture Butte AB T0K 1V0

Tel: 403-732-4302; *Fax:* 403-732-4703
e-mail: chamber@picturebutte.ca
Wes Brouwer, President
Corrine McInnis, Office Manager

Pigeon Lake Regional Chamber of Commerce (PLRCC)
#6B Village Drive, Westerose AB T0C 2V0
Tel: 780-586-6263; *Fax:* 780-586-3667
e-mail: plchambe@telusplanet.net
URL: www.pigeonlakechamber.ca
Affiliation(s): Alberta Chambers of Commerce
Darlene Kobeluck, Manager
Sharon Will, President

Pincher Creek & District Chamber of Economic Development
PO Box 2287, Pincher Creek AB T0K 1W0
Tel: 403-627-5199; *Fax:* 403-627-5850
e-mail: info@pincher-creek.com
URL: www.pincher-creek.com
Brian Wright, President

Ponoka & District Chamber of Commerce
PO Box 4188, Ponoka AB T4J 1R6
Tel: 403-783-3888; *Fax:* 403-783-3888
e-mail: chamber@ponoka.org
Irven Snider, Executive Manager
Judith Knutson, President

Provost & District Chamber of Commerce
PO Box 637, Provost AB T0B 3S0
Tel: 780-753-6643
e-mail: chamberofcommerce@provost.ca
Anne Fraser, Contact

Rainbow Lake Chamber of Commerce
PO Box 272, Rainbow Lake AB T0H 2Y0
Tel: 780-956-3030; *Fax:* 780-956-3882
e-mail: tschulter@rainbowcable.ca
John Watt, Mayor

Raymond Chamber of Commerce
General Delivery, Raymond AB T0K 2S0
Tel: 403-752-3057
Russell Court, President

Red Deer Chamber of Commerce
3017 Gaetz Ave., Red Deer AB T4N 5Y6
Tel: 403-347-4491; *Fax:* 403-343-6188
e-mail: rdchamber@reddeerchamber.com
URL: www.reddeerchamber.com
Mike Axworthy, President
Tim Creedon, Executive Director

Redwater & District Chamber of Commerce
c/o The Town Of Redwater Town Office, PO Box 322, 4924-47 St., Redwater AB T0A 2W0
Tel: 780-942-3519; *Fax:* 780-942-4321
Dave McRae, Project Manager
Anne Murland, Secretary
Linda Lawrence, Treasurer

Rimbey Chamber of Commerce
PO Box 87, Rimbey AB T0C 2J0
Tel: 403-843-2020; *Fax:* 403-843-2027
e-mail: rimbeychamber@rimbey.com
Audreyann Bresnahan, President

Rocky Mountain House & District Chamber of Commerce
PO Box 1374, Stn. 5406-48 St., Rocky Mountain House AB T4T 1B1
Tel: 403-845-5450; *Fax:* 403-845-7764
Toll-Free: 800-565-3793
e-mail: rmhcofc@rockychamber.org
URL: www.rockychamber.org
Affiliation(s): AB Chamber of Commerce; Canadian Chamber of Commerce
Tammy Cote, President
Muriel Finkbeiner, Manager

St Albert Chamber of Commerce
71 St. Albert Rd., St Albert AB T8N 6L5
Tel: 780-458-2833; *Fax:* 780-458-6515
e-mail: chamber@stalbertchamber.com
URL: www.stalbertchamber.com
Joe Becigneul, Chair
Lynda Moffat, President & CEO

St Paul & District Chamber of Commerce
PO Box 887, St Paul AB T0A 3A0
Tel: 780-645-6800; *Fax:* 780-645-6059
Toll-Free: 888-733-8367
e-mail: admin@stpaulchamber.ca
URL: www.stpaulchamber.ca
Affiliation(s): Alberta Chambers of Commerce
Rhea Labrie, Executive Director
Doug Lamb, President

Sedgewick Chamber of Commerce
PO Box 625, Sedgewick AB T0B 4C0
Tel: 780-384-3912; *Fax:* 780-384-3938
Jeanette Harris, President

Sexsmith & District Chamber of Commerce
PO Box 146, Sexsmith AB T0H 3C0
Tel: 780-568-4663; *Fax:* 780-568-4115
e-mail: chmbrtos@telusplanet.net
Freda King, President

Sherwood Park & District Chamber of Commerce
100 Ordze Ave., Sherwood Park AB T8B 1M6
Tel: 780-464-0801; *Fax:* 780-449-3581
Toll-Free: 866-464-0801
e-mail: admin.spchamber@shaw.ca
URL: www.sherwoodparkchamber.com
Bob Bittner, Contact, Member Services
Todd Banks, Executive Director

Slave Lake & District Chamber of Commerce
PO Box 190, Slave Lake AB T0G 2A0
Tel: 780-849-3222; *Fax:* 780-849-6894
e-mail: sldcc@telusplanet.net
URL: www.slavelakechamberofcommerce.ca
Fay Sand, President
Annie Aarts, Office Manager

Smoky Lake & District Chamber of Commerce
PO Box 635, Smoky Lake AB T0A 3C0
Tel: 780-656-3842; *Fax:* 780-451-3321
e-mail: wilddeer@mcsnet.ca
Wayne Taylor, President

Spruce Grove & District Chamber of Commerce
PO Box 4210, 99 Campsite Rd, Spruce Grove AB T7X 3B4
Tel: 780-962-2561; *Fax:* 780-962-4417
e-mail: info@sprucegrovechamber.com
URL: www.sprucegrovechamber.com
Charlene Bell, President
Paul J. Lepine, CHRP, Executive Director

Stettler Regional Board of Trade & Community Development
6606, 50th Ave., Stettler AB T0C 2L2
Tel: 403-742-3181; *Fax:* 403-742-3123
Toll-Free: 877-742-9499
e-mail: info@stettlerboardoftrade.com
URL: www.stettlerboardoftrade.com
Gail Peterson, President
Keith Ryder, Executive Director

Stony Plain & District Chamber of Commerce
4815 - 44 Ave., Stony Plain AB T7Z 1V5
Tel: 780-963-4545; *Fax:* 780-963-4542
e-mail: info@stonyplainchamber.ca
URL: www.stonyplainchamber.ca
Graeme Dawes, President
Glen McCalpin, 1st Vice President

Strathmore & District Chamber of Commerce
PO Box 2222, Strathmore AB T1P 1K2
Tel: 403-901-3175; *Fax:* 403-901-1785
e-mail: contactus@strathmoredistrictchamber.com
URL: strathmoredistrictchamber.com
Robert Desjardins, President
Vi Giesbrecht, Administrative Assistance

Sundre Chamber of Commerce
PO Box 1085, Sundre AB T0M 1X0
Tel: 403-638-3245
e-mail: info@sundrechamber.com
URL: www.sundrechamber.com
Heidi Overgard, Secretary
James Eklund, President

Swan Hills Chamber of Commerce
PO Box 149, Swan Hills AB T0G 2C0
Tel: 780-333-4477; *Fax:* 780-333-4547
e-mail: town@townofswanhills.com
Ken Pullen, President

Sylvan Lake Chamber of Commerce
4802, 48 St., Sylvan Lake AB T4S 1S6
Tel: 403-887-3048; *Fax:* 403-887-4944
e-mail: info@sylvanlakechamber.com
URL: www.sylvanlakechamber.com
Laurie Breeze, Administrator
Danine Weber, President

Taber & District Chamber of Commerce
4702 - 50 St., Taber AB T1G 2B6
Tel: 403-223-2265; *Fax:* 403-223-2291
e-mail: admin@taberchamber.com
URL: www.taberchamber.com
Louie Tams, President
Candace Karren, Manager

Thorhild Chamber of Commerce
PO Box 384, 638 - 6th Ave., Thorhild AB T0A 3J0
Tel: 780-398-2575; *Fax:* 780-398-2010
e-mail: thorhildchamber@telus.net
John Dickey, President
Ed Cowley, Secretary

Thorsby & District Chamber of Commerce
PO Box 197, Thorsby AB T0C 2P0
Tel: 780-789-2100; *Fax:* 780-789-2155
e-mail: jfhunter@netcom.ca
Clarence Kruger, President

Three Hills & District Chamber of Commerce
PO Box 277, Three Hills AB T0M 2A0
Tel: 780-662-4441; *Fax:* 780-443-7171
Timothy J. Shearlaw, President

Tofield & District Chamber of Commerce
PO Box 967, General Delivery, Tofield AB T0B 4J0
Tel: 780-661-4441; *Fax:* 780-662-3725
URL: www.tofieldalberta.ca/chamber.htm
David Williamson, President

Trochu Chamber of Commerce
PO Box 607, Trochu AB T0M 2C0
Tel: 403-442-2785
Linda Hayes, President

Two Hills & District Chamber of Commerce
PO Box 225, Two Hills AB T0B 4K0
Tel: 780-632-3395; *Fax:* 780-657-2158
e-mail: diane_zawalykut@digitalweb.net
Robert Marsh, President

Valleyview Chamber of Commerce
PO Box 270, Valleyview AB T0H 3N0
Tel: 780-524-5150; *Fax:* 780-524-2727
e-mail: valvadmn@telusplanet.net
URL: www.albertafirst.com/profiles/statspack/20479.html
Gary Peterson, Town Manager
Bob Hall, Regional Manager

Vegreville & District Chamber of Commerce
Civic Bldg., PO Box 877, 5009 - 50 Ave., Vegreville AB T9C 1R9
Tel: 780-632-2771; *Fax:* 780-632-6958
e-mail: vegchamb@telusplanet.net
URL: www.vegrevillechamber.com
Rhonda Tkachuk, President
Elaine Kucher, General Manager

Vermilion & District Chamber of Commerce
4606 - 52nd St., Vermilion AB T9X 0A1
Tel: 780-853-6593; *Fax:* 780-853-1740
e-mail: vermcofc@telusplanet.net
URL: www.vermilionchamber.ca
Marlene Beattie, President

Viking Economic Development Committee (VEDC)
PO Box 369, Viking AB T0B 4N0
Tel: 780-336-3466; *Fax:* 780-336-2660
e-mail: laura.arndt@town.viking.ab.ca
URL: www.town.viking.ab.ca
Doug Lefsrud, Chair
Rod Krips, Town Manager

Vulcan & District Chamber of Commerce
PO Box 1161, 115 Centre St., Vulcan AB T0L 2B0
Tel: 403-485-2994; *Fax:* 403-485-2878
e-mail: info@vulcantourism.com
URL: www.vulcantourism.com
Brenda Weber, President

Wabamun District Chamber of Commerce Society
PO Box 29, Wabamun AB T0E 2K0
Tel: 780-892-4665
URL: www.albertafirst.com/profiles/statspack/20590.html
Tom Harris, President

Wainwright & District Chamber of Commerce
PO Box 2997, Wainwright AB T9W 1S9
Tel: 780-842-4910; *Fax:* 780-842-6061
e-mail: exec@wdchamber.com
URL: www.wdchamber.com
Dave Neville, President
Marketta Fahnbulleh, Executive Director

Waterton Park Chamber of Commerce & Visitors Association
PO Box 55, Waterton Lakes National Park AB T0K 2M0
Tel: 403-859-2224; *Fax:* 403-859-2650
e-mail: waterton.info@pc.gc.ca
URL: www.watertonchamber.com
Rod Kretz, President

Westlock & District Chamber of Commerce
PO Box 5917, Westlock AB T7P 2P7

Wetaskiwin Chamber of Commerce (WCC)
4910 - 55A St., Wetaskiwin AB T9A 2R7
Tel: 780-352-8003; *Fax:* 780-352-6226
e-mail: wcoc@incentre.net
URL: www.wetaskiwinchamber.ca
Cindy Ekkel, Secretary
Harvey Loroff, Treasurer
Wayne DiLallo, President

Whitecourt & District Chamber of Commerce
PO Box 1011, 3002 - 33rd St., Whitecourt AB T7S 1N9
Tel: 780-778-5363; *Fax:* 780-778-2351
Toll-Free: 800-313-7383
e-mail: manager@whitecourtchamber.com
URL: www.whitecourtchamber.com
Affiliation(s): Alberta Chamber of Commerce
Pat VanderBurg, General Manager
Marc Chayer, President

Worsley Chamber of Commerce
PO Box 181, Worsley AB T0H 3W0
Tel: 780-685-3943; *Fax:* 780-685-2115
Doug Allen, President

British Columbia

Abbotsford Chamber of Commerce
#207, 32900 South Fraser Way, Abbotsford BC V2S 5A1
Tel: 604-859-9651; *Fax:* 604-850-6880
e-mail: acoc@telus.net
URL: www.abbotsfordchamber.com
James Barlow, President

Alberni Valley Chamber of Commerce
2533 Port Alberni Hwy., Port Alberni BC V9Y 8P2
Tel: 250-724-6535; *Fax:* 250-724-6560
e-mail: avcoc@alberni.net
URL: www.avcoc.com
Dewayne Parfitt, President
Mike Carter, Executive Director

Armstrong-Spallumcheen Chamber of Commerce
PO Box 118, 3550 Bridge St., Armstrong BC V0E 1B0
Tel: 250-546-8155; *Fax:* 250-546-8868
e-mail: armstrong_chamber@telus.net
URL: aschamber.com
Patti Noonan, Manager
Sandra Starke, President

Bamfield Chamber of Commerce
Bamfield BC V0R 1B0
Tel: 250-728-3006
e-mail: info@bamfieldchamber.com
URL: www.bamfieldchamber.com
Affiliation(s): Pacific Rim Tourism Association

Barriere & District Chamber of Commerce
PO Box 1190, Barriere BC V0E 1E0
Tel: 250-672-9221; *Fax:* 250-672-2159
e-mail: info@barrieredistrict.com
URL: www.barrieredistrict.com/
Affiliation(s): Canadian Chamber of Commerce
Lorne Richardson, Manager & Marketing Coordinator

Bowen Island Chamber of Commerce
432 Cardena Road, Bowen Island BC V0N 1G0
Tel: 604-947-9024; *Fax:* 604-947-0633
e-mail: info@bowenisland.org
URL: www.bowenisland.org
Tim Rhodes, President

Burnaby Board of Trade (BBOT)
#201, 4555 Kingsway, Burnaby BC V5H 4T8
Tel: 604-412-0100; *Fax:* 604-412-0102
e-mail: contact@burnabyboardoftrade.com
URL: www.bbot.ca
Darlene Gering, CEO

Burns Lake & District Chamber of Commerce
PO Box 339, Burns Lake BC V0J 1E0
Tel: 250-692-3773; *Fax:* 250-692-3493
e-mail: bldcoc@telus.net
URL: www.burnslakechamber.ca
Rise Johansen, President

Cache Creek Chamber of Commerce
PO Box 460, Cache Creek BC V0K 1H0
Tel: 250-457-9668; *Fax:* 250-457-9669
e-mail: jade@coppervalleybc.ca
Gordon Daily, President

Campbell River & District Chamber of Commerce
PO Box 400, 900 Alder St., Campbell River BC V9W 5B6
Tel: 250-287-4636; *Fax:* 250-286-6490
e-mail: chamber@campbellriverchamber.ca
URL: www.campbellriverchamber.ca
Gary Thulin, President

Castlegar & District Chamber of Commerce (CDCoC)
c/o Mark Melnyk, 652, 18th St., Castlegar BC V1N 4B7
Tel: 250-365-6313; *Fax:* 250-365-5778
e-mail: info@castlegar.com
URL: www.castlegar.com
Mark Melnyk, President

Chamber of Commerce of the City of Grand Forks
PO Box 1086, 1647 Central Ave., Grand Forks BC V0H 1H0
Tel: 250-442-2833; *Fax:* 250-442-5688
Toll-Free: 866-442-2833
e-mail: manager@grandforkschamber.com
URL: www.grandforkschamber.com
David Evdokimoff, President
Cher Wyers, Manager

Chase & District Chamber of Commerce
PO Box 592, 400 Shuswap Avenue, Chase BC V0E 1M0
Tel: 250-679-8432; *Fax:* 250-679-3120
e-mail: admin@chasechamber.com
URL: www.chasechamber.com/
Barbara Maher, President

Chemainus & District Chamber of Commerce
PO Box 575, 9796 Willow St., Chemainus BC V0R 1K0
Tel: 250-246-3944; *Fax:* 250-246-3251
e-mail: ccoc@islandnet.com
URL: www.chemainus.bc.ca

Chetwynd & District Chamber of Commerce
PO Box 870, Chetwynd BC V0C 1J0
Tel: 250-788-3345; *Fax:* 250-788-3655
e-mail: chetcham@pris.bc.ca
Jackie Drake, Manager
Barb Shirley, President

Chilliwack Chamber of Commerce
#16, 45966 Yale Rd., Chilliwack BC V2P 2M3
Tel: 604-793-4323; *Fax:* 604-793-4303
e-mail: info@chilliwackchamber.com
URL: www.chilliwackchamber.com
Tim McAlpine, President
Sue Attrill, Chief Executive Officer

Christina Lake Chamber of Commerce
Hwy. 3 & Kimura Rd., Christina Lake BC V0H 1E2
Tel: 250-447-6161
e-mail: info@christinalake.com
URL: www.christinalake.com

Clearwater & District Chamber of Commerce
PO Box 1988, RR#1, Clearwater BC V0E 1N0
Tel: 250-674-2646; *Fax:* 250-674-3693
e-mail: info@clearwaterbcchamber.com
URL: www.clearwaterbcchamber.com
Sheena vanDyk

Clinton & District Chamber of Commerce
PO Box 256, Clinton BC V0K 1K0
Tel: 250-459-2640; *Fax:* 250-459-2627
Susan Swan, President

Cloverdale & District Chamber of Commerce
17687 - 56A Ave., Surrey BC V3S 1G4
Tel: 604-574-9802; *Fax:* 604-574-9122
e-mail: clovcham@axion.net
URL: www.cloverdale.bc.ca
Ben Wevers, President

Columbia Valley Chamber of Commerce (CVCC)
PO Box 1019, Invermere BC V0A 1K0
Tel: 250-342-2844; *Fax:* 250-342-3261
URL: www.cvchamber.ca
Affiliation(s): British Columbia Chamber of Commerce

Comox Valley Chamber of Commerce (CVCC)
2040 Cliffe Ave., Courtenay BC V9N 2L3
Tel: 250-334-3234; *Fax:* 250-334-4908
Toll-Free: 888-357-4471
e-mail: membership@comoxvalleychamber.com
URL: www.comoxvalleychamber.com
Sean O'Gorman, President
Dianne Hawkins, Executive Director

Cowichan Lake District Chamber of Commerce
PO Box 824, 125C South Shore Rd., Lake Cowichan BC V0R 2G0
Tel: 250-749-3244; *Fax:* 250-749-0187
e-mail: info@cowichanlake.ca
URL: www.cowichanlake.ca
Affiliation(s): Canadian Chamber of Commerce
Jim Humphrey, President

Cranbrook & District Chamber of Commerce
PO Box 84, Cranbrook BC V1C 4H6
Tel: 250-426-5914
Toll-Free: 800-222-6174
e-mail: cbkchamber@cyberlink.bc.ca
URL: www.cranbrookchamber.com
Connor Stewart, President
Karin Penner, Manager

Cumberland Chamber of Commerce
PO Box 250, 2680 Dunsmuir Ave., Cumberland BC V0R 1S0
Tel: 250-336-8313; *Fax:* 250-336-2455
e-mail: cumbcham@shaw.ca
URL: www.cumberlandbc.org
Affiliation(s): North By Northwest Tourism Association of BC

Dawson Creek & District Chamber of Commerce
10201 - 10th St., Dawson Creek BC V1G 3T5
Tel: 250-782-4868; *Fax:* 250-782-2371
e-mail: info@dawsoncreekchamber.ca
URL: www.dawsoncreekchamber.ca
Affiliation(s): BC Chamber of Commerce
David Roch, President

Dease Lake & District Chamber of Commerce
PO Box 338, Dease Lake BC V0C 1L0
Tel: 250-771-3900; *Fax:* 250-771-3900
Lyonna Mroch, Secretary
Rich Mroch, President

Delta Chamber of Commerce
6201 - 60 Ave., Delta BC V4K 4E2
Tel: 604-946-4232; *Fax:* 604-946-5285
e-mail: info@deltachamber.com
URL: www.deltachamber.com
Peter Roaf, Executive Director
Greg Muirhead, President

Discovery Islands Chamber of Commerce
PO Box 190, Quathiaski Cove BC V0P 1N0
Tel: 250-285-2724
Toll-Free: 866-285-2724
e-mail: chamber@discoveryislands.ca
URL: www.discoveryislands.ca/chamber
Susan Wilson, President

Duncan-Cowichan Chamber of Commerce (DCCC)
381 Trans-Canada Hwy., Duncan BC V9L 3R5
Tel: 250-748-1111; *Fax:* 250-746-8222
Toll-Free: 888-303-3337
e-mail: manager@duncancc.bc.ca
URL: www.duncancc.bc.ca
Cathy Mailhot, Manager
Alison Philp, Coordinator, Visitor Services (Visitor Centre - Community & Tourism Informatio

Elkford Chamber of Commerce
PO Box 220, 4A Front St., Elkford BC V0B 1H0
Tel: 250-865-4614; *Fax:* 250-865-2442
Toll-Free: 877-355-9453
e-mail: info@tourismelkford.ca
URL: www.tourismelkford.ca
Susan Robitaille, Manager
Ian Benson, President

Enderby & District Chamber of Commerce
PO Box 1000, Enderby BC V0E 1V0
Tel: 250-838-6727; *Fax:* 250-838-0123
Toll-Free: 877-213-6509
e-mail: echamber@jetstream.net
URL: www.enderby.com/chamber

Esquimalt Chamber of Commerce
PO Box 36019, 1153 Esquimalt Rd., Victoria BC V9A 7J5
Tel: 250-704-2525; *Fax:* 250-380-6932
e-mail: info@esquimaltchamber.com
URL: www.esquimaltchamber.com
Ed Williams, President

Fernie Chamber of Commerce
102 Commerce Rd., Fernie BC V0B 1M5
Tel: 250-423-6868; *Fax:* 250-423-3811
Toll-Free: 877-433-7643

e-mail: info@ferniechamber.com
URL: www.ferniechamber.com
Affiliation(s): Economic Development Association of BC

Fort Nelson & District Chamber of Commerce
PO Box 196, 5315B, 50th Avenue S, Fort Nelson BC V0C 1R0
Tel: 250-774-2956; *Fax:* 250-774-2958
e-mail: info@fortnelsonchamber.com
URL: www.fortnelsonchamber.com
Geordie McLennan, President
Heather Sellors, Executive Director

Fort St. James Chamber of Commerce
PO Box 1164, Fort St James BC V0J 1P0
Tel: 250-996-7023; *Fax:* 250-996-7047
e-mail: fsjchamb@fsjames.com
URL: www.fortstjameschamber.com
Dennis Gladne, President
Carol Magnus, Manager

Fort St. John & District Chamber of Commerce
9325 - 100 St., Fort St John BC V1J 4N4
Tel: 250-785-6037; *Fax:* 250-785-7181
e-mail: info@fsjchamber.com
URL: www.fsjchamber.com
Annette Oak, Chamber Manager
Andy Ackerman, President

Gabriola Island Chamber of Commerce
PO Box 249, #3, 575 North Rd., Gabriola BC V0R 1X0
Tel: 250-247-9332; *Fax:* 250-247-9332
Toll-Free: 888-284-9332
e-mail: info@gabriolaisland.org, manager@gabriolaisland.org
URL: www.gabriolaisland.org
Affiliation(s): Tourism Association of Vancouver Island
Ken Wur, President

Galiano Island Chamber of Commerce
PO Box 73, Galiano BC V0N 1P0
Tel: 250-539-2233
e-mail: info@galianoisland.com
URL: www.galianoisland.com
Ken Smith, President

Gibsons & District Chamber of Commerce
PO Box 1190, #21, 900 Gibsons Way, Gibsons BC V0N 1V0
Tel: 604-886-2325; *Fax:* 604-886-2379
e-mail: gibsonsbcchamber@telus.net
URL: www.gibsonsbc.ca/chamber
Jeff Barringer, President
Cheryl Baron, Executive Director

Gold River Chamber of Commerce
PO Box 39, Gold River BC V0P 1G0
Tel: 250-283-7333
Gabriella Pentz, President
Craig Scott, Vice-President

Golden & District Chamber of Commerce (GDCC)
PO Box 1320, 500 - 10 North Ave., Golden BC V0A 1H0
Tel: 250-344-7125; *Fax:* 250-344-6688
Toll-Free: 800-622-4653
e-mail: info@goldenchamber.bc.ca
URL: www.goldenchamber.bc.ca
Ruth Kowalski, Manager
Michael Dalzell, President

Greater Kamloops Chamber of Commerce
1290 Trans Canada Hwy., Kamloops BC V2C 6R3
Tel: 250-372-7722; *Fax:* 250-828-9500
e-mail: mail@kamloopschamber.bc.ca
URL: www.kamloopschamber.bc.ca
Leslie Brochu, President
Deb McClelland, Executive Director

Greater Langley Chamber of Commerce
#1, 5761 Glover Rd., Langley BC V3A 8M8
Tel: 604-530-6656; *Fax:* 604-530-7066
e-mail: chamber@langleychamber.com
URL: www.langleychamber.com
Kevin Staples, President

Greater Nanaimo Chamber of Commerce
2133 Bowen Rd., Nanaimo BC V9S 1H8
Tel: 250-756-1191; *Fax:* 250-756-1584
e-mail: info@nanaimochamber.bc.ca
URL: www.nanaimochamber.bc.ca
Lee Mason, Executive Director & Coordinator, Special Events
Donna Hais, President
Scott Thomson, Treasurer

Greater Vernon Chamber of Commerce (GVCC)
701 Hwy. 97 South, Vernon BC V1B 3W4
Tel: 250-545-0771; *Fax:* 250-545-3114
e-mail: info@vernonchamber.ca
URL: www.vernonchamber.ca
Affiliation(s): Canadian Chamber of Commerce
Val Trevis, General Manager
David Fletcher, President

Greater Victoria Chamber of Commerce (GVCC)
#100, 852 Fort St., Victoria BC V8W 1H8
Tel: 250-383-7191; *Fax:* 250-385-3552
e-mail: chamber@gvcc.org
URL: www.victoriachamber.ca
Bruce Carter, CEO
Margaret Lucas, Chair
David Marshall, Treasurer

Harrison Agassiz Chamber of Commerce
PO Box 429, Harrison Hot Springs BC V0M 1K0
Tel: 604-796-1133; *Fax:* 604-796-3694
URL: www.harrison.ca
Robert Reyerse, President

Hope & District Chamber of Commerce
PO Box 588, 895, 3rd Avenue, Hope BC V0X 1L0
Tel: 604-869-3111; *Fax:* 604-869-8208
e-mail: info@hopechamber.bc.ca
URL: www.hopechamber.bc.ca
Victor Smith, President

Houston & District Chamber of Commerce
PO Box 396, 3289 Hwy. 16, Houston BC V0J 1Z0
Tel: 250-845-7640; *Fax:* 250-845-3682
e-mail: info@houstonchamber.ca
URL: www.houstonchamber.ca
Troy Reitsma, President
Maureen Czirfusz, Manager

Kaslo Chamber of Commerce
PO Box 329, Kaslo BC V0G 1M0
Toll-Free: 866-276-3212
e-mail: info@kaslochamber.com
URL: www.kaslochamber.com
Gary Cockerall, President

Kelowna Chamber of Commerce
544 Harvey Ave., Kelowna BC V1Y 6C9
Tel: 250-861-3627; *Fax:* 250-861-3624
e-mail: info@kelownachamber.org
URL: www.kelownachamber.org
Affiliation(s): BC Chamber of Commerce
Norm LeCavalier, President

Kimberley Bavarian Society Chamber of Commerce (KBSCC)
270 Kimberley Ave., Kimberley BC V1A 3N3
Tel: 250-427-3666; *Fax:* 250-427-5378
Toll-Free: 866-913-3666
e-mail: info@kimberleychamber.ca
URL: www.kimberleychamber.ca
Schaun Goodeve, President

Kitimat Chamber of Commerce
PO Box 214, Kitimat BC V8C 2G7
Tel: 250-632-6294; *Fax:* 250-632-4685
Toll-Free: 800-664-6554
e-mail: kitimatchamber@telus.net
URL: www.visitkitimat.com
Tony Brady, President

Kitsilano Chamber of Commerce (KCC)
PO Box 34369, Stn. D, Vancouver BC V6J 4P3
Tel: 604-731-4454
Toll-Free: 877-312-1898
e-mail: admin@kitsilanochamber.com
URL: www.kitsilanochamber.com/
Thomas B. DeSchutter, President

Kootenay Lake Chamber of Commerce
PO Box 120, Crawford Bay BC V0B 1E0
Tel: 250-227-9233
e-mail: info@kootenaylake.bc.ca
URL: www.kootenaylake.bc.ca
Paul Hindson, Treasurer

Ladysmith Chamber of Commerce
PO Box 598, 441B, 1st Ave., Ladysmith BC V9G 1A4
Tel: 250-245-2112; *Fax:* 250-245-2124
e-mail: info@ladysmithcofc.com
URL: www.ladysmithcofc.com
Affiliation(s): Cowichan Regional Valley
Heidi Derhousoff, Manager
Brian Bancroft, President

Lake Country Chamber of Commerce
#40, 9522 Main St., Lake Country BC V4V 2L9
Tel: 250-766-5670; *Fax:* 250-766-0170
Toll-Free: 888-766-5670
e-mail: admin@lakecountrychamber.com
URL: www.lakecountrychamber.com
Bill Clark, President
Linda Wilson, Manager

Likely & District Chamber of Commerce
PO Box 29, Likely BC V0L 1N0
Tel: 250-790-2127; *Fax:* 250-790-2323
e-mail: chamber@likely-bc.ca
URL: www.likely-bc.ca

Lillooet & District Chamber of Commerce
PO Box 650, Lillooet BC V0K 1V0
Tel: 250-256-3578; *Fax:* 250-256-4882
e-mail: deverell@telus.net
URL: www.lillooetchamberofcommerce.com
Bob Sheridan, President

Lumby & District Chamber of Commerce
PO Box 534, Lumby BC V0E 2G0
Tel: 250-547-2300; *Fax:* 250-547-2300
e-mail: lumbychamber@shaw.ca
URL: www.monasheetourism.com
Stephanie Sexsmith, Manager
Bill Maltman, President

Lytton & District Chamber of Commerce
PO Box 460, Lytton BC V0K 1Z0
Tel: 250-455-2523; *Fax:* 250-455-6669
e-mail: lyttoncc@goldtrail.com
URL: www.coastandmountains.bc.ca/page.cfm/650
Affiliation(s): Vancouver Coast & Mountains Tourism Region
Peggy Chute, Manager
Richard Forrest, President

Mackenzie Chamber of Commerce
PO Box 880, Mackenzie BC V0J 2C0
Tel: 250-997-5459; *Fax:* 250-997-6117
Toll-Free: 877-622-5360
e-mail: mackcoc@mackbc.com
URL: www.mackenziechamber.bc.ca
Affiliation(s): Retail Merchants Association of BC
Margaret Grant, Manager
Amber Hancock, President

Maple Ridge Pitt Meadows Chamber of Commerce
22238 Lougheed Hwy., Maple Ridge BC V2X 2T2
Tel: 604-463-3366; *Fax:* 604-463-3201
URL: www.ridgemeadowschamber.com
Affiliation(s): BC Chamber Executive; Canadian Chamber of Commerce; Southwestern BC Tourism
Jeff Cerpenter, President

Mayne Island Community Chamber of Commerce
PO Box 2, Mayne BC V0N 2J0
Tel: 250-539-9815
e-mail: info@mayneislandchamber.ca
URL: www.mayneislandchamber.ca
Richard Iredale, President
Joanie McCorry, Manager

McBride & District Chamber of Commerce
PO Box 2, McBride BC V0J 2E0
Tel: 250-569-3366; *Fax:* 250-569-2376
Toll-Free: 866-569-3366
e-mail: come2mcbride@telus.net
URL: www.mcbridebc.info
Vincent de Niet, President

Merritt & District Chamber of Commerce
PO Box 1649, 2185B Voght St., Merritt BC V1K 1B8
Tel: 250-378-5634; *Fax:* 250-378-6561
e-mail: manager@merrittchamber.com
URL: www.merrittchamber.com
Karen Fox, Executive Director

Mission Regional Chamber of Commerce
34033 Lougheed Hwy., Mission BC V2V 5X8
Tel: 604-826-6914; *Fax:* 604-826-5916
e-mail: manager@missionchamber.bc.ca
URL: www.missionchamber.bc.ca
Michelle Favero, Manager
Sean Melia, President

Nakusp & District Chamber of Commerce
PO Box 387, 92 - 6th. Ave. NW, Nakusp BC V0G 1R0
Tel: 250-265-4234; *Fax:* 250-265-3808
Toll-Free: 800-909-8819
e-mail: nakcom@telus.net
URL: www.nakusparrowlakes.com
Affiliation(s): Tourism British Columbia
Kim Reich, President

Nelson & District Chamber of Commerce
255 Hall St., Nelson BC V1L 5X4
Tel: 250-352-3433; *Fax:* 250-352-6355
Toll-Free: 877-663-5706
e-mail: info@discovernelson.com
URL: www.discovernelson.com
Affiliation(s): British Columbia Chamber of Commerce; Canadian Chamber of Commerce
Cal Renwick, President

New Westminster Chamber of Commerce
601 Queens Ave., New Westminster BC V3M 1L1
Tel: 604-521-7781; *Fax:* 604-521-0057
e-mail: nwcc@newwestchamber.com
URL: www.newwestchamber.com
David Brennan, Executive Director
Andrew Hopkins, President

North Shuswap Chamber of Commerce
PO Box 101, Celista BC V0E 1L0
Tel: 250-955-2113; *Fax:* 250-955-2113
Toll-Free: 888-955-1488
e-mail: requests@northshuswapbc.com
URL: www.northshuswapbc.com

North Vancouver Chamber of Commerce (NVCC)
#102, 124 - 1st St. West, Vancouver BC V7M 3N3
Tel: 604-987-4488; *Fax:* 604-987-8272
e-mail: info@nvchamber.bc.ca; events@nvchamber.ca
URL: www.nvchamber.bc.ca
Naomi Yamamoto, President & General Manager
Stephen Joyce, Chair
Misha Wilson, Manager, Visitor Centre

Okanagan Falls Chamber of Commerce
PO Box 246, Okanagan Falls BC V0H 1R0
e-mail: okfalls@img.net
Kevin Therrien, President

Osoyoos Chamber of Commerce
PO Box 277, Osoyoos BC V0H 1V0
Tel: 250-495-7142; *Fax:* 250-495-7132
e-mail: info@osoyooschamber.bc.ca
URL: www.osoyooschamber.bc.ca
CJ Rhodes, President

Parksville & District Chamber of Commerce
PO Box 99, 1275 East Island Hwy., Parksville BC V9P 2G3
Tel: 250-248-3613; *Fax:* 250-248-5210
URL: www.parksvillechamber.com
Peter Doukakis, Executive Director
Gary Child, President

Peachland Chamber of Commerce
5812 Beach Ave., Peachland BC V0H 1X7
Tel: 250-767-2455; *Fax:* 250-767-2420
Toll-Free: 866-955-2455
e-mail: peachlandchamber@shawcable.com
URL: www.peachlandchamber.bc.ca
Donna Weigelt, President

Pemberton Chamber of Commerce
PO Box 370, Pemberton BC V0N 2L0
Tel: 604-894-6477; *Fax:* 604-894-5571
e-mail: info@pembertonchamber.com
URL: www.pembertonchamber.com
Affiliation(s): Vancouver Board of Trade
Shirley Henry, Secretary
Paul Selina, President

Pender Harbour & Egmont Chamber of Commerce
PO Box 265, 1287 Madeira Park Rd., Madeira Park BC V0N 2H0
Tel: 604-883-2561; *Fax:* 604-883-2561
Toll-Free: 877-873-6337
e-mail: chamber@penderharbour.ca
URL: www.penderharbour.ca
Kerry Milligan, Secretary
Dave Milligan, President

Pender Island Chamber of Commerce
PO Box 123, Pender Island BC V0N 2M0
Tel: 250-629-3988
Toll-Free: 866-468-7924
e-mail: travel@penderislandchamber.com
URL: www.penderislandchamber.com

Penticton & Wine Country Chamber of Commerce
553 Railway St., Penticton BC V2A 8S3
Tel: 250-492-4103; *Fax:* 250-492-6119
Toll-Free: 800-663-5052
e-mail: membership@penticton.org
URL: www.penticton.org
Judy Poole, Manager
Joe Morelli, President

Port Hardy & District Chamber of Commerce
PO Box 249, Port Hardy BC V0N 2P0
Tel: 250-949-7622; *Fax:* 250-949-6653
e-mail: phcc@cablerocket.com
URL: www.ph-chamber.bc.ca
Sandra Boyd, President

Port McNeill & District Chamber of Commerce
PO Box 129, 1594 Beach Dr., Port McNeill BC V0N 2R0
Tel: 250-956-3131; *Fax:* 250-956-3132
Toll-Free: 888-956-3131
e-mail: pmccc@island.net
URL: www.portmcneill.net
Gaby Wickstrom, President
Gaby Wickstrom, President

Port Renfrew Chamber of Commerce
General Delivery, Port Renfrew BC V0S 1K0
Tel: 250-647-0009; *Fax:* 250-647-0058
e-mail: prcc@portrenfrew.com
URL: www.portrenfrewcommunity.com
Tim Cash, President
Brian Cameron, Vice-President

Powell River Chamber of Commerce
6807 Wharf St., Powell River BC V8A 2T9
Tel: 604-485-4051; *Fax:* 604-485-4272
e-mail: office@powellriverchamber.com
URL: www.powellriverchamber.com
Dave Formosa, President

Prince George Chamber of Commerce
890 Vancouver St., Prince George BC V2L 2P5
Tel: 250-562-2454; *Fax:* 250-562-6510
e-mail: chamber@pgchamber.bc.ca
URL: www.pgchamber.bc.ca
Sherry Sethen, Executive Director

Prince Rupert & District Chamber of Commerce (PRDCC)
PO Box 158, #100, 215 Cow Bay Rd., Prince Rupert BC V8J 1A2
Tel: 250-624-2296; *Fax:* 250-624-6105
Toll-Free: 800-667-1994
e-mail: manager@princerupertchamber.ca
URL: www.princerupertchamber.ca
Deb Stava, President
Maynard Angus, Vice-President
Lynne Graham, Chamber Manager

Princeton & District Chamber of Commerce
PO Box 540, Princeton BC V0X 1W0
Tel: 250-295-3103; *Fax:* 250-295-3255
e-mail: chamber@nethop.net
URL: www.princeton.ca
Lori Thomas, Manager

Qualicum Beach Chamber of Commerce
PO Box 159, 124 West 2nd Avenue, Qualicum Beach BC V9K 1S7
Tel: 250-752-0960; *Fax:* 250-752-2923
e-mail: chamber@qualicum.bc.ca
URL: www.qualicum.bc.ca
Affiliation(s): Oceanside Tourism Association
Judi Ainsworth, General Manager

Queen Charlotte Islands Chamber of Commerce
PO Box 448, Port Clements BC V0T 1R0
Tel: 250-557-4565; *Fax:* 250-557-4565
e-mail: chamber@qcislands.net
URL: www.qcislands.net/chamber
Maggie Bell Brown, Secretary

Quesnel & District Chamber of Commerce
679B, Hwy. 97 South, Quesnel BC V2J 4C7
Tel: 250-747-0125; *Fax:* 250-747-0126
e-mail: qchamber@quesnelbc.com
URL: www.quesnelchamber.com
Coralee Oakes, Manager
Keith Brookes, President

Radium Hot Springs Chamber of Commerce
PO Box 225, Radium Hot Springs BC V0A 1M0
Tel: 250-347-9331; *Fax:* 250-347-9127
Toll-Free: 800-347-9704
e-mail: info@RadiumHotSprings.com
URL: www.RadiumHotSprings.com
Kent Kebe, Manager
Douglas McIntosh, President

Revelstoke Chamber of Commerce
PO Box 490, 204 Campbell Avenue, Revelstoke BC V0E 2S0
Tel: 250-837-5345; *Fax:* 250-837-4223
e-mail: revelstokeinfo@telus.net
URL: revelstokechamber.com
Deenie Ottenbreit, President

Richmond Chamber of Commerce
South Tower, #101, 5811 Cooney Rd., Richmond BC V6X 3M1
Tel: 604-278-2822; *Fax:* 604-278-2972
e-mail: rcc@richmondchamber.ca
URL: www.richmondchamber.ca
Affiliation(s): Tourism Richmond; Sister Chamber - Kent, Washington
Carol Young, Manager, Administration & Events

Rossland Chamber of Commerce
PO Box 1385, Rossland BC V0G 1Y0
Tel: 250-362-5666; *Fax:* 250-362-5399
e-mail: commerce@rossland.com
URL: www.rossland.com/about
Maritza Reilly, Executive Director

Saanich Peninsula Chamber of Commerce (SPCOC)
#201, 2453 Beacon Ave., Sidney BC V8L 1X7
Tel: 250-656-3616; *Fax:* 250-656-7111
e-mail: info@peninsulachamber.ca
URL: www.peninsulachamber.ca
Eileen Leddy, Executive Director
Charles Hodgins, President

Salmo & District Chamber of Commerce
PO Box 400, 100 Fourth Street, Salmo BC V0G 1Z0
Tel: 250-357-2596
URL: www.salmo.net

Salmon Arm & District Chamber of Commerce (SACC)
PO Box 999, #101, 20 Hudson Avenue NE, Salmon Arm BC V1E 4P2
Tel: 250-832-6247; *Fax:* 250-832-8382
e-mail: info@sachamber.bc.ca
URL: www.sachamber.bc.ca
Dave Andrews, President

Salt Spring Island Chamber of Commerce
121 Lower Ganges Rd., Salt Spring Island BC V8K 2T1
Tel: 250-537-5252; *Fax:* 250-537-4276
Toll-Free: 866-216-2936
e-mail: chamber@saltspring.com
URL: www.saltspringtoday.com
Mafalda Hoogerdyk, President
Donna Powell, Manager

Sechelt & District Chamber of Commerce
PO Box 360, #102 - 5700 Cowrie St., Sechelt BC V0N 3A0
Tel: 604-885-0662; *Fax:* 604-885-0691
Toll-Free: 877-633-2963
e-mail: secheltchamber@dccnet.com
URL: www.secheltchamber.bc.ca
Jim Cleghorn, President
Colleen Clark, Executive Director

Seton Portage/Shalalth District Chamber of Commerce
PO Box 2067, Seton Portage BC V0N 3B0
Tel: 250-259-8312; *Fax:* 250-259-8213
e-mail: snor@uniserve.com
Ray Klassen, Vice-President

Sicamous & District Chamber of Commerce
PO Box 346, Sicamous BC V0E 2V0
Tel: 250-836-3313; *Fax:* 250-836-4368
e-mail: sicamouschamber@cablelan.net
URL: www.sicamouschamber.bc.ca
Charlotte Hutchinson, President
Doreen Favel, Manager

Slocan District Chamber of Commerce
PO Box 448, New Denver BC V0G 1S0
Tel: 250-358-2544; *Fax:* 250-358-7998
URL: www.slocanlake.com/chamber.html

Smithers District Chamber of Commerce
PO Box 2379, Smithers BC V0J 2N0
Tel: 250-847-5072; *Fax:* 250-847-3337
Toll-Free: 800-542-6673
e-mail: chamber@tourismsmithers.com
URL: www.tourismsmithers.com/chamber
Affiliation(s): Northern BC Tourism Association

Sooke Harbour Chamber of Commerce
PO Box 18, 6716 Westcoast Rd., Sooke BC V0S 1N0
Tel: 250-642-6112
e-mail: info@sookeharbourchamber.com
URL: www.sookeharbourchamber.com
Scott Gertsma, President

South Cariboo Chamber of Commerce
PO Box 2312, 100 Mile House BC V0K 2E0
Tel: 250-395-6124; *Fax:* 250-395-8974
e-mail: manager@scariboochamber.org
URL: www.scariboochamber.org
Affiliation(s): Canadian Chamber of Commerce
Howard McMillan, Manager
Chris Nickless, President

South Cowichan Chamber of Commerce (SCCC)
#368, 2720 Mill Bay Rd., Mill Bay BC V0R 2P1
Tel: 250-743-3566; *Fax:* 250-743-5332
e-mail: info@southcowichanchamber.org
URL: www.southcowichanchamber.org
Rosalie Power, Manager
Leslie Grills, President

South Okanagan Chamber Of Commerce
PO Box 460, 36205, 93rd St., Oliver BC V0H 1T0
Tel: 250-498-6321; *Fax:* 250-498-3156
Toll-Free: 888-498-6321
URL: www.sochamber.ca
Bonnie Dancey, Manager
Kenn Oldfield, President

South Shuswap Chamber of Commerce
PO Box 7, Blind Bay BC V0E 2W0
Tel: 250-675-3515; *Fax:* 250-675-3516
e-mail: sorrentochamber@telus.net
URL: www.southshuswapchamberofcommerce.org
Chris Emery, President
Nancy Kyle, Manager

Sparwood & District Chamber of Commerce
PO Box 1448, Aspen Dr., Sparwood BC V0B 2G0
Tel: 250-425-2423; *Fax:* 250-425-7130
Toll-Free: 877-485-8185
e-mail: administrator@sparwoodchamber.bc.ca
URL: www.sparwoodchamber.bc.ca
Muriel Stickney, President
Alayna Casselman, Administrator

Squamish Chamber of Commerce
Squamish Adventure Centre, #102, 38551 Loggers Lane, Squamish BC V8B 0H2
Tel: 604-815-4994; *Fax:* 604-815-4998
Toll-Free: 866-333-2010
e-mail: info@squamishchamber.com
URL: www.squamishchamber.com
Sameer Kajani, President
Kenny Music, Managing Director

Stewart-Hyder International Chamber of Commerce
PO Box 306, Stewart BC V0T 1W0
Tel: 250-636-9224; *Fax:* 250-636-2199
Toll-Free: 888-366-5999
e-mail: info@stewart-hyder.com
URL: www.stewart-hyder.com
Mary G. McKay, President
Gwen McKay, Manager

Summerland Chamber of Economic Development & Tourism (SCEDT)
PO Box 130, 15600 Hwy 97, Summerland BC V0H 1Z0
Tel: 250-494-2686; *Fax:* 250-494-4039
e-mail: info@summerlandchamber.com
URL: www.summerlandchamber.com
Affiliation(s): Economic Development Association of BC; Thompson/Okanagan Tourism Association
Scott Boswell, Executive Director
Juanita Gibney, President

Surrey Board of Trade (SBOT)
#101, 14439 - 104 Ave., Surrey BC V3R 1M1
Tel: 604-581-7130; *Fax:* 604-588-7549
Toll-Free: 866-848-7130
e-mail: info@businessinsurrey.com
URL: www.businessinsurrey.com
James Stewart, President
Anita Huberman, Chief Executive Officer

Tahsis Chamber of Commerce
PO Box 278, 36 Rugged Mountain Road, Tahsis BC V0P 1X0
Tel: 204-934-6425
e-mail: info@tahsischamberofcommerce.com
URL: www.tahsischamberofcommerce.com
Corrine Dahling, President
Jude Schooner, Secretary/Treasurer

Terrace & District Chamber of Commerce
4511 Keith Ave., Terrace BC V8G 1K1
Tel: 250-635-2063; *Fax:* 250-635-2573
Toll-Free: 800-499-1637
e-mail: executivedirector@terracechamber.com
URL: www.terracechamber.com
Stacey Mann, Executive Director

Tofino-Long Beach Chamber of Commerce
PO Box 249, Tofino BC V0R 2Z0
Tel: 250-725-3414; *Fax:* 250-725-3296
e-mail: info@tourismtofino.com
URL: www.tourismtofino.com
Larry Nicolay, President

Trail & District Chamber of Commerce
#200, 1199 Bay Ave., Trail BC V1R 4A4
Tel: 250-368-3144; *Fax:* 250-368-6427
e-mail: tcoc@netidea.com
URL: www.trailchamber.com
Shane McIntyre, President
Pam Lewin, Executive Director

Tri-Cities Chamber of Commerce Serving Coquitlam, Port Coquitlam & Port Moody
1209 Pinetree Way, Coquitlam BC V3B 7Y3
Tel: 604-464-2716; *Fax:* 604-464-6796
e-mail: info@tricitieschamber.com
URL: www.tricitieschamber.com
Dennis Marsden, President

Ucluelet Chamber of Commerce (UCOC)
PO Box 428, #3, 1645 Cedar Street, Ucluelet BC V0R 3A0
Tel: 250-726-4641; *Fax:* 250-726-4611
e-mail: marny@uclueletinfo.com
URL: www.uclueletinfo.com
Marny Saunders, General Manager

Valemount & Area Chamber of Commerce
PO Box 690, Valemount BC V0E 2Z0
Tel: 250-566-0061; *Fax:* 250-566-4244
URL: www.thevalleysentinel.com/chamber
Christine Latimer, President

Vanderhoof & District Chamber of Commerce
PO Box 126, 2353 Burrard Ave., Vanderhoof BC V0J 3A0
Tel: 250-567-2124; *Fax:* 250-567-3316
Toll-Free: 800-752-4094
e-mail: chamber@hwy16.com
URL: www.vanderhoofchamber.com
Affiliation(s): BC Chamber of Commerce
Stuart Sinclair, President
Erin Siemens, Manager

Wells & District Chamber of Commerce
PO Box 123, Wells BC V0K 2R0
Tel: 250-994-3223; *Fax:* 250-994-3223
Toll-Free: 877-451-9355
e-mail: marketing@wellsbc.com
URL: www.wellsbc.com
Norma Collins, President

West Shore Chamber of Commerce
2830 Aldwynd Rd., Victoria BC V9B 3S7
Tel: 250-478-1130; *Fax:* 250-478-1584
e-mail: chamber@westshore.bc.ca
URL: www.westshore.bc.ca
Mike Wicks, CEO
Leiha Snow, Manager, Membership
Lucinda French, Executive Assistant

West Vancouver Chamber of Commerce
1846 Marine Dr., West Vancouver BC V7V 1J6
Tel: 604-926-6614; *Fax:* 604-925-7220
e-mail: info@westvanchamber.com
URL: www.westvanchamber.com
Tom Young, Executive Director

Westbank & District Chamber of Commerce
#4, 2375 Pamela Rd., Westbank BC V4T 2H9
Tel: 250-768-3378; *Fax:* 250-768-3465
Toll-Free: 866-768-3378
e-mail: chamber@westbankchamber.com
URL: www.westbankchamber.com
Broc Braconnier, President
Leah Thordarson, Manager

Whistler Chamber of Commerce
#201, 4230 Gateway Dr., Whistler BC V0N 1B4
Tel: 604-932-5922; *Fax:* 604-932-3755
e-mail: chamber@whistlerchamber.com
URL: www.whistlerchamber.com
Dave Davenport, Chair
Fiona Famulak, President

White Rock & South Surrey Chamber of Commerce
#101, 2430 King George Hwy., Surrey BC V4B 1H5
Tel: 604-536-6844; *Fax:* 604-536-4994
e-mail: info@whiterockchamber.com
URL: www.whiterockchamber.com
Affiliation(s): BC Tourism
Dan Higgins, President

Williams Lake & District Chamber of Commerce
1660 Broadway South, Williams Lake BC V2G 2W4
Tel: 250-392-5025; *Fax:* 250-392-4214
Toll-Free: 877-967-5253
e-mail: info@williamslakechamber.com
URL: www.williamslakechamber.com
Affiliation(s): BC Chamber of Commerce; Canadian Chamber of Commerce; Cariboo Chilcotin Coast Tourism Association
Roger Solly, President
Claudia Blair, Executive Director

Zeballos Board of Trade
PO Box 208, Zeballos BC V0P 2A0
Tel: 250-761-4261; *Fax:* 250-761-4188
e-mail: boardoftrade@zeballos.com
URL: www.zeballos.com
Tom Weston, President
Debra Brown, Secretary

Manitoba

Altona & District Chamber of Commerce
PO Box 329, Altona MB R0G 0B0
Tel: 204-324-8793; *Fax:* 204-324-1314
e-mail: chamber@shopaltona.com
URL: www.shopaltona.com
Vic Loewen, President
Susan Yakabowich, Manager

Arborg Chamber of Commerce
PO Box 415, Arborg MB R0C 0A0
Tel: 204-376-2878; *Fax:* 204-376-2999
Lorne Floyd, President

Ashern & District Chamber of Commerce
PO Box 582, Ashern MB R0C 0E0
Tel: 204-768-2634; *Fax:* 204-768-2088
e-mail: info@ashern.ca
URL: www.ashern.ca
Glen Noordenbos, President

Assiniboia Chamber of Commerce (MB) (ACC)
PO Box 42122, Stn. Ferry Road, Winnipeg MB R3J 3X7
Tel: 204-774-4154; *Fax:* 204-774-4201
e-mail: info@assiniboiacc.mb.ca
URL: www.assiniboiacc.mb.ca
Ernie Nairn, Executive Director

Beausejour & District Chamber of Commerce
PO Box 224, Beausejour MB R0E 0C0
Tel: 204-268-3502; *Fax:* 204-268-3502
e-mail: chamber@mybeausejour.com
URL: mybeausejour.com/chamber/index.php
Carol Boychuk, Executive Director
Ken Zirk, President

Birtle & District Chamber of Commerce
PO Box 278, Birtle MB R0M 0C0
Tel: 204-842-3944
Alan Wong, Secretary
Steve Desjardins, President

Blue Water Chamber of Commerce
PO Box 11, St Georges MB R0E 1V0
Tel: 204-367-2762
Edward A Gaffray, President

Boissevain & District Chamber of Commerce
PO Box 734, Boissevain MB R0K 0E0
Tel: 204-534-6300; *Fax:* 204-534-6825
Ivan E.J. Strain, President
Donna Frasersik, Secretary

Brandon Chamber of Commerce
1043 Rosser Ave., Brandon MB R7A 0L5
Tel: 204-571-5340; *Fax:* 204-571-5347
e-mail: info@brandonchamber.ca
URL: www.brandonchamber.ca
Randy Brown, President
Marnie McGregor, General Manager

Carberry & District Chamber of Commerce
PO Box 101, Carberry MB R0K 0H0
Tel: 204-834-6616
e-mail: edo@townofcarberry.ca
Christinia Steen, President
Lori Scott, Secretary

Carman & Community Chamber of Commerce
PO Box 249, Carman MB R0G 0J0
Tel: 204-750-3050
e-mail: ccchamber@gmail.com
URL: www.carmanchamberofcommerce.com
Affiliation(s): Manitoba Chamber of Commerce

Heidi Sandulak, President
Jim Hay, Secretary

Chambre de commerce de Notre Dame
PO Box 107, Notre Dame de Lourdes MB R0G 1M0
Tel: 204-248-2582; *Fax:* 204-248-2731
Denis Collet, President
Joey Dupasquler, Secretary

La chambre de commerce de Saint-Malo & District
CP 328, Saint-Malo MB R0A 1T0
Joël Fouasse, Co-président
Gilles Maynard, Co-président

Chambre de commerce francophone de Saint-Boniface (CCFSB) / St-Boniface chamber of Commerce
CP 204, #212, 383, boul. Provencher, Saint-Boniface MB R2H 3B4
Tél: 204-235-1406; *Téléc:* 204-233-1017
Courriel: info@ccfsb.mb.ca
URL: www.ccfsb.mb.ca
Alain Laurencelle, Président

Churchill Chamber of Commerce
PO Box 176, Churchill MB R0B 0E0
Tel: 204-675-2022
Toll-Free: 888-389-2327
e-mail: churchillchamber@mts.net
URL: www.churchill.ca/chamber-of-commerce/
David Daley, President
Patricia Penwarden, Secretary

Crystal City & District Chamber of Commerce
PO Box 56, Crystal City MB R0K 0N0
Tel: 204-873-2523; *Fax:* 204-873-2456
e-mail: chamberofcommerce@crystalcitymb.ca
Sean Brooks, President
Keri Stevenson, Secretary

Cypress River Chamber of Commerce
PO Box 261, Cypress River MB R0K 0P0
Tel: 204-743-2119; *Fax:* 204-743-2339
URL: www.cypressriver.ca
Jim Cassels, President

Dauphin & District Chamber of Commerce
101 - 1st Ave. NW, #B, Dauphin MB R7N 1G8
Tel: 204-622-3140; *Fax:* 204-622-3141
e-mail: dauphinchamber@mts.net
Jason Yates, President

Deloraine & District Chamber of Commerce
PO Box 748, Deloraine MB R0M 0M0
Tel: 204-747-2842; *Fax:* 204-747-2856
Deb Calverley, President
Grant Cassils, Contact

Elie Chamber of Commerce
PO Box 175, Elie MB R0H 0H0
Tel: 204-353-2892; *Fax:* 204-353-2336
Maggy Leitgeb, Sec.-Treas.
Rick Desilets, President

Elkhorn Chamber of Commerce
PO Box 141, Elkhorn MB R0M 0N0
Tel: 204-845-2388; *Fax:* 204-845-2073
Kelly Martin, Secretary
Sharlean Bickerton, President

Eriksdale & District Chamber of Commerce
PO Box 434, Eriksdale MB R0C 0W0
Tel: 204-739-2641
URL: www.eriksdale.com
Phyllis Lamb, Secretary
Cindy Kinkead, President

Falcon/West Hawk Lakes Chamber of Commerce (FWHLCC)
PO Box 187, Falcon Beach MB R0E 0N0
Tel: 204-349-3134; *Fax:* 204-349-3134
e-mail: info@chamber-southwhiteshell.ca
URL: www.chamber-southwhiteshell.ca
Affiliation(s): Canadian Chamber of Commerce
Bob Harbottle, President

Fisher Branch Chamber of Commerce
PO Box 566, Fisher Branch MB R0C 0Z0
Tel: 204-372-6034; *Fax:* 204-372-8545
e-mail: fisher01@mts.net
Darcy Plett, President

Flin Flon & District Chamber of Commerce
#228, 35 Main St., Flin Flon MB R8A 1J7
Tel: 204-687-4518; *Fax:* 204-687-4456
e-mail: flinflonchamber@mts.net
URL: www.cityofflinflon.com/chamber
Randy Buie, President
Doug O'Brien, Secretary

Gilbert Plains & District Chamber of Commerce
PO Box 670, Gilbert Plains MB R0L 0X0
Tel: 204-548-2682; *Fax:* 204-548-2682
Brenda Kerns, President

Gillam Chamber of Commerce
PO Box 366, Gillam MB R0B 0L0
Tel: 204-652-5135; *Fax:* 204-652-5155
John Cullen, President

Grahamdale Chamber of Commerce
R.M. Of Grahamdale Administration Office, PO Box 160, 23 Government Rd., Moosehorn MB R0C 2E0
Tel: 204-768-2858; *Fax:* 204-768-3374
e-mail: info@grahamdale.ca
URL: www.grahamdale.ca
Karen Bittner, President

Grandview & District Chamber of Commerce
PO Box 28, Grandview MB R0L 0Y0
Tel: 204-546-2501
Linda Zazuliak, Secretary
Dennis Lukey, President

Grunthal & District Chamber of Commerce
PO Box 451, Grunthal MB R0A 0R0
Tel: 204-434-6750; *Fax:* 204-434-9353
e-mail: leonard@emergencyvehicles.ca
Leonard Hiebert, President

Hamiota Chamber of Commerce
PO Box 403, Hamiota MB R0J 1Z0
Tel: 204-764-2884
e-mail: info@hamiota.com
URL: www.hamiota.com/business.html
Larry Oakden, President
Bonnie Michaudville, Secretary

Hartney & District Chamber of Commerce
PO Box 224, Hartney MB R0M 0X0
Tel: 204-858-2089; *Fax:* 204-858-2089
URL: www.hartney.ca
Sharon Evans, Contact
Carol Thomas, President

Headingley Chamber of Commerce
5353 Portage Ave., Headingley MB R4H 1J9
Tel: 204-889-2132; *Fax:* 204-831-0816
e-mail: dwhitermofheadingley@mts.net
URL: www.rmofheadingley.ca/business/cofc.asp
Affiliation(s): Central Plains Development Corporation; White Horse Plains Development Corporation; Headingley Heritage Centre
Jill Ruth, President
Dave White, Executive Director

Killarney & District Chamber of Commerce
PO Box 809, Killarney MB R0K 1G0
Tel: 204-523-4202
e-mail: killarneychamber@hotmail.com
Mark Witherspoon, Chair
Dale Banman, Executive Director

Lac du Bonnet & District Chamber of Commerce
PO Box 598, Lac du Bonnet MB R0E 1A0
Tel: 204-345-8194; *Fax:* 204-345-8194
e-mail: kimbuhay@mts.net
URL: www.lacdubonnetchamber.com
Affiliation(s): Manitoba Chambers of Commerce
Donna Tschetter, President
Kim Buhay, Manager

Landmark & Community Chamber of Commerce
PO Box 469, Landmark MB R0A 0X0
Tel: 204-355-5200
e-mail: info@landmarkonline.ca
URL: www.landmarkonline.ca
Randy Wolgemuth, President

Leaf Rapids Chamber of Commerce
PO Box 26, Leaf Rapids MB R0B 1W0
Tel: 204-473-2491; *Fax:* 204-473-2284
e-mail: franklhd@mts.net
URL: www.townofleafrapids.ca
Vince Cmela, Secretary

Lundar Chamber of Commerce
PO Box 26, Lundar MB R0C 1Y0
Tel: 204-762-5611; *Fax:* 204-762-5551
Faye Goranson, President

MacGregor Chamber of Commerce
PO Box 685, MacGregor MB R0H 0R0
Tel: 204-685-2862; *Fax:* 204-685-2631
URL: www.macgregorchamber.com

Melita & District Chamber of Commerce
PO Box 666, Melita MB R0M 1L0
Tel: 204-522-3285; *Fax:* 204-522-3536
e-mail: ccagenci@mts.net
Murray Cameron, President

Minnedosa Chamber of Commerce
PO Box 857, Minnedosa MB R0J 1E0
Tel: 204-867-2951; *Fax:* 204-867-3641
e-mail: chamber@minnedosachamber.ca
URL: www.minnedosachamber.ca
Don Farr, President
Callie Mashtoler, Secretary

Morden Chamber of Commerce
311 North Railway St., Morden MB R6M 1S9
Tel: 204-822-5630; *Fax:* 204-822-2041
e-mail: chamber@mordenmb.com
URL: www.mordenchamber.com
Cheryl Link, Manager
Carol Fehr, President

Morris & District Chamber of Commerce
PO Box 98, Morris MB R0G 1K0
Tel: 204-746-6275; *Fax:* 204-746-6953
Pat Eidse, President
Barbara Wiebe, Secretary

Neepawa & District Chamber of Commerce
PO Box 726, 282 Hamilton St., Neepawa MB R0J 1H0
Tel: 204-476-5292; *Fax:* 204-476-5231
Toll-Free: 877-633-7292
e-mail: neepawachamber@mts.net
URL: www.neepawachamber.com
Dean Dietrich Vice, President
Michelle Gerrard, President

Niverville Chamber of Commerce
PO Box 157, Niverville MB R0A 1E0
Tel: 204-388-4325
e-mail: chamber@niverville.com
URL: www.niverville.com
Debbie Pearson, President
Jeannine Funk, Contact

North Interlake Chamber of Commerce
PO Box 160, 23 Government Rd., Moosehorn MB R0C 2E0
Tel: 204-768-2858; *Fax:* 204-768-3374
e-mail: rm606@tcmsnet.com
URL: www.grahamdale.ca
Gayle James, President
Carol Thurman, Secretary

Oakville & District Chamber of Commerce
PO Box 263, Oakville MB R0H 0Y0
Tel: 204-267-2048; *Fax:* 204-267-7015
e-mail: bingram@mts.net
Kam Blight, President
Barb Ingram, Contact

Pansy & District United Chamber of Commerce
PO Box 34, Pansy MB R0A 1J0
Tel: 204-425-3530; *Fax:* 204-425-3530
Theresa Narth, Secretary
Michael Narth, President

The Pas & District Chamber of Commerce
PO Box 996, The Pas MB R9A 1L1
Tel: 204-623-7256; *Fax:* 204-623-2589
e-mail: tpinfo@mts.net
URL: www.thepaschamber.com
Debbie Doucette, President

Pilot Mound & District Chamber of Commerce
PO Box 356, Pilot Mound MB R0G 1P0
Tel: 204-825-2587
e-mail: chamberofcommerce@pilotmound.com
URL: www.pilotmound.com
Jill Lints, Sec.-Treas.
Carolanne Bayne, President

Pinawa Chamber of Commerce
PO Box 544, Pinawa MB R0E 1L0
Tel: 204-753-2747
e-mail: chamber@granite.mb.ca
URL: www.pinawachamber.com
Rhonda Henschell, Secretary
Marsha Sheppard, President

Piney & District Chamber of Commerce
PO Box 50, Sprague MB R0A 1Z0
Tel: 204-437-2259; *Fax:* 204-437-2561
Dennis Konchak, President

Plum Coulee & District Chamber of Commerce
PO Box 392, Plum Coulee MB R0G 1R0
Tel: 204-829-3419; *Fax:* 204-829-3436
e-mail: wanderer@mts.net
June Letkeman, Secretary
June Alvinklassen, President

Portage & District Chamber of Commerce
11 - 2nd St. NE, Portage la Prairie MB R1N 1R8
Tel: 204-857-7778; *Fax:* 204-857-4095
e-mail: info@portagechamber.com
URL: www.portagechamber.com
Affiliation(s): Canadian Chamber of Commerce
Brent Budz, President

Rivers & District Chamber of Commerce
PO Box 795, Rivers MB R0K 1X0
Tel: 204-328-7316; *Fax:* 204-328-4460
e-mail: mbeever@mts.net
Marlin Beener, President
Jean Young, Manager

Riverton & District Chamber of Commerce
PO Box 258, Riverton MB R0C 2R0
Tel: 204-378-2084; *Fax:* 204-378-2085
e-mail: berniced@mts.net
URL: www.rivertoncanada.com
Bernice Danielson, President
Karen Donnellan-Fisher, Contact

Roblin & District Chamber of Commerce
PO Box 160, Roblin MB R0L 1P0
Tel: 204-937-3194
e-mail: rdcoc@mts.net
URL: www.roblinmanitoba.com
Colin Knight, President

Rossburn & District Chamber of Commerce
PO Box 579, Rossburn MB R0J 1V0
Tel: 204-859-3334; *Fax:* 204-859-3313
e-mail: wheatland@mts.net
Raymond Lysyshin, President
Val White, Secretary
Terence Waychyshin, First Vice President

Russell & District Chamber of Commerce
PO Box 155, Russell MB R0J 1W0
Tel: 204-773-2456
URL: www.russellmb.com/chamber.html
Brent Havelange, President

St. Pierre Chamber of Commerce
PO Box 71, St Pierre Jolys MB R0A 1V0
Tel: 204-433-7123; *Fax:* 204-433-3135
e-mail: st-pierre-jolys@mts.net
Sherry Stasiuk, Secretary
Luc Catellier, President

La Salle & District Chamber of Commerce
PO Box 608, La Salle MB R0G 1B0
Tel: 204-736-4555; *Fax:* 204-736-4363
Donna Bell, President
Ray Cormier, Treasurer

Selkirk & District Chamber of Commerce
100 Eaton Avenue, Selkirk MB R1A 0W6
Tel: 204-482-7176; *Fax:* 204-482-5448
e-mail: info@selkirkanddistrictchamber.ca
URL: www.selkirkanddistrictchamber.ca
Kelly Lewis, President
Bev Clegg, Executive Director

Shoal Lake & District Chamber of Commerce
PO Box 547, Shoal Lake MB R0J 1Z0
Tel: 204-759-3343; *Fax:* 204-759-2740
e-mail: nsims@simsco.mb.ca
Tara Patterson, Contact
Norman Sims, President

Somerset & District Chamber of Commerce
PO Box 353, Somerset MB R0G 2L0
Tel: 204-744-2088; *Fax:* 204-744-2153
Affiliation(s): Manitoba Chamber of Commerce
Jean Poiron, President
Bessette

Souris & Glenwood Chamber of Commerce
PO Box 939, Souris MB R0K 2C0
Tel: 204-483-3127; *Fax:* 204-483-2777
e-mail: robbin2@mts.net
Affiliation(s): Manitoba Chamber of Commerce
Sande Denbow, Contact
Colleen Robbins, President

Ste Rose & District Chamber of Commerce
PO Box 688, Ste Rose du Lac MB R0L 1S0
Tel: 204-447-2196; *Fax:* 204-447-2692
e-mail: storestarter@yahoo.ca
Trevor Gates, President
Monica Lambourne, Contact

Steinbach Chamber of Commerce
PO Box 1795, 225 Reimer Ave., Steinbach MB R5G 1N4
Tel: 204-326-9566; *Fax:* 204-346-6600
e-mail: stbcofc@mts.net
URL: www.steinbachchamberofcommerce.com
Paul Neustaedter, President

Stonewall & District Chamber of Commerce
PO Box 762, Stonewall MB R0C 2Z0
Tel: 204-467-8377
e-mail: info@stonewallchamber.com
URL: www.stonewallchamber.com
Don Lischka, President
Ryan Smith, CGA, Treasurer

Swan River Chamber of Commerce
PO Box 1540, Swan River MB R0L 1Z0
Tel: 204-734-3102; *Fax:* 204-734-4342
e-mail: srcc@svcn.mb.ca
Naomi Neufeld, President

Teulon Chamber of Commerce
PO Box 235, Teulon MB R0C 3B0
Tel: 204-294-6171; *Fax:* 204-886-3232
e-mail: president@teulonchamber.ca
Michael Ledarney, President
Debra Osbak, Secretary

Thompson Chamber of Commerce
PO Box 363, Thompson MB R8N 1N2
Tel: 204-677-4155; *Fax:* 204-677-3434
Toll-Free: 888-307-0103
e-mail: commerce@mts.net
URL: www.thompson.ca
Louise Hodder, President (Interim)

Treherne Chamber of Commerce
PO Box 344, Treherne MB R0G 2V0
Tel: 204-723-2774; *Fax:* 204-723-2719
Keith Sparling, President

Virden & District Chamber of Commerce
PO Box 899, 425 - 6th Ave. South, Virden MB R0M 2C0
Tel: 204-748-3955; *Fax:* 204-748-3467
e-mail: virdencc@mts.net
Affiliation(s): Virden Wallace Community Development Corp.; Virden Employment Skills Centre Inc., Virden Agricultural Society; Virden Indoor Rodeo
Deke Baley, President

Wasagaming Chamber of Commerce
PO Box 222, 110 Wasagaming Dr., Wasagaming MB R0J 2H0
Tel: 204-848-2742; *Fax:* 204-848-7712
e-mail: info@discoverclearlake.com
URL: www.discoverclearlake.com
Debb Geiler, President
Wayne Zachedniak, Treasurer

Winkler & District Chamber of Commerce
185 Main St., Winkler MB R6W 1B4
Tel: 204-325-9758; *Fax:* 204-325-8290
e-mail: chamber@winkleronline.com
URL: www.winklerchamber.com
Kenneth Thomas, President
Myrna Hildebrand, Vice-President
Brenda Storey, Executive Director
Dianne Frieson, Manager

Winnipeg Chamber of Commerce (WCC) / Chambre de commerce de Winnipeg
#100, 259 Portage Ave., Winnipeg MB R3B 2A9
Tel: 204-944-8484; *Fax:* 204-944-8492
e-mail: info@winnipeg-chamber.com
URL: www.winnipeg-chamber.com
Affiliation(s): Canadian Chamber of Commerce; Manitoba Chamber of Commerce
David Angus, President/CEO
Chuck Davidson, Vice President, Policy & Communications

New Brunswick

Albert County Chamber of Commerce
PO Box 3051, Hillsborough NB E4H 4W5
Tel: 506-389-6002; *Fax:* 506-387-8331
e-mail: kpower@nb.sympatico.ca
Brian Keirstead, President
Phyllis Sutherland, Secretary

Atlantic Provinces Chambers of Commerce (APCC) / Chambres de commerce des provinces de l'Atlantique
#21, 236 St. George St., Moncton NB E1C 1W1
Tel: 506-857-3980; *Fax:* 506-859-6131
e-mail: grace@apcc.ca
URL: www.apcc.ca
Bill Denyar, President & CEO
Jonathan T.T. Daniels, Chair

Bath Chamber of Commerce
163A Church St., Bath NB E7J 1A7
Tel: 506-278-5213; *Fax:* 506-278-5963
Michael Blanchard, President
Keith Sipprell, Secretary

Bouctouche Chamber of Commerce / Chambre de commerce de Bouctouche
PO Box 338, #301, 59, boul Irving, Bouctouche NB E4S 3J6
Tel: 506-743-2411; *Fax:* 506-743-8991
e-mail: chambouc@mon.auracom.com
Claude LeBlanc, President
Carole Léger, Staff

Campbellton Regional Chamber of Commerce / Chambre de commerce régional de Campbellton
PO Box 236, 18 Water St., Campbellton NB E3N 3G4
Tel: 506-759-7856; *Fax:* 506-759-7557
e-mail: crcc@nbnet.nb.ca
URL: www.campbelltonregionalchamber.ca
Affiliation(s): NB Chamber of Commerce; Atlantic Chamber of Commerce
Ginette Archambault, Secretary
Colleen Donnahee, Executive Director
Greg Davis, President

Central Carleton Chamber of Commerce
28 Palmer Rd., Waterville NB E7P 1B4
Tel: 506-375-4074
Dale Albright, President

Centreville Chamber of Commerce
PO Box 628, Centreville NB E7K 3H5
Tel: 506-276-4241; *Fax:* 506-276-9891
e-mail: centreville.chamber@aernet.ca
Kathy Simonson, Staff
Raymond Carmichael, President

Chambre de commerce de Clair
PO Box 1025, Clair NB E7A 2J5
Tel: 506-992-6030; *Fax:* 506-992-6041
e-mail: info@chambrecommerceclair.com
URL: www.chambrecommerceclair.com
Marie-Josée Michaud, Présidente

Chambre de commerce de Cocagne, Notre-Dame et Grande-Digue
CP 1090, Cocagne NB E4R 1N6
Tél: 506-576-6005; *Téléc:* 506-576-6073
Gilles Allain, Président

Chambre de commerce de Collette
60, rue des Arbres, Collette NB E4Y 1G4
Tél: 506-622-0752; *Téléc:* 506-622-0477
Maurice Desroches, Président

Chambre de commerce de Kent Centre Chamber of Commerce
#2, 9235 rue Main, Richibucto NB E4W 4C6
Tel: 506-523-1443; *Fax:* 506-523-6520
e-mail: kccc@richibucto.org
Richard Thébeau, Président

Chambre de commerce de la région d'Edmundston
1, ch Canada, Edmundston NB E3V 1T6
Tél: 506-737-1866; *Téléc:* 506-737-1862
Courriel: info@ccedmundston.com
URL: www.ccedmundston.com
Affiliation(s): Chambre de commerce du Nouveau-Brunswick; Chambre de commerce des Provinces Atlantiques; Chambre de commerce du Canada; Chambre de commerce Internationale
Lise Couturier, Présidente

Chambre de commerce de la region de Cap-Pelé
CP 1219, Cap-Pelé NB E4N 3B1
Tél: 506-577-4560; *Téléc:* 506-577-8900
Marcel Doiron, Président
Stéphane Dallaire, Secrétaire

Chambre de commerce de Lamèque
127, rue du Pêcheur nord, Lamèque NB E8T 1K6
Tél: 506-344-7246; *Téléc:* 506-336-3387
Rénald Haché, Secretary

Chambre de commerce de Rivière-du-Portage
5898B, RR#11, Rivière-du-Portage NB E9H 1X2
Tél: 506-393-1902
Courriel: jetta@nbnet.nb.ca
Claude G. Savoie, Président
Alice Thibodeau, Secrétaire

Chambre de commerce de Rogersville / Rogersville Chamber of Commerce
#5, 11101, rue Principale, Rogersville NB E4Y 2N2
Tél: 506-775-9378; *Téléc:* 506-775-1906
Lisa LeBlanc, Secrétaire
Yvon Doiron, Président

Chambre de Commerce de Saint Louis de Kent
#A, 83A Beauséjour, Saint-Louis-de-Kent NB E4X 1A6
Tel: 506-876-3475; *Fax:* 506-876-3477
René Côté, Présidente
Daniel Comeau, Secrétaire

Chambre de commerce de Saint-François
CP 378, Saint-François-de-Madawaska NB E7A 1G4
Tél: 506-992-6067; *Téléc:* 506-992-6049
Courriel: cdecsf@nb.aibn.com
Affiliation(s): Chambre de Commerce du Nouveau-Brunswick
Chantal Landry, Secrétaire
Luc L. Nadeau, Président

Chambre de commerce de Saint-Quentin Inc.
144D, rue Canada, Saint-Quentin NB E8A 1G7
Tél: 506-235-3666; *Téléc:* 506-235-1804
Courriel: n6chcomm@nb.aibn.com
URL: www.saintquentin.nb.ca
Jean-Guy R. Michaud, Président
Joyce Somers, Secrétaire

Chambre de commerce de Shippagan inc.
227, boul J.D. Gauthier, Shippagan NB E8S 3H1
Tél: 506-336-2207
Courriel: chambredecommerce@shippagan.com
Donald Hachey, Président

Chambre de commerce du Grand Caraquet Inc
#214, 220, boul St-Pierre ouest, Caraquet NB E1W 1B7
Tél: 506-727-2931; *Téléc:* 506-727-3191
Courriel: chambre@nb.alra.com
URL: www.acadie.net
Monique Godin, Présidente
Aline Landry, Directrice générale

Chipman Chamber of Commerce
237 Main St., Chipman NB E4E 1E5
Tel: 506-339-1821; *Fax:* 506-339-1823
Brian Harris, Chairman-Elect

East Restigouche Chamber of Commerce
389 Adelaide St., Dalhousie NB E8C 1B5
Tel: 506-684-5571; *Fax:* 506-684-4717
Paul Hayes, President

Eastern Charlotte Chamber of Commerce
#2, 21 Main St., St George NB E5C 3H9
Tel: 506-456-3951
e-mail: eccc@nbnet.nb.ca
Wanda MacLean, President
Irene Wright, Secretary

Florenceville Chamber of Commerce
PO Box 601, Florenceville NB E7L 1Y7
Tel: 506-392-0900; *Fax:* 506-392-0900
Scott Greer, Treasurer

Fredericton Chamber of Commerce / La Chambre de Commerce de Fredericton
PO Box 275, 270 Rookwood Ave., Fredericton NB E3B 4Y9
Tel: 506-458-8006; *Fax:* 506-451-1119
e-mail: fchamber@frederictonchamber.ca
URL: www.frederictonchamber.ca
Anthony Knight, CEO
Dale Dunphy, President
Jennifer English, Coordinator, Research & Communications

Gagetown & Area Chamber of Commerce
76 Babbit St., Gagetown NB E5M 1C8
Tel: 506-488-3281
Nancy MacQuade, President

Grand Falls/Grand Sault & District Chamber of Commerce
#300, 81 Burgess Street, Grand Falls NB E3Y 1C6
Tel: 506-473-1905; *Fax:* 506-475-7755
e-mail: gfcocgs@nbnet.nb.ca
Côme Ouellette, President
Linda N. Martin, Staff

Grand Manan Chamber of Commerce
1141 Rte. 776, Grand Manan NB E5G 4K9
Tel: 506-662-3442; *Fax:* 506-662-3593
Toll-Free: 888-525-1655
e-mail: info@grandmanannb.com
URL: www.grandmanannb.com
Joan Gallant, Staff
Theresa McFarland, President

Greater Bathurst Chamber of Commerce / Chambre de commerce du Grand Bathurst
CEI Bldg., 725 College St., Bathurst NB E2A 4B9
Tel: 506-548-8498; *Fax:* 506-548-2200
e-mail: bathcham@nbnet.nb.ca
URL: www.bathurstchamber.ca
Affiliation(s): Canadian Chamber of Commerce
Landry Donna, General Manager
Vilma Glidden, President
Gilles Deveaux, Treasurer

Greater Hillsborough Chamber of Commerce
PO Box 3051, Hillsborough NB E4H 4W5
Tel: 506-734-2851; *Fax:* 506-734-2244
Carole Coleman, Director

Greater Miramichi Chamber of Commerce
PO Box 342, Miramichi NB E1N 3A7
Tel: 506-622-5522; *Fax:* 506-622-5959
e-mail: mirchamber@nb.aibn.com
URL: www.miramichichamber.com
Véronique Arsenault, Executive Director
Dorothy Innes, President

Greater Moncton Chamber of Commerce (GMCC) / Chambre de commerce du Grand Moncton
#100, 910 Main St., Moncton NB E1C 1G6
Tel: 506-857-2883; *Fax:* 506-857-9209
e-mail: info@gmcc.nb.ca
URL: www.gmcc.nb.ca
Valerie Roy, CEO
André Pelletier, Chair
Norm Raynard, Sec.-Treas.

Greater Sackville Chamber of Commerce
#87, 8 Main St., Sackville NB E4L 4A9
Tel: 506-364-8911; *Fax:* 506-364-8082
e-mail: gscc@nbnet.nb.ca
URL: www.sackvillechamber.ca
Rebecca Maclean, Staff
Lisa Smith, President
Wayne Harper, Secretary

Greater Woodstock Chamber of Commerce
#2, 220 King St., Woodstock NB E7M 1Z8
Tel: 506-325-9049; *Fax:* 506-328-4683
e-mail: woodstockchamberofcommerce@nb.aibn.com
URL: www.town.woodstock.nb.ca
Peter Clark, Contact
Jeanne Langille, President

Hampton Area Chamber of Commerce (HACC)
PO Box 1829, #2, 17 Centennial Rd., Hampton NB E5N 6N3
Tel: 506-832-2559; *Fax:* 506-832-2559
e-mail: hacc@nbnet.nb.ca
URL: www.hamptonareachamber.org
Paige Banasik, President
Gail Kilpatrick, Secretary

Kennebecasis Valley Chamber of Commerce
PO Box 4455, #8, 53C Clark Rd., Rothesay NB E2E 5X2
Tel: 506-849-2860; *Fax:* 506-847-0996
e-mail: admin@kvbusiness.com
URL: www.kvbusiness.com
Phil Brodersen, President
Scott Cochrane, Secretary-Treasurer
Ann-Marie O'Neill, Administrator

Mactaquac County Chamber of Commerce
PO Box 1163, Nackawic NB E6G 2N1
Tel: 506-575-9622; *Fax:* 506-575-2035
e-mail: mccc@mactaquaccountry.com
URL: www.mactaquaccountry.com
Melanie Sloat, President
Dora Boudreau, Secretary

Oromocto & Area Chamber of Commerce
Oromocto Mall, PO Box 20124, Oromocto NB E2V 2R6
Tel: 506-446-6043; *Fax:* 506-446-6925
e-mail: oromotcochamber@nb.aibn.com
URL: www.oromoctochamber.nb.ca
Lloyd Chamber, President

Perth-Andover & Area Chamber of Commerce
11640 Route 105, Kilburn NB E7H 4W3
Tel: 506-273-6375; *Fax:* 506-273-6915
Jeff Walters-Gray, President
Elizabeth Davenport, Secretary

River Valley Chamber of Commerce (RVCC)
PO Box 3123, Grand Bay-Westfield NB E5K 4V4
Tel: 506-738-8666; *Fax:* 506-738-3697
Randy Bell, Secretary
Diane Bormke, President

St. Andrews Chamber of Commerce
46 Reed Ave., St Andrews NB E5B 1A1
Tel: 506-529-3555; *Fax:* 506-529-8095
e-mail: stachamb@nbnet.nb.ca
URL: www.standrewsby-the-sea.ca
Dave Bennett, President
Julie Crichton, Executive Director

St. Martins & District Chamber of Commerce
229 Main St., St Martins NB E5R 1B7
Tel: 506-833-2019; *Fax:* 506-833-2028
e-mail: fundytp@nbnet.nb.ca
Bruce Huttges, President
Brian Clark, Secretary

St. Stephen Area Chamber of Commerce
PO Box 457, 34 Milltown Blvd., St Stephen NB E3L 2X3
Tel: 506-466-7703; *Fax:* 506-466-7753
e-mail: chamber.ststephen@nb.aibn.com
URL: www.town.ststephen.nb.ca
Affiliation(s): Atlantic Chamber of Commerce; Canadian Chamber of Commerce
Diedre Rideout, President
Mary Gilmore, Staff

Sussex & District Chamber of Commerce
PO Box 5152, 66 Broad St., Sussex NB E4E 5L2
Tel: 506-433-1845; *Fax:* 506-433-1886
e-mail: sdcc@nbnet.nb.ca
URL: sdccinc.org
Affiliation(s): Atlantic Provinces Chambers of Commerce
Christine Philion, Administrative Officer
Kandy Mitton, President

Washademoak Region Chamber of Commerce
3359 Lower Cambridge, Cambridge-Narrows NB E4C 4P9
Tel: 506-488-2517; *Fax:* 506-488-2622
URL: www.w-rcc.ca/frameset.html
Tom Nisbet, President
Hertha Gebhardt, Vice-President

Newfoundland and Labrador

Argentia Area Chamber of Commerce
PO Box 109, 1 O'Reilly St., Placentia NL A0B 2Y0
Tel: 709-227-0003; *Fax:* 709-227-0016
e-mail: info@argentiachamber.org
URL: www.argentiachamber.org
Gerry Hynes, President
Frank Collins, Director

Arnolds Cove Area Chamber of Commerce
PO Box 411, Arnolds Cove NL A0B 1A0
Tel: 709-472-4151; *Fax:* 709-472-4182
Gloria Warren-Slade, President
Germaine Lynch, Treasurer

Baie Verte & Area Chamber of Commerce
PO Box 578, Baie Verte NL A0K 1B0
Tel: 709-532-4204; *Fax:* 709-532-4252
e-mail: bvachamber@nf.aibn.com
URL: www.bvachamber.com
Shannon Lewis, President

Bay St. George Chamber of Commerce
35 Carolina Ave., Stephenville NL A2N 3P8
Tel: 709-643-5854; *Fax:* 709-643-6398
e-mail: bsgcoc@wec-center.nl.ca
URL: www.bsgcc.org
Sheila Hawco, Executive Director
Cynthia Downey, President

Bonavista Area Chamber of Commerce (BACC)
PO Box 280, Bonavista NL A0C 1B0
Fax: 709-468-2495
e-mail: info@bacc.ca
URL: www.bacc.ca
Diane Thorpe, Secretary

Channel Port Aux Basques Chamber of Commerce
PO Box 1389, Channel-Port-aux-Basques NL A0M 1C0

Tel: 709-695-3688; *Fax:* 709-695-7925
e-mail: pabchamber@thezone.net
URL: www.pabchamber.com
Gary O'Brien, Secretary
Terry Anderson, President

Clarenville Area Chamber of Commerce
292A Memorial Dr., Clarenville NL A5A 1P1
Tel: 709-466-5800; *Fax:* 709-466-5803
Toll-Free: 866-466-5800
e-mail: info@clarenvillechamber.net
URL: www.clarenvilleareachamber.net
Bill Farrell, President
Michelle Frye, Office Manager

Conception Bay Area Chamber of Commerce
#3, 702 Conception Bay Hwy., Conception Bay South NL A1X 3A5
Tel: 709-834-5670; *Fax:* 709-834-5760
e-mail: info@cbachamber.com
URL: www.cbachamber.com
Glenda Noseworthy, Managing Director
Brenda Hollohan, Secretary
David Murphy, President

Deer Lake Chamber of Commerce
6 Cresent Street, Deer Lake NL A8A 1H6
Tel: 709-635-3260; *Fax:* 709-635-5857
e-mail: s-goulding@warp.nfld.net
Affiliation(s): Newfoundland Chambers of Commerce
Todd Lee, Treasurer
Susan Goulding, Executive Director
Jim Goudie, President

Exploits Regional Chamber of Commerce
PO Box 272, 16 High St., Grand Falls-Windsor NL A2A 2J7
Tel: 709-489-7512; *Fax:* 709-489-7532
e-mail: info@exploitschamber.com
URL: www.exploitschamber.com
Jason Thistle, President
Ron Aucoin, Executive Director

Gander & Area Chamber of Commerce (GACC)
109 Trans Canada Hwy., Gander NL A1V 1P6
Tel: 709-256-7110; *Fax:* 709-256-4080
e-mail: ganderchamber@ganderchamber.nf.ca
URL: www.ganderchamber.nf.ca
Hazel Bishop, Executive Director
Pat Kearney, President

Greater Corner Brook Board of Trade
PO Box 475, 11 Confederation Dr., Corner Brook NL A2H 6E6
Tel: 709-634-5831; *Fax:* 709-639-9710
e-mail: cbcc@thezone.net
URL: www.gcbbt.com
Charlene Woodford, Executive Director

Irish Loop Chamber of Commerce
PO Box 6, Trepassey NL A0A 4B0
Tel: 709-432-2662; *Fax:* 709-438-2892
Cathy Perry, President

Labrador North Chamber of Commerce (LNCC)
PO Box 460, Stn. B, 169 Hamilton River Rd., Happy Valley-Goose Bay NL A0P 1E0
Tel: 709-896-8787; *Fax:* 709-896-0585
Toll-Free: 877-920-8787
e-mail: admin@chamberlabrador.com
URL: www.chamberlabrador.com
Sterling Peyton, President
Brian Fowlow, Contact

Labrador South East Chamber of Commerce
PO Box 65, Port Hope Simpson NL A0K 4E0
Tel: 709-960-0510
e-mail: bfgillis@nf.sympatico.ca
Blair Gillis, President
Sharon Penney, Secretary

Labrador Straits Chamber of Commerce
PO Box 179, Forteau NL A0K 2P0
Tel: 709-931-2073; *Fax:* 709-931-2073
e-mail: chamber@labradorstraits.net
Kinza Trimm, Executive Director

Labrador West Chamber of Commerce
PO Box 273, Labrador City NL A2V 2K5
Tel: 709-944-3723; *Fax:* 709-944-4699
e-mail: lwc@crrstv.net
URL: www.labradorwestchamber.ca
Patsy Ralph, Business Manager

Lewisporte & Area Chamber of Commerce
PO Box 953, Lewisporte NL A0G 3A0
Tel: 709-535-2500; *Fax:* 709-535-2482
e-mail: lacc@superweb.ca
Cynthia Aylward, Executive Assistant

Marystown-Burin Area Chamber of Commerce
PO Box 728, Marystown NL A0E 2M0
Tel: 709-279-2080; *Fax:* 709-279-4492
e-mail: chamber@mbacc.nf.ca
URL: www.marystownburinchamber.com
Mike Graham, President
Kelly Pardy, Executive Director

Mount Pearl Chamber of Commerce
39 Commonwealth Ave., Mount Pearl NL A1N 1W7
Tel: 709-364-8513; *Fax:* 709-364-8500
e-mail: info@mtpearlchamber.com
URL: www.mtpearlchamber.com
Michelle Batterson, Executive Director

Pasadena Chamber of Commerce
c/o The Venture Centre, PO Box 149, Pasadena NL A0L 1K0
Tel: 709-686-2078; *Fax:* 709-686-2081
Derrick Anthony, President

St Anthony & Area Chamber of Commerce
PO Box 650, St Anthony NL A0K 4S0
Tel: 709-454-8898
e-mail: stanthonyandareachamber@yahoo.ca
Kaye Strickland, Coordinator
Marshall Dean, President

Springdale & Area Chamber of Commerce
PO Box 37, 151 Main St., Springdale NL A0J 1T0
Tel: 709-673-3837; *Fax:* 709-673-3897
e-mail: seabrightfinancial@aibn.com
Cyril Pelley, President
Glenn Seabright, Secretary

Straits-St. Barbe Chamber of Commerce
PO Box 119, Flowers Cove NL A0K 2N0
Tel: 709-456-2592; *Fax:* 709-456-2592
e-mail: straitsstbarbe@nf.aibn.com
Maggie Chambers, Secretary
Donna Doyle, President

Northwest Territories

Baffin Regional Chamber of Commerce (BRCC)
Igluvut Bldg., 2nd Fl., PO Box 59, Iqaluit NU X0A 0H0
Tel: 867-979-4656; *Fax:* 867-979-2929
URL: www.baffinchamber.ca
Hal Timar, Executive Director
Chris West, President
Frank May, Sec.-Treas.

Iqaluit Chamber of Commerce
PO Box 1107, Iqaluit NU X0A 0H0
Tel: 867-979-4095
e-mail: board@icoc.nu.ca
URL: www.icoc.nu.ca
David Fulgham, 2nd Vice-President

Kivalliq Chamber of Commerce
PO Box 147, Rankin Inlet NU X0C 0G0
Tel: 867-645-2718; *Fax:* 867-645-2483
e-mail: krmanson@arctic.ca
Ellie Camsill, President

Kugluktuk Chamber of Commerce
PO Box 307, Kugluktuk NU X0B 0E0
Tel: 867-982-3232; *Fax:* 867-982-3229
e-mail: coptours@polarnet.ca
Rachel Horn, President
Ruth Palmer, Office Manager

Nova Scotia

Amherst & Area Chamber of Commerce
PO Box 283, Amherst NS B4H 3Z4
Tel: 902-667-8186; *Fax:* 902-667-2270
e-mail: info@amherstchamber.ca
URL: www.amherstchamber.ca
David McNarin, President
Debbie Allen, Staff

Antigonish Chamber of Commerce
21B James St., Antigonish NS B2G 1R6
Tel: 902-863-6308; *Fax:* 902-863-2656
e-mail: contact@antigonishchamber.com
URL: www.antigonishchamber.com
Daniel Ross, President

Barrington & Area Chamber of Commerce
PO Box 110, Barrington NS B0W 1E0
Tel: 902-637-2625; *Fax:* 902-637-2075
e-mail: bcc@auracom.com
Wendy S. McGill, President
Debra Goreham, Staff

Bridgewater & Area Chamber of Commerce
PO Box 100, 200 North St., Bridgewater NS B4V 2W8
Tel: 902-543-4263; *Fax:* 902-527-1156
e-mail: bacc@eastlink.ca
URL: www.bridgewaterchamber.com
Ann O'Connell, Executive Director
Sandra Statton, President
Bernice Theriault, Secretary

Brier Island Chamber of Commerce
PO Box 74, Westport NS B0V 1H0
Tel: 902-839-2347; *Fax:* 902-839-2006
e-mail: akicita@ns.sympatico.ca
Harold Graham, President
Joan Riday, Secretary

Central Annapolis Valley Chamber of Commerce
PO Box 395, 831 Main St., Kingston NS B0P 1R0
Tel: 902-765-0344; *Fax:* 902-765-0141
e-mail: info@cavcoc.ca
URL: www.cavcoc.ca
Affiliation(s): World Trade Centre
Kenneth L. Bower, President
Melissa Robinson, Secretary

Chambre de commerce de Clare
CP 35, Pointe-de-l'Église NS B0W 1M0
Tél: 902-645-2368; *Téléc:* 902-645-2787
Courriel: chambredecommerce@hotmail.com
URL: www.commercedeclare.ca
Marc Robichaud, Président

Chester Municipal Chamber of Commerce
PO Box 831, #13, 4171, Highway 3, Chester NS B0J 1J0
Tel: 902-275-4709
e-mail: info@chesterns.com
URL: www.chesterns.com
Angela Jessome, Staff
Ben Wiper, President
Jim Barkhouse, Secretary

East Hants & District Chamber of Commerce
PO Box 1053, Lantz NS B2S 3G6
Tel: 902-883-1010; *Fax:* 902-883-7862
e-mail: info@ehcc.ca
URL: www.ehcc.ca
Heather Kerr, Manager
Stephen Pottie, President

Eastern Kings Chamber of Commerce (EKCC)
PO Box 314, Kentville NS B4N 3X1
Tel: 902-678-4634; *Fax:* 902-678-5448
e-mail: ekccbob@ns.aliantzinc.ca
URL: www.easternkingschamber.ns.ca
Bill Denyar, President
Judy Rafuse, Executive Director

Fort Simpson Chamber of Commerce
PO Box 244, Fort Simpson NT X0E 0N0
Tel: 867-695-3555; *Fax:* 867-695-3313
e-mail: commerce@fschamber.biz
URL: www.fschamber.biz
Duncan Canvin, President

Fort Smith Chamber of Commerce
PO Box 121, Fort Smith NT X0E 0P0
Tel: 867-872-4213; *Fax:* 867-872-9450
Fred Daniels, Director

Halifax Chamber of Commerce
#200, 656 Windmill Rd., Dartmouth NS B3B 1B8
Tel: 902-468-7111; *Fax:* 902-468-7333
e-mail: info@halifaxchamber.com
URL: www.halifaxchamber.com
Kim West, Chair
Valerie Payn, President

Hay River Chamber of Commerce
10K Gagnier St., Hay River NT X0E 1G1
Tel: 867-874-2565; *Fax:* 867-874-3631
e-mail: info@hayriverchamber.com
URL: www.hayriverchamber.com
Brian Lefebvre, President

Mahone Bay & Area Chamber of Commerce
PO Box 59, Mahone Bay NS B0J 2E0
Tel: 902-624-6151; *Fax:* 902-624-6152
Toll-Free: 888-624-6151
e-mail: info@mahonebay.com
URL: www.mahonebay.com
Allan O'Brien, President
Ray Morin, Secretary

Marie Raymond, Staff

Norman Wells & District Chamber of Commerce
PO Box 400, Norman Wells NT X0E 0V0
Tel: 867-587-6609; *Fax:* 867-587-2865
Chris Buist, Contact

Northeast Highlands Chamber of Commerce
PO Box 125, Ingonish Beach NS B0C 1L0
Tel: 902-285-2289; *Fax:* 902-285-2285
e-mail: alison.roper@pc.gc.ca
URL: www.northeasthighlands.com
Walter Lauffer, President
Mary Sue Mackinnon, Staff
Ann Hussey, Secretary

Northumberland Central Chamber of Commerce
Lower Level, Northumberland Mall, 1111 Elgin St. West, Cobourg NS K9A 5H7
Tel: 905-372-5831; *Fax:* 905-372-2411
e-mail: info@cobourgchamber.com
URL: www.cobourgchamber.com
K. Ward, Manager

Pictou County Chamber of Commerce
East River Plaza, 980 East River Rd., New Glasgow NS B2H 3S5
Tel: 902-755-3463; *Fax:* 902-755-2848
e-mail: info@pictouchamber.com
URL: www.pictouchamber.com
Barrie MacMillan, Executive Director
Gerald Green, President

Sheet Harbour & Area Chamber of Commerce
PO Box 239, Sheet Harbour NS B0J 3B0
Tel: 902-885-2595; *Fax:* 902-885-2708
e-mail: shcoc@ns.sympatico.ca
URL: coc.sheetharbour.ca
Myrene Keating-Owen, Secretary
Tom McInnis, President

Shelburne & Area Chamber of Commerce
PO Box 1150, Shelburne NS B0T 1W0
Tel: 902-875-0224; *Fax:* 902-875-3214
e-mail: info@shelburnechamber.com
URL: www.shelburnechamber.com
Sam Stewart, President
Ron Chute, Secretary

South Queens Chamber of Commerce
PO Box 1378, Liverpool NS B0K 1K0
Tel: 902-354-4163; *Fax:* 902-354-7388
e-mail: sqchambr@atcom.com
URL: www.southqueenschamber.com
Mark Sapp, Chair
Cheryl Beaton, Treasurer
Henry Sewuster, Chair

Springhill & Area Chamber of Commerce
PO Box 1030, Springhill NS B0M 1X0
Tel: 902-597-8462; *Fax:* 902-597-3839
e-mail: audrey@surrette.com
Adrien Baillargeon, President
Carys Messinger, Secretary

Strait Area Chamber of Commerce
#2, 4 MacIntosh Ave., Port Hawkesbury NS B9A 3K5
Tel: 902-625-1588; *Fax:* 902-625-5985
e-mail: straitareacoc@ns.sympatico.ca
URL: www.straitchamber.ca
Affiliation(s): Atlantic Provinces Chamber of Commerce
Shannon MacDougall, Executive Director
Bob MacEachern, President

Sydney & Area Chamber of Commerce (SACC)
PO Box 131, 275 Charlotte Street, Sydney NS B1P 1C6
Tel: 902-564-6453; *Fax:* 902-539-7487
e-mail: info@sydneyareachamber.ca
URL: www.sydneyareachamber.ca
Anne Marie Singler, Executive Secretary

Truro & District Chamber of Commerce (TDCOC)
PO Box 54, 605 Prince St., Truro NS B2N 1G2
Tel: 902-895-6328; *Fax:* 902-897-6641
e-mail: tdcoc@tru.eastlink.ca
URL: www.trurochamber.com
Tim Tucker, Executive Director
Ted Jordan, President

West Hants Chamber of Commerce
PO Box 2188, Windsor NS B0N 2T0
Tel: 902-798-5106
e-mail: info@whcc.ca
URL: www.whcc.ca
Gordon Winstone, President

Richard Cole, Vice-President

Yarmouth & Area Chamber of Commerce (YCC)
PO Box 532, #205, 310 Forest St., Yarmouth NS B5A 4B4
Tel: 902-742-3074; *Fax:* 902-749-1383
e-mail: info@yarmouthchamberofcommerce.com
URL: www.yarmouthchamberofcommerce.com
Ken Wheelans, President
Chris Atwood, 1st Vice-President
Gurdeep Brar, 2nd Vice-President

Yellowknife Chamber of Commerce
#21, 4910 - 50th Ave., 3rd Fl., Yellowknife NT X1A 3S5
Tel: 867-920-4944; *Fax:* 867-920-4640
e-mail: generalmanager@ykchamber.com
URL: www.ykchamber.com
Ellie Sasseville, Executive Director

Ontario

Aguasabon Chamber of Commerce
PO Box 695, Terrace Bay ON P0T 2W0
Tel: 807-825-4505; *Fax:* 807-825-9664
Toll-Free: 888-445-9999
e-mail: info@sncfdc.com
John Lubberdink, Chair
Robert Kirkpatrick, Director

Alliston & District Chamber of Commerce
519 Victoria St. East, Alliston ON L9R 1K1
Tel: 705-435-7921; *Fax:* 705-435-0289
Toll-Free: 888-835-3092
e-mail: info@adcc.ca
URL: www.adcc.ca
Geri English, Office Coordinator

Amherstburg Chamber of Commerce
PO Box 101, 268 Dalhousie St., Amherstburg ON N9V 2Z3
Tel: 519-736-2001; *Fax:* 519-736-9721
e-mail: acoc@mnsi.net
URL: www.amherstburgchamberofcommerce.ca
Ray Bezaire, President

Arthur & District Chamber of Commerce
PO Box 519, 146 George St., Arthur ON N0G 1A0
Tel: 519-848-5603; *Fax:* 519-848-5603
e-mail: achamber@wightman.ca
Jamie Couper, President

Atikokan Chamber of Commerce
PO Box 997, Atikokan ON P0T 1C0
Tel: 807-597-1599; *Fax:* 807-597-2726
Toll-Free: 888-334-2332
e-mail: info@atikokanchamber.com
URL: www.atikokanchamber.com
Affiliation(s): Canadian Chamber of Commerce
Judi Nault, President
Nancy Jordan, Office Manager

Aurora Chamber of Commerce
#321, 6 - 14845 Yonge St., Aurora ON L4G 6H8
Tel: 905-727-7262; *Fax:* 905-841-6217
e-mail: info@aurorachamber.on.ca
URL: www.aurorachamber.on.ca
Carla Adams, Executive Director

Bancroft & District Chamber of Commerce
PO Box 539, Bancroft ON K0L 1C0
Tel: 613-332-1513; *Fax:* 613-332-2119
e-mail: chamber@commerce.bancroft.on.ca
URL: www.commerce.bancroft.on.ca
Judy Edgar, General Manager

Bayfield & Area Chamber of Commerce
PO Box 2065, Bayfield ON N0M 1G0
Tel: 519-565-2499
Toll-Free: 800-565-2499
e-mail: info@villageofbayfield.com
URL: www.villageofbayfield.com
Janet Snider, President

Beaverton District Chamber of Commerce
PO Box 29, Beaverton ON L0K 1A0
Tel: 705-426-2051
e-mail: chamber@beavertononlakesimcoe.com
URL: www.beavertononlakesimcoe.com
Affiliation(s): Ontario Chamber of Commerce
Ted McCollum, President

Belleville & District Chamber of Commerce (BCC)
PO Box 726, 5 East Moira St., Belleville ON K8N 5B3
Tel: 613-962-4597; *Fax:* 613-962-3911
Toll-Free: 888-852-9992
e-mail: info@bellevillechamber.ca
URL: www.bellevillechamber.ca

Angela Genereaux, General Manager

Blenheim & District Chamber of Commerce
PO Box 1089, c/o 127 Malborough St. North, Blenheim ON N0P 1A0
Tel: 519-676-6555; *Fax:* 519-676-2622
Betty Russell, Admin. Secretary & Treasurer

Blind River Chamber of Commerce (BRCC)
PO Box 998, Blind River ON P0R 1B0
Tel: 705-356-2555; *Fax:* 705-356-3911
Toll-Free: 800-563-8719
e-mail: chamber@brchamber.ca
URL: www.brchamber.ca
Affiliation(s): Algoma Kinniwabi Travel Association
Betty-Ann Dunbar, President

Blue Mountains Chamber of Commerce
PO Box 477, Thornbury ON N0H 2P0
Tel: 519-599-1200; *Fax:* 519-599-3971
e-mail: info@bluemountainschamber.ca
URL: www.bluemountainschamber.ca
George Matamoros, President

Bobcaygeon & Area Chamber of Commerce
PO Box 388, 21 Canal St. East, Bobcaygeon ON K0M 1A0
Tel: 705-738-2202; *Fax:* 705-738-1534
Toll-Free: 800-318-6173
e-mail: chamber@bobcaygeon.org
URL: www.bobcaygeon.org
Affiliation(s): Kawartha Lakes Associated Chambers of Commerce
Tom Kupusa, President

Bracebridge Chamber of Commerce
#1, 1 Manitoba St., Bracebridge ON P1L 2A8
Tel: 705-645-5231; *Fax:* 705-645-7592
e-mail: chamber@bracebridgechamber.com
URL: www.bracebridgechamber.com
John Crawley, General Manager

Bradford & District Chamber of Commerce (BDCC)
PO Box 59, 100 Dissette St., Bradford ON L3Z 2A7
Tel: 905-775-3037; *Fax:* 905-775-6357
e-mail: info@bradfordchamber.on.ca
Deanna Stewart, General Manager

Brighton & District Chamber of Commerce
PO Box 880, 74 Main Street, Brighton ON K0K 1H0
Tel: 613-475-2775; *Fax:* 613-475-3777
Toll-Free: 877-475-2775
e-mail: info@brightonchamber.ca
URL: www.brightonchamber.ca
George Lucas, Administrator

Brockville & District Chamber of Commerce
#1, 3 Market St. West, Brockville ON K6V 7L2
Tel: 613-342-6553; *Fax:* 613-342-6849
e-mail: info@brockvillechamber.com
URL: www.brockvillechamber.com
Sueling Ching, Executive Director

Burlington Chamber of Commerce
#201, 414 Locust St., Burlington ON L7S 1T7
Tel: 905-639-0174; *Fax:* 905-333-3956
e-mail: info@burlingtonchamber.com
URL: www.burlingtonchamber.com
Janet Whitehouse, Chair

Caledon Chamber of Commerce
PO Box 626, Bolton ON L7E 5T5
Tel: 905-857-7393; *Fax:* 905-857-7405
Toll-Free: 888-599-9967
e-mail: info@caledonchamber.com
URL: www.caledonchamber.com
Affiliation(s): Canadian Chamber of Commerce; Ontario Chamber of Commerce
Kelly Darnley, President/CEO
Linda Bond, Chair

Caledonia Regional Chamber of Commerce
PO Box 2035, 1 Grand Trunk Lane, Caledonia ON N3W 2G6
Tel: 905-765-0377; *Fax:* 905-765-6730
e-mail: crcc@mountaincable.net
URL: www.caledonia-ontario.com
Barb Martindale, Executive Director

Cambridge Chamber of Commerce
750 Hespler Rd., Cambridge ON N3H 5L8
Tel: 519-622-2221; *Fax:* 519-622-0177
e-mail: cchamber@cambridgechamber.com
URL: www.cambridgechamber.com
Greg Durocher, General Manager

Carleton Place & District Chamber of Commerce
132 Coleman St., Carleton Place ON K7C 4M7

Tel: 613-257-1976; *Fax:* 613-257-8170
e-mail: manager@cpchamber.com
URL: www.cpchamber.com
Cathie McOrmond, Manager

Cayuga & District Chamber of Commerce
PO Box 118, 6 Cayuga St. North, Cayuga ON N0A 1E0
Tel: 905-772-5954; *Fax:* 905-772-2680
e-mail: info@cayugachamber.ca
URL: www.cayugachamber.ca
Bernadine Tompkins, President

Central Bruce Peninsula Chamber of Commerce
c/o Tourist Information Center, 2866 Hwy. 6, Wiarton ON N0H 2T0
Tel: 519-793-3178; *Fax:* 519-793-3296
e-mail: info@centralbrucepeninsula.ca
URL: www.centralbrucepeninsula.ca
Affiliation(s): Bruce Peninsula Tourism Association; Ontario Chamber of Commerce; Bruce County Tourism; Tobermory & District Chamber of Commerce; South Bruce Peninsula Chamber of Commerce; Sauble Beach Chamber of Commerce

Centre Wellington Chamber of Commerce
400 Tower St. South, Fergus ON N1M 2P7
Tel: 519-843-5140; *Fax:* 519-787-0983
Toll-Free: 877-242-6353
e-mail: chamber@ferguselora.com
URL: www.ferguselora.com
Affiliation(s): Canadian Chamber of Commerce
Deb Dalziel, General Manager

Chamber of Commerce of Brantford & Brant (BRCC)
PO Box 1294, 77 Charlotte St., Brantford ON N3T 5T6
Tel: 519-753-2617; *Fax:* 519-753-0921
e-mail: chamber@brcc.ca
URL: www.brcc.ca
Charlene Nicholson, Chief Executive Officer

Chatham-Kent Chamber of Commerce
54 Fourth St., Chatham ON N7M 2G2
Tel: 519-352-7540; *Fax:* 519-352-8741
e-mail: info@chatham-kentchamber.ca
URL: www.chatham-kentchamber.ca
G.A. (Gail) Antaya, President & CEO

Chesley & District Chamber of Commerce
PO Box 406, 112 - 1st Ave. South, Chesley ON N0G 1L0
Tel: 519-363-9837; *Fax:* 519-363-9838
e-mail: cdcc@bmts.com
URL: www.townofchesley.com
Stacy Charlton, Treasurer

Cobourg & District Chamber of Commerce
Northumberland Mall, 1111 Elgin St. West, Cobourg ON K9A 5H7
Tel: 905-372-5831; *Fax:* 905-372-2411
e-mail: info@cobourgchamber.com
URL: www.cobourgchamber.com
Kevin Ward, Manager

Collingwood Chamber of Commerce
PO Box 36, 25 Second St., Collingwood ON L9Y 1E4
Tel: 705-445-0221; *Fax:* 705-445-6858
e-mail: info@collingwoodchamber.com
URL: www.collingwoodchamber.com
Affiliation(s): Canadian Chamber of Commerce; Ontario Chamber of Commerce
David Ripley, President

Cornwall Chamber of Commerce
Commerce Court, #100, 113 Second St. East., Cornwall ON K6H 1Y5
Tel: 613-933-4004; *Fax:* 613-933-8466
URL: www.cornwallchamber.com
Debbie Rioux, President

Dryden District Chamber of Commerce (DDCC)
284 Government St., Dryden ON P8N 2P3
Tel: 807-223-2622; *Fax:* 807-223-2626
Toll-Free: 800-667-0935
e-mail: chamber@mail.drytel.net
URL: www.drydenchamber.ca
Affiliation(s): Sunset County Travel Association; Patricia Regional Tourist Council; Kenora District Camp Owners Association
Melina Jansen, Manager
Jamie Gould, Chair

Dunnville Chamber of Commerce
PO Box 124, 231 Chestnut Street, Dunnville ON N1A 2X1
Tel: 905-774-3183; *Fax:* 905-774-9281
e-mail: chamberofcommerce@mountaincable.net
URL: www.dunnvillechamberofcommerce.ca
Ron Speer, Office Manager

East Gwillimbury Chamber of Commerce
PO Box 199, 1590 Queensville Side Rd., Queensville ON L0G 1R0
Tel: 905-478-8447; *Fax:* 905-478-8786
e-mail: info@egcoc.org
URL: www.egcoc.org
Cindy Thiele, President

Eastern Ottawa Chamber of Commerce
#310, 2183 Ogilvie Road, Gloucester ON K1J 1C8
Tel: 613-745-3578; *Fax:* 613-745-8575
e-mail: info@easternottawa.com
URL: www.easternottawa.com
David Brault, President

Elliot Lake & District Chamber of Commerce
PO Box 81, Elliot Lake ON P5A 2J6
Tel: 705-848-3974; *Fax:* 705-848-7121
e-mail: elchamber@onlink.net
URL: www.elliotlakechamber.com
Peter Seidel, President

Emo Chamber of Commerce
PO Box 476, Emo ON P0W 1E0
Tel: 807-482-1811; *Fax:* 807-482-1813
e-mail: vennechenko@sympatico.ca
URL: www.twspemo.on.ca/chamber.html
Colleen Vennechenko, Contact
Paul Kyro, NOACC Representative
Dave Goodman, Vice-President

Englehart & District Chamber of Commerce
PO Box 171, Englehart ON P0J 1H0
Tel: 705-544-8580; *Fax:* 705-544-1964
e-mail: deacon@ntl.sympatico.ca
Annette Deacon, President

Espanola & District Chamber of Commerce
30 McCulloch, Espanola ON P5E 1J1
Tel: 705-869-3351; *Fax:* 705-869-4601
e-mail: rbheale@cyberbeach.net
Rob Heale, Contact

Fenelon Falls & District Chamber of Commerce
PO Box 28, 15 Oak St., Fenelon Falls ON K0M 1N0
Tel: 705-887-3409; *Fax:* 705-887-6912
e-mail: info@fenelonfallschamber.com
URL: www.fenelonfallschamber.com
Sandra Barrett, President

Flamborough Chamber of Commerce (FCC)
PO Box 1030, Waterdown ON L0R 2H0
Tel: 905-689-7650; *Fax:* 905-689-1313
e-mail: admin@flamboroughchamber.ca
URL: www.flamboroughchamber.ca
Affiliation(s): Ontario & Canadian Chamber of Commerce
Penny Gardiner, President

Fort Frances Chamber of Commerce
474 Scott St., Fort Frances ON P9A 1H2
Tel: 807-274-5773; *Fax:* 807-274-8706
Toll-Free: 800-820-3678
e-mail: thefort@nwonet.net
URL: www.fortfranceschamber.com
Affiliation(s): Ontario Chamber of Commerce; Canadian Chamber of Commerce
Dawn Booth, Chamber Coordinator
Christine Denby, President

Georgina Chamber of Commerce
22937 Woodbine Ave., RR#2, Keswick ON L4P 3E9
Tel: 905-476-7870; *Fax:* 905-476-6700
Toll-Free: 888-436-7446
e-mail: admin@georginachamber.com
URL: www.georginachamber.com
Christine Thomas, General Manager
Dan Fellini, President

Geraldton & District Chamber of Commerce
PO Box 128, Geraldton ON P0T 1M0
Tel: 807-854-1925
e-mail: ddumont42@sympatico.ca
URL: www.gdcc-on.ca
Stephane Parent, President
Gerard Dufour, Secretary
Katherine Russwurm, NOACC Representative

Goderich & District Chamber of Commerce
56 East Street, Goderich ON N7A 1N3
Tel: 519-440-0176; *Fax:* 519-440-0305
e-mail: info@goderichchamber.ca
URL: www.goderichchamber.ca
Laura Herman, President

Gogama Chamber of Commerce
PO Box 73, 59 Poupore St., Gogama ON P0M 1W0
Tel: 705-894-2111
e-mail: gogamachamber@vianet.ca
Eija MacDonald, Chair

Grand Bend & Area Chamber of Commerce
PO Box 248, #1, 81 Crescent St., Grand Bend ON N0M 1T0
Tel: 519-238-2001; *Fax:* 519-238-5201
Toll-Free: 888-338-2001
e-mail: info@grandbendtourism.com
URL: www.grandbendtourism.com
Eva Miller, Manager

Gravenhurst Chamber of Commerce/Visitors Bureau
#685, 2 Muskoka Rd. North, Gravenhurst ON P1P 1N5
Tel: 705-687-4432; *Fax:* 705-687-4382
e-mail: info@gravenhurstchamber.com
URL: www.gravenhurstchamber.com
Rosemary King, President

Greater Arnprior Chamber of Commerce (GACC)
PO Box 213, 16 Edward St., Arnprior ON K7S 3H2
Tel: 613-623-6817; *Fax:* 613-623-6826
e-mail: arnpriorchamberofcommerce@bellnet.ca
URL: www.gacc.ca
Lori Martin, Administrative Assistant
Joan Carey, President

Greater Barrie Chamber of Commerce
97 Toronto St., Barrie ON L4N 1V1
Tel: 705-721-5000; *Fax:* 705-726-0973
e-mail: chadmin@barriechamber.com
URL: www.barriechamber.com
Sybil Goruk, Executive Director

Greater Dufferin Area Chamber of Commerce
PO Box 101, Hwy. 10, Orangeville ON L9W 2Z5
Tel: 519-941-0490; *Fax:* 519-941-0492
e-mail: info@gdacc.ca
URL: www.gdacc.ca
Affiliation(s): Ontario Chamber of Commerce; Canadian Chamber of Commerce
Ron Munro, President

Greater Fort Erie Chamber of Commerce
#1, 660 Garrison Rd., Fort Erie ON L2A 6E2
Tel: 905-871-3803; *Fax:* 905-871-1561
e-mail: info@forteriechamber.com
URL: www.forteriechamber.com
Kimberly Walpole, President
Gina Ramkissoon, Vice-President

Greater Innisfil Chamber of Commerce (GICC)
7896 Yonge St., Innisfil ON L9S 1L5
Tel: 705-431-4199; *Fax:* 705-431-8020
Toll-Free: 866-575-0008
e-mail: info@innisfilchamber.com
URL: www.innisfilchamber.com
Affiliation(s): Alcona Business Association; South Innisfil Business & Community Association; Cookstown Chamber of Commerce; 400 Industrial Group
David Taylor, Secretary
Heather MacDonald, President

Greater Kingston Chamber of Commerce (GKCC)
67 Brock St., Kingston ON K7L 1R8
Tel: 613-548-4453; *Fax:* 613-548-4743
e-mail: bob@kingstonchamber.on.ca
URL: www.kingstonchamber.on.ca
Bob Scott, General Manager
David Phillips, Coordinator, New Membership

Greater Kitchener & Waterloo Chamber of Commerce
PO Box 2367, 80 Queen St. North, Kitchener ON N2H 6L4
Tel: 519-576-5000; *Fax:* 519-742-4760
Toll-Free: 888-672-4282
e-mail: admin@greaterkwchamber.com
URL: www.greaterkwchamber.com
Joan Fisk, President & CEO

Greater Nepean Chamber of Commerce
#1175, 2720 Queensview Dr., Ottawa ON K2B 1A5
Tel: 613-828-5556; *Fax:* 613-828-8022
e-mail: info@nepeanchamber.com
URL: www.nepeanchamber.com
Mary Pitt, Chair
Dan Laverdure, General Manager

Greater Oshawa Chamber of Commerce
#100, 44 Richmond St. West, Oshawa ON L1G 1C7
Tel: 905-728-1683; *Fax:* 905-432-1259
e-mail: info@oshawachamber.com
URL: www.oshawachamber.com

Affiliation(s): Ontario Chamber of Commerce; Canadian Chamber of Commerce
Bob Malcolmson, General Manager

Greater Peterborough Chamber of Commerce (GPCC)
175 George St. North, Peterborough ON K9J 3G6
Tel: 705-748-9771; *Fax:* 705-743-2331
Toll-Free: 887-640-4037
e-mail: info@peterboroughchamber.ca
URL: www.peterboroughinfo.com
Stuart Harrison, General Manager

Greater Sudbury Chamber of Commerce / Chambre de commerce du Grand Sudbury
#1, 40 Elm St., Sudbury ON P3C 1S8
Tel: 705-673-7133; *Fax:* 705-673-2944
e-mail: cofc@sudburychamber.ca
URL: www.sudburychamber.ca
Debbi M. Nicholson, President & CEO

Grimsby & District Chamber of Commerce
424 South Service Rd., RR#2, Grimsby ON L3M 4E8
Tel: 905-945-8319; *Fax:* 905-945-1615
e-mail: info@grimsbychamber.com
URL: www.grimsbychamber.com
Jinny Day, Executive Director

Guelph Chamber of Commerce (GCC)
PO Box 1268, #15, 485 Silvercreek Pkwy. North, Guelph ON N1H 6N6
Tel: 519-822-8081; *Fax:* 519-822-8451
e-mail: chamber@guelphchamber.com
URL: www.guelphchamber.com
Affiliation(s): Guelph Business Enterprise Centre; Guelph Partnership for Innovation
Lloyd Longfield, President and C.A.O.

Hagersville & District Chamber of Commerce
PO Box 1090, 24 Parkview Rd., Hagersville ON N0A 1H0
Tel: 905-768-3384
Brenda Moerschfelder, President

Haliburton Highlands Chamber of Commerce
PO Box 147, 5 Bobcaygeon Rd., Minden ON K0M 2K0
Tel: 705-286-7160; *Fax:* 705-286-6016
Toll-Free: 877-811-6111
e-mail: admin@hhchamber.on.ca
URL: www.hhchamber.on.ca
Nick Lawrence, President
Walter Schretter, Vice-President
Maria Micallef, Administrative Coordinator

Halton Hills Chamber of Commerce
328 Guelph St., Halton Hills ON L7G 4B5
Tel: 905-877-7119; *Fax:* 905-877-5117
e-mail: info@haltonhillschamber.on.ca
URL: www.haltonhillschamber.on.ca
Sue Walker, General Manager

Hamilton Chamber of Commerce (HCC)
555 Bay St. North, Hamilton ON L8L 1H1
Tel: 905-522-1151; *Fax:* 905-522-1154
e-mail: hdcc@hamiltonchamber.on.ca
URL: www.hamiltonchamber.on.ca
John Dolbec, CEO
Ruth Liebersbach, President

Hanover Chamber of Commerce
#1, 214 - 10th St., Hanover ON N4N 1N7
Tel: 519-364-5777; *Fax:* 519-364-6949
e-mail: koelschlagel@bdo.ca

Harrow & Colchester Chamber of Commerce
PO Box 888, Harrow ON N0R 1G0
Tel: 519-974-3200; *Fax:* 519-974-2222
e-mail: chamber@harrowchamber.ca
URL: www.harrowchamber.ca
Ginger Cooke, President

Havelock, Belmont, Methuen Chamber of Commerce
PO Box 779, Havelock ON K0L 1Z0
Tel: 705-778-2182; *Fax:* 705-778-2444
e-mail: info@havelockchamber.com
URL: www.havelockchamber.com
Rae McCutcheon, Secretary

Hawkesbury Chamber of Commerce / Chambre de Commerce de Hawkesbury
PO Box 36, 2 John St., Hawkesbury ON K6A 2R4
Tel: 613-632-8066; *Fax:* 613-632-3324
e-mail: info@hcoc.ca
URL: www.hcoc.ca
Richard Denis, President
Sylvain Labrie, Secretary-Treasurer

Hearst, Mattice - Val Côté Chamber of Commerce
PO Box 987, 523 Hwy. 11 East, Hearst ON P0L 1N0
Tel: 705-372-2838; *Fax:* 705-372-2840
Toll-Free: 800-655-5769
e-mail: hearstcoc@hearst.ca
URL: hearstcoc.com
Ghislain Jacques, President

Ingersoll District Chamber of Commerce
132 Thames St. South, Ingersoll ON N5C 2T4
Tel: 519-485-7333; *Fax:* 519-485-6606
e-mail: info@ingersollchamber.com
URL: www.ingersollchamber.com
Ann Campbell, General Manager

Iroquois Falls & District Chamber of Commerce
PO Box 840, 727 Synagogue Ave., Iroquois Falls ON P0K 1G0
Tel: 705-232-4656
e-mail: ifchamber@hotmail.com
URL: www.iroquoisfallschamber.com
Elizabeth King, President

Kawartha Lakes Chamber of Commerce
Eastern Region, PO Box 537, 12 Queen St., Lakefield ON K0L 2H0
Tel: 705-652-6963; *Fax:* 705-652-9140
Toll-Free: 888-565-8888
e-mail: info@kawarthachamber.ca
URL: www.kawarthachamber.ca
Scott Papp, Business Administrator

Kenora & District Chamber of Commerce
PO Box 471, Kenora ON P9N 3X5
Tel: 807-467-4646; *Fax:* 807-468-3056
e-mail: kenorachamber@kmts.ca
URL: www.kenorachamber.com
Laurene Manson-Sillery, Chamber Manager

Kincardine & District Chamber of Commerce
PO Box 115, Kincardine ON N2Z 2Y6
Tel: 519-396-9333; *Fax:* 519-396-5529
e-mail: kincardine.cofc@bmts.com
URL: www.kincardinechamber.com
Jackie Pawlikowski, Office Manager

Kirkland Lake District Chamber of Commerce (KLCC)
PO Box 966, 400 Government Rd. West, Kirkland Lake ON P2N 3N1
Tel: 705-567-5444; *Fax:* 705-567-1666
e-mail: klcofc@ntl.sympatico.ca
URL: kirklandlakechamber.com
Affiliation(s): Ontario Chamber of Commerce
Joanne Gorzalczynski, Secretary
Jim Taylor, President

The Land of Nipigon Chamber of Commerce
PO Box 760, 22 Third Street, Nipigon ON P0T 2J0
Tel: 807-887-0740; *Fax:* 807-887-5117
Toll-Free: 877-596-1359
e-mail: nipigonchamber@vianet.ca
URL: www.nipigon.net
Judi Bernard, President
Rebecca Lawrence, Director

Leamington District Chamber of Commerce
PO Box 321, 21 Talbot St., Leamington ON N8H 1L1
Tel: 519-326-2721; *Fax:* 519-326-3204
e-mail: christinec@leamingtonchamber.com
URL: www.leamingtonchamber.com
Chris Chopchik, General Manager

Lincoln Chamber of Commerce
4800 South Service Rd., Beamsville ON L0R 1B0
Tel: 905-563-5044; *Fax:* 905-563-7098
e-mail: lcoc@vaxxine.com
URL: www.lincolnchamber.ca
Cathy McNiven, General Manager

London Chamber of Commerce
#101, 244 Pall Mall St., London ON N6A 5P6
Tel: 519-432-7551; *Fax:* 519-432-8063
e-mail: gerry@londonchamber.com
URL: www.londonchamber.com
Kevin Switzer, President
Gerry MacCartney, General Manager & CEO

Longlac Chamber of Commerce
PO Box 877, 112 Hamel Ave., Longlac ON P0T 1A0
Tel: 807-876-2273; *Fax:* 807-876-2575
Lorraine Gagnon, Contact
Wayne Morris, President

Lucknow & District Chamber of Commerce
PO Box 313, Lucknow ON N0G 2H0
Tel: 519-528-2099

Lyndhurst Seeleys Bay & District Chamber of Commerce
PO Box 89, RR#1, Lyndhurst ON K0E 1N0
Tel: 613-387-3847
e-mail: info@lyndhurstseeleysbaychamber.com
URL: www.lyndhurstseeleysbaychamber.com
Charlie Kellington, President
Charles Shaw, Treasurer

Manitoulin Chamber of Commerce
PO Box 307, 6062 Hwy. 542, Mindemoya ON P0P 1S0
Tel: 705-377-7501; *Fax:* 705-377-7501
Toll-Free: 800-698-6681
e-mail: office@manitoulinchamber.com
URL: www.manitoulinchamber.com
Bob Taylor, President

Manitouwadge Chamber of Commerce
PO Box 2030, 1 Mississauga Dr., Manitouwadge ON P0T 2C0
Tel: 807-826-3227; *Fax:* 807-826-4592

Marathon Chamber of Commerce
PO Box 988, Marathon ON P0T 2E0
Tel: 807-229-3100; *Fax:* 807-229-1486
Affiliation(s): Northwestern Ontario Associated Chambers of Commerce
Bob Hancherow, Contact
George Macey, NOACC Representative

Markdale Chamber of Commerce
PO Box 177, 19 Toronto St. North, Markdale ON N0C 1H0
Tel: 519-986-4612; *Fax:* 519-986-4612
Toll-Free: 888-986-4612
e-mail: markdalechamber@cablerocket.com
URL: www.village.markdale.on.ca
Susan Roberts, Secretary

Maryborough Chamber of Commerce
PO Box 143, Moorefield ON N0G 2K0
Tel: 519-638-2971
e-mail: dcraven@wightman.net
Dennis Craven, President

Meaford & District Chamber of Commerce
PO Box 4836, 16 Trowbridge Street West, Meaford ON N4L 1X6
Tel: 519-538-1640; *Fax:* 519-538-5493
Toll-Free: 877-538-1640
e-mail: info@mdcc.ca
URL: www.mdcc.ca
Susan Lake, Manager

Milton Chamber of Commerce
#104, 251 Main St., Milton ON L9T 1P1
Tel: 905-878-0581; *Fax:* 905-878-4972
e-mail: info@chamber.milton.on.ca
URL: www.chamber.milton.on.ca
Sandy Martin, Executive Director

Minto Chamber of Commerce
PO Box 864, Harriston ON N0G 1Z0
Tel: 519-327-9619
e-mail: info@mintochamber.on.ca
URL: www.mintochamber.on.ca
John Burgess, President

Mount Forest District Chamber of Commerce
514 Main St. North, Mount Forest ON N0G 2L0
Tel: 519-323-4480; *Fax:* 519-323-1557
e-mail: mfchamber@wightman.ca
URL: www.mountforest.ca
Ron Forrest, President

Muskoka Lakes Chamber of Commerce
PO Box 536, 3181 Muskoka Rd. 169, Bala ON P0C 1A0
Tel: 705-762-5663; *Fax:* 705-762-5664
e-mail: info@muskokalakeschamber.com
URL: www.muskokalakeschamber.com
Tracy Owen, President
Jane Templeton, Manager

Napanee & District Chamber of Commerce
Napanee Business Centre, 47 Dundas St. East, Napanee ON K7R 1H7
Tel: 613-354-6601; *Fax:* 613-354-6848
Toll-Free: 877-354-6601
e-mail: info@napaneechamber.ca
URL: www.napaneechamber.ca
Dan Atkinson, President

Newmarket Chamber of Commerce
470 Davis Dr., Newmarket ON L3Y 2P3
Tel: 905-898-5900; *Fax:* 905-853-7271
e-mail: info@newmarketchamber.com
URL: www.newmarketchamber.com
Debra Scott, President & CEO

Niagara Falls Chamber of Commerce
4056 Dorchester Rd., Niagara Falls ON L2E 6M9
Tel: 905-374-3666; *Fax:* 905-374-2972
e-mail: info@niagarafallschamber.com
URL: www.niagarafallschamber.com
Carolyn Bones, President
Larry Vaughan, Chair

Niagara on the Lake Chamber of Commerce
PO Box 1043, 26 Queen St., Niagara-on-the-Lake ON L0S 1J0
Tel: 905-468-1950; *Fax:* 905-468-4930
e-mail: tourism@niagaraonthelake.com
URL: www.niagaraonthelake.com
Janice Thomson, Executive Director

North Bay & District Chamber of Commerce
PO Box 747, 1375 Seymour St., North Bay ON P1B 8J8
Tel: 705-472-8480; *Fax:* 705-472-8027
Toll-Free: 888-249-8998
e-mail: nbcc@northbaychamber.com
URL: www.northbaychamber.com
Patti Alcorn-Carr, Executive Director

North Grenville Chamber of Commerce
PO Box 1047, 5 Clothier St. East, Kemptville ON K0G 1J0
Tel: 613-258-4838; *Fax:* 613-258-3801
e-mail: info@northgrenvillechamber.com
URL: www.northgrenvillechamber.com
Pierre Blackburn, Chair

North Perth Chamber of Commerce
580 Main St., Listowel ON N4W 1A8
Tel: 519-291-1551; *Fax:* 519-291-4151
e-mail: info@npchamber.com
URL: www.npchamber.com
Tami Chauvin, General Manager

Northwestern Ontario Associated Chambers of Commerce (NOACC)
#102, 200 Syndicate Ave. South, Thunder Bay ON P7E 1C9
Tel: 807-624-2626; *Fax:* 807-622-7752
e-mail: chamber@tb-chamber.on.ca
URL: www.tb-chamber.on.ca
Affiliation(s): Ontario Chamber of Commerce
Lisa Sticca, Chair
Mary Long-Irwin, President

Oakville Chamber of Commerce
2521 Wyecroft Rd., Oakville ON L6L 6P8
Tel: 905-845-6613; *Fax:* 905-845-6475
e-mail: inquiries@oakvillechamber.com
URL: www.oakvillechamber.com
John Sawyer, President

Orillia & District Chamber of Commerce
150 Front St. South, Orillia ON L3V 4S7
Tel: 705-326-4424; *Fax:* 705-327-7841
e-mail: orilinfo@orillia.com
URL: www.orillia.com
Affiliation(s): Canadian Chamber of Commerce
Susan Lang, Managing Director

Orléans Chamber of Commerce / Chambre de commerce d'Orléans
2276A, boul St-Joseph., Orleans ON K1C 1E8
Tel: 613-824-9137; *Fax:* 613-824-0090
e-mail: contact@orleanschamber.ca
URL: www.orleanschamber.ca
Affiliation(s): National Capital Business Alliance
Peter Stewart, Executive Director

Oro-Medonte Chamber of Commerce
PO Box 100, 148 Line 7 South, Oro ON L0L 2X0
Tel: 705-487-7337; *Fax:* 705-487-0133
e-mail: info@oromedontecc.com
URL: www.oromedontecc.com
Carol Benedetti, Administrative Coordinator
Rick Dory, President
Anna Proctor, Vice-President
Bruce Chappell, Treasurer

Ottawa Chamber of Commerce (OCC)
1701 Woodward Dr., #LL-20, Ottawa ON K2C 0R4
Tel: 613-236-3631; *Fax:* 613-236-7498
e-mail: info@ottawachamber.ca
URL: www.ottawachamber.ca
Gail Logan, President

Owen Sound & District Chamber of Commerce
PO Box 1028, Owen Sound ON N4K 6K6
Tel: 519-376-6261; *Fax:* 519-376-5647
e-mail: bert@oschamber.com
URL: www.oschamber.com
David Moyer, President
Joanne Horton, Vice President

Paris Chamber of Commerce
c/o Williams Brant County Power, 65 Dundas St. East, Paris ON N3L 3H1
Tel: 519-758-5095
e-mail: sinjsswint@rogers.com
URL: www.pariscoc.ca
Tracey Palmer, President
Bryan Maude, President

Perth & District Chamber of Commerce
34 Herriott St., Perth ON K7H 1T2
Tel: 613-267-3200; *Fax:* 613-267-6797
Toll-Free: 888-319-3204
e-mail: welcome@perthchamber.com
URL: www.perthchamber.com
Affiliation(s): Canadian Chamber of Commerce; Ontario Chamber of Commerce
Dorothy Linden, President

Pointe-au-Baril Chamber of Commerce
PO Box 67, Pointe-au-Baril-Station ON P0G 1K0
Tel: 705-366-2331; *Fax:* 705-366-2331
e-mail: info@pointeaubarilchamber.com
URL: www.pointeaubarilchamber.com
Affiliation(s): Rainbow County Travel Association
Danielle Hill, President (interim)

Port Colborne-Wainfleet Chamber of Commerce
76 Main St. West, Port Colborne ON L3K 3V2
Tel: 905-834-9765; *Fax:* 905-834-1542
e-mail: office@pcwchamber.com
URL: www.pcwchamber.com
Donna Martens Gamm, President
Sherrie Fulbrook, Treasurer

Port Hope & District Chamber of Commerce
58 Queen St., Port Hope ON L1A 3Z9
Tel: 905-885-5519; *Fax:* 905-885-1142
e-mail: info@porthopechamber.com
URL: www.porthopechamber.com
Wendy Giroux, Manager

Prescott & District Chamber of Commerce
PO Box 2000, Prescott ON K0E 1T0
Tel: 613-925-2171; *Fax:* 613-925-4381
e-mail: prescottchamber@xplornet.com
URL: www.prescottanddistrictchamber.com
Debbie Lawless, Secretary

Prince Edward County Chamber of Tourism & Commerce (PECCTAC)
116 Main St., Picton ON K0K 2T0
Tel: 613-476-2421; *Fax:* 613-476-7461
Toll-Free: 800-640-4717
e-mail: pec@reach.net
URL: www.pecchamber.com
Jan Demille, Secretary/Manager

Quinte West Chamber of Commerce
97 Front St., Trenton ON K8V 4N6
Tel: 613-392-7635; *Fax:* 613-392-8400
Toll-Free: 800-930-3255
e-mail: info@quintewestchamber.on.ca
URL: www.quintewestchamber.on.ca
Suzanne Andrews, Manager

Rainy River & District Chamber of Commerce
PO Box 458, Rainy River ON P0W 1L0
Tel: 807-852-3343
URL: www.rainyriver.ca/chamber
Susan Carpenter, President

Ramara & District Chamber of Commerce
PO Box 144, 2304 Highway 12, Brechin ON L0K 1B0
Tel: 705-484-2141; *Fax:* 705-484-0161
e-mail: info@ramarachamber.com
URL: www.ramarachamber.com
Walt Meyers, President

Red Lake Chamber of Commerce
PO Box 430, Red Lake ON P0V 2M0
Tel: 807-727-3722; *Fax:* 807-727-3285
e-mail: chamber@goredlake.com
Rene Franczak, President
Kim Riddell, Staff

Renfrew & Area Chamber of Commerce
161 Raglan St. South, Renfrew ON K7V 1R2
Tel: 613-432-7015; *Fax:* 613-432-8645
Jon Pole, President

Richmond Hill Chamber of Commerce (RHCOC)
376 Church St. South, Richmond Hill ON L4C 9V8
Tel: 905-884-1961; *Fax:* 905-884-1962
e-mail: info@rhcoc.com
URL: www.rhcoc.com
Affiliation(s): Toronto Board of Trade
Earl Sky, Chair
Leslie Walker, CEO

Rideau Chamber of Commerce
PO Box 247, Manotick ON K4M 1A3
Tel: 613-692-6262; *Fax:* 613-822-4687
e-mail: info@rideauchamber.com
URL: www.rideauchamber.com
Affiliation(s): Ontario Chamber of Commerce
Salima Ismail, President

Ridgetown & District Chamber of Commerce
37 Main St. East, Ridgetown ON N0P 2C0
Tel: 519-674-0802; *Fax:* 519-674-0802
e-mail: ridgetownchamber@sympatico.ca
URL: www.ridgetown.com
Charlie Mitton, President
Sandra Dorner, General Manager

St Catharines-Thorold Chamber of Commerce
PO Box 940, #103, 1 St. Paul St., St Catharines ON L2R 6Z4
Tel: 905-684-2361; *Fax:* 905-684-2100
e-mail: info@scchamberofcommerce.com
URL: www.scthamber.com
Walter Sendzik, Executive Vice President

St. Catherine's-Thorold Chamber of Commerce
PO Box 940, #103, 1 St. Paul St., St. Catharines ON L2R 36Z4
Tel: 905-684-2361; *Fax:* 905-684-2100
e-mail: info@scchamberofcommerce.com
URL: www.thoroldchamber.com, www.sctchamber.com
Rob DePetris, President

St Thomas & District Chamber of Commerce
555 Talbot St., St Thomas ON N5P 1C5
Tel: 519-631-1981; *Fax:* 519-631-0466
e-mail: mail@stthomaschamber.on.ca
URL: www.stthomaschamber.on.ca
Affiliation(s): Ontario Chamber of Commerce; Canadian Chamber of Commerce
Bob Hammersley, President & CEO

Sarnia Lambton Chamber of Commerce
556 North Christina St., Sarnia ON N7T 5W6
Tel: 519-336-2400; *Fax:* 519-336-2085
e-mail: info@sarnialambtonchamber.com
URL: www.sarnialambtonchamber.com
Garry McDonald, President

Sauble Beach Chamber of Commerce
General Delivery, Sauble Beach ON N0H 2G0
Tel: 519-422-1262
e-mail: info@saublebeach.com
URL: www.saublebeach.com
Becky Knight, President
Shelley Elliott, Treasurer

Saugeen Shores Chamber Office
559 Goderich St., Port Elgin ON N0H 2C4
Tel: 519-832-2332; *Fax:* 519-389-3725
Toll-Free: 800-387-3456
e-mail: portelgininfo@saugeenshores.ca
URL: www.saugeenshores.ca
Gary Brown, President

Sault Ste Marie Chamber of Commerce (SSMCOC)
334 Bay St., Sault Ste Marie ON P6A 1X1
Tel: 705-949-7152; *Fax:* 705-759-8166
e-mail: comments@ssmcoc.com
URL: www.ssmcoc.com
Shelley Barich, General Manager

Scarborough Chamber of Commerce (SCC)
940 Progress Ave., Toronto ON M1G 3T5
Tel: 416-439-4140; *Fax:* 416-439-4147
e-mail: gbailey@bot.com
URL: www.bot.com
Gwen Bailey, Office Manager

Scugog Chamber of Commerce
PO Box 1282, #G1, 181 Perry St., Port Perry ON L9L 1A7

Tel: 905-985-4971; Fax: 905-985-7698
e-mail: info@scugogchamber.ca
URL: www.scugogchamber.ca
Affiliation(s): Joint Chambers of Durham Region; Durham Network for Excellence; Tourism Durham; Tourist Association of Durham Region; Durham Home & Small Business Association
Tony Janssen, President

Simcoe & District Chamber of Commerce
95 Queensway West, Chamber Plaza, Simcoe ON N3Y 2M8
Tel: 519-426-5867; Fax: 519-428-7718
e-mail: chamber@simcoechamber.on.ca
URL: www.simcoechamber.on.ca
Yvonne Di Pietro, General Manager

Sioux Lookout Chamber of Commerce
PO Box 577, 11 First Avenue South, Sioux Lookout ON P8T 1A8
Tel: 807-737-1937; Fax: 807-737-1778
e-mail: chamber@siouxlookout.com
URL: www.siouxlookout.com
Dean Woloshuck, President
Anne Reid, Staff Contact

South Bruce Peninsula Chamber of Commerce
PO Box 68, Wiarton ON N0H 2T0
Tel: 519-534-4009
e-mail: info@wiartonchamber.ca
URL: www.sbpcc.org
Affiliation(s): Wiarton BIA
John Aiken, Treasurer

South Dundas Chamber of Commerce
PO Box 288, Morrisburg ON K0C 1X0
Tel: 613-543-3443; Fax: 613-652-4120
e-mail: info@southdundaschamber.com
URL: sdcc.southdundas.com
Ed Kingsley, President

South Huron Chamber of Commerce
PO Box 550, 414 Main St. South, Exeter ON N0M 1S6
Tel: 519-235-4520; Fax: 519-235-3141
e-mail: office@shcc.on.ca
URL: www.shcc.on.ca
Hugh McMaster, President

South Stormont Chamber of Commerce
PO Box 489, Ingleside ON K0C 1M0
Tel: 613-537-8344; Fax: 613-537-9439
e-mail: info@sscc.on.ca
URL: www.sscc.on.ca
Lesley O'Gorman, President

Southeast Georgian Bay Chamber of Commerce
PO Box 70, 99 Lone Pine Rd., Port Severn ON L0K 1S0
Tel: 705-756-4863
e-mail: info@segbay.ca
URL: www.segbay.ca
Marianne Braid, Manager

Southern Georgian Bay Chamber of Commerce / Chambre de Commerce de la Baie Georgienne Sud
208 King St., Midland ON L4R 4C9
Tel: 705-526-7884; Fax: 705-526-1744
e-mail: info@sgbchamber.ca
URL: www.southerngeorgianbay.on.ca
Denise Hayes, General Manager

Stoney Creek Chamber of Commerce
21 Mountain Ave. South, Stoney Creek ON L8G 2V5
Tel: 905-664-4000; Fax: 905-664-7228
e-mail: sccc@bellnet.ca
URL: www.chamberstoneycreek.com
David Cage, Executive Director

Stratford & District Chamber of Commerce
55 Lorne Ave. East, Stratford ON N5A 6S4
Tel: 519-273-5250; Fax: 519-273-2229
e-mail: info@stratfordchamber.com
URL: www.stratfordchamber.com
Affiliation(s): Chamber of Commerce Executives of Canada
Garry Lobsinger, General Manager

Tavistock Chamber of Commerce
PO Box 670, Tavistock ON N0B 2R0
Tel: 519-655-2277
e-mail: b&croutly@rogers.com
Bob Routly, Secretary

Temagami & District Chamber of Commerce
PO Box 57, Stn. T, 7 Lakeshore Dr., Temagami ON P0H 2H0
Tel: 705-569-3344; Fax: 705-569-2834
Toll-Free: 800-661-7609
e-mail: cofc@temagami.ca
URL: www.temagamiinformation.com
Ann Richmond, Office Manager
Hendrika Krygsman, President

1,000 Islands Gananoque Chamber of Commerce
10 King St. East, Gananoque ON K7G 1E6
Tel: 613-382-3250; Fax: 613-382-1585
Toll-Free: 800-561-1595
e-mail: info@1000islandschamber.com
URL: www.1000islandsgananoque.com
Affiliation(s): Travel Media Association of Canada
Bonnie Ruddock, Operations Manager

Thunder Bay Chamber of Commerce (TBCC)
#102, 200 Syndicate Ave. South, Thunder Bay ON P7E 1C9
Tel: 807-624-2626; Fax: 807-622-7752
e-mail: chamber@tb-chamber.on.ca
URL: www.tb-chamber.on.ca
Affiliation(s): Northwestern Ontario Associated Chambers of Commerce; Ontario Chamber of Commerce; Canadian Chamber of Commerce
Harold Wilson, President
Barry Streib, NOACC Representative

Tilbury & District Chamber of Commerce
PO Box 1299, Tilbury ON N0P 2L0
Tel: 519-682-3040; Fax: 519-682-3123
e-mail: tbia.dcc@pppoe.ca
Carrie Sterling, Executive Director

Tillsonburg District Chamber of Commerce
PO Box 113, Tillsonburg ON N4G 4H3
Tel: 519-842-5571; Fax: 519-842-2941
e-mail: srenken@ody.ca
URL: www.tillsonburgchamber.ca

Timmins Chamber of Commerce / Chambre de Commerce de Timmins
PO Box 985, 76 McIntyre Rd., Timmins ON P4N 7H6
Tel: 705-360-1900; Fax: 705-360-1193
e-mail: info@timminschamber.on.ca
URL: www.timminschamber.on.ca
Keitha Robson, Manager
Rob Galloway, President

Tobermory & District Chamber of Commerce
7420 Hwy. 6, Box 250, Tobermory ON N0H 2R0
Tel: 519-596-2452; Fax: 519-596-2452
e-mail: chamber@tobermory.org
URL: www.tobermory.org
Affiliation(s): Central Bruce Peninsula Chamber of Commerce; South Bruce Peninsula Chamber of Commerce; Manitoulin Chamber of Commerce; Manitoulin Tourism Association; Sauble Beach Chamber of Commerce
Marilee S. Derby, Coordinator

Trent Hills & District Chamber of Commerce
PO Box 376, 51 Grand Road, Campbellford ON K0L 1L0
Tel: 705-653-1551; Fax: 705-653-1629
Toll-Free: 888-653-1556
e-mail: info@trenthillschamber.ca
URL: www.trenthillschamber.ca
Nancy Allanson, Executive Director

Tri-Town & District Chamber of Commerce
PO Box 811, 883356 Hwy. 65 East, New Liskeard ON P0J 1P0
Tel: 705-647-5771; Fax: 705-647-8633
Toll-Free: 866-947-5753
e-mail: chamber@ntl.sympatico.ca
URL: www.tritownchamber.ca
Ken Laffernier, President

Tweed Chamber of Commerce
PO Box 988, Tweed ON K0K 3J0
Tel: 613-813-2784
URL: www.tweed-chamber.ca
Richard Rashotte, President

Upper Ottawa Valley Chamber of Commerce
PO Box 1010, 611 TV Tower Rd., Pembroke ON K8A 6Y6
Tel: 613-732-1492; Fax: 613-732-5793
e-mail: manager@upperottawavalleychamber.com
URL: www.upperottawavalleychamber.com
Lorraine MacKenzie, Executive Director
Gail Richardson, President
Richard Hale, Vice-President

Uxbridge Chamber of Commerce
#810, 2 Campbell Dr., Uxbridge ON L9P 0A3
Tel: 905-852-7683; Fax: 905-852-2517
URL: www.uxcc.ca
Lee Ursel, Chairman

Vaughan Chamber of Commerce (VCC)
#2, 25 Edilcan Dr., Vaughan ON L4K 3S4
Tel: 905-761-1366; Fax: 905-761-1918
Toll-Free: 888-828-4426
e-mail: info@vaughanchamber.ca
URL: www.vaughanchamber.ca
Deborah Bonk, CEO

Walkerton & District Chamber of Commerce
PO Box 1344, 4 Park St., Walkerton ON N0G 2V0
Tel: 519-881-3413; Fax: 519-881-4009
Toll-Free: 888-820-9291
e-mail: chamberinfo@wightman.ca
URL: town.walkerton.on.ca/Chamber/chamber.html
Affiliation(s): Ontario Chamber of Commerce
Tracey Cassidy, Chamber Manager
Dennis Moran, President
Neil Kirstine, Vice-President

Wasaga Beach Chamber of Commerce
PO Box 394, 550 River Rd. West, Wasaga Beach ON L9Z 1A4
Tel: 705-429-2247; Fax: 705-429-1407
Toll-Free: 866-292-7242
e-mail: info@wasagainfo.com
URL: www.wasagainfo.com
Affiliation(s): Canadian Chamber of Commerce; Ontario Chamber of Commerce
Trudie McCrea, Office Manager/Special Events Coord

The Welland/Pelham Chamber of Commerce
32 East Main St., Welland ON L3B 3W3
Tel: 905-732-7515; Fax: 905-732-7175
URL: chamber.gurix.com
Dolores Fabiano, Executive Director

West Carleton District Chamber of Commerce
PO Box 179, Carp ON K0A 1L0
Tel: 613-839-5316; Fax: 613-839-1436
e-mail: rosemarylyall@hotmail.com
Rose Lyall, Secretary

West Elgin Chamber of Commerce
PO Box 276, Rodney ON N0L 2C0
Tel: 519-785-2217
e-mail: secretary@westelginchamber.ca
URL: www.westelginchamber.ca
Ted Uffen, Secretary

West Grey Chamber of Commerce
PO Box 800, 625 Garafraxa Rd. North, Durham ON N0G 1R0
Tel: 519-369-5750; Fax: 519-369-5750
e-mail: info@westgreychamber.ca
URL: www.westgreychamber.ca
Affiliation(s): Durham Business Improvement Association
Greta Kennedy, Sec.-Treas.

West Lincoln Chamber of Commerce
PO Box 555, 270 Station St., Smithville ON L0R 2A0
Tel: 905-957-1606; Fax: 905-957-4628
e-mail: wloffice@westlincolnchamber.com
URL: www.westlincolnchamber.com
Susan Wisniewski, President

Westport & Rideau Lakes Chamber of Commerce
PO Box 157, Westport ON K0G 1X0
Tel: 613-273-2929; Fax: 613-273-2929
e-mail: wrlcc@rideau.net
URL: www.westportrideaulakes.on.ca
Colin Horsfall, President

Whitby Chamber of Commerce (WCC)
128 Brock St. South, Whitby ON L1N 5Y4
Tel: 905-668-4506; Fax: 905-668-1894
e-mail: info@whitbychamber.org
URL: www.whitbychamber.org
Margot Weir, CEO

Whitchurch-Stouffville Chamber of Commerce
PO Box 1500, 6176 Main St., Stouffville ON L4A 8A4
Tel: 905-642-4227; Fax: 905-642-8966
e-mail: chamber@whitchurchstouffville.ca
URL: www.whitchurchstouffville.ca
Helene M. Johnson, President & CEO

Windsor & District Chamber of Commerce (WDCC)
2575 Ouellette Place, Windsor ON N8X 1L9
Tel: 519-966-3696; Fax: 519-966-0603
e-mail: info@windsorchamber.org
URL: www.windsorchamber.org
Linda E. Smith, President
John Thrasher, Membership Sales

Wingham & Area Chamber of Commerce
PO Box 1360, 273 Josephine St., Wingham ON N0G 2W0
Tel: 519-357-4990; Fax: 519-357-4847
e-mail: wacc@scsinternet.com
Kerri Herrfort, Manager

Woodstock District Chamber of Commerce
#3, 425 Dundas St., Woodstock ON N4S 1B8
Tel: 519-539-9411; *Fax:* 519-456-1611
e-mail: info@woodstockchamber.on.ca
URL: www.woodstockchamber.on.ca
Martha Dennis, General Manager

Zurich & Association District Chamber of Commerce
PO Box 189, Zurich ON N0M 2T0
Tel: 519-236-4717
URL: www.zurich-ontario-canada.com
Phillip Knight, President
Joyce McBeath, Secretary

Prince Edward Island

Chambre de commerce acadienne et francophone de l'Ile-du-Prince-Édouard
PO Box 67, Wellington PE C0B 2E0
Tel: 902-854-3439; *Fax:* 902-854-3099

Greater Charlottetown Chamber of Commerce
PO Box 67, 127 Kent St., Charlottetown PE C1A 7K2
Tel: 902-628-2000; *Fax:* 902-368-3570
e-mail: chamber@charlottetownchamber.com
URL: www.charlottetownchamber.com
Affiliation(s): Atlantic Provinces Chamber of Commerce
Douglas Coles, President
Kathy Hambly, Executive Director

Greater Summerside Chamber of Commerce (GSCC)
#10, 263 Harbour Dr., Summerside PE C1N 5P1
Tel: 902-436-9651; *Fax:* 902-436-8320
e-mail: info@chamber.summerside.ca
URL: www.chamber.summerside.ca
John J. MacDonald, Executive Director
Garth Doiron, President
Heather Matheson, Secretary
Patrick McSweeney, Treasurer

Kensington & Area Chamber of Commerce
PO Box 234, Kensington PE C0B 1M0
Tel: 902-836-3209
e-mail: kacc@pei.aibn.com
URL: www.kensington.ca/chamber
Glenna Lohnes, Executive Director
George Nelson, President

South Shore Chamber of Commerce
PO Box 127, Crapaud PE C0A 1J0
Tel: 902-437-2510
e-mail: wiseone@isn.net
URL: www.southshorechamber.pe.ca
Marion Miller, President

Southern Kings & Queens Chamber of Commerce (SKQCC)
PO Box 1593, Montague PE C0A 1R0
Tel: 902-838-4791; *Fax:* 902-838-0610
Tom Rath, President
Mary Elliot, Staff

West Prince Chamber of Commerce
455 Main St., Alberton PE C0B 1B0
Tel: 902-853-4555
John Lane, President
Elmer Arsenault, Vice-President

Québec

Association des gens d'affaires de Hâvre-Saint-Pierre
1235, de la Digue, RC 1, Hâvre-Saint-Pierre QC G0G 1P0

Chambre de commerce au Coeur de la Montérégie
675, rue St-Joseph, Marieville QC J3M 1H1
Tél: 450-460-4019; *Téléc:* 450-460-2362
Courriel: cccmonteregie@qc.aira.com
Gaétan Rozon, Président

Chambre de Commerce Bois-des-Filion - Lorraine
CP 72012, Bois-des-Filion QC J6Z 4N9
Tél: 450-471-4381
Courriel: info@ccbdfl.com
URL: www.ccbdfl.com
Danielle Dauphin, Trésorier

Chambre de commerce d'Amos-Région
CP 93, 487, 1e rue ouest, Amos QC J9T 3A5
Tél: 819-732-8100; *Téléc:* 819-732-8101
URL: www.ccar.qc.ca
Martin Veilleux, Directeur général

Chambre de commerce d'Amqui
CP 5056, Amqui QC G5J 3S5
Tél: 418-629-5715
Courriel: ccamqui@globetrotter.net
Carole Lacasse, Coordonnatrice

Chambre de commerce de Beauceville
CP 5142, Beauceville QC G5X 2P5
Tél: 418-774-1020
Courriel: cdecommercebeauceville@sogetel.net
Affiliation(s): Chambre de commerce du Québec; Chambre du commerce du Canada
Julien Boudreault, Président

Chambre de commerce de Bonaventure/St-Siméon/St-Élzear
CP 5006, 119, av Port-Royal, Bonaventure QC G0C 1E0
Tél: 418-392-9832
Pierre Gallant, Vice-président

Chambre de commerce de Brandon
117, rue Pacifique, Saint-Gabriel-de-Brandon QC J0K 2N0
Tél: 450-835-2105; *Téléc:* 450-835-2991
Ligne sans frais: 800-363-2788
Courriel: france.brisebois@qc.aira.com
Affiliation(s): Chambre de commerce du Québec
France Brisebois, Directrice générale

Chambre de Commerce de Cabano
CP 5028, Cabano QC G0L 1E0
Blandine Valentin, Contact

Chambre de Commerce de Cap-des-Rosiers
1127, Cap-des-Rosiers, Cap-des-Rosiers QC G4X 6G3
Gérard O'Connor, Secrétaire

Chambre de commerce de Carleton
629, boul Perron, Carleton QC G0C 1J0
Tél: 418-364-1004
Richard Gingras, Vice-président

Chambre de commerce de Causapscal
5, rue St-Jacques sud, Causapscal QC G0J 1J0
Tél: 418-756-6048
Marthe Gagnon, Contact

Chambre de commerce de Chandler
CP 129, 35, rue Commerciale, Chandler QC G0C 1K0
Tél: 418-689-6998
Michel Gagné, Président

Chambre de commerce de Charlevoix
#201, 6, rue St-Jean-Baptiste, Baie-Saint-Paul QC G3Z 1L7
Tél: 418-435-6187; *Téléc:* 418-435-5965
Courriel: info@creezdesliens.com
URL: www.creezdesliens.com
Guy Duchesne, Directeur général

Chambre de commerce de Chibougamau
#4, 600, 3e rue, Chibougamau QC G8P 1P1
Tél: 418-748-4827
Affiliation(s): Chambre de Commerce du Québec et du Canada
Louisette Tremblay, Agente de liaison

Chambre de commerce de Cowansville et région
#100B, 104, rue du Sud, Cowansville QC J2K 2X2
Tél: 450-266-1665; *Téléc:* 450-266-4117
Courriel: cccr@qc.aira.com
URL: www.chambre-cowansville.com
Michel Fleury, Directeur général

Chambre de commerce de Danville-Shipton
CP 599, 52, rue Daniel Johnson, Danville QC J0A 1A0
Tél: 819-839-2475; *Téléc:* 819-839-2446
Courriel: dgirard@interlinx.qc.ca
URL: www.villededanville.com/chambre.html

Chambre de commerce de Disraéli
CP 5008, 846, av Champlain, Disraéli QC G0N 1E0
Tél: 418-449-2955; *Téléc:* 418-449-1669
Courriel: chambcommdisraeli@tlb.sympatico.ca
URL: www.villededisraeli.com/chambredecommerce/index.html
Louise Aubert, Présidente

Chambre de commerce de Dolbeau-Mistassini
#300, 1341, boul Wallberg, Dolbeau-Mistassini QC G8L 1H3
Tél: 418-276-6638; *Téléc:* 418-276-9518
Courriel: info@cdcdm.com
URL: www.cdcdm.com
André Guy, Président

Chambre de commerce de East Angus et Région
221, St-Jean Ouest, East Angus QC J0B 1R0
Tél: 819-832-4950; *Téléc:* 819-832-1208
Courriel: info@cceastangus.com
URL: www.cceastangus.com
Véronique Bruneau, Directrice générale

Chambre de commerce de Ferme-Neuve
125, 12e rue, Ferme-Neuve QC J0W 1C0
Tél: 819-587-2727; *Téléc:* 819-587-2747
Courriel: c.ouellette@yahoo.ca
Céline Ouellette, Coordonnatrice

Chambre de Commerce de Fermont
CP 419, Fermont QC G0G 1J0
Tél: 418-287-3000; *Téléc:* 418-287-3001
Courriel: chambre.commerce@diffusionfermont.ca
URL: www.ccfermont.com
Johanne Nolin, Directrice générale

Chambre de commerce de Fleurimont
#204, 798, rue du Conseil, Sherbrooke QC J1F 1L2
Tél: 819-565-7991; *Téléc:* 819-565-3160
Courriel: ccfleurimont@bellnet.ca
URL: www.ccfleurimont.com
Sébastien Lussier, Directeur général

Chambre de commerce de Forestville
34, route 138 est, Forestville QC G0T 1E0

Chambre de commerce de Frampton
100, rue de la Coop, Frampton QC G0R 1M0
Rolande Lecours, Secrétaire

Chambre de commerce de Gaspé / Chambre of Commerce of Gaspé
27, boul. York Est, Gaspé QC G4X 2K9
Tél: 418-368-3521; *Téléc:* 418-368-8549
Courriel: adjoint@ccgaspe.ca
URL: www.ccgaspe.ca
Mélissa Plourde, Présidente

Chambre de commerce de Gatineau
#100, 45, rue de Villebois, Gatineau QC J8T 8J7
Tél: 819-243-2246; *Téléc:* 819-243-3346
Courriel: ccgatineau@ccgatineau.ca
URL: www.ccgatineau.ca
Karl Lavoie, Directeur général

Chambre de commerce de Grande-Rivière
256, rte 132, Pabos Mills QC G0C 2J0
Tél: 418-689-7515; *Téléc:* 418-689-7515
Courriel: evelynedube@globetrotter.net
Affiliation(s): Fédération des chambre de commerce du Québec
Evelyne Dubé, Présidente

Chambre de commerce de Hemmingford / Hemmingford Chamber of Commerce
#6, 505, rue Frontière, Hemmingford QC J0L 1H0
Tél: 450-247-3310; *Téléc:* 450-247-2389
Courriel: villagehford@b2b2c.ca
URL: www.hemmingford.org

Chambre de commerce de Jonquière
CP 211, 3568, boul Harvey, Jonquière QC G7X 7V9
Tél: 418-695-1362; *Téléc:* 418-695-6954
Courriel: info @ccjonq.qc.ca
URL: www.ccjonq.qc.ca

Chambre de commerce de l'Abitibi-Ouest
#203, 99, 5e Av est, La Sarre QC J9Z 3A8
Tél: 819-333-9836; *Téléc:* 819-333-5737
Courriel: ccao@ccao.qc.ca
URL: www.ccao.qc.ca
Julie Boudreau, Directrice

Chambre de Commerce de L'Assomption
CP 3027, 375, rue St-Pierre, L'Assomption QC J5W 4M9
Tél: 450-589-2405; *Téléc:* 450-589-9213
Courriel: cclassomption@qc.aira.com
URL: www.cclassomption.qc.ca
Ginette Blanchard, Directrice générale

Chambre de commerce de l'Est de la Beauce
CP 519, Saint-Prosper QC G0M 1Y0
Tél: 418-594-1219
Courriel: info@ccestbeauce.com
URL: www.ccestbeauce.com
Suzanne Lantagne, Présidente

Chambre de commerce de l'Est de Portneuf
CP 4031, Pont-Rouge QC G3H 3R4
Tél: 418-873-4085; *Téléc:* 418-873-4599
Courriel: ccep@globetrotter.net
URL: www.portneufest.com
Danielle Garneau, Agente de développement

Chambre de commerce de l'Ile d'Orléans (CCIO)
490, côte du Pont, Saint-Pierre-Ile-d'Orléans QC G0A 4E0
Tél: 418-828-0880; *Téléc:* 418-828-2335
Ligne sans frais: 866-941-9411

Courriel: ccio@videotron.ca
URL: www.cciledorleans.com
Affiliation(s): Chambre de commerce de Québec
Marie Langlois, Directrice générale

Chambre de commerce de l'Ouest-de-l'Ile de Montréal
207, Place Frontenac, Pointe-Claire QC H9R 4Z7
Tél: 514-697-4228; *Téléc:* 514-697-2562
Courriel: info@wimcc.ca
URL: www.ccoim.ca
Louise Hamelin, Directrice générale

Chambre de commerce de la Haute-Gaspésie
CP 6014, Sainte-Anne-des-Monts QC G4V 2Y3
Tél: 418-763-2200; *Téléc:* 418-763-3473
Courriel: dagneau.4@globetrotter.net
URL: www.cchg.qc.ca
Carol Dagneau, Directeur général

Chambre de commerce de la Haute-Matawinie
521, rue Brassard, Saint-Michel-des-Saints QC J0K 3B0
Tél: 450-833-1334
Courriel: infocchm@satelcom.qc.ca
URL: www.haute-matawinie.com
France Chapdelaine, Directrice générale

Chambre de Commerce de la Jacques-Cartier
4517, rte de Fossambault, RR#3, Ste-Catherine-de-la-J-Cartier QC G0A 3M0
Tél: 418-875-4103; *Téléc:* 418-875-2913
Stéphanie Bérard, Secrétaire

Chambre de commerce de la MRC de Rivière-du-Loup
298, boul. Armand-Thériault, Rivière-du-Loup QC G5R 4C2
Tél: 418-862-5243; *Téléc:* 418-862-5136
Courriel: info@ccmrcrdl.com
URL: www.ccmrcrdl.com
Pierre Lévesque, Directeur général

Chambre de commerce de la Région d'Acton
Édifice Gauthier, 1053, rue St-André, Acton Vale QC J0H 1A0
Tél: 450-546-0123; *Téléc:* 450-546-2709
URL: www.ccracton.qc.ca
Joanne Joannette, Directrice générale

Chambre de commerce de la région d'Asbestos
332, 1re av, Asbestos QC J1T 1Y9
Tél: 819-879-5768; *Téléc:* 819-879-5871
Courriel: ccra@qc.aira.com
URL: www.lccra.com

Chambre de commerce de la région de Berthier / D'Autray
CP 482, Berthierville QC J0K 1A0
Tél: 450-836-4689; *Téléc:* 450-836-4926
Courriel: ccregionberthier@hotmail.com
URL: www.ccberthier-dautray.com
Yves Rousseau, Président

Chambre de commerce de la région de Mont-Joli
#304, 1553, boul. Jacques-Cartier, Mont-Joli QC G5H 2V9
Tél: 418-775-4366; *Téléc:* 418-775-4366
Rémi Sénéchal, Président

Chambre de commerce de la région de Salaberry-de-Valleyfield
#400, 100, rue Sainte-Cécile, Salaberry-de-Valleyfield QC J6T 1M1
Tél: 450-373-8789; *Téléc:* 450-373-8642
Courriel: info@ccrsv.com
URL: www.ccrsv.com
Sylvie Villemure, Directrice générale

Chambre de commerce de la région de Weedon
280, 9e av, Weedon QC J0B 3J0
Tél: 819-560-8555; *Téléc:* 819-877-1111
Courriel: admin@ccweedon.com
URL: www.ccweedon.com
Affiliation(s): Chambre de Commerce du Québec
David Gauthier, Président

Chambre de commerce de Lac Brome
CP 723, Knowlton QC J0E 1V0
Tél: 450-242-2870; *Téléc:* 450-242-6896
URL: www.cclacbrome.com
Vivian Downing, Directrice générale

Chambre de commerce de Lévis
#225, 5700, rue JB Michaud, Lévis QC G6V 0B1
Tél: 418-837-3411; *Téléc:* 418-837-8497
Courriel: cclevis@cclevis.ca
URL: www.cclevis.com
Sylvie Girard, Directrice générale

Chambre de commerce de Malartic
CP 368, Malartic QC J0Y 1Z0
Tél: 819-757-2332
Dalila Dupuis, Secrétaire

Chambre de commerce de Manicouagan
#302, 67, place La Salle, Baie-Comeau QC G4Z 1K1
Tél: 418-296-2010; *Téléc:* 418-296-5397
Courriel: info@ccmanic.qc.ca
URL: www.ccmanic.qc.ca
Claude Théberge, Président

Chambre de commerce de Maria
CP 1098, Maria QC G0C 1Y0
Tél: 418-759-3468; *Téléc:* 418-759-5181
Daniel Leblanc, Président

Chambre de commerce de Mascouche
#240, 2822-A, ch Ste-Marie, Mascouche QC J7K 1N4
Tél: 450-966-1536; *Téléc:* 450-966 1531
Courriel: info@ccmascouche.com
URL: www.ccmascouche.com
Manon Brunelle, Directrice générale

Chambre de commerce de Mont-Laurier
445, du Pont, Mont-Laurier QC J9L 2R8
Tél: 819-623-3642; *Téléc:* 819-623-5220
Courriel: ccml@mont-laurier.net
URL: www.mont-laurier.net
Gina Constantin, Directrice exécutive

Chambre de commerce de Montmagny
#1, 17, rue St-Jean Baptiste ouest, Montmagny QC G5V 3B4
Tél: 418-248-3111; *Téléc:* 418-241-5779
Francis Lemieux, Directeur général

Chambre de commerce de Nicolet
30, rue Notre-Dame, Nicolet QC J3T 1G1
Tél: 819-293-4537; *Téléc:* 819-293-6092
Courriel: chambre@chambre-cnicolet.org
URL: www.chambre-cnicolet.org
Mylaine Paradis, Directrice générale

Chambre de commerce de Piedmont
685, rue Principale, Piedmont QC J0R 1K0
Tél: 450-227-5390; *Téléc:* 450-227-4187
Louisette Bernier, Présidente

Chambre de commerce de Port-Cartier
CP 82, Port-Cartier QC G5B 2G7
Tél: 418-766-8047; *Téléc:* 418-766-6367
Courriel: popco@globetrotter.net
Yves Desrosiers, Président

Chambre de commerce de Québec
17, rue St-Louis, Québec QC G1R 3Y8
Tél: 418-692-3853; *Téléc:* 418-694-2286
Courriel: info@ccquebec.ca
URL: www.ccquebec.ca
Affiliation(s): Chambre de commerce du Canada; Chambre de commerce du Québec
Alain Kirouac, Vice-président exécutif et directeu

Chambre de commerce de Radisson
CP 901, Radisson QC J0Y 2X0
Daniel Bellerose, Président

Chambre de commerce de Rawdon
3590, rue Metcalfe, Rawdon QC J0K 1S0
Tél: 450-834-2282; *Téléc:* 450-834-3084
Courriel: ccdr@bellnet.ca
URL: www.chambrecommercerawdon.ca
Benoit Forest, Président

Chambre de commerce de Rivière-au-Renard
CP 95, Gaspé QC G4X 1S0
Tél: 418-269-3328; *Téléc:* 418-269-7191
Isabelle Samuel, Contact

Chambre de commerce de Saint-Bruno
CP 123, Saint-Bruno-de-Montarville QC J3V 4P8
Tél: 450-653-0585; *Téléc:* 450-653-6967
Courriel: info@ccstbruno.ca
URL: www.ccstbruno.ca
Affiliation(s): Chambre de commerce du Québec; Chambre de commerce du Canada
Jacques Laliberté, Directeur général

Chambre de commerce de Saint-Côme
1661-A rue Principale, Saint-Côme QC J0K 2B0
Tél: 450-883-2730; *Téléc:* 450-883-3455
Courriel: info@stcomelanaudiere.com
URL: www.stcomelanaudiere.com
Sylvain Bourque, Président

Chambre de commerce de Ste-Croix
CP 488, Sainte-Croix QC G0S 2H0
Tél: 418-728-2131; *Téléc:* 418-728-4819
Lise Racette, Secrétaire-trésorière

Chambre de commerce de Sainte-Adèle
100, rue Morin, Sainte-Adèle QC J8B 2P7
Tél: 450-229-2644; *Téléc:* 450-229-1436
Courriel: chambredecommerce@sainte-adele.net
URL: www.sainte-adele.net
Marcelle Bergeron, Directrice générale

Chambre de Commerce de Saint-Ephrem
CP 2015, Saint-Éphrem QC G0M 1R0
Tél: 418-484-2681
Courriel: info@ccstephrem.com
URL: www.ccstephrem.com
Jean-François Busque, Président

Chambre de commerce de Ste-Julienne
1799, rte 125, Sainte-Julienne QC J0K 2T0
Tél: 819 831 3551; *Téléc:* 819-831-3551
Nicole Bourgie, Secrétaire

Chambre de commerce de Ste-Justine
167, rte 204, Sainte-Justine QC G0R 1Y0
Tél: 418-383-5397; *Téléc:* 418-383-5398
Courriel: sjustine@sogetel.net
Raymonde Lachance, Trésorière

Chambre de commerce de Sept-Iles
#237, 700, boul Laure, Sept-Iles QC G4R 1Y1
Tél: 418-968-3488; *Téléc:* 418-968-3432
Courriel: cadoretd@cgocable.ca
Luc Dion, Président

Chambre de commerce de Sherbrooke
#402, 75, rue Wellington nord, Sherbrooke QC J1H 5A9
Tél: 819-822-6151; *Téléc:* 819-822-6156
Courriel: info@ccsherbrooke.ca
URL: www.ccsherbrooke.ca
Louise Bourgault, Directrice générale

Chambre de commerce de St-Côme-Linière
1614, 6e rue, Saint-Côme-Linière QC G0M 1J0
Tél: 418-685-2630; *Téléc:* 418-685-2630
Courriel: chambredecommerce@stcomeliniere.com
URL: www.stcomeliniere.com/c_ccommerce.php
Sylvain Bourque, Président

Chambre de commerce de St-Donat
536A, rue Principale, Saint-Donat-de-Montcalm QC J0T 2C0
Tél: 819-424-2833; *Téléc:* 819-424-4366
Courriel: cc.st-donat@bellnet.ca
Diane Champagne, Agente de liaison

Chambre de commerce de St-Eugène-de-Guigues
CP 1013, 9, 1ere Avenue Ouest, Saint-Eugène-de-Guigues QC J0Z 3L0
Tél: 819-785-2057
Lillian Matteau, Secrétaire

Chambre de commerce de St-Frédéric
2166, rue Principale, Saint-Frédéric QC G0N 1P0
Tél: 418-426-3104; *Téléc:* 418-426-3357
Monique Morin-Cyr, Secrétaire
Andre Lessard, Président

Chambre de commerce de St-Georges
#310, 8585, boul Lacroix, Ville de Saint-Georges Beauce QC G5Y 5L6
Tél: 418-228-7879; *Téléc:* 418-228-8074
Courriel: administration@ccstgeorges.com
URL: www.ccstgeorges.com
Affiliation(s): Chambre de commerce du Québec; Chambre de commerce du Canada
Sabrina Gagné, Directrice générale

Chambre de commerce de St-Jean-de-Dieu
CP 392, Saint-Jean-de-Dieu QC G0L 3M0
Tél: 418-963-3205
Chantale Rioux, Secrétaire

Chambre de commerce de St-Joseph-de-Beauce
1021, av du Palais, Saint-Joseph-de-Beauce QC G0S 2V0
Tél: 418-397-4980; *Téléc:* 418-397-5982
Marielle Bertrand, Adjointe administrative

Chambre de commerce de St-Jules-de-Beauce
CP 81, 213, av Roy, Saint-Jules QC G0N 1R0
Tél: 418-397-1870
Sylvain Cloutier, Président

Chambre de commerce de St-Léonard
8370, boul. Lacordaire, Saint-Léonard QC H1R 3Y6

Tél: 514-325-4232; *Téléc:* 514-955-8544
Courriel: tmelita@citenet.net
URL: www.ccstleonard.qc.ca
Tony De Risi, Président

Chambre de Commerce de Terrebonne/Lachenaie
#301, 1025, montée Masson, Lachenaie QC J6W 5H9
Tél: 450-471-8779; *Téléc:* 450-471-5610
URL: www.ccterrebonne.qc.ca
Affiliation(s): Chambre de commerce du Canada; Chambre de commerce du Québec; Chambre de commerce régionale de Lanaudière; Réseau canadien de centres de services aux entreprises; Centre local de développement économique des Moulins (CLDEM); Centre local d'emploi de Terrebonne; Société de développement touristique des Moulins; Conseil de développement bioalimentaire de Lanaudière.
Robert Lalancette, Directeur général

Chambre de commerce de tourisme de la Vallée de St-Sauveur
#202, 228, rue Principal, St-Sauveur-des-Monts QC J0R 1R0
Tél: 450-227-2564; *Téléc:* 450-227-6480
Ligne sans frais: 877-528-2553
Courriel: chcommstso@qc.aira.com
URL: www.valleesaintsauveur.com/main.php?lang=fr
Pierre Urquhart, Relationniste

Chambre de commerce de Tring Jonction
184, av Commerciale, Tring-Jonction QC G0N 1X0
Tél: 418-427-3320; *Téléc:* 418-427-1466
Danye Vachon, Secrétaire

Chambre de commerce de Valcourt et Région
CP 900, Valcourt QC J0E 2L0
Tél: 450-532-3041; *Téléc:* 450-532-3041
Courriel: commerce@cooptel.qc.ca
Affiliation(s): Chambre de commerce régionale de l'Estrie
Ghislain D'Astous, Trésorier

Chambre de commerce de Val-d'Or
400, 3e av, Val-d'Or QC J9P 1R9
Tél: 819-825-3703; *Téléc:* 819-825-8599
Courriel: ccvd@cablevision.qc.ca
URL: www.ccvd.qc.ca
Anik Brochu, Directrice générale

Chambre de commerce de Villebois
1580, ch Selbaie, Villebois QC J0Z 3V0
Tél: 819-941-6302
Claude Côté, Président

Chambre de commerce de Ville-Marie
1, rue Industrielle, Ville-Marie QC J9V 1S3
Tél: 819-629-2918; *Téléc:* 819-622-1801
Courriel: chambredecommerce-vill@cablevision.qc.ca
Anne-Marie Demers, Secrétaire

Chambre de commerce des Iles-de-la-Madeleine (CCIM)
Édifice Fernand Cyr, #103, 735, ch Principal, Cap-aux-Meules QC G4T 1G8
Tél: 418-986-4111; *Téléc:* 418-986-4112
Courriel: info@ccim.qc.ca
URL: www.ccim.qc.ca
Claire Gaudet, Directrice générale

Chambre de commerce du Centre-de-la-Mauricie
900, 6e Avenue, Shawinigan-Sud QC G9P 1S4
Tél: 819-536-0777; *Téléc:* 819-536-0039
Courriel: info@cccmauricie.qc.ca
URL: www.cccmauricie.qc.ca
Isabele Rouette, Directrice générale

Chambre de commerce du district St-Rémi
CP 2578, 151, rue Perras, Saint-Rémi QC J0L 2L0
Tél: 450-454-3974; *Téléc:* 450-454-7320
Courriel: ccdstr@hotmail.com
Carole Cyr, Directrice générale

Chambre de commerce du Grand Joliette
500, rue Dollard, Joliette QC J6E 4M4
Tél: 450-759-6363; *Téléc:* 450-759-5012
Courriel: info@ccgj.qc.ca
URL: www.ccgj.qc.ca
André Hénault, Directeur général

Chambre de commerce du Grand Paspébiac
CP 1232, 6, boul Gérard D. Lévesque est, Paspébiac QC G0C 2K0
Tél: 418-752-3330; *Téléc:* 418-752-3330
Roger Horth, Secrétaire

Chambre de commerce du Haut St-Maurice
547-C, rue Commerciale, La Tuque QC G9X 3A7
Tél: 819-523-9933
Hélène Langlais, Directrice générale

Chambre de commerce du Haut-Richelieu
#232, 315, rue MacDonald, Saint-Jean-sur-Richelieu QC J3B 8J3
Tél: 450-346-2544; *Téléc:* 450-346-3812
Courriel: info@cchautrichelieu.qc.ca
URL: www.cchautrichelieu.qc.ca
Michel Fecteau, Président

Chambre de commerce du Lac des Deux-Montagnes (Pointe-Calumet, Saint-Joseph-du-Lac, Oka & Saint-Placide)
#400, 190 - 41e av, Pointe-Calumet QC J0N 1G2
Tél: 450-472-7535; *Téléc:* 450-472-0229
Courriel: c.c.lac2montagnes@videotron.ca
URL: www.cclac2montagnes.com
Affiliation(s): Chambre de Commerce du Québec
Denise Lemay, Directrice générale

Chambre de commerce du Lac Robertson
CP 100, Tête-à-la-Baleine QC G0G 2W0
Tél: 418-773-2659; *Téléc:* 418-773-2526
Gérald Organ, Secrétaire

Chambre de commerce du Montréal métropolitain / Board of Trade of Metropolitan Montréal
Niveau plaza, #6000, 380, rue St-Antoine ouest, Montréal QC H3Y 3X7
Tél: 514-871-4000; *Téléc:* 514-871-1255
Courriel: info@ccmm.qc.ca
URL: www.ccmm.qc.ca
Michel Leblanc, Président et chef de la direction

Chambre de commerce du Saguenay
194, rue Price ouest, Chicoutimi QC G7J 1H1
Tél: 418-543-5941; *Téléc:* 418-543-5576
Courriel: info@ccchic.qc.ca
URL: www.ccchic.qc.ca
Réjean Boucher, Directeur général

Chambre de commerce du secteur de Normandin
1048, rue St-Cyrille, Normandin QC G8M 4R9
Tél: 418-274-2004; *Téléc:* 418-274-7171
Courriel: ccnormandin@hotmail.com
URL: www.ville.normandin.qc.ca
Denise Paquette, Directrice générale

Chambre de commerce du Transcontinental
CP 2004, Rivière-Bleue QC G0L 2B0
Tél: 418-893-2347; *Téléc:* 418-893-2889
Courriel: cctrans@globetrotter.net
URL: pages.globetrotter.net/cctrans
Yves Thibault, Président

Chambre de commerce Duparquet
CP 369, Duparquet QC J0Z 1W0
Tél: 819-948-2030
Jasmine Therrien, Secrétaire

Chambre de commerce East Broughton
CP 916, East Broughton QC G0N 1G0
Tél: 418-427-5761; *Téléc:* 418-427-4032
Courriel: cceastbroughton@globetrotter.net
Annie Roy, Secrétaire

Chambre de commerce et d'industrie (St-Eustache / Deux-Montagnes / Ste-Marthe-sur-le-Lac)
67 A, boul. Industriel, Saint-Eustache QC J7R 5P2
Tél: 450-491-1991; *Téléc:* 450-491-1648
Courriel: info@chambrecommerce.com
URL: www.chambrecommerce.com
Michel Goyer, Directeur général

Chambre de commerce et d'industrie d'Argenteuil
#225, 580, rue Principale, Lachute QC J8H 1Y7
Tél: 450-562-1947; *Téléc:* 450-562-1896
Courriel: cci.argen@qc.aira.com
URL: www.cciargenteuil.qc.ca
Suzanne Gaudet, Directrice générale

Chambre de commerce et d'industrie de Bécancour
1045, av Nicolas Perrot, Bécancour QC G9H 3B7
Tél: 819-294-6010; *Téléc:* 819-294-6020
Courriel: info@ccibecancour.ca
URL: www.ccibecancour.ca
Jean-François Giroux, Président

Chambre de commerce et d'industrie de Châteauguay
#100, 15, boul Maple, Châteauguay QC J6J 3P7
Tél: 450-698-0027; *Téléc:* 450-698-0088
Courriel: ccic@qc.aira.com
URL: www.ccichateauguay.ca
Dorys Miousse, Directrice générale

Chambre de commerce et d'industrie de Drummond
CP 188, 234, rue Saint-Marcel, Drummondville QC J2B 6V7
Tél: 819-477-7822; *Téléc:* 819-477-2823
Courriel: info@ccid.qc.ca
URL: www.ccid.qc.ca
Alain Côté, Directeur général

Chambre de commerce et d'industrie de l'Est de l'Ile de Montréal
#201, 5790, av Pierre-de Coubertin, Montréal QC H1N 1R4
Tél: 514-354-5378; *Téléc:* 514-354-5340
Courriel: info@cciem.qc.ca
URL: www.ccieim.qc.ca
Manon Landry, Directrice générale

Chambre de commerce et d'industrie de la MRC de Maskinongé
396, Ste-Élisabeth, Louiseville QC J5V 1M7
Tél: 819-228-8582; *Téléc:* 819-228-8989
Courriel: info@cci-maskinonge.ca
URL: www.cci-maskinonge.ca
Marc H. Plante, Directeur général

Chambre de commerce et d'Industrie de la région de Coaticook (CCIRC)
150, rue Child, Coaticook QC J1A 2B3
Tél: 819-849-4733; *Téléc:* 819-849-6828
Courriel: ccrc@abacom.com
URL: www.ccircoaticook.ca
Sonia Montminy, Présidente

Chambre de commerce et d'industrie de la région de Richmond
CP 3119, Richmond QC J0B 2H0
Tél: 819-826-5854; *Téléc:* 819-826-2813
Courriel: ch.commerce@ville.richmond.qc.ca
URL: www.ville.richmond.qc.ca/chcom.htm
Rémi-Mario Mayette, Président

Chambre de commerce et d'industrie de la Rive-Sud
#101, 85, rue Saint-Charles ouest, Longueuil QC J4H 1C5
Tél: 450-463-2121; *Téléc:* 450-463-1858
Courriel: info@ccirs.qc.ca
URL: www.ccirs.qc.ca
Madeleine Ste-Marie, Directrice générale

Chambre de commerce et d'industrie de la Vallée-du-Richelieu
#102, 230, rue Brébeuf, Beloeil QC J3G 5P3
Tél: 450-464-3733; *Téléc:* 450-446-4163
Courriel: chambre@ccvr.qc.ca
URL: www.ccvr.qc.ca
Lise Lebel, Coordonnatrice

Chambre de commerce et d'industrie de Laval (CCIL)
#200, 1555, boul Chomedey, Laval QC H7V 3Z1
Tél: 450-682-5255; *Téléc:* 450-682-5735
Courriel: info@ccilaval.qc.ca
URL: www.ccilaval.qc.ca
Francine Cabral, Directrice générale

Chambre de commerce et d'industrie de Maniwaki (CCIM)
171, rue Principale sud, Maniwaki QC J9E 1Z8
Tél: 819-449-6627; *Téléc:* 819-449-7667
Ligne sans frais: 866-449-6728
Courriel: valeried@ccimki.ca
URL: www.ccimaniwaki.com
Claude Benoit, Président
Sophie Beaudoin, Directrice générale

Chambre de commerce et d'industrie de Mirabel
#208, 13479, boul du Curé Labelle, Mirabel QC J7J 1L2
Tél: 450-433-1944; *Téléc:* 450-433-5168
Courriel: info@ccmirabel.com
Yves Legault, Président

Chambre de commerce et d'industrie de Montréal-Nord (CRIMN)
#006A, 6000, boul Henri-Bourassa est, Montréal-Nord QC H1G 2T6
Tél: 514-329-4453; *Téléc:* 514-329-5373
Courriel: info@ccimn.qc.ca
URL: www.ccimn.qc.ca
Jean C. Touchette, Directeur général

Chambre de commerce et d'industrie de Rouyn-Noranda (CCIRN)
225, boul Rideau, Rouyn-Noranda QC J9X 5Y6
Tél: 819-797-2000; *Téléc:* 819-762-3091
Courriel: reseau@ccirn.qc.ca
URL: www.ccirn.qc.ca
Guy Veillet, Présidente

Chambre de commerce et d'industrie de Sorel-Tracy métropolitain
CP 568, 67, rue Georges, Sorel-Tracy QC J3P 1C2
Tél: 450-742-0018; *Téléc:* 450-742-7442
URL: www.ccstm.qc.ca
Rachel Doyon, Directrice générale

Chambre de commerce et d'industrie de St-Félicien
CP 34, 1209, boul Sacré-Coeur, Saint-Félicien QC G8K 2P8
Tél: 418-679-2097; *Téléc:* 418-679-4039
Courriel: ccistfe@ville.stfelicien.qc.ca
URL: www.chambre-sf.com
Jean-Paul Asselin, Directeur général

Chambre de commerce et d'industrie de St-Laurent
#204, 935, Décarie, Saint-Laurent QC H4L 3M3
Tél: 514-333-5222; *Téléc:* 514-333-0937
Courriel: info@ccstl.qc.ca
URL: www.ccstl.qc.ca
Robert Petit, Directeur général

Chambre de commerce et d'industrie de Varennes (CCIV)
2100, boul René Gaulthier, Varennes QC J3X 1P1
Tél: 450-652-4209; *Téléc:* 450-652-4244
Courriel: info@chambre-civ.com
URL: www.chambre-civ.com
Huguette Thivierge, Coordonnatrice

Chambre de commerce et d'industrie de Ville de La Baie
285, boul Grande Baie nord, La Baie QC G7B 3K4
Tél: 418-544-9861
Joanne Dubois, Directrice générale

Chambre de commerce et d'Industrie des Bois-Francs
122, rue Acqueduc, Victoriaville QC G6P 1M3
Tél: 819-758-6371; *Téléc:* 819-758-4604
URL: www.ccibf.qc.ca
Marc-Alexandre Brousseau, Directeur général

Chambre de commerce et d'industrie du bassin de Chambly (CCIB)
929, boul. de Périgny, Chambly QC J3L 5H5
Tél: 450-658-7598; *Téléc:* 450-658-6477
Courriel: info@ccibc.qc.ca
URL: www.ccibc.qc.ca
Johanne Garinther, Coordonnatrice administrative

Chambre de commerce et d'industrie du secteur Roberval (CCISR)
CP 115, Roberval QC G8H 2N4
Tél: 418-275-3504; *Téléc:* 418-275-0851
Courriel: info@ccisr.qc.ca
URL: www.ccisr.qc.ca
Affiliation(s): Chambre de Commerce du Québec; Chambre de Commerce du Canada
Érik Simard, Directeur général

Chambre de commerce et d'industrie Lac Saint-Jean-Est
625, rue Bergeron ouest, Alma QC G8B 1V3
Tél: 418-662-2734; *Téléc:* 418-669-2220
Courriel: cca@qc.aira.com
Madeleine Gagnon, Directrice générale

Chambre de commerce et d'industrie Magog-Orford
801, rue Principale Ouest, Magog QC J1X 2B4
Tél: 819-843-3494; *Téléc:* 819-843-4124
Courriel: info@ccimo.qc.ca
URL: www.ccimo.qc.ca
Francine Caya, Directrice générale

Chambre de commerce et d'industrie régionale de Saint-Léonard-d'Aston
#1, 370, rue Principale, Saint-Léonard-d'Aston QC J0C 1M0
Tél: 819-399-2020; *Téléc:* 819-399-3288
Courriel: ccistl@tlb.sympatico.ca
URL: www.ccst-leonard-daston.com
Marthe Proulx, Directrice générale

Chambre de commerce et d'industrie St-Jérôme (CCISJ)
309, rue De Villemure, Saint-Jérôme QC J7Z 5J5
Tél: 450-431-4339; *Téléc:* 450-431-1677
Courriel: rachel.roy@ccisj.qc.ca
URL: www.ccisj.qc.ca
Jocelyne Légaré, Directrice générale

Chambre de commerce et d'industries de Trois-Rivières
CP 1045, 168, rue Bonaventure, Trois-Rivières QC G9A 5K4
Tél: 819-375-9628; *Téléc:* 819-375-9083
Courriel: info@ccdtr.com
URL: www.ccdtr.com
Claude Durand, Directrice générale

Chambre de commerce et de l'industrie de l'Amiante
81, rue Notre-Dame sud, Thetford Mines QC G6G 1J4
Tél: 418-338-4551; *Téléc:* 418-335-2066
Charlotte Ferland, Directrice générale

Chambre de commerce et de l'industrie du Haut St-Laurent
CP 1914, 8, rue King, Huntingdon QC J0S 1H0
Tél: 450-264-5252; *Téléc:* 450-264-5111
Courriel: cdechsl@suroit.com
URL: ww.cdechsl.com
Kathleen Bisson, Présidente

Chambre de commerce et de l'industrie Les Maskoutains
780, av de L'Hôtel-de-ville, Saint-Hyacinthe QC J2S 5B2
Tél: 450-773-3474; *Téléc:* 450-773-9339
Courriel: chambre@chambrecommerce.ca
URL: www.chambrecommerce.ca
Nicole Laverrière, Directrice générale

Chambre de commerce et de l'industrie Rimouski-Neigette
CP 1296, #101, 125, rue de l'Évêché, Rimouski QC G5L 8M2
Tél: 418-722-4494; *Téléc:* 418-722-8402
Courriel: info@ccrimouski.com
URL: www.ccrimouski.com
Serge Barrette, Directeur principal

Chambre de commerce et de tourisme de Murdochville
CP 879, #29, 635 - 5e rue, Murdochville QC G0E 1W0
Tél: 418-784-2577; *Téléc:* 418-784-2597
Courriel: ccmurd.roy@globetrotter.net
URL: www.ccmurdochville.com
Francine Roy, Directrice générale

Chambre de commerce et de tourisme de St-Adolphe-d'Howard
CP 326, Saint-Adolphe-d'Howard QC J0T 2B0
Ligne sans frais: 888-710-4636
Courriel: info@st-adolphe.com
URL: www.st-adolphe.com
Albert Difruscia, Président

Chambre de commerce gaie du Québec (CCGQ) / The Québec Gay Chamber of Commerce
#302, 249, rue St-Jacques, Montréal QC H2Y 1M6
Tél: 514-522-1885; *Téléc:* 514-522-9468
Ligne sans frais: 888-595-8110
Courriel: info@ccgq.ca
URL: www.ccgq.ca
Hans Janiak, Président

Chambre de commerce Haute-Yamaska et Région
650, rue Principale, Granby QC J2G 8L4
Tél: 450-372-6100; *Téléc:* 450-372-3161
Courriel: info@chambredecommerce.org
URL: www.chambredecommerce.org
Céline Gagnon, Directrice générale

Chambre de commerce juive
1, carré Cummings, Montréal QC H3W 1M6
Tel: 514-345-2645; *Fax:* 514-345-2655
Kim Garzon, Directrice

Chambre de commerce Kamouraska-L'Islet (CCKL)
#208, 1000, 6e av, La Pocatière QC G0R 1Z0
Tél: 418-856-6227; *Téléc:* 418-856-6462
Ligne sans frais: 877-856-6227
Courriel: cckl@qc.aira.com
URL: www.cckl.org
Michel R. Henri, Directeur général

Chambre de commerce Notre-Dame-du-Lac
CP 147, Notre-Dame-du-Lac QC G0L 1X0
Tél: 418-899-6987
Jean-Paul Boucher, Trésorier

Chambre de commerce Notre-Dame-du-Nord
CP 517, Notre-Dame-du-Nord QC J0Z 3B0
Tél: 819-723-2814; *Téléc:* 819-723-2899
Ernest Laplante, Président

Chambre de commerce Nouvelle Beauce
CP 684, #C, 700, rue Notre-Dame nord, Sainte-Marie QC G6E 2K9
Tél: 418-387-2006; *Téléc:* 418-387-8223
Courriel: info@ccnb.ca
URL: www.nouvellebeauce.com/site.asp
Yannick Richard, Président
Johanne Côté, Directrice

Chambre de commerce Pierre-Le Gardeur De Repentigny
#151, 534, rue Notre-Dame, Repentigny QC J6A 2T8
Tél: 450-581-3010; *Téléc:* 450-581-5069
Courriel: info@ccrepentigny.qc.ca
URL: www.ccrepentigny.qc.ca
Linda Mallette, Directrice générale

Chambre de commerce région de Matane
CP 518, Matane QC G4W 3P5
Tél: 418-562-9344; *Téléc:* 418-562-7734
Courriel: info@ccmatane.com
URL: www.ccmatane.com
Yvon Gaudet, Directeur général

Chambre de commerce région de Mégantic
6346, rue Salaberry, Lac-Mégantic QC G6B 1J3
Tél: 819-583-5392; *Téléc:* 819-583-5457
Courriel: info@ccrmeg.com
URL: www.ccrmeg.com
Isabelle Gagnon, Directrice générale

Chambre de commerce régionale de St-Raymond (CCRSR)
#1, 100, av St-Jacques, Saint-Raymond QC G3L 3Y1
Tél: 418-337-4049; *Téléc:* 418-337-8017
Courriel: ccrsr@cite.net
URL: www.ccrsr.qc.ca
Isabelle Jobin, Directrice générale

Chambre de commerce régionale de Windsor
CP 115, Windsor QC J1S 2L7
Tél: 819-845-9121; *Téléc:* 819-845-9055
Courriel: info@voyagescorriveau.ca
Suzanne Grimard, Présidente

Chambre de commerce régionale des entrepreneurs de Québec (CCREQ)
#3200, 2700, boul Laurier, Sainte-Foy QC G1V 4K5
Tél: 418-651-7181; *Téléc:* 418-651-5248
Courriel: info@cceq.ca
Yvan Lachance, Vice-président exécutif

Chambre de commerce Ste-Émélie-de-l'Énergie
CP 272, Sainte-Émélie-de-l'Énergie QC J0K 2K0
Carmelle Tessier, Secrétaire

Chambre de commerce Saint-Lin-Laurentides
CP 3340, #101, 704, rue St-Isidore, Saint-Lin-Laurentides QC J5M 2V2
Tél: 450-439-3704; *Téléc:* 450-439-2066
Courriel: chambrecstlin@videotron.ca
André Corbeil, Président

Chambre de commerce secteur ouest de Portneuf
CP 2006, 1150, rue Principale, Saint-Marc-des-Carrières QC G0A 4B0
Tél: 418-268-5447; *Téléc:* 418-268-3532
Courriel: ccsop@globetrotter.net
URL: www.portneufouest.com
Émilie Savard, Agente de développement, Infographiste

Chambre de commerce St-Félix de Valois
15, ch Joliette, Saint-Félix-de-Valois QC J0K 2M0
Tél: 450-889-8161; *Téléc:* 450-889-1590
Courriel: ccst-flx@megacom.net
URL: www.stfelixdevalois.qc.ca
Josée Durand, Directrice générale

Chambre de commerce St-Jean-de-Matha
1159, rte Louis-Cyr, Saint-Jean-de-Matha QC J0K 2S0
Tél: 450-886-0599; *Téléc:* 450-886-3123
Courriel: info@chambrematha.com
URL: www.chambrematha.com
Régis Morissette, Président

Chambre de commerce St-Martin de Beauce
CP 31, 60, 5e av ouest, Saint-Martin QC G0M 1B0
Tél: 418-382-5549
Courriel: chambre@st-martin.qc.ca
URL: www.st-martin.qc.ca
Affiliation(s): Chambre de commerce du Québec; Chambre de commerce du Canada

Chambre de commerce Sud-Ouest de l'Ile de Montréal
#50, 410, av Lafleur, Montréal QC H8R 3H6
Tél: 514-365-4575; *Téléc:* 514-367-5462
Martine Mimeault, Responsable des communications

Chambre de commerce Vallée de la Missisquoi
858, rte de la Missisquoi, Bolton Centre QC J0E 1G0

Tél: 450-292-4217

Chambre de commerce Vallée de la Petite Nation
CP 93, Plaisance QC J0V 1S0
Tél: 819-427-6730; *Téléc:* 819-427-9849
Courriel: ccvpn@videotron.ca
URL: www.ccvpn.org
Michel Lavergne, Directeur

Chambre de commerce Vaudreuil-Dorion
#200, 417, av St-Charles, Vaudreuil-Dorion QC J7V 2M9
Tél: 450-424-9470; *Téléc:* 450-424-8759
Courriel: ccvd@qc.aira.com
URL: www.ccvdorion.qc.ca
Yvette Lefebvre, Secrétaire

Chambre de commerce Ville de Mont-Tremblant
990, rue Lauzon, Mont-Tremblant QC J8E 3J5
Tél: 819-425-8441; *Téléc:* 819-425-7949
Courriel: info@ccdemonttremblant.com
URL: www.ccdemonttremblant.com
Paul Bernier, Directeur général

Jeune chambre de commerce de Montréal (JCCM)
#203, 1010, rue Sherbrooke ouest, Montréal QC H3A 2R7
Tél: 514-845-4951; *Téléc:* 514-845-0587
Courriel: info@jccm.org
URL: www.jccm.org
Solange Blanchard, Directrice générale

Jeune chambre de commerce de Québec
#249, 4600, boul Henri-Bourassa, Charlesbourg QC G1H 3A5
Tél: 418-622-6937; *Téléc:* 418-628-7777
Courriel: jccq@jccq.qc.ca
URL: www.jccq.qc.ca/
Véronique Morin, Présidente

Regroupement des jeunes gens d'affaires du Québec (RJGAQ)
#900, 500 rue Sherbrooke ouest, Montréal QC H3A 3C6
Tél: 514-282-3836; *Téléc:* 514-844-7556
Sylvie Roberge, Adjointe administrative

Saskatchewan

Assiniboia Chamber of Commerce (SK)
PO Box 1803, 110 - 4th Ave. West, Assiniboia SK S0H 0B0
Tel: 306-642-5553; *Fax:* 306-642-3529
e-mail: aeda@assiniboia.net
Terry L. Sieffert, President
Sonia Dahlman, Treasurer
Bonnie Ruzicka, Executive Assistant

Battlefords Chamber of Commerce
PO Box 1000, North Battleford SK S9A 3E6
Tel: 306-445-6226; *Fax:* 306-445-6633
e-mail: b.chamber@sasktel.net
URL: www.battlefordschamber.com
Affiliation(s): Institution of Association Executives; Tourism Industry Association of Saskatchewan
Patti Acaster, President
Linda Machniak, Executive Director

Big River Chamber of Commerce
c/o Kangaroo Cottage, PO Box 351, Big River SK S0J 0E0
Tel: 306-469-2484; *Fax:* 306-469-2485
URL: www.bigriver.ca
Jeanette Wicinski-Dunn, President
Linda McKenzie, Secretary

Biggar & District Chamber of Commerce
c/o Bear Hills R.D.C., PO Box 327, 117 - 3rd Ave. West, Biggar SK S0K 0M0
Tel: 306-948-2295; *Fax:* 306-948-5050
e-mail: bearhills.rdc@sasktel.net
URL: townofbiggar.com
Garry Faye, Co-Chair
Diane Koenders, Sec.-Treas.

Blaine Lake & District Chamber of Commerce
PO Box 178, Blaine Lake SK S0J 0J0
Tel: 306-497-2695; *Fax:* 306-497-2402
e-mail: elhoe@sasktel.net
T.L. Bowie, President

Broadview Chamber of Commerce
PO Box 508, Broadview SK S0G 0K0
Tel: 306-696-3166
D.B. Norbeck, President
D.A. Massier, Secretary

Canora & District Chamber of Commerce
PO Box 1409, Canora SK S0A 0L0
Tel: 306-563-4123; *Fax:* 306-563-4124
Nick Martinuk, President
Dana Antonovitch, Secretary

Carlyle Chamber of Commerce
PO Box 365, Carlyle SK S0C 0R0
Tel: 306-453-6718; *Fax:* 306-453-2910
e-mail: blair.andrew@andrewagencies.com
Blair Andrew, President
S. Colpitts, Secretary

Choiceland & District Chamber of Commerce
c/o Grow Plan Fertilizers Ltd., PO Box 339, 115 Railway Ave. West, Choiceland SK S0J 0M0
Tel: 306-428-2300; *Fax:* 306-428-2526
Frank H. Bond, President
Colleen F Digness, Secretary

Coronach Community Chamber of Commerce
PO Box 577, Coronach SK S0H 0Z0
Tel: 306-267-2077; *Fax:* 306-267-2047
e-mail: marshalljackie@hotmail.com
Affiliation(s): Saskatchewan Chamber of Commerce
J. Marshall, President
S. Nelson, Secretary

Debden & District Chamber of Commerce
PO Box 91, Debden SK S0J 0S0
Tel: 306-724-2266; *Fax:* 306-724-4505
e-mail: p.demers@sasktel.net
Phil Demers, President
Denis Belair, Secretary

Eastend & District Chamber of Commerce
c/o L & E Farm Sales Ltd., PO Box 534, Eastend SK S0N 0T0
Tel: 306-295-3355; *Fax:* 306-295-3571
Bonnie Gleim, President
Stephanie Morris, Secretary

Eatonia & District Chamber of Commerce
PO Box 370, Eatonia SK S0L 0Y0
Tel: 306-967-2506; *Fax:* 306-967-2267
T. Drurey, President
Anne Rhodes, Secretary

Esterhazy & District Chamber of Commerce
PO Box 778, Esterhazy SK S0A 0X0
Tel: 306-745-5405; *Fax:* 306-745-6797
e-mail: esterhazy.ed@sasktel.net
T. Lippai, President
J. Parker, Secretary

Estevan Chamber of Commerce
#303, 1133 - 4th St., Estevan SK S4A 0W6
Tel: 306-634-2828; *Fax:* 306-634-6729
e-mail: estevanchamber@sasktel.net
URL: www.estevanchamber.ca
Carol Gress, Office Manager
Lynn Chipley, President
Michel Cyrenne, Community Development Manager

Fort Qu'Appelle & District Chamber of Commerce
c/o Mission Ridge, PO Box 1273, Fort Qu'appelle SK S0G 1S0
Tel: 306-332-5717; *Fax:* 306-332-1287
Denis Palmier, Secretary
K. Mattern, President

Fox Valley Chamber of Commerce
c/o Double L. Farms, PO Box 133, Fox Valley SK S0N 0V0
Tel: 306-666-4447; *Fax:* 306-666-4448
Lester N Lodoen, President
Delia E. Hughes, Secretary

Goodsoil & District Chamber of Commerce
PO Box 88, Main St., Goodsoil SK S0M 1A0
Tel: 306-238-2033; *Fax:* 306-238-4441
e-mail: joan.baer@goodsoil.cu.sk.ca
Lucille Martin, President
Joan Baer, Secretary

Gravelbourg Chamber of Commerce
PO Box 85, Gravelbourg SK S0H 1X0
Tel: 306-648-3182; *Fax:* 306-648-2311
e-mail: brouwerc@sasktel.net
G. Murray, Treasurer
Cees Brouwer, President

Greater Saskatoon Chamber of Commerce
#104, 202 - 4th Ave. N, Saskatoon SK S7K 0K1
Tel: 306-244-2151; *Fax:* 306-244-8366
e-mail: chamber@eboardoftrade.com
URL: www.eboardoftrade.com
Affiliation(s): Enterprise Centre; Leadership Saskatoon; Raj Manek Mentorship Program; Saskatchewan Agrivision Corporation; Saskatchewan Economic Development Authority; Saskatchewan Young Professionals & Entrepreneurs; Saskatoon Aboriginal Employment & Business Opportunities Inc., Saskatoon Air Services; Saskatoon Regional Economic Development Authority; Tourism Saskatoon; United Way of Saskatoon; Vision 2000
Kent Smith-Windsor, Executive Director
Marion Ghiglione, President

Herbert & District Chamber of Commerce
PO Box 700, Herbert SK S0H 2A0
Tel: 306-784-3475; *Fax:* 306-784-2801
e-mail: marniescoffeeshop@sasktel.net
Kevin Braun, President
Sandra MacArthur, Secretary

Hudson Bay Chamber of Commerce
PO Box 430, Hudson Bay SK S0E 0Y0
Tel: 306-865-2288; *Fax:* 306-865-2177
Tonia Jones, President
Liz Johnson, Secretary

Humboldt & District Chamber of Commerce
PO Box 1440, Humboldt SK S0K 2A0
Tel: 306-682-4990; *Fax:* 306-682-5203
e-mail: humboldtchamber@sasktel.net
URL: www.humboldtchamber.ca
Bonnie Classen, President
Lance Stockbrugger, Vice-President

Indian Head Chamber of Commerce
PO Box 1233, Indian Head SK S0G 2K0
Tel: 306-695-2238; *Fax:* 306-695-2307
e-mail: ihac@sasktel.net
Melanie Roth, Secretary

Kamsack & District Chamber of Commerce
PO Box 817, Kamsack SK S0A 1S0
Tel: 306-542-9694; *Fax:* 306-542-4396
e-mail: becenko@sasktel.net
Jack Koreluik, President
Wendy Becenko, Secretary

Kelvington & District Chamber of Commerce
c/o Kelvington Radio, PO Box 667, 107 Main St., Kelvington SK S0A 1W0
Tel: 306-327-4656
Jennifer L. Crawford, President
Don Ewing, Sec.-Treas.

Kenaston & District Chamber of Commerce
PO Box 70, Kenaston SK S0G 2N0
Tel: 306-252-2236; *Fax:* 306-252-2089
S. Anbolt, Sec.-Treas.
Mary Lou Whittles, President

Kerrobert Chamber of Commerce
PO Box 408, Kerrobert SK S0L 1R0
Tel: 306-834-5423
e-mail: kerrobert@sasktel.net
Myrna H. Kissick, President

Kindersley Chamber of Commerce
PO Box 1537, Kindersley SK S0L 1S0
Tel: 306-463-2320; *Fax:* 306-463-2312
e-mail: kindersleychamber@sasktel.net
URL: www.kindersleychamber.com
Richard Jones, President
Esther Redden, Office Manager

Kinistino & District Chamber of Commerce
PO Box 803, Kinistino SK S0J 1H0
Tel: 306-864-2275

Kipling Chamber of Commerce
PO Box 700, Kipling SK S0G 2S0
Tel: 306-736-8520; *Fax:* 306-736-2260
e-mail: ssauve.mib@sasktel.net
D.G. Balon, Secretary
K. Hassler, President

Lafleche & District Chamber of Commerce
PO Box 40, 41 Main St., Lafleche SK S0H 2K0
Tel: 306-472-3252; *Fax:* 306-472-5958
e-mail: lgs.cga@sasktel.net
L. Sutherland, President
Twyla Verhelst, Secretary

Langenburg & District Chamber of Commerce
PO Box 610, Langenburg SK S0A 2A0
Tel: 306-743-2231; *Fax:* 306-743-2873
R.J. Buchberger, President
Janice Fogg, Secretary

Macklin Chamber of Commerce
PO Box 642, Macklin SK S0L 2C0
Tel: 306-753-2221; *Fax:* 306-753-3585
e-mail: macklin.coop@sasktel.net
D.J. Lysitza, President

C.A. Moss, Treasurer

Maidstone & District Chamber of Commerce
PO Box 300, Maidstone SK S0M 1M0
Tel: 306-893-2461; *Fax:* 306-893-4222
e-mail: cheryl@elliottinsurance.ca
Cheryl D Jamieson, Secretary
Glenn Colley, President

Maple Creek Chamber of Commerce
PO Box 1766, Maple Creek SK S0N 1N0
Tel: 306-558-7055; *Fax:* 306-662-2422
e-mail: thedailygrind@sasktel.net
Tina Cresswell, President
Wayne Litke, Secretary

Meadow Lake & District Chamber of Commerce
c/o Northwest REDA, PO Box 1168, 106 - 1st St. East, Meadow Lake SK S9X 1Y8
Tel: 306-236-4447; *Fax:* 306-236-1833
e-mail: mltouristinfo@sasktel.net
Affiliation(s): Northwest Regional Economic Development Authority
Kirt Prete, President
Samantha L. Clarkson, Secretary

Melfort & District Chamber of Commerce
PO Box 2002, 102 Spruce Haven Rd., Melfort SK S0E 1A0
Tel: 306-752-4636; *Fax:* 306-752-9505
e-mail: melfortchamber@sasktel.net
URL: www.melfortchamber.com
Jim Thiessen, President
Lori Fettes, Executive Director

Melville & District Chamber of Commerce
c/o Chamber Office, PO Box 429, 420 Main St., Melville SK S0A 2P0
Tel: 306-728-4177; *Fax:* 306-728-5911
e-mail: melvillechamber@sasktel.net
URL: www.melvillechamber.com
Ron Walton, Manager
David Williams, President

Moose Jaw & District Chamber of Commerce
88 Saskatchewan St. East, Moose Jaw SK S6H 0V4
Tel: 306-692-6414; *Fax:* 306-694-6463
e-mail: chamber@mjchamber.com
URL: www.mjchamber.com
Brian Martynook, Executive Director
Darryl Pisio, President

Moosomin Chamber of Commerce
PO Box 819, Moosomin SK S0G 3N0
Tel: 306-435-2445; *Fax:* 306-435-3696
e-mail: world_spectator@sasktel.net
URL: www.moosomin.com/chamber
Kevin Weedmark, President
Bernie Nosterud, Sec.-Treas.

Nipawin & District Chamber of Commerce
PO Box 177, Nipawin SK S0E 1E0
Tel: 306-862-5252; *Fax:* 306-862-5350
e-mail: info@nipawinchamber.ca
URL: www.nipawinchamber.ca
Cindy M Murphy, Executive Director
Cliff Rose, President

Norquay & District Chamber of Commerce
PO Box 457, Norquay SK S0A 2V0
Tel: 306-594-2293; *Fax:* 306-594-2435
e-mail: nnjohnson@sasktel.net
Nina Johnson, President
Donna Lumley, Treasurer

Outlook & District Chamber of Commerce
PO Box 431, Outlook SK S0L 2N0
Tel: 306-867-9580; *Fax:* 306-867-9559
URL: www.town.outlook.sk.ca/chamber.htm
Lyle Rankin, President
Julie Haubrich, Secretary

Paradise Hill Chamber of Commerce
PO Box 118, Paradise Hill SK S0M 2G0
Tel: 306-344-2188; *Fax:* 306-344-4799
George H Palen, President
Sheila M Phillips, Secretary

Prince Albert Chamber of Commerce
#347, 1084 Central Avenue, Prince Albert SK S6V 7P3
Tel: 306-764-6222; *Fax:* 306-922-4727
e-mail: pachamber@sasktel.net
URL: www.princealbertchamber.com
Affiliation(s): Canadian Chamber of Commerce; Saskatchewan Chamber of Commerce
Allan Hopkins, Chair
Lyn Brown, CEO

Radisson & District Chamber of Commerce
PO Box 397, Radisson SK S0K 3L0
Tel: 306-827-4801; *Fax:* 306-827-2336
Lloyd E. Lorass, President
Cheryl D. Hamilton, Secretary

Radville Chamber of Commerce
PO Box 799, Radville SK S0C 2G0
Tel: 306-869-2610; *Fax:* 306-869-2859
e-mail: town.radville@sasktel.net
S.L. Scott, Sec.-Treas.
B.L. Loewen, President

Redvers Chamber of Commerce
PO Box 602, Redvers SK S0C 2H0
Tel: 306-452-3155; *Fax:* 306-452-3155
e-mail: rdaycare@sasktel.net
Tricia Martel, President
Tanis Chalmers, Director

Regina & District Chamber of Commerce
2145 Albert St., Regina SK S4P 2V1
Tel: 306-757-4658; *Fax:* 306-757-4668
e-mail: info@reginachamber.com
URL: www.reginachamber.com
Affiliation(s): Canadian Chamber of Commerce; Saskatchewan Chamber of Commerce
John Hopkins, CEO
Fred Titanich, President

Regina Beach & District Chamber of Commerce
PO Box 606, Regina Beach SK S0G 4C0
Tel: 306-729-4596
J. Cumbers, President
D. Needham, Secretary

La Ronge & District Chamber of Commerce
PO Box 179, La Ronge SK S0J 1L0
Tel: 306-425-3056
Toll-Free: 866-527-6643
e-mail: chamberofcommerce@townoflaronge.ca
B.A. Fenning, President
B.L. Bean, Secretary

Rosetown & District Chamber of Commerce
PO Box 744, Rosetown SK S0L 2V0
Tel: 306-882-1300; *Fax:* 306-882-1310
e-mail: e2000@sasktel.net
URL: www.rosetown.ca
Gerry Clark, Chair
Shirley Helgason, Executive Director

St. Walburg Chamber of Commerce
PO Box 501, St Walburg SK S0M 2T0
Tel: 306-248-3244; *Fax:* 306-248-3988
e-mail: townofstwalburg@sasktel.net
URL: www.stwalburg.com
M. Champigny, President
K. Rutherford, Treasurer

Shaunavon Chamber of Commerce
PO Box 820, Shaunavon SK S0N 2M0
Tel: 306-297-3462; *Fax:* 306-297-3420
URL: www.shaunavon.com/chamber.htm
Rick Schneider, President
Penny Schreiner, Secretary

Spiritwood Chamber of Commerce
PO Box 429, Spiritwood SK S0J 2M0
Tel: 306-883-2267; *Fax:* 306-883-2136
B. Fee, President
Yvette McGown, Secretary

Swift Current Chamber of Commerce
885 - 6th Ave. NE, Swift Current SK S9H 2M9
Tel: 306-773-7268; *Fax:* 306-773-5686
e-mail: info@swiftcurrentchamber.ca
URL: www.swiftcurrentchamber.ca
Affiliation(s): Saskatchewan Chamber of Commerce; Canadian Chamber of Commerce
Erin Kinney, President
Marianne Hawkins, Executive Director

Tisdale & District Chamber of Commerce
PO Box 219, Tisdale SK S0E 1T0
Tel: 306-873-4257; *Fax:* 306-873-4241
e-mail: tisdalechamber@sasktel.net
A.R. Freistadt, Manager
M.R. Kinar, President

Unity & District Chamber of Commerce
PO Box 834, Unity SK S0K 4L0
Tel: 306-228-2621
T.J. Schroh, President
Christine Gerein, Treasurer

Vonda Chamber of Commerce
c/o Vonda Hometown Insurance Brokers, PO Box 285, Vonda SK S0K 4N0
Tel: 306-258-2134; *Fax:* 306-258-2244
e-mail: rlalonde@sasktel.net
A. Bussiere, President
Robert Lalonde, Secretary

Waskesiu Chamber of Commerce
PO Box 216, Waskesiu Lake SK S0J 2Y0
Tel: 306-663-5140; *Fax:* 306-663-5448
e-mail: wakesiuchamber@sasktel.net
URL: www.waskesiulake.ca
G.A. Wilson, Manager
G.J.P. Bueckert, President

Watrous & District Chamber of Commerce
PO Box 906, Watrous SK S0K 4T0
Tel: 306-946-3353; *Fax:* 306-946-3966
E.T. Amendt, President
T. Frey, Secretary

Watson & District Chamber of Commerce
PO Box 686, Watson SK S0K 4V0
Tel: 306-287-3636; *Fax:* 306-287-3601
Michael Becker, President
Debbie A Schwartz, Treasurer

Weyburn Chamber of Commerce
#11, 3rd St. NE, Weyburn SK S4H OW5
Tel: 306-842-4738; *Fax:* 306-842-0520
e-mail: manager@weyburnchamber.com
URL: www.weyburnchamber.com
Affiliation(s): Saskatchewan Chamber of Commerce
Brent Allen, President
Jeff Richards, Manager

Wolseley & District Chamber of Commerce
PO Box 519, Wolseley SK S0G 5H0
Tel: 306-698-2252; *Fax:* 306-698-2750
S. Harris, Secretary
M.M. Dunn, President

Wynyard & District Chamber of Commerce
PO Box 508, Wynyard SK S0A 4T0
Tel: 306-554-2224; *Fax:* 306-554-3226
E.A. Zahayko, President
D. Johannesson, Secretary

Yorkton Chamber of Commerce
PO Box 1051, Hwy. 9 South, Yorkton SK S3N 2X3
Tel: 306-783-4368; *Fax:* 306-786-6978
e-mail: yorktonchamber@sasktel.net
URL: www.chamber.yorkton.sk.ca
Affiliation(s): Saskatchewan Economic Developers Association
Lori Walsh, President
Guy Gendreau, Exec. Vice-President

Yukon Territory

Dawson City Chamber of Commerce
PO Box 1006, Dawson YT Y0B 1G0
Tel: 867-993-5274; *Fax:* 867-993-6817
e-mail: dccc@dawson.net
Dina Grenon, President

St. Elias Chamber of Commerce
PO Box 5419, Haines Junction YT Y0B 1L0
Tel: 867-634-2916; *Fax:* 867-634-2034
e-mail: kluaneridin@yknet.ca
Wade Istchenko, President

Silver Trail Chamber of Commerce
PO Box 268, Mayo YT Y0B 1M0
Tel: 867-996-2827
e-mail: educate@nndfn.com
Nancy Hager, President

Southern Lakes Chamber of Commerce
PO Box 45, Carcross YT Y0B 1B0
Tel: 867-821-4372; *Fax:* 867-393-2436
e-mail: president@southernlakeschamber.com
URL: www.southernlakeschamber.com
Greg Kehoe, Contact

Teslin Regional Chamber of Commerce
PO Box 181, Teslin YT Y0A 1B0
Tel: 867-390-2521; *Fax:* 867-390-2687
e-mail: wes.wirth@northwestel.net
Wes Wirth, President

Watson Lake Chamber of Commerce
PO Box 591, Watson Lake YT Y0A 1C0

Tel: 867-536-2240; *Fax:* 867-536-7294
e-mail: wlchamberofcommerce@northwestel.net
Jennifer Anderson, Contact

Whitehorse Chamber of Commerce (WCC)
#101, 302 Steele St., Whitehorse YT Y1A 2C5
Tel: 867-667-7545; *Fax:* 867-667-4507
e-mail: business@whitehorsechamber.ca
URL: www.whitehorsechamber.ca
Affiliation(s): Yukon Chamber of Commerce; Tourism Industry Association of Yukon
Rick Karp, President

Credit Unions/Caisses Populaires

Credit unions and caisses populaires are owned and controlled by their members. These cooperative financial institutions are regulated at the provincial level. Credit unions, in most provinces, must engage external auditors to prepare financial statements. An annual inspection of credit unions is conducted by their provincial regulatory body.

The national trade association and central finance facility for Canadian credit unions is Credit Union Central of Canada. It is regulated under the Cooperative Credit Associations Act. In Québec, Mouvement des caisses Desjardins du Québec consists of a network of caisses. Fédération des caisses Desjardins du Québec is a cooperative which supports Mouvement des caisses Desjardins du Québec. Credit Unions are listed alphabetically.

1st Choice Savings & Credit Union Ltd.
1320 - 3 Ave. South
Lethbridge, AB T1J 0K5
403-320-4600
Fax: 403-329-6434
contact@1stchoicesavings.ca
www.1stchoicesavings.ca
Former Name: St. Patrick's Credit Union Ltd.; Southland Credit Union
Ownership: Public
Year Founded: 2001
Assets: $100-500 million

3M Employees' (London) Credit Union Limited
1840 Oxford St. East
London, ON N6A 4T1
519-452-6765
Fax: 519-452-6023
cuca-corporate@mmm.com
www.3mcreditunion.com

Acadian Credit Union
PO Box 250
15089 Cabot Trail
Cheticamp, NS B0E 1H0
902-224-2055
Fax: 902-224-3510
877-477-7724
www.acadiancreditu.ca
Former Name: Cheticamp Credit Union
Year Founded: 1936
Number of Employees: 12

ACE Credit Union Limited
#100, 2055 Albert St.
Regina, SK S4P 2T8
306-337-1700
Fax: 306-337-1719
info@ace.cu.sk.ca
www.acecreditunion.com
Year Founded: 1973

Adjala Credit Union Limited
7320 St. James Lane
Colgan, ON L0G 1W0
905-936-2761
Fax: 905-936-6391
adjalacreditunion@zing-net.ca
Year Founded: 1946

Advance Savings Credit Union (ASCU)
Corporate Office
10 Record St.
Moncton, NB E1C 0B2
506-853-1880
Fax: 506-382-3564
www.royal-cu.com
Former Name: Rexton Credit Union; Royal Credit Union; Trico Credit Union
Ownership: Member-owned
Year Founded: 2006
Assets: $50-100 million

Advantage Credit Union
PO Box 1657
118 Main St.
Melfort, SK S0E 1A0
306-752-2744
Fax: 306-752-1919
www.advantagecu.com
Former Name: Melfort Credit Union Ltd.
Ownership: Member-owned
Year Founded: 1943

Affinity Credit Union
309 - 22nd St. East
Saskatoon, SK S7K 0G7
306-934-4000
Fax: 306-934-5490
1-866-863-6237
questions@affinitycu.ca
www.affinitycu.com
Former Name: St. Mary's Credit Union Limited
Ownership: Member-owned
Year Founded: 1949
Assets: $1-10 billion

Agassiz Credit Union Limited
430 Stephen St.
Morden, MB R6M 1T6
204-822-4485
Fax: 204-822-6155
1-877-822-4485
admin@agassizcu.mb.ca
www.agassizcu.mb.ca
Ownership: Member-owned

Airline Financial Credit Union Limited
#120, 5955 Airport Rd.
Mississauga, ON L4V 1R9
905-673-7262
Fax: 905-676-8437
info@airlinecreditunion.com
www.airlinecreditunion.ca
Former Name: Airline (Malton) Credit Union Limited
Ownership: Member-owned
Year Founded: 1950
Number of Employees: 9
Assets: $10-50 million

Air-Toronto Credit Union
136 Florence Ave.
Toronto, ON M2N 1G3
416-359-9685
Fax: 416-512-2497
airtoronto@bellnet.ca
Year Founded: 1959

Aldergrove Credit Union
2941 - 272nd St.
Aldergrove, BC V4W 3R3
604-856-7724
Fax: 604-856-2565
www.aldergrovecu.ca
Former Name: Otter Farmers' Institute Credit Union
Year Founded: 1954

All Trans Financial Credit Union Limited
Administration Ctr.
#707, 3250 Bloor St. West
Toronto, ON M8X 2X9
416-231-8400
Fax: 416-231-8296
info@alltrans.com
www.alltrans.com
Year Founded: 1993
Number of Employees: 18

L'Alliance des caisses populaires de l'Ontario limitée
PO Box 3500
1870 Bond St.
North Bay, ON P1B 4V6
705-474-5634
Fax: 705-474-5326
support@acpol.com
www.caissealliance.com
Ownership: Member-owned.
Year Founded: 1979
Number of Employees: 240
Assets: $500m-1 billion
Revenues: $10-50 million

Alterna Savings & Credit Union Limited
400 Albert St.
Ottawa, ON K1R 5B2
613-560-0100
Fax: 613-560-0177
877-560-0100
Other Contact Information: 416/252-5621 (Toronto phone)
query@alterna.ca
www.alterna.ca
Former Name: Civil Service Co-operative Credit Society Ltd.
Ownership: Member-owned
Year Founded: 2005
Number of Employees: 600+
Assets: $1-10 billion

Anishinabek Nation Credit Union (ANCU)
7 Shingwauk St.
Garden River, ON P6A 6Z8
705-942-7655
Fax: 705-942-7613
866-775-2628
cu-info@ancu.ca
www.ancu.ca

Apex Credit Union Limited
Administration Office, TransCanada Centre
#210, 1440 - 52nd St. NE
Calgary, AB T2A 4T8
403-974-8640
Fax: 403-282-3099
1-877-273-9247
bsidhu@apexcu.com
www.apexcu.com
Ownership: Member-owned
Year Founded: 1940
Assets: $50-100 million

Apple Community Credit Union
406 North Cumberland St.
Thunder Bay, ON P7A 4P8
807-345-8153
Fax: 807-343-9271
info@applecu.com
www.applecu.com
Ownership: Private

Arctic Credit Union Ltd.
800 Central Ave., 9th Fl.
Prince Albert, SK S6V 6Z2
306-922-8252
Former Name: Arctic Savings & Credit Union Ltd.
Year Founded: 1939

Arnstein Community Credit Union Limited
PO Box 104
Port Loring, ON P0H 1Y0
705-757-2662
Fax: 705-757-2662
b.whitmell@thot.net
Year Founded: 1962

Assiniboine Credit Union Limited (ACU)
Corporate Office
PO Box 2, Main Stn. Main
200 Main St., 6th Fl.
Winnipeg, MB R3C 2G1
877-958-8588
Fax: 877-958-7348
Other Contact Information: 1-877-957-1587 (TTY Line for Hearing Impaired)
cu@assiniboine.mb.ca
www.assiniboine.mb.ca
Ownership: Member-owned
Year Founded: 1943
Number of Employees: 500
Assets: $1-10 billion

Austin Credit Union
PO Box 205
24 - 2nd Ave.
Austin, MB R0H 0H0
204-385-6140
Fax: 204-637-2204
www.austincreditunion.com
Year Founded: 1949

Auto Workers (Ajax) Credit Union Limited
PO Box 21115
290 Harwood Ave. South
Ajax, ON L1S 2J1
905-683-0791
Fax: 905-683-6047
Year Founded: 1968

Auto Workers' Community Credit Union Limited
322 King St. West
Oshawa, ON L1J 2J9

905-728-5187
Fax: 905-728-8727
800-268-8771
information@awccu.com
www.awccu.com

Ownership: Private. Cooperative
Year Founded: 1938
Number of Employees: 70
Revenues: $100-500 million

Battle River Credit Union Ltd.
5007 - 51 St.
Camrose, AB T4V 1S6

780-672-1175
Fax: 780-672-5996
brcu@battlerivercreditunion.com
www.battlerivercreditunion.com

Ownership: Member-owned
Year Founded: 1949
Number of Employees: 110
Assets: $100-500 million Year End: 20080930
Revenues: $1-5 million Year End: 20080930

Bay Credit Union Limited
142 Algoma St. South
Thunder Bay, ON P7B 3B8

807-345-7612
Fax: 807-345-8939
1-877-249-7076
info@baycreditunion.com
www.baycreditunion.com

Bay St Lawrence Credit Union
PO Box 112
3020 Bay St. Lawrence Rd.
Dingwall, NS B0C 1G0

902-383-2003

Year Founded: 1937
Number of Employees: 1

Bayshore Credit Union Ltd.
PO Box 878
191 North Front St.
Belleville, ON K8N 5B5

613-966-5550
Fax: 613-966-9523
www.bayshorecu.com

Bayview Credit Union
#400, 57 King St.
Saint John, NB E2L 1G5

506-634-1263
Fax: 506-634-1686
www.bayviewnb.com

Year Founded: 1938
Number of Employees: 115
Assets: $100-500 million

Beaubear Credit Union
PO Box 764
376 Water St.
Miramichi, NB E1V 3V4

506-622-4532
mdaley@beaubear.creditu.net
www.beaubear.ca

Ownership: Member-owned
Year Founded: 1938
Assets: $10-50 million

Beaumont Credit Union Limited
5007 - 50th Ave.
Beaumont, AB T4X 1E7

780-929-8561
Fax: 780-929-2999
800-307-8353
Other Contact Information: 1-800-561-7849 (Credit Card Balances); 306-566-1276 (Outside Canada)
cberube@alberta-cu.com
www.beaumontcu.com

Former Name: St Vital & Beaumont Savings & Credit Union
Year Founded: 1946

Beautiful Plains Credit Union
PO Box 99
239 Hamilton St.
Neepawa, MB R0J 1H0

204-476-3341
Fax: 204-476-3609
info@bpcu.mb.ca
www.bpcu.mb.ca

Year Founded: 1955

Belgian-Alliance Credit Union
1177 Portage Ave.
Winnipeg, MB R3G 0T2

204-927-0460
Fax: 204-927-0461
mail@alliancecu.ca
www.alliancecu.ca

Former Name: Alliance Credit Union; Adanac Credit Union Ltd; Communicators Credit Union; Progress Vera Credit Union
Year Founded: 2001

Bengough Credit Union Ltd.
260 Main St.
Bengough, SK S0C 0K0

306-268-2930
info@bengough.cu.sk.ca
www.bengough.cu.sk.ca

Year Founded: 1943

Bergengren Credit Union
257 Main St.
Antigonish, NS B2G 2C1

902-863-6600
Fax: 902-863-3031
888-273-3488
info@bergengrencu.com
www.bergengrencu.com

Year Founded: 1933
Number of Employees: 51

Blackville Credit Union
128 Main St.
Blackville, NB E9B 1P1

506-843-2219
Fax: 506-843-6773

Year Founded: 1936

Bow Valley Credit Union Limited
PO Box 876
Cochrane, AB T4C 1A9

403-932-4693
Fax: 403-932-9865
lbohn@bowvalleycu.com
www.bowvalleycu.com

Ownership: Member-owned

Brewers Warehousing Employees (Hamilton) Credit Union Limited
c/o Beer Store
673 Upper James St.
Hamilton, ON L9C 5R9

905-574-7652
Fax: 905-574-7652

Brewers Warehousing Employees (Kitchener) Credit Union Limited
53 Filbert St.
Kitchener, ON N2H 1Y1

519-576-7324

Brook Street Credit Union Ltd.
Millbrook Mall
PO Box 713
2 Herald Ave., Main Level
Corner Brook, NL A2H 6G7

709-634-4632
866-273-3488
brookstreet@brookstreet.creditu.net
www.bscu.ca

Ownership: Member-owned
Year Founded: 1963
Assets: $10-50 million

Bruno Savings & Credit Union Limited
PO Box 158
511 Main St.
Bruno, SK S0K 0S0

306-369-2901
Fax: 306-369-2225
www.brunocu.com

Ownership: Member-owned

Buduchnist Credit Union (BCU)
2280 Bloor St. West
Toronto, ON M6S 1N9

416-763-6883
Fax: 416-763-4512
800-461-5941
Other Contact Information: link@buduchnist.com (BCU Link); privacyofficer@buduchnist.com (Privacy Officer) info@buduchnist.com; help@buduchnist.com (Help Desk)
www.buduchnist.com

Ownership: Member-owned
Year Founded: 1952

Bulkley Valley Credit Union
PO Box 3637
3872 - 1st Ave.
Smithers, BC V0J 2N0

250-847-3255
Fax: 250-847-3012
infoadmin@bvcu.com
www.bvcu.com

Caisse centrale Desjardins du Québec (CCD)
#600, 1170 rue Peel
Montréal, QC H3B 0B1

514-281-7070
Fax: 514-281-7083
www.desjardins.com/ccd

Ownership: Cooperatively owned by the Fédération des caisses Desjardins du Québec
Year Founded: 1979

Caisse Horizon Credit Union Ltd.
PO Box 147
Girouxville, AB T0H 1S0

780-323-4600
Fax: 780-323-4545
866-758-6466
www.powerofmembers.ca

Also Known As: Horizon Credit Union
Ownership: Member-owned
Year Founded: 1956
Number of Employees: 58
Assets: $10-50 million

Caisse populaire de Saulnierville
RR#1
Saulnierville, NS B0W 2Z0

902-769-2574
Fax: 902-769-3555

Year Founded: 1953

Cambrian Credit Union Ltd.
***Also listed under:** Financing & Loan Companies*
225 Broadway
Winnipeg, MB R3C 5R4

204-925-2600
Fax: 204-231-1306
888-695-8900
ccuinfo@cambrian.mb.ca; ccuhead@cambrian.mb.ca
www.cambrian.mb.ca

Ownership: Member-owned
Year Founded: 1959
Assets: $1-10 billion

Campbell's Employees' (Toronto) Credit Union Limited
60 Birmingham St.
Toronto, ON M8V 2B8

416-251-1117
Fax: 416-253-8669

Canada Safeway Limited Employees Savings & Credit Union
1822 - 10th Ave. SW
Calgary, AB T3C 0J8

403-261-5681
Fax: 403-261-5748
877-723-2653
info@safewaycucalgary.com
www.safewaycucalgary.com

Ownership: Member-owned
Year Founded: 1952
Number of Employees: 10

Canada Sand Papers Employees' (Plattsville) Credit Union Limited
28 Albert St.
Plattsville, ON N0J 1S0

519-684-7441
Fax: 519-684-7210
savageo@execulink.com

Year Founded: 1954

Canadian Alternative Investment Cooperative
#111, 146 Laird Dr.
Toronto, ON M4G 3V7

416-467-7797
Fax: 416-467-8946
866-241-2242
caic@caic.ca
www.caic.ca

Year Founded: 1984

Canadian General Tower Employees (Galt) Credit Union Limited
Cambridge Place
#117, 73 Water St. North
Cambridge, ON N1R 7L6
519-623-2211
Fax: 519-623-2051
Ownership: Private
Number of Employees: 3

Canadian Transportation Employees' Credit Union Ltd.
PO Box 4
600 Ferguson Ave. North
Hamilton, ON L8L 4Z9
905-523-7385
Fax: 905-523-7556
Number of Employees: 3

Carleton Pioneer Credit Union
#1, 106 Richmond St.
Woodstock, NB E7M 2N9
506-328-8120
Fax: 506-328-3445
cpcu@nb.sympatico.ca
www.cpcu.coop
Year Founded: 1938
Number of Employees: 9

Carpathia Credit Union
952 Main St.
Winnipeg, MB R2W 3P4
204-989-7400
Fax: 204-589-2529
info@carpathiacu.mb.ca
www.carpathiacu.mb.ca
Ownership: Member-owned
Year Founded: 1940
Assets: $100-500 million

Casera Credit Union
1300 Plessis Rd.
Winnipeg, MB R2C 2Y6
204-958-6300
Fax: 204-222-6766
866-211-9233
www.caseracu.ca
Also Known As: Transcona Credit Union
Ownership: Member-owned
Year Founded: 1951

Cataract Savings & Credit Union Limited
7172 Dorchester Rd.
Niagara Falls, ON L2G 5V6
905-357-5222
Fax: 905-357-9366
www.cataractsavings.on.ca
Year Founded: 1949

CBC (Nfld) Credit Union Ltd.
PO Box 12010, A Stn. A
29-31 Pippy Place
St. John's, NL A1B 3T8
709-576-5407
Fax: 709-576-5409
cbccreditunion@cbccu.ca
www.cbccu.ca
Year Founded: 1965
Number of Employees: 3

CCB Employees' Credit Union Limited
46 Overlea Blvd.
Toronto, ON M4H 1B6
416-424-6280
Fax: 416-701-1944
Year Founded: 1973
Number of Employees: 2
Revenues: Under $1 million

CCEC Credit Union
2250 Commercial Dr.
Vancouver, BC V5N 5P9
604-254-4100
Fax: 604-254-6558
866-254-4100
info@ccec.bc.ca
www.ccec.bc.ca
Ownership: Cooperative
Year Founded: 1976

Central 1 Credit Union - British Columbia Region
1441 Creekside Dr.
Vancouver, BC V6J 4S7
604-734-2511
Fax: 604-734-5055
info@central1.com
www.cucbc.com
Former Name: Credit Union Central of British Columbia
Ownership: Member credit unions
Year Founded: 1944
Number of Employees: 475
Assets: $1-10 billion
Revenues: $10-50 million

Central 1 Credit Union - Ontario Region
2810 Matheson Blvd. East
Mississauga, ON L4W 4X7
905-238-9400
Fax: 905-238-8196
800-661-6813
Other Contact Information: 905-629-5711 (Help Desk Phone)
customerservice@central1.com
www.ontariocreditunions.com
Former Name: Credit Union Central of Ontario
Number of Employees: 125
Assets: $1-10 billion

Central Credit Union Limited
PO Box 279
512 Main St.
O'Leary, PE C0B 1V0
902-859-2266
Fax: 902-859-3219
central.cu@central.creditu.net
www.centralcreditu.com
Ownership: Member-owned
Year Founded: 1969
Number of Employees: 17

Church River Credit Union
305 Burnt Church Rd.
Burnt Church, NB E9G 4C8
506-776-3247
Fax: 506-776-3247

Churchbridge Savings & Credit Union
PO Box 260
103 Vincent Ave. East
Churchbridge, SK S0A 0M0
306-896-2544
Fax: 306-896-2325
877-890-2797
info@churchbridge.cu.sk.ca
www.churchbridgecu.ca
Year Founded: 1945

City Plus Credit Union Ltd.
Municipal Bldg.
PO Box 2100, M Stn. M
#8130, 800 MacLeod Trail SE, 5th Fl.
Calgary, AB T2P 2M5
403-268-2626
Fax: 403-268-4886
main@cpcu.ca
www.cpcu.ca
Former Name: Calgary Civic Employees Credit Union Limited
Ownership: Private
Year Founded: 1942
Number of Employees: 5

City Savings Financial Services
6002 Yonge St.
Toronto, ON M2M 3V9
416-225-7716
Fax: 416-225-7772
info@citysavingscu.com
www.citysavingscu.com
Former Name: City Savings & Credit Union Ltd.; The North York Municipal Employees' Credit Union
Year Founded: 1950

CN (London) Credit Union Limited
#301, 205 York St.
London, ON N6A 1B1
519-667-2326
Fax: 519-434-5687
cncucindy@ody.ca
www.cncu.ca
Year Founded: 1945
Number of Employees: 4

CNR Employees (Lakehead Terminal) Credit Union Limited
417 Fort William Rd.
Thunder Bay, ON P7B 2Z5
807-344-4096
Fax: 807-346-0595

Coady Credit Union
32 West Ave.
Glace Bay, NS B1A 6E9
902-849-7610
Fax: 902-842-0911
Year Founded: 1933

Coast Capital Savings Credit Union
Corporate Head Office
15117 - 101 Ave.
Surrey, BC V3R 8P7
604-517-7000
Fax: 604-517-7405
888-517-7000
Other Contact Information: 1-877-333-7736 (Technical Support); 604-517-7822 (Cantonese); 604-517-7823 (Mandarin); 604-517-7780 (Punjabi)
info@coastcapitalsavings.com
www.coastcapitalsavings.com
Ownership: Member-owned
Year Founded: 2000
Number of Employees: 2,000+

Coastal Community Credit Union
#21, 13 Victoria Cres.
Nanaimo, BC V9R 5B9
250-741-3200
Fax: 250-741-3223
888-741-1010
Other Contact Information: 1-888-741-4040 (Telephone Banking Toll-Free); 1-800-567-8111 (Lost Member Card, Canada & the USA); 1-800-567-8111 (Lost MasterCard, Canada & the USA)
www.cccu.ca
Ownership: Member-owned
Year Founded: 1946
Number of Employees: 600+
Assets: $1-10 billion

Coastal Financial Credit Union
2 Collins St.
Yarmouth, NS B5A 3C3
902-742-7322
Fax: 902-742-7476
rdoucette@coastalfinancial.ca
www.coastalfinancial.ca
Ownership: Member-owned
Year Founded: 2001
Number of Employees: 53
Assets: $50-100 million

Codroy Valley Credit Union
PO Box 29
Doyles, NL A0N 1J0
709-955-2402
Fax: 709-955-3081
www.codroyvalleycu.com

College Hill Credit Union
c/o University of New Brunswick, McConnell Hall
PO Box 4400
#107, 19 Bailey Dr.
Fredericton, NB E3B 5A3
506-455-3535
www.unb.ca/facilities/chcu

Columbia Valley Credit Union
PO Box 720
511 Main St.
Golden, BC V0A 1H0
250-344-2282
Fax: 250-344-2117
888-298-1777
Other Contact Information: 1-888-273-3488 (Online Banking Support); 1-866-344-7968 (Phone Banking)
www.cvcu.bc.ca
Ownership: Member-owned
Year Founded: 1955
Assets: $100-500 million

Communication Technologies Credit Union Limited
Eaton Centre
PO Box 501
#102, 220 Yonge St.
Toronto, ON M5B 2H1
416-598-1197
Fax: 416-598-0171
800-209-7444
member_services@comtechcu.com
www.comtechcu.com
Ownership: Member-owned
Number of Employees: 14
Assets: $50-100 million

Community Credit Union Ltd.
164 Main St.
Grunthal, MB R0A 0R0
204-434-6338
Fax: 204-434-9074
grunthal@communitycu.mb.ca
www.communitycu.mb.ca

Community Credit Union of Cumberland Colchester Limited
PO Box 578
#201, 32 Church St.
Amherst, NS B4H 4B8
902-667-7541
Fax: 902-667-0217
1-888-273-3488
www.communitycreditunion.ns.ca
Former Name: Amherst Credit Union; Colchester Credit Union
Ownership: Member-owned
Year Founded: 1999

Community First Credit Union Limited
289 Bay St.
Sault Ste Marie, ON P6A 1W7
705-942-1000
Fax: 705-946-2363
www.communityfirst-cu.com
Year Founded: 1948

Community Savings Credit Union
Central City Tower
#1600, 13450 - 102nd Ave., 16th Fl.
Surrey, BC V3T 5X3
604-654-2000
Fax: 604-586-5156
888-963-2000
www.comsavings.com
Former Name: IWA & Community Credit Union
Year Founded: 1944
Number of Employees: 500

Concentra Financial Corporate Banking
333 - 3rd Ave. North
Saskatoon, SK S7K 2M2
800-788-6311
servicecentre@concentrafinancial.ca
www.concentrafinancial.ca
Former Name: CUCORP Financial Services
Ownership: Private
Year Founded: 1997
Revenues: $1-10 billion

Conexus Credit Union
1960 Albert St.
Regina, SK S4P 2T4
306-780-1750
800-667-7477
information@conexuscu.com
www.conexuscu.com
Former Name: Assiniboia Credit Union Ltd.
Number of Employees: 1,000

Copperfin Credit Union
346 - 2nd St. South
Kenora, ON P9N 1G5
807-467-4400
Fax: 807-468-3500
888-710-6664
kenora@copperfin.ca
www.copperfin.ca
Former Name: Lakewood Credit Union Ltd.
Ownership: Member-owned
Year Founded: 1954
Number of Employees: 34

Cornerstone Credit Union Ltd.
PO Box 455
1202, 100th St.
Tisdale, SK S0E 1T0
306-873-2616
Fax: 306-873-4322
reception@cornerstone.cu.sk.ca
www.cornerstonecu.ca
Former Name: Tisdale Credit Union Ltd.
Ownership: Private. Member-owned
Year Founded: 1943
Number of Employees: 30
Assets: $100-500 million
Revenues: $1-5 million

Credit Union Atlantic (CUA)
#350, 7105 Chebucto Rd.
Halifax, NS B3L 4W8
902-492-6500
Fax: 902-492-6501
800-474-4282
Other Contact Information: 902-493-4800 (Teleservice); 1-800-963-4848 (TeleService Toll Free); 1-800-561-7849 (MasterCard Inquiries); 1-800-567-8111 (Lost MasterCards)
www.cua.com
Year Founded: 1948
Number of Employees: 115
Assets: $100-500 million

Credit Union Central Alberta Limited
#350N, 8500 MacLeod Trail South
Calgary, AB T2H 2N1
403-258-5900
Fax: 403-253-7720
email@albertacentral.com
www.albertacentral.com
Ownership: Owned by the credit unions of Alberta
Number of Employees: 230
Assets: $1-10 billion

Credit Union Central of Canada (CUCC)
#500, 300 The East Mall
Toronto, ON M9B 6B7
416-232-1262
Fax: 416-232-9196
cucc@cucentral.com
www.cucentral.ca
Ownership: Owned by the provincial credit union centrals
Year Founded: 1953

Credit Union Central of Manitoba (CUCM)
#400, 317 Donald St.
Winnipeg, MB R3B 2H6
204-985-4700
Fax: 204-957-0217
cuinfo@cucm.org
www.creditunion.mb.ca
Former Name: Cooperative Credit Society of Manitoba Ltd.
Ownership: Member-owned
Year Founded: 1950
Assets: $10-100 billion

Credit Union Central of New Brunswick (CUCNB)
663 Pinewood Rd.
Riverview, NB E1B 5R6
506-857-8184
800-332-3320
info@cucnb.nb.ca
www.creditunion.nb.ca
Year Founded: 1950

Credit Union Central of Nova Scotia
PO Box 9200
6074 Lady Hammond Rd.
Halifax, NS B3K 5N3
902-453-0680
Fax: 902-455-2437
800-668-2879
info@cucns.ca; humanresources@cucns.ca; communications@cucns.ca
www.ns-credit-unions.com
Year Founded: 1938

Credit Union Central of Prince Edward Island
PO Box 968
281 University Ave.
Charlottetown, PE C1A 7M4
902-566-3350
Fax: 902-368-3534
website@cucpei.com
www.peicreditunions.com
Year Founded: 1936
Number of Employees: 200
Assets: $500m-1 billion

Creston & District Credit Union
PO Box 215
140 - 11th Ave. North
Creston, BC V0B 1G0
250-428-5351
Fax: 250-428-5302
866-857-2802
cdcu@cdcu.com
www.cdcu.com
Ownership: Credit Union Central, BC
Year Founded: 1951

Croatian Toronto Credit Union Limited
19 Dundas St. West
Mississauga, ON L5B 1H2
905-276-1962
Fax: 905-532-0846
info@coatiancreditunion.ca
www.croatiancreditunion.ca
Year Founded: 1958

Crocus Credit Union
1016 Rosser Ave.
Brandon, MB R7A 0L6
204-729-4800
Fax: 204-729-4818
Other Contact Information: 1-800-567-8111 (Lost ATM Cards)
info@crocuscu.mb.ca
www.crocuscu.mb.ca
Former Name: Brandon Terminal Credit Union Society Limited
Ownership: Member-owned
Year Founded: 1952

Crosstown Civic Credit Union
171 Donald St.
Winnipeg, MB R3C 1M4
204-942-1277
Fax: 204-947-3108
Other Contact Information: 1-800-567-8111 (Lost ATM & Member Cards); 204-949-1048 (ExpressLine TeleService)
cu@crosstowncivic.mb.ca
www.crosstowncivic.mb.ca
Ownership: Member-owned
Year Founded: 1943
Assets: $1-10 billion Year End: 20081231

Crosstown Civic Credit Union Ltd.
171 Donald St.
Winnipeg, MB R3C 1M4
204-942-1277
Fax: 204-947-3108
cu@crosstowncivic.mb.ca
www.crosstowncivic.mb.ca
Former Name: Civic Credit Union Ltd.
Ownership: Member-owned
Year Founded: 1943

Crown Cork & Seal Employees Credit Union Limited
7250 Keele St.
Concord, ON L4K 1Z8
905-660-2537
ccsecu@on.aibn.com
Year Founded: 1955
Number of Employees: 2

Cut Knife Credit Union Ltd.
PO Box 308
205 Broad St.
Cut Knife, SK S0M 0N0
306-398-2544
Fax: 306-398-2744
Mitch.Rokochy@cutknife.cu.sk.ca
Year Founded: 1960
Number of Employees: 7

Cypress Credit Union Ltd.
PO Box 1060
115 Jasper St.
Maple Creek, SK S0N 1N0
306-662-2683
Fax: 306-662-3859
877-353-6311
contactus@cypresscu.sk.ca
www.cypresscu.sk.ca

Dana Canada Employees' (Ontario) Credit Union Limited
PO Box 85
Hayes Rd.
Thorold, ON L2V 3Y7
905-227-6645
Fax: 905-227-4103
dccu@sympatico.ca
Year Founded: 1951

Dauphin Plains Credit Union
PO Box 340
505 Main St. North
Dauphin, MB R7N 2V2
204-622-4500
Fax: 204-622-4530
1-866-372-4535
info@dauphinplainscu.mb.ca
www.dauphinplainscu.mb.ca
Year Founded: 1940

Desjardins Credit Union
Also listed under: *Credit Card Companies; Non-Depository Institutions*
East Tower, Whitby Mall
1615 Dundas St. East, 3rd Fl.
Whitby, ON L1N 2L1

905-743-5790
Fax: 905-743-6156
888-283-8333
www.desjardins.com

Ownership: Member-owned
Year Founded: 2002

Desjardins Gestion d'actifs/ Desjardins Asset Management
Also listed under: *Credit Card Companies; Non-Depository Institutions*
95 St Clair Ave. West
Toronto, ON M4V 1N7

Diamond North Credit Union
PO Box 2074
Nipawin, SK S0E 1E0

306-862-4651
Fax: 306-862-9611
877-881-2020
Other Contact Information: 306/862-2370 (Loans)
contactus@diamondnorthcu.com
www.diamondnorthcu.com, www.nipawincu.com

Year Founded: 2006
Assets: $100-500 million

Dodsland & District Credit Union Ltd.
PO Box 129
Dodsland, SK S0L 0V0

306-356-2155
Fax: 306-356-2202
james.duncan@dodsland.cu.sk.ca
www.dodslandcreditunion.com

Year Founded: 1961
Number of Employees: 7

Dominion Credit Union
94 Commercial St.
Dominion, NS B1G 1B4

902-849-8648
Fax: 902-842-0273

Year Founded: 1934

Domtar Newsprint Employees (Trenton) Credit Union Limited
PO Box 254
Trenton, ON K8V 5R5

613-392-2426
Fax: 613-392-6851
ldwannamaker@sympatico.ca

DUCA Financial Services Credit Union Ltd.
5290 Yonge St.
Toronto, ON M2N 5P9

416-223-8502
Fax: 416-223-2575
866-900-3822
duca.info@duca.com
www.duca.com

Former Name: Duca Community Credit Union Limited
Ownership: Member-owned
Year Founded: 1954
Number of Employees: 100
Assets: $500m-1 billion
Revenues: $10-50 million

Dundalk District Credit Union Limited
PO Box 340
79 Proton St. North
Dundalk, ON N0C 1B0

519-923-2400
Fax: 519-923-2950
jmason@dundalkdistrictcreditunion.ca
www.dundalkdistrictcreditunion.ca

Year Founded: 1943
Number of Employees: 11
Assets: $10-50 million
Revenues: Under $1 million

Dunnville & District Credit Union Ltd.
208 Broad St. East
Dunnville, ON N1A 1G2

905-774-7559
Fax: 905-774-4662
www.ddcu.com

Ownership: Member-owned
Number of Employees: 5

Dysart Credit Union Ltd.
PO Box 39
110 Main St.
Dysart, SK S0G 1H0

306-432-2211
donjeworski@sasktel.net

Year Founded: 1960

Eagle River Credit Union
PO Box 29
8 Branch Rd.
L'Anse au Loup, NL A0K 3L0

709-927-5524
Fax: 709-927-5759
877-377-3728
aobrien@eagleriver.creditu.net
www.eaglerivercu.com

Year Founded: 1984
Number of Employees: 40
Assets: $10-50 million
Revenues: Under $1 million

East Coast Credit Union
Admin. Office
305 Granville St.
Port Hawkesbury, NS B9A 2M5

902-625-5610
www.eastcoastcreditu.ca

Year Founded: 2003
Number of Employees: 104
Assets: $100-500 million

East Kootenay Community Credit Union
924 Baker St.
Cranbrook, BC V1C 1A5

250-426-6666
Fax: 250-426-0879
866-960-6666
reception@ekccu.com
www.ekccu.com

Number of Employees: 30

EasternEdge Credit Union
PO Box 2110
10 Factory Lane
St. John's, NL A1C 5H6

709-739-2920
Fax: 709-739-3728
800-716-7283
www.easternedgecu.com

Former Name: NewTel Credit Union
Year Founded: 1976
Assets: $10-50 million

Eckville District Savings & Credit Union Ltd.
PO Box 278
Eckville, AB T0M 0X0

403-746-2288
Fax: 403-746-3737
info@eckvillecu.com
www.eckvillecu.com

Ownership: Private
Year Founded: 1943
Number of Employees: 9

Edson Savings & Credit Union
PO Box 6118
4912 - 2nd Ave.
Edson, AB T7E 1T6

780-723-4468
Fax: 780-723-7973
edsoncu@alberta-cu.com
www.edsoncu.com

Year Founded: 1940

Electragas Credit Union
6070 Stairs St.
Halifax, NS B3K 2E5

902-454-6843
Fax: 902-453-5161

Electric Employees Credit Union
10 Lanceleve Cres.
Albert Bridge, NS B1K 3J3

902-564-9707
Fax: 902-564-0956

Employees of Dofasco (Hamilton) Credit Union Limited
Gate #17
PO Box 2460
1721 Burlington St. East
Hamilton, ON L8N 3J5

905-549-6506
Fax: 905-548-9216
www.edcu.ca

Year Founded: 1954
Number of Employees: 10
Assets: $10-50 million

Enderby & District Credit Union
PO Box 670
703 Mill St.
Enderby, BC V0E 1V0

250-838-6841
Fax: 250-838-9756
info@enderbycreditunion.com
www.enderbycreditunion.com

Entegra Credit Union
Corporate Head Office
1335 Jefferson Ave.
Winnipeg, MB R2P 1S7

204-949-7744
Fax: 204-949-5865
info@entegra.ca
www.entegra.ca

Former Name: Holy Spirit Credit Union
Year Founded: 1960
Number of Employees: 47
Assets: $100-500 million

Envision Credit Union
6470 - 201st St.
Langley, BC V2Y 2X4

604-539-7300
Fax: 604-539-7315
www.envisionfinancial.ca

Also Known As: Envision Financial
Ownership: Member-owned
Year Founded: 1946
Number of Employees: 779
Assets: $1-10 billion
Revenues: $100-500 million

Equity Financial Services
#3, 400 Eastern Ave.
Toronto, ON M4M 1B9

416-463-3173
Fax: 416-465-9984
1-800-263-9793
info@equityfs.ca
www.equitycreditunion.ca

Former Name: Unilever Employees Credit Union Limited; Equity Credit Union

Erickson Credit Union Limited
PO Box 100
24 Main St. West
Erickson, MB R0J 0P0

204-636-7771
Fax: 204-636-2498
info@ericksoncu.mb.ca
www.ericksoncu.mb.ca

Ownership: Member-owned
Year Founded: 1952

Eriksdale Credit Union Limited
PO Box 99, Railway Stn. Railway
Eriksdale, MB R0C 0W0

204-739-2137
Fax: 204-739-5409
info@eriksdalecu.mb.ca
www.eriksdalecu.mb.ca

Ownership: Member-owned
Year Founded: 1972
Number of Employees: 29

Espanola & District Credit Union Limited
91 Centre St.
Espanola, ON P5E 1S4

705-869-3001
www.espanolacu.com

Year Founded: 1958

Estonian (Toronto) Credit Union Limited
958 Broadview Ave.
Toronto, ON M4K 2R6

416-465-4659
Fax: 416-465-8442
866-844-3828
info@estoniancu.com
www.estoniancu.com

Year Founded: 1954
Number of Employees: 12

ETCU Financial
1 East Mall Cres.
Toronto, ON M9B 6G8

416-622-8500
Fax: 416-622-0610
877-337-8500
www.etcu.com

Former Name: Etobicoke Teachers' Credit Union Limited

Year Founded: 1951

Ethelbert Credit Union
109 Railway Ave.
Ethelbert, MB R0L 0T0
204-742-3529

Etobicoke Aluminum Employees' Credit Union Limited
15 Browns Line
Toronto, ON M8W 3S3
416-253-2319
Fax: 416-253-2396
Number of Employees: 1

Fairview & District Savings & Credit Union Ltd.
PO Box 459
10300 - 110 St.
Fairview, AB T0H 1L0
780-835-2914
Fax: 780-835-4214

Fédération des caisses Desjardins du Québec
100, av des Commandeurs
Lévis, QC G6V 7N5
418-835-8444
1-866-835-8444
www.desjardins.com
Former Name: Fédération des Caisses Populaires Desjardins du Québec

Fédération des caisses populaires acadiennes ltée
CP 5554
295, boul St-Pierre ouest
Caraquet, NB E1W 1B7
506-726-4000
Fax: 506-726-4001
info@acadie.com
www.acadie.com
Year Founded: 1946
Number of Employees: 227

Fédération des caisses populaires de l'Ontario
214 Montreal Rd.
Ottawa, ON K1L 8L8
613-746-3276
Fax: 613-746-6035
800-423-3276

Fédération des caisses populaires du Manitoba
#200, 605 Des Meurons St.
Winnipeg, MB R2H 2R1
204-237-8988
Fax: 204-233-6405
federation@caisse.biz
www.caisse.biz
Ownership: Member-owned
Year Founded: 1937
Number of Employees: 240

Fiberglas Employees (Guelph) Credit Union Limited
PO Box 3603
247 York Rd.
Guelph, ON N1E 3G4
519-824-2212
Fax: 519-824-1390
fiberglascu@bellnet.ca
Year Founded: 1953
Number of Employees: 1

First Calgary Savings & Credit Union Limited
#200, 510 - 16th Ave. NE
Calgary, AB T2E 1K4
403-230-2783
Fax: 403-276-6338
info@1stcalgary.com
www.1stcalgary.com
Ownership: Member-owned
Year Founded: 1987
Assets: $1-10 billion

FirstOntario Credit Union Limited
688 Queensdale Ave. East
Hamilton, ON L8V 1M1
905-387-0770
888-283-7835
contact@firstontariocu.com
www.firstontariocu.com
Former Name: Avestel Family Savings Credit Union Limited; Family Savings & Credit Union Limited
Year Founded: 1940
Number of Employees: 300
Assets: $500m-1 billion

Flin Flon Credit Union
36 Main St.
Flin Flon, MB R8A 1J6
204-687-6620
www.flinfloncu.mb.ca
Year Founded: 1940
Number of Employees: 3

Foam Lake Savings & Credit Union Ltd.
PO Box 160
326 Main St.
Foam Lake, SK S0A 1A0
306-272-3385
Fax: 306-272-4948
info@foamlake.cu.sk.ca
www.foamlake.cu.sk.ca
Year Founded: 1941

Food Family Credit Union
2044 Danforth Ave.
Toronto, ON M4C 1J6
416-424-4798
Fax: 416-424-4760
800-267-3663
info@foodfamilycreditunion.com
www.foodfamilycreditunion.com
Year Founded: 1964
Number of Employees: 3
Assets: $10-50 million

Forget Credit Union Ltd.
General Delivery
Stoughton, SK S0C 0X0
306-457-2747
Year Founded: 1950

Fort Erie Community Credit Union Limited
1201 Garrison Rd.
Fort Erie, ON L2A 1N8
905-994-1201
Fax: 905-994-1897
info@forteriecu.com
www.forteriecu.com

Fort York Community Credit Union Limited
Sunnyside East Wing
#207, 30 The Queensway
Toronto, ON M6R 1B5
416-530-6474
Fax: 416-530-6763
fyinfo@fortyork.com
www.fortyork.com
Year Founded: 1950

Frontline Financial Credit Union
365 Richmond Rd.
Ottawa, ON K2A 0E7
613-729-4312
Fax: 613-729-5075
www.911cu.com
Former Name: Ottawa Fire Fighters' Credit Union Ltd.
Year Founded: 1948

G & F Financial Group
Also listed under: *Financial Planning & Investment Management Companies; Insurance Companies*
7375 Kingsway
Burnaby, BC V3N 3B5
604-517-5100
Fax: 604-659-4025
www.gffg.com
Former Name: Gulf & Fraser Fishermen's Credit Union
Year Founded: 1941
Number of Employees: 175
Assets: $500m-1 billion
Revenues: $1-5 million

Ganaraska Financial Services Group
17 Queen St.
Port Hope, ON L1A 2Y8
905-885-8134
Fax: 905-885-8298
info@ganaraskacu.com
www.ganaraskacu.com
Former Name: Ganaraska Credit Union
Year Founded: 1945

Genfast Employees Credit Union Limited
Bldg. 5
PO Box 1690
225 Henry St.
Brantford, ON N3T 5V7
519-754-4400
Fax: 519-750-1428
Ownership: Private
Number of Employees: 1

Glace Bay Central Credit Union
598 Main St.
Glace Bay, NS B1A 4X8
902-849-7512
Fax: 902-842-9201
www.glacebaycentralcreditunion.com
Year Founded: 1932

Goderich Community Credit Union Limited
PO Box 66
39 St. David St.
Goderich, ON N7A 3Y5
519-524-8366
Fax: 519-524-1329
reception@gccu.on.ca
www.gccu.on.ca
Ownership: Member-owned
Year Founded: 1954
Number of Employees: 15

Goodsoil Credit Union Limited
PO Box 88
Goodsoil, SK S0M 1A0
306-238-2033
Fax: 306-238-4441
info@goodsoil.cu.sk.ca
www.goodsoilcu.com
Ownership: Member-owned
Year Founded: 1946
Number of Employees: 7
Assets: $10-50 million
Revenues: Under $1 million

Goodyear Employees (Bowmanville) Credit Union Limited
371 Orange Cres.
Oshawa, ON L1G 5X2
905-623-2606
Fax: 905-432-7590
Year Founded: 1966
Number of Employees: 1

Govan Credit Union Ltd.
PO Box 280
Govan, SK S0G 1Z0
306-484-2177
Fax: 306-484-4333
866-298-1336
govancreditunion@govan.cu.sk.ca
www.govancreditunion.ca
Year Founded: 1940

Grand Forks District Savings Credit Union
PO Box 2500
447 Market Ave.
Grand Forks, BC V0H 1H0
250-442-5511
Fax: 250-442-5644
866-442-5511
info@gfdscu.com
www.gfdscu.com
Year Founded: 1949

Grandview Credit Union
PO Box 159
405 Main St.
Grandview, MB R0L 0Y0
204-546-5200
Fax: 204-546-5219
info@grandviewcu.mb.ca
www.grandviewcu.mb.ca

Greater Vancouver Community Credit Union
1801 Willingdon Ave.
Burnaby, BC V5C 5R3
604-298-3344
Fax: 604-421-8949
info@gvccu.com
www.gvccu.com

Greater Victoria Savings Credit Union
1001 Blanshard St.
Victoria, BC V8W 2H4
250-388-4408
Fax: 250-384-4232
www.vancity.com
Year Founded: 1940

Grey Bruce Health Services Credit Union Ltd.
1939 - 8 Ave. East
Owen Sound, ON N4K 3C4
519-376-9336
Fax: 519-376-1719

creditunion@mbts.com
Former Name: Health Centre (Owen Sound) Employees Credit Union Limited
Year Founded: 1967

GSW (Fergus) Credit Union Limited
599 Hill St. West
Fergus, ON N1M 2X1

519-843-1616
Fax: 519-787-5533

Year Founded: 1951
Number of Employees: 2

Hald-Nor Community Credit Union Limited
PO Box 2135
22 Caithness St. East
Caledonia, ON N3W 2G6

905-765-4071
Fax: 905-765-0485
caledonia@hald-nor.on.ca
www.hald-nor.on.ca

Ownership: Member-owned
Year Founded: 1954
Assets: $50-100 million

Halifax Civic Credit Union
6070 Lady Hammond Rd.
Halifax, NS B3K 2R6

902-455-5489
Fax: 902-453-5491

Year Founded: 1938

Hamilton Community Credit Union Limited
698 King St. East
Hamilton, ON L8M 1A3

905-529-9445
Fax: 905-529-9016
hccu@sympatico.ca
www.hccu.on.ca

Number of Employees: 15

Health Care Credit Union Ltd.
PO Box 5375
800 Commissioners Rd. East
London, ON N6A 4G5

519-685-8353
Fax: 519-685-8153
creditunion@lhsc.on.ca
www.lhsc.on.ca/cr_union/

Year Founded: 1949

Healthcare & Municipal Employees Credit Union (HMECU)
209 Limeridge Rd. East
Hamilton, ON L9A 2S6

905-575-8888
Fax: 905-575-3104
866-808-2888
www.hmecu.com

Number of Employees: 9

Heritage Credit Union
#100, 630 - 17th St.
Castlegar, BC V1N 4G7

250-365-7232
Fax: 250-365-2913
hcu@heritagecu.ca
www.heritagecu.ca

Former Name: Castlegar Savings Credit Union
Ownership: Member-owned
Year Founded: 1948
Assets: $50-100 million

Hir-Walk Employees' (Windsor) Credit Union Limited
2072 Riverside Dr. East
Windsor, ON N8Y 4S5

519-561-5543
Fax: 519-971-5744
hir-walker.credit@bellnet.ca

Year Founded: 1949
Number of Employees: 4

Hobart Employees' (Owen Sound) Credit Union Limited
PO Box 278
Owen Sound, ON N4K 5P5

519-376-8886
Fax: 519-376-2955

Holy Angel's & St. Anne's Parish (St Thomas) Credit Union Limited
PO Box 20125
St Thomas, ON N5P 4H4

519-633-1710
Fax: 519-633-4024
lphoffer@bellnet.ca

Holy Name Parish (Pembroke) Credit Union Limited
667 Front St.
Pembroke, ON K8A 6J4

613-732-3181
Fax: 613-732-1903

Ownership: Member-owned
Year Founded: 1942
Number of Employees: 3
Assets: Under $1 million
Revenues: Under $1 million

Horizon Credit Union
PO Box 1900
136 - 3rd Ave. East
Melville, SK S0A 2P0

306-728-5425
Fax: 306-728-4520
866-522-1880
Other Contact Information: Telephone Banking: 306/728-1880
info@horizon.cu.sk.ca
www.horizon.cu.sk.ca

Former Name: Melville District Credit Union Ltd.; Aspen Prairie Credit Union Ltd.
Ownership: Co-operative. Member-owned
Year Founded: 1949
Number of Employees: 49

Hudson Bay Credit Union Ltd.
PO Box 538
208 Churchill St.
Hudson Bay, SK S0E 0Y0

306-865-2209
Fax: 306-865-2381
info@hudsonbay.cu.sk.ca
www.hudsonbaycu.com

Year Founded: 1954
Number of Employees: 17
Assets: $10-50 million
Revenues: $1-5 million

Industrial Savings & Credit Union Ltd.
PO Box 97
Hwy 16A & 17 St.
Edmonton, AB T5J 2G9

780-410-5502
Fax: 780-410-5391

Year Founded: 1964

Inglewood Savings & Credit Union
1328 - 9th Ave. SE
Calgary, AB T2G 0T3

403-265-5396
Fax: 403-265-1326
manager@inglewoodcu.com
www.inglewoodcu.com

Ownership: Member-owned
Year Founded: 1938
Assets: $10-50 million

Innovation Credit Union
PO Box 638
1202 - 102nd St.
North Battleford, SK S9A 2Y7

306-446-7000
Fax: 306-445-6086
Other Contact Information: 1-866-446-7001 (North Region Toll-Free); 1-800-381-5502 (South Region Toll-Free); 306-445-6086 (North Region Fax); 306-773-0294 (South Region Fax)
www.innovationcu.ca

Year Founded: 2007

iNova Credit Union
PO Box 8153, A Stn. A
6175 Almon St.
Halifax, NS B3K 5L9

902-453-1145
Fax: 902-453-0370
800-665-1145
ask@inovacreditunion.coop
www.nspostalcreditunion.com

Former Name: Nova Scotia Postal Employees Credit Union

Integris Credit Union
1532 - 6th Ave.
Prince George, BC V2L 5B5

250-612-3456
Fax: 250-612-3450
www.integriscu.ca

Former Name: Prince George Savings Credit Union; Nechako Valley Credit Union; Quesnel & District Credit Union
Year Founded: 2004

Interior Savings Credit Union
#300, 678 Bernard Ave.
Kelowna, BC V1Y 6P3

250-762-4355
Fax: 250-762-9581
info@interiorsavings.com
www.interiorsavings.com

Ownership: Member-owned
Assets: $100-500 million

Island Savings Credit Union
Also listed under: *Financing & Loan Companies*
#300, 499 Canada Ave.
Duncan, BC V9L 1T7

250-748-4728
Fax: 250-748-8831
info@iscu.com
www.iscu.com

Ownership: Member-owned
Year Founded: 1951
Number of Employees: 300
Assets: $500m-1 billion

Kakabeka Falls Community Credit Union Limited
115 Clergue St.
Kakabeka Falls, ON P0T 1W0

807-475-4276
Fax: 807-475-5990
kakabeka@tbaytel.net
www.kakabekacu.com

Kawartha Credit Union Limited
PO Box 116
1054 Monaghan Rd.
Peterborough, ON K9J 6Y5

705-743-3643
Fax: 705-749-1890
888-743-9966
info@kawarthacu.com
www.kawarthacu.com

Year Founded: 1952

Kellogg Employees Credit Union Limited
PO Box 5517
100 Kellogg Lane
London, ON N6A 4P9

519-452-6414
Fax: 519-452-6316
kelloggcu@kelloggcu.com
www.kelloggcu.com

Year Founded: 1953
Number of Employees: 3
Revenues: $10-50 million

Kelvington Credit Union Ltd.
PO Box 459
Kelvington, SK S0A 1W0

306-327-4728
Fax: 306-327-5100
info@kelvington.cu.sk.ca
www.kelvingtoncu.com

Year Founded: 1943

Kenaston Credit Union Ltd.
PO Box 70
607 - 3rd St.
Kenaston, SK S0G 2N0

306-252-2160
garth.lewis@kenaston.cu.sk.ca
www.kenaston.cu.sk.ca

Kenora District Credit Union Limited
PO Box 2200
101 Park St.
Kenora, ON P9N 3X8

807-467-4400
Fax: 807-468-6452
www.kdcu.on.ca

Kerrobert Credit Union Ltd.
PO Box 140
437 Pacific Ave.
Kerrobert, SK S0L 1R0

306-834-2611
Fax: 306-834-5558
info@kerrobert.cu.sk.ca
www.kerrobert.cu.sk.ca

Year Founded: 1963

Khalsa Credit Union (Alberta) Limited
#604, 4656 Westwinds Dr. NE
Calgary, AB T3J 3Z5

403-285-0707
Fax: 403-285-0771
khalsacu@telusplanet.net
www.khalsacu.ca

Year Founded: 1995
Number of Employees: 3
Assets: $1-5 million
Revenues: $1-5 million

King-York Newsmen Toronto Credit Union Limited
444 Front St. West
Toronto, ON M5V 2S9

416-585-5110
Fax: 416-585-5534
credit-union@globeandmail.ca

Ownership: Private
Year Founded: 1955
Assets: $1-5 million
Revenues: $1-5 million

Kootenay Savings Credit Union
#300, 1199 Cedar Ave.
Trail, BC V1R 4B8

250-368-2686
Fax: 250-368-5203
info@kscu.com
www.kscu.com

Ownership: Member-owned
Year Founded: 1969
Number of Employees: 208
Assets: $500m-1 billion

Korean (Toronto) Credit Union Limited
703 Bloor St. West
Toronto, ON M6G 1L5

416-535-4511
Fax: 416-535-9323
ktcul@rogers.com
www.koreancu.com

Korean Catholic Church Credit Union Limited
849 Don Mills Rd., 2nd Fl.
Toronto, ON M3C 1W1

416-447-7788
Fax: 416-447-5297
kcccu@on.aibn.com

Krek Slovenian Credit Union Ltd.
747 Brown's Line
Toronto, ON M8W 3V7

416-252-6527
Fax: 416-252-2092
main@krek.ca
www.krek.ca

Former Name: John E. Krek's Slovenian (Toronto) Credit Union Limited
Ownership: Private
Year Founded: 1953
Number of Employees: 17
Assets: $50-100 million

Ladysmith & District Credit Union
PO Box 430
330 First Ave.
Ladysmith, BC V9G 1A3

250-245-2247
Fax: 250-245-5913
info@ldcu.ca
www.ldcu.ca

Year Founded: 1944

LaFleche Credit Union Ltd.
105 Main St.
Lafleche, SK S0H 2K0

306-472-5215
Fax: 306-472-5545
info@lafleche.cu.sk.ca
www.laflechecu.com

Ownership: Member-owned
Year Founded: 1938
Number of Employees: 12
Assets: $10-50 million

Lake View Credit Union
800 - 102nd Ave.
Dawson Creek, BC V1G 2B2

250-782-4871
Fax: 250-782-5828
lvcu@lakeviewcreditunion.com
www.lakeviewcreditunion.com

Ownership: Private
Number of Employees: 36

Lakeland Credit Union
PO Box 8057
5016 - 50 Ave.
Bonnyville, AB T9N 2J3

780-826-3377
Fax: 780-826-6322
admin@lakelandcreditunion.com
www.lakelandcreditunion.com

Lambton Financial Credit Union Ltd.
1295 London Rd.
Sarnia, ON N7S 1P6

519-542-0483
Fax: 519-542-3778
866-380-8008
www.lambtonfinancial.ca

Former Name: Polysar Lambton Credit Union Limited
Ownership: Private
Year Founded: 1947
Number of Employees: 48
Assets: $100-500 million
Revenues: $5-10 milllon

Landis Credit Union Ltd.
PO Box 220
Landis, SK S0K 2K0

306-658-2152
Fax: 306-658-2153
owen.nicklin@landis.cu.sk.ca
www.landis.cu.sk.ca

Year Founded: 1942
Number of Employees: 4
Assets: $5-10 million
Revenues: Under $1 million

Lasco Employees' (Whitby) Credit Union Limited
1801 Hopkins St. South
Whitby, ON L1N 5T1

905-668-8811
Fax: 905-668-2807

Latvian Credit Union
4 Credit Union Dr.
Toronto, ON M4A 2N8

416-922-2551
Fax: 416-922-2758
www.kredsab.ca

Ownership: Member-owned
Number of Employees: 12

Lear Seating Canada Employees' (Kitchener) Credit Union Ltd.
PO Box 758
530 Manitou Dr.
Kitchener, ON

519-895-3213

Legacy Savings & Credit Union Ltd.
1940, 9 Ave.
Calgary, AB T2G 0V2

403-265-6050
Fax: 403-265-8010
admin@legacysavings.com
www.legacysavings.com

Lethbridge Legion Savings & Credit Union Ltd.
324 Mayor Magrath Dr.
Lethbridge, AB T1J 3L7

403-327-6417
Fax: 403-317-0122

Year Founded: 1958

Libro Financial Group
167 Central Ave., 2nd Fl.
London, ON N6A 1M6

519-672-0124
Fax: 519-672-7831
800-265-5935
service@libro.ca
www.libro.ca

Former Name: St. Willibrod Credit Union Limited; St. Willibrod Community Credit Union Limited
Ownership: 47,000 owners
Year Founded: 1951
Number of Employees: 300
Assets: $1-10 billion
Revenues: $500m-1 billion

Lintlaw Credit Union Ltd.
PO Box 190
212 Main St.
Lintlaw, SK S0A 2H0

306-325-2118
Fax: 306-325-4311

Year Founded: 1940

LIUNA Local 183 Credit Union Limited
#108, 1263 Wilson Ave.
Toronto, ON M3M 3G2

416-242-6643
Fax: 416-242-7852
info@local183cu.ca
www.local183cu.ca

London Civic Employees' Credit Union Limited
343 Dundas St.
London, ON N6B 1V5

519-661-4563
Fax: 519-663-9369
memberservices@lcecu.com
www.lcecu.com

Ownership: Private
Year Founded: 1948

London Diesel Employees' Credit Union Limited
#4B, 525 First St.
London, ON N5V 1Z5

519-451-9580
Fax: 519-451-1831
london_diesel@yahoo.com

Year Founded: 1951

London Fire Fighters' Credit Union Limited
400 Horton St. East
London, ON N6B 1L7

519-661-5635
Fax: 519-661-5635
info@lfdcreditunion.com
www.lfdcreditunion.com

Ownership: Private
Number of Employees: 2

Macklin Credit Union Ltd.
PO Box 326
4809 Herald St.
Macklin, SK S0L 2C0

306-753-2333
Fax: 306-753-2676
info@macklin.cu.sk.ca
www.macklin.cu.sk.ca

Number of Employees: 13

Macleod Savings & Credit Union Ltd.
PO Box 1659
5018 - 2nd St. West
Claresholm, AB T0L 0T0

403-625-2179
Fax: 403-625-4413
admin@macleodcu.com
www.macleodcu.com

Ownership: Member-owned
Year Founded: 1941
Number of Employees: 35
Assets: $50-100 million

Main-à-Dieu Credit Union
#3, 2886 Louis-Main-A-Dieu Rd.
Main-à-Dieu, NS B1C 1X5

902-733-2555
Fax: 902-733-2301

Ownership: Member-owned
Year Founded: 1935
Number of Employees: 2
Assets: $1-5 million
Revenues: Under $1 million

Mankota Credit Union
Main St.
Mankota, SK S0H 2W0

306-478-2284
Fax: 306-478-2277
Other Contact Information: Kikcaid Phone: 306-264-3822; Kincaid Office Fax: 306-264-5175
info@mankota.cu.sk.ca
www.mankotacu.ca

Number of Employees: 7

Mariposa Community Credit Union Limited
PO Box 129
2 King St. South
Little Britain, ON K0M 2C0

705-786-3524
Fax: 705-786-3568
mccu.littlebritain@sympatico.ca
www3.sympatico.ca/mccu.kinmount/

Ownership: Private
Year Founded: 1995
Number of Employees: 6

McMaster Savings & Credit Union Ltd.
Westdale Village
1005 King St. West
Hamilton, ON L8S 1L3
905-522-2903
Fax: 905-522-4467
mscuwestdale@maccu.com
www.maccu.com
Ownership: Member-owned
Year Founded: 1936

Media Group Financial Credit Union Limited
369 York St.
London, ON N6A 4G1
519-667-4505
Fax: 519-667-5522
creditunion@mediagroupfinancial.ca
www.mediagroupfinancial.ca

Me-Dian Credit Union
303 Selkirk Ave.
Winnipeg, MB R2W 2L8
204-943-9111
Fax: 204-942-3698
www.me-diancu.mb.ca

The Medical-Dental Financial, Savings & Credit Limited
c/o Credential, Ontario Regl. Office
#200, 3430 South Service Rd.
Burlington, ON L7N 3T9
905-632-9200
Fax: 905-632-0032

Member Savings Credit Union
55 Lakeshore Blvd. East
Toronto, ON M5E 1A4
416-864-2461
Fax: 416-864-6858
888-560-2218
membercu@membercu.com
www.membercu.com
Year Founded: 1949
Assets: $50-100 million

MemberOne Credit Union Ltd.
PO Box 35
200 Front St. West, Concourse Level
Toronto, ON M5V 3K2
416-344-4070
Fax: 416-344-4069
info@memberone.ca
www.memberone.ca
Former Name: WCB Credit Union Limited

Mendham-Burstall Credit Union
PO Box 69
Mendham, SK S0N 1P0
306-628-3257
Fax: 306-628-4284
mendham@sasktel.net
Ownership: Member-owned
Assets: $10-50 million
Revenues: Under $1 million

Mennonite Savings & Credit Union (Ontario) Limited
1265 Strasburg Rd.
Kitchener, ON N2R 1S6
519-746-1010
Fax: 519-746-1045
888-672-6728
info@mscu.com
www.mscu.com
Ownership: Member-owned
Year Founded: 1964
Number of Employees: 96
Assets: $500m-1 billion
Revenues: $50-100 million

Meridian Credit Union
College Park
777 Bay St., 26th Fl.
Toronto, ON M5G 2C8
416-597-4400
Fax: 416-597-5068
866-592-2226
www.meridiancu.ca
Former Name: HEPCOE Credit Union Limited
Ownership: Member-owned
Year Founded: 2005
Number of Employees: 1,000
Assets: $1-10 billion

Midale Credit Union Ltd.
PO Box 418
211 Main St.
Midale, SK S0C 1S0
306-458-2222
Fax: 306-458-2329
www.midalecu.com

Milestone Credit Union Ltd.
PO Box 144
118 Main St.
Milestone, SK S0G 3L0
306-436-2002
Fax: 306-436-2114
info@milestone.cu.sk.ca
Former Name: Milestone Savings & Credit Union Ltd.

Minnedosa Credit Union
PO Box 459
60 Main St.
Minnedosa, MB R0J 1E0
204-867-6350
Fax: 204-867-6391
877-663-7228
www.minnedosacu.mb.ca
Year Founded: 1947
Number of Employees: 20

Miracle Credit Union Ltd.
#22, 86 Guided Crt.
Toronto, ON M9V 4K6
416-740-7553
Fax: 416-740-3767
miracle@on.aibn.com
www.miraclecreditunion.ca

Mitchell & District Credit Union Limited
105 Ontario Rd.
Mitchell, ON N0K 1N0
519-348-8448
Fax: 519-348-8009
mitchell@mitchellcu.ca
www.mitchellcu.ca
Ownership: Private
Year Founded: 1960
Number of Employees: 33
Assets: $50-100 million
Revenues: $1-5 million

Molson Brewery Employees Credit Union Limited
1 Carlingview Dr.
Toronto, ON M9W 5E5
416-675-8710
Fax: 416-213-0518
dmccurdy@virtualonecu.com
www.virtualonecu.ca
Year Founded: 1956
Number of Employees: 2

Moore Employees' Credit Union Limited
6100 Vipond Dr.
Mississauga, ON L5T 2X1
416-241-7132
sylvia_murphy@ca.moore.com
Year Founded: 1962

Motor City Community Credit Union Limited
6701 Tecumseh Rd. East
Windsor, ON N8T 1E8
519-944-7333
Fax: 519-944-9765
info@mcccu.com
www.mcccu.com
Ownership: Member-owned
Assets: $100-500 million

Mount Lehman Credit Union
5889 Mount Lehman Rd.
Mount Lehman, BC V4X 1V7
604-856-7761
Fax: 604-856-1429
Other Contact Information: MemberCall: 604-856-7726
info@mtlehman.com
www.mtlehman.com
Year Founded: 1942
Number of Employees: 12

Mountain View Credit Union Ltd.
PO Box 3752
4920 - 50 Ave.
Olds, AB T4H 1P5
403-556-3306
Fax: 403-556-1050
mvcu@alberta-cu.com
www.mountainviewcreditunion.ca

Ownership: Member-owned
Number of Employees: 1977
Assets: $100-500 million

Mouvement des caisses Desjardins du Québec
Also listed under: *Financing & Loan Companies; Insurance Companies*
100, av des Commandeurs
Lévis, QC G6V 7N5
418-835-8444
Fax: 418-833-5873
www.desjardins.com
Ownership: Private.
Year Founded: 1901
Number of Employees: 38,000
Assets: $10-50 million

Mozart Savings & Credit Union Limited
PO Box 96
Mozart, SK S0A 2S0
306-554-2808
Fax: 306-554-2839
mozart@sasktel.net
Year Founded: 1940
Number of Employees: 3

Municipal Employees (Chatham) Credit Union Limited
301 Delaware Ave.
Chatham, ON N7L 2W9
519-354-9182
Year Founded: 1954
Number of Employees: 2
Assets: $1-5 million
Revenues: Under $1 million

Nasco Employees' Credit Union Limited
PO Box 2450
602 Kenilworth Ave. North
Hamilton, ON L8N 3J4
905-544-3311
Fax: 905-544-5449
nascocu@canada.com
Year Founded: 1946
Number of Employees: 2

NCR Employees' Credit Union Ltd.
6865 Century Ave.
Mississauga, ON L5N 2E2
905-819-4000
Year Founded: 1949

Nelson & District Credit Union
PO Box 350
501 Vernon St.
Nelson, BC V1L 5R2
250-352-7207
Fax: 250-352-9663
877-352-7207
enrichingyourlife@nelsoncu.com
www.nelsoncu.com
Number of Employees: 50

New Brunswick Teachers' Association Credit Union
PO Box 752
650 Montgomery St.
Fredericton, NB E3B 5R6
506-452-1724
Fax: 506-452-1732
800-565-5626
nbtacu@nbnet.nb.ca
www.nbtacu.nb.ca
Ownership: Private
Year Founded: 1971
Number of Employees: 12
Assets: $10-50 million

New Community Credit Union
321 - 20th St. West
Saskatoon, SK S7M 0X1
306-653-1300
Fax: 306-653-4711
info@newcommunity.cu.sk.ca
www.newcommunitycu.com
Former Name: New Community Savings & Credit Union Ltd.
Year Founded: 1939

New Glasgow Credit Union
175 Victoria St.
New Glasgow, NS B2H 4V3
902-752-3102
Fax: 902-755-5777

New Ross Credit Union
PO Box 32
56 Forties Rd.
New Ross, NS B0J 2M0
902-689-2949
Fax: 902-689-2597
www.newrosscreditunion.ca
Year Founded: 1956

New Waterford Credit Union
3462 Plummer Ave.
New Waterford, NS B1H 1Z6
902-862-6453
Fax: 902-862-9206
www.newwaterfordcreditunion.com
Year Founded: 1934
Number of Employees: 14
Assets: $10-50 million

Niverville Credit Union
PO Box 430
62 Main St.
Niverville, MB R0A 1E0
204-388-4747
Fax: 204-388-9970
info@nivervillecu.mb.ca
www.nivervillecu.mb.ca
Year Founded: 1949

North Peace Savings & Credit Union
10344 - 100th St.
Fort St John, BC V1J 3Z1
250-787-0361
Fax: 250-787-9704
800-561-7849
members@northpeacesavings.com
www.northpeacesavings.com
Ownership: Private
Number of Employees: 53

North Shore Credit Union
1112 Lonsdale Ave., 3rd Fl.
North Vancouver, BC V7M 2H2
604-982-8000
Fax: 604-985-6810
880-713-6728
www.nscu.ca
Year Founded: 1941

North Valley Credit Union Limited
PO Box 1389
516 Main St.
Esterhazy, SK S0A 0X0
306-745-6615
Fax: 306-745-2858
866-533-6828
www.northvalleycu.com
Former Name: Esterhazy Credit Union Limited
Ownership: Member-owned
Year Founded: 1998
Number of Employees: 14

Northern Credit Union
Also listed under: *Financial Planning & Investment Management Companies*
681 Pine St.
Sault Ste Marie, ON P6B 3G2
705-253-9868
Fax: 705-949-1056
www.northerncu.com
Year Founded: 1957
Assets: $500m-1 billion

Northern Lights Credit Union Limited
PO Box 876
97 Duke St.
Dryden, ON P8N 2Z5
807-223-5358
Fax: 807-223-8650
kimf@nlcu.on.ca
www.nlcu.on.ca
Number of Employees: 57

Northern Savings Credit Union
138 Third Ave. West
Prince Rupert, BC V8J 1K8
250-627-7571
Fax: 250-624-8297
info@northsave.com
www.northsave.com
Ownership: Member-owned

Northland Savings & Credit Union Limited
10 Cain Ave.
Kapuskasing, ON P5N 1S9
705-335-2348
Fax: 705-337-1070
kapcu@ntl.sympatico.ca
Ownership: Member-owned
Year Founded: 1939

Northridge Savings & Credit Union Ltd.
9 Second Ave. North
Sudbury, ON P3B 3L7
705-566-8540
Fax: 705-566-8480
www.northridgesavings.com

Oak Bank Credit Union
PO Box 217
686 Main St.
Oakbank, MB R0E 1J0
204-444-7200
Fax: 204-444-3513
info@oakbankcu.mb.ca
www.oakbankcu.mb.ca
Year Founded: 1946

Ogema District Credit Union Ltd.
PO Box 339
Ogema, SK S0C 1Y0
306-459-2266
info@ogema.cu.sk.ca
www.ogema.cu.sk.ca
Year Founded: 1950

Omista Credit Union
151 Cornhill St.
Moncton, NB E1C 6L3
506-857-3222
Fax: 506-857-2235
cornhillst@omista.com
www.omista.com
Ownership: Member-owned

ONR Employees' (North Bay) Credit Union Limited
555 Oak St. East
North Bay, ON P1B 9E5
705-472-1100
Fax: 705-472-0651
onrcu@ontc.on.ca
Year Founded: 1950

Ontario Civil Service Credit Union Limited
#1, 18 Grenville St.
Toronto, ON M4Y 3B3
416-314-6772
Fax: 416-314-1289
888-516-6664
memberassistance@mycreditunion.ca
www.mycreditunion.ca
Ownership: Cooperative
Year Founded: 1945
Assets: $100-500 million
Revenues: $5-10 million

Ontario Educational Credit Union Limited
PO Box 360
#1, 6435 Edwards Blvd.
Mississauga, ON L5T 2P7
905-795-1637
Fax: 905-795-0625
800-463-3602
www.oecu.on.ca
Year Founded: 1962
Number of Employees: 8

Ontario Provincial Police Association Credit Union Limited
123 Ferris Lane
Barrie, ON L4M 2Y1
705-726-5656
Fax: 705-726-1449
800-461-4288
gd@oppacu.com
www.oppacu.com
Also Known As: O.P.P.A Credit Union
Year Founded: 1971

Oregon Employees Credit Union Limited
505 Edinburgh Rd. North
Guelph, ON N1H 6L4
519-822-6870

Osoyoos Credit Union
PO Box 360
8312 Main St.
Osoyoos, BC V0H 1V0
250-495-6522
Fax: 250-495-3363
800-882-1966
contact@osoyooscreditunion.com
www.osoyooscreditunion.com
Ownership: Member-owned
Year Founded: 1946
Number of Employees: 20

Ottawa Police Credit Union Limited
#206, 474 Elgin St., 2nd Fl.
Ottawa, ON K2P 2J6
613-236-1222
Fax: 613-567-3760
www.opcu.com
Former Name: Ottawa-Carleton Police Credit Union Limited
Ownership: Private.
Year Founded: 1955
Number of Employees: 5
Revenues: $10-50 million

Ottawa Women's Credit Union Limited
Co-operative House
271 Bank St.
Ottawa, ON K2P 1X5
613-233-7711
Fax: 613-233-6413
info@owcu.on.ca
www.owcu.on.ca

Pace Savings & Credit Union Limited
#1, 8111 Jane St.
Vaughan, ON L4K 4L7
905-738-8900
Fax: 905-738-8283
pace.info@pacecu.com
www.pacecu.com
Ownership: Member-owned
Year Founded: 1984
Assets: $50-100 million
Revenues: $5-10 million

PACE Savings & Credit Union Ltd.
#1, 8111 Jane St.
Vaughan, ON L4K 4L7
905-738-8900
Fax: 905-738-8283
pace.info@pacecu.com
www.pacecu.com
Former Name: North York Community Credit Union Limited
Year Founded: 1955
Number of Employees: 20
Assets: $50-100 million

Parama Lithuanian Credit Union Limited
1573 Bloor St. West
Toronto, ON M6P 1A6
416-532-1149
Fax: 416-532-5595
info@parama.ca
www.parama.net
Year Founded: 1952
Number of Employees: 30
Assets: $100-500 million

Pedeco (Brockville) Credit Union Limited
2337 Parkedale Ave.
Brockville, ON K6V 5W5
613-342-4436
Fax: 613-342-6584
cmacdonald@ripnet.com
Year Founded: 1952

PenFinancial Credit Union
247 East Main St.
Welland, ON L3B 3X1
905-735-4801
Fax: 905-735-2983
www.penfinancial.com
Former Name: St Catharines Civic Employees' Credit Union Ltd.
Year Founded: 1951
Number of Employees: 57
Assets: $100-500 million

Peterborough Community Credit Union Limited
PO Box 1600
167 Brock St.
Peterborough, ON K9J 7S4
705-748-4481
Fax: 705-748-5520
www.pboccu.com
Year Founded: 1939

Peterborough Industrial Credit Union
890 High St.
Peterborough, ON K9J 5R2
705-743-4651
Fax: 705-743-9889

Pierceland Credit Union Ltd.
PO Box 10
181 Main St.
Pierceland, SK S0M 2K0
306-839-2071
Fax: 306-839-2292
info@pierceland.cu.sk.ca
Year Founded: 1941
Number of Employees: 8

Pincher Creek Credit Union Ltd.
PO Box 1660
750 Kettles St.
Pincher Creek, AB T0K 1W0
403-627-4431
Fax: 403-627-5331
www.pinchercreek-creditunion.com
Ownership: Member-owned
Year Founded: 1944
Number of Employees: 5

Plainsview Credit Union
PO Box 150
600 Main St.
Kipling, SK S0G 2S0
306-736-2549
Fax: 306-736-8290
info1@plainsview.cu.sk.ca
www.plainsview.com

The Police Credit Union Ltd.
#303, 3650 Victoria Park Ave.
Toronto, ON M2H 3P7
416-226-3353
Fax: 416-226-1565
800-561-2557
callcentre@tpcu.on.ca
www.tpcu.on.ca
Ownership: Member-owned
Year Founded: 1946

Polish Alliance (Brant) Credit Union Limited
126 Albion St.
Brantford, ON N3T 3M6
519-756-1070
Fax: 519-756-9885
pabcu@rogers.com
Year Founded: 1957
Number of Employees: 3
Assets: $5-10 million
Revenues: Under $1 million

Porcupine Credit Union Ltd.
PO Box 189
150 McAllister Ave.
Porcupine Plain, SK S0E 1H0
306-278-2181
Fax: 306-278-2944
info@porcupine.cu.sk.ca
www.porcupine.cu.sk.ca
Year Founded: 1946

Portuguese Canadian (Toronto) Credit Union Ltd.
1168 Dundas St. West
Toronto, ON M6J 1X4
416-533-9245
Fax: 416-533-2578
inforequest@pccufinancial.com
www.pccufinancial.com
Year Founded: 1966

Powell River Credit Union Financial Group
Also listed under: *Financial Planning & Investment Management Companies*
4721 Joyce Ave.
Powell River, BC V8A 3B5
604-485-6206
Fax: 604-485-7112
800-393-6733
www.prcu.com
Year Founded: 1939
Number of Employees: 46
Assets: $100-500 million
Revenues: $5-10 million

Prairie Centre Credit Union
PO Box 940
Rosetown, SK S0L 2V0
306-882-2693
Fax: 306-882-3326
comments@pccu.ca
www.pccu.ca
Ownership: Cooperative
Year Founded: 1993
Number of Employees: 75
Assets: $100-500 million
Revenues: $5-10 million

Prairie Diamond Credit Union
PO Box 819
123 Garfield St.
Davidson, SK S0G 1A0
306-567-2931
Fax: 306-567-5503
info@prairiediamond.cu.sk.ca
www.affinitycu.ca
Year Founded: 1994

Prairie Pride Credit Union
PO Box 37
Alameda, SK S0C 0A0
306-489-2131
Fax: 306-489-2188
info@prairiepride.cu.sk.ca
www.prairiepridecu.com
Former Name: Gainsborough Credit Union Ltd.
Year Founded: 2001
Number of Employees: 9

Prime Savings Credit Union
#201, 735 South Service Rd.
Stoney Creek, ON L8E 5Z2
905-643-2879
www.primecu.com
Former Name: Industrial Family (Hamilton) Credit Union Ltd.

Princess Credit Union
22 Fraser Ave.
Sydney Mines, NS B1V 2B7
902-736-9204
Fax: 902-736-2887

Progressive Credit Union
30 Hughes
Fredericton, NB E3A 2W3
506-458-9145
Fax: 506-459-0106
www.progressivecu.nb.ca
Former Name: Capital Credit Union
Year Founded: 1949

Prosperity ONE Credit Union
44 Main St. East
Milton, ON L9T 1N3
905-878-4168
Fax: 905-878-5500
info@prosperityone.ca
www.prosperityone.ca
Former Name: Halton Community Credit Union
Year Founded: 1957
Number of Employees: 36
Assets: $50-100 million

Province House Credit Union Ltd.
PO Box 1083
1724 Granville St.
Halifax, NS B3J 2X1
902-424-5712
Fax: 902-424-3662
888-484-0880
info@provincehouse.com
www.provincehouse.com

Provincial Alliance Credit Union Limited
1201 Wilson Ave.
Toronto, ON M3M 1J8
416-235-4373
Fax: 416-235-4225
877-523-7228
help@provincialalliance.com
www.provincialalliance.com
Year Founded: 1953
Number of Employees: 24

Public Service Credit Union Ltd.
403 Empire Ave.
St. John's, NL A1E 1W6
709-579-8210
Fax: 709-579-8233
800-563-6755
pscuadmin@pscu.creditu.net
www.pscu.ca
Ownership: Cooperative
Year Founded: 1936
Number of Employees: 18
Assets: $10-50 million
Revenues: $1-5 million

Public Service Employees Credit Union
141 Weldon St.
Moncton, NB E1C 5W1
506-853-8881
Fax: 506-856-8492
www.psecreditunion.ca

Quill Lake Credit Union Ltd.
PO Box 520
Quill Lake, SK S0A 3E0
306-383-4155
Fax: 306-383-2622
www.quilllake.cu.sk.ca
Year Founded: 1946

QuintEssential Credit Union Limited
293 Sidney St.
Belleville, ON K8P 3Z4
613-966-4111
Fax: 613-966-8909
info@qcu.ca
www.qcu.ca

Radville Credit Union Ltd.
PO Box 279
201 Main St.
Radville, SK S0C 2G0
306-869-2215
Fax: 306-869-2891
info@radville.cu.sk.ca
www.radville.cu.sk.ca
Year Founded: 1943

Railway Employees' (Sarnia) Credit Union Limited
431 Russell St. South
Sarnia, ON N7T 3N1
519-336-0093
Fax: 519-336-6945
info@recu.ca
www.recu.ca

Raymore Savings & Credit Union Ltd.
PO Box 460
121 Main St.
Raymore, SK S0A 3J0
306-746-2160
Fax: 306-746-5811
866-612-2300
info@raymore.cu.sk.ca
www.raymorecu.com
Year Founded: 1949

RBW Employees' (Owen Sound) Credit Union Limited
2049 - 20th St.
Owen Sound, ON N4K 5R2
519-376-8330
Fax: 519-376-1164
Number of Employees: 1

Reddy Kilowatt Credit Union Ltd.
Newfoundland Power Bldg.
PO Box 8910
50 Duffy Pl.
St. John's, NL A1B 3P6
709-737-5624
Fax: 709-737-2937
800-409-2887
rkcu@reddykilowatt.creditu.net
www.reddyk.net
Year Founded: 1956
Number of Employees: 6

Resurrection Parish (Toronto) Credit Union Limited
3 Resurrection Rd.
Toronto, ON M9A 5G1
416-532-3400
Fax: 416-532-4816
rpcul@rpcul.com
www.rpcul.com
Number of Employees: 13

River City Credit Union Ltd.
11715A - 108 Ave.
Edmonton, AB T5H 1B8
780-496-3482
Fax: 780-496-3477
rivercity@alberta-cu.com
www.river-citycu.com
Former Name: Edmonton Civic Employees Credit Union Ltd.

Rochdale Credit Union Limited
943 Dundas St.
Woodstock, ON N4S 1H2
519-539-4813
Fax: 519-539-8667
rochdale@rcu.com
www.rcu.com
Year Founded: 1942

Rocky Credit Union Ltd.
PO Box 1420
5035 - 49 St.
Rocky Mountain House, AB T4T 2A3
403-845-2861
Fax: 403-845-7295
rockycu@alberta-cu.com
www.rockycreditunion.com
Ownership: Public
Year Founded: 1944
Number of Employees: 40
Assets: $100-500 million
Revenues: $1-5 million

Rorketon & District Credit Union
PO Box 10
691 Main St.
Rorketon, MB R0L 1R0
204-732-2448
Fax: 204-732-2275
rorkinfo@rorketoncu.mb.ca
www.rorketoncu.mb.ca
Year Founded: 1961

Rosenort Credit Union Limited
PO Box 339
23 Main St.
Rosenort, MB R0G 1W0
204-746-2355
Fax: 204-746-2541
800-265-7925
info@rcu.mb.ca
www.rcu.mb.ca
Year Founded: 1940
Assets: $50-100 million

Rossignol Credit Union
PO Box 310
Brooklyn, NS B0J 1H0
902-354-2021
Ownership: Private
Year Founded: 1937
Number of Employees: 1
Assets: $1-5 million
Revenues: Under $1 million

Royglenor Savings & Credit Union Ltd.
Royal Alexander Hospital, Community Services Centre
#174, 10240 Kingsway Ave.
Edmonton, AB T5H 3V9
780-474-7724
Fax: 780-474-9043
www.royglenorcu.ca
Year Founded: 1956

St Gregor Credit Union Ltd.
PO Box 128
2 Main St.
St Gregor, SK S0K 3X0
306-366-2116
Fax: 306-366-2032

St Josaphat's Parish (Toronto) Credit Union Limited
12 Parkman Ave.
Toronto, ON M6P 3R5
416-536-2643
Fax: 416-536-4989
stjos@pathcom.com
Year Founded: 1950

St. Joseph's Credit Union
PO Box 159
3552 Hwy. 206
Petit de Grat, NS B0E 2L0
902-226-2288
Fax: 902-226-9855
866-876-3192
www.stjosephscreditu.ca
Year Founded: 1936
Number of Employees: 12

St Mary's (Toronto) Credit Union Limited
832 Bloor St. West
Toronto, ON M6G 1M2
416-537-2163
Fax: 416-537-7730
smcu@stmarys-cu.com
www.stmarys-cu.com
Year Founded: 1950

St. Mary's Paperworkers Credit Union
75 Huron St.
Sault Ste Marie, ON P6A 5P4
705-541-2438
Fax: 705-942-6427
baile_s@stmarys-paper.com
Ownership: Private. Closed Bond.
Year Founded: 1953
Number of Employees: 1
Assets: Under $1 million
Revenues: Under $1 million

St. Stanislaus & St. Casimir's Polish Parishes Credit Union Ltd.
220 Roncesvalles Ave.
Toronto, ON M6R 2L7
416-537-2181
Fax: 416-536-8525
info@polcu.com
www.polcan.com
Former Name: Polish (St Catharines) Credit Union Limited
Year Founded: 1951
Number of Employees: 3

Sandhills Credit Union
PO Box 249
Leader, SK S0N 1H0
306-628-3687
Fax: 306-628-3674
info@sandhills.cu.sk.ca
www.sandhillscu.com
Ownership: Member-owned

Sandy Lake Credit Union
PO Box 129
102 Main St.
Sandy Lake, MB R0J 1X0
204-585-2609
Fax: 204-585-2163
slcunion@slcu.mb.ca
www.slcu.mb.ca

Sanford Credit Union
7 Mellow St.
Sanford, MB R0G 2J0
204-736-2373
Fax: 204-736-4108
info@sanfordcu.mb.ca
www.sanfordcu.mb.ca
Year Founded: 1950

Saskatoon City Employees Credit Union
222 - 3rd Ave. North
Saskatoon, SK S7K 0J5
306-975-3280
Fax: 306-975-7806
www.scecu.com
Former Name: Saskatoon City Employee Credit Union Ltd.
Year Founded: 1947
Number of Employees: 9
Assets: $10-50 million
Revenues: $1-5 million

SaskCentral
PO Box 3030
2055 Albert St.
Regina, SK S4P 3G8
306-566-1200
Fax: 306-566-1372
1-866-403-7499
info@saskcentral.com
www.saskcu.com
Ownership: Owned by Saskatchewan credit unions
Assets: $1-10 billion

Saugeen Community Credit Union Limited
PO Box 708
118 Queen St. South
Durham, ON N0G 1R0
519-369-2931
Fax: 519-369-2994
durhamcu@saugeencreditunion.com
www.saugeencreditunion.com

Scarborough Hospitals Employees' Credit Union Ltd.
#504, 3050 Lawrence Ave. East
Toronto, ON M1O 2T7
416-438-2911
Fax: 416-431-8131
fran.carolyn@sympatico.ca
Year Founded: 1964

Servus Credit Union
#300, 8723 - 82 Ave.
Edmonton, AB T6C 0Y9
780-496-2000
Fax: 780-468-5220
877-496-2151
Other Contact Information: askafinancialplanner@servuscu.ca (Financial Planning); 780-450-9647 (TTY for the hearing impaired)
info@servuscu.ca; careers@servuscu.ca
www.servuscu.ca
Ownership: Member-owned
Year Founded: 1938
Assets: $1-10 billion

Sharons Credit Union
1055 Kingsway
Vancouver, BC V5V 3C7
604-873-6490
Fax: 604-873-6498
sharons@sharonscu.ca
www.sharonscu.ca
Year Founded: 1988
Number of Employees: 30
Assets: $100-500 million

Shaunavon Credit Union
399 Centre St.
Shaunavon, SK S0N 2N0
306-297-2635
Fax: 306-297-3137
800-667-0068
shaunavon.cu@sasktel.net
www.shaunavoncu.sk.ca
Ownership: Member-owned
Year Founded: 1944

Shell Employees Credit Union Limited
PO Box 100, M Stn. M
Calgary, AB T2P 2H5
403-691-3817
Fax: 403-262-4009
Other Contact Information: Toll Free: 1-877-582-6222 (AB only)
shellcu@shellcu.com
www.shellcu.com
Ownership: Member-owned
Year Founded: 1953

Sheridan Park Credit Union Ltd.
2251 Speakman Dr.
Mississauga, ON L5K 1B2
905-823-1263
Fax: 905-823-8661
spcu@primus.ca
www.spcu.ca

Smiths Falls Community Credit Union Limited
1 Beckwith St. North
Smiths Falls, ON K7A 2B2
613-283-3835
Fax: 613-283-9623
Year Founded: 1951

SOC Savings & Credit Union Ltd.
Eau Claire Place I
525 - 3 Ave. SW
Calgary, AB T2P 0G4
403-509-4078
Fax: 403-509-4299

So-Use Credit Union
2265 Bloor St. West
Toronto, ON M6S 1P1
416-763-5575
Fax: 416-761-9604
800-322-9274
so-use.info@so-use.com
www.so-use.com
Year Founded: 1950

South Calgary Savings & Credit Union Limited
4810 - 16th St. SW
Calgary, AB T2T 4J5
403-243-5224
Fax: 403-287-9189
Ownership: Member-owned

South Interlake Credit Union Ltd.
233 Main St.
Selkirk, MB R1A 1S1
204-785-7625
Fax: 204-785-7649
www.sicu.mb.ca

Ownership: Member-owned
Year Founded: 1944
Number of Employees: 106
Assets: $100-500 million

Southlake Regional Health Centre Employees' Credit Union Limited
596 Davis Dr.
Newmarket, ON L0G 1V0
905-895-4521
Fax: 905-853-2218
Former Name: York County Hospital Employees' (Newmarket) Credit Union Limited
Number of Employees: 1

Southwest Regional Credit Union
1205 Exmouth St.
Sarnia, ON N7S 1W7
519-383-8001
Fax: 519-383-8841
info@southwestcu.com
www.southwestcu.com
Year Founded: 1989
Number of Employees: 30

Spalding Savings & Credit Union Ltd.
111 Centre St.
Spalding, SK S0K 4C0
306-872-2050
Fax: 306-872-2100
Year Founded: 1941

Spiritwood Credit Union Ltd.
PO Box 129
Spiritwood, SK S0J 2M0
306-883-2250
Fax: 306-883-2223
877-288-1414
contactus@spiritwood.cu.sk.ca
www.spiritwoodcu.com
Ownership: Member-owned
Year Founded: 1938

Spruce Credit Union
879 Victoria St.
Prince George, BC V2L 2K7
250-562-5415
sprucecu@cucbc.com
www.sprucecu.bc.ca
Number of Employees: 30
Assets: $50-100 million

Squamish Credit Union
PO Box 1940
38085 - 2nd St.
Squamish, BC V0N 3G0
604-892-8355
Fax: 604-892-8377
877-892-5288
squamishsavings.com
Ownership: Private

Stanco Credit Union Ltd.
Chevron Plaza, Room 759
500 - 5 Ave. SW
Calgary, AB T2P 0L7
403-234-5300
Fax: 403-234-5823
info@stancocu.com
www.stancocu.com
Number of Employees: 1
Assets: $1-5 million
Revenues: Under $1 million

Standard Tube Employees' (Woodstock) Credit Union Limited
273 Ingersoll Ave.
Woodstock, ON N4S 4W7
519-537-8121
Fax: 519-537-8099
stucrun@execulink.com
Year Founded: 1948

Starbuck Credit Union
16 Main St.
Starbuck, MB R0G 2P0
204-735-2394
Fax: 204-735-4020
866-398-9642
info@starbuckcreditunion.com
www.starbuckcreditunion.com
Year Founded: 1940
Assets: $50-100 million

Starnews Credit Union Limited
1 Yonge St.
Toronto, ON M5E 1E5
416-366-5534
Fax: 416-366-6225
877-782-7639
inquiries@starnewscu.com
www.starnewscu.com

State Farm (Toronto) Credit Union Limited
333 First Commerce Dr.
Aurora, ON L4G 8A4
905-750-4100
Fax: 905-750-4487
Year Founded: 1968

Steel Centre Credit Union
340 Prince St.
Sydney, NS B1P 5K9
902-562-5559
Fax: 902-539-6024
www.sccu.ca
Year Founded: 1993

Steinbach Credit Union
305 Main St.
Steinbach, MB R5G 1B1
204-326-3495
Fax: 204-326-3102
800-728-6440
scu@scu.mb.ca
www.scu.mb.ca
Ownership: Member-owned
Year Founded: 1941
Assets: $1-10 billion
Revenues: $50-100 million

Stelco Finishing Works Credit Union Limited
1013 King St. East
Hamilton, ON L8M 1C9
905-547-8724
Fax: 905-547-4742
stelcocu@stelcocu.ca
www.stelcocu.ca

Stoughton Credit Union Ltd.
PO Box 420
Stoughton, SK S0G 4T0
306-457-2443
Fax: 306-457-2511
info@stoughton.cu.sk.ca
www.stoughtoncu.com
Year Founded: 1960
Number of Employees: 9
Assets: $10-50 million
Revenues: $1-5 million

Strathclair Credit Union
PO Box 246
Strathclair, MB R0J 2C0
204-365-4700
Fax: 204-365-4710
info@strathclaircu.mb.ca
www.strathclaircu.mb.ca

Strathfiner Credit Union Ltd.
PO Box 1020
Edmonton, AB T5J 2M1
780-449-8295
Fax: 780-449-8174
sfcu@datanet.ab.ca
Ownership: Member-owned. Closed bond.
Year Founded: 1954
Number of Employees: 1
Assets: $1-5 million
Revenues: Under $1 million

Sudbury Credit Union
Also listed under: *Financing & Loan Companies*
PO Box 662
1 Gribble St.
Copper Cliff, ON P0M 1N0
705-682-0641
Fax: 705-682-1348
info@sudburycu.com
www.sudburycu.com
Former Name: Sudbury Regional Credit Union
Ownership: Member-owned
Year Founded: 1951
Assets: $100-500 million

Summerland & District Credit Union
PO Box 750
13601 Victoria Rd. North
Summerland, BC V0H 1Z0
250-494-7181
Fax: 250-494-4261
sdcu@sdcu.com
www.sdcu.com
Year Founded: 1944
Number of Employees: 39

Sunnybrook Credit Union Limited
c/o Sunnybrook Health Sciences Centre
#CB02, 2075 Bayview Ave.
Toronto, ON M4N 3M5
416-480-4467
Fax: 416-480-5908
info@sunnybrookcu.com
www.sunnybrookcu.com
Year Founded: 1950

SunRise Credit Union
356 South Railway St.
Boissevain, MB R0K 0E0
204-534-2421
Fax: 204-534-6310
Former Name: Turtle Mountain Credit Union

Sunshine Coast Credit Union
Also listed under: *Financial Planning & Investment Management Companies*
PO Box 799
985 Sunshine Coast Hwy.
Gibsons, BC V0N 1V0
604-886-2122
Fax: 604-886-0797
1-866-886-2132
administration@sunshineccu.net
www.sunshineccu.com
Ownership: Member-owned
Year Founded: 1941
Number of Employees: 83
Assets: $100-500 million
Revenues: $100-500 million

Superior Credit Union Limited
318 South Syndicate Ave.
Thunder Bay, ON P7E 1E3
807-624-2255
info@supercu.com
www.supercu.com
Year Founded: 1997

Sydenham Community Credit Union Limited
32 Front St. East
Strathroy, ON N7G 1Y4
519-245-2530
Fax: 519-245-0167
info@sydenhamccu.on.ca
www.sydenhamccu.on.ca
Year Founded: 1957

Sydney Credit Union
PO Box 1386
95 Townsend St.
Sydney, NS B1P 6K3
902-562-5593
Fax: 902-539-8448
sydney@sydney.creditu.net
www.sydneycreditunion.com
Ownership: Member-owned
Year Founded: 1935

Taiwanese - Canadian Toronto Credit Union Limited
Also listed under: *Financing & Loan Companies*
Metro Square
#305, 3636 Steeles Ave. East
Markham, ON L3R 1K9
905-944-0981
Fax: 905-944-0982
866-889-8893
tcu@on.aibn.com
www.tctcu.com
Ownership: Member-owned
Year Founded: 1978
Number of Employees: 5
Assets: $5-10 million
Revenues: Under $1 million

Talka Lithuanian Credit Union Limited
830 Main St. East
Hamilton, ON L8M 1L6
905-544-7125
Fax: 905-544-7126
www.talka.ca
Former Name: Talka Hamilton Credit Union
Year Founded: 1955

Teachers Credit Union
75 James St. South
Hamilton, ON L8P 2Y9
905-525-8090
Fax: 905-525-7422
877-427-1281
www.teacherscu.on.ca
Former Name: Hamilton Teachers Credit Union Limited
Ownership: Private

Teachers Plus Credit Union
36 Brookshire Ct.
Bedford, NS B4A 4E9
902-477-5664
Fax: 902-477-4108
800-565-3103
info@teachersplus.ca
www.teachersplus.ca
Former Name: Nova Scotia Teachers Credit Union
Year Founded: 1956
Number of Employees: 11
Assets: $10-50 million

Thamesville Community Credit Union
84 London Rd.
Thamesville, ON N0P 2K0
519-692-3855
Fax: 519-692-9532
info@thamesvilleccu.ca
www.thamesvilleccu.ca
Ownership: Member-owned
Year Founded: 1955

Thorold Community Credit Union
63 Front St. South
Thorold, ON L2V 3Z3
905-227-1106
Fax: 905-227-1109
www.thoroldcu.com

Thunder Bay Elevators Employees' Credit Union Limited
417 Fort William Rd.
Thunder Bay, ON P7B 2Z5
807-345-2471
Fax: 807-344-0829
elevatorcreditunion@tbaytel.net
Year Founded: 1953

Toronto Catholic School Board Employees' Credit Union Ltd.
80 Sheppard Ave. East
Toronto, ON M2N 6E8
416-229-5315
Fax: 416-512-3427
tcsbecu-info@tcsbecu.com
www.tcsbecu.com
Former Name: Metropolitan Separate School Board Employees Credit Union Limited
Ownership: Private
Year Founded: 1972
Number of Employees: 7
Assets: $10-50 million

The Toronto Electrical Utilities Credit Union Limited
14 Carlton St.
Toronto, ON M5B 1K5
416-542-2522
Fax: 416-542-2735
teucu@teucu.com
www.teucu.com
Ownership: Member-owned
Year Founded: 1941
Number of Employees: 8

Toronto Municipal Employees' Credit Union Limited
City Hall
PO Box 30
100 Queen St. West, Main Fl.
Toronto, ON M5H 2N2
416-392-6868
Fax: 416-392-6895
www.tmecu.com
Year Founded: 1940

Tri-Island Credit Union
PO Box 580
1 Rink Rd.
Twillingate, NL A0G 4M0
709-884-2704
Fax: 709-884-2026
www.triislandcu.com
Year Founded: 1986
Number of Employees: 10

Turtleford Credit Union Ltd.
PO Box 370
208 Main St.
Turtleford, SK S0M 2Y0
306-845-2105
Fax: 306-845-3035
info@turtleford.cu.sk.ca
www.turtleford.cu.sk.ca

Twin Oak Credit Union Ltd.
PO Box 463
1045 Industry St.
Oakville, ON L6J 5A8
905-845-3441
Fax: 905-845-2155
877-894-6625
industry@twinoakcu.com
www.twinoakcu.com
Year Founded: 1954
Number of Employees: 11
Assets: $10-50 million

Ukrainian (St Catharines) Credit Union Limited (USCCU)
118 Niagara St.
St Catharines, ON L2R 4L4
905-684-5062
Fax: 905-684-3098
bruce@hroshi.com
www.hroshi.com
Year Founded: 1946

Unigasco Credit Union Limited
40 Keil Dr. South
Chatham, ON N7M 3G8
519-436-4590
Fax: 519-436-5451
800-592-9592
www.unigasco.com
Year Founded: 1952
Number of Employees: 23

Union Bay Credit Union
PO Box 158
313 McLeod Rd.
Union Bay, BC V0R 3B0
250-335-2122
Fax: 250-335-2131
www.unionbaycreditunion.com
Ownership: Member-owned
Year Founded: 1944

United Employees Credit Union Limited
964 Eastern Ave.
Toronto, ON M4L 1A6
416-461-9257
Fax: 416-461-8141
infounited@unitedcu.com
www.unitedcu.com
Year Founded: 1946
Number of Employees: 10

Unity Credit Union Ltd.
PO Box 370
120 - 2nd Ave. East
Unity, SK S0K 4L0
306-228-2688
Fax: 306-228-2185
info@unity.cu.sk.ca
www.unity.cu.sk.ca
Year Founded: 1941
Number of Employees: 31
Assets: $50-100 million
Revenues: $1-5 million

Unity Savings & Credit Union Limited
Central Management Support Office, Bayridge Centre West
775 Strand Blvd.
Kingston, ON K7P 2S7
613-389-9965
unityone@unitysavings.com
www.unitysavings.com
Number of Employees: 23

University Hospitals Staff Credit Union Ltd.
8440 - 112 St.
Edmonton, AB T6G 2B7
780-407-8151
Fax: 780-407-7557
chauah@telus.net
Year Founded: 1949
Number of Employees: 3
Assets: $5-10 million
Revenues: Under $1 million

Utilities Employees' (Windsor) Credit Union Limited
4545 Rhodes Dr.
Windsor, ON N8W 5T1
519-945-5141
Fax: 519-945-0347

Valley Credit Union
PO Box 70
5682 Hwy. #1
Waterville, NS B0P 1V0
902-538-4510
Fax: 902-538-4529
www.valleycreditunion.com
Year Founded: 1994

Valley First Financial Group
184 Main St., 3rd Fl.
Penticton, BC V2A 8G7
250-490-2720
Fax: 250-490-2721
800-567-8111
info@valleyfirst.com
www.valleyfirst.com
Also Known As: Valley Field Credit Union
Year Founded: 2001
Assets: $500m-1 billion

Van Tel/Safeway Credit Union
#2010, 4330 Kingsway
Burnaby, BC V5H 4G8
604-656-6200
Fax: 604-656-6167
800-663-1557
Former Name: Van Tel Credit Union
Year Founded: 1940
Number of Employees: 70+
Assets: $100-500 million

Vancouver City Savings Credit Union
PO Box 2120, Terminal Stn. Terminal
183 Terminal Ave.
Vancouver, BC V6B 5R8
604-877-7000
Fax: 604-877-7639
888-826-2489
vc_editor@vancity.com
www.vancity.com
Also Known As: VanCity Credit Union
Year Founded: 1946
Assets: $1-10 billion

Vanguard Credit Union
Also listed under: *Financing & Loan Companies; Investment Management*
PO Box 490
47 Main St.
Rossburn, MB R0J 1V0
204-859-5010
Fax: 204-859-5020
contact@vanguardcu.mb.ca
www.vanguardcu.mb.ca
Ownership: Member-owned
Year Founded: 1947
Number of Employees: 92
Assets: $100-500 million
Revenues: $5-10 million

Vermilion Credit Union Ltd.
5019 - 50 Ave.
Vermilion, AB T9X 1A7
780-853-2822
Fax: 780-853-4361
vermilion@alberta-cu.com
www.vermilioncreditunion.com

Vernon & District Credit Union
Also listed under: *Financing & Loan Companies; Investment Management*
3108 - 33rd Ave.
Vernon, BC V1T 2N7
250-545-9251
Fax: 250-545-8166
888-339-8328
info@vdcu.com
www.vdcu.com
Ownership: Co-operative. Member-owned.
Year Founded: 1944
Number of Employees: 45
Assets: $100-500 million
Revenues: $10-50 million

Victory Community Credit Union
#102, 2100 Lawrence Ave. West
Toronto, ON M9N 3W3

416-243-0686
Fax: 416-243-9614
creditunion@vccu.com
www.vccu.com

Year Founded: 1948
Number of Employees: 3
Revenues: $5-10 million

Victory Credit Union
PO Box 340, 41 Water St.
Windsor, NS B0N 2T0

902-798-1820
Fax: 902-798-1255
www.victorycreditunion.ca

Ownership: Cooperative
Number of Employees: 30
Revenues: $10-50 million

Virden Credit Union
PO Box 1660
220 - 7th Ave. South
Virden, MB R0M 2C0

204-748-2907
Fax: 204-748-1081
888-748-2907

Year Founded: 1940
Number of Employees: 58
Assets: $100-500 million

Virtual One Credit Union Ltd.
15 Bronte College Ct.
Mississauga, ON L5B 0E7

905-270-2223
Fax: 905-270-0902
info_cu@virtualonecu.com
www.virtualonecu.com

Year Founded: 1946
Assets: $50-100 million

Wainwright Credit Union
Administration Office
502 - 10 St.
Wainwright, AB T9W 1P4

780-842-9184
Fax: 780-842-2855
www.wainwright-cu.com

Ownership: Member-owned
Year Founded: 1943
Number of Employees: 84
Assets: $100-500 million
Revenues: $10-50 million

Wallace Barnes Employees' Credit Union Limited
3100 Mainway Dr.
Burlington, ON L7M 1A3

905-335-6688
Fax: 905-336-1336

Ownership: Private
Year Founded: 1943
Number of Employees: 1
Assets: Under $1 million
Revenues: Under $1 million

Westminster Savings Credit Union
Corporate Centre
#108, 960 Quayside Dr.
New Westminster, BC V3M 6G2

604-517-0100
Fax: 604-528-3812
www.wscu.com

Ownership: Member-owned
Year Founded: 1944
Number of Employees: 357
Assets: $1-10 billion
Revenues: $50-100 million

Westoba Credit Union Limited
#C, 220 - 10th St.
Brandon, MB R7A 4E8

204-729-2050
Fax: 204-729-8852
infowcul@westoba.com
www.westoba.com

Ownership: Member-owned
Year Founded: 1963
Number of Employees: 200
Assets: $500m-1 billion
Revenues: $10-50 million

Weyburn Credit Union Limited
PO Box 1117, 221 Coteau Ave.
Weyburn, SK S4H 2L3

306-842-6641
Fax: 306-842-6620
800-667-8842
info@weyburn.cu.sk.ca
www.weyburn.cu.sk.ca

Ownership: Member-owned
Year Founded: 1944
Assets: $1-5 million
Revenues: $1-5 million

Weymouth Credit Union
PO Box 411
4569 Hwy. #1
Weymouth, NS B0W 3T0

902-837-4089
Fax: 902-837-4089

William S. Gibson Employees' Credit Union (Mt. Dennis) Limited
1551 Weston Rd.
Toronto, ON M6M 4Y4

416-246-6704

Williams Lake & District Credit Union
139 North 3rd Ave.
Williams Lake, BC V2G 2A5

250-392-4135
Fax: 250-392-4361
info@wldcu.com
www.wldcu.com

Year Founded: 1952
Number of Employees: 12

Windsor Family Credit Union
2800 Tecumseth Rd East
Windsor, ON N8W 1G4

519-974-3100
Fax: 519-974-4077
info@windsorfamily.com
www.windsorfamily.com

Windsor-Essex County Catholic Parishes Credit Union Ltd.
2275 Wellesley Ave.
Windsor, ON N8W 2G1

519-256-7555
Fax: 519-256-6524
cathcu@mnsi.net

Winnipeg Police Credit Union Ltd.
300 William Ave.
Winnipeg, MB R3A 1P9

204-944-1033
Fax: 204-949-0821
866-491-7122
www.policecu.mb.ca

Year Founded: 1949

York Credit Union
494 Queen St.
Fredericton, NB E3B 1B6

506-458-8844
Fax: 506-452-8496
membersfirst@york.creditu.net
www.yorkcu.nb.ca

Year Founded: 1953

Your Credit Union Limited
14 Chamberlain Ave
Ottawa, ON K1S 1V9

613-238-8001
Fax: 613-238-2149
800-379-7757
info@yourcu.com
www.yourcu.com

Ownership: Member-owned

Your Neighbourhood Credit Union Ltd.
5415 Tecumseh Rd. East
Windsor, ON N8T 1C5

519-258-3890
Fax: 519-945-5933
info@yncu.com
www.yncu.com

Former Name: Windsor & Essex Educational Credit Union
Year Founded: 1953

Insurance Companies

Insurance companies are registered to conduct business under the federal Insurance Companies Act and/ or corresponding provincial legislation. Life insurance companies are registered to underwrite life insurance, accident and sickness insurance and annuity business. Property and casualty insurance companies are registered to underwrite insurance other than life insurance.

Included in these listings are federally and provincially incorporated insurance companies, reinsurance companies, fraternal benefit societies and reciprocal exchanges, with the classes of insurance they offer.

*Companies marked with an * are provincially incorporated. For provincially incorporated companies not listed below, contact the government agency for each province. For further information, please see the "Government Quick Reference" guide at the beginning of Section 7, and check under "Insurance".*

CLASSES OF INSURANCE
Classes of insurance indicated in the listings below may be one of more of the following: Accident, Auto, Aircraft, Boiler & Machinery, Credit, Fidelity, Fire, Hail & Crop, Legal Expense, Liability, Life, Marine, Personal Accident & Sickness, Property, Reinsurance, Surety, and Theft.

Accident

ACA Assurance
ACE INA Insurance
American Bankers Life Assurance Company of Florida
American Re-Insurance Company
Assumption Mutual Life Insurance Company
Ayr Farmers Mutual Insurance Company
Caisse Centrale de Réassurance
Canadian Professional Sales Association
CIGNA Life Insurance Company of Canada
The Citadel General Assurance Company
Connecticut General Life Insurance Co.
Constitution Insurance Company of Canada
Continental Casualty Company
CUMIS Life Insurance Company
Desjardins Financial Security
Echelon General Insurance Company
Empire Life Insurance Company
L'Entraide assurance, compagnie mutuelle
FaithLife Financial
Federated Insurance Company of Canada
Federation Insurance Company of Canada
Granite Insurance Company
The Guarantee Company of North America
Industrial Alliance Pacific Life Insurance Company
Life Insurance Company of North America
London & Midland General Insurance Company
The Nordic Insurance Company of Canada
OdysseyRe - Canadian Branch
Old Republic Insurance Company of Canada
Optimum Reassurance Company
Pacific Blue Cross
Peace Hills General Insurance Company
Pembridge Insurance Company
Promutuel Réassurance
Promutuel Vie inc
Québec Blue Cross
Saskatchewan Motor Club Insurance Company Ltd.
SGI CANADA Consolidated
Société de l'assurance automobile du Québec
South Easthope Mutual Insurance Co.
SSQ, Société d'assurances générales inc.
SSQ, Société d'assurance-vie inc
Tradition Mutual Insurance Company
Trillium Mutual Insurance Company
Union of Canada Life Insurance
Western Financial Group Inc.
Zurich Canada

Aircraft

ACE INA Insurance
American Home Assurance Company
Avemco Insurance Company
Aviation & General Insurance Company Limited
Aviva Canada Inc.
AXA Corporate Solutions Assurance
AXA General Insurance Company
AXA Insurance (Canada)
AXA Pacific Insurance Company
AXA RE Canada
Berkley Insurance Company
Caisse Centrale de Réassurance
Canadian Universities Reciprocal Insurance Exchange
Chubb Insurance Company of Canada
Commonwealth Insurance Company
Continental Casualty Company
Co-operators General Insurance Company
Eagle Star Insurance Company Ltd.
Elite Insurance Company
Employers Reinsurance Corporation
Everest Insurance Company of Canada
Everest Reinsurance Company
GCAN Insurance Company
General Reinsurance Corporation
Global Aerospace Underwriting Managers (Canada) Limited
Great American Insurance Company
Hannover Rückversicherungs AG
Hartford Fire Insurance Company
Henderson Insurance Inc.
Johnston Meier Insurance Agencies Group
Liberty Mutual Insurance Company
Liberty Mutual Insurance Company
Lloyd's Underwriters
Lombard General Insurance Company of Canada
Lombard Insurance Company
Mitsui Sumitomo Insurance Co., Limited.
OdysseyRe - Canadian Branch
Old Republic Insurance Company of Canada
Omega General Insurance Company
Oxford Mutual Insurance Company
Peace Hills General Insurance Company
The Personal Insurance Company
Revios Reinsurance
SGI CANADA Consolidated
State Farm Canada
TD General Insurance Company
Travelers - Canada
Wedgwood Insurance Limited
Western Assurance Company
XL Reinsurance America Inc.

Auto

ACE INA Insurance
Alberta Motor Association Insurance Co.
Algoma Insurance Group
Algoma Mutual Insurance Co.
Alliance Assurance
Allstate Insurance Company of Canada
L'ALPHA, compagnie d'assurances inc.
Alpine Insurance & Financial Inc.
American Home Assurance Company
American Re-Insurance Company
The American Road Insurance Company
Astro Insurance 1000 Inc.
Atlantic Insurance Company Limited
Aviva Canada Inc.
A-WIN Insurance Network
AXA Corporate Solutions Assurance
AXA General Insurance Company
AXA Insurance (Canada)
AXA Pacific Insurance Company
AXA RE Canada
Ayr Farmers Mutual Insurance Company
Bay of Quinte Mutual Insurance Co.
Belair Insurance Company Inc.
Berkley Insurance Company
Bertie and Clinton Mutual Insurance Company
Brant Mutual Insurance Company
British Columbia Automobile Association Insurance Agency
Butler Byers Insurance Ltd.
CAA Insurance Company (Ontario)
Caisse Centrale de Réassurance
Canadian Northern Shield Insurance Company
Canadian Petroleum Insurance Exchange Ltd.
Canadian Professional Sales Association
La Capitale General Insurance Inc.
Caradoc Delaware Mutual Fire Insurance Company
Carleton Mutual Insurance Company
Cavell Insurance Company Limited
Certas Direct Insurance Company
Chrysler Insurance Company
Chubb Insurance Company of Canada
The Citadel General Assurance Company
Coachman Insurance Company
Coastal Community Insurance Services (2007) Ltd.
La Compagnie d'Assurance Missisquoi
Constitution Insurance Company of Canada
Continental Casualty Company
Co-operators General Insurance Company
COSECO Insurance Company
Cowan Insurance Group Ltd.
Crowsnest Insurance Agencies Ltd.
CUMIS General Insurance Company
The CUMIS Group Limited
CUMIS Life Insurance Company
Desjardins assurances générales inc
The Dominion of Canada General Insurance Company
Dufferin Mutual Insurance Company
Dumfries Mutual Insurance Company
Eagle Star Insurance Company Ltd.
Ecclesiastical Insurance Office plc
Echelon General Insurance Company
Economical Mutual Insurance Company
Elite Insurance Company
Employers Reinsurance Corporation
Erie Mutual Fire Insurance Company
Everest Insurance Company of Canada
Everest Reinsurance Company
Farmers' Mutual Insurance Company (Lindsay)
Federal Insurance Company
Federated Insurance Company of Canada
Federation Insurance Company of Canada
Fenchurch General Insurance Company
First North American Insurance Company
Folksamerica Reinsurance Company
Fundy Mutual Insurance Company
GCAN Insurance Company
General Reinsurance Corporation
Germania Farmers' Mutual Fire Insurance Co.
Gibb's Agencies (1997) Ltd.
Glengarry Farmers' Mutual Fire Insurance Co.
Gore Mutual Insurance Company
Granite Insurance Company
Great American Insurance Company
Grenville Mutual Insurance Company
Grey & Bruce Mutual Insurance Co.
Le Groupe Estrie-Richelieu, compagnie d'assurance
The Guarantee Company of North America
Halwell Mutual Insurance Company
Hannover Rückversicherungs AG
Hartford Fire Insurance Company
Hay Mutual Insurance Company
Henderson Insurance Inc.
Howard Mutual Insurance Co.
Howick Mutual Insurance Company
Industrial Alliance Insurance & Financial Services Inc.
Insurance Company of Prince Edward Island
Insurance Corporation of British Columbia
Intact Insurance Company of Canada - Novex Group Insurance
JEVCO Insurance Company
Johnston Meier Insurance Agencies Group
Kent & Essex Mutual Insurance Company
Kingsway Financial Services Inc.
Kingsway General Insurance Company
Kirkham Insurance
Lambton Mutual Insurance Company
Lanark Mutual Insurance Company
Lennox & Addington Mutual Insurance Company
Liberty Mutual Insurance Company
Liberty Mutual Insurance Company
Lloyd's Underwriters
Lombard General Insurance Company of Canada
Lombard Insurance Company
London & Midland General Insurance Company
Manitoba Public Insurance
Markel Insurance Company of Canada
McFarlane & Company Financial Group Limited
McKillop Mutual Insurance Company
Mennonite Mutual Insurance Co. (Alberta) Ltd.
Metro General Insurance Corp.
Middlesex Mutual Insurance Co.
Millennium Insurance Corporation
Mitsui Sumitomo Insurance Co., Limited.
Motors Insurance Corporation
Munich Reinsurance Company of Canada
The Nordic Insurance Company of Canada
Norfolk Mutual Insurance Company
North Bleinheim Mutual Insurance Co.
North Blenheim Mutual Insurance Company
North Kent Mutual Fire Insurance Company
The North Waterloo Farmers Mutual Insurance Company
OdysseyRe - Canadian Branch
Old Republic Insurance Company of Canada
Ontario Mutual Insurance Association

Ontario School Boards' Insurance Exchange
Optimum Assurance Agricole inc
Optimum Général inc
Optimum Société d'Assurance inc
Oxford Mutual Insurance Company
Pafco Insurance Company
PartnerRe SA
PC Financial Insurance Agency
Peace Hills General Insurance Company
Peel Mutual Insurance Company
The Personal General Insurance Inc.
The Personal Insurance Company
Perth Insurance Company
Pilot Insurance Company
The Portage La Prairie Mutual Insurance Company
Primmum Insurance Company
Progressive Casualty Insurance Company
Protective Insurance Company
Québec Blue Cross
RBC General Insurance Company
RBC Insurance
Revios Reinsurance
Saskatchewan Auto Fund
Saskatchewan Mutual Insurance Company
Scottish & York Insurance Co. Limited
Security National Insurance Company
SGI CANADA Consolidated
Société de l'assurance automobile du Québec
South Easthope Mutual Insurance Co.
SSQ Financial Group
SSQ, Société d'assurances générales inc.
SSQ, Société d'assurance-vie inc
Stanley Mutual Insurance Company
State Farm Canada
Suecia Reinsurance Company
TD General Insurance Company
TD Home and Auto Insurance Company
Thomson-Schindle-Green Insurance & Financial Services Ltd.
The Tokio Marine & Nichido Fire Insurance Co., Ltd.
Town & Country Mutual Insurance
Townsend Farmers' Mutual Fire Insurance Company
Traders General Insurance Company
Tradition Mutual Insurance Company
Travelers - Canada
Trillium Mutual Insurance Company
Unifund Assurance Company
L'Union Canadienne Compagnie d'Assurances
United General Insurance Corporation
Virginia Surety Company, Inc.
Wabisa Mutual Insurance Company
Waterloo Insurance Company
The Wawanesa Mutual Insurance Company
Wedgwood Insurance Limited
West Elgin Mutual Insurance Company
West Wawanosh Mutual Insurance Company
Western Assurance Company
Western Financial Group Inc.
Westland Insurance
Westminster Mutual Insurance Company
XL Insurance Company Limited
XL Reinsurance America Inc.
Yarmouth Mutual Fire Insurance Company
York Fire & Casualty Insurance Company
Zenith Insurance Company
Zurich Canada

Boiler & Machinery

ACE INA Insurance
Affiliated FM Insurance Company
Algoma Insurance Group
Allstate Insurance Company of Canada
American Home Assurance Company
American Re-Insurance Company
The American Road Insurance Company
L'Assurance Mutuelle des Fabriques de Montréal
Atlantic Insurance Company Limited
Aviva Canada Inc.
AXA Corporate Solutions Assurance
AXA General Insurance Company
AXA Insurance (Canada)
AXA Pacific Insurance Company
AXA RE Canada
Ayr Farmers Mutual Insurance Company
Bay of Quinte Mutual Insurance Co.
Belair Insurance Company Inc.
Berkley Insurance Company
Bertie and Clinton Mutual Insurance Company
The Boiler Inspection & Insurance Company of Canada
Brant Mutual Insurance Company
Caisse Centrale de Réassurance
Canadian Farm Insurance Corp.
Caradoc Delaware Mutual Fire Insurance Company
Cavell Insurance Company Limited
Chubb Insurance Company of Canada
Commonwealth Insurance Company
La Compagnie d'Assurance Missisquoi
Continental Casualty Company
Co-operators General Insurance Company
CUMIS General Insurance Company
Desjardins assurances générales inc
Dufferin Mutual Insurance Company
Dumfries Mutual Insurance Company
Eagle Star Insurance Company Ltd.
Ecclesiastical Insurance Office plc
Economical Mutual Insurance Company
Elite Insurance Company
Employers Reinsurance Corporation
Erie Mutual Fire Insurance Company
Everest Insurance Company of Canada
Everest Reinsurance Company
Farmers' Mutual Insurance Company (Lindsay)
Federal Insurance Company
Federated Insurance Company of Canada
Federation Insurance Company of Canada
Fenchurch General Insurance Company
FM Global
Fundy Mutual Insurance Company
GCAN Insurance Company
General Reinsurance Corporation
Germania Farmers' Mutual Fire Insurance Co.
Glengarry Farmers' Mutual Fire Insurance Co.
Grain Insurance and Guarantee Company
Granite Insurance Company
Great American Insurance Company
Grenville Mutual Insurance Company
Grey & Bruce Mutual Insurance Co.
Le Groupe Estrie-Richelieu, compagnie d'assurance
The Guarantee Company of North America
Halwell Mutual Insurance Company
Hannover Rückversicherungs AG
Hartford Fire Insurance Company
Howick Mutual Insurance Company
Intact Insurance Company of Canada - Novex Group Insurance
Kent & Essex Mutual Insurance Company
Lambton Mutual Insurance Company
Lanark Mutual Insurance Company
Liberty Mutual Insurance Company
Liberty Mutual Insurance Company
Lloyd's Underwriters
Lombard General Insurance Company of Canada
Lombard Insurance Company
London & Midland General Insurance Company
Lumbermen's Underwriting Alliance
MAX Canada Insurance Company
McKillop Mutual Insurance Company
Mennonite Mutual Fire Insurance Company
Mitsui Sumitomo Insurance Co., Limited.
Motors Insurance Corporation
The Nordic Insurance Company of Canada
The North Waterloo Farmers Mutual Insurance Company
OdysseyRe - Canadian Branch
Omega General Insurance Company
Ontario School Boards' Insurance Exchange
Oxford Mutual Insurance Company
Peace Hills General Insurance Company
Peel Mutual Insurance Company
The Personal General Insurance Inc.
The Personal Insurance Company
Promutuel Réassurance
Red River Valley Mutual Insurance Co.
Revios Reinsurance
Saskatchewan Mutual Insurance Company
Scottish & York Insurance Co. Limited
SGI CANADA Consolidated
South Easthope Mutual Insurance Co.
Southeastern Mutual Insurance Company
Stanley Mutual Insurance Company
State Farm Canada
TD General Insurance Company
Temple Insurance Company
Town & Country Mutual Insurance
Townsend Farmers' Mutual Fire Insurance Company
Tradition Mutual Insurance Company
Travelers - Canada
Trillium Mutual Insurance Company
Virginia Surety Company, Inc.
The Wawanesa Mutual Insurance Company
West Wawanosh Mutual Insurance Company
Western Assurance Company
Western Financial Group Inc.
XL Insurance Company Limited
XL Reinsurance America Inc.
Zurich Canada

Credit

ACE INA Insurance
American Home Assurance Company
American Re-Insurance Company
The American Road Insurance Company
Assurance-Vie Banque Nationale
Assurant Solutions Canada
AXA Corporate Solutions Assurance
AXA Pacific Insurance Company
Berkley Insurance Company
Canadian Premier Life Insurance Company
CIGNA Life Insurance Company of Canada
Continental Casualty Company
CUMIS Life Insurance Company
Employers Reinsurance Corporation
L'Entraide assurance, compagnie mutuelle
Euler Hermes Canada
Everest Insurance Company of Canada
Everest Reinsurance Company
GCAN Insurance Company
General Reinsurance Corporation
Granite Insurance Company
The Guarantee Company of North America
Industrial Alliance Pacific Life Insurance Company
Intact Insurance Company of Canada - Novex Group Insurance
Lombard General Insurance Company of Canada
Lombard Insurance Company
Omega General Insurance Company
Peace Hills General Insurance Company
The PMI Group, Inc. Canada
Revios Reinsurance
Transatlantic Reinsurance Company
Zurich Canada

Fidelity

ACE INA Insurance
Affiliated FM Insurance Company
Allstate Insurance Company of Canada
American Home Assurance Company
American Re-Insurance Company
ATB Financial
Atlantic Insurance Company Limited
Aviva Canada Inc.
AXA Corporate Solutions Assurance
AXA General Insurance Company
AXA Insurance (Canada)
AXA Pacific Insurance Company
AXA RE Canada
Ayr Farmers Mutual Insurance Company
Bay of Quinte Mutual Insurance Co.
Belair Insurance Company Inc.
Berkley Insurance Company
Bertie and Clinton Mutual Insurance Company
Brant Mutual Insurance Company
Caisse Centrale de Réassurance
Canadian Farm Insurance Corp.
Cavell Insurance Company Limited
Chubb Insurance Company of Canada
The Citadel General Assurance Company
Commonwealth Insurance Company
La Compagnie d'Assurance Missisquoi
Constitution Insurance Company of Canada
Continental Casualty Company
Co-operators General Insurance Company
CUMIS General Insurance Company
CUMIS Life Insurance Company
Dufferin Mutual Insurance Company
Eagle Star Insurance Company Ltd.
Ecclesiastical Insurance Office plc
Echelon General Insurance Company
Elite Insurance Company
Employers Reinsurance Corporation
Erie Mutual Fire Insurance Company
Everest Reinsurance Company
Farmers' Mutual Insurance Company (Lindsay)
Federal Insurance Company
Federated Insurance Company of Canada
Federation Insurance Company of Canada
Folksamerica Reinsurance Company
GCAN Insurance Company
General Reinsurance Corporation
Germania Farmers' Mutual Fire Insurance Co.
Glengarry Farmers' Mutual Fire Insurance Co.
Grain Insurance and Guarantee Company
Granite Insurance Company
Great American Insurance Company
Grenville Mutual Insurance Company
The Guarantee Company of North America

Halwell Mutual Insurance Company
Hannover Rückversicherungs AG
Hartford Fire Insurance Company
Howard Mutual Insurance Co.
Howick Mutual Insurance Company
Intact Insurance Company of Canada - Novex Group Insurance
Kent & Essex Mutual Insurance Company
Lambton Mutual Insurance Company
Liberty Mutual Insurance Company
Liberty Mutual Insurance Company
Lloyd's Underwriters
Lombard General Insurance Company of Canada
Lombard Insurance Company
London & Midland General Insurance Company
MAX Canada Insurance Company
McKillop Mutual Insurance Company
Mitsui Sumitomo Insurance Co., Limited.
The Nordic Insurance Company of Canada
The North Waterloo Farmers Mutual Insurance Company
Omega General Insurance Company
Oxford Mutual Insurance Company
Peace Hills General Insurance Company
Peel Mutual Insurance Company
The Personal Insurance Company
Red River Valley Mutual Insurance Co.
Revios Reinsurance
Saskatchewan Mutual Insurance Company
Scottish & York Insurance Co. Limited
SGI CANADA Consolidated
State Farm Canada
Suecia Reinsurance Company
Swiss Reinsurance Company Canada
TD General Insurance Company
Town & Country Mutual Insurance
Tradition Mutual Insurance Company
Travelers - Canada
Trillium Mutual Insurance Company
Wabisa Mutual Insurance Company
West Elgin Mutual Insurance Company
West Wawanosh Mutual Insurance Company
Western Assurance Company
Western Financial Group Inc.
Western Surety Company
XL Reinsurance America Inc.
Zurich Canada

Fire

ACE INA Insurance
Affiliated FM Insurance Company
Alberta Motor Association Insurance Co.
Antigonish Farmers' Mutual Insurance Company
L'Assurance Mutuelle des Fabriques de Montréal
British Columbia Automobile Association Insurance Agency
Caisse Centrale de Réassurance
Carleton Mutual Insurance Company
The Citadel General Assurance Company
Clare Mutual Insurance Company
La Compagnie d'Assurance Missisquoi
Co-operators General Insurance Company
CUMIS General Insurance Company
CUMIS Life Insurance Company
The Dominion of Canada General Insurance Company
Echelon General Insurance Company
Federated Insurance Company of Canada
Federation Insurance Company of Canada
Germania Mutual Insurance Company
Glengarry Farmers' Mutual Fire Insurance Co.
Gore Mutual Insurance Company
Grain Insurance and Guarantee Company
Granite Insurance Company
Le Groupe Estrie-Richelieu, compagnie d'assurance
The Guarantee Company of North America
Hamilton Township Mutual Insurance Company
Hartford Fire Insurance Company
The Kings Mutual Insurance Company
Lloyd's Underwriters
Lombard Canada Ltd.
Lombard Insurance Company
London & Midland General Insurance Company
Mennonite Mutual Fire Insurance Company
Mennonite Mutual Insurance Co. (Alberta) Ltd.
The Mutual Fire Insurance Company of British Columbia
Norfolk Mutual Insurance Company
North Kent Mutual Fire Insurance Company
The North Waterloo Farmers Mutual Insurance Company
OdysseyRe - Canadian Branch
Ontario School Boards' Insurance Exchange
Optimum Assurance Agricole inc
Peace Hills General Insurance Company
Prince Edward Island Mutual Insurance Company
Promutuel Réassurance
RBC General Insurance Company
Red River Valley Mutual Insurance Co.
Revios Reinsurance
Security National Insurance Company
Southeastern Mutual Insurance Company
SSQ, Société d'assurances générales inc.
SSQ, Société d'assurance-vie inc
State Farm Canada
The Tokio Marine & Nichido Fire Insurance Co., Ltd.
Travelers - Canada
The Wawanesa Mutual Insurance Company
Western Financial Group Inc.
Zurich Canada

Hail & Crop

ACE INA Insurance
Agriculture Financial Services Corporation
American Home Assurance Company
American Re-Insurance Company
Astro Insurance 1000 Inc.
Aviva Canada Inc.
AXA Corporate Solutions Assurance
AXA General Insurance Company
AXA Insurance (Canada)
AXA Pacific Insurance Company
AXA RE Canada
Ayr Farmers Mutual Insurance Company
Berkley Insurance Company
Brant Mutual Insurance Company
Butler Byers Hail Insurance Ltd.
Cavell Insurance Company Limited
Clare Mutual Insurance Company
Continental Casualty Company
Co-operative Hail Insurance Company Ltd.
Co-operators General Insurance Company
Dumfries Mutual Insurance Company
Employers Reinsurance Corporation
Everest Insurance Company of Canada
Everest Reinsurance Company
Federation Insurance Company of Canada
Folksamerica Reinsurance Company
GCAN Insurance Company
General Reinsurance Corporation
Granite Insurance Company
Great American Insurance Company
The Guarantee Company of North America
Hannover Rückversicherungs AG
Hartford Fire Insurance Company
Hay Mutual Insurance Company
Henderson Insurance Inc.
Howard Mutual Insurance Co.
Howick Mutual Insurance Company
Lambton Mutual Insurance Company
Lanark Mutual Insurance Company
Lombard General Insurance Company of Canada
Lombard Insurance Company
Manitoba Agricultural Services Corporation - Insurance Corporate Office
McFarlane & Company Financial Group Limited
North Kent Mutual Fire Insurance Company
The North Waterloo Farmers Mutual Insurance Company
OdysseyRe - Canadian Branch
Oxford Mutual Insurance Company
Palliser Insurance Company Limited
Rain and Hail Insurance Corporation
Revios Reinsurance
Saskatchewan Crop Insurance Corporation
Saskatchewan Municipal Hail Insurance Association
Suecia Reinsurance Company
Thomson-Schindle-Green Insurance & Financial Services Ltd.
Town & Country Mutual Insurance
Townsend Farmers' Mutual Fire Insurance Company
Tradition Mutual Insurance Company
Trillium Mutual Insurance Company
West Elgin Mutual Insurance Company
Western Financial Group Inc.
XL Reinsurance America Inc.
Yarmouth Mutual Fire Insurance Company

Legal Expense

Allstate Insurance Company of Canada
Aviva Canada Inc.
AXA Corporate Solutions Assurance
AXA General Insurance Company
AXA Insurance (Canada)
AXA Pacific Insurance Company
Belair Insurance Company Inc.
Berkley Insurance Company
CAA Insurance Company (Ontario)
Caisse Centrale de Réassurance
La Compagnie d'Assurance Missisquoi
Constitution Insurance Company of Canada
Echelon General Insurance Company
Federation Insurance Company of Canada
Glengarry Farmers' Mutual Fire Insurance Co.
The Guarantee Company of North America
Intact Insurance Company of Canada - Novex Group Insurance
Lloyd's Underwriters
Lombard General Insurance Company of Canada
Lombard Insurance Company
The Nordic Insurance Company of Canada
Omega General Insurance Company
The Portage La Prairie Mutual Insurance Company
Scottish & York Insurance Co. Limited

Liability

ACE INA Insurance
ACE INA Life Insurance
Affiliated FM Insurance Company
Algoma Insurance Group
Alliance Assurance
Allstate Insurance Company of Canada
Alpine Insurance & Financial Inc.
American Home Assurance Company
American Re-Insurance Company
The American Road Insurance Company
Amherst Island Mutual Insurance Company
L'Assurance Mutuelle des Fabriques de Montréal
Astro Insurance 1000 Inc.
Atlantic Insurance Company Limited
Aviation & General Insurance Company Limited
Aviva Canada Inc.
A-WIN Insurance Network
AXA Corporate Solutions Assurance
AXA General Insurance Company
AXA Insurance (Canada)
AXA Pacific Insurance Company
AXA RE Canada
Ayr Farmers Mutual Insurance Company
Bay of Quinte Mutual Insurance Co.
Belair Insurance Company Inc.
Berkley Insurance Company
Bertie and Clinton Mutual Insurance Company
The Boiler Inspection & Insurance Company of Canada
Brant Mutual Insurance Company
CAA Insurance Company (Ontario)
Caisse Centrale de Réassurance
Canadian Direct Insurance Incorporated
Canadian Farm Insurance Corp.
Canadian Lawyers Liability Assurance Society
Canadian Northern Shield Insurance Company
Canadian Petroleum Insurance Exchange Ltd.
Canadian Universities Reciprocal Insurance Exchange
Canassurance Insurance Company
Caradoc Delaware Mutual Fire Insurance Company
Cavell Insurance Company Limited
Certas Direct Insurance Company
Chrysler Insurance Company
Chubb Insurance Company of Canada
The Citadel General Assurance Company
Commonwealth Insurance Company
La Compagnie d'Assurance Missisquoi
Constitution Insurance Company of Canada
Continental Casualty Company
Crowsnest Insurance Agencies Ltd.
Desjardins assurances générales inc
The Dominion of Canada General Insurance Company
Dufferin Mutual Insurance Company
Dumfries Mutual Insurance Company
Eagle Star Insurance Company Ltd.
Ecclesiastical Insurance Office plc
Echelon General Insurance Company
Elite Insurance Company
Employers Reinsurance Corporation
Erie Mutual Fire Insurance Company
Everest Insurance Company of Canada
Everest Reinsurance Company
Farmers' Mutual Insurance Company (Lindsay)
Federal Insurance Company
Federated Insurance Company of Canada
Federation Insurance Company of Canada
Fenchurch General Insurance Company
Folksamerica Reinsurance Company
Frank Cowan Company Limited
Fundy Mutual Insurance Company
GCAN Insurance Company
General Reinsurance Corporation
Germania Farmers' Mutual Fire Insurance Co.
Germania Mutual Insurance Company
Glengarry Farmers' Mutual Fire Insurance Co.
Global Aerospace Underwriting Managers (Canada) Limited
Gore Mutual Insurance Company

Grain Insurance and Guarantee Company
Granite Insurance Company
Great American Insurance Company
Grenville Mutual Insurance Company
Grey & Bruce Mutual Insurance Co.
Le Groupe Estrie-Richelieu, compagnie d'assurance
The Guarantee Company of North America
Halwell Mutual Insurance Company
Hannover Rückversicherungs AG
Hartford Fire Insurance Company
Hay Mutual Insurance Company
Henderson Insurance Inc.
Howard Mutual Insurance Co.
Howick Mutual Insurance Company
Intact Insurance Company of Canada - Novex Group Insurance
Kent & Essex Mutual Insurance Company
The Kings Mutual Insurance Company
Kingsway General Insurance Company
Lambton Mutual Insurance Company
Lanark Mutual Insurance Company
Lawyers' Professional Indemnity Company
Legacy General Insurance Company
Lennox & Addington Mutual Insurance Company
Liberty Mutual Insurance Company
Liberty Mutual Insurance Company
Lloyd's Underwriters
Lombard General Insurance Company of Canada
Lombard Insurance Company
MAX Canada Insurance Company
McFarlane & Company Financial Group Limited
McKillop Mutual Insurance Company
Mennonite Mutual Insurance Co. (Alberta) Ltd.
Metro General Insurance Corp.
Middlesex Mutual Insurance Co.
Mitsui Sumitomo Insurance Co., Limited.
Motors Insurance Corporation
Munich Reinsurance Company of Canada
Municipal Insurance Association of British Columbia
MUNIX Reciprocal
The Nordic Insurance Company of Canada
North Bleinheim Mutual Insurance Co.
North Blenheim Mutual Insurance Company
North Kent Mutual Fire Insurance Company
The North Waterloo Farmers Mutual Insurance Company
OdysseyRe - Canadian Branch
Old Republic Insurance Company of Canada
Omega General Insurance Company
Ontario School Boards' Insurance Exchange
Optimum Général inc
Optimum Société d'Assurance inc
Oxford Mutual Insurance Company
Peace Hills General Insurance Company
Peel Mutual Insurance Company
The Personal General Insurance Inc.
The Personal Insurance Company
Pictou Mutual Insurance Company
The Portage La Prairie Mutual Insurance Company
Premier Marine Insurance Managers Group
Prince Edward Island Mutual Insurance Company
Progressive Casualty Insurance Company
Promutuel Réassurance
Protective Insurance Company
Québec Blue Cross
RBC General Insurance Company
Real Estate Insurance Exchange
Red River Valley Mutual Insurance Co.
Revios Reinsurance
Saskatchewan Mutual Insurance Company
Scottish & York Insurance Co. Limited
SGI CANADA Consolidated
Southeastern Mutual Insurance Company
SSQ, Société d'assurances générales inc.
SSQ, Société d'assurance-vie inc
Stanley Mutual Insurance Company
State Farm Canada
Suecia Reinsurance Company
TD General Insurance Company
TD Home and Auto Insurance Company
Thomson-Schindle-Green Insurance & Financial Services Ltd.
Town & Country Mutual Insurance
Townsend Farmers' Mutual Fire Insurance Company
Tradition Mutual Insurance Company
Trans Global Insurance Company
Travelers - Canada
Trillium Mutual Insurance Company
Trisura Guarantee Insurance Company
Virginia Surety Company, Inc.
Wabisa Mutual Insurance Company
The Wawanesa Mutual Insurance Company
West Elgin Mutual Insurance Company
West Wawanosh Mutual Insurance Company
Western Assurance Company
Western Financial Group Inc.
Westland Insurance
Westminster Mutual Insurance Company
XL Insurance Company Limited
XL Reinsurance America Inc.
Yarmouth Mutual Fire Insurance Company
York Fire & Casualty Insurance Company
Zenith Insurance Company
Zurich Canada

Life

ACA Assurance
ACTRA Fraternal Benefit Society
Alberta Motor Association Insurance Co.
Allianz Life Insurance Company of North America
Alpine Insurance & Financial Inc.
American Bankers Life Assurance Company of Florida
American Health & Life Insurance Company
American Income Life Insurance Company
AMEX Assurance Company
Assumption Mutual Life Insurance Company
Assurance-Vie Banque Nationale
AVie, Financial Security Advisors
AXA RE Canada
BMO Life Assurance Company of Canada
British Columbia Automobile Association Insurance Agency
British Columbia Life & Casualty Company
Butler Byers Insurance Ltd.
CAA Insurance Company (Ontario)
Canada Life Financial Corporation
Canadian Premier Life Insurance Company
Canadian Professional Sales Association
Canadian Slovak League
Canassurance Insurance Company
La Capitale Civil Service Insurer Inc.
La Capitale Insurance & Financial Services
CIBC Life Insurance Company Limited
CIGNA Life Insurance Company of Canada
Combined Insurance Company of America
Connecticut General Life Insurance Co.
Co-operators General Insurance Company
Co-operators Life Insurance Company
Croatian Fraternal Union of America
The CUMIS Group Limited
CUMIS Life Insurance Company
Desjardins Financial Security
Empire Life Insurance Company
L'Entraide assurance, compagnie mutuelle
The Equitable Life Insurance Company of Canada
L'Excellence, Compagnie d'assurance-vie
FaithLife Financial
GAN Assurances Vie Compagnie française d'assurances vie mixte
General American Life Insurance Company
Gerber Life Insurance Company
The Grand Orange Lodge of British America Beneficent Fund
The Great-West Life Assurance Company
The Independent Order of Foresters
Industrial Alliance Insurance & Financial Services Inc.
Industrial Alliance Pacific Life Insurance Company
Insurance Company of Prince Edward Island
L'Internationale, compagnie d'assurance-vie
Johnston Meier Insurance Agencies Group
Knights of Columbus
Life Insurance Company of North America
London & Midland General Insurance Company
London Life Insurance Company
Manitoba Blue Cross
Manufacturers Life Insurance Company
Manulife Canada Ltd.
Manulife Financial
Massachusetts Mutual Life Insurance Company
McFarlane & Company Financial Group Limited
MD Life Insurance Company
Medavie Blue Cross
Metropolitan Life Insurance Company, Canadian Branch
Minnesota Life Insurance Company
Munich Reinsurance Company - Canada Life
The North West Commercial Travellers' Association of Canada
Optimum Reassurance Company
The Order of United Commercial Travelers of America
Pacific Blue Cross
PartnerRe SA
Penncorp Life Insurance Company
Primerica Life Insurance Company of Canada
Principal Life Insurance Company
Promutuel Vie inc
Québec Blue Cross
RBC Insurance
RBC Life Insurance Company
RBC Travel Insurance Company
Reliable Life Insurance Company
ReliaStar Life Insurance Company
Saskatchewan Blue Cross
SCOR Vie
Scotia Life Insurance Company
Sons of Scotland Benevolent Association
SSQ Financial Group
SSQ, Société d'assurance-vie inc
The Standard Life Assurance Company of Canada
Sun Life Assurance Company of Canada
Sun Life Financial Inc.
Supreme Council of the Royal Arcanum
La Survivance, compagnie mutuelle d'assurance vie
Swiss Re Frankona Rückversicherungs-Aktiengesellschaft
TD Life Insurance Company
Thomson-Schindle-Green Insurance & Financial Services Ltd.
Trans Global Life Insurance Company
Transamerica Life Canada
Ukrainian Fraternal Association of America
Ukrainian Fraternal Society of Canada
Ukrainian Mutual Benefit Association of St. Nicholas of Canada
Ukrainian National Association
Union of Canada Life Insurance
L'Union-Vie, compagnie mutuelle d'assurance
United American Insurance Company
Unity Life of Canada
The Wawanesa Life Insurance Company
Wedgwood Insurance Limited
Western Financial Group Inc.
Western Life Assurance Company
Woman's Life Insurance Society

Marine

ACE INA Insurance
American Re-Insurance Company
Antigonish Farmers' Mutual Insurance Company
Avemco Insurance Company
Aviva Canada Inc.
AXA RE Canada
Belair Insurance Company Inc.
Butler Byers Insurance Ltd.
CAA Insurance Company (Ontario)
Canadian Universities Reciprocal Insurance Exchange
Cavell Insurance Company Limited
Chubb Insurance Company of Canada
Commonwealth Insurance Company
Cowan Insurance Group Ltd.
Ecclesiastical Insurance Office plc
Elite Insurance Company
Everest Insurance Company of Canada
Farmers' Mutual Insurance Company (Lindsay)
Federal Insurance Company
GCAN Insurance Company
Great American Insurance Company
Hamilton Township Mutual Insurance Company
Henderson Insurance Inc.
Intact Insurance Company of Canada
Johnston Meier Insurance Agencies Group
Lennox & Addington Mutual Insurance Company
Lombard Canada Ltd.
Lombard Insurance Company
MAX Canada Insurance Company
Pacific Coast Fishermen's Mutual Marine Insurance Company
Peace Hills General Insurance Company
Pembridge Insurance Company
Premier Marine Insurance Managers Group
Revios Reinsurance
Swiss Reinsurance Company Canada
The Tokio Marine & Nichido Fire Insurance Co., Ltd.
Travelers - Canada
Trillium Mutual Insurance Company
Wedgwood Insurance Limited
Western Assurance Company
Zurich Canada

Personal Accident & Sickness

ACE INA Life Insurance
ACTRA Fraternal Benefit Society
Alberta Blue Cross
Alberta Motor Association Insurance Co.
Allianz Life Insurance Company of North America
Allstate Insurance Company of Canada
American Bankers Life Assurance Company of Florida
American Home Assurance Company
American Income Life Insurance Company
American Re-Insurance Company
AMEX Assurance Company
Amherst Island Mutual Insurance Company
Assumption Mutual Life Insurance Company

Assurance-Vie Banque Nationale
Avemco Insurance Company
AVie, Financial Security Advisors
Aviva Canada Inc.
AXA Corporate Solutions Assurance
AXA General Insurance Company
AXA Insurance (Canada)
AXA Pacific Insurance Company
AXA RE Canada
Ayr Farmers Mutual Insurance Company
Bay of Quinte Mutual Insurance Co.
Belair Insurance Company Inc.
Berkley Insurance Company
Bertie and Clinton Mutual Insurance Company
BMO Life Assurance Company of Canada
Brant Mutual Insurance Company
British Columbia Automobile Association Insurance Agency
British Columbia Life & Casualty Company
Butler Byers Insurance Ltd.
CAA Insurance Company (Ontario)
Canadian Direct Insurance Incorporated
Canadian Farm Insurance Corp.
Canadian Premier Life Insurance Company
Canadian Professional Sales Association
Canassurance Insurance Company
La Capitale Insurance & Financial Services
Caradoc Delaware Mutual Fire Insurance Company
Cavell Insurance Company Limited
Chubb Insurance Company of Canada
CIBC Life Insurance Company Limited
CIGNA Life Insurance Company of Canada
The Citadel General Assurance Company
Combined Insurance Company of America
Connecticut General Life Insurance Co.
Continental Casualty Company
Co-operators General Insurance Company
Co-operators Life Insurance Company
Croatian Fraternal Union of America
The CUMIS Group Limited
CUMIS Life Insurance Company
Desjardins Financial Security
Dufferin Mutual Insurance Company
Eagle Star Insurance Company Ltd.
Echelon General Insurance Company
Elite Insurance Company
Empire Life Insurance Company
Employers Reinsurance Corporation
L'Entraide assurance, compagnie mutuelle
Erie Mutual Fire Insurance Company
Everest Reinsurance Company
L'Excellence, Compagnie d'assurance-vie
FaithLife Financial
Farmers' Mutual Insurance Company (Lindsay)
Federal Insurance Company
Fenchurch General Insurance Company
First North American Insurance Company
GCAN Insurance Company
General Reinsurance Corporation
Germania Farmers' Mutual Fire Insurance Co.
Glengarry Farmers' Mutual Fire Insurance Co.
Global Aerospace Underwriting Managers (Canada) Limited
Gore Mutual Insurance Company
Granite Insurance Company
Great American Insurance Company
The Great-West Life Assurance Company
Green Shield Canada
Grenville Mutual Insurance Company
Grey & Bruce Mutual Insurance Co.
The Guarantee Company of North America
Hannover Rückversicherungs AG
Hartford Fire Insurance Company
Howard Mutual Insurance Co.
Howick Mutual Insurance Company
The Independent Order of Foresters
Industrial Alliance Insurance & Financial Services Inc.
Industrial Alliance Pacific Life Insurance Company
Intact Insurance Company of Canada - Novex Group Insurance
L'Internationale, compagnie d'assurance-vie
Kent & Essex Mutual Insurance Company
Lambton Mutual Insurance Company
Legacy General Insurance Company
Lennox & Addington Mutual Insurance Company
Liberty Mutual Insurance Company
Liberty Mutual Insurance Company
Life Insurance Company of North America
Lloyd's Underwriters
Lombard General Insurance Company of Canada
Lombard Insurance Company
London & Midland General Insurance Company
London Life Insurance Company
Manitoba Blue Cross
Manufacturers Life Insurance Company
Massachusetts Mutual Life Insurance Company
McKillop Mutual Insurance Company
Medavie Blue Cross
Metropolitan Life Insurance Company, Canadian Branch
Mitsui Sumitomo Insurance Co., Limited.
Munich Reinsurance Company - Canada Life
Omega General Insurance Company
Ontario Blue Cross
Ontario Mutual Insurance Association
Optimum Reassurance Company
The Order of United Commercial Travelers of America
Oxford Mutual Insurance Company
Pacific Blue Cross
PartnerRe SA
Penncorp Life Insurance Company
The Personal Insurance Company
Primerica Life Insurance Company of Canada
Principal Life Insurance Company
Promutuel Vie inc
Protective Insurance Company
Québec Blue Cross
RBC General Insurance Company
RBC Insurance
RBC Life Insurance Company
RBC Travel Insurance Company
Reliable Life Insurance Company
ReliaStar Life Insurance Company
Saskatchewan Blue Cross
SCOR Vie
Scotia Life Insurance Company
SecuriCan General Insurance Company
Security National Insurance Company
The Sovereign General Insurance Company
SSQ Financial Group
SSQ, Société d'assurance-vie inc
The Standard Life Assurance Company of Canada
Suecia Reinsurance Company
Sun Life Assurance Company of Canada
Supreme Council of the Royal Arcanum
La Survivance, compagnie mutuelle d'assurance vie
Swiss Re Frankona Rückversicherungs-Aktiengesellschaft
TD General Insurance Company
TD Life Insurance Company
Town & Country Mutual Insurance
Townsend Farmers' Mutual Fire Insurance Company
Trans Global Insurance Company
Trans Global Life Insurance Company
Transamerica Life Canada
Transatlantic Reinsurance Company

Ukrainian Mutual Benefit Association of St. Nicholas of Canada
Ukrainian National Association
L'Union-Vie, compagnie mutuelle d'assurance
United American Insurance Company
Unity Life of Canada
Wabisa Mutual Insurance Company
The Wawanesa Life Insurance Company
West Elgin Mutual Insurance Company
West Wawanosh Mutual Insurance Company
Western Assurance Company
Western Financial Group Inc.
Western Life Assurance Company
XL Insurance Company Limited
XL Reinsurance America Inc.
Zenith Insurance Company
Zurich Canada

Property

ACE INA Insurance
Affiliated FM Insurance Company
Alberta Motor Association Insurance Co.
Algoma Insurance Group
Algoma Mutual Insurance Co.
Alliance Assurance
Allstate Insurance Company of Canada
L'ALPHA, compagnie d'assurances inc.
Alpine Insurance & Financial Inc.
American Home Assurance Company
American International Underwriters, Canada
American Re-Insurance Company
The American Road Insurance Company
Amherst Island Mutual Insurance Company
Antigonish Farmers' Mutual Insurance Company
L'Assurance Mutuelle des Fabriques de Montréal
Astro Insurance 1000 Inc.
Atlantic Insurance Company Limited
Aviva Canada Inc.
A-WIN Insurance Network
AXA Corporate Solutions Assurance
AXA General Insurance Company
AXA Insurance (Canada)
AXA Pacific Insurance Company
AXA RE Canada
Ayr Farmers Mutual Insurance Company
Bay of Quinte Mutual Insurance Co.
Belair Insurance Company Inc.
Berkley Insurance Company
Bertie and Clinton Mutual Insurance Company
The Boiler Inspection & Insurance Company of Canada
Brant Mutual Insurance Company
British Columbia Automobile Association Insurance Agency
Butler Byers Insurance Ltd.
CAA Insurance Company (Ontario)
Caisse Centrale de Réassurance
Canadian Direct Insurance Incorporated
Canadian Farm Insurance Corp.
Canadian Northern Shield Insurance Company
Canadian Petroleum Insurance Exchange Ltd.
Canadian Professional Sales Association
Canadian Universities Reciprocal Insurance Exchange
Canassurance Insurance Company
La Capitale General Insurance Inc.
Caradoc Delaware Mutual Fire Insurance Company
Carleton Mutual Insurance Company
Cavell Insurance Company Limited
Certas Direct Insurance Company
Chrysler Insurance Company
Chubb Insurance Company of Canada
The Citadel General Assurance Company
Clare Mutual Insurance Company
Coastal Community Insurance Services (2007) Ltd.
Commonwealth Insurance Company
La Compagnie d'Assurance Missisquoi
Constitution Insurance Company of Canada
Continental Casualty Company
Co-operators General Insurance Company
Co-operators Life Insurance Company
COSECO Insurance Company
Cowan Insurance Group Ltd.
Crowsnest Insurance Agencies Ltd.
CUMIS General Insurance Company
The CUMIS Group Limited
CUMIS Life Insurance Company
Desjardins assurances générales inc
The Dominion of Canada General Insurance Company
Dufferin Mutual Insurance Company
Dumfries Mutual Insurance Company
Eagle Star Insurance Company Ltd.
Ecclesiastical Insurance Office plc
Echelon General Insurance Company
Economical Mutual Insurance Company
Elite Insurance Company
Employers Reinsurance Corporation
Erie Mutual Fire Insurance Company
Everest Insurance Company of Canada
Everest Reinsurance Company
Farmers' Mutual Insurance Company (Lindsay)
Federal Insurance Company
Federated Insurance Company of Canada
Federation Insurance Company of Canada
Fenchurch General Insurance Company
First North American Insurance Company
FM Global
Folksamerica Reinsurance Company
Fundy Mutual Insurance Company
GCAN Insurance Company
General Reinsurance Corporation
Germania Farmers' Mutual Fire Insurance Co.
Germania Mutual Insurance Company
Gibb's Agencies (1997) Ltd.
Glengarry Farmers' Mutual Fire Insurance Co.
Global Aerospace Underwriting Managers (Canada) Limited
Gore Mutual Insurance Company
Grain Insurance and Guarantee Company
Granite Insurance Company
Great American Insurance Company
Grenville Mutual Insurance Company
Grey & Bruce Mutual Insurance Co.
Le Groupe Estrie-Richelieu, compagnie d'assurance
The Guarantee Company of North America
Halwell Mutual Insurance Company
Hannover Rückversicherungs AG
Hartford Fire Insurance Company
Hay Mutual Insurance Company
Henderson Insurance Inc.
Howard Mutual Insurance Co.
Howick Mutual Insurance Company
Insurance Company of Prince Edward Island
Intact Insurance Company of Canada - Novex Group Insurance

JEVCO Insurance Company
Kent & Essex Mutual Insurance Company
The Kings Mutual Insurance Company
Kingsway Financial Services Inc.
Kingsway General Insurance Company
Kirkham Insurance
Lambton Mutual Insurance Company
Lanark Mutual Insurance Company
Legacy General Insurance Company
Lennox & Addington Mutual Insurance Company
Liberty Mutual Insurance Company
Liberty Mutual Insurance Company
Lloyd's Underwriters
Lombard General Insurance Company of Canada
Lombard Insurance Company
London & Midland General Insurance Company
Lumbermen's Underwriting Alliance
MAX Canada Insurance Company
McFarlane & Company Financial Group Limited
McKillop Mutual Insurance Company
Mennonite Mutual Fire Insurance Company
Mennonite Mutual Insurance Co. (Alberta) Ltd.
Metro General Insurance Corp.
Middlesex Mutual Insurance Co.
Millennium Insurance Corporation
Mitsui Sumitomo Insurance Co., Limited.
Munich Reinsurance Company of Canada
MUNIX Reciprocal
The Mutual Fire Insurance Company of British Columbia
The Nordic Insurance Company of Canada
Norfolk Mutual Insurance Company
North Bleinheim Mutual Insurance Co.
North Blenheim Mutual Insurance Company
North Kent Mutual Fire Insurance Company
The North Waterloo Farmers Mutual Insurance Company
OdysseyRe - Canadian Branch
Old Republic Insurance Company of Canada
Omega General Insurance Company
Ontario Mutual Insurance Association
Ontario School Boards' Insurance Exchange
Optimum Assurance Agricole inc
Optimum Général inc
Optimum Société d'Assurance inc
Oxford Mutual Insurance Company
PartnerRe SA
PC Financial Insurance Agency
Peace Hills General Insurance Company
Peel Mutual Insurance Company
Pembridge Insurance Company
The Personal General Insurance Inc.
The Personal Insurance Company
Perth Insurance Company
Pictou Mutual Insurance Company
Pilot Insurance Company
The Portage La Prairie Mutual Insurance Company
Premier Marine Insurance Managers Group
Primmum Insurance Company
Prince Edward Island Mutual Insurance Company
Progressive Casualty Insurance Company
Promutuel Réassurance
Protective Insurance Company
RBC General Insurance Company
RBC Insurance
Red River Valley Mutual Insurance Co.
Revios Reinsurance
Royal & SunAlliance Insurance Company of Canada
Saskatchewan Mutual Insurance Company
Scottish & York Insurance Co. Limited
Security National Insurance Company
SGI CANADA Consolidated
South Easthope Mutual Insurance Co.
Southeastern Mutual Insurance Company
The Sovereign General Insurance Company
SSQ, Société d'assurances générales inc.
SSQ, Société d'assurance-vie inc
Stanley Mutual Insurance Company
State Farm Canada
Suecia Reinsurance Company
Swiss Reinsurance Company Canada
TD General Insurance Company
TD Home and Auto Insurance Company
Temple Insurance Company
Thomson-Schindle-Green Insurance & Financial Services Ltd.
The Tokio Marine & Nichido Fire Insurance Co., Ltd.
Town & Country Mutual Insurance
Townsend Farmers' Mutual Fire Insurance Company
Traders General Insurance Company
Tradition Mutual Insurance Company
Trans Global Insurance Company
Transatlantic Reinsurance Company
Travelers - Canada
Trillium Mutual Insurance Company
Unifund Assurance Company
L'Union Canadienne Compagnie d'Assurances
Virginia Surety Company, Inc.
Wabisa Mutual Insurance Company
Waterloo Insurance Company
The Wawanesa Mutual Insurance Company
Wedgwood Insurance Limited
West Elgin Mutual Insurance Company
West Wawanosh Mutual Insurance Company
Western Assurance Company
Western Financial Group Inc.
Westland Insurance
Westminster Mutual Insurance Company
XL Insurance Company Limited
XL Reinsurance America Inc.
Yarmouth Mutual Fire Insurance Company
York Fire & Casualty Insurance Company
Zenith Insurance Company
Zurich Canada

Reinsurance

American Re-Insurance Company
General American Life Insurance Company
Kingsway Financial Services Inc.
Lloyd's Underwriters
London Life Insurance Company
Munich Reinsurance Company - Canada Life
OdysseyRe - Canadian Branch
Old Republic Insurance Company of Canada
Optimum Reassurance Company
Promutuel Réassurance
RGA Life Reinsurance Company of Canada
SCOR Canada Reinsurance Company
SGI CANADA Consolidated
Suecia Reinsurance Company
Swiss Reinsurance Company Canada
The Toa Reinsurance Company of America
Transatlantic Reinsurance Company
Travelers - Canada
L'Union-Vie, compagnie mutuelle d'assurance

Surety

ACE INA Insurance
Affiliated FM Insurance Company
Algoma Insurance Group
Allstate Insurance Company of Canada
L'ALPHA, compagnie d'assurances inc.
American Home Assurance Company
American Re-Insurance Company
The American Road Insurance Company
Atlantic Insurance Company Limited
Aviva Canada Inc.
AXA Corporate Solutions Assurance
AXA General Insurance Company
AXA Insurance (Canada)
AXA Pacific Insurance Company
AXA RE Canada
Belair Insurance Company Inc.
Berkley Insurance Company
CAA Insurance Company (Ontario)
Caisse Centrale de Réassurance
Canadian Farm Insurance Corp.
Cavell Insurance Company Limited
Certas Direct Insurance Company
Chrysler Insurance Company
Chubb Insurance Company of Canada
The Citadel General Assurance Company
Commonwealth Insurance Company
La Compagnie d'Assurance Missisquoi
Constitution Insurance Company of Canada
Continental Casualty Company
Co-operators General Insurance Company
Desjardins assurances générales inc
The Dominion of Canada General Insurance Company
Eagle Star Insurance Company Ltd.
Echelon General Insurance Company
Economical Mutual Insurance Company
Elite Insurance Company
Employers Reinsurance Corporation
Everest Insurance Company of Canada
Everest Reinsurance Company
Federal Insurance Company
Federated Insurance Company of Canada
Federation Insurance Company of Canada
Fenchurch General Insurance Company
Folksamerica Reinsurance Company
GCAN Insurance Company
General Reinsurance Corporation
Grain Insurance and Guarantee Company
Granite Insurance Company
Great American Insurance Company
The Guarantee Company of North America
Hannover Rückversicherungs AG
Hartford Fire Insurance Company
Intact Insurance Company of Canada
Intact Insurance Company of Canada - Novex Group Insurance
Johnston Meier Insurance Agencies Group
Kingsway General Insurance Company
Liberty Mutual Insurance Company
Liberty Mutual Insurance Company
Lloyd's Underwriters
Lombard General Insurance Company of Canada
Lombard Insurance Company
London & Midland General Insurance Company
McFarlane & Company Financial Group Limited
Mitsui Sumitomo Insurance Co., Limited.
The Nordic Insurance Company of Canada
OdysseyRe - Canadian Branch
Omega General Insurance Company
Peace Hills General Insurance Company
The Personal General Insurance Inc.
The Personal Insurance Company
Progressive Casualty Insurance Company
Promutuel Réassurance
Red River Valley Mutual Insurance Co.
Revios Reinsurance
St. Paul Guarantee Insurance Company
Scottish & York Insurance Co. Limited
SGI CANADA Consolidated
State Farm Canada
Swiss Reinsurance Company Canada
TD General Insurance Company
Transatlantic Reinsurance Company
Travelers - Canada
Trisura Guarantee Insurance Company
The Wawanesa Mutual Insurance Company
Western Assurance Company
Western Financial Group Inc.
Western Surety Company
XL Insurance Company Limited
XL Reinsurance America Inc.
Zurich Canada

Theft

Algoma Insurance Group
L'Assurance Mutuelle des Fabriques de Montréal
Canadian Petroleum Insurance Exchange Ltd.
The Citadel General Assurance Company
La Compagnie d'Assurance Missisquoi
Co-operators General Insurance Company
CUMIS General Insurance Company
CUMIS Life Insurance Company
The Dominion of Canada General Insurance Company
Federated Insurance Company of Canada
Germania Mutual Insurance Company
Glengarry Farmers' Mutual Fire Insurance Co.
Gore Mutual Insurance Company
Grain Insurance and Guarantee Company
Granite Insurance Company
The Guarantee Company of North America
Hartford Fire Insurance Company
Lanark Mutual Insurance Company
Lombard General Insurance Company of Canada
Lombard Insurance Company
London & Midland General Insurance Company
Mennonite Mutual Fire Insurance Company
Munich Reinsurance Company of Canada
North Kent Mutual Fire Insurance Company
Peace Hills General Insurance Company
Prince Edward Island Mutual Insurance Company
Promutuel Réassurance
RBC General Insurance Company
Red River Valley Mutual Insurance Co.
SSQ Financial Group
SSQ, Société d'assurances générales inc.
The Wawanesa Mutual Insurance Company
Western Financial Group Inc.
Zurich Canada

Federal & Provincial Insurance Companies

ACA Assurance
3050, boul St-Jean
Trois-Rivières, QC G9A 5E1
819-377-1777
Fax: 819-377-3587
1-800-567-9455
infocan@aca-assurance.org
www.aca-assurance.org
Classes of Insurance: Accident, Life

ACE INA Insurance
130 King St. West, 12th Fl.
Toronto, ON M5X 1A6
416-368-2911
Fax: 416-594-2600
www.ace-ina-canada.com
Classes of Insurance: Accident, Aircraft, Auto, Liability, Boiler & Machinery, Credit, Marine, Fidelity, Property, Fire, Surety, Hail & Crop

ACE INA Life Insurance/ Assurance-vie ACE INA
#1400, 25 York St.
Toronto, ON M5J 2V5
416-368-2911
Fax: 416-594-2600
Classes of Insurance: Personal Accident & Sickness, Liability

ACTRA Fraternal Benefit Society (AFBS)
1000 Yonge St.
Toronto, ON M4W 2K2
416-967-6600
Fax: 416-967-4744
800-387-8897
benefits@actrafrat.com
www.actrafrat.com
Classes of Insurance: Personal Accident & Sickness, Life

Affiliated FM Insurance Company
#500, 165 Commerce Valley Dr. West
Thornhill, ON L3T 7V8
905-763-5555
Fax: 905-763-5556
www.affiliatedfm.ca
Classes of Insurance: Liability, Boiler & Machinery, Fidelity, Property, Fire, Surety

Agriculture Financial Services Corporation (AFSC)
5718 - 56 Ave.
Lacombe, AB T4J 1R5
403-782-3000
Fax: 403-782-4226
www.afsc.ca
Classes of Insurance: Hail & Crop

AIG United Guaranty Mortgage Insurance Company Canada
#400, 1 Toronto St.
Toronto, ON M5C 2V6
416-640-8924
Fax: 416-640-8948
866-414-9109
Other Contact Information: 1-877-244-8422 (Toll Free underwriting related inquiries)
info@aigug.ca
www.aigug.ca

Alberta Blue Cross
Blue Cross Place
10009 - 108th St. NW
Edmonton, AB T5J 3C5
780-498-8000
Fax: 780-425-4627
800-661-6995
Other Contact Information: Travel Coverage: 780/498-8550; Individual Health & Dental Plans: 780/498-8008; Group Sales: 780/498-8500
www.ab.bluecross.ca
Classes of Insurance: Personal Accident & Sickness

Alberta Motor Association Insurance Co.
PO Box 8180, South Stn. South
Edmonton, AB T6H 5X9
780-430-5555
800-615-5897
Other Contact Information: Membership Inquiries Toll Free: 800-222-6400
www.ama.ab.ca
Classes of Insurance: Personal Accident & Sickness, Auto, Life, Property, Fire,

Algoma Insurance Group
#200, 855 Queen St. East
Sault Ste. Marie, ON P6A 2B3
705-949-6555
Fax: 705-949-3513
info@algomains.com
www.algomains.com
Classes of Insurance: Auto, Liability, Boiler & Machinery, Property, Surety, Theft

Algoma Mutual Insurance Co.
131 Main St.
Thessalon, ON P0R 1L0
705-842-3345
Fax: 705-842-3500
800-461-7260
www.amico.ca
Classes of Insurance: Auto, Property

Alliance Assurance
PO Box 7664
#200, 166 Broadway Blvd.
Grand Falls, NB E3Z 2J9
506-473-9400
Fax: 506-473-9401
800-939-9400
gffax@alliance-assurance.com
www.alliance-assurance.com
Classes of Insurance: Auto, Liability, Property

Allianz Life Insurance Company of North America
#700, 2005 Sheppard Ave. East
Toronto, ON M2J 5B4
Fax: 416-502-2555
Classes of Insurance: Personal Accident & Sickness, Life

Allstate Insurance Company of Canada/ Allstate du Canada, Compagnie d'assurance
#100, 27 Allstate Pkwy.
Markham, ON L3R 5P8
905-477-6900
Fax: 905-415-4831
800-255-7828
Other Contact Information: Claims Toll Free Numbers: 800-387-0462 (AB, BC, MB, ON, SK); 800-463-2813 (QC); 800-561-7222 (NS, NB, PE, NL)
www.allstate.ca
Classes of Insurance: Personal Accident & Sickness, Legal Expense, Auto, Liability, Boiler & Machinery, Fidelity, Property, Surety

L'ALPHA, compagnie d'assurances inc.
#119, 430, rue Saint-Georges
Drummondville, QC J2C 4H4
819-474-7958
Fax: 819-477-6139
drummond@assurance-alpha.com
www.assurance-alpha.com/alpha.php
Classes of Insurance: Auto, Property, Surety

Alpine Insurance & Financial Inc.
#203, 1026 - 16th Ave. NW
Calgary, AB T2M 0K6
403-270-8822
Fax: 403-270-0201
877-770-8822
calgary.info@alpineinsurance.ca
www.alpineinsurance.ca
Classes of Insurance: Auto, Liability, Life, Property

American Bankers Life Assurance Company of Florida
#500, 5160 Yonge St.
Toronto, ON M2N 7C7
416-733-3360
Fax: 416-733-7826
800-561-3232
www.assurant.com.br/canada/
Classes of Insurance: Accident, Personal Accident & Sickness, Life

American Health & Life Insurance Company
201 Queens Ave.
London, ON N6A 1J1
519-672-1070
Fax: 519-660-2625
Classes of Insurance: Life,

American Home Assurance Company
145 Wellington St. West
Toronto, ON M5J 1H8
416-596-3000
AHAC@aig.com
www.aigamericanhome.com
Classes of Insurance: Personal Accident & Sickness, Aircraft, Auto, Liability, Boiler & Machinery, Credit, Fidelity, Property, Surety, Hail & Crop

American Income Life Insurance Company
c/o McLean & Kerr
#2800, 130 Adelaide St. West
Toronto, ON M5H 3P5
416-364-5371
Fax: 416-366-8571
Classes of Insurance: Personal Accident & Sickness, Life

American International Underwriters, Canada
145 Wellington St. West
Toronto, ON M5J 2T4
416-596-3000
www.aig.com
Classes of Insurance: Property

American Re-Insurance Company
Munich Re Centre
390 Bay St., 22nd Fl.
Toronto, ON M5H 2Y2
416-591-8668
Classes of Insurance: Accident, Personal Accident & Sickness, Auto, Liability, Boiler & Machinery, Credit, Marine, Fidelity, Property, Surety, Hail & Crop, Reinsurance

The American Road Insurance Company
#2, 1145 Nicholson Rd.
Newmarket, ON L3Y 9C3
905-853-0858
Classes of Insurance: Auto, Liability, Boiler & Machinery, Credit, Property, Surety

AMEX Assurance Company/ AMEX Compagnie d'Assurance
c/o Focus Group Inc.
#500, 36 King St. East
Toronto, ON M5C 1E5
416-361-1728
Fax: 416-361-6113
Classes of Insurance: Personal Accident & Sickness, Life

Amherst Island Mutual Insurance Company
RR#1
Stella, ON K0H 2S0
613-389-2012
Fax: 613-389-9986
Classes of Insurance: Personal Accident & Sickness, Liability, Property

Antigonish Farmers' Mutual Insurance Company
188 Main St.
Antigonish, NS B2G 2B9
902-863-3544
Fax: 902-863-0664
Other Contact Information: Toll Free (Maritimes only): 1-800-565-3544
jchisolm@antigonish-mutual.com
www.antigonish-mutual.com
Classes of Insurance: Marine, Property, Fire

Ascentus Insurance Ltd.
10 Wellington St. East
Toronto, ON M5E 1L5
888-877-1710
Other Contact Information: Claims: 1-877-275-3698
www.ascentusinsurance.ca

Assumption Mutual Life Insurance Company/ Assomption Compagnie Mutuelle d'Assurance-Vie
Assumption Place
PO Box 160
770 Main St.
Moncton, NB E1C 8L1
506-853-6040
Fax: 506-853-5428
800-455-7337
Other Contact Information: Group Insurance, Phone: 506-869-9797; Toll Free: 1-888-869-9797; Individual Insurance, Toll Free: 1-800-343-5622; Mortgage Loans, Phone: 506-869-9755
comments@assumption.ca; financial.services@assumption.ca
www.assumption.ca
Classes of Insurance: Accident, Personal Accident & Sickness, Life

L'Assurance Mutuelle des Fabriques de Montréal
1071, rue de la Cathédrale
Montréal, QC H3B 2V4
514-395-4969
Fax: 514-861-8921
800-567-6586
info.general@amf-mtl.com

Classes of Insurance: Liability, Boiler & Machinery, Property, Fire, Theft

Assurance-Vie Banque Nationale/ National Bank Life Insurance Company
1100, rue University, 11e étage
Montréal, QC H3B 2G7

514-871-7500
Fax: 514-394-6604
877-871-7500
assurances@nbc.ca
www.nbc.ca

Classes of Insurance: Personal Accident & Sickness, Life, Credit

Assurant Solutions Canada
#500, 5160 Yonge St.
Toronto, ON M2N 7C7

416-733-3360
Fax: 416-733-7826
800-561-3232
shari.doherty@assurant.com
www.assurantsolutions.com/canada/

Classes of Insurance: Credit

Astro Insurance 1000 Inc.
#100, 542 - 7th St.
Lethbridge, AB T1J 2H1

403-328-1000
Fax: 403-320-1962
astroins@astro-insurance.com
www.astro-insurance.com

Classes of Insurance: Auto, Liability, Property, Hail & Crop

Atlantic Insurance Company Limited
64 Commonwealth Ave.
Mount Pearl, NL A1N 1W8

709-364-5209
Fax: 709-364-5262

Classes of Insurance: Auto, Liability, Boiler & Machinery, Fidelity, Property, Surety

Avemco Insurance Company
#401, 133 Richmond St. West
Toronto, ON M5H 2L3

416-363-6103
Fax: 416-363-7454

Classes of Insurance: Personal Accident & Sickness, Aircraft, Marine

Aviation & General Insurance Company Limited
#201, 3650 Victoria Park Ave.
Toronto, ON M2H 3P7

416-496-1148
Fax: 416-496-1089

Classes of Insurance: Aircraft, Liability

AVie, Financial Security Advisors/ AVie, Cabinet de conseillers en sécurité financière
Édifice Martin-J.-Légère
CP 5554
295, boul St-Pierre ouest
Caraquet, NB E1W 1B7

506-726-4203
Fax: 506-726-8204
888-822-2343
www.acadie.com; www.assumption.ca

Classes of Insurance: Personal Accident & Sickness, Life

Aviva Canada Inc./ Aviva, Compagnie d'Assurance du Canada
2206 Eglinton Ave. East
Toronto, ON M1L 4S8

416-288-1800
Fax: 416-288-5888
800-387-4518
www.avivacanada.com

Classes of Insurance: Personal Accident & Sickness, Aircraft, Legal Expense, Auto, Liability, Boiler & Machinery, Marine, Fidelity, Property, Surety, Hail & Crop

A-WIN Insurance Network
#200, 2417 - 51 Ave. SE
Calgary, AB T2C 0A2

403-278-1050
Fax: 403-225-0515
info1@awinins.ca
www.awinins.ca

Classes of Insurance: Auto, Liability, Property

AXA Canada Inc.
#700, 2020, rue University
Montréal, QC H3A 2A5

514-282-1914
Fax: 514-282-9588
www.axa.ca

AXA Corporate Solutions Assurance
#600, 2020, rue University
Montréal, QC H3A 2A5

514-392-6033
Fax: 514-392-7392
www.axa-corporatesolutions.com

Classes of Insurance: Personal Accident & Sickness, Aircraft, Legal Expense, Auto, Liability, Boiler & Machinery, Credit, Fidelity, Property, Surety, Hail & Crop

AXA General Insurance Company/ AXA Assurances générales
#1400, 5700 Yonge St.
Toronto, ON M2M 4K2

877-292-4968
www.axa.ca

Classes of Insurance: Personal Accident & Sickness, Aircraft, Legal Expense, Auto, Liability, Boiler & Machinery, Fidelity, Property, Surety, Hail & Crop

AXA Insurance (Canada)/ AXA Assurances (Canada)
#1400, 5700 Yonge St.
Toronto, ON M2M 4K2

8770292-4968
av.operations@axa-assurances.ca
www.axa-insurance.ca; www.axa.ca

Classes of Insurance: Personal Accident & Sickness, Aircraft, Legal Expense, Auto, Liability, Boiler & Machinery, Fidelity, Property, Surety, Hail & Crop

AXA Pacific Insurance Company/ AXA Pacifique Compagnie d'Assurance
PO Box 22
999 Hastings St. West, 2nd Fl.
Vancouver, BC V6C 2W2

604-669-4247
Fax: 604-682-6693
www.axa.ca

Classes of Insurance: Personal Accident & Sickness, Aircraft, Legal Expense, Auto, Liability, Boiler & Machinery, Credit, Fidelity, Property, Surety, Hail & Crop

AXA RE Canada
Place Montréal Trust
#2000, 1800, av McGill College
Montréal, QC H3A 3J6

514-842-9262
Fax: 514-842-9254
www.axa.com

Classes of Insurance: Personal Accident & Sickness, Aircraft, Auto, Liability, Boiler & Machinery, Life, Marine, Fidelity, Property, Surety, Hail & Crop

Ayr Farmers Mutual Insurance Company
PO Box 1170
1400 Northumberland St.
Ayr, ON N0B 1E0

519-632-7413
Fax: 519-632-8908
800-265-8792
www.ayrmutual.com

Classes of Insurance: Accident, Personal Accident & Sickness, Auto, Liability, Boiler & Machinery, Fidelity, Property, Hail & Crop

Bay of Quinte Mutual Insurance Co.
PO Box 6050
13379 Loyalist Pkwy.
Picton, ON K0K 2T0

613-476-2145
800-267-2126
info@bayofquintemutual.com
www.bayofquintemutual.com

Classes of Insurance: Personal Accident & Sickness, Auto, Liability, Boiler & Machinery, Fidelity, Property

Belair Insurance Company Inc./ La Compagnie d'Assurance Belair Inc.
#300, 7101, rue Jean-Talon est
Montréal, QC H1M 3T6

514-270-9111
888-270-9111
Other Contact Information: 888-280-8549, 888-270-9732 (Toll Free, Auto & Home); 1-877-874-5433 (Toll Free, Travel Insurance); 877-270-9124 (Toll Free, Claims Emergency)
belairdirect@belairdirect.com, belairdirect.ontario@belairdirect.com
www.belairdirect.com

Classes of Insurance: Personal Accident & Sickness, Legal Expense, Auto, Liability, Boiler & Machinery, Marine, Fidelity, Property, Surety

Berkley Insurance Company
#201, 3650 Victoria Park Ave.
Toronto, ON M2H 3P7

416-496-1148
Fax: 416-496-1089

Classes of Insurance: Personal Accident & Sickness, Aircraft, Legal Expense, Auto, Liability, Boiler & Machinery, Credit, Fidelity, Property, Surety, Hail & Crop

Bertie and Clinton Mutual Insurance Company
1789 Merrittville Hwy., RR#2
Welland, ON L3B 5N5

905-892-0606
Fax: 905-892-0365
800-263-0494
info@bertieandclinton.com
www.bertieandclinton.com

Classes of Insurance: Personal Accident & Sickness, Auto, Liability, Boiler & Machinery, Fidelity, Property

BMO Life Assurance Company of Canada
60 Yonge St.
Toronto, ON M5E 1H5

416-596-3900
Fax: 416-596-4143
877-742-5244
www4.bmo.com

Classes of Insurance: Personal Accident & Sickness, Life

The Boiler Inspection & Insurance Company of Canada (BI&I)
18 King St. East
Toronto, ON M5C 1C4

416-363-5491
Fax: 416-363-0538
corporate@biico.com
www.biico.com

Classes of Insurance: Liability, Boiler & Machinery, Property

Brant Mutual Insurance Company
207 Greenwich St.
Brantford, ON N3S 2X7

519-752-0088
Fax: 519-752-7917
solutions@brantmutual.com
www.brantmutual.com

Classes of Insurance: Personal Accident & Sickness, Auto, Liability, Boiler & Machinery, Fidelity, Property, Hail & Crop

British Columbia Automobile Association Insurance Agency
4567 Canada Way
Burnaby, BC V5G 4T1

604-268-5000
Fax: 604-268-5569
800-719-2224
Other Contact Information: Claims: 604-268-5260; Toll Free, TeleCentre: 1-877-325-8888; Toll Free, BCAA Advantage Home Policy: 310-2345; Customer Contact Centre: 604 268-5555
www.bcaa.com

Classes of Insurance: Personal Accident & Sickness, Auto, Life, Property, Fire,

British Columbia Life & Casualty Company
PO Box 7000
Vancouver, BC V6B 4E1

604-419-2000
Fax: 604-419-2990
888-275-4672
www.pbchbs.com

Classes of Insurance: Personal Accident & Sickness, Life

Butler Byers Hail Insurance Ltd.
PO Box 330
Saskatoon, SK S7K 3L5

306-652-4245
Fax: 306-652-8472
800-997-4245
sbyers@butlerbyers.com
www.butlerbyers.com

Classes of Insurance: Hail & Crop

Butler Byers Insurance Ltd.
301 - 4th Ave. North
Saskatoon, SK S7K 2L8

306-653-2233
www.butlerbyers.com

Classes of Insurance: Personal Accident & Sickness, Auto, Life, Marine, Property

CAA Insurance Company (Ontario)
60 Commerce Valley Dr. East
Thornhill, ON L3T 7P9

905-771-3000
Fax: 905-771-3101
800-268-3750
Other Contact Information: 877-222-3939 (Auto & Property); 800-387-2656 (Claims); 866-999-4222 (Health & Dental); 877-942-4222 (Group Life)
info@caasco.ca
www.caasco.on.ca/insurance
Classes of Insurance: Personal Accident & Sickness, Legal Expense, Auto, Liability, Life, Marine, Property, Surety

Caisse Centrale de Réassurance
#2110, 181 University Ave.
Toronto, ON M5H 3M7
416-644-0821
www.ccr.fr
Classes of Insurance: Accident, Aircraft, Legal Expense, Auto, Liability, Boiler & Machinery, Fidelity, Property, Fire, Surety

Canadian Direct Insurance Incorporated
#600, 750 Cambie St.
Vancouver, BC V6B 0A2
604-699-3838
Fax: 604-699-3860
888-225-5234
Other Contact Information: 888-261-8888 (Toll Free, Claims)
insurancegeneral@canadiandirect.com
www.canadiandirect.com
Classes of Insurance: Personal Accident & Sickness, Liability, Property

Canadian Farm Insurance Corp. (CFIC)
#310, 13220 St. Albert Trail
Edmonton, AB T5L 4W1
780-447-3276
Fax: 780-732-3607
877-909-3276
Other Contact Information: 24 hour Livestock Claims Assistance: 780-732-3692
www.cdnfarmins.com
Classes of Insurance: Personal Accident & Sickness, Liability, Boiler & Machinery, Fidelity, Property, Surety

Canadian Lawyers Insurance Association/ L'Association d'Assurance des Juristes Canadiens
#2900, 250 Yonge St.
Toronto, ON M5B 2L7
416-408-3721
800-268-9484
info@clia.ca
www.clia.ca

Canadian Lawyers Liability Assurance Society (CLLAS)
c/o Torys LLP
#3000, 79 Wellington St. West
Toronto, ON M5K 1N2
416-865-7337
Fax: 416-865-7380
cllas.ca
Classes of Insurance: Liability

Canadian Northern Shield Insurance Company (CNS)
#1900, 555 Hastings St. West
Vancouver, BC V6B 4N6
604-662-2911
Fax: 604-662-5698
corporate_service@cns.ca
www.cns.ca
Classes of Insurance: Auto, Liability, Property

Canadian Petroleum Insurance Exchange Ltd. (CPIX)
#500, 717 - 7th Ave. SW
Calgary, AB T2P 0Z3
403-261-6061
Fax: 403-261-6068
insurance@cpix.com
www.cpix.com
Classes of Insurance: Auto, Liability, Property, Theft

Canadian Premier Life Insurance Company
80 Tiverton Ct., 5th Fl.
Markham, ON L3R 0G4
905-479-7500
Fax: 905-479-3224
800-598-6918
www.canadianpremier.ca
Classes of Insurance: Personal Accident & Sickness, Life, Credit

Canadian Professional Sales Association (CPSA)
#800, 310 Front St. West
Toronto, ON M5V 3B5
416-408-2685
Fax: 416-408-2684
888-267-2772
www.cpsa.com
Classes of Insurance: Accident, Personal Accident & Sickness, Auto, Life, Property

Canadian Slovak League
#6, 259 Traders Blvd. East
Mississauga, ON L4Z 2E5
905-735-5624
Classes of Insurance: Life

Canadian Universities Reciprocal Insurance Exchange (CURIE)
#901, 5500 North Service Rd.
Burlington, ON L7L 6W6
905-336-3366
Fax: 905-336-3373
888-462-8743
inquiry@curie.org
www.curie.org
Classes of Insurance: Aircraft, Liability, Marine, Property

Canassurance Insurance Company
c/o Ontario Blue Cross
#610, 185 The West Mall
Toronto, ON M9C 5P1
866-732-2583
www.useblue.com
Classes of Insurance: Personal Accident & Sickness, Liability, Life, Property

La Capitale Civil Service Insurer Inc.
625, rue Saint-Amable
Québec, QC G1R 2G5
418-643-3884
Fax: 418-646-0370
866-227-2606
www.lacapitale.com
Classes of Insurance: Life

La Capitale General Insurance Inc./ La Capitale assurances générales inc.
Édifice Hector-Fabre
CP 17100
525, boul René-Lévesque est
Québec, QC G1K 9E2
888-522-5260
Other Contact Information: Claims: 800-461-0770
www.lacapitale.com
Classes of Insurance: Auto, Property

La Capitale Insurance & Financial Services/ La Capitale assurances et gestion du patrimoine
Édifice Le Delta II
#100, 2875, boul Laurier
Québec, QC G1V 2M2
418-644-4200
Fax: 418-644-5226
888-463-4856
collectif@lacapitale.com
www.lacapitale.com
Classes of Insurance: Personal Accident & Sickness, Life

Caradoc Delaware Mutual Fire Insurance Company
PO Box 460
22508 Adelaide Rd.
Mount Brydges, ON N0L 1W0
519-264-2298
Fax: 519-264-9101
877-707-2298
info@cdmins.com
www.cdmins.com
Classes of Insurance: Personal Accident & Sickness, Auto, Liability, Boiler & Machinery, Property

Carleton Mutual Insurance Company
301 Main St.
Florenceville, NB E7L 3G5
506-392-6041
Fax: 506-392-8243
800-561-1550
cmi@nb.aibn.com
www.carletonmutual.com
Classes of Insurance: Auto, Property, Fire

Cavell Insurance Company Limited
c/o D.M. Williams & Associates Ltd.
#201, 3650 Victoria Park Ave.
Toronto, ON M2H 3P7
416-496-1148
Fax: 416-496-1089
Classes of Insurance: Personal Accident & Sickness, Auto, Liability, Boiler & Machinery, Marine, Fidelity, Property, Surety, Hail & Crop

Certas Direct Insurance Company/ Certas Direct, compagnie d'assurances
PO Box 3500
6300, boul de la Rive-Sud
Lévis, QC G6V 6P9
905-306-3900
Fax: 418-835-5599
800-565-6020
www.certas.ca
Classes of Insurance: Auto, Liability, Property, Surety

Chicago Title Insurance Company Canada
2700 Argentia Rd.
Mississauga, ON L5N 5V4
905-816-4485
Fax: 902-816-4988
888-868-4853
info@chicagotitle.ca
www.ctic.ca

Chrysler Insurance Company (DCIC)
#400, East Tower, 2700 Matheson Blvd. East
Mississauga, ON L4W 4V9
905-629-6066
www.insurance.chrysler.com
Classes of Insurance: Auto, Liability, Property, Surety

Chubb Insurance Company of Canada/ Chubb du Canada Compagnie d'Assurance
One Financial Place
1 Adelaide St. East
Toronto, ON M5C 2V9
416-863-0550
Fax: 416-863-5010
www.chubb.com/international/canada
Classes of Insurance: Personal Accident & Sickness, Aircraft, Auto, Liability, Boiler & Machinery, Marine, Fidelity, Property, Surety

CIBC Life Insurance Company Limited/ Compagnie d'Assurance-Vie CIBC Limitée
#900, 3 Robert Speck Pkwy.
Mississauga, ON L4Z 2G5
905-306-4904
Fax: 905-306-4957
Classes of Insurance: Personal Accident & Sickness, Life

CIGNA Life Insurance Company of Canada
PO Box 14
#606, 55 Town Centre Ct.
Toronto, ON M1P 4X4
416-290-6666
Fax: 416-290-0732
www.cigna.com
Classes of Insurance: Accident, Personal Accident & Sickness, Life, Credit

The Citadel General Assurance Company
#1200, 1075 Bay St.
Toronto, ON M5S 2W5
416-928-8500
Fax: 416-928-1553
cit-web-info@citadel.ca
www.citadel.ca
Classes of Insurance: Accident, Personal Accident & Sickness, Auto, Liability, Fidelity, Property, Fire, Surety, Theft

Clare Mutual Insurance Company
3300 Hwy. 1
Belliveau Cove, NS B0W 1J0
902-837-4597
Fax: 902-837-7745
877-818-0887
claremutual@sympatico.ns.ca
www.claremutual.com
Classes of Insurance: Property, Fire, Hail & Crop

Coachman Insurance Company
802 The Queensway
Toronto, ON M8Z 1N5
416-255-3417
Fax: 416-255-3347
800-361-2622
inquiries@coachmanins.com
www.coachmaninsurance.ca
Classes of Insurance: Auto

Coast Underwriters Limited
#1610, 200 Granville St.
Vancouver, BC V6C 1S4
604-683-5631
Fax: 604-683-8561
www.coast-uw.com

Coastal Community Insurance Services (2007) Ltd.
#21, 13 Victoria Cres.
Nanaimo, BC V9R 5B9
250-741-3200
888-741-1010
Classes of Insurance: Auto, Property

Combined Insurance Company of America/ Compagnie d'assurance Combined d'Amérique
PO Box 3720, MIP Stn. MIP
7300 Warden Ave., 3rd. Fl.
Markham, ON L3R 0X3
905-305-1922
Fax: 905-305-8600
888-234-4466
www.combined.ca
Classes of Insurance: Personal Accident & Sickness, Life

Commonwealth Insurance Company
Bentall Tower III
PO Box 49115
#1500, 595 Burrard St.
Vancouver, BC V7X 1G4
604-683-5511
Fax: 604-683-8968
info@commonw.com
www.commonw.com
Classes of Insurance: Aircraft, Liability, Boiler & Machinery, Marine, Fidelity, Property, Surety

La Compagnie d'Assurance Missisquoi/ The Missisquoi Insurance Company
#500, 1000, rue de la Gauchetière ouest
Montréal, QC H3B 4W5
514-875-5790
Fax: 514-875-9769
800-361-7573
Classes of Insurance: Legal Expense, Auto, Liability, Boiler & Machinery, Fidelity, Property, Fire, Surety, Theft

Connecticut General Life Insurance Co. (CGLIC)
c/o CIGNA Life Insurance Company of Canada
#606, 55 Town Centre Ct.
Toronto, ON M1P 4X4
416-290-6666
Fax: 416-290-0732
800-668-7029
www.cigna.com
Classes of Insurance: Accident, Personal Accident & Sickness, Life

Constitution Insurance Company of Canada
#202, 1232C Lawrence Ave. East
Toronto, ON M3A 1B9
416-585-9876
Fax: 416-595-5302
Classes of Insurance: Accident, Legal Expense, Auto, Liability, Fidelity, Property, Surety

Continental Casualty Company
#1500, 250 Yonge St.
Toronto, ON M5B 2L7
416-542-7300
Fax: 416-542-7310
800-268-9399
www.cnacanada.ca/portal/
Classes of Insurance: Accident, Personal Accident & Sickness, Aircraft, Auto, Liability, Boiler & Machinery, Credit, Fidelity, Property, Surety, Hail & Crop

Co-operative Hail Insurance Company Ltd.
PO Box 777
2709 - 13th Ave.
Regina, SK S4P 3A8
306-522-8891
Fax: 306-352-9130
info@coophail.com
www.coophail.com
Classes of Insurance: Hail & Crop

Co-operators General Insurance Company
Priory Sq., 7th Fl.
Guelph, ON N1H 6P8
519-824-4400
Fax: 519-824-0599
877-795-7272
service@cooperators.ca
www.cooperators.ca
Classes of Insurance: Personal Accident & Sickness, Aircraft, Auto, Boiler & Machinery, Life, Fidelity, Property, Fire, Surety, Hail & Crop, Theft

Co-operators Life Insurance Company
1920 College Ave.
Regina, SK S4P 1C4
306-347-6200
Fax: 306-347-6806
800-454-8061
Other Contact Information: Group Benefits, Toll Free: 1-800-667-8164; Fax: 306-761-7373; Email: group_client_services@cooperators.ca; Travel, Toll Free: 1-800-869-6747
service@cooperators.ca; phs_individual_life@cooperators.ca
www.cooperators.ca
Classes of Insurance: Personal Accident & Sickness, Life, Property

COSECO Insurance Company
5600 Cancross Ct.
Mississauga, ON L5R 3E9
905-507-6156
Fax: 905-507-8661
service@cooperators.ca.
www.cooperators.ca
Classes of Insurance: Auto, Property

Cowan Insurance Group Ltd.
PO Box 1510
705 Fountain St. North
Cambridge, ON N1R 5T2
519-650-6360
Fax: 519-650-6366
866-912-6926
infocib@cowangroup.ca
www.cowangroup.ca
Classes of Insurance: Auto, Marine, Property

Croatian Fraternal Union of America
c/o Deloitte & Touche
#1400, 181 Bay St.
Toronto, ON M5J 2V1
416-601-6150
Fax: 416-601-6590
www.croatianfraternalunion.org
Classes of Insurance: Personal Accident & Sickness, Life

Crowsnest Insurance Agencies Ltd.
PO Box 88
12731 - 20th Ave.
Blairmore, AB T0K 0E0
403-562-8822
Fax: 403-562-8239
800-361-8658
info@crowsnestinsurance.com
crowsnestinsurance.com
Classes of Insurance: Auto, Liability, Property

Culross Mutual Insurance Company (CMI)
PO Box 173
28 Clinton St.
Teeswater, ON N0G 2S0
519-392-6260
Fax: 519-392-8177
888-800-8666
ken@culrossmutual.com
www.culrossmutual.com

CUMIS General Insurance Company
PO Box 5065
151 North Service Rd.
Burlington, ON L7R 4C2
905-632-1221
Fax: 905-632-9412
800-263-9120
www.cumis.com
Classes of Insurance: Auto, Boiler & Machinery, Fidelity, Property, Fire, Theft

The CUMIS Group Limited
PO Box 5065
151 North Service Rd.
Burlington, ON L7R 4C2
905-632-1221
Fax: 905-632-9412
800-263-9120
customer.service@cumis.com
www.cumis.com
Classes of Insurance: Personal Accident & Sickness, Auto, Life, Property

CUMIS Life Insurance Company
PO Box 5065
151 North Service Rd.
Burlington, ON L7R 4C2
905-632-1221
Fax: 905-632-9412
800-263-9120
customer.service@cumis.com
www.cumis.com
Classes of Insurance: Accident, Personal Accident & Sickness, Auto, Life, Credit, Fidelity, Property, Fire, Theft

Desjardins assurances générales inc/ Desjardins General Insurance Inc.
PO Box 3500
6300, boul de la Rive-Sud
Lévis, QC G6V 6P9
418-835-4850
Fax: 418-835-5599
800-277-8726
www.desjardinsassurancesgenerales.com
Classes of Insurance: Auto, Liability, Boiler & Machinery, Property, Surety

Desjardins Financial Security (DFS)/ Desjardins Sécurité financière
200, av des Commandeurs
Lévis, QC G6V 6R2
866-838-7553
info@desjardinssecuritefinanciere.com; grouppension@dsf.ca
www.dsf-dfs.com
Classes of Insurance: Accident, Personal Accident & Sickness, Life

Desjardins Groupe d'assurances générales inc/ Desjardins General Insurance Group Inc.
6300, boul de la Rive-Sud
Lévis, QC G6V 6P9
888-277-8726
www.dgag.ca

The Dominion of Canada General Insurance Company/ Compagnie d'assurance générale dominion du Canada
165 University Ave.
Toronto, ON M5H 3B9
416-362-7231
Fax: 416-362-9918
800-268-8447
www.thedominion.ca
Classes of Insurance: Auto, Liability, Property, Fire, Surety, Theft

Dufferin Mutual Insurance Company
712 Main St. East
Shelburne, ON L0N 1S0
519-925-2026
Fax: 519-925-3357
800-265-9115
info@dufferinmutual.com
www.dufferinmutual.com
Classes of Insurance: Personal Accident & Sickness, Auto, Liability, Boiler & Machinery, Fidelity, Property

Dumfries Mutual Insurance Company
12 Cambridge St.
Cambridge, ON N1R 3R7
519-621-4660
Fax: 519-740-8732
info@dumfriesmutual.com
www.dumfriesmutual.com
Classes of Insurance: Auto, Liability, Boiler & Machinery, Property, Hail & Crop

Eagle Star Insurance Company Ltd.
c/o Focus Group Inc.
#500, 36 King St. East
Toronto, ON M5C 1E5
416-361-1728
Fax: 416-361-6113
www.eaglestar.ie
Classes of Insurance: Personal Accident & Sickness, Aircraft, Auto, Liability, Boiler & Machinery, Fidelity, Property, Surety

Ecclesiastical Insurance Office plc/ Société des Assurances écclésiastiques
PO Box 2004
#2200, 20 Eglinton Ave. West
Toronto, ON M4R 1K8
416-484-4555
Fax: 416-484-6352
info@eccles-ins.com
www.eigcanada.com, www.ecclesiastical.co.uk

Classes of Insurance: Auto, Liability, Boiler & Machinery, Marine, Fidelity, Property

Echelon General Insurance Company
#310, 1550 Enterprise Rd.
Mississauga, ON L4W 4P4

905-564-9215
Fax: 905-565-7992
800-324-3566
www.echelon-insurance.ca

Classes of Insurance: Accident, Personal Accident & Sickness, Legal Expense, Auto, Liability, Fidelity, Property, Fire, Surety

The Economical Insurance Group
PO Box 2000
111 Westmount St. South
Waterloo, ON N2J 4S4

519-570-8200
Fax: 519-570-8389
800-265-2180
www.economicalinsurance.com

Economical Mutual Insurance Company
PO Box 2000
111 Westmount Rd. South
Waterloo, ON N2J 4S4

519-570-8200
Fax: 519-570-8389
800-265-2180
www.economicalinsurance.com

Classes of Insurance: Auto, Boiler & Machinery, Property, Surety

Elite Insurance Company
2206 Eglinton Ave. East
Toronto, ON M1L 4S8

416-288-1800
Fax: 416-288-5888
Other Contact Information: 800-590-5003 (Toll Free, After Hours Emergency Service, Atlantic Canada); 800-561-9899 (Toll Free, NB, 8am-5pm); 800-565-7153 (Toll Free, NS, PE, NL)
www.avivacanada.com

Classes of Insurance: Personal Accident & Sickness, Aircraft, Auto, Liability, Boiler & Machinery, Marine, Fidelity, Property, Surety

Empire Life Insurance Company/ Empire Vie
259 King St. East
Kingston, ON K7L 3A8

613-548-1881
800-561-1268
buildingempires@empire.ca
www.empire.ca

Classes of Insurance: Accident, Personal Accident & Sickness, Life

Employers Reinsurance Corporation
PO Box 50
#2200, 150 King St. West
Toronto, ON M5H 1J9

416-217-5555
Fax: 416-217-5566
www.swissre.com

Classes of Insurance: Personal Accident & Sickness, Aircraft, Auto, Liability, Boiler & Machinery, Credit, Fidelity, Property, Surety, Hail & Crop

L'Entraide assurance, compagnie mutuelle/ L'Entraide Assurance Mutual Company
CP 70226, Québec-Centre Stn. Québec-Centre
520, boul Charest est, 1er étage
Québec, QC G1K 7P5

418-658-0663
Fax: 418-658-5065
800-536-8724
service@lentraide.com
www.lentraide.com

Classes of Insurance: Accident, Personal Accident & Sickness, Life, Credit

The Equitable Life Insurance Company of Canada
1 Westmount Rd. North
Waterloo, ON N2J 4C7

519-886-5110
Fax: 519-883-7400
800-265-8878
webmaster@equitable.ca
www.equitable.ca

Classes of Insurance: Life

Erie Mutual Fire Insurance Company
711 Main St. East
Dunnville, ON N1A 2W5

905-774-8566
Fax: 905-774-6468
800-263-6484
www.eriemutual.com

Classes of Insurance: Personal Accident & Sickness, Auto, Liability, Boiler & Machinery, Fidelity, Property

Euler Hermes Canada
#1702, 1155, boul René-Lévesque ouest
Montréal, QC H3B 3Z7

514-876-9656
Fax: 514-876-9658
877-509-3224
canada.info@eulerhermes.com
www.eulerhermes.com/canada

Classes of Insurance: Credit

Everest Insurance Company of Canada/ La Compagnie d'assurance Everest du Canada
The Exchange Tower
PO Box 431
#2520, 130 King St. West
Toronto, ON M5X 1E3

416-862-1228
Fax: 416-366-5899
www.everestre.com

Classes of Insurance: Aircraft, Auto, Liability, Boiler & Machinery, Credit, Marine, Property, Surety, Hail & Crop

Everest Reinsurance Company
The Exchange Tower
PO Box 431
#2520, 130 King St. West
Toronto, ON M5X 1E3

416-862-1228
Fax: 416-366-5899
www.everestre.com

Classes of Insurance: Personal Accident & Sickness, Aircraft, Auto, Liability, Boiler & Machinery, Credit, Fidelity, Property, Surety, Hail & Crop

L'Excellence, Compagnie d'assurance-vie/ Excellence Life Insurance Company
#202, 5055, boul Métropolitain est
Montréal, QC H1R 1Z7

514-327-0020
800-465-5818
service@excellence.qc.ca
www.excellence.qc.ca

Classes of Insurance: Personal Accident & Sickness, Life

FaithLife Financial
470 Weber St. North
Waterloo, ON N2J 4G4

519-886-4610
Fax: 519-886-0350
moreinfo@faithlifefinancial.ca
www.faithlifefinancial.ca

Classes of Insurance: Accident, Personal Accident & Sickness, Life

Farmers' Mutual Insurance Company (Lindsay)
PO Box 28
336 Angeline St. South
Lindsay, ON K9V 4R8

705-324-2146
Fax: 705-324-2356
800-461-0310
www.farmerslindsay.com

Classes of Insurance: Personal Accident & Sickness, Auto, Liability, Boiler & Machinery, Marine, Fidelity, Property

Federal Insurance Company
One Financial Place
1 Adelaide St. East
Toronto, ON M5C 2V9

416-863-0550
Fax: 416-863-5010
gdamiano@chubb.com
www.chubb.com/international/canada

Classes of Insurance: Personal Accident & Sickness, Auto, Liability, Boiler & Machinery, Marine, Fidelity, Property, Surety

Federated Insurance Company of Canada
PO Box 5800
717 Portage Ave.
Winnipeg, MB R3C 3C9

204-786-6431
Fax: 204-784-6755
800-665-1934
webmaster@federated.ca
www.federated.ca

Classes of Insurance: Accident, Auto, Liability, Boiler & Machinery, Fidelity, Property, Fire, Surety, Theft

Federation Insurance Company of Canada/ La Fédération Compagnie d'Assurances du Canada
#500, 1000, rue de la Gauchetière ouest
Montréal, QC H3B 4W5

514-875-5790
Fax: 514-875-9769
800-361-7573
admin@federation.ca
www.federation.ca

Classes of Insurance: Accident, Legal Expense, Auto, Liability, Boiler & Machinery, Fidelity, Property, Fire, Surety, Hail & Crop

Fenchurch General Insurance Company (FGIC)
Promontory II
#115, 2655 North Sheridan Way
Mississauga, ON L5K 2P8

905-822-2282
Fax: 905-822-1282
info@fenchurchgeneral.com
www.fenchurchgeneral.com

Classes of Insurance: Personal Accident & Sickness, Auto, Liability, Boiler & Machinery, Property, Surety

First Canadian Title
2235 Sheridan Garden Dr.
Oakville, ON L6J 7Y5

905-287-1000
Fax: 905-287-2400
800-307-0370
www.firstcanadiantitle.com

First North American Insurance Company
#1600, 5650 Yonge St.
Toronto, ON M2M 4G4

800-668-0195
am_service@manulife.com
www.manulife.ca

Classes of Insurance: Personal Accident & Sickness, Auto, Property

FM Global
#500, 165 Commerce Valley Dr. West
Thornhill, ON L3T 7V8

905-763-5555
Fax: 905-763-5556
www.fmglobal.com

Classes of Insurance: Boiler & Machinery, Property

FNF Canada
2700 Argentia Rd.
Mississauga, ON L5N 5V4

905-821-2262
Fax: 905-821-7918
877-526-3232
info@fnf.ca
www.fnf.ca

Folksamerica Reinsurance Company
#1202, 80 Bloor St. West
Toronto, ON M5S 2V1

416-928-2430
Fax: 416-928-2459
marketing@folksamerica.com
www.folksamerica.com

Classes of Insurance: Auto, Liability, Fidelity, Property, Surety, Hail & Crop

Fonds d'assurance responsabilité professionnelle de la Chambre des notaires du Québec
#1500, 1200, av McGill College
Montréal, QC H3B 4G7

514-871-4999
Fax: 514-879-1781
www.cdnq.org

Fonds d'assurance responsabilité professionnelle du Barreau du Québec
#300, 445, boul Saint-Laurent
Montréal, QC H2Y 3T8

514-954-3452
Fax: 514-954-3454
Other Contact Information: Toll Free: 1-800-361-8495, poste 3452
assuranceresponsabilite@barreau.qc.ca
www.assurance-barreau.com

Frank Cowan Company Limited
4 Cowan St. East
Princeton, ON N0J 1V0

519-458-4331
Fax: 519-458-4366
800-265-4000
mail@frankcowan.com
www.frankcowan.com

Classes of Insurance: Liability

Fundy Mutual Insurance Company
1022 Main St.
Sussex, NB E4E 2M3

506-432-1535
Fax: 506-433-6788
800-222-9550
info@fundymutual.com
www.fundymutual.com

Classes of Insurance: Auto, Liability, Boiler & Machinery, Property

G & F Financial Group
7375 Kingsway
Burnaby, BC V3N 3B5

604-517-5100
Fax: 604-659-4025
www.gffg.com

GAN Assurances Vie Compagnie française d'assurances vie mixte
#1470, 1155, rue Metcalfe
Montréal, QC H3B 2V6

514-286-9007
eclark@bellnet.ca

Classes of Insurance: Life

GCAN Insurance Company (GCAN)/ GCAN compagnie d'assurances
#1000, 181 University Ave.
Toronto, ON M5H 3M7

416-682-5300
Fax: 416-682-9213
central.office@gcan.ca
www.gcan.ca

Classes of Insurance: Personal Accident & Sickness, Aircraft, Auto, Liability, Boiler & Machinery, Credit, Marine, Fidelity, Property, Surety, Hail & Crop

General American Life Insurance Company (GALIC)
c/o RGA Life Reinsurance Company of Canada
#1000, 1255, rue Peel
Montréal, QC H3B 2T9

514-985-5260
Fax: 514-985-3066
800-985-4326
mail@rgare.ca

Classes of Insurance: Life, Reinsurance

General Reinsurance Corporation
PO Box 471
#5705, 1 First Canadian Pl.
Toronto, ON M5X 1E4

416-869-0490
Fax: 416-360-2020
AskGenRe@genre.com
www.genre.com

Classes of Insurance: Personal Accident & Sickness, Aircraft, Auto, Liability, Boiler & Machinery, Credit, Fidelity, Property, Surety, Hail & Crop

Genworth Financial Mortgage Insurance Company Canada
#300, 2060 Winston Park Dr.
Oakville, ON L6H 5R7

800-511-8888
mortgage.info@genworth.com
www.gemortgage.ca

Gerber Life Insurance Company
PO Box 22265, BRM B Stn. BRM B
Toronto, ON M7Y 4A1

800-518-8884
www.gerberlife.ca

Classes of Insurance: Life

Germania Farmers' Mutual Fire Insurance Co.
PO Box 30
403 Mary St.
Ayton, ON N0G 1C0

519-665-7715
Fax: 519-665-7558
800-265-3433
info@germaniamutual.com
www.germaniamutual.com

Classes of Insurance: Personal Accident & Sickness, Auto, Liability, Boiler & Machinery, Fidelity, Property

Germania Mutual Insurance Company
127 Kaiser William Ave. East
Langenburg, SK S0A 2A0

306-743-5363
germania@sasktel.net

Classes of Insurance: Liability, Property, Fire, Theft

Gibb's Agencies (1997) Ltd.
Main St.
Barons, AB T0L 0G0

403-757-3820
Fax: 403-757-2083
888-974-4227
info@gibbsagencies.ca
www.gibbsagencies.com

Classes of Insurance: Auto, Property

Glengarry Farmers' Mutual Fire Insurance Co.
PO Box 159
3720 County Rd. 34
Alexandria, ON K0C 1A0

613-525-2557
Fax: 613-525-5162
800-263-7684
glenins@glenins.ca
www.glenins.ca

Classes of Insurance: Personal Accident & Sickness, Legal Expense, Auto, Liability, Boiler & Machinery, Fidelity, Property, Fire, Theft

Global Aerospace Underwriting Managers (Canada) Limited
#200, 100 Renfrew Dr.
Markham, ON L3R 9R6

905-479-2244
Fax: 905-479-0751
Jzigrossi@global-aero.com
www.global-aero.co.uk

Classes of Insurance: Personal Accident & Sickness, Aircraft, Liability, Property

Gore Mutual Insurance Company
PO Box 70, Galt Stn. Galt
252 Dundas St.
Cambridge, ON N1R 5T3

519-623-1910
800-265-8600
webserver@goremutual.ca
www.goremutual.ca

Classes of Insurance: Personal Accident & Sickness, Auto, Liability, Property, Fire, Theft

Grain Insurance and Guarantee Company
#1240, 1 Lombard Pl.
Winnipeg, MB R3B 0V9

204-943-0721
Fax: 204-943-6419
800-665-3351
infowinnipeg@graininsurance.com
www.graininsurance.com

Classes of Insurance: Liability, Boiler & Machinery, Fidelity, Property, Fire, Surety, Theft

The Grand Orange Lodge of British America Beneficent Fund
94 Sheppard Ave. West
Toronto, ON M2N 1M5

416-223-1690
Fax: 416-223-1324
800-565-6248
info@grandorangelodge.ca
www.grandorangelodge.ca

Classes of Insurance: Life

Granite Insurance Company
#200, 2 Eva Rd.
Toronto, ON M9C 2A8

416-622-0660
Fax: 416-622-8809
800-342-5243
dsymons@gorancapital.com

Classes of Insurance: Accident, Personal Accident & Sickness, Auto, Liability, Boiler & Machinery, Credit, Fidelity, Property, Fire, Surety, Hail & Crop, Theft

Great American Insurance Company
c/o Cassels, Brock & Blackwell, Scotia Plaza
#2100, 40 King St. West
Toronto, ON M5H 3C2

416-869-5300
Fax: 416-360-8877

Classes of Insurance: Personal Accident & Sickness, Aircraft, Auto, Liability, Boiler & Machinery, Marine, Fidelity, Property, Surety, Hail & Crop

The Great-West Life Assurance Company (GWL)/ Great-West, Compagnie d'Assurance Vie
100 Osborne St. North
Winnipeg, MB R3C 3A5

204-946-1190
Fax: 204-946-4159
800-665-5758
Other Contact Information: TTY, Toll Free: 1-800-990-6654
webmaster@gwl.ca
www.greatwestlife.com; www.grsaccess.com

Classes of Insurance: Personal Accident & Sickness, Life

Green Shield Canada
PO Box 1606
8677 Anchor Dr.
Windsor, ON N9A 6W1

519-739-1133
Fax: 519-739-0200
800-265-5615
www.greenshield.ca

Classes of Insurance: Personal Accident & Sickness

Grenville Mutual Insurance Company
PO Box 10
3005 County Rd. 21
Spencerville, ON K0E 1X0

613-658-2013
Fax: 613-658-3374
800-267-4400
mail@grenvillemutual.com
www.grenvillemutual.com

Classes of Insurance: Personal Accident & Sickness, Auto, Liability, Boiler & Machinery, Fidelity, Property

Grey & Bruce Mutual Insurance Co.
517 - 10th St.
Hanover, ON N4N 1R4

519-364-2250
Fax: 519-364-6067
800-265-5522
www.greybrucemutualinsurance.com

Classes of Insurance: Personal Accident & Sickness, Auto, Liability, Boiler & Machinery, Property

Le Groupe Estrie-Richelieu, compagnie d'assurance (GER)
770, rue Principale
Granby, QC J2G 2Y7

450-378-0101
Fax: 450-378-5189
ressources@ger.qc.ca
www.ger.qc.ca

Classes of Insurance: Auto, Liability, Boiler & Machinery, Property, Fire

Groupe Promutuel, Fédération de sociétés mutuelles d'assurance générale
1091, Grande Allée ouest
Québec, QC G1S 4Y7

866-999-2433
federation@promutuel.ca
www.promutuel.ca

The Guarantee Company of North America/ La Garantie, Compagnie d'Assurance de l'Amérique d
Madison Centre
#1400, 4950 Yonge St.
Toronto, ON M2N 6K1

416-223-9580
Fax: 416-223-6577
800-260-6617
www.gcna.com

Classes of Insurance: Accident, Personal Accident & Sickness, Legal Expense, Auto, Liability, Boiler & Machinery, Credit, Fidelity, Property, Fire, Surety, Hail & Crop, Theft

Halwell Mutual Insurance Company
PO Box 60
812 Woolwich St.
Guelph, ON N1H 6J6

519-836-2860
Fax: 519-836-2831
800-267-5706
reception@halwellmutual.com
www.halwellmutual.com

Classes of Insurance: Auto, Liability, Boiler & Machinery, Fidelity, Property

Hamilton Township Mutual Insurance Company
PO Box 201
1176 Division St.
Cobourg, ON K9A 4K5

905-372-0186
Fax: 905-372-1364
800-263-3935
info@htminsurance.ca
www.htminsurance.ca

Classes of Insurance: Marine, Fire

Hannover Rückversicherungs AG
#201, 3650 Victoria Park Ave.
Toronto, ON M2H 3P7
416-496-1148
Fax: 416-496-1089
www.hannover-rueck.de
Classes of Insurance: Personal Accident & Sickness, Aircraft, Auto, Liability, Boiler & Machinery, Fidelity, Property, Surety, Hail & Crop

Hartford Fire Insurance Company
121 King St. West
Toronto, ON M5H 3T9
416-733-9265
Fax: 416-733-0510
888-898-8334
Classes of Insurance: Personal Accident & Sickness, Aircraft, Auto, Liability, Boiler & Machinery, Fidelity, Property, Fire, Surety, Hail & Crop, Theft

Hay Mutual Insurance Company
PO Box 130
37868 Zurich-Hensall Rd.
Zurich, ON N0M 2T0
519-236-4381
Fax: 519-236-7681
www.haymutual.on.ca
Classes of Insurance: Auto, Liability, Property, Hail & Crop

Henderson Insurance Inc.
339 Main St. North
Moose Jaw, SK S6H 0W2
306-694-5959
Fax: 306-693-0117
888-661-5959
hii@hendersoninsurance.ca
www.hendersoninsurance.ca
Classes of Insurance: Aircraft, Auto, Liability, Marine, Property, Hail & Crop

Howard Mutual Insurance Co.
PO Box 398
20 Ebenezer St. West
Ridgetown, ON N0P 2C0
519-674-5434
Fax: 519-674-2029
howardmutual.com
Classes of Insurance: Personal Accident & Sickness, Auto, Liability, Fidelity, Property, Hail & Crop

Howick Mutual Insurance Company
PO Box 30
1091 Centre St.
Wroxeter, ON N0G 2X0
519-335-3561
Fax: 519-335-6416
800-265-3033
sedgar@howickmutual.com
www.howickmutual.com
Classes of Insurance: Personal Accident & Sickness, Auto, Liability, Boiler & Machinery, Fidelity, Property, Hail & Crop

The Independent Order of Foresters
789 Don Mills Rd.
Toronto, ON M3C 1T9
416-429-3000
Fax: 416-467-2516
800-828-1540
service@foresters.biz
www.foresters.biz
Classes of Insurance: Personal Accident & Sickness, Life

Industrial Alliance Insurance & Financial Services Inc./ Industrielle Alliance Assurance et Services Financ
CP 1907, Terminus Stn. Terminus
1080, ch Saint-Louis
Québec, QC G1K 7M3
418-684-5000
800-463-6236
info@inalco.com, customers@inalco.com
www.inalco.com
Classes of Insurance: Personal Accident & Sickness, Auto, Life

Industrial Alliance Pacific Life Insurance Company (IAP)
PO Box 5900
2165 West Broadway
Vancouver, BC V6B 5H6
604-734-1667
Fax: 604-734-8221
800-363-2166
intouch@iaplife.com
www.iaplife.com
Classes of Insurance: Accident, Personal Accident & Sickness, Life, Credit

Innovative Insurance Agencies
6351 Rideau Valley Dr. North
Ottawa, ON K4M 1B3
Fax: 613-692-0338
800-265-4275
info@innovativeinsurance.ca
www.innovativeinsurance.ca

Insurance Company of Prince Edward Island
14 Great George St.
Charlottetown, PE C1A 4J6
902-368-3675
Fax: 902-626-3529
inquiries@icpei.ca
www.icpei.ca
Classes of Insurance: Auto, Life, Property,

Insurance Corporation of British Columbia (ICBC)
151 West Esplanade
North Vancouver, BC V7M 3H9
604-661-2800
Fax: 604-646-7400
800-663-3051
www.icbc.com
Classes of Insurance: Auto

Intact Insurance Company of Canada
700 University Ave., 15th Fl.
Toronto, ON M5G 0A1
416-341-1464
Fax: 416-344-8030
877-341-1464
info@intact.net
www.intactinsurance.com
Classes of Insurance: Marine, Surety

Intact Insurance Company of Canada - Novex Group Insurance/ ING Novex Compagnie d'Assurance du Canada
700 University Ave., 15th Fl.
Toronto, ON M5G 0A1
416-341-1464
Fax: 416-344-8030
877-341-1464
info@intact.net
www.intactinsurance.com
Classes of Insurance: Personal Accident & Sickness, Legal Expense, Auto, Liability, Boiler & Machinery, Credit, Fidelity, Property, Surety

L'Internationale, compagnie d'assurance-vie/ The International Life Insurance Company
CP 696
142, rue Hériot
Montréal, QC J2B 6W9
514-281-0666
Fax: 514-281-6340
800-310-2166
courrier@linternationale.qc.ca
www.linternationale.qc.ca
Classes of Insurance: Personal Accident & Sickness, Life

JEVCO Insurance Company/ La Compagnie d'Assurances JEVCO
#100, 5250, boul Décarie
Montréal, QC H3X 2H9
514-284-9350
Fax: 514-289-9257
800-361-8500
Other Contact Information: 514-284-4823 (Commercial); 514-284-3805 (Claims); 514-284-3390 (Motoplan)
communications@jevco.ca
www.jevco.ca
Classes of Insurance: Auto, Property

Johnston Meier Insurance Agencies Group
1944 Como Lake Ave.
Coquitlam, BC V3J 3R3
604-937-3601
Fax: 604-937-5062
www.kbyinsurance.com
Classes of Insurance: Aircraft, Auto, Life, Marine, Surety

Kent & Essex Mutual Insurance Company
PO Box 356
10 Creek Rd.
Chatham, ON N7M 5K4
519-352-3190
Fax: 519-352-5344
800-265-5206
info@kentesexmutual.com
www.kentessexmutual.com
Classes of Insurance: Personal Accident & Sickness, Auto, Liability, Boiler & Machinery, Fidelity, Property

The Kings Mutual Insurance Company
220 Commercial St.
Berwick, NS B0P 1E0
902-538-3187
Fax: 902-538-7271
800-565-7220
info@kingsmutual.ns.ca
www.kingsmutual.ns.ca
Classes of Insurance: Liability, Property, Fire

Kingsway Financial Services Inc.
#800, 7210 Hurontario St.
Mississauga, ON L5W 0A9
905-629-7888
Fax: 905-629-5008
info@kingsway-financial.com
www.kingsway-financial.com
Classes of Insurance: Auto, Property, Reinsurance

Kingsway General Insurance Company
#700, 7120 Hurontario St.
Mississauga, ON L5W 0B1
905-677-8889
Fax: 905-677-5008
800-265-5458
kgmarketing@kingsway-general.com
www.kingsway-general.com
Classes of Insurance: Auto, Liability, Property, Surety

Kirkham Insurance
205 - 11th St. South
Lethbridge, AB T1J 4A6
403-328-1228
Fax: 403-380-4051
800-256-2155
www.kirkhaminsurance.com
Classes of Insurance: Auto, Property

Knights of Columbus
25 Campbell St.
Belleville, ON K8N 1S6
613-962-5347
Fax: 613-968-7359
kjs@sodenco.com
Classes of Insurance: Life

Lambton Mutual Insurance Company
PO Box 520
7873 Confederation Line
Watford, ON N0M 2S0
519-876-2304
Fax: 519-876-3940
800-561-4136
info@lambtonmutual.com
www.lambtonmutual.com
Classes of Insurance: Personal Accident & Sickness, Auto, Liability, Boiler & Machinery, Fidelity, Property, Hail & Crop

Lanark Mutual Insurance Company
96 South St., Scotch Line Rd.
Perth, ON K7H 0A2
613-267-5554
Fax: 613-267-6793
800-267-7908
lmadmin@LanarkMutual.com
www.lanarkmutual.com
Classes of Insurance: Auto, Liability, Boiler & Machinery, Property, Hail & Crop, Theft

Lawyers' Professional Indemnity Company (LAWPRO)
PO Box 3
#3101, 250 Yonge St.
Toronto, ON M5B 2L7
416-598-5800
Fax: 416-599-8341
800-410-1013
service@lawpro.ca
www.lawpro.ca
Classes of Insurance: Liability

Legacy General Insurance Company/ Compagnie d'Assurances Générales Legacy
80 Tiverton Ct., 5th Fl.
Markham, ON L3R 0G4
905-479-7500
Fax: 905-479-3224
www.canadianpremier.ca
Classes of Insurance: Personal Accident & Sickness, Liability, Property

Lennox & Addington Mutual Insurance Company
PO Box 174
32 Mill St.
Napanee, ON K7R 3M3
613-354-4810
Fax: 613-354-7112
800-267-7812
www.l-amutual.com
Classes of Insurance: Personal Accident & Sickness, Auto, Liability, Marine, Property

Liberty Mutual Insurance Company/ La Compagnie d'Assurance Liberté Mutuelle
Brookfield Place
#1000, 181 Bay St.
Toronto, ON M5J 2T3
416-307-4353
Fax: 416-365-7281
www.libertymutual.com
Classes of Insurance: Personal Accident & Sickness, Aircraft, Auto, Liability, Boiler & Machinery, Fidelity, Property, Surety

Liberty Mutual Insurance Company/ Société d'assurance mutuelle des employeurs de Wau
Brookfield Place
#1000, 181 Bay St.
Toronto, ON M5J 2T3
416-365-7587
Fax: 416-307-4372
www.liucanada.com
Classes of Insurance: Personal Accident & Sickness, Aircraft, Auto, Liability, Boiler & Machinery, Fidelity, Property, Surety

Life Insurance Company of North America (LINA)
#606, 55 Town Centre Ct.
Toronto, ON M1P 4X4
416-290-6666
Fax: 416-290-0726
www.cigna.com
Classes of Insurance: Accident, Personal Accident & Sickness, Life

Lloyd's Underwriters
#2220, 1155, rue Metcalfe
Montréal, QC H3B 2V6
514-861-8361
Fax: 514-861-0470
877-455-6937
info@lloyds.ca
www.lloyds.com
Classes of Insurance: Personal Accident & Sickness, Aircraft, Legal Expense, Auto, Liability, Boiler & Machinery, Fidelity, Property, Fire, Surety, Reinsurance

Lombard General Insurance Company of Canada
105 Adelaide St. West
Toronto, ON M5H 1P9
416-350-4400
Fax: 416-350-4412
Classes of Insurance: Personal Accident & Sickness, Aircraft, Legal Expense, Auto, Liability, Boiler & Machinery, Credit, Fidelity, Property, Surety, Hail & Crop, Theft

Lombard Insurance Company
105 Adelaide St. West
Toronto, ON M5H 1P9
416-350-4400
Fax: 416-350-4412
www.lombard.ca
Classes of Insurance: Personal Accident & Sickness, Aircraft, Legal Expense, Auto, Liability, Boiler & Machinery, Credit, Marine, Fidelity, Property, Fire, Surety, Hail & Crop, Theft

London & Midland General Insurance Company
201 Queens Ave.
London, ON N6A 1J1
519-672-1070
Fax: 519-660-2625
800-285-8623
Classes of Insurance: Accident, Personal Accident & Sickness, Auto, Boiler & Machinery, Life, Fidelity, Property, Fire, Surety, Theft

London Life Insurance Company/ London Life, Compagnie d'Assurance-Vie
255 Dufferin Ave.
London, ON N6A 4K1
519-432-5281
corporate.information@londonlife.com
www.londonlife.com
Classes of Insurance: Personal Accident & Sickness, Life, Reinsurance

The Loyalist Insurance Company
#107, 911 Golf Links Rd.
Ancaster, ON L9K 1H9
905-648-6767
Fax: 905-648-7220
info@loyalistinsurance.com
www.loyalistinsurance.com

Lumbermen's Underwriting Alliance
#300, 455, boul Fénélon
Montréal, QC H9S 5T8
514-631-2710
Fax: 514-631-9788
www.lumbermensunderwriting.com
Classes of Insurance: Boiler & Machinery, Property

Manitoba Agricultural Services Corporation - Insurance Corporate Office (MASC)
#400, 50 - 24th St. NW
Portage La Prairie, MB R1N 3V9
204-239-3246
Fax: 204-239-3401
mailbox@masc.mb.ca
www.masc.mb.ca
Classes of Insurance: Hail & Crop

Manitoba Blue Cross
PO Box 1046
599 Empress St.
Winnipeg, MB R3C 2X7
204-775-0151
Fax: 204-786-5965
888-873-2583
www.mb.bluecross.ca
Classes of Insurance: Personal Accident & Sickness, Life

Manitoba Public Insurance
PO Box 6300
Winnipeg, MB R3C 4A4
204-985-7000
800-665-2410
Other Contact Information: TTY/TDD: 204-985-8832
www.mpi.mb.ca
Classes of Insurance: Auto

Manufacturers Life Insurance Company/ La Compagnie d'Assurance-Vie Manufacturers
200 Bloor St. East
Toronto, ON M4W 1E5
888-626-8543
www.manulife.ca
Classes of Insurance: Personal Accident & Sickness, Life

Manulife Canada Ltd./ Manuvie Canada Ltée
PO Box 1669
500 King St. North
Waterloo, ON N2J 4Z6
888-626-8543
valued_customer_centre@manulife.com
www.manulife.ca
Classes of Insurance: Life

Manulife Financial
PO Box 1669
500 King St. North
Waterloo, ON N2J 4Z6
888-626-8543
valued_customer_centre@manulife.com
www.manulife.ca
Classes of Insurance: Life

Markel Insurance Company of Canada
#1500, 55 University Ave.
Toronto, ON M5J 2H7
416-364-7800
Fax: 416-364-5655
888-627-5351
letstalk@markel.ca
www.markel.ca
Classes of Insurance: Auto

Massachusetts Mutual Life Insurance Company
c/o Cassels Brock & Blackwell LLP, Scotia Plaza
#2100, 40 King St. West
Toronto, ON M5H 3C2
416-869-5745
Fax: 416-350-6955
www.massmutual.com
Classes of Insurance: Personal Accident & Sickness, Life

MAX Canada Insurance Company
140 Foundry St.
Baden, ON N3A 2P7
Fax: 519-634-5159
877-770-7729
www.mutualaidexchange.com
Classes of Insurance: Liability, Boiler & Machinery, Marine, Fidelity, Property,

McFarlane & Company Financial Group Limited
#430, 999 - 8th St. SW
Calgary, AB T2R 1J5
403-229-0466
Fax: 403-228-9784
888-224-0466
info@mcfarlaneco.com
www.mcfarlaneco.com
Classes of Insurance: Auto, Liability, Life, Property, Surety, Hail & Crop

McKillop Mutual Insurance Company
PO Box 819
91 Main St. South
Seaforth, ON N0K 1W0
519-527-0400
Fax: 519-527-2777
800-463-9204
mckillo@tcc.on.ca
www.mckillopmutual.com
Classes of Insurance: Personal Accident & Sickness, Auto, Liability, Boiler & Machinery, Fidelity, Property

MD Life Insurance Company
1870 Alta Vista Dr.
Ottawa, ON K1G 6R7
Classes of Insurance: Life

Medavie Blue Cross
PO Box 220
644 Main St.
Moncton, NB E1C 8L3
506-853-1811
Fax: 506-867-4651
800-667-4511
Other Contact Information: Group Benefits, Atlantic Provinces & Ontario: 1-888-227-3400; Group Benefits, Québec: 1-888-588-1212
www.medavie.bluecross.ca
Classes of Insurance: Personal Accident & Sickness, Life

Meloche Monnex Inc.
50, Place Crémazie, 12e étage
Montréal, QC H2P 1B6
514-382-6060
Fax: 514-385-2162
www.melochemonnex.com

Mennonite Mutual Fire Insurance Company
PO Box 190
Waldheim, SK S0K 4R0
306-945-2239
Fax: 306-945-4666
mmfi@sasktel.net
www.mmfi.com
Classes of Insurance: Boiler & Machinery, Property, Fire, Theft

Mennonite Mutual Insurance Co. (Alberta) Ltd. (MMI)
#300, 2946 - 32nd St. NE
Calgary, AB T1Y 6J7
403-275-6996
Fax: 403-291-6733
866-222-6996
office@mmiab.ca
www.mmiab.ca
Classes of Insurance: Auto, Liability, Property, Fire

Metro General Insurance Corp.
T.D. Place
PO Box 548
#700, 140 Water St.
St. John's, NL A1C 5K9
709-726-1922
Fax: 709-726-5207
Classes of Insurance: Auto, Liability, Property

Metropolitan Life Insurance Company, Canadian Branch
Constitution Square
#1750, 360 Albert St.
Ottawa, ON K1R 7X7
613-237-7171
Fax: 613-237-7585
ldumas@metlife.com
www.metlife.com
Classes of Insurance: Personal Accident & Sickness, Life

Middlesex Mutual Insurance Co.
PO Box 100
13271 Ilderton Rd.
Ilderton, ON N0M 2A0

519-666-0075
Fax: 519-666-0079
800-851-4045
mmic@middlesexmutual.on.ca
www.middlesexmutual.on.ca
Classes of Insurance: Auto, Liability, Property

Millennium Insurance Corporation
340 Sioux Rd.
Sherwood Park, AB T8A 3X6
780-467-1500
Fax: 780-467-0004
866-467-1245
info@millenniuminsurance.ca
www.directinsure.net
Classes of Insurance: Auto, Property

Minnesota Life Insurance Company/ Compagnie d'Assurance-vie Minnesota
c/o McLean & Kerr LLP
#2800, 130 Adelaide St. West
Toronto, ON M5H 3P5
416-364-5371
Fax: 416-366-8571
www.minnesotamutual.com
Classes of Insurance: Life

Mitsui Sumitomo Insurance Co., Limited.
Chubb Insurance Company of Canada, One Financial Place
#1500A, 1 Adelaide St. East
Toronto, ON M5C 2V9
416-863-0550
Fax: 416-863-3144
www.ms-ins.com/english/index.html
Classes of Insurance: Personal Accident & Sickness, Aircraft, Auto, Liability, Boiler & Machinery, Fidelity, Property, Surety

Motors Insurance Corporation
#400, 8500 Leslie St.
Thornhill, ON L3T 7M8
905-882-3900
Fax: 905-882-3955
Classes of Insurance: Auto, Liability, Boiler & Machinery

Mouvement des caisses Desjardins du Québec
100, av des Commandeurs
Lévis, QC G6V 7N5
418-835-8444
Fax: 418-833-5873
www.desjardins.com

Munich Reinsurance Company - Canada Life
Munich Re Centre
390 Bay St., 26th Fl.
Toronto, ON M5H 2Y2
416-359-2200
Fax: 416-361-0305
generalenquiries@munichre.ca
www.munichre.ca
Classes of Insurance: Personal Accident & Sickness, Life, Reinsurance

Munich Reinsurance Company of Canada
390 Bay St., 22nd Fl.
Toronto, ON M5H 2Y2
416-366-9206
Fax: 416-366-4330
800-444-5321
www.mroc.com
Classes of Insurance: Auto, Liability, Property, Theft

Municipal Insurance Association of British Columbia (MIA)
#390, 1050 Homer St.
Vancouver, BC V6E 2W9
604-683-6266
Fax: 604-683-6244
info@miabc.org
www.miabc.org
Classes of Insurance: Liability

MUNIX Reciprocal (MUNIX)
300-8616 51 Ave.
Edmonton, AB T6E 6E6
780-433-4431
Fax: 780-409-4314
www.auma.ca
Classes of Insurance: Liability, Property

The Mutual Fire Insurance Company of British Columbia
#201, 9366 - 200A St.
Langley, BC V1M 4B3
604-881-1250
Fax: 604-881-1440
www.mutualfirebc.com
Classes of Insurance: Property, Fire

La Mutuelle d'Église de l'Inter-ouest
180, boul du Mont-Bleu
Gatineau, QC J8Z 3J5
819-595-2678

The Nordic Insurance Company of Canada
181 University Ave., 7th Fl.
Toronto, ON M5H 3M7
416-941-5151
Fax: 416-941-5322
Classes of Insurance: Accident, Legal Expense, Auto, Liability, Boiler & Machinery, Fidelity, Property, Surety

Norfolk Mutual Insurance Company
PO Box 515
33 Park Rd.
Simcoe, ON N3Y 4L5
519-426-1294
Fax: 519-426-7594
800-304-5573
norins@norfolkmutualinsco.on.ca
www.norfolkmutualinsco.on.ca
Classes of Insurance: Auto, Property, Fire

North Bleinheim Mutual Insurance Co.
11 Baird St. North
Bright, ON N0J 1B0
519-454-8661
Fax: 519-454-8785
800-665-6888
north.blenheim@sympatico.ca
www.northblenheim.omia.com
Classes of Insurance: Auto, Liability, Property

North Blenheim Mutual Insurance Company
11 Baird St. North
Bright, ON N0J 1B0
519-454-8661
Fax: 519-454-8785
800-665-6888
info@northblenheim.com
www.northblenheim.ca
Classes of Insurance: Auto, Liability, Property

North Kent Mutual Fire Insurance Company
PO Box 478
29553 St. George St.
Dresden, ON N0P 1M0
519-683-4484
Fax: 519-683-4509
888-736-4705
nkm@northkentmutual.com
www.nkmutual.com
Classes of Insurance: Auto, Liability, Property, Fire, Hail & Crop, Theft

The North Waterloo Farmers Mutual Insurance Company
100 Erb St. East
Waterloo, ON N2J 1L9
519-886-4530
Fax: 519-746-0222
800-265-8813
insurance@nwfm.com
www.nwfm.com
Classes of Insurance: Auto, Liability, Boiler & Machinery, Fidelity, Property, Fire, Hail & Crop

The North West Commercial Travellers' Association of Canada (NWC)
PO Box 336
28 Queen Elizabeth Way
Winnipeg, MB R3C 2H6
204-284-8900
Fax: 204-284-8909
800-665-6928
nwcta@nwcta.com
www.nwcta.com
Classes of Insurance: Life

OdysseyRe - Canadian Branch
#1600, 55 University Ave.
Toronto, ON M5J 2H7
416-862-0162
Fax: 416-367-3248
www.odysseyre.com
Classes of Insurance: Accident, Aircraft, Auto, Liability, Boiler & Machinery, Property, Fire, Surety, Hail & Crop, Reinsurance

Old Republic Insurance Company of Canada/ L'Ancienne République, Compagnie d'Assurance du Ca
PO Box 557, LCD 1 Stn. LCD 1
100 King St. West
Hamilton, ON L8N 3K9
905-523-5936
Fax: 905-528-4685
Classes of Insurance: Accident, Aircraft, Auto, Liability, Property, Reinsurance

Omega General Insurance Company
#500, 36 King St. East
Toronto, ON M5C 1E5
416-361-1728
Fax: 416-361-6113
contactus@omegageneral.com
www.omegageneral.com
Classes of Insurance: Personal Accident & Sickness, Aircraft, Legal Expense, Liability, Boiler & Machinery, Credit, Fidelity, Property, Surety

Ontario Blue Cross
#610, 185 The West Mall
Toronto, ON M9C 5P1
416-626-1447
Fax: 416-626-0997
800-873-2583
bco.indhealth@ont.bluecross.ca
www.useblue.com
Classes of Insurance: Personal Accident & Sickness

Ontario Mutual Insurance Association
PO Box 3187
1305 Bishop St. North
Cambridge, ON N3H 4S6
519-622-9220
Fax: 519-622-9227
information@omia.com
www.omia.com
Classes of Insurance: Personal Accident & Sickness, Auto, Property

Ontario School Boards' Insurance Exchange (OSBIE)
91 Westmount Rd.
Guelph, ON N1H 5J2
519-767-2182
Fax: 519-767-0281
800-668-6724
info@osbie.on.ca
www.osbie.on.ca
Classes of Insurance: Auto, Liability, Boiler & Machinery, Property, Fire

Optimum Assurance Agricole inc/ Optimum Farm Insurance Inc.
#422, 25 rue des Forges
Trois-Rivières, QC G9A 6A7
819-373-2040
Fax: 819-373-2801
www.optimum-general.com
Classes of Insurance: Auto, Property, Fire

Optimum Général inc/ Optimum General Inc.
#1500, 425, boul de Maisonneuve ouest
Montréal, QC H3A 3G5
514-288-8725
Fax: 514-288-0760
www.optimum-general.com
Classes of Insurance: Auto, Liability, Property

Optimum Reassurance Company
#1200, 425, boul de Maisonneuve ouest
Montréal, QC H3A 3G5
514-288-1900
Fax: 514-288-8099
www.optimumre.ca
Classes of Insurance: Accident, Personal Accident & Sickness, Life, Reinsurance

Optimum Société d'Assurance inc (OSA)/ Optimum Insurance Company Inc.
#1500, 425, boul de Maisonneuve ouest
Montréal, QC H3A 3G5
514-288-8711
Fax: 514-288-8269
Classes of Insurance: Auto, Liability, Property

The Order of United Commercial Travelers of America (UCT)
#300, 901 Centre St. North
Calgary, AB T2E 2P6

403-277-0745
Fax: 403-277-6662
800-267-2371
www.uct.org
Classes of Insurance: Personal Accident & Sickness, Life

Ordre des Architectes du Québec
1825, boul René-Lévesque ouest
Montréal, QC H3H 1R4
514-937-6168
Fax: 514-933-0242
800-599-6168
info@oaq.com
www.oaq.com

Ordre des dentistes du Québec
625, boul René-Lévesque ouest, 15e étage
Montréal, QC H3B 1R2
514-875-8511
Fax: 514-393-9248
800-361-4887
com@odq.ac.ca
www.odq.qc.ca

Oxford Mutual Insurance Company
PO Box 430
RR#4
Thamesford, ON N0M 2M0
519-285-2916
Fax: 519-285-3099
800-461-6933
mail@oxfordmutual.com
www.oxfordmutual.com
Classes of Insurance: Personal Accident & Sickness, Aircraft, Auto, Liability, Boiler & Machinery, Fidelity, Property, Hail & Crop

Pacific Blue Cross
PO Box 7000
4250 Canada Way
Vancouver, BC V6B 4E1
604-419-2000
Fax: 604-419-2990
800-487-3228
www.pac.bluecross.ca
Classes of Insurance: Accident, Personal Accident & Sickness, Life

Pacific Coast Fishermen's Mutual Marine Insurance Company
3757 Canada Way
Burnaby, BC V5G 1G5
604-438-4240
Fax: 604-438-5756
Other Contact Information: Toll Free (BC only): 1-888-438-4242
info@mutualmarine.bc.ca
www.mutualmarine.bc.ca
Classes of Insurance: Marine

Pafco Insurance Company
#100, 27 Allstate Pkwy.
Markham, ON L3R 5P8
905-513-4000
Fax: 905-513-4026
877-216-6973
contactus@pafco.ca
www.pafco.ca
Classes of Insurance: Auto

Palliser Insurance Company Limited
PO Box 1358
Saskatoon, SK S7H 3N9
306-955-4814
Fax: 306-955-1317
info@palliserinsurance.com
www.palliserinsurance.com
Classes of Insurance: Hail & Crop

PartnerRe SA
PO Box 166
#2300, 130 King St. West
Toronto, ON M5X 1C7
416-861-0033
Fax: 416-861-0200
800-363-6800
www.partnerre.com
Classes of Insurance: Personal Accident & Sickness, Auto, Life, Property

PC Financial Insurance Agency
2202 Eglinton Ave. East
Toronto, ON M1L 4S8
866-660-9035
Other Contact Information: 1-866-472-2683 (Claims)
talktous@homeauto.pcinsurance.ca
www.pcinsurance.ca
Classes of Insurance: Auto, Property

Peace Hills General Insurance Company
#300, 10709 Jasper Ave., 3rd Fl.
Edmonton, AB T5J 3N3
780-424-3986
Fax: 780-424-0396
800-272-5614
phi@peacehillsinsurance.com
www.peacehillsinsurance.com
Classes of Insurance: Accident, Aircraft, Auto, Liability, Boiler & Machinery, Credit, Marine, Fidelity, Property, Fire, Surety, Theft

Peel Maryborough Mutual Insurance Company
PO Box 190
103 Wellington St.
Drayton, ON N0G 1P0
519-638-3304
Fax: 519-638-3521
800-265-2473
pmmutual@pmmutual.on.ca
www.pmmutual.on.ca

Peel Mutual Insurance Company
103 Queen St. West
Brampton, ON L6Y 1M3
905-451-2386
info@peelmutual.com
www.peelmutual.com
Classes of Insurance: Auto, Liability, Boiler & Machinery, Fidelity, Property

Pembridge Insurance Company
#100, 27 Allstate Pkwy.
Markham, ON L3R 5P8
905-513-4013
Fax: 905-513-4020
877-736-2743
www.pembridge.com
Classes of Insurance: Accident, Marine, Property

Penncorp Life Insurance Company
7150 Derrycrest Dr.
Mississauga, ON L5W 0E5
Fax: 905-795-2316
800-268-2835
cs@penncorp.ca
www.penncorp.ca
Classes of Insurance: Personal Accident & Sickness, Life

The Personal General Insurance Inc./ La Personnelle, assurances générales inc.
PO Box 3500
6300, boul de la Rive-Sud
Lévis, QC G6V 6P9
418-835-9040
Fax: 418-835-5599
800-463-6416
info@lapersonnelle.com
www.lapersonnelle.com
Classes of Insurance: Auto, Liability, Boiler & Machinery, Property, Surety

The Personal Insurance Company/ La Personnelle, compagnie d'assurances
PO Box 3500
6300, boul de la Rive-Sud
Lévis, QC G6V 6P9
905-306-3350
Fax: 418-835-5599
800-268-2620
www.thepersonal.com
Classes of Insurance: Personal Accident & Sickness, Aircraft, Auto, Liability, Boiler & Machinery, Fidelity, Property, Surety

Perth Insurance Company
#1600, 5700 Yonge St.
Toronto, ON M2M 4K2
416-590-0038
800-268-8801
www.economicalinsurance.com
Classes of Insurance: Auto, Property

Pictou Mutual Insurance Company
PO Box 130
368 Faulkland St.
Pictou, NS B0K 1H0
902-485-4542
Fax: 902-485-5136
888-485-4542
info@pictoumutual.com
www.pictoumutual.com
Classes of Insurance: Liability, Property

Pilot Insurance Company
2206 Eglinton Ave. East
Toronto, ON M1L 4S8
416-288-1800
Fax: 416-288-5888
800-387-4518
www.avivacanada.com
Classes of Insurance: Auto, Property

The PMI Group, Inc. Canada
520 Coronation Dr.
Toronto, ON M1E 5C7
416-286-2176
www.pmicgroupinc.ca
Classes of Insurance: Credit

The Portage La Prairie Mutual Insurance Company
PO Box 340
749 Saskatchewan Ave. East
Portage La Prairie, MB R1N 3B8
204-857-3415
Fax: 204-239-6655
800-567-7721
info@portagemutual.com
www.portagemutual.com
Classes of Insurance: Legal Expense, Auto, Liability, Property

Premier Marine Insurance Managers Group
#650, 625 Howe St.
Vancouver, BC V6C 2T6
604-669-5211
Fax: 604-669-2667
www.premiermarine.com
Classes of Insurance: Liability, Marine, Property

Primerica Life Insurance Company of Canada
Plaza V
#300, 2000 Argentia Rd.
Mississauga, ON L5N 2R7
905-812-2900
Fax: 905-813-5310
800-387-7876
www.primericacanada.ca
Classes of Insurance: Personal Accident & Sickness, Life

Primmum Insurance Company/ Primmum compagnie d'assurance
999, boul de Maisonneuve ouest, 3e étage
Montréal, QC H3A 3L4
514-954-2463
Fax: 514-874-0463
866-454-8911
www.primmum.com
Classes of Insurance: Auto, Property

Prince Edward Island Mutual Insurance Company
201 Water St.
Summerside, PE C1N 1B4
902-436-2185
Fax: 902-436-0148
800-565-5441
protect@peimutual.com
www.peimutual.com
Classes of Insurance: Liability, Property, Fire, Theft

Principal Life Insurance Company/ Compagnie d'assurance-vie Principal
c/o John Milnes & Associates
1300 Bay St., 4th Fl.
Toronto, ON M5R 3K8
416-964-0067
Fax: 416-964-3338
www.principal.com
Classes of Insurance: Personal Accident & Sickness, Life

Progressive Casualty Insurance Company
#1500-28, 5650 Yonge St.
Toronto, ON M2M 4G3
416-499-6599
Fax: 416-499-7478
www.progressive.com
Classes of Insurance: Auto, Liability, Property, Surety

Promutuel Réassurance
1091, Grande Allée ouest
Québec, QC G1S 1Y7
418-683-1212
Fax: 418-683-2559
800-463-4888
sylvain.fauchon@promutuel.ca
www.promutuel.ca
Classes of Insurance: Accident, Liability, Boiler & Machinery, Property, Fire, Surety, Theft, Reinsurance

Promutuel Vie inc
1091, Grande Allée ouest
Québec, QC G1S 4Y7
418-683-1212
Fax: 418-683-2559
federation@promutuel.ca
www.promutuel.ca
Classes of Insurance: Accident, Personal Accident & Sickness, Life

Protective Insurance Company
c/o John Milnes & Associates
1300 Bay St., 4th Fl.
Toronto, ON M5R 3K8
416-964-0067
Fax: 416-964-3338
www.protective.com
Classes of Insurance: Personal Accident & Sickness, Auto, Liability, Property

Québec Blue Cross/ Croix Bleue du Québec
#B9, 550, rue Sherbrooke ouest
Montréal, QC H3C 3S3
514-286-8403
Fax: 514-286-8358
877-909-7686
info@qc.bluecross.ca, info@qc.croixbleue.ca
www.qc.bluecross.ca, www.qc.croixbleue.ca
Classes of Insurance: Accident, Personal Accident & Sickness, Auto, Liability, Life

Rain and Hail Insurance Corporation
#200, 4303 Albert St.
Regina, SK S4S 3R6
306-584-8844
Fax: 306-584-3466
800-667-8084
regina@rainhail.com
www.rainhail.com/about/canada.htm
Classes of Insurance: Hail & Crop

RBC General Insurance Company/ Compagnie d'assurance generale RBC
6880 Financial Dr.
Mississauga, ON L5N 7Y5
905-816-2452
Fax: 905-816-2450
800-769-2526
www.rbcinsurance.com
Classes of Insurance: Personal Accident & Sickness, Auto, Liability, Property, Fire, Theft

RBC Insurance
Tower 1
6880 Financial Dr.
Mississauga, ON L5N 7Y5
905-949-3663
Fax: 905-813-4853
877-749-7224
www.rbcinsurance.com
Classes of Insurance: Personal Accident & Sickness, Auto, Life, Property

RBC Life Insurance Company
West Tower
6880 Financial Dr.
Mississauga, ON L5N 7Y5
905-606-1473
Fax: 905-813-4850
877-519-9501
Other Contact Information: 866-223-7113 (Toll Free, New Life Insurance Inquiries); 800-461-1413 (Toll Free, Existing Life Insurance Inquiries)
www.rbcinsurance.com
Classes of Insurance: Personal Accident & Sickness, Life

RBC Travel Insurance Company
West Tower
6880 Financial Dr., 5th Fl.
Mississauga, ON L5N 7Y5
905-816-2452
Fax: 905-813-4850
Other Contact Information: Toll Free, Trip Cancellation Insurance Claim: 800-387-2487; Mail Address, Trip Cancellation Insurance Claim: PO Box 97, Stn. A, Mississauga, L5A 2Y9
www.rbcinsurance.com/travel
Classes of Insurance: Personal Accident & Sickness, Life

Real Estate Insurance Exchange (REIX)
#205, 4954 Richard Rd. SW
Calgary, AB T3E 6L1
403-228-2667
Fax: 403-229-3466
877-462-7349
info@reix.ca
www.reix.ca
Classes of Insurance: Liability

Red River Valley Mutual Insurance Co.
PO Box 940
245 Centre Ave. East
Altona, MB R0G 0B0
204-324-6434
Fax: 204-324-1316
800-370-2888
info@redrivermutual.com
www.redrivermutual.com
Classes of Insurance: Liability, Boiler & Machinery, Fidelity, Property, Fire, Surety, Theft

Reliable Life Insurance Company
PO Box 557
100 King St. West
Hamilton, ON L8N 3K9
905-523-5587
Fax: 905-522-7211
800-465-0661
service@reliablelifeinsurance.com
www.reliablelifeinsurance.com
Classes of Insurance: Personal Accident & Sickness, Life

ReliaStar Life Insurance Company/ Compagnie d'Assurance-Vie ReliaStar
c/o D.M. Williams & Assoc. Ltd.
#201, 3650 Victoria Park Ave.
Toronto, ON M2H 3P7
416-496-1148
www.ing.com/us/reliastar
Classes of Insurance: Personal Accident & Sickness, Life

Revios Reinsurance
#1600, 480 University Ave.
Toronto, ON M5G 1V6
416-598-4677
Fax: 416-599-6390
Classes of Insurance: Aircraft, Auto, Liability, Boiler & Machinery, Credit, Marine, Fidelity, Property, Fire, Surety, Hail & Crop

RGA Life Reinsurance Company of Canada/ RGA Compagnie de réassurance-vie du Canada
#1100, 55 University Ave.
Toronto, ON M5J 2H7
416-682-0000
Fax: 416-777-9526
800-433-4326
www.rgare.com/global/canada.asp
Classes of Insurance: Reinsurance

Royal & SunAlliance Insurance Company of Canada
10 Wellington St. East
Toronto, ON M5E 1L5
416-366-7511
Fax: 416-367-9869
800-268-8406
www.royalsunalliance.ca
Classes of Insurance: Property

St. Paul Guarantee Insurance Company
PO Box 6
#300, 20 Queen St. West
Toronto, ON M5H 3R3
416-360-8183
Fax: 416-360-8267
Other Contact Information: Toll Free: 1-800-387-1581, 1-800-330-5033
www.stpaulguarantee.com
Classes of Insurance: Surety

Saskatchewan Auto Fund
2260 - 11th Ave.
Regina, SK S4P 0J9
306-751-1200
Fax: 306-565-8666
www.sgi.sk.ca
Classes of Insurance: Auto

Saskatchewan Blue Cross
PO Box 4030
516 - 2nd Ave. North
Saskatoon, SK S7K 3T2
306-244-2662
Fax: 306-652-5751
800-667-6853
www.sk.bluecross.ca
Classes of Insurance: Personal Accident & Sickness, Life

Saskatchewan Crop Insurance Corporation
PO Box 3000
484 Prince William Dr.
Melville, SK S0A 2P0
306-728-7200
Fax: 306-728-7268
888-935-0000
customer.service@scic.gov.sk.ca
www.saskcropinsurance.com
Classes of Insurance: Hail & Crop

Saskatchewan Motor Club Insurance Company Ltd.
200 Albert St. North
Regina, SK S4R 5E2
306-791-4321
Fax: 306-949-4461
www.caasask.sk.ca
Classes of Insurance: Accident

Saskatchewan Municipal Hail Insurance Association
2100 Cornwall St.
Regina, SK S4P 2K7
306-569-1852
Fax: 306-522-3717
877-414-7644
smhi@smhi.ca
www.smhi.ca
Classes of Insurance: Hail & Crop

Saskatchewan Mutual Insurance Company (SMI)
279 - 3 Ave. North
Saskatoon, SK S7K 2H8
306-653-4232
Fax: 306-653-3260
800-667-3067
headoffice@saskmutual.com
www.saskmutual.com
Classes of Insurance: Auto, Liability, Boiler & Machinery, Fidelity, Property

SCOR Canada Reinsurance Company/ SCOR Canada Compagnie de Réassurance
TD Canada Trust Tower, BCE Place
PO Box 615
#5000, 161 Bay St.
Toronto, ON M5J 2S1
416-869-3670
Fax: 416-365-9393
800-268-8207
ca@scor.com
www.scor.com
Classes of Insurance: Reinsurance

SCOR Vie/ SCOR Life - Canada Branch
TD Canada Trust Tower, BCE Place, Succursale du Canada
#5100, 161 Bay St.
Toronto, ON M5J 2S1
416-304-6536
Fax: 416-304-6574
cavie@scor.com
www.scor.com
Classes of Insurance: Personal Accident & Sickness, Life

Scotia Life Insurance Company/ Scotia-Vie Compagnie d'Assurance
#400, 100 Yonge St.
Toronto, ON M5H 1H1
416-866-5412
Fax: 416-866-5810
800-387-9844
www.scotiabank.com
Classes of Insurance: Personal Accident & Sickness, Life

Scottish & York Insurance Co. Limited
2206 Eglinton Ave. East
Toronto, ON M1L 4S8
416-288-1800
Fax: 416-288-5888
800-387-4518
info@avivacanada.com
www.avivacanada.com
Classes of Insurance: Legal Expense, Auto, Liability, Boiler & Machinery, Fidelity, Property, Surety

SecuriCan General Insurance Company
#200, 1200 Portage Ave.
Winnipeg, MB R3G 0T5
800-431-3132
info@securican.ca
www.securican.ca
Classes of Insurance: Personal Accident & Sickness

Security National Insurance Company/ Sécurité Nationale compagnie d'assurance
50, Place Crémazie, 12e étage
Montréal, QC H2P 1B6
514-382-6060
Fax: 514-385-2162
800-361-3821
www.melochemonnex.com
Classes of Insurance: Personal Accident & Sickness, Auto, Property, Fire

SGI CANADA Consolidated
2260 - 11th Ave.
Regina, SK S4P 0J9
306-751-1200
Fax: 306-565-8666
800-667-8015
sgiinquiries@sgi.sk.ca
www.sgi.sk.ca
Classes of Insurance: Accident, Aircraft, Auto, Liability, Boiler & Machinery, Fidelity, Property, Surety, Reinsurance

Société de l'assurance automobile du Québec
CP 19600, Terminus Stn. Terminus
333, boul Jean-Lesage
Québec, QC G1K 8J6
418-643-7620
800-361-7620
Other Contact Information: Montréal: 514/873-7620
www.saaq.gouv.qc.ca
Classes of Insurance: Accident, Auto

Sons of Scotland Benevolent Association
#202, 40 Eglinton Ave. East
Toronto, ON M4P 3A2
416-482-1250
Fax: 416-482-9576
800-387-3382
info@sonsofscotland.com
www.sonsofscotland.com
Classes of Insurance: Life

South Easthope Mutual Insurance Co.
PO Box 33
62 Woodstock St.
Tavistock, ON N0B 2R0
519-655-2011
Fax: 519-655-2021
seins@seins.on.ca
www.seins.on.ca
Classes of Insurance: Accident, Auto, Boiler & Machinery, Property

Southeastern Mutual Insurance Company
378 Coverdale Rd.
Riverview, NB E1B 3J7
506-386-9002
Fax: 506-386-3325
800-561-7223
www.semutual.nb.ca
Classes of Insurance: Liability, Boiler & Machinery, Property, Fire

The Sovereign General Insurance Company
#140, 6700 Macleod Trail SE
Calgary, AB T2H 0L3
403-298-4200
Fax: 403-298-4217
800-661-1652
www.cooperators.ca; www.sovereigngeneral.com
Classes of Insurance: Personal Accident & Sickness, Property

SSQ Financial Group
PO Box 10500, Sainte-Foy Stn. Sainte-Foy
2525, boul Laurier
Québec, QC G1V 4H6
418-651-7000
Fax: 418-688-7791
888-900-3457
communications@ssq.ca; mutuallife@ssq.ca
www.ssq.ca
Classes of Insurance: Personal Accident & Sickness, Auto, Life, Theft

SSQ, Société d'assurances générales inc./ SSQ General Insurance Company Inc.
Édifice Le Delta 2
CP 10530
2515, boul Laurier
Québec, QC G1V 0A5
418-683-0554
Fax: 418-683-5603
800-463-2343
email@ssqgenerale.com
www.ssqgenerale.com
Classes of Insurance: Accident, Auto, Liability, Property, Fire, Theft

SSQ, Société d'assurance-vie inc/ SSQ, Life Insurance Company Inc.
CP 10500
2525, boul Laurier
Québec, QC G1V 4H6
418-651-7000
Fax: 418-652-2739
www.ssq.ca
Classes of Insurance: Accident, Personal Accident & Sickness, Auto, Liability, Life, Property, Fire

The Standard Life Assurance Company of Canada
1245, rue Sherbrooke ouest
Montréal, QC H3G 1G3
514-499-8855
Fax: 514-499-4908
877-499-9555
information@standardlife.ca
www.standardlife.ca
Classes of Insurance: Personal Accident & Sickness, Life

Stanley Mutual Insurance Company
32 Irishtown Rd.
Stanley, NB E6B 1B6
506-367-2273
Fax: 506-367-3076
800-442-9714
info@stanleymutual.com
www.stanleymutual.com
Classes of Insurance: Auto, Liability, Boiler & Machinery, Property

State Farm Canada
333 First Commerce Dr.
Aurora, ON L4G 8A4
905-750-4100
www.statefarm.ca
Classes of Insurance: Aircraft, Auto, Liability, Boiler & Machinery, Fidelity, Property, Fire, Surety

Stewart Financial Services
1282 Cornwall Rd., #B
Oakville, ON L6J 7W5
905-845-0990
Fax: 905-845-2882
888-845-0990
drew@stewartfinancial.ca
www.stewartfinancial.ca

Stewart Title Guaranty Company
North Tower, Royal Bank Plaza
#2200, 200 Bay St.
Toronto, ON M5J 2J2
416-307-3300
Fax: 416-307-3305
888-667-5151
inquirycda@stewart.com
www.stewart.ca

Suecia Reinsurance Company
763 Pape Ave.
Toronto, ON M4K 3T2
416-361-0056
Classes of Insurance: Personal Accident & Sickness, Auto, Liability, Fidelity, Property, Hail & Crop, Reinsurance

Sun Life Assurance Company of Canada
Corporate Office
150 King St. West
Toronto, ON M5H 1J9
416-979-9966
Fax: 416-979-4853
corp_website@sunlife.com
www.sunlife.ca
Classes of Insurance: Personal Accident & Sickness, Life

Sun Life Financial Inc.
150 King St. West
Toronto, ON M5H 1J9
416-979-9966
Fax: 416-979-4853
www.sunlife.com
Classes of Insurance: Life

Supreme Council of the Royal Arcanum
PO Box 990
#400, 21 King St. West
Hamilton, ON L8N 3R1
905-528-8411
888-272-2686
www.royalarcanum.com
Classes of Insurance: Personal Accident & Sickness, Life

La Survivance, compagnie mutuelle d'assurance vie
CP 10 000
1555, rue Girouard ouest
Saint-Hyacinthe, QC J2S 7C8
450-773-6051
Fax: 450-773-6470
800-773-8404
info@lasurvivance.com
www.lasurvivance.com; www.lsmutual.com
Classes of Insurance: Personal Accident & Sickness, Life

Swiss Re Frankona Rückversicherungs-Aktiengesellschaft
#1000, 150 King St. West
Toronto, ON M5H 1J9
416-814-2272
Fax: 416-364-7308
Classes of Insurance: Personal Accident & Sickness, Life

Swiss Reinsurance Company Canada
PO Box 50
#2200, 150 King St. West
Toronto, ON M5H 1J9
416-408-0272
Fax: 416-408-4222
800-268-7116
www.swissre.com
Classes of Insurance: Marine, Fidelity, Property, Surety, Reinsurance

TD General Insurance Company
c/o Meloche Monnex Inc.
50, Place Crémazie, 12e étage
Montréal, QC H2P 1B6
www.tdcanadatrust.com/tdinsurance
Classes of Insurance: Personal Accident & Sickness, Aircraft, Auto, Liability, Boiler & Machinery, Fidelity, Property, Surety

TD Home and Auto Insurance Company/ Compagnie d'Assurance Habitation et Auto TD
2161 Yonge St., 4th Fl.
Toronto, ON M4S 3A6
800-338-0218
Other Contact Information: 866-955-5558 (Toll Free, Quotes); 866-322-5854 (Toll Free, Client Services); 866-482-1919 (Toll Free, Claims)
www.tdcanadatrust.com/tdinsurance, www.mytdigroup.com
Classes of Insurance: Auto, Liability, Property

TD Life Insurance Company/ TD, Compagnie d'assurance-vie
120 Adelaide St. West, 2nd Fl.
Toronto, ON M5H 1T1
416-982-3006
Fax: 416-944-5859
877-397-4187
TD.InsuranceLifeAndHealth@td.com
www.tdcanadatrust.com/tdinsurance/life
Classes of Insurance: Personal Accident & Sickness, Life

Temple Insurance Company
390 Bay St., 20nd Fl.
Toronto, ON M5H 2Y2
416-364-2851
Fax: 416-361-1163
877-364-2851
www.templeinsurance.ca
Classes of Insurance: Boiler & Machinery, Property

Thomson-Schindle-Green Insurance & Financial Services Ltd.
Chinook Place
#100, 623 - 4th St. SE
Medicine Hat, AB T1A 0L1
403-526-3283
Fax: 403-526-8082
800-830-9423
tsg@tsginsurance.com
www.tsginsurance.com
Classes of Insurance: Auto, Liability, Life, Property, Hail & Crop

The Toa Reinsurance Company of America
PO Box 17
#2420, 401 Bay St.
Toronto, ON M5H 2Y4
416-366-5888
Fax: 416-366-7444
info@toare.com
www.toare.com
Classes of Insurance: Reinsurance

The Tokio Marine & Nichido Fire Insurance Co., Ltd.
c/o Lombard Canada Ltd.
105 Adelaide St. West
Toronto, ON M5H 1P9
416-350-4400
Fax: 416-350-4412
Classes of Insurance: Auto, Marine, Property, Fire

Town & Country Mutual Insurance
79 Caradoc St. North
Strathroy, ON N7G 2M5
519-246-1132
Fax: 519-246-1115
888-868-5064
info@town-country-ins.ca
www.town-country-ins.ca
Classes of Insurance: Personal Accident & Sickness, Auto, Liability, Boiler & Machinery, Fidelity, Property, Hail & Crop

Townsend Farmers' Mutual Fire Insurance Company
Waterford Place Plaza
PO Box 1030
Waterford, ON N0E 1Y0
519-443-7231
Fax: 519-443-5198
888-302-6052
farmins@townsendfarmers.com
www.townsendfarmers.com
Classes of Insurance: Personal Accident & Sickness, Auto, Liability, Boiler & Machinery, Property, Hail & Crop

Traders General Insurance Company/ Compagnie d'Assurance Traders Générale
2206 Eglinton Ave. East
Toronto, ON M1L 4S8
416-288-1800
Fax: 416-288-5888
800-387-4518
info@avivacanada.com
www.avivacanada.com
Classes of Insurance: Auto, Property

Tradition Mutual Insurance Company
PO Box 10
264 Huron Rd.
Sebringville, ON N0K 1X0
519-393-6402
Fax: 519-393-5185
800-263-1961
www.traditionmutual.com
Classes of Insurance: Accident, Auto, Liability, Boiler & Machinery, Fidelity, Property, Hail & Crop

Trans Global Insurance Company (TGI)
c/o Fraser Milner Cosgrain LLP, First Canadian Place
100 King St. West, 42nd Fl.
Toronto, ON T5X 1B2
416-862-3418
Fax: 416-863-4592
Classes of Insurance: Personal Accident & Sickness, Liability, Property

Trans Global Life Insurance Company (TGLI)
c/o Fraser Milner Cosgrain LLP, First Canadian Place
100 King St. West, 42nd Fl.
Toronto, ON M5X 1B2
416-862-3418
Fax: 416-863-4592
Classes of Insurance: Personal Accident & Sickness, Life

Transamerica Life Canada
5000 Yonge St.
Toronto, ON M2N 7J8
416-883-5000
Fax: 416-883-5012
webmaster.canada@aegoncanada.ca
www.transamerica.ca
Classes of Insurance: Personal Accident & Sickness, Life

Transatlantic Reinsurance Company
145 Wellington St. West
Toronto, ON M5J 1H8
416-596-3960
Fax: 416-971-8782
www.transre.com
Classes of Insurance: Personal Accident & Sickness, Credit, Property, Surety, Reinsurance

Travelers - Canada
PO Box 5
#200, 20 Queen St. West
Toronto, ON M5H 3R3
416-366-8301
Fax: 416-366-0846
800-268-8481
www.travelerscanada.ca
Classes of Insurance: Aircraft, Auto, Liability, Boiler & Machinery, Marine, Fidelity, Property, Fire, Surety, Reinsurance

Trillium Mutual Insurance Company
1078 Bruce Rd. 12
Formosa, ON N0G 1W0
519-367-5600
Fax: 519-367-5681
800-265-3020
admin@trilliummutual.com
www.trilliummutual.com
Classes of Insurance: Accident, Auto, Liability, Boiler & Machinery, Marine, Fidelity, Property, Hail & Crop

Trisura Guarantee Insurance Company
#1100, 70 York St.
Toronto, ON M5J 1S9
416-214-2555
Fax: 416-214-9597
info@trisura.com
www.trisura.com
Classes of Insurance: Liability, Surety

Ukrainian Fraternal Association of America (UFA)
c/o Burns Hubley
#406, 2800 - 14 Ave.
Markham, ON L3R 0E4
416-495-1755
Fax: 416-495-1838
Classes of Insurance: Life

Ukrainian Fraternal Society of Canada
235 McGregor St.
Winnipeg, MB R2W 4W5
204-586-4482
Fax: 204-589-6411
800-988-8372
Classes of Insurance: Life

Ukrainian Mutual Benefit Association of St. Nicholas of Canada
804 Selkirk Ave.
Winnipeg, MB R2W 2N6
204-582-4882
Fax: 204-586-2095
866-582-4882
umbaofsn@mts.net
www.ukrainianmutual.com
Classes of Insurance: Personal Accident & Sickness, Life

Ukrainian National Association (UNA)
c/o Burns Hubley LLP
#406, 2800 - 14 Ave.
Markham, ON L3R 0E4
416-495-1755
Fax: 416-495-1838
www.unamember.com
Classes of Insurance: Personal Accident & Sickness, Life,

Unifund Assurance Company
PO Box 12049
95 Elizabeth Ave.
St. John's, NL A1B 1R7
709-737-1500
Fax: 709-737-1580
unifund@johnson.ca
www.unifund.ca
Classes of Insurance: Auto, Property

L'Union Canadienne Compagnie d'Assurances
2475, boul Laurier
Québec, QC G1T 1C4
418-651-3551
800-463-3382
www.unioncanadienne.com
Classes of Insurance: Auto, Property

Union of Canada Life Insurance
PO Box 717, B Stn. B
325 Dalhousie St.
Ottawa, ON K1P 5P8
613-241-3660
Fax: 613-241-7880
877-966-6676
union@on.aira.com
www.ucav.ca
Classes of Insurance: Accident, Life

L'Union-Vie, compagnie mutuelle d'assurance/ The Union Life, Mutual Assurance Company
CP 696
142, rue Hériot
Drummondville, QC J2B 6W9
819-478-1315
Fax: 819-474-1990
800-567-0988
direction@union-vie.qc.ca
www.union-vie.qc.ca
Classes of Insurance: Personal Accident & Sickness, Life, Reinsurance

United American Insurance Company (UA)
c/o McLean & Kerr LLP
#2800, 130 Adelaide St. West
Toronto, ON M5H 3P5
416-369-6624
Fax: 416-366-8571
www.unitedamerican.com
Classes of Insurance: Personal Accident & Sickness, Life

United General Insurance Corporation
860 Prospect St.
Fredericton, NB E3B 2T8
506-459-5120
Fax: 506-453-0882
don.dougherty@ugic.nb.ca
Classes of Insurance: Auto

Unity Life of Canada
#400, 100 Milverton Dr.
Mississauga, ON L5RL4W 5S8
905-219-8000
Fax: 905-219-8121
800-267-8777
info@unitylife.ca
www.unitylife.ca
Classes of Insurance: Personal Accident & Sickness, Life

Usborne & Hibbert Mutual Fire Insurance Company
507 Main St. South
Exeter, ON N0M 1S1
519-235-0350
Fax: 519-235-3623
usborne@on.aibn.com
www.usborne-ins.com

Virginia Surety Company, Inc. (VCS)/ Compagnie de Sûreté Virginia Inc.
#201, 3650 Victoria Park Ave.
Toronto, ON M2H 3P7
www.thewarrantygroup.com
Classes of Insurance: Auto, Liability, Boiler & Machinery, Property

Wabisa Mutual Insurance Company
PO Box 621
35 Talbot St. East
Jarvis, ON N0A 1J0
519-587-4454
Fax: 519-587-5470
wabisa@mountaincable.net
www.wabisa.omia.com
Classes of Insurance: Personal Accident & Sickness, Auto, Liability, Fidelity, Property

Waterloo Insurance Company
590 Riverbend Dr.
Kitchener, ON N2K 3S2
519-570-8335
Fax: 519-570-8312
800-265-4562
www.economicalinsurance.com
Classes of Insurance: Auto, Property

The Wawanesa Life Insurance Company
#200, 191 Broadway
Winnipeg, MB R3C 3P1
204-985-3940
Fax: 204-985-3872
800-263-6785
life@wawanesa.com
www.wawanesalife.com
Classes of Insurance: Personal Accident & Sickness, Life

The Wawanesa Mutual Insurance Company
#900, 191 Broadway
Winnipeg, MB R3C 3P1
204-985-3923
Fax: 204-942-7724
www.wawanesa.com

Classes of Insurance: Auto, Liability, Boiler & Machinery, Property, Fire, Surety, Theft

Wedgwood Insurance Limited
PO Box 13370, A Stn. A
85 Thorburn Rd.
St. John's, NL A1B 4B7

709-753-3210
Fax: 709-753-8238
800-706-2676
www.wedgwoodinsurance.com

Classes of Insurance: Aircraft, Auto, Life, Marine, Property

West Elgin Mutual Insurance Company
PO Box 130
274 Currie Rd.
Dutton, ON N0L 1J0

519-762-3530
Fax: 519-762-3801
800-265-7635
info@westelgin.com
www.westelgin.com

Classes of Insurance: Personal Accident & Sickness, Auto, Liability, Fidelity, Property, Hail & Crop

West Wawanosh Mutual Insurance Company
PO Box 130
81 Southampton St., RR#1
Dungannon, ON N0M 1R0

519-529-7921
Fax: 519-529-3211
800-265-5595
wawains@wwmic.com
www.wwmic.com

Classes of Insurance: Personal Accident & Sickness, Auto, Liability, Boiler & Machinery, Fidelity, Property

Western Assurance Company
Sheridan Insurance Centre
#1000, 2225 Erin Mills Pkwy.
Mississauga, ON L5K 2S9

905-403-3318
Fax: 905-403-3319
877-263-4442
www.royalsunalliance.ca

Classes of Insurance: Personal Accident & Sickness, Aircraft, Auto, Liability, Boiler & Machinery, Marine, Fidelity, Property, Surety

Western Financial Group Inc.
1010 - 24 St. SE
High River, AB T1V 2A7

403-652-2663
Fax: 403-652-2661
866-843-9378
info@westernfinancialgroup.net
www.westernfinancialgroup.net

Classes of Insurance: Accident, Personal Accident & Sickness, Auto, Liability, Boiler & Machinery, Life, Fidelity, Property, Fire, Surety, Hail & Crop, Theft

Western Life Assurance Company
1010 24th St. SE
High River, AB T1V 2A7

403-652-2663
Fax: 403-652-2673
866-843-9378
info@westernlife.com
www.westernlifeassurance.net

Classes of Insurance: Personal Accident & Sickness, Life

Western Surety Company
PO Box 527
#2000, 1874 Scarth St.
Regina, SK S4P 2G8

306-791-3735
Fax: 306-359-0929
800-475-4454
wscinfo@westernsurety.ca
www.westernsurety.ca

Classes of Insurance: Fidelity, Surety

Westland Insurance
#300, 5455 152nd St.
Surrey, BC V3S 5A5

604-543-7788
800-899-3093
contactus@westland-insurance.com
www.westland-insurance.com

Classes of Insurance: Auto, Liability, Property

Westminster Mutual Insurance Company
14122 Belmont Rd.
Belmont, ON N0L 1B0

519-644-1663
Fax: 519-644-0315
800-565-3523
westminster@westminstermutual.com
www.westminstermutual.com

Classes of Insurance: Auto, Liability, Property

Woman's Life Insurance Society
PO Box 234
1455 Lakeshore Rd.
Sarnia, ON N7S 2M4

519-542-2826
Fax: 810-985-6970
800-521-9292
www.womanslifeins.com

Classes of Insurance: Life

XL Insurance Company Limited (XL)
#1802, 100 Yonge St.
Toronto, ON M5C 2W1

416-928-5586
Fax: 416-928-8858
www.xlinsurance.com

Classes of Insurance: Personal Accident & Sickness, Auto, Liability, Boiler & Machinery, Property, Surety

XL Reinsurance America Inc.
Scotia Plaza
#1702, 100 Yonge St.
Toronto, ON M5C 2W1

416-598-1084
Fax: 416-598-1980
www.xlre.com

Classes of Insurance: Personal Accident & Sickness, Aircraft, Auto, Liability, Boiler & Machinery, Fidelity, Property, Surety, Hail & Crop

Yarmouth Mutual Fire Insurance Company
1229 Talbot St. East
St Thomas, ON N5P 1G9

519-631-1572
Fax: 519-631-6058
office@yarmouth-ins.com
www.yarmouth-ins.com

Classes of Insurance: Auto, Liability, Property, Hail & Crop

York Fire & Casualty Insurance Company
#400, 7120 Hurontario St.
Mississauga, ON L5W 0B2

905-677-9777
800-676-0967
yfmarketing@york-fire.com
www.york-fire.com

Classes of Insurance: Auto, Liability, Property

Zenith Insurance Company/ Compagnie d'Assurance Zenith
c/o Lombard Canada Ltd.
105 Adelaide St. West, 3rd Fl.
Toronto, ON M5H 1P9

416-350-4400
Fax: 416-350-4417
888-440-4876
inquiries@zenithinsurance.ca
www.zenithinsurance.ca

Classes of Insurance: Personal Accident & Sickness, Auto, Liability, Property

Zurich Canada
400 University Ave., 25th Fl.
Toronto, ON M5G 1S7

416-586-3000
Fax: 416-586-2525
800-387-5454
zurich.information@zurich.com
www.zurichcanada.com

Classes of Insurance: Accident, Personal Accident & Sickness, Auto, Liability, Boiler & Machinery, Credit, Marine, Fidelity, Property, Fire, Surety, Theft

Major Companies

Companies are listed under the following categories:

Agriculture

AG Growth Income Fund
1301 Kenaston Blvd., Winnipeg, MB R3P 2P2

204-489-1855 Fax: 204-488-6929 www.aggrowth.com
Ticker Symbol: AFN.UN
Company Type: Public

Profile: AG Growth Income Fund is involved in the manufacturing of grain handling, conditioning, & storage equipment. Products include belt conveyors, augers, grain storage bins, & grain aeration equipment.

Bennett Environmental Inc.
#208, 1540 Cornwall Rd., Oakville, ON L6J 7W5

905-339-1540 Fax: 905-339-0016 800-386-1388
info@bennettenv.com
www.bennettenv.com
Ticker Symbol: BEV
Company Type: Public

Profile: The company is engaged in contaminated soil remediation.

James Richardson International
#2800, 1 Lombard Pl., Winnipeg, MB R3B 0X8

204-934-5961 Fax: 204-942-4161
corporateaffairs@jri.ca
www.jri.ca
Company Type: Private

Profile: Offices of holding companies; Commodity contracts brokers and dealers

Newco Grain Ltd.
PO Box 717, Coaldale, AB T1M 1M6

Fax: 403-345-2040 800-661-2312
info@newcograin.com
www.newcograin.com
Company Type: Private

Profile: Newco Grain Ltd. purchases grains from producers throughout western Canada, & distributes these feed products.

Nexia Biotechnologies Inc.
c/o 70 St. George's Cres., Edmonton, AB T5N 3M7

780-486-2317 Fax: 780-486-9411 www.nexiabiotech.com
Ticker Symbol: NBL
Company Type: Public

Profile: Nexia is involved in transgenic goat husbandry & related research

Ridley Inc.
Ridley Feed Operations, 34 Terracon Pl., Winnipeg, MB R2J 4G7

507-388-9400 Fax: 507-388-9415
campbell@ridleyinc.com
www.ridleyinc.com
Ticker Symbol: RCL
Company Type: Public

Profile: The commercial animal nutrition company manufactures & distributes animal nutrition products. Products include feeds, supplements, health products, low-moisture blocks, & animal care & livestock handling equipment.

Stolt Sea Farm Inc.
#513, 4100 Yonge St., Toronto, ON M2P 2B5

416-221-0404 Fax: 416-221-4010
info@stoltseafarm.com
www.stoltseafarm.com
Company Type: Private

Profile: Agricultural production & animal aquaculture; Commercial fishing in fish hatcheries & preserves

Thompsons Limited
2 Hyland Dr., Blenheim, ON N0P 1A0

519-676-5411 Fax: 519-676-3185 800-265-5225
info@thompsonslimited.com
www.thompsonslimited.com
Company Type: Private

Profile: Thompsons Limited is a supplier of agricultural products & farm services to producers throughout Ontario, & a provider of grain handling facilities. Agricultural products include seed, fertilizer, & crop protectants. The company is also engaged in the purchasing, processing, packaging, & shipping of commercial corn, wheat, soybeans, & edible beans to both domestic & export markets.

United Farmers of Alberta Co-Operative Limited
PO Box 5350 A, #700, 4838 Richard Rd. SW, Calgary, AB T2H 2J9
866-333-3832
customer.support@ufa.com; grain@ufa.com
www.ufa.net
Company Type: Public
Profile: United Farmers of Alberta Co-Operative Limited has over 35 farm & ranch supply stores & more than 120 petroleum locations throughout Alberta. UFA is also a provider of construction services. The cooperative consists of over 110,000 members. United Farmers of Alberta Co-Operative Limited has an environmental program which involves the education of member-owners about environmentally sustainable farm practices, the replacement of older petroleum systems, the safe storage & distribution of crop-related chemicals, & the establishment of emergency response plans & training programs.

Viterra Inc.
2625 Victoria Ave., Regina, SK S4T 7T9
306-569-4411 Fax: 306-569-4400
investor@viterra.ca
www.viterra.ca
Ticker Symbol: VT
Company Type: Public
Profile: Viterra is the owner & operator of a large grain handling network. The agri-business is also engaged in livestock, agri-food processing, sales, & financial products. Operations & distribution capabilities are located throughout Canada, as well as in the United States Singapore, & Japan.

Business & Computer Services

20-20 Technologies
#2020, 400 Armand-Frappier Blvd., Laval, QC H7V 4B4
514-332-4110 Fax: 514-334-6043
investor@2020.net
www.2020technologies.com
Ticker Symbol: TWT
Company Type: Public
Profile: Provider of computer-aided design, sales & manufacturing software for the interior design industry

724 Solutions Inc.
4101 Yonge St., Toronto, ON M2P 1N6
416-226-2900 Fax: 416-226-4456 www.724.com
Ticker Symbol: SVN
Company Type: Public
Profile: Computer integrated systems design; Prepackaged software; Computer related services

ACD Systems International Inc.
#200, 1312 Blanshard St., Victoria, BC V8W 2J1
250-419-6700 Fax: 250-419-6745 www.acdcorporate.com
Ticker Symbol: ASA
Company Type: Public
Profile: Image management & technical illustration software

Actuate Corporation
Performance Management Center of Excellence, #600, 150 John St., Toronto, ON M5V 3E3
416-537-9336 800-449-3804
PMinfo@actuate.com
www.actuate.com
Ticker Symbol: ACTU
Company Type: Public
Profile: Actuate provides a full range of Business Intelligence & Reporting Tools (BIRT), professional services, & support.

Aditya Birla Minacs
180 Duncan Mill Rd., 7th Floor, Toronto, ON M3B 1Z6
416-380-3800 Fax: 416-380-3830 888-646-2271
info@minacs.adityabirla.com
www.minacs.adityabirla.com
Ticker Symbol: MXW
Company Type: Public
Profile: Business process outsourcing solutions in the following areas: contact center solutions, transaction & knowledge services, integrated marketing services & IT solutions & services

Adobe Systems Canada Inc.
343 Preston St., Ottawa, ON K1S 1N4
613-940-3600 Fax: 613-594-8886 866-341-2256
info@adobe.com
www.adobe.com/ca
Company Type: Public
Profile: Imaging, design & document technology software

Advanced Micro Devices
1 Commerce Valley Dr. East, Markham, ON L3T 7X6
905-882-2600 Fax: 905-882-2620 www.amd.com
Ticker Symbol: AMD
Company Type: Public
Profile: Computer integrated systems design; Commercial art & graphic design

Apple Canada Inc.
7495 Birchmount Rd., Markham, ON L3R 5G2
905-513-5800 Fax: 905-477-8668 www.apple.ca
Company Type: Private
Profile: Computer integrated systems design; computer related services

Averna
#140, 87, rue Prince, Montréal, QC H3C 2M7
514-842-7577 Fax: 514-842-7573 877-842-7577
info@averna.com; sales@averna.com
www.averna.com
Company Type: Public
Profile: The firm is engaged in test engineering. Averna works with OEMs in a variety of industries, in order to deliver solutions that have been tried & tested.

Axia NetMedia Corporation
#3300, 450 - 1st St. SW, Calgary, AB T2P 5H1
403-538-4000 Fax: 403-538-4100 866-773-3348
info@axia.com; sales@axia.com
www.axia.com
Ticker Symbol: AXX
Company Type: Public
Profile: The company is a provider of real broadband Internet Protocol services & solutions. Axia NetMedia plans, designs, develops, & operates Open Access Next Generation Networks.

Belzberg Technologies Inc.
#3400, 40 King St. West, Toronto, ON M5H 3Y2
416-360-1812 Fax: 416-360-0039 800-823-8631
sales@belzberg.com
www.belzberg.com
Ticker Symbol: BLZ
Company Type: Public
Profile: Provider of technology-based brokerage services

Book4golf Corporation
#302, 250 Ferrand Dr., Toronto, ON M3C 3G8
416-421-5501 Fax: 416-429-8457
info@book4.com
www.book4golf.com
Company Type: Public
Profile: Information retrieval services; Prepackaged software; Travel agencies

Burntsand Inc
#600, 185 The East Mall, Toronto, ON M9C 5L5
416-234-3800 Fax: 416-234-3801
info@burntsand.com
www.burntsand.com
Ticker Symbol: BRT
Company Type: Public
Profile: Computer integrated systems design

CDC Software
Guinness Tower, #800, 1055 West Hastings St., Vancouver, BC V6E 2E9
604-699-8000 Fax: 604-699-8001
info@cdcsoftware.com
www.cdcsoftware.com
Company Type: Private
Profile: CDC Software provides enterprise software applications & services. Industries served include healthcare, financial services, & food & beverage.

Cedara Software, a Merge Healthcare Company
6509 Airport Rd., Mississauga, ON L4V 1S7
905-672-2100 Fax: 905-672-2307
800-724-5970www.cedara.com
Ticker Symbol: CDE
Company Type: Public
Profile: Prepackaged medical imaging software; Computer integrated systems design; Commercial physical & biological research

Certicom Corp.
5520 Explorer Dr., 4th Fl., Mississauga, ON L4W 5L1
905-507-4220 Fax: 905-507-4230 800-561-6100
info@certicom.com
www.certicom.com
Company Type: Public
Profile: Manufacturers of computer peripheral equipment; programming services; integrated systems design

Compugen Systems Ltd.
25 Leek Cres., Richmond Hill, ON L4B 4B3
905-707-2000 Fax: 905-707-2020 800-387-5045
info@compugen.com
www.compugen.com
Company Type: Private
Profile: Information technology service providers; PC systems integrators

Constellation Software Inc.
#1200, 20 Adelaide St. East, Toronto, ON M5C 2T6
416-861-2279 Fax: 416-861-2287
info@csisoftware.com
www.csisoftware.com
Ticker Symbol: CSU
Company Type: Public
Profile: Constellation Software's area of expertise is the acquisition & management of industry specific software businesses. Specialized software solutions are provided to customers in more than 30 countries.

Corel Corporation
1600 Carling Ave., Ottawa, ON K1Z 8R7
613-728-8200 Fax: 613-725-2691 800-772-6735www.corel.com
Ticker Symbol: CRE
Company Type: Public
Profile: Software company selling to both consumers & corporations in 75 countries

CryptoLogic Limited
55 St. Clair Ave. West, 3rd Fl., Toronto, ON M4V 2Y7
416-545-1455 Fax: 416-545-1454
info@cryptologic.com
www.cryptologic.com
Ticker Symbol: CRY
Company Type: Public
Profile: Through its wholly-owned subsidiary, WagerLogic Ltd., CryptoLogic Limited is engaged in online gaming software industry. The company serves the Internet gaming market around the world.

Cyberplex Inc.
#400, 1255 Bay St., Toronto, ON M5R 2A9
416-597-8889 Fax: 416-597-2345 888-597-8889
investor@cyberplex.com
www.cyberplex.com
Ticker Symbol: CX
Company Type: Public
Profile: Web advertising solutions and online customer acquisition strategies

Cybersurf Corp.
#300, 1144 - 29 Ave. NE, Calgary, AB T2E 7P1
403-777-2000 Fax: 403-777-2003 888-858-8958
investor.relations@cybersurf.com
www.cybersurf.com
Company Type: Public
Profile: Computer programming services; Information retrieval services; Computer related services

Dialogic Corporation
9800, boul Cavendish, 5th Fl., Montréal, QC H4M 2V9
514-745-5500 Fax: 514-745-5588 www.dialogic.com
Company Type: Private
Profile: Prepackaged software; computer related services; manufacturers of computer terminals; IP Solutions

Diversinet Corp.
#1700, 2235 Sheppard Ave. East, Toronto, ON M2J 5B5
416-756-2324 Fax: 416-756-7346 800-357-7050
info@diversinet.com
www.diversinet.com
Company Type: Public
Profile: Solutions for securing and provisioning mobile business applications in healthcare and financial services

Divestco Inc.
#700, 707 - 7th Ave. SW, Calgary, AB T2P 3H6
403-237-9170 Fax: 403-269-7066 888-294-0081
info@divestco.com
www.divestco.com
Ticker Symbol: DVT
Company Type: Public
Profile: Divestco Inc. offers a portfolio of software, data, & consulting products & services. It serves the oil & gas industry.

EMJ, A Technology Solutions Division of SYNNEX
PO Box 1012 Main, Guelph, ON N1H 6N1
Fax: 877-801-6300 800-265-7212
info@emj.ca
www.emj.ca
Ticker Symbol: SNX
Company Type: Public
Profile: Niche market hardware and software products, including Auto-ID, Card Technology, Physical Security, Digital Signage, Video and Imaging, Kiosk solutions

Enghouse Systems Limited
#800, 80 Tiverton Ct., Markham, ON L3R 0G4
905-946-3200 Fax: 905-946-3201
info@enghouse.com
www.enghouse.com
Ticker Symbol: ESL
Company Type: Public
Profile: Enghouse Systems Limited provides enterprise software solutions. The company's divisions include Syntellect & Asset Management. Syntellect specializes in interactive voice response & voice & speech enabled systems. The Asset Management group develops & sells geographic (GIS) based asset management solutions.

Envoy Capital Group Inc.
172 John St., Toronto, ON M5T 1X5
416-593-1212 Fax: 416-593-4434 866-883-6869
info@envoy.to
www.envoy.to
Ticker Symbol: ECG
Company Type: Public
Profile: Advertising agencies; Commercial art & graphic design; Information retrieval services; Computer related services

Epic Data International Inc.
#300, 6300 River Rd., Richmond, BC V6X 1X5
604-273-9146 Fax: 604-273-1830 877-332-3792
info@epicdata.com
www.epicdata.com
Ticker Symbol: EKD
Company Type: Public
Profile: Computer programming services; Prepackaged software

Gemcom Software International Inc.
PO Box 12507, #1100, West Hastings St., Vancouver, BC V6E 3X1
604-684-6550 Fax: 604-684-3541
info@gemcomsoftware.com
www.gemcomsoftware.com
Company Type: Public
Profile: Gemcom Software International Inc. provides software & professional service solutions to the mining industry. Gemcom's technology & services help mining companies around the world increase productivity.

Hartco Corporation
9393, Louis H. Lafontaine, Montréal, QC H1J 1Y8
514-354-3810 Fax: 514-354-1998 www.hartco.com
Ticker Symbol: HCI:UN
Company Type: Public
Profile: Computer integrated systems design; retails-computer & computer software stores; retails-miscellaneous retail stores

IBM Cognos
PO Box 9707 T, 3755 Riverside Dr., Ottawa, ON K1G 4K9
613-738-1440 Fax: 613-738-0002
800-267-2777www.cognos.com
Ticker Symbol: COGN
Company Type: Public
Profile: Business intelligence (BI) and performance planning software

Intrinsyc Software International Inc.
700 West Pender St., 10th Fl., Vancouver, BC V6C 1G8
604-801-6461 Fax: 604-801-6417 800-474-7644
info@intrinsyc.com
www.intrinsyc.com
Ticker Symbol: ICS
Company Type: Public
Profile: Software solutions for mobile and embedded device development, and project management services to clients building wireless devices

L-1 Identity Solutions
505 Cochrane Dr., Markham, ON L3R 8E3
905-940-7750 Fax: 905-940-7642 www.l1id.com
Ticker Symbol: ID
Company Type: Public
Profile: Security systems services; Patent owners & lessors

LGS Group Inc.
#400, 1300, René-Lévesque ouest, Montréal, QC H3G 2W6
514-964-0939 Fax: 514-861-4114
infolgsmtl@lgs.com
www.lgs.com
Company Type: Private
Profile: Solutions for portals, content management, data warehousing, business intelligence, corporate and technological architecture, system implementation, security, work organization and change management. Offices in Montréal, Québec and Gatineau

Liquidation World Inc.
225 Henry Street, Brantford, ON N3S 7R4
519-758-8878 Fax: 866-237-3778
investorinfo@liquidationworld.com
www.liquidationworld.com
Ticker Symbol: LQW
Company Type: Public
Profile: Business services (various)

Logibec Groupe Informatique Ltée
#1500, 700 Wellington St., Montréal, QC H3C 3S4
514-766-0134 Fax: 514-766-9237 877-392-2486
marketing@logibec.com
www.logibec.com
Ticker Symbol: LGI
Company Type: Public
Profile: Logibec develops application software & implements information management systems. Management software is used by the health & social service sector. Related services include end-user training & system maintenance.

MacDonald, Dettwiler & Associates Ltd.
13800 Commerce Pkwy., Richmond, BC V6V 2J3
604-278-3411 Fax: 604-278-1837 888-780-6444
info@mdacorporation.com
www.mdacorporation.com
Ticker Symbol: MDA
Company Type: Public
Profile: The company offers advanced information solutions to capture & process great amounts of data for business & government organizations. Products include tailored information services, complex operational systems, & electronic information products.

Mad Catz Interactive Inc.
Brookfield Place, #2500, 181 Bay St., Toronto, ON M5J 2T7
416-368-4449 Fax: 416-368-7779 800-831-1442
mcz@jcir.com
www.madcatz.com
Ticker Symbol: MCZ
Company Type: Public
Profile: Mad Catz Interactive Inc. is a designer & marketer of accessories for video game systems. The company is also engaged in the publication of video game software. An example of Mad Catz' software is the GameShark brand of video game enhancements.

March Networks
303 Terry Fox Dr., Ottawa, ON K2K 3J1
613-591-8181 Fax: 613-591-7337 800-563-5564
info@marchnetworks.com
www.marchnetworks.com
Ticker Symbol: MN
Company Type: Public
Profile: March Networks Corporation provides IP video software & systems for risk mitigation, loss prevention, & improved security. The company's business analysis applications are used by organizations such as financial institutions, transportation authorities, & retailers. March Networks is ISO-certified.

Maximizer Software Inc.
1090 West Pender St., 10th Fl., Vancouver, BC V6E 2N7
604-601-8000 Fax: 604-601-8001 800-804-6299
info@maximizer.com
www.maximizer.com
Ticker Symbol: MAX
Company Type: Public
Profile: Maximizer Software provides accessible customer relationship management & mobile customer relationship management solutions. The company serves small & medium-sized businesses, as well as divisions of large organizations.

McKesson Canada
8625, rte Transcanadienne, Montréal, QC H4S 1Z6
514-725-2100 Fax: 514-745-2300
communication@mckesson.ca
www.mckesson.ca
Company Type: Private
Profile: Provider of logistics services, software applications and automation solutions to the Canadian healthcare sector

Mediagrif Interactive Technologies Inc.
Le Bienville Phase III, #800, 1010, rue de Sérigny, Longueuil, QC J4K 5G7
450-677-8797 Fax: 450-677-4612
info@mediagrif.com
www.mediagrif.com
Ticker Symbol: MDF
Company Type: Public
Profile: Established in 1996, Mediagrif Interactive Technologies Inc. operates e-business networks. Networks include Polygon, The Broker Forum, Telecom Finders, Global Wine & Spirits, & Power Source On-Line. The company's markets include North America, the Middle East, Europe, & Asia.

MediSolution Ltd.
110, boul Cremazie ouest, 10e étage, Montréal, QC H2P 1B9
514-850-5000 Fax: 514-850-5005 800-361-4187
careers@medisolution.com
www.medisolution.com
Company Type: Private
Profile: The information technology company provides ERP software & services to the North American healthcare & service sectors.

Mercer LLC
Brookfield Place, PO Box 501, 161 Bay St., Toronto, ON M5J 2S5
416-868-2000 Fax: 416-868-7671 www.mercer.com
Company Type: Private
Profile: The firm is engaged in human resources consulting & the provision of related financial advice, products, & services.

Microforum International
1 Woodborough Ave., Toronto, ON M6M 5A1
416-657-8548 Fax: 416-657-8621 866-737-0577
info@microforum.com; fab@microforum.com
www.microforuminternational.com
Company Type: Private
Profile: Microforum International is a developer & publisher of mobile games. Mobile gaming solutions are provided to the following: network operators, handset manufactures, media companies, services providers, & brand owners.

Microsoft Canada Inc.
1950 Meadowvale Blvd., Mississauga, ON L5N 8L9
905-568-0434 Fax: 905-568-1527
877-568-2495www.microsoft.ca
Company Type: Private
Profile: Microsoft Canada Inc. is a provider of software, services, & Internet technologies for both personal & business computing.

Microtec Enterprises Inc.
4780, rue Saint-Felix, St-Augustin-de-Desmaures, QC G3A 2J9
888-864-7918www.microtec.ca
Company Type: Private
Profile: Microtec is a large residential & commercial security monitoring company.

Mitel Networks Corporation
Corporate Headquarters, 350 Legget Dr., Kanata, ON K2K 2W7
613-592-2122 Fax: 613-592-4784 800-267-6244www.mitel.com
Company Type: Private
Profile: The organization provides a broad range of communications solutions, from basic business communications to tailored applications. Mitel is present in more than ninety countries.

MKS Inc.
410 Albert St., Waterloo, ON N2L 3V3
519-884-2251 Fax: 519-884-8861 800-265-2797
info@mks.com
www.mks.com
Ticker Symbol: MKX
Company Type: Public
Profile: MKS Inc. is a global application lifecycle management technology company. Through a single enterprise application, the MKS Integrity product enables support for software-related activities & assets.

NBS Technologies Inc.
#400, 703 Evans Ave., Toronto, ON M9C 5E9
416-621-1911 Fax: 416-621-8875
info@nbstech.com
www.nbstech.com
Ticker Symbol: MIS
Company Type: Public
Profile: NBS Technologies has a worldwide dealer network. Its Smart Card Solutions division develops & manufactures card personalization equipment & software, plus related products & services.

Netgraphe Inc
300, av Viger est, 7e étage, Montréal, QC H2X 3W4
514-847-9155 Fax: 514-847-9151
info@canoe.quebecor.com
www2.canoe.com
Ticker Symbol: WWW
Company Type: Public
Profile: Information retrieval services; Computer programming services

Northcore Technologies Inc.
#300, 302 The East Mall, Toronto, ON M9B 6C7
416-640-0400 888-287-7467
info@northcore.com
www.northcore.com

Ticker Symbol: NTI
Company Type: Public
Profile: Information retrieval services; Computer programming services; Retailing in miscellaneous stores

Nurun Inc.
711, rue de la Commune ouest, Montréal, QC H3C 1X6
514-392-1900 Fax: 514-392-0911 877-696-1292
montreal@nurun.com
www.nurun.com
Ticker Symbol: IFN
Company Type: Private
Profile: Nurun Inc. is a global interactive marketing agency. Working with a great range of companies & organizations, Nurun executes & measures interactive programs that use technologies.

OnX Enterprise Solutions Inc.
155 Commerce Valley Dr. East, Thornhill, ON L3T 7T2
905-482-2292 Fax: 905-482-2295 866-906-4669www.onx.com
Ticker Symbol: ON
Company Type: Private
Profile: OnX Enterprise Solutions Ltd. delivers high-impact, vendor neutral IT solutions & services. Offices are located in Canada, the United States, & Europe.

Open Solutions Canada
#200, 13571 Commerce Pkwy., Richmond, BC V6V 2R2
604-278-6470 Fax: 604-214-4900 www.ca.opensolutions.com
Company Type: Private
Profile: Open Solutions Canada serves the Canadian financial services industry by providing banking system outsourcing. The company designs, builds, integrates, & operates advanced banking & payment technologies. These technologies are used by financial institutions, retailers, independent sales organizations, processing centres, & third-party organizations.

Open Text Connectivity Solutions Group
38 Leek Cres., Richmond Hill, ON L4B 4N8
905-762-6400 Fax: 905-762-6407 877-359-4866
conninfo@opentext.com
connectivity.opentext.com
Company Type: Public
Profile: Designer of computer integrated systems; Wholesaler of computers, peripheral equipment & business software

Open Text Corporation
275 Frank Tompa Dr., Waterloo, ON N2L 0A1
519-888-7111 Fax: 519-888-0386 800-499-6544
sales@opentext.com; support@opentext.com
www.opentext.com
Ticker Symbol: OTC
Company Type: Public
Profile: Open Text Corporation provides Enterprise Content Management solutions to assist organizations manage their information assets.

Optimal Group Inc.
2 Place Alexis Nihon, #800, 3500, boul de Maisonneuve ouest, Montréal, QC H3Z 3C1
514-738-8885 Fax: 514-738-2284
info@optimalgrp.com
www.optimalgrp.com
Ticker Symbol: OPMR
Company Type: Public
Profile: Operates The Optimal Payments group of companies (secure electronic payment & risk management solutions for businesses delivering goods & services over the Internet); & The WowWee group of companies (technology-based consumer robotic, toy & electronic products)

Optimal Payments
2 Place Alexis Nihon, #700, 3500, boul de Maisonneuve ouest, Montréal, QC H3Z 3C1
514-380-2700 Fax: 514-380-2760
info@optimalpayments.com
www.optimalpayments.ca
Ticker Symbol: FIR
Company Type: Public
Profile: Customized solutions for payment processing. A subsidiary of CardOne Plus

Pason Systems Inc.
6130 - 3 St. SE, Calgary, AB T2H 1K4
403-301-3400 Fax: 403-301-3499
InvestorRelations@pason.com
www.pason.com
Ticker Symbol: PSI
Company Type: Public
Profile: Pason Systems Inc. specializes in the design & manufacture of specialized rental drilling instrumentation systems. These systems are used by the oilfield industry on land based drilling & service rigs. Operations are located in Canada, the United States, Mexico, South America, & Australia.

Peer 1 Network Enterprises Inc.
#100, 555 West Hastings St., Vancouver, BC V6B 4N5
604-683-7747 Fax: 604-683-4634 877-504-0091
investor@peer1.com
www.peer1.com
Ticker Symbol: PIX
Company Type: Public
Profile: PEER 1 Network Enterprises, Inc. is the parent company of PEER 1 Network Inc.. The company is an online information technology infrastructure provider.

Procom
#400, 2323 Yonge St., Toronto, ON M4P 2C9
416-483-0766 Fax: 416-483-8102 800-461-4878
toronto@procom.ca; montreal@procom.ca
www.procom.ca
Company Type: Private
Profile: Procom is a vendor of information technology staffing services. The organization maintains ISO 9001:2000 certification for its management and quality processes.

Q - Media Solutions Corporation
13566 Maycrest Way, Richmond, BC V6V 2J7
800-690-5881
info@qmscorp.com
qmsfife.com
Company Type: Private
Profile: The supply chain services company works with technology companies to provide documentation, software, & accessory kits to customers. Q - Media Solutions' services include planning, materials procurement, media replication, printing, package assembly, inventory management, & e-commerce.

Rand Worldwide
5285 Solar Dr., Mississauga, ON L4W 5B8
905-625-2000 Fax: 905-625-2012 877-726-3243www.rand.com
Company Type: Private
Profile: Rand Worldwide provides technology solutions & professional services to assist organizations with information technology & engineering design requirements.

Reliance Protectron Security Services
8481, boul Langelier, Montréal, QC H1P 2C3
514-323-5000 Fax: 514-323-6423
800-811-1818www.protectron.com
Company Type: Private
Profile: Reliance Protectron Security Services is a security monitoring & installation company. The company serves residential, commercial, industrial, & wholesale subscribers throughout Canada.

Resolve Business Outsourcing Income Fund
#1600, 2 Robert Speck Pkwy., Mississauga, ON L4Z 1H8
905-306-6200 Fax: 905-306-2904
866-678-6019www.resolve.com
Ticker Symbol: RBO.UN
Company Type: Public
Profile: Resolve Business Outsourcing Income Fund is involved in business process outsourcing. The firm serves businesses & governments throughout Canada, the United States, & Mexico.

Roxio
c/o Sonic Solutions, #110, 101 Rowland Blvd., Novato, CA
877-697-6946www.roxio.com
Company Type: Private
Profile: Roxio provides digital media creation applications for consumers. The division of Sonic Solutions also produces media products & services to help people in their creation, management, & sharing of digital media. Examples of products include Roxio Creator, Roxio Easy VHS to DVD, Roxio CinePlayer DVD Decoders, Roxio BackOnTrack Suite, Roxio Easy LP to MP3, & Easy DVD Copy 4 Premier.

Sandvine Corp.
408 Albert St., Waterloo, ON N2L 3V3
519-880-2600 Fax: 519-884-9892
investor_relations@sandvine.com
www.sandvine.com
Ticker Symbol: SVC
Company Type: Public
Profile: Sandvine Corporation is a developer & marketer of broadband network management products. Products are used by residential broadband service providers. Sandvine Incorporated is the wholly owned operating subsidiary of Sandvine Corporation.

Sierra Systems Group Inc.
#2500, 1177 West Hastings St., Vancouver, BC V6E 2K3
604-688-1371 Fax: 604-688-6482 877-688-1371
Marketing@SierraSystems.com
www.sierrasystems.com
Company Type: Private
Profile: Sierra Systems Group is an information technology & management consulting services company. Examples of the company's services include content & records management, human capital management, & finance & controlling. Sierra Systems serves the government, justice, transportation, health, energy, & financial services sectors.

Sun Microsystems of Canada Inc.
27 Allstate Pkwy., 7th Fl., Markham, ON L3R 5L7
905-477-6745 Fax: 905-477-9423 ca.sun.com
Company Type: Private
Profile: Provides software solutions, systems, and services, including Java technology, Solaris OS and the MySQL database management system

SXC Health Solutions, Inc.
555 Industrial Dr., Milton, ON L9T 5E1
905-876-4741 Fax: 905-878-8869
investors@sxc.com
www.sxc.com
Ticker Symbol: SXC
Company Type: Public
Profile: SXC Health Solutions Corp. serves the healthcare benefits management industry. Healthcare information technology solutions are among the professional services provided.

TECSYS Inc.
87, rue Prince, 5e étage, Montréal, QC H3C 2M7
514-866-0001 Fax: 514-866-1805 800-922-8649
info@tecsys.com
www.tecsys.com
Ticker Symbol: TCS
Company Type: Public
Profile: Prepackaged software

TELUS Health Solutions
#600, 1000, rue de Sérigny, Longueuil, QC J4K 5B1
450-928-6000 Fax: 450-928-6344
866-363-7447www.telushealth.com
Ticker Symbol: IFM
Company Type: Public
Profile: Implementation of information communication technology processes for healthcare: claims & benefit management, electronic health records, centralized warehousing of health data, telehealth, & other information processing solutions

Teranet Income Fund
#600, 1 Adelaide St. East, Toronto, ON M5C 2V9
416-360-5263 Fax: 416-360-5659 800-208-5263
info@teranet.ca
www.teranet.ca
Company Type: Public
Profile: The organization provides e-service solutions. Services are useful to the financial, legal, government, healthcare, & real estate markets. One of its applications, Teraview software, allows access to the Ontario Electronic Land Registration System.

The Descartes Systems Group Inc.
120 Randall Dr., Waterloo, ON N2V 1C6
519-746-8110 Fax: 519-747-0082 800-419-8495
info@descartes.com
www.descartes.com
Ticker Symbol: DSG
Company Type: Public
Profile: Prepackaged software; Computer programming services

Ventyx
10271 Shellbridge Way, Richmond, BC V6X 2W8
604-207-6000 Fax: 604-207-6060
800-294-6374www.ventyx.com
Company Type: Public
Profile: Service delivery management solutions for utility, communications and other commercial field service organizations; services include asset management, mobile workforce management, customer care, energy trading and risk management, energy operations, and energy analytics

Chemicals

Abbott Laboratories Ltd.
PO Box 6150 Centre-Ville, 8401, rte Trans-Canada, Saint-Laurent, QC H4S 1Z1
514-832-7000 Fax: 514-832-7800 800-361-7852www.abbott.ca
Company Type: Public
Profile: Manufacturers of pharmaceutical preparations

Acetex Corporation
World Trade Centre, #750, 999 Canada Pl., Vancouver, BC V6C 3E1

604-688-9600 Fax: 604-688-9620
invest@acetex.com
www.acetex.com
Company Type: Private
Profile: Manufacturers of various industrial organic chemicals, plastic materials, synthetic resins, & nonvulcanizable elastomers

Agrium Inc.
13131 Lake Fraser Dr. SE, Calgary, AB T2J 7E8
403-225-7000 Fax: 403-225-7609 877-247-4861
investor@agrium.com
www.agrium.com
Ticker Symbol: AGU
Company Type: Public
Profile: Agrium Inc. produces & markets major agricultural nutrients throughout the world. The company also supplies specialty fertilizers across North America. In North & South America, Agrium is engaged in the retail supply of agricultural products & services.

Ambrilia Biopharma Inc.
1000, chemin du Golf, Verdun, QC H3E 1H4
514-751-2003 Fax: 514-751-2502
info@ambrilia.com
www.ambrilia.com
Ticker Symbol: AMB
Company Type: Public
Profile: Commercial, physical & biological research

Angiotech Pharmaceuticals, Inc.
1618 Stanton St., Vancouver, BC V6A 1B6
604-221-7676 Fax: 604-221-2330
info@angio.com
www.angiotech.com
Ticker Symbol: ANP
Company Type: Public
Profile: Commercial physical & biological research

Apotex Inc., Canada
150 Signet Dr., Toronto, ON M9L 1T9
416-749-9300 Fax: 416-291-0049 800-268-4623
corpinfo@apotex.com
www.apotex.com
Company Type: Private
Profile: The largest Canadian-owned pharmaceutical company.

AstraZeneca Canada Inc.
1004 Middlegate Rd., Mississauga, ON L4Y 1M4
905-277-7111 Fax: 905-270-3248 800-565-5877
customer.relations1@astrazeneca.com
www.astrazeneca.ca
Company Type: Private
Profile: Global pharmaceutical company; therapeutic areas include gastrointestinal, cardiovascular, infection, neuroscience, oncology & respiratory; drug discovery centre based in Montréal, QC

Atrium Innovations Inc.
1405, boul du Parc-Technologique, Québec, QC G1P 4P5
418-652-1116 Fax: 418-652-0151
atrium@atrium-innov.com
www.atrium-bio.ca
Ticker Symbol: ATB
Company Type: Public
Profile: Atrium Innovations is engaged in the development & manufacture of products, which are marketed to the chemical, pharmaceutical, & nutrition industries.

Axcan Pharma Inc.
597, boul Laurier, Mont-Saint-Hilaire, QC J3H 6C4
450-467-5138 Fax: 450-464-9979 800-565-3255
axcan@axcan.com
www.axcan.com
Ticker Symbol: AXP
Company Type: Public
Profile: Pharmaceutical company specializing in the field of gastroenterology; products are marketed in North America & the European Union

BASF Canada
100 Milverton Dr., 5th Fl., Mississauga, ON L5R 4H1
289-360-1300 Fax: 289-360-6000 866-485-2273
noc_canada-webmaster@basf-corp.com
www.basf.ca
Company Type: Private
Profile: Manufacturers of: gum & wood chemicals, paints, lacquers, enamels & allied products, pesticides & agricultural chemicals, prepared feeds & feed ingredients for animals & fowls, industrial organic chemical, synthetic rubber, cyclic crudes, intermediates, organic dyes & pigments; Wholesalers of: chemicals & allied products, paints, agricultural products & nutrition, raw materials, reactants, solvents & catalysts, pigments, plastics, polyurethans, coatings

Baxter Corporation
#700, 4 Robert Speck Pkwy., Mississauga, ON L4Z 3Y4
905-270-1125 Fax: 905-281-6560 800-387-8399
business_development_canada@baxter.com
www.baxter.ca
Company Type: Private
Profile: Wholesalers of professional equipment & supplies; Manufacturers of pharmaceutical preparations

Bayer Inc.
77 Belfield Rd., Toronto, ON M9W 1G6
416-248-0771 800-622-2937
contactbayer@bayer.com
www.bayer.ca
Company Type: Private
Profile: Wholesalers of drugs, drug proprietaries & druggists' sundries, synthetic rubber, chemicals & allied products; Manufacturers of synthetic rubber; agriculture crop engineering

BioMS Medical Corp.
6030 - 88 Street, Edmonton, AB T6E 6G4
780-413-7152 Fax: 780-408-3040 866-701-6603
info@biomsmedical.com
www.biomsmedical.com
Ticker Symbol: MS
Company Type: Public
Profile: Commercial physical & biological research

Bioniche Life Sciences Inc.
PO Box 1570, 231 Dundas St. East, Belleville, ON K8N 5J2
613-966-8058 Fax: 613-966-4177 800-265-5464
info@bioniche.com
www.bioniche.com
Ticker Symbol: BNC
Company Type: Public
Profile: Manufacturers of pharmaceutical preparations; Commercial physical & biological research

Biovail Corporation
7150 Mississauga Rd., Mississauga, ON L5N 8M5
905-286-3000 Fax: 905-286-3050
ir@biovail.com
www.biovail.com
Ticker Symbol: BVF
Company Type: Public
Profile: Biovail Corporation formulates, tests, registers, manufactures, & commercializes pharmaceutical products. Canada & the United States are the company's main markets.

Biovail Corporation
7150 Mississauga Rd., Mississauga, ON L5N 8M5
905-286-3000 Fax: 905-286-3050
ir@biovail.com
www.biovail.com
Ticker Symbol: BVF
Company Type: Public
Profile: Manufacturers of pharmaceutical preparations; Wholesalers of drugs, drug proprietaries & druggists' sundries; Commercial physical & biological research; Patent owners & lessors

BXL Bulk Explosives Ltd
PO Box 5247 A, 5511 - 6 St. SE, Calgary, AB T2H 1X6
403-255-7776 Fax: 403-255-2226 www.explosives.com
Company Type: Private
Profile: Wholesales-chemicals and allied products; Mfrs-explosives

Canexus Income Fund
#600, 801 - 7th Ave. SW, Calgary, AB T2P 3P7
403-571-7300 Fax: 403-571-7800
canexus@canexus.ca
www.canexus.ca
Ticker Symbol: CUS.UN
Company Type: Public
Profile: Canexus Income Fund is an unincorporated open-ended trust. It is involved in the production of chlor-alkali & sodium chlorate products.

Cangene Corporation
#360, 180 Attwell Dr., Toronto, ON M9W 6A9
416-675-8300 Fax: 416-675-8301
ir@cangene.com
www.cangene.com
Ticker Symbol: CNJ
Company Type: Public
Profile: Cangene Corporation's areas of expertise are the developing, manufacturing, & marketing of biotechnology products & specialty hyperimmune plasma. Research & development operations are located in Canada & the United States.

Cardiome Pharma Corp.
6190 Agronomy Rd., 6th Fl., Vancouver, BC V6T 1Z3
604-677-6905 Fax: 604-677-6915 800-330-9928
phofman@cardiome.com
www.cardiome.com
Ticker Symbol: COM
Company Type: Public
Profile: Commercial physical & biological research

CCL Industries Inc.
#500, 105 Gordon Baker Rd., Toronto, ON M2H 3P8
416-756-8500 Fax: 416-756-8555
ccl@cclind.com
www.cclind.com
Ticker Symbol: CCL
Company Type: Public
Profile: CCL Industries Inc. is engaged in the development & provision of specialty packaging for producers of consumer brands. Products include labelling, plastic tubes, & aluminum containers.

Chemtrade Logistics Income Fund
#301, 111 Gordon Baker Rd., Toronto, ON M2H 3R1
416-496-5856 Fax: 416-496-9942
investor-relations@chemtradelogistics.com
www.chemtradelogistics.com
Ticker Symbol: CHE.UN
Company Type: Public
Profile: Chemtrade Logistics Income Fund supplies the following: sodium hydrosulphite, sulphuric acid, liquid sulphur dioxide, sodium chlorate, sulphur, & phosphorus pentasulphide. The organization is also a processor of spent acid & a producer of zinc oxide. Chemtrade distributes industrial chemicals & services to customers in North America & around the world.

DRAXIS Health, Inc.
#200, 6870 Goreway Dr., Mississauga, ON L4V 1P1
905-677-5500 Fax: 905-677-5494 877-441-1984
requestforinfo@draxis.com
www.draxis.com
Company Type: Public
Profile: Manufacturers of pharmaceutical preparations; Wholesalers of drugs, drug proprietaries & druggists' sundries; Patent owners & lessors; Commercial physical & biological research

DuPont Canada
PO Box 2200 Streetsville, 7070 Mississauga Rd., Mississauga, ON L5M 2H3
905-821-3300 Fax: 905-821-5057 800-387-2122
information@ca.dupont.com
www.ca.dupont.com
Ticker Symbol: DUP
Company Type: Public
Profile: Manufacturers of various industrial inorganic chemicals, manmade organic fibers & various organic chemicals; Wholesalers of chemicals & allied products

Eli Lilly Canada Inc.
3650 Danforth Ave., Toronto, ON M1N 2E8
416-694-3221 Fax: 416-694-0487 800-268-4446www.lilly.ca
Company Type: Private
Profile: Manufacturers of pharmaceutical preparations

Enerchem International Inc.
#1950, 777 - 8th Avenue SW, Calgary, AB T2P 3R5
780-980-1682 Fax: 780-980-2610
investors@enerchem.com
www.enerchem.com
Ticker Symbol: ECH
Company Type: Public
Profile: Supplier of specialty chemicals & hydrocarbon-based well-servicing fluids to the oil & gas industry

GlaxoSmithKline Inc.
7333 Mississauga Rd. North, Mississauga, ON L5N 6L4
905-819-3000 Fax: 905-819-3099 800-387-7374www.gsk.ca
Company Type: Private
Profile: Commercial physical & biological research; Manufacturers of pharmaceutical preparations

Haemacure Corporation
#100, 215, ave Redfern, Montréal, QC H3Z 3L5
514-282-3350 Fax: 514-282-3358
info@haemacurecorp.com
www.haemacure.com
Ticker Symbol: HAE
Company Type: Public
Profile: Manufacturers of pharmaceutical preparations; Commercial physical & biological research

Hanfeng Evergreen Inc.
#788, 20 Toronto St., Toronto, ON M5C 2B8
416-368-8588 Fax: 416-849-0075
info@hanfengevergreen.com
www.hanfengevergreen.com

Ticker Symbol: HF
Company Type: Public
Profile: Hanfeng Evergreen Inc.'s area of expertise is the production of slow & controlled release (S&CR) fertilizers. The company's fertilizers are used by China's agricultural sector. Hanfeng Evergreen owns production facilities in China.

Intellipharmaceutics International Inc.
30 Worcester Rd., Toronto, ON M9W 5X2
416-798-3001 Fax: 416-798-3007
info@intellipharmaceutics.com
www.intellipharmaceutics.com
Ticker Symbol: I
Company Type: Public
Profile: Intellipharmaceutics International Inc. designs, develops, & produces sophisticated controlled release pharmaceutical products. IntelliPharmaCeutics employs its patented HYPERMATRIX technology to bring finished drug products to market.

Kronos Canadian Systems Inc.
#800, 100 Milverton Dr., Mississauga, ON L5R 4H1
905-568-0101 Fax: 905-568-8510 www.kronos.com/canada/
Company Type: Private
Profile: Employee management software & solutions

Labopharm Inc.
480, boul Armand-Frappier, Laval, QC H7V 4B4
450-686-0207 Fax: 450-687-5860 888-686-1017
info@labopharm.com
www.labopharm.com
Ticker Symbol: DDS
Company Type: Public
Profile: Manufacturers of pharmaceutical preparations; Patent owners & lessors

Merck Canada
16711, rte Trans-Canada, Montréal, QC H9H 3L1
514-428-8600 800-567-2594
servicesmf_customer@merck.com
www.merckfrosst.ca
Company Type: Private
Profile: Merck Canada is a research-driven pharmaceutical company. It researches, develops, manufactures, & markets innovative pharmaceutical, consumer. & animal health products. Merck also publishes resources that provide general health information to consumers. The company supports sustainable access to life-saving medicines in developing countries, through its partnership with Health Partners International of Canada.

Methanex Corporation
Waterfront Centre, #1800, 200 Burrard St., Vancouver, BC V6C 3M1
604-661-2600 Fax: 604-661-2666
invest@methanex.com
www.methanex.com
Ticker Symbol: MX
Company Type: Public
Profile: Methanex Corporation is a producer & marketer of methanol.

Migao Corporation
#1108, 8 King St. East, Toronto, ON M5C 1B5
416-869-1108 Fax: 416-869-1101
info@migaocorp.com
www.migaocorp.com
Ticker Symbol: MGO
Company Type: Public
Profile: Migao Corporation is the the owner & operator of fertilizer production plants. Plants are situated across the People's Republic of China. Products are used by Chinese domestic agricultural markets.

MIGENIX Inc.
#400, 1727 West Broadway, Vancouver, BC V6J 4W6
604-221-9666 Fax: 604-221-9688
info@migenix.com
www.migenix.com
Ticker Symbol: MGI
Company Type: Public
Profile: MIGENIX Inc. develops & commercializes drugs for the treatment of infectious diseases.

Nova Chemicals Corporation
PO Box 2518, 1000 - 7th Ave. SW, Calgary, AB T2P 5C6
403-750-3600
invest@novachem.com; public@novachem.com
www.novachemicals.com
Company Type: Public
Profile: Chemicals & plastics are produced by the company.

Novartis Pharmaceuticals Canada Inc.
385, boul Bouchard, Montréal, QC H9S 1A9
514-631-6775 www.novartis.ca
Company Type: Private
Profile: Novartis Pharmaceuticals Canada is a healthcare company which is engaged in scientific research to discover, develop, & market innovative pharmaceutical products to prevent & cure diseases.

Nuvo Research Inc.
#10, 7560 Airport Rd., Mississauga, ON L4T 4H4
905-673-6980 Fax: 905-673-1842
888-398-3463www.nuvoresearch.com
Ticker Symbol: NRI
Company Type: Public
Profile: The Canadian pharmaceutical company is engaged in the research & development of drug products that are delivered to & through the skin, with the use of topical & transdermal drug delivery technologies.

Nymox Pharmaceutical Corporation
#306, 9900, boul Cavendish, Montréal, QC H4M 2V2
Fax: 514-332-2227 800-936-9669
info@nymox.com
www.nymox.com
Ticker Symbol: NYMX
Company Type: Public
Profile: Biopharmaceutical company specializing in research & development of therapeutics & diagnostics for an aging population

Oncolytics Biotech Inc
#210, 1167 Kensington Cres. NW, Calgary, AB T2N 1X7
403-670-7377 Fax: 403-283-0858
info@oncolyticsbiotech.com
www.oncolyticsbiotech.com
Ticker Symbol: ONC
Company Type: Public
Profile: The biotechnology company develops oncolytic viruses as potential cancer therapeutics. Oncolytics Biotech's clinical program includes a range of human trials.

Oncothyreon Inc.
#500, 2601 Fourth Ave., Seattle, WA
206-801-2100 Fax: 206-801-2101
ir@oncothyreon.com
www.oncothyreon.com
Ticker Symbol: ONTY
Company Type: Public
Profile: Commercial physical & biological research; Manufacturers of biological products; Wholesalers of drugs, drug proprietaries & druggists' sundries; Primary focus is on oncology products

Orbus Pharma Inc.
20 Konrad Cres., Markham, ON L3R 8T4
905-943-9444 Fax: 905-943-9878
info@orbus.ca
www.orbus.ca
Ticker Symbol: ORB
Company Type: Public
Profile: Develops & manufactures off-patent generic drugs & drug delivery systems

Paladin Labs Inc.
#102, 6111, av Royalmount, Montréal, QC H4P 2T4
514-340-1112 Fax: 514-344-4675
info@paladin-labs.com
www.paladin-labs.com
Ticker Symbol: PLB
Company Type: Public
Profile: The specialty pharmaceutical company acquires or in-licenses pharmaceutical products for the Canadian market.

Patheon Inc.
2100 Syntex Court, Mississauga, ON L5N 7K9
905-821-4001 Fax: 905-812-6705 888-728-4366
patheon@patheon.com
www.patheon.com
Ticker Symbol: PTI
Company Type: Public
Profile: Manufacturers of pharmaceutical preparations; Testing laboratories

PFB Corporation
#100, 2886 Sunridge Way NE, Calgary, AB T1Y 7H9
403-569-4300 Fax: 403-569-4075
mailbox@pfbcorp.com
www.pfbcorp.com
Ticker Symbol: PFB
Company Type: Public
Profile: Through its wholly-owned subsidiaries, PFB Corporation manufactures insulating building products, based on expanded polystyrene technology. Brands of insulating building products include Plasti-Fab EPS, Riverbend Timber Framing, Insulspan SIPS, & Advantage ICF. The company serves the construction, industrial, commercial, & residential markets throughout North America.

Pfizer Canada Inc.
17300, rte Trans-Canada, Montréal, QC H9R 2M5
514-695-0500 877-633-2001www.pfizer.ca
Ticker Symbol: PFE (NYSE)
Company Type: Public
Profile: Pfizer develops innovative medications & other products to prevent & treat diseases of both people & animals thoughout the world. Canadian locations include Kirkland, Quebec, where Pfizer Animal Health & Pfizer Global Pharmaceuticals are situated, as well as Calgary Alberta's distribution centre, & Mississauga Ontario's logistics centre. The company's environmental, health, & safety management system is consistent with international management standards, such as ISO 14001 & OHSAS 18001.

Pharmascience Inc.
#100, 6111, av Royalmount, Montréal, QC H4P 2T4
514-340-9800 Fax: 514-342-7764 800-363-8805
Corporate-Affairs@pharmascience.com
www.pharmascience.com
Company Type: Private
Profile: Pharmascience Inc. consists of the following commercial business units: pharmaceutical products (generics), consumer products (OTC), international, & hospital & institutional products. Products include a great range of drug therapies, such as anti-infectives & cholestorol reduction agents, as well as non-prescription, over-the-counter products. These products are marketed & sold to retail pharmacies & hospitals in Canada & internationally.

PPG Canada Inc.
2450 Bristol Way, Oakville, ON L6H 6P6
905-829-5074 Fax: 905-829-9498 www.ppg.com
Company Type: Private
Profile: PPG Canada is a manufacturer of coatings & specialty products & services. The manufacturer serves customers in the following areas: construction, industrial markets, consumer products, & transportation markets.

Procter & Gamble Inc.
PO Box 355 A, 4711 Yonge St., Toronto, ON M5W 1C5
800-668-1050www.pg.com
Company Type: Private
Profile: Procter & Gamble is a consumer product company. Some of the brands offered by the company include Bounce, CoverGirl, Crest toothpastes & toothbrushes, Duracell, Gillette, Ivory, Mr. Clean, Pampers, Pringles, Swiffer, Tide, & Vicks. Proctor & Gamble supports environmental management actions & scientific research to reduce environmental impacts, & it also participates in waste reduction initiatives.

ProMetic Life Sciences Inc.
8168, ch Montview, Montréal, QC H4P 2L7
514-341-2115 Fax: 514-341-6227
info@prometic.com; investor@prometic.com
www.prometic.com
Ticker Symbol: PLI
Company Type: Public
Profile: The biopharmaceutical company provides technologies for drug development, drug purification, the elimination of pathogens, & the study of proteins. ProMetic also develops therapeutic drugs for the treatment of nephrological & hematological disorders & cancer.

QLT Inc.
887 Great Northern Way, Vancouver, BC V5T 4T5
604-707-7000 Fax: 604-707-7001 800-663-5486
corpcomm@qltinc.com
www.qltinc.com
Ticker Symbol: QLT
Company Type: Public
Profile: Global biopharmaceutical company; Develops treatments for eye diseases & dermatological & urological conditions

Ratiopharm Inc.
6755 Mississauga Rd., 4th Fl., Mississauga, ON L5N 7Y2
905-858-9612 Fax: 905-858-9610 800-266-2584
clients@ratiopharm.ca
www.ratiopharm.ca
Company Type: Private
Profile: Ratiopharm provides Canadian pharmacists with a wide range of generic products. The company also offers pharmacists professional services, such as Rx solutions, a comprehensive technology & patient-focussed program.

Recochem Inc.
850, montée de Liesse, Montréal, QC H4T 1P4
514-341-3550 Fax: 514-341-1292
Consumerinquiry@recochem.com
www.recochem.com
Company Type: Private

Profile: Manufacturers of various chemicals & chemical preparations, specialty cleaning, polishing & sanitation preparations

Rohm & Haas Canada Inc.
2 Manse Rd., Toronto, ON M1E 3T9
416-284-4711 Fax: 416-287-4486 www.rohmhass.com
Company Type: Private
Profile: Rohm & Haas Canada Inc. is part of the architectural & functional coatings industry. It manufactures specialty chemical products that are used by industries such as the commercial & industrial paints & coatings sector, the industrial finishes sector, & printing inks & overprint varnishes companies. The Rohm & Haas facility in West Hill is the first chemical company to join Ontario's Environmental Leaders Program, because of its reduced emissions & its commitment to further reductions.

Sico Inc.
2505, rue de la Métropole, Longueuil, QC J4G 1E5
514-527-5111 Fax: 514-651-1257 800-463-7426
info@sico.ca
www.sico.ca
Company Type: Private
Profile: Sico develops, manufactures, & markets paints, coatings, & related products. Markets include the architectural business & industry.

Theratechnologies Inc.
2310, boul Alfred-Nobel, Montréal, QC H4S 2A4
514-336-7800 Fax: 514-336-7242
communications@theratech.com
www.theratech.com
Ticker Symbol: TH
Company Type: Public
Profile: Manufacturers of pharmaceutical preparations, in vitro & in vivo diagnostic substances, surgical & medical instruments & apparatus, dental equipment & supplies; Commercial physical & biological research; Wholesalers of drugs, drug proprietaries & druggists' sundries

Univar Canada Ltd.
9800 Van Horne Way, Richmond, BC V6X 1W5
604-273-1441 Fax: 604-273-2046 www.univarcanada.com
Company Type: Private
Profile: Univar provides chemicals & related chemical distribution services.

Communications

Allstream Corp.
#1400, 200 Wellington St. West, Toronto, ON M5V 3G2
204-225-5687 Fax: 204-949-1244 800-883-2054
brad.woods@mts.ca
www.allstream.com
Ticker Symbol: TEL
Company Type: Public
Profile: Telephone communications; Information retrieval services

Amtelecom Income Fund
PO Box 1800, 18 Sydenham St. East, Aylmer West, ON N5H 3E7
519-773-8441 Fax: 519-765-3200 800-440-7472
info@amtelecom.ca
www.amtelecom.ca
Ticker Symbol: ATM
Company Type: Public
Profile: Cable & other pay television services; Telephone communications; Internet services

Astral Media Inc
Maison Astral, #1000, 2100, rue Sainte-Catherine ouest, Montréal, QC H3H 2T3
514-939-5000 Fax: 514-939-1515
investorrelations@corp.astral.com
www.astral.com
Ticker Symbol: ACM
Company Type: Public
Profile: Astral Media focuses upon the following services: radio & outdoor advertising; & speciality, pay & pay-per-view television.

BCE Inc.
1 Carrefour Alexander-Graham-Bell, Montréal, QC H3B 3B3
514-870-8276 Fax: 514-786-3970 800-339-6353
investor.relations@bce.ca
www.bce.ca
Ticker Symbol: BCE
Company Type: Public
Profile: Radiotelephone, telephone, telegraph & other message communications services; Miscellaneous publishing; Special trade electrical work; Electrical & electronic repair shops; Retail stores

BCE Inc.
#3700, 1000, rue de la Gauchetière ouest, Montréal, QC H3B 4Y7
514-870-8777 Fax: 514-786-3970 800-339-6353
investor.relations@bce.ca
www.bce.ca
Ticker Symbol: BCE
Company Type: Public
Profile: BCE Inc. is a provider of communication services, such as internet access, IP-broadband services, phone services, direct-to-home satellite, & VDSL television services. Customers include residential & business customers across Canada.

Bell Aliant Inc.
PO Box 1430, Saint John, NB E2L 4K2
877-248-3113 Fax: 506-694-2722 866-425-4268
investors@bell.aliant.ca
www.bellaliant.ca
Ticker Symbol: BA.UN
Company Type: Public
Profile: Offices of holding companies; Telephone & various other communications services; Computer related services

Canadian Broadcasting Corporation
PO Box 3220 C, Ottawa, ON K1Y 1E4
613-288-6033 Fax: 613-724-5707
liaison@radio-canada.ca
www.cbc.ca
Company Type: Crown
Profile: Radio & television broadcasting stations; Theatrical producers & miscellaneous services; Motion picture & video tape production

CanWest Global Communications Corp.
CanWest Place, 201 Portage Ave., 31st Fl., Winnipeg, MB R3B 3L7
204-956-2025 Fax: 204-947-9841 www.canwestglobal.com
Ticker Symbol: CGS
Company Type: Public
Profile: The international media company owns the Global Television Network. The company also holds interests in newspapers, specialty cable channels, radio networks, advertising, & websites. Business is conducted in Canada, the United States, the United Kingdom, Turkey, Singapore, Australia, & New Zealand.

Cogeco Cable Inc.
#1700, 5 Place Ville-Marie, Montréal, QC H3B 0B3
514-764-4700 Fax: 514-874-2625
marie.carrier@cogeco.com
www.cogeco.ca
Ticker Symbol: CCA
Company Type: Public
Profile: The cable telecommunications company provides the following services: internet, telephony, audio, & analog & digital television.

COGECO Cable Inc.
#1700, 5, Place Ville-Marie, Montréal, QC H3B 0B3
514-764-4700 Fax: 514-874-2625
marie.carrier@cogeco.com
www.cogecocable.com
Ticker Symbol: CCA
Company Type: Public
Profile: The cable operator provides analogue & digital video & audio services, high-speed Internet access, & digital telephony service to residential & commercial customers.

COGECO Inc.
#915, 5, Place Ville-Marie, Montréal, QC H3B 3P2
514-874-2600 Fax: 514-874-2625 www.cogeco.com
Ticker Symbol: CGO
Company Type: Public
Profile: COGECO Inc. is a diversified telecommunication company which serves consumers & advertisers. It is engaged in broadcasting in Quebec & cable distribution in Canada & Portugal.

Copernic Inc.
388, rue St-Jacques ouest, 9e étage, Montréal, QC H2Y 1S1
514-844-2700 Fax: 514-844-3532
888-844-2372www.copernic.com
Ticker Symbol: CNIC
Company Type: Public
Profile: Software development; Internet, desktop and mobile search products; Web properties include mamma.com, and copernic.com

Corus Entertainment Inc.
Bay Wellington Tower, BCE Place, #1630, 181 Bay St., Toronto, ON M5J 2T3
416-642-3770 Fax: 416-642-3779
investor.relations@corusent.com
www.corusent.com
Ticker Symbol: CJR
Company Type: Public
Profile: The media & entertainment company is engaged in the following services: television broadcasting, specialty television, pay television, specialty radio, digital audio services, advertising, children's animation, & children's book publishing. Some of the companies & brands that comprise Corus Entertainment include the following: W Network, YTV, Treehouse, TELETOON, Nelvana, & Kids Can Press.

Cossette Communication Group Inc.
#200, 801, Grande Allée ouest, Québec, QC G1S 1C1
418-647-2727 Fax: 418-523-1689
infomaster@cossette.com
www.cossette.com
Ticker Symbol: KOS
Company Type: Public
Profile: Cossette Communication Group Inc. offers the following services: planning, researching, B2B communications, advertising, database marketing, direct marketing, ethnic marketing, alliance marketing, sports marketing, interactive marketing solutions, branding, sales promotion, product placement, & public relations. The full range of communication services are provided to clients of all sizes.

Cossette Communication Group Inc.
#200, 801 Grande Allee Ouest, Québec, QC G1S 1C1
418-647-2727 Fax: 418-647-2564
investor@cossette.com
www.cossette.com
Ticker Symbol: KOS
Company Type: Public
Profile: The company offers a full range of communication services to clients of all sizes.

CTV Inc.
9 Channel Nine Ct., Scarborough, ON M1S 4B5
416-332-5000 Fax: 416-332-5022 www.ctv.ca
Company Type: Public
Profile: Television broadcasting stations; Motion picture & video tape production

EastLink
PO Box 8660 A, NS, NL B3K 5M3
709-754-3775 Fax: 709-754-3883 888-345-1111www.eastlink.ca
Company Type: Private
Profile: EastLink services include telephone, high speed Internet, & cable & digital cable. Residential, business, & public sector customers are located throughout Canada.

Ericsson Canada Inc.
5255 Satellite Dr., Mississauga, ON L4W 5E3
905-629-6700 Fax: 905-629-6701 www.ericsson.ca
Company Type: Private
Profile: Provides mobile internet, wireless, IP & data systems, & consulting services

General Dynamics Canada
3785 Richmond Rd., Ottawa, ON K2H 5B7
613-596-7000 Fax: 613-596-7396
info@gdcanada.com
www.gdcanada.com
Company Type: Private
Profile: International supplier of maritime systems, integrating naval & airborne anti-submarine warfare systems

Glentel Inc.
8501 Commerce Ct., Burnaby, BC V5A 4N3
604-415-6500 Fax: 604-415-6565
tskidmore@glentel.com
www.glentel.com
Ticker Symbol: GLN
Company Type: Public
Profile: Glentel Inc. is a provider of telecommunications services & solutions, through its retail & business operating divisions. Products & services include wireless devices, wireless engineering, & wireless asset monitoring. Locations across Canada are known as Glentel Wireless Business Centres, The Telephone Booth / La Cabine Telephonique, WIRELESS, & WirelessWave.

Manitoba Telecom Services Inc.
PO Box 6666, #MP18C, 333 Main St., Winnipeg, MB R3C 3V6
204-941-8256 Fax: 204-772-6391 800-263-1174
investor.relations@mtsallstream.com
www.mts.ca
Ticker Symbol: MBT
Company Type: Public
Profile: Through its wholly-owned subsidiary MTS Allstream Inc., Manitoba Telecom Services Inc. provides television, voice, data, wireless, & wireline services. Both residential & business customers are served in Manitoba, while across Canada, business clients are served through a portfolio of information

technology consulting & security services, as well as voice & data connectivity services.

Newfoundland Capital Corporation Limited
745 Windmill Rd., Dartmouth, NS B3B 1C2
902-468-7557 Fax: 902-468-7558
ncc@ncc.ca
www.ncc.ca
Ticker Symbol: NCC
Company Type: Public
Profile: Newfoundland Capital Corporation Limited is the owner & operator of radio stations throughout Canada. Newcap Radio is a wholly owned subsidiary of Newfoundland Capital Corporation Limited. In addition to its involvement in radio broadcasting, Newfoundland Capital Corporation Limited also owns & operates the Glynmill Inn in Corner Brook, Newfoundland & Labrador.

Northwestel Inc.
PO Box 2727 Main, 301 Lambert St., Whitehorse, YT Y1A 4Y4
867-668-5300 Fax: 867-668-7079 888-423-2333
customerservice@nwtel.ca
www.nwtel.ca
Company Type: Private
Profile: Northwestel is engaged in the communications & entertainment industry. It offers innovative technology to customers in northern Canada. The following are some of Northwestel's services: cable television; advanced data communications, including high speed internet in some areas; long distance communications by microwave radio; & satellite & fibre optic cable.

Rainmaker Entertainment Inc.
#500, 2025 West Broadway, Vancouver, BC V6J 1Z6
604-714-2600 Fax: 604-714-2641 www.rainmaker.com
Ticker Symbol: RNK
Company Type: Public
Profile: Animated film production

Rogers Communications Inc.
333 Bloor St. East, 7th Floor, Toronto, ON M4W 1G9
888-764-3771
investor.relations@rogers.com
www.rogers.com
Ticker Symbol: RCI.A; RCI.B
Company Type: Private
Profile: Rogers Wireless is one of three business lines of Rogers Communications Inc., and Canada's largest wireless voice and data communications services provider

Rogers Communications Inc.
333 Bloor St. East, 7th Floor, Toronto, ON M4W 1G9
888-764-3771
investor.relations@rogers.com
www.rogers.com
Ticker Symbol: RCI.A; RCI.B
Company Type: Public
Profile: A diversified Canadian company with three main business lines: Rogers Wireless, Rogers Cable, and Rogers Media

SaskTel
PO Box 2121, Regina, SK S4P 4C5
866-727-5835www.sasktel.com
Company Type: Crown
Profile: SaskTel is a full service communications provider in Saskatchewan. Communications products & services include voice, cellular, data, wireless data, messaging, internet, entertainment, & directory services.

Score Media Inc.
#425, 370 King St. West, Toronto, ON M5V 1J9
416-977-6787 Fax: 416-977-7851 www.scoremedia.ca
Ticker Symbol: SCR
Company Type: Public
Profile: The media company delivers sports entertainment. Its primary asset is The Score Television Network, a national specialty television service. The company also operates a satellite radio network, known as Hardcore Sports Radio. Other assets include Score Mobile & theScore.com.

Shaw Communications Inc.
#900, 630 - 3rd Ave. SW, Calgary, AB T2P 4L4
403-750-4500 Fax: 403-750-4501
angela.haigh@sjrb.ca
www.shaw.ca
Ticker Symbol: SJR
Company Type: Public
Profile: The communications company provides broadband cable television, internet, digital phone, telecommunications services, & satellite direct-to-home services.

Shaw Direct
Shaw Satellite G.P., #100, 2400 -32 Ave. NE, Calgary, AB T2E 9A7
866-782-7932 Fax: 800-872-8219
investor.relations@sjrb.ca
www.shawdirect.ca
Company Type: Private
Profile: Shaw Direct supplies digital satellite television. The company offers more than 470 audio & video channels to over 870,000 subscribers. Subscribers also have access to pay per view movies & events.

Stratos Global Corporation
#210, 2650 Queensview Dr., Ottawa, ON K2B 8H6
613-230-4544 Fax: 613-230-4212 877-995-9901
investor@stratosglobal.com
www.stratosglobal.com
Company Type: Public
Profile: Offices of holding companies; Radiotelephone & various other communications services

Tata Communications
1555, rue Carrie-Derick, Montréal, QC H3C 6W2
514-868-7272 Fax: 514-868-7234 www.tatacommunications.com
Company Type: Public
Profile: Communications solutions and services, including transmission, IP, converged voice, mobility, managed network connectivity, hosting, storage, managed security, managed collaboration and business transformation, Internet, retail broadband, content services

Telesat Canada
1601 Telesat Ct., Gloucester, ON K1B 5P4
613-748-0123 Fax: 613-748-8712
info@telesat.ca
www.telesat.ca
Company Type: Private
Profile: Telesat manages satellite communications & systems.

TELUS Corp.
555 Robson St., Vancouver, BC V6B 3K9
800-667-4871 Fax: 604-899-9228
ir@telus.com
www.telus.com
Ticker Symbol: T
Company Type: Public
Profile: Communications products include internet protocol, data, voice, & video.

TVA Group Inc.
1600, boul de Maisonneuve est, Montréal, QC H2L 4P2
514-526-9251 Fax: 514-598-6085
denis.rozon@tva.ca
www.tva.canoe.ca
Ticker Symbol: TVA
Company Type: Public
Profile: The integrated communications company provides the following services: broadcasting, publishing, & producting & distributing audiovisual products. TVA Group owns French-language television stations, plus a specialty channel. It also publishes French-language magazines. The TVA Films subsidiary serves both Canada's English & French-language markets.

Télébec
625, av Godefroy, Bécancour, QC G9H 1S3
Fax: 819-233-6877 888-835-3232
telebec@telebec.com
www.telebec.com
Ticker Symbol: BA.UN
Company Type: Public
Profile: Provides range of integrated telecommunications services in the province of Québec. A member of the Bell Aliant Group

Videon CableSystems, Inc.
#900, 630 - 3rd Ave. SW, Calgary, AB T2P 4L4
403-750-4570 Fax: 403-750-7469 www.shaw.ca
Company Type: Public
Profile: Multi-system cable operator

Videotron Communications Ltd
300, av Viger est, Montréal, QC H2X 3W4
514-281-1232 Fax: 514-985-8834 www.videotron.com
Company Type: Private
Profile: Cable & other pay television services; Television broadcasting stations; Communications services (various)

Construction

Aecon Group Inc.
#800, 20 Carlson Ct., Toronto, ON M9W 7K6
416-293-7004 Fax: 416-293-0271
aecon@aecon.com
www.aecon.com
Ticker Symbol: ARE
Company Type: Public
Profile: Aecon Group is a construction & infrastructure development company. It serves both public & private sector clients through the provision of engineering, financing, procurement, construction, & project management services.

Badger Income Fund
#2820, 715 - 5th Ave. SW, Calgary, AB T2P 2X6
403-264-8500 Fax: 403-228-9773 800-465-4273
rlynas@badgerinc.com
www.badgerinc.com
Ticker Symbol: BAD
Company Type: Public
Profile: Badger Income Fund is an open-ended trust. It is involved in non-destructive excavating & slot trenching services. Services are provided to industries, such as petroleum, industrial, utility, industrial, & transportation.

Bechtel Canada Inc.
#910, 1500, rue Univesité, Montréal, QC H3A 3S7
514-871-1711 Fax: 514-871-1392 www.bechtel.com
Company Type: Private
Profile: Offices of holding companies; Management & public relations services; Engineering services

Bird Construction Income Fund
5403 Eglinton Ave. West, Toronto, ON M9C 5K6
416-620-7122 Fax: 416-620-1516
investor.relations@bird.ca
www.bird.ca
Ticker Symbol: BDT.UN
Company Type: Public
Profile: The organization is a national general contractor in the residential, institutional, & industrial markets.

Carma Corporation
4906 Richard Rd. SW, Calgary, AB T3E 6L1
403-231-8900 Fax: 403-231-8960
info@carma.ca
www.carma.ca
Company Type: Public
Profile: General contractors in residential buildings, & single family houses; Real estate land subdividers & developers

Churchill Corporation
11825 - 146 St., Edmonton, AB T5L 2J1
780-454-3667 Fax: 780-488-0194
inquiries@churchill-cuq.com
www.churchillcorporation.com
Ticker Symbol: CUQ
Company Type: Public
Profile: The Churchill Corporation is a provider of building construction, industrial construction, & related maintenance services. It operates in western Canada. The Churchill Corporation's subsidiaries are as follows: Triton Projects, Laird Electric, Stuart Olson Construction Ltd., & Insulation Holdings Inc. The company has policies, procedures, training programs, & compliance procedures in place to manage environmental issues & comply with legislation & regulations.

Dominion Construction Company Inc.
#130, 2985 Virtual Way, Vancouver, BC V5M 4X7
604-631-1000 Fax: 604-631-1100
reception@dominionco.com
www.dominionco.com
Company Type: Private
Profile: General contractors in industrial & non-residential buildings & warehouses; Offices located in Vancouver, Calgary, Edmonton, Regina, Saskatoon, Swift Current, Winnipeg & Thunder Bay

Eastern Construction Company Ltd.
#1100, 505 Consumers Rd., Toronto, ON M2J 5G2
416-497-7110 Fax: 416-497-7241
info@easternconstruction.com
www.easternconstruction.com
Company Type: Private
Profile: General contractors in industrial & non-residential buildings & warehouses

Ellis-Don Construction Ltd.
2045 Oxford St. West, London, ON N5V 2Z7
519-455-6770 Fax: 519-455-2944
bwaltham@ellisdon.com
www.ellisdon.com
Company Type: Private
Profile: General contractors of industrial buildings & warehouses, residential & non-residential buildings

Finning International Inc.
Park Place, #1000, 666 Burrard St., Vancouver, BC V6C 2X8
604-691-6444 Fax: 604-691-6440
investor_relations@finning.ca

www.finning.com
Ticker Symbol: FTT
Company Type: Public
Profile: The company sells, rents, & offers customer service for Caterpillar equipment. Business is conducted in Canada, South America, & the United Kingdom.

Fluor Canada Ltd.
Sundance Park, 55 Sunpark Plaza SE, Calgary, AB T2X 3R4
403-537-4000 Fax: 403-537-4222 www.fluor.com/canada
Company Type: Private
Profile: Engineering, architectural & surveying services; Management & public relations services; Oil & gas field exploration services

Lafarge Canada Inc.
#800, 606, rue Cathcart, Montréal, QC H3B 1L7
514-861-1411 Fax: 514-861-1123 www.lafarge-na.com
Company Type: Public
Profile: Supplier of construction materials

Ledcor Industries Inc.
#1200, 1067 West Cordova St., Vancouver, BC V61 1C7
604-681-7500 Fax: 604-895-4385
info@ledcor.com
www.ledcor.com
Company Type: Private
Profile: General contractors in nonresidential, industrial buildings & warehouses; Highway, bridge, tunnel, elevated highway & street construction; Water, sewer, pipeline, communications, power line construct; Various heavy construction; Special trade construction in excavation work

Les Entreprises Kiewit ltée
4333, Grande-Allée, Boisbriand, QC J7H 1M7
450-435-5756 Fax: 450-435-6764
info@kiewit.com
www.kiewit.ca
Company Type: Private
Profile: Offices of holding companies; Bridge, tunnel, elevated highway & various construction; Water, sewer, pipeline, communications & power line construction; Metal mining services in gold & copper ores; Coal mining services

Lockerbie & Hole Inc.
14940-121A Ave., Edmonton, AB T5V 1A3
780-452-1250 Fax: 780-452-1284 800-417-2329
mail@lockerbiehole.com
www.lockerbiehole.com
Company Type: Private
Profile: Construction services to industrial, municipal, commercial & institutional markets

Maple Reinders Constructors Ltd.
2660 Argentia Rd., Mississauga, ON L5N 5V4
905-821-4844 Fax: 905-821-4822
info@maple.ca
www.maple-reinders.com
Company Type: Private
Profile: The construction company is involved in green building in all regions of Canada.

Monarch Corporation
#200, 2550 Victoria Park Ave., Toronto, ON M2J 5A9
416-491-7440 www.monarchgroup.net
Company Type: Private
Profile: The construction company offers a range of housing options, from high-rise condominiums to single family homes.

PCL Constructors Inc.
5410 - 99 St., Edmonton, AB T6E 3P4
780-733-5000 Fax: 780-733-5075
pclinfo@pcl.com
www.pcl.com
Company Type: Private
Profile: PCL Constructors provides full service building operations & civil work. Construction management services & general contracting services are available for industrial companies, such as oil & gas, pulp & paper, & mining industries.

Seacliff Construction Corp.
Oceanic Plaza, 1066 West Hastings St., 23rd Fl., Vancouver, BC V6E 3X2
604-601-8206 Fax: 604-408-8893
info@seacliffconstruction.ca
www.seacliffconstruction.ca
Ticker Symbol: SDC
Company Type: Public
Profile: The diversified construction company provides services in the institutional infrastructure, light, & commercial sectors. Seacliff Construction's independently operated business units include Canem Systems & Dominion Construction. The company has locations in western Canada.

Steeplejack Industrial Group Inc.
8925 - 62 Ave., Edmonton, AB T6E 5L2
780-465-9016 Fax: 780-466-8584
request@steeplejack.ca
www.steeplejack.ca
Company Type: Public
Profile: Offices of holding companies; Special trade contractors in plastering, drywall, acoustical & insulation

Stuart Olson Construction Ltd.
#400 4954 Richard Rd. SW, Calgary, AB T3E 6L1
403-520-6565 Fax: 403-230-5323
info@stuartolson.com
www.stuartolson.com
Ticker Symbol: CUQ
Company Type: Private
Profile: General contractors in residential, non-residential & industrial buildings & warehouses

The Churchill Corporation
11825 - 149 St., Edmonton, AB T5L 2J1
780-454-3667 Fax: 780-488-0194
inquiries@churchill-cuq.com
www.churchillcorporation.com
Ticker Symbol: CUQ
Company Type: Public
Profile: Commercial building & industrial construction, insulation, industrial electical, maintenance & related services

Viceroy Homes Limited
Corporate Headquarters, 414 Croft St. East, Port Hope, ON L1A 4H1
905-885-8600
info@viceroy.com; careers@viceroy.com
www.viceroy.com
Company Type: Private
Profile: Viceroy Homes Limited designs, engineers, & manufactures custom home packages for owners & professional contractors. Viceroy ships its home packages to clients throughout the world.

Winalta Inc.
Kalwin Business Park, 26302 Township Rd. 531A, Acheson, AB T7X 5A3
780-960-6900 Fax: 780-960-9523
winalta@winaltainc.com
www.winaltainc.com
Ticker Symbol: WTA
Company Type: Public
Profile: Winalta Inc. is a land developer. The company is also involved in the production of manufacturered & modular homes & site built homes, as well as the manufacturing & renting of industrial trailers and camps. Operations take place in western Canada.

Distribution & Retail

A & B Sound Ltd.
13260 Delf Pl., Richmond, BC V6V 2A2
604-303-2900 Fax: 604-303-2932
webfeedback@absound.ca
www.absound.ca
Company Type: Private
Profile: A & B Sound Ltd. is a retailer of consumer electronics, as well as music & movies.

Acklands-Grainger Inc.
90 West Beaver Creek Rd., Richmond Hill, ON L4B 1E7
905-731-5516 Fax: 905-731-9677 800-668-8989
contact@agi.ca
www.acklandsgrainger.com
Company Type: Public
Profile: Distributes industrial, safety and fastener products, including hand tools, power tools, metalworking tools, electrical equipment, material handling equipment, shop equipment

Alimentation Couche-Tard inc
Tour B, #200, 1600, boul Saint-Martin est, Laval, QC H7G 4S7
450-662-6632 Fax: 450-662-6633
info@couche-tard.com
www.couche-tard.com
Ticker Symbol: ATD
Company Type: Public
Profile: In eastern, central, & western Canada, as well as in the United States, Alimentation Couche-Tard operates convenience stores. Some of these stores include motor fuel dispensing. In Canada, the businesses operate under the brands Couche-Tard & Mac's.

Avon Canada Inc.
5500, aut Transcanadienne, Montréal, QC H9R 1B6
514-695-3371 Fax: 514-630-5439 800-265-2866
questions@avon.com
www.avon.ca
Company Type: Private
Profile: Manufacturers of perfumes, cosmetics & other toilet preparations, costume jewelry & novelties; Retailing in miscellaneous retail stores

Birks & Mayors Inc.
1240 Phillips Sq., Montréal, QC H3B 3H4
514-397-2511 Fax: 514-397-2537
mrabinovitch@birksandmayors.com
www.birksandmayors.com
Ticker Symbol: BMJ
Company Type: Public
Profile: Birks & Mayors Inc. designs, manufactures, & retails fine jewellery, silverware, timepieces, & gitware. Brand names include Birks, Brinkhaus, & Mayors. Retail stores are located in Canada & the United States.

Black Photo Corporation
371 Gough Rd., Markham, ON L3R 4B6
905-475-2777 Fax: 905-475-8027 800-668-3826
support@blackphoto.com
www.blackphoto.com
Company Type: Private
Profile: Photograpy equipment & supplies retail stores

BMR Le Groupe
2375, rue de la Province, Longueuil, QC J4G 1G3
450-463-2441 Fax: 450-463-1766
info@bmr-legroupe.com
www.bmr-legroupe.com
Company Type: Private
Profile: Wholesale distributor of brick, stone, lumber, plywood, millwork & related construction materials

BMTC Group Inc.
8500, Place Marien, Montréal, QC H1B 5W8
514-648-5757 Fax: 514-881-4056
y.desgroseillers@braultmartineau.com
Ticker Symbol: GBT.A
Company Type: Public
Profile: BMTC Group is a holding company. Its subsidiaries include Ameublements Tanguay Inc. & Brault et Martineau Inc. These subsidiaries are engaged in the retail sale of furniture, electronic goods, & household appliances in Québec.

Calgary Co-Operative Association Ltd.
#110, 151 - 86th Ave. SE, Calgary, AB T2H 3A5
403-219-6025 Fax: 403-299-5445 www.calgarycoop.com
Company Type: Private
Profile: The Calgary Co-Operative Association Ltd. offers a range of retail services in the Calgary area, including grocery, pharmacy, petroleum, liquor, & travel.

Canada Safeway Ltd.
1020 - 64 Ave. NE, Calgary, AB T2E 7V8
403-730-3500 Fax: 403-730-3888
800-723-3929www.safeway.com
Company Type: Private
Profile: Manufacturers of fluid milk, bread & other bakery products, various other food preparations; Retailing in grocery stores

Canadian Tire Corporation, Limited
PO Box 770 K, 2180 Yonge St., Toronto, ON M4V 2V8
416-480-3000 Fax: 416-544-7715
investor.relations@cantire.com
www.canadiantire.ca
Ticker Symbol: CTC
Company Type: Public
Profile: Canadian Tire Corporation, Limited is engaged in retail, petroleum, & financial services.

Canon Canada Inc.
6390 Dixie Rd., Mississauga, ON L5T 1P7
905-795-1111 Fax: 905-795-2130
hrmississauga@canada.canon.com
www.canon.ca
Company Type: Private
Profile: Wholesales-photographic equipment & supplies; Wholesales-commercial equipment; Retails-camera & photographic supply stores

Canpotex Limited
PO Box 1600, #400, 111 - 2nd Ave. South, Saskatoon, SK S7K 3R7
306-931-2200 Fax: 306-653-5505
canpqlx.sasktelwebhosting.com
Company Type: Private
Profile: Exporter of Saskatchewan potash

CanWel Building Materials Income Fund
PO Box 10034, #1510, 700 West Georgia St., Vancouver, BC V7Y 1A1

604-432-1400 Fax: 604-436-6670
info@canwel.com
www.canwel.com
Ticker Symbol: CWX.UN
Company Type: Public
Profile: CanWel Building Materials Income Fund is involved in the distribution of building materials & related products. Business is conducted throughout Canada.

CanWel, Hardware Division
PO Box 5485, 3232 White Oak Rd., London, ON N6A 4G8
519-686-2200 www.canwel.com
Ticker Symbol: CWX.UN
Company Type: Public
Profile: Wholesalers of hardware

Cara Operations Limited
6303 Airport Rd., Mississauga, ON L4V 1R8
905-405-6500
info@cara.com
www.cara.com
Ticker Symbol: CAO
Company Type: Public
Profile: Retail eating places & gift, novelty & souvenir shops, news dealers & newsstands

Cargill Ltd.
PO Box 5900, #300, 240 Graham Ave., Winnipeg, MB R3C 4C5
204-947-0141 Fax: 204-947-6444 www.cargill.com
Company Type: Private
Profile: Wholesalers of grain & field beans, farm supplies, meat packing plants, sausages & other prepared meat products, prepared feeds & feed ingredients for animals & fowls, nitrogenous fertilizers, & phosphatic fertilizers

Cervus LP
#205, 120 Country Hills Landing NW, Calgary, AB T3K 5P3
403-567-0339 Fax: 403-567-0392 www.cervuslp.com
Ticker Symbol: CVL.UN
Company Type: Public
Profile: Cervus LP retails agricultural & industrial equipment. The company acquires & operates dealerships, such as John Deere, Bobcat, JLG, & JCB Construction equipment dealerships. Business is conducted in western Canada.

Co-op Atlantic
PO Box 750, 123 Halifax St., Moncton, NB E1C 8N5
506-858-6000 Fax: 506-858-6477 www.coopatlantic.ca
Profile: Wholesalers of general line groceries, farm supplies, grain & field beans, petroleum & petroleum products, hardware

Coast Wholesale Appliances Income Fund
8488 Main St., Vancouver, BC V5X 4W8
604-321-6644 Fax: 604-321-6782
invest@coastappliances.com
www.coastappliances.com
Ticker Symbol: CWA.UN
Company Type: Public
Profile: Coast Wholesale Appliances Income Fund is an unincorporated, open-ended limited purpose trust. The Fund indirectly owns 65% of Coast Wholesale Appliances LP (Coast). Coast Wholesale Appliances Income Fund is involved in the supply of household appliances. It serves retail customers, plus developers & builders of single family & multi-family housing. There are locations across Canada.

Commercial Solutions Inc.
4203 - 95th St., Edmonton, AB T6E 5R6
780-432-1611 Fax: 780-496-9172
info@csinet.ca
www.commercialsolutions.ca
Ticker Symbol: CSA
Company Type: Public
Profile: Commercial Solutions Inc. is a national distributor of the following products: forestry, mining & resource management equipment, bearing & power transmission supplies, & industrial safety equipment. In addition to these products & services, Commercial Solution Inc.'s group of companies also provides Business to Business services, such as electronic fund transfers, invoicing, & electronic data interchange. Commercial Solution Inc.'s subsidiaries are as follows: Cando Oilfield Supplies & Rentals Ltd., Commercial Bearing Service (1966) Ltd., & Impact Oilfield Supply Inc.. Divisions include Aim Supply, CFE Equipment, & Nisku Safety Service.

CoolBrands International Inc.
210 Shields Court, Markham, ON L3R 8V2
905-479-8762 Fax: 905-479-5235
info@coolbrandsinternational.com
www.coolbrandsinc.com
Ticker Symbol: COB
Company Type: Public
Profile: Retailing in eating places; Wholesalers of dairy products, frozen specialties, frozen fruits, fruit juices & vegetables; Manufacturers of ice cream & frozen desserts

Coopérative fédérée de Québec
#200, 9001, boul de L'Acadie, Montréal, QC H4N 3H7
514-384-6450 Fax: 514-384-7176
information@lacoop.coop
www.lacoop.coop
Company Type: NA
Profile: Wholesalers of meats & meat products, fresh fruits & vegetables, dairy products, petroleum & petroleum products

Costco Canada Inc.
415 West Hunt Club, Ottawa, ON K2E 1C5
613-221-2000 Fax: 613-221-2001 www.costco.com
Company Type: Private
Profile: Bulk retail store that provides members with discounts on items

easyhome Ltd.
10239 - 178 St., Edmonton, AB T5S 1M3
780-930-3000 Fax: 780-481-7426
leanne@easyhome.ca
www.easyhome.ca
Ticker Symbol: EH
Company Type: Public
Profile: easyhome Ltd. is a merchandise lease company. The company rents products, such as household furnishings, home entertainment products, electronics, appliances & computers. Customers may have the option to purchase products.

Forzani Group Ltd.
824 - 41 Ave. NE, Calgary, AB T2E 3R3
403-717-1400 Fax: 403-717-1490
cjordan@forzani.com (Investor Relations)
www.forzanigroup.com
Ticker Symbol: FGL
Company Type: Public
Profile: The Forzani Group Ltd. is involved in the retail of sporting goods. Its stores operate under the following corporate banners: National Sports, Coast Mountain Sports, Sport Chek, & Sport Mart. Franchised banners feature the following: Nevada Bob's, Intersport, Econosport, Fitness Source, Sports Experts, Pegasus, & Atmosphere.

Future Shop Ltd.
8800 Glenlyon Pkwy., Burnaby, BC V5J 5K3
604-435-8223 Fax: 604-412-5280 800-663-2275
service@futureshop.com
www.futureshop.ca
Company Type: Private
Profile: Retailing in radio, television & consumer electronics stores, computer & computer software stores, household appliance stores

Futuremed Healthcare Income Fund
277 Basaltic Rd., Concord, ON L4K 5V3
905-761-0068 Fax: 905-761-6079
800-387-7025www.futuremed.ca
Ticker Symbol: FMD.UN
Company Type: Public
Profile: Futuremed Healthcare Income Fund is involved in the distribution of medical supplies, equipment, & specialized furniture to long-term care facilities.

GLV Inc.
#2100, 2001, av McGill College, Montréal, QC H3A 1G1
514-284-2224 Fax: 514-284-2225
courrier@glv.com
www.glv.com
Ticker Symbol: GLV.A
Company Type: Public
Profile: GLV Inc. supplies technological solutions & services. Processes & equipment are used in pulp & paper production & for the treatment & recycling of municipal & industrial wastewater.

Grand & Toy Ltd.
33 Green Belt Dr., Toronto, ON M3C 1M1
416-445-7255 Fax: 416-445-7741
generalinquiries@grandtoy.com
www.grandandtoy.com
Company Type: Private
Profile: Commercial supplier of office supplies, furniture & technology products

Groupe BMTC inc
8500, Place Marien, Montréal, QC H1B 5W8
514-648-5757 Fax: 514-881-4056
service.clients@braultetmartineau.com
www.braultetmartineau.com
Ticker Symbol: GBT
Company Type: Public
Profile: Retailing furniture stores, household appliance stores, radio, television, & consumer electronics stores

Harry Rosen Inc.
#1600, 77 Bloor St. West, Toronto, ON M5S 1M2
416-935-9200 Fax: 416-515-7067 www.harryrosen.com
Company Type: Private
Profile: Retail menswear

Harry Winston Diamond Corporation
PO Box 4569 A, Toronto, ON M5W 4T9
416-362-2237 Fax: 416-362-2230
hw@harrywinston.com
investor.harrywinston.com
Ticker Symbol: HW
Company Type: Public
Profile: Harry Winston Diamond Corporation owns 40% interest in the Diavik Diamond Mine in the Northwest Territories. Rough diamonds are supplied to an international market. The specialist diamond enterprise is also the owner of a diamond jewelry & watch retailer, known as Harry Winston Inc. Retail salons are locatedd in cities around the world, such as Tokyo, Beijing, Paris, London, & New York.

Hart Stores Inc.
900, Place Paul Kane, Laval, QC H7C 2T2
450-661-4155 Fax: 450-661-6531
hartstoresinfo@hartstores.com
www.hartstores.com
Ticker Symbol: HIS
Company Type: Public
Profile: Hart Stores Inc. operates a network of mid-sized department stores. Its stores are located in Newfoundland, Nova Scotia, New Brunswick, Quebec, & Ontario. Hart Stores Inc.'s banners include Bargain Giant, Géant des Aubaines, & Hart.

Haworth Canada
10 SMED Lane SE, Calgary, AB T2C 4T5
403-203-6000 Fax: 403-203-6001 www.haworth.com
Company Type: Private
Profile: Haworth Canada manufactures & markets office furniture & workspaces. A factory is located in Quebec, and showrooms are situated in Toronto & Calgary.

Hudson's Bay Company
#500, 401 Bay St., Toronto, ON M5H 2Y4
416-861-6112 Fax: 416-861-4720 866-746-7422www.hbc.ca
Company Type: Public
Profile: Retailing in department stores; Short-term business credit institutions; Information retrieval services

Indigo Books & Music Inc.
#500, 468 King St. West, Toronto, ON M5V 1L8
416-364-4499 Fax: 416-364-0355 800-832-9124
InvestorRelations@indigo.ca
www.chapters.indigo.ca
Ticker Symbol: IDG
Company Type: Public
Profile: The book retailer operates in all provinces & one territory, under the following names: Indigo, Coles, Chapters, & the World's Biggest Bookstore. Indigo also operates chapters.indigo.ca, to retail books, music, & movies online. Indigo Books & Music Inc. is implementing an environmental paper policy in conjunction with Markets Initiative.

Itochu Canada Ltd
World Trade Centre, #770, 999 Canada Pl., Vancouver, BC V6C 3E1
604-331-5800 Fax: 604-688-9292 www.itochu.com
Company Type: Private
Profile: Wholesalers of electrical appliances, television & radio sets, commercial equipment, various durable & non-durable goods

Jace Holdings Ltd.
6649 Bulter Cres., Saanichton, BC V8M 1Z7
250-483-1600 Fax: 250-483-1601 800-667-8280
info@thriftyfoods.com
www.thriftyfoods.com
Company Type: Private
Profile: Isle Three Holdings Ltd. provides retail grocery stores & bakeries.

Jean Coutu Group (PJC) Inc.
530, rue Bériault, Longueuil, QC J4G 1S8
450-646-9760 Fax: 450-646-0550 www.jeancoutu.com
Ticker Symbol: PJC
Company Type: Public
Profile: Wholesalers of drugs, drug proprietaries & druggists' sundries; Retailing in drug stores & proprietary stores; Real estate operators of nonresidential buildings; Patent owners & lessors

Katz Group Canada Ltd.
Bell Tower, #1702, 10104 - 103 Ave., Edmonton, AB T5J 0H8

780-990-0505 Fax: 780-702-0647 877-378-4100
esilverman@katzgroup.ca
www.katzgroup.ca
Company Type: Private
Profile: Encompasses more than 1,800 pharmacies across North America; Canadian pharmacies include Rexall Drug Stores, Pharma Plus, Rexall Pharma Plus, Medicine Shoppe Pharmacy, Guardian, I.D.A., Herbie's/Payless Drug & Food, & Meditrust Pharmacy

La Senza Corporation
1604, boul St-Régis, Montréal, QC H9P 1H6
514-684-3651 Fax: 514-421-0381 888-527-3692
ir@lasenza.com
www.lasenza.com
Ticker Symbol: LTD
Company Type: Public
Profile: Retailing in women's clothing stores, women's accessory & specialty stores, miscellaneous apparel & accessory stores

Leon's Furniture Limited
PO Box 1100 B, 45 Gordon Mackay Rd., Toronto, ON M9L 2R8
416-243-7880 Fax: 416-243-7890
investors@leons.ca
www.leons.ca
Ticker Symbol: LNF
Company Type: Public
Profile: Through a chain of retail facilities & franchises across Canada, Leon's Furniture Limited is engaged in the sale of home furnishings, electronics, & appliances.

Liquor Control Board of Ontario
55 Lakeshore Blvd. East, Toronto, ON M5E 1A4
416-365-5900 Fax: 416-864-2596 800-668-5226
infoline@lcbo.com
www.lcbo.com
Company Type: Crown
Profile: Retailers in liquor stores

Loblaw Companies Limited
1 President's Choice Circle, Brampton, ON L6Y 5S5
905-459-2500 Fax: 905-861-2206
investor@loblaw.ca
www.loblaw.com
Ticker Symbol: L
Company Type: Public
Profile: Loblaw Companies Limited operates the following grocery stores: Loblaws, Your Independent Grocer, The Real Canadian Superstore, Fortinos, Atlantic Superstore, Atlantic SaveEasy, No Frills, SuperValu, Valumart, Extra Foods, Shop Easy Foods, Provigo, Zehrs, Cash & Carry, & Maxi.

Loeb Canada Inc
5559 Dundas St. W., Toronto, ON M9B 1B9
877-335-5632
loeb@metro.ca
www.loeb.ca
Company Type: Private
Profile: Retails-miscellaneous general merchandise stores; Wholesales-tobacco and tobacco products; Wholesales-confectionery; Wholesales-drugs, drug proprietaries and druggists' sundries; Wholesales-groceries, general line; Retails-fruit and vegetable markets; Retails-meat and fish markets, and freezer provisioners; Retails-dairy products stores

Mark's Work Wearhouse Ltd.
#30, 1035 - 64 Ave. SE, Calgary, AB T2H 2J7
403-255-9220 Fax: 403-255-6005 800-663-6275
karen.bentley@marks.com
www.marks.com
Company Type: Private
Profile: Incorporated on April 12, 1977, the company operates Mark's Work Wearhouse retail stores & has granted franchises to operate Mark's stores in Canada. At Dec. 30, 2006, there were 339 stores, 287 corporate & 52 franchise. The stores sell a wide range of men's, women's, unisex leisure, casual & workwear clothes & footwear, healthwear & uniforms. In Quebec, Mark's corporate & franchise stores operate under the name L'Equipeur. The company employs 4,600 people. It is a wholly-owned subsidiary of CTC Acquisition, a wholly-owned subsidiary of Canadian Tire Corporation, Limited. Mark's was purchased by CT on Feb. 1, 2002, & is now a private company.

Marubeni Canada Ltd.
#600, 40 University Ave., Toronto, ON M5J 1T1
416-368-1171 Fax: 416-947-9004 www.marubeni.com
Company Type: Private
Profile: Wholesalers of farm & garden machinery & equipment, automobile & other motor vehicles. Offices in Toronto & Vancouver

Metro Inc.
11011, boul Maurice-Duplessis, Montréal, QC H1C 1V6
514-643-1000 Fax: 514-643-1215
finance@metro.ca
www.metro.ca
Ticker Symbol: MRU
Company Type: Public
Profile: Metro Inc. operates food retail stores in Ontario & Québec, under the following names: Metro, Super C, A&P, Loeb, Food Basics, Marché Richelieu, AMI, Les 5 Saisons, & GEM. The company also distributes pharmaceutical products under the following banners: Brunet, Clini-Plus, The Pharmacy, & Drug Basics.

Metro Inc.
PO Box 68 A, Toronto, ON M5A 1A6
416-239-7171 Fax: 416-234-6581 877-763-7374www.metro.ca
Company Type: Private
Profile: Offices of holding companies; Retailing in grocery stores

Mitsubishi Canada Ltd.
#2800, 200 Granville St., Vancouver, BC V6C 1G6
604-654-8000 Fax: 604-654-8222 www.mitsubishi.ca
Company Type: Private
Profile: Wholesalers of automobiles & other motors vehicles, supplies & new parts; Divisions in electrical machinery, home appliances

Mitsui & Co. (Canada) Ltd.
#1400, 20 Adelaide St. East, Toronto, ON M5C 2T6
416-365-3800 Fax: 416-865-1486 www.mitsui.ca
Company Type: Private
Profile: Steel & metals; machinery; chemicals; energy; foods; consumer goods; transportation logistics

Nevada Bob's International Inc.
824 - 41st Ave. NE, Calgary, AB T2E 3R3
403-717-1400 Fax: 403-717-1491
cjordan@forzani.com
www.nevadabobs.ca; www.forzanigroup.com
Ticker Symbol: FGL; NBC
Company Type: Public
Profile: Owns and operates golf specialty shops

New Brunswick Liquor Corporation
PO Box 20787, 170 Wilsey Rd., Fredericton, NB E3B 5B8
506-452-6826 Fax: 506-462-2024
info@anbl.com
www.nbliquor.com
Company Type: Crown
Profile: A provincial Crown corporation responsible for the purchase, importation, distribution and retailing of all beverage alcohol in New Brunswick

North West Company Fund
Gibraltar House, 77 Main St., Winnipeg, MB R3C 2R1
204-943-0881 Fax: 204-934-1455 800-563-0002
nwc@northwest.ca
www.northwest.ca
Ticker Symbol: NWF
Company Type: Public
Profile: North West Company Fund is involved in the retail of food & daily products & services. Business is carried out in northern Canada, Alaska, the South Pacific, & the Caribbean.

Olco Petroleum Group Inc.
2775, av Georges Vanier, Montréal, QC H1L 6J7
514-645-6526 Fax: 514-645-8048 800-363-1120www.olco.ca
Company Type: Private
Profile: OLCO is engaged in the supply & marketing of petroleum products. Products include gasoline, propane, kerosene, ultra low-sulphur diesel, furnace oils, & various grades of residual oils. Environmentally friendly products are promoted, such as reusable propane tanks.

Pantorama Industries Inc.
2, rue Lake, Montréal, QC H9B 3H9
514-421-1850 Fax: 514-684-3159 www.pantorama.com
Ticker Symbol: PTA
Company Type: Private
Profile: Retailing in men's & boys' clothing & accessory stores, women's clothing stores & shoe stores

Parkland Income Fund
Riverside Office Plaza, #236, 4919 - 59th St., Red Deer, AB T4N 6C9
403-357-6400 Fax: 403-352-0042
corpinfo@parkland.ca
www.parkland.ca
Ticker Symbol: PKI
Company Type: Public
Profile: The Fund is engaged in the operation of retail & wholesale fuels, as well as convenience store businesses. These operations are carried out through independent branded dealers & the following brands: Fas Gas, Fas Gas Plus, Race Trac Fuels, & Short Stop Food Stores. Fuel is transported through the Petrohaul division. Parkland has implemented risk mitigation programs & emergency response procedures to prevent environmental risk in the handling & transportation of fuels, propane, & other products. Business is conducted in Ontario, Manitoba, Saskatchewan, Alberta, British Columbia, & the Yukon Territory.

Pet Valu Canada Inc.
121 McPherson St., Markham, ON L3R 3L3
905-946-1200 Fax: 905-946-0658 888-254-7824
hr@petvalue.com
www.petvalue.com
Ticker Symbol: PVC
Company Type: Public
Profile: Specialty retailer of pet food and pet-related supplies, with stores located in Ontario and Manitoba, as well as the US states of Maryland, Virginia, Pennsylvania and New Jersey

Pharmacy Won Inc.
7171 Yonge St., Thornhill, ON L3T 2A9
905-886-7171 Fax: 905-886-9605 www.pharmacy2.ca
Company Type: Private
Profile: Retailing in drug stores & proprietary stores, grocery stores & miscellaneous general merchandise stores

Pharmasave Drugs National Ltd.
#201, 8411 - 200th St., Langley, BC V2Y 0E7
604-455-2400 Fax: 604-455-2493 800-661-6106
info@bc.pharmasave.ca
www.pharmasave.com
Company Type: Private
Profile: Pharmasave Drugs National Ltd. is an independent pharmacy & drugstore retailer. Over 400 stores are located in nine provinces.

Premetalco Inc.
110 Belfield Rd., Toronto, ON M9W 1G1
416-245-7386 Fax: 416-242-2839 **Company Type:** Private
Profile: Wholesales-metals service centers and offices; Wholesales-chemicals and allied products; Wholesales-construction materials; Mfrs-miscellaneous fabricated wire products

Provigo Inc.
400, av Sainte-Croix, Saint-Laurent, QC H4N 3L4
514-383-8800 Fax: 514-383-3100 www.provigo.ca
Company Type: Private
Profile: The holding company is engaged in the wholesale & retail of groceries & general merchandise. Provigo owns or franchises supermarkets in Québec, under the Provigo banner. The company also owns or franchises discount stores, known as Maxi & Maxi & Cie.

Reitmans (Canada) Limited
250, rue Sauvé ouest, Montréal, QC H3L 1Z2
514-384-1140 Fax: 514-385-2669
info@reitmans.com
www.reitmans.com
Ticker Symbol: RET
Company Type: Public
Profile: Reitmans (Canada) Ltd. is the operator of clothing stores, which specialize in both women's & men's fashions & accessories. Stores are operated under the following names: Reitmans, RW & Co., Smart Set, Cassis, Pennington Superstores, Addition-Elle, & Thyme Maternity.

Richelieu Hardware Ltd.
7900, boul Henri-Bourassa ouest, Montréal, QC H4S 1V4
514-336-4144 Fax: 514-832-4002 866-832-4040
info@richelieu.com
www.richelieu.com
Ticker Symbol: RCH
Company Type: Public
Profile: Richelieu Hardware manufactures, imports, & distributes specialty hardware & complementary products. The company serves manufacturers & retailers throughout North America.

Ritchie Bros. Auctioneers Inc.
6500 River Rd., Richmond, BC V6X 4G5
604-273-7564 Fax: 604-273-2405 800-663-1739
info@rbauction.com
www.rbauction.com
Ticker Symbol: RBA
Company Type: Public
Profile: The company is an auctioneer of industrial equipment for the agricultural, mining, petroleum, forestry, construction, transportation, marine, & material handling industries. Ritchie Bros. Auctioneers has locations worldwide.

Roadking Travel Centres Inc.
26 Strathmoor Dr., Sherwood Park, AB T8H 2B6
780-464-1000 Fax: 780-464-1043
info@roadking.ca
www.roadking.ca
Ticker Symbol: RKG
Company Type: Public

Profile: Roadking Travel Centres Inc. operates travel facilities which offer hospitality & fuel services in Alberta. Centres include Roadking Inns, RK General Stores, RK Express Convenience Stores, restaurants, & fuel stations.

RONA Inc.
220, ch du Tremblay, Boucherville, QC J4B 8H7
514-599-5100 Fax: 514-599-5161
investor.relations@rona.ca
www.rona.ca
Ticker Symbol: RON
Company Type: Public
Profile: Hardware, home renovation, & gardening products are distributed & retailed by RONA Inc.

Sears Canada Inc.
222 Jarvis St., Toronto, ON M5B 2B8
416-941-4425 Fax: 416-941-4793
home@sears.ca
www.sears.ca
Ticker Symbol: SCC
Company Type: Public
Profile: Sears Canada Inc. is a general merchandise retailer, as well as a catalogue publisher.

Shnier
50 Kenview Blvd., Brampton, ON L6T 5S8
905-789-3755 Fax: 905-789-3757 800-970-2000www.shnier.ca
Company Type: Private
Profile: Markets floor covering products

Shoppers Drug Mart Corporation
243 Consumers Rd., Toronto, ON M2J 4W8
416-493-1220 Fax: 416-491-1022
investorrelations@shoppersdrugmart.ca
www.shoppersdrugmart.ca
Ticker Symbol: SC
Company Type: Public
Profile: Shoppers Drug Mart Corporation licenses retail drug stores, which operate under the name Shoppers Drug Mart, & Pharmaprix in Quebec. Shoppers Home Health Care stores are also owned & operated by Shoppers Drug Mart Corporation. In addition to these retail establishments, Shoppers Drug Mart Corporation also owns a provider of pharmaceutical products & services to long-term care facilities, which operates under the name MediSystem Technologies Inc.

Sleep Country Canada Income Fund
#1, 140 Wendell Ave., Toronto, ON M9N 3R2
416-242-4774 Fax: 416-242-9644 888-753-3788
investor@sleepcountry.ca
www.sleepcountry.ca
Company Type: Public
Profile: Sleep Country Canada Income Fund is engaged in the provision of mattresses & bedding related products. Its wholly-owned subsidiaries are as follows: Sleep Country Canada Inc., Sleep America, LLC, & Dormez-vous Sleep Centres Inc.

Sobeys Inc.
115 King St., Stellarton, NS B0K 1S0
902-752-8371
paul.jewer@sobeys.com
www.sobeys.com
Ticker Symbol: SBY
Company Type: Public
Profile: Sobeys is a national grocery retailer. Retail banners include Sobeys, Foodland, IGA, & Price Chopper. Its two operating divisions are Thrifty Foods & Lawtons Drugs.

Société des alcools du Québec
905, av de Lorimier, Montréal, QC H2K 3V9
514-254-2711 Fax: 514-864-3532 866-873-2020
info@saq.com
www.saq.com
Company Type: Crown
Profile: Regulation, licensing & inspection of miscellaneous commercial sectors

Somerset Entertainment Income Fund
#600, 20 York Mills Rd., Toronto, ON M2P 2C2
416-510-2800 Fax: 416-510-3070
information@somersetent.com
www.somersetent.com
Ticker Symbol: SOM.UN
Company Type: Public
Profile: Somerset Entertainment Income Fund is engaged in the production & distribution of specialty music. Music is sold internationally, through non-traditional retailers, using interactive displays.

Sony of Canada Ltd.
115 Gordon Baker Rd., Toronto, ON M2H 3R6
416-499-1414 Fax: 416-497-1774 877-899-7669
general_enquiries@sony.ca
www.sony.ca
Company Type: Private
Profile: Sony of Canada Ltd. is an entertainment company that offers electronics, movies, music, & games. Examples of Sony products include BRAVIA televisions, VAIO computers, Blu-ray Disc players, Handycam Camcorders, broadcast cameras, Cyber-shot digital cameras, & IPELA security cameras. Sony of Canada Ltd. is headquartered in Toronto. Sales offices are located in Montréal, Québec & Vancouver British Columbia. Distribution centres are situated in Whitby, Ontario & Coquitlam, British Columbia.

Sterling Shoes Income Fund
2580 Viscount Way, Richmond, BC V6V 1N1
604-270-6114 Fax: 604-278-7751
www.sterlingshoesincomefund.com
Ticker Symbol: SSI.UN
Company Type: Public
Profile: Through its interest in Sterling Shoes Limited Partnership, Sterling Shoes Income Fund is involved in the retailing of footwear. The following are the organization's retail banners: Sterling Shoes, Shoe Warehouse, Gia Shoes, Joneve Shoes, Freedman Shoes, & Sterling Outlet. There are more than 100 stores throughout Canada.

Summit Food Service Distributors Inc.
580 Industrial Rd., London, ON N5V 1V1
Fax: 519-453-5148 800-265-9267
headoffice@summitfoods.com
www.summitfoods.com
Company Type: Public
Profile: Wholesalers of packaged frozen foods & general line groceries

SunOpta Inc.
2838 Bovaird Dr. West, Brampton, ON L7A 0H2
905-455-1990 Fax: 905-455-2529
info@sunopta.com
www.sunopta.com
Ticker Symbol: STKL
Company Type: Public
Profile: SunOpta Inc. is focused upon sourcing, processing, & distributing healthy, environmentally responsible products. Products include organic food supplements & health & beauty products. The company consists of the following business segments: SunOpta Food Group, SunOpta BioProcess Inc., & Opta Minerals Inc.

The Brick Group Income Fund
16930 - 114 Ave., Edmonton, AB T5M 3S2
780-930-6000 Fax: 780-454-0969 877-843-2742
investor@thebrick.com
www.thebrick.com
Ticker Symbol: BRK.UN
Company Type: Public
Profile: The Brick Group Income Fund is an unincorporated, open-ended, limited purpose trust. The Fund indirectly acquired the limited partnership units of The Brick Warehouse LP. The Brick Warehouse LP owns the outstanding limited partnership units of United Furniture Warehouse LP (United Furniture) & the outstanding shares of First Oceans Trading Corporation. Through its subsidiaries, The Brick Group Income Fund is involved in retailing furniture, appliances, mattresses, & electronics.

The Winroc Corporation
4949 - 51 St. SE, Calgary, AB T2B 3S7
403-236-5383 Fax: 403-279-0372 www.winroc.com
Company Type: Private
Profile: Wholesalers of construction materials; Retailing in lumber & other building materials dealers

Toshiba of Canada Ltd.
191 McNabb St., Markham, ON L3R 8H2
905-470-3500 Fax: 905-470-3509 www.toshiba.ca
Company Type: Private
Profile: Wholesalers of office equipment, computers & peripheral equipment & software, electrical appliances, television & radio sets, electronic parts & equipment, medical, dental, hospital equipment & supplies

UAP Inc.
7025, rue Ontario est, Montréal, QC H1N 2B3
514-256-5031 Fax: 514-256-8469 www.uapinc.com
Company Type: Private
Profile: Wholesales-motor vehicle supplies and new parts; Retails-auto and home supply stores

Uni-Select Inc.
170, boul Industriel, Boucherville, QC J4B 2X3
450-641-2440 Fax: 450-449-4908
questions@uni-select.com
www.uni-select.com
Ticker Symbol: UNS
Company Type: Public
Profile: Uni-Select Inc. is a wholesale distributor & marketer of heavy duty tools, equipment, replacement parts, & accessories. The company serves the automotive industry.

Unilever Canada Inc.
#1500, 160 Bloor St. East, Toronto, ON M4W 3R2
416-964-1857 Fax: 416-963-5197
info.ca-unilever@unilever.com
www.unilever.ca
Company Type: Private
Profile: Consumer products company in foods, home & personal care products, food service industries

United Furniture Warehouse Ltd.
16930 - 114th Ave., Edmonton, AB T5M 3S2
Fax: 780-454-0969 866-508-7766
vp@ufw.com
www.ufw.com
Company Type: Private
Profile: The home furnishing retailer has warehouse-style shopping operations in British Columbia, Alberta, Saskatchewan, Manitoba, & Ontario.

Wajax Income Fund
3280 Wharton Way, Mississauga, ON L4X 2C5
905-212-3300 Fax: 905-624-6020
ir@wajax.com
www.wajax.com
Ticker Symbol: WJX
Company Type: Public
Profile: Through its subsidiaries, Wajax is involved in the sale & parts & service support of power systems, mobile equipment, & industrial components. Wajax serves the manufacturing, natural resources, utilities, construction, & industrial processing sectors. Branches are located throughout Canada.

Westfair Foods Ltd.
PO Box 300 M, 3225 - 12 St. NE, Calgary, AB T2P 2H9
403-291-7700 Fax: 403-291-7899 www.loblaw.ca
Ticker Symbol: WF
Company Type: Public
Profile: Retailing in grocery stores; Wholesalers of general line groceries. The division serves Western Canada and Northern Ontario

Electronics & Electrical Equipment

Aastra Technologies Limited
155 Snow Blvd., Concord, ON L4K 4N9
905-760-4200 Fax: 905-760-4233
investors@aastra.com
www.aastra.com
Ticker Symbol: AAH
Company Type: Public
Profile: The company develops, markets, & supports products for communication networks. Products include communication servers, gateways, wireless products, telephone terminals, & advanced software applications. Aastra Technologies Limited serves both the business & residential markets.

Ansen Corporation
100 Schneider Rd., Kanata, ON K2K 1Y2
613-599-6277 Fax: 613-599-6146 www.ansencorp.com
Ticker Symbol: AGT
Company Type: Public
Profile: Manufacturers of various measuring & controlling devices, & printed circuit boards

Ballard Power Systems Inc.
9000 Glenlyon Parkway, Burnaby, BC V5J 5J8
604-454-0900 Fax: 604-412-4700
investors@ballard.com
www.ballard.com
Ticker Symbol: BLD
Company Type: Public
Profile: Designers, developers & manufacturers of zero-emission proton exchange membrane fuel cells

Bell Canada International Inc.
#1200, 1000 rue de la Gauchetière ouest, Montréal, QC H3B 4Y8
514-392-2384 Fax: 514-392-2266
info@marcnon.qc.ca
Ticker Symbol: BI
Company Type: Public
Profile: Manufacturers of telephone & telegraph apparatus; Manufacturers of radio & television broadcasting & communications equipment; Special trade contracting in electrical work

Celestica Inc.
12 Concorde Place, 5th Fl., Toronto, ON M3C 3R8
416-448-5800 Fax: 416-448-5527 888-899-9998
corpinfo@celestica.com

www.celestica.com
Ticker Symbol: CLS
Company Type: Public
Profile: Manufacturers of various electronic components, printed circuit boards; Wholesalers in electronic parts & equipment

Cinram International Inc.
2255 Markham Rd., Scarborough, ON M1B 2W3
416-298-8190 Fax: 416-298-0612
lynefisher@cinram.com
www.cinram.com
Ticker Symbol: CRW
Company Type: Public
Profile: Manufacturers of phonograph records & prerecorded audio tapes & disks; Services allied to motion picture production; Motion picture & video tape distribution

CMC Electronics Inc.
600, boul Dr.-Frederik-Philips, Montréal, QC H4M 2S9
514-748-3148 Fax: 514-748-3100 www.cmcelectronics.ca
Company Type: Private
Profile: Manufacturers of aviation electronics, communications solutions, custom electronic products, CPS OEM products; Marine & land electronics sales & service; Customer support; Calibration

COM DEV International Ltd.
155 Sheldon Dr., Cambridge, ON N1R 7H6
519-622-2300 Fax: 519-622-1691
investor.relations@comdev.ca
www.comdev.ca
Ticker Symbol: CDV
Company Type: Public
Profile: COM DEV International engineers & manufactures custom-designed space hardware. The space technology company serves the commercial, civil, & military space hardware market. Facilities are located in Canada, the United States, & the United Kingdom.

Connex See Service
120 East Beaver Creek Rd., Richmond Hill, ON L4B 4V1
905-944-6500 Fax: 905-944-6520 866-429-4625
central@connexservice.ca
www.connexservice.ca
Company Type: Public
Profile: Manufacturers of radio & television broadcasting & communications equipment

Coretec Inc.
8150 Sheppard Ave. East, Toronto, ON M1B 5K2
416-208-2100 Fax: 416-208-2195
snemchin@coretec-inc.com
www.coretec-inc.com
Ticker Symbol: CYY
Company Type: Public
Profile: Manufacturers of printed circuit boards; Wholesalers of electronic parts & equipment

DALSA Corp.
605 McMurray Rd., Waterloo, ON N2V 2E9
519-866-6000 Fax: 519-866-8023
sales.americas@dalsa.com
www.dalsa.com
Ticker Symbol: CRC
Company Type: Public
Profile: Designers, developers, and manufacturers of digital imaging products & solutions. In addition engineers semiconductor components.

Descartes Systems Group Inc.
120 Randall Dr., Waterloo, ON N2V 1C6
519-746-8110 Fax: 519-747-0082 800-419-8495
info@descartes.com
www.descartes.com
Ticker Symbol: DSG
Company Type: Public
Profile: The Descartes Systems Group provides logistics management solutions. Solutions are used by the transportation logistics, distribution, manufacturing, & retail sectors.

Electrovaya Inc.
2645 Royal Windsor Dr., Mississauga, ON L5J 1K9
905-855-4610 Fax: 905-822-7953 800-388-2865
customerservice@electrovaya.com
www.electrovaya.com
Ticker Symbol: EFL
Company Type: Public
Profile: Manufacturers of storage batteries

Evertz Technologies Limited
5288 John Lucas Dr., Burlington, ON L7L 5Z9
905-335-3700 Fax: 905-335-3573
ir@evertz.com; sales@evertz.com
www.evertz.com
Ticker Symbol: ET
Company Type: Public
Profile: Evertz Technologies Limited is a high-technology company. It is engaged in the designing, manufacturing, & marketing of film production, post production, & broadcast equipment. This equipment is used in the film & television broadcast industry.

EXFO Electro-Optical Engineering Inc.
400, av Godin, Québec, QC G1M 2K2
418-683-0211 Fax: 418-683-2170 800-663-3936
info@exfo.com; ir@exfo.com
www.exfo.com
Ticker Symbol: EXF
Company Type: Public
Profile: Test, measurement, & monitoring products are designed & manufactured by EXFO Electro-Optical Engineering Inc.. The company's test & service assurance solutions are used by the global telecommunications industry.

Gamecorp Ltd.
#102, 3565 King Rd., King City, ON L7B 1M3
905-833-5844 Fax: 905-833-9847
jmoretto@gamecorp.comcom
www.gamecorp.com
Ticker Symbol: GGG
Company Type: Public
Profile: Manufacturers of telephone & telegraph apparatus; Computer integrated systems design

General Electric Canada Inc.
2300 Meadowvale Blvd., Mississauga, ON L5N 5P9
905-858-5100 Fax: 905-858-5106 www.ge.com/ca/en/
Company Type: Private
Profile: Manufactured products & services include power generation, water processing, aircraft engines, medical imaging, security technology, business & consumer financing, & media content

Genesis Microchip (Canada) Co.
165 Commerce Valley Dr. West, Thornhill, ON L3T 7V8
905-889-5400 Fax: 905-889-5422
sales-americas@gnss.com
www.gnss.com
Ticker Symbol: GNSS
Company Type: Public
Profile: Monitor products, analog video processors, digital TV processing

Gennum Corporation
4281 Harvester Road, Burlington, ON L7L 5M4
905-632-2996 Fax: 905-632-2055
corporate@gennum.com
www.gennum.com
Ticker Symbol: GND
Company Type: Public
Profile: Manufacturers & marketers of semiconductor components, electrical subsystems & solutions for the global video, audio & data communications markets

Hammond Power Solutions Inc.
595 Southgate Dr., Guelph, ON N1G 3W6
519-822-2441 Fax: 519-822-9701
cdncustservice@hammondpowersolutions.com
www.hammondpowersolutions.com
Ticker Symbol: HPS.A
Company Type: Public
Profile: Hammond Power Solutions Inc. engineers & manufactures custom & standard dry-type transformers & related magnetic products. The company's products are used by the global electrical industry.

Hemisphere GPS Inc.
4110 - 9 St. SE, Calgary, AB T2G 3C4
403-259-3311 Fax: 403-259-8866
info@hemispheregps.com
www.hemispheregps.com
Company Type: Public
Profile: Manufacturers of precision commercial GPS (Global Positioning System) technology

Hewlett-Packard (Canada) Ltd.
5150 Spectrum Way, Mississauga, ON L4W 5G1
905-206-4725 Fax: 905-206-4739 www.hp.ca
Company Type: Public
Profile: Hewlett-Packard (Canada) Ltd. is a technology solutions companys. It offers information technology infrastructure, personal computing & access devices, global services, imaging, & printing. for consumers & small & medium businesses.

Honeywell Ltd.
333 Unity Dr., Mississauga, ON L5L 3S6
905-608-6000 Fax: 905-608-6001 www.honeywell.ca
Company Type: Private
Profile: Provides aerospace technology & manufacturing products & services, control technologies for buildings, homes & industry, automotive products, power generation systems, specialty chemicals, fibers, plastics & advanced materials

Hydrogenics Corporation
5985 McLaughlin Rd., Mississauga, ON L5R 1B8
905-361-3660 Fax: 905-361-3626
investors@hydrogenics.com
www.hydrogenics.com
Ticker Symbol: HYG
Company Type: Public
Profile: Manufacturers of various electrical industrial apparatus, fuel cell systems for power generation; Fuel testing & diagnosis

L-3 Wescam
649 North Service Rd. West, Burlington, ON L7P 5B9
905-633-4000 Fax: 905-633-4100 800-668-4355
Sales.Wescam@L-3com.com
www.wescam.com
Company Type: Public
Profile: Manufacturers of gyrostabilized imaging turrets, digital & analogue reception & custom fitted system integration

Miranda Technologies Inc.
3499, rue Douglas B. Floreani, Montréal, QC H4S 2C6
514-333-1772 Fax: 514-333-9828
investorrelations@miranda.com
www.miranda.com
Ticker Symbol: MT
Company Type: Public
Profile: Miranda Technologies is a developer, manufacturer, & marketer of hardware & software. Products are used by the television broadcast industry.

Mitec Telecom Inc.
3299, boul. Jean-Baptiste-Deschamps, Lachine, QC H8T 3E4
514-694-9000 Fax: 514-630-8600
sales@mitectelecom.com
www.mitectelecom.com
Ticker Symbol: MTM
Company Type: Public
Profile: The company is a designer, manufacturer, & supplier of frequency products & solutions. Products power infrastructure in wireless communications, broadcast networks, & satellite communications. Facilities are operated in the United States & China.

Mobile Knowledge Corp.
308 Legget Dr., Kanata, ON K2K 1Y6
613-287-5020 Fax: 613-287-5021 866-624-5330
info@mobile-knowledge.com
www.mobile-knowledge.com
Company Type: Public
Profile: GPS, wireless and mobile data communications technology to serve the taxi, black car, and limousine industry

MOSAID Technologies Incorporated
#203, 11 Hines Rd., Ottawa, ON K2K 2X1
613-599-9539 Fax: 613-591-8148
communications@mosaid.com
www.mosaid.com
Ticker Symbol: MSD
Company Type: Public
Profile: MOSAID Technologies Incorporated specializes in the development & licensing of patented intellectual property. Products include semiconductors, & wireless & wired communications systems.

Norsat International Inc.
#110, 4020 Viking Way, Richmond, BC V6V 2N2
604-821-2800 Fax: 604-821-2801
info@norsat.com; sales@norsat.com
www.norsat.com
Ticker Symbol: NII
Company Type: Public
Profile: Norsat International, Inc. designs, engineers, & markets intelligent satellite solutions for high-speed data transmission. Examples of its portable satellite units include the GLOBETrekker & NewsLink models.

Nortel Networks Corporation
#100, 8200 Dixie Road, Brampton, ON L6T 5P6
905-863-0000 Fax: 905-863-8423 888-901-7286
investor@nortel.com
www.nortelnetworks.com
Ticker Symbol: NT
Company Type: Public
Profile: Offices of holding companies; Manufacturers of telephone & telegraph apparatus, radio & television broadcasting & communications equipment; Wholesalers of electrical apparatus & equipment, wiring supplies; Commercial physical & biological research

Philips Electronics Canada
281 Hillmount Rd., Markham, ON L6C 2S3
905-201-4100 Fax: 905-887-4241 888-744-5477
webmaster@philips.com
www.philips.ca
Company Type: Private
Profile: Philips Electronics manufactures & markets technological products in areas such as healthcare, household, entertainment, & personal care.

Research In Motion Limited
295 Phillip St., Waterloo, ON N2L 3W8
519-888-7465 Fax: 519-888-6906
investor_relations@rim.com; help@rim.com
www.rim.com
Ticker Symbol: RIM
Company Type: Public
Profile: Research in Motion Ltd. designs, manufactures, & markets wireless solutions for the mobile communications market.

Sierra Wireless, Inc.
13811 Wireless Way, Richmond, BC V6V 3A4
604-231-1100 Fax: 604-231-1109
info@sierrawireless.com
www.sierrawireless.com
Ticker Symbol: SW
Company Type: Public
Profile: Sierra Wireless, Inc. specializes in wireless solutions. It provides professional services to clients who require expertise in wireless design, integration, & carrier certification.

Softchoice Corporation
#200, 173 Dufferin St., Toronto, ON M6K 3H7
416-588-9002 Fax: 416-588-9004
investor_relations@softchoice.com
www.softchoice.com
Ticker Symbol: SO
Company Type: Public
Profile: Softchoice Corporation provides technology solutions & services. Organizations & businesses are assisted with their software & hardware technology resources.

Sonepar Canada
#1840, 1, Place Ville-Marie, Montréal, QC H3B 4A9
514-861-1155 Fax: 514-861-4453 www.sonepar.com
Company Type: Private
Profile: Electrical equipment, with emphasis on cable, wiring, fittings, HVAC & lighting. Sonepar Canada comprises Gescan, Texcan, Lumen, Osso Electric Supplies Inc., and Hagemeyer Canada Century Vallen divisions

Spectrum Signal Processing by Vecima
#300, 2700 Production Way, Burnaby, BC V5A 4X1
604-421-5422 Fax: 604-421-1764 800-663-8986
sales@spectrumsignal.com
www.spectrumsignal.com
Ticker Symbol: VCM
Company Type: Public
Profile: Developer of software defined radio (SDR) solutions for communications and intelligence gathering applications (rugged and semi-rugged military communications, modem solutions for infrastructure, signals intelligence, radar/sonar, industrial computing, electronic warfare)

SR Telecom & Co.
3200, rue Guénette, Montréal, QC H4S 2G5
514-335-1210 www.srtelecom.com
Company Type: Private
Profile: SR Telecom & Co. provides WiMAX & WiMAX-based wireless technologies for mobile, nomadic, & fixed networks. Clients include telecommunications companies & independent operating companies that deliver Internet & broadband data services.

Tri-Vision International Ltd.
41 Pullman Ct., Toronto, ON M1X 1E4
416-298-8551 Fax: 416-298-7976 888-298-8551
trivision@tri-vision.ca
www.tri-vision.ca
Ticker Symbol: TVL
Company Type: Public
Profile: Provides technologies & systems design, development & manufacture of hardward & software products for cable television & multimedia industries

TS Telecom Ltd.
180 Amber St., Markham, ON L3R 3J8
905-470-2282 Fax: 905-470-2273
tsinfo@tstelecom.com
www.tstelecom.com
Ticker Symbol: TOM
Company Type: Public
Profile: Manufacturers of telephone & telegraph apparatus

Tundra Semiconductor Corp.
603 March Rd., Ottawa, ON K2K 2M5
613-592-0714 Fax: 613-592-1320 800-267-7321
inquire@tundra.com
www.tundra.com
Ticker Symbol: TUN
Company Type: Public
Profile: Manufacturers of semiconductors & related devices; Wholesalers of electronic parts & equipment

Turbo Power Systems Inc.
#400, 350 Bay St., Toronto, ON M5H 2S6
905-690-1722 Fax: 905-690-1721
rak@turbopowersystems.com
www.turbopowersystems.com
Company Type: Public
Profile: Development and manufacture of electrical machines used in distributed and other power generation applications

Vecima Networks Inc.
4210 Commerce Circle, Victoria, BC V8Z 6N6
250-881 1982 Fax: 250-881-1974
invest@vecima.com
www.vecima.com
Ticker Symbol: VCM
Company Type: Public
Profile: Vecima Networks Inc. is a designer, manufacturer, & distributor of hardware products with embedded software that supports broadband access to cable, wireless, & telephony networks. Principal markets include Broadband Wireless & Converged Wired Solutions. Vecima Networks has ISO 9001:2000 certified manufacturing operations in Saskatoon, Saskatchewan.

Wi-LAN Inc.
#608, 11 Holland Ave., Ottawa, ON K1Y 4S1
613-688-4330 Fax: 613-688-4894
info@wi-lan.com; ir@wi-lan.com
www.wi-lan.com
Ticker Symbol: WIN
Company Type: Public
Profile: The company is a technology innovation & licensing company. Wi-LAN Inc.'s patent portfolio applies to products in the communications & consumer electronics markets.

Wireless Matrix Corporation
#1A, 3751 North Fraser Way, Burnaby, BC V5J 5G4
604-439-2444 Fax: 604-439-2447 888-843-8554
invest@wirelessmatrixcorp.com
www.wirelessmatrixcorp.com
Ticker Symbol: WRX
Company Type: Public
Profile: Wireless Matrix Corporation is engaged in the provision of software solutions to improve service fleet delivery metrics.

Zarlink Semiconductor Inc.
400 March Rd., Ottawa, ON K2K 3H4
613-592-0200 Fax: 613-592-5470 800-325-4927
corporate@zarlink.com
www.zarlink.com
Ticker Symbol: ZL
Company Type: Public
Profile: Zarlink Semiconductor Inc. focuses upon manufacturing & distributing microelectronic components. Products are used in the medical device & communications markets.

Engineering & Management

ADS Inc.
485, des Érables, Saint-Elzéar, QC G0S 2J0
418-387-3383 Fax: 418-387-8853
ads@adsinc.ca
www.adsinc.ca
Ticker Symbol: AAL
Company Type: Public
Profile: Offices of holding companies; Engineering services; General contractors in industrial buildings & warehouses

AECOM Canada Ltd.
#275, 3001 Wayburne Dr., Burnaby, BC V5G 4W3
604-438-5311 Fax: 604-438-5587
info@aecom.com
www.aecom.com
Company Type: Private
Profile: AECOM provides professional technical & management support services. The company serves a great range of markets, such as the energy, water, environmental, & transporation industries. AECOM has more than seventy offices across Canada. An example of its work is the Distant Early Warning Line Project, which remediates landfills in the Canadian North.

AEterna Zentaris Inc.
1405 du Parc-Technologique Blvd., Québec, QC G1P 4P5
418-652-8525 Fax: 418-652-0881 www.aeternazentaris.com
Ticker Symbol: AEL
Company Type: Public
Profile: Commercial physical & biological research

AMEC Inc.
4th Floor, 700 University Ave., Toronto, ON M5G 1X6
416-592-2102 Fax: 416-592-8284 www.amec.com
Company Type: Private
Profile: Engineering & management services; Heavy construction; Water, sewer, pipeline, communications, power line construct; Refuse systems; Prepackaged software; Real estate, Land subdividers & developers; Manufacturers of general industrial machinery & equipment

Armtec Infrastructure Income Fund
#3, 370 Speedvale Ave. West, Guelph, ON N1H 7M7
519-822-0210 Fax: 519-822-8894 www.armtecincomefund.com
Ticker Symbol: ARF.UN
Company Type: Public
Profile: Armtec Infrastructure Income Fund is an unincorporated, open-ended, limited purpose trust. It is involved in the manufacturing & marketing of engineered bridging solutions & drainage products. Products are used for infrastructure applications, such as residential & commercial building construction, agricultural drainage, & the natural resources industry.

Avcorp Industries Inc.
10025 River Way, Delta, BC V4G 1M7
604-582-1137 Fax: 604-582-2620
info@avcorp.com
www.avcorp.com
Ticker Symbol: AVP
Company Type: Public
Profile: Engineering services; Manufacturers of aircraft parts & auxiliary equipment, aircraft engines & engine parts

CAE Inc.
8585, ch de Côte-de-Liesse, Montréal, QC H4T 1G6
514-341-6780 Fax: 514-341-7699 866-999-6223
investor.relations@cae.com
www.cae.com
Ticker Symbol: CAE
Company Type: Public
Profile: CAE Inc. serves the civil aviation & defense forces, through the provision of simulation & modelling technologies, as well as integrated training solutions. The company's civil aviation & military training centres are located throughout the world. CAE Inc. has been granted the BOMA Go Green plan certification, & has implemented environmental programs such as the management of residual materials, recycling, pollution prevention, & residue exchange.

Calian Technology Ltd.
2 Beaverbrook Rd., Ottawa, ON K2K 1L1
613-599-8600 Fax: 613-592-7771
ir@calian.com
www.calian.com
Ticker Symbol: CTY
Company Type: Public
Profile: Calian Technologies Ltd. is comprised of a Technology Services Division & a Systems Engineering Division. It specializes in the satellite communications, telecommunications, manufacturing, defence, & aerospace markets. Technology services are sold to industry & government in Canada & internationally.

Cell-Loc Location Technologies Inc.
#1600, 37th St. SW, Calgary, AB T3C 3P1
403-569-5700 Fax: 403-569-5701
investors@cell-loc.com
www.cell-loc.com
Ticker Symbol: XCT
Company Type: Public
Profile: Commercial physical & biological research; Patent owners & lessors

CGI Group Inc.
1130, rue Sherbrooke ouest, 7e étage, Montréal, QC H3A 2M8
514-841-3200 Fax: 514-841-3299 www.cgi.com
Ticker Symbol: GIB
Company Type: Public
Profile: The information technology & business process services firm is engaged in the integration & customization of technologies & software applications, as well as the management of business processes & transactions.

Chromos Molecular Systems Inc.
PO Box 8, #220, 980 W 1st St., North Vancouver, BC V7P 3N4
604-985-7100 Fax: 604-980-2501
info@chromos.com
www.chromos.com

Ticker Symbol: CHR
Company Type: Public
Profile: Commercial physical & biological research

ConjuChem Inc.
#3950, 225, President Kennedy Ave., Montréal, QC H2X 3Y8
514-844-5558 Fax: 514-844-1119
lapointe@conjuchem.com
www.conjuchem.com
Ticker Symbol: CJB
Company Type: Public
Profile: Commercial physical & biological research

Conor Pacific Group Inc.
Four Bentall Centre, PO Box 49224, #3474, 1055 Dunsmuir St., Vancouver, BC V7X 1L2
604-669-3373 Fax: 604-669-3353
bob.nowack@conorpacific.com
www.conorpacific.com
Company Type: Public
Profile: Refuse systems

CPI Plastics Group Limited
151 Courtney Park Dr. West, Mississauga, ON L5W 1Y5
905-795-5505 Fax: 905-795-5523 800-663-9097
info@cpiplastics.com
www.cpiplastics.com
Ticker Symbol: CPI
Company Type: Public
Profile: Plastics processor & thermoplastic profile design, engineering & processing

CryoCath Technologies Inc.
16771, ch Sainte-Marie, Montréal, QC H9H 5H3
514-694-1212 Fax: 514-694-6279
customerservice@cryocath.com
www.cryocath.com
Company Type: Public
Profile: Commercial physical & biological research; Manufacturers of surgical & medical instruments & apparatus

Cymat Corp.
#6320, 2 Danville Rd., Mississauga, ON L5T 2L7
905-696-9900 Fax: 905-696-9300
info@cymat.com
www.cymat.com
Ticker Symbol: CYM
Company Type: Public
Profile: Commercial physical & biological research; Patent owners & lessors; Manufacturers of various primary metal products; Wholesalers of metals service centers & offices

Decoma International Inc.
50 Casmir Ct., Concord, ON L4K 4J5
905-669-2888 Fax: 905-669-5075
info@decoma.com
www.decoma.com
Company Type: Private
Profile: Engineering services; Manufacturers of motor vehicle parts & accessories, automotive stampings, various plastics products, coating, engraving & allied services

GE Water & Process Technologies
3239 Dundas St. West, Oakville, ON L6M 4B2
905-465-3030 Fax: 905-465-3050 www.zenon.com
Company Type: Private
Profile: ZENON is engaged in commercial physical & biological research. It manufactures various service industry machinery, general industrial machinery & equipment, & water treatment systems.

GENIVAR Income Fund
5858, ch de la Côte-des-Neiges, 4e étage, Montréal, QC H3S 1Z1
www.genivar.com
Ticker Symbol: GNV.UN
Company Type: Public
Profile: GENIVAR Income Fund is involved in consulting engineering. Projects are carried out in over 35 countries. Offices are located in Canada & the Caribbean. GENIVAR is an ISO 9001:2000 certified organization.

Hatch Ltd.
Sheridan Science & Technology Park, 2800 Speakman Dr., Mississauga, ON L5K 2R7
905-855-7600 Fax: 905-855-8270
webmaster@hatch.ca
www.hatch.ca
Company Type: Private
Profile: The consulting & technical design firm serves the global mining & metals, energy & infrastructure sectors.

Helix BioPharma Corp.
#3, 305 Industrial Pkwy. South, Aurora, ON L4G 6X7
905-841-2300 Fax: 905-841-2244
helix@helixbiopharma.com
www.helixbiopharma.com
Ticker Symbol: HBP
Company Type: Public
Profile: Commercial physical & biological research

Isotechnika Inc.
5120 - 75th St., Edmonton, AB T6E 6W2
780-487-1600 Fax: 780-484-4105 888-487-9944
investorrelations@isotechnika.com
www.isotechnika.com
Ticker Symbol: ISA
Company Type: Public
Profile: Commercial physical & biological research; Manufacturers of pharmaceutical preparations, in-vitro & in-vivo diagnostic substances

KHD Humboldt Wedag International Ltd.
#1620, 400 Burrard St., Vancouver, BC V6C 3A6
604-683-5767 Fax: 604-683-3205 www.khdhumboldt.com
Ticker Symbol: KHD
Company Type: Public
Profile: KHD Humboldt Wedag International Ltd. is engaged in designing & engineering services. It supplies proprietary technologies & equipment for the coal, cement, & minerals processing industry.

Linamar Corporation
287 Speedvale Ave. West, Guelph, ON N1H 1C5
519-836-7550 Fax: 519-836-9175
investorrelations@linamar.com
www.linamar.com
Ticker Symbol: LNR
Company Type: Public
Profile: Highly engineered products are developed, designed, & produced by thie manufacturing company. Linamar Corporation's divisions, Driveline & Powertrain, are engaged in the manufacture of components, modules, & systems for the automotive industry, & mobile industrial markets.

Marsulex Inc.
#300, 111 Gordon Baker Rd., Toronto, ON M2H 3R1
416-496-9655 Fax: 416-496-4155 800-387-5030
investor@marsulex.com
www.marsulex.com
Ticker Symbol: MLX
Company Type: Public
Profile: Marsulex Inc. provides the following industrial services: handling waste streams & industrial by-products; production of water treatment chemicals; environmental compliance solutions for air quality control; & production of sulphur-based industrial chemicals.

Neo Material Technologies Inc.
#1740, 121 King St. West, Toronto, ON M5H 3T9
416-367-8588 Fax: 416-367-5471
info@neomaterials.com
www.neomaterials.com
Ticker Symbol: NEM
Company Type: Public
Profile: Through its business divisions, Performance Materials & Magnaquench, Neo Material Technologies Inc. produces, processes, & develops zirconium, neodymium-iron-boron magnetic powders, & rare earths based engineered materials & applications. The products are used in many high technology products.

Neurochem Inc.
275, boul Armand-Frappier, Laval, QC H7V 4A7
450-680-4500 Fax: 450-680-4501 877-680-4500
webinfo@neurochem.com
www.neurochem.com
Ticker Symbol: NRM
Company Type: Public
Profile: Commercial physical & biological research

Sandwell International Inc.
Park Place, #1650, 666 Burrard St., Vancouver, BC V6C 2X8
604-684-0055 Fax: 604-684-7533
info@sandwell.com
www.sandwell.com
Company Type: Private
Profile: Engineering & management services

SNC-Lavalin Group Inc.
455, boul René-Lévesque ouest, Montréal, QC H2Z 1Z3
514-393-1000 Fax: 514-866-0795
investors@snclavalin.com
www.snclavalin.com
Ticker Symbol: SNC
Company Type: Public
Profile: The international engineering & construction organization owns infrastructure, & is engaged in the provision of operation & maintenance services. Examples of services include project financing, project management, procurement, engineering, & construction. The group is involved in sectors such as pharmaceuticals, petroleum, agrifood, the environment, transit, power, & mining.

Stantec Inc.
10160 - 112th St., Edmonton, AB T5K 2L6
780-917-7000 Fax: 780-917-7330
ir@stantec.com;
www.stantec.com
Ticker Symbol: STN
Company Type: Public
Profile: Stantec Inc. offers professional consulting services for infrastructure & facilities projects. The following services are provided: planning, project management, project economics, surveying & geomatics, engineering, architecture, landscape architecture, environmental science, & interior design.

Stressgen Biotechnologies Corporation
#350, 4243 Glanford Ave., Victoria, BC V8Z 4B9
250-744-2811 Fax: 250-744-3331
800-661-4978www.stressgen.com
Company Type: Public
Profile: Commercial physical & biological research; Manufacturers of pharmaceutical preparations

Thallion Pharmaceuticals Inc.
7150, rue Alexander-Fleming, Montréal, QC H4S 2C8
514-940-3600 Fax: 514-940-3622
info@thallion.com
www.thallion.com
Ticker Symbol: TLN
Company Type: Public
Profile: Commercial physical & biological research

The Goldfarb Corporation
#100, 18 Spadina Rd., Toronto, ON M5R 2S7
416-229-2070 Fax: 416-229-5392
info@goldfarbcorp.com
www.goldfarbcorp.com
Company Type: Public
Profile: Management consulting services; Wholesalers of industrial & personal service paper; General automotive repair shops; Automotive exhaust system repair shops

Virtek Vision International Inc.
785 Bridge St., Waterloo, ON N2V 2K1
519-746-7190 Fax: 519-746-3383
info@virtek.ca
www.virtek.ca
Company Type: Private
Profile: Virtek is a provider of precision laser-based templating, inspection, & CNC manufacturing solutions. The company serves customers in the automotive, aerospace, woodworking, metalworking, & transportation industries around the world.

Westaim Corporation
#1010, 144 - 4th Ave. SW, Calgary, AB T2P 3N4
403-237-7272 Fax: 403-237-8181
info@westaim.com
www.westaim.com
Ticker Symbol: WED
Company Type: Public
Profile: Commercial physical & biological research; Patent owners & lessors

Finance

Accord Financial Corp.
77 Bloor St. West, 18th Fl., Toronto, ON M5S 1M2
416-961-0007 Fax: 416-961-9443
info@accordfinancial.com
www.accordfinancial.com
Ticker Symbol: ACD
Company Type: Public
Profile: Through its subsidiaries, Accord Financial provides the following financial services to small & medium-sized businesses: record-keeping, financing, credit investigation, collection services, & guarantees.

AGF Management Limited
Toronto Dominion Bank Tower, 66 Wellington St. West, 31st Fl., Toronto, ON M5K 1E9
416-367-1900 Fax: 905-214-8243 800-268-8583
tiger@agf.com
www.agf.com
Ticker Symbol: AGF
Company Type: Public
Profile: AGF Management Limited comprises AGF Asset Management, AGF Investment Management, & AGF Trust. The financial services company has offices throughout Canada, as well as subsidiaries internationally.

Allbanc Split Corp.
Scotia Plaza, PO Box 4085 A, 40 King St. West, 26th Fl., Toronto, ON M5W 2X6
416-945-4171 Fax: 416-863-7425
mc_allbanc@scotiacapital.com
www.scotiamanagedcompanies.com
Ticker Symbol: ABK
Company Type: Public
Profile: Security brokers, dealers, & flotation companies; Unit investment trusts, certificate/closed-end management offices

Amalgamated Income Limited Partnership
#1, 606 Meredith Rd. NE, Calgary, AB T2E 5A8
403-265-6540 Fax: 403-206-7185 888-708-5757
info@aiun.ca
www.aiun.ca
Ticker Symbol: AI
Company Type: Public
Profile: Security brokers, dealers & flotation companies

Amisk Inc.
#101, 3633 rue Panet, Jonquière, QC G7X 8T7
418-546-1156 Fax: 418-546-0004 **Company Type:** Public
Profile: Miscellaneous business credit institutions

ATB Financial
9888 Jasper Ave. NW, Edmonton, AB T5J 1P1
780-408-7000 Fax: 780-422-4178 800-332-8383
atbinfo@atb.com
www.atb.com
Company Type: Crown
Profile: Provincially chartered banks &/or trust companies

AXA Canada
#700, 2020, rue University, Montréal, QC H3A 2A5
514-282-1914 Fax: 514-282-9588 www.axa.ca
Company Type: Private
Profile: Property/casualty insurance & financial services

B2B Trust
130 Adelaide St. West, Toronto, ON M5H 3P5
416-947-7427 Fax: 416-947-9476
800-263-8349www.b2b-trust.com
Ticker Symbol: BBT
Company Type: Public
Profile: Enables non-bank partners to provide banking & other financial services to their customers

Bank of Canada
234 Wellington St., Ottawa, ON K1A 0G9
613-782-8111 Fax: 613-782-7713 800-303-1282
info@bankofcanada.ca
www.bankofcanada.ca
Company Type: Crown
Profile: The Bank of Canada is a federal central bank.

Bank of Nova Scotia
Scotia Plaza, 40 King St. West, Toronto, ON M5H 1H1
416-866-6161 Fax: 416-866-3750
investor.relations@scotiabank.com
www.scotiabank.com
Ticker Symbol: BNS
Company Type: Public
Profile: The Bank of Nova Scotia's business includes personal & commercial banking, corporate & investment banking services & products, as well as wealth management services.

BMO Financial Group
First Canadian Place, 100 King St. West, 18th Fl., Toronto, ON M5X 1A1
416-867-6642 Fax: 416-867-3367 877-225-5266
steven.bonin@bmo.com
www.bmo.com
Ticker Symbol: BMO
Company Type: Public
Profile: BMO Financial Group offers a wide range of financial products & services, including retail banking, investment banking, & wealth management.

Business Development Bank of Canada
BDC Bldg., #400, 5, Place Ville Marie, Montréal, QC H3B 5E7
877-232-2269
info@bdc.ca
www.bdc.ca
Ticker Symbol: BDB
Company Type: Crown
Profile: Federal & federally sponsored credit agency; management consulting services; business consulting services

Canaccord Capital Inc.
#2200, 609 Granville St., Vancouver, BC V7Y 1H2
604-643-7300
katherine_young@canaccord.com
www.canaccord.com
Ticker Symbol: CCI
Company Type: Public
Profile: The full service investment dealer conducts operations in the following sectors: capital markets, & private client services.

Canada Life Financial Corporation
330 University Ave., Toronto, ON M5G 1R8
416-597-1456 Fax: 416-597-1940 888-252-1847
info@canadalife.com
www.canadalife.com
Ticker Symbol: CL.PR.B
Company Type: Public
Profile: Canada Life Assurance Company is the subsidiary of Canada Life Financial Corporation. It provides insurance, reinsurance services, unit trusts, & wealth management products & services. Clients are both individuals & groups in Canada, the United Kingdom, the United States, & the Republic of Ireland.

Canada Mortgage & Housing Corporation
700 Montreal Rd., Ottawa, ON K1A 0P7
613-748-2000 Fax: 613-748-2098
chic@cmhc-schl.gc.ca
www.cmhc-schl.gc.ca
Company Type: Crown
Profile: Administration of housing programs

Canadian Imperial Bank of Commerce
Commerce Court West, 199 Bay St., Toronto, ON M5L 1A2
416-980-2211 800-465-2422
investorrelations@cibc.com
www.cibc.com
Ticker Symbol: CM
Company Type: Public
Profile: CIBC provides financial products & services through CIBC Retail Markets and CIBC World Markets. Customers include individuals & small business clients, plus corporate & institutional clients.

Canadian Western Bank
#2300, 10303 Jasper Ave., Edmonton, AB T5J 3X6
780-423-8865 Fax: 780-423-8899 800-663-1124
InvestorRelations@cwbank.com
www.cwbankgroup.com
Ticker Symbol: CWB
Company Type: Public
Profile: The federally chartered, Schedule I, bank provides personal & commercial banking services across western Canada. Subsidiaries of Canadian Western Bank include Valiant Trust Company & Canadian Western Trust. These subsidiaries offer both personal & corporate trust services. Canadian Direct Insurance Inc., another of Canadian Western Bank's subsidiaries, is engaged in the provision of personal home & automobile insurance.

Carfinco Income Fund
#300, 4245 - 97 St., Edmonton, AB T6E 5Y7
780-413-7549 Fax: 780-450-1134
carfinco@carfinco.com
www.carfinco.com
Ticker Symbol: CFN.UN
Company Type: Public
Profile: Carfinco Income Fund is a specialty finance income fund. It is involved in the provision of consumer car loans to borrowers who are unable to obtain financing through traditional sources.

Cash Store Financial Services Inc.
17631 - 103 Ave., Edmonton, AB T5S 1N8
780-408-5118 Fax: 780-443-2155
gord@rentcash.ca
www.rentcash.ca
Ticker Symbol: CSF
Company Type: Public
Profile: The Cash Store Financial Services Inc. provides alternative financial products & services. It serves clients who seek short term loans. The company operates under the following banners: Instaloans & The Cash Store. There are over 400 branches across Canada.

Central 1 Credit Union
1441 Creekside Dr., Vancouver, BC V6J 4S7
604-734-2511 Fax: 604-737-5085
info@cucbc.com
www.cucbc.com
Company Type: Public
Profile: Provincially chartered credit union. Ontario regional office located at 2810 Matheson Blvd. E., Mississauga, ON L4W 4X7, (905) 238-9400.

Chrysler Financial Canada Inc.
2425 Matheson Blvd. East, 3rd Fl., Mississauga, ON L4W 5N7
905-629-6000 800-263-6920www.chryslerfinancial.ca
Company Type: Public
Profile: Personal credit & business credit institution

CI Financial Corp.
2 Queen St. East, 20th Fl., Toronto, ON M5C 2W7
416-364-1145 Fax: 416-364-4990 800-268-9374
mpanchal@ci.com
www.ci.com
Ticker Symbol: CIX
Company Type: Public
Profile: Through it wholly-owned subsidiaries, CI Investments Inc. & the Assante Corporation, CI Financial Income Fund manages mutual funds & other investment products.

Clairvest Group Inc.
#1700, 22 St. Clair Ave. East, Toronto, ON M4T 2S3
416-925-9270 Fax: 416-925-5753
lanar@clairvest.com
www.clairvest.com
Ticker Symbol: CVG
Company Type: Public
Profile: Clairvest Group Inc. is a merchant bank. Through Clairvest Equity Partners III Limited Partnership & Clairvest Equity Partners Limited Partnership, it provides equity financing to North American mid-market companies. Clairvest's goal is to build value in the businesses & to generate financial returns for investors.

Clarke Inc.
6009 Quinpool Rd., 9th Fl., Halifax, NS B3K 5J7
902-442-3000 Fax: 902-442-0187
bcook@clarkeinc.com
www.clarkeinc.com
Ticker Symbol: CKI
Company Type: Public
Profile: Clarke Inc. is an activist catalyst investment company, with several wholly-owned operating companies & divisions. The company has a diversified portfolio of investments. Clarke Inc.'s operating subsidiaries are as follows: Clarke Transport Inc., Clarke Road Transport Inc., Clarke IT Solutions Inc., La Traverse Rivière-du-Loup - St. Siméon Ltée., CIS Shipping International Inc., & Granby Industries.

Coast Capital Savings Credit Union
15117 - 101 Ave., Surrey, BC V3R 8P7
604-517-7000 888-517-7000www.coastcapitalsavings.com
Company Type: Private
Profile: Coast Capital Savings Credit Union is a provincially chartered credit union in British Columbia.

Credit Union Central of Saskatchewan
PO Box 3030, 2055 Albert St., Regina, SK S4P 3G8
306-566-1200 Fax: 306-566-1372 866-403-7499
info@saskcentral.com
www.saskcu.com; www.saskcentral.com
Company Type: Private
Profile: Credit Union Central of Saskatchewan is a provincially chartered credit union.

Davis + Henderson Income Fund
#201, 939 Eglington Ave. East, Toronto, ON M4G 4H7
416-696-7700 Fax: 416-696-9720 866-524-1470
investorrelations@dhltd.com
www.dhltd.com
Ticker Symbol: DHF.UN
Company Type: Public
Profile: The organization supplies programs to customers who offer lending & chequing account services in Canada.

Desjardins Trust Inc.
PO Box 34, 1, Complexe Desjardins, Montréal, QC H5B 1E4
514-286-9441 Fax: 514-286-1131
800-361-6840www.desjardins.com
Company Type: Public
Profile: Federally chartered bank & trust company

Deutsche Bank AG, Canada Branch
Commerce Court West, PO Box 263, #4700, 199 Bay St., Toronto, ON M5L 1E9
416-682-8400 Fax: 416-682-8383 www.db.com/canada/
Company Type: Private
Profile: Federally chartered bank; Branch of a foreign bank

DRI Capital Inc.
#200, 22 St. Clair Ave East, Toronto, ON M4T 2S5
416-863-1865 Fax: 416-863-5161
info@dricapital.com
www.dricapital.com
Company Type: Private
Profile: Patent owners & lessors; Personal credit institutions

DundeeWealth Inc.
Dundee Place, 1 Adelaide Street East, 27th Fl., Toronto, ON M5C 2V9
416-350-3250 888-332-2661
inquiries@dundeewealth.com

www.dundeewealth.com
Ticker Symbol: DW
Company Type: Public
Profile: Financial products and services, including securities, insurance, mortgages, banking

Equitable Group Inc.
#700, 30 St. Clair Ave. West, Toronto, ON M4V 3A1
416-515-7000 Fax: 416-515-7001
investor@equitablegroupinc.com
www.equitablegroupinc.com
Ticker Symbol: ETC
Company Type: Public
Profile: Through its wholly-owned subsidiary, The Equitable Trust Company, Equitable Group Inc. offers first mortgage financing & Guaranteed Investment Certificates to depositors. The Equitable Trust Company is a federally incorporated trust company.

Export Development Canada
151 O'Connor St., Ottawa, ON K1A 1K3
613-598-2500 Fax: 613-237-2690 800-267-8510www.edc.ca
Company Type: Crown
Profile: Export credit agency; offers assistance to Canadian exporters & investors to expand their international business

Farm Credit Canada
PO Box 4320, 1800 Hamilton St., Regina, SK S4P 4L3
306-780-8100 Fax: 306-780-5456 888-332-3301
csc@fcc-fac.ca
www.fcc-fac.ca
Company Type: Crown
Profile: Federal & federally sponsored credit agencies

Fiera Capital Inc.
#800, 1501, av McGill College, Montréal, QC H3A 3M8
514-954-3300 Fax: 514-954-5098 800-361-3499
info@fieracapital.com
www.fieracapital.com
Company Type: Private
Profile: Fiera Capital is an independent investment management firm. Its clientele consists of private clients, institutional investors, charitable organizations, & mutual funds.

Firm Capital Mortgage Investment Trust
1244 Caledonia Rd., Toronto, ON M6A 2X5
416-635-0221 Fax: 416-635-1713
mortgages@firmcapital.com
www.firmcapital.com
Ticker Symbol: FC
Company Type: Public
Profile: Through its mortgage banker, Firm Capital Corporation, Firm Capital Mortgage Investment Trust is a non-bank lender. It provides residential & commercial real estate finance.

Ford Credit Canada Limited
PO Box 5005, #800, 1275 North Service Rd., Oakville, ON L6M 3G4
905-845-2511 Fax: 866-868-1213
800-263-0582www.fordcredit.ca
Company Type: Public
Profile: Personal credit institution; Provides automotive financial services to manufacturers, dealers & customers

General Motors Acceptance Corp. of Canada Ltd.
Main Mailing Dept. CA1-002-002, 1908 Colonel Sam Dr., Oshawa, ON L1HÆ8P7
416-234-6600 Fax: 416-234-6607
800-268-2508www.gmcanada.com
Company Type: Public
Profile: Personal credit institutions; Short-term business credit institutions, except agricultural

Gluskin Sheff + Associates Inc.
Brookfield Place, PO Box 774, #4600, 181 Bay St., Toronto, ON M5J 2T3
416-681-6000 Fax: 416-681-6060 866-681-6001
shareholders@gluskinsheff.com
www.gluskinsheff.com
Ticker Symbol: GS
Company Type: Public
Profile: The wealth management firm serves institutional investors & high net worth private clients.

GMP Capital Trust
#300, 145 King St. West, Toronto, ON M5H 1J8
416-367-8600 Fax: 416-943-6175
investorrelations@gmpcapitaltrust.com
www.gmpcapitaltrust.com
Ticker Symbol: GMP
Company Type: Public
Profile: GMP Capital Trust is a Canadian independent investment dealer. Through its subsidiaries, GMP Capital Trust is involved in the following investment areas: alternative investments, capital markets, & wealth management. Individual, corporate, & institutional investor clients are served.

Great Eastern Corporation Limited
#2104, 1969 Upper Water St., Halifax, NS B3J 3R7
902-423-8414 Fax: 902-422-7701 **Ticker Symbol:** GTN.PR.A
Company Type: Public
Profile: The organization is an investment holding company. Great Eastern Corp. has a diversified investment portfolio.

Guardian Capital Group Limited
PO Box 201, #3100, Commerce Ct. West, Toronto, ON M5L 1E8
416-364-8341 Fax: 416-364-2067 **Ticker Symbol:** GCG
Company Type: Public
Profile: Through its businesses, Guardian Capital Group Limited is involved in the distribution of mutual funds, institutional & high net worth investment management, as well as other financial services. Guardian Capital LP is one wholly-owned division of Guardian Capital Group Limited.

Home Capital Group Inc.
#2300, 145 King St. West, Toronto, ON M5H 1J8
416-360-4663 Fax: 416-363-7611 800-990-7881
inquiry@homecapital.com
www.homecapital.com
Ticker Symbol: HCG.B
Company Type: Public
Profile: Home Capital Group Inc.'s subsidiary is Home Trust Company. It offers deposit services, retail credit, credit card issuing services, & mortgage lending. Offices are located in Nova Scotia, Québec, Ontario, Alberta, & British Columbia.

HSBC Bank Canada
#300, 885 West Georgia St., Vancouver, BC V6C 3E9
604-685-1000 Fax: 604-641-2506 888-310-4722
info@hsbc.ca
www.hsbc.ca
Ticker Symbol: HSB
Company Type: Public
Profile: Banking & financial services are offered by HSBC Bank Canada.

IGM Financial Inc.
One Canada Centre, 447 Portage Ave., Winnipeg, MB R3C 3B6
204-956-8532 Fax: 204-949-9594
corpsec@investorsgroup.com
www.igmfinancial.com
Ticker Symbol: IGM
Company Type: Public
Profile: IGM Financial Inc. is a managed asset, mutual fund, & personal financial services company. Its operating units include Investment Planning Counsel Inc., Mackenzie Financial Corporation, & Investors Group.

Investors Group Inc.
Canada Centre, #1, 447 Portage Ave., Winnipeg, MB R3C 3B6
204-943-0361 Fax: 204-947-1659
888-746-6344www.investorsgroup.com
Ticker Symbol: IGI
Company Type: Public
Profile: Provides personal financial planning services, mutual funds, other investment products including Registered Retirement Savings Plans, Registered Retirement Income Funds, Deferred Profit Sharing Plans, life and disability insurance, mortgages and Guaranteed Investment Certificates

Kingsway International Holdings Limited
Kingsway Capital of Canada Limited, #1400, 8 King St. East, Toronto, ON M5C 1B5
416-861-9584 Fax: 416-861-9027
toronot@kingswaygroup.com
www.kingswaygroup.com
Ticker Symbol: KIH
Company Type: Public
Profile: Boutique investment bank specializing in general business-to-Asia intermediation

Laurentian Bank of Canada
Tour Banque Laurentienne, #2085, 1981, av McGill College, Montréal, QC H3A 3K3
514-284-4500 Fax: 514-284-3916 800-522-1846
gladys.caron@banquelaurentienne.ca
www.laurentianbank.com
Ticker Symbol: LB
Company Type: Public
Profile: The schedule I chartered bank provides products & services across Canada through it bank branches, commercial banking centres, & brokerage offices.

LML Payment Systems Inc.
#1680, 1140 West Pender St., Vancouver, BC V6E 4G1
604-689-4440 Fax: 604-689-4413
info@lmlpayment.com
www.lmlpayment.com
Ticker Symbol: LMLP
Company Type: Public
Profile: Financial payment processor specializing in providing end-to-end cheque processing solutions to supermarkets, grocery stores, retailers

Macquarie Private Wealth Management
Bay Wellington Tower, Brookfield Place, #3200, 181 Bay St., Toronto, ON M5J 2T3
416-864-3600 Fax: 416-864-9024
866-775-7704www.macquarie.com
Company Type: Private
Profile: Macquarie's Banking & Financial Services Group in Canada comprises several businesses, including Macquarie Private Wealth Management, which offers clients tailored, independent investment advice. Macquarie Private Wealth Management has thirteen offices in Canada.

Manulife Financial Corporation
North Tower 3, 200 Bloor St. East, Toronto, ON M4W 1E5
416-926-3000 Fax: 416-926-5410 888-588-7999
investor_relations@manulife.com
www.manulife.ca
Ticker Symbol: MFC
Company Type: Public
Profile: Manulife Financial provides financial protection services & wealth management products.

MCAN Mortgage Corporation
#400, 200 King St. West, Toronto, ON M5H 3T4
416-591-5214 Fax: 416-598-4142 800-387-4405
mcanexecutive@mcanmortgage.com
www.mcanmortgage.com
Ticker Symbol: MKP
Company Type: Public
Profile: MCAN Mortgage is a mortgage investment corporation. Funds are invested in a portfolio of mortgages, as well as other types of loans & investments, real estate, & marketable securities.

National Bank of Canada
Tour de la Banque Nationale, 600, rue de la Gauchetière ouest, Montréal, QC H3B 4L2
514-394-5555 Fax: 514-394-6258 888-483-5628
investorrelations@nbc.ca
www.nbc.ca
Ticker Symbol: NA
Company Type: Public
Profile: Chartered under the Bank Act of Canada, the National Bank of Canada provides retail, commercial, corporate, international, & treasury banking services. Branches & offices are located across Canada & throughout the world. Subsidiaries of the National Bank of Canada are National Bank Financial & National Bank Trust.

Pyxis Capital Inc.
175 King St. East, 2nd Fl., Toronto, ON M5A 1J4
416-867-9079 Fax: 416-867-1961
info@pyxiscapital.ca
www.pyxiscapital.ca
Company Type: Public
Profile: Pyxis Capital is engaged in financial services.

Quest Capital Corp.
Bentall 5, PO Box 61, #1028, 550 Burrard St., Vancouver, BC V6C 2B5
604-687-8378 Fax: 604-682-3941 www.questcapcorp.com
Ticker Symbol: QC
Company Type: Public
Profile: The provision of mortgages in the real estate sector is the chief activity of Quest Capital Corp.

Rampart Mercantile Inc.
31 Sunset Trail, Toronto, ON M9M 1J4
416-744-7405 Fax: 416-744-7405 **Ticker Symbol:** YRH
Company Type: Public
Profile: Security brokers, dealers, & flotation companies

Renasant Financial Partners Ltd.
#800, 55 City Centre Dr., Mississauga, ON L5B 1M3
905-281-4760 Fax: 905-281-4761 www.renasant.ca
Company Type: Private
Profile: An independent financial service provider undertaking debt and equity investments in private and public companies

Royal Bank of Canada
Royal Bank Plaza, PO Box 1, 200 Bay St., Toronto, ON M5J 2J5
416-974-5151 Fax: 416-955-7800
invesrel@rbc.com
www.rbc.com

Ticker Symbol: RY
Company Type: Public
Profile: The Royal Bank of Canada is engaged in the following services: personal & commercial banking; corporate & investment banking, insurance; wealth management; & transaction processing services.

Royal Canadian Mint
320 Sussex Dr., Ottawa, ON K1A 0G8
613-993-8990 Fax: 613-998-4130 800-267-1871
info@mint.ca
www.rcmint.ca
Company Type: Crown
Profile: The Royal Canadian Mint is a for-profit Crown Corporation. Its responsibilities include the production of circulation & non-circulation coins, management of the domestic coinage system, & the provision of advice to the Minister of Finance on matters related to coinage.

Sceptre Investment Counsel Limited
26 Wellington St. East, 12th Fl., Toronto, ON M5E 1W4
416-601-9898 Fax: 416-367-8716
mail@sceptre.ca
www.sceptre.ca
Ticker Symbol: SZ
Company Type: Public
Profile: Investment advice & management for clients which include corporations, governments, hospitals, charitable foundations, endowments, universities & unions

Seamark Asset Management Ltd.
#310, 1801 Hollis St., Halifax, NS B3J 3N4
902-423-9367 Fax: 902-423-1518 888-303-5055
information@seamark.ca
www.seamark.ca
Ticker Symbol: SM
Company Type: Public
Profile: Investment management firm focusing on enhancing assets over a long term period

Sentry Select Capital Inc.
The Exchange Tower, #2850, 130 King St. West, Toronto, ON M5X 1A4
416-861-8729 Fax: 416-364-1197 888-246-6656
info@sentryselect.com
www.sentryselect.com
Ticker Symbol: SYI
Company Type: Public
Profile: Sentry Select Capital Inc. is a wealth management company. It offers investment products, such as mutual funds, closed-end trusts, & principal-protected notes. Offices are located in Toronto, Vancouver, & Montréal.

Split Yield Corporation
Royal Trust Tower, PO Box 341, #4500, 77 King St. West, Toronto, ON M5K 1K7
416-304-4443 Fax: 416-304-4441 877-478-237
info@quadravest.com
www.quadravest.com
Ticker Symbol: YLD
Company Type: Public
Profile: Split Yield Corporation provides quarterly dividends to each class of shareholder. It returns the original issue price to each shareholder on the maturity of the company. To generate additional income, Split Yield Corporation writes covered call options. The company's investment manager is Quadravest Capital Management Inc.

Sprott Inc.
South Tower, Royal Bank Plaza, #2700, 200 Bay St., Toronto, ON M5J 2J1
416-943-4065 Fax: 416-943-6497 888-362-7172
ir@sprott.com
www.sprottinc.com
Ticker Symbol: SII
Company Type: Public
Profile: Sprott Inc. was established to acquire all common shares of Sprott Asset Management Inc.. Sprott Asset Management is an asset management company, which provides investment management services for high net worth individuals & institutions.

Toronto-Dominion Bank
Toronto-Dominion Centre, PO Box 1, 66 Wellington St. West, Toronto, ON M5K 1A2
416-982-8222 866-756-8936
tdir@td.com; tdshinfo@td.com
www.td.com
Ticker Symbol: TD
Company Type: Public
Profile: The major Canadian bank offers a wide range of financial products & services.

TSX Group Inc.
The Exchange Tower, 130 King St. West, Toronto, ON M5X 1J2
416-947-4670 Fax: 416-947-4662 888-873-8392
info@tsx.com
www.tsx.com
Ticker Symbol: X
Company Type: Public
Profile: TMX Group is the owner & operator of the Toronto Stock Exchange, the TSX Venture Exchange, the Natural Gas Exchange (NGX), & Shorcan Brokers Limited. The Toronto Stock Exchange, a national stock exchange, serves the senior equity market. Another national stock exchange, the TSX Venture Exchange provides services for the public venture equity market. The Natural Gas Exchange is a North American exchange for the trading & clearing of natural gas & electricity contracts. Shorcan Brokers Limited is a fixed income inter-dealer broker. The Equicom Group Inc. is also owned by the TSX Group. It provides investor relations & corporate communications.

Urbana Corporation
#1702, 150 King St. West, Toronto, ON M5H 1J9
416-595-9106 Fax: 416-862-2498
investorrelations@urbanacorp.com
www.urbanacorp.com
Ticker Symbol: URB
Company Type: Public
Profile: Urbana Corporation is a non-redeemable investment fund. Urbana seeks & acquires investments for capital appreciation & income.

Vancouver City Savings Credit Union
PO Box 2120 Terminal, Vancouver, BC V6B 5R8
604-877-7000 888-826-2489www.vancity.com
Company Type: Private
Profile: The credit union serves over 400,000 members at almost sixty locations throughout British Columbia.

West Street Capital Corporation
Brookfield Place, #300, 181 Bay St., Toronto, ON M5J 2T3
416-359-8590 Fax: 416-365-9642 **Company Type:** Private
Profile: West Street Capital Corporation is an investment holding company. In 2009, West Street amalgamated with a wholly-owned subsidiary of Brookfield Asset Management Inc.

Western Financial Group Inc.
1010 - 24 St. SE, High River, AB T1V 2A7
403-652-2663 Fax: 403-652-2661 866-843-9378
info@westernfinancialgroup.net
www.westernfinancialgroup.net
Ticker Symbol: WES
Company Type: Public
Profile: Through Western Life Assurance & Bank West, Western Financial Group offers insurance, banking, & investment products. Financial services are provided to customers in western Canada. The company's other business unit is Marlin Travel.

Wilmington Capital Management Inc.
Brookfield Place, PO Box 762, #300, 181 Bay St., Toronto, ON M5J 2T3
416-867-9370 Fax: 416-363-2856 www.wilmingtoncapital.com
Ticker Symbol: WCM
Company Type: Public
Profile: The Canadian investment company holds cash & marketable securities. Wilmington Capital Management also owns land lease properties.

Food, Beverages & Tobacco

A&W Revenue Royalties Income Fund
#300, 171 Esplanade West, North Vancouver, BC V7M 3K9
604-988-2141 Fax: 604-988-5531
investorrelations@aw.ca
www.awincomefund.ca
Ticker Symbol: AW.UN
Company Type: Private
Profile: A&W Revenue Royalties Income Fund is a limited purpose trust. It invests in A&W Trade Marks Inc., which owns the trade-marks used in the A&W restaurant business in Canada. Through its subsidiary, A&W Trade Marks Inc., A&W Revenue Royalties licences trade-marks for royalty income.

Agropur cooperative
#600 - 101 boul. Roland-Therrien, Longueuil, QC J4H 4B9
450-646-1010 www.agropur.com
Company Type: NA
Profile: Manufacturers of fluid milk; creamery butter; natural, processed & imitation cheese; dry, condensed & evaporated dairy products; ice cream & frozen desserts

Andrew Peller Limited
697 South Service Rd., Grimsby, ON L3M 4E8
905-643-4131 Fax: 905-643-4944
info@andrewpeller.com
www.andrewpeller.com
Ticker Symbol: ADW.A
Company Type: Public
Profile: Andrew Peller Limited is the owner of wineries located in Nova Scotia, Ontario, & British Columbia. Through Vineco International Products Ltd. & Winexpert Inc., Andrew Peller Limited is also engaged in the production & marketing of wine kit products. The company also markets craft beer, under the Granville Island brand. Products are sold predominantly in Canada.

Arctic Glacier Income Fund
625 Henry Ave., Winnipeg, MB R3A 0V1
204-772-2473 Fax: 204-783-9857 888-573-9237
info@arcticglacierinc.com
www.arcticglacierinc.com
Ticker Symbol: AG.UN
Company Type: Public
Profile: Through its wholly-owned operating company, Arctic Glacier Inc., Arctic Glacier Income Fund produces, markets, & distributes packaged ice products. Products are marketed under the brand name, Arctic Glacier Premium Ice. Production & distribution take place throughout Canada, as well as in the western, central, & northeastern United States.

Barry Callebaut Canada Inc.
PO Box 398, 2950 rue Nelson, Saint-Hyacinthe, QC J2S 1Y7
450-774-9131 Fax: 450-774-8335
sthyacinthe@barry-callebaut.com
www.barry-callebaut.com
Company Type: Private
Profile: Producers of cocoa & chocolate products

Big Rock Brewery Income Trust
5555 - 76 Ave. SE, Calgary, AB T2C 4L8
403-720-3239 Fax: 403-236-7523 800-242-3107
beer@bigrockbeer.com
www.bigrockbeer.com
Ticker Symbol: BR.UN
Company Type: Public
Profile: Manufacturers of malt beverages; Wholesalers of beer & ale

Boston Pizza Royalties Income Fund
5500 Parkwood Way, Richmond, BC V6V 2M4
604-270-1108 Fax: 604-270-4168
investorrelations@bostonpizza.com
www.bpincomefund.com
Ticker Symbol: BPF.UN
Company Type: Public
Profile: Boston Pizza Royalties Income Fund is a limited purpose open-ended trust. Its purpose is to acquire certain trade marks & trade names used by Boston Pizza International Inc. (BPI) in its Boston Pizza restaurants in Canada.

Campbell Soup Company Ltd. of Canada
60 Birmingham St., Toronto, ON M8V 2B8
416-251-1131 Fax: 416-253-8611
800-575-7687www.campbellsoup.ca
Company Type: Private
Profile: Manufacturers of canned specialties, various food preparations, pickled fruits & vegetables, sauces, seasonings & dressings; Wholesalers of general line groceries

Canada Bread Company, Limited
Investor Relations Department, #1500, 30 St. Clair Ave. West, Toronto, ON M4V 3A2
416-926-2000 Fax: 416-926-2018 800-465-5515
Investorrelations@mapleleaf.ca
www.canadabread.ca
Ticker Symbol: CBY
Company Type: Public
Profile: Canada Bread Company, Limited manufactures & markets the following products: fresh bakery products, such as bread, bagels, & sweet goods; frozen unbaked & partially baked products, such as bread, rolls, & bagels; & specialty pasta & sauces. Brand names include Olafson's, Ben's, POM, Dempster's, & Olivieri. Operations are located throughout North America & in the United Kingdom.

Chai-Na-Ta Corp.
CNT Nutraceuticals Ltd., #100, 12051 Horseshoe Way, Richmond, BC V7A 4V4
604-272-4118 Fax: 604-272-4113 800-406-7668
info@chainata.com
www.chainata.com
Ticker Symbol: CCCFF
Company Type: Public
Profile: The world's largest grower and exporter of North American ginseng

Clearly Canadian Beverage Corporation
#11/12, 220 Viceroy Rd., Vaughan, ON L4K 3C2

800-735-7180
consumer.relations@clearly.ca
www.clearly.ca
Ticker Symbol: CCBEF
Company Type: Public
Profile: Marketer of bottled carbonated & noncarbonated waters; Patent owners & lessors

Corby Distilleries Limited
#1100, 225 King St. West, Toronto, ON M5V 3M2
416-479-2400 Fax: 416-369-9809
investors@corby.ca
www.corby.ca
Ticker Symbol: CDL
Company Type: Public
Profile: Corby Distilleries is a marketer of distilled spirits, whiskies, & liqueurs produced in Canada. In addition, imported wines, gin, cognac, scotch, & liqueurs are marketed by the organization. Its owned brands include Wiser's Canadian whiskies & Seagram Coolers. Corby Distilleries represents international brands, such as Jameson Irish whiskey & Wyndham Estate wines, through its affiliation with Pernod Ricard.

Cott Corporation
6525 Viscount Road, Mississauga, ON L4V 1H6
905-672-1900 Fax: 905-672-7504
investor_relations@cott.com
www.cott.com
Ticker Symbol: BCB
Company Type: Public
Profile: Manufacturers of retailer branded soft drinks & carbonated waters

Dover Industries Limited
4350 Harvester Rd., Burlington, ON L7L 5S4
905-333-1515 Fax: 905-333-1584
info@dovergrp.com
www.dovergrp.com
Ticker Symbol: DVI
Company Type: Public
Profile: Dover Industries Ltd. is made up up a food products division & a paper products division. Dover Flour operates flour mills in Saskatchewan, Ontario, & Nova Scotia. Dover Cone produces ice cream cones. Dover Cup manufactures hot & cold paper cups & related food containers.

Farmers Cooperative Dairy Ltd.
PO Box 8118, Halifax, NS B3K 5Y6
902-835-3373 Fax: 902-835-1583 800-565-1945
customer.services@farmersdairy.ca
www.farmersdairy.ca
Company Type: Private
Profile: Produces & distributes dairy & dairy-related products in Atlantic Canada

Forbes Medi-Tech Inc.
#200, 750 West Pender St., Vancouver, BC V6C 2T8
604-689-5899 Fax: 604-689-7641
info@forbesmedi.com
www.forbesmedi.com
Ticker Symbol: FMI
Company Type: Public
Profile: Develops and markets a portfolio of nutraceutical products, including functional foods and supplements

FP Resources Limited
PO Box 550, 70 O'Leary Ave., St. John's, NL A1C 5L1
709-570-0000 Fax: 709-570-0479 www.fpresources.ca
Company Type: Public
Profile: Harvests, processes, sources & markets seafood products

Freshxtend Technologies Corp.
#104, 334 East Kent Ave., Vancouver, BC V5X 4N6
604-322-0759 Fax: 604-322-0487 800-269-5269
info@freshxtend.com
www.freshxtend.com
Ticker Symbol: FXT
Company Type: Public
Profile: A leading provider of natural life extension technologies to the fresh produce and flower industries

Gay Lea Foods Co-Operative Ltd.
5200 Orbitor Dr., Mississauga, ON L4W 5B4
905-283-5300 Fax: 416-741-5384 800-268-0508
contact@gayleafoodmembers.com
www.gaylea.com
Company Type: Private
Profile: Manufacturers of fluid milk, creamery butter & dry, condensed & evaporated dairy products; Wholesalers of dairy products, groceries & related products

George Weston Limited
22 St Clair Ave. East, Toronto, ON M4T 2S7
416-922-2500 Fax: 416-922-4395
investor@weston.ca
www.weston.ca
Ticker Symbol: WN
Company Type: Public
Profile: George Weston Limited consists of Weston Foods & Loblaws. Weston Foods is involved in the baking & dairy industries. Operated by Loblaw Companies Limited, Loblaws is engaged in food distribution. Loblaws also offers drug store merchandise & general merchandise, as well as financial products & services.

High Liner Foods Incorporated
PO Box 910, 100 Battery Point, Lunenburg, NS B0J 2C0
902-634-8811 Fax: 902-634-4785
info@highlinerfoods.com
www.highlinerfoods.com
Ticker Symbol: HLF
Company Type: Public
Profile: High Liner Foods Incorporated specializes in processing & marketing prepared, frozen seafood products. Products are marketed under the following brands: High Liner, Sea Cuisine, Fisher Boy, Royal Sea, Mirabel, & FPI. Subsidiaries & divisions include High Liner Foods (USA) Incorporated & Fishery Products International (USA). The company serves the retail & food service markets throughout Canada, the United States, & Mexico.

Imperial Tobacco Canada Limited
3711, rue Saint-Antoine, Montréal, QC H4C 3P6
514-932-6161 Fax: 514-932-3993
www.imperialtobaccocanada.com
Company Type: Private
Profile: Manufacturers of cigarettes, chewing & smoking tobacco & snuff; Wholesalers of tobacco & tobacco products

Kraft Canada Inc.
95 Moatfield Dr., Toronto, ON M3B 3L6
416-441-5000 Fax: 416-441-5059
800-323-0768www.kraftcanada.com
Company Type: Private
Profile: Manufacturers of natural, processed & imitation cheese; cereal breakfast foods; canned fruits, vegetables, preserves, jams & jellies; various food preparations; pickled fruits & vegetables, sauces, seasonings, dressings; roasted coffee; chocolate & cocoa products

Lassonde Industries Inc.
755, rue Principale, Rougemont, QC J0L 1M0
450-469-4926 Fax: 450-469-1366 866-552-7643
info@lassonde.com
www.lassonde.com
Ticker Symbol: LAS
Company Type: Public
Profile: Through its subsidiaries, Lassonde Industries develops, manufactures, packages, & markets food products. The following products are manufactured: fruit juices, fruit beverages, canned corn, baked beans, barbecue sauces, dipping sauces, pasta sauces, meat marinades, bruschetta topping, tapenades, & fondue bouillon.

Leading Brands, Inc.
#1800, 1500 West Georgia, Vancouver, BC V6G 2Z6
604-685-5200 Fax: 604-685-5249 866-685-5200
info@lbix.com
www.leadingbrandsinc.com
Company Type: Public
Profile: Manufacturers of bottled & canned soft drinks & carbonated waters; wholesalers of groceries & related products

Lilydale Co-Operative Ltd.
7727 - 127 Ave., Edmonton, AB T5C 1R9
780-476-6261 Fax: 780-476-7253
webmaster@lilydale.com
www.lilydale.com
Company Type: NA
Profile: Wholesalers of poultry & poultry products

Liquor Stores Income Fund
#300, 10508 - 82 Ave., Edmonton, AB T6E 2A4
780-944-9994 Fax: 780-702-1999 www.liquorstoresgp.ca
Ticker Symbol: LIQ.UN
Company Type: Public
Profile: Liquor Stores Income Fund is involved in the operation of retail liquor stores in Alberta.

Magnotta Winery Corporation
271 Chrislea Rd., Vaughan, ON L4L 8N6
905-738-9463 Fax: 905-738-5551 800-461-9463
mailbox@magnotta.com
www.magnotta.com
Ticker Symbol: MGN
Company Type: Public
Profile: Magnotta Winery Corporation is licensed to produce & sell wine, beer & distilled products.

Maple Leaf Foods Inc.
#1500, 30 St Clair Ave. West, Toronto, ON M4V 3A2
416-926-2000 Fax: 416-926-2018 800-268-3708
investorrelations@mapleleaf.ca
www.mapleleaf.ca
Ticker Symbol: MFI
Company Type: Public
Profile: Maple Leaf Foods products include fresh & prepared meats, poultry, seafood, fresh & frozen bakery goods, & animal feed. Products are sold to wholesale, retail, & industrial customers around the world. Maple Leaf Foods has operations in Canada, the United States, Europe, & Asia.

McCain Foods (Canada)
107 Main St., Florenceville, NB E7L 1B2
800-563-7437 800-387-7321www.mccain.ca
Company Type: Private
Profile: McCain Foods in Canada produces food products. Products include frozen foods, such as potato products & beverages, as well as specialty items under brand names such as Wong Wing Foods & Charcuterie la Tour Eiffel. Food products are distributed throughout Canada & internationally.

McDonald's Restaurants of Canada Ltd.
McDonald's Place, Toronto, ON M3C 3L4
416-443-1000 Fax: 416-446-3443 www.mcdonalds.ca
Company Type: Private
Profile: McDonald's Canada consists of over 1,400 McDonald's restaurants across Canada. More than 77,000 Canadians are employed at McDonald's & its franchisees.

Molson Coors Brewing Company (Canada)
1555, rue Notre-Dame est, 4e étage, Montréal, QC H2L 2R5
514-597-1786 800-566-1786www.molsoncoorscanada.com
Ticker Symbol: TAP
Company Type: Public
Profile: Molson Coors Brewing Company (Canada) operates six breweries throughout Canada. Major markets are located in Canada, the United States, & the United Kingdom.

MTY Food Group Inc.
3465, boul Thimens, Montréal, QC H4R 1V5
514-336-8885 Fax: 514-336-9222
info@mtygroup.com
www.mtygroup.com
Ticker Symbol: MTY
Company Type: Public
Profile: MTY Food Group is an operator & franchisor of quick service restaurants. Brands include Thai Express, Vanellis, Yogen Früz, & Cultures.

Nestlé Canada Inc.
25 Sheppard Ave. West, Toronto, ON M2N 6S8
416-512-9000 Fax: 416-218-2654 800-387-4636
corporateaffairs@ca.nestle.com
www.nestle.ca
Company Type: Private
Profile: 27 facilities in Canada, including manufacturing sites, sales offices & distribution centres, employ 4,000 people; Producer of foods & beverages such as Carnation, Nescafé, Lean Cuisine, Good Start, Nestlé Baby Cereal, Powerbar, Nestlé Pure Life, Nestlé Drumstick, Kit Kat & Purina Beneful

Parmalat Canada Limite
Consumer Relations Department, 405 The West Mall, 10th Fl., Toronto, ON M9C 5J1
416-626-1973 Fax: 416-620-3123
800-563-1515www.parmalat.ca
Company Type: Private
Profile: Parmalat Canada produces & markets a variety of dairy products, fruit juices, table spreads, & cultured products to Canadians. Brand names include Balderson, Black Diamond, Beatrice, Astro, & Lantantia. Operating facilities are located across Canada.

PDM Royalties Income Fund
#400, 774 Main St., Moncton, NB E1C 9Y3
506-853-0990 Fax: 506-853-4131
blane@imvescor.ca
www.pdmfund.com
Ticker Symbol: PDM.UN
Company Type: Public
Profile: PDM Royalties Income Fund is an open-ended, limited purpose trust. The Fund is the indirect owner of the trade marks & other intellectual property for Mikes, Scores, Pizza Delight, & Baton Rouge. They are licensed to Imvescor Inc., which operates restaurants under the brand names Mikes, Scores, Pizza Delight, & Baton Rouge.

Pizza Pizza Royalty Income Fund
580 Jarvis St., Toronto, ON M4Y 2H9
416-967-1010 Fax: 416-967-5941
www.pizzapizzaroyaltyincomefund.com
Company Type: Public

Profile: Pizza Pizza Royalty Income Fund is a limited purpose, open-ended trust. The Fund acquired trademarks & trade names used by Pizza Pizza Limited in its restaurants. The trademarks are licensed to Pizza Pizza.

Premium Brands Income Fund
7720 Alderbridge Way, Richmond, BC V6X 2A2
604-656-3100 Fax: 604-656-3170
investor@premiumbrandsgroup.com
www.premiumbrandsincomefund.com
Ticker Symbol: PBI.UN
Company Type: Public
Profile: Premium Brands Income Fund is the owner of branded specialty food businesses. Manufacturing & distribution facilities are situated in Manitoba, Saskatchewan, Alberta, British Columbia, & Washington. The following are the brands within the Fund's family of businesses: Quality Fast Foods, McSweeney's, B&C Foods, Bread Garden, Grimm's, Made-Rite, Harlan's, Stuyver's, Harvest, Centennial, Harlan's, Gloria's, Hempler's, & Hygaard.

Prime Restaurants Royalty Income Fund
#600, 10 Kingsbridge Garden Circle, Mississauga, ON L5R 3K6
905-568-0000 Fax: 905-568-0080 www.primeincomefund.ca
Ticker Symbol: EAT.UN
Company Type: Public
Profile: Prime Restaurants Royalty Income Fund is a limited purpose trust. Its subsidiary is PRC Trademarks Inc.. The Fund receives royalties from pooled restaurants, under an agreement with Prime Restaurants of Canada Inc.. Prime Restaurants of Canada Inc. owns, operates, & franchises casual dining restaurants & pubs. Prime Restaurants of Canada's restaurants & pubs include Casey's, East Side Mario's, Bier Markt, Paddy Flaherty's & Fionn MacCool's.

Quaker Oats Company of Canada Ltd.
Consumer Relations, 14 Hunter St. East, Peterborough, ON K9J 7B2
800-267-6287www.quakeroats.ca
Company Type: Private
Profile: Quaker Oats Company of Canada provides the following products: oatmeal, cereals, granola bars, portion & lite snacks, & baking mixes.

Rothmans Inc.
1500 Don Mills Rd., Toronto, ON M3B 3L1
416-449-5525 Fax: 416-449-9601
ir@rothmansinc.ca
www.rothmansinc.ca
Ticker Symbol: ROC
Company Type: Public
Profile: The holding company owns 60% of Rothmans Bensons & Hedges Inc., which manufactures tobacco products.

Saputo Inc.
6869, boul Métropolitain est, Montréal, QC H1P 1X8
514-328-6662 Fax: 514-328-3310
saputo@saputo.com
www.saputo.com
Ticker Symbol: SAP
Company Type: Public
Profile: Saputo Inc. is engaged in the production, commercialization, & distribution of dairy products & grocery products. The company's brands include the following: Saputo, Dairyland De Lucia, Frigo, Stella, HOP&GO!, Rondeau, Alexis de Portneuf, DuVillage de Warwick, La Paulina, Treasure Cave, Armstrong, Nutrilait, Vachon, & Ricrem. Production facilities are situated in five countries.

Schneider Corporation
PO Box 130, 321 Courtland Ave. East, Kitchener, ON N2G 3X8
519-741-5000 Fax: 519-749-7420
877-567-5326www.schneiders.ca
Company Type: Private
Profile: Schneider Foods is a producer of meats & food products, such as Schneiders sliced meats & Schneiders Lunchmate & SmartSnax.

Scotsburn Dairy Group
PO Box 340, Scotsburn, NS B0K 1R0
902-485-8023 Fax: 902-485-4013 800-511-6455
consumerservices@scotsburn.com
www.scotsburn.com
Company Type: Private
Profile: Scotsburn Dairy Group manufactures & distributes ice cream & frozen novelties, such as fluid milk, ice cream, frozen yogourt, sherbet, sour cream, & butter. Retail customers are located throughout the world.

Second Cup Royalty Income Fund
6303 Airport Rd., Mississauga, ON L4V 1R8
905-405-6500 Fax: 905-405-6777
investor@secondcup.com
www.secondcupincomefund.com
Ticker Symbol: SCU.UN
Company Type: Public
Profile: Second Cup Royalty Income Fund is an open-ended trust. Through its wholly-owned subsidiary, Second Cup Royalty Income Fund holds The Second Cup cafés' trademarks & other intellectual property & rights. These trademarks are licenced by the Fund to The Second Cup Ltd. The Second Cup Ltd. is a retailer & franchisor of specialty coffee cafés throughout Canada.

Sepp's Gourmet Foods Ltd.
529 Annance Ct., Delta, BC V3M 6Y7
604-524-2540 Fax: 604-524-2941
dcullum@seppsfoods.com
www.seppsfoods.com
Company Type: Private
Profile: Sepp's Gourmet Foods Ltd. produces & markets food products. Products include frozen waffles, French toast, & wraps. The company serves the food service & retail grocery sectors in North America, South America, & Asia.

SIR Royalty Income Fund
#200, 5360 South Service Rd., Burlington, ON L7L 5L1
905-681-2997 Fax: 905-681-0394
info@sircorp.com
www.sircorp.com
Ticker Symbol: SRV.UN
Company Type: Public
Profile: Trademarks related to SIR Corp.'s restaurant brands are used under a license agreement with SIR Royalty Limited Partnership. A royalty is paid by SIR Corp. to SIR Royalty Limited Partnership. SIR Royalty Income Fund has an investment in SIR Royalty Limited Partnership. The Fund receives distribution income from this investment. Distributions are paid to unitholders by the Fund on a monthly basis. SIR Corp.'s restaurant brands include Alice Fazooli's, Jack Astor's Bar & Grill, Canyon Creek Chop House, Far Nienter / Soul of the Vine, & Loose Moose Tap & Grill.

Sleeman Breweries Ltd.
551 Clair Rd. West, Guelph, ON N1L 1E9
519-822-1834 Fax: 519-822-0148 800-268-8537
consumer.relations@sleeman.ca
www.sleeman.com
Company Type: Private
Profile: Sleeman Breweries Ltd. is a brewer & distributor of beer.

Smucker Foods of Canada Co.
Consumer Services Department, 80 Whitehall Dr., Markham, ON L3R 0P3
800-567-1897www.smuckers.ca
Company Type: Private
Profile: Smucker Foods of Canada manufactures & markets products such as fruit spreads, peanut butter, ice cream toppings, condiments, & shortening & oils. Brand names include Smuckers, Crisco, Robin Hood, Five Roses, Europe's Best, Bick's, Red River, & Double Fruit Spreads.

Sodexo Canada Ltd.
3350 South Service Rd., Burlington, ON L7N 3M6
514-866-7070 877-632-8592
Canada@sodexo.com
www.sodexoca.com
Company Type: Private
Profile: Sodexo Canada provides food & facilities management. Outsourcing solutions offered include food service, grounds keeping, housekeeping, laundry services, & plant operations & maintenance.

Sun-Rype Products Ltd.
1165 Ethel St., Kelowna, BC V1Y 2W4
250-860-7973 Fax: 250-762-3611
info@sunrype.com
www.sunrype.com
Ticker Symbol: SRF
Company Type: Public
Profile: Sun-Rype manufactures & markets fruit juices & fruit snacks. Products include 100% Pure Not From Concentrate Apple Juice & Fruit to Go.

Swiss Water Decaffeinated Coffee Co. Income Fund
3131 Lake City Way, Burnaby, BS V5A 3A3
604-420-4050 Fax: 604-420-8711 800-667-6181
info@swisswater.com
www.swisswater.com
Ticker Symbol: SWS.UN
Company Type: Public
Profile: Listed on the Toronto Stock Exchange in 2002, Swiss Water Decaffeinated Coffee Co. Income Fund is a limited purpose, open ended trust. Swiss Water Decaffeinated Coffee Company, Inc. (SWDCC) decaffeinates premium coffees. The organization is certified by the Organic Crop Improvement Association (OCIA), in accordance with National Organic Program (NOP) standards.

TDL Group Ltd.
874 Sinclair Rd., Oakville, ON L6K 2Y1
905-845-6511 Fax: 905-845-0265 888-601-1616
customer_service@timhortons.com
www.timhortons.com
Company Type: Private
Profile: Retail eating places; head office of Tim Hortons

The Keg Royalties Income Fund
10100 Shellbridge Way, Richmond, BC V6X 2W7
604-821-6416 Fax: 604-276-0138 www.kegincomefund.com
Ticker Symbol: KEG.UN
Company Type: Public
Profile: The Keg Royalties Income Fund is an unincorporated open-ended, limited purpose trust. The Fund is the owner of The Keg Rights LP, which owns the trademarks, names, & other intellectual property used by The Keg restaurants. The Keg Royalties Income Fund licenses Keg Restaurants Ltd. to use these rights.

The Spectra Hospitality Group Inc.
389 West 6th Ave., Vancouver, BC V5Y 1L1
604-714-6500 Fax: 604-730-5508 www.spectragroup.com
Company Type: Public
Profile: Retailing in eating places, alcoholic beverage drinking places; Patent owners & lessors

Van Houtte Inc.
8300, 19e av, Montréal, QC H1Z 4J8
514-593-7711 Fax: 514-593-8755
877-593-7722www.vanhoutte.com
Company Type: Private
Profile: Van Houtte Inc. roasts, markets, & distributes gourmet, flavoured, organic, & fair trade coffees throughout North America. Other activities include offering a coffee service & manufacturing single-cup equipment. The company also markets & distributes a range of water filtration systems for businesses.

Vincor Canada
441 Courtneypark Dr. East, Mississauga, ON L5T 2V3
905-564-6900 Fax: 905-564-6909
800-265-9463www.vincorinternational.com
Company Type: Private
Profile: Vincor Canada produces & markets wine & related products throughout Canada. Products are produced at wineries in New Brunswick, Québec, Ontario, & British Columbia. Examples of Vincor Canada's brands include Inniskillin, Jackson-Triggs, & Sawmill Creek.

Forestry & Paper

3M Canada Company
300 Tartan Dr., London, ON N6A 4T1
519-452-6765 Fax: 800-479-4453 888-364-3577www.3m.ca
Ticker Symbol: 3M CO
Company Type: Private
Profile: Manufacturers of packaging paper & coated & laminated plastics film, adhesives & sealants, photographic equipment & supplies, orthopedic, prosthetic & surgical appliances & supplies

Abitibi-Consolidated Inc.
#800, 1155, rue Metcalfe, Montréal, QC H3B 5H2
514-875-2160
contact@abitibiconsolidated.com
www.abitibiconsolidated.com
Ticker Symbol: A
Company Type: Public
Profile: Manufacturers in paper mills, pulp mills, logging, sawmills & general planing mills

Ainsworth Lumber Co. Ltd.
Bentall 4, PO Box 49307, #3194, 1055 Dunsmuir St., Vancouver, BC V7X 1L3
604-661-3200 Fax: 604-661-3201
info@ainsworth.ca
www.ainsworth.ca
Ticker Symbol: ANS
Company Type: Public
Profile: Manufacturers in logging, sawmills & general planing mills, hardwood & softwood veneer & plywood, reconstituted wood products, & various other wood products

Arbec Forest Products Inc.
#216, 8770, boul Langelier, St-Léonard, QC H1P 3C6
514-327-3350 Fax: 514-327-1966
information@arbec.ca
www.arbec.ca
Ticker Symbol: ABR.SV.A
Company Type: Public
Profile: The manufacturer of softwood lumber carries on business through mills in Port-Cartier & in the Péribonka area.

Canfor Pulp Income Fund
#100, 1700 - 75 Ave. West, Vancouver, BC V6P 6G2
604-661-5241 Fax: 604-661-5235
info@canfor.ca
www.canfor.com
Ticker Symbol: CFX.UN
Company Type: Public
Profile: Canfor Pulp Income Fund is an unincorporated, open-ended trust, which holds interest in the Canfor Pulp Limited Partnership. The Limited Partnership is an owner & operator of mills in British Columbia. NBSK pulp & fully bleached Kraft Paper are produced.

Cascades Inc.
PO Box 30, 404, boul Marie-Victorin, Kingsey Falls, QC J0A 1B0
819-363-5100 Fax: 819-363-5127
info@cascades.com
www.cascades.com
Ticker Symbol: CAS
Company Type: Public
Profile: Cascades Inc. is engaged in the production, transformation, & marketing of packaging & tissue products. Products are composed mainly of recycled fibres. Operations are situated throughout North America & Europe.

Catalyst Paper Corporation
3600 Lysander Lane, 2nd Fl., Richmond, BC V7B 1C3
604-247-4400 Fax: 604-247-0551
contactus@catalystpaper.com
www.catalystpaper.com
Ticker Symbol: CTL
Company Type: Public
Profile: Producer of mechanical printing papers & deinked & market kraft pulp; Owner of Western Canada's largest paper recycling facility

Commonwealth Plywood Co. Ltd.
PO Box 90, 15 boul Labelle, Sainte-Thérèse, QC J7E 4H9
450-435-6541 Fax: 450-435-3814
info@commonwealthplywood.com
www.commonwealthplywood.com
Company Type: Private
Profile: Manufacturers of hardwood veneer & plywood, softwood veneer & plywood, millwork; in sawmills & planing mills; wholesales hardwood & softwood lumber, plywood, millwork & wood panels

Concert Industries Ltd.
1680 rue Atmec, Gatineau, QC J8P 7G7
819-669-8100 Fax: 819-669-8161
info@concert.ca
www.concert.ca
Company Type: Public
Profile: Manufacturers sanitary paper products

Domtar Inc.
395, boul de Maisonneuve ouest, Montréal, QC H3A 1L6
514-848-5555 Fax: 514-848-5638
ir@domtar.com
www.domtar.com
Ticker Symbol: UFS
Company Type: Public
Profile: Manager of forestland in Canada & the USA; Producer of lumber & other wood products; Manufacturer of business, commercial printing, publication, technical & specialty papers

Eacom Timber Corp.
#425, 5600 Parkwood Way, Richmond, BC V6V 2M2
604-279-8511 Fax: 604-279-8711
800-315-3660www.eacomtimber.com
Ticker Symbol: ETR
Company Type: Public
Profile: Forestry and lumber company.

Federated Co-Operatives Ltd.
PO Box 1050 Main, 401 - 22 St. East, Saskatoon, SK S7K 0H2
306-244-3311 Fax: 306-244-3403
inquiries@fcl.ca
www.fcl.ca
Company Type: Private
Profile: Manufacturers in sawmills & planing mills, general; of millwork, prepared feeds & feed ingredients for animals & fowls, petroleum refining, dog & cat food; Wholesalers of general-line groceries & hardware; Retailing in lumber & other building materials dealers

Fortress Paper Ltd.
157 Chadwick Ct., 2nd Fl., North Vancouver, BC V7M 3K2
604-904-2328 Fax: 604-988-5327 888-820-3888
info@fortresspaper.com
www.fortresspaper.com
Ticker Symbol: FTP
Company Type: Public
Profile: Fortress Paper is engaged in the production of security & other specialty papers. It operates the following paper mills: the Dresden mill in Germany, & the Landqart Mill in Switzerland. Products include banknotes, visa & passport papers, technical papers, & wallpaper base products.

Goodfellow Inc.
225, rue Goodfellow, Delson, QC J5B 1V5
450-635-6511 Fax: 450-635-3730 800-361-6503
info@goodfellowinc.com
www.goodfellowinc.com
Ticker Symbol: GDL
Company Type: Public
Profile: Goodfellow Inc. re-manufactures, wholesales, & distributes wood & wood by-products, such as the following: dressed & rough lumber, sawn timber, composite & veneer based wood panel products, & prefinished & unfinished flooring. Customers are served in Canada & internationally. Goodfellow Inc. has implemented an environmental policy to conduct its business in an environmentally responsible manner.

Hardwoods Distribution Income Fund
#306, 9440 - 202 St., Langley, BC V1M 4A6
604-881-1999 Fax: 604-881-1995 www.hardwoods-inc.com
Ticker Symbol: HWD.UN
Company Type: Public
Profile: The Hardwoods Distribution Income Fund is an unincorporated open-ended limited purpose trust. The Fund holds interest in the securities of Hardwoods Specialty LP & Hardwoods Specialty Products USLP. The businesses distribute hardwood lumber, plywood, & specialty wood products to the woodworking industry. Distribution centres are located in Canada & the United States.

International Forest Products Ltd.
Bentall Tower Four, PO Box 49114, #3500, 1055 Dunsmuir St., Vancouver, BC V7X 1H7
604-689-6800 Fax: 604-689-6825
info@interfor.com
www.interfor.com
Ticker Symbol: IFP
Company Type: Public
Profile: Manufacturers in sawmills & general planing mills; of logging; special product sawmills; wholesalers of lumber, plywood, millwork & wood panels

Kitchen Craft of Canada Ltd.
1180 Springfield Rd., Winnipeg, MB R2C 2Z2
204-224-3211 Fax: 800-665-3495 800-463-9707
sales@kitchencraft.com
www.kitchencraft.com
Company Type: Private
Profile: Kitchen Craft of Canada is a manufacturer of wood kitchen cabinets.

Kruger Inc.
3285, ch Bedford, Montréal, QC H3S 1G5
514-737-1131 Fax: 514-343-3124
webadmin@kruger.com
www.kruger.com
Company Type: Private
Profile: Paperboard mills & paper mills; Manufacturers of packaging paper & plastics film, coated & laminated, corrugated & solid fiber boxes

Masonite International Corporation
6184, rue Notre-Dame, Lac-Mégantic, QC G6B 3B5
819-683-1550 Fax: 819-583-5902
immirh@megantic.ca
www.masonite.com
Ticker Symbol: MHM
Company Type: Private
Profile: Masonite International Corporation designs & markets interior doors.

Norwall Group Inc.
1055 Clark Blvd., Brampton, ON L6T 3W4
905-791-2787 Fax: 905-791-5281 800-268-0147
mmartin@norwallgroup.com
www.norwall.net
Ticker Symbol: NGI
Company Type: Public
Profile: Norwall Group Inc. is a manufacturer of residential wallcoverings & borders. Products are distributed to home centres, mass merchants, & specialty stores in Canada. In the United States, products are distributed through Norwall Group's wholly-owned operating subsidiary, Patton Wallcoverings.

PRT Forest Regeneration Income Fund
#101, 1006 Fort St., Victoria, BC V8V 3K4
250-381-1404 Fax: 250-381-0252 866-553-8733
investor_relations@prtgroup.com
www.prtgroup.com
Ticker Symbol: PRT.UN
Company Type: Private
Profile: PRT produces forest seedlings in nurseries located in Canada & the USA.

Quebecor Inc.
612, rue Saint-Jacques, Montréal, QC H3C 4M8
514-877-9777 Fax: 514-380-6097
webmaster@quebecor.com
www.quebecor.com
Ticker Symbol: QBR
Company Type: Public
Profile: Offices of holding companies; Manufacturers in pulp & paper mills, sawmills & planing mills; Newspaper, periodical & books: publishing & printing

Sino-Forest Corporation
#1208, 90 Burnhamthorpe Rd. West, Mississauga, ON L5B 3C3
905-281-8889 Fax: 905-281-3338
info@sinoforest.com
www.sinoforest.com
Ticker Symbol: TRE
Company Type: Public
Profile: Sino-Forest Corporation is an owner & cultivator of forest plantation trees. The company manufactures engineered-wood products & sells standing timber & harvested logs. Operations are carried out in China.

St. Mary's Paper Corp.
75 Huron St., Sault Ste Marie, ON P6A 5P4
705-942-6070 Fax: 705-541-2440 www.stmarys-paper.com
Company Type: Private
Profile: St. Marys Paper Corp. operates a paper mill in Sault Ste Marie, Ontario. It produces paper under the trade names Synpress, Sequence, & Sequel. The paper is sold mainly to magazine publishers & to retail companies for the production of catalogues.

Stella-Jones Inc.
#300, 3100 boul de la Côte-Vertu, Montréal, QC H4R 2J8
514-934-8666 Fax: 514-934-5327
ir@stella-jones.com
www.stella-jones.com
Ticker Symbol: SJ
Company Type: Public
Profile: Stella-Jones specializes in the production & marketing of industrial treated wood products. Products include the following: treated wood for bridges; pressure treated railway ties; marine & foundation pilings; construction timbers; highway guardrail posts; & wood poles for electrical utilities & telecommunications companies.

Supremex Income Fund
7213, rue Cordner, Lasalle, QC H8N 2J7
514-595-4045 Fax: 514-595-3092
investors@supremex.com
www.supremex.com
Ticker Symbol: SXP.UN
Company Type: Private
Profile: Supremex specializes in manufacturing & marketing stock & custom envelopes & related products. The company has an Enviro-logiX Program, which includes environmentally friendly bubble mailers, among other products.

Taiga Building Products Ltd.
PO Box 80329, #800, 4710 Kingsway, Burnaby, BC V5H 3X6
604-438-1471 Fax: 604-439-4242 800-663-1470
invest@taigabuilding.com
www.taigabuilding.com
Ticker Symbol: TBL
Company Type: Public
Profile: Taiga Building Products Ltd. distributes building products, such as lumber, engineered wood, mouldings, siding, flooring, & polyethylene sheeting. It is also involved in the production of treated wood, which reduces the use of timber resources. The company's customers are most often industrial manufacturers & building supply dealers.

Tembec Inc.
#1050, 800, boul René-Lévesque ouest, Montréal, QC H3B 1X9
514-871-0137 Fax: 514-397-0896 www.tembec.ca
Ticker Symbol: TMB
Company Type: Public
Profile: Forest products company with operations in North America & France

TimberWest Forest Corp.
PO Box 11101, #2300, 1055 West Georgia St., Vancouver, BC V6E 3P3
604-654-4600 Fax: 604-654-4662
invest@timberwest.com
www.timberwest.com

Ticker Symbol: TWF
Company Type: Public
Profile: Manufacturers of logging; in sawmills & general planing mills; Forestry-timber tracts

Uniboard Canada Inc
#500, 2540, boul Daniel-Johnson, Laval, QC H7T 2S3
450-682-5240 Fax: 450-682-0550 800-263-5240
sales.canada@uniboard.com
www.uniboard.com
Company Type: Private
Profile: Manufacturers in paperboard mills; of reconstituted wood products, converted paper & various paperboard products

West Fraser Timber Co. Ltd.
#501, 858 Beatty St., Vancouver, BC V6B 1C1
604-895-2700 Fax: 604-681-6061
shareholder@westfraser.com
www.westfrasertimber.ca
Ticker Symbol: WFT
Company Type: Public
Profile: Manufacturers in pulp mills, paper mills, paperboard mills, sawmills & general planing mills; Retailers in hardware stores, lumber & other building materials dealers

Western Forest Products Inc.
435 Trunk Rd., Duncan, BC V9L 2P9
250-748-3711 Fax: 250-748-6045
info@westernforest.com
www.westernforest.com
Ticker Symbol: WEF
Company Type: Public
Profile: Western Forest Products is a large woodland operator & lumber producer in the coastal region of British Columbia. Activities include timber harvesting, sawmilling logs into lumber & wood chips, value-added remanufacturing, & reforestation. Customers are served in North America & around the world.

Weyerhaeuser Company Limited
925 West Georgia St., 5th Fl., Vancouver, BC V6C 3L2
604-661-8000 800-525-5440www.weyerhaeuser.com
Company Type: Public
Profile: Weyerhaeuser is part of the forest products industry. The company grows & harvests trees & produces forestry products. Businesses include cellulose fibers, newsprint & specialty papers, hardwood products, & homes. It works to conduct its business in an environmentally sustainable & socially responsible manner.

Government Administration

Alberta Gaming & Liquor Commission
50 Corriveau Ave., St Albert, AB T8N 3T5
780-447-8600 Fax: 780-447-8918 800-272-8876
aglc_feedback@aglc.gov.ab.ca
www.aglc.gov.ab.ca
Company Type: Crown
Profile: The agent of the Government of Alberta oversees games of chance, gambling & sale & distribution of liquor in the province.

British Columbia Lottery Corporation
74 West Seymour St., Kamloops, BC V2C 1E2
250-828-5500 Fax: 250-828-5631 www.bclc.com
Company Type: Crown
Profile: BC Lottery Corp. is a gaming entertainment company.

Canada Post Corporation
2701 Riverside Dr., Ottawa, ON K1A 0B1
613-734-8440 Fax: 613-734-6084 866-607-6301
service@canadapost.ca
www.canadapost.ca
Company Type: Crown
Profile: Canadian postal service

Loto-Québec
500, rue Sherbrooke ouest, Montréal, QC H3A 3G6
514-282-8000 Fax: 514-873-8999
service_clientele@loto-quebec.com
www.loto-quebec.com
Company Type: Crown
Profile: Oversees games of chance & gambling; operates & monitors casinos, a video lottery terminal network, & network bingo activities

Manitoba Lotteries Corporation
830 Empress St., Winnipeg, MB R3G 3H3
204-957-2500 Fax: 204-957-3991
communications@mlc.mb.ca
www.mlc.mb.ca
Company Type: Crown
Profile: Manitoba Lotteries Corporation is the owner & operator of the Video Lottery Terminal (VLT) Network, Club Regent Casino, & McPhillips Station Casino. The crown corporation also distributes & sells tickets for lotteries operated by the Western Canada Lottery Corporation.

Ontario Lottery and Gaming Corporation
#800, 70 Foster Dr., Sault Ste. Marie, ON P6A 6V2
705-946-6464 800-387-0098www.olg.ca
Company Type: Crown
Profile: Oversees games of chance & gambling; Operates & monitors casinos: charity, aboriginal & commercial; Operates slotmachines at race tracks

Holding & Other Investment

ACE Aviation Holding Inc.
5100, boul de Maisonneuve ouest, Montréal, QC H4Y 1H4
514-422-5000 Fax: 514-422-5789
shareholders.actionnaires@aceaviation.com
www.aceaviation.com
Ticker Symbol: ACE
Company Type: Public
Profile: The investment holding company has interests in aviation companies such as Air Canada & Jazz Air.

AGF Master Limited Partnership
Toronto-Dominion Centre, PO Box 50, Toronto, ON M5K 1E9
416-367-1900 Fax: 905-214-8243 800-268-8583
info@agf.com
www.agf.com
Ticker Symbol: AFP
Company Type: Public
Profile: Offices of holding companies

AIC Diversified Canada Split Corp.
1375 Kerns Rd., Burlington, ON L7R 4X8
905-331-4286 Fax: 905-331-1321 800-263-2144
info@aic.com
www.aic.com
Ticker Symbol: ADC
Company Type: Public
Profile: Unit investment trusts, certificate/closed-end management offices

Argus Corporation Limited
10 Toronto St., Toronto, ON M5C 2B7
416-363-8721 Fax: 416-363-4187 **Ticker Symbol:** AR
Company Type: Public
Profile: Offices of holding companies

Avenir Diversified Income Trust
#300, 808 - 1st St. SW, Calgary, AB T2P 1M9
403-237-9949 Fax: 403-237-0903
info@avenirtrust.com
www.avenirtrust.com
Ticker Symbol: AVF.UN
Company Type: Public
Profile: The income trust has interests in the following sectors: financial services, energy, & real estate.

BAM Investments Corp.
Brookfield Place, #300, 181 Bay St., Toronto, ON M5J 2T3
416-359-8620 Fax: 416-365-9642 **Ticker Symbol:** BNB
Company Type: Public
Profile: BAM Investments Corp. is a leveraged investment company. It has a principal holding in Brookfield Asset Management.

BAM Split Corp.
Brookfield Place, PO Box 762, #300, 181 Bay St., Toronto, ON M5J 2T3
416-359-8620 Fax: 416-359-9642 www.bnnsplit.com
Ticker Symbol: BAM
Company Type: Public
Profile: Offices of holding companies

British Columbia Investment Management Corporation
PO Box 9910, Victoria, BC V8W 9R1
250-356-0263 Fax: 250-387-7874
communications@bcimc.com
www.bcimc.com
Company Type: Public
Profile: Investment funds management, with clients including public sector pension plans, the Province of British Columbia, Crown corporations and publicly administered trust funds; pooled investment funds and segregated funds

Brookfield Asset Management
Brookfield Place, #300, 181 Bay St., Toronto, ON M5J 2T3
416-363-9491 Fax: 416-365-9642 www.brookfield.com
Ticker Symbol: BAM
Company Type: Public
Profile: The global asset manager concentrates on property, infrastructure, & power assets.

C.I. Fund Management Inc.
2 Queen St. East, 20th Fl., Toronto, ON M5C 3G7
416-364-1145 Fax: 416-364-6299 800-268-9374
service@ci.com
www.cifunds.com
Ticker Symbol: CIX
Company Type: Public
Profile: Management investment offices, open-end

Canada Trust Income Investments
c/o TD Asset Management Inc., Canada Trust Tower, 161 Bay St., 35th Fl., Toronto, ON M5J 2T2
416-308-9049 Fax: 416-983-1729 866-888-3383
tdeft@tdam.com
www.tdcanadatrust.com
Company Type: Public
Profile: Unit investment trusts, certificate/closed-end management offices

Canadian Apartment Properties Real Estate Investment
#401, 11 Church St., Toronto, ON M5E 1W1
416-861-9404 Fax: 416-861-9209
ir@capreit.net
www.capreit.net
Ticker Symbol: CAR
Company Type: Public
Profile: Real estate investment trusts

Canadian Real Estate Investment Trust
North Tower, #500, 175 Bloor St. East, Toronto, ON M4W 3R8
416-628-7771 Fax: 416-628-7777
info@creit.ca
www.creit.ca
Ticker Symbol: REF
Company Type: Public
Profile: Canadian Real Estate Investment Trust is the owner of a portfolio of retail, office, & industrial properties.

Canadian Resources Income Trust
Scotia Plaza, PO Box 4085 A, #2600, 40 King St. West, Toronto, ON M5W 2X6
416-863-7144 Fax: 416-863-7425
mc_carit@scotiacapital.com
Company Type: Public
Profile: Unit investment trusts, certificate/closed-end management offices

Canadian World Fund Limited
10 Toronto St., Toronto, ON M5C 2B7
416-366-2931 Fax: 416-366-2729 866-443-6097
mma@mmainvestments.com
www.mmainvestments.com
Ticker Symbol: CWF
Company Type: Public
Profile: Unit investment trusts, certificate/closed-end management offices

Central Fund of Canada Limited
Hallmark Estates, #805, 1323 - 15th Ave. SW, Calgary, AB T3C 0X8
403-228-5861 Fax: 403-228-2222
info@centralfund.com
www.centralfund.com
Ticker Symbol: CEF, CEF.A
Company Type: Public
Profile: A Canadian company that passively holds gold and silver bullion on a secure basis for investors

Chesswood Income Fund
4077 Chesswood Dr., Toronto, ON M3J 2R8
416-386-3099 Fax: 416-386-3085
info@chesswoodfund.com
www.chesswoodfund.com
Ticker Symbol: CFU.UN
Company Type: Public
Profile: A financial services trust with operating businesses in both Canada & the USA

Cineplex Galaxy Income Fund
1303 Yonge St., Toronto, ON M4T 2Y9
416-323-6600 Fax: 416-323-6633
pat.marshall@cineplex.com
www.cineplex.com
Ticker Symbol: CGX.UN
Company Type: Public
Profile: The unincorporated, open-ended limited purpose trust owns approximately 97% of Cineplex Entertainment Limited Partnership.

Citadel Diversified Investment Trust
#1006, 141 Adelaide St. West, Toronto, ON M5H 3L5
416-361-9673 Fax: 416-361-0634 877-261-9674
investorrelations@citadelfunds.com

www.citadelfunds.com
Company Type: Public
Profile: Unit investment trusts, certificate/closed-end management offices

CML Healthcare Income Fund
#1, 60 Courtneypark Dr. West, Mississauga, ON L5W 0B3
905-565-0043 Fax: 905-565-2844
800-263-0801www.cmlhealthcare.com
Ticker Symbol: CLC
Company Type: Public
Profile: The open-ended investment trust is the owner of CML HealthCare Inc. The healthcare service provides laboratory testing & medical imaging services in Canada. HealthCare Income Fund also acquired American Radiology Services, Inc., which provides diagnostic medical imaging services in the United States.

Consolidated Mercantile Incorporated
106 Avenue Rd., Toronto, ON M5R 2H3
416-920-0500 Fax: 416-920-7851
info@consolidatedmercantile.com
www.consolidatedmercantile.com
Ticker Symbol: CMC
Company Type: Public
Profile: Offices of holding companies; Manufacturers of wood household & office furniture, various plastics products; Real estate land subdividers & developers; Investment management in furniture specialty covers, packaging, & real estate industries

Consumers' Waterheater Income Fund
80 Allstate Pkwy., 2nd Fl., Markham, ON L3R 6H3
905-943-6292 Fax: 905-943-6393 877-877-0142
info@consumerswaterheaters.com
www.consumerswaterheaters.com
Ticker Symbol: CWI.UN
Company Type: Public
Profile: Consumers Waterheater Income Fund is the owner of a portfolio of waterheaters, which are leased to residential customers in Ontario.

Counsel Corporation
Scotia Plaza, #3200, 40 King St. West, Toronto, ON M5H 3Y2
416-866-3000 Fax: 416-866-3061
info@counselcorp.com
www.counselcorp.com
Ticker Symbol: CXS
Company Type: Public
Profile: Counsel Corporation is an international asset management firm. It strives to take advantage of corporate & real estate investment opportunities.

Crew Gold Corporation
#400, 837 West Hastings St., Vancouver, BC V6C 3N6
604-683-7585 Fax: 604-682-0566
investorrelations@crewgold.com
www.crewgroup.com
Ticker Symbol: CRU
Company Type: Public
Profile: Offices of holding companies

DDJ High Yield Fund
CI Investments, 2 Queen St. East, 20th Fl., Toronto, ON M5C 3G7
416-364-1145 Fax: 416-364-6299 800-268-9374
service@ci.com
www.ci.com
Ticker Symbol: HYB
Company Type: Public
Profile: Unit investment trusts, certificate/closed-end management offices

Dundee Corporation
Dundee Place, 1 Adelaide St. East, 28th Fl., Toronto, ON M5C 2V9
416-863-6990 Fax: 416-363-4536
investor@dundeebancorp.com
www.dundeecorporation.com
Ticker Symbol: DC.A
Company Type: Public
Profile: The asset management company is engaged in real estate, private wealth management, & resources.

E-L Financial Corporation Limited
165 University Ave., 10th Fl., Toronto, ON M5H 3B8
416-947-2578 Fax: 416-362-0792 **Ticker Symbol:** ELF
Company Type: Public
Profile: The investment & insurance holding company consists of the following subsidiaries: E-L Financial Services Ltd., The Dominion of Canada General Insurance Company, & The Empire Life Insurance Company.

Economic Investment Trust Limited
165 University Ave., 10th Fl., Toronto, ON M5H 3B8
416-947-2578 Fax: 416-362-2592 **Ticker Symbol:** EVT
Company Type: Public
Profile: Unit investment trusts, certificate/closed-end management offices

Empire Company Limited
115 King St., Stellarton, NS B0K 1S0
902-755-4440 Fax: 902-755-6477
ir-empire@sobeys.com
www.empireco.ca
Ticker Symbol: EMP
Company Type: Public
Profile: The Empire Company Limited is engaged in food retailing, through its majority ownership of Sobeys Inc. Through wholly-owned companies, Empire Company is also involved in real estate.

EnerVest Diversified Income Trust
350 - 7th Ave. SW, 39th Fl., Calgary, AB T2P 3N9
403-571-5550 Fax: 403-571-5554 877-434-2796
info@enervest.com
www.enervest.com
Ticker Symbol: EIT
Company Type: Public
Profile: Unit investment trusts, certificate/closed-end management offices

Exchange Industrial Income Fund
1067 Sherwin Rd., Winnipeg, MB R3H 0T8
204-982-1852 Fax: 204-982-1855
dspencer@eig.ca
www.eiif.ca
Ticker Symbol: EIF.UN
Company Type: Public
Profile: Exchange Industrial Income Fund is a Canadian business trust. The Fund seeks acquisition opportunities in well-established, profitable companies in the industrial products & transportation markets. The following are the Fund's subsidiaries: Overlanders Manufacturing, Water Blast Manufacturing, Jasper Tank, Stainless Fabrication, Inc., Perimeter Air, & Keewatin Air.

Fairfax Financial Holdings Limited
#800, 95 Wellington St. West, Toronto, ON M5J 2N7
416-367-4941 Fax: 416-367-4946 www.fairfax.ca
Ticker Symbol: FFH
Company Type: Public
Profile: Through its subsidiaries, the financial services holding company is involved in insurance claims management, property & casualty insurance & reinsurance, & investment management. Subsidiaries include Northbridge Financial, Crum & Forster, Falcon Insurance, First Capital, OdysseyRe, Group Re, Hamblin Watsa Investment Counsel, & MFXchange.

First Asset Energy & Resource Fund
#1400, 95 Wellington St., Toronto, ON M5J 2N7
416-642-1289 Fax: 416-362-2199 877-642-1289
info@firstasset.com
www.firstasset.com
Ticker Symbol: TRF.UN
Company Type: Public
Profile: Unit investment trusts, certificate/closed-end management offices

Forest & Marine Investments Ltd.
#500, 345 Wallace St., Nanaimo, BC V9R 5B6
250-753-0141 Fax: 250-753-0173 877-772-0022
dhitch@forestandmarine.com
www.forestandmarine.com
Ticker Symbol: FME
Company Type: Public
Profile: Unit investment trusts, certificate/closed-end management offices

Freehold Royalty Trust
#400, 144 - 4th Ave. SW, Calgary, AB T2P 3N4
403-221-0802 Fax: 403-221-0888 888-257-1873
ir@freeholdtrust.com
www.freeholdtrust.com
Ticker Symbol: FRU
Company Type: Public
Profile: Open-ended management investment offices; Oil royalty traders

Garbell Holdings Limited
Standard Life Centre, PO Box 35, #1770, 121 King St. West, Toronto, ON M5H 3T9
416-947-1100 Fax: 416-947-0834
msimpson@garbell.on.ca
Company Type: Private
Profile: Garbell Holdings Limited is an investment holding company.

Gendis Inc.
1370 Sony Place, Winnipeg, MB R3C 3C3
204-474-5200 Fax: 204-474-5201
finance@gendis.ca
www.gendis.ca
Ticker Symbol: GDS
Company Type: Public
Profile: Offices of holding companies; Management services

Glendale International Corp.
353 Iroquois Shore Rd., Oakville, ON L6H 1M3
905-844-2870 Fax: 905-844-2907
info@glendaleint.com
www.glendaleint.com
Ticker Symbol: GIN
Company Type: Public
Profile: Glendale International Corp. manages a portfolio of companies involved in electronics, technology, & recreational vehicles.

GLP NT Corporation
Brookfield Place, PO Box 770, #300, 181 Bay St., Toronto, ON M5J 2T3
416-369-8268 Fax: 416-363-2856 **Ticker Symbol:** GP
Company Type: Public
Profile: Offices of holding companies

Great-West Lifeco Inc.
100 Osborne St. North, Winnipeg, MB R3C 3A5
204-946-8366 Fax: 204-946-4129
contactus@gwl.ca
www.greatwestlife.com
Ticker Symbol: GWO
Company Type: Public
Profile: The financial services holding company owns Great-West Life Assurance Co. of Winnipeg, Manitoba.

H&R Real Estate Investment Trust
#500, 3625 Dufferin St., Toronto, ON M3K 1N4
416-635-7520 Fax: 416-398-0040
info@hr-reit.com
www.hr-reit.com
Ticker Symbol: HR
Company Type: Public
Profile: The organization is a real estate investment trust.

Halterm Income Fund
PO Box 1057, 577 Marginal Rd., Halifax, NS B3J 2X1
902-421-1778 Fax: 902-429-3193
info@halterm.com
www.halterm.com
Ticker Symbol: HAL
Company Type: Public
Profile: Non-charitable, non-educational & non-religious trusts

IAT Air Cargo Facilities Income Fund
#2000, 5000 Miller Rd., Richmond, BC V7B 1K6
604-249-5100 Fax: 604-249-5101
mmitchell@amb.com
www.iat-yvr.com
Ticker Symbol: ACF
Company Type: Public
Profile: Unit investment trusts, certificate/closed-end management offices

IBI Income Fund
230 Richmond St. West, 5th Fl., Toronto, ON M5V 1V6
416-596-1930 Fax: 416-596-8024 www.ibigroup.com
Ticker Symbol: IBG.UN
Company Type: Public
Profile: IBI Income Fund holds interest in IBI Group. IBI Group provides service in the following areas of practice: facilities, systems, urban land, & transportation. Offices are situated in Canada, the United States, Europe, the Middle East, & Asia.

Income Financial Trust
Royal Trust Tower, PO Box 341, #4500, 77 King St. West, Toronto, ON M5K 1K7
416-304-4440 Fax: 416-304-4441 877-478-2372
info@quadravest.com
www.quadravest.com
Ticker Symbol: INC
Company Type: Public
Profile: Unit investment trusts, certificate/closed-end management offices; Investors

iUnits S&P/TSE 60 Index Participation Fund
Barclays Global Investors Canada Limited, BCE Plac, PO Box 614, #2500, 161 Bay St., Toronto, ON M5J 2S1
416-643-4080 Fax: 416-643-4039 877-468-6487
iunits@barclaysglobal.com
www.iunits.com
Ticker Symbol: XIU
Company Type: Public
Profile: Unit investment trusts, certificate/closed-end management offices

Labrador Iron Ore Royalty Income Fund
Scota Plaza, PO Box 4085 A, 40 King St. West, 26th Fl., Toronto, ON M5W 2X6
416-863-7133 Fax: 416-863-7425 www.labradorironore.com
Ticker Symbol: LIF
Company Type: Public
Profile: Labrador Iron Ore Royalty Income Fund is an unicorporated, limited purpose trust. Its wholly-owned subsidiaries include Hollinger-Hanna Limited & Labrador Mining Co Ltd. (Labmin). Through these subsidiaries, the Fund holds a 15.10% equity interest in Iron Ore Company of Canada (IOC).

Longview Capital Partners Inc.
1111 West Georgia St., 24th Fl., Vancouver, BC V6E 4M3
604-681-5755 Fax: 604-684-2990
info@longviewcp.com
www.longviewcp.com
Ticker Symbol: LV
Company Type: Public
Profile: The global resource group's portfolio of companies includes over ten different mineral commodities. The company commenced a Corporate Social Responsibility program to assess the environmental, social, & financial impacts of its operations.

MINT Income Fund
c/o Middlefield Fund Management Limited, PO Box 192, One First Canadian Pl., 58th Fl., Toronto, ON M5X 1A6
416-362-0714 Fax: 416-362-7925 888-890-1868
invest@middlefield.com
www.middlefield.com
Ticker Symbol: MIDUN
Company Type: Public
Profile: The closed-end investment trust invests in securities primarily of units of business trusts, power & pipeline trusts, & real estate investment trusts. It is managed by Middlefield Fund Management Limited.

Morgan Meighen & Associates
10 Toronto St., Toronto, ON M5C 2B7
416-366-2931 Fax: 416-366-2729 866-443-6097
mma@mmainvestments.com
www.mmainvestments.com
Ticker Symbol: CGI
Company Type: Public
Profile: Unit investment trusts, certificate/closed-end management offices

Morguard Real Estate Investment Trust
#1000, 55 City Centre Dr., Mississauga, ON L5B 1M3
905-281-4800 Fax: 905-281-4818
skaur@morguard.com
www.morguardreit.com
Ticker Symbol: MRT
Company Type: Public
Profile: The organization is a closed-end investment trust. The Morguard Real Estate Investment Trust has a portfolio of diversified real estate assets across Canada.

Mulvihill Capital Management Inc.
Standard Life Centre, #2600, 121 King St. West, Toronto, ON M5H 3T9
416-681-3900 Fax: 416-681-3901 800-725-7172
info@mulvihill.com
www.mulvihill.com
Company Type: Private
Profile: Mulvihill Capital Management is registered as a mutual fund dealer, limited market dealer, & investment counselor throughout Canada.

Mulvihill Premier Canada Income Fund
Mulvihill Capital Management, #2600, 121 King St. West, Toronto, ON M5H 3T9
416-681-3900 Fax: 416-681-3901 800-725-7172
hybrid@mulvihill.com
www.mulvihill.com
Ticker Symbol: GIP
Company Type: Public
Profile: Unit investment trusts, certificate/closed-end management offices

NAL Oil & Gas Trust
#1000, 550 - 6th Ave. SW, Calgary, AB T2P 0S2
403-294-3600 Fax: 403-294-3601 888-223-8792
investor.relations@nal.ca
www.nal.ca
Ticker Symbol: NAE.UN
Company Type: Public
Profile: NAL Oil & Gas Trust is an open-end investment trust. The Trust's distributions are generated by acquiring, developing, producing, & marketing oil, natural gas, & natural gas liquids.

NewGrowth Corp.
Scotia Plaza, Scotia Managed Companies Admin. Inc., PO Box 4085 A, 40 King St. West, 26th Fl., Toronto, ON M5W 2X6
416-862-3931 Fax: 416-863-7425
mc_newgrowth@scotiacapital.com
www.scotiamanagedcompanies.com
Ticker Symbol: NEW
Company Type: Public
Profile: The mutual fund corporation's investment portfolio consists of publicly-listed securities of selected Canadian chartered banks, pipelines, telecommunications companies, & utility issuers.

Northfield Capital Corporation
#301, 141 Adelaide St. West, Toronto, ON M5H 3L5
416-628-5901 Fax: 416-628-5911
info@northfieldcapital.com
www.northfieldcapital.com
Ticker Symbol: NFD.A
Company Type: Public
Profile: Formed in 1981, the investment company owns interests in diverse business activities. Major oil, gas, minining, & viticulture holdings include Ground Star Resources, GoldCorp Inc., Queenston Mining Inc., FNX Mining Corporation, Guyana Goldfields Inc., White Pine Resources Inc., Bear Lake Gold Ltd., & The Grange of Prince Edward Inc.

Northland Power Income Fund
c/o Iroquois Falls Power Management Inc., 30 St Clair Ave. West, 17th Fl., Toronto, ON M4V 3A2
416-962-6262 Fax: 416-962-6266
info@npifund.com
www.npifund.com
Ticker Symbol: NPI
Company Type: Public
Profile: Open-ended management investment offices; Owner & operator of independent power projects

Onex Corporation
PO Box 700, 161 Bay St., Toronto, ON M5J 2S1
416-362-7711 Fax: 416-362-5765
info@onex.com
www.onex.com
Ticker Symbol: OCX
Company Type: Public
Profile: Through Onex Partners & ONCAP families of funds, Onex Corporation makes private equity investments. The company is also engaged in the management of alternative asset platforms, which focuses on real estate & distressed credit.

Oppenheimer Holdings Inc.
PO Box 2015, #1110, 20 Eglinton Ave. West, Toronto, ON M4R 1K8
416-322-1515 Fax: 416-322-7007
investorrelations@opy.ca; info@opco.com
www.opco.com
Ticker Symbol: OPY
Company Type: Public
Profile: Oppenheimer Holdings Inc. is a holding company. Its subsidiaries provide the following financial services: investment banking, securities brokerage, asset management, & trust services. Offices are located in the United States, Latin America, England, & Israel.

Power Corp. of Canada
751, carré Victoria, Montréal, QC H2Y 2J3
514-286-7400 Fax: 514-286-7424 www.powercorporation.com
Ticker Symbol: POW
Company Type: Public
Profile: The main subsidiaries of this diversified international management & holding company include Gesca Ltee., Power Financial Corp., & Power Technology Investment Corp.

Power Financial Corp.
751, carré Victoria, Montréal, QC H2Y 2J3
514-286-7400 Fax: 514-286-7424 www.powerfinancial.com
Ticker Symbol: PWF
Company Type: Public
Profile: The holding & management company includes the following subsidiaries: IGM Financial Inc., Canada Life Assurance Company, Great-West Lifeco Inc., London Insurance Insurance Company, Investors Group Inc., Mackenzie Financial Corporation, & Putnam Investments, LLC.

Quadravest Capital Management Inc.
PO Box 341, #4500, 77 King St. West, Toronto, ON M5K 1K7
416-304-4440 Fax: 416-304-4441 877-478-2372
info@quadravest.com
www.quadravest.com
Company Type: Public
Profile: Unit investment trusts, certificate/closed-end management offices

R Split II Corporation
Scotia Plaza, PO Box 4085 A, 40 King St. West, 26th Fl., Toronto, ON M5W 2X6
416-945-5353 Fax: 416-863-7425
mc_rsplit2@scotiacapital.com
www.scotiamanagedcompanies.com
Ticker Symbol: RBS
Company Type: Public
Profile: Unit investment trusts, certificate/closed-end management offices; Investors

Ravensource Fund
Cinnamon Investments, 60 Bedford Rd., Toronto, ON M5R 2K2
416-922-9096 Fax: 416-921-3551 www.ravensource.ca
Company Type: Public
Profile: This company is a closed end fund which focuses on troubled business enterprises, including small capitalization stocks, income trusts, defualted bonds and restricted securities.

Richards Packaging Income Fund
6095 Ordan Dr., Mississauga, ON L4T 2M7
905-670-7760 Fax: 905-670-1961 www.richardspackaging.com
Ticker Symbol: RPI.UN
Company Type: Public
Profile: Richards Packaging Income Fund is an indirect owner of securities of Richards Packaging Inc. Richards Packaging is a plastic & glass container manufacturer & distributor. The company also distributes metal & plastic closures, as well as injection molded containers & packaging systems.

Rogers Sugar Income Fund
4026, rue Notre-Dame est, Montréal, QC H1W 2K3
514-940-4350 Fax: 514-527-1610
infos@rogerssugar.com
www.rogerssugar.com
Ticker Symbol: RSI
Company Type: Public
Profile: The open-ended, limited purpose trust holds the common shares & notes of Lantic Sugar Limited. Lantic refines, processes, distributes, & markets sugar products throughout Canada.

SCI Income Trust
#251, 6900 Airport Rd., Mississauga, ON L4V 1E8
905-671-1033 Fax: 905-671-0669
sci-investor-relations@simmonscanada.com
www.simmonscanada.com
Ticker Symbol: SMN.UN
Company Type: Public
Profile: Manufacturers of mattresses & foundations

Senvest Capital Inc.
#2400, 1000, rue Sherbrooke ouest, Montréal, QC H3A 3G4
514-281-8082 Fax: 514-281-0166 www.senvest.com
Ticker Symbol: SEC
Company Type: Public
Profile: Senvest Capital Inc.'s subsidiaries are involved in following sectors: asset management, merchant banking, real estate, & electronic security.

Sonor Investments Limited
PO Box 104, #2120, 130 Adelaide St. West, Toronto, ON M5H 3P5
416-369-1499 Fax: 416-369-0280 **Ticker Symbol:** SNI
Company Type: Public
Profile: Sonor Investments Limited is an investment holding company.

Superior Plus Income Fund
#2820, 605 - 5th Ave. SW, Calgary, AB T2P 3H5
403-218-2954 Fax: 403-218-2973
info@superiorplus.com
www.superiorplus.ca
Ticker Symbol: SPB
Company Type: Public
Profile: The limited purpose trust holds securities of Superior Plus Inc.. Distributions are made to holders of trust units of the Fund.

The Data Group Income Fund
9195 Torbram Rd., Brampton, ON L6S 6H2
905-791-3151 Fax: 905-791-3277 www.datagroup.ca
Ticker Symbol: DGI.UN
Company Type: Public
Profile: The Data Group Income Fund is the owner of The Data Group Limited Partnership. Document management solutions are provided, including printed products. Twenty-five facilities are operated throughout Canada.

The Health Care & Biotechnology Venture Fund
c/o Lumira Capital Corp., #770, 141 Adelaide St. West, Toronto, ON M5H 3L5
416-675-7661 Fax: 416-213-4232 www.lumiracapital.com
Company Type: Public

Profile: Unit investment trusts, certificate/closed-end management offices; Investors

The Jim Pattison Group
#1800, 1067 West Cordova St., Vancouver, BC V6C 1C7
604-688-6764 Fax: 604-687-2601
admin@jp-group.com
www.jimpattison.com
Company Type: Private
Profile: Periodical distribution; Radio & TV stations; Advertising display & signage; Retail food & fish harvesting & processing; Retail vehicle franchising; Export & financial services

Third Canadian General Investment Trust Limited
10 Toronto St., Toronto, ON M5C 2B7
416-366-2931 Fax: 416-366-2729 866-443-6097
mma@mmainvestments.com
www.mmainvestments.com
Ticker Symbol: THD
Company Type: Public
Profile: Offices of holding companies; Unit investment trusts, certificate/closed-end management offices

Thirty-Five Split Corp.
Scotia Plaza, PO Box 4085 A, 40 King St. West, 26th Fl., Toronto, ON M5W 2X6
416-945-4535 Fax: 416-863-7425
mc_thirtyfivesplit@scotiacapital.com
www.scotiamanagedcompanies.com
Ticker Symbol: TFS
Company Type: Public
Profile: Open-ended management investment offices

Triax Diversified High-Yield Trust
#1400, 95 Wellington St., Toronto, ON M5J 2N7
416-362-2929 Fax: 416-362-2199 800-407-0287
info@triaxcapital.com
www.triaxcapital.com
Ticker Symbol: TRH
Company Type: Public
Profile: Unit investment trusts, certificate/closed-end management offices

Unique Broadband Systems, Inc.
8250 Lawson Rd., Milton, ON L9T 5C6
905-660-8100 Fax: 905-669-0785
irinfo@uniquebroadband.com
www.uniquebroadband.com
Ticker Symbol: UBS
Company Type: Public
Profile: Unique Broadband Systems, Inc. is a publicly listed Canadian holding company.

United Corporations Limited
165 University Ave., 10th Fl., Toronto, ON M5H 3B8
416-947-2578 Fax: 416-362-2592 www.ucorp.ca
Ticker Symbol: UNC
Company Type: Public
Profile: Unit investment trusts, certificate/closed-end management offices

Utility Corp.
Scotia Plaza, PO Box 4085 A, 40 King St. West, 26th Fl., Toronto, ON M5W 2X6
416-863-7893 Fax: 416-863-7425
mc_utility@scotiacapital.com
www.scotiamanagedcompanies.com
Ticker Symbol: UTC
Company Type: Public
Profile: Utility Corp. is a mutual fund corporation whose investment portfolio consists of publicly listed securities of Canadian utility & telecommunications companies.

WesternOne Equity Income Fund
#910, 925 West Georgia St., Vancouver, BC V6C 3L2
604-678-4042 Fax: 604-681-5969
info@weq.ca
www.weq.ca
Ticker Symbol: WEQ.UN
Company Type: Public
Profile: WesternOne Equity Income Fund is an unincorporated, open-ended trust. It invests in mainly small & medium sized equipment & infrastructure related businesses. The Fund's businesses are located primarily in Saskatchewan, Alberta, & British Columbia.

Westshore Terminals Income Fund
#1800, 1067 West Cordova St., Vancouver, BC V6C 1C7
604-688-6764 Fax: 604-687-2601 www.westshore.com
Ticker Symbol: WTE
Company Type: Public
Profile: The open-ended trust owns all the limited partnership units of Westshore Terminals Limited Partnership. Westshore Terminals Limited is located in Roberts Bank, British Columbia, where it operates a coal storage & coal export facility. The Fund distributes available cash received from Westshore Terminals Limited to its unitholders. Westar Management Ltd. operates Westshore Terminals Limited for the Fund.

Insurance

Agriculture Financial Services Corporation
5718 - 56 Ave., Lacombe, AB T4L 1B1
403-782-8200 Fax: 403-782-4226 800-396-0215
afsc.webmaster@afsc.ca
www.afsc.ca
Company Type: Crown
Profile: Fire, marine & casualty insurance; Agricultural services, farm management services

Aviva Canada Inc.
2206 Eglinton Ave. East, Toronto, ON M1L 4S8
416-288-1800 800-387-4518www.avivacanada.com
Company Type: Private
Profile: Property & casualty insurance group

Canada Deposit Insurance Corporation
PO Box 2340 D, 50 O'Connor St., 17th Fl., Ottawa, ON K1P 5W5
Fax: 613-996-6095 800-461-2342
info@cdic.ca
www.cdic.ca
Company Type: Crown
Profile: Various insurance carriers; Public finance, taxation, & monetary policy

Co-operators General Insurance Company
Service Quality Department, Priory Square, 130 MacDonell St., Guelph, ON N1H 6P8
519-824-4400 Fax: 519-763-5152 800-265-2612
service@cooperators.ca
www.cooperators.ca
Ticker Symbol: CCS
Company Type: Public
Profile: Co-operators General Insurance Company provides home, automobile, farm, & commecial insurance services throughout Canada.

Cunningham Lindsey Group Inc.
#1000, 70 University Ave., Toronto, ON M5J 2M4
416-596-8020 Fax: 416-596-6510
corpservices@cl-na.com
www.cunninghamlindsey.com
Ticker Symbol: LIN
Company Type: Public
Profile: Offices of holding companies; Insurance agents, brokers & service

Desjardins Financial Corporation
PO Box 10500 Desjardins, #2822, 1 complexe Desjardins, Montréal, QC H5B 1J1
514-281-7070 Fax: 514-281-7083
info@desjardins.com
www.desjardins.com
Company Type: Public
Profile: Offices of holding companies; Life, fire, marine & casualty insurance

EGI Financial Holdings Inc.
#300, 2680 Matheson Blvd. East, Mississauga, ON L4W 0A5
905-214-7880 Fax: 905-214-8028 www.egi.ca
Ticker Symbol: EFH
Company Type: Public
Profile: Through its subsidiary, Echelon General Insurance, EGI Financial is involved in the property & casualty insurance industry in Canada. Specialty general insurance products include non-standard automobile insurance.

Equitable Life Insurance Company of Canada
1 Westmount Rd. North, Waterloo, ON N2J 4C7
519-886-5110 Fax: 519-883-7400 800-265-8878
headoffice@equitable.ca
www.equitable.ca
Company Type: Private
Profile: Individual life & health insurance & annuities, group life, health & pension plans; retirement savings; commercial mortgages & segregated funds

Gore Mutual Insurance Company
PO Box 70, 252 Dundas St. North, Cambridge, ON N1R 5T3
519-623-1910 Fax: 800-601-9773
800-265-8600www.goremutual.ca
Company Type: Private
Profile: Fire, marine surety & casualty insurance

Great-West Life Assurance Company
100 Osborne St. North, Winnipeg, MB R3C 3A5
204-946-1190 Fax: 204-946-4129 www.greatwestlife.com.
Ticker Symbol: GWL
Company Type: Public
Profile: The insurance company serves individuals, families, businesses, & organizations. Great-West Life Assurance Company also supplies specialty general insurance & reinsurance.

Hub International Limited
8 Nelson St. West, 6th Fl., Brampton, ON L6X 4J2
905-459-4000 Fax: 905-459-1401 800-387-2592
dennis.pauls@hubinternational.com
www.hubinternational.com
Company Type: Public
Profile: Insurance brokerage: property, casualty, life & health, employee benefits, investment & risk management & services

Industrial Alliance Insurance & Financial Services
PO Box 1907 Terminus, 1080, Grande Allée ouest, Québec, QC G1K 7M3
418-684-5000 Fax: 418-684-5294 800-463-6236
info@inalco.com; investors@inalco.com
www.inalco.com
Ticker Symbol: IAG
Company Type: Public
Profile: Industrial Alliance Insurance & Financial Services Inc. provides a great range of financial & insurance products & services, including life & health insurance, automobile & home insurance, RRSPs, savings & retirement plans, securities, mutual & segregated funds, & mortgage loans.

ING Canada Inc.
ING Tower, 700 University Ave., 15th Fl., Toronto, ON M5G 0A1
416-341-1464 Fax: 416-941-5320
info@ingcanada.com
www.ingcanada.com
Ticker Symbol: IIC
Company Type: Private
Profile: Through its subsidiaries, ING Canada Inc. provides the following types of insurance: property, liability, & automobile. The property & casualty insurance provider serves both individuals & businesses.

Insurance Corporation of British Columbia
151 West Esplanade, North Vancouver, BC V7M 3H9
604-661-2800 800-663-3051www.icbc.com
Company Type: Crown
Profile: Automobile insurance

Kingsway Financial Services Inc.
#800, 7120 Hurontario, Mississauga, ON L5W 0A9
905-696-1372 Fax: 905-696-1772
info@kingsway-financial.com
www.kingsway-financial.com
Ticker Symbol: KFS
Company Type: Public
Profile: Offices of holding companies; Fire, marine & casualty insurance

Lloyd's Canada Inc.
#1540, 1155, rue Metcalfe, Montréal, QC H3B 2V6
514-861-8361 Fax: 514-861-0470 877-455-6937
info@lloyds.ca
www.lloyds.com
Company Type: Private
Profile: Insurance market providing specialist insurance services to businesses

London Life Insurance Company
255 Dufferin Ave., London, ON N6A 4K1
519-432-5281 Fax: 519-435-7077 www.londonlife.com
Company Type: Public
Profile: London Life Insurance Company provides financial security advice & planning for individuals, businesses, & organizations. Products include life insurance, mortgages, & group retirement plans.

MARSH Canada Limited
Brookfield Place, #1400, 161 Bay St., Toronto, ON M5J 2S4
416-868-2600 www.marsh.ca
Company Type: Private
Profile: The broker & risk advisor offers advice & transactional capabilities. Services include mergers & acquisitions, risk management services, & alternative risk financing.

Northbridge Financial Corporation
105 Adelaide St. West, 7th Fl., Toronto, ON M5H 1P9
416-350-4300 Fax: 416-350-4307
investor.relations@norfin.com
www.norfin.com
Ticker Symbol: NB
Company Type: Public
Profile: Northbridge Financial Corporation provides automobile, property, general liability, & other commercial insurance products. Clients are businesses in Canada.

Optimum General Inc.
#1500, 425, boul de Maisonneuve ouest, Montréal, QC H3A 3G5
514-288-8725 Fax: 514-288-0760
direction@optimum-general.com
www.optimum-general.com
Ticker Symbol: OGI
Company Type: Public
Profile: Automobile, personal property, commercial property and liability insurance

Royal & Sun Alliance Insurance Company of Canada
10 Wellington St. East, Toronto, ON M5E 1L5
416-366-7511 Fax: 416-367-9869 800-268-8406
info@royalsunalliance.ca
www.royalsunalliance.ca
Company Type: Private
Profile: Automobile & personal property insurance; Marine, small business & custom risk products

SGI Canada
2260 - 11th Ave., Regina, SK S4P 0J9
306-751-1200 800-667-8015
sgiinquiries@sgi.sk.ca
www.sgi.sk.ca
Company Type: Crown
Profile: SGI Canada sells property & casualty insurance products. The company operates in the following provinces: Alberta, Saskatchewan, Manitoba, Ontario, New Brunswick, Nova Scotia, & Prince Edward Island. In Saskatchewan, the compulsory auto insurance program is the Saskatchewan Auto Fund. The Fund operates both the drivers' licensing & the vehicle registration systems. SGI Canada works with motor licence issuing outlets in Saskatchewan, plus insurance brokers in numerous provinces. The company also operates the Coachman Insurance Company in Toronto, & is a partner of the Insurance Company of Prince Edward Island.

State Farm Group Insurance Company
333 First Commerce Dr., Aurora, ON L4G 8A4
905-750-4573 Fax: 905-750-4834
info@statefarm.ca
www.statefarm.ca
Company Type: Private
Profile: Group of insurance companies

Sun Life Financial Inc.
150 King St. West, Toronto, ON M5H 1J9
416-979-9966 Fax: 416-585-7892 877-786-5433
investor.relations@sunlife.com
www.sunlife.com
Ticker Symbol: SLF
Company Type: Public
Profile: Sun Life Financial serves both individuals & corporate customers. It offers customers a broad range of protection & wealth management products & services.

The CUMIS Group Limited
PO Box 5065, 151 North Service Rd., Burlington, ON L7R 4C2
905-632-1221 Fax: 905-632-9412 800-263-9120
customer.service@cumis.com
www.cumis.com
Company Type: Private
Profile: Offices of holding companies; Life, accident, health, fire, marine & casualty insurance; Pension, health, & welfare funds

The Economical Insurance Group
PO Box 2000, 111 Westmount Rd. South, Waterloo, ON N2J 4S4
519-570-8200 Fax: 519-570-8389
800-265-2180www.economicalinsurance.com
Company Type: Private
Profile: Auto, property & casualty insurers

Wawanesa Insurance
#900, 191 Broadway, Winnipeg, MB R3C 3P1
204-985-3923 Fax: 204-942-7724 www.wawanesa.com
Company Type: Private
Profile: Property & casualty insurer

Workers' Compensation Board - Alberta
PO Box 2415, 9912 - 107 St., Edmonton, AB T5J 2S5
780-498-3999 Fax: 780-498-7999 866-922-9221www.wcb.ab.ca
Company Type: Private
Profile: Non-profit disability insurance system

Workplace Safety & Insurance Board of Ontario
200 Front St. West, Toronto, ON M5V 3J1
416-344-1000 Fax: 416-344-4684 800-387-5540
wsibcomm@wsib.on.ca
www.wsib.on.ca
Company Type: Crown
Profile: Oversees workplace safety education & training, provides disability benefits

Machinery

Anchor Lamina Inc.
2590 Ouellette Ave., Windsor, ON N8X 1L7
519-966-4431 Fax: 519-972-6862 800-265-5007
wineng@anchorlamina.com
www.anchorlamina.com
Company Type: Private
Profile: The company is a manufacturer of special dies & tools, die sets, jigs & fixtures, molds, & fabricated plate work.

Atlas Copco Canada Inc.
Atlas Copco Compressors Canada, 30, av Montrose, Dollard-des-Ormeaux, QC H9B 3J9
514-421-4121 Fax: 514-421-1950 800-513-3782
compressors.canada@ca.atlascopco.com
www.atlascopco.com
Company Type: Private
Profile: International industrial company, publicly listed under the laws of Sweden, with locations and contacts across Canada. Products and services include compressed air and gas equipment, generators, construction and mining equipment, industrial tools, assembly systems

ATS Automation Tooling Systems Inc.
PO Box 32100, 250 Royal Oak Rd., Cambridge, ON N3H 4R6
519-653-6500 Fax: 519-653-6533
info@atsautomation.com
www.atsautomation.com
Ticker Symbol: ATA
Company Type: Public
Profile: Producers of turn-key automated manufacturing & test systems, precision components, sub-assemblies, & solar power cells & panels

Bühler Industries Inc.
1260 Clarence Ave., Winnipeg, MB R3T 1T2
204-661-8711 Fax: 204-654-2503 888-524-1003
info@buhler.com
www.buhler.com
Ticker Symbol: BUI
Company Type: Public
Profile: The company manufactures farm machinery & equipment. Agricultural products include Buhler Farm King Grain Handling & Compact Implements, Buhler Versatile Tractors, Buhler Inland Hay Tools, & Buhler Allied Front-End Loaders.

CE Franklin Ltd.
#1900, 300 - 5th Ave. SW, Calgary, AB T2P 3C4
403-531-5600 Fax: 403-234-7698
ho-calgary@cefranklin.com
www.cefranklin.com
Ticker Symbol: CFT
Company Type: Public
Profile: CE Franklin Ltd. provides products & services to the oil & gas industry in Canada. Products include production equipment, pipes, valves, fittings, & flanges.

Collicutt Energy Services Ltd.
7550 Edgar Industrial Dr., Red Deer, AB T4P 3R2
403-358-3200 Fax: 403-358-3210 888-323-2217
inquiries@collicutt.com
www.collicutt.com
Ticker Symbol: COH
Company Type: Public
Profile: Manufacturers of air & gas compressors; Wholesalers of industrial machinery & equipment; Engineering services; Various oil & gas field services

Eagle Precision Technologies Inc.
31 Adams Blvd., Brantford, ON N3S 7V8
519-720-6800 www.eaglept.com
Company Type: Public
Profile: Manufacturers of machine tools, metal forming & cutting types

Enerflex Systems Income Fund
4700 - 47 St. SE, Calgary, AB T2B 3R1
403-236-6800 Fax: 403-236-6816
ir@enerflex.com
www.enerflex.com
Ticker Symbol: EFX
Company Type: Public
Profile: Enerflex Systems Income Fund supplies products & services to the international oil & gas production industry. Products include natural gas compression, power generation, & process equipment. Services include field maintenance & electrical, instrumentation, & controls services. In its operations, Enerflex follows industry & regional environmental guidelines, legislation, & regulations, & conducts environmental audits on a regular basis.

Exco Technologies Limited
130 Spy Ct., 2nd Fl., Markham, ON L3R 5H6
905-477-3065 Fax: 905-477-2449
excotech@compuserve.com
www.excocorp.com
Ticker Symbol: XTC
Company Type: Public
Profile: Manufacturers of special dies & tools, die sets, jigs & fixtures, molds, cutting tools, mach tool accessories, measuring devices, various industrial & commercial machinery & equipment, motor vehicle parts & accessories

Foremost Industries LP
1225 - 64 Ave. NE, Calgary, AB T2E 8P9
403-295-5800 Fax: 403-295-5832 800-661-9190
investorrelations@foremost.ca
www.foremost.ca
Ticker Symbol: FMO.UN
Company Type: Public
Profile: Foremost Income Fund is an unincorporated, open-ended unit trust, which holds manufacturing businesses. Through these holdings, Foremost is involved in the design, manufacture, sale, & service of oil treating systems, drilling equipment, petroleum storage tanks, gas separation equipment, compression equipment, pressure vessels, & off-road vehicles. Foremost Industries Ltd. is the administrator of the Fund.

Groupe Laperrière & Verreault inc
Le Bourg du Fleuve Bldg., #420, 25, rue Des Forges, Trois-Rivières, QC G9A 6A7
819-371-8265 Fax: 819-373-4439
courrier@glv.com
www.glv.com
Ticker Symbol: GLV
Company Type: Public
Profile: Manufacturers of general industrial machinery & equipment, paper industries machinery; Special trade installation/erection of building equipment

Husky Injection Molding Systems Ltd.
500 Queen St. South, Bolton, ON L7E 5S5
905-951-5000 Fax: 905-951-5337 888-884-8759
info@husky.ca
www.husky.ca
Company Type: Public
Profile: Manufacturers of special dies & tools, die sets, jigs & fixtures, molds, machine tools, metal cutting types; Wholesalers of various durable goods

IBM Canada Ltd.
3600 Steeles Ave. East, Markham, ON L3R 9Z7
905-316-5000 Fax: 905-316-2535 800-426-4968
canada_int@vnet.ibm.com
www.ibm.com/ca/
Company Type: Private
Profile: Manufacturers of electronic computers, & calculating & accounting machines; Repair shops & various related services; equipment rental & leasing

Ingersoll Rand Canada Inc.
1076 Lakeshore Rd. E., Mississauga, ON L5E 1E4
905-403-1800 Fax: 416-213-4616
IRS&SCanada@irco.com
www.irco.com
Company Type: Private
Profile: Manufacturers of general industrial machinery & equipment, pumps & pumping equipment, various special industry machinery, automatic controls regulating environment & appliances

Komatsu America Corp.
160 boul de l'Industrie, Candiac, QC J5R 1J3
450-659-1961 Fax: 450-659-3557 www.komatsuamerica.com; www.komatsu.com
Company Type: Private
Profile: Manufacturer of construction, mining and compact construction equipment, with distributors across Canada

Luxell Technologies Inc.
2145 Meadowpine Blvd., Mississauga, ON L5N 6R8
905-363-0325 Fax: 905-363-0336
info@luxell.com; careers@luxell.com
www.luxell.com
Company Type: Public
Profile: The company is engaged in the research & development of flat panel display enhancing technologies. Business activities are focussed on products & services for defence & aero-space applications, such as radar warning devices, field communications systems, & navigational displays.

NCR Canada Ltd.
6865 Century Ave., Mississauga, ON L5N 2E2
905-826-9000 www.ncr.com
Company Type: Private
Profile: Manufacturers of electronic computers, manifold business forms, calculating & accounting machines; Computer integrated systems design

Pitney Bowes Canada Ltd.
#200, 314 Harwood Ave., Ajax, ON L1S 2J1
800-672-6937
MrBowes.Canada@pb.com
www.pitneybowes.ca
Company Type: Private
Profile: Pitney Bowes Canada's activities focus upon mailing technology. Products include innovations that copy, scan, print, fax, insert, & seal. With Pitney Bowes' services, companies are able to manage the flow of information, mail, documents, & packages.

Reko International Group Inc.
5390 Brendan Lane, Oldcastle, ON N0R 1L0
519-737-6974 Fax: 519-737-6975
vpf@rekointl.com
www.rekointl.com
Ticker Symbol: REK
Company Type: Public
Profile: Manufacturers of special dies & tools, die sets, molds, jigs & fixtures; Engineering services

RPM Tech Inc.
184, rte 138, Cap-Santé, QC G0A 1L0
418-285-1811 Fax: 418-285-4289 800-463-3882
info@grouperpmtech.com
www.grouperpmtech.com
Ticker Symbol: RP
Company Type: Public
Profile: Manufacturers of construction machinery & equipment, industrial trucks, tractors, trailers & stackers, mining machinery & equipment; Repair shops & various related services; Wholesalers of farm & garden machinery & equipment

Skyjack Inc.
55 Campbell Rd., Guelph, ON N1H 1B9
519-837-0888 Fax: 519-837-8104 800-265-2738
skyjack@skyjack.com; service@skyjack.com
www.skyjackinc.com
Company Type: Public
Profile: Skyjack Inc. designs, manufactures, sells, & services self propelled aerial work platforms.

Strongco Income Fund
1640 Enterprise Rd., Mississauga, ON L4W 4L4
905-565-1899 Fax: 905-565-1907
info@strongco.com
www.strongco.com
Ticker Symbol: SQP.UN
Company Type: Public
Profile: Strongco Income Fund is involved in multi-line equipment distribution in Canada. Mobile industrial equipment is sold, rented, & serviced. The equipment is used in the following sectors: mining, forestry, construction, road building, & utilities. Business divisions include Strongco Equipment/Cranes & Strongco Engineered Systems. Among the equipment manufacturers represented by Strongco are Cedarapids, Case, Volvo, & Manitowoc.

Tesco Corporation
6204 - 6A St. SE, Calgary, AB T2H 2B7
403-692-5700 Fax: 403-692-5710
investor@tescocorp.com
www.tescocorp.com
Ticker Symbol: TESO
Company Type: Public
Profile: Tesco Corporation specializes in the design, manufacture, & service of technology. The company's technology based solutions are used in the upstream energy industry.

Toromont Industries Ltd.
Bldg. B, PO Box 5511, 3131 Hwy. 7 West, Concord, ON L4K 1B7
416-667-5511 Fax: 416-667-5555
pjewer@toromont.com
www.toromont.com
Ticker Symbol: TIH
Company Type: Public
Profile: The company is engaged in the design, engineering, & sale of specialized equipment & other heavy equipment. Its business segments are the Equipment Group & the Compression Group. Toromont Industries has implemented environmental practices, such as technology to recycle energy, reduce greenhouse gas emissions, & cleanse oil of contaminants.

Weir Canada Inc.
2360 Millrace Ct., Mississauga, ON L4N 1W2
905-812-7100 Fax: 905-812-1749
info@weirmaricas.com
www.weirservices.com
Company Type: Private
Profile: Manufacturers of pumps & pumping equipment, valves & pipe fittings, speed changers, industrial high-speed drives & gears, industrial trucks, tractors, trailers & stackers; Wholesalers of construction & mining machinery & equipment; Wholesalers of industrial machinery & equipment

Wenzel Downhole Tools Ltd.
#1000, 717 - 7th Ave. SW, Calgary, AB T2P 0Z3
403-262-3050 Fax: 403-265-8154
handre@wenzel-downhole.com
www.downhole.com
Ticker Symbol: WZL
Company Type: Public
Profile: Manufacturers of oil & gas field machinery & equipment; Wholesalers of construction & mining machinery & equipment; Equipment rental & leasing

Westport Innovations Inc.
#101, 1750 West 75th Ave., Vancouver, BC V6P 6G2
604-718-2000 Fax: 604-718-2001
info@westport.com
www.westport.com
Ticker Symbol: WPT
Company Type: Public
Profile: Develops technologies to allow commercial engine industry to shift from oil-based to gaseous fuels

Xerox Canada Inc.
5650 Yonge St., Toronto, ON M2M 4G7
416-229-3769 Fax: 416-229-6826 800-275-9376www.xerox.ca
Company Type: Public
Profile: To improve work processes, Xerox Canada provides document technologies, products, & services. The company has created waste-free products, & built in waste-free facilities, as part of its continuing remanufacturing initiatives.

Manufacturing, Miscellaneous

AFG Industries Ltd.
PO Box 628, 18544 - 9th Concession, Mount Albert, ON L0G 1M0
905-738-9400 Fax: 905-738-1177 800-661-7214www.afg.com
Company Type: Private
Profile: Manufacturers of flat glass, glass products (made of purchased glass); Wholesalers of construction materials

AirBoss of America Corp.
16441 Yonge St., Newmarket, ON L3X 2G8
905-751-1188 Fax: 905-751-1101
info@airbossofamerica.com
www.airbossofamerica.com
Ticker Symbol: BOS
Company Type: Public
Profile: The company is a developer, manufacturer, & seller of rubber compounds & specialty rubber moulded products. Products are used in the industrial, transportation, & defense industries.

Amcor PET Packaging-North America
910 Central Pkwy. West, Mississauga, ON L5C 2V5
905-275-1592 Fax: 905-275-1061
brigitte.sigwarth@amcor.com
www.amcor.com
Company Type: Private
Profile: Manufacturers of plastics packaging, rigid plastics & plastube packaging

Amisco Industries Ltd.
33 - 5e rue, L'Islet, QC G0R 2C0
800-361-6360 Fax: 800-232-6614
info@amisco.com
www.amisco.com
Ticker Symbol: IAC
Company Type: Public
Profile: Manufacturers of metal & wood household furniture

Armstrong World Industries Canada Ltd
6911, boul Decarie, Montréal, QC H3W 3E5
514-733-9981 www.armstrong.com
Company Type: Private
Profile: Manufacturers of linoleum, asphalted-felt-base, & other hard floorings, & mineral wool; Wholesalers of construction materials & home furnishings; Miscellaneous nonmetallic minerals mining & quarrying

ART Advanced Research Technologies Inc.
2300, boul Alfred-Nobel, Montréal, QC H4S 2A4
514-832-0777 Fax: 514-832-0778
info@art.ca
www.art.ca
Ticker Symbol: ARA
Company Type: Public
Profile: Canadian medical device company specializing in optical molecular imaging products for the healthcare & pharmaceutical industries.

Bestar Inc.
4220, rue Villeneuve, Lac-Mégantic, QC G6B 2C3
Fax: 819-583-5370 888-823-7827
service@bestar.ca
www.bestar.ca
Ticker Symbol: BES
Company Type: Public
Profile: Manufacturers of wood household furniture, wood tv, radio, phonograph & sewing machine cabinets; Wholesalers of furniture

Brampton Brick Limited
225 Wanless Dr., Brampton, ON L7A 1E9
905-840-1011 Fax: 905-840-1535
investor.relations@bramptonbrick.com
www.bramptonbrick.com
Ticker Symbol: BBL
Company Type: Public
Profile: Brampton Brick Limited manufactures the following products: concrete interlocking paving stone, clay brick, retaining walls, & related items. In Ontario & Nova Scotia, the company operates facilities for the destruction of biomedical & pharmaceutical waste. Brampton Brick Limited is an ISO 9001 certified company.

BW Technologies Ltd.
2840 - 2 Ave. SE, Calgary, AB T2A 7X9
403-248-9226 Fax: 403-273-3708 800-663-4164
info@gasmonitors.com
www.gasmonitors.com
Company Type: Public
Profile: Manufacturers of various measuring & controlling devices; Wholesalers of industrial machinery & equipment

Camco Inc.
PO Box 5345, #300, 5420 North Service Rd., Burlington, ON L7R 5B6
905-315-2300 Fax: 905-315-2451 888-566-6667
InvestorRelations@mabe.ca
www.geappliances.ca
Company Type: Public
Profile: Manufacturers of household cooking equipment, household refrigerators & home & farm freezers, household laundry equipment, various household appliances; Wholesalers of electrical appliances, television & radio sets

CGC Inc.
350 Burnhamthorpe Rd. West, 5th Fl., Mississauga, ON L5B 3J1
905-803-5600 Fax: 905-803-5688 800-565-6607
ckane@cgcinc.com
www.cgcinc.com
Company Type: Private
Profile: Manufacturers and distributors of gypsum wallboard products, interior finishing materials & suspended acoustical ceilings

Chevron Canada Ltd
#1500, 1050 West Pender St., Vancouver, BC V6E 3T4
604-668-5300 Fax: 604-668-5559 800-663-1650
cclinfo@chevron.com
www.chevron.ca
Company Type: Private
Profile: Manufacturers of petroleum refining; Wholesalers of petroleum, petroleum products, & bulk stations & terminals

CVTech Group Inc.
1975, rue Jean-Bérimens Michaud, Drummondville, QC J2C 0H2
819-479-7771 Fax: 819-479-8887
a.laramee@cvtech.ca
www.groupecvtech.com
Ticker Symbol: CVT
Company Type: Public
Profile: Through its subsidiaries, CVTech Group designs, manufactures, & sells continuously variable power transmission systems. The company's subsidiary, Thiro Ltd., is a general contracting firm, which specializes in the maintenance of transmission & distribution lines, electrical power houses, & substations.

Dorel Industries Inc.
#300, 1255, av Greene, Montréal, QC H3Z 2A4
514-934-3034 Fax: 514-934-9379
info@dorel.com; ir@dorel.com
www.dorel.com
Ticker Symbol: DII
Company Type: Public
Profile: Dorel Industries Inc. designs, manufactures, & markets juvenile products, bicycles, & home furnishings. The company

has facilities in seventeen countries, & sells its products throughout the world.

Dynetek Industries Ltd.
4410 - 46 Ave. SE, Calgary, AB T2B 3N7
403-720-0262 Fax: 403-720-0263 888-396-3835
contactus@dynetek.com
www.dynetek.com
Ticker Symbol: DNK
Company Type: Public
Profile: Manufacturer and supplier of lightweight storage cyliners for compressed gases, and complete systems.

Empire Industries Ltd.
717 Jarvis Ave., Winnipeg, MB R2W 3B4
204-589-9300 Fax: 204-582-8057 www.empind.com
Ticker Symbol: EIL
Company Type: Public
Profile: Empire Industries Ltd. is a designer & manufacturer of various industrial products & amusement park rides. The company is also engaged in erecting structural steel & offering structural & construction engineering services. Empire Industries Ltd. has a Health, Safety, & Environmental Policy, & adheres to regulations. Some of Empire Industries Ltd.'s subsidiaries include the following: Dynamic Structures, Empire Construction Services, Empire Iron Works, George Third & Son, Hopkins Steel Works, Lemax Machine & Welding, Parr Metal Fabricators, Sorge's Welding Ltd., Somerset Engineering, Tornado Technologies Inc., & Ward Industrial Equipment.

Essroc Canada Inc.
PO Box 620, Highway 49 South, Picton, ON K0K 2T0
613-476-3233 Fax: 613-476-8130
info@essroc.com
www.essroc.com
Company Type: Private
Profile: Manufacturers of cement and other building materials

General Donlee Income Fund
9 Fenmar Dr., Toronto, ON M9L 1L5
416-743-4417 Fax: 416-746-8998
info@generaldonlee.com
www.generaldonlee.com
Ticker Symbol: GDI.UN
Company Type: Public
Profile: General Donlee Income Fund is a trust that holds the securities of General Donlee Limited. General Donlee Limited manufactures precision-machined products. Products are used by the military, commercial, & general aviation industries, as well as the industrial products & power generation industries.

Global Alumina Corp.
245 Park Ave., 38th Fl., New York, NY
212-351-0000 Fax: 212-351-0001
info@globalalumina.com
www.globalalumina.com
Ticker Symbol: GLA.U
Company Type: Public
Profile: Incorporated in New Brunswick in 2004, Global Alumina is involved in alumina production & sales. It is developing an alumina refinery in the bauxite-rich region of in the Republic of Guinea.

GSW Inc.
599 Hill St. West, Fergus, ON N1M 2X1
519-843-1610 Fax: 519-787-5500
gswinfo@gsw-wh.com
www.gsw-wh.com
Company Type: Public
Profile: Offices of holding companies; Manufacturers of various household appliances, air-conditioning, warm air heating, refrigeration equipment, pumps & pumping equipment, fabricated plate work, various plastics products

Hanwei Energy Services Corp.
#902, 595 Howe St., Vancouver, BC V6C 2T5
604-685-2239 Fax: 604-677-5579
info@hanweienergy.com
www.hanweienergy.com
Ticker Symbol: HE
Company Type: Public
Profile: Hanwei Energy Services develops, manufactures, & sells high pressure fiberglass reinforced plastic products. Products are used mainly in the global energy sector. The company owns interest in Daqing Harvest Longwall High Pressure Pipe Co. Ltd. in China.

Heroux-Devtek Inc.
Tour Est, #658, 1111, rue Saint-Charles ouest, Longueuil, QC J4K 5G4
450-679-3330 Fax: 450-679-3666
ir@herouxdevtek.com
www.herouxdevtek.com
Ticker Symbol: HRX
Company Type: Public
Profile: Heroux-Devtek Inc. develops, designs, manufactures, repairs, & overhauls systems & components. The company has three divisions: The Landing Gear Division; The Aerostructure Division; & The Gas Turbine Components Division. Products are used in the aerospace market in both the commercial & military sectors, & in the industrial market for power generation & other machinery applications.

Holcim (Canada) Inc.
2300 Steeles Ave. West, 4th Fl., Concord, ON L4K 5X6
905-532-3000 Fax: 905-761-7200
communications-ca@holcim.com
www.holcim.ca
Company Type: Private
Profile: Holcim (Canada) Inc. is a producer & supplier of aggregates, concrete, & construction materials. It provides products & services for the construction industry throughout Canada. The building materials & construction company's divisions are Dufferin in Ontario & Demix in Québec. From Holcim's plant in Mississauga, Ontario, cement is shipped throughout Ontario, & to western Canada & the United States. From the Holcim plant in Joliette, Québec, cement is sent to locations in Québec, Atlantic Canada, & the United States.

Imax Corporation
Sheridan Science & Technology Park, 2525 Speakman Dr., Mississauga, ON L5K 1B1
905-403-6500 Fax: 905-403-6474
info@imax.com
www.imax.com
Ticker Symbol: IMX
Company Type: Public
Profile: Manufacturers of photographic equipment & supplies; Motion picture & video tape production & distribution; Motion picture theatres

INSCAPE Corporation
67 Toll Rd., Holland Landing, ON L9N 1H2
905-836-7676 Fax: 905-836-6000
info@inscapesolutions.com
www.inscapesolutions.com
Ticker Symbol: INQ
Company Type: Public
Profile: Manufacturers of wood & non-wood office furniture, wood & non-wood office & store fixtures & partitions; Wholesalers of furniture & office equipment

IPL Inc.
140, rue Commerciale, Saint-Damien, QC G0R 2Y0
418-789-2880 Fax: 418-789-2185 600-463-7083
info-ipl@ipl-plastics.com
www.ipl-plastics.com
Ticker Symbol: IPI
Company Type: Public
Profile: IPL Inc. specializes in manufacturing injection & extrusion moulded plastic products. Products, such as material & handling crates & rigid packaging containers & pails, are used by the following industries: recycling, automotive, transportation, construction, petrochemical, chemical, food, fishing, & forestry. The company is an ISO 14001 certified organization

JDS Uniphase Canada Ltd.
#210, 362 Terry Fox Dr., Kanata, ON K2K 2P5
613-599-4069 Fax: 613-271-2627 www.jdsu.com
Ticker Symbol: JDU
Company Type: Public
Profile: Designs & manufactures products for fiberoptic communications

Johnson Controls Ltd.
100 Townline Rd., Tillsonburg, ON N4G 2R7
519-842-5971 Fax: 519-842-3443 www.jci.com
Company Type: Private
Profile: Special trade contracting in plumbing, heating & air-conditioning; Manufacturers of automatic controls regulating environments & appliances

Lear Canada Ltd.
PO Box 9758, 530 Manitou Dr., Kitchener, ON N2G 4C2
519-895-1600 Fax: 519-895-3248 www.lear.com
Company Type: Private
Profile: Designs, tests & produces automotive interiors: seat systems, electronic products and electrical distribution systems

MAAX
600, rte Cameron, Sainte-Marie-de-Beauce, QC G6E 1B2
Fax: 418-387-8055 418-386-3487www.maax.com
Company Type: Private
Profile: MAAX is a designer of bathroom products, such as bathtubs, showers, & medicine cabinets.

Magna International Inc.
337 Magna Dr., Aurora, ON L4G 7K1
905-726-2462 Fax: 905-726-7164 www.magna.com
Ticker Symbol: MG.A
Company Type: Public
Profile: The automotive supplier designs, develops, & manufactures automotive systems, assemblies, modules, & components. Magna also engineers & assembles complete vehicles to sell to original equipment manufacturers of cars & trucks.

McCoy Corporation
#301, 9618 - 42 Ave., Edmonton, AB T6E 5Y4
780-453-8451 Fax: 780-453-8756 www.mccoycorporation.ca
Ticker Symbol: MCB
Company Type: Public
Profile: McCoy Corporation serves the transportation industry & the oil & gas sector. The following are some of the products & services provided by McCoy Corporation: trailer mounted hydrovac & vacuum tanks; heavy duty trailer manufacturing; parts & service for heavy-duty trucks & trailers; hydraulic power tongs for rigs; & coatings for the prevention of corrosion.

Nestlé Purina Petcare Company
2500 Royal Windsor Dr., Mississauga, ON L5J 1K8
905-822-1611 Fax: 905-855-5700 800-268-5345www.purina.ca
Company Type: Private
Profile: The pet care company provides the following brands in North America: Puppy Chow, Dog Chow, Alpo, Busy Bones, T-Bonz, Beggin Strips, Beneful, Kitten Chow, Cat Chow, Luvs, Friskies, Fancy Feast, Maxx Multi Cat, Kitty Litter, Purina Veterinary Diets, Pro Plan, & Purina One.

NovAtel Inc.
1120 - 68 Ave. NE, Calgary, AB T2E 8S5
403-295-4500 Fax: 403-295-4501 800-668-2835
sales@novatel.ca; support@novatel.com
www.novatel.com
Company Type: Private
Profile: NovAtel Inc. is an ISO 9001 certified company which provides Global Navigation Satellite System components & subsystems. Products include irmware, receivers, antennas, & enclosures, which are integrated into high precision positioning applications. Applications include Geographical Information System (GIS) mapping, surveying, port automation, & precision agriculture machine guidance.

Opta Minerals Inc.
PO Box 260, 407 Parkside Dr., Waterdown, ON L0R 2H0
905-689-7361 Fax: 905-689-0604 888-689-6661
info@optaminerals.com
www.optaminerals.com
Ticker Symbol: OPM
Company Type: Public
Profile: Opta Minerals Inc. is engaged in the recycling, manufacturing, production, & distribution of industrial minerals, specialty sands, & related products. The company's products are used mainly in the following industries: steel, foundry, roof shingle granules, loose abrasive cleaning, & municipal water filtration. Opta Minerals production facilities are located in Ontario, Quebec, Michigan, New York, Louisiana, Virginia, Maryland, South Carolina, Indiana, Ohio, & Texas, as well as France & Slovakia.

Owens-Corning Canada LP
3450 McNicoll Ave., Toronto, ON M1V 1Z5
416-292-4000 Fax: 416-412-6719 800-438-7465
non-managementdirectors@owenscorning.com
www.owenscorning.ca
Ticker Symbol: OC (NYSE: OC)
Company Type: Private
Profile: The home building products company is an innovator of glass fiber materials & glass fiber insulation. Glass fiber materials are used in applications such as automobiles, aircraft, boats, computers, telecommunications cables, & appliances.

Palliser Furniture Ltd
70 Lexington Park, Winnipeg, MB R2G 4H2
204-988-5600 Fax: 204-663-1776 www.palliser.com
Company Type: Private
Profile: Manufacturers of wood household furniture

Polyair Inter Pack Inc.
330 Humberline Dr., Toronto, ON M9W 1R5
416-679-6600 Fax: 416-740-7356 888-765-9247
marketing@polyair.com
www.polyair.com
Ticker Symbol: PPK
Company Type: Public
Profile: Manufacturers of plastic foam products, various plastics products, packaging paper & coated & laminated plastics film; Wholesalers of plastics materials & basic forms & shapes

PreMD Inc.
#242, 4211 Yonge St., Toronto, ON M2P 2A9
416-222-3449 Fax: 416-222-4533
info@premdinc.com

www.premdinc.com
Company Type: Public
Profile: Acquires & develops technologies for non-invasive predictive medical tests that detect early stage cardiovascular disease and cancer

Premier Tech Ltd.
International Corporate Office, 1, av Premier, Rivière-du-Loup, QC G5R 6C1
418-867-8883 Fax: 418-862-6642
info@premiertech.com
www.premiertech.com
Ticker Symbol: PTL
Company Type: Private
Profile: Premier Tech's develops, manufactures, & markets innovative solutions in the following areas: horticulture & agriculture, environmental technologies, & industrial equipment.

Royal Group, Inc.
1 Royal Gate Blvd., Woodbridge, ON L4L 8Z7
905-264-0701 Fax: 905-264-0702
www.royalbuildingproducts.com
Company Type: Private
Profile: Royal Group Inc. produces & markets vinyl-based construction, building, & home improvement products. The company consists of the following divisions: Royal Building Products, Royal Pipe Systems, Royal Mouldings, Royal Window & Door Profiles, & Royal Outdoor Products. Royal Group has locations in both Canada & the Unitd States. Customers include construction, renovation, & remodeling industries.

SACO Smartvision Inc
7809 Trans Canada Hwy, Montréal, QC H4S 1L3
514-745-0310 Fax: 514-745-0315
info@smartvision.com
www.smartvision.com
Ticker Symbol: SSV
Company Type: Public
Profile: Manufacturers of photographic equipment & supplies

Shermag Inc.
2171, rue King ouest, Sherbrooke, QC J1J 2G1
819-566-1515 Fax: 819-566-4104
info@shermag.com
www.shermag.com
Ticker Symbol: SMG
Company Type: Public
Profile: Manufacturers of wood household furniture, sawmills & general planing mills

Siemens Canada Limited
2185 Derry Rd. West, Mississauga, ON L5N 7A6
905-819-8000 Fax: 905-819-5777 888-303-3353
corporate.communications@siemens.com
www.siemens.ca
Company Type: Private
Profile: Provides innovative products and solutions in automation & control, power, transportation, medical, information & communications, & lighting

Sigma Industries Inc.
Tour Belle Cour, Place de la Cité, #380, 2590, boul Laurier, 3e étage, Québec, QC G1V 4M6
418-780-3903 Fax: 418-780-3909 www.sigmaventures.ca
Ticker Symbol: SIC
Company Type: Public
Profile: Sigma Industries Inc. manufactures plastic composites & metal products. Its markets include machinery, heavy duty truck, coach, bus & transit, train & subway, forestry, agriculture, & alternative energy.

Tarkett Inc.
1001, rue Yamaska est, Farnham, QC J2N 1J7
450-293-3173 Fax: 450-293-6644
800-465-4030www.tarkett-floors.com
Company Type: Private
Profile: Manufacturers of linoleum, felt-base & other vinyl floorings, hardwood dimension & flooring mills; Wholesalers of home furnishings

Teknion Corporation
1150 Flint Rd., Toronto, ON M3J 2J5
416-661-3370 Fax: 416-661-7970
info.can@teknion.com
www.teknion.com
Ticker Symbol: TKN
Company Type: Public
Profile: Manufacturers of wood & non-wood office furniture, public building & related furniture, wood & non-wood office & store fixtures, partitions, shelving etc.; Wholesalers of furniture

Trojan Technologies Inc.
3020 Gore Rd., London, ON N5V 4T7
519-457-3400 Fax: 519-457-3030
888-220-6118www.trojanuv.com
Company Type: Private
Profile: Trojan Technologies develops technology-based, environmentally responsible solutions to the water related problems of municipalities, industries, & residential consumers. For example, Trojan manufactures ultraviolet ray equipment for residential water disinfection applications.

VSM MedTech Ltd.
9 Burbidge St., Coquitlam, BC V6K 7B2
604-472-2300 Fax: 604-472-2301 877-876-8484
corp@vsmmedtech.com
www.vsmmedtech.com
Ticker Symbol: VSM
Company Type: Public
Profile: Produces diagnostic medical devices for the evaluation & treatment of neurological disorders & cardiovascular disease

Winpak Ltd.
100 Saulteaux Cres., Winnipeg, MB R3J 3T3
204-889-1015 Fax: 204-888-7806
info@winpak.com
www.winpak.com
Ticker Symbol: WPK
Company Type: Public
Profile: Manufacturing & distributing packaging materials & related packaging machines are the chief activities of Winpak Ltd. Products are used to protect perishable foods & beverages, as well as in health care applications. The company's facilities are located in Canada & the United States. Its services are offered in North America, Latin America, the Pacific Rim countries, & Europe.

Mining

Agnico-Eagle Mines Limited
#400, 145 King St. East, Toronto, ON M5C 2Y7
416-947-1212 Fax: 416-367-4681
info@agnico-eagle.com
www.agnico-eagle.com
Ticker Symbol: AEM
Company Type: Public
Profile: Agnico-Eagle Mines Limited is an international gold production company, which carries out exploration & development activities. Operations are conducted in Canada, the United States, Mexico, & Finland.

Alamos Gold Inc.
#2010, 120 Adelaide St. West, Toronto, ON M5H 1T1
416-368-9932 Fax: 416-368-2934 866-788-8801
info@alamosgold.com
www.alamosgold.com
Ticker Symbol: AGI
Company Type: Public
Profile: The mining company owns the Salamandra group of concessions. The group includes the Mulatos gold deposit in Sonora, Mexico.

Altius Minerals Corporation
PO Box 385, #300, 53 Bond St., St. John's, NL A1C 5J9
709-576-3440 Fax: 709-576-3441 877-576-2209
info@altiusminerals.com
www.altiusminerals.com
Company Type: Public
Profile: Altius Minerals Corporation is a natural resource project generation & royalty business. The company has royalty interest or equity stakes in several natural resource projects.

Amerigo Resources Ltd.
Three Bentall Centre, PO Box 49298, #3083, 595 Burrard St., Vancouver, BC V7X 1L3
604-681-2802 Fax: 604-682-2802
questions@amerigoresources.com
www.amerigoresources.com
Ticker Symbol: ARG
Company Type: Public
Profile: Amerigo Resources Ltd. specializes in the production of copper & molybdenum concentrates. The company is active in Chile. Amerigo's wholly-owned subsidiary is Minera Valle Central.

Andean American Mining Corp.
#1340, 1090 West Georgia St., Vancouver, BC V6E 3V7
604-681-6186 Fax: 604-681-3652
IR@andeanamerican.com
www.andeanamerican.com
Ticker Symbol: AAG
Company Type: Public
Profile: Metal mining in gold, silver & copper ores

Anvil Mining Limited
#2001, 1, Place Ville Marie. 20e étage, Montréal, QC H3B 2C4
514-448-6664 Fax: 514-448-6665
robertl@anvilmining.com
www.anvilmining.com
Ticker Symbol: AVM
Company Type: Public
Profile: The copper & silver producer focuses upon the exploration, acquisition, development, & mining of mineral properties.

Archon Minerals Ltd
#2801, 323 Jervis St., Vancouver, BC V6C 3P8
604-682-3303 Fax: 604-682-2919
sblusson@shaw.ca
Ticker Symbol: ACS
Company Type: Public
Profile: Mining & quarrying of miscellaneous nonmetallic minerals

Arehada Mining Limited
#1000, 36 Toronto St., Toronto, ON M5C 2C5
416-350-5133 Fax: 416-350-3510
info@arehada.com
www.arehadamining.com
Ticker Symbol: AHD
Company Type: Public
Profile: Arehada Mining Limited explores, develops, extracts, & refines base metals. Zinc & lead concentrates are produced & sold to smelters. Operations are carried out in Dongwuzhumuqinqi, Inner Mongolia, China.

Arizona Star Resource Corp.
Bldg. 152, #2700, 401 Bay St., Toronto, ON M5H 2Y4
416-359-7800 Fax: 416-359-7801
pparisotto@coniston.ca
www.arizonastar.com
Ticker Symbol: AZS
Company Type: Public
Profile: Metal mining gold, copper & miscellaneous metal ores

Ashton Mining of Canada Inc.
#116, 980 West 1st St., North Vancouver, BC V7P 3N4
604-983-7750 Fax: 604-987-7107 **Ticker Symbol:** ACA
Company Type: Public
Profile: Mining & quarrying of miscellaneous nonmetallic minerals

Atacama Minerals Corp.
#2101, 885 West Georgia St., Vancouver, BC V6C 3E8
604-689-7842 Fax: 604-689-4250
atacama@namdo.com
www.atacama.com
Ticker Symbol: AAM
Company Type: Public
Profile: Mining & quarrying of potash, soda & borate minerals

Aurizon Mines Ltd.
#3120, 666 Burrard St., Vancouver, BC V6C 2X8
604-687-6600 Fax: 604-687-3932
info@aurizon.com
www.aurizon.com
Ticker Symbol: ARZ
Company Type: Public
Profile: Aurizon Mines Ltd. specializes in gold exploration & production. Activity takes places in the Abitibi region of northwestern Quebec.

Azure Resources Corporation
#502, 815 Hornby St., Vancouver, BC V6Z 2E6
604-684-2401 Fax: 604-684-2407
azu@azure-res.com
www.azure-res.com
Ticker Symbol: TMI
Company Type: Public
Profile: Azure Resources Corporation is engaged in the exploration of copper & gold & the production of diamonds. A copper & gold project is located in Gilgit, Pakistan, & a diamond exploration project is situated in Kokong, Botswana.

Banro Corporation
First Canadian Place, PO Box 419, #7070, 100 King St. West, Toronto, ON M5X 1E3
416-366-2221 Fax: 416-366-7722
info@banro.com
www.banro.com
Ticker Symbol: BAA
Company Type: Public
Profile: Metal mining in gold ores

Barrick Gold Corporation
TD Canada Trust Tower, Brookfield Place, PO Box 212, #3700, 161 Bay St., Toronto, ON M5J 2S1
416-861-9911 Fax: 416-861-2492 800-720-7415
investor@barrick.com
www.barrick.com

Ticker Symbol: ABX
Company Type: Public
Profile: The gold mining company explores, develops, & operates mines in five continents.

Breakwater Resources Ltd.
#950, 95 Wellington St. West, Toronto, ON M5J 2N7
416-363-4798 Fax: 416-363-1315
investorinfo@breakwater.ca
www.breakwater.ca
Ticker Symbol: BWR
Company Type: Public
Profile: Breakwater Resources' area of expertise is the acquisition, exploration, development, & mining of base metal & precious metal deposits. Operations are carried out at the Myra Falls mine in British Columbia, the El Mochito mine in Honduras, & the El Toqui mine in Chile.

Caledonia Mining Corporation
#1201, 67 Yonge St., Toronto, ON M5E 1JB
416-369-9835 Fax: 416-369-0449
info@caledoniamining.com
www.caledoniamining.com
Ticker Symbol: CAL
Company Type: Public
Profile: Metal mining in copper, gold, silver & ferroalloy ores; Mining & quarrying in miscellaneous nonmetallic minerals

Cameco Corporation
2121 - 11 St. West, Saskatoon, SK S7M 1J3
306-956-6200 Fax: 306-956-6201 www.cameco.com
Ticker Symbol: CCO
Company Type: Public
Profile: The uranium producer conducts its exploration activities in North America, Australia, & Asia. Cameco Corp. holds a majority interest in Centerra Gold Inc. & a 31.6% interest in Bruce Power Limited Partnership.

Campbell Resources Inc.
#1101, 80 Berlioz Street, Montréal, QC H3E 1N9
514-766-4517 Fax: 514-765-9810
afortier@campbellresources.com
www.campbellresources.com
Ticker Symbol: CCH
Company Type: Public
Profile: Metal mining in gold & copper ores

Canadian Royalties Inc.
2772 chemin Sullivan, Val-d'Or, QC J0Y 2N0
819-824-1030 Fax: 819-824-1003 866-219-4678
info@canadianroyalties.com
www.canadianroyalties.com
Ticker Symbol: CZZ
Company Type: Public
Profile: Nickel exploration in Canada

Canadian Salt Company Limited
#700, 755, boul Saint-Jean, Montréal, QC H9R 5M9
514-630-0900 Fax: 514-694-2451
tferrara@windsorsalt.com
www.windsorsalt.com
Company Type: Private
Profile: Manufacturing and sale of salt & salt products

Canarc Resource Corp.
#301, 700 West Pender St., Vancouver, BC V6C 1G8
604-685-9700 Fax: 604-685-9744 877-684-9700
invest@canarc.net
www.canarc.net
Ticker Symbol: CCM
Company Type: Public
Profile: Metal mining in gold & silver ores

Capstone Mining Corp.
#1980, 1055 West Hastings St., Vancouver, BC V6E 2E9
604-684-8894 Fax: 604-688-2180 866-684-8894
info@capstonemining.com
www.capstonemining.com
Ticker Symbol: CS
Company Type: Public
Profile: Capstone Mining Corp. operates silver, zinc, lead, & copper mines. Activities are focused in Zacatecas State, Mexico.

Chapleau Resources Ltd.
#104, 135 - 10th Ave. South, Cranbrook, BC V1C 2N1
250-489-5156 Fax: 250-489-5185
info@chapleauresources.com
www.chapleauresources.com
Ticker Symbol: CHI
Company Type: Public
Profile: Acquisition, exploration & development of gold properties

Claude Resources Inc.
#200, 224 - 4th Ave. South, Saskatoon, SK S7K 5M5
306-668-7505 Fax: 306-668-7500
clauderesources@clauderesources.com
www.clauderesources.com
Ticker Symbol: CRJ
Company Type: Public
Profile: Metal mining in gold ores; Crude petroleum, natural gas & natural gas liquids extraction

Cogema Resources Inc.
PO Box 9204, 817 - 45 St. West, Saskatoon, SK S7K 3X5
306-343-4500 Fax: 306-653-3883 888-992-7382
publicrelations@cogema.ca
www.cogema.ca
Company Type: Private
Profile: Metal mining in uranium, radium, vanadium & gold ores

Continental Minerals Corporation
#1020, 800 West Pender St., Vancouver, BC V6C 2V6
604-684-6365 Fax: 604-684-8092
info@hdgold.com
www.hdgold.com/kmk/home.asp
Ticker Symbol: KMK
Company Type: Public
Profile: Exploration & mining company; Engaged in the advancement of the Xietongmen Project in Tibet, China

Crew Gold
#615, 800 West Pender St., Vancouver, BC V6C 2V6
604-681-8003 Fax: 604-662-3180
800-444-9284www.crewgroup.com
Ticker Symbol: CRU
Company Type: Public
Profile: Offices of holding companies; Mining & quarrying of gold

Crystallex International Corporation
#1210, 18 King St. East, Toronto, ON M5C 1C4
416-203-2448 Fax: 416-203-0099 800-738-1577
info@crystallex.com
www.crystallex.com
Ticker Symbol: KRY
Company Type: Public
Profile: Metal mining in gold ores

Cumberland Resources Ltd.
One Bentall Centre, PO Box 72, #950, 505 Burrard St., Vancouver, BC V7X 1M4
604-608-2557 Fax: 604-608-2559 **Company Type:** Public
Profile: Metal mining in gold ores

Denison Mines Corp.
Atrium on Bay, #402, 595 Bay St., Toronto, ON M5G 2C2
416-979-1991 Fax: 416-979-5893
blazare@denisonmines.com
www.denisonmines.com
Ticker Symbol: DML
Company Type: Public
Profile: Denison Mines Corp. is a uranium exploration & production company. Its active uranium mines are located in Canada & the United States. Denison Environmental Services (DES) was established to provide mine decommissioning, long-term care, & maintenance services to closed mining facilities.

Denison Mines Corporation
Atrium On Bay, #402, 595 Bay St., Toronto, ON M5G 2C2
416-979-1991 Fax: 416-979-5893 www.denisonmines.com
Ticker Symbol: DML
Company Type: Public
Profile: Metal mining in uranium, radium & vanadium ores

Dundee Precious Metals Inc.
South Tower, Royal Bank Plaza, #3060, 200 Bay St., Toronto, ON M5J 2J1
416-365-5191 Fax: 416-365-9080
info@dundeeprecious.com
www.dundeeprecious.com
Ticker Symbol: DPM
Company Type: Public
Profile: Dundee Precious Metals Inc. acquires, explores, develops, & mines precious metals properties. The company is active in Nunavut, Armenia, Bulgaria, & Serbia.

East Asia Minerals Corporation
#1980, 1055 West Hastings St., Vancouver, BC V6E 2E9
604-684-8894 Fax: 604-688-2180
patchettm@eaminerals.com
www.eaminerals.com
Ticker Symbol: EAS
Company Type: Public
Profile: The mineral acquisition & exploration company has gold & copper assets in Indonesia & uranium properties in Mongolia.

Eldorado Gold Corporation
Bentall 5, #1188, 550 Burrard St., Vancouver, BC V6C 2B5
604-687-4018 Fax: 604-687-4026 888-353-8166
info@eldoradogold.com
www.eldoradogold.com
Ticker Symbol: ELD
Company Type: Public
Profile: Eldorado Gold Corporation specializes in the exploration & development of gold properties. The gold producer has properties in Brazil, Greece, Turkey, & China. Industry best practices are implemented in each region in an effort to minimize environmental impacts.

Elk Valley Coal Corporation
#1000, 205 - 9th Ave., Calgary, AB T2G 0R3
403-260-9800 Fax: 403-265-8794
info@elkvalleycoal.ca
www.elkvalleycoal.ca
Company Type: Public
Profile: Coal mining in bituminous coal & lignite surface mining

Energold Drilling Corp.
#1100, 543 Granville St., Vancouver, BC V6C 1X8
604-681-9501 Fax: 604-605-3816
info@energold.com
www.energold.com
Ticker Symbol: EGD
Company Type: Public
Profile: The contract diamond drilling company serves the international mining sector. The driller strives to operate in an environmentally & socially sensitive manner. Canada's E3 Environmental Excellence in Exploration chose one of Energold's drill programs as a case study.

European Goldfields Ltd.
Registered Office, Financial Plaza, #200, 204 Lambert St., Whitehorse, YT Y1A 3T2
info@egoldfields.com
www.egoldfields.com
Ticker Symbol: EGU
Company Type: Public
Profile: European Goldfields Limited is engaged in the acquisition, exploration, & development of mineral properties. Operations take place in Greece, Romania, & southeastern Europe. The company implemented environmental initiatives such as improving the distribution system of mine water, installing a sprinkler system, removing old mining debris & waste, & switching from tailings slurry disposal to dry fitter cake disposal.

Excellon Resources Inc.
#900, 20 Victoria St., Toronto, ON M5C 2N8
416-364-1130 Fax: 416-364-6745
info@excellonresources.com
www.excellonresources.com
Ticker Symbol: EXN
Company Type: Public
Profile: The mineral exploration company is engaged in the production of silver, lead, & zinc. Its principal area of activity is Durango State, Mexico.

Farallon Resources Ltd.
#1020, 800 West Pender St., Vancouver, BC V6C 2V6
604-684-6365 Fax: 604-684-8092 800-667-2114
info@hdgold.com
www.farallonresources.com
Ticker Symbol: FAN
Company Type: Public
Profile: Metal mining in gold, silver, lead & zinc ores

First Quantum Minerals Ltd.
#800, 543 Granville St., Vancouver, BC V6C 1X8
604-688-6577 Fax: 604-688-3818 888-688-6577
info@fqml.com
www.first-quantum.com
Ticker Symbol: FM
Company Type: Public
Profile: Operations of the mining & metals company include mineral exploration, development, mining, smelting, & refining. First Quantum Minerals is engaged in copper & cobalt mining in Africa. The company also has interest in gold & cobalt production.

FNX Mining Company Inc.
#1500, 145 King St. West, Toronto, ON M5H 1J8
416-628-5929 Fax: 416-360-0550
info@fnxmining.com
www.fnxmining.com
Ticker Symbol: FNX
Company Type: Public
Profile: Metal mining & metal mining services

FNX Mining Company Inc.
#1500, 145 King St. West, Toronto, ON M5H 2B7
416-628-5929 Fax: 416-360-0550
info@fnxmining.com

www.fnxmining.com
Ticker Symbol: FNX
Company Type: Public
Profile: The company focuses upon the exploration, development, & production of copper, platinum, nickel, cobalt, gold, & palladium. Mining properties are situated in Sudbury, Ontario.

Formation Capital Corporation
#1510, 999 West Hastings St., Vancouver, BC V6C 2W2
604-682-6229 Fax: 604-682-6205
inform@formcap.com
www.formcap.com
Ticker Symbol: FCO
Company Type: Public
Profile: Formation Capital Corporation's area of expertise is mineral exploration, mine development, & refining. It has interests in base, precious metal, & uranium projects. The company also owns a hydrometallurgical complex & precious metals refinery in the United States, through its wholly-owned subsidiary, Essential Metals Corporation. The following are Formation Capital Corporation's areas of activity: Canada, the United States, & Mexico.

Fronteer Development Group Inc.
#1650, 1055 West Hastings St., Vancouver, BC V6E 2E9
604-632-4677 Fax: 604-632-4678 877-632-4677
info@fronteergroup.com
www.fronteergroup.com
Ticker Symbol: FRG
Company Type: Public
Profile: Fronteer Development Group is involved in exploration & development. Its portfolio includes the following: gold projects in Nevada; Aurora Energy Resources (42.2% interest); & gold & copper-gold projects in northwestern Turkey (40% interest).

Frontera Copper Corporation
#1000, 36 Toronto St., Toronto, ON M5C 2C5
602-667-3202 Fax: 602-424-5490
info@fronteracopper.com
www.fronteracopper.com
Ticker Symbol: FCC
Company Type: Public
Profile: Frontera Copper Corporation is a Canadian copper cathode producer. Its' principle area of activity is the Piedras Verdes project in Sonora, Mexico.

Gabriel Resources Ltd.
#1501, 110 Yonge St., Toronto, ON M5C 1T4
416-955-9200 Fax: 416-955-4661
info@gabrielresources.com
www.gabrielresources.com
Ticker Symbol: GBU
Company Type: Public
Profile: Metal mining in gold & silver ores

Gammon Gold Inc.
PO Box 2067 Summit Place, #402, 1601 Water St., Halifax, NS B3J 3P6
902-468-0614 Fax: 902-468-0631
info@gammongold.com
www.gammongold.com
Ticker Symbol: GAM
Company Type: Public
Profile: Owns gold-silver deposits at Ocampo, Mexico

Glencairn Gold Corp.
#500, 6 Adelaide St. E, Toronto, ON M5C 1H6
416-860-0919 Fax: 416-367-0182 **Company Type:** Public
Profile: Metal mining in gold & silver ores

GobiMin Inc.
#1250, 120 Adelaide St. West, Toronto, ON M5H 1T1
416-915-0133 Fax: 416-915-2908
info@gobimin.com
www.gobimin.com
Ticker Symbol: GMN
Company Type: Public
Profile: GobiMin Inc. is engaged in mineral exploration & development. The junior mining company has nickel, copper, & sulphide operations in northwestern China. In addition to the Chinese properties, GobiMin has set up a joint venture for exploration of metal properties in Indonesia. GobiMin Inc.'s subsidiaries include Hami Jubao Resources Co. Ltd. & Xinjiang Yakesi Resources Co. Ltd.

Goldcorp Inc.
Park Place, #3400, 666 Burrard St., Vancouver, BC 86C 2X8
604-696-3000 Fax: 604-696-3001 800-567-6223
info@goldcorp.com
www.goldcorp.com
Ticker Symbol: G
Company Type: Public
Profile: Goldcorp Inc. is a gold mining company. Its development projects & operations are located throughout North & South America.

Golden Queen Mining Co. Ltd.
6411 Imperial Ave., Vancouver, BC V7W 2J5
604-921-7570 Fax: 604-921-9446
mintoexpl@telus.net
www.goldenqueen.com
Ticker Symbol: GQM
Company Type: Public
Profile: Metal mining in gold & silver ores

Great Basin Gold Ltd.
#1020, 800 West Pender St., Vancouver, BC V6C 2V6
604-684-6365 Fax: 604-684-8092 800-667-2114
info@hdgold.com
www.greatbasingold.com
Ticker Symbol: GBG
Company Type: Public
Profile: Mid-tier gold producer with mines in South Africa and the United States

Harry Winston Diamond Corporation
PO Box 4569 A, Toronto, ON M5W 4T9
416-362-2237 Fax: 416-362-2230
hw@harrywinston.com
www.harrywinston.com; investor.harrywinston.com
Ticker Symbol: ABZ
Company Type: Public
Profile: Mining & quarrying of miscellaneous nonmetallic minerals

High River Gold Mines Ltd.
#1700, 155 University Ave., Toronto, ON M5H 3B7
416-947-1440 Fax: 416-360-0010
info@hrg.ca
www.hrg.ca
Ticker Symbol: HRG
Company Type: Public
Profile: Metal mining in gold ores

High River Gold Mines Ltd.
#1700, 155 University Ave., Toronto, ON M5H 3B7
416-947-1440 Fax: 416-360-0010
highrivergold@hrg.ca
www.hrg.ca
Ticker Symbol: HRG
Company Type: Public
Profile: Metal mining in gold ores

Horizon North Logistics Inc.
#1600, 505 - 3rd St. SW, Calgary, AB T2P 3E6
403-517-4654 Fax: 403-517-4678
888-366-5558www.horizonnorth.ca
Ticker Symbol: HNL
Company Type: Public
Profile: Services are provided to natural resource development projects. Horizon North Logistics Inc.'s services include marine transportation & logistics, mobile structures, & matting solutions. Projects take place in oil & gas exploration & development areas & the oil sands of western & northern Canada & Alaska.

HudBay Minerals Inc.
Dundee Place, #2501, 1 Adelaide St. East, Toronto, ON M4S 2E2
416-362-0615 Fax: 416-362-7844
investor.relations@hbms.ca
www.hudbayminerals.com
Ticker Symbol: HBM
Company Type: Private
Profile: Zinc, copper, & precious metals are produced by the mining & smelting company.

IAMGOLD Corporation
PO Box 153, #3200, 401 Bay St., Toronto, ON M5H 2Y4
416-360-4710 Fax: 416-360-4750 888-464-9999
info@iamgold.com
www.iamgold.com
Ticker Symbol: IMG
Company Type: Public
Profile: Metal mining in gold & miscellaneous ores

IAMGOLD Corporation
PO Box 153, #3200, 401 Bay St., Toronto, ON M5H 2Y4
416-360-4710 Fax: 416-360-4750 888-464-9999
info@iamgold.com
www.iamgold.com
Ticker Symbol: IMG
Company Type: Public
Profile: The company is engaged in metal mining in gold ores.

Imperial Metals Corporation
#200, 580 Hornby St., Vancouver, BC V6C 3B6
604-669-8959 Fax: 604-687-4030
info@imperialmetals.com
www.imperialmetals.com
Ticker Symbol: III
Company Type: Public
Profile: Imperial Metals Corporation explores, develops, operates, & maintains mine properties.

Inco Limited
#1500, 145 King St. West, Toronto, ON M5H 4B7
416-361-7511 Fax: 416-361-7781
inco@inco.com
www.inco.com
Company Type: Public
Profile: Metal mining in ferroalloy, copper & gold ores; Manufacturers of primary smelting & refining of nonferrous metals, various industrial inorganic chemicals, secondary smelting & refining of nonferrous metals, nonferrous forgings

Inmet Mining Corporation
#1000, 330 Bay St., Toronto, ON M5H 2S8
416-361-6400 Fax: 416-368-4692
ir@inmetmining.com
www.inmetmining.com
Ticker Symbol: IMN
Company Type: Public
Profile: The mining company produces gold, copper, & zinc.

International Royalty Corporation
#104, Inverness Dr. East, Englewood, CO 80112
303-799-9020 Fax: 303-799-9017 800-496-1629
info@internationalroyalty.com
www.internationalroyalty.com
Ticker Symbol: IRC
Company Type: Public
Profile: The global mineral royalty company holds more than 60 royalties. It is listed on the Toronto Stock Exchange. Its legal counsel & transfer agent are also in Toronto.

Ivanhoe Mines Ltd.
World Trade Centre, #654, 999 Canada Pl., Vancouver, BC V6C 3E1
604-688-5755 Fax: 604-682-2060 888-273-9999
info@ivanhoemines.com
www.ivanhoemines.com
Ticker Symbol: IVN
Company Type: Public
Profile: Metal mining in copper, iron, gold, silver, lead & zinc ores

Ivernia Inc.
#300, 44 Victoria St., Toronto, ON M5C 1Y2
416-867-9298 Fax: 416-867-9384
investor@ivernia.ca
www.ivernia.com
Ticker Symbol: IVW
Company Type: Public
Profile: Offices of holding companies; Metal mining in lead & zinc ores

Kinross Gold Corporation
Scotia Plaza, 40 King St. West, 52nd Fl., Toronto, ON M5H 3Y2
416-365-5123 Fax: 416-363-6622 866-561-3636
info@kinross.com
www.kinross.com
Ticker Symbol: K
Company Type: Public
Profile: Kinross Gold Corporation explores, acquires, mines, & processes gold & silver ore in North & South America.

Kirkland Lake Gold Inc.
Macassa Mine, PO Box 370 Main, 1360 Government Road West, Kirkland Lake, ON P2N 3J1
705-567-5208 Fax: 705-568-6444
info@klgold.com
www.klgold.com
Ticker Symbol: KGI
Company Type: Public
Profile: Gold mining

Lakota Resources Inc.
#600, 15 Toronto St., Toronto, ON M5C 2E3
416-368-1447 Fax: 416-368-8957
info@lakotaresources.ca
www.lakotaresources.ca
Ticker Symbol: YLA
Company Type: Public
Profile: Gold exploration in Tanzania

Leader Mining International Inc.
#2806, 505 - 6th St. SW, Calgary, AB T2P 1X5
403-234-7501 Fax: 403-539-9490
gen-info@leadermining.com
www.leadermining.com

Ticker Symbol: LMN
Company Type: Public
Profile: Magnesium & tantalum mining

Lundin Mining Corporation
PO Box 38, #1500, 150 King St. West, Toronto, ON M5H 1J9
416-342-5560 Fax: 416-348-0303
info@lundinmining.com
www.lundinmining.com
Ticker Symbol: LUN
Company Type: Public
Profile: Lundin Mining Corporation is engaged in the exploration, mining, & production of base metal mineral resources, such as copper, nickel, zinc, & lead. Operations are located in Spain, Portugal, & Sweden. The corporation also holds a development project pipeline & an equity stake in a copper & cobalt project in the Democratic Republic of Congo.

Madison Minerals Inc.
Guinness Tower, #2000, 1055 West Hastings St., Vancouver, BC V6E 2E9
604-331-8772 Fax: 604-331-8773 877-529-8475
dscott@mine-tech.com
www.madison-enterprises.com
Ticker Symbol: MNP
Company Type: Public
Profile: The company is engaged in metal mining of gold, silver & copper ores.

Major Drilling Group International Inc.
#100, 111 St George St., Moncton, NB E1C 1T7
506-857-8636 Fax: 506-857-9211
info@majordrilling.com
www.majordrilling.com
Ticker Symbol: MDI
Company Type: Public
Profile: Major Drilling Group International's drilling operations are carried out in the following areas: Canada, the United States, Central America, South America, Africa, Armenia, Indonesia, & Australia. Drilling services include geotechnical, environmental drilling, surface & underground coring, reverse circulation, & coal-bed methane. The company primarily serves the mining industry.

Mazarin Inc.
696, rue Monfette est, Thetford Mines, QC G6G 7G9
418-338-3669 Fax: 418-338-0229
jleboutillier@mazarin-inc.com
Ticker Symbol: MAZ.H
Company Type: Public
Profile: The company manages several mining sites. Mazarin Inc. is also engaged in the development of tailings.

Mediterranean Resources Ltd.
#890, 885 Dunsmuir St., Vancouver, BC V6C 1N5
604-669-3397 Fax: 604-669-3357
charpestad@medresources.ca
www.medresources.ca
Ticker Symbol: MNR
Company Type: Public
Profile: Mediterranean Resources Ltd. develops gold deposits in Turkey.

Metalex Ventures Ltd.
2600 B Enterprise Way, Kelowna, BC V1X 7Y5
250-860-8599 Fax: 250-860-1362 www.metalexventures.com
Ticker Symbol: MTX
Company Type: Public
Profile: Exploration & mining diamonds in Ontario & Quebec and oversees projects in Angola, Greenland, Mali and Morocco

Minefinders Corporation Ltd.
#2288, 1177 West Hastings St., Vancouver, BC V6E 2K3
604-687-6263 Fax: 604-687-6267 866-687-6263
ilianne@minefinders.com
www.minefinders.com
Ticker Symbol: MFL
Company Type: Public
Profile: Metal mining in gold & silver ores

Mountain Province Diamonds Inc.
PO Box 152, #2700, 401 Bay St., Toronto, ON M5H 2Y4
416-361-3562 Fax: 416-603-8565
p.evans@mountainprovince.com
www.mountainprovince.com
Ticker Symbol: MPV
Company Type: Public
Profile: Mountain Province Diamonds Inc. is engaged in diamond exploration & development. The Gahcho Kué diamond project in the Northwest Territories is the company's main asset, in a joint venture partnership with De Beers Canada.

NEMI Northern Energy & Mining Inc.
2500 - 555 W. Hastings St., Vancouver, BC V6B 4N5
604-689-0277 Fax: 604-688-5210
info@nemi-energy.com
www.nemi-energy.com
Ticker Symbol: NNE.A
Company Type: Public
Profile: Mine development company focused on the exploration and development of metallurgical coal assets in northeast British Columbia

Neo Material Technologies
#1740, 121 King St. West, Toronto, ON M5H 3T9
416-367-8588 Fax: 416-367-5471
info@neomaterials.com
www.neomaterials.com
Ticker Symbol: NEM
Company Type: Public
Profile: Metal mining in miscellaneous ores; Manufacturing of various industrial inorganic chemicals

Nevsun Resources Ltd.
#800, 1075 West Georgia St., Vancouver, BC V6E 3C9
604-623-4700 Fax: 604 623 4701 888-600-2200
nevsuninfo@nevsun.com
www.nevsun.com
Ticker Symbol: NSU
Company Type: Public
Profile: Metal mining in gold & miscellaneous metal ores

New Gold Inc.
#3110, 666 Burrard St., Vancouver, BC V6C 2X8
604-639-0022 Fax: 604-696-4110 888-315-9715
info@newgold.com
www.newgold.com
Company Type: Public
Profile: The intermediate gold mining company has assets in Canada, Alaska, Mexico, Brazil, & Australia.

Newmont Mining Corporation of Canada Ltd.
Cambridge Bay Expediting Building, PO Box 1203, Cambridge Bay, NU X0B 0C0
604-759-3450 Fax: 506-759-0318
canadahr@newmont.com
www.newmont.com
Ticker Symbol: NEM
Company Type: Public
Profile: Newmont Mining Corporation of Canada Ltd. is engaged in gold exploration & production. Current activity takes place in the Hope Bay greenstone belt area of the Arctic.

NGEx Resources Inc.
#2101, 885 West Georgia St., Vancouver, BC V6C 3E8
604-689-7842 Fax: 604-689-4250
ngexresources@namdo.com
www.ngexresources.com
Ticker Symbol: NGQ
Company Type: Public
Profile: Metal mining in gold, copper, lead & zinc ores

Noranda Income Fund
c/o Xstrata Canada Inc., First Canadian Place, PO Box 403, #6900, 100 King St. West, Toronto, ON 5X 1E33
416-775-1500 Fax: 416-775-1749 www.norandaincomefund.com
Ticker Symbol: NIF.UN
Company Type: Public
Profile: The Fund's main asset is Canadian Electrolytic Zinc Limited, a zinc processing facility in Salaberry-de-Valleyfield, Québec. The facility has obtained ISO 9001 & ISO 14001 certification to cover all environmental processes at the plant.

North American Palladium Ltd.
#2116, 130 Adelaide St. West, Toronto, ON M5H 3P5
416-360-7590 Fax: 416-360-7709
info@napalladium.com
www.napalladium.com
Ticker Symbol: PDL
Company Type: Public
Profile: Metal mining in gold, copper, ferroalloy & miscellaneous metal ores

Northgate Minerals Corporation
#406, 815 Hornby St., Vancouver, BC V6Z 2E6
604-681-4004 Fax: 604-681-4003
ngx@northgateminerals.com
www.northgateminerals.com
Ticker Symbol: NGX
Company Type: Public
Profile: Northgate Minerals Corp. is engaged in the production of gold & copper. The company's exploration properties, development projects, & mining operations are located in Canada & Australia.

Northrock Resources Inc.
Pacific Centre, PO Box Box 10322, #1588, 609 Granville St., Vancouver, BC V7Y 1G5
604-689-7422 Fax: 604-689-7442 www.northrockresources.com
Ticker Symbol: NRK
Company Type: Public
Profile: The company is engaged in the exploration & development of mineral properties.

NovaGold Resources Inc
Granville Square, PO Box 24, #2300, 200 Granville St., Vancouver, BC V6C 1S4
604-669-6227 Fax: 604-669-6272 866-669-6227
info@novagold.net
www.novagold.net
Ticker Symbol: NG
Company Type: Public
Profile: Metal mining-gold ores; Metal mining-miscellaneous metal ores

Olympus Pacific Minerals Inc.
#500, 10 King St. East, Toronto, ON M5C 1C3
416-572-2525 Fax: 416-572-4202 888-902-5522
info@olympuspacific.com
www.olympuspacific.com
Ticker Symbol: OYM
Company Type: Public
Profile: Production & exploration for gold in Vietnam & SE Asia

Orsu Metals Corporation
c/o Vanguard Shareholder Solutions Inc., #1205, 1095 West Pender St., Vancouver, BC
604-608-0824 Fax: 604-608-0854 866-448-0780
info@orsumetals.com
www.orsumetals.com
Ticker Symbol: OSU
Company Type: Public
Profile: Metal mining gold & silver ores; Oil royalty traders

Orvana Minerals Corp.
#1530, 320 Bay St., Toronto, ON M5H 4A6
416-369-1629 Fax: 416-369-1402
mking@orvana.com
www.orvana.com
Ticker Symbol: ORV
Company Type: Public
Profile: The Canadian gold mining & exploration company evaluates, develops, & mines precious & base metals deposits. Orvana Minerals is the owner & operator of the Don Mario gold mine in Bolivia.

OZ Minerals Limited
#200, 1159 Alloy Dr., Thunder Bay, ON P7B 6M8
807-346-1668 Fax: 807-345-8708
866-690-9653www.ozminerals.com
Ticker Symbol: OZL.AX
Company Type: Public
Profile: Mining exploration & development, with operations around the world, including 2,600 km of exploration area in the Slave Region of Nunavut. Through the acquisition of Wolfden Resources Limited in 2007, OZ Minerals now owns the High Lake and Izok Lake projects

Pacific Rim Mining Corp.
#1050, 625 Howe St., Vancouver, BC V6C 2T6
604-689-1976 Fax: 604-689-1978 888-775-7097
general@pacrim-mining.com
www.pacrim-mining.com
Ticker Symbol: PMU
Company Type: Public
Profile: Pacific Rim Mining is a gold exploration company. The company's main asset is the El Dorado gold project in El Salvador. Salvadoran & U.S. subsidiaries include Pac Rim Cayman LLC, Pacific Rim El Salvador, S.A. de C.V., & Dorado Exploraciones, S.A. de C.V..

Pan American Silver Corp.
#1500, 625 Howe St., Vancouver, BC V6C 2T6
604-684-1175 Fax: 604-684-0147
info@panamericansilver.com
www.panamericansilver.com
Ticker Symbol: PAA
Company Type: Public
Profile: The silver producer conducts its mining & exploration activities in Mexico, Bolivia, Peru, & Argentina.

Pelangio Exploration Inc.
440 Harrop Dr., 2nd Fl, Milton, ON L9T 3H2
905-875-3828 Fax: 905-875-3829 877-746-1632
info@pelangio.com
www.pelangio.com
Ticker Symbol: PX
Company Type: Public
Profile: Pelangio Exploration Inc. is a junior gold exploration company. Its exploration & development operations are conducted on mineral properties in Canada & Ghana.

Philex Gold Inc.
#1200, 95 Wellington St. West, Toronto, ON M5J 2Z9
416-864-9700 Fax: 416-941-8852 www.philexgold.com
Ticker Symbol: PGI
Company Type: Public
Profile: Philex Gold is engaged in gold & copper exploration in the Philippines. The company's interests include the former Bulawan gold mine, the Silangan Project, the Lascogon, Danao, & other gold prospects. Philex adheres to the Community-Based Development & Environmental Management Program.

Potash Corporation of Saskatchewan Inc.
PCS Tower, #500, 122 - 1st Ave. South, Saskatoon, SK S7K 7G3
306-933-8500 Fax: 306-652-2699 800-667-0403
corporate.relations@potashcorp.com
www.potashcorp.com
Ticker Symbol: POT
Company Type: Public
Profile: The fertilizer enterprise produces the following plant nutrients: potash, nitrogen, & phosphate. Potash Corporation of Saskatchewan supplies the agriculture, animal nutrition, & industrial chemical markets.

Quadra Mining Ltd.
Four Bentall Centre, PO Box 49185, #2414, 1055 Dunsmuir St., Vancouver, BC V7X 1K8
604-689-8550 Fax: 604-689-8556
info@quadramining.com
www.quadramining.com
Ticker Symbol: QUA
Company Type: Public
Profile: Quadra Mining Ltd. owns & operates the Robinson copper mine in Nevada. The base metal producer also holds a 100% interest in the Carlota Copper Project, which is under construction in Arizona, plus an 82% interest in International Molybdenum & its Malmbjerg Project.

Redcorp Ventures Ltd.
#800, 1281 West Georgia St., Vancouver, BC V6E 3J7
604-639-0135 Fax: 604-669-5330 888-669-4775
info@redcorp-ventures.com
www.redcorp-ventures.com
Ticker Symbol: RDV
Company Type: Public
Profile: The company is engaged in metal mining of gold, silver, copper, lead & zinc ores. It is listed on the TSX.

Rex Diamond Mining Corporation
#1900, 25 Adelaide St. East, Toronto, ON M5C 3A1
416-867-8800
info@rexmining.com
www.rexmining.com
Company Type: Public
Profile: Rex Diamond Mining Corporation is a Canadian incorporated, public company which is currently seeking new business opportunities.

Richmont Mines Inc.
110, av Principale, Rouyn-Noranda, QC J9X 4P2
819-797-2465 Fax: 819-797-0166
info@richmont-mines.com
www.richmont-mines.com
Ticker Symbol: RIC
Company Type: Public
Profile: Richmont Mines Inc. specializes in gold exploration, development, & mining. Operations take place in Ontario, Quebec, & Newfoundland & Labrador.

Rochester Resources Ltd.
#1305, 1090 West Georgia St., Vancouver, BC V6E 3V7
604-685-9316 Fax: 604-683-1585
info@rochesterresources.com
www.rochesterresources.com
Ticker Symbol: RCT
Company Type: Public
Profile: Rochester Resources Ltd. is engaged in the exploration & development of gold & silver properties. Operations take place in the state of Nayarit, Mexic, where the Mina Real Property & the Santa Fe Project are located.

Sabina Silver Corporation
#202, 930 West 1st St., North Vancouver, BC V7P 3N4
604-998-4175 Fax: 604-998-1051 888-648-4218
info@sabinasilver.com
www.sabinasilver.com
Ticker Symbol: SBB
Company Type: Public
Profile: Sabina Silver Corporation specializes in acquiring, exploring, & developing precious metal properties. The company's assets are as follows: the Del Norte project in the Stewart-Eskay Creek Mining District; the Hackett River silver-zinc project in the Canadian Arctic; & many projects in the Red Lake gold camp.

Seabridge Gold Inc.
#400, 106 Front St. East, Toronto, ON M5A 1E1
416-367-9292 Fax: 416-367-2711
info@seabridgegold.net
www.seabridgegold.net
Ticker Symbol: SEA
Company Type: Public
Profile: Has gold interests in North America; Does not operate mines

SEMAFO Inc.
#375, 750, boul Marcel-Laurin, Montréal, QC H4M 2M4
514-744-4408 Fax: 514-744-2291
info@semafo.com
www.semafo.com
Ticker Symbol: SMF
Company Type: Public
Profile: Metal mining in gold, lead & zinc ores

Sherritt International Corporation
Investor Relations, 1133 Yonge St., 5th Fl., Toronto, ON M4T 2Y7
416-924-4551 Fax: 416-924-5015 800-704-6698
info@sherritt.com; investor@sherritt.com
www.sherritt.com
Ticker Symbol: S
Company Type: Public
Profile: Sherrit International Corporation has interests in a nickel & cobalt metals business, thermal coal production, electricity generation, & oil & gas exploration, development, & production. The company conducts its operations in Canada & internationally.

Shore Gold Inc.
#300, 224 - 4th Ave. South, Saskatoon, SK S7K 5M5
306-664-2202 Fax: 306-664-7181
shoregold@shoregold.com
www.shoregold.com
Ticker Symbol: SGF
Company Type: Public
Profile: Shore Gold Inc. specializes in mineral exploration & development. Operations take place in Saskatchewan.

Silver Standard Resources Inc.
#1180, 999 West Hastings St., Vancouver, BC V6C 2W2
604-689-3846 Fax: 604-689-3847 888-338-0046
invest@silverstandard.com
www.silverstandard.com
Ticker Symbol: SSO
Company Type: Public
Profile: Metal mining in gold & silver ores

Silver Wheaton Corp.
#3150, 666 Burrard St., Vancouver, BC V6C 2X8
604-684-9648 Fax: 604-684-3123 800-380-8687
info@silverwheaton.com
www.silverwheaton.com
Ticker Symbol: SLW
Company Type: Public
Profile: Silver Wheaton Corp. is engaged in silver production. The company purchases silver production from mines in the United States, Mexico, Peru, Sweden, & Greece.

Silvercorp Metals Inc.
#1378, 200 Granville St., Vancouver, BC V6C 1S4
604-669-9397 Fax: 604-669-9387 888-224-1881
info@silvercorp.ca; ir@silvercorp.ca
www.silvercorp.ca
Ticker Symbol: SVM
Company Type: Public
Profile: Silvercorp Metals acquires, explores, & mines silver-related properties located in the People's Republic of China. The company has implemented a range of employee safety measures & environmental protection measures.

Southwestern Resources Corp.
PO Box 10102, #1650, 701 West Georgia St., Vancouver, BC V7Y 1C6
604-669-2525 Fax: 604-688-5175
swg@swgold.com
www.swgold.com
Ticker Symbol: SWG
Company Type: Public
Profile: Metal mining in gold, silver & miscellaneous metal ores; Mining & quarrying of miscellaneous nonmetallic minerals

St. Andrew Goldfields Ltd.
#212, 1540 Cornwall Rd., Oakville, ON L6J 7W5
905-815-9855 Fax: 905-815-9437 800-463-5139
info@standrewgoldfields.com
www.standrewgoldfields.com
Ticker Symbol: SAS
Company Type: Public
Profile: Metal mining of gold ores

Sterlite Gold Ltd.
PO Box 25, 199 Bay St., Toronto, ON M5L 1A9
416-863-2753 Fax: 416-863-2653 **Company Type:** Private
Profile: Metal mining in gold & ferroalloy ores

Stratic Energy Corporation
#17, 100 - 6th Ave. SW, Calgary, AB T2P 0P5
403-698-8897 Fax: 403-410-7797
yash.chapanery@straticenergy.com
www.straticenergy.com
Ticker Symbol: SE
Company Type: Public
Profile: Metal mining in gold ores

Tahera Diamond Corporation
PO Box 1020 T.D.C., 77 King St. West, Toronto, ON M5K 1P2
416-777-1998 Fax: 416-777-1898 877-777-2004
investor_relations@tahera.com
www.tahera.com
Ticker Symbol: TAH
Company Type: Public
Profile: Publicly traded on the Toronto Stock Exchange, the company is a diamond mine explorer, developer, & operator.

Tan Range Exploration Corporation
#1400, 355 Burrard St., Vancouver, BC V6C 2G8
604-669-5598 Fax: 604-669-8915 800-811-3855
investors@tanrange.com
www.tanrange.com
Ticker Symbol: TNX
Company Type: Public
Profile: Exploration & mining gold in Tanzania

Taseko Mines Limited
#200, 900 West Pender St., Vancouver, BC V6C 1L6
604-684-6365 Fax: 604-684-8092 800-667-2114
info@hdgold.com
www.tasekomines.com
Ticker Symbol: TKO
Company Type: Public
Profile: Taseko Mines Limited is a mineral exploration & mining company. The company is engaged in the following main projects in British Columbia: the Prosperity gold-copper project; the Gibraltar copper-molybdenum mine; & the Harmony gold prospect.

Teck Cominco Ltd.
Bentall 5, #3300, 550 Burrard St., Vancouver, BC V6C 0B3
604-699-4000 Fax: 604-699-4718
info@teck.com
www.teck.com
Ticker Symbol: TCK
Company Type: Public
Profile: The mining, smelting, & refining company produces zinc, copper, metallurgical coal, & gold.

Thompson Creek Metals Company Inc.
PO Box 118, #2010, 401 Bay St., Toronto, ON M5H 2Y4
416-860-1438 Fax: 416-860-0813
info@tcrk.com
www.thompsoncreekmetals.com
Ticker Symbol: TCM
Company Type: Public
Profile: The molybdenum producer owns the Thompson Creek open-pit molybdenum mine & mill in Idaho, a metallurgical roasting facility in Pennsylvania, as well as 75% of northern British Columbia's Endako open-pit mine, mill, & roasting facility.

Tiberon Minerals Ltd.
Scotia Plaza, #1101, 100 Yonge St., Toronto, ON M5C 2W1
416-214-1877 Fax: 416-214-0091 866-616-2404
info@tiberon.com
www.tiberon.com
Ticker Symbol: TBR
Company Type: Public
Profile: Exploration & production, mainly in Vietnam

TVI Pacific Inc.
#2000, 736 - 6th Ave. SW, Calgary, AB T2P 3T7
403-265-4356 Fax: 403-264-7028
tvi-info@tvipacific.com
www.tvipacific.com
Ticker Symbol: TVI
Company Type: Public
Profile: Precious & base metal producer & explorer; contract drilling services in SE Asia & the Philippines

Uranium One Inc.
#900, 1285 West Pender Street, Vancouver, BC V6E 4B1
604-601-5620 Fax: 604-601-5621
chris.sattler@uranium1.com
www.uranium1.com
Ticker Symbol: UUU
Company Type: Public
Profile: Metal mining in uranium, radium & vanadium ores

Uruguay Mineral Exploration
#101, Richmond St. East, Toronto, ON M5C 1N7
416-848-7744 Fax: 416-848-0790 www.uruguayminerals.com
Ticker Symbol: UME
Company Type: Public
Profile: The gold exploration & production company is active in South America. Uruguay Mineral Exploration Inc. also has a portfolio of diamond & base metal prospects.

Vista Gold Corp.
Waterfront Centre, PO Box 48600, #900, 200 Burrard St., Vancouver, BC V7X 1T2
720-981-1185 Fax: 720-981-1186 www.vistagold.com
Ticker Symbol: VGZ
Company Type: Public
Profile: Evaluates & acquires gold & precious metal projects

Wesdome Gold Mines Ltd.
#1305, 8 King St. East, Toronto, ON M5C 1B5
416-360-3743 Fax: 416-360-7620
info@wesdome.com
www.wesdome.com
Ticker Symbol: WDO
Company Type: Public
Profile: Metal mining in gold ores

Western Copper Corporation
#2050, 1111 West Georgia St., Vancouver, BC V6E 4M3
604-684-9497 Fax: 604-669-2926 888-966-9995
info@westerncoppercorp.com
www.westerncoppercorp.com
Ticker Symbol: WRN
Company Type: Public
Profile: Metal mining in copper ores

Xstrata Canada Corporation
PO Box 403, #6900, 100 King St. West, Toronto, ON M5X 1E3
416-775-1556 Fax: 416-775-1740
info@xstrata.com
www.xstrata.com
Ticker Symbol: FAL
Company Type: Public
Profile: Xstrata is engaged in the production of thermal coal, copper, mined nickel, & zinc.

Yamana Gold Inc.
#1102, 150 York St., Toronto, ON M5H 3S5
416-815-0220 Fax: 416-815-0021
investor@yamana.com
www.yamana.com
Ticker Symbol: YRI
Company Type: Public
Profile: Yamana Gold Inc. is engaged in the exploration & production of gold, copper, & other precious metals. Development projects & operating mines are located in Mexico, Central America, Brazil, & Argentina.

Oil & Gas

Addax Petroleum Corporation
#3400, 350 - 7th Ave. SW, Calgary, AB
22 -702-9400 Fax: 22 -702-9590
investor.relations@addaxpetroleum.com
www.addaxpetroleum.com
Ticker Symbol: AXC
Company Type: Public
Profile: The oil & gas exploration & production company carries out activities in Africa & the Middle East.

Advantage Oil & Gas Ltd.
Canterra Tower, #700, 400 - 3rd Ave. SW, Calgary, AB T2P 4H2
403-718-8000 Fax: 403-718-8300 866-393-0393
ir@advantageog.com; hr@advantageog.com
www.advantageog.com
Ticker Symbol: AAV
Company Type: Public
Profile: The intermediate oil & natural gas corporation has properties in western Canada, including the Montney natural gas resource at Glacier, Alberta.

Akita Drilling Ltd.
#900, 311 - 6 Ave. SW, Calgary, AB T2P 3H2
403-292-7979 Fax: 403-292-7990
akitainfo@akita-drilling.com
www.akita-drilling.com
Ticker Symbol: AKT
Company Type: Public
Profile: Akita Drilling Ltd. serves the oil & gas industry by providing contract drilling services. Western Canada, Canada's northern territories, & Alaska are the principal areas of activity.

Apache Canada Ltd.
700 - 9 Ave. SW, Calgary, AB T2P 3V4
403-261-1200 Fax: 403-266-5987 www.apachecorp.com
Company Type: Private
Profile: Crude petroleum & natural gas extraction; oil & gas fields exploration services

ARC Energy Trust
#2100, 440 - 2nd Ave. SW, Calgary, AB T2P 5E9
403-503-8600 Fax: 403-509-6417 888-272-4900
ir@arcresources.com
www.arcenergytrust.com
Ticker Symbol: AET
Company Type: Public
Profile: ARC Energy Trust offers investors indirect ownership in oil & gas assets.

Arogosy Energy Inc.
#2100, 500 - 4th Ave. SW, Calgary, AB T2P 2V6
403-269-8846 Fax: 403-269-8366
investor@argosyenergy.com
www.argosyenergy.com
Ticker Symbol: GSY
Company Type: Public
Profile: Argosy Engery Inc. was formed in conjunction with Pengrowth Energy Trust's acquisition of Accrete Energy Inc.. The company commenced trading on the Toronto Stock Exchange in 2008. The junior oil & gas company acquires, explores, & develops oil & gas properties. Areas of operation include Claresholm, Granum, Pearce, Edson, & Saxon in southern & north central Alberta.

Barrick Energy Inc.
Watermark Tower, #1400, 530 - 8th Ave. SW, Calgary, AB T2P 3S8
403-290-3400 Fax: 403-290-3447 www.barrick.com
Company Type: Public
Profile: Crude petroleum, natural gas & natural gas liquids extraction

Baytex Energy Ltd.
Bow Valley Square II, #2200, 205 - 5th Ave. SW, Calgary, AB T2P 2V7
403-269-4282 Fax: 403-205-3845 800-524-5521
investor@baytex.ab.ca
www.baytex.ab.ca
Ticker Symbol: BTE.UN
Company Type: Public
Profile: The organization is a conventional oil & gas income trust. It is engaged in internal property development, maintenance of production, & delivery of consistent returns to unitholders. Baytex Energy Trust has a formal policy to ensure environmental health & safety policies are carried out in the course of its operations.

Baytex Energy Trust
Bow Valley Square II, 2200, 205 - 5th Ave. SW, Calgary, AB T2P 2V7
403-269-4282 Fax: 403-205-3845 800-524-5521
helpdesk@baytex.ab.ca
www.baytex.ab.ca
Ticker Symbol: BTE.UN
Company Type: Public
Profile: Baytex Energy Trust is an energy income trust. Its portfolio of heavy oil, light oil, & natural gas assets is focused in the Western Canadian Sedimentary Basin & the United States. In addition to establishing its own health, safety and environmental policies & procedures, Baytex Energy Trust also participates in the Canadian Association of Petroleum Producer's Environment, Health, & Safety Stewardship program.

Berkana Energy Corp.
#2100, 801 - 6th Ave. SW, Calgary, AB T2P 3W2
403-221-7700 Fax: 403-221-7719
info@berkanaenergy.com
www.berkanaenergy.com
Ticker Symbol: BEC
Company Type: Public
Profile: Crude petroleum, natural gas & natural gas liquids extraction

BJ Services Company Canada
4839 - 90 Ave. SE, Calgary, AB T2C 2S8
403-531-5300 Fax: 403-236-8740 www.bjservices.com
Company Type: Private
Profile: Oil & gas field services; Manufacturers of oil & gas field machinery & equipment

Bonavista Energy Trust
#700, 311 - 6th Ave. SW, Calgary, AB T2P 3H2
403-213-4300 Fax: 403-262-5184
inv_rel@bonavistaenergy.com
www.bonavistaenergy.com
Ticker Symbol: BNP.UN
Company Type: Public
Profile: Bonavista Energy Trust is an oil & gas royalty trust. Operations are carried out in Alberta, Saskatchewan, & northeastern British Columbia.

Bonterra Oil & Gas Ltd.
#901, 1015 - 4th St. SW, Calgary, AB T2R 1J4
403-262-5307 Fax: 403-265-7488
info@bonterraenergy.com
www.bonterraenergy.com
Ticker Symbol: BNE
Company Type: Public
Profile: Bonterra Oil & Gas Ltd. is engaged in acquiring, exploring, & developing oil & natural gas properties. Activities are conducted in Saskatchewan & Alberta.

Bow Valley Energy Ltd.
#1200, 333 - 7th Ave. SW, Calgary, AB T2P 2Z1
403-232-0292 Fax: 403-232-8920
bve@bvenergy.com
www.bvenergy.com
Ticker Symbol: BVX
Company Type: Public
Profile: The company is engaged in acquiring, exploring, & developing natural gas properties. Operations take place in Alaska & the United Kingdom.

Breaker Energy Ltd.
#2300, 635 - 8th Ave. SW, Calgary, AB T2P 3M3
403-215-5264 Fax: 403-263-8665
info@breakerenergy.com
www.breakerenergy.com
Ticker Symbol: WAV.A
Company Type: Public
Profile: Breaker Energy Ltd. is a junior exploration & production company. Its specialty is the exploration, development, & production of oil & gas. Operations are carried out primarily in northern & southern Alberta, & northeastern British Columbia.

Brownstone Ventures Inc.
The Exchange Tower, #2500, 130 King Street West, Toronto, ON M5X 1A9
416-941-8900 Fax: 416-941-1090
www.brownstoneventures.com
info@brownstoneventures.com
Ticker Symbol: BWN
Company Type: Public
Profile: Brownstone Ventures Inc. is a Canadian based investment company, which has direct interests in oil & gas assets. Its portfolio includes diverse energy-based projects throughout the world.

Calfrac Well Services Ltd.
411 - 8th Ave. SW, Calgary, AB T2P 1E3
403-266-6000 Fax: 403-266-7381 866-770-3722
info@calfrac.com
www.calfrac.com
Ticker Symbol: CFW
Company Type: Public
Profile: Calfrac Well Services Ltd. is engaged in the provision of oilfield services, such as cementing, fracturing, & well stimulation services. Operations are situated in western Canada, the United States, Mexico, Argentina, & Russia.

Calpine Canada
#210, 1011 - 1st St., SW, Calgary, AB T2R 1J2
403-296-1410 Fax: 403-266-3896
public-relations@calpine.com
www.calpine.com
Company Type: Public
Profile: Electricity production using natural gas, geothermal steam, geothermal energy

Calvalley Petroleum Inc.
#700, 600 - 6th Ave. SW, Calgary, AB T2P 0S5
403-297-0490 Fax: 403-297-0499
inquiries@calvalleypetroleum.com
www.calvalleypetroleum.com
Ticker Symbol: CVI.A
Company Type: Public
Profile: Calvalley Petroleum's area of expertise is acquiring, exploring, & developing oil & gas properties. Activity takes place in the Republic of Yemen.

Canadex Resources Ltd.
10 Sun Pac Blvd., Brampton, ON L6S 4R5
905-792-2700 Fax: 905-792-8490 **Company Type:** Public
Profile: Extraction of crude petroleum, natural gas & natural gas liquids; School buses; Local trucking with storage; General warehousing & storage; Truck rental & leasing

Canadian Energy Services L.P.
East Tower, Energy Plaza, #300, 311 - 6th Ave. SW, Calgary, AB T2P 3H2

403-269-2800 Fax: 403-266-5708 888-785-6695
info@ceslp.ca
www.canadianenergyservices.ca
Ticker Symbol: CEU.UN
Company Type: Public

Profile: Canadian Energy Services L.P. is a designer of drilling fluid systems. Products are delivered to the oil & natural gas industry in the Western Canadian Sedimentary Basin & the United States. The company's subsidiary is AES Drilling Fluids, LLC.

Canadian Imperial Venture Corp.
Fortis Bldg., PO Box 6232, 139 Water St., St. John's, NL A1C 6J9
709-739-6700 Fax: 709-739-6605
info@canadianimperial.com
www.canadianimperial.com
Ticker Symbol: CQV
Company Type: Public

Profile: Crude petroleum, natural gas & natural gas liquids extraction

Canadian Natural Resources Limited
#2500, 855 - 2nd St. SW, Calgary, AB T2P 4J8
403-517-6700 Fax: 403-517-7370
ir@cnrl.com
www.cnrl.com
Ticker Symbol: CNQ
Company Type: Public

Profile: Canadian Natural Resources Limited is engaged in the exploration, development, & production of oil & natural gas. Operations are carried out in western Canada, the North Sea, & offshore west Africa.

Canadian Oil Sands Trust
First Canadian Centre, #2500, 350 - 7th Ave. SW, Calgary, AB T2P 3N9
403-218-6200 Fax: 403-218-6201
investor_relations@cos-trust.com
www.cos-trust.com
Ticker Symbol: COS.UN
Company Type: Public

Profile: The trust holds a 36.74% working interest in the Syncrude Project.

Canadian Superior Energy Inc.
#2700, 605 - 5th Ave. SW, Calgary, AB T2P 3H5
403-294-1411 Fax: 403-216-2374 www.cansup.com
Ticker Symbol: SNG
Company Type: Public

Profile: Extraction of crude petroleum, natural gas & natural gas liquids

Canetic Resources Trust
#1900, 255 - 5th Ave. SW, Calgary, AB T2P 3G6
403-539-6300 Fax: 403-539-6499 877-539-6300
info@canetictrust.com
canetictrust.com
Ticker Symbol: CNE.UN
Company Type: Public

Profile: Unit investment trusts, certificate/closed-end management offices; Extraction of crude petroleum, natural gas & natural gas liquids

Cathedral Energy Services Trust
#1700, 715 - 5th Ave. SW, Calgary, AB T2P 2X6
403-265-2560 Fax: 403-262-4682
www.cathedralenergyservices.com
Ticker Symbol: CET.UN
Company Type: Public

Profile: Cathedral Energy Services Income Trust is a limited purpose trust. The Trust is the owner of the securities of Cathedral Energy Services Ltd. & Cathedral Energy Services Limited Partnership. Cathedral is engaged in the provision of oilfield services to oil & natural gas companies. Activities take place in western Canada & the Rocky Mountain area of the United States.

CCS Income Trust
#2400, 530 - 8th Ave. SW, Calgary, AB T2P 3S8
403-233-7565 Fax: 403-261-5612
info@ccsincometrust.com
www.ccsincometrust.com
Ticker Symbol: CCR
Company Type: Public

Profile: Various oil & gas fields services; Refuse systems

Celtic Exploration Ltd.
#500, 505 - 3rd St. SW, Calgary, AB T2P 3E6
403-201-9153 Fax: 403-201-9163
invest@celticex.com
www.celticex.com
Ticker Symbol: CLT
Company Type: Public

Profile: Celtic Exploration Ltd. specializes in the exploration & production of oil & gas.

Centurion Energy International Inc.
Bow Valley Square II, #1700, 205 - 5th Ave. SW, Calgary, AB T2P 2V7
403-263-6002 **Company Type:** Public

Profile: Extraction of crude petroleum, natural gas & natural gas liquids

Compton Petroleum Corporation
East Tower, Fifth Avenue Place, #3300, 425 - 1st St. SW, Calgary, AB T2P 3L8
403-237-9400 Fax: 403-237-9410
investorinfo@comptonpetroleum.com
www.comptonpetroleum.com
Ticker Symbol: CMT
Company Type: Public

Profile: Compton Petroleum Corporation explores for, develops, & produces natural gas, natural gas liquids, & crude oil. Activities are carried out in western Canada's sedimentary basin.

Connacher Oil & Gas Limited
#900, 332 - 6th Ave. SW, Calgary, AB T2P 0B2
403-538-6201 Fax: 403-538-6225
inquiries@connacheroil.com
www.connacheroil.com
Ticker Symbol: CLL
Company Type: Public

Profile: Connacher Oil & Gas Limited is involved in the exploration, development, & production of oil & natural gas. The company's operations are carried out in western Canada, where its principal asset is oil sands leases in the Great Divide & Halfway Creek regions near Fort McMurray, Alberta. It is also the owner & operator of a refinery in Montana.

Conoco Phillips Canada
Gulf Canada Square, PO Box 130 M, 401 - 9 Ave. SW, Calgary, AB T2P 2H7
403-233-4000 Fax: 403-233-5143 www.conocophillips.ca
Company Type: Private

Profile: Extraction of crude petroleum, natural gas & natural gas liquids

Corridor Resources Inc.
#301, 5475 Spring Garden Rd., Halifax, NS B3J 3T2
902-429-4511 Fax: 902-429-0209 888-429-4511
info@corridor.ca
www.corridor.ca
Ticker Symbol: CDH
Company Type: Public

Profile: Corridor Resources Inc. is a junior resource company, which is engaged in the exploration & development of oil & gas properties. Activities are carried out onshore in Prince Edward Island, New Brunswick, & Québec, & offshore in the Gulf of St. Lawrence.

Crescent Point Energy Trust
#2800, 111 - 5th Ave. SW, Calgary, AB T2P 3Y6
403-693-0020 Fax: 403-693-0070 www.crescentpointenergy.com
Ticker Symbol: CPG
Company Type: Public

Profile: Conventional oil & gas income trust

Crew Energy Inc.
#1400, 425 First St. SW, Calgary, AB T2P 3L8
403-266-2088 Fax: 403-266-6259
investor@crewenergy.com
www.crewenergy.com
Ticker Symbol: CR
Company Type: Public

Profile: The junior oil & natural gas producer carries out its activities in northeastern British Columbia & central Alberta.

Destiny Resource Services Corp.
#300, 444 - 58th Ave. SE, Calgary, AB T2H 0P4
403-237-6437 Fax: 403-233-8714
destiny@destiny-resources.com
www.destiny-resources.com
Ticker Symbol: DSC
Company Type: Public

Profile: Extraction services in drilling oil & gas wells; Oil & gas fields exploration services

Devon Canada Corporation
#2000, 400 - 3rd Ave. SW, Calgary, AB T2P 4H2
403-232-7100 Fax: 403-232-7221 www.devonenergy.com
Ticker Symbol: DVN
Company Type: Public

Profile: Crude petroleum, natural gas & natural gas liquids extraction

Duvernay Oil Corp.
#1500, 202 - 6th Ave. SW, Calgary, AB T2P 2R9
403-571-3600 Fax: 403-269-6510 **Ticker Symbol:** DDQ
Company Type: Public

Profile: Duvernay Oil acquires, explores, & develops crude oil & natural gas properties in the sedimentary basin of Alberta & northeastern British Columbia.

Enbridge Inc.
Fifth Avenue Place, #3000, 425 - 1st St. SW, Calgary, AB T2P 3L8
403-231-3900 Fax: 403-231-3920 877-420-8800
investor.relations@enbridge.com
www.enbridge.com
Ticker Symbol: ENB
Company Type: Public

Profile: Enbridge Inc. is engaged in the following businesses: natural gas pipelines, crude oil & liquids pipelines, & natural gas distribution. The company;s pipeline system is located in Canada & the United States. International activity includes energy projects & renewable energy.

EnCana Corporation
PO Box 2850, #1800, 855 - 2nd St. SW, Calgary, AB T2P 2S5
403-645-2000 Fax: 403-645-2091
investor.relations@encana.com
www.encana.com
Ticker Symbol: ECA
Company Type: Public

Profile: The company is engaged in oil & gas production.

Enerplus Resources Fund
The Dome Tower, #3000, 333 - 7th Ave. SW, Calgary, AB T2P 2Z1
403-298-2200 Fax: 403-298-2211
investorrelations@enerplus.com
www.enerplus.com
Ticker Symbol: ERF.UN
Company Type: Public

Profile: Enerplus Resources Fund has a portfolio of oil & natural gas producing properties. Properties are situated in western Canada & the United States.

Ensign Energy Services Inc.
#1000, 400 - 5th Ave. SW, Calgary, AB T2P 0L6
403-262-1361 Fax: 403-262-8215
info@ensignenergy.com
www.ensignenergy.com
Ticker Symbol: ESI
Company Type: Public

Profile: Oilfield services are provided throughout the world to the oil & natural gas industry. Some of Ensign Energy Services's principal operating subsidiaries include Arctic Ensign Drilling Ltd., Big Sky Drilling Inc., Encore Coring & Drilling Inc., Opsco Energy Industries Ltd., Rockwell Servicing Inc., & Gwich'in Ensign Oilfield Services Inc.

Enterra Energy Corp.
#2700, 500 - 4th Ave. SW, Calgary, AB T2P 2V6
403-263-0262 Fax: 403-294-1197 877-263-0262
info@enterraenergy.com
www.enterraenergy.com
Company Type: Public

Profile: Crude petroleum, natural gas & natural gas liquids extraction

Eurogas Corporation
#250, 435 - 4 Ave. SW, Calgary, AB T2P 3A8
403-264-4985 Fax: 403-262-8299
eurogas@eurogascorp.com
www.eurogascorp.com
Ticker Symbol: EUG
Company Type: Public

Profile: Extraction of crude petroleum, natural gas & natural gas liquids, natural gas storage

Eveready Inc.
14904 - 121A Ave., Edmonton, AB T5V 1A3
780-451-6075 Fax: 780-451-2142 877-661-6689
investorrelations@evereadyinc.com
www.evereadyinc.com
Ticker Symbol: EIS
Company Type: Public

Profile: Eveready Inc. serves the energy, resource, & industrial sectors. The company provides industrial & oilfield maintenance & production services in Canada & internationally.

Fairborne Energy Ltd.
#3400, 450 - 1st St. SW, Calgary, AB T2P 5H1
403-290-7750 Fax: 403-290-7724
info@fairborne-energy.com
www.fairborne-energy.com
Ticker Symbol: FEL
Company Type: Public

Profile: Fairborne Energy Ltd. develops oil & gas properties. The company's main operating areas are as follows: Central Alberta; West Pembina/Brazeau; Columbia/Harlech; Deep Basin;

Peace River Arch in Alberta; & Sinclair in southwestern Manitoba. The company has implemented a comprehensive health, safety, & environmental program.

First Calgary Petroleums Ltd.
#500, 1414 - 8th St. SW, Calgary, AB T2R 1J6
403-264-6697 Fax: 403-264-3955
info@fcpl.ca
www.fcpl.ca
Ticker Symbol: FCP
Company Type: Public
Profile: Extraction of crude petroleum, natural gas & natural gas liquids

Flint Energy Services Ltd.
Stock Exchange Bldg., #700, 300 - 5th Ave. SW, Calgary, AB T2P 3C4
403-218-7100 Fax: 403-215-5481
gcocquyt@flint-energy.com
www.flint-energy.com
Ticker Symbol: FES
Company Type: Public
Profile: The company serves North America's energy & resource industries through the provision of integrated midstream production services. Flint Energy Services employs a Corporate Manager of Occupational Health, Safety & the Environment to monitor regulatory requirements & implement compliance procedures.

Fort Chicago Energy Partners L.P.
Livingston Place, #440, 222 - 3rd Ave. SW, Calgary, AB T2P 0B4
403-296-0140 Fax: 403-213-3648
investor-relations@fortchicago.com
www.fortchicago.com
Ticker Symbol: FCE
Company Type: Public
Profile: Fort Chicago Energy Partners L.P. invests in natural gas liquids extraction, power, & pipeline transportation businesses throughout North America.

Galleon Energy Inc.
West Tower, Livingston Place, #400, 250 - 2nd St. SW, Calgary, AB T2P 0C1
403-261-6012 Fax: 403-262-5561
information@galleonenergy.com
www.galleonenergy.com
Ticker Symbol: GO
Company Type: Public
Profile: Galleon Energy is a mid-sized oil & natural gas explorer & producer. It specializes in the acquisition, exploration, & development of petroleum & natural gas properties. Activities are carried out in western Canada.

Halliburton Canada Inc.
#1600, 645 - 7 Ave. SW, Calgary, AB T2P 4G8
403-231-9300 Fax: 403-261-9420 www.halliburton.com
Company Type: Public
Profile: Offices of holding companies; Various & oil & gas fields services; Engineering services; Equipment rental & leasing

Harvest Energy Trust
Calgary Place, #2100, 330 - 5th Ave. SW, Calgary, AB T2P 0L4
403-265-1178 Fax: 403-265-3490 www.harvestenergy.ca
Ticker Symbol: HTE.UN
Company Type: Private
Profile: Crude petroleum, natural gas & natural gas liquids extraction

Heritage Oil Corporation
#2000, 633 - 6th Avenue SW, Calgary, AB T2P 2Y5
403-234-9974 Fax: 403-261-1941
info@heritageoilcorp.com
www.heritageoilcorp.com
Ticker Symbol: HOC.A
Company Type: Public
Profile: Oil & gas exploration, development & production in Africa & Middle East

Hunt Oil Company of Canada, Inc.
Transcanada Tower, #3100, 450 First St. SW, Calgary, AB T2P 5H1
403-531-1430 Fax: 403-531-1539
877-444-9295www.huntoil.com
Company Type: Private
Profile: Crude petroleum, natural gas & natural gas liquids extraction

Husky Energy Inc.
PO Box 6525 D, 707 - 8 Ave. SW, Calgary, AB T2P 3G7
403-298-6111 Fax: 403-298-7464
investor.relations@huskyenergy.ca
www.huskyenergy.ca
Ticker Symbol: HSE
Company Type: Public
Profile: Husky Energy Inc. is engaged in the exploration & development of crude oil & natural gas, as well as the production, transportation & marketing of petroleum products.

Imperial Oil Limited
PO Box 2480 M, 237 Fourth Ave. SW, Calgary, AB T2P 3M9
800-567-3776 Fax: 800-367-0585 www.imperialoil.ca
Ticker Symbol: IMO
Company Type: Public
Profile: The company is a producer of crude oil & natural gas. Imperial Oil also refines & markets petroleum products.

Integrated Production Services Ltd.
#1900, 840 - 7th Ave. SW, Calgary, AB T2P 3G2
403-266-0908 Fax: 403-266-1639 www.ipsadvantage.com
Company Type: Private
Profile: Various oil & gas fields services

Inter Pipeline Fund
#2600, 237 - 4th Ave. SW, Calgary, AB T2P 4K3
403-290-6000 Fax: 403-290-6092 866-716-7473
investorrelations@interpipelinefund.com
www.interpipelinefund.com
Ticker Symbol: IPL.UN
Company Type: Public
Profile: Services included petroleum transportation, bulk liquid storage & natural gas liquids extraction; Owner & operator of energy infrastructure assets in Western Canada, the United Kingdom, Germany & the Republic of Ireland

Ivanhoe Energy Inc.
#654, 999 Canada Place, Vancouver, BC V6C 3E1
604-688-8323 Fax: 604-682-2060
info@ivanhoeenergy.com
www.ivanhoeenergy.com
Ticker Symbol: IE
Company Type: Public
Profile: Extraction of crude petroleum, natural gas & natural gas liquids

Jura Energy Corporation
#227, 200 Barclay Parade SW, Calgary, AB T2P 4R5
403-266-6364 Fax: 403-266-6365
info@juraenergy.com
www.juraenergy.com
Ticker Symbol: JEC
Company Type: Public
Profile: Petroleum & natural gas exploration & production, primarily conducted in Pakistan

Kinder Morgan Canada
#2700, 300 - 5th Ave., Calgary, AB T2P 5J2
403-514-6400 Fax: 403-514-6401 800-535-7219
info@kindermorgan.com
www.kindermorgan.com
Company Type: Public
Profile: Crude petroleum & refined petroleum pipelines

Nabors Drilling (Canada)
#2800, 500 - 4th Ave. SW, Calgary, AB T2P 2V6
403-263-6777 Fax: 403-269-7352
ndl.marketing@nabors.com
www.nabors.com
Company Type: Private
Profile: Nabors is engaged in the exploration & development of oil, gas, & geothermal wells. A variety of land rigs & ancillary services are marketed by Nabors Canada throughout the country.

Nexen Inc.
801 - 7 Ave. SW, Calgary, AB T2P 3P7
403-699-4000 Fax: 403-699-5800
ir@nexeninc.com
www.nexeninc.com
Ticker Symbol: NXY
Company Type: Public
Profile: The energy company carries out operations in the Athabasca oil sands of Alberta, the Gulf of Mexico, offshore West Africa, & the Middle East.

Niko Resources Ltd.
4600 Canterra Tower, #4600, 400 - 3 Ave. SW, Calgary, AB T2P 4H2
403-262-1020 Fax: 403-263-2686
nikocalgary@nikoresources.com
www.nikoresources.com
Ticker Symbol: NKO
Company Type: Public
Profile: Extraction of crude petroleum, natural gas & natural gas liquids

North American Energy Partners Inc.
Zone 3, Acheson Industrial Area, #2, 53016 Hwy. 60, Acheson, AB T7X 5A7
780-960-4531 Fax: 780-960-7103
IR@nacg.caca
www.nacg.ca
Ticker Symbol: NOA
Company Type: Public
Profile: North American Energy Partners Inc. is the corporate parent of North American Construction Group Inc. The following services are provided by North American Energy Partners Inc.: pipeline, piling, heavy construction, & mining. Large oil, natural gas, & resource companies are the main recipients of these services. The principal area of activity is the Canadian oil sands.

NuVista Energy Ltd.
#700, 311 - 6th Ave. SW, Calgary, AB T2P 3H2
403-538-8500 Fax: 403-538-8505
inv_rel@nuvistaenergy.com
www.nuvistaenergy.com
Ticker Symbol: NVA
Company Type: Public
Profile: Nuvista Energy is a Canadian oil & gas company, which acquires, explores, & develops oil & gas properties. The company is active in the Western Canadian Sedimentary Basin.

Oilexco Inc.
#3200, 715 - 5th Ave. SW, Calgary, AB T2P 2X6
403-262-5441 Fax: 403-263-3251
info@oilexco.com
www.oilexco.com
Ticker Symbol: OIL
Company Type: Public
Profile: Oilexco Inc. specializes in the exploration, development, & production of oil & gas.

Open Range Energy Corp.
#1100, 645 - 7 Ave. SW, Calgary, AB T2P 4G8
403-262-2936 Fax: 403-262-3924
sbuick@tempestenergy.com
www.openrangeenergy.com
Ticker Symbol: ONR
Company Type: Public
Profile: Oil & gas exploration, development & production, primarily in Alberta

Pacific Northern Gas Ltd.
#950, 1185 West Georgia St., Vancouver, BC V6E 4E6
604-691-5680 Fax: 604-697-6210
info@png.ca
www.png.ca
Ticker Symbol: PNG
Company Type: Public
Profile: Pacific Northern Gas delivers natural gas to its residential, commercial, & industrial customers. Customers are situated in west-central British Columbia. The company's subsidiary, Pacific Northern Gas (N.E.) Ltd., is engaged in the delivery of natural gas to customers in northeastern British Columbia.

Pacific Rubiales Energy
#1400, 220 Bay St., Toronto, ON M5J 2W4
416-362-7735 Fax: 416-360-7783 www.petrorubiales.com
Ticker Symbol: PRE
Company Type: Public
Profile: Pacific Rubiales Energy is engaged in the production of heavy crude oil & natural gas. It is the owner of Meta Petroleum Limited, which is a Colombian oil operator.

Pan Orient Energy Corp.
#1505, 505 - 3rd St. SW, Calgary, AB T2P 3E6
403-294-1770 Fax: 403-294-1780 www.panorient.ca
Ticker Symbol: POE
Company Type: Public
Profile: The oil & gas exploration & production company's areas of activity are western Canada & Thailand.

Pantera Drilling Income Trust
#600, 407 - 8th Ave. SW, Calgary, AB T2P 1E5
403-515-8400 Fax: 403-515-8405
info@panteradrilling.com
www.panteradrilling.com
Ticker Symbol: RIG.UN
Company Type: Public
Profile: Pantera Drilling Income Trust is an open-ended, investment trust. The Trust is involved in the provision of contract drilling services. It serves oil & gas exploration & production companies in the Western Canadian Sedimentary Basin.

Paramount Resources Ltd.
Bankers Hall West, #4700, 888 - 3rd St. SW, Calgary, AB T2P 5C5

403-290-3600 Fax: 403-262-7994
info@paramountres.com
www.paramountres.com
Ticker Symbol: POU
Company Type: Public
Profile: The oil & natural gas exploration, development, & production company carries out its operations in western Canada.

Peak Energy Services Trust Ltd.
#900, 222 - 3rd Ave. SW, Calgary, AB T2P 0B4
403-543-7325 Fax: 403-543-7335 800-661-3803
mjhuber@pesl.com
www.peak-energy.com
Ticker Symbol: PES
Company Type: Public
Profile: Offices of holding companies; Various oil & gas fields services; Manufacturers of oil & gas field machinery & equipment; Equipment rental & leasing

Pebercan Inc.
#106, 750, boul Marcel Laurin, Saint-Laurent, QC H4M 2M4
514-286-5200 Fax: 514-286-5177
info@pebercan.com
www.pebercan.com
Ticker Symbol: PBC
Company Type: Public
Profile: Pebercan Inc. is engaged in the exploration, development, & operation of oil & gas fields in the Republic of Cuba. Its wholly-owned subsidiary is Peberco Limited.

Pembina Pipeline Income Fund
#2000, 700 - 9th Ave. SW, Calgary, AB T2P 3V4
403-231-7500 Fax: 403-237-0254
investor-relations@pembina.com
www.pembina.com
Ticker Symbol: PIF
Company Type: Public
Profile: Through its subsidiaries, Pembina Pipeline Income Fund is involved in the transportation of light conventional & synthetic crude oil, & condensate & natural gas liquids. Operations are carried out in western Canada.

Pengrowth Energy Trust
#2100, 222 - 3rd Ave. SW, Calgary, AB T2P 0B4
403-233-0224 Fax: 866-433-5224
pengrowth@pengrowth.com
www.pengrowth.com
Ticker Symbol: PGF
Company Type: Public
Profile: The energy royalty trust invests in crude oil & natural gas properties.

Penn West Energy Trust
#200, 207 - 9th Ave. SW, Calgary, AB T2P 1K3
403-777-2500 Fax: 403-777-2699 866-693-2707
investor_relations@pennwest.com
www.pennwest.com
Ticker Symbol: PWT.UN, PWE
Company Type: Public
Profile: Penn West Petroleum Ltd. is a conventional oil & natural gas producing income trust. It operates throughout the Western Canadian Sedimentary Basin. The organization strives to meet & exceed regulatory environmental codes & guidelines.

Petro-Canada
PO Box 2844, 150 - 6th Ave. SW, Calgary, AB T2P 3E3
403-296-8000 Fax: 403-296-3030
investor@petro-canada.ca
www.petro-canada.ca
Ticker Symbol: PCA
Company Type: Public
Profile: Petro-Canada is engaged in the development, production, & marketing of crude oil & natural gas. Petroleum products are also refined & distributed by the company.

Petrobank Energy & Resources Ltd.
#2600, 240 - 4th Ave. SW, Calgary, AB T2P 4H4
403-750-4400 Fax: 403-266-5794
ir@petrobank.com
www.petrobank.com
Ticker Symbol: PBG
Company Type: Public
Profile: The company is engaged in the acquisition, exploration, & development of natural gas & oil properties. Operations are carried out in western Canada & Colombia.

Petrolifera Petroleum Limited
#900, 332 - 6th Ave. SW, Calgary, AB T2P 0B2
403-538-6201 Fax: 403-538-6225
inquiries@petrolifera.ca
www.petrolifera.ca
Ticker Symbol: PDP
Company Type: Public
Profile: The oil & natural gas exploration & production company is active in Peru, Argentina, & Columbia. Connacher Oil and Gas Limited owns part of Petrolifera's shares.

Peyto Energy Trust
#2900, 450 - 1st St. SW, Calgary, AB T2P 5H1
403-261-6081 Fax: 403-261-8976
info@peyto.com
www.peyto.com
Ticker Symbol: PEY
Company Type: Public
Profile: The exploration & development of oil & gas properties take place in western Canada.

Phoenix Technology Income Fund
#630, 434 - 4th Ave. SW, Calgary, AB T2P 3A8
403-543-4466 Fax: 403-543-4485
investor@phoenixcan.com
www.phoenixcan.com
Ticker Symbol: PHX.UN
Company Type: Public
Profile: Phoenix Technology Income Fund is involved in the provision of directional & horizontal drilling services & technology. The organization serves the oil & natural gas producing sectors in Canada & the United States. Phoenix Technology Income Fund works through the following companies: Phoenix Technology Services LP in Canada; & Nevis Energy Services Inc. in the United States.

Precision Drilling Trust
#4200, 150 - 6th Ave. SW, Calgary, AB T2P 3Y7
403-716-4500 Fax: 403-264-0251
info@precisiondrilling.com
www.precisiondrilling.com
Ticker Symbol: PD.UN
Company Type: Public
Profile: The energy services company consists of the following business segments: contract drilling, & completion & production.

Progress Energy Resources Corp.
#1200, 205 - 5th Ave. SW, Calgary, AB T2P 2V7
403-216-2510 Fax: 403-216-2514
ir@progressenergy.com
www.progressenergy.com
Ticker Symbol: PRQ
Company Type: Public
Profile: Progress Energy Resources Corp. is a natural gas & crude oil exploration & production organization.

Provident Energy Trust
#2100, 250 - 2nd St. SW, Calgary, AB T2P 0C1
403-296-2233 Fax: 403-294-0111
info@providentenergy.com
www.providentenergy.com
Ticker Symbol: PVE.UN
Company Type: Public
Profile: The open-ended income trust has a diversified portfolio of energy infrastructure assets & upstream oil & gas assets.

Pulse Data Inc.
#2400, 639 - 5th Ave. SW, Calgary, AB T2P 0M9
403-237-5559 Fax: 403-531-0688 877-460-5559
info@pulsedatainc.com
www.pulsedatainc.com
Ticker Symbol: PSD
Company Type: Public
Profile: Specializing in data ownership through acquisition, marketing & information management, with current focus on the energy sector

Sabretooth Energy Ltd.
#702, 2303 - 4th St. SW, Calgary, AB T2S 2S7
403-229-3050 Fax: 403-229-0603
info@sabretooth.ca
www.sabretooth.ca
Ticker Symbol: SAB
Company Type: Public
Profile: Production of oil, natural gas, & natural gas liquids. The company holds interest in properties in Alberta & British Columbia

Savanna Energy Services Corp.
#1800, 311 - 6th Ave. SW, Calgary, AB T2P 3H2
403-503-9990 Fax: 403-267-6749 877-568-2344
info@savannaenergy.com
www.savannaenergy.com
Ticker Symbol: SVY
Company Type: Public
Profile: The company is a North American energy services provider. Savanna Energy Services has partnerships with several Aboriginal communities in western Canada. It uses PLC-controlled service rigs & patented hybrid drilling rigs in its operations.

Saxon Energy Services Inc.
#1700, 700 - 4th Ave. SW, Calgary, AB T2P 3J4
403-716-4150 Fax: 403-716-4151 www.saxonservices.com
Ticker Symbol: SES
Company Type: Public
Profile: Saxon Energy Services Inc. is engaged in oil & gas drilling, & well servicing. The company serves multinational & national oil & gas exploration & production companies. Saxon Energy Services is active in Canada, the United States, Mexico, Ecuador, Venezuela, & Columbia.

Schlumberger Canada Ltd.
525 - 3rd Ave. SW, Calgary, AB T2P 0G4
403-509-4000 Fax: 403-509-4021 www.slb.com
Company Type: Private
Profile: Schlumberger Canada is an oilfield services provider, with offices in Calgary, Alberta & Mount Pearl, Newfoundland. It offers a great range of products & services, from well cementing to information management services. The company has research & engineering facilities throughout the world to develop innovative technology for the oil & gas industry. Schlumberger has high standards for health & safety & the protection of the environment in the communities in which it works.

ShawCor Ltd.
25 Bethridge Rd., Toronto, ON M9W 1M7
416-743-7111 Fax: 416-743-9123
glove@shawcor.com
www.shawcor.com
Ticker Symbol: SCL.A
Company Type: Public
Profile: ShawCor Ltd. is a provider of technology-based products & services for the pipeline & pipe services market, as well as the petrochemical & industrial market. Facilities are located in over twenty countries.

Shell Canada Limited
PO Box 100 M, 400 - 4th Ave. SW, Calgary, AB T2P 2H5
403-691-3537 Fax: 403-691-3696 800-661-1600
questions@shell.ca
www.shell.ca
Company Type: Private
Profile: Shell Canada is an integrated oil & gas company. The following are the company's activities: exploration & production of oil & gas; delivery of gas projects; production of petrochemicals for industrial customers; the sale of petroleum-based products for domestic, transport, & industrial use; & the extraction of bitumen, at the company's Athabasca Oil Sands Project in Alberta, & its conversion to synthetic crude oil.

Stoneham Drilling Trust
#1230, 335 - 8th Ave. SW, Calgary, AB T2P 1C9
403-264-7777 Fax: 403-264-7766
bjones@stonehamdrilling.ca
www.stonehamdrilling.com
Ticker Symbol: SDG.UN
Company Type: Public
Profile: Contract drilling services are provided by Stoneham Drilling Trust. It serves oil & natural gas exploration & production companies in the Western Canada Sedimentary Basin & the Anadarko Basin of Oklahoma. The company's operating practices comply with provincial standards for oilfield waste management.

Storm Exploration Inc.
#800, 205 - 5th Ave. SW, Calgary, AB T2P 2V7
403-264-3520 Fax: 403-264-3552
info@stormexploration.com
www.stormexploration.com
Ticker Symbol: SEO
Company Type: Public
Profile: Storm Exploration Inc. focuses upon exploring, acquiring, & developing oil & natural gas reserves in Alberta & British Columbia.

Suncor Energy Inc.
PO Box 38, 112 - 4 Ave. SW, Calgary, AB T2P 2V5
403-269-8100 Fax: 403-269-6217 866-786-2671
info@suncor.com
www.suncor.com
Ticker Symbol: SU
Company Type: Public
Profile: Suncor Energy Inc. is engaged in natural gas production in western Canada, with a focus on the oil sands. Refinement & marketing operations are carried out in Ontario & Colorado. The company also invests in renewable energy, especially ethanol production & wind power.

Sword Energy Inc.
#400, 321 - 6th Ave. SW, Calgary, AB T2P 3H3
403-294-1635 Fax: 403-232-1317
info@swordenergy.com

www.thunderenergy.com
Company Type: Public
Profile: Crude petroleum, natural gas & natural gas liquids extraction

Syncrude Canada Ltd.
PO Box 4023 Main, 9911 MacDonald Ave., Fort McMurray, AB T9H 3H5
780-790-5911 Fax: 780-790-6215 800-667-9494
info@syncrude.com
www.syncrude.com
Company Type: Private
Profile: Crude petroleum & natural gas extraction

Talisman Energy Inc.
#3400, 888 - 3rd St. SW, Calgary, AB T2P 5C5
403-237-1234 Fax: 403-237-1210
tlm@talisman-energy.com
www.talisman-energy.com
Ticker Symbol: TLM
Company Type: Public
Profile: Talisman Energy carries out its operations as an oil & gas producer in Canada. The company's subsidiaries has operations in the United States, Trinidad & Tobago, North Africa, the North Sea, Southeast Asia, & Australia.

Tanganyika Oil Company Ltd.
#700, 444 - 7th Ave. SW, Calgary, AB T2P 0X8
403-663-2999 Fax: 403-261-1007
info@tanganyikaoil.com
www.tanganyikaoil.com
Ticker Symbol: TYK
Company Type: Public
Profile: The international oil & gas exploration, development, & production company has interests in properties in Syria.

TAQA North Ltd.
#5100, 150 - 6th Ave. SW, Calgary, AB T2P 3Y7
403-724-5000 Fax: 403-724-5025
ir@taqaglobal.com
www.taqa.ae/en/canada.html
Company Type: Private
Profile: TAQA North Ltd. is engaged in oil & gas exploration. It is active in the following regions: the Northwest Territories, northern British Columbia & Alberta; west central & southern Alberta, & southeastern & southwestern Saskatchewan.

Taylor NGL Limited Partnership
#2200, 800 - 5th Ave. SW, Calgary, AB T2P 3T6
403-781-8181 Fax: 403-777-1907 **Company Type:** Private
Profile: Extraction of natural gas liquids; Processing of natural gas

Terasen Gas Inc.
16705 Fraser Hwy., Surrey, BC V4N 0E8
604-576-7000 800-773-7001
websupport@terasengas.com
www.terasengas.com
Company Type: Public
Profile: Natural gas transmission & distribution; Gas & other services combined; Refined petroleum pipelines

Total Energy Services Trust
#2550, 300 - 5th Ave. SW, Calgary, AB T2P 3C4
403-216-3939 Fax: 403-234-8731 877-818-6825
investorrelations@totalenergy.ca
www.totalenergy.ca
Ticker Symbol: TOT
Company Type: Public
Profile: The oil & gas service income trust is involved in drilling & production services. Total Energy Services Trust serves western & northern Canada's oil & gas industry.

Trans Québec & Maritimes Pipeline Inc.
#525, 6300, av Auteuil, Brossard, QC J4Z 3P2
450-462-5300 Fax: 450-462-5388
tqm@gazoductqm.com
www.gazoductqm.com
Company Type: Public
Profile: Natural gas transmission & distribution

TransCanada PipeLines Limited
450 - 1 St. SW, Calgary, AB T2P 5H1
403-920-2000 Fax: 403-920-2200 800-661-3805
communications@transcanada.com
www.transcanada.com
Ticker Symbol: TCA
Company Type: Public
Profile: The energy infrastructure company is engaged in natural gas transmission & power services.

TransGlobe Energy Corporation
#2500, 605 - 5th Ave. SW, Calgary, AB T2P 3H5
403-264-9888 Fax: 403-264-9898
contact@trans-globe.com
www.trans-globe.com
Ticker Symbol: TGL
Company Type: Public
Profile: TransGlobe Energy acquires, explores, & develops oil & gas properties. The Alberta-based oil & gas exploration & development company focuses its production activities in the Arab Republic of Egypt, & the Republic of Yemen.

Trican Well Service Ltd.
#2900, 645 - 7th Ave. SW, Calgary, AB T2P 4G8
403-266-0202 Fax: 403-237-7716
info@trican.ca; sales@trican.ca
www.trican.ca
Ticker Symbol: TCW
Company Type: Public
Profile: Trican Well Service Ltd. is a provider of products, equipment, & services, which are employed in the exploration & development of oil & gas reserves. The company conducts its operations in Canada, the United States, & Russia.

Trinidad Drilling Ltd.
#2500, 700 - 9th Ave. SW, Calgary, AB T2P 3V4
403-265-6525 Fax: 403-265-4168
info@trinidaddrilling.com
www.trinidaddrilling.com
Ticker Symbol: TDG
Company Type: Public
Profile: The company specializes in drilling, well servicing, & barge drilling operations within the North American oil & gas industry. Trinidad Drilling Ltd.incorporates environmental protection measures into its procedures for site inspections, products, equipment, & waste disposal.

True Energy Trust
#2300, 530 - 8th Avenue SW, Calgary, AB T2P 3S8
403-266-8670 Fax: 403-264-8163
general.info@trueenergy.ab.ca
www.trueenergytrust.com
Ticker Symbol: TUI.UN
Company Type: Public

TUSK Energy Corp.
#1900, 700 - 4th Ave. SW, Calgary, AB T2P 3J4
403-264-8875 Fax: 403-263-4247
tusk@tusk-energy.com
www.tusk-energy.com
Ticker Symbol: TSK
Company Type: Public
Profile: Crude petroleum, natural gas & natural gas liquids extraction

Ultra Petroleum Corp.
#1200, 363 North Sam Houston Pkwy. East, Houston, TX 77060
281-876-0120 Fax: 281-876-2831
info@ultrapetroleum.com
www.ultrapetroleum.com
Ticker Symbol: UPL
Company Type: Public
Profile: Incorporated in British Columbia in 1979, Ultra Petroleum Corp. is engaged in the exploration & development of oil & gas properties in the Green River Basin of Wyoming. The company's transfer agent is Computershare Trust Company of Canada & Computershare Trust Company, Inc.

Ultramar Ltd.
2200, av McGill College, Montréal, QC H3A 3L3
514-499-6111 800-363-6949
publicaffairs@ultramar.ca
www.ultramar.ca
Company Type: Private
Profile: Ultramar Ltd. is engaged in the provision of clean-burning, environmentally sound petroleum fuels at the industrial, commercial, & retail levels in North America. The company has a network of service stations, including car washes & stores, located throughout eastern Ontario, Québec, & the Atlantic provinces. Ultramar Ltd. also provides home heating & air conditioning services.

Union Gas Limited
PO Box 2001, 50 Keil Dr. North, Chatham, ON N7M 5M1
519-352-3100 Fax: 519-436-4566 800-265-5230
customerrelations@uniongas.com
www.uniongas.com
Ticker Symbol: UNG
Company Type: Public
Profile: The natural gas storage, transmission, & distribution company provides services in northern, southwestern, & eastern Ontario to commercial, industrial, & residential customers. In Quebec, Ontario, & the United States, Union Gas Limited also offers natural gas storage & transportation services to other utilities.

UPI Energy LP
#200, #105 Silvercreek Pkwy. North, Guelph, ON N1H 8M1
519-821-2667 Fax: 519-821-4919 800-396-2667
info@upi.on.ca; customers@upi.on.ca
www.upienergylp.com
Company Type: Public
Profile: UPI Energy LP provides environmentally friendly energy products & related services. Examples of products & services offered to farms & businesses include gasolines, diesel fuels, propane, & lubricants. The company serves consumers & motorists in rural Ontario.

UTS Energy Corporation
#1000, 350 - 7th Ave. SW, Calgary, AB T2P 3N9
403-538-7030 Fax: 403-538-7033
mail@uts.ca
www.uts.ca
Ticker Symbol: UTS
Company Type: Public
Profile: The company is engaged in the exploration & development of oil sands leases, such as the Fort Hills Project.

Vermilion Energy Trust
#2800, 400 - 4th Ave. SW, Calgary, AB T2P 0J4
403-269-4884 Fax: 403-264-6306 866-895-8101
investor_relations@vermilionenergy.com
www.vermilionenergy.com
Ticker Symbol: VET
Company Type: Public
Profile: The international energy trust is engaged in acquiring, developing, & optimizing producing properties. Activities take place in western Canada, western Europe, & Australia.

Vero Energy Inc.
#1400, 333 - 5th Ave. SW, Calgary, AB T2P 3B6
403-218-2063 Fax: 403-218-2064 866-709-8376
general.info@veroenergy.ca
www.veroenergy.ca
Ticker Symbol: VRO
Company Type: Public
Profile: Vero Energy Inc. specializes in oil & natural gas exploration, development, & production.

Westcoast Energy Inc
#2600, 425 - 1st St. SW, Calgary, AB T2P 3L8
403-699-1999 Fax: 403-699-1998 www.spectraenergy.com
Ticker Symbol: W.PR.J
Company Type: Public
Profile: Operating under the name, Spectra Energy Transmission, the company owns & operates businesses which are engaged in natural gas gathering, processing, storage, transmission, & distribution.

Winstar Resources Ltd.
#845, 401 - 9th Ave. SW, Calgary, AB T2P 3C5
403-205-3722 Fax: 403-205-2722 800-875-1217
info@winstar.ca
www.winstar.ca
Ticker Symbol: WIX
Company Type: Public
Profile: Winstar Resources Ltd. is an oil & gas exploration & development company. Operations are carried out in Canada, Romania, Hungary, & Tunisia.

Zargon Energy Trust
#700, 333 - 5th Ave. SW, Calgary, AB T2P 3B6
403-264-9992 Fax: 403-265-3026
zargon@zargon.ca
www.zargon.ca
Ticker Symbol: ZAR
Company Type: Public
Profile: Zargon Energy Trust is involved in oil & natural gas exploration, development, & production. The organization is active in the Alberta plains, west central Alberta, & the Williston Basin core area.

ZCL Composites Inc.
6907 - 36 St., Edmonton, AB T6B 2Z6
Fax: 780-466-6126 800-661-8265
ir@zcl.com
www.zcl.com
Ticker Symbol: ZCL
Company Type: Public
Profile: ZCL Composites Inc. designs, manufactures & distributes fiberglass tank systems. The environmentally friendly liquid handling solutions are used by the petroleum industry.

Port Authorities

Halifax Port Authority
PO Box 336, 1215 Marginal Rd., Halifax, NS B3H 4P8
902-426-8222 Fax: 902-426-7335 www.portofhalifax.ca
Company Type: Crown
Profile: Cargo: Bulk Cargo (Oil, Fuel, Gypsum) - 8.8 million metric tones Breakbulk Cargo (Iron/Steel, Machinery, Rubber) - 136,000 metric tones Roll-on, Roll-off Cargo (Cars and Trucks) -

216,000 metric tones Containerized Cargo - 4.6 million metric tones

Hamilton Port Authority
605 James St. North, 6th Floor, Hamilton, ON L8L 1K1
905-525-4330 Fax: 905-528-6554 800-263-2131
cargo@hamiltonport.ca
www.hamiltonport.ca
Company Type: Crown

Montreal Port Authority
Édifice du port de Montréal, 2100, av Pierre-Dupuy, Aile #1, Montréal, QC H3C 3R5
514-283-7011 Fax: 514-283-0829 www.port-montreal.com
Company Type: Crown
Profile: The Montreal port offers year-round access to major markets in central Canada, & the midwestern & northeastern United States.

Nanaimo Port Authority
PO Box 131, 104 Front St., Nanaimo, BC V9R 5K4
250-753-4146 Fax: 250-753-4899
info@npa.ca
www.npa.ca/en/index.htm
Company Type: Crown
Profile: The harbour, waters, & foreshore of the Georgia Strait are administered, controlled, & managed by the Nanimo Port Authority.

Port Alberni Port Authority
2750 Harbour Rd., Port Alberni, BC V9Y 7X2
250-723-5312 Fax: 250-723-1114
bfilipchuk.papa@portalberni.ca
www.portalberniportauthority.ca
Company Type: Crown
Profile: Under the Canada Marine Act, the Port Alberni Port Authority has jurisdiction of the Alberni Inlet, from the Somass River to Tzartus Island. The Inlet offers a direct shipping route to the Pacific Rim & can accommodate Panama size vessels.

Port of Belledune
112, Shannon Dr., Belledune, NB E8G 2W2
506-522-1200 Fax: 506-522-0803
info@portofbelledune.ca
www.portofbelledune.ca
Company Type: Crown
Profile: The Port of Belledune is a year-round marine transport facility, offering access to north-eastern & global markets. The port serves shipping companies, importers, & exporters.

Prince Rupert Port Authority
#200, 215 Cow Bay Rd., Prince Rupert, BC V8J 1A2
250-627-8899 Fax: 250-627-8980 www.rupertport.com
Company Type: Crown
Profile: The Prince Rupert Port Authority operates the port in the Prince Rupert Harbour, under the Canada Marine Act, & Letters Patent issued under the Act. The Authority facilitates the movement of cargo & passengers through the port in a safe & environmentally sound manner. Its responsibilities include the planning, development, marketing, & management of the commercial port facilities.

Québec Port Authority
PO Box 80 Haute-Ville, 150, rue Dalhousie, Québec, QC G1R 4M8
418-648-3640 Fax: 418-649-6414
marketing@portquebec.ca
www.portquebec.ca
Company Type: Crown
Profile: The Québec Port Authority is an independent federal agency which serves the economic interests of Québec & Canada by developing & promoting maritime trade. The port authority is involved in commercial exchanges with countries around the world.

Saguenay Port Authority
6600, rue Quai-Marcel-Dionne, La Baie, QC G7B 3N9
418-697-0250 Fax: 418-697-0243
info@portsaguenay.ca
www.portsaguenay.ca
Company Type: Crown
Profile: Under the Canada Marine Act, the Saguenay Port Authority provides services that promote & expand Canada's foreign trade. The port authority also works to develop the port's hinterland, especially the area of Saguenay-Lac-Saint-Jean-Chibougamau-Chapais. The Saguenay Port Authority consists of the Grande-Anse Marine Terminal, for the reception & transshipment of general cargo, & the Albert Maltais Oil Terminal, for the reception of oil.

Saint John Port Authority
111 Water St., Saint John, NB E2L 0B1
506-636-4869 Fax: 506-636-4443
port@sjport.com
www.sjport.com
Company Type: Crown
Profile: The Port of Saint John is an international seaport which accommodates a variety of shipping services, from shipping lines to cruise ships & ferry services. The port is important to New Brunswick's import & export trade, handling an average of 27 million metric tonnes of cargo each year.

Sept-Iles Port Authority
1 Quai Mgr-Blanche, Sept-Iles, QC G4R 5P3
418-968-1231 Fax: 418-962-4445
www.portsi.com/eg/default.htm
Company Type: Crown

Toronto Port Authority
60 Harbour St., Toronto, ON M5J 1B7
416-863-2000 Fax: 416-863-4830 www.torontoport.com
Company Type: Crown
Profile: Maintains a paved facility of over 50 acres centrally located, adjacent to downtown Toronto. The yard provides convenience, with excellent access to the railroads, as well as all major highways. This facility is fully bonded and has 24-hour security

Vancouver Fraser Port Authority
999 Canada Place, 100 The Pointe, Vancouver, BC V6C 3T4
604-665-9000 Fax: 866-284-4271 www.nfpa.ca/engindex.html
Company Type: Crown
Profile: In 2008, the Vancouver Port Authority, the Fraser River Port Authority, & the North Fraser Port Authority combined to create the Vancouver Fraser Port Authority. The port authority offers twenty-eight marine cargo terminals, plus three Class 1 railroads to serve the international shipping community.

Windsor Port Authority
#502, 251 Goyeau St., Windsor, ON N9A 6V2
519-258-5741 Fax: 519-258-5905 www.portwindsor.com
Company Type: Crown
Profile: Located on the Great Lakes / St. Lawrence Seaway System, the Windsor Port Authority carries out the following activities: administration of federal lands within the port; representation of port users at the municipal, provincial, & federal levels; facilitation of economic development & trade; development & promotion of the port; provision of general security; & ensuring safety & environmental responsibility in all operations.

Printing & Publishing

Canadian Bank Note Company, Limited
145 Richmond Rd., Ottawa, ON K1Z 1A1
613-722-3421 Fax: 613-722-2548
headoffice@cbnco.com
www.cbnco.com
Ticker Symbol: CBK
Company Type: Public
Profile: Manufacturers of security-printed products; production divisions include: Lottery Systems, Identification Systems, Payment Systems, and Shareholder Services

Datamark Systems Group Inc.
2800, av Francis-Hughes, Laval, QC H7L 3Y7
450-663-8716 Fax: 450-663-7720
888-360-0470www.datamark.ca
Ticker Symbol: DMK
Company Type: Public
Profile: Manufacturers of manifold business forms, various, gravure & lithographic commercial printing

FP Newspapers Income Fund
1355 Mountain Ave., Winnipeg, MB R2X 3B6
204-697-7364 Fax: 204-697-7344 www.fpnewspapers.com
Ticker Symbol: FP.UN
Company Type: Public
Profile: FP Newspapers Income Fund is an unincorporated, open-ended, limited purpose trust. It owns indirect interests in FP Canadian Newspapers Limited Partnership (FPLP). The Winnipeg Free Press & the Brandon Sun are two of the newspapers owned & published by FP Canadian Newspapers Limited Partnership.

Glacier Media Inc.
1970 Alberta St., Vancouver, BC V5Y 3X4
604-872-8565 Fax: 604-879-1483 www.glacierventures.com
Ticker Symbol: GVC
Company Type: Public
Profile: Glacier Media Inc. provides information & related services through print, electronic, & online media. The Business & Professional Group consists of organizations such as CD-Pharma, Eco Log ERIS, & Fundata. The Newspaper & Trade Group is comprised of organizations such as Western Producer Publications, Farm Business Communications, & the Business Information Group.

GVIC Communications Corp.
275 West 4th Ave., Vancouver, BC V5Y 1G8
604-872-8565 Fax: 604-879-1483
osmysnuik@madison.ca
Ticker Symbol: GCT
Company Type: Public
Profile: GVIC Communications is an information communications company. It owns local newspapers in western Canada, as well as trade, business, & professional information businesses.

Hollinger Inc.
#512, 120 Adelaide Street West, Toronto, ON M5H 1T1
416-363-8721 Fax: 416-363-4187 www.hollingerinc.com
Ticker Symbol: HLG
Company Type: Public
Profile: Offices of holding companies; Information retrieval services; Media broadcasting; Publishing & printing of newspapers & periodicals

McGraw-Hill Ryerson Limited
300 Water St., Whitby, ON L1N 9B6
905-430-5000 Fax: 905-430-5020 800-463-5885
gordond@mcgrawhill.ca
www.mcgrawhill.ca
Ticker Symbol: MHR
Company Type: Public
Profile: McGraw-Hill Ryerson publishes & distributes educational, technical, & professional books & reference materials. The publishing company also provides multi-media products & services.

MDC Partners
45 Hazelton Ave., Toronto, ON M5R 2E3
416-960-9000 Fax: 416-960-9555 www.mdc-partners.com
Ticker Symbol: MDZ
Company Type: Public
Profile: A portfolio of marketing communications companies

Metro Label Company Inc.
99 Progress Ave., Toronto, ON M1B 6J1
416-292-6600 Fax: 416-292-6133 800-668-4405
sales@metrolabel.com; jobs@metrolabel.com
www.metrolabel.com
Company Type: Private
Profile: Metro Label Company Inc. is a manufacturer of pressure sensitive labels.

PLM Group
210 Duffield Dr., Markham, ON L6G 1C9
416-848-8500 Fax: 416-848-8501 866-848-8500
contact_us@plmgroup.com
www.plmgroup.com
Company Type: Private
Profile: The commercial printing company delivers innovative print solutions. PLM Group serves agencies & corporations such as those in the promotional & print-for-one markets. Brand names include Mailer Magic & Optium.

Pollard Banknote Income Fund
1499 Buffalo Pl., Winnipeg, MB R3T 1L7
204-474-2323 Fax: 204-453-1375
winnipeg@pollardbanknote.com
www.pollardbanknote.com
Ticker Symbol: PBL.UN
Company Type: Public
Profile: Pollard Banknote Income Fund is an unincorporated, open-ended, limited purpose trust. It holds indirectly an investment in Pollard Holdings Limited Partnership. The Fund is involved in the printing of instant-win scratch tickets & break open/pull tab tickets, as well as the provision of related services to the lottery & charitable gaming industry.

Quebecor World Inc.
612, rue Saint-Jacques, Montréal, QC H3C 4M8
514-954-0101 Fax: 514-954-9624 800-567-7070
webmaster@quebecorworldinc.com
www.quebecorworldinc.com
Ticker Symbol: IQW
Company Type: Public
Profile: Manufacturers of lithographic, gravure & various commercial printing, paper mills & book printing

Technicolor Canada Inc.
40 Lesmill Rd., Don Mills, ON M3B 2T5
Fax: 416-449-3001 www.technicolor.com
Company Type: Public
Profile: Full port production, transfer, editing, visual effects, lab service & audio

Thomson Reuters
Toronto-Dominion Bank Tower, 66 Wellington St. West, Toronto, ON M5K 1A1
416-360-8700
investor.relations@thomsonreuters.com

www.thomsonreuters.com
Ticker Symbol: TRI
Company Type: Public
Profile: Thomson Reuters provides intelligent information for businesses & professionals.

Torstar Corporation
#600, 1 Yonge St., Toronto, ON M5E 1P9
416-869-4010 Fax: 416-869-4183
torstar@thestar.ca
www.torstar.com
Ticker Symbol: TS
Company Type: Public
Profile: The media company includes the following businesses: Star Media Group, which features the Toronto Star & Torstar Digital; Metroland Media Group, which publishes community & daily newspapers throughout Ontario; & Harlequin Enterprises, which publishes books for women. Torstar Corporation also owns parts of CTVglobemedia Inc. & Black Press.

Transcontinental Inc.
#3315, 1, Place Ville Marie, Montréal, QC H3B 3N2
514-954-4000 Fax: 514-954-4016
info@transcontinental.ca
www.transcontinental.com
Ticker Symbol: TCL.A
Company Type: Public
Profile: The company is engaged in the printing & publishing of consumer magazines & community newspapers, as well as direct marketing, & distribution of advertising material. Transcontinental Inc. has worked to address environmental issues, by programs such as the implementation of the Transcontinental Paper Purchasing Policy.

Yellow Pages Income Fund
Ile des Soeurs, 16, Place du Commerce, Verdun, QC H3E 2A5
514-934-2611 877-909-9356
ir.info@ypg.com
www.ypg.com
Ticker Symbol: YLO
Company Type: Public
Profile: Yellow Pages Income Fund indirectly holds 97% ownership interest in Yellow Pages Group & Trader Corporation. Yellow Pages Group publishes telephone directories. The Trader Corporation is engaged in print & online vertical media.

Real Estate

Accommodation and Real Estate Services
3350 Douglas St., Victoria, BC V8Z 3L1
250-952-8500 Fax: 250-952-8295
ARES@gov.bc.ca
www.accommodationandrealestate.gov.bc.ca
Company Type: Crown
Profile: Real estate operators of nonresidential buildings; General contractors of nonresidential buildings; Real estate agents & managers; Management services

Allied Hotel Properties Inc.
#300, 515 West Pender St., Vancouver, BC V6B 6H5
604-669-5335 Fax: 604-682-8131
info@alliedhotels.com
www.alliedhotels.com
Ticker Symbol: AHP
Company Type: Public
Profile: Allied Hotel Properties Inc. owns first class business hotels in Canadian urban centres. The organization's principal hotel properties are the Crowne Plaza Chateau Lacombe Hotel & the Crowne Plaza Toronto Don Valley Hotel.

Allied Properties Real Estate Investment Trust
255 Adelaide St. West, Toronto, ON M5H 1X9
416-977-9002 Fax: 416-977-9053
info@alliedpropertiesreit.com
www.alliedpropertiesreit.com
Ticker Symbol: AP.UN
Company Type: Public
Profile: Allied Properties REIT is the owner of office properties. Properties are located in Winnipeg, Toronto, Montréal, & Québec.

Altus Group Income Fund
#7, 17075 Leslie St., Newmarket, ON L3Y 8E1
905-953-9948 Fax: 905-953-0018 877-953-9948
info@altusgroup.com
www.altusgroupincomefund.com
Ticker Symbol: AIF.UN
Company Type: Public
Profile: Altus Group Income Fund is involved in the provision of independent real estate consulting & advisory services. The following are the organization's business units: cost consulting; research, valuation, & advisory; environmental & forestry services; & geomatics.

Amica Mature Lifestyles Inc.
1111 Melville St., 10th Fl., Vancouver, BC V6E 3V6
604-608-6777 Fax: 604-608-6717 877-447-4827
mail@amica.ca
www.amica.ca
Ticker Symbol: ACC
Company Type: Public
Profile: Amica Mature Lifestyles Inc. is a designer, developer, manager, & marketer of seniors' retirement residences & services. Amica has locations in Ontario & British Columbia.

Anthem Works Ltd.
#300, 550 Burrard St., Vancouver, BC V6C 2B5
604-689-3040 Fax: 604-689-5642 800-926-8436
info@anthemproperties.com
www.anthemproperties.com
Ticker Symbol: ANT
Company Type: Private
Profile: Real estate agents & managers; real estate land subdividers & developers

Artis Real Estate Investment Trust
#300, 360 Main St., Winnipeg, MB R3C 3Z3
204-947-1250 Fax: 204-947-0453
info@artisreit.com
www.artisreit.com
Ticker Symbol: AX.UN
Company Type: Public
Profile: Artis REIT is an open-end real estate investment trust. It produces distributions for unitholders from its ownership & management of retail, commercial, & industrial properties. Properties are located in western Canada.

Aspen Properties Ltd.
#1200, 833 - 4th Ave. SW, Calgary, AB T2P 3T5
403-216-2660 Fax: 403-216-2661
apl@aspenpropertiesltd.com
www.aspenpropertiesltd.com
Company Type: Private
Profile: Real estate agents & managers; Real estate land subdividers & developers

Bentall LP
Four Bentall Centre, PO Box 49001, #1800, 1055 Dunsmuir St., Vancouver, BC V7X 1B1
604-661-5000 Fax: 604-661-5055
info@bentall.com
www.bentall.com
Company Type: Private
Profile: Provides real estate investment management services, property development & merchant banking

Berwick Retirement Communities Ltd.
1162 Fort St., Victoria, BC V8V 3K8
250-385-1505 Fax: 250-385-9851 866-397-5463
mail@berwickrc.com
www.berwickrc.com
Ticker Symbol: BWK
Company Type: Public
Profile: Residential care; Real estate operators of non-apartment building dwellings

Boardwalk Real Estate Income Trust
#200, 1501 - 1st St. SW, Calgary, AB T2R 0W1
403-531-9255 Fax: 403-531-9565
investor@bwalk.com
www.bwalk.com
Ticker Symbol: BEI.UN
Company Type: Public
Profile: Real estate operators of apartment buildings; Real estate real estate agents & managers

Boston Development Corp.
#201, 3550 Taylor St. East, Saskatoon, SK S7H 5H9
306-955-6012 Fax: 306-955-3446
neil@bostoncorp.com
www.bostoncorp.com
Ticker Symbol: BTN
Company Type: Private
Profile: Real estate operators of apartment buildings

BPO Properties Ltd.
Brookfield Place, PO Box 770, #330, 181 Bay St., Toronto, ON M5J 2T3
416-359-8555 Fax: 416-359-8596
info@bpoproperties.com
www.bpoproperties.com
Ticker Symbol: BPP
Company Type: Public
Profile: The Canadian commercial real estate company is engaged in the ownership, development, & management of office properties. BPO Properties has endeavoured to develop several environmental initiatives in its properties, such as energy savings programs, environmentally sensitive fittings & finishes, & recycling.

Brookfield Properties Corporation
Brookfield Place, #330, 181 Bay St., Toronto, ON M5J 2T3
416-369-2300 Fax: 416-369-2301
melissa.coley@brookfieldproperties.com
www.brookfieldproperties.com
Ticker Symbol: BPO
Company Type: Public
Profile: The corporation owns, develops and manages office properties. Brookfield's portfolio includes the following places: Bankers Hall in Calgary, BCE Place in Toronto, World Financial Center in New York, & Bank of America Plaza in Los Angeles. The company is working towards developing properties that are sustainable & environmentally friendly, by ensuring that all future developments are built to a Leadership in Energy & Environmental Design (LEED) Gold standard.

Brookfield Real Estate Services Fund
39 Wynford Dr., Toronto, ON M3C 3K5
416-510-5853 Fax: 416-446-0050
info@brookfieldres.com
www.brookfieldres.com
Ticker Symbol: BRE.UN
Company Type: Public
Profile: Brookfield Real Estate Services Fund is involved in the provision of services to residential real estate franchisees & agents across Canada. Cash flow is generated from franchise royalties & service fees from realtors. Realtors operate under the brand names Royal LePage, La Capitale Real Estate Network, & Johnston & Daniel.

Cadillac Fairview Corporation Limited
20 Queen St. West, 5th Fl., Toronto, ON M5H 3R4
416-598-8200 Fax: 416-598-8607 www.cadillacfairview.com
Company Type: Private
Profile: Real estate operators of nonresidential buildings; Real estate agents & managers; Real estate land subdividers & developers

Calloway Real Estate Investment Trust
#200, 700 Applewood Cres., Vaughan, ON L4K 5X3
905-326-6400 Fax: 905-326-0783
investorrelations@callowayreit.com
www.callowayreit.com
Ticker Symbol: CWT.UN
Company Type: Public
Profile: Calloway REIT is an unincorporated, open-end real estate investment trust. It focuses on owning & developing high quality retail properties. Its portfolio consists of leaseable area throughout Canada.

Charlwood Pacific Group
#900, 1199 West Pender St., Vancouver, BC V6E 2R1
604-718-2600 Fax: 604-718-2678 **Company Type:** Private
Profile: Travel & real estate franchising company made up of brands such as Uniglobe Travel International, Century 21 Canada and Centum Financial Group.

CML Global Capital Ltd.
#1200, 833 - 4th Ave. SW, Calgary, AB T2P 3T5
403-216-3850 Fax: 403-216-2661 **Company Type:** Private
Profile: Offices of holding companies; Real estate land subdividers & developers; Automobile parking

CMN International Inc.
#1910, 200 Granville St., Vancouver, BC V6C 2R6
604-681-4111 Fax: 604-661-0849 www.colliersmn.com
Company Type: Public
Profile: Commercial real estate services: brokerage, property management, valuation and market research

Cominar Real Estate Investment Trust
455, rue du Marais, Québec, QC G1M 3A2
418-681-8151 Fax: 418-681-2946
info@cominar.com
www.cominar.com
Ticker Symbol: CUF
Company Type: Public
Profile: The unincorporated closed-end investment trust owns & manages commercial property in the Quebec City, Montreal, & Ottawa region.

Consolidated HCI Holdings Corporation
#3, 100 Strada Dr., Woodbridge, ON L4L 5V7
905-851-7741 Fax: 416-253-5074
ewdl@sympatico.ca
Ticker Symbol: CXA
Company Type: Public
Profile: The Ontario-based real estate company invests in syndicated mortgage loans. Through joint ventures, it is also engaged in housebuilding & the leasing of commercial & industrial properties.

Crombie Real Estate Investment Trust
115 King St., Stellarton, NS B0K 1S0
902-755-8100 Fax: 902-752-5136
investing@crombie.ca
www.crombiereit.ca
Ticker Symbol: CRR.UN
Company Type: Public
Profile: Crombie REIT owns & manages properties across Saskatchewan, Ontario, Quebec, & Atlantic Canada. Office buildings & shopping centres are the organizations's main properties.

Dundee Real Estate Investment Trust
State Street Financial Centre, #1600, 30 Adelaide St. East, Toronto, ON M5C 3H1
416-365-3535 Fax: 416-365-6565
info@dundeereit.com
www.dundeereit.com
Ticker Symbol: D.UN
Company Type: Public
Profile: Dundee REIT is engaged in acquiring, owning, managing, & leasing mid-sized urban & suburban offices & industrial properties across Canada.

Extendicare Real Estate Investment Trust
#700, 3000 Steeles Ave. East, Markham, ON L3R 9W2
905-470-4000 Fax: 905-470-5588
hgould@extendicare.com
www.extendicare.com
Ticker Symbol: EXE
Company Type: Public
Profile: Through its wholly owned subsidiaries, Extendicare REIT owns & operates retirement, assisted living, & nursing homes. In Canada, Extendicare REIT's wholly owned subsidiary is Extendicare (Canada) Inc. (ECI), & its division is ParaMed Home Health Care.

First Capital Realty Inc.
#400, 85 Hanna Ave., Toronto, ON M6K 3S3
416-504-4114 Fax: 416-941-1655
investor.relations@firstcapitalrealty.ca
www.firstcapitalrealty.ca
Ticker Symbol: FCR
Company Type: Public
Profile: First Capital Realty Inc. owns, develops, & operates shopping centres, anchored by supermarkets & drug stores. Properties are located mainly in metropolitan areas.

FirstService Corporation
#4000, 1140 Bay St., Toronto, ON M5S 2B4
416-960-9500 Fax: 416-960-5333
info@firstservice.com
www.firstservice.com
Ticker Symbol: FSV
Company Type: Public
Profile: FirstService Corporation is involved in residential property management, property improvement services, & commerical real estate.

Genesis Land Development Corp.
#200, 3115 - 12 St. NE, Calgary, AB T2E 7J2
403-265-8079 Fax: 403-266-0746 800-341-7211
genesis@genesisland.com
www.genesisland.com
Ticker Symbol: GDC
Company Type: Public
Profile: The community development company operates in British Columbia & Alberta. Most of the land is situated in & around Calgary. Activities include land development, single-family & multi-family home building, & commercial development & leasing.

Homburg Invest Inc.
#600, 1741 Brunswick St., Halifax, NS B3J 3X8
902-468-3395 Fax: 902-468-2457
sjedynak@homburg.com
www.homburginvest.com
Ticker Symbol: HII
Company Type: Public
Profile: The company is the owner, developer, & operator of residential & commercial real estate, including townhouses, apartments, offices, & retail properties. Properties are located in Canada, the United States, Germany, & The Netherlands.

InnVest Real Estate Investment Trust
#700, 5090 Explorer Dr., Mississauga, ON L4W 4T9
905-206-7100 Fax: 905-206-7114 877-209-3429
investor@innvestreit.com
www.innvestreit.com
Ticker Symbol: INN.UN
Company Type: Public
Profile: InnVest Real Estate Investment Trust holds a portfolio of hotels. The portfolio of limited service & full service hotel properties operate under the following brands: Holiday Inn, Radisson, Travelodge, Best Western, Comfort Inn, Quality Suites, Delta, & Hilton.

Intrawest ULC
#800, 200 Burrard St., Vancouver, BC V6C 3L6
604-669-9777 Fax: 604-669-0605
intrainfo@intrawest.com
www.intrawest.com
Ticker Symbol: ITW
Company Type: Public
Profile: Development and management of experiential destination resorts

Ivanhoe Cambridge
Centre CDP Capital, #C-500, 1001 square Victoria, Montréal, QC H2Z 2B5
514-841-7600 Fax: 514-841-7762
communications@ivanhoecambridge.com
www.ivanhoecambridge.com
Company Type: Private
Profile: Property owners, managers & developers of shopping centres in urban areas

King George Financial Corporation
#604, 905 West Pender St., Vancouver, BC V6C 1L6
604-687-8882 Fax: 604-687-1476
billc@kinggeorge.ca
Ticker Symbol: KGF
Company Type: Public
Profile: Real estate-operators of nonresidential buildings; Real estate-operators of apartment buildings; Real estate-land subdividers & developers

Kruger Capital Corp.
#300, 550 Burrard St., Vancouver, BC V6C 2B5
604-689-3040 Fax: 604-689-5642 **Company Type:** Public
Profile: Offices of holding companies; Real estate agents & managers

Madison Pacific Properties Inc.
389 West 6th Ave., Vancouver, BC V5Y 1L1
604-732-6540 Fax: 604-732-6550
reception@madisonpacific.ca
www.madisonpacific.ca
Ticker Symbol: MPC
Company Type: Public
Profile: Madison Pacific Properties Inc. is a real estate investment & development company. Its properties are located in Greater Vancouver.

Mainstreet Equity Corp.
#100, 1122 - 8th Ave. SW, Calgary, AB T2P 1J5
403-215-6060 Fax: 403-266-8867
mainstreet@mainst.biz
www.mainst.biz
Ticker Symbol: MEQ
Company Type: Public
Profile: Real estate operators of apartment buildings; Real estate agents & managers

Melcor Developments Ltd.
#900, 10310 Jasper Ave., Edmonton, AB T5J 1Y8
780-423-6931 Fax: 780-426-1796
info@melcor.ca
www.melcor.ca
Ticker Symbol: MRD
Company Type: Public
Profile: Melcor Developments acquires land to develop & sell for multi-family sites, residential communities, & commercial sites. The organization is also the owner, developer, & manager of commercial income properties & golf courses.

MI Developments Inc.
455 Magna Dr., Aurora, ON L4G 7A9
905-713-6322 Fax: 905-713-6332
ir@midevelopments.com
www.midevelopments.com
Ticker Symbol: MIM.A
Company Type: Public
Profile: The real estate company is the owner, leaser, developer, & manager of industrial & commercial properties. MI Developments Inc.'s real estate properties are located in North America & Europe. The company also holds a controlling interest in Magna Entertainment Corp.

Mont Saint-Sauveur International Inc.
350, av Saint-Denis, Saint-Sauveur, QC J0R 1R3
450-227-4671 Fax: 450-227-2065 800-363-2426
webmaster@mssi.ca
www.montsaintsaveur.com
Ticker Symbol: MSX
Company Type: Public
Profile: Ski resorts, hotels & motels; real estate

Morguard Corporation
#1000, 55 City Centre Dr., Mississauga, ON L5B 1M3
905-281-3800 Fax: 905-281-5890
info@morguard.com
www.morguard.com
Ticker Symbol: MRC
Company Type: Public
Profile: Morguard Corporation is a real estate & property management company. Through its investments in Morguard REIT & Revenue Properties Company Limited, the corporation has a diversified portfolio of residential, office, retail, & industrial properties owned or under management. Through Morguard Investments Limited, management services to institutional & other investors for residential & commercial real estate are offered.

MP Western Properties Inc.
389 West 6th Ave., Vancouver, BC V5Y 1L1
604-732-6540 Fax: 604-732-6550
reception@madisonpacific.ca
Ticker Symbol: MPW.H
Company Type: Public
Profile: Real estate operators of nonresidential buildings; Real estate operators of apartment buildings; Real estate land subdividers & developers

Northern Property Real Estate Investment Trust
#110, 6131 - 6th St. SE, Calgary, AB T2H 1L9
403-531-0720 Fax: 403-531-0727
info@npreit.com
www.npreit.com
Ticker Symbol: NPR
Company Type: Public
Profile: Northern Property Real Estate Investment Trust is an unincorporated, open-end real estate investment trust. The Trust invests in mainly residential income-producing properties. Commercial buildings & executive suites are also owned by the Trust. Properties are situated in Newfoundland & Labrador, Alberta, northeastern British Columbia, Nunavut & the Northwest Territories.

Oxford Properties Group Inc.
Oxford Tower, #1100, 130 Adelaide St. West, Toronto, ON M5H 3P5
416-865-8300 Fax: 416-868-3751 www.oxfordproperties.com
Company Type: Private
Profile: Commercial real estate investment firm; Owner & manager of a portfolio of office, retail, industrial & multi-family residential properties across Canada; Holder of interests in real estate assets abroad

Pacific & Western Credit Corp.
#2002, 140 Fullarton St., London, ON N6A 5P2
519-645-1919 Fax: 519-645-2060
investorrelations@pwbank.com
www.pwbank.com
Ticker Symbol: PWC
Company Type: Public
Profile: Banking & financial services

Parkbridge Lifestyle Communities Inc.
#700, 505 - 3rd St. SW, Calgary, AB T2P 3E6
403-215-2100 Fax: 403-215-2115
info@parkbridge.ca
www.parkbridge.ca
Ticker Symbol: PRK
Company Type: Public
Profile: Parkbridge Lifestyle Communities Inc. owns, develops, & operates land use communities. Communities are located in British Columbia, Alberta, Ontario, & Quebec. Parkbridge specializes in the following sectors: marinas, family & senior communities, chalets, cottage & RV communities, & lifestyle communities.

Plazacorp Retail Properties Ltd.
#200, 527 Queen St., Fredericton, NB E3B 1B8
506-451-1826 Fax: 506-451-1802
info@plaza.ca
www.plaza.ca
Ticker Symbol: PLZ
Company Type: Public
Profile: Plazacorp Retail Properties Ltd. is engaged in the acquisition, development, & re-development of enclosed mall shopping centres, strip centres, & freestanding retail properties. Operations take place in Ontario, Québec, New Brunswick, Nova Scotia, Prince Edward Island, & Newfoundland.

Retrocom Mid-Market Real Estate Investment Trust
PO Box 204, #214, 4025 Yonge St., Toronto, ON M2P 2E3
416-741-7999 Fax: 416-741-7993
info@rmmreit.com
www.rmmreit.com
Ticker Symbol: RMM.UN
Company Type: Public

Profile: The Retrocom Mid-Market REIT acquires & owns mid-market commercial properties in cities throughout Canada.

Revenue Properties Company Limited
#800, 55 City Centre Dr., Mississauga, ON L5B 1M3
905-281-3800 Fax: 905-281-5890
pmiatello@morguard.com
www.revprop.com
Ticker Symbol: RPC
Company Type: Public
Profile: Real estate operators of nonresidential buildings, apartment buildings & other dwellings; Land subdividers and developers

RioCan Real Estate Investment Trust
RioCan Yonge Eglinton Centre, PO Box 2386, #500, 2300 Yonge St., Toronto, ON M4P 1E4
416-866-3033 Fax: 416-866-3020 800-465-2733
inquiries@riocan.com; ir@riocan.com
www.riocan.com
Ticker Symbol: REI
Company Type: Public
Profile: The Trust owns a portfolio of retail properties throughout Canada.

Royal Host Real Estate Investment Trust
#103, 808 - 42 Ave. SE, Calgary, AB T2G 1Y9
403-259-9800 Fax: 403-259-8580
investorinfo@royalhost.com
www.royalhost.com
Ticker Symbol: RYL
Company Type: Public
Profile: The open-end unincorporated investment trust invests in & manages hotel properties. Royal Host REIT owns the master franchise rights for Thriftlodge & Travelodge in Canada.

United Communities Inc.
#200, 808 - 4 Ave. SW, Calgary, AB T2P 3E8
403-265-6180 Fax: 403-265-6270
info@unitedcommunities.com
www.unitedcommunities.com
Company Type: Private
Profile: The real estate development company has operations in the following areas: Calgary & Edmonton, Alberta, Sacramento, California, & Kimberley, British Columbia. United Communities Inc. builds architecturally controlled & themed communities to satisfy the needs of families.

Wall Financial Corporation
#3502, 1088 Burrard St., Vancouver, BC V6Z 2R9
604-893-7131 Fax: 604-893-7179 **Ticker Symbol:** WFC
Company Type: Public
Profile: The corporation is engaged in the following acitivites: real estate development; investment in properties; management of residential rental apartments & hotel properties; & development & construction of residential housing for resale.

Services, Miscellaneous

Arbor Memorial Services Inc.
#211, 2 Jane St., Toronto, ON M6S 4W8
416-763-4531 Fax: 416-763-4821
lhowe@arbormemorial.com
www.arbormemorial.com
Ticker Symbol: ABO
Company Type: Public
Profile: Arbor Memorial Services Inc. is the owner of the following: reception centres, crematoria, funeral homes, & cemeteries. Services are available in all Canadian provinces, except Prince Edward Island & Newfoundland & Labrador.

Atlantic Lottery Corporation Inc.
PO Box 5500, 922 Main St., Moncton, NB E1C 8W6
506-867-5825 800-561-3942
info@alc.ca
www.alc.ca
Company Type: Public
Profile: Amusement and recreation services (various)

BFI Canada Income Fund
#300, 135 Queens Plate Dr., Toronto, ON M9W 6V1
416-741-5221 Fax: 416-741-4565
investorrelations@bficanada.com
www.bficanada.com
Ticker Symbol: BFC
Company Type: Public
Profile: The waste management company provides non-hazardous solid waste collection & landfill disposal services. BFI Canada serves residential, commercial, industrial, & municipal customers in Canada & the United States.

Boyd Group Income Fund
3570 Portage Ave., Winnipeg, MB R3K 0Z8
204-895-1244 Fax: 204-895-1283
info@boydgroup.com
www.boydgroup.com
Ticker Symbol: BYD
Company Type: Public
Profile: Boyd Group Income Fund is an unincorporated, open-ended mutual fund trust. The Fund has an interest in the Boyd Group Inc. & its subsidiaries. Boyd Group Inc. operates collision repair facilities. Operations are situated in western Canada & the United States. The organization's trade names include Boyd Autobody & Glass & Service Collision Repair & Gerber Collision & Glass.

Canadian Commercial Corporation
50 O'Connor St., 11th Floor, Ottawa, ON K1A 0S6
613-996-0034 Fax: 613-995-2121 800-748-8191
info@ccc.ca
www.ccc.ca
Company Type: Crown
Profile: The organization is engaged in the administration of general economic programs.

Canlan Ice Sports Corp
6501 Sprott St., Burnaby, BC V5B 3B8
604-736-9152 Fax: 604-736-9170
info@icesports.com
www.canlanicesports.com
Ticker Symbol: ICE
Company Type: Public
Profile: Amusement and recreation services (various)

ClubLink Corporation
15675 Dufferin St., King City, ON L7B 1K5
905-841-3730 Fax: 905-841-1134 800-661-1818
invest@clublink.ca
www.clublink.ca
Ticker Symbol: LNK
Company Type: Public
Profile: ClubLink Corporation owns, develops, & operates member golf clubs, daily fee golf clubs, & resorts.

Compass Group Canada
#400, 5560 Explorer Dr., Mississauga, ON L4W 5M3
905-568-4636 Fax: 905-568-9392 905-568-9392
info@compass-canada.com
www.compass-canada.com
Company Type: Private
Profile: Catering & retail eating places

Fairmont Hotels & Resorts Inc.
Canadian Pacific Tower, PO Box 40 TD Centre, #1600, 100 Wellington St. West, Toronto, ON M5K 1B7
416-874-2600 Fax: 416-874-2601
communications@fairmont.com
www.fairmont.com
Company Type: Public
Profile: Hotels & motels; Real estate operators of nonresidential buildings

First National AlarmCap
#810, 112 - 4th St. SW, Calgary, AB T2R 1M1
403-299-2299 Fax: 403-299-2209 www.alarmcap.ca
Ticker Symbol: FNA.UN
Company Type: Public
Profile: First National AlarmCap Income Fund is involved in the provision of electronic security alarm monitoring & services. It indirectly owns & operates Microtec Security & Securex. The full-service alarm organization serves both residential & commercial subscribers.

Four Seasons Hotels Inc.
1165 Leslie St., Toronto, ON M3C 2K8
416-449-1750 Fax: 416-441-4374
investors@fourseasons.com
www.fourseasons.com
Ticker Symbol: FSH
Company Type: Public
Profile: Hotels & motels

Gamehost Income Fund
#400, 4406 - 50 Ave., Red Deer, AB T4N 3Z5
403-346-4545 Fax: 403-340-0683
info@gamehost.ca
www.gamehost.ca
Ticker Symbol: GH.UN
Company Type: Public
Profile: Gamehost Income Fund is an unincorporated open-ended limited purpose trust. It is involved in gaming, hospitality, & hotel services in Alberta. Operations include the Boomtown Casino in Fort McMurray, the Great Northern Casino in Grande Prairie, & Service Plus Inns & Suites in Grand Prairie. The Fund is also a joint venture partner in the Stampede Casino & the Deerfoot Inn & Casino Inc. in Calgary.

Garda World Security Corporation
1390, rue Barré, Montréal, QC H3C 1N4
514-281-2811 Fax: 514-281-2860 800-859-1599
info@garda.ca
www.garda.ca
Ticker Symbol: GW
Company Type: Public
Profile: Garda World Security Corporation's areas of expertise are consulting, investigation & security. The firm's operations are located in Canada, the United States, Latin America, Europe, Africa, the Middle East, & Asia.

Great Canadian Gaming Corporation
#200, 13775 Commerce Pkwy., Richmond, BC V6V 2V4
604-303-1000 Fax: 604-279-8605
info@gcgaming.com
www.gcgaming.com
Ticker Symbol: GC
Company Type: Public
Profile: Great Canadian Gaming Corporation is a gaming & entertainment operator. Operations include entertainment facilities, such as casinos, racetracks, & show theatres. Business is conducted in Nova Scotia, Ontario, British Columbia, & Washington State.

Helix Hearing Care of America Corp.
#203, 815 Taylor Creek Dr., Cumberland, ON K1C 1T1
613-824-1154 Fax: 613-824-1109
info@helixhca.com
www.helixhca.com
Ticker Symbol: HCA
Company Type: Public
Profile: Hearing care practitioners: audiologists and hearing instrument specialists

K-Bro Linen Income Fund
#103, 15023 - 123 Ave., Edmonton, AB T5V 1J7
780-453-5218 Fax: 780-455-6676 www.k-brolinen.com
Ticker Symbol: KBL.UN
Company Type: Public
Profile: Through its wholly-owned subsidiary, K-Bro Linen Systems, K-Bro Linen Income Fund is involved in the operation of laundry & linen processing facilities. It serves industrial & commercial sectors, such as hospitality & healthcare. Facilities are located in Toronto, Edmonton, Calgary, Vancouver, & Victoria.

Keystone North America Inc.
#1900, 400 North Ashley Dr., Tampa, FL
813-225-4650 Fax: 813-225-4655
www.keystonenorthamerica.ca
Ticker Symbol: KNA.UN
Company Type: Public
Profile: Keystone North America Inc. owns & operates funeral homes & cemeteries in Ontario & the United States.

Lions Gate Entertainment Corp.
#2200, 1055 West Hastings St., Vancouver, BC V6E 2E9
604-983-5555 Fax: 604-983-5554
pwilkes@lgf.com
www.lgf.com
Ticker Symbol: LGF
Company Type: Public
Profile: Lions Gate Entertainment Corp. is a developer, producer, & distributor of television, motion picture, family entertainment, home entertainment, video-on-demand, & digitally delivered content. The company is made up of the following operating divisions: Motion Pictures, Television, Animation, & Studio Facilities.

Lorus Therapeutics Inc.
2 Meridian Rd., Toronto, ON M9W 4Z7
416-798-1200 Fax: 416-798-2200
info@lorusthera.com; ir@lorusthera.com
www.lorusthera.com
Ticker Symbol: LOR
Company Type: Public
Profile: The biopharmaceutical company is engaged in the research & development of anticancer therapies.

Loto-Québec
500, rue Sherbrooke ouest, Montréal, QC H3A 3G6
514-282-8000 Fax: 514-873-8999
service_clientele@loto-quebec.com
www.loto-quebec.com
Company Type: Crown
Profile: Oversees games of chance & gambling; operates & monitors casinos, and a video lottery terminal network

MDS Inc.
West Tower, #300, 2700 Matheson Blvd. E., Mississauga, ON L4W 4V9
416-675-6777 Fax: 416-675-0688
info@mdsinc.com

www.mdsinc.com
Ticker Symbol: MDS
Company Type: Public
Profile: MDS Inc. provides products & services for the development of drugs, & the diagnosis & treatment of disease. Products include radiotherapeutics, medical isotopes for molecular imaging, & analytical instruments.

Morneau Sobeco Income Fund
One Morneau Sobeco Centre, #700, 895 Don Mills Rd., Toronto, ON M3C 1W3
416-445-2700 Fax: 416-445-4688
info@morneausobeco.com
www.morneausobeco.com
Ticker Symbol: MSI.UN
Company Type: Public
Profile: Morneau Sobeco Income Fund is involved in the provision of human resource consulting & outsourcing services. The firm assists employers with the management of pension & benefit plans for employees.

Newalta Income Fund
211 - 11th Ave. SW, Calgary, AB T2R 0C6
403-806-7000 Fax: 403-806-7348 800-774-8466
info@newalta.com
www.newalta.com
Ticker Symbol: NAL
Company Type: Public
Profile: Newalta Income Fund is part of the Canadian industrial waste management & environmental services industry. Newalta is involved in the recovery of saleable products & recycling, as well as the environmentally sound disposal of solid, non-hazardous industrial waste.

Peace Arch Entertainment Group Inc.
#650, 1867 Yonge St., Toronto, ON M4S 1Y5
416-783-8383 Fax: 416-783-8384 888-588-3608
ryon@trilogy-capital.com
www.peacearch.com
Ticker Symbol: PAE
Company Type: Public
Profile: Offices of holding companies; Motion picture & video tape production

Service Corporation International (Canada) Limited
1835 Hastings St. E., Vancouver, BC V5L 1T3
604-806-4100 Fax: 604-806-4111 www.sci-corp.com
Company Type: Private
Profile: Network of funeral homes, crematoria & cemeteries

Speedy Corporation
#303, 21 St. Clair Ave. East, Toronto, ON M4T 1L9
416-961-1133 800-387-1410www.speedy.com
Ticker Symbol: SMK
Company Type: Private
Profile: Speedy specializes in services for cars, light trucks, & SUVs. The company also sells tires & conducts road safety inspections. Speedy Corporation has a wholly owned susidiary called Minute Muffler.

TLC Vision Corporation
#100, 5280 Solar Dr., Mississauga, ON L4W 5M8
800-852-1033 Fax: 905-602-2025 877-852-2020
investor.relations@tlcvision.com
www.tlcv.com
Ticker Symbol: TLC
Company Type: Public
Profile: Offices & clinics of doctors of medicine

Waste Services, Inc.
#600, 1122 International Blvd., Burlington, ON L7L 6Z8
www.wasteservicesinc.com
Company Type: Private
Profile: Waste Services, Inc. is a non-hazardous solid waste services company. It provides collection, transfer, landfill disposal, & recycling services. The company serves residential, commercial, & industrial customers in Ontario, Saskatchewan, Alberta, British Columbia, & the United States.

Steel & Metal

ADF Group Inc.
300, rue Henry-Bessemer, Terrebonne, QC J6Y 1T3
450-965-1911 Fax: 450-965-8558
infos@adfgroup.com
www.adfgroup.com
Ticker Symbol: DRX
Company Type: Public
Profile: ADF Group Inc. specializes in the design, engineering, fabrication & installation of steel superstructures, architectural, & miscellaneous metals. The company serves the non-residential construction market.

Alcan Inc.
1188 Sherbrook St., Montréal, QC H3A 3G2
514-848-8000 Fax: 514-848-8115
media.relations@alcan.com
www.alcan.com
Ticker Symbol: AL
Company Type: Public
Profile: Manufacturers of aluminum sheet, plate & foil, aluminum rolling & drawing, primary production of aluminum, aluminum foundries, various industrial inorganic chemicals; Metal mining of miscellaneous metal ores

American Iron & Metal Co. Inc.
9100, boul Henri-Bourassa est, Montréal, QC H1E 2S4
514-494-2000 Fax: 514-494-3008
info@scrapmetal.net
www.scrapmetal.net
Company Type: Private
Profile: The company is engaged in secondary smelting & refining of nonferrous metals. It is a wholesaler of scrap & waste materials.

Arcelor Mittal Dofasco Inc.
PO Box 2460, 1330 Burlington St. East, Hamilton, ON L8N 3J5
905-544-3761 Fax: 905-545-3236 800-363-2726
general@dofasco.ca
www.dofasco.ca
Company Type: Public
Profile: Manufacturers of steel works, blast furnaces, coke ovens, rolling mills, cold-rolled steel sheet, strip & bars, steel pipe & tubes

Babcock & Wilcox Canada, Ltd.
581 Coronation Blvd., Cambridge, ON N1R 5V3
519-621-2130 Fax: 519-621-9681 www.babcock.com/bwc
Company Type: Private
Profile: Manufacturers of fabricated plate work

Ball Packaging Products Canada, Inc.
1121 Walkers Line, Burlington, ON L7N 2G4
905-335-4780 Fax: 905-319-4083
info@ball.com
www.ball.com
Company Type: Private
Profile: Ball Packaging Products Canada manufactures metal & plastic packaging for food & beverages. It is also involved in aerospace & other technologies.

Canam Group Inc.
#500, 11505 - 1e av, Saint-Georges, QC G5Y 7H5
418-228-8031 Fax: 418-228-1750
infocanamcanada@canam.ws
www.canamgroup.ws
Ticker Symbol: CAM
Company Type: Public
Profile: Canam Group Inc. is engaged in the design & fabrication of construction products & solutions.

Crown Cork & Seal Canada Inc.
7900 Keele St., Concord, ON L4K 2A3
905-669-1401 Fax: 905-669-1692 www.crowncork.com
Company Type: Private
Profile: Manufacturers of metal cans, crowns & closures

ESSAR Steel Algoma Inc.
105 West St., Sault Ste Marie, ON P6A 7B4
705-945-2351 Fax: 705-945-2203 www.algoma.com
Ticker Symbol: AGA
Company Type: Public
Profile: The company manufactures steel works, blast furnaces, coke ovens, rolling mills, sheet & plate.

Flex-N-Gate Corporation Canada
538 Blanchard Park Dr., Tecumseh, ON N8N 2L9
519-727-3931
mchadwick@flexngate.com
www.flex-n-gate.com
Company Type: Private
Profile: Supplier of truck bumpers & accessories

Foster Wheeler Ltd.
#200, 4954 Richard Rd. SE, Calgary, AB T3E 6L1
403-255-3447 Fax: 403-259-4558
rcampbell@fwfhl.com
www.fwc.com
Company Type: Private
Profile: Foster Wheeler Ltd. is a manufacturer of fabricated plate work, & general industrial machinery & equipment.

Garneau Inc.
2003 - 5 St., Nisku, AB T9E 7X4
780-955-2396 Fax: 780-955-7715
darlened@garneau-inc.com
www.garneau-inc.com
Ticker Symbol: GAR
Company Type: Public
Profile: Manufacturers of coating, engraving & allied services, various fabricated metal products

Gerdau Ameristeel Corporation
Hopkins St. South, Whitby, ON L1N 5T1
416-297-3700 Fax: 416-297-3740 800-263-2662
basmith@gerdauameristeel.com
www.gerdauameristeel.com
Ticker Symbol: GNA
Company Type: Public
Profile: Gerdau Ameristeel Corporation manufactures steel products for the automotive, construction, appliance, & machinery industries. Steel scrap is also sourced, traded, & processed by the company.

Groupe Bocenor inc
274, rue Duchesnay, Sainte-Marie, QC G6E 3C2
418-387-7723 Fax: 418-387-3904
corpo@bocenor.com
www.bocenor.com
Ticker Symbol: GBO
Company Type: Public
Profile: Manufacturers of metal doors, sash, frames, molding & trim, millwork, windows; Retail in lumber & other building materials dealers, hardware stores

H. Paulin & Co., Limited
55 Milne Ave., Toronto, ON M1L 4N3
416-694-3351 Fax: 416-694-1869 800-268-4000
investor@hpaulin.com
www.hpaulin.com
Ticker Symbol: PAP
Company Type: Public
Profile: Manufacturers of bolts, nuts, screws, rivets, washers, valves & pipe fittings, various hardware; Wholesalers of motor vehicle supplies & new parts, industrial supplies; Collection of end cuts & short lengths for recycling

Haley Industries Limited
634 Magnesium Rd., Haley, ON K0J 1Y0
613-432-8841 Fax: 613-432-0743
info.haley@magellan.aero
Company Type: Private
Profile: Manufacturers of aluminum foundries, primary smelting & refining of nonferrous metals

Harris Steel Group Inc.
#404, 4120 Yonge St., Toronto, ON M2P 2B8
416-590-9549 Fax: 416-590-9560
info@harrissteel.com
www.harrissteel.com
Company Type: Private
Profile: Fabrication & processing steel training business; installation of steel products

ITW Canada
120 Travail Rd., Markham, ON L3S 3J1
800-387-9692
info@itwconstruction.ca
www.itw.com
Company Type: Private
Profile: Offices of holding companies; Manufacturers of various fabricated metal products; Wholesalers of industrial supplies, industrial machinery & equipment, chemicals & allied products

Martinrea International Inc.
30 Aviva Park Dr., Vaughan, ON L4L 9C7
416-749-0314 Fax: 905-264-2937
info@martinrea.com; HR@martinrea.com
www.martinrea.com
Ticker Symbol: MRE
Company Type: Public
Profile: Martinrea International Inc. specializes in the production of metal parts, assemblies & modules, & fluid management systems. The company supplies the automotive industry & other industrial sectors. Divisions are located in Canada, the United States, Mexico, & Europe.

Meridian Lightweight Technologies Inc.
25 MacNab Ave., Strathroy, ON N7G 4H6
519-246-9600 Fax: 519-245-6605
hr@meridian-mag.com
www.meridian-mag.com
Company Type: Private
Profile: The company is engaged in magnesium die casting design & manufacturing. Components & assemblies are supplied to the global automotive market.

QIT-Fer & Titane inc
1625, rue Marie-Victorin, Sorel-Tracy, QC J3R 1M6
450-746-3000 Fax: 450-746-4438
info@qit.com

www.qit.com
Company Type: Private
Profile: Manufacturers of steel works, blast furnaces & coke ovens, rolling mills

Russel Metals Inc.
#210, 1900 Minnesota Ct., Mississauga, ON L5N 3C9
905-819-7777 Fax: 905-819-7409
info@russelmetals.com
www.russelmetals.com
Ticker Symbol: RUS
Company Type: Public
Profile: The metal processor & distributor operates in North America. The company implemented environmental standards & an ongoing audit process.

Samuel Manu-Tech Inc.
#1500, 185 The West Mall, Toronto, ON M9C 5L5
416-626-2190 Fax: 416-626-5969
smt@samuelmanutech.com
www.samuelmanutech.com
Ticker Symbol: SMT
Company Type: Public
Profile: Samuel Manu-Tech Inc. produces steel, plastic, & related industrial products. The company has locations in Canada, the United States, & Mexico.

TenarisAlgomaTubes
#800, 440 - 2nd Ave. SW, Calgary, AB T2P 5E9
403-514-2276 Fax: 403-290-0619 www.tenaris.com
Company Type: Public
Profile: Manufacturers of fabricated pipe & pipe fittings; Wholesalers in metals service centres & offices

Timminco Limited
Sun Life Financial Tower, #2401, 150 King St. West, Toronto, ON M5H 1J9
416-364-5171 Fax: 416-364-3451
info@timminco.com
www.timminco.com
Ticker Symbol: TIM
Company Type: Public
Profile: Manufacturers of rolling, drawing & extruding of nonferrous metals, secondary smelting & refining of nonferrous metals; Wholesalers of metals service centers & offices

Tree Island Wire Income Fund
3933 Boundary Rd., Richmond, BC V6V 1T8
604-524-3744 Fax: 604-524-2657
800-663-0955www.treeisland.com
Ticker Symbol: TIL.UN
Company Type: Public
Profile: Tree Island Wire Income Fund is an unincorporated open ended limited purpose trust. It owns Tree Island Industries Ltd.. The company serves the following industries: residential construction, commercial construction, industrial, & agriculture. Products include the following: bright, galvanized, & stainless steel wire; fabricated wire products, such as fencing; stucco; engineered structural mesh; & bulk, packaged, & collated nails.

U.S. Steel Canada
PO Box 2030, 386 Wilcox St., Hamilton, ON L8N 3T1
905-528-2511 Fax: 905-308-7002 800-263-9305
infocanada@uss.com
www.ussteelcanaca.com
Company Type: Public
Profile: Manufacturers of steel works, blast furnaces, coke ovens, rolling mills, hot & cold-rolled steel sheet, bars, steel pipe & tubes, wire & wire products

Valdor Technology International Inc.
#480, 789 West Pender St., Vancouver, BC V6C 1H2
604-687-3775 Fax: 604-689-7654
info@valdor.com; sales@valdor.com
www.valdortech.com
Ticker Symbol: VTI
Company Type: Public
Profile: Valdor Technology International is a high technology fiber optic components company. It specializes in designing & manufacturing optical & optoelectronic components, such as new generation fiber optic connectors. Connectors incorporate the environmentally friendly Impact Mount technology.

Velan Inc.
7007, ch de la Côte-de-Liesse, Montréal, QC H4T 1G2
514-748-7743 Fax: 514-748-8635
sales@velan.com
www.velan.com
Ticker Symbol: VLN
Company Type: Public
Profile: Velan Inc. manufactures industrial steel valves. Manufacturing plants are located in Canada, the United States, Europe, & Asia. Velan valves are used in numerous industries, such as oil & gas, chemical & petrochemical, pulp & paper, mining, & power generation. The company also offers aftermarket services.

Vicwest Income Fund
1296 South Service Rd. West, Oakville, ON L6L 5T7
905-469-5702 Fax: 905-825-1090
IR@vicwestfund.com
www.vicwestfund.com
Ticker Symbol: VIC.UN
Company Type: Public
Profile: Vicwest Income Fund is involved in supplying metal roofing, siding & other building products to the residential, commercial, institutional, & industrial sectors. The organization also supplies steel containers used in the petroleum, grain, & fertilizer industries.

Textiles, Apparel & Leather

Algo Group Inc.
5555, rue Cypihot, Montréal, QC H4S 1R3
514-382-1240 Fax: 514-385-0163
info@algo.com
www.algo.com
Company Type: Public
Profile: Manufacturers of various men's & boys' clothing, women's, misses' & juniors' dresses, misses' & juniors' suits, skirts, coats & various outerwear; manufacturers of broadwoven fabric and manmade fiber & silk, home furnishings

Beaulieu Canada
335, rue de Roxton, Acton Vale, QC J0H 1A0
450-546-5000 Fax: 450-546-5027
800-853-9048beaulieucanada-com.rebeltrail.com
Company Type: Private
Profile: Manufacture & distribution of broadloom carpets

Consoltex Inc.
8555, rte Transcanadienne, Saint-Laurent, QC H4S 1Z6
514-333-8800 Fax: 514-335-7013 800-736-2743
solutions@consoltex.com
www.consoltex.com
Company Type: Public
Profile: Offices of holding companies; Manufacturers of circular weft, knit fabric mills; Finishers of broadwoven fabrics of manmade fiber & silk; Wholesalers of piece goods, notions & other dry goods

Danier Leather Inc.
2650 St Clair Ave. West, Toronto, ON M6N 1M2
416-762-8175 Fax: 416-762-4570
info@danier.com
www.danier.com
Ticker Symbol: DL
Company Type: Public
Profile: Manufacturers of leather & sheepskin-lined clothing, leather gloves & mittens, personal leather goods; Retailing luggage & leather goods stores

Gildan Activewear Inc.
600, boul de Maisonneuve ouest, Montréal, QC H3A 3J2
514-735-2023 Fax: 514-735-6810 866-755-2023
info@gildan.com
www.gildan.com
Ticker Symbol: GIL
Company Type: Public
Profile: Gildan Activewear manufactures & markets activewear, athletic socks, & underwear. The company serves both North American & international markets.

Intertape Polymer Group Inc.
999 Cavendish Blvd. 2nd Fl., Montréal, QC H4M 2X5
514-731-7591 Fax: 514-731-5039
info@intertapeipg.com
www.intertapepolymer.com
Ticker Symbol: ITP
Company Type: Public
Profile: Manufacturers of coated fabrics, not rubberized, packaging paper & plastics film, coated & laminated

Le Château Inc.
8300, boul Decarie, Montréal, QC H4P 2P5
514-738-7000 Fax: 514-738-3670
comments@lechateau.ca
www.lechateau.ca
Ticker Symbol: CTU
Company Type: Public
Profile: Le Château Inc. is a designer & manufacturer of clothing. The company operates retail stores in Canada & United States. Le Château stores sell ladieswear, menswear, footwear, & accessories.

Transportation & Travel

Admiral Marine Inc.
#207-7035 Maxwell Rd., Mississauga, ON L5S 1R5
905-564-8788 Fax: 905-564-1440
admiral@admiralmarine.ca
www.admiralmarine.ca
Company Type: Public
Profile: Canstar Ocean Line, through Admiral Marine, operate a regular break-bulk/conventional service from North America to Europe, with transshipment via Antwerp to Eastern Europe, the Middle East and Africa.

Air Canada
PO Box 14000 St-Laurent, Saint-Laurent, QC H4Y 1H4
514-422-5000 Fax: 514-422-5909
denis.biro@aircanada.ca
www.aircanada.ca
Ticker Symbol: AC
Company Type: Public
Profile: The Canadian-based international air carrier provides scheduled & chartered air transportation for both passengers & cargo.

Algoma Central Corporation
#600, 63 Church St., St Catharines, ON L2R 3C4
905-687-7888 Fax: 905-687-7840
svaughan@heenan.ca
www.algonet.com
Ticker Symbol: ALC
Company Type: Public
Profile: Algoma Central Corporation is a Canadian-flag ship owner on the Great Lakes - St. Lawrence Waterway. The company owns both dry-bulk carriers & product tankers. As well as the operation of vessels, ship & diesel engine repair & fabrication are part of Algoma Central's operations.

American Cartage Ltd.
#101 - 9366, 200A St., Langley, BC V1M 4B3
604-513-3681 Fax: 604-513-3677 www.americancartage.com
Company Type: Private
Profile: American Cartage Ltd. delivers marine containers to & from Vancouver's waterfront terminals.

American President Lines Ltd.
#728, 185 The West Mall, Toronto, ON M9C 5L5
416-620-7790 Fax: 416-620-7723 www.apl.com
Company Type: Public
Profile: APL provides customers around the world with container transportation services.

Atlas Cold Storage Income Trust
5255 Yonge St., Toronto, ON M2N 5P8
416-512-2352 Fax: 416-512-2353 888-642-3333
inquiries@atlascold.com
www.atlascold.com
Ticker Symbol: FZR
Company Type: Public
Profile: Refrigerated warehousing & storage

ATS Andlauer Income Fund
ATS Toronto (Head Office), 96 Disco Rd., Toronto, ON M9W 0A3
416-679-7979 Fax: 416-679-7845 www.ats.ca
Company Type: Public
Profile: ATS Andlauer Income Fund is involved in the provision of integrated trucking, courier, & air freight transportation & distribution solutions. It serves major consumer companies in Canada.

AutoCanada Income Fund
#200, 15505 Yellowhead Trail, Edmonton, AB T5H 3P9
780-732-3135 Fax: 780-447-0651
yporter@autocan.ca
www.autocan.ca
Ticker Symbol: ACQ.UN
Company Type: Public
Profile: Through its interest in AutoCanada LP, AutoCanada Income Fund is involved in the operation & management of franchised automobile dealerships across Canada. Both sales & repair services are provided by AutoCanada.

Automodular Corporation
#420, 20 Toronto St., Toronto, ON M5C 2B8
416-861-0662 Fax: 416-861-0063
info@Automodular.com; hr@Automodular.net
www.automodular.com
Ticker Symbol: AM
Company Type: Public
Profile: Automodular Corporation is engaged in automotive parts sequencing & sub-assembly. Components & modules are installed in vehicles made by North American Original Equipment Manufacturers in Canada & the United States.

Bombardier Inc.
800, boul René-Lévesque ouest, 29e étage, Montréal, QC H3B 1Y8
514-861-9481 Fax: 514-861-2629
investors@bombardier.com
www.bombardier.com
Ticker Symbol: BBD
Company Type: Public
Profile: Bombardier Inc. manufactures transportation solutions, such as rail equipment & commercial aircraft.

British Columbia Ferry Services Inc.
1112 Fort St., Victoria, BC V8V 4V2
250-386-3431 Fax: 250-388-7754
888-223-3779www.bcferries.com
Company Type: Private
Profile: Operates a fleet of 36 ferries serving 47 destinations in British Columbia

British Columbia Railway Company
#600, 221 West Esplanade Ave, North Vancouver, BC V7M 3J3
604-678-4735 Fax: 604-678-4736
westerhouts@bcrco.com
www.bcrco.com
Company Type: Crown
Profile: Offices of holding companies; Real estate operators of nonresidential buildings; Real estate agents & managers; Railroads, line-haul operating; Marine cargo handling

Bulk Carriers (PEI) Ltd.
PO Box 153, 779 Bannockburn Rd., Cornwall, PE C0A 1H0
902-675-2600 Fax: 902-675-3100
info@bulkcarrierspei.com
www.bulkcarrierspei.com
Company Type: Private
Profile: With a fleet made up of reefer trailers, the company hauls mainly food products throughout Canada & the United States.

Canada Steamship Lines Inc.
759 Victoria Square, Montréal, QC H2Y 2K3
514-982-3800 Fax: 514-982-3801
info@cslmtl.com
www.csl.ca
Company Type: Public

Canadian American Transportation Inc.
4 rue du Transport, Coteau-du-Lac, QC J0P 1B0
450-763-6363 Fax: 450-763-2400 800-363-5313
cat@cat.ca
www.cat.ca
Company Type: Private
Profile: Canadian American Transportation Inc. offers logistics services & a partnership program with other transportation companies.

Canadian Helicopters Income Fund
1215, montee Pilon, Les Cèdres, QC J7T 1G1
450-452-3000 Fax: 450-452-3057 www.canadianhelicopters.com
Ticker Symbol: CHL.UN
Company Type: Public
Profile: Through Canadian Helicopters Limited, Canadian Helicopters Income Fund is a helicopter transportation services company. In addition to transportation services, the company also operates flight schools & offers repair & maintenance services. Canadian Helicopters serves the following sectors: emergency medical services, mining, construction, oil & gas, infrastructure maintenance, & utilities.

Canadian National Railway Company
935, rue de la Gauchetière ouest, Montréal, QC H3B 2M9
514-399-6591 Fax: 514-399-4296 888-888-5909
CNPQATL@cn.ca; CNON@cn.ca; CNSKMB@cn.ca
www.cn.ca
Ticker Symbol: CNR
Company Type: Public
Profile: Crossing the North American continent, the Canadian National Railway Company serves ports on the Atlantic, Pacific, & Gulf coasts.

Canadian Pacific Railway Limited
Gulf Canada Square, #500, 401 - 9th Ave. SW, Calgary, AB T2P 4Z4
403-319-7000 Fax: 403-319-7567 888-333-6370
investor@cpr.ca
www.cpr.ca
Ticker Symbol: CP
Company Type: Public
Profile: The transcontinental carrier operates in Canada & the United States.

Cargojet Income Fund
#5&6, 350 Britannia Rd. East, Mississauga, ON L4Z 1X9
905-501-7373 Fax: 905-501-8228 www.cargojet.com
Ticker Symbol: CJT.UN
Company Type: Public
Profile: Cargojet Income Fund is involved in the provision of overnight air cargo services.

Celtic Maritime
1066 Thierry, La Salle, QC H8N 2Y6
514-932-6464 Fax: 514-932-6565
info@celticmaritime.com
www.celticmaritime.com
Company Type: Public

Challenger Motor Freight Inc.
300 Maple Grove Rd., Cambridge, ON N3E 1B7
519-653-6226 Fax: 519-653-9810 800-265-6358
ginfo@challenger.com
www.challenger.com
Company Type: Private

CHC Helicopter Corporation
4740 Agar Dr., Richmond, BC V7B 1A3
604-276-7500 Fax: 604-232-8359
communications@chc.ca
www.chc.ca
Company Type: Public
Profile: CHC Helicopter Corporation offers helicopter transportation services throughout the world. It specializes in offshore support to serve the oil & gas industry. Other services include search & rescue & helicopter training. Through its Heli-One division, leasing, logistics, repair, & overhaul services are available. CHC Helicopters's systems & procedures meet or exceed ISO 9001, ISO 14001, & OHSAS 18001 specifications.

Chrysler Canada Inc.
One Riverside Drive West, Windsor, ON N9A 5K3
519-973-2000 Fax: 519-973-2950 www.chryslercanada.ca
Company Type: Private
Profile: Marketing & sale of Chrysler, Dodge & Jeep vehicles; Operates the Automotive Research & Development Centre with University of Windsor

Contrans Income Fund
1179 Ridgeway Rd., Woodstock, ON N4V 1E3
519-421-4600 Fax: 519-539-9220
info@contrans.ca
www.contrans.ca
Ticker Symbol: CSS
Company Type: Public
Profile: The organization is involved in trucking & logistics services. Services are provided across Canada & the United States.

CRS-Express Inc.
2100, 95e rue, Saint-Georges, QC G5Y 8J3
418-227-7379 Fax: 418-227-7381
800-807-7379www.crs-express.com
Company Type: Private

CSL Group Inc.
759, carré Victoria, 6e étage, Montréal, QC H2Y 2K3
514-982-3800 Fax: 514-982-3920
ships@cslmtl.com
www.csl.ca
Company Type: Private
Profile: Specializes in bulk transportation & self-loading technology

Discovery Air Inc.
106 Dickens St., Yellowknife, NT X1A 2R3
Fax: 519-913-2204 866-903-3247www.discoveryair.com
Ticker Symbol: DA.A
Company Type: Public
Profile: Incorporated in 2004, Discovery Air Inc. created an alliance of aviation companies to provide safe, professional air transportation in selected niche markets. The following are Discovery Air's subsidiaries: Great Slave Helicopters Ltd., Discovery Mining Services Ltd., Hicks & Lawrence Limited, Top Aces Inc., & Air Tindi Ltd.

Essen Transport Ltd.
PO Box 2229, Winkler, MB R6W 4B9
204-325-5200 Fax: 204-325-5252
800-760-3776www.essentransport.com
Company Type: Private
Profile: Essen Transport Ltd. provides supply chain management. It uses logistics to track inbound & outbound shipments for companies in Canada and the United States.

F.K. Warren Ltd.
Cogswell Tower, #920, 2000 Barrington St., Halifax, NS B3J 2X1
902-423-8136 Fax: 902-429-1326 www.fkwarren.ca
Company Type: Public
Profile: F.K. Warren provides a comprehensive range of Marine Agency Services at all ports throughout Atlantic Canada.

Fednav Limited
#3500, 1000, rue de la Gauchetière ouest, Montréal, QC H3B 4W5
514-878-6500 Fax: 514-878-6642
info@fednav.com
www.fednav.com
Company Type: Private
Profile: Deep sea foreign transportation of freight; Freight transportation on the Great Lakes - St.Lawrence Seaway; Marine cargo handling

Ford Motor Company of Canada, Limited
PO Box 2000, The Canadian Rd., Oakville, ON L6J 5E4
Fax: 905-845-7016 800-565-3673www.ford.ca
Company Type: Private
Profile: Manufacturers of motor vehicles & passenger car bodies; wholesalers of automobiles & other motor vehicles, motor vehicle supplies & new parts

General Motors of Canada Limited
Main Mailing Dept. CA1-002-002, 1908 Colonel Sam Dr., Oshawa, ON L1H 8P7
905-644-5000 Fax: 905-644-6273
800-263-3777www.gmcanada.com
Company Type: Private
Profile: Manufacturers of motor vehicles & passenger car bodies, truck & bus bodies, motor vehicle parts & accessories, railroad equipment

Ghost Transportation Services
715E-46th St. West, Saskatoon, SK S7L 6A1
306-249-3515 Fax: 306-249-3335
customerservice@ghosttrans.com
www.ghosttrans.com
Company Type: Private
Profile: Ghost Transportation Services offers warehousing, shipment of raw materials, & transportation or distribution of finished products.

Global Railway Industries Ltd.
PO Box 5484, 1255 Brydges St., London, ON N5W 2C2
585-419-9720 Fax: 585-385-6790
info@globalrailway.com
www.globalrailway.com
Ticker Symbol: GBI
Company Type: Public
Profile: Global Railway Industries Ltd. is a designer, manufacturer, & marketer of railway equipment. The company is also engaged in remanufacturing locomotives & repairing rail cars. Global Railway Industries Ltd.'s products are provided through the following operating subsidiaries: CAD Railway Industries Ltd., Bach-Simpson Corporation, & G&B Specialties, Inc.. Operations are located in Canada & the United States.

GN Transport
163 Bowes Rd., Concord, ON L4K 1H3
905-760-2888 Fax: 905-760-2040 866-738-6661
info@gntransport.com
www.gntransport.com
Company Type: Private

Go Transport Ltd.
57 Braid St., New Westminster, BC V3L 3P2
604-525-0840 Fax: 604-525-3684 888-363-6699
dispatch@gotransport.ca
www.gotransport.ca
Company Type: Private

Greyhound Canada Transportation Corp.
877 Greyhound Way SW, Calgary, AB T3C 3V8
403-260-0877 Fax: 403-260-0779
canada.info@greyhound.ca
www.greyhound.ca
Company Type: Private
Profile: Intercity & rural bus transportation; travel agencies; courier services

Grimshaw Trucking LP
PO Box 960, 11510-151 St., Edmonton, AB T5M 3N6
780-414-2880 Fax: 780-455-7818
888-414-2850www.grimshaw-trucking.com
Company Type: Private
Profile: Grimshaw Trucking LP is a transportation company in western Canada.

Group Express Inc.
170 Main St. N., Alexandria, ON K0C 1A0
613-525-1275 Fax: 613-525-1278 800-387-6691
traffic@groupexpress.ca
www.groupexpress.ca
Company Type: Private

Groupe Desgagnés Inc.
21 Marché-Champlain St., Québec, QC G1K 8Z8
418-692-1000 Fax: 418-692-6044
info@degagnes.com
www.groupedesgagnes.com
Company Type: Public
Profile: Groupe Desgagnés' entire history has been marked by sustained, carefully orchestrated efforts that have helped ensure its growth & maintain its position as a shipping industry leader.

Harold Newell & Son Trucking Ltd.
R.R. #1, Barrington, NS B0W 1E0
902-637-2243 Fax: 902-637-1563
trucking@ns.sympatico.ca
www.tcfb.com/trucking
Company Type: Private

Holmes Maritime Inc.
1345 Hollis St., Halifax, NS B3J 1T8
902-422-0400 Fax: 902-422-9439
info@holmesmaritime.com
www.holmesmaritime.com
Company Type: Public
Profile: Holmes Maritime Inc. is a privately owned Canadian company, headquartered in Halifax, Nova Scotia. It provides port agency & logistics services to international ship owners & operators throughout eastern Canada & along the Great Lakes.

Honda Canada Inc.
715 Milner Ave., Toronto, ON M1B 2K8
416-284-8110 Fax: 416-286-1322 888-946-6329www.honda.ca
Company Type: Private
Profile: Manufacturers of motor vehicles & passenger car bodies; Wholesalers of automobiles & other motor vehicles, motor vehicle supplies & new parts

Hyundai Canada Inc.
75 Frontenac Dr., Markham, ON L3R 6H2
905-948-6712 Fax: 905-477-3820 800-461-8242
cr@hyundaicanada.com
www.hyundaicanada.com
Company Type: Private
Profile: Wholesalers of motor vehicle supplies & new parts

Jay's Moving & Storage
PO Box 4560, Regina, SK S4P 3Y3
306-569-9369 Fax: 306-721-4641
jaysreg@sasktel.net
Company Type: Private
Profile: Jay's Moving & Storage is a multi-branch moving & storage firm which serves the prairie provinces. A freight division provides services in Saskatchewan.

Jazz Air Income Fund
Halifax International Airport, 310 Goudey Dr., Enfield, NS B2T 1E4
902-873-5094 Fax: 902-873-2098 www.flyjazz.ca
Ticker Symbol: JAZ.UN
Company Type: Public
Profile: Jazz Air Income Fund is an unincorporated, open-ended trust. Its purpose is to hold an interest in the outstanding limited partnership units of Jazz Air LP.

Kindersley Transport Inc.
660 Aldford Ave., Delta, BC V3M 6X1
604-522-4002 Fax: 604-525-2955
customerservice@kindersleytransport.com
www.kindersleytransport.com
Company Type: Private
Profile: The fleet, based in western Canada, provides truckload & less-than-truckload services through a network of service centers in Canada & the United States.

KO Transport Inc.
651 Burlington St. E., Hamilton, ON L8L 4J5
905-544-9000 **Company Type:** Private
Profile: Established in 1933, KO Transport services the southern Ontario region & points beyond.

Kooi Trucking Inc.
PO Box 70, Scotland, ON N0E 1R0
519-446-3333 Fax: 519-446-3999
info@kooitruckinginc.com
www.kooitruckinginc.com
Company Type: Private
Profile: Kooi Trucking Inc. is a freight company, which specializes in the transportatoin needs of North American importers & exporters.

Lark Transport Inc.
2880 Saskatchewan Ave. W., Portage la Prairie, MB R1N 3B9
888-444-5257 Fax: 888-246-9365 www.larktransport.com
Company Type: Private
Profile: Lark Transport Inc. is a Canadian based freight transportation company.

Lighthouse Transport Services Ltd.
PO Box 38010, #2-150 Wright Ave., Dartmouth, NS B3B 1X2
902-468-3696 Fax: 902-468-5267 800-770-5457
colleen@lighthousetransport.com
www.lighthousetransport.com
Company Type: Private
Profile: Lighthouse Transport Services Ltd. offers the following services: FTL & LTL transport, container transport, warehousing & crating, oversized cargo moves, pilot car services, flatbed moves, deconsolidations, & exclusive deliveries.

Logistec Corporation
#1500, 360, rue Saint-Jacques, Montréal, QC H2Y 1P5
514-844-9381 Fax: 514-985-2314
corp@logistec.com
www.logistec.com
Ticker Symbol: LGT
Company Type: Public
Profile: Logistec Corporation & its subsidiaries serve the marine & industrial sectors. Cargo-handling services are offered at port terminals situated in eastern Canada & the United States, & on the Great Lakes. Other services include agency services to foreign ship-owners & operators at Canadian ports, marine transportation services, & on-site decontamination services.

Marine Atlantic Inc.
Baine Johnston Centre, #802, 10 Fort William Pl., St. John's, NL A1C 1K4
709-772-8957 Fax: 709-772-8956 800-341-7981
info@marine-atlantic.ca
www.marine-atlantic.ca
Company Type: Crown
Profile: Deep sea domestic transportation of freight; Ferries; Various water transportation of passengers

Mazda Canada Inc.
55 Vogell Rd., Richmond Hill, ON L4B 3K5
905-787-7000 Fax: 905-787-7125 800-263-4680www.mazda.ca
Company Type: Private
Profile: Wholesalers of automobiles & other motor vehicles, motor vehicle supplies & new parts

Mercedes-Benz Canada Inc.
98 Vanderhoof Ave., Toronto, ON M4G 4C9
800-387-0100www.mercedes-benz.ca
Company Type: Private
Profile: Wholesalers of automobiles & other motor vehicles, motor vehicle supplies & new parts; Retailers in new & used motor vehicle dealers

Montship Inc.
#1000, 360, rue Saint-Jacques, Montréal, QC H2Y 1R2
514-286-4646 Fax: 514-286-4650 www.montship.ca
Company Type: Public
Profile: The Canadian shipping agent has the capability of handling most any type of cargo movement. Montship Inc. has six offices located across the country.

N.M. Paterson & Sons Limited
PO Box 24, GRP 210, RR2 ., Winnipeg, MB R3C 2E6
204-694-4445 Fax: 204-694-4446
winnipeg_terminal@patersongrain.com
www.patersongrain.com
Company Type: Private
Profile: Freight transportation on the Great Lakes - St. Lawrence Seaway

NAV Canada
PO Box 3411 D, 77 Metcalfe St., Ottawa, ON K1P 5L6
613-563-5588 Fax: 613-563-3426 800-876-4693
service@navcanada.ca
www.navcanada.ca
Company Type: Private
Profile: Canada's civil air navigation services provider. Provides air traffic control, flight information, weather briefings, aeronautical information services, airport advisory services and electronic aids to navigation

Nissan Canada Inc.
5290 Orbitor Dr., Mississauga, ON L4W 4Z5
Fax: 905-629-6553 800-387-0122
information.centre@nissancanada.com
www.nissan.ca
Company Type: Private
Profile: Manufacturers of motor vehicles & passenger car bodies; Provides vehicles to Meals-on-Wheels agencies

Oceanex Inc.
#2550, 630, boul René-Lévesque ouest, Montréal, QC H3B 1S6
514-875-9244 Fax: 514-392-0200
bookings@oceanex.com
www.oceanex.com
Company Type: Public
Profile: Inter-modal transportation, with emphasis on container/roroship operations; door-to-door freight servies from any point of origin in North America to destinations in Newfoundland and Labrador

Overland West Freight Lines
#300, 10362 King George Hwy., Surrey, BC V3T 2W5
604-580-4600 Fax: 604-580-4601 800-698-2111
admin@overlandwest.ca
www.overlandwest.ca
Company Type: Private
Profile: Overland West Freight Lines operates as a full service carrier in British Columbia. It serves the retail, commercial, municipal construction, forestry, & mineral sectors.

Pacific Coast Express Ltd.
10299 Grace Rd., Surrey, BC V3V 3V7
604-582-3230 Fax: 604-588-7906 800-667-6061
service@pcx.ca; dispatch@pcx.ca
www.pcx.ca
Company Type: Private
Profile: Pacific Coast Express provides services related to the movement of goods across North America.

Phantom Freightlines
5300 - 86 Ave. SE, Calgary, AB T2C 47L
403-219-1008 Fax: 403-219-1016 www.phantomfreightlines.com
Company Type: Private
Profile: Phantom Freightlines specializes in the transportation of time sensitive & delicate materials, such as flowers, & fresh & frozen goods. Business is conducted across Canada & the United States.

Premium Trucking Ltd.
PO Box 39, 449 Lower Rd., Arichat, NS B0E 1A0
902-226-3474 Fax: 902-226-0026
www.premiumseafoods.ns.ca/ptrucking.php
Company Type: Private
Profile: Premium Trucking Ltd. transports fish & other products for Premium Seafoods Ltd. & for other companies that require dependable transportation services.

Prevost Car Inc.
35, boul Gagnon, Sainte-Claire, QC G0R 2V0
418-883-3391 Fax: 418-883-4157
prevostcar@volvo.com
www.prevostcar.com
Company Type: Private
Profile: Manufacturers of intercity coaches & coach shells for motorhomes & specialty conversion

Public Storage Canadian Properties
One First Canadian Place, #6600, 100 King St. West, Toronto, ON M5X 1B8
866-772-2623www.publicstoragecanada.com
Ticker Symbol: PUB
Company Type: Public
Profile: Public Storage Canadian Properties invests in self-storage facilities located throughout Canada. The facilities operate under the trade name "Public Storage". Canadian Mini-Warehouse Properties Company (CMP) is the General Partner of Public Storage Canadian Properties. CMP manages the facilities owned by Public Storage Canadian Properties.

Purolator Courier Ltd.
5995 Avebury Rd., Mississauga, ON L5R 3T8
888-744-7123www.purolator.com
Company Type: Private
Profile: The courier company has facilities throughout Canada. Purolator also provides international delivery services.

Rigel Shipping Canada Inc.
PO Box 5151, Shediac, NB E4P 8T9
506-533-9000 Fax: 506-533-9010
admin@rigelcanada.com
www.rigelcanada.com
Company Type: Private
Profile: Rigel Shipping Canada Inc. offers marine tanker solutions for petroleum & petro-chemical transportation. It serves the Canadian petroleum industry by providing safe, secure, & environmentally friendly shipping services.

Rockman Trucking Inc.
#56, 10765, ch de Côte-de-Liesse, Dorval, QC H9P 1A7
514-422-1085 Fax: 514-422-1083 800-565-1085
info@rockman.ca
www.rockman.ca
Company Type: Private
Profile: The licensed Canadian trucking company is a container, truckload, & LTL carrier. Rockman Trucking offers shipping in Canada & to the United States.

Rolls Right Industries
2864 Norland Ave., Burnaby, BC V5B 3A6

604-298-0080 Fax: 604-298-1366
info@rollsright.ca
www.rollsright.ca
Company Type: Private

Profile: The Canadian owned & operated carrier company has a fleet of more than eighty trucks. Rolls Right Industries provides truck & van delivery (LTL), trailer loads (FTL), & container hauling.

Seaway Marine Transport
#300, 20 Corporate Park Dr., St. Catharines, ON L2S 3W2
905-988-2600 Fax: 905-988-1803
www.seawaymarinetransport.com
Company Type: Private

Profile: Seaway Marine Transport, Inc. manages a fleet of gearless bulk carriers & self-unloading vessels, which carry products such as iron ore, coal, potash, grain, gypsum, & salt. A grain marketing office is located in the Richardson Building in Winnipeg, Manitoba.

Shadow Lines Transportation Group
9818 - 198B St., Langley, BC V1M 2X5
604-888-2928 Fax: 604-888-2794 800-663-1421
trucking@shadowlines.com
www.shadowlines.com
Company Type: Private

Profile: The transporation company operates from British Columbia to Ontario & throughout the United States. Shadow Lines Transportation Group's container fleet of trucks operates from the Langley, British Columbia terminal, where it serves Vancouver, Seattle, & Tacoma ports. The company's divisions include Heavy Haul / Line Haul & Logistics Solutions. Offices are also located in Edmonton & Calgary, Alberta & Regina & Saskatoon, Saskatchewan.

Spar Aerospace Limited
Edmonton International Airport, PO Box 9864, Edmonton, AB T5J 2T2
780-890-6300 Fax: 780-890-6652 www.spar.ca
Company Type: Private

Profile: Aviation services: aircraft programs; Component maintenance, repair & operation; Support services

Subaru Canada, Inc.
560 Suffolk Ct., Mississauga, ON L5R 4J7
Fax: 905-568-8087 800-894-4212www.subaru.ca
Company Type: Private

Profile: Manufacturers & retailers of motor vehicles

The Toronto Transit Commission
1900 Yonge St., Toronto, ON M4S 1Z2
416-393-4000 Fax: 416-482-0478 www.ttc.ca
Company Type: Crown

Profile: Operates & maintains the Toronto urban transit system: buses, subways, streetcars & trolleys, and Wheel-Trans accessible transit

TMT Freight System
14 Cadetta Rd., Brampton, ON L6T 3Z8
905-794-9845 Fax: 905-794-9846 888-817-4410
info@tmtfreight.com
www.tmtfreight.com
Company Type: Private

Profile: TMT Freight System is a container carrier.

Toyota Canada Inc.
1 Toyota Pl., Toronto, ON M1H 1H9
416-438-6320 Fax: 416-431-1867 888-869-6828www.toyota.ca
Company Type: Private

Profile: Wholesalers of automobiles & other motor vehicles, motor vehicle supplies & new parts, industrial machinery & equipment

Transat A.T. Inc.
Place du Parc, #600, 300, rue Léo-Pariseau, Montréal, QC H2X 4C2
514-987-1660 Fax: 514-987-8035 800-387-2672
info@transat.com
www.transat.com
Ticker Symbol: TRZ
Company Type: Public

Profile: Transat A.T. is an integrated tour operator, which organizes & markets holiday travel. Tour operators are based in Canada & France.

TransForce Income Fund
#300, 8585, rte Trans-Canada, Montréal, QC H4S 1Z6
514-331-4000 Fax: 514-337-4200
administration@transforce.ca
www.transforce.ca
Ticker Symbol: TFI
Company Type: Public

Profile: The Fund invests in organizations that provide trucking & transportation logistics services.

TransForce Income Fund
#300, 8585 Trans-Canada Highway, Saint-Laurent, QC H4S 1Z6
514-331-4000 Fax: 514-337-4200
administration@transforce.ca
www.transforce.ca
Company Type: Private

Profile: TransForce Income Fund invests in a network of independent operating companies. The Fund, through these subsidiaries, is involved in Canada's transportation & logistics industry.

Trappers Transport Ltd.
2475 Day St., Winnipeg, MB R2C 2Z2
204-697-7647 Fax: 204-633-5569
info@trapperstransport.com
www.trapperstransport.com
Company Type: Private

Profile: Trappers Transport Ltd. specializes in the transportation of refrigerated LTL or full Loads throughout North America.

Tri-White Corporation
#1400, 1 University Ave., Toronto, ON M5J 2P1
416-367-6877 Fax: 416-367-6890 www.tri-white.com
Ticker Symbol: TWH
Company Type: Public

Profile: Tri-White Corporation is the owner & operator of White Pass & Yukon Route. Port facilities, the passenger tourist railway, & related services operate in British Columbia, the Yukon Territory, & Alaska. Tri-White Corporation is also involved in merchant banking in Canada.

Trimac Income Fund
#1700, 800 - 5th Ave. SW, Calgary, AB T2P 5A3
403-298-5100 Fax: 403-298-5146
investors@trimac.com
www.trimacincomefund.com
Ticker Symbol: TMA.UN
Company Type: Public

Profile: Trimac Income Fund is an unincorporated, open-ended limited purpose trust. Through its subsidiary, Trimac Transportation Services Limited Partnership, Trimac Income Fund is involved in the provision of bulk trucking services.

Uniglobe Travel International L.P.
#900, 1199 West Pender St., Vancouver, BC V6E 2R1
604-718-2600 Fax: 604-718-2678
info@uniglobetravel.com
www.uniglobetravel.com
Company Type: Private

Profile: Travel franchise specializing in corporate travel services for small to medium accounts as well as individual travelers.

Upper Lakes Group Inc.
49 Jackes Ave., Toronto, ON M4T 1E2
416-920-7610
inquires@upperlakes.com
www.upperlakes.com
Company Type: Public

Profile: Upper Lakes Group Inc. moves, handles, & stores wet & dry bulk commodities & containerized cargoes. Areas of operation include the Great Lakes, Canada, & around the world. The company operates a large fleet of ships on the Great Lakes & the St. Lawrence Seaway, & it owns & operates grain terminal facilities throughout the Great Lakes & the St. Lawrence Seaway System. Upper Lakes Group Inc. is also involved in property development.

Vector Aerospace Corporation
#300, 105 Bedford Rd., Toronto, ON M5R 2K4
416-925-1143 Fax: 416-925-7214
info@vectoraerospace.com
www.vectoraerospace.com
Ticker Symbol: RNO
Company Type: Public

Profile: Vector Aerospace Corporation provides aviation maintenance, repair & overhaul services. Services are offered to both commercial & military customers, with fixed wing & rotary wing aircraft. Facilities are located in Canada, the United States, & the United Kingdom.

VersaCold
2115 Commissioner St., Vancouver, BC V5L 1A6
604-255-4656 Fax: 604-255-4330 800-563-2653
info@versacold.com
www.versacold.com
Company Type: Public

Profile: Refrigerated warehousing & logistics

VIA Rail Canada Inc.
Customer Relations, PO Box 8116 A, Montréal, QC H3C 3N3
514-871-6000 Fax: 514-871-6104 888-842-7245
customer_relations@viarail.ca
www.viarail.ca
Company Type: Crown

Profile: On behalf of the Government of Canada, VIA Rail Canada operates a safe, efficient, & environmentally responsible passenger rail service. VIAÆRail serves 450 communities across Canada.

Vitran Corporation Inc.
#701, 185 The West Mall, Toronto, ON M9C 5L5
416-596-7664 Fax: 416-596-8039
webmaster@vitran.com
www.vitran.com
Ticker Symbol: VTN
Company Type: Public

Profile: Vitran Corporation provides freight surface transportation & related logistics services in Canada & the United States. Services include logistics, less-than-truckload, & truckload services.

Volvo Cars of Canada Corp.
Customer Service, 175 Gordon Baker Rd., Toronto, ON M2H 2N7
800-663-8255
customerservice@volvo.com
www.volvocanada.com
Company Type: Private

Profile: Volvo Cars of Canada is an automotive manufacturer, which focuses on safety, quality, & environmental care.

Wallenius Wilhelmsen Logistics Vehicle Svs Canada Ltd
Annacis Auto Terminals, #100, 820 Dock Rd., Delta, BC V3M 6A3
604-521-6681 Fax: 604-522-7783
cms@2wglobal.com
www.2wglobal.com
Company Type: Private

Profile: Wallenius Wilhelmsen Logistics is engaged in the provision of global factory-to-dealer transport solutions. The company serves the automotive, construction equipment, & agricultural industries. Innovative solutions have been developed to reduce the impact of the company's operations on the environment. In British Columbia, the company operates an automotive terminal located on the Fraser River. It handles Mercedes Benz, BMW, Subaru, Kia, Mitsubishi, Honda, Nissan, & Hyundai.

WestJet Airlines Ltd.
5055 - 11 St. NE, Calgary, AB T2E 8N4
403-444-2600 Fax: 403-444-2261
investor_relations@westjet.com
www.westjet.com
Ticker Symbol: WJA
Company Type: Public

Profile: Scheduled passenger airline transportation is provided by WestJet Airlines.

World Point Terminals Inc.
#110, 1981, av McGill College, Montréal, QC H3A 3C1
403-261-3700
broy@wpo.ca
www.wpo.ca
Ticker Symbol: WPO
Company Type: Public

Profile: World Point Terminals Inc. & its subsidiaries are involved in the ownership & operation of oil terminaling facilities. The facilities tranship crude oil, refined petroleum, & other liquid products. Bulk storage is also offered. Liquid bulk storage & terminal facilities are situated in North America, the Bahamas, & the Netherlands.

Yanke Group of Companies
2815 Lorne Ave., Saskatoon, SK S7J 0S5
306-955-4221 Fax: 306-955-5663 800-667-7988
yanke_sales@yanke.ca
www.yanke.ca
Company Type: Private

Profile: Yanke Group of Companies is an international transportation company. It offers eight terminals across Canada. The company specializes in moving products such as agri-chemicals, temperature sensitive commodities, hazardous materials, & food stuffs.

Zeena Transport
PO Box 759, Morden, MB R6M 1A7
204-822-4915 Fax: 204-822-4687
info@zeenatransport.com
www.zeenatransport.com
Company Type: Private

Profile: Zeena Transport provides refrigerated & dry van service. The company also offers a brokerage service to ensure that freight is moved effectively.

Transportation Manufacturers & Services

Héroux-Devtek inc
Tour est, Complexe Saint-Charles, #658, 1111, rue Saint-Charles, Longueuil, QC J4K 5G4
450-679-3330 Fax: 450-679-3666
ir@herouxdevtek.com
www.herouxdevtek.com
Ticker Symbol: HRX
Company Type: Public
Profile: Manufacturers of aircraft parts & auxiliary equipment; Wholesalers of transportation equipment & supplies; Airports, flying fields & airport terminal services

Magellan Aerospace Corporation
3160 Derry Rd. East, Mississauga, ON L4T 1A9
905-677-1889 Fax: 905-677-5658
info@magellanaerospace.com
www.magellanaerospace.com
Ticker Symbol: MAL
Company Typo: Public
Profile: Manufacturers of aircraft parts & auxiliary equipment, aircraft engines & engine parts

Northstar Aerospace
 # 3430, 695 Bishop St. N, Cambridge, ON N3H 4V2
519-653-5774 Fax: 519-653-7190
infocambridge@nsaero.com
www.nsaero.com
Ticker Symbol: NAS
Company Type: Public
Profile: Manufacturers of motor vehicle parts & accessories, aircraft parts & auxiliary equipment, speed changers, industrial high-speed drives, gears, aircraft engines & engine parts; Airports, flying fields & airport terminal services

Pratt & Whitney Canada
1000, boul Marie-Victorin, Longueuil, QC J4G 1A1
450-677-9411 800-268-8000
maria.mandato@pwc.ca (Media Relations)
www.pwc.ca
Company Type: Private
Profile: Pratt & Whitney Canada is a designer & manufacturer of aircraft engines. The company also sells, rents, & repairs its products. Pratt & Whitney Canada's new generation engines surpass ICAO standards for low emissions & low noise. With research & manufacturing facilities throughout Canada & around the globe, Pratt & Whitney Canada is a major research & development investor in the Canadian aerospace industry.

Rolls-Royce Canada Ltd.
9500, ch de Côte-de-Liesse, Montréal, QC H8T 1A2
514-636-0964 Fax: 514-636-9969 www.rolls-royce.com
Company Type: Private
Profile: Canadian operations consist of engineering, repair, & overhaul within the diversified aerospace, industrial engine, & energy businesses. Facilities are situated in Montréal, Quebec & Vancouver, British Columbia. Customers include airlines, government bodies, & corporate operators around the world.

Wescast Industries Inc.
150 Savannah Oaks Dr., Brantford, ON N3T 5L8
519-750-0000 Fax: 519-720-1629
investor.relations@wescast.com
www.wescast.com
Ticker Symbol: WCS.A
Company Type: Public
Profile: Manufacturers of motor vehicle parts & accessories; Wholesalers of motor vehicle supplies & new parts

Trucking Companies

AMJ Campbell Inc.
1445 Courtneypark Dr., Mississauga, ON L5T 2E3
905-795-3785 Fax: 905-670-3787 www.amjcampbell.com
Ticker Symbol: AMJ
Company Type: Public
Profile: Local trucking with storage; Trucking, except local

Can-Truck Inc.
655 Bloor St. West, Oshawa, ON L1J 5Y6
905-404-6622 Fax: 905-404-6620
donf@can-truck.com
www.can-truck.com
Company Type: Private
Profile: Concentrates mainly on truckload freight including consolation and distribution throughout North America

Canadian Freightways
Lake City Industrial Park, 7867 Express St., Burnaby, BC V5A 1S8
604-420-4044 Fax: 604-420-4312 http://cf.cfmvmt.com
Company Type: Private
Profile: North American Coverage: Canadian Freightways provides services to 25,000 points across Canada and the U.S. through an integrated network of regional carriers including sister companies Epic Express and Click Express and strategic partners Averitt Express, New England Motor Freight, Midwest Motor Express and the Connection Company. Regional Expertise: Each partner in their North American network is a regional specialist providing overnight and second day service within their region. Partners operate local Service Centers and are represented by professional drivers and sales teams in key economic communities.

Challenger Motor Freight Inc.
300 Maple Grove Rd., Cambridge, ON N3E 1B7
519-653-6226 Fax: 519-653-9810 800-265-6358
info1@challenger.com
www.challenger.com
Company Type: Private
Profile: Challenger transports goods between Canada and anywhere in North America. Has a full range of transportation, warehousing and logistics services

International Truck and Engine Corporation Canada
5500 North Service Rd., 4th Fl., Burlington, ON L7L 5H7
905-332-3323 Fax: 905-332-2965 www.internationaldelivers.com
Company Type: Private
Profile: Dealers of trucks, buses, vans: engines, parts, services & financing

Motrux Inc.
731 Belgrave Way, Delta, BC V3M 5R8
604-527-1000 Fax: 604-527-1002 800-663-3436
info@motrux.com
www.motrux.com
Company Type: Private
Profile: Motrux is a carrier which serves a wide range of industries throughout North America. In addition to its head office in Delta, British Columbia, it also has an office in Oakville, Ontario.

Mullen Group Income Fund
PO Box 87, 1 Maple Leaf Rd., Aldersyde, AB T0L 0A0
403-652-8888 Fax: 403-601-8301
ir@mullentransportation.com
www.mullen-group.com
Ticker Symbol: MTL
Company Type: Public
Profile: Offices of holding companies; Long-distance trucking; Local trucking with storage; Various oil & gas fields services

Polar Express Transportation Ltd.
#4, 10097 - 201 St., Langley, BC V1M 3G4
604-888-3729 Fax: 604-888-3759
accounting@polarexpresstrans.com
www.polarexpresstrans.com
Company Type: Private
Profile: Polar Express Transportation is a Canadian & USA bonded carrier, which meets customers' distribution needs. Full & LTL loads are hauled between British Columbia, western Canada, & the United States.

Swift Dispatch Service Ltd.
32 West 5th Ave., Vancouver, BC V5Y 1H5
604-873-5422 Fax: 604-879-2311
info@swiftdispatch.com
www.swiftdispatch.com
Company Type: Private

TLI FlatDecks Inc.
1260 Cliveden Ave., Delta, BC V3M 6Y1
877-517-1177 Fax: 604-527-1175 www.tliflatdecks.net
Company Type: Private
Profile: The international flat deck specialized carrier is based in Delta BC. It services all North America.

Utilities

Algonquin Power Income Fund
2845 Bristol Circle, Oakville, ON L6H 7H7
905-465-4500 Fax: 905-465-4514
apif@algonquinpower.com
www.algonquinpower.com
Ticker Symbol: APF
Company Type: Public
Profile: Algonquin Power Income Fund is an open-ended investment trust. It owns or has interests in a portfolio of renewable power & sustainable infrastructure assets throughout Canada & the United States. The Trust's facilities include the following: hydroelectric generation, wind energy, energy from waste, landfill gas, biomass-fired generation, natural gas cogeneration, water distribution, & wastewater treatment.

AltaGas Income Trust
#1700, 355 - 4th Ave. SW, Calgary, AB T2P 0J1
403-691-7575 Fax: 403-691-7576 888-890-2715
feedback@altagas.ca
www.altagas.ca
Ticker Symbol: ALA
Company Type: Public
Profile: The energy infrastructure organization acquires, grows, & optimizes gas & power infrastructure. AltaGas Income Trust focuses upon renewable energy sources.

AltaGas Utility Group Inc.
#540, 355 - 4 Ave. SW, Calgary, AB T2P 0J1
403-806-3310 Fax: 403-806-3311
information@altagasutility.com
www.altagasutilitygroup.com
Ticker Symbol: AUI
Company Type: Public
Profile: AltaGas Utility Group Inc. is involved in the natural gas distribution marketplace. The company invests in infrastructure-based utility & related businesses. It holds interest in the following companies: AltaGas Utilities Inc., Inuvik Gas Ltd., Heritage Gas Limited, & Ikhil Joint Venture.

ATCO Ltd.
#1400, 909 - 11th Ave. SW, Calgary, AB T2R 1N6
403-292-7500 Fax: 403-292-7623
info@atco.com
www.atco.com
Ticker Symbol: ACO
Company Type: Public
Profile: The management holding company consists of the following main divisions: utilities, which includes natural gas & electricity transmission & distribution; power generation, which features the operation of hydroelectric, coal, & natural gas fired power plants; & global enterprises, which comprises ATCO Frontec, ATCO Midstream, ATCO Structures, ATCO Travel, ATCO I-Tek, & ATCO Noise Management.

Atomic Energy of Canada Limited
2251 Speakman Dr., Mississauga, ON L5K 1B2
905-823-9040 Fax: 905-823-1290 866-886-2325
info@aecl.ca
www.aecl.ca
Company Type: Crown
Profile: Manufacturers of various industrial inorganic chemicals, measuring & controlling devices, special industry machinery; Commercial physical & biological research; Management services; Electric services

Bell Aliant Regional Communications Income Fund
1 Brunswick Sq., 5th Fl., Saint John, NB E2L 4L4
877-248-3113 Fax: 877-498-2464
investors@bell.aliant.ca
www.bell.aliant.ca
Ticker Symbol: BA.UN
Company Type: Public
Profile: The wireline company operates in Atlantic Canada, Quebec, & Ontario.

Boralex Inc.
36, rue Lajeunesse, Kingsey Falls, QC J0A 1B0
819-363-5860 Fax: 819-363-5866
info@boralex.com
www.boralex.com
Ticker Symbol: BLX
Company Type: Public
Profile: The electricity producer provides the following types of power generation: natural gas cogeneration, hydroelectric, wind power, & wood-residue.

BP Canada Energy Company
240-4th Ave., SW, Calgary, AB T2P 2H8
403-233-1313 www.bp.com
Company Type: Public
Profile: BP is an energy company which provides its customers with fuel for transportation, energy for heat & light, retail services, & petrochemical products.

Brantford Power Inc.
84 Market St. 3rd Fl., Brantford, ON N3T 5N8
519-751-3522 Fax: 519-753-6130
brantfordpower@brantford.ca
www.brantfordpower.com
Company Type: Public
Profile: Brantford Power strives to provide safe, reliable, & competitively priced services to customers, while providing value for municipal shareholder.

British Columbia Hydro
6911 Southpoint Dr., Burnaby, BC V3N 4X8
604-224-9376 Fax: 604-528-3137
800-224-9376www.bchydro.com
Company Type: Crown
Profile: Electric services

British Columbia Utilities Commission
PO Box 250, 900 Howe St., Vancouver, BC V6Z 2N3
604-660-4700 Fax: 604-660-1102 800-663-1385
commission.secretary@bcuc.com
www.bcuc.com
Company Type: Public
Profile: The British Columbia Utilities Commission is an independent regulatory agency of the Provincial Government. The Commission's primary responsibility is the regulation of British Columbia's natural gas & electricity utilities. It also regulates intra-provincial pipelines & universal compulsory automobile insurance.

Cambridge & North Dumfries Hydro Inc.
PO Box 1060, 1500 Bishop St., Cambridge, ON N1R 5X6
519-621-3530 Fax: 519-621-0383 **Company Type:** Public
Profile: Cambridge & North Dumfries Hydro Inc. is a local distribution company which delivers electricity to the community on a not-for-profit basis. Local distribution rates are approved by the Ontario Energy Board.

Canadian Hydro Developers, Inc.
#500, 1324 - 17 Ave. SW, Calgary, AB T2T 5S8
403-269-9379 Fax: 403-244-7388
canhydro@canhydro.com
www.canhydro.com
Ticker Symbol: KHD
Company Type: Public
Profile: Canadian Hydro Developers, Inc. owns, develops, & operates generating facilities, which are certified, or slated for certification, under Environment Canada's EcoLogo Program. Renewable power generation facilities are situated in Quebec, Ontario, Alberta, & British Columbia. The renewable generation portfolio includes water, wind, & biomass technologies. The company's wholly-owned subsidiary is Canadian Renewable Energy Corporation.

Canadian Utilities Limited
#1400, 909 - 11th Ave. SW, Calgary, AB T2R 1N6
403-292-7500 Fax: 403-292-7623
investors@canadian-utilities.com
www.canadian-utilities.com
Ticker Symbol: CU
Company Type: Public
Profile: Part of the ATCO Group of Companies, Canadian Utilities Limited is engaged in natural gas & electricity transmission & distribution, as well as technology, logistics, & energy services.

CU Inc.
#1600, 909 - 11 Ave. SW, Calgary, AB T2R 1N6
403-292-7500 Fax: 403-292-7532 www.canadian-utilities.com
Ticker Symbol: CIU.PR.A
Company Type: Public
Profile: A wholly owned subsidiary of Canadian Utilities Limited, CU Inc. is involved in natural gas & electricity transmission & distribution, as well as power generation. CU Inc.'s subsidiaries include CU Water Limited, ATCO Gas & Pipelines Ltd., ATCO Electric Ltd., & Alberta Power (2000) Ltd.

Emera Incorporated
Barrington Tower, Scotia Square, PO Box 910, 1894 Barrington St., 18th Fl., Halifax, NS B3J 2W5
902-450-0507 Fax: 902-428-6112 888-450-0507
investors@emera.com
www.emera.com
Ticker Symbol: EMA
Company Type: Public
Profile: The holding company is involved in the energy sector. Emera Inc.'s subsidiaries include Bangor Hydro-Electric Company, Nova Scotia Power Inc., Emera Energy, Maritimes & Northeast Pipeline, Brunswick Pipeline, Emera Utility Services, & Grand Bahama Power Ltd.

Enbridge Income Fund
Fifth Avenue Place, #3000, 425 - 1st St. SW, Calgary, AB T2P 3L8
403-231-3900 Fax: 403-231-3920
webmaster@enbridgeincomefund.com
www.enbridgeincomefund.com
Ticker Symbol: ENF.UN
Company Type: Public
Profile: The unincorporated, open-ended trust is the owner of the following organizations: Enbridge Pipelines (Saskatchewan) Inc. (Saskatchewan System); NRGreen Power Limited Partnership (50% interest); wind power projects; & Alliance Canada Pipeline (50% interest). Enbridge is also developing electrical generation opportunities with waste heat. Operations are conducted in western Canada.

Energy Savings Income Fund
#2630, 100 King St. West, Toronto, ON M5X 1E1
416-367-2998 Fax: 416-367-4749
fundinfo@energysavingsincomefund.com
www.esif.ca
Ticker Symbol: SIF
Company Type: Public
Profile: The open-ended, limited purpose trust is involved in the sale of natural gas & electricity to both residential & commercial customers. Operating affiliates inlcude Ontario Energy Savings L.P., Energy Savings (Manitoba) L.P., Energy Savings (Quebec) L.P., ES (B.C.) Limited Partnership, Alberta Energy Savings L.P., Illinois Energy Savings Corp., New York Energy Savings Corp., Indiana Energy Savings Corp., & Energy Savings Texas Corp.

Enersource Hydro Mississauga
3240 Mavis Rd., Mississauga, ON L5C 3K1
905-273-9050 Fax: 905-566-2731
info@enersource.com
www.enersource.com
Company Type: Private
Profile: Provides electricity to the City of Mississauga

ENMAX Corporation
141 - 50 Ave. SE, Calgary, AB T2G 4S7
403-514-3000 Fax: 403-310-2010 877-571-7111
customercare@enmax.com
www.enmax.com
Company Type: Public
Profile: ENMAX Corporation provides electricity & natural gas energy services in Alberta.

EPCOR Power Equity Ltd.
Investor Relations, EPCOR Centre, 10065 Jasper Ave., Edmonton, AB T5J 3B1
780-412-4297 Fax: 780-412-3808 866-896-4636
InvestorInquiries@epcorpowerlp.ca
www.epcor.ca
Ticker Symbol: EPP.PR.A
Company Type: Public
Profile: EPCOR's business & power generation assets, plus other assets in the United States, are indirectly held by EPCOR Power Equity Ltd.

EPCOR Power L.P.
EPCOR Centre, 10065 Jasper Ave., 20th Fl., Edmonton, AB T5J 3B1
780-412-4297 Fax: 780-412-3808 866-896-4636
investorinquiries@epcorpowerlp.ca
www.epcorpowerlp.ca
Ticker Symbol: EP.UN
Company Type: Public
Profile: EPCOR Power L.P. is a limited partnership, which is involved in the generation of electricity & steam, through it ownership & operation of a portfolio power plants. Earnings & cash flows are derived from this activity. The Partnership's wholly-owned power generation assets are situated in Canada & the United States. The General Partner of the Partnership, EPCOR Power Services Ltd., is responsible for management of the Partnership.

Fortis Inc.
Fortis Bldg., PO Box 8837, #1201, 139 Water St., St. John's, NL A1B 3T2
709-737-2800 Fax: 709-737-5307
investorrelations@fortisinc.com
www.fortisinc.com
Ticker Symbol: FTS
Company Type: Public
Profile: Fortis Inc. is an international distribution utility holding company, which serves gas & electricity customers. The company also owns hotels & commercial real estate in Canada.

FortisAlberta
320 17th Avenue SW, Calgary, AB T2S 2V1
403-514-4000 Fax: 403-514-4001
866-717-3113www.fortisalberta.com
Company Type: Public
Profile: FortisAlberta provides power to various communities in Alberta. It is affliated with the Fortis Family of Companies.

FortisOntario
PO Box 1218, 1130 Bertie St., Fort Erie, ON L2A 5Y2
905-871-0330 www.cornwallelectric.com
Company Type: Public
Profile: FortisOntario is an innovative growth company with core businesses focused on electricity distribution, transmission, & generation. It is 100% Canadian owned & is affliated with the Fortis Family of Companies.

Gaz Métro inc
1717, rue du Havre, Montréal, QC H2K 2X3
514-598-3444 Fax: 514-598-3144 800-361-4005
info@gazmetro.com
www.gazmetro.com
Ticker Symbol: GZM
Company Type: Public
Profile: Offices of holding companies; Natural gas transmission & distribution; Retail in household appliance stores; Equipment rental & leasing

Gaz Métro Limited Partnership
1717, rue du Havre, Montréal, QC H2K 2X3
514-598-3444 Fax: 514-598-3144
investors@gazmetro.com
www.gazmetro.com
Ticker Symbol: GZM
Company Type: Public
Profile: Gaz Métro Limited Partnership focuses upon the distribution of natural gas, through its interests in natural gas transmission companies. The company is also engaged in the sale of goods in the energy & fiber optics fields, as well as the diagnosis & rehabilitation of drinking water & wastewater infrastructures. In order to reduce greenhouse gas emissions, Gaz Métro has adopted an environmental policy, an environmental management system, & energy efficiency programs.

Great Lakes Hydro Income Fund
#200, 480, boul de la Cité, Gatineau, QC J8T 8R3
819-561-2722 Fax: 819-561-7188 888-327-2722
unitholderenquiries@greatlakeshydro.com
www.greatlakeshydro.com
Ticker Symbol: GLH
Company Type: Public
Profile: Electric services; Open-ended management investment offices.

Grimsby Power Incorporated
231 Roberts Rd., Grimsby, ON L3M 5N2
905-945-5437 Fax: 905-945-9933
info@grimsbypower.com
www.grimsbypower.com
Company Type: Public
Profile: Grimsby Power Incorporated provides customers in Grimsby with electricity.

Guelph Hydro Electric Systems Inc.
395 Southgate Dr., Guelph, ON N1G 4Y1
519-822-3010 Fax: 519-822-0960
bbagley@guelphhydro.com
www.guelphhydro.com
Company Type: Public
Profile: Guelph Hydro Electric Systems Inc. is Guelph's and Rockwood's electricity distribution company. They deliver electricity, maintain the lines to homes and businesses provide 24-hr emergency service and ensure that the local distribution system meets Guelph's and Rockwood's growing needs.

Hydro One Inc.
483 Bay St., 15th Fl., Toronto, ON M5G 2P5
416-345-6867 Fax: 416-345-6225 877-955-1155
investor.relations@hydroone.com
www.hydroone.com
Company Type: Public
Profile: HydroOne is the largest electricity delivery company in Ontario. It is a holding company for various subsidiaries. It provides electric services in Toronto.

Hydro-Québec
75, boul René-Lévesque ouest, Montréal, QC H2Z 1A4
514-289-2211 Fax: 514-289-5773
800-790-2424www.hydroquebec.com
Company Type: Crown
Profile: Electricity services in Quebec

Independent Electricity System Operator
PO Box 4474 A, Toronto, ON M5W 4E5
905-403-6900 Fax: 905-403-6921
customer.relations@ieso.ca
www.ieso.ca
Company Type: Public
Profile: The IESO balances the supply of & demand for electricity in Ontario & then directs its flow across the province's transmission lines. The IESO works at the heart of Ontario's power system, connecting all participants that produce electricity, transmitters that send it across the province, retailers that buy & sell it, industries & businesses that use it in large quantities, & local distribution companies that deliver it to homes.

Innergex Renewable Energy Inc.
#1255, 1111, rue Saint-Charles ouest, Longueuil, QC J4K 5G4
450-928-2550 Fax: 450-928-2544
jtrudel@innergex.com
www.innergex.com
Ticker Symbol: INE
Company Type: Public
Profile: Innergex Renewable Energy develops & operates renewable power generating facilities. If focuses upon the wind power & hydroelectric sectors.

Kenora Hydro Electric Corp. Ltd
City Hall, 1 Main St. South, Kenora, ON P9N 3X2
807-467-2000
service@kenora.ca
Company Type: Private
Profile: Distributes electricity to the towns of Kenora and Keewatin; has 12 employees dedicated to the delivery of electricity to its customers

Keyera Facilities Income Fund
#600, 144 - 4 Ave. SW, Calgary, AB T2P 3N4
403-205-8300 Fax: 403-205-8303
ir@keyera.com
www.keyera.com
Ticker Symbol: KEY.UN
Company Type: Public
Profile: The Keyera Facilities Income Fund is an unincorporated open-ended trust. It owns 100% interest in Keyera Energy Canada Partnership. Keyera is engaged in the following activities: gathering & processing natural gas; storing & transporting natural gas liquids & crude oil; & marketing natural gas liquids.

London Hydro
111 Horton St., London, ON N6A 4J8
519-661-5503 Fax: 519-661-5838
admin@londonhydro.com
www.londonhydro.com
Company Type: Public
Profile: The sole shareholder of London Hydro is the City of London. London Hydro provides London residents & businesses with electricity, through a network of overhead & underground power lines.

Manitoba Hydro
PO Box 815 Main, 360 Portage Ave., Winnipeg, MB R3C 2P4
204-480-5900 Fax: 204-475-0069 888-624-9376
publicaffairs@hydro.mb.ca
www.hydro.mb.ca
Company Type: Crown
Profile: Manitoba Hydro is a major energy utility. It serves electric & natural gas customers in Manitoba.

Maritime Electric
c/o Island Customer Service Centre, PO Box 1328, 180 Kent St., Charlottetown, PE C1A 7N2
Fax: 902-629-3630 800-670-1012
customerservice@maritimeelectric.com
www.maritimeelectric.com
Company Type: Public
Profile: Maritime Electric operates according to the Electric Power Act & the Renewable Energy Act to deliver electricity on Prince Edward Island.

MAXIM Power Corp.
#1210, 715 - 5th Ave. SW, Calgary, AB T2P 2X6
403-263-3021 Fax: 403-263-9125
maxim@maximpowercorp.com
www.maximpowercorp.com
Ticker Symbol: MXG
Company Type: Public
Profile: MAXIM Power Corp. is an independent power producer. The company is involved in the acquisition, development, ownership, & operation of environmentally responsible power projects. Its assets include coal & natural gas powered generators in western Canada, the United States, & France.

Medicine Hat Electric
2172 Brier Park Place NW, Medicine Hat, AB T1C 1S6
403-529-8262 Fax: 403-502-8060
elecdist@medicinehat.ca
Company Type: Private
Profile: Responsible for providing electrical power, natural gas, water treatment & supply, and waste management services to the city of Medicine Hat

New Brunswick Power Distribution & Customer Svs. Corp
PO Box 2000, 515 King St., Fredericton, NB E3B 4X1
506-458-4444 Fax: 506-458-4000 800-663-6272
customerservices@nbpower.com
www.nbpower.com
Company Type: Crown
Profile: NB Power provides safe & sustainable energy services to homes, businesses, & facilities in New Brunswick. Electricity is generated at sixteen facilities.

Newfoundland & Labrador Hydro
Hydro Place, PO Box 12400, 500 Columbus Dr., St.John's, NL A1B 4K7
709-737-1400 Fax: 709-737-1800 888-737-1296
hydro@nlh.nl.ca; tenders@nlh.nl.ca
www.nlh.nl.ca
Company Type: Public
Profile: Newfoundland & Labrador Hydro is the primary generator of safe & reliable electricity to residents, utilities, & industries across the province. The company's assets include hydroelectric generating stations, high-voltage terminal stations, lower-voltage interconnected distribution stations, diesel plants, gas turbines, transmission & distribution lines, & an oil-fired plant.

Newfoundland Power Inc.
PO Box 8910, 55 Kenmount Rd., St. John's, NL A1B 3P6
709-737-2802 Fax: 709-737-2903 800-663-2802
contactus@newfoundlandpower.com
www.newfoundlandpower.com
Company Type: Public
Profile: Newfoundland Power Inc. is engaged in the operation of an integrated generation, transmission, & distribution system. Safe, reliable electricity is supplied to the island portion of Newfoundland & Labrador.

Niagara Peninsula Energy Inc.
PO Box 120, 7447 Pin Oak Dr., Niagara Falls, ON L2E 6S9
905-356-2681 Fax: 905-356-0118 877-270-3938
info@npei.ca
www.npei.ca
Company Type: Public
Profile: Niagara Peninsula Energy Inc. provides local electricity distribution & related services in the Township of West Lincoln, the City of Niagara Falls, the Town of Pelham, & the Town of Lincoln. It serves both business & residential customers.

Northwest Territories Power Corporation
4 Capital Dr., Hay River, NT X0E 1G2
867-874-5200
info@ntpc.com
www.ntpc.com
Company Type: Crown
Profile: Northwest Territories Power Corporation generates & delivers power across the Northwest Territories. The corporation operates 28 separate power systems. Northwest Territories Power Corporation attempts to reduce its environmental impact with natural gas engines in Inuvik, rather than shipping in diesel.

Nova Scotia Power Inc.
PO Box 910, #1800, 1894 Barrington St., Halifax, NS B3J 2W5
902-450-0507 Fax: 902-428-6112 800-428-6230
investors@emera.com
www.nspower.ca
Ticker Symbol: NSI
Company Type: Public
Profile: Nova Scotia Power Inc. is engaged in the generation, transmission, & distribution of electric power across Nova Scotia.

Ontario Power Generation Inc.
700 University Ave., Toronto, ON M5G 1X6
416-592-2555 877-592-2555
investor.relations@opg.com; media@opg.com
www.opg.com; mypowercareer@opg.com
Company Type: Crown
Profile: The electricity generation company operates in a safe & environmentally responsible manner to generate & sell electricity throughout Ontario. Assets include sixty-five hydroelectric generating stations, five fossil generating stations, & three nuclear generating stations.

Oshawa PUC Networks Inc.
100 Simcoe St. South, Oshawa, ON L1H 7M7
905-723-4623 Fax: 905-743-5222
contactus@opuc.on.ca
www.opuc.on.ca
Company Type: Private
Profile: Oshawa PUC Networks distributes electricity to homes & businesses in Oshawa.

Peterborough Utilities Group
PO Box 4125 Main, 1867 Ashburnham Dr., Peterborough, ON K9J 6Z5
705-748-9300 Fax: 705-748-6761
info@peterboroughutilities.ca
www.peterboroughutilities.ca
Company Type: Public
Profile: Peterborough Utilities Group delivers & sells utility-related products & services.

Powerex Corp.
#1400, 666 Burrard St., Vancouver, BC V6C 2X8
604-891-5000 Fax: 604-891-6060 800-220-4907
Brian.Moghadam@powerex.com (Business Dev)
www.powerex.com
Company Type: Public
Profile: As a wholly-owned subsidiary of BC Hydro, Powerex markets BC Hydro's surplus electricity. Powerex is a participant in energy markets across North America, where it supplies & buys wholesale power, natural gas, ancillary services, & environmental products.

Saint John Energy
PO Box 850, Saint John, NB E2L 4C7
506-658-5252 Fax: 506-658-0868
877-907-5550www.sjenergy.com
Company Type: Private
Profile: Responsible for providing electricity to the city of Saint John. Other services include tree trimming, rental of water heaters, street light repair

Saskatoon Light & Power
322 Brand Rd., Saskatoon, SK S7K 0J5
306-975-2414 Fax: 306-975-3057
www.city.saskatoon.sk.ca/org/electrical
Company Type: Private
Profile: Founded in 1906, Saskatoon Light & Power distributes electrical services to citizens & businesses of the Saskatoon area that lies roughly within the 1958 boundary. The utility is also responsible for the street light system for the city.

SaskEnergy Incorporated
1777 Victoria Ave., Regina, SK S4P 4K5
306-777-9225 800-567-8899www.saskenergy.com
Company Type: Crown
Profile: The natural gas distribution company is a provincial Crown corporation. SaskEnergy Incorporated delivers safe & environmentally friendly natural gas to customers throughout Saskatchewan. The company also works with independent natural gas retailers to offer natural gas appliances, maintenance, & financing.

Spectra Energy Inc.
#1000, 1055 West Georgia St., Vancouver, BC V6E 3K9
604-488-8000 Fax: 604-488-8500 www.duke-energy.com
Company Type: Public
Profile: Natural gas transmission & distribution; Electric services; Crude petroleum, natural gas & natural gas liquids extraction; Natural gas transmission; Special warehousing & storage.

Terasen Gas
PO Box 6666 Terminal, Vancouver, BC V6B 6M9
250-979-4900 Fax: 888-224-2720 888-224-2710
customerservice@tersengas.com
www.terasengas.com
Company Type: Public
Profile: Tersan Gas delivers natural gas & piped propane to homes & businesses throughout BC. It has approximately 900,000 customers in 125 communities & provides service to 95% of BC's natural gas customers.

Toronto Hydro Corporation
14 Carlton St., Toronto, ON M5B 1K5
416-542-3100 Fax: 416-542-3452
contactus@torontohydro.com
www.torontohydro.com
Company Type: Crown
Profile: Offices of holding companies; Electric services; Natural gas distribution.

TransAlta Corporation
PO Box 1900 M, 110 - 12 Ave. SW, Calgary, AB T2P 2M1
403-267-7110 Fax: 403-267-2590
investor_relations@transalta.com
www.transalta.com
Ticker Symbol: TA
Company Type: Public
Profile: TansAlta Corporation is engaged in coal & gas-fired generation. The company carries out its activities in Canada, the United States, Mexico, & Australia.

TransAlta Power, L.P.
PO Box 1900 M, 110 - 12 Ave. SW, Calgary, AB T2P 2M1
403-267-7110 Fax: 403-267-2590
investor_relations@transalta.com
www.transalta.com
Ticker Symbol: TA
Company Type: Public
Profile: Unit investment trusts, certificate/closed-end management offices; Electric services

TransCanada Corp.
450 - 1 St. SW, Calgary, AB T2P 5H1
403-920-2000 Fax: 403-920-2200
communications@transcanada.com
www.transcanada.com
Ticker Symbol: TRP
Company Type: Public
Profile: TransCanada Corporation is engaged in the pipelines & energy business. Pipelines are located in Canada, the United States, & Mexico. Power operations & natural gas storage are part of the energy segment.

Utilities Kingston
PO Box 790, Kingston, ON K7L 4X7

613-456-0000
info@utilitieskingston.com
www.utilitieskingston.com
Company Type: Private

Profile: Utilities Kingston is responsible for supplying, distributing and metering electricity and natural gas in the City Central. Also responsible for supplying, distributing and metering water and for collecting, pumping and treating sewage for the entire city of Kingston

Wellington North Power Inc.
PO Box 359, 290 Queen St. West, Mount Forest, ON N0G 1A0

519-323-1710 Fax: 519-323-2425
wnp@wellingtonnorthpower.com
www.wellingtonnorthpower.com
Company Type: Public

Profile: The distribution company delivers electricity & maintains service to residents & businesses. Wellington North Power Inc. serves the areas of Arthur, Mount Forest, & Holstein in Ontario.

Westario Power Inc.
24 Eastridge Rd., RR#2, Walkerton, ON N0G 2V0

519-507-6937 866-978-2746
customer.service@westario.com
www.westario.com
Company Type: Public

Profile: Westario Power Inc. is engaged in the safe & reliable delivery of electricity. It is owned by the municipalities it serves. FortisOntario also has a 10% interest in Westario Power.

Yukon Electrical Company Limited
#100, 1100 - 1st Ave., Whitehorse, YT Y1A 3T4

867-633-7000 Fax: 867-668-6692
800-661-0513www.yukonelectrical.com
Company Type: Private

Profile: The Yukon Electrical Company Limited is a private, investor-owned utility which provides electrical services to Yukoners. The company works to design & construct its facilities in a way that reduces pollution & the impact of operations upon the environment.
@CHAPTER CODE = Business & Finance

Stock Exchanges

Stock exchanges are organized alphabetically by exchange name.

Canadian National Stock Exchange (CNSX)
c/o CNSX Markets Inc.
220 Bay St., 9th Fl.
Toronto, ON M5J 2W4

416-572-2000
Fax: 416-572-4160
www.cnsx.ca

Former Name: Canadian Trading & Quotation System Inc.
Also Known As: CNSX
Year Founded: 2004

Canadian Unlisted Board Inc.
The Exchange Tower, Trading Services, Toronto Stock Exchange
130 King St. West
Toronto, ON M5X 1J2

416-947-4705
Fax: 416-947-4280
cubadmin@cub.ca
www.cub.ca

Also Known As: CUB
Year Founded: 2000

ICE Futures Canada, Inc.
Commodity Exchange Tower
#400, 360 Main St.
Winnipeg, MB R3C 3Z4

204-925-5000
Fax: 204-943-5448
Other Contact Information: 204-925-5017 (Phone, ICE Clear Canada)
www.theice.com

Former Name: Winnipeg Commodity Exchange Inc.
Ownership: Wholly owned subsidiary of IntercontinentalExchange (ICE), Atlanta, GA, USA
Year Founded: 1887

Montréal Exchange Inc. (MX)/ Bourse de Montréal Inc.
Tour de la Bourse
CP 61
800, square Victoria
Montréal, QC H4Z 1A9

514-871-2424
Fax: 514-871-3514
800-361-5353
Other Contact Information: 00.800.36.15.35.35 (Toll-free from Great Britain & France); rh@m-x.ca (HR); marketdata@m-x.ca (Market Data); reg@m-x.ca (Regulation / Registration) info@m-x.ca; communications@m-x.ca; finances@m-x.ca; legal@m-x.ca
www.m-x.ca

Also Known As: MX
Year Founded: 1874

Natural Gas Exchange Inc. (NGX)
#2330, 140 - 4 St. SW
Calgary, AB T2P 3N3

403-974-1700
Fax: 403-974-1719
Other Contact Information: Ops@ngx.com (NGX Help Desk & Operations);
Clearing@ngx.com; Marketing@ngx.com
www.ngx.com

Also Known As: NGX
Ownership: Wholly owned by TMX Group Inc., Toronto, ON.
Year Founded: 1994

NEX Board
PO Box 11633
#2700, 650 West Georgia St.
Vancouver, BC V6B 4N9

604-689-3334
Fax: 604-844-7502
866-344-5639
nex@tsxventure.com
www.tsx.com/en/nex

Also Known As: NEX
Year Founded: 2003

TMX Group Inc.
PO Box 450
130 King St. West, 3rd Fl.
Toronto, ON M5X 1J2

416-947-4670
Fax: 416-947-4662
888-873-8392
Other Contact Information: Couriered deliveries to TMX Group Inc.: c/o Plus One Inc., First Canadian Place, 77 Adelaide St. West, Toronto, ON, M5X 1A4
info@tsx.com (TSX); information@tsxventure.com (TSX Venture)
www.tsx.com

Former Name: TSX Group Inc.
Also Known As: TSX-X

The Toronto Stock Exchange (TSX)
The Exchange Tower
PO Box 450
130 King St. West , 3rd Fl.
Toronto, ON M5X 1J2

416-947-4670
Fax: 416-947-4770
888-873-8392
Other Contact Information: marketregs@tsx.com (Investor Services); disclosure@tsx.com (Compliance & disclosure); queries@tsxdatalinx.com (TSX Datalinx)
info@tsx.com; listedissuers@tsx.com;
issuersupport@tsxconnect.com
www.tsx.com

Also Known As: TSX
Ownership: Subsidiary of TMX Group Inc., Toronto, ON
Year Founded: 1861

TSX Venture Exchange
PO Box 450
130 King St. West, 3rd Fl.
Toronto, ON M5X 1J2

416-365-2200
Fax: 416-365-2224
877-421-2369
Other Contact Information: 888-873-8392 (Toll Free, Business Development); complianceanddisclosure@tsxventure.com (E-mail, Concerns regarding listed issuers)
information@tsxventure.com
www.tsxventure.com

Former Name: Canadian Venture Exchange
Ownership: Subsidiary of TMX Group Inc., Toronto, ON

Trust Companies

Trust Companies are regulated under the federal Trust and Loan Companies Act and operate under either provincial or federal legislation. The business of trust companies includes activities like those of a bank, plus fiduciary functions. Trust Companies are listed alphabetically.

AGF Trust Company
Toronto-Dominion Centre
66 Wellington St. West, 31st Fl.
Toronto, ON M5K 1E9

416-216-5353
800-244-8457
trust@agf.com
www.agf.com/mortgages

Ownership: Wholly owned subsidiary of AGF Management Limited.
Year Founded: 1988

All Nations Trust Company
#208, 345 Yellowhead Hwy.
Kamloops, BC V2H 1H1

250-828-9770
Fax: 250-372-2585
800-663-2959
antco@antco.bc.ca
www.antco.bc.ca

Ownership: Private
Year Founded: 1984
Number of Employees: 13

B2B Trust
130 Adelaide St. West
Toronto, ON M5H 3P5

416-947-7427
Fax: 416-947-9476
800-263-8349
www.b2b-trust.com

Former Name: Sun Life Trust Company
Ownership: Private. Subsidiary of Laurentian Bank of Canada, Montréal, QC.
Year Founded: 1991
Number of Employees: 258
Assets: $1-10 billion
Revenues: $50-100 million

The Bank of Nova Scotia Trust Company
Scotia Plaza
44 King St. West
Toronto, ON M5H 1H1

416-866-6161
Fax: 416-866-3750

Also Known As: Scotiatrust
Ownership: Private. Subsidiary of Bank of Nova Scotia
Year Founded: 1993
Number of Employees: 450

BMO Trust Company
55 Bloor St. West, 12th Fl.
Toronto, ON M4W 3N5

416-867-6784
AATinvestmentservices@bmo.com
www.advisorsadvantagetrust.com

Former Name: The Trust Company of Bank of Montréal
Also Known As: Advisor's Advantage Trust
Ownership: Wholly owned subsidiary of Bank of Montréal. Member of BMO Financial Group.

BNY Trust Company of Canada
#1101, 4 King St. West
Toronto, ON M5H 1B6

www.bankofny.com

Ownership: Wholly owned subsidiary of the Bank of New York Company Inc.
Year Founded: 2001

The Canada Trust Company
Toronto Dominion Centre
PO Box 1, TD Centre Stn. TD Centre
55 King St. West, 12th Fl.
Toronto, ON M5K 1A2

888-222-3456
www.tdcanadatrust.com

Year Founded: 1855

Canadian Western Trust Co. (CWT)
#600, 750 Cambie St.
Vancouver, BC V6B 0A2

604-685-2081
Fax: 604-669-6069
800-663-1124
informationservices@cwt.ca
www.cwt.ca

Ownership: Wholly owned subsidiary of Canadian Western Bank

CIBC Mellon Trust Company
320 Bay St., 4th Fl.
Toronto, ON M5H 4A6

416-643-5000
Fax: 416-643-6409
www.cibcmellon.ca
Ownership: Parent companies are Canadian Imperial Bank of Commerce & Mellon Financial Corporation
Year Founded: 1978
Number of Employees: 350
Assets: $500m-1 billion

CIBC Trust Corporation
#900, 55 Yonge St.
Toronto, ON M5E 1J4
800-465-3863
www.cibc.com

Citizens Trust Company
#401, 815 West Hastings St.
Vancouver, BC V6B 1B4
604-682-7171
Fax: 604-708-7790
800-663-1435
www.citizensbank.ca

Clarica Trustco Company
PO Box 1601, Waterloo Stn. Waterloo
227 King St. South
Waterloo, ON N2J 4C5
888-864-5463
service@clarica.com
www.clarica.ca
Former Name: Mutual Trust Co.
Ownership: Subsidiary of Sun Life Assurance Company of Canada
Year Founded: 1918

Community Trust Company
2271 Bloor St. West
Toronto, ON M6S 1P1
416-763-2291
Fax: 416-763-2444
officepresident@communitytrust.ca
Ownership: Private
Year Founded: 1975

Computershare Trust Company of Canada
100 University Ave., 11th Fl.
Toronto, ON M5J 2Y1
416-263-9200
Fax: 416-263-9261
800-663-9097
www.computershare.com
Former Name: Montreal Trust
Ownership: Public. Listed on the Australian Stock Exchange
Year Founded: 2000
Number of Employees: 1,400
Revenues: $1-5 million

The Effort Trust Company
240 Main St. East
Hamilton, ON L8N 1H5
905-528-8956
Fax: 905-528-8182
www.efforttrust.ca
Ownership: Private. Wholly owned subsidiary of Effort Corporation.
Year Founded: 1978
Number of Employees: 100
Assets: $100-500 million
Revenues: $10-50 million

The Equitable Trust Company
#700, 30 St. Clair Ave. West
Toronto, ON M4V 3A1
416-515-7000
Fax: 416-515-7001
mortgage@equitabletrust.com
www.equitabletrust.com
Ownership: Wholly-owned subsidiary of Equitable Group Inc.
Year Founded: 1970

Equity Transfer & Trust Company
#400, 200 University Ave.
Toronto, ON M5H 4H1
416-361-0152
Fax: 416-361-0470
866-393-4891
Other Contact Information: newbusiness@equitytransfer.com (New Business); investor@equitytransfer.com (Investor Inquiries); clientservices@equitytransfer.com (Client Services) info@equitytransfer.com, trustservices@equitytransfer.com
www.equitytransfer.com
Ownership: Wholly owned subsidiary of Grey Horse Capital Corporation.
Year Founded: 1990

Fiduciary Trust Company of Canada
Also listed under: *Financial Planning & Investment Management Companies*
#3000, 350 Seventh Ave. SW
Calgary, AB T2P 3N9
403-543-3950
Fax: 403-543-3955
800-574-3822
www.fiduciarytrust.ca
Former Name: Bissett & Associates Investment Management Ltd.
Year Founded: 1982

Fiducie Desjardins/ Desjardins Trust
Also listed under: *Investment Fund Companies*
CP 34, Desjardins Stn. Desjardins
1, Complexe Desjardins
Montréal, QC H5B 1E4
514-286-9441
Fax: 514-286-1131
800-361-6840
Other Contact Information: 514-286-3225 (Business Centre Phone); 514-286-3100 (Asset Custody Service Phone); 514-499-8440 (Immigrant Investors Program Phone)
info@immigrantinvestor.com
www.fiduciedesjardins.com
Ownership: Part of the Desjardins Group.
Year Founded: 1963
Number of Employees: 850

Home Trust Company
Also listed under: *Credit Card Companies*
#2300, 145 King St. West
Toronto, ON M5H 1J8
416-360-4663
Fax: 416-360-0401
800-990-7881
inquiry@hometrust.ca
www.hometrust.ca
Ownership: Public. Principal subsidiary of Home Capital Group Inc.
Year Founded: 1977
Number of Employees: 296
Assets: $1-10 billion
Revenues: $100-500 million

HSBC Trust Company (Canada)
620, 885 West Georgia St.
Vancouver, BC V6C 3E9
604-641-1122
Fax: 604-641-1138
888-887-3388
www.hsbc.ca
Ownership: Private. Wholly owned subsidiary of HSBC Bank Canada
Year Founded: 1972
Number of Employees: 28

IBT Trust Company (Canada)
PO Box 231, First Canadian Place Stn. First Canadian Place
#2800, 100 King St. West
Toronto, ON M5X 1C8
416-363-6427
Fax: 416-861-8989
Other Contact Information: 416-861-8983 (Sales phone)
www.ibtco.com
Ownership: Subsidiary of Investors Bank & Trust, Boston, MA
Year Founded: 1993

Industrial Alliance Trust Inc.
1080, Grande Allée ouest
Québec, QC G1K 7M3
418-684-5000
www.inalco.com
Former Name: Industrial-Alliance Trust Company
Year Founded: 2000

Investors Group Trust Co. Ltd./ La Compagnie de Fiducie du Groupe Investors Ltée
One Canada Centre
447 Portage Ave.
Winnipeg, MB R3C 3B6
204-943-0361
Fax: 204-949-1340
888-746-6344
www.investorsgroup.com
Ownership: Subsidiary of Investors Group Inc.
Year Founded: 1968

Laurentian Trust of Canada Inc.
1981, av McGill College
Montréal, QC H3A 3K3
514-284-4500
Fax: 514-284-3396
mail@laurentianbank.ca
www.laurentianbank.com
Ownership: Private. Wholly owned subsidiary of the Laurentian Bank of Canada.
Year Founded: 1939
Assets: $500m-1 billion
Revenues: $10-50 million

LBC Trust
130 Adelaide St. West
Toronto, ON M5H 3P5
800-522-1846
www.laurentianbank.ca
Ownership: Wholly-owned subsidiary of Laurentian Bank

Legacy Private Trust
PO Box 1
#800, 1 Toronto St.
Toronto, ON M5C 2V6
416-868-0001
Fax: 416-868-6541
Other Contact Information: 416-868-4205 (Corporate Secretary Phone)
rlw@legacyprivatetrust.com
www.legacyprivatetrust.com
Ownership: Private
Year Founded: 2002

Maple Trust Company/ Compagnie Maple Trust
TD Waterhouse Tower, Toronto-Dominion Centre
PO Box 349
#3500, 79 Wellington St. West
Toronto, ON M5K 1K7
416-350-7400
Fax: 416-350-7441
800-307-8341
Other Contact Information: 416-350-7488 (Client Services Hotline); 416-350-7498 (Client Services Fax); MTMortgageAdministration@mapletrust.com (Mortgage Email)
MTTrustServices@mapletrust.com,
MTDepositServices@mapletrust.com
www.mapletrust.com
Former Name: London Trust and Savings Corporation
Ownership: Private. Member of the Scotiabank Group.
Year Founded: 1999
Assets: $1-10 billion

Mennonite Trust Limited
PO Box 40
3005 Central Ave.
Waldheim, SK S0K 4R0
306-945-2080
Fax: 306-945-2225
mtl@sasktel.ca
www.mennonitetrust.com
Year Founded: 1917

M.R.S. Trust Company
#2100, 777 Bay St.
Toronto, ON M5G 2N4
416-964-0028
Fax: 416-413-1723
800-387-2087
Other Contact Information: mortgages@mrs.com (Email MRS Mortgages); 888-677-5363 (Mortgage Toll-Free); 416-926-0570 (Mortgage Information Phone)
accounthelp@mrs.com
www.mackenziefinancial.com
Former Name: Mackenzie Trust Company
Also Known As: MRS Trust
Ownership: Subsidiary of Mackenzie Financial Corporation.
Year Founded: 1979

NATCAN Trust Company
National Bank
1100, rue University, 12e étage
Montréal, QC H3B 2G7
514-871-7633
Fax: 514-871-7580
800-235-5566
Ownership: Wholly owned by National Bank Acquisition Holding Inc.

National Bank Trust/ Trust Banque National
1100, rue University, 10e étage
Montréal, QC H3B 2G7
514-871-7240
800-463-6643
www.nbc.ca

Northern Trust Company, Canada
PO Box 526
#1510, 145 King St. West
Toronto, ON M5H 1J8

416-365-7161
Fax: 416-365-9484
www.ntrs.com
Ownership: Subsidiary of Northern Trust Company, Chicago, USA
Number of Employees: 31

Oak Trust Company
One London Place
#1770, 255 Queens Ave.
London, ON N6A 5R8
519-433-6629
Fax: 519-433-6652
866-973-6631
Other Contact Information: 519-979-2338 (Windsor/Essex Phone)
www.oaktrust.ca
Year Founded: 2004

Olympia Trust Company
#2300, 125 - 9th Ave. SW
Calgary, AB T2G 0P6
403-261-0900
Fax: 403-265-1455
800-727-4493
info@olympiatrust.com
www.olympiatrust.com
Ownership: Wholly owned subsidiary of Olympia Financial Group Inc.

Pacific Corporate Trust Company
510 Burrard St., 2nd Fl.
Vancouver, BC V6C 3B9
604-689-9853
Fax: 604-689-8144
pacific@pctc.com
www.pctc.com
Former Name: Pacific Corporate Services Limited
Ownership: Private
Year Founded: 1981

Peace Hills Trust Company
Samson Mall, Samson Cree Nation Reserve
PO Box 60
Hobbema, AB T0C 1N0
780-585-3013
Fax: 780-585-2216
pht@peacehills.com
www.peacehills.com
Ownership: Private
Year Founded: 1981
Number of Employees: 120
Assets: $100-500 million
Revenues: $10-50 million

Peoples Trust Company
Also listed under: *Financing & Loan Companies*
888 Dunsmuir St., 14th Fl.
Vancouver, BC V6C 3K4
604-683-2881
Fax: 604-331-3469
people@peoplestrust.com
www.peoplestrust.com
Ownership: Private
Year Founded: 1985

RBC Dexia Investor Services Trust
Royal Trust Tower, Toronto Dominion Centre
77 King St. West, 35th Fl.
Toronto, ON M5W 1P9
416-955-5907
www.rbcdexia-is.com
Ownership: Wholly-owned subsidiary of RBC Dexia Investor Services
Year Founded: 2006

ResMor Trust Company
Also listed under: *Financing & Loan Companies*
#400, 555 - 4th Ave. SW
Calgary, AB T2P 3E7
403-539-4920
Fax: 403-539-4921
866-333-7030
www.resmor.com
Former Name: Equisure Trust Company
Ownership: Private. ResMor Capital Corporation.
Year Founded: 1964
Number of Employees: 195
Assets: $100-500 million
Revenues: $10-50 million

The Royal Trust Company
Also listed under: *Financial Planning & Investment Management Companies*
Royal Bank
1, Place Ville-Marie, 6e étage sud
Montréal, QC H3B 2B2
514-874-7222
800-668-1990
Other Contact Information: 866-553-5585 (Eastern Canada Toll Free); 888-299-5290 (Western Canada Toll Free); 866-474-4344 (Québec Toll Free); tradvmtl@rbc.com (Québec Email) tradvtor@rbc.com (East), tradvcal@rbc.com (West)
www.rbc.com
Ownership: Part of RBC Financial Group.
Year Founded: 1899

Standard Life Trust Company
#206, 1245, rue Sherbrooke ouest
Montréal, QC H3G 1G3
888-841-6633
www.standardlife.ca
Former Name: Bonaventure Trust Company of Canada
Ownership: Private
Year Founded: 1825

State Street Bank & Trust Company - Canada
Also listed under: *Foreign Banks: Schedule III*
#1100, 30 Adelaide St. East
Toronto, ON M5C 3G6
416-362-1100
Fax: 416-956-2525
888-287-8639
www.statestreet.com
Former Name: State Street Trust Company Canada
Ownership: State Street Corporation
Year Founded: 1990
Number of Employees: 700

Sun Life Financial Trust Inc.
PO Box 1601, Waterloo Stn. Waterloo
227 King St. South
Waterloo, ON N2J 4C5
877-786-5433
www.sunlife.com

Trimark Trust/ Fiducie Trimark
#900, 5140 Yonge St.
Toronto, ON M2N 6X7
416-590-0036
800-631-7008
inquiries@aimtrimark.com
www.aimtrimark.com
Former Name: Bayshore Trust
Ownership: AIM Trimark Investments, Toronto, ON.
Year Founded: 1977

The Trust Company of London Life
One Canada Centre
447 Portage Ave.
Winnipeg, MB R3C 3B6
204-956-8470

Valiant Trust Company
#600, 750 Cambie St.
Vancouver, BC V6B 0A2
604-699-4880
Fax: 604-681-3067
877-699-4880
inquiries@valianttrust.com
www.valianttrust.com
Ownership: Subsidiary of Canadian Western Bank

Western Pacific Trust Company
#500, 1130 West Pender St.
Vancouver, BC V6E 4A4
604-683-0455
Fax: 604-669-6978
www.westernpacifictrust.com
Ownership: Public
Year Founded: 1964

SECTION 6
EDUCATION

Arranged by Province, and each Province includes the following categories. Each category is further arranged by specific subcategories, as applicable to each Province.

Government Agencies

School Boards/Districts/Divisions
Public; Protestant; Catholic; French; School Authorities

Schools: Specialized
Charter; First Nations; Hearing Impaired; Distance Education; Special Education

Schools: Independent & Private

Universities & Colleges

Post Secondary/Technical

Alberta

Government Agencies

Edmonton: Alberta Advanced Education
Communications Branch
10155 - 102 St., 7th Fl. Edmonton, T5J 4L5 Canada
780-422-4495, Fax: 780-422-1263,
AdvanceEducation.Contact@gov.ab.ca
www.advancededucation.gov.ab.ca

School Boards/Districts/Divisions

Public

Airdrie: Rocky View School Division #41
2651 Chinook Winds Dr. Airdrie, T4B 0B4 Canada
403-945-4000, Fax: 403-945-4001,
www.rockyview.ab.ca

Enrollment: 16000
Sylvia Eggerer, Chair
seggerer@rockyview.ab.ca

Athabasca: Aspen View Regional Division #19
3600 - 48 Ave. Athabasca, T9S 1M8 Canada
780-675-7080, Fax: 780-675-3660, 1-888-488-0288
aspenview@aspenview.org
www.aspenview.org

Grades: Kindergarten - 12
Paul Ponich, Board Chair, 780-525-2288
paul.ponich@aspenview.org
Derm Madden, Superintendent, Schools
derm.madden@aspenview.org
Bernie Giacobbo, Associate Superintendent
bernie.giacobbo@aspenview.org
Brian LeMessurier, Associate Superintendent
brian.lemessurier@aspenview.org
Mark Francis, Director, Education Initiatives
mark.francis@aspenview.org
Dave Holler, Director, Business Services
dave.holler@aspenview.org

Barrhead: Pembina Hills Regional Division #7
5310 - 49 St. Barrhead, T7N 1P3 Canada
780-674-8500, Fax: 780-674-3262,
info@phrd.ab.ca
www.phrd.ab.ca

Enrollment: 4355
Richard Harvey, Superintendent

Bonnyville: Northern Lights School Division #69
6005 - 50 Ave. Bonnyville, T9N 2L4 Canada
780-826-3145, Fax: 780-826-4600,
www.nlsd.ab.ca

Grades: K.-12
Enrollment: 5885
This division is an amalgamation of the Lac La Biche School Division and the Lakeland Public School District.
Roger Nippard, Supt.
roger.nippard@nlsd.ab.ca
Beverley Topylki, Sec.-Treas.
beverley.topyki@nlsd.ab.ca

Brooks: Grasslands Regional Division #6
745 - 2nd Ave. East Brooks, T1R 1L2 Canada
403-793-6700, Fax: 403-362-8225,
www.grasslands.ab.ca

Grades: Kindergarten - 12; Alternative Ed.
Number of Schools: 13 schools; 7 Hutterite colony schools
Susan Chomistek, Superintendent
Scott Brandt, Assistant Superintendent
David Steele, Deputy Superintendent
David Steele, Deputy Superintendent
Shane Harahus, Director, Finance
Michael Nielsen, Director, Technology
Alan Kloepper, Manager, Facilities & Maintenance

Calgary: Calgary Board of Education
515 Macleod Trail SE Calgary, T2G 2L9 Canada
403-294-8255,
Trustees: 403-294-8487; Aboriginal Education: 403-777-8970
www.cbe.ab.ca

Grades: Kindergarten - 12; Continuing Ed.
Enrollment: 102376
Number of Schools: 128 elementary schools; 26 junior high schools; 24 elementary / middle / junior high schools; 16 senior high schools; 14 unique settings; 6 junior / senior high schools; 4 outreach programs
Naomi Johnson, Chief Superintendent, Schools, 403-294-8100
David Stevenson, Deputy Chief Superintendent, Schools, 403-294-8100
Deborah Meyers, Chief Financial Officer, Business & Finance S, 403-294-8392
Frank Coppinger, Superintendent, Facilities & Environment Serv, 403-214-1119
Cathy Faber, Superintendent, Learning Innovation, 403-294-8154
John G. Johnston, Superintendent, Human Resources, 403-294-8189
Deborah Lewis, Superintendent, Learning Support, 403-294-8118
Diane Yee, Director, Area I, 403-777-8710
Susan Church, Director, Area II, 403-777-8720
Darlene Selby, Director, Area III, 403-777-6233
Jim Langley, Director, Area IV, 403-777-8750
Jane Rogerson, Director, Area V, 403-777-8780

Calgary: Francophone Regional Authority (South)
#230, 6940 Fisher Rd. SE Calgary, T2H 0W3 Canada
403-686-6998, Fax: 403-686-2914, 1-877-245-7686

Enrollment: 2008
Number of Schools: 13
Anne-Marie Bocher, Contact, 403-686-6998
Diane Boutin, Contact
403-685-9881

Camrose: Battle River Regional Division #31
5402 - 48A Ave. Camrose, T4V 0L3 Canada
780-672-6131, Fax: 780-672-6137, 1-800-262-4869
www.brrd.ab.ca

Enrollment: 6700
Cheryl Smith, Board Chair, 780-678-3265
csmith@brsd.ab.ca
Dr. Larry Payne, Superintendent, Schools, 780-672-4718 5227
LPayne@brsd.ab.ca
Ray Bosh, Deputy Superintendent, Sc, 780-672-4718 5011
RBosh@brsd.ab.ca
Rick Jarret, Assistant Superintendent, 780-672-4718 5238
RJarrett@brsd.ab.ca
Bill Schulte, Assistant Superintendent, 780-672-4718 5229
BSchulte@brsd.ab.ca
Greg Friend, Director, Personnel, 780-672-4718 5247
GFriend@brsd.ab.ca
Brenda Johnson, Director, Transportation, 780-672-4718 5245
BJohnson@brsd.ab.ca
Maureen Parker, Director, Curriculum, 780-672-4718 5223
MParker@brsd.ab.ca
Percy Roberts, Director, Maintenance & O, 780-672-4718 5246
PRoberts@brsd.ab.ca
Diane Hutchinson, Coordinator, Communicatio, 780-672-4718 5248
DHutchinson@brsd.ab.ca

Canmore: Canadian Rockies Public Schools
618 - 7th St. Canmore, T1W 2H5 Canada
403-609-6072, Fax: 403-609-6071,
hr@crps.ab.ca (Human Resources)
www.crps.ab.ca

Grades: Kindergarten - 12
Enrollment: 2042
Number of Schools: 6
Brian Callaghan, Superintendent, Schools
D. MacKenzie, Secretary-Treasurer

Cardston: Westwind School Division #74
P.O. Box 10
445 Main St. Cardston, T0K 0K0 Canada
403-653-4991, Fax: 403-653-4641, 800-655-4991
www.westwind.ab.ca

Grades: Pre-K.-12
Enrollment: 4249
Ken Summerfeldt, Supt.
Dexter Durfey, Sec.-Treas.
Lance Miller, Chair., 403-634-4770

Claresholm: Livingstone Range School Division #68
P.O. Box 69
5202 - 5 St. East Claresholm, T0L 0T0 Canada
403-625-3356, Fax: 403-325-2424, 800-310-6579
centraloffice@lrsd.ab.ca
www.lrsd.ab.ca

Grades: Pre.-12
Enrollment: 3845
Ellie Elliot, Supt. of Schools

Dunmore: Prairie Rose Regional Division #8
P.O. Box 204
918 - 2 Ave. Dunmore, T0J 1A0 Canada
403-527-5516, Fax: 403-528-2264,
www.prrd.ab.ca

Enrollment: 3380
Doug Nicholls, Superintendent

Edmonton: Edmonton School District #7
Centre for Education
One Kingsway Ave. Edmonton, T5H 4G9 Canada
780-429-8000, Fax: 780-429-8318,
info@epsb.ca
www.epsb.ca

Enrollment: 82447

Edmonton: Greater North Central Francophone Education Region No.2
Conseil scolaire Centre-Nord
#322, 8627 - 91st St. (Marie-Anne-Gaboury St.) Edmonton, T6C 3N1 Canada
780-468-6440, Fax: 780-440-1631, 1-800-248-6886
conseil@centrenord.ab.ca
www.centrenord.ab.ca

Grades: Kindergarten - 12
Enrollment: 2400
Number of Schools: 14 francophone (Catholic or public) schools
Claude Duret, Chair
cduret@centrenord.ab.ca
Henrie Lemire, Superintendent
hlemire@centrenord.ab.ca
Nicole Bugeaud, Associate Superintendent
nbugeaud@centrenord.ab.ca
Josée Devaney, Secretary-Treasurer
jdevaney@centrenord.ab.ca
Jean-Marc Cloutier, Director, Technological Services, 780-432-4654
jmcloutier@centrenord.ab.ca
Denise Lauzon Dempsey, Coordinator, Transportation
dldempsey@centrenord.ab.ca
Denise Lavallée, Coordinator, Communications
dlavallee@centrenord.ab.ca
Suzanne Amyotte, Associate, Human Ressources & Finance
samyotte@centrenord.ab.ca

Edson: Grande Yellowhead Public School Division No. 77
3656 - 1st Ave. Edson, T7E 1S8 Canada
780-723-2414, Fax: 780-723-2414, 1-800-723-2564
escgyrd@gyrd.ab.ca
www.gyrd.ab.ca

Grades: Elementary - Secondary
Enrollment: 5000
Number of Schools: 18. Number of Employees: 800
Dean Lindquist, Superintendent, Schools, 780-723-4471 103
deanlind@gyrd.ab.ca
Cory Gray, Deputy Superintendent, Leadership & Human Res, 780-723-4471 106
corygray@gyrd.ab.ca
Ed Latka, Assistant Superintendent, Business Services, 780-723-4471 102
edlatk@gyrd.ab.ca
Nancy Spencer-Poitras, Assistant Superintendent, Learning Services, 780-723-4471 116
nancspen@gyrd.ab.ca
Ken Baluch, Director, Facility Services, 780-723-4471 119
kenbalu@gyrd.ab.ca
Leigh McDonald, Director, Transportation Services, 780-723-4471 121
leigmcdo@gyrd.ab.ca
Kathleen Gardiner, Manager, Financial Services, 780-723-4471 112
kathgard@gyrd.ab.ca
Nikki Gilks, Manager, Communications, 780-723-4471 142
nikkgilk@gyrd.ab.ca
Jody Beck, Supervisor, Learning Services - Student Progr, 780-723-4471
jodybeck@gyrd.ab.ca
Kurt Scobie, Supervisor, Learning Services - Special Progr, 780-865-5692
kurtscob@gyrd.ab.ca
Sharon Styles, Supervisor, Learning Services - Curriculum &, 780-723-4471
sharstyl@gyrd.ab.ca

Fort McMurray: Fort McMurray Public School District
District Office, Clearwater Public Education Cent
231 Hardin St. Fort McMurray, T9H 2G2 Canada
780-799-7900,
www.fortmcmurraypsd.sharpschool.com

Grades: ECS - 12
Number of Schools: 9 elementary schools; 3 high schools
Jeff Thompson, Board Chair, 780-743-3798, fax: 780-743-4542
Paula.Ogonoski@fmpsd.ab.ca
Dennis Parsons, Superintendent, Schools, 780-799-7903
Dennis.Parsons@fmpsd.ab.ca
Allan Kallal, Associate Superintendent, Business & Finance, 780-799-7908
Allan.Kallal@fmpsd.ab.ca

Phil Meagher, Associate Superintendent, Education & Adminis, 780-799-7909
Phil.Meagher@fmpsd.ab.ca
Amgad Rushdy, Associate Superintendent, Human Resources & A, 780-799-7902
Amgad.Rushdy@fmpsd.ab.ca
Dr. Brenda Sautner, Director, Special Education, 780-792-5656
Brenda.Sautner@fmpsd.ab.ca
Leslie Ann Booker, Coordinator, Early Childhood Programs, 780-799-7928
Leslie.Booker@fmpsd.ab.ca
Ray Campbell, Coordinator, Education - Curriculum, 780-799-7925
Ray.Campbell@fmpsd.ab.ca
Lyndel Donald, Coordinator, Special Education Staffing, 780-788-8008
Lyndel.Donald@fmpsd.ab.ca
Malcolm Fedoretz, Coordinator, Student Information Systems, 780-799-7928
Malcolm.Fedoretz@fmpsd.ab.ca
Myrna Matheson, Coordinator, Literacy, 780-799-7906
Myrna.Matheson@fmpsd.ab.ca
Paula Ogonoski, Coordinator, Communications, 780-788-8009
Paula.Ogonoski@fmpsd.ab.ca
Ali Syed, Coordinator, Educational Technology, 780-799-7923
Ali.Syed@fmpsd.ab.ca
Lori Weinberger, Coordinator, District Numeracy, 780-788-8007
Lori.Weinberger@fmpsd.ab.ca

Fort Vermilion: Fort Vermilion School Division No. 52
P.O. Box 1
5213 River Rd. Fort Vermilion, T0H 1N0 Canada
780-927-3766, Fax: 780-927-4625,
info@fvsd.ab.ca
www.fvsd.ab.ca

Grades: Kindergarten - 12
Number of Schools: 15 schools; 4 learning stores (storefront schools)
Wally Schroeder, Chair
wallys@fvsd.ab.ca
Roger Clarke, Superintendent, Schools, 780-927-3766
rogerc@fvsd.ab.ca
Rick Cusson, Assistant Superintendent, Operations, 780-927-3766
rickc@fvsd.ab.ca
Kathryn Kirby, Assistant Superintendent, Teaching & Learning, 780-927-3766
kathrynk@fvsd.ab.ca
Bob Barrett, Manager, Information Technology, 780-926-4693
robertb@fvsd.ab.ca
Dan Dyck, Manager, Maintenance, 780-928-3013
dand@fvsd.ab.ca
Dave Elias, Manager, Transportation, 780-928-3860
davee@fvsd.ab.ca
Joanne Smith, Administrator, Payroll, 780-927-3766
joannes@fvsd.ab.ca

Grande Prairie: Grande Prairie School District
10213 - 99 St. Grande Prairie, T8V 2H3 Canada
780-532-4491, Fax: 780-539-4265,
www.gppsd.ab.ca

Grades: Kindergarten - 12
Enrollment: 6300
Number of Schools: 14
Karen Prokopowich, Chair, 780-532-1575
Chris Gonnet, Superintendent
chris.gonnet@gppsd.ab.ca
Dr. Roger Mestinsek, Deputy Superintendent
roger.mestinsek@gppsd.ab.ca
Lance Therrien, Assistant Superintendent, Curriculum
lance.therrien@gppsd.ab.ca
Christina Farquharson, Assistant Superintendent, Student Services
chris.farquharson@gppsd.ab.ca
Barry Bodner, Director, Operations
barry.bodner@gppsd.ab.ca
Frank Canavan, Director, Psychological Services
frank.canavan@gppsd.ab.ca
Sharron Graham, Director, Instruction
sharron.graham@gppsd.ab.ca
Sandy McDonald, Director, Education Technology
Sandy.McDonald@gppsd.ab.ca
Justin Vickers, Director, Information Technology
justin.vickers@gppsd.ab.ca
Wade Webb, Director, Finance
wade.webb@gppsd.ab.ca
Lorna Nordhagen, Manager, Human Resources
lorna.nordhagen@gppsd.ab.ca

Grande Prairie: Peace Wapiti Public School Division #76
8611A - 108 St. Grande Prairie, T8V 4C5 Canada
780-532-8133, Fax: 780-532-4234,
www.pwsd76.ab.ca

Enrollment: 5600
Sheldon Rowe, Superintendent

Hanna: Prairie Land Regional Division #25
P.O. Box 1400
Hanna, T0J 1P0 Canada
403-854-4481, Fax: 403-854-2803, 800-601-3898
lana.campbell@plrd.ab.ca
www.plrd.ab.ca

Enrollment: 1625
Wes Neumeier, Superintendent
wes.neumeier@plrd.ab.ca

High Prairie: High Prairie School Division #48
P.O. Box 870
High Prairie, T0G 1E0 Canada
780-523-3337, Fax: 780-523-4639, 877-523-3337
www.hpsd48.ab.ca

Enrollment: 3600
Laura Poloz, Superintendent
lpoloz@hpsd48.ab.ca

High River: Foothills School Division
P.O. Box 5700
120 - 5th Ave. West High River, T1V 1M7 Canada
403-652-3001, Fax: 403-652-4204,
www.fsd38.ab.ca

Grades: Kindergarten - 12; French Immersion
Number of Schoools: 27
Doug Gardner, Chair, 403-652-7842
gardnerd@fsd38.ab.ca
Denise Rose, Chief Executive Officer & Superintendent, Sch, 403-652-6522
Del Litke, Deputy Superintendent
Louise Ascah, Manager, Communications, 403-652-6522

Innisfail: Chinook's Edge School Division #73
4904 - 50 St. Innisfail, T4G 1W4 Canada
403-227-7070, Fax: 403-227-3652, 1-800-561-922
division.office@chinooksedge.ab.ca
www.chinooksedge.ab.ca

Enrollment: 11000

Lethbridge: Lethbridge School District #51
433 - 15 St. South Lethbridge, T1J 2Z5 Canada
403-380-5300, Fax: 403-327-4387,
www.lethsd.ab.ca

Grades: K-12
Enrollment: 8000
Gary Bartlett, Chair

Lethbridge: Palliser Regional Division #26
#101, 3305 - 18 Ave. North Lethbridge, T1H 5S1 Canada
403-328-4111, Fax: 403-380-6890, 877-667-1234
www.pallisersd.ab.ca

Enrollment: 6300
Kevin Gietz, Superintendent

Lloydminster: Lloydminster School Division #99
5017 - 46 St. Lloydminster, T9V 1R4 Canada
780-875-5541, Fax: 780-875-7829,
www.lpsd.ca

Grades: K.-12
Enrollment: 3862
Dr. Michael Diachuk, Dir.
michael.diachuk@lpsd.ca
Walter Hardy, Supt. of Admin., 780-808-2523
walter.hardy@lpsd.ca

Medicine Hat: Medicine Hat School District #76
601 - 1 Ave. SW Medicine Hat, T1A 4Y7 Canada
403-528-6700, Fax: 403-529-5339,
www.sd76.ab.ca

Grades: K.-12
Enrollment: 6275
Linda Rossler, Supt. of Schools
linda.rossler@sd76.ab.ca
Jerry Labossiere, Sec.-Treas.

Morinville: Sturgeon School Division #24
9820 - 104 St. Morinville, T8R 1L8 Canada
780-939-4341, Fax: 780-939-5520,
www.sturgeon.ab.ca

Grades: Kindergarten - 12
Enrollment: 5000
Number of Schools: 16 (including a school on the Morinville Hutterite Colony & a school operated in conjunction with the Oak Hill Boys' Ranch, plus 3 outreach learning centres)
Dr. Michèle Dick, Superintendent, 780-939-4341
mdick@sturgeon.ab.ca
Wolfgang Jeske, Director, Curriculum & Instruction

Nisku: Black Gold Regional Division #18
1101 - 5 St., 3rd Fl. Nisku, T9E 7N3 Canada
780-955-6025, Fax: 780-955-6050,
www.blackgold.ab.ca

Grades: Junior Kindergarten - Secondary
Barb Martinson, Chair, Board of Education
barb.martinson@blackgold.ca
Stuart Evans, Superintendent, 780-955-6026
stuart.evans@blackgold.ca
Neil Fenske, Associate Superintendent, 780-955-6028
neil.fenske@blackgold.ca
Dennis Nosyk, Associate Superintendent, 780-955-6032
dennis.nosyk@blackgold.ca
Dianne Butler, Director, Student Services, 780-955-6037
dianne.butler@blackgold.ca
Peter Balding, Administrator, Division Technology, 780-955-6037
dianne.butler@blackgold.ca
Dan Borys, Manager, Operations & Maintenance, 780-955-6068
dan.borys@blackgold.ca
Laurel Kvarnberg, Manager, Finance, 780-955-6059
laurel.kvarnberg@blackgold.ca
Sue Timmermans, Manager, Transportation, 780-955-6034
sue.timmermans@blackgold.ca
Warren Watson, Manager, Projects, 780-955-6062
warren.watson@blackgold.ca

Peace River: Northland School Division #61
P.O. Box 1400
9809 - 77 Ave. Peace River, T8S 1V2 Canada
780-624-2060, Fax: 780-624-5914, 800-362-1360
central.office@northland61.ab.ca
www.northland61.ab.ca

Grades: K.-12
Enrollment: 2600
Donald Tessier, Supt. 6102
don.tessier@northland61.ab.ca
Dennis Walsh, Dir. of Finance 6141
dennis.walsh@northland61.ab.ca
Delores Pruden, Coordinator, Aboriginal Programs 6161

Peace River: Peace River School Division #10
10018 - 101 St. Peace River, T8S 2A5 Canada
780-624-3601, Fax: 780-624-5941,
peaceriversd@prsd.ab.ca
www.prsd.ab.ca

Enrollment: 3100
Nan Bartlett, Chair

Ponoka: Wolf Creek School Division #72
6000 Hwy. 2A Ponoka, T4J 1P6 Canada
403-783-3473, Fax: 403-783-3483,
info@wolfcreek.ab.ca
www.wolfcreek.ab.ca

Grades: K.-12
Enrollment: 7500
Larry Jacobs, Supt.
ljacobs@wolfcreek.ab.ca
Joe Henderson, Sec.-Treas., 403-783-5441 1229
jhenderson@wolfcreek.ab.ca
Lorrie Jess, Chair

Red Deer: Red Deer School District #104
4747 - 53 St. Red Deer, T4N 2E6 Canada
403-343-1405, Fax: 403-347-8190,
info@rdpsd.ab.ca
www.rdpsd.ab.ca

Enrollment: 9000
Don Falk, Superintendent

Rocky Mountain House: Wild Rose School Division #66
4912 - 43 St. Rocky Mountain House, T4T 1P4 Canada
403-845-3376, Fax: 403-845-3850,
www.wrsd.ca

Grades: K.-12
Enrollment: 5469
Brian Celli, Supt.
brian.celli@wrsd.ca
Gordon Majeran, Sec.-Treas.
gordon.majeran@wrsd.ca
Keith Warren, Chair
keith.warren@wrsd.ca

Sherwood Park: Elk Island Public Schools Regional Division #14
683 Wye Rd. Sherwood Park, T8B 1N2 Canada
780-464-3477, Fax: 780-417-8181, 1-800-905-347
communications@ei.educ.ab.ca
www.ei.educ.ab.ca

Enrollment: 16200

***St Isidore:* Conseil scolaire du Nord-Ouest No. 1**
P.O. Box 1220
St Isidore, T0H 3B0 Canada
780-624-8855, Fax: 780-624-8554, 866-624-8855
conseil@csno.ab.ca
www.csno.ab.ca
Enrollment: 279

***St Paul:* East Central Francophone Education Region #3**
P.O. Box 249
4537 - 50 Ave. St Paul, T0A 3A0 Canada
780-645-3888, Fax: 780-645-2045,
cen3@atrium.ca
www.cen3.ab.ca
Enrollment: 493

***St Paul:* St. Paul Education Regional Division #1**
4313 - 48th Ave. St Paul, T0A 3A3 Canada
780-645-3323, Fax: 780-645-5789,
www.stpauleducation.ab.ca
Grades: Kindergarten - 12
Enrollment: 3988
Number of Schools: 18 (including 5 kindergarten to grade 12 schools, 2 Hutterite colonies, 2 outreach schools, & a virtual education campus). Number of Employees: 270 teaching staff; 346 support staff
Darrell Younghans, Chair, 780-943-2460
Glen Brodziak, Superintendent, 780-645-3323
Patricia Gervais, Assistant Superintendent, 780-645-3323
Patrick Rivard, Assistant Superintendent, 780-645-3323
Glenda Bristow, Coordinator, Program, 780-645-3323
Janice Muench, Coordinator, Special Education, 780-645-3323
Jean Champagne, Secretary-Treasurer, 780-645-3323

***Stettler:* Clearview School Division #71**
4704 - 55 St. Stettler, T0C 2L2 Canada
403-742-3331, Fax: 403-742-1388,
www.clearview.ab.ca
Enrollment: 2628

***Stony Plain:* Parkland School Division #70**
4603 - 48 St. Stony Plain, T7Z 2A8 Canada
780-963-4010, Fax: 780-963-4169,
www.psd70.ab.ca
Enrollment: 9454

***Strathmore:* Golden Hills School Division #75**
435A Hwy. #1 Strathmore, T1P 1J4 Canada
403-934-5121, Fax: 403-934-5125, 1-800-320-3739
www.ghsd75.ca
Grades: ECS - 12
Ron Kenworthy, Chair, 403-823-8802, fax: 403-823-8819
ron.kenworthy@ghsd75.ca
Dianne McBeth, Superintendent, Schools, 403-934-5121 2013
Edwin Holt, Associate Superintendent, Schools, 403-934-5121 2016
Dr. Kandace Jordan, Associate Superintendent, Schools, 403-934-5121 2014
Bevan Daverne, Division Principal, 403-934-5121 2005
Richard Armstrong, Manager, Financial Services, 403-934-5121 2022
Don Hartman, Manager, Facilities & Maintenance, 403-934-5121 2053
Ken MacLean, Supervisor, Transportation, 877-442-4340
Tahra Sabir, Secretary-Treasurer, 403-934-5121 2024

***Taber:* Horizon School Division #67**
6302 - 56 St. Taber, T1G 1Z9 Canada
403-223-3547, Fax: 403-223-2999,
www.horizon.ab.ca
Enrollment: 3500
Marie Logan, Chair

***Wainwright:* Buffalo Trail Public Schools Regional Division No. 28**
Central Office
1041 - 10A St. Wainwright, T9W 2R4 Canada
780-842-6144, Fax: 780-842-3255,
www.btps.ca
Grades: Kindergarten - 12
Enrollment: 4500
Number of Schools: 19 schools, with varying grade combinations, from ECS to grade 12; 7 Hutterite Colony schools, 1 outreach site, 1 distance learning site. Number of Employees: 281 FTE teachers + 236 support staff
Darcy Eddleston, Chair, 780-745-2370
darcy.eddleston@btps.ca
Bob Allen, Superintendent, Schools, 780-842-6144
superintendent@btps.ca
Nick Radujko, Assistant Superintendent, 780-806-2059
nick.radujko@btps.ca
Bob Brown, Secretary-Treasurer, 780-806-2050
bob.brown@btps.ca
Daryl Hoey, Director, Technology, 780-806-2065
daryl.hoey@btps.ca
Randy Huxley, Director, Facilities, 780-806-2064
randy.huxley@btps.ca
Chrysti Mannix, Director, Transportation, 780-806-2051
chrysti.mannix@btps.ca
Shannon Melin, Director, Human Resources, 780-806-2062
shannon.melin@btps.ca
Crystal Tower, Director, Student Services, 780-806-2056
crystal.tower@btps.ca
Hugh Forrester, Curriculum Lead, 780-872-1885
hugh.forrester@btps.ca

***Wetaskiwin:* Wetaskiwin Regional Division #11**
5515 - 47A Ave. Wetaskiwin, T9A 3S3 Canada
780-352-6018, Fax: 780-352-7886,
wrps@wrps.ab.ca
www.wrps.ab.ca
Grades: Pre-K.-12
Enrollment: 4081
Terry Pearson, Supt.
Sherri Senger, Dir., Bus. Services
Robert Reimer, Chair

***Whitecourt:* Northern Gateway Regional Division #10**
P.O. Box 840
4104 Kepler St. Whitecourt, T7S 1M8 Canada
780-778-2800, Fax: 780-778-6719, 800-262-8674
www.ngrd.ab.ca
Grades: K.-12
Enrollment: 5300
Kevin Andrea, Supt.
Mike Gramatovich, Sec.-Treas.
mgramatovich@ngrd.ab.ca

Protestant

***St Albert:* St. Albert Protestant Separate School District #6**
60 Sir Winston Churchill Ave. St Albert, T8N 0G4 Canada
780-460-3712, Fax: 780-460-7686,
www.spschools.org
Enrollment: 6600
Barry Wowk, Superintendent

Catholic

***Bonnyville:* Lakeland Roman Catholic Separate School District #150**
4810 - 46 St. Bonnyville, T9N 1B5 Canada
780-826-3764, Fax: 780-826-7576,
www.lcsd150.ab.ca
Enrollment: 2200
Bernadette Provost, Superintendent

***Calgary:* Calgary Catholic School District**
Catholic School Centre
1000 - 5th Ave. SW Calgary, T2P 4T9 Canada
403-500-2000,
Communications: 403-500-2763; Trustees: 403-500-2761
communications@cssd.ab.ca; trustees@cssd.ab.ca
www.cssd.ab.ca
Grades: Kindergarten - 12
Enrollment: 45066
Number of Schools: 52 elementary schools; 34 elementary / junior high schools; 9 senior high schools; 6 junior high schools; 2 junior / senior high schools; 2 congregated special education schools. Number of Employees: 3,143 instructional staff; 1,202 support staff; 314 caretaking staff; 144 exempt staff; 9 senior officers
Dr. Lucy Miller, EdD, Chief Superintendent
John Deausy, Superintendent, Finance & Business, & Secreta
Craig Foley, Superintendent, Human Resources
Judy MacKay, Superintendent, Specialized Schools/Instructi
Dr. Andra McGinn, Superintendent, Area A Schools
Luba Diduch, Superintendent, Area B Schools
Mark Rawlek, Superintendent, Area C Schools
Gary Strother, Superintendent, Area D Schools & Information
Michael Barbero, Superintendent, Area E Schools & Support Serv
Tania Younker, Director, Communications, 403-500-2763, fax: 403-500-2927
communications@cssd.ab.ca

***Edmonton:* Edmonton Catholic Separate School District #7**
9807 - 106 St. Edmonton, T5K 1C2 Canada
780-441-6000, Fax: 780-425-8759,
www.ecsd.net
Enrollment: 32000

***Fort McMurray:* Fort McMurray Roman Catholic Board of Education**
Fort McMurray Catholic Education Centre
9809 Main St. Fort McMurray, T9H 1T7 Canada
780-799-5700, Fax: 780-799-5706,
Service Support Centre, Phone: 780-799-5714
district@fmcsd.ab.ca
www.fmcsd.ab.ca
Grades: Kindergarten - 12; French Immersion
Enrollment: 4300
Number of Schools: 9. Number of Employees: 260 teachers; 160 support staff
Geraldine Carbery, Chair
Kim Jenkins, Superintendent, Schools, 780-799-5799 5001
kjenkins@fmcsd.ab.ca
George McGuigan, Deputy Superintendent, 780-799-5799 5020
gmcguigan@fmcsd.ab.ca
Francois Gagnon, Associate Superintendent, Business & Finance, 780-799-5700
fgagnon@fmcsd.ab.ca
Norena Hart, Director, Facilities, 780-799-5714
NHart@fmcsd.ab.ca
Monica Mankowski, Director, Student Services, 780-799-5799 5041
mmankowski@fmcsd.ab.ca
Kathleen Murray House, Director, School Based Administration, & Ment, 780-799-5799 5001
kmurphy@fmcsd.ab.ca
Betty-Lou Cahill, Coordinator, Human Resources, 780-799-5799 5021
BCahill@fmcsd.ab.ca

***Grande Prairie:* Grande Prairie & District Catholic Schools**
Catholic Education Centre
9902 - 101 St. Grande Prairie, T8V 2P4 Canada
780-532-3013, Fax: 780-532-3430, 1-800-661-2568
Transportation & Maintenance, Phone: 780-513-1220
cec@gpcsd.ca (Catholic Ed. Ctr.); support@gpcsd.ca (Tech Support)
www.gpcsd.ca
Grades: JK - 12; French Immersion; Outreach
Enrollment: 3900
Number of Schools: 12. Number of Employees: 400
Karl Germann, Superintendent, Schools, 780-532-3013
Ed Buckle, Assistant Superintendent, Human Resources, 780-532-3013 121
Marlene Stefura, Assistant Superintendent, Curriculum & Assess, 780-532-3013 122
Bryan Turner, Associate Superintendent, Business Operations, 780-532-3013 123
Pauline Ruel-Wyant, Director, Student Services, 780-532-3013 403
Clint Carrell, Administrator, Information Systems, 780-532-3013 300
John Dooley, Supervisor, Maintenance, 780-513-1220
Randy Lester, Supervisor, Transportation & Custodians, 780-513-1220

***Leduc:* St. Thomas Aquinas Roman Catholic Separate Regional Division #38**
4906 - 49th Ave. Leduc, T9E 6W6 Canada
780-986-2500, Fax: 780-986-8620, 1-800-583-0688
feedback@starcatholic.ab.ca
www.faithinyourfuture.ca
Grades: Kindergarten - 12; Catholicism
Enrollment: 2500
Number of Schools: 9 schools; 1 outreach centre. Number of Employees: 140 full-time teachers; 100 support staff
Maria Lentz, Board Chair
Jamie McNamara, Superintendent, Schools
jamie.mcnamara@starcatholic.ab.ca
Troy Davies, Assistant Superintendent
troy.davies@starcatholic.ab.ca
Jeanne Fontaine, Secretary-Treasurer
jeanne.fontaine@starcatholic.ab.ca
Tara-Ann Drexler, Coordinator, Transportation, & Accounting Cle
tadrexler@starcatholic.ab.ca
Marilyn Kunitz, Coordinator, Student Services
marilyn.kunitz@starcatholic.ab.ca
Pius MacLean, Coordinator, Curriculum & Instruction
pius.maclean@starcatholic.ab.ca
Michael Marien, Coordinator, Faith Life & Curriculum
michael.marien@starcatholic.ab.ca
David Scribner, Coordinator, Facilites
david.scribner@starcatholic.ab.ca
Dan Svitich, Coordinator, Information Technology
david.scribner@starcatholic.ab.ca

Susan Baudin, Officer, Human Resouces & Payroll
susan.baudin@starcatholic.ab.ca
Wendy Hoguen, Liaison, Communications
wendy.hogue@starcatholic.ab.ca

***Lethbridge:* Holy Spirit Roman Catholic Separate Regional Division #4**
620 - 12B St. North Lethbridge, T1H 2L7 Canada
403-327-9555, Fax: 403-327-9595,
www.holyspirit.ab.ca
Enrollment: 4400
Christopher Smeaton, Superintendent

***Lloydminster:* Lloydminster Roman Catholic Separate School Division #89**
6611B - 39th St. Lloydminster, T9V 2Z4 Canada
780-808-8585, Fax: 780-808-8787,
information@lcsd.ca
www.lcsd.ca
Grades: K.-12
Doug Robertson, Dir.
Tom Schinold, Supt. of Admin.
tschinold@lcsd.ca

***Medicine Hat:* Medicine Hat Catholic Separate School Regional Division #20**
1251 - 1 Ave. SW Medicine Hat, T1A 8B4 Canada
403-527-2292, Fax: 403-529-0917, 866-864-0013
www.mhcbe.ab.ca
Grades: Pre-K.-12
Enrollment: 2800
David Leahy, Supt. of Schools

***Okotoks:* Christ the Redeemer Catholic Separate Regional Division #3**
46 Elma St. West Okotoks, T1S 1J7 Canada
403-938-2659, Fax: 403-938-4575,
www.redeemer.ab.ca
Enrollment: 6200

***Peace River:* Holy Family Catholic Regional Division #37**
10307 - 99 St. Peace River, T8S 1R5 Canada
780-624-3956, Fax: 780-624-1154, 800-285-8712
www.hfcrd.ab.ca
Enrollment: 2000
Betty Turpin, Superintendent

***Red Deer:* Red Deer Catholic Regional Division #39**
5210 - 61 St. Red Deer, T4N 6N8 Canada
403-343-1055, Fax: 403-347-6410,
info@rdcrd.ab.ca
www.rdcrd.ab.ca
Enrollment: 5923
Paulette Hanna, Superintendent

***Sherwood Park:* Elk Island Catholic Separate Regional Division #41**
160 Festival Way Sherwood Park, T8A 5Z2 Canada
780-467-8896, Fax: 780-467-5469,
www.eics.ab.ca
Enrollment: 5600

***Spruce Grove:* Evergreen Catholic Separate Regional Division No. 2**
Holy Trinity Church
P.O. Box 4265
200 Boundry Rd., 2nd Fl. Spruce Grove, T7X 3B4 Canada
780-962-5627, Fax: 780-962-4664, 1-800-825-7152
www.ecsrd.ca
Grades: ECS - 12
Enrollment: 3481
Number of Schools: 9
Gerald Bernakevitch, Board Chair
Dr. Cindi Vaselenak, Superintendent
Michael Hauptman, Deputy Superintendent
Sime Fatovic, Director, Facilities & Technology
Sheila Shumate, Director, Student Services
Karen Koester, Coordinator, Religious Education
Marlene Fehr, Treasurer
Al Brettnell, Network Administrator

***St Albert:* Greater St. Albert Catholic Schools**
6 St. Vital Ave. St Albert, T8N 1K2 Canada
780-459-7711, Fax: 780-458-3213,
pgerhardt@gsacrd.ab.ca (Exec. Asst, Office of the Superintendent)
www.gsacrd.ab.ca
Grades: Kindergarten - 12
Enrollment: 6251
Number of Schools: 17. Number of Employees: 666 staff in schools; 48 staff in division operations
David Keohane, Superintendent
dkeohane@gsacrd.ab.ca
Steve Bayus, Deputy Superintendent
sbayus@gsacrd.ab.ca
David Quick, Assistant Superintendent, Learning Services
dquick@gsacrd.ab.ca
Therese deChamplain-Good, Director, Curriculum & Instruction
tdecgood@gsacrd.ab.ca
Ren Giesbrecht, Director, Technology Services
rgiesbrecht@gsacrd.ab.ca
Tony McClellan, Director, Student Services
tmcclellan@gsacrd.ab.ca
Trevor Gough, Supervisor, Operations Services
tgough@gsacrd.ab.ca
Deb Schlag, Secretary-Treasurer
dschlag@gsacrd.ab.ca

***Wainwright:* East Central Alberta Catholic Separate School Regional Division #16**
1018 - 1st Ave. Wainwright, T9W 1G9 Canada
780-842-3992, Fax: 780-842-5322,
www.ecacs16.ab.ca
Enrollment: 3300

***Whitecourt:* Living Waters Catholic Regional Division #42**
P.O. Box 1949
4204 Kepler St. Whitecourt, T7S 1P6 Canada
780-778-5666, Fax: 780-778-2727, 888-434-7348
www.livingwaters.ab.ca
Grades: Pre.-12
Enrollment: 1723

First Nations

***Brownvale:* Duncan's First Nation Education**
P.O. Box 148
Brownvale, T0H 0L0 Canada
780-597-3777, Fax: 780-597-3920,
www.duncansfn.ca
Duncan's First Nation is a small band situated southwest of Peace River, Alberta. A Child Development Centre offers daycare & a head start program. The head start program, for children from age three to five, includes a Cree language & cultural program. School buses transport Duncan's First Nation students to Berwyn, Grimshaw, & Peace River to enter a public school system.
Don Testawich, Chief, Duncan's First Nation

***Chard:* Chipewyan Prairie Dene First Nation Education Authority**
General Delivery Chard, T0P 1G0 Canada
780-559-2259, Fax: 780-559-2213
Number of Schools: 1

***Chateh:* Dene Tha' First Nation Education Department**
P.O. Box 120
Chateh, T0H 0S0 Canada
780-321-3886, Fax: 780-321-3775, 877-336-3842
info@denetha.ca
www.denetha.ca
Grades: Jr. Kindergarten-10; Dene language
Enrollment: 450
Number of Schools: 1 (Dene Tha' Community School). The Dene Tha' First Nation Education Department oversees education, counselling, transportation, & accommodation for Dene Tha' First Nation band members. Through its association with the North Peace Tribal Council, the Dene Tha' First Nation Education Department also directs post-secondary student services.
Adrienne Beaulieu, Coordinator, Post-Secondary Student Services, 780-926-2786, fax: 780-926-6652
Adrienne.Beaulieu@denetha.ca
Debbie Ahkimnachie, Clerk, Education Program, 780-321-3405
Debbie.Ahkimnachie@denetha.ca

***Duffield:* Paul Band Education Authority**
P.O. Box 89
Duffield, T0E 0N0 Canada
780-892-2675, Fax: 780-892-4436
Grades: Pre.-12

***Enoch:* Kitaskinaw Education Authority**
P.O. Box 90
Enoch, T7X 3Y3 Canada
780-470-5657
Grades: Nursery - 9
Number of Schools: 1 (Kitaskinaw School). The Kitaskinaw Education Authority oversees education for the Enoch Cree Nation.

***Fort Vermilion:* Tallcree First Nation School Division**
P.O. Box 310
Fort Vermilion, T0H 1N0 Canada
780-927-3803,
tallcreesd@gmail.com
Grades: K4 - 6
Enrollment: 100
Number of Schools: 2 (Chief Tallcree North School & Chief Tallcree South School)
Vic Dikaitis, Director, Education

***Goodfish:* Whitefish Lake Education Authority**
P.O. Box 274
Goodfish, T0A 1R0 Canada
780-636-2525, Fax: 780-636-3101
Grades: Pre.-9

***Hobbema:* Kiseputinow Education Dept.**
P.O. Box 1290
Hobbema, T0C 1N0 Canada
780-585-4065, Fax: 780-585-2037
Grades: Pre.-6

***Hobbema:* Nipisihkopahk Education Authority**
P.O. Box 658
Hobbema, T0C 1N0 Canada
780-585-2211, Fax: 780-585-3857,
www.wtc.ab.ca/nipisihkopahk
Grades: 1-12

***John D'Or Prairie:* Little Red River Board of Education**
P.O. Box 90
John D'Or Prairie, T0H 3X0 Canada
780-759-3780, Fax: 780-759-3848,
www.lrrbe.ab.ca
Grades: Kindergarten - 12; Special Ed.
Enrollment: 1050
Number of Schools: 3 (Jean Baptiste Sewepagaham School; John D'Or Prairie School; & Sister Gloria School). Number of Employees: 110+. The Little Red River Board of Education administers the provision of educational programming for First nation students of the Little Red River Cree Nation. Cultural programming is part of the students' education. The Board also offers adult upgrading & trades training.
Gloria Cardinal, Director, Education
glocardinal@gmail.com
Leah Blesse, Financial Controller

***Lac La Biche:* Beaver Lake Education Authority**
P.O. Box 5000
Lac La Biche, T0A 2C0 Canada
780-623-4549, Fax: 780-623-4523,
Amisk Community School, Phone: 780-623-4548; Fax: 780-623-4659
amiskcommunityschool@yahoo.ca
www.beaverlakecreenation.ca
Grades: Early Childhood Svs.-Jr. Secondary
Number of Schools: 1. The Beaver Lake Education Authority operates the Amisk Community School. The school is led by a nine member management team which is supervised by the Beaver Lake Cree Nation Band Council Education Portfolio Holder.
Councillor Germaine Anderson, Beaver Lake Cree Nation Council Education Por

***Morinville:* Alexander First Nation Education Authority**
P.O. Box 3449
Morinville, T8R 1S3 Canada
780-939-3868, Fax: 780-939-3991
The Alexander First Nation Education Authority operates the Kipohtakaw Education Centre.
Raymond Soetaert, Principal, Kipohtakaw Education Centre

***Morley:* Stoney Education Authority**
P.O. Box 238
Morley, T0L 1N0 Canada
403-881-2743, Fax: 403-881-4252,
www.stoneynation.com
Grades: Kindergarten - 12; Stoney language
Enrollment: 1100
Number of Schools: 3 (Morley Community School; Ta Otha Community School; & Chief Jacob Bearspaw School). The Stoney Education Authority, located west of Calgary, Alberta, provides education to members of the Stoney Nakoda First Nation. Education includes cultural programs.
Nadeem Altaf, Administrator, Education, 403-881-2776

***Rocky Mountain House:* Sunchild First Nation Band Education Authority**
P.O. Box 1149
Rocky Mountain House, T4T 1A8 Canada

403-989-3476, Fax: 403-989-3614
Grades: Kindergarten - 12
Number of Schools: 1 (Sunchild First Nation School). Number of Employees: 50+ full-time & part-time personnel
Caroline Bigchild, Chair
Nelson Daychief, Director, Education
administrator@sunchildschool.com

***Saddle Lake:* Saddle Lake Education Authority**
P.O. Box 130
Saddle Lake, T0A 3T0 Canada
780-726-4009, Fax: 780-726-4141
Grades: 1-12

***Siksika:* Siksika Board of Education**
P.O. Box 1099
Siksika, T0J 3W0 Canada
403-734-5220, Fax: 403-734-2505
Grades: Pre.-12

***Stand Off:* Kainaiwa Board of Education**
P.O. Box 240
Stand Off, T0L 1Y0 Canada
403-737-3966, Fax: 403-737-2361
Grades: 7-12

***Tsuu T'ina Sarcee:* Tsuu T'ina Nation Board of Education**
#250, 9911 Chiila Blvd. SW Tsuu T'ina Sarcee, T2W 6H6 Canada
403-238-5484,
www.tsuutina.ca
Grades: K4 - 12; Adult Upgrading
Enrollment: 299
Number of Schools: 3 (Chiila Elementary School; Tsuu T'ina Junior Senior High School; & Tsuu T'ina Bullhead Adult Education Centre)

***Valleyview:* Sturgeon Lake First Nation, Band #154, Education Authority**
P.O. Box 5
Valleyview, T0H 3N0 Canada
780-524-4590
Grades: Kindergarten - 12
Enrollment: 230
Number of Schools: 1 (Sturgeon Lake School)

***Wabasca:* Bigstone Cree Nation Education Authority**
P.O. Box 870
Wabasca, T0G 2K0 Canada
780-891-3825, Fax: 780-891-3021, 1-800-661-3891
www.bigstone.ca
Grades: Elementary
Enrollment: 247
Number of Schools: 1 (Oski Pasikoniwew Kamik, also known as the Bigstone Community School)
P. Ray Peters, Director, Education
ray.peters@bigstone.ca
Priscilla Auger, Counsellor, Post-Secondary Education, 877-458-2447, fax: 866-801-3021
priscilla.auger@bigstone.ca

Schools: Specialized

Charter

***Calgary:* Almadina Language Charter Academy**
225 - 28 St. SE Calgary, T2A 5K4 Canada
403-543-5070, Fax: 403-543-5073,
www.esl-almadina.com
Grades: 1-9
Enrollment: 600

***Calgary:* Calgary Arts Academy Society**
4931 Grove Hill Rd. S.W. Calgary, T3E 4G4 Canada
403-532-3020, Fax: 403-217-0965,
info@calgaryartsacademy.com
www.calgaryartsacademy.com
Enrollment: 279

***Calgary:* Calgary Girls' School - Bel Aire Campus**
1011 Beverley Blvd. SW Calgary, T2V 2C4 Canada
403-253-3785, Fax: 403-253-0430,
www.calgarygirlsschool.com
Grades: 4-9
Lakeview Campus: 6304 Larkspur Way SW, (403) 220-0745.

***Calgary:* Calgary Girls' School - Lakeview Campus**
6304 Larkspur Way SW Calgary, T3E 5P7 Canada
403-220-0745, Fax: 403-217-1371,
www.calgarygirlsschool.com
Grades: 4-9
Enrollment: 460
Bel Aire Campus: 1011 Beverley Blvd. SW, (403) 253-3785.
Caroline Parker, Principal

***Calgary:* Calgary Science School Society**
5915 Lewis Dr. SW Calgary, T3E 5Z4 Canada
403-282-2890, Fax: 403-282-2896,
www.calgaryscienceschool.com
Enrollment: 343

***Calgary:* Foundations for the Future Charter Academy**
Charter School Society
311, 5940 MacLeod Trail South Calgary, T2H 2G4 Canada
403-520-3206, Fax: 403-520-3209,
www.ffca-calgary.com
Grades: 1-9
Enrollment: 1896

***Calgary:* Westmount Charter School Society**
2519 Richmond Rd. SW Calgary, T3E 4M2 Canada
403-217-0426, Fax: 403-217-0252,
admin@westmountcharter.com
www.westmountcharter.com
Grades: K-12
Enrollment: 880

***Edmonton:* Aurora Charter School Ltd.**
8755 - 170 St. Edmonton, T5R 5Y6 Canada
780-735-5502, Fax: 780-735-2598,
aurorasc@telusplanet.net
www.auroraschool.com
Grades: 1-9
Enrollment: 437

***Edmonton:* Boyle Street Education Centre**
10312 - 105 Ave. Edmonton, T5J 1E6 Canada
780-428-1420, Fax: 780-429-1428,
www.bsec.ab.ca
Grades: 7-12
Enrollment: 105

***Edmonton:* Suzuki Charter School Society**
7211 - 96A Ave. Edmonton, T6B 1B5 Canada
780-468-2598, Fax: 780-463-8630,
www.suzukischool.ca
Grades: 1-6
Enrollment: 176

***Fort McMurray:* Moberly Hall School Society**
194B Grenfell Cres. Fort McMurray, T9H 2M6 Canada
780-743-8409, Fax: 780-743-9407,
moberlyhall@shaw.ca
moberlyhallschool.com
Grades: 1-12
Enrollment: 85

***Medicine Hat:* Centre for Academic & Personal Excellence Institute - CAPE**
830A Balmoral St. SE Medicine Hat, T1A 0W9 Canada
403-528-2983, Fax: 403-528-3048,
tdininno@capeisgreat.org
www.capeisgreat.org
Grades: 1-9
Enrollment: 135

***Sherwood Park:* New Horizons Charter School Society**
3 Spruce Ave. Sherwood Park, T8A 2B6 Canada
780-467-6409, Fax: 780-417-1786,
administration@newhorizons.ab.ca
www.newhorizons.ab.ca
Grades: K-9
Enrollment: 160

***Wabamun:* Mother Earth's Children's Charter School Society**
P.O. Box 1150
Wabamun, T0E 2K0 Canada
780-892-7222, Fax: 780-892-7223,
admin@meccs.ca
www.meccs.ca

First Nations

***Atikameg:* Whitefish Lake First Nation**
General Delivery Atikameg, T0G 0C0 Canada
780-767-3914, Fax: 780-767-3814
Grades: 1-12

***Brocket:* Peigan Band**
P.O. Box 130
Brocket, T0K 0H0 Canada
403-965-3910, Fax: 403-965-3713

***Cadotte Lake:* Woodland Cree First Nation**
General Delivery Cadotte Lake, T0H 0N0 Canada
780-629-3803, Fax: 780-629-3898
Grades: Gr. 1-12

***Chard:* Chipewyan Prairie Dene High School / CPDHS**
Chipewyan Prairie Education Multi-Plex
General Delivery Chard, T0P 1G0
780-559-2478
Grades: Secondary
Enrollment: 30
The band operated high school is situated south of Fort McMurray, Alberta, where it provides education for the Chipewyan Prairie Dene First Nation.

***Chateh:* Dene Tha' Community School / DTCS**
P.O. Box 30
Chateh, T0H 0S0
780-321-3940, Fax: 780-321-3800,
reception@chateh-education.net; info@denetha.ca
www.denetha.ca
Grades: Jr. Kindergarten-10; Dene language
Enrollment: 450
Dene Tha' Community School provides education that follows Alberta's kindergarten to grade 10 curriculum, as well as programs such as an early literacy program, a special education program, & Dene language & culture programs.
Lori Aliche, Principal, 780-321-3940, fax: 780-926-0500
Virginia Alarcon, Vice-Principal, Junior High, 780-321-3940, fax: 780-926-1412
Rosalie Metchooyeah, Elder, 780-321-3940
Hayley Natannah, Office Manager, 780-321-3940
Hayley.Natannah@denetha.ca
Ann Austin, Librarian, 780-321-3940
Helen Metchooyeah, Instructor, Dene Language, 780-321-3940
Tyler Metchooyeah, Instructor, Dene, 780-321-3940
Shane Providence-Toho, Instructor, Dene, 780-321-3940

***Driftpile:* Driftpile Community School**
P.O. Box 240
Driftpile, T0G 0V0 Canada
780-355-3615, Fax: 780-355-2135,
www.driftpilecreenation.com
Grades: K-4, K-5 - 8; Cree language
Enrollment: 75
Driftpile Community School offers a full academic program, as well as a Cree language & cultural program with traditional music, folklore, & crafts.
Daisy McGee, Principal
Josephine Willier, Secretary
Janice Chalifoux, Family School Wellness Worker
Leonard Isadore, Contact, Cultural Appreciation

***Enoch:* Kitaskinaw School**
P.O. Box 90
Enoch, T7X 3Y3
780-470-5657, Fax: 780-470-5687
Grades: Nursery - 9
Kitaskinaw School is part of the Kitaskinaw Education Authority. The school educates members of the Enoch Cree Nation.

***Enoch:* Yellowhead Tribal Council**
P.O. Box 150
Enoch, T7X 3Y3 Canada
780-470-3454, Fax: 780-470-3541
Grades: 7-12

***Fox Lake:* Jean Baptiste Sewepagaham School**
P.O. Box 270
Fox Lake, T0H 1R0
780-659-3820,
jbssch@telusplanet.net
www.lrrbe.ab.ca
Grades: Kindergarten - 12; Cree language
Enrollment: 600
Jean Baptiste Sewepagaham School is one of three schools in the Little Red River Board of Education. The school serves members of the Little Red River Cree Nation, located approximately 125 kilometres east of High Level, Alberta.

***Frog Lake:* Frog Lake First Nation**
General Delivery Frog Lake, T0A 1M0 Canada
780-943-3918, Fax: 780-943-2336, 1-800-816-873
Grades: Pre.-12; Special Ed.

***Garden River:* Sister Gloria School**
P.O. Box 90
Garden River, T0H 4G0
780-659-3644, Fax: 780-659-3890
The Little Red River Board of Education consists of three schools, including Sister Gloria School. Sister Gloria School

provides education to First Nation students of the Little Red River Cree Nation. The Alberta community is situated approximately 125 kilometres east of High Level.
Garry Wilson, Principal
wilson_garry@hotmail.com

***Glenevis:* Alexis Nakota Sioux First Nation School**
P.O. Box 27
Glenevis, T0E 0X0 Canada
780-967-4878,
www.alexised.ca
Grades: Elementary - Junior Secondary

***Hobbema:* Meskanahk Ka-Nipa-Wit School**
P.O. Box 129
Hobbema, T0C 1N0 Canada
780-585-2799, Fax: 780-585-2264
Grades: Pre.-9

***Hobbema:* Miyo Wahkohtowin Community Education Authority**
P.O. Box 248
Hobbema, T0C 1N0 Canada
780-585-2118, Fax: 780-585-2116,
www.miyo.ca
Grades: Pre.-9

***Hythe:* Horse Lake First Nation**
P.O. Box 303
Hythe, T0H 2C0 Canada
780-356-2248, Fax: 780-356-3666

***John D'Or Prairie:* John D'Or Prairie School**
P.O. Box 120
John D'Or Prairie, T0H 3X0
780-759-3772,
www.lrrbe.ab.ca
John D'Or Prairie School is part of the Little Red River Board of Education. Education is provided to the Little Red River Cree Nation, located approximately 865 kilometres north of Edmonton, Alberta.

***Kehewin:* Kehewin Cree Nation**
P.O. Box 30
Kehewin, T0A 1C0 Canada
780-826-6200, Fax: 780-826-5919
Grades: Pre.-12

***Kinuso:* Swan River First Nation School**
P.O. Box 120
Kinuso, T0G 1K0
780-775-2177, Fax: 780-775-2155
Grades: 7 - 12
Enrollment: 100
The Swan River First Nation School operates on the Swan River First Nation Reserve in Kinuso, Alberta.

***Lac La Biche:* Amisk Community School**
P.O. Box 5000
Lac La Biche, T0A 2C0
780-623-4548, Fax: 780-623-4659,
www.beaverlakecreenation.ca
Grades: Early Childhood Svs.-Jr. Secondary
Operated by the Beaver Lake Education Authority, the Amisk Community School provides education to the Beaver Lake Cree Nation.

***Lac La Biche:* Heart Lake First Nation**
P.O. Box 469
Lac La Biche, T0A 2C0 Canada
780-623-2330, Fax: 780-623-3505
Grades: Pre.-12

***Longview:* Chief Jacob Bearspaw School**
P.O. Box 116
100 Center St. SW Longview, T0L 1H0
403-558-2480, Fax: 403-558-3618,
www.stoney-nation.com
Chief Jacob Bearspaw School, located on the Eden Valley Reserve in Alberta, is part of the Stoney Education Authority.
Bill Shade, Principal

***Morley:* Morley Community School**
P.O. Box 238
Morley Morley, T0L 1N0
403-881-2755, Fax: 403-881-2333,
www.stoney-nation.com
Grades: K4 - 12; Stoney language
The Stoney Education Authority oversees the Morley Community School. The First Nations school serves members of the Nakoda First Nation, situated west of Calgary, Alberta.

***Rocky Mountain House:* O'chiese Education Authority**
P.O. Box 337
Rocky Mountain House, T4T 1A3 Canada
403-989-3911, Fax: 403-989-2122
Grades: K-12

***Rocky Mountain House:* Sunchild First Nation School**
P.O. Box 1149
Rocky Mountain House, T4T 1A8
403-989-3476, Fax: 403-989-3614,
www.sunchildschool.com
Grades: Kindergarten - 12
The Sunchild First Nation School is part of the Sunchild First Nation Band Education Authority.
Martin Sacher, Principal
sacher@sccyber.net
Susan Collicutt, Vice-Principal
collicutts@yahoo.ca

***Tsuu T'ina Sarcee:* Chiila Elementary School**
#250, 991 Chiila Blvd. SW Tsuu T'ina Sarcee, T2W 6H6
403-238-5484,
www.tsuutina.ca
Grades: K4 - 5
Chiila Elementary School is part of the Tsuu T'ina Nation Board of Education.

***Tsuu T'ina Sarcee:* Tsuu T'ina Junior Senior High School**
#250, 991 Chiila Blvd. SW Tsuu T'ina Sarcee, T2W 6H6
403-251-9555, Fax: 403-251-9833,
www.tsuutina.ca
Grades: 6 - 12
The Tsuu T'ina Nation Board of Education oversees the operations of the Tsuu T'ina Junior Senior High School.

***Valleyview:* Sturgeon Lake School**
P.O. Box 5
Valleyview, T0H 3N0
780-524-4590, Fax: 780-524-3696
Grades: Kindergarten - 12
Enrollment: 230
The Sturgeon Lake School is part of the Sturgeon Lake First Nation, Band #154, Education Authority. The First Nation school serves the Sturgeon Lake Cree Nation.

***Wabasca:* Bigstone Cree Nation Community School Oski Pasikoniwew Kamik**
P.O. Box 930
Wabasca, T0G 2K0
780-891-3830, Fax: 780-891-3831,
www.bigstone.ca
Grades: Preschool - 6
Enrollment: 247
The Bigstone Community School operates under the direction of the Bigstone Cree Nation Education Authority. The school strives to maintain traditional values as its educational foundation.

Schools: Independent & Private

Catholic

***Calgary:* Clear Water Academy**
2521 Dieppe Ave. SW Calgary, T3E 7J9 Canada
403-217-8448, Fax: 403-217-8043,
administration@clearwateracademy.com
www.clearwateracademy.com
Grades: Pre.-12
An independent Catholic school.
Paul Hudec, Principal

Special Education

***Edmonton:* Edmonton Academy**
10231 - 120 St. Edmonton, T5K 2A4 Canada
780-482-5449, Fax: 780-482-0902,
lizrich@telusplanet.net
www.edmontonacademy.com
Grades: 7-12
Founded in 1983; provides specialized teaching for students with learning disabilities.
Liz Richards, Executive Director

***Edmonton:* Elves Child Development Centre**
10825 - 142 St. Edmonton, T5N 3Y7 Canada
780-454-5310, Fax: 780-454-5889,
elvessoc@telusplanet.net
www.elves-society.com
Grades: Pre.-12
The Elves Special Needs Society offers programs for pre-school and older children, youth and adults who are severely developmentally delayed and/or medically fragile, as well as outreach to students unable to attend school for extended periods of time.
Cristina Molina, Executive Director

***Edmonton:* John Howard Society of Edmonton**
#301, 10526 Jasper Ave. Edmonton, T5J 1Z7 Canada
780-428-7590, Fax: 780-425-1549,
info@edm.johnhoward.org
www.johnhoward.ab.ca; www.johnhoward.org
Grades: To Gr. 9
The Edmonton John Howard Society's Adult Transition Learning Centre offers courses to clients at every stage of learning, including: literacy, GED & college preparation, language arts, math & computer basics, personal development, & life skills (addictions, anger management, mental health; all aspects of employment preparation). The Centre is located at 10010 105th St., Suite 401, in Edmonton.

Independent & Private Schools

***Airdrie:* Airdrie Koinonia Christian School**
2104 Big Hill Springs Rd., RR#1 Airdrie, T4B 2A3 Canada
403-948-5100, Fax: 403-948-5563,
adminoffice@akcs.com
Grades: Pre.-12

***Banff:* Banff Mountain Academy**
P.O. Box 369 Main
1 Mount Norquay Banff, T1L 1A5 Canada
403-760-4101
Grades: 9-12
Enrollment: 40
Banff Mountain Academy is a residential, co-educational school. It offers a flexible program for athletes.

***Bow Island:* Cherry Coulee Christian Academy / CCCA**
P.O. Box 10370
Bow Island, T0K 0G0 Canada
403-545-2107, Fax: 403-545-2944,
www.cherrycoulee.ca
Grades: Kindergarten - 9
Kim Dolan, Administrator

***Brant:* Brant Christian School**
P.O. Box 130
Brant, T0L 0L0 Canada
403-684-3752, Fax: 403-684-3894,
www.brantchristianschool.com
Grades: Kindergarten - 12
Corry Brown, Principal
Susan McLean, Librarian

***Brooks:* Newell Christian School / NCS**
P.O. Box 100
Brooks, T1R 1B2 Canada
403-378-4448, Fax: 403-378-3991,
www.newellchristianschool.com
Grades: Kindergarten - 9
The Alberta curriculum is taught from a Christian perspective.
Dale Rempel, Chair
Ron Cousins, Principal

***Calgary:* Akiva Academy**
140 Haddon Rd. SW Calgary, T2V 2Y3 Canada
403-258-1312, Fax: 403-258-3812,
office@akiva.ca
www.akiva.ca
Grades: Pre.-6
Jemmie Silver, Principal

***Calgary:* Banbury Crossroads Private School**
#201, 2451 Dieppe Ave. SW Calgary, T3E 7K1 Canada
403-270-7787, Fax: 403-270-7486,
general@banburycrossroads.com
www.banburycrossroads.com
Banbury Crossroads Private School offers education to children aged 3 to 18.
Diane Swiatek, Principal
Karen Harrison, Vice Principal

***Calgary:* Bearspaw Christian School / BCS**
15001 - 69th St. NW Calgary, T3R 1C5 Canada
403-295-2566, Fax: 403-275-8170,
info@bearspawschool.com
www.bearspawschool.com
Grades: Kindergarten - 12
Enrollment: 500
Kelly Blake, President
kblake@bearspawschool.com
Judy Huffman, Principal
jhuffman@bearspawschool.com

Jennifer Lockhart, Vice Principal, Elementary
jlockhart@bearspawschool.com
Lara Melashenko, Vice Principal, Secondary
lmelashenko@bearspawschool.com

Calgary: Bethel Christian Academy
2220 - 39th Ave. NE Calgary, T2E 5T4 Canada
403-735-3335, Fax: 403-219-3059,
tbetts@encountergod.org
www.encountergod.org
Grades: Kindergarten - 12

Calgary: Calgary Academy
9400 - 17th Ave. SW Calgary, T3H 4A6 Canada
403-686-6444, Fax: 403-240-3427,
info@calgaryacademy.com; careers@calgaryacademy.com
(Employment)
www.calgaryacademy.com
Grades: 2 - 12
Enrollment: 625
Peter Istvanffy, President/CEO
Joanne Endacott, Director, Admissions
jendacott@calgaryacademy.com

Calgary: Calgary Chinese Alliance School
Calgary Chinese Alliance Church
150 Beddington Blvd. NE Calgary, T3K 2E2 Canada
403-274-6925, Fax: 403-275-7799
Grades: 10 - 12
Enrollment: 500
Alex Hung, President
Mimi Fong, Principal
mimiefong@hotmail.com

Calgary: Calgary Chinese Private School
599 Northmount Dr. NW Calgary, T2K 3J6 Canada
403-264-2233, Fax: 403-263-3895
Grades: 10 - 12
The Calgary Chinese Private School works to maintain Chinese heritage & culture in the community.

Calgary: Calgary Christian School
North Bldg.
5029 - 26th Ave. SW Calgary, T3E 0R5 Canada
403-242-2896, Fax: 403-242-6682,
www.calgarychristianschool.com
Grades: Preschool - 12
Calgary Christian School has an elementary campus & a secondary campus.
Scott Hickling, Executive Director
Harry Fritschy, Principal, Elementary
Gwen Uittenbosch, Principal, Secondary
Glenda Jullion, Vice Principal, Elementary
Jason Kupery, Vice Principal, Secondary

Calgary: Calgary French & International School / CFIS
700 - 77th St. SW Calgary, T3H 5R1 Canada
403-240-1500, Fax: 403-249-5899,
inquiries@cfis.com
www.cfis.com
Grades: Preschool - 12
Calgary French & International School offers French Immersion education.
John McVicar, Chair & President
societyboard@cfis.com
Dr. Richard Slevinsky, Headmaster, 403-240-1500 130
rslevinsky@cfis.com
Michele Gariépy, Vice Principal, Junior High School
mgariepy@cfis.com
Cecile Triggle, Vice Principal, Elementary School, 403-240-1500 210
ctriggle@cfis.com
Janice Jalving, Director, Child Care Centre, 403-246-4708
childcare@cfis.com
Katharine Ray, Officer, Admissions, 403-240-1500 329
kray@cfis.com

Calgary: Calgary Islamic Private School / CIS
2612 - 37th Ave. NE Calgary, T1Y 5L2 Canada
403-248-2773,
www.calgaryislamicschool.com
Grades: Kindergarten - 9
Enrollment: 490
Calgary Islamic School offers the regular curriculum, as well as a Quran recitation & memorization curriculum, an Arabic language curriculum, an Islamic Studies curriculum.

Calgary: Calgary Jewish Academy / CJA
6700 Kootenay St. SW Calgary, T2V 1P7 Canada
403-253-3992, Fax: 403-255-0842,
info@cja.ab.ca
www.cja.ab.ca
Grades: Preschool - 9
Ben Karmel, Principal
KarmelB@cja.ab.ca
Barbara Dare, Associate Principal, Alberta Curriculum
dareb@cja.ab.ca
Shoshana Kirmayer, Associate Principal, Judaic Studies
kirmayers@cja.ab.ca

Calgary: Calgary Quest School
c/o Spruce Cliff Elementary
3405 Spruce Dr. SW Calgary, T3C 0A5 Canada
403-253-0003, Fax: 403-253-0025,
info@calgaryquestschool.com
www.calgaryquestschool.com
Calgary Quest School offers a program for children with special challenges.
Kathy Peron, Chair

Calgary: Calgary Waldorf School
515 Cougar Ridge Dr. SW Calgary, T3H 5G9 Canada
403-287-1868, Fax: 403-287-3414,
info@calgarywaldorf.org
www.calgarywaldorf.org
Grades: Preschool - 9
Calgary Waldorf School also offers a Parent-and-Tot program.
Cathie Foote, School Administrator
Kathy Brunetta, Pedagogical Administrator
Dinah Clark, Financial Administrator
Laureen Loree, Principal
Sandra Langlois, Manager, Admissions & Facility

Calgary: The Chinese Academy
John G. Diefenbaker Senior High School
6620 - 4th St. NW Calgary, T2K 1C2 Canada
403-777-7663, Fax: 403-777-7669,
admin@chineseacademy.ca; chineseacademy@telus.net
www.chineseacademy.ca
Grades: Kindergarten - 12
Enrollment: 1925
Kindergarten, Level 1, begins for children aged 3.5 years at the Sir John A. Macdonald Junior High School, 6600 - 4th St. NW in Calgary. The goal of the school is to promote Chinese language & culture. Cantonese & Mandarin classes, as well as Chinese as a Second Language for beginners in Cantonese & Mandarin.
Martina Lui, President
Judy Fung, School Superintendent
Elaine Chan, BSc., M.A. (Ed. Admin.), Principal

Calgary: Chinook Winds Adventist Academy / CWAA
10101 - 2nd Ave. SW Calgary, T3B 5T2 Canada
403-286-5686, Fax: 403-247-1623,
cwaa2@cwaa.net
www.cwaa.net
Grades: Kindergarten - 12
The Seventh-day Adventist school also features music, outdoor education, Bible instruction, & mission trips for senior high students.
Murray McLeod, BA, Principal
Marilyn Kelloway, BEd., Vice Principal
Samuel Millen, MDiv., Chaplain

Calgary: Community Connections School
225 - 37 St. NW Calgary, T2N 4N6 Canada
403-283-6361, Fax: 403-283-5741,
brenda@homeeducation.ca
Grades: 1-12

Calgary: Delta West Academy
414 - 11A St. NE Calgary, T2E 4P3 Canada
403-290-0767, Fax: 403-290-0768,
info@deltawestacademy.ca
Grades: Pre.-12; Special Ed.

Calgary: Eastside Christian Academy
1320 Abbeydale Dr. SE Calgary, T2A 7L8 Canada
403-569-1039, Fax: 403-569-1023,
admin@ecaab.ca
Grades: Pre.-12

Calgary: Edge School for Athletes
700 - 77 St. SW Calgary, T3H 5R1 Canada
403-246-6432, Fax: 403-217-8463
Grades: 1-12

Calgary: Educere International College
#1500, 910 - 7 Ave. SW Calgary, T2P 3N8 Canada
403-232-8551, Fax: 403-233-0239,
educere@educere.ca
Grades: 10-12

Calgary: Equilibrium International Educational Institute
707 - 14 St. NW Calgary, T2N 2A4 Canada
403-283-1111, Fax: 403-270-7786,
school@equilibrium.ab.ca
Grades: 10-12

Calgary: Foothills Academy
745 - 37 St. NW Calgary, T2N 4T1 Canada
403-270-9400, Fax: 403-270-9438
Grades: 1-12; Special Ed.

Calgary: Froebel's Garden of Children
119 Pinetown Pl. NE Calgary, T1Y 5J1 Canada
403-280-4855,
froebel@shaw.ca
Grades: Pre.-6

Calgary: Glenmore Christian Academy
16520 - 24th St. Calgary, T2Y 4W2 Canada
403-254-9050, Fax: 403-256-9695,
admin@glenmorechristian.com
Grades: Pre.-9; Special Ed.
Derrick Mohamed, Principal

Calgary: Greek Community School
1 Tamarac Cres. SW Calgary, T3C 3B7 Canada
403-246-4553, Fax: 403-246-8191,
school@calgaryhellenic.com
Grades: 1-12

Calgary: Heritage Christian Academy
2003 McKnight Blvd. NE Calgary, T2E 6L2 Canada
403-219-3201, Fax: 403-219-3210,
hca@telus.net
www.hcacalgary.com
Grades: Pre.-12
Enrollment: 500
LaVerne Pue, Principal

Calgary: International School of Excellence
3915 - 34 St. NE Calgary, T1Y 6Z8 Canada
403-234-0453, Fax: 403-250-2401,
isoe@shaw.ca
Grades: Pre.-12

Calgary: Italian School of Calgary
24 Beddington Way NE Calgary, T3K 1N9 Canada
403-264-6349
Grades: 7-12

Calgary: Janus Academy
71 Edgebrook Circle NW Calgary, T3A 5A4 Canada
403-262-3333, Fax: 403-693-2345
Grades: Pre.-9

Calgary: Language School
German Canadian Club
2626 - 23 St. NE Calgary, T2E 8L2 Canada
403-248-0994
Grades: 10-12

Calgary: Lycée Louis Pasteur
4099, boul Garrison sud-ouest Calgary, T2T 6G2 Canada
403-243-5420, Fax: 403-287-2245,
office@lycee.ca
www.lycee.ca
Grades: Mat./Prim.
Benjamin Orillon, Chef d'établissement

Calgary: Master's Academy
4414 Crowchild Trail SW Calgary, T2T 5J4 Canada
403-242-7034, Fax: 403-242-4629
Grades: Pre.-12

Calgary: Menno Simons Christian School
7000 Elkton Dr. SW Calgary, T3H 4Y7 Canada
403-531-0745, Fax: 403-531-0747,
office@mennosimons.ab.ca
Grades: Pre.-9

Calgary: Montessori School of Calgary
2201 Cliff St. SW Calgary, T2S 2G4 Canada
403-229-1011,
msofc@telusplanet.net
www.montessorischoolofcalgary.com
Grades: Preschool / Elementary
Enrollment: 100
The children at the Montessori School of Calgary range in age from 2.5 to 12. Both the Montessori program & the Alberta Programme of Studies are followed.
Nancy Lowden, Head of School

Calgary: Mountain View Academy / MVA
#B4, 2452 Battleford Ave. SW Calgary, T3E 7K9 Canada
403-217-4346, Fax: 403-249-4312,
www.mountainviewacademy.ca
Grades: Preschool - 12

Jitka Smuszko, Director
Lenka Popplestone, Principal
Colleen Ryan, Vice Principal
Jane Lizotte, Assistant Principal

Calgary: Renfrew Educational Services
Main School & Administrative Centre
2050 - 21st St. NE Calgary, T2E 6S5 Canada
403-291-5038, Fax: 403-291-2499,
renfrew@renfreweducation.org
www.renfreweducation.org
Grades: Preschool - Elementary
Enrollment: 700
Renfrew Educational Services offers specialized educational programs for preschool & elementary students. The not-for-profit society also develops programs for children with special needs.
Tom Buchanan, Chair
Janice McTighe, Executive Director
Kim LaCourse, Associate Executive Director
Cathy Gable, Director, Community Services
Mary lou Hill, Director, Education
Bruce Monnery, Director, Finance & Administration

Calgary: Rundle College Academy
4330 - 16 St. SW Calgary, T2J 4H9 Canada
403-250-2965, Fax: 403-250-2914,
www.rundle.ab.ca
Grades: 1-12

Calgary: Rundle College Elementary School
2634 - 12 Ave. NW Calgary, T2N 1K6 Canada
403-282-8411, Fax: 403-282-4460,
johnston@rundle.ab.ca
www.rundle.ab.ca
Grades: Pre.-6

Calgary: Rundle College Junior High School
7375 - 17 Ave/ SW Calgary, T3H 3W5 Canada
403-250-7180, Fax: 403-250-7184,
baird@rundle.ab.ca
Grades: 7-9

Calgary: Rundle College Senior High School
7375 - 17 Ave. SW Calgary, T3H 3W5 Canada
403-250-7180, Fax: 403-250-7184,
bridal@rundle.ab.ca
www.rundle.ab.ca
Grades: 7-12
Mr. Hauk, Headmaster
hauk@rundle.ab.ca

Calgary: St. John Bosco Private School
712 Fortalice Cres. SE Calgary, T2A 2E1 Canada
403-248-3664, Fax: 403-273-8012,
stjohnbosco@shaw.ca
www.stjohnboscoprivateschool.com
Grades: Pre.-9

Calgary: Third Academy
B4 Bldg., Currie Barracks
2452 Battleford Ave. SW Calgary, T3E 7K1 Canada
403-288-5335, 1-877-508-5335
info@thirdacademy.com
www.thirdacademy.com
Grades: 1 - 12
The Third Academy offers an Individualized Program Plan for students with special needs to remediate of compensate for their learning disorder. There is a Calgary North location, a Calgary South location, & a Red Deer location.
Jitka Smuszko, Chair
Dr. S. Lal Mattu, CEO & Founder
Sunil Mattu, LLB (Hons) Law, BEd, Chief Operating Officer
David Lambe, Vice President, Business & Community Relation
Kathleen Colmant, Coordinator, Special Events
Rehana Mattu, BEd, Master Teacher
Liz Wray, Registrar

Calgary: The Timothy Centre for Scholarship
P.O. Box 49096
7740 - 18th St. SE Calgary, T2C 3W5 Canada
403-230-0702,
info@timothycentre.com
www.timothycentre.com
Grades: Kindergarten - 12
The Timothy Centre for Scholarship offers a classical Christian education for Calgary homeschoolers.
Laurel Roberts, Principal

Calgary: Trinity Christian School / TCS
#100, 295 Midpark Way SE Calgary, T2X 2A8 Canada
403-254-6682, Fax: 403-254-9843,
403-254-6716 (Phone, Business Office)
trinity@tcskids.com
www.tcskids.com
Grades: Kindergarten - 9
Merle Rayner, Chair
James Sijpheer, Principal
james.sijpheer@tcskids.com
George Graffunder, Vice Principal
ggraffunder@tcskids.com
Tania Spears, Manager, Business
Sandy Stasko, Coordinator, Resources

Calgary: Truth Academy
615 Northmount Dr. NW Calgary, T2K 3J6 Canada
403-282-0238, Fax: 403-289-8356
Grades: Preschool - 12

Calgary: Webber Academy
1515 - 93rd St. SW Calgary, T3H 4A8 Canada
403-277-4700, Fax: 403-277-2770,
www.webberacademy.ca
Grades: Junior Kindergarten - 12
Webber Academy is a coeducational, non-denominational university preparatory school.
Dr. Neil Webber, Head of School
nwebber@webberacademy.ca
Barbara Webber, Vice-President, Administration
bwebber@webberacademy.ca
Dianne Lever, Contact, Admissions
admissions@webberacademy.ca

Calgary: West Island College / WIC
7410 Blackfoot Trail SE Calgary, T2H 1M5 Canada
403-255-5300, Fax: 403-252-1434,
admissions@westislandcollege.ab.ca (E-mail, Admissions)
office@westislandcollege.ab.ca
www.westislandcollege.ab.ca
Grades: 7 - 12
West Island College provides pre-university training. Programs include English & French communication skills & the arts.
Carol Grant-Watt, Head of School, 403-255-5300 238
Boyd Belisle, Head, Junior School, 403-255-5300 277
Claire Allen, Director, International Studies, 403-255-5300 302
Scott Bennett, Director, Faculty Development, 403-255-5300 501
Roland Chalifoux, Director, Programme Studies, 403-255-5300 237
Todd Larsen, Director, Co-Curricular Programmes, 403-255-5300 231
Murray Marran, Director, Admissions & Bursar, 403-255-5300 285
Pierre Poitras, Director, Technology, 403-255-5300 260
Malcolm Rennie, Director, Post-Secondary Placement, 403-255-5300 286

Canmore: Mountain Gate Community School
P.O. Box 8287
Canmore, T1W 2V1 Canada
403-609-2105, Fax: 403-609-8355,
mgsc@monarch.net
Grades: 1 - 6

Cardston: Red Crow Community College / RCCC
P.O. Box 1258
Cardston, T0K 0K0 Canada
403-737-2400, Fax: 403-737-2101, 866-937-2400
webmaster@redcrowcollege.com
www.redcrowcollege.com
Mi'Kai'sto Red Crow Community College is a post-secondary institution whcih offers Diploma, Degree and Masters programs. The College partners with Mount Royal, Lethbridge Community College, SAIT, the University of Lethbridge, & the University of Calgary.
Dr. Marie Smallface-Marule, President

Caroline: Living Faith Christian School
P.O. Box 100
Caroline, T0M 0M0 Canada
403-722-2225, Fax: 403-722-2459,
lfcs@telusplanet.net
Grades: 1-12

Champion: Hope Christian School
P.O. Box 235
Champion, T0L 0R0 Canada
403-897-3019, Fax: 403-897-2392,
hopec@telusplanet.net
Grades: 1-12

Coaldale: Coaldale Christian School
2008 - 8 St. Coaldale, T1M 1L1 Canada
403-345-4055, Fax: 403-345-6436,
ccsoffic@telusplanet.net
Grades: Pre.-12; Special Ed.

Cold Lake: Lakeland Christian Academy
P.O. Box 8397
Cold Lake, T9M 1N2 Canada
780-639-2077, Fax: 780-639-4151,
lca@hlvc.org
Grades: 1-12

Cold Lake: Trinity Christian School
5731 - 50th Ave. Cold Lake, T9M 1T1 Canada
780-594-2205, Fax: 780-594-3737,
trinity@cablerocket.com
Grades: Preschool - 12
Richard Schienbein, Principal

Devon: Devon Christian School
P.O. Box 5390
Devon, T9G 1Y1 Canada
780-987-4157, Fax: 780-987-3323,
dcs@devonchristianschool.com
Grades: Pre.-9

Edmonton: Alberta Centre for Chinese Studies
13719 - 133 Ave. Edmonton, T5L 3T3 Canada
780-453-3968,
louisho@telus.net
Grades: 10-12

Edmonton: Columbus Academy
6770 - 129 Ave. Edmonton, T5C 1V7 Canada
780-440-0708, Fax: 780-440-0760,
cci@telusplanet.net
Grades: 7-12

Edmonton: Concordia Continuing Education High School
10537 - 44 St. Edmonton, T6A 1W1 Canada
780-413-7800, Fax: 780-466-9394,
gerrie.cameron@concordia.ab.ca
www.hs.concordia.ab.ca
Grades: 10-12

Edmonton: Concordia High School
7128 Ada Blvd. Edmonton, T5B 4E4 Canada
780-479-9391, Fax: 780-479-5050,
www.concordiahighschool.com
Grades: 10-12

Edmonton: Coralwood Adventist Academy
12218 - 135 St. NW Edmonton, T5L 1X1 Canada
780-454-2173, Fax: 780-455-6946,
corlwood@telusplanet.net
Grades: Pre.-12

Edmonton: Dante Alighieri Italian School
c/o Archbishop O'Leary High
8760 - 132 Ave. Edmonton, T5E 0X8 Canada
780-474-1787, Fax: 780-451-0669,
aristidem@shaw.ca
Grades: 10-12

Edmonton: Don Bosco Academy
6770 - 129 Ave. Edmonton, T5C 1V7 Canada
780-922-4790, Fax: 780-922-3290,
admin@boscohomes.ca
Grades: 1-12

Edmonton: Edmonton Bible Heritage Christian School
13054 - 112 St. NW Edmonton, T5E 6E6 Canada
780-454-3672, Fax: 780-488-3672
Grades: 1-12

Edmonton: Edmonton Islamic Academy
14525 - 127 St. Edmonton, T6V 0B3 Canada
780-454-4573, Fax: 780-454-3498,
eia@islamicschool.ca
www.islamicacademy.ca
Grades: K.-9
Enrollment: 700
Abdullah A. Omar, Principal

Edmonton: Edmonton Menorah Academy
10735 McQueen Rd. NW Edmonton, T5N 3L1 Canada
780-451-1848, Fax: 780-451-2254,
ema613@yahoo.ca
Grades: Pre.-9

Edmonton: Faith Lutheran School
11515 - 36 St. Edmonton, T5W 2A9 Canada
780-496-9302, Fax: 780-496-3556,
faithschool@shaw.ca
Grades: Pre.-9

***Edmonton:* German Language School Society of Edmonton**
c/o Rio Terrace School
7608 - 154 St. Edmonton, T5R 1R7 Canada
780-435-7540,
kerstin.buelow@shaw.ca
www.germanschooledmonton.org
Grades: 10-12
Judith Meyers, Administrator
judith.meyers@gmx.de

***Edmonton:* Gil Vicente School**
8830 - 132 Ave. Edmonton, T5E 0X8 Canada
780-474-7242,
cpereira@gsacrd.ab.ca
Grades: 10-12

***Edmonton:* Headway School Society of Alberta**
3530 - 91 St. Edmonton, T6E 6P1 Canada
780-461-7683, Fax: 780-485-0507,
headway@telusplanet.net
www.members.shaw.ca/worman/
Grades: Pre.-12

***Edmonton:* Ivan Franko Ukrainian School**
14535 - 52 St. Edmonton, T5A 4N1 Canada
780-476-7529,
lsukhy@hotmail.com
Grades: 10-12

***Edmonton:* Meadowlark Christian School**
9825 - 158 St. Edmonton, T5P 2X4 Canada
780-483-6476, Fax: 780-487-8992,
mdlkchr@telusplanet.net
www.k-9christian.com
Grades: Pre.-9

***Edmonton:* Parkland Immanuel Christian School**
21304 - 35 Ave. NW Edmonton, T6M 2P6 Canada
780-444-6443, Fax: 780-444-6448,
info@parklandimmanuel.ca
www.parklandimmanuel.ca
Grades: Pre.-12

***Edmonton:* Phoenix Academy**
6770 - 129 Ave. Edmonton, T5C 1V7 Canada
780-440-0708, Fax: 780-440-0760,
admin@boscohomes.ca
Grades: K.-12
School for students who struggle with behavioural disorders and learning disabilities

***Edmonton:* Progressive Academy**
13212 - 106 Ave. Edmonton, T5N 1A3 Canada
780-455-8344, Fax: 780-455-1425,
info@progressiveacademy.ca
www.progressiveacademy.ca
Grades: Junior Kindergarten - 12
The school offers small classes & the flexibility for students to progress through grades at an irregular pace. Progressive Academy is licensed by Applied Scholastics International & accredited by Alberta Education.

***Edmonton:* St. George's Hellenic Language School**
10831 - 124 St. Edmonton, T5M 0H4 Canada
780-452-1455, Fax: 780-452-1455
Grades: 10-12

***Edmonton:* Solomon College**
#228, 10621 - 100 Ave. Edmonton, T5J 0B3 Canada
780-431-1515, Fax: 780-431-1644,
info@solomoncollege.ca
www.solomoncollege.ca
Grades: 10-12

***Edmonton:* Tempo School**
5603 - 148 St. Edmonton, T6H 4T7 Canada
780-434-1190, Fax: 780-430-6209,
admin@temposchool.org
www.temposchool.org
Grades: Pre.-12
Enrollment: 380
P. Mitchell, Headmaster

***Edmonton:* Victory Christian School / VCS**
11520 Ellerslie Rd. Edmonton, T6W 1A2 Canada
780-988-5433, Fax: 780-988-5280,
info@victorychristianschool.ca
www.victorychristianschool.ca
Grades: Preschool - 12
Enrollment: 120
Victory Christian School's preschool offers curriculum suited to the developmental stages of four year old children.

***Edson:* Yellowhead Koinonia Christian School**
430 - 72 St. Edson, T7E 1N3 Canada
780-723-3850, Fax: 780-723-7566,
ykcs@yellowhead.com
Grades: Pre.-12

***Fort McMurray:* Fort McMurray Christian School**
190 Tamarack Way Fort McMurray, T9K 1A1 Canada
780-743-1079, Fax: 780-743-1379
Grades: Pre.-9

***Grande Prairie:* Grande Prairie Christian School**
8202 - 110 St. Grande Prairie, T8W 1M3 Canada
780-539-4566, Fax: 780-539-4748,
diana.krahn@gppsd.ab.ca
www.gppsd.ab.ca/school/gpchristian
Grades: Pre.-12
Enrollment: 220
John Bueckert, Principal

***Grande Prairie:* Hillcrest Christian School**
10306 - 102 St. Grande Prairie, T8V 2W3 Canada
780-539-9161, Fax: 780-532-6932,
hcsgp@telus.net
Grades: Pre.-12

***High Level:* High Level Christian Academy**
P.O. Box 1100
10701 - 100 Ave. High Level, T0H 1Z0 Canada
780-926-2360, Fax: 780-926-3245,
hlca@telusplanet.net
www.highlevelchristianacademy.ca
Grades: Pre.-12
Vera Bartlett, Vice Principal

***Hobbema:* Maskwachees Cultural School**
P.O. Box 360
Hobbema, T0C 1N0 Canada
780-585-3925, Fax: 780-585-2080,
mcc@wtc.ab.ca
Grades: 10-12

***Joussard:* North Country School**
1 Joussard, T0G 1J0 Canada
780-776-2215
Grades: Kindergarten - 12

***Kingman:* Cornerstone Christian Academy**
P.O. Box 99
Kingman, T0B 2M0 Canada
780-672-7197, Fax: 780-608-1420,
corner@cable-lynx.net
www.cornerstonekingman.ca
Grades: Pre.-12; Special Ed.
Core subjects are taught; Bible Studies.
Steve Ioanidis, Principal

***Lacombe:* Central Alberta Christian High School / CACHS**
22 Eagle Rd. Lacombe, T4L 1G7 Canada
403-782-4535, Fax: 403-782-5425,
office@cachs.ca
www.cachs.ca
Grades: Secondary
Bernie TenHove, Chair
Jack Vanden Pol, Principal
Wendy Barnes, Business Administrator
office@cachs.ca

***Lacombe:* College Heights Christian School**
5201 College Ave. Lacombe, T4L 1Z6 Canada
403-782-6212, Fax: 403-782-7507
Grades: Pre.-9

***Lacombe:* Lacombe Christian School**
5206 - 58 St. Lacombe, T4L 1G9 Canada
403-782-6531, Fax: 403-782-5760,
office@lacs.ca
Grades: Pre.-9

***Lacombe:* Parkview Adventist Academy**
5505 College Ave. Lacombe, T4L 2E7 Canada
403-782-3381, Fax: 403-782-7308,
www.paa.ca
Grades: 10-12
Christian boarding school affiliated with Canadian University College

***Leduc:* Covenant Christian School**
P.O. Box 3827 Main
Leduc, T9E 6M7 Canada
780-986-8353, Fax: 780-986-8360,
www.covenantchristian.ca
Grades: Pre.-9; Special Ed.
Enrollment: 165
Christ-centered education within a curriculum of core subjects.
Gayle Monsma, Principal
gayle.monsma@blackgold.ca

***Lethbridge:* Immanuel Christian Elementary School**
2010 - 5 Ave. North Lethbridge, T1H 0N5 Canada
403-317-7860, Fax: 403-317-7862,
icesoffice@gmail.com
Grades: Pre.-6

***Lethbridge:* Immanuel Christian High School**
802 - 6 Ave. North Lethbridge, T1H 0S1 Canada
403-328-4783, Fax: 403-327-6333
Grades: 7-12

***Linden:* Kneehill Christian School**
P.O. Box 370
Linden, T0M 1J0 Canada
403-546-3781, Fax: 403-546-3181
Grades: 1-9

***Medicine Hat:* Cornerstone Christian School**
P.O. Box 40043
355 Southridge Dr. SE Medicine Hat, T1B 3M6 Canada
403-529-6169, Fax: 403-529-6169,
ccschool@canopycanada.net
Grades: Pre.-9

***Medicine Hat:* Medicine Hat Christian School**
68 Rice Dr. SE Medicine Hat, T1B 3X2 Canada
403-526-3246, Fax: 403-528-9048,
mhcs@shockware.com
Grades: Pre.-9

***Monarch:* Calvin Christian School**
P.O. Box 40
Monarch, T0L 1M0 Canada
403-381-3030, Fax: 403-381-4241,
office@ccschool.ca

***Monarch:* Providence Christian School**
P.O. Box 68
Monarch, T0L 1M0 Canada
403-381-4418, Fax: 403-381-4418,
provchr@telusplanet.net
Grades: Preschool - 12

***Morinville:* Morinville Christian School**
10515 - 100 Ave. Morinville, T8R 1A2 Canada
780-939-2987,
mcfs@telus.net
www.morinvillechristian.com
Lou Brunelle, Director of School

***Neerlandia:* Covenant Canadian Reformed School**
P.O. Box 67
Neerlandia, T0G 1R0 Canada
780-674-4774, Fax: 780-401-3295,
ccrs@xplornet.com
www.ccrs.110mb.com
Grades: Pre.-12; Special Ed.
Enrollment: 170
Students are members of the Canadian Reformed or United Reformed churchesLocation: 3030 Township Rd. 615A, Neerlandia.
Harry VanDelden, Principal

***Okotoks:* Edison School**
Box 2, Site 11, RR#2 Okotoks, T1S 1A2 Canada
403-938-7670, Fax: 403-938-7224,
office@edisonschool.ca
Grades: Pre.-12

***Okotoks:* Strathcona-Tweedsmuir School**
RR#2 Okotoks, T1S 1A2 Canada
403-938-4431, Fax: 403-938-8343,
advancement@sts.ab.ca
www.sts.ab.ca
Grades: 1-12

***Olds:* Horizon School Special Education**
5401 - 53 St. Olds, T4H 1T3 Canada
403-556-6310, Fax: 403-556-1640,
shorizon@telusplanet.net
Grades: Pre., Special Ed.

***Olds:* Olds Koinonia Christian School**
P.O. Box 4039
Olds, T4H 1P7 Canada
403-556-4038, Fax: 403-556-8770,
www.oldskoinonia.com
Grades: Pre.-12
Enrollment: 300

Dwayne Brown, Administrator/Principal
dwaynebrown@chinooksedge.ab.ca

***Ponoka:* Ponoka Christian School**
6300 - 50 St. Ponoka, T4J 1V3 Canada
403-783-6563, Fax: 403-783-6687,
ponxsch@telus.net
www.ponokachristianschool.com
Grades: Pre.-9
Robert Morris, Principal

***Ponoka:* Woodlands Adventist School**
PO Box 16, Site 2, RR#3 Ponoka, T4J 1R3 Canada
403-783-2640, Fax: 403-783-2640,
woodlds@telusplanet.net
Grades: Pre.-9

***Purple Springs:* Tween Valley Christian School**
P.O. Box 96
Purple Springs, T0K 1X0 Canada
403-223-9571, Fax: 403-224-9594,
tvcs.principal@hotmail.com
Grades: 1 - 12

***Raymond:* Mennonite School**
P.O. Box 768
Raymond, T0K 2S0 Canada
403-756-2277

***Red Deer:* Destiny Christian School Society**
Box 30, Site 4, RR#4 Red Deer, T4N 5E4 Canada
403-343-6510, Fax: 403-343-8480,
info@destinyschool.ca
Grades: Pre.-9

***Red Deer:* Koinonia Christian School of Red Deer**
6014 - 57 Ave. Red Deer, T4N 4S9 Canada
403-346-1818, Fax: 403-347-3013,
info@koinonia.ca
Grades: Pre.-12

***Red Deer:* Parkland School Special Education**
6016 - 45 Ave. Red Deer, T4N 3M4 Canada
403-347-3911, Fax: 403-342-2677,
prkland@shaw.ca
www.parklandschool.org
Grades: Special Ed.
Monica Lawes, Principal

***Red Deer:* South Side Christian School**
P.O. Box 219
Red Deer, T4N 5E8 Canada
403-886-2266, Fax: 403-886-5026,
office@southsidechristianschool.ca
www.southsidechristianschool.ca
Grades: Pre.-10
Affiliated with the Seventh-day Adventist Church

***Rimbey:* Echo Valley Christian School**
General Delivery Rimbey, T0C 2J0 Canada
403-843-4555
Grades: 1-9

***Rimbey:* Rimbey Christian School**
P.O. Box 90
4522 - 54th Ave. Rimbey, T0C 2J0 Canada
403-843-4790, Fax: 403-843-3904,
office@rimbeychristianschool.com
www.rimbeychristianschool.com
Grades: Kindergarten - 9
Enrollment: 84
The Alberta Provincial Program of Studies is taught from a Christian perspective.
Tambourine Simpson, Principal
principal@rimbeychristianschool.com

***Rocky Mountain House:* Rocky Christian School / RCS**
5204 - 54 Ave. Rocky Mountain House, T4T 1S5 Canada
403-845-3516, Fax: 403-845-4370,
office@rockycs.com
www.rockycs.com
Grades: Kindergarten - 9
Enrollment: 105
The interdenominational school provides a Biblically based curriculum, which reflects Alberta Learning requirements.
Dave Simmelink, Chair
Rob Duiker, Principal

***Saddle Lake:* Saddle Lake Full Gospel School**
P.O. Box 69
Saddle Lake, T0A 3T0 Canada
780-636-3736, Fax: 780-636-3994,
slcs@telusplanet.net
Grades: 1-12

***Siksika:* Old Sun Community College**
P.O. Box 1250
Siksika, T0J 3W0 Canada
403-734-3862, Fax: 403-734-5363,
admin@oldsuncollege.net
www.oldsuncollege.net
Grades: College
Amelia Clark, B.A., M.A., President/Post-Secondary Director, 403-734-3862 222
amelia@oldsuncollege.net

***Slave Lake:* Slave Lake Koinonia Christian**
P.O. Box 1548
Slave Lake, T0G 2A0 Canada
780-849-5400, Fax: 780-849-5460,
koinonia@telusplanet.net
Grades: 1-9

***Spirit River:* Northern Lights School**
Box 19, Site 4, RR#1 Spirit River, T0H 3G0 Canada
780-351-2242, Fax: 780-351-2280
Grades: 1 - 9
The Northern Lights Church of God in Christ Mennonite congregation operates the Northern Lights School.

***Spruce Grove:* Harvest Baptist Academy**
26404 Hwy.16 West Spruce Grove, T7X 3H5 Canada
780-960-0235, Fax: 780-960-9235, 888-960-0235
hba@ibces.org
www.ibces.org
Grades: Pre.-12

***Spruce Grove:* Living Waters Christian Academy**
5 Grove Dr. West Spruce Grove, T7X 3X8 Canada
780-962-3331, Fax: 780-962-3958,
www.lwca.ab.ca
Grades: Pre.-12

***St Paul:* Blue Quills First Nations College / BQFNC**
P.O. Box 279
3 Airport Rd. North St Paul, T0A 3A0 Canada
780-645-4455, Fax: 780-645-5215, 1-888-645-4455
www.bluequills.ca
Dr. Leona Makokis, BAdm, BEd, MA, EdD, President
Bernadine Houle-Steinhauer, BA, PRdip, Director, Special Projects
Dr. Patricia Makokis, EdD, Director, Curriculum Development
Dr. Halia Boychuk, BEd, MA, PhD, Coordinator, University Transfer
Sherri Chisan, BMgmt, MA, Coordinator, Leadership & Management
Sharon Steinhauer, BSW, RSW, Coordinator, Social Work Diploma
Lena Lapatrack, Registrar
registrar@bluequills.ca

***Stony Plain:* St. John's School of Alberta**
RR#5 Stony Plain, T7Z 1X5 Canada
780-789-4826, Fax: 780-848-2395,
info@sjsa.ab.ca
www.sjsa.ab.ca
Grades: 7-12

***Stony Plain:* St. Matthew Lutheran School**
5014 - 53 Ave. Stony Plain, T7Z 1R8 Canada
780-963-2715, Fax: 780-963-7324,
school@st-matthew.com
Grades: Pre.-9
Glen Schmitke, Principal
glen@st-matthew.com

***Sundre:* Olds Mountain View Christian School**
Box 2, Site 8, RR#2 Sundre, T4H 1P3 Canada
403-556-1551, Fax: 403-556-5936,
principal@omvcs.ca
www.omvcs.ca
Grades: K-12

***Sylvan Lake:* Lighthouse Christian School**
PO Box 1078, RR#1 Sylvan Lake, T4S 1X6 Canada
403-887-2166, Fax: 403-887-5729,
lightca@telusplanet.net
Grades: Pre.-12

***Three Hills:* Prairie Christian Academy**
P.O. Box 68
Three Hills, T0M 2A0 Canada
403-443-4220, Fax: 403-443-7005,
pcasecondary@ghsd75.ca
pca.ghsd75.ca
Grades: 7-12

***Three Hills:* Prairie Christian Academy**
P.O. Box 4451
1025 - 4th St. North Three Hills, T0M 2N0 Canada
403-443-3006, Fax: 403-443-3076,
jsept@goldenhills-schools.com
www.pca3hills.ca
Grades: Pre.-9; Special Ed.

Post Secondary/Technical

***Calgary:* Columbia College**
802 Manning Rd. NE Calgary, T2E 7N8 Canada
403-235-9300, Fax: 403-272-3805,
columbia@columbia.ab.ca
www.columbia.ab.ca
Grades: 10-12; Special Ed.
Adult education & continuing education. Professional programmes (business management, dental assisting, paramedic, health care aide, practical nurse); ESL; bridging programmes/university preparation; academic upgrading. ISO 9001:2000 certified.

Universities & Colleges

Universities

***Athabasca:* Athabasca University**
1 University Dr. Athabasca, T9S 3A3 Canada
780-675-6100, Fax: 780-675-6437, 800-788-9041
www.athabascau.ca
Enrollment: 39700
An open university offering any student access to university-level study.
James D'Arcy, Registrar, 780-675-6302, fax: 780-675-6174
registrar@athabascau.ca
Dr Frits Pannekcoek, President
auprez@athabascau.ca
Dr Margaret Haughey, Vice-Pres., Academic
mhaughey@athabascau.ca
Dr Ray Block, Vice-Pres., Finance/Admin.
rblock@athabascau.ca
Lori Van Rooijen, Vice-Pres., Advancement
loriv@athabascau.ca
Brian Stewart, Chief Information Officer
brians@athabascau.ca
Greg Wiens, Dir., Facilities/Services
gregw@athabascau.ca
David Hrenewich, Dir., Computing Services
daveh@athabascau.ca
Elizabeth Munroe, Assoc. Dir., Human Resources
elizabeth@athabascau.ca
Steve Schafer, Dir., Library Services
steves@athabascau.ca

Schools
Centre for Global & Social Analysis
Dr David Gregory, Chair
davidg@athabascau.ca

Centre for Distance Education
Dr Mohamed Ally, Director
mohameda@athabascau.ca

Centre for Innovative Management
Kay Devine, Director
kay_devine@mba.athabascau.ca

Centre for Language & Literature
Kathy Williams, Chair
kathyw@athabascau.ca

Centre for Science
Dr Norman Temple, Chair
normant@athabascau.ca

Centre for Nursing & Health Studies
Dr Donna Romyn, Dean, Health Disciplines
dromyn@athabascau.ca

Centre for Psychology
Dr Cheryl Kier, Chair
cherylk@athabascau.ca

Centre for State & Legal Studies
Dr Evelyn Ellerman, Co-Chair
evelyne@athabascau.ca
Dr Alvin Finkel, Co-Chair
alvinf@athabascau.ca

Centre for Work & Community Studies
Dr Lynda Ross, Chair
lyndar@athabascau.ca

Centre for Learning Accreditation
Dr Dianne Conrad, Director
diannec@athabascau.ca

Centre of Computing & Information Systems
Dr Kinshuk, Director
kinshuk@athabascau.ca

Centre for World Indigenous Knowledge
Dr Tracey Lindberg, Director
traceyl@athabascau.ca

Centre for Integrated Studies
Dr Mike Gismondi, Director
mikeg@athabascau.ca

Centre for Graduate Education in Applied Psychology
Dr Sandra Collins, Director
sandrac@athabascau.ca

Publications
The Voice Magazine
Published by the Athabasca University Students' Union
Tamra Ross, Editor-In-Chief
voice@voicemagazine.org

Calgary: The University of Calgary
2500 University Dr. NW Calgary, T2N 1N4 Canada
403-220-5110, Fax: 403-282-8413,
www.ucalgary.ca

Enrollment: 24141
Joanne Cuthbertson, Chancellor
Jack Perraton, Chair
Harvey P. Weingarten, B.Sc., M.Sc., M.Phil., Ph, President & Vice-Chancellor
David B. Johnston, B.A., M.A., Registrar
Alan Harrison, Vice-President & Provost
Jonathan (Jake) Gebert, Interim Vice-President
Dennis R. Salahub, B.Sc., Ph.D., F.R.S.C., Vice-President
Dr. Ann Davies, Director
Rhonda M. Williams, B.A. (Hons.), Director
Roman Cooney, B.A., M.C.S., Vice-President

Faculties
Continuing Education

Dr. Scott McLean, Ph.D., Director

Education
Dr. Dennis Sumara, B.Ed., M.Ed., Ph.D., Dean

Engineering
M. Elizabeth Cannon, P.Eng, FCAE, FRSC, Dean

Environmental Design
Prof. Loraine Fowlow, Dean

Fine Arts
Ann E. Calvert, B.A., Dip.Ed., M.Ed., Ph., Dean

Graduate Studies & Assoc. Vice-President, Graduate & Post-Degree Progams
Dr. Fred Hall, Ph.D., Dean

Humanities
Dan Maher, Interim Dean

Law
Alastair R. Lucas, Q.C., Dean

Medicine
Dr. Tom Feasby, M.D., B.Sc., Dean

Nursing
Dianne Tapp, M.N., Ph.D., Dean

Kinesiology
Dr. Wayne Giles, Ph.D., Dean

Science
Dr. J.S. Murphree, B.Sc., Ph.D., Dean

Social Sciences
Dr. Kevin McQuillan, B.A., M.A., Ph.D., Dean

Social Work
Gayla Rogers, B.A., B.SW., R.SW., Ph.D., Dean

Communication & Culture
Wisdom Tettey, B.A. (Hons.), M.A., Ph.D., Interim Dean

Haskayne School of Business
Leonard Waverman, Dean

Publications
Alumni Magazine

The Gauntlet

Edmonton: University of Alberta
114 St. - 89 Ave. Edmonton, T6G 2E1 Canada
780-492-3111,
www.ualberta.ca

Enrollment: 36962
Linda Hughes, Chancellor
Dr. Indira Samarasekera, O.C., President & Vice-Chancellor
Brian Heidecker, Chair
Carl Amrhein, Ph.D., Provist & Vice-President
P. Clark, M.A., Vice-President
Sandra Conn, Vice-President
D. Hickey, P.Eng., Vice-President
Lee Elliott, Director
C. Byrne, M.B.A., Vice-Provost & Registrar
M. Craige, C.P.P., Director
T. Anderson, Director
K. Adams, Director
Frank Robinson, Interim Vice-Provost & Dean
L. Babiuk, Ph.D., Vice-President

Faculties
Agriculture, Forestry & Home Economics
John Kennelly, Ph.D., Dean

Arts
C. Skidmore, Ph.D., Interim Dean

Business
M. Percy, Ph.D., Dean

Education
Fern Snart, Ph.D., Dean

Engineering
D. Lynch, Ph.D., Dean

Extension
K. Campbell, Ph.D., Dean

Graduate Studies & Research
M. Shirvani, Ph.D., Dean

Law
P. Bryden, B.A., B.C.L., LL.M., Dean

Medicine & Dentistry
Philip Baker, D.M., FRCOG, Dean

Nursing
Dr. Anita Molzahn, Ph.D., Dean

Pharmacy & Pharmaceutical Sciences
F. Pasutto, Ph.D., Dean

Physical Education & Recreation
M. Mahon, Ph.D., Dean

Rehabilitation Medicine

M. Ferguson-Pell, Ph.D., Dean

School of Native Studies
E. Beilawski, Ph.D., Dean

Science
G. Taylor, Ph.D., Dean

Campus Saint-Jean
M. Arnal, Ph.D., Dean

Campuses
Augustana Faculty
R. Epp

St. Joseph's College
University of Alberta
Edmonton, T6G 2J5 Canada
780-492-7681, Fax: 780-492-8145,
www.ualberta.ca/~stjoseph
The College, located at the University of Alberta, was established by the Roman Catholic Archdiocese of Edmonton. It offers courses in Christian theology & philosophy.
Fr. Timothy Scott, President
timothy.scott@ualberta.ca
Kenneth J. Munro, Academic Dean
ken.munro@ualberta.ca

St. Stephen's College
University of Alberta Campus
8810, 112 St. Edmonton, T6G 1J6 Canada
780-439-7311, Fax: 780-433-8875, 1-800-661-4956
ststephn@ualberta.ca
www.ualberta.ca/st.stephens/

Earle Sharam, Dean
esharam@ualberta.ca
Shelley Westermann, Registrar
westerma@ualberta.ca

Publications
Gateway

New Trail
c/o Alumni Association
430 Athabasca Hall Edmonton, T6G 2E8 Canada

Folio

Lethbridge: University of Lethbridge
4401 University Dr. Lethbridge, T1K 3M4 Canada
403-329-2111, Fax: 403-329-2097,
inquiries@uleth.ca
www.uleth.ca

Enrollment: 8000
Bill Cade, Ph.D., President & Vice-Chancellor
Chris Horbachewski, Vice-President
Seamus O'Shea, Vice-President
Andrew Hakin, Vice-President
Dennis Fitzpatrick, Vice-President
Daryl Schacher, Manager
Annette Bright, Manager
Nancy Walker, Vice-President

Faculties
Arts & Science
Chris Nicol, Dean

Education
Jane O'Dea, Dean

Fine Arts
Dr. Desmond Rochfort, Dean

Management
Murray Lindsay, Dean

Schools
Graduate Studies
Dr. Jo-Anne Fiske, Dean

Health Sciences
Christopher Hosgood, Dean

Publications
The Meliorist
Student newspaper at the University of Lethbridge

Colleges

Calgary: Alberta College of Art & Design / ACAD
1407 - 14 Ave. NW Calgary, T2N 4R3 Canada
403-284-7600, Fax: 403-289-6682,
registrar@acad.ca
www.acad.ca

Enrollment: 1115
Lance Carlson, President & CEO
lance.carlson@acad.ca
Marc Scholes, Dean of Undergraduate Studies
marc.scholes@acad.ca

Calgary: Ambrose Unviersity College
Canada Centre Building
#630, 833 - 4th Ave. SW Calgary, T2P 3T5 Canada
403-410-2000, Fax: 403-571-2556, 800-461-1222
www.ambrose.edu

Enrollment: 508
Formerly Alliance University College/Nazarene University College
Dr. George Durance, President
Dr. R. Riley Coulter, President

Calgary: Bow Valley College
332 - 6 Ave. SE Calgary, T2G 4S6 Canada
403-410-1400, Fax: 403-297-4887, 1-866-428-2669
TDD: 403-410-1412
info@bowvalleycollege.ca
www.bowvalleycollege.ca

Sharon Carry, President & CEO
Katherine Cormack, Director, Marketing, Communications & Recruit
kcormack@bowvalleycollege.ca
Val Hoey, Director, Development

Calgary: Calgary Campus
2700 - 3rd Ave. SE Calgary, T2A 7W4 Canada
403-235-3450, 800-363-5558
www.devry.edu/calgary

Calgary: St. Mary's University College
14500 Bannister Rd. SE Calgary, T2X 1Z4 Canada
403-531-9130, Fax: 403-531-9136,
Tamara.Acheson@stmu.ab.ca
www.stmu.ab.ca

The post-secondary institution operates in the tradition of Catholic scholarship in Canada. Liberal arts & sciences are taught.

Most Rev. Frederick Henry, DD, Chancellor
Dr. Terrence Downey, Vice-Chancellor & President, 403-254-3701
Tamara Acheson, Registrar, 403-254-3732

Edmonton: Concordia University College of Alberta
7128 Ada Blvd. Edmonton, T5B 4E4 Canada
780-479-8481, Fax: 780-474-1933, 866-479-5200
www.concordia.ab.ca

Enrollment: 1700
Dr. Gerald Krispin, President
Dr. Richard Willie, Vice-President Academic & Provost
Patricia Warmington, Vice-President, Advancement
Jerry Reglin, Vice-President, Finance
Judy Kruse, Registrar

Edmonton: Grant MacEwan Community College
P.O. Box 1796
Edmonton, T5J 2P2 Canada
780-497-5712, Fax: 780-497-5720,
www.gmcc.ab.ca/

Enrollment: 40791
Enrolment figure includes full-time & part-time students
Dr. Paul Byrne, President

Edmonton: The King's University College
9125 - 50 St. Edmonton, T6B 2H3 Canada
780-465-3500, Fax: 780-465-3534, 800-661-8582
www.kingsu.ca

Enrollment: 652
Dr. J. Harry Fernhout, President

Edmonton: NorQuest College
Downtown Campus, Main Bldg.
10215 - 108 St. Edmonton, T5J 1L6 Canada
780-644-6000, Fax: 780-644-6013, 1-866-534-7218
info@norquest.ca
www.norquest.ca

Enrollment: 10800

Edmonton: Taylor University College & Seminary
11525 - 23 Ave. Edmonton, T6J 4T3 Canada
780-431-5200, Fax: 780-436-9416, 800-567-4988
admissions@taylor-edu.ca
www.taylor-edu.ca

David Williams, President
Craig Weston, Registrar
Terry Opperman, Director of Student Development
Tom Berekoff, Vice President of Development

Fort McMurray: Keyano College
8115 Franklin Ave. Fort McMurray, T9H 2H7 Canada
780-791-4800, Fax: 780-791-1555, 800-251-1408
www.keyanoc.ab.ca

Enrollment: 1200
5000 part-time enrollment
Jim Foote, President
Al Adibi, Vice-President, Finance & Administration
Marylea Jarvis, Vice-President, Instruction

Grande Prairie: Grande Prairie Regional College
10726 - 106 Ave. Grande Prairie, T8V 4C4 Canada
780-539-2944, Fax: 780-539-2832, 888-539-4772
studentinfo@gprc.ab.ca
www.gprc.ab.ca

Enrollment: 2000
Don Gnatiuk, President
dgnatiuk@gprc.ab.ca
Doug Hart, Vice-President, Special Projects
dhart@gprc.ab.ca

Lac La Biche: Portage College
P.O. Box 417
Lac La Biche, T0A 2C0 Canada
780-623-5551, Fax: 780-623-5639,
info@portagecollege.ca
www.portagecollege.ca

Business Career; Human Services; Native Arts & Culture; Health & Wellness; Trades & Technical; Academic Upgrading programs
William (Bill) Persley, President

Lacombe: Canadian University College
5415 College Ave. Lacombe, T4L 2E5 Canada
403-782-3381, 800-661-8129
admissions@cauc.ca
www.cauc.ca

Enrollment: 400
Lawrence Murrin, Registrar
lmurrin@cauc.ca

Lethbridge: Lethbridge College
3000 College Dr. South Lethbridge, T1K 1L6 Canada
403-320-3200, Fax: 403-320-1461, 800-572-0103
info@lethbridgecollege.ab.ca
www.lethbridgecollege.ab.ca

Enrollment: 7200
Tracy L. Edwards, President, 403-320-3209
tracy.edwards@lethbridgecollege.ab.ca

Olds: Olds College
4500 - 50th St. Olds, T4H 1R6 Canada
403-556-8281, Fax: 403-556-4711, 1-800-661-6537
Continuing Education: 403-507-7956; Registrar: 403-556-8281
info@oldscollege.ca; library@oldscollege.ca
www.oldscollege.ca

Enrollment: 1309
Olds College features the following schools: School of Agriculture, Business & Technology; School of Animal Science; School of Applied Arts & Career Studies; School of Horticulture; School of Land Sciences; School of Innovation; & Continuing Education.
Bill Quinney, Chair
H.J. (Tom) Thompson, President/CEO

Campuses
Calgary Campus
640 - 14th Ave. SE Calgary, T2G 1E8

Slave Lake: Northern Lakes College
1201 Main St. SE Slave Lake, T0G 2A3 Canada
780-849-8600, Fax: 780-849-2570, 1-866-652-3456
Grouard Phone: 780-751-3200; Library (Slave Lake): 780-849-8670
info@northernlakescollege.ca;
webmaster@northernlakescollege.ca
www.northernlakescollege.ca

Distance learning is an important part of the college education. Northern Lakes College reaches full-time & part-time students in 30 rural communities in north central Alberta.
Trevor W. Gladue, Chair
Rick Neidig, President/CEO, 780-751-3260

Vermilion: Lakeland College
Vermillion Campus
5707 - 47 Ave. West Vermilion, T9X 1K5 Canada
780-853-8400, Fax: 780-853-7355,
admissions@lakelandc.ab.ca
www.lakelandcollege.ca

Enrollment: 7000
Glenn Charlesworth, President & CEO

Campuses
Lloyminster Campus
2602-59 Ave. Bag 6000 Lloydminster, S9V 1Z3 Canada
Fax: 780-875-5136, 1-800-661-6490
admissions@lakelandc.ab.ca
www.lakelandcollege.ca

Strathcona County Learning Centre
Broadmoore Place IV
#172, 2257 Premier Way Sherwood Park, T8H 2M8 Canada
1-800-661-6490
admissions@lakelandc.ab.ca
www.lakelandcollege.ca

Post Secondary/Technical

Colleges

Calgary: Mount Royal College
Lincoln Park Campus
4825 Mount Royal Gate SW Calgary, T3E 6K6 Canada
403-440-6111, Fax: 403-440-5938, 1-877-440-5001
externalrelations@mtroyal.ca; international@mtroyal.ca
www.mtroyal.ca

Enrollment: 11992
Sixty-eight credit programs are offered by the college.
Cathy Williams, Chair
Dr. David Marshall, President, 403-440-6393, fax: 403-440-6040
president@mtroyal.ca
Dr. Robin Fisher, Provost & Vice-President, Academic

Campuses
Holy Cross Campus
2204 - 2nd St. SW Calgary, T2P 1S5
403-503-4886

Sprinkbank Campus
143 MacLaurin Dr. Springbank
403-288-9551

Paul Tigchelaar, B.Sc., B.Ed., M.Ed., Principal
Grace Lo-Voo, B.Sc., M.Ed., Vice Principal
Dan Dowber, H.R. Management Diploma o, Director, Development
Elsy TerMaat, B.A., Business Administrator

Edmonton: Grant MacEwan College
City Centre Campus
10700 - 104 Ave. Edmonton, T5J 4S2 Canada
780-497-5401, Fax: 780-497-5405,
www.macewan.ca

Dr. Paul Byrne, President
byrnep@macewan.ca

Campuses
Alberta College Campus
10050 MacDonald Dr. Edmonton, T5J 0S3 Canada

Centre for the Arts
10045 - 156 St. Edmonton, T5P 2P7 Canada
Fax: 780-497-4300

City Centre Campus
10700 - 104 Ave. Edmonton, T5J 4S2 Canada
Fax: 780-497-5045

South Campus
7319 - 29 Ave. Edmonton, T6K 2P1 Canada
Fax: 780-497-4045

Publications
The Intercamp

The Interpreter
c/o Students' Association
P.O. Box 1796
Edmonton, T5J 2P2 Canada

The MacEwan Journalist
10700 - 104 St Edmonton, T5J 4S2 Canada
Fax: 780-497-5630

Fort McMurray: Keyano College
8115 Franklin Ave. Fort McMurray, T9H 2H7 Canada
780-791-4800, Fax: 780-791-1555, 1-800-251-140
registrar@keyano.ca
www.keyano.ca

Jim Foote, President

Publications
Student Connection

Lethbridge: Lethbridge Community College
3000 College Dr. South Lethbridge, T1K 1L6 Canada
403-320-3200, Fax: 403-320-1461, 1-800-572-010
info@lethbridgecollege.ab.ca
www.lethbridgecollege.ab.ca

Enrollment: 4100
Dr. Tracy Edwards, Ed.D., President/CEO

Medicine Hat: Medicine Hat College
299 College Dr. SE Medicine Hat, T1A 3Y6 Canada
403-529-3811, Fax: 403-504-3517,
info@mhc.ab.ca
www.mhc.ab.ca

Ralph Weeks, Ph.D., President
weeks@mhc.ab.ca

Campuses
Brooks Campus
200 Horticultural Rd. East Brooks, T1R 1E5 Canada
Fax: 403-362-1474

Publications
Express This

Red Deer: Red Deer College
P.O. Box 5005
100 College Blvd. Red Deer, T4N 5H5 Canada
403-342-3300, Fax: 403-340-8940,
www.rdc.ab.ca

Ron Woodward, President
ron.woodward@rdc.ab.ca

Publications
Bricklayer

Post Secondary/Technical

Banff: The Banff Centre
P.O. Box 1020
Banff, T1L 1H5 Canada
403-762-6100, Fax: 403-762-6444,
Telex: Artsbanff 03-826657
www.banffcentre.ca

Mary E. Hofstetter, President/CEO
Melanie Busby, Director

Banff: Banff Centre for Management
P.O. Box 1020 45
Banff, T0L 0C0 Canada
403-762-6133, Fax: 403-762-6422, 1-800-590-979
bcm@banffcentre.ca
www.banffcentre.ab.ca

Banff: **Banff School of Advanced Management**
P.O. Box 1020 5
Banff, T1L 1H5 Canada
403-762-6127, Fax: 403-762-6499, 1-888-762-612
bsam@banffcentre.ab.ca
Offers a 28-day executive development program for high potential & advancing managers

Calgary: **CDI College of Business, Technology & Healthcare**
Trimac House
#100, 800 5th Ave. SW Calgary, T2P 3T6OW7 Canada
403-232-6410, Fax: 403-266-0830,
www.cdicollege.com
Career training; 5 locations in Alberta

Calgary: **Enform**
1538 - 25 Ave. NE Calgary, T2E 8Y3 Canada
403-250-9606, Fax: 403-291-9408, 1-800-667-555
pschoenhals@enform.ca
www.enform.ca
Paul Schoenhals, President/CEO

Calgary: **The Southern Alberta Institute of Technology**
1301 - 16th Ave. NW Calgary, T2M 0L4 Canada
403-284-7248, Fax: 403-284-7112, 1-877-284-7248
advising@sait.ca
www.sait.ca
Canada's premier technical institute by 2010
Irene Lewis, President & CEO

Publications
The Emery Weal

Edmonton: **The Northern Alberta Institute of Technology**
11762 - 106 St. Edmonton, T5G 2R1 Canada
780-471-7400, Fax: 780-471-8583,
registrar@nait.ca
www.nait.ca

Campuses
Fairview Campus
P.O. Box 3000
11235 - 98 Ave. Fairview, T0H 1L0 Canada
Fax: 780-835-6698, 1-888-999-7882

Grande Prairie Campus
10632 - 102 Ave. Grande Prairie, T8V 6J8 Canada
Fax: 780-539-2081

High Level Campus
P.O. Box 810
10901 - 93 St. High Level, T0H 1Z0 Canada
Fax: 780-926-2264

Peace River Campus
P.O. Box 3500
8106 - 99 Ave. Peace River, T8S 1V9 Canada
Fax: 780-624-4532

St. Albert Campus
506B St. Albert Rd. St Albert, T8N 5Z1 Canada
Fax: 780-458-6495

Publications
The Nugget

Edmonton: **Northern Alberta Institute of Technology**
11762 - 106 St. NW Edmonton, T5G 3H1 Canada
780-471-7400,
www.nait.ab.ca/
D. Warwick, Environmental Training Coordinator, 780-471-7769
davew@nait.ab.ca

Grande Prairie: **Mayfair College**
#305, 9804 - 100 Ave. Grande Prairie, T8V 0T8 Canada
780-539-5090, Fax: 780-539-7089,
mayfair@telusplanet.net
Computer training.

Lloydminster: **Reeves College**
P.O. Box 51
5012 - 49 St. Lloydminster, S9V 0X9 Canada
780-875-3308, Fax: 780-875-9209,
www.reevescollege.ab.ca
Secretarial, accounting training; 4 campuses

Red Deer: **Academy of Professional Hair Design**
4929 - 49 St. Red Deer, T4N 1Z1 Canada
403-347-2018, Fax: 403-342-4244,
www.academyofprofessionalhairdesign.com
Esthetics, hair design.

Vermilion: **Alberta Fire Training School**
5704 - 47 Ave. Vermilion, T9X 1K4 Canada
780-853-5800, Fax: 780-853-3008, 1-888-863-238
aftsinfor@afts.ab.ca
www.afts.ab.ca

British Columbia

Government Agencies

Victoria: **Ministry of Advanced Education**
P.O. Box 9059 Prov Govt
Victoria, V8W 9E2 Canada
Fax: 250-356-2598, 1-888-664-225
AVED.WEBMASTER@gov.bc.ca
Hon. Murray Coell, Minister
Moura Quayle, Deputy Minister

Victoria: **Ministry of Education**
Parliament Bldgs.
P.O. Box 9150 Prov Govt
Victoria, V8V 9H1 Canada
250-356-8156, Fax: 250-356-5945
Hon. Shirley Bond, Minister

School Boards/Districts/Divisions

Public

Abbotsford: **Abbotsford School District #34**
2790 Tims St. Abbotsford, V2T 4M7 Canada
604-859-4891, Fax: 604-852-8587,
Facilities, Phone: 604-852-9494; Fax: 604-852-4876
info@sd34.bc.ca
www.sd34.bc.ca
Grades: Kindergarten - Secondary
Enrollment: 18500
Julie MacRae, Superintendent, 604-859-4891 1230
Kevin Godden, Secretary-Treasurer, 604-859-4891 1241
Judy Chapman, Director, Curriculum, 604-504-0026
judy_chapman@sd34.bc.ca
Deb Peters, Director, Instruction, 604-504-4610
Debbie_PetersLSS@sd34.bc.ca
Lisa Pleadwell, Director, Finance, 604-859-4891 1287
Lisa_Pleadwell@sd34.bc.ca
Marnie Wright, Director, Human Resources, 604.859.4891 1249
marnie_wright@sd34.bc.ca
Dave Stephen, Manager, Communications, 604-859-4891 1206
dave_stephen@sd34.bc.ca

Ashcroft: **Gold Trail School District #74**
P.O. Box 250
400 Hollis Rd. Ashcroft, V0K 1A0 Canada
250-453-9101, Fax: 250-453-2425,
www.sd74.bc.ca
Grades: Kindergarten - Secondary
Enrollment: 1800
Number of Schools: 12. Number of Employees: 150 teachers & support staff
Valerie Adrian, Chair
vadrian@gw.sd74.bc.ca
Alison Sidow, Superintendent, Education, 250-453-9101 208
asidow@gw.sd74.bc.ca
Teresa Downs, District Principal, 250-453-9101 234
tdowns@gw.sd74.bc.ca
Marianne Munro, Manager, Information Technology, 250-453-9101 222
mmunro@gw.sd74.bc.ca
Patrice Barth, District Teacher, Learner Support, 250-453-9101 210
pbarth@gw.sd74.bc.ca
Wendy Blaskovic, District Resource Teacher, Trades, 250-453-9101 235
wblaskovic@gw.sd74.bc.ca
Lynda Minnabarriet, Secretary-Treasurer, 250-453-9101 200
lminnab@gw.sd74.bc.ca

Burnaby: **Burnaby School District #41**
5325 Kincaid St. Burnaby, V5G 1W2 Canada
604-664-8441, Fax: 604-664-8382,
www.sd41.bc.ca
Grades: Kindergarten - 12; Continuing Ed.
Enrollment: 24000
Number of Schools: 40 elementary schools (including 7 community schools); 8 secondary schools. Number of Employees: 4,000+
Diana Mumford, Chair, 604-434-9757
Claudio Morelli, Superintendent, Schools, 604-664-8393
claudio.morelli@sd41.bc.ca
Elliott Grieve, Associate Superintendent, 604-664-8385
Elliott.Grieve@sd41.bc.ca
Kevin Kaardal, Assistant Superintendent, 604-664-8377
kevin.kaardal@sd41.bc.ca
Gina Niccoli-Moen, Assistant Superintendent, 604-664-8365
Gina.Niccoli-Moen@sd41.bc.ca
Doug Berardine, Director, Employee Relations, 604-664-8362
doug.berardine@sd41.bc.ca
Bonda Bitzer, Director, Human Resources, 604-664-8353
Bonda.Bitzer@sd41.bc.ca
Phil Shepherd, Director, Facility Services, 604-664-8383
phil.shepherd@sd41.bc.ca
Greg Frank, Secretary-Treasurer, 604-664-8387
Greg.Frank@sd41.bc.ca

Campbell River: **Campbell River School District #72**
425 Pinecrest Rd. Campbell River, V9W 3P2 Canada
250-830-2300, Fax: 250-287-2616,
www.sd72.bc.ca
Grades: Kindergarten-12; Continuing Ed; ESL
Enrollment: 5874
Number of Schools: 15 elementary schools; 2 middle schools; 2 secondary schools. Number of Employees: 750
Tom Longridge, Superintendent, Schools, 250-830-2398
Jim Ansell, Assistant Superintendent, Schools, 250-830-2398
Nevenka Fair, Director, Instructional Programs, 250-830-2339
Sheila Johnsrude, Director, Student Services, 250-286-4400 2253
Diane Rhenisch, Director, Leadership Support, 250-830-2327
Yves Vachon, Manager, Human Resources, 250-830-2310
Geoff Wilson, Manager, Information Technology, 250-830-2390
Steve Woods, Manager, Operations, 250-830-2334
Greg Johnson, District Principal, Aboriginal Education, 250-923-4902 2216
Sean Toal, District Principal, Robron Centre, 250-923-4918
Lyle Boyce, Secretary-Treasurer, 250-830-2302
Ruth Kine, District Teacher Librarian, 250-830-2322

Chilliwack: **Chilliwack School District #33**
8430 Cessna Dr. Chilliwack, V2P 7K4 Canada
604-792-1321, Fax: 604-792-9665
Enrollment: 12794
Jacquie Taylor, Supt.
jacquie_taylor@sd33.bc.ca
Jim Alkins, Sec.-Treas.
Brenda Point, Aboriginal Education Contact, 604-824-6173, fax: 604-824-0721
brenda_point@sd33.bc.ca

Coquitlam: **Coquitlam School District #43**
550 Poirier St. Coquitlam, V3J 6A7 Canada
604-939-9201, Fax: 604-939-7828
Enrollment: 32838
Laureen Doerksen, Supt.
ldoerksen@sd43.bc.ca
Lorcan O'Melinn, Sec.-Treas.
Margaret Mary Deck, Aboriginal Education Contact, 604-945-7386, fax: 604-945-7395
mdeck@sd43.bc.ca

Courtenay: **Comox Valley School District #71**
607 Cumberland Rd. Courtenay, V9N 7G5 Canada
250-334-5500, Fax: 250-334-4472
Enrollment: 9659
Bryan Morgan, Supt.
bryan.morgan@sd71.bc.ca
Len Ibbs, Sec.-Treas.
Lynn Joseph, Aboriginal Education Contact, 250-334-5502, fax: 250-334-4472

Cranbrook: **Southeast Kootenay School District #5**
940 Industrial Rd. No. 1 Cranbrook, V1C 4C6 Canada
250-426-4201, Fax: 250-489-5460,
www.sd5.bc.ca
Enrollment: 6204
Bill Gook, Superintendent
bill.gook@sd5.bc.ca
Robert Norum, Sec.-Treas.
Doug McPhee, Aboriginal Education Contact, 250-489-3480
doug.mcphee@sd5.bc.ca

Dawson Creek: **Peace River South School District #59**
11600, 7th St. Dawson Creek, V1G 4R8 Canada
250-782-8571, Fax: 250-782-3204,
www.sd59.bc.ca
Enrollment: 4855
Kathy Sawchuk, Superintendent
Gerry Slykhuis, Sec.-Treas.
Cammy-Jo Plummer, Aboriginal Education Contact

Dease Lake: **Stikine School District #87**
P.O. Box 190
Dease Lake, V0C 1L0 Canada
250-771-4440, Fax: 250-771-4441
Grades: Kindergarten - 12; Alternative Ed.
Enrollment: 260

Number of Schools: 4 elementary schools; 3 high schools; 1 alternative school. Number of Employees: 71
Bryan Ennis, Superintendent, Schools
bennis@sd87.bc.ca

Delta: Delta School District #37
4585 Harvest Dr. Delta, V4K 5B4 Canada
604-946-4101, Fax: 604-952-5375

Enrollment: 17426
Dr. John L. Anderson, Interim Supt.
jcalder@deltasd.bc.ca
Grant McRadu, Sec.-Treas.
Kathy Guild, Aboriginal Education Contact, 604-946-4101, fax: 604-946-7803
kguild@deltasd.bc.ca

Duncan: Cowichan Valley School District #79
2557 Beverly St. Duncan, V9L 2X3 Canada
250-748-0321, Fax: 250-748-6591

Enrollment: 9801
Peter Porte, Supt.
pporte@sd79.bc.ca
Phil Turin, Sec.-Treas.
Ted Cadwallader, Aboriginal Education Contact, 250-748-0321 ext.216, fax: 250-748-6591

Fort Nelson: Fort Nelson School District #81
P.O. Box 87
5104 Airport Dr. Fort Nelson, V0C 1R0 Canada
250-774-2591, Fax: 250-774-2598,
www.sd81.bc.ca

Grades: Kindergarten - 12
Enrollment: 889
Number of Schools: 5. Number of Employees: 100
Linda Dolen, Chair
ldolen@sd81.bc.ca
Diana Samchuck, Superintendent
dsamchuck@sd81.bc.ca
Ray Irwin, Director, Instruction
rirwin@sd81.bc.ca
Patti Burt, District Vice Principal, Technology / Distrib
pburt@sd81.bc.ca
Margaret-Anne Hall, Secretary-Treasurer
mhall@sd81.bc.ca
Darryl Low, Supervisor, Maintenance
dlow@sd81.bc.ca

Fort St John: Peace River North School District #60
10112 - 105 Ave. Fort St John, V1J 4S4 Canada
250-262-6000, Fax: 250-262-6048,
www.prn.bc.ca

Enrollment: 5792
Larry Espe, Superintendent
lespe@prn.bc.ca
Doug Boyd, Sec.-Treas.
Brenda Paul, Aboriginal Education Contact, 250-785-8324, fax: 250-785-0846

Gibsons: Sunshine Coast School District #46
P.O. Box 220
494 South Fletcher Rd. Gibsons, V0N 1V0 Canada
604-886-8811, Fax: 604-886-4652,
Questions@sd46.bc.ca; board@sd46.bc.ca
www.sd46.bc.ca

Grades: Kindergarten - 12; Alternative Ed.
Enrollment: 3600
Number of Schools: 9 elementary schools; 4 secondary schools
Silas White, Chair
silas@nightwoodeditions.com
Deborah Palmer, Superintendent, Schools
dpalmer@sd46.bc.ca
Tom Hierck, Assistant Superintendent
thierck@sd46.bc.ca
Debbie Amaral, District Principal, Student Support Services
damaral@sd46.bc.ca
Kerry Mahlman, District Principal, Aboriginal Programs & Svs
cmahlman@sd46.bc.ca
Maurice Arduin, Manager, Facilities & Transportation
marduin@sd46.bc.ca
Diane Ready, Secretary-Treasurer
dready@sd46.bc.ca
Tara Sweet, Officer, Human Resources
hr@sd46.bc.ca

Gold River: Vancouver Island West School District #84
P.O. Box 100
2 Hwy. 28 Gold River, V0P 1G0 Canada
250-283-2241, Fax: 250-283-7352,
www.sd84.bc.ca

Grades: Kindergarten - 12
Enrollment: 466
Number of Schools: 5
Jessie Smith, Chair
Lawrence Tarasoff, Superintendent, Schools, & Secretary-Treasure
Annie James, Administrator, Human Resources

Grand Forks: Boundary School District #51
P.O. Box 640
1021 Central Ave. Grand Forks, V0H 1H0 Canada
250-442-8258, Fax: 250-442-8800,
info@sd51.bc.ca
www.sd51.bc.ca

Grades: Kindergarten - 12; Alternate Ed.
Teresa Rezansoff, Board Chair, 250-442-2240
teresa.rezansoff@sd51.bc.ca
Michael Strukoff, Superintendent, Schools
michael.strukoff@sd51.bc.ca
Jeanette Hanlon, Secretary-Treasurer
jeanette.hanlon@sd51.bc.ca
Maxine Ruzicka, Director, Instruction
maxine.ruzicka@sd51.bc.ca
Dean Higashi, Manager, Operations
dean.higashi@sd51.bc.ca
John Popoff, Manager, Technology
john.popoff@sd51.bc.ca

Hagensborg: Central Coast School District #49
PO Bag 130 Hagensborg, V0T 1H0 Canada
250-982-2691, Fax: 250-982-2319,
www.sd49.bc.ca

Grades: Kindergarten - 12
Enrollment: 200
Number of Schools: 5
Robyn Willis, Chair, Board of Trustees
rwillis@sd49.bc.ca
Denise Perry, CEO, Superintendent of Schools, & Secretary-T
dperry@sd49.bc.ca
Sheldon Lee, CMA, Director, Business Operations
Sheldon.Lee.SDBOC@telus.net
Lela Walkus, Coordinator, Aboriginal Studies
lwalkus@sd49.bc.ca
Jeremy Baillie, Principal, Sir Alexander Mackenzie Secondary
jbaillie@sd49.bc.ca
Nam Nguyen, Principal, Bella Coola Elementary School
nnguyen@sd49.bc.ca
Erin Chapman, District Librarian
echapman@sd49.bc.ca
Debbie Gibson, Comptroller
dgibson@sd49.bc.ca
Mark Chatham, Lead Hand, Maintenance
mchatham@sd49.bc.ca
Stephen Sheppard, Lead Hand, Transportation
ssheppard@sd49.bc.ca

Hope: Fraser Cascade School District No. 78
650 Kawkawa Lake Rd. Hope, V0X 1L4 Canada
604-869-2411, Fax: 604-869-7400,
Agassiz Phone: 604-796-2225
www.sd78.bc.ca

Grades: Kindergarten - 12
Number of Schools: 12
Linda McMullan, Chair
Dr. Karen Nelson, Superintendent, Schools
Dr. Scott Benwell, Assistant Superintendent
Natalie Lowe-Zucchet, CA, Secretary-Treasurer
Donna Barner, Speech Pathologist
Dan Landrath, Supervisor, Transportation
Mike Repstock, Supervisor, Maintenance
Pat Marsh, Assistant, First Nations Education

Invermere: Rocky Mountain School District #6
P.O. Box 430
620, 4th St. Invermere, V0A 1K0 Canada
250-342-9243, Fax: 250-342-6966,
www.sd6.bc.ca

Enrollment: 3823
Paul Carriere, Superintendent
pcarriere@sd6.bc.ca
Cameron Dow, Sec.-Treas.

Kamloops: Kamloops-Thompson School District #73
1383 - 9 Ave. Kamloops, V2C 3X7 Canada
250-374-0679, Fax: 250-372-1183,
www.sd73.bc.ca

Enrollment: 15087
Dr. Terry Sullivan, Superintendent
tsullivan@sd73.bc.ca
Jim Sheldon, Sec.-Treas.
Debora Draney, Aboriginal Education Principal, 250-374-0679

Kelowna: Central Okanagan School District #23
1940 Underhill St. Kelowna, V1X 5X7 Canada
250-860-8888, Fax: 250-860-9799,
www.sd23.bc.ca

Grades: Kindergarten - 12; Alternate Ed.
Rolli Cacchioni, Chair, 250-470-3216, fax: 250-860-9799
board@sd23.bc.ca
Hugh Gloster, Superintendent, 250-470-3256, fax: 250-860-9799
hgloster@sd23.bc.ca
Terry Lee Beaudry, Assistant Superintendent, 250-470-3225, fax: 250-870-5025
tbeaudry@sd23.bc.ca
Norm Bradley, Co-Director, Instruction K-12, 250-470-3271, fax: 250-870-5053
gthomson@sd23.bc.ca
Jim Colquhoun, Director, Human Resources - Labour Relations, 250-470-3237, fax: 250-870-5088
jcolquho@sd23.bc.ca
Alan Cumbers, Director, Operations, 250-491-4001, fax: 250-870-5094
acumbers@sd23.bc.ca
Ross Dumontet, Director, Instruction - Human Resources, 250-470-3237, fax: 250-870-5088
rdumonte@sd23.bc.ca
Lisa McCullough, Co-Director, Instruction K-12, 250-470-3210, fax: 250-870-5021
bbrowns@sd23.bc.ca
Peter Molloy, Director, Student Support Services, 250-470-3267, fax: 250-470-3272
bericksо@sd23.bc.ca
Jon Rever, Co-Director, Instruction K-12, 250-860-9729 4688, fax: 250-870-5086
lgradidg@sd23.bc.ca
Eileen Sadlowski, Director, Finance, 250-470-3224, fax: 250-470-3274
esadlows@sd23.bc.ca
Clara Sulz, Co-Director, Instruction K-12, 250-470-3217, fax: 250-870-5027
lpaziuk@sd23.bc.ca

Langley: Langley School District #35
4875 - 222 St. Langley, V3A 3Z7 Canada
604-534-7891, Fax: 604-533-1115,
www.sd35.bc.ca

Enrollment: 18000
Cheryle Beaumont, Superintendent
cbeaumont@sd35.bc.ca
Peter Greenwood, Sec.-Treas.
Dave Coutu, Aboriginal Program Administrator, 604-534-7891, fax: 604-532-1458
dcoutu@sd35.bc.ca

Maple Ridge: Maple Ridge School District #42
22225 Brown Ave. Maple Ridge, V2X 8N6 Canada
604-463-4200, Fax: 604-463-4181,
www.sd42.ca

Grades: K.-12
Enrollment: 15559
Jan Unwin, Supt.
junwin@sd42.ca
Wayne Jefferson, Sec.-Treas.
wjefferson@sd42.ca
Doug Hoey, Principal, Aboriginal Education, 604-466-6265
dhoey@sd42.ca

Merritt: Nicola-Similkameen School District #58
P.O. Box 4100 Main
1550 Chapman St. Merritt, V1K 1B8 Canada
250-378-5161, Fax: 250-378-6263,
www.sd58.bc.ca

Grades: K.-12
Enrollment: 2500
Dr Robert Peacock, Supt.
rpeacock@sd58.bc.ca
H. Bruce Tisdale, Sec.-Treas.
btisdale@sd58.bc.ca
Shelley Oppenheim-Lacerte, Principal, Aboriginal Education 1111
so-lacerte@sd58.bc.ca

Mission: Mission School District #75
33046 - 4 Ave. Mission, V2V 1S5 Canada
604-826-6286, Fax: 604-826-4517,
www.mpsd.ca

Grades: Pre-K.-12
Enrollment: 6311
Frank Dunham, Supt.
frank.dunham@mpsd.ca
Roy Daykin, Sec.-Treas.
roy.daykin@mpsd.ca
Colleen Hannah, Aboriginal Education Contact, 604-826-3103, fax: 604-820-2850
colleen.hannah@sd75.mission.bc.ca

Nakusp: Arrow Lakes School District #10
P.O. Box 340
98 - 6th Ave. NW Nakusp, V0G 1R0 Canada

250-265-3638, Fax: 250-265-3701,
sdchanges@sd10.bc.ca
www.sd10production.bcelearner.ca
Grades: Kindergarten - 12
Enrollment: 589
Walter Posnikoff, District Superintendent & Secretary-Treasurer, 250-265-3638 25, fax: 250-265-3701
wposnikoff@sd10.bc.ca
George Harding, District Facilitator & Coordinator, Instructi, 250-265-3638, fax: 250-265-3081
gharding@sd10.bc.ca
Alistair Skey, Manager, District Technology, 250-265-3638 26, fax: 250-265-3701
askey@sd10.bc.ca
Natalie Verigin, District Financial Comptroller, 250-265-3638, fax: 250-265-3701
nverigin@sd10.bc.ca

***Nanaimo:* Nanaimo-Ladysmith School District #68**
395 Wakesiah Ave. Nanaimo, V9R 3K6 Canada
250-754-5521, Fax: 250-741-5248,
info@sd68.bc.ca
www.sd68.bc.ca
Grades: Pre-K.-12
Enrollment: 14500
Michael J. Munro, Supt./CEO
mmunro@sd68.bc.ca
J. David Green, Sec.-Treas., 250-754-5521
dgreen@sd68.bc.ca
Stella Bates, District Principal, Aboriginal Education, 250-741-5318
sbates@sd68.bc.ca

***Nelson:* Kootenay Lake School District #8**
570 Johnstone Rd. Nelson, V1L 6J2 Canada
250-352-6681, Fax: 250-352-6686,
www.sd8.bc.ca
Grades: K-12
Enrollment: 6113
Pat Dooley, Superintendent
Monica Schulte, Sec.-Treas.
Nancy Cobra, Aboriginal Education Co-ordinator, 250-428-2217, fax: 250-428-4990
ncobra@sd8.bc.ca

***New Aiyansh:* Nisga'a School District #92**
P.O. Box 240
5201 Tait Ave. New Aiyansh, V0J 1A0 Canada
250-633-2228, Fax: 250-633-2401,
www.nisgaa.bc.ca
Grades: K.-12
Enrollment: 480
Keith Spencer, Supt. 1102
kspencer@nisgaa.bc.ca
Bruce Matthews, Sec.-Treas. 1104, fax: 250-633-2425
bmatthews@nisgaa.bc.ca
Tina Jules, Aboriginal Education Contact 1107
tjules@nisgaa.bc.ca

***New Westminster:* New Westminster School District #40**
1001 Columbia St. New Westminster, V3M 1C4 Canada
604-517-6240, Fax: 604-517-6390,
district.sd40.bc.ca
Grades: K.-12
Enrollment: 6095
John Woudzia, Supt., 604-517-6328
rbennett@sd40.bc.ca
Brian Sommerfeldt, Sec.-Treas., 604-517-6320
bsommerfeldt@sd40.bc.ca
Bertha Lansdowne, Aboriginal Education Contact, 604-517-6316, fax: 604-517-6204
blansdow@sd40.bc.ca

***North Vancouver:* North Vancouver School District #44**
721 Chesterfield Ave. North Vancouver, V7M 2M5 Canada
604-903-3444, Fax: 604-903-3445,
www.nvsd44.bc.ca
Grades: K.-12
Enrollment: 16917
John Lewis, Supt., 604-903-3449, fax: 604-903-3448
jlewis@nvsd44.bc.ca
Irene Young, Sec.-Treas.
iyoung@nvsd44.bc.ca
Brad Baker, Aboriginal Education Contact, 604-903-3463, fax: 604-903-3778
bbaker@nvsd44.bc.ca

***Oliver:* Okanagan Similkameen School District #53**
P.O. Box 1770
35061, 101 St. Oliver, V0H 1T0 Canada
250-498-3481, Fax: 250-498-4070,
www.sd53.bc.ca
Enrollment: 2800
Juleen McElgunn, Superintendent
jmcelgunn@sd53.bc.ca
Richard Goodwein, Sec.-Treas.
Jim Insley, Asst. Superintendent, 250-498-3481 117

***Parksville:* Qualicum School District #69**
P.O. Box 430
Parksville, V9P 2G5 Canada
250-248-4241, Fax: 250-248-5767,
www.sd69.bc.ca
Enrollment: 5322
Candice Morgan, Superintendent
cmorgan@sd69.bc.ca
Bernice Hannam, Sec.-Treas.
Rosie McLeod-Shannon, Aboriginal Education Contact, 250-954-3024, fax: 250-954-3027

***Penticton:* Okanagan Skaha School District #67**
425 Jermyn Ave. Penticton, V2A 1Z4 Canada
250-770-7700, Fax: 250-770-7730,
sd67@summer.com
www.sd67.bc.ca
Enrollment: 7411
Wendy Hyer, Superintendent
whyer@summer.com
Ron Shongrunden, Sec.-Treas.
rs@summer.com
Kathy Pierre, Aboriginal Education Contact, 250-770-7703, fax: 250-770-7732

***Port Alberni:* School District #70 (Alberni)**
4690 Roger St. Port Alberni, V9Y 3Z4 Canada
250-723-3565, Fax: 250-723-0318,
www.sd70.bc.ca
Grades: Kindergarten - Secondary
Cam Pinkerton, Superintendent, 250-720-2770
cpinkerton@sd70.bc.ca
Jerry Linning, Secretary-Treasurer, 250-720-2756
jlinning@sd70.bc.ca
Jack Hitchings, Director, Curriculum, 250-720-2779
Harry Eberts, Manager, Operations, 250-723-8821
heberts@sd70.bc.ca

***Port Hardy:* Vancouver Island North School District #85**
Administration Office
P.O. Box 90
6975 Rupert St. Port Hardy, V0N 2P0 Canada
250-949-6618, Fax: 250-949-8792,
msalski@sd85.bc.ca
www.sd85.bc.ca
Grades: Kindergarten - 12
Enrollment: 1550
Number of Schools: 12
Kathy Bedard, Superintendent, Schools, & Chief Executive Of, 250-949-6618 2236
kbedard@sd85.bc.ca
John Martin, Secretary-Treasurer, 250-949-6618 2222
jmartin@sd85.bc.ca
Katherine McIntosh, Director, Instruction (Curriculum), 250-949-6618 2234
kmcintosh@sd85.bc.ca
Kaleb Child, District Principal, FN Programs, Initiatives, 250-949-6618 2233
kchild@sd85.bc.ca
Wally Wright, District Principal, Special Programs, 250-949-6618 2229
wwright@sd85.bc.ca
Wendy Glos, Speech-Language Pathologist, 250-949-6618 2244
wglos@sd85.bc.ca
Jennifer Holme, District Teacher. Literacy & Early Learning, 250-949-6618 2228
jholme@sd85.bc.ca
Charleen Purdy, District Counsellor, Elementary Schools, 250-949-6618 2251
cpurdy@sd85.bc.ca
Randy Ball, Manager, Operations & Maintenance, 250-949-8155 229

***Powell River:* Powell River School District #47**
4351 Ontario Ave. Powell River, V8A 1V3 Canada
604-485-6271, Fax: 604-485-6435
Enrollment: 2500
Jay Yule, Superintendent
jyule@sd47.bc.ca
Steve Hopkins, Sec.-Treas.
Wayne Pielle, Aboriginal Education Contact, 604-485-6271, fax: 250-483-3127
wpielle@sd47.bc.ca

***Prince George:* Prince George School District #57**
2100 Ferry Ave. Prince George, V2L 4R5 Canada
250-561-6800, Fax: 250-561-6801,
sd57@sd57.bc.ca
www.sd57.bc.ca
Enrollment: 15260
Brian Pepper, Superintendent
bpepper@sd57.bc.ca
Bryan Mix, Sec.-Treas.
Charlotte Henay, Aboriginal Education Contact, 250-561-6800 ext.315, fax: 250-561-6820

***Prince Rupert:* Prince Rupert School District #52**
634 - 6 Ave. East Prince Rupert, V8J 1X1 Canada
250-624-6717, Fax: 250-624-6517
Enrollment: 2937
Lynn Hauptman, Superintendent
Cam McIntyre, Sec.-Treas.
Debbie Leighton-Stephens, Aboriginal Education Contact, 250-627-1536 ext.221, fax: 250-624-6572
debbiels@sd52.bc.ca

***Queen Charlotte:* Haida Gwaii / Queen Charlotte School District No. 50**
P.O. Box 69
107 - 3rd Ave. Queen Charlotte, V0T 1S0 Canada
250-559-8471, Fax: 250-559-8849, 1-888-771-3131
trustees@sd50.bc.ca
www.sd50.bc.ca
Grades: Elementary-Secondary; Aboriginal Ed
Number of Schools: 6 (Agnes L. Mathers Elementary Jr. Secondary School; Sk'aadgaa Naay Elementary School; Queen Charlotte Secondary School; Port Clements Elementary School; Tahayghen Elementary School; George M. Dawson Secondary School)
Wayne Wilson, Chair, 250-559-4760, fax: 250-559-4773
wwilson@sd50.bc.ca
Angus Wilson, Superintendent, Schools
Ken Campbell, Secretary-Treasurer
Tawni Davidson, Coordinator, Early Learning
Alison Gear, Coordinator, Early Learning
Joanne Yovanovich, Principal, Aboriginal Education

***Quesnel:* Quesnel School District #28**
401 North Star Rd. Quesnel, V2J 5K2 Canada
250-992-8802, Fax: 250-992-7652,
www.sd28.bc.ca
Enrollment: 4360
Sue-Ellen Miller, Superintendent
Teri Stoneman, Sec.-Treas.
Holly Toews, Aboriginal Education Contact

***Revelstoke:* Revelstoke School District #19**
P.O. Box Bag 5800
1121 Vernon Ave. Revelstoke, V0E 2S0 Canada
250-837-2101, Fax: 250-837-9335,
www.sd19.bc.ca
Enrollment: 1200
Anne Cooper, Superintendent
acooper@sd19.bc.ca
Barbara Ross, Sec.-Treas.
Shan Jorgenson-Adam, Aboriginal Education Contact, 250-837-2101, fax: 250-837-9335

***Richmond:* French Education Authority of British Columbia**
Conseil scholaire francophone de la Columbie-Britannique
#180, 10200 Shellbridge Way Richmond, V6X 2W7 Canada
604-214-2600, Fax: 604-214-9881, 1-888-715-2200
info@csf.bc.ca
www.csf.bc.ca
Marie Bourgeois, President
Pierre Claveau, Director, Public Relations, 604-214-2617
pclaveau@csf.bc.ca

***Richmond:* Richmond School District #38**
7811 Granville Ave. Richmond, V6Y 3E3 Canada
604-668-6000, Fax: 604-668-6006,
www.sd38.bc.ca
Enrollment: 23092
Monica Pamer, Superintendent
Mark De Mello, Sec.-Treas.
Mike Akiwenzie, Aboriginal Education Contact, 604-668-6068, fax: 604-668-6697
mike_akiwenzie@richmond.sd38.bc.ca

***Saanichton:* Saanich School District #63**
2125 Keating Cross Rd. Saanichton, V8M 2A5 Canada
250-652-7300, Fax: 250-652-6421,
www.sd63.bc.ca
Enrollment: 9081

Dr. Keven Elder, Superintendent
kelder@sd63.bc.ca
Joan Axford, Sec.-Treas.
jaxford@sd63.bc.ca
Sheila Austin, Aboriginal Education Contact, 250-652-7331, fax: 250-652-7361
saustin@sd63.bc.ca

Salmon Arm: North Okanagan-Shuswap School District #83
P.O. Box 129
220 Shuswap St. NE Salmon Arm, V1E 4N2 Canada
250-832-2157, Fax: 250-832-9428,
supt@sd83.bc.ca
www.sd83.bc.ca

Grades: K.-12
Enrollment: 6723
Doug Pearson, Supt.
supt@sd83.bc.ca
Bruce Hunt, Sec.-Treas., 250-804-7830
bhunt@sd83.bc.ca
Irene LaPierre, Principal, Aboriginal Education, 250-832-8223, fax: 250-832-4456
ilapierr@sd83.bc.ca

Salt Spring Island: Gulf Islands School District #64
112 Rainbow Rd. Salt Spring Island, V8K 2K3 Canada
250-537-5548, Fax: 250-537-4200,
dfennell@sd64.bc.ca (Assistant, Dawne Fennell)
www.sd64.bc.ca

Grades: Kindergarten-12; International Ed.
Member of Schools: 10 (Galiano Community; Mayne Island; Pender Islands; Saturna Island; Fernwood; Fulford Community; Phoenix; Gulf Islands Secondary; Salt Spring Elementary; Saltspring Island Middle)
May McKenzie, Chair, 250-539-2530
mayonmayne@shaw.ca
Jeff Hopkins, Superintendent
jhopkins@sd64.bc.ca
Sheila Miller, Director, Instruction, 250-537-9441 206
sheilamiller@sd64.bc.ca
Linda Underwood, Director, Human Resources
lunderwood@sd64.bc.ca
Rob Scotvold, Secretary-Treasurer
rscotvold@sd64.bc.ca
Dr. Holly Smith, District Psychologist, 250-537-9441
hsmith@sd64.bc.ca

Smithers: Bulkley Valley School District #54
P.O. Box 758
1235 Montreal St. Smithers, V0J 2N0 Canada
250-877-6820, Fax: 250-877-6835,
info@sd54.bc.ca; contact-sd54@sd54.bc.ca
www.sd54.bc.ca

Grades: Elementary - Secondary
Number of Schools: 7 elementary schools; 2 secondary schools
Les Kearns, Board Chair, 250-845-7859
Beverly Young, Superintendent, Schools
Chris van der Mark, Assistant Superintendent
Steven Richards, Secretary-Treasurer
Toni Perreault, Administrator, Human Resources
Barb Guillon, Administrator, Payroll
Ed Hildebrandt, Supervisor, Operations

Squamish: Howe Sound School District #48
P.O. Box 250
37866 Second Ave. Squamish, V8B 0A2 Canada
604-892-5228, Fax: 604-892-1038,
tfarina@sd48.bc.ca
www.sd48.bc.ca

Enrollment: 4536
Dr. Rick Erickson, Superintendent
ricke@sd48.bc.ca
John Hetherington, Sec.-Treas.
jhetherington@sd48.bc.ca
Juanita Coltman, Aboriginal Education Administrator
jcoltman@sd48.bc.ca

Surrey: Surrey School District #36
14225 - 56th Ave. Surrey, V3X 3A3 Canada
604-596-7733, Fax: 604-596-4197,
www.sd36.bc.ca

Grades: Kindergarten - 12; Adult Education
Enrollment: 67293
Number of Schools: 99 elementary schools; 19 secondary schools; 5 student learning centres; 4 adult education centres.
Number of Employees: 8,700 (including approximately 5,000 teachers)
Laurae McNally, Chair, 604-531-1091, fax: 604-542-2613
mcnally_laurae@sd36.bc.ca
Mike McKay, Superintendent, Schools, 604-596-7733 469
Sharon Cohen, Deputy Superintendent, 604-596-7733 469
Rick Fabbro, Assistant Superintendent, 604-596-7733 470
Alan Jones, Assistant Superintendent, 604-596-7733 471
John Ormond, Assistant Superintendent, 604-596-7733 478
David Paul, Assistant Superintendent, 604-596-7733 471
Rick Ryan, Assistant Superintendent, 604-596-7733 470
Brett Raycroft, District Principal, 604-596-7733 435
Wayne D. Noye, Secretary-Treasurer, 604-596-7733 416

Terrace: Coast Mountains School District #82
3211 Kenney St. Terrace, V8G 3E9 Canada
250-635-4931, Fax: 250-635-4287

Enrollment: 6379
Randy Smalbrugge, Supt.
rsmalbrugge@cmsd.bc.ca
Marcel Aboriginal, Sec.-Treas.
Rob Greenwood, Aboriginal Education Contact, 250-638-4403, fax: 250-638-4287

Trail: Kootenay-Columbia School District #20
#120, 1290 Esplanade Trail, V1R 4T2 Canada
250-368-6434, Fax: 250-364-2470, 888-316-3338
www.sd20.bc.ca

Enrollment: 4926
Jean Borsa, Superintendent
jborsa@sd20.bc.ca
Kim Morris, Sec.-Treas.
Christine Marsh, Aboriginal Education Program Coordinator, 250-364-1275 241

Vancouver: Vancouver School District #39
1580 West Broadway Ave. Vancouver, V6J 5K8 Canada
604-713-5000, Fax: 604-713-5049,
info@vsb.bc.ca
www.vsb.bc.ca

Grades: K.-12
Enrollment: 59182
Steve Cardwell, Supt., 604-713-5100, fax: 604-713-5412
scardwell@vsb.bc.ca
Brenda Ng, Sec.-Treas., 604-713-5080, fax: 604-713-5049
bng@vsb.bc.ca
Debra Martel, Aboriginal Education Contact, 604-713-5682, fax: 604-713-5076
dmartel@vsb.bc.ca

Vanderhoof: Nechako Lakes School District #91
P.O. Box 129
153 E. Connaught St. Vanderhoof, V0J 3A0 Canada
250-567-2284, Fax: 250-567-4639,
www.sd91.bc.ca

Grades: K.-12
Enrollment: 5500
Ray LeMoigne, Supt.
rlemoigne@mail.sd91.bc.ca
Sterling Olson, Sec.-Treas.
solson@mail.sd91.bc.ca
Libby McDiarmid, Aboriginal Education Contact, 250-567-2284, fax: 250-567-4639

Vernon: Vernon School District #22
1401 - 15 St. Vernon, V1T 8S8 Canada
250-542-3331, Fax: 250-549-9200,
district_web@sd22.bc.ca
www.sd22.bc.ca

Grades: Pre-K.-12
Enrollment: 9047
Bev Rundell, Supt., 250-549-9226
brundell@sd22.bc.ca
Randy Hoffman, Sec.-Treas., 250-549-9205
rhoffman@sd22.bc.ca
Sandra Lynxleg, Aboriginal Education Contact, 250-542-3331
slynxleg@sd22.bc.ca

Victoria: Greater Victoria School District #61
556 Boleskine Rd. Victoria, V8Z 1E8 Canada
250-475-3212, Fax: 250-475-6161,
Alternative Ed., Phone: 250-360-4321; Continuing Ed: 250-360-4332
Trustees@sd61.bc.ca
www.sd61.bc.ca

Grades: Kindergarten - 12; Continuing Ed.
Enrollment: 20000
Number of School: 26 elementary schools; 10 middle schools; 7 secondary schools
Tom Ferris, Board Chair, 250-889-0689
tferris@sd61.bc.ca
John Gaiptman, Superintendent, Schools
Sherri Bell, Associate Superintendent
Pat Duncan, Associate Superintendent
Chris Harvey, Associate Superintendent
Deborah Courville, District Principal
Ted Pennell, Director, Information Technology
Jim Soles, Supervisor, Building Projects
Ross Walker, Supervisor, Construction
George Ambeault, Secretary-Treasurer

Victoria: Sooke School District #62
3143 Jacklin Rd. Victoria, V9B 5R1 Canada
250-474-9800, Fax: 250-474-9825,
info@sd62.bc.ca
www.sd62.bc.ca

Enrollment: 8500
Jim Cambridge, Superintendent
jcambridge@sd62.bc.ca
David Lockyer, Sec.-Treas.
Kathleen King-Hunt, Aboriginal Education Contact, 250-474-9879, fax: 250-474-9825

West Vancouver: West Vancouver School District #45
1075 - 21st St. West Vancouver, V7V 4A9 Canada
604-981-1000, Fax: 604-981-1001,
info@sd45.bc.ca
www.sd45.bc.ca

Grades: K.-12
Enrollment: 6758
Geoff Jopson, Supt., 604-981-1034
gjopson@sd45.bc.ca
Ellen Forsyth, Sec.-Treas., 604-981-1048
eforsyth@sd45.bc.ca
Jody Langlois, Aboriginal Education Contact, 604-981-1095, fax: 604-981-1096
jlanglois@sd45.bc.ca

Williams Lake: Cariboo-Chilcotin School District #27
School Administration Office
350 - 2nd Ave. North Williams Lake, V2G 1Z9 Canada
250-398-3833, Fax: 250-392-3600,
www.sd27.bc.ca

Grades: Kindergarten - 12; Adult Education
Enrollment: 6800
Number of Employees: 1,000+
Wayne Rodier, Chair, 250-305-7981
wayne.rodier@sd27.bc.ca
Diane Wright, Superintendent, Schools, 250-398-3824, fax: 250-392-3600
diane.wright@sd27.bc.ca
Harj Manhas, Assistant Superintendent, 250-398-3810, fax: 250-398-7871
harjinder.manhas@sd27.bc.ca
Mark Wintjes, Director, Instruction for Human Resources
mark.wintjes@sd27.bc.ca
Doug Gorcak, Manager, Facilities & Transportation, 250-398-3877, fax: 250-392-2202
doug.gorcak@sd27.bc.ca
Ken Matieshen, District Principal, Information Technology, 250-305-7955
Bonnie Roller, Secretary-Treasurer, 250-398-3801, fax: 250-392-3600
bonnie.roller@sd27.bc.ca

Schools: Specialized

Hearing Impaired

Burnaby: BC Provincial School for the Deaf
c/o Burnaby South Secondary School
5455 Rumble St. Burnaby, V5J 2B7 Canada
604-664-8560, Fax: 604-664-8561

Grades: 1-12
Enrollment: 75
M. Henderson, Principal
mhenders@south.sd41.bc.ca

Distance Education

Chilliwack: Fraser Valley Distance Education
49520 Prairie Central Rd. Chilliwack, V2P 6H3 Canada
604-794-7310, Fax: 604-795-8480, 800-663-3381
www.fvdes.com

Grades: K.-12
Enrollment: 537
Trish Williams, Principal
twilliams@fvdes.com

Courtenay: North Island Distance Education
2505 Smith Rd. Courtenay, V9J 1T6 Canada
250-898-8999, Fax: 250-898-8883, 800-663-7925
principal@nides.bc.ca
www.nides.bc.ca

Grades: K.-12
Enrollment: 466
Sheila Shanahan, Principal
sshanahan@nides.bc.ca

Creston: SelfDesign Learning Community
P.O. Box 747
Creston, V0B 1G0 Canada

604-224-3640, Fax: 604-224-3662,
info@selfdesign.org
www.selfdesign.org

Grades: K.
Enrollment: 652
Brent Cameron, Principal
brentcameron@selfdesign.org

Fort St John: **Northern BC Distance Education**
10511 - 99 Ave. Fort St John, V1J 1V6 Canada
250-261-5660, Fax: 250-785-1188, 800-663-9511
info@nbcdes.com
www.des.prn.bc.ca

Grades: K.-12
Enrollment: 228
Randy Pauls, Principal

Grindrod: **Christian Homelearner's eStreams**
P.O. Box 162
Grindrod, V0E 1Y0 Canada
250-838-5979, Fax: 250-838-5979, 877-777-1547
info@estreams.ca
www.estreams.ca

Grades: K.-12
Enrollment: 211
H. Hunt, Principal

Kelowna: **Heritage Christian Online School**
905 Badke Rd. Kelowna, V1X 5Z5 Canada
250-862-2376, Fax: 250-762-9277, 877-862-2375
info@onlineschool.ca
www.onlineschool.ca

Grades: K.-12
Enrollment: 864
Greg Bitgood, Superintendent

Merritt: **South Central Interior Distance Education School**
P.O. Box 4700 Main
2475 Merritt Ave. Merritt, V1K 1B8 Canada
250-378-4245, Fax: 250-378-1447, 800-663-3536
www.scides.com

Grades: K.-12
Enrollment: 137
Al Mackay-Smith, Principal, 800-663-3536 1200

Nelson: **Distance Education School of the Kootenays**
811 Stanley St. Nelson, V1L 1N8 Canada
250-354-4311, Fax: 250-505-7007, 800-663-4614
www.desk.bc.ca

Grades: K-12
Dan Dalgaard, Principal

Prince George: **Central Interior Distance Education**
P.O. Box 7400
1270 - 2nd Ave. Prince George, V2L 3B3 Canada
250-563-1818, Fax: 250-563-1150, 800-661-7515
www.cides.sd57.bc.ca

Grades: K.-12
Enrollment: 188
Steve Fleck, Principal

Salmon Arm: **Anchor Academy**
7201 Hurst Rd. Salmon Arm, V1E 4R8 Canada
250-832-2754, Fax: 250-832-4379, 888-917-3783
anchor@ark.net
www.ark.net

Grades: K.-12
Enrollment: 405
Howard Hunt, Principal & Missions Coordinator

Surrey: **Traditional Learning Academy (DL)**
6225C - 136 St. Surrey, V3X 1H3 Canada
604-572-3441, Fax: 604-572-7832, 866-576-3001
principal@schoolathome.ca
www.schoolathome.ca

Grades: K.-12
Enrollment: 334
Karen Gledhill, Principal

Terrace: **North Coast Distance Education**
P.O. Box 5000
3211 Kenney St. Terrace, V8G 5K2 Canada
250-635-7944, Fax: 250-638-2399, 800-663-3865
www.ncdes.ca

Grades: K.-12
Enrollment: 220
Cindy Sousa, Principal
Cindy.Sousa@cmsd.bc.ca

Vancouver: **Vancouver Learning Network**
530 East 41st Ave. Vancouver, V5W 1P3 Canada
604-713-5520, Fax: 604-713-5528,
vln@vsb.bc.ca
www.gvdes.com

Grades: K.-12
Enrollment: 578
Cindy Gauthier, Principal
cgauthier@gvdes.com

Victoria: **South Island Distance Education**
4575 Wilkinson Rd. Victoria, V8Z 7E8 Canada
250-704-4979, Fax: 250-479-9870, 800-663-7610
sides@sides.ca
www.sides.sd63.bc.ca

Grades: K.-12
Enrollment: 626
Kevin White, Principal

Schools: Independent & Private

Catholic

Burnaby: **Holy Cross Elementary**
1450 Delta Ave. Burnaby, V5B 3G2 Canada
604-299-3530, Fax: 604-299-3534,
hcoffice@telus.net
www.holycrosselementary.ca

Grades: K.-7
Enrollment: 224
Dino Alberti, Principal

North Vancouver: **Holy Trinity Elementary School**
128 - 27 St. West North Vancouver, V7N 2H1 Canada
604-987-4454, Fax: 604-987-0360,
holyt@telus.net
www.holytschool.org; www.holytrinityparish.ca

Grades: K.-7
Enrollment: 233
Kevin Smith, Principal

Penticton: **Holy Cross Elementary School**
1298 Main St. Penticton, V2A 5G2 Canada
250-492-4480, Fax: 250-490-4602,
www.holyc.com

Grades: K.-7
Enrollment: 145
Jeff Brophy, Principal

Port Coquitlam: **Archbishop Carney Regional Secondary School**
1335 Dominion Ave. Port Coquitlam, V3B 8G7 Canada
604-942-7465, Fax: 604-942-5289,
admin@acrss.org
www.acrss.org

Grades: 8-12
Enrollment: 720
Lorraine Paruzzolo, Principal
paruzzol@acrss.org

Powell River: **Assumption Catholic School**
7091 Glacier St. Powell River, V8A 1R8 Canada
604-485-9894, Fax: 604-485-7984,
assump.office@shaw.ca
www.assumpschool.com

Grades: K.-9
Enrollment: 186
Accredited by the B.C. Min. of Education. Curriculum includes math, sciences, social studies, physical education, languages, music, art, drama, & relgion.
Mimi Richardson, Principal

Surrey: **Cloverdale Catholic School**
17511 - 59th Ave. Surrey, V3S 1P3 Canada
604-574-5151, Fax: 604-574-5160,
office@ccsunited.ca
ccsunited.ca

Grades: Preschool; K.-7
Enrollment: 245
Jason Borkowski, Principal

Vancouver: **Corpus Christi School**
6344 Nanaimo St. Vancouver, V5P 4K7 Canada
604-321-1117, Fax: 604-321-1410,
mkcc@telus.net
www.corpuschristi-school.ca

Grades: K.-7
Enrollment: 241
Rosa Natola, Principal

First Nations

Iskut: **Klappan Independent Day School**
P.O. Box 60
Iskut, V0J 1K0 Canada
250-234-3561, Fax: 250-234-3562,
www.bced.gov.bc.ca

Grades: K.-9
Enrollment: 41
Serving students of Iskut First Nation.
Carolyn Ann Doody, Principal
carolyn_ann_doody@hotmail.com

Independent & Private Schools

100 Mile House: **Cariboo Christian School**
P.O. Box 670
550 Exeter Truck Rd. 100 Mile House, V0K 2E0 Canada
250-395-4637

Grades: Kindergarten - 9

Abbotsford: **Abbotsford Christian School**
35011 Old Clayburn Rd. Abbotsford, V2S 7L7 Canada
604-850-5730, Fax: 604-850-6978,
administration@abbotsfordchristian.com
www.abbotsfordchristian.com

Grades: K.-12
Enrollment: 1014
Daryl Verbeek, Executive Director

Abbotsford: **Cornerstone Christian School**
P.O. Box 520 Main
Abbotsford, V2S 5Z5 Canada
604-859-7867, Fax: 604-859-7860,
principal@cornerstoneschool.ca

Grades: K.-12
Enrollment: 176
M. Dana, Principal

Abbotsford: **Dasmesh Punjabi School**
33094 South Fraser Way Abbotsford, V2S 2A9 Canada
604-852-8986, Fax: 604-852-8924,
dastaff@telus.net

Grades: K.-10
Enrollment: 397
Dalip Singh Gill, Principal

Abbotsford: **Mennonite Educational Institute / MEI**
4081 Clearbrook Rd. Abbotsford, V4X 2M8 Canada
604-859-3700, Fax: 604-859-9206,
www.meisoc.com

Grades: Preschool - 12
Enrollment: 1774
The British Columbia curriculum is taught from a Biblical perspective.
Tim Regehr, President
Peter Froese, Superintendent
Ernest Janzen, Principal, Elementary
Dave Loewen, Principal, Chilliwack
David Neufeld, Principal, Secondary
dneufeld@meisoc.com
Heather Smith, Principal, Middle
Jeff Gamache, Vice Principal, Elementary
Rick Thiessen, Vice Principal, Secondary
rthiessen@meisoc.com
Grant Wardle, Vice Principal, Middle
Mr. M. Friesen, Business Adminstrator

Abbotsford: **St. James School**
2767 Townline Rd. Abbotsford, V2T 5E1 Canada
604-852-1788, Fax: 604-850-5376

Grades: K.-7
Enrollment: 219
J. Lindenbach, Principal
principal.stjames@shaw.ca

Abbotsford: **St. John Brebeuf**
2747 Townline Rd. Abbotsford, V2T 5E1 Canada
604-855-0571, Fax: 604-855-0572,
office@stjohnbrebeuf.ca
www.stjohnbrebeuf.com

Grades: 8-12
Enrollment: 347
C. Blesch, Principal

Abbotsford: **Valley Christian School / VCS**
32721 Cherry Ave. Abbotsford, V2V 2T8 Canada
604-826-1388, Fax: 604-826-2744,
info@valleychristianschool.ca
www.valleychristianschool.ca

Grades: Preschool - 9
The preschool program works with children, ages three & four. A home school program is supported by the interdenominational school.
Ken Keis, Chair, Board of Directors
Bill Humphreys, Principal
Bob Barclay, Business Administrator

***Agassiz:* Agassiz Christian School**
7571 Morrow Rd. Agassiz, V0M 1A2 Canada
604-796-9310, Fax: 604-796-9519,
agchris@shawcable.com
Grades: K.-7
Enrollment: 58
J. Zuidhof, Principal

***Agassiz:* Seabird Island Community School**
P.O. Box 930
5 Chowat Rd. Agassiz, V0M 1A0 Canada
604-796-3061, Fax: 604-796-3068,
principal@seabirdschool.ca
Grades: K.-12
Enrollment: 162
M. Point, Principal

***Ahousat:* Maaqtusiis School**
General Delivery Ahousat, V0R 1A0 Canada
250-670-9589, Fax: 250-670-9543
Grades: K.-12
Enrollment: 217
Gregory Louie, Principal
gwl_princeapple@yahoo.com

***Aldergrove:* Aldergrove Christian Academy**
4057 - 248 St. Aldergrove, V4W 1E3 Canada
604-856-2577, Fax: 604-857-0088,
academy@rosbc.com
Grades: K.-12
Enrollment: 335
G. Wickens, Principal

***Aldergrove:* Fraser Valley Adventist Academy**
P.O. Box 249
Aldergrove, V4W 2T8 Canada
604-607-3822, Fax: 604-856-1002,
fvaa@fvaa.net
Grades: K.-12
Enrollment: 307
K. Honey, Principal

***Alert Bay:* T'lisalagi'lakw School**
P.O. Box 50
Alert Bay, V0N 1A0 Canada
250-974-5591, Fax: 250-974-2475,
gloriaa@namgis.bc.ca
Grades: K.-11
Enrollment: 79
G. Alfred, Principal

***Armstrong:* North Okanagan Junior Academy**
4699 South Grandview Flats Rd. Armstrong, V0E 1B5 Canada
250-546-8330, Fax: 250-546-8343,
info@noja.ca
www.noja.ca
The Academy is operated by the Seventh-day Adventist Church.
Marilyn Ilchuk, B.Sc., Principal
marilynilchuk@aol.com
Sharon Trussell, B.Sc., M.A., Vice Principal
shrbet@shaw.ca
Cameron Koronko, Pastor
koronkoc@hotmail.com

***Bella Coola:* Acwsalcta Band School**
P.O. Box 778
Bella Coola, V0T 1C0 Canada
250-799-5911, Fax: 250-799-5576,
principal@acwsalcta.com
Grades: K.-12
Enrollment: 127
V. Latvala, Principal

***Bowen Island:* Island Pacific School**
P.O. Box 128
671 Carter Rd. Bowen Island, V0N 1G0 Canada
604-947-9311, Fax: 604-947-9366,
info@islandpacific.org
Grades: 6-9
Enrollment: 50
E. Spear, Principal

***Burnaby:* Deer Lake SDA School**
5550 Gilpin St. Burnaby, V5G 2H6 Canada
604-434-5844, Fax: 604-434-5845,
office@deerlakeschool.ca
Grades: K.-10
Enrollment: 192
C. Erickson, Principal

***Burnaby:* John Knox Christian School**
8260 - 13 Ave. Burnaby, V3N 2G5 Canada
604-522-1410, Fax: 604-522-4606,
admin@johnknoxbc.org
Grades: K.-7
Enrollment: 310
A. Ferguson, Principal

***Burnaby:* Kenneth Gordon School**
7855 Meadow Ave. Burnaby, V3N 2V8 Canada
604-524-5224, Fax: 604-524-8297
Grades: Elem. Ungraded
Enrollment: 85
Eithne Harrison, Principal
joniharrison@shaw.ca

***Burnaby:* Our Lady of Mercy School**
7481 - 10 Ave. Burnaby, V3N 2S1 Canada
604-526-7121, Fax: 604-520-3194,
admin@ourladyofmercy.ca
www.ourladyofmercy.ca
Grades: K.-7
Enrollment: 240
N. Grout, Principal

***Burnaby:* St. Francis de Sales School**
6656 Balmoral St. Burnaby, V5E 1J1 Canada
604-435-5311, Fax: 604-434-4798
Grades: K.-7
Enrollment: 217
Cecilia McLaren, Principal
cmclaren@cisva.bc.ca

***Burnaby:* St. Helen's School**
3894 Triumph St. Burnaby, V5C 1Y7 Canada
604-299-2234, Fax: 604-299-3565,
sthelens@telus.net
Grades: K.-7
Enrollment: 352
Waldemar Sambor, Principal

***Burnaby:* St. Michaels School**
9387 Holmes St. Burnaby, V3N 4C3 Canada
604-526-9768, Fax: 604-540-9799,
ckennedy@cisva.bc.ca
Grades: K.-7
Enrollment: 216
C. Kennedy, Principal

***Burnaby:* St. Thomas More Collegiate**
7450 - 12 Ave. Burnaby, V3N 2K1 Canada
604-521-1801, Fax: 604-520-0725,
www.stmc.bc.ca
Grades: 8-12
Enrollment: 666
D. Hall, Principal
principal@stmc.bc.ca

***Burnaby:* Vancouver Christian School, Carver Christian High School**
7650 Sapperton Ave. Burnaby, V3N 4E1
604-523-1580, Fax: 604-523-9646,
www.vancouverchristian.org; www.carverchristian.org
Grades: 9 - 12

***Campbell River:* Campbell River Christian School / CRCS**
250 South Dogwood St. Campbell River, V9W 6Y7 Canada
250-287-4266, Fax: 250-287-3130,
crcs@oberon.ark.com
www.crcs.bc.ca
Grades: Kindergarten - 12
Neil Steinke, Principal
ns-admin-crcs@uniserve.com

***Chemainus:* St. Joseph's School**
9735 Elm St. Chemainus, V0R 1K0 Canada
250-246-3191, Fax: 250-246-2921,
sjc@cisdv.bc.ca
Grades: K.-7
Enrollment: 115
B. Cleary, Principal

***Chetwynd:* Peace Christian School**
P.O. Box 2050
5124, 46th Ave. Chetwynd, V0C 1J0 Canada
250-788-2044, Fax: 250-788-2579,
pcs@persona.ca
Grades: K.-10
Enrollment: 74
S. Lee, Principal

***Chilliwack:* Highroad Academy**
46641 Chilliwack Central Rd. Chilliwack, V2P 1K3 Canada
604-792-4680, Fax: 604-792-2465,
info@highroadacademy.com
www.highroadacademy.com
Grades: K.-12
Enrollment: 430
Dave Shinness, Principal
dshinness@highroadacademy.com

***Chilliwack:* John Calvin School**
4268 Stewart Rd. Chilliwack, V2R 5G3 Canada
604-823-6814, Fax: 604-823-6791,
office@jcss.ca
Grades: K.-7
Enrollment: 170
Pieter H. Torenvliet, Principal

***Chilliwack:* Mount Cheam Christian School**
48988 Yale Rd. East Chilliwack, V2P 6H4 Canada
604-794-3072, Fax: 604-794-3078,
office@mccsbc.com
Grades: Kindergarten - 12
Enrollment: 360
Adrian Stoutjesdyk, B.Ed. M.Ed., Principal

***Chilliwack:* St. Mary's School**
8909 Mary St. Chilliwack, V2P 4J4 Canada
604-792-7715, Fax: 604-792-7031,
principalstmary@telus.net
Grades: K.-7
Enrollment: 183
M. McDermott, Principal

***Chilliwack:* Timothy Christian School**
50420 Castleman Rd. Chilliwack, V2P 6H4 Canada
604-794-7114, Fax: 604-794-3520,
office@tcs.chilliwack.bc.ca
Grades: Kindergarten - 12
Enrollment: 367
Doug Stam, Principal

***Chilliwack:* Unity Christian School, Elementary Campus / UCS**
Elementary Campus
P.O. Box 371
9750 McNaught Rd. Chilliwack, V2P 6J4 Canada
604-792-4171, Fax: 604-792-0640,
elementary@unitychristian.ca; general@unitychristian.ca
www.unitychristian.ca
Grades: Preschool - 6
A Christ-centered education is provided by Unity Christian School.
Ed Noot, Principal
Jeanette Berkenbosch, Vice Principal

***Chilliwack:* Unity Christian School, Secondary Campus / UCS**
Secondary Campus
P.O. Box 371
50950 Hack-Brown Rd. Chilliwack, V2P 6J4
604-794-7797, Fax: 604-794-7667,
general@unitychristian.ca
www.unitychristian.ca
Grades: 7 - 12
Unity Christian School offers a Christ-centered education.

***Cobble Hill:* Evergreen Independent School**
P.O. Box 166
Cobble Hill, V0R 1L0 Canada
250-743-2433, Fax: 250-743-2570,
evergreen@evergreenbc.net
Grades: K.-6
Enrollment: 63
J. Ovans, Principal

***Coquitlam:* Coquitlam College**
516 Brookmere Ave. Coquitlam, V3J 1W9 Canada
604-939-6633, Fax: 604-939-0336,
admiss@coquitlamcollege.com
www.coquitlamcollege.com
Grades: 11-12
Enrollment: 85
W. Eckford, Principal

***Coquitlam:* Eagle Ridge Montessori Elementary**
2541 Quay Pl. Coquitlam, V3S 3H7 Canada
604-469-9166, Fax: 604-469-9168,
info@ermontessori.com
Grades: K.-6
Enrollment: 38
V. Lawrie, Principal

***Coquitlam:* Mediated Learning Academy**
550 Thompson Ave. Coquitlam, V3J 3Z8 Canada

604-937-3641, Fax: 604-937-3642,
info@mediatedlearningacademy.org
Grades: K.-12
Enrollment: 84
K. Jeffrey, Principal

Coquitlam: **Our Lady of Fatima School**
315 Walker St. Coquitlam, V3K 4C7 Canada
604-936-4228, Fax: 604-936-4403,
info@fatimaschool.ca
www.fatimaschool.ca
Grades: K.-7
Enrollment: 388
Maria Katsionis, Principal

Coquitlam: **Queen of All Saints Elementary School / QAS**
1405 Como Lake Ave. Coquitlam, V3J 3P4 Canada
604-931-9071, Fax: 604-931-9089,
queenofallsaintsschool@shawcable.com
www.queenofallsaintsschool.ca
Grades: Kindergarten - 7
Queen of All Saints Elementary School was established by the Roman Catholic Archdiocese of Vancouver. The school belongs to All Saints Parish.
Oscar Pozzolo, Principal
Mrs. J. Sussex, Vice Principal
Father Tien Tran, Pastor

Coquitlam: **Traditional Learning Academy / TLA**
1189 Rochester Ave. Coquitlam, V3K 2X3 Canada
604-931-7265, Fax: 604-931-3432,
tlaprincipal@traditionallearning.com (E-mail, Principal)
tlaoffice@traditionallearning.com
www.traditionallearning.com
Traditional Learning Academy encourages students to know the Catholic faith.
Allan Garneau, Administrator

Cranbrook: **Kootenay Christian Academy**
1200 Kootenay St. North Cranbrook, V1C 5X1 Canada
250-426-0166, Fax: 250-426-0186,
kca12@shaw.ca
Grades: K.-9
Enrollment: 142
J. Markuson, Principal

Cranbrook: **St. Mary's Catholic Independent School**
1701 - 5 St. South Cranbrook, V1C 1K1 Canada
250-426-5017, Fax: 250-426-5076,
jmacneil@cintek.com
Grades: K.-6
Enrollment: 143
J. Macneil, Principal

Dawson Creek: **Mountain Christian School / MCS**
11501 - 17th St. Dawson Creek, V1G 4S7 Canada
250-782-9528, Fax: 250-782-3888,
mcs@shawcable.com
www.mcsed.ca
Grades: Kindergarten - 12
Enrollment: 94
Trevor Ragan, Principal

Dawson Creek: **Notre Dame School**
925 - 104th Ave. Dawson Creek, V1G 2H8 Canada
250-782-4923, Fax: 250-782-4388,
www.notredamedc.org/notre-dame-school
Grades: Kindergarten - 7
Enrollment: 150
Notre Dame School provides a Catholic education.
Mrs. Terri Haynal, Principal

Dawson Creek: **Ron Pettigrew Christian School**
1761 - 110th Ave. Dawson Creek, V1G 4X4 Canada
250-782-4580, Fax: 250-782-9805,
rpcs@pris.ca
Grades: Kindergarten - 12
Enrollment: 75
Phyllis Roch, Principal

Delta: **Delta Christian School**
4789 - 53 St. Delta, V4K 2Y9 Canada
604-946-2514, Fax: 604-946-2589,
deltachristian@telus.net
Grades: K.-7
Enrollment: 169
G. de Vos, Principal

Delta: **Immaculate Conception School**
8840 - 119 St. Delta, V4C 6M4 Canada
604-596-6116, Fax: 604-596-4338,
immaculate_conception_school@hotmail.com
Grades: K.-7
Enrollment: 473
W. MacCormack, Principal

Delta: **Sacred Heart School**
P.O. Box 10 Main
3900 Arthur Dr. Delta, V4K 3N5 Canada
604-946-2611, Fax: 604-946-0598,
office@shsdelta.org
www.shsdelta.org
Grades: K.-7
Enrollment: 400
D. Schollen, Principal
dschollen@shsdelta.org

Delta: **Southpointe Academy**
1741 - 56 St. Delta, V4L 2B2 Canada
604-948-8826, Fax: 604-948-8853,
school@spacademy.ca
www.southpointeacademy.ca
Grades: K.-12
Enrollment: 425
G. Baldwin, Principal
graham.baldwin@spacademy.ca

Duncan: **Duncan Christian School**
495 Beech Ave. Duncan, V9L 3J8 Canada
250-746-3654, Fax: 250-746-3615,
office@duncanchristianschool.ca
Grades: K.-12
Enrollment: 276
C. Davis, Principal

Duncan: **Island Oak High School**
P.O. Box 873 Main
Duncan, V9L 3Y2 Canada
250-701-0400, Fax: 250-701-0400,
mail@islandoak.org
Grades: 9-12
Enrollment: 40
R. Tibbetts, Principal

Duncan: **Queen Margaret's School / QMS**
660 Brownsey Ave. Duncan, V9L 1C2 Canada
250-746-4185, Fax: 250-746-4187,
www.qms.bc.ca
Grades: Junior Kindergarten - 12
Queen Margaret's School consists of a coeducational junior school for students from junior kindergarten to grade seven. The school also consists of an All-Girls High School, which offers a university preparatory program. An English as a Second Language Program is available for beginner & advanced students.
Michael DeBeck, Chair
Ms. Pat Rowantree, Head of School
prowantree@qms.bc.ca
Chad Holtum, Deputy Head, Operations
choltum@qms.bc.ca
Sharon Klein, Deputy Head, Student Life & Senior School Pri
sklein@qms.bc.ca
Stuart Hall, Junior School Principal
shall@qms.bc.ca
Celina Mason, Director, Residential Life & Student Support
Julie Scurr, Director, Finance & Privacy Officer
Shannon Peck, Coordinator, Admissions & Marketing
Cheryl Skinn, Coordinator, Student Life

Duncan: **Queen of Angels Catholic School**
2085 Maple Bay Rd. Duncan, V9L 5L9 Canada
250-746-5919, Fax: 250-746-8689,
info@queenofangels.ca
www.queenofangels.ca
Grades: Preschool - 9
Tina Campagne, Chair, Local School Council
Art Therrien, Principal
Ciaran McLaverty, Vice Principal
Lana Durand, Coordinator, Special Education
Denika Osmond, Secretary

Duncan: **Sunrise Waldorf School**
4344 Peters Rd. Duncan, V9L 6M3 Canada
250-743-7253, Fax: 250-743-7245,
mail@sunrisewaldorfschool.org
www.sunrisewaldorfschool.org
Grades: K.-8
Enrollment: 162
J. Canty, Principal

Fernie: **Fernie Academy**
P.O. Box 2677
Fernie, V0B 1M0 Canada
250-423-0212, Fax: 250-423-4799
Grades: K.-7
Enrollment: 97
J. Sombrowski, Principal
jsombrowski@fernieacademy.com

Fort Nelson: **Chalo School**
Mile 293, RR#1 Fort Nelson, V0C 1R0 Canada
250-774-7655, Fax: 250-774-7651,
chalo@gmail.com
www.chaloschool.bc.ca
Grades: Preschool - 12
Enrollment: 200
Fort Nelson First Nation owns & operates Chalo School.
Celine Kotchea, Chair

Fort St James: **Nak'albun Elementary School**
P.O. Box 1390
Fort St James, V0J 1P0 Canada
250-996-8441, Fax: 250-996-2229,
www.nakalbun.com
Grades: Kindergarten - 7
Enrollment: 60
The elementary school is operated under the jurisdiction of Nak'azdli Band.
Rick Aucoin, Principal
nkbprincipal@fsjames.com

Fort St John: **Christian Life School**
8923 - 112th Ave. Fort St John, V1J 5H8 Canada
250-785-1437, Fax: 250-785-4852,
office@christianlifeschool.ca
www.christianlifeschool.ca
Grades: Kindergarten - 12; Christianity
Lynette Kovacs, Chair, 250-785-1437
Don Irwin, Principal
dirwin@christianlifeschool.ca

Fort St John: **Maccabee Christian School**
P.O. Box 6771 Main
Fort St John, V1J 4J2 Canada
250-772-5010, Fax: 250-772-5009
F. Roscher, Principal

Fort Ware: **Aatse Davie School**
P.O. Box 79
Fort Ware, V0J 3B0 Canada
250-471-2002, Fax: 250-471-2080,
aatse@pris.bc.ca
www.kwadacha.com
Grades: K.-12
Enrollment: 84
The school serves the Kwadacha First Nation. In addition to the standard humanities & sciences curriculum, classes in the Tsek'ene language are taught.
Andreas Rohrbach, Principal

Hazelton: **Kispiox Junior Secondary School**
RR#1, SK C 128 Hazelton, V0J 1Y0 Canada
250-842-6148, Fax: 250-842-5799,
kispiox@bc.firstnationschools.ca
Grades: K.-8
Enrollment: 86
R. Steinbeisser, Principal

Houston: **Houston Christian School**
P.O. Box 237
Houston, V0J 1Z0 Canada
250-845-7736, Fax: 250-845-7738,
hcschool@telus.net
Grades: K.-12
Enrollment: 131
Jack Vanden Born, Principal

Kamloops: **Kamloops Christian School**
750 Cottonwood Ave. Kamloops, V2B 3X2 Canada
250-376-6900, Fax: 250-376-6904,
heatherb@kamcs.org
Grades: K.-12
Enrollment: 363
T. Rogers, Principal

Kamloops: **Our Lady of Perpetual Help School**
235 Poplar St. Kamloops, V2B 4B9 Canada
250-376-2343, Fax: 250-376-2361,
rose@olphschool.ca
www.olphschool.ca
Grades: K.-7
Enrollment: 181
Rose Nowicki, Principal
rose@olphschool.ca

Kamloops: **St. Ann's Academy**
205 Columbia St. Kamloops, V2C 2S7 Canada

250-372-5452, Fax: 250-372-5257, www.stannsacademy.bc.ca
Grades: K.-12
Enrollment: 480
S. Chisholm, Principal
principal@stannsacademy.bc.ca

Kelowna: First Lutheran Christian School
4091 Lakeshore Rd. Kelowna, V1W 1V7 Canada
250-764-3111, Fax: 250-764-3129
Grades: K.-6
Enrollment: 64
T. Hennig, Principal
thennig@firstlutheran.ca

Kelowna: Heritage Christian School
907 Badke Rd. Kelowna, V1X 5Z5 Canada
250-862-2377, Fax: 250-862-4943, office@heritagechristian.ca
www.heritagechristian.ca
Grades: K.-12
Enrollment: 308
Greg Bitgood, Principal
gbitgood@heritagechristian.ca

Kelowna: Immaculata Catholic Regional High School
1493 K.L.O. Rd. Kelowna, V1W 3N8 Canada
250-762-2730, Fax: 250-861-3028, secretary@immaculatakelowna.ca
www.immaculatakelowna.ca
Grades: Secondary; Religious education
Enrollment: 350
Number of Employees: 26 (including 14 teachers)
John Campbell, B.Sc., Dip.Ed. M.Ed., Principal
principal@immaculatakelowna.ca
Edward Frison, B.Ed., Vice-Principal
vice_principal@immaculatakelowna.ca
Fr. Wayne Pfliger, Chaplain
chaplain@immaculatakelowna.ca
Mary Gallagher, B.Ed, Coordinator, Religious Education
religion@immaculatakelowna.ca
Nadine Casorso, Librarian
ncasorso@immaculatakelowna.ca
Chris Schmidt, Librarian
cschmidt@immaculatakelowna.ca
Lois Ehman, B.Ed., Contact, Special Education Department
lhorizons@immaculatakelowna.ca

Kelowna: Kelowna Christian School
2870 Benvoulin Rd. Kelowna, V1W 2E3 Canada
250-861-3238, Fax: 250-861-4844, berne.watters@kelownachristian.ca
Grades: K.-12
Enrollment: 802
B. Watters, Principal

Kelowna: Kelowna Christian School
2870 Benvoulin Rd. Kelowna, V1W 2E3 Canada
250-861-3238, Fax: 250-861-4844
Grades: K.-9
Enrollment: 195
B. Watters, Principal
berne.watters@kelownachristian.ca

Kelowna: Kelowna Waldorf School
PO Box 29093, RPO Okanagan Mission Kelowna, V1W 4A7 Canada
250-764-4130, Fax: 250-764-4139, info@kelownawaldorfschool.com
Grades: K.-7
Enrollment: 107
D. Lane, Principal

Kelowna: Okanagan Adventist Academy
1035 Hollywood Rd. Kelowna, V1X 4N3 Canada
250-860-5305, Fax: 250-868-9703, okaa@shaw.ca
www.okaa.ca
Grades: K.-12
Enrollment: 135
Don Straub, Principal
dstraub@okaa.ca

Kelowna: St. Joseph Elementary School
839 Sutherland Ave. Kelowna, V1Y 5X4 Canada
250-763-3371, Fax: 250-763-2740, school@stjosephkelowna.ca
www.stjosephkelowna.ca
Grades: K.-7
Enrollment: 316
R. Smith, Principal

Kelowna: Vedanta Academy
1180 Houghton Rd. Kelowna, V1X 2C9 Canada
250-868-8816, Fax: 250-868-8836, www.vedantaacademy.com
Grades: Kindergarten - 12
C. Belliveau, Principal

Kitimat: St. Anthony's School
1750 Nalabila Blvd. Kitimat, V8C 1E6 Canada
250-632-6313, Fax: 250-632-6313, stanthonys@citywest.ca
Grades: K.-7
Enrollment: 150
Most Rev. P. Cornthwaite, Principal

Ladysmith: Stu"ate Lelum Secondary School
P.O. Box 730
Ladysmith, V9G 1A5 Canada
250-245-3522, Fax: 250-245-8263, len.merriman@cfnation.com
Grades: GA
Enrollment: 76
L. Merriman, Principal

Langley: Credo Christian Schools
21846 - 52 Ave. Langley, V2Y 2M7 Canada
604-530-5396, Fax: 604-530-8965, H.Moes@Credochs.com
Grades: K.-12
Enrollment: 470
H. Moes, Principal

Langley: Langley Christian School
21789 - 50 Ave. Langley, V3A 3T2 Canada
604-533-2222, Fax: 604-533-7276, elem@langleychristian.com
Grades: K.-12
Enrollment: 813
H. Vanderveen, Principal

Langley: Langley Montessori School
19785 - 55A Ave. Langley, V3A 3X1 Canada
604-534-1556, Fax: 604-532-4358, langleymontessori@telus.net
Grades: K.
Enrollment: 65
U. Hodgson, Principal

Langley: St. Catherines School
20244 - 32 Ave. Langley, V2Z 2E1 Canada
604-534-6564, Fax: 604-534-4871, www.stcatherines.ca
Grades: K.-7
Enrollment: 229
A. Castellon, Principal
acastellon@stcatherines.ca

Langley: Whytecliff Agile Learning Centre-Langley
20561 Logan Ave. Langley, V3A 7R3 Canada
604-532-1268, Fax: 604-532-1269, mlinski@focusbc.org
Grades: 7-11
Enrollment: 49
M. Linski, Principal

Lantzville: Aspengrove School
7660 Clark Dr. Lantzville, V0R 2H0 Canada
250-390-2201, Fax: 250-390-2281, cgrunlund@aspengroveschool.ca
aspengroveschool.ca
Grades: K.-12
Enrollment: 190
Accredited International Baccalaureate programs for primary and middle years; core academic subjects, as well as performing arts, physical and outdoor education, community service.
Zinda Fitzgerald, Head of School

Lax Kw'Alaams: Lax Kw Alaams Academy
11 Lagaic St. Lax Kw'Alaams, V0V 1H0 Canada
604-625-3207, Fax: 604-625-3425, principal@laxkwalaamsacademy.net
Grades: K.-10
Enrollment: 152
S. Campbell, Principal

Lillooet: Fountainview Academy
P.O. Box 500
Lillooet, V0K 1V0 Canada
250-256-5400, Fax: 250-256-5499
Grades: 9-12
Enrollment: 58
B. Corrigan, Principal
bcorrigan@fountainview.ca

Lister: Bountiful Elementary - Secondary School
P.O. Box 226
1070 JRB Rd. Lister, V0B 1Y0 Canada
250-428-4679, Fax: 250-428-4789, bountifulschool@gmail.com
www.bountifulschool.org
Grades: Kindergarten - 12
Bountiful Elementary - Secondary School prrovides education for members of the FLDS faith.
Merrill R. Palmer, Principal

Lister: Mormon Hills Elementary Secondary School
P.O. Box 725
Lister, V0B 1Y0 Canada
250-428-4800, Fax: 250-428-4810, mormonhillsschool@yahoo.ca
Grades: Kindergarten - 11
Enrollment: 191
Jeff Banman, Principal

Lytton: Stein Valley Nlakapamux School
PO Bag 300 Lytton, V0K 1Z0 Canada
250-455-2522, Fax: 250-455-2512, steinvalleyschool@yahoo.com
Grades: K.-12
Enrollment: 109
C. Holmes, Principal

Mackenzie: Mackenzie Christian Academy
P.O. Box 2406
Mackenzie, V0J 2C0 Canada
250-997-4000, Fax: 250-997-3800, ward@ljcc.ca
Grades: K.-8
Enrollment: 36
W. McGowan, Principal

Mansons Landing: Linnaea School
P.O. Box 98
Mansons Landing, V0P 1K0 Canada
250-935-6747, Fax: 250-935-6413, school@linneafarm.org
Grades: K.-8
Enrollment: 57
D. Bracewell, Principal

Maple Ridge: James Cameron School
P.O. Box 157 Del Ctr.
Maple Ridge, V2X 7G1 Canada
604-465-8444, Fax: 604-465-4561, jcsadmin@jcs.bc.ca
Grades: 2-7
Enrollment: 55
G. Storteboom, Principal

Maple Ridge: Maple Ridge Christian School
12140 - 203 St. Maple Ridge, V2X 2S5 Canada
604-465-4442, Fax: 604-465-1685, jroxburgh@mrcs.ca
Grades: K.-12
Enrollment: 322
R. Roxburgh, Principal

Maple Ridge: Meadowridge School
12224 - 240th St. Maple Ridge, V4R 1N1 Canada
604-467-4444, Fax: 604-467-4989
Grades: K.-12
Enrollment: 450
H. Burke, Principal
hburke@meadowridge.bc.ca

Maple Ridge: St. Patrick's School
22589 - 121 Ave. Maple Ridge, V2X 3T5 Canada
604-467-1571, Fax: 604-467-2686
Grades: K.-7
Enrollment: 214
Irene Wihak, Principal
iwihak@cisva.bc.ca

Merritt: Lower Nicola Band School
181 Nawishaskin Lane Merritt, V1K 1N2 Canada
250-378-5527, Fax: 250-378-6389
Grades: K.-12
Enrollment: 60
D. Sterling, Principal
dsterling@lnib.net

Merville: Comox Valley Christian School
P.O. Box 425
Merville, V0R 2M0 Canada
250-337-5335, Fax: 250-337-5632, cvcs4u@island.net
Grades: K.-9
Enrollment: 112

R. Janzen, Principal

Mill Bay: Brentwood College School
2735 Mount Baker Rd. Mill Bay, V0R 2P1 Canada
250-743-5521, Fax: 250-743-2911,
admissions@brentwood.bc.ca
www.brentwood.bc.ca

Grades: 9 - 12
Brentwood College School is a co-educational university prep school.
Andrea Pennells, Head, Brentwood College School
amp@brentwood.bc.ca
John Allpress, Deputy Head, Advancement
allpress@brentwood.bc.ca
Marius Felix, Assistant Head, Campus Life
marius.felix@brentwood.bc.ca
John Garvey, Assistant Head, Administration
garveyj@brentwood.bc.ca
Clayton Johnston, Director, Admissions
clayton.johnston@brentwood.bc.ca
Dave McCarthy, Director, Academics
mccarthd@brentwood.bc.ca
Gerry Pennells, Director, University Planning
pennells@brentwood.bc.ca

Milner: King's School
21783 - 76B Ave. Milner, V0X 1T0 Canada
604-888-0969, Fax: 604-888-0977,
school@tkc.com
Grades: K.-12
Enrollment: 141
P. Thomas, Principal

Nanaimo: Malaspina International High School
900 Fifth St. Nanaimo, V9R 5S5 Canada
250-740-6317, Fax: 250-740-6470,
lewist@mala.bc.ca
Grades: 10-12
Enrollment: 121
T. Lewis, Principal

Nanaimo: Nanaimo Christian School / NCS
198 Holland Rd. Nanaimo, V9R 6W2 Canada
250-754-4512, Fax: 250-754-4271,
inquiries.ncs@shaw.ca
www.nanaimochristianschool.ca
Grades: Preschool - 12
John Reems, Principal
Brian De Schiffart, Vice Principal
Sue De Schiffart, Coordinator, Special Education

Nanoose Bay: Beacon Christian School
2210 Morello Rd. Nanoose Bay, V9P 9A9 Canada
250-468-9433, Fax: 250-468-7748,
beaconchristian@shaw.ca
Grades: Kindergarten - 3
Enrollment: 12
Barbara Judd, Principal
beacon.principal@shaw.ca

Nelson: Nelson Waldorf School
P.O. Box 165 Main
Nelson, V1L 5P9 Canada
250-352-6919, Fax: 250-352-6887,
info@nelsonwaldorf.org
www.nelsonwaldorf.org
Grades: Kindergarten - 8
The school offers Waldorf education to children in the West Kootenay area.
Beverley Barcham, General Administrator & Principal
Lisa Bramson, Coordinator, Special Needs
Diana Finley, Coordinator, Social Inclusion
Andromeda Drake, Bookkeeper

Nelson: St. Joseph's School
523 Mill St. Nelson, V1L 4S2 Canada
250-352-3041, Fax: 250-352-9188,
office@stjosephnelson.ca
www.stjosephnelson.ca

Grades: K.-6
Enrollment: 122
L. Luck, Principal

New Westminster: Purpose Independent Secondary School
40 Begbie St. New Westminster, V3M 3L9 Canada
604-526-2522, Fax: 604-526-6546,
info@purposesociety.org
www.purposesociety.org/purpose
Grades: 10 - 12
The program at The Purpose School is designed for students, aged fifteen to nineteen, who are unable to succeed in the traditional school system. A Purpose Secondary School education leads to a Standard Dogwood Diploma.
Phill Esau, Principal

North Vancouver: Bodwell High School
955 Harbourside Dr. North Vancouver, V7P 3S4 Canada
604-924-5056, Fax: 604-924-5058,
www.bodwell.edu/highschool

Grades: 8 - 12
Bodwell High School is a co-educational day & boarding school.
Stephen Smith, B.A., Dip. Ed., M.A., M.E, Principal
Cathy Lee, B.S.Sc., M.S.W., Director, Admissions

North Vancouver: L'École française internationale de Vancouver
French International School of Vancouver
4343 Starlight Way North Vancouver, V7N 3N8 Canada
604-924-2457, Fax: 604-924-4483,
info@efiv.org
www.efiv.org

Grades: Mat./Prim.
Enrollment: 125
Programme du Ministère de l'Éducation Nationale Français, enrichi par des cours d'histoire, de géographie et des cultures du Canada.
Jérémy Harrison, Directeur (par intérim)

North Vancouver: Lions Gate Christian Academy
420 Seymour River Pl. North Vancouver, V7H 1S8 Canada
604-984-8226, Fax: 604-984-8254,
lgca@telus.net
Grades: K.-7
Enrollment: 181
D. North, Principal

North Vancouver: St. Edmund's School
535 Mahon Ave. North Vancouver, V7M 2R7 Canada
604-988-7364, Fax: 604-988-7350,
www.stedmunds.ca
Grades: K.-7
Enrollment: 204
Michael Field, Principal
mfield@stedmunds.ca

North Vancouver: St. Pius X Elementary School
1150 Mount Seymour Rd. North Vancouver, V7G 1R6 Canada
604-929-0345, Fax: 604-929-5051,
stpiusxschool@telus.net
Grades: K.-7
Enrollment: 227
Fabio Battisti, Principal

North Vancouver: St. Thomas Aquinas School
541 Keith Rd. West North Vancouver, V7M 1M5 Canada
604-987-4431, Fax: 604-987-7816,
office@aquinas.org
www.aquinas.org
Grades: 8-12
Enrollment: 601
F. Dragojevich, Principal
dragojevich@aquinas.org

North Vancouver: Vancouver Waldorf School
2725 St. Christophers Rd. North North Vancouver, V7K 2B6 Canada
604-985-7435, Fax: 604-985-4948,
board@vws.ca (E-mail, Board of Trustees)
reception@vws.ca
www.vws.ca
Grades: Preschool - 12
Vancouver Waldorf School integrates the movement arts & artistic activities throughout the curriculum.
Rea Gill, Administrator
Robert Adams, Administrator, High School
Mary Paradis, Director, Development
Fiona Thatcher, Director, Admissions, 604-985-7435 200
admissions@vws.ca

Oliver: Sen Pok Chin
#2 McKinney Rd. Oliver, V0H 1T0 Canada
250-498-2019, Fax: 250-498-3096,
office@senpokchin.com
www.senpokchin.com
Grades: K.-7
Enrollment: 36
R. Laurie, Principal
principal@senpokchin.com

Penticton: Penticton Community Christian School
P.O. Box 910 Main
Penticton, V2A 6J9 Canada
250-493-5233, Fax: 250-276-4124,
office@pentictonchristianschool.ca
www.pentictonchristianschool.ca
Grades: K.-12
Enrollment: 54
K. Boehmer, Principal
kboehmer@pentictonchristianschool.ca

Port Alberni: Haahuupayak School
6000 Santu Dr. Port Alberni, V9Y 7M2 Canada
250-724-5542, Fax: 250-724-7335,
ha-ak-sap@hotmail.com
www.haahuupayak.com
Grades: K.-6
Enrollment: 79
Tricia McAuley, Principal

Port Alberni: Port Alberni Christian School
4283 Glenside Rd. Port Alberni, V9Y 5W9 Canada
250-723-2700, Fax: 250-723-5799
Grades: K.-7
Enrollment: 36
M. Walker, Principal

Port Coquitlam: British Columbia Christian Academy
1019 Fernwood Ave. Port Coquitlam, V3B 5A8 Canada
604-941-8426, Fax: 604-945-6455,
admissions@bcchristianacademy.ca
www.bcchristianacademy.ca
Grades: Preschool - 12
British Columbia Christian Academy is an interdenominational Christian school.
Mr. I. Jarvie, Head Principal
ijarvie@bcchristianacademy.ca
Mr. T. Bryerton, Elementary Principal
tbryerton@bcchristianacademy.ca
Ms. T. Cota, Director, Preschool, Out Of School, Daycare
tcota@bcchristianacademy.ca
Mr. D. Dowell, Director, Foreign Studies & Continuing Educat
ddowell@bcchristianacademy.ca
Ms. Tko, Librarian
library@bcchristianacademy.ca

Port Coquitlam: Hope Lutheran Elementary
3151 York St. Port Coquitlam, V3B 4A7 Canada
604-942-5322, Fax: 604-942-5311
Grades: K.-8
Enrollment: 190
M. Towriss, Principal
mtowriss@hopelutheranschool.com

Port Coquitlam: Our Lady of the Assumption School
2255 Fraser Ave. Port Coquitlam, V3B 6G8 Canada
604-942-5522, Fax: 604-942-8313,
info@assumptionschool.com
www.assumptionschool.com
Grades: K.-7
Enrollment: 244
J. Brophy, Principal

Port Hardy: Avalon Adventist Junior Academy
P.O. Box 974
Port Hardy, V0N 2P0 Canada
250-949-8243, Fax: 250-949-6770,
www.aaja.ca
Grades: Kindergarten - 10
Wesley Bradford, P.E., Principal
wbradford@vandercook.edu
Karen Wallace, Vice Prinicipal
karenwallace1166@gmail.com

Port Hardy: Gwa'sala-'Nakwaxda'xw School
P.O. Box 1799
Port Hardy, V0N 2P0 Canada
250-949-7743, Fax: 250-949-7422,
www.gwanak.bc.ca
Grades: K.-7
Enrollment: 82
Independent First Nation's school
Barry Prong, Principal

Prince George: Cedars Christian School
701 North Nechako Rd. Prince George, V2K 1A2 Canada
250-564-0707, Fax: 250-564-0729,
www.cedars.bc.ca
Grades: Preschool - 12
Cedars Christian School is a non-denominational school.
Judy Serup, Chair

Prince George: Gateway Christian School
P.O. Box 1089
Prince George, V2L 4V2 Canada

250-563-8585, Fax: 250-563-3488,
gcsadmin@telus.net

Grades: K.-12
Enrollment: 126
M. Kostamo, Principal

Prince George: Immaculate Conception School
3285 Cathedral Ave. Prince George, V2N 5R2 Canada
250-964-4362, Fax: 250-964-9465,
iconceptoffice@shawcable.com

Grades: K.-7
Enrollment: 181
D. O'Callaghan, Principal

Prince George: Sacred Heart School
785 Patricia Blvd. Prince George, V2L 3V5 Canada
250-563-5201, Fax: 250-563-5201,
shspg@netbistro.com
www.shspg.com

Grades: K.-7
Enrollment: 104
K. Harnish, Principal
kharnish@netbistro.com

Prince George: St. Mary's School
1088 Gillett St. Prince George, V2M 2V3 Canada
250-563-7502, Fax: 250-563-7818,
coachbrent@stmaryspg.org
www.stmaryspg.org

Grades: K.-7
Enrollment: 199
B. Arsenault, Principal

Prince George: Westside Academy
3791 Hwy. 16 West Prince George, V2N 5P8 Canada
250-964-9600,
waoffice@telus.net; webmaster@westsideacademy.ca
www.westsideacademy.ca

Grades: Kindergarten - 12
Westside Academy is a ministry of Westside Family Fellowship.
Robert Tower, School Principal
rob@westsideacademy.ca
Donna Rosenbaum, School Dean
drosenbaum@westsideacademy.ca
Shannon Dimler, School Secretary & Admissions Coordinator
shannon@westsideacademy.ca

Prince Rupert: Annunciation School
627 - 5 Ave. West Prince Rupert, V8J 1V1 Canada
250-624-5873, Fax: 250-627-4486,
annun@citytel.net

Grades: K.-7
Enrollment: 197
M. McDermott, Principal

Quesnel: North Cariboo Christian School / NCCS
2876 Red Bluff Rd. Quesnel, V2J 6C7 Canada
250-747-4417, Fax: 250-747-4410,
office@nccschool.ca
www.nccschool.ca

Grades: Kindergarten - 9
Enrollment: 63
The North Cariboo Christian School is a non-denominational school.
John Hengen, Principal

Quesnel: St. Ann's School
150 Sutherland Ave. Quesnel, V2J 2J5 Canada
250-992-6237, Fax: 250-992-6234,
principal.stanns@shawcable.com

Grades: K.-7
Enrollment: 71
R. Nieman, Principal

Richmond: BC Muslim School
12300 Blundell Rd. Richmond, V6W 1B3 Canada
604-270-2511, Fax: 604-270-2679,
admin@bcmuslimschool.ca
www.bcmuslimschool.ca

Grades: Kindergarten - 7
BC Muslim School offers an accredited Arabic program.
Farida Wahab, Principal

Richmond: Choice School
Main Campus
20451 Westminster Hwy. North Richmond, V6V 1B3 Canada
604-273-2418, Fax: 604-273-2419,
info@choiceschool.org
www.choiceschool.org

Grades: Pre-Kindergarten - 8
Choice School offers gifted education to talented & gifted children.
Ken Affolder, Principal

Richmond: Cornerstone Christian Academy
7890 No. 5 Rd. Richmond, V6Y 2V2 Canada
604-303-9181, Fax: 604-303-9187,
cca@cebccanada.com
www.cebccanada.com

Grades: K.-7
Enrollment: 141
Associated with the Cornerstone Evangelical Baptist Church located on the same property.
W. Kushnir, Principal

Richmond: Richmond Christian School / RCS
5240 Woodwards Rd. Richmond, V7E 1H1 Canada
604-272-5720, Fax: 604-272-7370,
info@richmondchristian.ca
www.richmondchristian.ca

Grades: Preschool - 5
Enrollment: 400
The Richmond Christian Elementary School is an independent school, which offers a Christ-centered curriculum.
Richard Macdonald, Chair
Roger Grose, Systems & Elementary Campus Principal
Hugh Mawby, Vice Principal, Elementary Campus
Aza Nakagawa, Business Manager
Darlene Neufeld, Coordinator, Educational Support Services
Judy Sawatsky, Secretary, Elementary Campus & Admissions

Richmond: Richmond Christian School / RCS
10200 No. 5 Rd. Richmond, V7A 4E5
604-274-1122, Fax: 604-274-1128,
info@richmondchristian.ca
www.richmondchristian.ca

Grades: 6 - 8
Enrollment: 200
The Richmond Christian Middle School provides a Christ-centred community for students.

Richmond: Richmond Christian School / RCSS
10260 No. 5 Rd. Richmond, V7A 4E5
604-274-1122, Fax: 604-274-1128,
info@richmondchristian.ca
www.richmondchristian.ca

Grades: 9 - 12
Enrollment: 233
The Richmond Christian Secondary School is an independent school, where students grow academically, physically, & spiritually.

Richmond: Richmond Jewish Day School / RJDS
8760 No. 5 Rd. Richmond, V6Y 2V4 Canada
604-275-3393, Fax: 604-275-9322,
www.rjds.ca

Grades: Preschool - 7
Richmond Jewish Day School incorporates Hebrew & Judaic studies with the British Columbia curriculum.
Jeff Moss, Co-President, Board of Directors
Alan Seltzer, Co-President, Board of Directors
Rebecca Coen, Head of School
rcoen@rjds.ca
Dee Jacobs, Director, Preschool
djacobs@rjds.ca
Mary Jane Brown, Business Manager
mjbrown@rjds.ca
Malki Moshkovitz, Counsellor
mmoshkovitz@rjds.ca
Kelly Koyanagi, Administrative Assistant
kkoyanag@rjds.ca.ca

Richmond: St. Joseph the Worker School
4451 Williams Rd. Richmond, V7E 1J7 Canada
604-277-1115, Fax: 604-272-5214,
office@stjo.richmond.bc.ca

Grades: K.-7
Enrollment: 222
M. Jacob, Principal

Richmond: St. Paul's School
8251 St. Alban's Rd. Richmond, V6Y 2L2 Canada
604-277-4487, Fax: 604-277-1810,
principal@stpaulschool.ca
www.stpaulschool.ca

Grades: K.-7
Enrollment: 241
Nicole Regush, Principal

Salmon Arm: King's Christian School
350B - 30th St. NE Salmon Arm, V1E 1J2 Canada
250-832-5200, Fax: 250-832-5201,
info@kingschristianschool.com

Grades: K.-12
Enrollment: 214
D. Demeter, Principal

Shawnigan Lake: Maxwell International Baha'i School
P.O. Box 1000
Shawnigan Lake, V0R 2W0 Canada
250-743-7144, Fax: 250-743-3522

Grades: 7-12
Enrollment: 145
D. Vaillancourt, Principal
danv@maxwell.bc.ca

Shawnigan Lake: Shawnigan Lake School
RR#1, 1975 Renfrew Rd. Shawnigan Lake, V0R 2W0 Canada
250-743-5516, Fax: 250-743-6200,
info@sls.bc.ca

Grades: 8-12
Enrollment: 444
D. Robertson, Principal

Smithers: Bulkley Valley Christian School / BVCS
Secondary Campus
P.O. Box 3635
Smithers Smithers, V0J 2N0 Canada
250-847-4238,
250-857-9833 (Elementary); 250-847-4238 (Distributed Learning)
www.bvcs.ca

Grades: Elementary / Secondary
Bulkley Valley Christian School offers an program for international students.
Klaas Kort, Principal, Elementary Campus, 250-857-9833
Chris Steenhof, Principal, Distributed Learning, 250-847-4238
Hugo VanderHoek, Principal, Secondary Campus, 250-847-4238
Glenda Posthuma, Business Adminstrator, 250-847-4238
John Buikema, Director, Development, Academic Cousellor, &, 250-847-4238

Smithers: Ebenezer Canadian Reformed School
P.O. Box 3700
1685 Lower Viewmount Rd. Smithers, V0J 2N0 Canada
250-847-3492, Fax: 250-847-3912,
ebenezer@bulkley.net

Grades: K.-12
Enrollment: 133
D. Stoffels, Principal

Smithers: Moricetown Elementary School
#2, 205 Beaver Rd., RR#1 Smithers, V0J 2N1 Canada
250-847-3166, Fax: 250-877-5092,
school@moricetown.ca
www.moricetown.ca

Grades: Elementary

Smithers: St. Joseph's School
P.O. Box 454
4054 Broadway Ave. Smithers, V0J 2N0 Canada
250-847-9414, Fax: 250-847-9402,
stjosephs@telus.net

Grades: K.-7
Enrollment: 191
S. Forbrigger, Principal

South Hazelton: Gitsegukla Elementary School
21 Seymour Ave., RR#1 South Hazelton, V0J 2R0 Canada
250-849-5739, Fax: 250-849-5276,
roy.sakata@gitsegukla.org
www.gitsegukla.org

Grades: K.-7
Enrollment: 60
Tuskasa Sakata, Principal

Summerland: Glenfir School
P.O. Box 1800
7808 Pierre Dr. Summerland, V0H 1Z0 Canada
250-494-0004, Fax: 250-494-0058, 1-866-494-0005
www.glenfir.com

Grades: Junior Kindergarten - 12
Dr. Justin Naude, Chair
justinnaude@shaw.ca
Craig Dunbar, Head of School
Mary Taylor, Managing Director
mtaylor@glenfir.com
Nikki Johnson, Director, Admissions
nikkijohnson@glenfir.com

Surrey: Bibleway Christian Academy / BCA
18603 - 60th Ave. Surrey, V3S 7P4 Canada
604-576-8188, Fax: 604-576-1370,
www.biblewayacademy.org

Grades: Kindergarten - 9
Julius Briner, President
Randall Timmermans, Principal

Surrey: Cornerstone Kindergarten
14724 - 84 Ave. Surrey, V3S 2M5 Canada

604-599-9918, Fax: 604-597-0468, corstone@telus.net
Grades: K.-7
Enrollment: 121
Rita Gausman, Principal

Surrey: Diamond Elementary
18620 - 56th Ave. Surrey, V3S 1G1 Canada
604-576-1146, Fax: 604-574-9831, relevantschool@shawlink.ca
Grades: K.-7
Enrollment: 159
Douglas Smith, Principal

Surrey: Fraser Valley Christian High School
15353 - 92 Ave. Surrey, V3R 1C3 Canada
604-581-1033, Fax: 604-581-1712, fvchs@fvchs.bc.ca
Grades: 8-12
Enrollment: 454
D. de Groot, Principal

Surrey: Heritage Christian School
3487 King George Hwy. Surrey, V4P 1B7 Canada
604-536-5967, Fax: 604-536-6073, hcs@telus.net
Grades: K.-12
Enrollment: 198
T. Bryerton, Principal

Surrey: Holy Cross Regional High School
16193 - 88 Ave. Surrey, V4N 1G3 Canada
604-581-3023, Fax: 604-583-4795, jfraser@idmail.com
Grades: 8-12
Enrollment: 797
Robert Dejulius, Principal

Surrey: Iqra School
14590 - 116A Ave. Surrey, V3R 2V1 Canada
604-583-7530, Fax: 604-583-7510, info@iqraschool.com
Grades: K.-8
Enrollment: 306
W. Ramadan, Principal

Surrey: Khalsa School (Surrey)
6933 - 124th St. Surrey, V3W 3W6 Canada
604-591-2248, Fax: 604-591-3396
Grades: K.-10
Enrollment: 1468
J. Bhatia, Principal
jsbhatia@khalsaschool.ca

Surrey: Our Lady of Good Counsel School
10504 - 139 St. Surrey, V3T 4L5 Canada
604-581-3154, Fax: 604-588-1633, olgcprincipal@shaw.ca
www.ourladyofgoodcounselschool.ca
Grades: K.-7
Enrollment: 245
G. Wright, Principal

Surrey: Pacific Academy
10238 - 168 St. Surrey, V4N 1Z4 Canada
604-581-5353, Fax: 604-581-0087, contact@papcs.com
www.pacificacademy.net
Grades: K.-12
Enrollment: 1450
Private Christian School
T. Kooy, Principal
tkooy@papcs.com

Surrey: Regent Christian Academy / RCA
15100 - 66A Ave. Surrey, V3S 2A6 Canada
604-599-8171, Fax: 604-599-8175, www.regent.bc.ca
Grades: Preschool - 13
Enrollment: 550
Regent Christian Academy is a coeducational school, which offers primary, middle, high school, English as a Second Language, & international programs.
Paul Johnson, Principal
Linda Mehus-Barber, Administrator, Middle Division
Allan Visser, Administrator, International Division
Amanda Whone, Administrator, Primary Division
Maureen Sayler, Registrar & Secretary

Surrey: Relevant Schools' Society
18620 Hwy. #10 Surrey, V3S 1G1 Canada
604-574-4736, Fax: 604-574-9831, relevantschool@shawlink.ca
www.relevanthighschool.ca
Grades: 8 - 12
Relevant High School is coeducational, non-denominational secondary school.

Surrey: Relevant Schools' Society
18620 Hwy. #10 Surrey, V3S 1G1
604-576-1146, Fax: 604-574-9831, diamondschool@shawlink.ca
www.relevanthighschool.ca
Grades: Kindergarten - 7

Surrey: Roots & Wings Montessori Place
5438 - 152nd St. Surrey, V3S 5J9 Canada
604-574-5399, Fax: 604-574-5319, info@rootsandwingsbc.com
www.rootsandwingsbc.com
Grades: Preschool - Elementary
Primary Montessori programs are offered for children between the ages of 2.5 & 5. The senior program at the school is designed for students from age 9 to 12.

Surrey: St. Bernadette School
13130 - 65B Ave. Surrey, V3W 9M1 Canada
604-596-1101, Fax: 604-596-1550, kkozack@cisva.bc.ca
Grades: K.-7
Enrollment: 227
K. Kozack, Principal

Surrey: Southridge Senior School
2656 - 160 St. Surrey, V3S 0B7 Canada
604-535-5056, Fax: 604-535-3676
Grades: 8-12
Enrollment: 260
M. Ayotte, Head of Senior School
mayotte@southridge.bc.ca

Surrey: Star of the Sea School
15024 - 24 Ave. Surrey, V4A 2H8 Canada
604-531-6316, Fax: 604-531-0171, www.starofthesea.bc.ca/school
Grades: K.-7
Enrollment: 316
L. Balsevich, Principal
lbalsevich@starofthesea.bc.ca

Surrey: Surrey Christian School
9115 - 160 St. Surrey, V4N 2X7 Canada
604-581-2474, Fax: 604-581-5211, primaryoffice@surreychristian.org
www.surreychristian.org
Grades: K.-8
Enrollment: 608
A. Stegeman, Principal

Surrey: White Rock Christian Academy
2265 - 152 St. Surrey, V4A 4P1 Canada
604-531-9186, Fax: 604-531-1727, wrca@wrca.bc.ca
Grades: K.-12
Enrollment: 308
L. Baerg, Principal

Surrey: William of Orange Christian School
P.O. Box 34090
17790 Hwy. 10 Surrey, V3S 8C4 Canada
604-576-2144, Fax: 604-576-0975, admin@wofo.org
Grades: K.-7
Enrollment: 106
J. Siebenga, Principal

Surrey: Zion Lutheran
5950 - 179 St. Surrey, V3S 4J9 Canada
604-576-6313, Fax: 604-576-1399, zionschool@telus.net
Grades: K.-9
Enrollment: 162
D. Davis, Principal

Terrace: Centennial Christian School
3608 Sparks St. Terrace, V8G 2V6 Canada
250-635-6173, Fax: 250-635-9385, ccs@telus.net
www.centennialchristian.ca
Grades: Preschool - 12
Curtis Tuininga, Principal
Edgars Veldman, Vice Principal

Terrace: Veritas Catholic School
4836 Straume Ave. Terrace, V8G 4G3 Canada
250-635-3035, Fax: 250-635-7588, www.veritascatholicschool.com
Grades: Kindergarten - 7
Colleen LeBlanc, Chair
Glen Palahicky, Principal
veritas.principal@telus.net
Isabel DeMedeiros, Secretary
veritas.class@telus.net

Trail: St. Michael's Elementary School
1329 - 4 Ave. Trail, V1R 1S3 Canada
250-368-6151, Fax: 250-368-9962, stmichaelsschool@shaw.ca
Grades: K.-7
Enrollment: 179
D. Nowicki, Principal

Vancouver: Blessed Sacrament School École Saint Sacrement
3020 Heather St. Vancouver, V5Z 3K3 Canada
604-876-7211, Fax: 604-876-7280, admin@ess.vancouver.bc.ca
moodle.ess.vancouver.bc.ca/moodle
Grades: Kindergarten - 7
Michael Yaptinchay, Director
michael.yaptinchay@ess.vancouver.bc.ca

Vancouver: Canadian College International
#200, 1050 Alberni St. Vancouver, V6E 1A3 Canada
604-688-9366, Fax: 604-688-9322, study@canadiancollege.com
www.canadiancollege.com
Enrollment: 300
Jim Clark, President & Owner
jim.clark@canadiancollege.com
Jeff Carter, Director, Academic
jeff.carter@canadiancollege.com
Cindy Kwon, Director, Marketing
cindy.kwon@canadiancollege.com

Vancouver: Century High School / CHS
#300, 1788 West Broadway Vancouver, V6J 1Y1 Canada
604-730-8138, Fax: 604-731-9542, admission@centuryhighschool.ca
www.centuryhighschool.ca
Grades: 8 - 12

Vancouver: Columbia College
#500, 555 Seymour St. Vancouver, V6B 6J9 Canada
604-683-8360, Fax: 604-682-7191, admin@columbiacollege.ca
www.columbiacollege.ca
Enrollment: 57
A liberal arts college offering 1st & 2nd year university transfer courses, associate degrees, university preparation programmes, adult secondary school completion, & English language instruction geared to international students.
Dr. Trevor Toone, Principal

Vancouver: Crofton House School
3200 - 41 Ave. West Vancouver, V6N 3E1 Canada
604-263-3255, Fax: 604-263-4941, www.croftonhouse.ca
Grades: Elem./Sec.; girls
Enrollment: 667
Patricia J. Dawson, Head of School
pdawson@croftonhouse.ca

Vancouver: Fraser Academy
2294 - 10 Ave. West Vancouver, V6K 2H8 Canada
604-736-5575, Fax: 604-736-5578, enesling@fraser-academy.bc.ca
Grades: 1-12
Enrollment: 188
E. Nesling, Principal

Vancouver: Immaculate Conception School
3745 - 28 Ave. West Vancouver, V6S 1S6 Canada
604-224-5012, Fax: 604-224-3721, chit-ics@shaw.ca
Grades: K.-7
Enrollment: 196
C. Riviere, Principal

Vancouver: Khalsa School (Vancouver)
5987 Prince Albert St. Vancouver, V5W 3E2 Canada
604-321-1226, Fax: 604-321-2709, khalsa13@telus.net
Grades: K.-7
Enrollment: 207
Amar Dhaliwal, Principal

Vancouver: King David High School
5718 Willow St. Vancouver, V5Z 4S9 Canada
604-263-9700, Fax: 604-263-4848
Grades: 8-12
Enrollment: 140

E. Seidelman, Principal
pseidelman@telus.net

Vancouver: Kingston High School
2026 - 12th Ave. West Vancouver, V6J 2G2 Canada
604-738-6273, Fax: 604-738-6974
Grades: Gr. 10-12
Enrollment: 138
Dr. K. Skau, Principal
kskau@exchange.kingston.edu

Vancouver: Little Flower Academy
4195 Alexandra St. Vancouver, V6J 4C6 Canada
604-738-9016, Fax: 604-738-5749,
lfa@lfabc.com
Grades: 8-12
Enrollment: 469
M. DeFreitas, Principal

Toronto: LSC Toronto
#400, 124 Eglinton Ave. West Toronto, M4R 2G8 Canada
416-488-2200, Fax: 416-488-2225,
toronto@lsc-canada.com
www.lsc-canada.com
David S. Diplock, Director

Calgary: LSC Calgary
140 4th Ave. SW. Suite 300, North Tower Calgary, T2P 3N3 Canada
403-662-2200, Fax: 403-662-2201,
calgary@lsc-canada.com
www.lsc-canada.com

Montréal: LSC Montréal
1610 Ste-Catherine W. Suite 401 Montréal, H3H 2S2 Canada
514-939-9911, Fax: 514-939-2223,
montreal@lsc-canada.com
www.lsc-canada.com

Vancouver: LSC Vancouver
570 Dusmuir St. Vancouver, V6B 1Y1 Canada
604-683-1199, Fax: 604-683-6088,
vancouver@lsc-canada.com
www.lsc-canada.com

Vancouver: Notre Dame Regional Secondary School
2855 Parker St. Vancouver, V5K 2T8 Canada
604-255-5454, Fax: 604-255-2115,
www.ndrs.ca
Grades: 8 - 12
Enrollment: 620
Notre Dame Regional Secondary School is a Catholic school.
Mr. R. DesLauriers, Principal
Mr. R. Gabriele, Vice Principal
Mr. G. Oswald, Vice Principal
Mrs. M. Grant, Manager, Office

Vancouver: Our Lady of Perpetual Help School
2550 Camosun St. Vancouver, V6R 3W6 Canada
604-228-8811, Fax: 604-224-6822
Grades: K.-7
Enrollment: 406
Lora Clarke, Acting Principal

Vancouver: Our Lady of Sorrows School
575 Slocan St. Vancouver, V5K 3X5 Canada
604-253-2434, Fax: 604-253-1523,
ourladyofsorrows1@telus.net
www.ourladyofsorrows.ca
Grades: K.-7
Enrollment: 231
P. Balletta, Principal

Vancouver: Pacific Spirit School
Jericho Hill Centre
4196 West 4th Ave. Vancouver, V6J 4J5 Canada
604-222-1900, Fax: 604-222-1934,
info@pacificspiritschool.org
www.pacificspiritschool.org
Grades: K.-7
Enrollment: 227
Formerly Life Song School, Pacific Spirit School is the flagship for the New Learning Society, which promotes and supports the growth of the whole child.
Ingrid Price, Ph.D., Executive Director

Vancouver: Royal Canadian College
8610 Ash St. Vancouver, V6P 3M2 Canada
604-738-2221, Fax: 604-738-2282,
info@royalcanadiancollege.com
Grades: 10-12
Enrollment: 52
H. Jiang, Principal

Vancouver: St. Andrew's School
450 - 47th Ave. East Vancouver, V5W 2B4 Canada
604-325-6317, Fax: 604-325-0920,
saintandrews@telus.net
Grades: K.-7
Enrollment: 227
M. Mailley, Principal

Vancouver: St. Anthony of Padua
1370 - 73rd Ave. West Vancouver, V6P 3E8 Canada
604-261-4043, Fax: 604-261-4036,
office@stanthonyofpaduaschool.ca
www.stanthonyofpaduaschool.ca
Grades: K.-7
Enrollment: 209
C. Kraemer, Principal

Vancouver: St. Augustine's School
2145 - 8 Ave. West Vancouver, V6K 2A5 Canada
604-731-8024, Fax: 604-739-1712,
info@faithandfoundation.com
www.faithandfoundation.com
Grades: K.-7
Enrollment: 224
Catherine Oberndorf, Principal

Vancouver: St. Francis of Assisi School
870 Victoria Dr. Vancouver, V5L 4E7 Canada
604-253-7311, Fax: 604-253-7375,
sfaprincipal@telus.net
Grades: K.-7
Enrollment: 191
Joan Sandberg, Principal

Vancouver: St. Francis Xavier School
428 Great Northern Way Vancouver, V5T 4S5 Canada
604-254-2714, Fax: 604-254-2514,
sfxs@telus.net
Grades: K.-7
Enrollment: 327
B. Krivuzoff, Principal

Vancouver: St. George's School
4175 - 29 Ave. West Vancouver, V6S 1V1 Canada
604-224-1304, Fax: 604-224-7066,
sradmin@stgeorges.bc.ca
www.stgeorges.bc.ca
Grades: 1-12
Enrollment: 1123
Day and boarding school for boys
Nigel Toy, Headmaster

Vancouver: St. John's International
1885 West Broadway Vancouver, V6J 1Y5 Canada
604-683-4572, Fax: 604-683-4679,
general@stjohnsis.com
www.stjohnsis.com
Grades: 8-12
Enrollment: 76
L. Fast, Principal

Vancouver: St. John's School
2215 - 10 Ave. West Vancouver, V6K 2J1 Canada
604-732-4434, Fax: 604-732-1074,
info@stjohns.bc.ca
www.stjohns.bc.ca
Grades: K.-12
Enrollment: 342
University prep school
S. Hutchison, Headmaster
shutchison@stjohns.bc.ca

Vancouver: St. Joseph's School
3261 Fleming St. Vancouver, V5N 3V6 Canada
604-872-5715, Fax: 604-872-5700,
stjosephsvancouver@telus.net
www.stjoesschool-vancouver.org
Grades: K.-7
Enrollment: 210
Dierdre O'Callaghan, Principal

Vancouver: St. Jude's School
2953 - 15 Ave. East Vancouver, V5M 2K7 Canada
604-434-1633, Fax: 604-434-8677,
stjude@shawcable.com
Grades: K.-7
Enrollment: 221
M. Perry, Principal

Vancouver: St. Mary's School
5239 Joyce St. Vancouver, V5R 4G8 Canada
604-437-1312, Fax: 604-437-1193
Grades: K.-7
Enrollment: 230
K. Smith, Principal
ksmith@cisva.bc.ca

Vancouver: St. Patrick Regional Secondary School
115 - 11 Ave. East Vancouver, V5T 2C1 Canada
604-874-6422, Fax: 604-874-5176,
administration@stpats.bc.ca
Grades: 8-12
Enrollment: 501
J. Bevacqua, Principal
jbevacqua@stpats.bc.ca

Vancouver: St. Patrick's Elementary School
2850 Quebec St. Vancouver, V5T 3A9 Canada
604-879-4411, Fax: 604-879-3737
Grades: K.-7
Enrollment: 249
M. Boreham, Principal
mboreham@shaw.ca

Vancouver: Stratford Hall
3000 Commercial Dr. Vancouver, V5N 4E2 Canada
604-436-0608, Fax: 604-436-0616,
info@stratfordhall.ca
www.stratfordhall.ca
Grades: K.-12
Enrollment: 370
J. McConnell, Principal

Vancouver: Vancouver Christian School / VCS
3496 Mons Dr. Vancouver, V5M 3E6 Canada
604-435-3113, Fax: 604-430-1591,
604-523-1580 (Phone, Carver Christian High School)
office@vancouverchristian.org
www.vancouverchristian.org
Grades: Kindergarten - 12
Vancouver Christian School is an independent, interdenominational school. Grades nine to twelve are offered at Carver Christian High School.
Mrs. E. Freestone, Principal
Mrs. Wiebe, Vice Principal, Kindergarten - Grade 5
Miss Wong, Vice Principal, Grades 6 to 8

Vancouver: Vancouver College
5400 Cartier St. Vancouver, V6M 3A5 Canada
604-261-4285, Fax: 604-261-2284,
info@vc.bc.ca
www.vc.bc.ca
Grades: Kindergarten - 12
Enrollment: 1000
Vancouver College consists of an elementary school, a middle school, & a senior school.
John McFarland, Principal
jmcfarland@vc.bc.ca
Mary-Joy Derouin, Assistant Principal, Senior School
Michel DesLauriers, Assistant Principal, Middle School
Barbara Seppelt, Assistant Principal, Elementary School
Kelly Lattimer, Business Manager
Ronith Cogswell, Athletic Director & Communications Officer
Mr. Kim Findlay, Chief Development Officer
Rev. John Horgan, Chaplain
Margaret Vossen, Registrar
Wade Anderson, Department Head, Physical Education
Monica Beck, Department Head, Student Services
Henry Budai, Department Head, Second Languages
Anne Field, Department Head, English
Br. Charles Gattone, Department Head, Religion
Marilia Marghetti, Department Head, Sciences
Enzo Nardi, Department Head, Mathematics
Larry Olson, Department Head, Applied / Fine Arts
Lilian Vernier, Department Head, Social Studies

Vancouver: Vancouver Hebrew Academy
1545 West 62nd Ave. Vancouver, V6P 2E8 Canada
604-266-1245, Fax: 604-264-0648,
vha@vhebrewacademy.com
www.vhebrewacademy.com
Grades: Preschool - 10
Vancouver Hebrew Academy is an Orthodox Jewish school which offers Judaic & general studies.
Rabbi Don Pacht, Head of School
Patricia Haslop, Principal
Nancy Scambler, Administrative Secretary

Vancouver: Vancouver Montessori School
8650 Barnard St. Vancouver, V6P 5G5 Canada
604-261-0315,
www.vancouvermontessorischool.com
Grades: Preschool - Elementary
Preschool (Casa) programs are available for three to six year old children. Elementary classes are offered for children from age six to twelve.
Prasannata Runkel, Principal

Roni (Bamendine) Jones, Administrator, School Operations
Chrystle Williams, Registrar & Administration Assistant

Vancouver: Vancouver Talmud Torah School / VTT
998 West 26th Ave. Vancouver, V5Z 2G1 Canada
604-736-7307, Fax: 604-736-9754,
info@talmudtorah.com
sites.google.com/a/vttschool.ca/vtt1/Home
Grades: Preschool - 7
Enrollment: 500
Vancouver Talmud Torah School is a Jewish day school.
Cathy Lowenstein, B.Ed., M.Ed., Principal
Janice St. Helene, Vice Principal, General Studies
Judith Wolfman, Vice Principal, Judaic Studies
Adam Gelmon, Director, Admissions & School-Wide Programs
Gaby Lutrin, Director, Preschool
Mark Maibauer, Director, Operations
Jessica Neville, Director, Student Services
Jennifer Shecter-Balin, Director, Communications

Vancouver: West Coast Christian School / WCCS
15 North Renfrew St. Vancouver, V5K 3N6 Canada
604-255-2990, Fax: 604-255-2103,
school@wccf.bc.ca
www.westcoastchristianschool.ca
Grades: Kindergarten - 12
Enrollment: 100
The school is a ministry of West Coast Christian Fellowship. It offers a Christian approach to learning.
David Ferguson, Principal
Marcellina Arnold, Secretary

Vancouver: West Point Grey Academy / WPGA
4125 West 8th Ave. Vancouver, V6R 4P9 Canada
604-222-8750, Fax: 604-222-8756,
604-224-1332 (Phone, Senior School)
admissions@wpga.ca
www.wpga.ca
Grades: Preschool - 12
Enrollment: 905
West Point Grey Academy demonstrates a belief in Humanism in its community of Renaissance learners. The pre-kindergarten class is for four year old children.
Robert Standerwick, Chair
boardchair@wpga.ca
Clive S.K. Austin, Headmaster
headmaster@wpga.ca
Stephen Anthony, Head, Senior School
headmaster@wpga.ca

Vancouver: York House School
4176 Alexandra St. Vancouver, V6J 2V6 Canada
604-736-6551, Fax: 604-736-6530,
info@yorkhouse.ca
Grades: K.-12
Enrollment: 598
G. Ruddy, Principal

Vanderhoof: Northside Christian School
3337 Voth Rd., RR#2 Vanderhoof, V0J 3A2 Canada
250-567-9335, Fax: 250-567-9332,
ncadmin@telus.net
Grades: 1 - 12
Enrollment: 67
Michael Shenk, Principal

Vanderhoof: Rainbow Christian School
P.O. Box 710
2994 Burrard Ave. Vanderhoof, V0J 3A0 Canada
250-567-3127, Fax: 250-567-3167,
rcschool@telus.net
Grades: Kindergarten - 8
Enrollment: 80
The day school offers a Christ-centered learning environment.

Vanderhoof: St. Joseph's School
P.O. Box 1429
Vanderhoof, V0J 3A0 Canada
250-567-2794, Fax: 250-567-2333,
gillis.stjoes1@telus.net
Grades: K.-7
Enrollment: 92
G. Gillis, Principal

Vernon: Pleasant Valley Christian Academy
1802 - 45th Ave. Vernon, V1T 3M7 Canada
250-545-7852, Fax: 250-545-9230,
pvadmin@shaw.ca
Grades: K.-9
Enrollment: 30
Affiliated with the Seventh-day Adventist Church
R. Tiller, Principal

Vernon: St. James School
2700 - 28 Ave. Vernon, V1T 1V7 Canada
250-542-4081, Fax: 250-542-5696,
principalsjs@shaw.ca
Grades: K.-7
Enrollment: 106
G. Higginson, Principal

Vernon: Vernon Christian School
Elementary Campus
6890 Pleasant Valley Rd. Vernon, V1B 3R5 Canada
250-545-7345, Fax: 250-545-0254,
info@vcs.ca
www.vcs.ca
Grades: Kindergarten - 12
Enrollment: 350
TVernon Christian School is an interdenominational school. The school's secondary campus is located at 6920 Pleasant Valley Road.
Karen Wiseman, Chair
kwiseman@vcs.ca
Larry Simpson, Principal
lsimpson@vcs.ca
Matt Driediger, Assistant Principal, Secondary Campus
mdriediger@vcs.ca
Steve Onsorge, Assistant Principal, Elementary Campus
sonsorge@vcs.ca

Victoria: Christ Church Cathedral School / CCCS
Cathedral Memorial Hall
912 Vancouver St. Victoria, V8V 3V7 Canada
250-383-5125, Fax: 250-383-5128,
cathedralschool@cathedralschool.ca (office)
www.cathedralschool.ca
Grades: Kindergarten - 8
Enrollment: 155
Christ Church Cathedral School is an Anglican school attached to a cathedral.
Mary Hendy, President
Charles Peacock, Head of School
head@cathedralschool.ca
Tobi Blue, Assistant Head, Elementary Grades
Marylee McKeown, Assistant Head, Middle & Intermediate Grades

Victoria: Glenlyon Norfolk School
801 Bank St. Victoria, V8S 4A8 Canada
250-370-6800, Fax: 250-370-6840,
gns@mygns.ca
www.glenlyonnorfolk.bc.ca
Grades: K.-12
Enrollment: 643
Simon Bruce-Lockhart, Head of School

Victoria: Greater Victoria Christian Academy
98 Cadillac Ave. Victoria, V8Z 1T4 Canada
250-475-2977, Fax: 250-475-2988,
deborah.arcuri@gvca.ca
Grades: K.-12
Enrollment: 179
L. Makaroff, Principal

Victoria: Lakeview Christian School
729 Cordova Bay Rd. Victoria, V8Y 1P7 Canada
250-658-5082, Fax: 250-658-5072,
lakeviewschool@shaw.ca
Grades: K.-7
Enrollment: 71
A. Oosterhof, Principal

Victoria: Lighthouse Christian Academy
1289 Parkdale Dr. Victoria, V9B 4G9 Canada
250-474-5311, Fax: 250-474-5021,
info@lighthousechristianacademy.com
Grades: K.-9
Enrollment: 70
D. Hunwick, Principal

Victoria: Maria Montessori Academy
4052 Wilkinson Rd. Victoria, V8Z 5A5 Canada
250-479-4746, Fax: 250-744-1925,
mma@montessori.bc.ca
Grades: K.-7
Enrollment: 95
B. McDermitt, Principal

Victoria: Pacific Christian School
654 Agnes St. Victoria, V8Z 2E7 Canada
250-479-9365, Fax: 250-479-3685,
www.pacificchristian.ca
Grades: K.-12
Enrollment: 1000
B. Helmus, Principal
bhelmus@pacificchristian.ca

Victoria: St. Andrew's Regional High School
880 Mckenzie Ave. Victoria, V8X 3G5 Canada
250-479-1414, Fax: 250-479-5356,
wjamieson@cisdv.bc.ca
www.standrewshigh.ca
Grades: 8-12
Enrollment: 469
W. Jamieson, Principal

Victoria: St. Andrew's School
1002 Pandora Ave. Victoria, V8V 3P5 Canada
250-382-3815, Fax: 250-385-3830,
kpollard@cisdv.bc.ca
Grades: K.-7
Enrollment: 188
K. Pollard, Principal

Victoria: St. Joseph's Catholic School
757 Burnside Rd. West Victoria, V8Z 1M9 Canada
250-479-1232, Fax: 250-479-1907,
sdicastri@cisdv.bc.ca
Grades: K.-7
Enrollment: 203
S. Di Castri, Principal

Victoria: St. Margaret's School
1080 Lucas Ave. Victoria, V8X 3P7 Canada
250-479-7171, Fax: 250-479-3244,
stmarg@stmarg.ca
www.stmarg.ca
Grades: K.-12
Enrollment: 325
L. Mcgregor, Principal
lmcgregor@stmarg.ca

Victoria: St. Michael's University School (Junior)
820 Victoria Ave. Victoria, V8S 4N3 Canada
250-598-3922, Fax: 250-592-0783,
nrichards@smus.ca
www.smus.ca
Grades: K.-5
Enrollment: 160
University prep boarding school
Nancy Richards, Principal

Victoria: St. Michael's University School (Middle)
3400 Richmond Rd. Victoria, V8P 4P5 Canada
250-592-3549, Fax: 250-592-3942,
www.smus.bc.ca
Grades: 6-8
Enrollment: 204
X. Abrioux, Principal
xabrioux@smus.bc.ca

Victoria: St. Michael's University School (Senior)
3400 Richmond Rd. Victoria, V8P 4P5 Canada
250-592-2411, Fax: 250-592-2812,
www.smus.bc.ca
Grades: 9-12
Enrollment: 573
K. Roth, Principal
kathy.roth@smus.bc.ca

Victoria: St. Patrick's School
2368 Trent St. Victoria, V8R 4Z3 Canada
250-592-6713, Fax: 250-592-6717,
pmckenna@cisdv.bc.ca
Grades: K.-7
Enrollment: 355
P. McKenna, Principal

Victoria: Selkirk Montessori School
2970 Jutland Rd. Victoria, V8T 5K2 Canada
250-384-3414, Fax: 250-384-3449,
office@selkirkmontessori.ca
www.selkirkmontessori.ca
Grades: K.
Enrollment: 202
G. Henry, Interim Academic Head

Victoria: West-Mont School
4075 Metchosin Rd. Victoria, V9C 4A4 Canada
250-474-2626, Fax: 250-478-8944,
info@west-mont.ca
www.west-mont.ca
Grades: Preschool - 7
West-Mont School provides a Montessori preschool to grade three. For students in grades four to seven, an enriched British Columbia curriculum is offered. The school is operated by the Western Communities Montessori Society.
Bruce Laurie, Principal

Cory Meausette, Vice Principal
Barbara Kennelly, Manager, Business
bkennelly@west-mont.ca
Barb Lewis, Head, Admissions
admissions@west-mont.ca

Waglisla: Bella Bella Community School / BBCS
General Delivery Waglisla, V0T 1Z0 Canada
250-957-2391, Fax: 250-957-2691,
Brendah@bellabella.net
www.bellabella.ca

Grades: Nursery - Secondary
Brenda Humchitt, Principal
Jason Cobey, Vice Principal
Frances Brown, Head, Heiltsuk Language Program

West Vancouver: Collingwood School
70 Morven Dr. West Vancouver, V7S 1B2 Canada
604-925-3331, Fax: 604-925-3862,
jonna.mcguinness@collingwood.org

Grades: K.-12
Enrollment: 1196
R. Wright, Principal

West Vancouver: Mulgrave School
2330 Cypress Lane West Vancouver, V7S 3H9 Canada
604-922-3223, Fax: 604-922-3328,
info@mulgrave.com
www.mulgrave.com

Grades: Kindergarten - 12
The coeducational, non-denominational school is an IB World School.
Donald Kirkwood, Chair
Tony Macoun, Head of School
tmacoun@mulgrave.com
Derek Muzyka, Head, Finance
dmuzyka@mulgrave.com
Graham Gilley, Director, Educational Technology
ggilley@mulgrave.com
Martin Jones, Director, Summer Camp Programmes
mjones@mulgrave.com
Luke Lawson, Director, University Counselling
Tony Macoun, Director, Advancement
tmacoun@mulgrave.com
Mark Steffens, Director, Community Relations
msteffens@mulgrave.com
Lesley Tetiker, Director, Admissions
ltetiker@mulgrave.com

West Vancouver: St. Anthony's School
595 Keith Rd. West Vancouver, V7T 1L8 Canada
604-922-0011, Fax: 604-922-3196,
office@saswv.ca
www.saswv.ca

Grades: K.-7
Enrollment: 204
Laila Maravillas, Principal
principal@saswv.ca

Westbank: Our Lady of Lourdes Elementary School
2547 Hebert Rd. Westbank, V4T 2J6 Canada
250-768-9008, Fax: 250-768-0168,
adminolol@telus.net
www.ourladyoflourdeswestbank.com

Grades: K.-7
Enrollment: 132
M. Manton, Principal

Westbank: Sensisyusten House of Learning
1920 Quail Lane Westbank, V4T 2H3 Canada
250-768-2802, Fax: 250-768-5462,
school@wfn.ca

Grades: K.-6
Enrollment: 36
R. Howardson, Principal

Williams Lake: Cariboo Adventist Academy
1405 South Lakeside Dr. Williams Lake, V2G 3A7 Canada
250-392-4741,
cacademy@yahoo.com
www.caribooadventistacademy.ca

Grades: Kindergarten - 12
The Cariboo Adventist Academy is operated by the Seventh-day Adventist Church.

Williams Lake: Maranatha Christian School
1278 Lakeview Cres. Williams Lake, V2G 1A3 Canada
250-392-7410, Fax: 250-392-2823,
maranatha@telus.net

Grades: K.-12
Enrollment: 128
C. Klaue, Principal

Williams Lake: Sacred Heart Catholic School
455 Pigeon Ave. Williams Lake, V2G 4R5 Canada
250-398-7770, Fax: 250-398-7725,
principal.shcs@telus.net

Grades: K.-7
Enrollment: 84
Donna Ameerali, Principal

Universities & Colleges

Universities

Abbotsford: Summit Pacific College
P.O. Box 1700
35235 Straiton Rd. Abbotsford, V2S 7E7 Canada
604-853-7491, Fax: 604-853-8951, 1-800-976-8388
www.summitpacific.ca

Formerly Western Pentecostal Bible College

Burnaby: Simon Fraser University
8888 University Dr. Burnaby, V5A 1S6 Canada
604-291-3111,
www.sfu.ca

Enrollment: 30313
Dr. Brandt C. Louie, Chancellor
Dr. Michael Stevenson, B.A., M.A, Ph.D., President & Vice-Chancellor
Dr. Jon Driver, Vice-President
Pat Hibbitts, B.A., M.B.A., Vice-President
Mario Pinto, Vice-President
William Krane, B.A., M.A., Ph.D., Assoc. Vice-President
Kate Ross, Registrar
Lynn Copeland, B.Sc., M.A., M.L.S., University Librarian & Dean
R. Szczotko, Manager
Biff Savoie, B.A., Director
Gregg Macdonald, B.A., M.A., Executive Director
Warren Gill, B.A., M.A., Ph.D., Vice-President
Joe Weinberg, Assoc. Vice-President
Judith Osborne, LL.B., M.A., LL.M., Vice-President
Joanne Curry, B.Sc., Ph.D., Executive Director
Cathy Daminato, Vice-President

<u>Faculties</u>
Applied Sciences
Brian Lewis, B.A., M.A., Ph.D., Dean

Arts
John T. Pierce, B.A., M.A., Ph.D., Dean

Business Administration
Daniel Shapiro, B.A., M.A., Ph.D., Dean

Continuing Studies
John Labrie, Ph.D., Dean

Education
Paul Shaker, B.A., M.A., Ph.D., Dean

Graduate Studies
Wade Parkhouse, B.P.E., M.P.E., Ph.D., Dean

Health Sciences
David MacLean, Ph.D., Dean

Science
Michael Plischke, B.Sc., M.Phil., Ph.D., Dean

<u>Publications</u>
Alumni Journal
c/o Simon Fraser University
8888 University Dr. Burnaby, V5A 1S6 Canada

The Peak

Kamloops: Thompson Rivers University
P.O. Box 3010
900 McGill Rd. Kamloops, V2C 5N3 Canada
250-828-5000, Fax: 250-828-5086, 800-663-1663
admissions@tru.ca
www.tru.ca

Enrollment: 7632
With distance-learning, enrolment figures swell to over 25,000 students.
The Hon Nancy Greene Raine, Chancellor
Dr Roger H. Barnsley, Interim President & Vice-chancellor, 250-828-5001
president@tru.ca
Dr Ulrich Scheck, Provost & Vice-Pres., Academic, 250-377-6126
uscheck@tru.ca
Cliff Neufeld, Vice-Pres., Admin. & Finance, 250-828-5012
Christopher Seguin, Vice-Pres., Advancement, 250-574-0474
cseguin@tru.ca
Judith Murray, Vice-Pres., Open Learning, 250-828-5007
judithmurray@tru.ca

<u>Faculties</u>
Arts
250-371-5566, Fax: 250-371-5510,
baadvising@tru.ca

Dr Michael Mehta, Dean, 250-852-7275
mmehta@tru.ca

Science
Dr Tom Dickinson, Dean, 250-852-7137
tdickinson@tru.ca

Human, Social, and Educational Development
Dr. Charles F. Webber, Dean, 250-828-5249
cwebber@tru.ca

Law
Chris Axworthy, QC, Dean, 250-852-7267
caxworthy@tru.ca

<u>Schools</u>
Business and Economics / SoBE
Dr. Murray Young, Dean, 250-828-5217
myoung@tru.ca

Nursing
Barbara Paterson, Dean, 250-852-7288
bpaterson@tru.ca

Tourism
Harold Richins, Dean, 250-852-7138
hrichins@tru.ca

Trades & Technology
Lindsay Langill, Dean, 250-828-5110
lblangill@tru.ca

<u>Campuses</u>
100 Mile House Centre
P.O. Box 2109
485 South Birch Ave. 100 Mile House, V0K 2E0 Canada
250-395-3115, Fax: 250-395-2894

Robin Bercowski, Coordinator
rbercowski@tru.ca

Ashcroft/Cache Creek Centre
P.O. Box 1419
310 Railway Ave. Ashcroft, V0K 1A0 Canada
250-453-9999, Fax: 250-453-2518

Sloane Hammond, Coordinator
shammond@tru.ca

Barriere Centre
629 Barriere Town Rd. Barriere, V0E 1E0 Canada
250-672-9875, Fax: 250-672-9875

Susan Ross, Coordinator
sross@tru.ca

Clearwater Centre
751 Clearwater Village Rd., RR#1 Clearwater, V0E 1N0 Canada
250-674-3530, Fax: 250-674-3540

Sylvia Arduini, Coordinator
sarduini@tru.ca

Lillooet Centre
P.O. Box 339
#10, 155 Main St. Lillooet, V0K 1V0 Canada
250-256-4296, Fax: 250-256-4278

Jane Bryson, Coordinator
jbryson@tru.ca

Williams Lake Campus
1250 Western Ave. Williams Lake, V2G 1H7 Canada
250-392-8000, Fax: 250-392-4984, 800-663-4936
wlmain@tru.ca

Open Learning Division
P.O. Box 3010
900McGill Rd. Kamloops, V2C 5N3 Canada
250-852-7000, Fax: 250-852-6405, 1-800-663-1663
student@tru.ca

<u>Publications</u>
The Omega
250-372-1272, Fax: 250-372-5331,
theomega.ca

Sadie Cox, Editor-In-Chief
editorofomega@gmail.com

Langley: The Associated Canadian Theological Schools of Trinity Western University
7600 Glover Rd. Langley, V2Y 1Y1 Canada
604-888-6045, Fax: 604-513-2045,
acts@twu.ca

Langley: Canadian Baptist Seminary
7600 Glover Rd. Langley, V2Y 1Y1 Canada
604-513-2015, Fax: 604-513-2078,
canadianbaptistseminary.com

Enrollment: 23
This institution is one of six seminaries representative of other denominations forming a consortium called Associated Canadian Theological Seminaries (ACTS). It is located on the Trinity Western University campus.

Langley: Canadian Pentecostal Seminary
Fosmark Bldg.
7600 Glover Rd. Langley, V2Y 1Y1 Canada
604-513-2161, Fax: 604-513-2078,
cps@twu.ca
canadianpentecostalseminary.ca
This institution is in partnership with Trinity Western University, and with five other denominations, to form ACTS, the Associated Canadian Theological Schools. It is located on the Trinity Western U. campus.

Langley: Canadian Theological Seminary
7600 Glover Rd. Langley, V2Y 1Y1 Canada
604-888-7511

Langley: Mennonite Brethren Biblical Seminary - BC
7600 Glover Rd. Langley, V2Y 1Y1 Canada
604-513-2133

Langley: Northwest Baptist Seminary
P.O. Box 790
Langley, V1M 2S2 Canada
604-888-3310

Langley: Trinity Western University
7600 Glover Rd. Langley, V2Y 1Y1 Canada
604-888-7511, Fax: 604-513-2061,
admissions@twu.ca
www.twu.ca
Enrollment: 2510
Dr Jonathan S. Raymond, President
president@twu.ca
Paul Weme, Vice-Pres., Strategic Advancement
paul.weme@twu.ca
David Coons, Vice-Pres., Developemnt
david.coons@twu.ca
Jim Poulsen, Vice-Pres., Finance
poulsen@twu.ca
Joan van Dyck, Vice-Pres., University Communications
joan.vandyck@twu.ca
Dennis Jameson, Provost
jameson@twu.ca
Alma Barranco-Mendoza, Exec. Dir., Information Technology
alma.barranco@twu.ca
Janis Ryder, Exec. Dir., Human Resources
janis.ryder@twu.ca
Scott Henderson, Dir., University Enterprises
scott.henderson@twu.ca
Grant McMillan, Registrar, 604-513-2070, fax: 604-513-2096
registrar@twu.ca

Faculties
Natural & Applied Sciences
Dr Ka Yin Leung, Dean
kayin.leung@twu.ca

Humanities & Social Sciences
Dr Robert K. Burkinshaw, Dean
burkinsh@twu.ca

Professional Studies & Performing Arts

David Squires, Dean
david.squires@twu.ca

Schools
Graduate Studies
604-513-2019, Fax: 604-513-2064, 888-468-6898
gradadmissions@twu.ca
Dr William R. Acton, Interim Dean
william.acton@twu.ca

Business
Andrea Soberg, Dean, 604-513-2137, fax: 604-513-2042
andreas@twu.ca

Education
Dr Kimberly Franklin, Dean, 604-513-2105
kimberly.franklin@twu.ca

Human Kinetics
Dr Blair Whitmarsh, Dean, 604-513-2121 2114
whitmars@twu.ca

Nursing
Dr Landa Terblanche, Dean, 604-888-7511 3268, fax: 604-513-2012
landa.terblanche@twu.ca

Affiliations
Associated Canadian Theological Seminaries of Trinity Western University / ACTS
7600 Glover Rd. Langley, V2Y 1Y1 Canada
604-513-2044, Fax: 604-513-2078,
acts@twu.ca
acts.twu.ca
Dr John W. Auxier, Acting President & Dean
auxier@twu.ca

Canadian Baptist Seminary
7600 Glover Rd. Langley, V2Y 1Y1 Canada
604-513-2015, Fax: 604-513-2078,
canadianbaptistseminary.com
Dr Ed Stuckey, Interim President
estuckey@journeycentre.ca
Cal Netterfield, D.Min., Vice-Pres., Development 3805
cal.netterfield@twu.ca
Dr Daryl Busby, Dean 3833
daryl@twu.ca
Wendell Phillips, Registrar 3807
phillips@twu.ca

Canadian Pentecostal Seminary
7600 Glover Rd. Langley, V2Y 1Y1 Canada
604-513-2161, Fax: 604-513-2078,
cps@twu.ca
canadianpentecostalseminary.ca
Dr. Jim Lucas, President
jim@clcc.ca
Dr Joanne Pepper, Dean

Mennonite Brethren Biblical Seminary - BC
7600 Glover Rd. Langley, V2Y 1Y1 Canada
604-513-2044, Fax: 604-513-2078
Dr Lynn Jost, Acting-President

Northwest Baptist Seminary
7600 Glover Rd. Langley, V2Y 1Y1 Canada
604-888-7592, Fax: 604-637-3212,
www.nbseminary.ca
Dr Larry Perkins, President 3861
Loren Warkentin, Registrar 3866

Trinity Western Seminary
7600 Glover Rd. Langley, V2Y 1Y1 Canada
604-513-2044, Fax: 604-513-2078
Dr John Auxier, Acting-President

Pacific Summit College
P.O. Box 1700
35235 Straiton Rd. Abbotsford, V2S 7E7 Canada
604-853-7491, Fax: 604-853-8951, 800-976-8388
pr@summitpacific.ca
www.summitpacific.ca
Formerly Western Pentecostal Bible College
Dr Dave Demchuk, President
ddemchuk@summitpacific.ca
Melody Deeley, Registrar
registrar@summitpacific.ca

North Vancouver: Capilano University
Lynmour Campus
2055 Purcell Way North Vancouver, V7J 3H5 Canada
604-986-1911, Fax: 604-984-4985,
TDD: 604-990-7848
www.capilanou.ca
Enrollment: 14500
Peter Ufford, Chancellor
Dr. Kris Bulcroft, President/Vice-Chancellor, 604-984-4925
kbulcrof@capilanou.ca
Cindy Turner, VP, Finance & Administration, 604-984-4937
cturner@capilanou.ca
Dr Jacalyn Snodgrass, VP, Education - Academic & Arts Programs, 604-984-1740
jsnodgra@capilanou.ca
Catherine Vertesi, VP, Education - Mgmt. & International Program, 604-990-7894
cvertesi@capilanou.ca
Dr Patrick Donahoe, VP, Student and Institutional Support, 604-984-4975
pdonahoe@capilanou.ca
Mike Arbogast, VP, Human Resources, 604-984-4991
marbogas@capilanou.ca
Cheryl Helm, Acting Registrar, 604-983-7506
chelm@capilanou.ca

Faculties
Arts & Science
Dr Robert Campbell, Dean, 604-984-4976
robertc@capilanou.ca

Business
Graham Fane, Dean, 604-984-4988
gfane@capilanou.ca

Fine & Applied Arts
Jennifer Moore, Dean, 604-990-7801
jmoore2@capilanou.ca

Health & Education
Jean Bennett, Dean, 604-990-7982
jbennett@capilanou.ca

Tourism & Outdoor Recreation
Dr Chris Bottrill, Dean, 604-983-7586
cbottril@capilanou.ca

Campuses
Squamish
P.O. Box 1538
1150 Carson Pl. Squamish, V8B 0B1 Canada
604-892-5322, Fax: 604-892-9274,
squamish@capilanou.ca

Sunshine Coast
P.O. Box 1609
5627 Inlet Ave. Sechelt, V0N 3A0 Canada
604-885-9310, Fax: 604-885-9350

Publications
Capilano Courier

Prince George: University of Northern British Columbia / UNBC
3333 University Way Prince George, V2N 4Z9 Canada
250-960-5555, Fax: 250-960-5794,
www.unbc.ca
Enrollment: 3675
Dr. George Iwama, President
Nancy Black, Acting University Librarian
Dr. Mark R.T. Dale, Vice-President
John DeGrace, University Secretariat & Registrar
Eileen Bray, Vice-President
John DeGrace, Registrar
Dr. Gail Fondahl, Vice-President
Rob van Adrichem, Director

Faculties
Arts, Social & Health Sciences
Dr. John Young, Acting Dean

Graduate Programs
Dr. Ian Hartley, Dean

Science & Management

Dr. William McGill, Dean

Publications
Over the Edge
Student newspaper at the University of Northern British Columbia

Vancouver: University of British Columbia
2329 West Mall Vancouver, V6T 1Z4 Canada
604-822-2211,
Telex: 04-51233
www.ubc.ca
Enrollment: 48610
Bill Levine, Chair
Sarah Morgan-Silvester, Chancellor
Dr Stephen J. Toope, President & Vice-Chancellor, 604-822-8300 604-822-50
presidents.office@ubc.ca
Dr David H. Farrar, Provost & Vice-Pres., Academic, 604-822-4948
david.farrar@ubc.ca
Pierre Ouillet, Vice-Pres., Finance, Resources & Operations, 604-822-6317
carolina.cerna@ubc.ca
Barbara Miles, Vice-Pres., Development & Alumni Engagement, 604-822-1585
barbara.miles@ubc.ca
Stephen Owen, Vice-Pres., External, Legal & Community Relat, 604-822-5017
stephen.owen@ubc.ca
Dr John Hepburn, Vice-Pres., Research & International, 604-822-1995
vpr@exchange.ubc.ca
Brian D. Sullivan, Vice-Pres., Students, 604-822-3955
vpstudents@exchange.ubc.ca
James Ridge, Assoc. Vice-Pres. & Registrar, 604-822-3265
james.ridge@ubc.ca

Faculties
Applied Science

www.apsc.ubc.ca
Dr Tyseer Aboulnasr, Dean, 604-822-6413, fax: 604-822-7006
info@apsc.ubc.ca

Arts

www.arts.ubc.ca

Dr Gage Averill, Dean, 604-822-3751
mtw@mail.arts.ubc.ca

Dentistry

www.dentistry.ubc.ca

Dr Charles Shuler, Dean, 604-822-0738, fax: 604-822-4532
foddo@interchange.ubc.ca

Education

www.educ.ubc.ca

Dr Jon shapiro, Interim Dean, 604-822-5214, fax: 604-822-6501
jon.shapiro@ubc.ca

Forestry

www.forestry.ubc.ca

Dr John Innes, Dean, 604-822-3542
john.innes@ubc.ca

Graduate Studies

www.grad.ubc.ca

Barbara Evans, Dean, 604-827-5547
barbara.evans@ubc.ca

Land & Food Systems

www.landfood.ubc.ca
Murray B. Isman, Dean, 604-822-1219, fax: 604-822-6394
dean.landfood@ubc.ca

Law

www.law.ubc.ca

Mary Ann Bobinski, Dean, 604-822-6335
deansoffice@law.ubc.ca

Medicine

www.med.ubc.ca
Dr Gavin Stuart, Dean, 604-822-2421, fax: 604-822-6061
fomdo_reception@medd.med.ubc.ca

Pharmaceutical Sciences

www.pharmacy.ubc.ca
Robert Sindelar, Dean, 604-822-2343, fax: 604-822-3035
sindelar@interchange. ubc.ca

Sciences

www.science.ubc.ca
Dr Simon Peacock, Dean, 604-822-3336, fax: 604-822-5558
scidean@science.ubc.ca

Schools

Architecture & Landscape Architecture
604-822-2779, Fax: 604-822-3808,
arch1@interchange.ubc.ca; larc@interchange.ubc.ca
www.sala.ubc.ca

Leslie Van Duzer, Director
vanduzer@interchange.ubc.ca

Audiology & Speech Sciences
604-822-5591, Fax: 604-822-6569,
inquiry@audiospeech.ubc.ca
www.audiospeech.ubc.ca

Valter Ciocca, Director
director@audiospeech.ubc.ca

Community & Regional Planning
604-822-3276, Fax: 604-822-3787,
www.scarp.ubc.ca

Dr Penny Gurstein, Director
gurstein@interchange.ubc.ca

Continuing Studies
604-822-1444, Fax: 604-822-1599,
www.cstudies.ubc.ca

Dr Judith Plessis, Executive Director

Human Kinetics
604-822-3838, Fax: 604-822-6842,
www.hkin.educ.ubc.ca

Dr Robert E.C. Sparks, Director
robert.sparks@ubc.ca

Library, Archival & Information Studies
604-822-2404, Fax: 604-822-6006,
slais@interchange.ubc.ca
www.slais.ubc.ca

Terry Eastwood, Interim Director
eastwood@interchange.ubc.ca

Music
604-822-3113, Fax: 604-822-4884,
www.music.ubc.ca

Dr Richard Kurth, Director
richard.kurth@ubc.ca

Nursing
604-822-7417, Fax: 604-822-7466,
www.nursing.ubc.ca

Dr Sally Thorne, Director
sally.thorne@nursing.ubc.ca

Population & public Health
604-822-2772, Fax: 604-822-4994,
www.spph.ubc.ca

Dr Martin Schechter, Director
martin.schechter@ubc.ca

Journalism
604-822-6688, Fax: 604-822-6707,
journal@interchange.ubc.ca
www.journalism.ubc.ca

Dr Mary Lynn Young, Director

Social Work
604-822-2255, Fax: 604-822-8656,
www.socialwork.ubc.ca

Dr Kwong-leung Tang, Director
kltang@interchange.ubc.ca

Sauder School of Business
604-822-8868, Fax: 604-822-8468,
www.sauder.ubc.ca

Dr Daniel Muzyka, Dean
daniel.muzyka@sauder.ubc.ca

Environmental Health
604-822-9595, Fax: 604-822-9588,
soeh@interchange.ubc.ca
www.soeh.ubc.ca

Christie Hurrell, Exeuctive Director
hurrell@interchange.ubc.ca

College of Health Disciplines
604-822-5571, Fax: 604-822-2495,
chd@interchange.ubc.ca
www.health-disciplines.ubc.ca

Louise Nasmith, Principal
louise.nasmith@ubc.ca

College of Interdisciplinary Studies

www.cfis.ubc.ca

Michael Burgess, Principal, 604-827-5262
cfis.principal@ubc.ca

Campuses

UBC Okanagan Campus
3333 University Way Kelowna, V1V 1V7 Canada
250-807-8000, 866-596-0767
askme@ubc
www.ubc.ca/okanagan

UBC Robson Square Campus
800 Robson St. Vancouver, V6Z 3B7
604-822-3333, Fax: 604-822-0070,
robson.info@ubc.ca
www.robsonsquare.ubc.ca

Great Northern Way Campus
577 Great Northern Way Vancouver, V5T 1E1
778-370-1001, Fax: 778-370-1045,
admin@gnwc.ca
www.gnwc.ca

Affiliations

Regent College
5800 University Blvd. Vancouver, V6T 2E4 Canada
604-224-3245, Fax: 604-224-3097, 1-800-663-8664
Regent Bookstore, Toll Free: 1-800-334-3279
admissions@regent-college.edu; registrar@regent-college.edu
www.regent-college.edu

Dr Rod J.K. Wilson, President
presidentsoffice@regent-college.edu

St. Mark's College
5935 Iona Dr. Vancouver, V6T 1J7 Canada
604-822-4463, Fax: 604-822-4659,
stmarks@stmarkscollege.ca
www.stmarkscollege.ca

Dr. J. Stapleton, Interim Principal
Dr. Marjorie Budnikas, Registrar
registrar@stmarkscollege.ca

Carey Theological College
5920 Iona Dr. Vancouver, V6T 1J6
604-224-4308, Fax: 604-224-5014,
info@careytheologicalcollege.ca
www.careycentre.com

Vancouver School of Theology
6000 Iona Dr. Vancouver, V6T 1L4
604-822-0824, Fax: 604-822-9212,
possibilities@vst.edu
www.vst.edu

Publications

Perspectives

perspectives.ubc.ca
An English-Chinese bilingual student paper
KaGeen Cheung, Editor-In-Chief
editor@perspectives.ubc.ca

Discorder Magazine

discorder.ca/discorder-magazine
Jordie Yow, Editor-In-Chief
editor.discorder@gmail.com

The Graduate Magazine
Published by the Graduate Student Society

The Point

thepoint@rec.ubc.ca
www.thepoint.ubc.ca
Focusing on recreational activities, health and lifestyle news

The Thunderbird

thethunderbird.ca
A student publication of the Graduate School of Journalism

The Ubyssey

ubyssey.ca
Justin McElroy, Coordinating Editor
coordinating@ubyssey.ca

Trek Magazine

www.alumni.ubc.ca/trekmagazine/index.php
Published by UBC Alumni Affairs
Chris Petty, Editor
chris.petty@ubc.ca

Victoria: Royal Roads University

2005 Sooke Rd. Victoria, V9B 5Y2 Canada
250-391-2511, Fax: 250-391-2500, 1-800-788-8028
info@royalroads.ca .ca
www.royalroads.ca

Enrollment: 4130
Royal Roads University offers: Doctoral degrees in Social Sciences; Masters degrees in Arts, Business Admin., Science; Bachelor degrees in Arts, Commerce, Science; Graduate Certificates; Graduate Diplomas.
Peter Robinson, Chair & Chancellor
Dr Allan Cahoon, President & Vice-Chancellor, 250-391-2517
allan.cahoon@royalroads.ca
Thomas Chase, Vice-Pres., Academic & Provost, 250-391-2545
thomas.chase@royalroads.ca
Dan Tulip, Vice-Pres. & CFO, 250-391-2521
dan.tulip@royalroads.ca
Cyndi McLeod, Vice-Pres., Marketing, Recruitment & Business, 250-391-2516
cyndi.mcleod@royalroads.ca
Steve Grundy, Registrar, CIO & Assoc. Vice-Pres., Program D, 250-391-2606
steve.grundy@royalroads.ca

Victoria: University of Victoria

P.O. Box 1700 CSC
Victoria, V8W 2Y2 Canada
250-721-7211, Fax: 250-721-7212,
www.uvic.ca

Enrollment: 16961
Murray Farmer, B.A., Chancellor
David H. Turpin, B.Sc., Ph.D., President
James L. Cassels, B.A., LL.B., LL.M., Vice-President
Gayle Gorrill, B.B.A., C.A., C.B.V., Vice-President
Julia Eastman, B.A., M.A., Ph.D., University Secretary
Vacant, Administrative Registrar
Bruce Kilpatrick, B.A., Director
J. Howard Brunt, B.A., A.D.N., M.Sc.N., Ph, Vice-President
Valerie Kuehne, B.Sc.N., M.Ed., M.A., Ph., Vice-President

Faculties

Business

Ali Dastmalchian, B.Sc., M.Sc., Ph.D., Dean

Continuing Studies
Maureen MacDonald, B.A., LL.B., M.B.A., D.Ph, Dean

Education
Ted Riecken, B.A., M.Ed., Ph.D., Dean

Engineering
Thomas Tiedje, B.Sc., M.Sc., Ph.D., Dean

Fine Arts
Sarah Blackstone, B.A., M.A., Ph.D., Dean

Graduate Studies
Aaron H. Devor, B.A., M.A., Ph.D., Dean

Human & Social Development
Mary Ellen Purkis, B.S.N., M.Sc., Ph.D., Dean

Humanities
Andrew Rippin, B.A., M.A., Ph.D., Dean

Law
Donna Greschner, B.Comm., LL.B., Dean

Science
Tom Pedersen, B.Sc., Ph.D., Dean

Social Sciences
Peter Keller, B.A., M.A., Ph.D., Dean

Publications

The Martlet
Independent weekly student newspaper at the University of Victoria

The Ring
The University of Victoria's monthly newspaper

Standard
The University of Victoria's monthly newspaper

The UVic Torch
P.O. Box 3060
3775 Haro Rd Victoria, V8W 3R4 Canada
Fax: 250-721-8955
Alumni magazine

Colleges

Castlegar: Selkirk College
Castlegar Campus
301 Frank Beinder Way Castlegar, V1N 4L3 Canada
250-365-6601, Fax: 250-365-6568, 1-888-953-1133
www.selkirk.ca
The regional community college consists of the following schools: Kootenay School of the Arts; School of Adult Basic Education & Transitional Training; School of Business & Aviation; School of Digital Media & Music; School of Health & Human Services; School of Hospitality & Tourism; School of Industry & Trades Training; School of Renewable Resources; School of University Arts & Sciences; & Selkirk International.
Christian Schadendorf, Chair
Marilyn Luscombe, President

Campuses

Grand Forks Campus
486 - 72nd Ave. Grand Forks, V0H 1H0 Canada
250-442-2704, Fax: 250-442-2877,

Kaslo Centre
421 Front St. Kaslo, V0G 1M0 Canada
250-353-2618, Fax: 250-353-7121

Kootenay School of the Arts (KSA) Campus
606 Victoria St. Nelson, V1L 4K9
250-352-2821, Fax: 250-352-1625, 1-877-552-2821

Nakusp Centre
311 Broadway Nakusp, V0H 1R0 Canada
250-265-4077, Fax: 250-265-3195,
Adult Basic Education: 250-265-3640

Silver King Campus
2001 Silver King Rd. Nelson, V1L 1C8 Canada
250-352-6601, Fax: 250-352-3180, 1-866-301-6601

Tenth Street Campus
820 Tenth St. Nelson, V1L 3C7 Canada
250-352-6601, Fax: 250-352-5716, 1-866-301-6601

Trail Campus
900 Helena St. Trail, V1R 4S6 Canada
250-368-5236, Fax: 250-368-4983

Courtenay: North Island College
Comox Valley Campus
2300 Ryan Rd. Courtenay, V9N 8N6 Canada
250-334-5000, Fax: 250-334-5018, 800-715-0914
www.northislandcollege.ca
Enrollment: 8253
Dr. Lou Dryden, President
Susan Toresdahl, Director

Campuses

Campbell River Campus
1685 South Dogwood St. Campbell River, V9W 8C1 Canada
250-923-9700, Fax: 250-923-9703, 1-800-715-0914
www.northislandcollege.ca

Comox Valley Campus
2300 Ryan Rd. Courtenay, V9N 8N6 Canada
250-334-5000, Fax: 250-334-5018, 1-800-715-0914
www.northislandcollege.ca

Port Alberni Campus
3699 Roger St. Port Alberni, V9Y 8E3 Canada
250-724-8711, Fax: 250-724-8700, 1-800-715-0914
www.northislandcollege.ca

Port Hardy Campus
P.O. Box 901
9300 Trustee Rd. Port Hardy, V0N 2P0 Canada
250-949-7912, Fax: 250-949-2617, 1-800-715-0914
www.northislandcollege.ca

Vigar Vocational Centre
2780 Vigar Rd. Campbell River, V9W 6A3 Canada
250-923-9794, Fax: 250-830-0816, 1-800-715-0914
www.northislandcollege.ca

Tebo Vocational Centre
4781 Tebo Ave. Port Alberni, V9Y 6X7 Canada
1-800-715-0914
www.northislandcollege.ca

Cranbrook: College of the Rockies
P.O. Box 8500
2700 College Way Cranbrook, V1C 5L7 Canada
250-489-2751, Fax: 250-489-1790, 1-877-489-2687
ask@cotr.bc.ca
www.cotr.bc.ca
Enrollment: 2000
Donna Kraus-Hagerman, Manager
Dr. Nick Rubidge, President

Campuses

Creston Campus
P.O. Box 1978
301-16th Ave. Creston, V0B 1G0 Canada
250-428-5332, Fax: 250-428-4314, 1-877-489-2687
creston@cotr.bc.ca
www.cotr.bc.ca/creston/

Invermere Campus
#2, 1535 - 14th St., RR#4 Invermere, V0A 1K4 Canada
250-342-3210, Fax: 250-342-9221, 1-877-489-2687
invermere@cotr.bc.ca
www.cotr.bc.ca/invermere/

Elk Valley-Fernie Campus
P.O. Box 1770
342-3rd Ave. Fernie, V0B 1M0 Canada
250-423-4691, Fax: 250-423-3932, 1-866-423-4691
fernie@cotr.bc.ca
www.cotr.bc.ca/fernie/

Golden Campus
P.O. Box 376
1305 South 9th St. Golden, V0A 1H0 Canada
250-344-5901, Fax: 250-344-5745, 1-877-489-2687
golden@cotr.bc.ca
www.cotr.bc.ca/golden/

Kimberley Campus
555 McKenzie St. Kimberley, V1A 2C1 Canada
250-427-7116, Fax: 250-427-3034, 1-877-489-2687
peet@cotr.bc.ca
http://www.cotr.bc.ca/kimberley/

Dawson Creek: Northern Lights College
Regional Administration
11401 - 8th St. Dawson Creek, V1G 4G2 Canada
250-782-5251, Fax: 250-782-5233, 1-866-463-6652
appinfo@nlc.bc.ca; webmaster@nlc.bc.ca
www.nlc.bc.ca
Kate O'Neil, Board Chair
D. Jean Valgardson, CEO
jvalgardson@nlc.bc.ca

Campuses

Atlin Campus
P.O. Box 29
Atlin, V0W 1A0
250-651-7762,
ljancek@nlc.bc.ca (Campus Clerk); dthorn@nlc.bc.ca (Literacy)
The campus offers continuing education in academic & pre-professional studies, development & upgrading, distance education, & industrial & workforce training.
Richard Macdonald, Chair
Roger Grose, Systems Principal
Bob White, Principal, Secondary Campus
Henry Au, Vice Principal, Secondary Campus
Aza Nakagawa, Business Manager
Blondie Enns, Secretary, High School

Chetwynd Campus
P.O. Box 1180
5132 - 50th St. Chetwynd, V0C 1J0 Canada
250-788-2248, Fax: 250-788-9706,
mmeunier@nlc.bc.ca (Administrator)
Enrollment: 400
Programs offered include applied business technology, teacher assistant training, social services worker training, forestry, hospitality & tourism operations, continuing education, adult basic education, university transfer, & adult special education.
Mark Meunier, Campus Administrator

Dawson Creek Campus
11401 - 8 St. Dawson Creek, V1G 4G2 Canada
Fax: 250-782-5251, 250-784-7563
Continuing Education Coordinator, Phone: 250-784-7509
dpatterson@nlc.bc.ca (Administrator)
The campus features technical, academic, trades, & vocational programs.
Doug Patterson, Campus Administrator

Dease Lake Campus
P.O. Box 220
Commercial Dr. Dease Lake, V0C 1L0
250-771-5500, Fax: 250-771-5510, 1-800-324-8203
mpharand@nlc.bc.ca (Stikine Administrator)
Enrollment: 625
The campus serves full-time & part-time vocational and continuing education students in Atlin, Telegraph Creek, Lower Post, Iskut, & Good Hope Lake.
Tiffany Scobie, Head of School, 905-565-8707 10
tscobie@rotherglen.com
Laura Rossi, Office Manager, 905-565-8707 10
lrossi@rotherglen.com

Fort Nelson Campus
P.O. Box 860
5201 Simpson Trail Fort Nelson, V0C 1R0 Canada
Fax: 250-774-2741, 250-774-2750
ssandvik@nlc.bc.ca (Administrator)
Continuing education programs are provided.
Vacant, Campus Administrator

Fort St. John Campus
P.O. Box 1000
9820 - 120 St. Fort St John, V1J 6K1 Canada
250-785-6981, Fax: 250-785-1294
Enrollment: 1800
Academic, apprenticeship, career/technical, vocational, & international students students are served by the Fort St. John campus.
Ed Benoit, Campus Administrator

Hudson's Hope Campus
Perkes Centre
P.O. Box 268
10801 Dudley Dr. Hudson's Hope
250-783-5711, Fax: 250-783-5788,
vrowsell@nlc.bc.ca (Continuing Education Coordinator)
Adult basic education & continuing education programs are offered in Hudson's Hope.
Jacinta Snyder, Head of School
jsnyder@rotherglen.com

Tumbler Ridge Campus
High School Bldg.
180 Southgate Tumbler Ridge, V0C 2W0
250-242-5591, Fax: 250-242-3109,
mmeunier@nlc.bc.ca (Administrator)
Adult basic education is offered in Tumbler Ridge.
Tracey Chong, Administrator
tchong@rotherglen.com

Kelowna: Okanagan University College
North Kelowna Campus
3333 College Way Kelowna, V1V 1V7 Canada
250-762-5445, Fax: 250-470-6004,
www.ouc.bc.ca/

Campuses

The Phoenix

Langley: Trinity Western Seminary
7600 Glover Rd. Langley, V2Y 1Y1 Canada
604-513-2019, Fax: 604-513-2045,
www.acts.twu.ca

Publications

Mars' Hill
Official student newspaper of Trinity Western University

***Nanaimo:* Vancouver Island University**
900 - 5th St. Nanaimo, V9R 5S5 Canada
250-753-3245, 888-920-2221
info@viu.ca
www.viu.ca

Enrollment: 19124
Formerly Malaspina University College.
Ralph Nilson, President, 250-740-6102
ralph.nilson@viu.ca

***Prince George:* College of New Caledonia**
3330 - 22 Ave. Prince George, V2N 1P8 Canada
250-562-2131, Fax: 250-561-5861, 1-800-371-811
www.cnc.bc.ca/

Enrollment: 5000
John Bowman, President
bowmanj@cnc.bc.ca

***Surrey:* Kwantlen Polytechnic University**
12666 - 72nd Ave. Surrey, V3W 2M8 Canada
604-599-2100, Fax: 604-599-2068,
inquiry@kwantlen.ca
www.kwantlen.ca

Enrollment: 11000
Formerly known as Kwantlen University College; 6,000 part-time enrollment
David Atkinson, President, 604-599-2078
david.atkinson@kwantlen.ca
Joshua Mitchell, Director, Enrolment Services, 604-599-2474
joshua.mitchell@kwantlen.ca

***Terrace:* Northwest Community College**
College Services
5331 McConnell Ave. Terrace, V8G 4X2 Canada
250-635-6511, Fax: 250-635-5432, 1-877-277-2288
www.nwcc.bc.ca

Stephanie Forsyth, President

Campuses
Hazelton Campus
P.O. Box 338
4815 Swannell Dr. Hazelton, V0J 1Y0 Canada
250-842-5291, Fax: 250-842-5813,
www.nwcc.bc.ca

Houston Campus
P.O. Box 1277
3221 - 14 St.W. Houston, V0J 1Z0 Canada
250-845-7266, Fax: 250-845-5629,
www.nwcc.bc.ca

Kitimat Campus
606 Mountainview Sq. Kitimat, V8C 2N2 Canada
250-632-4766, Fax: 250-632-5069,
www.nwcc.bc.ca

Prince Rupert Campus
353 - 5th St. Prince Rupert, V8J 3L6 Canada
250-624-6054, Fax: 250-624-3923,
www.nwcc.bc.ca

Queen Charlotte City Campus
P.O. Box 67
138 Bay St. Queen Charlotte Village, V0T 1S0 Canada
250-559-8222, Fax: 250-559-8219,
www.nwcc.bc.ca

Smithers Campus
P.O. Box 3606
3966 - 2nd Ave. Smithers, V0J 2N0 Canada
250-847-4461, Fax: 250-847-4568,
www.nwcc.bc.ca

Stewart Campus
P.O. Box 919
Stewart, V0T 1W0 Canada
250-636-9184, Fax: 250-636-2770,
www.nwcc.bc.ca

Terrace Campus
5331 McConnell Ave. Terrace, V8G 4X2 Canada
250-635-6511, Fax: 250-638-5432

Masset Campus
P.O. Box 559
1730 Hodges Masset, V0T 1M0 Canada
250-626-3670, Fax: 250-626-3680,
www.nwcc.bc.ca

***Victoria:* Camosun College**
Lansdowne Campus, 3100 Foul Bay Rd. Victoria, V8P 5J2 Canada
250-370-3000, Fax: 250-370-3551, 877-554-7555
info@camosun.bc.ca
www.camosun.bc.ca/

Enrollment: 7200
Dr. Liz Ashton, President

***Victoria:* Lester B. Pearson College of the Pacific**
650 Pearson College Dr. Victoria, V9C 4H7 Canada
250-391-2411, Fax: 250-391-2412,
admin@pearsoncollege.ca
www.pearsoncollege.ca

Enrollment: 200
David B. Hawley, College Director

Post Secondary/Technical

Universities

***Abbotsford:* University of the Fraser Valley**
33844 King Rd. Abbotsford, V2S 7M8 Canada
604-504-7441, Fax: 604-855-7614, 888-504-7441
info@ufv.ca
www.ucfv.ca

Enrollment: 10000
Dr Brian Minter, Chancellor
Dr Mark Evered, President & Vice-Chancellor, 604-864-4608, fax: 604-853-7341
jill.smith@ufv.ca
Dr Brian Minter, Chancellor
Dr Eric Davis, Provost & Vice-Pres., Academic, 604-864-4642
eric.davis@ufv.ca
Eleanor Busse-Klassen, Exec. Ass't to Vice-Pres., Administration
eleanor.busse@ufv.ca
Bill Cooke, Registrar 2820
bill.cooke@ufv.ca

Faculties
Arts
Dr Jacqueline Nolte
jacqueline.nolte@ufv.ca

Science
Ora Stein, Interim Dean
ora.steyn@ufv.ca

Professional Studies
Dr Rosetta Khalideen, Dean
rosetta.khalideen@ufv.ca

Trades & Technology
Harv McCullough, Dean
harv.mccullough@ufv.ca

Access & Continuing Studies
Dr Karen Evans
karen.evans@ufv.ca

Schools
Graduate Studies
Yvon Dandurand, Assoc. Vice-President
yvon.dandurand@ufv.ca

Campuses
Chilliwack Campus
45635 Yale Rd. Chilliwack, V2P 6T4 Canada
604-792-0025, Fax: 604-792-2388

Chilliwack, Trades & Tech Centre
Canada Education Park
5579 Tyson Rd. Chilliwack, V2R 0H9 Canada
Fax: 604-824-7931, 888-504-7441

UFV Aerospace Centre
Abbotsford Airport
30645 Firecat Ave. Abbotsford, V2T 6H5 Canada
Fax: 604-852-7399, 888-504-7441
aerospace@ufv.ca

Hope Centre
1250 7th Ave. Hope, V0X 1L4 Canada
604-869-9991, Fax: 604-869-7431

Mission Campus
Heritage Park Centre
33700 Prentis Ave. Mission, V2V 7B1 Canada
604-557-7603, Fax: 604-826-0681

Abbotsford, Marshall Rd. Annex
34194 Marshall Rd. Abbotsford, V2S 5E4
604-851-6324

UFV India Office
SD College Chandigarh
Sector 32C Chandigarth, 160030 India
(0)172 500 1048
ufv.india@ufv.ca
www.ufv.ca/chandigarh

Publications
The Cascade
ufvcascade.ca

***Nanaimo:* Vancouver Island University**
900 Fifth St. Nanaimo, V9R 5S5 Canada
250-753-3245, Fax: 250-740-6473, 888-920-2221
info@viu.ca
www.viu.ca

Enrollment: 18000
VIU offers a variety of certificate, diploma, and degree programs.
Chief Shawn A. Atleo, Chancellor
Dr Ralph Nilson, President & Vice-chancellor, 250-740-6101, fax: 250-740-6555
president@viu.ca
Pat Eager, Vice-Pres., Admin. & Finance
ralph.nilson@viu.ca
David Witty, Vice-Pres., Academic & Provost
david.witty@viu.ca
Fred Jacklin, Registrar, 250-753-3245 2283
david.witty@viu.ca

Campuses
Cowichan Campus
222 Cowichan Way Duncan, V9L 6P4 Canada
250-746-3500, Fax: 250-746-3529

Parksville-Qualicum Centre
100 Jensen Ave. East Parksville, V9P 2G3 Canada
250-248-2096, Fax: 250-248-9792,
pqcampus@viu.ca

Powell River Campus
3960 Selkirk Ave. Powell River, V8A 3C6 Canada
604-485-2878, Fax: 604-485-2868, 877-888-8890

Publications
Navigator
editor@thenav.ca
thenav.mala.bc.ca

***Surrey:* Kwantlen Polytechnic University**
12666 - 72 Ave. Surrey, V3W 2M8 Canada
604-599-2100, Fax: 604-599-2068,
switchboard@kwantlen.ca
www.kwantlen.bc.ca

Enrollment: 17000
Arvinder Singh Bubber, Chancellor
David W. Atkinson, President & Vice-Chancellor, 604-599-2078, fax: 604-599-2235
sandy.kuzyk@kwantlen.ca
Judith McGillivray, Provost & Vice-Pres., Academic, 604-599-2363
judith.mcgillivray@kwantlen.ca
Robert Hensley, Registrar, 604-599-2018
robert.hensley@kwantlen.ca

Faculties
Humanities
Dr Mazen Guirguis, Dean, 604-599-2672
humanities.dean@kwantlen.ca

Social Sciences
Dr Robert Adamoski, Dean, 604-599-3068, fax: 604-599-2966
robert.adamoski@kwantlen.ca

Design
Barbara Duggan, Dean, 604-599-2525
barbara.duggan@kwantlen.ca

Community & Health Studies
Jean Nicolson-Church, Interim Dean, 604-599-2266
jean.nicolson-church@kwantlen.ca

Academic & Career Advancement
Dr Arthur Coren, Interim Dean, 604-599-3252
arthur.coren@kwantlen.ca

Trades & Technology
Wayne Tebb, Dean, 604-599-6101
wayne.tebb@kwantlen.ca

Science, Mathematics & Applied Sciences
Dr Brian G. Carr, Dean, 604-599-2244, fax: 604-599-2435
brian.carr@kwantlen.ca

Business
Dr Arthur Coren, Dean, 604-599-3252
arthur.coren@kwantlen.ca

Schools
Horticulture
David Davidson, Assoc. Dean, 604-599-3254
horticulture@kwantlen.ca

Campuses
Surrey Campus
12666 - 72 Ave. Surrey, V3T 5H8 Canada
Fax: 604-599-2068

Richmond Campus
8771 Lansdowne Rd. Richmond, V6X 3V8 Canada
Fax: 604-599-2578

Cloverdale Campus
5500 - 180 St. Surrey, V3S 4K5 Canada

Langley Campus
20901 Langley Bypass Langley, V3A 8G9 Canada
Fax: 604-599-3242

Publications
Kwantlen Chronicle

www.kwantlenchronicle.ca

Colleges

Kelowna: Okanagan College
1000 KLO Rd. Kelowna, V1Y 4X8 Canada
250-762-5445,
www.okanagan.bc.ca

Enrollment: 4850
Jim Hamilton, President

Campuses
Penticton Campus
583 Duncan Ave. West Penticton, V2A 8E1 Canada
Fax: 250-490-3950

Donna Lomas, Regional Dean

Salmon Arm Campus
P.O. Box 189
Salmon Arm, V1E 4N3 Canada
Fax: 250-804-8850

Lynda Wilson, Regional Dean

Kalamalka Campus
7000 College Way Vernon, V1B 2N5 Canada
Fax: 250-545-3277

Tony Sellars, Regional Dean

South Kelowna Campus
1000 KLO Rd. Kelowna, V1Y 4X8 Canada
Heather Schneider, Regional Dean

Publications
The Phoenix

New Westminster: Douglas College
P.O. Box 2503
New Westminster, V3L 5B2 Canada
604-527-5400, Fax: 604-527-5095,
registrar@douglas.bc.ca
www.douglas.bc.ca/

Enrollment: 7000
Susan R. Witter, President

Campuses
New Westminster Campus
700 Royal Ave. New Westminster, V3M 5Z5 Canada

David Lam Campus
1250 Pinetree Way Coquitlam, V3B 7X3 Canada

Publications
Other Press

North Vancouver: Capilano College
2055 Purcell Way North Vancouver, V7J 3H5 Canada
604-986-1911, Fax: 604-984-4985,
switchboard@capcollege.bc.ca
www.capcollege.bc.ca

Enrollment: 5537
Dr. Greg Lee, B.Sc., M.Sc., Ph.D., President

Publications
Capilano Courier

Prince George: College of New Caledonia
3330 - 22nd Ave. Prince George, V2N 1P8 Canada
250-562-2131, Fax: 250-561-5816, 1-800-371-811
askcnc@cnc.bc.ca
www.cnc.bc.ca

Enrollment: 5250
John Bowman, President, 250-561-5825
Bruce Sutherland, Chair

Campuses
Lakes District Campus
P.O. Box 5000
545 Hwy. 16 West Burns Lake, V0J 1E0 Canada
250-692-1700, Fax: 250-692-1750, 866-692-1943
lksdist@cnc.bc.ca

Joan Ragsdale, Director, 250-692-1715
ragsdale@cnc.bc.ca

Mackenzie Campus
P.O. Box 2110
540 Mackenzie Blvd. Mackenzie, V0J 2C0 Canada
250-997-7200, Fax: 250-997-3779,
cncmackenzie@cnc.bc.ca

Carole L'Herault, Director, 250-997-7203
lherault@cnc.bc.ca

Quesnel Campus
100 Campus Way Quesnel, V2J 7K1 Canada
250-991-7500, Fax: 250-991-7502, 866-680-7523
quesnel@cnc.bc.ca

Lynda Williams, Associate Director, 250-991-7622
williamsl2@cnc.bc.ca

Nechako Campus
3231 Hospital Rd. Vanderhoof, V0J 3A2 Canada
250-567-3200, Fax: 250-567-3217,
nechako@cnc.bc.ca

Maureen Mallais, Director, 250-567-3200
mallais@cnc.bc.ca

Fort St. James Campus
P.O. Box 1557
179 Douglas St. Fort St. James, V0J 1P0
250-996-7019, Fax: 250-996-7014,
cncfsj@cnc.bc.ca

Ann McCormick, Campus Supervisor
mccormicka@cnc.bc.ca

Valemount Campus
P.O. Box 789
99 Gorse St. Valemount, V0E 2Z0 Canada
250-566-4601, Fax: 250-566-4602, 888-690-4422
valemount@cnc.bc.ca

Sandra Craig, Program Clerk
craigs@cnc.bc.ca

Fraser Lake Campus
298 McMillan Ave. Fraser Lake, V0J 1S0
250-699-6249, Fax: 250-699-6247,
cncfl@cnc.bc.ca

Wendy Galvin, Program Assistant
galvinw@cnc.bc.ca

Publications
The Confluence

cncsn@cnc.bc.ca

Vancouver: Langara College
100 West 49th Ave. Vancouver, V5Y 2Z6 Canada
604-323-5511, Fax: 604-323-5555,
geninfo@langara.bc.ca
www.langara.bc.ca

Enrollment: 12218
Linda Holmes, President

Publications
Gleaner

The Voice

Vancouver: Vancouver Community College
1155 East Broadway Vancouver, V5T 4V5 Canada
604-871-7000, Fax: 604-871-7100,
www.vcc.ca

Dale Dorn, President
L. Martin, Vice-President
Alan Davis, Vice-President
Peter Legg, Interim Vice-President

Campuses
City Centre Campus
250 West Pender St. Vancouver, V6B 1S9 Canada
Fax: 604-443-8588

King Edward Campus
1155 East Broadway Vancouver, V5T 4V5 Canada
Fax: 604-871-7100

Publications
The Gleaner

V.C.C. Voice
100 - 49th Ave. West Vancouver, V5Y 2Z6 Canada

Victoria: Camosun College
Lansdowne Campus
3100 Foul Bay Rd. Victoria, V8P 5J2 Canada
250-370-3550, Fax: 250-370-3551,
www.camosun.bc.ca

Dr. Elizabeth Ashton, President

Campuses
Interurban Campus
4461 Interurban Rd., RR#3 Victoria, V9E 2C1 Canada
Fax: 250-370-3750

Publications
Nexus

Post Secondary/Technical

Burnaby: BC Institute of Technology
3700 Willingdon Ave. Burnaby, V5G 3H2 Canada
604-434-5734, Fax: 604-431-6917,
www.bcit.ca

Dr. Tony Knowles, President
Marshall Heinekey, Acting Vice President
Dr. Verna Magee-Shepherd, Vice President

Campuses
Burnaby Campus
3700 Willingdon Ave. Burnaby, V5G 3H2 Canada

Aircraft Technology Campus
5301 Airport Rd. South Richmond, V7B 1B5 Canada

Downtown Campus
555 Seymour St. Vancouver, V6B 3H6 Canada

Marine Campus
265 West Esplanade North Vancouver, V7M 1A5 Canada

Publications
Great Northern Way Campus
555 Great Northern Way Vancouver, V5T 1E2 Canada

Burnaby: British Columbia Institute of Technology
3700 Willingdon Ave. Burnaby, V5G 3H2 Canada
604-434-5734, Fax: 604-434-6243,
www.bcit.bc.ca/

Burnaby: CDI College of Business, Technology & Healthcare
#211, 4603 Kingsway Burnaby, V5H 4M4 Canada
604-437-8585, Fax: 604-437-8595,
www.cdicollege.com

Computers, accounting & business training; 7 locations across BC

Burnaby: Institute of Indigenous Government
#200, 4355 Mathissi Place Burnaby, V5G 4S8 Canada
604-602-9555, Fax: 604-602-3400,
iig@all-nations.ca
www.all-nations.ca

Burnaby: Jennings Institute for Performing Artists Inc.
1870 Sperling Ave. Burnaby, V5B 4K5 Canada
604-420-3213, Fax: 604-420-3210,
forperformingartists@hotmail.com

Representation & management of performers, training in dance, music, drama, speech arts & theoretical subjects

Burnaby: Pacific Vocational College Ltd.
4064 McConnell Dr. Burnaby, V5A 3A8 Canada
604-421-5255, Fax: 604-421-7445,
pvc@telus.net
www.pacificvocationalcollege.com

Piping trades, gas fitting, sprinkler fitting, welding
Robert F. Bradbury, President

Burnaby: ProCare Institute Inc.
#240, 4411 Hastings St. Burnaby, V5C 2K1 Canada
604-291-0030, Fax: 604-291-0003, 1-800-282-003
procare@telus.net
www.procare.ca

Health care programs

Coquitlam: Barkel Business School Ltd.
#223, 3030 Lincoln Ave. Coquitlam, V3B 6B4 Canada
604-464-8717, Fax: 604-942-6355
Secretarial, bookkeeping, computer training & management

Coquitlam: Personal Growth Consulting Training Centre
#4, 1111 Austin Ave. Coquitlam, V3K 3P4 Canada
604-939-1760,
breathwork.citysoup.ca

Susan Hewins, Master Teacher

Coquitlam: Sprott-Shaw Community College
#104, 2748 Lougheed Hwy. Coquitlam, V3B 6P2 Canada
604-552-7686, Fax: 604-552-6986, 1-800-310-447
info@sprott-shaw.com
www.sprottshaw.com

21 campuses in BC; 1 in Calgary; 1 in Edmonton; 3 international colleges in India & Jordan

Courtenay: Comox Valley Beauty School
911 McPhee Ave. Courtenay, V9N 3A1 Canada

250-338-9982, Fax: 250-338-0199,
cvbeautyschool.com/

Beauty, cosmetology, esthetics

Kelowna: Fine-Art Bartending School
2979 Pandosy St. Kelowna, V1Y 1W1 Canada
250-363-6392, Fax: 250-860-0998, 1-866-881-669
info@fineart.ca
www.fineart.ca

Kelowna: Kelowna College of Professional Counselling
#101, 251 Lawrence Ave. Kelowna, V1Y 6L2 Canada
250-717-0412, Fax: 250-717-0427, 1-800-667-327
cti@uniserve.com
www.counselortraining.com

Counselling practice training
Dr. Libby Stowers, Program Director

Kelowna: Trend College Kelowna Ltd.
546 Leon Ave. Kelowna, V1Y 6J6 Canada
250-763-7400, Fax: 250-763-9948, 1-888-763-740
info@trendcollege.com
www.trendcollege.com

Computer technology, business & management, specialty careers, health care, beauty & trade

Langley: New Directions
#101, 20570 - 56 Ave. Langley, V3A 3Z1 Canada
604-530-4555

Career counselling, ESL, general upgrading, life skills
Annemieke Vrijmoed, ELSA Coordinator

Langley: RCABC Roofing Institute
9734 - 201st St. Langley, V1M 3E8 Canada
604-882-9734, Fax: 604-882-1744,
registrar@rcabc.org
www.rcabc.org

Roofing training
Brian Hofler, Exec. Vice-President

Maple Ridge: Justice Institute - Fire & Safety Training Centre
13500 - 256 St. Maple Ridge, V4R 1C9 Canada
604-462-1000, Fax: 604-462-9149,
www.jibc.bc.ca

Courses offered on marine & industrial firefighting, emergency response to incidents involving hazardous materials, fire service training from recruit to chief officer.
Dan Murphy, Manager

Maple Ridge: Ridge Meadows College
22610 Dewdney Trunk Rd. Maple Ridge, V2X 3J9 Canada
604-466-6577, Fax: 604-467-7548,
rmc@sd42.ca
www.rmcollege.ca

Business, Education, Health Care, Hospitality, Recreation, Trades & Corporate Contract Training: Admin. Asst., Computer Accounting, Family Daycare, ECE, SETA, TESL, Dental Reception, FoodSafe Programs, Home Health Aide, Medical Asst., Hospitality Operation.

Campuses

Arthur Peake Centre
23125 - 116th Ave. Maple Ridge, V2X 3M6 Canada
Fax: 604-467-4143

Thomas Haney Centre
23000C - 116th Ave. Maple Ridge, V2X 0T8 Canada
Fax: 604-463-5437

Merritt: Nicola Valley Institute of Technology
4155 Belshaw St. Merritt, V1K 1R1 Canada
250-378-3300, Fax: 250-378-3332, 1-877-682-330
www.nvit.bc.ca

Enrollment: 800
Certificate & diploma programs, adult basic education, collaborative degrees & on-campus, in-community & online delivery
Casey Sheridan, President
Ken Tourand, Director
Dr. Gerry William, Dean
Verna Billy-Minnabarriet, Dean

New Westminster: Canadian Electrolysis College Ltd.
712 - 6th St. New Westminster, V3L 3C5 Canada
604-519-1101, 1-888-561-441
www.canadianelectrolysis.com/

Electrolysis thermolysis, blend + multiple needle, & advanced computerized epilation; 13 weeks, 500 hrs.
Ruth Struve, Owner

New Westminster: Justice Institute of B.C.
715 McBride Blvd. New Westminster, V3L 5T4 Canada
604-525-5422, Fax: 604-528-5518, 1-88-865-7764
infodesk@jibc.ca
www.jibc.bc.ca

Jack McGee, President

Campuses

Chilliwack Campus
1092 Caen Rd. Chilliwack, V2R 5X6 Canada
604-847-0881,
infodesk@jibc.ca
www.jibc.ca

Downtown Vancouver
Education Centre
400 Burrard St., 18th Fl. Vancouver, V6C 3A6 Canada
Fax: 604-528-5653

Maple Ridge Campus
13500 - 256 St. Maple Ridge, V4R 1C9 Canada
604-462-1000, Fax: 604-462-9149,
infodesk@jibc.ca
www.jibc.ca

Okanagan Campus
825 Walrod St. Kelowna, V1Y 2S4 Canada
250-469-6020, Fax: 250-469-6022,
infodesk@jibc.ca
www.jibc.ca

Anyone shipping good to this campus should contact the Facilities Adinistrator at 250-469-6020.

Victoria Campus
#101, 910 Government St. Victoria, V8W 1X3 Canada
250-405-3500, Fax: 250-405-3500,
infodesk@jibc.ca
www.jibc.ca

North Vancouver: Academy of Learning
#300, 1221 Lonsdale Ave. North Vancouver, V7M 2H5 Canada
604-987-4277, Fax: 604-987-4213,
www.academyoflearning.com

Computer & business skills; 24 locations across BC

Port Moody: BC Office
#108, 135 Balmoral Dr. Port Moody, V3H 1X7 Canada
604-461-7132,
wmtcbc@telus.net
westernmontessori.ca

Campuses

AB Office
P.O. Box 1120
Bragg Creek, T0L 0K0 Canada
403-949-2238, Fax: 403-949-2238,
WMTCab@telus.net
westernmontessori.ca

Revelstoke: Canadian Avalanche Association
P.O. Box 2759
Revelstoke, V0E 2S0 Canada
250-837-2435, Fax: 250-837-4624,
Toll Free: 1-800-667-1105 (Voice Bulletins)
canav@avalanche.ca
www.avalanche.ca

Observing weather, snowpack conditions, forecasting snow stability, organizing training courses in all aspects of avalanche hazard control for professionals

Richmond: Automotive Training Centre
#210, 13460 Smallwood Pl. Richmond, V6V 1W8 Canada
604-270-6121, Fax: 604-270-6123, 1-888-546-288
vancouver@autotrainingcentre.com
www.autotrainingcentre.com

Richmond: Richmond Campus
8057 Anderson Rd. Richmond, V6Y 1S2 Canada
604-276-8202,
www.hairdressing.ca

Hairstyling courses

Campuses

Maple Ridge Campus
11922 - 227 St. Maple Ridge, V2X 6J2 Canada
604-467-0222, Fax: 604-467-0218,
www.hairdressing.ca

New Westminster Campus
333 - 6th St. New Westminster, V3L 4H2 Canada
604-520-3989,
www.hairdressing.ca

Sechelt: Sunshine Coast Computer College
P.O. Box 2429
5797 Ebbtide St. Sechelt, V0N 3A0 Canada
604-885-3386, Fax: 604-885-7123,
b_pap@uniserve.com
www.homestead.com/computercollege/

Surrey: Hilltop Security Academy
#119, 9801 King George Hwy. Surrey, V3T 5H5 Canada
604-930-8377,
info@hilltopsecurity.com
www.hilltopsecurity.com/

Private security training; software quality assurance

Surrey: West Coast College of Health Care
#210, 2383 King George Hwy. Surrey, V4A 5A4 Canada
604-951-6644, Fax: 604-951-6608, 1-800-807-855
admin@westcoastcollege.com
www.westcoastcollege.com

Enrollment: 220
Pharmacy Technician, Community Support/Justice Worker, Veterinary Assistant, Medical Lab Assistant, Resident Care Attendant, Certified Dental Assistant

Vancouver: Blanche Macdonald Centre
#100, 555 West 12th Ave. Vancouver, V5Z 3X7 Canada
604-685-0347, Fax: 604-669-1415,
info@blanchemacdonald.com
www.blanchemacdonald.com

Fashion merchandising & design, make-up artistry, esthetics programs, professional nail technology programs

Vancouver: BM Chan International Cosmetology College
2951 Kingsway Vancouver, V5R 5J4 Canada
604-437-3109,
info@bmchan.com
www.bmchan.com

Hair, esthetics & nail courses
Monita Chan, Founder/President/Director

Vancouver: Canadian Business English Institute
#400, 1130 West Pender St. Vancouver, V6E 4A4 Canada
604-685-0291, Fax: 604-685-0294,
info@cbei.com
www.cbei.com

ESL, TOEFL, business English, TEFL training, student internships

Vancouver: Canadian Family Resource Institute & Career College
L-1 Broadway Plaza
600 West Broadway Vancouver, V5Z 4C2 Canada
604-879-2291, Fax: 604-879-2082,
info@fricollege.com
www.fricollege.com

Nurse's aides training

Vancouver: Canadian Institute of Gemmology
P.O. Box 57010
Vancouver, V5K 5G6 Canada
604-530-8569, Fax: 604-530-8569, 1-800-294-221
www.cigem.ca

Diamond grading, jewellery, history & design, gem identification

Vancouver: Columbia Academy, Digital Entertainment & Communications Training
1295 West Broadway Vancouver, V6H 3X8 Canada
604-736-3316, Fax: 604-731-5458, 1-800-665-928
administration@columbia-academy.com
www.columbia-academy.com

10-month programs in Broadcast Performing Arts (Radio/TV), Audio Recording/Sound Design & Digital Video Production

Vancouver: EJ Canada College
520 Hornby St. Vancouver, V6C 2E7 Canada
604-689-1079, Fax: 604-689-1649,
info@ejcanadacollege.com
www.ejcanadacollege.com

ESL

Vancouver: Emily Carr Institute of Art & Design
1399 Johnston St. Vancouver, V6H 3R9 Canada
604-844-3800, Fax: 604-844-3801, 1-800-832-778
www.eciad.ca/

Enrollment: 1173
Dr. Ronald Burnett, President

Vancouver: Erickson College
2021 Columbia St. Vancouver, V5Y 3C9 Canada
604-879-5600, 1-800-665-694
info@erickson.edu
www.erickson.edu

Psychotherapy & counselling, personal & professional empowerment & growth
Marilyn Atkinson, President

***Vancouver:* Eurocentres Vancouver**
#250, 815 West Hastings St. Vancouver, V6C 1B4 Canada
604-688-7942, Fax: 604-688-7985,
info@languagecanada.com
www.languagecanada.com
English as a Second Language training

***Vancouver:* Gateway Careers Inc.**
395 West Broadway Vancouver, V5Y 1A7 Canada
604-738-0285, Fax: 604-738-0994,
info@gatewaycareers.ca
www.gatewaycareers.ca
Resident care; long-term care aide training

***Vancouver:* Granville Business College**
#725, 570 Dunsmuir St. Vancouver, V6B 1Y1 Canada
604-683-8850, Fax: 604-682-7115, 1-800-661-988
vetassistant@telus.net
www.vet-assistant.com
Veterinary Office Assistants

***Vancouver:* Helen Lefeaux Inc. School of Fashion Design**
#100, 247 Abbott St. Vancouver, V6B 2K7 Canada
604-687-3352, Fax: 604-687-3356,
info@helenlefeaux.com
www.helenlefeaux.com
Fashion design

***Vancouver:* Institute of Forest Engineering of BC**
Forintek Building University of British Columbia
2665 East Mall Vancouver, V6T 1W5 Canada
604-224-7800, Fax: 604-224-7010,
ifebc@interchg.ubc.ca

***Vancouver:* Joji's Academy of Hair Fashion International**
1126 Commercial Dr. Vancouver, V5L 3X2 Canada
604-255-5809, Fax: 604-255-5803,
enroll@jojishair.com
www.jojishairschool.com

***Vancouver:* MTI Vancouver Campus**
#290, 220 Cambie St. Vancouver, V6B 2M9 Canada
604-682-6020, Fax: 604-682-6468, 1-866-682-6020
vancouver@mticc.com
www.metrocollege.net
ECCE; Residential Care; Long Term Care Aide; Community Support Worker; Internet Development; MCSE

Campuses
Surrey King George Campus
10072 King George Hwy. Surrey, V3T 2W4 Canada
604-583-6020, Fax: 604-583-6019,
surrey@mticc.com
www.metrocollege.net

Coquitlam Campus
#223- 3030 Lincoln Ave. Coquitlam, V3B 6B4 Canada
604-464-8718, Fax: 604-942-6355,
coquitlam@mticc.com
www.metrocollege.net

Burnaby Campus
#100-6446 Nelson Ave. Burnaby, V5H 3J5 Canada
604-437-6030, Fax: 604-437-6036,
burnaby@mticc.com
www.metrocollege.net

Chilliwack Campus
#107-7491 Vedder Rd. Chilliwack, V2R 4E7 Canada
604-824-6081, Fax: 604-824-6084,
chilliwack@mticc.com
www.metrocollege.net

***Vancouver:* Native Education Centre**
285 East 5th Ave. Vancouver, V5T 1H2 Canada
604-873-3772, Fax: 604-873-9152,
admissions@necvancouver.org
www.necvancouver.org
Family counselling, ECE, office administration, criminal justice studies, aboriginal tourism & aboriginal land stewardship

***Vancouver:* Pacific Gateway Vancouver**
1155 Robson St., 3rd Fl. Vancouver, V6E 1B5 Canada
604-687-3595, Fax: 604-687-3586,
info@pacificgateway.net
www.pacificgateway.net

Campuses
Brisbane Campus
Level 1, 232 Adelaise St. Brisbane, Queensland, 4000 Australia
Fax: 617-322- 027,
61-7-3220-0144
study@pacificgateway.net.au
www.pacificgateway.net.au

Pacific Gateway Toronto
80 Bloor St. West, 9th Fl. Toronto, M5S 2V1 Canada
416-413-0511, Fax: 416-413-9044,
toronto@pacificgateway.net
www.pacificgateway.net

Pacific Gateway Victoria
1012 Douglas St., 3rd. Fl. Victoria, V8W 2C3 Canada
250-381-6630, Fax: 250-381-6631,
victoria@pacificgateway.net
www.pacificgateway.net

Sydney Campus
Level 7, 190 George St. The Rocks Sydney NSW, 2000
029-247-1744, Fax: 029-247-1644,
study@pacificgateway.net.au
www.pacificgateway.net.au

***Vancouver:* Rhodes Wellness College**
#280, 1125 Howe St. Vancouver, V6Z 2K8 Canada
604-708-4416, Fax: 604-708-4418,
admin@rhodescollege.ca
www.rhodescollege.ca
Wellness, lifeskills, coaching & counselling diplomas & certificates; PCTIA accredited

***Vancouver:* Spectrum College & Consulting Services Ltd.**
#301, 1010 Beach Ave. Vancouver, V6E 1T7 Canada
604-685-5100, Fax: 604-685-5199,
flong@knowplace.ca
knowplace.ca
Provides online courses, workshops and conferences online

***Vancouver:* Tourism Training Institute**
#301, 1245 West Broadway Vancouver, V6H 1G7 Canada
604-736-7008, Fax: 604-736-7723,
info@tourismti.com
www.tourismti.com
Travel & tourism; hotel management; cruise hospitality

***Vancouver:* Vancouver Campus**
#501-1755 West Broadway Vancouver, V6J 4S5 Canada
604-736-8000, Fax: 604-731-9819, 1-800-668-9301
vancouver@tourismcollege.com
www.tourismcollege.com
Travel, tourism & hospitality

Campuses
Surrey
#320-10362 King Surrey, V3R 8X8 Canada
Fax: 604-583-4092,
www.tourismcollege.com

***Vancouver:* Vancouver Campus**
#200, 1111 Melville St. Vancouver, V6E 3V6 Canada
604-684-4467, Fax: 604-689-4430, 1-87-STENBERG
vanadmin@stenbergcollege.com
www.stenbergcollege.com
Resident care attendant; community support worker; nursing unit clerk, medical office assistant; institutional aid; veterinary assistant; practical nursing program; automotive technician

Campuses
Surrey Campus at Central City
#750-13450 - 102nd Ave. Surrey, V3T 5X3 Canada
604-580-2772, Fax: 604-580-2774, 1-87-STENBERG
admin@stenbergcollge.com
www.stenbergcollege.com

***Vancouver:* Vancouver School of Theology**
6000 Iona Dr. Vancouver, V6T 1L4 Canada
604-822-9031, Fax: 604-822-9212, 1-866-822-903
possibilities@vst.edu
www.vst.edu
Multi-denominational graduate school educating leaders for the church, service agencies & businesses
Rev. Dr. Wendy Fletcher, Principal

***Vancouver:* Western Imperial College of Canada**
#201, 2460 Commercial Dr. Vancouver, V5H 4T9 Canada
604-872-1236, Fax: 604-872-1275,
teachabroad@telus.net
wiccbc.tripod.com/index.html
Specializes in offering Aspen University's Master's Degree Programs to international & North American students; also runs & manages ESL International - an educational centre that specializes in the training of individuals to teach English as a Second/For
Henry Yeo, Executive Director

***Victoria:* Academy of Excellence**
#303, Goldstream Ave. Victoria, V9B 2W4 Canada
604-386-7843, Fax: 250-386-0090,
excellence@telus.net
www.academyofexcellencevictoria.com

***Victoria:* Aveda Institute Victoria**
660 Johnson St. Victoria, V8W 1M6 Canada
250-386-7985, Fax: 250-386-7945,
admissions@pauldacostainstitute.ca
www.avedainstitutevictoria.ca
Enrollment: 81
Cosmetology & esthiology

***Victoria:* BC School of Art Therapy**
1941 Lee Ave. Victoria, V8R 4W9 Canada
250-598-6434, Fax: 250-598-6449,
info@bcsat.com
bcsat.com
Graduate level clinical training in art therapy
Aira Welwood, Program Director

***Victoria:* Canadian Acupressure College Inc.**
#301, 733 Johnson St. Victoria, V8W 3C7 Canada
250-388-7475, Fax: 250-383-3647, 1-877-909-224
cai@islandnet.com
www.acupressureshiatsuschool.com
Training in acupressure & shiatsu diploma programs

***Victoria:* Canadian College of Business & Language**
16 Bastion Sq. Victoria, V8W 1H9 Canada
250-383-3933, Fax: 250-383-2292,
admin@cdncollege.bc.ca
www.canadiancollege.ca
Gerald La Belle, President

***Victoria:* Canadian College of Performing Arts**
1701 Elgin Rd. Victoria, V8R 5L7 Canada
250-595-9970, Fax: 250-595-0779,
admin@ccpacanada.com
www.ccpacanada.com
Enrollment: 65
Two, 1-year extensive training programs in acting, voice, dance & career management

***Victoria:* Lester B. Pearson College of the Pacific**
650 Pearson College Dr. Victoria, V9C 4H7 Canada
250-391-2411, Fax: 250-391-2412,
admin@pearsoncollege.ca
www.pearsoncollege.ca
Stuart Walker, Director

***Victoria:* Western Academy of Photography**
755A Queens Ave. Victoria, V8T 1M2 Canada
250-383-1522, Fax: 250-383-1534,
wap-office@shaw.ca
www.westernacademyofphotography.com
Professional Photography & Journalism/Photojournalism

***West Vancouver:* ABC Occupational First Aid Training**
1057 Millstream Rd. West Vancouver, V7S 2C8 Canada
604-925-1057, Fax: 604-596-2999,
www.abcfirstaidtraining.com
Industrial first aid
Alison Spears
alison_abc@shaw.ca

***West Vancouver:* The Anna Wyman School of Dance Arts**
1457 Marine Dr. West Vancouver, V7T 1B8 Canada
604-926-6535, Fax: 604-926-6912,
info@annawyman.com
www.annawyman.com
Offering professional dance training to dedicated students for over 30 years

***West Vancouver:* Vancouver Art Therapy Institute**
#350, 1425 Marine Dr. West Vancouver, V7T 1B9 Canada
604-926-9381, Fax: 604-926-5728,
vatimail@telus.net
www.vati.bc.ca

Manitoba

Government Agencies

***Winnipeg:* Manitoba Advanced Education & Training**
Legislative Bldg.
#156, 450 Broadway Winnipeg, R3C 0V8 Canada
204-945-0825, Fax: 204-948-2216,
www.edu.gov.mb.ca/aet/
Hon. Diane McGifford, Minister
Dwight Botting, Acting Deputy Minister

Winnipeg: Manitoba Education, Citizenship & Youth
#168, 450 Broadway Winnipeg, R3C 0Y8 Canada
204-945-3720, Fax: 204-945-1291,
minedu@leg.gov.mb.ca
www.edu.gov.mb.ca
Gerald Farthing, Acting Deputy Minister
Hon. Peter Bjornson, Minister

School Boards/Districts/Divisions

Public

Altona: Border Land School Division
P.O. Box 390
120 - 9th St. NW Altona, R0G 0B0 Canada
204-324-6491, Fax: 204-324-1664, 1-866-324-6491
Transportation Office: 204-427-2091; Maintenance: 204-324-9536
www.borderland.ca
Grades: Kindergarten - 12; French Immersion
Krista Curry, Chief Executive Officer / Superintendent, 204-324-6491 1010, fax: 204-324-1664
Carol Braun, Assistant Superintendent, 204-324-6491 1011, fax: 204-324-1664
Anne Malyon, Secretary-Treasurer, 204-324-6491 1012, fax: 204-324-1664
Todd Nichols, Coordinator, Transportation, 204-427-2091 1510, fax: 204-427-2531
Julie Weber, Coordinator, Student Services, 204-427-2091 1013, fax: 204-427-2531

Beausejour: Sunrise School Division
Sunrise Education Center
P.O. Box 1206
344 Second St. North Beausejour, R0E 0C0 Canada
204-268-6500, Fax: 204-268-6545, 1-866-444-5559
Transportation, Phone: 204-444-2498; Business, Fax: 204-268-4149
kwold@sunrisesd.ca (Kathy Wold, Reception)
www.sunrisesd.ca
Grades: Kindergarten - 12; Adult Education
Number of Schools: 24
Don Nichol, Chair, 204-348-2818
dnichol@sunrisesd.ca
Wayne Leckie, Superintendent & Chief Executive Officer, 204-268-6507
wleckie@sunrisesd.ca
Paul Barnard, Assistant Superintendent, People Services, 204-268-6538
pbarnard@sunrisesd.ca
Paul Magnan, Assistant Superintendent, Student Learning, 204-268-6517
pmagnan@sunrisesd.ca
Lesley Eblie Trudel, Division Principal, Student Support Programs, 204-268-6535
leblie@sunrisesd.ca
Joan Badger, Leader, Middle Years & ICt Program, 204-268-6543
jbadger@sunrisesd.ca
Karen David, Leader, Early Years Program, 204-268-6527
kdavid@sunrisesd.ca
Kevin Doell, Leader, Music Program, 204-444-2473
kdoell@sunrisesd.ca
Marie Josee Morneau, Leader, Senior Years Program, 204-268-6532
mjmorneau@sunrisesd.ca
Fran King, Manager, Purchasing, 204-268-6531
fking@sunrisesd.ca
Roger Hardman, Secretary-Treasurer, 204-268-6514
rhardman@sunrisesd.ca

Birtle: Park West School Division
P.O. Box 68
1161 St. Claire St. Birtle, R0M 0C0 Canada
204-842-2100, Fax: 204-842-2110, 877-418-5320
cbonner@pwsd.ca
www.pwsd.ca
Enrollment: 1800
Joe Arruda, Chief Executive Officer

Brandon: Brandon School Division
Administration Office
1031 - 6th St. Brandon, R7A 4K5 Canada
204-729-3100, Fax: 204-727-2217,
info@brandonsd.mb.ca; human.resources@brandonsd.mb.ca
www.brandonsd.mb.ca
Grades: Kindergarten - 12; French Immersion
Enrollment: 7200
George Buri, Chair, 204-727-3156
buri.george@brandonsd.mb.ca
Dr. Donna Michaels, Chief Executive Officer & Superintendent of S
michaels.donna@brandonsd.mb.ca
Greg Malazdrewicz, Associate Superintendent
malazdrewicz.greg@brandonsd.mb.ca
Gerald F. Barnes, Secretary-Treasurer
barnes.gerald@brandonsd.mb.ca

Carman: Prairie Rose School Division
45 Main St. South Carman, R0G 0J0 Canada
204-745-2003, Fax: 204-745-3699, 866-745-3699
prsd@prsdmb.ca
www.prsdmb.ca
Enrollment: 2278
Bruce Wood, Superintendent

Dauphin: Mountain View School Division
P.O. Box 715
Dauphin, R7N 3B3 Canada
204-638-3001, Fax: 204-638-7250,
www.mvsd.ca
Grades: K.-12
Enrollment: 3300
Jack Sullivan, Supt.
jsullivan@mvsd.ca
Bart Michaleski, Sec.-Treas.
michale@mvsd.ca

Eriksdale: Lakeshore School Division
P.O. Box 100
Eriksdale, R0C 0W0 Canada
204-739-2101, Fax: 204-739-2145,
admin@lakeshoresd.mb.ca
www.lakeshoresd.mb.ca
Enrollment: 1304
Janet Martell, Superintendent

Flin Flon: Flin Flon School Division
9 Terrace Ave. Flin Flon, R8A 1S2 Canada
204-681-3413, Fax: 204-681-3417,
www.ffsd.mb.ca
Grades: Kindergarten - 12; Alternative Ed.
Enrollment: 1378
Number of Schools: 3 elementary schools; 2 secondary schools
Trish Sattelberger, Chair
Blaine Veitch, Superintendent
bveitch@ffsd.mb.ca
Dean Grove, Assistant Superintendent
dgrove@ffsd.mb.ca
Debbie Bongfeldt, Secretary-Treasurer
dbongfeldt@ffsd.mb.ca
Bruce Fidler, Supervisor, Maintenance
bfidler@ffsd.mb.ca

Gimli: Evergreen School Division
Education Support Centre
P.O. Box 1200
140 Centre Ave. West Gimli, R0C 1B0 Canada
204-642-6260, Fax: 204-642-7273,
info@esd.mb.ca
www.esd.mb.ca
Grades: Kindergarten - 12; Continuing Ed.
Enrollment: 1671
Number of Schools: 8. Number of Employees: 273
Ruth Ann Furgala, Chair, 204-378-2901
rfurgala@esd.mb.ca
Paul Cuthbert, Superintendent & Chief Executive Officer, 204-642-6278
pcuthbert@esd.mb.ca
Roza Gray, Assistant Superintendent, 204-642-6267
rgray@esd.mb.ca
Daniel Howe, Director, Operations, 204-642-6269
dhowe@esd.mb.ca
Fay Cassidy, Coordinator, Student Services, 204-642-6279
fcassidy@esd.mb.ca
Brenda Chapman, Officer, Safety, 204-641-1365
bchapman@esd.mb.ca
Charlie Grieve, Secretary-Treasurer, 204-642-6266
cgrieve@esd.mb.ca

Gladstone: Pine Creek School Division
P.O. Box 420
Gladstone, R0J 0T0 Canada
204-385-2216, Fax: 204-385-2825,
pcsddo@pinecreeksd.mb.ca
www.pinecreeksd.mb.ca
Enrollment: 1200
Brian Gouriluk, Superintendent
bgouriluk@pinecreeksd.mb.ca

Killarney: Turtle Mountain School Division
P.O. Box 280
435 Williams Ave. Killarney, R0K 1G0 Canada
204-523-7531, Fax: 204-523-7269,
dbo@tmsd.mb.ca
www.tmsd.mb.ca
Grades: Kindergarten - 12; Continuing Ed.
Number of Schools: 4 Hutterian schools; 1 elementary / middle years schools; 2 kindergarten to grade 12 schools; 2 adult education campuses
Larry Rainnie, Superintendent
lrainnie@tmsd.mb.ca
Tanya Edgar, Assistant Superintendent, Student Services
tedgar@tmsd.mb.ca
Kathy Siatecki, Secretary-Treasurer
Julie Dyck, Administrator, Payroll & Benefits
jdyck@tmsd.mb.ca
John Reimer, Supervisor, Transportation
jreimer@tmsd.mb.ca
Ken Rose, Supervisor, Buildings & Maintenance
krose@tmsd.mb.ca

Lorette: Division Scolaire franco-manitobaine
P.O. Box 204
1263, ch Dawson Lorette, R0A 0Y0 Canada
204-878-9399, Fax: 204-878-9407,
dsfm@atrium.ca
Enrollment: 4572
Gérard Auger, Supt.

Lorette: Seine River School Division
475A Senez St. Lorette, R0A 0Y0 Canada
204-878-4713, Fax: 204-878-4717,
www.srsd.mb.ca
Enrollment: 3500
Michael Borgfjord, Superintendent

McCreary: Turtle River School Division
P.O. Box 309
808 Burrows Rd. McCreary, R0J 1B0 Canada
204-835-2067, Fax: 204-835-2426,
trsd32.mb.ca
Grades: Kindergarten - 12
Enrollment: 771
Number of Schools: 7. Number of Staff: 63 teachers; 52 support staff
Allan Trotter, Chair, Board of Trustees
Bev Szymesko, Superintendent, Student Services
bevs@trsd32.mb.ca
Richard Bidzinski, Secretary-Treasurer
Richard@trsd32.mb.ca
Dean Bluhm, Supervisor, Transportation & Maintenance
deanb@trsd32.mb.ca
Shannon Desjardins, Accountant
shannon@trsd32.mb.ca
Helen Sommer, Speech / Language Pathologist
helen@trsd32.mb.ca
Jeff Fudge, Information & Communication Technology Techni
jeff@trsd32.mb.ca

Melita: Southwest Horizon School Division
P.O. Box 370
Melita, R0M 1L0 Canada
204-483-5533, Fax: 204-483-5535,
www.shsd.mb.ca
Enrollment: 1793
Brad Kyle, Superintendent

Minnedosa: Rolling River School Division
P.O. Box 1170
Minnedosa, R0J 1E0 Canada
204-867-2754, Fax: 204-867-2037,
rrsd@rrsd.mb.ca
www.rrsd.mb.ca
Enrollment: 1882
Reg Klassen, Superintendent
rklassen@rrsd.mb.ca

Morden: Western School Division
75 Thornhill St., #4 Morden, R6M 1P2 Canada
204-822-4448, Fax: 204-822-4262,
divoff@westernsd.mb.ca
www.westernsd.mb.ca
Grades: K.-12
Enrollment: 1600
Stephen Ross, Supt.
sross@westernsd.mb.ca
Carl Pedersen, Sec.-Treas.
cpedersen@westernsd.mb.ca
Dr David McAndrew, Chair
dmcandrew@westernsd.mb.ca

Morris: Red River Valley School Division
P.O. Box 400
233 Main St. Morris, R0G 1K0 Canada

204-746-2317, Fax: 204-746-2785,
rrvsd@rrvsd.ca
www.rrvsd.ca

Enrollment: 2196
Kelly Barkman, Superintendent

Neepawa: Beautiful Plains School Division
P.O. Box 700
Neepawa, R0J 1H0 Canada
204-476-2388, Fax: 204-476-3606,
bpsd@bpsd.mb.ca
www.bpsd.mb.ca

Grades: Kindergarten - 12; Special Ed.
Enrollment: 1500
Jason Young, Superintendent
jyoung@bpsd.mb.ca
Gord Olmstead, Secretary-Treasurer
golmstead@bpsd.mb.ca
Melanie Burnett, Coordinator, Student Services
mburnett@bpsd.mb.ca
Melanie Nordstrom, Coordinator, Technology
mordstrom@bpsd.mb.ca
Jennifer Donais, Speech Language Pathologist
jdonais@bpsd.mb.ca

Pilot Mound: Prairie Spirit School Division
P.O. Box 77
152 Broadway Ave. West Pilot Mound, R0G 1P0 Canada
204-825-2721, Fax: 204-825-2725,
prspirit@mts.net
www.prairiespirit.mb.ca

Enrollment: 2479
Don Hurton, Superintendent

Pinawa: Whiteshell School District
P.O. Box 130
Pinawa, R0E 1L0 Canada
204-753-8366, Fax: 204-753-2237,
derousie@sdwhiteshell.mb.ca
sdwhiteshell.mb.ca

Grades: K.-12
Enrollment: 206
Bob Derousie, Supt./CEO
derousie@sdwhiteshell.mb.ca
Jenny Petersen, Sec.-Treas.
petersenj@sdwhiteshell.mb.ca
Rob Murray, Chair
murrayr@sdwhiteshell.mb.ca

Portage la Prairie: Portage la Prairie School Division
535 - 3 St. NW Portage la Prairie, R1N 2C4 Canada
204-857-8756, Fax: 204-239-5998,
div0024@merlin.mb.ca
www.plpsd.mb.ca

Enrollment: 3486
Hazen Barrett, Superintendent

Selkirk: Lord Selkirk School Division
205 Mercy St. Selkirk, R1A 2C8 Canada
204-482-5942, Fax: 204-482-3000, 866-433-5942
lssd.boardoffice@lssd.ca
www.lssd.ca

Grades: K.-12
Enrollment: 5000
The schools celebrate the heritage and culture of the region - including the Brokenhead Ojibway Nation, the Scottish pioneers, the French Canadian voyageurs and the Ukrainian settlers.
Scott Kwasnitza, Supt./CEO
Bruce Cairns, Sec. Treas.

Steinbach: Hanover School Division
5 Chrysler Gate Steinbach, R5G 0E2 Canada
204-326-6471, Fax: 204-326-9901,
hsdadmin@hsd.ca
www.hsd.ca

Enrollment: 7400
Ken Klassen, Superintendent

Stonewall: Interlake School Division
192 - 2nd Ave. North Stonewall, R0C 2Z0 Canada
204-467-5100, Fax: 204-467-8334,
www.isd21.mb.ca

Enrollment: 3040
Ross Metcalfe, Superintendent
rmetcalfe@isd21.mb.ca

Swan River: Swan Valley School Division
John Kastrukoff Building
1481 - 3rd St. North Swan River, R0L 1Z0 Canada
204-734-4531,
www.svsd.ca

Grades: JK - 12; French Immersion
Number of Schools: 9
Bryon Fried, Chair
M. Marquis-Forster, Superintendent
R. Rausch, Secretary-Treasurer
D. Coulthart, Supervisor, Transportation
L. Delaurier, Supervisor, Maintenance
D. Burnside, Coordinator, Student Services

The Pas: Kelsey School Division
P.O. Box 4700
322 Edwards Ave. The Pas, R9A 1R4 Canada
204-623-6421, Fax: 204-623-7704,
kelsey@merlin.mb.ca
www.ksd.mb.ca

Enrollment: 1733
Doug Long, Superintendent
douglong@ksd.mb.ca

Thompson: Mystery Lake School District
408 Thompson Dr. North Thompson, R8N 0C5 Canada
204-677-6150, Fax: 204-677-9528,
sdml@mysterynet.mb.ca
www.mysterynet.mb.ca

Grades: K.-12
Enrollment: 3000
Beverly Hammond, Supt./CEO
Arnie Assoignon, Sec.-Treas.
aassoignon@mysterynet.mb.ca

Virden: Fort la Bosse School Division
P.O. Box 1420
523 - 9th Ave. South Virden, R0M 2C0 Canada
204-748-2692, Fax: 204-748-2436,
flbsd@flbsd.mb.ca
www.flbsd.mb.ca

Grades: Kindergarten - 12
Enrollment: 1400
Number of Schools: 11
Gary E. Draper, Chair
Barry Pitz, Superintendent
Vaughn Wilson, Supervisor, Operations
Kent Reid, Secretary-Treasurer
Judy Dandridge, Coordinator, Student Services
Dr. Robert Paulet, School Psychologist

Winkler: Garden Valley School Division
P.O. Box 1330
750 Triple E Blvd. Winkler, R6W 4B3 Canada
204-325-8335, Fax: 204-325-4132,
gvsd@gvsd.ca
www.gvsd.ca

Grades: Kindergarten - Secondary
Enrollment: 4100
Hilda Froese, Board Chair
Vern Reimer, Chief Executive Officer & Superintendent of S
Todd Monster, Assistant Superintendent
Debra Loewen, Assistant Superintendent, Student Services
Jenn Sager Hlady, Manager, Human Resources
Ken Bergen, Supervisor, Operations
Abe Wiebe, Supervisor, Capital Projects
James Reimer, Coordinator, Technology
Terry Penner, Secretary-Treasurer

Winnipeg: Frontier School Division
30 Speers Rd. Winnipeg, R2J 1L9 Canada
204-775-9741, Fax: 204-775-9940,
frontier@frontiersd.mb.ca
www.frontiersd.mb.ca

Enrollment: 6869
Number of Schools: 41
Linda Ballantyne, Chair
Gordon Shead, Chief Superintendent
Bradley Hampson, Assistant Superintendent, Technology
Don McCaskill, Assistant Superintendent, Senior Years & Care
Arnold Dysart, Superintendent, Area 1
Karen Crozier, Superintendent, Area 2
Cam Giavedoni, Superintendent, Area 3
Catherine Fidierchuk, Superintendent, Area 4
David Swanson, Superintendent, Area 5
Lena McAlinden, Director, Human Resources
Gerald Cattani, Secretary-Treasurer

Winnipeg: Louis Riel School Division
900 St. Mary's Rd. Winnipeg, R2M 3R3 Canada
204-257-7827, Fax: 204-256-8553,
www.lrsd.net

Grades: K.-12
Enrollment: 14464
The is an amalgamation of the St. Boniface and St. Vital School Divisions.
Terry D. Borys, Supt./CEO

Winnipeg: Pembina Trails School Division
181 Henlow Bay Winnipeg, R3Y 1M7 Canada
204-488-1757, Fax: 204-487-3667,
ptsdwebinfo@pembinatrails.ca
www.pembinatrails.ca

Enrollment: 13385
Lawrence Lussier, Superintendent

Winnipeg: River East Transcona School Division
589 Roch St. Winnipeg, R2K 2P7 Canada
204-667-7130, Fax: 204-661-5618,
www.retsd.mb.ca

Enrollment: 17000
Dennis Pottage, Superintendent

Winnipeg: St. James-Assiniboia School Division
2574 Portage Ave. Winnipeg, R3J 0H8 Canada
204-888-7951, Fax: 204-831-0859,
Continuing Ed., Phone: 204-832-9637; Intl. Program: 204-837-1331
inquiries@sjsd.net; mnachtigall@sjsd.net (administration & board)
www.sjsd.net

Grades: Kindergarten - Senior 4
Number of Schools: 15 early years schools; 6 middle years schools; 5 senior years schools
Bruce Chegus, Chair, 204-888-9498
bchegus@sjsd.net
Ron K. Weston, Chief Superintendent
Brett J. Lough, Assistant Superintendent, Administration, Pla
Greg Mutter, Assistant Superintendent, Personnel & Human R
Tanis C.M. Pshebniski, Assistant Superintendent, Program & Curriculu
Dennis G. Dart, Manager, Facilities & Maintenance
Carrol A. Harvey, Manager, Human Resources (MANTE & excluded)
Cindy Labaty, Manager, Human Resources (CUPE)
P. Elsworth, Officer, Information
pelsworth@sjsd.net
B. Neufeld, Officer, Purchasing
bneufeld@sjsd.net
Michael J. Friesen, Secretary-Treasurer

Winnipeg: Seven Oaks School Division
830 Powers St. Winnipeg, R2V 4E7 Canada
204-586-8061, Fax: 204-589-2504,
communitybeginshere@7oaks.org
www.7oaks.org

Enrollment: 8950
Brian O'Leary, Superintendent

Winnipeg: Winnipeg School Division
1577 Wall St. East Winnipeg, R3E 2S5 Canada
204-775-0231, Fax: 204-772-6464,
adminofc@wsd1.org
ww.wsd1.org

Grades: Pre-K.-12
Enrollment: 32000
Pauline Clarke, Chief Supt.
pclarke@wsd1.org
Rene Appelmans, Sec.-Treas.
rappelmans@wsd1.org
Val Georges, Dir., Aboriginal Ed., 204-788-0203, fax: 204-772-3911
vgeorges@wsd1.org

First Nations

Ebb & Flow: Ebb & Flow Eduction Authority
P.O. Box 160
Ebb & Flow, R0L 0R0
204-448-2438, Fax: 204-448-2393,
eandf@mts.net

Grades: Elementary - Secondary
Number of Schools: 1 (Ebb & Flow School). The Ebb & Flow Eduction Authority serves the Ebb & Flow First Nation in Manitoba
Arlene Mousseau, Director, Education

Gods River: Amos Okemow Memorial Education Authority
Building 1D
103 Gods River, R0B 0N0 Canada
204-366-2070, Fax: 204-366-2105

Grades: Kindergarten - 9
Enrollment: 170
The Amos Okemow Memorial Education Authority serves the Manto Sipi Cree Nation through operation of the Amos Okemow Memorial School. To continue their secondary school education, students must leave the community.
A. Jane Tuesday, Director, Education
ajanet25@hotmail.com
Alan Pogson, Principal

Oxford House: **Oxford House First Nation Board of Education**
General Delivery Oxford House, R0B 1C0
204-538-2051
Grades: Elementary - S4
Enrollment: 675
Number of Schools: 2 (Oxford House Elementary School & 1972 Memorial High School). The Oxford House First Nation Board of Education serves the Bunibonibee Cree Nation of Oxford House, which is situated 600 km north of Winnipeg, Manitoba.
Alvin Grieves, Director, Education, Oxford House First Natio
argrieves@hotmail.com

Pelican Rapids: **Sapotaweyak Education Authority**
General Delivery Pelican Rapids, R0L 1L0
204-587-2045, Fax: 204-587-2341
Grades: Nursery - 12
Enrollment: 350
Number of Schools: 1 (Neil Dennis Kematch Memorial School). Number of Employees: 50. The Sapotaweyak Education Authority is responsible for the provision of education for the Sapotaweyak Cree Nation, near the towns of Swan River & The Pas in Manitoba.
Diane Genaille, Director, Education
school@ndkms.com

Pine Falls: **Sagkeeng Education Authority**
P.O. Box 1610
Pine Falls, R0E 1M0 Canada
204-367-2287, Fax: 204-367-4315, 1-866-878-2911
Grades: Elementary - Secondary
Number of Schools: 3 (Anicinabe Community School; Sagkeeng Junior High School; & Sagkeeng Anicinabe High School)
Eva Courchene, Education Director
Alan Courchene, Principal, Sagkeeng Anicinabe High School, 204-367-2243, fax: 204-367-4566
Rick Fewchuck, Principal, Anicinabe Community School, 204-367-2285, fax: 204-367-9205
Claude Guimond, Principal, Sagkeeng Junior High School, 204-367-2588, fax: 204-367-9231

Winnipeg: **Southeast Tribal Division for Schools Inc.**
#301, 208 Edmonton St. Winnipeg, R3C 1R7 Canada
204-943-7412, Fax: 204-947-8386

Schools: Specialized

First Nations

Beulah: **Chan Kagha Otina Dakota Wayawa Tipi School**
P.O. Box 40
Beulah, R0M 0B0 Canada
204-568-4757, Fax: 204-568-4762,
www.frontiersd.mb.ca
Grades: birdtailschool@gmail.ca
Enrollment: 130
The Chan Kagha Otina Dakota Wayawa Tipi School serves the Birdtail Sioux Dakota Nation. It is part of Manitoba's Frontier School Division.
Karen Crozier, Superintendent, Frontier School Division (Dau, 204-638-6839
jacqueline_birdtail@yahoo.ca
Michael Gamblin, Principal

Birch River: **Chief Charles Thomas Audy Memorial School**
P.O. Box 307
Birch River, R0L 0E0 Canada
204-236-4783, Fax: 204-236-4779
Grades: Nursery - 8
Chief Charles Thomas Audy Memorial School serves the Wuskwi Sipihk First Nation.

Bloodvein: **Miskooseepi School**
General Delivery Bloodvein, R0C 0J0 Canada
204-395-2012, Fax: 204-395-2189
Grades: Pre.-9

Camperville: **Pine Creek School**
P.O. Box 130
Camperville, R0L 0J0 Canada
204-524-2318, Fax: 204-524-2177
Grades: Pre.-11

Crane River: **Donald Ahmo School**
P.O. Box 91
Crane River, R0L 0M0 Canada
204-732-2548, Fax: 204-732-2753
The Donald Ahmo School is a band-operated First Nation school which serves the O-Chi-Chak-Ko-Sipi First Nation in Crane River, Manitoba.
Peter McKay, Director of Education & Principal
mckay_pj@hotmail.com

Cross Lake: **Mikisew Middle School**
P.O. Box 370
Cross Lake, R0B 0J0 Canada
204-676-3030, Fax: 204-676-2798
Grades: 5-8

Cross Lake: **Otter Nelson River**
P.O. Box 370
Cross Lake, R0B 0J0 Canada
204-676-2050, Fax: 204-676-2464,
sch1991@merlin.mb.ca
Grades: Pre.-12

Dakota Tipi: **Dakota Tipi School**
2000A Dakota Dr. Dakota Tipi, R1N 3P1 Canada
204-857-7190
Enrollment: 60
Located outside the city of Portage La Prairie, Manitoba, the Dakota Tipi School is a First Nations band operated school. The school serves the Dakota Tipi First Nation.

Easterville: **Chemawawin School**
P.O. Box 10
Easterville, R0C 0V0 Canada
204-329-2115, Fax: 204-329-2214
Located on the southern shore of Cedar Lake, 300 kilometres north of Winnipeg, Manitoba, the Chemawawin School provides education to the Chemawawin Cree Nation.
Melvin George, Director, Education
Amie Martin, Principal
amiemd@gmail.com

Ebb & Flow: **Ebb & Flow School**
P.O. Box 160
Ebb & Flow, R0L 0R0 Canada
204-448-2012, Fax: 204-448-2393,
eandf@mts.net
Grades: Elementary - Secondary
The Ebb & Flow School is a band-operated school in Manitoba which provides education to the Ebb & Flow First Nation.
Paul Monchka, Principal

Edwin: **Dakota Plains School**
P.O. Box 120
Edwin, R0H 0G0 Canada
204-252-2895, Fax: 204-252-2188
Grades: Elementary
The Dakota Plains School serves the Dakota Plains Wahpeton Nation.
Donald R. Smoke, Director, Education

Elphinstone: **Keeseekoowenin School**
P.O. Box 129
Elphinstone, R0J 0N0 Canada
204-625-2062, Fax: 204-625-2418
Grades: Pre.-8

Fairford: **Pinaymootang School**
Fairford Reserve
Fairford, R0C 0X0 Canada
204-659-2045, Fax: 204-659-2270,
sch1972@merlin.mb.ca
Grades: Pre.-12

Fisher River: **Charles Sinclair School**
P.O. Box 109
Fisher River, R0C 1S0 Canada
204-645-2206, Fax: 204-645-2614,
www.csschool.mb.ca
Part of the Fisher River Board of Education, Charles Sinclair School provides education to the Fisher River Cree Nation.
Davin Dumas, Principal, 204-645-2206, fax: 204-645-2614
davin@csschool.mb.ca
Jennifer Garson, Vice-Principal, 204-645-2206, fax: 204-645-2614
jennifer@csschool.mb.ca

Gillam: **Fox Lake Native Spiritual School**
P.O. Box 279
Gillam, R0B 0L0 Canada
204-486-2307, Fax: 204-486-2606
Grades: Pre.-4

Ginew: **Ginew School**
P.O. Box 10
Ginew, R0A 2R0 Canada
204-427-2490, Fax: 204-427-2398
Grades: Pre.-10

Gods Lake Narrows: **God's Lake Narrows First Nation School**
General Delivery Gods Lake Narrows, R0B 0M0 Canada
204-335-2003, Fax: 204-335-2440
Grades: Pre.-8

Gods River: **Amos Okemow Memorial School**
Building 1D
103 Gods River, R0B 0N0
204-366-2312, Fax: 204-366-2105, 866-896-4255
Grades: Kindergarten - 9
Enrollment: 170
Under the direction of the Amos Okemow Memorial Education Authority, the Amos Okemow Memorial School serves the Manto Sipi Cree Nation. Students must leave the community to continue their secondary school education.

Griswold: **Sioux Valley School**
P.O. Box 99
Griswold, R0M 0S0 Canada
204-855-2536, Fax: 204-855-3204,
sioux2@escape.ca
Grades: Pre.-12

Gypsumville: **Dauphin River School**
P.O. Box 140
Gypsumville, R0C 1J0 Canada
204-659-5268, Fax: 204-659-5790
Grades: Elementary
Dauphin River First Nation is located at the junction of Dauphin River & Lake Winnipeg. A Dauphin River Mature Student Program is also available.

Gypsumville: **Lake St. Martin School**
P.O. Box 2020
Gypsumville, R0C 1J0 Canada
204-659-2699, Fax: 204-659-5739,
narrowsed@xplornet.ca
Grades: Nursery - 9
Enrollment: 120
The Lake St. Martin School provides elementary education to the Lake St. Martin First Nation in Manitoba's Interlake Region.
Roselyn Beardy, Principal

Gypsumville: **Little Saskatchewan School**
P.O. Box 5050
Gypsumville, R0C 1J0 Canada
204-659-2672, Fax: 204-659-5763,
sch1216@merlin.mb.ca
Grades: Pre.-10

Hodgson: **Lawrence Sinclair Memorial School**
P.O. Box 359
Hodgson, R0C 1N0 Canada
204-394-2314, Fax: 204-394-2431,
lawrencesinclairmemorialschool@hotmail.com
Grades: Nursery - 10
Lawrence Sinclair Memorial School is a band operated school which serves members of the Kinonjeoshtegon First Nation.
Adeline Traverse, Principal

Island Lake: **Garden Hill First Nations High School**
General Delivery Island Lake, R0B 0T0 Canada
204-456-2886, Fax: 204-456-2894
Grades: 7-12

Island Lake: **Kistiganwacheeng Elementary School**
General Delivery Island Lake, R0B 0T0 Canada
204-456-2391, Fax: 204-456-2350
Grades: Gr. N.-6

Lac Brochet: **Petit Casimir Memorial School**
General Delivery Lac Brochet, R0B 2E0 Canada
204-337-2278, Fax: 204-337-2078
Grades: Pre.-12

Marius: **Isaac Beaulieu Memorial**
Marius Post Office
Marius, R0H 0T0 Canada
204-843-2407, Fax: 204-843-2269,
sch1402@merlin.mb.ca
Grades: Pre.-12

Negginan: **Poplar River School**
Stn Negginan Negginan, R0B 0Z0 Canada
204-244-2113, Fax: 204-244-2259,
prfn@mb.sympatico.ca
Grades: Pre.-9

Nelson House: **Nisichawayasihk Neyo Ohtinwak**
General Delivery Nelson House, R0B 1A0 Canada
204-484-2095, Fax: 204-484-2257
Grades: 9-12

***Nelson House:* Otetiskewin Kiskinwamahtowekamik**
General Delivery Nelson House, R0B 1A0 Canada
204-484-2242, Fax: 204-484-2002,
sch1413@merlin.mb.ca
Grades: Pre.-8

***O'Hanly:* Little Black River School**
General Delivery O'Hanly, R0E 1K0 Canada
204-367-8298, Fax: 204-367-2266
Grades: Kindergarten - 12
Enrollment: 242
Members of the Little Black River First Nation are educated at the Little Black River School in O'Hanley, Manitoba. The First Nation community is situated approximately 150 kilometres north of Winnipeg.
Sheldon Kent, Chief

***Opaskwayak:* Joe A. Ross School**
c/o Opaskwayak Education Authority
P.O. Box 10160
Opaskwayak, R0B 2J0 Canada
204-623-4286, Fax: 204-623-4442
Grades: Pre.-12

***Oxford House:* 1972 Memorial High School**
General Delivery Oxford House, R0B 1C0 Canada
204-538-2020, Fax: 204-538-2075, 1-888-377-8520
Oxford House First Nation Bd. of Ed., Phone: 204-538-2051
www.ohboe.ca
Grades: 7 - S4
Enrollment: 225
Under the Oxford House First Nation Board of Education, the 1972 Memorial High School serves the Bunibonibee Cree Nation of Oxford House.
Alvin Grieves, Director, Education, Oxford House First Natio
argrieves@hotmail.com
Lawrence Einarsson, Principal
l.einarsson@hotmail.com

***Oxford House:* Oxford House Elementary School**
General Delivery Oxford House, R0B 1C0 Canada
204-538-2318, Fax: 204-538-2782, 1-888-377-8520
Oxford House First Nation Bd. of Ed., Phone: 204-538-2051
www.ohboe.ca
Grades: Elementary
Enrollment: 450
Under the Oxford House First Nation Board of Education, the Oxford House Elementary School serves the Bunibonibee Cree Nation of Oxford House.
Alvin Grieves, Director, Education, Oxford House First Natio
argrieves@hotmail.com
Wilfred Wood, Principal
wilfred.wood@ohboe.ca

***Peguis First Nation:* Peguis Central School**
P.O. Box 670
Peguis First Nation, R0C 3J0 Canada
204-645-2164, Fax: 204-645-2270
Grades: 6-12

***Pelican Rapids:* Neil Dennis Kematch Memorial School / NDKMS**
General Delivery Pelican Rapids, R0L 1L0 Canada
204-587-2045, Fax: 204-587-2341,
school@ndkms.com
www.ndkms.com
Grades: Nursery - 12
Enrollment: 350
The Neil Dennis Kematch Memorial School serves the citizens of Sapotaweyak Cree First Nation in a community located approximately 120 kilometres north of Swan River, Manitoba. The school is administered by the Sapotaweyak Education Authority.
Lorna Carter, Principal
principal@ndkms.com

***Pine Falls:* Anicinabe Community School**
P.O. Box 219
Pine Falls, R0E 1M0
204-367-2285, Fax: 204-367-9205
Anicinabe Community School serves the Sagkeeng First Nation. It operates under the direction of the Sagkeeng Education Authority.
Rick Fewchuck, Principal

***Pine Falls:* Sagkeeng Anicinabe High School**
P.O. Box 1610
Pine Falls, R0E 1M0
204-367-2243, Fax: 204-367-4566
Grades: Secondary
The Sagkeeng Education Authority operates the Sagkeeng Anicinabe High School, which educates secondary school students of the Sagkeeng First Nation.
Alan Courchene, Principal

***Pine Falls:* Sagkeeng Junior High School**
P.O. Box 1610
Pine Falls, R0E 1M0
204-367-2588, Fax: 204-367-9231
Sagkeeng Junior High School serves the Sagkeeng First Nation. The school operates under the Sagkeeng Education Authority.
Claude Guimond, Principal

***Pipestone:* Wambdi Iyotaka School**
P.O. Box 146
Pipestone, R0M 1T0 Canada
204-854-2975, Fax: 204-854-2933,
wambdi_iyotaka@live.ca
The Wambdi Iyotaka School serves members of the Canupawakpa Dakota Nation in Manitoba.
Anna Bone, Principal

***Portage la Prairie:* Long Plain School**
P.O. Box 430
Portage la Prairie, R1N 3B7 Canada
204-252-2326, Fax: 204-252-2786
Grades: Pre.-9

***Pukatawagan:* Sakastew School**
P.O. Box 319
Pukatawagan, R0B 1G0 Canada
204-553-2163, Fax: 204-553-2225,
pukschol@cancom.net
Grades: K.-12

***Red Sucker Lake:* Red Sucker Lake School**
General Delivery Red Sucker Lake, R0B 1H0 Canada
204-469-5302, Fax: 204-469-5436
Grades: Pre.-12

***Scanterbury:* Sergeant Tommy Prince School**
General Delivery Scanterbury, R0E 1W0 Canada
204-766-2636, Fax: 204-766-2809,
bone2@mb.sympatico.ca
Grades: K.-12

***Shamattawa:* Abraham Beardy Memorial School**
General Delivery Shamattawa, R0B 1K0 Canada
204-565-2022, Fax: 204-565-2122
Grades: Kindergarten - 10
Enrollment: 350
Abraham Beardy Memorial School serves the Cree First Nation of Shamattawa. To attend grades 11 & 12, students must enroll in educational institutions outside the community.
Ron Miles, Director, Education
Roberto Romero, Principal
r_romero@hotmail.com

***Shortdale:* Chief Clifford Lynxleg Anishinabe School**
General Delivery Shortdale, R0L 1W0 Canada
204-546-2641, Fax: 204-546-3120
Chief Clifford Lynxleg Anishinabe School is located on the Tootinawaziibeeng (Valley River) Reserve, where it provides education to the Tootinaowaziibeeng First Nation.
Madeline Whitehawk, Director, Education, & Principal
cclas@live.ca

***Split Lake:* Chief Sam Cook Mahmuwee Education Centre**
General Delivery Split Lake, R0B 1P0 Canada
204-342-2134, Fax: 204-342-2139,
teduauthority@mts.net
Grades: Nursery - 12
Chief Sam Cook Mahmuwee Education Centre serves the Tataskweyak Cree Nation. The Tataskweyak reserve is located approximately 150 kilometres northeast of Thompson, Manitoba.
Alfred Beardy, Director, Education
Dan Beardy, Principal, Grades 7 - 12
Thelma Spence, Principal, Nursery - Grade 6
Blake Symons, Principal, Middle Years

***St Theresa Point:* St. Theresa Point School**
General Delivery St Theresa Point, R0B 1J0 Canada
204-462-2600, Fax: 204-462-2341
Grades: K.-12

***Swan Lake:* Indian Springs School**
P.O. Box 145
Swan Lake, R0G 2S0 Canada
204-836-2332, Fax: 204-836-2317,
isprings@mb.sympatico.ca
Grades: Pre.-8

***Tadoule Lake:* Peter Yassie Memorial School**
General Delivery Tadoule Lake, R0B 2C0 Canada
204-684-2279, Fax: 204-684-2130
Grades: K.-12

***Vogar:* Lake Manitoba School**
P.O. Box 1250
Vogar, R0C 3C0 Canada
204-768-2728, Fax: 204-768-2194
Grades: Nursery - 8
Lake Manitoba School provides education to the Lake Manitoba First Nation.
Freda Missayabit, Principal

***Waasagomach:* George Knott School**
General Delivery Waasagomach, R0B 1Z0 Canada
204-457-2485, Fax: 204-457-2273,
sch2067@merlin.mb.ca
Grades: Pre.-12

***Waywayseecappo:* Waywayseecappo Community School**
P.O. Box 9
Waywayseecappo, R0J 1S0 Canada
204-859-2811, Fax: 204-859-2992,
waywayschool@yahoo.ca
Grades: Nursery - 8
Enrollment: 457
Number of Employees: 21 teachers; 6 teacher assistants; 8 bus drivers; 3 custodians. The Waywayseecappo Community School is a band operated elementary school, which provides education to members of Manitoba's Waywayseecappo First Nation. The First Nation community is situated appoximately thirty-four kilometres east of Russell. Secondary school students from Waywayseecappo First Nation are transported to Russell's Major Pratt School.
Patrick Anderson, Principal

***York Landing:* George Saunders Memorial School**
General Delivery York Landing, R0B 2B0 Canada
204-341-2118, Fax: 204-341-2235
Grades: Pre.-12

Special Education

***Brandon:* Child & Adolescent Treatment Centre**
1240 - 10th St. Brandon, R7A 7L6 Canada
204-727-3445, Fax: 204-727-3451
Grades: 4-12

***Portage la Prairie:* Gladys Cook Educational Centre**
P.O. Box 1342
Portage la Prairie, R1N 3A9 Canada
204-239-3029, Fax: 204-239-3025,
sch1219@merlin.mb.ca
Grades: 1-12

***Winnipeg:* Behavioural Health Foundation**
35 av de la Digue Winnipeg, R3V 1L6 Canada
204-261-3312, Fax: 204-275-8847
Grades: K-S4

***Winnipeg:* Manitoba School for the Deaf**
242 Stradford St. Winnipeg, R2Y 2C9 Canada
204-945-8934, Fax: 204-945-1767,
sch1570@merlin.mb.ca
Grades: K.-12

***Winnipeg:* Manitoba Youth Centre**
170 Doncaster St. Winnipeg, R3N 1X9 Canada
204-475-2010, Fax: 204-945-3112,
sch1049@merlin.mb.ca
Grades: K.-12

***Winnipeg:* Marymound School**
442 Scotia St. Winnipeg, R2V 1X4 Canada
204-336-5285, Fax: 204-338-4690,
school@marymound.com
Grades: 3-10

***Winnipeg:* St. Amant School**
440 River Rd. Winnipeg, R2M 3Z9 Canada
204-256-4301, Fax: 204-257-4349
Grades: K.-12

Schools: Independent & Private

Protestant

***Austin:* Edrans Christian School**
P.O. Box 1
RR #1 Austin, R0H 0C0 Canada
204-466-2865, Fax: 204-466-2994,
www.echurchnet.ca
Grades: K.-12
Dwight Kinley, Contact

Stonewall: **Faith Academy - Stonewall Campus**
P.O. Box 1669
539 - 4th Ave. South Stonewall, R0C 2Z0 Canada
204-467-5833, Fax: 204-467-5833,
www.faithacademy.ca
Grades: K.-8
Bill Cavey, Executive Director
FA_ceo@shaw.ca

Winnipeg: **Faith Academy - Winnipeg Campus**
437 Matheson Ave. Winnipeg, R2W 0E1 Canada
204-582-3400, Fax: 204-582-2616,
www.faithacademy.ca
Grades: K.-12
Enrollment: 520
Faith Academy is a conservative, evangelical, Christian, revival-based educational institution open to any Manitoba student willing and able to follow the established school guide. Winnipeg Middle School located at 600 Jefferson Ave., (204) 338-6150; Pritchard Campus located at 220 Pritchard Ave., (204) 589-6885.
Bill Cavey, Executive Director
FA_ceo@shaw.ca

Catholic

Winnipeg: **Holy Cross School**
300 Dubuc St. Winnipeg, R2H 1E4 Canada
204-237-4936, Fax: 204-237-7433
Grades: K.-8
Enrollment: 159
John Talaga, Principal

Independent & Private Schools

Altona: **Sunflower Valley Christian School**
P.O. Box 2484
Altona, R0G 0B0 Canada
204-324-1564, Fax: 204-327-5505
Grades: 1-9

Arborg: **Interlake Mennonite Fellowship School**
P.O. Box 388
Arborg, R0C 0A0 Canada
204-364-2328
Grades: K.-12

Arborg: **Lake Centre Mennonite Fellowship School**
P.O. Box 838
Arborg, R0C 0A0 Canada
204-364-2201
Grades: 1-9

Arborg: **Morweena Christian School / MCS**
P.O. Box 1030
Arborg, R0C 0A0 Canada
204-364-2466, Fax: 204-364-3117
Grades: Kindergarten - 12

Austin: **Austin Christian Academy**
P.O. Box 460
Austin, R0H 0C0 Canada
204-637-2303, Fax: 204-637-2529,
aca@escape.ca
Grades: Kindergarten - 12
Enrollment: 50

Austin: **Austin Mennonite School**
P.O. Box 267
Austin, R0H 0C0 Canada
204-637-2008
Grades: 1 - 12

Austin: **Pine Creek School**
Pine Creek Colony
P.O. Box 370
Austin, R0H 0C0 Canada
204-466-2925, Fax: 204-466-2698
Grades: K.-10

Austin: **Pine Creek School**
P.O. Box 74
Austin, ROH OCO Canada
204-385-3025
Grades: K.-10

Beausejour: **Willow Grove School**
P.O. Box 59
Beausejour, R0E 0C0 Canada
204-268-4035
Grades: 2-8

Birnie: **Shady Oak Christian School**
P.O. Box 14
Birnie, R0J 0J0 Canada
204-966-3477, Fax: 204-966-3479
Grades: 1-9

Brandon: **Christian Heritage School**
Heritage Campus
2025 - 26 St. Brandon, R7B 3Y2 Canada
204-725-3209, Fax: 204-728-9641,
chs@westman.wave.ca
Grades: K.-8
Enrollment: 103

Carman: **Dufferin Christian School**
Box 1450 Carman, R0G 0J0 Canada
204-745-2278, Fax: 204-745-3441,
dufferin@mb.sympatico.ca
Grades: K.-12
Enrollment: 210

Cartwright: **Cartwright Community Independent School / CCIS**
P.O. Box 419
Cartwright, R0K 0L0 Canada
204-529-2357, Fax: 204-529-2455
Grades: 12 (Senior 4)

Cartwright: **Rock Lake School**
P.O. Box 69
Cartwright, R0K 0L0 Canada
204-529-2349, Fax: 204-529-2184
Grades: 1 - 9

Elie: **Huron Christian Academy**
Elie, R0H 0H0 Canada
204-353-4120
Grades: 1-12

Elie: **Milltown Academy**
P.O. Box 250
Elie, R0H 0H0 Canada
204-353-4111, Fax: 204-353-2224
Grades: Kindergarten - 12

Elm Creek: **Wingham HB School**
P.O. Box 45
RR #1 Elm Creek, R0G 0N0 Canada
204-436-3231, Fax: 204-436-3230
Grades: K.-12

Elma: **Riverside School**
P.O. Box 136
Elma, R0E 0Z0 Canada
204-348-2686, Fax: 204-348-7181
Grades: 1 - 9

Elma: **Twin Rivers Country School**
P.O. Box 30
Elma, R0E 0Z0 Canada
204-426-5611, Fax: 204-426-5611
Grades: 1 - 9

Fairford: **Interlake Christian Academy**
Fairford, R0C 0X0 Canada
204-659-5359
Grades: 1-10

Grandview: **Poplar Grove School**
P.O. Box 70
Grandview, R0L 0Y0 Canada
204-546-2691
Grades: 1-9

Gretna: **Mennonite Collegiate Institute**
P.O. Box 250
Gretna, R0G 0V0 Canada
204-327-5891, Fax: 204-327-5872,
mciblues@mb.sympatico.ca
Grades: 9-12
Enrollment: 170

Grunthal: **Mennonite Christian Academy**
P.O. Box 149
Grunthal, R0A 0R0 Canada
204-434-9315
Grades: K.-11

Hodgson: **Hodgson Christian Academy**
P.O. Box 220
Hodgson, R0C 1N0 Canada
204-372-8483
Grades: 1-9

Horndean: **Horndean Christian Day School**
P.O. Box 79
Horndean, R0G 0Z0 Canada
204-829-3354
Grades: 1-10

Kenville: **Riverdale School**
RR#1 Kenville, R0L 0Z0 Canada
204-539-2660
Grades: 1 - 9

Killarney: **Lakeside Christian School**
P.O. Box 894
Killarney, R0K 1G0 Canada
204-523-8240, Fax: 204-523-8351,
ics@mb.sympatico.ca
Grades: K.-9

Kleefeld: **New Hope Christian School**
P.O. Box 120
Kleefeld, R0A 0V0 Canada
204-377-4204
Grades: 1 - 12

Kleefeld: **Wild Rose School**
P.O. Box 167
Kleefeld, R0A 0V0 Canada
204-377-4778
Grades: 1-8

Kola: **Kola Community School**
P.O. Box 553
Kola, R0M 1B0 Canada
204-556-2488, Fax: 204-556-2600
Grades: K.-1

Lorette: **Daystar Christian Academy**
PO Box 5, Grp. 100, RR#2 Lorette, R0A 0Y0 Canada
204-878-3044
Grades: 2-9

MacGregor: **Grace Christian Academy**
P.O. Box 331
MacGregor, R0H 0R0 Canada
204-685-2867, Fax: 204-685-2867
Grades: 1-12

MacGregor: **H.B. Community Baker Colony School**
P.O. Box 40
MacGregor, R0H 0R0 Canada
204-252-2178, Fax: 204-252-2381,
bakercs@mb.sympatico.ca
Grades: K.-12

Minnedosa: **Odanah Colony School**
P.O. Box 990
Minnedosa, R0J 1E0 Canada
204-867-5074, Fax: 204-867-2037
Grades: K.-12

Neepawa: **Living Hope School**
P.O. Box 2158
Neepawa, R0J 1H0 Canada
204-966-3274
Grades: 3-12

Pine Falls: **Christian Faith Academy**
P.O. Box 459
Pine Falls, R0E 1M0 Canada
204-367-2056, Fax: 204-367-2056,
cfa@granite.mb.ca
Grades: 1 - 12

Pine River: **Pine River School**
P.O. Box 242
Pine River, R0L 1M0 Canada
204-263-2617, Fax: 204-263-2184
Grades: K.-9

Plum Coulee: **Christ Full Gospel Academy**
P.O. Box 107
75 Elm St. Plum Coulee, R0G 1R0 Canada
204-829-3506, Fax: 204-829-7937,
204-829-7937 (Phone, Pastor's study)
cfgf@mts.net
www.christfullgospel.org/main/academy.html
Grades: Kindergarten - 12
Christ Full Gospel Academy uses the Accelerated Christian Education curriculum.

Plum Coulee: **Prairie Mennonite School**
P.O. Box 53
Plum Coulee, R0G 1R0 Canada
204-829-3336
Grades: 1-11

Portage la Prairie: **Airport Colony School**
P.O. Box 967
Portage la Prairie, R1N 3C4 Canada
204-274-2412
Grades: K.-10
Location: NE 2-13-8 W, MacDonald, MB.

Portage la Prairie: **Lighthouse Christian School**
P.O. Box 1360
Portage la Prairie, R1N 3N9 Canada
204-428-5332, Fax: 204-428-5386
Grades: K.-12

Portage la Prairie: **Westpark School**
P.O. Box 91
2375 Saskatchewan Ave. West Portage la Prairie, R1N 3B2 Canada
204-857-3726,
office@westpark.mb.ca
www.westpark.mb.ca
Grades: Kindergarten - 12 (Senior 1 - 4)
Enrollment: 220
The school is a ministry of Portage Alliance Church.
Akaps Mweemba, Principal
Heather Boddy, Vice Principal

Roblin: **Parkland Christian School**
P.O. Box 480
Roblin, R0L 1P0 Canada
204-937-2870
Grades: 1-9

Rosenort: **Prairie View School**
P.O. Box 117
112 River Rd. North Rosenort, R0G 1W0 Canada
204-746-8837, Fax: 204-746-8517
Grades: 1 - 9

Sinclair: **Stony Creek School**
P.O. Box 5
Sinclair, R0M 2A0 Canada
204-662-4409, Fax: 204-662-4539
Grades: 1-9

Sperling: **Silverwinds School**
P.O. Box 130
Sperling, R0G 2M0 Canada
204-626-3378, Fax: 204-626-3397
Grades: K.-12

Ste. Anne: **Greenland School**
P.O. Box 224
RR#1 Ste. Anne, R5H 1R1 Canada
204-355-4922, Fax: 204-355-9280
Grades: 1-9

Steinbach: **Church of God Sunrise Academy**
P.O. Box 3368
Steinbach, R5G 1P6 Canada
204-434-6643, Fax: 204-326-6681
Grades: K.-9

Steinbach: **Country View School**
P.O. Box 3910
Steinbach, R5G 1P9 Canada
204-326-1481
Grades: 1-9

Steinbach: **Steinbach Christian Academy**
P.O. Box 20629
Steinbach, R5G 1S1 Canada
204-326-5553
Grades: K.-12

Steinbach: **Steinbach Christian High School**
50 Pth 12 North Steinbach, R5G 1T4 Canada
204-326-3537, Fax: 204-326-5164,
schs@schs.ca
www.schs.ca
Grades: 7-12
Enrollment: 161
Christian High School with Mennonite affiliation

Stonewall: **Northern Shield Academy**
P.O. Box 1039
Stonewall, R0C 2Z0 Canada
204-467-5547, Fax: 204-467-2571
Grades: 6 - 12
Enrollment: 50
This is a private Christian school.

Stuartburn: **Border View Christian Day School**
P.O. Box 11
Stuartburn, R0A 2B0 Canada
204-427-2932
Grades: 1 - 10

Swan River: **Community Bible Fellowship Christian School**
P.O. Box 1630
Swan River, R0L 1Z0 Canada
204-734-2174, Fax: 204-734-5706
Grades: K.-8
Enrollment: 25

Swan River: **Solid Rock Christian School**
P.O. Box 1239
Swan River, R0L 1Z0 Canada
204-734-2651
Grades: K.-12

Swan River: **Solid Rock Christian School**
P.O. Box 1239
Swan River, R0L 1Z0 Canada
204-734-2651
Grades: K.-12

Wawanesa: **Green Acres Colony High School**
P.O. Box 190
Wawanesa, R0K 2G0 Canada
204-824-2340, Fax: 204-824-2112
Grades: 9-12

Winkler: **Grace Valley Mennonite Academy**
P.O. Box 839
Winkler, R6W 4A9 Canada
204-829-3301, Fax: 204-829-3038
Grades: 1-12

Winkler: **Schoenweise Christian School**
P.O. Box 663
Group 11 Winkler, R6W 4A1 Canada
204-325-5401
Grades: 1-11

Winkler: **Valley Mennonite Academy**
P.O. Box 139
Grp. 7, RR#1 Winkler, R6W 4A1 Canada
204-325-8172, Fax: 204-331-3199
Grades: Kindergarten - 12
Enrollment: 134
Two private schools are operated by the Valley Mennonite Academy.

Winnipeg: **Alhijra Islamic School**
410 Desalaberry Ave. Winnipeg, R2L 0Y7 Canada
204-489-1300, Fax: 204-489-1323,
alhijraschool@hotmail.com
Grades: K.-9
Enrollment: 196

Winnipeg: **Balmoral Hall School**
630 Westminster Ave. Winnipeg, R3C 3S1 Canada
204-784-1600,
TDD: 1-866-373-2611
www.balmoralhall.com
Grades: Nursery - 5
Balmoral Hall School specializes in education for girls. It also offers a child care program for girls, aged 2 & 3.
Corrine Scott, Chair
Dr. Linda Schwartz, Head
Tina Alto, Director, Advancement, 204-784-1600
Pamela McGhie, Director, Admissions, 204-784-1621

Winnipeg: **Beautiful Savior Lutheran School / BSLS**
52 Birchdale Ave. Winnipeg, R2H 1R9 Canada
204-984-9600, Fax: 204-984-9607,
admin@bsls.ca; admissions@bsls.ca; preschool@bsls.ca
www.bsls.ca
Grades: Nursery - 8
Beautiful Savior Lutheran School also offers a daycare program & before & after school care.
Jennifer McCrea, Principal
Heather Burnett, Director, Child Care Services

Winnipeg: **Calvin Christian School**
Collegiate Campus
706 Day St. Winnipeg, R2C 1B6 Canada
204-222-7910, Fax: 204-222-8511,
204-338-7981 (Elementary phone); 204-339-3280 (Elementary fax)
www.calvinchristian.mb.ca
Grades: Kindergarten - 12
Rob Booy, Chair & Staff Liaison
David Taylor, Principal, Collegiate Campus
Hank Vande Kraats, Principal, Elementary Campus
Rod Harris, Vice Principal, Collegiate Campus
Maureen Vaags-Nyhof, Vice Principal, Elementary Campus

Winnipeg: **Christ the King School**
12 Lennox Ave. Winnipeg, R2M 1A6 Canada
204-257-0027, Fax: 204-257-2129,
www.ctkschool.ca
Grades: Junior Kindergarten - 8
Brian Steeves, Chair
brian@steeves.ca
Maria Coutu, Principal
mcoutu@ctkschool.ca
Mrs. S. Finnigan, Accountant
sfinnigan@ctkschool.ca
Ms. S. Barnert, Administrative Secretary
sbarnert@ctkschool.ca

Winnipeg: **The Collegiate at the University of Winnipeg**
515 Portage Ave. Winnipeg, R3B 2E9 Canada
204-786-9221, Fax: 204-775-1942,
collegiate@uwinnipeg.ca
www.uwinnipeg.ca/index/collegiate-index
Grades: 9 - 12
The independent secondary school is a division of The University of Winnipeg.
Robert Bend, Dean, 204-786-9843
r.bend@uwinnipeg.ca
Claude Garand, Associate Dean, 204-786-9842
c.garand@uwinnipeg.ca
Heather Singer, Associate Dean, 204-786-9258
h.singer@uwinnipeg.ca
Kathy Cullen, Registrar & International Student Advisor, 204-786-9901
k.cullen@uwinnipeg.ca

Winnipeg: **Gray Academy of Jewish Education**
A100, 123 Doncaster St. Winnipeg, R3N 2B4 Canada
204-477-7410, Fax: 204-477-7474,
info@grayacademy.ca
www.grayacademy.ca
Grades: K.-12
The largest independent Jewish day school in Western Canada. Co-educational. General subjects & Jewish studies programmes.
Rory Paul, Head of School

Winnipeg: **Holy Ghost School**
319 Selkirk Ave. Winnipeg, R2W 2L8 Canada
204-582-1053, Fax: 204-582-4870
Grades: K.-8
Enrollment: 239

Winnipeg: **Immaculate Heart of Mary School**
650 Flora Ave. Winnipeg, R2W 2S5 Canada
204-582-5698, Fax: 204-586-6698,
ihms@ihms.mb.ca
Grades: K.-8
Enrollment: 235

Winnipeg: **Immanuel Christian School**
215 Rougeau Ave. Winnipeg, R2C 3Z9 Canada
204-661-8937, Fax: 204-669-7013,
sch1274@merlin.mb.ca
Grades: K.-12
Enrollment: 188

Winnipeg: **Indian & Métis Holiness**
610 Selkirk Ave. Winnipeg, R2W 2N1 Canada
204-586-9484
Grades: K.-10

Winnipeg: **Islamic Academy of Manitoba**
Académie islamique du Manitoba
340 Provencher Blvd. Winnipeg, R2H 0G7 Canada
204-231-4441, Fax: 204-231-3240,
www.miaonline.org
Grades: K.-6
Program & instruction Arabic, English & French. Daily Qur'an studies.
Dr. Taib Soufi, Principal

Winnipeg: **The King's School**
851 Panet Rd. Winnipeg, R2K 4C9 Canada
204-989-6581, Fax: 204-989-6584,
www.thekingsschool.ca
Grades: Kindergarten - 12
Enrollment: 250
The King's School is a co-educational school, which is a ministry of Gateway Christian Community Church.
Peter Todd, BA (Hons), PGCE, Principal

Winnipeg: **The Laureate Academy**
100 Villa Maria Pl. Winnipeg, R3V 1A9 Canada
204-831-7107, Fax: 204-885-3217,
www.laureateacademy.com
Grades: Kindergarten - 12

Winnipeg: Linden Christian School
877 Wilkes Ave. Winnipeg, R3P 1B8 Canada
204-989-6730, Fax: 204-487-7068
Grades: K.-12
Enrollment: 741

Winnipeg: Mennonite Brethren Collegiate Institute
180 Riverton Ave. Winnipeg, R2L 2E8 Canada
204-667-8210, Fax: 204-661-5091,
mbci@mbci.mb.ca
Grades: 1-12
Enrollment: 532

Winnipeg: Montessori Learning Centre / MLC
Asland School
170 Ashland Ave. Winnipeg, R3L 1L1 Canada
204-475-1039, Fax: 204-452-4643,
mlcmont@mts.net
www.mlcwinnipeg.ca
Grades: Preschool - Kindergarten
The Centre's preschool program is designed for children from age 3 to 5.

Winnipeg: Oholei Torah School
2095 Sinclair St. Winnipeg, R2V 3K2 Canada
204-339-8737, Fax: 204-586-0487,
sch1997@merlin.mb.ca
Grades: Gr. N.-8
Enrollment: 13

Winnipeg: Ohr Hatorah School
620 Brock St. Winnipeg, R3N 0Z4 Canada
204-489-1147, Fax: 204-489-5899
Grades: Gr. N.-4

Winnipeg: Our Lady of Victory School
249 Arnold Ave. Winnipeg, R3L 0W4 Canada
204-452-7632, Fax: 204-453-3081,
olv@shawbiz.ca
www.victoryedu.com
Grades: Pre K.-8
Enrollment: 117
A. Cap, Principal

Winnipeg: Red River Valley Junior Academy / RRVJA
56 Grey St. Winnipeg, R2L 1V3 Canada
204-667-2383, Fax: 204-667-1396,
info@rrvja.ca
info@rrvja.ca
www.rrvja.ca
Grades: Junior Kindergarten - 10
Red River Valley Junior Academy is owned & operated by the Seventh Day Adventist Church.
Ian Mighty, M.A., B.Ed., PBCE, Admin., Principal
imight@rrvja.ca
Daniel NcGuire, B.Ed., Vice Principal & Middle Years Specialist
dmcguire@rrvja.ca
Lora Troop, Administrative Assistant
ltoop@rrvja.ca

Winnipeg: St. Aidan's Christian School
418 Aberdeen Ave. Winnipeg, R2W 1V7 Canada
204-586-6792, Fax: 204-582-4729
Grades: K.-8
Enrollment: 30

Winnipeg: St. Alphonsus School
343 Munroe Ave. Winnipeg, R2K 1H2 Canada
204-667-6271, Fax: 204-663-4187,
info@stalphonsusschool.ca
www.stalphonsusschool.ca
Grades: K.-8
Enrollment: 230

Winnipeg: St. Boniface Diocesan High School
282 Dubuc St. Winnipeg, R2H 1E4 Canada
204-987-1560, Fax: 204-237-9891,
www.sbdhs.net
admin@sbdhs.net
Grades: S1-S4
Enrollment: 150
Jeff Beaudin, Principal

Winnipeg: St. Charles Interparochial School
331 St. Charles St. Winnipeg, R3K 1T6 Canada
204-837-1520, Fax: 204-837-2326,
sec@stccs.ca
www.stccs.ca
Grades: K.-8
Enrollment: 206
Dr. Penny Parzyjagla, Principal

Winnipeg: St. Edward's School
836 Arlington St. Winnipeg, R3E 2E4 Canada
204-774-8773, Fax: 204-775-0011,
sch1430@merlin.mb.ca
Grades: K.-6
Enrollment: 191

Winnipeg: St. Emile School
552 St. Anne's Rd. Winnipeg, R2M 3G4 Canada
204-989-5020, Fax: 204-989-5026,
www.stemileschool.ca
Grades: K.-8
Enrollment: 236

Winnipeg: St. Gerard School
40 Foster St. Winnipeg, R2L 1V7 Canada
204-667-4862, Fax: 204-668-7932,
stgerard@shaw.ca
Grades: Gr. N.-8
Enrollment: 240

Winnipeg: St. Ignatius School
239 Harrow St. Winnipeg, R3M 2Y3 Canada
204-475-1386, Fax: 204-475-3961,
sch1829@merlin.mb.ca
Grades: K.-8
Enrollment: 245

Winnipeg: St. John Brebeuf School
605 Renfrew St. Winnipeg, R3N 1J8 Canada
204-489-2115, Fax: 204-489-6097,
sch1729@merlin.mb.ca
Grades: K.-8
Enrollment: 221

Winnipeg: St. John's-Ravenscourt School
400 South Dr. Winnipeg, R3T 3K5 Canada
204-477-2400, Fax: 204-477-2429,
sch1155@merlin.mb.ca
Grades: K.-12
Enrollment: 780

Winnipeg: St. Joseph the Worker School
505 Brewster St. Winnipeg, R2C 2W6 Canada
204-222-1841, Fax: 204-222-1769,
stjoesch@mts.net
www.stjosephtheworkerschool.ca
Grades: K.-6
Enrollment: 129
Brian Hargrave, Principal

Winnipeg: St. Mary's Academy
550 Wellington Cres. Winnipeg, R3M 0C1 Canada
204-477-0244, Fax: 204-453-2417
Grades: 7-12
Enrollment: 550

Winnipeg: St. Mary's Montessori School Inc.
150 Pacific Ave. Winnipeg, R3B 3K8 Canada
204-956-1622, Fax: 204-956-7088
Grades: Gr. N.-K.
Enrollment: 74

Winnipeg: St. Maurice School
1639 Pembina Hwy. Winnipeg, R3T 2G6 Canada
204-452-2873, Fax: 204-452-4050,
admin@stmaurice.mb.ca
www.stmaurice.mb.ca
Grades: K.-12
Enrollment: 585
G. Caligiuri, Principal

Winnipeg: St. Michael's School
174 Maple St. North Winnipeg, R2W 3L4 Canada
204-334-8763
Grades: 1-12

Winnipeg: St. Paul's High School
2200 Grant Ave. Winnipeg, R3P 0P8 Canada
204-831-2300, Fax: 204-831-2340,
contact-us@stpauls.mb.ca
www.stpauls.mb.ca
Grades: 9-12
Enrollment: 582
Jesuit University prep school for boys
Tom Lussier, Principal

Winnipeg: Southeast College
1301 Lee Blvd. Winnipeg, R3T 5W8 Canada
204-261-3551, Fax: 204-269-7880,
ilinklater@secollege.ca
www.secollege.ca
Grades: S1-S4
Irene Linklater, Principal

Winnipeg: Springs Christian Academy
#2, 595 Lagimodiere Blvd. Winnipeg, R2J 3X2 Canada
204-235-0863, Fax: 204-235-0390,
sch1942@merlin.mb.ca
www.springschurch.com/sca
Grades: K.-12
Enrollment: 689
Affiliated with Springs Church

Winnipeg: Twelve Tribes School
89 East Gate Winnipeg, R3C 2C2 Canada
204-779-1118
Grades: 1 - 8

Winnipeg: Westgate Mennonite Collegiate
86 West Gate Winnipeg, R3C 2E1 Canada
204-775-7111, Fax: 204-786-1651,
www.westgatemennonite.ca
Grades: 7 - 12
Enrollment: 315
The Christian school is based upon the Anabaptist Mennonite tradition.
Bob Hummelt, Principal

Winnipeg: Winnipeg Mennonite Elementary School
Bedson Campus
250 Bedson St. Winnipeg, R3K 1R7 Canada
204-885-1032, Fax: 204-897-4068,
wmes@wmes.ca
Grades: K.-8
Enrollment: 450

Winnipeg: Winnipeg Montessori School Inc.
1525 Willson Pl. Winnipeg, R3T 4H1 Canada
204-452-3315, Fax: 204-452-3315,
sch2093@merlin.mb.ca
Grades: Gr. N.-K.

Winnipeg: Winnipeg South Academy
870 Scotland Ave. Winnipeg, R3M 1X8 Canada
204-488-5046, Fax: 204-452-6563
Grades: Gr. N.-4
Enrollment: 107

Universities & Colleges

Universities

Brandon: Brandon University
270 - 18th St. Brandon, R7A 6A9 Canada
204-728-9520, Fax: 204-726-4573,
www.brandonu.ca
Enrollment: 2625
Dr. Deborah C. Poff, Pres./Vice-Chancellor
president@brandonu.ca
Scott J.B. Lamont, Vice-Pres., Admin./Finance
lamont@brandonu.ca
Dr. Scott Grills, Vice-Pres., Academic
grillss@brandonu.ca
Bruce Strang, Dean, Arts
artsdean@brandonu.ca
Dr Cam Symons, Dean, Education
symonsc@Brandonu.ca
Dr W. Dean Care, Dean, Health Studies
cared@brandonu.ca
Dr Austin F. Gulliver, Dean, Science
gulliver@brandonu.ca
Dr. Lawrence VanBeek, Registrar, 204-727-7310
vanbeekl@brandonu.ca

Faculties

Arts
S. Grills, Dean

Education
Jerrie Storie, Acting Dean

Science
Dr. Austin Gulliver, Acting Dean

Student & International Affairs
Dr. Janet Wright, Dean

Schools

Health Studies
L. Ross, Dean

Music
G. Carruthers, Dean

Publications
Quill

Winnipeg: Canadian Mennonite University
500 Shaftsbury Blvd. Winnipeg, R3P 2N2 Canada
204-487-3300, Fax: 204-487-3858, 877-231-4570
info@cmu.ca
www.cmu.ca

Enrollment: 1600
Gerald Gerbrandt, President
ggerbrandt@cmu.ca
Earl Davey, Vice-Pres., Academic
edavey@cmu.ca
Wesley Toews, Registrar & Assistant VP
wtoews@cmu.ca
Gordon Matties, Dean, Humanities & Sciences
gmatties@cmu.ca
Dietrich Bartel, Dean, School of Music
dbartel@cmu.ca
Paul Redekop, Dean, Social Sciences
p.redekop@uwinnipeg.ca
Paul Kroeker, Dean, International Programs
pkroeker@cmu.ca
Ruth Taronno, Assoc. Vice-Pres., MSC
rtaronno@cmu.ca

Winnipeg: Prairie Theatre Exchange
300-393 Portage Ave., #Y Winnipeg, R3B 2H6 Canada
204-942-7291, Fax: 204-942-1774,
www.pte.mb.ca

Winnipeg: Salvation Army William & Catherine Booth University College
447 Webb Pl. Winnipeg, R3B 2P2 Canada
204-947-6701, Fax: 204-942-3856, 877-942-6684
admissions@boothcollege.ca
www.boothcollege.ca

Enrollment: 500
Enrollment number includes on-campus and distance students.

Winnipeg: University College
#203, 220 Dysart Rd. Winnipeg, R3T 2M8 Canada
204-474-9751, Fax: 204-261-0021,
ucsecr@cc.umanitoba.ca
umanitoba.ca/colleges/uc/
Affiliated with the University of Manitoba

Winnipeg: University of Manitoba
134 Services Building
97 Dafoe Rd. Winnipeg, R3T 2N2 Canada
204-474-8880,
www.umanitoba.ca

Enrollment: 29932
William Norrie, C.M., O.M., Q.C., B.A., L, Chancellor
Dr. David T. Barnard, B.Sc., M.Sc., Ph.D., Dip., President & Vice-Chancellor
Bob Raeburn, B.Sc., Executive Assistant to the President
Deborah J. McCallum, B.Sc., Vice-President
Digvir Jayas, Ph.D., Vice-President
Joanne C. Keselman, B.A., M.A., Ph.D., Vice-President
P. Dueck, Director
Alan Simms, B.Comm.(Hons.), L.L.B., Assoc. Vice-President
Peter Cattini, B.Sc.(Hons.), Ph.D., Assoc. Vice-President
David R. Morphy, B.A., M.A., Ph.D., Vice-Provost
Karen R. Grant, B.A., M.A., Ph.D., Vice-Provost
Richard A. Lobdell, B.A., M.A., Ph.D., Vice-Provost
Terry Voss, B.Comm. (Hons.), C.H.R.P., Exec. Director
Karen Adams, B.A., M.L.S., Director
John G. Alho, B.A.(Hons.), Assoc. Vice-President
B. Hanchard, Manager
Peter A. Cattini, B.Sc., Ph.D., Assoc. Vice-President
Elaine V. Goldie, Cert.Ed., Vice-President
Gerry Miller, B.Sc., Exec. Director
A. Simms, L.L.B., Exec. Director
James S. Gardner, B.Sc., M.Sc., Ph.D., Exec. Director
Jeffrey M. Leclerc, B.Ed., University Secretary

Faculties
Agricultural & Food Sciences
Michael Trevan, Dean

Architecture
Richard Perron, Acting Dean

Arts
Richard Sigurdson, Dean

Continuing Education
A. Percival, Dean

Dentistry
Anthony Iacopino, Dean

Education
John Wiens, Dean

Engineering
Douglas Ruth, Dean

Environment
Clayton H. Riddell, Dean

Graduate Studies
Jay Doering, Dean

Human Ecology
Gustaaf P. Sevenhuysen, Dean

I.H. Asper School of Business
Glenn Feltham, Dean

Law
Chris Axworthy, Q.C., Dean

Medicine
Dean Sandham, Dean

Music
Edmund Dawe, Dean

Nursing
Ruth Anne Kinsman, Dean

Pharmacy

David M. Collins, Dean

Physical Education & Recreation Studies
Dr. Jane Watkinson, Dean

Science
Mark Whitmore, Dean

Social Work
Harvy Frankel, Dean

University 1
Christine Blais, Dean

Schools
Agriculture
Mervyn K. Pritchard, Director

Art
Prof. Celia Rabinovitch, Director

Dental Hygiene
Salme Lavigne, Director

Extended Education Division
Anne Percival, Director

Medical Rehabilitation
Emily Etcheverry, Director

Affiliations
Collège universitaire de Saint-Boniface
200, av de la Cathédrale Winnipeg, R2H 0H7 Canada
204-233-0210
Raymonde Gagné, B.A., Cert.Ed., M.B.A., Rectrice
rgagne@ustboniface.mb.ca

St. John's College
92 Dysart Rd. Winnipeg, R3T 2M5 Canada
204-474-8531, Fax: 204-474-7610, 1-800-432-1960
Stjohns_College@umanitoba.ca
www.umanitoba.ca/colleges/st_johns
Affiliated with the Anglican Church of Canada, St. John's College is located on the University of Manitoba campus.
Dr. Janet Hoskins, Warden & Vice-Chancellor
j_hoskins@umanitoba.ca
Erin Palamar, Registrar
e_palamar@umanitoba.ca

St. Paul's College
70 Dysart Rd. Winnipeg, R3T 2M6 Canada
204-474-8575,
stpauls@umanitoba.ca
www.umanitoba.ca/stpauls
The Roman Catholic College is located on the University of Manitoba campus.
Denic C. Bracken, Rector
bracken@cc.umanitoba.ca
Christine Butterill, Dean of Studies
butteri@cc.umanitoba.ca

University College
500 Dysart Rd. Winnipeg, R3T 2M8 Canada
204-474-9388
Dr. Richard Sigurdson, B.A., M.A. Ph.D., Acting Provost

William & Catherine Booth Bible College
447 Webb Pl. Winnipeg, R3B 2P2 Canada
204-947-6701
Dr. Donald Burke, President, 204-924-4868
president@boothcollege.ca
Denise Young, BBA, MPA, Director, College Admin., 204-924-4864
dyoung@boothcollege.ca
Deborah Knight, Financial Coordinator, 204-924-4853
dknight@boothcollege.ca

Prairie Theatre Exchange
300-393 Portage Ave., #Y Winnipeg, R3B 2H6 Canada
204-942-7291
Robert Metcalfe, Artistic Director
ad@pte.mb.ca

Publications
Alumni Journal
180 Dafoe Rd Winnipeg, R3T 2N2 Canada

The Gradzette

The Manitoban

Winnipeg: University of Winnipeg
515 Portage Ave. Winnipeg, R3B 2E9 Canada
204-786-7811,
www.uwinnipeg.ca

Enrollment: 9460
Robert Silver, Chancellor
Lloyd Axworthy, President & Vice-Chancellor, 204-786-9214
president@uwinnipeg.ca
John Corlett, Vice-Pres., Academic, 204-786-9120
j.corlett@uwinnipeg.ca
Bill Balan, Vice-Pres., Finance & Administration, 204-786-9229
b.balan@uwinnipeg.ca
Laurel Repski, Vice-Pres., Human Resources, 204-789-1451
l.repski@uwinnipeg.ca
Neil Besner, Vice-Pres., Students & International, 204-786-8656
n.besner@uwinnipeg.ca

Faculties
Arts
David Fitzpatrick, Dean, 204-786-9943
d.fitzpatrick@uwinnipeg.ca

Business & Economics
Michael Benarroch, Dean, 204-786-9268
m.benarroch@uwinnipeg.ca

Education
Ken Mccluskey, Dean, 204-786-9470
k.mccluskey@uwinnipeg.ca

Science
Rodney Hanley, Dean, 204-786-9862
r.hanley@uwinnipeg.ca

Theology
Dr James Christie, Dean, 204-786-9247
j.christie@uwinnipeg.ca

Affiliations
Menno Simons College
520 Portage Ave. Winnipeg, R3C 0G2 Canada
204-953-3855, Fax: 207-783-3699,
msc@uwinnipeg.ca
mscollege.ca
A college of the Canadian Mennonite University, maintaining an affiliation with the University of Winnipeg. It is located on the campus of the U. of W.
Dr. Earl Davey, Vice-President, Academic (CMU), 204-953-3873
e.davey@uwinnipeg.ca
Dr. Paul Redekop, Dean, MSC/Faculty of Social Sciences (CMU), 204-953-3858
p.redekop@uwinnipeg.ca

Publications
The Uniter
204-786-9790, Fax: 204-786-9497,
uniter@uniter.ca
uniter.ca

Colleges

Brandon: Assiniboine Community College
1430 Victoria Ave. East Brandon, R7A 2A9 Canada
204-725-8700, Fax: 204-725-8740, 1-800-862-6307
info@assiniboine.net
www.assiniboine.net

Enrollment: 2500
Joel Ward, President
wardj@assiniboine.net
Karen Barclay, Associate Registrar
barclay@assiniboine.net

Campuses
Parkland Campus
P.O. Box 4000
520 Whitmore Ave. East Dauphin, R7N 2V5 Canada

204-622-2023, Fax: 204-638-3941,
info@assiniboine.net
www.assiniboine.net

***Saint-Boniface:* Collège universitaire de Saint-Boniface**
200, av de la Cathédrale Saint-Boniface, R2H 0H7 Canada
204-233-0210, Fax: 204-237-3240, 1-888-233-5112
sci@ustboniface.mb.ca
www.ustboniface.mb.ca
Raymonde Gagné, B.A., Cert.Ed., M.B.A., Rectrice
rgagne@ustboniface.mb.ca

***Saint-Boniface:* École technique et professionnelle**
c/o Collège universitaire de Saint-Boniface
200, av de la Cathédrale Saint-Boniface, R2H 0H7 Canada
204-233-0210, Fax: 204-237-3240, 1-888-233-5112
sci@ustboniface.mb.ca
www.ustboniface.mb.ca
Raymonde Gagné, Rectrice

***The Pas:* University College of the North**
P.O. Box 3000
436 - 7 St. East The Pas, R9A 1M7 Canada
204-627-8500, Fax: 204-623-7316, 866-627-8500
admissions@ucn.ca
www.ucn.ca
Enrollment: 3500
Denise K. Henning, President & Vice-Chancellor
Carol Girling, Registrar & Director, Enrolment Services, 204-627-8553
cgirling@ucn.ca

***Winnipeg:* Collège universitaire de Saint-Boniface**
200, av de la Cathédrale Winnipeg, R2H 0H7 Canada
204-233-0210, Fax: 204-237-3240, 1-888-233-5112
sci@ustboniface.mb.ca
www.ustboniface.mb.ca

Publications
Le Réveil

***Brandon:* Office of the Fire Commissioner (Brandon)**
1601 Vanhorne Ave. East Brandon, R7A 7K2 Canada
204-726-6855, Fax: 204-948-2089, 1-800-282-806
firecomm@gov.mb.ca
www.firecomm.gov.mb.ca
The college is a broad-based emergency services training organizationwhich offers a full-time program for those interested in a career in the EMS field.
Rick Negrich, 204-945-3330

***Winnipeg:* Office of the Fire Commissioner (Winnipeg)**
508-401 York Ave. Winnipeg, R3C 0P8 Canada
204-945-3322, Fax: 204-948-2089, 1-800-282-8069
firecomm@gov.mb.ca
www.firecomm.gov.mb.ca
The college is a broad-based emergency services training organizationwhich offers a full-time program for those interested in a career in the EMS field.

***Winnipeg:* Red River College of Applied Arts, Science & Technology**
2055 Notre Dame Ave. Winnipeg, R3H 0J9 Canada
204-632-3960,
register@rrc.mb.ca; cde@rrc.mb.ca; intled@rrc.mb.ca
www.rrc.mb.ca
Enrollment: 32000
Al Morin, Chair
Jeff Zabudsky, PhD, President/CEO

Campuses
Gimli Campus
Gimli Industrial Park
P.O. Box 190
234 Tudor Lane Gimli, R0C 1B0
204-642-5496, Fax: 204-642-4189,
gimli@rrc.mb.ca

Portage Campus
180 Centennaire Dr. Southport, R0H 1N0
204-428-6322, Fax: 204-428-6337,
portage@rrc.mb.ca

Steinbach Campus
#2, 385 Loewen Blvd. Steinbach, R5G 0B3
204-320-2500, Fax: 204-346-0178,
steinbach@rrc.mb.ca
The Steinbach Campus has community learning centres in Steinbach (204-320-2500) and in St. Pierre (204-433-7404).

Winkler Campus
#100, 561 Main St. Winkler, R6W 1E8
204-325-9672, Fax: 204-325-4947,
Winkler Community Learning Centre, Phone: 204-325-4997
winkler@rrc.mb.ca; winklerlearningcentre@rrc.mb.ca

***Winnipeg:* St. Andrew's College**
29 Dysart Rd. Winnipeg, R3T 2M7 Canada
204-474-8895, Fax: 204-474-7624,
st_andrews@umanitoba.ca
www.umanitoba.ca/colleges/st_andrews
Affiliated with the University of Manitoba, St. Andrew's College is an institution of the Ukrainian Orthodox Church of Canada. It works to promote spiritual, academic, cultural, & moral leadership.
His Eminence John Stinka, Chancellor
V. Rev. Fr. Roman Bozyk, Chair, Dean of Theology, Acting Principal, &

Post Secondary/Technical

Post Secondary/Technical

***Winnipeg:* Winnipeg Branch**
300 Oak Point Hwy. Winnipeg, R2R 1V1 Canada
204-925-1580, Fax: 204-925-1587, 1-888-883-7483
learn@transportdriver.com
www.transportdriver.com
Class 1 air brake licence training

***Brandon:* Brandon Branch**
1731 B Middleton Ave. Brandon, R7A 1A7 Canada
204-729-0240, 1-888-883-7483
learn@transportdriver.com
www.transportdriver.com

***Dauphin:* Academy of Learning**
Village Mall
P.O. Box 603
1430 Main St. South Dauphin, R7N 2V4 Canada
204-622-9999, Fax: 204-622-9998,
www.academyoflearning.com
Computer & business training; other locations in Brandon, Steinbach, Swan River, Winnipeg - North, Winnipeg - South

***McCreary:* Canadian College of Taxidermy**
419 - First Ave. McCreary, R0J 1B0 Canada
204-835-2639, Fax: 204-835-2764,
tledoux@sympatico.ca

***Otterburne:* Providence College & Theological Seminary**
Otterburne, R0A 1G0 Canada
204-433-7488, Fax: 204-433-7158, 1-800-668-776
info@prov.ca
www.prov.ca
Enrollment: 717
Institution for Christian higher education

***Winnipeg:* Canadian School of Floral Art**
569 St. Mary's Rd. Winnipeg, R2M 3L6 Canada
204-233-2426, Fax: 204-237-7301

***Winnipeg:* CDI College of Business, Technology & Healthcare**
280 Main St. Winnipeg, R3C 1A9 Canada
204-942-1773, Fax: 204-944-0752
Computer & business training

***Winnipeg:* European School of Esthetics**
241 Vaughan St. Winnipeg, R3C 1T6 Canada
204-943-3440,
idonils.mts.net
www.idonails.ca
Esthetics

***Winnipeg:* Herzing College**
723 Portage Ave. Winnipeg, R3G 0M8 Canada
204-775-8175, Fax: 204-783-8107,
info@wpg.herzing.edu
www.herzing.edu/winnipeg
Bill Riches, President

***Winnipeg:* Mid Ocean School of Media Arts**
1588 Erin St. Winnipeg, R3E 2T1 Canada
204-775-3308, Fax: 204-775-9231,
info@midoceanschool.ca
www.midoceanschool.ca
Audio engineer, audio in media

***Winnipeg:* National Screen Institute**
#206, 70 Arthur St. Winnipeg, R3B 1G7 Canada
204-956-7800, Fax: 204-956-5811,
info@nsi-canada.ca
www.nsi-canada.ca
Professional training & development for Canadian film & television writers, directors & producers
Susan Millican, CEO
Glynis Corkal, Manager
Paul Moreau, Director

***Winnipeg:* Panache Agency Models School**
#106, 897 Corydon Ave. Winnipeg, R3M 0W7 Canada
204-982-6150, Fax: 204-474-2687,
panache_jane@mts.net
www.panachemanagement.com
Models training

***Winnipeg:* Patal Vocational Preparation Schools Ltd.**
264 Portage Ave. Winnipeg, R3C 0B6 Canada
204-944-8202, Fax: 204-944-8207, 1-877-829-807
www.patalvocational.mb.ca
Life skills, upgrading, PC service, computerized accounting, purchasing/inventory, service/parts/inventory; internet technical support; customer service training for the customer contact industry; cooking

***Winnipeg:* Reimer Express Driver Training Institute Inc.**
50 Milner St. Winnipeg, R2X 2X3 Canada
204-958-5100, Fax: 204-958-3034, 1-888-866-7623
wayne.hartle@reimerexpress.com
www.reimerdrivertraining.com
Class 1S driver training.
Wayne Hartle, Manager

***Winnipeg:* Robertson College Winnipeg**
265 Notre Dame Ave. Winnipeg, R3B 1N9 Canada
204-943-5661, Fax: 204-926-8320, 1-877-880-8789
info@robertsoncollege.com
www.robertsoncollege.com
Wayne Palendat, Registrar

Campuses
Robertson College Calgary
Edinburgh Pl.
300-417 14th St. NW Calgary, T2N 2A1 Canada
403-920-0070, Fax: 403-543-1245, 1-866-920-0070
Calgary@RobertsonCollege.com
www.robersoncollege.com

Robertson College Brandon
Town Centre
800 Rosser Ave. Brandon, R7A 6N5 Canada
204-725-7205, Fax: 204-725-7218, 1-877-757-7575
info@robertsoncollege.com
www.robertsoncollege.com

***Winnipeg:* School of Recording Arts of Manitoba**
275 Selkirk Ave. Winnipeg, R2W 2L5 Canada
204-586-8057, Fax: 204-582-8397,
studio@magic.mb.ca, info@worldwidesunshine.com
www.sunshinerecords.com
Studio recording

***Winnipeg:* Scientific-Marvel School of Hairstyling & Esthetics**
269 Kennedy St. 2nd Fl. Winnipeg, R3C 1T2 Canada
204-943-2145, Fax: 204-943-2445,
winnipeghairstylingesthetics@marvelschools.com
www.marvelschools.com
Skin care & hairstyling

***Winnipeg:* Winnipeg Campus**
105-260 St. Mary Ave. Winnipeg, R3C 0M6 Canada
204-925-2790,
learn@anokiiwin.com
www.anokiiwin.com/learn
Aboriginally owned and operated training company committed to providing culturally sensitive, high quality training to First Nation communinities.

Campuses
Thompson Campus
203-3 Station Rd. Thompson, R8N 0R2 Canada
204-778-5937,
learn@anokiiwin.com
www.anokiiwin.com/learn
Aboriginally owned and operated training company committed to providing culturally sensitive, high quality training to First Nation communinities.

***Winnipeg:* Winnipeg Technical College**
130 Henlow Bay Winnipeg, R3Y 1G4 Canada
204-989-6500, Fax: 204-488-4152,
sch1956@merlin.mb.ca
Enrollment: 1200
Dave Thorlakson, Director

New Brunswick

Government Agencies

Fredericton: **Department of Education**
P.O. Box 6000
Place 2000 Fredericton, E3B 5H1 Canada
506-453-3678, Fax: 506-453-3111,
www.gnb.ca/000/index-e.asp
Barry Lydon, Director, 506-453-2155
barry.lydon@gnb.ca
Marcel Lavoie, Director, 506-453-2743
marcel.lavoie@gnb.ca

Fredericton: **Department of Post-Secondary Education & Training / asp**
Chestnut Complex
P.O. Box 6000
Fredericton, E3B 5H1 Canada
506-453-2597, Fax: 506-453-3618,
www.gnb.ca/0105/index-e.asp
Margaret-Ann Blaney, Minister
Barbara Leger, Manager
Félixine Thériault, Administrator

School Boards/Districts/Divisions

Public

Campbellton: **District Scolaire #5**
21, rue King Campbellton, E3N 1C5 Canada
506-789-2255, Fax: 506-789-2269
Enrollment: 5934
Monelle Perron, Dir. de l'éducation
monelle.perron@gnb.ca
Jean-Guy Levesque, Dir. gén.
jean-guy.levesque@gnb.ca

Dalhousie: **School District #15**
464 Montgomery St. Dalhousie, E8C 2A6 Canada
506-684-7557, Fax: 506-684-7552, 888-950-1515
district15@gnb.ca
www.district15.nbed.nb.ca
Enrollment: 3982
Nancy Boucher, Director of Education
John McLaughlin, Superintendent
john.mclaughlin@gnb.ca

Dieppe: **District Scolaire #1**
425, rue Champlain Dieppe, E1A 1P2 Canada
506-856-3225, Fax: 506-856-3254
Enrollment: 7056
Anne-Marie LeBlanc, Dir. gén.
anne-marie.leblanc@gnb.ca
Maurice Langlais, Dir. de l'éducation
maurice.langlais@gnb.ca

Edmundston: **District Scolaire #3**
298, rue Martin Edmundston, E3V 5E5 Canada
506-737-4550, Fax: 506-737-4569
Enrollment: 6966
Bertrand Beaulieu, Dir. gén.
bertrand.beaulieu@gnb.ca
Lise Aubut, Dir. de l'éducation
lise.aubut@gnb.ca

Fredericton: **School District #18**
P.O. Box 10
1135 Prospect St. Fredericton, E3B 4Y4 Canada
506-453-5454, Fax: 506-444-5264,
www.district18.nbed.nb.ca
Enrollment: 12000
Dianne Wilkins, Director of Education
dianne.wilkins@gnb.ca
Alex Dingwall, Superintendent
alex.dingwall@gnb.ca

Miramichi: **School District #16**
78 Henderson St. Miramichi, E1N 2R7 Canada
506-778-6075, Fax: 506-778-6090,
www.district16.nbed.nb.ca
Enrollment: 8100
Richard Walsh, Director of Education
richard.walsh@gnb.ca
Laurie Keoughan, Superintendent
laurie.keoughan@gnb.ca

Moncton: **School District #2**
1077 St. George Blvd. Moncton, E1E 4C9 Canada
506-856-3222, Fax: 506-856-3224,
www.district2.nbed.nb.ca
Enrollment: 16000
Gregg Ingersoll, Director of Education
Gregg.Ingersoll@gnb.ca
Karen Branscombe, Superintendent
karen.branscombe@gnb.ca

Oromocto: **School District #17**
17 Miramichi Rd. Oromocto, E2V 2P6 Canada
506-357-4010, Fax: 506-357-4011
Enrollment: 5200
David McTimoney, Superintendent
Rick Demmings, Director of Education

Richibucto: **District Scolaire #11**
#2, 10, rue Commerciale Richibucto, E4W 3X6 Canada
506-523-7655, Fax: 506-523-7659
Enrollment: 6093
Ronald Caissie, Dir. gén.
ronald.caissie@gnb.ca
Yolande McLaughlin, Dir. de l'éducation
yolande.mclaughlin@gnb.ca

Rothesay: **School District #6**
70B Hampton Rd. Rothesay, E2E 5Y2 Canada
506-847-6262, Fax: 506-847-6211,
www.district6.nbed.nb.ca
Enrollment: 10200
Andrew Hopper, Director of Education
andrew.hopper@gnb.ca
Zoë Watson, Superintendent
zoe.watson@gnb.ca

Saint John: **School District #8**
490 Woodward Ave. Saint John, E2K 5N3 Canada
506-658-5300, Fax: 506-658-5399,
www.district8.nbed.nb.ca
Enrollment: 13000
Susan Tipper, Superintendent
susan.tipper@gnb.ca
Beverly MacDonald, Director of Education
bev.macdonald@gnb.ca

St Stephen: **School District #10**
11 School St. St Stephen, E3L 2N4 Canada
506-466-7300, Fax: 506-466-7309,
d10webadmin@gnb.ca
www.district10.nbed.nb.ca
Enrollment: 4340
Jenny MacDougall, Director of Education
Jenny.MacDougall@gnb.ca
Derek O'Brien, Superintendent
derek.o'brien@nbed.nb.ca

Tracadie-Sheila: **District Scolaire #9**
P.O. Box 3668 Bureau chef
3376, rue Principale Tracadie-Sheila, E1X 1G5 Canada
506-394-3400, Fax: 506-394-3455
Enrollment: 7412
Philip Chiasson, Dir. de l'éducation
philip.chiasson@gnb.ca
Solange Haché, Dir. gén.
solange.hache@gnb.ca

Woodstock: **School District #14**
138 Chapel St. Woodstock, E7M 1H3 Canada
506-325-4432, Fax: 506-325-4490,
www.district14.nbed.nb.ca
Enrollment: 8511
Loree Kaye, Director of Education (Acting)
loree.kaye@gnb.ca
Lisa Gallagher, Superintendent
lisa.gallagher@gnb.ca

Schools: Specialized

First Nations

Burnt Church: **Burnt Church School**
626 Bayview Dr. Burnt Church, E9G 2A8 Canada
506-776-1206, Fax: 506-776-1226,
lflanagan@burntchurchschool.ca
burntchurchschool.ca
Grades: Kindergarten - 8
Enrollment: 120
The Burnt Church School, located northeast of the City of Miramichi, is part of School District #16. The school serves the Burnt Church First Nation.
Robert Bowes, Principal

Eel Ground: **Eel Ground First Nation School**
55 Church St. Eel Ground, E1V 4E6 Canada
506-627-4615, Fax: 506-627-4624,
www.eelgroundschool.ca
Grades: Kindergarten - 8; Mi'kmaq language
Eel Ground First Nation School operates as part of School District #16 in Miramichi, New Brunswick. The school provides education to the Eel Ground First Nation, a Mi'kmaq community in northeastern New Brunswick.
Donald Donahue, Principal

Eel River Bar: **Eel River Bar First Nation Pre-School**
Eel River Bar First Nation
P.O. Box 4007
#201, 11 Main St. Eel River Bar, E8C 1A1 Canada
506-684-6307, Fax: 506-684-6282
Grades: Pre-School (K4)
Eel River Bar First Nation Pre-School is a First Nations band operated school in a Mi'kmaq village on New Brunswick's north shore.
Priscilla Pictou, Principal

Elsipogtog: **Elsipogotg School**
356 Big Cove Rd. Elsipogtog, E4W 2S6 Canada
506-523-8240, Fax: 506-523-8235,
kitpo@nbnet.nb.ca
www.elsipogtogschool.ca
Grades: Kindergarten - 8
Part of Miramichi, New Brunswick's School District #16, the Elsipogtog School provides education to the Elsipogtog First Nation.
Levi Sock, Superintendent
Ivan Augustine, Principal
Stan Drillen, Vice-Principal
Laurie Donovan, Program Coordinator, Resources
lauried@elsipogtogschool.ca

Fredericton: **Chief Harold Sappier Memorial Elementary School**
c/o St. Mary's Maliseet First Nation
305 Maliseet Dr. Fredericton, E3A 5R8 Canada
506-462-9683, Fax: 506-462-9686,
chsmesjf@nb.aibn.com
www.firstnationhelp.com/stmarys
Grades: K4 - K5; 1 - 5; Maliseet language
In addition to providing elementary education beginning with kindergarten, the Chief Harold Sappier Memorial Elementary School provides education about the Maliseet language & culture.
Allison Brooks, Principal
Judith Fullarton, Office Manager

Fredericton: **Wulastukw Elementary School**
Kingsclear First Nation
712 Church St. Fredericton, E3E 1K8 Canada
506-363-3019
Grades: K4; 1-5
Enrollment: 45
Allan McIntyre, Principal

Red Bank: **Metepanagiag - Red Bank School**
1926 MicMac Rd. Red Bank, E9E 1B3 Canada
506-836-6160,
rbedu@nbt.aibn.com
Grades: K4; 1-6
Enrollment: 41
Maureen Donovan, Principal

Tobique First Nation: **Mah-Sos School**
270 Main St. Tobique First Nation, E7H 2Y8 Canada
506-273-5407
Grades: K4; 1-5
Enrollment: 115
Paula Pirie, Principal
paula_pirie@hotmail.com

Woodstock First Nation: **Woodstock First Nation Pre-School**
6 Eagles Nest Dr. Woodstock First Nation, E7M 4J3 Canada
506-328-4332
June Tomah, Principal
Janet Paul, Principal

Schools: Independent & Private

Independent & Private Schools

Fredericton: **Devon Park Christian School**
P.O. Box 3510 B
145 Clark St. Fredericton, E3A 5J8 Canada
506-458-9379, Fax: 506-458-8702
Grades: K.-12
Enrollment: 179
Randy Fox, Principal

Moncton: **Moncton Christian Academy / MCA**
945 St. George Blvd. Moncton, E1E 2C9 Canada

506-855-5403, Fax: 506-857-9016,
www.monctonchristianacademy.com

Grades: Kindergarten - 12
Enrollment: 120
Moncton Christian Academy is an interdenominational school.
Willie Brownlee, Administrator
Esther Flanagan, Assistant

Plaster Rock: Apostolic Christian School
123 Main St. Plaster Rock, E7G 2H2 Canada
506-356-8690, Fax: 506-356-9996

Grades: K.-12
Enrollment: 64
Sanford Goodine, Principal

Rothesay: Rothesay Netherwood School / RNS
40 College Hill Rd. Rothesay, E2E 5H1 Canada
506-847-8224, Fax: 506-848-0851,
education@rns.cc; admission@rns.cc; bursar@rns.cc;
alumni@rns.cc
www.rns.cc

Grades: 6 - 12
Rothesay Netherwood School is a day & boarding school.
Sylvia MacVey, Chair
Paul G. Kitchen, Head of School, 506-848-0863
kitchenp@rns.cc
Paul McLellan, Director, Senior School & Assistant Head of S, 506-848-0864
mclellanp@rns.cc
Dean Van Doleweerd, Director, Middle School & Assistant Head of S, 506-847-8224
vandoleweerdd@rns.cc
Jayne Fillman, Director, Admission, 506-848-0859
fillmanj@rns.cc
David Keeping, Director, Finance & Operations, 506-848-0855
keepingd@rns.cc
Linda MacDonald, Director, Residential Life, 506-848-8224
macdonaldl@rns.cc
Geoffrey McCullogh, Director, Athletics, 506-848-0852
mcculloghg@rns.cc
Brian Murray, Director, Student Life, 506-848-0876
murrayb@rns.cc
Tammy Earle, Head, Information Technology & Coordinator IB, 506-848-1739
earlet@rns.cc

Rothesay: Valley Christian Academy / VCA
P.O. Box 4722
30 Vincent Rd. Rothesay, E2E 5X4 Canada
506-848-6373, Fax: 506-848-6379,
vca@nbnet.nb.ca
www.valleychristianacademy.com

Grades: Preschool - 9
Valley Christian Academy is a ministry of Rothesay Baptist Church. The preschool accepts children as young as three years of age.
Elizabeth MacDonald, Principal
vcaprinc@nbnet.nb.ca

Somerville: Somerville Christian Academy
2608, rte 103 Somerville, E7P 3A9 Canada
506-375-4327, Fax: 506-375-4406

Grades: K.-5
Enrollment: 63
Angela Mabey, Principal

Sussex: Sussex Christian School
45 Chapman Dr. Sussex, E4E 1M4 Canada
506-433-4005, Fax: 506-433-3402,
scs@sussexchristianschool.com
www.sussexchristianschool.com

Grades: Jr. K.-12
Enrollment: 67
Marsha Boyd-Mitchell, Principal

Universities & Colleges

Universities

Fredericton: Maritime College of Forest Technology
Hugh John Flemming Forestry Centre
1350 Regent St. Fredericton, E3C 2G6 Canada
506-458-0653, Fax: 506-458-0652,
info@mcft.ca
www.mcft.ca

Enrollment: 150

Fredericton: St. Thomas University
Fredericton, E3B 5G3 Canada
506-452-0532, Fax: 506-452-0617,
www.stu.ca

Most Rev. Faber MacDonald, B.Comm., Chancellor
Dr. Daniel W. O'Brien, B.Comm., M.S.W., Adv.Dip., President & Vice-Chancellor, 506-452-0537
obrien@stu.ca
Dr. Patrick Malcolmson, B.Ed., M.A., Ph.D., Vice-President, 506-452-0417
pmalcolm@stu.ca
Lawrence H. Durling, B.B.A., C.A., Vice-President, 506-452-0533
ldurling@stu.ca
Kathryn Monti, B.A., Director, 506-452-0532
monti@stu.ca
Derryl Smith, B.A., B.Ed., M.Ed., Director, 506-452-0539
dsmith@stu.ca
Robert B. Edgett, B.A., C.F.R.E., Director, 506-452-0512
Rev. John Keoughan, B.A., B.Ed., M.Ed., Chaplain, 506-452-0643
Reginald J. Gallant, B.B.A., C.A., Comptroller, 506-452-0631
gallant@stu.ca
Fred Wallace, Manager, 506-452-0606
Jane McGinn-Giberson, P.Eng., Director, 506-452-0638
jmcginn@stu.ca
Lawrence A. Batt, B.A., M.A., Registrar, 506-452-0530
lbatt@stu.ca
Peter Dielissen, ISP., Director, 506-460-0363
peterd@stu.ca
Kathy Wishart, B.A., B.Ed., Coordinator, 506-452-0529
wishart@stu.ca
Ilkay Silk, N.S.C.D., L.U.D., L.R.A.M, Coordinator, 506-452-0605
silk@stu.ca
Colleen Comeau, B.A., B.Ed., Director, 506-452-0630
ccomeau@stu.ca
Ryan Sullivan, B.A., Coordinator, 506-460-0343
sullivan@stu.ca
Karen Taylor, B.A., M.P.A., C.S.W., Director, 506-452-0445
taylor@stu.ca
Dale Dasset, B.A., Multimedia Coordinator, 506-460-0320
dasset@stthomas.ca
Jeffrey Carleton, B.A., M.A., Director, 506-452-0522
carleton@stu.ca

Publications
Aquinian

Fredericton: University of New Brunswick
P.O. Box 4400 A
Fredericton, E3B 5A3 Canada
506-453-4666, Fax: 506-453-5158,
trudya@unb.ca
www.unb.ca

Enrollment: 9000
Richard J. Currie, O.C., M.B.A., L.L.D., P.E, Chancellor
John D. McLaughlin, B.Sc.E., M.Sc.E., Ph.D., President & Vice-Chancellor
jdm@unb.ca
Angelo Belcastro, B.A., B.PE., M.Sc., Ph.D., Vice-President
abelcas@unb.ca
Daniel V. Murray, C.A., B.Comm., Vice-President
dmurray@unb.ca
Larry J. Guitard, B.A., L.L.B., C.A., Asst. Vice-President, Finance & Corporate Ser
lguitard@unb.ca
S. Strople, B.A., M.A., University Secretary
sstrople@unb.ca
David Hinton, B.Sc., M.Sc., Registrar
hinton@unb.ca
Peter McDougall, B.A., M.I.R., C.H.R.P., Associate Vice-President
pmcdouga@unb.ca
C. Anne Forrestall, B.A., M.A., Director
caf@unb.ca
W. Brewer, Procurement Manager
wbrewer@unb.ca
S. Fillmore, Manager
fillmore@unb.ca
Kathryn E. Hamer, B.A., M.A., Ph.D., Vice-President
khamer@unbsj.ca
Gregory Kealey, B.A., M.A., Ph.D., F.R.S., Vice-President
gkealey@unb.ca
Thomas Buckley, B.A., B.Ed., Registrar
buckleyt@unbsj.ca
K. Bonner, B.A., M.Ed., Director
kbonner@unbsj.ca
P. Joas, Manager
joas@unbsj.ca

Faculties
Arts
James Murray, B.A., M.A., Ph.D., Dean
arts@unb.ca

Arts (Saint John)
Robert MacKinnon, B.A., M.A., Ph.D., Dean

Business (Saint John)
Shelley Rinehart, B.A., M.B.A., Ph.D., Dean

Business Administration
Daniel Coleman, B.A., Ph.D., Dean
fadmin@unb.ca

Computer Science
Virendra Bhavsar, B.Eng., M.Tech., Ph.D., Dean

Education
Sharon Rich, Ed.D., M.Ed., B.A., Dean
educ@unb.ca

Engineering
David Coleman, B.Sc.E., Ph.D., P.Eng., M, Dean
deaneng@unb.ca

Forestry & Environmental Management
D. MacLean, B.Sc., Ph.D., Dean
forem@unb.ca

Kinesiology
Terry Haggerty, B.A., B.P.H.E., Dip.Educ., Dean
cls@unb.ca

Law
Philip Bryden, B.A., B.C.L., L.L.M., Dean
law@unb.ca

Nursing
C.H. Gibson, B.N., M.Sc.N., Ph.D., Dean
nursing@unb.ca

School of Graduate Studies
Gwendolyn Davies, B.A., M.A., Ph.D., Cert.E, Dean
gradschl@unb.ca

Science
A.R. Sharp, B.Sc., M.Sc., Ph.D., Dean
science@unb.ca

Science, Applied Science & Engineering (Saint John)
Deborah MacLatchy, B.Sc., Ph.D., Dean
sci-eng@unbsj.ca

Campuses
Renaissance College
P.O. Box 4400
Fredericton, E3B 5A3 Canada
Fax: 506-447-3274

Pierre Zundel, Dean

Saint John Campus
P.O. Box 5050
Saint John, E2L 4L5 Canada
Fax: 506-648-5528

K.E. Hamer, Vice-President

Affiliations
Maritime College of Forest Technology
1350 Regent St. Fredericton, E3C 2G6 Canada
506-458-0653, Fax: 506-458-0652,
info@mcft.ca
www.mcft.ca

Robert A. Whitney, Acting Executive Director
rwhitney@mcft.ca
Jason A. Thibodeau, MFRS, Recruitment Officer
jthibodeau@mcft.ca

Publications
Baron (St. John campus)

Brunswickan

Moncton: Université de Moncton
Campus de Moncton
Moncton, E1A 3E9 Canada
506-858-4000, Fax: 506-858-4544, 1-800-363-8336
info@umoncton.ca
www.umoncton.ca

Une institution d'enseignement exclusivement de langue française; campus: Edmunston, Moncton et Shippagan
Louis R. Comeau, C.M., Chancelier
Yvon Fontaine, Recteur et Vice-Chancelier
recteur@umoncton.ca
Lynne Castonguay, Secrétaire générale
Nassir El-Jabi, Vice-recteur à l'administration et aux ressou
eljabin@umoncton.ca
Linda Schofield, Dir. gén.
schofil@umoncton.ca
Daniel Godbout, Directeur
godboud@umoncton.ca
Roger Boulay, Directeur
boulayr@umoncton.ca
vacant, Bibliothécaire en chef
Janique Léger, Directrice
legerja@umoncton.ca

Rhéal Belliveau, Directeur
bellivr@umoncton.ca
Paul-Emile Benoit, Directeur
benoitpe@umoncton.ca
Thérèse Thériault, Directrice
theriat@umoncton.ca
Gaston LeBlanc, Doyen
Isabelle McKee-Allain, Doyenne
chiassz@umoncton.ca
Andrew Boghen, Doyen
Anne Lowe, Doyenne
Charles Bourque, Doyen
Lise Caron, Doyenne
Marie-France Albert, Doyenne
Paul Chiasson, Doyen
Régina Robichaud, Directrice
Sylvie Robichaud-Ekstrand, Directrice
Paul Bourque, Directeur
Normand Gionet, Directeur
Paul Albert, Vice-recteur
Jocelyne Roy-Vienneau, Vice-rectrice
Normand Gionet, Doyen (par intérim)
Nasser Baccouche, Directeur
Zénon Chiasson, Directeur
chiassz@umoncton.ca
Terrance J. LeBlanc, Director
leblanct@umoncton.ca
Marc Boudreau, Directeur
boudrema@umoncton.ca
Neil Boucher, Vice-recteur à l'enseignement et à la recherc
bouchen@umoncton.ca

Publications
Le Front

***Sackville:* Mount Allison University**
65 York St. Sackville, E4L 1E4 Canada
506-364-2300,
www.mta.ca
John L. Bragg, O.C., B. Comm., B.Ed., LL, Chancellor
Kenneth L. Ozmon, O.C., Ph.D., B.A., M.A., President & Vice-Chancellor
Brian G. Johnston, B. Comm., LL.B., Q.C., Chair
John F. Read, B.Sc., Ph.D., Vice-President
David Stewart, B.Sc., LL.B., Vice-President
Carrie MacMillan, B.A., M.A., Ph.D., Dean
Robert Summerby-Murray, B.A., M.A., Ph.D., A.T.C., Dean
Chris Parker, B.F.A., Registrar
Charles W. F. Hunter, B.A., M.A., B.Ed., Associate Vice-President
Margaret Beattie, B.Sc., M.Sc., Ph.D., Dean
Bruno Gnassi, B.A., M.A., M.L.S., University Librarian

Publications
Argosy Weekly

Colleges

***Bathurst:* New Brunswick Community College (Bathurst)**
Collège communautaire du Nouveau-Brunswick (Bathurst)
P.O. Box 266
725, rue du Collège Bathurst, E2A 3Z2 Canada
506-547-2145, Fax: 506-547-2741, 1-800-552-5483
www.bathurst.ccnb.nb.ca
Jeanne A. Comeau, Principal
jeanne.a.comeau@gnb.ca

***Campbellton:* Collège communautaire du Nouveau-Brunswick - Campbellton**
P.O. Box 309
47, av Village Campbellton, E3N 3G7 Canada
506-789-2377, Fax: 506-789-2433, 1-888-648-4111
yves.chouinard2@gnb.ca
campbellton.ccnb.nb.ca
Yves Chouinard, Directeur général

***Dieppe:* Collège Communautaire du Nouveau-Brunswick - Dieppe**
505, rue du Collège Dieppe, E1A 7H9 Canada
506-856-2200, Fax: 506-856-2847, 1-800-561-7162
cheryl.mclaughlin-basque@gnb.ca
www.ccnb.nb.ca/college/campus/dieppe
Claude Allard, Directeur
claude.allard@gnb.ca

***Edmundston:* New Brunswick Community College (Edmundston)**
Collège communautaire du Nouveau-Brunswick (Edmundston)
225, rue Pouvoir Edmundston, E3V 3K7 Canada
506-735-2500, Fax: 506-735-2717, 1-888-695-2262
infoccnb@gnb.ca
www.edmundston.ccnb.nb.ca
Richard Doiron, Principal
richard.doiron@gnb.ca

***Fredericton:* New Brunswick Community College (Fredericton)**
Collège communautaire du Nouveau-Brunswick (Fredericton)
P.O. Box 6000
457 Queen St. Fredericton, E3B 5H1 Canada
506-453-2305, Fax: 506-457-7352,
nbccd.email@gnb.ca
www.nbccd.nbcc.nb.ca
Bronwen Cunningham, Principal
bronwen.cunningham@gnb.ca

***Miramichi:* New Brunswick Community College (Miramichi)**
Collège communautaire du Nouveau-Brunswick (Miramichi)
P.O. Box 1053
80 University Ave. Miramichi, E1N 3W4 Canada
506-778-6000, Fax: 506-778-6001,
www.nbcc.nb.ca
Karen White-O'Connell, Principal
karen.white-o'connell@gnb.ca

***Moncton:* New Brunswick Community College (Moncton)**
Collège communautaire du Nouveau-Brunswick (Moncton)
1234 Mountain Rd. Moncton, E1C 8H9 Canada
506-856-2220, Fax: 506-856-3288, 1-888-664-1477
student.services@gnb.ca
www.nbcc.nb.ca/
Enrollment: 3500
Darren Ros, Principal
darren.rose@gnb.ca

***Saint John:* New Brunswick Community College (Saint John)**
Collège communautaire du Nouveau-Brunswick (Saint John)
P.O. Box 2270
950 Grandview Ave. Saint John, E2L 3V1 Canada
506-658-6600, Fax: 506-658-6792,
studentservices.nbccsj@gnb.ca
www.nbcc.nb.ca
Annette Albert, Principal
annette.albert@gnb.ca

***Shippagan:* New Brunswick Community College (Péninsule acadienne)**
Collège communautaire du Nouveau-Brunswick (Péninsule acad
232A, avenue de l'Église Shippagan, E8S 1P6 Canada
506-336-3073, Fax: 506-336-3075, 1-866-299-9900
info_ccnbpa@gnb.ca
Thérèse Finn-McGraw, Principal
therese.finn-mcgraw@gnb.ca

***St Andrews:* New Brunswick Community College (St. Andrews)**
Collège communautaire du Nouveau-Brunswick (St. Andrews)
99 Augustus St. St Andrews, E5B 2E9 Canada
506-529-5024, Fax: 506-529-5078,
webinquiries@gnb.ca
www.nbcc.nb.ca
Enrollment: 300
Diane Burt, Principal
diane.burt@gnb.ca

***Woodstock:* New Brunswick Community College (Woodstock)**
Collège communautaire du Nouveau-Brunswick (Woodstock)
100 Broadway St. Woodstock, E7M 5C5 Canada
506-325-4400, Fax: 506-328-8426,
debbie.antworth@gnb.ca
www.nbcc.nb.ca
Joy Dion, Principal
joy.dion@gnb.ca

Post Secondary/Technical

Post Secondary/Technical

***Fredericton:* Maritime Forest Ranger School**
1350 Regent St. Fredericton, E3C 2G6 Canada
506-458-0199, Fax: 506-458-0652
Established 1946. Identical francophone program offered at the Bathurst, NB campus. A minimum 12-month pre-admission apprenticeship in woods work or forestry is required. In addition to course work, students are required to work a minimum 12-week practic
J.S. Hoyt, Director

***Fredericton:* New Brunswick Community Colleges**
Collèges communautaires du Nouveau-Brunswick
284 Smythe St. Fredericton, E3B 3C9 Canada
506-453-3641, Fax: 506-453-7944,
www.gov.nb.ca/ael/nbcc/

***Moncton:* McKenzie College**
100 Cameron St. Moncton, E1C 5Y6 Canada
506-384-6460, Fax: 506-384-6224,
info@mckenzie.edu
www.mckenzie.edu
Multimedia, animation & information technology training.

***Fredericton:* Atlantic Business College - Fredericton Campus**
1115 Regent St. Fredericton, E3B 3Z2 Canada
506-450-1408, Fax: 506-450-8388, 1-800-983-292
atlantic@abc.nb.ca
www.abc.nb.ca
Day school programs, continuing education courses, corporate training; also in Moncton.
Jacqueline Devine, Principal

***Moncton:* Moncton Campus**
100 Cameron St. 2nd Fl. Moncton, E1C 5Y6 Canada
506-857-3011, Fax: 506-857-4885, 1-800-442-3111
TDD: 1-800-442-3011
moncton@abc.nb.ca
www.abc.nb.ca
Day school programs, continuing education courses, corporate training; also in Moncton.

***Saint John:* Academy of Learning**
245 Union St. Saint John, E2L 1B2 Canada
506-652-8973, Fax: 506-634-1997,
learn@aolnb.com
ww.aolnb.com
Computer & business skills training; 2 other locations in New Brunswick
Sumbal Sheikh, Manager

Newfoundland & Labrador

Government Agencies

***St. John's:* Department of Education**
P.O. Box 8700
St. John's, A1B 4J6 Canada
709-729-5097, Fax: 709-729-5896,
education@gov.nl.ca
www.gov.nl.ca/edu
Rick Hayward, Asst. Deputy Minister, 709-729-3025
rhayward@gov.nl.ca
Rachelle Cochrane, Asst. Deputy Minister, 709-729-3026
rachellecochrane@gov.nl.ca
Tony Cornect, District Assistant, 709-729-5096
tonycornect@gov.nl.ca

School Boards/Districts/Divisions

Public

***Corner Brook:* Western School District**
P.O. Box 368
10 Wellington St. Corner Brook, A2H 6G9 Canada
709-637-4000, Fax: 709-634-1828,
www.wnlsd.ca
Grades: K.-12
Enrollment: 14737
This district is an amalgation of school districts 2, 3, and 4.
Ross Elliott, PhD, Dir., 709-634-8349
Donald Brown, Chair

***Gander:* Nova Central - School District 3**
203 Elizabeth Dr. Gander, A1V 1H6 Canada
709-256-2547, Fax: 709-651-3044,
www.ncsd.ca
Enrollment: 13000
Cynthia Fleet, Director of Education
cfleet@ncsd.ca

***Happy Valley-Goose Bay:* District Office (Lab. East)**
P.O. Box 1810 B
16 Strathcona Happy Valley-Goose Bay, A0P 1E0 Canada

709-896-2431, Fax: 709-896-9638,
bpardy@lsb.ca
www.lsb.ca

Cindy Fleet, Director

Regional Office (Lab.West)
669 Tamarack Dr. Labrador City, A2V 2V2 Canada
709-944-7628, Fax: 709-944-3480,
sthibeau@lsb.ca
www.lsb.ca

Happy Valley-Goose Bay: Labrador - School district 1

P.O. Box 1810 B
16 Strathcona St. Happy Valley-Goose Bay, A0P 1E0 Canada
709-896-2431, Fax: 709-896-9638,
www.lsb.ca

Grades: K-12
Enrollment: 5000
Bruce Vey, Director of Education
bvey@lsb.ca

St. Jean: Conseil scolaire francophone provincial de Terre-Neuve-et-Labrador

#212, 65, ch Ridge St. Jean, A1B 4P5 Canada
709-722-6324, Fax: 709-722-6325, 888-794-6324
conseil@csfp.nf.ca
www.csfp.nf.ca

Dr. Ahmed Derradji-Aouat, Président du Conseil

St. John's: Eastern - School District 4

#601 Atlantic Place
P.O. Box 64-66
215 Water St. St. John's, A1C 6C9 Canada
709-758-2372, Fax: 709-758-2706,
www.esdnl.ca

Dr. Darin King, Dir. of Education

Schools: Specialized

First Nations

Conne River: Se't A'newey Kina'magino'kuom School

P.O. Box 100
Conne River, A0H 1J0 Canada
709-882-2747, Fax: 709-882-2528,
www.k12.nf.ca/stannes/

Grades: K.-12
Craig Benoit, Principal

Natuashish: Mushuau Innu Natuashish

P.O. Box 189
Natuashish, A0P 1A0 Canada
709-478-8972, Fax: 709-478-8989,
www.natuashish.K12.nf.ca

Robert Myers
rmyers122@hotmail.com

Hearing Impaired

St. John's: Newfoundland School for the Deaf

425 Topsail Rd. St. John's, A1E 5N7 Canada
709-364-1234, Fax: 709-729-5848,
regmacdonald@gov.nl.ca
www.nsd.nf.ca/

Grades: K.-3, 5, 7-12
Reginald MacDonald, Principal

Schools: Independent & Private

Independent & Private Schools

Churchill Falls: Eric G. Lambert All-Grade School

P.O. Box 40
Churchill Falls, A0R 1A0 Canada
709-925-3371, Fax: 709-925-3364,
aclarke@nlh.nf.ca
www.k12.nf.ca/eglambert

Grades: K.-12
Enrollment: 156
Adrian Clarke, Principal
aclarke@nlh.nf.ca

St. John's: Lakecrest - St. John's Independent School

58 Patrick St. St. John's, A1E 2S7 Canada
709-738-1212, Fax: 709-738-1701,
www.lakecrest.ca

Grades: K.-9
Enrollment: 129
Ron Pellerin, Principal

St. John's: St. Bonaventure's College

Bonaventure Ave. St. John's, A1C 6B3 Canada
709-726-0024, Fax: 709-726-0148,
principal@stbonaventurescollege.ca
www.stbonaventurescollege.ca/

Grades: K.-12
Enrollment: 325
Catholic school in the Jesuit tradition
Cecil Critch, Principal
ccritch@stbonaventurescollege.ca

Universities & Colleges

Universities

St. John's: Memorial University of Newfoundland

P.O. Box 4200
230 Elizabeth Ave. St. John's, A1C 5S7 Canada
709-737-8000, Fax: 709-737-4569,
www.mun.ca

Enrollment: 17300
The Hon. Edward Roberts, O.N.L., B.A., LL.B., LL.D, Official Visitor
Gen. Rick Hillier, Chancellor
Dr. H.E.A. Campbell, Acting President & Vice-Chancellor
Dr. Chris Loomis, Vice-President
vpacad@mun.ca
Kent Decker, B.Comm. (Hons.), C.A., Vice-President
kdecker@mun.ca
Christopher W. Loomis, B.Sc., M.Sc., Ph.D., Vice-President
cwloomis@mun.ca
Glenn Collins, B.Sc., B.Ed., M.Sc., Registrar
gcollins@mun.ca
Deborah Collis, Acting Director
dcollis@mun.ca
Robert E. Simmonds, QC, Chair
Wilf Nicholls, B.Sc., Ph.D., Director
John Hanchar, Ph.D., Director
Charles Randell, P.Eng., B.Eng., M.A.Sc., President/CEO
Bill Morrissey, B.A.(Ed.), M.Ed., Director
Kenneth M. LeDez, M.B., Ch.B., F.R.C.T.C., Director
Graham Mowbray, B.Sc., Director
Peter Cornish, B.Sc., M.A., Ph.D., Director
Karen Hollett, B.A., L.L.B., Director
Martin Lovelace, B.A., M.A., Ph.D., Director
Bonnie Simmons, B.Comm., M.B.A., Director
David King, B.Comm., M.B.A., C.A., President & CEO
Lisa Hollett, B.A., M.I.R., Director
James A. Tuck, A.B., Ph.D., F.R.S.C., Director
Ron Sparkes, Ed.D., Interim Director
Richard H. Ellis, B.A., M.L.S., University Librarian
rhellis@mun.ca
Heather Wareham, B.A., Archivist
Peter Pope, B.A., M.A., Ph.D., Director
B.J. Veitch, B.Eng., M.Eng., L.Tech., Director
Ian Fleming, Ph.D., Director
Barbara Cox, B.A., Director
Norman Lee, B.M.S., M.D., C.C.F.P., Director
Sheila Devine, B.A., B.Ed., LL.B., Director
Robert Sheppard, B.Eng., M.B.A., M.Eng., P, Director
Victoria Collins, B.A., Director
Darrell Miles, P.Eng., Director
L. Husa, M.V.Dr., Director
Susan Vaughan, B.A., M.B.A., Director
Georgina Hedges, M.D., Acting Chair
Michael Collins, M.Sc., M.Ed., Ph.D., Assoc. Vice-President
collinsm@mun.ca
Penny Blackwood, B.Sc., M.Sc., Ph.D., Director
Paul Chancey, B.Sc., B.Comm., Director
Gerald Pocius, B.Sc., M.A., Ph.D., Director
Robert Shea, B.A., B.S.W., M.Ed., R.S., Director
Keith Storey, B.A., M.A., Ph.D., Director
Christine Burke, B.Comm., M.B.A., Director
J. Beal (Britain), B.A.(Hons.), Ph.D., Director
Anthony B. Dickinson, B.Sc., B.Ed., M.Sc., M.A., Acting Exec. Director
James Feehan, B.A., M.Sc., Ph.D., Director
Claude Horlick, B.Comm., Director
Bruce Belbin, B.A., B.Ed., M.Ed., Director
Dr. Lilly Walker, B.A., M.A., Ph.D., Dean
lwalker@mun.ca
Robert Greenwood, B.A.(Hons.), M.A., Ph.D., Director

Faculties
Arts
Reeta Tremblay, Ph.D., Dean

Business Administration
Gary Gorman, B.B.A., M.B.A., Ph.D., Dean

Education
Alice Collins, B.A., B.Ed., M.A., Ph.D., Dean

Engineering & Applied Science
Ray Gosine, B.Eng., Ph.D., P.Eng., Dean

Graduate Studies
Chet Jablonski, B.Sc., Ph.D., F.C.I.C., Dean

Medicine
James Rourke, M.D., C.C.F.P. (EM), F.C., Dean

Science
Robert Lucas, B.Sc., M.Sc., D.Phil., F., Dean

Schools
Division of Lifelong Learning
Doreen Whalen, Dip. A.A., C.T.T., B.Voc., Director

Distance Education & Learning Technologies
Anne Marie Vaughan, B.A., B.Ed., M.Ed., M.A., Director

Human Kinetics & Recreation
Mary Bluechardt, B.P.H.D., M.Sc., Ph.D., Director

Marine Institute
Glenn Blackwood, B.Sc. (Hon.), M.A., Executive Director

Music
Tom Gordon, B.A., B.Mus., M.A., Ph.D., Director

Nursing
Sandra LeFort, B.A., B.N., M.N., Ph.D., Director

Pharmacy
Linda Hensman, B.Sc.(Pharm.), S.U.N.Y., Director

Social Work
Shelly Birnie-Lefcovitch, B.A., M.S.W., Ph.D., Director

Affiliations
Fisheries & Marine Institute of Memorial University of Newfoundland
P.O. Box 4920
St. John's, A1C 5R3 Canada
709-778-0200, Fax: 709-778-0672, 1-800-563-5799
Registrar, Phone: 709-778-0492
public.relations@mi.mun.ca; admissions@mi.mun.ca
www.mi.mun.ca

Glenn Blackwood, Executive Director
Carey Bonnell, Head, MI School of Fisheries

Harlow Campus Trust
The Maltings, St. John's Walk, Market St., Old Harl Essex, CM17 0AJ England

Phone: (0)1279-455900; Fax: (0)1279-455921
hcampus@hcampus.inty.net
www.mun.ca/harlow

Sandra Wright, General Manager

Queen's College
c/o The Provost, Faculty of Theology
#3000, 210 Prince Philip Dr. St. John's, A1B 3R6 Canada
709-753-0116, Fax: 709-753-1214, 1-877-753-0116
queens@mun.ca
www.mun.ca/queens

The Rev. Dr. John Mellis, Provost & Vice-Chancellor & Associate Profess
jmellis@mun.ca

Sir Wilfred Grenfell College
1 University Dr. Corner Brook, A2H 6P9 Canada
709-637-6200,
info@swgc.mun.ca; helpdesk@swgc.mun.ca;
webadmin@swgc.mun.ca
www.swgc.mun.ca

The College features the following divisions: Arts, Fine Arts, Science, & Social Science.
E. Holly Pike, Ph.D., Acting Principal, 709-637-6200 6231
hpike@swgc.mun.ca

Publications
The Muse

Colleges

Stephenville: College of the North Atlantic

P.O. Box 5400
Stephenville, A2N 2Z6 Canada
709-643-7701, Fax: 709-643-7808, 888-982-2268
info@cna.nl.ca
www.cna.nl.ca

Enrollment: 20000
Bruce Hollett, Interim President, 709-643-7701, fax: 709-643-7808
bruce.hollet@cna.nl.
John Hutchings, Vice-Pres., Finance & Administration, 709-643-7704
john.hutchings@cna.nl.ca

Cyril Organ, Vice-Pres., Academic & Learner Services, 709-643-7732
cyril.organ@cna.nl.ca
Corinne Dunne, Vice-Pres., Development/College Advancement, 709-758-7652
corinne.dunne@cna.nl.ca
Greg Chaytor, Vice-Pres., Qatar Project, 709-643-7702
greg.chaytor@cna.nl.ca
Linda Dunne, Registrar, 709-643-0827, fax: 709-643-7843
linda.dunne@cna.nl.ca

Schools

Academics
Brenda Tobin, Dean, 709-292-5636, fax: 709-643-0518

Applied Arts
Brenda Tobin, Dean, 709-292-5636, fax: 709-489-0518

Business
Mary Vaughan, Dean, 709-649-7970, fax: 709-643-8454

Engineering Technology
Arthur Leung, Dean, 709-758-7100, fax: 709-758-7126

Health Sciences
Jane Gamberg, Dean, 709-758-7624, fax: 709-758-7634

Industrial Trades
Norris Eaton, Dean, 709-637-8523, fax: 709-634-8767

Information Technology
Mary Vaughan, Dean, 709-649-7970, fax: 709-643-8454

Tourism & Natural Resources
Brent Howell, Dean, 709-637-8608, fax: 709-634-2126

Campuses

Baie-Verte Campus
1 Terra Nova Rd. Baie Verte, A0K 1B0 Canada
709-532-8066, Fax: 709-532-4624
Emily Foster, Campus Administrator, 709-532-8066, fax: 709-532-4624
emily.foster@cna.nl.ca

Bay St. George Campus - Headquarters
DSB Fowlow Bldg.
P.O. Box 5400
432 Massachussetts Dr. Stephenville, A2N 2Z6 Canada
709-643-7838, Fax: 709-643-7734
Chris Dohaney, Campus Administrator, 709-643-7916, fax: 709-643-7827
chris.dohaney@cna.nl.ca

Bonavista Campus
P.O. Box 670
301 Confederation Dr. Bonavista, A0C 1B0 Canada
709-468-2610, Fax: 709-468-2004
Marilyn Coles-Hayley, Campus Administrator, 709-468-1700, fax: 709-468-2004
marilyn.hayley@cna.nl.ca

Burin Campus
P.O. Box 370
105 Main St. Burin Bay, A0E 1G0 Canada
709-891-5600, Fax: 709-891-2256, 800-838-0976
ask.burin@cna.nl.ca
Mike Graham, Campus Administrator, 709-891-5602, fax: 709-891-2256
mike.graham@cna.nl.ca

Carbonear Campus
4 Pike's Lane Carbonear, A1Y 1A7 Canada
709-596-6139, Fax: 709-596-2688
Gary Myrden, Campus Administrator, 709-596-6139, fax: 709-596-2688
gary.myrden@cna.nl.ca

Clarenville Campus
69 Pleasant St. Clarenville, A5A 1V9 Canada
709-466-6900, Fax: 709-466-2771
Maisie Caines, Campus Administrator, 709-466-6931, fax: 709-466-2771
maisie.caines@cna.nl.ca

Corner Brook Campus
P.O. Box 822
41 O'Connell Dr. Corner Brook, A2H 6H6 Canada
709-637-8530, Fax: 709-634-2126
Chad Simms, Campus Administrator, 709-637-8549, fax: 709-634-2126
chad.simms@cna.nl.ca

Gander Campus
P.O. Box 395
1 Magee Rd. Gander, A1V 1W8 Canada
709-651-4800, Fax: 709-651-3376
Bob Dwyer, Campus Administrator, 709-651-4803, fax: 709-651-3376
bob.dwyer@cna.nl.ca

Grand Falls-Windsor Campus
P.O. Box 413
5 Cromer Ave. Grand Falls-Windsor, A2A 1X3 Canada
709-292-5600, Fax: 709-489-4180
Joan Pynn, Campus Administrator, 709-292-5625, fax: 709-489-5765
joan.pynn@cna.nl.ca

Happy Valley Campus
P.O. Box 1720 B
219 Hamilton River Rd. Happy Valley-Goose Bay, A0P 1E0 Canada
709-896-6300, Fax: 709-896-3733
Paul Motty, Campus Administrator, 709-896-6312, fax: 709-896-9533
paul.motty@cna.nl.ca

Labrador West Campus
1 Campbell Dr. Labrador City, A2V 2Y1 Canada
709-944-7210, Fax: 709-944-6581
Richard Sawyer, Campus Administrator, 709-944-6814, fax: 709-944-5413
richard.sawyer@cna.nl.ca

Placentia Campus
P.O. Box 190
1 Roosevelt Ave. Placentia, A0B 2Y0 Canada
709-227-2037, Fax: 709-227-7185
Darrell Clarke, Campus Administrator, 709-227-2037, fax: 709-227-7185
darrell.clarke@cna.nl.ca

Port-aux-Basques Campus
P.O. Box 760
59 Grand Bay Rd. Port-aux-Basques, A0M 1C0 Canada
709-695-3582, Fax: 709-695-2963
Mr Jan Peddle, Campus Administrator, 709-695-3582, fax: 709-695-2963
jan.peddle@cna.nl.ca

Prince Philip Drive Campus - St. John's
P.O. Box 1693
1 Prince Philip Dr. St. John's, A1C 5P7 Canada
709-758-7284, Fax: 709-758-7304
Trudy Barnes, Campus Administrator, 709-758-7418, fax: 709-758-7235
trudy.barnes@cna.nl.ca

Ridge Road Campus
P.O. Box 1150
St. John's, A1C 6L8
709-758-7000, Fax: 709-758-7059
John Oates, Campus Administrator, 709-758-7517, fax: 709-758-7126
john.oates@cna.nl.ca

Seal Cove Campus
P.O. Box 19003 Seal Cove
1670 Conception Bay Highway Conception Bay South, A1X 5C7 Canada
709-744-2047, Fax: 709-744-3929
Chris Patey, Campus Administrator, 709-744-1041, fax: 709-744-3929
chris.patey@cna.nl.ca

St. Anthony Campus
P.O. Box 550
83-93 East St. St Anthony, A0K 4S0 Canada
709-454-3559, Fax: 709-454-8808
Fred Russell, Campus Administrator, 709-454-2884, fax: 709-454-8808
frederick.russell@cna.nl.ca

Qatar Campus
P.O. Box 24449
Doha Qatar
974-495-2222

The Troubadour
709-643-7746,
the.troubador@cna.nl.ca
www.cna.nl.ca/troubadour

Post Secondary/Technical

Post Secondary/Technical

Badger: **Central Training Academy**
P.O. Box 400
6 - 3rd Ave. Badger, A0H 1A0 Canada
709-539-5150, Fax: 709-539-5145, 1-800-563-515
cta@nf.aibn.com
Training in commercial transport, heavy equipment operation

Bay Roberts: **Canadian Training Institute**
P.O. Box 479
Bay Roberts, A0A 1G0 Canada
709-786-2400, Fax: 709-786-1215
Arthur Dominix

Conception Bay South: **Woodford Training Centre Inc.**
P.O. Box 17145 Kelligrews
Conception Bay South, A1X 3H1 Canada
709-834-7000, Fax: 709-834-9663,
info@woodfordtraining.com
www.woodfordtraining.com
Cosmetology & barbering
Sharon Woodford

Corner Brook: **Corner Brook / VON**
Corner Brook District
31 Wellington St. Corner Brook, A2H 5H5 Canada
709-634-2042, Fax: 709-634-2517,
pitchere@von.ca
www.von.ca/branch/nf_cornerbrook/
Eileen Pitcher

Campuses

Gander District / VON
Gander Medical Bldg.
177 Elizabeth Dr. Gander, A1V 1H6 Canada
709-256-2924, Fax: 709-256-2905,
vongander@nf.aibn.com
www.von.ca/branch/nf_gander

St.John's / VON
39 Campbell Ave. St.John's, A1E 2Z3 Canada
709-726-8597, Fax: 709-726-4228,
von@nf.aibn.com
www.von.ca/branch/nf_stjohns

Corner Brook: **Corner Brook Campus**
2 University Dr. Corner Brook, A2H 5G4 Canada
709-637-2100, Fax: 709-637-2123,
www.academycanada.com
M.A.Ed. Michael Barrett, President

Campuses

St. John's Campus
167-169 Kenmount Rd. St. John's, A1B 3P9 Canada
709-739-6767, Fax: 709-739-6797,
www.academycanada.com

Trades College
37-45 Harding Rd. St. John's, A1C 5R4 Canada
709-722-9151, Fax: 709-722-9197,
www.academycanada.com

Creston: **Centrac College of Business, Trades & Technology**
P.O. Box 160
Creston, A0E 1K0 Canada
709-891-1995, Fax: 709-891-5272, 1-800-563-191
admissions@centraccollege.ca
www.centraccollege.ca

Gander: **Centrac College of Business, Trades & Technology**
P.O. Box 473
Gander, A1V 1W8 Canada
709-256-2670, Fax: 709-256-3697, 1-888-336-872
Campuses in Gander, Marystown, St. John's & Springdale.

Gander: **Gander Flight Training**
P.O. Box 355
Gander, A1V 1W7 Canada
709-256-7484, Fax: 709-256-7953, 1-888-926-766
admin@gft.ca
www.gft.ca
Patrick White, President & CEO

Grand Falls-Windsor: **Corona Training Institute**
P.O. Box 819
60 Hardy Ave. Grand Falls-Windsor, A2A 2P7 Canada
709-489-7825, Fax: 709-489-5001, 1-888-926-766
admin@coronacollege.com
www.coronacollege.com
Bernice Walker

Holyrood: **Boilermakers Industrial Training Centre**
P.O. Box 250
Holyrood, A0A 2R0 Canada
709-229-7958, Fax: 709-229-7300
Tom Welsh

Holyrood: **Operating Engineers, Education & Development Inc.**
P.O. Box 389
Holyrood, A0A 2R0 Canada
709-229-6464, Fax: 709-229-6469,
oec@oecollege.com
www.oecollege.com
Larry Connolly

Lewisporte: **DieTrac Technical Institute**
P.O. Box 970
82 Premier Dr. Lewisporte, A0G 3A0 Canada
709-535-0550, Fax: 709-535-6101,
admin@dietrac.com
www.dietrac.com

Mount Pearl: **Iron Workers Education & Training Co. Inc.**
38 Sagona St. Mount Pearl, A1N 4R3 Canada
709-747-2158, Fax: 709-747-1042
Tom Woodward

Paradise: **Carpenters Millwrights College Inc.**
P.O. Box 3040
Paradise, A1L 3W2 Canada
709-364-5586, Fax: 709-364-5587,
kpower@nlrc.ca
www.nlrc.ca
John Pitcher

St. John's: **Association for New Canadians**
P.O. Box 2031
St. John's, A1C 5R6 Canada
709-722-9680, Fax: 709-754-4407,
www.anc-nf.cc
ESL
Bridget Foster, Executive Director

St. John's: **Atlantic Aviation Academy**
St. John's International Airport
Hangar #2 St. John's, A1A 5B5 Canada
709-576-3420, Fax: 709-576-3427,
snoseworthy@provair.com

St. John's: **Atlantic Construction Training Centre**
P.O. Box 236
41-44 Harding Rd. St. John's, A1G 1H2 Canada
709-726-6264, Fax: 709-726-6255,
jpoirier@actc.nf.ca
John Poirier, Training Co-ordinator

St. John's: **Avalon Educational Systems**
65 Whiteway St. St. John's, A1B 1K5 Canada
709-739-5507, Fax: 709-754-3212
Custom-designed programs

St. John's: **Graduate Centre of Applied Technology**
P.O. Box 6345 C
275 Duckworth St. St. John's, A1C 6J9 Canada
709-758-5770, 1-800-247-575
gcat@graduatecentre.com
www.graduatecentre.com
Cal Burton

St. John's: **Highland College of Trades & Technology**
P.O. Box 21323
St. John's, A1A 5G6 Canada
709-747-0171, Fax: 709-747-0172,
www.highlandcollege.com
Secina Brown

St. John's: **Judy Knee Dance College Ltd.**
27 Mayor Ave. St. John's, A1C 4N4 Canada
709-579-3233, Fax: 709-579-3392,
jknee@avint.net
Judy Knee

St. John's: **Keyin College**
KeyCorp Incorporated, Head Office Keyin College
P.O. Box 13609 A
44 Austin St. St. John's, A1B 4G1 Canada
709-579-1061, Fax: 709-579-6002, 1-800-563-8989
lori@keyin.com
www.coredynamic.com/keyin/about.asp
Industry-directed education
Gwen Tucker, Founder

Campuses
Carbonear Campus
81 LeMarchant St. Carbonear, A1Y 1A9 Canada
709-596-6472, Fax: 709-596-0217, 800-563-8989
margdrover@hotmail.com (Principal Margaret Drover)
www.coredynamic.com/keyin/about.asp
Ken Drover, Principal

Clarenville Campus
Cormack Bldg.
221B Memorial Dr. Clarenville, A5A 1R3 Canada
709-466-7115, Fax: 709-466-1290, 1-800-563-8989
paula@keyinclarenville.com (Principal Paula Benson)
www.coredynamic.com/keyin/about.asp
Paula Benson, Principal

Fortune Adult Learning Centre Campus
8 Benson St. Fortune, A0E 1P0 Canada
709-279-5090, Fax: 709-279-5091, 1-800-563-8989
marc.coady@personainternet.ca (Principal Marc Coady)
www.coredynamic.com/keyin/about.asp

Gander Campus
175 Airport Blvd. Gander, A1V 1K6 Canada
709-651-8560, Fax: 709-651-8565, 1-800-563-8989
ebabstock@keyincentral.nf.ca (Principal Elsie Babstock)
www.coredynamic.com/keyin/about.asp
Elise Babstock, Principal

Grand Falls-Windsor Campus
3 Hardy Ave. Grand Falls-Windsor, A2A 2P8 Canada
709-489-8560, Fax: 709-489-8565, 1-800-563-8989
bhanlon@keyincentral.nf.ca (Principal Bill Hanlon)
www.coredynamic.com/keyin/about.asp
Bill Hanlon, Principal

Lamaline Adult Learning Centre Campus
GLADA Bldg.
P.O. Box 39
Lamaline, A0E 2C0 Canada
709-279-5090, Fax: 709-279-5091, 1-800-563-8989
marc.coady@personainternet.com (Principal Marc Coady)
www.coredynamic.com/keyin/about.asp

Lewisporte Adult Learning Centre Campus
395 Main St. Lewisporte, A0G 3A0 Canada
709-535-3946, Fax: 709-535-3946, 1-800-563-8989
brian@keyincentral.nf.ca
www.coredynamic.com/keyin/about.asp
Brian Caravan, Principal

Marystown Campus
P.O. Box 1327
414 Ville Marie Dr. Marystown, A0E 2M0 Canada
709-279-8090, Fax: 709-279-5091, 1-800-563-8989
marc.coady@personainternet.com (Principal Marc Coady)
www.coredynamic.com/keyin/about.asp
Marc Coady, Principal

St. John's Campus
P.O. Box 13609 A
44 Austin St. St. John's, A1B 4G1 Canada
709-579-1061, Fax: 709-579-6002, 1-800-563-8989
lori@keyin.com (Principal Lori Caines)
www.coredynamic.com/keyin/about.asp

St. John's: **Lawrence College Inc.**
120 LeMarchant Rd. St. John's, A1C 2H2 Canada
709-738-1053, Fax: 709-738-3350, 1-888-738-105
Brenda Steele, Principal

St. John's: **LeMoine's School of Hair Design**
P.O. Box 5744
St. John's, A1C 5X3 Canada
709-576-2148, Fax: 709-579-1134,
lemoines@nl.rogers.com
www.lemoines.com
Hair dressing and esthetics school.
Allan LeMoine

St. John's: **T & R Goldshield Security Services**
300 Topsail Rd. St. John's, A1E 2B5 Canada
709-726-0160, Fax: 709-726-0133
Don Ross

St.John's: **United Association of Journeymen & Apprentices of the Plumbing and Pipefitti / UA**
P.O. Box 8583 A
St.John's, A1B 3P2 Canada
709-747-0364, Fax: 709-747-2861,
bshea@local74.nf.net (Betty Shea: Executive Secretary)
www.ualocal740.ca
Official name: "United Association of Journeymen & Apprentices of the Plumbing and Pipefitting Industry of the United States and Canada".
Larry Slaney

Northwest Territories

Government Agencies

Yellowknife: **Department of Education, Culture & Employment**
P.O. Box 1320
Yellowknife, X1A 2L9 Canada
867-920-6240, Fax: 867-873-0338,
www.ece.gov.nt.ca
Pauline Gordon, Asst. Deputy Minister
Dan Daniels, Deputy Minister

School Boards/Districts/Divisions

Public

Fort Simpson: **Dehcho Divisional Education Council**
P.O. Box 376
Fort Simpson, X0E 0N0 Canada
867-695-7308
Nolan Swartzentruber, Supt.

Fort Smith: **South Slave Divisional Education Council**
P.O. Box 510
Fort Smith, X0E 0P0 Canada
867-872-5701, Fax: 867-872-2150,
jmurray@ssdec.nt.ca
www.ssdec.nt.ca
Curtis Brown, Superintendent
cbrown@ssdec.nt.ca

Inuvik: **Beaufort Delta Divisional Education Council**
c/o Bag Service No. 12 Inuvik, X0E 0T0 Canada
867-777-7136, Fax: 867-777-2469,
www.bdec.nt.ca
Grades: Kindergarten - 12
Enrollment: 1800
Roy Cole, Superintendent, Schools, 867-777-7332
roy_cole@bdec.learnnet.nt.ca
Gayle Strikes With A Gun, Assistant Superintendent, 867-777-7176
gaylestrikeswithagun@bdec.learnnet.nt.ca
Grey Storey, Supervisor, Schools, 867-777-7131
greg_storey@bdec.learnnet.nt.ca
Austin Abbott, Coordinator, Skills Programs, 867-777-7367
austin_abbott@bdec.learnnet.nt.ca
Camellia Gray, Coordinator, Public Affairs, 867-777-7322
camellia_gray@bdec.learnnet.nt.ca
Liz Hansen, Coordinator, Gwich'in Aboriginal Language & C, 867-777-7101
liz_hansen@bdec.learnnet.nt.ca
Rose Marie Kirby, Coordinator, Inuvialuit Aboriginal Language &, 867-777-7371
rosemarie_kirby@bdec.learnnet.nt.ca

Norman Wells: **Sahtu Divisional Education Council**
P.O. Box 64
Norman Wells, X0E 0V0 Canada
867-587-3450,
info@sahtudec.ca
www.sahtudec.ca
Seamus Quigg, Superintendent

Rae Edzo: **Tłįchǫ Community Services Agency**
Bag Service #5 Rae Edzo, X0E 0Y0 Canada
867-392-3000, Fax: 867-392-3001,
tcsa@tlicho.net
www.tlicho.ca
Lucy Lafferty, Superintendent

Yellowknife: **Commission scolaire francophone des Territoires du Nord-Ouest**
P.O. Box 1980
4920, 51e Rue Yellowknife, X1A 2P5 Canada
867-873-6555, Fax: 867-873-5644,
csftno@gov.nt.ca
www.csftno.com
Philippe Brûlot, Directeur général

Yellowknife: **Yellowknife Catholic Schools**
5124 - 49 St. Yellowknife, X1A 2P4 Canada
867-766-7400, Fax: 867-766-7401,
www.ycs.nt.ca
Grades: K.-12
Enrollment: 1450
Claudia Parker, Supt.
Mike Huvenaars, Asst. Supt., Business
Dianne Lafferty, Coordinator, Aboriginal Ed.

Yellowknife: **Yellowknife Education District No. 1**
P.O. Box 788
5402 - 50th Ave. Yellowknife, X1A 2N6 Canada
867-766-5050, Fax: 867-873-5051,
yk1@yk1.nt.ca
www.yk1.nt.ca/#Scene_1
Grades: K.-12
Enrollment: 2000
Metro Huculak, Supt./CEO, 867-766-5064
metro.huculak@yk1.nt.ca
Metro Huculak, Supt./CEO, 867-766-5064
metro.huculak@yk1.nt.ca
Myrna Pokiak, Coordinator, Aboriginal Ed., 867-766-5054
myrna.pokiak@yk1.nt.ca

Universities & Colleges

Colleges

Inuvik: **Aurora College**
P.O. Box 1290
199 McDougal Inuvik, X0E 0P0 Canada
867-872-7009, Fax: 867-872-4730,
www.auroracollege.nt.ca
Maurice Evans, President

Campuses
Aurora Campus
P.O. Box 1008
Inuvik, X0E 0T0 Canada
Fax: 867-777-2850
Miki O'Kane, Campus Director

Thebacha Campus
P.O. Box 600
Fort Smith, X0E 0P0 Canada
Fax: 867-872-4511
Kathleen E. Purchase, Campus Director

Yellowknife Campus
Bag Service 9700 Yellowknife, X1A 2R3 Canada
Fax: 867-873-0333
Sarah Wright, Campus Director

Nova Scotia

Government Agencies

Halifax: **Department of Education**
P.O. Box 578
2021 Brunswick St. Halifax, B3J 2S9 Canada
902-424-5168, Fax: 902-424-0511,
www.ednet.ns.ca
Margelaine Holding, Executive Director, 902-424-3927
Ann Blackwood, Director, 902-424-5745

School Boards/Districts/Divisions

Public

Berwick: **Annapolis Valley Regional School Board**
P.O. Box 340
121 Orchard St. Berwick, B0P 1E0 Canada
902-538-4600, Fax: 902-538-4630, 1-800-850-3887
communications@avrsb.ednet.ns.ca
www.avrsb.ca
Grades: Elementary - Secondary
Enrollment: 16000
Margo Tait, Superintendent, Schools, 902-538-4606, fax: 902-538-4634
superintendent@avrsb.ednet.ns.ca
Allen Hume, Director, Human Resources, 902-538-4610, fax: 902-538-4635
allen.hume@avrsb.ca
Stuart Jamieson, Director, Finance & Operations, 902-538-4607, fax: 902-538-4657
stuart.jamieson@avrsb.ca
Dave Jones, Director, Programs & Services, 902-538-4611, fax: 902-538-4630
dave.jones@avrsb.ca

Bridgewater: **South Shore Regional School Board**
130 North Park St. Bridgewater, B4V 4G9 Canada
902-543-2468, Fax: 902-541-3051, 888-252-2217
tsmith@ssrsb.ca
www.ssrsb.ca
Enrollment: 7400
Elliott Payzant, Chair
Nancy Pynch-Worthylake, Superintendent
npynch-worthylake@ssrsb.ca

Dartmouth: **Halifax Regional School Board**
90 Alderney Dr. Dartmouth, B2Y 4S8 Canada
902-464-2000,
www.hrsb.ns.ca
Grades: Primary - 12
Enrollment: 52000
Number of Schools: 85 elementary schools; 28 junior high schools; 15 senior high schools; 9 primary to grade 9 schools.
Number of Employees: 8,000 (including 3,478 teachers & school administrators
Irvine Carvery, Chair, 902-464-2000 4445
icarvery@hrsb.ns.ca
Carole Olsen, Superintendent
Geoff Cainen, Director, Program
Mike Christie, Director, Human Resource Services
Charles Clattenburg, Director, Operations Services
Danielle McNeil-Hessian, Director, School Administration
Richard Morris, Director, Financial Services
Heather Chandler, Coordinator, Diversity Management
Gerard Costard, Coordinator, Information Technology
Doug Hadley, Coordinator, Communications
Kim Matheson, Coordinator, Policy & Research
Tracey O'Kroneg, Coordinator, Human Resource Services
Jim Gunn, Corporate Secretary

Port Hastings: **Strait Regional School Board**
16 Cemetery Rd. Port Hastings, B9A 1K6 Canada
902-625-2191, Fax: 902-625-2281, 1-800-650-4448
srsb@srsb.ca; cathy.rankin@srsb.ca (Receptionist)
ls-strait.ednet.ns.ca/srsb/SRSBoard.nsf/MainFrameSet
Grades: Primary - 12
Number of Schools: 25
Mary Jess MacDonald, Chair
Jack Beaton, Superintendent, Schools, 902-625-7065
jack.beaton@srsb.ca
William J. Cormier, Director, Finance, 902-625-7050
william.cormier@srsb.ca
Terry Doyle, Director, Operations, 902-747-3647
terry.doyle@srsb.ca
Sherman England, Director, Human Resources, 902-625-7081
sherman.england@srsb.ca
Monica Williams, Director, Programs & Student Services, 902-625-7083
monica.williams@srsb.ca
Anita Cameron, Manager, Labour Relations, 902-747-3647
anita.cameron@srsb.ca
Tara Gaskell, Manager, Occupational Health & Safety Program, 902-747-3647
tara.gaskell@srsb.ca
Deanna Gillis, Manager, Communications & Community Relations, 902-625-7093
deanna.gillis@srsb.ca
Shirley Hart, Manager, Purchasing, 902-625-7050
shirley.hart@srsb.ca
Carleton MacNeil, Manager, Facilities, 902-747-3647
carleton.macneil@srsb.ca
Philip Hall, Coordinator, Information Technology & Integra, 902-625-7083
philip.hall@srsb.ca
Kathy Rhodes-Langille, Coordinator, Race Relations & Cross Cultural, 902-625-7112
kathy.rhodeslangille@srsb.ca
Joan Bona, Board Secretary, 902-625-7065
joan.bona@srsb.ca

Saulnierville: **Conseil scolaire acadien provincial**
P.O. Box 88
Saulnierville, B0W 2Z0 Canada
902-769-5458, Fax: 902-769-5459, 888-533-2727
madeleine.ferron@csap.ednet.ns.ca
csap.ednet.ns.ca
Enrollment: 4059
Adresse civique: 9248, rte 1, La Butte, Meteghan River, N-É.
Darrell Samson, Directeur général
Madeleine Ferron, Secrétaire du Conseil
madeleine.ferron@csap.ednet.ns.ca

Sydney: **Cape Breton-Victoria Regional School Board**
275 George St. Sydney, B1P 1J7 Canada
902-564-8293, Fax: 902-564-0123
Grades: Elementary - Secondary; Adult Ed.
Enrollment: 16006
Number of Schools: 61
Lorne Green, Chair
Ed Davis, Superintendent
Charles Sheppard, Coordinator, School Services

Truro: **Chignecto-Central Regional School Board**
60 Lorne St. Truro, B2N 3K3 Canada
902-897-8900, Fax: 902-897-8989, 1-800-770-000
www.ccrsb.ednet.ns.ca
Enrollment: 25722
Gary Miller, Supt.
Trudy Thompson, Chair

Yarmouth: **Tri-County Regional School Board**
79 Water St. Yarmouth, B5A 1L4 Canada
902-749-5696, Fax: 902-749-5697, 1-800-915-0113
www.tcrsb.ca
Grades: Primary - 12
Number of Schools: 30
Faye Haley, Chair
Phil Landry, Superintendent, Schools, 902-749-5682
plandry@tcrsb.ca
Trevor Cunningham, Director, Programs & Student Services, 902-749-5675
tcunning@tcrsb.ca
Gerry Purdy, Director, Human Resources, 902-749-5684
gpurdy@tcrsb.ca
Steve Stoddart, Director, Operations, 902-749-5691
sstoddar@tcrsb.ca
Wade Tattrie, Director, Finance, 902-541-3009
wtattrie@ssrsb.ca
Steve Adams, Manager, Transportation, 902-749-2804
sadams@tcrsb.ca
Mark Albert, Manager, Technology Services, 902-749-5689
mark.albert@tcrsb.ca
Dave Buckland, Coordinator, Monitoring & Evaluation, 902-749-5814
dbuckland@tcrsb.ca
Craig Crosby, Coordinator, Property Services, 902-749-2827
ccrosby@tcrsb.ca
Jason Curtis, Coordinator, Information Systems, 902-749-5186
jcurtis@tcrsb.ca
Lisa Doucet, Coordinator, Student Services, 902-749-5196
ldoucet@tcrsb.ca
Steven Gaudet, Coordinator, French Programs, 902-749-5680
sgaudet@tcrsb.ca
Gerry Pitman, Coordinator, Community Learning, 902-749-5679
gpitman@tcrsb.ca
Gerry Randell, Coordinator, Programs 7 - 12, 902-749-5197
grandell@tcrsb.ca
Gerry Stockman, Coordinator, Programs P - 6, 902-749-2826
kstockman@tcrsb.ca

First Nations

Eskasoni: **Eskasoni First Nation School Board**
P.O. Box 7959
4645 Shore Rd. Eskasoni, B1W 1B8
902-379-2507, Fax: 902-379-2273,
www.eskasonischoolbd.com
eskasoni@schoolbd.ca
Grades: Day Care - Secondary; Mi'kmaq
Enrollment: 1249
Number of Schools: 4 (Eskasoni Ksite'taqnk Day Care; Eskasoni Unama'ki Training & Education Centre; Eskasoni Elementary & Middle School, & Chief Allison Bernard Memorial High School).
Number of Employees: 175. Situated on eastern Cape Breton Island, Eskasoni First Nation is a large Mi'kmaq community. Education in the community is directed by the Eskasoni First Nation School Board, which is overseen by the Eskasoni Band Council.
John F. Toney, Chair
Patricia Marshall, Director, Education, 902-379-2507, fax: 902-379-2273
patriciamarshall@schoolbd.ca
Patrick Johnson, Director, Mi'kmaq Student Services at Cape Br, 902-379-2507, fax: 902-379-2273
patriciamarshall@schoolbd.ca
Terry Lynn Marshall, Contact, Finance, 902-379-2507, fax: 902-379-2273
terrylynnmarshall@schoolbd.ca
Barbara Sylliboy, Contact, Language, 902-379-2507, fax: 902-379-2273
barbsylliboy@schoolbd.ca
Belinda Stevens, Clerk, Post-Secondary Program, 902-379-2507, fax: 902-379-2273
belindastevens@schoolbd.ca

Schools: Specialized

First Nations

Chapel Island: **Mi'kmaway School**
P.O. Box 538
RR#1, Richmond County Chapel Island, B0E 3B0 Canada
902-535-2307, Fax: 902-535-3428,
mikmawey@auracom.com
www.kinu.ns.ca/chapel
Grades: Primary - 6; Mi'kmaq language
Enrollment: 73

The Mi'kmaway School is administered by the Potlotek Board of Education. The school serves the Chapel Island First Nation.
Nancy MacLeod, Director, Potlotek Education Office, fax: 902-535-3164
nmacleod@potlotek.ca

Eskasoni: Chief Allison Bernard Memorial High School
P.O. Box 7969
4673 Shore Rd. Eskasoni, B1W 1B8 Canada
902-379-3000, Fax: 902-379-3011,
www.eskasonischoolbd.com
Grades: 10 - 12; Mi'kmaq language & culture
Enrollment: 200
Chief Allison Bernard Memorial High School operates under the direction of the Eskasoni First Nation School Board. The First Nation secondary school is situated in the Mi'kmaq community of Eskasoni in Cape Breton Island. Chief Allison Bernard Memorial High School follows the Nova Scotia Curriculum Guide & also offers Mi'kmaq studies.
John Googoo, Principal
johndgoogoo@hotmail.com
Newell Johnson, Vice-Principal

Eskasoni: Eskasoni Elementary & Middle School
P.O. Box 7970
4675 Shore Rd. Eskasoni, B1W 1B8 Canada
902-379-2825, Fax: 902-379-2886,
eems@eskasonischool.ca
www.eskasonischool.ca
Grades: Kindergarten - 9; Mi'kmaq language
Eskasoni Elementary & Middle School is a Mi'kmaq First Nation school, which operates under the direction of the Eskasoni First Nation School Board. Mi'kmaq immersion classes are offered from kindergarten to grade 3.
Philomena Moore, Principal
philmoore46@hotmail.com
Cameron Frost, Vice-Principal

Eskasoni: Eskasoni Ksite'taqnk Day Care
c/o Eskasoni First Nation School Board
P.O. Box 7959
4645 Shore Rd. Eskasoni, B1W 1B8
902-379-2017,
www.eskasonischoolbd.com
Grades: Pre-School
Number of Employees: 1 coordinator, 6 early childhood educators; 1 cook / day care worker. The Eskasoni Ksite'taqnk Day Care operates under the administration of the Eskasoni First Nation School Board. The day care offers a Mi'kmaq educational program, taught in the Mi'kmaq language.
Miranda Bernard, Contact

Eskasoni: Eskasoni Unama'ki Training & Education Centre / TEC
P.O. Box 7010
Eskasoni, B1L 1A1 Canada
902-379-2758, Fax: 902-379-2586,
www.unamakitec.ca; www.eskasonischoolbd.com
Grades: Adult & Alternative Education
Enrollment: 75
Number of Employees: 1 principal; 1 teaching vice-principal; 5 teachers; 1 guidance counsellor; 1 secretary; 1 teaching assistant; 1 janitor. Activities of the Unama'ki Training & Education Centre are guided by the Eskasoni First Nation School Board.
Michelle Marshall-Johnson, Principal
Joanne MacDonald, Vice-Principal

Micmac: Indian Brook School
Micmac Post Office Micmac, B0N 1W0 Canada
902-758-1229, Fax: 902-758-1492
Grades: K.-12
Randy Kelly, Principal
kellyr2@staff.ednet.ns.ca

Sydney: Membertou Elementary School
Wallace Bernard Memorial
45 Maillard St. Sydney, B1S 2P5 Canada
902-562-2205, Fax: 902-562-4561
Grades: K.-6
Darrell Syms, Principal
dsyms@membertouschool.ca

Trenton: Pictou Landing First Nations Elementary School
P.O. Box 116
43 Maple St., Pictou Landing, Site 6, RR#2 Trenton, B0K 1X0 Canada
902-755-9954, Fax: 902-752-4916,
firstnationhelp.com/pictou
Grades: K.-6
Sheila Francis, Director
sheilaf@pchg.net

Wagmatcook: Wagmatcookewey School
P.O. Box 30018
Wagmatcook, B0E 3N0 Canada
902-295-3491,
wagmatco@auracom.com
Grades: Primary - 12; Mi'kmaq Studies
Located on the Wagmatcook First Nation Reserve in Cape Breton, Nova Scotia, the Wagmatcookewey School provides education to Mi'Kmaq First Nation students.
Wayne Morris, Principal

Whycocomagh: We'koqma'q Elementary School
P.O. Box 209
15 Reservation Rd. Whycocomagh, B0E 3M0 Canada
902-756-9000, Fax: 902-756-2171
Grades: K.-6
Joanne Alex, Principal
joanna@wfnes.ca

Whycocomagh: We'koqma'q School Secondary Education
P.O. Box 209
9231 Trans Canada Hwy. Whycocomagh, B0E 3M0 Canada
902-756-3002, Fax: 902-756-2017
Grades: 7-12
John Leonard, Principal
Lisa Lunney, Vice-Principal

Special Education

Halifax: Atlantic Provinces Special Education Authority / APSEA
5940 South St. Halifax, B3H 1S6 Canada
902-424-8500, Fax: 902-424-0543,
apsea@apsea.ca
www.apsea.ca
Deborah Pottie, Supt.

Schools: Independent & Private

Independent & Private Schools

Bedford: Sandy Lake Academy
435 Hammond's Plains Rd. Bedford, B4B 1Y2 Canada
902-835-8548, Fax: 902-835-9752,
info@sandylakeacademy.ca
www.sandylakeacademy.ca
Grades: Pre.-12
Enrollment: 76
A Seventh-day Adventist Christian School
Chris Dupuis, Principal

Cambridge Station: Kings County Christian School
6185 Hwy. 1, RR#1 Cambridge Station, B0P 1G0 Canada
902-679-6641,
www.kccschool.ca
Grades: Pre.-9
Enrollment: 65
Barbara C. Billings, Principal

Halifax: Armbrae Academy
1400 Oxford St. Halifax, B3H 3Y8 Canada
902-423-7920, Fax: 902-423-9731,
office@armbrae.ns.ca
www.armbrae.ns.ca
Grades: Pre.-12
Enrollment: 245
Gary O'Meara, Headmaster
omeara@armbrae.ednet.ns.ca

Halifax: Halifax Christian Academy
114 Downs Ave. Halifax, B3N 1Y6 Canada
902-475-1441, Fax: 902-477-4922,
office@halifaxchristianacademy.ca
www.halifaxchristianacademy.ca
Grades: Pre.-12
Enrollment: 243
Jo-an Dennis, Principal

Halifax: Halifax Grammar School
945 Tower Rd. Halifax, B3H 2Y2 Canada
902-423-9312, Fax: 902-423-9315,
info@hgs.ns.ca
www.hgs.ns.ca
Grades: Pre.-12
Enrollment: 410
Blayne Addley, Headmaster

Halifax: Maritime Muslim Academy
6225 Chebucto Rd. Halifax, B3L 1K7 Canada
902-429-9067, Fax: 902-429-0136,
www.maritimemuslimacademy.ca/
Grades: Pre.-12; Islamic studies; Arabic la
Enrollment: 78
Dr. M.A. Salah, Principal

Halifax: Sacred Heart School of Halifax
5820 Spring Garden Rd. Halifax, B3H 1X8 Canada
902-422-4459, Fax: 902-423-7691,
admin@shsh.ca
www.sacredheartschool.ns.ca
Grades: Pre.-12
Enrollment: 444
Patricia Donnelly, Headmistress
pdonnelly@sacredheartschool.ns.ca

Halifax: Shambhala School
5450 Russell St. Halifax, B3K 1W9 Canada
902-454-6100, Fax: 902-454-6157,
director@shambhalaschool.org
www.shambhalaschool.org
Grades: Preschool - 12
Enrollment: 160
This is a non-denominational school, which offers an enriched curriculum.
Steve Mustain, Director

Tantallon: Crossroads Academy
15 French Village Station Rd. Tantallon, B3Z 1H3 Canada
902-826-1805, Fax: 902-826-1867,
ca@crossroadsacademy.ca
www.crossroadsacademy.ca/
Grades: Pre.-6
Sylvia Luffman, Principal

Truro: Colchester Christian Academy
P.O. Box 393
15 Elm St. Truro, B2N 5C5 Canada
902-895-6520, Fax: 902-893-3727
Grades: Pre.-12
Enrollment: 132
Steve Vanderkwaak, Principal

Tusket: Living Waters Christian Academy
P.O. Box 175
Tusket, B0W 3M0 Canada
902-648-2676, Fax: 902-648-2676
Grades: Pre.-9
Enrollment: 44
Mardee Nickerson, Acting Principal

Windsor: Kings-Edgehill School
33 King's-Edgehill Lane Windsor, B0N 2T0 Canada
902-798-2278, Fax: 902-798-2105,
admissions@kes.ns.ca
www.kes.ns.ca
Grades: 1-12
Enrollment: 282
David R. Penaluna, Headmaster

Wolfville: Landmark East School
708 Main St. Wolfville, B4P 1G4 Canada
902-542-2237, Fax: 902-542-4147,
gmitchell@landmarkeast.org
www.landmarkeast.org
Grades: 4-12
Enrollment: 57
Tim Moore, Headmaster

Universities & Colleges

Universities

Antigonish: St. Francis Xavier University
P.O. Box 5000
Antigonish, B2G 2W5 Canada
902-863-3300, Fax: 902-867-5153,
Admissions: 902-867-2219
admit@stfx.ca
www.stfx.ca
Enrollment: 4200
The university is primarily an undergraduate university, offering education in the arts, science, business & information systems, & applied programs.
Sean E. Riley, Ph.D., President
sriley@stfx.ca
Dr. Mary B. McGillivray, Vice-President, Academic & Provost
Peter Fardy, Vice-President, University Advancement
Ramsay Duff, Vice-President, Finance & Operations
Mary Coyle, Vice-President & Director, Coady Internationa
Danny McInnis, Acting Registrar
John Blackwell, Director, Research Grants
Lynne Murphy, Librarian

Faculties
Arts
Dr. Steve Baldner, Dean

Science
Dr. William Marshall, Dean

Students
Joe MacDonald, Dean

Schools
Coady International Institute

Mary Coyle, Director
mcoyle@stfx.ca

Enterprise Development Centre
Sue McNeil, Interim Director

Halifax: Atlantic School of Theology
660 Francklyn St. Halifax, B3H 3B5 Canada
902-423-6939, Fax: 902-492-4048,
www.astheology.ns.ca

Enrollment: 150
The Rev. Canon Eric Beresford, President, 902-423-6801
Rev. Dr. David MacLachlan, Academic Dean & Registrar, 902-496-7941
David Myatt, Chief Admin. Officer, 902-496-7946
Joyce Thomson, Library Director, 902-496-7948

Halifax: Dalhousie University
Henry Hicks Academic Administration Bldg.
6299 South St. Halifax, B3H 4H6 Canada
902-494-2211, Fax: 902-494-1630,
communications.marketing@dal.ca
www.dal.ca

Enrollment: 16000
Dalhousie University is a comprehensive teaching & research university located in Atlantic Canada. Dalhousie places special emphasis on Ocean Studies & Health Studies & has a growing involvement in Advanced Technical Studies.
Dr Fred Fountain, Chancellor
Dr Tom Traves, Vice-Chancellor & President, 902-494-2511, fax: 902-494-1658
tom.traves@dal.ca
Dr Carolyn Watters, Acting Vice-Pres., Academic & Provost, 902-494-2586
carolyn.watters@dal.ca
Ken Burt, Vice-Pres., Finance & Admin., 902-494-3862
ken.burt@dal.ca
Floyd Dykeman, Vice-Pres., External, 902-494-2238
floyd.dykeman@dal.ca
Dr Bonnie Neuman, Vice-Pres., Student Services, 902-494-8021
bonnie.neuman@dal.ca
Dr Martha Crago, Vice-Pres., Research, 902-494-8075, fax: 902-494-1595
martha.crago@dal.ca

Faculties
Architecture & Planning
902-494-3971, Fax: 902-423-6672,
arch.office@dal.ca
Christine Macy, Dean

Arts & Social Sciences
902-494-1440, Fax: 902-494-1957,
fass@dal.ca
Dr Robert Summerby-Murray, Dean

Computer Science
902-494-2093, Fax: 902-492-1517,
inquiries@cs.dal.ca
Dr Michael Shephard, Dean

Dentistry
902-494-2824, Fax: 902-494-2527
Dr Thomas Boran, Dean
thomas.boran@dal.ca

Engineering
902-494-6217, Fax: 902-429-3011
Dr L. Joshua Leon, Dean
joshua.leon@dal.ca

Graduate Studies
902-494-2485, Fax: 902-494-8797
Sunny Marche, Acting Dean
sunny.marche@dal.ca

Health Professions
902-494-3327, Fax: 902-494-1966
Dr William G. Webster, Dean
will.webster@dal.ca

Management
902-494-2582, Fax: 902-494-1195
Peggy Cunningham, Dean
managementdean@dal.ca

Medicine
902-494-6592, Fax: 902-494-7119
Dr Thomas J. Marrie, Dean
dean.medicine@dal.ca

Science
902-494-3540, Fax: 902-494-1123,
science@dal.ca
Chris Moore, Dean

Schools
Atlantic Health Promotion Research Centre
902-494-2240, Fax: 902-494-3594,
ahprc@dal.ca
Sandra J. Crowell, Managing Director

Business Administration
902-494-7080, Fax: 902-494-1107
Dr Greg Hebb, Director
gregory.hebb@dal.ca

Canadian Institute of Fisheries Technology
902-494-6030, Fax: 902-494-0219,
cift@dal.ca
Dr Tom Gill, Director

Centre for Foreign Policy Studies
902-494-3769, Fax: 902-494-3825,
centre@dal.ca
David R. Black, Director

College of Continuing Education
902-494-2526, Fax: 902-494-3662,
ducceinf@dal.ca
Andrew Cochrane, Dean

College of Pharmacy
902-494-2378, Fax: 902-494-1396,
pharmacy@dal.ca
Rita Caldwell, Director

Dental Hygiene
Nancy Neish, Director, 902-494-8864
nancy.neish@dal.ca

Division of Medical Education
902-494-1845, Fax: 902-494-2278,
dme@dal.ca
Dr. Frank Blye, Director

Health & Human Performance
902-494-2152, Fax: 902-494-5120,
hahp@dal.ca
Dr Fred McGinn, Interim Director

Health Administration
902-494-7097, Fax: 902-494-6849,
healthadmin@dal.ca
Dr Joseph M. Byrne, Director

Human Communication Disorders
902-494-7052, Fax: 902-494-5151,
hucd@dal.ca
Dr. Joy Armson, Director

Information Management
902-494-3656, Fax: 902-494-2451,
sim@dal.ca
Fiona Black, Director

International Research & Development
902-494-2038, Fax: 902-494-1216,
ird@dal.ca
Pat Rodee, Director

Neuroscience Institute
902-494-1251, Fax: 902-494-2050,
neurosci@dal.ca
Dr Alan Fine, Director

Nursing
902-494-2535, Fax: 902-494-3487,
nursing@dal.ca
Dr. Patricia Sullivan, Director

Occupational Therapy
902-494-8804, Fax: 902-494-1229,
occupational.therapy@dal.ca
Dr Fazley Siddiq, Director

Physiotherapy
902-494-2524, Fax: 902-494-1941,
physiotherapy@dal.ca
Dr Sandy Rennie, Director

Public Administration
902-494-3742, Fax: 902-494-7023,
dalmpa@dal.ca

Resource & Environmental Studies
902-494-3632, Fax: 902-494-3728,
sres@dal.ca
Dr. Peter Duinker, Director

Schulich School of Law
902-494-3495, Fax: 902-494-1316,
Kim R. Brooks, Dean
lawdean@dal.ca

Social Work
902-494-3760, Fax: 902-494-6709,
social.work@dal.ca
Dr. Wanda Thomas Bernard, Director

Transition Year Program
Prof. Patricia Doyle-Bedwell, Director, 902-494-8810, fax: 902-494-2135
patricia.doyle.bedwell@dal.ca

Affiliations
Nova Scotia Agricultural College
P.O. Box 550
Truro, B2N 5E3 Canada
902-893-6600,
reg@nsac.ca
www.nsac.ns.ca

Enrollment: 900
NSAC has the following academic departments: Business & Social Sciences, Engineering, Environmental Sciences, & Plant & Animal Sciences; as well as, these academic units: Continuing & Distance Education, Research.
Carol Goodwin, Chair
Dr. Bernie Macdonald, Co-President & VP, Admin.
Dr. Leslie MacLaren, Co-President & VP, Academic

University of King's College
6350 Coburg Rd. Halifax, B3H 2A1 Canada
902-422-1271, Fax: 902-423-3357,
www.ukings.ns.ca

Enrollment: 1170
The Hon. Michael A. Meighen, QC, Chancellor
Dr William Barker, President & Vice-Chancellor 121
Elizabeth Yeo, Registrar 122
elizabeth.yeo@ukings.ns.ca

Publications
Dalhousie Gazette
6136 University Ave. Halifax, B3H 4J2
902-128-0,
www.dalgazette.com
Josh Boyter, Editor-In-Chief
editor.dalgazatte.com

Halifax: Mount Saint Vincent University
166 Bedford Hwy. Halifax, B3M 2J6 Canada
902-457-6117, Fax: 902-457-6498,
www.msvu.ca

Enrollment: 4900
Kathryn E. Laurin, M.Mus., President & Vice-Chancellor
Donna Woolcott, Vice-President
Brigitte MacInnes, Registrar
Amanda Whitewood, C.M.A., C.H.E., Vice-President
Sr. Donna Geernaert, Chancellor

Faculties
Arts & Sciences
Susan Mumm, Ph.D., Dean

Education
Jim Sharpe, Ph.D., Dean

Professional Studies
Mary Lyon, Ph.D., Dean

Publications
Jargon

Picaro

Halifax: NSCAD University
5163 Duke St. Halifax, B3J 3J6 Canada
902-444-9600, Fax: 902-425-2420,
admiss@nscad.ca
www.nscad.ca

Enrollment: 1025
Prof. David B. Smith, President
Kenn Gardner Honeychurch, Sr. Vice-President
Peter Flemming, Vice-President
Dr. Laurelle LeVert, Registrar & Director
Deborah Carver, Executive Director

Halifax: Saint Mary's University
923 Robie St. Halifax, B3H 3C3 Canada
902-420-5400,
Students Closure/Cancellation Hotline: 902-491-6263

public.affairs@smu.ca; webmaster@smu.ca; helpdesk@smu.ca
www.smu.ca
Enrollment: 8500
Offering a wide range of both undergraduate & graduate programs, Saint Mary's University has a student-faculty ratio of 21-1.
Most Rev. Terrence Prendergast, Chancellor
Most Rev. Claude Champagne, Vice-Chancellor
Dr. J. Colin Dodds, President
Gabrielle Morrison, Vice-President, Administration
Dr. Terry Murphy, Vice-President, Academic & Research

Faculties
Arts
Dr. Esther Enns, Dean

Commerce
Dr. David Wicks, Dean

Continuing Education
Betty MacDonald, Director
betty.macdonald@smu.ca

Graduate Studies & Research
Dr. Kevin Vessey, Dean

Science
Dr. Malcolm Butler, Dean

Pointe-de-L'Église: Université Sainte-Anne
1695, Route 1 Pointe-de-L'Église, B0W 1M0 Canada
902-769-2114, Fax: 902-769-2930, 1-888-338-8337
mario.dushesne@usaintanne.ca
www.usainteanne.ca
La seule institution d'enseignement post-secondaire de langue française en Nouvelle-Écosse. Programmes: administration des affaires, éducation, sciences humaines, science pures, programmes professionnels. Campus: Pointe-de-L'Église, Halifax, Petit-de-Grat, Saint-Joseph-du Moine, et Tusket
Christiane Rabier, Vice-rectrice (Enseignement et Recherche)
Murielle Comeau, Registraire
Éric Tufts, Vice-recteur (Administrations)
Hughie Batherson, Vice-recteur (Affaires étudiantes)
Allister Surette, Vice-recteur (Développement & partenariats)
André Roberge, Recteur
andre.roberge@usaintanne.ca

Campuses
Campus de Halifax
1589 Walnut St. Halifax, B3H 3S1 Canada
902-424-2630, Fax: 902-424-3607,
pachalifax@usaintanne.ca
www.usainteanne.ca
Donald Kenny, Contact

Campus de Petit-de-Grat
3433 rte 206 Petit-de-Grat, N.-É., B0E 2L0 Canada
902-226-3900,
lisa.berthier@usainteanne.ca
www.usainteanne.ca
Lisa Berthier

Campus de Saint-Joseph-du-Moine
12521 Cabot Trail Grand-Étang, N.-É., B0E 3A0 Canada
902-244-4100,
rene.aucoin@usainteanne.ca
www.usaintanne.ca
René Aucoin, Contact

Campus de Wellington
48 Chemin Mill Wellington, C0B 2E0 Canada
902-854-7286,
colette@socedipe.org
www.usainteanne.ca
Colette Aucoin, Contact

Campus de Tusket
1 Slocumb Cres. Tusket, B0W 3M0 Canada
902-648-3524,
peter.boudreau@usainteanne.ca
www.usainteanne.ca
Peter Boudreau, Contact

Sydney: Cape Breton University
P.O. Box 5300
1250 Grand Lake Rd. Sydney, B1P 6L2 Canada
902-539-5300, Fax: 902-562-0119, 888-959-9995
welcome@cbu.ca; registrar@cbu.ca
www.capebretonu.ca
Enrollment: 3110
The university is also home to Unama'ki College which offers Mi'kmaw programs and services, such as teacher training, court worker certification, business, Mi'kmaw language, health careers, and natural resources. Email: mci@cbu.ca
Annette Verschuren, Chancellor
H. John Harker, President & Vice-Chancellor, 902-563-1333
john_harker@cbu.ca
Gordon MacInnis, Vice-Pres., Finance & Operations, 902-563-1128
gordon_macinnis@cbu.ca
Robert Baily, Vice-Pres., Academic & Research, 902-563-1980
robert_bailey@cbu.ca
Roger Winn, Vice-Pres., Academic
roger_winn@cbu.ca
Brown Keith, Vice-Pres., External, 902-563-1859
keith_brown@cbu.ca
Dr Ross McCurdy, COO, 902-563-1392
ross_mccurdy@cbu.ca
Debbie Rudderham, CIO, 902-563-1446
debbie_rudderham@cbu.ca
Alexis Manley, Registrar/VP, Student Services, 902-563-1650
registrar@cbu.ca

Faculties
Arts & Social Studies
Dr Roderick Nicholls, Dean, 902-563-1354
rod_nicholls@cbu.ca

Science & Technology
Dr Allen Britten, Dean, 902-563-1262
allen_britten@cbu.ca

Schools
Shannon School of Business
John MacKinnon, Dean, 902-563-1221
john_mackinnon@cbu.ca

School of Professional & Graduate Studies
Robert Baily, Interim Dean, 902-563-1304
brenda_leloup@cbu.ca

Publications
Caper Times
Suzanne MacNeil, Editor-In-Chief, 902-563-1473
editor@capertimes.ca

The 60th Meridian

Wolfville: Acadia Divinity College
31 Horton Ave. Wolfville, B4P 2R6 Canada
902-585-2210, Fax: 902-585-2233, 866-875-8975
adc.acadiau.ca
Enrollment: 160
Dr Harry G. Gardner, President/Dean, Theology
Dr Bruce Fawcett, Academic Dean/Dir., Doctoral Studies
Shawna Peverill, Registrar, 902-585-2216
shawna.peverill@acadiau.ca

Wolfville: Acadia University
Wolfville, B4P 2R6 Canada
902-542-2201, Fax: 902-585-1072,
agi@acadiau.ca
www.acadiau.ca
Enrollment: 3620
Ray Ivany, Pres./Vice-Chancellor 1218
Dr. Tom Herman, Vice-Pres., Academic 1357
Dr Akivah Starkman, Vice-Pres., Admin.
Rosemary Jotcham, Registrar
registrar@acadiau.ca
Scott Roberts, Exec. Dir., Communications & Public Affairs 1705
scott.roberts@acadiau.ca

Faculties
Arts
Robert Perrins, B.A., M.A., Ph.D., Dean 1782

Professional Studies
Dr Heather Hemming, B.Sc., M.Sc., D.P.E., Dean 1133

Pure & Applied Science
Dr Peter Williams, B.Sc., M.Sc., Ph.D., Dean 1472

Theology
Dr Harry Gardner, B.A., B.D., Th.M., Ph.D., Dean 2212

Schools
Business Administration
Dr Ian Hutchinson, Director 1205

Computer Science
Dr Daniel Silver, Director 1331

Education
Dr. Ann Vibert, Director 1229

Engineering
Andrew Mitchell, Dip.Eng., B.Eng., M.A.Sc., Director 1206

Music
Dr Jeff Hennessy, Director 1512

Nutrition & Dietetics
Barb Anderson, Director 1346

Recreation, Management & Kinesiology
Dr Rene Murphy, Director 1559

Publications
The Athenaeum
The official student newspaper
Tim Hansen, Editor-in-Chief

Colleges

Halifax: Nova Scotia Community College / NSCC
P.O. Box 220
Halifax, B3J 2M4 Canada
902-491-4911, Fax: 902-491-3514, 1-866-679-6722
TDD: 1-866-288-7034Toll Free Fax: 1-866-329-6722
admissions@nscc.ca
www.nscc.ca
The college has the following institutes: The Aviation Institute, located in the Halifax Regional Municipality at Shearwater, the Centre of Geographic Sciences in Lawrencetown, & the Nautical Institute in Port Hawkesbury & the School of Fisheries at Pictou.
Sandra Greer, Chair
Joan McArthur-Blair, President, 902-491-6701, fax: 902-491-4825
Ronald Farrell, Dean, Trades & Technology
Ken Jones, Dean, Business Development
Judith Limkilde, Dean, Health & Human Services
Claudine Lowry, Dean, Organizational Learning
George MacDonald, Dean, Access
Bruce Tawse, Dean, Applied Arts & New Media
Bill Walsh, Dean, Business

Campuses
Akerley Campus
21 Woodlawn Rd. Dartmouth, B3W 2R7 Canada
902-491-4940, Fax: 902-491-4903,
Centre for Student Success, Phone: 902-491-4940
akadmissions@nscc.ca
Enrollment: 4000
Graham MacDermott, Principal

Amherst Community Learning Centre
902-661-3180,
Deborah.MacPhail@nscc.ca

Annapolis Valley Campus, Lawrencetown
50 Elliott Rd. Lawrencetown, B0S 1M0
902-825-3491, Fax: 902-825-2285,
Centre for Student Success, Phone: 902-825-2930
avc.info@nscc.ca
www.annapolis.nscc.ca
Enrollment: 900
Jim Stanley, Principal

Annapolis Valley Campus, Middleton
295 Commercial St. Middleton, B0S 1P0 Canada
902-825-3491,
Centre for Student Success, Phone: 902-825-2930
avc.info@nscc.ca
www.annapolis.nscc.ca
Enrollment: 900
The Applied Geomatics Research Centre is located at the Middleton location.
Jim Stanley, Principal

Burridge Campus
372 Pleasant St. Yarmouth, B5A 2L2 Canada
902-742-0760, Fax: 902-749-2402,
Centre for Student Success, Phone: 902-742-0760
buadmissions@nscc.ca
www.burridge.nscc.ca
Enrollment: 950
Marcel Cottreau, Principal

Cumberland Campus
P.O. Box 550
1 Main St. Springhill, B0M 1X0 Canada
902-597-3737, Fax: 902-597-8548,
Centre for Student Success, Phone: 902-597-4101
cuadmissions@nscc.ca
Enrollment: 400
Shelley Carter-Rose, Principal

Digby Community Learning Centre
902-245-7211,
Deborah.Fox@nscc.ca

Institute of Technology Campus
P.O. Box 2210
5685 Leeds St. Halifax, B3J 3C4 Canada
902-491-6722, Fax: 902-491-4800,
Centre for Student Success, Phone: 902-491-4752
inadmissions@nscc.ca
Enrollment: 5200
Daurene Lewis, Principal

Kingstec Campus
236 Belcher St. Kentville, B4N 0A6 Canada

902-678-7341, Fax: 902-679-1141,
Centre for Student Success, Phone: 902-679-7361;
902-679-7359
kiadmissions@nscc.ca
Enrollment: 1750
Don Bureaux, Principal

Liverpool Community Learning Centre
902-543-8261,
Cecile.Mansfield@nscc.ca

Lunenburg Campus
75 High St. Bridgewater, B4V 1V8 Canada
902-543-4608, Fax: 902-543-0190, 1-866-346-4608
Centre for Student Success, Phone: 902-543-2295
luadmissions@nscc.ca
Enrollment: 850
Craig Collins, Principal

Marconi Campus
P.O. Box 1042
1240 Grand Lake Rd. Sydney, B1P 6J7 Canada
902-563-2450, Fax: 902-563-3440,
Centre for Student Success, Phone: 902-563-2464
maadmissions@nscc.ca
Enrollment: 2300
Dave MacLean, Principal

New Glasgow Community Learning Centre
902-755-7209,
David.Freckelton@nscc.ca

Pictou Campus
P.O. Box 820
39 Acadia Ave. Stellarton, B0K 1S0 Canada
902-752-2002, Fax: 902-752-5446,
Centre for Student Success, Phone: 902-755-7299
piadmissions@nscc.ca
Enrollment: 1675
Dave Freckelton, Principal

Shelburne Campus
P.O. Box 760
1575 Lake Rd. Shelburne, B0T 1W0 Canada
902-875-8640, Fax: 902-875-3797,
Centre for Student Success, Phone: 902-875-8640
shadmissions@nscc.ca
Enrollment: 350
Marcel Cottreau, Principal

Strait Area Campus
226 Reeves St. Port Hawkesbury, B9A 2A2 Canada
902-625-4017, Fax: 902-625-0193,
Centre for Student Success, Phone: 902-625-4017
stadmissions@nscc.ca
Enrollment: 800
The Nautical Institute is located on the Strait Area Campus.
Bert Lewis, Principal

Truro Campus
36 Arthur St. Truro, B2N 1X5 Canada
902-893-5385, Fax: 902-893-5610,
Centre for Student Success, Phone: 902-893-5346
tradmissions@nscc.ca
www.truro.nscc.ca
Enrollment: 1300
Kevin Quinlan, Principal

Waterfront Campus
80 Mawiomi Pl. Dartmouth, B2Y 0A5
902-491-1100, Fax: 902-491-1795,
Centre for Student Success, Phone: 902-491-1793
watadmissions@nscc.ca
Enrollment: 4300
Cathy MacLean, Principal

Halifax: University of King's College
6350 Coburg Rd. Halifax, B3H 2A1 Canada
902-422-1271, Fax: 902-423-3357,
www.ukings.ns.ca
Enrollment: 1100

Publications
Watch
Student newspaper at University of King's College

Post Secondary/Technical

Post Secondary/Technical

Bedford: C.L. Douglas & Associates Inc.
1142 Bedford Hwy. Bedford, B4A 1B8 Canada
902-835-8880, Fax: 902-835-6751,
info@cldouglas.com
www.cldouglas.com
Computer software, network management training.
Paul Cudmore

East Dover: Atlantic Home Building & Renovation Sector Council
53 Leary's Cove Rd. East Dover, B3Z 3W7 Canada
902-852-2151, Fax: 902-852-3193,
info@ahbrsc.com
www.ahbrsc.com/courses/index.html
Atlantic Home Warranty Program Training; Nova Scotia Home Builder's Association Certified Builder Training Program; Training for Employment Insurance Recipients; Renovation Sector Skills Development

Englishtown: Gaelic College of Celtic Arts & Crafts
P.O. Box 80
Englishtown, B0C 1H0 Canada
902-295-3411, Fax: 902-295-2912,
info@gaeliccollege.edu
www.gaeliccollege.edu

Halifax: Atlantic Media Institute / AMI
#300, 7071 Bayers Rd. Halifax, B3L 2C2 Canada
902-457-0002, Fax: 902-457-4503,
ami@theami.com
www.theami.com

Halifax: CDI College of Business, Technology & Health Care
P.O. Box 111
5657 Spring Garden Rd. Halifax, B3J 3R4 Canada
902-429-7373, Fax: 902-422-0576
Anne Miller

Halifax: Halifax Campus
800 Sackville Dr. Halifax, B4E 1R8 Canada
902-865-8283, Fax: 902-865-0285, 1-800-662-3991
halifax@thinksuccess.ca
www.thinksuccess.ca
Work related programs.
Hazel Matthews

Campuses
Truro Campus
100 Victoria St. Truro, B2N 1Y8 Canada
902-893-2400, Fax: 902-893-7875, 1-866-897-0349
Work related programs.

Halifax: Maritime Conservatory of Performing Arts
6199 Chebucto Rd. Halifax, B3L 1K7 Canada
902-423-6995, Fax: 902-423-6029,
admin@maritimeconservatory.com
www.maritimeconservatory.com
Ifan Williams, Director

North Sydney: Mactech Distance Education
P.O. Box 457
North Sydney, B2A 3M3 Canada
Fax: 902-794-1414, 1-888-622-8324
administration@homeed.com
www.homeed.com
Distance education

Truro: Institute for Human Services Education
#1, 60 Lorne St., 2nd Fl. Truro, B2N 3K3 Canada
902-893-3342, Fax: 902-895-4487,
admin@inst-hse.ca
www.inst-hse.ca
Early Childhood Education Diploma, Public School Program Assistants Certificate, Special Education Diploma, Youth Worker Diploma
Kimberly Elliott, B.Comm., Executive Director
Anna MacDonell, CDSA IV, B.A., M.Ed., Program Director
Debbie Connoly, CDSA IV, BBA, Student Services Coordinator

Nunavut

Government Agencies

Iqaluit: Department of Education
P.O. Box 1000 980
Iqaluit, X0A 0H0 Canada
867-975-5600, Fax: 867-975-5605,
www.gov.nu.ca/education/eng/
Pam Hine, Deputy Minister

School Boards/Districts/Divisions

Public

Arctic Bay: Arctic Bay District Education Authority
P.O. Box 90
Arctic Bay, X0A 0A0 Canada
867-439-8843
Grades: Kindergarten - 12

Arviat: Arviat District Education Authority
P.O. Box 180
Arviat, X0C 0E0 Canada
867-857-2885, Fax: 867-857-2622

Baker Lake: Baker Lake District Education Authority
P.O. Box 119
Baker Lake, X0C 0A0 Canada
867-793-4657, Fax: 867-793-4659

Baker Lake: Kivalliq School Operations
P.O. Box 90
Baker Lake, X0C 0A0 Canada
867-793-2803, Fax: 867-793-2996,
http://kivalliq.edu.nu.ca

Cambridge Bay: Cambridge Bay District Education Authority
P.O. Box 9
Cambridge Bay, X0B 0C0 Canada
867-983-2510, Fax: 867-983-2515
Karen Wilford, Chair

Cape Dorset: Cape Dorset District Education Authority
P.O. Box 210
Cape Dorset, X0A 0C0 Canada
867-897-8826
Grades: Kindergarten - 12; Inuktitut

Chesterfield Inlet: Chesterfield Inlet District Education Authority
P.O. Box 6
Chesterfield Inlet, X0C 0B0 Canada
867-898-9007, Fax: 867-898-9143
Annie Amuyak, Chair

Clyde River: Clyde River District Education Authority
General Delivery Clyde River, X0A 0E0 Canada
867-924-6309, Fax: 867-924-6247
Jacob Jaypoody

Coral Harbour: Coral Harbour District Education Authority
P.O. Box 129
Coral Harbour, X0C 0C0 Canada
867-925-8637, Fax: 867-925-9000
Dino Bruce, Chair

Gjoa Haven: Gjoa Haven District Education Authority
General Delivery Gjoa Haven, X0E 1J0 Canada
867-360-7414, Fax: 867-360-7314
Raymond Kamookak, Chair

Grise Fiord: Grise Fiord District Education Authority
General Delivery Grise Fiord, X0A 0J0 Canada
867-980-9921

Hall Beach: Hall Beach District Education Authority
P.O. Box 83
Hall Beach, X0A 0K0 Canada
867-928-8839
Grades: Kindergarten - 12

Igloolik: Igloolik District Education Authority
P.O. Box 150
Igloolik, X0A 0L0 Canada
867-934-8909, Fax: 867-934-8571
Lucasi Ivvalu, Chair

Iqaluit: Apex District Education Authority
P.O. Box 1420
Iqaluit, X0A 0H0 Canada
867-979-6597

Iqaluit: La Commission scolaire francophone du Nunavut
P.O. Box 11008
Iqaluit, X0A 1H0 Canada
867-979-5849, Fax: 867-979-5878,
info.ecoletrois-soleils@csfn.ca
www.trois-soleils.ca
Martine St-Louis, Directrice

Iqaluit: Iqaluit District Education Authority
P.O. Box 235
Iqaluit, X0A 0H0 Canada
867-979-5314, Fax: 867-979-0330
Christa Kunnuk, Chair

Kimmirut: **Kimmirut District Education Authority**
General Delivery Kimmirut, X0A 0N0 Canada
867-939-2221, Fax: 867-939-2334
Pudloo Akavak, Chair

Kugaaruk: **Kugaaruk District Education Authority**
c/o Kugaaruk Iliniarvik
P.O. Box 53
Kugaaruk, X0B 1K0 Canada
867-769-6211, Fax: 867-769-6116
Remi Krikort, Chair

Kugluktuk: **Kitikmeot School Operations**
P.O. Box 287
Kugluktuk, X0B 0E0 Canada
867-982-7220, Fax: 867-982-3054,
kitikmeot.edu.nu.ca

Kugluktuk: **Kugluktuk District Education Authority**
P.O. Box 273
Kugluktuk, X0B 0E0 Canada
867-982-5001, Fax: 867-982-5706
Simon Kuliktana, Chair

Pangnirtung: **Pangnirtung District Education Authority**
P.O. Box 54
Pangnirtung, X0A 0R0 Canada
867-473-8810, Fax: 867-473-8718
Tim Evic, Chair

Pond Inlet: **Pond Inlet District Education Authority**
General Delivery Pond Inlet, X0A 0S0 Canada
867-899-8779, Fax: 867-899-8780
Norman Simonie, Chair

Pond Inlet: **Qikiqtani School Operations**
P.O. Box 429
Pond Inlet, X0A 0S0 Canada
867-899-7350, Fax: 867-899-7334,
qikiqtani.edu.nu.ca
Trudy Pettigrew, Executive Director

Qikiqtarjuaq: **Qikiqtarjuaq District Education Authority**
P.O. Box 7
Qikiqtarjuaq, X0A 0B0 Canada
867-927-8938, Fax: 867-927-8067
Toomasie Newkingnak, Chair

Rankin Inlet: **Rankin Inlet District Education Authority**
PO Bag 002 Rankin Inlet, X0C 0G0 Canada
867-645-2642, Fax: 867-645-2209
Darrin Nichol, Chair

Repulse Bay: **Repulse Bay District Education Authority**
P.O. Box 105
Repulse Bay, X0C 0H0 Canada
867-462-4045, Fax: 867-462-4232
Elizabeth Kidlapik, Chair

Resolute Bay: **Resolute Bay District Education Authority**
P.O. Box 120
Resolute Bay, X0A 0V0 Canada
867-252-3888, Fax: 867-252-3690
Zipporah K. Aronsen, Chair

Sanikiluaq: **Sanikiluaq District Education Authority**
General Delivery Sanikiluaq, X0A 0W0 Canada
867-266-8816, Fax: 867-266-8843
Lucassie Arragutainaq, Chair

Taloyoak: **Taloyoak District Education Authority**
c/o Netsilik Ilihakvik
P.O. Box 9
Taloyoak, X0B 1B0 Canada
867-561-6706, Fax: 867-561-5036
Johnny Kootook, Chair

Whale Cove: **Whale Cove District Education Authority**
P.O. Box 90
Whale Cove, X0C 0J0 Canada
867-896-9300, Fax: 867-896-9005
Grades: K.-12
Enrollment: 110
Imelda Angotialuk, Chair

Post Secondary/Technical

Post Secondary/Technical

Arviat: **Nunavut Arctic College**
P.O. Box 230
Arviat, X0C 0E0 Canada
867-857-8608, Fax: 867-857-8623, 866-988-4636
www.arcticcollege.ca
Daniel Vandermeulen, President
dan.vandermeulen@arcticcollege.ca
Linda Pemik, Director, Academic Affairs, 867-857-8603, fax: 867-857-8623
linda.pemik@arcticcollege.ca
Penny Dominix-Nadeau, Registrar, 866-979-7222, fax: 867-979-7103
penny.dominix-nadeau@arcticcollege.ca

Campuses
Kitikmeot Campus - Cambridge Bay
P.O. Box 54
Cambridge Bay, X0B 0C0 Canada
867-983-4107, Fax: 867-983-4106, 866-988-4636
Fiona Buchan-Corey, Director

Kivalliq Campus - Rankin Inlet
P.O. Box 002
Rankin Inlet, X0C 0G0 Canada
867-645-5500, Fax: 867-645-2387
Mike Shouldice, Director, 866-988-4636, fax: 867-645-2387

Nunatta Campus - Iqaluit
P.O. Box 600
Iqaluit, X0A 0H0 Canada
867-979-7200, Fax: 867-979-7102
Peesee Pitsiulak-Stephens, Director, 867-979-7216, fax: 867-979-7102

Ontario

Government Agencies

Brampton: **Ontario Environmental Training Consortium / OETC**
37 George St. North Suite 206 Brampton, L6X 1R5 Canada
905-796-2851, Fax: 905-796-8744, 1-877-796-2851
info@oetc.on.ca
www.oetc.on.ca
The OETC represents the Ontario Colleges of Applied Arts & Technology in developing & delivering province-wide environmental training, education & certification programs. OETC can provide a single point of contact with experts in all areas of environment
Gary Cronkwright, Executive Director

Toronto: **Ministry of Education & Training**
c/o Public Inquiries Unit
2nd Fl., 880 Bay St. Toronto, M7A 1N3 Canada
416-325-2929, Fax: 416-325-4153, 1-800-268-5755
TDD: 1-800-263-2892
info@edu.gov.on.ca
www.edu.gov.on.ca
Ginette Plourde, Director, 416-325-2127
Marie-Lison Fougère, Director, 416-325-2660

Campuses
Barrie
20 Rose St., 2nd Fl. Barrie, L4M 2T2 Canada
Fax: 705-725-7635, 800-471-0713

London
#207, 217 York St. London, N6A 5P9 Canada
Fax: 519-667-9769, 800-265-4221

North Bay/Sudbury
#211, 447 McKeown Ave. North Bay, P1B 9S9 Canada
Fax: 705-497-6896, 800-461-9570

Ottawa
#504, 1580 Merivale Rd. Nepean, K2G 4B5 Canada
Fax: 613-225-2881, 800-267-1067

Thunder Bay
#336, 435 James St. South Thunder Bay, P7E 6S9 Canada
Fax: 807-475-1550, 800-465-5020

Toronto & Area
880 Bay St., 2nd Fl. Toronto, M7A 1N3 Canada
Fax: 416-325-4190, 800-268-5755

Toronto: **Ministry of Training, Colleges & Universities**
c/o Public Inquiries Unit
880 Bay St., 2nd Fl. Toronto, M7A 1N3 Canada
416-325-2929, Fax: 416-325-6348,
TDD: 1-800-263-289
info@edu.gov.on.ca
www.edu.gov.on.ca

Toronto: **Ontario Agricultural Training Institute**
#405, 491 Eglinton Ave. West Toronto, M5N 1A8 Canada
416-485-3677, Fax: 416-485-5661, 1-800-668-628
infooati@oati.com

School Boards/Districts/Divisions

Public

Aurora: **York Region District School Board**
The Education Centre
60 Wellington St. West Aurora, L4G 3H2 Canada
905-727-3141, Fax: 905-727-1931,
feedback@yrdsb.edu.on.ca
www.yrdsb.edu.on.ca
Grades: Pre-K.-12
Enrollment: 112000
Ken Thurston, Dir.
ken.thurston@yrdsb.edu.on.ca
Bruce Richardson, Assoc. Dir., Bus. Services
bruce.richardson@yrdsb.edu.on.ca
Diane Giangrande, Chair, 905-770-0826
diane.giangrande@yrdsb.edu.on.ca

Belleville: **Hastings & Prince Edward District School Board**
156 Ann St. Belleville, K8N 1N9 Canada
613-966-1170, Fax: 613-966-6023, 800-267-4350
information@hpedsb.on.ca
www.hpedsb.on.ca
Grades: JK-12
Enrollment: 15700
Kathy Soule, Director of Education
Carl Pitman, Chair

Brantford: **Grand Erie District School Board**
Education Centre
349 Erie Ave. Brantford, N3T 5V3 Canada
519-756-6301, Fax: 519-756-9181, 1-888-548-8878
www.granderie.ca
Grades: JK - 12; Special Ed; Continuing Ed.
Enrollment: 28226
Number of Schools: 64 elementary schools; 18 secondary schools
Jane Angus, Chair, 519-753-2530
jane.angus@granderie.ca
Jim Wibberley, Director, Education, & Secretary, 519-756-6301 281137
Sharon Bell, Manager, Human Resources, 519-756-6301 281289
Kevin Holly, Manager, Information Technology Services, 519-754-0696 287033
Kathy Kirby, Manager, Business Services, 519-754-0696 281123
Phil Kuckyt, Manager, Transportation Services, 519-751-7532 282202
Michael Tancredi, Manager, Facilities Services, 519-751-7532 281161
Wayne Hobbs, Executive Supervisor, Student Support Service, 519-754-0696 287237
Jamie Gunn, Treasurer, 519-756-6301 281142

Brockville: **Upper Canada District School Board**
Administration Building
225 Central Ave. West Brockville, K6V 5X1 Canada
613-342-0371, 1-800-267-7131
inquiries@ucdsb.on.ca
www.ucdsb.on.ca
Grades: K-12; Alternative Ed; Continuing Ed
Enrollment: 30825
Number of Schools: 100 elementary & secondary schools (alternative & continuing education available at more than 30 campuses); Number of Employees: 5,000
David K. Thomas, Director, Education, 613-342-0371 1234, fax: 613-342-6084
david.thomas@ucdsb.on.ca
Ian Carswell, Associate Director, 613-342-0371 1397, fax: 613-342-0277
ian.carswell@ucdsb.on.ca
David Coombs, Superintendent, School Effectiveness, 613-933-5256 4279, fax: 613-933-5275
david.coombs@ucdsb.on.ca
Susan Edwards, Superintendent, Student Engagement, 877-485-1211
susan.edwards@ucdsb.on.ca
Rick Gales, Superintendent, Business, 613-342-0371 1255, fax: 613-343-0277
rick.gales@ucdsb.on.ca

Ted Kennedy, Superintendent, School Operations, 613-258-9393 2551, fax: 613-258-6321
ted.kennedy@ucdsb.on.ca
Linda Lumsden, Superintendent, School Effectiveness, 613-342-0371 1414, fax: 613-342-6084
linda.lumsden@ucdsb.on.ca
Charlotte Patterson, Superintendent, Human Resources, 613-342-0371 1240, fax: 613-342-0277
charlotte.patterson@ucdsb.on.ca
Jeremy Hobbs, Chief Information & Facilities Officer, 613-342-0371 1126, fax: 613-498-0291
jeremy.hobbs@ucdsb.on.ca
Terry Davies, Officer, Accountability & Alignment, 613-342-0371 1274, fax: 613-342-6084
terry.davies@ucdsb.on.ca
Terry Simzer, Manager, Communications, 613-342-0371 1119, fax: 613-342-0277
terry.simzer@ucdsb.on.ca
Frances Boomhouwer, Trustee Liaison, 613-342-0371 1279, fax: 613-342-6084
frances.boomhouwer@ucdsb.on.ca

Burlington: Halton District School Board
J.W. Singleton Education Centre
P.O. Box 5005 LCD 1
2050 Guelph Line Burlington, L7R 3Z2 Canada
905-335-3663, Fax: 905-335-9802,
Special Ed. Ctr., Student Svs., & Programs, Phone: 905-631-6120
inquiry@haltonbus.ca (student transportation)
www.hdsb.ca

Grades: Elementary - Secondary
Enrollment: 54000
Number of Schools: 80 elementary schools; 17 secondary schools. Number of Employees: 3,244 teachers; 1,350 non-teaching & support staff; 181 principals & vice-principals
Bruce Jones, Chair, 905-257-5926, fax: 905-257-5923
jonesbr@hdsb.ca
David Euale, Director, Education, fax: 905-335-4447
director@hdsb.ca
Ruth Peden, Acting Associate Director, Education, 905-335-3663 3352, fax: 905-335-4447
pedenr@hdsb.ca
Marnie Denton, Manager, Communication Services, fax: 905-335-4447
dentonm@hdsb.ca
Gail Gortmaker, Manager, Director's Office, fax: 905-335-4447
gortmakerg@hdsb.ca
Suzanne Muir, Coordinator, Diversity, 905-631-6120 434, fax: 905-335-4447
muirs@hdsb.ca
Jacki Oxley, Liaison, School & Community, fax: 905-335-4447
oxleyj@hdsb.ca

Chesley: Bluewater District School Board
P.O. Box 190
351 - 1st Ave. North Chesley, N0G 1L0 Canada
519-363-2014, Fax: 519-370-2909, 1-800-661-7509
communications@bwdsb.on.ca
www.bwdsb.on.ca

Grades: Elementary - Secondary; Special Ed.
Enrollment: 19454
Jennifer Yenssen, Chair
Mary Ann Alton, Director, Education
Brenda Booth, Treasurer & Superintendent, Business
Marnie Coke, Superintendent, Elementary Education
Alana Murray, Superintendent, Secondary Education
Jean Stephenson, Superintendent, Student Success
Lori Wilder, Superintendent, Student Services
Jacqui Traverse-Thomas, Principal, Program
Richard Thomas, Coordinator, Communications

Fort Frances: Rainy River District School Board
522 Second St. East Fort Frances, P9A 1N4 Canada
807-274-9855, Fax: 807-274-5078, 800-214-1753
www.rrdsb.com

Enrollment: 3080
Heather Campbell, Director of Education
Dan Belluz, Chair

Guelph: Upper Grand District School Board
Main Office
500 Victoria Rd. North Guelph, N1E 6K2 Canada
519-822-4420, Fax: 519-822-4487, 1-800-321-4025
inquiry@ugdsb.on.ca
www.ugdsb.on.ca

Grades: JK - 12; Continuing Education
Martha Rogers, Director, Education, & Secretary-Treasurer, 519-822-4420 720
martha.rogers@ugdsb.on.ca
Maggie McFadzen, Officer, Communications, 519-822-4420 275, fax: 519-826-9534
maggie.mcfadzen@ugdsb.on.ca

Hamilton: Hamilton-Wentworth District School Board
P.O. Box 2558
100 Main St. West Hamilton, L8N 3L1 Canada
905-527-5092, Fax: 905-521-2536,
www.hwdsb.on.ca

Enrollment: 50000
John Malloy, Director of Education
Jessica Brennan, Chair

Kenora: Keewatin-Patricia District School Board
100 First Ave. West Kenora, P9N 3Z7 Canada
807-468-5571, Fax: 807-468-3857, 877-275-7771
www.kpdsb.on.ca

Enrollment: 7000
Larry Hope, Director of Education
David Penney, Chair

Kingston: Limestone District School Board
P.O. Box Bag 610
220 Portsmouth Ave. Kingston, K7L 4X4 Canada
613-544-6920, Fax: 613-544-6804, 800-267-0935
TDD: 613-548-0279Automated: 613-544-6925
inq@limestone.on.ca
www.limestone.on.ca

Grades: JK-12
Enrollment: 22000
Brenda Hunter, Director of Education
Helen Chadwick, Chair

Kitchener: Waterloo Region District School Board
51 Ardelt Ave. Kitchener, N2C 2R5 Canada
519-570-0003, Fax: 519-742-1364,
www.wrdsb.on.ca

Grades: Pre-K.-12
Enrollment: 60000
Linda Fabi, Dir. 4222
Colin Harrington, Chair 4224

Lindsay: Trillium Lakelands District School Board
Corporate Office
P.O. Box 420
300 County Rd. 36 Lindsay, K9V 4S4 Canada
705-324-6776, Fax: 705-328-2036, 1-888-526-5552
Bracebridge Office, Phone: 705-645-8704; Haliburton: 705-457-1980
info@tldsb.on.ca
www.tldsb.on.ca

Grades: K-12; French Immersion; Adult Ed.
Enrollment: 18000
Number of Schools: 41 elementary schools; 7 secondary schools; 6 education centres. Number of Employees: 1,216 elementary school staff, including 772 teachers; 626 secondary school staff, including 440 teachers; 55 adult education centre staff, including 36 teachers; 158 other staff, including 26 teachers
Larry Hope, Director, Education, 705-324-6776
Bruce Barrett, Superintendent, Secondary School Improvement/, 705-324-6776
Kevin Cutler, Superintendent, Special Education, 705-645-8704
Bob Kaye, Superintendent, Business, 705-324-6776
Dianna Scates, Superintendent, ICT & Secondary Operations, 705-324-6776
Gale Sherin, Superintendent, Elementary School Improvement, 705-324-6776
Andrea Gillespie, District Principal, Elementary School Improve, 705-645-8704
Greg Ingram, District Principal, Secondary School Improvem, 705-324-6776
Shelley Woon, District Principal, Special Education, 705-324-6776
Earl Manners, Administrator, Human Resources, 705-324-6776
Jeanne Pengelly, Officer, Communications, 888-526-5552 22129
jeanne.pengelly@tldsb.on.ca

London: Thames Valley District School Board
P.O. Box 5888
1250 Dundas St. London, N5W 5P2 Canada
519-452-2000, Fax: 519-452-2395,
info@tvdsb.on.ca
www.tvdsb.on.ca

Grades: JK - 12; Adult Ed.; Alternative Ed.
Enrollment: 76864
Number of Schools: 148 elementary schools; 32 secondary schools. Number of Employees: 4,920 teachers; 297 principals & vice-principals; 2,645 support staff
Bill Tucker, Director, Education & Secretary, 519-452-2000 20001
Karen Dalton, Executive Superintendent, Operations, 519-452-2000 20083
Laura Elliott, Executive Superintendent, Program Services, 519-452-2000 20380
Brian Greene, Executive Superintendent, Business Services, 519-452-2000 20343
Michael Sereda, Executive Superintendent, Human Resources, 519-452-2000 20254
C. Bourbonnais Macdonald, Superintendent, Education - Operations Servic, 519-452-2000 20376
Karen Edgar, Superintendent, Education - Operations Svs. /, 519-452-2000 20275
Lynne Griffith-Jones, Superintendent, Education - HR Services / Ope, 519-452-2000 20250
Scott Hughes, Superintendent, Education - Operations Svs. /, 519-452-2000 20082
Marion Moynihan, Superintendent, Education - Operations Servic, 519-452-2000 20075
Valerie Neilsen, Superintendent, Education - Operations Svs. /, 519-452-2000 20387
Mary Ellen Smith, Superintendent, Education - Operations Servic, 519-452-2000 20251
Barbara Sonier, Superintendent, Education - Operations Servic, 519-452-2000 20078
Paul Tufts, Superintendent, Education - Operations Servic, 519-452-2000 20073
Karen Wilkinson, Superintendent, Education - Operations Servic, 519-452-2000 20501

Marathon: Superior-Greenstone District School Board
12 Hemlo Dr., Postal Bag A Marathon, P0T 2E0 Canada
807-229-0436, Fax: 807-229-1471,
boardoffice@sgdsb.on.ca
www.sgdsb.on.ca

Grades: Elementary - Secondary
Number of Schools: 12 elementary schools; 5 secondary schools
Julie Sparrow, Board Chair
jsparrow@sgdsb.on.ca
Patti Pella, Director, Education
ppella@sgdsb.on.ca
Cathy Tsubouchi, Superintendent, Business, & Treasurer
Wayne Chiupka, Manager, Plant Services
wchiupka@sgdsb.on.ca
Barb Draper, Coordinator, Human Resources
bdraper@sgdsb.on.ca
Val Newton, Coordinator, Student Success
vnewton@sgdsb.on.ca
Marc Paris, Coordinator, Maintenance & Safety
mparis@sgdsb.on.ca
Bradley Ross, Coordinator, Systems & Information Technology
bross@sgdsb.on.ca

Midhurst: Simcoe County District School Board
1170 Hwy. 26 Midhurst, L0L 1X0 Canada
705-728-7570, Fax: 705-728-2265,
www.scdsb.on.ca

Enrollment: 50000
Kathi Wallace, Director of Education
Brad Saunders, Chair

Mississauga: Peel District School Board
5650 Hurontario St. Mississauga, L5R 1C6 Canada
905-890-1099, Fax: 905-890-6747, 800-668-1146
communications@peelsb.com
www.peel.edu.on.ca

Enrollment: 150000
Tony Pontes, Director of Education
Janet McDougald, Chair

Nepean: Ottawa-Carleton District School Board
133 Greenbank Rd. Nepean, K2H 6L3 Canada
613-721-1820, Fax: 613-820-6968,
www.ocdsb.edu.on.ca

Enrollment: 72436
Cathy Curry, Chair
Dr. Lyall M. Thompson, Director of Education

North Bay: Near North District School Board
P.O. Box 3110
963 Airport Rd. North Bay, P1B 8H1 Canada
705-472-8170, Fax: 705-472-9927, 800-278-4922
info@nearnorthschools.ca
www.nearnorthschools.ca

Grades: Pre-K.-12
Enrollment: 4895
Heli Vail, Dir. 5050
vailh@nearnorthschools.ca
Al Bottomley, Chair, 705-384-5267
bottomleya@nearnorthschools.ca

Pembroke: Renfrew County District School Board
1270 Pembroke St. West Pembroke, K8A 4G4 Canada
613-735-0151, Fax: 613-735-6315,
www.renfrew.edu.on.ca

Enrollment: 10537

Roger Clarke, Director of Education
Roy C. Reiche, Chair

***Peterborough:* Kawartha Pine Ridge District School Board**
P.O. Box 7190
1994 Fisher Dr. Peterborough, K9J 7A1 Canada
705-742-9773, Fax: 705-742-7801, 877-741-4577
kpr_info@kpr.edu.on.ca
www.kpr.edu.on.ca

Enrollment: 37156
W.R. (Rusty) Hick, Director of Education
Diane Lloyd, Chair

***Sarnia:* Lambton Kent District School Board**
P.O. Box 2091
200 Wellington St. Sarnia, N7T 7L2 Canada
519-336-1500, Fax: 519-336-0992, 800-754-7125
www.lkdsb.net

Enrollment: 24000
Jim Costello, Director
Carmen McGregor, Chair

***Sault Ste Marie:* Algoma District School Board**
Central Board Office, Education Centre
644 Albert St. East Sault Ste Marie, P6A 2K7 Canada
705-945-7111, 1-888-393-3639
Northern Office: 705-856-2309; Eastern Office: 705-848-3661
vanders@adsb.on.ca (Susan Vandermolen)
www.adsb.on.ca

Grades: Kindergarten - 12; Adult Education
Mario Turco, Director, Education
Wanda McQueen, Chair

***Seaforth:* Avon Maitland District School Board**
62 Chalk St. North Seaforth, N0K 1W0 Canada
519-527-0111, Fax: 519-527-0222, 1-800-592-5437
info@fc.amdsb.ca
www.avonmaitland.on.ca

Grades: JK - Secondary; Continuing Ed.
Enrollment: 17000
Jenny Versteeg, Chair, Board of Trustees, 519-335-3623
jennvers@fc.amdsb.ca
Chuck Reid, Director, Education & Secretary of the Board, 519-527-0111 106
chucreid@fc.amdsb.ca
Mike Ash, Superintendent, Education - School Operations, 519-527-0111 113
Janet Baird-Jackson, Superintendent, Business, 519-527-0111 206
Jodie Baker, Superintendent, Education - Learning Services, 519-527-0111 109
Ted Doherty, Superintendent, Education - Human Resources, 519-527-0111 208
Patricia Stanley, Superintendent, Education - Curriculum & Asse, 519-527-0111 116
Steve Howe, Manager, Communications, 519-527-0111 132

***St Catharines:* District School Board of Niagara**
191 Carleton St. St Catharines, L2R 7P4 Canada
905-641-1550, Fax: 905-685-8511,
www.dsbn.edu.on.ca

Enrollment: 15749
Warren Hoshizaki, Dir.
Kevin Maves, Chair

***Sudbury:* Rainbow District School Board**
69 Young St. Sudbury, P3E 3G5 Canada
705-674-3171, Fax: 705-647-9112, 866-421-2661
www.rainbowschools.ca

Enrollment: 14762
Norm Blaseg, Director of Education
Tyler Campbell, Chair

***Thunder Bay:* Lakehead District School Board**
The Jim McCuaig Education Centre
2135 Sills St. Thunder Bay, P7E 5T2 Canada
807-625-5100, Fax: 807-622-0961,
www.lakeheadschools.ca

Enrollment: 10906
Catherine Siemieniuk, Director of Education
Deborah Massaro, Chair

***Timmins:* District School Board Ontario North East**
P.O. Box 1020
Timmins, P4N 7H7 Canada
705-360-1151, Fax: 705-268-7100, 1-800-381-728
comments@dsb1.edu.on.ca
www.dsb1.edu.on.ca

Enrollment: 4316
Linda Knight, Dir.
Juergen Leukert, Chair

***Toronto:* Toronto District School Board**
5050 Yonge St. Toronto, M2N 5N8 Canada
416-397-3000,
Public Affairs, Phone: 416-395-2721
communications@tdsb.on.ca
www.tdsb.on.ca

Grades: K - 12; Adult Ed.; French Immersion
Enrollment: 260000
Number of Schools: 565. Number of Employees: 37,000
Chris Spence, Director, Education
chris.spence@tdsb.on.ca
Sue Pfeffer, Superintendent, Region NE1, 416-396-9172
Sue.Pfeffer@tdsb.on.ca
Peter Chang, Superintendent, Region NE2, 416-396-9180
p.chang@tdsb.on.ca
Sandy Spyropoulos, Superintendent, Region NE3, 416-396-9176
sandy.spyropoulos@tdsb.on.ca
Colleen Russell, Superintendent, Region NE4, 416-396-9178
Colleen.Russell@tdsb.on.ca
Kathleen Meighan, Superintendent, Region NE5, 416-396-9174
Kathleen.Meighan@tdsb.on.ca
Johanne Messner, Superintendent, Region NE6, 416-396-9182
johanne.messner@tdsb.on.ca
Rauda Dickinson, Superintendent, Region SE1, 416-396-9186
Rauda.Dickinson@tdsb.on.ca
Kerry-Lynn Stadnyk, Superintendent, Region SE2, 416-396-9188
Kerry-Lynn.Stadnyk@tdsb.on.ca
Don McLean, Superintendent, Region SE3, 416-396-9190
Don.McLean@tdsb.on.ca
Allan Wolch, Superintendent, Region SE4, 416-396-9192
Allan.Wolch@tdsb.on.ca
Anne Kerr, Superintendent, Region SE5, 416-396-9194
Anne.Kerr@tdsb.on.ca
Kathy Cowan, Superintendent, Region SE6, 416-396-9196
Kathy.Cowan@tdsb.on.ca
Jim Spyropoulos, Superintendent, Region SW1, 416-394-2042
Jim.Spyropoulos@tdsb.on.ca
Manon Gardner, Superintendent, Region SW2, 416-394-2044
Manon.Gardner@tdsb.on.ca
Michael Smith, Superintendent, Region SW3, 416-394-2046
Michael.Smith@tdsb.on.ca
Ian Allison, Superintendent, Region SW4, 416-394-2048
Ian.Allison@tdsb.on.ca
Andrea Alimi, Superintendent, Region SW5, 416-394-2050
Andrea.Alimi@tdsb.on.ca
Karen Falconer, Superintendent, Region SW6, 416-394-2052
karen.falconer@tdsb.on.ca
Annie Appleby, Superintendent, Region NW1, 416-394-2028
Annie.Appleby@tdsb.on.ca
Glenford Duffus, Superintendent, Region NW2, 416-394-2030
Glenford.Duffus@tdsb.on.ca
John Chasty, Superintendent, Region NW3, 416-394-2032
john.chasty@tdsb.on.ca
Jeff Hainbuch, Superintendent, Region NW4, 416-394-2034
Jeff.Hainbuch@tdsb.on.ca
Leila Girdhar, Superintendent, Region NW5, 416-394-2036
Leila.Girdhar@tdsb.on.ca
Susan Winter, Superintendent, Region NW6, 416-394-2038
Susan.Winter@tdsb.on.ca

***Whitby:* Durham District School Board**
400 Taunton Rd. East Whitby, L1R 2K6 Canada
905-666-5500, Fax: 905-666-6474, 1-800-265-3968
TDD: 905-666-6943Trustees' Administrative Assistant, Phone: 905-666-6363
douglas_karen@durham.edu.on.ca (Executive Assistant to Diretor)
www.durham.edu.on.ca

Grades: K - 12; Special Ed.; Continuing Ed.
Enrollment: 69086
Number of Schools: 109 elementary schools; 26 secondary schools & learning centres. Number of Employees: 2,760 elementary teachers; 1,663 secondary teachyers; 208 elementary administrators; 77 secondary administrators; 2,665 educational services staff (including educational assistants, clerical, custodial, maintenance, & lunchroom supervisors)
Martyn Beckett, Director, Education, 905-666-5500, fax: 905-666-6318
beckett_martyn@durham.edu.on.ca
Luigia Ayotte, Superintendent, Education (Programs), 905-666-5500, fax: 905-666-6946
ayotte_luigia@durham.edu.on.ca
John Beatty, Superintendent, Education (Brock, Uxbridge, &, 905-666-6905
beatty_john@durham.edu.on.ca
John Bowyer, Superintendent, Education (Whitby), 905-666-6373
bowyer_john@durham.edu.on.ca
Doug Crichton, Superintendent, Education (Special Education), 905-666-6371
crichton_doug@durham.edu.on.ca
Janet Edwards, Superintendent, Education (Ajax), 905-666-6379
edwards_janet@durham.edu.on.ca
Ed Hodgins, Superintendent, Education & Business, & Treas, 905-666-6402, fax: 905-666-6969
hodgins_ed@durham.edu.on.ca
Mark Joel, Superintendent, Education (Ops, Transportatio, 905-666-5500, fax: 905-666-6376
joel_mark@durham.edu.on.ca
Jeannine Joubert, Superintendent, Education (Oshawa), 905-666-6369
joubert_jeannine@durham.edu.on.ca
Lisa Millar, Superintendent, Education (Pickering), 905-666-6486
millar_lisa@durham.edu.on.ca
Lou Vavougios, Superintendent, Education (Employee Services), 905-666-6332, fax: 905-666-6908
vavougios_lou@durham.edu.on.ca
David Visser, Superintendent, Education (Facilities Service, 905-666-6426, fax: 905-666-6439
visser_david@durham.edu.on.ca
Denise Gilbert, Executive Director, Schoolhouse Playcare Cent, 905-666-6487
gilbert_denise@durham.edu.on.ca
Andrea Pidwerbecki, Manager, Communications, 905-666-6313
pidwerbecki_andrea@durham.edu.on.ca

***Windsor:* Greater Essex County District School Board**
P.O. Box 210
451 Park St. West Windsor, N9A 6K1 Canada
519-255-3200,
Adult & Continuing Education, Phone: 519-253-5006
www.gecdsb.on.ca

Grades: Jr Kindergarten-12; Alternative Ed.
Enrollment: 35350
Number of Schools: 61 elementary schools; 16 secondary schools; 5 agency schools
Warren Kennedy, Director, Education, 519-255-3200 10250
Penny Allen, Superintendent, Business, 519-255-3200 10210
Paul Antaya, Superintendent, Secondary Schools, 519-255-3200 10254
Clara Howitt, Superintendent, Program & Instructional Servi, 519-255-3200 10255
John Howitt, Superintendent, Operations & Information Tech, 519-255-3200 10253
Heather Liffiton, Superintendent, Education, 519-255-3200 10251
Terry Lyons, Superintendent, Accommodations & Safe Schools, 519-255-3200 10223
Donne Petryshyn, Superintendent, Human Resources, 519-255-3200 10264
Sharon Pyke, Superintendent, Special Education, 519-255-3200 10222
Mary Guthrie, Chief Information Officer, 519-255-3200 10260

Catholic

***Aurora:* York Catholic District School Board**
320 Bloomington Rd. West Aurora, L4G 0M1 Canada
905-713-1211, Fax: 905-713-1272,
www.ycdsb.ca

Grades: Pre-K.-12
Enrollment: 54580
Susan LaRosa, Dir.
susan.larosa@ycdsb.ca
John Sabo, Assoc. Dir./Board Treas. 12300
john.sabo@ycdsb.ca
Elizabeth Crowe, Chair
elizabeth.crowe@ycdsb.ca

***Barrie:* Simcoe Muskoka Catholic District School Board**
46 Alliance Blvd. Barrie, L4M 5K3 Canada
705-722-3555, Fax: 705-722-6534,
www.smcdsb.on.ca

Enrollment: 22000
Michael. O'Keefe, Director of Education
John Grisé, Chair

***Brantford:* Brant Haldimand Norfolk Catholic District School Board**
P.O. Box 217
322 Fairview Dr. Brantford, N3T 5M8 Canada
519-756-6505, Fax: 519-756-9913,
webmaster@bhncdsb.ca
www.bhncdsb.edu.on.ca

Grades: Elementary - Secondary; Special Ed.
Enrollment: 10653
Number of Schools: 31 Catholic elementary schools; 3 Catholic secondary schools. Number of Employees: 700+ teachers; 300+ non-academic staff
June Szeman, Chair, 519-753-9198
jszeman@bhncdsb.ca

Cathy Horgan, Director, Education & Secretary, 519-756-6505 223
William Chopp, Superintendent, Education, 519-756-6505 244
Patricia (Trish) Kings, Superintendent, Education, 519-756-6505 242
Chris Roehrig, Superintendent, Education, 519-756-6505 240
Wally Easton, Associate Director, Corporate Services, & Tre, 519-756-6505 272
Mary Gallo, Principal, Secondary Program, 519-756-6505 251
Terre Slaght, Principal, Special Education Program, 519-759-8862 402
Leslie Telfer, Principal, School Effectiveness, 519-756-6505 264
Maureen Wills, Principal, Elementary Program, 519-756-6505 256
Tony Castagna, Manager, Information Technology, 519-758-5924 342
Paula Dunn, Manager, Human Resources, 519-756-6505 235
Phillip Kuckyt, Manager, Transportation Services, 519-751-7532 28220
Pat Petrella, Manager, Finance, 519-756-6505 228
Don Zelem, Manager, Facilities & Construction Projects, 519-759-3555 15
Tracey Austin, Coordinator, Communications & Community Relat, 519-756-6505 234
taustin@bhncdsb.ca

Burlington: Halton Catholic District School Board
Education Center
802 Drury Lane Burlington, L7R 2Y2 Canada
905-632-6300, Fax: 905-333-4661, 1-800-741-8382
Special Education Services, E-mail: speced@hcdsb.org
comments@hcdsb.org; communications@hcdsb.org; business@hcdsb.org
www.haltonrc.edu.on.ca

Grades: Elementary-Secondary; Continuing Ed
Enrollment: 29000
Number of Schools: 40 elementary schools; 8 secondary schools; 2 continuing education centres
Michael Pautler, Director, Education, 905-632-6314 110, fax: 905-333-4661
director@hcdsb.org
Erica vanRoosmalen, Chief Officer, Research & Development Service, 905-632-6314 367
Joseph O'Hara, Executive Officer, Human Resources, 905-632-6314 104
Giacomo Corbacio, Superintendent, Facilities Services, 905-632-6314 170
Jacqueline Herman, Superintendent, Education, 905-632-6314 161
John Langill, Superintendent, School Services, 905-632-6314 183
Richard MacDonald, Superintendent, Curriculum Services, 905-632-6314 122
Fiammetta Mazzetti, Superintendent, Education, 905-632-6314 216
Paul McMahon, Superintendent, Business Services, 905-632-6314 130
Suzanne Rossini, Superintendent, Special Education Services, 905-632-6314 128
James Rowles, Superintendent, Education, 905-632-6314 180
Mary Tessari, Superintendent, Education, Staff Dev. & Faith, 905-632-6314 118
Wayne Elshof, Senior Administrator, Information Technology, 905-632-6314 550
Scott Bland, Administrator, Planning Services, 905-632-6314 107
Christopher Jewell, Administrator, Communication Services, 905-632-6314 157

Dublin: Huron-Perth Catholic District School Board
P.O. Box 70
87 Mill St. Dublin, N0K 1E0 Canada
519-345-2440, Fax: 519-345-2449,
www.hpcdsb.edu.on.ca

Enrollment: 1753
Martha Dutrizac, Director of Education
Mike Miller, Chair

Dubreuilville: Conseil des écoles séparées catholiques de Dubreuilville
P.O. Box 69
149, av du Parc Dubreuilville, P0S 1B0 Canada
705-884-2309, Fax: 705-884-2062,
www.dubreuilville.ca

Enrollment: 138
Guy Pelletier, Président du Conseil

Fort Frances: Northwest Catholic District School Board
555 Flinders Ave. Fort Frances, P9A 3L2 Canada
807-274-2931, Fax: 807-274-8792,
www.tncdsb.on.ca

Enrollment: 1434
Mary-Catherine Kelly, Director of Education
Anne-Marie Fitzgerald, Chair
amfitzgerald@tncdsb.on.ca

Guelph: Wellington Catholic District School Board
75 Woolwich St. Guelph, N1H 6N6 Canada
519-821-4600, Fax: 519-824-3088,
andrew_duszczyszyn@wellingtoncssb.edu.on.ca
www.wellingtoncssb.edu.on.ca

Grades: Pre-K.-12
Enrollment: 61000
Don Drone, Dir., 519-821-4640, fax: 519-837-4156
ddrone@wellingtoncdsb.ca
Dan Duszczyszyn, Supt. of Corp. Services/Treas., fax: 519-837-4154
dduszczyszyn@wellingtoncdsb.ca
Rev Dennis J. Noon, Chair, 519-824-3951, fax: 519-824-1920
dnoon@dionet.ca

Hamilton: Hamilton-Wentworth Catholic District School Board
P.O. Box 2012
90 Mulberry St. Hamilton, L8N 3R9 Canada
905-525-2930, Fax: 905-525-1724,
Summer fax: 905-525-2914
www.hwcdsb.edu.on.ca/

Grades: K-12
Enrollment: 30000
Patricia Amos, Director of Education, 905-525-2930 2180
Patrick J. Daly, Chair, 905-525-2930 2162

Hanover: Bruce-Grey Catholic District School Board
799 - 16th Ave. Hanover, N4N 3A1 Canada
519-364-5820, Fax: 519-364-5882,
bruce_grey@bgcdsb.org
www.bgcdsb.org

Grades: Kindergarten-12; Religious Ed.; ESL
Enrollment: 3524
Number of Schools: 13
Norman Bethune, Chair, 519-376-8315
Bruce MacPherson, Director, Education
Gerald Casey, Superintendent, Education
Catherine Montreuil, Superintendent, Education
Cathy Colton, Superintendent, Business
Jim Aitken, Supervisor, Maintenance
Joyce Benninger, Supervisor, Payroll & Health & Safety
Doreen Rogers, Coordinator, Community Relations & Outreach
Ann-Marie Deas, Social Worker
Alecia Lantz, Financial Analyst
Brenda Leahy, Speech Language Pathologist
Catherine Penner, Psychometrist

Kemptville: Catholic District School Board of Eastern Ontario
c/o Kemptville Board Office
P.O. Box 2222
2755 Hwy. 43 Kemptville, K0G 1J0 Canada
613-258-7757, Fax: 613-258-7134, 1-800-443-4562
Western Ed. Ctr.: 613-283-5007; Eastern Ed. Ctr.: 613-933-1720
mail@cdsbeo.on.ca
www.cdsbeo.on.ca

Grades: Elementary - Secondary
Enrollment: 15000
Number of Schools: 40 elementary schools; 10 secondary schools. Number of Employees: 850 teachers; 450 support staff
Ronald Eamer, Chair, 613-931-2369
Ronald.Eamer@cdsbeo.on.ca
Dr. Donaleen Hawes, Superintendent, Education, 613-283-5007 234, fax: 613-283-5783
Donaleen.Hawes@cdsbeo.on.ca
Mark Musca, Superintendent, Human Resources, 613-258-7757, fax: 613-258-3610
Mark.Musca@cdsbeo.on.ca
Marg Shea-Lawrence, Superintendent, Religious & Family Life Educa, 613-258-7757 207, fax: 613-258-3610
Marg.Shea@cdsbeo.on.ca
Bernie Kehoe, Manager, Plant & Maintenance, 613-258-7757 227, fax: 613-258-3610
Bernie.Kehoe@cdsbeo.on.ca
Nicole Makinson, Manager, Transportation & Assessment, 613-258-7757 107, fax: 613-258-3610
Nicole.Makinson@cdsbeo.on.ca
Bonnie Norton, Manager, Finance, 613-258-7757 238, fax: 613-258-3610
Bonnie.Norton@cdsbeo.on.ca
James Proulx, Manager, ICT Services, 613-258-7757 555, fax: 613-258-3610
James.Proulx@cdsbeo.on.ca
Sheila Farris, Supervising Principal, Student Success Initia, 613-283-5007, fax: 613-283-5783
Sheila.Farris@cdsbeo.on.ca
Tom Jordan, Principal, Special Education, 613-283-5007 205, fax: 613-283-5783
Tom.Jordan@cdsbeo.on.ca
Jim Roberts, Principal, Religious Education, 613-258-7757 246, fax: 613-258-3610
jim.roberts@cdsbeo.on.ca
Charlotte Rouleau, Principal, Curriculum, 613-933-1720 377, fax: 613-933-7966
charlotte.rouleau@cdsbeo.on.ca

Kenora: Kenora Catholic District School Board
200 First St. North Kenora, P9N 2K4 Canada
807-468-9851, Fax: 807-468-8094,
mcunningham@kcdsb.on.ca
www.kcdsb.on.ca

Enrollment: 1475
Phyllis Eikre, Director of Education
Darryl Michaluk, Chair

Kitchener: Waterloo Catholic District School Board
P.O. Box 91116
35 Weber St. W, #A Kitchener, N2G 4G2 Canada
519-578-3660, Fax: 519-578-5291,
info@wcdsb.ca
www.wcdsb.ca

Grades: Pre-K.-12
Enrollment: 40000
Roger Lawler, Dir.
roger.lawler@wcdsb.ca
Shesh Maharaj, CFO
shesh.maharaj@wcdsb.ca
Wayne Buchholtz, Chair

L'Orignal: Conseil scolaire de district catholique de l'Est ontarien
875, ch de comté 17 L'Orignal, K0B 1K0 Canada
613-675-4691, Fax: 613-675-2921, 800-204-4098
bur-central@csdceo.on.ca
www.csdceo.ca

Enrollment: 3718
Céline Cadieux, Directrice de l'éducation/Sec.
Michel Pilon, Président du Conseil

London: London District Catholic School Board
Catholic Education Centre
P.O. Box 5474
5200 Wellington Rd. South London, N6A 4X5 Canada
519-663-2088,
communications@ldcsb.on.ca
www.ldcsb.on.ca

Grades: Jr Kindergarten - 12; Continuing Ed
Enrollment: 21000
Number of Schools: 48 elementary schools; 8 secondary schools
Bill Hall, Chair, Board of Trustees
Wilma de Rond, Director, Education, & Secretary-Treasurer, 519-663-2088 40002, fax: 519-663-9250
w.derond@ldcsb.on.ca
Terry Grand, Superintendent, Education
Vince MacDonald, Superintendent, Education
John Mombourquette, Superintendent, Education
Tamara Nugent, Superintendent, Education
Sharon Wright-Evans, Superintendent, Education

Mississauga: Dufferin-Peel Catholic District School Board
40 Matheson Blvd. West Mississauga, L5R 1C5 Canada
905-890-1221, Fax: 905-890-7610,
www.dpcdsb.org

Enrollment: 80000
Michael Bator, Dir.
mike.bator@dpcdsb.org
Arthur Peters, Chair

Napanee: Algonquin & Lakeshore Catholic District School Board
151 Dairy Ave. Napanee, K7R 4B2 Canada
613-354-2255, 1-800-581-1116
info@alcdsb.on,
www.alcdsb.on.ca

Grades: Elementary - Secondary
Enrollment: 12397
Michael Schmitt, Director, Education, 613-354-6257 448
schmitt@alcdsb.on.ca
Bob Koubsky, Superintendent, Finance & Business Services, 613-354-6257 436
koubsky@alcdsb.on.ca
Lori Bryden, Coodinator, Student Services, 613-354-6257 434
bryden@alcdsb.on.ca
Bronek Korczynski, Coodinator, Religous & Family Life Education, 613-354-6257 462
Bronek.Korczynski@alcdsb.on.ca

Louise Lannan, Coodinator, Curriculum & Staff Development, 613-354-6257 402
lannan@alcdsb.on.ca

Nepean: Ottawa-Carleton Catholic District School Board
570 Hunt Club Rd. West Nepean, K2G 3R4 Canada
613-224-2222, Fax: 613-224-5063,
www.occdsb.on.ca

Enrollment: 39000
Julian Hanlon, Director of Education & Sec.-Treas.
Gordon Butler, Chair

North Bay: Conseil scolaire catholique Franco-Nord
681-C, rue Chippewa ouest North Bay, P1B 6G8 Canada
705-472-1702, Fax: 705-474-3824,
information@franco-nord.ca
www.franco-nord.edu.on.ca

Enrollment: 3400
Cynthia Roveda, Directrice de l'éducation/Sec.-trésorière
Ronald Demers, Président du Conseil

North Bay: Nipissing-Parry Sound Catholic District School Board
1000 High St. North Bay, P1B 6P2 Canada
705-472-1201, Fax: 705-472-0507,
www.npsc.edu.on.ca

Grades: Pre_K.-12
Enrollment: 3438
Anna Marie Bitonti, Dir.
Joanne Bénard, Supt.
Donald B. Houle, Chair

Oshawa: Durham Catholic District School Board
650 Rossland Rd. West Oshawa, L1J 7C4 Canada
905-576-6150, Fax: 905-576-0953,
www.durhamrc.edu.on.ca

Enrollment: 26069
Patricia Manson, Dir.
patricia.manson@idirect.com
Mary Ann Martin, Chair

Ottawa: Conseil des écoles catholiques du Centre-Est
4000, rue Labelle Ottawa, K1J 1A1 Canada
613-744-2555, Fax: 613-746-3081, 888-230-5131
ecolecatholique@ecolecatholique.ca
www.ceclf.edu.on.ca

Enrollment: 18000
Diane Doré, Présidente du Conseil
Bernard Roy, Directeur de l'éducation/Sec.-trésorier

Pembroke: Renfrew County Catholic District School Board
499 Pembroke St. West Pembroke, K8A 5P1 Canada
613-735-1031, Fax: 613-735-2649, 800-267-0191
www.rccdsb.edu.on.ca

Enrollment: 5000
Michele Arbour, Director
Bob Schreader, Chair

Peterborough: Peterborough Victoria Northumberland & Clarington Catholic District School B
1355 Lansdowne St. West Peterborough, K9J 7M3 Canada
705-748-4861, Fax: 705-748-9734, 800-461-8009
www.pvnccdsb.on.ca

Enrollment: 14678
John Mackle, Director of Education & Sec./Treas.
David Bernier, Chair

Sault Ste Marie: Huron-Superior Catholic District School Board
90 Ontario Ave. Sault Ste Marie, P6B 6G7 Canada
705-945-5400, Fax: 705-945-5575, 800-267-0754
www.hscdsb.on.ca

Enrollment: 6795
John Stadnyk, Director of Education
Marchy Bruni, Chair

Sudbury: Conseil scolaire catholique du Nouvel-Ontario
201, rue Jogues Sudbury, P3C 5L7 Canada
705-673-5626, Fax: 705-669-1270, 800-259-5567
info@nouvelon.ca
www.nouvelon.ca

Enrollment: 7500
Marcel Montpellier, Président du Conseil
Lyse-Anne Papineau, Directrice de l'éducation

Sudbury: Sudbury Catholic District School Board
Catholic Education Centre
165A D'Youville St. Sudbury, P3C 5E7 Canada
705-673-5620, Fax: 705-673-6670,
Transportation, Phone: 705-521-1234
employment@sudburycatholicschools.ca
www.scdsb.edu.on.ca

Grades: JK - 12; French Immersion; Adult Ed
Enrollment: 6595
Number of Schools: 20 elementary schools; 5 secondary schools (including an all-girls school & the St. Albert Adult Learning Centre)
Catherine McCullough, Director, Education, & Secretary of the Board, 705-673-5620 242, fax: 705-688-1781
Catherine.McCullough@sudburycatholicschools.ca
Rossella Bagnato, Superintendent, Special Education & Academic, 705-673-5620 238, fax: 705-688-1781
Rossella.Bagnato@sudburycatholicschools.ca
Dennis Bazinet, Superintendent, Business & Finance, 705-673-5620 238, fax: 705-688-1781
Dennis.Bazinet@sudburycatholicschools.ca
Jean McHarg, Superintendent, Programs (K-12), 705-673-5620 238, fax: 705-688-1781
Jean.McHarg@sudburycatholicschools.ca
Roland Muzzatti, Superintendent, Student Success & 7-12 School, 705-673-5620 238, fax: 705-688-1781
Roland.Muzzatti@sudburycatholicschools.ca
Suzanne Dubien, Senior Manager, Human Resources, 705-673-5620 312
Denis Faucher, Manager, Facility Services, 705-673-5620 415
Gerry Robillard, Manager, Information Management Services, 705-673-5620 371
Gina Tullio, Coordinator, Outreach & Media Relations, 705-673-5620 244

Terrace Bay: Superior North Catholic District School Board
P.O. Box 610
21 Simcoe Plaza Terrace Bay, P0T 2W0 Canada
807-825-3209, Fax: 807-825-3885,
BoardOffice@sncdsb.on.ca; Board@sncdsb.on.ca
www.sncdsb.on.ca

Grades: Elementary; Religious Program
Number of Schools: 9 elementary schools
Valerie Pichette, Director, Education
vpichette@sncdsb.on.ca
Mary Anne Baker, Superintendent, Education
mbaker@sncdsb.on.ca
Sherry Bortolotti, Superintendent, School Effectiveness
sbortolotti@sncdsb.on.ca
Scott Adams, Manager, Finance
sadams@sncdsb.on.ca
Dan Bourgeault, Manager, Operations
dbourgeault@sncdsb.on.ca
Laureen Kay, Officer, Payroll & Human Resources, 807-825-3209 25, fax: 807-825-3885
lkay@sncdsb.on.ca
Maria Lapenskie, Officer, Transportation
mlapenskie@sncdsb.on.ca

Thunder Bay: Conseil scolaire de district catholique des Aurores boréales
175, rue High nord Thunder Bay, P7A 8C7 Canada
807-344-2266, Fax: 807-344-3734, 800-367-0874
info@csdcab.on.ca
www.csdcab.on.ca

Enrollment: 652
Sylvianne Mauro, Directrice de l'éducation
Angèle Brunelle, Présidente du Conseil

Thunder Bay: Thunder Bay Catholic District School Board
Catholic Education Centre
459 Victoria Ave. West Thunder Bay, P7C 0A4 Canada
807-625-1555,
jsheriff@tbcdsb.on.ca
www.tbcdsb.on.ca

Grades: Jr. Kindergarten-12; Alternative Ed
Enrollment: 8606
Number of Schools: 16 elementary schools; 3 senior elementary schools; 2 secondary schools. Number of Employees: 366 elementary school teachers; 194 secondary school teachers; 283 non-teaching staff
John De Faveri, Director, Education, 807-625-1567, fax: 807-623-2167
jdefaver@tbcdsb.on.ca
Tom Mustapic, Associate Director & Superintendent, Business, 807-625-1508, fax: 807-625-1583
tmustapi@tbcdsb.on.ca
Rob Kruse, Superintendent, Education (St. Ignatius HS &, 807-625-1590, fax: 807-625-1560
dsebesta@tbcdsb.on.ca
Joan Powell, Superintendent, Education - Special Education, 807-625-1573, fax: 807-625-1560
jpowell@tbcdsb.on.ca
David Bragnalo, Officer, Education, 807-625-1585, fax: 807-625-1560
dbragnal@tbcdsb.on.ca
Michael Thompson, Officer, Communications, 807-625-1587, fax: 807-623-2187
mthompso@tbcdsb.on.ca
Garry Grgurich, Manager, Employee Services, 807-625-1577, fax: 807-625-8601
jwillis@tbcdsb.on.ca

Timmins: Conseil des écoles séparées catholiques de Foleyet
52, pl Theodore Timmins, P4N 7P6 Canada
705-267-3521, Fax: 705-267-3691,
www.afocsc.org

Enrollment: 15
Lisa Côté, Sec.-Treas.
Suzanne Roch, Chair

Timmins: Conseil scolaire catholique de district des Grandes Rivières
896, promenade Riverside Timmins, P4N 3W2 Canada
705-267-1421, Fax: 705-267-7247,
www.cscdgr.on.ca

Enrollment: 2668
Isabelle Charbonneau, Présidente du Conseil
charbonneau@cscdgr.on.ca
Lorraine Presley, Directrice de l'éducation

Timmins: Northeastern Catholic District School Board
101 Spruce St. North Timmins, P4N 6M9 Canada
705-268-7443, Fax: 705-267-3590, 877-422-9322
www.ncdsb.on.ca

Grades: Pre-K.-12
Enrollment: 2373
Glenn Sheculski, Dir., fax: 705-268-7499
gsheculski@ncdsb.on.ca
Tricia Stefanic Weltz, Supt., fax: 705-266-9144
tricia.weltz@ncdsb.on.ca

Toronto: Conseil scolaire de district catholique Centre-Sud
110, av Drewry Toronto, M2M 1C8 Canada
416-397-6564, Fax: 416-397-6576, 800-274-3764
commentaires@csdccs.edu.on.ca
www.csdccs.edu.on.ca

Enrollment: 12000
Réjean Sirois, Directeur de l'éducation/Sec.-trésorier
Mikale-Andrée Joly, Directrice des communications stratégiques

Toronto: Toronto Catholic District School Board
80 Sheppard Ave. East Toronto, M2N 6E8 Canada
416-222-8282, Fax: 416-229-5345,
Public Relations, Phone: 416-222-8282, ext. 5314
webmaster@tcdsb.org; helpdesk@tcdsb.org (technical difficulties)
www.tcdsb.org

Grades: Kindergarten - 12; Adult Education
Enrollment: 93054
Number of Schools: 168 elementary schools; 31 secondary schools; 2 combined elementary & secondary (Cardinal Carter Academy for the Arts & St. Michael's Choir). Number of Employees: 5,997 teachers; 2,806 support & academic staff; 356 principals & vice-principals; 202 administrative personnel
Ann Perron, Director, Education, 416-222-8282 2296
ann.perron@tcdsb.org
Angela Gauthier, Associate Director, Academic Services, 416-222-8282 2641
angela.gauthier@tcdsb.org
Sandra Pessione, Associate Director, Business Services, CFO, &, 416-222-8282 2641
sandra.pessione@tcdsb.org
Angelo Sangiorgio, Associate Director, Planning & Facilities, 416-222-8282 2349
Josie DiGiovanni, Superintendent, Curriculum & Accountability &, 416-222-8282 2490
josie.digiovanni@tcdsb.org
Lori DiMarco, Superintendent, Schools - Area 4ountability &, 416-222-8282 2267
lori.dimarco@tcdsb.org
Richard Francki, Superintendent, Facilities Services, 416-222-8282 2349
richard.francki@tcdsb.org
Geoffrey Grant, Superintendent, Schools - Area 8, 416-222-8282 2730
geoffrey.grant@tcdsb.org
Patrick Keyes, Superintendent, Student Success, Equity & Inc, 416-222-8282 5370
patrick.keyes@tcdsb.org
Rory McGuckin, Superintendent, Safe Schools & Parent & Commu, 416-222-8282
rory.mcguckin@tcdsb.org

Michael McMorrow, Superintendent, Schools - Area 6, 416-222-8282 5371
michael.mcmorrow@tcdsb.org
Josie Nespolo, Superintendent, Schools - Area 2, 416-222-8282 2732
josephine.nespolo@tcdsb.org
Loretta Notten, Superintendent, Schools - Area 1, 416-222-8282 2732
loretta.notten@tcdsb.org
Anthony Petitti, Superintendent, Schools - Area 7, 416-222-8282 2730
anthony.petitti@tcdsb.org
Frank Piddisi, Superintendent, Special Services & Parent Eng, 416-222-8282 2486
frank.piddisi@tcdsb.org
Gary Poole, Superintendent, Human Resources, 416-222-8282 2304
gary.poole@tcdsb.org
Vidyia Rego, Superintendent, Business Services, 416-222-8282 2257
vidyia.rego@tcdsb.org
Jim Saraco, Superintendent, Schools - Area 5, 416-222-8282 5371
jim.saraco@tcdsb.org
Doug Yack, Superintendent, Schools - Area 3, 416-222-8282 2267
douglas.yack@tcdsb.org
Barbara McMorrow, Executive Corporate Secretary & Board Liaison, 416-222-8282 2080
barbara.mcmorrow@tcdsb.org
Mary Jo Dieghan, Coordinator, Communications, 416-222-8282 5314
maryjo.deighan@tcdsb.org; commdept@tcdsb.org

***Wallaceburg:* St. Clair Catholic District School Board**
Catholic Education Centre
420 Creek St. Wallaceburg, N8A 4C4 Canada
519-627-6762, Fax: 519-627-8230, 1-866-336-6139
media@st-clair.net
www.st-clair.ne
Grades: Elementary - Secondary
Number of Schools: 29 elementary schools; 3 secondary schools. Number of Employees: 1,100+
Anita Labadie, Chair, 519-360-9254
Paul Wubben, Director, Education, Chief Executive Officer, 519-627-6762 241
James McKenzie, Associate Director & Treasurer
Deb Crawford, Superintendent, Education
Dr. Frank Leddy, Superintendent, Education
Ann Sutton, Superintendent, Education
Steven Mitchell, Chief Information Officer
Carol Ann Bélanger, Assistant Superintendent, Catholic Curriculum
Lisa Demers, Principal, Special Education
Cindy Waddick, Leader, Elementary Chaplaincy
cindy.waddick@st-clair.net
Karen Dolson, Manager, Planning Services
Bruce Hannah, Manager, Facility Services
Amy Janssens, Manager, Financial Services
Todd Lozon, Supervisor, Communications & Community Relati, 519-627-6762 243
todd.lozon@st-clair.net

***Welland:* Niagara Catholic District School Board**
427 Rice Rd. Welland, L3C 7C1 Canada
905-735-0240, Fax: 905-734-8828,
info@ncdsb.com
www.niagararc.com
Grades: Pre-K.-12
Enrollment: 25000
John Crocco, Dir./Sec.-Treas. 220
john.crocco@ncdsb.com
Kathy Burtnik, Chair

***Windsor:* Conseil scolaire de district des écoles catholiques du Sud-Ouest**
7515, promenade Forest Glade Windsor, N8T 3P5 Canada
519-948-9227, Fax: 519-948-1091, 888-768-2219
www.csdecso.on.ca
Enrollment: 1412
Janine Griffore, Directrice générale

***Windsor:* Windsor-Essex Catholic District School Board**
1325 California Ave. Windsor, N9B 3Y6 Canada
519-253-2481, Fax: 519-253-8397,
www.wecdsb.on.ca
Grades: Pre-K.-12
Enrollment: 27518
Joseph Berthiaume, Dir. 1201
joseph_berthiaume@wecdsb.on.ca
Mario Iatonna, Supt. of Business 1211
mario_iatonna@wecdsb.on.ca
Fred Alexander, Chair, 519-735-8664
fred_alexander@wecdsb.on.ca

French

***North Bay:* Conseil scolaire public du Nord-Est de l'Ontario**
310 , av Algonquin North Bay, P1B 9T5 Canada
705-472-3443, Fax: 705-472-5757, 888-591-5656
information@csdne.edu.on.ca
www.csdne.edu.on.ca
Enrollment: 1725
Timmins: 111, av Wilson, (705) 264-1119.
Roch Gallien, Directeur de l'éducation
Robert Poirier, Président du Conseil

***Ottawa:* Conseil des écoles publiques de l'Est de l'Ontario**
2445, boul Saint-Laurent Ottawa, K1G 6C3 Canada
613-747-3802, Fax: 613-747-3810, 888-332-3736
www.cepeo.on.ca
Rachid El Keurti, Directeur exécutif
rachid.elkeurti@cepeo.on.ca
Georges Orfal, Président du Conseil
georges.orfali@cepeo.on.ca

***Sudbury:* Conseil scolaire public Grand Nord de l'Ontario**
296, rue Van Horne Sudbury, P3B 1H9 Canada
705-671-1533, Fax: 705-671-1720, 800-465-5993
www.cspgno.ca
Enrollment: 902
Pierre Riopel, Directeur général (par intérim)
Jean-Marc Aubin, Président

***Toronto:* Conseil scolaire de district du Centre-Sud-Ouest**
116, Cornelius Pkwy. Toronto, M6L 2K5 Canada
416-614-0844, Fax: 416-397-2012, 888-538-1702
www.csdcso.on.ca
Enrollment: 7700
Jean-Luc Bernard, Directeur de l'éducation
Ronald Marion, Président du Conseil

School Authorities

***Armstrong:* Northern District School Area Board**
P.O. Box 98
1 Hwy. 527 Armstrong, P0T 1A0 Canada
807-583-2010, Fax: 807-583-2614,
esip.edu.gov.on.ca/english/profiles/board_directory.asp?ID=B15245
Grades: Pre-K.-8
Enrollment: 123
Fred Porter, Supervisory Officer, 807-475-6989
fporter@resourcenorth.com
Yolanda Wanakamik, Chair

***Hornepayne:* Hornepayne Roman Catholic Separate School Board**
P.O. Box 430
200 Front St. Hornepayne, P0M 1Z0 Canada
807-868-2010, Fax: 807-868-3026
Enrollment: 86
Julie Roy, Sec.
Carol MacEachern, Chair

***Madawaska:* Murchison & Lyell District School Area Board**
c/o G. Breshnahan, Major Lake Rd.
P.O. Box 10
Madawaska, K0J 2C0 Canada
613-637-1349, Fax: 613-637-1349,
esip.edu.gov.on.ca/english/profiles/board_directory.asp?ID=B15229
Grades: Pre-K.-8
Enrollment: 21
Elaine Hare, Vice-Chair/Trustee

***Mine Centre:* Mine Centre District Area School Board**
P.O. Box 128
Mine Centre, P0W 1H0 Canada
807-599-2836, Fax: 807-599-2815,
esip.edu.gov.on.ca/english/profiles/board_directory.asp?ID=B15172
Grades: Pre-K.-8
Enrollment: 84
Sheila McMillen, Sec.-Treas.
Genevieve Bliss, Chair

***Moose Factory:* Moose Factory Island District School Area Board**
P.O. Box 160
Moose Factory, P0L 1W0 Canada
705-658-4571, Fax: 705-658-4768,
esip.edu.gov.on.ca/english/profiles/board_directory.asp?ID=B15199
Grades: Pre-K.-8
Enrollment: 362
Brenda J. Chilton-Jeffries, Sec.-Treas.
Irene Hunter, Chair

***Moosonee:* James Bay Lowlands Secondary School Board**
P.O. Box 157
1 Keewatin Dr. Moosonee, P0L 1Y0 Canada
705-336-2903, Fax: 705-336-0234
Enrollment: 179
Charles Faries, Adm.
Bernice Morrison, Chair

***Moosonee:* Moosonee District School Area Board**
P.O. Box 250
Moosonee, P0L 1Y0 Canada
705-336-2300, Fax: 705-336-0334,
esip.edu.gov.on.ca/english/profiles/board_directory.asp?ID=B15202
Grades: Pre-K.-8
Enrollment: 328
Barbara Faries, Sec.-Treas.
Dianne Wynne, Chair

***Moosonee:* Moosonee Roman Catholic Separate School Board**
P.O. Box 340
Moosonee, P0L 1Y0 Canada
705-336-2605, Fax: 705-336-2881,
esip.edu.gov.on.ca/english/profiles/board_directory.asp?ID=B16063
Grades: Pre-K-8
Enrollment: 109
Kathy Hallett, Supervisory Officer

***Oshawa:* Campbell Children's School Authority**
600 Towline Rd. South Oshawa, L1H 7K6 Canada
905-576-8403, Fax: 905-576-4414,
ccs@grtc.ca
Grades: Specialized programs
Campbell Children's School serves students from the local district school boards with communication or multiple disabilities.
Lynda Schuler, Chair

***Ottawa:* Ottawa Children's Treatment Centre School Authority**
395 Smyth Rd. Ottawa, K2H 8L2 Canada
613-737-0871, Fax: 613-523-5167
Enrollment: 23
Neil Wilson, Chair

***Parry Sound:* Parry Sound Roman Catholic Separate School Board**
#203, 60 James St. Parry Sound, P2A 1T5 Canada
705-746-6231, Fax: 705-746-7568
Enrollment: 208
Brian McLeod, Chair

***Penetanguishene:* Penetanguishene Protestant Separate School Board**
2 Poyntz St. Penetanguishene, L9M 1M2 Canada
705-549-6422, Fax: 705-549-2768,
pssbp@bellnet.ca
www.pssb.ca
Enrollment: 261
Lynne Cousens, Chair

***Red Lake:* Red Lake Area Combined Roman Catholic Separate School Board**
P.O. Box 888
54 Discovery Rd. Red Lake, P0V 2M0 Canada
807-727-3470, Fax: 807-727-3211
Enrollment: 119
Nora Kolmel, Secretary
Vaughan Blab, Chair

***St Catharines:* Niagara Peninsula Children's Centre School Authority**
567 Glenridge Ave. St Catharines, L2T 4C2 Canada
905-688-3550, Fax: 905-688-1055, 800-896-5496
info@npcc.on.ca
www.npcc.on.ca
Enrollment: 84
A non-profit, charitable organization aiming to provide programs

and services to enable children and youth with physical or communicative challenges to maximize their independence.
Oksana Fisher, CEO
Tim Wright, Exec. Dir.

***Timmins:* Missarenda District School Area Board**
869 Denise St. Timmins, P6N 7M5 Canada
705-268-6217, Fax: 705-268-6217,
esip.edu.gov.on.ca/english/profiles/board_directory.asp?ID=B15180
Enrollment: 3
Jody Charette, Sec.
Lise Anglehart, Chair

***Toronto:* Bloorview School Authority**
150 Kilgour Rd. Toronto, M4G 1R8 Canada
416-424-3831, Fax: 416-425-2981,
school@bloorview.ca
www.bloorviewschool.ca
Bloorview School Authority provides school programs to children & youth with special needs.
Rachee Allen, Trustee
Dr. Doug Biggar, Trustee
Earl Campbell, Trustee
Mary Campbell, Trustee
Brenda Keleher, Trustee
James McCarron, Trustee
Richard Volpe, Trustee

***Waterloo:* KidsAbility School Authority Board**
500 Hallmark Dr. Waterloo, N2K 3P5 Canada
519-886-8886, Fax: 519-885-6222,
www.kidsability.ca
KidsAbility School Authority Board serves children with a wide range of special needs. Programs & services include a kindergarten program, individual education plans, composite classes, communication classes, & language classes.
Justin Heimpel, Chair
Linda Rogers, Principal & Secretary to the Board
Joanne Cotter, Secretary-Treasurer

***Windsor:* John McGivney Children's Centre School Authority**
3945 Matchette Rd. Windsor, N9C 4C2 Canada
519-252-7281, Fax: 519-252-5873,
www.jmccentre.ca
The John McGivney Children's Centre School Authority governs the John McGivney Children's Centre School, formerly known as the Children's Rehabilitation Centre School. The school provides a post trauma / post operative rehabilitation program for students from ages four to twenty-one, who live in Windsor / Essex County.
Carolyn Tavolieri, Chair
Adelina Irvine, Vice-Chair
Dr. Brenda Roberts-Santarossa, Secretary
Karen McConnell, Treasurer

First Nations

***Attawapiskat:* Attawapiskat First Nation Education Authority**
General Delivery Attawapiskat, P0L 1A0 Canada
705-997-2114, Fax: 705-997-2357,
psinfo@afnea.com; recruit@afnea.com (Recruitment)
www.afnea.com
Grades: Junior Kindergarten-12; Special Ed.
Enrollment: 800
Number of Schools: 2 (J.R. Nakogee School & Vezina Secondary School)
John B. Nakogee, Director, Education
Andrew Hirst, Chair

***Big Trout Lake:* Kitchenuhmaykoosib Education Authority**
General Delivery Big Trout Lake, P0V 1G0 Canada
807-537-2553, Fax: 807-537-2316,
kifirstnation@knet.ca
www.bigtroutlake.firstnation.ca
Grades: Junior Kindergarten-11; Special Ed.
Enrollment: 275
Number of Schools: 1 (Aglace Chapman Education Centre). Number of Employees: 30. The Kitchenuhmaykoosib Education Authority serves the Kitchenuhmaykoosib Inninnuwug First Nation, formerly known as Big Trout Lake First Nation, located north of Thunder Bay, Ontario. Secondary programs are also available through computer, radio, & television.

***Christian Island:* Beausoleil First Nation Education Authority**
Administration Building
1 O'Gema St., Main Level Christian Island, L0K 1C0 Canada
705-247-2051, Fax: 705-247-2239,
p.mcgregor@beausoleil-education.ca
www.beausoleil-education.ca
Grades: Junior Kindergarten - 8; Special Ed
Number of Schools: 1 (Christian Island Elementary School). The Beausoleil First Nation Education Authority serves the Chippewas of the Beausoleil First Nation by operating the Christian Island Elementary School. For secondary education, students attend high schools in the Simcoe County District School Board or the Simcoe Muskoka Catholic School Board.
Peggy McGregor, Director, Education
p.mcgregor@beausoleil-education.ca
Mike Lucas, Principal, Christian Island Elementary School
m.lucas@beausoleil-education.ca
Peter Dimoff, Manager, Human Resources
pdimoff@chimnissing.ca
Herb Connell, Coordinator, Adult Education, 705-247-2825
Karen King, Coordinator, Parental Engagement
Angela Phillips, Teacher, Special Education
Nancy Assance, Contact, Post-Secondary Student Assistance Pr
n.assance@beausoleil-education.ca

***Constance Lake:* Constance Lake First Nation Education Authority**
P.O. Box 4000
Constance Lake, P0L 1B0 Canada
705-463-4511, Fax: 705-463-2222,
www.clfn.on.ca
Grades: Daycare - JK - 12; Adult Education
Enrollment: 257
Number of Schools: 1 (Mamawmatawa Holistic Education Center). Located in the District of Cochrane, the Constance Lake First Nation Education Authority provides education to community members of Cree & Ojibway ancestry. The Constance Lake First Nation Education Authority is supported by the Matawa Education Department in Thunder Bay, Ontario.
Ronnie Martin, President, Board of Diretors
Ron Wesley, Councillor (Education, Day care, Finance, & A
Ken Neegan, Administrator, Education
Veronica Ramadan, Manager, Finance
Lizzie Sutherland, Librarian & Secretary

***Cornwall:* Ahkwesahsne Mohawk Board of Education**
P.O. Box 819
169 International Rd. Cornwall, K6H 5T7 Canada
613-933-0409, Fax: 613-933-9262,
www.akwesasne.ca
Grades: Pre-Kindergarten-8; Alternative Ed.
The Ahkwesahsne Mohawk Board of Education operates three elementary schools. Since the Ahkwesahsne Mohawk Board of Education does not have a secondary school, there is an agreement with the Upper Canada Public School Board to provide secondary education.
Barry M. Montour, Director, Education, 613-933-0409
bmontour@akwesasne.ca
Deborah Terrance, Associate Director
Lillian Macias, Coordinator, Curriculum, 613-933-3366
Val Mitchell, Coordinator, Alternative Education Program, 613-575-1969
Sandra Rourke, Coordinator, Student Services
Norma Sunday, Coordinator, Post Secondary Program
Alice King, Supervisor, Head Start Program
Dwayne Thomas, Supervisor, Transportation
Gerald Thompson, Supervisor, Operation & Maintenance
Anneke Fischer-Fey, Psychometrist, 613-932-3366

***Deer Lake:* Deer Lake Education Authority**
P.O. Box 69
Deer Lake, P0V 1N0
807-775-2055, Fax: 807-751-9225,
TDD: 1-888-751-9225
www.deerlake.firstnation.ca
Grades: K4 - K5; 1 - 9; Special Education
Number of Schools: 1 (Deer Lake School). The Deer Lake Education Authority oversees education for the Deer Lake First Nation, an Oji-Cree community situated about 180 kilometres north of Red Lake, Ontario. Deer Lake School provides education to grade nine. The Authority coordinates the enrollment & boarding for students who leave the reserve for schooling beyond ninth grade, in places such as Ear Falls, Sioux Lookout, Red Lake, Thunder Bay, & Winnipeg.
Leonard Mamakeesic, Director, Education

***Dinorwic:* Wabigoon Lake Ojibway Nation Education Authority**
P.O. Box 24
Site 112 Dinorwic, P0V 1P0 Canada
807-938-6684, Fax: 807-938-1166
Grades: Junior Kindergarten - 8
Number of Schools: 1 (Wabsnki-Penasi School). Elementary education is provided in a school operated by the Wabigoon Lake Ojibway Nation. Secondary school students are bused to nearby Dryden, Ontario.

***Eabamet Lake:* Eabametoong (Fort Hope) First Nation Education Authority**
P.O. Box 294
Eabamet Lake, P0T 1L0 Canada
807-242-1305, Fax: 807-242-1313,
Education Coordinator, Phone: 807-242-1305, ext. 24
efnea64@gmail.com
www.eabametoong.firstnation.ca
Grades: Kindergarten - 10; Special Ed.
Enrollment: 380
Number of Schools: 1 (John C. Yesno Education Centre). Number of Employees: 25 teachers; 10 teaching assistants & tutor escorts; 3 counsellors. Eabametoong (Fort Hope) is a fly-in Ojibwe First Nations community located approximately 360 kilometres northeast of Thunder Bay, Ontario. The Eabametoong (Fort Hope) First Nation Education Authority consists of a Board of Directors & a head office staff. The Matawa Education Department in Thunder, Bay, Ontario supports the education authority.
Sharon Allan, Education Coordinator, Eabametoong First Nati
sharon-nate@hotmail.com

***Eagle River:* Migisi Sah Gai Gun Education Authority**
P.O. Box 10
Eagle River, P0V 1S0 Canada
807-755-5350, Fax: 807-755-5696
Grades: Elem.
Enrollment: 44
Leonard Gardner, Dir.

***Fort Albany:* Mundo Peetabeck Education Authority**
P.O. Box 31
Fort Albany, P0L 1H0 Canada
705-278-3390, Fax: 705-278-1049,
www.onlink.net/~stannes/staff/
Grades: Elem.
Enrollment: 150
Daniel Metatawabin, Administrator

***Fort Severn:* Wasaho Education Authority**
General Delivery Fort Severn, P0V 1W0 Canada
807-478-9548, Fax: 807-478-2573
Enrollment: 120
Number of Schools: 1. The Wasaho Education Authority provides education to members of the Fort Severn First Nation. The Fort Severn First Nation Reserve is situated in northern Ontario, near the mouth of the Severn River.

***Heron Bay:* Pic River First Nation Education Authority**
General Delivery Heron Bay, P0T 1R0 Canada
807-229-1749, Fax: 807-229-1944
Grades: Elem.
Enrollment: 94
Cindy Fisher, Dir.

***Kasabonika:* Sineonokway Education Authority**
P.O. Box 102
Kasabonika, P0V 1Y0 Canada
807-535-1117, Fax: 807-535-1152
Grades: Elem.
Enrollment: 250
Ida Morris, Chair
Josie Semple, Dir.

***Kashechewan:* Hishkoonikun Education Authority**
P.O. Box 235
Kashechewan, P0L 1S0 Canada
705-275-4538, Fax: 705-275-4515
Grades: Elem.
Enrollment: 500
Jonathan Solomon, Dir.
Elkina Hughie, Chair

***Keewaywin:* Keewaywin Education Authority**
General Delivery Keewaywin, P0V 3G0 Canada
807-771-1125, Fax: 807-774-1067
Enrollment: 78
Lorraine Kakegamic, Dir.

***Kejick:* Shoal Lake Chief & Council: Education Authority**
General Delivery Kejick, P0X 1E0 Canada
807-733-2315, Fax: 807-733-3115
Grades: Elem.
Enrollment: 50
Kelvin Redsky, Administrator

Kenora: Northwest Angle #33 Education Authority
P.O. Box 1490
Kenora, P9N 3X7 Canada
807-733-2200, Fax: 807-733-3148
Grades: Elem.
Enrollment: 16
Josephine Sandy, Education Counsellor

Kingfisher: Kingfisher Lake Education Authority
General Delivery Kingfisher, P0V 1Z0 Canada
807-532-2067, Fax: 807-532-2153
Grades: Elem.
Enrollment: 100
Solomon Mamakwa, Dir.

Lac Seul: Obishikokaang Education Authority
General Delivery Lac Seul, P0V 2A0 Canada
807-582-3420, Fax: 807-582-3430
Grades: Elem./Sec.
Enrollment: 97
Karen Ningewance, Chair
Richard Morris, Dir.

Longlac: Long Lake #58 & Ginoogaming First Nations Education Authority
P.O. Box 89
Longlac, P0T 2A0
807-876-4914
Grades: JK-12; Special Ed; Ojibway language
Enrollment: 173
Number of Schools: 2 (Migizsi Wazisin Elementary School & Nimiki Migizsi Secondary School). Number of Employees: 24 teachers, board administrative personnel, support staff, & custodial personnel. The Long Lake #58 & Ginoogaming First Nations Education Authority consists of three board members from Long Lake #58 First Nation & three board members from Ginoogaming First Nation (formerly the Long Lake #77 First Nation). Both First Nations are members of Matawa First Nations, so that educational support services for the Long Lake #58 & Ginoogaming First Nations Education Authority are provided by the Matawa Education Department in Thunder Bay, On
Claire Onabigon, Director, Education, 807-876-1270
conabigo@lakeheadu.ca
Fred Simoniatis, Principal

M'Chigeeng: West Bay Board of Education
P.O. Box 297
M'Chigeeng, P0P 1J0 Canada
705-377-5611, Fax: 705-377-5080
Grades: Elem.
Enrollment: 180
Melvina Corbiere, Education Coordinator

MacDiarmid: Rocky Bay First Nation Education Authority
71 Macdonald Ave. MacDiarmid, P0T 2B0 Canada
807-885-3401, Fax: 807-885-3266
Grades: Elem.
Enrollment: 41

Morson: Big Grassy River (Mishkosiimiiniiziibig) Education Authority
P.O. Box 453
Beach Rd. Morson, P0W 1J0 Canada
807-488-5916, Fax: 807-488-5345,
bgschool@bgfn.onca
www.bgfn.on.ca
Grades: Jr. Kindergarten - 8; Special Ed.
Enrollment: 61
Number of Schools: 1 (Pegamigaabo Elementary School)

Muncey: Chippewas of the Thames First Nation Board of Education
330 Chippewa Rd. Muncey, N0L 1Y0 Canada
519-289-0621, Fax: 519-289-0633,
www.chippewa-ed.on.ca
Grades: Elementary
Number of Schools: 1 elementary school (Antler River Elementary School)
Kristin Hendrick, Council Liaison
Joanne Henry, Coordinator, Eucation Administration
joann.henry@chippewa-ed.on.ca
Jody Joseph, Contact, Post-Secondary Program & Guidance, 519-289-0621, fax: 519-289-0633
postsecondary@chippewa-ed.on.ca
Starr McGahey-Albert, Contact, Education Finance
postsecondary@chippewa-ed.on.ca

Muskrat Dam: Muskrat Dam First Nation Education Authority
P.O. Box 140
Muskrat Dam, P0V 3B0 Canada
807-471-2524, Fax: 807-471-2649,
Whasa Distant Education Centre, Phone: 807-471-2619
Grades: Junior Kindergarten - 8
Number of Schools: 1 (Samson Beardy Memorial School). The Muskrat Dam First Nation community is situated approximately 370 kilometres north of Sioux Lookout. Oji-Cee & English are spoken. The community features an elementary school, plus the Wahsa Distance Education Centre to support secondary & post-secondary students attending schools in towns & cities.
Vernon Morris, Chief, Muskrat Dam First Nation

New Osnaburgh: Mishkeegogamang Education Authority
General Delivery New Osnaburgh, P0V 2H1 Canada
807-928-2137, Fax: 807-928-2077
Grades: Elem./Sec.; 3 schools
Enrollment: 255
Ida Mackuck, Education Coordinator
Isabe Skunk, Secretary

North Spirit Lake: North Spirit Lake Education Authority
General Delivery North Spirit Lake, P0V 2G0 Canada
807-776-0001, Fax: 807-776-0003
Grades: Elem.
Enrollment: 50
Luke Rae, Dir.

Ogoki Post: Marten Falls (Ogoki) First Nation Education Authority
Education Administration Office
General Delivery Ogoki Post, P0T 2L0 Canada
807-349-2628, Fax: 807-349-2511
Grades: Kindergarten - 8
Number of Schools: 1 (Henry Coaster Memorial School). The Marten Falls (Ogoki) First Nation Education Authority offers elementary education in the Cree-Ojibwe community. Members of the First Nation board in Thunder Bay, Ontario to attend secondary school. The Matawa Education Department provides educational support services to the Marten Falls (Ogoki) First Nation Education Authority.
Maria Baxter, Education Administrator, 807-349-2509, fax: 807-349-2602
maria.baxter@martenfallsfn.ca

Pawitik: Whitefish Bay: Northwest Angle Education Authority
General Delivery Pawitik, P0X 1L0 Canada
807-226-5710, Fax: 807-226-1066
Grades: Elem./Sec.
Enrollment: 300
Isobel White, Dir.

Peawanuck: Weenusk First Nation Education Services
P.O. Box 2
Peawanuck, P0L 2H0 Canada
705-473-2527, Fax: 705-473-2528
Grades: Elem.
Enrollment: 60
Abraham Hunter Sr., Chair
George Hunter, Dir.

Pikangikum: Pikangikum Education Authority
c/o Eenchokay Birchstick School
General Delivery Pikangikum, P0V 2L0 Canada
807-773-1093, Fax: 807-773-1014,
http://forcedata.net/pea/
Grades: Elem./Sec.
Enrollment: 750
Charlie Pascal, Dir.
George Suggashie, Chair

Rama: Mnjikaning First Nation Education Authority
#200, 5884 Rama Rd. Rama, L0K 1T0 Canada
705-325-3611, Fax: 705-327-7029
Enrollment: 126
Tracey Sharpe, Manager
Myrna Watson, Manager

Sandy Lake: Sandy Lake Board of Education
P.O. Box 8
Sandy Lake, P0V 1V0 Canada
807-774-1135, Fax: 807-774-1166,
www.sandylake.firstnation.ca
Grades: Kindergarten - 10; Adult Ed.
Enrollment: 514
Number of Schools: 3 (Thomas Fiddler Memorial Elementary School; Thomas Fiddler Memorial High School; Gabbius Goodman Memorial Adult Learning Centre). The Sandy Lake Board of Education oversees the management of schools which serve students of Sandy Lake First Nation.
Christina Meekis, Director, Education
Troy Kakepetum, Assistant Director, Education
Russell Kakepetum, Band Councillor, Education Portfolio
Florance Ballentyne, Officer, Finance

Sarnia: Aamjiwnaang First Nation Education Administration
978 Tashmoo Ave. Sarnia, N7T 7H5 Canada
519-336-8410, Fax: 519-336-0382,
www.aamjiwnaang.ca
Formerly Chippewas of Sarnia, the community of Aamjiwnaang First Nation is located in the city limits of Sarnia, Ontario.
Jodi Branton, Coordinator, Education Services, 519-336-0382 247
Diane Aiken, Assistant, Education Services, 519-336-0382 246

Sioux Lookout: Sioux Lookout Education Authority
P.O. Box 1118
Sioux Lookout, P8T 1B7 Canada
807-727-1488, Fax: 807-737-1732
Enrollment: 600
Dennis Nestrovich, Dir.

Sioux Lookout: Windigo Education Authority
P.O. Box 299
Sioux Lookout, P8T 1A3 Canada
807-737-1064, Fax: 807-737-3452,
wea@windigo.on.ca
www.windigoeducation.on.ca
Grades: JK-8; Aboriginal language & culture
Enrollment: 445
Number of Schools: 4 (Michikan Lake School; Titotay Memorial School; Martin McKay Memorial School; & Bimaychikamah School). Windigo Education Authority consists of the following First Nation members: Bearskin Lake First Nation, Cat Lake First Nation, Sachigo Lake First Nation, & Slate Falls Nation. The language of each First Nation community is Ojibway or Oji-Cree.
Lana Bighead, Education Coordinator, Bimaychikamah School, 807-737-5701, fax: 807-347-1299
James Chapman, Education Coordinator, Martin McKay Memorial, 807-595-2527, fax: 807-595-1119
Vince Ostberg, Education Coordinator, Michikan Lake School, 807-363-1011, fax: 807-363-2519
Marie Stewart, Education Coordinator, Titotay Memorial Schoo, 807-347-2102, fax: 807-347-2057

Sioux Narrows: Northwest Angle #37 Education Authority
P.O. Box 267
Sioux Narrows, P0X 1N0 Canada
807-733-3284, Fax: 807-226-1164

Southwold: Onyota'a:ka Kalthuny Nihtsla Tehatilihutakwas (OKT) Education Authority
RR#2 Southwold, N0L 2G0 Canada
519-652-1580, Fax: 519-652-3219
Grades: Elem.
Enrollment: 185
Neil Cornelius, Chair
Lynda Doxtator, Education Adm.

Thunder Bay: Matawa Education Department
c/o Matawa First Nations Management
233 South Court St. Thunder Bay, P7B 2X9 Canada
807-344-4575, Fax: 807-344-2977, 1-800-463-2249
learningcentre@matawa.on.ca
www.education.matawa.on.ca
Grades: JK - Secondary; Adult Education
Number of Schools: 9 (Johnny Therriault School, Aroland First Nation; Mamawmatawa Holistic Education Centre, Constance Lake First Nation; John C. Yesno Education Centre, Eabametoong First Nation; Nibinamik Education Centre, Nibinamik First Nation; Migizi Wazisin Elementary School, Long Lake #58 First Nation; Henry Coaster Memorial School, Marten Falls First Nation; Nimiki Migizi Secondary School, Ginoogaming First Nation; Neskantaga Education Centre, Neskantaga First Nation; & Simon Jacob Memorial Education Centre, Webequie First Nation). The Matawa Education Department delivers educational support services to local education authorities. Edu
Murray L. Wavoose, Manager, Education Department
mwaboose@matawa.on.ca
Georgette O'Nabigon, Coordinator, Post Secondary Program
gonabigon@matawa.on.ca
Steve Chase, Developer, E-Learning
schase@matawa.on.ca

Tyendinaga Mohawk Territory: Tyendinaga Mohawk Education, Culture, & Language Department
Administration Building
13 Old York Rd. Tyendinaga Mohawk Territory, K0K 1X0 Canada
613-396-3424, Fax: 613-396-3627
Educational programs available for the Mohawks of the Bay of Quinte include the Eksa'okon:'a Child Care Centre, the

Tahatikonhsotontie Head Start Program, a Post-Secondary Education Program, a Native Student Liaison Program, an Employment & Training Program, the Ka:nhiote Public Library, & Mohawk Bus Lines. Mohawk language & cultural instruction is part of Tahatikonhsotontie Head Start, an early childhood education program.
Tracey Gazley, Manager, Tahatikonhsotontie Head Start Progra, 613-396-6716
traceyg@mbq-tmt.org
Cheryl Lavigne, Manager, Day Care (Eksa'okon:'a Child Care Ce, 613-967-4401
daycare@tyendinaga.net
Bruce Maracle, Manager, Mohawk Bus Lines, 613-396-2000
Karen Lewis, Librarian, Ka:nhiote Public Library, 613-967-6264
karenl@tyendinaga.net
Patti Brinklow, Coordinator, Post-Secondary Education, 613-396-3424 119
pattig@mbq-tmt.org
Betty Maracle, Teacher, Culture, 613-396-6716
bettym@mbq-tmt.org
Melissa Maracle, Teacher, Mohawk Language
Sandra Sero, Counsellor, Employment & Training Program, 613-968-1122 141
sandys@mbq-tmt.org

Wallaceburg: Walpole Island Elementary School
RR#3 Wallaceburg, N8A 4K9 Canada
519-627-0712, Fax: 519-627-8596
Grades: Junior Kindergarten - 8
The Walpole Island Elementary School is a First Nation operated school which serves members of the Walpole Island First Nation community. School employees are required to have knowledge & understanding of the Anishinaabeg culture. The education program is administered by the Walpole Island First Nation Board of Education. For secondary education, students from Walpole Island First Nation are transported to the nearby communities of Sarnia, Chatham, & Wallaceburg.

Wallaceburg: Walpole Island First Nation Board of Education
RR#3 Wallaceburg, N8A 4K9
519-627-1481, Fax: 519-627-0440
Grades: Junior Kindergarten - 8
Number of Schools: 1 (Walpole Island Elementary School). Secondary school students from the Walpole Island First Nation community are transported to Chatham, Sarnia, & Wallaceburg to attend school.
Joseph Gilbert, Chief
Bill Tooshkenig, Chair
Cynthia Williams, Officer, Human Resources
cynthia.williams@wifn.org

Weagamow Lake: North Caribou Lake First Nation Education Office
P.O. Box 155
Weagamow Lake, P0V 2Y0 Canada
807-469-1222, Fax: 807-469-1351
Grades: Elem.
Enrollment: 136
Saul Williams, Dir.

Webequie: Webequie First Nation Education Authority
P.O. Box 102
Webequie, P0T 3A0
807-353-9942, Fax: 807-353-9966,
webequieeducation@knet.ca
info@webequie.ca
Grades: K-10; Native Language; Special Ed.
Enrollment: 200
Number of Schools: 1 (Simon Jacob Memorial Education Centre). The Webequie First Nation Education Authority is located in a Oji-Cree community on the Winisk River in northern Ontario. The education authority receives educational support services from the Matawa Education Department in Thunder Bay, Ontario. Programs include special education, native education, distance education, & post-secondary education support services.
Ennis Jacob, Director, Education
ennisjacob@hotmail.com
Paul Quisses, Administrator, Finance

Whitedog: Wabaseemoong Education Authority
General Delivery Whitedog, P0X 1P0 Canada
807-927-2062, Fax: 807-927-2176
Grades: JK - 12; Cultural activities
Enrollment: 300
Number of Schools: 1 (Wabaseemoong School). The Wabaseemoong Education Authority oversees education in the Wabaseemoong First Nation community located approximately 100 kilometres northwest of Kenora, Ontario.

Wiarton: Chippewas of Nawash Unceded First Nation Board of Education
6 Harbour Rd., RR#5, Cape Croker Reserve Wiarton, N0H 2T0 Canada
519-534-0882, Fax: 519-534-5138,
cnbdofed@bmts.com
www.nawash.ca
Number of Schools: 1. The board of education serves the Chippewas of Nawash Unceded First Nation band members of the Neyaashiinigmiing Indian Reserve No. 27. The reserve is situated on the eastern shore of the Saugeen (Bruce) Peninsula in Ontario, approximately 26 kilometres from Wiarton. The Chippewas of Nawash Unceded First Nation Board of Education strives to offer a culturally & community based education, based upon traditional values.
Pamela J. Keeshig, Chair & Curriculum & Program Development Port
Judy Nadjiwan, Education Administrator, 519-534-0882
nawashed.administrator@gbtel.ca
Jennifer Linklater, Coordinator, Nawash Post-Secondary Education
nawashed.postsec@gbtel.ca
Lisa Pedoniquotte, Education Counsellor, Secondary Student Servi
nawashed.edcounsellor@gbtel.ca
Vanessa M. Keeshig, Contact, Administrative Support
nawashed.vkeeshig@gbtel.ca

Wikwemikong: Wikwemikong Board of Education
P.O. Box 112
34 Henry St Wikwemikong, P0P 2J0 Canada
705-859-3864, Fax: 705-859-3787,
speltier@wiky.net
Grades: Elem./Sec.; 3 schools
Enrollment: 486
Margaret Manitowabi, Chair
Sara Peltier, Dir.

Wunnummin Lake: Wunnumin Lake Education Authority
P.O. Box 105
Wunnummin Lake, P0V 2Z0 Canada
807-442-2559, Fax: 807-442-2627
Grades: Elem.
Enrollment: 146
Samuel Mamokwa, Chair
Matthew Angees, Dir.

Schools: Specialized

First Nations

Neskantaga First Nation Education Centre
P.O. Box 106
Lansdowne House , P0T 1Z0
807-479-1170, Fax: 807-479-1178,
www.education.matawa.on.ca
Grades: JK - 9; Native culture & language
The Neskantaga First Nation Education Centre is situated in a community approximately 180 kilometres north of Pickle Lake in northern Ontario. The elementary school is a Matawa First Nations community school which receives educational support services from the Matawa Education Department.
Tony Sakanee, Member, Matawa Regional Committee on Educatio
tonysakanee@hotmail.com

Aroland: Johnny Therriault Memorial School
c/o Aroland First Nation
General Delivery Aroland, P0T 1B0
807-329-5470, Fax: 807-329-5472,
www.education.matawa.on.ca
Grades: Junior Kindergarten - 9
Enrollment: 120
The Johnny Therriault School serves the Aroland First Nation School, which is located approximately 350 kilometres northeast of Thunder Bay, Ontario. The school is supported by the Matawa Education Department. Tuition agreements are in place with the Superior-Greenstone District School Board, so that Aroland First Nation students can attend grades 10 to 12 in the communities of Nakina & Geraldton.
Sam Kashkeesh, Chief, Aroland First Nation
Patricia Magiskan, Member, Matawa Regional Committee on Educatio
Stephanie Ash, Communications Officer, Aroland First Nation, 807-767-4443

Attawapiskat: J.R. Nakogee Elementary School
P.O. Box 15
Attawapiskat, P0L 1A0
705-997-2114, Fax: 705-997-1259,
www.afnea.com
Grades: Junior Kindergarten - 8; Special Ed
J.R. Nakogee Elementary School is located in the Ontario Cree fly-in only community of Attawapiskat. It is part of the Attawapiskat First Nation Education Authority.

Attawapiskat: Vezina Secondary School
P.O. Box 219
Attawapiskat, P0L 1A0
705-997-2117, Fax: 705-997-2357,
www.afnea.com
Grades: 9 - 12
Attawapiskat First Nation Education Authority operates the high school on the west coast of James Bay.

Bearskin Lake: Michikan Lake School
General Delivery Bearskin Lake, P0V 1E0
www.windigoeducation.on.ca
Grades: JK-8; Aboriginal language & culture
Enrollment: 140
Operations of the Michikan Lake School are overseen by the Windigo Education Authority. The school provides elementary education to young people of the Bearskin Lake First Nation. The First Nation community is located about 425 kilometres north of Sioux Lookout, Ontario.
Nona Sinclair, Principal, 807-363-2570, fax: 807-363-1078

Big Trout Lake: Aglace Chapman Education Centre
P.O. Box 168
Big Trout Lake, P0V 1G0 Canada
807-537-2264, Fax: 807-537-1067,
kifirstnation@knet.ca
www.aglacechapmaneducationcentre.myknet.org
Grades: Junior Kindergarten-11; Special Ed.
Enrollment: 275
The Kitchenuhmaykoosib Education Authority oversees operations of the Aglace Chapman Education Centre. The centre is located about 270 air miles north of Sioux Lookout, Ontario, where it provides education to the Kitchenuhmaykoosib Inninnuwug First Nation.

Brantford: Six Nations of the Grand River
Indian & Northern Affairs
P.O. Box 1960
Brantford, N3T 5W5 Canada
519-758-2405, Fax: 519-754-0639
Grades: Elem.; 5 schools
Enrollment: 1328
Kathy Knott

Cat Lake: Titotay Memorial School
P.O. Box 80
Cat Lake, P0V 1J0
807-347-2102, Fax: 807-347-2057,
www.titotayschool.myknet.org; www.windigoeducation.on.ca
Grades: JK-8; Aboriginal language & culture
Enrollment: 135
The Titotay Memorial School is one of four schools within the Windigo Education Authority. The First Nation School provides elementary education to members of the Cat Lake First Nation. The school is situated about 180 kilometres north of Sioux Lookout, Ontario.
Ruby Keesiquayash, Principal, 807-347-2102, fax: 807-347-2057

Christian Island: Christian Island Elementary School
67 Kate Kegwin St. Christian Island, L0K 1C0
705-247-2011,
l.monague@beausoleil-education.ca
ASSISTANT)
WWW.BEAUSOLEIL-EDUCATION.CA
Grades: Junior Kindergarten - 8; Special Ed
Under the Beausoleil First Nation Education Authority, the Christian Island Elementary School provides education to the Chippewas of the Beausoleil First Nation.
Mike Lucas, Principal
m.lucas@beausoleil-education.ca
Sylvia Norton-Sutherland, Native Student Advisor

Constance Lake: Mamawmatawa Holistic Education Center
P.O. Box 4000
Constance Lake, P0L 1B0
705-463-1199, Fax: 705-463-2077,
www.clfn.on.ca
Grades: Daycare - JK - 12; Adult Education
Enrollment: 257
The Mamawmatawa Holistic Education Center educates members of the Constance Lake First Nation, who live west of Hearst, Ontario. The school operates under the direction of the Constance Lake First Nation Education Authority.
Zandra Bear-Lowen, Principal
Karen Wesley, Administrator, Daycare
Pamela Dalcourt, Teacher, Literacy Resources

Judy Hewitt, Teacher, Special Education
Florrie Sutherland, Teacher, Native Language
Vivian Bird, Counsellor, Attendance & Guidance
Linda Chum, Counsellor, Child & Youth
Leo Grezla, Counsellor, Guidance
Susan Sutherland, Contact, Adult Education, ILC, & Co-op

Deer Lake: Deer Lake School
P.O. Box 69
Deer Lake, P0V 1N0 Canada
807-775-2055, Fax: 807-775-2148, 1-888-751-9225
www.dls.firstnationschools.ca
Grades: K4 - K5; 1 - 9; Special Education
The Deer Lake School also offers native language instruction.
Leonard Mamakeesic, Director, Education
Elizabeth Rae, Finance Officer
Loretta Cameron, Teacher, Special Education
Victoria Meekis, Senior Instructor, Native Language

Dinorwic: Wabsnki-Penasi School
P.O. Box 24
Site 112 Dinorwic, P0V 1P0
807-938-6684, Fax: 807-938-1166
Grades: Junior Kindergarten - 8
The First Nation elementary school is part of the Wabigoon Lake Ojibway Nation Education Authority. For secondary school education, students are transported thirty kilometres west to Dryden, Ontario.

Fort Hope: John C. Yesno Education Centre
P.O. Box 297
Fort Hope, P0T 1L0 Canada
807-242-8421, Fax: 807-242-1592
Grades: Kindergarten - 10; Special Ed.
Enrollment: 380
The John C. Yesno Education Centre serves the Eabametoong First Nation. The Ojibwe First Nations community is located on the north shore of northern Ontario's Eabamet Lake. Eabametoong First Nation students, continuing their education beyond tenth grade, attend schools in Thunder Bay, Sault Ste. Marie, & Sioux Lookout.

Fort Severn: Wasaho First Nations School
P.O. Box 165
Fort Severn, P0V 1W0
807-478-9548, Fax: 807-478-2573
Enrollment: 120
The Wasaho First Nations School is part of the Wasaho Education Authority. The school serves members of the Fort Severn First Nation in northern Ontario.

Longlac: Migizi Wazisin Elementary School
P.O. Box 240
Martin Rd. Longlac, P0T 2A0
807-876-4482, Fax: 807-876-4128,
www.education.matawa.on.ca
Grades: JK - 7; Special Ed; Native language
The Migizi Wazisin Elementary School is located in Long Lake #58 First Nation, an Anishinaabe (Ojibway) First Nation near Geraldton, Ontario. It serves students from both the Long Lake #58 First Nation & the Ginoogaming First Nation. Operations of the elementary school are administered by the Long Lake #58 & Ginoogaming First Nations Education Authority.

Longlac: Nimiki Migizi Secondary School
P.O. Box 360
100 Balsam St. Longlac, P0T 2A0
807-876-1270, Fax: 807-876-4151,
www.education.matawa.on.ca; www.ginoogaming.ca
Grades: 8 - 12; Ojibway language
The Nimiki Migizi Secondary School is located in the Ginoogaming First Nation, which is an Anishnawbe (Ojibway) First Nation near Geraldton, Ontario. The high school serves students from both the Ginoogaming First Nation & Long Lake #58 First Nation. Nimiki Migizi Secondary School operates with support from the Long Lake #58 & Ginoogaming First Nations Education Authority.

Muskrat Dam: Samson Beardy Memorial School
P.O. Box 43
Muskrat Dam, P0V 3B0
807-471-2524, Fax: 807-471-2649
Grades: Junior Kindergarten - 8
The Samson Beardy Memorial School is a First Nation operated school administered by the Muskrat Dam First Nation Education Authority. Secondary & post-secondary students attend schools outside the remote First Nation community.

Nordegg: Ta Otha Community School
P.O. Box 39
Nordegg, T0M 2H0
403-721-3989, Fax: 403-721-2174,
www.stoney-nation.com
The Ta Otha School is part of the Stoney Education Authority. The school serves members of the Stoney Nakoda First Nation.

Ogoki Post: Henry Coaster Memorial School
General Delivery Ogoki Post, P0T 2L0
807-349-2509, Fax: 807-349-2511,
maria.baxter@martenfallsfn.ca (Education Administrator)
www.education.matawa.on.ca
Grades: Junior Kindergarten - 8
Enrollment: 90
Henry Coaster Memorial School is located in Marten Falls Nation, on the north side of the Albany River in northern Ontario. The First Nation school offers traditional culture & language programming. The elementary school operates with support from the Marten Falls (Ogoki) First Nation Education Authority.

Sachigo Lake: Martin McKay Memorial School
General Delivery Sachigo Lake, P0V 2P0 Canada
www.windigoeducation.on.ca
Grades: JK-8; Aboriginal language & culture
Enrollment: 115
The Martin McKay Memorial School serves students of the Sachigo Lake First Nation. The First Nation community is situated approximately 150 kilometres west of Big Trout Lake, Ontario. Activities of the Sachigo Lake First Nation school are administered by the Windigo Education Authority.
Doug St. Laurent, Principal, 807-595-2526, fax: 807-595-1305

Sarnia: Aamjiwnaang Junior Kindergarten (Aamjiwnaang Binoojiinyag Kino Maagewgamgoon
1900 Virgil Ave. Sarnia, N7T 8A7
519-344-4132, Fax: 519-344-6956
Grades: Junior Kindergarten
Under the Aamjiwnaang First Nation Education Administration, education is offered to members of the Aamjiwnaang First Nation.
Kim Henry, Principal
Muriel Joseph-Plain, Supervisor, 519-344-5831

Slate Falls: Bimaychikamah School
General Delivery Slate Falls, P0V 3C0
Grades: JK-8; Aboriginal language & culture
Enrollment: 55
Education for members of the Slate Falls Nation is provided by the Bimaychikamah School. The elementary school is situated in the Slate Falls Nation community north of Sioux Lookout, Ontario. Operations of Bimaychikamah School are overseen by the Windigo Education Authority.
Mary Anne Ketchemonia, Principal, 807-737-5701, fax: 807-347-1299

Summer Beaver: Nibinamik First Nation Education Centre
General Delivery Summer Beaver, P0T 3B0
807-593-2195, Fax: 807-593-2198,
www.education.matawa.on.ca
Grades: JK - 10; Native Language
The Nibinamik First Nation Education Centre is a Matawa First Nations community school which receives educational support services from the Matawa Education Department. The Nibinamik First Nation is located approximately 185 kilometres northwest of Pickle Lake in northern Ontario.

Whitedog: Wabaseenmoong School
General Delivery Whitedog, P0X 1P0 Canada
807-927-2062, Fax: 807-927-2176
Grades: JK - 12; Alternative Education
Enrollment: 300
Elementary & secondary education is provided to Wabaseemoong First Nation students living in a community situated about 100 kilometres northwest of Kenora, Ontario. The school focuses upon academics as well as cultural education. School activities are overseen by the Wabaseemoong Education Authority.
Ron R. McDonald, Principal, 807-927-2000 264

Wiarton: Cape Croker Elementary School
17 School Rd., RR#5 Wiarton, N0H 2T0
519-534-0719, Fax: 519-534-1592,
ccfnes@bmts.com
www.nawash.ca
Grades: Pre-Kindergarten - 8
Part of the Chippewas of Nawash Unceded First Nation Board of Education, the Cape Croker Elementary School provides a culturally-based education, which includes the history of the Anishnabek, band sovereignty, & communication & language arts in Anishinaabemowin & English.
Judy Nadjiwan, Education Administrator, Board of Education, 519-534-0882
nawashed.administrator@gbtel.ca
Debra Chegahno, Prinicpal, Cape Croker Elementary School, 519-534-0719, fax: 519-534-1592
nawashed.principal@gbtel.ca
Juanita Pheasant, Ojibway Language Resource Teacher

Hearing Impaired

Belleville: The Sir James Whitney School
350 Dundas St. West Belleville, K8P 1B2 Canada
613-967-2823, Fax: 613-967-2841
Lauraine Milligan

Brantford: The W. Ross Macdonald School
350 Brant Ave. Brantford, N3T 3J9 Canada
519-759-0730, Fax: 519-759-4741
Donald Neale

London: The Robarts School
P.O. Box 7300 E
1090 Highbury Ave. London, N5Y 4V9 Canada
519-453-4400, Fax: 519-453-4193
Paul Cowley

Milton: The Ernest C. Drury School
255 Ontario St. Milton, L9T 2N5 Canada
905-878-2851, Fax: 905-878-9261
Nancy Syer

Special Education

Belleville: Sir James Whitney/Sagonaska School
350 Dundas St. West Belleville, K8P 1B2 Canada
613-967-2830, Fax: 613-967-2482
Lindi Pierce, Principal

London: The Amethyst School
P.O. Box 7300
1090 Highbury Ave. London, N5Y 4V9 Canada
519-453-4400, Fax: 519-453-2160
Clive Hodder, Principal

Milton: E.C. Drury/Trillium Demonstration School Elementary
347 Ontario St. South Milton, L9T 3X9 Canada
905-878-2851, Fax: 905-878-4278

Ottawa: Centre Jules-Léger
281, av Lanark Ottawa, K1Z 6R8 Canada
613-761-9300, Fax: 613-761-9301,
ATS: 613-761-9302
www.centrejulesleger.com
Services aux enfants (et leurs familles) en difficultés d'apprentissage, avec ou sans déficit d'attention/hyperactivité, qui sont sourds ou malentendant, qui sont aveugles ou en basse vision, ou qui sont sourds et aveugles.
Lillian Patry, Surintendante

Schools: Independent & Private

Catholic

Richmond Hill: Holy Trinity School
c/o The Head of School
11300 Bayview Ave. Richmond Hill, L4S 1L4 Canada
905-737-1114, Fax: 905-737-5187, 866-727-7580
Grades: Elem./Sec.
Enrollment: 694
George Rutherford, Head of School

First Nations

Pikangikum: Eenchokay Birchstick School
General Delivery Pikangikum, P0V 2L0 Canada
807-773-5561, Fax: 807-773-5958
Grades: K./Elem./Sec.
Enrollment: 166
Serving students of the Pikangikum First Nation.
Jonah Strang, Chief, Pikangikum First Nation, 807-773-5578

Special Education

Richmond Hill: Academy for Gifted Children
12 Bond Cres. Richmond Hill, L4E 3K2 Canada
905-773-0997, Fax: 905-773-4722,
www.pace.on.ca
Grades: Elem./Sec.
Enrollment: 284
P.A.C.E. - Programming for Academic & Creative Excellence. A non-denominational, co-ed, private day school, with programmes focussing on basic skills, with a strong emphasis on math & science, accelerated learning & individual instruction.
Barbara Rosenberg, Founder & Principal

Independent & Private Schools

***Ajax:* Faithway Baptist Church School**
1964 Salem Rd. Ajax, L1T 4V3 Canada
905-686-0951, Fax: 905-686-1450
Grades: K./Elem./Sec.
Enrollment: 65
L. Homan

***Ajax:* Montessori Learning Centre of Ajax**
250 Bayly St. West Ajax, L1S 3V4 Canada
905-428-3122,
www.montessorilearningcentreofajax.ca
Grades: Preschool / Elementary
Montessori Learning Centre of Ajax offers a toddler program for children from 18 months to 3 years, as well as a Casa program for 3 to 6 year old children. Elementary education is provided for children from age 6 to 12.
Camilla Graziani, Principal

***Ajax:* Pickering Christian School**
162 Rossland Rd. East Ajax, L1T 4V2 Canada
905-427-3120, Fax: 905-427-0211,
office@pickeringcs.on.ca
www.pickeringcs.on.ca
Grades: Elem.
Enrollment: 219
Dr. Paul Douglas Ogborne, Principal

***Alliston:* Alliston Community Christian School**
4428 Adjala-Tecumseth Townline, RR#4 Alliston, L9R 1V4 Canada
705-434-2227, Fax: 705-435-0126,
info@allistonchristianschool.com
www.allistonccs.ca
Grades: K./Elem.
Enrollment: 113
Cathy Lubbers, Principal

***Ancaster:* Hamilton District Christian High School**
92 Glancaster Rd., RR#1 Ancaster, L9G 3K9 Canada
905-648-6655, Fax: 905-648-3139,
www.hdch.org
info@hdch.org
Grades: Sec.
Enrollment: 600
George VanKampen, Principal
gvankampen@hdch.org

***Aurora:* Aurora Montessori School & Private School**
330 Industrial Pkwy. North Aurora, L4G 4C3 Canada
905-841-0065, Fax: 905-841-2022,
info@auroramontessori.com;
admissions@auroramontessori.com
www.auroramontessori.com
Grades: 1-8
Aurora Montessori School & Private School also offers a toddler program for children from ages 18 months to 3 years. Casa programs are for children from ages 2.5 to 6 years.
Brenda Glashan, Principal

***Aurora:* Foundations Private School**
81 Industrial Pkwy North Aurora, L4G 4C4 Canada
905-713-1141
Grades: Elem.
Enrollment: 159
Ellen Powers

***Aurora:* St. Andrew's College**
15800 Yonge St. North Aurora, L4G 3H7 Canada
905-727-3178, Fax: 905-841-6911,
info@sac.on.ca
www.sac.on.ca
Grades: 6-12
Enrollment: 560
All-boys boarding and day school
Kevin McHenry, Headmaster

***Aylmer:* Immanuel Christian School Society**
75 Caverly Rd. Aylmer, N5H 2P6 Canada
519-773-8476, Fax: 519-773-8315
Grades: K./Elem.
Enrollment: 152
Marianne Vangoor

***Aylmer:* Mount Salem Christian School / MSCS**
c/o Evangelical Mennonite Church
6576 Springfield Rd., RR#6 Aylmer, N5H 2R5 Canada
519-765-3555, Fax: 519-765-3879,
mscsch@amtelecom.net
www.mountsalemchristianschool.ca
Grades: Junior Kindergarten - 12
Mount Salem Christian School is an interdenominational school, using a BEKA curriculum.
Judy Wiebe, Principal

***Aylmer:* Old Colony Christian School**
P.O. Box 127
Aylmer, N5H 2R8 Canada
519-765-1138
Grades: Elem./Sec.
Enrollment: 288
Anna Ens

***Bancroft:* Bancroft Christian Academy**
P.O. Box 657
160 South Baptiste Lake Rd. Bancroft, K0L 1C0 Canada
613-332-3670
Grades: Elementary / Secondary

***Barrie:* Heritage Christian Academy**
79 Ardagh Rd. Barrie, L4N 9B6 Canada
705-733-0112, Fax: 705-733-2054
Grades: JK.-12
Enrollment: 75
Pastor Brett Pennell, Principal

***Barrie:* Timothy Christian School**
750 Essa Rd. Barrie, L4N 9E9 Canada
705-726-6621, Fax: 705-726-8571,
tcsgen@timothychristianschool.ca
www.timothychristianschool.ca
Grades: Junior Kindergarten - 8
Timothy Christian School is an interdenominational school.
Kevin Eisses, Chair
Andrew Straatsma, Principal
Brenda Goodnough, Vice Principal
Ina VanHouten, Director, Development

***Beamsville:* Great Lakes Christian College**
4875 King St. Beamsville, L0R 1B0 Canada
905-563-5374, Fax: 905-563-0818,
www.glchs.on.ca
Grades: Sec.
Enrollment: 130
Don Rose, President
drose@glchs.on.ca

***Belleville:* Albert College**
160 Dundas St. West Belleville, K8P 1A6 Canada
613-968-5726, Fax: 613-968-9651,
info@albertcollege.ca
www.albertc.on.ca
Grades: Elem./Sec.
Enrollment: 298
Heather Kidd, Director of Admission
hkidd@albertc.on.ca

***Belleville:* Belleville District Christian School / BCS**
18 Christian School Rd., RR#5 Belleville, K8N 4Z5 Canada
613-962-7849, Fax: 613-962-6440,
bellevillechristianschool@yahoo.com
www.bellevillechristianschool.ca
Grades: Junior Kindergarten - 8
Jennifer Richmond, Principal

***Belleville:* Quinte Christian High School / QCHS**
138 Wallbridge-Loyalist Rd. Belleville, K8N 4Z2 Canada
613-968-7870, Fax: 613-968-7970,
admin@qchs.ca; finance@qchs.ca
www.qchs.ca
Grades: Secondary
Johan Cooke, Principal

***Bethany:* The Bethany Hills School**
P.O. Box 10
727 Bethany Hills Rd. Bethany, L0A 1A0 Canada
705-277-2866, Fax: 705-277-2455,
info1@bethanyhills.on.ca
www.bethanyhills.on.ca
Grades: Jr. K.-12
Enrollment: 80
Co-educational day school for all grades and girls-only boarding school for grades 7-12
Andrew Wallace

***Bloomingdale:* Koinonia Christian Academy**
850 Sawmill Rd. Bloomingdale, N0B 1K0 Canada
519-744-7447, Fax: 519-744-6745
Enrollment: 157
David J. Champion

***Bolton:* Countryside Montessori Private School**
1 Loring Dr. Bolton, L7E 1Y1 Canada
905-951-3359, Fax: 905-951-3920
Enrollment: 257
Rose Sampogna

***Bowmanville:* Durham Christian High School**
340 Scugog St. Bowmanville, L1C 3K2 Canada
905-623-5940, Fax: 905-623-6258
Grades: Sec.
Enrollment: 164
Fred Spoelstra

***Bowmanville:* Knox Christian School**
410 Scugog St., RR#1 Bowmanville, L1C 3K2 Canada
905-623-5871, Fax: 905-623-8877
Grades: K./Elem.
Enrollment: 339
George Petrusma

***Brampton:* Brampton-Georgetown Montessori School / BGMS**
1030 Queen St. West Brampton, L6X 0B2 Canada
905-457-2496,
info@bgmschool.com
www.bgmschool.com
Grades: Casa / Elementary
Brampton-Georgetown Montessori School provides programs for children from ages 2.5 to 11.

***Brampton:* Canada Christian Academy**
22 Abbey Rd. Brampton, L6W 2T8 Canada
905-789-5841, Fax: 905-789-0645,
www.canadachristianacademy.com
Grades: Junior Kindergarten - 12
Enrollment: 100

***Brampton:* John Knox Christian School**
82 McLaughlin Rd. South Brampton, L6Y 2C7 Canada
905-451-3236, Fax: 905-451-3448
Grades: K./Elem.
Enrollment: 336
Ed Boelens

***Brampton:* Rowntree Montessori School**
3 Sunforest Dr. Brampton, L6Z 2Z2 Canada
905-790-3838, Fax: 905-790-5686,
www.rowntreemontessori.com
Dr. Yamil H. Alonso

***Brampton:* Tall Pines School**
8525 Torbram Rd. Brampton, L6T 5K4 Canada
905-458-6770, Fax: 905-458-7967,
info@tallpinesschool.com
www.tallpinesschool.com
Grades: Elem.
Enrollment: 519
Private Montessori and Progressive school
Elaine Flett, Principal

***Brantford:* Braemar House School**
36 Baxter St. Brantford, N3R 2V8 Canada
519-753-2929, Fax: 519-753-1235,
admin@braemarhouseschool.ca
www.braemarhouseschool.ca
Grades: Junior Kindergarten - 8
Enrollment: 92
Braemar House School also offers a Montessori Casa program.
Annette Minutillo, Executive Director

***Brantford:* Brantford Christian Collegiate**
North Park Plaza
P.O. Box 28116
452 Grey St. Brantford, N3R 7X5 Canada
519-753-4900,
information@brantfordchristiancollegiate.org
www.brantfordchristiancollegiate.org
Grades: 9 - 12
Jeff Gillmore, Principal
Rev. Ron Humphries, Faculty Member

***Brantford:* Brantford Christian School / BCS**
7 Calvin St. Brantford, N3S 3E4 Canada
519-752-0433, Fax: 519-752-6088,
www.bcsbrantford.ca
Grades: Junior Kindergarten - 8
Walter Hartholt, Principal
whartholt@bcsbrantford.ca
Heather Murray, Vice Principal
hmurray@bcsbrantford.ca
Audrey Reitsma, Vice Principal
areitsma@bcsbrantford.ca

***Brantford:* Central Baptist Academy / CBA**
300 Fairview Dr. Brantford, N3R 2X6 Canada
519-754-4806, Fax: 519-754-4201,
cbaoffice@centralbaptistbrantford.com
www.centralbaptistbrantford.com
Grades: Junior Kindergarten - 8
Rev. Minne Bouma, Principal

Brantford: Montessori House of Children
85 Charlotte St. Brantford, N3T 2X2 Canada
519-759-7290, Fax: 519-759-6774,
admissions@montessorihouseofchildren.com (Admission inquiries)
mails@montessorihouseofchildren.com
www.montessorihouseofchildren.com
Brantford's Montessori House of Children provides programs for children from 2.5 to 9 years of age.
Nahida Hamam, Principal

Breslau: St. John's-Kilmarnock School
P.O. Box 179
2201 Shantz Station Rd. Breslau, N0B 1M0 Canada
519-648-2183, Fax: 519-648-2186,
info@sjkschool.org
www.sjkschool.org
Grades: Jr. K.-12
Enrollment: 505
Ian Hornsby

Breslau: Woodland Christian High School
1058 Spitzig Rd. R.R.# 1 Breslau, N0B 1M0 Canada
519-648-2114, Fax: 519-648-3402,
office@woodland.on.ca
www.woodland.on.ca
Grades: Sec.
Enrollment: 194
Gary VanArragon

Brockville: Grenville Christian College
P.O. Box 610
Brockville, K6V 5V8 Canada
613-345-5521, Fax: 613-345-3826
Grades: K./Elem./Sec.
Enrollment: 301
Rev. Gordon G. Mintz, Head Master

Burlington: Burlington Christian Academy / BCA
521 North Service Rd. West Burlington, L7P 5C3 Canada
905-639-7364, Fax: 905-639-1657,
info@burlingtonchristian.net
www.burlingtonchristian.net
Grades: Junior Kindergarten - 8
Enrollment: 130
Gord McNeice, Principal
Heather Crossing, Vice Principal (Part-time)
Jessica Purdy, Vice Principal (Part-time)
Jann Schlett, Coordinator, Advancement & Recruitment

Burlington: Halton Waldorf School / HWS
2193 Orchard Rd. Burlington, L7R 3X5 Canada
905-331-4387, Fax: 905-331-3231,
enrollment@haltonwaldorf.com
www.waldorfschool.net
Grades: Preschool - 8
Enrollment: 160
The school provides Waldorf education.

Burlington: John Calvin Christian School
607 Dynes Rd. Burlington, L7N 2V4 Canada
905-634-8015, Fax: 905-634-9772
Grades: K./Elem.
Enrollment: 141
Jane Holtvluwer

Burlington: Niagara Montessori School
3132 South Dr. Burlington, L7N 1H7 Canada
905-632-2374, Fax: 905-632-9959
Grades: Preschool - Kindergarten
The Montessori School offers programs for children from age 2.5 to 6.
Jacqueline Gaskin, Principal

Burlington: Trinity Christian School
2170 Itabashi Way Burlington, L7M 5B3 Canada
905-634-3052, Fax: 905-634-9382,
trinity@tcsonline.ca
www.tcsonline.ca
Grades: Junior Kindergarten - 8
Juliette Lamb, Chair
Rick Schenk, Principal
principal@tcsonline.ca
Sara Flokstra, Vice Principal
Cheri VanderBrook, Bookkeeper

Caledon: Brampton Christian School / BCS
12480 Hurontario St. Caledon, L7C 2B6 Canada
905-846-3771, Fax: 905-843-2929,
admin@bramptoncs.org
www.bramptoncs.org
Grades: Elementary/Junior High/Senior High
R. Andrews, Principal
randrews@bramptoncs.org
A. Cabral, Division Head, Senior High
afcabral@bramptoncs.org
C. Doggart, Division Head, Elementary
cdoggart@bramptoncs.org
J. Miller, Division Head, Junior High
jmiller@bramptoncs.org

Cambridge: Cambridge Christian School / CCS
229 Myers Rd. Cambridge, N1R 7H3 Canada
519-623-2261, Fax: 519-623-4042,
cc2@bellnet.ca
www.cambridgechristianschool.com
Grades: Kindergarten - 8
Derek Frank, Chair
Jules de Jager, Principal
ccsprincipal@bellnet.ca

Cambridge: Temple Baptist Christian Academy
400 Holiday Inn Dr. Cambridge, N3C 3T1 Canada
519-658-9001, Fax: 519-658-9426,
academy@tbca.ca
www.tbca.ca
Grades: Jr. K-8
Enrollment: 267
Evelyn Hewitt, Principal

Campbellville: Hitherfield Preparatory School
2439 - 10th Side Rd. Campbellville, L0P 1B0 Canada
905-854-0890, Fax: 905-854-3155
Grades: Elem./Sec.
Enrollment: 115
Ann J. Scott

Carp: Venta Preparatory School
2013 Old Carp Rd. Carp, K0A 1L0 Canada
613-839-2175, Fax: 613-839-1956,
info@ventapreparatoryschool.com
www.ventapreparatoryschool.com
Grades: 1 - 10
Venta Preparatory School is a day & boarding school. The maximum class size is twelve students.
Marilyn Mansfield, Principal, 613-839-2175 223
Sean Hopper, Dean, Students, 613-839-2175 225
Shaun Quinn, Director, Studies, 613-839-2175 224
Tracey Quinn, Director, Enrollment, 613-839-2175 240

Chatham: Chatham Christian High School / CCHS
475 Keil Dr. South Chatham, N7M 6L8 Canada
519-352-4980, Fax: 519-352-4041,
rayverburg@chathamchristian.ca (Vice Principal)
chathamchristian@chathamchristian.ca
www.chathamchristian.ca
Grades: 9 - 12
Enrollment: 140

Chatham: Chatham Christian School
475 Keil Dr. South Chatham, N7M 6L8 Canada
519-352-4980, Fax: 519-352-4041,
philteeuwsen@chathamchristian.ca (Head Administrator)
chathamchristian@chathamchristian.ca
www.chathamchristian.ca
Grades: Junior Kindergarten - 8
Enrollment: 300

Chatham: Eben-Ezer Christian School
485 McNaughton Ave. East Chatham, N7L 2H2 Canada
519-354-1142, Fax: 519-354-2159
Grades: Elem.
Enrollment: 51
Carlos Bos

Clinton: Clinton & District Christian School
P.O. Box 658
87 Percival St. Clinton, N0M 1L0 Canada
519-482-7851, Fax: 519-482-7448
Grades: K./Elem.
Enrollment: 205
Clarence Bos

Cobourg: Northumberland Christian School
8861 Danforth Rd., RR#5 Cobourg, K9A 4J8 Canada
905-372-8766, Fax: 905-372-6299,
ncsoffice@bellnet.ca
www.northumberlandchristianschool.com
Grades: Junior Kindergarten - 8
Northumberland Christian School is an interdenominational school.
Cindy Warr

Cookstown: Thor College
4073 - 4th Line Innisfil Cookstown, L0L 1L0
705-458-9705,
www.thorcollege.ca
Grades: Preschool - 12
W.H. Madden, BA, BPHE, BEd, Director
Michael J. Madden, Headmaster

Copetown: Rehoboth Christian School - Copetown / RCS
P.O. Box 70
198 Inksetter Rd. Copetown, L0R 1J0 Canada
905-627-5977, Fax: 905-628-4422,
office@rehoboth.on.ca
www.rehoboth.on.ca
Grades: Kindergarten - 12
Rehoboth Free Reformed Christian School Society of Copetown owns & operates the school. Education is provided with a Reformed Christian view.
Jack Westerink, B.Sc., M.Sc., CSPC, Principal
jwesterink@rehoboth.on.ca
Dick Naves, B.A., C.S.P.C., Vice Principal
dnaves@rehoboth.on.ca

Cornwall: Islamic Institute Al-Rashid
RR#1 Cornwall, K6H 5R5 Canada
613-931-2895
Grades: Elem./Sec.
Enrollment: 66
M.M. Alam

Deep River: The Deep River Science Academy / DRSA
20 Forest Ave. Deep River, K0J 1P0 Canada
613-584-4541,
info@drsa.ca
www.drsa.ca
Grades: Secondary
The Deep River Science Academy partners with Atomic Energy of Canada, Ltd. to offer science camps. Students must have completed a grade 10 or higher science high school credit. Hhigh school credits are awarded.

Deer Lake: David Meekis Memorial School
P.O. Box 69
Deer Lake, P0V 1N0 Canada
807-775-2055, Fax: 807-775-2148,
www.dmms.firstnationschools.ca/
Grades: Sec.
Enrollment: 236
Leonard Mamakeesic, Dir.

Drayton: Community Christian School / CCS
P.O. Box 141
35 High St. Drayton, N0G 1P0 Canada
519-638-2935, Fax: 519-638-3373,
ccsdray@bellnet.ca
www.ccsdray.org
Grades: Junior Kindergarten - 8

Dresden: Dresden Private Mennonite School
P.O. Box 1210
RR#2 Dresden, N0P 1M0 Canada
519-683-6610, Fax: 519-683-6610
Grades: Elem.
Enrollment: 69
Anna Friesen

Dundas: Calvin Christian School - Dundas
542 Ofield Rd. North Dundas, L9H 5E2 Canada
905-627-1411, Fax: 905-627-8004,
www.dccs.ca
Grades: Kindergarten - 8
Enrollment: 180
Rick Dykstra, Principal
rdykstra@dccs.ca
Mrs. I. Vos, Coordinator, Curriculum
ivos@dccs.ca
Corrie Zandstra, Administrator, Office
office@dccs.ca

Dunnville: Attercliffe Canadian Reformed Elementary School
75785 Canborough Rd., RR#1 Dunnville, N1A 2W1 Canada
905-774-9009
Grades: Kindergarten - 8
This is a coducational school.
Ed Slaa, Principal

Dunnville: Dunnville Christian School
37 Robinson Rd Dunnville, N1A 2W1 Canada
905-774-5142, Fax: 905-774-5519
Grades: K./Elem.
Enrollment: 129
Arie Vanderstoel

Etobicoke: Al-Ashraf Islamic School
23 Brydon Dr. Etobicoke, M9W 4M7 Canada
416-740-1495

Grades: Elem./Sec.
Enrollment: 157
Riyad Khan, Principal

***Etobicoke:* Kingsway College School**
4600 Dundas St. West Etobicoke, M9A 1A5 Canada
416-234-5073, Fax: 416-234-8386

Grades: Elem.
Enrollment: 180
Glenn Zederayko

***Etobicoke:* Madresatul Banaat Almuslimaat**
10 Vulcan St. Etobicoke, M9W 1L2 Canada
416-244-8600

Grades: Elem./Sec.
Enrollment: 152
Syed Quadri

***Etobicoke:* Richmond Hill Christian Academy**
Administration
96 Antioch Dr. Etobicoke, M9B 5V4 Canada
416-621-4100, Fax: 416-621-0930,
905-770-4055 (Phone, RHCA Campus); 905-770-6255 (Fax, Campus)
rhca@rogers.com
www.rhcaweb.ca

Grades: Junior Kindergarten - 8
Enrollment: 339
Richmond Hill Christian Academy is a non-denominational school, which is a member of the Association of Christian Schools International. The A Beka curriculum is used. Its campus is located at 9711 Bayview Avenue in Richmond Hill.
Brian R. Hayes, B.Com., C.F.A., Administrator
Madeline J. Hayes, B.A., M.Ed., Principal

***Fergus:* Emmanuel Christian High School**
RR#3 Fergus, N1M 2W4 Canada
519-843-3029, Fax: 519-843-3029

Grades: Elem./Sec.
Enrollment: 110
Henk Nobel

***Fergus:* Maranatha Christian School**
RR#3 Fergus, N1M 2W4 Canada
519-843-3029, Fax: 519-843-3029

Grades: Elem.
Enrollment: 146
Henk Nobel

***Fort Erie:* Niagara Christian Community of Schools / NCC**
2619 Niagara Pkwy. Fort Erie, L2A 5M4 Canada
905-871-6980, Fax: 905-871-9260,
ncc@niagaracc.com
www.niagaracc.com

Grades: Junior Kindergarten - 12
Kevin Bayne, Principal, Secondary School
kbayne@niagaracc.com
Cari Dean, Principal, Elementary School & Middle School
cdean@niagaracc.com
Mark Thiessen, Principal, Secondary School
mthiess@niagaracc.com
Tom Auld, Director, Student Life
tomauld@niagaracc.com
Vivian Pengelly, Business Administrator
vivianp@niagaracc.com

***Fort Frances:* Lac La Croix High School**
P.O. Box 640
Fort Frances, P9A 3M9 Canada
807-485-2402, Fax: 807-485-2558

Grades: 9-12

***Fort Frances:* Seven Generations Education Institute School**
P.O. Box 297
Fort Frances, P9A 3M6 Canada
807-274-2796, Fax: 807-274-8761,
www.7generations.org/

Dan Bird

***Fruitland:* John Knox Christian School**
795 Hwy. #8 Fruitland, L8E 5J3 Canada
905-643-2460, Fax: 905-643-5875,
www.nace.ca

Grades: K./Elem.
Enrollment: 185
The Niagara Ass'n for Christian Education (NACE).
Bonnie Desjardins, Principal
bdesjardins@nace.ca

***Georgetown:* Halton Hills Christian School**
11643 Trafalgar Rd. Georgetown, L7G 4S4 Canada
905-877-4221, Fax: 905-877-1483,
office@haltonhillschristianschool.org
www.haltonhillschristianschool.org

Grades: K./Elem.
Enrollment: 228
Formerly known as Georgetown District Christian School
Marianne Vangoor, Principal

***Gloucester:* Life Christian Academy**
2214 Innes Rd. Gloucester, K1B 4C4 Canada
613-834-6588, Fax: 613-834-6589

Grades: Elem./Sec.
Enrollment: 130
Jason Courteau

***Grassy Narrows:* Sakatcheway-Anishinabe**
P.O. Box 213
General Delivery Grassy Narrows, P0X 1B0 Canada
807-925-2626, Fax: 807-925-2855

***Guelph:* Crestwicke Christian Academy**
400 Speedvale Ave. East Guelph, N1E 1N9 Canada
519-836-5395, Fax: 519-836-2139

Grades: K./Elem.
Enrollment: 330
Sharon Dow

***Guelph:* Elora Road Christian School**
5696 Wellington Rd.7, RR #5 Guelph, N1H 6J2 Canada
519-824-1890, Fax: 519-821-3518,
school@ercf.ca
www.eloraroad.ca

Grades: K./Elem.
Enrollment: 99
Jason Wryghte

***Guelph:* John Calvin Christian School**
286 Water St. Guelph, N1G 1B8 Canada
519-824-8860, Fax: 519-824-2105

Grades: K./Elem.
Enrollment: 188
Jake Vriend

***Hamilton:* Calvin Christian School / CCS**
547 West 5th St. Hamilton, L9C 3P7 Canada
905-388-2645, Fax: 905-388-2769,
www.ccshamilton.ca

Grades: Junior Kindergarten - 8
Enrollment: 450
Ted Postma, Principal

***Hamilton:* Columbia International College of Canada**
1003 Main St. West Hamilton, L8S 4P3 Canada
905-572-7883, Fax: 905-572-9332

Grades: Sec.
Enrollment: 1285
Anna Skholnik

***Hamilton:* Guido de Bres Christian High School**
P.O. Box 30013
1576 Upper James St. Hamilton, L9B 1K0 Canada
905-574-4011, Fax: 905-574-8662,
office@guidodebres.org
www.guidodebres.org

Grades: Sec.
Enrollment: 400
J.G. Vandooren, Principal

***Hamilton:* Hamilton Hebrew Academy Zichron Meir School**
60 Dow Ave. Hamilton, L8S 1W4 Canada
905-528-0330, Fax: 905-528-0544,
school@hamiltonhebrewacademy.ca
www.hamiltonhebrewacademy.ca

Grades: Elem.
Enrollment: 132
Rivka Shaffir, Principal
principal@hamiltonhebrewacademy.ca

***Hamilton:* Hillfield - Strathallan College**
299 Fennell Ave. West Hamilton, L9C 1G3 Canada
905-389-1367, Fax: 905-389-6366

Grades: K./Elem./Sec.
Enrollment: 1173
William Matthews

***Hamilton:* Islamic School of Hamilton / ISH**
1545 Stonechurch Rd. East Hamilton, L8W 3P8 Canada
905-383-7786, Fax: 905-667-4797

Enrollment: 170
The school also teaches the Arabic language, Quran, & Islam Studies.
Zakir Patel, Principal

***Hamilton:* Southern Ontario College**
430 York Blvd. Hamilton, L8R 3K8 Canada
905-546-1500, Fax: 905-538-5494,
info@mysoc.ca
www.mysoc.ca

Grades: Sec.
Enrollment: 181
International Secondary School specializing in ESL and University prep.
Brian Inglis, Director

***Hamilton:* Timothy Canadian Reformed School**
430 East 25th St. Hamilton, L8V 3B4 Canada
905-385-3953, Fax: 905-385-8073

Grades: Kindergarten - 8
The school is affiliated with the Canadian Reformed Church.
Hendrik Plug, Principal

***Hawkesville:* Countryside Christian School**
P.O. Box 67
Hawkesville, N0B 1X0 Canada
519-699-5793, Fax: 519-699-4576

Grades: K./Elem./Sec.
Enrollment: 119
Howard Lichty

***Islington:* Kingsley Primary School**
516 The Kingsway Islington, M9A 3W6 Canada
416-233-0150, Fax: 416-233-5971

Grades: K./Elem.
Enrollment: 52
Ursula Morton

***Jarvis:* Jarvis District Christian School**
P.O. Box 520
Jarvis, N0A 1J0 Canada
519-587-4444, Fax: 519-587-2985

Grades: K./Elem.
Enrollment: 178
Garry Glasbergen

***Jordan Station:* Heritage Christian School**
P.O. Box 400
2850 Fourth Ave. Jordan Station, L0R 1S0 Canada
905-562-7303, Fax: 905-562-0020

Grades: Elem./Sec.
Enrollment: 501
Ben Harsvoort, Principal

***Jordan Station:* Jordan Christian School**
P.O. Box 69
4171 - 15 St. South Jordan Station, L0R 1S0 Canada
905-562-4023, Fax: 905-562-4024

Enrollment: 132
Mark Fintelman

***Kasabonika Lake:* Chief Simeon McKay Education Centre**
P.O. Box 120
Kasabonika Lake, P0V 1Y0 Canada
807-535-2574, Fax: 807-535-1108

***King:* The Country Day School / CDS**
13415 Dufferin St. King, L7B 1K5 Canada
905-833-1220, Fax: 905-833-1350,
www.cds.on.ca

Grades: Junior Kindergarten - 12
The co-educational school is non-denominational.
Paul C. Duckett, Headmaster
David Huckvale, Director, Admission

***King City:* St. Thomas of Villanova College School**
P.O. Box 133
2480 15th Sideroad King City, L7B 1A4 Canada
905-833-1909, Fax: 905-833-1915,
www.villanovacollege.net

Grades: 5-12
Enrollment: 450
Paul Paradiso

***Kingston:* Kingston Christian School**
1212 Woodbine Rd. Kingston, K7L 4V2 Canada
613-384-9572, Fax: 613-384-9580

Grades: K./Elem.
Enrollment: 145
Karl Reid

***Kingsville:* Old Colony Christian Academy**
Kingsville Campus
1521 County Rd. 4 West, RR#2 Kingsville, N9Y 2E5 Canada
519-733-8308, Fax: 519-733-2167

Grades: Elem./Sec.
Enrollment: 194
Peter Klassen

Kitchener: **Fellowship Christian School**
1780 Glascow St. Kitchener, N2G 3W7 Canada
519-746-0008, Fax: 519-746-4206
Grades: Elem.
Enrollment: 84
Marilyn Lambert

Kitchener: **Kitchener-Waterloo Montessori School**
194 Allen St. East Kitchener, N2J 1K1 Canada
519-742-1051, Fax: 519-742-1051
Grades: K./Elem.

Kitchener: **Laurentian Hills Christian School**
11 Laurentian Dr. Kitchener, N2E 1C1 Canada
519-576-6700, Fax: 519-576-2583
Grades: K./Elem.
Enrollment: 333
Hugo Marcus

Kitchener: **Rockway Mennonite Collegiate Inc.**
110 Doon Rd. Kitchener, N2G 3C8 Canada
519-743-5209, Fax: 519-743-5935,
www.rockway.on.ca
Grades: 7 - 12
Enrollment: 350
Rockway Mennonite Collegiate is an inspected & accredited private school, with students from Mennonite congregations & Christian denominations.
Gloria Eby, Chair
Betsy Petker, Principal
Dennis Wikerd, Assistant Principal
Tom Bileski, Director, Community Relations
Bernie Burnett, Director, Development
Barry Bishop, Business Manager

Kitchener: **Sunshine Montessori School**
10 Boniface Ave. Kitchener, N2C 1L9 Canada
519-744-1423, Fax: 519-744-9929,
admin@sunshinemontessori.on.ca
www.sunshinemontessori.on.ca
Grades: Jr. K.-8
Enrollment: 209
Roshmina Shamji, Principal/Administrator

Kleinburg: **Calvary Christian School**
6950 Nashville Rd. Kleinburg, L0J 1C0 Canada
905-893-7211,
ccs.behosted.ca
Grades: Junior Kindergarten - 8
Garry Zondervan, Principal
LeeAnn Major, Head, Junior Department

Lakefield: **Lakefield College School**
4391 County Rd. 29 Lakefield, K0L 2H0 Canada
705-652-3324, Fax: 705-652-6320,
www.lcs.on.ca
Grades: Elem./Sec.
Enrollment: 321
Founded 1879; co-ed boarding and day school, for grades 9-12 and 7-12 respectively; core academics, athletics, and co-curricular arts programmes.
David Thompson, Head of School
Kathy Green, Board Secretary
kgreen@lcs.on.ca

Laurel: **Dufferin Area Christian School**
General Delivery Laurel, L0N 1L0 Canada
519-941-4368, Fax: 519-941-3748
Grades: Elem.
Enrollment: 122
Nick Mans

Leamington: **United Mennonite Educational Institute / UMEI**
614 Mersea Rd. 6, RR#5 Leamington, N8H 3V8 Canada
519-326-7448, Fax: 519-326-0278,
umei@mnsi.net
www.umei.on.ca
Grades: 9 - 12
United Mennonite Educational Institute is a secondary school which provides an education that incorporates an Anabaptist / Mennonite world view.
Victor J. Winter, Principal
umeiadmi@mnsi.net
Jane Klassen, Secretary

Lindsay: **Heritage Christian School**
159 Colborne St. West Lindsay, K9V 5Z8 Canada
705-324-8363, Fax: 705-324-8363,
hcs_office@bellnet.ca
Grades: K./Elem.
Enrollment: 102
John Frederick

Listowel: **Listowel Christian School**
P.O. Box 151
Listowel, N4W 3H2 Canada
519-291-3086, Fax: 519-291-3086
Grades: K./Elem.
Enrollment: 142
Garth Bierma

London: **Al-Taqwa Islamic Schools**
Elementary School
35 Jim Ashton St. London, N5V 3H4 Canada
519-951-1414, Fax: 519-951-1092, 866-812-9127
ischool@altaqwa.org
www.altaqwa.org
Grades: Elem./Sec.
Enrollment: 163
The elementary school is located at 35 Jim Ashton St.; the secondary school is located at 1697 Trafalgar St., (519) 452-3366, secondary@altaqwa.org.
Siham Kaloti, Principal

London: **Faith Community Christian School**
7 Howard Ave. London, N6P 1B3 Canada
519-652-1250, Fax: 519-652-1296
Grades: K./Elem.
Enrollment: 85
Mel Finch

London: **London Christian Academy / LCA**
85 Charles St. London, N6H 1H1 Canada
519-473-3332, Fax: 519-473-9843,
www.londonchristianacademy.ca
Grades: Junior Kindergarten - 8
London Christian Academy is an interdenominational, Christian school.
Glen Smeltzer, Chair
chairman@londonchristianacademy.ca
Ron Hesman, Principal
principal@londonchristianacademy.ca
Steve Gaunt, Vice Principal
sgaunt@londonchristianacademy.ca

London: **London Community Hebrew Day School**
247 Epworth Ave. London, N6A 2M2 Canada
519-439-8419, Fax: 519-439-0404
Grades: K./Elem.
Enrollment: 75
Janet Nish-Lapidus

London: **London District Christian Secondary School**
24 Braesyde Ave. London, N5W 1V3 Canada
519-455-4360, Fax: 519-455-4364
Grades: Sec.
Enrollment: 363
Henry Kooy

London: **London Islamic School**
151 Oxford St. West London, N6H 1S3 Canada
519-679-9920, Fax: 519-679-6842
Enrollment: 187
Patricia Zabian

London: **London Parental Christian School**
202 Clarke Rd. London, N5W 5E4 Canada
519-455-0360, Fax: 519-455-6717
Grades: K./Elem.
Enrollment: 217
Mary Haven

London: **London Waldorf School**
7 Beaufort St. London, N6G 1A5 Canada
519-858-8862, Fax: 519-858-8863
Grades: K./Elem.
Enrollment: 109
Peter von Holtzendorff

London: **Matthews Hall Private School**
1370 Oxford St. West London, N6H 1W2 Canada
519-471-5942, Fax: 519-471-4765
Grades: K./Elem./Sec.
Enrollment: 233
Patricia Doig

London: **Montessori House of Children**
711 Waterloo St. London, N6A 3W1 Canada
519-433-9121, Fax: 519-433-8941,
reception@montessori.on.ca
www.montessori.on.ca
Grades: 1 - 8
London's Montessori House of Children also offers a toddler program for children from 18 to 30 months & a Casa program, for children from ages 2.5 to 6.
Margaret Whitley, Director
mwhitley@montessori.on.ca
Kim Clarke, Coordinator, Communications
kclarke@montessori.on.ca
Kristen Crouse, Coordinator, Elementary & Junior High
kcrouse@montessori.on.ca
Marianne Rutledge, Coordinator, Admissions
registrar@montessori.on.ca
Kathy Work-Schlattman, Coordinator, Casa
kwork@montessori.on.ca
Shonagh Stevenson-Ramsay, Directress, Toddler Program
sstevenson@montessori.on.ca
Walter Iwanowski, Controller
wki@montessori.on.ca

Lucknow: **Lucknow & District Christian School**
PO Box 550 Lucknow, N0G 2H0 Canada
519-528-2016, Fax: 519-528-2095
Grades: K./Elem.
Lawrence Uyl

Markham: **Somerset Academy**
7700 Brimley Rd. Markham, L3R 0E5 Canada
905-940-8990, Fax: 905-940-8992,
administration@somersetacademy.ca
www.somersetacademy.ca
Grades: Jr. K.-8
Enrollment: 172
Maureen VanLoon

Markham: **Town Centre Montessori Private Schools / TCMPS**
Main Campus
155 Clayton Dr. Markham, L3R 7P3 Canada
905-470-1200, Fax: 905-470-0184,
905-474-3434 (Phone, Preschool & Grade 1)
admin@tcmps.com
www.tcmps.com
Grades: Preschool - 8
The preschool program accepts children as young as two years of age.
Marianne Vanderlugt, Principal

Markham: **Town Centre Private High School / TCPHS**
155 Clayton Dr. Markham, L3R 7P3
905-470-1200, Fax: 905-470-1721,
www.tcphs.com
Grades: 9 - 12
This is a coeducational school which provides university bound & advanced placement courses.

Markham: **Trillium School**
4277 - 14th Ave. Markham, L3R 0J2 Canada
905-946-1181, Fax: 905-946-8267,
info@trilliumschool.ca
www.trilliumschool.ca
Grades: Preschool - 8
Trillium School is a coeducational, non-denominational school. It features a pre-Casa program for toddlers & a Casa program.
Lily Moon, Principal

Markham: **Wesley Christian Academy**
22 Heritage Rd. Markham, L3P 1M4 Canada
905-201-8461, Fax: 905-201-6438,
office@wesleychristianacademy.com
www.wesleychristianacademy.com
Grades: Senior Kindergarten - 8
Wesley Christian Academy offers an academic program within the context of Christian principles.

Markham: **Wishing Well Montessori School**
#30, 455 Cochrane Dr. Markham, L3R 9R4 Canada
905-470-9751, Fax: 905-470-0496
Grades: K./Elem.
Enrollment: 432
Connie Xuereb

Metcalfe: **Community Christian School**
2681 Glen St. Metcalfe, K0A 2P0 Canada
613-821-3669, Fax: 613-821-6135,
info@communitychristianschool.ca
www.communitychristianschool.ca
Grades: Elem.
Enrollment: 77
Gayle Freeburn, Principal

Millgrove: **Covenant Christian School**
P.O. Box 2
497 Millgrove Side Rd. Millgrove, L0R 1V0 Canada
905-689-3191, Fax: 905-689-0191,
covenant@on.aibn.com
Grades: Elem.
Enrollment: 119
George Hofsink, Principal

***Mississauga:* Bronte College of Canada**
88 Bronte College Ct. Mississauga, L5B 1M9 Canada
905-270-7788, Fax: 905-270-7828,
info@brontecollege.ca; admissions@brontecollege.ca
www.brontecollege.ca
Grades: 9 - 12
Bronte College of Canada is a co-educational, international day & boarding school. The school also offers University of Guelph & Bronte College first year university courses, an advanced placement program, & English as a Second Language (ESL).

***Mississauga:* Froebel Education Centre**
1576 Dundas St. West Mississauga, L5C 1E5 Canada
905-277-9371, Fax: 905-277-9402,
office@froebel.com
www.froebel.com
Grades: K.-8
Enrollment: 89
Education based on the principle's of Friedrich Froebel: working in partnership with the child's family, tranformation of creative play into creative work, & making connections with others, the world & God.
Barbara E. Corbett, B.A., Ed.D., Director of Education

***Mississauga:* IQRA Islamic School**
5753 Coopers Ave. Mississauga, L4Z 1R9 Canada
905-507-6688, Fax: 905-507-9243
Enrollment: 150
Ghzala Khan

***Mississauga:* ISNA Islamic School**
1525 Sherway Dr. Mississauga, L4X 1C5 Canada
905-272-4303, Fax: 905-272-4311
Grades: K./Elem.
Enrollment: 306
Osama Ghanim

***Mississauga:* Khalsa Community School**
7280 Airport Rd. Mississauga, L4T 2H3 Canada
905-678-0603, Fax: 905-678-9133
Enrollment: 187
Ripsodhak Grewal

***Mississauga:* Mentor College**
Main Campus
40 Forest Ave. Mississauga, L5G 1L1 Canada
905-271-3393, Fax: 905-271-8367,
56cayuga@mentorcollege.edu (E-mail, Primary campus)
40forest@mentorcollege.edu (Main campus)
www.mentorcollege.edu
Grades: Junior Kindergarten - 12
Ken Philbrook, Director

***Mississauga:* Mississauga Christian Academy / MCA**
Gananoque Campus
2720 Gananoque Dr. Mississauga, L5N 2R2 Canada
905-826-4114, Fax: 905-567-5874,
office@mississaugachristianacademy.com
www.mississaugachristianacademy.com
Grades: Junior Kindergarten - 8
The Mississauga Christian Academy also operates a licensed day care.

***Mississauga:* Northstar Montessori**
4900 Tomken Rd. Mississauga, L4W 1J8 Canada
905-890-7827, Fax: 905-890-6771,
admin@northstarmontessori.com
www.northstarmontessori.com
Grades: Preschool / Elementary
Northstar Montessori offers the following programs: toddlers, pre-Casa, primary, & elementary. Ages of children range from 18 months to 12 years.
Virginia Ramirez, Principal
Sherry Gosal, Vice Principal
Rick Ramirez, Manager, Business
Rose Sta. Ana, Office Administrator

***Mississauga:* Rotherglen School**
929 Old Derry Rd. Mississauga, L5W 1A1
905-565-8707, Fax: 905-565-0485,
www.rotherglen.com
Grades: Preschool - 8
The Casa program is designed for children from age three to five. Rotherglen school has over 1,200 students who attend the school's four campuses.

***Mississauga:* Rotherglen School**
3553 South Common Crt. Mississauga, L5L 2B3
905-820-9445, Fax: 905-569-1569,
www.rotherglen.com
Grades: Preschool - 6
The Erin Mills campus provides a Montessori program for its students, from Casa to grade six.

***Mississauga:* Sherwood Heights School**
3065 Glen Erin Dr. Mississauga, L5L 1J3 Canada
905-569-8999, Fax: 905-569-9034,
info@sherwoodheights.com
www.sherwoodheights.com
Grades: Elem.
Enrollment: 206
Anthony H. Mutlak

***Mississauga:* Sommerville Manor Private School**
1135 Central Pkwy. West Mississauga, L5C 3J2 Canada
905-277-1085, Fax: 905-277-3801,
info@sommervillemanor.com
www.sommervillemanor.com
Grades: K.-8
Enrollment: 283
Winefride Johnson

***Mississauga:* Springfield Preparatory School**
1444 Dundas Cres. Mississauga, L5C 1E9 Canada
905-273-9717, Fax: 905-273-9717,
info@springfieldprep.ca
www.springfieldprep.ca
Grades: Jr. K.-6
Enrollment: 66
Janet Murphy

***Mississauga:* TEAM School**
275 Rudar Rd. Mississauga, L5A 1S2 Canada
905-279-7200, Fax: 905-279-1561,
www.teamschool.com
Grades: K./Elem./Spec. Ed.
Enrollment: 299
Chuck MacDonald, Principal

***Mississauga:* Toronto Ability School**
1146 Clarkson Rd. North Mississauga, L5J 2W2 Canada
905-855-3800
Grades: Preschool - 8

***Mississauga:* White Oaks Montessori School Ltd.**
Vanier Campus
1200 Vanier Dr. Mississauga, L5H 4C7 Canada
905-278-4454, Fax: 905-278-5184,
905-855-2321 (Phone, Clarkson Campus)
admin@woms.ca
www.woms.ca
Grades: Preschool - Elementary
White Oaks Montessori School is a fully accredited Canadian Council of Montessori Administrators school. The youngest children are offered toddler programs. Casa programs are provided for children from age three to five. The Clarkson Campus is located at the following address: 1338 Clarkson Road North, Mississauga.
Barbara S. Ward, AMI, Founder & Chief Administrative Officer
Irene Stathoukos, BSc., AMI, Principal
Daniel Ward, Information Technologist

***Mount Forest:* Farewell Parochial**
9173 Concession 11 Mount Forest, N0G 2L0 Canada
Grades: Elem.
Florence Martin

***Mount Hope:* Grandview Adventist Academy**
3975 Hwy. 6 Mount Hope, L0R 1W0 Canada
905-679-4492, Fax: 905-679-4492,
grandview@mountaincable.net
www.grandviewschool.ca
Grades: Elem./Sec.
Enrollment: 58
Gisela I. Hoelzel

***Nepean:* Ottawa Islamic School**
10 Coral Ave. Nepean, K2E 5Z6 Canada
613-727-5066, Fax: 613-727-8486,
info@ottawaislamicschool.org
www.ottawaislamicschool.org
Grades: JK-12
Enrollment: 246
Mohamed Sheik Ahmed (Dalmar, Principal
msahmed@islamicschool.on.ca

***Nepean:* Rambam Day School**
25 Esquimault Ave. Nepean, K2H 6Z5 Canada
613-820-9484, Fax: 613-820-0029,
613-820-9484, ext. 348 (Phone, Admissions & Judaica)
www.rambam.ca
Grades: Preschool - 8
The RAMBAM Day School offers general & Judaic studies, in Hebrew, French, & English.
Rabbi Dovid Hayes, Executive Director, 613-820-9484 350
Chana Hayes, Principal & Head, Judaica
Susan Spence, Vice Principal & Head, General Studies
Rabbi Yaakov Wilschanski, Educational Director, 613-820-9484 351

***Nepean:* Redeemer Christian High School / RCHS**
82 Colonnade Rd. North Nepean, K2E 7L2 Canada
613-723-9262, Fax: 613-723-9321,
info@rchs.on.ca
www.rchs.on.ca
Grades: 9 - 12
Redeemer Christian High School offers a Christ-centered education. The school also provides programs for students with learning disabilities.
William Van Dyke, Principal
principal@rchs.on.ca
J. David Naftel, B.Ed., B.Sc., Vice Principal
dnaftel@rchs.on.ca
Mary Joustra, Contact, Finance & Admissions
info@rchs.on.ca
Cheryl Sullivan, Secretary
office@rchs.on.ca

***Nestor Falls:* Mikinaak Onigaming School**
P.O. Box 160
Nestor Falls, P0X 1K0 Canada
807-484-2162, Fax: 807-484-2737
Grades: Junior Kindergarten - 12
Enrollment: 100
Mikinaak Onigaming School is a band operated school, providing education for the Ojibways of Onigaming First Nation.
Owen Zoccole, Director, Education

***Newmarket:* Holland Marsh District Christian School**
18955 Dufferin St. Newmarket, L3Y 4V9 Canada
905-775-3701, Fax: 905-775-2395
Grades: K./Elem.
Enrollment: 279
Rod Berg

***Newmarket:* Newmarket & District Christian Academy / NDCA**
P.O. Box 297
221 Carlson Dr. Newmarket, L3Y 4X1 Canada
905-895-1199, Fax: 905-895-4353,
ndca@rogers.com
www.ndca.ca
Grades: Kindergarten - 8
Steve Klassen, Chair
Jane MacLachlan, Principal

***Newmarket:* Pickering College**
16945 Bayview Ave. Newmarket, L3Y 4X2 Canada
905-895-1700, Fax: 905-895-9076, 877-895-1700
info@pickeringcollege.on.ca
www.pickeringcollege.on.ca
Grades: Jr. K.-University Prep
Enrollment: 415
Day and Boarding School
Peter C. Sturrup, Headmaster

***Niagara Falls:* Niagara Community Church School**
9527 McLeod St., RR#2 Niagara Falls, L2E 6S5 Canada
905-357-9519
Grades: Kindergarten - 8
Chris Schmoll, Principal

***Nobleton:* The Montessori Country School**
Nobleton Campus
P.O. Box 455
6185 - 15th Sideroad Nobleton, L0G 1N0 Canada
905-859-4739, Fax: 905-859-5696, 1-866-557-2272
admin@mcs-nobleton.com
www.montessoricountryschool.ca
Grades: Preschool / Elementary
The Montessori Country School offers a toddler program, a Casa program, & an elementary program. Children range in age from 12 months to 12 years.
Jack Rice, Director, Education
Joanne Hastie, Director, Curriculum & Instruction
Gregory Dixon, Administrator

***North York:* Scarborough Christian School**
95 Jonesville Cres. North York, M4A 1H2 Canada
416-750-7515, Fax: 905-750-7720,
info@scarboroughchristianschool.com
www.scarboroughchristianschool.com
Grades: K./Elem./Sec.
Enrollment: 276
Martin D. Sandford, Principal

***North York:* Willow Wood School**
55 Scarsdale Rd. North York, M3B 2R3 Canada
416-444-7644, Fax: 416-444-1801
Grades: Elem./Sec./Spec. Ed.
Joy Kurtz

***North York:* Willowdale Christian School**
60 Hilda Ave. North York, M2M 1V5 Canada
416-222-1711, Fax: 416-222-1939
Grades: K./Elem.
Enrollment: 191
Mary Jansen

***Norwich:* Rehoboth Christian School - Norwich**
P.O. Box 220
43 Main St. East Norwich, N0J 1P0 Canada
519-863-2403, Fax: 519-863-3984, office@rcsnorwich.com
Grades: Kindergarten - 12
Enrollment: 600
J. Heikoop, Principal
Martien Vanderspek, Vice Principal
mvanterspek@nor-del.com

***Oakville:* Al-Falah Islamic School**
391 Burnhamthorpe Rd. East Oakville, L6H 7B4 Canada
905-257-5782, Fax: 905-257-0848, office@al-falah.org
www.al-falah.org
Grades: Elem.
Enrollment: 215
Accredited by the Ontario Min. of Education; curriculum also includes programmes in the arts, computers, physicial education, Arabic language, & Quran studies.
Nafees Khan, Principal

***Oakville:* Appleby College**
540 Lakeshore Rd. West Oakville, L6K 3P1 Canada
905-845-4681, Fax: 905-845-9828, info@appleby.on.ca
www.appleby.on.ca
Grades: Elem./Sec.
Enrollment: 740
Independent, co-educational school for boarding & day students in Grandes 7 through 12.
Guy S. McLean, Principal

***Oakville:* Chisholm Educational Centre**
1484 Cornwall Rd. Oakville, L6J 7W5 Canada
905-844-3240, www.chisholmcentre.com
Grades: Secondary / Post Secondary
Chisholm Educational Centre consists of the Academy High School & the Collegiate.
Dr. Howard Bernstein, C. Psych., Executive Director
Dr. Shirley Bryntwick, C. Psych., Director, Professional Services
Frances Hatcher, Dip. Math., Post Grad. Ed, Head, Chisholm Collegiate
C. David Jowett, M.Ed., Principal, Chisholm Academy
Sylvia Moyssakos, M.Sc.Ed., O.C.T., Head, Tutorial & Remedial Services
Karen Boyd, Manager, Office

***Oakville:* Dearcroft Montessori School**
1167 Lakeshore Rd. East Oakville, L6J 1L3 Canada
905-844-2114, Fax: 905-844-3529
Grades: K./Elem.
Enrollment: 138
Barbara Phippen

***Oakville:* Fern Hill School**
3300 Ninth Line Rd. Oakville, L6H 7A8 Canada
905-257-0022, www.fernhillschool.com
Grades: Elem.
Enrollment: 542
Co-educational. Burlington Campus: 801 North Service Rd., (905) 634-8652.
Wendy Derrick, Director/Co-founder
Joanne McLean, Director/Co-founder

***Oakville:* Glenburnie School**
2035 Upper Middle Rd. East Oakville, L6J 7G6 Canada
905-338-6236, Fax: 905-338-2654, admin@glenburnieschool.com
www.glenburnieschool.com
Grades: K./Elem.
Enrollment: 361
Melissa Leduc, Principal
mleduc@glenburnieschool.com

***Oakville:* John Knox Christian School**
2232 Sheridan Garden Dr. Oakville, L6J 7T1 Canada
905-829-8048, Fax: 905-829-8056
Grades: Elem.
Enrollment: 382
Lorna Keith

***Oakville:* John Knox Christian School**
2232 Sheridan Garden Dr. Oakville, L6J 7T1 Canada
905-829-8048, Fax: 905-829-8056, www.jkcs-oakville.org
Grades: K./Elem.
Enrollment: 256
William Barneveld

***Oakville:* King's Christian College**
528 Burnhamthorpe Rd. West Oakville, L6M 4K6 Canada
905-257-5464
Grades: Sec.
Enrollment: 152
Jim Vanderkooy

***Oakville:* MacLachlan College**
337 Trafalgar Rd. Oakville, L6J 3H3 Canada
905-844-0372, Fax: 905-844-9369
Grades: Elem./Sec.
Enrollment: 375
John H. Bailey

***Oakville:* Oakville Christian School / OCS**
112 Third Line Oakville, L6L 3Z6 Canada
905-825-1247, ocsadmissions@ocsonline.org
www.ocsonline.org
Grades: Junior Kindergarten - 8
Enrollment: 245
Jeff Kennedy, Principal

***Oakville:* Rotherglen School**
2050 Neyagawa Blvd. Oakville, L6H 6R2 Canada
905-849-1897, Fax: 905-849-1354, www.rotherglen.com
Grades: 1 - 8
The school features the Rotherglen Education in Active Leadership initiative for its grade eight students. Over 1,200 students attend Rotherglen School's four campuses in Oakville & Mississauga.
Tracey Du Preez, Coordinator, Admissions
tdupreez@rotherglen.com

***Oakville:* Rotherglen School**
2045 Sixth Line Oakville, L6H 1X9
905-338-3528, Fax: 905-338-9599, www.rotherglen.com
Grades: Preschool - 1
The Casa program is designed for children as young as three years of age. The school includes students from age three to six.

***Oakville:* St. Mildred's - Lightbourn School**
1080 Linbrook Rd. Oakville, L6J 2L1 Canada
905-845-2386, Fax: 905-845-4799, info@smls.on.ca
www.smls.on.ca/
Grades: Jr. K.-12
Enrollment: 600
All-girls school
Jane Wightman, Principal
jwightman@smls.on.ca

***Orangeville:* Hillcrest School**
#74A, 90 Lawrence Ave. Orangeville, L9W 4J3 Canada
519-942-3251, Fax: 519-942-3251
Grades: K./Elem./Sec.
Enrollment: 66
Gail P. Hooper

***Orangeville:* The Maples Independent Country School**
RR#4 Orangeville, L9W 2Z1 Canada
519-942-3310, Fax: 519-942-8041, info@TheMaplesSchool.com
www.themaplesschool.com
Grades: Preschool - 8
Enrollment: 120

***Orillia:* Orillia Christian School**
P.O. Box 862
505 Gill St. Orillia, L3V 6K8 Canada
705-326-0532, Fax: 705-327-9856, www.ocswebsite.com
Grades: K./Elem.
Enrollment: 120
Bill Freeman

***Oshawa:* College Park Elementary School**
220 Townline Rd. North Oshawa, L1H 8L7 Canada
905-723-0163, Fax: 905-723-2984
Grades: K./Elem.
Enrollment: 200
Cathy Dan, Principal

***Oshawa:* Durham Christian Academy**
615 Ridgeway Ave. Oshawa, L1J 2W3 Canada
905-436-6354, Fax: 905-436-9852
Grades: K./Elem.
Enrollment: 95
David Burns

***Oshawa:* Immanuel Christian School**
849 Rossland Rd. West Oshawa, L1J 8R5 Canada
905-728-9071, Fax: 905-728-0604
Grades: K./Elem.
Enrollment: 143
Jasper Hoogendam, Principal

***Oshawa:* Kingsway College**
1200 Leland Rd. Oshawa, L1K 2H4 Canada
905-433-1144, Fax: 905-433-1156
Grades: Sec.
Enrollment: 186
John C. Janes

***Ottawa:* Abraar School**
P.O. Box 332
1568 Merivale Rd. Ottawa, K2G 5Y7 Canada
613-820-0044, Fax: 613-820-1495, info@abraarschool.com
www.abraarschool.com
Grades: Elem.
Enrollment: 212
Islamic school. Location: 1085 Grenon Ave., Ottawa.
Moussa Ouarou, Principal

***Ottawa:* Ashbury College**
362 Mariposa Ave. Ottawa, K1M 0T3 Canada
613-749-5954, Fax: 613-749-9724
Grades: Elem./Sec.
Enrollment: 648
Tam Mathews

***Ottawa:* Bishop Hamilton School**
2199 Regency Terrace Ottawa, K2C 1H2 Canada
613-596-4013, Fax: 613-596-4971, bhswest@bhsmontessori.ca
www.bhsmontessori.ca
Grades: Toddler/Casa/Elementary/Junior High
Bishop Hamilton School is a Christian Montessori school for children from ages 18 months to 14 years.
Heather Smith, Chair
Alison Goss, B.A., AMI., M.Ed., Principal

***Ottawa:* Canadian Montessori Academy / CMA**
70 Fieldrow St. Ottawa, K2G 2Y7 Canada
613-727-9427, Fax: 613-723-1035, info@montessori-academy.com; office@montessori-academy.com
www.montessori-academy.com
Canadian Montessori Academy is a bilingual school, with both English & French Montessori teachers.
Renette Sasouni, Chief Administrative Officer
Sherie de Mel, Principal
Sabena de Mel, Vice Principal & Head, Primary Department
Jackie Lalumiere, Head, Infant / Toddler Department
Dylan McLaughlin, Head, Elementary & Middle School
Libby Glencross, Coordinator, Corpore Sano Programme

***Ottawa:* Counterpoint Academy Inc.**
149 King George St. Ottawa, K1K 1V2 Canada
613-748-1052, Fax: 613-748-8234, dpribyl@counterpointacademy.com
www.counterpointacademy.com
Grades: K.-6
Enrollment: 163
Enriched curriculum, including early literacy, spelling/phonics/grammar, writing skills, math, science, English & French language arts, public speaking, art, music, drama, computers, & physical education. Counterpoint Academy West: 35 Beaufort Dr., Kanata, (613) 271-6356 (Ms. C. Kim, B.A., B.Ed., Principal & Registrar). Day care centres at both locations.
Laura W. Tilson, B.A., B.Ed., M.Ed., Principal

***Ottawa:* Elmwood School**
Rockcliffe Park
261 Buena Vista Rd. Ottawa, K1M 0V9 Canada
613-749-6761, Fax: 613-741-8210
Grades: K./Elem./Sec.
Enrollment: 564
Helen Hirsh Spence

***Ottawa:* Fern Hill School (Ottawa) Inc.**
50 Vaughan St. Ottawa, K1M 1X1 Canada
613-746-0255, Fax: 613-746-7514, www.fernhillottawa.com
Grades: Pre./K./Elem.
Enrollment: 99
Enriched academic programme; before/after school care & after school programmes; Extended French programme.

Elizabeth Milligan, Principal
principal@fernhillottawa.com

Ottawa: Hillel Academy
31 Nadolny Sachs Private Ottawa, K2A 1R9 Canada
613-820-5602, Fax: 613-722-0020
Grades: K./Elem./Sec.
Enrollment: 421
Borch Perton

Ottawa: Joan of Arc Academy
2221 Elmira Dr. Ottawa, K2C 1H3 Canada
613-728-6364, Fax: 613-728-2935
Grades: K./Elem.; Girls
Enrollment: 160
Suzanne Lebrun-Lamoureux

Ottawa: Lycée Claudel
1635, prom Riverside Ottawa, K1G 0E5 Canada
613-733-8522, Fax: 613-733-3782,
www.claudel.org
Grades: Mat./Prim./Sec.
Enrollment: 887
Joëlle Émorine, Proviseure
proviseure@claudel.org

Ottawa: Ottawa Christian School
2191 Benjamin Ave. Ottawa, K2A 1P6 Canada
613-722-5836, Fax: 613-722-5836,
info@ocschool.org
www.ocschool.org
Grades: K./Elem.
Enrollment: 237
Paul Triemstra, Principal

Ottawa: Ottawa Languages Institute Ltd.
1990 Leslie Ave. Ottawa, K1H 5M3 Canada
613-521-3331, Fax: 613-521-6482
Grades: Sec.
Tin S. Yap

Ottawa: Ottawa Montessori School
335 Lindsay St. Ottawa, K1G 0L6 Canada
613-521-5185, Fax: 613-521-6796,
info@ottawamontessori.com
www.ottawamontessori.com/
Grades: K./Elem.
Enrollment: 400
Pat Gere, Dir.

Ottawa: Parsifal Waldorf School
1644 Bank St. Ottawa, K1V 7Y6 Canada
613-733-2668, Fax: 613-733-6774
Grades: K./Elem.
Rachel Montgomery

Ottawa: Turnbull School
1132 Fisher Ave. Ottawa, K1Z 6P7 Canada
613-729-9940, Fax: 613-729-1636,
admin@turnbull.ca
www.turnbull.ca
Grades: Junior Kindergarten - 8
Mary Ann S. Turnbull, B.Sc. (Psychology), Director
Gareth Reid, Principal
Buddy Clinch, Vice Principal, Junior School
Craig Dunn, Vice Principal, Senior School
Liz Doran, Head, Academic Studies (Primary Division)
Christine Ferris, Head, Academic Studies (Senior Division)
Katie Horton, Head, Academic Studies (Junior Division)
Jane Minty, Head, School Life
Sally Swan, Head, Community Service
Joyce Walker-Steed, Registrar
jwalker-steed@turnbull.ca

Ottawa: Westboro Academy
Académie Westboro
200 Brewer Way Ottawa, K1S 5R2 Canada
613-737-9543,
Westboro@WestboroAcademy.com
www.westboroacademy.com
Grades: Junior Kindergarten - 8
Westboro Academy is a coeducational school, which offers an enriched bilingual education.
Marcel Papineau, Principal

Owen Sound: Riverforest Montessori School
1595 - 3rd Ave. West Owen Sound, N4K 4R2 Canada
519-371-2313, Fax: 519-371-1178,
riverforestmontessori@hotmail.com
www.riverforestmontessori.com
Grades: Preschool - 6
The Casa program is offered for children from age 2.5 to 6.

Owen Sound: Timothy Christian School / TCS
1735 - 4th Ave. West Owen Sound, N4K 4X7 Canada
519-371-9151, Fax: 519-371-8607,
timothy@timothycs.org
www.timothycs.org
Grades: Junior Kindergarten - 8
Matthew Bittel, Principal
Kendra VanSchepen, Bookkeeper

Pawitik: Baibombeh Anishinabe School
Whitefish Bay First Nation
General Delivery Pawitik, P0X 1L0 Canada
807-226-5698, Fax: 807-226-1089,
bbbschool@hotmail.com; bbbschool@kmts.ca
www.kmts.ca/~baibombe
Grades: Junior Kindergarten - 12
Baibombeh Anishinabe School is a band operated Ojibway school.

Peterborough: Grace Christian Academy
575 Centreline Peterborough, K9J 7Y4 Canada
705-745-4400, Fax: 705-745-5427
Grades: K./Elem.
Enrollment: 92
Kim T. Bolton

Peterborough: Rhema Christian School
29 County Rd. 4 Peterborough, K9L 1B8 Canada
705-743-1400, Fax: 705-743-1415,
office@rhema.ca
www.rhema.ca
Grades: Junior Kindergarten - 8
Rhema Christian School is a day school which offers a Christ-centered education.
Joel Slofstra, Principal
Joel Slofstra, Principal
Joanne Brethour, Business Administrator
Rena Ridley, Office Administrator

Pickering: Blaisdale Montessori School
415 Toynevale Rd. Pickering, L1W 2G9 Canada
905-509-5005, Fax: 905-509-1959,
info@blaisdale.com
www.blaisdale.com
Grades: Toddler/Casa/Elementary/Renaissance
Blaisdale Montessori School offers programs for ages 12 months to 14 years, including pre-toddler.
Heather Wilson, Principal & Administrator, 905-509-5005 107
hwilson@blaisdale.com

Pickering: Montessori Learning Centre of Pickering / MLCP
401 Kingston Rd. Pickering, L1V 1A3 Canada
905-509-1722, Fax: 905-509-8283,
info@montessorilearningcentre.com
www.mlcp.ca
Grades: Preschool / Elementary
Enrollment: 240
Montessori Learning Centre of Pickering provides the following programs: infants, pre-Casa, Casa, & elementary.

Picton: Sonrise Christian Academy
P.O. Box 845
58 Johnson St. Picton, K0K 2T0 Canada
613-476-7883, Fax: 613-476-4202,
office@sonrisechristianacademy.com
www.sonrisechristianacademy.com
Grades: Elem.
Enrollment: 62
Julie Scrivens, Principal

Poole: Fair Haven Christian Day School
RR#1 Poole, N0K 1S0 Canada
519-595-4568
Grades: K./Elem.
Enrollment: 66
Howard Bean

Port Hope: Trinity College School / TCS
55 Deblaquire St. North Port Hope, L1A 4K7 Canada
905-885-3217, Fax: 905-885-9690,
info@tcs.on.ca; communications@tcs.on.ca;
admissions@tcs.on.ca
www.tcs.on.ca
Grades: 5 - 12
Enrollment: 600
The school is a coeducational boarding / day school. The senior school has approximately 500 students. Over 100 students attend the junior school.
Stuart K.C. Grainger, Headmaster
Jeffrey Prince, Secretary

Prince Albert: Scugog Christian School
P.O. Box 3308
14480 Old Simcoe Rd. Prince Albert, L9L 1C3 Canada
905-985-3741, Fax: 905-985-7153,
scugogchristianschool@powergate.ca
www.scugogchristianschool.com
Grades: K.-8
Enrollment: 53
Grace van Niejenhuis, Principal

Richmond Hill: Century Montessori School
Regent Campus
71 Regent St. Richmond Hill, L4C 9Y1 Canada
905-737-9494, Fax: 905-737-1014,
Info@CenturyMontessori.com
www.centurymontessori.com
Grades: Casa / PresSchool - 8
Century Montessori School offers education for children from age 2.5 to grade 8.

Richmond Hill: Richmond Hill Montessori & Elementary School / RHMS
Hillsview Campus
118 Hillsview Dr. Richmond Hill, L4C 1T2 Canada
905-508-2228, Fax: 905-508-2229,
reception@rhms.org
www.rhms.org
Grades: Preschool - 8
The school's preschool program is Montessori based. The junior program includes three & four year old children. The senior program is designed for children who are four & five year olds.
Walter Ribeiro, Director
w.ribeiro@rhms.org
Janet Darbey, Principal, Hillsview Campus
jdarbey@rhms.org
Anita Gonzalez, Principal, 16th Avenue Campus
agonzalez@rhms.org
Dino D'Amato, Vice Principal, Hillsview Campus
ddamato@rhms.org
Rose Chitiz, Administrator
rchitiz@rhms.org
Catherine Evans, Administrator
cevans@rhms.org
Sarah Salvatore, Administrator
ssalvatore@rhms.org
Claude Rodrigues, Contact, Purchasing & Finance
crodrigues@rhms.org

Richmond Hill: Toronto Montessori Schools / TMS
8569 Bayview Ave. Richmond Hill, L4B 3M7
905-889-6882, Fax: 905-886-6516,
tmshr@torontomontessori.ca (E-mail, Human Resources)
admissions@torontomontessori.ca;
alumni@torontomontessori.ca
www.torontomontessori.ca
Grades: Preschool - 12

Rosseau: Rosseau Lake College / RLC
1967 Bright St. Rosseau, P0C 1J0 Canada
705-732-4351, Fax: 705-732-6319, 800-265-0569
info@rlc.on.ca; advancement@rlc.on.ca; admissions@rlc.on.ca
www.rosseaulakecollege.com
Enrollment: 150
Rosseau Lake College is a coeducational day & boarding school. The average class size is twelve.
Graham Hookey, Head of School

Ruthven: Emmanuel Christian Academy
P.O. Box 34
294 County Rd. East, RR#2 Ruthven, N0P 2G0 Canada
519-839-4874, Fax: 519-839-4875
Grades: K./Elem.
Enrollment: 22
Benna Nicolai

Sandy Lake: Thomas Fiddler Memorial Elementary School
P.O. Box 8
Sandy Lake, P0V 1V0 Canada
807-744-4491, Fax: 807-774-1324,
www.sandylake.firstnation.ca
Grades: Kindergarten - 6; Special Ed.
Enrollment: 390
Number of Employees: 53. The Thomas Fiddler Memorial Elementary School is part of the Sandy Lake Board of Education. The elementary school educates members of Sandy Lake First Nation. From kindergarten to grade four, Thomas Fiddler Memorial Elementary School provides a native immersion program.
Rose Yesno, Principal
roseyesno@hotmail.com
Doreen Fiddler, Social Counsellor

Andrew Mamakeesic, Social Counsellor

***Sandy Lake:* Thomas Fiddler Memorial High School**
P.O. Box 8
Sandy Lake, P0V 1V0
807-774-1229, Fax: 807-774-1228,
www.sandylake.firstnation.ca
Grades: 7 - 10
Enrollment: 124
The activities of Thomas Fiddler Memorial High School are overseen by the Sandy Lake Board of Education. The secondary school serves students of the Sandy Lake First Nation.

***Sarnia:* Sarnia Christian School**
1273 Exmouth St. Sarnia, N7S 1W9 Canada
519-383-7750, Fax: 519-383-6304,
info@sarniachristian.com
www.sarniachristian.com
Grades: K.-8
Enrollment: 164
Len Smit, Principal
len.smit@sarniachristian.com

***Sarnia:* Temple Christian Academy**
1410 Quinn Dr. Sarnia, N7T 7H4 Canada
519-542-9563, Fax: 519-542-9889,
office@templechristianacademy.ca
www.templechristianacademy.ca
Grades: Jr. K.-8
Enrollment: 84
P. Wes Harding, Principal

***Scarborough:* Agbu Zaroukian School**
930 Progress Ave. Scarborough, M1G 3T5 Canada
416-439-3900, Fax: 416-431-2510
Grades: K./Elem.
Enrollment: 91
Hasmik Kurdian

***Scarborough:* Ellesmere Montessori School Incn Campus**
37 Marchington Circle Scarborough, M1R 3M6 Canada
416-447-1059, Fax: 416-447-1059
Grades: K./Elem.
Enrollment: 76
Jill Weinberger

***Scarborough:* Ellington Montessori**
2102 Lawrence Ave. East Scarborough, M1R 2Z9 Canada
416-759-8363, Fax: 416-759-2162
Grades: Elem.
Enrollment: 81
Deborah Renwick

***Scarborough:* Madinatul-Uloom Academy**
670 Progress Ave Scarborough, M1H 3A4 Canada
416-332-1810
Grades: Elem./Sec.
Enrollment: 358
Mohammed Wajiduddin

***Scarborough:* Madison Academy**
#1, 700 Progress Ave. Scarborough, M1H 2Z7 Canada
416-439-8991
Grades: Sec.
Enrollment: 177
Sheileen Krone

***Scarborough:* Salaheddin Islamic School**
741 Kennedy Rd. Scarborough, M1K 2C6 Canada
416-264-9495
Grades: Elem.
Enrollment: 185
Laila Maarouf

***Scarborough:* Whitefield Christian Schools**
5808 Finch Ave. East Scarborough, M1B 4Y6 Canada
416-297-1212, Fax: 416-291-4632
Grades: Elem.
Enrollment: 330
Dr. Ruth E. Slade

***Sebringville:* Stratford District Christian School**
130 Huron Rd., RR#1 Sebringville, N0K 1X0 Canada
519-393-5675, Fax: 519-393-6306
Grades: K./Elem.
Enrollment: 90
Edward J. Petrusma

***Simcoe:* Bethel Baptist Christian School**
P.O. Box 752
4059 Hwy. #3 East Simcoe, N3Y 4T2 Canada
519-426-8421, Fax: 519-426-8426,
www.bethelsimcoe.addr.com/school.html
Grades: Junior Kindergarten - 12
Dr. Michael Glowacki, Principal

***Sioux Lookout:* New Life Christian Academy**
P.O. Box 697
28 - 1st Ave. Sioux Lookout, P8T 1B1 Canada
807-737-0020, Fax: 807-737-4281

***Sioux Lookout:* Pelican Falls First Nation High School**
P.O. Box 4127
Sioux Lookout, P8T 1J9 Canada
807-737-1110, Fax: 807-737-1449, 1-800-378-911
pelican@nnec.on.ca
www.nnec.on.ca/pffnhs/
Grades: Sec.
Enrollment: 143
Desta Buswa, Principal

***Sioux Lookout:* Wahsa Distance Education Centre**
P.O. Box 1118
74 Front St. Sioux Lookout, P8T 1B7 Canada
807-737-1488, Fax: 807-737-1732
Grades: 9 - 12
Enrollment: 950
The Wahsa Distance Education Centre allows students in northern Ontario communities across the Sioux Lookout District to complete their secondary school education at home. Courses & services are developed in consultation with First Nation communities. The Centre is operated by the Northern Nishnawbe Education Council.
Norma Kejick

***Smithville:* Covenant Christian School**
6470 Regional Rd. #14 Smithville, L0R 2A0 Canada
905-957-7796, Fax: 905-957-7794,
www.nace.ca
Grades: Elem.
Enrollment: 226
The Niagara Ass'n for Christian Education (NACE).
Sid Bakker, Principal
sbakker@nace.ca

***Smithville:* John Calvin Private School**
P.O. Box 280
320 Station St. Smithville, L0R 2A0 Canada
905-957-2341, Fax: 905-957-2342
Grades: K./Elem.
Enrollment: 275
Frank C. Ludwig

***Smithville:* Smithville District Christian High School**
P.O. Box 40
6488 Smithville Rd. Smithville, L0R 2A0 Canada
905-957-3255, Fax: 905-957-3431,
sdoffice@sdch.on.ca
www.sdch.on.ca
Grades: Sec.
Enrollment: 224
Ted Harris, Administrator

***St Catharines:* Beacon Christian Schools**
Bldg. A & Bldg. B
300 Scott St. St Catharines, L2N 1J3 Canada
905-937-7411, Fax: 905-937-1130,
admissions@beaconchristian.org
www.beaconchristian.org
Grades: Elementary / Secondary
Dwayne Bulthuis, Principal, Secondary School
dbulthuis@beaconchristian.org
Karen Gerritsma, Principal, Elementary School
kgerritsma@beaconchristian.org
Ralph Pot, Vice Principal, Elementary School

***St Catharines:* Grey Gables School**
1 Dexter St. St Catharines, L2S 2L4 Canada
905-685-4577, Fax: 905-685-5102
Grades: K./Elem./Sec.
Enrollment: 176
Kathleen Miller

***St Catharines:* Ridley College**
P.O. Box 3013
2 Ridley Rd. St Catharines, L2R 7C3 Canada
905-684-1889, Fax: 905-684-8875,
admission@ridleycollege,com
www.ridley.on.ca
Enrollment: 607
Ridley College is a university preparatory school, which features both a lower school & an uppper school. Boarding is available. Over 30% of students are international students.
John R. Anderson, President, Board of Governors
Jonathan Leigh, Headmaster
headmaster@ridleycollege.com
Brian Iggulden, Deputy Headmaster, 905-684-1889 2211
brian_iggulden@ridleycollege.com
Jay Goulart, Executive Director, Advancement
jay_goulart@ridleycollege.com
Cynthia A. Weedon, Executive Director, Finance & Operations
cynthia_weedon@ridleycollege.com
Don Rickers, Director, External Relations
don_rickers@ridleycollege.com
Stephen Clarke, Assistant Head, Academics, 905-684-1889 2301
stephen_clarke@ridleycollege.com
Margaret Lech, Assistant Headmaster, Student Affairs
margaret_lech@ridleycollege.com
James Milligan, Assistant Head, Lower School
jim_milligan@ridleycollege.com

***St Catharines:* St Catharines Montessori School**
238 Geneva St. St Catharines, L2R 4P8 Canada
905-684-6110,
stcathmontessori@hotmail.com
Grades: K./Elem.
Susan Bowslaugh

***St Catharines:* Wheatley School of Montessori Education Inc.**
497 Scott St. St Catharines, L2M 3X3 Canada
905-641-3012, Fax: 905-641-1443,
mail@wheatleyschool.com
www.wheatleyschool.com
Grades: Preschool - 8
The coeducational, non-denominational school provides Montessori programs for children from preschool to grade four. The Wheatley School's preschool program accepts children as young as two years of age. For upper elementary students in grades five to eight, a traditional, enriched program is offered.
Eda Varalli, Principal

***St Thomas:* Faith Christian Academy**
109 Chestnut St. St Thomas, N5R 2B1 Canada
519-633-0943, Fax: 519-633-6848
Grades: K./Elem.
Enrollment: 163
Barry E. Pearce

***St Thomas:* St. Thomas Community School**
77 Fairview Ave. St Thomas, N5R 4X7 Canada
519-633-0690, Fax: 519-633-0019,
info@stthomaschristian.org
www.stthomaschristian.org
Grades: Jr. K.-8
Enrollment: 789
John Lunshof

***Stittsville:* Ottawa Waldorf School**
1 Goulbourn St. Stittsville, K2S 1N9 Canada
613-836-1547, Fax: 613-831-4447,
ottawawaldorf@bellnet.ca
www.waldorf.cyberus.ca
Grades: K./Elem.
Enrollment: 91
Karen Ann McKinna

***Stouffville:* Stouffville Christian School**
12485 Tenth Line Stouffville, L4A 7X3 Canada
905-640-3297, Fax: 905-640-7845,
stouffville_cs@bellnet.ca
www.stouffvillechristianschool.org
Grades: Jr. K.-8
Enrollment: 70
Jake Vriend, Principal

***Strathroy:* Strathroy Community Christian School**
7880 Walkers Dr., RR#2 Strathroy, N7G 3H4 Canada
519-245-1934, Fax: 519-245-4424,
sccs@sympatico.ca
www.sccs.ca
Grades: Jr. K.-8
Enrollment: 200
Henry Wiersema

***Thornhill:* As-Sadiq Islamic School**
9000 Bathurst St. Thornhill, L4J 8A7 Canada
905-771-9917, Fax: 905-771-9778
Enrollment: 165
William Lahey

***Thornhill:* Associated Hebrew Schools of Toronto — The Kamin Education Centre**
300 Atkinson Ave. Thornhill, L4J 8A2 Canada
905-889-3998, Fax: 905-889-5183,
www.associatedhebrewschools.com
Grades: K./Elem.
Enrollment: 1415

Bet Hayeled: Eynat Katz, Vice Principal; Brenda Dzalov, Preschool Coordinator.
Sandy Rabinowitz, Principal
srabinowitz@ahschools.com

Thornhill: Central Montessori School of Thornhill / CMS
72 Steels Ave. West Thornhill, L4J 1A1 Canada
416-889-0012, Fax: 905-889-0422,
info@cmschool.net
www.cmschool.net

Grades: Toddlers - 8
Central Montessori School is a co-educational, non-denominational school. The early childhood education program is designed for children from 18 months to 2.5 years.
Minno Mohajer

Thornhill: The Leo Baeck Day School
North Campus
36 Atkinson Ave. Thornhill, L4J 8C9 Canada
905-709-3636, Fax: 905-709-1999,
info@leobaeck.ca
www.leobaeck.ca

Grades: Preschool - 8
The Leo Baeck Day School is a Reform Jewish day school. Students experience Judaism from a Reform perspective.
Brian Simon, President
board@leobaeck.ca
Dennis H. Grubbs, Interim Director of School
dgrubbs@leobaeck.ca
Robyn Buchmam, Director, Admission
rbuchman@leobaeck.ca
Howard Laderman, Principal, North Campus
hladerman@leobaeck.ca
Eric Petersiel, M.A., B. Ed., RJE, Principal, South Campus, 416-787-9899, fax: 416-787-9838
epetersiel@leobaeck.ca

Thornhill: Ner Israel Yeshiva College
250 Bathurst Glen Dr. Thornhill, L4J 8A7 Canada
905-731-1224, Fax: 905-731-2104

The college provides undergraduate & graduate religious degrees.

Thornhill: Netivot HaTorah Day School
18 Atkinson Ave. Thornhill, L4J 8C8 Canada
905-771-1234, Fax: 905-771-1807,
webregistration@netivothatorah.com
www.netivot.com

Grades: Elementary
Enrollment: 600
Netivot HaTorah is an orthodox Jewish school. Its program includes Judaic & general studies.
Dr. Reuven Stern, Head of School
rstern@netivothatorah.com
Rabbi Elliott Diamond, Vice-Principal, Judaic Studies
ediamond@netivothatorah.com
Robyn Shiner, Vice-Principal, General Studies
rshiner@netivothatorah.com
Eileen Goldstein, Director, ECE Department
egoldstein@netivothatorah.com
Alan Steinfeld, Director, Development
asteinfeld@netivothatorah.com
Carol Weir, Director, Podolski NESS Department
cweir@netivothatorah.com

Thornhill: Or Haemet Sefaradic School
7026 Bathurst St. Thornhill, L4J 8K3 Canada
905-669-7653, Fax: 905-669-5138,
orhaemet@kehilacentre.com

Grades: K./Elem.
Enrollment: 181
Sarah Wasserman

Thornhill: Toronto Waldorf School / TWS
9100 Bathurst St. Thornhill, L4J 8C7 Canada
905-881-1611, Fax: 905-881-6710,
www.torontowaldorfschool.com

Grades: Preschool - Secondary
Bill Harlow, Chair
Michèle Andrews, Administrative Director
Katharina Dannenberg, High School Administrator
Natalie Semenov, Financial Administrator
Darlene Gregoire, Manager, Business
Paul Sheardown, Manager, Facilities
Aileen Stewart, Coordinator, Admissions

Thorold: Grand River Academy of Christian Education
29 Claremont St. Thorold, L2V 1R4 Canada
905-227-7507

Grades: Elem./Sec.
Enrollment: 125
Terrence Edwards

Thunder Bay: Thunder Bay Christian School / TBCS
37 Cooper Rd. Thunder Bay, P7C 4V1 Canada
807-939-1209, Fax: 807-939-2843,
tbcs@tbaytel.net
www.tbaychristianschool.ca

Grades: Junior Kindergarten - 10
Enrollment: 165
Thunder Bay Christian School is an interdenominational school operated by parents.
Bea Hayen, Principal

Toronto: Alan Howard Waldorf School / AHWS
250 Madison Ave. Toronto, M4V 2W6 Canada
416-962-6447, Fax: 416-975-5513,
admin@ahws.org
www.ahws.org

Grades: Elem.
Enrollment: 169
Einat Bar Yosef, Enrolment Manager
admissions@ahws.org

Toronto: Archer Preparatory College
1440 Don Mills Rd. Toronto, M3B 3M1 Canada
416-512-7143,
www.archereducation.com

Grades: 3 - 12
Archer Preparatory College was formerly Toronto Academic School. The coeducational high school is operated by Archer Education Group. Advanced academic programs are offered for students in grades three to eight. High school credits are offered for students in grades nine to twelve. English as a Second Language is also provided.
Ivan Davis, Principal

Toronto: ARS Armenian Private School
45 Hallcrown Pl. Toronto, M2J 4Y4 Canada
416-491-2675, Fax: 416-491-8559,
www.arsdayschool.ca

Grades: K.-12
Enrollment: 363
Armen Martirossian, Principal

Toronto: Associated Hebrew Schools of Toronto
Hurwich Education Centre
252 Finch Ave. West Toronto, M2R 1M9 Canada
416-494-7666, Fax: 416-494-2925,
www.associatedhebrewschools.com

Grades: K.-8
Enrollment: 1700
A community day school with a focus on Torah-values & high academic standards. Locations in Toronto & Thornhill.
Dr. Mark Smiley, Director of Education
msmiley@ahschools.com

Toronto: Bais Yaakov Elementary School
15 Saranac Blvd. Toronto, M6A 2G4 Canada
416-256-4436, Fax: 416-783-4688

Grades: Pre-school - 8
Enrollment: 400
Bais Yaakov Elementary School is a school for girls.
Magda Simon, Principal, 416-783-6181
Devorah Drebin, Junior High Principal, 416-783-6181

Toronto: Bannockburn School
12 Bannockburn Ave. Toronto, M5M 2M8 Canada
416-789-7855, Fax: 416-789-7963,
bannockburn@bannockburn.ca
www.bannockburn.ca

Grades: Toddler / Preschool / Elementary
Bannockburn School offers Montessori education.
Adalove Gorrie, Principal, Elementary Program, 416-789-7855 303
agorrie@bannockburn.caa
Helen Traicus, Vice Principal, Toddler & Primary Program, 416-789-7855 306
htraicus@bannockburn.ca
Terry Gorrie, Director, Business, 416-789-7855 302
tgorrie@bannockburn.ca

Toronto: Bayview Glen
275 Duncan Mill Rd. Toronto, M3B 3H9 Canada
416-443-1030, Fax: 416-443-1032,
jmaxwell@bayviewglen.ca
www.bvg.on.ca

Grades: Preschool - 12
Enrollment: 1011
Preschool education at Bayview Glen starts at age 2. The school includes lower school, prep school, & upper school.
Eileen Daunt, Head
Vince Haines, Director, Finance
vhaines@bayviewglen.ca
Dara Kahane, Director, Summer Camp
darak@bayviewglen.ca
Judy Maxwell, Director, Admissions
jmaxwell@bayviewglen.ca

Toronto: Beth Jacob High School
410 Lawrence Ave. West Toronto, M5M 1C2 Canada
416-787-4949, Fax: 416-787-0453

Grades: Secondary
Beth Jacob High School is a school for Orthodox Jewish girls.

Toronto: Bialik Hebrew Day School
2760 Bathurst St. Toronto, M6B 3A1 Canada
416-783-3346,
info@bialik.ca; boardsecretary@bialik.on.ca
www.bialik.ca

Grades: Junior kindergarten - 8
Enrollment: 800
Sonia Shron, Executive Director
Shana Harris, Head
Benjamin Cohen, Principal, General Studies
Simona Dayan, Principal, Jewish Studies
simona_dayan@bialik.on.ca
Anita Eckhaus, Vice Principal, Elementary Division
Rochelle Wise, Vice Principal, Preschool Division
Beverley Young, Vice Principal, Senior Division

Toronto: The Bishop Strachan School / BSS
298 Lonsdale Rd. Toronto, M4V 1X2 Canada
416-483-4325, Fax: 416-481-5632,
strachan@bss.on.ca
www.bss.on.ca

Grades: Junior Kindergarten - 12
The Bishop Strachan School educates girls.
Kate Berghuis, Chair, Board of Governors
Sarah Kavanagh, Chair, Board of Trustees
Deryn Lavell, Head of School
Catherine Hart, Director, Admissions
admissions@bss.on.ca
Rachel Yeager, Director, Marketing & Communications
ryeager@bss.on.ca ca

Toronto: Bnei Akiva Schools
45 Canyon Ave. Toronto, M3H 3S4 Canada
416-630-5434, Fax: 416-638-7905,
bneiakivaschools.org

Grades: 9-12
Enrollment: 283
Bnei Akiva Schools serves the Jewish community.
Jeff Shumacher, President
Frank Samuels, Principal, General Studies
Rabbi Scot A. Berman, Headmaster
Jay Shiel, Director, Operations
Jerry Solomon, MSW, Director, Development

Toronto: Bond International College
720 Midland Ave. Toronto, M1K 4C9 Canada
416-266-8878, Fax: 416-266-3898,
info@bondcollege.com
www.bondcollege.com

Grades: Secondary
Bond International College prepares international students for colleges & universities in Canada, the United States, the United Kingdom, & Australia.
Jeffrey Farber, Principal

Toronto: Branksome Hall
10 Elm Ave. Toronto, M4W 1N4 Canada
416-920-9741, Fax: 416-920-5390,
attendance@branksome.on.ca
www.branksome.on.ca

Grades: Junior Kindergarten - 12
Branksome Hall is an independent day & boarding school for girls & an International Baccalaureate (IB) World School.
Karen Murton, Principal
kmurton@branksome.on.ca
Sarah Craig, Head, Junior School
scraig@branksome.on.ca
Karrie Weinstock, Head, Senior / Middle School & Admissions
kweinstock@branksome.on.ca
Terence Carty, Director, Information Technology
tcarty@branksome.on.ca
Joanne Colwell, Director, Student Life
jcolwell@branksome.on.ca
Julia Drake, Director, Communications & Marketing
jdrake@branksome.on.ca
Rosemary Evans, Director, Academic Studies
revans@branksome.on.ca
Judy Gordon, Director, Finance & Administration
jgordon@branksome.on.ca
Nanci Smith, Director, Residence & Athletics
nsmith@branksome.on.ca

***Toronto:* Cambridge International College of Canada / CICC**
35 Ourland Ave. Toronto, M8Z 4E1 Canada
416-252-9195
Grades: Secondary
The school for foreign students specializes in TOEFL / ESL & preparation courses for university.

***Toronto:* Cathedral Christian Academy**
c/o The Prayer Palace Ministries
1111 Arrow Rd. Toronto, M9N 3B3 Canada
416-241-1100, Fax: 416-241-4404,
generalinfo@th[rayerpalace.com
www.theprayerpalace.com/cds
Grades: Junior Kindergarten - 12

***Toronto:* Children's Garden Junior School / CGS**
670 Eglinton Ave. East Toronto, M4G 2K4 Canada
416-423-5017,
info@childrensgardenschool.com
www.childrensgardenschool.com
Grades: Pre- Kindergarten - 6
Kelly Shimizu, Director, Admissions, 416-423-5017 43
kshimizu@childrensgardenschool.com
Zandee Toovey, Executive Assistant, 416-423-5017 44
ztoovey@childrensgardenschool.com

***Toronto:* City Academy**
3080 Yonge St. Toronto, M4N 3N1 Canada
416-482-2521, Fax: 416-482-2496,
info@cityacademy.ca
www.cityacademy.ca
Grades: Sec.
Enrollment: 230
Sheila Dever, Principal

***Toronto:* Community Hebrew Academy of Toronto / CHAT**
200 Wilmington Ave. Toronto, M3H 5J8 Canada
416-636-5984, Fax: 416-636-7717,
info@tanenbaumchat.org
www.chat-edu.ca
Grades: Sec.
Enrollment: 800
Co-educational high school of the Greater Toronto Jewish community. Campuses in Toronto and Vaughan. Programmes include core subjects and Jewish studies.
Paul Shaviv, M.A., M.Phil., Director of Education

***Toronto:* Crawford Adventist Academy**
531 Finch Ave. West Toronto, M2R 3X2 Canada
416-633-0090, Fax: 416-633-0467
Grades: K./Elem./Sec.
Enrollment: 526
Vernon Langdon

***Toronto:* Crescent School**
2365 Bayview Ave. Toronto, M2L 1A2 Canada
416-449-2556, Fax: 416-449-7950,
info@crescentschool.org
www.crescentschool.org
Grades: 3 - 12
Crescent School is a day school for boys.
Geoff Roberts, Headmaster
Mark Hord, Head, Middle School
Ross MacDonald, Head, Lower School
Christopher White, Director, Admissions

***Toronto:* Crestwood Preparatory College**
217 Brookbanks Dr. Toronto, M3A 2T7 Canada
416-391-1441, Fax: 416-444-0949,
dcarrotte@crestwoodprepco.com
www.crestwoodprepco.com
Grades: Elem./Sec.
Enrollment: 391
Vince Pagano, Principal

***Toronto:* Crestwood School**
411 Lawrence Ave. East Toronto, M3C 1N9 Canada
416-444-5858, Fax: 416-444-2127
Grades: Elem.
Enrollment: 416
Dalia Eisen

***Toronto:* De La Salle College**
131 Farnham Ave. Toronto, M4V 1H7 Canada
416-969-8771, Fax: 416-969-9175,
info@delasalle.toronto.on.ca
www2.delasalle.toronto.on.ca/
Grades: Elem./Sec.
Enrollment: 578
Br. Domenic Viggiani

***Toronto:* Dominion College**
343 Jones Ave. Toronto, M4J 3G4 Canada
416-348-8708, Fax: 416-348-8805
Grades: Sec.
Enrollment: 83
David Tech

***Toronto:* Dr. Abraham Shore She'Arim Hebrew Day School**
4588 Bathurst St. Toronto, M2R 1W6 Canada
416-633-8247, Fax: 416-633-4783
Grades: Elem./Spec. Ed.
Enrollment: 67
Kathy Manoim

***Toronto:* Eitz Chaim Schools**
475 Patricia Ave. Toronto, M2R 2N1 Canada
416-225-1187, Fax: 416-225-3732
Grades: K./Elem./Sec.
Enrollment: 831
Robert W. Pletsch

***Toronto:* Fieldstone Day School**
2999 Dufferin St. Toronto, M6B 3T4 Canada
416-487-7381, Fax: 416-487-8190,
office@fieldstonedayschool.org
www.fieldstonedayschool.org
Grades: K.-12
Enrollment: 244
Enriched curriculum.
Melissa Volekaert, Head of Lower School
mvol@fieldstonedayschool.org
Sue Johnson, Ass't Head of Lower School
sjohnson@fieldstonedayschool.org

***Toronto:* The Giles School L'École Giles**
80 Scarsdale Rd. Toronto, M3C 2C3 Canada
416-446-0825, Fax: 416-446-0846,
info@gilesschool.ca
www.gilesschool.ca
Grades: Pre-Kindergarten - 12
The Giles School is a co-educational school which offers an enriched French immersion program. Students are introduced to a third language in grade one.
Kemp Rickett, Headmaster
kemp_rickett@gilesschool.ca
Sue Vijh, Deputy Headmaster
sue_vijh@gilesschool.ca
Harry Giles, Director, Education
Rosine Dika Balotoken, Manager, Administration
rosine_dika@gilesschool.ca
Bob Spencer, Manager, Special Projects
rgspencer@rogers.com

***Toronto:* Great Lakes College of Toronto / GLCT**
Toronto Campus
323 Keele St. Toronto, M6P 2K6 Canada
416-763-4121, Fax: 416-763-5225,
query@glctschool.com
www.glctschool.com
Grades: 10 - 12
The school is an international high school, which offers a pre-university program. English as a Second Language courses are also provided.
Tom Tidey, B.A., M.Ed., Principal

***Toronto:* Havergal College**
1451 Avenue Rd. Toronto, M5N 2H9 Canada
416-483-3843, Fax: 416-483-6796,
www.havergal.on.ca
Grades: K./Elem./Sec.
Enrollment: 956
University-preparatory day and boarding school for girls.
Dr. Susan R. Groesbeck, Principal

***Toronto:* Hawthorn School for Girls**
101 Scarsdale Rd. Toronto, M3B 2R2 Canada
416-444-3054, Fax: 416-449-2891,
www.hawthornschool.com
Grades: Elem./Sec.
Enrollment: 222
Eliza Trotter, School Head

***Toronto:* High Park Centennial Montessori School**
35 High Park Gdns. Toronto, M6R 1S8 Canada
416-763-6097, Fax: 416-763-0380
Grades: K./Elem.
Enrollment: 332
Tracy Grisdale

***Toronto:* Humberside Montessori School**
121 Kennedy Ave Toronto, M6S 2X8 Canada
416-762-8888, Fax: 416-766-1211
Grades: Elem./Ungraded
Enrollment: 81
Felix Bednarski

***Toronto:* Imperial College of Toronto**
20 Queen Elizabeth Blvd. Toronto, M8Z 1L8 Canada
416-251-4970, Fax: 416-251-0259
Grades: Sec.
Enrollment: 114
Jon Austin

***Toronto:* Institute of Child Study**
45 Walmer Rd. Toronto, M5R 2X2 Canada
416-934-4509, Fax: 416-978-6485
Grades: Elem.
Enrollment: 176
Elizabeth Morley

***Toronto:* Islamic Foundation School**
441 Nugget Ave. Toronto, M1V 5E1 Canada
416-321-3776, Fax: 416-321-1078
Grades: Elem.
Enrollment: 327
Yahya Qurechi

***Toronto:* The Japanese School of Toronto Shokokai Inc.**
c/o McMurrich Junior Public Shool
115 Winnona Dr. Toronto, M6G 3S8 Canada
416-656-4822, Fax: 416-658-8931,
www.torontohoshuko.ca
This is a Japanese Saturday school

***Toronto:* Junior Academy**
2454 Bayview Ave. Toronto, M2L 1A6 Canada
416-425-4567, Fax: 416-425-7379,
www.junioracademy.com
Grades: Kindergarten - 8
Pat Kendall, B.A., Graduate Diploma in, Administrator
Dianne Johnson, Principal
Julie Stewart, Vice Principal
Cathy Hibbert, Director, Physical Education
Susan Jones, Director, Middle School
Kris Potter, Director, Student Affairs

***Toronto:* Leonardo Da Vinci Academy of Arts & Sciences**
100 Allanhurst Dr. Toronto, M9A 4K4 Canada
416-247-6137, Fax: 416-247-6138,
ldva@ldva.on.ca
www.ldva.on.ca/
Grades: K./Elem.
Salvatore Ritacca, Principal

***Toronto:* The Linden School**
10 Rosehill Ave. Toronto, M4T 1G5 Canada
416-966-4406,
www.lindenschool.ca
Grades: 1 - 12
The Linden School provides education for girls.
Alana Bell, BA (Honours) (English), M, Co-Principal
Dawn Chan, B.Sc. (Biology), M.Sc. (S, Co-Principal
Ina Székely, B.A., M.A., B.Ed., Co-Principal
Kate Raven, B.A. (Honours), Post-Grad, Coordinator, Communications

***Toronto:* Lycée Français de Toronto**
2327, rue Dufferin Toronto, M6E 3S5 Canada
416-924-1789, Fax: 416-924-9078,
samia.farahat@lft.ca
www.lft.ca
Grades: Prim./Sec.
Enrollment: 340
M. Dominique Duthel, Proviseur

***Toronto:* The Mabin School**
50 Poplar Plains Rd. Toronto, M4V 2M8 Canada
416-964-9594, Fax: 416-964-3643,
admissions@mabin.com
www.mabin.com
Grades: Junior Kindergarten - 6
The Mabin School provides a full day, non-denominational program for girls & boys.
Lynn Seligman, Principal

***Toronto:* Maria Montessori School**
125 Brentcliffe Rd. Toronto, M4G 3Y7 Canada
416-423-9123, Fax: 416-423-7819
Grades: Elem.
Enrollment: 196
James Brand

Toronto: McDonald International Academy
920 Yonge St., 2nd Fl. Toronto, M4W 3C7 Canada
416-322-1502, Fax: 416-322-5775
Enrollment: 753
Fraser Rose

Toronto: Metropolitan Preparatory Academy
49 Mobile Dr. Toronto, M4A 1H5 Canada
416-285-0870, Fax: 416-285-0873,
www.metroprep.com
Grades: 6 - 12
Metropolitan Preparatory Academy offers a middle & high school program for university-oriented students.
William Wayne McKelvey, Hons. B.A., M.A., Dip. Ed, Principal
Debra McKelvey-Cleveland, Vice Principal & Head, Guidance
dmckelvey@MetroPrep.com
Jason Van Allen, Administrator, Information Technology
lvanallen@MetroPrep.com

Toronto: Montcrest School
4 Montcrest Blvd. Toronto, M4K 1J7 Canada
416-469-2008, Fax: 416-469-0934,
info@montcrest.on.ca
www.montcrest.on.ca
Grades: Junior Kindergarten - 8
Enrollment: 300
Montcrest School is a co-educational, nondenominational school. The school also offers special education classes for students with learning disabilities.
Stephen Beatty, Head of School

Toronto: MPS Etobicoke / MPS
30 Barrhead Cres. Toronto, M9W 3Z7 Canada
416-745-1328, Fax: 416-745-4168,
mpsinfo@rogers.com
www.mpsontario.com
Grades: Junior Kindergarten - 12
Gabrielle Bush, Director

Toronto: National Ballet School / NBS
400 Jarvis St. Toronto, M4Y 2G6 Canada
416-964-3780, Fax: 416-964-5133, 1-800-387-0785
careers@nbs-enb.ca
www.nbs-enb.ca
The school offers elite ballet training, academic instruction, & residential care.
Judith Gelber, Chair
Jeff Melanson, Executive Director & Co-Chief Executive Offic
Mavis Staines, Artistic Director & Co-Chief Executive Office
Katharine Harris, Officer, Media Relations & Communications, 416-964-3780 2117
kharris@nbs-enb.ca

Toronto: North Toronto Christian School / NTCS
50 Page Ave. Toronto, M2K 2B4 Canada
416-226-3366,
www.yorkland.on.ca
Grades: Junior Kindergarten - 6
Enrollment: 380

Toronto: Northmount School
26 Mallard Rd. Toronto, M3B 1S3 Canada
416-449-8823, Fax: 416-449-1244,
Lolita.Pereira@northmount.com
www.northmount.com
Grades: Junior Kindergarten - 8
Northmount School specializes in the education of boys.
Dr. Carmen Mombourquette, Head of School

Toronto: P.T. Montessori School
280 Culford Rd. Toronto, M6L 2V3 Canada
416-242-3725,
ptmontessori@look.ca
Grades: Elem.
Enrollment: 51
Linda Harrison, Administrator

Toronto: People's Christian Academy
374 Sheppard Ave. East Toronto, M2N 3B6 Canada
416-222-3341, Fax: 416-222-3344,
info@pca.ca
www.pca.ca
Grades: Jr. K.-12
Enrollment: 808
Rev. Reg Andrews, Director of Operations and Ministry

Toronto: Queensway Christian College School / QCC
1536 The Queensway Toronto, M8Z 1T5 Canada
416-255-6033, Fax: 416-255-7389,
www.qccollege.com
Grades: Junior Kindergarten - 12
Queensway Christian College os a non-denominational Christian school, which consists of a high school, a middle school, & a junior school.
David Broomer, Executive Director
John Allardyce, Supervising Principal
Tim Bramer, Elementary Vice Principal
Sue Broomer, Secretary

Toronto: Royal St. George's College
120 Howland Ave. Toronto, M5R 3B5 Canada
416-533-9481, Fax: 416-533-0028,
contactus@rsgc.on.ca
www.rsgc.on.ca/
Grades: Elem./Sec.; Boys
Enrollment: 430
Hal Hannaford

Toronto: St. Clement's School
21 St. Clement's Ave. Toronto, M4R 1G8 Canada
416-483-4835, Fax: 416-483-8242,
admissions@scs.on.ca
www.scs.on.ca/
Grades: 1-12
Enrollment: 450
All-girl's school affiliated with the Anglican church
Patricia Parisi, Principal

Toronto: St. Michael's College School
1515 Bathurst St. Toronto, M5P 3H4 Canada
416-653-3180, Fax: 416-653-7704,
info@smcsmail.com; privacyofficer@smcsmail.com (privacy officer)
www.stmichaelscollegeschool.com
Grades: 7-12
Enrollment: 1100
St. Michael's College School provides Catholic, Liberal Arts eductaion for young men.
Fr. Tim Scott, C.S.B., Chair, Board of Directors
Rev. John Malo, C.S.B., Superior
Fr. Joseph Redican, C.S.B., President, 416-653-3180 174
Terence Sheridan, Principal, 416-653-3180 139
Emile John, Vice-Principal, 416-653-3180 156
David Lee, Vice-Principal
Kimberley Bailey, Director, Advancement, 416-653-3180 118
Michael De Pellegrin, Director, Communications, 416-653-3180 292
Fr. John Malo, C.S.B., Director, Pastoral Care, 416-653-3180 229
Greg Paolini, Director, Admissions, 416-653-3180 195
Fr. John Reddy, C.S.B., Director, Faith Development, 416-653-3180 217
Bill Smith, Director, Plant, 416-653-3180 129
Gino Saccone, Corporate Controller, 416-653-3180 239

Toronto: School of Liberal Arts / SOLA
#200, 36 Eglinton Ave. West Toronto, M4R 1A1 Canada
416-489-7652, Fax: 416-489-2074,
www.solaprep.com
Grades: Sec.
Enrollment: 251
University Preparatory School
David L. Ferguson

Toronto: Shmuel Zahavy Cheder Chabad of Toronto
#203, 900 Alness St. Toronto, M3J 2H6 Canada
416-663-1972, Fax: 416-650-9404,
www.chederchabad.com
Students at Shmuel Zahavy Cheder Chabad of Toronto also receive education in Torah scholarship & classic Jewish values.
Rabbi Yona Shur, Director
Rabbi Baruch Zaltzman, Principal

Toronto: Sidney Ledson School Ltd.
#107, 220 Duncan Mill Rd. Toronto, M3B 3J5 Canada
416-447-5355, Fax: 416-447-5283,
www.sidneyledsoninstitute.com
Grades: K./Elem.
Enrollment: 50
Sidney Ledson

Toronto: Sterling Hall School of Toronto / SHS
99 Cartwright Ave. Toronto, M6A 1V4 Canada
416-785-3410, Fax: 416-785-6616,
shsadmin@sterlinghall.com
www.sterlinghall.com
Grades: Junior Kindergarten - 8
Enrollment: 300
Sterling Hall School of Toronto educates boys.
Ian Robinson, Principal
Claire Reed, Director, Admissions
admissions@sterlinghall.com

Toronto: Sunnybrook School
469 Merton St. Toronto, M4S 1B4 Canada
416-487-5308, Fax: 416-487-5381,
sbmail@sunnybrookschool.com
www.sunnybrookschool.com
Grades: Jr. K.-6
Enrollment: 134
Dr. Irene Davy, Ph.D., Director

Toronto: Three Fishes Christian Elementary School
Miracle Family Temple
1100 Bellamy Rd. North Toronto, M1H 1H2 Canada
416-284-9003,
3fishes@threefishes.org
www.threefishes.org
Grades: Junior Kindergarten - 8
Three Fishes Christian Elementary School offers a Christ-centered & academically demanding program.
Laurel Ann Mirams, Principal
dmirams@sympatico.ca

Toronto: Timothy Christian School (Rexdale) / TCS
28 Elmhurst Dr. Toronto, M9W 2J5 Canada
416-741-5770, Fax: 416-741-3359,
www.timothycs.com
Grades: Junior Kindergarten - 8
Enrollment: 100
Timothy Christian School in Rexdale offers a Christ-centred education.
Margareth Lise, Principal
Bobbie Van Ysseldyk, Finance Administrator & Administrative Assist

Toronto: Toronto Cheder School
3995 Bathurst St. Toronto, M3H 5V3 Canada
416-636-2987
Enrollment: 200
Toronto Cheder School is an Orthodox school for boys.
Rabbi D. Engel, Principal

Toronto: Toronto French School / TFS
Toronto Campus
306 Lawrence Ave. East Toronto, M4N 1T7 Canada
416-484-6533, Fax: 416-488-3090,
admissions@tfs.ca
www.tfs.ca
Grades: Preschool - 12
Toronto French School is a co-educational, non-denominational school, which offers bilingual education.
Lena Sarkissian, Chair
board@tfs.ca
John Godfrey, Headmaster
Alain Delaune, Principal, Mississauga School
Heidi Gollert, Principal, Senior School
Mirna Hafez, Principal, Junior School

Toronto: The Toronto Heschel School
819 Sheppard Ave. West Toronto, M3H 3J7 Canada
416-635-1876, Fax: 416-635-1800,
info@torontoheschel.org
www.torontoheschel.org
Grades: Junior Kindergarten - 8
Enrollment: 300
The Jewish day school combines the teaching of Judaism with a general studies curriculum.
Ashira Gobrin, Board Co-Chair
Ken Kraft, Board Co-Chair
Mark Abramsohn, Executive Director
Gail Baker, Head of School & Principal
Rav Eliot Feldman, Vice Principal
Greg Beiles, Director, Curriculum & Training

Toronto: United Synagogue Day School / USDS
Administration House
3072 Bayview Ave. Toronto, M2N 5L3 Canada
416-224-8737, Fax: 416-225-9108,
bayview.campus@usds.ca (E-mail, Bayview Campus)
admin.house@usds.ca; bathurst.campus@usds.ca (Bathurst Campus)
www.usds.ca
Grades: Preschool - 8
Enrollment: 700
United Synagogue Day School is a Conservative Jewish day school. It offers a program of Jewish & general studies.
Gail Silver, Principal, Bayview Campus, 416-225-1143 201
gails@usds.ca
Ashley Waltman, Principal, Bathurst Campus, 416-781-5658 301
awaltman@usds.ca
Sheila Miller, Director, Development, 416-224-8737 140
sheilam@usds.ca
Michele Viner, Director, Admissions, 416-224-8737 137
mviner@usds.ca

Toronto: University of Toronto Schools / UTS
371 Bloor St. West Toronto, M5S 2R7 Canada

416-978-3212, Fax: 416-978-6775,
416-946-7995 (Phone, Admissions); 416-978-7325 (Student Services)
info@utschools.ca
www.utschools.ca
Grades: 7 - 12
Enrollment: 640
UTS is a coeducational school, affiliated with the University of Toronto.
Robert E. Lord, Chair
UTSBoard@utschools.ca
Michaele Robertson, Principal

Toronto: Upper Canada College / UCC
200 Lonsdale Rd. Toronto, M4V 1W6 Canada
416-488-1125, Fax: 416-484-8611,
416-488-1125, ext. 2313 (Phone, Office of Advancement)
admission@ucc.on.ca; administration@ucc.on.ca
www.ucc.on.ca
Grades: Senior Kindergarten - 12
The Preparatory School has over 400 boys from Senior Kindergarten to grade seven. The Upper School offers a five year secondary education.
Michael MacMillan, Chair, Board of Governors
Jim Power, Principal, 416-488-1125 4010
Steve Griffin, Head, Upper School
sgriffin@ucc.on.ca
David Matthews, Asst. Head, University Relations & Sec., Boar, 416-488-1125 2260
dmatthews@ucc.on.ca
Andrea Aster, Associate Director, Marketing & Communication
416-488-1125, ext. 3355

Toronto: Yeshiva Bnei Zion of Bobov
44 Champlain Blvd. Toronto, M3H 2Z1 Canada
416-633-6332, Fax: 416-633-6704
Grades: K./Elem.; Boys
Enrollment: 146
David Kessler

Toronto: Yeshiva Yesodei Hatorah
77 Glen Rush Blvd. Toronto, M5N 2T8 Canada
416-787-1101, Fax: 416-787-9044
Grades: K./Elem.; Boys
Enrollment: 422
Rabbi Asher A. Bornstein

Toronto: Yeshivas Nachalas Zvi
475 Lawrence Ave. West Toronto, M5M 1C6 Canada
416-782-8912, Fax: 416-782-8517
Grades: Elem./Sec.
Enrollment: 90
Bruce Graham

Toronto: The York School
1320 Yonge St. Toronto, M4T 1X2 Canada
416-926-1325,
416-646-5275 (Phone, Admissions)
www.yorkschool.com
Grades: Junior Kindergarten - 12
Enrollment: 593
The York School is co-educational & non-denominational. It is an International Baccalaureate World School, which offers PYP, MYP, & Diploma programs.
Jason Hanson, Chair
Ezio Crescenzi, Head of School, 416-646-5271
ezio_crescenzi@tys.on.ca
Susan Charron, Principal, Lower School, 416-646-5273
susan_charron@tys.on.ca
David Hamilton, Principal, Upper School, 416-646-5272
david_hamilton@tys.on.ca
Marilyn Andrews, Director, External Relations
Conor Jones, Director, Admission
Robin Kester, Director, Advancement
Annette Whiteley, Director, Business & Finance

Toronto: The Yorkland School / TYS
255 Yorkland Blvd. Toronto, M2J 1S3 Canada
416-491-7667, Fax: 416-491-3806,
admin@yorkland.on.ca
www.yorkland.on.ca
Grades: 7 - 12
The Yorkland School is the middle & upper school division of the North Toronto Christian School, The school is commited to Biblical principles & values. The Yorkland School helps its students achieve both academically & athletically.
Kevin Ko, Principal

Trenton: Trenton Christian School
340 Second Dug Hill Rd. Trenton, K8V 5P7 Canada
613-392-3600, Fax: 613-392-6316,
tcs@reach.net
www.trentonchristianschool.com
Grades: Junior Kindergarten - 8
Linda Wikkerink, Chair
Allen Bron, Principal
Laurie Tuckey, Vice Principal
Mrs. K. Whitley, Director, Development
tcsdvdr@reach.net

Unionville: Unionville Montessori School / UMS
9302 Kennedy Rd. Unionville, L6C 1N6 Canada
905-474-9888, Fax: 905-474-5767,
www.unionvillemontessori.com
Grades: Preschool - 8
Unionville Montessori School is a coeducational, non-denominational school. The Casa program is available for children from age two to six.
Kevin R. McCarthy, Principal
B.A, B.Sc., M.Ed.

Utterson: Muskoka Christian School
P.O. Box 150
2483 Old Muskoka Rd. Utterson, P0B 1M0 Canada
705-385-2847, Fax: 705-385-1756,
mcs@muskoka.com
www.muskokachristianschool.com
Grades: Junior Kindergarten - 8
The school is owned and operated by the Muskoka Association for Christian Education.
Lauralyn Mercer, Principal

Vaughan: Community Hebrew Academy of Toronto / CHAT
9600 Bathurst St. Vaughan, L4A 3Z8 Canada
905-787-8772, Fax: 905-787-8773,
info@tanenbaumchat.org
www.chat-edu.ca
Grades: Sec.
Enrollment: 600
Paul Shaviv, M.A., M.Phil., Director of Education

Wallaceburg: Wallaceburg Christian Private School / WCS
693 Albert St. Wallaceburg, N8A 1Y8 Canada
519-627-6013, Fax: 519-627-5051,
admin@wallaceburgchristianschool.com
www.wallaceburgchristianschool.com
Grades: Junior Kindergarten - 8
The school is a member of the Ontario Alliance of Christian Schools & Christian Schools International. It is independent of the Ministry of Education, although the school is registerd with the Ministry.
Andy J. Alblas, Principal

Wasaga Beach: Silvercrest Christian School
3267 Mosley St. Wasaga Beach, L0L 2P0 Canada
705-429-4303, Fax: 705-429-0417,
silvercrest@rogers.com
www.silvercrestchristianschool.com
Grades: Jr. K.-8
Enrollment: 52
Heidi Kerssies, Principal

Waterloo: Kitchener Waterloo Bilingual School
600 Erb St. West Waterloo, N2J 3Z4 Canada
519-886-6510, Fax: 519-886-4053
Grades: K./Elem.
Enrollment: 320
Michel Poinot

Waterloo: St. Jude's School Inc.
420 Weber St. Waterloo, N2R 1K4 Canada
519-888-0807, Fax: 519-884-0316,
director2@stjudes.com
www.stjudes.com
Grades: 1-12
Enrollment: 172
Founded in 1980 for students with learning difficulties. Also offers an after-hours Tutoring School and Second Language School
Toni Fouse

Webequie: Simon Jacob Memorial Education Centre
P.O. Box 265
Webequie, P0T 3A0 Canada
807-353-6491, Fax: 807-353-1306,
www.education.matawa.on.ca
Grades: K-10; Native Language; Special Ed.
The Simon Jacob Memorial Education Centre serves members of the Webequie First Nation, in a community about 540 kilometres northeast of Thunder Bay, Ontario. The education centre operates on a schedule, which is sensitive to the Webequie First Nation culture. The school is administered by the Webequie First Nation Education Authority.
Mary Gardiner, Principal
Stephanie Jones, Teacher, Special Education
Lois Whitehead, Instuctor, Native Language

Wellandport: Robert Land Academy
6726 South Chippawa Rd., RR#3 Wellandport, L0R 2J0 Canada
905-386-6203, Fax: 905-386-6607,
www.robertlandacademy.com
Grades: 6 - 12
Enrollment: 165
Robert Land Academy is a highly structured military boarding school, which provides education for previously under-achieving boys with potential.
Major (retired) G. Scott Bowman, Founder & Headmaster

Wellandport: Wellandport Christian Private School
P.O. Box 123
84008 Wellandport Rd. Wellandport, L0R 2J0 Canada
905-386-6272, Fax: 905-386-7184,
wcs@wellandportchristianschool.ca
www.wellandportchristianschool.ca
Grades: Preschool - 8
Wellandport Christian Private School is a day school which offers Christ-centred programs. The Christian preschool program is for four year old children.

Wheatley: Old Colony Christian Academy
21311 Campbell Rd., RR#1 Wheatley, N0P 2P0 Canada
519-825-9188, Fax: 519-825-9122
Grades: Elem.
Enrollment: 252
Abe Thiessen

Whitby: Trafalgar Castle School
401 Reynolds St. Whitby, L1N 3W9 Canada
905-668-3358, Fax: 905-668-4136,
www.castle-ed.com
Grades: 6 - 12
The day & boarding school educates young women.
Brian McClure, Principal, 905-668-3358 225
mcclureb@castle-ed.com
Gillian Martin, Vice Principal, School Life, 905-668-3358 228
mcclureb@castle-ed.com
Tim Southwell, Vice Principal, Academics, 905-668-3358 229
southwellt@castle-ed.com
Marguerita Dykstra, Director, Finance, 905-668-3358 232
dykstram@castle-ed.com
Martha Cassidy, Administrator, Office, 905-668-3358 221
cassidym@castle-ed.com
Rhonda Daley, Officer, Marketing & Development, 905-668-3358 247
daleyr@castle-ed.com
Irene Talent, Officer, Admissions & Administrative Assistan, 905-668-3358 227
talenti@castle-ed.com

Whitby: Whitby Montessori & Elementary School
95 Taunton Rd. East Whitby, L1R 3L3 Canada
905-430-8201
Grades: Preschool - Elementary
Whitby Montessori & Elementary School educates children from age thirteen months to fourteen years.
Cathy Barber, Principal

Williamsburg: Timothy Christian School
P.O. Box 179
12600 County Rd. 18 Williamsburg, K0C 2H0 Canada
613-535-2687, Fax: 613-535-1074,
www.tcswilliamsburg.ca
Grades: Junior Kindergarten - 8
Enrollment: 130
Gary Postma, Principal
Principal@tcswilliamsburg.ca
Truusje Berkelaar, Administrative Assistant
office@tcswilliamsburg.ca

Windsor: Académie Ste. Cécile International School
925 Cousineau Rd. Windsor, N9G 1V8 Canada
519-969-1291, Fax: 519-969-7953,
info@stececile.ca
www.stececile.ca
Grades: Pre./Elem./Sec.
Enrollment: 250
Affiliated with the Univ. of Windsor. Programmes include the Ontario Sec. School Programme, the International Bacc. Programme, Advanced Placement; emphasis on music, dance, art, & performing arts, as well as programmes in technology; ESL, FSL & TOEFL courses; summer school.
Thérèse H. Gadoury, Principal

Windsor: An-Noor Private School
1480 Janette Ave. Windsor, N8X 1Z4 Canada
519-966-4422

Grades: Elem.
Enrollment: 158
Cassim Parak, Principal

Windsor: First Lutheran Christian Academy
3850 Locke St. Windsor, N9G 1S1 Canada
519-250-7888, Fax: 519-250-7715

Enrollment: 201
Suzanne Eberhard

Windsor: Maranatha Christian Academy
939 Northwood St. Windsor, N9E 2B4 Canada
519-966-7424, Fax: 519-966-9519

Grades: K./Elem.
Enrollment: 252
William Van Dyke

Windsor: Windsor Christian Fellowship Academy
4490 - 7th Concession, RR#1 Windsor, N9A 6J3 Canada
519-972-5986, Fax: 519-972-5643

Grades: Elem.
Enrollment: 81
Patti Banks

Woodbridge: Credo Christian Private School
8260 Huntington Rd., RR#1 Woodbridge, L4L 1A5 Canada
905-851-1620, Fax: 905-851-1620

Grades: K./Elem.
Enrollment: 74
L.P. Maat

Woodbridge: Maple Leaf Montessori School Inc.
8286 Islington Ave. Woodbridge, L4L 1W8 Canada
905-856-3359

Grades: Elem.
Enrollment: 178
Johanna Madeley

Woodbridge: Toronto District Christian High School
377 Woodbridge Ave. Woodbridge, L4L 2V7 Canada
905-851-1772, Fax: 905-851-9992,
info@tdchristian.ca; admissions@tdchristian.ca
www.tdchristian.ca

Grades: Secondary
Ren Siebenga, Principal
principal@tdchristian.ca
Tim Bentum, Vice Principal, Admissions & Students
bentum@tdchristian.ca
Justin De Moor, Vice Principal, Communications
demoor@tdchristian.ca
William Groot, Vice Principal, Scheduling
groot@tdchristian.ca
Meg Cate, Financial Administrator
cate@tdchristian.ca

Wunnummin Lake: Lydia Lois Beardy Memorial School
P.O. Box 108
General Delivery Wunnummin Lake, P0V 2Z0 Canada
807-442-2575, Fax: 807-442-2640

Grades: Elem./Sec.
Enrollment: 150
Mary Angees

Wyoming: John Knox Christian School of Wyoming
P.O. Box 81
Wyoming, N0N 1T0 Canada
519-845-3112, Fax: 519-845-1404

Grades: K./Elem.
Enrollment: 140
Ymko Boersma

Universities & Colleges

Universities

Guelph: University of Guelph
50 Stone Rd. East Guelph, N1G 2W1 Canada
519-824-4120, Fax: 519-767-1693,
www.uoguelph.ca

Enrollment: 19408
Pamela Wallin, O.C., S.O.M., Chancellor
chancellor@uoguelph.ca
Alastair J.S. Summerlee, President & Vice-Chancellor
president@uoguelph.ca
Maureen Mancuso, Provost & Vice-President (Academic)
Nancy Sullivan, Vice-President (Finance & Administration)
Martha Harley, Asst. Vice-President (Human Resources)
Brenda Whiteside, Assoc. Vice-President (Student Affairs)
Serge Desmarais, Assoc. Vice-President (Academic)
Michael Ridley, Chief Librarian & Chief Information Officer

Faculties
Arts

Jacqueline Murray, Dean

Biological Science
Michael Emes, Dean

Environmental Sciences
Josef Ackerman, Dean

Graduate Studies
Isobel Heathcote, Dean

Management & Economics
Chris McKenna, Dean

Ontario Agricultural College
Craig Pearson, Dean

Ontario Veterinary College
Elizabeth Stone, Interim Dean

Physical & Engineering Science
Peter Tremaine, Dean

Social & Applied Sciences
Alun Joseph, Dean

Schools
College d'Alfred
Marcel Couture, Acting Director

Engineering
Richard Zynter, Acting Director

Environmental Design & Rural Development
Robert Brown, Acting Director

Fine Arts & Music
John Kissick, Director

Hospitality & Tourism Management
Marion Joppe, Director

Kemptville College
Michael Goss, Director

Ridgetown College
Ron Pitblado, Acting Director

School of English & Theatre Studies
David Murray, Acting Director

Publications
At Guelph

Guelph Peak

The Ontarion

Hamilton: McMaster University
1280 Main St. West Hamilton, L8S 4L8 Canada
905-525-9140, Fax: 905-521-9183,
www.mcmaster.ca

Enrollment: 23325
Lynton (Red) Wilson, Chancellor 24340
Peter George, President & Vice-Chancellor 24340

Engineering
David S. Wilkinson, Dean

Graduate Studies
F.L. Hall, Dean

Health Sciences
John G. Kelton, Dean

Humanities
Suzanne Crosta, Dean

Science
John P. Capone, Dean

Social Sciences
Charlotte A.B. Yates, Dean

Schools
DeGroote School of Business
Paul Bates, Dean

Arts & Science Program
Gary Warner, Director

Indigenous Studies Program
Dawn Martin-Hill, Director

Institute on Globalization and the Human Condition
Robert O'Brien, Director

Affiliations
McMaster Divinity College
1280 Main St. W. Hamilton, L8S 4K1 Canada
905-525-9140, Fax: 090-577-4782,
divinity@mcmaster.ca
www.macdiv.ca

Enrollment: 300
Stanley E. Porter, Principal & Dean
Bill Marshall, Director of Finance, 905-525-9140 24685
marshaw@mcmaster.ca
Dr. Phil Zylla, Academic Dean, 905-525-9140 20104
zyllap@mcmaster.ca

Publications
Community Report

McMaster Times

vanraay@mcmaster.ca

Alumni magazine.

McMaster Update
c/o Office of Public Relations, Room 111, Chester
1280 Main St. West Hamilton, L8S 4L9 Canada
905-525-9140,
update@mcmaster.ca

Hearst: Université de Hearst
60, 9e Rue Hearst, P0L 1N0 Canada
705-372-1781, 1-800-887-1781
info_gen@uhearst.ca
www.uhearst.ca

Kemptville: Kemptville Campus
P.O. Box 2003
830 Prescott St. Kemptville, K0G 1J0 Canada
613-258-8336, Fax: 613-258-8384,
kcampus@kemptvillec.uoguelph.ca
www.kemptvillec.uoguelph.ca

Dr. Michael Goss

Kingston: Queen's University
99 University Ave. Kingston, K7L 3N6 Canada
613-533-2000, Fax: 613-533-6300,
www.queensu.ca

Enrollment: 21607
David A. Dodge, Chancellor
Dr. Tom Williams, B.Sc., M.A., Ph.D., Principal & Vice-Chancellor
Leora Jackson, B.Sc.H, Rector
Sean Conway, B.A., Vice-Principal
Bill Bryck, Vice-Principal
Jo-Anne Brady, B.A., M.B.A., University Registrar
Georgina Moore, B.A., Secretary of the Senate, University & Board
Richard P. Seres, B.Comm., Director
Peggy Watkin, Secretary of the University Council
Mike Stefano, Director
Chris Tabor, Bookstore Manager
Dr. Patrick Deane, Ph.D., Vice-Principal
Dr. Kerry Rowe, B.Sc., B.E., Ph.D., D.Eng, Vice-Principal
Roderick Morrison, B.A., M.B.A., M.I.R., Vice-Principal

Faculties
Applied Science
Dr. K. Woodhouse, Ph.D., P.Eng., Dean

Arts & Science
Dr. A. MacLean, Ph.D., C.Psych., Dean

Business
Dr. David Saunders, Ph.D., Dean

Education
Dr. Rosa Bruno-Jofré, Ph.D., Dean

Graduate Studies & Research
Dr. J. Deakin, Ph.D., Dean

Health Sciences
Dr. David M.C. Walker, M.D., F.R.C.P.(C), Dean

Law
William F. Flanagan, J.D., D.E.A., LL.M., Dean

Schools
Centre for International Relations
Charles Pentland, B.A., M.A., Ph.D., Director

English
Amanda Marshall, Acting Co-Chair
Barbara Yates, Acting Co-Chair

Institute of Intergovernmental Relations

Sean Conway, Director

Music
Gordon E. Smith, A.R.C.T., B.A., M.A., Ph., Director

Nursing
Cynthia Baker, M.N., Ph.D., Director

Physical & Health Education
Janice Deakin, B.A., B.P.H.E., M.Sc., Director

Policy Studies
Arthur Sweetman, B.Eng., M.A., Ph.D., Director

Rehabilitation Therapy
Sandra J. Olney, B.Sc., Ph.D., M.Ed., Director

Theological College
Jean Stairs, Mus.Bac., M.Div., D.Min., Principal

Urban & Regional Planning
Hok-Lin Leung, B.Arch., M.C.P., M.Sc., P, Director

Computing
James Cordy, B.Sc., M.Sc., Ph.D., P.En, Director

Publications
antiThesis

Golden Words

Queen's Alumni Review
79 Stuart St Kingston, K7L 3N6 Canada
Fax: 613-545-6777

Queen's Journal

Kingston: Royal Military College of Canada
Collège militaire royal du Canada
P.O. Box 17000 Forces
Kingston, K7K 7B4 Canada
613-541-6000, Fax: 613-542-3565, 1-866-762-2672
Undergraduate Programs: 613-541-6000, ext. 6797
liaison@rmc.ca; transcripts@rmc.ca; webmaster@rmc.ca
www.rmc.ca

Individuals must be a Canadian citizen in possession of the necessary academic qualifications. Applicants must also be one of the following: an MOC ((Military Occupation Classification) qualified member of the Canadian Forces; an applicant for the Regular Officer Training Plan (ROTP) or the Reserve Entry Training Plan (RETP); an employee of the Department of National Defence; or the spouse of a member of the Canadian Forces.
Dr. Joel Sokolsky, BA, MA, PhD, Principal
principals.office@rmc.ca
Dr. James Downey, OC, PhD, DHL, DLitt, LLD, Chair
Brigadier-Gener Tom Lawson, O.M.M., C.D., Commandant
Colonel J.G.B. Ouellette, CD, Director, Cadets
Lieutenant-Colo R.R.(Rod) McDonald, CD, Registrar, 613-541-6000 4790

Faculties
Arts
J.J. Sokolsky, BA, MA, PhD, Dean
sokolsky-j@rmc.ca

Continuing Studies
M.A. Hennessy, BA, MA, PhD., Dean
hennessy-m@rmc.ca

Engineering
Dr. John A. Stewart, Dean
stewart_j@rmc.ca

Graduate Studies & Research

Dr. B.J. Fugère, Dean
fugere-j@rmc.ca

Science
Dr. Richard Marsden, Dean
marsden-r@rmc.ca

London: Brescia University College
1285 Western Rd. London, N6G 1H2 Canada
519-432-8353, Fax: 519-858-5137,
brescia@uwo.ca
www.brescia.uwo.ca

Enrollment: 1005
A women's university affiliated with the University of Western Ontario

London: Huron University College
1349 Western Rd. London, N6G 1H3 Canada
519-438-7224, Fax: 519-438-3938,
www.huronuc.on.ca

Enrollment: 1100

London: King's University College
266 Epworth Ave. London, N6A 2M3 Canada
519-433-3491, Fax: 519-433-2227, 1-800-265-4406
kings@uwo.ca
www.uwo.ca/kings/

Enrollment: 3650

London: University of Western Ontario
#2, 1151 Richmond St. London, N6A 5B8 Canada
519-661-2111,
www.uwo.ca

Enrollment: 25000
Dr. Amit Chakma, President & Vice-Chancellor
Frank Angeletti, Vice-Chair
Fred Longstaffe, Provost & Vice-President
Gitta Kulczycki, Vice-President
Ted Garrard, Vice-President
Ted Hewitt, Vice-President
Irene Birrell, Secretary
Valerie Smith, Director
G. Blazak, Director
D. Jones, Director
G.E. Hutchinson, Director
Therese Quigley, Director
S. Grindrod, Assoc. Vice-President
J. Schroeder, Director
Joyce Garnett, Director
V. Smith, Director
R. Moore, Director
Susan Hoddinott, Director
S. Bantock, Director
Michael Mics, Manager
D. Estok, Director
Alan Weedon, Vice-Provost
Carole A. Orchard, Director
Roma Harris, Vice-Provost & Registrar
Tyrrel de Langley, Director
D. Dawson, Director
Alex Navarre, Director
Steve Alb, Director
F. Bauer, Ombudsman
Michele Noble, Chair
John Thompson, Chancellor

Faculties
Arts & Humanities

Education

Julia O'Sullivan, Dean

Engineering
Amit Chakma, Dean

Graduate Studies
Alan C. Weedon, Dean

Health Sciences
William James Weese, Dean

Information & Media Studies
Dr. Thomas Carmichael, Dean

Law
Ian Holloway, Dean

Medicine & Dentistry
Carol Herbert, Dean

Music
Robert Wood, Dean

Richard Ivey School of Business
Carol Stephenson, Dean

Science
David M. Wardlaw, Dean

Social Science
Brian Timney, Dean

Schools
Applied Electrostatics Research Centre
I. Inculet, Director

Boundary Layer Wind Tunnel Laboratory
A.G. Davenport, Director

Canadian Centre for Activity & Aging
Clara Fitzgerald, Director

Centre for Cognitive Science
Z.W. Pylyshyn, Director

Centre for Health & Well-Being
W. Avison, Director

Centre for Interdisciplinary Studies in Chemical Physics
M. Stillman, Director

Centre for Mass Media Studies
A.M. Osler, Director

Centre for Research & Teaching of Canadian Native Languages
R. Darnell, Director

Centre for Studies in Family Medicine
M. Stewart, Director

Centre for the Study of International Economic Relations
J. Whalley, Director

Centre for the Study of Theory & Criticism
T. Rajan, Director

Centre for Textual Scholarship
R.J. Shroyer, Director

Centre for Women's Studies & Feminist Research
Katherine McKenna, Director

Chemical Reactor Engineering Centre
H. de Lasa, Director

Continuing Studies
Kim Miller, Acting Director

Geotechnical Research Centre
K. Lo, Director

International Centre for Olympic Studies
R. Barney, Director

John P. Robarts Research Institute
M. Poznansky, Director
poznansky@admin.rri.uwo.ca

London Museum of Archaeology
Robert Pearce, Director

National Centre for Management Research & Development
K. Hardy, Director

National Tax Centre
T.W. Edgar, Director

Population Studies Centre
Rajulton Fernando, Director

Research Centre in Tribology
W.K. Wan, Director

Surface Science Western
Leo Lau, Director

Affiliations
Brescia University College
1285 Western Rd. London, N6G 1H2 Canada
519-432-8553, Fax: 519-679-6489
Dr Colleen Hanycz, Principal 28263
chanycz@uwo.ca
Dr John B. Mitchell, Academic Dean 28116
jbmitche@uwo.ca
Marianne Simm, Registrar 28266
msimm@uwo.ca

Huron University College
1349 Western Rd. London, N6G 1H3 Canada
519-438-7224, Fax: 519-438-3938
Dr. Ramona Lumpkin, Principal, 519-438-7224 307
rlumpkin@huron.uwo.ca
Bonnie Crocker, Registrar, 519-438-7224 285
bcrocke2@huron.uwo.ca
Rev. Susan Baldwin, Acting Dean, 519-438-7224 251
ssteers2@huron.uwo.ca

King's College
266 Epworth Ave. London, N6A 2M3 Canada
519-433-3491, Fax: 519-433-2227
Dr. Gerald Killan, Principal, 519-433-3491 4300
gkillian@uwo.ca
Dr. Desmond Dutrizac, Academic Dean, 519-433-3491 4303
dutrizac@uwo.ca
Marilyn Mason, Registrar, 519-433-3491 4308
mmason@uwo.ca

Publications
Alumni Gazette

The Gazette
Rm. 244, University Community Centre
London, N6A 3K7 Canada
Fax: 519-661-3816

Western Alumni Gazette
#11, Alumni Hall, University of Western Ontario
Richmond St. N London, N6A 5B9 Canada
Fax: 519-661-3948

Western News

North Bay: Nipissing University
P.O. Box 5002
100 College Dr. North Bay, P1B 8L7 Canada
705-474-3450, Fax: 705-474-1947,
nuinfo@nipissingu.ca
www.nipissingu.ca

Enrollment: 4800
David Brian Liddle, Chancellor
Dr. Lesley Lovett-Doust, President & Vice-Chancellor
Peter Gavan, Chair

Vicky Paine-Mantha, Vice-Pres., Finance & Administration 4289
vickyp@nipissingu.ca
Dr. Katharine M. Bergman, Vice-Pres., Academic & Research 4254
kmb@nipissingu.ca
Lisa Drinkwalter, Acting Exec. Dir., University Advancement 4327
lisad@nipissingu.ca
Brian Nettlefold, Exec. Dir., Library Services 4220
briann@nipissingu.ca
Heather Brown, Associate Registrar 4521, fax: 705-495-1772
registrar@nipissingu.ca

Faculties

Applied & Professional Studies
Rick Vanderlee, Dean
rickv@nipissingu.ca

Arts & Science
Dr. Craig Cooper, Dean 4290
craigc@nipissingu.ca

Schulich School of Education
Dr. Sharon Rich, Dean
sharonr@nipissingu.ca

Campuses

Brantford
50 Wellington St. Brantford, N3T 2L6
519-752-1524, Fax: 519-752-8372,
brant@nipissingu.ca.
Dr Maria Cantalini-Williams, Interim Assoc. Dean
mariac@nipissingu.ca

Muskoka
125 Wellington St. Bracebridge, P1L 1E2
705-645-2921, Fax: 705-645-2922,
muskoka@nipissingu.ca
Jan Lucy, Campus Administrator
janl@nipissingu.ca

Oshawa: University of Ontario Institute of Technology / UOIT

2000 Simcoe St. North Oshawa, L1H 7K4 Canada
905-721-8668, Fax: 905-721-3178,
admissions@uoit.ca
www.uoit.ca

Enrollment: 6500
Hon. Perrin Beatty, B.A., Chancellor
Dr. Ronald Bordessa, B.A., Ph.D, L.LD. (Hons.), President & Vice-Chancellor, 905-721-8668 3212
ron.bordessa@uoit.ca
Richard Marceau, B.Eng., M.Sc.A., Ph.D., F, Provost, 905-721-8668 3147, fax: 905-721-3210
richard.marceau@uoit.ca
MaryLynn West-Moynes, B.Sc. (Hons.), M.A., Vice-President, External Relations, 905-721-8668 3135
marylynn.west-moynes@uoit.ca
Ralph Aprile, B.Tech., M.B.A., Vice-President, Facilities & Ancillary Servic, 905-721-8668 3024
ralph.aprile@dc-uoit.ca
Tom Austin, B.A., C.M.A., Vice-President, Finance & CFO, 905-721-8668 3796
tom.austin@uoit.ca
Margaret Greenley, B.Ed., M.A., Vice-President, Student Affairs, 905-721-8668 2340
margaret.greenley@uoit.ca
Pamela Drayson, B.A., M.A., Ph.D., Chief Librarian, 905-721-8668 2348
pamela.drayson@uoit.ca
Victoria Choy, B.A. (Hons.), M.A., Registrar, 905-721-8668 2988
victoria.choy@uoit.ca

Faculties

Faculty of Business & Information Technology
2000 Simcoe St. N. Oshawa, L1H 7K4 Canada
905-721-3181,
www.businessandit.uoit.ca
Pamela Ritchie, B.A., M.Sc., Ph.D., Dean, 905-721-8668 3160
pamela.ritchie@uoit.ca

Faculty of Criminology, Justice, and Policy Studies (Social Sciences & Human
2000 Simcoe St. N. Oshawa, L1H 7K4 Canada
905-721-3234,
www.criminologyandjustice.uoit.ca/
Nawal Ammar, B.Sc. (Hons.), M.Sc., Ph., Dean, 905-721-8668 3159
nawal.ammar@uoit.ca

Faculty of Education
2000 Simcoe St. N. Oshawa, L1H 7K4 Canada
905-721-3181,
kim.mitchell@uoit.ca (Receptionist, Faculty of Education)
http://education.uoit.ca/
Jim Greenlaw, B.A., B.Ed., M.A.(T), Ph., Dean, 905.721.8668 3158
jim.greenlaw@uoit.ca

Faculty of Energy Systems & Nuclear Science
2000 Simcoe St. N. Oshawa, L1H 7K4 Canada
905-721-8668, Fax: 905-721-3046,
admissions@uoit.ca
nuclear.uoit.ca/
George Bereznai, B.Eng., M.Eng., Ph.D., Dean, 905-721-8668 3142
george.bereznai@uoit.ca

Faculty of Engineering & Applied Science
Ontario Power Generation Engineering Bldg.
2000 Simcoe St.N. Oshawa, L1H 7K4 Canada
905-721-3268, Fax: 905-721-3370,
engineering@uoit.ca
www.engineering.uoit.ca
George Bereznai, B.Eng., M.Eng., Ph.D., Dean, 905-721-8668 3142
george.bereznai@uoit.ca

Faculty of Health Sciences
2000 Simcoe St. N. Oshawa, L1H 7K4 Canada
905-721-3166,
viven.ricard@uoit.ca
www.healthsciences.uoit.ca
Mary Bluechardt, E.M.T., B.PHE, M.Sc., Ph., Dean, 905-721-8668 2518
mary.bluechardt@uoit.ca

Faculty of Science
Science Bldg. UA4000
2000 Simcoe St.N. Oshawa, L1H 7K4 Canada
905-721-3050, Fax: 905-721-3304,
facultyofscience@uoit.ca
www.science.uoit.ca
William Smith, B.A.Sc., M.A.Sc., M.Sc., Dean, 905-721-8668 3235
william.smith@uoit.ca

Office of Graduate Studies
Business and It Bldg.
2nd Fl., 2000 Simcoe St.N. Oshawa, L1H 7K4 Canada
905-721-8668, Fax: 905-721-3242,
gradstudies@uoit.ca
gradstudies.uoit.ca/
Address as of August 20th, 2007.
Brian Campbell, Dean, 905-721-8668 2650
brian.campbell@uoit.ca

Ottawa: Carleton University

1125 Colonel By Dr. Ottawa, K1S 5B6 Canada
613-520-7400, Fax: 613-520-7858,
info@carleton.ca
www.carleton.ca

Grades: 25200
Herb Gray, Chancellor
Dr. Roseann O'Reilly Runte, President & Vice-Chancellor, 613-520-3801
presidents_office@carleton.ca
Peter Ricketts, Provost & Vice-President, 613-520-3884
provost@carleton.ca
Duncan Watt, Vice-Pres., Finance & Administration, 613-520-3804
duncan_watt@carleton.ca
Kimberly Matheson, Vice-Pres., Research & International, 613-520-7838
vpri@carleton.ca
Gisele Samson-Verreault, Chair, 613-520-3811
governors@carleton.ca
Suzanne Blanchard, Registrar, 613-520-2874, fax: 613-520-4410
registrar@carleton.ca

Faculties

Arts & Social Sciences
John Osborne, Dean, 613-520-2355, fax: 613-520-4481
fassod@carleton.ca

Engineering & Design

Dr Rafik Goubran, Dean, 613-520-5790, fax: 613-520-7481
info_engdesign@carleton.ca

Graduate & Postdoctoral Affairs
John Shepard, Dean, 613-520-2525, fax: 613-520-4049
graduate_studies@carleton.ca

Public Affairs
John ApSimon, Interim Dean, 613-520-3741, fax: 613-520-3742
odfpa@carleton.ca

Science
Malcolm Butler, Dean, 613-520-4388, fax: 613-520-4389
odscience@carleton.ca

Azrieli School of Architecture and Urbanism
Sheryl Boyle, Director, 613-520-2855, fax: 613-520-2849
architecture@carleton.ca

Schools

School for Studies in Art & Culture
Brian Foss, Director, 613-520-2600 3791, fax: 613-520-3575
brian_foss@carleton.ca

Linguistics & Language Studies
Lynne Young, Acting Director, 613-520-6612, fax: 613-520-6641
slals@carleton.ca

Sprott School of Business
Dr. Jerry Tomberlin, Dean, 613-520-2388, fax: 613-520-4427
info@sprott.carleton.ca

Canadian Studies
André Loiselle, Director, 613-520-2366, fax: 613-520-3903
canadian_studies@carleton.ca

Computer Science
Dr Douglas Howe, Director, 613-520-4333, fax: 613-520-4334
howescs.carleton.ca

Technology, Society, Environment Studies
Dr. John Buschek, Chair, 613-520-4483
john_buschek@carleton.ca

Industrial Design
Thomas Garvey, Director, 613-520-5672, fax: 613-520-4465
diane_smyth@carleton.ca

Information Technology
Dr Anthony Whitehead, Director, 613-520-5644, fax: 613-520-6623
info@bitdegree.ca

Journalism & Communication
Christopher Waddell, Director, 613-520-7404, fax: 613-520-6690
journalism@carleton.ca

Norman Paterson School of International Affairs
Bryan Henderson, Director, 613-520-6655, fax: 613-520-2889
international_affairs@carleton.ca

Public Policy & Administration
Dr. Susan Phillips, Director, 613-520-2547, fax: 613-520-2551
sppa@carleton.ca

Social Work
Hugh Shewell, Director, 613-520-5601, fax: 613-520-7496
karen_spencer@carleton.ca

Mathematics & Statistics
Yiqiang Zhao, Director, 613-520-3531
ms-dir@math.carleton.ca

Institute for Comparative Studies in Literature, Art & Culture
Paul Théberge, Director, 613-520-2177
icslac@carleton.ca

Institute of African Studies
Blair Rutherford, Director, 613-520-2600 2220, fax: 613-520-2363
african_studies@carleton.ca

Institute of Cognitive Science
Dr Jo-Anne Lefevre, Director, 613-520-2368, fax: 613-520-3985
jo-anne_lefevre@carleton.ca

Institute of Interdisciplinary Studies
Fran Cherry, Director, 613-520-2368, fax: 613-520-3985
iis@carleton.ca

Pauline Jewett Institute of Women's & Gender Studies
Katharine Kelly, Director, 613-520-6645, fax: 613-520-2622
womens_studies@carleton.ca

Institute of Criminology & Criminal Justice
Joanna Pozzulo, Director, 613-520-2588, fax: 613-520-6654
criminology@carleton.ca

Institute of European, Russian & Eurasian Studies
Dr Jeff Sahadeo, Director, 613-520-2888, fax: 613-520-7501
jeff_sahadeo@carleton.ca

Institute of Political Economy
Prof Janet Siltanen, Director, 613-520-7414, fax: 613-520-2154
political_economy@carleton.ca

Institute of Biochemistry
John Vierula, Director, 613-520-2478, fax: 613-520-3539
biochem@carleton.ca

Institute of Environmental Science
Dr Frederick A. Michel, Director, 613-520-2600 4461, fax: 613-520-3422
environmentalscience@carelton.ca

Integrated Science Institute
Pam Wolff, Director, 613-520-2600 4461, fax: 613-520-3422
integratedscience@carleton.ca

Publications
Carleton University Magazine
613-520-3636, Fax: 613-520-3587,
advancement@carleton.ca
magazine.carleton.ca
Fateema Sayani, Editor
fateema_sayani@carleton.ca

The Charlatan
613-520-6680,
charlatan@charlatan.ca
www.charlatan.ca
An independent student newspaper since 1945
Julia Johnson, Editor-In-Chief
editor@charlatan.ca

Ottawa: Dominican University College
Collège Universitaire Dominicain
96 Empress Ave. Ottawa, K1R 7G3 Canada
613-233-5696, Fax: 613-233-6064,
info@dominicancollege.ca
www.collegedominicain.ca
Enrollment: 110
Yvon Pomerleau, O.P., Chancellor
Gabor Csepregi, President & Regent of Studies
Michel Gourges, O.P., Vice-President
Peter Foy, Sec.-Treas.
Francis Peddle, Master of Studies
Daniel Cadrin, Chair, Institute of Pastoral Studies
Marie-Thérèse Nadeau, C.N.D., Dean, Faculty of Theology
Jean-François Méthot, Dean, Philosophy

Ottawa: Saint Paul University
Université Saint-Paul
223 Main St. Ottawa, K1S 1C4 Canada
613-236-1393, Fax: 613-782-3005, 1-800-637-6859
info@ustpaul.ca; studentservices@ustpaul.ca;
bookstore@ustpaul.ca
www.ustpaul.ca
Federated with the University of Ottawa, the Catholic & bilingual institution offers faculties of Canon Law, Human Sciences, Philosophy, & Theology.
Rev. Dale Schlitt, Rector
Prof. Achiel Peelman, Acting Vice-Rector, Academic
Prof. Chantal Beauvais, Vice-Rector, Administration
Rev. Andrea Spatafora, Dean, Faculty of Theology

Ottawa: University of Ottawa
Université d'Ottawa
75 Laurier Ave E. Ottawa, K1N 6N5 Canada
613-562-5700, Fax: 613-562-5103, 1-877-868-8292
www.uottawa.ca
Enrollment: 35548
Huguette Labelle, O.C., B.Sc.N.Ed., B.Ed., Chancellor
Allan Rock, B.A., P.C., President & Vice-Chancellor
François Hule, Vice-President, Academic & Provost
Sylvie Lauzon, B.Sc., M.Sc., Ph.D., Assoc. Vice-President
Victor Simon, B.A., M.A., Vice-President
Louis de Melo, B.A., C.M.A., Vice-President
Pierre Mercier, B.A., M.A., Ph.D., Assoc. Vice-President
Pamela Harrod, Secretary
François Chapleau, B.Sc., M.Sc., Ph.D., Registrar & Assoc. Vice-President
Leslie Weir, B.A., M.L.S., Chief Librarian
Lyse Huot, B.A., Director
Kathryn Prud'homme, B.A., LL.B., Legal Counsel
Mona Nemer, Vice-President
Nicolas Georganas, Ph.D., F.I.E.E., F.R.S.Ca, Assoc. Vice-President
Adele Reinhart, B.A., M.A., Ph.D., Assoc. Vice-President
Paul Boult, B.A., Director

Faculties
Management
Micheál J. Kelly, A.B., M.A., Ph.D., Dean

Arts
Antoni Lewkowicz, B.A., M.A., Ph.D., Dean

Education
Marie Josée Berger, B.Ed., M.Ed. Ph.D., Dean

Engineering
Claude Laguë, Dean

Health Sciences
Denis Prud'homme, B.Sc., M.Sc., PR.D., M.D., Dean

Law, Common Law Section
Bruce Feldthusen, Dean

Law, Civil Law Section
Sébastien Grammond, Dean

Medicine
Jacques Bradwejn, Dean

Science
André Lalonde, B.Sc., M.Sc., Ph.D., Dean

Social Sciences
Catherine M. Lee, Ph.D., Acting Dean

Graduate Studies & Postdoctoral
Gary Slater, B.Sc., M.Sc., Ph.D., Dean

Publications
Tabaret Magazine

The Fulcrum

La Rotonde

Peterborough: Trent University
1600 West Bank Dr. Peterborough, K9J 7B8 Canada
705-748-1011, Fax: 705-748-1246, 1-888-739-8885
www.trentu.ca
Enrollment: 7475
David L. Morton, B.A., M.B.A., LL.D., Chair
Tom Jackson, O.C., LL.D (Hon.), Chancellor
Dr. Steven E. Franklin, Ph.D., President & Vice-Chancellor
Don F. O'Leary, B.B.A., Vice-President
Colin Taylor, M.A., Ph.D., Dean
Dianne Lister, Vice-President
Christopher Michael, B.A., LL.B., Registrar
Julie E. Smith, LL.B., Secretary of the Senate
Leonard Conolly, M.A., Ph.D.., Principal
Michael Peterman, A.B., M.A., Ph.D., Principal
Stephen Brown, M.A., Ph.D., F.S.A., Master
A.A. Krüger, STAATSEXAMEN, Principal
Ian Storey, M.A., Ph.D., Head
Dr. Jocelyn Aubrey, Assoc. Dean of Arts & Science
Garth Brownscombe, B.A., CGA, Director
Lorraine Hayes, B.Sc., Manager
Don Cumming, B.A., Senior Director
Bill Byrick, B.A., Director
D'Arcy Legros, Bookstore Manager
Dr. Christine McKinnon, B.A. (Hons.), B.Phil., D., Vice-President
James Parker, B.A., M.A., Ph.D., Assoc. Vice-President
David Poole, B.Sc., M.Sc., Ph.D., Associate Dean

Publications
Arthur

St Catharines: Brock University
500 Glenridge Ave. St Catharines, L2S 3A1 Canada
905-688-5550, Fax: 905-688-2789,
www.brocku.ca
Enrollment: 17493
Dr Ned Goodman, Chancellor
Dr Jack N. Lightstone, President & Vice-Chancellor
Dr Murray Knuttila, Provost/Vice-Pres., Academic
Steven Pillar, Vice-Pres., Finance/Admin.
David Petis, Vice-Pres., Advancement
Ian Brindle, Vice-Pres., Research
Barb Anderson, Registrar 3566
bdavis@brocku.ca

Faculties
Business
Barbara Sainty, Interim Dean 3182
bsainty@brocku.ca

Education
James Heap, Dean 5190
jheap@brocku.ca

Humanities
Rosemary Hale, Dean 4562
rhale@brocku.ca

Social Sciences

Thomas Dunk, Dean 3426
tdunk@brocku.ca

Mathematics & Sciences
Richard Cheel, Interim Dean 3421
dean.fms@brocku.ca

Applied Health Sciences
John Corlett, Dean 3385
john.corlett@brocku.ca

Graduate Studies
Marilyn Rose, Dean 5152
mrose@brocku.ca

Publications
Brock Press
Katherine Gottli, Editor-In-Chief 3269
editor@brockpress.com

Sudbury: Huntington University
935 Ramsey Lake Rd. Sudbury, P3E 2C6 Canada
705-673-4126, Fax: 705-673-6917, 800-461-6366
www.huntingtonu.ca
Liberal Arts University specializing in Communication Studies, Ethics, Gerontology, Religious studies and Theology.

Sudbury: Laurentian University of Sudbury
Université Laurentienne de Sudbury
935 Ramsey Lake Rd. Sudbury, P3E 2C6 Canada
705-675-1151, Fax: 705-675-4891, 800-461-4030
admissions@laurentian.ca
www.laurentian.ca
Enrollment: 8270
Teaching is in French & English. Certain faculties offer parallel programs in both languages.
Dominic Giroux, MBA, President
Susan Silverton, Ph.D., M.D., Vice-President
Harley d'Entremont, M.A., Ph.D., Vice-President
R. Bertoli, Director
D. Mayer, M.Sc., Assoc. Vice-President
R. Smith, B.Sc., Registrar
L. Bonin, B.A., M.L.S., Director
Gerry Labelle, B.Comm., C.A., Director

Faculties
Humanities & Social Sciences
Donald Dennie, B.A., M.A., Ph.D., Dean

Management
Huguette Blanco, M.B.A., Ph.D., Dean

Professional Schools
Anne-Marie Mawhiney, B.A., B.S.W., M.S.W., Ph., Dean

Sciences & Engineering
R. Haq, B.Sc., M.Sc., Ph.D., Dean

Schools
Commerce
Ozhand Ganjavi, M.M.Sc., Ph.D., Director

Education (English)
John Lundy, Ed.D., Director

Education (French)
Serge Demers, Ph.D., Director

Engineering
Anis Farah, Ph.D., Director

Graduate Studies

Paul Colilli, M.A., Ph.D., Director

Human Kinetics
Roger Couture, M.A., Ph.D., Director

Nursing
Sharolyn Mossey, M.Sc.N., Director

Social Work
Duncan Matheson, M.S.W., Ph.D., Director

Sports Administration
K. Lefroy, B.Ed., M.Ed., Ed.D., Director

Affiliations
University of Sudbury
Université de Sudbury
935 Ramsey Lake Rd. Sudbury, P3E 2C6 Canada
705-673-5661, Fax: 705-673-4912,
Registrar, E-mail: registrar@usudbury.ca
usudreg@usudbury.ca; usudburyalumni@usudbury.ca (Alumni)
www.usudbury.com
Founded in 1913 as Collège du Sacré-Coeur, the University of Sudbury operates in the Jesuit tradition. The bilingual university is committed to the English, French, & First Nations cultures. Courses include Religious Studies, Philosophy, Communications, French-Canadian Folklore, & Native Studies.
André Lacroix, Q.C., LL.D., Chancellor
Robert L. Fabbro, LL.B., Chair, Board of Regents
Dr. Pierre Zundel, Ph.D., President & Vice-Chancellor
pzundel@usudbury.ca
Sylvie Renault, H.B.Com., Registrar & Director, Recruitment & Communica
srenault@usudbury.ca
Shelley R. Machum, B.Com., C.A., Treasurer & Director, Administrative Services
smachum@usudbury.ca
Gerry Copeman, B.A., S.T.B., B.Th., Director, Spiritual Services
gcopeman@usudbury.ca
Paul Laverdure, Ph.D., Director, Library Services
plaverdure@usudbury.ca
Rachel Haliburton, Chair, Philosophy
rhaliburton@usudbury.ca
Jack Laughlin, Chair, Religious Studies
jlaughlin@usudbury.ca
Roger Spielmann, Chair, Native Studies
rspielmann@usudbury.ca

Pierre Brideau, Manager, Facilities & Security
pbrideau@usudbury.ca

Huntington University
Ramsey Lake Rd. Sudbury, P3E 2C6 Canada
705-673-4126
Kevin McCormick, President & Vice-Chancellor
kmccormick@huntingtonu.ca

Thorneloe University at Laurentian University
935 Ramsey Lake Rd. Sudbury, P3E 2C6 Canada
705-673-1730, Fax: 705-673-4979, 1-866-846-7635
smoores@laurentian.ca (Susan Moores, Administrative Secretary)
www.thorneloe.laurentian.ca
Affiliated with the Anglican Church, Thorneloe University features the departments of Religious Studies, Classical Studies, Theatre Arts, & Women's Studies.
The Rev. Dr. Robert A. Derrenbacker, PhD., President, Provost, & Chaplain
rderrenbacker@laurentian.ca
Dr. Ian Maclennan, Registrar
imaclennan@laurentian.ca
Adam Sauve, Dean
ay_sauve@laurentian.ca
David Macdonald, Coordinator, Distance Education & Learning Te, 705-673-1730 33, fax: 705-673-4979
dmacdonald@laurentian.ca
Janine Moutsatsos, Librarian
jmoutsatsos@laurentian.ca

Collège Universitaire de Hearst
Hearst, P0L 1N0 Canada
705-372-1781
Raymond Tremblay, B.A., B.Sc., M.A., Ph.D., Recteur
Pierre Ouellette, B.A., M.A., Vice-recteur
Manon Cyr, B.A., M.B.A., Secrétaire générale

Publications
Lambda

L'Original déchainé

Sudbury: Thorneloe University
935 Ramsey Lake Rd. Sudbury, P3E 2C6 Canada
705-673-1730, Fax: 705-673-4979, 866-846-7635
smoores@laurentian.ca
thorneloe.laurentian.ca

Sudbury: University of Sudbury
Ramsey Lake Rd Sudbury, P3E 2C6 Canada
705-673-5661,
registrar@usudbury.ca
www.usudbury.ca

Thunder Bay: Lakehead University
955 Oliver Rd. Thunder Bay, P7B 5E1 Canada
807-343-8110, Fax: 807-343-8023,
www.lakeheadu.ca

Enrollment: 8050
L.G. Everett, Chancellor
Frederick F. Gilbert, President & Vice-Chancellor
K. Roche, Registrar & Secretary of Senate
A.E. Deighton, University Librarian
R. Blais, Controller
G. Wojda, Director
J. Podd, Director
J. Smith, Director
C. Calvert, Director
K.L. Clarke, Director
T. Warden, Director
L. Hayes, Vice-President
E.G. Walsh, Executive Director
M. Pawlowski, Vice-President
B. Sabourin, Vice-Provost
E. Abaya, Director
B. Moore, Director
S. Jafri, Director
R. Wang, Vice-President

Faculties
Business Administration
B. Dadgostar, Dean

Education
J. O'Sullivan, Dean

Engineering
H.T. Saliba, Dean

Forestry & the Forest Environment
U. Runesson, Dean

Graduate & International Studies
P. Hicks, Dean

Northern Ontario School of Medicine
J. Lanphear, West Campus Dean

Professional Schools
I. Newhouse, Dean

Science & Environmental Studies
A.P. Dean, Dean

Schools
Kinesiology

J. Farrell, Director

Nursing
K. Poole, Director

Outdoor Recreation
B. Cuthbertson, Director

Social Work
D. Tranter, Director

Publications
The Argus

Toronto: Emmanuel College
75 Queen's Park Cres. East Toronto, M5S 1K7 Canada
416-585-4539, Fax: 416-585-4516,
ec.office@utoronto.ca
www.vicu.utoronto.ca/emmanuel.htm

Enrollment: 173
Theological college affiliated with the United Church of Canada

Toronto: Innis College
2 Sussex Ave. Toronto, M5S 1J6 Canada
416-978-2513, Fax: 416-978-5503,
www.utoronto.ca/innis/

Enrollment: 1480
Constituent college of the University of Toronto
Janet Paterson, Principal, 416-978-2510
principal.innis@utoronto.ca
Donald Boere, Assistant Principal & Registrar, 416-978-2513
donald.boere@utoronto.ca

Toronto: Knox College
59 St. George St. Toronto, M5S 2E6 Canada
416-978-4500, Fax: 416-971-2133,
knox.college@utoronto.ca
www.utoronto.ca/knox/
Theological college at the University of Toronto affiliated with the Presbyterian Church in Canada

Toronto: Massey College
4 Devonshire Pl. Toronto, M5S 2E1 Canada
416-978-2895, Fax: 416-946-7890,
massey.porter@gmail.com
masseycollege.ca

Enrollment: 130

Toronto: Ontario College of Art & Design / OCAD
100 McCaul St. Toronto, M5T 1W1 Canada
416-977-6000, Fax: 416-977-0235,
www.ocad.ca

Enrollment: 3467
Sara Diamond, President
Dr. Sarah McKinnon, Vice-President
Peter Caldwell, Vice-President
Josephine Polera, Director
Simone Jones, Asst. Dean
Dr. Anthony Cahalan, Dean
Blake Fitzpatrick, Dean
Wendy Coburn, Asst. Dean
Steve Quinlan, Asst. Dean
Peter Fraser, Director
Colleen Reid, Asst. Dean
Rosemary Donegan, Asst. Dean
Jill Patrick, Director
Alastair MacLeod, Director
Christine Swiderski, Exhibitions Coordinator
Cindy Ball, Director
Marian Ruston, Manager
Jan Sage, Director
Nicky Davis, Director
Peter Lashko, Director
Ted Rickard, Manager
Sarah Mulholand, Coordinator
Laura Matthews, Director
Charles Reeve, Curator
Lance Straun, Manager
Dr. Kathryn Shailer, Dean
Vladimir Spicanovic, Asst. Dean
Doreen Balabanoff, Asst. Dean

Toronto: Ryerson University
350 Victoria St. Toronto, M5B 2K3 Canada
416-979-5000,
inquire@ryerson.ca
www.ryerson.ca

Enrollment: 25600
Peter Lukasiewicz, Chair
G. Raymond Chang, Chancellor
Sheldon Levy, President & Vice-Chancellor
Sheldon Levy, Provost & Vice-President
Michael Dewson, Vice-Provost
Dr. Linda Grayson, Vice-President
Keith Alnwick, Registrar
Janice Winton, Executive Director
Marion Creery, Sr. Director
Renée Lemieux, Sr. Director
Shirley Lewchuk, Secretary of the Board of Governors
Ian Marlatt, Sr. Director
Peter Lukasiewicz, Vice-Chair
Dr. Anastasios (Tas) Venetsanopoulos, Vice-President
Judith Sandys, Assoc. Vice-President

Faculties
Arts
Dr. Carla Cassidy, Dean

Business
Dr. Ken Jones, Ph.D., Dean

Communication & Design
Dr. Daniel Doz, Dean

Community Services
Dr. Usha George, Ph.D., Dean

Engineering & Applied Science
Dr. Mohamed Lachemi, Interim Dean

Engineering & Applied Science, Research, Development & New Science Programs
Steven Liss, Assoc. Dean

Engineering & Applied Science, Undergraduate Programs & Student Affairs
Zouheir Fawaz, Assoc. Dean

The G. Raymond Chang School of Continuing Education
Anita Shilton, Dean

Graduate Studies

Publications
The Eyeopener

The Ryerson Rambler
350 Victoria St Toronto, M5B 2K3 Canada

Ryersonian

NightViews

Toronto: University College
15 King's College Circle Toronto, M5S 3H7 Canada
416-978-3170, Fax: 416-978-6019

Toronto: University of Guelph Humber
207 Humber College Blvd. Toronto, M9W 5L7 Canada
416-798-1331, Fax: 416-798-1991,
info@guelphhumber.ca
www.guelphhumber.ca
John Walsh, Vice-Provost, Chief Academic & Executive Offi
Dalia Smith, Librarian
dalia.smith@guelphhumber.ca
Jock Phippen, Manager, Registrarial Services
jock.phippen@guelphhumber.ca
Gabrielle Bernardi-Dengo, Manager, Finance & Administration Services
gabrielle.bernardi-dengo@guelphhumber.ca

Toronto: University of Toronto
21 King's College Circle Toronto, M5S 1A1 Canada
416-978-2011,
www.utoronto.ca

Enrollment: 45009
The Hon. David Peterson, Chancellor
Dr. David Naylor, President
Cheryl Misak, Vice-President & Provost
Edith Hillan, Vice-Provost
John Challis, Assoc. Provost & Vice-President
Safwat Zaky, Vice-Provost
Rivi Frankle, Asst. Vice-President & Chief Operations Offic
Angela Hildyard, Vice-President
Catherine J. Riggall, Vice-President
Tim McTiernan, Asst. Vice-President, Research & Executive Di
Joan E. Foley, University Ombudsperson
Karel Swift, University Registrar & Director
Avon McFarlane, Acting Asst. Vice-President
Catharine Whiteside, Vice-Provost
Robert Steiner, Asst. Vice-President
Jonathan Freedman, Deputy Provost

John F. (Jack) Petch, Chair of the Governing Council
Sheila Brown, CFO
Judith Wolfson, Vice-President

Faculties
Applied Science & Engineering
Prof. Cristina Amon, Dean

Architecture, Landscape & Design
George Baird, Dean

Arts & Science
Meric Gertler, Dean

Dentistry
Prof. David Mock, Dean

Forestry
Tattersall Smith, Dean

Information Studies

Ross Seamus, Dean

Law
Mayo Moran, Dean

Management
Roger L. Martin, Dean

Medicine
Catharine Whiteside, Dean

Music
Russell Hartenberger, Dean

Nursing
Sioban Nelson, Dean

OISE/UT
Jane Gaskell, Dean

Pharmacy
Henry Mann, Dean

Physical Education & Health
Bruce Kidd, Dean

School of Graduate Studies
Brian Corman, Dean

Social Work
Cheryl Regehr, Dean

Schools
Asian Institute
Joseph Wong, Director

Canadian Institute for Theoretical Astrophysics
Norm Murray, Director

Centre for Comparative Literature
Neil ten Kortenaar, Director

Centre for Environmental Studies
Ingrid Leman Stefanovic, Director

Centre for European, Russian, and Eurasian Studies
Jeffrey Kopstein, Director

Centre for Industrial Relations
Anil Verma, Interim Director

Centre for International Studies
Prof. Louis W. Pauly, Director

Centre for Medieval Studies
Andrew Orchard, Director

Centre for Reformation & Renaissance Studies
Olga Pugliese, Director

Centre for Research in Women's Health
Heather Maclean, Director

Centre for South Asian Studies
Chelva Kanaganayekam, Director

Centre for the Study of Pain
Michael Salter, Director

Centre for Urban & Community Studies
David Hulchanski, Director

Centre of Criminology
Anthony Doob, Acting Director

Computing in the Humanities & Social Sciences
Chris Leowski, Director

David Dunlap Observatory
Sold to Metrus Development in 2008, operated by The Royal Astronomical Society of Canada

Fields Institute for Research in Mathematical Sciences
Sold to Metrus Development in 2008, operated by The Royal Astronomical Society of Canada
Barbara Keyfitz, Director

Frank Iacobucci Centre for Italian Canadian Studies
Sold to Metrus Development in 2008, operated by The Royal Astronomical Society of Canada
Salvatore Bancheri, Acting Director

Graduate Centre for Study of Drama
Sold to Metrus Development in 2008, operated by The Royal Astronomical Society of Canada
Prof. John Astington, Director

Institute for Aerospace Studies
Sold to Metrus Development in 2008, operated by The Royal Astronomical Society of Canada
D.W. Zingg, Director

Institute for History & Philosophy of Science & Technology
Sold to Metrus Development in 2008, operated by The Royal Astronomical Society of Canada
Paul Thompson, Director

Institute for Human Development, Life Course & Aging
Sold to Metrus Development in 2008, operated by The Royal Astronomical Society of Canada
L. McDonald, Director

Institute for Policy Analysis
Sold to Metrus Development in 2008, operated by The Royal Astronomical Society of Canada
Wendy Dobson, Director

Institute for Women's Studies & Gender Studies
Sold to Metrus Development in 2008, operated by The Royal Astronomical Society of Canada
Bonnie McElhinny, Director

Institute of Aboriginal People's Health
Sold to Metrus Development in 2008, operated by The Royal Astronomical Society of Canada
Jeff Reading, Director

Institute of Biomaterials & Biomedical Engineering
Sold to Metrus Development in 2008, operated by The Royal Astronomical Society of Canada
Paul Santerre, Director

Institute of Child Study
Sold to Metrus Development in 2008, operated by The Royal Astronomical Society of Canada
Kang Lee, Director

Institute of Medical Science
Sold to Metrus Development in 2008, operated by The Royal Astronomical Society of Canada
Ori D. Rothstein, Director

Institute of Population & Public Health
Sold to Metrus Development in 2008, operated by The Royal Astronomical Society of Canada
John Frank, Director

Institute on Human Development, Child & Youth Health
Sold to Metrus Development in 2008, operated by The Royal Astronomical Society of Canada
Michael Kramer, Director

Knowledge Media Design Institute
Sold to Metrus Development in 2008, operated by The Royal Astronomical Society of Canada
Ron Baecker, Interim Director

Masters of Mathematical Finance
Sold to Metrus Development in 2008, operated by The Royal Astronomical Society of Canada
Robert Almgren, Director

McLuhan Program in Culture & Technology
Sold to Metrus Development in 2008, operated by The Royal Astronomical Society of Canada
Derrick de Kerckhove, Director

Museum Studies Program
Sold to Metrus Development in 2008, operated by The Royal Astronomical Society of Canada
John Fleming, Interim Director

Pontifical Institute of Medieval Studies
Sold to Metrus Development in 2008, operated by The Royal Astronomical Society of Canada
James K. McConica, Director

Toronto School of Theology
Sold to Metrus Development in 2008, operated by The Royal Astronomical Society of Canada
Alan Hayes, Director

Transitional Year Program
Sold to Metrus Development in 2008, operated by The Royal Astronomical Society of Canada
Rhonda Love, Director

U of T Joint Program in Transportation
Sold to Metrus Development in 2008, operated by The Royal Astronomical Society of Canada
Eric Miller, Director

Affiliations
University of Toronto Mississauga
3359 Mississauga Rd. Mississauga, L5L 1C6 Canada
905-569-4455,
Admissions, Phone: 905-828-5400; Public Affairs: 905-828-5214
hrserv.utm@utoronto.ca (human resources)
www.utm.utoronto.ca

Enrollment: 11430
The University of Toronto Mississauga provides undergraduate education to approximately 11,000 students & graduate studies to about 430 graduate students. With 14 academic departments, the school employs 700 faculty & staff.
Professor Hargurdeep Saini, Vice-President & Principal
Lynda Collins, Director, Human Resources, 905-828-5210
lynda.collins@utoronto.ca

Massey College
4 Devonshire Pl. Toronto, M5S 2E1 Canada
416-978-2891, Fax: 416-946-7890
John Fraser, Master/CAO, 416-978-2549
Mary Graham, Registrar, 416-978-2891, fax: 416-971-3032
mary.graham@utoronto.ca
Anna Luengo, College Administrator, 416-978-6606
anna.luengo@utoronto.ca

New College
300 Huron Toronto, M5S 3J6 Canada
416-978-2460, Fax: 416-978-0554
Prof. Yves Roberge, Principal, 416-978-2461, fax: 416-978-4345
nc.principal@utoronto.ca
Prof. Cheryl Misak, Vice-Principal

University of Toronto Scarborough
1265 Military Trail Toronto, M1C 1A4 Canada
416-287-8872,
stuaff@utsc.utoronto.ca (student affairs)
www.utsc.utoronto.ca

Enrollment: 10131
Number of Employees: 189 academic staff & librarians; 373 non-academic staff. Number of Programs: 242
Professor Franco J. Vaccarino, Vice-President, U of T, & Principal, U of T S
Professor Rick Halpern, Vice-Principal & Dean, Academic
deanadmin@utsc.utoronto.ca
Professor Malcolm Campbell, MA (Oxon), PhD, Vice-Principal, Research
vpresearch@utsc.utoronto.ca
Tom Nowers, Dean, Student Affairs
Professor William Gough, Vice-Dean, Graduate Education & Program Devel
Professor John Scherk, Vice-Dean, Undergraduate
Lesley Lewis, Assistant Dean
Andrew Arifuzzaman, Chief Strategy Officer
Kim McLean, Chief Administrative Officer
Georgette Zinaty, Executive Director, Development & Alumni Rela
gzinaty@utsc.utoronto.ca
Kim Burbine Richard, Director, Human Resource Services
Rita Pearsall, Director, Enrollment Services
Professor John Bassili, Chair, Department of Psychology
Professor William Bowen, Chair, Department of Humanities
Professor Donald Cormack, Chair, Department of Physical & Environmental
Professor Vassos Hadzilacos, Chair, Department of Computer & Mathematical
Professor Michael Krashinsky, Chair, Department of Management
Professor Ted Relph, Chair, Department of Social Sciences
Professor Greg Vanlerberghe, Chair, Department of Biological Sciences

University College
15 King's College Circle Toronto, M5S 3H7 Canada
416-978-3170, Fax: 416-978-6019
Paul Perron, Principal

Woodsworth College
119 Saint George St. Toronto, M5S 1A1 Canada
416-978-4444, Fax: 416-978-4088
Joseph R. Desloges, Principal
Mary Choi, CAO
Cheryl Shook, Registrar

St. Michael's College
81 St. Mary St. Toronto, M4S 1J4 Canada
416-926-1300,
www.utoronto.ca/stmikes
Fully federated with the University of Toronto, St. Michael's College has a large Faculty of Theology. It also features the

Canadian Catholic Bioethics Institute & the Pontifical Institute of Mediaeval Studies.
Anne Anderson, Interim President
Mark McGowan, Principal

Trinity College in the University of Toronto
6 Hoskin Ave. Toronto, M5S 1H8 Canada
416-978-2522, Fax: 416-978-2797,
Bursar's Office, E-mail: fees@trinity.utoronto.ca
deanofstudents@trinity.utoronto.ca; chaplain@trinity.utoronto.ca
www.trinity.utoronto.ca

Enrollment: 1840
Trinity College educates approximately 1,700 undergraduate students in the Faculty of Arts & Science, plus 140 students in the Faculty of Divinity. Founded in 1851, it is Canada's oldest Anglican theological school.
The Hon. Bill Graham, Chancellor
Professor Andy Orchard, Provost & Vice-Chancellor, 416-978-2689
provost@trinity.utoronto.ca
Bruce Bowden, B.A., M.A., Ph.D. (Tor.), Registrar & Director, Student Services, 416-978-2687, fax: 416-978-2831
bowden@trinity.utoronto.ca; registrar@trinity.utoronto.ca
Linda W. Corman, A.B. (Vassar), M.A. (Chi., College Librarian, 416-978-4398, fax: 416-978-2797
linda.corman@utoronto.ca
Jill Willard, Officer, Personnel
jwillard@trinity.utoronto.ca

Victoria University
73 Queen's Park Cres. East Toronto, M5S 1K9 Canada
416-585-4524, Fax: 416-585-4584,
www.vicu.utoronto.ca

Paul W. Gooch, President, 416-585-4511
vic.president@utoronto.ca
Susan McDonald, Registrar, 416-585-4405
s.mcdonald@utoronto.ca
Kelly Castle, Dean of Students, 416-585-4495
jason.hunter@utoronto.ca

Emmanuel College
75 Queen's Park Cres. East Toronto, M5S 1K7 Canada
416-585-4539, Fax: 416-585-4516,
ec.office@utoronto.ca

Mark G. Toulouse, Principal
Wanda Chin, Registrar
wanda.chin@utoronto.ca

Knox College
59 Saint George St. Toronto, M5S 2E6 Canada
416-978-4500, Fax: 416-971-2133

Rev. Dr. J. Dorcas Gordon, Principal
Rev. Beth McCutcheon, Director, Academic Programs
mb.mccutcheon@utoronto.ca

Wycliffe College
5 Hoskin Ave. Toronto, M5S 1H7 Canada
416-979-3535, Fax: 416-946-3545

Rev. Dr. George Sumner, Principal

Regis College
15 St. Mary St. Toronto, M4Y 2R5 Canada
416-922-5474, Fax: 416-922-2898,
www.regiscollege.ca

Regis is a Roman Catholic college in the Jesuit tradition. It is a federated college of the University of Toronto.
Very Reverend Adolfo Nicolas, S.J., Chancellor , Ecclesiastical Faculty
Joseph G. Schner, S.J., President & Rector

Publications
The Bulletin
Dept. of Public Affairs
21 King's College Circle Toronto, M5S 1A1 Canada

The Newspaper
#245, 1 Spadina Cres Toronto, M5S 1A1 Canada
Fax: 416-593-0552

The Toike Oike

University of Toronto Magazine
Dept. of Public Affairs
21 King's College Circle Toronto, M5S 1A1 Canada
Fax: 416-978-7430

Varsity

Toronto: Victoria University
73 Queen's Park Cres. Toronto, M5S 1K7 Canada
416-585-4508, Fax: 416-585-4459,
vic.registrar@utoronto.ca
www.vicu.utoronto.ca

Enrollment: 2300
Although the university is located within the University of Toronto campus, it has its own independent administration, faculty and governing body.

Toronto: Woodsworth College
119 Saint George St. Toronto, M5S 1A9 Canada
416-978-4444, Fax: 416-978-6111,
wdwregistrar@utoronto.ca
wdw.utoronto.ca

Enrollment: 6000

Toronto: Wycliffe College
5 Hoskin Ave. Toronto, M5S 1H7 Canada
416-979-3535, Fax: 416-946-3545,
www.wycliffecollege.ca

Seminary at the University of Toronto affiliated with the Anglican Church of Canada

Toronto: York University
4700 Keele St. Toronto, M3J 1P3 Canada
416-736-2100, Fax: 416-736-5700,
www.yorku.ca

Enrollment: 45890
Marshall Cohen, Chair of the Board
Roland (Roy) McMurty, O.C., O.O., B.A., LL.B., Chancellor
Mahmoud Shoukri, B.Sc., M.Eng., Ph.D., President & Vice-Chancellor
S.M. Embleton, B.Sc., M.Sc., Ph.D., Vice-President
John Lennox, Assoc. Vice-President
G. Brewer, Vice-President
S. Shapson, B.Sc., M.A., Ph.D., Vice-President
H.I. Lewis, B.A., M.A., LL.B., University Secretary & General Counsel
Sylvia Schippke, Asst. Vice-President
Trudy Pound-Curtis, CFO & Asst. Vice-President
Michael Graham, Asst. Vice-President
P. Cantor, B.A., L.L.B., F.I.C.B., Chair
N. White, Director
Luana Jursza, CIO & Executive Director
Norman Ahmet, Asst. Vice-President
B. Purves, President
B. Miller, Director
J. Meikle, Director
P. Murray, B.P.H.E., M.Sc., Director
R. Woodhouse, Academic Director
T. Mohammed, B.Sc., M.Sc., P.Eng., Director
P. Monk, Director/Curator
M. Scheepers, B.A., Director
J. Briggs, Director
B. Bellissimo, Director
R. Thompson, B.A., Director
P. Yu, B.Sc., Director
K. Irani, B.E., P.Eng., Director
D.L. Glass, B.A., B.Ed., M.E.D., Director
E.S. Spence, Director
B. Abner, B.A., M.A., Assoc. Vice-President
M. Chan, Director
Robert J. Tiffin, Vice-President
C. Archer, University Librarian
N. Gouda, Director
Calum MacKechnie, Director
K. Swartz, B.A., B.S.W., M.S.W., Director
Joanne Duklas, University Registrar
B. Brown, Director
S. MacDonald, Director
R.A. Webb, Assoc. Vice-President
A. Shubert, Assoc. Vice-President
A. Wickens, Asst. Vice-President
S. Spence, Director
B. Woodward, Director
R. Faverin, Director
Suzanne MacDonald, Assoc. Vice-President

Faculties
Arts
Bob Drummond, Dean

Joseph E. Atkinson College
Rhonda Lenton, Dean

Education
Paul Axelrod, Dean

Environmental Studies
David Morley, Dean

Fine Arts
Phillip Silver, B.A., Dean

Glendon College
K. McRoberts, B.A., M.A., Ph.D., Principal

Graduate Studies
Ronald Pearlman, Dean

Health
Harvey Skinner, Dean

Law School, Osgoode Hall
Patrick Monahan, Dean

Schulich School of Business
Dezsö J. Horvath, Dean

Science & Engineering
Nick Cercone, Dean

Schools
Canadian Centre for German & European Studies
Kurt Huebner, Acting Director

Centre for Applied Sustainability
D.V.J. Bell, B.A., A.M., Ph.D., Director

Centre for Atmospheric Chemistry
G.W. Harris, B.Sc., Ph.D., Director

Centre for International & Security Studies
D.B. Dewitt, B.A., M.A., Ph.D., Director

Centre for Jewish Studies
M. Lockshin, Director

Centre for Practical Ethics
Shirley Katz, Acting Director

Centre for Public Law & Public Policy
Bruce Ryder, Director

Centre for Refugee Studies
Susan McGrath, Director

Centre for Research in Earth & Space Science
G.G. Shepherd, B.Sc., M.Sc., Ph.D., F.R., Director

Centre for Research in Mass Spectrometry
M. Siu, Director

Centre for Research on Latin America & the Caribbean
Viviana Patroni, Director

Centre for Research on Work & Society
N. Pupo, Director

Centre for Vision Research
J. Tsotsos, B.A., M.Sc., Ph.D., Director

Institute for Research & Innovation in Sustainability
David Wheeler, Director

Institute for Research on Learning Technologies
Ron Owston, Director

Institute for Social Research
M.D. Ornstein, B.Sc., Ph.D., Director

Jack & Mae Nathanson Centre for the Study of Organized Crime & Corruption
M. Beare, B.A., M.A., M.P.H.L., Ph., Director

La Marsh Centre for Research on Violence & Conflict Resolution
Anne Marie Wall, Acting Director

Robarts Centre for Canadian Studies
S. Feldman, Director

York Centre for Asian Research
P. Vandergeest, Director

York Centre for Feminist Research
V. Agnew, Director

York Institute for Health Research
M. Rioux, Director

Campuses
Glendon Campus
2275 Bayview Ave. Toronto, M4N 3M6 Canada

Publications
Atkinsonian

Excalibur

Lexicon

MacMedia (McLaughlin College)

Obiter Dicta (Osgoode Hall)

The Pro Tem (Glendon College)

Waterloo: Conrad Grebel University College
140 Westmount Rd. North Waterloo, N2L 3G6 Canada
519-885-0220, Fax: 519-885-0014,
congreb@uwaterloo.ca
grebel.uwaterloo.ca

Enrollment: 3894

Waterloo: University of Waterloo
200 University Ave. West Waterloo, N2L 3G1 Canada
519-888-4567, Fax: 519-884-8009,
www.uwaterloo.ca/

Enrollment: 26457
V. Prem Watsa, Chancellor

Bob Harding, Chair
D.L. Johnston, C.C., A.B., L.L.B., President & Vice-Chancellor
Bruce Mitchell, B.Sc., M.Sc., Ph.D., Vice-President
Meg Beckell, B.A., M.B.A., Vice-President
W.B. Mitchell, B.A., M.A., Ph.D., Associate Provost
P.D. Guild, B.A., M.A., D.Phil., Vice-President
A.C. Scott, B.A., Associate Provost
D.E. Huber, B.B.A., C.M.A., Vice-President
L.H.P. Claxton, B.A., B.L.S., M.L.S., Secretary of the University
K.A. Lavigne, B.A., Registrar
G. Cuthbert Brandt, B.A., M.A., Ph.D., Associate Vice-President
J.D. Walker, B.A., M.A.Sc., Director
J.A. George, B.Sc., M.Sc., Ph.D., F.R., Vice-President, University Research & Associa

Faculties

Applied Health Sciences
R.C. Mannell, B.A., M.P.E., Ph.D., Dean

Arts
Ken Coates, Dean

Engineering
A.S. Sedra, B.Sc., M.A.Sc., Ph.D., Dean

Environmental Studies
H.S. (Deep) Saini, B.Sc., M.Sc., Ph.D., Dean

Graduate Studies
R. Bird, B.Sc., M.Sc., Ph.D., Dean

Mathematics
T.F. Coleman, Ph.D., Dean

Science
Terry McMahon, Dean

Affiliations

Conrad Grebel University College
Waterloo, N2L 3G6 Canada
519-885-0220
Henry Paetkau, B.A., M.A., Ph.D., Principal, 519-885-0220 24237
cgcpres@uwaterloo.ca
E. Paul Penner, Dir., Operations, 519-885-0220 24231
eppenner@uwaterloo.ca
Dr James Pankratz, Academic Dean, 519-885-0220 24232
pankratz@uwaterloo.ca

Renison College
240 Westmount Rd. North Waterloo, N2L 3G4 Canada
519-884-4400, Fax: 519-884-5135,
www.renison.uwaterloo.ca
College programs lead to a Bachelor of Arts or an Honours Bachelor of Social Work degree of the University of Waterloo.
John Crossley, B.A., M.A., Ph.D., Principal

St. Jerome's University
290 Westmount Rd. North Waterloo, N2L 3G3 Canada
519-884-8110, Fax: 519-884-5759,
webmaster@sju.uwaterloo.ca
www.sju.ca
Enrollment: 1019
Federated with the University of Waterloo, St. Jerome's University is a public Catholic university. Education in the Arts & Mathematics is provided.
Peter Naus, Chancellor
David Perrin, President & Vice-Chancellor, 519-884-8111 28253
dperrin@sju-serv1.uwaterloo.ca

St. Paul's United College
University of Waterloo
190 Westmount Rd. North Waterloo, N2L 3G5 Canada
519-885-1460, Fax: 519-885-6364,
stpauls@uwaterloo.ca
www.stpauls.uwaterloo.ca
The residential teaching institution is affiliated with the University of Waterloo. It features the international development program.
Dr. Mark Seasons, Chair
Graham Brown, Principal
ggbrown@uwaterloo.ca
Peter Frick, Academic Dean
Rod McAllister, Dean of Students

Publications

Imprint
Student newspaper at the University of Waterloo

UW Gazette
Newspaper published by the Office of Information and Public Affairs

Waterloo: Wilfrid Laurier University
75 University Ave. West Waterloo, N2L 3C5 Canada
519-884-0710, Fax: 519-886-9351,
www.wlu.ca
Enrollment: 12239
Dr. Max Blouw, President
Dr. Deborah MacLatchy, Vice-President
dmaclatchy@wlu.ca
Jim Butler, Vice-President
jbutler@wlu.ca
Ray Darling, Registrar
rdarling@wlu.ca
Robert Donelson, Vice-President
rdonelson@wlu.ca
Sharon Brown, University Librarian
sbrown@wlu.ca

Faculties

Arts
Dr. David Docherty, Dean

Brantford Campus
73 George St. Brantford, N3T 2Y3 Canada
519-756-8228, Fax: 519-759-2172
Dr. Bruce Arai, Dean
barai@wlu.ca

Graduate Studies & Research
73 George St. Brantford, N3T 2Y3 Canada
519-756-8228, Fax: 519-759-2172
Dr. Joan Norris, Dean

Music
73 George St. Brantford, N3T 2Y3 Canada
519-756-8228, Fax: 519-759-2172
Charles Morrison, Dean
cdmorris@wlv.ca

School of Business & Economics
73 George St. Brantford, N3T 2Y3 Canada
519-756-8228, Fax: 519-759-2172,
Ginny Dybenko, Dean
gdybenko@wlv.ca

Science
73 George St. Brantford, N3T 2Y3 Canada
519-756-8228, Fax: 519-759-2172
Dr. Peter Tiidus, Acting Dean
ptiidus@wlv.ca

Social Work
73 George St. Brantford, N3T 2Y3 Canada
519-756-8228, Fax: 519-759-2172
Lesley Cooper, Dean

Waterloo Lutheran Seminary
73 George St. Brantford, N3T 2Y3 Canada
519-756-8228, Fax: 519-759-2172
Dr. David Pfrimmer, Principal-Dean
dpfrimmer@wlu.ca

Publications

The Cord Weekly
Student newspaper at Wilfrid Laurier University

Windsor: Iona College
208 Sunset Ave. Windsor, N9B 3A7 Canada
519-253-3000, Fax: 519-973-7050,
office@ionacollege.edu
www.ionacollege.edu
Affiliate College to the University of Windsor, affiliated with the United Church of Canada designed to promote theological educaion, social justice and Chaplaincy.
Rev. Dr. BoJeong Kim, Principal & Chaplain Emeritus
principal@ionacollege.edu
Rev. Dr. Lloyd Smith, Chancellor
Dr. Norman King, Director, School of Theology
theology@ionacollege.edu

Windsor: University of Windsor
401 Sunset Ave. Windsor, N9B 3P4 Canada
519-253-3000,
www.uwindsor.ca/
Enrollment: 13496
Plus 3,387 part-time students
Amanda Gellman, Vice-President, University Advancement

Faculties

Arts & Social Sciences
Cecil Houston, B.A., M.A., Ph.D., Dean

Education
Pat Rogers, B.A., M.Sc., Ph.D., Dean

Engineering
Graham Reader, B.Tech. (Hons.), B.A., Ph, Dean

Graduate Studies & Research
Jim Frank, Dean

Human Kinetics
Bob Boucher, B.H.K., M.H.K., Ph.D., Dean

Law
Bruce Elman, B.Sc., L.L.B., L.L.M., Dean

Nursing
Elaine Duffy, B.A.Sc., M.N., Ph.D., Reg, Dean

Odette School of Business
Dr. Allan Conway, Dean

Science
Richard Caron, Dean

Schools

Athletics & Recreational Services
Gord Grace, Head

Biological Sciences
William Crosby, Head

Chemistry & Biochemistry
Douglas Stephan, Head

Civil & Environmental Engineering
Ram Balachandar, B.E., Ph.D., P.Eng., Head

Classical & Modern Languages
Dietmar Lage, B.A., M.A., Ph.D., Head

Communication Studies
James Wittebols, Head

Dramatic Art
Lionel Walsh, Head

Earth Sciences
Ihsan Al-Aasm, Head

Economics, Mathematics & Statistics
Ronald Meng, Head

Electrical & Computer Engineering
Maher Sid-Ahmed, Head

English
Karl Jirgens, Head

History
Christina Simmons, Head

Industrial & Manufacturing Systems Engineering
Leo Oriet, Head

Intelligent Manufacturing Systems
Hoda ElMaraghy, B.Eng., M.Eng., Ph.D., Head
Waguih ElMaraghy, B.Eng., M.Eng., Ph.D., Head

Languages, Literatures, Cultures
Dietmar Lage, Head

Mechanical, Automotive & Materials Engineering
Robert Gaspar, B.A.Sc., M.A.Sc., Ph.D., Head

Philosophy
Jeffrey Noonan, Head

Physics
Gordon Drake, B.Sc., M.Sc., Ph.D., Head

Political Science
Tom Najem, Head

Psychology
Shelagh Towson, B.A., M.A., Ph.D., Head

Social Work
Brent Angell, Head

Sociology & Anthropology
Lynne Phillips, B.A., M.A., Ph.D., Head

Student Health Services
Maria Blass, M.D., Head

Visual Arts
Brenda Pelkey, Head

Women's Studies
Anne Forrest, Head

Affiliations

Assumption University
2629 Riverside Dr. West Windsor, N9B 1B4 Canada
519-973-7033, Fax: 519-973-7089,
cbertrand@assumptionu.ca
www.assumptionu.ca
Most Rev. Ronald P. Fabbro, C.S.B., D.D.Bishop of Lon, Chancellor
Fr William A. Riefel, C.S.B., Treas./Dir., Operations
Dr. Lois Smedick, Chair
Rev. Dr. Paul Rennick, C.S.B., Pres./Vice-Chancellor
Dr Anne Snowdon, Dir., Centre for Religion & Culture
Anne Shore, Prog. Dir., Dept. of Theology

Canterbury College
2500 University Ave. West Windsor, N9B 3Y1 Canada
519-971-3646, Fax: 519-971-3645,
canter@uwindsor.ca
www.uwindsor.ca/canterbury

Canterbury College offers the following courses: Doctor of Ministry Degree (in affiliation with Ashland Theological Seminary at Ashland University); certificate courses for the Anglican Community of Deacons & interested lay people; & professional courses for the community.
Dr. Gordon W.F. Drake, Principal
Crystal Martens, Head of College
Brenda Smith, Coordinator, Residence Admissions
brsmith@uwindsor.ca

Iona College
208 Sunset Ave. Windsor, N9B 3A7 Canada
519-973-7039

Publications
The Lance

The Uniter

Colleges

Barrie: Georgian College
One Georgian Dr. Barrie, L4M 3X9 Canada
705-728-1968, Fax: 705-722-5123,
inquire@georgianc.on.ca
www.georgianc.on.ca

Enrollment: 9000
Plus 28,000 part-time & continuing education students
Brian Tamblyn, President

Campuses
Collingwood Campus
49 Huron St. Collingwood, L9Y 1L5 Canada

Midland Campus
649 Prospect Blvd. Midland, L4R 4L3 Canada

Muskoka Campus
4440 Ecclestone Dr. Bracebridge, P1L 1Z6 Canada

Orangeville Campus
5 Armstrong St. Orangeville, L9W 3H6 Canada

Orillia Campus
P.O. Box 2316
825 Memorial Ave. Orillia, L3V 6S2 Canada

Owen Sound Campus
1450 - 8th St. East Owen Sound, N4K 5R4 Canada

Port Colborne Campus
2193 Barber Dr. Port Colborne, L3K 5X7 Canada

Publications
The Georgian Eye

Belleville: Loyalist College of Applied Arts & Technology
P.O. Box 4200
Wallbridge-Loyalist Rd. Belleville, K8N 5B9 Canada
613-969-1913, Fax: 613-962-1376, 888-569-2547
www.loyalistcollege.com

Jeff MacNab, Registrar 2366
jmacnab@loyalistc.on.ca
Aatos Lehtila, Dean ext-2332

Hamilton: Mohawk College
P.O. Box 2034
Hamilton, L8N 3T2 Canada
905-575-1212, Fax: 905-575-2378,
www.mohawkcollege.ca

Enrollment: 13000
Plus 40,000 part-time students
MaryLynn West-Moynes, President
Rosemary Knechtel, Vice President, Academic
Dale Schenk, Vice President, Finance & Administration

Campuses
Brantford Campus
411 Elgin St. Brantford, N3T 5V2 Canada
Fax: 519-758-6043

Fennell Campus
P.O. Box 2034
Fennell Ave. & West 5th Hamilton, L8N 3T2 Canada
Fax: 905-575-2378

Mohawk - McMaster Institute for Applied Health Sciences
1400 Main St. West Hamilton, L8S 1C7 Canada
Fax: 905-528-4198

Stoney Creek Campus
P.O. Box 9901
481 Barton St. East Stoney Creek, L8G 3Y4 Canada
Fax: 905-575-2549

Wentworth Campus
196 Wentworth St. North Hamilton, L8L 5V7 Canada
Fax: 905-523-8504

Publications
The Satellite

Kingston: St. Lawrence College
100 Portsmouth Ave. Kingston, K7L 5A6 Canada
613-544-5400, Fax: 613-545-3923, 866-276-6601
dreamit@sl.on.ca
www.sl.on.ca

Enrollment: 6500
Chris Whitaker, President & CEO
Glenn Vollebregt, Sr. Vice-Pres., Finance & Administration 1591
Gordon MacDougall, Vice-Pres., Student Services & External Affai 1298
Lorraine Carter, Vice-Pres., Academic 1446

Campuses
Brockville Campus
2288 Parkedale Ave. Brockville, K6V 5X3 Canada
613-345-0660, Fax: 613-345-0124, 888-622-8880
Beverlie Dietze, Campus Dean 3260
bdietze@sl.on.ca

Cornwall Campus
2 Belmont St. Cornwall, K6H 4Z1 Canada
613-933-6080, Fax: 613-937-1524, 866-276-6600
Don Fairweather, Campus Dean 2223
dfairweather@sl.on.ca

Kitchener: Conestoga College Institute of Technology & Advanced Learning
299 Doon Valley Dr. Kitchener, N2G 4M4 Canada
519-748-5220, Fax: 519-748-3505,
www.conestogac.on.ca/

Enrollment: 6900
With an additional 38,000 part-time students
Dr. John W. Tibbits, President
jtibbits@conestogac.on.ca

Publications
Spoke

London: Fanshawe College
P.O. Box 7005
1001 Fanshawe College Blvd. London, N5Y 5R6 Canada
519-452-4430, Fax: 519-452-4420,
www.fanshawec.ca

Enrollment: 15000
Plus 5,000 part-time students
Dr. Howard W. Rundle, President
hrundle@fanshawec.ca
Janice Lamoureux, Registrar
jlamoureux@fanshawec.ca

Publications
The Interrobang

North Bay: Canadore College of Applied Arts & Technology
P.O. Box 5001
100 College Dr. North Bay, P1B 8K9 Canada
705-474-7600, Fax: 705-474-2384,
info@canadorec.on.ca
www.canadorec.on.ca

Enrollment: 3500
Barbara Taylor, President & CEO

Oakville: Sheridan College Institute of Technology & Advanced Learning
Trafalgar Road Campus
1430 Trafalgar Rd. Oakville, L6H 2L1 Canada
905-845-9430,
infosheridan@sheridaninstitute.ca; tours@sheridaninstitute.ca
www1.sheridaninstitute.ca

Enrollment: 14472
The polytechnic institute offers pre-apprenticeship & apprenticeship training, one-year certificate & graduate certificates, two & three-year diplomas, & Bachelor's degrees in applied areas of study. Collaborative degree progrmas are provided through partnerships with the following universities: Brock University, University of Toronto at Mississauga, & York University.
Dr. Robert W. Turner, President/CEO

Campuses
Davis Campus
P.O. Box 7500
7899 McLaughlin Rd. Brampton, L6V 1G6 Canada
Fax: 905-459-7533

Skills Training Centre
407 Iroquois Shore Rd. Oakville, L6H 1M3 Canada
Fax: 905-845-9430

St. Joseph Secondary School
5555 Creditview Rd. Mississaugua, L5V 2B9 Canada
This is an additional continuing education location.

Oshawa: Durham College
P.O. Box 385
2000 Simcoe St. North Oshawa, L1H 7L7 Canada
905-721-2000, Fax: 905-721-3113,
www.durhamcollege.ca

Enrollment: 6000
Plus 23,000 part-time enrolment
Don Lovisa, President
Ralph Aprile, Vice-President, Facilities & Ancillary Servic
Ruth MacKay, Director, Institutional Research & Government
David Chambers, President, Foundation & Vice-President, Advan
Judy Robinson, Vice-President, Academic
Margaret Greenley, Vice-President, Student Affairs
Donna MacFarlane, Vice-President, Communications & Marketing
Ken Robb, Vice-President, Human Resources
Gerry Pinkney, Vice-President, Information Technology Servic

Publications
The Chronicle
P.O. Box 385
Oshawa, L1H 7L7 Canada
Fax: 905-436-9774

Ottawa: Algonquin College of Applied Arts & Technology
1385 Woodroffe Ave. Ottawa, K2G 1V8 Canada
613-727-4723, Fax: 613-727-7743,
www.algonquincollege.com/

Enrollment: 16000
Robert Gillett, President

Peterborough: Sir Sandford Fleming College
Sutherland Campus
599 Brealey Dr. Peterborough, K9J 7B1 Canada
705-749-5530, Fax: 705-749-5507, 1-866-353-6464
info@flemingc.on.ca; admissions@flemingc.on.ca
www.flemingc.on.ca

Enrollment: 3500
The College consists of the following schools: School of Business & Technology; School of Environmental & Natural Resource Sciences; School of Health & Wellness; School of Interdisciplinary Studies; School of Law, Justice & Community Services; School of Continuing Education & Skilled Trades; & the Haliburton School of The Arts.
Murray Rodd, Chair
G.A. (Tony) Tilly, Ph.D., President

Campuses
Cobourg Campus
1005 Elgin St. West Cobourg, K9A 5J4
905-372-6865, 1-866-353-6464
info@flemingc.on.ca
The Cobourg Campus offers academic upgrading & part time studies, as well as esthetician studies.

Frost Campus
P.O. Box 8000
200 Albert St. South Lindsay, K9V 5E6 Canada
705-324-9144, Fax: 705-878-9331, 1-866-353-6464
Enrollment: 1500
The Frost Campus features Fleming College's School of Environmental & Natural Resource Sciences, The Centre for Alternative Wastewater Treatment, The Centre for Heavy Equipment Technology, & The Geomatics Institute.

Haliburton Campus
P.O. Box 839
297 College Dr. Haliburton, K0M 1S0 Canada
705-457-1680, 1-866-353-6464
info@flemingc.on.ca
The Haliburton Campus features the Haliburton School of The Arts & Fleming's Ecotourism & Adventure Tourism Management program.

McRae Campus
P.O. Box 4350
555 Bonnacord St. Peterborough, K9J 7B1
705-749-5530, Fax: 705-741-3279, 1-888-269-6929
info@flemingc.on.ca
This campus offers specialized programs in skilled trades, apprenticeships, & several part-time studies.
Michael N. Durisin, Chair
Dr. Glenn Zederayko, Head of Schools
Ann Bianco-Harvey, Director, Marketing & Communications
webmaster@torontomontessori.ca; editor@torontomontessori.ca
Silvana Fazzari, Director, Admissions, 905-889-6882 230
Sharron Cooper, Registrar, 905-889-6882 254

Norwood - Eastern Ontario Fire Academy
36 Industrial Dr. Norwood, K0L 2V0
705-639-2121

Sarnia: Lambton College of Applied Arts & Technology
1457 London Rd. Sarnia, N7S 6K4 Canada
519-542-7751, Fax: 519-541-2418,
www.lambton.on.ca
Enrollment: 2500
Catherine Holden, Registrar, 519-542-7751 3310
cathie@lambton.on.ca
Tony Hanlon, President

Publications
Lion's Tale

Sault Ste Marie: Sault College of Applied Arts & Technology
443 Northern Ave. Sault Ste Marie, P6A 5L3 Canada
705-759-2554, Fax: 705-759-3273, 1-800-461-2260
studentrecruitment@saultcollege.ca; registrar@saultcollege.ca
www.saultcollege.ca
Enrollment: 6000
The College offers education & training to full-time & part-time students in post-secondary, apprenticeship, adult retraining, continuing education, & contract training programs.
Joe Nardi, Chair
Dr. Ron Common, President
Max S. Liedke, Sec.-Treas.

Sault Ste. Marie: Algoma University College
1520 Queen St. E Sault Ste. Marie, P6A 2G4 Canada
705-949-2301, Fax: 705-949-6583, 888-254-6628
info@algomau.ca
www.algomau.ca
Enrollment: 1207
Became wholly independent as of June, 2008
Dr Richard Myers, President
Dr. Arthur H. Perlini, Academic Dean 4116
dean@algomau.ca.
David Marasco, Registrar 4218
registrar@algomau.ca

Scarborough: Centennial College of Applied Arts & Technology
P.O. Box 631 A
Scarborough, M1K 5E9 Canada
416-289-5000, Fax: 416-439-7358, 800-268-4419
Telex: 06-963824
www.centennialcollege.ca
Enrollment: 40000
Ann Buller, President

Publications
Siren

Sudbury: Cambrian College of Applied Arts & Technology
1400 Barrydowne Rd. Sudbury, P3A 3V8 Canada
705-566-8101, Fax: 705-524-7334, 800-461-7145
info@cambriancollege.ca
www.cambriancollege.ca
Enrollment: 4300
Sylvia Barnard, President

Publications
The Shield

Thunder Bay: Confederation College
P.O. Box 398
1450 Nakina Dr. Thunder Bay, P7C 4W1 Canada
807-475-6110, Fax: 807-623-4512, 800-465-5493
www.confederationc.on.ca/
Enrollment: 4160
Plus 17,000 part-time & continuing education students
Patricia Lang, President, 807-475-6350
plang@confederationc.on.ca
Brian Campbell, Director, Resource Development, 807-475-6582
campbell@confederationc.on.ca
Reg Jones, Vice-President, Corporate Services, 807-475-6173
jones@confederationc.on.ca

Publications
Opus

Polar Press

Talon

Timmins: Northern College of Applied Arts & Technology
P.O. Box 3211
Timmins, P4N 8R6 Canada
705-235-3211, Fax: 705-235-7279,
hansonth@northernc.on.ca (Registrar)
www.northernc.on.ca

Toronto: Elliott Allen Institute for Theology & Ecology
81 St. Mary's St. Toronto, M5S 1J4 Canada
416-926-1300, Fax: 416-926-7294,
ext. 3408
eaite.contact@utoronto.ca
www.utoronto.ca/stmikes/eaite/
Dr. Dennis Patrick O'Hara, Director, 416-926-1300 3408

Campuses
Theology & Ecology Certificate of Specialization
Eight courses & one seminar. The Institute cooperates with the Tornot School of Theology, Holy Cross Centre for Ecology Y spirituality, Institute for Environmental Studies (Universsity of Toronto), Transformative Learning Centres (OISE), Faculty of Enviornmental Studues (York University).

Toronto: George Brown College
P.O. Box 1015 B
Toronto, M5T 2T9 Canada
416-415-2000, Fax: 416-415-4493, 800-265-2002
info@georgebrown.ca
www.georgebrown.ca
Enrollment: 15000
Plus 60,000 part-time & continuing education students
Anne Sado, President

Publications
Dialog Newspaper

Toronto: Humber Institute of Technology and Advanced Learning
North Campus
205 Humber College Blvd. Toronto, M9W 5L7 Canada
416-675-5005, Fax: 416-675-2427,
enquiry@humber.ca
www.humber.ca
Enrollment: 29000
Over 65,000 Part-time enrollment
Michael Hatton, Vice-President, Academic 4510
michael.hatton@humber.ca
John Mason, Vice-President, Student & Corporate Services 5041
john.mason@humber.ca
Rani K. Dhaliwal, Vice-President, Finance & Administrative Serv 5062
rani.dhaliwal@humber.ca
John Davies, President 5070
john.davies@humber.ca

Campuses
Humber Canadian Plastics Training Centre
#NB102, 205 Humber College Blvd. Toronto, M9W 5L7 Canada
Fax: 416-213-0927

Lakeshore Campus
3199 Lakeshore Blvd. West Toronto, M8V 1K8 Canada
Fax: 416-252-8842

Sailing & Powerboating Centre (SPC)
Humber Bay Park West (Lakeshore Blvd. West of Park Toronto, M8V 3X7 Canada
Fax: 416-252-5393

Transportation Training Centre (TTC)
55 Woodbine Downs Blvd. Toronto, M9W 6N5 Canada
Fax: 416-798-0307

Publications
Etcetera

Toronto: New College
300 Huron St. Toronto, M5S 3J6 Canada
416-978-2460, Fax: 416-978-0554,
newcollege.registrar@utoronto.ca
www.newcollege.utoronto.ca/site6.aspx
Enrollment: 4300

Toronto: Seneca College of Applied Arts & Technology
Newnham Campus
1750 Finch Ave. East Toronto, M2J 2X5 Canada
416-491-5050,
Newnham Campus Library Circulation: 416.491.5050, ext. 2099
admissions@senecac.on.ca;
InternationalAdmissions@senecac.on.ca
www.senecac.on.ca
The polytechnic educational institution consists of the following faculties: Faculty of Applied Arts & Health Sciences; Faculty of Applied Science & Engineering Technology; Faculty of Business; Faculty of Information Arts & Technology; Faculty of Continuing Education & Training; & Faculty of Workforce Skills Development
Jean Anne McLeod, B.A. (Hon.), Chair
Dr. Rick Miner, President, 416-491-5050 2261, fax: 416-491-7745
president@senecac.on.ca

Campuses
Buttonville Campus
Hangers 6, 7, & 8, Buttonville Airport
P.O. Box 190
2833 16th Ave. Markham, L3R 0P8 Canada
416-491-5050, Fax: 905-477-8103

Jane Campus
21 Beverley Hills Dr. Toronto, M3L 1A2 Canada
416-491-5050, Fax: 416-235-0462

King Campus
13990 Dufferin St. King City, L7B 1B3 Canada
905-833-3333,
King Campus Library, Circulation: 416-491-5050, ext. 5108

Markham Campus
10 Allstate Pkwy. Markham, L3R 5Y1 Canada
416-491-5050

Newmarket Campus
Weston Produce Plaza
#3, 16655 Yonge St. Newmarket, L3X 1V6 Canada
905-898-6199

Seneca @ York Campus
70 The Pond Rd. Toronto, M3J 3M6 Canada
416-491-5050,
Student Services: 416-491-5050, ext. 3000

Yorkgate Campus
1 York Gate Blvd. Toronto, M3N 3A1 Canada
416-493-4144,

Welland: Niagara College
Welland Campus
300 Woodlawn Rd. Welland, L3C 7L3 Canada
905-735-2211, Fax: 905-736-6020,
Grimsby Phone: 905-563-3254
infocentre@niagaracollege.ca (Welland Campus InfoCentre)
www.niagarac.on.ca
Enrollment: 6300
In addition to its full time student enrollment, the college has more than 15,000 continuing education registrants each year. Niagara College offers over 90 post-secondary diploma & graduate certificate programs, skills & apprenticeship training programs, plus two bachelor degree programs.
Jim Ryan, Chair
Dan Patterson, President, 905-641-2252 4040
dpatterson@niagaracollege.ca

Campuses
Maid of the Mist Campus
5881 Dunn St. Niagara Falls, L2G 2N9 Canada
Fax: 905-374-7454

Niagara-on-the-Lake Campus
135 Taylor Rd. Niagara-on-the-Lake, L0S 1J0 Canada
Fax: 905-641-2252

Ontario Street Satellite Site - Niagara Health System
155 Ontario St., St. Catharines, L2R 5K3
905-641-2252

Windsor: St. Clair College
South Campus
2000 Talbot Rd. West Windsor, N9A 6S4 Canada
519-966-1656, Fax: 519-972-3811, 1-800-387-0524
info@stclaircollege.ca
www.stclaircollege.ca
Enrollment: 5000
The College consists of the following schools of specialization: School of Liberal Arts & Sciences; School of Business & Information Technology; School of Academic Studies; School of Community Studies; School of Media, Art & Design; School of Engineering Technologies; School of Health Sciences; & School of Skilled Trades.
Vince Marcotte, Chair
John A. Strasser, Ph.D., President, 519-972-2701
jstrasser@stclaircollege.ca
Sherry Sharon, Registrar, 519-972-2727 4260
ssharon@stclaircollege.ca

Campuses
Thames Campus
1001 Grand Ave. West Chatham, N7M 5W4 Canada
519-354-9100, Fax: 519-354-6941, 1-800-387-0524
Registrar's Office: 519-354-9100, ext. 3238
info@stclaircollege.ca
The campus provides specialized training from the Schools of Business & Technology, & Health & Community Studies.

Wallaceburg Campus - James A. Burgess Skills Centre
920 Elgin St. Wallaceburg, N9A 3E1 Canada

519-627-8336, Fax: 519-627-5950, 1-800-387-0524
info@stclaircollege.ca
The campus features the Technical Industry Education Partnership.

Windsor - Riverside Dr. - St. Clair Centre for the Arts
201 Riverside Dr. West Windsor, N9A 5K4
519-252-8311, Fax: 519-973-4976, 1-800-387-0524
info@stclaircollege.ca
Enrollment: 500
The campus features the School of Media, Art & Design.
Ed Noot, Principal
Mike Campbell, Vice Principal & Counsellor

Post Secondary/Technical

Post Secondary/Technical

Northern Ontario School of Medicine
807-766-7300,
noms@normed.ca
www.normed.ca
4-year MD program
Dr. Roger Strasser, Founding Dean

Campuses
East Campus / NORMED
935 Ramsey Lake Rd. Sudbury, P3E 2C6 Canada
705-675-4883, Fax: 705-675-4858,
nos@normed.ca
www.normed.ca

West Campus / NORMED
955 Oliver Rd. Thunder Bay, P7B 5E1 Canada
807-766-7300, Fax: 807-766-7370,
nos@normed.ca
www.normed.ca

Ajax: **Diamond Institute of Business & Computer Technology**
Ajax GO Station
100 Westney Rd. S. Ajax, L1S 7H3 Canada
905-427-1922, Fax: 905-427-2558, 1-888-25-LEARN
info@diamondinstitute.ca
www.diamondinstitute.ca
Computer service technician, computer service/network engineer, computer programmer/analyst.

Alfred: **Collège d'Alfred de l'Université de Guelph**
31, rue St-Paul, CP 580 Alfred, K0B 1A0 Canada
613-679-2218, Fax: 613-679-2423,
www.alfredc.uoguelph.ca
Agriculture, horticulture, techniques de diététique, développement international, techniques soins vétérinaires
Marcel Couture, Directeur

Ancaster: **Redeemer University College**
777 Garner Rd. East Ancaster, L9K 1J4 Canada
905-648-2131, Fax: 905-648-2134,
mvanbev@redeemer.ca
www.redeemer.ca
Enrollment: 816
Justin D. Cooper, Ph.D., President
Jacob P. Ellens, Ph.D., Vice-President
William van Staalduinen, M.A., Vice-President
Ineke VanBruinessen, C.G.A., Senior Director
Marian Ryks-Szelekovszky, M.Ed., Senior Director, Admissions & Student Service
Mark Van Beveren, M.B.A., Media & Public Relations Director
Doug Loney, Ph.D., Dean
Doug Needham, Ph.D., Dean

Publications
The Crown

Belleville: **Loyalist College**
P.O. Box 4200
Belleville, K8N 5B9 Canada
613-969-1913, Fax: 613-962-1376,
liaison@loyalistc.on.ca
www.loyalistcollege.com
Douglas A.L. Auld, President

Publications
The Pioneer

Brantford: **Medical Radiation Technology**
c/o Ontario Association of Medical Radiation Tech
P.O. Box 1054
Brantford, N3T 5S7 Canada
519-753-6037, Fax: 519-753-6408, 1-800-387-467
inquiries@oamrt.on.ca
www.oamrt.on.ca

Burks Falls: **Outward Bound Canada**
996 Chetwynd Rd., RR#2 Burks Falls, P0A 1C0 Canada
705-382-5454, Fax: 705-382-5959, 1-888-688-9273
dave_wolfenden@outwardbound.ca (Exec.Dir.)
www.outwardbound.ca
Enrollment: 440
Fiona Hugh, Executive Director

Burlington: **Charles Sturt University, Ontario**
Bay Area Learning Centre
860 Harrington Ct. Burlington, L7N 3N4 Canada
905-333-4955, Fax: 905-333-6562,
canada@csu.edu.au
www.csu.edu.au
1-year teacher education program

Burlington: **Luba Mera School of Aesthetics, Cosmetology & Aromatherapy**
515 John St. Burlington, L7R 2L1 Canada
905-681-7882, Fax: 905-681-1494, 1-888-809-5559
info@lubamera.com
www.lubamera.com
Aesthetics training.

Burlington: **Syms Travel School**
Mount Royal Plaza
2049A Mount Forest Dr. Burlington, L7P 1H4 Canada
905-335-0125, Fax: 905-335-4880, 1-888-306-922
symsts@bellnet.ca
www.symstravelschool.ca
Travel industry training

Concord: **RCC College of Technology**
2000 Steeles Ave. West Concord, L4K 4N1 Canada
905-669-0544, Fax: 905-669-0551, 1-800-268-9098
www.rcc.on.ca
Electronics & computer networks engineering technology training & programs

Dundas: **Dundas Valley School of Art**
21 Ogilvie St. Dundas, L9H 2S1 Canada
905-628-6357, Fax: 905-628-1087,
dvsa@cogeco.net
www.dvsa.ca
Arthur Greenblatt, Director

Guelph: **Canadian Academy of Floral Art**
#103, 355 Elmira Rd. North Guelph, N1K 1S5 Canada
519-836-5495, Fax: 519-836-7529, 1-800-698-011
cafa@cafachat.com
www.cafachat.com
Floral designing & business program
Maija Asaris, Pres.

Guelph: **OATI Learning Group**
#101, 450 Speedvale Ave. West Guelph, N1H 7Y6 Canada
519-763-3160, Fax: 519-763-9585,
info@oatilearninggroup.com
Ian Barrett, Executive Director

Guelph: **Ontario Agricultural College**
OAC Dean's Office, Univ. of Guelph
103 Johnston Hall Guelph, N1G 2W1 Canada
519-824-4120, Fax: 519-766-1423,
oacinfo@uoguelph.ca
www.oac.uoguelph.ca
Heather Renwick, Executive Assistant, 519-824-4120 ext.56513
hrenwick@oac.uoguelph.ca
Dr. Craig J. Pearson, Dean, 519-824-4120 ext.52285
cpearson@uoguelph.ca

Hamilton: **Canadian Institute for NDE**
135 Fennell Ave. West Hamilton, L8N 3T2 Canada
905-387-1655, Fax: 905-574-6080,
info@cinde.ca
www.cinde.ca
Nondestructive testing/nondestructive examination
Douglas Marshall, Managing Director

Hamilton: **Grand Health Academy - Hamilton Campus - King Street East**
760 King St. East Hamilton, L8M 1A6 Canada
905-577-7707, Fax: 905-577-7738,
info@grandhealthacademy.com
www.grandhealthacademy.com
Personal support worker; CPR; first-aid courses
Janine K. Grand-Wilewski, Director

Hamilton: **Grand Health Academy - Hamilton - Concession Street**
574 Concession St. Hamilton, L8V 1B1 Canada
905-385-7727, Fax: 905-385-7477,
info@grandhealthacademy.com
www.grandhealthacademy.com

Hamilton: **Medical Laboratory Technology**
The Canadian Society for Medical Laboratory Scien
P.O. Box 2830
Hamilton, L8N 3N8 Canada
905-528-8642, Fax: 905-528-4968,
kurtd@csmls.org
www.csmls.org
Kurt H. Davis, Executive Director

London: **AlphaLogic Career College**
280 King Edward Ave. London, N5Z 3V3 Canada
519-858-0010, Fax: 519-858-0089,
info@alphalogic.net
www.alphalogic.net
Computer software applications, information technology programs
Jerry Vandergoot, President

London: **Elegance Schools Inc.**
#302, 219 Oxford St. West London, N6H 1S5 Canada
519-434-1181, Fax: 519-434-1182,
elegance@eleganceschools.on.ca
www.eleganceschools.on.ca
Esthetics & electrolysis.
Lisa Hakim, Director

London: **St. Peter's Seminary**
1040 Waterloo St. North London, N6A 3Y1 Canada
519-432-1824, Fax: 519-432-0964,
stpeters@uwo.ca
www.stpetersseminary.ca
Rev. W.T. McGrattan, B.E.Sc., M.Div., S.T.L., Rector
Rev. T.F. O'Connor, M.A., M.T.S., M.Th., Spiritual Director
Rev. Brian Dunn, Dean
Rev. John Comiskey, B.A., M.Div., H.E.L., H.E, Vice Rector & Registrar
Gabriella Catolino, D.M.C., M.Div., Executive Director

London: **Westervelt College**
1060 Wellington Rd. London, N6E 3W5 Canada
519-668-2000, Fax: 519-668-1616, 1-877-668-200
info@westerveltcollege.com
www.westerveltcollege.com
Business, travel, law, policing & computers
Donna M. Doerr, President & Chair

Markham: **CMS Training**
#725, 7305 Woodbine Ave. Markham, L3R 3V7 Canada
416-236-6332, 1-800-477-957
www.cmstraining.com
Home study in computer programming

Mississauga: **Credit Institute of Canada**
#216C, 219 Dufferin St. Mississauga, M6K 3J1 Canada
905-572-2615, Fax: 905-572-2619,
generalinformation@creditedu.org
www.creditedu.org
E. Keith Devolin, President & Dean
Geoff Wilkinson, General Manager

Burlington: **HBI College - Burlington Campus / HBI**
#26, 460 Brant St. Burlington, L7R 4B6 Canada
905-637-3415, Fax: 905-637-2843,
info@hbicollege.com
www.hbicollege.com
Administrative & computer programs.

Mississauga: **HBI College - Mississauga Campus / HBI**
Mississauga Executive Centre
Suite 120, 2 Robert Speck Parkway Mississauga, L4Z 1H8 Canada
905-949-9900,
infogta@hbicollege.com
www.hbicollege.com
Administrative & computer programs.

Mississauga: **The Investment Funds Institute of Canada**
3660 Huronatrio St. Mississauga, L5B 3C4 Canada
416-865-1237, 1-888-865-2437
ifse@ifse.ca
www.myinvestmentfunds.ca; www.cifp.ca
Keith Costello, Managing Director

Campuses
Québec Branch
#1800, 1010, rue Sherbrooke ouest Montréal, H3A 2R7 Canada
Fax: 514-985-5113

Mississauga: **Quality Management Institute / QMI**
#300, 90 Burnhamthorpe Rd. West Mississauga, L5B 3C3 Canada

905-272-3920, Fax: 905-272-3942

Campuses
Calgary Office
Manulife Centre
#710, 603 - 7 Ave. SW Calgary, T2P 2T5 Canada
Fax: 403-261-4075

Moncton Office
#400, 1133 George St. Moncton, E1E 4E1 Canada
Fax: 506-858-9302

Montréal Office
865, rue Ellingham Pointe-Claire, H9R 5E8 Canada
Fax: 514-694-9697

Vancouver Office
13799 Commerce Pkwy. Richmond, V6V 2N9 Canada
Fax: 604-244-6810

Niagara Falls: Niagara Parks Botanical Gardens & School of Horticulture
P.O. Box 150
Niagara Falls, L2E 6T2 Canada
905-356-8554, Fax: 905-356-5488,
schoolofhorticulture@niagaraparks.com
www.niagaraparks.com; www.schoolofhorticulture.com
Tom Laviolette, Supt.
Liz Klose, Supt.

North Bay: Canadore College of Applied Arts & Technology
P.O. Box 5001
100 College Dr. North Bay, P1B 8K9 Canada
705-474-7600, Fax: 705-474-2384,
info@canadorec.on.ca
www.canadorec.on.ca
Enrollment: 2977
Barbara Taylor, President

North York: Tyndale University College & Seminary
25 Ballyconnor Ct. North York, M2M 4B3 Canada
416-226-6380, Fax: 416-226-6746, 1-877-896-3253
info@tyndale.ca; admissions@tyndale.ca
www.tyndale.ca
A Christian College and Seminary whose mission is to educate and equip Christians to serve the world with passion for Jesus Christ.
Archie McLean, Chair
Dr. Brian C. Stiller, President
The Hon. Jake Epp, Chancellor

Ohsweken: Six Nations Polytechnic
P.O. Box 700
Ohsweken, N0A 1M0 Canada
519-445-0023, Fax: 519-445-4416,
www.snpolytechnic.com
Linda Staats, CEO

Ottawa: Algonquin Careers Academy
1644 Bank St. Ottawa, K1V 7Y6 Canada
613-722-7811, Fax: 613-722-4494, 1-888-722-781
www.algonquinacademy.com
Travel & Hospitality; Healthcare; Business

Ottawa: Canadian Police College Collège canadien de police
P.O. Box 8900
Ottawa, K1G 3J2 Canada
613-993-9500, Fax: 613-990-9738,
cpc-cpc@rcmp.gc.ca
www.cpc.gc.ca
Mike Saunders, Director general

Ottawa: La Cité collégiale
801, promenade de l'Aviation Ottawa, K1K 4R3 Canada
613-742-2483, Fax: 613-742-2481, 1-800-267-2483
info@lacitec.on.ca
www.lacitecollegiale.com
Enrollment: 3500
Andrée Lortie, Président

Ottawa: International Academy Health Education Centre
380 Forest St. Ottawa, K2B 8E6 Canada
613-820-0318, Fax: 613-820-7478, 1-800-267-873
info@intlacademy.com
www.intlacademy.com
Nutrition; herbs; iridology; reflexology; aromatherapy; homeopathy; shiatsu/accupressure; massage
Dorothy Marshall, Ph.D., N.D., C.H.H.P., N., Executive Director

Ottawa: International Academy of Natural Health Sciences
380 Forest St. Ottawa, K2B 8E6 Canada
613-820-0318, Fax: 613-820-7478, 1-800-267-873
naturalhealth@intlacademy.com
www.intlacademy.com
Nutrition; herbs; iridology; reflexology

Ottawa: Mican Business College
1825 Woodward Dr. Ottawa, K2C 0P9 Canada
613-224-6211, Fax: 613-224-2739,
nicki@lcancollege.com
www.micancollege.com
Nicki Wilmore, President

Ottawa: Natural Resources Canada
Office of Energy Efficiency
580 Booth St., 18th Fl. Ottawa, K1A 0E4 Canada
613-995-6839, Fax: 613-947-4121,
www.emr.ca/home/nrcanhpe.htm
Philip B. Jago, Chief
pjago@nrcan.gc.ca

Ottawa: Ottawa School of Art
35 George St. Ottawa, K1N 8W5 Canada
613-241-7471, Fax: 613-241-4391,
info@artottawa.ca
www.artottawa.ca
Fine arts training.
Jeff Stellick, Executive Director

Ottawa: Pères Montfortains (Residence des étudiants)
463 Riverdale Ave. Ottawa, K1S 1S1 Canada
613-731-2271
Cor Kauffman, s.m.m., Superior

Ottawa: Transport Canada Training Institute
c/o Coast Guard Emergencies, Canada Bldg.
#941, 344 Slater Ottawa, K1A 0N7 Canada
613-990-3400, Fax: 613-995-4700,

Ottawa: Versailles Academy of Make-Up Arts, Esthetics, Hair
#1, 1930 Bank St. Ottawa, K1V 7Z8 Canada
613-521-4155, Fax: 613-521-6945,
www.versaillesacademy.com
Cosmetic, esthetic & hair trades courses since 1981

Ottawa: Willis College of Business & Technology
85 O'Connor St. Ottawa, K1P 5M6 Canada
613-233-1128, Fax: 613-233-9286,
ottawa@williscollege.com
www.williscollege.com
E-business & IT training.
Rima Aristocrat, President/CEO

Owen Sound: Creative Career Systems Inc.
RR#5 Owen Sound, N4K 5N7 Canada
519-376-7396, Fax: 519-376-6772, 1-800-463-045
info@creative.on.ca
www.creative.on.ca
Health care aide program.

Pickering: Pickering Campus
#220, 1099 Kingston Rd. Pickering, L1V 1B5 Canada
905-427-3010, Fax: 905-420-6752,
geninfo@staff.dbcc.on.ca
www.dbcc.on.ca
Business; Information Technology; Health Care; Corporate Training
Farid Jenabieh, President

Campuses
Oshawa Campus
#111, 50 Richmond St. Oshawa, L1G 7C7 Canada
905-443-3010, Fax: 905-443-3011,
geninfo@staff.dbcc.on.ca
www.dbcc.on.ca
Business; Information Technology; Health Care; Corporate Training

Toronto Campus
#203, 1457 McCowan Rd. Scarborough, M1E 2S2 Canada
416-724-1053, Fax: 416-724-5258,
geninfo@staff.dbcc.on.ca
www.dbcc.on.ca
Business; Information Technology; Health Care; Corporate Training

Richmond Hill: Academy of Learning
10235 Yonge St. Richmond Hill, L4C 3B4 Canada
905-508-5791, Fax: 905-508-9409,
www.academyoflearning.com
Computer & business skills training; 40 locations across Ontario

Ridgetown: Ridgetown College - University of Guelph
Ridgetown, N0P 2C0 Canada
519-674-1500, Fax: 519-674-1515
Ron E. Pitblado, B.Sc.(Agr.), M.Sc., Ph.D., Acting Director
rpitblad@ridgetownc.uoguelph.ca
J.M. Brooks, Executive Officer
jbrooks@ridgetownc.uoguelph.ca

Scarborough: St. Augustine's Seminary of Toronto
2661 Kingston Rd. Scarborough, M1M 1M3 Canada
416-261-7207, Fax: 416-261-2529,
info@staugustines.on.ca
www.staugustines.on.ca
Enrollment: 95
Rev. Msgr. A. Robert Nusca, B.A., M.Div., S.T.B., S.S, Rector
Rev. Thomas A. Lynch, B.A., M.Div., S.T.L., S.T, Dean

Scarborough: Scarborough Campus
1371 Neilson Rd., Suite 413 Scarborough, M1B 4Z8 Canada
416-283-8252, Fax: 416-283-3796,
admin.scar@cjcollege.com
www.cjcollege.com
Health care related program.
Cynthia Cooper, President

Campuses
Etobicoke Campus
365 Evans Ave. Etobicoke, M8Z 1K2 Canada
Fax: 416-247-8927

Scarborough: Toronto Institute of Pharmaceutical Technology
#200, 55 Town Centre Ct. Scarborough, M1P 4X4 Canada
416-296-1478, Fax: 416-296-7077,
info@tipt.com
www.tipt.com
Alexander MacGregor, Dean

Sudbury: Collège Boréal
21, boul Lasalle Sudbury, P3A 6B1 Canada
705-560-6673, Fax: 705-560-7641, 1-800-361-667
www.borealc.on.ca
Enrollment: 1500
Denis Hubert, Président

Timmins: Northern College
P.O. Box 3211
Hwy. 101 East, South Porcupine Timmins, P4N 8R6 Canada
705-235-3211, Fax: 705-235-7279, 1-866-736-587
info@northern.on.ca
www.northernc.on.ca
Enrollment: 1489
Michael Hill, President, fax: 705-235-7277

Campuses
Haileybury Campus
640 Latchford Haileybury, P0J 1K0 Canada
Fax: 705-672-2014,
www.northernc.on.ca

Kirkland Lake Campus
140 Government Rd. East Kirkland Lake, P2N 3L8 Canada
Fax: 705-568-8186

Timmins Campus
P.O. Box 3211
Hwy. 101 East, South Porcupine Timmins, P4N 8R6 Canada
Fax: 705-235-7279

Toronto: Benns International Schools Inc.
#490, 20 Eglinton Ave. East Toronto, M4P 1A9 Canada
416-489-8246, Fax: 416-489-1662,
benns@tesolandtesl.com
www.tesolandtesl.com
Enrollment: 125
TESL & ECE teacher training
Sandra Benns

Toronto: Canadian Business College
Head Office
2 Bloor St. West, 22nd Fl. Toronto, M4W 3E2 Canada
416-925-9929, Fax: 416-925-9220, 1-888-925-992
www.cbstraining.com
Business, technology, health care & digital graphics

Toronto: Canadian Churches' Forum for Global Ministries
47 Queen's Park Cres. East Toronto, M5S 2C3 Canada
416-924-9351, Fax: 416-978-7821,
director@ccforum.ca
www.ccforum.ca
Cross cultural orientation programs for church related personnel & volunteers involved in global mission & ministry

***Toronto:* The Canadian College of Naturopathic Medicine**
1255 Sheppard Ave. East Toronto, M2K 1E2 Canada
416-498-1255, Fax: 416-498-1576, 1-866-241-226
info@ccnm.edu
www.ccnm.edu
Naturopathic medical education, research & clinical practice; 4,500+ hours of classroom & clinical training
Catherine Kenwell, Director
Bob Bernhardt, President & CEO

***Toronto:* Canadian Institute of Health Care & Business**
#303, 7 Hayden St. Toronto, M4Y 2P2 Canada
416-925-4417,
best-care@sympatico.ca
www.infobest-care.com
Personal Support Worker; Live-in Caregiver; Travel & Tourism; Pharmacy Technician

***Toronto:* Canadian Jewellers Institute / CJI**
#600, 27 Queen St. East Toronto, M5C 2M6 Canada
416-368-7616, Fax: 416-368-1986, 1-800-580-0942
cji@canadianjewellers.com
www.canadianjewellers.com/html/cji.htm
Wide range of jewellry education.

***Toronto:* Canadian Memorial Chiropractic College**
6100 Leslie St. Toronto, M2H 3J1 Canada
416-482-2340, Fax: 416-482-9745,
communications@cmcc.ca
www.cmcc.ca
Undergraduate and graduate Chiropratic College.
J.A. Moss, D.C., M.B.A., President
president@cmcc.ca

***Toronto:* Canadian School of Private Investigation & Security Ltd.**
2828 Dufferin St. Toronto, M6B 3S3 Canada
416-785-5701, Fax: 416-785-6064,
cspis@cspis.com
www.cspis.com
Private investigation, paralegal, security, law enforcement & police foundations training.
Carl Franco, Founder & Principle Instructor

***Toronto:* Canadian Securities Institute**
200 Wellington St. W., 15th Fl. Toronto, M5V 3C7 Canada
416-364-9130, Fax: 866-866-2660, 1-866-866-2601
customer_support@csi.ca
www.csi.ca

Campuses
Montréal Office
1155, rue University, Suite 600 Montréal, H3B 3A7 Canada
Fax: 866-866-2660, 1-866-866-2601
customer_support@csi.ca
www.csi.ca

***Toronto:* CDI College of Business, Technology & Healthcare**
#200, 424 Yonge St. Toronto, M5B 2H4 Canada
416-963-8633, Fax: 416-963-5919
Computers, accounting & business training; 23 locations across Ontario

***Toronto:* The Certified General Accountants Association of Ontario**
240 Eglinton Ave. East Toronto, M4P 1K8 Canada
416-322-6520, Fax: 416-322-5594, 1-800-668-1454
info@cga-ontario.org
www.cga-ontario.org/

***Toronto:* Commercial Business College**
2327 Dufferin St., 1st Fl. Toronto, M6E 3S5 Canada
416-480-1545,
info@policefoundations-cbc.com
Police & law enforcement courses

***Toronto:* Complections International - The Make-Up School**
85 St. Nicholas St. Toronto, M4Y 1W8 Canada
416-968-6739, Fax: 416-968-7340,
info@complectionsmake-up.com
www.complectionsmake-up.com
Professional make-up artistry training for stage, TV & film, special effects & fashion

***Toronto:* Constellation College of Hospitality**
808 Mount Pleasant Rd. Toronto, M4P 2L2 Canada
416-675-2175, Fax: 416-675-6477,
admiss@constellationcollege.com
www.constellationcollege.com
Hotel & Restaurant Operations; Culinary Arts
Sharon Turner, Director

***Toronto:* Frontier College**
35 Jackes Ave. Toronto, M4T 1E2 Canada
416-923-3591, Fax: 416-323-3522, 1-800-555-652
information@frontiercollege.ca
www.frontiercollege.ca
Volunteer-based, literacy organization.
John Daniel O'Leary, President

***Toronto:* The Glenn Gould School of the Royal Conservatory of Music**
90 Croatia St. Toronto, M6H 1K9 Canada
416-408-2824, Fax: 416-408-3096,
glenngouldschool@rcmusic.ca
www.rcmusic.ca
Enrollment: 130
Professional training in music performance & pedagogy at the bachelor & graduate levels
Rennie Regehr, Dean

***Toronto:* Global Village**
#202, 180 Bloor St. West Toronto, M5S 2V6 Canada
416-968-1405, Fax: 416-968-6667,
toronto@gvenlish.com
www.gvenglish.com
Geneviève Bouchard, Director

***Toronto:* Granton Institute of Technology**
263 Adelaide St. West Toronto, M5H 1Y3 Canada
416-977-3929, Fax: 416-977-5612,
info@grantoninstitute.com
www.grantoninstitute.com
Distance education courses

***Toronto:* Herzing College**
#202, 220 Yonge St. Toronto, M5B 2H1 Canada
416-599-6996, Fax: 416-599-0192,
mark@tor.herzing.edu
www.herzing.edu/toronto
Information technology programs (programming, networking, database management & microprocessor technology), healthcare & legal.

***Toronto:* Institute of Technical Trades Ltd.**
749 Warden Ave. Toronto, M1L 4A8 Canada
416-750-1950, Fax: 416-750-4702,
technicaltrade@rogers.com
www.technicaltrade.ca
Welding & CNC machine setup operation.

***Toronto:* International Academy of Design & Technology**
39 John St. Toronto, M5V 3G6 Canada
041-692-2366, 1-800-361-6664
www.iadt.ca
Accredited diploma programs in Computer Graphics, Interior Design, Multimedia Web Design & Development & Network & Internet Technologies.

***Toronto:* National Institute of Broadcasting**
1498 Yonge St. Toronto, M4T 1Z6 Canada
416-922-2556, Fax: 416-922-5470, 1-800-216-6247
info@nibtv.com
www.nibtraining.com
Radio & television broadcast training.

***Toronto:* New Skills Health College**
720 Midland Ave. Toronto, M1K 4C9 Canada
416-261-8988, Fax: 416-261-8488, 1-877-227-229
info@newskillshealth.ca
www.newskillshealth.ca
Personal Support Worker diploma program

***Toronto:* Ontario Institute for Studies in Education**
252 Bloor St. West Toronto, M5S 1V6 Canada
416-923-6641, Fax: 416-926-4725,
www.oise.utoronto.ca
Jane Gaskell, Dean

***Toronto:* The RCM Community School at The Royal Conservatory of Music**
90 Croatia St. Toronto, M6H 1K9 Canada
416-408-2825, Fax: 416-408-3096,
communityschool@rcmusic.ca
www.rcmusic.ca
Enrollment: 6000
Music lessons for people of all ages & levels of ability; recognized for its Early Childhood Education programs & its commitment to life-long learning
Jeff Melanson, Dean

***Toronto:* Rets PLC Training**
2084 Danforth Ave. Toronto, M4C 1J9 Canada
416-698-5287, Fax: 416-689-5288,
rets@canada.com
www.rets.ca
PLC automation; engineering technology; government regulated & approved.

***Toronto:* The Royal Conservatory of Music**
90 Croatia St. Toronto, M6H 1K9 Canada
416-408-2824, Fax: 416-408-3096,
www.rcmusic.ca
The largest & oldest independent arts educator in Canada, committed to developing human potential through leadership in music & arts education
Peter Simon, President

***Toronto:* St. Basil's College**
95 St. Joseph St. Toronto, M5S 2R9 Canada
416-925-4368
Part of the University of Toronto.

***Toronto:* School of Makeup Art Ltd.**
25 Yorkville Ave. Toronto, M4W 1L1 Canada
416-340-1300, Fax: 416-640-4491,
info@schoolofmakeup.com
www.schoolofmarkupart.com
Professional make-up training: beauty; film & TV; special effects.

***Toronto:* Shiatsu School of Canada Inc.**
547 College St. Toronto, M6G 1A9 Canada
416-323-1818, Fax: 416-323-1681, 1-800-263-170
info@shiatsucanada.com
www.shiatsucanada.com
2,200-hour program has the highest standard in the world outside of Japan
Enza Ierullo, Director

***Toronto:* The Society of Management Accountants of Ontario**
#300, 70 University Ave. Toronto, M5J 2M4 Canada
416-977-7741, Fax: 416-977-6079, 1-800-387-299
www.cma-canada.org/ontario/default.asp
David Hipgrave, President & CEO

***Toronto:* Sutherland Chan School & Teaching Clinic**
#400, 330 Dupont St. Toronto, M5R 1V9 Canada
416-924-1107, Fax: 416-924-9413,
admissions@sutherland-chan.com
www.sutherland-chan.com
Massage therapy.
Grace Chan, President
Nicole Blake Perryman, Admissions & Student Services Coordinator

***Toronto:* Toronto Art Therapy Institute**
216 St. Clair Ave. West Toronto, M4V 1R2 Canada
416-924-6221, Fax: 416-924-0156,
info@tati.on.ca
www.tati.on.ca
Gilda Grossman, M.S.W., R.S.W., R.C.A.T., Director

***Toronto:* Toronto Baptist Seminary & Bible College**
130 Gerrard St. East Toronto, M5A 3T4 Canada
416-925-3263, Fax: 416-925-8305,
info@tbs.edu
www.tbs.edu
Michael Haykin, Principal

***Toronto:* Toronto Campus**
Head Office
#300, 700 Lawrence Ave. West Toronto, M6A 3B4 Canada
416-630-8021, Fax: 416-630-9790, 1-877-736-3349
dboyes@medixschool.ca
www.medixschool.ca
Health care programs
Randy Henry, President

Campuses
Brantford Campus
39 King George Rd. Brantford, N3R 5K2 Canada
519-752-4859, Fax: 519-752-2217, 1-877-736-3349
www.medixschool.ca

Kitchener
#14, 248 Stirling Ave. Kitchener, N2G 4L1 Canada
519-895-0013, Fax: 519-772-0107, 1-877-736-3349
www.medixschool.ca

London
1299 Oxford St. East London, N5Y 4W5 Canada
519-659-4822, Fax: 519-659-2516, 1-877-736-3349
www.medixschool.ca

Scarborough
#205, 2130 Lawrence Avenue East Scarborough, M1R 3A6 Canada

416-701-1201, Fax: 416-701-0855, 1-877-736-3349
www.medixschool.ca

***Toronto:* Toronto Centre**
152 Norseman St. Toronto, M8Z 2R4 Canada
416-231-7227, Fax: 416-231-2753, 1-800-458-7473
toronto@autotrainingcentre.com
www.autotrainingcentre.com
Private college specializing in automotive training

Campuses
Montreal Campus
3900, rue Jean-Talon est Montréal, H3R 2G8 Canada
514-725-6026, Fax: 514-725-1630, 1-877-725-6026
Montreal@AutoTraiingCentre.com
www.autotrainingcentre.com

Richmond Campus
210-13460 Smallwood Place Richmond, V6V 1W8 Canada
604-270-6121, Fax: 604-270-6123, 1-888-546-2886
Vancouver@AutoTrainingCentre.com
www.autotrainingcentre.com

Surrey Campus
#4 12372 - 84th Ave. Surrey, V3W 0J5 Canada
604-270-6121, Fax: 604-270-6123, 1-888-546-2886
Surry@AutoTrainingCentre.com
www.autotrainingcentre.com

***Toronto:* Toronto Office / iitravel**
#302, 1240 Bay St. Toronto, M5R 2A7 Canada
416-924-2271, Fax: 416-924-5667,
iit@ica.net
www.iitravel.com
Travel & tourism training including "Learning at Seas Seminars".

Campuses
Brampton Campus
#200, 341 Main St. North Brampton, L6X 1N5 Canada
Fax: 905-459-7463
Travel & tourism training including "Learning at Seas Seminars".

London Campus
2031 Dundas St. East London, N5V 1P6 Canada
Fax: 519-452-1058
Travel & tourism training including "Learning at Seas Seminars".

Mississauga Campus
1550 South Gatway Rd. Suite 310 Mississauga, L4W 5G6 Canada
905-624-8600, Fax: 905-624-4992,
iit@ica.net
www.iitravel.com
Travel & tourism training including "Learning at Seas Seminars".

Scarborough Campus
#309, 80 Corporate Dr. Scarborough, M1H 3G5 Canada
416-924-9132, Fax: 416-289-3342,
iit@ica.net
www.ittravel.com
Travel & tourism training including "Learning at Seas Seminars".

***Toronto:* Toronto School**
5 Park Home Ave., 6th Fl. Toronto, M2N 6L4 Canada
416-223-7855, Fax: 416-224-1641,
toronto@omnicomtrans.com
www.omnicomtrans.com
Ivan Markiet, Director

Campuses
Calgary School
#100, 840 - 6 Ave. SW Calgary, T2P 3E5 Canada
403-265-6936, Fax: 403-265-6926,
calgary@omnicomstudy.com
www.omnicomstudy.com

***Toronto:* Townshend College of Business & Computers**
#202, 1711 McCowan Rd. Toronto, M1S 2Y3 Canada
416-297-5627, Fax: 416-297-0210,
info@townshendcollege.com
www.townshendcollege.com
Accounting, payroll, administration, healthcare & technology training programs
Jerry Townshend, Dir. of Education
Sandra Townshend, Principal

***Toronto:* Travel Training Career Centre Ltd.**
#201, 16 Spadina Rd. Toronto, M5R 2S7 Canada
416-481-2265, Fax: 416-487-5428,
travelcollege@sympatico.ca
www.travelcollege.ca
Travel & tourism industry courses, customer service.

***Toronto:* Trebas Institute**
149 College St. Toronto, M5T 1P5 Canada
416-966-3066, Fax: 416-966-0030,
info@trebas.com
www.trebas.com
Enrollment: 400
Audio Engineering & Production/DJ Arts, Entertainment Management, Film/Television Production
Peter Di Santo, Director

***Toronto:* Yorkville College**
2nd Fl., 1835 Yonge St. Toronto, M5S 1X8 Canada
416-929-0121, 1-888-868-9688
mail@yorkvillecollege.com
www.yorkvillecollege.com
Computer & technical programs.
Fred Fisher, President

***Waterloo:* Shad International**
8 Young St. East Waterloo, N2J 2L3 Canada
519-884-8844, Fax: 519-884-8191,
info@shad.ca
www.shad.ca
Four week summer enrichment program for students in grades 11 or 12, secondaire V or CEGEP I for Quebec students, or the international equivalent. The program includes the sciences, technology, and entrepreneurship.
Barry Bisson, President
Mary Dever, National Director of Development

***Windsor:* MicroAge Learning Centre**
#920, 4510 Rhodes Dr. Windsor, N8W 5K5 Canada
519-945-9900, Fax: 519-945-9777, 1-800-946-266
info@learning-centre.com
www.learning-centre.com
Software training.

Prince Edward Island

Government Agencies

***Charlottetown:* Department of Education**
P.O. Box 2000
Charlottetown, C1A 7N8 Canada
902-368-4600, Fax: 902-368-4663,
www.gov.pe.ca/educ/
Clayton Coe, Acting Director
Imelda M. Arsenault, Director, 902-368-4477
Carolyn Simpson, Administrator

School Boards/Districts/Divisions

Public

***Abram Village:* French Language School Board of Prince Edward Island**
La Commission scolaire de langue française de l'le-du-Prin
P.O. Box 124
1596 rte. 124 Abram Village, C0B 2E0 Canada
902-854-2975, Fax: 902-854-2981,
cslf@edu.pe.ca
www.edu.pe.ca/cslf
Grades: 1 - 12
Number of Schools: 6
Robert Maddix, Chair
Gilles Benoit, Chief Executive Officer
gjbenoit@edu.pe.ca
Paul Cyr, Director, Instruction
pacyr@edu.pe.ca
Louise Gallant, Director, Accounting
lzgallant@edu.pe.ca
Brad Samson, Director, Administration
blsamson@edu.pe.ca
Michel Gagnon, Manager, Information Systemes & Communication
mgagnon@edu.pe.ca
Élise Milligan, Secretary
emmilligan@edu.pe.ca

***Charlottetown:* Eastern School District**
P.O. Box 8600
Charlottetown, C1A 8V7 Canada
902-368-6990, Fax: 902-368-6960
Enrollment: 14309
David MacDonald, Secretary
Dr. Robert Clow, Chair
Mary Lou Morrison, Director
Ronald Lee, Vice-Chair
Ricky Hood, Director

***Summerside:* Western School Board**
272 MacEwen Rd. Summerside, C1N 2P7 Canada
902-888-8400, Fax: 902-888-8449,
www.edu.pe.ca/wsb
Grades: K.-12
Enrollment: 6244
Dale Sabean, Supt.
dcsabean@edu.pe.ca
Harvey MacEwen, Dir., Bus. Services
hfmacewen@edu.pe.ca
Gary Doucette, Chair

Schools: Specialized

First Nations

***Lennox Island:* John J. Sark Memorial School**
P.O. Box 124
Lennox Island, C0B 1P0 Canada
902-831-2777, Fax: 902-831-3153,
johnjsms@auracom.com
www.lennoxisland.com/portal/com_education.htm
Grades: K.-6
Alan Gillis, Director

Schools: Independent & Private

Independent & Private Schools

***Charlottetown:* Fair Isle Adventist School**
20 Lapthorne Ave. Charlottetown, C1A 2M2 Canada
902-894-9301
Grades: 1-9; Seventh-day Adventist
Enrollment: 7
Deanna Fall

***Charlottetown:* Full Circle Co-operative**
219 Kent St. Charlottetown, C1A 1P1 Canada
902-628-6174,
fullcircleloop@easlink.ca
users.eastlink.ca/~fullcirclecoop/
Grades: 5-12
Enrollment: 15
Scott Davidson, B.A., B.Ed., Principal

***Charlottetown:* Grace Christian School**
50 Kirkdale Rd. Charlottetown, C1E 1N6 Canada
902-628-1668, Fax: 902-628-1668,
gbc@gracechristianschool.ca
www.gracechristianschool.ca
Grades: K.-12
Enrollment: 190
A ministry of Grace Baptist Church
Jason Biech, Principal
principal@gracechristianschool.ca

***Charlottetown:* Immanuel Christian School**
65 Kirkwood Dr. Charlottetown, C1A 8C3 Canada
902-628-6465,
ics@pei.aibn.com
www.immanuelchristianschool.ca/
Grades: K-9
Enrollment: 28
Ruth Van Eyk, Principal

Universities & Colleges

Universities

***Charlottetown:* University of Prince Edward Island**
550 University Ave. Charlottetown, C1A 4P3 Canada
902-566-0439, Fax: 902-566-0420,
www.upei.ca
Enrollment: 3500
H. Wade MacLaughlan, B.B.A., LL.B., LL.M., President & Vice-Chancellor
William G. (Bill Andrew, Chancellor
Fred Hyndman, Chair of the Board
Alan Buchannan, B.A., M.A., Registrar & University Secretary
Dr. Rosemary Herbert, Ph.D., Acting Vice-President
Roger Cook, Purchasing Agent
Kevin Rogers, Manager
Kevin Lewis, B.B.A., M.B.A., Chief Development Officer
Gary Bradshaw, Vice-President
Katherine Schultz, Vice-President
Mark Leggott, B.Sc., M.Sc, M.L.I.S., University Librarian

Faculties
Arts
Richard Kurial, B.A., M.A., Ph.D., Dean

Business Administration
Roberta MacDonald, B.A., Dean

Education
J. Tim Goddard, Ph.D., Dean

Nursing
Dr. Kim Critchley, Dean

Science
Christian Lacroix, B.Sc., M.Sc., Dean

Veterinary Medicine
Dr. Donald L. Reynolds, Dean

Publications
The Cadre

Panther Prints

X-Press

Post Secondary/Technical

Post Secondary/Technical

Charlottetown: **Holland College of Applied Arts and Technology**
Administrative Services
140 Weymouth St. Charlottetown, C1A 4Z1 Canada
902-629-4217, Fax: 902-629-4239,
info@hollandc.pe.ca
www.hollandc.pe.ca/

Alex MacAulay, President

Campuses
Atlantic Police Academy
P.O. Box 156
Slemon Park, C0A 2A0 Canada
Fax: 902-888-6725,

Marine Training Centre
100 Water St. Summerside, C1N 1A9 Canada
Fax: 902-888-6404

Royalty Centre
40 Enman Cres. Charlottetown, C1E 1E6 Canada
Fax: 902-566-9323

Souris Centre
Main St. Plaza
P.O. Box 429
Souris, C0B 2B0 Canada
Fax: 902-687-3543

East Prince Centre
223 Water St. Summerside, C1N 1B4 Canada
Fax: 902-888-6402

Montague Centre
Montague, C0A 1R0 Canada
Fax: 902-838-3518

Atlantic Technology Centre
140 Weymouth St. Charlottetown, C1A 4Z1 Canada

Culinary Institute of Canada
4 Sydney St. Charlottetown, C1A 1E9 Canada
Fax: 902-894-6801, 877-475-2844

Tourism and Culinary Centre
4 Sydney St. Charlottetown, C1A 1E9 Canada
Fax: 902-894-6801, 877-475-2844

Charlottetown Centre
140 Weymouth St. Charlottetown, C1A 4Z1 Canada
Fax: 902-566-9505

Georgetown Centre
117 Kent St. Georgetown, C0A 1L0 Canada
Fax: 902-652-2424

Atlantic Technology Centre
140 Weymouth St. Charlottetown, C1A 4Z1 Canada

Assessment & Counselling Service
140 Weymouth St. Charlottetown, C1A AZ1 Canada
Fax: 902-566-9639, 800-446-5265

Publications
The Surveyor

Summerside: **The College of Piping & Celtic Performing Arts of Canada**
619 Water St. East Summerside, C1N 4H8 Canada
902-436-5377, Fax: 902-436-4930, 1-877-224-747
info@collegeofpiping.com
www.collegeofpiping.com

Scott MacAulay, Director

Québec

Government Agencies

Québec: **Ministère de l'Éducation, du Loisir et du Sport**
Direction des communications
1035, rue De La Chevrotière, 28e étage Québec, G1R 5A5 Canada
418-643-7095, Fax: 418-646-6561, 866-747-6626
www.mels.gouv.qc.ca

Line Beauchamp, Ministre
Christiane Barbe, Sous-ministre

Campuses
Directions régionales 1 & 11: Bas St-Laurent/Gaspésie-Iles-de-la-Madeleine
337, rue Moreault, bureau 2.04, 2e étage Rimouski, G5L 0A5 Canada
418-727-3600, Fax: 418-727-3557,
dr-01@mels.gouv.qc.ca

Gérard Bédard, Directeur régional

Direction régionale 2: Saguenay—Lac-Saint-Jean
2220, rue Saint-David Jonquière, G7X 0L3 Canada
418-695-7982, Fax: 418-695-7990,
dr-02@mels.gouv.qc.ca

François Paquette, Directeur régional

Directions régionales 3 & 12: Capitale-Nationale et Chaudière-Appalaches
1020, rte de l'Église, 3e étage Québec, G1V 3V9 Canada
418-643-7934, Fax: 418-643-0972,
dr-03-mels.gouv.qc.ca

Marie-Sylvie Descôteau, Directrice régionale

Directions régionales 4 & 17: Mauricie et Centre-du-Québec
Édifice Capitanal
#213, 100, rue Laviolette Trois-Rivières, G9A 5S9 Canada
819-371-6711, Fax: 819-371-6075,
dr-04@mels.gouv.qc.ca

Claude Lamarre, Directeur régional

Direction régionale 5: Estrie
#3.05, 200, rue Belvédère nord Sherbrooke, J1H 4A9 Canada
819-820-3382, Fax: 819-820-3947,
dr-05@mels.gouv.qc.ca

Diane Lamothe, Directrice régionale

Direction régionale 6: Montréal
600, rue Fullum, 10e étage Montréal, H2K 4L1 Canada
514-873-4630, Fax: 514-873-0620,
dr-063@mels.gouv.qc.ca

Gilles Lamirande, Directeur régional

Direction régionale 7: Outaouais
170, rue de l'Hôtel-de-Ville, 4e étage Gatineau, J8X 4C2 Canada
819-772-3382, Fax: 819-772-3955,
dr-07@mels.gouv.qc.ca

Hélène Audet, Directrice régionale

Directions régionales 8 & 10: Abitibi-Témiscamingue et Nord-du-Québec
215, boul Rideau, 1er étage Rouyn-Noranda, J9X 5Y6 Canada
819-763-3001, Fax: 819-763-3017,
dr-08@mels.gouv.qc.ca

Louise Bilodeau, Directrice régionale (par intérim)

Direction régionale 9: Côte-Nord (Services adm. et gén.)
Édifice Paul-Provencher
#1.812, 625, boul Laflèche Baie-Comeau, G5C 1C5 Canada
418-295-4400, Fax: 418-295-4467,
dr09-bc@mels.gouv.qc.ca

Lucy de Mendonça, Directrice régionale

Direction régionale 9: Côte-Nord (Services éducatifs)
#201, 106, rue Napoléon Sept-Iles, G4R 3L7 Canada
418-964-8420, Fax: 418-964-8504,
dr09-si@mels.gouv.qc.ca

Lucy de Mendoça, Directrice régionale

Directions régionales 13, 14 et 15: Laval, Lanaudière, et Laurentides
#200, 300, rue Sicard Sainte-Thérèse, J7E 3X5 Canada
450-430-3611, Fax: 450-430-4005,
dr-061@mels.gouv.qc.ca

Lauraine Langlois, Directrice régionale

Direction régionale 16: Montérégie
Édifice Montval
201, place Charles-Le Moyne, 6e étage Longueuil, J4K 2T5 Canada
450-928-7438, Fax: 450-928-7451,
dr-062@mels.gouv.qc.ca

Francis Culée, Directeur régional

School Boards/Districts/Divisions

Public

Aylmer: **Commission scolaire Western Québec Western Québec School Board**
15, rue Katimavik Aylmer, J9J 0E9 Canada
819-684-2336, Fax: 819-684-1328, 800-363-9111
wqsb@wqsb.qc.ca
www.wqsb.qc.ca

Michael Dawson, Directeur général

Châteauguay: **Commission scolaire New Frontiers New Frontiers School Board**
214, rue McLeod Châteauguay, J6J 2H4 Canada
450-691-1440, Fax: 450-691-0643,
secgen@csnewfrontiers.qc.ca
www.csnewfrontiers.qc.ca

Wayne Goldthorp, Directeur général

Dorval: **Commission scolaire Lester-B.-Pearson Lester B. Pearson School Board**
1925, av Brookdale Dorval, H9P 2Y7 Canada
514-422-3000,
info@lbpsb.qc.ca
www.lbpsb.qc.ca

Robert T. Mills, Directeur général

Magog: **Commission scolaire Eastern Townships Eastern Townships School Board**
#205, 101, rue Du Moulin Magog, J1X 6H8 Canada
819-868-3100, Fax: 819-868-2286,
priests@etsb.qc.ca
www.etsb.qc.ca

Chantal C. Beaulieu, Directrice générale

Montréal: **Commission scolaire English-Montréal English Montréal School Board**
6000, av Fielding Montréal, H3X 1T4 Canada
514-483-7200, Fax: 514-483-7324,
webmaster@emsb.qc.ca
www.emsb.qc.ca

Robert Stocker, Directeur général

New Carlisle: **Commission scolaire Eastern Shores Eastern Shores School Board**
40, rue Mount Sorrel New Carlisle, G0C 1Z0 Canada
418-752-2247, Fax: 418-752-6447,
info@essb.qc.ca
www.essb.qc.ca

Dave Royal, Directeur général
dave.royal@essb.qc.ca

Québec: **Commission scolaire Central Québec Central Québec School Board**
2046, ch Saint-Louis Québec, G1T 1P4 Canada
418-688-8730, Fax: 418-682-5891, 800-249-5573
cqsb@dqsb.qc.ca
www.cqsb.qc.ca

Ronald Corriveau, Directeur général

Rosemère: **Commission scolaire Sir-Wilfrid-Laurier Sir Wilfrid Laurier School Board**
235, montée Lesage Rosemère, J7A 4Y6 Canada
450-621-5600, Fax: 450-621-7929, 866-621-5600
www.swlauriersb.qc.ca

Anne-Marie Lepage, Directrice générale

Saint-Lambert: **Commission scolaire Riverside Riverside School Board**
299, boul Sir Wilfrid-Laurier Saint-Lambert, J4R 2V7 Canada
450-672-4010, Fax: 450-465-8809,
rsb@rsb.qc.ca
www.rsb.qc.ca

Stephen Lessard, Directeur général
slessard@rsb.qc.ca

French

Alma: **Commission scolaire du Lac-Saint-Jean**
350, boul Champlain sud Alma, G8B 5W2 Canada
418-669-6000, Fax: 418-669-6351,
www.cslacst-jean.qc.ca

Eric Blackburn, Directeur général
dglstjean@cslacst-jean.qc.ca

Amos: **Commission scolaire Harricana**
341, rue Principale nord Amos, J9T 2L8 Canada
819-732-6561, Fax: 819-732-1623,
communications@csharricana.qc.ca
www.csharricana.qc.ca

Guy Baril, Directeur général

Amqui: **Commission scolaire des Monts-et-Marées**
93, rue du Parc Amqui, G5J 2L8 Canada
418-629-6200, Fax: 418-629-6234,
www.csmm.qc.ca
Centre de services de Matane: 530, av Saint-Jérôme, 418-566-2500.
Pierre Berthelet, Directeur général

Baie-Comeau: **Commission scolaire de l'Estuaire**
771, boul Joliet Baie-Comeau, G5C 1P3 Canada
418-589-0806, Fax: 418-589-2711, 877-589-0806
www.csestuaire.qc.ca
Alain Ouellet, Directeur général

Beauharnois: **Commission scolaire de la Vallée-des-Tisserands**
630, rue Ellice Beauharnois, J6N 3S1 Canada
450-225-2788, Fax: 450-225-0691, 877-225-2788
info@csvt.qc.ca
www.csvt.qc.ca
Carole Houle, Directrice générale
dg@csvt.qc.ca

Beauport: **Commission scolaire des Premières-Seigneuries**
643, av du Cénacle Beauport, G1E 1B3 Canada
418-666-4666, Fax: 418-666-9783,
sic@csdps.qc.ca
www.csdps.qc.ca
Serge Pelletier, Directeur général
dg@csdps.qc.ca

Bonaventure: **Commission scolaire René-Lévesque**
145, av Louisbourg Bonaventure, G0C 1E0 Canada
418-534-3003, Fax: 418-534-3220,
www.cs-renelevesque.qc.ca
Chantal Bourdages, Directrice générale

Cabano: **Commission scolaire du Fleuve-et-des-Lacs**
14, rue du Vieux-Chemin Cabano, G0L 1E0 Canada
418-854-2370, Fax: 418-854-2715,
info@csfl.qc.ca
www.csfl.qc.ca
Serge Pelletier, Directeur général

Chibougamau: **Commission scolaire de la Baie-James**
596, 4e rue Chibougamau, G8P 1S3 Canada
418-748-7621, Fax: 418-748-2440,
www.csbj.qc.ca
Michèle Perron, Directrice générale

Chicoutimi: **Commission scolaire des Rives-du-Saguenay**
36, rue Jacques-Cartier est Chicoutimi, G7H 1W2 Canada
418-698-5000, Fax: 418-698-5262,
www.csrsaguenay.qc.ca
Centre de services La Baie: 3111, rue Mgr Dufour, La Baie, 418-544-3307. Service informatique: 475, rue Lafontaine, Chicoutimi, 418-541-7799.
Yvon Pelletier, Directeur général

Donnacona: **Commission scolaire de Portneuf**
310, rue de l'Église Donnacona, G3M 1Z8 Canada
418-285-2600, Fax: 418-285-2738,
www.csportneuf.qc.ca
Jean-Pierre Soucy, Directeur général
jeanpsoucy@csdp.qc.ca

Drummondville: **Commission scolaire des Chênes**
P.O. Box 846
457, rue des Écoles Drummondville, J2B 6X1 Canada
819-478-6700, Fax: 819-478-6777,
commentaires@csdeschenes.qc.ca
www.csdeschenes.qc.ca
Yvan Aubé, Directeur général

East Angus: **Commission scolaire des Hauts-Cantons**
308, rue Palmer East Angus, J0B 1R0 Canada
819-832-4953, Fax: 819-832-4863,
www.cshc.qc.ca
Bernard Lacroix, Directeur général

Gaspé: **Commission scolaire des Chic-Chocs**
102, rue Jacques-Cartier Gaspé, G4X 2S9 Canada
418-368-3499, Fax: 418-368-6531,
commission.scolaire@cschic-chocs.net
www.cschic-chocs.net
Jean Letarte, Directeur général

Gatineau: **Commission scolaire au Coeur-des-Vallées**
582, rue MacLaren est Gatineau, J8L 2W2 Canada
819-986-8511, Fax: 819-986-9283, 800-958-9966
info@cscv.qc.ca
www.cscv.qc.ca
Maurice Groulx, Directeur général

Gatineau: **Commission scolaire des Draveurs**
200, boul Maloney est Gatineau, J8P 1K3 Canada
819-663-9221, Fax: 819-663-6176,
reception@csdraveurs.qc.ca
www.csdraveurs.qc.ca
François Jetté, Directeur général
dg@csdraveurs.qc.ca

Gatineau: **Commission scolaire des Portages-de-l'Outaouais**
225, rue St-Rédempteur Gatineau, J8X 2T3 Canada
819-771-4548, Fax: 819-771-6964,
www.cspo.qc.ca
Jean-Claude Bouchard, Directeur général
dgcspo@cspo.qc.ca

Granby: **Commission scolaire du Val-des-Cerfs**
P.O. Box 9000
55, rue Court Granby, J2G 9H7 Canada
450-372-0221, Fax: 450-372-3150,
descerfs@csvdc.qc.ca
www.csvdc.qc.ca
André Messier, Directeur général

Ha@vre-Saint-Pierre: **Commission scolaire de la Moyenne-Côte-Nord**
1235, rue de la Digue Ha@vre-Saint-Pierre, G0G 1P0 Canada
418-538-3044, Fax: 418-538-3268,
www.csmcn.qc.ca
Marius Richard, Directeur général

Jonquière: **Commission scolaire De La Jonquière**
P.O. Box 1600
3644, rue St-Jules Jonquière, G7X 7X4 Canada
418-542-7551, Fax: 418-542-1505,
info@csjonquiere.qc.ca
www.csjonquiere.qc.ca
Raynald Thibeault, Directeur général

L'Étang-du-Nord: **Commission scolaire des Iles**
1419, ch de l'Étang-du-Nord L'Étang-du-Nord, G4T 3B9 Canada
418-986-5511, Fax: 418-986-3552,
info@csdesiles.qc.ca
www.csdesiles.qc.ca
Diane Arsenault, Directrice générale

La Malbaie: **Commission scolaire de Charlevoix**
575, boul de Comporté La Malbaie, G5A 1T5 Canada
418-665-3765, Fax: 418-665-6805,
www.cscharlevoix.qc.ca
Robert Labbé, Directeur général
robert.labbe@cscharlevoix.qc.ca

La Prairie: **Commission scolaire des Grandes-Seigneuries**
50, boul Taschereau La Prairie, J5R 4V3 Canada
514-380-8899, Fax: 514-380-8345,
www.csdgs.qc.ca
Michelle Fournier, Directrice générale
directiongenerale@csdgs.qc.ca

La Sarre: **Commission scolaire du Lac-Abitibi**
500, rue Principale La Sarre, J9Z 2A2 Canada
819-333-5411, Fax: 819-333-3044,
www.csdla.qc.ca
Huguette Théberge, Directrice générale

Laval: **Commission scolaire de Laval**
955, boul Saint-Martin ouest Laval, H7S 1M5 Canada
450-662-7000, Fax: 450-625-2042,
www2.cslaval.qc.ca
Claude Sabourin, Directeur général
directiongenerale@cslaval.qc.ca

Longueuil: **Commission scolaire Marie-Victorin**
13, rue St-Laurent est Longueuil, J4H 4B7 Canada
450-670-0730, Fax: 450-670-0902,
info@csmv.qc.ca
www.csmv.qc.ca
André Byette, Directeur général

Magog: **Commission scolaire des Sommets**
449, rue Percy Magog, J1X 1B5 Canada
819-847-1610, Fax: 819-847-2065, 888-847-1610
info@csdessommets.qc.ca
www.csdessommets.qc.ca
Christian Provencher, Directeur général

Maniwaki: **Commission scolaire des Hauts-Bois-de-l'Outaouais**
331, rue du Couvent Maniwaki, J9E 1H5 Canada
819-449-7866, Fax: 819-449-2636, 888-831-9606
info@cshbo.qc.ca
www.cshbo.qc.ca
Harold Sylvain, Directeur général

Mont-Laurier: **Commission scolaire Pierre-Neveu**
525, rue de la Madone Mont-Laurier, J9L 1S4 Canada
819-623-4310, Fax: 819-623-7979, 866-334-4114
cspn@cspn.qc.ca
www.cspn.qc.ca
Normand Bélanger, Directeur général
belanger.normand@cspn.qc.ca

Montmagny: **Commission scolaire de la Côte-du-Sud**
157, rue Saint-Louis Montmagny, G5V 4N3 Canada
418-248-1001,
info@cscotesud.qc.ca
www.cscotesud.qc.ca
Jocelyn Carrier, Directeur général

Montréal: **Commission scolaire de la Pointe-de-l'Ile**
550, 53e av Montréal, H1A 2T7 Canada
514-642-9520, Fax: 514-642-1590,
www.cspi.qc.ca
Antonio Bernardelli, Directeur général

Montréal: **Commission scolaire de Montréal**
3737, rue Sherbrooke est Montréal, H1X 3B3 Canada
514-596-6000, Fax: 514-596-7570,
info@csdm.qc.ca
www.csdm.qc.ca
Gilles Petitclerc, Directeur général

Nicolet: **Commission scolaire de la Riveraine**
375, rue de Monseigneur-Brunault Nicolet, J3T 1Y6 Canada
819-293-5821, Fax: 819-293-8691,
csdlrweb@admin.csriveraine.qc.ca
www.csriveraine.qc.ca
Jean-René Dubois, Directeur général

Québec: **Commission scolaire de la Capitale**
1900, rue Côté Québec, G1N 3Y5 Canada
418-686-4040, Fax: 418-686-4032,
adm2@cscapitale.qc.ca
www.cscapitale.qc.ca
Berthe Bernatchez, Directrice générale

Québec: **Commission scolaire des Découvreurs**
945, av Wolfe Québec, G1V 4E2 Canada
418-652-2121, Fax: 418-652-2146,
www.csdecou.qc.ca
Reynald Deraspe, Directeur général
dirgen@csdecou.qc.ca

Repentigny: **Commission scolaire des Affluents**
80, rue Jean-Baptiste-Meilleur Repentigny, J6A 6C5 Canada
450-492-9400, Fax: 450-492-3720,
info@csaffluents.qc.ca
www.csaffluents.qc.ca
Thomas Duzyk, Directeur général
thomas.duzyk@dg.csaffluents.qc.ca

Rimouski: **Commission scolaire des Phares**
435, av Rouleau Rimouski, G5L 8V4 Canada
418-723-5927, Fax: 418-724-3350,
dgphares@csphares.qc.ca
www.csphares.qc.ca
Jacques Poirier, Directeur général
jpoirier@csphares.qc.ca

Rivière-du-Loup: **Commission scolaire de Kamouraska—Rivière-du-Loup**
464, rue Lafontaine Rivière-du-Loup, G5R 3C2 Canada
418-868-8201, Fax: 418-862-0964,
web.cskamloup.qc.ca
Yvan Tardif, Directeur général

Roberval: **Commission scolaire du Pays-des-Bleuets**
828, boul Saint-Joseph Roberval, G8H 2L5 Canada
418-275-4136, Fax: 418-275-6217,
www.cspaysbleuets.qc.ca
Secteur Dolbeau-Mistassini: 1950, boul Sacré-Coeur, Dolbeau-Mistassini, 418-276-2012.
Serge Bergeron, Directeur général

Rouyn-Noranda: **Commission scolaire de Rouyn-Noranda**
P.O. Box 908
70, rue des Oblats est Rouyn-Noranda, J9X 5C9 Canada
819-762-8161, Fax: 819-764-7170,
dgcsrn@csrn.qc.ca
www.csrn.qc.ca
Richard Gauthier, Directeur général

Saint-Eustache: **Commission scolaire de la Seigneurie-des-Mille-Iles**
430, boul Arthur-Sauvé Saint-Eustache, J7R 6V6 Canada
450-974-7000, Fax: 450-974-6977,
info@cssmi.qc.ca
www.cssmi.qc.ca
Jean-François Lachance, Directeur général

Saint-Félix-de-Valois: **Commission scolaire des Samares**
4671, rue Principale Saint-Félix-de-Valois, J0K 2M0 Canada
450-758-3500, Fax: 450-889-8604,
sq@cssamares.qc.ca
www.cssamares.qc.ca
Richard Fiset, Directeur général

Saint-Hyacinthe: **Commission scolaire de Saint-Hyacinthe**
2255, av Sainte-Anne Saint-Hyacinthe, J2S 5H7 Canada
450-773-8401, Fax: 450-773-3262,
webcorp.cssh.qc.ca
Yvan Gauthier, Directeur général
yvan.gauthier@cssh.qc.ca

Saint-Jean-sur-Richelieu: **Commission scolaire des Hautes-Rivières**
210, rue Notre-Dame Saint-Jean-sur-Richelieu, J3B 6N3 Canada
450-359-6411, Fax: 450-359-4623,
casegen@csdhr.qc.ca
www.csdhr.qc.ca
Mme Claude Boivin, Directrice générale

Saint-Jérôme: **Commission scolaire de la Rivière-du-Nord**
995, rue Labelle Saint-Jérôme, J7Z 5N7 Canada
450-438-3131, Fax: 450-436-5277,
csrdn@csrdn.qc.ca
www.csrdn.qc.ca
Centre administratif II: 795, rue Melançon, 450-438-3131.
Lise Allaire, Directrice générale

Saint-Laurent: **Commission scolaire Marguerite-Bourgeoys**
1100, boul de la Côte-Vertu Saint-Laurent, H4L 4V1 Canada
514-855-4500, Fax: 514-855-4749,
www.csmb.qc.ca
Yves Sylvain, Directeur général

Saint-Romuald: **Commission scolaire des Navigateurs**
1860, 1e rue Saint-Romuald, G6W 5M6 Canada
418-839-0500, Fax: 418-839-0536,
dg@csnavigateurs.qc.ca
www.csdn.qc.ca
Joanne Plourde, Directrice générale

Sainte-Agathe-des-Monts: **Commission scolaire des Laurentides**
13, rue Saint-Antoine Sainte-Agathe-des-Monts, J8C 2C3 Canada
819-326-0333, Fax: 819-326-2121,
beattiej@cslaurentides.qc.ca
www.cslaurentides.qc.ca
Claude Pouliot, Directeur général

Sept-Iles: **Commission scolaire du Fer**
30, rue Comeau Sept-Iles, G4R 4N2 Canada
418-968-9901, Fax: 418-962-7760,
www.csdufer.qc.ca
Robert Smith, Directeur général

Sept-Iles: **Commission scolaire du Littoral**
789, rue Beaulieu Sept-Iles, G4R 1P8 Canada
418-962-5559, Fax: 418-968-2942, 877-745-7226
www.csdulittoral.qc.ca
Lucy de Mendonça, Administratrice
dglittoral@csdulittoral.qc.ca

Shawinigan: **Commission scolaire de l'Énergie**
P.O. Box 580
2072, rue Gignac Shawinigan, G9N 6V7 Canada
819-539-6971, Fax: 819-539-7797,
cse@csenergie.qc.ca
www.csenergie.qc.ca
Denis Lemaire, Directeur général

Sherbrooke: **Commission scolaire de la Région-de-Sherbrooke**
2955, boul de l'Université Sherbrooke, J1K 2Y3 Canada
819-822-5540, Fax: 819-822-5530,
www.csrs.qc.ca
Claude St-Cyr, Directeur général

Sorel-Tracy: **Commission scolaire de Sorel-Tracy**
41, av de l'Hôtel-Dieu Sorel-Tracy, J3P 1L1 Canada
450-746-3990, Fax: 450-746-4474,
www.cs-soreltracy.qc.ca
Jean Morin, Directeur général
dgen@cs-soreltracy.qc.ca

St-Bruno-de-Montarville: **Commission scolaire des Patriotes**
1740, rue Roberval St-Bruno-de-Montarville, J3V 3R3 Canada
450-441-2919, Fax: 450-441-0838,
courriel@csp.qc.ca
www.csp.qc.ca
Normande Lemieux, Directrice générale

St-Georges: **Commission scolaire de la Beauce-Etchemin**
1925, 118e rue St-Georges, G5Y 7R7 Canada
418-228-5541, Fax: 418-228-5549,
secretariat.general@csbe.qc.ca
www.csbe.qc.ca
Normand Lessard, Directeur général

Thetford Mines: **Commission scolaire des Appalaches**
650, rue Lapierre Thetford Mines, G6G 7P1 Canada
418-338-7800, Fax: 418-338-7845,
ghebert@csappalaches.qc.ca
www.csappalaches.qc.ca
Camil Turmel, Directeur général

Trois-Rivières: **Commission scolaire du Chemin-du-Roy**
1515, rue Ste-Marguerite Trois-Rivières, G9A 5E7 Canada
819-379-6565, Fax: 819-379-2068,
info@csduroy.qc.ca
www.csduroy.qc.ca
Michel Morin, Directeur général
dgduroy@csduroy.qc.ca

Val-d'Or: **Commission scolaire de l'Or-et-des-Bois**
799, boul Forest Val-d'Or, J9P 2L4 Canada
819-825-4220, Fax: 819-825-5305,
info@csob.qc.ca
www.csob.qc.ca
Jean Denommé, Directeur général

Vaudreuil-Dorion: **Commission scolaire des Trois-Lacs**
400, av St-Charles Vaudreuil-Dorion, J7V 6B1 Canada
514-477-7000,
dgenerale@cstrois-lacs.qc.ca
www.cstrois-lacs.qc.ca
Sophie Proulx, Directrice générale

Victoriaville: **Commission scolaire des Bois-Francs**
40, boul Bois-Francs nord Victoriaville, G6P 6S5 Canada
819-758-6453, Fax: 819-758-4925,
info@csbf.qc.ca
www.csbf.qc.ca
François Labbé, Directeur général

Ville-Marie: **Commission scolaire du Lac-Témiscamingue**
2, rue Maisonneuve Ville-Marie, J9V 1V4 Canada
819-629-2472, Fax: 819-629-2791,
courrier@cslactem.qc.ca
www.cslactem.qc.ca
Éric Larivière, Directeur général
eric.lariviere@cslactem.qc.ca

First Nations

Lac-Simon: **Conseil de l'Éducation du Lac-Simon**
1013, av Amikwiche Lac-Simon, J0Y 3M0 Canada
819-736-2121,
ecole_amikwiche@hotmail.com
Grades: Elem./Sec.

Mistissini: **Commission scolaire Crie**
Cree School Board
203, rue Principale Mistissini, G0W 1C0 Canada
418-923-2764, Fax: 418-923-2072,
www.cscree.qc.ca
Abraham Jolly, Directeur général
ajolly@cscree.qc.ca

Saint-Laurent: **Commission scolaire Kativik**
Kativik School Board
#400, 9800, boul Cavendish Saint-Laurent, H4M 2V9 Canada
514-482-8220, Fax: 514-482-8496,
www.kativik.qc.ca
Annie Grenier, Directrice générale

Schools: Cégep

Cégep

Baie-Comeau: **Cégep de Baie-Comeau**
537, boul Blanche Baie-Comeau, G5C 2B2 Canada
418-589-5707, Fax: 418-589-9842, 1-800-463-2030
fraduval@cegep-baie-comeau.qc.ca
www.cegep-baie-comeau.qc.ca
Grades: Préuniv., Techniques, Form. cont.
Danielle Delorme, Directrice générale

Publications
D.E.C. express

Chicoutimi: **Cégep de Chicoutimi**
534, rue Jacques-Cartier est Chicoutimi, G7H 1Z6 Canada
418-549-9520, Fax: 418-549-1315,
dirgene@cegep-chicoutimi.qc.ca
www.cegep-chicoutimi.qc.ca
Grades: Préuniv., Techniques, Form. cont.
Ginette Sirois, Directrice générale

Publications
La Grenouille

Le Nénu phare

Drummondville: **Cégep de Drummondville**
960, rue St-Georges Drummondville, J2C 6A2 Canada
819-478-4671, Fax: 819-474-6859,
dg@cdrummond.qc.ca
www.cdrummond.qc.ca
Grades: Préuniv., Techniques
Enrollment: 1900
Normand W. Bernier, Directeur général

Publications
Mouton Noir

Gaspé: **Cégep de la Gaspésie et des Iles**
96, rue Jacques-Cartier Gaspé, G4X 2S8 Canada
418-368-2201, Fax: 418-368-7003, 1-866-424-3341
infogaspe@cgaspesie.qc.ca
www.cgaspesie.qc.ca
Grades: Préuniv., Techniques, Form. cont.
Enrollment: 1140
Roland Auger, Directeur général

Gatineau: **Cégep de l'Outaouais**
Campus Gabrielle-Roy
333, boul de la Cité-des-Jeunes Gatineau, J8Y 6M4 Canada
819-770-4012, Fax: 819-770-8167,
www.cegepoutaouais.qc.ca
Enrollment: 4418
Marielle Poirier, Directrice générale
dirgen@cegepoutaouais.qc.ca

Publications
La Brise

L'Entremetteur

Granby: **Cégep de Granby Haute-Yamaska**
P.O. Box 7000
235, rue St-Jacques Granby, J2G 9H7 Canada
450-372-6614, Fax: 450-372-6565,
lfalvarez@cegepgranby.qc.ca
www.cegepgranby.qc.ca
Marie-Johanne Lacroix, Directrice générale

Publications
de Fouille-moi

Jonquière: **Cégep de Jonquière**
2505, rue St-Hubert Jonquière, G7X 7W2 Canada
418-547-2191, Fax: 418-547-3359,
cegep@cjonquiere.qc.ca
www.cjonquiere.qc.ca
Michel Gravel, Directeur général

Publications
La Pige

***La Pocatière:* Cégep de La Pocatière**
140, 4e av La Pocatière, G0R 1Z0 Canada
418-856-1525, Fax: 418-856-4589,
information@cegeplapocatiere.qc.ca
www.cegeplapocatiere.qc.ca
Enrollment: 900
Claude Harvey, Directeur général

Publications
Le Nordet

***Lasalle:* Cégep André-Laurendeau**
1111, rue Lapierre Lasalle, H8N 2J4 Canada
514-364-3320, Fax: 514-364-7130,
courrier@claurendeau.qc.ca
www.claurendeau.qc.ca
Grades: Préuniv., Tech., Form. continue
Enrollment: 2700
Hervé Pilon, Directeur général

Publications
Vox-Populi

***Lévis:* Cégep de Lévis-Lauzon**
205, rte Mgr Bourget Lévis, G6V 6Z9 Canada
418-833-5110, Fax: 418-833-7323,
julie.talbot@clevislauzon.qc.ca
www.clevislauzon.qc.ca
Enrollment: 2885
Guy Demers, Directeur général

Publications
Le Forcep

***Matane:* Cégep de Matane**
616, av St-Rédempteur Matane, G4W 1L1 Canada
418-562-1240, Fax: 418-566-2115,
information@cegep-matane.qc.ca
www.cegep-matane.qc.ca
Émery Béland, Directeur général

Publications
La Criée

***Montréal:* Cégep de Saint-Laurent**
625, av Ste-Croix Montréal, H4L 3X7 Canada
514-747-6521, Fax: 514-748-1249,
webmestre@cegep-st-laurent.qc.ca
www.cegep-st-laurent.qc.ca
Enrollment: 2500
Paul-Émile Bourque, Directeur général
pebourque@cegep-st-laurent.qc.ca

Publications
La Minerve

***Montréal:* Cégep du Vieux Montréal**
255, rue Ontario est Montréal, H2X 1X6 Canada
514-982-3437, Fax: 514-982-3400,
gestionnairew3@cvm.qc.ca
www.cvm.qc.ca
Enrollment: 6000
Jacques Roussil, Directeur général
jroussil@cvm.qc.ca

Publications
Le République

***Montréal:* Cégep Marie-Victorin**
7000, rue Marie-Victorin Montréal, H1G 2J6 Canada
514-325-0150, Fax: 514-328-3830,
promotion@collegemv.qc.ca
www.collegemv.qc.ca
Enrollment: 3082
Nicole Rouillier, Directrice générale

***Québec:* Cégep de Sainte-Foy**
2410, ch Ste-Foy Québec, G1V 1T3 Canada
418-659-6600, Fax: 418-659-4563,
info@cegep-ste-foy.qc.ca
www.cegep-ste-foy.qc.ca
Grades: Préuniv., Techniques, Form. cont.
Enrollment: 8000
Denis Juneau, Directeur général

Publications
Éclosion

***Québec:* Cégep François-Xavier-Garneau**
1660, boul de l'Entente Québec, G1S 4S3 Canada
418-688-8310, Fax: 418-681-9384,
communications@cegep-fxg.qc.ca
www.cegep-fxg.qc.ca
Grades: Préuniv., Bacc. int'l, Tech.
Enrollment: 9000
Yves Blouin, Directeur général

Publications
La Crise

***Québec:* Cégep Limoilou**
1300, 8e av Québec, G1J 5L5 Canada
418-647-6600, Fax: 418-647-6798,
info@climoilou.qc.ca
www.climoilou.qc.ca
Enrollment: 4470
Pierre Malouin, Directeur général

Publications
L'Interdit

***Repentigny:* Cégep régional de Lanaudière**
781, rue Notre-Dame Repentigny, J5Y 1B4 Canada
450-470-0911, Fax: 450-581-1567,
infocom@collanaud.qc.ca
www.collanaud.qc.ca
Bernard Lachance, Directeur général

Campuses
L'Assomption
180, rue Dorval L'Assomption, J5W 6C1 Canada
Fax: 450-589-8926

Joliette
20, rue Saint-Charles sud Joliette, J6E 4T1 Canada
Fax: 450-759-4468

Terrebonne
2505, boul des Entreprises Terrebonne, J6X 5S5 Canada

Publications
L'Alinéa

***Rimouski:* Cégep de Rimouski**
60, rue de l'Évêché ouest Rimouski, G5L 4H6 Canada
418-723-1880, Fax: 418-724-4961,
infoscol@cegep-rimouski.qc.ca
www.cegep-rimouski.qc.ca
Enrollment: 4000
Jean-Pierre Villeneuve, Directeur général

Publications
Le Calvaire

***Rivière-du-Loup:* Cégep de Rivière-du-Loup**
80, rue Frontenac Rivière-du-Loup, G5R 1R1 Canada
418-862-6903, Fax: 418-862-4959,
sercom@cegep-rdl.qc.ca
www.cegep-rdl.qc.ca
Grades: Préuniv., Techniques, Form. cont.
Enrollment: 2200
André Morin, Directeur général

Publications
L'Ulcère

***Rouyn-Noranda:* Cégep de l'Abitibi-Témiscamingue**
425, boul du Collège Rouyn-Noranda, J9X 5E5 Canada
819-762-0931, Fax: 819-762-2071, 1-866-234-3728
cegepat.qc.ca
Grades: Préuniv., Techniques, Form. cont.
Enrollment: 2400
Daniel Marcotte, Directeur général
daniel.marcotte@cegepat.qc.ca

Publications
Le Profane

***Saint-Félicien:* Cégep de St-Félicien**
P.O. Box 7300
1105, boul Hamel Saint-Félicien, G8K 2R8 Canada
418-679-5412, Fax: 418-679-0238,
info@cstfelicien.qc.ca
www.cstfelicien.qc.ca
Grades: Préuniv., Techniques
Enrollment: 1000
Louis Lefebvre, Directeur général

Publications
Le Sentier

***Saint-Hyacinthe:* Cégep de Saint-Hyacinthe**
3000, av Boullé Saint-Hyacinthe, J2S 1H9 Canada
450-773-6800, Fax: 450-773-9971,
info@cegepsth.qc.ca
www.cegepsth.qc.ca
Grades: Préuniv., Techniques, Form. cont.
Enrollment: 3200
Roger Sylvestre, Directeur général

Publications
L'Électic

***Saint-Jean-sur-Richelieu:* Cégep Saint-Jean-sur-Richelieu**
P.O. Box 1018
30, boul du Séminaire Saint-Jean-sur-Richelieu, J3B 7B1 Canada
450-347-5301, Fax: 450-347-3329,
communications@cstjean.qc.ca
www.cstjean.qc.ca
Grades: Préuniv., Techniques, Form. cont.
Enrollment: 3600
Chantal Denis, Directrice générale

Publications
L'Hermes

***Saint-Jérôme:* Cégep de Saint-Jérôme**
455, rue Fournier Saint-Jérôme, J7Z 4V2 Canada
450-436-1580, Fax: 450-436-1756,
communications-et-promotion@cstj.qc.ca
www.cegep-st-jerome.qc.ca
Enrollment: 3300
Serge Tessier, Directeur général

***Sainte-Anne-de-Bellevue:* Cégep John Abbott College**
21275, rue Lakeshore Sainte-Anne-de-Bellevue, H9X 3L9 Canada
514-457-6610, Fax: 514-457-4730,
webmaster@johnabbott.qc.ca
www.johnabbott.qc.ca
Enrollment: 7600
Keith W. Henderson, Directeur général

Publications
Bandersnatch

***Sept-Iles:* Cégep de Sept-Iles**
175, rue De La Vérendrye Sept-Iles, G4R 5B7 Canada
418-962-9848, Fax: 418-962-2458,
info@cegep-sept-iles.qc.ca
www.cegep-sept-iles.qc.ca
Donald Bhérer, Directeur général
donald.bherer@cegep-sept-iles.qc.ca

Publications
D'Épiderme

***Sherbrooke:* Cégep de Sherbrooke**
475, rue du Cégep Sherbrooke, J1E 4K1 Canada
819-564-6350, Fax: 819-564-1579,
communications@cegepsherbrooke.qc.ca
www.cegepsherbrooke.qc.ca
Grades: Préuniv., Techniques, Form. cont.
Enrollment: 6000
Sylvain Saint-Cyr, Directeur général

Publications
in Extremis

***Sorel-Tracy:* Cégep de Sorel-Tracy**
3000, boul Tracy Sorel-Tracy, J3R 5B9 Canada
450-742-6651, Fax: 450-742-1878,
info@cegep-sorel-tracy.qc.ca
www.cegep-sorel-tracy.qc.ca
Grades: Préuniv., Techniques, Form. cont.
Fabienne Desroches, Directrice générale

Publications
L'Exemplaire

***St-Georges:* Cégep Beauce-Appalaches**
1055, 116e rue St-Georges, G5Y 3G1 Canada
418-228-8896, Fax: 418-228-0562,
info@cegepbceapp.qc.ca
www.cegepbceapp.qc.ca
Enrollment: 1424
Charles Garneau, Directeur général
cgarneau@cegepbceapp.qc.ca

***Thetford Mines:* Cégep de Thetford**
671, boul Frontenac ouest Thetford Mines, G6G 1N1 Canada
418-338-8591, Fax: 418-338-6691,
www.cegep-ra.qc.ca
Enrollment: 1000
François Dornier, Directeur général

***Trois-Rivières:* Cégep de Trois-Rivières**
P.O. Box 97
3500, rue De Courval Trois-Rivières, G9A 5E6 Canada
819-376-1721, Fax: 819-693-8023,
webmestre@cegeptr.qc.ca
www.cegeptr.qc.ca

Grades: Préuniv., Techniques, Form. cont.
Enrollment: 9475
Jean-Denis Leduc, Directeur général

Publications
La Gifle

***Victoriaville:* Cégep de Victoriaville**
475, rue Notre-Dame est Victoriaville, G6P 4B3 Canada
819-758-6401, Fax: 819-758-6026, 1-888-284-9476
information@cgpvicto.qc.ca
www.cgpvicto.qc.ca
Vincent Guay, Directeur général
guay.vincent@cgpvicto.qc.ca

Publications
La Réplique

Schools: Specialized

First Nations

***Betsiamites:* École Nussim du conseil de bande de Betsiamites**
P.O. Box 70
4, rue Pulis Betsiamites, G0H 1B0 Canada
418-567-2215
Grades: K./Elem.

***Betsiamites:* École secondaire Uashkaikan du conseil de bande de Betsiamites**
63, rue Messek Betsiamites, G0H 1B0 Canada
418-567-2271
Grades: Sec.

***Côte-Nord-du-Golfe-du-Saint-Lau:* École Olamen du Conseil des Montagnais (La Romaine)**
P.O. Box 222
Côte-Nord-du-Golfe-du-Saint-Lau, G0G 1M0 Canada
418-229-2450
Grades: K./Elem./Sec.

***Kawawachikamach:* École Jimmy Sandy Memorial**
P.O. Box 5115
Kawawachikamach, G0G 2Z0 Canada
418-585-3811
Grades: K./Elem./Sec.

***Manawan:* École Otapi**
470, rue Otapi Manawan, J0K 1M0 Canada
819-971-1379,
lucpatin@hotmail.com
www.monecole-myschool.com/otapi/
Grades: Sec.

***Manawan:* École Simon P. Ottawa**
150, rue Wapoc Manawan, J0K 1M0 Canada
819-971-8817, Fax: 819-871-8872
Grades: K./Elem./Sec.

***Mashteuiatsh:* École Amishk**
1725, rue Amishk Mashteuiatsh, G0W 2H0 Canada
418-275-2473
Grades: K./Elem.

***Mashteuiatsh:* École secondaire Kassinu Mamu**
1711, rue Amishk Mashteuiatsh, G0W 2H0 Canada
418-275-2473,
kassinumamu@monecole-myschool.com
www.monecole-myschool.com/kassinumamu/
Grades: Sec.

***Natashquan:* École Uauitshitun Natashquan**
Pointe-Parent
Natashquan, G0G 2E0 Canada
418-726-3368
Grades: K./Elem./Sec.

***Obedjiwan:* École primaire Niska**
70, rue Niska Obedjiwan, G0W 3B0 Canada
819-974-8842
Grades: K./Elem.

***Obedjiwan:* École secondaire Mikisiw**
92, rue Tcikatnaw Obedjiwan, G0W 3B0 Canada
819-974-1221
Grades: Sec.

***Pikogan:* École Mikwan**
P.O. Box 36
RR#4 Pikogan, J9T 3A3 Canada
819-732-5213,
ecole@pikogan.com
Grades: Gr. K./Elem.

***Sept-Iles:* École Johnny-Pilot du conseil des Montagnais de Sept-Iles et Maliotenam**
1, rue Ukuiass Sept-Iles, G4R 5V2 Canada
418-968-1550
Grades: K./Elem.

***Sept-Iles:* École Manikanetish du conseil des Montagnais de Sept-Iles et Maliotenam**
P.O. Box 8000
1, rue Ukuiass Sept-Iles, G4R 2N5 Canada
418-968-1550
Grades: Sec.

***Sept-Iles:* École Tshishteshinu du conseil des Montagnais de Sept-Iles et Maliotenam**
P.O. Box 430
Sept-Iles, G0G 2B0 Canada
418-927-2956
Grades: K./Elem.

***Shefferville:* Kanatamat Tsitipenitamunu**
P.O. Box 1000
224, rue Lorraine Shefferville, G0G 2T0 Canada
418-585-2116
Grades: K./Elem./Sec.

***St-Augustin:* École Pakuashipi**
P.O. Box 68
St-Augustin, G0G 2R0 Canada
418-947-2729
Grades: Gr. K./Elem./Sec.

***Wendake:* École Hetaie**
20, rue de l'Ours Wendake, G0A 4V0 Canada
418-842-3740
Grades: K./Elem.

***Weymontachie:* École primaire Seskitin**
P.O. Box 214 A
Weymontachie, G0X 3R0 Canada
819-666-2226,
ericniquay@hotmail.com
http://www.monecole-myschool.com/seskitin/
Grades: Elem.

***Weymontachie:* École secondaire Waratinak**
P.O. Box 222 B
Weymontachie, G0X 3R0 Canada
819-666-2232,
waratinak@monecole-myschool.com
www.monecole-myschool.com/waratinak/

Schools: Independent & Private

Catholic

***Ayer's Cliff:* Collège Notre-Dame des Servites**
470, rue Main Ayer's Cliff, J0B 1C0 Canada
819-838-4221, Fax: 819-838-4222,
courrier@cnds.qc.ca
www.cnds.qc.ca
Grades: Sec.; Pens. & Ext.
Confessionnelle catholique.
Éric Faucher, Directeur général
dirgen@cnds.qc.ca

***Baie-Comeau:* École secondaire Jean-Paul II**
20, av de Ramezay Baie-Comeau, G4Z 1B2 Canada
418-296-6212, Fax: 418-296-3654,
admjpii@globetrotter.net
www.jpii.ca
Grades: Sec.
Dorsay Talaï, Directrice générale

***Coaticook:* Collège Rivier**
343, rue St-Jacques nord Coaticook, J1A 2R2 Canada
819-849-4833, Fax: 819-849-3621,
crivier@crivier.qc.ca
www.crivier.qc.ca
Grades: Sec.; Pens. & Ext.
Enrollment: 250
École catholique, privée et mixte.
Benoit Hélie, Directeur général

***Dolbeau-Mistassini:* Juvénat Saint-Jean**
200, boul Wallberg Dolbeau-Mistassini, G8L 6A5 Canada
418-276-3340, Fax: 418-276-1757,
juvenatstjean@hotmail.com
www.juvenatstjean.ca
Grades: Sec.; Pens. & Ext.
Marc Tremblay, Directeur général

***Grenville-sur-la-Rouge:* Séminaire du Sacré-Coeur**
2738, rte 148 Grenville-sur-la-Rouge, J0V 1B0 Canada
819-242-0957, Fax: 819-242-4089,
administration@seminairedusacrecoeur.qc.ca
www.seminairedusacrecoeur.qc.ca
Grades: Sec.; Pens. & Ext.
Richard Dupuis, Directeur

***Lan-Saint-Jean:* Séminaire Marie-Reine-du-Clergé**
1569, rte 169 Métabetchouan-Lac-à-la-Croix Lan-Saint-Jean, G8G 1A8 Canada
418-349-2816, Fax: 418-349-8055,
direction@smrc.qc.ca
www.smrc.qc.ca
Grades: Sec.; Pens. & Ext.
Jacques Ménard, Directeur général

***Lévis:* École Sainte-Famille (Fraternité St-Pie X) inc.**
10425, boul de la Rive-Sud Lévis, G6V 7M5 Canada
418-837-3028, Fax: 418-837-7070,
fspx@ecolestefamille.ca
Grades: Prim./Sec.
Jean de l'Estourbeillon, Directeur

***Montréal:* Collège de Montréal**
1931, rue Sherbrooke ouest Montréal, H3H 1E3 Canada
514-933-7397, Fax: 514-933-3225,
cdm@college-montreal.qc.ca
www.college-montreal.qc.ca
Grades: Sec.
École catholique privée.
Jacques Giguère, Directeur général

***Montréal:* École Augustin Roscelli inc.**
11960, boul de l'Acadie Montréal, H3M 2T7 Canada
514-334-0057, Fax: 514-334-4060,
info@ecoleaugustinroscelli.com
www.ecoleaugustinroscelli.com
Grades: Mat./Prim.
École Catholique, privée, mixte.
Sr. Rosa Rossi, Soeur Supérieure

***Montréal:* École Marie-Clarac**
3530, boul Gouin est Montréal, H1H 1B7 Canada
514-322-1161, Fax: 514-322-4364,
dcormier@marie-clarac.qc.ca
www.ecolemarie-clarac.qc.ca
Grades: Mat./Prim./Sec.; mixte; filles
Enrollment: 1300
Garderie et préscolaire/primaire (mixte); secondaire (filles); dirigée par les Soeurs de Charité de Sainte-Marie.
Sr. Martine Côté, Directrice générale

***Montréal:* École Saint-Joseph (1985) inc.**
4080, rue De Lorimier Montréal, H2K 3X7 Canada
514-526-8288, Fax: 514-526-5498,
secretariat@stjoseph.qc.ca
www.stjoseph.qc.ca
Grades: Mat./Prim.
Marc Tremblay, Directeur général
mtremblay@stjoseph.qc.ca

***Montréal:* Externat Mont-Jésus-Marie**
2755, ch de la Côte-Ste-Catherine Montréal, H3T 1B5 Canada
514-272-1035,
www.montjesusmarie.com
Grades: Mat./Prim.
Sylvie Gagné, Directrice générale

***Montréal:* Pensionnat du Saint-Nom-de-Marie**
628, ch de la Côte Ste-Catherine Montréal, H2V 2C5 Canada
514-735-5261, Fax: 514-735-5266,
admission@psnm.qc.ca
www.psnm.qc.ca
Grades: Sec.; filles; Pens. & Ext.
Enrollment: 1020
Sr. Kathleen Caissy, Directrice
kcaissy@psnm.qc.ca

***Montréal:* The Sacred Heart School of Montreal**
3635, av Atwater Montréal, H3H 1Y4 Canada
514-937-2845, Fax: 514-937-8214,
admissions@sacredheart.qc.ca
www.sacredheart.qc.ca
Grades: Sec.; Girls; Eng.; Res & Day
One of Canada's oldest, independent Catholic schools for girls.
Mr. Shawn O'Donnell, Head of School

***Montréal-Nord:* École secondaire Marie-Victorin inc.**
10748, boul Saint-Vital Montréal-Nord, H1H 4T3 Canada
514-322-8111, Fax: 512—,
dg@marievictorin.qc.ca
www.marievictorin.qc.ca
Grades: Sec.
Louise Bergeron, Directrice

Publications
Le Matulu

Québec: **Collège Jésus-Marie de Sillery**
2047, ch St-Louis Québec, G1T 1P3 Canada
418-687-9250, Fax: 418-687-9847,
dir.gen@cjmds.qc.ca
www.cjmds.qc.ca
Grades: Prim./Sec.; filles; Pens. & Ext.
Dirigé par la Congrégation des Religieuses de Jésus-Marie; programme enrichi au primaire, programme d'éducation internationale au secondaire.
Sr. Odile Fortin, Directrice

Québec: **Collège Saint-Charles-Garnier**
1150, boul René-Lévesque ouest Québec, G1S 1V7 Canada
418-681-0107, Fax: 418-681-9631,
cscg@collegegarnier.qc.ca
www.collegegarnier.qc.ca
Grades: Sec.
Propriétaire du Collège des Jésuites.
Mario Gagnon, Directeur général
mgagnon@collegegarnier.qc.ca

Québec: **Externat Saint-Coeur de Marie**
30, av des Cascades Québec, G1E 2J8 Canada
418-663-0605, Fax: 418-663-9484,
richard.morin@pscm.ca
www.pscm.ca
Grades: Prim.; Pens. & Ext.
Enrollment: 411
Richard Morin, Directeur général

Rosemère: **Externat Sacré-Coeur**
535, rue Lefrançois Rosemère, J7A 4R5 Canada
450-621-6720, Fax: 450-621-1525,
courrier@externat.qc.ca
www.externat.qc.ca
Grades: Sec.
Enrollment: 1000
Denyse Hébert, Directrice générale

Saint-Augustin-de-Desmaures: **Séminaire Saint-François**
4900, rue Saint-Félix Saint-Augustin-de-Desmaures, G3A 1X3 Canada
418-872-0611, Fax: 418-872-5845,
l.lessard@ss-f.com
www.ss-f.com
Grades: Sec.; Pens. & Ext.
Père Jean-Marc Boulé, Directeur général/Directeur des élèves
jmb@ss-f.com

Saint-Hyacinthe: **École secondaire Saint-Joseph de Saint-Hyacinthe**
2875, av Bourdages nord Saint-Hyacinthe, J2S 5S3 Canada
450-774-3775, Fax: 450-774-6340,
www.essj.qc.ca
Grades: Sec.; Pens. & Ext.
Pierre Duclos, Directeur général
pduclos@essj.qc.ca

Saint-Laurent: **École bilingue Notre-Dame de Sion**
1775, boul Décarie Saint-Laurent, H4L 3N5 Canada
514-747-3895, Fax: 514-747-5492,
cnicolet@ebnds.ca
www.ebnds.ca
Grades: Mat./Prim.; Fr./Angl.
Véronique Lemieux-Boyer, Directrice générale

Saint-Michel-de-Bellechasse: **Collège Dina-Bélanger**
1, rue St-Georges Saint-Michel-de-Bellechasse, G0R 3S0 Canada
418-884-2360, Fax: 418-884-3274,
colldb@globetrotter.net
www.collegedina-belanger.qc.ca
Grades: Sec.; Pens. & Ext.
Enrollment: 300
Dirigé par les Relgieuses de Jésus-Marie.
Sr Yvette Rioux, Directrice générale

Sherbrooke: **Collège du Sacré-Coeur**
155, rue Belvédère nord Sherbrooke, J1H 4A7 Canada
819-569-9457, Fax: 819-820-0636,
info@cscoeur.ca
www.college-sacre-coeur.qc.ca
Grades: Sec.; filles
Enrollment: 500
Daniel Léveillé, Directeur général

St-Bruno-de-Montarville: **Séminaire Sainte-Trinité**
1475, ch des Vingt St-Bruno-de-Montarville, J3V 4P6 Canada
450-653-2409, Fax: 450-441-4786,
secretariat@ste-trinite.qc.ca
www.ste-trinite.qc.ca
Grades: Sec.
Guy Saumure, Directeur général

Trois-Rivières: **Séminaire Saint-Joseph**
858, rue Laviolette Trois-Rivières, G9A 5S3 Canada
819-376-4459, Fax: 819-378-0607,
andrem@ssj.qc.ca
www.ssj.qc.ca
Grades: Sec.; garçons; Pens. & Ext.
Michel Trépanier, Directeur général

Special Education

Montréal: **L'École à Pas de Géant (Montréal)**
Giant Steps School (Montréal)
5460, av Connaught Montréal, H4V 1X7 Canada
514-935-1911,
info@giantstepsmontreal.com
giantstepsmontreal.com
Grades: Mat./Prim./Sec; Éd. spéc.
Favoriser l'éducation et l'insertion scolaire et sociale des jeunes autistes.
Pierre Martin, Président, Conseil d'administration

Montréal: **École orale de Montréal pour les sourds inc.**
Montreal Oral School for the Deaf Inc.
4670, rue Sainte-Catherine ouest Montréal, H3Z 1S5 Canada
514-488-4946, Fax: 514-488-0802,
info@montrealoralschool.com
www.montrealoralschool.com
Grades: Mat./Prim.; Éd. spéc.
Mission: enseigner aux enfants sourds à parler & à communiquer verbalement. Programmes d'études et programmes d'intégration; services cliniques; counseling.
Martha Pérusse, Directrice

Montréal: **École Peter Hall inc.**
Peter Hall School
Campus Côte-Vertu & Centre administratif
840, boul de la Côte-Vertu Montréal, H4L 1Y4 Canada
514-747-4075, Fax: 514-747-0164,
cote-vertu@peterhall.qc.ca
www.peterhall.qc.ca
Grades: Mat./Prim./Sec.; Fr./Angl.;Éd.Spec.
Services éducatifs pour des élèves de 4 à 21 ans présentant une déficience intellectuelle. Campus Ouimet: 1200, rue Ouimet, St-Laurent, 514-748-1050, courriel: ouimet@peterhall.qc.ca.
Jean Laliberté, Directeur général

Saint-Laurent: **Summit School**
École le Sommet
1750, rue Deguire Saint-Laurent, H4L 1M7 Canada
514-744-2867, Fax: 514-744-6410,
admin@summit-school.com
www.summit-schol.com
Grades: Pre./Elem./Sec.; Spec. Ed.; Eng.
Enrollment: 450
Educational services for special needs students, from ages 4 to 21, with developmental disabilities such as autism, behavioral disturbances and other associated problems.
Lucy Orsini, Registrar

Independent & Private Schools

Baie-d'Urfé: **École internationale allemande Alexander von Humboldt inc. / AvH**
Alexander von Humboldt German International School Inc.
216, rue Victoria Baie-d'Urfé, H9X 2H9 Canada
514-457-2886, Fax: 514-457-2885,
avh@avh.montreal.qc.ca
www.avh.montreal.qc.ca
Grades: Mat./Prim./Sec.; Deutsche/Fr./Eng.
Environnement multilingue: allemand, anglais, français; sciences naturelles & sociales; arts; Dipl. d'études sec. du Québec & bacc. allemand international; Deutsches Sprachdiplom der Kultusministerkonferenz.
Dr. Jörg Klinkert, Directeur

Beauceville: **École Jésus-Marie de Beauceville**
670, 9e av est Beauceville, G5X 3P6 Canada
418-774-3709, Fax: 418-774-5749,
secretariat@ejm.qc.ca
ww.ejm.qc.ca
Grades: Sec.; Pens. & Ext.
Enrollment: 80
Monique Lambert, Directrice générale

Boisbriand: **L'Académie des jeunes filles Beth Tziril**
241, av Beth Halevy Boisbriand, J7E 4H4 Canada
450-419-4085, Fax: 418-434-5440,
cpetash@yahoo.com
Grades: Mat./Prim./Sec.
Abraham Halpern, Directeur

Boucherville: **École Les Trois Saisons**
570, boul de Mortagne Boucherville, J4B 5E4 Canada
450-641-2000,
3saisons@biz.videotron.ca
Grades: Prim.
Monique Mathieu, Directrice générale

Brossard: **Académie Marie-Laurier**
Marie-Laurier Academy
1555, av Stravinski Brossard, J4X 2H5 Canada
450-923-2787, Fax: 450-923-2291,
academie@marielaurier.com
www.marielaurier.com
Grades: Mat./Prim./Sec.; Fr./Angl.
Enseignement bilingue.
Monique Bergeron, Directrice

Châteauguay: **Collège Héritage de Châteauguay inc.**
P.O. Box 80036
270, boul d'Youville Châteauguay, J6J 5X2 Canada
450-692-5578, Fax: 450-692-5579,
info@collegeheritage.ca
www.collegeheritage.ca
Grades: Prim./Sec.
Enrollment: 570
Jean-Guy Brais, Directeur

Chicoutimi: **École Apostolique de Chicoutimi / 2A3**
913, rue Jacques-Cartier est Chicoutimi, G7H 2A3 Canada
418-549-3302, Fax: 418-615-2030,
ecole.apostolique@globetrotter.net
www.soeursantoniennes.org
Grades: Prim.
Janick Dumas, Directrice

Chicoutimi: **Le Lycée du Saguenay**
658, rue Racine est Chicoutimi, G7H 1V1 Canada
418-543-4448, Fax: 418-543-1716
Grades: Sec.
Jean-François Gagné, Directeur

Chicoutimi: **Séminaire de Chicoutimi**
679, rue Chabanel Chicoutimi, G7H 1Z7 Canada
418-549-0190, Fax: 418-549-1524,
lycee.seminaire@lyce-sdec.qc.ca
www.sdec.qc.ca
Grades: Sec.
Marcel Bergeron, Directeur

Compton: **École primaire Des Arbrisseaux**
6288, rte Louis-S.-St-Laurent Compton, J0B 1L0 Canada
819-835-9503, Fax: 819-835-9506,
direction@arbrisseaux.qc.ca
www.arbrisseaux.qc.ca
Grades: Prim.; Pens. & Ext.
Brigitte Raymond, Directrice

Côte Saint-Luc: **L'Académie Hébraïque Inc.**
Hebrew Academy
5700, av Kellert Côte Saint-Luc, H4W 1T4 Canada
514-489-5321, Fax: 514-489-8607,
www.ha-mtl.org
Grades: Mat./Prim./Sec.; Angl./Fr.
Linda Lehrer, Directrice
director@ha-montreal.org

Dollard-des-Ormeaux: **Collège de l'Ouest de l'Ile**
West Island College
851, rue Tecumseh Dollard-des-Ormeaux, H9B 2L2 Canada
514-683-4660, Fax: 514-683-1702,
office@westislandcollege.qc.ca
www.westislandcollege.qc.ca
Grades: Sec.; Fr./Angl.
Martin Bailly, Directeur des services éducatifs

Dollard-des-Ormeaux: **Emmanuel Christian School**
École chrétienne Emmanuel
4698, boul St-Jean Dollard-des-Ormeaux, H9H 4S5 Canada
514-696-6430, Fax: 514-696-3687,
ladirection@emmanuelchristianschool.qc.ca
www.emmanuelchristianschool.qc.ca
Grades: Pre./Elem./Sec.; Eng./Fr.
Enrollment: 300
A Christian education, with instruction in English & French.
Jack Bauer, Director

***Dollard-des-Ormeaux:* Hebrew Foundation School**
École de formation hébraïque
2, rue Hope Dollard-des-Ormeaux, H9A 2V5 Canada
514-684-6270, Fax: 514-684-1998,
hebrewfoundation@total.net
206.132.176.122/BJEC_HebrewFoundation/index.php
Grades: Pre./Elem.; Eng./Fr.
Programmes include M.E.L.S. French Immersion, traditional Jewish subjects, as well as the standard curriculum, dance & visual arts; instruction in English, French & Hebrew.
Rabbi Zev Lanton, Principal

***Dorval:* Queen of Angels Academy**
100, boul Bouchard Dorval, H9S 1A7 Canada
514-636-0900,
jdion@qaa.qc.ca
www.qaa.qc.ca
Grades: Sec.; Girls; Eng.
Joanne Dion, Directrice

***Drummondville:* Collège Saint-Bernard**
25, av des Frères Drummondville, J2B 6A2 Canada
819-478-3330, Fax: 819-478-2582,
csb@csb.qc.ca
www.csb.qc.ca
Grades: Prim./Sec.; Pens. & Ext.
Alexandre Cusson, Directeur général

***Gatineau:* Collège Saint-Alexandre**
2425, rue Saint-Louis Gatineau, J8V 1E7 Canada
819-561-3812, Fax: 819-561-5205,
www.college-stalexandre.qc.ca
Grades: Sec.
Mario Vachon, Directeur général
mario.vachon@i-alex.qc.ca

***Gatineau:* Collège Saint-Joseph de Hull**
174, rue Notre-Dame-de-l'Ile Gatineau, J8X 3T4 Canada
819-776-3123, Fax: 819-776-0992,
direction@collegestjoseph.ca
www.collegestjoseph.ca
Grades: Sec.; filles
Sandra Beauchamp, Directrice générale

***Gatineau:* École Montessori de l'Outaouais inc.**
161, rue Principale Gatineau, J9H 7H4 Canada
819-682-3299, Fax: 819-682-7484,
info.montessori@videotron.ca
www.montessori-outaouais.qc.ca
Grades: Mat./Prim.
Paul Dumetz, Directeur

***Granby:* Collège Mont-Sacré-Coeur**
210, rue Denison est Granby, J2G 8E3 Canada
450-372-6882, Fax: 450-372-9219,
info@college-msc.qc.ca
www.college-msc.qc.ca
Grades: Sec.
Enrollment: 870
Programme Exploration; Programme sports instensifs; Programme anglais intensif.
Claude Lacroix, S.C., Directeur général

***Granby:* École secondaire du Verbe Divin**
P.O. Box 786
1021, rue Cowie Granby, J2G 8W8 Canada
450-378-1074, Fax: 450-378-4566,
pedagogie@verbedivin.com
www.verbedivin.com
Grades: Sec.
Programmes - Immersion anglaise; Sports-Élite; Arts-Élite; Voyages; Programme Découverte.
Pierre Labbé, Directeur

***Joliette:* Académie Antoine Manseau**
P.O. Box 410
20, rue St-Charles-Borromée sud Joliette, J6E 3Z9 Canada
450-753-4271, Fax: 450-753-3661,
courier@aamanseau.qc.ca
www.amanseau.qc.ca
Grades: Sec.
Alain Bergmans, Directeur général

***Joliette:* École les Mélèzes**
393, rue de Lanaudière Joliette, J6E 3L9 Canada
450-752-4433, Fax: 450-752-4337,
info@lesmelezes.qc.ca
www.lesmelezes.qc.ca
Grades: Mat./Prim.; filles; Pens. & Ext.
Renée Champagne, Directrice générale

***Kirkland:* Académie Marie-Claire**
18190, boul Elkas Kirkland, H9J 3Y4 Canada
514-697-9995, Fax: 514-697-5575,
academie@academiemarieclaire.qc.ca
www.academiemarie-claire.qc.ca
Grades: Mat./Prim.
1ère année à 6ème année. Enseignement bilingue.
Marie-Claire Martin, Directrice

***Kirkland:* Kuper Academy**
#2 & #4, 2975, rue Edmond Kirkland, H9H 5K5 Canada
514-426-3007, Fax: 514-426-0377,
admissions@kuperacademy.ca
www.kuperacademy.ca
Grades: K./Prim./Sec.; Eng.
Liberal arts, mathematics, sciences, social sciences, & creative & performing arts.
Joan Salette, Director

***L'Assomption:* Collège de l'Assomption**
270, boul de l'Ange-Gardien L'Assomption, J5W 1R7 Canada
450-589-5621, Fax: 450-589-2910,
dirgen@classomption.qc.ca
www.classomption.qc.ca
Grades: Sec.
Robert Corriveau, Directeur général

***La Pocatière:* Collège de Sainte-Anne-de-la-Pocatière**
100, 4e av La Pocatière, G0R 1Z0 Canada
418-856-3012, Fax: 418-856-5611,
info@leadercsa.com
www.leadercsa.com
Grades: Sec.; Pens. & Ext.
Enrollment: 600
Le programme Leader est offert.
Martine Dubé, Directrice générale

***La Prairie:* Collège Jean de la Mennais**
870, ch de St-Jean La Prairie, J5R 2L5 Canada
450-659-7657, Fax: 450-659-3717,
administration@jeandelamennais.qc.ca
www.jeandelamennais.qc.ca
Grades: Prim./Sec.
Enrollment: 1400
Serge Courtemanche, Directeur général

***Laval:* Académie Lavalloise**
5290, boul des Laurentides Auteuil Laval, H7K 2J8 Canada
450-628-1430, Fax: 450-628-1431,
info@academielavalloise.com
www.academielavalloise.com
Grades: Mat./Prim.
Enrollment: 300
David C. Zakaïb, Directeur
david.zakaib@academielavalloise.com

***Laval:* Collège Laval**
275, rue Laval Laval, H7C 1W8 Canada
450-661-7714, Fax: 450-661-7146,
secretariat@collegelaval.qc.ca
www.collegelaval.qc.ca
Grades: Sec.
Centre sportif, salle de théâtre, laboratoires informatiques, bibliothèque.
Richard Roy, Directeur

***Laval:* Collège Letendre**
1000, boul de l'Avenir Laval, H7N 6J6 Canada
450-688-9933, Fax: 450-688-3591,
info@collegeletendre.qc.ca
www.collegeletendre.com
Grades: Sec.
Yves Legault, Directeur

***Laval:* École Charles-Perrault (Laval)**
1750, boul de la Concorde est Laval, H7G 2E7 Canada
450-975-2233, Fax: 450-975-2248,
direction@charles-perrault-laval.com
www.ecolecharlesperrault.com/laval/
Grades: Mat./Prim./Sec.
Enrollment: 380
Denis Faber, Directeur général (Pierrefonds)

***Laval:* École Démosthène**
1565, boul Saint-Martin ouest Laval, H7S 1N1 Canada
450-972-1800, Fax: 450-972-1345
Grades: Mat./Prim.
Enrollment: 218
École privée de la communauté greque orthodoxe de Laval; formation générale; langues d'enseignement: française, greque.
Liza Henry, Directrice
liza.demonsthene@videotron.ca

***Laval:* École Notre-Dame de Nareg**
555, 67E Av Laval, H7V 2M3 Canada
450-680-1168,
naregvarjaran@hotmail.com
Grades: Mat./Prim.
L'Abbé Paul Kazandjian, Directeur

***Lévis:* Juvénat Notre-Dame du Saint-Laurent**
30, rue du Juvénat Lévis, G6V 6P5 Canada
418-839-9592, Fax: 418-839-5605,
juvenat@jnd.qc.ca
www.jnd.qc.ca
Grades: Sec.
Claude Gélinas, Directeur général
cgelinas@jnd.qc.ca

***Longueuil:* Collège Charles-Lemoyne inc.**
901, ch Tiffin Longueuil, J4P 3G6 Canada
514-875-0505, Fax: 450-463-4494,
college@cclemoyne.edu
www.cclemoyne.edu
Grades: Sec.
Enrollment: 2700
Campus Longueuil II: 2301, boul Fernand-Lafontaine; Campus Ville de Sainte-Catherine: 125, place Charles-Lemoyne.
Réjean Palardy, Directeur général

***Longueuil:* Collège Français - Primaire Longueuil**
1391, rue Beauregard Longueuil, J4K 2M3 Canada
514-495-2581, Fax: 514-279-5131,
info@collegefrancais.ca
www.collegefrancais.ca
Grades: Mat./Prim.

***Longueuil:* Collège Notre-Dame-de-Lourdes**
845, ch Tiffin Longueuil, J4P 3G5 Canada
450-670-4740, Fax: 450-670-2800,
collegendl@ndl.qc.ca
www.ndl.qc.ca
Grades: Sec.
Enrollment: 950
Lucie D'Amour, Directrice générale

***Mont-Saint-Hilaire:* Collège Saint-Hilaire inc.**
800, rue Rouillard Mont-Saint-Hilaire, J3G 4S6 Canada
450-467-7001, Fax: 450-467-9040,
info@csh.qc.ca
www.csh.qc.ca
Grades: Sec.
Enrollment: 600
Diane Lavoie, Directrice générale

***Montebello:* Sedbergh School**
École Sedbergh
810, Côte Azélie Montebello, J0V 1L0 Canada
819-423-5523, Fax: 819-423-5769,
admissions@sedbergh.com
www.sedberghschool.ca
Grades: Elem./Sec.; Eng.; Res. & Day
Enrollment: 80
A co-educational boarding school, with a focus on academics, athletics & outdoor programs, & environmental education.
Andrew Blair, Headmaster

***Montréal:* Académie Beth Rivkah**
5001, rue Vézina Montréal, H3W 1C2 Canada
514-731-3681, Fax: 514-342-4956,
info@bethrivkah.com
www.bethrivkah.com
Grades: Mat./Prim./Sec.; filles
Enrollment: 500
Une école pour filles juives, fondée en 1956 par le Rebbe Menachem Schneerson de Loubavitch.
Rabbin Leib Kramer, Directeur

***Montréal:* Académie Kells**
Kells Academy
6865, boul Maisonneuve ouest Montréal, H4B 1T1 Canada
514-485-8565, Fax: 514-485-8505,
kadmin@kells.ca
www.kells.ca
Grades: Prim./Sec.; Fr./Angl.; Éd. spéc.
École mixte. Enseignement bilingue.
Irene Woods, Directrice

***Montréal:* Académie Louis-Pasteur**
7220, rue Marie-Victorin Montréal, H1G 2J5 Canada
514-322-6123, Fax: 514-322-6787,
info@academielouispasteur.com
www.academielouispasteur.com
Grades: Mat./Prim.
École primaire privée qui accueille des enfants de la maternelle à la 6e année.

Gisèle Bisaillon, Directrice générale

***Montréal:* Académie Michèle-Provost inc.**
1517, av des Pins ouest Montréal, H3G 1B3 Canada
514-934-0596, Fax: 514-934-2390,
info@academiemicheleprovost.qc.ca
www.academiemicheleprovost.qc.ca
Grades: Prim./Sec.; Pens. & Ext.
Michèle Provost, Directrice
m.provost@academiemicheleprovost.qc.

***Montréal:* Académie Saint-Louis de France**
4430, rue Bélanger est Montréal, H1T 1B3 Canada
514-725-0340, Fax: 514-725-1460,
pascal.foucault@academiesldf.ca
academiestlouisdefrance.googlepages.com
Grades: Mat./Prim.
Pascal Foucault, Directeur

***Montréal:* Centennial Academy L'Académie Centennale**
3641, av Prud'homme Montréal, H4A 3H6 Canada
514-486-5533, Fax: 514-486-1401,
aburgos@centennial.qc.ca
www.centennial.qc.ca
Grades: Sec.; Eng.
Angéla Burgos, Directrice

***Montréal:* Centre d'intégration scolaire inc.**
6361, 6e av Montréal, H1Y 2R7 Canada
514-374-8490, Fax: 514-374-3978,
pallard@cisi.qc.ca
www.cisi.qc.ca
Grades: Prim./Sec.; Éd. spéc.
Patrice Allard, Directeur général

***Montréal:* Centre François-Michelle**
10095, rue Meunier Montréal, H3L 2Z1 Canada
514-381-4418, Fax: 514-381-2895,
dsormany@francois-michelle.qc.ca
www.francois-michelle.qc.ca
Grades: Mat./Prim./Sec.; Éd. spéc.
Danielle Sormany, Directrice générale

***Montréal:* Collège Beaubois**
4901, rue du Collège Beaubois Montréal, H8Y 3T4 Canada
514-684-7642, Fax: 514-684-3011,
info@collegebeaubois.qc.ca
www.collegebeaubois.qc.ca
Grades: Mat./Prim./Sec.
Daniel Trottier, Directeur général

***Montréal:* Collège Charlemagne inc.**
5000, rue Pilon Montréal, H9K 1G4 Canada
514-626-7060, Fax: 514-626-1654,
admin@collegecharlemagne.com
www.collegecharlemagne.com
Grades: Mat./Prim./Sec.
Julie Beaudet, Directrice générale
jbeaudet@collegecharlemagne.com
Claudette Bélanger, Registraire
cbelanger@collegecharlemagne.com

***Montréal:* Collège Français - Secondaire Montréal**
185, av Fairmount ouest Montréal, H2T 2M6 Canada
514-495-2581, Fax: 514-279-2823,
info@collegefrancais.ca
www.collegefrancais.ca
Grades: Sec.; Pens. & Ext.
Colette Portal, Directrice

***Montréal:* Collège international Marie de France**
4635, ch Queen Mary Montréal, H3W 1W3 Canada
514-737-1177, Fax: 514-737-0789,
college@mariedefrance.qc.ca
www.mariedefrance.qc.ca
Grades: Mat./Prim./Sec.
Enrollment: 1800
Brigitte Peytier, Directrice générale

***Montréal:* Collège Jean-Eudes**
3535, boul Rosemont Montréal, H1X 1K7 Canada
514-376-5740, Fax: 514-376-4325,
info@jeaneudes.qc.ca
www.jeaneudes.qc.ca
Grades: Sec.
Enrollment: 1700
Louis Laliberté, Directeur général
llaliberte@jeaneudes.qc.ca

***Montréal:* Collège Mont-Royal**
2165, rue Baldwin Montréal, H1L 5A7 Canada
514-351-7851, Fax: 514-351-3124,
mradm@collegemont-royal.qc.ca
www.collegemont-royal.qc.ca
Grades: Sec.
Anne-Marie Blais, Directrice générale

***Montréal:* Collège Mont-Saint-Louis**
1700, boul Henri-Bourassa est Montréal, H2C 1J3 Canada
514-382-1560, Fax: 514-382-5886,
jldesrosiers@msl.qc.ca
www.msl.qc.ca
Grades: Sec.
André Lacroix, Directeur général
alacroix@msl.qc.ca

***Montréal:* Collège Notre-Dame**
3791, ch Queen Mary Montréal, H3V 1A8 Canada
514-739-3371, Fax: 514-739-4833,
info@collegenotre-dame.qc.ca
www.collegenotre-dame.qc.ca
Grades: Sec., Pens. & Ext.
Yvon Lafrenière, Directeur général

***Montréal:* College Prep International**
7475, rue Sherbrooke ouest Montréal, H4B 1S3 Canada
514-489-7287, Fax: 514-489-7280,
info@prepinternational.com
www.prepinternational.com
Grades: Elem./Sec.; Eng.
A private, non-sectarian & co-educational school.
Ursulene T. Mora, CEO

***Montréal:* Collège rabbinique du Canada**
6405, av Westbury Montréal, H3W 2X5 Canada
514-735-2201, Fax: 514-345-0275,
nicoleytt@vl.videotron.ca
Grades: Mat./Prim./Sec.; garçons
Enrollment: 350
École juive orthodoxe.
Linda Rosenblum, Directrice
lindaytt@vl.videotron.ca

***Montréal:* Collège Rachel**
5030, rue Jeanne-Mance Montréal, H2V 4J8 Canada
514-287-1944, Fax: 514-287-7523,
collegerachel@qc.aira.com
www.collegerachel.qc.ca
Grades: Sec.
Enrollment: 250
Véronique Geoffrion, Directrice générale

***Montréal:* Collège Regina Assumpta**
1750, rue Sauriol est Montréal, H2C 1X4 Canada
514-382-4121, Fax: 514-387-7825,
info@reginaassumpta.qc.ca
www.reginaassumpta.qc.ca
Grades: Sec.
Enrollment: 2200
Programme de musique; danse; centre culturel & sportif; chapelle.
Pierre Carle, Directeur général

***Montréal:* Collège Reine-Marie**
9300, boul Saint-Michel Montréal, H1Z 3H1 Canada
514-382-0484, Fax: 514-858-1401,
secretariat@reine-marie.qc.ca
www.reine-marie.qc.ca
Grades: Sec.; filles
Enrollment: 500
Johanne Kenyon, Directrice générale

***Montréal:* Collège Sainte-Anne de Lachine**
1250, boul St-Joseph Montréal, H8S 2M8 Canada
514-637-3571, Fax: 514-637-8906,
larivierd@college-sainte-anne.qc.ca
www.college-sainte-anne.qc.ca
Grades: Sec.
Ugo Cavenaghi, M.Éd., M.B.A., Directeur général
cavenaghiu@college-sainte-anne.qc.ca

***Montréal:* Collège Sainte-Marcelline**
9155, boul Gouin ouest Montréal, H4K 1C3 Canada
514-334-9651, Fax: 514-334-0210,
information@college.marcelline.qc.ca
college.marcelline.qc.ca
Grades: Mat./Prim/Sec.
Enseignement préscolaire et primaire pour garçons et filles; et l'enseignement secondaire pour filles.
Sr. Marielle Dion, Directrice

***Montréal:* Collège St-Jean-Vianney**
12630, boul Gouin est Montréal, H1C 1B9 Canada
514-648-3821, Fax: 514-648-8401,
college@st-jean-vianney.qc.ca
www.st-jean-vianney.qc.ca
Grades: Sec.
Enrollment: 1350
Yves Lacroix, Directeur général

***Montréal:* Collège Ville-Marie**
2850, rue Sherbrooke est Montréal, H2K 1H3 Canada
514-525-2516, Fax: 514-525-7675,
college@cvmarie.qc.ca
www.cvmarie.qc.ca
Grades: Sec.
Programme d'Éducation internationale.
Hélène Sirois, Directrice générale

***Montréal:* L'école Ali Ibn Abi Talib**
1610, rue de Beauharnois ouest Montréal, H4N 1J5 Canada
514-744-0801, Fax: 514-387-3457,
info@ecoleali.com
www.ecoleali.com
Grades: Mat./Prim./Sec.
Bilal Jundi, Directeur

***Montréal:* L'École arménienne Sourp Hagop**
3400, rue Nadon Montréal, H4J 1P5 Canada
514-332-1373, Fax: 514-332-8303,
direction@sourphagop.com
www.sourphagop.com
Grades: Mat./Prim./Sec.
Enrollment: 700
Hagop Boulgarian, Directeur

***Montréal:* École au Jardin Bleu inc.**
1690, rue Sauvé est Montréal, H2C 2A8 Canada
514-388-4949, Fax: 514-388-1970,
ecole@ecoleaujardinbleu.ca
www.ecoleaujardinbleu.ca
Grades: Mat./Prim.
École privée française d'allégeance catholique.
Nicole Auclair Normand, Directrice

***Montréal:* École Charles-Perrault (Pierrefonds)**
106, rue Cartier Montréal, H8Y 1G8 Canada
514-684-5043, Fax: 514-684-5048,
info@ecolecharlesperrault.com
www.ecolecharlesperrault.com/pierrefonds/
Grades: Mat./Prim.
Denis Faber, Directeur général

***Montréal:* L'École des Premières Lettres**
5155, av de Gaspé Montréal, H2T 2A1 Canada
514-272-2229, Fax: 514-272-3330,
info@premiereslettres.com
www.premiereslettres.com
Grades: Mat./Prim.
Anne Deguilhem, Directrice
adeguilhem@premiereslettres.com

***Montréal:* École Maïmonide**
Campus Jacob Safra
1900, rue Bourdon Montréal, H4M 2X7 Canada
514-744-5300, Fax: 514-744-4838,
admin@maimonide.ca
www.maimonide.ca
Grades: Mat./Prim./Sec.
École de la communauté Sépharade de Montréal. Campus Parkhaven: 5615, rue Parkhaven, Côte Saint-Luc, 514-488-9224 (Michelle Serano, Directrice).
Lucienne Azoulay, Directrice générale

***Montréal:* École Montessori Ville-Marie inc.**
6520, boul Gouin ouest Montréal, H4K 1B2 Canada
514-335-6688, Fax: 514-333-8988,
emvm76@hotmail.com
ecolemontessorivillemarie.org
Grades: Mat./Prim.
Campus Saint-Laurent: 760, rue St-Germain; Campus Laval-Duvernay: 755, rue Roland-Forget. Enseignement bilingue.
Claudette Debbané, Directrice

***Montréal:* École Pasteur**
12345, av de la Miséricorde Montréal, H4J 2E8 Canada
514-331-0850, Fax: 514-331-2312,
www.ecolepasteur.qc.ca
Grades: Mat./Prim./Sec.
Enrollment: 800
Volta Ramirez, Directeur général

***Montréal:* École première Mesifta du Canada**
2355, av Ekers Montréal, H3S 1C6 Canada
514-738-1738,
eelbaz@myway.com

Grades: Mat./Prim./Sec.
École juive.
Rabbin Chesky Buchinger, Directeur général

Montréal: **École primaire Socrates Socrates School**
5777, av Wilderton Montréal, H3S 2K8 Canada
514-738-2421, Fax: 514-906-0764,
www.hcm-chm.org
Grades: Mat./Prim.
Langues d'enseignement: française, greque et anglaise.
Chris Adamopoulos, Directeur général
chis.adamopoulos@hcm-chm.org

Montréal: **École Rudolf Steiner de Montréal**
4855, av Kensington Montréal, H3X 3S6 Canada
514-481-5686, Fax: 514-481-5072,
info@ersm.org
www.ersm.org
Grades: Mat./Prim./Sec.
Pédagogie Waldorf.
Anne Lange, Directrice

Montréal: **École Sainte-Anne**
6855, 13e av Montréal, H1X 2Z3 Canada
514-725-4179, Fax: 514-725-9962,
admin@ecolesainte-anne.qc.ca
Grades: Mat./Prim.
Sr. Monique Cloutier, Directrice

Montréal: **École secondaire Duval**
260, boul Henri-Bourassa est Montréal, H3L 1B8 Canada
514-382-6070, Fax: 514-382-7207,
info@ecoleduval.com
www.ecoleduval.com
Grades: Sec.
École sec. pour élèves qui ont abandonné leurs études régulières mais désirent obtenir leur diplôme dans les plus brefs délais, ou qui désirent satisfaire aux préalables d'un programme ou suivre un cours pour l'admission au collégial; cours individualisés ou cours de groupe.
Jacques Duval, Directeur

Montréal: **École secondaire Jeanne-Normandin**
690, boul Crémazie est Montréal, H2P 1E9 Canada
514-381-3945, Fax: 514-381-1695,
mtremblay@jeanne-normandin.qc.ca
www.jeanne-normandin.qc.ca
Grades: Sec.; filles
Marie Robert, Directrice générale

Montréal: **Les écoles communautaires Skver**
1235, av Ducharme Montréal, H2V 1E2 Canada
514-274-6133, Fax: 514-274-1468
Grades: Mat./Prim./Sec.; Fr./Eng.
Ruth Bensimhon, Directrice
bensimhon@btmtl.ca

Montréal: **Écoles musulmanes de Montréal**
Campus Secondaire
2255, boul Cavendish Montréal, H4B 2L7 Canada
514-484-5084, Fax: 514-484-5439,
info@emms.ca
www.emms.ca
Grades: Prim./Sec.
Campus Primaire: 7445, av Chester, (514) 484-8845 (Radjouh Idriss, directeur).
Fouzi Belaiboud, Directeur, Campus Secondaire

Montréal: **Greaves Adventist Academy**
2330, av West Hill Montréal, H4B 2S3 Canada
514-486-5092, Fax: 514-486-0515,
www.greavesadventistacademy.com
Grades: Pre./Elem./Sec.; Eng.

Montréal: **Jewish People's Schools & Peretz Schools Inc.**
Les Écoles juives populaires et Les Écoles Peretz inc.
6502, ch Kildare Montréal, H4W 3B8 Canada
514-731-2944, Fax: 514-731-0343,
info@jppsbialik.ca
www.jppsbialik.ca
Grades: Pre./Elem./Sec.; Eng./Fr.
One educational system retaining the names of both founding schools, united in 1971. JPPS-Bialik is a Jewish day school system in Montréal, comprising: Bialik High School, 6500, ch Kildare, 514-481-2736; JPPS Elementary School, 5170, av Van Horne, 514-731-6456; and JPPS Children's Centre, 7950 ch Wavell, 514-488-1232. Instruction in English, French & Hebrew, with language programmes in French, Hebrew, Yiddish; mathematics, sciences & technology, Judaic Studies, Social Sciences, Arts; athletics; library.
Arnold Cohen, President
Elaine Wisenthal Milech, Principal, Bialik High School
Ms. Randy Zucker, Director, JPPS Children's Centre
Adina Matas, Principal/Educational Director, JPPS

Montréal: **Lower Canada College**
4090, av Royale Montréal, H4A 2M5 Canada
514-482-9916, Fax: 514-482-0195,
admin@lcc.ca
www.lcc.ca
Grades: Sec.; Eng./Fr.
Christopher J. Shannon, Headmaster

Montréal: **Loyola High School**
7272, rue Sherbrooke ouest Montréal, H4B 1R2 Canada
514-486-1101, Fax: 514-486-7266,
admin@loyola.ca
www.loyola.ca/index.htm
Grades: Sec.; Boys; Eng.
Éric McLean, Directeur

Montréal: **Pensionnat Notre-Dame-des-Anges**
5680, boul Rosemont Montréal, H1T 2H2 Canada
514-254-6447, Fax: 514-254-6261,
pnda@pnda.qc.ca
www.pnda.qc.ca/
Grades: Prim.
France Mailloux, Directrice générale

Montréal: **The Priory School inc.**
3120 The Boulevard Montréal, H3Y 1R9 Canada
514-935-5966, Fax: 514-935-1428,
info@priory.qc.ca
www.priory.qc.ca
Grades: Pre./Elem.; Eng.
John Marinelli, Directeur

Montréal: **St. George's School of Montreal**
3100, The Boulevard Montréal, H3Y 1R9 Canada
514-937-9289, Fax: 514-933-3621,
www.stgeorges.qc.ca
Grades: Pre./Elem./Sec.; Eng.
A co-educational, non-denominational school.
James A. Officer, Head of School
james.officer@stgeorges.qc.ca

Montréal: **Solomon Schechter Academy Académie Solomon Schechter**
5555, ch de la Côte-St-Luc Montréal, H3X 2C9 Canada
514-485-0866, Fax: 514-485-2267,
info@solomonschechter.ca
www.ssa.koumbit.org
Grades: Pre./Prim.; Eng./Fr.
Committed to the values of Conservative Judaism; affiliated with the Shaare Zion Synagogue. Pre-Kindergarten to Gr. 6. Instruction in English, French & Hebrew.
Dr. Shimshon Hamerman, B.A., M.Sc., Ph.D., Principal

Montréal: **Trafalgar School for Girls**
3495, rue Simpson Montréal, H3G 2J7 Canada
514-935-2644, Fax: 514-935-2359,
admin1@trafalgar.qc.ca
www.trafalgar.qc.ca/
Grades: Sec.; Girls; Eng.
Geoffrey Dowd, Director

Montréal: **United Talmud Torahs of Montréal Talmud Torahs Unis de Montréal**
4840, av Saint-Kevin Montréal, H3W 1P2 Canada
514-739-2294, Fax: 514-739-2296,
www.herzliahsnowdon.qc.ca
Grades: Pre./Elem./Sec.; Eng./Fr.
Instruction in Hebrew, French & English; college preparatory programme; Judaic Studies; athletics; arts; library.
Linda Leiberman, Campus Director
lleiberman@utt.qc.ca

Montréal: **Villa Maria**
4245, boul Décarie Montréal, H4A 3K4 Canada
514-484-4950, Fax: 514-484-4492,
secretariat@villamaria.qc.ca
www.villamaria.qc.ca
Grades: Sec.; Girls; Eng./Fr.
Enrollment: 600
Committed to students' proficiency in French & English; programmes include languages; arts (visual arts, drama, music); mathematics & sciences; technology; social sciences; ethics & religious culture; physical education & health.
Claire Drolet, Director General

Montréal: **Yechivat or Torah**
4605, rue Mackenzie Montréal, H3W 1B2 Canada
514-341-9459, Fax: 514-341-0594,
jhassan-yavne@qc.aira.com
Grades: Pre./Elem./Sec.
Irène Waller, Directrice

Montréal: **Yeshiva Gedola Merkaz Hatorah**
6155, ch Deacon Montréal, H3S 2P4 Canada
514-735-6611, Fax: 513-343-0083
Grades: Pre./Elem./Sec.; Eng./Fr.
Rabbin Moshe Glustein, Directeur

Montréal-Nord: **Centre Académique Fournier**
10339, av du Parc-Georges Montréal-Nord, H1H 4Y4 Canada
514-321-2642, Fax: 514-321-0278,
paola.gravino@academiefournier.qc.ca
www.academiefournier.qc.ca
Grades: Prim./Sec.; Éd. spéc.
Paola Gravino, Directrice générale
paola.gravino@academiefournier.qc.ca

Montréal-Nord: **École Michelet**
10550, av Pelletier Montréal-Nord, H1H 3R5 Canada
514-321-9551, Fax: 514-321-9111,
michelet@qc.aira.com
www.ecolemichelet.com
Grades: Prim.
Lucienne Mortier, Directrice

Nicolet: **Collège Notre-Dame-de-l'Assomption**
225, rue St-Jean-Baptiste Nicolet, J3T 0A2 Canada
819-293-4500, Fax: 819-293-2099,
snault@cnda.qc.ca
www.cnda.qc.ca
Grades: Sec.; Pens. & Ext.
École privée mixte.
Robert Cyr, Directeur général

Outremont: **Belz Community School École communautaire Belz**
1495, av Ducharme Outremont, H2V 1E8 Canada
514-271-0611, Fax: 514-271-9329,
belz@belzschool.org
Grades: Pre./Elem./Sec.; Fr./Eng.; girls
Belz Boys School: 6508, Durocher, Outremont, (514) 270-5086.
Helen Liberman, Principal

Outremont: **Beth Jacob School Inc. École Beth Jacob inc.**
1750, av Glendale Outremont, H2V 1B3 Canada
514-739-3614, Fax: 514-739-0172,
bjdrh@hotmail.com
Grades: Pre./Elem./Sec.; Eng./Fr.; Girls
Rabbin S. Aisenstark, Directeur

Outremont: **Collège Stanislas**
780, boul Dollard Outremont, H2V 3G5 Canada
514-273-9521, Fax: 514-273-3409,
direction@stanislas.qc.ca
www.stanislas.qc.ca
Grades: Mat./Prim./Sec./Coll.
Enrollment: 2150
Henri-Laurent Brusa, Directeur général

Outremont: **École Buissonnière, centre de formation artistique inc.**
215, av de l'Épée Outremont, H2V 3T3 Canada
514-272-4739, Fax: 514-907-5094,
infos@ecolebuissonniere.ca
www.ecolebuissonniere.ca
Grades: Mat./Prim.
Intégration des arts aux programmes du Min. de l'Éducation; arts plastiques, musique, danse, art dramatique.
Hélène Bourduas, Directrice générale

Québec: **Académie Saint-Louis (Québec)**
1500, rue de La Rive-Boisée sud Québec, G2C 2B3 Canada
418-845-5121, Fax: 418-845-5244,
www.aslouis.qc.ca
Grades: Sec.
Enrollment: 800
Programmes: Concentration Langues; Études-Sports: Hockey, Golf, Natation, Football, Cheerleading, et Soccer féminin.
Jocelyn Lee, Directeur général

Québec: **Centre Psycho-Pédagogique de Québec inc. (École Saint-François)**
1000, rue du Joli-Bois Québec, G1V 3Z6 Canada
418-650-1171, Fax: 418-650-1145,
adm@cppq.qc.ca
www.cppq.qc.ca
Grades: Prim./Sec./; Éd. spéc.
Enrollment: 200
Favoriser l'intégration sociale de filles et garçons présentant des difficultés d'adaptation scolaire.
Jean-Marie Guay, Directeur

***Québec:* Collège de Champigny**
1400, rte de l'Aéroport Québec, G2G 1G6 Canada
418-872-0508, Fax: 418-872-1002,
www.collegedechampigny.com
Grades: Sec.
Robert Laperle, Directeur
rlaperle@collegechampigny.com

***Québec:* L'École des Ursulines de Québec et de Loretteville**
P.O. Box 820
4, rue du Parloir Québec, G1R 4S7 Canada
418-692-2612, Fax: 418-692-1240,
secrectariat_euq@ursulinesquebec.com
www.ursulinesquebec.com
Grades: Prim./Sec.; filles; Pens. & Ext.
Enrollment: 580
Loretteville: 63, rue Racine, (418) 842-2949.
Serge Goyette, Directeur

***Québec:* École Montessori de Québec inc.**
1265, av Du Buisson Québec, G1T 2C4 Canada
418-688-7646, Fax: 418-687-5282,
montessori_qc@yahoo.ca
www.montessori-qc.net
Grades: Mat./Prim.
Benoît Dubuc, Directeur

***Québec:* École Saint-Louis-de-Gonzague**
980, rue Richelieu Québec, G1R 1L5 Canada
418-692-1072, Fax: 418-692-5965,
secretariat@eslg.qc.ca
www.eslg.qc.ca
Grades: Prim.; garçons
Enrollment: 300
Programme d'éducation internationale.
Patrick L'Heureux, Directeur général
dirgen@eslg.qc.ca

***Québec:* École secondaire François-Bourrin**
50, av des Cascades Québec, G1E 6B3 Canada
418-661-6978, Fax: 418-661-4778,
efb@fbourrin.qc.ca
www.fbourrin.qc.ca
Grades: Sec.
M. Magella Beaulieu, Directeur général

***Québec:* Externat Saint-Jean-Eudes**
650, av du Bourg-Royal Québec, G2L 1M8 Canada
418-627-1550, Fax: 418-627-0770,
info@sje.qc.ca
www.sje.qc.ca
Grades: Sec.
Édouard Malenfant, Directeur général

***Québec:* Externat St-Jean-Berchmans**
2303, ch Saint-Louis Québec, G1T 1R5 Canada
418-687-5871, Fax: 418-687-5886,
sec@externatsjb.com
www.externatsjb.com
Grades: Mat./Prim.
Alain Roy, Directeur général

***Québec:* Institut St-Joseph**
Pavillon Saint-Vallier
550, ch Ste-Foy Québec, G1S 2J5 Canada
418-688-0736, Fax: 418-688-0737,
jean-guy_lussier@fc.st-joseph.qc.ca
www.st-joseph.qc.ca
Grades: Mat./Prim.
Jean-Guy Lussier, Directeur général

***Québec:* Le Petit Séminaire de Québec**
6, rue de la Vielle-Université Québec, G1R 5X8 Canada
418-694-1020, Fax: 418-694-1072,
admission@psq.qc.ca
www.psq.qc.ca
Grades: Sec.
Réjean Lemay, Directeur général

***Québec:* Séminaire des Pères Maristes**
2315, ch Saint-Louis Québec, G1T 1R5 Canada
418-651-4944, Fax: 418-651-6841,
spmecole@spmaristes.qc.ca
www.spmaristes.qc.ca
Grades: Sec.
Jean-François Bussières, Directeur général

***Rawdon:* Collège Champagneur**
3713, rue Queen Rawdon, J0K 1S0 Canada
450-834-5401, Fax: 450-834-6500,
direction@champagneur.qc.ca
www.champagneur.qc.ca
Grades: Sec.; Pens. & Ext.
Privée mixte.
Richard Fiola, Directeur
brab@pandore.qc.ca

***Rawdon:* École et Pensionnat Marie-Anne**
4567, rue du Mont-Pontbriand Rawdon, J0K 1S0 Canada
450-834-4668, Fax: 450-834-2800,
ema@intermonde.net
www.ecolemarieanne.qc.ca
Grades: Mat./Prim.; Pens. & Ext.
Carole Lalancette, Directrice

***Repentigny:* Académie François-Labelle**
1227, rue Notre-Dame Repentigny, J5Y 3H2 Canada
450-582-2020, Fax: 450-582-9732,
afl@classomption.qc.ca
www.academiefrancoislabelle.qc.ca
Grades: Mat./Prim.
Michèle Beaudry, Directrice générale

***Repentigny:* Centre Académique de Lanaudière**
930, boul L'Assomption Repentigny, J6A 5H5 Canada
450-654-5026,
drn@lecadl.com
www.lecadl.com
Grades: Mat./Prim.
Denise Normandin, Directrice

***Rigaud:* Collège Bourget**
65, rue St-Pierre Rigaud, J0P 1P0 Canada
450-451-0815, Fax: 450-451-4171,
dg@collegebourget.qc.ca
www.collegebourget.qc.ca
Grades: Prim./Sec.; Pens. & Ext.
Jean-Marc St-Jacques, c.s.v., Directeur général

***Rivière-du-Loup:* Collège Notre-Dame**
P.O. Box 820
56, rue Saint-Henri Rivière-du-Loup, G5R 3Z5 Canada
418-862-8257, Fax: 418-862-8495,
info@collegenotredame.ca
collegenotredame.ca
Grades: Sec.
Abbé Fernand Chouinard, Directeur général

***Saint-Augustin-de-Desmaures:* Collège Saint-Augustin**
4950, rue Lionel-Groulx Saint-Augustin-de-Desmaures, G3A 1V2 Canada
418-872-0954, Fax: 418-872-8249,
fouc@globetrotter.net
Grades: Sec.; Pens. & Ext.
Charles Fournier, Directeur

***Saint-Bruno-de-Montarville:* Pensionnat des Sacrés-Coeurs**
1575, ch des Vingt Saint-Bruno-de-Montarville, J3V 4P6 Canada
450-653-3681, Fax: 450-653-0816,
info@psscc.qc.ca
www.psscc.qc.ca
Grades: Mat./Prim.; Pens. & Ext.
Guy Saumure, Directeur général

***Saint-Gabriel-de-Valcartier:* École secondaire Mont-Saint-Sacrement**
200, boul St-Sacrement Saint-Gabriel-de-Valcartier, G0A 4S0 Canada
418-844-3771, Fax: 418-844-2926,
secretariat@mss.qc.ca
www.mss.qc.ca
Grades: Sec.
Programme Baccalauréat international; Programme Magellan.
Pierre Lantier, Directeur général

***Saint-Guillaume:* Juvénat Saint-Louis-Marie**
96, rue Saint-Jean-Baptiste Saint-Guillaume, J0C 1L0 Canada
819-396-2076, Fax: 819-396-3331,
info@juvenat.ca
www.juvenat.ca
Grades: Sec.; Pens. & Ext.
Martin Girard, Directeur

***Saint-Hyacinthe:* Collège Antoine-Girouard**
700, rue Girouard est Saint-Hyacinthe, J2S 2Y2 Canada
514-773-4334, Fax: 450-773-8011,
admin@antoine-girouard.qc.ca
www.antoine-girouard.qc.ca
Grades: Sec.
M. Dominique Lestage, Directeur général

***Saint-Hyacinthe:* Collège Saint-Maurice**
630, rue Girouard ouest Saint-Hyacinthe, J2S 2Y3 Canada
450-773-7478, Fax: 450-773-1413,
info.college@csm.qc.ca
www.csm.qc.ca
Grades: Sec.; filles; Pens. & Ext.
École secondaire pour filles; Programme d'éducation internationale.
Jean-Pierre Jeannotte, Directeur général

***Saint-Hyacinthe:* La Petite Académie**
1090, av Pratte Saint-Hyacinthe, J2S 4B6 Canada
450-771-0644, Fax: 450-771-7242,
info@lapetiteacademie.qc.ca
www.lapetiteacademie.qc.ca
Grades: Mat./Prim.
Lise Thiboutot, Directrice générale

***Saint-Jacques:* Collège Esther-Blondin**
101, rue Ste-Anne Saint-Jacques, J0K 2R0 Canada
450-839-3672, Fax: 450-839-3951,
admin@collegeblondin.qc.ca
www.collegeblondin.qc.ca
Grades: Sec.; Pens. & Ext.
Enrollment: 1100
Membre, Soc. des établissements du bacc. international du Québec, et Org. du bacc. international; le collège est reconnu École Verte Brundtland.
Julie Pothier, Directrice générale

***Saint-Jean-sur-Richelieu:* École secondaire Marcellin-Champagnat**
14, ch des Patriotes est Saint-Jean-sur-Richelieu, J2X 5P9 Canada
450-347-5343, Fax: 450-347-2423,
webmaster@esmc.qc.ca
www.esmc.qc.ca
Grades: Sec.
F. Jacques Bélisle, Directeur général

***Saint-Jérôme:* Académie Lafontaine**
2171, boul Maurice Saint-Jérôme, J7Y 4M7 Canada
450-431-3733, Fax: 450-431-7390,
info@academielafontaine.qc.ca
www.academielafontaine.qc.ca
Grades: Mat./Prim./Sec.
Camps du jour; piscine; cantine.
Claude Potvin, Directeur général

***Saint-Lambert:* Collège Durocher Saint-Lambert**
Pavillon Durocher
857, rue Riverside Saint-Lambert, J4P 1C2 Canada
450-465-7213, Fax: 450-465-0860,
johanne.tremblay@cdsl.qc.ca
www.cdsl.qc.ca
Grades: Sec.
Enrollment: 2230
Pavillon Saint-Lambert: 375, rue Riverside, 450-671-5585.
Carmen Poirier, Directrice générale

***Saint-Laurent:* École Alex Manoogian**
755, rue Manoogian Saint-Laurent, H4N 1Z5 Canada
514-744-5636, Fax: 514-744-2785,
armenque@qc.aira.com
www.alexmanoogian.qc.ca
Grades: Mat./Prim./Sec.; Fr./Eng./Armenian
Enrollment: 550
La première école arménienne au Canada; école privée.
Dr. Robert Marc Kechayan, Directeur

***Saint-Laurent:* École Vanguard Québec ltée (École primaire interculturelle)**
Vanguard Québec School
1150, rue Deguire Saint-Laurent, H4L 1M2 Canada
514-747-3711, Fax: 514-747-2831,
cccaputo@vanguardquebec.qc.ca
www.vanguardquebec.qc.ca
Grades: Prim./Sec.; Fr./Angl.; Éd. spéc.
Services adaptés à des élèves présentant des difficultés graves d'apprentissage. École Vanguard Primaire Interculturelle: 1150, rue Deguire, (514) 747-3711 (Denise Bédard, directrice). École Vanguard Secondaire Francophone: 83, boul des Prairies, Laval, (450) 972-6268 (François Papineau, directeur). École Vanguard Secondaire Interculturelle: 175, rue Metcalfe, (514) 932-9770 (Maryse Bessette, directrice).
Carolyn Coffin-Caputo, Directrice générale, 514-747-5500

***Saint-Laurent:* Education Plus**
1275, rue Hodge Saint-Laurent, H4N 2B1 Canada
514-733-9600, Fax: 514-733-3060,
www.edplus.ca
Grades: Grs. 10 & 11
Enrollment: 40

Relationship-based education, flexible structure, informal environment; Life Skills courses; drama; arts; English & French language skills.
James Watts, Director
j.watts@sympatico.ca

Sainte-Thérèse: Académie Ste-Thérèse
Campus Ste-Thérèse
425, rue Blainville est Sainte-Thérèse, J7E 1N7 Canada
450-434-1130, Fax: 450-434-0010,
infostetherese@academie.ste-therese.com
www.academie.ste-therese.com
Grades: Mat./Prim./Sec.; Pens. & Ext.
Campus Rosemère: 1, ch des Écoliers, Rosemère, 450-434-1130.
Rose De Angelis, Directrice générale

Sept-Iles: Institut d'enseignement de Sept-Iles inc.
737, av Gamache Sept-Iles, G4R 2J8 Canada
418-962-9104, Fax: 418-962-8561,
direction@ecolepriveesi.com
ecolepriveesi.com
Grades: Sec.
Richard Savignac, Directeur général

Shawinigan: Institution secondaire Montfort
1805, rang St-Mathieu est Shawinigan, G9N 6T5 Canada
819-536-2544, Fax: 819-536-3609,
montfort@bellnet.ca
Grades: Sec.
Guy Lefort, Directeur

Shawinigan: Séminaire Sainte-Marie
5655, boul des Hêtres Shawinigan, G9N 4V9 Canada
819-539-5493, Fax: 819-539-1749,
apsssm@ssm1950.qc.ca
www.seminairestemarie.com
Grades: Prim./Sec.
Marc St-Onge, Directeur général

Sherbrooke: Bishop's College School, Inc. / BCS
P.O. Box 5001 Lennoxville
80, ch Moulton Hill Sherbrooke, J1M 1Z8 Canada
819-566-0227, Fax: 819-822-8917,
admissions@bishopscollegeschool.com
www.bishopscollegeschool.com
Grades: 7-12
Bishop's College School is a bilingual boarding & day school.
Ian Watt, Headmaster, 819-566-0227 201
Charles de Sainte Marie, Director, Development, 819-566-0227 203
François de Sainte Marie, Director, Finance & Operations, 819-566-0227 205
Valerie Scullion, Director, Admissions, 819-566-0227 248

Sherbrooke: Collège du Mont-Sainte-Anne
2100, ch Ste-Catherine Sherbrooke, J1N 3V5 Canada
819-823-3003, Fax: 819-569-9636, 877-823-3003
msa@collegemsa.qc.ca
www.college-mont-sainte-anne.qc.ca
Grades: Sec.; garçons; Pens. & Ext.
André Ricard, Directeur général

Sherbrooke: Collège Mont Notre-Dame de Sherbrooke inc.
114, rue de la Cathédrale Sherbrooke, J1H 4M1 Canada
819-563-4104, Fax: 819-563-8689,
cmnd@mont-notre-dame.qc.ca
www.mont-notre-dame.qc.ca
Grades: Mat./Prim./Sec; filles
Programme d'éducation international; école de musique; école de danse; Espagnol; sports.
Richard Custeau, Directeur général

Sherbrooke: École Plein Soleil (Association coopérative)
300, rue de Montréal Sherbrooke, J1H 1E5 Canada
819-569-8359, Fax: 819-569-3979,
info@pleinsoleil.qc.ca
www.pleinsoleil.qc.ca
Grades: Mat./Prim.
Programme d'éducation internationale.
Marie-Josée Mayrand, Directrice générale
mjmayrand@pleinsoleil.qc.ca

Sherbrooke: École secondaire de Bromptonville
125, rue du Frère-Théode Sherbrooke, J1C 0S3 Canada
819-846-2738, Fax: 819-846-4808,
esb@esb-fsc.ca
www.esb.bromptonville.qc.ca
Grades: Sec.; garçons; Pens. & Ext.
Fr. Jean-Guy Beaulieu, Directeur général
dirgen@esb-fsc.ca

Sherbrooke: Séminaire de Sherbrooke
195, rue Marquette Sherbrooke, J1H 1L6 Canada
819-563-2050, Fax: 819-562-8261,
courrier@seminaire-sherbrooke.qc.ca
www.seminaire-sherbrooke.qc.ca
Grades: Sec.
Secondaire et collégial; formation continue.
André Métras, Recteur-Directeur général

Sherbrooke: Séminaire Salésien
135, rue Don Bosco nord Sherbrooke, J1L 1E5 Canada
819-566-2222, Fax: 819-566-6969,
salesien@seminairesalesien.org
www.seminairesalesien.org
Grades: Sec.
Raymond Lepage, Directeur

St-Augustin-de-Desmaures: Réseau VISION
Maître Franchiseur Vision inc.
4920, rue Pierre-Georges-Roy St-Augustin-de-Desmaures, G3A 1V7 Canada
418-653-3547, Fax: 418-653-6435, 866-553-3547
info@visionschools.com
www.visionschools.com
Grades: Mat./Prim./Sec.
Le réseau regroupe huit écoles VISION (immersion) et deux écoles Once Upon a Time (préscolaire; apprentissage de l'anglais ou de l'espagnol).
Richard Dumais, Président

Stanstead: Stanstead College
450, rue Dufferin Stanstead, J0B 3E0 Canada
819-876-2223, Fax: 819-876-5891,
admissions@stansteadcollege.com
www.stansteadcollege.com
Grades: Sec.; Eng.; Res. & Day
Enrollment: 200
Co-educational; curriculum/instruction in English, with programmes in French, arts, music, drama; athletics.
Michael Wolfe, Headmaster

Terrebonne: Collège Saint-Sacrement
901, rue St-Louis Terrebonne, J6W 1K1 Canada
450-471-6615, Fax: 450-471-5904,
css@collegesaintsacrement.qc.ca
www.collegesaintsacrement.qc.ca
Grades: Sec.
Luc St-Louis, Directeur général
lst-louis@collegesaintsacrement.qc.ca

Trois-Rivières: Collège Marie-de-l'Incarnation
725, rue Hart Trois-Rivières, G9A 5S3 Canada
819-379-3223, Fax: 819-379-3226,
ecole@cmitr.qc.ca
www.cmitr.qc.ca
Grades: Mat./Prim./Sec.; Pens. & Ext.
École pour filles; école de musique.
Martine Talbot, Directrice, Services éducatifs du secondaire
martine.talbot@cmitr.qc.ca
Carolyne Gagnon, Directrice, Services éducatifs du préscolaire
carolyne.gagnon@cmitr.qc.ca

Trois-Rivières: Institut secondaire Keranna (1992) inc.
6205, boul des Chenaux Trois-Rivières, G9A 5S3 Canada
819-378-4833, Fax: 819-378-2417,
keranna@keranna.qc.ca
keranna.qc.ca
Grades: Sec.; filles; Pens. & Ext.
Julie L'Heureux, Directrice générale

Trois-Rivières: Val Marie
88, ch du Passage Trois-Rivières, G8T 2M3 Canada
819-379-8040, Fax: 819-378-8559,
sgoyette@ecolevalmarie.qc.ca
www.ecolevalmarie.qc.ca
Grades: Mat./Prim.; Pens. & Ext.
Serge Goyette, Directeur

Val-Morin: Académie Laurentienne
1200, 14e av Val-Morin, J0T 2R0 Canada
819-322-2913, Fax: 819-322-7086,
info@al.qc.ca
www.academielaurentienne.com
Grades: Prim./Sec.; Pens. & Ext.
Programmes académiques et sportifs; installations sportives: piscines, palestre, gymnase double; terrains de jeux, de tennis; centre équestre.
Guy Richard, Directeur
richard.guy@al.qc.ca

Varennes: Centre Éducatif Chante Plume
104, boul de la Marine Varennes, J3X 1Z5 Canada
450-652-6869, Fax: 450-652-5773,
varennes@visionschools.com
varennes.visionschools.com
Grades: Mat./Prim.
Colette Cardin, Directrice

Varennes: Collège Saint-Paul
235, rue Sainte-Anne Varennes, J3X 1P9 Canada
450-652-2941, Fax: 450-652-4461,
reception@college-st-paul.qc.ca
www.college-st-paul.qc.ca
Grades: Sec.
Programme de formation générale; Programme d'éducation internationale.
André Langevin, Directeur général

Victoriaville: Collège Clarétain
663, rue Gamache Victoriaville, G6R 0W3 Canada
819-752-4571, Fax: 819-752-4572,
administration@collegeclaretain.com
www.collegeclaretain.com
Grades: Sec.; Pens. & Ext.
École privée mixte.
Jean-Roch Gagné, Directeur général

Waterville: Collège François-Delaplace
365, rue Compton est Waterville, J0B 3H0 Canada
819-837-2882, Fax: 819-837-0625,
dir@college-francois-delaplace.qc.ca
www.college-francois-delaplace.qc.ca
Grades: Sec.; filles
École Verte Brundtland; école secondaire privée pour filles (pensionnaires & externes).
Josée Hamel, Directrice générale

Westmount: The Akiva School
450, av Kensington Westmount, H3Y 3A2 Canada
514-939-2430, Fax: 514-939-2432,
suzanna@akivaschool.com
www.akivaschool.com
Grades: Pre-K./Gr. 6; Eng./Fr./Hebrew
Jewish community school; programmes include English Language Arts, Français, Judaic Studies, Music, Mathematics, Art, Media & Technology, Physical Education, & Ethics & Religious Cultures.
Frances Levy, Head of School

Westmount: Miss Edgar's & Miss Cramp's School / ECS
525, av Mount Pleasant Westmount, H3Y 3H6 Canada
514-935-6357, Fax: 514-935-1099,
www.ecs.qc.ca
Grades: Pre./Elem./Sec.; Girls; Eng.
Enrollment: 344
University-preparatory programme, to Gr. 11; French Immersion junior school; arts, athletics, math, sciences, languages, citizenship education; extended day programme; library.
Katherine Nikidis, B.Ed., MHSc, Head of School
nikidisk@ecs.qc.ca

Westmount: Selwyn House
École Selwyn House
95, ch Côte-St-Antoine Westmount, H3Y 2H8 Canada
514-931-9481, Fax: 514-931-6118,
admission@selwyn.ca
www.selwyn.ca
Grades: Pre./Elem./Sec.; Eng.; Boys
Enrollment: 570
Hal Hannford, Headmaster

Westmount: The Study
3233, The Boulevard Westmount, H3Y 1S4 Canada
514-935-9352, Fax: 514-935-1721,
info@thestudy.qc.ca
www.thestudy.qc.ca
Grades: Pre./Elem./Sec.; Eng.; Girls
Committed to best practices in education, with a focus on proficiency in both English & French, academics & athletics. The school is the first in Québec to introduce a Mandarin language program at the primary level.
Elizabeth Falco, M.Ed., MBA, Head of School

Westmount: Villa Sainte-Marcelline
815, av Upper Belmont Westmount, H3Y 1K5 Canada
514-488-2528, Fax: 514-488-5384,
srmathilde@villa.marcelline.qc.ca
Grades: Mat./Prim./Sec.; filles
Sr. Mathilde Fantone, Directrice

Universities & Colleges

Universities

Chicoutimi: Université du Québec à Chicoutimi
555, boul de l'Université Chicoutimi, G7H 2B1 Canada
418-545-5011, Fax: 418-545-5012,
info_programmes@uqac.ca
www.uqac.ca

Publications
La Petite Caisse

Gatineau: Université du Québec en Outaouais
Pavillion Alexandre-Taché
283, boul Alexandre-Taché Gatineau, J9A 1L8 Canada
819-595-3900, Fax: 819-595-3924, 1-800-567-1283
questions@uqo.ca
www.uqo.ca

Enrollment: 5200

Publications
Le Canard Déchaine

Le Virus

Laval: Institut Armand-Frappier
531, boul des Prairies Laval, H7V 1B7 Canada
450-687-5010, Fax: 450-686-5501,
www.iaf.inrs.ca

Lennoxville: Université Bishop's
P.O. Box 5000
Lennoxville, J1M 1Z7 Canada
819-822-9600, Fax: 819-822-9661, 1-800-567-279
liaison@ubishops.ca
www.ubishops.ca

Enrollment: 2206
Scott Griffin, B.A., D.C.L., Chancellor
Philip Matthews, B.A., LL.B., President of Corporation
Yves Jodoin, B.A., B.Sp. Adm., M.B.A., Registrar
Joan Stadelman, B.Sc., M.Sc., Vice-President of Corporation
Sam Elkas, Chair
Robert Poupart, B.A., B.Ph., M.Ps., D.Ps., Principal & Vice-Chancellor
Mark McLaughlin, B.B.A., C.A., Vice-Principal
Tony Addona, B.Sc., Dip.Ed., M.Sc., Director
Cathy Beauchamp, B.A., Dip.Ed., M.A., Ph.D, Director
Hans Rouleau, B.A., Liaison Coordinator
Damien Roy, B.A., Director
Suzanne Meeson, B.B.A., Continuing Education Coordinator
Pam McPhail, B.A., Director
Matt McBrine, B.A., Alumni Relations Coordinator
Patricia MacAulay, Manager
Jonathan Rittenhouse, B.A., M.A., Ph.D., Vice-Principal

Faculties
Business Administration
W. Robson, B.Com., M.B.A., Dean

Humanities
Stephen Sheeran, B.A., M.A., Dean

Natural Sciences & Mathematics
Brad Willms, B.Math, M.M. Ph.D., Dean

Social Sciences
Andrew Johnson, B.A., M.A., Ph.D., Dean

Student Affairs
Bruce Stevenson, B.A., Dip.Ed., M.Ed., Dean

Williams School of Business

Sylvie Béquet, M.Sc., Dean

Publications
The Campus

Montréal: Concordia University
Université Concordia
Sir George Williams Campus
1455, boul de Maisonneuve ouest Montréal, H3G 1M8 Canada
514-848-2424,
www.concordia.ca

Enrollment: 44000
Please refer to main French record for more details.
Judith Woodsworth, President & Vice-Chancellor
David Graham, Provost & Vice-President, Academic
Kathy Assayag, Vice-President, Advancement and Alumni Relati
Bram Freedman, Vice-President, External Relations and Secret
Patrick Kelley, CFO
Louise Dandurand, Vice-President, Research and Graduate Studies
Michael Di Grappa, Vice-President, Services
Philippe Beauregard, CCO

Faculties
Arts & Science
Dr. David Graham, Dean

Engineering & Computer Science
Nabil Esmail, Dean

Fine Arts
Catherine Wild, Dean

Graduate Studies & Research
Elizabeth Saccà, Dean

John Molson School of Business (JMSB)
Jerry Tomberlin, Dean

Campuses
Loyola Campus
7141, rue Sherbrooke ouest Montréal, H4B 1R6 Canada

Sir George Williams Campus
1455, boul de Maisonneuve ouest Montréal, H3G 1M8 Canada

Publications
Concordia University Magazine
Office of Alumni Affairs
#BC-101, 1455, boul de Maisonneuve ouest Montréal, H3G 1M8 Canada
Fax: 514-848-2826

The Concordian

The Link

The Sting

Thursday Report

CAS

Montréal: École de technologie supérieure
1100, rue Notre-Dame ouest Montréal, H3C 1K3 Canada
514-396-8800, Fax: 514-396-8950, 1-888-394-7888
admission@etsmtl.ca
www.etsmtl.ca

Enrollment: 4800

Publications
Le Jets

Montréal: HEC Montréal
Université de Montréal
3000, ch de la Côte-Sainte-Catherine Montréal, H3T 2A7 Canada
514-340-6000, Fax: 514-340-6411,
webmestre@hec.ca
www.hec.ca

Enrollment: 12000
HEC Montréal est la première école de gestion au Canada. Affaires internationales; finance; gestion des opérations/logistique; gestion des ressources humaines; management; marketing; méthodes quantitatives de gestion; sciences comptables; technologies de l'information; économie appliquée. Édifice Decelles: 5255, av Decelles. Campus Laval: 2572, boul Daniel-Johnson, (450) 973-7741. Campus Longueuil: 101, place Charles-Lemoyne, (450) 651-5458. Bureau international à Paris: 15, rue du Louvre, 75001 Paris, 33(0)1 42 33 43 40.
Michel Patry, Directeur

Montréal: McGill University
845, rue Sherbrooke ouest Montréal, H3A 2T5 Canada
514-398-4455, Fax: 514-398-4455,
www.mcgill.ca

Enrollment: 32510
Arnold Steinberg, Chancellor
Robert Rabinovitch, Ph.D., M.A., B.Com., Chair of Board
Heather Munroe-Blum, O.C. Ph.D. FRSC, Principal & Vice-Chancellor
Anthony C. Masi, Provost
Morty Yalovsky, Vice-Principal
Sylvia Franke, CIO
Denis Therien, Vice-Principal
Johanne Pelletier, Secretary General
Sylvia Franke, Registrar & Exec. Director
Jennifer Robinson, Assoc. Vice-Principal
Kim Bartlett, Director
Howard Tontini, Director
Ann Dowsett Johnston, Vice-Principal

Faculties
Agricultural & Environmental Sciences
Chandra A. Madramootoo, B.Sc., M.Sc., Ph.D., Dean

Arts
John Galaty, Dean

Centre for Continuing Education
Robin Eley, Director

Dentistry
James Percy Lund, B.D.S., Ph.D., Dean

Education
Dr. Roger Slee, Dean

Engineering
Pierre Christophe, Dean

Graduate & Post-Doctoral Studies
Dr. James Nemes, Dean

Law
Prof. Nicholas Kasirer, Dean

Management
Peter Todd, Dean

Medicine
Abraham Fuks, B.Sc., M.D., C.M., Dean

Music

Don McLean, Dean

Religious Studies
B. Barry Levy, B.A., B.R.E., M.A., Ph.D., Dean

Science
Martin Grant, Dean

Schools
Architecture
David Covo, B.Sc.Arch., M.B.Arch., O., Director

Communication Sciences & Disorders
Dr. Shari R. Baum, Director

Computer Science
Sue Whitesides, Director

Dietetics & Human Nutrition
Dr. Kristine G. Koski, Director

International Executive Institute
Peter Todd, Director

Library & Information Studies
France Bouthillier, Director

Nursing
Dr. Hélène Ezer, Acting Director

Physical & Occupational Therapy
Dr. Maureen J. Simmonds, Director

Social Work
Dr. Wendy Thomson, Director

Urban Planning
David Brown, Director

Affiliations
Macdonald Campus
21111, ch Bord-du-Lac Sainte-Anne-de-Bellevue, H9X 3V9 Canada
514-398-7707, Fax: 514-398-7766,
info.macdonald@mcgill.ca
www.mcgill.ca/macdonald/

Established in 1905, Macdonald College began as Canada's foremost institution for agricultural education. In 1972, it became the Macdonald Campus of McGill University & is the home of the University's Faculty of Agricultural & Environmental Sciences, the McGill School of Environment, & the School of Dietetics & Human Nutrition. Programmes leading to the degree of B.Sc.(Agr.), as well as graduate programs in agriculture, food, natural sciences, applied economics, environment, & engineering are offered.
Chandra A. Madramootoo, B.Sc., M.Sc., Ph.D., Dean, Fac. of Agricultural & Environmental Sc

The Montreal Diocesan Theological College
3475, rue University Montréal, H3A 2A8 Canada
514-849-3004, Fax: 514-849-4113,
info@dio-mdtc.ca
www.dio-mdtc.ca

An Anglican theological college founded in 1873. Affiliated with McGill Univ. & l'Univ. de Montréal. Degree courses: B.Th., Dip.Min, M.Div. Advanced degrees, offered through McGill: S.T.M, M.A., Ph.D. Distance education courses leading to the Cert. in Theology, or Licentiate in Theology also available.
The Rev. Canon John Simons, Principal

The Presbyterian College
Collège Presbytérien
3495, rue University Montréal, H3A 2A8 Canada
514-288-5256, Fax: 514-288-8072,
email@presbyteriancollege.ca
www.presbyteriancollege.ca

Founded in 1867 & affiliated with McGill Univ.
Rev. Dr. John A. Vissers, B.A., M.Div., Th.M., Th.D, Principal
jvissers@presbyteriancollege.ca
Rev. Dr. Dale Woods, B.A., M.C.S., M.Div., D.M, Director, Pastoral Studies
dwoods@presbyteriancollege.ca

Royal Victoria College
3425, rue University Montréal, H3A 2A8 Canada
514-398-6378, Fax: 514-398-4445,
www.mcgill.ca/residences/undergraduate/tour/rvc/
Enrollment: 266
Royal Victoria College is McGill's only all women's residence.

The United Theological College
Le Séminaire Uni
3521, rue University Montréal, H3A 2A9 Canada
514-849-2042, 888-849-2042
admin@utc.ca
www.utc.ca
A college of the United Church of Canada, committed to the training of persons, regardless of race, economic status, sexual orientation & gender identity, for various Christian ministries. Instruction in English & French is offered.
Philip L. Joudrey, M.Div., D.Min., Principal
pjoudrey@utc.ca
Michael Ryneveld, Registrar
mryneveld@utc.ca
Elisabeth Jones, M.Div., Th.M, Director of Studies
erjones@utc.ca

Publications
Debit Memo

The Faucet

The McGill News
c/o Graduates' Society
3605 Mountain St Montréal, H3G 2M1 Canada
Fax: 514-398-7338

The Reporter

The Tablet

Montréal: Télé-Université (Montréal)
#100, 4750, Henri-Julien Montréal, H2T 3E4 Canada
514-843-2015, Fax: 514-843-2160, 1-800-665-4333
info@teluq.ugam.ca
www.teluq.uquebec.ca
20,000 students in distance learning

Montréal: The United Theological College Le Séminaire Uni
3521, rue University Montréal, H3A 2A9 Canada
514-849-2042, Fax: 514-849-8634, 888-849-2042
admin@utc.ca
www.utc.ca

Montréal: Université de Montréal
Pavillon J-A.-DeSève
P.O. Box 6205
2332, boul Édouard-Montpetit Montréal, H3C 3T5 Canada
514-343-7076, Fax: 514-343-5788,
www.umontreal.ca
Enrollment: 55000
Facultés: Aménagement; Arts/Sciences; Droit; Éducation permanente; Études supérieures/postdoctorales; Médecine; Médecine dentaire; Médecine vétérinaire; Musique; Pharmacie; Sciences de l'éducation; Sciences infirmières; Théologie; Kinésiologie; Optometrie; Santé publique. Campus régionaux: Terrebonne; Ville de Laval; Longueuil; Québec.
Guy Breton, Recteur, 514-343-6776
guy.breton@umontreal.ca

Affiliations
École Polytechnique de Montréal
P.O. Box 6079 Centre-ville
Montréal, H3C 3A7 Canada
514-340-4711,
www.polymtl.ca
Enrollment: 4000
Fondée en 1873, Le Polytechnique est une école d'ingénierie de classe internationale; programmes au baccalauréat, cycles supérieurs, formation continue; recherche; l'École se trouve à 2900, boul Édouard-Montpetit, Campus de l'Univ. de Montréal, 2500 ch de Polytechnique.
Christophe Guy, ing., Ph.D., MACG, Directeur général

HEC Montréal
3000, ch de la Côte-Sainte-Catherine Montréal, H3T 2A7 Canada
514-340-6000, Fax: 514-340-6411,
www.hec.ca
Michel Patry, Directeur

Circuit
Presses de l'Université de Montréal
P.O. Box 6128 Centre-ville
Montréal, H3C 3J7
514-343-6388, Fax: 514-343-5727,
info@revuecircuit.ca
www.pum.umontreal.ca; www.revuecircuit.ca
Circuit, créée en 1989, publie des articles sur la musique contemporaine québécoise et internationale. Trois fois par année.
Jonathan Goldman, Rédacteur en chef

Études françaises
Presses de l'Université de Montréal
P.O. Box 6128 Centre-ville
Montréal, H3C 3J7
514-343-6933, Fax: 514-343-2232,
www.pum.umontreal.ca
Fondée en 1965; littératures de langue française, québécoises et internationales; critique et théorie. Trois fois par année.
Francis Gingras, Directeur

Pigeon Dissident
#A-2412, 3200, rue Jean-Brillant Montréal, H3T 1N8
514-343-6111, Fax: 514-343-5929,
info@pigeondissident.com
www.pigeondissident.com
Le journal des étudiants de la Faculté de droit, l'Université de Montréal. Six fois par année.
Takwa Souissi, Rédactrice en chef

Quartier Libre
P.O. Box 6128 Centre-ville
2350, boul Édouard-Montpetit Montréal, H3C 3J7
514-343-7630, Fax: 514-343-7744,
quartierlibre@hotmail.com
www.ql.umontreal.ca
Quartier Libre est le journal des étudiants de l'Université de Montréal, publié par Les Publications du Quartier Libre, une corporation sans but lucratif créée par des étudiants en 1992. Le version papier (bimensuel) est distribué gratuitement sur tout le campus de l'UM et dans ses environs.
Mikaëlle Monfort, Directrice
monfortmikaelle@hotmail.com

Montréal: Université du Québec à Montréal / UQAM
P.O. Box 8888 Centre-Ville
Montréal, H3C 3P8 Canada
514-987-3000,
general@uqam.ca
www.uqam.ca

Publications
L'Action

Journal U.Q.A.M

Le Temporel

Transactions

Unité

Uquam

Suites

Québec: École nationale d'administration publique
555, boul Charest est Québec, G1K 9E5 Canada
418-641-3000, Fax: 418-641-3060,
info@enap.ca
www.enap.ca
Enrollment: 1832
Campus: Québec, Montréal, Gatineau, Saguenay, Trois-Rivières

Québec: Institut national de la recherche scientifique (INRS)
490, rue de la Couronne Québec, G1K 9A9 Canada
418-654-4677, Fax: 418-654-2525,
lise.roy@adm.inrs.ca
www.inrs.uquebec.ca

Québec: Université du Québec
475, rue de l'Église Québec, G1K 9H7 Canada
418-657-3551, Fax: 418-657-2132,
cscuq@uqss.uquebec.ca
www.uquebec.ca
Guy Massicotte, Directeur
Pierre Moreau, Président
Michel Quimper, Secrétaire général
Serge Cabana, Directeur
Pierre Chenard, Directeur

Affiliations
Université du Québec en Abitibi-Témiscamingue
445, boul de l'Université Rouyn-Noranda, J9X 5E4 Canada
819-762-0971, Fax: 819-797-4727,
www.uqat.ca
Johanne Jean, Rectrice
Jean Turgeon, Secrétaire généal

Université du Québec à Chicoutimi
555, boul de l'Université Chicoutimi, G7H 2B1 Canada
418-545-5011, Fax: 418-545-5012,
www.uqac.uquebec.ca
Michel Belley, Recteur

Université du Québec en Outaouais
Pavillon Alexandre-Taché
P.O. Box 1250 Hull
283, boul Alexandre-Taché Gatineau, J8X 3X7 Canada
819-595-3900, Fax: 819-595-3924,
www.uqo.ca
Jean Vaillancourt, Recteur

Université du Québec à Montréal
P.O. Box 8888 Centre-Ville
Montréal, H3C 3P8 Canada
514-987-3000,
www.uqam.ca
Claude Corbo, Recteur

Université du Québec à Rimouski
300, allée des Ursulines Rimouski, G5L 3A1 Canada
418-723-1986,
uqar@uqar.qc.ca
www.uqar.qc.ca
Michel Ringuet, Recteur

Université du Québec à Trois-Rivières
P.O. Box 500 Bureau-chef
3351, boul des Forges Trois-Rivières, G9A 5H7 Canada
819-376-5011, Fax: 819-376-5012,
www.uqtr.ca
Ghislain Bourque, Recteur

École nationale d'administration publique
555, boul Charest est Québec, G1K 9E5 Canada
418-641-3000, Fax: 418-641-3055,
www.enap.ca
Marcel Proulx, Directeur général

École de technologie supérieure
1100, rue Notre-Dame ouest Montréal, H3C 1K3 Canada
514-396-8800, Fax: 514-396-8950,
www.etsmtl.ca
Yves Beauchamp, Directeur général

Institut Armand-Frappier
531, boul des Prairies Laval, H7V 1B7 Canada
450-687-5010, Fax: 450-686-5501,
www.iaf.inrs.ca

Institut national de la recherche scientifique (INRS)
490, rue de la Couronne Québec, G1K 9A9 Canada
418-654-4677, Fax: 418-654-2525
Lise Roy, Communications
lise.roy@adm.inrs.ca
Yvonne Boisvert, Registraire
yvonne.boisvert@adm.inrs.ca

Télé-université
P.O. Box 4800 Terminus
455, rue de l'Église Québec, G1K 9H5 Canada
418-657-2747, Fax: 418-657-2094,
info@teluq.uquebec.ca
www.teluq.uquebec.ca/
Louise Bertrand, Directrice générale

Télé-Université (Montréal)
#100, 4750, Henri-Julien Montréal, H2T 3E4 Canada
514-843-2015, Fax: 514-843-2160

Publications
Réseau/U.Q. Network

Québec: Université Laval
Cité universitaire Québec, G1K 7P4 Canada
418-656-3333, Fax: 418-656-5920, 1-877-785-2825
info@ulaval.ca
www.ulaval.ca
Enrollment: 38500
Première université francophone d'Amerique, ouverte sur le monde et animée d'une culture de l'exigence, l'Université Laval contribue au développement de la société par la formation de personnes compétentes, responsables et promotrice de changement, par l'avancement et le partage des connaissances, dans un environnement dynamique de recherche et de création
Denis Brière, Recteur

Campuses
Service des communications
Pavillon Alphonse-Desjardins.
#3577, Université de Laval Laval, G1K 7P4 Canada
Fax: 418-656-2809
Richard Fournier, Directeur

Publications
Au Fil des Evénements
#214, Tour des Arts Québec, G1K 7P4 Canada
Fax: 418-529-0649

Impact Campus

Rimouski: Université du Québec à Rimouski
P.O. Box 3300 A
300, allée des Ursulines Rimouski, G5L 3A1 Canada
418-723-1986, Fax: 041-872-4152, 1-800-511-3382
uqar@uqar.qc.ca
www.uqar.ca

Publications
U.Q.A.R. Information

Uquarium

Rouyn-Noranda: Université du Québec en Abitibi-Témiscamingue
445, boul de l'Université Rouyn-Noranda, J9X 5E4 Canada
819-762-0971, Fax: 819-797-4727,
www.uqat.ca

Publications
Le Voyeur

Sainte-Anne-de-Bellevue: Macdonald Campus
21111, ch Bord-du-Lac Sainte-Anne-de-Bellevue, H9X 3V9 Canada
514-398-7707, Fax: 514-398-7766,
info.macdonald@mcgill.ca
www.mcgill.ca/macdonald/
Houses McGill University's Faculty of Agricultural & Environmental Sciences.

Sherbrooke: Bishop's University
2600 College St. Sherbrooke, J1M 1Z7 Canada
819-822-9600, Fax: 819-822-9661,
www.ubishops.ca
Enrollment: 2263
Michael Goldbloom, Principal/Vice-Chancellor 2611
principal@ubishops.ca
Isabelle Goyette, Dir., Finance 2656
isablle.goyette@ubishops.ca
Yves Jodoin, Registrar/Sec.-General 2676
yves.jodoin@ubishops.ca

Sherbrooke: Université de Sherbrooke
2500, boul de l'Université Sherbrooke, J1K 2R1 Canada
819-821-7686,
information@usherbrooke.ca
www.usherbrooke.ca

Denis Marceau, Vice-recteur
Edwin Bourget, Vice-recteur
Jean Desclos, Vice-recteur
Martin Buteau, Vice-recteur
Roger Noël, Doyen
Bruno-Marie Béchard, Recteur
Luce Samoisette, Rectrice adjointe et vice-rectrice à l'admini
Daniel Proulx, Doyen
Céline Garant, Doyenne
Paul Deshaies, Doyen
Linda Bellalite, Doyenne
Dr. Réjean Hébert, Doyen
Donald Thomas, Doyen
Gérard Lachiver, Doyen
Marc Dumas, Doyen
Sylvie Belzile, Directrice
Jacques Labrecque, Directeur
Christian Gagnon, Directeur
Serge Cabana, Directeur
Renald Mercier, Directeur
René Alarie, Directeur
Luc Bédard, Directeur
Pierre Lemieux, Directeur
France Myette, Registraire
Lise Grenier, Directrice
Gilles Bilodeau, Directeur
Daniel Dupont, Directeur
Mario Laforest, Directeur
Michèle Desrochers, Directrice
Denis Marceau, Directeur (par interim)
Serge Fortier, Directeur
François Dubé, Directeur (par intérim)

Publications
Bilan

La Sagace

Liaison

Sommets
2500, boul de l'Université Sherbrooke, J1K 2R1 Canada
Fax: 819-821-7900

Trois-Rivières: Université du Québec à Trois-Rivières
P.O. Box 500
3351, boul des Forges Trois-Rivières, G9A 5H7 Canada
819-376-5011, Fax: 819-376-5210, 1-800-365-0922
communications@uqtr.ca
www.uqtr.ca
Enrollment: 11000

Publications
En Tete

Le Voyeur

Colleges

Alma: Collège d'Alma
675, boul Auger ouest Alma, G8B 2B7 Canada
418-668-2387, Fax: 418-668-7336,
college@calma.qc.ca
www.calma.qc.ca
Grades: Préuniv., Techniques, Form. cont.
Jean Paradis, Directeur générale

Publications
Le Majeur

Gatineau: Heritage College
325, boul Cité des Jeunes Gatineau, J8Y 6T3 Canada
819-778-2270, Fax: 819-778-7364,
www.cegep-heritage.qc.ca
Enrollment: 1387
Career Programs (Nursing; Early Childhood Ed.; New Media & Publication Design; Electronics; Computer Science); Pre-University Programs: Liberal Arts, Sciences, Commerce, Social Sciences, Visual Arts; Continuing Ed.: French as a Second Language; Distance Education; Corporate Training.
Louise Brunet, Director General
dg@cegep-heritage.qc.ca

La Pocatière: Institut de technologie agroalimentaire
Campus de La Pocatière
401, rue Poiré La Pocatière, G0R 1Z0 Canada
418-856-1110, Fax: 418-856-1719,
scitalp@mapaq.gouv.qc.ca
www.ita.qc.ca
Enrollment: 1000
Spécialisé en agroalimentaire; Campus de Saint-Hyacinthe: 3230, rue Sicotte, (450) 778-6504; Collège Macdonald, Univ. McGill.
Rosaire Ouellet, Directeur général

Campuses
Campus de Saint-Hyacinthe
P.O. Box 70
3230, rue Sicotte Saint-Hyacinthe, J2S 7B3 Canada
450-778-6504, Fax: 450-778-6536,
ita.st.hyacinthe@mapaq.gouv.qc.ca
www.ita.qc.ca

Laval: Collège Montmorency
475, boul de l'Avenir Laval, H7N 5H9 Canada
450-975-6100, Fax: 450-975-6116,
info.programmes@cmontmorecy.qc.ca
www.cmontmorency.qc.ca
Denyse Blanchet, Directrice générale

Publications
Le Zèle

Lévis: Collège de Lévis
9, rue Monseigneur Gosselin Lévis, G6V 5K1 Canada
418-833-1249, Fax: 418-833-1974,
info@collegedelevis.qc.ca
www.collegedelevis.qc.ca
Grades: Sec.
David Lehoux, Directeur général

Publications
Le Script

Longueuil: Collège Édouard-Montpetit
945, ch de Chambly Longueuil, J4H 3M6 Canada
450-679-2631, Fax: 450-679-5570,
communications@college-em.qc.ca
www.college-em.qc.ca
Serge Brasset, Directeur général

Publications
Le Motdit

Montréal: Collège Ahuntsic
9155, rue St-Hubert Montréal, H2M 1Y8 Canada
514-389-5921, Fax: 514-389-5762,
www.collegeahuntsic.qc.ca
Enrollment: 10100
Roch Tremblay, Directeur général

Publications
L'Attribut

Le Misanthrope

Montréal: Collège Dawson
3040, rue Sherbrooke ouest Montréal, H3Z 1A4 Canada
514-931-8731, Fax: 514-931-5181,
www.dawsoncollege.qc.ca
Enrollment: 10000
Richard Filion, Dir. gén.

Publications
Plant

Montréal: Collège de Bois-de-Boulogne
10555, av de Bois-de-Boulogne Montréal, H4N 1L4 Canada
514-332-3000, Fax: 514-332-5857,
communications@bdeb.qc.ca
www.bdeb.qc.ca
Grades: Préuniv., Techniques, Form. cont.
Maurice Piché, Directeur général

Publications
L'Infomane

Montréal: Collège de Maisonneuve
3800, rue Sherbrooke est Montréal, H1X 2A2 Canada
514-254-7131, Fax: 514-253-7637,
communic@cmaisonneuve.qc.ca
www.cmaisonneuve.qc.ca
Grades: Préuniv., Techniques
Enrollment: 3398
Pierre Harrison, Directeur général

Publications
Le Trait d'Union

Montréal: Collège de Rosemont
6400, 16e av Montréal, H1X 2S9 Canada
514-376-1620, Fax: 514-376-1440,
regist@crosemont.qc.ca
www.crosemont.qc.ca
Patricia Hanigan, Directrice générale

Publications
République étudiante

Montréal: Collège Jean-de-Brébeuf inc.
3200, ch Côte Ste-Catherine Montréal, H3T 1C1 Canada
514-342-9342, Fax: 514-342-6607,
diradm@brebeuf.qc.ca
www.brebeuf.qc.ca
Grades: Sec., Collégial
Michel April, Directeur, Services administratifs

Publications
Le Grafitti

Montréal: École Polytechnique de Montréal
Université de Montréal
2900, boul Édouard-Montpetit Montréal, H3T 1J4 Canada
514-340-4711,
www.polymtl.ca
Enrollment: 4000
Fondée en 1873, le Polytechnique est une école d'ingénierie de classes internationale; programmes au baccalauréat, cycles supérieures, formation continue; recherche. Adresse postale: CP 6079, succ. Centre-ville, Montréal, QC H3C 3A7.

Publications
Le Polyscope

Montréal: HEC Montréal
3000, ch de la Côte-Sainte-Catherine Montréal, H3T 2A7 Canada
514-340-6000, Fax: 514-340-6411,
webmestre@hec.ca
www.hec.ca
Grades: Bacc., MBA, LL.M., M.Sc., Ph.D.
Enrollment: 12000
La première école de gestion au Canada, fondée en 1907

Publications
Le Caducée
#310, 3333 Queen Mary Rd Montréal, H3V 1A2 Canada
Fax: 514-340-6508

L'Intérêt

Montréal: Institut de tourisme et d'hôtellerie du Québec
3535, rue Saint-Denis Montréal, H2X 3P1 Canada
514-282-5108, Fax: 514-282-5126,
administration@ithq.qc.ca
www.ithq.qc.ca
Lucille Daoust, Directrice

Montréal: The Montreal Diocesan Theological College
3475, rue University Montréal, H3A 2A8 Canada
514-849-3004, Fax: 514-849-4113,
info@dio-mdtc.ca
www.dio-mdtc.ca

Montréal: The Presbyterian College Collège Presbytérien
3495, rue University Montréal, H3A 2A8 Canada
514-288-5256, Fax: 514-288-8072,
email@presbyteriancollege.ca
www.presbyteriancollege.ca
Enrollment: 70

Québec: Direction générale du Conservatoire de musique et d'art dramatique du Québec
Bloc C
225, Grande Allée est, 3e étage Québec, G1R 5G5 Canada
418-380-2327, Fax: 418-380-2328,
info@conservatoire.gouv.qc.ca
www.conservatoire.gouv.qc.ca

Campuses
Conservatoire de musique de Saguenay
202, rue Jacques-Cartier est Chicoutimi, G7H 6R8 Canada
Fax: 418-698-3521,
info@conservatoire.gouv.qc.ca
www.conservatoire.gouv.qc.ca/saguenay/index.asp
Jacques Clément, Directeur

Conservatoire de musique de Gatineau
430, boul Alexandre-Taché Gatineau, J9A 1M7 Canada
819-772-3283, Fax: 819-772-3346,
info@conservatoire.gouv.qc.ca
www.conservatoire.gouv.qc.ca/gatineau/index.asp
Danielle Dubé, Directrice

Conservatoire de musique de Montréal
4750, av Henri-Julien Montréal, H2T 2C8 Canada
514-873-4031, Fax: 514-873-4601,
info@conservatoire.gouv.qc.ca
http://www.conservatoire.gouv.qc.ca/montreal/index.asp
Isolde Lagacé, Directrice

Conservatoire de musique de Québec
270, rue St-Amable Québec, G1R 5G1 Canada
418-643-2190, Fax: 418-644-9658,
info@conservatoire.gouv.qc.ca
www.conservatoire.gouv.qc.ca/quebec/index.asp
André Picard, Directeur

Conservatoire de musique de Rimouski
22, rue Sainte-Marie Rimouski, G5L 4E2 Canada
418-727-3706, Fax: 418-727-3818,
info@conservatoire.gouv.qc.ca
www.conservatoire.gouv.qc.ca/rimouski/
Benoît Plourde, Directeur

Conservatoire de musique de Trois-Rivières
587, rue Radisson Trois-Rivières, G9A 2C8 Canada
Fax: 819-371-6955,
info@conservatoire.gouv.qc.ca
www.conservatoire.gouv.qc.ca/trois-rivieres
Pierre Normandin, Directeur

Conservatoire de musique de Val-d'Or
88, rue Allard Val-d'Or, J9P 2Y1 Canada
819-354-4585, Fax: 819-354-4297,
info@conservatoire.gouv.qc.ca
www.conservatoire.gouv.qc.ca/val-dor/
Jean Saint-Jules, Directeur

Conservatoire d'art dramatique de Montréal
4750, av Henri-Julien Montréal, H2T 2C8 Canada
514-873-4283, Fax: 514-873-4601,
info@conservatoire.gouv.qc.ca
www.conservatoire.gouv.qc.ca/cadm/
Gilbert Lepage, Directeur

Conservatoire d'art dramatique de Québec
31, rue Mont-Carmel Québec, G1R 4A6 Canada
Fax: 418-646-9255,
info@conservatoire.gouv.qc.ca
www.conservatoire.gouv.qc.ca/cadq/
André Jean, Directeur (par intérim)

Saint-Laurent: Vanier College
821, av Ste-Croix Saint-Laurent, H4L 3X9 Canada
514-744-7500, Fax: 514-744-7505,
info@vaniercollege.qc.ca
www.vaniercollege.qc.ca
Enrollment: 6100
An English Cégep.
Gilbert Héroux, Dir. gén.
John McMahon, Dean

Publications
The Echo

Vanier Phoenix

The Vanier Vandoo

Sainte-Geneviève: Collège Gérald-Godin
15615, boul Gouin ouest Sainte-Geneviève, H9H 5K8 Canada
514-626-2666, Fax: 514-626-6866,
information@cgodin.qc.ca
www.college-gerald-godin.qc.ca
Enrollment: 1125
Pierre Schetagne, Directeur général

Sainte-Thérèse: Le Collège Lionel-Groulx
100, rue Duquet Sainte-Thérèse, J7E 3G6 Canada
450-430-3120, Fax: 450-971-7883,
info@clg.qc.ca
www.clg.qc.ca
Grades: Préuniv., Techniques, Form. cont.
Enrollment: 4109
Monique Laurin, Directrice générale

Publications
L'Écorché

Salaberry-de-Valleyfield: Collège de Valleyfield
169, rue Champlain Salaberry-de-Valleyfield, J6T 1X6 Canada
450-373-9441, Fax: 450-377-7719,
courrier@colval.qc.ca
www.colval.qc.ca
Jacques Turgeon, Directeur général

Publications
Pars ailleurs

Shawinigan: Collège Shawinigan
P.O. Box 610
2263, av du Collège Shawinigan, G9N 6V8 Canada
819-539-6401, Fax: 819-539-8819,
information@collegeshawinigan.qc.ca
www.collegeshawinigan.qc.ca
Enrollment: 1500
Jean Lefebvre, Directeur général par intérim

Publications
Journal l'actif

Sherbrooke: Champlain Regional College
P.O. Box 5000
1301, boul Portland Sherbrooke, J1H 5N1 Canada
819-564-3600, Fax: 819-564-3639,
lmillette@abacom.com
www.champlaincollege.qc.ca
Gerald R. Cutting, Directeur général

Campuses
Campus Lennoxville
P.O. Box 5003
2580 College St. Lennoxville, J1M 0C8 Canada
819-564-3666, Fax: 819-564-5171,
admissions@crc-lennox.qc.ca
www.crc-lennox.qc.ca

Campus St. Lambert
900, av Riverside Saint-Lambert, J4P 3P2 Canada
450-672-7360, Fax: 450-672-9299,
InfoCenter@champlaincollege.qc.ca
www.champlainonline.com

Campus St. Lawrence
790, rue Nérée-Tremblay Sainte-Foy, G1V 4K2 Canada
418-656-6921, Fax: 418-656-6925,
slccegep@slc.qc.ca
www.slc.qc.ca

Post Secondary/Technical

Post Secondary/Technical

Brossard: Academy of Arts and Design Académie des arts et de design
7305, Marie-Victorin, 2e étage Brossard, J4W 1A6 Canada
514-875-9777, 800-268-9777
www.aadmtl.com
Fashion Design, Fashion Merchandising, Interior Design, Advertising & Web Design, Animation Design. Instruction in French & English.
Serge Landry, Directeur général

Drummondville: Collège Ellis
235, rue Moisan Drummondville, J2C 1W9 Canada
819-477-3113, Fax: 819-477-4556,
www.ellis.qc.ca
Les installations du Pensionnat de Drummondville passent au Collège Ellis en 2006. Campus Trois-Rivières: 90, rue Dorval, (819) 691-2600.
Alain Scalzo, Directeur général

Laval: Collège CDI Administration. Technologie. Santé / ICD
#400, 3, place Laval Laval, H7N 1A2 Canada
450-662-9090, Fax: 450-662-0741, 1-800-961-417
martin.gascon@cdi.ca
www.cicdi.ca
Enrollment: 380
Martin Gascon, Directeur

Campuses
Montréal
#700, 416, boul de Maisonneuve ouest Montréal, H3A 1L2 Canada
Fax: 514-849-9034

Québec
#20, 905, av Honoré-Mercier Québec, G1R 5M6 Canada
Fax: 418-694-9082

Montréal: Les Ateliers de danse moderne de Montréal
#201, 372, rue Ste-Catherine ouest Montréal, H3B 1A2 Canada
514-866-9814, Fax: 514-866-5887,
reception@ladmmi.com
www.ladmmi.com
Christine Bouchard, Directrice générale

Montréal: CDI College of Business, Technology & Healthcare
416, boul De Maisonneuve ouest, 7e étage Montréal, H3A 1L2 Canada
514-849-4757, Fax: 514-849-9034,
www.cdicollege.com
Computers, accounting & business training; 5 locations across Québec

Montréal: Collège André-Gasset
1001 Crémazie est Montréal, H2M 1M3 Canada
514-381-4293, Fax: 514-381-7421,
inform@grasset.qc.ca
www.grasset.qc.ca/index.htm
Pascal Nadon

Montréal: Collège d'enseignement en immobilier inc.
255, boul Crémazie est Montréal, H2M 1M2 Canada
514-905-1551, Fax: 514-904-1453,
info@enseignementimmobilier.com
Shirley Soulard, Directeur général
ssoulard@enseignementimmobilier.com

Montréal: Collège d'informatique Marsan
1001, boul de Maisonneuve est, 9e étage Montréal, H2L 4P9 Canada
514-525-3030, Fax: 514-525-3314,
info@collegemarsan.qc.ca
www.collegemarsan.qc.ca
Carlos Richer, Directeur général

Montréal: Collège de photographie Marsan
1001, boul de Maisonneuve est, 9e étage Montréal, H2L 4P9 Canada
514-525-2352, Fax: 514-525-3314,
info@collegemarsan.qc.ca
www.collegemarsan.qc.ca
Carlos Richer, Directeur général

Montréal: College Inter Dec
2120, rue Ste-Catherine ouest Montréal, H3H 1M7 Canada

514-939-4444, Fax: 514-939-0762,
InterdecInfo@clasalle.com
www.interdec.qc.ca
Chrystel Jacquot-Donnat, Dir.

***Montréal:* Collège Jean-de-Brébeuf**
3200, ch Sainte-Catherine Montréal, H3T 1C1 Canada
514-342-1320, Fax: 514-342-7169,
sadm@brebeuf.qc.ca
www.brebeuf.qc.ca
Jean-Claude Gaudet, Directeur général

***Montréal:* Collège LaSalle**
2000, rue Sainte-Catherine ouest Montréal, H3H 2T2 Canada
514-939-2006, Fax: 514-939-2015,
admission@clasalle.com
www.clasalle.qc.ca/fr/index.html
Jacques Marchand, Directeur général

***Montréal:* Collège Salette**
418, rue Sherbrooke Est, 3e étage Montréal, H2L 1J6 Canada
514-388-5725, Fax: 514-388-5957,
info@collegesalette.qc.ca
www.collegesalette.qc.ca
Graphic design & computer graphics

***Montréal:* L'École Du Show-Business**
#3010, 5505, boul Saint-Laurent Montréal, H2T 1S6 Canada
514-271-2244, Fax: 514-271-2434,
info@ecoledushowbusiness.com
www.ecoledushowbusiness.com
Richard Blin, Directeur général

***Montréal:* École nationale de cirque**
National Circus School
8181, 2e av Montréal, H1Z 4N9 Canada
514-982-0859, Fax: 514-982-6025,
info@enc.qc.ca
www.enc.qc.ca
Marc Lalonde, Dir.

***Montréal:* École nationale de l'humour**
2120, rue Sherbrooke est, 7e étage Montréal, H2K 1C3 Canada
514-849-7876, Fax: 514-849-3307,
humour@enh.qc.ca
www.enh.qc.ca
Formation professionnelle aux humoristes & aux auteurs. Reconnue par le Min. de l'Éducation, du Loisir & du Sport du Québec.
Louise Richer, Directrice générale

***Montréal:* École supérieure de ballet contemporain**
4816, rue Rivard Montréal, H2J 2N6 Canada
514-849-4929, Fax: 514-849-6107,
info@enbc.org
www.enbc.org
Didier Chirpaz, Dir. gén.

***Montréal:* Herzing College**
1616, boul René-Lévesque ouest Montréal, H3H 1P8 Canada
450-686-7494, Fax: 450-933-6182,
info@mtl.herzing.edu
www.herzing.edu/campus_info/
Career training programs
Hayat Drinali, Directeur général

***Montréal:* Institut de création artistique et de recherche en infographie ICARI inc.**
55, av Mont Royal ouest, 5e étage Montréal, H2T 2S6 Canada
514-982-0922, Fax: 514-982-0288,
info@icari.com
www.icari.qc.ca
Mariam Ladha, Directrice générale

***Montréal:* Institut supérieur d'informatique I.S.I.**
#100, 255, boul Crémazie est Montréal, H2M 1M2 Canada
514-842-2426, Fax: 514-842-2084,
info@isi-mtl.com
www.isi-mtl.com
Henriette Morin

***Montréal:* Institut supérieur de design de mode I.S.D.M. inc.**
6920, rue St-Hubert, 2e étage Montréal, H2S 2H2 Canada
514-274-1092, Fax: 514-270-0333,
info@isdm-mode.com
www.isdm-mode.com
Phuc Tran-Huu, Directeur général
phuctran@aei.ca

***Montréal:* Institut Teccart (2003)**
3030, rue Hochelaga Montréal, H1W 1G2 Canada
514-526-2501, Fax: 514-526-9192,
nehajibi@teccart.qc.ca
www.teccart.qc.ca
Nour-Eddine Hajibi

***Montréal:* The International College of Spiritual & Psychic Sciences**
P.O. Box 1445 H
1974, boul de Maisonneuve ouest Montréal, H3G 2N3 Canada
514-937-8359, Fax: 514-937-5380,
iiihs@iiihs.org
www.iiihs.org
Dr. Marilyn Zwaig Rossner, Ph.D., Dean
mrossner@iiihs.org

***Montréal:* Marianopolis College**
3880, Côte-des-Neiges Montréal, H3H 1W1 Canada
514-931-8792, Fax: 514-931-8790,
www.marianopolis.edu
Sr. Françoise Boisvert, Dir. gén.

Publications
The Papercut

***Montréal:* National Theatre School of Canada**
École nationale de théâtre du Canada
5030, rue St-Denis Montréal, H2J 2L8 Canada
514-842-7954, Fax: 514-842-5661, 1-866-547-732
info@ent-nts.qc.ca
www.ent-nts.qc.ca
Enrollment: 160
Offers training in acting, playwriting, directing, set & costume design & technical production in both English & French.
Simon Brault, O.C., CEO

***Montréal:* Trebas Institute**
Institut Trebas
Tour Est
550, rue Sherbrooke ouest, 6e étage Montréal, H3A 1B9 Canada
514-845-4141, Fax: 514-845-2581,
infomtl@trebas.com
www.trebas.com
Enrollment: 200
David P. Leonard, Président

***Outremont:* École de Musique Vincent d'Indy**
628, ch Côte Ste-Catherine Outremont, H2V 2C5 Canada
514-735-5261, Fax: 514-735-5266,
info@isdm-mode.com
www.emvi.qc.ca
Kathleen Caissy, Directrice générale

***Québec:* Collège Mérici**
755, ch St-Louis Québec, G1S 1C1 Canada
418-683-1591, Fax: 418-682-8938,
information@college-merici.qc.ca
www.college-merici.qc.ca
Pierre L'Heureux, Directeur général

***Québec:* Collège radio télévision de Québec inc.**
751, côte d'Abraham Québec, G1R 1A2 Canada
418-647-2095, Fax: 418-522-5456,
christian.lavoie@crtq.net
www.crtq.net
Christian Lavoie, Dir.

***Québec:* L'École de danse de Québec**
#214, 310, boul Langelier Québec, G1K 5N3 Canada
418-649-4715, Fax: 418-649-4702,
info.edq@qc.aira.com
www.ecolededansedequebec.qc.ca
Professional training in contemporary dance performance, 3-year, full-time, post-secondary level
Dominique Turcotte, Director

***Saint-Hubert:* Académie de l'Entrepreneurship Québécois inc.**
4619, rue de Niverville Saint-Hubert, J3Y 9G6 Canada
450-676-5826, Fax: 450-676-2261,
info@academieentrepreneurship.com
www.academieentrepreneurship.com
Johanne Bouchard

***Trois-Rivières:* Collège Laflèche**
1687, boul du Carmel Trois-Rivières, G8Z 3R8 Canada
819-375-7346, Fax: 819-375-7347,
college@clafleche.qc.ca
www.clafleche.qc.ca
Marcel Côté, Directeur général

***Verdun:* Collège de l'immobilier du Québec**
600, ch du Golf Verdun, H3E 1A8 Canada
514-762-1862, Fax: 514-762-4975,
francine.forget@cigm.qc.ca
www.collegeimmobilier.com
Francine Forget, Directrice générale

***Ville Mont-Royal:* Collège Technique de Montréal**
#204, Royalmount Ville Mont-Royal, H4P 1H7 Canada
514-932-6444, Fax: 514-932-6448,
info@mtccollege.com
www.mtccollege.com

***Westmount:* International Career School Canada**
#610, 245 Victoria Ave. Westmount, H3Z 2M6 Canada
514-482-6951, Fax: 514-482-6868, 1-888-427-2400
info@icslearn.ca
www.icslearn.ca
Enrollment: 12875
At-home training in 50 career fields.

Saskatchewan

Government Agencies

***Regina:* Saskatchewan Advanced Education & Employment**
2220 College Ave. Regina, S4P 4V9 Canada
306-787-6030, Fax: 306-798-2045, 1-888-775-327
www.aee.gov.sk.ca

***Regina:* Saskatchewan Learning**
2220 College Ave. Regina, S4P 4V9 Canada
306-787-6030, Fax: 306-798-2045, 1-888-775-3276
learninginquiry@sasked.gov.sk.ca
www.sasklearning.gov.sk.ca

Campuses
Region One
4635 Wascana Parkway Regina, S4P 3A3 Canada
306-798-6071, Fax: 306-787-6139
Tom Chell, Regional Director

Region Two
350 Cheadle St. West Swift Current, S9H 4G3 Canada
306-778-8249, Fax: 306-778-8583
Wanda Biffart, Regional Director

Region Three
4635 Wascana Pkwy. Regina, S4P 3V7 Canada
306-787-6075, Fax: 306-787-6139
Wayne Back, Regional Director

Region Four
Sturdy Stone Bldg.
122 - 3 Ave. North, 8th Fl. Saskatoon, S7K 2H6 Canada
306-933-5028, Fax: 306-933-7469
Crandall Hrynkiw, Regional Director

Region Five
P.O. Box 6500
107 Crawford Ave. East Melfort, S0E 1A0 Canada
306-752-6166, Fax: 306-752-6168
Darlene Thompson, Regional Director

Region Six
1146 - 102 St. North Battleford, S9A 1E9 Canada
306-446-7435, Fax: 306-446-7586
Dr. Lois Duffee, Regional Director

Northern Region Office- La Ronge
P.O. Box 5000
La Ronge, S0J 1L0 Canada
306-425-4380, Fax: 306-425-4383, 1-800-667-4380
Kevin (Toby Greschner, Regional Director

School Boards/Districts/Divisions

Public

***Creighton:* Creighton School Division #111**
P.O. Box 158
325 Main St. Creighton, S0P 0A0 Canada
306-688-5825, Fax: 306-688-3131
Enrollment: 394
Austin Gerein, Dir.
Shirley Owen, Sec.-Treas.

***Englefeld:* Engelfeld Protestant Separate School Division #132**
P.O. Box 100
Englefeld, S0K 1N0 Canada
306-287-3568, Fax: 306-287-3569
Enrollment: 107
Jim Martin, Sec.-Treas.

Harvey Bowers, Dir.

Ile-a-la-Crosse: Ile a la Crosse School Division #112
P.O. Box 89
Ile-a-la-Crosse, S0M 1C0 Canada
306-833-2141, Fax: 306-833-2104

Enrollment: 469
Christine Arnett, Sec.-Treas.
carnett@icsd.ca
Lon Borgerson, Director of Education
lborgerson@icsd.ca

La Ronge: Northern Lights School Division #113
Bag Service #6500 La Ronge, S0J 1L0 Canada
306-425-3302, Fax: 306-425-3377,
centraloffice@nlsd113.net
www.nlsd113.com

Grades: K.-12
Enrollment: 4168
Ralph Pilz, Dir.
ralphpilz@nlsd113.net
Charlie McCloud, Sec.-Treas.
charliemccloud@nlsd113.net
Julius Park, First Nations/Metis Education Consultant
juliuspark@nlsd113.net

Langian: Horizon School Division #205
P.O. Box 100
110 main st. Langian, S0K 2M0 Canada
306-365-4888, Fax: 306-365-2808, 877-365-4888
www.hzsd.ca

Enrollment: 6992
Marc Danylchuk, Director of Education
Philip Benson, Sec.-Treas.

Melfort: North East School Division #200
P.O. Box 6000
402 Main St. Melfort, S0E 1A0 Canada
306-752-5741, Fax: 306-752-1933, 888-752-5741
www.nesd.ca

Grades: Pre-K.-12
Enrollment: 5317
Don Rempel, Dir.
Ralph Paquin, Supt. of Bus. Admin., 306-752-1211, fax: 306-752-4580

Melville: St. Henry's Roman Catholic Separate School Division #5
P.O. Box 1930
633 Main St. Melville, S0A 2P0 Canada
306-728-4426, Fax: 306-728-2351

Enrollment: 309
This division amalgamated with Yorkton RCSSD #86, St. Theodore RCSSD #138 Melville Rural RCSSD #217 and Yorkton Rural RCSSD #216 to form the new Christ the Teacher Roman Catholic Separate School Division #212.
Brian Boechler, Dir.
Wilfred Hotsko, Sec.-Treas.

Moose Jaw: Holy Trinity Roman Catholic Separate School Division #22
P.O. Box 1087
502 - 6 Ave. NE Moose Jaw, S6H 4P8 Canada
306-694-5333, Fax: 306-692-2238,
www.htcsd.ca

Enrollment: 2080
Celeste York, Director of Education
Gerry Gieni, Sec.-Treas.

Moose Jaw: Prairie South School Division #210
15 Thatcher Dr. East Moose Jaw, S6J 1L8 Canada
306-694-1200, Fax: 306-694-4955, 877-434-1200
www.prairiesouth.ca

Enrollment: 6931
Brenda Edwards, Director of Education
Gordon Stewart, Chair

North Battleford: Living Sky School Division #202
509 Pioneer Ave. North Battleford, S9A 4A5 Canada
306-937-7702, Fax: 306-445-4332,
office@lskysd.ca
www.lskysd.ca

Grades: K.-12
Enrollment: 5550
Ron Ford, Dir., 306-937-7909
ron.ford@lskysd.ca
Ray Kopera, CFO, 306-937-7702
ray.kopera@lskysd.ca

North Battleford: North West Roman Catholic Separate School Division #16
9301 - 19 Ave. North Battleford, S9A 3N5 Canada
306-445-6158, Fax: 306-445-3993,
loccsd@loccsd.ca
www.loccsd.ca

Grades: Pre-K.-12
Enrollment: 1968
This school division is an amalgamation of 4 boards: North Battleford RCSSD#16, Wilkie St. George RCSSD#85, Unity RCSSD#88 and Spiritwood RCSSD#82.
Herb Sutton, Dir.
h.sutton@loccsd.ca
Guy Denton, Supt. of Admin.
g.denton@loccsd.ca

Prince Albert: Prince Albert Roman Catholic Separate School Division #6
118 - 11 St. East Prince Albert, S6V 1A1 Canada
306-953-7500, Fax: 306-763-1723,
info@cec.pacsd6.sk.ca
www.pacsd6.sk.ca

Enrollment: 3121
Tim Jelinski, Director of Education
Don Orr, Sec.-Treas.

Prince Albert: Saskatchewan Rivers School Division #119
545 - 11 St. East Prince Albert, S6V 1B1 Canada
306-764-1571, Fax: 306-763-4460,
www.srsd119.ca

Enrollment: 9200
Dr. William O. Cooke, Director of Education
D. A.. Moniuk, Sec.-Treas.

Regina: Division scolaire francophone #310
#200, 3850 Hillsdale St. Regina, S4S 7J5 Canada
306-757-7541, Fax: 306-757-2040,
www.dsf.sk.ca/

Enrollment: 1095
Denis Ferré, Dir.
Lise Gareau, Sec.-Treas.

Regina: Prairie Valley School Division #208
P.O. Box 1937
3080 Albert St. North Regina, S4P 3E1 Canada
306-949-3366, Fax: 306-543-1771,
reception@pvsd.ca
www.pvsd.ca

Enrollment: 8292
Ben J. Grebinski, Director
Michael Back, Sec.-Treas.

Regina: Regina Roman Catholic Separate School Division #81
2160 Cameron St. Regina, S4T 2V6 Canada
306-791-7200, Fax: 306-347-7699,
rcs@rcs.sk.ca
www.rcsd.ca

Grades: K-12
Enrollment: 10000
Gwen Keith, Director
Curt Van Parys, Sec.-Treas.

Regina: Regina School Division #4
1600 - 4 Ave. Regina, S4R 8C8 Canada
306-523-3000, Fax: 306-532-3031,
info@rbe.sk.ca
www.rbe.sk.ca

Enrollment: 20678
Don Hoium, Director
Debra Burnett, Sec.-Treas.

Rosetown: Sun West School Division #207
P.O. Box 700
Rosetown, S0L 2V0 Canada
306-882-2677, Fax: 306-882-3366, 1-866-375-2677
info@sunwestsd.ca
www.sunwestsd.ca

Grades: Kindergarten - 12
Enrollment: 4500
Number of Schools: 14 kindergarten to grade 12 schools; 15 Hutterite colony schools; 7 elementary schools; 3 secondary schools; 1 distance education centre
Lorne Ulven, Chair
Janet Casswell-Beckmann, Director, Education, 306-882-2677
janet.casswell-beckmann@sunwestsd.ca
Tony Baldwin, Superintendent, Education
Cheryl Bashutski, Superintendent, Education
Tracy Dollansky, Superintendent, Education
Lynne Dressler, Superintendent, Education
Maureen Sample, Superintendent, Business
Mike Fedyk, Officer, Communications
Michelle Leith, Officer, Human Resources
Doug Klassen, Supervisor, Technology
Earl McKnight, Supervisor, Transportation
Rob Minion, Supervisor, Facilities
Rhonda Saathoff, Supervisor, Business

Saskatoon: Greater Saskatoon Catholic Schools
420 - 22nd St. East Saskatoon, S7K 1X3 Canada
306-659-7000,
Learning Services, Phone: 306-659-2010; HR Services: 306-659-2012
info@gscs.sk.ca
www.scs.sk.ca

Grades: K-12; French, Cree, & Ukrainian
Enrollment: 15000
Number of Schools: 37 elementary schools; 6 secondary schools; 2 associate schools (Co-manager of Humboldt Collegiate Institute, with Horizon School Division). Number of Employees: 1,900+
Diane Boyko, Board Chair, 306-382-2832
DLBoyko@gscs.sk.ca
Beverley Hanson, Director, Education, 306-659-7001
Darryl Bazylak, Superintendent, Education, 306-659-7040
Al Boutin, Superintendent, Human Resource Services, 306-659-7048
Greg Chatlain, Superintendent, Education, 306-659-7090
Dr. Donald Lloyd, Superintendent, Administrative Services, 306-659-7021
Gordon Martell, Superintendent, Education, 306-659-7056
John McAuliffe, Superintendent, Education, 306-659-7044
Joanne Weninger, Superintendent, Education, 306-659-7041
Donella Hoffman, Consultant, Communications, 306-659-7077
dhoffman@gscs.sk.ca

Saskatoon: Saskatoon School Division #13
310 - 21st St. East Saskatoon, S7K 1M7 Canada
306-683-8200, Fax: 306-657-3900,
totht@spsd.sk.ca
www.spsd.sk.ca

Enrollment: 20000
George Rathwell, Director of Education
Garry Benning, Chief Financial Officer

Swift Current: Chinook School Division No. 211
P.O. Box 1809
Swift Current, S9H 4J8 Canada
306-778-9200, Fax: 306-773-8011

Enrollment: 6329
Liam Choo-Foo, Director
Rod Quintin, Sec.-Treas.

Turtleford: Northwest School Division #203
P.O. Box 280
Turtleford, S0M 2Y0 Canada
306-845-2150, Fax: 306-845-3392,
www.nwsd.ca

Enrollment: 4910
Glen Winkler, Director of Education
Greg Gerwing, Sec.-Treas.

Viscount: St. Alphonse Roman Catholic Separate School Division #2
P.O. Box 71
Viscount, S0K 4M0 Canada
306-944-4446, Fax: 306-944-4446

Enrollment: 21
Joseph Kammermayer, Dir.
Mary Comeault, Sec.-Treas.

Warman: Prairie Spirit School Division #206
P.O. Box 809
121 Klassen St. East Warman, S0K 4S0 Canada
306-683-2800, Fax: 306-934-8221,
www.spiritsd.ca

Enrollment: 8787
Evelyn Novak, Director of Education
Jim Shields, Superintendent

Weyburn: Holy Family R.C.S.S.D. #140
110 Souris Ave., 3rd Fl. Weyburn, S4H 2Z8 Canada
306-842-7025, Fax: 306-842-7033,
www.holyfamilyrcssd.ca

Enrollment: 981
Shelley Rowein, Director of Education
Bruno Tuchscherer, Chair

Weyburn: South East Cornerstone School Division #209
80A - 18 St. NE Weyburn, S4H 2W4 Canada
306-848-0080, Fax: 306-848-4747, 888-938-0080
contactus@cornerstonesd.ca
www.cornerstonesd.ca

Enrollment: 7862
Marc Casavant, Director of Education
Lionel Diederichs, Chief Financial Officer

Yorkton: Christ the Teacher RCSSD No. 212
45A Palliser Way Yorkton, S3N 4C5 Canada
306-783-8787, Fax: 306-783-4992,
www.christtheteacher.ca

Grades: Pre-K.-12
Enrollment: 1800
This division is an amalgamation of St. Henry's RCSSD #5, Yorkton RCSSD #86, St. Theodore RCSSD #138, Melville Rural RCSSD #217 and Yorkton Rural RCSSD #216.
Darrell Zaba, Dir.
Wilfred Hotsko, Sec.-Treas.
Del Killick, Chair

Yorkton: Good Spirit School Division #204
Fairview Education Centre
63 King St. East Yorkton, S3N 0T7 Canada
306-786-5500, Fax: 306-783-0355, 1-866-390-0773
GSSD Distance Learning Center, Toll-Free Phone: 1-877-988-1122
feedback@mail.gssd.ca
www.gssd.ca

Grades: Junior Kindergarten - 12
Enrollment: 5935
Number of Schools: 28
Raymond Sass, Chair
Dwayne Reeve, Director, Education
Juanita Brown, Assistant Superintendent, Learning
Withman Jaigobin, Superintendent, Schools
Thom Koroluk, Superintendent, Student Services
Susan Maserek, Superintendent, Schools
Alan Sharp, Superintendent, Program Development
Sherry Todosichuk, Superintendent, Business Administration

Yorkton: Yorkton Roman Catholic Separate School Division #86
259 Circlebrooke Dr. Yorkton, S3N 2S8 Canada
306-783-8787, Fax: 306-783-4992

Enrollment: 1451
This division amalgamated with St. Henry's RCSSD #5 in Melville, St. Theodore RCSSD #138 in Theodore, and the two rural divisions around the cities of Yorkton and Melville to become Christ the Teacher Roman Catholic Separate School Division #212.
Brian Boechler, Dir.
Wilfred R. Maier, Sec.-Treas.
Tim Molnar, Chair

Protestant

Englefeld: Englefeld Protestant Separate School District #132
P.O. Box 190
Englefeld, S0K 1N0 Canada
306-287-3568, Fax: 306-287-3569

Enrollment: 113
Harvey Bowers, Dir.
Jim Martin, Sec.-Treas.

Schools: Specialized

Special Education

Pilot Butte: Schaller School
P.O. Box 570
Pilot Butte, S0G 3Z0 Canada
306-781-1829, Fax: 306-757-0599

Grades: K.-12
Enrollment: 192
Marion MacIver, Principal

Regina: Cornwall Alternative School
40 Dixon Cres. Regina, S4N 1V4 Canada
306-522-0044, Fax: 306-359-0720,
unis.ca@sasktel.net
www.saskschools.ca/schoolinfo/44.htm

Enrollment: 30
Eunice Cameron, Principal
eunice@sk.sympatico.ca

Saskatoon: Radius Community Centre for Education & Employment
P.O. Box 1812
#6 Bateman Crest. Saskatoon, S7H 3C2 Canada
306-665-0362, Fax: 306-665-5579,
info@radiuscentre.com
www.radiuscentre.com

Gail McKenzie-Wilcox, Principal

Schools: Independent & Private

Independent & Private Schools

Battleford: Heritage Christian School
P.O. Box 490
11 - 20th St. West Battleford, S0M 0E0 Canada
306-446-3188, Fax: 306-446-3187,
hcs@bsd.sk.ca

Grades: K.-12; Days only
Enrollment: 59
Peter Halvorsen, Principal

Caronport: Caronport High School / CHS
c/o Briercrest College & Seminary
510 College Dr. Caronport, S0H 0S0 Canada
306-756-3200,
info@briercrest.ca
www.briercrest.ca/chs

Grades: 9 - 12
Deborah Ike, Principal
deborahi@briercrest.ca
David Frostad, Vice Principal
dfrostad@briercrest.ca
George Willatt, Vice Principal
gwillatt@briercrest.ca
Vi Thiessen, Office Administrator
vthiessen@briercrest.ca

Moose Jaw: Cornerstone Christian School
43 Iroquois St. East Moose Jaw, S6H 4S9 Canada
306-693-2937,
office@ccsmj.ca
www.ccsmj.ca

Grades: K.-12; Day only
Enrollment: 300
Scott Robertson, Principal

Outlook: Lutheran Collegiate Bible Institute
P.O. Box 459
Outlook, S0L 2N0 Canada
306-867-8971, Fax: 306-867-9947,
lcbi@outlet.sk.ca
www.lcbi.sk.ca

Grades: 10-12; Residential only
Philip Guebert, Principal

Pilot Butte: Schaller School
P.O. Box 570
Pilot Butte, S0G 3Z0 Canada
306-781-1838, Fax: 306-757-0599

Grades: K.-12
Enrollment: 190
Marion MacIver, Principal

Prince Albert: Rivier Academy
1405 Bishop Pascal Pl. Prince Albert, S6V 5J1 Canada
306-764-6289, Fax: 306-763-1442,
rivier.academy_rivier@saskschools.ca
www.saskschools.ca/~rivier

Grades: 7 - 12
An associate school of the Prince Albert Roman Catholic School Division 6, Rivier Academy is an independent, Catholic high school for young women. It provides a full course, as prescribed by Saskatchewan Learning.
Sr. Mary Woodward, Principal
Claude Jalbert, Vice Principal

Regina: Harvest City Christian Academy
Harvest City Church
2202 - 8th Ave. North Regina, S4R 7T9 Canada
306-569-1935, Fax: 306-359-9047,
hcc.office@harvestcity.sk.ca
www.harvestcity.sk.ca

Grades: K.-12 (Non-Denom.); Day only
Enrollment: 172
Todd Harrison, Principal

Regina: Luther College High School
1500 Royal St. Regina, S4T 5A5 Canada
306-791-9150

Grades: 9-12
Berbel Knoll, Principal

Regina: Regina Christian School / RCS
2505 - 23rd Ave. Regina, S4S 7K7 Canada
306-775-0919, Fax: 306-775-3070,
development@reginachristianschool.org (E-mail, Development)
office@reginachristianschool.org
www.reginachristianschool.org

Grades: Preschool - 12
Enrollment: 504
The interdenominational school's academic program is offered with an evangelical Christian view.
Darryl Brown, Board Chair
Rod Rilling, B.Ed., B.A. (Hons), Principal
principal@reginachristianschool.org
Krista Munson, B.Ed., B.A., Vice Principal
krista.munson@rbe.sk.ca
Doreen Brace, B.Ed., Learning Leader & Resource Teacher
doreen.brace@rbe.sk.ca

Regina: Regina Huda School
40 Sheppard St. Regina, S4R 3M6 Canada
306-565-1988,
www.hudaschool.regina.sk.ca

Grades: Preschool - 12
Regina Huda School strives to preserve the Islamic identity, by offering Islamic & Arabic studies for the Muslim community.
Dr. Ayman Aboguddah, Board President
aboguddah@gmail.com
Twila Wilson, Principal
twila.wilson@rbe.sk.ca
Diane Szabo, School Secretary
secretary@hudaschool.regina.sk.ca

Rosthern: Rosthern Junior College
410 - 6th Ave. Rosthern, S0K 3R0 Canada
306-232-4222, Fax: 306-232-5250,
office@rjc.sk.ca
www.rjc.sk.ca

Grades: 10 - 12
The Christian secondary school operates within a Mennonite school community, for students of any faith. Completion of enriched courses leads to a Saskatchewan senior matriculation.
Gail Schellenberg, Principal
Lloyd Schmidt, Academic Coordinator
Holly Epp, Dean, Women
Matt Love, Dean, Men
Kathy Powley, Dean, Women
Graeme Rinholm, Dean, Men
Dave Feick, Contact, Admissions & Relations
Dave Feick, Contact, Admissions

Saskatoon: Christian Centre Academy / CCA
102 Pinehouse Dr. Saskatoon, S7K 5H7 Canada
306-242-7141,
academy@christiancentre.ca
www.christiancentre.ca/academy

Grades: Kindergarten - 12
The Accelerated Christian Education curriculum is used from kindergarten to grade 9 at the Christian Centre Academy. From grade 10 to 12, Saskatchewan Association of Independent Church Schools materials are used.

Saskatoon: Saskatoon Christian School
Site 510, Box 8, RR#5 Saskatoon, S7K 3J8 Canada
306-343-1494, Fax: 306-343-0366,
ssce@saskatoonchristianschool.ca
www.saskatoonchristianschool.ca

Grades: K.-12; Day only
Doug Wiebe, Principal
wiebedo@spsd.sk.ca

Wilcox: Athol Murray College of Notre Dame
P.O. Box 100
49 Main St. Wilcox, S0G 5E0 Canada
306-732-2080, Fax: 306-732-4409,
info@notredame.ca
www.notredame.sk.ca

Grades: 9-12
Enrollment: 350
Athol Murray College of Notre Dame is an international coeducational & residential college preparatory school. It is dedicated to Catholic Christian education.
Rob Palmarin, B.Ed., M.Th., President, 306-732-1230
Bob Baumuller, B.Ed., Director, Student Services, 306-732-1221
Dave Kenney, B.A., M.Ed., Director, Admissions, MarComm, & Alumni Relat, 306-732-2080 221
Hugh Lambert, B.Ed, B.Sc., Director, Academics, 306-732-2080 143

Universities & Colleges

Universities

Caronport: Briercrest College & Seminary
510 College Dr. Caronport, S0H 0S0 Canada
306-756-3200, Fax: 306-756-5500, 800-667-5199
info@briercrest.ca
www.briercrest.ca

Enrollment: 640
The institution also operates the Caronport High School.

Regina: Campion College
University of Regina
3737 Wascana Pkwy. Regina, S4S 0A2 Canada
306-586-4242, Fax: 306-359-1200, 800-667-7282
campion.college@uregina.ca
www.campioncollege.sk.ca

Enrollment: 1000

Regina: First Nations University of Canada
1 First Nations Way Regina, S4S 7K2 Canada
306-790-5950, Fax: 306-790-5999,
www.firstnationsuniversity.ca

Enrollment: 760

Regina: Luther College
University of Regina Campus
Regina, S4S 0A2 Canada
306-585-5333, Fax: 306-585-2949, 800-588-4378
www.luthercollege.edu

Enrollment: 1000
While administratively independent, Luther is academically integrated with the University of Regina.

Regina: The University of Regina
3737 Wascana Pkwy. Regina, S4S 0A2 Canada
306-585-4402, Fax: 306-585-4997,
communications@uregina.ca
www.uregina.ca

Enrollment: 11554
Lt. Gov. The Ho L.M. Haverstock, Visitor
Garth Fredrickson, Chairman
William F. Ready, Chancellor
Dr. Vianne Timmins, B.A., B.Ed., M.Ed., Ph.D., President & Vice-Chancellor
Dr. Gary Boire, Ph.D., Vice-President
Dave Button, M.Sc., P.Eng., P.M.P., Vice-President
Annette Revet, B.Sc.(Hons.), MBA, University Secretary
Barbara Pollock, B.A., B.Ed., Vice-President
Bev Liski, Registrar
Dr. Lynn Wells, B.A. (Hons.), M.A., Ph.D., Assoc. Vice-President
John D. Smith, Assoc. Vice-President
Allan Cahoon, B.A., M.Sc., Ph.D., Vice-President
Kelly Kummerfield, B.Admin., Assoc. Vice-President
Nelson Wagner, Assoc. Vice-President
Dale Schoffer, Assoc. Vice-President

Faculties
Arts
Dr. Lynn Wells, B.A. (Hons.), M.A., Ph.D., Acting Dean

Business Administration
Dr. Anne Lavack, Ph.D, Dean

Education
Dr. James McNinch, B.A., Ph.D., Dean

Engineering
Dr. Paitoon Tontiwachwuthikul, B.A., B.Eng. (Hons.), M.E, Dean

Fine Arts
Dr. Sheila Petty, B.A. (Hons.), L ès L, M è, Dean

Graduate Studies & Research
Dr. Rodney A. Kelln, B.Sc. (Hons.), Ph.D., Dean

Kinesiology & Health Studies
Dr. Craig Chamberlin, B.P.E., M.P.E., Ph.D., Dean

Science
Dr. Brien Maguire, B.Sc., M.Sc., Ph.D., Dean

Social Work
Dr. David Schantz, Ph.D., Dean

Schools
Canadian Plains Research Center
Dr. Polo Diaz, Ph.D., Executive Director

Centre for Continuing Education/Conservatory of Performing Arts
Dr. Harvey King, Ph.D., Director

Counselling Services
Dr. Brian Sveinson, B.A., M.A., Ph.D., Director

Graduate School of Business
Anne Lavack, B.Sc., M.B.A., Ph.D., Director

Graduate School of Public Policy
Dr. Michael Atkinson, B.A., M.A., Ph.D., Executive Director

School of Journalism
Mitch Diamantopoulos, B.A. Hons., M.A., Department Head

Affiliations
Campion College
c/o University of Regina
3737 Wascana Pkwy. Regina, S4S 0A2 Canada
306-586-4242, Fax: 306-359-1200, 1-800-667-7282
campion.college@uregina.ca
www.campioncollege.sk.ca

Enrollment: 1000
Number of Employees: 21 full-time professors; 12 full-time staff members; 1 campus minister
Fr. Benjamin Fiore, SJ, Ph.D., President, 306-359-1212
benjamin.fiore@uregina.ca
Fred Marcia, Exec. Dir., Administrative Services, 306-359-1231
fred.marcia@uregina.ca
Joanne Kozlowski, Dir., Admissions & Communications, 306-359-1244
joanne.kozlowski@uregina.ca
Kenneth Yanko, Dir. Facilities & Operations, 306-359-1249
ken.yanko@uregina.ca
Stephanie Molloy, Dir., Pastoral Studies, 306-359-1235
stephanie.molloy@uregina.ca
Frank Obrigewitsch, Dean, 306-359-1237
frank.obrigewitsch@uregina.ca
Nancy McNeill, Coordinator, Library, 306-359-1233
nancy.mcNeill@uregina.ca
Deborah Morrison, Registrar, 306-359-1226
deborah.morrison@uregina.ca

First Nations University of Canada
1 First Nations Way Regina, S4S 7K2 Canada
306-790-5950, Fax: 306-790-5999,
Human Resources, E-mail: mseveright@firstnationsuniversity.ca
tpelletier@firstnationsuniversity.ca (Communications)
www.firstnationsuniversity.ca

Enrollment: 2190
At the First Nations University of Canada, students have the opportunity to learn in an environment of First Nations languages, traditions, & values.
Dr. Shauneen Pete, President, 306-790-5950 2105
spete@firstnationsuniversity.ca
Dr. Herman Michell, Vice-President, Academic
Joely BigEagle, Chair
Tina Pelletier, Officer, Communications

Gabriel Dumont Institute
#2, 604 - 22nd St. West Saskatoon, S7M 5W1 Canada
306-242-5297, Fax: 306-242-0002,
www.gdins.org

Luther College
c/o University of Regina
Regina, S4S 0A2 Canada
306-585-5333,
www.luthercollege.edu/

Bruce Perlson, President, 306-585-5024
bruce.perlson@luthercollege.edu
Mark Duke, Dir. of Finance, 306-585-5023
mark.duke@luthercollege.edu
Mary Vetter, Academic Dean, 306-585-5036
mary.vetter@luthercollege.edu

Publications
The Carillon

Cityside
Regina, S4S 0A2 Canada

Saskatoon: College of Emmanuel & St. Chad
114 Seminary Cres. Saskatoon, S7N 0X3 Canada
306-975-3753, Fax: 306-934-2683,
emmanuel.stchad@usask.ca
www.usask.ca/stu/emmanuel

Saskatoon: Lutheran Theological Seminary
114 Seminary Cres. Saskatoon, S7N 0X3 Canada
306-966-7850, Fax: 306-966-7852,
lutheran.seminary@usask.ca
www.usask.ca/stu/luther

Enrollment: 142
Theological college at the University of Saskatchewan affiliated with the Evangelical Lutheran Church in Canada

Saskatoon: St. Thomas More College
1437 College Dr. Saskatoon, S7N 0W6 Canada
306-966-8900, Fax: 306-966-8904, 800-667-2019
info@stmcollege.ca
stmcollege.ca

Enrollment: 2294

Saskatoon: University of Saskatchewan
105 Admin. Place Saskatoon, S7N 5A2 Canada
306-966-4343, Fax: 306-966-4530,
www.usask.ca

Enrollment: 15228
The Hon. G. Barnhart, Lt. Governor of Saskatche, Visitor
Dr. Vera Pezer, Ph.D., Chancellor
Art Dumont, B.E.(ME), Chair
R.P. MacKinnon, Q.C., B.A., LL.B., LL.M., President
Dr. Brett Fairbairn, B.A. (Hons.), D.Phil., Provost & Vice-President
Richard Florizone, B.Sc., M.Sc., Ph.D., Vice-President
L. Pennock, B.A., M.A., Ph.D., University Secretary
Kelly McInnes, B.Sc., B.Ed., Registrar
L. Kennedy, B. Comm., C.A., Assoc. Vice-President & Controller
Karen Chad, Ph.D., Acting Vice-President
R. Bunt, B.Sc., M.Sc., Ph.D., Assoc. Vice-President
D. Hannah, B.Ed., M.Ed. Ph.D., Assoc. Vice-President
Jim Germida, B.S., M.S., Ph.D., Vice-Provost
Barb Daigle, B.Comm., M.B.A., C.H.R.P., Assoc. Vice-President

Faculties
Agriculture
Dr. G.J. Scoles, B.Sc., M.Sc., Ph.D., Acting Dean

Arts & Science
J. Dillon, A.R.C.T., B.Sc., M.Sc., P, Dean

Commerce
G.E. Isaac, B.A., M.A., Ph.D., Dean

Dentistry
G. Uswak, Dean

Education
C. Reynolds, B.A., M.A., Ph.D., Dean

Engineering
J.A. Kozinski, B.S., M.Eng., Ph.D., Dean

Extension
W. Archer, B.A., B.Ed., M.A., Ph.D., Dean

Graduate Studies & Research
L. Martz, B.Sc., M.Sc., Ph.D., Dean

Kinesiology
Carol Rodgers, Ph.D., B.P.E., M.H.K., Dean

Law
B. Cotter, B.Comm., LL.B., LL.M., Dean

Medicine
W. Albritton, M.D., Ph.D., FRCPC, Dean

Nursing
L. Butler, B.S.N., M.N., Ph.D., Dean

Pharmacy & Nutrition
D.K.J. Gorecki, B.S.P., Ph.D., Dean

Physical Therapy & Interprofessional Health Sciences Education
E.L. Harrison, Assoc. Dean

Veterinary Medicine
C. Rhodes, B.Sc., D.V.M., M.Sc., Dean

Schools
Physical Therapy
A. Busch, B.P.T., M.Sc., Ph.D., Director

Affiliations
Briercrest Bible College & Biblical Seminary
510 College Dr. Caronport, S0H 0S0 Canada
306-756-3200

Dr Dwayne Uglem, President
Glenn Werner, Chair

Central Pentecostal College
1303 Jackson Ave. Saskatoon, S7H 2M9 Canada
306-374-6655, Fax: 306-373-6968

Dr. Gordon Griesbrecht, President
Deborah McConkey, Registrar
Dr. David Munk, B.A., B.R.E., M.A., Ph.D., Academic Dean

College of Emmanuel & St. Chad
1337 College Dr Saskatoon, S7N 0W6 Canada
306-975-3753, Fax: 306-934-2683

The Rev Derek Hoskin, Chancellor
Rev. Dr Bill Richards, Vice-Chancellor
The Rt. Rev Greg Kerr-Wilson, President
The Rt. Rev. Dr Jane Alexander, Vice-President
Colleen Walker, Registrar
colleen.walker@usask.ca

Gabriel Dumont College
#2, 604 - 22nd St. West Saskatoon, S7M 5W1 Canada
306-934-4941, Fax: 306-242-0002,
www.gdins.org/GDC.shtml

Geordy McCaffrey, Executive Director, 306-657-2231
geordy.mccaffrey_dti@sasktel.net

Lutheran Theological Seminary
114 Seminary Cres. Saskatoon, S7N 0X3 Canada
306-966-7850, Fax: 306-966-7852

Kevin Ogilvie, President
Gordon Jensen, Dean of Studies
Susan Avant, Registrar
Debbie Thiessen, Office Manager

St. Andrew's College
1121 College Dr. Saskatoon, S7N 0W3 Canada
306-966-8970, Fax: 306-966-8981, 1-877-644-8970
standrews.registrar@usask.ca
www.usask.ca/stu/standrews
The College is a theological school of The United Church of Canada.
Vic Wiebe, Chair
vbwiebe@sasktel.net
Laura Balas, Acting Principal, 306-966-8975
laura.balas@usask.ca

St. Peter's College
P.O. Box 40
Muenster, S0K 2Y0 Canada
306-682-7888, Fax: 306-682-4402,
spc@stpeters.sk.ca
www.stpeterscollege.ca
Affiliated with the University of Saskatchewan, the College provides Arts & Science, Agriculture, & Commerce courses to first and second year students.
Robert Harasymchuk, President
Grant McConnell, Coordinator, Fine Arts, Conexus Community Art
Barbara Langhorst, Coordinator, Humanities, Academic Centre for

St. Thomas More College
1437 College Dr. Saskatoon, S7N 0W6 Canada
306-966-8900, Fax: 306-966-8904, 1-800-667-2019
www.stmcollege.ca
Enrollment: 2000
St. Thomas More College is a Catholic, liberal arts college, federated with the University of Saskatchewan. The college has 31 full-time tenure track faculty, 3 full-time term faculty, & 42 sessional faculty.
George Smith, President, 306-966-8903
gsmith@stmcollege.ca
Carl Still, Dean & Associate Professor, 306-966-8950
cstill@stmcollege.ca
Patricia McDougall, Associate Dean & Associate Professor, 306-966-8919
pmcdougall@stmcollege.ca
Derrin Raffey, Chief Financial Officer & Director, Administr, 306-966-8912
draffey@stmcollege.ca
Rod Antonichuk, Director, External Relations, 306-966-2955
rantonichuk@stmcollege.ca
Donna Brockmeyer, Director, Library, 306-966-8962
dbrockmeyer@stmcollege.ca
Kathie Jeffrey, Manager, Human Resources, 306-966-6467
kjeffrey@stmcollege.ca
Kerry Stefaniuk, Manager, Accounting, 306-966-2191
kstefaniuk@stmcollege.ca
Stacy Stillwell, Manager, Information Technology, 306-966-8920
sstillwell@stmcollege.ca
Richard Medernach, Coordinator, Student Services, 306-966-8946
rmedernach@stmcollege.ca
Luke Muller, Coordinator, Development & Alumni Affairs, 306-966-8918
lmuller@stmcollege.ca
David Peacock, Coordinator, Engaged Learning, 306-966-4828
dpeacock@stmcollege.ca
Gertrude Rompre, Campus Minister, 306-966-8929
grompre@stmcollege.ca

Publications
The Green & White
234 Kirk Hall Saskatoon, S7N 0W0 Canada
Fax: 306-966-8717

The Sheaf

Colleges

Saskatoon: **Gabriel Dumont Institute**
#2, 604 - 22nd St. West Saskatoon, S7M 5W1 Canada
306-934-4941, Fax: 306-244-0252, 888-344-0445
general@gdi.gdins.org
www.gdins.org
Has partnerships with University of Saskatchewan & University of Regina; Educational arm of the Métis Nation-Saskatchewan

Saskatoon: **Horizon College & Seminary**
1303 Jackson Ave. Saskatoon, S7H 2M9 Canada
306-374-6655, Fax: 306-373-6968,
inquiries@horizon.edu
www.horizon.edu

Post Secondary/Technical

Post Secondary/Technical

Air Ronge: **Northlands College**
P.O. Box 1000
Air Ronge, S0J 3G0 Canada
306-425-4480, Fax: 306-425-3002, 1-888-311-1185
www.northlandscollege.sk.ca
Program Centers are located in La Ronge (306-425-4353), Buffalo Narrows (306-235-1765), & Creighton (306-688-8838).
Bill McLaughlin, CEO, 306-425-4273

Biggar: **Prairie West Regional College**
P.O. Box 700
701 Dominion St. Biggar, S0K 0M0 Canada
306-948-3363, Fax: 306-948-2094,
rosetown.office@prairiewestcollege.ca
www.prairiewestcollege.ca
Bruce Probert, CEO

Humboldt: **Carlton Trail Regional College**
P.O. Box 720
623 - 7 St. Humboldt, S0K 2A0 Canada
306-682-2623, Fax: 306-682-3101, 1-800-667-2623
humboldt@ctrc.sk.ca
www.ctrc.sk.ca/ctrc/
Rob Barber, CEO

Melville: **Parkland Regional College**
P.O. Box 790
200 Block 9th Ave. East Melville, S0A 2P0 Canada
306-728-4471, Fax: 306-728-2576, 1-866-783-6766
info@parklandcollege.sk.ca
www.parklandcollege.sk.ca
Fay Myers, CEO

North Battleford: **North West Regional College**
10702 Diefenbaker Dr. North Battleford, S9A 4A8 Canada
306-937-5100, Fax: 306-445-1575,
www.nwrc.sk.ca
Enrollment: 823
Bryan Nylander, CEO

Regina: **Academy of Learning**
2721 Avonhurst Dr. Regina, S4R 3J3 Canada
306-757-8973, Fax: 306-757-2544,
admissions@aolregina.com
www.aolregina.com
Office admin.; accounting; IT training; other locations in: Lloydminster, Estevan, Fort Qu'Appelle, Moose Jaw, North Battleford, Meadow Lake, Prince Albert, Saskatoon, Yorkton & Swift Current
Chris Bourassa, Director
cbourassa@aolregina.com

Regina: **INtouch Career Advancement Training**
633 Park St. Regina, S4N 5N1 Canada
306-781-0366, Fax: 306-781-0369,
info@intouchcareercollege.com
www.intouchcareercollege.com
Academic upgrading, employment preparation, computer education & business programs
Donna Singer, Principal
dsinger@intouchcareercollege.com

Saskatoon: **Academy of Fashion Design**
218-B Ave. B South Saskatoon, S7M 1M4 Canada
306-978-9088, Fax: 306-933-9362, 1-877-978-9088
fashiondesign@sasktel.net
www.aofdesign.com
Heather J. Brigidear, Principal & Manager

Saskatoon: **CDI College of Business, Technology & Healthcare**
#107, 119 4th Ave. South Saskatoon, S7K 5X2 Canada
306-244-8585, Fax: 306-244-0788,
www.cdicollege.com
Computer Programming, Networking Technology & Business Applications programs; also Regina campus
Peter Hubbs, Director
peter.hubbs@cdi.ca

Saskatoon: **McKay Career Training Inc.**
226 - 20th St. East Saskatoon, S7K 0A6 Canada
306-652-7878, Fax: 306-653-1808, 1-800-205-8140
registrar@careercampus.ca
www.careercampus.ca
Medical & veterinary office assistant, graphic art/electronic prepress, multi media, massage therapy.
Gordon McKay

Saskatoon: **Redhouse College of Animation**
148 2nd Ave. North Saskatoon, S7K 2B2 Canada
306-668-0013, Fax: 306-668-0073, 1-877-264-6867
info@redhousecollege.com
www.redhousecollege.com
Three year animation program which includes basic animation principles and the process of writing, directing, and animating ones own film.
Gord Groat, Principal & Manager

Saskatoon: **Regency College**
233-4th Ave. South Saskatoon, S7K 1N1 Canada
306-651-1700, Fax: 306-651-1702, 1-800-667-4771
regencycollege@sasktel.net
www.regencycollege.com
Private vocational college which specializes in training hospitality industry and business employees.
Karen Butcher, Principal & Manager

Saskatoon: **Saskatchewan Indian Institute of Technologies**
c/o Asimakaniseekan Askiy Reserve
#118, 335 Packham Ave. Saskatoon, S7N 4S1 Canada
306-244-4444, Fax: 306-244-1391,
www.siit.sk.ca
Ray Ahenakew, Acting President
Paul Ledoux, Registrar
Darlene Arcand, Director of Admission

Saskatoon: **Saskatchewan Institute of Applied Science & Technology / SIAST**
Administrative Offices
400-119, 4th Ave. South Saskatoon, S7K 5X2 Canada
306-933-7331, Fax: 306-933-7323, 1-866-467-4278
HR.Admin.Offices@siast.sk.ca
www.siast.sk.ca
Dr. Bob McCulloch, President & CEO
Claude Naud, Vice-President
Patricia Gillies, Director
Cheryl McMillan, Acting CFO

Campuses
SIAST Kelsey Campus
P.O. Box 1520
Saskatoon, S7K 3R5 Canada
306-933-7331, Fax: 306-933-8403, 1-866-467-4278
HR.Kelsey@siast.sk.ca
www.siast.sk.ca
Gerry Bonsal, Director

SIAST Palliser Campus
P.O. Box 1420
Moose Jaw, S6H 4R4 Canada
306-694-3200, Fax: 306-693-3271, 1-866-467-4278
palliserjobs@siat.sk.ca
www.siast.sk.ca
Don Shanner, Director

SIAST Wascana Campus
HR.Wascana@siast.sk.ca
P.O. Box 556
Regina, S4P 3A3 Canada
306-798-4356, Fax: 306-798-8113, 1-866-467-4278
HR.Wascana@siast.sk.ca
www.siast.sk.ca
Noel Selinger, Director

SIAST Woodland Campus
P.O. Box 3003
1100 - 15 St. East Prince Albert, S6V 6G1 Canada
306-953-7094, Fax: 306-953-7168, 1-866-467-4278
HR.Woodland@siast.sk.ca
www.siast.sk.ca
Larry Fladager, Director

Saskatoon: **Saskatchewan Institute of Applied Science & Technology**
Administrative Offices, S.J. Cohen Centre
#400, 119 4th Ave. South Saskatoon, S7K 5X2 Canada
306-933-7331,
www.siast.sk.ca

Saskatoon: **Saskatoon Business College**
221 Third Ave. North Saskatoon, S7K 2H7 Canada
306-244-6333, Fax: 306-652-4888, 1-800-679-771
www.saskbusinesscollege.com
Business, health care, computer courses
Beth Shewkenek, Principal & Manager

Saskatoon: **Saskatoon Campus**
1223 Idylwyld Dr. North Saskatoon, S7L 1A1 Canada
306-955-4412, Fax: 306-955-5337, 1-866-755-5551
info@newmediacampus.com
www.newmediacampus.com
Multimedia; 3D animation.
Gary Lawrence, Principal

Campuses
Regina Campus
1831 College Ave., 3rd Fl. Regina, S4P 4V5 Canada
Fax: 306-721-1461,
info@newmediacampus.com
www.newmediacampus.com
Janea Bailey, Principal

Saskatoon: **Universal Career College**
226 - 20th St. East Saskatoon, S7K 0A6 Canada
306-652-7878, Fax: 306-653-1808, 1-800-205-8140
registrar@careercampus.ca
www.careercampus.ca
Office & business management, travel & tourism
Laurette McCaig, Manager

Saskatoon: **Western Academy Broadcasting College**
1222 Alberta Ave. Saskatoon, S7K 4E5 Canada
306-665-1771, Fax: 306-244-1219,
wabc@shaw.ca
www.wabcwesternacademy.com
Don Scott, Manager

Swift Current: **Cypress Hills Regional College**
P.O. Box 5000
129 - 2 Ave. NE Swift Current, S9H 4G3 Canada
306-773-1531, Fax: 306-773-2384, 1-866-296-2472
info@cypresshillscollege.sk.ca
www.cypresshillscollege.sk.ca
Mark Frison, CEO

Gravelbourg: **Gravelbourg Campus**
P.O. Box 652
7 Athabasca St. Gravelbourg, S0H 1X0 Canada
306-648-3244, Fax: 306-648-2983, 1-866-296-2472
margarets@cypresshillscollege.sk.ca (Attn: Margaret Schafer)
www.cypresshillscottage.sk.ca

Maple Creek: **Maple Creek Campus**
P.O. Box 1738
20 Pacific Ave. Maple Creek, S0N 1N0 Canada
306-662-3829, Fax: 306-662-3849, 1-866-296-2472
path@cypresshillscollege.sk.ca (Attn: Pat Hlady)
www.cypresshillscollege.sk.ca

Shaunavon: **Shaunavon Campus**
P.O. Box 1478
23-4th Ave. W. Shaunavon, S0N 2M0 Canada
306-297-3462, Fax: 306-297-3420, 1-866-296-2472
maryjaneb@cypresshillcollege.sk.ca (Attn: Mary Jane Benesh)
www.cypresshillscollege.sk.ca

Nipawin: **Nipawin Campus**
P.O. Box 2225
501 - 6th St. East Nipawin, S0E 1E0 Canada
306-862-9833, Fax: 306-862-4940,
crc.nipawin@cumberlandcollege.sk.ca
www.cumberlandcollege.sk.ca
Valerie Mushinski, CEO

Melfort: **Melfort Campus**
P.O. Box 2320
400 Burns Ave. E. Melfort, S0E 1A0 Canada
306-752-2786, Fax: 306-752-3484,
crc.melfort@cumberlandcollege.sk.ca
www.cumberlandcollege.sk.ca

Hudson Bay: **Hudson Bay Campus**
P.O. Box 207
501 Prince St. Hudson Bay, S0E 0Y0 Canada
306-865-2175, Fax: 306-865-2314,
crc.hudsonbay@cumberlandcollege.sk.ca
www.cumberlandcollege.sk.ca

Tisdale: **Tisdale Campus**
800-101 St. Tisdale, S0E 1T0 Canada
306-873-2525, Fax: 306-873-4450,
tisdale@cumberlandcollege.sk.ca
www.cumberlandcollege.sk.ca

Weyburn: **Southeast Regional College**
P.O. Box 2003
629 King St. Weyburn, S4H 0M4 Canada
306-848-2520, Fax: 306-848-2517, 1-866-999-7372
www.southeastcollege.org
Graham Mickleborough, President

Yukon Territory

Government Agencies

Whitehorse: **Department of Education**
P.O. Box 2703
1000 Lewes Blvd. Whitehorse, Y1A 2C6 Canada
867-667-5141, Fax: 867-393-6254,
contact.education@gov.yk.ca
www.education.gov.yk.ca
Brent Slobodin, Asst. Deputy Minister
Lee Kubica, Supt. of Schools/Asst. Deputy Minister
John Edzerza, Minister

School Boards/Districts/Divisions

Public

Whitehorse: **Yukon Francophone School Board**
P.O. Box 3983
3151C - 3rd Ave. Whitehorse, Y1A 5M6 Canada
867-667-8680, Fax: 867-393-6946, 800-661-0408
Grades: Pre-K.-12
Enrollment: 165
The board operates the Yukon's only French first language school, École Émilie-Tremblay.
André Bourcier, President

Universities & Colleges

Colleges

Whitehorse: **Yukon College**
P.O. Box 2799
500 College Dr. Whitehorse, Y1A 5K4 Canada
867-668-8800, Fax: 867-668-8890, 800-661-0504
www.yukoncollege.yk.ca
Terry Weninger, President
Karen Barnes, Vice-President (Education & Training)
Wayne Coghill, Director, Administrative Services
Jock Bryce, Director, Human Resources

Schools: Specialized

Overseas Schools/Programs

Antigua: **Picadilly: Island Academy**
Medical School Rd. Picadilly Antigua
026-856-2620, Fax: 026-846-3758,
mwayne@hotmail.com
Accredited with the Ontario Ministry of Education (allowing the school to offer the Ontario Secondary School Diploma). Island Academy opened its doors to students in September, 2001 at Piccadilly, Antigua
Wayne MacInnis, Principal

Canada: **Beijing: Beijing Tsinghua Zhiqing High School**
North Road of Zhongguancun Beijing, 100086 Canada
086-106-2974, Fax: 086-106-2976,
sotino@sina.com

Canada: **Vancouver: Dalian Maple Leaf International School**
#400-601 Broadway West Vancouver, V5Z 4C2 Canada
604-675-6910, Fax: 604-675-6911,
don@mapleleafschool.com
http://mapleleafschools.org
Grades: 9-12
Enrollment: 1616
Maple Leaf Educational Systems is a Chinese firm that currently operates 12 schools in China enrolling approximately 5,000 students. Maple Leaf's High Schools (Grade 10-12) programs and its Foreign Nationals Schools (K-9) are taught in English by British Columbia, Canada certified teachers. These programs are inspected and certified by British Columbia's Ministry of Eductation. Grade 12 graduates receive both the Chinese and British Columbia graduation certificates
C. Savage, Principal

Canada: **Vancouver: Grand Canadian Academy**
2026 West 12th Ave. Vancouver, V6J 2G2 Canada
604-738-6273, Fax: 604-738-6974,
office@gcahighschool.ca
www.gcahighschool.ca
Grades: 10-12
Enrollment: 135
Certified by the Ministry of Education, Province of British Columbia. British Columbia's High School Graduation Program includes Grades 10, 11 and 12. Courses numbered 10, 11 and 12 earn credits toward graduation. To graduate, students must complete a minimum of 80 credits over the three-year Graduation Program
G. Batt, Principal

Canada: **Vancouver: Jiangdu International School**
c/o 1262 - 13th Ave. East Vancouver, V5T 2M1 Canada
604-874-3386, Fax: 604-874-3386,
quincy_dai@yahoo.ca
Grades: 11
Enrollment: 13
Dr. R. Fransila, Principal

Canada: **Vancouver: Shanxi Sino-Canadian School**
c/o 1719 Trutch St. Vancouver, V6K 4G2 Canada
604-738-5777, Fax: 604-737-9969,
pm83@hotmail.com
Grades: 10
Enrollment: 50
Offers B.C. Grade 10,11, & 12
P. McManus, Principal

Canada: **Harrison Hot Springs: Sino-Canadian High School**
c/o PO Box 523 Harrison Hot Springs, V0M 1K0 Canada
604-796-2368, Fax: 604-796-2378,
butcherm218@yahoo.com
Grades: 10-12
Enrollment: 287
A. Butcher, Principal

China: **Jiangmen City: Boren Sino - Canadian School**
65 Shuanglong Ave. Jiangmen City, 529030 China
086-750-3217, Fax: 086-750-3219,
mryan1274@hotmail.com
Boren Sino-Canadian School is a privately funded education initiative with authorization from the Ministries of Education in the provinces of Guangdong, The People's Republic of China, and Ontario, Canada. As such, it adheres strictly to curricular re quirements and grants education credits in the pursuit of high school diplomas in both countries. The Chinese curriculum is designed to prepare students for national academic examinations qualifying students for university and college entrance. At the same time, the Ontario curriculum of the school is both demanding and exciting and requires a high level of aptitude and dedication
Carol Dubeau, Principal

China: **Quanzhou City: The Canadian Trillium College**
#7 High School, 46 Tian Hou Rd. Quanzhou City China
086-595-2203, Fax: 086-595-2202
CTC is a private Canadian School that offers an Ontario Secondary School curriculum to students in China. After passing their Chinese Middle School program and completing the necessary Ontario Secondary School courses students may be granted an Ontario Secondary School Diploma (OSSD). The granting of an OSSD is based on the total educational experience the student has acquired over their entire educational history in China
Don Folz, Principal

China: **Changsha: Changjun Education Group, Changsha, Hunan, China**
9th Section of Wang Yue Village Changsha China
086-731-8883, Fax: 086-731-8883,
Caifanganne@yahoo.com.cn

China: **Ranghulu District, Daqing: Daqing - Bond International College Daqing High School**
192 Zhongyong Da Jie Ranghulu District, Daqing China
086-459-6346, Fax: 045-963-4652

China: **Tianjin: Harbor View School**
#71, 3rd Avenue South Tianjin, 300457 China
086-226-2226, Fax: 086-222-4992,
liling@thehomeworld.com.cn
Harbor View School is a private-run boarding school owned and managed by Home World Corporation and certified with the Ministry of Education of Ontario. The school has been approved by the Tianjin Education Committee under whose great support - in cooperation with various other administrative departments in TEDA - was founded under its new name and in its new location in the year 2000. Harbor View School received the consent of the Tianjin Education Committee and was licensed as a private school in March and April of 2001. Construction was completed on June 10th 2003
Bill McInerney

China: **Huanggu District, Shenyang: Liaodong Canadian International School of China**
89 Huanghe South St. Huanggu District, Shenyang, 110031 China

086-417-2615, Fax: 086-417-2615,
jennysue0104@hotmail.com
Canadian international school in China, located in Yingkou

China: Longkou: Shandong Canada China Donghai School
Donghai Development Zone
P.O. Box 265713
Longkou China
086-535-8606, Fax: 086-535-8606
Terry Lynch, Principal

China: Shenzhen City, Futian District: Shenzhen Fujing Foreign Language School
Jingtian North, Futian District Shenzhen City, Futian District China
086-755-3910, Fax: 086-755-3921,
sunwenjin0208@hotmail.com
Enrollment: 108
The International Program at Fujing Foreign Languages School is accredited with the Ministry of Education and Training, Ontario and can grant credits leading to the Ontario Secondary School Diploma. All teachers teaching Ontario credit courses are qualified Ontario teachers. The program is inspected annually by the Ministry to ensure that all credit courses follow the prescribe Ontario courses of study and that assessment and evaluation follows the expectations of the Ministry as defined in the Ministry document, Ontario Secondary Schools, Program and Diploma Requirements, 1999. They offer a Dual Diploma Program which is currently in its thir
James Fish, Principal

China: WuQing District, Tianjin: Yinghua - Bond International College
P.O. Box 307100
Yong Yang West Road WuQing District, Tianjin China
086-225-9611, Fax: 086-225-9611,
elizabeth.jarrell@hotmail.com
Elizabeth Jarrell

China 510520: Guangzhou, Guangdong Province: Huamei-Bond International College
Longdong, Tianhe District Guangzhou, Guangdong Province China 510520
085-227-8229, Fax: 086-208-7210,
hmoacprincipal@yahoo.com
Huamei-Bond International College (HBIC) is operated jointly by Bond International College (Toronto) and Huamei International School (China). HBIC is accredited by and inspected by the Ontario Ministry of Education, Canada. The school offers Ontario secondary school academic courses as well as a Chinese high school curriculum leading to an Ontario Secondary School Diploma and a Chinese High School Diploma. With these two diplomas, graduates can apply directly to universities in China or overseas
Jim Burns, Principal
burnsjamesW@hotmail.com

Egypt: Zone 4, New Greater Cairo: Canadian International School
El Tagamosa El Khames Zone 4, New Greater Cairo Egypt
001-120-2758, Fax: 001-120-2758,
ser.sha@ie-eg.com
CISE is a Junior Kindergarten to Grade Twelve International School in Cairo (Kattameya - New Cairo) approved by the Egyptian Ministry of Education and licensed as a Canadian School by the Ontario Ministry of Education. Its administration and over 85% of its teachers are trained and licensed (certified) in Canada. The school uses a Canadian curriculum, teaching and classroom management techniques and Canadian learning materials (text books, computer software and audio-visual aids). The school opened its doors in September 2002
John Trafford, Principal

Hong Kong: Aberdeen: Canadian International School
36 Nam Long Shan Rd. Aberdeen Hong Kong
085-225-2570, Fax: 085-225-2575,
schoolinfo@cdnis.edu.hk
www.cdnis.edu.hk
Enrollment: 1332
Offers kindergarten, primary & secondary education
Barbara McKenzie, Principal

Hong Kong: Quarry Bay: Delia School of Canada
Tai Fung Rd., Taikoo Shing Quarry Bay Hong Kong
085-228-8441, Fax: 085-228-8578,
dscstk@delia.edu.hk
www.delia.edu.hk
Enrollment: 909
Delia School of Canada is a private school. Delia School of Canada is a member of the Delia Group of Schools. It follows the curriculum offered in Ontario. Delia School of Canada is accredited with the Ministry of Education in Ontario and registered with the Hong Kong Education and Manpower Bureau. The school meets the appropriate regulations put forth by the Education Department of Ontario and the Hong Kong Education and Manpower Bureau. Delia School of Canada was established in 1987
Jack Merner Saddler, Principal

Hong Kong: Shamshuipo, Kowloon: Phoenix International School
5 Tonkin St. Shamshuipo, Kowloon Hong Kong
085-227-0822, Fax: 085-227-0820,
info@phoenix.edu.hk
Enrollment: 369
Hugh McKeown, Principal

India: Bangalore 560 092: Canadian International School
14/1 Kodighalli Main Rd., Sahakar Nagar Bangalore 560 092 India
091-803-4384, Fax: 091-803-4364,
csib@vsnl.com
Enrollment: 212
Provides a learning experience to mainly expatriate and Indian students, representing over 25 nationalities from Pre indergarten to Grade 12. The school is accredited by the International Baccalaureate Organization and Ontario Ministry of Education, and is a member of the Council of International Schools
Brian Tinker, Principal

Italy: Lanciano, Chieti: Canadian College Italy - The Renaissance
via Cavour 13 Lanciano, Chieti Italy
039-087-2714, Fax: 039-087-2450,
cciren@tin.it
www.ccilanciano.com
Enrollment: 115
CCI debuted among Europe's private schools as the first private school in Italy to offer a Canadian high school program. The School offers grades 10 through high school graduation, and students may enroll for a single semester or for up to three academic years (two semesters per year). CCI is inspected by the province of Ontario, whose requirements parallel or exceed most other North American jurisdictions, and is a member of ECIS, the European Council of International Schools
Marisa DiCarlo D'Alessandr, Principal

Japan: Saitama 359-0027, Tokyo: Columbia International School of Japan
153 Matsugo, Tokorozawa Saitama 359-0027, Tokyo Japan
042-946-1911, Fax: 042-946-1955,
office@columbia-ca.co.jp
Enrollment: 112
Prepares students for the post secondary education overseas with a world recognized and accepted Ontario Secondary School Diploma (grade 12) of Canada. CIS admits students regardless of their nationality nor ethnic origin. CIS is accredited and annually inspected by the Ontario Ministry of Education, and follows the Ontario curriculum
Barrie McCliggott, Principal

Malaysia: Petaling Jaya, Selanger Darul E: Canadian International Matriculation Programme
P.O. Box 46150
No. 5 Jalan Kolej, Bandar Sunway Petaling Jaya, Selanger Darul E Malaysia
060-374-9186, Fax: 060-356-3586,
rosemaryg@sunway.edu.my
Enrollment: 649
CIMP is an Ontario Curriculum, developed according to the requirements of the Ontario Ministry of Education, Canada. It is identical to the programme offered in Ontario, which upon completion, students will receive the Ontario Secondary School Diploma (OSSD). Establised in 1990, the Canadian International Matriculation Programme (CIMP) has grown to become the largest Canadian Matriculation programme in the world
Rosemary Gannon, Principal

Malaysia: Selangor: Taylor's College
No. 1, Jalan SS15/8, 47500 Subang Jaya Selangor Malaysia
060-356-3626, Fax: 060-356-3452,
admission@taylors.edu.my
Enrollment: 490
For over three decades, Taylor's University College has been recognised as Malaysia's leading private college of higher learning. International Canadian Pre-University (ICPU) programme: Students choose this programme for its flexibility and wide-ranging subjects. Accepted for university entry internationally, ICPU students at Taylor's University College are constantly exposed to the latest developments in education and the global experiences provided by a team of qualified Malaysian and Canadian lecturers
Frank Meagher, Principal

Netherlands: AFNORTH International School
Ferdinand Bolstraat 1, 6445EE Brunssum Netherlands
000-314-5527, Fax: 000-314-5527,
Charmaine.Martel@eu.dodea.edu
Enrollment: 215
The AFNORTH International School was founded in September 1967 and provides education for about 1400 Children of Allied Forces Northern Europe (AFNORTH) and other NATO personnel serving at the Headquarters and nearby commands
Charmaine Martel, Principal

Netherlands Antilles: St. Maarten: Caribbean International Academy
#4 Tigres Rd., Dutch Lowlands St. Maarten Netherlands Antilles
001-159-9545, Fax: 001-159-9545,
admission@carib-international.org
To meet the Ministry of Ontario OSSD (Ontario Secondary School Diploma) graduation requirements, the Principal of the school and 80% of the secondary teaching staff must be certified by the Ontario College of Teachers. Opened in September 2003
Liz Shuttleworth

Rep. Of Trinidad & Tob: Montrose, Chaguanas: Trillium International School
#6 Maraj St. Montrose, Chaguanas Rep. Of Trinidad & Tob
A private school offering the Ontario Ministry of Education Curriculum to Elementary and Secondary school students

Singapore: Singapore 289 759: Canadian International School
71 Bukit Tinggi Rd. Singapore 289 759 Singapore
065-687-5151, Fax: 065-687-5151,
secondary@cis.edu.sg
www.cis.edu.sg
Enrollment: 977
Accredited by the Ontario Ministry of Education, and the International Baccalaureate programmes. Their graduates receive the Ontario Secondary Diploma or the IB Diploma, both of which are recognized around the world by major universities. Associate member in the Council of International Schools (CIS)
James Dalziel, Principal

Switzerland: Neuchâtel: Neuchâtel Jr. College
P.O. Box 2002
Crêt-Taconnet, 4 Neuchâtel Switzerland
041-327-2527, Fax: 041-327-2442,
principal@njc.ch
www.njc.ch/school/
Enrollment: 116
Member of the Canadian Association of Independent Schools (CAIS). Neuchâtel Junior College is a Swiss non-profit foundation of the Ville de Neuchâtel. As such, NJC has a governing council comprising two Boards of Governors, one in Switzerland (Le Conseil de Fondation), and the other in Canada. The members of the Conseil are appointed by the Neuchâtel City Council and come largely from the fields of education and business. The Canadian Board members are alumni of NJC and/or parents of recent students. The Boards are responsible for the selection of the Principal, the financial operation of the College, and the general direction of NJC's curric
Norman Southward, Principal

Trinidad: Petit Valley: Maple Leaf International School
Alyce Heights Dr., Alyce Glen Petit Valley Trinidad
086-863-2957, Fax: 086-863-3306,
mlis@tstt.net.tt
www.mapleleaf-school.com
Enrollment: 509
Maple Leaf International School opened on September 5, 1994 and offers a Canadian International Education Program in Port of Spain, Trinidad. The curriculum follows the guidelines established by the Province of Ontario Ministry of Education and Training, offering advanced level courses leading to university and college entrance. Maple Leaf is a private coeducational school that accepts students from Junior Kindergarten (3 years of age) through to Grade 12 (age 19)
Janet Pomeroy, Principal

United Arab Emirates: Abu Dhabi: The Sheikh Zayed Private Academy for Girls
P.O. Box 42989
Abu Dhabi United Arab Emirates
097-1 2- 446, Fax: 097-1 2- 443,
tszpaafg@emirates.net.ae
www.szpag.com
The Sheikh Zayed Private Academy for Girls is a school based in Abu Dhabi providing international education for students from KG1 through to Year 12. The Academy offers a holistic, international education programme based on the Canadian Curriculum
Natalie Little, Principal

Yemen: Sana: Canadian International School
P.O. Box 16621
Hadda Street - Diplomatic Area in front of Al Rahma Sana
Yemen
097-641-8510, Fax: 097-651-8510

SECTION 7
GOVERNMENT/FEDERAL & PROVINCIAL

Government Quick Reference Guide

ABORIGINAL AFFAIRS

Canadian Heritage, 15 Eddy St., Gatineau, K1A 0M5 QC
819-997-0055, 866-811-0055, info@pch.gc.ca
Indian & Northern Affairs Canada, 10 Wellington St., North Tower, Gatineau, K1A 0H4 QC
819-997-0380, Fax: 819-953-3017, 866-817-3977, infopubs@ainc-inac.gc.ca
Indian Claims Commission, Minto Enterprise Bldg., #400, 427 Laurier Ave. West, PO Box 1750 B,Ottawa, K1P 1A2 ON
613-943-2737, Fax: 613-943-0157, feedback@indianclaims.ca
Office of Intergovernmental Affairs, c/o Privy Council Office, #1000, 85 Slater St., Ottawa, K1A 0A3 ON
613-957-5153, Fax: 613-957-5043, info@pco-bcp.gc.ca

Alberta

Alberta Aboriginal Relations, Commerce Place, 19th Fl., 10155 - 102 St., Edmonton, T5J 4G8 AB
780-422-4144, Fax: 780-644-8389
Métis Settlements Appeal Tribunal, 14605 - 134 St., Edmonton, AB T5L 4S9
780-422-1541, Fax: 780-422-0019, 800-661-8864

British Columbia

Ministry of Aboriginal Relations & Reconciliation, 2957 Jutland Rd., PO Box 9100 Prov Govt,Victoria, V8W 9B1 BC
250-387-6121, 800-663-7867, abrinfo@gov.bc.ca

Manitoba

Manitoba Aboriginal & Northern Affairs, 59 Elizabeth Dr., PO Box 37, Thompson, R8N 1X4 MB
204-677-6607, Fax: 204-677-6753, amartin@gov.mb.ca
Aboriginal Affairs Secretariat, #200, 500 Portage Ave., Winnipeg, R3C 3X1 MB
204-945-2510, Fax: 204-945-3689

New Brunswick

Aboriginal Affairs Secretariat, Kings Place, #237, 440 King St., PO Box 6000, Fredericton, E3B 5H1 NB
506-462-5177, Fax: 506-444-5142

Newfoundland & Labrador

Department of Labrador & Aboriginal Affairs, Confederation Bldg., East Block, 6th Fl., PO Box 8700, St. John's, A1B 4J6 NL
709-729-4776, Fax: 709-729-4900, 877-788-8822, laa@gov.nl.ca

Northwest Territories

Department of Aboriginal Affairs & Intergovernmental Relations, 4910 - 52nd St., PO Box 1320, Yellowknife, X1A 2L9 NT
867-873-7143, Fax: 867-873-0233, 877-838-8194, nancy_gardiner @gov.nt.ca

Nunavut

Department of Culture, Language, Elders & Youth, PO Box 1000 800,Iqaluit, X0A 0H0 NU
867-975-5500, Fax: 867-975-5504, 866-934-2035

Ontario

Ministry of Aboriginal Affairs, 720 Bay St., 4th Fl., Toronto, M5G 2K1 ON
416-326-4740, Fax: 416-326-4017

Quebec

Secrétariat aux affaires autochtones, 905, av Honoré-Mercier, 1er étage, Québec, G1R 5M6 QC
418-643-3166, Fax: 418-646-4918

Saskatchewan

Saskatchewan First Nations & Métis Relations, #210, 1855 Victoria Ave., Regina, S4P 3T2 SK
306-787-6250, Fax: 306-787-5832

ACTS & REGULATIONS

Justice Canada, East Memorial Bldg., 284 Wellington St., Ottawa, K1A 0H8 ON
613-957-4222, Fax: 613-954-0811, webadmin@justice.gc.ca

New Brunswick

Legislative Services, Centennial Bldg., #418, 670 King St., PO Box 6000, Fredericton, E3B 5H1 NB
506-453-2855, Fax: 506-457-7342

Newfoundland & Labrador

Department of Justice, Confederation Bldg., East Block, 4th Fl., PO Box 8700, St. John's, A1B 4J6 NL
709-729-5942, Fax: 709-729-2129, justice@gov.nl.ca
Department of Transportation & Works, Confederation Bldg., West Block, 6th Fl., PO Box 8700, St. John's, A1B 4J6 NL
709-729-3679, Fax: 709-729-4285, twminister@gov.nl.ca

Northwest Territories

Department of Justice, Courthouse, 4903 - 49th St., 6th Fl., PO Box 1320, Yellowknife, X1A 2L9 NT
867-920-6197

Nova Scotia

Department of Service Nova Scotia & Municipal Relations, 1505 Barrington St., PO Box 216, Halifax, B3J 2M4 NS
902-424-4141, Fax: 902-424-0581, public-enquiries@gov.ns.ca

Ontario

Ministry of the Attorney General, McMurtry-Scott Bldg., 720 Bay St., 11th Fl., Toronto, M5G 2K1 ON
416-326-2220, Fax: 416-326-4007, 800-518-7901

Prince Edward Island

Office of the Attorney General, Shaw Building, North, 105 Rochford St., 4th Fl., PO Box 2000, Charlottetown, C1A 7N8 PE
902-368-5152, Fax: 902-368-4910

Quebec

Les Publications du Québec, #500, 1000 rte de l'Eglise, Québec, G1V 3V9 QC
418-643-5150, Fax: 418-643-6177, 800-463-2100, publicationsduquebec@cspq.gouv.qc.ca

Yukon Territory

Yukon Justice, PO Box 2703, Whitehorse, Y1A 2C6 YT
867-667-8655, Fax: 867-393-5790

AGRICULTURE

See Also: Land Resources
Agriculture & Agri-Food Canada, 1341 Baseline Rd., Ottawa, K1A 0C5 ON
613-773-1000, Fax: 613-773-2772, 866-345-7972, info@agr.gc.ca
Canadian Grain Commission, #600, 303 Main St., Winnipeg, R3C 3G8 MB
204-983-2770, Fax: 204-983-2751, 800-853-6705, contact@grainscanada.gc.ca
Canadian Wheat Board, 423 Main St., PO Box 816 Main,Winnipeg, R3C 2P5 MB
204-983-0239, Fax: 204-983-3841, 800-275-4292, questions@cwb.ca
National Farm Products Council, Canada Bldg., 344 Slater St., 10th Fl., Ottawa, K1R 7Y3 ON
613-995-6752, Fax: 613-995-2097, fpcc-cpac@agr.gc.ca
Plant Biotechnology Institute, 110 Gymnasium Pl., Saskatoon, S7N 0W9 SK
306-975-5248, Fax: 306-975-4839, pbi-info@nrc-cnrc.gc.ca

Alberta

Alberta Agriculture & Rural Development, J.G. O'Donoghue Bldg., 7000 - 113 St., 1st Fl., Edmonton, T6H 5T6 AB
780-427-2727, Fax: 780-427-2861, 866-882-7677,
Agriculture Financial Services Corporation, 5718 - 56 Ave., Lacombe, AB T4L 1B1
403-782-8200, Fax: 403-782-4226, 800-396-0215

British Columbia

Ministry of Agriculture & Lands, PO Box 9120 Prov Govt,Victoria, V8W 9E2 BC
250-387-5121, Fax: 250-387-1522

Manitoba

Agricultural Societies, 1129 Queens Ave., Brandon, MB R7A 1L9
204-726-6195, Fax: 204-726-6260
Manitoba Agriculture, Food & Rural Initiatives, Norquay Bldg., 401 York Ave., Winnipeg, R3C 0P8 MB
Food Development Centre, 810 Phillips St., PO Box 1240, Portage la Prairie, MB R1N 3J9
204-239-3150, Fax: 204-239-3180, 800-870-1044

New Brunswick

Department of Agriculture & Aquaculture, PO Box 6000, Fredericton, E3B 5H1 NB
506-453-2666, Fax: 506-453-7170, DAA-MAA@gnb.ca

Newfoundland & Labrador

Agrifoods Branch, Provincial Agriculture Bldg., Brookfield Rd., PO Box 8700, St. John's, A1B 4J6 NL
709-729-6588, Fax: 709-729-2674

Northwest Territories

Department of Environment & Natural Resources, PO Box 1320, Yellowknife, X1A 2L9 NT

Nova Scotia

Department of Agriculture, 1741 Brunswick St., 3rd Fl., PO Box 2223, Halifax, B3J 3C4 NS
902-424-4560, Fax: 902-424-4671

Ontario

Ministry of Agriculture, Food & Rural Affairs, 1 Stone Rd. West, Guelph, N1G 4Y2 ON
519-826-3100, 888-466-2372

Prince Edward Island

Department of Agriculture, Jones Bldg., 11 Kent St., PO Box 2000, Charlottetown, C1A 7N8 PE
902-368-4880, Fax: 902-368-4857

Quebec

Ministère de l'Agriculture, des Pêcheries et de l'Alimentation, 200, ch Sainte-Foy, Québec, G1R 4X6 QC
418-380-2110, 888-222-6272

Saskatchewan

Saskatchewan Agriculture, Walter Scott Bldg., 3085 Albert St., Regina, S4S 0B1 SK
306-787-5140, 866-457-2377, aginfo@gov.sk.ca

AGRICULTURE & FOOD

Agriculture & Agri-Food Canada, 1341 Baseline Rd., Ottawa, K1A 0C5 ON
613-773-1000, Fax: 613-773-2772, 866-345-7972, info@agr.gc.ca
Market & Industry Services Branch, Tower 5, 1341 Baseline Rd., Ottawa, K1A 0C5 ON
613-759-1000, Fax: 613-773-1755
Plant Biotechnology Institute, 110 Gymnasium Pl., Saskatoon, S7N 0W9 SK
306-975-5248, Fax: 306-975-4839, pbi-info@nrc-cnrc.gc.ca
Research Branch, Tower 5, 1341 Baseline Rd., Ottawa, K1A 0C5 ON
613-759-1000, Fax: 613-773-1866
Strategic Policy Branch, Tower 7, 1341 Baseline Rd., Ottawa, K1A 0C5 ON
613-759-1000, Fax: 613-773-2111

Alberta

Alberta Agriculture & Rural Development, J.G. O'Donoghue Bldg., 7000 - 113 St., 1st Fl., Edmonton, T6H 5T6 AB
780-427-2727, Fax: 780-427-2861, 866-882-7677
Agriculture Financial Services Corporation, 5718 - 56 Ave., Lacombe, AB T4L 1B1
403-782-8200, Fax: 403-782-4226, 800-396-0215
Farmers' Advocate of Alberta, 7000 - 113 St., 3rd Fl., Edmonton, AB T6H 5T6
780-427-2433, Fax: 780-427-3913, farmers.advocate@gov.ab.ca
Irrigation Council, Provincial Bldg., 200 - 5 Ave. South, 3rd Fl., PO Bag 3014, Lethbridge, AB T1J 4L1
403-381-5176, Fax: 403-382-4406

British Columbia

Agricultural Land Commission, #133, 4940 Canada Way, Burnaby, BC V5G 4K6
604-660-7000, Fax: 604-660-7033
Ministry of Agriculture & Lands, PO Box 9120 Prov Govt,Victoria, V8W 9E2 BC
250-387-5121, Fax: 250-387-1522

Manitoba

Agricultural Societies, 1129 Queens Ave., Brandon, MB R7A 1L9
204-726-6195, Fax: 204-726-6260
Manitoba Agriculture, Food & Rural Initiatives, Norquay Bldg., 401 York Ave., Winnipeg, R3C 0P8 MB
Farm Lands Ownership Board, #812, Norquay Bldg., 401 York Ave., Winnipeg, MB R3C 0P8
204-945-3149, Fax: 204-945-1489, 800-282-8069, robert.mckenzie@gov.mb.ca
Farm Machinery Board, Norquay Bldg., #812, 401 York Ave., Winnipeg, MB R3C 0P8
204-945-3856, Fax: 204-948-2844, randy.ozunko@gov.mb.ca
Manitoba Agricultural Services Corporation, #100, 1525 First St. South, Brandon, MB R7A 7A1
204-726-6850, Fax: 204-726-6849, mailbox@masc.mb.ca

New Brunswick

New Brunswick Crop Insurance Commission, PO Box 6000, Fredericton, NB E3B 5H1
506-453-2185, Fax: 506-453-7406
New Brunswick Farm Products Commission, c/o Department of Agriculture & Aquaculture, PO Box 6000, Fredericton, NB E3B 5H1
506-453-3647, Fax: 506-444-5969

Newfoundland & Labrador

Agrifoods Branch, Provincial Agriculture Bldg., Brookfield Rd., PO Box 8700, St. John's, A1B 4J6 NL
709-729-6588, Fax: 709-729-2674
Department of Natural Resources, Natural Resources Bldg., 50 Elizabeth Ave., 7th Fl., PO Box 8700, St. John's, A1B 4J6 NL
709-729-2920, Fax: 709-729-0059

Nova Scotia
Department of Agriculture, 1741 Brunswick St., 3rd Fl., PO Box 2223, Halifax, B3J 3C4 NS
902-424-4560, Fax: 902-424-4671

Ontario
AGRICORP, 1 Stone Rd. West, PO Box 3660 Central, Guelph, ON N1H 8M4
Fax: 519-826-4118, 888-247-4999, cac@agricorp.com
Agricultural Research Institute of Ontario, 1 Stone Rd. West, 2nd Fl. NW, Guelph, ON N1G 4Y2
519-826-4199, Fax: 519-826-4211
Agriculture, Food & Rural Affairs Tribunal, 1 Stone Rd. West, 1st Fl., Guelph, ON N1G 4Y2
519-826-3433, Fax: 519-826-4232, appeals.tribunal@omafra.gov.on.ca
Ministry of Agriculture, Food & Rural Affairs, 1 Stone Rd. West, Guelph, N1G 4Y2 ON
519-826-3100, 888-466-2372

Prince Edward Island
Agricultural Insurance Corporation, 29 Indigo Cres., PO Box 1600, Charlottetown, PE C1A 7N3
902-368-4842, Fax: 902-368-6677, peiaic@gov.pe.ca
Department of Agriculture, Jones Bldg., 11 Kent St., PO Box 2000, Charlottetown, C1A 7N8 PE
902-368-4880, Fax: 902-368-4857
Food Technology Centre, 101 Belvedere Ave., PO Box 2000, Charlottetown, PE C1A 7N8
902-368-5548, Fax: 902-368-5549, 877-368-5548, ftcweb@gov.pe.ca

Quebec
Ministère de l'Agriculture, des Pêcheries et de l'Alimentation, 200, ch Sainte-Foy, Québec, G1R 4X6 QC
418-380-2110, 888-222-6272
Commission de protection du territoire agricole du Québec, 200, ch Ste-Foy, 2e étage, Québec, QC G1R 4X6
418-643-3314, Fax: 418-643-2261, 800-667-5294, info@cptaq.gouv.qc.ca
Régie des marchés agricoles et alimentaires du Québec, 201, boul Crémazie est, 5e étage, Montréal, QC H2M 1L3
514-873-4024, Fax: 514-873-3984, rmaaqc@rmaaq.gouv.qc.ca

Saskatchewan
Saskatchewan Agriculture, Walter Scott Bldg., 3085 Albert St., Regina, S4S 0B1 SK
306-787-5140, 866-457-2377, aginfo@gov.sk.ca
Saskatchewan Crop Insurance Corporation, 484 Prince William Dr., PO Box 3000, Melville, SK S0A 2P0
306-728-7200, Fax: 306-728-7268, 888-935-0000, customer.service@scic.gov.sk.ca

Yukon Territory
Yukon Environment, PO Box 2703, Whitehorse, Y1A 2C6 YT
867-667-5652, Fax: 867-393-7197, 800-661-0408, environmentyukon@gov.yk.ca

AIR POLLUTION

See Also: Environment
Environmental Stewardship Branch, 351 boul St-Joseph, Gatineau, K1A 0H3 QC
819-997-1575, Fax: 819-953-9452
International Joint Commission, 234 Laurier Ave. West, 22nd Fl., Ottawa, K1P 6K6 ON
613-947-1420, Fax: 613-993-5583, beckhoffb@ottawa.ijc.org
Meteorological Service of Canada, 4905 Dufferin St., Toronto, M3H 5T4 ON
416-739-4770, Fax: 416-739-4232

Alberta
Alberta Environment, South Tower, Petroleum Plaza, 9915 - 108 St., 10th Fl., Edmonton, T5K 2G8 AB
780-427-2700, Fax: 780-422-4086, env.infocent@gov.ab.ca
Environmental Assurance Division, Petroleum Plaza ST, 9915 - 108 St., 10th Fl., Edmonton, T5K 2G8 AB

British Columbia
Ministry of Environment, PO Box 9339 Prov Govt,Victoria, V8W 9M1 BC
250-387-1161, Fax: 250-387-5669, www.envmail@gov.bc.ca

Manitoba
Manitoba Conservation, 200 Saulteaux Cres., Winnipeg, R3J 3W3 MB
204-945-6784, 800-214-6497, mincon@leg.gov.mb.ca

New Brunswick
Department of the Environment, Marysville Place, 20 McGloin St., PO Box 6000, Fredericton, E3B 5H1 NB
506-453-2690, Fax: 506-457-4991, env-info@gnb.ca
Environmental Management, Marysville Place, 20 McGloin St., PO Box 6000, Fredericton, E3B 5H1 NB
506-444-5119, Fax: 506-457-7333
Department of Natural Resources, PO Box 6000, Fredericton, E3B 5H1 NB
506-453-2510, Fax: 506-444-5839, dnrweb@gnb.ca
Sciences & Planning, Marysville Place, 20 McGloin St., 2nd Fl., PO Box 6000, Fredericton, E3B 5H1 NB
506-453-2862, Fax: 506-453-2265

Newfoundland & Labrador
Department of Environment & Conservation, Confederation Bldg., West Block, 4th Fl., PO Box 8700, St. John's, A1B 4J6 NL
709-729-2664, Fax: 709-729-6639, 800-563-6181, info@gov.nl.ca

Northwest Territories
Department of Environment & Natural Resources, PO Box 1320, Yellowknife, X1A 2L9 NT

Nova Scotia
Department of Environment, 5151 Terminal Rd., 5th Fl., PO Box 442, Halifax, B3J 2T8 NS
902-424-3600, Fax: 902-424-0503, 877-936-8476

Nunavut
Department of Environment, PO Box 1000 1300,Iqaluit, X0A 0H0 NU
867-975-7700, Fax: 867-975-7742, 866-222-9063, environment@gov.nu.ca

Ontario
Ministry of Environment, 135 St. Clair Ave. West, Toronto, M4V 1P5 ON
416-325-4000, Fax: 416-325-3159, 800-565-4923

Prince Edward Island
Department of Environment, Energy & Forestry, Jones Bldg., 11 Kent St., 4th & 5th Fl., PO Box 2000, Charlottetown, C1A 7N8 PE
902-368-5000, Fax: 902-368-5830

Quebec
Ministère du Développement durable, de l'Environnement et des Parcs, Édifice Marie-Guyart, 675, boul René-Lévesque est, 29e étage, Québec, G1R 5V7 QC
418-521-3830, Fax: 418-646-5974, 800-561-1616, info@mddep.gouv.qc.ca

Saskatchewan
Saskatchewan Environment, 3211 Albert St., 2nd Fl., Regina, S4S 5W6 SK
306-953-3750, Fax: 306-787-9544, 800-567-4224, inquiry@serm.gov.sk.ca

Yukon Territory
Yukon Environment, PO Box 2703, Whitehorse, Y1A 2C6 YT
867-667-5652, Fax: 867-393-7197, 800-661-0408, environmentyukon@gov.yk.ca

AIRPORTS & AVIATION

See Also: Transportation
Canadian Air Transport Security Authority, 99 Bank St., 13th Fl., Ottawa, ON K1P 6B9
Fax: 613-991-6726, 888-294-2202
Institute for Aerospace Research, 1200 Montreal Rd., Ottawa, K1A 0R6 ON
613-990-0765, Fax: 613-952-7214
Transport Canada, Place de Ville, 330 Sparks St., Tower C, Ottawa, K1A 0N5 ON
613-990-2309, Fax: 613-954-4731, minTC@tc.gc.ca
Transportation Appeal Tribunal of Canada, 333 Laurier Ave. West, 12th Fl., Ottawa, ON K1A 0N5
613-990-6906, Fax: 613-990-9153, info@tatc.gc.ca

Newfoundland & Labrador
Department of Transportation & Works, Confederation Bldg., West Block, 6th Fl., PO Box 8700, St. John's, A1B 4J6 NL
709-729-3679, Fax: 709-729-4285, twminister@gov.nl.ca

Northwest Territories
Airports, YK Centre, 4922 - 28th St., 4th fl., PO Box 1320, Yellowknife, X1A 2L9 NT
867-873-7725, Fax: 867-873-0297
Department of Transportation, Lahm Ridge Bldg., 4501 50 Ave., PO Box 1320, Yellowknife, X1A 2L9 NT
867-920-3460, Fax: 867-873-0363

Nunavut
Department of Community & Government Services, J.G. Brown Bldg., PO Box 1000 700,Iqaluit, X0A 0H0 NU
867-975-5400, Fax: 867-975-5305

Ontario
Ministry of Transportation, Ferguson Block, 77 Wellesley St. West, 3rd Fl., Toronto, M7A 1Z8 ON
416-235-4686, Fax: 416-327-9185, 800-268-4686,

Saskatchewan
Saskatchewan Highways & Infrastructure, 1855 Victoria Ave., Regina, S4P 3T2 SK
306-787-4800

Yukon Territory
Yukon Highways & Public Works, PO Box 2703, Whitehorse, Y1A 2C6 YT
867-393-7193, Fax: 867-393-6218, 800-661-0408, hpw-info@gov.yk.ca

APPRENTICESHIP PROGRAMS

Canadian Council of Directors of Apprenticeship, 140 Promenade du Portage, 5th Fl, Phase IV, Gatineau, QC K1A 0J9
819-953-7443, Fax: 819-994-0202, redseal-sceaurouge@hrsdc-rhdcc.gc.ca

Alberta
Alberta Advanced Education & Technology, Legislature Bldg., #324, 10800 - 97 Ave., Edmonton, T5K 2B6 AB
780-422-5400, Fax: 780-422-1263,-310-0000, aet.info@gov.ab.ca
Community, Learner & Industry Connections Division, Phipps-McKinnon Bldg., 5th Fl., 10020 - 101A Ave., Edmonton, T5J 3G2 AB
780-427-8517

New Brunswick
Apprenticeship & Occupational Certification Board, PO Box 6000, Fredericton, NB E3B 5H1
506-453-2260, Fax: 506-453-5317
Department of Post-Secondary Education, Training & Labour, 470 York St., PO Box 6000, Fredericton, E3B 5H1 NB
506-453-2597, Fax: 506-453-3618, dpetlinfo@gnb.ca

Northwest Territories
Northwest Territories Apprenticeship, Trade & Occupations Certification Board, PO Box 1320, Yellowknife, NT X1A 2L9
867-873-7357, Fax: 867-873-0200

Prince Edward Island
Community & Labour Development, Shaw Bldg., 105 Rochford St., 5th Fl., PO Box 2000, Charlottetown, C1A 7N8 PE
902-368-4244, Fax: 902-368-4242

Quebec
Conseil consultatif du travail et de la main d'oeuvre, #9.400, 500, boul René-Lévesque ouest, Montréal, QC H2Z 1W7
514-873-2880, Fax: 514-873-1129, cctm@cctm.gouv.qc.ca

Saskatchewan
Saskatchewan Advanced Education & Employment, 2220 College Ave., Regina, S4P 4V9 SK
306-787-9478, aeeinquiry@gov.sk.ca

Yukon Territory
Yukon Education, PO Box 2703, Whitehorse, Y1A 2C6 YT
867-667-5141, Fax: 867-393-6254

ARCTIC & NORTHERN AFFAIRS

Canadian Polar Commission, Constitution Square, #1710, 360 Albert St., Ottawa, K1R 7X7 ON
613-943-8605, Fax: 613-943-8607, 888-765-2701, mail@polarcom.gc.ca
Indian & Northern Affairs Canada, 10 Wellington St., North Tower, Gatineau, K1A 0H4 QC
819-997-0380, Fax: 819-953-3017, 866-817-3977, infopubs@ainc-inac.gc.ca

British Columbia
Northern Development Initiative Trust, #301, 1268 Fifth Ave., Prince George, BC V2L 3L2
250-561-2525, Fax: 250-561-2563, admin@nditrust.ca

Manitoba
Manitoba Aboriginal & Northern Affairs, 59 Elizabeth Dr., PO Box 37, Thompson, R8N 1X4 MB
204-677-6607, Fax: 204-677-6753, amartin@gov.mb.ca

Newfoundland & Labrador
Department of Labrador & Aboriginal Affairs, Confederation Bldg., East Block, 6th Fl., PO Box 8700, St. John's, A1B 4J6 NL
709-729-4776, Fax: 709-729-4900, 877-788-8822, laa@gov.nl.ca

Northwest Territories
Department of Environment & Natural Resources, PO Box 1320, Yellowknife, X1A 2L9 NT

Northwest Territories Business Development & Investment Corporation, #701, 5201 - 50 Ave., Yellowknife, NT X1A 3S9
867-920-6455, Fax: 867-765-0652, bdicinfo@gov.nt.ca

Nunavut

Department of Executive & Intergovernmental Affairs, 1084 Aeroplex bldg., PO Box 1000 200,Iqaluit, X0A 0H0 NU
867-975-6000, Fax: 867-975-6090

Ontario

Northern Development Division, Roberta Bondar Place, #200, 70 Foster Dr., Sault Ste Marie, P6A 6V8 ON
705-945-5900, Fax: 705-945-5931, 800-461-2287

Ministry of Northern Development, Mines & Forestry, 99 Wellesley St. West, Toronto, M7A 1W3 ON
416-327-0633, Fax: 416-327-0665

Saskatchewan

Saskatchewan Northern Affairs, Mistasinihk Place, 1328 La Ronge Ave., PO Box 5000, La Ronge, S0J 1L0 SK
306-425-4207, Fax: 306-425-4349, 866-663-4065, admin@sna.gov.sk.ca

Yukon Territory

Yukon Economic Development, PO Box 2703, Whitehorse, Y1A 2C6 YT
867-393-7191, Fax: 867-395-7199, 800-661-0408

ARTS & CULTURE

Canada Council for the Arts, 350 Albert St., PO Box 1047, Ottawa, K1P 5V8 ON
613-566-4414, Fax: 613-566-4390, 800-263-5588, info@canadacouncil.ca

Canada Place Corporation, 504 - 999 Canada Place, Vancouver, V6C 3E1 BC
604-775-7200, Fax: 604-775-6251, administration@canadaplace.ca

Canadian Artists & Producers Professional Relations Tribunal, C.D. Howe Bldg., 240 Sparks St., 1st Fl., West Tower, Ottawa, K1A 1A1 ON
613-996-4052, Fax: 613-947-4125, 800-263-ARTS, info@capprt-tcrpap.gc.ca

Canadian Broadcasting Corporation, 181 Queen St., PO Box 3220 C,Ottawa, K1Y 1E4 ON
613-288-6033, liaison@radio-canada.ca

Canadian Heritage, 15 Eddy St., Gatineau, K1A 0M5 QC
819-997-0055, 866-811-0055, info@pch.gc.ca

Canadian Museum of Civilization, 100 Laurier St., PO Box 3100 B,Gatineau, J8X 4H2 QC
819-776-7000, Fax: 819-776-8300, 800-555-5621

Canadian Museum of Nature, PO Box 3443 D,Ottawa, K1P 6P4 ON
613-566-4700, Fax: 613-364-4021, 800-263-4433, enquiries@mus-nature.ca

Library of Parliament, Parliamentary Bldgs., 111 Wellington St., Ottawa, K1A 0A9 ON
613-992-4793, Fax: 613-943-6383, 866-599-4999

National Arts Centre, 53 Elgin St., PO Box 1534 B,Ottawa, K1P 5W1 ON
613-947-7000, Fax: 613-996-9578, info@nac-cna.ca

National Film Board of Canada, 3155, rue Côte de Liesse, CP 1600 Centre-ville,Saint-Laurent, H4N 2N4 QC
514-283-9000, Fax: 514-283-7564, 800-267-7710

National Gallery of Canada, 380 Sussex Dr., PO Box 427 A,Ottawa, K1N 9N4 ON
613-990-1985, Fax: 613-993-4385, 800-319-2787, info@gallery.ca; info@beaux-arts.ca

Parks Canada, 25 Eddy St., Gatineau, K1A 0M5 QC
613-860-1251, 888-773-8888, information@pc.gc.ca

Telefilm Canada, #500, 360, rue Saint-Jacques, Montréal, H2Y 1P5 QC
514-283-6363, Fax: 514-283-2365, 800-567-0890, info@telefilm.gc.ca

Alberta

Alberta Foundation for the Arts, Standard Life Centre, #901, 10405 Jasper Ave., Edmonton, AB T5J 4R7
780-427-9968, Fax: 780-422-1162

British Columbia

ActNow BC, 800 Johnson St., 1st Fl., PO Box 9898 Prov Govt,Victoria, V8W 1N3 BC
Fax: 250-387-8720

British Columbia Film Commission, #201, 865 Hornby St., Vancouver, BC V6Z 2G3
604-660-2732, Fax: 604-660-4790, info@bcfilmcommission.com

Islands Trust, #200, 1627 Fort St., Victoria, BC V8R 1H8
250-405-5151, Fax: 250-405-5155, information@islandstrust.bc.ca

Provincial Capital Commission, 613 Pandora Ave., Victoria, BC V8W 1N8
250-953-8800, Fax: 250-386-1303, info.pcc@bcpcc.com

Ministry of Small Business & Revenue, 1810 Blanshard St., 3rd Fl., PO Box 9432 Prov Govt,Victoria, V8W 9N6 BC
250-387-6206, Fax: 250-952-0712, MSBROffice@gov.bc.ca

Manitoba

Communications Services Manitoba, 155 Carlton St., 10th Fl., Winnipeg, R3C 3H8 MB
204-945-3765, Fax: 204-948-2147

Manitoba Culture, Heritage, Tourism & Sport, Legislative Building, #118, 450 Broadway Ave., Winnipeg, R3C 0V8 MB
204-945-3729, Fax: 204-945-5223, mincht@leg.gov.mb.ca

Heritage Grants Advisory Council, 213 Notre Dame Ave., 3rd Fl., Winnipeg, MB R3B 1N3
204-945-2213, Fax: 204-948-2086

Le Centre Culturel franco-manitobain/Franco-Manitoban Cultural Centre, 340, boul Provencher, St Boniface, MB R2H 0G7
204-233-8972, Fax: 204-233-3324, ccfm@ccfm.mb.ca

Manitoba Arts Council, #525, 93 Lombard Ave., Winnipeg, MB R3B 3B1
204-945-2237, Fax: 204-945-5925, 866-994-2787, info@artscouncil.mb.ca

Manitoba Centennial Centre Corporation, 555 Main St., Winnipeg, MB R3B 1C3
204-956-1360, Fax: 204-944-1390

Manitoba Film Classification Board, #216, 301 Weston St., Winnipeg, MB R3E 3H4
204-945-8962, Fax: 204-945-0890, 866-612-2399, mfcb@gov.mb.ca

Manitoba Heritage Council, 213 Notre Dame Ave., Main Fl., Winnipeg, MB R3B 1N3
204-945-2118, Fax: 204-948-2384, hrb@gov.mb.ca

Manitoba Museum, 190 Rupert Ave., Winnipeg, MB R3B 0N2
204-956-2830, Fax: 204-942-3679, info@manitobamuseum.mb.ca

Multiculturalism Secretariat, 213 Notre Dame Ave., 4th Fl., Winnipeg, MB R3B 1N3
204-945-1156, Fax: 204-948-2323

New Brunswick

Ministerial Advisory Committee on Multiculturalism, PO Box 6000, Fredericton, NB E3B 5H1

New Brunswick Arts Board, #300, 634 Queen St., Fredericton, NB E3B 1C2
506-444-4444, Fax: 506-444-5543, 1-866-460-2787

New Brunswick Film, Assumption Pl., 770 Main St., 16th Fl., PO Box 5001, Moncton, NB E1C 8R3
506-869-6868, Fax: 506-869-6840, nbfilm@gnb.ca

Department of Social Development, Sartain MacDonald Bldg., 551 King St., PO Box 6000, Fredericton, E3B 5H1 NB
506-453-2001, Fax: 506-453-7478

Department of Wellness, Culture & Sport, Place 2000, 250 King St., 4th Fl., PO Box 6000, Fredericton, E3B 5H1 NB
506-453-2909, Fax: 506-453-6548

Newfoundland & Labrador

Provincial Information & Library Resources Board, 48 St. George's Ave, Stephenville, NL A2H 1K9
709-643-0900, Fax: 709-643-0925

Department of Tourism, Culture & Recreation, Confederation Bldg., West Block, 2nd Fl., PO Box 8700, St. John's, A1B 4J6 NL
709-729-0862, Fax: 709-729-0870, tcrinfo@gov.nl.ca

Northwest Territories

Department of Education, Culture & Employment, PO Box 1320, Yellowknife, X1A 2L9 NT
867-669-2399, Fax: 867-873-0431, 866-606-5627

NWT Arts Council, PO Box 1320 Main, Yellowknife, NT X1A 2L9
867-920-6370, Fax: 867-873-0205

Nova Scotia

Culture Division, #601, 1800 Argyle St., PO Box 456, Halifax, B3J 2R5 NS
Fax: 902-424-0710

Department of Education, Trade Mart Bldg., 2021 Brunswick St., 4th Fl., PO Box 578, Halifax, B3J 2S9 NS
902-424-5168, Fax: 902-424-0680

Film Nova Scotia, Collins Bank Bldg., 1869 Upper Water St., 3rd Fl., Halifax, NS B3J 1S9
902-424-7177, Fax: 902-424-0617, 888-360-2111, connorkm@gov.ns.ca

Nova Scotia Tourism Partnership Council, World Trade & Convention Centre, #603, 1800 Argyle St., Halifax, NS B3J 3N8
902-424-0048, Fax: 902-424-0723, pashermc@gov.ns.ca

Nunavut

Department of Culture, Language, Elders & Youth, PO Box 1000 800,Iqaluit, X0A 0H0 NU
867-975-5500, Fax: 867-975-5504, 866-934-2035

Ontario

Art Gallery of Ontario, 317 Dundas St. West, Toronto, ON M5T 1G4
416-977-0414, Fax: 416-979-6646

Culture Policy, Programs & Services Division, 400 University Ave., 5th Fl., Toronto, M7A 2R9 ON
416-314-7265, Fax: 416-314-7461

Ministry of Culture, Mowat Block, 900 Bay St., 5th Fl., Toronto, M7A 1L2 ON
416-325-1660, Fax: 416-325-1726, 866-454-0049

McMichael Canadian Art Collection, 10365 Islington Ave., Kleinburg, ON L0J 1C0
905-893-1121, Fax: 905-893-0692, 888-213-1121, info@mcmichael.com

Minister's Advisory Council for Arts & Culture, 400 University Ave., 5th Fl., Toronto, ON M7A 2R9
416-314-8321, Fax: 416-314-7091, 866-888-5829

Ontario Arts Council, 151 Bloor St. West, 5th Fl., Toronto, ON M5S 1T6
416-961-1660, Fax: 416-961-7796

Ontario Heritage Trust, 10 Adelaide St. East, Toronto, ON M5C 1J3
416-325-5000, Fax: 416-325-5071, marketing@heritagefdn.on.ca

Ontario Library Service - North, 334 Regent St., Sudbury, ON P3C 4E2
705-675-6467, Fax: 705-675-2285, 800-461-6348

Ontario Media Development Corporation, South Tower, #501, 175 Bloor St. East, Toronto, ON M4W 3R8
416-314-6858, Fax: 416-314-6876, mail@omdc.on.ca

Ontario Northland, 555 Oak St. East, North Bay, ON P1B 8L3
705-472-4500, Fax: 705-476-5598, 800-363-7512, info@ontc.on.ca

Ontario Place Corporation, 955 Lake Shore Blvd. West, Toronto, ON M6K 3B9
416-314-9900, Fax: 416-314-9992

Ontario Tourism Marketing Partnership Corporation, Hearst Block, 900 Bay St., 10th Fl., Toronto, ON M7A 2E1
416-212-0757, Fax: 416-325-6004, 800-668-2746

Ontario Trillium Foundation, 45 Charles St. East, 5th Fl., Toronto, ON M4Y 1S2
416-963-4927, Fax: 416-963-8781, 800-263-2887, trillium@trilliumfoundation.org

Ottawa Congress Centre, 55 Colonel By Dr., Ottawa, ON K1N 9J2
613-563-1984, Fax: 613-563-7646

Royal Ontario Museum, 100 Queen's Park Cres., Toronto, ON M5S 2C6
416-586-5549, Fax: 416-586-5685, info@rom.on.ca

Southern Ontario Library Service, #902, 111 Peter St., Toronto, ON M5V 2H1
416-961-1669, Fax: 416-961-5122, 800-387-5765

Ministry of Tourism, Hearst Block, 900 Bay St., 9th Fl., Toronto, M7A 2E1 ON
416-326-9326, Fax: 416-314-7854, 800-668-2746

Prince Edward Island

Department of Communities, Cultural Affairs & Labour, Shaw Bldg., 95 Rochford St., 4th Fl., PO Box 2000, Charlottetown, C1A 7N8 PE
902-368-5250, Fax: 902-368-4121

PEI Museum & Heritage Foundation, 2 Kent St., PO Box 2000, Charlottetown, PE C1A 1M6
902-368-6600, Fax: 902-368-6608, mhpei@gov.pe.ca

Quebec

Bibliothèque et Archives nationales du Québec (BAnQ), 475, boul De Maisonneuve est, Montréal, H2L 5C4 QC
514-873-1100, Fax: 514-873-9312, 800-363-9028,

Commission de reconnaissance des associations d'artistes et des associations de producteurs, #14.60, 500, boul René-Lévesque ouest, Montréal, H2Z 1W7 QC
514-873-6012, Fax: 514-873-6267, tribunal@craaap.gouv.qc.ca

Commission des biens culturels du Québec, Bloc A-RC, 225, Grande Allée est, Québec, G1R 5G5 QC
418-643-8378, Fax: 418-643-8591, info@cbcq.gouv.qc.ca

Conseil des arts et des lettres du Québec, #320, 79, boul René-Lévesque est, Québec, G1R 5N5 QC
418-643-1707, Fax: 418-643-4558, 800-897-1707, info@calq.gouv.qc.ca

Conseil des relations interculturelles, #10.04, 500, boul René-Lévesque ouest, Montréal, QC H2Z 1W7
514-873-8501, Fax: 514-873-3469

Ministère de la Culture, des Communications & de la Condition féminine, 225, Grande Allée est, Québec, G1R 5G5 QC
Fax: 418-380-2364, 888-380-8882, infos@mcccf.gouv.qc.ca

Curateur public du Québec, 600, boul René-Lévesque ouest, 10e étage, Montréal, QC H3B 4W9
514-873-4074, Fax: 514-873-5033, 800-363-9020, information@curateur.gouv.qc.ca

Musée d'art contemporain de Montréal, 185, rue Ste-Catherine ouest, Montréal, H2X 3X5 QC
514-847-6226, Fax: 514-847-6290
Musée de la civilisation, 85, rue Dalhousie, CP 155 B,Québec, G1K 7A6 QC
418-643-2158, Fax: 418-646-9705, 866-710-8031, mcqweb@mcq.org
Musée national des beaux-arts du Québec, Parc des Champs-de-Bataille, 1, av Wolfe-Montcalm, Québec, G1R 5H3 QC
418-643-2150, Fax: 418-646-3330, 866-220-2150, webmestre@mnba.qc.ca
Régie du cinéma, #100, 390, rue Notre-Dame ouest, Montréal, H2Y 1T9 QC
514-873-2371, Fax: 514-873-2142, 800-463-2463, regieducinema@rcq.gouv.qc.ca
Secrétariat à la politique linguistique, 225 Grande-Allée est, 4e étage, Québec, G1R 5G5 QC
418-643-4248, Fax: 418-646-7832, info@spl.gouv.qc.ca
Société de développement des entreprises culturelles, #800, 215, rue Saint-Jacques, Montréal, H2Y 1M6 QC
514-841-2200, Fax: 514-841-8606, 800-363-0401, info@sodec.gouv.qc.ca
Société de la Place des Arts de Montréal, 260, boul de Maisonneuve ouest, Montréal, H2X 1Y9 QC
514-285-4200, Fax: 514-285-1968, info@pda.qc.ca
Société de télédiffusion du Québec (Télé-Québec), 1000, rue Fullum, Montréal, H2K 3L7 QC
514-521-2424, Fax: 514-873-7739, 800-361-4301, info@telequebec.tv
Société du Grand Théâtre de Québec, 269, boul René-Lévesque est, Québec, G1R 2B3 QC
418-644-8921, Fax: 418-646-7670

Saskatchewan

Saskatchewan Archives Board, University of Regina, 3303 Hillsdale St., Regina, S4S 0A2 SK
306-787-4068, Fax: 306-787-1197, info.regina@archives.gov.sk.ca
Royal Saskatchewan Museum, 2445 Albert St., Regina, SK S4P 4W7
306-787-2815, Fax: 306-787-2820, info@royalsaskmuseum.ca
Sask Film, 1831 College Ave., Regina, SK S4P 3V7
306-798-3456, Fax: 306-798-7768, 800-561-9933
Saskatchewan Archives Board, University of Regina, 3303 Hillsdale St., Regina, SK S4S 0A2
306-787-4068, Fax: 306-787-1197, info.regina@archives.gov.sk.ca
Saskatchewan Arts Board, 2135 Broad St., Regina, SK S4P 3V7
306-787-4056, Fax: 306-787-4199, 800-667-7526, sab@artsboard.sk.ca
Saskatchewan Communications Network, #313E, 2440 Broad St., Regina, SK S4P 0A5
306-787-0490, Fax: 306-787-0496, 800-667-5055, inquiries@scn.ca
Saskatchewan Film & Video Classification Board, #500, 1919 Saskatchewan Dr., Regina, SK S4P 4H2
306-787-5550, Fax: 306-787-9779, 888-374-4636, adwyer@justice.gov.sk.ca
Saskatchewan Tourism, Parks, Culture, & Sport, 1919 Saskatchewan Dr., 4th Fl., Regina, S4P 4H2 SK
306-787-5729, Fax: 306-787-8560
Wanuskewin Heritage Park, RR#4, Saskatoon, SK S7K 3J7
306-931-6767, Fax: 306-931-4522, wanuskewin@wanuskewin.com

Yukon Territory

Yukon Tourism & Culture, PO Box 2703, Whitehorse, Y1A 2C6 YT
867-667-5036, Fax: 867-667-3546

AUDITORS-GENERAL

Auditor General of Canada, 240 Sparks St., Ottawa, K1A 0G6 ON
613-995-3708, Fax: 613-957-0474, 888-761-5953, communications@oag-bvg.gc.ca; infomedia@oag-bvg.gc.ca

Alberta

Alberta Office of the Auditor General, 9925 - 109 St., 8th Fl., Edmonton, T5K 2J8 AB
780-427-4222, Fax: 780-422-9555, info@oag.ab.ca

British Columbia

Office of the Auditor General, 8 Bastion Sq., Victoria, V8V 1X4 BC
250-387-6803, Fax: 250-387-1230, info@bcauditor.com

Manitoba

Office of the Auditor General, #500, 330 Portage Ave., Winnipeg, R3C 0C4 MB
204-945-3790, Fax: 204-945-2169, contact@oag.mb.ca

New Brunswick

Office of the Auditor General, HSBC Place, 520 King St., 6th Fl., Fredericton, E3B 6G3 NB
506-453-2243, Fax: 506-453-3067

Newfoundland & Labrador

Office of the Auditor General, Viking Bldg., 3rd Fl., PO Box 8700, St. John's, A1B 4J6 NL
709-729-2700, Fax: 709-729-5970, oag@gov.nl.ca

Nova Scotia

Office of the Auditor General, #302, 1888 Brunswick St., Halifax, B3J 3J8 NS
902-424-5907, Fax: 902-424-4350

Ontario

Office of the Provincial Auditor, 20 Dundas St. West, 15th Fl., PO Box 105, Toronto, M5G 2C2 ON
416-327-2381, Fax: 416-327-9862, comments@auditor.on.ca

Prince Edward Island

Office of the Auditor General, Shaw Bldg., 105 Rochford St, 2nd Fl., PO Box 2000, Charlottetown, C1A 7N8 PE
902-368-4520, Fax: 902-368-4598

Quebec

Vérificateur général du Québec, 750, boulevard Charest est, 3e étage, Québec, G1K 9J6 QC
418-691-5900, Fax: 418-644-4460, verificateur.general@vgq.gouv.qc.

Saskatchewan

Provincial Auditor Saskatchewan, #1500, 1920 Broad St., Regina, S4P 3V2 SK
306-787-6398, Fax: 306-787-6383, info@auditor.sk.ca

AUTOMOBILE INSURANCE

See Also: Insurance (Life, Fire Property)

Alberta

Automobile Insurance Rate Board, Terrace Bldg., #200, 9515 - 107 St. NW, Edmonton, AB T5K 2C3
780-415-1126, Fax: 780-644-7771, airb@gov.ab.ca

British Columbia

Insurance Corporation of British Columbia, 151 West Esplanade, North Vancouver, V7M 3H9 BC
604-661-2800, 800-663-3051

Manitoba

Manitoba Public Insurance, #820, 234 Donald St., PO Box 6300, Winnipeg, R3C 4A4 MB
204-985-7000, Fax: 204-943-9851, 800-665-2410

New Brunswick

Department of Justice & Consumer Affairs, Centennial Bldg., 670 King St., PO Box 6000, Fredericton, E3B 5H1 NB
506-462-5100, Fax: 506-453-3651, justice.comments@gnb.ca

Northwest Territories

Department of Finance, YK Center, 3rd Fl., PO Box 1320, Yellowknife, X1A 2L9 NT
867-669-2311, Fax: 867-873-0385

Nova Scotia

Nova Scotia Utility and Review Board, Summit Place, 1601 Lower Water St., 3rd Fl., Halifax, NS B3J 3P6
902-424-4448, uarb.board@gov.ns.ca

Ontario

Financial Services Commission of Ontario, 5160 Yonge St., PO Box 85, Toronto, ON M2N 6L9
416-250-7250, Fax: 416-590-7070, 800-668-0128

Quebec

Société de l'assurance automobile du Québec, 333, boul Jean-Lesage, CP 19600 Terminus, Québec, QC G1K 8J6
418-643-7620, Fax: 418-644-0339, 800-361-7620, courrier@saaq.gouv.qc.ca

Saskatchewan

Saskatchewan Government Insurance, 2260 - 11th Ave., Regina, S4P 0J9 SK
306-751-1200, Fax: 306-787-7477, 800-667-8015, sgiinquiries@sgi.sk.ca

Yukon Territory

Yukon Justice, PO Box 2703, Whitehorse, Y1A 2C6 YT
867-667-8655, Fax: 867-393-5790

BANKING & FINANCIAL INSTITUTIONS

Bank of Canada, 234 Wellington St., Ottawa, K1A 0G9 ON
613-782-8111, Fax: 613-782-7713, 800-303-1282, info@bankofcanada.ca; communications@bankofcanada.ca (Media)
Business Development Bank of Canada, #400, 5, Place Ville-Marie, Montréal, H3B 5E7 QC
514-283-5904, Fax: 514-283-2872, 877-232-2269
Canada Deposit Insurance Corporation, 50 O'Connor St., 17th Floor, PO Box 2340 D,Ottawa, K1P 5W5 ON
613-996-2081, Fax: 613-996-6095, 800-461-2342, info@cdic.ca; info@sadc.ca
Finance Canada, L'esplanade Laurier, 140 O'Connor St., Ottawa, K1A 0G5 ON
613-992-1573, Fax: 613-943-0938, finpub@fin.gc.ca
Financial Consumer Agency of Canada, 427 Laurier Ave. West, 6th Fl., Ottawa, K1R 1B9 ON
Fax: 613-941-1436, info@fcac-acfc.gc.ca
Office of the Superintendent of Financial Institutions, Kent Square, 255 Albert St., Ottawa, K1A 0H2 ON
613-990-7788, Fax: 613-990-5591, 800-385-8647, information@osfi-bsif.gc.ca
Treasury Management, Terrace Building, 9515 - 107 St., 3rd Fl., Edmonton, T5K 2C3 AB

Alberta

ATB Financial, 9888 Jasper Ave., Edmonton, AB T5J 1P1
780-408-7000, 800-332-8383
Credit Union Deposit Guarantee Corporation, 10130 - 103 St., 18th Fl., Edmonton, AB T5J 3N9
780-428-6680, Fax: 780-428-7571, 800-661-0351, mail@cudgc.ab.ca
Alberta Finance & Enterprise, Terrace Building, #426, 9515 - 107 St., Edmonton, T5K 2C3 AB
780-427-3035, Fax: 780-427-1147, tra.revenue@gov.ab.ca
Alberta Treasury Board, Legislature Bldg., #204, 10800 - 97 Ave., Edmonton, T5K 2B6 AB
780-415-4855, Fax: 780-422-4853

British Columbia

Ministry of Finance, PO Box 9048 Prov Govt,Victoria, V8W 9E2 BC
250-387-3751, Fax: 250-387-5594, Fin.Minister@gov.bc.ca
Financial Institutions Commission, #1200, 13450 - 102 Ave., Surrey, BC V3T 5X3
604-953-5300, Fax: 604-953-5301, 866-206-3030, FICOM@ficombc.ca; HR@ficombc.ca

Manitoba

Credit Union Deposit Guarantee Corporation, #390, 200 Graham Ave., Winnipeg, MB R3C 4L5
204-942-8480, Fax: 204-947-1723, 800-697-4447, mail@cudgc.com
Financial Institutions Regulation Branch, #1115, 405 Broadway, Winnipeg, R3C 3L6 MB
204-945-2542, Fax: 204-948-2268

New Brunswick

New Brunswick Credit Union Deposit Insurance Corp., PO Box 6000, Fredericton, NB E3B 5H1
506-457-4852, Fax: 506-453-7474

Newfoundland & Labrador

Credit Union Deposit Guarantee Corporation, PO Box 340, Marystown, NL A0E 2M0
709-279-0170, Fax: 709-279-0177, 877-279-0170

Northwest Territories

Department of Finance, YK Center, 3rd Fl., PO Box 1320, Yellowknife, X1A 2L9 NT
867-669-2311, Fax: 867-873-0385

Nunavut

Nunavut Business Credit Corporation, PO Box 224, Cape Dorset, NU X0A 0C0
867-897-3647, 800-758-0038

Ontario

Deposit Insurance Corporation of Ontario, #700, 4711 Yonge St., Toronto, ON M2N 6K8
416-325-9444, Fax: 416-325-9722, 800-268-6653
Ministry of Finance, Frost Bldg. South, 7 Queen's Park Cres., 7th Fl., Toronto, M7A 1Y7 ON
416-325-0333, Fax: 905-433-6777, 800-263-7965, financecommunications.fin@ontario.ca
Financial Services Commission of Ontario, 5160 Yonge St., PO Box 85, Toronto, ON M2N 6L9
416-250-7250, Fax: 416-590-7070, 800-668-0128
Ministry of Revenue, Frost Bldg. South, 7 Queen's Park Cres., 6th Fl., Toronto, M7A 1Y7 ON
Fax: 866-888-3850, 866-668-8297

Prince Edward Island

Consumer, Corporate & Insurance Division, Shaw Building, 95 Rochford St., 4th Fl., PO Box 2000, Charlottetown, C1A 7N8 PE
902-368-4580, Fax: 902-368-5283, 800-658-1799

Quebec

Caisse de dépôt et placement du Québec, 1000, place Jean-Paul-Riopelle, Montréal, QC H2Z 2B3
514-842-3261, Fax: 514-842-4833, 866-330-3936, info@lacaisse.com

Registraire des entreprises, 787, boul. Lebourgneuf, Québec, G2J 1C3 QC
418-644-4545, Fax: 418-528-5703, 877-644-4545, registre@servicesquebec.gouv.qc.ca

Saskatchewan

Saskatchewan Finance, 2350 Albert St., Regina, S4P 4A6 SK
306-787-6768, Fax: 306-787-0241

Saskatchewan Financial Services Commission, #601, 1919 Saskatchewan Dr., Regina, SK S4P 4H2
306-787-5645, Fax: 306-787-5899

Yukon Territory

Yukon Finance, PO Box 2703, Whitehorse, Y1A 2C6 YT
867-667-5343, Fax: 867-393-6217

BILINGUALISM

Canadian Heritage, 15 Eddy St., Gatineau, K1A 0M5 QC
819-997-0055, 866-811-0055, info@pch.gc.ca

Office of the Commissioner of Official Languages, 344 Slater St., 3rd fl., Ottawa, K1A 0T8 ON
613-996-6368, Fax: 613-993-5082, 877-996-6368,

Manitoba

Le Centre Culturel franco-manitobain/Franco-Manitoban Cultural Centre, 340, boul Provencher, St Boniface, MB R2H 0G7
204-233-8972, Fax: 204-233-3324, ccfm@ccfm.mb.ca

Northwest Territories

Office of the Languages Commissioner, PO Box 1320, Yellowknife, X1A 2L9 NT
867-873-7034, Fax: 888-305-7353, 800-661-0889

Nunavut

Department of Culture, Language, Elders & Youth, PO Box 1000 800,Iqaluit, X0A 0H0 NU
867-975-5500, Fax: 867-975-5504, 866-934-2035

Ontario

Office of Francophone Affairs, 777 Bay St., 6th Fl., Toronto, M7A 2J4 ON
416-325-4949, Fax: 416-325-4980, 800-268-7507, ofa@ontario.ca

Quebec

Secrétariat à la politique linguistique, 225 Grande-Allée est, 4e étage, Québec, G1R 5G5 QC
418-643-4248, Fax: 418-646-7832, info@spl.gouv.qc.ca

BIOTECHNOLOGY

Biotechnology Research Institute, 6100, av Royalmount, Montréal, H4P 2R2 QC
514-496-6100, Fax: 514-496-1928, bri-info@cnrc-nrc.gc.ca

Plant Biotechnology Institute, 110 Gymnasium Pl., Saskatoon, S7N 0W9 SK
306-975-5248, Fax: 306-975-4839, pbi-info@nrc-cnrc.gc.ca

BOARDS OF REVIEW

Canada Industrial Relations Board, 240 Sparks St., 4th Floor West, Ottawa, K1A 0X8 ON
613-947-5440, Fax: 613-995-9493, 800-575-9696, info@cirb-ccri.gc.ca

Canadian International Trade Tribunal, Standard Life Centre, 333 Laurier Ave. West, 17 Floor, Ottawa, K1A 0G7 ON
613-990-2452, Fax: 613-990-2439

Canadian Nuclear Safety Commission, 280 Slater St., PO Box 1046 B,Ottawa, K1P 5S9 ON
613-995-5894, Fax: 613-995-5086, 800-668-5284, info@cnsc-ccsn.gc.ca

Commission for Public Complaints Against the Royal Canadian Mounted Police, #102, 7337 137 St., Surrey, BC V3W 1A4
Fax: 613-952-8045, 800-665-6878, org@cpc-cpp.gc.ca

Homelessness Partnering Secretariat, 165, rue Hôtel-de-Ville, Gatineau, K1A 0J2 QC

Immigration & Refugee Board of Canada, Canada Bldg, 344 Slater St., 12th Fl., Ottawa, K1A 0K1 ON
613-995-6486, Fax: 613-943-1550, info@irb-cisr.gc.ca

Mackenzie Valley Environmental Impact Review Board, 200 Scotia Centre, 5102 - 50th Ave., PO Box 938, Yellowknife, NT X1A 2N7
867-766-7050, Fax: 867-766-7074, 866-912-3472, tcharlo@reviewboard.ca

Merchant Seamen Compensation Board, Secretary, Merchant Seamen Compensation Board, Phase II, Place du Portage, 10th Fl., Gatineau, QC K1A 0J2
819-953-8001, Fax: 819-994-5368

National Energy Board, 444 - 7 Ave. SW, Calgary, T2P 0X8 AB
403-292-4800, Fax: 403-292-5503, 800-899-1265, info@neb-one.gc.ca

Nunavut Impact Review Board, PO Box 1360, Cambridge Bay, NU X0B 0C0
867-983-4600, Fax: 867-983-2594, 866-233-3033, info@nirb.ca

Nunavut Water Board, PO Box 119, Gjoa Haven, NU X0B 1J0
867-360-6338, Fax: 867-360-6369

Patented Medicine Prices Review Board, Standard Life Centre, #1400, 333 Laurier Ave. West, PO Box L40, Ottawa, K1P 1C1 ON
613-952-7360, Fax: 613-952-7626, 877-861-2350, pmprb@pmprb-cepmb.gc.ca

Porcupine Caribou Management Board, PO Box 31723, Whitehorse, YT Y1A 6L3
867-633-4780, Fax: 867-393-3904, pcmb@taiga.net

Public Service Staffing Tribunal, 240 Sparks St., 6th Fl., Ottawa, K1A 0A5 ON
613-949-6516, Fax: 613-949-6551, 866-637-4491, info@psst-tdfp.gc.ca

Royal Canadian Mounted Police External Review Committee, PO Box 1159 B, Ottawa, ON K1P 5R2
613-998-2134, Fax: 613-990-8969, org@erc-cee.gc.ca

Rural & Co-operatives Secretariat, Tower 7, 1341 Baseline Rd., Ottawa, K1A 0C5 ON
613-759-1000, Fax: 613-773-2727

Security Intelligence Review Committee, Jackson Bldg., 122 Bank St., 4th Fl., PO Box 2430 D,Ottawa, K1P 5W5 ON
613-990-8441, Fax: 613-990-5230, ellardm@sirc-csars.gc.ca

Veterans Review & Appeal Board, Daniel J. MacDonald Bldg., 161 Grafton St., PO Box 9900, Charlottetown, PE C1A 8V7
902-566-8751, Fax: 902-566-7850, 800-450-8006, vrab_tacra@vac-acc.gc.ca

Alberta

Alberta Review Board, Oxford Tower, 10235 - 101 St., 11th Fl., Edmonton, AB T5J 3E9
780-422-5994, Fax: 780-427-1762

British Columbia

British Columbia Review Board, #1020, 510 Burrard St., Vancouver, BC V6C 3A8
604-660-8789, Fax: 604-660-8809, 877-305-2277

Manitoba

Manitoba Review Board, 408 York Ave., 2nd Fl., Winnipeg, MB R3C 0P9
204-945-4438, Fax: 204-945-5751

Northwest Territories

Legal Services Board of the Northwest Territories, PO Box 1320, Yellowknife, NT X1A 2L9
867-873-7450, Fax: 867-873-5320, www-jus-tice

Territorial Board of Revision, PO Box 1320, Yellowknife, NT X1A 2L9
867-873-7125, Fax: 867-873-0609

Ontario

Animal Care Review Board, 77 Grenville St., 8th Fl., Toronto, ON M5S 1B3
416-314-3509, Fax: 416-314-3518

Medical Eligibility Committee, 370 Select Dr., PO Box 168, Kingston, ON K7M 8T4
613-548-6405

Ontario Film Review Board, 1075 Millwood Rd., Toronto, ON M4G 1X6
416-314-3626, Fax: 416-314-3632

Ontario Municipal Board & Board of Negotiation, 655 Bay St., 15th Fl., Toronto, ON M5G 1E5
416-326-6800, Fax: 416-326-5370

Ontario Review Board, 151 Bloor St. West, 10th Fl., Toronto, ON M5S 2T5
416-327-8866, Fax: 416-327-8867

Quebec

Bureau d'audiences publiques sur l'environnement, Édifice Lomer-Gouin, #2.10, 575, rue Saint-Amable, 2e étage, Québec, QC G1R 6A6
418-643-7447, Fax: 418-643-9474, 800-463-4732, communication@bape.gouv.qc.ca

Saskatchewan

Public & Private Rights Board, 23-3085 Albert St., Regina, SK S4S 0B1
306-787-4071, Fax: 306-787-0088

Saskatchewan Film & Video Classification Board, #500, 1919 Saskatchewan Dr., Regina, SK S4P 4H2
306-787-5550, Fax: 306-787-9779, 888-374-4636, adwyer@justice.gov.sk.ca

Surface Rights Board of Arbitration, 113 - 2nd Ave. East, PO Box 1597, Kindersley, SK S0L 1S0
306-463-5447, Fax: 306-463-5449, SurfaceRightsBoard@gov.sk.ca

BROADCASTING

Canadian Broadcasting Corporation, 181 Queen St., PO Box 3220 C,Ottawa, K1Y 1E4 ON
613-288-6033, liaison@radio-canada.ca

Canadian Radio-Television & Telecommunications Commission, Central Office, 1, Promenade du Portage, Les Terrasses de la Chaudière, Gatineau, J8X 4B1 QC
819-997-0313, Fax: 819-994-0218, 877-249-2782,

Alberta

Alberta Public Affairs Bureau, Park Plaza, 10611 - 98 Ave., 6th Fl., Edmonton, T5K 2P7 AB
403-427-9261, Fax: 403-422-4168

Manitoba

Manitoba News Media Services, #29, Legislative Bldg., 450 Broadway, Winnipeg, R3C 0V8 MB
204-945-3746, Fax: 204-945-3988, nmservices@leg.gov.mb.ca

New Brunswick

Communications New Brunswick, Wilcom Bldg., 225 King St., 2nd Fl., PO Box 6000, Fredericton, E3B 5H1 NB
506-453-2240, Fax: 506-453-5329

Nova Scotia

Communications Nova Scotia, 1723 Hollis St., PO Box 608, Halifax, B3J 2R7 NS
902-424-7690, Fax: 902-424-0515

Quebec

Société de télédiffusion du Québec (Télé-Québec), 1000, rue Fullum, Montréal, H2K 3L7 QC
514-521-2424, Fax: 514-873-7739, 800-361-4301, info@telequebec.tv

Saskatchewan

Saskatchewan Communications Network, #313E, 2440 Broad St., Regina, S4P 0A5 SK
306-787-0490, Fax: 306-787-0496, 800-667-5055, inquiries@scn.ca

BUDGET PLANNING

Alberta

Enterprise Division, Commerce Place, 10155 - 102 St., 6th Fl., Edmonton, T5J 4L6 AB

British Columbia

Provincial Treasury, 620 Superior St., PO Box 9414 Prov Govt,Victoria, V8V 9V1 BC
250-387-4541, Fax: 250-356-3041, Jim.Hopkings@gov.bc.ca

New Brunswick

Budget & Financial Management, Centennial Bldg., #250, 670 King St., PO Box 6000, Fredericton, E3B 5H1 NB
506-453-2808, Fax: 506-444-4499

Northwest Territories

Department of Finance, YK Center, 3rd Fl., PO Box 1320, Yellowknife, X1A 2L9 NT
867-669-2311, Fax: 867-873-0385

Financial Management Board Secretariat, c/o Secretary of the FMB / Comptroller General, 5003 - 49 St., PO Box 1320, Yellowknife, X1A 2L9 NT
867-873-7211, Fax: 867-873-0112

Nova Scotia

Department of Finance, Provincial Bldg., 1723 Hollis St., 7th Fl., PO Box 187, Halifax, B3J 2N3 NS
902-424-5554, Fax: 902-424-0635, FinanceWeb@gov.ns.ca

Nunavut

Department of Finance, Bldg. 1079, 1st Fl., PO Box 1000 Stn 330,Iqaluit, X0A 0H0 NU
867-975-5800, Fax: 867-975-5805

Prince Edward Island

Department of the Provincial Treasury, Shaw Bldg., 95 Rochford St., 2nd Fl. South, PO Box 2000, Charlottetown, C1A 7N8 PE
902-368-4050, Fax: 902-368-6575

BUSINESS & FINANCE

Atlantic Canada Opportunities Agency, Blue Cross Centre, 644 Main St., 3rd Fl., PO Box 6051, Moncton, E1C 9J8 NB
506-851-2271, Fax: 506-851-7403, 800-561-7862, information@acoa-apeca.gc.ca

Auditor General of Canada, 240 Sparks St., Ottawa, K1A 0G6 ON
613-995-3708, Fax: 613-957-0474, 888-761-5953, communications@oag-bvg.gc.ca; infomedia@oag-bvg.gc.ca

Bank of Canada, 234 Wellington St., Ottawa, K1A 0G9 ON
613-782-8111, Fax: 613-782-7713, 800-303-1282,

info@bankofcanada.ca; communications@bankofcanada.ca (Media)
Business Development Bank of Canada, #400, 5, Place Ville-Marie, Montréal, H3B 5E7 QC
514-283-5904, Fax: 514-283-2872, 877-232-2269
Calgary, Home Oil Tower, #606, 3240 - 8 Ave. SW, Calgary, T2P 2Z2 AB
403-537-9800, Fax: 403-537-9811
Canada Business, 235 Queen St., Ottawa, K1A 0H5 ON
Fax: 888-417-0442, 888-576-4444
Canada Deposit Insurance Corporation, 50 O'Connor St., 17th Floor, PO Box 2340 D,Ottawa, K1P 5W5 ON
613-996-2081, Fax: 613-996-6095, 800-461-2342, info@cdic.ca; info@sadc.ca
Canada Economic Development for Québec Regions, Édifice Dominion Square, #900, 1255, rue Peel, Montréal, H3B 2T9 QC
514-283-6412, Fax: 514-283-3302, 866-385-6412
Canada Investment & Savings, #900, 110 Yonge St., Toronto, ON M5C 1T4
416-952-1252, Fax: 416-952-1270, 800-575-5151, csb@csb.gc.ca
Canada Mortgage & Housing Corporation, 700 Montreal Rd., Ottawa, K1A 0P7 ON
613-748-2000, Fax: 613-748-2098, 800-668-2642, chic@cmhc-schl.gc.ca
Canada Pension Plan Investment Board, #2600, 1 Queen St. East, PO Box 101, Toronto, M5C 2W5 ON
416-868-4075, Fax: 416-868-8689, 866-557-9510, csr@cppib.ca
Canada Revenue Agency, 875 Heron Rd., Ottawa, K1A 0L5 ON
613-952-0384, 800-267-6999
Canadian Commercial Corporation, 50 O'Connor St., 11th Fl., Ottawa, K1A 0S6 ON
613-996-0034, Fax: 613-995-2121, 800-748-8191
Canadian International Development Agency, 200, Promenade du Portage, Gatineau, K1A 0G4 QC
819-997-5006, Fax: 819-953-6088, 800-230-6349, info@acdi-cida.gc.ca
Cape Breton Development Fund Corporation, Silicon Island, 70 Crescent St., PO Box 1264, Sydney, NS B1P 6T7
902-564-3600, Fax: 902-564-3825, 800-705-3926
Competition Bureau, Place du Portage, Phase I, 50, rue Victoria, 21e étage, Ottawa, K1A 0C9 ON
613-997-4282, Fax: 613-997-0324, 800-348-5358, compbureau@ic.gc.ca
Competition Tribunal, Thomas D'Arcy McGee Bldg., #600, 90 Sparks St., Ottawa, ON K1P 5B4
613-957-3172, Fax: 613-957-3170, tribunal@ct-tc.gc.ca
Corporate Support Division, Telus Plaza NT, 10025 Jasper Ave., 19th Fl., Edmonton, T5J 1S6 AB
Electronic Commerce Branch, 300 Slater St., Ottawa, ON K1A 0C8
613-990-4268, Fax: 613-941-0178, 800-328-6189
Enterprise Cape Breton Corporation, Silicon Island, 70 Crescent St., Sydney, NS B1S 2Z7
902-564-3600, Fax: 902-564-3825, 800-705-3926,information@ecbc-secb.gc.ca
Export Development Canada, 151 O'Connor St., Ottawa, K1A 1K3 ON
613-598-2500, Fax: 613-598-3811, 800-267-8510
Farm Credit Canada, 1800 Hamilton St., PO Box 4320, Regina, S4P 4L3 SK
306-780-8100, Fax: 306-780-8919, 888-332-3301, csc@fcc-fac.ca
Finance Canada, L'esplanade Laurier, 140 O'Connor St., Ottawa, K1A 0G5 ON
613-992-1573, Fax: 613-943-0938, finpub@fin.gc.ca
Office of the Superintendent of Financial Institutions, Kent Square, 255 Albert St., Ottawa, K1A 0H2 ON
613-990-7788, Fax: 613-990-5591, 800-385-8647, information@osfi-bsif.gc.ca
Financial Transactions & Reports Analysis Centre of Canada, 234 Laurier Ave. West, 24th Fl., Ottawa, ON K1P 1H7
Fax: 613-943-7931, 866-346-8722, guidelines-lignesdirectrices@fintrac-canafe.gc.ca
Foreign Affairs & International Trade Canada, 125 Sussex Dr., Ottawa, K1A 0G2 ON
613-944-4000, Fax: 613-996-9709, 800-267-8376, enqserv@international.gc.ca
Freshwater Fish Marketing Corporation, 1199 Plessis Rd., Winnipeg, R2C 3L4 MB
204-983-6601, Fax: 204-983-6497, sandi.cain@freshwaterfish.com
Global Operations & Chief Trade Commissioner, 125 Sussex Dr,, Ottawa, K1A 0G2 ON
613-944-2697, Fax: 613-996-1667
Industry Canada, 235 Queen St., Ottawa, K1A 0H5 ON
Fax: 613-954-6436, 800-328-6189, info@ic.gc.ca
National Round Table on the Environment & Economy, #200, 344 Slater St., Ottawa, K1R 7Y3 ON
613-992-7189, Fax: 613-992-7385, admin@nrtee-trnee.ca
North American Free Trade Agreement (NAFTA) Secretariat, Canadian Section, #705, 90 Sparks St., Ottawa, K1P 5B4 ON
613-992-9388, Fax: 613-992-9392, webmaster@nafta-alena.gc.ca
Public Sector Pension Investment Board, #200, 440 Laurier Ave. West, Ottawa, ON K1R 7X6
613-782-3095, Fax: 613-782-6864, info@investpsp.ca
Royal Canadian Mint, 320 Sussex Dr., Ottawa, K1A 0G8 ON
613-993-3500, Fax: 613-993-4092, 800-267-1871
Statistics Canada, R.H. Coats Bldg., Tunney's Pasture, 100 Tunney's Pasture Driveway, Ottawa, K1A 0T6 ON
613-951-8116, Fax: 877-287-4369, 800-263-1136, infostats@statcan.ca
Treasury Board of Canada, 300 Laurier Ave. West, 10th Fl., Ottawa, K1A 0R5 ON
613-957-2400, Fax: 613-941-4000, 877-636-0656, info@tbs-sct.gc.ca
Treasury Management, Terrace Building, 9515 - 107 St., 3rd Fl., Edmonton, T5K 2C3 AB
Western Economic Diversification Canada, Canada Place, #1500, 9700 Jasper Ave. NW, Edmonton, T5J 4H7 AB
780-495-4164, Fax: 780-495-4557, 888-338-9378

Alberta

Agriculture Financial Services Corporation, 5718 - 56 Ave., Lacombe, AB T4L 1B1
403-782-8200, Fax: 403-782-4226, 800-396-0215
Alberta Capital Finance Authority, Canadian Western Bank Place, #2450, 10303 Jasper Ave., Edmonton, AB T5J 3N6
780-427-9711, Fax: 780-422-2175, webacfa@gov.ab.ca
Alberta Securities Commission, 300 - 5 Ave. SW, 4th Fl., Calgary, AB T2P 3C4
403-297-6454, Fax: 403-297-6156, 877-355-0585, inquiries@asc.ca
ATB Financial, 9888 Jasper Ave., Edmonton, AB T5J 1P1
780-408-7000, 800-332-8383
Alberta Office of the Auditor General, 9925 - 109 St., 8th Fl., Edmonton, T5K 2J8 AB
780-427-4222, Fax: 780-422-9555, info@oag.ab.ca
Automobile Insurance Rate Board, Terrace Bldg., #200, 9515 - 107 St. NW, Edmonton, AB T5K 2C3
780-415-1126, Fax: 780-644-7771, airb@gov.ab.ca
Credit Union Deposit Guarantee Corporation, 10130 - 103 St., 18th Fl., Edmonton, AB T5J 3N9
780-428-6680, Fax: 780-428-7571, 800-661-0351, mail@cudgc.ab.ca
Alberta Finance & Enterprise, Terrace Building, #426, 9515 - 107 St., Edmonton, T5K 2C3 AB
780-427-3035, Fax: 780-427-1147, tra.revenue@gov.ab.ca
Intergovernmental Relations, Commerce Place, 10155 - 102 St., 12th Fl., Edmonton, T5J 4L8 AB
Alberta Treasury Board, Legislature Bldg., #204, 10800 - 97 Ave., Edmonton, T5K 2B6 AB
780-415-4855, Fax: 780-422-4853

British Columbia

Asia Pacific Foundation of Canada, #666, 999 Canada Pl., Vancouver, BC V6C 3E1
604-684-5986, info@asiapacific.ca; researchgrants@asiapacific.ca
Auditor Certification Board, 940 Blanshard St., 2nd Fl., PO Box 9431 Prov Govt, Victoria, BC V8W 9V3
250-356-8658, Fax: 250-356-9422, sherrilyn.johnson@gov.bc.ca
Office of the Auditor General, 8 Bastion Sq., Victoria, V8V 1X4 BC
250-387-6803, Fax: 250-387-1230, info@bcauditor.com
British Columbia Innovation Council, 1188 West Georgia St., 9th Fl., Vancouver, BC V6E 4A2
604-683-2724, Fax: 604-683-6567, 800-665-7222, info@bcic.ca
British Columbia Pension Corporation, 2995 Jutland Rd., PO Box 9460, Victoria, BC V8W 9V8
250-387-1002, Fax: 250-953-0429, 800-663-8823, PensionCorp@pensionsbc.ca; Retired.Members@pensionsbc.ca
British Columbia Securities Commission, Pacific Centre, 701 West Georgia St., 12th Fl., PO Box 10142, Vancouver, BC V7Y 1L2
604-899-6500, Fax: 604-899-6506, 800-373-6393, inquiries@bcsc.bc.ca
Crown Agencies Secretariat, #400, 1675 Douglas St,, PO Box 9300 Prov Govt, Victoria, BC V8W 9N2
250-952-0750, Fax: 250-952-0777, 800-663-7867, Trena.Huson@gov.bc.ca
Ministry of Finance, PO Box 9048 Prov Govt,Victoria, V8W 9E2 BC
250-387-3751, Fax: 250-387-5594, Fin.Minister@gov.bc.ca
Financial Institutions Commission, #1200, 13450 - 102 Ave., Surrey, BC V3T 5X3
604-953-5300, Fax: 604-953-5301, 866-206-3030, FICOM@ficombc.ca; HR@ficombc.ca
Insurance Corporation of British Columbia, 151 West Esplanade, North Vancouver, V7M 3H9 BC
604-661-2800, 800-663-3051
Insurance Council of British Columbia, #300, 1040 West Georgia St., PO Box 7, Vancouver, BC V6E 4H1
604-688-0321, Fax: 604-662-7767, 877-688-0321
International Financial Centre British Columbia, Park Place, #1170, 666 Burrard St., Vancouver, BC V6C 2X8
604-683-6626, Fax: 604-683-6646, info@ifcvancouver.com
Office of the Superintendent of Motor Vehicles, 940 Blanshard St., PO Box 9254 Prov Govt,Victoria, V8W 9J2 BC
250-387-7747, Fax: 250-387-4891, OSMV.Mailbox@gov.bc.ca
Provincial Capital Commission, 613 Pandora Ave., Victoria, BC V8W 1N8
250-953-8800, Fax: 250-386-1303, info.pcc@bcpcc.com
Public Sector Employers' Council Secretariat, #210, 880 Douglas St., PO Box 9400 Prov Govt, Victoria, BC V8V 9V1
250-387-0842, Fax: 250-387-6258
Ministry of Small Business & Revenue, 1810 Blanshard St., 3rd Fl., PO Box 9432 Prov Govt,Victoria, V8W 9N6 BC
250-387-6206, Fax: 250-952-0712, MSBROffice@gov.bc.ca
Timber Export Advisory Committee, 1520 Blanshard St., 2nd Fl., PO Box 9514 Prov Govt, Victoria, BC V8W 9C2
250-387-8916, Fax: 250-387-5050

Manitoba

Office of the Auditor General, #500, 330 Portage Ave., Winnipeg, R3C 0C4 MB
204-945-3790, Fax: 204-945-2169, contact@oag.mb.ca
Claimant Adviser Office, #200, 330 Portage Ave., Winnipeg, MB R3C 0C4
204-945-7413, Fax: 204-948-3157
Communities Economic Development Fund, #100, 23 Station Rd., Thompson, MB R8N 0N6
204-778-4138, Fax: 204-778-4313, 800-561-4315
Manitoba Competitiveness, Training & Trade, International Business Centre, The Paris Building, 259 Portage Ave., Winnipeg, R3B 3P4 MB
204-945-2475, Fax: 204-945-3977, minctt@leg.gov.mb.ca
Comptroller Division, #715, 401 York Ave., Winnipeg, R3C 0P8 MB
204-945-4920, Fax: 204-945-2394
Credit Union Deposit Guarantee Corporation, #390, 200 Graham Ave., Winnipeg, MB R3C 4L5
204-942-8480, Fax: 204-947-1723, 800-697-4447, mail@cudgc.com
Crown Corporations Council, #1130, 444 St. Mary Ave., Winnipeg, MB R3C 3T1
204-949-5270, Fax: 204-949-5283, crowncc@mts.net
Manitoba Development Corporation, #555, 155 Carlton St., Winnipeg, R3C 3H8 MB
204-945-7626, Fax: 204-945-1193
Federal-Provincial Relations & Research Division, #910, 386 Broadway, Winnipeg, R3C 3R6 MB
204-945-3757, Fax: 204-945-5051
Manitoba Finance, #109, Legislative Bldg., Winnipeg, R3C 0V8 MB
204-945-3754, Fax: 204-945-8316, minfin@leg.gov.mb.ca
Heritage Grants Advisory Council, 213 Notre Dame Ave., 3rd Fl., Winnipeg, MB R3B 1N3
204-945-2213, Fax: 204-948-2086
Manitoba Public Insurance, #820, 234 Donald St., PO Box 6300, Winnipeg, R3C 4A4 MB
204-985-7000, Fax: 204-943-9851, 800-665-2410
Manitoba Intergovernmental Affairs, #301, 450 Broadway Ave., Winnipeg, R3C 0V8 MB
Fax: 204-945-1383, mnia@leg.gov.mb.ca
Manitoba Agricultural Services Corporation, #100, 1525 First St. South, Brandon, MB R7A 7A1
204-726-6850, Fax: 204-726-6849, mailbox@masc.mb.ca
Manitoba Bureau of Statistics, #824, 155 Carlton St., Winnipeg, R3C 3H9 MB
204-945-2406, Fax: 204-945-0695
Manitoba Round Table for Sustainable Development, #160, 123 Main St., Winnipeg, R3C 1A5 MB
204-945-1671, Fax: 204-948-2357, mrtsd@gov.mb.ca
Manitoba Securities Commission, #500, 400 St. Mary Ave., Winnipeg, MB R3C 4K5
204-945-2548, Fax: 204-945-0330, 800-655-5244, securities@gov.mb.ca
Mineral Resources Division, #360, 1395 Ellice Ave., Winnipeg, R3G 3P2 MB
Fax: 204-945-8427

Pension Commission of Manitoba, #1004, 401 York Ave., Winnipeg, MB R3C 0P8
204-945-2740, Fax: 204-948-2375, pensions@gov.mb.ca
Manitoba Treasury Board Secretariat, #200, 386 Broadway, Winnipeg, R3C 3R6 MB
204-945-4150, Fax: 204-948-4878

New Brunswick

Office of the Auditor General, HSBC Place, 520 King St., 6th Fl., Fredericton, E3B 6G3 NB
506-453-2243, Fax: 506-453-3067
Department of Business New Brunswick, Centennial Bldg., 670 King St., PO Box 6000, Fredericton, E3B 5H1 NB
506-444-5228, Fax: 506-453-5428
Office of the Comptroller, Centennial Bldg., 670 King St., Fredericton, E3B 1G1 NB
506-453-2565, Fax: 506-453-2917, wwwooc@gnb.ca
Corporate Services, Centennial Bldg., 670 King St., 5th Fl., PO Box 6000, Fredericton, E3B 5H1 NB
506-453-3707, Fax: 506-453-3993
Finance & Administration, Centennial Bldg., #373, 670 King St., PO Box 6000, Fredericton, E3B 5H1 NB
506-457-6863, Fax: 506-444-4724
Department of Finance, 670 King St., PO Box 6000, Fredericton, E3B 5H1 NB
506-453-2451, Fax: 506-444-4724
New Brunswick Credit Union Deposit Insurance Corp., PO Box 6000, Fredericton, NB E3B 5H1
506-457-4852, Fax: 506-453-7474
New Brunswick Crop Insurance Commission, PO Box 6000, Fredericton, NB E3B 5H1
506-453-2185, Fax: 506-453-7406
New Brunswick Expropriations Advisory Office, Phoenix Square Bldg., 371 Queen St., Fredericton, NB E3B 1B1
506-453-7771, Fax: 506-453-9600
New Brunswick Farm Products Commission, c/o Department of Agriculture & Aquaculture, PO Box 6000, Fredericton, NB E3B 5H1
506-453-3647, Fax: 506-444-5969
New Brunswick Investment Management Corporation, York Tower, #581, 440 King St., Fredericton, NB E3B 5H8
506-444-5800, Fax: 506-444-5025, comments@nbimc.com
New Brunswick Lotteries & Gaming Corporation, Centennial Bldg., 670 King St., PO Box 6000, Fredericton, NB E3B 5H1
506-453-2451, Fax: 506-457-4989
New Brunswick Municipal Finance Corporation, #376, 670 King St., PO Box 6000, Fredericton, NB E3B 5H1
506-453-3952, Fax: 506-453-2053
New Brunswick Round Table on Environment & Economy, 20 McGloin St., PO Box 6000, Fredericton, NB E3B 5H1
506-453-3703, Fax: 506-453-3876
Regional Development Corporation, RDC Bldg., 836 Churchill Row, PO Box 428, Fredericton, E3B 5R4 NB
506-453-2277, Fax: 506-453-7988
Department of Supply & Services, PO Box 6000, Fredericton, E3B 5H1 NB
506-453-3742, Fax: 506-444-4400, Reception.Marysville@gnb.ca

Newfoundland & Labrador

Office of the Auditor General, Viking Bldg., 3rd Fl., PO Box 8700, St. John's, A1B 4J6 NL
709-729-2700, Fax: 709-729-5970, oag@gov.nl.ca
Department of Business, Confederation Bldg., East Block, 6th Fl., PO Box 8700, St. John's, A1B 4J6 NL
709-729-3254, Fax: 709-729-3306, business@gov.nl.ca
Credit Union Deposit Guarantee Corporation, PO Box 340, Marystown, NL A0E 2M0
709-279-0170, Fax: 709-279-0177, 877-279-0170
Department of Finance, Confederation Bldg., PO Box 8700, St. John's, A1B 4J6 NL
709-729-6310, finance@gov.nl.ca
Department of Innovation, Trade & Rural Development, West Block, Confederation Bldg., PO Box 8700, St. John's, A1B 4J6 NL
709-729-7000, Fax: 709-729-0654, 800-563-2299, itrd@gov.nl.ca
Ireland Business Partnership, PO Box 8700, St. John's, NL A1B 4J6
709-729-1684, Fax: 709-729-2236
Department of Labrador & Aboriginal Affairs, Confederation Bldg., East Block, 6th Fl., PO Box 8700, St. John's, A1B 4J6 NL
709-729-4776, Fax: 709-729-4900, 877-788-8822, laa@gov.nl.ca
Nearshore Atlantic, 84 Elizabeth Ave., 1st Fl., St. John's, NL A1A 1W7
709-772-8324, Fax: 709-757-6284, info@nearshoreatlantic.com
Newfoundland & Labrador Municipal Financing Corporation, Confederation Bldg., PO Box 8700, St. John's, NL A1B 4J6
709-729-6686, Fax: 709-729-2095

Northwest Territories

Department of Finance, YK Center, 3rd Fl., PO Box 1320, Yellowknife, X1A 2L9 NT
867-669-2311, Fax: 867-873-0385
Financial Management Board Secretariat, c/o Secretary of the FMB / Comptroller General, 5003 - 49 St., PO Box 1320, Yellowknife, X1A 2L9 NT
867-873-7211, Fax: 867-873-0112
Northwest Territories Business Development & Investment Corporation, #701, 5201 - 50 Ave., Yellowknife, NT X1A 3S9
867-920-6455, Fax: 867-765-0652, bdicinfo@gov.nt.ca
Department of Public Works & Services, PO Box 1320, Yellowknife, X1A 2L9 NT
867-873-7114, Fax: 867-873-0226

Nova Scotia

Office of the Auditor General, #302, 1888 Brunswick St., Halifax, B3J 3J8 NS
902-424-5907, Fax: 902-424-4350
Department of Economic & Rural Development, Centennial Building, #600, 1660 Hollis St., PO Box 2311, Halifax, B3J 1V7 NS
902-424-0377, Fax: 902-424-7008, comm@gov.ns.ca
Department of Finance, Provincial Bldg., 1723 Hollis St., 7th Fl., PO Box 187, Halifax, B3J 2N3 NS
902-424-5554, Fax: 902-424-0635, FinanceWeb@gov.ns.ca
Nova Scotia Business Inc., World Trade & Convention Centre, #701, 1800 Argyle St., PO Box 2374, Halifax, NS B3J 3E4
902-424-6650, Fax: 902-424-5739, 800-260-6682, info@nsbi.ca
Nova Scotia Securities Commission, Joseph Howe Bldg., 1690 Hollis St., 2nd Fl., PO Box 458, Halifax, NS B3J 2P8
902-424-7768, Fax: 902-424-4625
Pension Regulation Division, PO Box 2531, Halifax, B3J 3N5 NS
902-424-8915, Fax: 902-424-0662

Nunavut

Department of Finance, Bldg. 1079, 1st Fl., PO Box 1000 Stn 330,Iqaluit, X0A 0H0 NU
867-975-5800, Fax: 867-975-5805
Nunavut Legal Registries Division, Brown Bldg., 1st Fl., PO Box 1000 570,Iqaluit, X0A 0H0 NU
867-975-6190, Fax: 867-975-6194

Ontario

Advertising Review Board, Macdonald Block, #M2-56, 900 Bay St., 2nd Fl., Toronto, ON M7A 1N3
416-327-2183, Fax: 416-327-2179
Agriculture, Food & Rural Affairs Tribunal, 1 Stone Rd. West, 1st Fl., Guelph, ON N1G 4Y2
519-826-3433, Fax: 519-826-4232, appeals.tribunal@omafra.gov.on.ca
Office of the Provincial Auditor, 20 Dundas St. West, 15th Fl., PO Box 105, Toronto, M5G 2C2 ON
416-327-2381, Fax: 416-327-9862, comments@auditor.on.ca
Deposit Insurance Corporation of Ontario, #700, 4711 Yonge St., Toronto, ON M2N 6K8
416-325-9444, Fax: 416-325-9722, 800-268-6653
Ministry of Economic Development & Trade, Hearst Block, 900 Bay St., 8th Fl., Toronto, M7A 2E1 ON
416-325-6666, Fax: 416-325-6688, 866-668-4249, info@edt.gov.on.ca
Ministry of Finance, Frost Bldg. South, 7 Queen's Park Cres., 7th Fl., Toronto, M7A 1Y7 ON
416-325-0333, Fax: 905-433-6777, 800-263-7965, financecommunications.fin@ontario.ca
Financial Services Commission of Ontario, 5160 Yonge St., PO Box 85, Toronto, ON M2N 6L9
416-250-7250, Fax: 416-590-7070, 800-668-0128
Ministry of Government Services, Whitney Block, #4320, 99 Wellesley St. West, 4th Fl., Toronto, M7A 1W3 ON
416-326-1234, Fax: 416-327-3790, 800-268-1142
Grain Financial Protection Board, 1 Stone Rd. West, PO Box 3660, Guelph, ON N1H 8M4
519-826-3949, Fax: 519-826-3367
Infrasutucture Ontario, 777 Bay St., 9th Fl., Toronto, M5G 2C8 ON
416-212-7289, Fax: 416-325-4646, info@infrastructureontario.ca
Licence Appeal Tribunal (LAT), 1 St. Clair Ave. West, 12th Fl., Toronto, ON M4V 1K6
416-314-4260, Fax: 416-314-4270, 800-255-2214
Livestock Financial Protection Board, 1 Stone Rd. West, 5th Fl. NW, Guelph, ON N1G 4Y2
519-826-3886, Fax: 519-826-4375, jim.wideman@omaf.gov.on.ca
Metro Toronto Convention Centre Corporation, 255 Front St. West, Toronto, ON M5V 2W6
416-585-8000, Fax: 416-585-8270, info@mtcc.com
Normal Farm Practices Protection Board, 1 Stone Rd. West, 3rd Fl., Northeast, Guelph, ON N1G 4Y2
519-826-3549, Fax: 519-826-6611
Ontario Electricity Financial Corporation, #1400, 1 Dundas St. West, Toronto, ON M7A 1Y7
416-325-8000, Fax: 416-325-8005
Ontario Farm Products Marketing Commission, 1 Stone Rd. West, 5th Fl., Guelph, ON N1G 4Y2
519-826-4220, Fax: 519-826-3400
Ontario Financing Authority, #1400, 1 Dundas St. West, Toronto, ON M7A 1Y7
416-325-8000, Fax: 416-325-8005
Ontario Food Terminal Board, 165 The Queensway, Toronto, ON M8Y 1H8
416-259-5479, Fax: 416-259-4303
Ontario Place Corporation, 955 Lake Shore Blvd. West, Toronto, ON M6K 3B9
416-314-9900, Fax: 416-314-9992
Ontario Securities Commission, #1903, 20 Queen St. West, PO Box 55, Toronto, ON M5H 3S8
416-597-0681, Fax: 416-593-8122
Ottawa Congress Centre, 55 Colonel By Dr., Ottawa, ON K1N 9J2
613-563-1984, Fax: 613-563-7646
Pay Equity Commission, 400 University Ave., 11th Fl., Toronto, ON M7A 1T7
416-314-1896, Fax: 416-314-8741, 800-387-8813
Ministry of Revenue, Frost Bldg. South, 7 Queen's Park Cres., 6th Fl., Toronto, M7A 1Y7 ON
Fax: 866-888-3850, 866-668-8297,
Ministry of Small Business & Customer Services, Whitney Block, #1306 - 99 Wellesley St. W., Toronto, M7A 1W2 ON
416-325-6000, Fax: 416-326-1947, 866-668-4249, info.sbe@ontario.ca
Stadium Corporation of Ontario Ltd., 33 King St. West, 6th Fl., Oshawa, ON L1H 8H5
416-314-5158, Fax: 905-433-6688

Prince Edward Island

Agricultural Insurance Corporation, 29 Indigo Cres., PO Box 1600, Charlottetown, PE C1A 7N3
902-368-4842, Fax: 902-368-6677, peiaic@gov.pe.ca
Office of the Auditor General, Shaw Bldg., 105 Rochford St, 2nd Fl., PO Box 2000, Charlottetown, C1A 7N8 PE
902-368-4520, Fax: 902-368-4598
Department of Innovation & Advanced Learning, Shaw Bldg., 105 Rochford St., 5th Fl., PO Box 2000, Charlottetown, C1A 7N8 PE
902-368-4240, Fax: 902-368-4242
Island Investment Development Inc., 94 Euston St., 2nd Fl., Charlottetown, PE C1A 1W4
902-894-0351, Fax: 902-368-5886
Prince Edward Island Business Development Inc., 94 Euston St., 1st & 2nd Fl., PO Box 910, Charlottetown, PE C1A 7L9
902-368-6300, Fax: 902-368-6301, 800-563-3734, business@gov.pe.ca
Prince Edward Island Lending Agency, Confederation Court Office Tower, #201, 134 Kent St., PO Box 1420, Charlottetown, PE C1A 7N1
902-368-6200, Fax: 902-368-6201
Prince Edward Island Lotteries Commission, Office of the Deputy Provincial Treasurer, 95 Rochford St., PO Box 2000, Charlottetown, PE C1A 7N8
902-368-4053, Fax: 902-368-6575
Department of the Provincial Treasury, Shaw Bldg., 95 Rochford St., 2nd Fl. South, PO Box 2000, Charlottetown, C1A 7N8 PE
902-368-4050, Fax: 902-368-6575

Quebec

Autorité des marchés financiers, Tour de la Bourse, 800, Square Victoria, 22e étage, Montréal, QC H4Z 1G3
514-395-0337, Fax: 514-873-3090, 877-525-0337
Caisse de dépôt et placement du Québec, 1000, place Jean-Paul-Riopelle, Montréal, QC H2Z 2B3
514-842-3261, Fax: 514-842-4833, 866-330-3936, info@lacaisse.com
Ministère des Finances, Édifice Gérard-D.-Lévesque, 12, rue Saint-Louis, Québec, G1R 5L3 QC
418-528-9323, Fax: 418-646-1631, info@finances.gouv.qc.ca
Fonds de la recherche en santé du Québec, #800, 500, rue Sherbrooke ouest, Montréal, QC H3A 3C6
514-873-2114, Fax: 514-873-8768
Innovatech Québec, #120, 925, Grande Allée ouest, Québec, QC G1S 1C1
418-528-9770, Fax: 418-528-9783, 866-605-1676, info@innovatech-regions.qc.ca

Le Protecteur du Citoyen, #1.25, 525, boul René-Lévesque est, Québec, G1R 5Y4 QC
418-643-2688, Fax: 418-643-8759, 800-463-5070
Loto-Québec, 500, rue Sherbrooke ouest, Montréal, QC H3A 3G6
514-282-8000, Fax: 514-873-8999
Registraire des entreprises, 787, boul. Lebourgneuf, Québec, G2J 1C3 QC
418-644-4545, Fax: 418-528-5703, 877-644-4545, registre@servicesquebec.gouv.qc.ca
Ministère des Relations internationales, Édifice Hector-Fabre, 525, boul Réne-Lévesque est, Québec, G1R 5R9 QC
418-649-2300, Fax: 418-649-2656, communications@mri.gouv.qc.ca
Revenu Québec, Direction des relations publiques/Communications, 3800, rue de Marly, Québec, G1X 4A5 QC
418-652-6831, Fax: 418-646-0167
Régie des rentes du Québec, CP 5200, Sainte-Foy, QC G1K 7S9
418-643-5185, rrq@rrq.gouv.qc.ca
Société du Centre des congrès de Québec, 900, boul René-Lévesque est, 2e étage, Québec, QC G1R 2B5
418-644-4000, Fax: 418-644-6455, 888-679-4000
Société générale de financement du Québec, #1500, 600, rue de La Gauchetière ouest, Montréal, QC H3B 4L8
514-876-9290, Fax: 514-395-8055, info@sgfqc.com
Société générale de financement du Québec, #1500, 600, rue de La Gauchetière ouest, Montréal, QC H3B 4L8
514-876-9290, Fax: 514-395-8055, info@sgfqc.com
Secrétariat du Conseil du trésor, 875, Grande Allée est, 3e étage, secteur 100, Québec, G1R 5R8 QC
418-643-1529, Fax: 418-643-9226, 866-552-5158, communication@sct.gouv.qc.ca
Vérificateur général du Québec, 750, boulevard Charest est, 3e étage, Québec, G1K 9J6 QC
418-691-5900, Fax: 418-644-4460, verificateur.general@vgq.gouv.qc.

Saskatchewan

Provincial Auditor Saskatchewan, #1500, 1920 Broad St., Regina, S4P 3V2 SK
306-787-6398, Fax: 306-787-6383, info@auditor.sk.ca
Board of Revenue Commissioners, #480, 2151 Scarth St., Regina, SK S4P 2H8
306-787-6221, Fax: 306-787-1610
Crown Investments Corporation of Saskatchewan, #400, 2400 College Ave., Regina, S4P 1C8 SK
306-787-6851, Fax: 306-787-8125
Saskatchewan Energy & Resources, #300, 2103 - 11th Ave., Regina, S4P 3Z8 SK
306-787-2528, Fax: 306-787-0395, 866-727-5427
Saskatchewan Finance, 2350 Albert St., Regina, S4P 4A6 SK
306-787-6768, Fax: 306-787-0241
Saskatchewan Government Insurance, 2260 - 11th Ave., Regina, S4P 0J9 SK
306-751-1200, Fax: 306-787-7477, 800-667-8015, sgiinquiries@sgi.sk.ca
Saskatchewan Crop Insurance Corporation, 484 Prince William Dr., PO Box 3000, Melville, SK S0A 2P0
306-728-7200, Fax: 306-728-7268, 888-935-0000, customer.service@scic.gov.sk.ca
Saskatchewan Development Fund Corporation, #300, 2400 College Ave., Regina, SK S4P 1C8
306-787-1645, 800-667-7543
Saskatchewan Financial Services Commission, #601, 1919 Saskatchewan Dr., Regina, SK S4P 4H2
306-787-5645, Fax: 306-787-5899
Saskatchewan Trade & Export Partnership, #320, 1801 Hamilton St., PO Box 1787, Regina, SK S4P 3C6
306-787-9210, Fax: 306-787-6666, 877-313-7244, inquire@sasktrade.sk.ca

Yukon Territory

Yukon Finance, PO Box 2703, Whitehorse, Y1A 2C6 YT
867-667-5343, Fax: 867-393-6217
Yukon Lottery Commission, 312 Wood St., Whitehorse, YT Y1A 2E6
867-633-7890, Fax: 867-668-7561, lotteriesyukon@gov.yk.ca

BUSINESS DEVELOPMENT

See Also: Industry; Science & Technology
Atlantic Canada Opportunities Agency, Blue Cross Centre, 644 Main St., 3rd Fl., PO Box 6051, Moncton, E1C 9J8 NB
506-851-2271, Fax: 506-851-7403, 800-561-7862, information@acoa-apeca.gc.ca
Business Development Bank of Canada, #400, 5, Place Ville-Marie, Montréal, H3B 5E7 QC
514-283-5904, Fax: 514-283-2872, 877-232-2269
Canada Business, 235 Queen St., Ottawa, K1A 0H5 ON
Fax: 888-417-0442, 888-576-4444
Canada Economic Development for Québec Regions, Édifice Dominion Square, #900, 1255, rue Peel, Montréal, H3B 2T9 QC
514-283-6412, Fax: 514-283-3302, 866-385-6412
Cape Breton Development Fund Corporation, Silicon Island, 70 Crescent St., PO Box 1264, Sydney, NS B1P 6T7
902-564-3600, Fax: 902-564-3825, 800-705-3926
Enterprise Cape Breton Corporation, Silicon Island, 70 Crescent St., Sydney, NS B1S 2Z7
902-564-3600, Fax: 902-564-3825, 800-705-3926,information@ecbc-secb.gc.ca
Export Development Canada, 151 O'Connor St., Ottawa, K1A 1K3 ON
613-598-2500, Fax: 613-598-3811, 800-267-8510
Global Operations & Chief Trade Commissioner, 125 Sussex Dr,, Ottawa, K1A 0G2 ON
613-944-2697, Fax: 613-996-1667
Industry Canada, 235 Queen St., Ottawa, K1A 0H5 ON
Fax: 613-954-6436, 800-328-6189, info@ic.gc.ca
Market & Industry Services Branch, Tower 5, 1341 Baseline Rd., Ottawa, K1A 0C5 ON
613-759-1000, Fax: 613-773-1755
Western Economic Diversification Canada, Canada Place, #1500, 9700 Jasper Ave. NW, Edmonton, T5J 4H7 AB
780-495-4164, Fax: 780-495-4557, 888-338-9378

Alberta

Alberta Economic Development Authority, McDougall Centre, 455 - 6 St. SW, Calgary, AB T2P 4E8
403-297-3022, Fax: 403-297-6435

British Columbia

Asia Pacific Foundation of Canada, #666, 999 Canada Pl., Vancouver, BC V6C 3E1
604-684-5986, info@asiapacific.ca; researchgrants@asiapacific.ca
British Columbia Innovation Council, 1188 West Georgia St., 9th Fl., Vancouver, BC V6E 4A2
604-683-2724, Fax: 604-683-6567, 800-665-7222, info@bcic.ca
British Columbia Progress Board, #730, 999 Canada Pl., Vancouver, BC V6C 3E1
604-775-1664, Fax: 604-775-2129, ideas@bcprogressboard.com
Columbia Basin Trust, Southwest Basin, 5400, 445 - 13 Ave., Castlegar, BC V1N 1G1
250-365-6633, Fax: 250-365-6670, 800-505-8998, cbt@cbt.org
Economic Competitiveness Division, 1810 Blanshard St., 7th Fl., PO Box 9327 Prov Govt,Victoria, V8W 9N3 BC
250-952-0367, Fax: 250-952-0137
International Financial Centre British Columbia, Park Place, #1170, 666 Burrard St., Vancouver, BC V6C 2X8
604-683-6626, Fax: 604-683-6646, info@ifcvancouver.com
Northern Development Initiative Trust, #301, 1268 Fifth Ave., Prince George, BC V2L 3L2
250-561-2525, Fax: 250-561-2563, admin@nditrust.ca
Ministry of Small Business & Revenue, 1810 Blanshard St., 3rd Fl., PO Box 9432 Prov Govt,Victoria, V8W 9N6 BC
250-387-6206, Fax: 250-952-0712, MSBROffice@gov.bc.ca
Small Business BC, #82, 601 West Cordova St., Vancouver, BC V6B 1G1
800-775-5525, Fax: 604-775-5520, 800-667-2272, askus@smallbusinessbc.ca
Ministry of Small Business, Technology & Economic Development, 1810 Blanshard St., PO Box 9324 Prov Govt,Victoria, V8W 9N3 BC
250-356-7411, Fax: 250-356-6376, Feedback.CSE@gov.bc.ca

Manitoba

Manitoba Competitiveness, Training & Trade, International Business Centre, The Paris Building, 259 Portage Ave., Winnipeg, R3B 3P4 MB
204-945-2475, Fax: 204-945-3977, minctt@leg.gov.mb.ca
Manitoba Development Corporation, #555, 155 Carlton St., Winnipeg, R3C 3H8 MB
204-945-7626, Fax: 204-945-1193

New Brunswick

Department of Business New Brunswick, Centennial Bldg., 670 King St., PO Box 6000, Fredericton, E3B 5H1 NB
506-444-5228, Fax: 506-453-5428
Regional Development Corporation, RDC Bldg., 836 Churchill Row, PO Box 428, Fredericton, E3B 5R4 NB
506-453-2277, Fax: 506-453-7988

Newfoundland & Labrador

Department of Business, Confederation Bldg., East Block, 6th Fl., PO Box 8700, St. John's, A1B 4J6 NL
709-729-3254, Fax: 709-729-3306, business@gov.nl.ca
Department of Innovation, Trade & Rural Development, West Block, Confederation Bldg., PO Box 8700, St. John's, A1B 4J6 NL
709-729-7000, Fax: 709-729-0654, 800-563-2299, itrd@gov.nl.ca
Ireland Business Partnership, PO Box 8700, St. John's, NL A1B 4J6
709-729-1684, Fax: 709-729-2236
Department of Labrador & Aboriginal Affairs, Confederation Bldg., East Block, 6th Fl., PO Box 8700, St. John's, A1B 4J6 NL
709-729-4776, Fax: 709-729-4900, 877-788-8822, laa@gov.nl.ca

Northwest Territories

Department of Industry, Tourism & Investment, PO Box 1320, Yellowknife, X1A 2L9 NT
Fax: 867-873-0306, info@iti.ca
Northwest Territories Business Development & Investment Corporation, #701, 5201 - 50 Ave., Yellowknife, NT X1A 3S9
867-920-6455, Fax: 867-765-0652, bdicinfo@gov.nt.ca

Nova Scotia

Department of Economic & Rural Development, Centennial Building, #600, 1660 Hollis St., PO Box 2311, Halifax, B3J 1V7 NS
902-424-0377, Fax: 902-424-7008, comm@gov.ns.ca
InNOVACorp, #1400, 1801 Hollis St., Halifax, NS B3J 3N4
902-424-8670, Fax: 902-424-4679, 800-565-7051, communications@innovacorp.ca
Nova Scotia Business Inc., World Trade & Convention Centre, #701, 1800 Argyle St., PO Box 2374, Halifax, NS B3J 3E4
902-424-6650, Fax: 902-424-5739, 800-260-6682, info@nsbi.ca
Trade Centre Limited, 1800 Argyle St., PO Box 955, Halifax, NS B3J 2V9
902-421-8686, Fax: 902-422-2922

Nunavut

Department of Economic Development & Transportation, #1104 Inuksugait Plaza, PO Box 1000 1500,Iqaluit, X0A 0H0 NU
867-975-7800, Fax: 867-975-7870, 888-975-5999, edt@gov.nu.ca

Ontario

Ministry of Economic Development & Trade, Hearst Block, 900 Bay St., 8th Fl., Toronto, M7A 2E1 ON
416-325-6666, Fax: 416-325-6688, 866-668-4249, info@edt.gov.on.ca
Northern Development Division, Roberta Bondar Place, #200, 70 Foster Dr., Sault Ste Marie, P6A 6V8 ON
705-945-5900, Fax: 705-945-5931, 800-461-2287
Ministry of Research & Innovation, Ferguson Block, 77 Wellesley St. West, 12th Fl., Toronto, M7A 1N3 ON
416-325-5181, Fax: 416-325-3877, 866-446-5216
Ministry of Small Business & Customer Services, Whitney Block, #1306 - 99 Wellesley St. W., Toronto, M7A 1W2 ON
416-325-6000, Fax: 416-326-1947, 866-668-4249, info.sbe@ontario.ca

Prince Edward Island

Department of Innovation & Advanced Learning, Shaw Bldg., 105 Rochford St., 5th Fl., PO Box 2000, Charlottetown, C1A 7N8 PE
902-368-4240, Fax: 902-368-4242
Prince Edward Island Business Development Inc., 94 Euston St., 1st & 2nd Fl., PO Box 910, Charlottetown, PE C1A 7L9
902-368-6300, Fax: 902-368-6301, 800-563-3734, business@gov.pe.ca

Quebec

Ministère du Développement économique, de l'Innovation et de l'Exportation, 710, place D'Youville, 3e étage, Québec, G1R 4Y4 QC
418-691-5950, Fax: 418-644-0118, 866-680-1884

Saskatchewan

Saskatchewan Energy & Resources, #300, 2103 - 11th Ave., Regina, S4P 3Z8 SK
306-787-2528, Fax: 306-787-0395, 866-727-5427
Enterprise Saskatchewan, #200, 3085 Albert St., Regina, S4S 0B1 SK
Fax: 306-798-0629, 800-265-2001, Webmaster@enterprisesask.ca

Yukon Territory

Yukon Development Corporation, PO Box 2703 D-1,Whitehorse, Y1A 2C6 YT
867-393-5337, Fax: 867-393-5401

Yukon Economic Development, PO Box 2703, Whitehorse, Y1A 2C6 YT
867-393-7191, Fax: 867-395-7199, 800-661-0408

BUSINESS REGULATIONS

Canada Revenue Agency, 875 Heron Rd., Ottawa, K1A 0L5 ON
613-952-0384, 800-267-6999
Industry Canada, 235 Queen St., Ottawa, K1A 0H5 ON
Fax: 613-954-6436, 800-328-6189, info@ic.gc.ca

Alberta
Technology Services, John E. Brownlee Bldg., 10365 - 97 St., 8th Fl., Edmonton, T5J 3W7 AB
780-422-8545

British Columbia
Corporate & Ministry Support Services, 617 Government St., 3rd Fl., PO Box 9415 Prov Govt,Victoria, V8W 9V1 BC
250-356-1787, Fax: 250-356-7326

Manitoba
Companies Office, #1010, 405 Broadway, Winnipeg, R3C 3L6 MB
204-945-2500, Fax: 204-945-1459, companies@gov.mb.ca

Northwest Territories
Northwest Territories Business Development & Investment Corporation, #701, 5201 - 50 Ave., Yellowknife, NT X1A 3S9
867-920-6455, Fax: 867-765-0652, bdicinfo@gov.nt.ca

Nova Scotia
Nova Scotia Business Inc., World Trade & Convention Centre, #701, 1800 Argyle St., PO Box 2374, Halifax, NS B3J 3E4
902-424-6650, Fax: 902-424-5739, 800-260-6682, info@nsbi.ca

Nunavut
Department of Finance, Bldg. 1079, 1st Fl., PO Box 1000 Stn 330,Iqaluit, X0A 0H0 NU
867-975-5800, Fax: 867-975-5805,

Ontario
ServiceOntario, College Park, 777 Bay St., 15th fl., Toronto, M7A 2J3 ON
416-326-6205, Fax: 416-326-5106

Prince Edward Island
Consumer, Corporate & Insurance Division, Shaw Building, 95 Rochford St., 4th Fl., PO Box 2000, Charlottetown, C1A 7N8 PE
902-368-4580, Fax: 902-368-5283, 800-658-1799

Quebec
Registraire des entreprises, 787, boul. Lebourgneuf, Québec, G2J 1C3 QC
418-644-4545, Fax: 418-528-5703, 877-644-4545, registre@servicesquebec.gouv.qc.ca

CABINETS & EXECUTIVE COUNCILS

See Also: Government (General Information); Parliament
The Canadian Ministry, Information Service, Parliament of Canada, Ottawa, K1A 0A9 ON
613-992-4793, 866-599-4999, info@parl.gc.ca

Alberta
Executive Council, Legislature Bldg., 10800 - 97 Ave., Edmonton, T5K 2B6 AB
780-427-2251, Fax: 780-427-1349

British Columbia
Executive Council, Parliament Bldgs., Victoria, V8V 1X4 BC

Manitoba
Executive Council, Legislative Building, 450 Broadway Ave., Winnipeg, R3C 0V8 MB

New Brunswick
Executive Council, Centennial Bldg., 670 King St., PO Box 6000, Fredericton, E3B 5H1 NB
506-453-2144, Fax: 506-453-7407, Shawn.Graham@gnb.ca

Newfoundland & Labrador
Executive Council, c/o Communications Branch, East Block, Confederation Bldg., 10th Fl., St. John's, A1B 4J6 NL
709-729-5645, info@gov.nl.ca

Northwest Territories
Executive Council, PO Box 1320, Yellowknife, X1A 2L9 NT
executive@gov.nt.ca

Nova Scotia
Executive Council, One Government Place, PO Box 2125, Halifax, B3J 3B7 NS
902-424-5970, Fax: 902-424-0667

Nunavut
Executive Council, Legislative Bldg., 2nd Fl., Box 2410, Iqaluit, X0A 0H0 NU
867-975-5090, Fax: 867-975-5095

Ontario
Executive Council, Whitney Block, Queen's Park, 99 Wellesley St. West, 6th Fl., Toronto, M7A 1A1 ON
416-325-5721, Fax: 416-314-1551

Prince Edward Island
Executive Council, Shaw Bldg., 5th Fl., PO Box 2000, Charlottetown, C1A 7N8 PE
902-368-4502, Fax: 902-368-6118

Quebec
Ministère du Conseil exécutif, 875, Grande Allée est, Québec, G1R 4Y8 QC
418-646-3021, Fax: 418-528-9242

Saskatchewan
Executive Council, Legislative Bldg., 2405 Legislative Dr., Regina, S4S 0B3 SK
306-787-7448

Yukon Territory
Executive Council, PO Box 2703, Whitehorse, Y1A 2C6 YT
867-667-5800, Fax: 867-393-6202, 800-040-8 ex, eco@gov.yk.ca

CANADIANS & SOCIETY

Beverly & Qamanirjuaq Caribou Management Board, Secretariat, PO Box 629, Stonewall, MB R0C 2Z0
204-467-2438, rossthompson@mymts.net
British Columbia Treaty Commission, #203, 1155 West Pender St., Vancouver, BC V6E 2P4
604-482-9200, Fax: 604-482-9222, 800-665-8330, info@bctreaty.net
Canada Council for the Arts, 350 Albert St., PO Box 1047, Ottawa, K1P 5V8 ON
613-566-4414, Fax: 613-566-4390, 800-263-5588, info@canadacouncil.ca
Canada Lands Company Ltd., #1200, 1 University Ave., Toronto, M5J 2P1 ON
416-952-6111, Fax: 416-952-6115, 888-252-5263
Canadian Heritage, 15 Eddy St., Gatineau, K1A 0M5 QC
819-997-0055, 866-811-0055, info@pch.gc.ca
Canadian Human Rights Commission, 344 Slater St., 8th Fl., Ottawa, K1A 1E1 ON
613-995-1151, Fax: 613-996-9661, 888-214-1090, info.com@chrc-ccdp.ca
Canadian Human Rights Tribunal, 160 Elgin St., 11th Fl., Ottawa, K1A 1J4 ON
613-995-1707, Fax: 613-995-3484, registrar@chrt-tcdp.gc.ca
Canadian Race Relations Foundation, #701, 4576 Yonge St., Toronto, M2N 6N4 ON
416-952-3500, Fax: 416 952-3326, 888-240-4936, info@crr.ca
Citizenship & Immigration Canada, Jean Edmonds, South Tower, 365 Laurier Ave. West, Ottawa, K1A 1L1 ON
613-954-9019, Fax: 613-954-2221, 888-242-2100
First Nations Tax Commission, #200, 160 Grorge St., Ottawa, ON K1N 9M2
613-789-5000, Fax: 613-789-5008, mail@fntc.ca
Foreign Affairs & International Trade Canada, 125 Sussex Dr., Ottawa, K1A 0G2 ON
613-944-4000, Fax: 613-996-9709, 800-267-8376, enqserv@international.gc.ca
Government of Canada, c/o Canada Enquiry Centre, Service Canada, Ottawa, K1A 0J9 ON
613-941-1827, 800-622-6232, sitecanadasite@canada.gc.ca
Historic Sites & Monuments Board of Canada, Terrasses de la Chaudière, 25 Eddy St., Gatineau, QC K1A 0M5
819-997-4059, Fax: 819-934-1115, hsmbc-clmhc@pc.gc.ca
Homelessness Partnering Secretariat, 165, rue Hôtel-de-Ville, Gatineau, K1A 0J2 QC
Human Resources & Skills Development Canada, 140 Promenade du Portage, Ottawa, K1A 0J9 ON
Immigration & Refugee Board of Canada, Canada Bldg, 344 Slater St., 12th Fl., Ottawa, K1A 0K1 ON
613-995-6486, Fax: 613-943-1550, info@irb-cisr.gc.ca
Indian & Northern Affairs Canada, 10 Wellington St., North Tower, Gatineau, K1A 0H4 QC
819-997-0380, Fax: 819-953-3017, 866-817-3977, infopubs@ainc-inac.gc.ca
Indian Claims Commission, Minto Enterprise Bldg., #400, 427 Laurier Ave. West, PO Box 1750 B,Ottawa, K1P 1A2 ON
613-943-2737, Fax: 613-943-0157, feedback@indianclaims.ca
National Advisory Council on Aging, Jeanne Mance Bldg., 8th Fl., Postal Locator 1908 A1, Ottawa, K1A 0K9 ON
613-957-1968, Fax: 613-957-7627
National Battlefields Commission, 390, av de Bernières, Québec, G1R 2L7 QC
418-648-3506, Fax: 418-648-3638, information@ccbn-nbc.gc.ca
National Capital Commission, #202, 40 Elgin St., Ottawa, K1P 1C7 ON
613-239-5555, Fax: 613-239-5063, 800-704-8227, info@ncc-ccn.ca
National Round Table on the Environment & Economy, #200, 344 Slater St., Ottawa, K1R 7Y3 ON
613-992-7189, Fax: 613-992-7385, admin@nrtee-trnee.ca
Nunavut Impact Review Board, PO Box 1360, Cambridge Bay, NU X0B 0C0
867-983-4600, Fax: 867-983-2594, 866-233-3033, info@nirb.ca
Nunavut Planning Commission, PO Box 2101, Cambridge Bay, NU X0B 0C0
867-983-4625, Fax: 867-983-4626, staptuna@nunavut.ca
Nunavut Water Board, PO Box 119, Gjoa Haven, NU X0B 1J0
867-360-6338, Fax: 867-360-6369
Office of the Prime Minister (Conservative Party of Canada), Langevin Block, 80 Wellington St., Ottawa, K1A 0A2 ON
613-992-4211, Fax: 613-941-6900, pm@pm.gc.ca
Office of the Commissioner of Official Languages, 344 Slater St., 3rd fl., Ottawa, K1A 0T8 ON
613-996-6368, Fax: 613-993-5082, 877-996-6368
Passport Canada, Le 70 Crémazie, 70 Crémazie St., Gatineau, K1A 0G3 QC
Fax: 819-953-5856, 800-567-6868
Porcupine Caribou Management Board, PO Box 31723, Whitehorse, YT Y1A 6L3
867-633-4780, Fax: 867-393-3904, pcmb@taiga.net
Privacy Commissioner of Canada, Tower B, Place de Ville, 112 Kent St., 3rd Fl., Ottawa, K1A 1H3 ON
613-995-8210, Fax: 613-947-6850, 800-282-1376, info@privcom.gc.ca
Secteur du Québec de la Force terrestre, Montréal,QC
514-252-2777
Seniors Services Division, Standard Life Centre, 10405 Jasper Ave., 6th Fl., Edmonton, T5J 4R7 AB
780-427-7876
Social Sciences & Humanities Research Council of Canada, Constitution Sq., 350 Albert St., PO Box 1610 B,Ottawa, K1P 6G4 ON
613-992-0691, Fax: 613-992-1787, info@sshrc.ca
Status of Women Canada, 123 Slater St., 10th Fl., Ottawa, K1P 1H9 ON
613-995-7835, Fax: 613-947-0761, 866-902-2719, infonational@swc-cfc.gc.ca
Veterans Affairs Canada, 161 Grafton St., PO Box 7700, Charlottetown, C1A 8M9 PE
902-566-8888, information@vac-acc.gc.ca
Veterans Review & Appeal Board, Daniel J. MacDonald Bldg., 161 Grafton St., PO Box 9900, Charlottetown, PE C1A 8V7
902-566-8751, Fax: 902-566-7850, 800-450-8006, vrab_tacra@vac-acc.gc.ca

Alberta
Alberta Human Rights & Citizenship Commission, Northern Regional Office, Standard Life Centre, #800, 10405 Jasper Ave., Edmonton, AB T5J 4R7
780-427-7661, Fax: 780-427-6013,-310-0000, humanrights@gov.ab.ca.
Alberta Sport, Recreation, Parks & Wildlife Foundation, Standard Life Centre, 10405 Jasper Ave., 9th Fl., Edmonton, AB T5J 4R7
780-415-1167, Fax: 780-415-0308
Alberta Children and Youth Services, Sterling Place, 9940 - 106 St., 12th Fl., Edmonton, T5K 2N2 AB
780-422-3004, Fax: 780-422-3071, 866-714-5437, cs.communications@gov.ab.ca
Government House Foundation, 12845 - 102 Ave., Edmonton, AB T5N 0M6
780-427-2281, Fax: 780-422-6508
Alberta Health & Wellness, Telus Plaza NT, 10025 Jasper Ave., 22nd Fl., PO Box 1360 Main,Edmonton, T5J 2N3 AB
780-427-7164, health.ahinform@gov.ab.ca
Labour Relations Board, #503, 10808 - 99 Ave., Edmonton, AB T5K 0G5
780-422-5926, Fax: 780-422-0970, 800-463-2572, alrbinfo@lab.gov.ab.ca
Premier's Council on the Status of Persons with Disabilities, HSBC Bldg., #1110, 10055 - 106 St., Edmonton, AB T5J 2Y2
780-422-1095, 800-272-8841, pcspd@gov.ab.ca
Alberta Seniors & Community Supports, Standard Life Centre, 10405 Jasper Ave., Main Fl., Edmonton, T5J 4R7 AB
780-427-7876, Fax: 780-422-6301, 800-642-3853
Seniors Advisory Council for Alberta, Standard Life Centre, #600, 10405 Jasper Ave., Edmonton, AB T5J 4R7
780-422-2321, Fax: 780-422-8762

Alberta Tourism, Parks, Recreation & Culture, Communications Branch, Standard Life Centre, 10405 Jasper Ave., 7th Fl., Edmonton, T5J 4R7 AB
780-427-6530, Fax: 780-427-1496, Comdev.Communications@gov.ab.ca

British Columbia

Ministry of Children & Family Development, PO Box 9770 Prov Govt,Victoria, V8W 9S5 BC
250-387-7027, 877-387-7027, MCF.CorrespondenceManagement@gov.bc.ca

Ministry of Community & Rural Development, 800 Johnson St., 6th Fl., PO Box 9490 Prov Govt,Victoria, V8W 9N7 BC
250-387-2283, Fax: 250-387-4312, Feedback@gov.bc.ca

Local Government Department, 800 Johnson St., 6th Fl., PO Box 9490 Prov Govt,Victoria, V8W 9N7 BC
lgd_feedback@gov.bc.ca

Native Economic Development Advisory Board, c/o Director, Economic Initiatives, 2955 Jutland Rd., PO Box 9100 Prov Govt, Victoria, BC V8W 9B1
250-387-2536, Fax: 250-356-9467

Manitoba

Manitoba Aboriginal & Northern Affairs, 59 Elizabeth Dr., PO Box 37, Thompson, R8N 1X4 MB
204-677-6607, Fax: 204-677-6753, amartin@gov.mb.ca

Aboriginal Affairs Secretariat, #200, 500 Portage Ave., Winnipeg, R3C 3X1 MB
204-945-2510, Fax: 204-945-3689

Communications Services Manitoba, 155 Carlton St., 10th Fl., Winnipeg, R3C 3H8 MB
204-945-3765, Fax: 204-948-2147

Communities Economic Development Fund, #100, 23 Station Rd., Thompson, MB R8N 0N6
204-778-4138, Fax: 204-778-4313, 800-561-4315

Manitoba Culture, Heritage, Tourism & Sport, Legislative Building, #118, 450 Broadway Ave., Winnipeg, R3C 0V8 MB
204-945-3729, Fax: 204-945-5223, mincht@leg.gov.mb.ca

Manitoba Family Services & Housing, #219, 114 Garry St., Winnipeg, R3C 4V6 MB
204-945-3242, Fax: 204-945-2156, minfam@leg.gov.mb.ca

Heritage Grants Advisory Council, 213 Notre Dame Ave., 3rd Fl., Winnipeg, MB R3B 1N3
204-945-2213, Fax: 204-948-2086

Manitoba Human Rights Commission, 175 Hargrave St., 7th Fl., Winnipeg, R3C 3R8 MB
204-945-3007, Fax: 204-945-1292, 888-884-8681, hrc@gov.mb.ca

Le Centre Culturel franco-manitobain/Franco-Manitoban Cultural Centre, 340, boul Provencher, St Boniface, MB R2H 0G7
204-233-8972, Fax: 204-233-3324, ccfm@ccfm.mb.ca

Manitoba Centennial Centre Corporation, 555 Main St., Winnipeg, MB R3B 1C3
204-956-1360, Fax: 204-944-1390

Manitoba Film Classification Board, #216, 301 Weston St., Winnipeg, MB R3E 3H4
204-945-8962, Fax: 204-945-0890, 866-612-2399, mfcb@gov.mb.ca

Manitoba Heritage Council, 213 Notre Dame Ave., Main Fl., Winnipeg, MB R3B 1N3
204-945-2118, Fax: 204-948-2384, hrb@gov.mb.ca

Multiculturalism Secretariat, 213 Notre Dame Ave., 4th Fl., Winnipeg, MB R3B 1N3
204-945-1156, Fax: 204-948-2323

Primary Care & Healthy Living, 300 Carlton St., 2nd Floor, Winnipeg, R3B 3M9 MB

Manitoba Seniors & Healthy Aging Secretariat, #822, 155 Carlton St., Winnipeg, R3C 3H8 MB
204-945-6565, Fax: 204-948-2514, 800-665-6565, seniors@gov.mb.ca

New Brunswick

Premier's Council on the Status of Disabled Persons, Kings Place, #648, 440 King St., Fredericton, E3B 5H8 NB
506-444-3000, Fax: 506-444-3001, 800-442-4412, pcsdp@gnb.ca

Department of Health, PO Box 5100, Fredericton, E3B 5G8 NB
506-457-4800, Fax: 506-453-5243, dh-ms@dh-ms.ca

New Brunswick Human Rights Commission, PO Box 6000, Fredericton, E3B 5H1 NB
506-453-2301, Fax: 506-453-2653, 888-471-2233, hrc.cdp@gnb.ca

Department of Intergovernmental Affairs, Centennial Bldg., #274, 670 King St., PO Box 6000, Fredericton, E3B 5H1 NB
506-444-5418, Fax: 506-453-2995, iga@gnb.ca

Ministerial Advisory Committee on Multiculturalism, PO Box 6000, Fredericton, NB E3B 5H1

Regional Development Corporation, RDC Bldg., 836 Churchill Row, PO Box 428, Fredericton, E3B 5R4 NB
506-453-2277, Fax: 506-453-7988

Department of Social Development, Sartain MacDonald Bldg., 551 King St., PO Box 6000, Fredericton, E3B 5H1 NB
506-453-2001, Fax: 506-453-7478

New Brunswick Advisory Council on Youth, Frederick Square, #130, 77 Westmorland St., PO Box 6000, Fredericton, E3B 5H1 NB
506-453-3271, Fax: 506-444-4413, 888-830-5588, nbacy-ccjnb@gnb.ca

Newfoundland & Labrador

C.A. Pippy Park Commission, Mount Scio House, 15 Mount Scio Rd., St. John's, NL A1B 3T2
709-737-3655, Fax: 709-737-3303, 877-477-3655, pippyparkinfo@nf.aibn.com

Department of Human Resources, Labour & Employment, Confederation Bldg., PO Box 8700, St. John's, A1B 4J6 NL
709-729-2478, Fax: 709-729-6996, hreweb@gov.nl.ca

Newfoundland & Labrador Human Rights Commission, PO Box 8700, St. John's, A1B 4J6 NL
709-729-2709, Fax: 709-729-0790, 800-563-5808, humanrights@mail.gov.nl.ca

Department of Labrador & Aboriginal Affairs, Confederation Bldg., East Block, 6th Fl., PO Box 8700, St. John's, A1B 4J6 NL
709-729-4776, Fax: 709-729-4900, 877-788-8822, laa@gov.nl.ca

Provincial Advisory Council on the Status of Women, #103, 15 Hallett Cres., St. John's, A1B 4C4 NL
709-753-7270, Fax: 709-753-2606, 877-753-7270, info@pacsw.ca

Department of Tourism, Culture & Recreation, Confederation Bldg., West Block, 2nd Fl., PO Box 8700, St. John's, A1B 4J6 NL
709-729-0862, Fax: 709-729-0870, tcrinfo@gov.nl.ca

Northwest Territories

Department of Aboriginal Affairs & Intergovernmental Relations, 4910 - 52nd St., PO Box 1320, Yellowknife, X1A 2L9 NT
867-873-7143, Fax: 867-873-0233, 877-838-8194, nancy_gardiner @gov.nt.ca

Department of Municipal & Community Affairs, PO Box 1320, Yellowknife, X1A 2L9 NT
867-873-7118, Fax: 867-873-0309

Office of the Languages Commissioner, PO Box 1320, Yellowknife, X1A 2L9 NT
867-873-7034, Fax: 888-305-7353, 800-661-0889

Status of Women Council of the Northwest Territories, PO Box 1320, Yellowknife, X1A 2L9 NT
867-920-6177, Fax: 867-873-0285, 888-234-4485, council@statusofwomen.nt.ca

Nova Scotia

Department of Community Services, Nelson Place, 5675 Spring Garden Rd., 3rd Fl., PO Box 696, Halifax, B3J 2T7 NS
902-424-4304, Fax: 902-428-0618

Nova Scotia Human Rights Commission, Joseph Howe Bldg., 1690 Hollis St., 6th Fl., Halifax, B3J 3C4 NS
902-424-4111, Fax: 902-424-0596

Nova Scotia Advisory Commission on AIDS, Dennis Bldg., 1740 Granville St., 6th Fl., Halifax, NS B3J 1X5
902-424-5730, Fax: 902-424-4727

Nova Scotia Disabled Persons Commission, PO Box 222 CRO, Halifax, NS B3J 2M4
902-424-8280, Fax: 902-424-0592, 800-565-8280

Pay Equity Commission, 5151 Terminal Rd., 7th Fl., PO Box 697, Halifax, NS B3J 2T8
902-424-2385, Fax: 902-424-0575

Seniors' Secretariat, Dennis Bldg., 1740 Granville St., 4th Fl., PO Box 2065, Halifax, NS B3J 2Z1
902-424-0065, Fax: 902-424-0561, 800-670-0065, scs@gov.ns.ca

Department of Service Nova Scotia & Municipal Relations, 1505 Barrington St., PO Box 216, Halifax, B3J 2M4 NS
902-424-4141, Fax: 902-424-0581, public-enquiries@gov.ns.ca

Nova Scotia Advisory Council on the Status of Women, PO Box 745, Halifax, B3J 2T3 NS
902-424-8662, Fax: 902-424-0573, 800-565-8663, nsacsw@gov.ns.ca

Ontario

Ministry of Aboriginal Affairs, 720 Bay St., 4th Fl., Toronto, M5G 2K1 ON
416-326-4740, Fax: 416-326-4017

Citizenship & Immigration Division, 400 University Ave., 3rd Fl., Toronto, M7A 2R9 ON
416-314-7541, Fax: 416-314-7599

Ministry of Citizenship & Immigration, 400 University Ave., 6th Fl., Toronto, M7A 2R9 ON
416-327-2422, Fax: 416-314-4965, 800-267-7329

Ministry of Community & Social Services, Hepburn Block, 80 Grosvenor St., 6th Fl., Toronto, M7A 1E9 ON
416-325-5666, Fax: 416-325-5172, 888-789-4199

Office of Francophone Affairs, 777 Bay St., 6th Fl., Toronto, M7A 2J4 ON
416-325-4949, Fax: 416-325-4980, 800-268-7507, ofa@ontario.ca

Ministry of Government Services, Whitney Block, #4320, 99 Wellesley St. West, 4th Fl., Toronto, M7A 1W3 ON
416-326-1234, Fax: 416-327-3790, 800-268-1142

Ontario Human Rights Commission, 180 Dundas St. West, 7th Fl., Toronto, M7A 2R9 ON
416-314-4500, Fax: 416-326-9520, 800-387-9080, info@ohrc.on.ca

Information & Privacy Commissioner of Ontario, #1400, 2 Bloor St. East, Toronto, M4W 1A8 ON
416-326-3333, Fax: 416-325-9195, 800-387-0073, info@ipc.on.ca

McMichael Canadian Art Collection, 10365 Islington Ave., Kleinburg, ON L0J 1C0
905-893-1121, Fax: 905-893-0692, 888-213-1121, info@mcmichael.com

Ontario Arts Council, 151 Bloor St. West, 5th Fl., Toronto, ON M5S 1T6
416-961-1660, Fax: 416-961-7796

Ontario Heritage Trust, 10 Adelaide St. East, Toronto, ON M5C 1J3
416-325-5000, Fax: 416-325-5071, marketing@heritagefdn.on.ca

Ontario Northland, 555 Oak St. East, North Bay, ON P1B 8L3
705-472-4500, Fax: 705-476-5598, 800-363-7512, info@ontc.on.ca

Royal Ontario Museum, 100 Queen's Park Cres., Toronto, ON M5S 2C6
416-586-5549, Fax: 416-586-5685, info@rom.on.ca

Social Benefits Tribunal, 1075 Bay St., 7th Fl., Toronto, ON M5S 2B1
416-326-0978, Fax: 416-325-5135, 800-753-3895

Ontario Women's Directorate, 777 Bay St., 6th Fl., Toronto, M7A 2J4 ON
416-314-0300, Fax: 416-314-0247, 866-510-5902, info.mci@ontario.ca

Prince Edward Island

Advisory Council on the Status of Women, Sherwood Business Centre, 161 St. Peter's Rd., PO Box 2000, Charlottetown, PE C1A 7N8
902-368-4510, Fax: 902-368-4516, peistatusofwomen@eastlink.ca

PEI Public Archives & Records Office, PO Box 1000, Charlottetown, C1A 7M4 PE
902-368-4290, Fax: 902-368-6327, archives@gov.pe.ca

Department of Communities, Cultural Affairs & Labour, Shaw Bldg., 95 Rochford St., 4th Fl., PO Box 2000, Charlottetown, C1A 7N8 PE
902-368-5250, Fax: 902-368-4121

Prince Edward Island Human Rights Commission, 53 Water St., PO Box 2000, Charlottetown, C1A 7N8 PE
902-368-4180, Fax: 902-368-4236, 800-237-5031, lbuell@peihumanrights.ca

Quebec

Secrétariat aux affaires autochtones, 905, av Honoré-Mercier, 1er étage, Québec, G1R 5M6 QC
418-643-3166, Fax: 418-646-4918

Commission administrative des régimes de retraite et d'assurances (Québec), 475, rue Saint-Amable, Québec, QC G1R 5X3
418-643-4881, Fax: 418-644-3839, 800-463-5533

Commission des biens culturels du Québec, Bloc A-RC, 225, Grande Allée est, Québec, G1R 5G5 QC
418-643-8378, Fax: 418-643-8591, info@cbcq.gouv.qc.ca

Conseil de la famille et de l'enfance, #800, 900, boul René-Lévesque est, Montréal, QC G1R 6B5
514-646-7678, Fax: 514-643-9832, 877-221-7024

Conseil des arts et des lettres du Québec, #320, 79, boul René-Lévesque est, Québec, G1R 5N5 QC
418-643-1707, Fax: 418-643-4558, 800-897-1707, info@calq.gouv.qc.ca

Conseil des aînés, #810, 900, boul René-Lévesque est, 8e étage, Québec, QC G1R 2B5
418-643-0071, Fax: 418-643-1916, 877-657-2463, aines@conseil-des-aines.qc.ca

Conseil des relations interculturelles, #10.04, 500, boul René-Lévesque ouest, Montréal, QC H2Z 1W7
514-873-8501, Fax: 514-873-3469

Conseil du statut de la femme, 800, place D'Youville, 3e étage, Québec, QC G1R 6E2
418-643-4326, Fax: 418-643-8926, 800-463-2851, csf@csf.gouv.qc.ca

Ministère de la Culture, des Communications & de la Condition féminine, 225, Grande Allée est, Québec, G1R 5G5 QC
Fax: 418-380-2364, 888-380-8882, infos@mcccf.gouv.qc.ca
Curateur public du Québec, 600, boul René-Lévesque ouest, 10e étage, Montréal, QC H3B 4W9
514-873-4074, Fax: 514-873-5033, 800-363-9020, information@curateur.gouv.qc.ca
Ministère de l'Emploi et de la Solidarité sociale, 425, rue St-Amable, 4e étage, Québec, G1R 4Z1 QC
418-643-4721, 888-643-4721
Fonds québécois de la recherche sur la société et la culture, #470, 140, Grande Allée est, Québec, QC G1R 5M8
418-643-7582, Fax: 418-644-5248, fqrsc@fqrsc.gouv.qc.ca
Ministère de l' Immigration et des Communautés culturelles, 360, rue McGill, 4e étage, Montréal, H2Y 2E9 QC
514-864-9191, Fax: 514-864-2899
Office des personnes handicapées du Québec, 309, rue Brock, Drummondville, QC J2B 1C5
819-475-8585, Fax: 819-475-8767, 800-567-1465
Ministère des Relations internationales, Édifice Hector-Fabre, 525, boul Réne-Lévesque est, Québec, G1R 5R9 QC
418-649-2300, Fax: 418-649-2656, communications@mri.gouv.qc.ca
Ministère de la Santé et des Services sociaux, Direction des communications et Renseignements généraux, 1075, ch Sainte-Foy, Québec, G1S 2M1 QC
418-266-8900, 800-707-3380, regisseur.web@msss.gouv.qc.ca
Secrétariat aux Affaires intergouvernementales canadiennes, 875, Grande Allée est, 3e étage, Québec, G1R 4Y8 QC
418-643-4011, Fax: 418-528-0052
Secrétariat à la politique linguistique, 225 Grande-Allée est, 4e étage, Québec, G1R 5G5 QC
418-643-4248, Fax: 418-646-7832, info@spl.gouv.qc.ca
Société de développement des entreprises culturelles, #800, 215, rue Saint-Jacques, Montréal, H2Y 1M6 QC
514-841-2200, Fax: 514-841-8606, 800-363-0401, info@sodec.gouv.qc.ca
Tribunal administratif du Québec, 575, rue Saint-Amable, Québec, QC G1R 5R4
418-643-3418, Fax: 418-643-5335

Saskatchewan
Saskatchewan First Nations & Métis Relations, #210, 1855 Victoria Ave., Regina, S4P 3T2 SK
306-787-6250, Fax: 306-787-5832
Saskatchewan Government Relations, 1855 Victoria Ave., Regina, S4P 3T2 SK
306-787-2635
Saskatchewan Human Rights Commission, Saskatoon Office, Sturdy Stone Bdg., #816, 122 - 3 Ave. North, 8th Fl., Saskatoon, S7K 2H6 SK
306-933-5952, Fax: 306-933-7863, 800-667-9249, shrc@shrc.gov.sk.ca
Information & Privacy Commissioner of Saskatchewan, #503, 1801 Hamilton St., Regina, S4P 4B4 SK
306-787-8350, Fax: 306-798-1603, 877-748-2298, info@oipc.sk.ca
Sask Heritage Foundation, 1919 Saskatchewan Dr., 9th Fl., Regina, SK S4P 3V7
306-787-4188, Fax: 306-787-0069,
Saskatchewan Social Services, 1920 Broad St., Regina, S4P 3V6 SK
306-787-3700
Saskatchewan Tourism, Parks, Culture, & Sport, 1919 Saskatchewan Dr., 4th Fl., Regina, S4P 4H2 SK
306-787-5729, Fax: 306-787-8560

Yukon Territory
Yukon Community Services, PO Box 2703, Whitehorse, Y1A 2C6 YT
867-667-5811, Fax: 867-393-6295, 800-661-0408, inquiry@gov.yk.ca
Yukon Health & Social Services, PO Box 2703, Whitehorse, Y1A 2C6 YT
867-667-3673, Fax: 867-667-3096, 800-661-0408, hss@gov.yk.ca
Yukon Women's Directorate, PO Box 2703, Whitehorse, Y1A 2C6 YT
867-667-3030, Fax: 867-393-6270
Yukon Human Rights Commission, #201, 211 Hawkins St., Whitehorse, YT Y1A 1X3
867-667-6226, Fax: 867-667-2662, 800-661-0535, humanrights@yhrc.yk.ca

CAREER PLANNING

Alberta
Workforce Supports Division, Labour Building, 10808 - 99 Ave., 10th Fl., Edmonton, T5K 0G5 AB
780-722-0010

Ontario
Ministry of Training, Colleges & Universities, Mowat Block, 900 Bay St., 3rd Fl., Toronto, M7A 1L2 ON
416-325-1600, Fax: 416-325-2934

Saskatchewan
Saskatchewan Education, 2220 College Ave., Regina, S4P 4V9 SK
306-787-6030, 888-775-3276, learninginquiry@sasked.gov.sk.ca

CENSORSHIP (MEDIA)

Canadian Broadcasting Corporation, 181 Queen St., PO Box 3220 C,Ottawa, K1Y 1E4 ON
613-288-6033, liaison@radio-canada.ca
Canadian Radio-Television & Telecommunications Commission, Central Office, 1, Promenade du Portage, Les Terrasses de la Chaudière, Gatineau, J8X 4B1 QC
819-997-0313, Fax: 819-994-0218, 877-249-2782

Manitoba
Manitoba Film Classification Board, #216, 301 Weston St., Winnipeg, MB R3E 3H4
204-945-8962, Fax: 204-945-0890, 866-612-2399, mfcb@gov.mb.ca

Nunavut
Department of Community & Government Services, J.G. Brown Bldg., PO Box 1000 700,Iqaluit, X0A 0H0 NU
867-975-5400, Fax: 867-975-5305

Ontario
Ontario Film Review Board, 1075 Millwood Rd., Toronto, ON M4G 1X6
416-314-3626, Fax: 416-314-3632

Quebec
Régie du cinéma, #100, 390, rue Notre-Dame ouest, Montréal, H2Y 1T9 QC
514-873-2371, Fax: 514-873-2142, 800-463-2463, regieducinema@rcq.gouv.qc.ca

Saskatchewan
Saskatchewan Film & Video Classification Board, #500, 1919 Saskatchewan Dr., Regina, SK S4P 4H2
306-787-5550, Fax: 306-787-9779, 888-374-4636, adwyer@justice.gov.sk.ca

CHEMICALS

Institute for Chemical Process & Environmental Technology, Bldg. M-12, 1200 Montreal Rd., Ottawa, K1A 0R6 ON
613-993-4041, Fax: 613-957-8231

CHILD WELFARE

See Also: Day Care Services

British Columbia
Integrated Policy & Legislation, 765 Broughton St., 5th Fl., PO Box 9766 Prov Govt,Victoria, V8W 9S5 BC
250-387-3006, Fax: 250-356-6534

New Brunswick
Program Development & Monitoring, Sartain MacDonald Bldg., #4007, 551 King St., PO Box 6000, Fredericton, E3B 5H1 NB
506-453-2181, Fax: 506-453-3829

Northwest Territories
Department of Health & Social Services, Centre Square Tower, PO Box 1320, Yellowknife, X1A 2L9 NT
Fax: 867-873-0266

Nunavut
Department of Health & Social Services, Sivummut bldg., PO Box 1007 1000,Iqaluit, X0A 0H0 NU
867-975-5700, Fax: 867-975-5705, health@gov.nu.ca

Ontario
Ministry of Children & Youth Services, 56 Wellesley St. West, 14th Fl., Toronto, M5S 2G3 ON
Fax: 416-325-5191, 866-821-7770

Prince Edward Island
Department of Social Services & Seniors, Jones Bldg., 11 Kent St., 2nd Fl., PO Box 2000, Charlottetown, C1A 7N8 PE
902-620-3777, Fax: 902-894-0242

Quebec
Conseil de la famille et de l'enfance, #800, 900, boul René-Lévesque est, Montréal, QC G1R 6B5
514-646-7678, Fax: 514-643-9832, 877-221-7024

CITIZENSHIP

Immigration & Refugee Board of Canada, Canada Bldg, 344 Slater St., 12th Fl., Ottawa, K1A 0K1 ON
613-995-6486, Fax: 613-943-1550, info@irb-cisr.gc.ca

Manitoba
Manitoba Education, Citizenship & Youth, #168, Legislative Bldg., 450 Broadway, Winnipeg, R3C 0V8 MB
204-945-3720, Fax: 204-945-1291, minedu@leg.gov.mb.ca

Ontario
Ministry of Citizenship & Immigration, 400 University Ave., 6th Fl., Toronto, M7A 2R9 ON
416-327-2422, Fax: 416-314-4965, 800-267-7329,

CLIMATE & WEATHER

Canadian Space Agency, 6767, rte de l'Aéroport, Saint-Hubert, J3Y 8Y9 QC
450-926-4800, Fax: 450-926-4352, webmaster@space.gc.ca
Meteorological Service of Canada, 4905 Dufferin St., Toronto, M3H 5T4 ON
416-739-4770, Fax: 416-739-4232

CLIMATE CHANGE

Manitoba
Energy Climate Change & Green Strategy Initiatives Branch, #1202 - 155 Carlton St., Winnipeg, R3C 3H8 MB
204-945-7382, Fax: 204-948-3739, ccinfo@gov.mb.ca

Quebec
Ministère du Développement durable, de l'Environnement et des Parcs, Édifice Marie-Guyart, 675, boul René-Lévesque est, 29e étage, Québec, G1R 5V7 QC
418-521-3830, Fax: 418-646-5974, 800-561-1616, info@mddep.gouv.qc.ca

COAL

See Also: Energy

Alberta
Energy Resources Conservation Board, #1000, 250 - 5 Ave. SW, Calgary, AB T2P 0R4
403-297-8311, Fax: 403-297-7336, inquiries@ercb.ca

New Brunswick
New Brunswick Power Group of Companies, 515 King St., PO Box 2000, Fredericton, E3B 4X1 NB
506-458-4444, Fax: 506-458-4000, questions@nbpower.com

Ontario
Ontario Power Generation, 700 University Ave., Toronto, M5G 1X6 ON
416-592-2555, 877-592-2555

Saskatchewan
Saskatchewan Power Corporation (SaskPower), 2025 Victoria Ave., Regina, S4P 0S1 SK
306-566-2121, Fax: 306-566-2330, 800-667-4749

COMMUNICATIONS

See: Telecommunications
Canada Post Corporation, Corporate Secretariat, 2701 Riverside Dr., Ottawa, K1A 0B1 ON
613-734-8440, Fax: 613-734-6084, 800-267-1177, service@mailposte.ca
Canadian Broadcasting Corporation, 181 Queen St., PO Box 3220 C,Ottawa, K1Y 1E4 ON
613-288-6033, liaison@radio-canada.ca
Canadian Radio-Television & Telecommunications Commission, Central Office, 1, Promenade du Portage, Les Terrasses de la Chaudière, Gatineau, J8X 4B1 QC
819-997-0313, Fax: 819-994-0218, 877-249-2782
Chief Informatics Office, 235 Queen St., Ottawa, ON K1A 0H5
613-954-3570, Fax: 613-941-1938
Communications Research Centre Canada, 3701 Carling Ave., PO Box 11490 H, Ottawa, ON K2H 8S2
613-991-3313, Fax: 613-998-5355, info@crc.ca
Global Operations & Chief Trade Commissioner, 125 Sussex Dr,, Ottawa, K1A 0G2 ON
613-944-2697, Fax: 613-996-1667
Institute for Information Technology, Bldg. M-50, 1200 Montreal Rd., Ottawa, K1A 0R6 ON
613-991-3373, Fax: 613-952-0074, 877-672-2672
Spectrum, Information Technologies & Telecommunications, Journal Tower North, 300 Slater St., 20th Fl., Ottawa, K1A 0C8 ON
613-998-0368, Fax: 613-952-1203

Alberta
Alberta Public Affairs Bureau, Park Plaza, 10611 - 98 Ave., 6th Fl., Edmonton, T5K 2P7 AB
403-427-9261, Fax: 403-422-4168

Manitoba
Communications Services Manitoba, 155 Carlton St., 10th Fl., Winnipeg, R3C 3H8 MB
204-945-3765, Fax: 204-948-2147

Manitoba News Media Services, #29, Legislative Bldg., 450 Broadway, Winnipeg, R3C 0V8 MB
204-945-3746, Fax: 204-945-3988, nmservices@leg.gov.mb.ca

Manitoba Telecom Services Inc., 333 Main St., PO Box 6666, Winnipeg, R3C 3V6 MB
204-941-4111, Fax: 204-772-6391

New Brunswick

Business Development, Centennial Bldg., 670 King St., 5th Fl., PO Box 6000, Fredericton, E3B 5H1 NB
506-453-2111, Fax: 506-444-4182

Communications New Brunswick, Wilcom Bldg., 225 King St., 2nd Fl., PO Box 6000, Fredericton, E3B 5H1 NB
506-453-2240, Fax: 506-453-5329

Legislative Services, Centennial Bldg., #418, 670 King St., PO Box 6000, Fredericton, E3B 5H1 NB
506-453-2855, Fax: 506-457-7342

Ontario

Ontario Library Service - North, 334 Regent St., Sudbury, ON P3C 4E2
705-675-6467, Fax: 705-675-2285, 800-461-6348

Quebec

Ministère de la Culture, des Communications & de la Condition féminine, 225, Grande Allée est, Québec, G1R 5G5 QC
Fax: 418-380-2364, 888-380-8882, infos@mcccf.gouv.qc.ca

Saskatchewan

Saskatchewan Communications Network, #313E, 2440 Broad St., Regina, S4P 0A5 SK
306-787-0490, Fax: 306-787-0496, 800-667-5055, inquiries@scn.ca

Saskatchewan Telecommunications (SaskTel), 2121 Saskatchewan Dr., 7th Fl., Regina, S4P 3Y2 SK
306-777-3737, Fax: 306-359-7854, 800-727-5835

COMMUNITY & MUNICIPAL DEVELOPMENT

Atlantic Canada Opportunities Agency, Blue Cross Centre, 644 Main St., 3rd Fl., PO Box 6051, Moncton, E1C 9J8 NB
506-851-2271, Fax: 506-851-7403, 800-561-7862, information@acoa-apeca.gc.ca

Canada Economic Development for Québec Regions, Édifice Dominion Square, #900, 1255, rue Peel, Montréal, H3B 2T9 QC
514-283-6412, Fax: 514-283-3302, 866-385-6412

Western Economic Diversification Canada, Canada Place, #1500, 9700 Jasper Ave. NW, Edmonton, T5J 4H7 AB
780-495-4164, Fax: 780-495-4557, 888-338-9378

Alberta

Alberta Tourism, Parks, Recreation & Culture, Communications Branch, Standard Life Centre, 10405 Jasper Ave., 7th Fl., Edmonton, T5J 4R7 AB
780-427-6530, Fax: 780-427-1496, Comdev.Communications@gov.ab.ca

British Columbia

Local Government Department, 800 Johnson St., 6th Fl., PO Box 9490 Prov Govt,Victoria, V8W 9N7 BC
lgd_feedback@gov.bc.ca

Manitoba

Manitoba Aboriginal & Northern Affairs, 59 Elizabeth Dr., PO Box 37, Thompson, R8N 1X4 MB
204-677-6607, Fax: 204-677-6753, amartin@gov.mb.ca

Community Land Use Planning Services, #604, 800 Portage Ave., Winnipeg, R3G 0N4 MB

Provincial-Municipal Support Services, #508, 800 Portage Ave., Winnipeg, R3G 0N4 MB

New Brunswick

Regional Development Corporation, RDC Bldg., 836 Churchill Row, PO Box 428, Fredericton, E3B 5R4 NB
506-453-2277, Fax: 506-453-7988

Newfoundland & Labrador

Department of Health & Community Services, West Block, Confederation Bldg., PO Box 8700, St. John's, A1B 4J6 NL
709-729-5021, Fax: 709-729-5824

Northwest Territories

Department of Municipal & Community Affairs, PO Box 1320, Yellowknife, X1A 2L9 NT
867-873-7118, Fax: 867-873-0309

Nova Scotia

Department of Service Nova Scotia & Municipal Relations, 1505 Barrington St., PO Box 216, Halifax, B3J 2M4 NS
902-424-4141, Fax: 902-424-0581, public-enquiries@gov.ns.ca

Nunavut

Department of Community & Government Services, J.G. Brown Bldg., PO Box 1000 700,Iqaluit, X0A 0H0 NU
867-975-5400, Fax: 867-975-5305

Ontario

Ministry of Municipal Affairs & Housing, 777 Bay St., 17th Fl., Toronto, M5G 2E5 ON
416-585-7041, Fax: 416-585-6227, 866-220-2290, mininfo.mah@ontario.ca

Prince Edward Island

Community & Labour Development, Shaw Bldg., 105 Rochford St., 5th Fl., PO Box 2000, Charlottetown, C1A 7N8 PE
902-368-4244, Fax: 902-368-4242

Quebec

Ministère des Affaires municipales et Occupation du territoire, Aile Chaveau, 10, rue Pierre-Olivier-Chauveau, 3e étage, Québec, G1R 4J3 QC
418-691-2019, Fax: 418-643-7385, communications@mamrot.gouv.qc.ca

Ministère du Développement économique, de l'Innovation et de l'Exportation, 710, place D'Youville, 3e étage, Québec, G1R 4Y4 QC
418-691-5950, Fax: 418-644-0118, 866-680-1884

Saskatchewan

Enterprise Saskatchewan, #200, 3085 Albert St., Regina, S4S 0B1 SK
Fax: 306-798-0629, 800-265-2001, Webmaster@enterprisesask.ca

COMMUNITY FINANCING

Atlantic Canada Opportunities Agency, Blue Cross Centre, 644 Main St., 3rd Fl., PO Box 6051, Moncton, E1C 9J8 NB
506-851-2271, Fax: 506-851-7403, 800-561-7862, information@acoa-apeca.gc.ca

Business Development Bank of Canada, #400, 5, Place Ville-Marie, Montréal, H3B 5E7 QC
514-283-5904, Fax: 514-283-2872, 877-232-2269

Canada Economic Development for Québec Regions, Édifice Dominion Square, #900, 1255, rue Peel, Montréal, H3B 2T9 QC
514-283-6412, Fax: 514-283-3302, 866-385-6412

Canada Investment & Savings, #900, 110 Yonge St., Toronto, ON M5C 1T4
416-952-1252, Fax: 416-952-1270, 800-575-5151, csb@csb.gc.ca

Finance Canada, L'esplanade Laurier, 140 O'Connor St., Ottawa, K1A 0G5 ON
613-992-1573, Fax: 613-943-0938, finpub@fin.gc.ca

Western Economic Diversification Canada, Canada Place, #1500, 9700 Jasper Ave. NW, Edmonton, T5J 4H7 AB
780-495-4164, Fax: 780-495-4557, 888-338-9378

Alberta

Alberta Capital Finance Authority, Canadian Western Bank Place, #2450, 10303 Jasper Ave., Edmonton, AB T5J 3N6
780-427-9711, Fax: 780-422-2175, webacfa@gov.ab.ca

Manitoba

Communities Economic Development Fund, #100, 23 Station Rd., Thompson, MB R8N 0N6
204-778-4138, Fax: 204-778-4313, 800-561-4315

Provincial-Municipal Support Services, #508, 800 Portage Ave., Winnipeg, R3G 0N4 MB

New Brunswick

New Brunswick Municipal Finance Corporation, #376, 670 King St., PO Box 6000, Fredericton, NB E3B 5H1
506-453-3952, Fax: 506-453-2053

Newfoundland & Labrador

Newfoundland & Labrador Municipal Financing Corporation, Confederation Bldg., PO Box 8700, St. John's, NL A1B 4J6
709-729-6686, Fax: 709-729-2095

Nova Scotia

Nova Scotia Municipal Finance Corporation, Maritime Centre, 1505 Barrington St., 10th Fl. South, PO Box 850 M, Halifax, NS B3J 2V2
902-424-4590, Fax: 902-424-0525

Prince Edward Island

Community & Labour Development, Shaw Bldg., 105 Rochford St., 5th Fl., PO Box 2000, Charlottetown, C1A 7N8 PE
902-368-4244, Fax: 902-368-4242

Quebec

Ministère des Affaires municipales et Occupation du territoire, Aile Chaveau, 10, rue Pierre-Olivier-Chauveau, 3e étage, Québec, G1R 4J3 QC
418-691-2019, Fax: 418-643-7385, communications@mamrot.gouv.qc.ca

Yukon Territory

Yukon Economic Development, PO Box 2703, Whitehorse, Y1A 2C6 YT
867-393-7191, Fax: 867-395-7199, 800-661-0408

COMMUNITY SERVICES

Alberta

Alberta Tourism, Parks, Recreation & Culture, Communications Branch, Standard Life Centre, 10405 Jasper Ave., 7th Fl., Edmonton, T5J 4R7 AB
780-427-6530, Fax: 780-427-1496, Comdev.Communications@gov.ab.ca

British Columbia

Ministry of Community & Rural Development, 800 Johnson St., 6th Fl., PO Box 9490 Prov Govt,Victoria, V8W 9N7 BC
250-387-2283, Fax: 250-387-4312, Feedback@gov.bc.ca

Manitoba

Local Government Development Division, 59 Elizabeth Dr., PO Box 33, Thompson, R8N 1X4 MB
204-677-6794, Fax: 204-677-6525

New Brunswick

Department of Social Development, Sartain MacDonald Bldg., 551 King St., PO Box 6000, Fredericton, E3B 5H1 NB
506-453-2001, Fax: 506-453-7478

Newfoundland & Labrador

Department of Health & Community Services, West Block, Confederation Bldg., PO Box 8700, St. John's, A1B 4J6 NL
709-729-5021, Fax: 709-729-5824,

Northwest Territories

Department of Municipal & Community Affairs, PO Box 1320, Yellowknife, X1A 2L9 NT
867-873-7118, Fax: 867-873-0309

Nova Scotia

Department of Community Services, Nelson Place, 5675 Spring Garden Rd., 3rd Fl., PO Box 696, Halifax, B3J 2T7 NS
902-424-4304, Fax: 902-428-0618

Nunavut

Department of Community & Government Services, J.G. Brown Bldg., PO Box 1000 700,Iqaluit, X0A 0H0 NU
867-975-5400, Fax: 867-975-5305

Ontario

Ministry of Community & Social Services, Hepburn Block, 80 Grosvenor St., 6th Fl., Toronto, M7A 1E9 ON
416-325-5666, Fax: 416-325-5172, 888-789-4199

Prince Edward Island

Department of Communities, Cultural Affairs & Labour, Shaw Bldg., 95 Rochford St., 4th Fl., PO Box 2000, Charlottetown, C1A 7N8 PE
902-368-5250, Fax: 902-368-4121

Saskatchewan

Saskatchewan Social Services, 1920 Broad St., Regina, S4P 3V6 SK
306-787-3700

Yukon Territory

Yukon Community Services, PO Box 2703, Whitehorse, Y1A 2C6 YT
867-667-5811, Fax: 867-393-6295, 800-661-0408, inquiry@gov.yk.ca

CONFLICT OF INTEREST

Office of the Ethics Commissioner, 66 Slater St., 22nd Fl., Ottawa, K1A 0A6 ON
613-995-0721, Fax: 613-995-7308, ciec-ccie@parl.gc.ca

Alberta

Alberta Office of the Ethics Commissioner, #1250, 9925 - 109 St., Edmonton, T5K 2J8 AB
780-422-2273, Fax: 780-422-2261, generalinfo@ethicscommissioner.ab.ca

British Columbia

Office of the Conflict of Interest Commissioner, #101, 431 Menzies St., Victoria, V8V 1X4 BC
250-356-0750, Fax: 250-356-6580, ConflictofInterest@gov.bc.ca

Ontario

Office of the Integrity Commissioner, #2101, 2 Bloor St. East, Toronto, M4W 1A8 ON
416-314-8983, Fax: 416-314-8987, integrity.mail@oico.on.ca

CONSERVATION & ECOLOGY

See Also: Heritage Resources; Natural Resources

Canadian Heritage, 15 Eddy St., Gatineau, K1A 0M5 QC
819-997-0055, 866-811-0055, info@pch.gc.ca

Canadian Polar Commission, Constitution Square, #1710, 360 Albert St., Ottawa, K1R 7X7 ON
613-943-8605, Fax: 613-943-8607, 888-765-2701, mail@polarcom.gc.ca
Environment Canada, 10 Wellington St., Gatineau, K1A 0H3 QC
819-997-2800, Fax: 819-994-1412, 800-668-6767, enviroinfo@ec.gc.ca
Commission for Environmental Cooperation, Secretariat, #200, 393, rue St-Jacques ouest, Montréal, H2Y 1N9 QC
514-350-4300, Fax: 514-350-4314, info@cec.org
Fisheries Resource Conservation Council, PO Box 2001 D, Ottawa, ON K1P 5W3
613-998-0433, Fax: 613-998-1146, info@frcc-ccrh.ca
Natural Resources Canada, 580 Booth St., Ottawa, K1A 0E4 ON
613-995-0947, Fax: 613-992-7211
Parks Canada, 25 Eddy St., Gatineau, K1A 0M5 QC
613-860-1251, 888-773-8888, information@pc.gc.ca

Alberta

Alberta Environmental Appeals Board, Peace Hills Trust Tower, #306, 10011 - 109 St. NW, Edmonton, AB T5J 3S8
780-427-6207, Fax: 780-427-4693
Alberta Special Areas Board, 212 - 2nd Ave. West, PO Box 820, Hanna, AB T0J 1P0
403-854-5600, Fax: 403-854-5527, specarea@telusplanet.net
Alberta Used Oil Management Association, Scotia One, Scotia Place, #1050, 10060 Jasper Ave., Edmonton, AB T5J 3R8
780-414-1510, Fax: 780-414-1519, reception@usedoilrecycling.ca
Beverage Container Management Board, #750, 10707 - 100 Ave., Edmonton, AB T5J 3M1
780-424-3193, Fax: 780-428-4620, 888-424-7671, info@bcmb.ab.ca
Clean Air Strategic Alliance, Centre West Bldg, 10035 - 108 St., 10th Fl., Edmonton, AB T5J 3E1
780-427-9793, Fax: 780-422-3127, casa@casahome.org
Alberta Environment, South Tower, Petroleum Plaza, 9915 - 108 St., 10th Fl., Edmonton, T5K 2G8 AB
780-427-2700, Fax: 780-422-4086, env.infocent@gov.ab.ca
Natural Resources Conservation Board, Sterling Place, 9940 - 106 St., 4th Fl., Edmonton, AB T5K 2N2
780-422-1977, Fax: 780-427-0607, 866-383-6722

British Columbia

British Columbia Assessment Authority, 1537 Hillside Ave., Victoria, BC V8T 4Y2
250-595-6211, Fax: 250-595-6222, info@bcassessment.ca
Ministry of Environment, PO Box 9339 Prov Govt,Victoria, V8W 9M1 BC
250-387-1161, Fax: 250-387-5669, www.envmail@gov.bc.ca
Environmental Appeal Board, 747 Fort St., 4th Fl., PO Box 9425 Prov Govt, Victoria, BC V8W 9V1
250-387-3464, Fax: 250-356-9923, eabinfo@gov.bc.ca
Environmental Stewardship Division, 2975 Jutland Rd., 5th Fl., PO Box 9339 Prov Govt,Victoria, V8T 5J9 BC
250-356-0121, Fax: 250-953-3414
Forest Practices Board, 1675 Douglas St., 3rd Fl., PO Box 9905 Prov Govt, Victoria, BC V8W 9R1
250-387-7964, Fax: 250-387-7009, 800-994-5899, fpboard@gov.bc.ca
Fraser Basin Council, Central Office, 470 Granville St., 1st Fl., Vancouver, BC V6C 1V5
604-488-5350, Fax: 604-488-5351, info@fraserbasin.bc.ca
Mediation & Arbitration Board, #310, 9900 - 100 Ave., Fort St John, BC V1J 5S7
250-787-3403, Fax: 250-787-3228, mab.office@gov.bc.ca
Northern Interior, 1011 - 4 Ave., 5th Fl., Prince George, V2L 3H9 BC
250-565-6100, Fax: 250-565-6671, www.for.gov.bc.ca/rni

Manitoba

Clean Environment Commission, #305, 155 Carlton St., Winnipeg, MB R3C 3H8
204-945-0594, Fax: 204-945-0090
Manitoba Conservation, 200 Saulteaux Cres., Winnipeg, R3J 3W3 MB
204-945-6784, 800-214-6497, mincon@leg.gov.mb.ca
Ecological Reserves Advisory Committee, c/o Manitoba Conservation, Parks & Natural Areas Branch, 200 Saulteaux Cres., Winnipeg, MB R3J 3W3
204-945-4148, Fax: 204-945-0012, hhernandez@gov.mb.ca
Manitoba Conservation Districts Commission, Secretariat c/o Planning & Coordination Branch, 123 Main St., PO Box 20000, Neepawa, MB R0J 1H0
204-476-7033, Fax: 204-476-7539, whildebran@gov.mb.ca

New Brunswick

Assessment & Planning Appeal Board, #201, 435 King St., PO Box 6000, Fredericton, NB E3B 5H1
506-453-2126, Fax: 506-444-4881
Department of the Environment, Marysville Place, 20 McGloin St., PO Box 6000, Fredericton, E3B 5H1 NB
506-453-2690, Fax: 506-457-4991, env-info@gnb.ca

Newfoundland & Labrador

Department of Environment & Conservation, Confederation Bldg., West Block, 4th Fl., PO Box 8700, St. John's, A1B 4J6 NL
709-729-2664, Fax: 709-729-6639, 800-563-6181, info@gov.nl.ca

Northwest Territories

Department of Environment & Natural Resources, PO Box 1320, Yellowknife, X1A 2L9 NT

Nova Scotia

Environmental & Natural Areas Management, PO Box 697, Halifax, B3J 3T8 NS
902-424-3571
Department of Natural Resources, Founder's Square, 1701 Hollis St., 3rd Fl., PO Box 698, Halifax, B3J 2T9 NS
902-424-5935, Fax: 902-424-0594, 800-565-2224

Ontario

Ministry of Environment, 135 St. Clair Ave. West, Toronto, M4V 1P5 ON
416-325-4000, Fax: 416-325-3159, 800-565-4923
Ministry of Natural Resources, Whitney Block, #6630, 99 Wellesley St. West, 6th Fl., Toronto, M7A 1W3 ON
800-667-1940
Niagara Escarpment Commission, 232 Guelph St., Georgetown, L7G 4B1 ON
905-877-5191, Fax: 905-873-7452

Prince Edward Island

Department of Environment, Energy & Forestry, Jones Bldg., 11 Kent St., 4th & 5th Fl., PO Box 2000, Charlottetown, C1A 7N8 PE
902-368-5000, Fax: 902-368-5830
Environmental Advisory Council, 11 Kent St., PO Box 2000, Charlottetown, PE C1A 7N8
Department of Tourism, PO Box 2000, Charlottetown, C1A 7N8 PE
800-463-4734

Quebec

Comité consultatif de l'environnement Kativik, CP 930, Kuujjuaq, QC J0M 1C0
819-964-2961, Fax: 819-964-0694, ndea@krg.ca
Ministère du Développement durable, de l'Environnement et des Parcs, Édifice Marie-Guyart, 675, boul René-Lévesque est, 29e étage, Québec, G1R 5V7 QC
418-521-3830, Fax: 418-646-5974, 800-561-1616, info@mddep.gouv.qc.ca
Fondation de la faune du Québec, Place Iberville II, #420, 1175, av Lavigerie, Québec, QC G1V 4P1
418-644-7926, Fax: 418-643-7655, 877-639-0742, ffq@riq.qc.ca
Société de développement de la Baie James, 110, boul Matagami, CP 970, Matagami, QC J0Y 2A0
819-739-4717, Fax: 819-739-4329
Société québécoise de récupération et de recyclage, Siège social, #200, 420, boul Charest est, Québec, QC G1K 8M4
418-643-0394, Fax: 418-643-6507, 866-523-8290, info@recyc-quebec.gouv.qc.ca

Saskatchewan

Saskatchewan Assessment Management Agency, #200, 2201 - 11th Ave., Regina, S4P 0J8 SK
306-924-8000, Fax: 306-924-8070, 800-667-7262, info.request@sama.sk.ca
Saskatchewan Environment, 3211 Albert St., 2nd Fl., Regina, S4S 5W6 SK
306-953-3750, Fax: 306-787-9544, 800-567-4224, inquiry@serm.gov.sk.ca
Saskatchewan Conservation Data Centre, 3211 Albert St., Regina, SK S4S 5W6
306-787-9038, Fax: 306-787-9544
Saskatchewan Watershed Authority, 111 Fairford St. East, Moose Jaw, SK S6H 7X9
306-694-3900, Fax: 306-694-3465, comm@swa.ca

Yukon Territory

Alsek Renewable Resource Council, PO Box 2077, Haines Junction, YT Y0B 1L0
867-634-2524, Fax: 867-634-2527
Carmacks Renewable Resource Council, PO Box 122, Carmacks, YT Y0B 1C0
867-863-6838, Fax: 867-863-6429, carmacksrrc@lscfn.ca
Dawson District Renewable Resource Council, PO Box 1380, Dawson City, YT Y0B 1G0
867-993-6976, Fax: 867-993-6093, dawsonrrc@yknet.yk.ca
Yukon Environment, PO Box 2703, Whitehorse, Y1A 2C6 YT
867-667-5652, Fax: 867-393-7197, 800-661-0408, environmentyukon@gov.yk.ca
Mayo District Renewable Resources Council, PO Box 249, Mayo, YT Y0B 1M0
867-996-2942, Fax: 867-996-2948, mayorrc@yknet.yk.ca
North Yukon Renewable Resources Council, PO Box 80, Old Crow, YT Y0B 1N0
vgrrc@yknet.yk.ca
Selkirk Renewable Resources Council, PO Box 32, Pelly Crossing, YT Y0B 1P0
867-537-3937, Fax: 867-537-3939, selkirkrre@yknet.yk.ca
Teslin Renewable Resource Council, PO Box 186, Teslin, YT Y0A 1B0
867-390-2323, Fax: 867-390-2919, teslinrrc@yknet.yk.ca
Yukon Land Use Planning Council, #201, 307 Jarvis St., Whitehorse, YT Y1A 2H3
867-667-7397, Fax: 867-667-4624, ylupc@planyukon.ca

CONSTRUCTION

Canada Mortgage & Housing Corporation, 700 Montreal Rd., Ottawa, K1A 0P7 ON
613-748-2000, Fax: 613-748-2098, 800-668-2642, chic@cmhc-schl.gc.ca
Defence Construction Canada, Constitution Square, 350 Albert St., 19th Fl., Ottawa, K1A 0K3 ON
613-998-9548, Fax: 613-998-1061, 800-514-3555, info@dcc-cdc.gc.ca
Infrastructure Canada, 90 Sparks St., 6th Fl., Ottawa, K1P 5B4 ON
613-948-1148, Fax: 613-946-9888, 800-622-6232, info@infc.gc.ca
Institute for Research in Construction, Bldg. M-24, 1500 Montreal Rd., Ottawa, K1A 0R6 ON
613-993-2607, Fax: 613-952-7673, Irc.Client-Services@nrc-cnrc.gc.ca
Policy & Corporate Services Division, Twin Atria Building, 4999 - 98 Ave., 3rd Fl., Edmonton, T6B 2X3 AB

Alberta

Alberta Infrastructure, Infrastructure Building, 6950 - 101 St., 3rd Fl., Edmonton, T6H 5V7 AB
780-415-0507, Fax: 780-427-2187,-310-0000

Manitoba

Construction & Maintenance Branch, #1610, 215 Garry St., Winnipeg, R3C 3Z1 MB
Fax: 204-945-3841

Newfoundland & Labrador

Department of Transportation & Works, Confederation Bldg., West Block, 6th Fl., PO Box 8700, St. John's, A1B 4J6 NL
709-729-3679, Fax: 709-729-4285, twminister@gov.nl.ca

Nova Scotia

Labour Relations Board & Construction Industry Panel, 5151 Terminal Rd.,7th Fl., PO Box 697, Halifax, NS B3J 2T8
902-424-6730, Fax: 902-424-1744

Nunavut

Department of Community & Government Services, J.G. Brown Bldg., PO Box 1000 700,Iqaluit, X0A 0H0 NU
867-975-5400, Fax: 867-975-5305

Ontario

Building Code Commission, 777 Bay St., 2nd Fl., Toronto, ON M5G 2E5
416-585-6503, Fax: 416-585-7531
Building Materials Evaluation Commission, 777 Bay St., 2nd Fl., Toronto, ON M5G 2E5
416-585-4234, Fax: 416-585-7531

Quebec

Commissaire de l'industrie de la construction, 150, boul René-Lévesque est, 18e étage,, Québec, QC G1R 5B1
418-646-7200, Fax: 418-644-9977
Commission de la construction du Québec, 3530, rue Jean-Talon ouest, Montréal, QC H3R 2G3
514-341-7740, Fax: 514-341-6354, 888-842-8222
Régie du bâtiment du Québec, 545, boul Crémazie est, 4e étage, Montréal, QC H2M 2V2
514-873-0976, Fax: 514-864-2903, 800-361-0761, crc@rbq.gouv.qc.ca

CONSUMER PROTECTION

See Also: Public Safety

Financial Consumer Agency of Canada, 427 Laurier Ave. West, 6th Fl., Ottawa, K1R 1B9 ON
Fax: 613-941-1436, info@fcac-acfc.gc.ca

Alberta

Registries Services, John E. Brownlee Bldg., 10365 - 97 St., 3rd Fl., Edmonton, T5J 3W7 AB

Nova Scotia
Department of Service Nova Scotia & Municipal Relations, 1505 Barrington St., PO Box 216, Halifax, B3J 2M4 NS
902-424-4141, Fax: 902-424-0581, public-enquiries@gov.ns.ca

Nunavut
Department of Community & Government Services, J.G. Brown Bldg., PO Box 1000 700,Iqaluit, X0A 0H0 NU
867-975-5400, Fax: 867-975-5305

CORONERS

British Columbia
Coroners Service of British Columbia, Metrotower II, #800, 4720 Kingsway, Burnaby, BC V5H 4N2
604-660-7745, Fax: 604-660-7766, BC.CorSer@gov.bc.ca

Manitoba
Office of the Chief Medical Examiner, #210, 1 Wesley Ave., Winnipeg, MB R3C 4C6
204-945-2088, Fax: 204-945-2442, 800-282-9069

Nova Scotia
Nova Scotia Medical Examiner Service, Halifax Insurance Bldg., #701, 5670 Spring Garden Rd., Halifax, NS B3J 1H7
902-424-2722, Fax: 902-424-0607, 888-424-4336

Nunavut
Office of the Chief Coroner, PO Box 1000 590, Iqaluit, NU X0A 0H0

Quebec
Bureau du coroner, #390, 2875, boul Laurier, Sainte-Foy, QC G1V 5B1
418-643-1845, Fax: 418-643-6174, clientele.coroner@msp.gouv.qc.ca

CORRECTIONAL SERVICES

Office of the Correctional Investigator, PO Box 3421 D,Ottawa, K1P 6L4 ON
Fax: 613-990-9091, 877-885-8848, org@oci-bec.gc.ca
Correctional Service Canada, 340 Laurier Ave. West, Ottawa, K1A 0P9 ON
613-992-5891, Fax: 613-943-1630

British Columbia
Corrections Branch, 1001 Douglas St., 7th Fl., PO Box 9278 Prov Govt,Victoria, V8W 9J7 BC
250-387-5059, Fax: 250-387-5698

Manitoba
Corrections Division, #810, 405 Broadway Ave., Winnipeg, R3C 3L6 MB
204-945-7291

Nunavut
Baffin Correctional Centre, 1550 Federal Rd., PO Box 368, Iqaluit, NU X0A 0H0
867-979-8100, Fax: 867-979-4646

Saskatchewan
Saskatchewan Corrections, Public Safety & Policing, 1874 Scarth St., Regina, S4P 4B3 SK
306-787-7872, Fax: 306-787-8747

CRIMES COMPENSATION

Communications Branch, 284 Wellington St., Ottawa, K1A 0H8 ON
Fax: 613-941-2329

Alberta
Criminal Injuries Review Board, J.E. Brownlee Bldg., 10365 - 97 St., 5th Fl., Edmonton, AB T5J 3W7
780-427-7330, Fax: 780-427-7347, ciab@just.gov.ab.ca

Manitoba
Compensation for Victims of Crime, 1410 - 405 Broadway, Winnipeg, MB R3C 3L6
204-945-0899, Fax: 204-948-3071, 800-262-9344

Northwest Territories
Victims Assistance Committee, c/o Community Justice Division, PO Box 1320, Yellowknife, NT X1A 2L9
867-920-6911, Fax: 867-873-0299

Ontario
Criminal Injuries Compensation Board, 439 University Ave., 4th Fl., Toronto, ON M5G 1Y8
416-326-2900, Fax: 416-326-2883, 800-372-7463
Office for Victims of Crime, 700 Bay St., 3rd Fl., Toronto, ON M5G 1Z6
416-326-1682, Fax: 416-326-2343, 887-435-7661
Ontario Victim Services Secretariat, 18 King St. E, 7th Fl., Toronto, M5C 1C4 ON
416-325-3265, Fax: 416-212-1091

CULTURE & HERITAGE

See: Arts & Culture
Canadian Heritage, 15 Eddy St., Gatineau, K1A 0M5 QC
819-997-0055, 866-811-0055, info@pch.gc.ca
Historic Sites & Monuments Board of Canada, Terrasses de la Chaudière, 25 Eddy St., Gatineau, QC K1A 0M5
819-997-4059, Fax: 819-934-1115, hsmbc-clmhc@pc.gc.ca
Indian & Northern Affairs Canada, 10 Wellington St., North Tower, Gatineau, K1A 0H4 QC
819-997-0380, Fax: 819-953-3017, 866-817-3977, infopubs@ainc-inac.gc.ca

Alberta
Alberta Sport, Recreation, Parks & Wildlife Foundation, Standard Life Centre, 10405 Jasper Ave., 9th Fl., Edmonton, AB T5J 4R7
780-415-1167, Fax: 780-415-0308
Alberta International & Intergovernmental Relations, Commerce Place, 10155 - 102 St., 12th Fl., Edmonton, T5J 4G8 AB
780-422-1510, Fax: 780-427-0699

British Columbia
Ministry of Community & Rural Development, 800 Johnson St., 6th Fl., PO Box 9490 Prov Govt,Victoria, V8W 9N7 BC
250-387-2283, Fax: 250-387-4312, Feedback@gov.bc.ca

Manitoba
Manitoba Culture, Heritage, Tourism & Sport, Legislative Building, #118, 450 Broadway Ave., Winnipeg, R3C 0V8 MB
204-945-3729, Fax: 204-945-5223, mincht@leg.gov.mb.ca
Manitoba Heritage Council, 213 Notre Dame Ave., Main Fl., Winnipeg, MB R3B 1N3
204-945-2118, Fax: 204-948-2384, hrb@gov.mb.ca

New Brunswick
Department of Wellness, Culture & Sport, Place 2000, 250 King St., 4th Fl., PO Box 6000, Fredericton, E3B 5H1 NB
506-453-2909, Fax: 506-453-6548,

Newfoundland & Labrador
Department of Tourism, Culture & Recreation, Confederation Bldg., West Block, 2nd Fl., PO Box 8700, St. John's, A1B 4J6 NL
709-729-0862, Fax: 709-729-0870, tcrinfo@gov.nl.ca

Northwest Territories
Department of Aboriginal Affairs & Intergovernmental Relations, 4910 - 52nd St., PO Box 1320, Yellowknife, X1A 2L9 NT
867-873-7143, Fax: 867-873-0233, 877-838-8194, nancy_gardiner @gov.nt.ca
Department of Education, Culture & Employment, PO Box 1320, Yellowknife, X1A 2L9 NT
867-669-2399, Fax: 867-873-0431, 866-606-5627

Nova Scotia
Culture Division, #601, 1800 Argyle St., PO Box 456, Halifax, B3J 2R5 NS
Fax: 902-424-0710

Ontario
Ontario Trillium Foundation, 45 Charles St. East, 5th Fl., Toronto, ON M4Y 1S2
416-963-4927, Fax: 416-963-8781, 800-263-2887, trillium@trilliumfoundation.org

Saskatchewan
Saskatchewan First Nations & Métis Relations, #210, 1855 Victoria Ave., Regina, S4P 3T2 SK
306-787-6250, Fax: 306-787-5832
Saskatchewan Government Relations, 1855 Victoria Ave., Regina, S4P 3T2 SK
306-787-2635

CURRENCY

Bank of Canada, 234 Wellington St., Ottawa, K1A 0G9 ON
613-782-8111, Fax: 613-782-7713, 800-303-1282, info@bankofcanada.ca; communications@bankofcanada.ca (Media)
Royal Canadian Mint, 320 Sussex Dr., Ottawa, K1A 0G8 ON
613-993-3500, Fax: 613-993-4092, 800-267-1871

CUSTOMS

Canada Border Services Agency, Headquarters, 191 Laurier Ave. West, Ottawa, K1A 0L8 ON
800-461-9999, CBSA-ASFC@canada.gc.ca; communications@ps.gc.ca (Public Safety)

DAIRY INDUSTRY

Canadian Dairy Commission, Central Experimental Farm, NCC Driveway, Bldg. 55, 960 Carling Ave., Ottawa, K1A 0Z2 ON
613-792-2000, Fax: 613-792-2009, cdc-ccl@agr.gc.ca

Manitoba
Manitoba Milk Prices Review Commission, c/o Boards, Commissions & Legislation Branch, #812, 401 York Ave., Winnipeg, MB R3C 0P8
204-945-3854, Fax: 204-948-2844, randy.ozunko@gov.mb.ca

Prince Edward Island
Department of Agriculture, Jones Bldg., 11 Kent St., PO Box 2000, Charlottetown, C1A 7N8 PE
902-368-4880, Fax: 902-368-4857

DANGEROUS GOODS & HAZARDOUS MATERIALS

See Also: Occupational Safety; Waste Management
Hazardous Materials Information Review Commission, 427 Laurier Ave. West, 7th Fl., Ottawa, ON K1A 1M3
613-993-4331, Fax: 613-993-4686, hmirc-ccrmd@hc-sc.gc.ca

British Columbia
Ministry of Transportation & Infrastructure, 940 Blanshard St., PO Box 9850 Prov Govt,Victoria, V8W 9T5 BC
250-387-3198, Fax: 250-356-7706, tran.webmaster@gov.bc.ca

Northwest Territories
Department of Transportation, Lahm Ridge Bldg., 4501 50 Ave., PO Box 1320, Yellowknife, X1A 2L9 NT
867-920-3460, Fax: 867-873-0363

Nova Scotia
Department of Transportation & Infrastructure Renewal, Johnston Bldg., 1672 Granville St., 2nd Fl., PO Box 186, Halifax, B3J 2N2 NS
902-424-2297, Fax: 902-424-0171, 888-432-3233, tpwpaff@gov.ns.ca

Ontario
Ministry of Transportation, Ferguson Block, 77 Wellesley St. West, 3rd Fl., Toronto, M7A 1Z8 ON
416-235-4686, Fax: 416-327-9185, 800-268-4686

Prince Edward Island
Department of Transportation & Public Works, Jones Bldg., 11 Kent St., PO Box 2000, Charlottetown, C1A 7N8 PE
902-368-5100, Fax: 902-368-5395

Quebec
Ministère du Développement durable, de l'Environnement et des Parcs, Édifice Marie-Guyart, 675, boul René-Lévesque est, 29e étage, Québec, G1R 5V7 QC
418-521-3830, Fax: 418-646-5974, 800-561-1616, info@mddep.gouv.qc.ca

Saskatchewan
Saskatchewan Highways & Infrastructure, 1855 Victoria Ave., Regina, S4P 3T2 SK
306-787-4800

Yukon Territory
Yukon Highways & Public Works, PO Box 2703, Whitehorse, Y1A 2C6 YT
867-393-7193, Fax: 867-393-6218, 800-661-0408, hpw-info@gov.yk.ca

DAY CARE SERVICES

See Also: Child Welfare

British Columbia
Corporate Services, 765 Broughton St., 3rd Fl., PO Box 9738 Prov Govt,Victoria, V8W 9S2 BC
250-387-5954, Fax: 250-387-2481

Ontario
Ministry of Children & Youth Services, 56 Wellesley St. West, 14th Fl., Toronto, M5S 2G3 ON
Fax: 416-325-5191, 866-821-7770

DEBT MANAGEMENT

Finance Canada, L'esplanade Laurier, 140 O'Connor St., Ottawa, K1A 0G5 ON
613-992-1573, Fax: 613-943-0938, finpub@fin.gc.ca

British Columbia
Provincial Treasury, 620 Superior St., PO Box 9414 Prov Govt,Victoria, V8V 9V1 BC
250-387-4541, Fax: 250-356-3041, Jim.Hopkings@gov.bc.ca

New Brunswick
Treasury, Centennial Bldg., #376, 670 King St., PO Box 6000, Fredericton, E3B 5H1 NB
506-453-3952, Fax: 506-453-2053

DEFENCE

See Also: Emergency Response; Public Safety

Canadian Forces Grievance Board, 60 Queen St., 10th Fl., Ottawa, K1P 5Y7 ON
613-996-8529, Fax: 613-996-6491, 877-276-4193
Defence Construction Canada, Constitution Square, 350 Albert St., 19th Fl., Ottawa, K1A 0K3 ON
613-998-9548, Fax: 613-998-1061, 800-514-3555, info@dcc-cdc.gc.ca
Defence Research & Development Canada, 305 Rideau St., Ottawa, K1A 0K2 ON
613-992-7237, info@drdc-rddc.gc.ca
Military Police Complaints Commission, 270 Albert St., 10th Fl., Ottawa, ON K1P 5G8
613-947-5625, Fax: 613-947-5713, 800-632-0566, commission@mpcc-cppm.gc.ca
National Defence Canada, Major-General George R. Pearkes Bldg., 101 Colonel By Dr., Ottawa, K1A 0K2 ON
613-995-2534, Fax: 613-992-4739, 800-856-8488

DISABLED PERSONS SERVICES

Canadian Human Rights Commission, 344 Slater St., 8th Fl., Ottawa, K1A 1E1 ON
613-995-1151, Fax: 613-996-9661, 888-214-1090, info.com@chrc-ccdp.ca

Alberta

Persons with Developmental Disabilities Boards, c/o PDD Program Branch, Peace Hills Trust Tower, #404, 10011 - 109 St., Edmonton, AB T5J 3S8
780-427-1177, Fax: 780-427-1220, 800-310-0000
Premier's Council on the Status of Persons with Disabilities, HSBC Bldg., #1110, 10055 - 106 St., Edmonton, AB T5J 2Y2
780-422-1095, 800-272-8841, pcspd@gov.ab.ca
Alberta Seniors & Community Supports, Standard Life Centre, 10405 Jasper Ave., Main Fl., Edmonton, T5J 4R7 AB
780-427-7876, Fax: 780-422-6301, 800-642-3853

Manitoba

Disabilities Issues Office, #630, 240 Graham Ave., Winnipeg, MB R3C 0J7
204-945-7613, Fax: 204-948-2896, dio@gov.mb.ca

New Brunswick

Premier's Council on the Status of Disabled Persons, Kings Place, #648, 440 King St., Fredericton, E3B 5H8 NB
506-444-3000, Fax: 506-444-3001, 800-442-4412, pcsdp@gnb.ca

Nova Scotia

Nova Scotia Disabled Persons Commission, PO Box 222 CRO, Halifax, NS B3J 2M4
902-424-8280, Fax: 902-424-0592, 800-565-8280

Nunavut

Department of Culture, Language, Elders & Youth, PO Box 1000 800,Iqaluit, X0A 0H0 NU
867-975-5500, Fax: 867-975-5504, 866-934-2035

Quebec

Office des personnes handicapées du Québec, 309, rue Brock, Drummondville, QC J2B 1C5
819-475-8585, Fax: 819-475-8767, 800-567-1465

DISCRIMINATION & EMPLOYMENT EQUITY

Canadian Human Rights Commission, 344 Slater St., 8th Fl., Ottawa, K1A 1E1 ON
613-995-1151, Fax: 613-996-9661, 888-214-1090, info.com@chrc-ccdp.ca
Canadian Human Rights Tribunal, 160 Elgin St., 11th Fl., Ottawa, K1A 1J4 ON
613-995-1707, Fax: 613-995-3484, registrar@chrt-tcdp.gc.ca

Alberta

Labour Relations Board, #503, 10808 - 99 Ave., Edmonton, AB T5K 0G5
780-422-5926, Fax: 780-422-0970, 800-463-2572, alrbinfo@lab.gov.ab.ca

British Columbia

British Columbia Human Rights Tribunal, #1170, 605 Robson St., Vancouver, BC V6B 5J3
604-775-2000, Fax: 604-775-2020, 888-440-8844, BCHumanRightsTribunal@gov.bc.ca

Manitoba

Manitoba Human Rights Commission, 175 Hargrave St., 7th Fl., Winnipeg, R3C 3R8 MB
204-945-3007, Fax: 204-945-1292, 888-884-8681, hrc@gov.mb.ca

New Brunswick

New Brunswick Human Rights Commission, PO Box 6000, Fredericton, E3B 5H1 NB
506-453-2301, Fax: 506-453-2653, 888-471-2233, hrc.cdp@gnb.ca

Newfoundland & Labrador

Newfoundland & Labrador Human Rights Commission, PO Box 8700, St. John's, A1B 4J6 NL
709-729-2709, Fax: 709-729-0790, 800-563-5808, humanrights@mail.gov.nl.ca

Nova Scotia

Nova Scotia Human Rights Commission, Joseph Howe Bldg., 1690 Hollis St., 6th Fl., Halifax, B3J 3C4 NS
902-424-4111, Fax: 902-424-0596

Ontario

Ontario Human Rights Commission, 180 Dundas St. West, 7th Fl., Toronto, M7A 2R9 ON
416-314-4500, Fax: 416-326-9520, 800-387-9080, info@ohrc.on.ca

Prince Edward Island

Prince Edward Island Human Rights Commission, 53 Water St., PO Box 2000, Charlottetown, C1A 7N8 PE
902-368-4180, Fax: 902-368-4236, 800-237-5031, lbuell@peihumanrights.ca

Quebec

Commission de l'équité salariale, 200, ch Ste-Foy, 4e étage, Québec, QC G1R 6A1
418-528-8765, Fax: 418-528-6999, 888-528-8765, equite.salariale@ces.gouv.qc.ca

Saskatchewan

Saskatchewan Human Rights Commission, Saskatoon Office, Sturdy Stone Bdg., #816, 122 - 3 Ave. North, 8th Fl., Saskatoon, S7K 2H6 SK
306-933-5952, Fax: 306-933-7863, 800-667-9249, shrc@shrc.gov.sk.ca

Yukon Territory

Yukon Human Rights Commission, #201, 211 Hawkins St., Whitehorse, YT Y1A 1X3
867-667-6226, Fax: 867-667-2662, 800-661-0535, humanrights@yhrc.yk.ca

DIVORCE

Justice Canada, East Memorial Bldg., 284 Wellington St., Ottawa, K1A 0H8 ON
613-957-4222, Fax: 613-954-0811, webadmin@justice.gc.ca

DRIVERS' LICENCES

Alberta

Technology Services, John E. Brownlee Bldg., 10365 - 97 St., 8th Fl., Edmonton, T5J 3W7 AB
780-422-8545,

British Columbia

Ministry of Transportation & Infrastructure, 940 Blanshard St., PO Box 9850 Prov Govt,Victoria, V8W 9T5 BC
250-387-3198, Fax: 250-356-7706, tran.webmaster@gov.bc.ca

Manitoba

Manitoba Infrastructure & Transportation, Legislative Building, #203, 450 Broadway Ave., Winnipeg, R3C 0V8 MB
204-945-3723, Fax: 204-945-7610

Northwest Territories

Road Licensing & Safety, 4510 - 50 Ave., 1st fl., PO Box 1320, Yellowknife, X1A 2L9 NT
867-873-7972, Fax: 867-873-0120

Ontario

Licence Appeal Tribunal (LAT), 1 St. Clair Ave. West, 12th Fl., Toronto, ON M4V 1K6
416-314-4260, Fax: 416-314-4270, 800-255-2214
Ministry of Transportation, Ferguson Block, 77 Wellesley St. West, 3rd Fl., Toronto, M7A 1Z8 ON
416-235-4686, Fax: 416-327-9185, 800-268-4686

Prince Edward Island

Department of Transportation & Public Works, Jones Bldg., 11 Kent St., PO Box 2000, Charlottetown, C1A 7N8 PE
902-368-5100, Fax: 902-368-5395

Quebec

Société de l'assurance automobile du Québec, 333, boul Jean-Lesage, CP 19600 Terminus, Québec, QC G1K 8J6
418-643-7620, Fax: 418-644-0339, 800-361-7620, courrier@saaq.gouv.qc.ca

Saskatchewan

Saskatchewan Government Insurance, 2260 - 11th Ave., Regina, S4P 0J9 SK
306-751-1200, Fax: 306-787-7477, 800-667-8015, sgiinquiries@sgi.sk.ca

Yukon Territory

Driver Control Board, 308 Steele St., PO Box 2703, Whitehorse, YT Y1A 2C6
867-667-3774, Fax: 867-393-6483, dcb@gov.yk.ca

DRUGS & ALCOHOL

See Also: Liquor Control
Canadian Centre on Substance Abuse, #300, 75 Albert St., Ottawa, K1P 5E7 ON
613-235-4048, Fax: 613-235-8101

Alberta

Alberta Health Services, Manulife Place, 10180 - 101 St., Edmonton, AB T5J 3S4
780-342-2000, Fax: 780-342-2060, 888-342-2471

British Columbia

Ministry of Health Services, 1515 Blanshard St., Victoria, V8W 3C8 BC
250-952-1742, Fax: 250-356-9587, 800-465-4911, hlth.health@gems1.gov.bc.ca

Quebec

Bureau des projets Centres hospitaliers universitaires de Montréal, CHUM, CUSM et CHU Sainte-Justine, #10.049, 2021, rue Union, Montréal, QC H3A 2S9
514-864-9883, Fax: 514-873-7362
Ministère de la Santé et des Services sociaux, Direction des communications et Renseignements généraux, 1075, ch Sainte-Foy, Québec, G1S 2M1 QC
418-266-8900, 800-707-3380, regisseur.web@msss.gouv.qc.ca

EDUCATION

Canada School of Public Service, 373 Sussex Dr., Ottawa, K1N 6Z2 ON
819-953-5400, Fax: 819-953-7953, 866-703-9598, info@csps-efpc.gc.ca
Canadian Council of Directors of Apprenticeship, 140 Promenade du Portage, 5th Fl, Phase IV, Gatineau, QC K1A 0J9
819-953-7443, Fax: 819-994-0202, redseal-sceaurouge@hrsdc-rhdcc.gc.ca
Canadian Forces College, Toronto,ON
416-482-6800
Canadian Police College, PO Box 8900, Ottawa, K1G 3J2 ON
613-993-9500, Fax: 613-990-9738, cpc-ccp@rcmp-grc.gc.ca
RCMP Training Academy, 6101 Dewdney Ave., Regina, S4P 3J7 SK
306-780-5002, Fax: 306-780-7940
Royal Military College, Kingston,ON
613-541-6000

Alberta

Alberta Advanced Education & Technology, Legislature Bldg., #324, 10800 - 97 Ave., Edmonton, T5K 2B6 AB
780-422-5400, Fax: 780-422-1263,-310-0000, aet.info@gov.ab.ca
Alberta Apprenticeship & Industry Training Board, South Tower, 10030 - 107 St., 7th Fl., Edmonton, AB T5J 4X7
780-427-8517, Fax: 780-422-3734, 800-232-7215
Alberta Council on Admissions & Transfer, Commerce Place, 10155 - 102 St., 11th Fl., Edmonton, AB T5J 4L5
780-422-9021, Fax: 780-422-3688, 800-232-7215, acat@gov.ab.ca
Alberta Learning Information Service, City Centre, 10242 - 105 St., Edmonton, AB T5J 3L5
780-427-9674,-310-0000, info@alis.gov.ab.ca
Campus Alberta Quality Council, Commerce Place, 10155 - 102 St., 11th Fl., Edmonton, AB T5J 4L5
780-427-8921, Fax: 780-427-0423, caqc@gov.ab.ca
Community, Learner & Industry Connections Division, Phipps-McKinnon Bldg., 5th Fl., 10020 - 101A Ave., Edmonton, T5J 3G2 AB
780-427-8517
Council on Alberta Teaching Standards, 10044 - 108 St., Edmonton, AB T5J 5E6
780-427-2045, Fax: 780-422-4199
Alberta Education, Commerce Place, 10155 - 102 St., 7th Fl., Edmonton, T5J 4L5 AB
780-427-7219, Fax: 780-427-0591
Private Vocational Schools Advisory Council, Commerce Place, 10155 - 102 St., 10th Fl., Edmonton, AB T5J 4L5
780-427-5609, Fax: 780-427-5920

British Columbia

Ministry of Advanced Education & Labour Market Development, PO Box 9059 Prov Govt,Victoria, V8W 9E2 BC
250-356-2771, Fax: 250-356-3000, ALMD.WEBMASTER@gov.bc.ca
Auditor Certification Board, 940 Blanshard St., 2nd Fl., PO Box 9431 Prov Govt, Victoria, BC V8W 9V3

250-356-8658, Fax: 250-356-9422, sherrilyn.johnson@gov.bc.ca
Degree Quality Assessment Board, Degree Quality Assessment Board Secretariat, 835 Humboldt St., 1st Fl., PO Box 9177 Prov Govt, Victoria, BC V8V 4W8
250-387-5163, aved.dqabsecretariat@gov.bc.ca
Ministry of Education, PO Box 9146 Prov Govt,Victoria, V8W 9H1 BC
250-387-1977, Fax: 250-387-3200, 888-879-1166
Leading Edge Endowment Fund Board, 1188 West Georgia St., 9th Fl., Vancouver, BC V6E 4A2
604-438-3220, Fax: 604-438-6564, contact@leefbc.ca
Premier's Technology Council, #730, 999 Canada Pl., Vancouver, BC V6C 3E1
604-775-2122, Fax: 604-775-2129, premiers.technologycouncil@gov.bc.ca
Private Career Training Institutions Agency, #300, 5172 Kingsway, Burnaby, BC V5H 2E8
604-660-4400, Fax: 604-660-3312, 800-661-7441, info@pctia.bc.ca

Manitoba
Manitoba Advanced Education & Literacy, Legislative Building, #162, 450 Broadway Ave., Winnipeg, R3C 0V8 MB
204-945-0825, Fax: 204-948-2216, minaed@leg.gov.mb.ca
Division du Bureau de l'éducation française, #509, 1181 av Portage, Winnipeg, R3C 0T3 MB
204-945-6916, Fax: 204-945-1625
Manitoba Education, Citizenship & Youth, #168, Legislative Bldg., 450 Broadway, Winnipeg, R3C 0V8 MB
204-945-3720, Fax: 204-945-1291, minedu@leg.gov.mb.ca
Manitoba Education, Research & Learning Information Networks, #100 - 135 Innovation Dr., University of Manitoba, Winnipeg, MB R3T 6A8
204-474-7800, Fax: 204-474-7830, 800-430-6404
Public Schools Finance Board, #506, 1181 Portage Ave., Winnipeg, MB R3G 0T3
204-945-6628, Fax: 204-948-2001
School Programs Division, #307, 1181 Portage Ave., Winnipeg, R3G 0T3 MB
Fax: 204-945-8303,

New Brunswick
Apprenticeship & Occupational Certification Board, PO Box 6000, Fredericton, NB E3B 5H1
506-453-2260, Fax: 506-453-5317
Department of Education, Place 2000, 250 King St., PO Box 6000, Fredericton, E3B 5H1 NB
506-453-3678, Fax: 506-453-3325
Maritime Provinces Higher Education Commission, PO Box 6000, Fredericton, E3B 5H1 NB
506-453-2844, Fax: 506-453-2106, info@mphec.ca
Department of Post-Secondary Education, Training & Labour, 470 York St., PO Box 6000, Fredericton, E3B 5H1 NB
506-453-2597, Fax: 506-453-3618, dpetlinfo@gnb.ca

Newfoundland & Labrador
Department of Education, West Block, Confederation Bldg., 100 Prince Philip Dr., 3rd Fl., PO Box 8700, St. John's, A1B 4J6 NL
709-729-5097, Fax: 709-729-5896, education@gov.nl.ca

Northwest Territories
Aurora Research Institute, 191 MacKenzie Rd., PO Box 1450, Inuvik, X0E 0T0 NT
867-777-3298, Fax: 867-777-4264, webmaster@nwtresearch.com
Department of Education, Culture & Employment, PO Box 1320, Yellowknife, X1A 2L9 NT
867-669-2399, Fax: 867-873-0431, 866-606-5627

Nova Scotia
Council of Ministers of Education & Training, PO Box 2044, Halifax, NS B3J 2Z1
902-424-5352, Fax: 902-424-8976, camet_camef@cap-cpma.ca
Department of Education, Trade Mart Bldg., 2021 Brunswick St., 4th Fl., PO Box 578, Halifax, B3J 2S9 NS
902-424-5168, Fax: 902-424-0680
Nova Scotia Apprenticeship Board, 2021 Brunswick St., PO Box 578, Halifax, NS B3J 2S9
902-424-0872, Fax: 902-428-0605, apprenticeboard@ednet.ns.ca

Nunavut
Department of Education, PO Box 1000 910,Iqaluit, X0A 0H0 NU
867-975-5600, Fax: 867-975-5605, 888-531-1456

Ontario
Academic & Experience Requirements Committee of the Association of Ontario Land Surveyors, 1043 McNicoll Ave., Toronto, ON M1W 3W6
416-491-9020, Fax: 416-491-2576, 800-268-0718, admin@aols.org
College Compensation & Appointments Council, #1102, 2 Carlton St., Toronto, ON M5B 1J3
416-325-2914, Fax: 416-325-2917
College of Veterinarians of Ontario, 2106 Gordon St., Guelph, ON N1L 1G6
519-824-5600, Fax: 519-824-6497, 800-424-2856
Ministry of Education, Mowat Block, 900 Bay St., 22nd. Fl., Toronto, M7A 1L2 ON
416-325-2929, Fax: 416-325-2934, 800-387-5514, info@edu.gov.on.ca
Elementary/Secondary Business & Finance Division, Mowat Block, 900 Bay St., 20th fl., Toronto, M7A 1L2 ON
416-325-6127, Fax: 416-327-1182
Ontario Graduate Scholarship Program Selection Board, 189 Red River Rd., 4thFl., PO Box 4500, Thunder Bay, ON P7B 6G9
807-343-7257, Fax: 807-343-7278, 800-465-3957
Ontario Student Assistance Appeal Board, Mowat Block, 900 Bay St., 7th Fl., Toronto, ON M7A 1L2
416-314-0714, Fax: 416-325-3096
Postsecondary Education Quality Assessment Board, #1511, 2 Carlton St., Toronto, ON M5B 1J3
416-325-1686, Fax: 416-325-1711
Strategic Planning & Elementary/Secondary Programs Division, Mowat Block, 900 Bay st., 22nd fl., Toronto, M7A 1L2 ON
416-325-2135, Fax: 416-327-1182
Ministry of Training, Colleges & Universities, Mowat Block, 900 Bay St., 3rd Fl., Toronto, M7A 1L2 ON
416-325-1600, Fax: 416-325-2934

Prince Edward Island
Department of Education & Early Childhood Development, Sullivan Bldg., 16 Fitzroy St., 2nd Fl., PO Box 2000, Charlottetown, C1A 7N8 PE
902-368-4600, Fax: 902-368-4663

Quebec
Commission consultative de l'enseignement privé, 1035, rue De La Chevrotière, 14e étage, Québec, QC G1R 5A5
418-646-1249, Fax: 418-643-7752
Commission d'évaluation de l'enseignement collégial, 800, place d'Youville, 18e étage, Québec, QC G1R 5P4
418-643-9938, Fax: 418-643-9019, info@ceec.gouv.qc.ca
Commission de l'éducation en langue anglaise, 600, rue Fullum, 9e étage, Montréal, QC H2K 4L1
514-873-5656, Fax: 514-864-4181, cela-abee@mels.gouv.qc.ca
Commission des programmes d'études, #1.85, 525, boul René-Lévesque est, Québec, QC G1R 5Z4
418-646-0133, Fax: 418-643-5431, cpe@mels.gouv.qc.ca
Conseil supérieur de l'éducation, #180, 1175, av Lavigerie, Sainte-Foy, QC G1V 5B2
418-643-3850, Fax: 418-644-2530, panorama@cse.gouv.qc.ca
Ministère de l'Éducation, du Loisir et du Sport, 1035, rue De La Chevrotière, 28e étage, Québec, G1R 5A5 QC
418-643-7095, Fax: 418-646-6561, 866-747-6626

Saskatchewan
Saskatchewan Advanced Education & Employment, 2220 College Ave., Regina, S4P 4V9 SK
306-787-9478, aeeinquiry@gov.sk.ca
Saskatchewan Education, 2220 College Ave., Regina, S4P 4V9 SK
306-787-6030, 888-775-3276, learninginquiry@sasked.gov.sk.ca
Saskatchewan Research Council, #125, 15 Innovation Blvd., Saskatoon, S7N 2X8 SK
306-933-5400, Fax: 306-933-7446, info@src.sk.ca

Yukon Territory
Yukon Education, PO Box 2703, Whitehorse, Y1A 2C6 YT
867-667-5141, Fax: 867-393-6254

EDUCATION & TRAINING

Human Resources & Skills Development Canada, 140 Promenade du Portage, Ottawa, K1A 0J9 ON
Department of Labour & Workforce Development, 5151 Terminal Rd., 6th Fl., PO Box 697, Halifax, B3J 2T8 NS
902-424-5301, Fax: 902-424-0575

Alberta
Alberta Employment & Immigration, Minister's Office, Legislature Bldg., #208, 10800 - 97 Ave., Edmonton, T5K 2B6 AB
780-644-5135, Fax: 780-422-9556, 866-644-5135, eii.communications@gov.ab.ca

British Columbia
Ministry of Labour, PO Box 9052 Prov Govt,Victoria, V8W 9E2 BC
250-356-6348, Fax: 250-356-6595, LCS.Minister@gov.bc.ca
Private Career Training Institutions Agency, #300, 5172 Kingsway, Burnaby, BC V5H 2E8
604-660-4400, Fax: 604-660-3312, 800-661-7441, info@pctia.bc.ca

New Brunswick
Department of Post-Secondary Education, Training & Labour, 470 York St., PO Box 6000, Fredericton, E3B 5H1 NB
506-453-2597, Fax: 506-453-3618, dpetlinfo@gnb.ca

Northwest Territories
Department of Education, Culture & Employment, PO Box 1320, Yellowknife, X1A 2L9 NT
867-669-2399, Fax: 867-873-0431, 866-606-5627

Ontario
Ministry of Labour, 400 University Ave., 14th Fl., Toronto, M7A 1T7 ON
416-326-7770, 800-268-8013

Saskatchewan
Saskatchewan Advanced Education & Employment, 2220 College Ave., Regina, S4P 4V9 SK
306-787-9478, aeeinquiry@gov.sk.ca

ELECTED OFFICIALS & CONSTITUENCIES

Fortieth Parliament - Canada, House of Commons, Parliament Buildings, Ottawa, K1A 0A9 ON
Thirty-ninth Parliament - Ontario, Clerk's Office, Legislative Bldg., Queen's Park, Toronto, M7A 1A2 ON
416-325-7500, Fax: 416-325-7489

Alberta
Twenty-seventh Legislature - Alberta, Legislature Bldg., 10800 - 97 Ave., Edmonton, T5K 2B6 AB
780-427-2826, Fax: 780-427-1623, laocommunications@assembly.ab.ca

British Columbia
Thirty-Eighth Legislature - British Columbia, Parliament Bldgs., Victoria, V8V 1X4 BC
250-387-3785, Fax: 250-387-0942, ClerkHouse@leg.bc.ca

Manitoba
Thirty-ninth Legislature - Manitoba, Legislative Building, 450 Broadway Ave., Winnipeg, R3C 0V8 MB
204-945-3636, Fax: 204-948-2507, clerkla@leg.gov.mb.ca

New Brunswick
Fifty-sixth Legislature - New Brunswick, Legislative Assembly of New Brunswick, 706 Queen St., PO Box 6000, Fredericton, E3B 5H1 NB
506-453-2506, Fax: 506-453-7154

Newfoundland & Labrador
Forty-sixth House of Assembly - Newfoundland & Labrador, PO Box 8700, St. John's, A1B 4J6 NL
709-729-3405, ClerkHOA@gov.nl.ca

Northwest Territories
Sixteenth Legislature - Northwest Territories, PO Box 1320, Yellowknife, X1A 2L9 NT
867-669-2200, Fax: 867-920-4735, 800-661-0784

Nova Scotia
Sixtieth Assembly - Nova Scotia, Province House, PO Box 1617, Halifax, B3J 2Y3 NS
902-424-5978, Fax: 902-424-0632

Nunavut
Second Legislature - Nunavut, PO Box 1200, Iqaluit, X0A 0H0 NU

Prince Edward Island
Sixty-third General Assembly - Prince Edward Island, Province House, 165 Richmond St., 1st Fl., PO Box 2000, Charlottetown, C1A 7N8 PE
902-368-5970, Fax: 902-368-5175, 877-315-5518

Quebec
Trente-huitième législature, Hôtel du Parlement, 1045, rue des Parlementaires, Québec, G1A 1A4 QC
418-643-7239, Fax: 418-646-4271, 866-337-8837

Saskatchewan
Twenty-sixth Legislature - Saskatchewan, #123, Legislative Bldg., 2405 Legislative Dr., Regina, S4S 0B3 SK
306-787-2376, Fax: 306-787-1558, info@legassembly.sk.ca

Yukon Territory
Thirty-Second Legislature - Yukon Territory, PO Box 2703, Whitehorse, Y1A 2C6 YT
867-667-5498

ELECTIONS

Elections Canada, The Jackson Bldg., 257 Slater St., Ottawa, K1A 0M6 ON
613-993-2975, Fax: 613-954-8584, 800-463-6868

Alberta
Alberta Office of the Chief Electoral Officer/Elections Alberta, #100, 11510 Kingsway Ave., Edmonton, T5G 2Y5 AB
780-427-7191, Fax: 780-422-2900, info@electionsalberta.ab.ca

British Columbia
Elections British Columbia, PO Box 9275 Prov Govt,Victoria, V8W 9J6 BC
250-387-5305, Fax: 250-387-3578, 800-661-8683, electionsbc@elections.bc.ca

Manitoba
Elections Manitoba, #120, 200 Vaughan St., Winnipeg, R3C 1T5 MB
204-945-3225, Fax: 204-945-6011, 866-628-6837, election@elections.mb.ca

New Brunswick
Office of the Chief Electoral Officer, PO Box 6000, Fredericton, E3B 5H1 NB
506-453-2218, Fax: 506-457-4926, 800-308 2922

Newfoundland & Labrador
Office of the Chief Electoral Officer, 39 Hallett Cr., St. John's, A1B 4C4 NL
709-729-0712, Fax: 709-729-0679, 877-729-7987, oceo@gov.nl.ca

Northwest Territories
Elections NWT/Plebiscite Office, PO Box 1320, Yellowknife, X1A 2L9 NT
867-920-6999, Fax: 867-873-0366, 800-661-0796

Nova Scotia
Elections Nova Scotia, 3667 Strawberry Hill St., PO Box 2246, Halifax, B3J 3C8 NS
902-424-8584, Fax: 902-424-6622, 800-565-1504, elections@gov.ns.ca

Nunavut
Legislative Assembly, Legislative Assembly Bldg., 3rd Fl., PO Box 1200, Iqaluit, X0A 0H0 NU
867-975-5000, Fax: 867-975-5190, 877-334-7266, leginfo@assembly.nu.ca

Ontario
Elections Ontario, 51 Rolark Dr., Toronto, M1R 3B1 ON
416-326-6300, Fax: 416-326-6200, 888-668-8683, info@elections.on.ca

Prince Edward Island
Elections Prince Edward Island, J. Angus MacLean Bldg., 94 Great George St., PO Box 774, Charlottetown, C1A 7L3 PE
902-368-5895, Fax: 902-368-6500

Quebec
Directeur général des Élections du Québec, Édifice René-Lévesque, 3460, rue de La Pérade, Québec, G1X 3Y5 QC
418-528-0422, Fax: 418-643-7291, 888-353-2846, info@electionsquebec.qc.ca

Saskatchewan
Elections Saskatchewan, 1702 Park St., Regina, S4N 6B2 SK
306-787-4000, Fax: 306-787-4052, 877-958-VOTE, info@elections.sk.ca

EMERGENCY MEASURES

Environment Canada, 10 Wellington St., Gatineau, K1A 0H3 QC
819-997-2800, Fax: 819-994-1412, 800-668-6767, enviroinfo@ec.gc.ca

National Search & Rescue Secretariat, #400, 275 Slater St., Ottawa, K1A 0K2 ON
613-992-0054, Fax: 613-996-3746, 800-727-9414, inquiry@nss.gc.ca

Public Safety Canada, 269 Laurier Ave. West, Ottawa, K1A 0P8 ON
613-944-4875, Fax: 613-954-5186, 866-222-3006, communications@ps.gc.ca

Alberta
Alberta Environment, South Tower, Petroleum Plaza, 9915 - 108 St., 10th Fl., Edmonton, T5K 2G8 AB
780-427-2700, Fax: 780-422-4086, env.infocent@gov.ab.ca

British Columbia
British Columbia Provincial Emergency Program, PO Box 9201 Prov Govt,Victoria, V8W 9J1 BC
250-952-4913, Fax: 250-952-4888, 888-257-4777

Manitoba
Emergency Measures Organization, 405 Broadway Ave., 15th Floor, Winnipeg, R3C 3L6 MB
204-945-4772, Fax: 204-945-4929, 888-267-8298, emo@gov.mb.ca

New Brunswick
New Brunswick Emergency Measures Organization, Victoria Health Centre, 65 Brunswick Ave., Fredericton, NB E3B 1G5
506-453-2133, Fax: 506-453-5513, 800-561-4034, emo@gnb.ca

Newfoundland & Labrador
Newfoundland & Labrador Emergency Measures Organization, PO Box 8700, St. John's, A1B 4J6 NL
709-729-3703, Fax: 709-729-3857

Nova Scotia
Nova Scotia Emergency Management Office, PO Box 2581, Halifax, B3J 3N5 NS
902-424-5620, Fax: 902-424-5376, 866-424-5620, emo@gov.ns.ca

Nunavut
Nunavut Emergency Management, PO Box 1000 700,Iqaluit, X0A 0H0 NU
867-975-5403, Fax: 867-979-4221, 800-693-1666

Ontario
Emergency Management Ontario, 77 Wellesley St. W, PO Box 222, Toronto, M7A 1N3 ON
416-314-3723, Fax: 416-314-3758

Prince Edward Island
Prince Edward Island Emergency Measures Organization, National Bank Tower, #600, 134 Kent St., PO Box 2000, Charlottetown, C1A 7N8 PE
902-894-0385, Fax: 902-368-6362

Saskatchewan
Saskatchewan Emergency Management Organization, #100, 1855 Victoria Ave., Regina, S4P 3V7 SK
306-787-9563, Fax: 306-787-1694, infosafety@cps.gov.sk.ca

Yukon Territory
Emergency Measures Organization, PO Box 2703, Whitehorse, Y1A 2C6 YT
867-667-5220, Fax: 867-393-6266, 800-661-0408, emo.yukon@gov.yk.ca

EMPLOYMENT

Alberta
Alberta Employment & Immigration, Minister's Office, Legislature Bldg., #208, 10800 - 97 Ave., Edmonton, T5K 2B6 AB
780-644-5135, Fax: 780-422-9556, 866-644-5135, eii.communications@gov.ab.ca

British Columbia
Ministry of Housing & Social Development, PO Box 9058 Prov Govt,Victoria, V8W 9E2 BC
250-356-7750, Fax: 250-356-7292, EIA.Minister@gov.bc.ca; EnquiryBC@gov.bc.ca

Manitoba
Manitoba Labour & Immigration, Legislative Building, 317, 450 Broadway Ave., Winnipeg, R3C 0V8 MB
204-945-4079, Fax: 204-945-8312, minlab@leg.gov.mb.ca

New Brunswick
Office of Human Resources, Centennial Bldg, #345, 670 King St., PO Box 6000, Fredericton, E3B 5H1 NB
506-453-2264, Fax: 506-453-7195

Newfoundland & Labrador
Department of Human Resources, Labour & Employment, Confederation Bldg., PO Box 8700, St. John's, A1B 4J6 NL
709-729-2478, Fax: 709-729-6996, hreweb@gov.nl.ca

Northwest Territories
Department of Human Resources, PO Box 1320, Yellowknife, X1A 2L9 NT
867-920-3409, Fax: 867-873-0306, 866-475-8162, HRHelpDesk@gov.nt.ca

Nunavut
Department of Human Resources, PO Box 1000 400,Iqaluit, X0A 1H0 NU
867-975-6200, Fax: 867-975-6216, 888-668-9993, gnhr@gov.nu.ca

Quebec
Ministère de l'Emploi et de la Solidarité sociale, 425, rue St-Amable, 4e étage, Québec, G1R 4Z1 QC
418-643-4721, 888-643-4721

Emploi-Québec, #2800, 800, rue du Square-Victoria, Montréal, H4Z 1B7 QC
514-873-1892, 888-367-5647

Ministère du Travail, 200, ch Sainte-Foy, 6e étage, Québec, G1R 5S1 QC
418-643-4817, Fax: 418-528-0559, 800-643-4817, service_clientele@travail.gouv.qc.ca

Saskatchewan
Saskatchewan Advanced Education & Employment, 2220 College Ave., Regina, S4P 4V9 SK
306-787-9478, aeeinquiry@gov.sk.ca

EMPLOYMENT INSURANCE

Canada Employment Insurance Commission, 140, Promenade du Portage, Phase IV, Gatineau, QC K1A 0J9
800-206-7218

Saskatchewan
Saskatchewan Advanced Education, Employment & Labour, 1945 Hamilton St., Regina, S4P 2C8 SK
306-787-9478, Fax: 306-787-2315

ENERGY

See Also: Natural Resources

Atomic Energy of Canada Limited, Head Office, Sheridan Science & Technology Park, 2251 Speakman Dr., Mississauga, L5K 1B2 ON
905-823-9040, 866-886-2325, librarycr@aecl.ca (Library); speakers@aecl.ca (Community speakers)

Canadian Nuclear Safety Commission, 280 Slater St., PO Box 1046 B,Ottawa, K1P 5S9 ON
613-995-5894, Fax: 613-995-5086, 800-668-5284, info@cnsc-ccsn.gc.ca

Indian Oil & Gas Canada, #100, 9911 Chula Blvd., Tsuu T'ina (Sarcee), AB T2W 6H6
403-292-5625, Fax: 403-292-5618, ContactIOGC@inac-ainc.gc.ca

National Energy Board, 444 - 7 Ave. SW, Calgary, T2P 0X8 AB
403-292-4800, Fax: 403-292-5503, 800-899-1265, info@neb-one.gc.ca

Alberta
Energy Resources Conservation Board, #1000, 250 - 5 Ave. SW, Calgary, AB T2P 0R4
403-297-8311, Fax: 403-297-7336, inquiries@ercb.ca

Alberta Energy, North Petroleum Plaza, 9945 - 108 St., 10th Fl., Edmonton, T5K 2G6 AB
780-427-8050, Fax: 780-422-0698, 780-310-0000,

British Columbia
Ministry of Energy, Mines & Petroleum Resources, PO Box 9318 Prov Govt,Victoria, V8W 9N3 BC
250-952-0241

British Columbia Hydro, 333 Dunsmuir St., 18th Fl., Vancouver, V6B 5R3 BC
604-224-9376, Fax: 604-623-4467, 800-224-9376

Oil & Gas Commission, #100, 10003 - 110 Ave., Fort St John, BC V1J 6M7
250-261-5700, 800-663-7867

Powerex Corp., #1400, 666 Burrard St., Vancouver, BC V6C 2X8
604-891-5000, Fax: 604-891-6060, 800-220-4907, customer.service@bchydro.com

Powertech Labs Inc., 12388 - 88 Ave., Surrey, BC V8W 7R7
604-590-7500, Fax: 604-590-5347, info@powertechlans.com

British Columbia Utilities Commission, 900 Howe St., 6th Fl., PO Box 250, Vancouver, V6Z 2N3 BC
604-660-4700, Fax: 604-660-1102, 800-663-1385, commission.secretary@bcuc.com

Manitoba
Manitoba Hydro, PO Box 815 Main,Winnipeg, R3C 2P4 MB
204-474-3311, Fax: 204-475-0069, publicaffairs@hydro.mb.ca

Petroleum, #360, 1395 Ellice Ave., Winnipeg, R3G 3P2 MB
204-945-6577, Fax: 204-945-0586

Manitoba Science, Technology, Energy & Mines, #333, 450 Broadway, Winnipeg, R3C 0V8 MB

New Brunswick
Efficiency NB, #101, 33 Charlotte St., Saint John, NB E2L 2H3
506-643-7826, Fax: 506-643-7835, 866-643-8833

Department of Energy, Brunswick Square, #100M, 1 Germain St., PO Box 5001, Saint John, E2L 4Y9 NB
506-658-3180, Fax: 506-658-3191

Department of Natural Resources, PO Box 6000, Fredericton, E3B 5H1 NB
506-453-2510, Fax: 506-444-5839, dnrweb@gnb.ca

New Brunswick Power Group of Companies, 515 King St., PO Box 2000, Fredericton, E3B 4X1 NB
506-458-4444, Fax: 506-458-4000, questions@nbpower.com

Newfoundland & Labrador
Canada-Newfoundland Offshore Petroleum Board, TD Place, 140 Water St., 5th Fl., St. John's, NL A1C 6H6
709-778-1400, Fax: 709-778-1473, postmaster@cnlopb.nl.ca

Churchill Falls (Labrador) Corporation Limited, Hydro Place, 500 Columbus Dr., PO Box 12500, St. John's, A1B 4K7 NL
709-737-1859, Fax: 709-737-1816

Newfoundland & Labrador Hydro, Hydro Place, Columbus Dr., PO Box 12400, St. John's, A1B 4K7 NL
709-737-1400, Fax: 709-737-1800

Newfoundland & Labrador Board of Commissioners of Public Utilities, PO Box 21040, St. John's, A1A 5B2 NL
709-726-8600, Fax: 709-726-9604, 866-782-0006, ito@pub.nf.ca

Twin Falls Power Corporation, PO Box 12500, St. John's, A1B 3T5 NL

Northwest Territories

Department of Environment & Natural Resources, PO Box 1320, Yellowknife, X1A 2L9 NT

Northwest Territories Power Corporation, 4 Capital Dr., Hay River, X0E 1G2 NT
867-874-5200, Fax: 867-874-5229, info@ntpc.com

Nova Scotia

Canada-Nova Scotia Offshore Petroleum Board, TD Centre, 1791 Barrington St., 6th Fl., Halifax, NS B3J 3K9
902-422-5588, Fax: 902-422-1799, postmaster@cnsopb.ns.ca

Department of Energy, Bank of Montreal Bldg., #400, 5151 George St., PO Box 2664, Halifax, B3J 3P7 NS
902-424-4575, Fax: 902-424-0528, energyinfo@gov.ns.ca

Nova Scotia Utility & Review Board, 1601 Lower Water St., 3rd Fl., PO Box 1692 M,Halifax, B3J 3S3 NS
902-424-4448, Fax: 902-424-3919, uarb.board@gov.ns.ca

Ontario

Ministry of Energy and Infrastructure, Hearst Block, 900 Bay St., 4th Fl., Toronto, M7A 2E1 ON
416-327-6758, Fax: 416-327-6754, 888-668-4636

Ministry of Environment, 135 St. Clair Ave. West, Toronto, M4V 1P5 ON
416-325-4000, Fax: 416-325-3159, 800-565-4923

Hydro One Inc., North Tower, 483 Bay St., Toronto, M5G 2P5 ON
416-345-5000, 877-955-1155, webmaster@HydroOne.com

Independent Electricity System Operator, PO Box 4474 A,Toronto, M5W 4E5 ON
905-403-6900, Fax: 905-403-6921, 888-448-7777, customer.relations@ieso.ca

Ontario Energy Board, #2700, 2300 Yonge St., Toronto, ON M4P 1E4
416-481-1967, Fax: 416-440-7656, 888-632-6273

Ontario Power Authority, #1600, 120 Adelaide St. West, Toronto, ON M5H 1T1
416-967-7474, Fax: 416-967-1947, info@powerauthority.on.ca

Ontario Power Generation, 700 University Ave., Toronto, M5G 1X6 ON
416-592-2555, 877-592-2555

Prince Edward Island

Department of Environment, Energy & Forestry, Jones Bldg., 11 Kent St., 4th & 5th Fl., PO Box 2000, Charlottetown, C1A 7N8 PE
902-368-5000, Fax: 902-368-5830

PEI Energy Corporation, Jones Bldg., 11 Kent St., 4th Fl., PO Box 2000, Charlottetown, PE C1A 7N8
902-894-0288, Fax: 902-368-0290

Quebec

Agence de l'efficacité énergétique, #B-405, 5700, 4e av ouest, Québec, QC G1H 6R1
418-627-6379, Fax: 418-643-5828, 877-727-6655, aee@aee.gouv.qc.ca

Hydro-Québec, 75, boul René-Lévesque ouest, 20e étage, Montréal, H2Z 1A4 QC
514-289-2211

Régie de l'énergie, Tour de la Bourse, #255, 800, Place Victoria, CP 1, Montréal, QC H4Z 1A2
514-873-2452, Fax: 514-873-2070, 888-873-2452, secretariat@regie-energie.qc.ca

Société d'énergie de la Baie-James, 888, de Maisonneuve est, 2e étage, Montréal, H2L 5B2 QC
514-286-2020

Saskatchewan

Saskatchewan Energy & Resources, #300, 2103 - 11th Ave., Regina, S4P 3Z8 SK
306-787-2528, Fax: 306-787-0395, 866-727-5427

Saskatchewan Power Corporation (SaskPower), 2025 Victoria Ave., Regina, S4P 0S1 SK
306-566-2121, Fax: 306-566-2330, 800-667-4749

SaskEnergy Incorporated, 1777 Victoria Ave., Regina, S4P 4K5 SK
306-777-9225, Fax: 306-777-9200, 800-567-8899

Yukon Territory

Yukon Energy, Mines & Resources, PO Box 2703, Whitehorse, Y1A 2C6 YT
867-667-5466, Fax: 867-667-8601, 800-661-0408, emr@gov.yk.ca

ENGINEERING & CONSULTING

Canadian Environmental Assessment Agency, Place Bell Canada, 160 Elgin St., 22nd Fl., Ottawa, K1A 0H3 ON
613-957-0700, Fax: 613-957-0862, 866-582-1884, info@ceaa-acee.gc.ca

Defence Construction Canada, Constitution Square, 350 Albert St., 19th Fl., Ottawa, K1A 0K3 ON
613-998-9548, Fax: 613-998-1061, 800-514-3555, info@dcc-cdc.gc.ca

Natural Sciences & Engineering Research Council of Canada, Constitution Square, Tower II, 350 Albert St., Ottawa, K1A 1H5 ON
613-995-4273, Fax: 613-943-1624, marie-josee.duval@nserc-crsng.gc.ca

British Columbia

Transportation Planning & Policy Department, #5C, 940 Blanshard St., PO Box 9850 Prov Govt,Victoria, V8W 9T5 BC
250-387-5062, Fax: 250-387-6431

Manitoba

Manitoba Infrastructure & Transportation, Legislative Building, #203, 450 Broadway Ave., Winnipeg, R3C 0V8 MB
204-945-3723, Fax: 204-945-7610,

Northwest Territories

Highways, 4510 - 50 Ave., 2nd fl., PO Box 1320, Yellowknife, X1A 2L9 NT
867-920-8771, Fax: 867-873-0288

Saskatchewan

Saskatchewan Highways & Infrastructure, 1855 Victoria Ave., Regina, S4P 3T2 SK
306-787-4800

ENVIRONMENT

Environment Canada, 10 Wellington St., Gatineau, K1A 0H3 QC
819-997-2800, Fax: 819-994-1412, 800-668-6767, enviroinfo@ec.gc.ca

National Round Table on the Environment & Economy, #200, 344 Slater St., Ottawa, K1R 7Y3 ON
613-992-7189, Fax: 613-992-7385, admin@nrtee-trnee.ca

Alberta

Alberta Environment, South Tower, Petroleum Plaza, 9915 - 108 St., 10th Fl., Edmonton, T5K 2G8 AB
780-427-2700, Fax: 780-422-4086, env.infocent@gov.ab.ca

Alberta Sustainable Resource Development, Information Centre, 9920 - 108 St., Main Fl., Edmonton, T5K 2M4 AB
780-944-0313, Fax: 780-427-4407, 877-944-0313, srd.infocent@gov.ab.ca

British Columbia

Ministry of Environment, PO Box 9339 Prov Govt,Victoria, V8W 9M1 BC
250-387-1161, Fax: 250-387-5669, www.envmail@gov.bc.ca

Manitoba

Manitoba Conservation, 200 Saulteaux Cres., Winnipeg, R3J 3W3 MB
204-945-6784, 800-214-6497, mincon@leg.gov.mb.ca

Manitoba Water Stewardship, 200 Saulteaux Cres., PO Box 11, Winnipeg, R3J 3W3 MB
204-945-6398, 800-282-8069, wsd@gov.mb.ca

New Brunswick

Department of the Environment, Marysville Place, 20 McGloin St., PO Box 6000, Fredericton, E3B 5H1 NB
506-453-2690, Fax: 506-457-4991, env-info@gnb.ca

Newfoundland & Labrador

Department of Environment & Conservation, Confederation Bldg., West Block, 4th Fl., PO Box 8700, St. John's, A1B 4J6 NL
709-729-2664, Fax: 709-729-6639, 800-563-6181, info@gov.nl.ca

Northwest Territories

Department of Environment & Natural Resources, PO Box 1320, Yellowknife, X1A 2L9 NT

Nova Scotia

Department of Environment, 5151 Terminal Rd., 5th Fl., PO Box 442, Halifax, B3J 2T8 NS
902-424-3600, Fax: 902-424-0503, 877-936-8476

Nunavut

Department of Environment, PO Box 1000 1300,Iqaluit, X0A 0H0 NU
867-975-7700, Fax: 867-975-7742, 866-222-9063, environment@gov.nu.ca

Ontario

Ministry of Environment, 135 St. Clair Ave. West, Toronto, M4V 1P5 ON
416-325-4000, Fax: 416-325-3159, 800-565-4923

Environmental Commissioner of Ontario, #605, 1075 Bay St., Toronto, M5S 2B1 ON
416-325-3377, Fax: 416-325-3370, 800-701-6454, commissioner@eco.on.ca

Prince Edward Island

Department of Environment, Energy & Forestry, Jones Bldg., 11 Kent St., 4th & 5th Fl., PO Box 2000, Charlottetown, C1A 7N8 PE
902-368-5000, Fax: 902-368-5830

Quebec

Bureau d'audiences publiques sur l'environnement, Édifice Lomer-Gouin, #2.10, 575, rue Saint-Amable, 2e étage, Québec, QC G1R 6A6
418-643-7447, Fax: 418-643-9474, 800-463-4732, communication@bape.gouv.qc.ca

Ministère du Développement durable, de l'Environnement et des Parcs, Édifice Marie-Guyart, 675, boul René-Lévesque est, 29e étage, Québec, G1R 5V7 QC
418-521-3830, Fax: 418-646-5974, 800-561-1616, info@mddep.gouv.qc.ca

Saskatchewan

Saskatchewan Environment, 3211 Albert St., 2nd Fl., Regina, S4S 5W6 SK
306-953-3750, Fax: 306-787-9544, 800-567-4224, inquiry@serm.gov.sk.ca

ENVIRONMENT DEPARTMENTS/MINISTRIES

Environment Canada, 10 Wellington St., Gatineau, K1A 0H3 QC
819-997-2800, Fax: 819-994-1412, 800-668-6767, enviroinfo@ec.gc.ca

Alberta

Alberta Environment, South Tower, Petroleum Plaza, 9915 - 108 St., 10th Fl., Edmonton, T5K 2G8 AB
780-427-2700, Fax: 780-422-4086, env.infocent@gov.ab.ca

British Columbia

Ministry of Environment, PO Box 9339 Prov Govt,Victoria, V8W 9M1 BC
250-387-1161, Fax: 250-387-5669, www.envmail@gov.bc.ca

Manitoba

Manitoba Conservation, 200 Saulteaux Cres., Winnipeg, R3J 3W3 MB
204-945-6784, 800-214-6497, mincon@leg.gov.mb.ca

New Brunswick

Department of the Environment, Marysville Place, 20 McGloin St., PO Box 6000, Fredericton, E3B 5H1 NB
506-453-2690, Fax: 506-457-4991, env-info@gnb.ca

Newfoundland & Labrador

Department of Environment & Conservation, Confederation Bldg., West Block, 4th Fl., PO Box 8700, St. John's, A1B 4J6 NL
709-729-2664, Fax: 709-729-6639, 800-563-6181, info@gov.nl.ca

Northwest Territories

Department of Environment & Natural Resources, PO Box 1320, Yellowknife, X1A 2L9 NT

Nova Scotia

Department of Environment, 5151 Terminal Rd., 5th Fl., PO Box 442, Halifax, B3J 2T8 NS
902-424-3600, Fax: 902-424-0503, 877-936-8476

Nunavut

Department of Environment, PO Box 1000 1300,Iqaluit, X0A 0H0 NU
867-975-7700, Fax: 867-975-7742, 866-222-9063, environment@gov.nu.ca

Ontario

Ministry of Environment, 135 St. Clair Ave. West, Toronto, M4V 1P5 ON
416-325-4000, Fax: 416-325-3159, 800-565-4923

Prince Edward Island

Department of Environment, Energy & Forestry, Jones Bldg., 11 Kent St., 4th & 5th Fl., PO Box 2000, Charlottetown, C1A 7N8 PE
902-368-5000, Fax: 902-368-5830,

Quebec

Ministère du Développement durable, de l'Environnement et des Parcs, Édifice Marie-Guyart, 675, boul René-Lévesque est, 29e étage, Québec, G1R 5V7 QC
418-521-3830, Fax: 418-646-5974, 800-561-1616, info@mddep.gouv.qc.ca

Saskatchewan
Saskatchewan Environment, 3211 Albert St., 2nd Fl., Regina, S4S 5W6 SK
306-953-3750, Fax: 306-787-9544, 800-567-4224, inquiry@serm.gov.sk.ca

Yukon Territory
Yukon Environment, PO Box 2703, Whitehorse, Y1A 2C6 YT
867-667-5652, Fax: 867-393-7197, 800-661-0408, environmentyukon@gov.yk.ca

ENVIRONMENTAL ASSESSMENT

Canadian Environmental Assessment Agency, Place Bell Canada, 160 Elgin St., 22nd Fl., Ottawa, K1A 0H3 ON
613-957-0700, Fax: 613-957-0862, 866-582-1884, info@ceaa-acee.gc.ca

British Columbia
British Columbia Environmental Assessment Office, 836 Yates St., 1st Fl., PO Box 9426 Prov Govt,Victoria, V8W 9V1 BC
250-356-7441, Fax: 250-356-7440, eaoinfo@gov.bc.ca

New Brunswick
Environmental Management, Marysville Place, 20 McGloin St., PO Box 6000, Fredericton, E3B 5H1 NB
506-444-5119, Fax: 506-457-7333

EROSION CONTROL

Research Branch, Tower 5, 1341 Baseline Rd., Ottawa, K1A 0C5 ON
613-759-1000, Fax: 613-773-1866

Quebec
Commission de protection du territoire agricole du Québec, 200, ch Ste-Foy, 2e étage, Québec, QC G1R 4X6
418-643-3314, Fax: 418-643-2261, 800-667-5294, info@cptaq.gouv.qc.ca

Saskatchewan
Saskatchewan Agriculture, Walter Scott Bldg., 3085 Albert St., Regina, S4S 0B1 SK
306-787-5140, 866-457-2377, aginfo@gov.sk.ca

EXPORT DEVELOPMENT

Business Development Bank of Canada, #400, 5, Place Ville-Marie, Montréal, H3B 5E7 QC
514-283-5904, Fax: 514-283-2872, 877-232-2269
Export Development Canada, 151 O'Connor St., Ottawa, K1A 1K3 ON
613-598-2500, Fax: 613-598-3811, 800-267-8510
Global Operations & Chief Trade Commissioner, 125 Sussex Dr,, Ottawa, K1A 0G2 ON
613-944-2697, Fax: 613-996-1667
Industry Canada, 235 Queen St., Ottawa, K1A 0H5 ON
Fax: 613-954-6436, 800-328-6189, info@ic.gc.ca
Western Economic Diversification Canada, Canada Place, #1500, 9700 Jasper Ave. NW, Edmonton, T5J 4H7 AB
780-495-4164, Fax: 780-495-4557, 888-338-9378

New Brunswick
Business Development, Centennial Bldg., 670 King St., 5th Fl., PO Box 6000, Fredericton, E3B 5H1 NB
506-453-2111, Fax: 506-444-4182

Northwest Territories
Northwest Territories Business Development & Investment Corporation, #701, 5201 - 50 Ave., Yellowknife, NT X1A 3S9
867-920-6455, Fax: 867-765-0652, bdicinfo@gov.nt.ca

Ontario
Ministry of Economic Development & Trade, Hearst Block, 900 Bay St., 8th Fl., Toronto, M7A 2E1 ON
416-325-6666, Fax: 416-325-6688, 866-668-4249, info@edt.gov.on.ca

Saskatchewan
Saskatchewan Energy & Resources, #300, 2103 - 11th Ave., Regina, S4P 3Z8 SK
306-787-2528, Fax: 306-787-0395, 866-727-5427
Saskatchewan Trade & Export Partnership, #320, 1801 Hamilton St., PO Box 1787, Regina, SK S4P 3C6
306-787-9210, Fax: 306-787-6666, 877-313-7244, inquire@sasktrade.sk.ca

EXPROPRIATION

Canada Lands Company Ltd., #1200, 1 University Ave., Toronto, M5J 2P1 ON
416-952-6111, Fax: 416-952-6115, 888-252-5263
Justice Canada, East Memorial Bldg., 284 Wellington St., Ottawa, K1A 0H8 ON
613-957-4222, Fax: 613-954-0811, webadmin@justice.gc.ca
National Defence Canada, Major-General George R. Pearkes Bldg., 101 Colonel By Dr., Ottawa, K1A 0K2 ON
613-995-2534, Fax: 613-992-4739, 800-856-8488

Alberta
Land Compensation/Surface Rights Board, Phipps-McKinnon Bldg., 10020 - 101A Ave., 18th Fl., Edmonton, AB T5J 3G2
780-427-2444, Fax: 780-427-5798

Manitoba
Manitoba Land Value Appraisal Commission, 800 Portage Ave., Winnipeg, MB R3G 0N4
204-945-2941, Fax: 204-948-2235

New Brunswick
New Brunswick Expropriations Advisory Office, Phoenix Square Bldg., 371 Queen St., Fredericton, NB E3B 1B1
506-453-7771, Fax: 506-453-9600

Quebec
Ministère de la Justice, Édifice Louis-Philippe-Pigeon, 1200, rte de l'Église, Québec, G1V 4M1 QC
418-643-5140, 866-536-5140, informations@justice.gouv.qc.ca
Ministère des Transports, 700, boul René-Lévesque est, 27e étage, Québec, G1R 5H1 QC
418-643-6980, Fax: 418-643-2011, 888-355-0511, communications@mtq.gouv.qc.ca

Saskatchewan
Saskatchewan Government Services, Century Plaza, 1920 Rose St., Regina, S4P 0A9 SK
306-787-6911, Fax: 306-787-1061
Public & Private Rights Board, 23-3085 Albert St., Regina, SK S4S 0B1
306-787-4071, Fax: 306-787-0088

FAMILY BENEFITS

See Also: Income Security; Social Services
Social Development, L'esplanade Laurier, Level 2, 300 Laurier Ave. West, Ottawa, K1A 0J6 ON
613-990-5100, Fax: 613-990-5091,

Alberta
Alberta Children and Youth Services, Sterling Place, 9940 - 106 St., 12th Fl., Edmonton, T5K 2N2 AB
780-422-3004, Fax: 780-422-3071, 866-714-5437, cs.communications@gov.ab.ca

British Columbia
Ministry of Children & Family Development, PO Box 9770 Prov Govt,Victoria, V8W 9S5 BC
250-387-7027, 877-387-7027, MCF.CorrespondenceManagement@gov.bc.ca

Manitoba
Manitoba Family Services & Housing, #219, 114 Garry St., Winnipeg, R3C 4V6 MB
204-945-3242, Fax: 204-945-2156, minfam@leg.gov.mb.ca

New Brunswick
Family Income Security Appeal Board, PO Box 6000, Fredericton, NB E3B 5H1
506-525-4007, Fax: 506-525-4008
Department of Social Development, Sartain MacDonald Bldg., 551 King St., PO Box 6000, Fredericton, E3B 5H1 NB
506-453-2001, Fax: 506-453-7478

Newfoundland & Labrador
Department of Human Resources, Labour & Employment, Confederation Bldg., PO Box 8700, St. John's, A1B 4J6 NL
709-729-2478, Fax: 709-729-6996, hreweb@gov.nl.ca

Northwest Territories
Department of Education, Culture & Employment, PO Box 1320, Yellowknife, X1A 2L9 NT
867-669-2399, Fax: 867-873-0431, 866-606-5627

Prince Edward Island
Department of Social Services & Seniors, Jones Bldg., 11 Kent St., 2nd Fl., PO Box 2000, Charlottetown, C1A 7N8 PE
902-620-3777, Fax: 902-894-0242

Quebec
Conseil de la famille et de l'enfance, #800, 900, boul René-Lévesque est, Montréal, QC G1R 6B5
514-646-7678, Fax: 514-643-9832, 877-221-7024
Ministère de l'Emploi et de la Solidarité sociale, 425, rue St-Amable, 4e étage, Québec, G1R 4Z1 QC
418-643-4721, 888-643-4721
Ministère de la Famille et des Aînés, 425, rue Saint-Amable, 1er étage, Québec, G1R 4Z1 QC
877-216-6202

FEDERAL-PROVINCIAL AFFAIRS

Canadian Intergovernmental Conference Secretariat, 222 Queen St., 10th Fl., PO Box 488 A,Ottawa, K1N 8V5 ON
613-995-2341, Fax: 613-996-6091, info@scics.gc.ca
Office of Intergovernmental Affairs, c/o Privy Council Office, #1000, 85 Slater St., Ottawa, K1A 0A3 ON
613-957-5153, Fax: 613-957-5043, info@pco-bcp.gc.ca

Alberta
Alberta International & Intergovernmental Relations, Commerce Place, 10155 - 102 St., 12th Fl., Edmonton, T5J 4G8 AB
780-422-1510, Fax: 780-427-0699

British Columbia
Intergovernmental Relations Secretariat, 548 Michigan St., 1st Fl., PO Box 9433 Prov Govt,Victoria, V8W 9V3 BC
250-387-0783, Fax: 250-387-1920, igrs@gov.bc.ca

New Brunswick
Department of Intergovernmental Affairs, Centennial Bldg., #274, 670 King St., PO Box 6000, Fredericton, E3B 5H1 NB
506-444-5418, Fax: 506-453-2995, iga@gnb.ca

Newfoundland & Labrador
Intergovernmental Affairs Secretariat, Confederation Bldg., East Block, 7th Fl., PO Box 8700, St. John's, A1B 4J6 NL
709-729-3164, Fax: 709-729-5038, iga@gov.nl.ca

Northwest Territories
Department of Aboriginal Affairs & Intergovernmental Relations, 4910 - 52nd St., PO Box 1320, Yellowknife, X1A 2L9 NT
867-873-7143, Fax: 867-873-0233, 877-838-8194, nancy_gardiner @gov.nt.ca

Nova Scotia
Department of Intergovernmental Affairs, Joseph Howe Bldg., 1690 Hollis St., 7th Fl., PO Box 1617, Halifax, B3J 2Y3 NS
902-424-5153, Fax: 902-424-0728, iga@gov.ns.ca

Nunavut
Department of Executive & Intergovernmental Affairs, 1084 Aeroplex bldg., PO Box 1000 200,Iqaluit, X0A 0H0 NU
867-975-6000, Fax: 867-975-6090

Ontario
Ministry of Intergovernmental Affairs, 77 Wellesley St. West, Toronto, M7A 1N3 ON
416-325-4800, Fax: 416-325-4787

Quebec
Secrétariat aux Affaires intergouvernementales canadiennes, 875, Grande Allée est, 3e étage, Québec, G1R 4Y8 QC
418-643-4011, Fax: 418-528-0052

Saskatchewan
Canadian Intergovernmental Relations, #800, 1919 Saskatchewan Dr., Regina, S4P 4H2 SK
Fax: 306-787-7317

FILM PRODUCTION & COLLECTIONS

Canadian Broadcasting Corporation, 181 Queen St., PO Box 3220 C,Ottawa, K1Y 1E4 ON
613-288-6033, liaison@radio-canada.ca
National Film Board of Canada, 3155, rue Côte de Liesse, CP 1600 Centre-ville,Saint-Laurent, H4N 2N4 QC
514-283-9000, Fax: 514-283-7564, 800-267-7710
Telefilm Canada, #500, 360, rue Saint-Jacques, Montréal, H2Y 1P5 QC
514-283-6363, Fax: 514-283-2365, 800-567-0890, info@telefilm.gc.ca

Alberta
Alberta Film Commission, 10155 - 102 St., 5th Fl., Edmonton, AB T5J 4L6
780-422-8584, Fax: 780-422-8582, 888-813-1738

British Columbia
British Columbia Film Commission, #201, 865 Hornby St., Vancouver, BC V6Z 2G3
604-660-2732, Fax: 604-660-4790, info@bcfilmcommission.com

Manitoba
Manitoba Film & Sound Recording Development Corporation, #410, 93 Lombard Ave., Winnipeg, MB R3B 3B1
204-947-2040, Fax: 204-956-5261, carole@mbfilmsound.mb.ca

New Brunswick
New Brunswick Film, Assumption Pl., 770 Main St., 16th Fl., PO Box 5001, Moncton, NB E1C 8R3
506-869-6868, Fax: 506-869-6840, nbfilm@gnb.ca

Newfoundland & Labrador
Newfoundland & Labrador Film Development Corporation, 12 King's Bridge Rd., St. John's, NL A1C 3K3

709-738-3456, Fax: 709-739-1680, 877-738-3456, info@nlfdc.ca

Nova Scotia
Film Nova Scotia, Collins Bank Bldg., 1869 Upper Water St., 3rd Fl., Halifax, NS B3J 1S9
902-424-7177, Fax: 902-424-0617, 888-360-2111, connorkm@gov.ns.ca

Ontario
Ontario Media Development Corporation, South Tower, #501, 175 Bloor St. East, Toronto, ON M4W 3R8
416-314-6858, Fax: 416-314-6876, mail@omdc.on.ca

Saskatchewan
Sask Film, 1831 College Ave., Regina, SK S4P 3V7
306-798-3456, Fax: 306-798-7768, 800-561-9933

FINANCE

See Also: Banking & Financial Institutions
Finance Canada, L'esplanade Laurier, 140 O'Connor St., Ottawa, K1A 0G5 ON
613-992-1573, Fax: 613-943-0938, finpub@fin.gc.ca

Alberta
Alberta Finance & Enterprise, Terrace Building, #426, 9515 - 107 St., Edmonton, T5K 2C3 AB
780-427-3035, Fax: 780-427-1147, tra.revenue@gov.ab.ca
Alberta Treasury Board, Legislature Bldg., #204, 10800 - 97 Ave., Edmonton, T5K 2B6 AB
780-415-4855, Fax: 780-422-4853

British Columbia
Ministry of Finance, PO Box 9048 Prov Govt,Victoria, V8W 9E2 BC
250-387-3751, Fax: 250-387-5594, Fin.Minister@gov.bc.ca

Manitoba
Manitoba Finance, #109, Legislative Bldg., Winnipeg, R3C 0V8 MB
204-945-3754, Fax: 204-945-8316, minfin@leg.gov.mb.ca

New Brunswick
Department of Finance, 670 King St., PO Box 6000, Fredericton, E3B 5H1 NB
506-453-2451, Fax: 506-444-4724

Newfoundland & Labrador
Department of Finance, Confederation Bldg., PO Box 8700, St. John's, A1B 4J6 NL
709-729-6310, finance@gov.nl.ca

Northwest Territories
Department of Finance, YK Center, 3rd Fl., PO Box 1320, Yellowknife, X1A 2L9 NT
867-669-2311, Fax: 867-873-0385

Nova Scotia
Department of Finance, Provincial Bldg., 1723 Hollis St., 7th Fl., PO Box 187, Halifax, B3J 2N3 NS
902-424-5554, Fax: 902-424-0635, FinanceWeb@gov.ns.ca

Nunavut
Department of Finance, Bldg. 1079, 1st Fl., PO Box 1000 Stn 330,Iqaluit, X0A 0H0 NU
867-975-5800, Fax: 867-975-5805

Ontario
Ministry of Finance, Frost Bldg. South, 7 Queen's Park Cres., 7th Fl., Toronto, M7A 1Y7 ON
416-325-0333, Fax: 905-433-6777, 800-263-7965, financecommunications.fin@ontario.ca
Ministry of Revenue, Frost Bldg. South, 7 Queen's Park Cres., 6th Fl., Toronto, M7A 1Y7 ON
Fax: 866-888-3850, 866-668-8297

Prince Edward Island
Department of the Provincial Treasury, Shaw Bldg., 95 Rochford St., 2nd Fl. South, PO Box 2000, Charlottetown, C1A 7N8 PE
902-368-4050, Fax: 902-368-6575

Quebec
Ministère des Finances, Édifice Gérard-D.-Lévesque, 12, rue Saint-Louis, Québec, G1R 5L3 QC
418-528-9323, Fax: 418-646-1631, info@finances.gouv.qc.ca

Saskatchewan
Saskatchewan Finance, 2350 Albert St., Regina, S4P 4A6 SK
306-787-6768, Fax: 306-787-0241

Yukon Territory
Yukon Finance, PO Box 2703, Whitehorse, Y1A 2C6 YT
867-667-5343, Fax: 867-393-6217

FINANCING & LOANS

See Also: Investment
Business Development Bank of Canada, #400, 5, Place Ville-Marie, Montréal, H3B 5E7 QC
514-283-5904, Fax: 514-283-2872, 877-232-2269
Canada Mortgage & Housing Corporation, 700 Montreal Rd., Ottawa, K1A 0P7 ON
613-748-2000, Fax: 613-748-2098, 800-668-2642, chic@cmhc-schl.gc.ca
Farm Credit Canada, 1800 Hamilton St., PO Box 4320, Regina, S4P 4L3 SK
306-780-8100, Fax: 306-780-8919, 888-332-3301, csc@fcc-fac.ca

Alberta
Alberta Capital Finance Authority, Canadian Western Bank Place, #2450, 10303 Jasper Ave., Edmonton, AB T5J 3N6
780-427-9711, Fax: 780-422-2175, webacfa@gov.ab.ca
ATB Financial, 9888 Jasper Ave., Edmonton, AB T5J 1P1
780-408-7000, 800-332-8383

British Columbia
International Financial Centre British Columbia, Park Place, #1170, 666 Burrard St., Vancouver, BC V6C 2X8
604-683-6626, Fax: 604-683-6646, info@ifcvancouver.com
Provincial Treasury, 620 Superior St., PO Box 9414 Prov Govt,Victoria, V8V 9V1 BC
250-387-4541, Fax: 250-356-3041, Jim.Hopkings@gov.bc.ca

Manitoba
Manitoba Agricultural Services Corporation, #100, 1525 First St. South, Brandon, MB R7A 7A1
204-726-6850, Fax: 204-726-6849, mailbox@masc.mb.ca

New Brunswick
New Brunswick Electric Finance Corporation, #376, 670 King St., PO Box 6000, Fredericton, NB E3B 5H1
506-453-3952, Fax: 506-453-2053

Newfoundland & Labrador
Department of Finance, Confederation Bldg., PO Box 8700, St. John's, A1B 4J6 NL
709-729-6310, finance@gov.nl.ca

Northwest Territories
Department of Industry, Tourism & Investment, PO Box 1320, Yellowknife, X1A 2L9 NT
Fax: 867-873-0306, info@iti.ca

Nova Scotia
Nova Scotia Farm Loan Board, PO Box 550, Truro, NS B2N 5E3
902-893-6506, Fax: 902-895-7693, flb@gov.ns.ca

Nunavut
Nunavut Business Credit Corporation, PO Box 224, Cape Dorset, NU X0A 0C0
867-897-3647, 800-758-0038

Ontario
Ontario Electricity Financial Corporation, #1400, 1 Dundas St. West, Toronto, ON M7A 1Y7
416-325-8000, Fax: 416-325-8005,
Ontario Financing Authority, #1400, 1 Dundas St. West, Toronto, ON M7A 1Y7
416-325-8000, Fax: 416-325-8005

Prince Edward Island
Prince Edward Island Lending Agency, Confederation Court Office Tower, #201, 134 Kent St., PO Box 1420, Charlottetown, PE C1A 7N1
902-368-6200, Fax: 902-368-6201

Quebec
Caisse de dépôt et placement du Québec, 1000, place Jean-Paul-Riopelle, Montréal, QC H2Z 2B3
514-842-3261, Fax: 514-842-4833, 866-330-3936, info@lacaisse.com
La financière agricole de Québec, 1400, boul de la Rive-Sud, Saint-Romuald, QC G6W 8K7
418-838-5602, Fax: 418-833-3871, 800-749-3646, dir.comm@fadq.qc.ca
Société générale de financement du Québec, #1500, 600, rue de La Gauchetière ouest, Montréal, QC H3B 4L8
514-876-9290, Fax: 514-395-8055, info@sgfqc.com
Société générale de financement du Québec, #1500, 600, rue de La Gauchetière ouest, Montréal, QC H3B 4L8
514-876-9290, Fax: 514-395-8055, info@sgfqc.com

Saskatchewan
Saskatchewan Trade & Export Partnership, #320, 1801 Hamilton St., PO Box 1787, Regina, SK S4P 3C6
306-787-9210, Fax: 306-787-6666, 877-313-7244, inquire@sasktrade.sk.ca

Yukon Territory
Yukon Economic Development, PO Box 2703, Whitehorse, Y1A 2C6 YT
867-393-7191, Fax: 867-395-7199, 800-661-0408

FIRE PREVENTION

British Columbia
Emergency Management BC, 525 Fort St., 2nd Fl., PO Box 9223 Prov Govt,Victoria, V8W 9J1 BC
250-953-4002, Fax: 250-953-4081, BC.CorSer@gov.bc.ca (Coroner); OFC@gov.bc.ca (Fire Commissioner)

Manitoba
Office of the Fire Commissioner, #508, 401 York Ave., Winnipeg, MB R3C 0P8
204-945-3322, Fax: 204-948-2089, 800-282-8069, firecomm@gov.mb.ca

Newfoundland & Labrador
Office of the Fire Commissioner, 2 Wellon Dr., Deer Lake, NL A8A 2G5
709-635-4153, Fax: 709-635-4163

Northwest Territories
Department of Municipal & Community Affairs, PO Box 1320, Yellowknife, X1A 2L9 NT
867-873-7118, Fax: 867-873-0309

Nunavut
Nunavut Emergency Management, PO Box 1000 700,Iqaluit, X0A 0H0 NU
867-975-5403, Fax: 867-979-4221, 800-693-1666

Ontario
Fire Safety Commission, Place Nouveau Bldg., 5775 Yonge St., 7th Fl., Toronto, ON M2M 4J1
416-325-3100, Fax: 416-314-1217

Quebec
Commissariat des incendies, 455, rue Dupont, Québec, QC G1K 6N2
418-529-5706, Fax: 418-529-9922

Saskatchewan
Lands & Forests Division, 3211 Albert St., 5th fl., Regina, S4S 5W6 SK
306-787-5407, Fax: 306-787-2947

Yukon Territory
Fire Marshal's Office, PO Box 2703, Whitehorse, Y1A 2C6 YT
867-667-5811, Fax: 867-393-6295, inquiry@gov.yk.ca

FIREARMS

Canada Firearms Centre, Ottawa, ON K1A 1M6
Fax: 613-825-0297, 800-731-4000, cfp-pcaf@rcmp-grc.gc.ca

British Columbia
Ministry of the Attorney General, PO Box 9044 Prov Govt,Victoria, V8W 9E2 BC
250-387-1866, Fax: 250-387-6411

FISHERIES

Fisheries & Oceans Canada, 200 Kent St., Ottawa, K1A 0E6 ON
613-993-0999, Fax: 613-996-1866, info@dfo-mpo.gc.ca
Fisheries Resource Conservation Council, PO Box 2001 D, Ottawa, ON K1P 5W3
613-998-0433, Fax: 613-998-1146, info@frcc-ccrh.ca
Freshwater Fish Marketing Corporation, 1199 Plessis Rd., Winnipeg, R2C 3L4 MB
204-983-6601, Fax: 204-983-6497, sandi.cain@freshwaterfish.com
Gulf Fisheries Centre, 343, av Université, 5th Fl., Moncton, E1C 9B6 NB
506-851-3886, Fax: 506-851-7732

British Columbia
Ministry of Agriculture & Lands, PO Box 9120 Prov Govt,Victoria, V8W 9E2 BC
250-387-5121, Fax: 250-387-1522
Oceans & Marine Fisheries Division, 2975 Jutland Rd., 3rd Fl., PO Box 9309, Victoria, V8W 9N1 BC
250-387-0389, Fax: 250-953-3401, fishstats@gov.bc.ca; fishinfo@gov.bc.ca

New Brunswick
Department of Agriculture & Aquaculture, PO Box 6000, Fredericton, E3B 5H1 NB
506-453-2666, Fax: 506-453-7170, DAA-MAA@gnb.ca
Department of Business New Brunswick, Centennial Bldg., 670 King St., PO Box 6000, Fredericton, E3B 5H1 NB
506-444-5228, Fax: 506-453-5428

Newfoundland & Labrador
Department of Fisheries & Aquaculture, Petten Bldg., 30 Strawberry Marsh Rd., PO Box 8700, St. John's, A1B 4J6 NL
709-729-3723, Fax: 709-729-6082, fishaqwebmaster@gov.nl.ca

Northwest Territories

Department of Environment & Natural Resources, PO Box 1320, Yellowknife, X1A 2L9 NT

Nova Scotia

Fisheries & Aquaculture Loan Board, PO Box 2223, Halifax, NS B3J 3C4
902-424-4560, Fax: 902-424-1766

Department of Fisheries & Aquaculture, 1741 Brunswick St., 3rd Fl., PO Box 2223, Halifax, B3J 3C4 NS
902-424-4560, Fax: 902-424-4671

Ontario

Fish & Wildlife Heritage Commission, Robinson Pl., 300 Water St., PO Box 7000, Peterborough, ON K9J 8M5
Fax: 705-755-5093

Natural Resources Management Division, Whitney Block, #6540, 99 Wellesley St. West, Toronto, M7A 1W3 ON
416-314-2000, Fax: 416-314-1994,

Prince Edward Island

Department of Agriculture, Jones Bldg., 11 Kent St., PO Box 2000, Charlottetown, C1A 7N8 PE
902-368-4880, Fax: 902-368-4857

FISHERIES & WILDLIFE

Beverly & Qamanirjuaq Caribou Management Board, Secretariat, PO Box 629, Stonewall, MB R0C 2Z0
204-467-2438, rossthompson@mymts.net

Fisheries & Oceans Canada, 200 Kent St., Ottawa, K1A 0E6 ON
613-993-0999, Fax: 613-996-1866, info@dfo-mpo.gc.ca

Natural Resources Canada, 580 Booth St., Ottawa, K1A 0E4 ON
613-995-0947, Fax: 613-992-7211

Porcupine Caribou Management Board, PO Box 31723, Whitehorse, YT Y1A 6L3
867-633-4780, Fax: 867-393-3904, pcmb@taiga.net

Alberta

Alberta Environment, South Tower, Petroleum Plaza, 9915 - 108 St., 10th Fl., Edmonton, T5K 2G8 AB
780-427-2700, Fax: 780-422-4086, env.infocent@gov.ab.ca

British Columbia

Ministry of Environment, PO Box 9339 Prov Govt,Victoria, V8W 9M1 BC
250-387-1161, Fax: 250-387-5669, www.envmail@gov.bc.ca

Strategic Industry Development, 808 Douglas St., 5th Fl., PO Box 9120 Prov Govt,Victoria, V8W 9B4 BC
250-356-1821, Fax: 250-356-7279

Manitoba

Endangered Species Advisory Committee, 200 Saulteaux Cres., PO Box 24, Winnipeg, MB R3J 3W3
204-945-7465, Fax: 204-945-3077

Manitoba Habitat Heritage Corporation, #200, 1555 St. James St., Winnipeg, MB R3H 1B5
204-784-4350, Fax: 204-784-7359, mhhc@mhhc.mb.ca

New Brunswick

Department of Agriculture & Aquaculture, PO Box 6000, Fredericton, E3B 5H1 NB
506-453-2666, Fax: 506-453-7170, DAA-MAA@gnb.ca

Newfoundland & Labrador

Department of Fisheries & Aquaculture, Petten Bldg., 30 Strawberry Marsh Rd., PO Box 8700, St. John's, A1B 4J6 NL
709-729-3723, Fax: 709-729-6082, fishaqwebmaster@gov.nl.ca

Forest Resources, Fortis Bldg., PO Box 2006, Corner Brook, A2H 6J8 NL
709-637-2284, Fax: 709-634-4378

Northwest Territories

Department of Environment & Natural Resources, PO Box 1320, Yellowknife, X1A 2L9 NT

Nova Scotia

Department of Natural Resources, Founder's Square, 1701 Hollis St., 3rd Fl., PO Box 698, Halifax, B3J 2T9 NS
902-424-5935, Fax: 902-424-0594, 800-565-2224

Ontario

Ministry of Natural Resources, Whitney Block, #6630, 99 Wellesley St. West, 6th Fl., Toronto, M7A 1W3 ON
800-667-1940

Prince Edward Island

Department of Environment, Energy & Forestry, Jones Bldg., 11 Kent St., 4th & 5th Fl., PO Box 2000, Charlottetown, C1A 7N8 PE
902-368-5000, Fax: 902-368-5830

Department of Tourism, PO Box 2000, Charlottetown, C1A 7N8 PE
800-463-4734

Quebec

Ministère de l'Agriculture, des Pêcheries et de l'Alimentation, 200, ch Sainte-Foy, Québec, G1R 4X6 QC
418-380-2110, 888-222-6272

Yukon Territory

Yukon Environment, PO Box 2703, Whitehorse, Y1A 2C6 YT
867-667-5652, Fax: 867-393-7197, 800-661-0408, environmentyukon@gov.yk.ca

Yukon Fish & Wildlife Management Board, 106 Main St., Whitehorse, YT Y1A 5P7
867-667-3754, Fax: 867-393-6947, yfwmbadmin@yknet.yk.ca

FOREST RESOURCES

Alberta

Alberta Prion Research Institute, Scotia Place, Tower 2, #2001, 10060 Jasper Ave., Edmonton, AB T5J 3R8
780-638-3790, Fax: 780-643-1432

British Columbia

Ministry of Forests & Range, PO Box 9529 Prov Govt,Victoria, V8W 9C3 BC
250-387-4809, Fax: 250-953-3687

New Brunswick

Forest Protection Limited, 2502 Hwy. 102, Lincoln, NB E3B 7E6
506-446-6930, Fax: 506-446-6934, info@forestprotectionlimited.com

New Brunswick Forest Products Commission, PO Box 6000, Fredericton, NB E3B 5H1
506-453-2196, Fax: 506-457-4966

Newfoundland & Labrador

Forest Resources, Fortis Bldg., PO Box 2006, Corner Brook, A2H 6J8 NL
709-637-2284, Fax: 709-634-4378

Nova Scotia

NS Primary Forest Products Marketing Board, #804, 45 Alderney Dr., Dartmouth, NS B2Y 2N6
902-424-7598, Fax: 902-424-6965

Nunavut

Department of Environment, PO Box 1000 1300,Iqaluit, X0A 0H0 NU
867-975-7700, Fax: 867-975-7742, 866-222-9063, environment@gov.nu.ca

Ontario

Algonquin Forestry Authority - Huntsville, 222 Main St. West, Huntsville, ON P1H 1Y1
705-789-9647, Fax: 705-789-3353

Algonquin Forestry Authority - Pembroke, Victoria Centre, 84 Isabella St., 2nd Fl., Pembroke, ON K8A 5S5
613-735-0173, Fax: 613-735-4192

Forests Division, Roberta Bondar Place, #400, 70 Foster Dr., Sault Ste Marie, P6A 6V5 ON
Fax: 705-945-5977, 800-667-1940

Quebec

Forêt Québec, 880, ch Ste-Foy, 10e étage, Québec, G1S 4X4 QC
418-627-8652, Fax: 418-528-1278, foretquebec@mrnf.gouv.qc.ca

Saskatchewan

Lands & Forests Division, 3211 Albert St., 5th fl., Regina, S4S 5W6 SK
306-787-5407, Fax: 306-787-2947

Yukon Territory

Yukon Energy, Mines & Resources, PO Box 2703, Whitehorse, Y1A 2C6 YT
867-667-5466, Fax: 867-667-8601, 800-661-0408, emr@gov.yk.ca

Yukon Environment, PO Box 2703, Whitehorse, Y1A 2C6 YT
867-667-5652, Fax: 867-393-7197, 800-661-0408, environmentyukon@gov.yk.ca

FORESTRY & PAPER

Natural Resources Canada, 580 Booth St., Ottawa, K1A 0E4 ON
613-995-0947, Fax: 613-992-7211

Alberta

Alberta Prion Research Institute, Scotia Place, Tower 2, #2001, 10060 Jasper Ave., Edmonton, AB T5J 3R8
780-638-3790, Fax: 780-643-1432

British Columbia

Forest Practices Board, 1675 Douglas St., 3rd Fl., PO Box 9905 Prov Govt, Victoria, BC V8W 9R1
250-387-7964, Fax: 250-387-7009, 800-994-5899, fpboard@gov.bc.ca

Ministry of Forests & Range, PO Box 9529 Prov Govt,Victoria, V8W 9C3 BC
250-387-4809, Fax: 250-953-3687

Timber Export Advisory Committee, 1520 Blanshard St., 2nd Fl., PO Box 9514 Prov Govt, Victoria, BC V8W 9C2
250-387-8916, Fax: 250-387-5050

New Brunswick

Forest Protection Limited, 2502 Hwy. 102, Lincoln, NB E3B 7E6
506-446-6930, Fax: 506-446-6934, info@forestprotectionlimited.com

New Brunswick Forest Products Commission, PO Box 6000, Fredericton, NB E3B 5H1
506-453-2196, Fax: 506-457-4966

Newfoundland & Labrador

Forest Resources, Fortis Bldg., PO Box 2006, Corner Brook, A2H 6J8 NL
709-637-2284, Fax: 709-634-4378

Department of Forest Resources, Natural Resources Bldg., 50 Elizabeth Ave., 7th Fl., PO Box 8700, St. John's, A1B 4J6 NL
709-729-2920, Fax: 709-729-0059

Nova Scotia

Department of Natural Resources, Founder's Square, 1701 Hollis St., 3rd Fl., PO Box 698, Halifax, B3J 2T9 NS
902-424-5935, Fax: 902-424-0594, 800-565-2224

Ontario

Algonquin Forestry Authority - Huntsville, 222 Main St. West, Huntsville, ON P1H 1Y1
705-789-9647, Fax: 705-789-3353

Algonquin Forestry Authority - Pembroke, Victoria Centre, 84 Isabella St., 2nd Fl., Pembroke, ON K8A 5S5
613-735-0173, Fax: 613-735-4192

Ministry of Natural Resources, Whitney Block, #6630, 99 Wellesley St. West, 6th Fl., Toronto, M7A 1W3 ON
800-667-1940

Quebec

Ministère du Développement durable, de l'Environnement et des Parcs, Édifice Marie-Guyart, 675, boul René-Lévesque est, 29e étage, Québec, G1R 5V7 QC
418-521-3830, Fax: 418-646-5974, 800-561-1616, info@mddep.gouv.qc.ca

Saskatchewan

Saskatchewan Environment, 3211 Albert St., 2nd Fl., Regina, S4S 5W6 SK
306-953-3750, Fax: 306-787-9544, 800-567-4224, inquiry@serm.gov.sk.ca

Yukon Territory

Yukon Environment, PO Box 2703, Whitehorse, Y1A 2C6 YT
867-667-5652, Fax: 867-393-7197, 800-661-0408, environmentyukon@gov.yk.ca

GEOLOGICAL SERVICES

Geological Survey of Canada, 601 Booth St., Ottawa, K1A 0E8 ON
613-996-3919, Fax: 613-943-8742, esic@nrcan.gc.ca

Alberta

Energy Resources Conservation Board, #1000, 250 - 5 Ave. SW, Calgary, AB T2P 0R4
403-297-8311, Fax: 403-297-7336, inquiries@ercb.ca

British Columbia

Ministry of Energy, Mines & Petroleum Resources, PO Box 9318 Prov Govt,Victoria, V8W 9N3 BC
250-952-0241

Manitoba

Manitoba Geological Survey, #360, 1394 Ellice Ave., Winnipeg, R3G 3P2 MB
Fax: 204-945-1406, 800-223-5215, minesinfo@gov.mb.ca

Nova Scotia

Nova Scotia Geomatics Centre, 160 Willow St., Amherst, B4H 3W3 NS
902-667-7231, Fax: 902-667-6008, 800-798-0706, info@nsgc.gov.ns.ca

GOVERNMENT

Auditor General of Canada, 240 Sparks St., Ottawa, K1A 0G6 ON
613-995-3708, Fax: 613-957-0474, 888-761-5953, communications@oag-bvg.gc.ca; infomedia@oag-bvg.gc.ca

Bank of Canada, 234 Wellington St., Ottawa, K1A 0G9 ON
613-782-8111, Fax: 613-782-7713, 800-303-1282, info@bankofcanada.ca; communications@bankofcanada.ca (Media)

British Columbia Treaty Commission, #203, 1155 West Pender St., Vancouver, BC V6E 2P4

604-482-9200, Fax: 604-482-9222, 800-665-8330, info@bctreaty.net
Business Development Bank of Canada, #400, 5, Place Ville-Marie, Montréal, H3B 5E7 QC
514-283-5904, Fax: 514-283-2872, 877-232-2269
Canada Economic Development for Québec Regions, Édifice Dominion Square, #900, 1255, rue Peel, Montréal, H3B 2T9 QC
514-283-6412, Fax: 514-283-3302, 866-385-6412
Canada Lands Company Ltd., #1200, 1 University Ave., Toronto, M5J 2P1 ON
416-952-6111, Fax: 416-952-6115, 888-252-5263
Canada Revenue Agency, 875 Heron Rd., Ottawa, K1A 0L5 ON
613-952-0384, 800-267-6999
Canadian Intergovernmental Conference Secretariat, 222 Queen St., 10th Fl., PO Box 488 A,Ottawa, K1N 8V5 ON
613-995-2341, Fax: 613-996-6091, info@scics.gc.ca
Canadian Nuclear Safety Commission, 280 Slater St., PO Box 1046 B,Ottawa, K1P 5S9 ON
613-995-5894, Fax: 613-995-5086, 800-668-5284, info@cnsc-ccsn.gc.ca
Defence Construction Canada, Constitution Square, 350 Albert St., 19th Fl., Ottawa, K1A 0K3 ON
613-998-9548, Fax: 613-998-1061, 800-514-3555, info@dcc-cdc.gc.ca
Elections Canada, The Jackson Bldg., 257 Slater St., Ottawa, K1A 0M6 ON
613-993-2975, Fax: 613-954-8584, 800-463-6868
Finance Canada, L'esplanade Laurier, 140 O'Connor St., Ottawa, K1A 0G5 ON
613-992-1573, Fax: 613-943-0938, finpub@fin.gc.ca
First Nations Tax Commission, #200, 160 Grorge St., Ottawa, ON K1N 9M2
613-789-5000, Fax: 613-789-5008, mail@fntc.ca
Foreign Affairs & International Trade Canada, 125 Sussex Dr., Ottawa, K1A 0G2 ON
613-944-4000, Fax: 613-996-9709, 800-267-8376, enqserv@international.gc.ca
Fortieth Parliament - Canada, House of Commons, Parliament Buildings, Ottawa, K1A 0A9 ON
Government of Canada, c/o Canada Enquiry Centre, Service Canada, Ottawa, K1A 0J9 ON
613-941-1827, 800-622-6232, sitecanadasite@canada.gc.ca
Governor General & Commander-in-Chief of Canada, Rideau Hall, 1 Sussex Dr., Ottawa, K1A 0A1 ON
613-993-8200, Fax: 613-998-8760, 800-465-6890, info@gg.ca
House of Commons, Canada, House of Commons, Parliament Buildings, Ottawa, K1A 0A6 ON
613-992-4793, 866-599-4999, info@parl.gc.ca
Indian & Northern Affairs Canada, 10 Wellington St., North Tower, Gatineau, K1A 0H4 QC
819-997-0380, Fax: 819-953-3017, 866-817-3977, infopubs@ainc-inac.gc.ca
Industry Canada, 235 Queen St., Ottawa, K1A 0H5 ON
Fax: 613-954-6436, 800-328-6189, info@ic.gc.ca
Office of Intergovernmental Affairs, c/o Privy Council Office, #1000, 85 Slater St., Ottawa, K1A 0A3 ON
613-957-5153, Fax: 613-957-5043, info@pco-bcp.gc.ca
International Development Research Centre, 150 Kent St., PO Box 8500, Ottawa, K1P 0B2 ON
613-236-6163, Fax: 613-238-7230, info@idrc.ca
Justice Canada, East Memorial Bldg., 284 Wellington St., Ottawa, K1A 0H8 ON
613-957-4222, Fax: 613-954-0811, webadmin@justice.gc.ca
National Defence Canada, Major-General George R. Pearkes Bldg., 101 Colonel By Dr., Ottawa, K1A 0K2 ON
613-995-2534, Fax: 613-992-4739, 800-856-8488
North American Free Trade Agreement (NAFTA) Secretariat, Canadian Section, #705, 90 Sparks St., Ottawa, K1P 5B4 ON
613-992-9388, Fax: 613-992-9392, webmaster@nafta-alena.gc.ca
Nunavut Impact Review Board, PO Box 1360, Cambridge Bay, NU X0B 0C0
867-983-4600, Fax: 867-983-2594, 866-233-3033, info@nirb.ca
Nunavut Planning Commission, PO Box 2101, Cambridge Bay, NU X0B 0C0
867-983-4625, Fax: 867-983-4626, staptuna@nunavut.ca
Office of the Leader, Bloc Québécois, 111 Wellington St., Ottawa, K1A 0A6 ON
613-992-6779, Fax: 613-954-2121
Office of the Leader, New Democratic Party (NDP), 111 Wellington St., Ottawa, K1A 0A6 ON
613-995-7224, Fax: 613-995-4565
Office of the Prime Minister (Conservative Party of Canada), Langevin Block, 80 Wellington St., Ottawa, K1A 0A2 ON
613-992-4211, Fax: 613-941-6900, pm@pm.gc.ca
Office of the Commissioner of Official Languages, 344 Slater St., 3rd fl., Ottawa, K1A 0T8 ON
613-996-6368, Fax: 613-993-5082, 877-996-6368
Privy Council Office, #1000, 85 Sparks St., Ottawa, K1A 0A3 ON
613-957-5153, Fax: 613-997-5043, info@pco-bcp.gc.ca
Public Service Commission, West Tower, 300 Laurier Ave. West, Ottawa, K1A 0M7 ON
613-992-9562, Fax: 613-992-9352, infocom@psc-cfp.gc.ca
Public Service Staffing Tribunal, 240 Sparks St., 6th Fl., Ottawa, K1A 0A5 ON
613-949-6516, Fax: 613-949-6551, 866-637-4491, info@psst-tdfp.gc.ca
Public Works & Government Services Canada, Place du Portage, Phase III, 11, rue Laurier, Ottawa, K1A 0S5 ON
819-997-6363, Fax: 819-956-9062, 800-622-6232, questions@tpsgc-pwgsc.gc.ca
Royal Canadian Mint, 320 Sussex Dr., Ottawa, K1A 0G8 ON
613-993-3500, Fax: 613-993-4092, 800-267-1871
Senate of Canada, Ottawa, K1A 0A4 ON
613-995-1900
Statistics Canada, R.H. Coats Bldg., Tunney's Pasture, 100 Tunney's Pasture Driveway, Ottawa, K1A 0T6 ON
613-951-8116, Fax: 877-287-4369, 800-263-1136, infostats@statcan.ca
The Canadian Ministry, Information Service, Parliament of Canada, Ottawa, K1A 0A9 ON
613-992-4793, 866-599-4999, info@parl.gc.ca
Thirty-ninth Parliament - Ontario, Clerk's Office, Legislative Bldg., Queen's Park, Toronto, M7A 1A2 ON
416-325-7500, Fax: 416-325-7489
Treasury Board of Canada, 300 Laurier Ave. West, 10th Fl., Ottawa, K1A 0R5 ON
613-957-2400, Fax: 613-941-4000, 877-636-0656, info@tbs-sct.gc.ca

Alberta

Alberta Apprenticeship & Industry Training Board, South Tower, 10030 - 107 St., 7th Fl., Edmonton, AB T5J 4X7
780-427-8517, Fax: 780-422-3734, 800-232-7215
Alberta Gaming & Liquor Commission, 50 Corriveau Ave., St Albert, AB T8N 3T5
780-447-8600, Fax: 780-447-8911, 800-272-8876
Alberta Pensions Services Corporation, 5103 Windermere Blvd. SW, Edmonton, AB T6W 0S9
780-427-5101, Fax: 780-421-1652, 800-358-0840, apa.info@gov.ab.ca; memberservices@apsc.ca
Alberta Review Board, Oxford Tower, 10235 - 101 St., 11th Fl., Edmonton, AB T5J 3E9
780-422-5994, Fax: 780-427-1762
Alberta Special Areas Board, 212 - 2nd Ave. West, PO Box 820, Hanna, AB T0J 1P0
403-854-5600, Fax: 403-854-5527, specarea@telusplanet.net
Alberta Office of the Auditor General, 9925 - 109 St., 8th Fl., Edmonton, T5K 2J8 AB
780-427-4222, Fax: 780-422-9555, info@oag.ab.ca
Alberta Office of the Chief Electoral Officer/Elections Alberta, #100, 11510 Kingsway Ave., Edmonton, T5G 2Y5 AB
780-427-7191, Fax: 780-422-2900, info@electionsalberta.ab.ca
Alberta Office of the Ethics Commissioner, #1250, 9925 - 109 St., Edmonton, T5K 2J8 AB
780-422-2273, Fax: 780-422-2261, generalinfo@ethicscommissioner.ab.ca
Executive Council, Legislature Bldg., 10800 - 97 Ave., Edmonton, T5K 2B6 AB
780-427-2251, Fax: 780-427-1349
Alberta Finance & Enterprise, Terrace Building, #426, 9515 - 107 St., Edmonton, T5K 2C3 AB
780-427-3035, Fax: 780-427-1147, tra.revenue@gov.ab.ca
Government of Alberta, 9718 - 107 St., Edmonton, T5K 1E4 AB
Alberta Office of the Information & Privacy Commissioner, #410, 9925 - 109 St., Edmonton, T5K 2J8 AB
780-422-6860, Fax: 780-422-5682, 888-878-4044, generalinfo@oipc.ab.ca
Alberta Infrastructure, Infrastructure Building, 6950 - 101 St., 3rd Fl., Edmonton, T6H 5V7 AB
780-415-0507, Fax: 780-427-2187,-310-0000
Alberta International & Intergovernmental Relations, Commerce Place, 10155 - 102 St., 12th Fl., Edmonton, T5J 4G8 AB
780-422-1510, Fax: 780-427-0699
Legislative Assembly, Legislature Annex Bldg., 9718 - 107 St., Edmonton, T5K 1E4 AB
780-427-2826, Fax: 780-427-1623, laocommunications@assembly.ab.ca
Office of the Lieutenant Governor, Legislature Bldg., 10800 - 97 Ave., 3rd Fl., Edmonton, T5K 2B6 AB
780-427-7243, Fax: 780-422-5134, ltgov@gov.ab.ca
Alberta Municipal Affairs, Communications Branch, Commerce Place, 10155 - 102 St., 18th Fl., Edmonton, T5J 4L4 AB
780-427-2732, Fax: 780-422-1419, comments@gov.ab.ca
Alberta Office of the Ombudsman, Canadian Western Bank Bldg., #2800, 10303 Jasper Ave., Edmonton, T5J 5C3 AB
780-427-2756, Fax: 780-427-2759, info@ombudsman.ab.ca
Office of the Premier, Legislature Bldg., #307, 10800 - 97 Ave., Edmonton, T5K 2B6 AB
780-427-2251, Fax: 780-427-1349
Alberta Public Affairs Bureau, Park Plaza, 10611 - 98 Ave., 6th Fl., Edmonton, T5K 2P7 AB
403-427-9261, Fax: 403-422-4168
Registries Services, John E. Brownlee Bldg., 10365 - 97 St., 3rd Fl., Edmonton, T5J 3W7 AB
Alberta Treasury Board, Legislature Bldg., #204, 10800 - 97 Ave., Edmonton, T5K 2B6 AB
780-415-4855, Fax: 780-422-4853
Twenty-seventh Legislature - Alberta, Legislature Bldg., 10800 - 97 Ave., Edmonton, T5K 2B6 AB
780-427-2826, Fax: 780-427-1623, laocommunications@assembly.ab.ca

British Columbia

Agricultural Land Commission, #133, 4940 Canada Way, Burnaby, BC V5G 4K6
604-660-7000, Fax: 604-660-7033
Office of the Auditor General, 8 Bastion Sq., Victoria, V8V 1X4 BC
250-387-6803, Fax: 250-387-1230, info@bcauditor.com
BC Pavilion Corporation (PavCo), 777 Pacific Blvd., Vancouver, BC V6B 4Y8
604-482-2200, Fax: 604-681-9017, info@bcpavco.com
British Columbia Assessment Authority, 1537 Hillside Ave., Victoria, BC V8T 4Y2
250-595-6211, Fax: 250-595-6222, info@bcassessment.ca
Client Services, 525 Superior St., 2nd Fl., PO Box 9472 Prov Govt,Victoria, V8W 9W6 BC
250-952-6861, Fax: 250-952-6803
Office of the Conflict of Interest Commissioner, #101, 431 Menzies St., Victoria, V8V 1X4 BC
250-356-0750, Fax: 250-356-6580, ConflictofInterest@gov.bc.ca
Court Services Branch, 850 Burdett Ave., 6th Fl., PO Box 9249 Prov Govt,Victoria, V8W 9J2 BC
250-356-1550, Fax: 250-356-8152
Crown Agencies Secretariat, #400, 1675 Douglas St,, PO Box 9300 Prov Govt, Victoria, BC V8W 9N2
250-952-0750, Fax: 250-952-0777, 800-663-7867, Trena.Huson@gov.bc.ca
Elections British Columbia, PO Box 9275 Prov Govt,Victoria, V8W 9J6 BC
250-387-5305, Fax: 250-387-3578, 800-661-8683, electionsbc@elections.bc.ca
Executive Council, Parliament Bldgs., Victoria, V8V 1X4 BC
Government of British Columbia, Parliament Bldgs., Victoria, V8V 1X4 BC
EnquiryBC@gov.bc.ca
Office of the Information & Privacy Commissioner for British Columbia, 756 Fort St., 3rd Fl., PO Box 9038 Prov Govt,Victoria, V8W 9A4 BC
250-387-5629, Fax: 250-387-1696, 800-663-7867, info@oipc.bc.ca
Legislative Assembly, Clerk's Office, #221, Parliament Bldgs., Victoria, V8V 1X4 BC
250-387-3785, Fax: 250-387-0942, ClerkHouse@leg.bc.ca
Office of the Lieutenant Governor, Government House, 1401 Rockland Ave., Victoria, V8S 1V9 BC
250-387-2080, Fax: 250-387-2078, ghinfo@gov.bc.ca
Office of the Ombudsman, 756 Fort St., 2nd Fl., PO Box 9039 Prov Govt,Victoria, V8W 9A5 BC
250-387-5855, Fax: 250-387-0198, 800-567-3247, systems@ombudsman.bc.ca (Information technology inquiries)
Office of the Premier, West Annex, Parliament Bldgs., PO Box 9041 Prov Govt,Victoria, V8W 9E1 BC
250-387-1715, Fax: 250-387-0087, premier@gov.bc.ca
BC Public Service Agency, #4, 810 Blanshard St., PO Box 9404 Prov Govt,Victoria, V8W 9V1 BC
250-356-6830, Fax: 250-356-7074
Thirty-Eighth Legislature - British Columbia, Parliament Bldgs., Victoria, V8V 1X4 BC
250-387-3785, Fax: 250-387-0942, ClerkHouse@leg.bc.ca
British Columbia Utilities Commission, 900 Howe St., 6th Fl., PO Box 250, Vancouver, V6Z 2N3 BC
604-660-4700, Fax: 604-660-1102, 800-663-1385, commission.secretary@bcuc.com

Manitoba

Aboriginal Affairs Secretariat, #200, 500 Portage Ave., Winnipeg, R3C 3X1 MB
204-945-2510, Fax: 204-945-3689
Office of the Auditor General, #500, 330 Portage Ave., Winnipeg, R3C 0C4 MB
204-945-3790, Fax: 204-945-2169, contact@oag.mb.ca

Civil Service Commission Board, #935, 155 Carlton St., Winnipeg, MB R3C 3H8
204-945-1435, Fax: 204-945-1486
Manitoba Civil Service Commission, #935, 155 Carlton St., Winnipeg, R3C 3H8 MB
204-945-2332, Fax: 204-945-1486, 800-282-8069, cschrp@gov.mb.ca
Crown Corporations Council, #1130, 444 St. Mary Ave., Winnipeg, MB R3C 3T1
204-949-5270, Fax: 204-949-5283, crowncc@mts.net
Elections Manitoba, #120, 200 Vaughan St., Winnipeg, R3C 1T5 MB
204-945-3225, Fax: 204-945-6011, 866-628-6837, election@elections.mb.ca
Executive Council, Legislative Building, 450 Broadway Ave., Winnipeg, R3C 0V8 MB
Federal-Provincial Relations & Research Division, #910, 386 Broadway, Winnipeg, R3C 3R6 MB
204-945-3757, Fax: 204-945-5051
Government of Manitoba, Legislative Building, Rm. 237, Winnipeg, R3C 0V8 MB
204-945-3636, Fax: 204-948-2507, clerkla@leg.gov.mb.ca
Manitoba Intergovernmental Affairs, #301, 450 Broadway Ave., Winnipeg, R3C 0V8 MB
Fax: 204-945-1383, mnia@leg.gov.mb.ca
Legislative Assembly, c/o Clerk's Office, Legislative Bldg., #237, 450 Broadway, Winnipeg, R3C 0V8 MB
204-945-3636, Fax: 204-948-2507, clerkla@leg.gov.mb.ca
Office of the Lieutenant Governor, Legislative Building, #235, 450 Broadway Ave., Winnipeg, R3C 0V8 MB
204-945-2753, Fax: 204-945-4329, ltgov@leg.gov.mb.ca
Local Government Development Division, 59 Elizabeth Dr., PO Box 33, Thompson, R8N 1X4 MB
204-677-6794, Fax: 204-677-6525
Manitoba Civil Service Commission, #935, 155 Carlton St., Winnipeg, MB R3C 3H8
204-945-2332, Fax: 204-945-1486, cschrp@gov.mb.ca
Manitoba Land Value Appraisal Commission, 800 Portage Ave., Winnipeg, MB R3G 0N4
204-945-2941, Fax: 204-948-2235
Manitoba Municipal Board, #1144, 363 Broadway, Winnipeg, MB R3C 3N9
204-945-2941, Fax: 204-948-2235
Mineral Resources Division, #360, 1395 Ellice Ave., Winnipeg, R3G 3P2 MB
Fax: 204-945-8427
Manitoba News Media Services, #29, Legislative Bldg., 450 Broadway, Winnipeg, R3C 0V8 MB
204-945-3746, Fax: 204-945-3988, nmservices@leg.gov.mb.ca
Manitoba Office of the Ombudsman, 750 - 500 Portage Ave., Winnipeg, R3C 3X1 MB
204-982-9130, Fax: 204-942-7803, 800-665-0531, ombudsma@ombudsman.mb.ca
Office of the Premier, Legislative Building, #204, 450 Broadway Ave., Winnipeg, R3C 0V8 MB
204-945-3714, Fax: 204-949-1484, premier@leg.gov.mb.ca
Provincial-Municipal Support Services, #508, 800 Portage Ave., Winnipeg, R3G 0N4 MB
Residential Tenancies Commission, #1650, 155 Carlton St., Winnipeg, MB R3C 3H8
204-945-2028, Fax: 204-945-5453, 800-782-8403, rtc@gov.mb.ca
Thirty-ninth Legislature - Manitoba, Legislative Building, 450 Broadway Ave., Winnipeg, R3C 0V8 MB
204-945-3636, Fax: 204-948-2507, clerkla@leg.gov.mb.ca
Manitoba Treasury Board Secretariat, #200, 386 Broadway, Winnipeg, R3C 3R6 MB
204-945-4150, Fax: 204-948-4878

New Brunswick

Office of the Auditor General, HSBC Place, 520 King St., 6th Fl., Fredericton, E3B 6G3 NB
506-453-2243, Fax: 506-453-3067
Communications New Brunswick, Wilcom Bldg., 225 King St., 2nd Fl., PO Box 6000, Fredericton, E3B 5H1 NB
506-453-2240, Fax: 506-453-5329
Office of the Comptroller, Centennial Bldg., 670 King St., Fredericton, E3B 1G1 NB
506-453-2565, Fax: 506-453-2917, wwwooc@gnb.ca
Corporate Services, Centennial Bldg., 670 King St., 5th Fl., PO Box 6000, Fredericton, E3B 5H1 NB
506-453-3707, Fax: 506-453-3993
Office of the Chief Electoral Officer, PO Box 6000, Fredericton, E3B 5H1 NB
506-453-2218, Fax: 506-457-4926, 800-308-2922
Executive Council, Centennial Bldg., 670 King St., PO Box 6000, Fredericton, E3B 5H1 NB
506-453-2144, Fax: 506-453-7407, Shawn.Graham@gnb.ca
Fifty-sixth Legislature - New Brunswick, Legislative Assembly of New Brunswick, 706 Queen St., PO Box 6000, Fredericton, E3B 5H1 NB
506-453-2506, Fax: 506-453-7154
Finance & Administration, Centennial Bldg., #373, 670 King St., PO Box 6000, Fredericton, E3B 5H1 NB
506-457-6863, Fax: 506-444-4724
Government of New Brunswick, PO Box 6000, Fredericton, E3B 5H1 NB
Department of Intergovernmental Affairs, Centennial Bldg., #274, 670 King St., PO Box 6000, Fredericton, E3B 5H1 NB
506-444-5418, Fax: 506-453-2995, iga@gnb.ca
Legislative Assembly of New Brunswick, Centre Block, Legislative Bldg., 706 Queen St., PO Box 6000, Fredericton, E3B 5H1 NB
506-453-2506, Fax: 506-453-7154, wwwleg@gnb.ca
Office of the Lieutenant-Governor, Old Government House, 51 Woodstock Rd., PO Box 6000, Fredericton, E3B 5H1 NB
506-453-2505, Fax: 506-444-5280
Office of the Ombudsman, 767 Brunswick St., PO Box 6000, Fredericton, E3B 5H1 NB
506-453-2789, Fax: 506-453-5599, 800-465-1100, nbombud@gnb.ca
Office of the Premier, Centennial Bldg., 670 King St., PO Box 6000, Fredericton, E3B 5H1 NB
506-453-2144, Fax: 506-453-7407, premier@gnb.ca
Department of Supply & Services, PO Box 6000, Fredericton, E3B 5H1 NB
506-453-3742, Fax: 506-444-4400, Reception.Marysville@gnb.ca

Newfoundland & Labrador

Office of the Auditor General, Viking Bldg., 3rd Fl., PO Box 8700, St. John's, A1B 4J6 NL
709-729-2700, Fax: 709-729-5970, oag@gov.nl.ca
Office of the Chief Electoral Officer, 39 Hallett Cr., St. John's, A1B 4C4 NL
709-729-0712, Fax: 709-729-0679, 877-729-7987, oceo@gov.nl.ca
Executive Council, c/o Communications Branch, East Block, Confederation Bldg., 10th Fl., St. John's, A1B 4J6 NL
709-729-5645, info@gov.nl.ca
Forty-sixth House of Assembly - Newfoundland & Labrador, PO Box 8700, St. John's, A1B 4J6 NL
709-729-3405, ClerkHOA@gov.nl.ca
Government of Newfoundland & Labrador, Confederation Bldg., St. John's, A1B 4J6 NL
info@gov.nl.ca
Department of Government Services, PO Box 8700, St. John's, A1B 4J6 NL
709-729-4860
House of Assembly, c/o Clerk's Office, Confederation Bldg., PO Box 8700, St. John's, A1B 4J6 NL
709-729-3405, Fax: 709-729-4820
Office of the Lieutenant Governor, Government House, Military Rd., PO Box 5517, St. John's, A1C 5W4 NL
709-729-4494, Fax: 709-729-2234, governmenthouse@gov.nl.ca
Department of Municipal Affairs, West Block, Main Fl., Confederation Bldg., PO Box 8700, St. John's, A1B 4J6 NL
709-729-3053
Newfoundland & Labrador Municipal Financing Corporation, Confederation Bldg., PO Box 8700, St. John's, NL A1B 4J6
709-729-6686, Fax: 709-729-2095
Office of the Premier, East Block, Confederation Bldg., 8th F., PO Box 8700, St. John's, A1B 4J6 NL
709-729-3570, Fax: 709-729-5875, premier@gov.nl.ca

Northwest Territories

Department of Aboriginal Affairs & Intergovernmental Relations, 4910 - 52nd St., PO Box 1320, Yellowknife, X1A 2L9 NT
867-873-7143, Fax: 867-873-0233, 877-838-8194, nancy_gardiner @gov.nt.ca
Office of the Commissioner, #803 Northwest Tower, PO Box 1320, Yellowknife, X1A 2L9 NT
867-873-7400, Fax: 867-873-0223, 888-270-3318, commissioner@gov.nt.ca
Executive Council, PO Box 1320, Yellowknife, X1A 2L9 NT
executive@gov.nt.ca
Financial Management Board Secretariat, c/o Secretary of the FMB / Comptroller General, 5003 - 49 St., PO Box 1320, Yellowknife, X1A 2L9 NT
867-873-7211, Fax: 867-873-0112
Government of the Northwest Territories, PO Box 1320, Yellowknife, X1A 2L9 NT
Legislative Assembly, c/o Clerk's Office, PO Box 1320, Yellowknife, X1A 2L9 NT
867-669-2299, Fax: 867-920-4735, 800-661-0784
Office of the Premier, Legislative Assembly Bldg., PO Box 1320, Yellowknife, X1A 2L9 NT
867-669-2311, Fax: 867-873-0385, premier@gov.nt.ca
Department of Public Works & Services, PO Box 1320, Yellowknife, X1A 2L9 NT
867-873-7114, Fax: 867-873-0226
Sixteenth Legislature - Northwest Territories, PO Box 1320, Yellowknife, X1A 2L9 NT
867-669-2200, Fax: 867-920-4735, 800-661-0784

Nova Scotia

Office of the Auditor General, #302, 1888 Brunswick St., Halifax, B3J 3J8 NS
902-424-5907, Fax: 902-424-4350
Council of Atlantic Premiers, Council Secretariat, #1006, 5161 George St., PO Box 2044, Halifax, B3J 2Z1 NS
902-424-7590, Fax: 902-424-8976, info@cap-cpma.ca
Crown Lands Record Centre, Founders Square, #501, 1701 Hollis St., PO Box 698, Halifax, NS B3J 2T9
902-424-8681
Elections Nova Scotia, 3667 Strawberry Hill St., PO Box 2246, Halifax, B3J 3C8 NS
902-424-8584, Fax: 902-424-6622, 800-565-1504, elections@gov.ns.ca
Executive Council, One Government Place, PO Box 2125, Halifax, B3J 3B7 NS
902-424-5970, Fax: 902-424-0667
Government of Nova Scotia, Province House, Halifax, B3J 2T3 NS
Legislative House of Assembly, c/o Clerk's Office, Province House, 1st Fl., PO Box 1617, Halifax, B3J 2Y3 NS
902-424-5978, Fax: 902-424-0632
Office of the Lieutenant Governor, Government House, 1451 Barrington St., Halifax, B3J 1Z2 NS
902-424-7001, Fax: 902-424-0537
Office of the Ombudsman, #700, 5670 Spring Garden Rd., PO Box 2152, Halifax, B3J 3B7 NS
902-424-6780, Fax: 902-424-6675, 800-670-1111
Office of the Premier, One Government Place, 1700 Granville St., PO Box 726, Halifax, B3J 2T3 NS
902-424-6600, Fax: 902-424-7648, 800-267-1993, premier@gov.ns.ca
Department of Service Nova Scotia & Municipal Relations, 1505 Barrington St., PO Box 216, Halifax, B3J 2M4 NS
902-424-4141, Fax: 902-424-0581, public-enquiries@gov.ns.ca
Sixtieth Assembly - Nova Scotia, Province House, PO Box 1617, Halifax, B3J 2Y3 NS
902-424-5978, Fax: 902-424-0632
Nova Scotia Treasury & Policy Board, 1700 Granville St., 5th Fl., PO Box 1617, Halifax, B3J 2Y3 NS
902-424-8910, Fax: 902-424-7638, tpbenquiries@gov.ns.ca
Nova Scotia Utility & Review Board, 1601 Lower Water St., 3rd Fl., PO Box 1692 M,Halifax, B3J 3S3 NS
902-424-4448, Fax: 902-424-3919, uarb.board@gov.ns.ca

Nunavut

Department of Community & Government Services, J.G. Brown Bldg., PO Box 1000 700,Iqaluit, X0A 0H0 NU
867-975-5400, Fax: 867-975-5305
Department of Culture, Language, Elders & Youth, PO Box 1000 800,Iqaluit, X0A 0H0 NU
867-975-5500, Fax: 867-975-5504, 866-934-2035
Department of Education, PO Box 1000 910,Iqaluit, X0A 0H0 NU
867-975-5600, Fax: 867-975-5605, 888-531-1456
Nunavut Emergency Management, PO Box 1000 700,Iqaluit, X0A 0H0 NU
867-975-5403, Fax: 867-979-4221, 800-693-1666
Department of Environment, PO Box 1000 1300,Iqaluit, X0A 0H0 NU
867-975-7700, Fax: 867-975-7742, 866-222-9063, environment@gov.nu.ca
Department of Executive & Intergovernmental Affairs, 1084 Aeroplex bldg., PO Box 1000 200,Iqaluit, X0A 0H0 NU
867-975-6000, Fax: 867-975-6090
Executive Council, Legislative Bldg., 2nd Fl., Box 2410, Iqaluit, X0A 0H0 NU
867-975-5090, Fax: 867-975-5095
Department of Finance, Bldg. 1079, 1st Fl., PO Box 1000 Stn 330,Iqaluit, X0A 0H0 NU
867-975-5800, Fax: 867-975-5805
Government of the Nunavut Territory, PO Box 1200, Iqaluit, X0A 0H0 NU
888-252-9869
Department of Health & Social Services, Sivummut bldg., PO Box 1007 1000,Iqaluit, X0A 0H0 NU
867-975-5700, Fax: 867-975-5705, health@gov.nu.ca
Department of Human Resources, PO Box 1000 400,Iqaluit, X0A 1H0 NU
867-975-6200, Fax: 867-975-6216, 888-668-9993, gnhr@gov.nu.ca

Department of Justice, Sivummut, 1st Fl., PO Box 1000 500,Iqaluit, X0A 0H0 NU
867-975-6170, Fax: 867-975-6195
Legislative Assembly, Legislative Assembly Bldg., 3rd Fl., PO Box 1200, Iqaluit, X0A 0H0 NU
867-975-5000, Fax: 867-975-5190, 877-334-7266, leginfo@assembly.nu.ca
Office of the Commissioner, PO Box 2379, Iqaluit, X0A 0H0 NU
867-975-5120, Fax: 867-975-5123, nunavutcommissioner@gov.nu.ca
Office of the Premier, Legislative Assembly Bldg., 2nd Fl., PO Box 2410, Iqaluit, X0A 0H0 NU
867-975-5050, Fax: 867-975-5051
Second Legislature - Nunavut, PO Box 1200, Iqaluit, X0A 0H0 NU

Ontario

Office of the Provincial Auditor, 20 Dundas St. West, 15th Fl., PO Box 105, Toronto, M5G 2C2 ON
416-327-2381, Fax: 416-327-9862, comments@auditor.on.ca
Cancer Care Ontario, 620 University Ave., 15th Fl., Toronto, ON M5G 2L7
416-971-9800, Fax: 416-971-6888
Elections Ontario, 51 Rolark Dr., Toronto, M1R 3B1 ON
416-326-6300, Fax: 416-326-6200, 888-668-8683, info@elections.on.ca
Executive Council, Whitney Block, Queen's Park, 99 Wellesley St. West, 6th Fl., Toronto, M7A 1A1 ON
416-325-5721, Fax: 416-314-1551
Government of Ontario, Queen's Park, Toronto, M7A 1A2 ON
416-326-1234, 800-267-8097
Healing Arts Radiation Protection Commission, 5700 Yonge St., 3rd Fl., Toronto, ON M2M 4K5
416-327-7952, Fax: 416-327-8805
Office of the Integrity Commissioner, #2101, 2 Bloor St. East, Toronto, M4W 1A8 ON
416-314-8983, Fax: 416-314-8987, integrity.mail@oico.on.ca
Ministry of Intergovernmental Affairs, 77 Wellesley St. West, Toronto, M7A 1N3 ON
416-325-4800, Fax: 416-325-4787
Legislative Assembly, c/o Clerk's Office, #104, Legislative Bldg., Queen's Park, Toronto, M7A 1A2 ON
416-325-7340, Fax: 416-325-7344, assembly@ontla.ola.org
Office of the Lieutenant Governor, Room 131, Legislative Bldg., Queen's Park, Toronto, M7A 1A1 ON
416-325-7780, Fax: 416-325-7787, ltgov@gov.on.ca
Ministry of Municipal Affairs & Housing, 777 Bay St., 17th Fl., Toronto, M5G 2E5 ON
416-585-7041, Fax: 416-585-6227, 866-220-2290, mininfo.mah@ontario.ca
Niagara Falls Bridge Commission, PO Box 395, Niagara Falls, L2E 6T8 ON
905-354-5641, Fax: 905-353-6644
Office of the Ombudsman, 483 Bay St., 10th Fl., Toronto, M5G 2C9 ON
416-586-3300, Fax: 416-586-3485, 800-263-1830, info@ombudsman.on.ca
Ontario Housing Corporation, 777 Bay St., 2nd Fl., Toronto, ON M5G 2E5
Ontario Mental Health Foundation, #508, 489 College St., Toronto, ON M6G 1A5
416-920-7721, Fax: 416-920-0026, grants@omhf.on.ca
Ontario Northland, 555 Oak St. East, North Bay, ON P1B 8L3
705-472-4500, Fax: 705-476-5598, 800-363-7512, info@ontc.on.ca
Ontario Pension Board, #1100, 1 Adelaide St. East, Toronto, ON M5C 2X6
416-364-8558, Fax: 416-364-7578, 800-668-6203, office.services@opb.on.ca
Ottawa Office, #1209, 350 Sparks St., Ottawa, K1R 7S8 ON
613-233-9890, Fax: 613-233-2543, lcooper@gov.nu.ca
Office of the Premier, Legislative Bldg., #281, 1 Queen's Park Cres. South, Toronto, M7A 1A1 ON
416-325-1941, Fax: 416-325-3745, webprem@gov.on.ca

Prince Edward Island

PEI Public Archives & Records Office, PO Box 1000, Charlottetown, C1A 7M4 PE
902-368-4290, Fax: 902-368-6327, archives@gov.pe.ca
Elections Prince Edward Island, J. Angus MacLean Bldg., 94 Great George St., PO Box 774, Charlottetown, C1A 7L3 PE
902-368-5895, Fax: 902-368-6500
Executive Council, Shaw Bldg., 5th Fl., PO Box 2000, Charlottetown, C1A 7N8 PE
902-368-4502, Fax: 902-368-6118,
Government of Prince Edward Island, PO Box 2000, Charlottetown, C1A 7N8 PE
902-368-4000, Fax: 902-368-5544, island@gov.pe.ca
Legislative Assembly, c/o Clerk's Office, Province House, Richmond St., PO Box 2000, Charlottetown, C1A 7K7 PE
902-368-5970, Fax: 902-368-5175
Office of the Premier, Shaw Bldg., 95 Rochford St., 5th Fl. South, PO Box 2000, Charlottetown, C1A 7N8 PE
902-368-4400, Fax: 902-368-4416
Sixty-third General Assembly - Prince Edward Island, Province House, 165 Richmond St., 1st Fl., PO Box 2000, Charlottetown, C1A 7N8 PE
902-368-5970, Fax: 902-368-5175, 877-315-5518
Department of the Provincial Treasury, Shaw Bldg., 95 Rochford St., 2nd Fl. South, PO Box 2000, Charlottetown, C1A 7N8 PE
902-368-4050, Fax: 902-368-6575

Quebec

Ministère des Affaires municipales et Occupation du territoire, Aile Chaveau, 10, rue Pierre-Olivier-Chauveau, 3e étage, Québec, G1R 4J3 QC
418-691-2019, Fax: 418-643-7385, communications@mamrot.gouv.qc.ca
Bureau du coroner, #390, 2875, boul Laurier, Sainte-Foy, QC G1V 5B1
418-643-1845, Fax: 418-643-6174, clientele.coroner@msp.gouv.qc.ca
Centre de recherche industrielle du Québec, 333, rue Franquet, Québec, QC G1P 4C7
418-659-1550, Fax: 418-652-2251, 800-667-2386, infocriq@criq.qc.ca
Comité de déontologie policière, Tour du Saint-Laurent, #A-200, 2525, boul Laurier, 2e étage, Québec, QC G1V 4Z6
418-646-1936, Fax: 418-528-0987, comite.deontologie@msp.gouv.qc.ca
Commissaire à la déontologie policière, 1200, rte de l'Église, R-C20, Sainte-Foy, QC G1V 4Y9
418-643-7897, Fax: 418-528-9473, 877-237-7897
Commissariat des incendies, 455, rue Dupont, Québec, QC G1K 6N2
418-529-5706, Fax: 418-529-9922
Commission de la fonction publique (Québec), 800, Place d'Youville, 7e étage, Québec, QC G1R 3P4
418-643-1425, 800-432-0432, cfp@cfp.gouv.qc.ca
Commission québecoise des libérations conditionnelles, #1.32A, 300, boul Jean-Lesage, Québec, QC G1K 8K6
418-646-8300, Fax: 418-643-7217, liberation.conditionnel@msp.gouv.
Ministère du Conseil exécutif, 875, Grande Allée est, Québec, G1R 4Y8 QC
418-646-3021, Fax: 418-528-9242
Direction générale de la Sûreté du Québec, 1701, rue Parthenais, Montréal, QC H2K 3S7
514-598-4488, Fax: 514-598-4957, info@surete.qc.ca
Commission des droits de la personne et des droits de la jeunesse, 360, rue St-Jacques, 2e étage, Montréal, H2Y 1P5 QC
514-873-5146, Fax: 514-873-6032, 800-361-6477, webmestre@cdpdj.qc.ca
Ministère du Développement économique, de l'Innovation et de l'Exportation, 710, place D'Youville, 3e étage, Québec, G1R 4Y4 QC
418-691-5950, Fax: 418-644-0118, 866-680-1884
Commission de la fonction publique, 800, Place D'Youville, 7e étage, Québec, G1R 3P4 QC
418-643-1425, Fax: 418-643-7264, 800-432-0432, cfp@cfp.gouv.qc.ca
Gouvernement du Québec, Hôtel du Parlement, 1045, rue des Parlementaires, Québec, G1A 1A4 QC
418-643-7239, Fax: 418-646-4271, 866-337-8837
Ministère de l' Immigration et des Communautés culturelles, 360, rue McGill, 4e étage, Montréal, H2Y 2E9 QC
514-864-9191, Fax: 514-864-2899
Institut de la statistique du Québec, 200, ch Ste-Foy, 3e étage, Québec, QC G1R 5T4
418-691-2401, Fax: 418-643-4129, 800-463-4090, direction@stat.gouv.qc.ca
L'Assemblée nationale, Hôtel du Parlement, 1045, rue des Parlementaires, Québec, G1A 1A4 QC
418-643-7239, Fax: 418-646-4271, 866-337-8837, responsable.contenu@assnat.qc.ca
Cabinet du Lieutenant-gouverneur, Édifice André-Laurendeau, 1050, rue des Parlementaires R.C., Québec, G1A 1A1 QC
418-643-5385, Fax: 418-644-4677, 866-791-0766
Cabinet du premier ministre, Édifice Honoré-Mercier, 835, boul René-Lévesque est, 3e étage, Québec, G1A 1B4 QC
418-643-5321, Fax: 418-643-3924
Ministère des Relations internationales, Édifice Hector-Fabre, 525, boul Réne-Lévesque est, Québec, G1R 5R9 QC
418-649-2300, Fax: 418-649-2656, communications@mri.gouv.qc.ca
Ministère des Ressources naturelles et de la Faune, 880, ch Sainte-Foy, Québec, G1S 4X4 QC
418-627-8600, Fax: 418-644-6513, 866-248-6936, services.clientele@mrnf.gouv.qc.ca
Régie des alcools, des courses et des jeux, 560, boul Charest est, Québec, QC G1K 3J3
418-643-7667, Fax: 418-643-5971, 800-363-0320, racj.quebec@racj.gouv.qc.ca
Secrétariat aux Affaires intergouvernementales canadiennes, 875, Grande Allée est, 3e étage, Québec, G1R 4Y8 QC
418-643-4011, Fax: 418-528-0052
Société des alcools du Québec, 905, av De Lorimier, Montréal, QC H2K 3V9
514-873-2020, Fax: 514-873-6788, 866-873-2020, info@saq.com
Société générale de financement du Québec, #1500, 600, rue de La Gauchetière ouest, Montréal, QC H3B 4L8
514-876-9290, Fax: 514-395-8055, info@sgfqc.com
Trente-huitième législature, Hôtel du Parlement, 1045, rue des Parlementaires, Québec, G1A 1A4 QC
418-643-7239, Fax: 418-646-4271, 866-337-8837
École nationale de police du Québec, 350, rue Marguerite-d'Youville, Nicolet, QC J3T 1X4
819-293-8631, Fax: 819-293-4018, courriel@enpq.qc.ca
Directeur général des Élections du Québec, Édifice René-Lévesque, 3460, rue de La Pérade, Québec, G1X 3Y5 QC
418-528-0422, Fax: 418-643-7291, 888-353-2846, info@electionsquebec.qc.ca

Saskatchewan

Provincial Auditor Saskatchewan, #1500, 1920 Broad St., Regina, S4P 3V2 SK
306-787-6398, Fax: 306-787-6383, info@auditor.sk.ca
Board of Revenue Commissioners, #480, 2151 Scarth St., Regina, SK S4P 2H8
306-787-6221, Fax: 306-787-1610
Saskatchewan Communications Network, #313E, 2440 Broad St., Regina, S4P 0A5 SK
306-787-0490, Fax: 306-787-0496, 800-667-5055, inquiries@scn.ca
Elections Saskatchewan, 1702 Park St., Regina, S4N 6B2 SK
306-787-4000, Fax: 306-787-4052, 877-958-VOTE, info@elections.sk.ca
Executive Council, Legislative Bldg., 2405 Legislative Dr., Regina, S4S 0B3 SK
306-787-7448
Government of Saskatchewan, Regina, S4S 0B3 SK
Saskatchewan Government Relations, 1855 Victoria Ave., Regina, S4P 3T2 SK
306-787-2635
Saskatchewan Government Services, Century Plaza, 1920 Rose St., Regina, S4P 0A9 SK
306-787-6911, Fax: 306-787-1061
Legislative Assembly, c/o Clerk's Office, Legislative Bldg., #123, 2405 Legislative Dr., Regina, S4S 0B3 SK
306-787-2376, Fax: 306-787-1558, info@legassembly.sk.ca
Office of the Lieutenant Governor, Government House, 4607 Dewdney Ave., Regina, S4P 1B7 SK
306-787-4070, Fax: 306-787-7716, lgo@ltgov.sk.ca
Saskatchewan Ombudsman, #150, 2401 Saskatchewan Dr., Regina, S4P 4H8 SK
306-787-6211, Fax: 306-787-9090, 800-667-7180
Office of the Premier, Legislative Bldg., #226, 2405 Legislative Dr., Regina, S4S 0B3 SK
306-787-9433, Fax: 306-787-0885, premier@gov.sk.ca
Saskatchewan Public Service Commission, 2100 Broad St., Regina, S4P 1Y5 SK
306-787-7575, Fax: 306-787-7578, 866-319-5999, webmaster@psc.gov.sk.ca
Saskatchewan Development Fund Corporation, #300, 2400 College Ave., Regina, SK S4P 1C8
306-787-1645, 800-667-7543
Saskatchewan Tourism, Parks, Culture, & Sport, 1919 Saskatchewan Dr., 4th Fl., Regina, S4P 4H2 SK
306-787-5729, Fax: 306-787-8560
Twenty-sixth Legislature - Saskatchewan, #123, Legislative Bldg., 2405 Legislative Dr., Regina, S4S 0B3 SK
306-787-2376, Fax: 306-787-1558, info@legassembly.sk.ca

Yukon Territory

Office of the Commissioner, 1098 First Ave., Whitehorse, Y1A 0C1 YT
867-667-5121, Fax: 867-393-6201, commissioner@gov.yk.ca
Executive Council, PO Box 2703, Whitehorse, Y1A 2C6 YT
867-667-5800, Fax: 867-393-6202, 800-040-8 ex, eco@gov.yk.ca
Government of the Yukon Territory, PO Box 2703, Whitehorse, Y1A 2C6 YT
867-667-5811, 800-661-0408
Legislative Assembly, c/o Clerk's Office, PO Box 2703, Whitehorse, Y1A 2C6 YT
867-667-5498, Fax: 867-393-6280

Office of the Premier, 2071 Second Ave., PO Box 2703, Whitehorse, Y1A 1B2 YT
867-667-8660, Fax: 867-393-6252, premier@gov.yk.ca
Yukon Public Service Commission, PO Box 2703, Whitehorse, Y1A 2C6 YT
867-667-5252, Fax: 867-667-6705
Thirty-Second Legislature - Yukon Territory, PO Box 2703, Whitehorse, Y1A 2C6 YT
867-667-5498

GOVERNMENT (GENERAL INFORMATION)

Auditor General of Canada, 240 Sparks St., Ottawa, K1A 0G6 ON
613-995-3708, Fax: 613-957-0474, 888-761-5953, communications@oag-bvg.gc.ca; infomedia@oag-bvg.gc.ca
Canada Business, 235 Queen St., Ottawa, K1A 0H5 ON
Fax: 888-417-0442, 888-576-4444
Citizenship & Immigration Canada, Jean Edmonds, South Tower, 365 Laurier Ave. West, Ottawa, K1A 1L1 ON
613-954-9019, Fax: 613-954-2221, 888-242-2100
Communications & Consultations Branch, Tower 7, 1341 Baseline Rd., Ottawa, K1A 0C7 ON
613-759-1000, Fax: 613-773-2772
Communications Branch, 284 Wellington St., Ottawa, K1A 0H8 ON
Fax: 613-941-2329
Consultations & Communications Branch, East Tower, 140 O'Connor St., 19th Fl., Ottawa, K1A 0G5 ON
613-992-1573, consltcomm@fin.gc.ca
Correctional Service Canada, 340 Laurier Ave. West, Ottawa, K1A 0P9 ON
613-992-5891, Fax: 613-943-1630
Environment Canada, 10 Wellington St., Gatineau, K1A 0H3 QC
819-997-2800, Fax: 819-994-1412, 800-668-6767, enviroinfo@ec.gc.ca
Fisheries & Oceans Canada, 200 Kent St., Ottawa, K1A 0E6 ON
613-993-0999, Fax: 613-996-1866, info@dfo-mpo.gc.ca
Foreign Affairs & International Trade Canada, 125 Sussex Dr., Ottawa, K1A 0G2 ON
613-944-4000, Fax: 613-996-9709, 800-267-8376, enqserv@international.gc.ca
Health Canada, Tunney's Pasture, Ottawa, K1A 0K9 ON
613-957-2991, Fax: 613-941-5366, Info@hc-sc.gc.ca
House of Commons, Canada, House of Commons, Parliament Buildings, Ottawa, K1A 0A6 ON
613-992-4793, 866-599-4999, info@parl.gc.ca
Human Resources & Skills Development Canada, 140 Promenade du Portage, Ottawa, K1A 0J9 ON
Indian & Northern Affairs Canada, 10 Wellington St., North Tower, Gatineau, K1A 0H4 QC
819-997-0380, Fax: 819-953-3017, 866-817-3977, infopubs@ainc-inac.gc.ca
Industry Canada, 235 Queen St., Ottawa, K1A 0H5 ON
Fax: 613-954-6436, 800-328-6189, info@ic.gc.ca
National Defence Canada, Major-General George R. Pearkes Bldg., 101 Colonel By Dr., Ottawa, K1A 0K2 ON
613-995-2534, Fax: 613-992-4739, 800-856-8488
Office of the Prime Minister (Conservative Party of Canada), Langevin Block, 80 Wellington St., Ottawa, K1A 0A2 ON
613-992-4211, Fax: 613-941-6900, pm@pm.gc.ca
Service Canada, 140, Promenade du Portage, Gatineau, K1A 0J9 QC
800-622-6232
Statistics Canada, R.H. Coats Bldg., Tunney's Pasture, 100 Tunney's Pasture Driveway, Ottawa, K1A 0T6 ON
613-951-8116, Fax: 877-287-4369, 800-263-1136, infostats@statcan.ca
Transport Canada, Place de Ville, 330 Sparks St., Tower C, Ottawa, K1A 0N5 ON
613-990-2309, Fax: 613-954-4731, minTC@tc.gc.ca
Treasury Board of Canada, 300 Laurier Ave. West, 10th Fl., Ottawa, K1A 0R5 ON
613-957-2400, Fax: 613-941-4000, 877-636-0656, info@tbs-sct.gc.ca
Veterans Affairs Canada, 161 Grafton St., PO Box 7700, Charlottetown, C1A 8M9 PE
902-566-8888, information@vac-acc.gc.ca

Alberta
Alberta Public Affairs Bureau, Park Plaza, 10611 - 98 Ave., 6th Fl., Edmonton, T5K 2P7 AB
403-427-9261, Fax: 403-422-4168
Alberta Service Alberta, John E. Brownlee Bldg., 10365 - 97 St., Mezzanine Fl., Edmonton, T5J 3W7 AB
780-427-2711, 877-427-4088, government.services@gov.ab.ca

British Columbia
Chief Information Office, 4000 Seymour Pl., PO Box 9412 Prov Govt,Victoria, V8W 9V1 BC
250-356-7970, Fax: 250-387-1940

New Brunswick
Communications New Brunswick, Wilcom Bldg., 225 King St., 2nd Fl., PO Box 6000, Fredericton, E3B 5H1 NB
506-453-2240, Fax: 506-453-5329

Newfoundland & Labrador
Department of Government Services, PO Box 8700, St. John's, A1B 4J6 NL
709-729-4860

Nova Scotia
Department of Service Nova Scotia & Municipal Relations, 1505 Barrington St., PO Box 216, Halifax, B3J 2M4 NS
902-424-4141, Fax: 902-424-0581, public-enquiries@gov.ns.ca

Nunavut
Department of Executive & Intergovernmental Affairs, 1084 Aeroplex bldg., PO Box 1000 200,Iqaluit, X0A 0H0 NU
867-975-6000, Fax: 867-975-6090

Ontario
ServiceOntario, College Park, 777 Bay St., 15th fl., Toronto, M7A 2J3 ON
416-326-6205, Fax: 416-326-5106

Quebec
Services Québec, Bureau de la qualité, 800, place D'Youville, 20e étage, Québec, G1R 3P4 QC
418-646-4011, Fax: 418-528-9341

Yukon Territory
Government Inquiry Office, Yukon Government Administration Building, 2071 Second Ave., PO Box 2703, Whitehorse, Y1A 2C6 YT
867-667-5811, information@gov.yk.ca

GRANTS & SUBSIDIES

See Also: Student Aid
Atlantic Canada Opportunities Agency, Blue Cross Centre, 644 Main St., 3rd Fl., PO Box 6051, Moncton, E1C 9J8 NB
506-851-2271, Fax: 506-851-7403, 800-561-7862, information@acoa-apeca.gc.ca
Business Development Bank of Canada, #400, 5, Place Ville-Marie, Montréal, H3B 5E7 QC
514-283-5904, Fax: 514-283-2872, 877-232-2269
Canada Council for the Arts, 350 Albert St., PO Box 1047, Ottawa, K1P 5V8 ON
613-566-4414, Fax: 613-566-4390, 800-263-5588, info@canadacouncil.ca
Canada Economic Development for Québec Regions, Édifice Dominion Square, #900, 1255, rue Peel, Montréal, H3B 2T9 QC
514-283-6412, Fax: 514-283-3302, 866-385-6412
Canada Mortgage & Housing Corporation, 700 Montreal Rd., Ottawa, K1A 0P7 ON
613-748-2000, Fax: 613-748-2098, 800-668-2642, chic@cmhc-schl.gc.ca
Canadian Institutes of Health Research, 160 Elgin St., 9th Fl., Ottawa, K1A 0W9 ON
613-941-2672, Fax: 613-954-1800, 888-603-4178, info@cihr-irsc.gc.ca
International Development Research Centre, 150 Kent St., PO Box 8500, Ottawa, K1P 0B2 ON
613-236-6163, Fax: 613-238-7230, info@idrc.ca
National Film Board of Canada, 3155, rue Côte de Liesse, CP 1600 Centre-ville,Saint-Laurent, H4N 2N4 QC
514-283-9000, Fax: 514-283-7564, 800-267-7710
Natural Sciences & Engineering Research Council of Canada, Constitution Square, Tower II, 350 Albert St., Ottawa, K1A 1H5 ON
613-995-4273, Fax: 613-943-1624, marie-josee.duval@nserc-crsng.gc.ca
Western Economic Diversification Canada, Canada Place, #1500, 9700 Jasper Ave. NW, Edmonton, T5J 4H7 AB
780-495-4164, Fax: 780-495-4557, 888-338-9378

Alberta
Local Government Services Division, Commerce Place, 10155 - 102 St., 17th Fl., Edmonton, T5J 4L4 AB

Newfoundland & Labrador
Newfoundland & Labrador Municipal Financing Corporation, Confederation Bldg., PO Box 8700, St. John's, NL A1B 4J6
709-729-6686, Fax: 709-729-2095

Nova Scotia
Department of Finance, Provincial Bldg., 1723 Hollis St., 7th Fl., PO Box 187, Halifax, B3J 2N3 NS
902-424-5554, Fax: 902-424-0635, FinanceWeb@gov.ns.ca

Ontario
Culture Policy, Programs & Services Division, 400 University Ave., 5th Fl., Toronto, M7A 2R9 ON
416-314-7265, Fax: 416-314-7461,

Prince Edward Island
Department of the Provincial Treasury, Shaw Bldg., 95 Rochford St., 2nd Fl. South, PO Box 2000, Charlottetown, C1A 7N8 PE
902-368-4050, Fax: 902-368-6575

Saskatchewan
Saskatchewan Energy & Resources, #300, 2103 - 11th Ave., Regina, S4P 3Z8 SK
306-787-2528, Fax: 306-787-0395, 866-727-5427

HAZARDOUS MATERIALS

Hazardous Materials Information Review Commission, 427 Laurier Ave. West, 7th Fl., Ottawa, ON K1A 1M3
613-993-4331, Fax: 613-993-4686, hmirc-ccrmd@hc-sc.gc.ca
Institute for Chemical Process & Environmental Technology, Bldg. M-12, 1200 Montreal Rd., Ottawa, K1A 0R6 ON
613-993-4041, Fax: 613-957-8231

British Columbia
British Columbia Provincial Emergency Program, PO Box 9201 Prov Govt,Victoria, V8W 9J1 BC
250-952-4913, Fax: 250-952-4888, 888-257-4777

Manitoba
Emergency Measures Organization, 405 Broadway Ave., 15th Floor, Winnipeg, R3C 3L6 MB
204-945-4772, Fax: 204-945-4929, 888-267-8298, emo@gov.mb.ca

Ontario
Ministry of Environment, 135 St. Clair Ave. West, Toronto, M4V 1P5 ON
416-325-4000, Fax: 416-325-3159, 800-565-4923
Pesticides Advisory Committee, #1203, 2300 Yonge St., 12th Fl., Toronto, ON M4P 1E4
416-314-9230, Fax: 416-314-9237

HEALTH

Canadian Centre for Occupational Health & Safety, 135 Hunter St. East, Hamilton, L8N 1M5 ON
905-572-2981, Fax: 905-572-2206, 800-668-4284, clientservices@ccohs.ca
Canadian Centre on Substance Abuse, #300, 75 Albert St., Ottawa, K1P 5E7 ON
613-235-4048, Fax: 613-235-8101
Canadian Food Inspection Agency, 1400 Merivale Rd., Ottawa, K1A 0Y9 ON
613-225-2342, Fax: 613-228-6629, 800-442-2342
Corporate Support Division, Telus Plaza NT, 10025 Jasper Ave., 19th Fl., Edmonton, T5J 1S6 AB
Hazardous Materials Information Review Commission, 427 Laurier Ave. West, 7th Fl., Ottawa, ON K1A 1M3
613-993-4331, Fax: 613-993-4686, hmirc-ccrmd@hc-sc.gc.ca
Health Canada, Tunney's Pasture, Ottawa, K1A 0K9 ON
613-957-2991, Fax: 613-941-5366, Info@hc-sc.gc.ca
Health Workforce Division, Telus Plaza NT, 10025 Jasper Ave., 10th Fl., Edmonton, T5J 1S6 AB
National Advisory Council on Aging, Jeanne Mance Bldg., 8th Fl., Postal Locator 1908 A1, Ottawa, K1A 0K9 ON
613-957-1968, Fax: 613-957-7627
Patented Medicine Prices Review Board, Standard Life Centre, #1400, 333 Laurier Ave. West, PO Box L40, Ottawa, K1P 1C1 ON
613-952-7360, Fax: 613-952-7626, 877-861-2350, pmprb@pmprb-cepmb.gc.ca
Public Health Agency of Canada, 130 Colonnade Rd., Ottawa, ON K1A 0K9
Seniors Services Division, Standard Life Centre, 10405 Jasper Ave., 6th Fl., Edmonton, T5J 4R7 AB
780-427-7876

Alberta
Alberta Health Services, Manulife Place, 10180 - 101 St., Edmonton, AB T5J 3S4
780-342-2000, Fax: 780-342-2060, 888-342-2471
Alberta Health & Wellness, Telus Plaza NT, 10025 Jasper Ave., 22nd Fl., PO Box 1360 Main,Edmonton, T5J 2N3 AB
780-427-7164, health.ahinform@gov.ab.ca
Health Disciplines Board, Telus Plaza NT, Health Professions Branch, 10025 Jasper Ave., 17th Fl., Edmonton, AB T5J 2N3
780-415-0486, Fax: 780-422-2880
Health Facilities Review Committee, First Edmonton Place, #590, 10665 Jasper Ave., Edmonton, AB T5J 3S9
780-427-2791, Fax: 780-427-0806
Occupational Health & Safety Council, Labour Bldg, 10808 - 99 Ave., 9th Fl., Edmonton, AB T5K 0G5
780-415-0599, Fax: 780-422-8944

Premier's Council on the Status of Persons with Disabilities, HSBC Bldg., #1110, 10055 - 106 St., Edmonton, AB T5J 2Y2
780-422-1095, 800-272-8841, pcspd@gov.ab.ca
Alberta Seniors & Community Supports, Standard Life Centre, 10405 Jasper Ave., Main Fl., Edmonton, T5J 4R7 AB
780-427-7876, Fax: 780-422-6301, 800-642-3853
Seniors Advisory Council for Alberta, Standard Life Centre, #600, 10405 Jasper Ave., Edmonton, AB T5J 4R7
780-422-2321, Fax: 780-422-8762

British Columbia
Ministry of Health Services, 1515 Blanshard St., Victoria, V8W 3C8 BC
250-952-1742, Fax: 250-356-9587, 800-465-4911, hlth.health@gems1.gov.bc.ca

Manitoba
Addictions Foundation of Manitoba, 1031 Portage Ave., Winnipeg, MB R3G 0R8
204-944-6200, Fax: 204-786-7768, library@afm.mb.ca
Manitoba Health & Healthy Living, #100, 300 Carlton St., Winnipeg, R3B 3M9 MB
204-786-7191, minhlt@leg.gov.mb.ca
Manitoba Council on Aging, #822, 155 Carlton St., Winnipeg, MB R3C 3H8
204-945-6565, Fax: 204-948-2514, 800-665-6565
Manitoba Drug Standards & Therapeutics Committee, #1014, 300 Carlton St., Winnipeg, MB R3B 3M9
204-786-7317, Fax: 204-942-2030
Office of the Chief Medical Examiner, #210, 1 Wesley Ave., Winnipeg, MB R3C 4C6
204-945-2088, Fax: 204-945-2442, 800-282-9069
Primary Care & Healthy Living, 300 Carlton St., 2nd Floor, Winnipeg, R3B 3M9 MB

New Brunswick
Premier's Council on the Status of Disabled Persons, Kings Place, #648, 440 King St., Fredericton, E3B 5H8 NB
506-444-3000, Fax: 506-444-3001, 800-442-4412, pcsdp@gnb.ca
Department of Health, PO Box 5100, Fredericton, E3B 5G8 NB
506-457-4800, Fax: 506-453-5243, dh-ms@dh-ms.ca
Workplace Health, Safety & Compensation Commission of New Brunswick, 1 Portland St., PO Box 160, Saint John, E2L 3X9 NB
506-632-2200, 800-222-9775, communications@ws-ts.nb.ca

Newfoundland & Labrador
Department of Health & Community Services, West Block, Confederation Bldg., PO Box 8700, St. John's, A1B 4J6 NL
709-729-5021, Fax: 709-729-5824
Newfoundland & Labrador Health Boards Associations, Board of Trade Bldg., #202, 66 Kenmount Rd., St. John's, NL A1B 3V7
709-364-7701, Fax: 709-364-6460, nlhba@nlhba.nf.ca

Northwest Territories
Department of Health & Social Services, Centre Square Tower, PO Box 1320, Yellowknife, X1A 2L9 NT
Fax: 867-873-0266

Nova Scotia
Department of Health, Joseph Howe Bldg., 1690 Hollis St., 4th Fl., PO Box 488, Halifax, B3J 2R8 NS
902-424-5818, Fax: 902-424-0730, 800-387-6665, DoHweb@gov.ns.ca
Nova Scotia Advisory Commission on AIDS, Dennis Bldg., 1740 Granville St., 6th Fl., Halifax, NS B3J 1X5
902-424-5730, Fax: 902-424-4727
Nova Scotia Medical Examiner Service, Halifax Insurance Bldg., #701, 5670 Spring Garden Rd., Halifax, NS B3J 1H7
902-424-2722, Fax: 902-424-0607, 888-424-4336
Occupational Health & Safety Advisory Council, PO Box 697, Halifax, NS B3J 2T8
902-424-2484, Fax: 902-424-5640,
Occupational Health & Safety Appeal Panel, 5151 Terminal Rd., 7th Fl., PO Box 697, Halifax, NS B3J 2T8
902-424-6730

Nunavut
Department of Culture, Language, Elders & Youth, PO Box 1000 800,Iqaluit, X0A 0H0 NU
867-975-5500, Fax: 867-975-5504, 866-934-2035
Department of Health & Social Services, Sivummut bldg., PO Box 1007 1000,Iqaluit, X0A 0H0 NU
867-975-5700, Fax: 867-975-5705, health@gov.nu.ca
Office of the Chief Coroner, PO Box 1000 590, Iqaluit, NU X0A 0H0

Ontario
Cancer Care Ontario, 620 University Ave., 15th Fl., Toronto, ON M5G 2L7
416-971-9800, Fax: 416-971-6888
Consent & Capacity Board, 151 Bloor St. West, 10th Fl., Toronto, ON M5S 2T5
416-327-4142, Fax: 416-327-4207
Healing Arts Radiation Protection Commission, 5700 Yonge St., 3rd Fl., Toronto, ON M2M 4K5
416-327-7952, Fax: 416-327-8805
Ministry of Health & Long-Term Care, Hepburn Block, 80 Grosvenor St., 10th Fl, Toronto, M7A 2C4 ON
416-327-4327, 800-268-1153
Health Boards Secretariat, 151 Bloor St. West, 9th Fl., Toronto, ON M5S 2T5
416-327-8512, Fax: 416-327-8524
Ministry of Health Promotion, 777 Bay Street, 18th Fl., Toronto, M7A 1S5 ON
416-326-8475, Fax: 416-326-4864, info@mhp.gov.on.ca
Medical Eligibility Committee, 370 Select Dr., PO Box 168, Kingston, ON K7M 8T4
613-548-6405
Ontario Mental Health Foundation, #508, 489 College St., Toronto, ON M6G 1A5
416-920-7721, Fax: 416-920-0026, grants@omhf.on.ca
Ontario Review Board, 151 Bloor St. West, 10th Fl., Toronto, ON M5S 2T5
416-327-8866, Fax: 416-327-8867
Pesticides Advisory Committee, #1203, 2300 Yonge St., 12th Fl., Toronto, ON M4P 1E4
416-314-9230, Fax: 416-314-9237
Smart Systems for Health, #1900, 415 Yonge St., Toronto, ON M5B 2E7
416-586-6500, Fax: 416-586-4363
Trillium Gift of Life Network, #1440, 155 University Ave., Toronto, ON M5H 3B7
416-363-4001, Fax: 416-363-4002

Prince Edward Island
Food Technology Centre, 101 Belvedere Ave., PO Box 2000, Charlottetown, PE C1A 7N8
902-368-5548, Fax: 902-368-5549, 877-368-5548, ftcweb@gov.pe.ca
Department of Health, Jones Bldg., 11 Kent St., 2nd Fl., PO Box 2000, Charlottetown, C1A 7N8 PE
902-368-4900, Fax: 902-368-4974

Quebec
Agence d'évaluation des technologies et des modes d'intervention en santé, #10.083, 2021, av Union, Montréal, QC H3A 2S9
514-873-2563, Fax: 514-873-1369
Bureau des projets Centres hospitaliers universitaires de Montréal, CHUM, CUSM et CHU Sainte-Justine, #10.049, 2021, rue Union, Montréal, QC H3A 2S9
514-864-9883, Fax: 514-873-7362
Bureau du coroner, #390, 2875, boul Laurier, Sainte-Foy, QC G1V 5B1
418-643-1845, Fax: 418-643-6174, clientele.coroner@msp.gouv.qc.ca
Commissaire à la santé et du bien-être, #700, 1020, rte de l'Église, Québec, QC G1V 3V9
418-643-3040, Fax: 418-644-0654, csbe@csbe.gouv.qc.ca
Commission de la santé et de la sécurité du travail, 425, rue du Pont, CP 4900 Terminus, Québec, QC G1K 7S6
418-266-4000, Fax: 418-266-4015, 800-668-6811
Conseil des aînés, #810, 900, boul René-Lévesque est, 8e étage, Québec, QC G1R 2B5
418-643-0071, Fax: 418-643-1916, 877-657-2463, aines@conseil-des-aines.qc.ca
Conseil du médicament, #100, 1195, av Lavigerie, Sainte-Foy, QC G1V 4N3
418-644-8103, Fax: 418-644-8120, cdm@cdm.gouv.qc.ca
Corporation d'hébergement du Québec, 2535, boul Laurier, 5e étage, Québec, QC G1V 4M3
418-644-3600, Fax: 418-644-3609, danielle.dussault@chq.gouv.qc.ca
Fonds de la recherche en santé du Québec, #800, 500, rue Sherbrooke ouest, Montréal, QC H3A 3C6
514-873-2114, Fax: 514-873-8768
Institut national de santé publique du Québec, 945, av Wolfe, Québec, QC G1V 5B3
418-650-5115, Fax: 418-646-9328, info@inspq.qc.ca
Régie de l'assurance maladie du Québec, 1125, Grande Allée ouest, Québec, QC G1S 1E7
418-646-4636
Commission de la santé et de la sécurité du travail du Québec, 524, rue Bourdages, CP 1200 Terminus postal,Québec, G1K 7E2 QC
418-266-4850, Fax: 418-266-4398, 866-302-2778
Ministère de la Santé et des Services sociaux, Direction des communications et Renseignements généraux, 1075, ch Sainte-Foy, Québec, G1S 2M1 QC
418-266-8900, 800-707-3380, regisseur.web@msss.gouv.qc.ca
Secrétariat à l'accès aux services en langue anglaise et aux communautés ethnoculturelles, #840, 2021, av Union, Montréal, QC H3A 2S9
514-873-5130, Fax: 514-873-9876
Urgences-santé Québec, 3232, rue Bélanger, Montréal, QC H1Y 3H5
514-723-5600, info@urgences-sante.qc.ca

Saskatchewan
Health Quality Council, 241, 111 Research Dr., Saskatoon, SK S7N 3R2
306-668-8810, Fax: 306-668-8820
Saskatchewan Health, T.C. Douglas Bldg., 3475 Albert St., Regina, S4S 6X6 SK
306-787-0146, 800-667-7766, info@health.gov.sk.ca

Yukon Territory
Yukon Health & Social Services, PO Box 2703, Whitehorse, Y1A 2C6 YT
867-667-3673, Fax: 867-667-3096, 800-661-0408, hss@gov.yk.ca

HEALTH & SAFETY

Canadian Centre for Occupational Health & Safety, 135 Hunter St. East, Hamilton, L8N 1M5 ON
905-572-2981, Fax: 905-572-2206, 800-668-4284, clientservices@ccohs.ca
Canadian Coast Guard, Centennial Towers, #6S018, 200 Kent St., Ottawa, K1A 0E6 ON
613-998-1573, Fax: 613-990-2780
Canadian Environmental Assessment Agency, Place Bell Canada, 160 Elgin St., 22nd Fl., Ottawa, K1A 0H3 ON
613-957-0700, Fax: 613-957-0862, 866-582-1884, info@ceaa-acee.gc.ca
Canadian Food Inspection Agency, 1400 Merivale Rd., Ottawa, K1A 0Y9 ON
613-225-2342, Fax: 613-228-6629, 800-442-2342
Canadian Food Inspection Agency, 1400 Merivale Rd., Ottawa, ON K1A 0Y9
613-225-2342, Fax: 613-228-6601, 800-442-2342
Hazardous Materials Information Review Commission, 427 Laurier Ave. West, 7th Fl., Ottawa, ON K1A 1M3
613-993-4331, Fax: 613-993-4686, hmirc-ccrmd@hc-sc.gc.ca
Health Canada, Tunney's Pasture, Ottawa, K1A 0K9 ON
613-957-2991, Fax: 613-941-5366, Info@hc-sc.gc.ca
Human Resources & Skills Development Canada, 140 Promenade du Portage, Ottawa, K1A 0J9 ON
Department of Labour & Workforce Development, 5151 Terminal Rd., 6th Fl., PO Box 697, Halifax, B3J 2T8 NS
902-424-5301, Fax: 902-424-0575
National Defence Canada, Major-General George R. Pearkes Bldg., 101 Colonel By Dr., Ottawa, K1A 0K2 ON
613-995-2534, Fax: 613-992-4739, 800-856-8488
Policy & Corporate Services Division, Twin Atria Building, 4999 - 98 Ave., 3rd Fl., Edmonton, T6B 2X3 AB
Public Safety Canada, 269 Laurier Ave. West, Ottawa, K1A 0P8 ON
613-944-4875, Fax: 613-954-5186, 866-222-3006, communications@ps.gc.ca
Transportation Safety Board of Canada, 200 Promenade du Portage, 4th Fl., Ottawa, K1A 1K8 ON
819-994-3741, Fax: 819-997-2239, 800-387-3557

Alberta
Alberta Employment & Immigration, Minister's Office, Legislature Bldg., #208, 10800 - 97 Ave., Edmonton, T5K 2B6 AB
780-644-5135, Fax: 780-422-9556, 866-644-5135, eii.communications@gov.ab.ca
Alberta Health & Wellness, Telus Plaza NT, 10025 Jasper Ave., 22nd Fl., PO Box 1360 Main,Edmonton, T5J 2N3 AB
780-427-7164, health.ahinform@gov.ab.ca
Alberta Workers' Compensation Board, 9912 - 107 St., PO Box 2415, Edmonton, AB T5J 2S5
780-498-3999, 866-922-9221
Occupational Health & Safety Council, Labour Bldg, 10808 - 99 Ave., 9th Fl., Edmonton, AB T5K 0G5
780-415-0599, Fax: 780-422-8944
Transportation Safety Board, Twin Atria Bldg., 4999 - 98 Ave., Main Fl., Edmonton, AB T6B 2X3
780-427-7178, Fax: 780-422-9739

British Columbia
Ministry of Health Services, 1515 Blanshard St., Victoria, V8W 3C8 BC
250-952-1742, Fax: 250-356-9587, 800-465-4911, hlth.health@gems1.gov.bc.ca
Ministry of Labour, PO Box 9052 Prov Govt,Victoria, V8W 9E2 BC
250-356-6348, Fax: 250-356-6595, LCS.Minister@gov.bc.ca

British Columbia Provincial Emergency Program, PO Box 9201 Prov Govt,Victoria, V8W 9J1 BC
250-952-4913, Fax: 250-952-4888, 888-257-4777

Workers' Compensation Board of British Columbia, PO Box 5350 Terminal,Vancouver, V6B 5L5 BC
604-276-3100, Fax: 604-244-6490, 888-621-7233

Manitoba

Advisory Council on Workplace Safety & Health, #200, 401 York Ave., Winnipeg, MB R3C 0P8
204-945-3446, Fax: 204-945-4556

Emergency Measures Organization, 405 Broadway Ave., 15th Floor, Winnipeg, R3C 3L6 MB
204-945-4772, Fax: 204-945-4929, 888-267-8298, emo@gov.mb.ca

Manitoba Health & Healthy Living, #100, 300 Carlton St., Winnipeg, R3B 3M9 MB
204-786-7191, minhlt@leg.gov.mb.ca

Manitoba Labour & Immigration, Legislative Building, 317, 450 Broadway Ave., Winnipeg, R3C 0V8 MB
204-945-4079, Fax: 204-945-8312, minlab@leg.gov.mb.ca

Workplace Safety & Health Division, #200, 401 York Ave., Winnipeg, R3C 0P8 MB
204-945-3446, Fax: 204-948-2209, wshcompl@gov.mb.ca

New Brunswick

Department of Health, PO Box 5100, Fredericton, E3B 5G8 NB
506-457-4800, Fax: 506-453-5243, dh-ms@dh-ms.ca

Department of Post-Secondary Education, Training & Labour, 470 York St., PO Box 6000, Fredericton, E3B 5H1 NB
506-453-2597, Fax: 506-453-3618, dpetlinfo@gnb.ca

Workplace Health, Safety & Compensation Commission of New Brunswick, 1 Portland St., PO Box 160, Saint John, E2L 3X9 NB
506-632-2200, 800-222-9775, communications@ws-ts.nb.ca

Newfoundland & Labrador

Newfoundland & Labrador Emergency Measures Organization, PO Box 8700, St. John's, A1B 4J6 NL
709-729-3703, Fax: 709-729-3857

Department of Environment & Conservation, Confederation Bldg., West Block, 4th Fl., PO Box 8700, St. John's, A1B 4J6 NL
709-729-2664, Fax: 709-729-6639, 800-563-6181, info@gov.nl.ca

Department of Health & Community Services, West Block, Confederation Bldg., PO Box 8700, St. John's, A1B 4J6 NL
709-729-5021, Fax: 709-729-5824

Newfoundland & Labrador Workplace Health, Safety & Compensation Commission, 146 - 148 Forest Rd., PO Box 9000, St. John's, A1A 3B8 NL
709-778-1000, Fax: 709-738-1714, 800-563-9000, general.inquiries@whscc.nl.ca

Northwest Territories

Department of Health & Social Services, Centre Square Tower, PO Box 1320, Yellowknife, X1A 2L9 NT
Fax: 867-873-0266

Northwest Territories & Nunavut Workers' Compensation Board, Centre Square Tower, 5022 - 49th St., 5th Fl., PO Box 8888, Yellowknife, X1A 2R3 NT
867-920-3888, Fax: 867-873-4596, 800-661-0792, wcb@wcb.nt.ca

Nova Scotia

Nova Scotia Emergency Management Office, PO Box 2581, Halifax, B3J 3N5 NS
902-424-5620, Fax: 902-424-5376, 866-424-5620, emo@gov.ns.ca

Department of Health, Joseph Howe Bldg., 1690 Hollis St., 4th Fl., PO Box 488, Halifax, B3J 2R8 NS
902-424-5818, Fax: 902-424-0730, 800-387-6665, DoHweb@gov.ns.ca

Occupational Health & Safety Advisory Council, PO Box 697, Halifax, NS B3J 2T8
902-424-2484, Fax: 902-424-5640

Occupational Health & Safety Appeal Panel, 5151 Terminal Rd., 7th Fl., PO Box 697, Halifax, NS B3J 2T8
902-424-6730

Ontario

Ministry of Government Services, Whitney Block, #4320, 99 Wellesley St. West, 4th Fl., Toronto, M7A 1W3 ON
416-326-1234, Fax: 416-327-3790, 800-268-1142

Ministry of Health & Long-Term Care, Hepburn Block, 80 Grosvenor St., 10th Fl, Toronto, M7A 2C4 ON
416-327-4327, 800-268-1153

Ministry of Labour, 400 University Ave., 14th Fl., Toronto, M7A 1T7 ON
416-326-7770, 800-268-8013

Road User Safety Division, #191, Bldg A, 1201 Wilson Ave., Toronto, M3M 1J8 ON
416-235-2999, Fax: 416-235-4153

Prince Edward Island

Prince Edward Island Emergency Measures Organization, National Bank Tower, #600, 134 Kent St., PO Box 2000, Charlottetown, C1A 7N8 PE
902-894-0385, Fax: 902-368-6362

Department of Health, Jones Bldg., 11 Kent St., 2nd Fl., PO Box 2000, Charlottetown, C1A 7N8 PE
902-368-4900, Fax: 902-368-4974

Prince Edward Island Workers Compensation Board, 14 Weymouth St., PO Box 757, Charlottetown, C1A 7L7 PE
902-368-5680, Fax: 902-368-5705, 800-237-5049

Quebec

Commission de la santé et de la sécurité du travail du Québec, 524, rue Bourdages, CP 1200 Terminus postal,Québec, G1K 7E2 QC
418-266-4850, Fax: 418-266-4398, 866-302-2778

Ministère de la Santé et des Services sociaux, Direction des communications et Renseignements généraux, 1075, ch Sainte-Foy, Québec, G1S 2M1 QC
418-266-8900, 800-707-3380, regisseur.web@msss.gouv.qc.ca

Ministère de la Sécurité publique, Tour des Laurentides, 2525, boul Laurier, 5e étage, Québec, G1V 2L2 QC
418-643-2112, Fax: 418-646-6168, 866-644-6826

Ministère du Travail, 200, ch Sainte-Foy, 6e étage, Québec, G1R 5S1 QC
418-643-4817, Fax: 418-528-0559, 800-643-4817, service_clientele@travail.gouv.qc.ca

Saskatchewan

Saskatchewan Advanced Education, Employment & Labour, 1945 Hamilton St., Regina, S4P 2C8 SK
306-787-9478, Fax: 306-787-2315

Saskatchewan Health, T.C. Douglas Bldg., 3475 Albert St., Regina, S4S 6X6 SK
306-787-0146, 800-667-7766, info@health.gov.sk.ca

Yukon Territory

Emergency Measures Organization, PO Box 2703, Whitehorse, Y1A 2C6 YT
867-667-5220, Fax: 867-393-6266, 800-661-0408, emo.yukon@gov.yk.ca

Yukon Health & Social Services, PO Box 2703, Whitehorse, Y1A 2C6 YT
867-667-3673, Fax: 867-667-3096, 800-661-0408, hss@gov.yk.ca

Yukon Workers' Compensation Health & Safety Board, 401 Strickland St., Whitehorse, Y1A 5N8 YT
867-667-5645, Fax: 867-393-6279, 800-661-0443, worksafe@gov.yk.ca

HEALTH CARE INSURANCE

Health Canada, Tunney's Pasture, Ottawa, K1A 0K9 ON
613-957-2991, Fax: 613-941-5366, Info@hc-sc.gc.ca

Health Workforce Division, Telus Plaza NT, 10025 Jasper Ave., 10th Fl., Edmonton, T5J 1S6 AB

British Columbia

Medical Services Commission, 1515 Blanshard St., 3rd Fl., Victoria, BC V8W 3C8
250-952-3073, Fax: 250-952-3131

Newfoundland & Labrador

Department of Health & Community Services, West Block, Confederation Bldg., PO Box 8700, St. John's, A1B 4J6 NL
709-729-5021, Fax: 709-729-5824,

Northwest Territories

Department of Health & Social Services, Centre Square Tower, PO Box 1320, Yellowknife, X1A 2L9 NT
Fax: 867-873-0266

Nunavut

Department of Health & Social Services, Sivummut bldg., PO Box 1007 1000,Iqaluit, X0A 0H0 NU
867-975-5700, Fax: 867-975-5705, health@gov.nu.ca

Prince Edward Island

Department of Health, Jones Bldg., 11 Kent St., 2nd Fl., PO Box 2000, Charlottetown, C1A 7N8 PE
902-368-4900, Fax: 902-368-4974

Quebec

Régie de l'assurance maladie du Québec, 1125, Grande Allée ouest, Québec, QC G1S 1E7
418-646-4636

HEALTH SERVICES

See Also: Health Care Insurance; Occupational Safety

Canadian Centre for Occupational Health & Safety, 135 Hunter St. East, Hamilton, L8N 1M5 ON
905-572-2981, Fax: 905-572-2206, 800-668-4284, clientservices@ccohs.ca

Canadian Institutes of Health Research, 160 Elgin St., 9th Fl., Ottawa, K1A 0W9 ON
613-941-2672, Fax: 613-954-1800, 888-603-4178, info@cihr-irsc.gc.ca

Health Canada, Tunney's Pasture, Ottawa, K1A 0K9 ON
613-957-2991, Fax: 613-941-5366, Info@hc-sc.gc.ca

Alberta

Alberta Health & Wellness, Telus Plaza NT, 10025 Jasper Ave., 22nd Fl., PO Box 1360 Main,Edmonton, T5J 2N3 AB
780-427-7164, health.ahinform@gov.ab.ca

British Columbia

Ministry of Health Services, 1515 Blanshard St., Victoria, V8W 3C8 BC
250-952-1742, Fax: 250-356-9587, 800-465-4911, hlth.health@gems1.gov.bc.ca

Medical Services Commission, 1515 Blanshard St., 3rd Fl., Victoria, BC V8W 3C8
250-952-3073, Fax: 250-952-3131

Manitoba

Manitoba Health & Healthy Living, #100, 300 Carlton St., Winnipeg, R3B 3M9 MB
204-786-7191, minhlt@leg.gov.mb.ca

Manitoba Healthy Child Office, #219, 114 Garry St., Winnipeg, R3C 1G1 MB
204-945-2266, 888-848-0140, healthychild@gov.mb.ca

Manitoba Health Appeal Board, #4011, 300 Carlton St., Winnipeg, MB R3B 3M9
204-788-6704, Fax: 204-948-2024, 866-744-3257

New Brunswick

Department of Health, PO Box 5100, Fredericton, E3B 5G8 NB
506-457-4800, Fax: 506-453-5243, dh-ms@dh-ms.ca

Newfoundland & Labrador

Department of Health & Community Services, West Block, Confederation Bldg., PO Box 8700, St. John's, A1B 4J6 NL
709-729-5021, Fax: 709-729-5824

Northwest Territories

Department of Health & Social Services, Centre Square Tower, PO Box 1320, Yellowknife, X1A 2L9 NT
Fax: 867-873-0266

Nova Scotia

Department of Health Promotion & Protection, Summit Place, 1601 Lower Water St., 5th Fl., PO Box 487, Halifax, B3J 2R7 NS
902-424-4807, Fax: 902-424-4716, 866-231-3882, healthpromotion@gov.ns.ca

Department of Health, Joseph Howe Bldg., 1690 Hollis St., 4th Fl., PO Box 488, Halifax, B3J 2R8 NS
902-424-5818, Fax: 902-424-0730, 800-387-6665, DoHweb@gov.ns.ca

Nunavut

Department of Health & Social Services, Sivummut bldg., PO Box 1007 1000,Iqaluit, X0A 0H0 NU
867-975-5700, Fax: 867-975-5705, health@gov.nu.ca

Ontario

Ministry of Health Promotion, 777 Bay Street, 18th Fl., Toronto, M7A 1S5 ON
416-326-8475, Fax: 416-326-4864, info@mhp.gov.on.ca

Prince Edward Island

Department of Health, Jones Bldg., 11 Kent St., 2nd Fl., PO Box 2000, Charlottetown, C1A 7N8 PE
902-368-4900, Fax: 902-368-4974

Quebec

Institut national de santé publique du Québec, 945, av Wolfe, Québec, QC G1V 5B3
418-650-5115, Fax: 418-646-9328, info@inspq.qc.ca

Ministère de la Santé et des Services sociaux, Direction des communications et Renseignements généraux, 1075, ch Sainte-Foy, Québec, G1S 2M1 QC
418-266-8900, 800-707-3380, regisseur.web@msss.gouv.qc.ca

Saskatchewan

Saskatchewan Health, T.C. Douglas Bldg., 3475 Albert St., Regina, S4S 6X6 SK
306-787-0146, 800-667-7766, info@health.gov.sk.ca

HERITAGE RESOURCES

See Also: Land Resources; Parks

Canadian Heritage, 15 Eddy St., Gatineau, K1A 0M5 QC
819-997-0055, 866-811-0055, info@pch.gc.ca

Parks Canada, 25 Eddy St., Gatineau, K1A 0M5 QC
613-860-1251, 888-773-8888, information@pc.gc.ca

Alberta
Alberta Historical Resources Foundation, Old St. Stephen's College, 8820 - 112 St., Edmonton, AB T6G 2P8
780-431-2300

Manitoba
Manitoba Culture, Heritage, Tourism & Sport, Legislative Building, #118, 450 Broadway Ave., Winnipeg, R3C 0V8 MB
204-945-3729, Fax: 204-945-5223, mincht@leg.gov.mb.ca
Heritage Grants Advisory Council, 213 Notre Dame Ave., 3rd Fl., Winnipeg, MB R3B 1N3
204-945-2213, Fax: 204-948-2086
Manitoba Heritage Council, 213 Notre Dame Ave., Main Fl., Winnipeg, MB R3B 1N3
204-945-2118, Fax: 204-948-2384, hrb@gov.mb.ca

Nova Scotia
Heritage Division, 1747 Summer St., Halifax, B3H 3A6 NS
902-424-7344, Fax: 902-424-0560, 800-632-1114, heritage@gov.ns.ca

Nunavut
Department of Culture, Language, Elders & Youth, PO Box 1000 800,Iqaluit, X0A 0H0 NU
867-975-5500, Fax: 867-975-5504, 866-934-2035

Ontario
Conservation Review Board, 400 University Ave. 4th Fl., Toronto, ON M7A 2R9
416-314-7137, Fax: 416-314-7175
Ontario Heritage Trust, 10 Adelaide St. East, Toronto, ON M5C 1J3
416-325-5000, Fax: 416-325-5071, marketing@heritagefdn.on.ca

Quebec
Commission des biens culturels du Québec, Bloc A-RC, 225, Grande Allée est, Québec, G1R 5G5 QC
418-643-8378, Fax: 418-643-8591, info@cbcq.gouv.qc.ca

Saskatchewan
Saskatchewan Archives Board, University of Regina, 3303 Hillsdale St., Regina, S4S 0A2 SK
306-787-4068, Fax: 306-787-1197, info.regina@archives.gov.sk.ca
Sask Heritage Foundation, 1919 Saskatchewan Dr., 9th Fl., Regina, SK S4P 3V7
306-787-4188, Fax: 306-787-0069
Saskatchewan Tourism, Parks, Culture, & Sport, 1919 Saskatchewan Dr., 4th Fl., Regina, S4P 4H2 SK
306-787-5729, Fax: 306-787-8560

Yukon Territory
Yukon Tourism & Culture, PO Box 2703, Whitehorse, Y1A 2C6 YT
867-667-5036, Fax: 867-667-3546

HISTORY & ARCHIVES

Canada Council for the Arts, 350 Albert St., PO Box 1047, Ottawa, K1P 5V8 ON
613-566-4414, Fax: 613-566-4390, 800-263-5588, info@canadacouncil.ca
Library & Archives Canada, 395 Wellington St., Ottawa, K1A 0N4 ON
613-996-5115, Fax: 613-995-6274, 866-578-7777, reference@lac-bac.ca
Library of Parliament, Parliamentary Bldgs., 111 Wellington St., Ottawa, K1A 0A9 ON
613-992-4793, Fax: 613-943-6383, 866-599-4999

Alberta
Culture & Community Development Division, Standard Life Centre, 10405 Jasper Ave., 9th Fl., Edmonton, T5J 4R7 AB
780-415-1167, Fax: 780-422-2891

Nova Scotia
Culture Division, #601, 1800 Argyle St., PO Box 456, Halifax, B3J 2R5 NS
Fax: 902-424-0710

Ontario
Archives of Ontario, 77 Grenville St., 3rd Fl., Toronto, M5S 1B3 ON
416-327-1600, Fax: 416-327-1999, 800-668-9933

Prince Edward Island
PEI Public Archives & Records Office, PO Box 1000, Charlottetown, C1A 7M4 PE
902-368-4290, Fax: 902-368-6327, archives@gov.pe.ca

Quebec
Bibliothèque et Archives nationales du Québec (BAnQ), 475, boul De Maisonneuve est, Montréal, H2L 5C4 QC
514-873-1100, Fax: 514-873-9312, 800-363-9028

Saskatchewan
Saskatchewan Archives Board, University of Regina, 3303 Hillsdale St., Regina, S4S 0A2 SK
306-787-4068, Fax: 306-787-1197, info.regina@archives.gov.sk.ca

HOSPITALS

See Also: Health Care Insurance

Alberta
Alberta Health & Wellness, Telus Plaza NT, 10025 Jasper Ave., 22nd Fl., PO Box 1360 Main,Edmonton, T5J 2N3 AB
780-427-7164, health.ahinform@gov.ab.ca

British Columbia
Ministry of Health Services, 1515 Blanshard St., Victoria, V8W 3C8 BC
250-952-1742, Fax: 250-356-9587, 800-465-4911, hlth.health@gems1.gov.bc.ca
Hospital Appeal Board, 747 Fort St., 4th Fl., PO Box 9425 Prov Govt, Victoria, BC V8W 9V1
250-387-3464, Fax: 250-356-9923, 800-663-7867, hab@gov.bc.ca

Northwest Territories
Department of Health & Social Services, Centre Square Tower, PO Box 1320, Yellowknife, X1A 2L9 NT
Fax: 867-873-0266

Nunavut
Department of Health & Social Services, Sivummut bldg., PO Box 1007 1000,Iqaluit, X0A 0H0 NU
867-975-5700, Fax: 867-975-5705, health@gov.nu.ca

Prince Edward Island
Department of Health, Jones Bldg., 11 Kent St., 2nd Fl., PO Box 2000, Charlottetown, C1A 7N8 PE
902-368-4900, Fax: 902-368-4974

Quebec
Ministère de la Santé et des Services sociaux, Direction des communications et Renseignements généraux, 1075, ch Sainte-Foy, Québec, G1S 2M1 QC
418-266-8900, 800-707-3380, regisseur.web@msss.gouv.qc.ca

HOUSING

Canada Mortgage & Housing Corporation, 700 Montreal Rd., Ottawa, K1A 0P7 ON
613-748-2000, Fax: 613-748-2098, 800-668-2642, chic@cmhc-schl.gc.ca

British Columbia
Local Government Department, 800 Johnson St., 6th Fl., PO Box 9490 Prov Govt,Victoria, V8W 9N7 BC
lgd_feedback@gov.bc.ca

Manitoba
Employment, Income & Housing Division, #201, 280 Broadway Ave., Winnipeg, R3C 0R8 MB
Manitoba Housing Authority - Public Housing, #2100, 185 Smith St., Winnipeg, MB R3C 3G4
204-945-4663, Fax: 204-948-2013, 800-661-4663

New Brunswick
Department of Local Government, Marysville Place, 20 McGloin St., PO Box 6000, Fredericton, E3B 5H1 NB
506-453-2807, Fax: 506-453-3988
Department of Social Development, Sartain MacDonald Bldg., 551 King St., PO Box 6000, Fredericton, E3B 5H1 NB
506-453-2001, Fax: 506-453-7478

Newfoundland & Labrador
Newfoundland & Labrador Housing Corporation, Sir Brian Dunfield Bldg., 2 Canada Dr., PO Box 220, St. John's, A1C 5J2 NL
709-724-3000, Fax: 709-724-3250, jmbowering@nsmail.nlhc.nl.ca

Northwest Territories
Northwest Territories Housing Corporation, Scotia Centre, 5102 50th Ave., PO Box 2100, Yellowknife, X1A 2P6 NT
867-873-7853, Fax: 867-873-9426

Nova Scotia
Department of Service Nova Scotia & Municipal Relations, 1505 Barrington St., PO Box 216, Halifax, B3J 2M4 NS
902-424-4141, Fax: 902-424-0581, public-enquiries@gov.ns.ca

Nunavut
Department of Community & Government Services, J.G. Brown Bldg., PO Box 1000 700,Iqaluit, X0A 0H0 NU
867-975-5400, Fax: 867-975-5305,
Nunavut Housing Corporation, PO Box 1000, Arviat, X0C 0E0 NU
867-857-3000, Fax: 867-857-3040

Quebec
Société d'habitation du Québec, Aile St-Amable, 1054, rue Louis-Alexandre-Taschereau, 3e étage, Québec, QC G1R 5E7
418-643-4035, Fax: 418-643-4560, 800-463-4315

Yukon Territory
Yukon Housing Corporation, 410H Jarvis St., Whitehorse, Y1A 2H5 YT
867-667-5759, Fax: 867-667-3664, 800-661-0408, ykhouse@housing.yk.ca

HUMAN RIGHTS

See Also: Boards of Review
Canadian Human Rights Commission, 344 Slater St., 8th Fl., Ottawa, K1A 1E1 ON
613-995-1151, Fax: 613-996-9661, 888-214-1090, info.com@chrc-ccdp.ca
Canadian Human Rights Tribunal, 160 Elgin St., 11th Fl., Ottawa, K1A 1J4 ON
613-995-1707, Fax: 613-995-3484, registrar@chrt-tcdp.gc.ca

British Columbia
British Columbia Human Rights Tribunal, #1170, 605 Robson St., Vancouver, BC V6B 5J3
604-775-2000, Fax: 604-775-2020, 888-440-8844, BCHumanRightsTribunal@gov.bc.ca

Manitoba
Manitoba Human Rights Commission, 175 Hargrave St., 7th Fl., Winnipeg, R3C 3R8 MB
204-945-3007, Fax: 204-945-1292, 888-884-8681, hrc@gov.mb.ca

New Brunswick
New Brunswick Human Rights Commission, PO Box 6000, Fredericton, E3B 5H1 NB
506-453-2301, Fax: 506-453-2653, 888-471-2233, hrc.cdp@gnb.ca

Newfoundland & Labrador
Newfoundland & Labrador Human Rights Commission, PO Box 8700, St. John's, A1B 4J6 NL
709-729-2709, Fax: 709-729-0790, 800-563-5808, humanrights@mail.gov.nl.ca

Nova Scotia
Nova Scotia Human Rights Commission, Joseph Howe Bldg., 1690 Hollis St., 6th Fl., Halifax, B3J 3C4 NS
902-424-4111, Fax: 902-424-0596

Ontario
Ontario Human Rights Commission, 180 Dundas St. West, 7th Fl., Toronto, M7A 2R9 ON
416-314-4500, Fax: 416-326-9520, 800-387-9080, info@ohrc.on.ca

Prince Edward Island
Prince Edward Island Human Rights Commission, 53 Water St., PO Box 2000, Charlottetown, C1A 7N8 PE
902-368-4180, Fax: 902-368-4236, 800-237-5031, lbuell@peihumanrights.ca

Quebec
Commission des droits de la personne et des droits de la jeunesse, 360, rue St-Jacques, 2e étage, Montréal, H2Y 1P5 QC
514-873-5146, Fax: 514-873-6032, 800-361-6477, webmestre@cdpdj.qc.ca

Saskatchewan
Saskatchewan Human Rights Commission, Saskatoon Office, Sturdy Stone Bdg., #816, 122 - 3 Ave. North, 8th Fl., Saskatoon, S7K 2H6 SK
306-933-5952, Fax: 306-933-7863, 800-667-9249, shrc@shrc.gov.sk.ca

Yukon Territory
Yukon Human Rights Commission, #201, 211 Hawkins St., Whitehorse, YT Y1A 1X3
867-667-6226, Fax: 867-667-2662, 800-661-0535, humanrights@yhrc.yk.ca
Yukon Human Rights Panel of Adjudication, #202, 407 Black St., Whitehorse, YT Y1A 2N2
867-667-5412, Fax: 867-633-6952

HYDRO, ELECTRIC POWER

National Energy Board, 444 - 7 Ave. SW, Calgary, T2P 0X8 AB
403-292-4800, Fax: 403-292-5503, 800-899-1265, info@neb-one.gc.ca

Alberta
Energy Resources Conservation Board, #1000, 250 - 5 Ave. SW, Calgary, AB T2P 0R4
403-297-8311, Fax: 403-297-7336, inquiries@ercb.ca
Alberta Utilities Consumer Advocate, TD Tower, 10088 - 102 Ave., Edmonton, T5J 2Z1 AB
780-644-5130, Fax: 780-644-5129, 866-714-4455, UtilitiesConsumerAdvocate@gov.ab.

British Columbia
British Columbia Hydro, 333 Dunsmuir St., 18th Fl., Vancouver, V6B 5R3 BC
604-224-9376, Fax: 604-623-4467, 800-224-9376
Powertech Labs Inc., 12388 - 88 Ave., Surrey, BC V8W 7R7
604-590-7500, Fax: 604-590-5347, info@powertechlans.com

Manitoba
Manitoba Hydro, PO Box 815 Main,Winnipeg, R3C 2P4 MB
204-474-3311, Fax: 204-475-0069, publicaffairs@hydro.mb.ca

New Brunswick
New Brunswick Electric Finance Corporation, #376, 670 King St., PO Box 6000, Fredericton, NB E3B 5H1
506-453-3952, Fax: 506-453-2053
New Brunswick Power Group of Companies, 515 King St., PO Box 2000, Fredericton, E3B 4X1 NB
506-458-4444, Fax: 506-458-4000, questions@nbpower.com

Newfoundland & Labrador
Churchill Falls (Labrador) Corporation Limited, Hydro Place, 500 Columbus Dr., PO Box 12500, St. John's, A1B 4K7 NL
709-737-1859, Fax: 709-737-1816
Newfoundland & Labrador Hydro, Hydro Place, Columbus Dr., PO Box 12400, St. John's, A1B 4K7 NL
709-737-1400, Fax: 709-737-1800
Twin Falls Power Corporation, PO Box 12500, St. John's, A1B 3T5 NL

Northwest Territories
Northwest Territories Power Corporation, 4 Capital Dr., Hay River, X0E 1G2 NT
867-874-5200, Fax: 867-874-5229, info@ntpc.com

Nova Scotia
Nova Scotia Utility & Review Board, 1601 Lower Water St., 3rd Fl., PO Box 1692 M,Halifax, B3J 3S3 NS
902-424-4448, Fax: 902-424-3919, uarb.board@gov.ns.ca

Ontario
Hydro One Inc., North Tower, 483 Bay St., Toronto, M5G 2P5 ON
416-345-5000, 877-955-1155, webmaster@HydroOne.com
Independent Electricity System Operator, PO Box 4474 A,Toronto, M5W 4E5 ON
905-403-6900, Fax: 905-403-6921, 888-448-7777, customer.relations@ieso.ca
Ontario Power Authority, #1600, 120 Adelaide St. West, Toronto, ON M5H 1T1
416-967-7474, Fax: 416-967-1947, info@powerauthority.on.ca
Ontario Power Generation, 700 University Ave., Toronto, M5G 1X6 ON
416-592-2555, 877-592-2555

Quebec
Hydro-Québec, 75, boul René-Lévesque ouest, 20e étage, Montréal, H2Z 1A4 QC
514-289-2211
Société d'énergie de la Baie-James, 888, de Maisonneuve est, 2e étage, Montréal, H2L 5B2 QC
514-286-2020,

Saskatchewan
Saskatchewan Power Corporation (SaskPower), 2025 Victoria Ave., Regina, S4P 0S1 SK
306-566-2121, Fax: 306-566-2330, 800-667-4749

IMMIGRATION

See Also: Citizenship
Citizenship & Immigration Canada, Jean Edmonds, South Tower, 365 Laurier Ave. West, Ottawa, K1A 1L1 ON
613-954-9019, Fax: 613-954-2221, 888-242-2100
Immigration & Refugee Board of Canada, Canada Bldg, 344 Slater St., 12th Fl., Ottawa, K1A 0K1 ON
613-995-6486, Fax: 613-943-1550, info@irb-cisr.gc.ca
Passport Canada, Le 70 Crémazie, 70 Crémazie St., Gatineau, K1A 0G3 QC
Fax: 819-953-5856, 800-567-6868

Manitoba
Immigration & Multiculturalism Division, 213 Notre Dame Ave., 5th Floor, Winnipeg, R3B 1N3 MB
204-945-6300, Fax: 204-948-2148, immigratemanitoba@gov.mb.ca

IMPORTS

See Also: Trade
Canada Border Services Agency, Headquarters, 191 Laurier Ave. West, Ottawa, K1A 0L8 ON
800-461-9999, CBSA-ASFC@canada.gc.ca; communications@ps.gc.ca (Public Safety)
Canadian International Trade Tribunal, Standard Life Centre, 333 Laurier Ave. West, 17 Floor, Ottawa, K1A 0G7 ON
613-990-2452, Fax: 613-990-2439
North American Free Trade Agreement (NAFTA) Secretariat, Canadian Section, #705, 90 Sparks St., Ottawa, K1P 5B4 ON
613-992-9388, Fax: 613-992-9392, webmaster@nafta-alena.gc.ca

New Brunswick
Investment & Export Development, Centennial Bldg., 670 King St., 5th F., PO Box 6000, Fredericton, E3B 5H1 NB
506-453-2875, Fax: 506-444-4277

Quebec
Revenu Québec, Direction des relations publiques/Communications, 3800, rue de Marly, Québec, G1X 4A5 QC
418-652-6831, Fax: 418-646-0167

INCOME SECURITY

See Also: Social Services

Alberta
Workforce Supports Division, Labour Building, 10808 - 99 Ave., 10th Fl., Edmonton, T5K 0G5 AB
780-722-0010

British Columbia
Community Living British Columbia, Airport Square, #700, 1200 West 73rd Ave., Vancouver, BC V6P 6G5
604-664-0101, Fax: 604-664-0765, 877-660-2522, info@communitylivingbc.ca
Management Services Division, 614 Humboldt St., 7th Fl., PO Box 9940 Prov Govt,Victoria, V8W 1A4 BC
250-387-3159, Fax: 250-387-2418

Manitoba
Employment, Income & Housing Division, #201, 280 Broadway Ave., Winnipeg, R3C 0R8 MB

New Brunswick
Family Income Security Appeal Board, PO Box 6000, Fredericton, NB E3B 5H1
506-525-4007, Fax: 506-525-4008

Ontario
Ministry of Community & Social Services, Hepburn Block, 80 Grosvenor St., 6th Fl., Toronto, M7A 1E9 ON
416-325-5666, Fax: 416-325-5172, 888-789-4199

Yukon Territory
Yukon Health & Social Services, PO Box 2703, Whitehorse, Y1A 2C6 YT
867-667-3673, Fax: 867-667-3096, 800-661-0408, hss@gov.yk.ca

INCORPORATION OF COMPANIES & ASSOCIATIONS

Alberta
Technology Services, John E. Brownlee Bldg., 10365 - 97 St., 8th Fl., Edmonton, T5J 3W7 AB
780-422-8545

New Brunswick
Service New Brunswick, Westmorland Place, #200, 82 Westmorland St., PO Box 1998, Fredericton, E3B 5G4 NB
506-457-3581, Fax: 506-457-7520, 888-762-8600, snb@snb.ca

Northwest Territories
Department of Justice, Courthouse, 4903 - 49th St., 6th Fl., PO Box 1320, Yellowknife, X1A 2L9 NT
867-920-6197

Nova Scotia
Department of Economic & Rural Development, Centennial Building, #600, 1660 Hollis St., PO Box 2311, Halifax, B3J 1V7 NS
902-424-0377, Fax: 902-424-7008, comm@gov.ns.ca
Registry of Joint Stock Companies, Martime Centre, 1505 Barrington St., 9th Fl., Halifax, B3J 3K5 NS
902-424-7770, Fax: 902-424-4633, 800-225-8227, joint-stock@gov.ns.ca

Nunavut
Nunavut Legal Registries Division, Brown Bldg., 1st Fl., PO Box 1000 570,Iqaluit, X0A 0H0 NU
867-975-6190, Fax: 867-975-6194

Ontario
ServiceOntario, College Park, 777 Bay St., 15th fl., Toronto, M7A 2J3 ON
416-326-6205, Fax: 416-326-5106

Prince Edward Island
Consumer, Corporate & Insurance Division, Shaw Building, 95 Rochford St., 4th Fl., PO Box 2000, Charlottetown, C1A 7N8 PE
902-368-4580, Fax: 902-368-5283, 800-658-1799

Quebec
Registraire des entreprises, 787, boul. Lebourgneuf, Québec, G2J 1C3 QC
418-644-4545, Fax: 418-528-5703, 877-644-4545, registre@servicesquebec.gouv.qc.ca

Yukon Territory
Yukon Community Services, PO Box 2703, Whitehorse, Y1A 2C6 YT
867-667-5811, Fax: 867-393-6295, 800-661-0408, inquiry@gov.yk.ca

INDUSTRY

See Also: Business Development
Agriculture & Agri-Food Canada, 1341 Baseline Rd., Ottawa, K1A 0C5 ON
613-773-1000, Fax: 613-773-2772, 866-345-7972, info@agr.gc.ca
Atlantic Canada Opportunities Agency, Blue Cross Centre, 644 Main St., 3rd Fl., PO Box 6051, Moncton, E1C 9J8 NB
506-851-2271, Fax: 506-851-7403, 800-561-7862, information@acoa-apeca.gc.ca
Atomic Energy of Canada Limited, Head Office, Sheridan Science & Technology Park, 2251 Speakman Dr., Mississauga, L5K 1B2 ON
905-823-9040, 866-886-2325, librarycr@aecl.ca (Library); speakers@aecl.ca (Community speakers)
Canada Mortgage & Housing Corporation, 700 Montreal Rd., Ottawa, K1A 0P7 ON
613-748-2000, Fax: 613-748-2098, 800-668-2642, chic@cmhc-schl.gc.ca
Canadian Dairy Commission, Central Experimental Farm, NCC Driveway, Bldg. 55, 960 Carling Ave., Ottawa, K1A 0Z2 ON
613-792-2000, Fax: 613-792-2009, cdc-ccl@agr.gc.ca
Canadian Food Inspection Agency, 1400 Merivale Rd., Ottawa, K1A 0Y9 ON
613-225-2342, Fax: 613-228-6629, 800-442-2342
Canadian Grain Commission, #600, 303 Main St., Winnipeg, R3C 3G8 MB
204-983-2770, Fax: 204-983-2751, 800-853-6705, contact@grainscanada.gc.ca
Canadian International Development Agency, 200, Promenade du Portage, Gatineau, K1A 0G4 QC
819-997-5006, Fax: 819-953-6088, 800-230-6349, info@acdi-cida.gc.ca
Canadian International Trade Tribunal, Standard Life Centre, 333 Laurier Ave. West, 17 Floor, Ottawa, K1A 0G7 ON
613-990-2452, Fax: 613-990-2439
Canadian Nuclear Safety Commission, 280 Slater St., PO Box 1046 B,Ottawa, K1P 5S9 ON
613-995-5894, Fax: 613-995-5086, 800-668-5284, info@cnsc-ccsn.gc.ca
Canadian Radio-Television & Telecommunications Commission, Central Office, 1, Promenade du Portage, Les Terrasses de la Chaudière, Gatineau, J8X 4B1 QC
819-997-0313, Fax: 819-994-0218, 877-249-2782
Canadian Space Agency, 6767, rte de l'Aéroport, Saint-Hubert, J3Y 8Y9 QC
450-926-4800, Fax: 450-926-4352, webmaster@space.gc.ca
Canadian Tourism Commission, #1400, 1055 Dunsmuir St., PO Box 49230, Vancouver, BC V7X 1L2
604-638-8300, Fax: 604-638-8425, ctc_feedback@businteractive.com
Canadian Wheat Board, 423 Main St., PO Box 816 Main,Winnipeg, R3C 2P5 MB
204-983-0239, Fax: 204-983-3841, 800-275-4292, questions@cwb.ca
Cape Breton Development Fund Corporation, Silicon Island, 70 Crescent St., PO Box 1264, Sydney, NS B1P 6T7
902-564-3600, Fax: 902-564-3825, 800-705-3926
Centre for Surface Transportation Technology, 2320 Lester Rd., Ottawa, K1V 1S2 ON
613-998-9639, Fax: 613-957-0831, inquiries.cstt@nrc-cnrc.gc.ca
Chief Informatics Office, 235 Queen St., Ottawa, ON K1A 0H5
613-954-3570, Fax: 613-941-1938
Communications Research Centre Canada, 3701 Carling Ave., PO Box 11490 H, Ottawa, ON K2H 8S2
613-991-3313, Fax: 613-998-5355, info@crc.ca

Competition Bureau, Place du Portage, Phase I, 50, rue Victoria, 21e étage, Ottawa, K1A 0C9 ON
613-997-4282, Fax: 613-997-0324, 800-348-5358, compbureau@ic.gc.ca
Competition Tribunal, Thomas D'Arcy McGee Bldg., #600, 90 Sparks St., Ottawa, ON K1P 5B4
613-957-3172, Fax: 613-957-3170, tribunal@ct-tc.gc.ca
Defence Construction Canada, Constitution Square, 350 Albert St., 19th Fl., Ottawa, K1A 0K3 ON
613-998-9548, Fax: 613-998-1061, 800-514-3555, info@dcc-cdc.gc.ca
Enterprise Cape Breton Corporation, Silicon Island, 70 Crescent St., Sydney, NS B1S 2Z7
902-564-3600, Fax: 902-564-3825, 800-705-3926,information@ecbc-secb.gc.ca
Office of the Ethics Commissioner, 66 Slater St., 22nd Fl., Ottawa, K1A 0A6 ON
613-995-0721, Fax: 613-995-7308, ciec-ccie@parl.gc.ca
Export Development Canada, 151 O'Connor St., Ottawa, K1A 1K3 ON
613-598-2500, Fax: 613-598-3811, 800-267-8510
Farm Credit Canada, 1800 Hamilton St., PO Box 4320, Regina, S4P 4L3 SK
306-780-8100, Fax: 306-780-8919, 888-332-3301, csc@fcc-fac.ca
Office of the Superintendent of Financial Institutions, Kent Square, 255 Albert St., Ottawa, K1A 0H2 ON
613-990-7788, Fax: 613-990-5591, 800-385-8647, information@osfi-bsif.gc.ca
Fisheries & Oceans Canada, 200 Kent St., Ottawa, K1A 0E6 ON
613-993-0999, Fax: 613-996-1866, info@dfo-mpo.gc.ca
Foreign Affairs & International Trade Canada, 125 Sussex Dr., Ottawa, K1A 0G2 ON
613-944-4000, Fax: 613-996-9709, 800-267-8376, enqserv@international.gc.ca
Freshwater Fish Marketing Corporation, 1199 Plessis Rd., Winnipeg, R2C 3L4 MB
204-983-6601, Fax: 204-983-6497, sandi.cain@freshwaterfish.com
Hazardous Materials Information Review Commission, 427 Laurier Ave. West, 7th Fl., Ottawa, ON K1A 1M3
613-993-4331, Fax: 613-993-4686, hmirc-ccrmd@hc-sc.gc.ca
Indian Oil & Gas Canada, #100, 9911 Chula Blvd., Tsuu T'ina (Sarcee), AB T2W 6H6
403-292-5625, Fax: 403-292-5618, ContactIOGC@inac-ainc.gc.ca
Industry Canada, 235 Queen St., Ottawa, K1A 0H5 ON
Fax: 613-954-6436, 800-328-6189, info@ic.gc.ca
Institute for Aerospace Research, 1200 Montreal Rd., Ottawa, K1A 0R6 ON
613-990-0765, Fax: 613-952-7214
Institute for Information Technology, Bldg. M-50, 1200 Montreal Rd., Ottawa, K1A 0R6 ON
613-991-3373, Fax: 613-952-0074, 877-672-2672
National Energy Board, 444 - 7 Ave. SW, Calgary, T2P 0X8 AB
403-292-4800, Fax: 403-292-5503, 800-899-1265, info@neb-one.gc.ca
National Farm Products Council, Canada Bldg., 344 Slater St., 10th Fl., Ottawa, K1R 7Y3 ON
613-995-6752, Fax: 613-995-2097, fpcc-cpac@agr.gc.ca
National Film Board of Canada, 3155, rue Côte de Liesse, CP 1600 Centre-ville,Saint-Laurent, H4N 2N4 QC
514-283-9000, Fax: 514-283-7564, 800-267-7710
National Research Council Canada, Bldg. M-58, 1200 Montreal Rd., Ottawa, K1A 0R6 ON
613-993-9101, Fax: 613-952-7928, 877-672-2672, info@nrc-cnrc.ca
National Round Table on the Environment & Economy, #200, 344 Slater St., Ottawa, K1R 7Y3 ON
613-992-7189, Fax: 613-992-7385, admin@nrtee-trnee.ca
Natural Resources Canada, 580 Booth St., Ottawa, K1A 0E4 ON
613-995-0947, Fax: 613-992-7211
Natural Sciences & Engineering Research Council of Canada, Constitution Square, Tower II, 350 Albert St., Ottawa, K1A 1H5 ON
613-995-4273, Fax: 613-943-1624, marie-josee.duval@nserc-crsng.gc.ca
North American Free Trade Agreement (NAFTA) Secretariat, Canadian Section, #705, 90 Sparks St., Ottawa, K1P 5B4 ON
613-992-9388, Fax: 613-992-9392, webmaster@nafta-alena.gc.ca
Patented Medicine Prices Review Board, Standard Life Centre, #1400, 333 Laurier Ave. West, PO Box L40, Ottawa, K1P 1C1 ON
613-952-7360, Fax: 613-952-7626, 877-861-2350, pmprb@pmprb-cepmb.gc.ca
Spectrum, Information Technologies & Telecommunications, Journal Tower North, 300 Slater St., 20th Fl., Ottawa, K1A 0C8 ON
613-998-0368, Fax: 613-952-1203
Standards Council of Canada, #200, 270 Albert St., Ottawa, K1P 6N7 ON
613-238-3222, Fax: 613-569-7808, info@scc.ca
Telefilm Canada, #500, 360, rue Saint-Jacques, Montréal, H2Y 1P5 QC
514-283-6363, Fax: 514-283-2365, 800-567-0890, info@telefilm.gc.ca
Western Economic Diversification Canada, Canada Place, #1500, 9700 Jasper Ave. NW, Edmonton, T5J 4H7 AB
780-495-4164, Fax: 780-495-4557, 888-338-9378

Alberta

Alberta Agriculture & Rural Development, J.G. O'Donoghue Bldg., 7000 - 113 St., 1st Fl., Edmonton, T6H 5T6 AB
780-427-2727, Fax: 780-427-2861, 866-882-7677
Alberta Economic Development Authority, McDougall Centre, 455 - 6 St. SW, Calgary, AB T2P 4E8
403-297-3022, Fax: 403-297-6435
Alberta Gaming & Liquor Commission, 50 Corriveau Ave., St Albert, AB T8N 3T5
780-447-8600, Fax: 780-447-8911, 800-272-8876
Alberta Grain Commission, 7000 - 113 St., 3rd Fl., Edmonton, AB T6H 5T6
780-427-7329, Fax: 780-422-9690
Alberta Science & Research Authority, Phipps-McKinnon Bldg., #500, 10020 - 101A Ave., Edmonton, AB T5J 3G2
780-427-1488, Fax: 780-427-0979, asra@gov.ab.ca
Community, Learner & Industry Connections Division, Phipps-McKinnon Bldg., 5th Fl., 10020 - 101A Ave., Edmonton, T5J 3G2 AB
780-427-8517
Energy Resources Conservation Board, #1000, 250 - 5 Ave. SW, Calgary, AB T2P 0R4
403-297-8311, Fax: 403-297-7336, inquiries@ercb.ca
Alberta Energy, North Petroleum Plaza, 9945 - 108 St., 10th Fl., Edmonton, T5K 2G6 AB
780-427-8050, Fax: 780-422-0698, 780-310-0000
Alberta Environment, South Tower, Petroleum Plaza, 9915 - 108 St., 10th Fl., Edmonton, T5K 2G8 AB
780-427-2700, Fax: 780-422-4086, env.infocent@gov.ab.ca
Farmers' Advocate of Alberta, 7000 - 113 St., 3rd Fl., Edmonton, AB T6H 5T6
780-427-2433, Fax: 780-427-3913, farmers.advocate@gov.ab.ca
Intergovernmental Relations, Commerce Place, 10155 - 102 St., 12th Fl., Edmonton, T5J 4L8 AB
Land Compensation/Surface Rights Board, Phipps-McKinnon Bldg., 10020 - 101A Ave., 18th Fl., Edmonton, AB T5J 3G2
780-427-2444, Fax: 780-427-5798

British Columbia

Agricultural Land Commission, #133, 4940 Canada Way, Burnaby, BC V5G 4K6
604-660-7000, Fax: 604-660-7033
Ministry of Agriculture & Lands, PO Box 9120 Prov Govt,Victoria, V8W 9E2 BC
250-387-5121, Fax: 250-387-1522,
British Columbia Farm Industry Review Board, 1007 Fort St., 3rd Fl., PO Box 9129 Prov Govt, Victoria, BC V8W 9B5
250-356-8945, Fax: 250-356-5131, firb@gov.bc.ca
Ministry of Energy, Mines & Petroleum Resources, PO Box 9318 Prov Govt,Victoria, V8W 9N3 BC
250-952-0241
Financial Institutions Commission, #1200, 13450 - 102 Ave., Surrey, BC V3T 5X3
604-953-5300, Fax: 604-953-5301, 866-206-3030, FICOM@ficombc.ca; HR@ficombc.ca
Forest Practices Board, 1675 Douglas St., 3rd Fl., PO Box 9905 Prov Govt, Victoria, BC V8W 9R1
250-387-7964, Fax: 250-387-7009, 800-994-5899, fpboard@gov.bc.ca
Ministry of Forests & Range, PO Box 9529 Prov Govt,Victoria, V8W 9C3 BC
250-387-4809, Fax: 250-953-3687
British Columbia Hydro, 333 Dunsmuir St., 18th Fl., Vancouver, V6B 5R3 BC
604-224-9376, Fax: 604-623-4467, 800-224-9376
Industry Training Authority, #1223, 13351 Commerce Pkwy., Richmond, BC V6V 2X7
604-214-8700, Fax: 604-214-8701, 866-660-6011, info@itabc.ca; customerservice@itabc.ca
Insurance Council of British Columbia, #300, 1040 West Georgia St., PO Box 7, Vancouver, BC V6E 4H1
604-688-0321, Fax: 604-662-7767, 877-688-0321
Ministry of Labour, PO Box 9052 Prov Govt,Victoria, V8W 9E2 BC
250-356-6348, Fax: 250-356-6595, LCS.Minister@gov.bc.ca
Oil & Gas Commission, #100, 10003 - 110 Ave., Fort St John, BC V1J 6M7
250-261-5700, 800-663-7867
Real Estate Council of British Columbia, #900, 750 West Pender St., Vancouver, BC V6C 2T8
604-683-9664, Fax: 604-683-9017, 877-683-9664, info@recbc.ca
Ministry of Small Business, Technology & Economic Development, 1810 Blanshard St., PO Box 9324 Prov Govt,Victoria, V8W 9N3 BC
250-356-7411, Fax: 250-356-6376, Feedback.CSE@gov.bc.ca
Strategic Industry Development, 808 Douglas St., 5th Fl., PO Box 9120 Prov Govt,Victoria, V8W 9B4 BC
250-356-1821, Fax: 250-356-7279
British Columbia Utilities Commission, 900 Howe St., 6th Fl., PO Box 250, Vancouver, V6Z 2N3 BC
604-660-4700, Fax: 604-660-1102, 800-663-1385, commission.secretary@bcuc.com

Manitoba

Manitoba Aboriginal & Northern Affairs, 59 Elizabeth Dr., PO Box 37, Thompson, R8N 1X4 MB
204-677-6607, Fax: 204-677-6753, amartin@gov.mb.ca
Advisory Council on Workplace Safety & Health, #200, 401 York Ave., Winnipeg, MB R3C 0P8
204-945-3446, Fax: 204-945-4556
Agricultural Societies, 1129 Queens Ave., Brandon, MB R7A 1L9
204-726-6195, Fax: 204-726-6260
Manitoba Agriculture, Food & Rural Initiatives, Norquay Bldg., 401 York Ave., Winnipeg, R3C 0P8 MB
Community & Economic Development Committee of Cabinet Secretariat, #648, 155 Carlton St., Winnipeg, R3C 3H8 MB
204-945-8221, Fax: 204-945-8229
Manitoba Competitiveness, Training & Trade, International Business Centre, The Paris Building, 259 Portage Ave., Winnipeg, R3B 3P4 MB
204-945-2475, Fax: 204-945-3977, minctt@leg.gov.mb.ca
Crown Corporations Council, #1130, 444 St. Mary Ave., Winnipeg, MB R3C 3T1
204-949-5270, Fax: 204-949-5283, crowncc@mts.net
Manitoba Development Corporation, #555, 155 Carlton St., Winnipeg, R3C 3H8 MB
204-945-7626, Fax: 204-945-1193
Manitoba Education, Citizenship & Youth, #168, Legislative Bldg., 450 Broadway, Winnipeg, R3C 0V8 MB
204-945-3720, Fax: 204-945-1291, minedu@leg.gov.mb.ca
Employment, Income & Housing Division, #201, 280 Broadway Ave., Winnipeg, R3C 0R8 MB
Farm Lands Ownership Board, #812, Norquay Bldg., 401 York Ave., Winnipeg, MB R3C 0P8
204-945-3149, Fax: 204-945-1489, 800-282-8069, robert.mckenzie@gov.mb.ca
Farm Machinery Board, Norquay Bldg., #812, 401 York Ave., Winnipeg, MB R3C 0P8
204-945-3856, Fax: 204-948-2844, randy.ozunko@gov.mb.ca
Manitoba Hydro, PO Box 815 Main,Winnipeg, R3C 2P4 MB
204-474-3311, Fax: 204-475-0069, publicaffairs@hydro.mb.ca
Manitoba Labour & Immigration, Legislative Building, 317, 450 Broadway Ave., Winnipeg, R3C 0V8 MB
204-945-4079, Fax: 204-945-8312, minlab@leg.gov.mb.ca
Manitoba Lotteries Corporation, 830 Empress St., Winnipeg, R3G 3H3 MB
204-957-2500, Fax: 204-957-3991, communications@casinosofwinnipeg.com
Manitoba Agricultural Services Corporation, #100, 1525 First St. South, Brandon, MB R7A 7A1
204-726-6850, Fax: 204-726-6849, mailbox@masc.mb.ca
Manitoba Bureau of Statistics, #824, 155 Carlton St., Winnipeg, R3C 3H9 MB
204-945-2406, Fax: 204-945-0695
Manitoba Habitat Heritage Corporation, #200, 1555 St. James St., Winnipeg, MB R3H 1B5
204-784-4350, Fax: 204-784-7359, mhhc@mhhc.mb.ca
Manitoba Labour Board, A.A. Heaps Bldg., #402, 258 Portage Ave., Winnipeg, MB R3C 0B6
204-945-3783, Fax: 204-945-1296, mlb@gov.mb.ca
Manitoba Minimum Wage Board, 614 - 401 York Ave., Winnipeg, MB R3C 0P8
204-945-4889, Fax: 204-948-2085, mw@gov.mb.ca
Public Utilities Board, #400, 330 Portage Ave., Winnipeg, MB R3C 0C4
204-945-2638, Fax: 204-945-2643, 866-854-3698, publicutilities@gov.mb.ca
Taxicab Board, #200, 301 Weston St., Winnipeg, MB R3E 3H4
Fax: 204-948-2315
Tourism Secretariat & Travel Manitoba, 155 Carlton St., 7th Fl., Winnipeg, R3C 3H8 MB
800-665-0040
Manitoba Workers' Compensation Board, 333 Broadway Ave., Winnipeg, R3C 4W3 MB

204-954-4321, Fax: 204-954-4999, 800-362-3340, wcb@wcb.mb.ca
Workplace Safety & Health Division, #200, 401 York Ave., Winnipeg, R3C 0P8 MB
204-945-3446, Fax: 204-948-2209, wshcompl@gov.mb.ca

New Brunswick
Department of Agriculture & Aquaculture, PO Box 6000, Fredericton, E3B 5H1 NB
506-453-2666, Fax: 506-453-7170, DAA-MAA@gnb.ca
Board of Examiners under the Scaler's Act, 1350 Regent St. South, PO Box 6000, Fredericton, NB E3B 5H1
506-453-2441, Fax: 506-453-6689
Department of Business New Brunswick, Centennial Bldg., 670 King St., PO Box 6000, Fredericton, E3B 5H1 NB
506-444-5228, Fax: 506-453-5428
Corporate Services, Centennial Bldg., 670 King St., 5th Fl., PO Box 6000, Fredericton, E3B 5H1 NB
506-453-3707, Fax: 506-453-3993
Department of the Environment, Marysville Place, 20 McGloin St., PO Box 6000, Fredericton, E3B 5H1 NB
506-453-2690, Fax: 506-457-4991, env-info@gnb.ca
Forest Protection Limited, 2502 Hwy. 102, Lincoln, NB E3B 7E6
506-446-6930, Fax: 506-446-6934, info@forestprotectionlimited.com
Investment & Export Development, Centennial Bldg., 670 King St., 5th F., PO Box 6000, Fredericton, E3B 5H1 NB
506-453-2875, Fax: 506-444-4277
New Brunswick Liquor Corporation, 170 Wilsey Rd., PO Box 20787, Fredericton, E3B 5B8 NB
506-452-6826, Fax: 506-462-2024, info@anbl.com
Department of Natural Resources, PO Box 6000, Fredericton, E3B 5H1 NB
506-453-2510, Fax: 506-444-5839, dnrweb@gnb.ca
New Brunswick Crop Insurance Commission, PO Box 6000, Fredericton, NB E3B 5H1
506-453-2185, Fax: 506-453-7406
New Brunswick Farm Products Commission, c/o Department of Agriculture & Aquaculture, PO Box 6000, Fredericton, NB E3B 5H1
506-453-3647, Fax: 506-444-5969
New Brunswick Film, Assumption Pl., 770 Main St., 16th Fl., PO Box 5001, Moncton, NB E1C 8R3
506-869-6868, Fax: 506-869-6840, nbfilm@gnb.ca
New Brunswick Industrial Development Board, Business New Brunswick, Centennial Bldg., 670 King St., PO Box 6000, Fredericton, NB E3B 5H1
506-453-4200, Fax: 506-444-4182
New Brunswick Real Estate Association, #1, 22 Durelle St., Fredericton, NB E3C 1N8
506-459-8055, Fax: 506-459-8057, 800-762-1677, info@nbrea.ca
New Brunswick Round Table on Environment & Economy, 20 McGloin St., PO Box 6000, Fredericton, NB E3B 5H1
506-453-3703, Fax: 506-453-3876
New Brunswick Power Group of Companies, 515 King St., PO Box 2000, Fredericton, E3B 4X1 NB
506-458-4444, Fax: 506-458-4000, questions@nbpower.com
Regional Development Corporation, RDC Bldg., 836 Churchill Row, PO Box 428, Fredericton, E3B 5R4 NB
506-453-2277, Fax: 506-453-7988
New Brunswick Research & Productivity Council, 921 College Hill Rd., Fredericton, E3B 6Z9 NB
506-452-1212, Fax: 506-452-1395, info@rpc.ca
Department of Social Development, Sartain MacDonald Bldg., 551 King St., PO Box 6000, Fredericton, E3B 5H1 NB
506-453-2001, Fax: 506-453-7478
Workplace Health, Safety & Compensation Commission of New Brunswick, 1 Portland St., PO Box 160, Saint John, E2L 3X9 NB
506-632-2200, 800-222-9775, communications@ws-ts.nb.ca

Newfoundland & Labrador
Canada-Newfoundland Offshore Petroleum Board, TD Place, 140 Water St., 5th Fl., St. John's, NL A1C 6H6
709-778-1400, Fax: 709-778-1473, postmaster@cnlopb.nl.ca
Department of Fisheries & Aquaculture, Petten Bldg., 30 Strawberry Marsh Rd., PO Box 8700, St. John's, A1B 4J6 NL
709-729-3723, Fax: 709-729-6082, fishaqwebmaster@gov.nl.ca
Newfoundland & Labrador Housing Corporation, Sir Brian Dunfield Bldg., 2 Canada Dr., PO Box 220, St. John's, A1C 5J2 NL
709-724-3000, Fax: 709-724-3250, jmbowering@nsmail.nlhc.nl.ca
Newfoundland & Labrador Hydro, Hydro Place, Columbus Dr., PO Box 12400, St. John's, A1B 4K7 NL
709-737-1400, Fax: 709-737-1800
Department of Innovation, Trade & Rural Development, West Block, Confederation Bldg., PO Box 8700, St. John's, A1B 4J6 NL
709-729-7000, Fax: 709-729-0654, 800-563-2299, itrd@gov.nl.ca
Labour Relations Board, Beothuck Bldg., 20 Crosbie Pl., 5th Fl., PO Box 8700, St. John's, NL A1B 4J6
709-729-2707, Fax: 709-729-5738
Department of Labrador & Aboriginal Affairs, Confederation Bldg., East Block, 6th Fl., PO Box 8700, St. John's, A1B 4J6 NL
709-729-4776, Fax: 709-729-4900, 877-788-8822, laa@gov.nl.ca
Department of Natural Resources, Natural Resources Bldg., 50 Elizabeth Ave., 7th Fl., PO Box 8700, St. John's, A1B 4J6 NL
709-729-2920, Fax: 709-729-0059
Newfoundland & Labrador Municipal Financing Corporation, Confederation Bldg., PO Box 8700, St. John's, NL A1B 4J6
709-729-6686, Fax: 709-729-2095
Newfoundland Labrador Liquor Corporation, 90 Kenmount Rd., PO Box 8750 A, St. John's, NL A1B 3V1
709-724-1100, Fax: 709-754-0321, info@nfliquor.com
Professional Fish Harvesters Certification Board, 15 Hallett Cres., PO Box 8541, St. John's, NL A1B 3P2
709-722-8170, Fax: 709-722-8201, pfh@pfhcb.com
Newfoundland & Labrador Board of Commissioners of Public Utilities, PO Box 21040, St. John's, A1A 5B2 NL
709-726-8600, Fax: 709-726-9604, 866-782-0006, ito@pub.nf.ca

Northwest Territories
Department of Environment & Natural Resources, PO Box 1320, Yellowknife, X1A 2L9 NT
Highways, 4510 - 50 Ave., 2nd fl., PO Box 1320, Yellowknife, X1A 2L9 NT
867-920-8771, Fax: 867-873-0288
Northwest Territories Housing Corporation, Scotia Centre, 5102 50th Ave., PO Box 2100, Yellowknife, X1A 2P6 NT
867-873-7853, Fax: 867-873-9426
Department of Industry, Tourism & Investment, PO Box 1320, Yellowknife, X1A 2L9 NT
Fax: 867-873-0306, info@iti.ca
Northwest Territories Business Development & Investment Corporation, #701, 5201 - 50 Ave., Yellowknife, NT X1A 3S9
867-920-6455, Fax: 867-765-0652, bdicinfo@gov.nt.ca
Northwest Territories Liquor Commission, #201, 31 Capital Dr., Hay River, NT X0E 1G2
867-874-2100, Fax: 867-874-2180
Northwest Territories Liquor Licensing & Enforcement, #210, 31 Capital Dr., Hay River, NT X0E 1G2
867-874-2906, Fax: 867-874-6011
Northwest Territories Liquor Licensing Board, #210, 31 Capital Dr., Hay River, NT X0E 1G2
867-874-2906, Fax: 867-874-6011, delilah_st-arneault@gov.nt.ca
Northwest Territories Power Corporation, 4 Capital Dr., Hay River, X0E 1G2 NT
867-874-5200, Fax: 867-874-5229, info@ntpc.com

Nova Scotia
Department of Agriculture, 1741 Brunswick St., 3rd Fl., PO Box 2223, Halifax, B3J 3C4 NS
902-424-4560, Fax: 902-424-4671
Canada-Nova Scotia Offshore Petroleum Board, TD Centre, 1791 Barrington St., 6th Fl., Halifax, NS B3J 3K9
902-422-5588, Fax: 902-422-1799, postmaster@cnsopb.ns.ca
Crane Operators Appeal Board, 5151 Terminal Rd., 7th Fl., PO Box 697, Halifax, NS B3J 2T8
902-424-8595, Fax: 902-424-0217, fraserej@gov.ns.ca
Department of Economic & Rural Development, Centennial Building, #600, 1660 Hollis St., PO Box 2311, Halifax, B3J 1V7 NS
902-424-0377, Fax: 902-424-7008, comm@gov.ns.ca
Film Nova Scotia, Collins Bank Bldg., 1869 Upper Water St., 3rd Fl., Halifax, NS B3J 1S9
902-424-7177, Fax: 902-424-0617, 888-360-2111, connorkm@gov.ns.ca
InNOVACorp, #1400, 1801 Hollis St., Halifax, NS B3J 3N4
902-424-8670, Fax: 902-424-4679, 800-565-7051, communications@innovacorp.ca
Department of Natural Resources, Founder's Square, 1701 Hollis St., 3rd Fl., PO Box 698, Halifax, B3J 2T9 NS
902-424-5935, Fax: 902-424-0594, 800-565-2224
Nova Scotia Crop & Livestock Insurance Commission, MacRae Library Bldg., #2, 137 College Rd., PO Box 1092, Truro, NS B2N 5G9
902-893-7755, Fax: 902-895-4622, 800-565-6371, nsclic@gov.ns.ca
Nova Scotia Farm Loan Board, PO Box 550, Truro, NS B2N 5E3
902-893-6506, Fax: 902-895-7693, flb@gov.ns.ca
Nova Scotia Liquor Corporation, Bayers Lake Business Park, 93 Chain Lake Dr., Halifax, B3S 1A3 NS
902-450-6752, 800-567-5874
Trade Centre Limited, 1800 Argyle St., PO Box 955, Halifax, NS B3J 2V9
902-421-8686, Fax: 902-422-2922
Nova Scotia Utility & Review Board, 1601 Lower Water St., 3rd Fl., PO Box 1692 M,Halifax, B3J 3S3 NS
902-424-4448, Fax: 902-424-3919, uarb.board@gov.ns.ca
Waterfront Development Corporation Ltd., 1751 Lower Water St., 2nd Fl., Halifax, NS B3J 1S5
902-422-6591, Fax: 902-422-7582, info@wdcl.ca

Nunavut
Department of Economic Development & Transportation, #1104 Inuksugait Plaza, PO Box 1000 1500,Iqaluit, X0A 0H0 NU
867-975-7800, Fax: 867-975-7870, 888-975-5999, edt@gov.nu.ca
Nunavut Liquor Licensing Board, Bag 002, Rankin Inlet, NU X0C 0G0
Fax: 867-645-3327

Ontario
AGRICORP, 1 Stone Rd. West, PO Box 3660 Central, Guelph, ON N1H 8M4
Fax: 519-826-4118, 888-247-4999, cac@agricorp.com
Agricultural Research Institute of Ontario, 1 Stone Rd. West, 2nd Fl. NW, Guelph, ON N1G 4Y2
519-826-4199, Fax: 519-826-4211
Ministry of Agriculture, Food & Rural Affairs, 1 Stone Rd. West, Guelph, N1G 4Y2 ON
519-826-3100, 888-466-2372
Building Code Commission, 777 Bay St., 2nd Fl., Toronto, ON M5G 2E5
416-585-6503, Fax: 416-585-7531
Building Materials Evaluation Commission, 777 Bay St., 2nd Fl., Toronto, ON M5G 2E5
416-585-4234, Fax: 416-585-7531
Ministry of Economic Development & Trade, Hearst Block, 900 Bay St., 8th Fl., Toronto, M7A 2E1 ON
416-325-6666, Fax: 416-325-6688, 866-668-4249, info@edt.gov.on.ca
Ministry of Environment, 135 St. Clair Ave. West, Toronto, M4V 1P5 ON
416-325-4000, Fax: 416-325-3159, 800-565-4923
Environmental Commissioner of Ontario, #605, 1075 Bay St., Toronto, M5S 2B1 ON
416-325-3377, Fax: 416-325-3370, 800-701-6454, commissioner@eco.on.ca
Ministry of Government Services, Whitney Block, #4320, 99 Wellesley St. West, 4th Fl., Toronto, M7A 1W3 ON
416-326-1234, Fax: 416-327-3790, 800-268-1142
Hydro One Inc., North Tower, 483 Bay St., Toronto, M5G 2P5 ON
416-345-5000, 877-955-1155, webmaster@HydroOne.com
Independent Electricity System Operator, PO Box 4474 A,Toronto, M5W 4E5 ON
905-403-6900, Fax: 905-403-6921, 888-448-7777, customer.relations@ieso.ca
Industry Division, Hearst Block, 900 Bay St., 7th fl., Toronto, M7A 2E1 ON
416-325-6964, Fax: 416-325-2102
Ministry of Labour, 400 University Ave., 14th Fl., Toronto, M7A 1T7 ON
416-326-7770, 800-268-8013
Ministry of Municipal Affairs & Housing, 777 Bay St., 17th Fl., Toronto, M5G 2E5 ON
416-585-7041, Fax: 416-585-6227, 866-220-2290, mininfo.mah@ontario.ca
Ministry of Natural Resources, Whitney Block, #6630, 99 Wellesley St. West, 6th Fl., Toronto, M7A 1W3 ON
800-667-1940
Ministry of Northern Development, Mines & Forestry, 99 Wellesley St. West, Toronto, M7A 1W3 ON
416-327-0633, Fax: 416-327-0665
Office of the Employer Advisor, #704, 151 Bloor St. West., Toronto, ON M5S 1S4
416-327-0020, Fax: 416-327-0726, 800-387-0774
Ontario Media Development Corporation, South Tower, #501, 175 Bloor St. East, Toronto, ON M4W 3R8
416-314-6858, Fax: 416-314-6876, mail@omdc.on.ca
Ontario Power Generation, 700 University Ave., Toronto, M5G 1X6 ON
416-592-2555, 877-592-2555
ServiceOntario, College Park, 777 Bay St., 15th fl., Toronto, M7A 2J3 ON
416-326-6205, Fax: 416-326-5106
Ministry of Small Business & Customer Services, Whitney Block, #1306 - 99 Wellesley St. W., Toronto, M7A 1W2 ON
416-325-6000, Fax: 416-326-1947, 866-668-4249, info.sbe@ontario.ca
Ministry of Tourism, Hearst Block, 900 Bay St., 9th Fl., Toronto, M7A 2E1 ON
416-326-9326, Fax: 416-314-7854, 800-668-2746

Workplace Safety & Insurance Board, 200 Front St. West, Ground Fl., Toronto, M5V 3J1 ON
416-344-1000, Fax: 416-344-4684, 800-387-0750

Prince Edward Island

Agricultural Insurance Corporation, 29 Indigo Cres., PO Box 1600, Charlottetown, PE C1A 7N3
902-368-4842, Fax: 902-368-6677, peiaic@gov.pe.ca

Department of Agriculture, Jones Bldg., 11 Kent St., PO Box 2000, Charlottetown, C1A 7N8 PE
902-368-4880, Fax: 902-368-4857

Community & Labour Development, Shaw Bldg., 105 Rochford St., 5th Fl., PO Box 2000, Charlottetown, C1A 7N8 PE
902-368-4244, Fax: 902-368-4242

Employment Development Agency, Sullivan Bldg., 1st Fl., PO Box 2000, Charlottetown, PE C1A 7N8
902-368-5805, Fax: 902-368-5909

Employment Standards Board, 161 St. Peters Rd., PO Box 2000, Charlottetown, PE C1A 7N8
902-368-5550, Fax: 902-368-5476

Food Technology Centre, 101 Belvedere Ave., PO Box 2000, Charlottetown, PE C1A 7N8
902-368-5548, Fax: 902-368-5549, 877-368-5548, ftcweb@gov.pe.ca

Grain Elevators Corporation, PO Box 250, Kensington, PE C0B 1M0
902-836-8929

Department of Innovation & Advanced Learning, Shaw Bldg., 105 Rochford St., 5th Fl., PO Box 2000, Charlottetown, C1A 7N8 PE
902-368-4240, Fax: 902-368-4242

Island Investment Development Inc., 94 Euston St., 2nd Fl., Charlottetown, PE C1A 1W4
902-894-0351, Fax: 902-368-5886

Prince Edward Island Liquor Control Commission, 3 Garfield St., PO Box 967, Charlottetown, C1A 7M4 PE
902-368-5710, Fax: 902-368-5735

Prince Edward Island Business Development Inc., 94 Euston St., 1st & 2nd Fl., PO Box 910, Charlottetown, PE C1A 7L9
902-368-6300, Fax: 902-368-6301, 800-563-3734, business@gov.pe.ca

Technology PEI Inc., 94 Euston St., 2nd Fl., PO Box 340, Charlottetown, PE C1A 7K7
902-368-6300, Fax: 902-368-6301, techpei@gov.pe.ca

Department of Tourism, PO Box 2000, Charlottetown, C1A 7N8 PE
800-463-4734

Department of Transportation & Public Works, Jones Bldg., 11 Kent St., PO Box 2000, Charlottetown, C1A 7N8 PE
902-368-5100, Fax: 902-368-5395

Prince Edward Island Workers Compensation Board, 14 Weymouth St., PO Box 757, Charlottetown, C1A 7L7 PE
902-368-5680, Fax: 902-368-5705, 800-237-5049

Quebec

Agence de l'efficacité énergétique, #B-405, 5700, 4e av ouest, Québec, QC G1H 6R1
418-627-6379, Fax: 418-643-5828, 877-727-6655, aee@aee.gouv.qc.ca

Ministère de l'Agriculture, des Pêcheries et de l'Alimentation, 200, ch Sainte-Foy, Québec, G1R 4X6 QC
418-380-2110, 888-222-6272

Centre de recherche industrielle du Québec, 333, rue Franquet, Québec, QC G1P 4C7
418-659-1550, Fax: 418-652-2251, 800-667-2386, infocriq@criq.qc.ca

Comité conjoint de chasse, de pêche et de piégeage, #C220, 383 rue Saint-Jacques, Montréal, QC H2Y 1N9
514-284-2151, Fax: 514-284-0039, hftcc@bellnet.ca

Commissaire de l'industrie de la construction, 150, boul René-Lévesque est, 18e étage,, Québec, QC G1R 5B1
418-646-7200, Fax: 418-644-9977

Commission de protection du territoire agricole du Québec, 200, ch Ste-Foy, 2e étage, Québec, QC G1R 4X6
418-643-3314, Fax: 418-643-2261, 800-667-5294, info@cptaq.gouv.qc.ca

Conseil consultatif du travail et de la main d'oeuvre, #9.400, 500, boul René-Lévesque ouest, Montréal, QC H2Z 1W7
514-873-2880, Fax: 514-873-1129, cctm@cctm.gouv.qc.ca

Ministère de la Culture, des Communications & de la Condition féminine, 225, Grande Allée est, Québec, G1R 5G5 QC
Fax: 418-380-2364, 888-380-8882, infos@mcccf.gouv.qc.ca

Ministère du Développement durable, de l'Environnement et des Parcs, Édifice Marie-Guyart, 675, boul René-Lévesque est, 29e étage, Québec, G1R 5V7 QC
418-521-3830, Fax: 418-646-5974, 800-561-1616, info@mddep.gouv.qc.ca

Ministère du Développement économique, de l'Innovation et de l'Exportation, 710, place D'Youville, 3e étage, Québec, G1R 4Y4 QC
418-691-5950, Fax: 418-644-0118, 866-680-1884

Hydro-Québec, 75, boul René-Lévesque ouest, 20e étage, Montréal, H2Z 1A4 QC
514-289-2211

Innovatech Québec, #120, 925, Grande Allée ouest, Québec, QC G1S 1C1
418-528-9770, Fax: 418-528-9783, 866-605-1676, info@innovatech-regions.qc.ca

La financière agricole de Québec, 1400, boul de la Rive-Sud, Saint-Romuald, QC G6W 8K7
418-838-5602, Fax: 418-833-3871, 800-749-3646, dir.comm@fadq.qc.ca

Office de la sécurité du revenu des chasseurs et piègeurs cris, Édifice Champlain, #1110, 2700, boul Laurier, Sainte-Foy, QC G1V 4K5
418-643-7300, Fax: 418-643-6803, courrier@osrcpc.ca

Régie des marchés agricoles et alimentaires du Québec, 201, boul Crémazie est, 5e étage, Montréal, QC H2M 1L3
514-873-4024, Fax: 514-873-3984, rmaaqc@rmaaq.gouv.qc.ca

Régie du bâtiment du Québec, 545, boul Crémazie est, 4e étage, Montréal, QC H2M 2V2
514-873-0976, Fax: 514-864-2903, 800-361-0761, crc@rbq.gouv.qc.ca

Société d'habitation du Québec, Aile St-Amable, 1054, rue Louis-Alexandre-Taschereau, 3e étage, Québec, QC G1R 5E7
418-643-4035, Fax: 418-643-4560, 800-463-4315

Société de développement des entreprises culturelles, #800, 215, rue Saint-Jacques, Montréal, H2Y 1M6 QC
514-841-2200, Fax: 514-841-8606, 800-363-0401, info@sodec.gouv.qc.ca

Société des alcools du Québec, 905, av De Lorimier, Montréal, QC H2K 3V9
514-873-2020, Fax: 514-873-6788, 866-873-2020, info@saq.com

Société générale de financement du Québec, #1500, 600, rue de La Gauchetière ouest, Montréal, QC H3B 4L8
514-876-9290, Fax: 514-395-8055, info@sgfqc.com

Société générale de financement du Québec, #1500, 600, rue de La Gauchetière ouest, Montréal, QC H3B 4L8
514-876-9290, Fax: 514-395-8055, info@sgfqc.com

Société québécoise de récupération et de recyclage, Siège social, #200, 420, boul Charest est, Québec, QC G1K 8M4
418-643-0394, Fax: 418-643-6507, 866-523-8290, info@recyc-quebec.gouv.qc.ca

Ministère du Tourisme, #400, 900, boul René-Lévesque est, Québec, G1R 2B5 QC
418-643-5959, Fax: 418-646-8723, 800-482-2433

Saskatchewan

Agri-Food Council, #302, 3085 Albert St., Regina, SK S4S 0B1
306-787-5139, Fax: 306-787-5134, james.kettel@gov.sk.ca

Saskatchewan Agriculture, Walter Scott Bldg., 3085 Albert St., Regina, S4S 0B1 SK
306-787-5140, 866-457-2377, aginfo@gov.sk.ca

Crown Investments Corporation of Saskatchewan, #400, 2400 College Ave., Regina, S4P 1C8 SK
306-787-6851, Fax: 306-787-8125

Saskatchewan Energy & Resources, #300, 2103 - 11th Ave., Regina, S4P 3Z8 SK
306-787-2528, Fax: 306-787-0395, 866-727-5427

Saskatchewan Environment, 3211 Albert St., 2nd Fl., Regina, S4S 5W6 SK
306-953-3750, Fax: 306-787-9544, 800-567-4224, inquiry@serm.gov.sk.ca

Farm Stress Unit, #329, 3085 Albert St., Regina, SK S4S 0B1
306-787-5196, Fax: 306-798-3042, 800-667-4442, ken.imhoff@gov.sk.ca

Labour Relations Board, #1600, 1920 Broad St., Regina, SK S4P 3V2
306-787-2406, Fax: 306-787-2664, mbaldwin@lrb.gov.sk.ca

Saskatchewan Liquor & Gaming Authority, 2500 Victoria Ave., PO Box 5054, Regina, S4P 3M3 SK
306-787-4213, Fax: 306-787-8468

Saskatchewan Power Corporation (SaskPower), 2025 Victoria Ave., Regina, S4P 0S1 SK
306-566-2121, Fax: 306-566-2330, 800-667-4749

Prairie Agricultural Machinery Institute, Hwy#5 West, PO Box 1900, Humboldt, SK S0K 2A0
306-682-2555, Fax: 306-682-5080, 800-567-7264, humboldt@pami.ca

Saskatchewan Crop Insurance Corporation, 484 Prince William Dr., PO Box 3000, Melville, SK S0A 2P0
306-728-7200, Fax: 306-728-7268, 888-935-0000, customer.service@scic.gov.sk.ca

Saskatchewan Lands Appeal Board, #202, 3085 Albert St., Regina, SK S4S 0B1
306-787-4693, Fax: 306-787-1315, dbrooks@agr.gov.sk.ca

Saskatchewan Trade & Export Partnership, #320, 1801 Hamilton St., PO Box 1787, Regina, SK S4P 3C6
306-787-9210, Fax: 306-787-6666, 877-313-7244, inquire@sasktrade.sk.ca

Saskatchewan Water Corporation (SaskWater), #200, 111 Fairford St. East, Moose Jaw, S6H 1C8 SK
306-694-3098, Fax: 306-694-3207, 888-230-1111, comm@saskwater.com

Saskatchewan Workers' Compensation Board, #200, 1881 Scarth St., Regina, SK S4P 4L1
306-787-4370, Fax: 306-787-7582, 800-667-7590, internet_clientsvc@wcbsask.com

SaskEnergy Incorporated, 1777 Victoria Ave., Regina, S4P 4K5 SK
306-777-9225, Fax: 306-777-9200, 800-567-8899

Saskatchewan Workers' Compensation Board, #200, 1881 Scarth St., Regina, S4P 4L1 SK
306-787-4370, Fax: 306-787-7582, 800-667-7590, internet_clientsvc@wcbsask.com

Yukon Territory

Yukon Development Corporation, PO Box 2703 D-1,Whitehorse, Y1A 2C6 YT
867-393-5337, Fax: 867-393-5401,

Yukon Economic Development, PO Box 2703, Whitehorse, Y1A 2C6 YT
867-393-7191, Fax: 867-395-7199, 800-661-0408

Yukon Environment, PO Box 2703, Whitehorse, Y1A 2C6 YT
867-667-5652, Fax: 867-393-7197, 800-661-0408, environmentyukon@gov.yk.ca

Yukon Housing Corporation, 410H Jarvis St., Whitehorse, Y1A 2H5 YT
867-667-5759, Fax: 867-667-3664, 800-661-0408, ykhouse@housing.yk.ca

Yukon Liquor Corporation, 9031 Quartz Rd., Whitehorse, Y1A 4P9 YT
867-667-5245, Fax: 867-393-6306, yukon.liquor@gov.yk.ca

Yukon Tourism & Culture, PO Box 2703, Whitehorse, Y1A 2C6 YT
867-667-5036, Fax: 867-667-3546

INDUSTRY & TRADE

Atlantic Canada Opportunities Agency, Blue Cross Centre, 644 Main St., 3rd Fl., PO Box 6051, Moncton, E1C 9J8 NB
506-851-2271, Fax: 506-851-7403, 800-561-7862, information@acoa-apeca.gc.ca

Business Development Bank of Canada, #400, 5, Place Ville-Marie, Montréal, H3B 5E7 QC
514-283-5904, Fax: 514-283-2872, 877-232-2269

Defence Construction Canada, Constitution Square, 350 Albert St., 19th Fl., Ottawa, K1A 0K3 ON
613-998-9548, Fax: 613-998-1061, 800-514-3555, info@dcc-cdc.gc.ca

Export Development Canada, 151 O'Connor St., Ottawa, K1A 1K3 ON
613-598-2500, Fax: 613-598-3811, 800-267-8510

Foreign Affairs & International Trade Canada, 125 Sussex Dr., Ottawa, K1A 0G2 ON
613-944-4000, Fax: 613-996-9709, 800-267-8376, enqserv@international.gc.ca

Industrial Materials Institute, 75, boul de Mortagne, Boucherville, J4B 6Y4 QC
450-641-5000, Fax: 450-641-5101, Imi-Info@cnrc-nrc.gc.ca

Industry Canada, 235 Queen St., Ottawa, K1A 0H5 ON
Fax: 613-954-6436, 800-328-6189, info@ic.gc.ca

Institute for Research in Construction, Bldg. M-24, 1500 Montreal Rd., Ottawa, K1A 0R6 ON
613-993-2607, Fax: 613-952-7673, Irc.Client-Services@nrc-cnrc.gc.ca

London - Centre for Automotive Materials and Manufacturing, 800 Collip Circle, London, N6G 4X8 ON
519-430-7166, Fax: 519-430-7064, John.Lyons@nrc-cnrc.gc.ca

Market & Industry Services Branch, Tower 5, 1341 Baseline Rd., Ottawa, K1A 0C5 ON
613-759-1000, Fax: 613-773-1755

Standards Council of Canada, #200, 270 Albert St., Ottawa, K1P 6N7 ON
613-238-3222, Fax: 613-569-7808, info@scc.ca

Western Economic Diversification Canada, Canada Place, #1500, 9700 Jasper Ave. NW, Edmonton, T5J 4H7 AB
780-495-4164, Fax: 780-495-4557, 888-338-9378

Alberta

Alberta Economic Development Authority, McDougall Centre, 455 - 6 St. SW, Calgary, AB T2P 4E8
403-297-3022, Fax: 403-297-6435

British Columbia

Timber Export Advisory Committee, 1520 Blanshard St., 2nd Fl., PO Box 9514 Prov Govt, Victoria, BC V8W 9C2
250-387-8916, Fax: 250-387-5050

Manitoba

Manitoba Competitiveness, Training & Trade, International Business Centre, The Paris Building, 259 Portage Ave., Winnipeg, R3B 3P4 MB
204-945-2475, Fax: 204-945-3977, minctt@leg.gov.mb.ca

New Brunswick

Board of Examiners under the Scaler's Act, 1350 Regent St. South, PO Box 6000, Fredericton, NB E3B 5H1
506-453-2441, Fax: 506-453-6689

Department of Business New Brunswick, Centennial Bldg., 670 King St., PO Box 6000, Fredericton, E3B 5H1 NB
506-444-5228, Fax: 506-453-5428

New Brunswick Industrial Development Board, Business New Brunswick, Centennial Bldg., 670 King St., PO Box 6000, Fredericton, NB E3B 5H1
506-453-4200, Fax: 506-444-4182

Regional Development Corporation, RDC Bldg., 836 Churchill Row, PO Box 428, Fredericton, E3B 5R4 NB
506-453 2277, Fax: 506-453-7988

Newfoundland & Labrador

Department of Innovation, Trade & Rural Development, West Block, Confederation Bldg., PO Box 8700, St. John's, A1B 4J6 NL
709-729-7000, Fax: 709-729-0654, 800-563-2299, itrd@gov.nl.ca

Department of Labrador & Aboriginal Affairs, Confederation Bldg., East Block, 6th Fl., PO Box 8700, St. John's, A1B 4J6 NL
709-729-4776, Fax: 709-729-4900, 877-788-8822, laa@gov.nl.ca

Northwest Territories

Department of Environment & Natural Resources, PO Box 1320, Yellowknife, X1A 2L9 NT

Northwest Territories Business Development & Investment Corporation, #701, 5201 - 50 Ave., Yellowknife, NT X1A 3S9
867-920-6455, Fax: 867-765-0652, bdicinfo@gov.nt.ca

Nova Scotia

Department of Agriculture, 1741 Brunswick St., 3rd Fl., PO Box 2223, Halifax, B3J 3C4 NS
902-424-4560, Fax: 902-424-4671

Department of Economic & Rural Development, Centennial Building, #600, 1660 Hollis St., PO Box 2311, Halifax, B3J 1V7 NS
902-424-0377, Fax: 902-424-7008, comm@gov.ns.ca

Labour Relations Board & Construction Industry Panel, 5151 Terminal Rd.,7th Fl., PO Box 697, Halifax, NS B3J 2T8
902-424-6730, Fax: 902-424-1744

Labour Standards Tribunal, 5151 Terminal Rd., 7th Fl., PO Box 697, Halifax, NS B3J 2T8
902-424-6730, Fax: 902-424-1744, noeljl@gov.ns.ca

Pay Equity Commission, 5151 Terminal Rd., 7th Fl., PO Box 697, Halifax, NS B3J 2T8
902-424-2385, Fax: 902-424-0575

Workers' Compensation Board of Nova Scotia, 5668 South St., PO Box 1150, Halifax, B3J 2Y2 NS
902-491-8999, Fax: 902-491-8002, 800-870-3331, info@wcb.gov.ns.ca

Ontario

Ministry of Economic Development & Trade, Hearst Block, 900 Bay St., 8th Fl., Toronto, M7A 2E1 ON
416-325-6666, Fax: 416-325-6688, 866-668-4249, info@edt.gov.on.ca

Ministry of Northern Development, Mines & Forestry, 99 Wellesley St. West, Toronto, M7A 1W3 ON
416-327-0633, Fax: 416-327-0665

Prince Edward Island

Department of Innovation & Advanced Learning, Shaw Bldg., 105 Rochford St., 5th Fl., PO Box 2000, Charlottetown, C1A 7N8 PE
902-368-4240, Fax: 902-368-4242

Quebec

Commission des lésions professionnelles, #700, 900, Place d'Youville, Québec, QC G1R 3P7
418-644-7777, Fax: 418-644-6443, 800-463-1591

Innovatech Québec, #120, 925, Grande Allée ouest, Québec, QC G1S 1C1
418-528-9770, Fax: 418-528-9783, 866-605-1676, info@innovatech-regions.qc.ca

Société générale de financement du Québec, #1500, 600, rue de La Gauchetière ouest, Montréal, QC H3B 4L8
514-876-9290, Fax: 514-395-8055, info@sgfqc.com

Saskatchewan

Saskatchewan Energy & Resources, #300, 2103 - 11th Ave., Regina, S4P 3Z8 SK
306-787-2528, Fax: 306-787-0395, 866-727-5427

Saskatchewan Trade & Export Partnership, #320, 1801 Hamilton St., PO Box 1787, Regina, SK S4P 3C6
306-787-9210, Fax: 306-787-6666, 877-313-7244, inquire@sasktrade.sk.ca

Tourism Saskatchewan, 1922 Park St., Regina, SK S4N 7M4
306-787-9600, 877-237-2273

Yukon Territory

Yukon Development Corporation, PO Box 2703 D-1,Whitehorse, Y1A 2C6 YT
867-393-5337, Fax: 867-393-5401

INFORMATION & PRIVACY COMMISSIONER

Office of the Information Commissioner of Canada, Place de Ville, Tower B, 112 Kent St., 7th Fl., Ottawa, K1A 1H3 ON
613-995-2410, Fax: 613-947-7294, 800-267-0441, general@infocom.gc.ca

Privacy Commissioner of Canada, Tower B, Place de Ville, 112 Kent St., 3rd Fl., Ottawa, K1A 1H3 ON
613-995-8210, Fax: 613-947-6850, 800-282-1376, info@privcom.gc.ca

Ontario

Information & Privacy Commissioner of Ontario, #1400, 2 Bloor St. East, Toronto, M4W 1A8 ON
416-326-3333, Fax: 416-325-9195, 800-387-0073, info@ipc.on.ca

Saskatchewan

Information & Privacy Commissioner of Saskatchewan, #503, 1801 Hamilton St., Regina, S4P 4B4 SK
306-787-8350, Fax: 306-798-1603, 877-748-2298, info@oipc.sk.ca

INFORMATION RESOURCES

Industry Canada, 235 Queen St., Ottawa, K1A 0H5 ON
Fax: 613-954-6436, 800-328-6189, info@ic.gc.ca

Public Works & Government Services Canada, Place du Portage, Phase III, 11, rue Laurier, Ottawa, K1A 0S5 ON
819-997-6363, Fax: 819-956-9062, 800-622-6232, questions@tpsgc-pwgsc.gc.ca

Statistics Canada, R.H. Coats Bldg., Tunney's Pasture, 100 Tunney's Pasture Driveway, Ottawa, K1A 0T6 ON
613-951-8116, Fax: 877-287-4369, 800-263-1136, infostats@statcan.ca

New Brunswick

Service New Brunswick, Westmorland Place, #200, 82 Westmorland St., PO Box 1998, Fredericton, E3B 5G4 NB
506-457-3581, Fax: 506-457-7520, 888-762-8600, snb@snb.ca

Nova Scotia

Nova Scotia Geomatics Centre, 160 Willow St., Amherst, B4H 3W3 NS
902-667-7231, Fax: 902-667-6008, 800-798-0706, info@nsgc.gov.ns.ca

Ontario

Ontario Geographic Names Board, Robinson Place, 300 Water St., 2nd Fl., PO Box 7000, Peterborough, ON K9J 8M5
705-755-2134, Fax: 705-755-2131

Science & Information Resources Division, Robinson Place, North Tower, 300 Water St., 2nd Fl., Peterborough, K9J 8M5 ON
705-755-2000, Fax: 705-755-2802, 800-667-1940

Saskatchewan

Saskatchewan Conservation Data Centre, 3211 Albert St., Regina, SK S4S 5W6
306-787-9038, Fax: 306-787-9544

INSURANCE

New Brunswick

New Brunswick Insurance Board, Saint John Mercantile Centre, #600, 55 Union St., Saint John, NB E2L 5B7
506-643-7710, Fax: 506-652-5011, info@nbib-canb.org

INSURANCE (LIFE, FIRE, PROPERTY)

See Also: Automobile Insurance; Health Care Insurance

Canada Deposit Insurance Corporation, 50 O'Connor St., 17th Floor, PO Box 2340 D,Ottawa, K1P 5W5 ON
613-996-2081, Fax: 613-996-6095, 800-461-2342, info@cdic.ca; info@sadc.ca

Office of the Superintendent of Financial Institutions, Kent Square, 255 Albert St., Ottawa, K1A 0H2 ON
613-990-7788, Fax: 613-990-5591, 800-385-8647, information@osfi-bsif.gc.ca

Office of Budget & Fiscal Planning, Terrace Building, 9515 - 107 St., 4th Fl., Edmonton, T5K 2C3 AB

British Columbia

Insurance Council of British Columbia, #300, 1040 West Georgia St., PO Box 7, Vancouver, BC V6E 4H1
604-688-0321, Fax: 604-662-7767, 877-688-0321

Manitoba

Financial Institutions Regulation Branch, #1115, 405 Broadway, Winnipeg, R3C 3L6 MB
204-945-2542, Fax: 204-948-2268

Manitoba Public Insurance, #820, 234 Donald St., PO Box 6300, Winnipeg, R3C 4A4 MB
204-985-7000, Fax: 204-943-9851, 800-665-2410

Manitoba Agricultural Services Corporation, #100, 1525 First St. South, Brandon, MB R7A 7A1
204-726-6850, Fax: 204-726-6849, mailbox@masc.mb.ca

New Brunswick

New Brunswick Credit Union Deposit Insurance Corp., PO Box 6000, Fredericton, NB E3B 5H1
506-457-4852, Fax: 506-453-7474

New Brunswick Crop Insurance Commission, PO Box 6000, Fredericton, NB E3B 5H1
506-453-2185, Fax: 506-453-7406

New Brunswick Insurance Board, Saint John Mercantile Centre, #600, 55 Union St., Saint John, NB E2L 5B7
506-643-7710, Fax: 506-652-5011, info@nbib-canb.org

Northwest Territories

Department of Finance, YK Center, 3rd Fl., PO Box 1320, Yellowknife, X1A 2L9 NT
867-669-2311, Fax: 867-873-0385

Nova Scotia

Nova Scotia Utility and Review Board, Summit Place, 1601 Lower Water St., 3rd Fl., Halifax, NS B3J 3P6
902-424-4448, uarb.board@gov.ns.ca

Ontario

Deposit Insurance Corporation of Ontario, #700, 4711 Yonge St., Toronto, ON M2N 6K8
416-325-9444, Fax: 416-325-9722, 800-268-6653

Financial Services Commission of Ontario, 5160 Yonge St., PO Box 85, Toronto, ON M2N 6L9
416-250-7250, Fax: 416-590-7070, 800-668-0128

Prince Edward Island

Agricultural Insurance Corporation, 29 Indigo Cres., PO Box 1600, Charlottetown, PE C1A 7N3
902-368-4842, Fax: 902-368-6677, peiaic@gov.pe.ca

Quebec

Commission administrative des régimes de retraite et d'assurances (Québec), 475, rue Saint-Amable, Québec, QC G1R 5X3
418-643-4881, Fax: 418-644-3839, 800-463-5533

Saskatchewan

Saskatchewan Government Insurance, 2260 - 11th Ave., Regina, S4P 0J9 SK
306 751-1200, Fax: 306-787-7477, 800-667-8015, sgiinquiries@sgi.sk.ca

Saskatchewan Crop Insurance Corporation, 484 Prince William Dr., PO Box 3000, Melville, SK S0A 2P0
306-728-7200, Fax: 306-728-7268, 888-935-0000, customer.service@scic.gov.sk.ca

Saskatchewan Financial Services Commission, #601, 1919 Saskatchewan Dr., Regina, SK S4P 4H2
306-787-5645, Fax: 306-787-5899

INTELLECTUAL PROPERTY

Canadian Intellectual Property Office, Place du Portage I, 50, rue Victoria, Gatineau, K1A 0C9 QC
819-997-1936, Fax: 819-953-7620, 866-997-1936

London - Centre for Automotive Materials and Manufacturing, 800 Collip Circle, London, N6G 4X8 ON
519-430-7166, Fax: 519-430-7064, John.Lyons@nrc-cnrc.gc.ca

INTERNATIONAL AFFAIRS

See Also: Trade

Canadian International Development Agency, 200, Promenade du Portage, Gatineau, K1A 0G4 QC
819-997-5006, Fax: 819-953-6088, 800-230-6349, info@acdi-cida.gc.ca

Canadian International Trade Tribunal, Standard Life Centre, 333 Laurier Ave. West, 17 Floor, Ottawa, K1A 0G7 ON
613-990-2452, Fax: 613-990-2439

Foreign Affairs & International Trade Canada, 125 Sussex Dr., Ottawa, K1A 0G2 ON
613-944-4000, Fax: 613-996-9709, 800-267-8376, enqserv@international.gc.ca

International Development Research Centre, 150 Kent St., PO Box 8500, Ottawa, K1P 0B2 ON
613-236-6163, Fax: 613-238-7230, info@idrc.ca
National Defence Canada, Major-General George R. Pearkes Bldg., 101 Colonel By Dr., Ottawa, K1A 0K2 ON
613-995-2534, Fax: 613-992-4739, 800-856-8488

Alberta
Alberta International & Intergovernmental Relations, Commerce Place, 10155 - 102 St., 12th Fl., Edmonton, T5J 4G8 AB
780-422-1510, Fax: 780-427-0699

British Columbia
Intergovernmental Relations Secretariat, 548 Michigan St., 1st Fl., PO Box 9433 Prov Govt,Victoria, V8W 9V3 BC
250-387-0783, Fax: 250-387-1920, igrs@gov.bc.ca

Manitoba
Manitoba Intergovernmental Affairs, #301, 450 Broadway Ave., Winnipeg, R3C 0V8 MB
Fax: 204-945-1383, mnia@leg.gov.mb.ca

New Brunswick
Department of Intergovernmental Affairs, Centennial Bldg., #274, 670 King St., PO Box 6000, Fredericton, E3B 5H1 NB
506-444-5418, Fax: 506-453-2995, iga@gnb.ca

Ontario
Ministry of Intergovernmental Affairs, 77 Wellesley St. West, Toronto, M7A 1N3 ON
416-325-4800, Fax: 416-325-4787

Quebec
Ministère des Relations internationales, Édifice Hector-Fabre, 525, boul Réne-Lévesque est, Québec, G1R 5R9 QC
418-649-2300, Fax: 418-649-2656, communications@mri.gouv.qc.ca

Saskatchewan
Trade & International Relations, #800, 1919 Saskatchewan Dr., Regina, S4P 4H2 SK
306-787-6445, Fax: 306-787-7317

INTERNATIONAL AID

Canadian International Development Agency, 200, Promenade du Portage, Gatineau, K1A 0G4 QC
819-997-5006, Fax: 819-953-6088, 800-230-6349, info@acdi-cida.gc.ca
International Development Research Centre, 150 Kent St., PO Box 8500, Ottawa, K1P 0B2 ON
613-236-6163, Fax: 613-238-7230, info@idrc.ca

INVESTMENT

See Also: Business Development; Industry
Canada Economic Development for Québec Regions, Édifice Dominion Square, #900, 1255, rue Peel, Montréal, H3B 2T9 QC
514-283-6412, Fax: 514-283-3302, 866-385-6412
Canada Investment & Savings, #900, 110 Yonge St., Toronto, ON M5C 1T4
416-952-1252, Fax: 416-952-1270, 800-575-5151, csb@csb.gc.ca
Canada Pension Plan Investment Board, #2600, 1 Queen St. East, PO Box 101, Toronto, M5C 2W5 ON
416-868-4075, Fax: 416-868-8689, 866-557-9510, csr@cppib.ca
Finance Canada, L'esplanade Laurier, 140 O'Connor St., Ottawa, K1A 0G5 ON
613-992-1573, Fax: 613-943-0938, finpub@fin.gc.ca
Global Operations & Chief Trade Commissioner, 125 Sussex Dr,, Ottawa, K1A 0G2 ON
613-944-2697, Fax: 613-996-1667
Industry Canada, 235 Queen St., Ottawa, K1A 0H5 ON
Fax: 613-954-6436, 800-328-6189, info@ic.gc.ca
Public Sector Pension Investment Board, #200, 440 Laurier Ave. West, Ottawa, ON K1R 7X6
613-782-3095, Fax: 613-782-6864, info@investpsp.ca
Tax & Revenue Administration, Sir Frederick W. Haultain Building, 9811 - 109 St., 2nd Fl., Edmonton, T5K 2L5 AB
780-427-3044

Alberta
Intergovernmental Relations, Commerce Place, 10155 - 102 St., 12th Fl., Edmonton, T5J 4L8 AB

British Columbia
Forestry Innovation Investments, #1200, 1130 West Pender St., Vancouver, BC V6E 4A4
604-685-7507, Fax: 604-685-5373, info@bcfii.ca
Technology, Research & Innovation Division, #730, 999 Canada Place, Vancouver, V6C 3E1 BC
Fax: 604-775-2070

New Brunswick
Investment & Export Development, Centennial Bldg., 670 King St., 5th F., PO Box 6000, Fredericton, E3B 5H1 NB
506-453-2875, Fax: 506-444-4277
New Brunswick Investment Management Corporation, York Tower, #581, 440 King St., Fredericton, NB E3B 5H8
506-444-5800, Fax: 506-444-5025, comments@nbimc.com

Northwest Territories
Department of Industry, Tourism & Investment, PO Box 1320, Yellowknife, X1A 2L9 NT
Fax: 867-873-0306, info@iti.ca
Northwest Territories Business Development & Investment Corporation, #701, 5201 - 50 Ave., Yellowknife, NT X1A 3S9
867-920-6455, Fax: 867-765-0652, bdicinfo@gov.nt.ca

Nova Scotia
InNOVACorp, #1400, 1801 Hollis St., Halifax, NS B3J 3N4
902-424-8670, Fax: 902-424-4679, 800-565-7051, communications@innovacorp.ca

Ontario
Investment & Trade Division, Hearst Block, 900 Bay St., 5th fl., Toronto, M7A 2E1 ON
416-325-9802, Fax: 416-325-5617

Prince Edward Island
Island Investment Development Inc., 94 Euston St., 2nd Fl., Charlottetown, PE C1A 1W4
902-894-0351, Fax: 902-368-5886
Prince Edward Island Business Development Inc., 94 Euston St., 1st & 2nd Fl., PO Box 910, Charlottetown, PE C1A 7L9
902-368-6300, Fax: 902-368-6301, 800-563-3734, business@gov.pe.ca

Quebec
Société générale de financement du Québec, #1500, 600, rue de La Gauchetière ouest, Montréal, QC H3B 4L8
514-876-9290, Fax: 514-395-8055, info@sgfqc.com

JUSTICE DEPARTMENTS

Justice Canada, East Memorial Bldg., 284 Wellington St., Ottawa, K1A 0H8 ON
613-957-4222, Fax: 613-954-0811, webadmin@justice.gc.ca

Alberta
Alberta Justice & Attorney General, Communications, Bowker Bldg., 9833 - 109 St., 3rd Fl., Edmonton, T5K 2E8 AB
780-427-2745, Fax: 780-427-6821,-310-0000

British Columbia
Ministry of the Attorney General, PO Box 9044 Prov Govt,Victoria, V8W 9E2 BC
250-387-1866, Fax: 250-387-6411

Manitoba
Manitoba Justice, Legislative Building, #104, 405 Broadway Ave., Winnipeg, R3C 3L6 MB
204-945-3728, Fax: 204-945-2517, minjus@gov.mb.ca

New Brunswick
Department of Justice & Consumer Affairs, Centennial Bldg., 670 King St., PO Box 6000, Fredericton, E3B 5H1 NB
506-462-5100, Fax: 506-453-3651, justice.comments@gnb.ca

Newfoundland & Labrador
Department of Justice, Confederation Bldg., East Block, 4th Fl., PO Box 8700, St. John's, A1B 4J6 NL
709-729-5942, Fax: 709-729-2129, justice@gov.nl.ca

Northwest Territories
Department of Justice, Courthouse, 4903 - 49th St., 6th Fl., PO Box 1320, Yellowknife, X1A 2L9 NT
867-920-6197

Nova Scotia
Department of Justice, 5151 Terminal Rd., 4th Fl., PO Box 7, Halifax, B3J 2L6 NS
902-424-4030, Fax: 902-424-0510, webbermj@gov.ns.ca

Nunavut
Department of Justice, Sivummut, 1st Fl., PO Box 1000 500,Iqaluit, X0A 0H0 NU
867-975-6170, Fax: 867-975-6195

Ontario
Ministry of the Attorney General, McMurtry-Scott Bldg., 720 Bay St., 11th Fl., Toronto, M5G 2K1 ON
416-326-2220, Fax: 416-326-4007, 800-518-7901

Prince Edward Island
Office of the Attorney General, Shaw Building, North, 105 Rochford St., 4th Fl., PO Box 2000, Charlottetown, C1A 7N8 PE
902-368-5152, Fax: 902-368-4910

Quebec
Ministère de la Justice, Édifice Louis-Philippe-Pigeon, 1200, rte de l'Église, Québec, G1V 4M1 QC
418-643-5140, 866-536-5140, informations@justice.gouv.qc.ca

Saskatchewan
Saskatchewan Justice, 1874 Scarth St., Regina, S4P 4B3 SK
306-787-7872, Fax: 306-787-3874

Yukon Territory
Yukon Justice, PO Box 2703, Whitehorse, Y1A 2C6 YT
867-667-8655, Fax: 867-393-5790

LABOUR

Canada Industrial Relations Board, 240 Sparks St., 4th Floor West, Ottawa, K1A 0X8 ON
613-947-5440, Fax: 613-995-9493, 800-575-9696, info@cirb-ccri.gc.ca
Canadian Artists & Producers Professional Relations Tribunal, C.D. Howe Bldg., 240 Sparks St., 1st Fl., West Tower, Ottawa, K1A 1A1 ON
613-996-4052, Fax: 613-947-4125, 800-263-ARTS, info@capprt-tcrpap.gc.ca
Canadian Council of Directors of Apprenticeship, 140 Promenade du Portage, 5th Fl, Phase IV, Gatineau, QC K1A 0J9
819-953-7443, Fax: 819-994-0202, redseal-sceaurouge@hrsdc-rhdcc.gc.ca
Human Resources & Skills Development Canada, 140 Promenade du Portage, Ottawa, K1A 0J9 ON
Department of Labour & Workforce Development, 5151 Terminal Rd., 6th Fl., PO Box 697, Halifax, B3J 2T8 NS
902-424-5301, Fax: 902-424-0575
Merchant Seamen Compensation Board, Secretary, Merchant Seamen Compensation Board, Phase II, Place du Portage, 10th Fl., Gatineau, QC K1A 0J2
819-953-8001, Fax: 819-994-5368
National Joint Council, C.D. Howe Bldg., 240 Sparks St. West, 7th Fl., PO Box 1525 B,Ottawa, K1P 5V2 ON
613-990-1805, Fax: 613-990-7071, email.courrier@njc-cnm.gc.ca
Public Service Commission, West Tower, 300 Laurier Ave. West, Ottawa, K1A 0M7 ON
613-992-9562, Fax: 613-992-9352, infocom@psc-cfp.gc.ca
Public Service Labour Relations Board, CD Howe Building, 240 Sparks St., 6th Fl., PO Box 1525 B, Ottawa, ON K1P 5V2
613-990-1800, Fax: 613-990-1849, 866-931-3454, mail.courrier@pslrb-crtfp.gc.ca
Public Service Staffing Tribunal, 240 Sparks St., 6th Fl., Ottawa, K1A 0A5 ON
613-949-6516, Fax: 613-949-6551, 866-637-4491, info@psst-tdfp.gc.ca
Workers' Compensation Appeals Tribunal, #1002, 5670 Spring Garden Rd., Halifax, NS B3J 1H6
902-424-2250, Fax: 902-424-2321, 800-274-8281

Alberta
Alberta Apprenticeship & Industry Training Board, South Tower, 10030 - 107 St., 7th Fl., Edmonton, AB T5J 4X7
780-427-8517, Fax: 780-422-3734, 800-232-7215
Community, Learner & Industry Connections Division, Phipps-McKinnon Bldg., 5th Fl., 10020 - 101A Ave., Edmonton, T5J 3G2 AB
780-427-8517
Alberta Employment & Immigration, Minister's Office, Legislature Bldg., #208, 10800 - 97 Ave., Edmonton, T5K 2B6 AB
780-644-5135, Fax: 780-422-9556, 866-644-5135, eii.communications@gov.ab.ca
Health Disciplines Board, Telus Plaza NT, Health Professions Branch, 10025 Jasper Ave., 17th Fl., Edmonton, AB T5J 2N3
780-415-0486, Fax: 780-422-2880
Labour Relations Board, #503, 10808 - 99 Ave., Edmonton, AB T5K 0G5
780-422-5926, Fax: 780-422-0970, 800-463-2572, alrbinfo@lab.gov.ab.ca
Occupational Health & Safety Council, Labour Bldg, 10808 - 99 Ave., 9th Fl., Edmonton, AB T5K 0G5
780-415-0599, Fax: 780-422-8944

British Columbia
British Columbia Labour Relations Board, Oceanic Plaza, #600, 1066 West Hastings St., Vancouver, BC V6E 3X1
604-660-1300, Fax: 604-660-1892, information@lrb.bc.ca
Employment Standards Tribunal, Oceanic Plaza, #650, 1066 West Hastings St., Vancouver, BC V6E 3X1
604-775-3512, Fax: 604-775-3372, registrar.est@bcest.bc.ca
Ministry of Housing & Social Development, PO Box 9058 Prov Govt,Victoria, V8W 9E2 BC
250-356-7750, Fax: 250-356-7292, EIA.Minister@gov.bc.ca; EnquiryBC@gov.bc.ca

Ministry of Labour, PO Box 9052 Prov Govt,Victoria, V8W 9E2 BC
250-356-6348, Fax: 250-356-6595, LCS.Minister@gov.bc.ca
Workers' Compensation Appeal Tribunal, #150, 4600 Jacombs Rd., Richmond, BC V6V 3B1
604-664-7800, Fax: 604-664-7898, 800-663-2782
Workers' Compensation Board of British Columbia, PO Box 5350 Terminal,Vancouver, V6B 5L5 BC
604-276-3100, Fax: 604-244-6490, 888-621-7233

Manitoba

Advisory Council on Workplace Safety & Health, #200, 401 York Ave., Winnipeg, MB R3C 0P8
204-945-3446, Fax: 204-945-4556
Civil Service Commission Board, #935, 155 Carlton St., Winnipeg, MB R3C 3H8
204-945-1435, Fax: 204-945-1486
Manitoba Civil Service Commission, #935, 155 Carlton St., Winnipeg, R3C 3H8 MB
204-945-2332, Fax: 204-945-1486, 800-282-8069, cschrp@gov.mb.ca
Manitoba Education, Citizenship & Youth, #168, Legislative Bldg., 450 Broadway, Winnipeg, R3C 0V8 MB
204-945-3720, Fax: 204-945-1291, minedu@leg.gov.mb.ca
Manitoba Labour & Immigration, Legislative Building, 317, 450 Broadway Ave., Winnipeg, R3C 0V8 MB
204-945-4079, Fax: 204-945-8312, minlab@leg.gov.mb.ca
Manitoba Civil Service Commission, #935, 155 Carlton St., Winnipeg, MB R3C 3H8
204-945-2332, Fax: 204-945-1486, cschrp@gov.mb.ca
Manitoba Labour Board, A.A. Heaps Bldg., #402, 258 Portage Ave., Winnipeg, MB R3C 0B6
204-945-3783, Fax: 204-945-1296, mlb@gov.mb.ca
Manitoba Minimum Wage Board, 614 - 401 York Ave., Winnipeg, MB R3C 0P8
204-945-4889, Fax: 204-948-2085, mw@gov.mb.ca
Pension Commission of Manitoba, #1004, 401 York Ave., Winnipeg, MB R3C 0P8
204-945-2740, Fax: 204-948-2375, pensions@gov.mb.ca
Manitoba Workers' Compensation Board, 333 Broadway Ave., Winnipeg, R3C 4W3 MB
204-954-4321, Fax: 204-954-4999, 800-362-3340, wcb@wcb.mb.ca
Workplace Safety & Health Division, #200, 401 York Ave., Winnipeg, R3C 0P8 MB
204-945-3446, Fax: 204-948-2209, wshcompl@gov.mb.ca

New Brunswick

Apprenticeship & Occupational Certification Board, PO Box 6000, Fredericton, NB E3B 5H1
506-453-2260, Fax: 506-453-5317
Department of Post-Secondary Education, Training & Labour, 470 York St., PO Box 6000, Fredericton, E3B 5H1 NB
506-453-2597, Fax: 506-453-3618, dpetlinfo@gnb.ca
Workplace Health, Safety & Compensation Commission of New Brunswick, 1 Portland St., PO Box 160, Saint John, E2L 3X9 NB
506-632-2200, 800-222-9775, communications@ws-ts.nb.ca

Newfoundland & Labrador

Department of Human Resources, Labour & Employment, Confederation Bldg., PO Box 8700, St. John's, A1B 4J6 NL
709-729-2478, Fax: 709-729-6996, hreweb@gov.nl.ca
Labour Relations Board, Beothuck Bldg., 20 Crosbie Pl., 5th Fl., PO Box 8700, St. John's, NL A1B 4J6
709-729-2707, Fax: 709-729-5738
Newfoundland & Labrador Workplace Health, Safety & Compensation Commission, 146 - 148 Forest Rd., PO Box 9000, St. John's, A1A 3B8 NL
709-778-1000, Fax: 709-738-1714, 800-563-9000, general.inquiries@whscc.nl.ca

Northwest Territories

Department of Education, Culture & Employment, PO Box 1320, Yellowknife, X1A 2L9 NT
867-669-2399, Fax: 867-873-0431, 866-606-5627
Northwest Territories Apprenticeship, Trade & Occupations Certification Board, PO Box 1320, Yellowknife, NT X1A 2L9
867-873-7357, Fax: 867-873-0200
Northwest Territories & Nunavut Workers' Compensation Board, Centre Square Tower, 5022 - 49th St., 5th Fl., PO Box 8888, Yellowknife, X1A 2R3 NT
867-920-3888, Fax: 867-873-4596, 800-661-0792, wcb@wcb.nt.ca

Nova Scotia

Labour Relations Board & Construction Industry Panel, 5151 Terminal Rd.,7th Fl., PO Box 697, Halifax, NS B3J 2T8
902-424-6730, Fax: 902-424-1744
Labour Standards Tribunal, 5151 Terminal Rd., 7th Fl., PO Box 697, Halifax, NS B3J 2T8
902-424-6730, Fax: 902-424-1744, noeljl@gov.ns.ca
Nova Scotia Advisory Board on Colleges & Universities, 2021 Brunswick St., PO Box 2086 M, Halifax, NS B3J 3B7
902-424-6992, Fax: 902-424-0651
Occupational Health & Safety Advisory Council, PO Box 697, Halifax, NS B3J 2T8
902-424-2484, Fax: 902-424-5640
Pay Equity Commission, 5151 Terminal Rd., 7th Fl., PO Box 697, Halifax, NS B3J 2T8
902-424-2385, Fax: 902-424-0575
Nova Scotia Public Service Commission, One Government Place, 1700 Granville St., PO Box 943, Halifax, B3J 2V9 NS
902-424-7660
Workers' Advisers Program, #502, 5670 Spring Garden Rd., PO Box 1063, Halifax, NS B3J 2X1
902-424-5050, Fax: 902-424-0530, 800-774-4712
Workers' Compensation Board of Nova Scotia, 5668 South St., PO Box 1150, Halifax, B3J 2Y2 NS
902-491-8999, Fax: 902-491-8002, 800-870-3331, info@wcb.gov.ns.ca

Nunavut

Department of Human Resources, PO Box 1000 400,Iqaluit, X0A 1H0 NU
867-975-6200, Fax: 867-975-6216, 888-668-9993, gnhr@gov.nu.ca

Ontario

Ministry of Education, Mowat Block, 900 Bay St., 22nd. Fl., Toronto, M7A 1L2 ON
416-325-2929, Fax: 416-325-2934, 800-387-5514, info@edu.gov.on.ca
Ministry of Labour, 400 University Ave., 14th Fl., Toronto, M7A 1T7 ON
416-326-7770, 800-268-8013
Office of the Employer Advisor, #704, 151 Bloor St. West., Toronto, ON M5S 1S4
416-327-0020, Fax: 416-327-0726, 800-387-0774
Office of the Worker Advisor, #1300, 123 Edward St., Toronto, ON M5G 1E2
416-325-8570, Fax: 416-325-4830, 800-435-8980
Ontario Labour Relations Board, 505 University Ave., 2nd Fl., Toronto, ON M5G 2P1
416-326-7500, Fax: 416-326-7531, 877-339-3335
Pay Equity Commission, 400 University Ave., 11th Fl., Toronto, ON M7A 1T7
416-314-1896, Fax: 416-314-8741, 800-387-8813
Ministry of Training, Colleges & Universities, Mowat Block, 900 Bay St., 3rd Fl., Toronto, M7A 1L2 ON
416-325-1600, Fax: 416-325-2934
Workplace Safety & Insurance Board, 200 Front St. West, Ground Fl., Toronto, M5V 3J1 ON
416-344-1000, Fax: 416-344-4684, 800-387-0750

Prince Edward Island

Employment Development Agency, Sullivan Bldg., 1st Fl., PO Box 2000, Charlottetown, PE C1A 7N8
902-368-5805, Fax: 902-368-5909
Employment Standards Board, 161 St. Peters Rd., PO Box 2000, Charlottetown, PE C1A 7N8
902-368-5550, Fax: 902-368-5476
Labour Relations Board, PO Box 2000, Charlottetown, PE C1A 7N8
902-368-5550, Fax: 902-368-5476
Prince Edward Island Workers Compensation Board, 14 Weymouth St., PO Box 757, Charlottetown, C1A 7L7 PE
902-368-5680, Fax: 902-368-5705, 800-237-5049

Quebec

Commission de l'équité salariale, 200, ch Ste-Foy, 4e étage, Québec, QC G1R 6A1
418-528-8765, Fax: 418-528-6999, 888-528-8765, equite.salariale@ces.gouv.qc.ca
Commission de la construction du Québec, 3530, rue Jean-Talon ouest, Montréal, QC H3R 2G3
514-341-7740, Fax: 514-341-6354, 888-842-8222
Commission des lésions professionnelles, #700, 900, Place d'Youville, Québec, QC G1R 3P7
418-644-7777, Fax: 418-644-6443, 800-463-1591
Commission des normes du travail, Hall Est, 400, boul Jean-Lesage, 7e étage, Québec, QC G1K 8W1
418-644-0817, Fax: 418-643-5132, 800-563-9058
Commission des partenaires du marché du travail, #2800, 800, rue du Square-Victoria, CP 100, Montréal, QC H4Z 1B7
514-873-5252, Fax: 514-864-8005, partenaires@messf.gouv.qc.ca
Conseil consultatif du travail et de la main d'oeuvre, #9.400, 500, boul René-Lévesque ouest, Montréal, QC H2Z 1W7
514-873-2880, Fax: 514-873-1129, cctm@cctm.gouv.qc.ca
Conseil des services essentiels du Québec, 800, tour de la place-Victoria, 25e étage, CP 365, Montréal, QC H4Z 1H9
514-873-7246, Fax: 514-873-3839, 800-337-7246, info@cses.gouv.qc.ca
Office des professions du Québec, 800, place D'Youville, 10e étage, Québec, G1R 5Z3 QC
418-643-6912, Fax: 418-643-0973, 800-643-6912, courrier@opq.gouv.qc.ca
Régie du bâtiment du Québec, 545, boul Crémazie est, 4e étage, Montréal, QC H2M 2V2
514-873-0976, Fax: 514-864-2903, 800-361-0761, crc@rbq.gouv.qc.ca
Commission de la santé et de la sécurité du travail du Québec, 524, rue Bourdages, CP 1200 Terminus postal,Québec, G1K 7E2 QC
418-266-4850, Fax: 418-266-4398, 866-302-2778
Ministère du Travail, 200, ch Sainte-Foy, 6e étage, Québec, G1R 5S1 QC
418-643-4817, Fax: 418-528-0559, 800-643-4817, service_clientele@travail.gouv.qc.ca

Saskatchewan

Saskatchewan Advanced Education, Employment & Labour, 1945 Hamilton St., Regina, S4P 2C8 SK
306-787-9478, Fax: 306-787-2315
Saskatchewan Education, 2220 College Ave., Regina, S4P 4V9 SK
306-787-6030, 888-775-3276, learninginquiry@sasked.gov.sk.ca
Labour Relations Board, #1600, 1920 Broad St., Regina, SK S4P 3V2
306-787-2406, Fax: 306-787-2664, mbaldwin@lrb.gov.sk.ca
Minimum Wage Board, #400, 1870 Albert St., Regina, SK S4P 4W1
306-787-2391, Fax: 306-787-7229, webmaster@lab.gov.sk.ca
Office of the Worker's Advocate, #400, 1870 Albert St., Regina, SK S4P 4W1
306-787-2456, Fax: 306-787-0249, 877-787-2456
Saskatchewan Public Service Commission, 2100 Broad St., Regina, S4P 1Y5 SK
306-787-7575, Fax: 306-787-7578, 866-319-5999, webmaster@psc.gov.sk.ca
Saskatchewan Workers' Compensation Board, #200, 1881 Scarth St., Regina, SK S4P 4L1
306-787-4370, Fax: 306-787-7582, 800-667-7590, internet_clientsvc@wcbsask.com
Saskatchewan Workers' Compensation Board, #200, 1881 Scarth St., Regina, S4P 4L1 SK
306-787-4370, Fax: 306-787-7582, 800-667-7590, internet_clientsvc@wcbsask.com

Yukon Territory

Yukon Public Service Commission, PO Box 2703, Whitehorse, Y1A 2C6 YT
867-667-5252, Fax: 867-667-6705
Yukon Workers' Compensation Health & Safety Board, 401 Strickland St., Whitehorse, Y1A 5N8 YT
867-667-5645, Fax: 867-393-6279, 800-661-0443, worksafe@gov.yk.ca

LAND RESOURCES

See Also: Agriculture; Forest Resources; Parks
Canada Lands Company Ltd., #1200, 1 University Ave., Toronto, M5J 2P1 ON
416-952-6111, Fax: 416-952-6115, 888-252-5263
Natural Resources Canada, 580 Booth St., Ottawa, K1A 0E4 ON
613-995-0947, Fax: 613-992-7211
Parks Canada, 25 Eddy St., Gatineau, K1A 0M5 QC
613-860-1251, 888-773-8888, information@pc.gc.ca

Alberta

Alberta Special Areas Board, 212 - 2nd Ave. West, PO Box 820, Hanna, AB T0J 1P0
403-854-5600, Fax: 403-854-5527, specarea@telusplanet.net

British Columbia

Crown Land Administration, 808 Douglas St., 5th Fl., PO Box 9120 Prov Govt,Victoria, V8W 9B4 BC
250-356-3076, Fax: 250-356-7279

Manitoba

Farm Lands Ownership Board, #812, Norquay Bldg., 401 York Ave., Winnipeg, MB R3C 0P8
204-945-3149, Fax: 204-945-1489, 800-282-8069, robert.mckenzie@gov.mb.ca
Manitoba Conservation Districts Commission, Secretariat c/o Planning & Coordination Branch, 123 Main St., PO Box 20000, Neepawa, MB R0J 1H0
204-476-7033, Fax: 204-476-7539, whildebran@gov.mb.ca
Manitoba Land Value Appraisal Commission, 800 Portage Ave., Winnipeg, MB R3G 0N4
204-945-2941, Fax: 204-948-2235

New Brunswick
Service New Brunswick, Westmorland Place, #200, 82 Westmorland St., PO Box 1998, Fredericton, E3B 5G4 NB
506-457-3581, Fax: 506-457-7520, 888-762-8600, snb@snb.ca

Northwest Territories
Department of Environment & Natural Resources, PO Box 1320, Yellowknife, X1A 2L9 NT
Department of Municipal & Community Affairs, PO Box 1320, Yellowknife, X1A 2L9 NT
867-873-7118, Fax: 867-873-0309

Nunavut
Department of Environment, PO Box 1000 1300,Iqaluit, X0A 0H0 NU
867-975-7700, Fax: 867-975-7742, 866-222-9063, environment@gov.nu.ca

Ontario
Natural Resources Management Division, Whitney Block, #6540, 99 Wellesley St. West, Toronto, M7A 1W3 ON
416-314-2000, Fax: 416-314-1994

Prince Edward Island
Department of Environment, Energy & Forestry, Jones Bldg., 11 Kent St., 4th & 5th Fl., PO Box 2000, Charlottetown, C1A 7N8 PE
902-368-5000, Fax: 902-368-5830

Quebec
Commission de protection du territoire agricole du Québec, 200, ch Ste-Foy, 2e étage, Québec, QC G1R 4X6
418-643-3314, Fax: 418-643-2261, 800-667-5294, info@cptaq.gouv.qc.ca
Foncier Québec, #E306, 5700, 4e av ouest, Québec, G1H 6R1 QC
418-643-3582, Fax: 418-528-8721, 866-226-0977, assistance.clientele@mrnf.registrefoncier.gouv.qc.ca
Territoire, #A313, 5700, 4e av ouest, Québec, G1H 6R1 QC
418-627-6256, Fax: 418-528-2075, territoire@mrnf.gouv.qc.ca

Saskatchewan
Saskatchewan Government Services, Century Plaza, 1920 Rose St., Regina, S4P 0A9 SK
306-787-6911, Fax: 306-787-1061
Saskatchewan Lands Appeal Board, #202, 3085 Albert St., Regina, SK S4S 0B1
306-787-4693, Fax: 306-787-1315, dbrooks@agr.gov.sk.ca

Yukon Territory
Yukon Land Use Planning Council, #201, 307 Jarvis St., Whitehorse, YT Y1A 2H3
867-667-7397, Fax: 867-667-4624, ylupc@planyukon.ca

LAND TITLES

See Also: Real Estate
Canada Lands Company Ltd., #1200, 1 University Ave., Toronto, M5J 2P1 ON
416-952-6111, Fax: 416-952-6115, 888-252-5263

British Columbia
British Columbia Assessment Authority, 1537 Hillside Ave., Victoria, BC V8T 4Y2
250-595-6211, Fax: 250-595-6222, info@bcassessment.ca

New Brunswick
Service New Brunswick, Westmorland Place, #200, 82 Westmorland St., PO Box 1998, Fredericton, E3B 5G4 NB
506-457-3581, Fax: 506-457-7520, 888-762-8600, snb@snb.ca

Nova Scotia
Registry of Deeds, PO Box 2205, Halifax, B3J 3C4 NS
Fax: 902-424-5872

Nunavut
Nunavut Legal Registries Division, Brown Bldg., 1st Fl., PO Box 1000 570,Iqaluit, X0A 0H0 NU
867-975-6190, Fax: 867-975-6194

LANDLORD & TENANT REGULATIONS

Alberta
Alberta Justice & Attorney General, Communications, Bowker Bldg., 9833 - 109 St., 3rd Fl., Edmonton, T5K 2E8 AB
780-427-2745, Fax: 780-427-6821,-310-0000

Northwest Territories
Northwest Territories Housing Corporation, Scotia Centre, 5102 50th Ave., PO Box 2100, Yellowknife, X1A 2P6 NT
867-873-7853, Fax: 867-873-9426

Nunavut
Nunavut Housing Corporation, PO Box 1000, Arviat, X0C 0E0 NU
867-857-3000, Fax: 867-857-3040

Ontario
Ontario Rental Housing Tribunal, 777 Bay St., 12th Fl., Toronto, ON M5G 2E5
416-585-7295, Fax: 416-585-6363, 888-332-3234

Prince Edward Island
Island Regulatory & Appeals Commission, National Bank Tower, #501, 134 Kent St., PO Box 577, Charlottetown, C1A 7L1 PE
902-892-3501, Fax: 902-566-4076, 800-501-6268, irac@irac.pe.ca

Quebec
Régie du logement du Québec, Pyramide Ouest, #2360, 5199, rue Sherbrooke est, Montréal, QC H1T 3X1
514-873-6575, Fax: 514-873-6805, 800-683-2245

Saskatchewan
Provincial Mediation Board, #120, 2151 Scarth St., Regina, SK S4P 2H8
306-787-5387, Fax: 306-787-5574, 888-215-2222

LANDS & SOILS

Agriculture & Agri-Food Canada, 1341 Baseline Rd., Ottawa, K1A 0C5 ON
613-773-1000, Fax: 613-773-2772, 866-345-7972, info@agr.gc.ca
Canada Centre for Remote Sensing - Geomatics Canada, 588 Booth St., Ottawa, K1A 0Y7 ON
613-995-0947, Fax: 613-947-1382
Indian & Northern Affairs Canada, 10 Wellington St., North Tower, Gatineau, K1A 0H4 QC
819-997-0380, Fax: 819-953-3017, 866-817-3977, infopubs@ainc-inac.gc.ca
Natural Resources Canada, 580 Booth St., Ottawa, K1A 0E4 ON
613-995-0947, Fax: 613-992-7211

Alberta
Irrigation Council, Provincial Bldg., 200 - 5 Ave. South, 3rd Fl., PO Bag 3014, Lethbridge, AB T1J 4L1
403-381-5176, Fax: 403-382-4406
Land Compensation/Surface Rights Board, Phipps-McKinnon Bldg., 10020 - 101A Ave., 18th Fl., Edmonton, AB T5J 3G2
780-427-2444, Fax: 780-427-5798

British Columbia
Ministry of Environment, PO Box 9339 Prov Govt,Victoria, V8W 9M1 BC
250-387-1161, Fax: 250-387-5669, www.envmail@gov.bc.ca
Forest Practices Board, 1675 Douglas St., 3rd Fl., PO Box 9905 Prov Govt, Victoria, BC V8W 9R1
250-387-7964, Fax: 250-387-7009, 800-994-5899, fpboard@gov.bc.ca
Timber Export Advisory Committee, 1520 Blanshard St., 2nd Fl., PO Box 9514 Prov Govt, Victoria, BC V8W 9C2
250-387-8916, Fax: 250-387-5050

Manitoba
Manitoba Geological Survey, #360, 1394 Ellice Ave., Winnipeg, R3G 3P2 MB
Fax: 204-945-1406, 800-223-5215, minesinfo@gov.mb.ca

New Brunswick
Assessment & Planning Appeal Board, #201, 435 King St., PO Box 6000, Fredericton, NB E3B 5H1
506-453-2126, Fax: 506-444-4881
Department of the Environment, Marysville Place, 20 McGloin St., PO Box 6000, Fredericton, E3B 5H1 NB
506-453-2690, Fax: 506-457-4991, env-info@gnb.ca
Department of Natural Resources, PO Box 6000, Fredericton, E3B 5H1 NB
506-453-2510, Fax: 506-444-5839, dnrweb@gnb.ca

Newfoundland & Labrador
Department of Government Services, PO Box 8700, St. John's, A1B 4J6 NL
709-729-4860

Northwest Territories
Department of Environment & Natural Resources, PO Box 1320, Yellowknife, X1A 2L9 NT

Nova Scotia
Department of Natural Resources, Founder's Square, 1701 Hollis St., 3rd Fl., PO Box 698, Halifax, B3J 2T9 NS
902-424-5935, Fax: 902-424-0594, 800-565-2224

Prince Edward Island
Department of Environment, Energy & Forestry, Jones Bldg., 11 Kent St., 4th & 5th Fl., PO Box 2000, Charlottetown, C1A 7N8 PE
902-368-5000, Fax: 902-368-5830
Department of Tourism, PO Box 2000, Charlottetown, C1A 7N8 PE
800-463-4734

Quebec
Ministère du Développement durable, de l'Environnement et des Parcs, Édifice Marie-Guyart, 675, boul René-Lévesque est, 29e étage, Québec, G1R 5V7 QC
418-521-3830, Fax: 418-646-5974, 800-561-1616, info@mddep.gouv.qc.ca
Territoire, #A313, 5700, 4e av ouest, Québec, G1H 6R1 QC
418-627-6256, Fax: 418-528-2075, territoire@mrnf.gouv.qc.ca

Saskatchewan
Saskatchewan Assessment Management Agency, #200, 2201 - 11th Ave., Regina, S4P 0J8 SK
306-924-8000, Fax: 306-924-8070, 800-667-7262, info.request@sama.sk.ca
Saskatchewan Government Services, Century Plaza, 1920 Rose St., Regina, S4P 0A9 SK
306-787-6911, Fax: 306-787-1061

Yukon Territory
Carmacks Renewable Resource Council, PO Box 122, Carmacks, YT Y0B 1C0
867-863-6838, Fax: 867-863-6429, carmacksrrc@lscfn.ca
Yukon Environment, PO Box 2703, Whitehorse, Y1A 2C6 YT
867-667-5652, Fax: 867-393-7197, 800-661-0408, environmentyukon@gov.yk.ca
Selkirk Renewable Resources Council, PO Box 32, Pelly Crossing, YT Y0B 1P0
867-537-3937, Fax: 867-537-3939, selkirkrrc@yknet.yk.ca
Yukon Land Use Planning Council, #201, 307 Jarvis St., Whitehorse, YT Y1A 2H3
867-667-7397, Fax: 867-667-4624, ylupc@planyukon.ca

LAW & JUSTICE

Auditor General of Canada, 240 Sparks St., Ottawa, K1A 0G6 ON
613-995-3708, Fax: 613-957-0474, 888-761-5953, communications@oag-bvg.gc.ca; infomedia@oag-bvg.gc.ca
Canadian Forces Grievance Board, 60 Queen St., 10th Fl., Ottawa, K1P 5Y7 ON
613-996-8529, Fax: 613-996-6491, 877-276-4193
Canadian Human Rights Commission, 344 Slater St., 8th Fl., Ottawa, K1A 1E1 ON
613-995-1151, Fax: 613-996-9661, 888-214-1090, info.com@chrc-ccdp.ca
Canadian Human Rights Tribunal, 160 Elgin St., 11th Fl., Ottawa, K1A 1J4 ON
613-995-1707, Fax: 613-995-3484, registrar@chrt-tcdp.gc.ca
Canadian International Trade Tribunal, Standard Life Centre, 333 Laurier Ave. West, 17 Floor, Ottawa, K1A 0G7 ON
613-990-2452, Fax: 613-990-2439
Canadian Judicial Council, 150 Metcalfe St., 15th Fl., Ottawa, K1A 0W8 ON
613-288-1566, Fax: 613-288-1575
Canadian Police College, PO Box 8900, Ottawa, K1G 3J2 ON
613-993-9500, Fax: 613-990-9738, cpc-ccp@rcmp-grc.gc.ca
Canadian Radio-Television & Telecommunications Commission, Central Office, 1, Promenade du Portage, Les Terrasses de la Chaudière, Gatineau, J8X 4B1 QC
819-997-0313, Fax: 819-994-0218, 877-249-2782
Canadian Security Intelligence Service, PO Box 9732 T,Ottawa, K1G 4G4 ON
613-993-9620
Commission for Public Complaints Against the Royal Canadian Mounted Police, #102, 7337 137 St., Surrey, BC V3W 1A4
Fax: 613-952-8045, 800-665-6878, org@cpc-cpp.gc.ca
Copyright Board of Canada, #800, 56 Sparks St., Ottawa, K1A 0C9 ON
613-952-8621, Fax: 613-952-8630, secretariat@cb-cda.gc.ca
Office of the Correctional Investigator, PO Box 3421 D,Ottawa, K1P 6L4 ON
Fax: 613-990-9091, 877-885-8848, org@oci-bec.gc.ca
Correctional Service Canada, 340 Laurier Ave. West, Ottawa, K1A 0P9 ON
613-992-5891, Fax: 613-943-1630
Defence Research & Development Canada, 305 Rideau St., Ottawa, K1A 0K2 ON
613-992-7237, info@drdc-rddc.gc.ca
Office of the Ethics Commissioner, 66 Slater St., 22nd Fl., Ottawa, K1A 0A6 ON
613-995-0721, Fax: 613-995-7308, ciec-ccie@parl.gc.ca
Office of the Commissioner for Federal Judicial Affairs, 99 Metcalfe St., 8th Fl., Ottawa, K1A 1E3 ON
613-995-5140, Fax: 613-995-5615, 877-583-4266, info@fja.gc.ca
Financial Transactions & Reports Analysis Centre of Canada, 234 Laurier Ave. West, 24th Fl., Ottawa, ON K1P 1H7

Fax: 613-943-7931, 866-346-8722, guidelines-lignesdirectrices@fintrac-canafe.gc.ca
Immigration & Refugee Board of Canada, Canada Bldg, 344 Slater St., 12th Fl., Ottawa, K1A 0K1 ON
613-995-6486, Fax: 613-943-1550, info@irb-cisr.gc.ca
International Joint Commission, 234 Laurier Ave. West, 22nd Fl., Ottawa, K1P 6K6 ON
613-947-1420, Fax: 613-993-5583, beckhoffb@ottawa.ijc.org
Justice Canada, East Memorial Bldg., 284 Wellington St., Ottawa, K1A 0H8 ON
613-957-4222, Fax: 613-954-0811, webadmin@justice.gc.ca
Legal Services Division, Bowker Building, 9833 - 109 St., 2nd Fl., Edmonton, T5K 2E8 AB
780-422-0500
Military Police Complaints Commission, 270 Albert St., 10th Fl., Ottawa, ON K1P 5G8
613-947-5625, Fax: 613-947-5713, 800-632-0566, commission@mpcc-cppm.gc.ca
National Parole Board, 410 Laurier Ave. West, Ottawa, K1A 0R1 ON
613-954-7474, Fax: 613-995-4380, 800-874-2652, info@npb-cnlc.gc.ca
Passport Canada, Le 70 Crémazie, 70 Crémazie St., Gatineau, K1A 0G3 QC
Fax: 819-953-5856, 800-567-6868
Privacy Commissioner of Canada, Tower B, Place de Ville, 112 Kent St., 3rd Fl., Ottawa, K1A 1H3 ON
613-995-8210, Fax: 613-947-6850, 800-282-1376, info@privcom.gc.ca
RCMP Training Academy, 6101 Dewdney Ave., Regina, S4P 3J7 SK
306-780-5002, Fax: 306-780-7940
Royal Canadian Mounted Police, 1200 Vanier Pkwy., Ottawa, K1A 0R2 ON
613-993-7267, Fax: 613-993-0260
Royal Canadian Mounted Police External Review Committee, PO Box 1159 B, Ottawa, ON K1P 5R2
613-998-2134, Fax: 613-990-8969, org@erc-cee.gc.ca
Security Intelligence Review Committee, Jackson Bldg., 122 Bank St., 4th Fl., PO Box 2430 D,Ottawa, K1P 5W5 ON
613-990-8441, Fax: 613-990-5230, ellardm@sirc-csars.gc.ca
Transportation Appeal Tribunal of Canada, 333 Laurier Ave. West, 12th Fl., Ottawa, ON K1A 0N5
613-990-6906, Fax: 613-990-9153, info@tatc.gc.ca
Transportation Safety Board of Canada, 200 Promenade du Portage, 4th Fl., Ottawa, K1A 1K8 ON
819-994-3741, Fax: 819-997-2239, 800-387-3557
Veterans Review & Appeal Board, Daniel J. MacDonald Bldg., 161 Grafton St., PO Box 9900, Charlottetown, PE C1A 8V7
902-566-8751, Fax: 902-566-7850, 800-450-8006, vrab_tacra@vac-acc.gc.ca
Workers' Compensation Appeals Tribunal, #1002, 5670 Spring Garden Rd., Halifax, NS B3J 1H6
902-424-2250, Fax: 902-424-2321, 800-274-8281

Alberta

Alberta Gaming & Liquor Commission, 50 Corriveau Ave., St Albert, AB T8N 3T5
780-447-8600, Fax: 780-447-8911, 800-272-8876
Alberta Human Rights & Citizenship Commission, Northern Regional Office, Standard Life Centre, #800, 10405 Jasper Ave., Edmonton, AB T5J 4R7
780-427-7661, Fax: 780-427-6013,-310-0000, humanrights@gov.ab.ca.
Alberta Review Board, Oxford Tower, 10235 - 101 St., 11th Fl., Edmonton, AB T5J 3E9
780-422-5994, Fax: 780-427-1762
Criminal Injuries Review Board, J.E. Brownlee Bldg., 10365 - 97 St., 5th Fl., Edmonton, AB T5J 3W7
780-427-7330, Fax: 780-427-7347, ciab@just.gov.ab.ca
Alberta Office of the Ethics Commissioner, #1250, 9925 - 109 St., Edmonton, T5K 2J8 AB
780-422-2273, Fax: 780-422-2261, generalinfo@ethicscommissioner.ab.ca
Fatality Review Board - Calgary, Medical Examiner's Office, 4070 Bowness Rd. NW, Calgary, AB T3B 3R7
403-297-8123, Fax: 403-297-3429
Alberta Justice & Attorney General, Communications, Bowker Bldg., 9833 - 109 St., 3rd Fl., Edmonton, T5K 2E8 AB
780-427-2745, Fax: 780-427-6821,-310-0000
Land Compensation/Surface Rights Board, Phipps-McKinnon Bldg., 10020 - 101A Ave., 18th Fl., Edmonton, AB T5J 3G2
780-427-2444, Fax: 780-427-5798
Law Enforcement Review Board, John E. Brownlee Bldg., 10365 - 97th St., Edmonton, AB T5J 3W7
780-422-9376, Fax: 780-422-4782, lerb@gov.ab.ca
Alberta Office of the Ombudsman, Canadian Western Bank Bldg., #2800, 10303 Jasper Ave., Edmonton, T5J 5C3 AB
780-427-2756, Fax: 780-427-2759, info@ombudsman.ab.ca
Public Security Division, 10365 - 97 St., Edmonton, T5J 3W7 AB
Fax: 780-427-1194
Registries Services, John E. Brownlee Bldg., 10365 - 97 St., 3rd Fl., Edmonton, T5J 3W7 AB
Alberta Solicitor General & Public Security, John E. Browntree Bldg, 10365 - 97 St., 10th Fl., Edmonton, T5J 3W7 AB
780-427-3441, Fax: 780-427-2789,-310-0000

British Columbia

Ministry of the Attorney General, PO Box 9044 Prov Govt,Victoria, V8W 9E2 BC
250-387-1866, Fax: 250-387-6411
British Columbia Office of the Police Complaint Commissioner, 756 Fort St., 3rd Fl., PO Box 9895 Prov Govt, Victoria, BC V8W 9T8
250-356-7458, Fax: 250-356-6503, 800-663-7867, info@opcc.bc.ca
British Columbia Review Board, #1020, 510 Burrard St., Vancouver, BC V6C 3A8
604-660-8789, Fax: 604-660-8809, 877-305-2277
Office of the Conflict of Interest Commissioner, #101, 431 Menzies St., Victoria, V8V 1X4 BC
250-356-0750, Fax: 250-356-6580, Conflictofinterest@gov.bc.ca
Court Services Branch, 850 Burdett Ave., 6th Fl., PO Box 9249 Prov Govt,Victoria, V8W 9J2 BC
250-356-1550, Fax: 250-356-8152
British Columbia Environmental Assessment Office, 836 Yates St., 1st Fl., PO Box 9426 Prov Govt,Victoria, V8W 9V1 BC
250-356-7441, Fax: 250-356-7440, eaoinfo@gov.bc.ca
Judicial Council of British Columbia, Pacific Centre, #602, 700 West Georgia St., PO Box 10287, Vancouver, BC V7Y 1E8
604-660-2864, Fax: 604-660-1108
Legal Services Society, #400, 510 Burrard St., Vancouver, BC V6C 3A8
604-601-6000, communications@lss.bc.ca
Management Services Branch, 910 Government St., 5th Fl., PO Box 9256 Prov Govt,Victoria, V8W 9J4 BC
250-387-5258, Fax: 250-387-0081
Mediation & Arbitration Board, #310, 9900 - 100 Ave., Fort St John, BC V1J 5S7
250-787-3403, Fax: 250-787-3228, mab.office@gov.bc.ca
Office of the Representative for Children & Youth, 1019 Wharf St., PO Box 9207 Prov Govt, Victoria, BC V8W 9J1
250-356-6710, Fax: 250-356-0837, 800-476-3933, rcy@rcybc.ca
Office of the Ombudsman, 756 Fort St., 2nd Fl., PO Box 9039 Prov Govt,Victoria, V8W 9A5 BC
250-387-5855, Fax: 250-387-0198, 800-567-3247, systems@ombudsman.bc.ca (Information technology inquiries)
Public Guardian & Trustee of British Columbia, #700, 808 West Hastings St., Vancouver, BC V6C 3L3
604-660-4444, Fax: 604-660-0374, mail@trustee.bc.ca

Manitoba

Advisory Council on Workplace Safety & Health, #200, 401 York Ave., Winnipeg, MB R3C 0P8
204-945-3446, Fax: 204-945-4556
Office of the Auditor General, #500, 330 Portage Ave., Winnipeg, R3C 0C4 MB
204-945-3790, Fax: 204-945-2169, contact@oag.mb.ca
Automobile Injury Compensation Appeal Commission, #301, 428 Portage Ave.., Winnipeg, MB R3C 0E2
204-945-4155, Fax: 204-948-2402, autoinjury@gov.mb.ca
Compensation for Victims of Crime, 1410 - 405 Broadway, Winnipeg, MB R3C 3L6
204-945-0899, Fax: 204-948-3071, 800-262-9344
Comptroller Division, #715, 401 York Ave., Winnipeg, R3C 0P8 MB
204-945-4920, Fax: 204-945-2394
Highway Traffic Board/Motor Transport Board, #200, 301 Weston St., Winnipeg, MB R3E 3H4
204-945-8912, Fax: 204-783-6529
Manitoba Human Rights Commission, 175 Hargrave St., 7th Fl., Winnipeg, R3C 3R8 MB
204-945-3007, Fax: 204-945-1292, 888-884-8681, hrc@gov.mb.ca
Manitoba Justice, Legislative Building, #104, 405 Broadway Ave., Winnipeg, R3C 3L6 MB
204-945-3728, Fax: 204-945-2517, minjus@gov.mb.ca
Law Enforcement Review Agency, #420, 155 Carlton St., Winnipeg, MB R3C 3H8
204-945-8667, Fax: 204-948-1014, 800-282-8069, lera@gov.mb.ca
Law Reform Commission, #432, 405 Broadway, Winnipeg, MB R3C 3L6
204-945-2896, Fax: 204-948-2184, lawreform@gov.mb.ca
Legal Aid Manitoba, 402 - 294 Portage Ave., Winnipeg, MB R3C 0B9
204-985-8500, Fax: 204-944-8582, 800-261-2960, info@legalaid.mb.ca
License Suspension Appeal Board/Medical Review Committee, #200, 301 Weston St., Winnipeg, MB R3E 3H4
204-945-7350, Fax: 204-948-2682
Manitoba Film Classification Board, #216, 301 Weston St., Winnipeg, MB R3E 3H4
204-945-8962, Fax: 204-945-0890, 866-612-2399, mfcb@gov.mb.ca
Manitoba Labour Board, A.A. Heaps Bldg., #402, 258 Portage Ave., Winnipeg, MB R3C 0B6
204-945-3783, Fax: 204-945-1296, mlb@gov.mb.ca
Manitoba Land Value Appraisal Commission, 800 Portage Ave., Winnipeg, MB R3G 0N4
204-945-2941, Fax: 204-948-2235,
Manitoba Liquor Control Commission, 1555 Buffalo Pl., PO Box 1023, Winnipeg, MB R3C 2X1
204-284-2501, Fax: 204-475-7666, info@mlcc.mb.ca
Manitoba Minimum Wage Board, 614 - 401 York Ave., Winnipeg, MB R3C 0P8
204-945-4889, Fax: 204-948-2085, mw@gov.mb.ca
Manitoba Review Board, 408 York Ave., 2nd Fl., Winnipeg, MB R3C 0P9
204-945-4438, Fax: 204-945-5751
Manitoba Securities Commission, #500, 400 St. Mary Ave., Winnipeg, MB R3C 4K5
204-945-2548, Fax: 204-945-0330, 800-655-5244, securities@gov.mb.ca
Office of the Chief Medical Examiner, #210, 1 Wesley Ave., Winnipeg, MB R3C 4C6
204-945-2088, Fax: 204-945-2442, 800-282-9069
Office of the Fire Commissioner, #508, 401 York Ave., Winnipeg, MB R3C 0P8
204-945-3322, Fax: 204-948-2089, 800-282-8069, firecomm@gov.mb.ca
Office of the Public Trustee, #500, 155 Carlton St., Winnipeg, MB R3C 5R9
204-945-2700, Fax: 204-948-2251, publictrustee@gov.mb.ca
Manitoba Office of the Ombudsman, 750 - 500 Portage Ave., Winnipeg, R3C 3X1 MB
204-982-9130, Fax: 204-942-7803, 800-665-0531, ombudsma@ombudsman.mb.ca
Residential Tenancies Commission, #1650, 155 Carlton St., Winnipeg, MB R3C 3H8
204-945-2028, Fax: 204-945-5453, 800-782-8403, rtc@gov.mb.ca
Manitoba Workers' Compensation Board, 333 Broadway Ave., Winnipeg, R3C 4W3 MB
204-954-4321, Fax: 204-954-4999, 800-362-3340, wcb@wcb.mb.ca
Workplace Safety & Health Division, #200, 401 York Ave., Winnipeg, R3C 0P8 MB
204-945-3446, Fax: 204-948-2209, wshcompl@gov.mb.ca

New Brunswick

Assessment & Planning Appeal Board, #201, 435 King St., PO Box 6000, Fredericton, NB E3B 5H1
506-453-2126, Fax: 506-444-4881
Board of Examiners under the Scaler's Act, 1350 Regent St. South, PO Box 6000, Fredericton, NB E3B 5H1
506-453-2441, Fax: 506-453-6689
New Brunswick Human Rights Commission, PO Box 6000, Fredericton, E3B 5H1 NB
506-453-2301, Fax: 506-453-2653, 888-471-2233, hrc.cdp@gnb.ca
Department of Justice & Consumer Affairs, Centennial Bldg., 670 King St., PO Box 6000, Fredericton, E3B 5H1 NB
506-462-5100, Fax: 506-453-3651, justice.comments@gnb.ca
New Brunswick Liquor Corporation, 170 Wilsey Rd., PO Box 20787, Fredericton, E3B 5B8 NB
506-452-6826, Fax: 506-462-2024, info@anbl.com
New Brunswick Real Estate Association, #1, 22 Durelle St., Fredericton, NB E3C 1N8
506-459-8055, Fax: 506-459-8057, 800-762-1677, info@nbrea.ca
Office of the Ombudsman, 767 Brunswick St., PO Box 6000, Fredericton, E3B 5H1 NB
506-453-2789, Fax: 506-453-5599, 800-465-1100, nbombud@gnb.ca
New Brunswick Police Commission, Fredericton City Centre, #202, 435 King St., Fredericton, E3B 1E5 NB
506-453-2069, Fax: 506-457-3542
Department of Public Safety, 364 Argyle St., PO Box 6000, Fredericton, E3B 5H1 NB
506-453-3992, Fax: 506-453-3870, DPS-MSP.Information@gnb.ca
Workplace Health, Safety & Compensation Commission of New Brunswick, 1 Portland St., PO Box 160, Saint John, E2L 3X9

NB
506-632-2200, 800-222-9775, communications@ws-ts.nb.ca

Newfoundland & Labrador

Newfoundland & Labrador Human Rights Commission, PO Box 8700, St. John's, A1B 4J6 NL
709-729-2709, Fax: 709-729-0790, 800-563-5808, humanrights@mail.gov.nl.ca

Department of Justice, Confederation Bldg., East Block, 4th Fl., PO Box 8700, St. John's, A1B 4J6 NL
709-729-5942, Fax: 709-729-2129, justice@gov.nl.ca

Newfoundland & Labrador Legal Aid Commission, Cormack Bldg., 2 Steers Cove, PO Box 399 C, St. John's, NL A1C 5J9
709-753-7860, Fax: 709-753-6226, 800-563-9911

Royal Newfoundland Constabulary Public Complaints Commission, Bally Rou Place, #E-160, 280 Torbay Rd., St. John's, NL A1A 3W8
709-729-0950, Fax: 709-729-1302

Northwest Territories

Assessment Appeal Tribunal of the Northwest Territories, #500, 5201 - 50th Ave., PO Box 1320, Yellowknife, NT X1A 2L9
867-873-7125, Fax: 867-873-0609

Judicial Council, PO Box 188, Yellowknife, NT X1A 2N2
867-873-7105, Fax: 867-873-0287

Department of Justice, Courthouse, 4903 - 49th St., 6th Fl., PO Box 1320, Yellowknife, X1A 2L9 NT
867-920-6197

Legal Services Board of the Northwest Territories, PO Box 1320, Yellowknife, NT X1A 2L9
867-873-7450, Fax: 867-873-5320, www-jus-tice

Northwest Territories Liquor Commission, #201, 31 Capital Dr., Hay River, NT X0E 1G2
867-874-2100, Fax: 867-874-2180

Northwest Territories Liquor Licensing & Enforcement, #210, 31 Capital Dr., Hay River, NT X0E 1G2
867-874-2906, Fax: 867-874-6011

Northwest Territories Liquor Licensing Board, #210, 31 Capital Dr., Hay River, NT X0E 1G2
867-874-2906, Fax: 867-874-6011, delilah_st-arneault@gov.nt.ca

Territorial Board of Revision, PO Box 1320, Yellowknife, NT X1A 2L9
867-873-7125, Fax: 867-873-0609

Victims Assistance Committee, c/o Community Justice Division, PO Box 1320, Yellowknife, NT X1A 2L9
867-920-6911, Fax: 867-873-0299

Northwest Territories & Nunavut Workers' Compensation Board, Centre Square Tower, 5022 - 49th St., 5th Fl., PO Box 8888, Yellowknife, X1A 2R3 NT
867-920-3888, Fax: 867-873-4596, 800-661-0792, wcb@wcb.nt.ca

Nova Scotia

Nova Scotia Human Rights Commission, Joseph Howe Bldg., 1690 Hollis St., 6th Fl., Halifax, B3J 3C4 NS
902-424-4111, Fax: 902-424-0596

Department of Justice, 5151 Terminal Rd., 4th Fl., PO Box 7, Halifax, B3J 2L6 NS
902-424-4030, Fax: 902-424-0510, webbermj@gov.ns.ca

Labour Relations Board & Construction Industry Panel, 5151 Terminal Rd.,7th Fl., PO Box 697, Halifax, NS B3J 2T8
902-424-6730, Fax: 902-424-1744

Labour Standards Tribunal, 5151 Terminal Rd., 7th Fl., PO Box 697, Halifax, NS B3J 2T8
902-424-6730, Fax: 902-424-1744, noeljl@gov.ns.ca

Nova Scotia Legal Aid Commission, #102, 137 Chain Lake Dr., Halifax, NS B3S 1B3
902-420-6573, Fax: 902-420-3471, nsla.exec@ns.sympatico.ca

Nova Scotia Medical Examiner Service, Halifax Insurance Bldg., #701, 5670 Spring Garden Rd., Halifax, NS B3J 1H7
902-424-2722, Fax: 902-424-0607, 888-424-4336

Nova Scotia Police Commission, #300, 1601 Lower Water St., PO Box 1573, Halifax, NS B3J 2Y3
902-424-3246, Fax: 902-424-3919, uarb.polcom@gov.ns.ca

Office of the Ombudsman, #700, 5670 Spring Garden Rd., PO Box 2152, Halifax, B3J 3B7 NS
902-424-6780, Fax: 902-424-6675, 800-670-1111

Pay Equity Commission, 5151 Terminal Rd., 7th Fl., PO Box 697, Halifax, NS B3J 2T8
902-424-2385, Fax: 902-424-0575

Workers' Compensation Board of Nova Scotia, 5668 South St., PO Box 1150, Halifax, B3J 2Y2 NS
902-491-8999, Fax: 902-491-8002, 800-870-3331, info@wcb.gov.ns.ca

Nunavut

Baffin Correctional Centre, 1550 Federal Rd., PO Box 368, Iqaluit, NU X0A 0H0
867-979-8100, Fax: 867-979-4646

Department of Justice, Sivummut, 1st Fl., PO Box 1000 500,Iqaluit, X0A 0H0 NU
867-975-6170, Fax: 867-975-6195

Legal Services Board of Nunavut, PO Box 125, Gjoa Haven, NU X0A 0H0
Fax: 867-360-6112

Nunavut Legal Registries Division, Brown Bldg., 1st Fl., PO Box 1000 570,Iqaluit, X0A 0H0 NU
867-975-6190, Fax: 867-975-6194

Nunavut Liquor Licensing Board, Bag 002, Rankin Inlet, NU X0C 0G0
Fax: 867-645-3327

Office of the Chief Coroner, PO Box 1000 590, Iqaluit, NU X0A 0H0

Young Offenders, 1548 Federal Rd., PO Box 1439, Iqaluit, NU X0A 0H0
867-979-4452, Fax: 867-979-5506

Ontario

Alcohol & Gaming Commission of Ontario, 20 Dundas St. West, Toronto, ON M5G 2N6
416-326-8700, Fax: 416-326-5555, 800-522-2876

Assessment Review Board, Eaton Tower, 250 Yonge St., 29th Fl., Toronto, ON M5B 2L7
416-314-6900, Fax: 416-314-3717

Association of Ontario Land Surveyors, 1043 McNicoll Ave., Toronto, ON M1W 3W6
416-491-9020, Fax: 416-491-2576, admin@aols.org

Ministry of the Attorney General, McMurtry-Scott Bldg., 720 Bay St., 11th Fl., Toronto, M5G 2K1 ON
416-326-2220, Fax: 416-326-4007, 800-518-7901,

Chief Inquiry Officer - Expropriations Act, 720 Bay St., 8th Fl., Toronto, ON M5G 2K1
416-326-4093

Ministry of Community Safety & Correctional Services, George Drew Bldg., 25 Grosvenor St., 18th Fl., Toronto, M7A 1Y6 ON
416-326-5000, Fax: 416-325-6067, 866-517-0571, jus.g.sgcs.webmaster@jus.gov.on.ca

Criminal Injuries Compensation Board, 439 University Ave., 4th Fl., Toronto, ON M5G 1Y8
416-326-2900, Fax: 416-326-2883, 800-372-7463

Ontario Human Rights Commission, 180 Dundas St. West, 7th Fl., Toronto, M7A 2R9 ON
416-314-4500, Fax: 416-326-9520, 800-387-9080, info@ohrc.on.ca

Information & Privacy Commissioner of Ontario, #1400, 2 Bloor St. East, Toronto, M4W 1A8 ON
416-326-3333, Fax: 416-325-9195, 800-387-0073, info@ipc.on.ca

Office of the Integrity Commissioner, #2101, 2 Bloor St. East, Toronto, M4W 1A8 ON
416-314-8983, Fax: 416-314-8987, integrity.mail@oico.on.ca

Judicial Appointments Advisory Committee, 720 Bay St., 3rd Fl., Toronto, ON M5G 2K1
416-326-4060, Fax: 416-212-7316

Legal Aid Ontario, #404, 375 University Ave., Toronto, ON M5G 2G1
416-979-1446, Fax: 416-979-8669, 800-668-8258, info@lao.on.ca

Licence Appeal Tribunal (LAT), 1 St. Clair Ave. West, 12th Fl., Toronto, ON M4V 1K6
416-314-4260, Fax: 416-314-4270, 800-255-2214

Office for Victims of Crime, 700 Bay St., 3rd Fl., Toronto, ON M5G 1Z6
416-326-1682, Fax: 416-326-2343, 887-435-7661

Office of the Ombudsman, 483 Bay St., 10th Fl., Toronto, M5G 2C9 ON
416-586-3300, Fax: 416-586-3485, 800-263-1830, info@ombudsman.on.ca

Ontario Civilian Commission on Police Services, 25 Grosvenor St., 1st Fl., Toronto, ON M7A 1Y6
416-326-1189, Fax: 416-314-2036, 888-515-5005

Ontario Film Review Board, 1075 Millwood Rd., Toronto, ON M4G 1X6
416-314-3626, Fax: 416-314-3632

Ontario Labour Relations Board, 505 University Ave., 2nd Fl., Toronto, ON M5G 2P1
416-326-7500, Fax: 416-326-7531, 877-339-3335

Ontario Municipal Board & Board of Negotiation, 655 Bay St., 15th Fl., Toronto, ON M5G 1E5
416-326-6800, Fax: 416-326-5370

Ontario Parole & Earned Release Board, 415 Yonge St., Toronto, ON M5B 2E7
416-325-4480, Fax: 416-325-4485

Ontario Police Arbitration Commission, George Drew Bldg., 25 Grosvenor St., 1st Fl., Toronto, ON M7A 1Y6
416-314-3520, Fax: 416-314-3522

Ontario Racing Commission, 20 Dundas St. West, 9th Fl., Toronto, ON M5G 2C2
416-327-0520, Fax: 416-325-3478, orcinqry@cbs.gov.on.ca

Ontario Review Board, 151 Bloor St. West, 10th Fl., Toronto, ON M5S 2T5
416-327-8866, Fax: 416-327-8867

OPSEU Pension Trust, #1200, 1 Adelaide St. East, Toronto, ON M5C 3A7
416-681-6161, Fax: 416-681-6175

Road User Safety Division, #191, Bldg A, 1201 Wilson Ave., Toronto, M3M 1J8 ON
416-235-2999, Fax: 416-235-4153

ServiceOntario, College Park, 777 Bay St., 15th fl., Toronto, M7A 2J3 ON
416-326-6205, Fax: 416-326-5106

Social Benefits Tribunal, 1075 Bay St., 7th Fl., Toronto, ON M5S 2B1
416-326-0978, Fax: 416-325-5135, 800-753-3895

Workplace Safety & Insurance Board, 200 Front St. West, Ground Fl., Toronto, M5V 3J1 ON
416-344-1000, Fax: 416-344-4684, 800-387-0750

Prince Edward Island

Office of the Attorney General, Shaw Building, North, 105 Rochford St., 4th Fl., PO Box 2000, Charlottetown, C1A 7N8 PE
902-368-5152, Fax: 902-368-4910

Office of the Auditor General, Shaw Bldg., 105 Rochford St, 2nd Fl., PO Box 2000, Charlottetown, C1A 7N8 PE
902-368-4520, Fax: 902-368-4598

Employment Standards Board, 161 St. Peters Rd., PO Box 2000, Charlottetown, PE C1A 7N8
902-368-5550, Fax: 902-368-5476

Prince Edward Island Human Rights Commission, 53 Water St., PO Box 2000, Charlottetown, C1A 7N8 PE
902-368-4180, Fax: 902-368-4236, 800-237-5031, lbuell@peihumanrights.ca

Labour Relations Board, PO Box 2000, Charlottetown, PE C1A 7N8
902-368-5550, Fax: 902-368-5476

Prince Edward Island Liquor Control Commission, 3 Garfield St., PO Box 967, Charlottetown, C1A 7M4 PE
902-368-5710, Fax: 902-368-5735

Island Regulatory & Appeals Commission, National Bank Tower, #501, 134 Kent St., PO Box 577, Charlottetown, C1A 7L1 PE
902-892-3501, Fax: 902-566-4076, 800-501-6268, irac@irac.pe.ca

Prince Edward Island Workers Compensation Board, 14 Weymouth St., PO Box 757, Charlottetown, C1A 7L7 PE
902-368-5680, Fax: 902-368-5705, 800-237-5049

Quebec

Bureau du coroner, #390, 2875, boul Laurier, Sainte-Foy, QC G1V 5B1
418-643-1845, Fax: 418-643-6174, clientele.coroner@msp.gouv.qc.ca

Comité de déontologie policière, Tour du Saint-Laurent, #A-200, 2525, boul Laurier, 2e étage, Québec, QC G1V 4Z6
418-646-1936, Fax: 418-528-0987, comite.deontologie@msp.gouv.qc.ca

Commissaire à la déontologie policière, 1200, rte de l'Église, R-C20, Sainte-Foy, QC G1V 4Y9
418-643-7897, Fax: 418-528-9473, 877-237-7897

Commissariat des incendies, 455, rue Dupont, Québec, QC G1K 6N2
418-529-5706, Fax: 418-529-9922

Commission des lésions professionnelles, #700, 900, Place d'Youville, Québec, QC G1R 3P7
418-644-7777, Fax: 418-644-6443, 800-463-1591

Commission des services juridiques, Tour de l'Est, #1404, 2, Complexe Desjardins, Montréal, QC H5B 1B3
514-873-3562, Fax: 514-873-8762, info@csj.qc.ca

Commission québecoise des libérations conditionnelles, #1.32A, 300, boul Jean-Lesage, Québec, QC G1K 8K6
418-646-8300, Fax: 418-643-7217, liberation.conditionnel@msp.gouv.

Conseil de la justice administrative, #RC-01, 575, rue Saint-Amable, Québec, QC G1R 2G4
418-644-6279, Fax: 418-528-8471, 888-848-2581, courrier@cja.gouv.qc.ca

Conseil de la magistrature, #5.12, 300, boul Jean-Lesage, Québec, QC G1K 8K6
418-644-2196, Fax: 418-528-1581, information@cm.gouv.qc.ca

Direction générale de la Sûreté du Québec, 1701, rue Parthenais, Montréal, QC H2K 3S7
514-598-4488, Fax: 514-598-4957, info@surete.qc.ca

Commission des droits de la personne et des droits de la jeunesse, 360, rue St-Jacques, 2e étage, Montréal, H2Y 1P5 QC
514-873-5146, Fax: 514-873-6032, 800-361-6477, webmestre@cdpdj.qc.ca

Fonds d'aide aux recours collectifs, #10.30, 1, rue Notre-Dame est, Montréal, QC H2Y 1B6
514-393-2087, Fax: 514-864-2998, farc@justice.gouv.qc.ca
Ministère de la Justice, Édifice Louis-Philippe-Pigeon, 1200, rte de l'Église, Québec, G1V 4M1 QC
418-643-5140, 866-536-5140, informations@justice.gouv.qc.ca
Le Protecteur du Citoyen, #1.25, 525, boul René-Lévesque est, Québec, G1R 5Y4 QC
418-643-2688, Fax: 418-643-8759, 800-463-5070
Registraire des entreprises, 787, boul. Lebourgneuf, Québec, G2J 1C3 QC
418-644-4545, Fax: 418-528-5703, 877-644-4545, registre@servicesquebec.gouv.qc.ca
Régie des alcools, des courses et des jeux, 560, boul Charest est, Québec, QC G1K 3J3
418-643-7667, Fax: 418-643-5971, 800-363-0320, racj.quebec@racj.gouv.qc.ca
Société des alcools du Québec, 905, av De Lorimier, Montréal, QC H2K 3V9
514-873-2020, Fax: 514-873-6788, 866-873-2020, info@saq.com
Société québécoise d'information juridique, 715, carré Victoria, 8e étage, Montréal, QC H2Y 2H7
514-842-8741, Fax: 514-844-8984, 800-363-6718, info@soquij.qc.ca
Ministère de la Sécurité publique, Tour des Laurentides, 2525, boul Laurier, 5e étage, Québec, G1V 2L2 QC
418-643-2112, Fax: 418-646-6168, 866-644-6826
Tribunal administratif du Québec, 575, rue Saint-Amable, Québec, QC G1R 5R4
418-643-3418, Fax: 418-643-5335
Vérificateur général du Québec, 750, boulevard Charest est, 3e étage, Québec, G1K 9J6 QC
418-691-5900, Fax: 418-644-4460, verificateur.general@vgq.gouv.qc.
École nationale de police du Québec, 350, rue Marguerite-d'Youville, Nicolet, QC J3T 1X4
819-293-8631, Fax: 819-293-4018, courriel@enpq.qc.ca

Saskatchewan

Agricultural Implements Board, #202, 3085 Albert St., Regina, SK S4S 0B1
306-787-4693, Fax: 306-787-1315
Saskatchewan Human Rights Commission, Saskatoon Office, Sturdy Stone Bdg., #816, 122 - 3 Ave. North, 8th Fl., Saskatoon, S7K 2H6 SK
306-933-5952, Fax: 306-933-7863, 800-667-9249, shrc@shrc.gov.sk.ca
Information & Privacy Commissioner of Saskatchewan, #503, 1801 Hamilton St., Regina, S4P 4B4 SK
306-787-8350, Fax: 306-798-1603, 877-748-2298, info@oipc.sk.ca
Saskatchewan Justice, 1874 Scarth St., Regina, S4P 4B3 SK
306-787-7872, Fax: 306-787-3874
Law Reform Commission of Saskatchewan, 410 26th St. West, Saskatoon, SK S7L 0H9
306-665-6428, mjfinley@shaw.ca
Saskatchewan Liquor & Gaming Authority, 2500 Victoria Ave., PO Box 5054, Regina, S4P 3M3 SK
306-787-4213, Fax: 306-787-8468
Saskatchewan Ombudsman, #150, 2401 Saskatchewan Dr., Regina, S4P 4H8 SK
306-787-6211, Fax: 306-787-9090, 800-667-7180
Provincial Mediation Board, #120, 2151 Scarth St., Regina, SK S4P 2H8
306-787-5387, Fax: 306-787-5574, 888-215-2222
Public & Private Rights Board, 23-3085 Albert St., Regina, SK S4S 0B1
306-787-4071, Fax: 306-787-0088
Saskatchewan Farm Land Security Board, #207, 3988 Albert St., Regina, SK S4S 3R1
306-787-5047, Fax: 306-787-8599, inquiries@farmland.gov.sk.ca
Saskatchewan Farm Security Programs, #207, 3988 Albert St., Regina, SK S4S 3R1
306-787-5047, Fax: 306-787-8599
Saskatchewan Film & Video Classification Board, #500, 1919 Saskatchewan Dr., Regina, SK S4P 4H2
306-787-5550, Fax: 306-787-9779, 888-374-4636, adwyer@justice.gov.sk.ca
Saskatchewan Financial Services Commission, #601, 1919 Saskatchewan Dr., Regina, SK S4P 4H2
306-787-5645, Fax: 306-787-5899
Saskatchewan Legal Aid Commission, #502, 201 - 21 St. East, Saskatoon, SK S7K 2H6
306-933-5300, Fax: 306-933-6764, 800-667-3764, central@legalaid.gov.sk.ca
Saskatchewan Police Commission, 600 - 1874 Scarth St., Regina, SK S4P 4B3
306-787-6518, Fax: 306-787-0136
Saskatchewan Public Complaints Commission, #300, 1919 Saskatchewan Dr., Regina, SK S4P 4H2
306-787-6519, Fax: 306-787-6528, 866-256-6194
Surface Rights Board of Arbitration, 113 - 2nd Ave. East, PO Box 1597, Kindersley, SK S0L 1S0
306-463-5447, Fax: 306-463-5449, SurfaceRightsBoard@gov.sk.ca
Saskatchewan Workers' Compensation Board, #200, 1881 Scarth St., Regina, S4P 4L1 SK
306-787-4370, Fax: 306-787-7582, 800-667-7590, internet_clientsvc@wcbsask.com

Yukon Territory

Driver Control Board, 308 Steele St., PO Box 2703, Whitehorse, YT Y1A 2C6
867-667-3774, Fax: 867-393-6483, dcb@gov.yk.ca
Law Society of Yukon - Discipline Committee, #201, 302 Steele St., Whitehorse, YT Y1A 2C5
867-668-4231, Fax: 867-667-7556, lsy@yknet.yk.ca
Law Society of Yukon - Executive, #202, 302 Steele St., Whitehorse, YT Y1A 2C5
867-668-4231, Fax: 867-667-7556, lsy@yknet.yk.ca
Yukon Liquor Corporation, 9031 Quartz Rd., Whitehorse, Y1A 4P9 YT
867-667-5245, Fax: 867-393-6306, yukon.liquor@gov.yk.ca
Yukon Workers' Compensation Health & Safety Board, 401 Strickland St., Whitehorse, Y1A 5N8 YT
867-667-5645, Fax: 867-393-6279, 800-661-0443, worksafe@gov.yk.ca
Yukon Human Rights Commission, #201, 211 Hawkins St., Whitehorse, YT Y1A 1X3
867-667-6226, Fax: 867-667-2662, 800-661-0535, humanrights@yhrc.yk.ca
Yukon Human Rights Panel of Adjudication, #202, 407 Black St., Whitehorse, YT Y1A 2N2
867-667-5412, Fax: 867-633-6952
Yukon Judicial Council, PO Box 31222, Whitehorse, YT Y1A 5PT
867-667-5438, Fax: 867-393-6400
Yukon Law Foundation, #202, 302 Steele St., Whitehorse, YT Y1A 2C5
867-668-4231, Fax: 867-667-7556, lsy@yknet.yk.ca
Yukon Legal Services Society/Legal Aid, #203, 2131 - 2nd Ave., Whitehorse, YT Y1A 1C3
867-667-5210, Fax: 867-667-8649, legalaid@yknet.yk.ca
Yukon Motor Transport Board, PO Box 2703, Whitehorse, YT Y1A 2C6
867-667-5782, Fax: 867-393-6408, Laurie.Hrynuik@gov.yk.ca

LEGAL & REGULATORY

Canadian Coast Guard, Centennial Towers, #6S018, 200 Kent St., Ottawa, K1A 0E6 ON
613-998-1573, Fax: 613-990-2780
Commission for Environmental Cooperation, Secretariat, #200, 393, rue St-Jacques ouest, Montréal, H2Y 1N9 QC
514-350-4300, Fax: 514-350-4314, info@cec.org
Institute for National Measurement Standards, Bldg. M-36, 1500 Montreal Rd., Ottawa, K1A 0R6 ON
613-998-7018, Fax: 613-954-1473, alexandra.shaw@nrc-cnrc.gc.ca
Standards Council of Canada, #200, 270 Albert St., Ottawa, K1P 6N7 ON
613-238-3222, Fax: 613-569-7808, info@scc.ca

British Columbia

British Columbia Environmental Assessment Office, 836 Yates St., 1st Fl., PO Box 9426 Prov Govt,Victoria, V8W 9V1 BC
250-356-7441, Fax: 250-356-7440, eaoinfo@gov.bc.ca
Mediation & Arbitration Board, #310, 9900 - 100 Ave., Fort St John, BC V1J 5S7
250-787-3403, Fax: 250-787-3228, mab.office@gov.bc.ca

New Brunswick

Board of Examiners under the Scaler's Act, 1350 Regent St. South, PO Box 6000, Fredericton, NB E3B 5H1
506-453-2441, Fax: 506-453-6689
Environmental Management, Marysville Place, 20 McGloin St., PO Box 6000, Fredericton, E3B 5H1 NB
506-444-5119, Fax: 506-457-7333

Northwest Territories

Assessment Appeal Tribunal of the Northwest Territories, #500, 5201 - 50th Ave., PO Box 1320, Yellowknife, NT X1A 2L9
867-873-7125, Fax: 867-873-0609

Nova Scotia

Crane Operators Appeal Board, 5151 Terminal Rd., 7th Fl., PO Box 697, Halifax, NS B3J 2T8
902-424-8595, Fax: 902-424-0217, fraserej@gov.ns.ca
Labour Relations Board & Construction Industry Panel, 5151 Terminal Rd.,7th Fl., PO Box 697, Halifax, NS B3J 2T8
902-424-6730, Fax: 902-424-1744
Labour Standards Tribunal, 5151 Terminal Rd., 7th Fl., PO Box 697, Halifax, NS B3J 2T8
902-424-6730, Fax: 902-424-1744, noeljl@gov.ns.ca
Occupational Health & Safety Advisory Council, PO Box 697, Halifax, NS B3J 2T8
902-424-2484, Fax: 902-424-5640
Pay Equity Commission, 5151 Terminal Rd., 7th Fl., PO Box 697, Halifax, NS B3J 2T8
902-424-2385, Fax: 902-424-0575
Workers' Advisers Program, #502, 5670 Spring Garden Rd., PO Box 1063, Halifax, NS B3J 2X1
902-424-5050, Fax: 902-424-0530, 800-774-4712
Workers' Compensation Board of Nova Scotia, 5668 South St., PO Box 1150, Halifax, B3J 2Y2 NS
902-491-8999, Fax: 902-491-8002, 800-870-3331, info@wcb.gov.ns.ca

Ontario

Ministry of Community Safety & Correctional Services, George Drew Bldg., 25 Grosvenor St., 18th Fl., Toronto, M7A 1Y6 ON
416-326-5000, Fax: 416-325-6067, 866-517-0571, jus.g.sgcs.webmaster@jus.gov.on.ca
Environmental Commissioner of Ontario, #605, 1075 Bay St., Toronto, M5S 2B1 ON
416-325-3377, Fax: 416-325-3370, 800-701-6454, commissioner@eco.on.ca
Environmental Review Tribunal, #1700, 2300 Yonge St., PO Box 2382, Toronto, ON M4P 1E4
416-314-4600, Fax: 416-314-4506
Road User Safety Division, #191, Bldg A, 1201 Wilson Ave., Toronto, M3M 1J8 ON
416-235-2999, Fax: 416-235-4153

Prince Edward Island

Island Regulatory & Appeals Commission, National Bank Tower, #501, 134 Kent St., PO Box 577, Charlottetown, C1A 7L1 PE
902-892-3501, Fax: 902-566-4076, 800-501-6268, irac@irac.pe.ca

LEGAL AID SERVICES

Alberta

Court Services Division, Bowker Building, 9833 - 109 St., 2nd Fl., Edmonton, T5K 2E8 AB
780-427-4992, Fax: 780-422-6613

British Columbia

Legal Services Society, #400, 510 Burrard St., Vancouver, BC V6C 3A8
604-601-6000, communications@lss.bc.ca

Manitoba

Legal Aid Manitoba, 402 - 294 Portage Ave., Winnipeg, MB R3C 0B9
204-985-8500, Fax: 204-944-8582, 800-261-2960, info@legalaid.mb.ca

New Brunswick

Department of the Attorney General, Centennial Bldg., #412, 670 King St., PO Box 6000, Fredericton, E3B 5H1 NB
506-453-3132, Fax: 506-453-3651, justice.comments@gnb.ca

Newfoundland & Labrador

Newfoundland & Labrador Legal Aid Commission, Cormack Bldg., 2 Steers Cove, PO Box 399 C, St. John's, NL A1C 5J9
709-753-7860, Fax: 709-753-6226, 800-563-9911

Northwest Territories

Legal Services Board of the Northwest Territories, PO Box 1320, Yellowknife, NT X1A 2L9
867-873-7450, Fax: 867-873-5320, www-jus-tice

Nova Scotia

Nova Scotia Legal Aid Commission, #102, 137 Chain Lake Dr., Halifax, NS B3S 1B3
902-420-6573, Fax: 902-420-3471, nsla.exec@ns.sympatico.ca

Ontario

Legal Aid Ontario, #404, 375 University Ave., Toronto, ON M5G 2G1
416-979-1446, Fax: 416-979-8669, 800-668-8258, info@lao.on.ca

Quebec

Fonds d'aide aux recours collectifs, #10.30, 1, rue Notre-Dame est, Montréal, QC H2Y 1B6
514-393-2087, Fax: 514-864-2998, farc@justice.gouv.qc.ca

Saskatchewan

Saskatchewan Legal Aid Commission, #502, 201 - 21 St. East, Saskatoon, SK S7K 2H6

306-933-5300, Fax: 306-933-6764, 800-667-3764, central@legalaid.gov.sk.ca

Yukon Territory
Yukon Legal Services Society/Legal Aid, #203, 2131 - 2nd Ave., Whitehorse, YT Y1A 1C3
867-667-5210, Fax: 867-667-8649, legalaid@yknet.yk.ca

LEGISLATIVE ASSEMBLIES/NATIONAL ASSEMBLIES/HOUSE OF COMMONS

See Also: uses

House of Commons, Canada, House of Commons, Parliament Buildings, Ottawa, K1A 0A6 ON
613-992-4793, 866-599-4999, info@parl.gc.ca

Alberta
Legislative Assembly, Legislature Annex Bldg., 9718 - 107 St., Edmonton, T5K 1E4 AB
780-427-2826, Fax: 780-427-1623, laocommunications@assembly.ab.ca

British Columbia
Legislative Assembly, Clerk's Office, #221, Parliament Bldgs., Victoria, V8V 1X4 BC
250-387-3785, Fax: 250-387-0942, ClerkHouse@leg.bc.ca

Manitoba
Legislative Assembly, c/o Clerk's Office, Legislative Bldg., #237, 450 Broadway, Winnipeg, R3C 0V8 MB
204-945-3636, Fax: 204-948-2507, clerkla@leg.gov.mb.ca

New Brunswick
Legislative Assembly of New Brunswick, Centre Block, Legislative Bldg., 706 Queen St., PO Box 6000, Fredericton, E3B 5H1 NB
506-453-2506, Fax: 506-453-7154, wwwleg@gnb.ca

Newfoundland & Labrador
House of Assembly, c/o Clerk's Office, Confederation Bldg., PO Box 8700, St. John's, A1B 4J6 NL
709-729-3405, Fax: 709-729-4820

Northwest Territories
Legislative Assembly, c/o Clerk's Office, PO Box 1320, Yellowknife, X1A 2L9 NT
867-669-2299, Fax: 867-920-4735, 800-661-0784

Nova Scotia
Legislative House of Assembly, c/o Clerk's Office, Province House, 1st Fl., PO Box 1617, Halifax, B3J 2Y3 NS
902-424-5978, Fax: 902-424-0632

Nunavut
Legislative Assembly, Legislative Assembly Bldg., 3rd Fl., PO Box 1200, Iqaluit, X0A 0H0 NU
867-975-5000, Fax: 867-975-5190, 877-334-7266, leginfo@assembly.nu.ca

Ontario
Legislative Assembly, c/o Clerk's Office, #104, Legislative Bldg., Queen's Park, Toronto, M7A 1A2 ON
416-325-7340, Fax: 416-325-7344, assembly@ontla.ola.org

Prince Edward Island
Legislative Assembly, c/o Clerk's Office, Province House, Richmond St., PO Box 2000, Charlottetown, C1A 7K7 PE
902-368-5970, Fax: 902-368-5175

Quebec
L'Assemblée nationale, Hôtel du Parlement, 1045, rue des Parlementaires, Québec, G1A 1A4 QC
418-643-7239, Fax: 418-646-4271, 866-337-8837, responsable.contenu@assnat.qc.ca

Saskatchewan
Legislative Assembly, c/o Clerk's Office, Legislative Bldg., #123, 2405 Legislative Dr., Regina, S4S 0B3 SK
306-787-2376, Fax: 306-787-1558, info@legassembly.sk.ca

Yukon Territory
Legislative Assembly, c/o Clerk's Office, PO Box 2703, Whitehorse, Y1A 2C6 YT
867-667-5498, Fax: 867-393-6280

LEISURE CRAFT & VEHICLE REGULATIONS

Alberta
Technology Services, John E. Brownlee Bldg., 10365 - 97 St., 8th Fl., Edmonton, T5J 3W7 AB
780-422-8545

Northwest Territories
Road Licensing & Safety, 4510 - 50 Ave., 1st fl., PO Box 1320, Yellowknife, X1A 2L9 NT
867-873-7972, Fax: 867-873-0120

Nova Scotia
Department of Transportation & Infrastructure Renewal, Johnston Bldg., 1672 Granville St., 2nd Fl., PO Box 186, Halifax, B3J 2N2 NS
902-424-2297, Fax: 902-424-0171, 888-432-3233, tpwpaff@gov.ns.ca

Ontario
Ministry of Transportation, Ferguson Block, 77 Wellesley St. West, 3rd Fl., Toronto, M7A 1Z8 ON
416-235-4686, Fax: 416-327-9185, 800-268-4686

Quebec
Ministère des Transports, 700, boul René-Lévesque est, 27e étage, Québec, G1R 5H1 QC
418-643-6980, Fax: 418-643-2011, 888-355-0511, communications@mtq.gouv.qc.ca

Saskatchewan
Saskatchewan Government Insurance, 2260 - 11th Ave., Regina, S4P 0J9 SK
306-751-1200, Fax: 306-787-7477, 800-667-8015, sgiinquiries@sgi.sk.ca

LIBRARIES

Library & Archives Canada, 395 Wellington St., Ottawa, K1A 0N4 ON
613-996-5115, Fax: 613-995-6274, 866-578-7777, reference@lac-bac.ca

Library of Parliament, Parliamentary Bldgs., 111 Wellington St., Ottawa, K1A 0A9 ON
613-992-4793, Fax: 613-943-6383, 866-599-4999

New Brunswick
Legislative Assembly of New Brunswick, Centre Block, Legislative Bldg., 706 Queen St., PO Box 6000, Fredericton, E3B 5H1 NB
506-453-2506, Fax: 506-453-7154, wwwleg@gnb.ca

Newfoundland & Labrador
Provincial Information & Library Resources Board, 48 St. George's Ave, Stephenville, NL A2H 1K9
709-643-0900, Fax: 709-643-0925

Nova Scotia
Legislative House of Assembly, c/o Clerk's Office, Province House, 1st Fl., PO Box 1617, Halifax, B3J 2Y3 NS
902-424-5978, Fax: 902-424-0632

Nunavut
Department of Culture, Language, Elders & Youth, PO Box 1000 800,Iqaluit, X0A 0H0 NU
867-975-5500, Fax: 867-975-5504, 866-934-2035

Ontario
Ontario Library Service - North, 334 Regent St., Sudbury, ON P3C 4E2
705-675-6467, Fax: 705-675-2285, 800-461-6348

Southern Ontario Library Service, #902, 111 Peter St., Toronto, ON M5V 2H1
416-961-1669, Fax: 416-961-5122, 800-387-5765

Quebec
Bibliothèque et Archives nationales du Québec (BAnQ), 475, boul De Maisonneuve est, Montréal, H2L 5C4 QC
514-873-1100, Fax: 514-873-9312, 800-363-9028

Saskatchewan
Saskatchewan Tourism, Parks, Culture, & Sport, 1919 Saskatchewan Dr., 4th Fl., Regina, S4P 4H2 SK
306-787-5729, Fax: 306-787-8560

LIQUOR CONTROL

See Also: Drugs & Alcohol

Alberta
Alberta Gaming & Liquor Commission, 50 Corriveau Ave., St Albert, AB T8N 3T5
780-447-8600, Fax: 780-447-8911, 800-272-8876

British Columbia
Liquor Distribution Branch, 2625 Rupert St., Vancouver, V5M 3T5 BC
604-252-3000, Fax: 604-252-3026

Manitoba
Manitoba Liquor Control Commission, 1555 Buffalo Pl., PO Box 1023, Winnipeg, MB R3C 2X1
204-284-2501, Fax: 204-475-7666, info@mlcc.mb.ca

New Brunswick
New Brunswick Liquor Corporation, 170 Wilsey Rd., PO Box 20787, Fredericton, E3B 5B8 NB
506-452-6826, Fax: 506-462-2024, info@anbl.com

Newfoundland & Labrador
Newfoundland Labrador Liquor Corporation, 90 Kenmount Rd., PO Box 8750 A, St. John's, NL A1B 3V1
709-724-1100, Fax: 709-754-0321, info@nfliquor.com

Northwest Territories
Northwest Territories Liquor Commission, #201, 31 Capital Dr., Hay River, NT X0E 1G2
867-874-2100, Fax: 867-874-2180

Northwest Territories Liquor Licensing & Enforcement, #210, 31 Capital Dr., Hay River, NT X0E 1G2
867-874-2906, Fax: 867-874-6011

Northwest Territories Liquor Licensing Board, #210, 31 Capital Dr., Hay River, NT X0E 1G2
867-874-2906, Fax: 867-874-6011, delilah_st-arneault@gov.nt.ca

Nova Scotia
Alcohol & Gaming Division, Alderney Gate, 40 Alderney Dr., 5th Fl., PO Box 545, Dartmouth, B2Y 3Y8 NS
902-424-6160, Fax: 902-424-6313, 877-565-0556

Nova Scotia Liquor Corporation, Bayers Lake Business Park, 93 Chain Lake Dr., Halifax, B3S 1A3 NS
902-450-6752, 800-567-5874

Nunavut
Nunavut Liquor Licensing Board, Bag 002, Rankin Inlet, NU X0C 0G0
Fax: 867-645-3327

Ontario
Alcohol & Gaming Commission of Ontario, 20 Dundas St. West, Toronto, ON M5G 2N6
416-326-8700, Fax: 416-326-5555, 800-522-2876

Prince Edward Island
Prince Edward Island Liquor Control Commission, 3 Garfield St., PO Box 967, Charlottetown, C1A 7M4 PE
902-368-5710, Fax: 902-368-5735

Quebec
Régie des alcools, des courses et des jeux, 560, boul Charest est, Québec, QC G1K 3J3
418-643-7667, Fax: 418-643-5971, 800-363-0320, racj.quebec@racj.gouv.qc.ca

Société des alcools du Québec, 905, av De Lorimier, Montréal, QC H2K 3V9
514-873-2020, Fax: 514-873-6788, 866-873-2020, info@saq.com

Saskatchewan
Saskatchewan Liquor & Gaming Authority, 2500 Victoria Ave., PO Box 5054, Regina, S4P 3M3 SK
306-787-4213, Fax: 306-787-8468

Yukon Territory
Yukon Liquor Corporation, 9031 Quartz Rd., Whitehorse, Y1A 4P9 YT
867-667-5245, Fax: 867-393-6306, yukon.liquor@gov.yk.ca

LOTTERIES & GAMING

Alberta
Alberta Gaming & Liquor Commission, 50 Corriveau Ave., St Albert, AB T8N 3T5
780-447-8600, Fax: 780-447-8911, 800-272-8876

British Columbia
British Columbia Lottery Corporation, 74 West Seymour St., Kamloops, BC V2C 1E2
250-828-5500, Fax: 250-828-5631, 866-815-0222,

Manitoba
Manitoba Lotteries Corporation, 830 Empress St., Winnipeg, R3G 3H3 MB
204-957-2500, Fax: 204-957-3991, communications@casinosofwinnipeg.com

Manitoba Gaming Control Commission, #800, 215 Garry St., Winnipeg, MB R3C 3P3
204-954-9400, Fax: 204-954-9450, 800-782-0363, information@mgcc.mb.ca

New Brunswick
New Brunswick Lotteries & Gaming Corporation, Centennial Bldg., 670 King St., PO Box 6000, Fredericton, NB E3B 5H1
506-453-2451, Fax: 506-457-4989

Newfoundland & Labrador
Department of Government Services, PO Box 8700, St. John's, A1B 4J6 NL
709-729-4860

Nova Scotia
Alcohol & Gaming Division, Alderney Gate, 40 Alderney Dr., 5th Fl., PO Box 545, Dartmouth, B2Y 3Y8 NS
902-424-6160, Fax: 902-424-6313, 877-565-0556

Nunavut
Department of Community & Government Services, J.G. Brown Bldg., PO Box 1000 700,Iqaluit, X0A 0H0 NU
867-975-5400, Fax: 867-975-5305

Ontario
Alcohol & Gaming Commission of Ontario, 20 Dundas St. West, Toronto, ON M5G 2N6
416-326-8700, Fax: 416-326-5555, 800-522-2876
Ontario Racing Commission, 20 Dundas St. West, 9th Fl., Toronto, ON M5G 2C2
416-327-0520, Fax: 416-325-3478, orcinqry@cbs.gov.on.ca

Prince Edward Island
Consumer, Corporate & Insurance Division, Shaw Building, 95 Rochford St., 4th Fl., PO Box 2000, Charlottetown, C1A 7N8 PE
902-368-4580, Fax: 902-368-5283, 800-658-1799
Prince Edward Island Lotteries Commission, Office of the Deputy Provincial Treasurer, 95 Rochford St., PO Box 2000, Charlottetown, PE C1A 7N8
902-368-4053, Fax: 902-368-6575

Quebec
Loto-Québec, 500, rue Sherbrooke ouest, Montréal, QC H3A 3G6
514-282-8000, Fax: 514-873-8999
Régie des alcools, des courses et des jeux, 560, boul Charest est, Québec, QC G1K 3J3
418-643-7667, Fax: 418-643-5971, 800-363-0320, racj.quebec@racj.gouv.qc.ca

Saskatchewan
Saskatchewan Liquor & Gaming Authority, 2500 Victoria Ave., PO Box 5054, Regina, S4P 3M3 SK
306-787-4213, Fax: 306-787-8468

Yukon Territory
Yukon Lottery Commission, 312 Wood St., Whitehorse, YT Y1A 2E6
867-633-7890, Fax: 867-668-7561, lotteriesyukon@gov.yk.ca

MAPS, CHARTS & AERIAL PHOTOGRAPHS

Canada Centre for Remote Sensing - Geomatics Canada, 588 Booth St., Ottawa, K1A 0Y7 ON
613-995-0947, Fax: 613-947-1382

Nova Scotia
Nova Scotia Geomatics Centre, 160 Willow St., Amherst, B4H 3W3 NS
902-667-7231, Fax: 902-667-6008, 800-798-0706, info@nsgc.gov.ns.ca

Ontario
Association of Ontario Land Surveyors, 1043 McNicoll Ave., Toronto, ON M1W 3W6
416-491-9020, Fax: 416-491-2576, admin@aols.org

MARINE NAVIGATION

Atlantic Pilotage Authority, Cogswell Tower, #910, 2000 Barrington St., Halifax, B3J 3K1 NS
902-426-2550, Fax: 902-426-4004, 877-272-3477, dispatch@atlanticpilotage.com
Great Lakes Pilotage Authority, 202 Pitt St., 2nd fl., PO Box 95, Cornwall, K6H 5R9 ON
613-933-2991, Fax: 613-932-3793, administration@glpa-apgl.com
Pacific Pilotage Authority Canada, #1000, 1130 Pender St. West, Vancouver, V6E 4A4 BC
604-666-6771, Fax: 604-666-1647, info@ppa.gc.ca
St. Lawrence Seaway Management Corporation, 202 Pitt St., Cornwall, K6J 3P7 ON
613-932-5170, Fax: 613-932-7286, marketing@seaway.ca

MINERALS & MINING

Alberta
Resource Development Policy Division, Petroleum Plaza NT, 9945 - 108 St., Edmonton, T5K 2G6 AB

British Columbia
Mining & Minerals, 1675 Douglas St., 7th Fl., PO Box 9320 Prov Govt,Victoria, V8W 9N3 BC
250-952-0596, Fax: 250-952-0491

Manitoba
Mines Branch, #360, 1395 Ellice Ave., Winnipeg, R3G 3P2 MB
Fax: 204-948-2578
Mining Board, #360, 1395 Ellice Ave., Winnipeg, MB R3G 3P2
204-489-0018

Northwest Territories
Department of Industry, Tourism & Investment, PO Box 1320, Yellowknife, X1A 2L9 NT
Fax: 867-873-0306, info@iti.ca

Nova Scotia
Department of Energy, Bank of Montreal Bldg., #400, 5151 George St., PO Box 2664, Halifax, B3J 3P7 NS
902-424-4575, Fax: 902-424-0528, energyinfo@gov.ns.ca

Nunavut
Department of Environment, PO Box 1000 1300,Iqaluit, X0A 0H0 NU
867-975-7700, Fax: 867-975-7742, 866-222-9063, environment@gov.nu.ca

Ontario
Mines & Minerals Division, Willet Green Miller Centre, 933 Ramsey Lake Rd., 6th Fl., Sudbury, P3E 6B5 ON
705-670-5755, Fax: 705-670-5818

Quebec
Mines, RC, 880, ch Ste-Foy, Québec, G1S 4X4 QC
418-627-6278, Fax: 418-418-6432, 800-363-7233, service.mines@mrnf.gouv.qc.ca
Énergie, #B401, 5700, 4e av ouest, Québec, G1H 6R1 QC
418-627-6377, Fax: 418-643-0701

Saskatchewan
Saskatchewan Energy & Resources, #300, 2103 - 11th Ave., Regina, S4P 3Z8 SK
306-787-2528, Fax: 306-787-0395, 866-727-5427,

Yukon Territory
Yukon Energy, Mines & Resources, PO Box 2703, Whitehorse, Y1A 2C6 YT
867-667-5466, Fax: 867-667-8601, 800-661-0408, emr@gov.yk.ca

MINES & MINERALS

Alberta
Resource Development Policy Division, Petroleum Plaza NT, 9945 - 108 St., Edmonton, T5K 2G6 AB

Alberta
Alberta Sport, Recreation, Parks & Wildlife Foundation, Standard Life Centre, 10405 Jasper Ave., 9th Fl., Edmonton, AB T5J 4R7
780-415-1167, Fax: 780-415-0308

British Columbia
Ministry of Energy, Mines & Petroleum Resources, PO Box 9318 Prov Govt,Victoria, V8W 9N3 BC
250-952-0241

Manitoba
Manitoba Geological Survey, #360, 1394 Ellice Ave., Winnipeg, R3G 3P2 MB
Fax: 204-945-1406, 800-223-5215, minesinfo@gov.mb.ca
Mining Board, #360, 1395 Ellice Ave., Winnipeg, MB R3G 3P2
204-489-0018

Northwest Territories
Department of Environment & Natural Resources, PO Box 1320, Yellowknife, X1A 2L9 NT

Ontario
Mines & Minerals Division, Willet Green Miller Centre, 933 Ramsey Lake Rd., 6th Fl., Sudbury, P3E 6B5 ON
705-670-5755, Fax: 705-670-5818
Ministry of Northern Development, Mines & Forestry, 99 Wellesley St. West, Toronto, M7A 1W3 ON
416-327-0633, Fax: 416-327-0665

Quebec
Mines, RC, 880, ch Ste-Foy, Québec, G1S 4X4 QC
418-627-6278, Fax: 418-418-6432, 800-363-7233, service.mines@mrnf.gouv.qc.ca

MINIMUM WAGES

See Also: Labour

British Columbia
Ministry of Labour, PO Box 9052 Prov Govt,Victoria, V8W 9E2 BC
250-356-6348, Fax: 250-356-6595, LCS.Minister@gov.bc.ca

Quebec
Commission des normes du travail, Hall Est, 400, boul Jean-Lesage, 7e étage, Québec, QC G1K 8W1
418-644-0817, Fax: 418-643-5132, 800-563-9058

Saskatchewan
Minimum Wage Board, #400, 1870 Albert St., Regina, SK S4P 4W1
306-787-2391, Fax: 306-787-7229, webmaster@lab.gov.sk.ca

MULTICULTURALISM

Canadian Race Relations Foundation, #701, 4576 Yonge St., Toronto, M2N 6N4 ON
416-952-3500, Fax: 416-952-3326, 888-240-4936, info@crr.ca

Manitoba
Manitoba Ethnocultural Advisory & Advocacy Council, 215 Notre Dame Ave. 4th Fl., Winnipeg, MB R3B 1N3
204-945-2339, Fax: 204-948-2323, 800-665-8332, meaac@gov.mb.ca
Multiculturalism Secretariat, 213 Notre Dame Ave., 4th Fl., Winnipeg, MB R3B 1N3
204-945-1156, Fax: 204-948-2323

New Brunswick
Ministerial Advisory Committee on Multiculturalism, PO Box 6000, Fredericton, NB E3B 5H1

Northwest Territories
Department of Education, Culture & Employment, PO Box 1320, Yellowknife, X1A 2L9 NT
867-669-2399, Fax: 867-873-0431, 866-606-5627

Nova Scotia
Department of Tourism, Culture & Heritage, World Trade & Convention Centre, 1800 Argyle St., 6th Fl., PO Box 456, Halifax, B3J 2R5 NS
902-424-5000, Fax: 902-424-4872, 800-565-0000, tns@gov.ns.ca

Ontario
Culture Policy, Programs & Services Division, 400 University Ave., 5th Fl., Toronto, M7A 2R9 ON
416-314-7265, Fax: 416-314-7461

Prince Edward Island
Department of Education & Early Childhood Development, Sullivan Bldg., 16 Fitzroy St., 2nd Fl., PO Box 2000, Charlottetown, C1A 7N8 PE
902-368-4600, Fax: 902-368-4663

Quebec
Conseil des relations interculturelles, #10.04, 500, boul René-Lévesque ouest, Montréal, QC H2Z 1W7
514-873-8501, Fax: 514-873-3469
Ministère de la Culture, des Communications & de la Condition féminine, 225, Grande Allée est, Québec, G1R 5G5 QC
Fax: 418-380-2364, 888-380-8882, infos@mcccf.gouv.qc.ca

MUNICIPAL & RURAL AFFAIRS

Canada Economic Development for Québec Regions, Édifice Dominion Square, #900, 1255, rue Peel, Montréal, H3B 2T9 QC
514-283-6412, Fax: 514-283-3302, 866-385-6412
Canada Mortgage & Housing Corporation, 700 Montreal Rd., Ottawa, K1A 0P7 ON
613-748-2000, Fax: 613-748-2098, 800-668-2642, chic@cmhc-schl.gc.ca
Indian & Northern Affairs Canada, 10 Wellington St., North Tower, Gatineau, K1A 0H4 QC
819-997-0380, Fax: 819-953-3017, 866-817-3977, infopubs@ainc-inac.gc.ca
Mackenzie Valley Environmental Impact Review Board, 200 Scotia Centre, 5102 - 50th Ave., PO Box 938, Yellowknife, NT X1A 2N7
867-766-7050, Fax: 867-766-7074, 866-912-3472, tcharlo@reviewboard.ca
Nunavut Impact Review Board, PO Box 1360, Cambridge Bay, NU X0B 0C0
867-983-4600, Fax: 867-983-2594, 866-233-3033, info@nirb.ca
Nunavut Planning Commission, PO Box 2101, Cambridge Bay, NU X0B 0C0
867-983-4625, Fax: 867-983-4626, staptuna@nunavut.ca

Alberta
Alberta Agriculture & Rural Development, J.G. O'Donoghue Bldg., 7000 - 113 St., 1st Fl., Edmonton, T6H 5T6 AB
780-427-2727, Fax: 780-427-2861, 866-882-7677
Alberta Municipal Government Board, Commerce Place, 10155 - 102 St., 15th Fl., Edmonton, AB T5J 4L4
780-427-4864, Fax: 780-427-0986,
Alberta Municipal Affairs, Communications Branch, Commerce Place, 10155 - 102 St., 18th Fl., Edmonton, T5J 4L4 AB
780-427-2732, Fax: 780-422-1419, comments@gov.ab.ca
Alberta Tourism, Parks, Recreation & Culture, Communications Branch, Standard Life Centre, 10405 Jasper Ave., 7th Fl., Edmonton, T5J 4R7 AB
780-427-6530, Fax: 780-427-1496, Comdev.Communications@gov.ab.ca

British Columbia
Local Government Department, 800 Johnson St., 6th Fl., PO Box 9490 Prov Govt,Victoria, V8W 9N7 BC
lgd_feedback@gov.bc.ca

Manitoba

Manitoba Aboriginal & Northern Affairs, 59 Elizabeth Dr., PO Box 37, Thompson, R8N 1X4 MB
204-677-6607, Fax: 204-677-6753, amartin@gov.mb.ca

Community Land Use Planning Services, #604, 800 Portage Ave., Winnipeg, R3G 0N4 MB

Manitoba Intergovernmental Affairs, #301, 450 Broadway Ave., Winnipeg, R3C 0V8 MB
Fax: 204-945-1383, mnia@leg.gov.mb.ca

Manitoba Municipal Board, #1144, 363 Broadway, Winnipeg, MB R3C 3N9
204-945-2941, Fax: 204-948-2235

New Brunswick

Assessment & Planning Appeal Board, #201, 435 King St., PO Box 6000, Fredericton, NB E3B 5H1
506-453-2126, Fax: 506-444-4881

Department of Health, PO Box 5100, Fredericton, E3B 5G8 NB
506-457-4800, Fax: 506-453-5243, dh-ms@dh-ms.ca

Regional Development Corporation, RDC Bldg., 836 Churchill Row, PO Box 428, Fredericton, E3B 5R4 NB
506-453-2277, Fax: 506-453-7988

Newfoundland & Labrador

Department of Health & Community Services, West Block, Confederation Bldg., PO Box 8700, St. John's, A1B 4J6 NL
709-729-5021, Fax: 709-729-5824

Department of Labrador & Aboriginal Affairs, Confederation Bldg., East Block, 6th Fl., PO Box 8700, St. John's, A1B 4J6 NL
709-729-4776, Fax: 709-729-4900, 877-788-8822, laa@gov.nl.ca

Department of Municipal Affairs, West Block, Main Fl., Confederation Bldg., PO Box 8700, St. John's, A1B 4J6 NL
709-729-3053

Northwest Territories

Department of Municipal & Community Affairs, PO Box 1320, Yellowknife, X1A 2L9 NT
867-873-7118, Fax: 867-873-0309

Nova Scotia

Department of Service Nova Scotia & Municipal Relations, 1505 Barrington St., PO Box 216, Halifax, B3J 2M4 NS
902-424-4141, Fax: 902-424-0581, public-enquiries@gov.ns.ca

Department of Transportation & Infrastructure Renewal, Johnston Bldg., 1672 Granville St., 2nd Fl., PO Box 186, Halifax, B3J 2N2 NS
902-424-2297, Fax: 902-424-0171, 888-432-3233, tpwpaff@gov.ns.ca

Ontario

Ministry of Agriculture, Food & Rural Affairs, 1 Stone Rd. West, Guelph, N1G 4Y2 ON
519-826-3100, 888-466-2372

Ministry of Municipal Affairs & Housing, 777 Bay St., 17th Fl., Toronto, M5G 2E5 ON
416-585-7041, Fax: 416-585-6227, 866-220-2290, mininfo.mah@ontario.ca

Northern Development Division, Roberta Bondar Place, #200, 70 Foster Dr., Sault Ste Marie, P6A 6V8 ON
705-945-5900, Fax: 705-945-5931, 800-461-2287

Ministry of Northern Development, Mines & Forestry, 99 Wellesley St. West, Toronto, M7A 1W3 ON
416-327-0633, Fax: 416-327-0665

Prince Edward Island

Department of Transportation & Public Works, Jones Bldg., 11 Kent St., PO Box 2000, Charlottetown, C1A 7N8 PE
902-368-5100, Fax: 902-368-5395

Quebec

Ministère des Affaires municipales et Occupation du territoire, Aile Chaveau, 10, rue Pierre-Olivier-Chauveau, 3e étage, Québec, G1R 4J3 QC
418-691-2019, Fax: 418-643-7385, communications@mamrot.gouv.qc.ca

Comité consultatif de l'environnement Kativik, CP 930, Kuujjuaq, QC J0M 1C0
819-964-2961, Fax: 819-964-0694, ndea@krg.ca

Commission municipale du Québec, Mezzanine, aile Chauveau, 10, rue Pierre-Olivier-Chauveau, Tour 5e étage, Québec, QC G1R 4J3
418-691-2014, Fax: 418-644-4676, 866-353-6767, cmq@mamr.gouv.qc.ca

Ministère du Développement économique, de l'Innovation et de l'Exportation, 710, place D'Youville, 3e étage, Québec, G1R 4Y4 QC
418-691-5950, Fax: 418-644-0118, 866-680-1884

Saskatchewan

Saskatchewan Northern Affairs, Mistasinihk Place, 1328 La Ronge Ave., PO Box 5000, La Ronge, S0J 1L0 SK
306-425-4207, Fax: 306-425-4349, 866-663-4065, admin@sna.gov.sk.ca

Yukon Territory

Yukon Community Services, PO Box 2703, Whitehorse, Y1A 2C6 YT
867-667-5811, Fax: 867-393-6295, 800-661-0408, inquiry@gov.yk.ca

MUNICIPAL AFFAIRS

Alberta

Alberta Municipal Affairs, Communications Branch, Commerce Place, 10155 - 102 St., 18th Fl., Edmonton, T5J 4L4 AB
780-427-2732, Fax: 780-422-1419, comments@gov.ab.ca

British Columbia

Local Government Department, 800 Johnson St., 6th Fl., PO Box 9490 Prov Govt,Victoria, V8W 9N7 BC
lgd_feedback@gov.bc.ca

Manitoba

Manitoba Aboriginal & Northern Affairs, 59 Elizabeth Dr., PO Box 37, Thompson, R8N 1X4 MB
204-677-6607, Fax: 204-677-6753, amartin@gov.mb.ca

Manitoba Intergovernmental Affairs, #301, 450 Broadway Ave., Winnipeg, R3C 0V8 MB
Fax: 204-945-1383, mnia@leg.gov.mb.ca

Local Government Development Division, 59 Elizabeth Dr., PO Box 33, Thompson, R8N 1X4 MB
204-677-6794, Fax: 204-677-6525

Manitoba Municipal Board, #1144, 363 Broadway, Winnipeg, MB R3C 3N9
204-945-2941, Fax: 204-948-2235

Provincial-Municipal Support Services, #508, 800 Portage Ave., Winnipeg, R3G 0N4 MB

New Brunswick

Department of Local Government, Marysville Place, 20 McGloin St., PO Box 6000, Fredericton, E3B 5H1 NB
506-453-2807, Fax: 506-453-3988

Regional Development Corporation, RDC Bldg., 836 Churchill Row, PO Box 428, Fredericton, E3B 5R4 NB
506-453-2277, Fax: 506-453-7988

Newfoundland & Labrador

Department of Municipal Affairs, West Block, Main Fl., Confederation Bldg., PO Box 8700, St. John's, A1B 4J6 NL
709-729-3053

Newfoundland & Labrador Municipal Financing Corporation, Confederation Bldg., PO Box 8700, St. John's, NL A1B 4J6
709-729-6686, Fax: 709-729-2095

Northwest Territories

Department of Municipal & Community Affairs, PO Box 1320, Yellowknife, X1A 2L9 NT
867-873-7118, Fax: 867-873-0309

Nova Scotia

Nova Scotia Municipal Finance Corporation, Maritime Centre, 1505 Barrington St., 10th Fl. South, PO Box 850 M, Halifax, NS B3J 2V2
902-424-4590, Fax: 902-424-0525

Department of Service Nova Scotia & Municipal Relations, 1505 Barrington St., PO Box 216, Halifax, B3J 2M4 NS
902-424-4141, Fax: 902-424-0581, public-enquiries@gov.ns.ca

Nunavut

Department of Community & Government Services, J.G. Brown Bldg., PO Box 1000 700,Iqaluit, X0A 0H0 NU
867-975-5400, Fax: 867-975-5305

Ontario

Economic Development Division, 1 Stone Road W., 2nd Fl., Guelph, N1G 4Y2 ON
519-826-6636, Fax: 519-826-4328

Ministry of Municipal Affairs & Housing, 777 Bay St., 17th Fl., Toronto, M5G 2E5 ON
416-585-7041, Fax: 416-585-6227, 866-220-2290, mininfo.mah@ontario.ca

Prince Edward Island

Department of Communities, Cultural Affairs & Labour, Shaw Bldg., 95 Rochford St., 4th Fl., PO Box 2000, Charlottetown, C1A 7N8 PE
902-368-5250, Fax: 902-368-4121

Quebec

Ministère des Affaires municipales et Occupation du territoire, Aile Chaveau, 10, rue Pierre-Olivier-Chauveau, 3e étage, Québec, G1R 4J3 QC
418-691-2019, Fax: 418-643-7385, communications@mamrot.gouv.qc.ca

MUSEUMS

Canadian Heritage, 15 Eddy St., Gatineau, K1A 0M5 QC
819-997-0055, 866-811-0055, info@pch.gc.ca

Canadian Museum of Civilization, 100 Laurier St., PO Box 3100 B,Gatineau, J8X 4H2 QC
819-776-7000, Fax: 819-776-8300, 800-555-5621

Canadian Museum of Nature, PO Box 3443 D,Ottawa, K1P 6P4 ON
613-566-4700, Fax: 613-364-4021, 800-263-4433, enquiries@mus-nature.ca

National Gallery of Canada, 380 Sussex Dr., PO Box 427 A,Ottawa, K1N 9N4 ON
613-990-1985, Fax: 613-993-4385, 800-319-2787, info@gallery.ca; info@beaux-arts.ca

Alberta

Culture & Community Development Division, Standard Life Centre, 10405 Jasper Ave., 9th Fl., Edmonton, T5J 4R7 AB
780-415-1167, Fax: 780-422-2891

British Columbia

Ministry of Healthy Living & Sport, PO Box 9067 Prov Govt,Victoria, V8W 9E2 BC
250-387-3504, Fax: 250-387-3420, Feedback@gov.bc.ca

Royal BC Museum Corporation, 675 Belleville St., Victoria, BC V8W 9W2
250-356-7226, Fax: 250-387-5674, 888-447-7977, reception@royalbcmuseum.bc.ca

Manitoba

Manitoba Museum, 190 Rupert Ave., Winnipeg, MB R3B 0N2
204-956-2830, Fax: 204-942-3679, info@manitobamuseum.mb.ca

Newfoundland & Labrador

Department of Fisheries & Aquaculture, Petten Bldg., 30 Strawberry Marsh Rd., PO Box 8700, St. John's, A1B 4J6 NL
709-729-3723, Fax: 709-729-6082, fishaqwebmaster@gov.nl.ca

Nova Scotia

Culture Division, #601, 1800 Argyle St., PO Box 456, Halifax, B3J 2R5 NS
Fax: 902-424-0710

Ontario

Ministry of Culture, Mowat Block, 900 Bay St., 5th Fl., Toronto, M7A 1L2 ON
416-325-1660, Fax: 416-325-1726, 866-454-0049

Royal Ontario Museum, 100 Queen's Park Cres., Toronto, ON M5S 2C6
416-586-5549, Fax: 416-586-5685, info@rom.on.ca

Prince Edward Island

PEI Museum & Heritage Foundation, 2 Kent St., PO Box 2000, Charlottetown, PE C1A 1M6
902-368-6600, Fax: 902-368-6608, mhpei@gov.pe.ca

Quebec

Ministère de la Culture, des Communications & de la Condition féminine, 225, Grande Allée est, Québec, G1R 5G5 QC
Fax: 418-380-2364, 888-380-8882, infos@mcccf.gouv.qc.ca

Musée d'art contemporain de Montréal, 185, rue Ste-Catherine ouest, Montréal, H2X 3X5 QC
514-847-6226, Fax: 514-847-6290

Musée de la civilisation, 85, rue Dalhousie, CP 155 B,Québec, G1K 7A6 QC
418-643-2158, Fax: 418-646-9705, 866-710-8031, mcqweb@mcq.org

Musée national des beaux-arts du Québec, Parc des Champs-de-Bataille, 1, av Wolfe-Montcalm, Québec, G1R 5H3 QC
418-643-2150, Fax: 418-646-3330, 866-220-2150, webmestre@mnba.qc.ca

Saskatchewan

Royal Saskatchewan Museum, 2445 Albert St., Regina, SK S4P 4W7
306-787-2815, Fax: 306-787-2820, info@royalsaskmuseum.ca

Western Development Museum, 2935 Melville St., Saskatoon, SK S7J 5A6
306-934-1400, Fax: 306-934-4467, 800-363-6345, info@wdm.ca

Yukon Territory

Yukon Tourism & Culture, PO Box 2703, Whitehorse, Y1A 2C6 YT
867-667-5036, Fax: 867-667-3546

NATIVE PEOPLES & NORTHERN AFFAIRS

British Columbia

Northern Interior, 1011 - 4 Ave., 5th Fl., Prince George, V2L 3H9 BC
250-565-6100, Fax: 250-565-6671, www.for.gov.bc.ca/rni

New Brunswick

Aboriginal Affairs Secretariat, Kings Place, #237, 440 King St., PO Box 6000, Fredericton, E3B 5H1 NB
506-462-5177, Fax: 506-444-5142

Yukon Territory

Yukon Development Corporation, PO Box 2703 D-1,Whitehorse, Y1A 2C6 YT
867-393-5337, Fax: 867-393-5401

Yukon Land Use Planning Council, #201, 307 Jarvis St., Whitehorse, YT Y1A 2H3
867-667-7397, Fax: 867-667-4624, ylupc@planyukon.ca

NATURAL RESOURCES

Canadian Museum of Nature, PO Box 3443 D,Ottawa, K1P 6P4 ON
613-566-4700, Fax: 613-364-4021, 800-263-4433, enquiries@mus-nature.ca

Natural Resources Canada, 580 Booth St., Ottawa, K1A 0E4 ON
613-995-0947, Fax: 613-992-7211

Alberta

Natural Resources Conservation Board, Sterling Place, 9940 - 106 St., 4th Fl., Edmonton, AB T5K 2N2
780-422-1977, Fax: 780-427-0607, 866-383-6722

Alberta Sustainable Resource Development, Information Centre, 9920 - 108 St., Main Fl., Edmonton, T5K 2M4 AB
780-944-0313, Fax: 780-427-4407, 877-944-0313, srd.infocent@gov.ab.ca

British Columbia

Ministry of Energy, Mines & Petroleum Resources, PO Box 9318 Prov Govt,Victoria, V8W 9N3 BC
250-952-0241,

Ministry of Environment, PO Box 9339 Prov Govt,Victoria, V8W 9M1 BC
250-387-1161, Fax: 250-387-5669, www.envmail@gov.bc.ca

Ministry of Forests & Range, PO Box 9529 Prov Govt,Victoria, V8W 9C3 BC
250-387-4809, Fax: 250-953-3687

Manitoba

Manitoba Conservation, 200 Saulteaux Cres., Winnipeg, R3J 3W3 MB
204-945-6784, 800-214-6497, mincon@leg.gov.mb.ca

Manitoba Conservation Districts Commission, Secretariat c/o Planning & Coordination Branch, 123 Main St., PO Box 20000, Neepawa, MB R0J 1H0
204-476-7033, Fax: 204-476-7539, whildebran@gov.mb.ca

New Brunswick

Department of Natural Resources, PO Box 6000, Fredericton, E3B 5H1 NB
506-453-2510, Fax: 506-444-5839, dnrweb@gnb.ca

Newfoundland & Labrador

Department of Natural Resources, Natural Resources Bldg., 50 Elizabeth Ave., 7th Fl., PO Box 8700, St. John's, A1B 4J6 NL
709-729-2920, Fax: 709-729-0059

Northwest Territories

Department of Environment & Natural Resources, PO Box 1320, Yellowknife, X1A 2L9 NT

Nova Scotia

Department of Natural Resources, Founder's Square, 1701 Hollis St., 3rd Fl., PO Box 698, Halifax, B3J 2T9 NS
902-424-5935, Fax: 902-424-0594, 800-565-2224

Nunavut

Department of Environment, PO Box 1000 1300,Iqaluit, X0A 0H0 NU
867-975-7700, Fax: 867-975-7742, 866-222-9063, environment@gov.nu.ca

Ontario

Ministry of Natural Resources, Whitney Block, #6630, 99 Wellesley St. West, 6th Fl., Toronto, M7A 1W3 ON
800-667-1940

Ministry of Northern Development, Mines & Forestry, 99 Wellesley St. West, Toronto, M7A 1W3 ON
416-327-0633, Fax: 416-327-0665

Prince Edward Island

Department of Agriculture, Jones Bldg., 11 Kent St., PO Box 2000, Charlottetown, C1A 7N8 PE
902-368-4880, Fax: 902-368-4857

Department of Environment, Energy & Forestry, Jones Bldg., 11 Kent St., 4th & 5th Fl., PO Box 2000, Charlottetown, C1A 7N8 PE
902-368-5000, Fax: 902-368-5830

Quebec

Ministère du Développement durable, de l'Environnement et des Parcs, Édifice Marie-Guyart, 675, boul René-Lévesque est, 29e étage, Québec, G1R 5V7 QC
418-521-3830, Fax: 418-646-5974, 800-561-1616, info@mddep.gouv.qc.ca

Ministère des Ressources naturelles et de la Faune, 880, ch Sainte-Foy, Québec, G1S 4X4 QC
418-627-8600, Fax: 418-644-6513, 866-248-6936, services.clientele@mrnf.gouv.qc.ca

Saskatchewan

Saskatchewan Energy & Resources, #300, 2103 - 11th Ave., Regina, S4P 3Z8 SK
306-787-2528, Fax: 306-787-0395, 866-727-5427

Saskatchewan Environment, 3211 Albert St., 2nd Fl., Regina, S4S 5W6 SK
306-953-3750, Fax: 306-787-9544, 800-567-4224, inquiry@serm.gov.sk.ca

Yukon Territory

Yukon Energy, Mines & Resources, PO Box 2703, Whitehorse, Y1A 2C6 YT
867-667-5466, Fax: 867-667-8601, 800-661-0408, emr@gov.yk.ca

Yukon Environment, PO Box 2703, Whitehorse, Y1A 2C6 YT
867-667-5652, Fax: 867-393-7197, 800-661-0408, environmentyukon@gov.yk.ca

NUCLEAR ENERGY

Atomic Energy of Canada Limited, Head Office, Sheridan Science & Technology Park, 2251 Speakman Dr., Mississauga, L5K 1B2 ON
905-823-9040, 866-886-2325, librarycr@aecl.ca (Library); speakers@aecl.ca (Community speakers)

Canadian Nuclear Safety Commission, 280 Slater St., PO Box 1046 B,Ottawa, K1P 5S9 ON
613-995-5894, Fax: 613-995-5086, 800-668-5284, info@cnsc-ccsn.gc.ca

Alberta

Alberta Energy, North Petroleum Plaza, 9945 - 108 St., 10th Fl., Edmonton, T5K 2G6 AB
780-427-8050, Fax: 780-422-0698, 780-310-0000

Ontario

Ontario Power Generation, 700 University Ave., Toronto, M5G 1X6 ON
416-592-2555, 877-592-2555

Quebec

Hydro-Québec, 75, boul René-Lévesque ouest, 20e étage, Montréal, H2Z 1A4 QC
514-289-2211

NUTRITION

Alberta

Health Workforce Division, Telus Plaza NT, 10025 Jasper Ave., 10th Fl., Edmonton, T5J 1S6 AB

Research Branch, Tower 5, 1341 Baseline Rd., Ottawa, K1A 0C5 ON
613-759-1000, Fax: 613-773-1866

Manitoba

Manitoba Healthy Child Office, #219, 114 Garry St., Winnipeg, R3C 1G1 MB
204-945-2266, 888-848-0140, healthychild@gov.mb.ca

Primary Care & Healthy Living, 300 Carlton St., 2nd Floor, Winnipeg, R3B 3M9 MB

Newfoundland & Labrador

Department of Health & Community Services, West Block, Confederation Bldg., PO Box 8700, St. John's, A1B 4J6 NL
709-729-5021, Fax: 709-729-5824

Northwest Territories

Department of Health & Social Services, Centre Square Tower, PO Box 1320, Yellowknife, X1A 2L9 NT
Fax: 867-873-0266

Nunavut

Department of Health & Social Services, Sivummut bldg., PO Box 1007 1000,Iqaluit, X0A 0H0 NU
867-975-5700, Fax: 867-975-5705, health@gov.nu.ca

Ontario

Ministry of Health & Long-Term Care, Hepburn Block, 80 Grosvenor St., 10th Fl, Toronto, M7A 2C4 ON
416-327-4327, 800-268-1153

Prince Edward Island

Department of Health, Jones Bldg., 11 Kent St., 2nd Fl., PO Box 2000, Charlottetown, C1A 7N8 PE
902-368-4900, Fax: 902-368-4974

Quebec

Ministère de la Santé et des Services sociaux, Direction des communications et Renseignements généraux, 1075, ch Sainte-Foy, Québec, G1S 2M1 QC
418-266-8900, 800-707-3380, regisseur.web@msss.gouv.qc.ca

Saskatchewan

Saskatchewan Health, T.C. Douglas Bldg., 3475 Albert St., Regina, S4S 6X6 SK
306-787-0146, 800-667-7766, info@health.gov.sk.ca

OCCUPATIONAL SAFETY

See Also: Dangerous Goods & Hazardous Materials

Canadian Centre for Occupational Health & Safety, 135 Hunter St. East, Hamilton, L8N 1M5 ON
905-572-2981, Fax: 905-572-2206, 800-668-4284, clientservices@ccohs.ca

Alberta

Occupational Health & Safety Council, Labour Bldg, 10808 - 99 Ave., 9th Fl., Edmonton, AB T5K 0G5
780-415-0599, Fax: 780-422-8944

Workplace Standards Division, Labour Bldg., 10808 - 99 Ave., 8th Fl., Edmonton, T5K 0G5 AB
780-415-9057, Fax: 780-644-2100

British Columbia

Ministry of Labour, PO Box 9052 Prov Govt,Victoria, V8W 9E2 BC
250-356-6348, Fax: 250-356-6595, LCS.Minister@gov.bc.ca

Workers' Compensation Board of British Columbia, PO Box 5350 Terminal,Vancouver, V6B 5L5 BC
604-276-3100, Fax: 604-244-6490, 888-621-7233

Manitoba

Advisory Council on Workplace Safety & Health, #200, 401 York Ave., Winnipeg, MB R3C 0P8
204-945-3446, Fax: 204-945-4556

Workplace Safety & Health Division, #200, 401 York Ave., Winnipeg, R3C 0P8 MB
204-945-3446, Fax: 204-948-2209, wshcompl@gov.mb.ca

New Brunswick

Workplace Health, Safety & Compensation Commission of New Brunswick, 1 Portland St., PO Box 160, Saint John, E2L 3X9 NB
506-632-2200, 800-222-9775, communications@ws-ts.nb.ca

Newfoundland & Labrador

Newfoundland & Labrador Workplace Health, Safety & Compensation Commission, 146 - 148 Forest Rd., PO Box 9000, St. John's, A1A 3B8 NL
709-778-1000, Fax: 709-738-1714, 800-563-9000, general.inquiries@whscc.nl.ca

Northwest Territories

Northwest Territories & Nunavut Workers' Compensation Board, Centre Square Tower, 5022 - 49th St., 5th Fl., PO Box 8888, Yellowknife, X1A 2R3 NT
867-920-3888, Fax: 867-873-4596, 800-661-0792, wcb@wcb.nt.ca

Nova Scotia

Occupational Health & Safety Advisory Council, PO Box 697, Halifax, NS B3J 2T8
902-424-2484, Fax: 902-424-5640

Workers' Compensation Board of Nova Scotia, 5668 South St., PO Box 1150, Halifax, B3J 2Y2 NS
902-491-8999, Fax: 902-491-8002, 800-870-3331, info@wcb.gov.ns.ca

Ontario

Workplace Safety & Insurance Board, 200 Front St. West, Ground Fl., Toronto, M5V 3J1 ON
416-344-1000, Fax: 416-344-4684, 800-387-0750

Prince Edward Island

Prince Edward Island Workers Compensation Board, 14 Weymouth St., PO Box 757, Charlottetown, C1A 7L7 PE
902-368-5680, Fax: 902-368-5705, 800-237-5049

Quebec

Commission des lésions professionnelles, #700, 900, Place d'Youville, Québec, QC G1R 3P7
418-644-7777, Fax: 418-644-6443, 800-463-1591

Commission de la santé et de la sécurité du travail du Québec, 524, rue Bourdages, CP 1200 Terminus postal,Québec, G1K 7E2 QC
418-266-4850, Fax: 418-266-4398, 866-302-2778

Saskatchewan
Office of the Worker's Advocate, #400, 1870 Albert St., Regina, SK S4P 4W1
306-787-2456, Fax: 306-787-0249, 877-787-2456
Saskatchewan Workers' Compensation Board, #200, 1881 Scarth St., Regina, S4P 4L1 SK
306-787-4370, Fax: 306-787-7582, 800-667-7590, internet_clientsvc@wcbsask.com

Yukon Territory
Yukon Workers' Compensation Health & Safety Board, 401 Strickland St., Whitehorse, Y1A 5N8 YT
867-667-5645, Fax: 867-393-6279, 800-661-0443, worksafe@gov.yk.ca

OCCUPATIONAL TRAINING

Canada School of Public Service, 373 Sussex Dr., Ottawa, K1N 6Z2 ON
819-953-5400, Fax: 819-953-7953, 866-703-9598, info@csps-efpc.gc.ca

Alberta
Community, Learner & Industry Connections Division, Phipps-McKinnon Bldg., 5th Fl., 10020 - 101A Ave., Edmonton, T5J 3G2 AB
780-427-8517

British Columbia
Ministry of Labour, PO Box 9052 Prov Govt,Victoria, V8W 9E2 BC
250-356-6348, Fax: 250-356-6595, LCS.Minister@gov.bc.ca

Manitoba
Manitoba Advanced Education & Literacy, Legislative Building, #162, 450 Broadway Ave., Winnipeg, R3C 0V8 MB
204-945-0825, Fax: 204-948-2216, minaed@leg.gov.mb.ca

New Brunswick
Office of Human Resources, Centennial Bldg, #345, 670 King St., PO Box 6000, Fredericton, E3B 5H1 NB
506-453-2264, Fax: 506-453-7195
Department of Post-Secondary Education, Training & Labour, 470 York St., PO Box 6000, Fredericton, E3B 5H1 NB
506-453-2597, Fax: 506-453-3618, dpetlinfo@gnb.ca

Ontario
Ministry of Training, Colleges & Universities, Mowat Block, 900 Bay St., 3rd Fl., Toronto, M7A 1L2 ON
416-325-1600, Fax: 416-325-2934

Quebec
École nationale de police du Québec, 350, rue Marguerite-d'Youville, Nicolet, QC J3T 1X4
819-293-8631, Fax: 819-293-4018, courriel@enpq.qc.ca
École nationale des pompiers du Québec, #3.08, 2800, boul Saint-Martin ouest, Laval, QC H7T 2S9
450-680-6800, Fax: 450-680-6818, 866-680-3677, enpq@enpq.gouv.qc.ca

OCEANOGRAPHY

Bayfield Institute, 867 Lakeshore Rd., PO Box 5050, Burlington, L7R 4A6 ON
905-336-6240
Bedford Institute of Oceanography, 1 Challenger Dr., PO Box 1006, Dartmouth, B2Y 4A2 NS
902-426-3492, Fax: 902-426-8484
Fisheries & Oceans Canada, 200 Kent St., Ottawa, K1A 0E6 ON
613-993-0999, Fax: 613-996-1866, info@dfo-mpo.gc.ca
Institut Maurice-Lamontagne, 850, rte de le Mer, CP 1000, Mont-Joli, G5H 3Z4 QC
418-775-0555, Fax: 418-775-0730
Institute for Marine Biosciences, 1411 Oxford St., Halifax, B3H 3Z1 NS
902-426-8332, Fax: 902-426-9413, communications.imb@nrc-cnrc.gc.ca
Institute for Ocean Technology, Kerwin Pl. & Arctic Ave., PO Box 12093, St. John's, A1B 3T5 NL
709-772-4939, Fax: 709-772-2462, Noel.Murphy@nrc-cnrc.gc.ca
Institute of Ocean Sciences, 9860 West Saanich Rd., PO Box 6000, Sidney, V8L 4B2 BC
250-363-6517, Fax: 250-363-6390

OIL & NATURAL GAS RESOURCES

See Also: Energy; Natural Resources
Indian Oil & Gas Canada, #100, 9911 Chula Blvd., Tsuu T'ina (Sarcee), AB T2W 6H6
403-292-5625, Fax: 403-292-5618, ContactIOGC@inac-ainc.gc.ca
National Energy Board, 444 - 7 Ave. SW, Calgary, T2P 0X8 AB
403-292-4800, Fax: 403-292-5503, 800-899-1265, info@neb-one.gc.ca

Alberta
Energy Resources Conservation Board, #1000, 250 - 5 Ave. SW, Calgary, AB T2P 0R4
403-297-8311, Fax: 403-297-7336, inquiries@ercb.ca
Alberta Energy, North Petroleum Plaza, 9945 - 108 St., 10th Fl., Edmonton, T5K 2G6 AB
780-427-8050, Fax: 780-422-0698, 780-310-0000

British Columbia
Ministry of Energy, Mines & Petroleum Resources, PO Box 9318 Prov Govt,Victoria, V8W 9N3 BC
250-952-0241
Oil & Gas Commission, #100, 10003 - 110 Ave., Fort St John, BC V1J 6M7
250-261-5700, 800-663-7867
British Columbia Utilities Commission, 900 Howe St., 6th Fl., PO Box 250, Vancouver, V6Z 2N3 BC
604-660-4700, Fax: 604-660-1102, 800-663-1385, commission.secretary@bcuc.com

Manitoba
Petroleum, #360, 1395 Ellice Ave., Winnipeg, R3G 3P2 MB
204-945-6577, Fax: 204-945-0586
Surface Rights Board, #360, 1395 Ellice Ave., Winnipeg, MB R3G 3P2
204-945-0731, Fax: 204-948-2578, 800-282-8069, bmiskimmin@gov.mb.ca

Newfoundland & Labrador
Canada-Newfoundland Offshore Petroleum Board, TD Place, 140 Water St., 5th Fl., St. John's, NL A1C 6H6
709-778-1400, Fax: 709-778-1473, postmaster@cnlopb.nl.ca

Nova Scotia
Canada-Nova Scotia Offshore Petroleum Board, TD Centre, 1791 Barrington St., 6th Fl., Halifax, NS B3J 3K9
902-422-5588, Fax: 902-422-1799, postmaster@cnsopb.ns.ca
Nova Scotia Utility & Review Board, 1601 Lower Water St., 3rd Fl., PO Box 1692 M,Halifax, B3J 3S3 NS
902-424-4448, Fax: 902-424-3919, uarb.board@gov.ns.ca

Nunavut
Department of Environment, PO Box 1000 1300,Iqaluit, X0A 0H0 NU
867-975-7700, Fax: 867-975-7742, 866-222-9063, environment@gov.nu.ca

Ontario
Ministry of Natural Resources, Whitney Block, #6630, 99 Wellesley St. West, 6th Fl., Toronto, M7A 1W3 ON
800-667-1940

Saskatchewan
SaskEnergy Incorporated, 1777 Victoria Ave., Regina, S4P 4K5 SK
306-777-9225, Fax: 306-777-9200, 800-567-8899

OIL SPILLS

Canadian Coast Guard, Centennial Towers, #6S018, 200 Kent St., Ottawa, K1A 0E6 ON
613-998-1573, Fax: 613-990-2780

Newfoundland & Labrador
Canada-Newfoundland Offshore Petroleum Board, TD Place, 140 Water St., 5th Fl., St. John's, NL A1C 6H6
709-778-1400, Fax: 709-778-1473, postmaster@cnlopb.nl.ca

OMBUDSMEN

Office of the Correctional Investigator, PO Box 3421 D,Ottawa, K1P 6L4 ON
Fax: 613-990-9091, 877-885-8848, org@oci-bec.gc.ca
Office of the Commissioner of Official Languages, 344 Slater St., 3rd fl., Ottawa, K1A 0T8 ON
613-996-6368, Fax: 613-993-5082, 877-996-6368
Privacy Commissioner of Canada, Tower B, Place de Ville, 112 Kent St., 3rd Fl., Ottawa, K1A 1H3 ON
613-995-8210, Fax: 613-947-6850, 800-282-1376, info@privcom.gc.ca

Alberta
Alberta Office of the Ombudsman, Canadian Western Bank Bldg., #2800, 10303 Jasper Ave., Edmonton, T5J 5C3 AB
780-427-2756, Fax: 780-427-2759, info@ombudsman.ab.ca

British Columbia
Office of the Ombudsman, 756 Fort St., 2nd Fl., PO Box 9039 Prov Govt,Victoria, V8W 9A5 BC
250-387-5855, Fax: 250-387-0198, 800-567-3247, systems@ombudsman.bc.ca (Information technology inquiries)

Manitoba
Manitoba Office of the Ombudsman, 750 - 500 Portage Ave., Winnipeg, R3C 3X1 MB
204-982-9130, Fax: 204-942-7803, 800-665-0531, ombudsma@ombudsman.mb.ca

New Brunswick
Office of the Ombudsman, 767 Brunswick St., PO Box 6000, Fredericton, E3B 5H1 NB
506-453-2789, Fax: 506-453-5599, 800-465-1100, nbombud@gnb.ca

Nova Scotia
Office of the Ombudsman, #700, 5670 Spring Garden Rd., PO Box 2152, Halifax, B3J 3B7 NS
902-424-6780, Fax: 902-424-6675, 800-670-1111

Ontario
Office of the Ombudsman, 483 Bay St., 10th Fl., Toronto, M5G 2C9 ON
416-586-3300, Fax: 416-586-3485, 800-263-1830, info@ombudsman.on.ca

Quebec
Le Protecteur du Citoyen, #1.25, 525, boul René-Lévesque est, Québec, G1R 5Y4 QC
418-643-2688, Fax: 418-643-8759, 800-463-5070

Saskatchewan
Saskatchewan Ombudsman, #150, 2401 Saskatchewan Dr., Regina, S4P 4H8 SK
306-787-6211, Fax: 306-787-9090, 800-667-7180

PARKS & RECREATION

Canadian Heritage, 15 Eddy St., Gatineau, K1A 0M5 QC
819-997-0055, 866-811-0055, info@pch.gc.ca
Historic Sites & Monuments Board of Canada, Terrasses de la Chaudière, 25 Eddy St., Gatineau, QC K1A 0M5
819-997-4059, Fax: 819-934-1115, hsmbc-clmhc@pc.gc.ca
Parks Canada, 25 Eddy St., Gatineau, K1A 0M5 QC
613-860-1251, 888-773-8888, information@pc.gc.ca

Alberta
Alberta Special Areas Board, 212 - 2nd Ave. West, PO Box 820, Hanna, AB T0J 1P0
403-854-5600, Fax: 403-854-5527, specarea@telusplanet.net
Alberta Sport, Recreation, Parks & Wildlife Foundation, Standard Life Centre, 10405 Jasper Ave., 9th Fl., Edmonton, AB T5J 4R7
780-415-1167, Fax: 780-415-0308
Parks, Conservation, Recreation & Sport Division, Oxbridge Place, 9820 - 106 St., 2nd Fl., Edmonton, T5K 2J6 AB
780-427-3582, Fax: 780-427-5980, 866-427-3582

British Columbia
Ministry of Environment, PO Box 9339 Prov Govt,Victoria, V8W 9M1 BC
250-387-1161, Fax: 250-387-5669, www.envmail@gov.bc.ca

Manitoba
Manitoba Competitiveness, Training & Trade, International Business Centre, The Paris Building, 259 Portage Ave., Winnipeg, R3B 3P4 MB
204-945-2475, Fax: 204-945-3977, minctt@leg.gov.mb.ca
Ecological Reserves Advisory Committee, c/o Manitoba Conservation, Parks & Natural Areas Branch, 200 Saulteaux Cres., Winnipeg, MB R3J 3W3
204-945-4148, Fax: 204-945-0012, hhernandez@gov.mb.ca

New Brunswick
Department of Business New Brunswick, Centennial Bldg., 670 King St., PO Box 6000, Fredericton, E3B 5H1 NB
506-444-5228, Fax: 506-453-5428
Department of Tourism & Parks, Centennial Bldg., 670 King St., Fredericton, E3B 1G1 NB
506-444-5205, Fax: 506-457-4984, taponlinedirectory@gnb.ca

Newfoundland & Labrador
Department of Tourism, Culture & Recreation, Confederation Bldg., West Block, 2nd Fl., PO Box 8700, St. John's, A1B 4J6 NL
709-729-0862, Fax: 709-729-0870, tcrinfo@gov.nl.ca

Northwest Territories
Department of Environment & Natural Resources, PO Box 1320, Yellowknife, X1A 2L9 NT

Nova Scotia
Department of Economic & Rural Development, Centennial Building, #600, 1660 Hollis St., PO Box 2311, Halifax, B3J 1V7 NS
902-424-0377, Fax: 902-424-7008, comm@gov.ns.ca

Nunavut
Department of Environment, PO Box 1000 1300,Iqaluit, X0A 0H0 NU
867-975-7700, Fax: 867-975-7742, 866-222-9063, environment@gov.nu.ca

Ontario

Ministry of Economic Development & Trade, Hearst Block, 900 Bay St., 8th Fl., Toronto, M7A 2E1 ON
416-325-6666, Fax: 416-325-6688, 866-668-4249, info@edt.gov.on.ca

Prince Edward Island

Department of Innovation & Advanced Learning, Shaw Bldg., 105 Rochford St., 5th Fl., PO Box 2000, Charlottetown, C1A 7N8 PE
902-368-4240, Fax: 902-368-4242

Department of Tourism, PO Box 2000, Charlottetown, C1A 7N8 PE
800-463-4734

Quebec

Ministère du Développement durable, de l'Environnement et des Parcs, Édifice Marie-Guyart, 675, boul René-Lévesque est, 29e étage, Québec, G1R 5V7 QC
418-521-3830, Fax: 418-646-5974, 800-561-1616, info@mddep.gouv.qc.ca

Société des établissements en plein air du Québec, Place de la Cité, #250, 2640, boul Laurier, Sainte-Foy, QC G1V 5C2
418-890-6527, Fax: 418-528-6025, 800-665-6527, inforeservation@sepaq.com

Saskatchewan

Tourism Saskatchewan, 1922 Park St., Regina, SK S4N 7M4
306-787-9600, 877-237-2273

Yukon Territory

Yukon Tourism & Culture, PO Box 2703, Whitehorse, Y1A 2C6 YT
867-667-5036, Fax: 867-667-3546

PARLIAMENT

See Also: Government (General Information; Protocol (State)

Fortieth Parliament - Canada, House of Commons, Parliament Buildings, Ottawa, K1A 0A9 ON

Library of Parliament, Parliamentary Bldgs., 111 Wellington St., Ottawa, K1A 0A9 ON
613-992-4793, Fax: 613-943-6383, 866-599-4999

Office of the Leader, Bloc Québécois, 111 Wellington St., Ottawa, K1A 0A6 ON
613-992-6779, Fax: 613-954-2121

Office of the Leader, New Democratic Party (NDP), 111 Wellington St., Ottawa, K1A 0A6 ON
613-995-7224, Fax: 613-995-4565

Office of the Prime Minister (Conservative Party of Canada), Langevin Block, 80 Wellington St., Ottawa, K1A 0A2 ON
613-992-4211, Fax: 613-941-6900, pm@pm.gc.ca

Privy Council Office, #1000, 85 Sparks St., Ottawa, K1A 0A3 ON
613-957-5153, Fax: 613-997-5043, info@pco-bcp.gc.ca

The Canadian Ministry, Information Service, Parliament of Canada, Ottawa, K1A 0A9 ON
613-992-4793, 866-599-4999, info@parl.gc.ca

Alberta

Legislative Assembly, Legislature Annex Bldg., 9718 - 107 St., Edmonton, T5K 1E4 AB
780-427-2826, Fax: 780-427-1623, laocommunications@assembly.ab.ca

British Columbia

Legislative Assembly, Clerk's Office, #221, Parliament Bldgs., Victoria, V8V 1X4 BC
250-387-3785, Fax: 250-387-0942, ClerkHouse@leg.bc.ca

Manitoba

Legislative Assembly, c/o Clerk's Office, Legislative Bldg., #237, 450 Broadway, Winnipeg, R3C 0V8 MB
204-945-3636, Fax: 204-948-2507, clerkla@leg.gov.mb.ca

New Brunswick

Legislative Assembly of New Brunswick, Centre Block, Legislative Bldg., 706 Queen St., PO Box 6000, Fredericton, E3B 5H1 NB
506-453-2506, Fax: 506-453-7154, wwwleg@gnb.ca

Northwest Territories

Legislative Assembly, c/o Clerk's Office, PO Box 1320, Yellowknife, X1A 2L9 NT
867-669-2299, Fax: 867-920-4735, 800-661-0784

Nova Scotia

Legislative House of Assembly, c/o Clerk's Office, Province House, 1st Fl., PO Box 1617, Halifax, B3J 2Y3 NS
902-424-5978, Fax: 902-424-0632

Nunavut

Legislative Assembly, Legislative Assembly Bldg., 3rd Fl., PO Box 1200, Iqaluit, X0A 0H0 NU
867-975-5000, Fax: 867-975-5190, 877-334-7266, leginfo@assembly.nu.ca

Ontario

Legislative Assembly, c/o Clerk's Office, #104, Legislative Bldg., Queen's Park, Toronto, M7A 1A2 ON
416-325-7340, Fax: 416-325-7344, assembly@ontla.ola.org

Prince Edward Island

Legislative Assembly, c/o Clerk's Office, Province House, Richmond St., PO Box 2000, Charlottetown, C1A 7K7 PE
902-368-5970, Fax: 902-368-5175

Quebec

L'Assemblée nationale, Hôtel du Parlement, 1045, rue des Parlementaires, Québec, G1A 1A4 QC
418-643-7239, Fax: 418-646-4271, 866-337-8837, responsable.contenu@assnat.qc.ca

Saskatchewan

Legislative Assembly, c/o Clerk's Office, Legislative Bldg., #123, 2405 Legislative Dr., Regina, S4S 0B3 SK
306-787-2376, Fax: 306-787-1558, info@legassembly.sk.ca

Yukon Territory

Legislative Assembly, c/o Clerk's Office, PO Box 2703, Whitehorse, Y1A 2C6 YT
867-667-5498, Fax: 867-393-6280

PAROLE BOARDS

See Also: Correctional Services

Alberta

Criminal Justice Division, Bowker Building, 9833 - 109 St., 2nd Fl., Edmonton, T5K 2E8 AB

National Parole Board, 410 Laurier Ave. West, Ottawa, K1A 0R1 ON
613-954-7474, Fax: 613-995-4380, 800-874-2652, info@npb-cnlc.gc.ca

Manitoba

Corrections Division, #810, 405 Broadway Ave., Winnipeg, R3C 3L6 MB
204-945-7291

New Brunswick

Department of Public Safety, 364 Argyle St., PO Box 6000, Fredericton, E3B 5H1 NB
506-453-3992, Fax: 506-453-3870, DPS-MSP.Information@gnb.ca

Ontario

Ontario Parole & Earned Release Board, 415 Yonge St., Toronto, ON M5B 2E7
416-325-4480, Fax: 416-325-4485

Quebec

Commission québecoise des libérations conditionnelles, #1.32A, 300, boul Jean-Lesage, Québec, QC G1K 8K6
418-646-8300, Fax: 418-643-7217, liberation.conditionnel@msp.gouv.

PASSPORT INFORMATION

See Also: Citizenship; Immigration

Passport Canada, Le 70 Crémazie, 70 Crémazie St., Gatineau, K1A 0G3 QC
Fax: 819-953-5856, 800-567-6868

PATENTS & COPYRIGHT

Copyright Board of Canada, #800, 56 Sparks St., Ottawa, K1A 0C9 ON
613-952-8621, Fax: 613-952-8630, secretariat@cb-cda.gc.ca

PAY EQUITY

Human Resources & Skills Development Canada, 140 Promenade du Portage, Ottawa, K1A 0J9 ON

British Columbia

Employment Standards Tribunal, Oceanic Plaza, #650, 1066 West Hastings St., Vancouver, BC V6E 3X1
604-775-3512, Fax: 604-775-3372, registrar.est@bcest.bc.ca

Ministry of Labour, PO Box 9052 Prov Govt,Victoria, V8W 9E2 BC
250-356-6348, Fax: 250-356-6595, LCS.Minister@gov.bc.ca

New Brunswick

Office of Human Resources, Centennial Bldg, #345, 670 King St., PO Box 6000, Fredericton, E3B 5H1 NB
506-453-2264, Fax: 506-453-7195

Nova Scotia

Pay Equity Commission, 5151 Terminal Rd., 7th Fl., PO Box 697, Halifax, NS B3J 2T8
902-424-2385, Fax: 902-424-0575

Ontario

Pay Equity Commission, 400 University Ave., 11th Fl., Toronto, ON M7A 1T7
416-314-1896, Fax: 416-314-8741, 800-387-8813

Prince Edward Island

Labour Relations Board, PO Box 2000, Charlottetown, PE C1A 7N8
902-368-5550, Fax: 902-368-5476

Quebec

Commission de l'équité salariale, 200, ch Ste-Foy, 4e étage, Québec, QC G1R 6A1
418-528-8765, Fax: 418-528-6999, 888-528-8765, equite.salariale@ces.gouv.qc.ca

PENSIONS

Canada Pension Plan Investment Board, #2600, 1 Queen St. East, PO Box 101, Toronto, M5C 2W5 ON
416-868-4075, Fax: 416-868-8689, 866-557-9510, csr@cppib.ca

Finance Canada, L'esplanade Laurier, 140 O'Connor St., Ottawa, K1A 0G5 ON
613-992-1573, Fax: 613-943-0938, finpub@fin.gc.ca

Office of the Superintendent of Financial Institutions, Kent Square, 255 Albert St., Ottawa, K1A 0H2 ON
613-990-7788, Fax: 613-990-5591, 800-385-8647, information@osfi-bsif.gc.ca

Office of the Commissioner of Review Tribunals, PO Box 8250 T, Ottawa, ON K1G 5S5
613-954-1313, Fax: 613-946-1588, 800-363-0076, info@ocrt-bctr.gc.ca

Pension Appeals Board, PO Box 8567 T, Ottawa, ON K1G 3H9
613-995-0612, Fax: 613-995-6834, 888-640-8001, info@pab-cap.gc.ca

Public Sector Pension Investment Board, #200, 440 Laurier Ave. West, Ottawa, ON K1R 7X6
613-782-3095, Fax: 613-782-6864, info@investpsp.ca

Veterans Review & Appeal Board, Daniel J. MacDonald Bldg., 161 Grafton St., PO Box 9900, Charlottetown, PE C1A 8V7
902-566-8751, Fax: 902-566-7850, 800-450-8006, vrab_tacra@vac-acc.gc.ca

Alberta

Alberta Pensions Services Corporation, 5103 Windermere Blvd. SW, Edmonton, AB T6W 0S9
780-427-5101, Fax: 780-421-1652, 800-358-0840, apa.info@gov.ab.ca; memberservices@apsc.ca

British Columbia

British Columbia Pension Corporation, 2995 Jutland Rd., PO Box 9460, Victoria, BC V8W 9V8
250-387-1002, Fax: 250-953-0429, 800-663-8823, PensionCorp@pensionsbc.ca; Retired.Members@pensionsbc.ca

Manitoba

Pension Commission of Manitoba, #1004, 401 York Ave., Winnipeg, MB R3C 0P8
204-945-2740, Fax: 204-948-2375, pensions@gov.mb.ca

Teachers' Retirement Allowances Fund Board, #330 Johnston Terminal, 35 Forks Market Rd., Winnipeg, MB R3C 4S8
204-949-0048, Fax: 204-944-0361

Nova Scotia

Pension Regulation Division, PO Box 2531, Halifax, B3J 3N5 NS
902-424-8915, Fax: 902-424-0662,

Ontario

Financial Services Commission of Ontario, 5160 Yonge St., PO Box 85, Toronto, ON M2N 6L9
416-250-7250, Fax: 416-590-7070, 800-668-0128

Ontario Pension Board, #1100, 1 Adelaide St. East, Toronto, ON M5C 2X6
416-364-8558, Fax: 416-364-7578, 800-668-6203, office.services@opb.on.ca

OPSEU Pension Trust, #1200, 1 Adelaide St. East, Toronto, ON M5C 3A7
416-681-6161, Fax: 416-681-6175

Prince Edward Island

Office of the Attorney General, Shaw Building, North, 105 Rochford St., 4th Fl., PO Box 2000, Charlottetown, C1A 7N8 PE
902-368-5152, Fax: 902-368-4910

Quebec

Commission administrative des régimes de retraite et d'assurances (Québec), 475, rue Saint-Amable, Québec, QC G1R 5X3
418-643-4881, Fax: 418-644-3839, 800-463-5533

Régie des rentes du Québec, CP 5200, Sainte-Foy, QC G1K 7S9
418-643-5185, rrq@rrq.gouv.qc.ca

Saskatchewan
Crown Investments Corporation of Saskatchewan, #400, 2400 College Ave., Regina, S4P 1C8 SK
306-787-6851, Fax: 306-787-8125
Saskatchewan Financial Services Commission, #601, 1919 Saskatchewan Dr., Regina, SK S4P 4H2
306-787-5645, Fax: 306-787-5899

PESTICIDES, HERBICIDES

Farm Financial Programs Branch, Tower 7, 1341 Baseline Rd., Ottawa, K1A 0C5 ON
613-759-1000, Fax: 613-773-2121
Pest Management Regulatory Agency, 2720 Riverside Dr., Ottawa, ON K1A 0K9
613-736-3401, Fax: 613-736-3798

New Brunswick
Environmental Management, Marysville Place, 20 McGloin St., PO Box 6000, Fredericton, E3B 5H1 NB
506-444-5119, Fax: 506-457-7333

Ontario
Pesticides Advisory Committee, #1203, 2300 Yonge St., 12th Fl., Toronto, ON M4P 1E4
416-314-9230, Fax: 416-314-9237

PIPELINES

National Energy Board, 444 - 7 Ave. SW, Calgary, T2P 0X8 AB
403-292-4800, Fax: 403-292-5503, 800-899-1265, info@neb-one.gc.ca

Alberta
Energy Resources Conservation Board, #1000, 250 - 5 Ave. SW, Calgary, AB T2P 0R4
403-297-8311, Fax: 403-297-7336, inquiries@ercb.ca
Alberta Energy, North Petroleum Plaza, 9945 - 108 St., 10th Fl., Edmonton, T5K 2G6 AB
780-427-8050, Fax: 780-422-0698, 780-310-0000

British Columbia
British Columbia Hydro, 333 Dunsmuir St., 18th Fl., Vancouver, V6B 5R3 BC
604-224-9376, Fax: 604-623-4467, 800-224-9376

Northwest Territories
Department of Environment & Natural Resources, PO Box 1320, Yellowknife, X1A 2L9 NT

Nova Scotia
Department of Energy, Bank of Montreal Bldg., #400, 5151 George St., PO Box 2664, Halifax, B3J 3P7 NS
902-424-4575, Fax: 902-424-0528, energyinfo@gov.ns.ca
Nova Scotia Utility & Review Board, 1601 Lower Water St., 3rd Fl., PO Box 1692 M,Halifax, B3J 3S3 NS
902-424-4448, Fax: 902-424-3919, uarb.board@gov.ns.ca

Saskatchewan
SaskEnergy Incorporated, 1777 Victoria Ave., Regina, S4P 4K5 SK
306-777-9225, Fax: 306-777-9200, 800-567-8899
TransGas Limited, 1777 Victoria Ave, Regina, S4P 4K5 SK
Fax: 306-352-8892

POLICING SERVICES

Royal Canadian Mounted Police, 1200 Vanier Pkwy., Ottawa, K1A 0R2 ON
613-993-7267, Fax: 613-993-0260

Alberta
Public Security Division, 10365 - 97 St., Edmonton, T5J 3W7 AB
Fax: 780-427-1194

British Columbia
Management Services Branch, 910 Government St., 5th Fl., PO Box 9256 Prov Govt,Victoria, V8W 9J4 BC
250-387-5258, Fax: 250-387-0081

Manitoba
Manitoba Justice, Legislative Building, #104, 405 Broadway Ave., Winnipeg, R3C 3L6 MB
204-945-3728, Fax: 204-945-2517, minjus@gov.mb.ca
Law Enforcement Review Agency, #420, 155 Carlton St., Winnipeg, MB R3C 3H8
204-945-8667, Fax: 204-948-1014, 800-282-8069, lera@gov.mb.ca

New Brunswick
New Brunswick Police Commission, Fredericton City Centre, #202, 435 King St., Fredericton, E3B 1E5 NB
506-453-2069, Fax: 506-457-3542

Newfoundland & Labrador
Royal Newfoundland Constabulary Public Complaints Commission, Bally Rou Place, #E-160, 280 Torbay Rd., St. John's, NL A1A 3W8
709-729-0950, Fax: 709-729-1302

Nova Scotia
Nova Scotia Police Commission, #300, 1601 Lower Water St., PO Box 1573, Halifax, NS B3J 2Y3
902-424-3246, Fax: 902-424-3919, uarb.polcom@gov.ns.ca

Nunavut
Department of Justice, Sivummut, 1st Fl., PO Box 1000 500,Iqaluit, X0A 0H0 NU
867-975-6170, Fax: 867-975-6195

Ontario
Ontario Provincial Police, Lincoln M. Alexander Bldg., 777 Memorial Ave., Orillia, L3V 7V3 ON
705-329-6111, 888-310-1122

Prince Edward Island
Office of the Attorney General, Shaw Building, North, 105 Rochford St., 4th Fl., PO Box 2000, Charlottetown, C1A 7N8 PE
902-368-5152, Fax: 902-368-4910,

Quebec
Direction générale de la Sûreté du Québec, 1701, rue Parthenais, Montréal, QC H2K 3S7
514-598-4488, Fax: 514-598-4957, info@surete.qc.ca

Saskatchewan
Saskatchewan Police Commission, 600 - 1874 Scarth St., Regina, SK S4P 4B3
306-787-6518, Fax: 306-787-0136
Saskatchewan Public Complaints Commission, #300, 1919 Saskatchewan Dr., Regina, SK S4P 4H2
306-787-6519, Fax: 306-787-6528, 866-256-6194

Yukon Territory
Yukon Justice, PO Box 2703, Whitehorse, Y1A 2C6 YT
867-667-8655, Fax: 867-393-5790

POLITICS & SOCIETY

Auditor General of Canada, 240 Sparks St., Ottawa, K1A 0G6 ON
613-995-3708, Fax: 613-957-0474, 888-761-5953, communications@oag-bvg.gc.ca; infomedia@oag-bvg.gc.ca
Canadian International Development Agency, 200, Promenade du Portage, Gatineau, K1A 0G4 QC
819-997-5006, Fax: 819-953-6088, 800-230-6349, info@acdi-cida.gc.ca
Commission for Environmental Cooperation, Secretariat, #200, 393, rue St-Jacques ouest, Montréal, H2Y 1N9 QC
514-350-4300, Fax: 514-350-4314, info@cec.org
Finance Canada, L'esplanade Laurier, 140 O'Connor St., Ottawa, K1A 0G5 ON
613-992-1573, Fax: 613-943-0938, finpub@fin.gc.ca
Foreign Affairs & International Trade Canada, 125 Sussex Dr., Ottawa, K1A 0G2 ON
613-944-4000, Fax: 613-996-9709, 800-267-8376, enqserv@international.gc.ca
International Development Research Centre, 150 Kent St., PO Box 8500, Ottawa, K1P 0B2 ON
613-236-6163, Fax: 613-238-7230, info@idrc.ca
International Joint Commission, 234 Laurier Ave. West, 22nd Fl., Ottawa, K1P 6K6 ON
613-947-1420, Fax: 613-993-5583, beckhoffb@ottawa.ijc.org
National Capital Commission, #202, 40 Elgin St., Ottawa, K1P 1C7 ON
613-239-5555, Fax: 613-239-5063, 800-704-8227, info@ncc-ccn.ca
National Defence Canada, Major-General George R. Pearkes Bldg., 101 Colonel By Dr., Ottawa, K1A 0K2 ON
613-995-2534, Fax: 613-992-4739, 800-856-8488
National Round Table on the Environment & Economy, #200, 344 Slater St., Ottawa, K1R 7Y3 ON
613-992-7189, Fax: 613-992-7385, admin@nrtee-trnee.ca
Public Safety Canada, 269 Laurier Ave. West, Ottawa, K1A 0P8 ON
613-944-4875, Fax: 613-954-5186, 866-222-3006, communications@ps.gc.ca
Public Works & Government Services Canada, Place du Portage, Phase III, 11, rue Laurier, Ottawa, K1A 0S5 ON
819-997-6363, Fax: 819-956-9062, 800-622-6232, questions@tpsgc-pwgsc.gc.ca
Strategic Policy Branch, Tower 7, 1341 Baseline Rd., Ottawa, K1A 0C5 ON
613-759-1000, Fax: 613-773-2111

Alberta
Alberta International & Intergovernmental Relations, Commerce Place, 10155 - 102 St., 12th Fl., Edmonton, T5J 4G8 AB
780-422-1510, Fax: 780-427-0699
Alberta Public Affairs Bureau, Park Plaza, 10611 - 98 Ave., 6th Fl., Edmonton, T5K 2P7 AB
403-427-9261, Fax: 403-422-4168

British Columbia
Ministry of Community & Rural Development, 800 Johnson St., 6th Fl., PO Box 9490 Prov Govt,Victoria, V8W 9N7 BC
250-387-2283, Fax: 250-387-4312, Feedback@gov.bc.ca

Manitoba
Manitoba Round Table for Sustainable Development, #160, 123 Main St., Winnipeg, R3C 1A5 MB
204-945-1671, Fax: 204-948-2357, mrtsd@gov.mb.ca

New Brunswick
New Brunswick Round Table on Environment & Economy, 20 McGloin St., PO Box 6000, Fredericton, NB E3B 5H1
506-453-3703, Fax: 506-453-3876
Department of Supply & Services, PO Box 6000, Fredericton, E3B 5H1 NB
506-453-3742, Fax: 506-444-4400, Reception.Marysville@gnb.ca

Newfoundland & Labrador
Department of Government Services, PO Box 8700, St. John's, A1B 4J6 NL
709-729-4860
Department of Transportation & Works, Confederation Bldg., West Block, 6th Fl., PO Box 8700, St. John's, A1B 4J6 NL
709-729-3679, Fax: 709-729-4285, twminister@gov.nl.ca

Northwest Territories
Department of Aboriginal Affairs & Intergovernmental Relations, 4910 - 52nd St., PO Box 1320, Yellowknife, X1A 2L9 NT
867-873-7143, Fax: 867-873-0233, 877-838-8194, nancy_gardiner @gov.nt.ca
Department of Public Works & Services, PO Box 1320, Yellowknife, X1A 2L9 NT
867-873-7114, Fax: 867-873-0226

Nova Scotia
Nova Scotia Emergency Management Office, PO Box 2581, Halifax, B3J 3N5 NS
902-424-5620, Fax: 902-424-5376, 866-424-5620, emo@gov.ns.ca

Ontario
Environmental Commissioner of Ontario, #605, 1075 Bay St., Toronto, M5S 2B1 ON
416-325-3377, Fax: 416-325-3370, 800-701-6454, commissioner@eco.on.ca
Environmental Review Tribunal, #1700, 2300 Yonge St., PO Box 2382, Toronto, ON M4P 1E4
416-314-4600, Fax: 416-314-4506

Prince Edward Island
Prince Edward Island Emergency Measures Organization, National Bank Tower, #600, 134 Kent St., PO Box 2000, Charlottetown, C1A 7N8 PE
902-894-0385, Fax: 902-368-6362
Department of Health, Jones Bldg., 11 Kent St., 2nd Fl., PO Box 2000, Charlottetown, C1A 7N8 PE
902-368-4900, Fax: 902-368-4974
Department of the Provincial Treasury, Shaw Bldg., 95 Rochford St., 2nd Fl. South, PO Box 2000, Charlottetown, C1A 7N8 PE
902-368-4050, Fax: 902-368-6575

Saskatchewan
Saskatchewan First Nations & Métis Relations, #210, 1855 Victoria Ave., Regina, S4P 3T2 SK
306-787-6250, Fax: 306-787-5832
Saskatchewan Government Relations, 1855 Victoria Ave., Regina, S4P 3T2 SK
306-787-2635

Yukon Territory
Emergency Measures Organization, PO Box 2703, Whitehorse, Y1A 2C6 YT
867-667-5220, Fax: 867-393-6266, 800-661-0408, emo.yukon@gov.yk.ca

POPULATION

See Also: Statistics
Statistics Canada, R.H. Coats Bldg., Tunney's Pasture, 100 Tunney's Pasture Driveway, Ottawa, K1A 0T6 ON
613-951-8116, Fax: 877-287-4369, 800-263-1136, infostats@statcan.ca

Alberta
Registries Services, John E. Brownlee Bldg., 10365 - 97 St., 3rd Fl., Edmonton, T5J 3W7 AB

Manitoba
Manitoba Bureau of Statistics, #824, 155 Carlton St., Winnipeg, R3C 3H9 MB
204-945-2406, Fax: 204-945-0695,

Nunavut
Department of Executive & Intergovernmental Affairs, 1084 Aeroplex bldg., PO Box 1000 200,Iqaluit, X0A 0H0 NU
867-975-6000, Fax: 867-975-6090

Quebec
Institut de la statistique du Québec, 200, ch Ste-Foy, 3e étage, Québec, QC G1R 5T4
418-691-2401, Fax: 418-643-4129, 800-463-4090, direction@stat.gouv.qc.ca

POSTAL SERVICE

Canada Post Corporation, Corporate Secretariat, 2701 Riverside Dr., Ottawa, K1A 0B1 ON
613-734-8440, Fax: 613-734-6084, 800-267-1177, service@mailposte.ca

PREMIERS & LEADERS

See Also: Cabinets & Executive Councils; Government (General Info)

Office of the Prime Minister (Conservative Party of Canada), Langevin Block, 80 Wellington St., Ottawa, K1A 0A2 ON
613-992-4211, Fax: 613-941-6900, pm@pm.gc.ca

Alberta
Office of the Premier, Legislature Bldg., #307, 10800 - 97 Ave., Edmonton, T5K 2B6 AB
780-427-2251, Fax: 780-427-1349

British Columbia
Office of the Premier, West Annex, Parliament Bldgs., PO Box 9041 Prov Govt,Victoria, V8W 9E1 BC
250-387-1715, Fax: 250-387-0087, premier@gov.bc.ca

Manitoba
Office of the Premier, Legislative Building, #204, 450 Broadway Ave., Winnipeg, R3C 0V8 MB
204-945-3714, Fax: 204-949-1484, premier@leg.gov.mb.ca

New Brunswick
Office of the Premier, Centennial Bldg., 670 King St., PO Box 6000, Fredericton, E3B 5H1 NB
506-453-2144, Fax: 506-453-7407, premier@gnb.ca

Newfoundland & Labrador
Office of the Premier, East Block, Confederation Bldg., 8th F., PO Box 8700, St. John's, A1B 4J6 NL
709-729-3570, Fax: 709-729-5875, premier@gov.nl.ca

Northwest Territories
Office of the Premier, Legislative Assembly Bldg., PO Box 1320, Yellowknife, X1A 2L9 NT
867-669-2311, Fax: 867-873-0385, premier@gov.nt.ca

Nova Scotia
Office of the Premier, One Government Place, 1700 Granville St., PO Box 726, Halifax, B3J 2T3 NS
902-424-6600, Fax: 902-424-7648, 800-267-1993, premier@gov.ns.ca

Nunavut
Office of the Premier, Legislative Assembly Bldg., 2nd Fl., PO Box 2410, Iqaluit, X0A 0H0 NU
867-975-5050, Fax: 867-975-5051

Ontario
Office of the Premier, Legislative Bldg., #281, 1 Queen's Park Cres. South, Toronto, M7A 1A1 ON
416-325-1941, Fax: 416-325-3745, webprem@gov.on.ca

Prince Edward Island
Office of the Premier, Shaw Bldg., 95 Rochford St., 5th Fl. South, PO Box 2000, Charlottetown, C1A 7N8 PE
902-368-4400, Fax: 902-368-4416

Quebec
Cabinet du premier ministre, Édifice Honoré-Mercier, 835, boul René-Lévesque est, 3e étage, Québec, G1A 1B4 QC
418-643-5321, Fax: 418-643-3924

Saskatchewan
Office of the Premier, Legislative Bldg., #226, 2405 Legislative Dr., Regina, S4S 0B3 SK
306-787-9433, Fax: 306-787-0885, premier@gov.sk.ca

Yukon Territory
Office of the Premier, 2071 Second Ave., PO Box 2703, Whitehorse, Y1A 1B2 YT
867-667-8660, Fax: 867-393-6252, premier@gov.yk.ca

PROPERTY ASSESSMENT

Alberta
Registries Services, John E. Brownlee Bldg., 10365 - 97 St., 3rd Fl., Edmonton, T5J 3W7 AB

British Columbia
British Columbia Assessment Authority, 1537 Hillside Ave., Victoria, BC V8T 4Y2
250-595-6211, Fax: 250-595-6222, info@bcassessment.ca

New Brunswick
Assessment & Planning Appeal Board, #201, 435 King St., PO Box 6000, Fredericton, NB E3B 5H1
506-453-2126, Fax: 506-444-4881

Newfoundland & Labrador
Department of Municipal Affairs, West Block, Main Fl., Confederation Bldg., PO Box 8700, St. John's, A1B 4J6 NL
709-729-3053

Northwest Territories
Assessment Appeal Tribunal of the Northwest Territories, #500, 5201 - 50th Ave., PO Box 1320, Yellowknife, NT X1A 2L9
867-873-7125, Fax: 867-873-0609

Prince Edward Island
Island Regulatory & Appeals Commission, National Bank Tower, #501, 134 Kent St., PO Box 577, Charlottetown, C1A 7L1 PE
902-892-3501, Fax: 902-566-4076, 800-501-6268, irac@irac.pe.ca

Saskatchewan
Saskatchewan Assessment Management Agency, #200, 2201 - 11th Ave., Regina, S4P 0J8 SK
306-924-8000, Fax: 306-924-8070, 800-667-7262, info.request@sama.sk.ca

PROTOCOL (STATE)

See Also: Parliament

Governor General & Commander-in-Chief of Canada, Rideau Hall, 1 Sussex Dr., Ottawa, K1A 0A1 ON
613-993-8200, Fax: 613-998-8760, 800-465-6890, info@gg.ca

Prince Edward Island
Office of the Lieutenant Governor, Government House, PO Box 846, Charlottetown, C1A 7L9 PE
902-368-5480, Fax: 902-368-5481,

PUBLIC SAFETY

See Also: Occupational Safety

Canadian Coast Guard, Centennial Towers, #6S018, 200 Kent St., Ottawa, K1A 0E6 ON
613-998-1573, Fax: 613-990-2780

Canadian Security Intelligence Service, PO Box 9732 T,Ottawa, K1G 4G4 ON
613-993-9620

Canadian Transportation Agency, Les Terrasses de la Chaudière, 15, rue Eddy, Gatineau, K1A 0N9 QC
819-997-0344, Fax: 819-997-6727, 888-222-2592, info@otc-cta.gc.ca

Communications Security Establishment, PO Box 9703 Terminal, Ottawa, ON K1G 3Z4
613-991-7600

National Defence Canada, Major-General George R. Pearkes Bldg., 101 Colonel By Dr., Ottawa, K1A 0K2 ON
613-995-2534, Fax: 613-992-4739, 800-856-8488

Office of the Communications Security Establishment Commissioner, PO Box 1984 B, Ottawa, ON K1P 5R5
613-992-3044

Public Safety Canada, 269 Laurier Ave. West, Ottawa, K1A 0P8 ON
613-944-4875, Fax: 613-954-5186, 866-222-3006, communications@ps.gc.ca

Royal Canadian Mounted Police, 1200 Vanier Pkwy., Ottawa, K1A 0R2 ON
613-993-7267, Fax: 613-993-0260

Alberta
Public Security Division, 10365 - 97 St., Edmonton, T5J 3W7 AB
Fax: 780-427-1194

British Columbia
Ministry of Public Safety & Solicitor General, PO Box 9282 Prov Govt,Victoria, V8W 9J7 BC
250-387-6121, 800-663-7867, pssgwebfeedback@gov.bc.ca

New Brunswick
Department of Public Safety, 364 Argyle St., PO Box 6000, Fredericton, E3B 5H1 NB
506-453-3992, Fax: 506-453-3870, DPS-MSP.Information@gnb.ca

Northwest Territories
Department of Justice, Courthouse, 4903 - 49th St., 6th Fl., PO Box 1320, Yellowknife, X1A 2L9 NT
867-920-6197

Nunavut
Department of Justice, Sivummut, 1st Fl., PO Box 1000 500,Iqaluit, X0A 0H0 NU
867-975-6170, Fax: 867-975-6195

Prince Edward Island
Prince Edward Island Emergency Measures Organization, National Bank Tower, #600, 134 Kent St., PO Box 2000, Charlottetown, C1A 7N8 PE
902-894-0385, Fax: 902-368-6362

Quebec
Ministère de la Sécurité publique, Tour des Laurentides, 2525, boul Laurier, 5e étage, Québec, G1V 2L2 QC
418-643-2112, Fax: 418-646-6168, 866-644-6826

Saskatchewan
Saskatchewan Corrections, Public Safety & Policing, 1874 Scarth St., Regina, S4P 4B3 SK
306-787-7872, Fax: 306-787-8747

PUBLIC SERVICES

Canada Deposit Insurance Corporation, 50 O'Connor St., 17th Floor, PO Box 2340 D,Ottawa, K1P 5W5 ON
613-996-2081, Fax: 613-996-6095, 800-461-2342, info@cdic.ca; info@sadc.ca

Canada Post Corporation, Corporate Secretariat, 2701 Riverside Dr., Ottawa, K1A 0B1 ON
613-734-8440, Fax: 613-734-6084, 800-267-1177, service@mailposte.ca

Canadian Broadcasting Corporation, 181 Queen St., PO Box 3220 C,Ottawa, K1Y 1E4 ON
613-288-6033, liaison@radio-canada.ca

Canadian Centre for Occupational Health & Safety, 135 Hunter St. East, Hamilton, L8N 1M5 ON
905-572-2981, Fax: 905-572-2206, 800-668-4284, clientservices@ccohs.ca

Canadian Coast Guard, Centennial Towers, #6S018, 200 Kent St., Ottawa, K1A 0E6 ON
613-998-1573, Fax: 613-990-2780

Canadian Security Intelligence Service, PO Box 9732 T,Ottawa, K1G 4G4 ON
613-993-9620

Citizenship & Immigration Canada, Jean Edmonds, South Tower, 365 Laurier Ave. West, Ottawa, K1A 1L1 ON
613-954-9019, Fax: 613-954-2221, 888-242-2100

Commission for Public Complaints Against the Royal Canadian Mounted Police, #102, 7337 137 St., Surrey, BC V3W 1A4
Fax: 613-952-8045, 800-665-6878, org@cpc-cpp.gc.ca

Correctional Service Canada, 340 Laurier Ave. West, Ottawa, K1A 0P9 ON
613-992-5891, Fax: 613-943-1630

Health Workforce Division, Telus Plaza NT, 10025 Jasper Ave., 10th Fl., Edmonton, T5J 1S6 AB

Human Resources & Skills Development Canada, 140 Promenade du Portage, Ottawa, K1A 0J9 ON

Immigration & Refugee Board of Canada, Canada Bldg, 344 Slater St., 12th Fl., Ottawa, K1A 0K1 ON
613-995-6486, Fax: 613-943-1550, info@irb-cisr.gc.ca

Legal Services Division, Bowker Building, 9833 - 109 St., 2nd Fl., Edmonton, T5K 2E8 AB
780-422-0500

Military Police Complaints Commission, 270 Albert St., 10th Fl., Ottawa, ON K1P 5G8
613-947-5625, Fax: 613-947-5713, 800-632-0566, commission@mpcc-cppm.gc.ca

National Capital Commission, #202, 40 Elgin St., Ottawa, K1P 1C7 ON
613-239-5555, Fax: 613-239-5063, 800-704-8227, info@ncc-ccn.ca

National Defence Canada, Major-General George R. Pearkes Bldg., 101 Colonel By Dr., Ottawa, K1A 0K2 ON
613-995-2534, Fax: 613-992-4739, 800-856-8488

National Parole Board, 410 Laurier Ave. West, Ottawa, K1A 0R1 ON
613-954-7474, Fax: 613-995-4380, 800-874-2652, info@npb-cnlc.gc.ca

National Search & Rescue Secretariat, #400, 275 Slater St., Ottawa, K1A 0K2 ON
613-992-0054, Fax: 613-996-3746, 800-727-9414, inquiry@nss.gc.ca

Public Service Commission, West Tower, 300 Laurier Ave. West, Ottawa, K1A 0M7 ON
613-992-9562, Fax: 613-992-9352, infocom@psc-cfp.gc.ca

Public Service Staffing Tribunal, 240 Sparks St., 6th Fl., Ottawa, K1A 0A5 ON
613-949-6516, Fax: 613-949-6551, 866-637-4491, info@psst-tdfp.gc.ca

Public Works & Government Services Canada, Place du Portage, Phase III, 11, rue Laurier, Ottawa, K1A 0S5 ON

819-997-6363, Fax: 819-956-9062, 800-622-6232, questions@tpsgc-pwgsc.gc.ca
Royal Canadian Mounted Police, 1200 Vanier Pkwy., Ottawa, K1A 0R2 ON
613-993-7267, Fax: 613-993-0260
Royal Canadian Mounted Police External Review Committee, PO Box 1159 B, Ottawa, ON K1P 5R2
613-998-2134, Fax: 613-990-8969, org@erc-cee.gc.ca
Security Intelligence Review Committee, Jackson Bldg., 122 Bank St., 4th Fl., PO Box 2430 D,Ottawa, K1P 5W5 ON
613-990-8441, Fax: 613-990-5230, ellardm@sirc-csars.gc.ca
Seniors Services Division, Standard Life Centre, 10405 Jasper Ave., 6th Fl., Edmonton, T5J 4R7 AB
780-427-7876
Veterans Affairs Canada, 161 Grafton St., PO Box 7700, Charlottetown, C1A 8M9 PE
902-566-8888, information@vac-acc.gc.ca
Veterans Review & Appeal Board, Daniel J. MacDonald Bldg., 161 Grafton St., PO Box 9900, Charlottetown, PE C1A 8V7
902-566-8751, Fax: 902-566-7850, 800-450-8006, vrab_tacra@vac-acc.gc.ca

Alberta

Alberta Capital Finance Authority, Canadian Western Bank Place, #2450, 10303 Jasper Ave., Edmonton, AB T5J 3N6
780-427-9711, Fax: 780-422-2175, webacfa@gov.ab.ca
Alberta Health Services, Manulife Place, 10180 - 101 St., Edmonton, AB T5J 3S4
780-342-2000, Fax: 780-342-2060, 888-342-2471
Alberta Municipal Government Board, Commerce Place, 10155 - 102 St., 15th Fl., Edmonton, AB T5J 4L4
780-427-4864, Fax: 780-427-0986
Alberta Pensions Services Corporation, 5103 Windermere Blvd. SW, Edmonton, AB T6W 0S9
780-427-5101, Fax: 780-421-1652, 800-358-0840, apa.info@gov.ab.ca; memberservices@apsc.ca
Alberta Children and Youth Services, Sterling Place, 9940 - 106 St., 12th Fl., Edmonton, T5K 2N2 AB
780-422-3004, Fax: 780-422-3071, 866-714-5437, cs.communications@gov.ab.ca
Energy Resources Conservation Board, #1000, 250 - 5 Ave. SW, Calgary, AB T2P 0R4
403-297-8311, Fax: 403-297-7336, inquiries@ercb.ca
Alberta Infrastructure, Infrastructure Building, 6950 - 101 St., 3rd Fl., Edmonton, T6H 5V7 AB
780-415-0507, Fax: 780-427-2187,-310-0000
Labour Relations Board, #503, 10808 - 99 Ave., Edmonton, AB T5K 0G5
780-422-5926, Fax: 780-422-0970, 800-463-2572, alrbinfo@lab.gov.ab.ca
Alberta Municipal Affairs, Communications Branch, Commerce Place, 10155 - 102 St., 18th Fl., Edmonton, T5J 4L4 AB
780-427-2732, Fax: 780-422-1419, comments@gov.ab.ca
Public Security Division, 10365 - 97 St., Edmonton, T5J 3W7 AB
Fax: 780-427-1194
Alberta Tourism, Parks, Recreation & Culture, Communications Branch, Standard Life Centre, 10405 Jasper Ave., 7th Fl., Edmonton, T5J 4R7 AB
780-427-6530, Fax: 780-427-1496, Comdev.Communications@gov.ab.ca

British Columbia

British Columbia Assessment Authority, 1537 Hillside Ave., Victoria, BC V8T 4Y2
250-595-6211, Fax: 250-595-6222, info@bcassessment.ca
British Columbia Transit, 520 Gorge Rd. East, PO Box 610, Victoria, BC V8W 2P3
250-385-2551, Fax: 250-995-5639
Ministry of Children & Family Development, PO Box 9770 Prov Govt,Victoria, V8W 9S5 BC
250-387-7027, 877-387-7027, MCF.CorrespondenceManagement@gov.bc.ca
Client Services, 525 Superior St., 2nd Fl., PO Box 9472 Prov Govt,Victoria, V8W 9W6 BC
250-952-6861, Fax: 250-952-6803
Community Living British Columbia, Airport Square, #700, 1200 West 73rd Ave., Vancouver, BC V6P 6G5
604-664-0101, Fax: 604-664-0765, 877-660-2522, info@communitylivingbc.ca
British Columbia Ferry Services Inc., 1112 Fort St., Victoria, V8V 4V2 BC
250-381-1401, 888-223-3779
Local Government Department, 800 Johnson St., 6th Fl., PO Box 9490 Prov Govt,Victoria, V8W 9N7 BC
lgd_feedback@gov.bc.ca
Management Services Branch, 910 Government St., 5th Fl., PO Box 9256 Prov Govt,Victoria, V8W 9J4 BC
250-387-5258, Fax: 250-387-0081
Office of the Representative for Children & Youth, 1019 Wharf St., PO Box 9207 Prov Govt, Victoria, BC V8W 9J1
250-356-6710, Fax: 250-356-0837, 800-476-3933, rcy@rcybc.ca
British Columbia Provincial Emergency Program, PO Box 9201 Prov Govt,Victoria, V8W 9J1 BC
250-952-4913, Fax: 250-952-4888, 888-257-4777
BC Public Service Agency, #4, 810 Blanshard St., PO Box 9404 Prov Govt,Victoria, V8W 9V1 BC
250-356-6830, Fax: 250-356-7074

Manitoba

Advisory Council on Workplace Safety & Health, #200, 401 York Ave., Winnipeg, MB R3C 0P8
204-945-3446, Fax: 204-945-4556
Office of the Auditor General, #500, 330 Portage Ave., Winnipeg, R3C 0C4 MB
204-945-3790, Fax: 204-945-2169, contact@oag.mb.ca
Automobile Injury Compensation Appeal Commission, #301, 428 Portage Ave.., Winnipeg, MB R3C 0E2
204-945-4155, Fax: 204-948-2402, autoinjury@gov.mb.ca
Civil Service Commission Board, #935, 155 Carlton St., Winnipeg, MB R3C 3H8
204-945-1435, Fax: 204-945-1486
Manitoba Civil Service Commission, #935, 155 Carlton St., Winnipeg, R3C 3H8 MB
204-945-2332, Fax: 204-945-1486, 800-282-8069, cschrp@gov.mb.ca
Credit Union Deposit Guarantee Corporation, #390, 200 Graham Ave., Winnipeg, MB R3C 4L5
204-942-8480, Fax: 204-947-1723, 800-697-4447, mail@cudgc.com
Manitoba Culture, Heritage, Tourism & Sport, Legislative Building, #118, 450 Broadway Ave., Winnipeg, R3C 0V8 MB
204-945-3729, Fax: 204-945-5223, mincht@leg.gov.mb.ca
Emergency Measures Organization, 405 Broadway Ave., 15th Floor, Winnipeg, R3C 3L6 MB
204-945-4772, Fax: 204-945-4929, 888-267-8298, emo@gov.mb.ca
Employment, Income & Housing Division, #201, 280 Broadway Ave., Winnipeg, R3C 0R8 MB
Manitoba Family Services & Housing, #219, 114 Garry St., Winnipeg, R3C 4V6 MB
204-945-3242, Fax: 204-945-2156, minfam@leg.gov.mb.ca
Manitoba Health & Healthy Living, #100, 300 Carlton St., Winnipeg, R3B 3M9 MB
204-786-7191, minhlt@leg.gov.mb.ca
Manitoba Human Rights Commission, 175 Hargrave St., 7th Fl., Winnipeg, R3C 3R8 MB
204-945-3007, Fax: 204-945-1292, 888-884-8681, hrc@gov.mb.ca
Manitoba Hydro, PO Box 815 Main,Winnipeg, R3C 2P4 MB
204-474-3311, Fax: 204-475-0069, publicaffairs@hydro.mb.ca
Manitoba Infrastructure & Transportation, Legislative Building, #203, 450 Broadway Ave., Winnipeg, R3C 0V8 MB
204-945-3723, Fax: 204-945-7610
Manitoba Public Insurance, #820, 234 Donald St., PO Box 6300, Winnipeg, R3C 4A4 MB
204-985-7000, Fax: 204-943-9851, 800-665-2410
Manitoba Justice, Legislative Building, #104, 405 Broadway Ave., Winnipeg, R3C 3L6 MB
204-945-3728, Fax: 204-945-2517, minjus@gov.mb.ca
Manitoba Labour & Immigration, Legislative Building, 317, 450 Broadway Ave., Winnipeg, R3C 0V8 MB
204-945-4079, Fax: 204-945-8312, minlab@leg.gov.mb.ca
Local Government Development Division, 59 Elizabeth Dr., PO Box 33, Thompson, R8N 1X4 MB
204-677-6794, Fax: 204-677-6525
Manitoba Bureau of Statistics, #824, 155 Carlton St., Winnipeg, R3C 3H9 MB
204-945-2406, Fax: 204-945-0695
Manitoba Film Classification Board, #216, 301 Weston St., Winnipeg, MB R3E 3H4
204-945-8962, Fax: 204-945-0890, 866-612-2399, mfcb@gov.mb.ca
Manitoba Housing & Renewal Corporation, 280 Broadway, Winnipeg, MB R3C 0R8
204-945-4895, Fax: 204-945-5710
Manitoba Housing Authority - Public Housing, #2100, 185 Smith St., Winnipeg, MB R3C 3G4
204-945-4663, Fax: 204-948-2013, 800-661-4663
Manitoba Labour Board, A.A. Heaps Bldg., #402, 258 Portage Ave., Winnipeg, MB R3C 0B6
204-945-3783, Fax: 204-945-1296, mlb@gov.mb.ca
Manitoba Land Value Appraisal Commission, 800 Portage Ave., Winnipeg, MB R3G 0N4
204-945-2941, Fax: 204-948-2235
Manitoba Minimum Wage Board, 614 - 401 York Ave., Winnipeg, MB R3C 0P8
204-945-4889, Fax: 204-948-2085, mw@gov.mb.ca
Manitoba News Media Services, #29, Legislative Bldg., 450 Broadway, Winnipeg, R3C 0V8 MB
204-945-3746, Fax: 204-945-3988, nmservices@leg.gov.mb.ca
Office of the Fire Commissioner, #508, 401 York Ave., Winnipeg, MB R3C 0P8
204-945-3322, Fax: 204-948-2089, 800-282-8069, firecomm@gov.mb.ca
Primary Care & Healthy Living, 300 Carlton St., 2nd Floor, Winnipeg, R3B 3M9 MB
Provincial-Municipal Support Services, #508, 800 Portage Ave., Winnipeg, R3G 0N4 MB
Public Utilities Board, #400, 330 Portage Ave., Winnipeg, MB R3C 0C4
204-945-2638, Fax: 204-945-2643, 866-854-3698, publicutilities@gov.mb.ca
Manitoba Seniors & Healthy Aging Secretariat, #822, 155 Carlton St., Winnipeg, R3C 3H8 MB
204-945-6565, Fax: 204-948-2514, 800-665-6565, seniors@gov.mb.ca
Manitoba Telecom Services Inc., 333 Main St., PO Box 6666, Winnipeg, R3C 3V6 MB
204-941-4111, Fax: 204-772-6391
Manitoba Workers' Compensation Board, 333 Broadway Ave., Winnipeg, R3C 4W3 MB
204-954-4321, Fax: 204-954-4999, 800-362-3340, wcb@wcb.mb.ca
Workplace Safety & Health Division, #200, 401 York Ave., Winnipeg, R3C 0P8 MB
204-945-3446, Fax: 204-948-2209, wshcompl@gov.mb.ca

New Brunswick

Communications New Brunswick, Wilcom Bldg., 225 King St., 2nd Fl., PO Box 6000, Fredericton, E3B 5H1 NB
506-453-2240, Fax: 506-453-5329
Premier's Council on the Status of Disabled Persons, Kings Place, #648, 440 King St., Fredericton, E3B 5H8 NB
506-444-3000, Fax: 506-444-3001, 800-442-4412, pcsdp@gnb.ca
Family Income Security Appeal Board, PO Box 6000, Fredericton, NB E3B 5H1
506-525-4007, Fax: 506-525-4008
Department of Health, PO Box 5100, Fredericton, E3B 5G8 NB
506-457-4800, Fax: 506-453-5243, dh-ms@dh-ms.ca
New Brunswick Human Rights Commission, PO Box 6000, Fredericton, E3B 5H1 NB
506-453-2301, Fax: 506-453-2653, 888-471-2233, hrc.cdp@gnb.ca
Legislative Services, Centennial Bldg., #418, 670 King St., PO Box 6000, Fredericton, E3B 5H1 NB
506-453-2855, Fax: 506-457-7342
New Brunswick Municipal Finance Corporation, #376, 670 King St., PO Box 6000, Fredericton, NB E3B 5H1
506-453-3952, Fax: 506-453-2053,
Office of the Ombudsman, 767 Brunswick St., PO Box 6000, Fredericton, E3B 5H1 NB
506-453-2789, Fax: 506-453-5599, 800-465-1100, nbombud@gnb.ca
Department of Post-Secondary Education, Training & Labour, 470 York St., PO Box 6000, Fredericton, E3B 5H1 NB
506-453-2597, Fax: 506-453-3618, dpetlinfo@gnb.ca
New Brunswick Power Group of Companies, 515 King St., PO Box 2000, Fredericton, E3B 4X1 NB
506-458-4444, Fax: 506-458-4000, questions@nbpower.com
Department of Social Development, Sartain MacDonald Bldg., 551 King St., PO Box 6000, Fredericton, E3B 5H1 NB
506-453-2001, Fax: 506-453-7478

Newfoundland & Labrador

C.A. Pippy Park Commission, Mount Scio House, 15 Mount Scio Rd., St. John's, NL A1B 3T2
709-737-3655, Fax: 709-737-3303, 877-477-3655, pippyparkinfo@nf.aibn.com
Newfoundland & Labrador Emergency Measures Organization, PO Box 8700, St. John's, A1B 4J6 NL
709-729-3703, Fax: 709-729-3857
Department of Government Services, PO Box 8700, St. John's, A1B 4J6 NL
709-729-4860
Department of Human Resources, Labour & Employment, Confederation Bldg., PO Box 8700, St. John's, A1B 4J6 NL
709-729-2478, Fax: 709-729-6996, hreweb@gov.nl.ca
Income & Employment Support Appeal Board, Confederation Bldg., PO Box 8700, St. John's, NL A1B 4J6
709-729-2479, Fax: 709-729-5139
Department of Municipal Affairs, West Block, Main Fl., Confederation Bldg., PO Box 8700, St. John's, A1B 4J6 NL
709-729-3053
Newfoundland & Labrador Legal Aid Commission, Cormack Bldg., 2 Steers Cove, PO Box 399 C, St. John's, NL A1C 5J9
709-753-7860, Fax: 709-753-6226, 800-563-9911

Newfoundland Labrador Liquor Corporation, 90 Kenmount Rd., PO Box 8750 A, St. John's, NL A1B 3V1
709-724-1100, Fax: 709-754-0321, info@nfliquor.com
Office of the Fire Commissioner, 2 Wellon Dr., Deer Lake, NL A8A 2G5
709-635-4153, Fax: 709-635-4163
Newfoundland & Labrador Public Service Commission, 2 Canada Dr., 3rd Fl., PO Box 8700, St. John's, A1B 4J6 NL
709-729-5810, Fax: 709-729-6234
Royal Newfoundland Constabulary Public Complaints Commission, Bally Rou Place, #E-160, 280 Torbay Rd., St. John's, NL A1A 3W8
709-729-0950, Fax: 709-729-1302
Department of Transportation & Works, Confederation Bldg., West Block, 6th Fl., PO Box 8700, St. John's, A1B 4J6 NL
709-729-3679, Fax: 709-729-4285, twminister@gov.nl.ca

Northwest Territories

Department of Health & Social Services, Centre Square Tower, PO Box 1320, Yellowknife, X1A 2L9 NT
Fax: 867-873-0266
Northwest Territories Housing Corporation, Scotia Centre, 5102 50th Ave., PO Box 2100, Yellowknife, X1A 2P6 NT
867-873-7853, Fax: 867-873-9426
Department of Municipal & Community Affairs, PO Box 1320, Yellowknife, X1A 2L9 NT
867-873-7118, Fax: 867-873-0309
Northwest Territories Power Corporation, 4 Capital Dr., Hay River, X0E 1G2 NT
867-874-5200, Fax: 867-874-5229, info@ntpc.com
Department of Public Works & Services, PO Box 1320, Yellowknife, X1A 2L9 NT
867-873-7114, Fax: 867-873-0226
Victims Assistance Committee, c/o Community Justice Division, PO Box 1320, Yellowknife, NT X1A 2L9
867-920-6911, Fax: 867-873-0299
Northwest Territories Water Board, 5114 - 49th St., PO Box 1326, Yellowknife, X1A 1N9 NT
867-765-0106, Fax: 867-765-0114, info@nwtwb.com

Nova Scotia

Alcohol & Gaming Division, Alderney Gate, 40 Alderney Dr., 5th Fl., PO Box 545, Dartmouth, B2Y 3Y8 NS
902-424-6160, Fax: 902-424-6313, 877-565-0556
Department of Community Services, Nelson Place, 5675 Spring Garden Rd., 3rd Fl., PO Box 696, Halifax, B3J 2T7 NS
902-424-4304, Fax: 902-428-0618
Nova Scotia Emergency Management Office, PO Box 2581, Halifax, B3J 3N5 NS
902-424-5620, Fax: 902-424-5376, 866-424-5620, emo@gov.ns.ca
Department of Health, Joseph Howe Bldg., 1690 Hollis St., 4th Fl., PO Box 488, Halifax, B3J 2R8 NS
902-424-5818, Fax: 902-424-0730, 800-387-6665, DoHweb@gov.ns.ca
Nova Scotia Disabled Persons Commission, PO Box 222 CRO, Halifax, NS B3J 2M4
902-424-8280, Fax: 902-424-0592, 800-565-8280
Nova Scotia Legal Aid Commission, #102, 137 Chain Lake Dr., Halifax, NS B3S 1B3
902-420-6573, Fax: 902-420-3471, nsla.exec@ns.sympatico.ca
Nova Scotia Police Commission, #300, 1601 Lower Water St., PO Box 1573, Halifax, NS B3J 2Y3
902-424-3246, Fax: 902-424-3919, uarb.polcom@gov.ns.ca
Department of Transportation & Infrastructure Renewal, Johnston Bldg., 1672 Granville St., 2nd Fl., PO Box 186, Halifax, B3J 2N2 NS
902-424-2297, Fax: 902-424-0171, 888-432-3233, tpwpaff@gov.ns.ca
Workers' Advisers Program, #502, 5670 Spring Garden Rd., PO Box 1063, Halifax, NS B3J 2X1
902-424-5050, Fax: 902-424-0530, 800-774-4712

Nunavut

Department of Community & Government Services, J.G. Brown Bldg., PO Box 1000 700,Iqaluit, X0A 0H0 NU
867-975-5400, Fax: 867-975-5305
Nunavut Emergency Management, PO Box 1000 700,Iqaluit, X0A 0H0 NU
867-975-5403, Fax: 867-979-4221, 800-693-1666
Department of Finance, Bldg. 1079, 1st Fl., PO Box 1000 Stn 330,Iqaluit, X0A 0H0 NU
867-975-5800, Fax: 867-975-5805
Department of Health & Social Services, Sivummut bldg., PO Box 1007 1000,Iqaluit, X0A 0H0 NU
867-975-5700, Fax: 867-975-5705, health@gov.nu.ca

Ontario

Advertising Review Board, Macdonald Block, #M2-56, 900 Bay St., 2nd Fl., Toronto, ON M7A 1N3
416-327-2183, Fax: 416-327-2179
Ministry of the Attorney General, McMurtry-Scott Bldg., 720 Bay St., 11th Fl., Toronto, M5G 2K1 ON
416-326-2220, Fax: 416-326-4007, 800-518-7901
Ministry of Community & Social Services, Hepburn Block, 80 Grosvenor St., 6th Fl., Toronto, M7A 1E9 ON
416-325-5666, Fax: 416-325-5172, 888-789-4199
Ministry of Community Safety & Correctional Services, George Drew Bldg., 25 Grosvenor St., 18th Fl., Toronto, M7A 1Y6 ON
416-326-5000, Fax: 416-325-6067, 866-517-0571, jus.g.sgcs.webmaster@jus.gov.on.ca
Deposit Insurance Corporation of Ontario, #700, 4711 Yonge St., Toronto, ON M2N 6K8
416-325-9444, Fax: 416-325-9722, 800-268-6653
Fire Safety Commission, Place Nouveau Bldg., 5775 Yonge St., 7th Fl., Toronto, ON M2M 4J1
416-325-3100, Fax: 416-314-1217
Human Rights Tribunal of Ontario, 400 University Ave., 7th Fl., Toronto, ON M7A 1T7
416-314-8419, Fax: 416-314-8743, 800-668-3946, hrto.registrar@jus.gov.on.ca
Hydro One Inc., North Tower, 483 Bay St., Toronto, M5G 2P5 ON
416-345-5000, 877-955-1155, webmaster@HydroOne.com
Independent Electricity System Operator, PO Box 4474 A,Toronto, M5W 4E5 ON
905-403-6900, Fax: 905-403-6921, 888-448-7777, customer.relations@ieso.ca
Ministry of Municipal Affairs & Housing, 777 Bay St., 17th Fl., Toronto, M5G 2E5 ON
416-585-7041, Fax: 416-585-6227, 866-220-2290, mininfo.mah@ontario.ca
Office of the Employer Advisor, #704, 151 Bloor St. West., Toronto, ON M5S 1S4
416-327-0020, Fax: 416-327-0726, 800-387-0774
Office of the Worker Advisor, #1300, 123 Edward St., Toronto, ON M5G 1E2
416-325-8570, Fax: 416-325-4830, 800-435-8980
Ontario Housing Corporation, 777 Bay St., 2nd Fl., Toronto, ON M5G 2E5
Ontario Pension Board, #1100, 1 Adelaide St. East, Toronto, ON M5C 2X6
416-364-8558, Fax: 416-364-7578, 800-668-6203, office.services@opb.on.ca
Ontario Rental Housing Tribunal, 777 Bay St., 12th Fl., Toronto, ON M5G 2E5
416-585-7295, Fax: 416-585-6363, 888-332-3234
Ontario Power Generation, 700 University Ave., Toronto, M5G 1X6 ON
416-592-2555, 877-592-2555
Public Safety Division, George Drew bldg, 25 Grosvenor St., 12th fl., Toronto, M7A 2H3 ON
416-314-3000, Fax: 416-314-4037
Social Benefits Tribunal, 1075 Bay St., 7th Fl., Toronto, ON M5S 2B1
416-326-0978, Fax: 416-325-5135, 800-753-3895
Southern Ontario Library Service, #902, 111 Peter St., Toronto, ON M5V 2H1
416-961-1669, Fax: 416-961-5122, 800-387-5765
Ministry of Transportation, Ferguson Block, 77 Wellesley St. West, 3rd Fl., Toronto, M7A 1Z8 ON
416-235-4686, Fax: 416-327-9185, 800-268-4686,

Prince Edward Island

Office of the Attorney General, Shaw Building, North, 105 Rochford St., 4th Fl., PO Box 2000, Charlottetown, C1A 7N8 PE
902-368-5152, Fax: 902-368-4910
Department of Communities, Cultural Affairs & Labour, Shaw Bldg., 95 Rochford St., 4th Fl., PO Box 2000, Charlottetown, C1A 7N8 PE
902-368-5250, Fax: 902-368-4121
Community & Labour Development, Shaw Bldg., 105 Rochford St., 5th Fl., PO Box 2000, Charlottetown, C1A 7N8 PE
902-368-4244, Fax: 902-368-4242
Prince Edward Island Emergency Measures Organization, National Bank Tower, #600, 134 Kent St., PO Box 2000, Charlottetown, C1A 7N8 PE
902-894-0385, Fax: 902-368-6362
Department of Health, Jones Bldg., 11 Kent St., 2nd Fl., PO Box 2000, Charlottetown, C1A 7N8 PE
902-368-4900, Fax: 902-368-4974
Island Waste Management Corporation, 110 Watts Ave., Charlottetown, PE C1E 2C1
902-894-0330, Fax: 902-894-0331, 888-280-8111, reception@iwmc.pe.ca; info@iwmc.pe.ca

Quebec

Ministère des Affaires municipales et Occupation du territoire, Aile Chaveau, 10, rue Pierre-Olivier-Chauveau, 3e étage, Québec, G1R 4J3 QC
418-691-2019, Fax: 418-643-7385, communications@mamrot.gouv.qc.ca
Bureau des projets Centres hospitaliers universitaires de Montréal, CHUM, CUSM et CHU Sainte-Justine, #10.049, 2021, rue Union, Montréal, QC H3A 2S9
514-864-9883, Fax: 514-873-7362
Commissariat des incendies, 455, rue Dupont, Québec, QC G1K 6N2
418-529-5706, Fax: 418-529-9922
Commission administrative des régimes de retraite et d'assurances (Québec), 475, rue Saint-Amable, Québec, QC G1R 5X3
418-643-4881, Fax: 418-644-3839, 800-463-5533
Commission de la fonction publique (Québec), 800, Place d'Youville, 7e étage, Québec, QC G1R 3P4
418-643-1425, 800-432-0432, cfp@cfp.gouv.qc.ca
Commission municipale du Québec, Mezzanine, aile Chauveau, 10, rue Pierre-Olivier-Chauveau, Tour 5e étage, Québec, QC G1R 4J3
418-691-2014, Fax: 418-644-4676, 866-353-6767, cmq@mamr.gouv.qc.ca
Conseil des services essentiels du Québec, 800, tour de la place-Victoria, 25e étage, CP 365, Montréal, QC H4Z 1H9
514-873-7246, Fax: 514-873-3839, 800-337-7246, info@cses.gouv.qc.ca
Ministère de l'Emploi et de la Solidarité sociale, 425, rue St-Amable, 4e étage, Québec, G1R 4Z1 QC
418-643-4721, 888-643-4721
Hydro-Québec, 75, boul René-Lévesque ouest, 20e étage, Montréal, H2Z 1A4 QC
514-289-2211
Institut de la statistique du Québec, 200, ch Ste-Foy, 3e étage, Québec, QC G1R 5T4
418-691-2401, Fax: 418-643-4129, 800-463-4090, direction@stat.gouv.qc.ca
Office des personnes handicapées du Québec, 309, rue Brock, Drummondville, QC J2B 1C5
819-475-8585, Fax: 819-475-8767, 800-567-1465
Palais des congrès de Montréal, 159, rue Saint-Antoine ouest, 9é étage, Montréal, QC H2Z 1H2
514-871-8122, Fax: 514-871-3188, 800-268-8122, pcmcomm@congresmtl.com
Régie de l'assurance maladie du Québec, 1125, Grande Allée ouest, Québec, QC G1S 1E7
418-646-4636
Régie du logement du Québec, Pyramide Ouest, #2360, 5199, rue Sherbrooke est, Montréal, QC H1T 3X1
514-873-6575, Fax: 514-873-6805, 800-683-2245
Ministère de la Santé et des Services sociaux, Direction des communications et Renseignements généraux, 1075, ch Sainte-Foy, Québec, G1S 2M1 QC
418-266-8900, 800-707-3380, regisseur.web@msss.gouv.qc.ca
Société d'habitation du Québec, Aile St-Amable, 1054, rue Louis-Alexandre-Taschereau, 3e étage, Québec, QC G1R 5E7
418-643-4035, Fax: 418-643-4560, 800-463-4315
Société de l'assurance automobile du Québec, 333, boul Jean-Lesage, CP 19600 Terminus, Québec, QC G1K 8J6
418-643-7620, Fax: 418-644-0339, 800-361-7620, courrier@saaq.gouv.qc.ca
Société immobilière du Québec, 1075, rue de l'Amérique-Française, Québec, QC G1R 5P8
418-646-1766, Fax: 418-646-6911, 877-747-9911, courrier@siq.gouv.qc.ca
Ministère de la Sécurité publique, Tour des Laurentides, 2525, boul Laurier, 5e étage, Québec, G1V 2L2 QC
418-643-2112, Fax: 418-646-6168, 866-644-6826
Urgences-santé Québec, 3232, rue Bélanger, Montréal, QC H1Y 3H5
514-723-5600, info@urgences-sante.qc.ca
Vérificateur général du Québec, 750, boulevard Charest est, 3e étage, Québec, G1K 9J6 QC
418-691-5900, Fax: 418-644-4460, verificateur.general@vgq.gouv.qc.
École nationale des pompiers du Québec, #3.08, 2800, boul Saint-Martin ouest, Laval, QC H7T 2S9
450-680-6800, Fax: 450-680-6818, 866-680-3677, enpq@enpq.gouv.qc.ca

Saskatchewan

Saskatchewan Assessment Management Agency, #200, 2201 - 11th Ave., Regina, S4P 0J8 SK
306-924-8000, Fax: 306-924-8070, 800-667-7262, info.request@sama.sk.ca
Provincial Auditor Saskatchewan, #1500, 1920 Broad St., Regina, S4P 3V2 SK
306-787-6398, Fax: 306-787-6383, info@auditor.sk.ca

Crown Investments Corporation of Saskatchewan, #400, 2400 College Ave., Regina, S4P 1C8 SK
306-787-6851, Fax: 306-787-8125

Saskatchewan Government Insurance, 2260 - 11th Ave., Regina, S4P 0J9 SK
306-751-1200, Fax: 306-787-7477, 800-667-8015, sgiinquiries@sgi.sk.ca

Saskatchewan Ombudsman, #150, 2401 Saskatchewan Dr., Regina, S4P 4H8 SK
306-787-6211, Fax: 306-787-9090, 800-667-7180

Saskatchewan Power Corporation (SaskPower), 2025 Victoria Ave., Regina, S4P 0S1 SK
306-566-2121, Fax: 306-566-2330, 800-667-4749

Saskatchewan Legal Aid Commission, #502, 201 - 21 St. East, Saskatoon, SK S7K 2H6
306-933-5300, Fax: 306-933-6764, 800-667-3764, central@legalaid.gov.sk.ca

Saskatchewan Water Corporation (SaskWater), #200, 111 Fairford St. East, Moose Jaw, S6H 1C8 SK
306-694-3098, Fax: 306-694-3207, 888-230-1111, comm@saskwater.com

SaskEnergy Incorporated, 1777 Victoria Ave., Regina, S4P 4K5 SK
306-777-9225, Fax: 306-777-9200, 800-567-8899

Saskatchewan Social Services, 1920 Broad St., Regina, S4P 3V6 SK
306-787-3700

Yukon Territory

Yukon Community Services, PO Box 2703, Whitehorse, Y1A 2C6 YT
867-667-5811, Fax: 867-393-6295, 800-661-0408, inquiry@gov.yk.ca

Emergency Measures Organization, PO Box 2703, Whitehorse, Y1A 2C6 YT
867-667-5220, Fax: 867-393-6266, 800-661-0408, emo.yukon@gov.yk.ca

Yukon Health & Social Services, PO Box 2703, Whitehorse, Y1A 2C6 YT
867-667-3673, Fax: 867-667-3096, 800-661-0408, hss@gov.yk.ca

Yukon Housing Corporation, 410H Jarvis St., Whitehorse, Y1A 2H5 YT
867-667-5759, Fax: 867-667-3664, 800-661-0408, ykhouse@housing.yk.ca

Yukon Public Service Commission, PO Box 2703, Whitehorse, Y1A 2C6 YT
867-667-5252, Fax: 867-667-6705

Yukon Utilities Board, #19, 1114 - 1st Ave., PO Box 31728, Whitehorse, YT Y1A 6L3
867-667-5058

PUBLIC TRUSTEE

British Columbia

Public Guardian & Trustee of British Columbia, #700, 808 West Hastings St., Vancouver, BC V6C 3L3
604-660-4444, Fax: 604-660-0374, mail@trustee.bc.ca

Manitoba

Office of the Public Trustee, #500, 155 Carlton St., Winnipeg, MB R3C 5R9
204-945-2700, Fax: 204-948-2251, publictrustee@gov.mb.ca

New Brunswick

Department of Justice & Consumer Affairs, Centennial Bldg., 670 King St., PO Box 6000, Fredericton, E3B 5H1 NB
506-462-5100, Fax: 506-453-3651, justice.comments@gnb.ca

Newfoundland & Labrador

Department of Justice, Confederation Bldg., East Block, 4th Fl., PO Box 8700, St. John's, A1B 4J6 NL
709-729-5942, Fax: 709-729-2129, justice@gov.nl.ca

Nova Scotia

Public Trustee Office, #201, 5151 Terminal Rd., PO Box 385, Halifax, NS B3J 2T3
902-424-7760, Fax: 902-424-0616,

Quebec

Curateur public du Québec, 600, boul René-Lévesque ouest, 10e étage, Montréal, QC H3B 4W9
514-873-4074, Fax: 514-873-5033, 800-363-9020, information@curateur.gouv.qc.ca

PUBLIC UTILITIES

Alberta

Energy Resources Conservation Board, #1000, 250 - 5 Ave. SW, Calgary, AB T2P 0R4
403-297-8311, Fax: 403-297-7336, inquiries@ercb.ca

Alberta Utilities Consumer Advocate, TD Tower, 10088 - 102 Ave., Edmonton, T5J 2Z1 AB
780-644-5130, Fax: 780-644-5129, 866-714-4455, UtilitiesConsumerAdvocate@gov.ab.

British Columbia

British Columbia Hydro, 333 Dunsmuir St., 18th Fl., Vancouver, V6B 5R3 BC
604-224-9376, Fax: 604-623-4467, 800-224-9376

British Columbia Transmission Corporation, Four Bentall Centre, #1100, 1055 Dunsmuir St., PO Box 49260, Vancouver, V7X 1V5 BC
604-699-7300, Fax: 604-699-7333, 866-647-3334, contact.us@bctc.com

British Columbia Utilities Commission, 900 Howe St., 6th Fl., PO Box 250, Vancouver, V6Z 2N3 BC
604-660-4700, Fax: 604-660-1102, 800-663-1385, commission.secretary@bcuc.com

Manitoba

Manitoba Hydro, PO Box 815 Main,Winnipeg, R3C 2P4 MB
204-474-3311, Fax: 204-475-0069, publicaffairs@hydro.mb.ca

Public Utilities Board, #400, 330 Portage Ave., Winnipeg, MB R3C 0C4
204-945-2638, Fax: 204-945-2643, 866-854-3698, publicutilities@gov.mb.ca

New Brunswick

NB Board of Commissioners of Public Utilities, #1400, 15 Market Sq., PO Box 5001, Saint John, NB E2L 4Y9
506-658-2504, Fax: 506-643-7300, 866-766-2782, general@pub.nb.ca

New Brunswick Power Group of Companies, 515 King St., PO Box 2000, Fredericton, E3B 4X1 NB
506-458-4444, Fax: 506-458-4000, questions@nbpower.com

Newfoundland & Labrador

Churchill Falls (Labrador) Corporation Limited, Hydro Place, 500 Columbus Dr., PO Box 12500, St. John's, A1B 4K7 NL
709-737-1859, Fax: 709-737-1816

Newfoundland & Labrador Hydro, Hydro Place, Columbus Dr., PO Box 12400, St. John's, A1B 4K7 NL
709-737-1400, Fax: 709-737-1800

Newfoundland & Labrador Board of Commissioners of Public Utilities, PO Box 21040, St. John's, A1A 5B2 NL
709-726-8600, Fax: 709-726-9604, 866-782-0006, ito@pub.nf.ca

Northwest Territories

Northwest Territories Power Corporation, 4 Capital Dr., Hay River, X0E 1G2 NT
867-874-5200, Fax: 867-874-5229, info@ntpc.com

Northwest Territories Water Board, 5114 - 49th St., PO Box 1326, Yellowknife, X1A 1N9 NT
867-765-0106, Fax: 867-765-0114, info@nwtwb.com

Nova Scotia

Nova Scotia Utility & Review Board, 1601 Lower Water St., 3rd Fl., PO Box 1692 M,Halifax, B3J 3S3 NS
902-424-4448, Fax: 902-424-3919, uarb.board@gov.ns.ca

Ontario

Hydro One Inc., North Tower, 483 Bay St., Toronto, M5G 2P5 ON
416-345-5000, 877-955-1155, webmaster@HydroOne.com

Independent Electricity System Operator, PO Box 4474 A,Toronto, M5W 4E5 ON
905-403-6900, Fax: 905-403-6921, 888-448-7777, customer.relations@ieso.ca

Ontario Power Generation, 700 University Ave., Toronto, M5G 1X6 ON
416-592-2555, 877-592-2555

Prince Edward Island

Island Regulatory & Appeals Commission, National Bank Tower, #501, 134 Kent St., PO Box 577, Charlottetown, C1A 7L1 PE
902-892-3501, Fax: 902-566-4076, 800-501-6268, irac@irac.pe.ca

Quebec

Hydro-Québec, 75, boul René-Lévesque ouest, 20e étage, Montréal, H2Z 1A4 QC
514-289-2211

Régie de l'énergie, Tour de la Bourse, #255, 800, Place Victoria, CP 1, Montréal, QC H4Z 1A2
514-873-2452, Fax: 514-873-2070, 888-873-2452, secretariat@regie-energie.qc.ca

Saskatchewan

Saskatchewan Power Corporation (SaskPower), 2025 Victoria Ave., Regina, S4P 0S1 SK
306-566-2121, Fax: 306-566-2330, 800-667-4749

Saskatchewan Water Corporation (SaskWater), #200, 111 Fairford St. East, Moose Jaw, S6H 1C8 SK
306-694-3098, Fax: 306-694-3207, 888-230-1111, comm@saskwater.com

SaskEnergy Incorporated, 1777 Victoria Ave., Regina, S4P 4K5 SK
306-777-9225, Fax: 306-777-9200, 800-567-8899

Yukon Territory

Yukon Utilities Board, #19, 1114 - 1st Ave., PO Box 31728, Whitehorse, YT Y1A 6L3
867-667-5058

PUBLIC WORKS

Public Works & Government Services Canada, Place du Portage, Phase III, 11, rue Laurier, Ottawa, K1A 0S5 ON
819-997-6363, Fax: 819-956-9062, 800-622-6232, questions@tpsgc-pwgsc.gc.ca

Alberta

Alberta Infrastructure, Infrastructure Building, 6950 - 101 St., 3rd Fl., Edmonton, T6H 5V7 AB
780-415-0507, Fax: 780-427-2187,-310-0000

British Columbia

Ministry of Labour, PO Box 9052 Prov Govt,Victoria, V8W 9E2 BC
250-356-6348, Fax: 250-356-6595, LCS.Minister@gov.bc.ca

Manitoba

Manitoba Infrastructure & Transportation, Legislative Building, #203, 450 Broadway Ave., Winnipeg, R3C 0V8 MB
204-945-3723, Fax: 204-945-7610

Newfoundland & Labrador

Department of Transportation & Works, Confederation Bldg., West Block, 6th Fl., PO Box 8700, St. John's, A1B 4J6 NL
709-729-3679, Fax: 709-729-4285, twminister@gov.nl.ca

Northwest Territories

Department of Public Works & Services, PO Box 1320, Yellowknife, X1A 2L9 NT
867-873-7114, Fax: 867-873-0226

Nova Scotia

Department of Transportation & Infrastructure Renewal, Johnston Bldg., 1672 Granville St., 2nd Fl., PO Box 186, Halifax, B3J 2N2 NS
902-424-2297, Fax: 902-424-0171, 888-432-3233, tpwpaff@gov.ns.ca

Nunavut

Department of Community & Government Services, J.G. Brown Bldg., PO Box 1000 700,Iqaluit, X0A 0H0 NU
867-975-5400, Fax: 867-975-5305

Prince Edward Island

Department of Transportation & Public Works, Jones Bldg., 11 Kent St., PO Box 2000, Charlottetown, C1A 7N8 PE
902-368-5100, Fax: 902-368-5395,

Quebec

Ministère des Services gouvernementaux, 4e étage, Secteur 500, 875, Grande Allée est, Québec, G1R 5R8 QC
418-643-8383, Fax: 418-528-6153, communication@msg.gouv.qc.ca

Saskatchewan

Saskatchewan Government Services, Century Plaza, 1920 Rose St., Regina, S4P 0A9 SK
306-787-6911, Fax: 306-787-1061

Yukon Territory

Yukon Highways & Public Works, PO Box 2703, Whitehorse, Y1A 2C6 YT
867-393-7193, Fax: 867-393-6218, 800-661-0408, hpw-info@gov.yk.ca

PUBLICATIONS

Public Works & Government Services Canada, Place du Portage, Phase III, 11, rue Laurier, Ottawa, K1A 0S5 ON
819-997-6363, Fax: 819-956-9062, 800-622-6232, questions@tpsgc-pwgsc.gc.ca

Manitoba

Statutory Publications, #20, 200 Vaughan St., Winnipeg, R3C 1T5 MB
204-945-3101, Fax: 204-945-7172, 800-321-1203, statpub@gov.mb.ca

New Brunswick

Legislative Services, Centennial Bldg., #418, 670 King St., PO Box 6000, Fredericton, E3B 5H1 NB
506-453-2855, Fax: 506-457-7342

Newfoundland & Labrador

Office of the Queen's Printer, Queen's Printer-Earl Tucker, Ground Fl., Confederation Blg., PO Box 8700, St. John's,

A1B 4J6 NL
709-729-3649, Fax: 709-729-1900, queensprinter@gov.nl.ca

Nova Scotia
Communications Nova Scotia, 1723 Hollis St., PO Box 608, Halifax, B3J 2R7 NS
902-424-7690, Fax: 902-424-0515
Department of Service Nova Scotia & Municipal Relations, 1505 Barrington St., PO Box 216, Halifax, B3J 2M4 NS
902-424-4141, Fax: 902-424-0581, public-enquiries@gov.ns.ca

Nunavut
Legislative Assembly, Legislative Assembly Bldg., 3rd Fl., PO Box 1200, Iqaluit, X0A 0H0 NU
867-975-5000, Fax: 867-975-5190, 877-334-7266, leginfo@assembly.nu.ca

Quebec
Ministère de la Culture, des Communications & de la Condition féminine, 225, Grande Allée est, Québec, G1R 5G5 QC
Fax: 418-380-2364, 888-380-8882, infos@mcccf.gouv.qc.ca

Yukon Territory
Yukon Highways & Public Works, PO Box 2703, Whitehorse, Y1A 2C6 YT
867-393-7193, Fax: 867-393-6218, 800-661-0408, hpw-info@gov.yk.ca

PURCHASING

Alberta
Alberta Infrastructure, Infrastructure Building, 6950 - 101 St., 3rd Fl., Edmonton, T6H 5V7 AB
780-415-0507, Fax: 780-427-2187,-310-0000

British Columbia
Ministry of Labour, PO Box 9052 Prov Govt,Victoria, V8W 9E2 BC
250-356-6348, Fax: 250-356-6595, LCS.Minister@gov.bc.ca

Manitoba
Government Services, Legislative Bldg., #332, 450 Broadway, Winnipeg, R3C 0V8 MB

Newfoundland & Labrador
Department of Government Services, PO Box 8700, St. John's, A1B 4J6 NL
709-729-4860

Northwest Territories
Department of Public Works & Services, PO Box 1320, Yellowknife, X1A 2L9 NT
867-873-7114, Fax: 867-873-0226

Nunavut
Department of Community & Government Services, J.G. Brown Bldg., PO Box 1000 700,Iqaluit, X0A 0H0 NU
867-975-5400, Fax: 867-975-5305

Prince Edward Island
Department of Transportation & Public Works, Jones Bldg., 11 Kent St., PO Box 2000, Charlottetown, C1A 7N8 PE
902-368-5100, Fax: 902-368-5395

Saskatchewan
Saskatchewan Government Services, Century Plaza, 1920 Rose St., Regina, S4P 0A9 SK
306-787-6911, Fax: 306-787-1061

RAIL TRANSPORTATION

See Also: Transportation
Transportation Safety Board of Canada, 200 Promenade du Portage, 4th Fl., Ottawa, K1A 1K8 ON
819-994-3741, Fax: 819-997-2239, 800-387-3557
Via Rail Canada Inc., #500, 3, Place Ville-Marie, Montréal, H3B 2C9 QC
514-871-6000, Fax: 514-871-6768

Manitoba
Manitoba Infrastructure & Transportation, Legislative Building, #203, 450 Broadway Ave., Winnipeg, R3C 0V8 MB
204-945-3723, Fax: 204-945-7610

New Brunswick
Department of Transportation, Kings Pl., 440 KingSt., PO Box 6000, Fredericton, E3B 5H8 NB
506-453-3939, Fax: 506-453-2900, Transportation.Web@gnb.ca

Newfoundland & Labrador
Department of Transportation & Works, Confederation Bldg., West Block, 6th Fl., PO Box 8700, St. John's, A1B 4J6 NL
709-729-3679, Fax: 709-729-4285, twminister@gov.nl.ca

Nova Scotia
Department of Transportation & Infrastructure Renewal, Johnston Bldg., 1672 Granville St., 2nd Fl., PO Box 186, Halifax, B3J 2N2 NS
902-424-2297, Fax: 902-424-0171, 888-432-3233, tpwpaff@gov.ns.ca

Ontario
GO Transit, #600, 20 Bay St., Toronto, ON M5J 2W3
416-869-3600, Fax: 416-869-1755, 888-438-6646

Quebec
Société du port ferroviaire Baie-Comeau-Hauterive, 18, rte Maritime, Baie-Comeau, QC G4Z 2L6
418-296-6785, Fax: 418-296-2377, soport@globetrotter.qc.ca
Ministère des Transports, 700, boul René-Lévesque est, 27e étage, Québec, G1R 5H1 QC
418-643-6980, Fax: 418-643-2011, 888-355-0511, communications@mtq.gouv.qc.ca

Saskatchewan
Saskatchewan Highways & Infrastructure, 1855 Victoria Ave., Regina, S4P 3T2 SK
306-787-4800

REAL ESTATE

See Also: Land Titles
Canada Mortgage & Housing Corporation, 700 Montreal Rd., Ottawa, K1A 0P7 ON
613-748-2000, Fax: 613-748-2098, 800-668-2642, chic@cmhc-schl.gc.ca

Alberta
Technology Services, John E. Brownlee Bldg., 10365 - 97 St., 8th Fl., Edmonton, T5J 3W7 AB
780-422-8545

British Columbia
Real Estate Council of British Columbia, #900, 750 West Pender St., Vancouver, BC V6C 2T8
604-683-9664, Fax: 604-683-9017, 877-683-9664, info@recbc.ca

New Brunswick
New Brunswick Real Estate Association, #1, 22 Durelle St., Fredericton, NB E3C 1N8
506-459-8055, Fax: 506-459-8057, 800-762-1677, info@nbrea.ca

Nova Scotia
Department of Service Nova Scotia & Municipal Relations, 1505 Barrington St., PO Box 216, Halifax, B3J 2M4 NS
902-424-4141, Fax: 902-424-0581, public-enquiries@gov.ns.ca

Nunavut
Nunavut Legal Registries Division, Brown Bldg., 1st Fl., PO Box 1000 570,Iqaluit, X0A 0H0 NU
867-975-6190, Fax: 867-975-6194

Prince Edward Island
Consumer, Corporate & Insurance Division, Shaw Building, 95 Rochford St., 4th Fl., PO Box 2000, Charlottetown, C1A 7N8 PE
902-368-4580, Fax: 902-368-5283, 800-658-1799

Quebec
Société immobilière du Québec, 1075, rue de l'Amérique-Française, Québec, QC G1R 5P8
418-646-1766, Fax: 418-646-6911, 877-747-9911, courrier@siq.gouv.qc.ca

RECREATION

See Also: Tourism & Tourist Information
Canada Place Corporation, 504 - 999 Canada Place, Vancouver, V6C 3E1 BC
604-775-7200, Fax: 604-775-6251, administration@canadaplace.ca
Canadian Heritage, 15 Eddy St., Gatineau, K1A 0M5 QC
819-997-0055, 866-811-0055, info@pch.gc.ca
Canadian Tourism Commission, #1400, 1055 Dunsmuir St., PO Box 49230, Vancouver, BC V7X 1L2
604-638-8300, Fax: 604-638-8425, ctc_feedback@businteractive.com
National Battlefields Commission, 390, av de Bernières, Québec, G1R 2L7 QC
418-648-3506, Fax: 418-648-3638, information@ccbn-nbc.gc.ca
Parks Canada, 25 Eddy St., Gatineau, K1A 0M5 QC
613-860-1251, 888-773-8888, information@pc.gc.ca

Alberta
Alberta Gaming & Liquor Commission, 50 Corriveau Ave., St Albert, AB T8N 3T5
780-447-8600, Fax: 780-447-8911, 800-272-8876
Alberta Sport, Recreation, Parks & Wildlife Foundation, Standard Life Centre, 10405 Jasper Ave., 9th Fl., Edmonton, AB T5J 4R7
780-415-1167, Fax: 780-415-0308

British Columbia
British Columbia 2010 Olympic & Paralympic Games Secretariat, 3585 Graveley St., 7th Fl., Vancouver, BC V5K 5J5
604-660-2010, Fax: 604-660-3437, 877-604-2010, bcsecretariat@gov.bc.ca
British Columbia Lottery Corporation, 74 West Seymour St., Kamloops, BC V2C 1E2
250-828-5500, Fax: 250-828-5631, 866-815-0222
Office of the Superintendent of Motor Vehicles, 940 Blanshard St., PO Box 9254 Prov Govt,Victoria, V8W 9J2 BC
250-387-7747, Fax: 250-387-4891, OSMV.Mailbox@gov.bc.ca
Ministry of Small Business & Revenue, 1810 Blanshard St., 3rd Fl., PO Box 9432 Prov Govt,Victoria, V8W 9N6 BC
250-387-6206, Fax: 250-952-0712, MSBROffice@gov.bc.ca
Sport Branch, 800 Johnson St., 1st Fl., PO Box 9820 Prov Govt,Victoria, V8W 9W3 BC
Fax: 250-387-8720

Manitoba
Manitoba Competitiveness, Training & Trade, International Business Centre, The Paris Building, 259 Portage Ave., Winnipeg, R3B 3P4 MB
204-945-2475, Fax: 204-945-3977, minctt@leg.gov.mb.ca
Manitoba Lotteries Corporation, 830 Empress St., Winnipeg, R3G 3H3 MB
204-957-2500, Fax: 204-957-3991, communications@casinosofwinnipeg.com
Manitoba Horse Racing Commission, c/o Boards, Commissions & Legislation Branch, #812, 401 York Ave., Winnipeg, MB R3C 0P8
204-945-4495, Fax: 204-948-2844, gordon.mackenzie@gov.mb.ca
Tourism Secretariat & Travel Manitoba, 155 Carlton St., 7th Fl., Winnipeg, R3C 3H8 MB
800-665-0040

New Brunswick
Department of Business New Brunswick, Centennial Bldg., 670 King St., PO Box 6000, Fredericton, E3B 5H1 NB
506-444-5228, Fax: 506-453-5428
Investment & Export Development, Centennial Bldg., 670 King St., 5th F., PO Box 6000, Fredericton, E3B 5H1 NB
506-453-2875, Fax: 506-444-4277
New Brunswick Lotteries & Gaming Corporation, Centennial Bldg., 670 King St., PO Box 6000, Fredericton, NB E3B 5H1
506-453-2451, Fax: 506-457-4989
Department of Wellness, Culture & Sport, Place 2000, 250 King St., 4th Fl., PO Box 6000, Fredericton, E3B 5H1 NB
506-453-2909, Fax: 506-453-6548

Newfoundland & Labrador
C.A. Pippy Park Commission, Mount Scio House, 15 Mount Scio Rd., St. John's, NL A1B 3T2
709-737-3655, Fax: 709-737-3303, 877-477-3655, pippyparkinfo@nf.aibn.com
Department of Tourism, Culture & Recreation, Confederation Bldg., West Block, 2nd Fl., PO Box 8700, St. John's, A1B 4J6 NL
709-729-0862, Fax: 709-729-0870, tcrinfo@gov.nl.ca

Nova Scotia
Alcohol & Gaming Division, Alderney Gate, 40 Alderney Dr., 5th Fl., PO Box 545, Dartmouth, B2Y 3Y8 NS
902-424-6160, Fax: 902-424-6313, 877-565-0556

Ontario
Alcohol & Gaming Commission of Ontario, 20 Dundas St. West, Toronto, ON M5G 2N6
416-326-8700, Fax: 416-326-5555, 800-522-2876
Ministry of Economic Development & Trade, Hearst Block, 900 Bay St., 8th Fl., Toronto, M7A 2E1 ON
416-325-6666, Fax: 416-325-6688, 866-668-4249, info@edt.gov.on.ca
Metro Toronto Convention Centre Corporation, 255 Front St. West, Toronto, ON M5V 2W6
416-585-8000, Fax: 416-585-8270, info@mtcc.com
Niagara Parks Commission, 7400 Portage Rd. South, PO Box 150, Niagara Falls, ON L2E 6T2
905-356-2241, Fax: 905-354-6041, 877-642-7275
Ontario Film Review Board, 1075 Millwood Rd., Toronto, ON M4G 1X6
416-314-3626, Fax: 416-314-3632
Ontario Place Corporation, 955 Lake Shore Blvd. West, Toronto, ON M6K 3B9
416-314-9900, Fax: 416-314-9992
Ontario Racing Commission, 20 Dundas St. West, 9th Fl., Toronto, ON M5G 2C2
416-327-0520, Fax: 416-325-3478, orcinqry@cbs.gov.on.ca

Ottawa Congress Centre, 55 Colonel By Dr., Ottawa, ON K1N 9J2
613-563-1984, Fax: 613-563-7646
St. Lawrence Parks Commission, RR#1, Morrisburg, ON K0C 1X0
613-543-3704, Fax: 613-543-2847, 800-437-2233,
Ministry of Tourism, Hearst Block, 900 Bay St., 9th Fl., Toronto, M7A 2E1 ON
416-326-9326, Fax: 416-314-7854, 800-668-2746

Prince Edward Island

Department of Communities, Cultural Affairs & Labour, Shaw Bldg., 95 Rochford St., 4th Fl., PO Box 2000, Charlottetown, C1A 7N8 PE
902-368-5250, Fax: 902-368-4121
Department of Innovation & Advanced Learning, Shaw Bldg., 105 Rochford St., 5th Fl., PO Box 2000, Charlottetown, C1A 7N8 PE
902-368-4240, Fax: 902-368-4242
Maritime Provinces Harness Racing Commission, 5 Gerald McCarville Dr., PO Box 128, Kensington, PE C0B 1M0
902-836-5500, Fax: 902-836-5390, dwalsh@mphrc.ca
Prince Edward Island Lotteries Commission, Office of the Deputy Provincial Treasurer, 95 Rochford St., PO Box 2000, Charlottetown, PE C1A 7N8
902-368-4053, Fax: 902-368-6575
Department of Tourism, PO Box 2000, Charlottetown, C1A 7N8 PE
800-463-4734

Quebec

Comité conjoint de chasse, de pêche et de piégeage, #C220, 383 rue Saint-Jacques, Montréal, QC H2Y 1N9
514-284-2151, Fax: 514-284-0039, hftcc@bellnet.ca
Loto-Québec, 500, rue Sherbrooke ouest, Montréal, QC H3A 3G6
514-282-8000, Fax: 514-873-8999
Régie des alcools, des courses et des jeux, 560, boul Charest est, Québec, QC G1K 3J3
418-643-7667, Fax: 418-643-5971, 800-363-0320, racj.quebec@racj.gouv.qc.ca
Société des établissements en plein air du Québec, Place de la Cité, #250, 2640, boul Laurier, Sainte-Foy, QC G1V 5C2
418-890-6527, Fax: 418-528-6025, 800-665-6527, inforeservation@sepaq.com

Saskatchewan

Saskatchewan Liquor & Gaming Authority, 2500 Victoria Ave., PO Box 5054, Regina, S4P 3M3 SK
306-787-4213, Fax: 306-787-8468
Saskatchewan Science Centre, 2903 Powerhouse Dr., Regina, SK S4N 0A1
306-522-4629, Fax: 306-525-0194, 800-667-6300, info@sasksciencecentre.com
Saskatchewan Tourism, Parks, Culture, & Sport, 1919 Saskatchewan Dr., 4th Fl., Regina, S4P 4H2 SK
306-787-5729, Fax: 306-787-8560
Western Development Museum, 2935 Melville St., Saskatoon, SK S7J 5A6
306-934-1400, Fax: 306-934-4467, 800-363-6345, info@wdm.ca

Yukon Territory

Yukon Tourism & Culture, PO Box 2703, Whitehorse, Y1A 2C6 YT
867-667-5036, Fax: 867-667-3546
Yukon Lottery Commission, 312 Wood St., Whitehorse, YT Y1A 2E6
867-633-7890, Fax: 867-668-7561, lotteriesyukon@gov.yk.ca

RECYCLING

Alberta

Alberta Recycling Management Authority, Scotia Tower 1, #1310, 10060 Jasper Ave., PO Box 189, Edmonton, AB T5J 2J1
780-990-1111, Fax: 780-990-1122, 888-999-8762, info@albertarecycling.ca

Newfoundland & Labrador

Multi-Materials Stewardship Board, PO Box 8131 A, St. John's, NL A1B 3M9
709-753-0948, Fax: 709-753-0974

RESEARCH & DEVELOPMENT

Bayfield Institute, 867 Lakeshore Rd., PO Box 5050, Burlington, L7R 4A6 ON
905-336-6240
Bedford Institute of Oceanography, 1 Challenger Dr., PO Box 1006, Dartmouth, B2Y 4A2 NS
902-426-3492, Fax: 902-426-8484
Biotechnology Research Institute, 6100, av Royalmount, Montréal, H4P 2R2 QC
514-496-6100, Fax: 514-496-1928, bri-info@cnrc-nrc.gc.ca
Canada Centre for Remote Sensing - Geomatics Canada, 588 Booth St., Ottawa, K1A 0Y7 ON
613-995-0947, Fax: 613-947-1382
Canadian Hydraulics Centre, 1200 Montreal Rd., Ottawa, K1A 0R6 ON
613-993-9381, Fax: 613-952-7679, info.chc@nrc-cnrc.gc.ca
Canadian Space Agency, 6767, rte de l'Aéroport, Saint-Hubert, J3Y 8Y9 QC
450-926-4800, Fax: 450-926-4352, webmaster@space.gc.ca
Centre for Surface Transportation Technology, 2320 Lester Rd., Ottawa, K1V 1S2 ON
613-998-9639, Fax: 613-957-0831, inquiries.cstt@nrc-cnrc.gc.ca
Fisheries Resource Conservation Council, PO Box 2001 D, Ottawa, ON K1P 5W3
613-998-0433, Fax: 613-998-1146, info@frcc-ccrh.ca
Freshwater Institute, 501 University Cres., Winnipeg, R3T 2N6 MB
204-983-5000, Fax: 204-983-6285
Herzberg Institute of Astrophysics, 5071 West Saanich Rd., Victoria, V9E 2E7 BC
250-363-0001, Fax: 250-363-0045, hia-www@nrc-cnrc.gc.ca
Industrial Materials Institute, 75, boul de Mortagne, Boucherville, J4B 6Y4 QC
450-641-5000, Fax: 450-641-5101, Imi-Info@cnrc-nrc.gc.ca
Institut Maurice-Lamontagne, 850, rte de le Mer, CP 1000, Mont-Joli, G5H 3Z4 QC
418-775-0555, Fax: 418-775-0730
Institute for Aerospace Research, 1200 Montreal Rd., Ottawa, K1A 0R6 ON
613-990-0765, Fax: 613-952-7214
Institute for Biological Sciences, Bldg. M-54, 1200 Montreal Rd., Ottawa, K1A 0R6 ON
613-993-5812, Fax: 613-957-7867
Institute for Chemical Process & Environmental Technology, Bldg. M-12, 1200 Montreal Rd., Ottawa, K1A 0R6 ON
613-993-4041, Fax: 613-957-8231
Institute for Marine Biosciences, 1411 Oxford St., Halifax, B3H 3Z1 NS
902-426-8332, Fax: 902-426-9413, communications.imb@nrc-cnrc.gc.ca
Institute for National Measurement Standards, Bldg. M-36, 1500 Montreal Rd., Ottawa, K1A 0R6 ON
613-998-7018, Fax: 613-954-1473, alexandra.shaw@nrc-cnrc.gc.ca
Institute for Ocean Technology, Kerwin Pl. & Arctic Ave., PO Box 12093, St. John's, A1B 3T5 NL
709-772-4939, Fax: 709-772-2462, Noel.Murphy@nrc-cnrc.gc.ca
Institute for Research in Construction, Bldg. M-24, 1500 Montreal Rd., Ottawa, K1A 0R6 ON
613-993-2607, Fax: 613-952-7673, Irc.Client-Services@nrc-cnrc.gc.ca
Institute of Ocean Sciences, 9860 West Saanich Rd., PO Box 6000, Sidney, V8L 4B2 BC
250-363-6517, Fax: 250-363-6390
London - Centre for Automotive Materials and Manufacturing, 800 Collip Circle, London, N6G 4X8 ON
519-430-7166, Fax: 519-430-7064, John.Lyons@nrc-cnrc.gc.ca
National Institute of Nanotechnology, Bldg. NINT, University of Alberta, 11421 Saskatchewan Dr., Edmonton, T6G 2M9 AB
780-641-1600, Fax: 780-641-1601, nintinfo@nrc.gc.ca
National Research Council Canada, Bldg. M-58, 1200 Montreal Rd., Ottawa, K1A 0R6 ON
613-993-9101, Fax: 613-952-7928, 877-672-2672, info@nrc-cnrc.gc.ca
Natural Sciences & Engineering Research Council of Canada, Constitution Square, Tower II, 350 Albert St., Ottawa, K1A 1H5 ON
613-995-4273, Fax: 613-943-1624, marie-josee.duval@nserc-crsng.gc.ca
Pacific Biological Station, 3190 Hammond Bay Rd., Nanaimo, V9T 6N7 BC
250-756-7000, Fax: 250-756-7053
Plant Biotechnology Institute, 110 Gymnasium Pl., Saskatoon, S7N 0W9 SK
306-975-5248, Fax: 306-975-4839, pbi-info@nrc-cnrc.gc.ca
Research Branch, Tower 5, 1341 Baseline Rd., Ottawa, K1A 0C5 ON
613-759-1000, Fax: 613-773-1866
St. Andrews Biological Station, 531 Brandy Cove Rd., St Andrews, E5B 2L9 NB
506-529-8854, Fax: 506-529-5862, XMARSABS@mar.dfo-mpo.gc.ca

Alberta

Alberta Science & Research Authority, Phipps-McKinnon Bldg., #500, 10020 - 101A Ave., Edmonton, AB T5J 3G2
780-427-1488, Fax: 780-427-0979, asra@gov.ab.ca

British Columbia

Powertech Labs Inc., 12388 - 88 Ave., Surrey, BC V8W 7R7
604-590-7500, Fax: 604-590-5347, info@powertechlans.com

New Brunswick

New Brunswick Research & Productivity Council, 921 College Hill Rd., Fredericton, E3B 6Z9 NB
506-452-1212, Fax: 506-452-1395, info@rpc.ca
Service New Brunswick, Westmorland Place, #200, 82 Westmorland St., PO Box 1998, Fredericton, E3B 5G4 NB
506-457-3581, Fax: 506-457-7520, 888-762-8600, snb@snb.ca

Newfoundland & Labrador

Department of Innovation, Trade & Rural Development, West Block, Confederation Bldg., PO Box 8700, St. John's, A1B 4J6 NL
709-729-7000, Fax: 709-729-0654, 800-563-2299, itrd@gov.nl.ca

Northwest Territories

Aurora Research Institute, 191 MacKenzie Rd., PO Box 1450, Inuvik, X0E 0T0 NT
867-777-3298, Fax: 867-777-4264, webmaster@nwtresearch.com

Ontario

Ministry of Research & Innovation, Ferguson Block, 77 Wellesley St. West, 12th Fl., Toronto, M7A 1N3 ON
416-325-5181, Fax: 416-325-3877, 866-446-5216
Science & Information Resources Division, Robinson Place, North Tower, 300 Water St., 2nd Fl., Peterborough, K9J 8M5 ON
705-755-2000, Fax: 705-755-2802, 800-667-1940

Prince Edward Island

Agricultural Insurance Corporation, 29 Indigo Cres., PO Box 1600, Charlottetown, PE C1A 7N3
902-368-4842, Fax: 902-368-6677, peiaic@gov.pe.ca
Food Technology Centre, 101 Belvedere Ave., PO Box 2000, Charlottetown, PE C1A 7N8
902-368-5548, Fax: 902-368-5549, 877-368-5548, ftcweb@gov.pe.ca

Quebec

Centre de recherche industrielle du Québec, 333, rue Franquet, Québec, QC G1P 4C7
418-659-1550, Fax: 418-652-2251, 800-667-2386, infocriq@criq.qc.ca
Fonds de la recherche en santé du Québec, #800, 500, rue Sherbrooke ouest, Montréal, QC H3A 3C6
514-873-2114, Fax: 514-873-8768
Fonds québécois de la recherche sur la nature et les technologies, #450, 140, Grande Allée est, Québec, QC G1R 5M8
418-643-8560, Fax: 418-643-1451, info@fqrnt.gouv.qc.ca
Innovatech Québec, #120, 925, Grande Allée ouest, Québec, QC G1S 1C1
418-528-9770, Fax: 418-528-9783, 866-605-1676, info@innovatech-regions.qc.ca
Société générale de financement du Québec, #1500, 600, rue de La Gauchetière ouest, Montréal, QC H3B 4L8
514-876-9290, Fax: 514-395-8055, info@sgfqc.com

Saskatchewan

Saskatchewan Power Corporation (SaskPower), 2025 Victoria Ave., Regina, S4P 0S1 SK
306-566-2121, Fax: 306-566-2330, 800-667-4749
Saskatchewan Research Council, #125, 15 Innovation Blvd., Saskatoon, S7N 2X8 SK
306-933-5400, Fax: 306-933-7446, info@src.sk.ca

ROUND TABLES

National Round Table on the Environment & Economy, #200, 344 Slater St., Ottawa, K1R 7Y3 ON
613-992-7189, Fax: 613-992-7385, admin@nrtee-trnee.ca

Manitoba

Manitoba Round Table for Sustainable Development, #160, 123 Main St., Winnipeg, R3C 1A5 MB
204-945-1671, Fax: 204-948-2357, mrtsd@gov.mb.ca

New Brunswick

New Brunswick Round Table on Environment & Economy, 20 McGloin St., PO Box 6000, Fredericton, NB E3B 5H1
506-453-3703, Fax: 506-453-3876

SALES TAX

Alberta

Financial Sector Regulation & Policy, Terrace Building, 9515 - 107 St., 4th Fl., Edmonton, T5K 2C3 AB

Manitoba

Taxation Division, #101, 401 York Ave., Winnipeg, R3C 0P8 MB 204-945-6444, Fax: 204-948-2360

New Brunswick

Revenue & Taxation, Centennial Bldg., #671, 670 King St., PO Box 3000, Fredericton, E3B 5G5 NB 506-444-2826, Fax: 506-444-4920

Northwest Territories

Department of Finance, YK Center, 3rd Fl., PO Box 1320, Yellowknife, X1A 2L9 NT 867-669-2311, Fax: 867-873-0385

Nova Scotia

Tax Commission, Maritime Centre, 1505 Barrington St., Halifax, B3J 3K5 NS 902-424-5200, Fax: 902-424-0720, 800-670-4357

Nunavut

Department of Finance, Bldg. 1079, 1st Fl., PO Box 1000 Stn 330,Iqaluit, X0A 0H0 NU 867-975-5800, Fax: 867-975-5805

Prince Edward Island

Department of the Provincial Treasury, Shaw Bldg., 95 Rochford St., 2nd Fl. South, PO Box 2000, Charlottetown, C1A 7N8 PE 902-368-4050, Fax: 902-368-6575

Quebec

Centre de perception fiscale, 3800, rue de Marly, Secteur 6-4-3, Québec, G1X 4A5 QC

SCIENCE & NATURE

Agriculture & Agri-Food Canada, 1341 Baseline Rd., Ottawa, K1A 0C5 ON 613-773-1000, Fax: 613-773-2772, 866-345-7972, info@agr.gc.ca

Atomic Energy of Canada Limited, Head Office, Sheridan Science & Technology Park, 2251 Speakman Dr., Mississauga, L5K 1B2 ON 905-823-9040, 866-886-2325, librarycr@aecl.ca (Library); speakers@aecl.ca (Community speakers)

Beverly & Qamanirjuaq Caribou Management Board, Secretariat, PO Box 629, Stonewall, MB R0C 2Z0 204-467-2438, rossthompson@mymts.net

Canada Centre for Remote Sensing - Geomatics Canada, 588 Booth St., Ottawa, K1A 0Y7 ON 613-995-0947, Fax: 613-947-1382

Canadian Institutes of Health Research, 160 Elgin St., 9th Fl., Ottawa, K1A 0W9 ON 613-941-2672, Fax: 613-954-1800, 888-603-4178, info@cihr-irsc.gc.ca

Canadian Nuclear Safety Commission, 280 Slater St., PO Box 1046 B,Ottawa, K1P 5S9 ON 613-995-5894, Fax: 613-995-5086, 800-668-5284, info@cnsc-ccsn.gc.ca

Canadian Polar Commission, Constitution Square, #1710, 360 Albert St., Ottawa, K1R 7X7 ON 613-943-8605, Fax: 613-943-8607, 888-765-2701, mail@polarcom.gc.ca

Canadian Space Agency, 6767, rte de l'Aéroport, Saint-Hubert, J3Y 8Y9 QC 450-926-4800, Fax: 450-926-4352, webmaster@space.gc.ca

Centre for Surface Transportation Technology, 2320 Lester Rd., Ottawa, K1V 1S2 ON 613-998-9639, Fax: 613-957-0831, inquiries.cstt@nrc-cnrc.gc.ca

Electronic Commerce Branch, 300 Slater St., Ottawa, ON K1A 0C8 613-990-4268, Fax: 613-941-0178, 800-328-6189,

Environment Canada, 10 Wellington St., Gatineau, K1A 0H3 QC 819-997-2800, Fax: 819-994-1412, 800-668-6767, enviroinfo@ec.gc.ca

Commission for Environmental Cooperation, Secretariat, #200, 393, rue St-Jacques ouest, Montréal, H2Y 1N9 QC 514-350-4300, Fax: 514-350-4314, info@cec.org

Fisheries & Aquaculture Management, 200 Kent St., Ottawa, K1A 0E6 ON

Fisheries & Oceans Canada, 200 Kent St., Ottawa, K1A 0E6 ON 613-993-0999, Fax: 613-996-1866, info@dfo-mpo.gc.ca

Fisheries Resource Conservation Council, PO Box 2001 D, Ottawa, ON K1P 5W3 613-998-0433, Fax: 613-998-1146, info@frcc-ccrh.ca

Geological Survey of Canada, 601 Booth St., Ottawa, K1A 0E8 ON 613-996-3919, Fax: 613-943-8742, esic@nrcan.gc.ca

Hazardous Materials Information Review Commission, 427 Laurier Ave. West, 7th Fl., Ottawa, ON K1A 1M3 613-993-4331, Fax: 613-993-4686, hmirc-ccrmd@hc-sc.gc.ca

Indian & Northern Affairs Canada, 10 Wellington St., North Tower, Gatineau, K1A 0H4 QC 819-997-0380, Fax: 819-953-3017, 866-817-3977, infopubs@ainc-inac.gc.ca

Indian Oil & Gas Canada, #100, 9911 Chula Blvd., Tsuu T'ina (Sarcee), AB T2W 6H6 403-292-5625, Fax: 403-292-5618, ContactIOGC@inac-ainc.gc.ca

Institute for Aerospace Research, 1200 Montreal Rd., Ottawa, K1A 0R6 ON 613-990-0765, Fax: 613-952-7214

Institute for Information Technology, Bldg. M-50, 1200 Montreal Rd., Ottawa, K1A 0R6 ON 613-991-3373, Fax: 613-952-0074, 877-672-2672

International Development Research Centre, 150 Kent St., PO Box 8500, Ottawa, K1P 0B2 ON 613-236-6163, Fax: 613-238-7230, info@idrc.ca

Mackenzie Valley Environmental Impact Review Board, 200 Scotia Centre, 5102 - 50th Ave., PO Box 938, Yellowknife, NT X1A 2N7 867-766-7050, Fax: 867-766-7074, 866-912-3472, tcharlo@reviewboard.ca

National Energy Board, 444 - 7 Ave. SW, Calgary, T2P 0X8 AB 403-292-4800, Fax: 403-292-5503, 800-899-1265, info@neb-one.gc.ca

National Research Council Canada, Bldg. M-58, 1200 Montreal Rd., Ottawa, K1A 0R6 ON 613-993-9101, Fax: 613-952-7928, 877-672-2672, info@nrc-cnrc.ca

National Round Table on the Environment & Economy, #200, 344 Slater St., Ottawa, K1R 7Y3 ON 613-992-7189, Fax: 613-992-7385, admin@nrtee-trnee.ca

Natural Resources Canada, 580 Booth St., Ottawa, K1A 0E4 ON 613-995-0947, Fax: 613-992-7211

Natural Sciences & Engineering Research Council of Canada, Constitution Square, Tower II, 350 Albert St., Ottawa, K1A 1H5 ON 613-995-4273, Fax: 613-943-1624, marie-josee.duval@nserc-crsng.gc.ca

Nunavut Impact Review Board, PO Box 1360, Cambridge Bay, NU X0B 0C0 867-983-4600, Fax: 867-983-2594, 866-233-3033, info@nirb.ca

Nunavut Water Board, PO Box 119, Gjoa Haven, NU X0B 1J0 867-360-6338, Fax: 867-360-6369

Pest Management Regulatory Agency, 2720 Riverside Dr., Ottawa, ON K1A 0K9 613-736-3401, Fax: 613-736-3798

Porcupine Caribou Management Board, PO Box 31723, Whitehorse, YT Y1A 6L3 867-633-4780, Fax: 867-393-3904, pcmb@taiga.net

Science Sector, 200 Kent St., Ottawa, K1A 0E6 ON

Social Sciences & Humanities Research Council of Canada, Constitution Sq., 350 Albert St., PO Box 1610 B,Ottawa, K1P 6G4 ON 613-992-0691, Fax: 613-992-1787, info@sshrc.ca

Alberta

Alberta Agriculture & Rural Development, J.G. O'Donoghue Bldg., 7000 - 113 St., 1st Fl., Edmonton, T6H 5T6 AB 780-427-2727, Fax: 780-427-2861, 866-882-7677

Alberta Agricultural Research Institute, Phipps-McKinnon Bldg., #500, 10020 - 101A Ave., Edmonton, AB T5J 3G2 780-427-1956, Fax: 780-427-3252, aarimail@gov.ab.ca

Alberta Environmental Appeals Board, Peace Hills Trust Tower, #306, 10011 - 109 St. NW, Edmonton, AB T5J 3S8 780-427-6207, Fax: 780-427-4693

Alberta Ingenuity Fund, 250 Karl Clark Rd., Edmonton, AB T6N 1E4 780-450-5111, Fax: 780-450-5333, info@albertaingenuity.ca

Alberta Innovates - Health Solutions, #1500, 10104 - 103 Ave, Edmonton, AB T5J 4A7 780-423-5727, Fax: 780-429-3509, 877-423-5727, health@albertainnovates.ca

Alberta Recycling Management Authority, Scotia Tower 1, #1310, 10060 Jasper Ave., PO Box 189, Edmonton, AB T5J 2J1 780-990-1111, Fax: 780-990-1122, 888-999-8762, info@albertarecycling.ca

Alberta Science & Research Authority, Phipps-McKinnon Bldg., #500, 10020 - 101A Ave., Edmonton, AB T5J 3G2 780-427-1488, Fax: 780-427-0979, asra@gov.ab.ca

Alberta Special Areas Board, 212 - 2nd Ave. West, PO Box 820, Hanna, AB T0J 1P0 403-854-5600, Fax: 403-854-5527, specarea@telusplanet.net

Alberta Sport, Recreation, Parks & Wildlife Foundation, Standard Life Centre, 10405 Jasper Ave., 9th Fl., Edmonton, AB T5J 4R7 780-415-1167, Fax: 780-415-0308

Alberta Used Oil Management Association, Scotia One, Scotia Place, #1050, 10060 Jasper Ave., Edmonton, AB T5J 3R8 780-414-1510, Fax: 780-414-1519, reception@usedoilrecycling.ca

Beverage Container Management Board, #750, 10707 - 100 Ave., Edmonton, AB T5J 3M1 780-424-3193, Fax: 780-428-4620, 888-424-7671, info@bcmb.ab.ca

Clean Air Strategic Alliance, Centre West Bldg, 10035 - 108 St., 10th Fl., Edmonton, AB T5J 3E1 780-427-9793, Fax: 780-422-3127, casa@casahome.org

Alberta Energy, North Petroleum Plaza, 9945 - 108 St., 10th Fl., Edmonton, T5K 2G6 AB 780-427-8050, Fax: 780-422-0698, 780-310-0000

Alberta Environment, South Tower, Petroleum Plaza, 9915 - 108 St., 10th Fl., Edmonton, T5K 2G8 AB 780-427-2700, Fax: 780-422-4086, env.infocent@gov.ab.ca

Farmers' Advocate of Alberta, 7000 - 113 St., 3rd Fl., Edmonton, AB T6H 5T6 780-427-2433, Fax: 780-427-3913, farmers.advocate@gov.ab.ca

Informatics Circle of Research Excellence, 3608 - 33 St. NW, Calgary, AB T2L 2A6 780-450-5111, Fax: 403-210-5337, techfutures@albertainnovates.ca

Irrigation Council, Provincial Bldg., 200 - 5 Ave. South, 3rd Fl., PO Bag 3014, Lethbridge, AB T1J 4L1 403-381-5176, Fax: 403-382-4406

Land Compensation/Surface Rights Board, Phipps-McKinnon Bldg., 10020 - 101A Ave., 18th Fl., Edmonton, AB T5J 3G2 780-427-2444, Fax: 780-427-5798

Natural Resources Conservation Board, Sterling Place, 9940 - 106 St., 4th Fl., Edmonton, AB T5K 2N2 780-422-1977, Fax: 780-427-0607, 866-383-6722

Alberta Sustainable Resource Development, Information Centre, 9920 - 108 St., Main Fl., Edmonton, T5K 2M4 AB 780-944-0313, Fax: 780-427-4407, 877-944-0313, srd.infocent@gov.ab.ca

British Columbia

Agricultural Land Commission, #133, 4940 Canada Way, Burnaby, BC V5G 4K6 604-660-7000, Fax: 604-660-7033

Ministry of Agriculture & Lands, PO Box 9120 Prov Govt,Victoria, V8W 9E2 BC 250-387-5121, Fax: 250-387-1522

British Columbia Farm Industry Review Board, 1007 Fort St., 3rd Fl., PO Box 9129 Prov Govt, Victoria, BC V8W 9B5 250-356-8945, Fax: 250-356-5131, firb@gov.bc.ca

Emergency Management BC, 525 Fort St., 2nd Fl., PO Box 9223 Prov Govt,Victoria, V8W 9J1 BC 250-953-4002, Fax: 250-953-4081, BC.CorSer@gov.bc.ca (Coroner); OFC@gov.bc.ca (Fire Commissioner)

Ministry of Energy, Mines & Petroleum Resources, PO Box 9318 Prov Govt,Victoria, V8W 9N3 BC 250-952-0241

Ministry of Environment, PO Box 9339 Prov Govt,Victoria, V8W 9M1 BC 250-387-1161, Fax: 250-387-5669, www.envmail@gov.bc.ca

Environmental Appeal Board, 747 Fort St., 4th Fl., PO Box 9425 Prov Govt, Victoria, BC V8W 9V1 250-387-3464, Fax: 250-356-9923, eabinfo@gov.bc.ca

British Columbia Environmental Assessment Office, 836 Yates St., 1st Fl., PO Box 9426 Prov Govt,Victoria, V8W 9V1 BC 250-356-7441, Fax: 250-356-7440, eaoinfo@gov.bc.ca

Environmental Protection Division, 2975 Jutland Rd., 5th Fl., PO Box 9339, Victoria, V8W 9M1 BC 250-387-1288, Fax: 250-387-5669

Environmental Stewardship Division, 2975 Jutland Rd., 5th Fl., PO Box 9339 Prov Govt,Victoria, V8T 5J9 BC 250-356-0121, Fax: 250-953-3414

Forest Appeals Commission, 747 Fort St., 4th Fl., PO Box 9425 Prov Govt, Victoria, BC V8W 9V1 250-387-3464, Fax: 250-356-9923, facinfo@gov.bc.ca

Forest Practices Board, 1675 Douglas St., 3rd Fl., PO Box 9905 Prov Govt, Victoria, BC V8W 9R1 250-387-7964, Fax: 250-387-7009, 800-994-5899, fpboard@gov.bc.ca

Forestry Innovation Investments, #1200, 1130 West Pender St., Vancouver, BC V6E 4A4 604-685-7507, Fax: 604-685-5373, info@bcfii.ca

Ministry of Forests & Range, PO Box 9529 Prov Govt,Victoria, V8W 9C3 BC 250-387-4809, Fax: 250-953-3687

Fraser Basin Council, Central Office, 470 Granville St., 1st Fl., Vancouver, BC V6C 1V5 604-488-5350, Fax: 604-488-5351, info@fraserbasin.bc.ca

Islands Trust, #200, 1627 Fort St., Victoria, BC V8R 1H8
250-405-5151, Fax: 250-405-5155,
information@islandstrust.bc.ca
Oil & Gas Commission, #100, 10003 - 110 Ave., Fort St John, BC V1J 6M7
250-261-5700, 800-663-7867
Operations, 1520 Blanshard St., 3rd Fl., PO Box 9525 Prov Govt,Victoria, V8W 9C3 BC
250-387-1236, Fax: 250-953-3687,
Forests.OperationsDivisionExecutiveOffice@gov.bc.ca
Timber Export Advisory Committee, 1520 Blanshard St., 2nd Fl., PO Box 9514 Prov Govt, Victoria, BC V8W 9C2
250-387-8916, Fax: 250-387-5050

Manitoba

Manitoba Aboriginal & Northern Affairs, 59 Elizabeth Dr., PO Box 37, Thompson, R8N 1X4 MB
204-677-6607, Fax: 204-677-6753, amartin@gov.mb.ca
Aboriginal Affairs Secretariat, #200, 500 Portage Ave., Winnipeg, R3C 3X1 MB
204-945-2510, Fax: 204-945-3689
Agricultural Societies, 1129 Queens Ave., Brandon, MB R7A 1L9
204-726-6195, Fax: 204-726-6260
Manitoba Agriculture, Food & Rural Initiatives, Norquay Bldg., 401 York Ave., Winnipeg, R3C 0P8 MB
Clean Environment Commission, #305, 155 Carlton St., Winnipeg, MB R3C 3H8
204-945-0594, Fax: 204-945-0090
Manitoba Conservation, 200 Saulteaux Cres., Winnipeg, R3J 3W3 MB
204-945-6784, 800-214-6497, mincon@leg.gov.mb.ca
Ecological Reserves Advisory Committee, c/o Manitoba Conservation, Parks & Natural Areas Branch, 200 Saulteaux Cres., Winnipeg, MB R3J 3W3
204-945-4148, Fax: 204-945-0012, hhernandez@gov.mb.ca
Endangered Species Advisory Committee, 200 Saulteaux Cres., PO Box 24, Winnipeg, MB R3J 3W3
204-945-7465, Fax: 204-945-3077
Farm Lands Ownership Board, #812, Norquay Bldg., 401 York Ave., Winnipeg, MB R3C 0P8
204-945-3149, Fax: 204-945-1489, 800-282-8069,
robert.mckenzie@gov.mb.ca
Farm Machinery Board, Norquay Bldg., #812, 401 York Ave., Winnipeg, MB R3C 0P8
204-945-3856, Fax: 204-948-2844, randy.ozunko@gov.mb.ca
Manitoba Hydro, PO Box 815 Main,Winnipeg, R3C 2P4 MB
204-474-3311, Fax: 204-475-0069,
publicaffairs@hydro.mb.ca
Local Government Development Division, 59 Elizabeth Dr., PO Box 33, Thompson, R8N 1X4 MB
204-677-6794, Fax: 204-677-6525
Manitoba Habitat Heritage Corporation, #200, 1555 St. James St., Winnipeg, MB R3H 1B5
204-784-4350, Fax: 204-784-7359, mhhc@mhhc.mb.ca

New Brunswick

Department of Agriculture & Aquaculture, PO Box 6000, Fredericton, E3B 5H1 NB
506-453-2666, Fax: 506-453-7170, DAA-MAA@gnb.ca
Board of Examiners under the Scaler's Act, 1350 Regent St. South, PO Box 6000, Fredericton, NB E3B 5H1
506-453-2441, Fax: 506-453-6689
Business Development, Centennial Bldg., 670 King St., 5th Fl., PO Box 6000, Fredericton, E3B 5H1 NB
506-453-2111, Fax: 506-444-4182
Department of the Environment, Marysville Place, 20 McGloin St., PO Box 6000, Fredericton, E3B 5H1 NB
506-453-2690, Fax: 506-457-4991, env-info@gnb.ca
Forest Protection Limited, 2502 Hwy. 102, Lincoln, NB E3B 7E6
506-446-6930, Fax: 506-446-6934,
info@forestprotectionlimited.com
Department of Natural Resources, PO Box 6000, Fredericton, E3B 5H1 NB
506-453-2510, Fax: 506-444-5839, dnrweb@gnb.ca
New Brunswick Crop Insurance Commission, PO Box 6000, Fredericton, NB E3B 5H1
506-453-2185, Fax: 506-453-7406
New Brunswick Farm Products Commission, c/o Department of Agriculture & Aquaculture, PO Box 6000, Fredericton, NB E3B 5H1
506-453-3647, Fax: 506-444-5969
New Brunswick Round Table on Environment & Economy, 20 McGloin St., PO Box 6000, Fredericton, NB E3B 5H1
506-453-3703, Fax: 506-453-3876
New Brunswick Research & Productivity Council, 921 College Hill Rd., Fredericton, E3B 6Z9 NB
506-452-1212, Fax: 506-452-1395, info@rpc.ca
Service New Brunswick, Westmorland Place, #200, 82 Westmorland St., PO Box 1998, Fredericton, E3B 5G4 NB
506-457-3581, Fax: 506-457-7520, 888-762-8600,
snb@snb.ca

Newfoundland & Labrador

C.A. Pippy Park Commission, Mount Scio House, 15 Mount Scio Rd., St. John's, NL A1B 3T2
709-737-3655, Fax: 709-737-3303, 877-477-3655,
pippyparkinfo@nf.aibn.com
Canada-Newfoundland Offshore Petroleum Board, TD Place, 140 Water St., 5th Fl., St. John's, NL A1C 6H6
709-778-1400, Fax: 709-778-1473, postmaster@cnlopb.nl.ca
Department of Environment & Conservation, Confederation Bldg., West Block, 4th Fl., PO Box 8700, St. John's, A1B 4J6 NL
709-729-2664, Fax: 709-729-6639, 800-563-6181,
info@gov.nl.ca
Department of Fisheries & Aquaculture, Petten Bldg., 30 Strawberry Marsh Rd., PO Box 8700, St. John's, A1B 4J6 NL
709-729-3723, Fax: 709-729-6082,
fishaqwebmaster@gov.nl.ca
Department of Innovation, Trade & Rural Development, West Block, Confederation Bldg., PO Box 8700, St. John's, A1B 4J6 NL
709-729-7000, Fax: 709-729-0654, 800-563-2299,
itrd@gov.nl.ca
Department of Natural Resources, Natural Resources Bldg., 50 Elizabeth Ave., 7th Fl., PO Box 8700, St. John's, A1B 4J6 NL
709-729-2920, Fax: 709-729-0059
Professional Fish Harvesters Certification Board, 15 Hallett Cres., PO Box 8541, St. John's, NL A1B 3P2
709-722-8170, Fax: 709-722-8201, pfh@pfhcb.com

Northwest Territories

Aurora Research Institute, 191 MacKenzie Rd., PO Box 1450, Inuvik, X0E 0T0 NT
867-777-3298, Fax: 867-777-4264,
webmaster@nwtresearch.com
Department of Environment & Natural Resources, PO Box 1320, Yellowknife, X1A 2L9 NT

Nova Scotia

Department of Agriculture, 1741 Brunswick St., 3rd Fl., PO Box 2223, Halifax, B3J 3C4 NS
902-424-4560, Fax: 902-424-4671
Canada-Nova Scotia Offshore Petroleum Board, TD Centre, 1791 Barrington St., 6th Fl., Halifax, NS B3J 3K9
902-422-5588, Fax: 902-422-1799,
postmaster@cnsopb.ns.ca
Crown Lands Record Centre, Founders Square, #501, 1701 Hollis St., PO Box 698, Halifax, NS B3J 2T9
902-424-8681
Department of Natural Resources, Founder's Square, 1701 Hollis St., 3rd Fl., PO Box 698, Halifax, B3J 2T9 NS
902-424-5935, Fax: 902-424-0594, 800-565-2224
Nova Scotia Crop & Livestock Insurance Commission, MacRae Library Bldg., #2, 137 College Rd., PO Box 1092, Truro, NS B2N 5G9
902-893-7755, Fax: 902-895-4622, 800-565-6371,
nsclic@gov.ns.ca
Nova Scotia Farm Loan Board, PO Box 550, Truro, NS B2N 5E3
902-893-6506, Fax: 902-895-7693, flb@gov.ns.ca
Nova Scotia Geomatics Centre, 160 Willow St., Amherst, B4H 3W3 NS
902-667-7231, Fax: 902-667-6008, 800-798-0706,
info@nsgc.gov.ns.ca

Nunavut

Department of Environment, PO Box 1000 1300,Iqaluit, X0A 0H0 NU
867-975-7700, Fax: 867-975-7742, 866-222-9063,
environment@gov.nu.ca

Ontario

Advisory Council on Drinking Water Quality & Testing Standards, 40 St. Clair Ave. West, 3rd Fl., Toronto, ON M4V 1M2
416-212-7779, Fax: 416-212-7595
Ministry of Agriculture, Food & Rural Affairs, 1 Stone Rd. West, Guelph, N1G 4Y2 ON
519-826-3100, 888-466-2372
Algonquin Forestry Authority - Huntsville, 222 Main St. West, Huntsville, ON P1H 1Y1
705-789-9647, Fax: 705-789-3353
Algonquin Forestry Authority - Pembroke, Victoria Centre, 84 Isabella St., 2nd Fl., Pembroke, ON K8A 5S5
613-735-0173, Fax: 613-735-4192
Animal Care Review Board, 77 Grenville St., 8th Fl., Toronto, ON M5S 1B3
416-314-3509, Fax: 416-314-3518
Association of Ontario Land Surveyors, 1043 McNicoll Ave., Toronto, ON M1W 3W6
416-491-9020, Fax: 416-491-2576, admin@aols.org
Cancer Care Ontario, 620 University Ave., 15th Fl., Toronto, ON M5G 2L7
416-971-9800, Fax: 416-971-6888
Conservation Review Board, 400 University Ave. 4th Fl., Toronto, ON M7A 2R9
416-314-7137, Fax: 416-314-7175
Crown Timber Board of Examiners, Roberta Bondar Place, #400, 70 Foster Dr., Sault Ste Marie, ON P6A 6V5
705-945-6643
Ministry of Environment, 135 St. Clair Ave. West, Toronto, M4V 1P5 ON
416-325-4000, Fax: 416-325-3159, 800-565-4923
Environmental Commissioner of Ontario, #605, 1075 Bay St., Toronto, M5S 2B1 ON
416-325-3377, Fax: 416-325-3370, 800-701-6454,
commissioner@eco.on.ca
Environmental Review Tribunal, #1700, 2300 Yonge St., PO Box 2382, Toronto, ON M4P 1E4
416-314-4600, Fax: 416-314-4506
Fish & Wildlife Heritage Commission, Robinson Pl., 300 Water St., PO Box 7000, Peterborough, ON K9J 8M5
Fax: 705-755-5093
Lake of the Woods Control Board, c/o Executive Engineer, Ottawa, ON K1A 0H3
Fax: 819-953-4666, 800-661-5922, secretariat@lwcb.ca
Livestock Medicines Advisory Committee, 1 Stone Rd. West, 3rd Fl. NE, Guelph, ON N1G 4Y2
519-826-4110, Fax: 519-826-3254
Mines & Minerals Division, Willet Green Miller Centre, 933 Ramsey Lake Rd., 6th Fl., Sudbury, P3E 6B5 ON
705-670-5755, Fax: 705-670-5818
Ministry of Natural Resources, Whitney Block, #6630, 99 Wellesley St. West, 6th Fl., Toronto, M7A 1W3 ON
800-667-1940
Niagara Parks Commission, 7400 Portage Rd. South, PO Box 150, Niagara Falls, ON L2E 6T2
905-356-2241, Fax: 905-354-6041, 877-642-7275
Ministry of Northern Development, Mines & Forestry, 99 Wellesley St. West, Toronto, M7A 1W3 ON
416-327-0633, Fax: 416-327-0665
Ontario Clean Water Agency, 1 Yonge St., 17th Fl., Toronto, ON M5E 1E5
416-314-5600, Fax: 416-314-8300, 800-667-6292
Ontario Geographic Names Board, Robinson Place, 300 Water St., 2nd Fl., PO Box 7000, Peterborough, ON K9J 8M5
705-755-2134, Fax: 705-755-2131
Ontario Moose & Bear Allocation Advisory Committee, PO Box 964, Sioux Lookout, ON P8T 1B3
807-737-2615, Fax: 807-737-4173
Ontario Science Centre, 770 Don Mills Rd., Toronto, ON M3C 1T3
416-696-1000, Fax: 416-696-3124
Pesticides Advisory Committee, #1203, 2300 Yonge St., 12th Fl., Toronto, ON M4P 1E4
416-314-9230, Fax: 416-314-9237
Rabies Advisory Committee, Trent University Science Complex, PO Box 4840, Peterborough, ON K9J 8N8
705-755-2270
Royal Botanical Gardens, 680 Plains Rd. West, Burlington, ON L7T 4H4
905-527-1158, Fax: 905-577-0375, 800-694-4769
Science & Information Resources Division, Robinson Place, North Tower, 300 Water St., 2nd Fl., Peterborough, K9J 8M5 ON
705-755-2000, Fax: 705-755-2802, 800-667-1940
Science North, 100 Ramsey Lake Rd., Sudbury, ON P3E 5S9
705-522-3701, Fax: 705-522-4954, 800-461-4898
Shibogama Interim Planning Board, PO Box 105, Wunnumin, ON P0V 2Z0
807-442-2559, Fax: 807-442-2627
St. Lawrence Parks Commission, RR#1, Morrisburg, ON K0C 1X0
613-543-3704, Fax: 613-543-2847, 800-437-2233
Windigo Interim Planning Board, PO Box 299, Sioux Lookout, ON P8T 1A3
807-737-1585, Fax: 807-737-3133

Prince Edward Island

Agricultural Insurance Corporation, 29 Indigo Cres., PO Box 1600, Charlottetown, PE C1A 7N3
902-368-4842, Fax: 902-368-6677, peiaic@gov.pe.ca
Department of Agriculture, Jones Bldg., 11 Kent St., PO Box 2000, Charlottetown, C1A 7N8 PE
902-368-4880, Fax: 902-368-4857
Grain Elevators Corporation, PO Box 250, Kensington, PE C0B 1M0
902-836-8929
PEI Energy Corporation, Jones Bldg., 11 Kent St., 4th Fl., PO Box 2000, Charlottetown, PE C1A 7N8
902-894-0288, Fax: 902-368-0290

Quebec
Ministère de l'Agriculture, des Pêcheries et de l'Alimentation, 200, ch Sainte-Foy, Québec, G1R 4X6 QC
418-380-2110, 888-222-6272
Bureau d'audiences publiques sur l'environnement, Édifice Lomer-Gouin, #2.10, 575, rue Saint-Amable, 2e étage, Québec, QC G1R 6A6
418-643-7447, Fax: 418-643-9474, 800-463-4732, communication@bape.gouv.qc.ca
Comité consultatif de l'environnement Kativik, CP 930, Kuujjuaq, QC J0M 1C0
819-964-2961, Fax: 819-964-0694, ndea@krg.ca
Conseil de la science et de la technologie, 1150, Grande Allée ouest, RC, Québec, QC G1S 4Y9
418-691-5986, cst@cst.gouv.qc.ca
Fondation de la faune du Québec, Place Iberville II, #420, 1175, av Lavigerie, Québec, QC G1V 4P1
418-644-7926, Fax: 418-643-7655, 877-639-0742, ffq@riq.qc.ca
Fonds québécois de la recherche sur la nature et les technologies, #450, 140, Grande Allée est, Québec, QC G1R 5M8
418-643-8560, Fax: 418-643-1451, info@fqrnt.gouv.qc.ca
Ottawa River Regulation Planning Board, 351 St Joseph Blvd., Gatineau, QC J8Y 3Z5
613-997-1735, 800-778-1246, secretariat@ottawariver.ca
Ministère des Ressources naturelles et de la Faune, 880, ch Sainte-Foy, Québec, G1S 4X4 QC
418-627-8600, Fax: 418-644-6513, 866-248-6936, services.clientele@mrnf.gouv.qc.ca
Régie de l'énergie, Tour de la Bourse, #255, 800, Place Victoria, CP 1, Montréal, QC H4Z 1A2
514-873-2452, Fax: 514-873-2070, 888-873-2452, secretariat@regie-energie.qc.ca
Société de développement de la Baie James, 110, boul Matagami, CP 970, Matagami, QC J0Y 2A0
819-739-4717, Fax: 819-739-4329

Saskatchewan
Agri-Food Council, #302, 3085 Albert St., Regina, SK S4S 0B1
306-787-5139, Fax: 306-787-5134, james.kettel@gov.sk.ca
Agricultural Implements Board, #202, 3085 Albert St., Regina, SK S4S 0B1
306-787-4693, Fax: 306-787-1315
Saskatchewan Agriculture, Walter Scott Bldg., 3085 Albert St., Regina, S4S 0B1 SK
306-787-5140, 866-457-2377, aginfo@gov.sk.ca
Enterprise Saskatchewan, #200, 3085 Albert St., Regina, S4S 0B1 SK
Fax: 306-798-0629, 800-265-2001, Webmaster@enterprisesask.ca
Saskatchewan Environment, 3211 Albert St., 2nd Fl., Regina, S4S 5W6 SK
306-953-3750, Fax: 306-787-9544, 800-567-4224, inquiry@serm.gov.sk.ca
Farm Stress Unit, #329, 3085 Albert St., Regina, SK S4S 0B1
306-787-5196, Fax: 306-798-3042, 800-667-4442, ken.imhoff@gov.sk.ca
Health Quality Council, 241, 111 Research Dr., Saskatoon, SK S7N 3R2
306-668-8810, Fax: 306-668-8820
Saskatchewan Northern Affairs, Mistasinihk Place, 1328 La Ronge Ave., PO Box 5000, La Ronge, S0J 1L0 SK
306-425-4207, Fax: 306-425-4349, 866-663-4065, admin@sna.gov.sk.ca
Prairie Agricultural Machinery Institute, Hwy#5 West, PO Box 1900, Humboldt, SK S0K 2A0
306-682-2555, Fax: 306-682-5080, 800-567-7264, humboldt@pami.ca
Saskatchewan Research Council, #125, 15 Innovation Blvd., Saskatoon, S7N 2X8 SK
306-933-5400, Fax: 306-933-7446, info@src.sk.ca
Saskatchewan Conservation Data Centre, 3211 Albert St., Regina, SK S4S 5W6
306-787-9038, Fax: 306-787-9544
Saskatchewan Crop Insurance Corporation, 484 Prince William Dr., PO Box 3000, Melville, SK S0A 2P0
306-728-7200, Fax: 306-728-7268, 888-935-0000, customer.service@scic.gov.sk.ca
Saskatchewan Farm Land Security Board, #207, 3988 Albert St., Regina, SK S4S 3R1
306-787-5047, Fax: 306-787-8599, inquiries@farmland.gov.sk.ca
Saskatchewan Farm Security Programs, #207, 3988 Albert St., Regina, SK S4S 3R1
306-787-5047, Fax: 306-787-8599
Saskatchewan Lands Appeal Board, #202, 3085 Albert St., Regina, SK S4S 0B1
306-787-4693, Fax: 306-787-1315, dbrooks@agr.gov.sk.ca
Saskatchewan Watershed Authority, 111 Fairford St. East, Moose Jaw, SK S6H 7X9
306-694-3900, Fax: 306-694-3465, comm@swa.ca
Surface Rights Board of Arbitration, 113 - 2nd Ave. East, PO Box 1597, Kindersley, SK S0L 1S0
306-463-5447, Fax: 306-463-5449, SurfaceRightsBoard@gov.sk.ca

Yukon Territory
Alsek Renewable Resource Council, PO Box 2077, Haines Junction, YT Y0B 1L0
867-634-2524, Fax: 867-634-2527
Carmacks Renewable Resource Council, PO Box 122, Carmacks, YT Y0B 1C0
867-863-6838, Fax: 867-863-6429, carmacksrrc@lscfn.ca
Dawson District Renewable Resource Council, PO Box 1380, Dawson City, YT Y0B 1G0
867-993-6976, Fax: 867-993-6093, dawsonrrc@yknet.yk.ca
Yukon Development Corporation, PO Box 2703 D-1,Whitehorse, Y1A 2C6 YT
867-393-5337, Fax: 867-393-5401
Yukon Environment, PO Box 2703, Whitehorse, Y1A 2C6 YT
867-667-5652, Fax: 867-393-7197, 800-661-0408, environmentyukon@gov.yk.ca
Mayo District Renewable Resources Council, PO Box 249, Mayo, YT Y0B 1M0
867-996-2942, Fax: 867-996-2948, mayorrc@yknet.yk.ca
North Yukon Renewable Resources Council, PO Box 80, Old Crow, YT Y0B 1N0
vgrrc@yknet.yk.ca
Selkirk Renewable Resources Council, PO Box 32, Pelly Crossing, YT Y0B 1P0
867-537-3937, Fax: 867-537-3939, selkirkrre@yknet.yk.ca
Teslin Renewable Resource Council, PO Box 186, Teslin, YT Y0A 1B0
867-390-2323, Fax: 867-390-2919, teslinrrc@yknet.yk.ca
Yukon Fish & Wildlife Management Board, 106 Main St., Whitehorse, YT Y1A 5P7
867-667-3754, Fax: 867-393-6947, yfwmbadmin@yknet.yk.ca
Yukon Land Use Planning Council, #201, 307 Jarvis St., Whitehorse, YT Y1A 2H3
867-667-7397, Fax: 867-667-4624, ylupc@planyukon.ca

SCIENCE & TECHNOLOGY

See Also: Business Development
Bedford Institute of Oceanography, 1 Challenger Dr., PO Box 1006, Dartmouth, B2Y 4A2 NS
902-426-3492, Fax: 902-426-8484
Biotechnology Research Institute, 6100, av Royalmount, Montréal, H4P 2R2 QC
514-496-6100, Fax: 514-496-1928, bri-info@cnrc-nrc.gc.ca
Canada Centre for Remote Sensing - Geomatics Canada, 588 Booth St., Ottawa, K1A 0Y7 ON
613-995-0947, Fax: 613-947-1382
Canadian Food Inspection Agency, 1400 Merivale Rd., Ottawa, K1A 0Y9 ON
613-225-2342, Fax: 613-228-6629, 800-442-2342
Canadian Hydraulics Centre, 1200 Montreal Rd., Ottawa, K1A 0R6 ON
613-993-9381, Fax: 613-952-7679, info.chc@nrc-cnrc.gc.ca
Canadian Institutes of Health Research, 160 Elgin St., 9th Fl., Ottawa, K1A 0W9 ON
613-941-2672, Fax: 613-954-1800, 888-603-4178, info@cihr-irsc.gc.ca
Canadian Space Agency, 6767, rte de l'Aéroport, Saint-Hubert, J3Y 8Y9 QC
450-926-4800, Fax: 450-926-4352, webmaster@space.gc.ca
Freshwater Institute, 501 University Cres., Winnipeg, R3T 2N6 MB
204-983-5000, Fax: 204-983-6285
Herzberg Institute of Astrophysics, 5071 West Saanich Rd., Victoria, V9E 2E7 BC
250-363-0001, Fax: 250-363-0045, hia-www@nrc-cnrc.gc.ca
Industrial Materials Institute, 75, boul de Mortagne, Boucherville, J4B 6Y4 QC
450-641-5000, Fax: 450-641-5101, Imi-Info@cnrc-nrc.gc.ca
Institut Maurice-Lamontagne, 850, rte de le Mer, CP 1000, Mont-Joli, G5H 3Z4 QC
418-775-0555, Fax: 418-775-0730
Institute for Biological Sciences, Bldg. M-54, 1200 Montreal Rd., Ottawa, K1A 0R6 ON
613-993-5812, Fax: 613-957-7867
Institute for Chemical Process & Environmental Technology, Bldg. M-12, 1200 Montreal Rd., Ottawa, K1A 0R6 ON
613-993-4041, Fax: 613-957-8231
Institute for Marine Biosciences, 1411 Oxford St., Halifax, B3H 3Z1 NS
902-426-8332, Fax: 902-426-9413, communications.imb@nrc-cnrc.gc.ca
Institute for National Measurement Standards, Bldg. M-36, 1500 Montreal Rd., Ottawa, K1A 0R6 ON
613-998-7018, Fax: 613-954-1473, alexandra.shaw@nrc-cnrc.gc.ca
Institute for Ocean Technology, Kerwin Pl. & Arctic Ave., PO Box 12093, St. John's, A1B 3T5 NL
709-772-4939, Fax: 709-772-2462, Noel.Murphy@nrc-cnrc.gc.ca
Institute for Research in Construction, Bldg. M-24, 1500 Montreal Rd., Ottawa, K1A 0R6 ON
613-993-2607, Fax: 613-952-7673, Irc.Client-Services@nrc-cnrc.gc.ca
Institute of Ocean Sciences, 9860 West Saanich Rd., PO Box 6000, Sidney, V8L 4B2 BC
250-363-6517, Fax: 250-363-6390
International Development Research Centre, 150 Kent St., PO Box 8500, Ottawa, K1P 0B2 ON
613-236-6163, Fax: 613-238-7230, info@idrc.ca
National Research Council Canada, Bldg. M-58, 1200 Montreal Rd., Ottawa, K1A 0R6 ON
613-993-9101, Fax: 613-952-7928, 877-672-2672, info@nrc-cnrc.ca
Natural Sciences & Engineering Research Council of Canada, Constitution Square, Tower II, 350 Albert St., Ottawa, K1A 1H5 ON
613-995-4273, Fax: 613-943-1624, marie-josee.duval@nserc-crsng.gc.ca
Pacific Biological Station, 3190 Hammond Bay Rd., Nanaimo, V9T 6N7 BC
250-756-7000, Fax: 250-756-7053
Plant Biotechnology Institute, 110 Gymnasium Pl., Saskatoon, S7N 0W9 SK
306-975-5248, Fax: 306-975-4839, pbi-info@nrc-cnrc.gc.ca
Science Sector, 200 Kent St., Ottawa, K1A 0E6 ON
Spectrum, Information Technologies & Telecommunications, Journal Tower North, 300 Slater St., 20th Fl., Ottawa, K1A 0C8 ON
613-998-0368, Fax: 613-952-1203
St. Andrews Biological Station, 531 Brandy Cove Rd., St Andrews, E5B 2L9 NB
506-529-8854, Fax: 506-529-5862, XMARSABS@mar.dfo-mpo.gc.ca

Alberta
Alberta Science & Research Authority, Phipps-McKinnon Bldg., #500, 10020 - 101A Ave., Edmonton, AB T5J 3G2
780-427-1488, Fax: 780-427-0979, asra@gov.ab.ca

British Columbia
Leading Edge Endowment Fund Board, 1188 West Georgia St., 9th Fl., Vancouver, BC V6E 4A2
604-438-3220, Fax: 604-438-6564, contact@leefbc.ca
Powertech Labs Inc., 12388 - 88 Ave., Surrey, BC V8W 7R7
604-590-7500, Fax: 604-590-5347, info@powertechlans.com
Premier's Technology Council, #730, 999 Canada Pl., Vancouver, BC V6C 3E1
604-775-2122, Fax: 604-775-2129, premiers.technologycouncil@gov.bc.ca

Manitoba
Industrial Technology Centre, #200, 78 Innovation Dr., Winnipeg, MB R3T 6C2
Manitoba Education, Research & Learning Information Networks, #100 - 135 Innovation Dr., University of Manitoba, Winnipeg, MB R3T 6A8
204-474-7800, Fax: 204-474-7830, 800-430-6404
Manitoba Science, Technology, Energy & Mines, #333, 450 Broadway, Winnipeg, R3C 0V8 MB

New Brunswick
Business Development, Centennial Bldg., 670 King St., 5th Fl., PO Box 6000, Fredericton, E3B 5H1 NB
506-453-2111, Fax: 506-444-4182
New Brunswick Research & Productivity Council, 921 College Hill Rd., Fredericton, E3B 6Z9 NB
506-452-1212, Fax: 506-452-1395, info@rpc.ca
Sciences & Planning, Marysville Place, 20 McGloin St., 2nd Fl., PO Box 6000, Fredericton, E3B 5H1 NB
506-453-2862, Fax: 506-453-2265

Northwest Territories
Aurora Research Institute, 191 MacKenzie Rd., PO Box 1450, Inuvik, X0E 0T0 NT
867-777-3298, Fax: 867-777-4264, webmaster@nwtresearch.com

Nova Scotia
InNOVACorp, #1400, 1801 Hollis St., Halifax, NS B3J 3N4
902-424-8670, Fax: 902-424-4679, 800-565-7051, communications@innovacorp.ca

Ontario
Ontario Science Centre, 770 Don Mills Rd., Toronto, ON M3C 1T3
416-696-1000, Fax: 416-696-3124
Ministry of Research & Innovation, Ferguson Block, 77 Wellesley St. West, 12th Fl., Toronto, M7A 1N3 ON
416-325-5181, Fax: 416-325-3877, 866-446-5216
Science North, 100 Ramsey Lake Rd., Sudbury, ON P3E 5S9
705-522-3701, Fax: 705-522-4954, 800-461-4898

Prince Edward Island
Department of Environment, Energy & Forestry, Jones Bldg., 11 Kent St., 4th & 5th Fl., PO Box 2000, Charlottetown, C1A 7N8 PE
902-368-5000, Fax: 902-368-5830

Quebec
Centre de recherche industrielle du Québec, 333, rue Franquet, Québec, QC G1P 4C7
418-659-1550, Fax: 418-652-2251, 800-667-2386, infocriq@criq.qc.ca
Conseil de la science et de la technologie, 1150, Grande Allée ouest, RC, Québec, QC G1S 4Y9
418-691-5986, cst@cst.gouv.qc.ca
Fonds québécois de la recherche sur la nature et les technologies, #450, 140, Grande Allée est, Québec, QC G1R 5M8
418-643-8560, Fax: 418-643-1451, info@fqrnt.gouv.qc.ca
Société générale de financement du Québec, #1500, 600, rue de La Gauchetière ouest, Montréal, QC H3B 4L8
514-876-9290, Fax: 514-395-8055, info@sgfqc.com

Saskatchewan
Saskatchewan Research Council, #125, 15 Innovation Blvd., Saskatoon, S7N 2X8 SK
306-933-5400, Fax: 306-933-7446, info@src.sk.ca

Yukon Territory
Yukon Energy, Mines & Resources, PO Box 2703, Whitehorse, Y1A 2C6 YT
867-667-5466, Fax: 867-667-8601, 800-661-0408, emr@gov.yk.ca

SECURITIES ADMINISTRATION

See Also: Finance

Alberta
Alberta Securities Commission, 300 - 5 Ave. SW, 4th Fl., Calgary, AB T2P 3C4
403-297-6454, Fax: 403-297-6156, 877-355-0585, inquiries@asc.ca

British Columbia
British Columbia Securities Commission, Pacific Centre, 701 West Georgia St., 12th Fl., PO Box 10142, Vancouver, BC V7Y 1L2
604-899-6500, Fax: 604-899-6506, 800-373-6393, inquiries@bcsc.bc.ca

Manitoba
Manitoba Securities Commission, #500, 400 St. Mary Ave., Winnipeg, MB R3C 4K5
204-945-2548, Fax: 204-945-0330, 800-655-5244, securities@gov.mb.ca

New Brunswick
New Brunswick Securities Commission, #300, 85 Charlotte St., Saint John, NB E2L 2J2
506-658-3060, Fax: 506-658-3059, 866-933-2222, information@nbsc-cvmnb.ca

Northwest Territories
Department of Justice, Courthouse, 4903 - 49th St., 6th Fl., PO Box 1320, Yellowknife, X1A 2L9 NT
867-920-6197

Nova Scotia
Nova Scotia Securities Commission, Joseph Howe Bldg., 1690 Hollis St., 2nd Fl., PO Box 458, Halifax, NS B3J 2P8
902-424-7768, Fax: 902-424-4625

Ontario
Ontario Securities Commission, #1903, 20 Queen St. West, PO Box 55, Toronto, ON M5H 3S8
416-597-0681, Fax: 416-593-8122

Quebec
Autorité des marchés financiers, Tour de la Bourse, 800, Square Victoria, 22e étage, Montréal, QC H4Z 1G3
514-395-0337, Fax: 514-873-3090, 877-525-0337

Saskatchewan
Saskatchewan Financial Services Commission, #601, 1919 Saskatchewan Dr., Regina, SK S4P 4H2
306-787-5645, Fax: 306-787-5899

SENIOR CITIZENS SERVICES

National Advisory Council on Aging, Jeanne Mance Bldg., 8th Fl., Postal Locator 1908 A1, Ottawa, K1A 0K9 ON
613-957-1968, Fax: 613-957-7627
Office of the Commissioner of Review Tribunals, PO Box 8250 T, Ottawa, ON K1G 5S5
613-954-1313, Fax: 613-946-1588, 800-363-0076, info@ocrt-bctr.gc.ca

Alberta
Alberta Seniors & Community Supports, Standard Life Centre, 10405 Jasper Ave., Main Fl., Edmonton, T5J 4R7 AB
780-427-7876, Fax: 780-422-6301, 800-642-3853
Seniors Advisory Council for Alberta, Standard Life Centre, #600, 10405 Jasper Ave., Edmonton, AB T5J 4R7
780-422-2321, Fax: 780-422-8762

British Columbia
Rural Development, 800 Johnson St., 6th Fl., PO Box 9824 Prov Govt,Victoria, V8W 9W4 BC
250-953-3005, Fax: 250-387-7935

Manitoba
Manitoba Seniors & Healthy Aging Secretariat, #822, 155 Carlton St., Winnipeg, R3C 3H8 MB
204-945-6565, Fax: 204-948-2514, 800-665-6565, seniors@gov.mb.ca

New Brunswick
New Brunswick Advisory Council on Seniors, #620, 440 King St., Fredericton, NB E3B 5H8
506-444-5757, Fax: 506-446-784, 888-762-5411
Program Development & Monitoring, Sartain MacDonald Bldg., #4007, 551 King St., PO Box 6000, Fredericton, E3B 5H1 NB
506-453-2181, Fax: 506-453-3829

Nova Scotia
Seniors' Secretariat, Dennis Bldg., 1740 Granville St., 4th Fl., PO Box 2065, Halifax, NS B3J 2Z1
902-424-0065, Fax: 902-424-0561, 800-670-0065, scs@gov.ns.ca

Nunavut
Department of Culture, Language, Elders & Youth, PO Box 1000 800,Iqaluit, X0A 0H0 NU
867-975-5500, Fax: 867-975-5504, 866-934-2035

Ontario
Ontario Seniors' Secretariat, Ferguson Block, #601C, 777 Bay St., Toronto, M7A 2J4 ON
416-326-7076, Fax: 416-326-7078, 888-910-1999, infoseniors@ontario.ca

Prince Edward Island
Department of Social Services & Seniors, Jones Bldg., 11 Kent St., 2nd Fl., PO Box 2000, Charlottetown, C1A 7N8 PE
902-620-3777, Fax: 902-894-0242

Quebec
Conseil des aînés, #810, 900, boul René-Lévesque est, 8e étage, Québec, QC G1R 2B5
418-643-0071, Fax: 418-643-1916, 877-657-2463, aines@conseil-des-aines.qc.ca
Ministère de la Famille et des Aînés, 425, rue Saint-Amable, 1er étage, Québec, G1R 4Z1 QC
877-216-6202
Ministère de la Santé et des Services sociaux, Direction des communications et Renseignements généraux, 1075, ch Sainte-Foy, Québec, G1S 2M1 QC
418-266-8900, 800-707-3380, regisseur.web@msss.gouv.qc.ca

Saskatchewan
Community Living Division, 1920 Broad St., 10th fl., Regina, S4P 3V6 SK
306-787-7803, Fax: 306-798-4450

Yukon Territory
Yukon Health & Social Services, PO Box 2703, Whitehorse, Y1A 2C6 YT
867-667-3673, Fax: 867-667-3096, 800-661-0408, hss@gov.yk.ca

SEXUALLY TRANSMITTED DISEASE CONTROL

See Also: AIDS

Prince Edward Island
Department of Health, Jones Bldg., 11 Kent St., 2nd Fl., PO Box 2000, Charlottetown, C1A 7N8 PE
902-368-4900, Fax: 902-368-4974,

SOCIAL AFFAIRS

Ontario
Ontario Trillium Foundation, 45 Charles St. East, 5th Fl., Toronto, ON M4Y 1S2
416-963-4927, Fax: 416-963-8781, 800-263-2887, trillium@trilliumfoundation.org

SOCIAL SERVICES

See Also: Community Services
Homelessness Partnering Secretariat, 165, rue Hôtel-de-Ville, Gatineau, K1A 0J2 QC
Social Development, L'esplanade Laurier, Level 2, 300 Laurier Ave. West, Ottawa, K1A 0J6 ON
613-990-5100, Fax: 613-990-5091

Alberta
Alberta Children and Youth Services, Sterling Place, 9940 - 106 St., 12th Fl., Edmonton, T5K 2N2 AB
780-422-3004, Fax: 780-422-3071, 866-714-5437, cs.communications@gov.ab.ca
Alberta Seniors & Community Supports, Standard Life Centre, 10405 Jasper Ave., Main Fl., Edmonton, T5J 4R7 AB
780-427-7876, Fax: 780-422-6301, 800-642-3853

British Columbia
Board of Registration for Social Workers in BC, #302, 1765 West 8th Ave., Vancouver, BC V6J 5C6
604-737-4916, Fax: 604-737-6809, brsw@brsw.bc.ca
Ministry of Community & Rural Development, 800 Johnson St., 6th Fl., PO Box 9490 Prov Govt,Victoria, V8W 9N7 BC
250-387-2283, Fax: 250-387-4312, Feedback@gov.bc.ca

Manitoba
Social Services Appeal Board, 175 Hargrave St., 7th Fl., Winnipeg, MB R3C 3R8
204-945-3003, Fax: 204-945-1736, 800-282-8069

New Brunswick
Department of Social Development, Sartain MacDonald Bldg., 551 King St., PO Box 6000, Fredericton, E3B 5H1 NB
506-453-2001, Fax: 506-453-7478

Newfoundland & Labrador
Department of Human Resources, Labour & Employment, Confederation Bldg., PO Box 8700, St. John's, A1B 4J6 NL
709-729-2478, Fax: 709-729-6996, hreweb@gov.nl.ca

Northwest Territories
Department of Health & Social Services, Centre Square Tower, PO Box 1320, Yellowknife, X1A 2L9 NT
Fax: 867-873-0266

Nunavut
Department of Health & Social Services, Sivummut bldg., PO Box 1007 1000,Iqaluit, X0A 0H0 NU
867-975-5700, Fax: 867-975-5705, health@gov.nu.ca

Ontario
Program Management Division, Hepburn Block, 80 Grosvenor St., 6th Fl., Toronto, M7A 1E9 ON
416-325-5581, Fax: 416-325-5432

Prince Edward Island
Department of Social Services & Seniors, Jones Bldg., 11 Kent St., 2nd Fl., PO Box 2000, Charlottetown, C1A 7N8 PE
902-620-3777, Fax: 902-894-0242

Quebec
Ministère de la Santé et des Services sociaux, Direction des communications et Renseignements généraux, 1075, ch Sainte-Foy, Québec, G1S 2M1 QC
418-266-8900, 800-707-3380, regisseur.web@msss.gouv.qc.ca

Saskatchewan
Saskatchewan Social Services, 1920 Broad St., Regina, S4P 3V6 SK
306-787-3700

SOIL RESOURCES

Soils & Crops Research & Development Centre, 2560, boul Hochelaga, Québec, G1V 2J3 QC
418-657-7980, Fax: 418-648-2402

Quebec
Commission de protection du territoire agricole du Québec, 200, ch Ste-Foy, 2e étage, Québec, QC G1R 4X6
418-643-3314, Fax: 418-643-2261, 800-667-5294, info@cptaq.gouv.qc.ca

SOLICITORS GENERAL

Alberta
Alberta Solicitor General & Public Security, John E. Browntree Bldg, 10365 - 97 St., 10th Fl., Edmonton, T5J 3W7 AB
780-427-3441, Fax: 780-427-2789,-310-0000

British Columbia

Ministry of Public Safety & Solicitor General, PO Box 9282 Prov Govt,Victoria, V8W 9J7 BC
250-387-6121, 800-663-7867, pssgwebfeedback@gov.bc.ca

Manitoba

Manitoba Justice, Legislative Building, #104, 405 Broadway Ave., Winnipeg, R3C 3L6 MB
204-945-3728, Fax: 204-945-2517, minjus@gov.mb.ca

Newfoundland & Labrador

Department of Justice, Confederation Bldg., East Block, 4th Fl., PO Box 8700, St. John's, A1B 4J6 NL
709-729-5942, Fax: 709-729-2129, justice@gov.nl.ca

Nova Scotia

Department of Justice, 5151 Terminal Rd., 4th Fl., PO Box 7, Halifax, B3J 2L6 NS
902-424-4030, Fax: 902-424-0510, webbermj@gov.ns.ca

Ontario

Ministry of Community Safety & Correctional Services, George Drew Bldg., 25 Grosvenor St., 18th Fl., Toronto, M7A 1Y6 ON
416-326-5000, Fax: 416-325-6067, 866-517-0571, jus.g.sgcs.webmaster@jus.gov.on.ca

Quebec

Ministère de la Sécurité publique, Tour des Laurentides, 2525, boul Laurier, 5e étage, Québec, G1V 2L2 QC
418-643-2112, Fax: 418-646-6168, 866-644-6826

Yukon Territory

Yukon Justice, PO Box 2703, Whitehorse, Y1A 2C6 YT
867-667-8655, Fax: 867-393-5790

SPACE & ASTRONOMY

Canadian Space Agency, 6767, rte de l'Aéroport, Saint-Hubert, J3Y 8Y9 QC
450-926-4800, Fax: 450-926-4352, webmaster@space.gc.ca

Herzberg Institute of Astrophysics, 5071 West Saanich Rd., Victoria, V9E 2E7 BC
250-363-0001, Fax: 250-363-0045, hia-www@nrc-cnrc.gc.ca

Institute for Aerospace Research, 1200 Montreal Rd., Ottawa, K1A 0R6 ON
613-990-0765, Fax: 613-952-7214

STANDARDS

Institute for National Measurement Standards, Bldg. M-36, 1500 Montreal Rd., Ottawa, K1A 0R6 ON
613-998-7018, Fax: 613-954-1473, alexandra.shaw@nrc-cnrc.gc.ca

Standards Council of Canada, #200, 270 Albert St., Ottawa, K1P 6N7 ON
613-238-3222, Fax: 613-569-7808, info@scc.ca

STATISTICS

See Also: Vital Statistics

Statistics Canada, R.H. Coats Bldg., Tunney's Pasture, 100 Tunney's Pasture Driveway, Ottawa, K1A 0T6 ON
613-951-8116, Fax: 877-287-4369, 800-263-1136, infostats@statcan.ca

British Columbia

Client Services, 525 Superior St., 2nd Fl., PO Box 9472 Prov Govt,Victoria, V8W 9W6 BC
250-952-6861, Fax: 250-952-6803

Manitoba

Manitoba Bureau of Statistics, #824, 155 Carlton St., Winnipeg, R3C 3H9 MB
204-945-2406, Fax: 204-945-0695

Nunavut

Department of Executive & Intergovernmental Affairs, 1084 Aeroplex bldg., PO Box 1000 200,Iqaluit, X0A 0H0 NU
867-975-6000, Fax: 867-975-6090

Ontario

Registrar General Branch, 189 Red River Rd., PO Box 4600, Thunder Bay, P7B 6L8 ON
807-343-7414, Fax: 807-343-7411, 800-461-2156

Prince Edward Island

Department of Health, Jones Bldg., 11 Kent St., 2nd Fl., PO Box 2000, Charlottetown, C1A 7N8 PE
902-368-4900, Fax: 902-368-4974

Quebec

Institut de la statistique du Québec, 200, ch Ste-Foy, 3e étage, Québec, QC G1R 5T4
418-691-2401, Fax: 418-643-4129, 800-463-4090, direction@stat.gouv.qc.ca

STATISTICS (ENVIRONMENTAL)

Statistics Canada, R.H. Coats Bldg., Tunney's Pasture, 100 Tunney's Pasture Driveway, Ottawa, K1A 0T6 ON
613-951-8116, Fax: 877-287-4369, 800-263-1136, infostats@statcan.ca

STUDENT AID

Nunavut

Department of Education, PO Box 1000 910,Iqaluit, X0A 0H0 NU
867-975-5600, Fax: 867-975-5605, 888-531-1456

Quebec

Secteur du Soutien à la mission et l'Aide financière aux études, 1035, rue De La Chevrotière, Québec, G1R 5A5 QC
418-643-3750, 877-643-3750

Saskatchewan

Saskatchewan Education, 2220 College Ave., Regina, S4P 4V9 SK
306-787-6030, 888-775-3276, learninginquiry@sasked.gov.sk.ca

SUSTAINABLE DEVELOPMENT

Manitoba

Manitoba Round Table for Sustainable Development, #160, 123 Main St., Winnipeg, R3C 1A5 MB
204-945-1671, Fax: 204-948-2357, mrtsd@gov.mb.ca

Quebec

Ministère du Développement durable, de l'Environnement et des Parcs, Édifice Marie-Guyart, 675, boul René-Lévesque est, 29e étage, Québec, G1R 5V7 QC
418-521-3830, Fax: 418-646-5974, 800-561-1616, info@mddep.gouv.qc.ca

TAXATION

See Also: Sales Tax

Canada Revenue Agency, 875 Heron Rd., Ottawa, K1A 0L5 ON
613-952-0384, 800-267-6999

Financial Sector Regulation & Policy, Terrace Building, 9515 - 107 St., 4th Fl., Edmonton, T5K 2C3 AB

First Nations Tax Commission, #200, 160 Grorge St., Ottawa, ON K1N 9M2
613-789-5000, Fax: 613-789-5008, mail@fntc.ca

Manitoba

Taxation Division, #101, 401 York Ave., Winnipeg, R3C 0P8 MB
204-945-6444, Fax: 204-948-2360

New Brunswick

Revenue & Taxation, Centennial Bldg., #671, 670 King St., PO Box 3000, Fredericton, E3B 5G5 NB
506-444-2826, Fax: 506-444-4920

Nova Scotia

Tax Commission, Maritime Centre, 1505 Barrington St., Halifax, B3J 3K5 NS
902-424-5200, Fax: 902-424-0720, 800-670-4357

Quebec

Centre de perception fiscale, 3800, rue de Marly, Secteur 6-4-3, Québec, G1X 4A5 QC

Saskatchewan

Board of Revenue Commissioners, #480, 2151 Scarth St., Regina, SK S4P 2H8
306-787-6221, Fax: 306-787-1610

TELECOMMUNICATIONS

See Also: Broadcasting

Canadian Broadcasting Corporation, 181 Queen St., PO Box 3220 C,Ottawa, K1Y 1E4 ON
613-288-6033, liaison@radio-canada.ca

Canadian Radio-Television & Telecommunications Commission, Central Office, 1, Promenade du Portage, Les Terrasses de la Chaudière, Gatineau, J8X 4B1 QC
819-997-0313, Fax: 819-994-0218, 877-249-2782

Communications Research Centre Canada, 3701 Carling Ave., PO Box 11490 H, Ottawa, ON K2H 8S2
613-991-3313, Fax: 613-998-5355, info@crc.ca

Spectrum, Information Technologies & Telecommunications, Journal Tower North, 300 Slater St., 20th Fl., Ottawa, K1A 0C8 ON
613-998-0368, Fax: 613-952-1203

Manitoba

Manitoba Telecom Services Inc., 333 Main St., PO Box 6666, Winnipeg, R3C 3V6 MB
204-941-4111, Fax: 204-772-6391

Prince Edward Island

Department of Innovation & Advanced Learning, Shaw Bldg., 105 Rochford St., 5th Fl., PO Box 2000, Charlottetown, C1A 7N8 PE
902-368-4240, Fax: 902-368-4242

Quebec

Ministère de la Culture, des Communications & de la Condition féminine, 225, Grande Allée est, Québec, G1R 5G5 QC
Fax: 418-380-2364, 888-380-8882, infos@mcccf.gouv.qc.ca

Société de télédiffusion du Québec (Télé-Québec), 1000, rue Fullum, Montréal, H2K 3L7 QC
514-521-2424, Fax: 514-873-7739, 800-361-4301, info@telequebec.tv

Saskatchewan

Saskatchewan Telecommunications (SaskTel), 2121 Saskatchewan Dr., 7th Fl., Regina, S4P 3Y2 SK
306-777-3737, Fax: 306-359-7854, 800-727-5835

TOURISM & TOURIST INFORMATION

Canadian Tourism Commission, #1400, 1055 Dunsmuir St., PO Box 49230, Vancouver, BC V7X 1L2
604-638-8300, Fax: 604-638-8425, ctc_feedback@businteractive.com

Parks Canada, 25 Eddy St., Gatineau, K1A 0M5 QC
613-860-1251, 888-773-8888, information@pc.gc.ca

British Columbia

British Columbia 2010 Olympic & Paralympic Games Secretariat, 3585 Graveley St., 7th Fl., Vancouver, BC V5K 5J5
604-660-2010, Fax: 604-660-3437, 877-604-2010, bcsecretariat@gov.bc.ca

Ministry of Healthy Living & Sport, PO Box 9067 Prov Govt,Victoria, V8W 9E2 BC
250-387-3504, Fax: 250-387-3420, Feedback@gov.bc.ca

Tourism British Columbia, 1803 Douglas St., 3rd Fl., Victoria, BC V8W 9W5
250-356-6363, research@tourismbc.com; superhost@tourismbc.com

Manitoba

Tourism Secretariat & Travel Manitoba, 155 Carlton St., 7th Fl., Winnipeg, R3C 3H8 MB
800-665-0040

New Brunswick

Department of Tourism & Parks, Centennial Bldg., 670 King St., Fredericton, E3B 1G1 NB
506-444-5205, Fax: 506-457-4984, taponlinedirectory@gnb.ca

Newfoundland & Labrador

Department of Tourism, Culture & Recreation, Confederation Bldg., West Block, 2nd Fl., PO Box 8700, St. John's, A1B 4J6 NL
709-729-0862, Fax: 709-729-0870, tcrinfo@gov.nl.ca

Northwest Territories

Department of Industry, Tourism & Investment, PO Box 1320, Yellowknife, X1A 2L9 NT
Fax: 867-873-0306, info@iti.ca

Ontario

Ministry of Tourism, Hearst Block, 900 Bay St., 9th Fl., Toronto, M7A 2E1 ON
416-326-9326, Fax: 416-314-7854, 800-668-2746

Prince Edward Island

Department of Tourism, PO Box 2000, Charlottetown, C1A 7N8 PE
800-463-4734

Quebec

Société des établissements en plein air du Québec, Place de la Cité, #250, 2640, boul Laurier, Sainte-Foy, QC G1V 5C2
418-890-6527, Fax: 418-528-6025, 800-665-6527, inforeservation@sepaq.com

Ministère du Tourisme, #400, 900, boul René-Lévesque est, Québec, G1R 2B5 QC
418-643-5959, Fax: 418-646-8723, 800-482-2433

Saskatchewan

Tourism Saskatchewan, 1922 Park St., Regina, SK S4N 7M4
306-787-9600, 877-237-2273

Yukon Territory

Yukon Tourism & Culture, PO Box 2703, Whitehorse, Y1A 2C6 YT
867-667-5036, Fax: 867-667-3546

TRADE

See Also: Business Development; Imports

Business Development Bank of Canada, #400, 5, Place Ville-Marie, Montréal, H3B 5E7 QC
514-283-5904, Fax: 514-283-2872, 877-232-2269
Canadian Commercial Corporation, 50 O'Connor St., 11th Fl., Ottawa, K1A 0S6 ON
613-996-0034, Fax: 613-995-2121, 800-748-8191
Canadian International Trade Tribunal, Standard Life Centre, 333 Laurier Ave. West, 17 Floor, Ottawa, K1A 0G7 ON
613-990-2452, Fax: 613-990-2439
Canadian Wheat Board, 423 Main St., PO Box 816 Main,Winnipeg, R3C 2P5 MB
204-983-0239, Fax: 204-983-3841, 800-275-4292, questions@cwb.ca
Commission for Environmental Cooperation, Secretariat, #200, 393, rue St-Jacques ouest, Montréal, H2Y 1N9 QC
514-350-4300, Fax: 514-350-4314, info@cec.org
Export Development Canada, 151 O'Connor St., Ottawa, K1A 1K3 ON
613-598-2500, Fax: 613-598-3811, 800-267-8510
Global Operations & Chief Trade Commissioner, 125 Sussex Dr,, Ottawa, K1A 0G2 ON
613-944-2697, Fax: 613-996-1667
International Trade Canada, 125 Sussex Dr., Ottawa, K1A 0G2 ON
613-995-2901, Fax: 613-996-8924
Market & Industry Services Branch, Tower 5, 1341 Baseline Rd., Ottawa, K1A 0C5 ON
613-759-1000, Fax: 613-773-1755
North American Free Trade Agreement (NAFTA) Secretariat, Canadian Section, #705, 90 Sparks St., Ottawa, K1P 5B4 ON
613-992-9388, Fax: 613-992-9392, webmaster@nafta-alena.gc.ca

Alberta

Intergovernmental Relations, Commerce Place, 10155 - 102 St., 12th Fl., Edmonton, T5J 4L8 AB

British Columbia

Asia Pacific Trade Council, #730, 999 Canada Pl., Vancouver, BC V6C 3E1
604-775-2100, Fax: 604-775-2070
Economic Competitiveness Division, 1810 Blanshard St., 7th Fl., PO Box 9327 Prov Govt,Victoria, V8W 9N3 BC
250-952-0367, Fax: 250-952-0137
Ministry of Small Business & Revenue, 1810 Blanshard St., 3rd Fl., PO Box 9432 Prov Govt,Victoria, V8W 9N6 BC
250-387-6206, Fax: 250-952-0712, MSBROffice@gov.bc.ca
Technology, Research & Innovation Division, #730, 999 Canada Place, Vancouver, V6C 3E1 BC
Fax: 604-775-2070

Manitoba

Manitoba Competitiveness, Training & Trade, International Business Centre, The Paris Building, 259 Portage Ave., Winnipeg, R3B 3P4 MB
204-945-2475, Fax: 204-945-3977, minctt@leg.gov.mb.ca

New Brunswick

Department of Business New Brunswick, Centennial Bldg., 670 King St., PO Box 6000, Fredericton, E3B 5H1 NB
506-444-5228, Fax: 506-453-5428

Newfoundland & Labrador

Department of Innovation, Trade & Rural Development, West Block, Confederation Bldg., PO Box 8700, St. John's, A1B 4J6 NL
709-729-7000, Fax: 709-729-0654, 800-563-2299, itrd@gov.nl.ca

Nova Scotia

Department of Economic & Rural Development, Centennial Building, #600, 1660 Hollis St., PO Box 2311, Halifax, B3J 1V7 NS
902-424-0377, Fax: 902-424-7008, comm@gov.ns.ca

Ontario

Investment & Trade Division, Hearst Block, 900 Bay St., 5th fl., Toronto, M7A 2E1 ON
416-325-9802, Fax: 416-325-5617

Prince Edward Island

Department of Innovation & Advanced Learning, Shaw Bldg., 105 Rochford St., 5th Fl., PO Box 2000, Charlottetown, C1A 7N8 PE
902-368-4240, Fax: 902-368-4242

Quebec

Ministère du Développement économique, de l'Innovation et de l'Exportation, 710, place D'Youville, 3e étage, Québec, G1R 4Y4 QC
418-691-5950, Fax: 418-644-0118, 866-680-1884
Ministère des Relations internationales, Édifice Hector-Fabre, 525, boul Réne-Lévesque est, Québec, G1R 5R9 QC
418-649-2300, Fax: 418-649-2656, communications@mri.gouv.qc.ca

Saskatchewan

Saskatchewan Trade & Export Partnership, #320, 1801 Hamilton St., PO Box 1787, Regina, SK S4P 3C6
306-787-9210, Fax: 306-787-6666, 877-313-7244, inquire@sasktrade.sk.ca
Trade & International Relations, #800, 1919 Saskatchewan Dr., Regina, S4P 4H2 SK
306-787-6445, Fax: 306-787-7317

Yukon Territory

Yukon Economic Development, PO Box 2703, Whitehorse, Y1A 2C6 YT
867-393-7191, Fax: 867-395-7199, 800-661-0408

TRAINING, ENVIRONMENTAL

Alberta

Community, Learner & Industry Connections Division, Phipps-McKinnon Bldg., 5th Fl., 10020 - 101A Ave., Edmonton, T5J 3G2 AB
780-427-8517

TRANSPORTATION

Atlantic Pilotage Authority, Cogswell Tower, #910, 2000 Barrington St., Halifax, B3J 3K1 NS
902-426-2550, Fax: 902-426-4004, 877-272-3477, dispatch@atlanticpilotage.com
Canadian Air Transport Security Authority, 99 Bank St., 13th Fl., Ottawa, ON K1P 6B9
Fax: 613-991-6726, 888-294-2202
Canadian Coast Guard, Centennial Towers, #6S018, 200 Kent St., Ottawa, K1A 0E6 ON
613-998-1573, Fax: 613-990-2780
Canadian Transportation Agency, Les Terrasses de la Chaudière, 15, rue Eddy, Gatineau, K1A 0N9 QC
819-997-0344, Fax: 819-997-6727, 888-222-2592, info@otc-cta.gc.ca
Centre for Surface Transportation Technology, 2320 Lester Rd., Ottawa, K1V 1S2 ON
613-998-9639, Fax: 613-957-0831, inquiries.cstt@nrc-cnrc.gc.ca
Federal Bridge Corporation Limited, #1210, 55 Metcalfe St., Ottawa, ON K1P 6L5
613-993-6880, Fax: 613-993-6945, info@federalbridge.ca
Great Lakes Pilotage Authority, 202 Pitt St., 2nd fl., PO Box 95, Cornwall, K6H 5R9 ON
613-933-2991, Fax: 613-932-3793, administration@glpa-apgl.com
Institute for Aerospace Research, 1200 Montreal Rd., Ottawa, K1A 0R6 ON
613-990-0765, Fax: 613-952-7214
Laurentian Pilotage Authority Canada, #1501, 555, boul René-Lévesque ouest, Montréal, H2Z 1B1 QC
514-283-6320, Fax: 514-496-2409, administration@apl.gc.ca
Marine Atlantic Inc., Baine Johnston Centre, #302, 10 Fort William Place, St. John's, A1C 1K4 NL
709-772-8957, Fax: 709-772-8956, 800-341-7981, info@marine-atlantic.ca
Old Port of Montréal Corporation Inc., 333, rue de la Commune ouest, Montréal, H2Y 2E2 QC
514-283-5256, Fax: 514-283-8423
Pacific Pilotage Authority Canada, #1000, 1130 Pender St. West, Vancouver, V6E 4A4 BC
604-666-6771, Fax: 604-666-1647, info@ppa.gc.ca
Parc Downsview Park Inc., #1, 35 Carl Hall Rd., Toronto, M3K 2B6 ON
613-952-2222, Fax: 613-952-2225, info@pdp.ca
Policy & Corporate Services Division, Twin Atria Building, 4999 - 98 Ave., 3rd Fl., Edmonton, T6B 2X3 AB
St. Lawrence Seaway Management Corporation, 202 Pitt St., Cornwall, K6J 3P7 ON
613-932-5170, Fax: 613-932-7286, marketing@seaway.ca
Transport Canada, Place de Ville, 330 Sparks St., Tower C, Ottawa, K1A 0N5 ON
613-990-2309, Fax: 613-954-4731, minTC@tc.gc.ca
Transportation & Civil Engineering, Twin Atria Building, 4999 - 98 Ave., 2nd Fl., Edmonton, T6B 2X3 AB
Transportation Appeal Tribunal of Canada, 333 Laurier Ave. West, 12th Fl., Ottawa, ON K1A 0N5
613-990-6906, Fax: 613-990-9153, info@tatc.gc.ca
Transportation Safety Board of Canada, 200 Promenade du Portage, 4th Fl., Ottawa, K1A 1K8 ON
819-994-3741, Fax: 819-997-2239, 800-387-3557
Transportation Safety Services, Twin Atria Building, 4999 - 98 Ave., Main Fl., Edmonton, T6B 2X3 AB
Via Rail Canada Inc., #500, 3, Place Ville-Marie, Montréal, H3B 2C9 QC
514-871-6000, Fax: 514-871-6768

Alberta

Automobile Insurance Rate Board, Terrace Bldg., #200, 9515 - 107 St. NW, Edmonton, AB T5K 2C3
780-415-1126, Fax: 780-644-7771, airb@gov.ab.ca
Alberta Infrastructure, Infrastructure Building, 6950 - 101 St., 3rd Fl., Edmonton, T6H 5V7 AB
780-415-0507, Fax: 780-427-2187,-310-0000
Transportation Safety Board, Twin Atria Bldg., 4999 - 98 Ave., Main Fl., Edmonton, AB T6B 2X3
780-427-7178, Fax: 780-422-9739

British Columbia

British Columbia Ferry Commission, PO Box 1497, Comox, BC V9M 8A2
250-339-2714, info@bcferrycommission.com
British Columbia Transit, 520 Gorge Rd. East, PO Box 610, Victoria, BC V8W 2P3
250-385-2551, Fax: 250-995-5639
British Columbia Ferry Services Inc., 1112 Fort St., Victoria, V8V 4V2 BC
250-381-1401, 888-223-3779
Passenger Transportation Board, #202, 940 Blanshard St., PO Box 9850 Prov Govt, Victoria, BC V8W 9T5
250-953-3777, Fax: 250-953-3788, ptboard@gov.bc.ca
Ministry of Transportation & Infrastructure, 940 Blanshard St., PO Box 9850 Prov Govt,Victoria, V8W 9T5 BC
250-387-3198, Fax: 250-356-7706, tran.webmaster@gov.bc.ca
Transportation Planning & Policy Department, #5C, 940 Blanshard St., PO Box 9850 Prov Govt,Victoria, V8W 9T5 BC
250-387-5062, Fax: 250-387-6431

Manitoba

Highway Traffic Board/Motor Transport Board, #200, 301 Weston St., Winnipeg, MB R3E 3H4
204-945-8912, Fax: 204-783-6529
Manitoba Infrastructure & Transportation, Legislative Building, #203, 450 Broadway Ave., Winnipeg, R3C 0V8 MB
204-945-3723, Fax: 204-945-7610
License Suspension Appeal Board/Medical Review Committee, #200, 301 Weston St., Winnipeg, MB R3E 3H4
204-945-7350, Fax: 204-948-2682,
Taxicab Board, #200, 301 Weston St., Winnipeg, MB R3E 3H4
Fax: 204-948-2315

New Brunswick

New Brunswick Transportation Authority, Kings Place, 440 King St., PO Box 6000, Fredericton, NB E3B 5H1
506-453-3939, Fax: 506-453-2900
Department of Transportation, Kings Pl., 440 KingSt., PO Box 6000, Fredericton, E3B 5H8 NB
506-453-3939, Fax: 506-453-2900, Transportation.Web@gnb.ca

Newfoundland & Labrador

Department of Transportation & Works, Confederation Bldg., West Block, 6th Fl., PO Box 8700, St. John's, A1B 4J6 NL
709-729-3679, Fax: 709-729-4285, twminister@gov.nl.ca

Northwest Territories

Highways, 4510 - 50 Ave., 2nd fl., PO Box 1320, Yellowknife, X1A 2L9 NT
867-920-8771, Fax: 867-873-0288
Department of Transportation, Lahm Ridge Bldg., 4501 50 Ave., PO Box 1320, Yellowknife, X1A 2L9 NT
867-920-3460, Fax: 867-873-0363

Nova Scotia

Department of Transportation & Infrastructure Renewal, Johnston Bldg., 1672 Granville St., 2nd Fl., PO Box 186, Halifax, B3J 2N2 NS
902-424-2297, Fax: 902-424-0171, 888-432-3233, tpwpaff@gov.ns.ca

Nunavut

Department of Community & Government Services, J.G. Brown Bldg., PO Box 1000 700,Iqaluit, X0A 0H0 NU
867-975-5400, Fax: 867-975-5305
Department of Economic Development & Transportation, #1104 Inuksugait Plaza, PO Box 1000 1500,Iqaluit, X0A 0H0 NU
867-975-7800, Fax: 867-975-7870, 888-975-5999, edt@gov.nu.ca

Ontario

GO Transit, #600, 20 Bay St., Toronto, ON M5J 2W3
416-869-3600, Fax: 416-869-1755, 888-438-6646
Licence Appeal Tribunal (LAT), 1 St. Clair Ave. West, 12th Fl., Toronto, ON M4V 1K6
416-314-4260, Fax: 416-314-4270, 800-255-2214
Niagara Falls Bridge Commission, PO Box 395, Niagara Falls, L2E 6T8 ON
905-354-5641, Fax: 905-353-6644

Ontario Highway Transport Board, 151 Bloor St. West, 10th Fl., Toronto, ON M5S 2T5
416-326-6732, Fax: 416-326-6738, ohtb@mto.gov.on.ca
Owen Sound Transportation Company Ltd., RR#5, Hwy 6 & 21, Owen Sound, ON N4K 5N7
519-376-8740
Road User Safety Division, #191, Bldg A, 1201 Wilson Ave., Toronto, M3M 1J8 ON
416-235-2999, Fax: 416-235-4153
Ministry of Transportation, Ferguson Block, 77 Wellesley St. West, 3rd Fl., Toronto, M7A 1Z8 ON
416-235-4686, Fax: 416-327-9185, 800-268-4686

Prince Edward Island
Department of Transportation & Public Works, Jones Bldg., 11 Kent St., PO Box 2000, Charlottetown, C1A 7N8 PE
902-368-5100, Fax: 902-368-5395

Quebec
Abitibi-Témiscamingue-Nord-du-Québec, 80, av Québec, Rouyn-Noranda, J9X 6R1 QC
819-763-3271, Fax: 819-763-3493, datnq@mtq.gouv.qc.ca
Bas-Saint-Laurent-Gaspésie-Iles-de-la-Madeleine, #101, 92, 2e rue ouest, Rimouski, G5L 8E6 QC
418-727-3674, Fax: 418-727-3673, dtbgi@mtq.gouv.qc.ca
Capitale-Nationale, 475, boul de l'Atrium, 2e étage, Québec, G1H 7H9 QC
418-643-1911, Fax: 418-646-0003, dcnat@mtq.gouv.qc.ca
Chaudière-Appalaches, 1156, boul de la Rive-Sud, Saint-Romuald, G6W 5M6 QC
418-839-5581, Fax: 418-834-7338, dtca@mtq.gouv.qc.ca
Commission des transports du Québec, 200, ch Sainte-Foy, 7e étage, Québec, QC G1R 5V5
Fax: 418-644-8034, 888-461-2433, courrier@ctq.gouv.qc.ca
Côte-Nord, #110, 625, boul Laflèche, Baie-Comeau, G5C 1C5 QC
418-295-4765, Fax: 418-295-4766, dtcn@mtq.gouv.qc.ca
Est-de-la-Montérégie, 201, place Charles-Lemoyne, 5e étage, Longueuil, J4K 2T5 QC
450-677-3413, Fax: 450-442-1317, dtem@mtq.gouv.qc.ca
Estrie, #2.02, 200, rue Belvédère nord, Sherbrooke, J1H 4A9 QC
819-820-3280, Fax: 819-820-3118, dte@mtq.gouv.qc.ca
Ile-de-Montréal, 440, boul René-Lévesque ouest, 10e étage, Montréal, H2Z 2A6 QC
514-873-7781, Fax: 514-864-3867, dtim@mtq.gouv.qc.ca
Laurentides-Lanaudière, 222, rue Saint-Georges, 2e étage, Saint-Jérôme, J7Z 4Z9 QC
450-569-3057, Fax: 450-569-3072, dll@mtq.gouv.qc.ca
Laval-Mille-Iles, 1725, boul Le Corbusier, Laval, H7S 2K7 QC
450-680-6330, Fax: 450-973-4959, dtlmi@mtq.gouv.qc.ca
Mauricie-Centre-du-Québec, 100, rue Laviolette, 4e étage, Trois-Rivières, G9A 5S9 QC
819-371-6896, Fax: 819-371-6136, dmcq@mtq.gouv.qc.ca
Ouest-de-la-Montérégie, #200, 180, boulevard d'Anjou, Châteauguay, J6K 1C4 QC
450-698-3400, Fax: 450-698-3452, dtom@mtq.gouv.qc.ca
Outaouais, #5.110, 170, rue de l'Hôtel-de-Ville, Gatineau, J8X 4C2 QC
819-772-3849, Fax: 819-772-3338, dto@mtq.gouv.qc.ca
Saguenay-Lac-Saint-Jean-Chibougamau, 3950, boul Harvey, Jonquière, G7X 8L6 QC
418-695-7916, Fax: 418-695-7926, dt.slsjc@mtq.gouv.qc.ca
Société de l'assurance automobile du Québec, 333, boul Jean-Lesage, CP 19600 Terminus, Québec, QC G1K 8J6
418-643-7620, Fax: 418-644-0339, 800-361-7620, courrier@saaq.gouv.qc.ca
Société des traversiers du Québec, 250, rue Saint-Paul, Québec, QC G1K 9K9
418-643-2019, Fax: 418-643-7308, stq@traversiers.gouv.qc.ca
Société du port ferroviaire Baie-Comeau-Hauterive, 18, rte Maritime, Baie-Comeau, QC G4Z 2L6
418-296-6785, Fax: 418-296-2377, soport@globetrotter.qc.ca
Ministère des Transports, 700, boul René-Lévesque est, 27e étage, Québec, G1R 5H1 QC
418-643-6980, Fax: 418-643-2011, 888-355-0511, communications@mtq.gouv.qc.ca

Saskatchewan
Saskatchewan Highways & Infrastructure, 1855 Victoria Ave., Regina, S4P 3T2 SK
306-787-4800
Saskatchewan Highway Traffic Board, 1550 Saskatchewan Dr., Regina, SK S4P 0E4
306-775-6674

Yukon Territory
Yukon Community Services, PO Box 2703, Whitehorse, Y1A 2C6 YT
867-667-5811, Fax: 867-393-6295, 800-661-0408, inquiry@gov.yk.ca
Driver Control Board, 308 Steele St., PO Box 2703, Whitehorse, YT Y1A 2C6
867-667-3774, Fax: 867-393-6483, dcb@gov.yk.ca
Yukon Highways & Public Works, PO Box 2703, Whitehorse, Y1A 2C6 YT
867-393-7193, Fax: 867-393-6218, 800-661-0408, hpw-info@gov.yk.ca
Yukon Motor Transport Board, PO Box 2703, Whitehorse, YT Y1A 2C6
867-667-5782, Fax: 867-393-6408, Laurie.Hrynuik@gov.yk.ca

TRANSPORTATION OF DANGEROUS GOODS

Nova Scotia
Department of Transportation & Infrastructure Renewal, Johnston Bldg., 1672 Granville St., 2nd Fl., PO Box 186, Halifax, B3J 2N2 NS
902-424-2297, Fax: 902-424-0171, 888-432-3233, tpwpaff@gov.ns.ca

Ontario
Road User Safety Division, #191, Bldg A, 1201 Wilson Ave., Toronto, M3M 1J8 ON
416-235-2999, Fax: 416-235-4153

Prince Edward Island
Department of Transportation & Public Works, Jones Bldg., 11 Kent St., PO Box 2000, Charlottetown, C1A 7N8 PE
902-368-5100, Fax: 902-368-5395,

Saskatchewan
Saskatchewan Highways & Infrastructure, 1855 Victoria Ave., Regina, S4P 3T2 SK
306-787-4800

TRAPPING & FUR INDUSTRY

Ontario
Ontario Moose & Bear Allocation Advisory Committee, PO Box 964, Sioux Lookout, ON P8T 1B3
807-737-2615, Fax: 807-737-4173

Quebec
Comité conjoint de chasse, de pêche et de piégeage, #C220, 383 rue Saint-Jacques, Montréal, QC H2Y 1N9
514-284-2151, Fax: 514-284-0039, hftcc@bellnet.ca
Office de la sécurité du revenu des chasseurs et piègeurs cris, Édifice Champlain, #1110, 2700, boul Laurier, Sainte-Foy, QC G1V 4K5
418-643-7300, Fax: 418-643-6803, courrier@osrcpc.ca

Saskatchewan
Saskatchewan Environment, 3211 Albert St., 2nd Fl., Regina, S4S 5W6 SK
306-953-3750, Fax: 306-787-9544, 800-567-4224, inquiry@serm.gov.sk.ca

TREASURY SERVICES

See Also: Finance
Treasury Board of Canada, 300 Laurier Ave. West, 10th Fl., Ottawa, K1A 0R5 ON
613-957-2400, Fax: 613-941-4000, 877-636-0656, info@tbs-sct.gc.ca

British Columbia
Provincial Treasury, 620 Superior St., PO Box 9414 Prov Govt,Victoria, V8V 9V1 BC
250-387-4541, Fax: 250-356-3041, Jim.Hopkings@gov.bc.ca

New Brunswick
Treasury, Centennial Bldg., #376, 670 King St., PO Box 6000, Fredericton, E3B 5H1 NB
506-453-3952, Fax: 506-453-2053

Nova Scotia
Nova Scotia Treasury & Policy Board, 1700 Granville St., 5th Fl., PO Box 1617, Halifax, B3J 2Y3 NS
902-424-8910, Fax: 902-424-7638, tpbenquiries@gov.ns.ca

Nunavut
Department of Finance, Bldg. 1079, 1st Fl., PO Box 1000 Stn 330,Iqaluit, X0A 0H0 NU
867-975-5800, Fax: 867-975-5805

Prince Edward Island
Department of the Provincial Treasury, Shaw Bldg., 95 Rochford St., 2nd Fl. South, PO Box 2000, Charlottetown, C1A 7N8 PE
902-368-4050, Fax: 902-368-6575

Quebec
Secrétariat du Conseil du trésor, 875, Grande Allée est, 3e étage, secteur 100, Québec, G1R 5R8 QC
418-643-1529, Fax: 418-643-9226, 866-552-5158, communication@sct.gouv.qc.ca

URBAN RENEWAL & DESIGN

See Also: Municipal Affairs

Alberta
Local Government Services Division, Commerce Place, 10155 - 102 St., 17th Fl., Edmonton, T5J 4L4 AB

Newfoundland & Labrador
Newfoundland & Labrador Housing Corporation, Sir Brian Dunfield Bldg., 2 Canada Dr., PO Box 220, St. John's, A1C 5J2 NL
709-724-3000, Fax: 709-724-3250, jmbowering@nsmail.nlhc.nl.ca

Northwest Territories
Department of Municipal & Community Affairs, PO Box 1320, Yellowknife, X1A 2L9 NT
867-873-7118, Fax: 867-873-0309

Ontario
Ministry of Municipal Affairs & Housing, 777 Bay St., 17th Fl., Toronto, M5G 2E5 ON
416-585-7041, Fax: 416-585-6227, 866-220-2290, mininfo.mah@ontario.ca

Prince Edward Island
Community & Labour Development, Shaw Bldg., 105 Rochford St., 5th Fl., PO Box 2000, Charlottetown, C1A 7N8 PE
902-368-4244, Fax: 902-368-4242

Quebec
Société d'habitation du Québec, Aile St-Amable, 1054, rue Louis-Alexandre-Taschereau, 3e étage, Québec, QC G1R 5E7
418-643-4035, Fax: 418-643-4560, 800-463-4315

VETERANS AFFAIRS

Veterans Affairs Canada, 161 Grafton St., PO Box 7700, Charlottetown, C1A 8M9 PE
902-566-8888, information@vac-acc.gc.ca

VICE-REGAL REPRESENTATIVES

Governor General & Commander-in-Chief of Canada, Rideau Hall, 1 Sussex Dr., Ottawa, K1A 0A1 ON
613-993-8200, Fax: 613-998-8760, 800-465-6890, info@gg.ca

Alberta
Office of the Lieutenant Governor, Legislature Bldg., 10800 - 97 Ave., 3rd Fl., Edmonton, T5K 2B6 AB
780-427-7243, Fax: 780-422-5134, ltgov@gov.ab.ca

British Columbia
Office of the Lieutenant Governor, Government House, 1401 Rockland Ave., Victoria, V8S 1V9 BC
250-387-2080, Fax: 250-387-2078, ghinfo@gov.bc.ca

Manitoba
Office of the Lieutenant Governor, Legislative Building, #235, 450 Broadway Ave., Winnipeg, R3C 0V8 MB
204-945-2753, Fax: 204-945-4329, ltgov@leg.gov.mb.ca

New Brunswick
Office of the Lieutenant-Governor, Old Government House, 51 Woodstock Rd., PO Box 6000, Fredericton, E3B 5H1 NB
506-453-2505, Fax: 506-444-5280

Newfoundland & Labrador
Office of the Lieutenant Governor, Government House, Military Rd., PO Box 5517, St. John's, A1C 5W4 NL
709-729-4494, Fax: 709-729-2234, governmenthouse@gov.nl.ca

Northwest Territories
Office of the Commissioner, #803 Northwest Tower, PO Box 1320, Yellowknife, X1A 2L9 NT
867-873-7400, Fax: 867-873-0223, 888-270-3318, commissioner@gov.nt.ca

Nova Scotia
Office of the Lieutenant Governor, Government House, 1451 Barrington St., Halifax, B3J 1Z2 NS
902-424-7001, Fax: 902-424-0537

Nunavut
Office of the Commissioner, PO Box 2379, Iqaluit, X0A 0H0 NU
867-975-5120, Fax: 867-975-5123, nunavutcommissioner@gov.nu.ca

Ontario
Office of the Lieutenant Governor, Room 131, Legislative Bldg., Queen's Park, Toronto, M7A 1A1 ON
416-325-7780, Fax: 416-325-7787, ltgov@gov.on.ca

Prince Edward Island
Office of the Lieutenant Governor, Government House, PO Box 846, Charlottetown, C1A 7L9 PE
902-368-5480, Fax: 902-368-5481

Quebec
Cabinet du Lieutenant-gouverneur, Édifice André-Laurendeau, 1050, rue des Parlementaires R.C., Québec, G1A 1A1 QC
418-643-5385, Fax: 418-644-4677, 866-791-0766

Saskatchewan
Office of the Lieutenant Governor, Government House, 4607 Dewdney Ave., Regina, S4P 1B7 SK
306-787-4070, Fax: 306-787-7716, lgo@ltgov.sk.ca

Yukon Territory
Office of the Commissioner, 1098 First Ave., Whitehorse, Y1A 0C1 YT
867-667-5121, Fax: 867-393-6201, commissioner@gov.yk.ca

VIOLENCE

See Also: policing Services

Alberta
Alberta Children and Youth Services, Sterling Place, 9940 - 106 St., 12th Fl., Edmonton, T5K 2N2 AB
780-422-3004, Fax: 780-422-3071, 866-714-5437, cs.communications@gov.ab.ca

New Brunswick
Department of Social Development, Sartain MacDonald Bldg., 551 King St., PO Box 6000, Fredericton, E3B 5H1 NB
506-453-2001, Fax: 506-453-7478

Nova Scotia
Department of Community Services, Nelson Place, 5675 Spring Garden Rd., 3rd Fl., PO Box 696, Halifax, B3J 2T7 NS
902-424-4304, Fax: 902-428-0618

VITAL STATISTICS

Vital Statistics, 254 Portage Ave., Winnipeg, R3C 0B8 MB
204-945-3701, Fax: 204-948-3128, 800-282-8063, vitalstats@gov.mb.ca

British Columbia
Vital Statistics, 818 Fort St., Victoria, V8W 1H8 BC
250-952-2681, Fax: 250-952-2587

Northwest Territories
Vital Statistics, Bag #9, Inuvik, X0E 0T0 NT
867-777-7400, Fax: 867-777-3197, 800-661-0830, hsa@gov.nt.ca

Nova Scotia
Vital Statistics, Joseph Howe Bldg., 1690 Hollis St., Ground Floor, PO Box 157, Halifax, B3J 2M9 NS
902-424-4071, Fax: 902-424-0678, 877-848-2578, vstat@gov.ns.ca

Ontario
Registrar General Branch, 189 Red River Rd., PO Box 4600, Thunder Bay, P7B 6L8 ON
807-343-7414, Fax: 807-343-7411, 800-461-2156

Prince Edward Island
Department of Health, Jones Bldg., 11 Kent St., 2nd Fl., PO Box 2000, Charlottetown, C1A 7N8 PE
902-368-4900, Fax: 902-368-4974

Quebec
Directeur de l'état civil, 2535, boul Laurier, Québec, QC G1V 5C5
418-643-3900, Fax: 418-646-3255, 800-567-3900, etatcivil@gouv.qc.ca

WASTE & GARBAGE

Newfoundland & Labrador
Department of Government Services, PO Box 8700, St. John's, A1B 4J6 NL
709-729-4860
Department of Municipal Affairs, West Block, Main Fl., Confederation Bldg., PO Box 8700, St. John's, A1B 4J6 NL
709-729-3053

Ontario
Ministry of Environment, 135 St. Clair Ave. West, Toronto, M4V 1P5 ON
416-325-4000, Fax: 416-325-3159, 800-565-4923

Quebec
Bureau d'audiences publiques sur l'environnement, Édifice Lomer-Gouin, #2.10, 575, rue Saint-Amable, 2e étage, Québec, QC G1R 6A6
418-643-7447, Fax: 418-643-9474, 800-463-4732, communication@bape.gouv.qc.ca
Société québécoise de récupération et de recyclage, Siège social, #200, 420, boul Charest est, Québec, QC G1K 8M4
418-643-0394, Fax: 418-643-6507, 866-523-8290, info@recyc-quebec.gouv.qc.ca

WASTE MANAGEMENT

See Also: Dangerous Goods & Hazardous Materials

Alberta
Alberta Recycling Management Authority, Scotia Tower 1, #1310, 10060 Jasper Ave., PO Box 189, Edmonton, AB T5J 2J1
780-990-1111, Fax: 780-990-1122, 888-999-8762, info@albertarecycling.ca
Alberta Used Oil Management Association, Scotia One, Scotia Place, #1050, 10060 Jasper Ave., Edmonton, AB T5J 3R8
780-414-1510, Fax: 780-414-1519, reception@usedoilrecycling.ca
Beverage Container Management Board, #750, 10707 - 100 Ave., Edmonton, AB T5J 3M1
780-424-3193, Fax: 780-428-4620, 888-424-7671, info@bcmb.ab.ca
Alberta Environment, South Tower, Petroleum Plaza, 9915 - 108 St., 10th Fl., Edmonton, T5K 2G8 AB
780-427-2700, Fax: 780-422-4086, env.infocent@gov.ab.ca

New Brunswick
Department of Local Government, Marysville Place, 20 McGloin St., PO Box 6000, Fredericton, E3B 5H1 NB
506-453-2807, Fax: 506-453-3988,

Newfoundland & Labrador
Multi-Materials Stewardship Board, PO Box 8131 A, St. John's, NL A1B 3M9
709-753-0948, Fax: 709-753-0974

Northwest Territories
Department of Municipal & Community Affairs, PO Box 1320, Yellowknife, X1A 2L9 NT
867-873-7118, Fax: 867-873-0309

Prince Edward Island
Island Waste Management Corporation, 110 Watts Ave., Charlottetown, PE C1E 2C1
902-894-0330, Fax: 902-894-0331, 888-280-8111, reception@iwmc.pe.ca; info@iwmc.pe.ca

Quebec
Société québécoise de récupération et de recyclage, Siège social, #200, 420, boul Charest est, Québec, QC G1K 8M4
418-643-0394, Fax: 418-643-6507, 866-523-8290, info@recyc-quebec.gouv.qc.ca

Saskatchewan
Saskatchewan Environment, 3211 Albert St., 2nd Fl., Regina, S4S 5W6 SK
306-953-3750, Fax: 306-787-9544, 800-567-4224, inquiry@serm.gov.sk.ca

Yukon Territory
Yukon Environment, PO Box 2703, Whitehorse, Y1A 2C6 YT
867-667-5652, Fax: 867-393-7197, 800-661-0408, environmentyukon@gov.yk.ca

WATER & WASTEWATER

Bedford Institute of Oceanography, 1 Challenger Dr., PO Box 1006, Dartmouth, B2Y 4A2 NS
902-426-3492, Fax: 902-426-8484
Canadian Hydraulics Centre, 1200 Montreal Rd., Ottawa, K1A 0R6 ON
613-993-9381, Fax: 613-952-7679, info.chc@nrc-cnrc.gc.ca
Environment Canada, 10 Wellington St., Gatineau, K1A 0H3 QC
819-997-2800, Fax: 819-994-1412, 800-668-6767, enviroinfo@ec.gc.ca
Fisheries & Oceans Canada, 200 Kent St., Ottawa, K1A 0E6 ON
613-993-0999, Fax: 613-996-1866, info@dfo-mpo.gc.ca
Freshwater Institute, 501 University Cres., Winnipeg, R3T 2N6 MB
204-983-5000, Fax: 204-983-6285
Institut Maurice-Lamontagne, 850, rte de le Mer, CP 1000, Mont-Joli, G5H 3Z4 QC
418-775-0555, Fax: 418-775-0730
Institute for Marine Biosciences, 1411 Oxford St., Halifax, B3H 3Z1 NS
902-426-8332, Fax: 902-426-9413, communications.imb@nrc-cnrc.gc.ca
Institute for Ocean Technology, Kerwin Pl. & Arctic Ave., PO Box 12093, St. John's, A1B 3T5 NL
709-772-4939, Fax: 709-772-2462, Noel.Murphy@nrc-cnrc.gc.ca
Institute of Ocean Sciences, 9860 West Saanich Rd., PO Box 6000, Sidney, V8L 4B2 BC
250-363-6517, Fax: 250-363-6390
Nunavut Water Board, PO Box 119, Gjoa Haven, NU X0B 1J0
867-360-6338, Fax: 867-360-6369

Alberta
Alberta Environment, South Tower, Petroleum Plaza, 9915 - 108 St., 10th Fl., Edmonton, T5K 2G8 AB
780-427-2700, Fax: 780-422-4086, env.infocent@gov.ab.ca
Irrigation Council, Provincial Bldg., 200 - 5 Ave. South, 3rd Fl., PO Bag 3014, Lethbridge, AB T1J 4L1
403-381-5176, Fax: 403-382-4406

British Columbia
Ministry of Environment, PO Box 9339 Prov Govt,Victoria, V8W 9M1 BC
250-387-1161, Fax: 250-387-5669, www.envmail@gov.bc.ca
British Columbia Utilities Commission, 900 Howe St., 6th Fl., PO Box 250, Vancouver, V6Z 2N3 BC
604-660-4700, Fax: 604-660-1102, 800-663-1385, commission.secretary@bcuc.com

Manitoba
Manitoba Conservation, 200 Saulteaux Cres., Winnipeg, R3J 3W3 MB
204-945-6784, 800-214-6497, mincon@leg.gov.mb.ca
Manitoba Water Services Board, PO Box 22080, Brandon, MB R7A 6Y9
204-726-6076, Fax: 204-726-6290

New Brunswick
Department of the Environment, Marysville Place, 20 McGloin St., PO Box 6000, Fredericton, E3B 5H1 NB
506-453-2690, Fax: 506-457-4991, env-info@gnb.ca
Department of Natural Resources, PO Box 6000, Fredericton, E3B 5H1 NB
506-453-2510, Fax: 506-444-5839, dnrweb@gnb.ca

Newfoundland & Labrador
Department of Environment & Conservation, Confederation Bldg., West Block, 4th Fl., PO Box 8700, St. John's, A1B 4J6 NL
709-729-2664, Fax: 709-729-6639, 800-563-6181, info@gov.nl.ca
Newfoundland & Labrador Board of Commissioners of Public Utilities, PO Box 21040, St. John's, A1A 5B2 NL
709-726-8600, Fax: 709-726-9604, 866-782-0006, ito@pub.nf.ca

Northwest Territories
Department of Environment & Natural Resources, PO Box 1320, Yellowknife, X1A 2L9 NT
Northwest Territories Water Board, 5114 - 49th St., PO Box 1326, Yellowknife, X1A 1N9 NT
867-765-0106, Fax: 867-765-0114, info@nwtwb.com

Nova Scotia
Department of Natural Resources, Founder's Square, 1701 Hollis St., 3rd Fl., PO Box 698, Halifax, B3J 2T9 NS
902-424-5935, Fax: 902-424-0594, 800-565-2224
Nova Scotia Utility & Review Board, 1601 Lower Water St., 3rd Fl., PO Box 1692 M,Halifax, B3J 3S3 NS
902-424-4448, Fax: 902-424-3919, uarb.board@gov.ns.ca
Waterfront Development Corporation Ltd., 1751 Lower Water St., 2nd Fl., Halifax, NS B3J 1S5
902-422-6591, Fax: 902-422-7582, info@wdcl.ca

Ontario
Ministry of Environment, 135 St. Clair Ave. West, Toronto, M4V 1P5 ON
416-325-4000, Fax: 416-325-3159, 800-565-4923
Lake of the Woods Control Board, c/o Executive Engineer, Ottawa, ON K1A 0H3
Fax: 819-953-4666, 800-661-5922, secretariat@lwcb.ca
Ministry of Natural Resources, Whitney Block, #6630, 99 Wellesley St. West, 6th Fl., Toronto, M7A 1W3 ON
800-667-1940
Ontario Clean Water Agency, 1 Yonge St., 17th Fl., Toronto, ON M5E 1E5
416-314-5600, Fax: 416-314-8300, 800-667-6292
Walkerton Clean Water Centre, PO Box 160, Walkerton, ON N0G 2V0
519-881-2003, Fax: 519-881-4947, inquiry@wcwc.ca

Prince Edward Island
Department of Environment, Energy & Forestry, Jones Bldg., 11 Kent St., 4th & 5th Fl., PO Box 2000, Charlottetown, C1A 7N8 PE
902-368-5000, Fax: 902-368-5830
Department of Tourism, PO Box 2000, Charlottetown, C1A 7N8 PE
800-463-4734

Quebec
Ministère du Développement durable, de l'Environnement et des Parcs, Édifice Marie-Guyart, 675, boul René-Lévesque est, 29e étage, Québec, G1R 5V7 QC

418-521-3830, Fax: 418-646-5974, 800-561-1616, info@mddep.gouv.qc.ca

Saskatchewan

Saskatchewan Environment, 3211 Albert St., 2nd Fl., Regina, S4S 5W6 SK
306-953-3750, Fax: 306-787-9544, 800-567-4224, inquiry@serm.gov.sk.ca

Saskatchewan Water Corporation (SaskWater), #200, 111 Fairford St. East, Moose Jaw, S6H 1C8 SK
306-694-3098, Fax: 306-694-3207, 888-230-1111, comm@saskwater.com

Saskatchewan Watershed Authority, 111 Fairford St. East, Moose Jaw, SK S6H 7X9
306-694-3900, Fax: 306-694-3465, comm@swa.ca

Yukon Territory

Yukon Environment, PO Box 2703, Whitehorse, Y1A 2C6 YT
867-667-5652, Fax: 867-393-7197, 800-661-0408, environmentyukon@gov.yk.ca

WATER RESOURCES

See Also: Oceanography

Alberta

Environmental Management Division, Petroleum Plaza ST, 9915 - 108 St., 10th Fl., Edmonton, T5K 2G8 AB

Environmental Stewardship Branch, 351 boul St-Joseph, Gatineau, K1A 0H3 QC
819-997-1575, Fax: 819-953-9452

Freshwater Institute, 501 University Cres., Winnipeg, R3T 2N6 MB
204-983-5000, Fax: 204-983-6285

International Joint Commission, 234 Laurier Ave. West, 22nd Fl., Ottawa, K1P 6K6 ON
613-947-1420, Fax: 613-993-5583, beckhoffb@ottawa.ijc.org

Nunavut Water Board, PO Box 119, Gjoa Haven, NU X0B 1J0
867-360-6338, Fax: 867-360-6369

Alberta

Alberta Environment, South Tower, Petroleum Plaza, 9915 - 108 St., 10th Fl., Edmonton, T5K 2G8 AB
780-427-2700, Fax: 780-422-4086, env.infocent@gov.ab.ca

British Columbia

Environmental Protection Division, 2975 Jutland Rd., 5th Fl., PO Box 9339, Victoria, V8W 9M1 BC
250-387-1288, Fax: 250-387-5669

Water Stewardship Division, 2975 Jutland Rd., 5th Fl., PO Box 9339 Prov Govt,Victoria, V8W 9M1 BC
250-356-9443, Fax: 250-953-3414

Manitoba

Manitoba Water Services Board, PO Box 22080, Brandon, MB R7A 6Y9
204-726-6076, Fax: 204-726-6290

Office of Drinking Water, 1007 Century St., Winnipeg, R3H 0W4 MB
204-945-5762, Fax: 204-945-1365

Manitoba Water Stewardship, 200 Saulteaux Cres., PO Box 11, Winnipeg, R3J 3W3 MB
204-945-6398, 800-282-8069, wsd@gov.mb.ca

New Brunswick

Department of the Environment, Marysville Place, 20 McGloin St., PO Box 6000, Fredericton, E3B 5H1 NB
506-453-2690, Fax: 506-457-4991, env-info@gnb.ca

Environmental Management, Marysville Place, 20 McGloin St., PO Box 6000, Fredericton, E3B 5H1 NB
506-444-5119, Fax: 506-457-7333

Department of Local Government, Marysville Place, 20 McGloin St., PO Box 6000, Fredericton, E3B 5H1 NB
506-453-2807, Fax: 506-453-3988

Sciences & Planning, Marysville Place, 20 McGloin St., 2nd Fl., PO Box 6000, Fredericton, E3B 5H1 NB
506-453-2862, Fax: 506-453-2265

Northwest Territories

Northwest Territories Water Board, 5114 - 49th St., PO Box 1326, Yellowknife, X1A 1N9 NT
867-765-0106, Fax: 867-765-0114, info@nwtwb.com

Nova Scotia

Department of Agriculture, 1741 Brunswick St., 3rd Fl., PO Box 2223, Halifax, B3J 3C4 NS
902-424-4560, Fax: 902-424-4671

Nunavut

Department of Health & Social Services, Sivummut bldg., PO Box 1007 1000,Iqaluit, X0A 0H0 NU
867-975-5700, Fax: 867-975-5705, health@gov.nu.ca

Ontario

Advisory Council on Drinking Water Quality & Testing Standards, 40 St. Clair Ave. West, 3rd Fl., Toronto, ON M4V 1M2
416-212-7779, Fax: 416-212-7595

Ontario Clean Water Agency, 1 Yonge St., 17th Fl., Toronto, ON M5E 1E5
416-314-5600, Fax: 416-314-8300, 800-667-6292

Walkerton Clean Water Centre, PO Box 160, Walkerton, ON N0G 2V0
519-881-2003, Fax: 519-881-4947, inquiry@wcwc.ca

Quebec

Ministère du Développement durable, de l'Environnement et des Parcs, Édifice Marie-Guyart, 675, boul René-Lévesque est, 29e étage, Québec, G1R 5V7 QC
418-521-3830, Fax: 418-646-5974, 800-561-1616, info@mddep.gouv.qc.ca

Saskatchewan

Saskatchewan Environment, 3211 Albert St., 2nd Fl., Regina, S4S 5W6 SK
306-953-3750, Fax: 306-787-9544, 800-567-4224, inquiry@serm.gov.sk.ca

Saskatchewan Water Corporation (SaskWater), #200, 111 Fairford St. East, Moose Jaw, S6H 1C8 SK
306-694-3098, Fax: 306-694-3207, 888-230-1111, comm@saskwater.com

Saskatchewan Watershed Authority, 111 Fairford St. East, Moose Jaw, SK S6H 7X9
306-694-3900, Fax: 306-694-3465, comm@swa.ca

Yukon Territory

Yukon Environment, PO Box 2703, Whitehorse, Y1A 2C6 YT
867-667-5652, Fax: 867-393-7197, 800-661-0408, environmentyukon@gov.yk.ca

WEIGHTS & MEASURES

Standards Council of Canada, #200, 270 Albert St., Ottawa, K1P 6N7 ON
613-238-3222, Fax: 613-569-7808, info@scc.ca

WILDLIFE RESOURCES

Alberta

Alberta Sport, Recreation, Parks & Wildlife Foundation, Standard Life Centre, 10405 Jasper Ave., 9th Fl., Edmonton, AB T5J 4R7
780-415-1167, Fax: 780-415-0308

British Columbia

Environmental Stewardship Division, 2975 Jutland Rd., 5th Fl., PO Box 9339 Prov Govt,Victoria, V8T 5J9 BC
250-356-0121, Fax: 250-953-3414

Manitoba

Endangered Species Advisory Committee, 200 Saulteaux Cres., PO Box 24, Winnipeg, MB R3J 3W3
204-945-7465, Fax: 204-945-3077

Newfoundland & Labrador

Forest Resources, Fortis Bldg., PO Box 2006, Corner Brook, A2H 6J8 NL
709-637-2284, Fax: 709-634-4378

Nunavut

Department of Environment, PO Box 1000 1300,Iqaluit, X0A 0H0 NU
867-975-7700, Fax: 867-975-7742, 866-222-9063, environment@gov.nu.ca

Ontario

Ministry of Environment, 135 St. Clair Ave. West, Toronto, M4V 1P5 ON
416-325-4000, Fax: 416-325-3159, 800-565-4923,

Fish & Wildlife Heritage Commission, Robinson Pl., 300 Water St., PO Box 7000, Peterborough, ON K9J 8M5
Fax: 705-755-5093

Quebec

Fondation de la faune du Québec, Place Iberville II, #420, 1175, av Lavigerie, Québec, QC G1V 4P1
418-644-7926, Fax: 418-643-7655, 877-639-0742, ffq@riq.qc.ca

Ministère des Ressources naturelles et de la Faune, 880, ch Sainte-Foy, Québec, G1S 4X4 QC
418-627-8600, Fax: 418-644-6513, 866-248-6936, services.clientele@mrnf.gouv.qc.ca

WOMEN'S ISSUES

See Also: Pay Equity

Status of Women Canada, 123 Slater St., 10th Fl., Ottawa, K1P 1H9 ON
613-995-7835, Fax: 613-947-0761, 866-902-2719, infonational@swc-cfc.gc.ca

Alberta

Alberta Tourism, Parks, Recreation & Culture, Communications Branch, Standard Life Centre, 10405 Jasper Ave., 7th Fl., Edmonton, T5J 4R7 AB
780-427-6530, Fax: 780-427-1496, Comdev.Communications@gov.ab.ca

British Columbia

Rural Development, 800 Johnson St., 6th Fl., PO Box 9824 Prov Govt,Victoria, V8W 9W4 BC
250-953-3005, Fax: 250-387-7935

Manitoba

Manitoba Women's Advisory Council, #301, 155 Carlton St., Winnipeg, MB R3C 3H8
204-945-6281, Fax: 204-945-6511, 800-282-8069, 001women@gov.mb.ca

Status of Women, #409, 401 York Ave., Winnipeg, R3C 0P8 MB
204-945-3476, Fax: 204-945-0013, 800-263-0234, mwd@gov.mb.ca

New Brunswick

Department of Social Development, Sartain MacDonald Bldg., 551 King St., PO Box 6000, Fredericton, E3B 5H1 NB
506-453-2001, Fax: 506-453-7478

New Brunswick Advisory Council on the Status of Women, 236 King St., Fredericton, E3B 1E2 NB
506-444-4101, Fax: 506-444-4318, 800-332-3087, acswcccf@gnb.ca

Newfoundland & Labrador

Provincial Advisory Council on the Status of Women, #103, 15 Hallett Cres., St. John's, A1B 4C4 NL
709-753-7270, Fax: 709-753-2606, 877-753-7270, info@pacsw.ca

Nova Scotia

Nova Scotia Advisory Council on the Status of Women, PO Box 745, Halifax, B3J 2T3 NS
902-424-8662, Fax: 902-424-0573, 800-565-8663, nsacsw@gov.ns.ca

Nunavut

Department of Culture, Language, Elders & Youth, PO Box 1000 800,Iqaluit, X0A 0H0 NU
867-975-5500, Fax: 867-975-5504, 866-934-2035

Ontario

Ontario Women's Directorate, 777 Bay St., 6th Fl., Toronto, M7A 2J4 ON
416-314-0300, Fax: 416-314-0247, 866-510-5902, info.mci@ontario.ca

Prince Edward Island

Advisory Council on the Status of Women, Sherwood Business Centre, 161 St. Peter's Rd., PO Box 2000, Charlottetown, PE C1A 7N8
902-368-4510, Fax: 902-368-4516, peistatusofwomen@eastlink.ca

Quebec

Ministère de la Famille et des Aînés, 425, rue Saint-Amable, 1er étage, Québec, G1R 4Z1 QC
877-216-6202

Saskatchewan

Status of Women, #400, 1870 Albert St., Regina, SK S4P 4W1
306-787-7401, Fax: 306-787-2058

Yukon Territory

Yukon Women's Directorate, PO Box 2703, Whitehorse, Y1A 2C6 YT
867-667-3030, Fax: 867-393-6270

WORKERS' COMPENSATION

Merchant Seamen Compensation Board, Secretary, Merchant Seamen Compensation Board, Phase II, Place du Portage, 10th Fl., Gatineau, QC K1A 0J2
819-953-8001, Fax: 819-994-5368

Alberta

Appeals Commission for Alberta Workers' Compensation, Energy Square Bldg., #901, 10109 - 106th St., Edmonton, AB T5J 3L7
780-412-8700, Fax: 780-412-8701

British Columbia

Workers' Compensation Appeal Tribunal, #150, 4600 Jacombs Rd., Richmond, BC V6V 3B1
604-664-7800, Fax: 604-664-7898, 800-663-2782

Workers' Compensation Board of British Columbia, PO Box 5350 Terminal,Vancouver, V6B 5L5 BC
604-276-3100, Fax: 604-244-6490, 888-621-7233

Manitoba

Manitoba Workers' Compensation Board, 333 Broadway Ave., Winnipeg, R3C 4W3 MB

204-954-4321, Fax: 204-954-4999, 800-362-3340, wcb@wcb.mb.ca

New Brunswick
Workplace Health, Safety & Compensation Commission of New Brunswick, 1 Portland St., PO Box 160, Saint John, E2L 3X9 NB
506-632-2200, 800-222-9775, communications@ws-ts.nb.ca

Newfoundland & Labrador
Newfoundland & Labrador Workplace Health, Safety & Compensation Commission, 146 - 148 Forest Rd., PO Box 9000, St. John's, A1A 3B8 NL
709-778-1000, Fax: 709-738-1714, 800-563-9000, general.inquiries@whscc.nl.ca

Northwest Territories
Northwest Territories & Nunavut Workers' Compensation Board, Centre Square Tower, 5022 - 49th St., 5th Fl., PO Box 8888, Yellowknife, X1A 2R3 NT
867-920-3888, Fax: 867-873-4596, 800-661-0792, wcb@wcb.nt.ca

Nova Scotia
Workers' Compensation Board of Nova Scotia, 5668 South St., PO Box 1150, Halifax, B3J 2Y2 NS
902-491-8999, Fax: 902-491-8002, 800-870-3331, info@wcb.gov.ns.ca

Ontario
Workplace Safety & Insurance Board, 200 Front St. West, Ground Fl., Toronto, M5V 3J1 ON
416-344-1000, Fax: 416-344-4684, 800-387-0750

Prince Edward Island
Prince Edward Island Workers Compensation Board, 14 Weymouth St., PO Box 757, Charlottetown, C1A 7L7 PE
902-368-5680, Fax: 902-368-5705, 800-237-5049

Quebec
Commission des lésions professionnelles, #700, 900, Place d'Youville, Québec, QC G1R 3P7
418-644-7777, Fax: 418-644-6443, 800-463-1591
Commission de la santé et de la sécurité du travail du Québec, 524, rue Bourdages, CP 1200 Terminus postal,Québec, G1K 7E2 QC
418-266-4850, Fax: 418-266-4398, 866-302-2778

Saskatchewan
Saskatchewan Workers' Compensation Board, #200, 1881 Scarth St., Regina, S4P 4L1 SK
306-787-4370, Fax: 306-787-7582, 800-667-7590, internet_clientsvc@wcbsask.com

Yukon Territory
Yukon Workers' Compensation Health & Safety Board, 401 Strickland St., Whitehorse, Y1A 5N8 YT
867-667-5645, Fax: 867-393-6279, 800-661-0443, worksafe@gov.yk.ca

YOUNG OFFENDERS

Justice Canada, East Memorial Bldg., 284 Wellington St., Ottawa, K1A 0H8 ON
613-957-4222, Fax: 613-954-0811, webadmin@justice.gc.ca

Alberta
Alberta Justice & Attorney General, Communications, Bowker Bldg., 9833 - 109 St., 3rd Fl., Edmonton, T5K 2E8 AB
780-427-2745, Fax: 780-427-6821,-310-0000

British Columbia
Ministry of the Attorney General, PO Box 9044 Prov Govt,Victoria, V8W 9E2 BC
250-387-1866, Fax: 250-387-6411
Office of the Representative for Children & Youth, 1019 Wharf St., PO Box 9207 Prov Govt, Victoria, BC V8W 9J1
250-356-6710, Fax: 250-356-0837, 800-476-3933, rcy@rcybc.ca

Northwest Territories
Department of Justice, Courthouse, 4903 - 49th St., 6th Fl., PO Box 1320, Yellowknife, X1A 2L9 NT
867-920-6197

Nova Scotia
Department of Justice, 5151 Terminal Rd., 4th Fl., PO Box 7, Halifax, B3J 2L6 NS
902-424-4030, Fax: 902-424-0510, webbermj@gov.ns.ca

Nunavut
Young Offenders, 1548 Federal Rd., PO Box 1439, Iqaluit, NU X0A 0H0
867-979-4452, Fax: 867-979-5506

Ontario
Ministry of the Attorney General, McMurtry-Scott Bldg., 720 Bay St., 11th Fl., Toronto, M5G 2K1 ON
416-326-2220, Fax: 416-326-4007, 800-518-7901

Prince Edward Island
Office of the Attorney General, Shaw Building, North, 105 Rochford St., 4th Fl., PO Box 2000, Charlottetown, C1A 7N8 PE
902-368-5152, Fax: 902-368-4910

YOUTH SERVICES

British Columbia
Provincial Services, #203, 940 Blanshard St., PO Box 9717 Prov Govt,Victoria, V8W 9S1 BC
250-387-0978, Fax: 250-356-2079

New Brunswick
New Brunswick Advisory Council on Youth, Frederick Square, #130, 77 Westmorland St., PO Box 6000, Fredericton, E3B 5H1 NB
506-453-3271, Fax: 506-444-4413, 888-830-5588, nbacy-ccjnb@gnb.ca

Nunavut
Department of Culture, Language, Elders & Youth, PO Box 1000 800,Iqaluit, X0A 0H0 NU
867-975-5500, Fax: 867-975-5504, 866-934-2035

Ontario
Ministry of Children & Youth Services, 56 Wellesley St. West, 14th Fl., Toronto, M5S 2G3 ON
Fax: 416-325-5191, 866-821-7770

Prince Edward Island
Department of Social Services & Seniors, Jones Bldg., 11 Kent St., 2nd Fl., PO Box 2000, Charlottetown, C1A 7N8 PE
902-620-3777, Fax: 902-894-0242

Quebec
Ministère de la Santé et des Services sociaux, Direction des communications et Renseignements généraux, 1075, ch Sainte-Foy, Québec, G1S 2M1 QC
418-266-8900, 800-707-3380, regisseur.web@msss.gouv.qc.ca

ZONING

Alberta
Local Government Services Division, Commerce Place, 10155 - 102 St., 17th Fl., Edmonton, T5J 4L4 AB

British Columbia
Ministry of Community & Rural Development, 800 Johnson St., 6th Fl., PO Box 9490 Prov Govt,Victoria, V8W 9N7 BC
250-387-2283, Fax: 250-387-4312, Feedback@gov.bc.ca

Manitoba
Manitoba Municipal Board, #1144, 363 Broadway, Winnipeg, MB R3C 3N9
204-945-2941, Fax: 204-948-2235

New Brunswick
Department of Local Government, Marysville Place, 20 McGloin St., PO Box 6000, Fredericton, E3B 5H1 NB
506-453-2807, Fax: 506-453-3988

Quebec
Commission municipale du Québec, Mezzanine, aile Chauveau, 10, rue Pierre-Olivier-Chauveau, Tour 5e étage, Québec, QC G1R 4J3
418-691-2014, Fax: 418-644-4676, 866-353-6767, cmq@mamr.gouv.qc.ca

Government of Canada

c/o Canada Enquiry Centre, Service Canada, Ottawa, ON K1A 0J9
613-941-1827, 800-622-6232
sitecanadasite@canada.gc.ca
www.canada.gc.ca

All political authority in Canada is divided between the federal & provincial governments, according to the provisions of the Constitution Act, 1867. Local municipalities are a concern of the provinces, & derive their authority from Acts of provincial legislation. The Parliament of Canada consists of Her Majesty Queen Elizabeth II (represented in Canada by the Governor General, His Excellency the Right Honourable David Johnston), an Upper House called the Senate, & an elected House of Commons.

Governor General & Commander-in-Chief of Canada / Gouverneur général et Commandant en chef du Canada

Rideau Hall, 1 Sussex Dr., Ottawa, ON K1A 0A1
613-993-8200, Fax: 613-998-8760, 800-465-6890
info@gg.ca
www.gg.ca

Canada is a constitutional monarchy. Under the terms of its Constitution, Her Majesty Queen Elizabeth II is the Head of State. The duties of the Head of State in Canada are undertaken by the Governor General as the Crown's representative. He is also Commander-in-Chief of the Canadian Forces, Chancellor & Principal Companion of the Order of Canada, Chancellor & Commander of the Order of Military Merit, & Head of the Canadian Heraldic Authority. The Office of the Governor General encompasses a number of responsibilities, both constitutional & traditional in nature. The Governor General of Canada exercises powers & responsibilities belonging to the Sovereign, with the advice of members of the Privy Council. He is involved in the promotion of Canadian sovereignty at home & represents Canada abroad. Canadian values, diversity, inclusion, culture, & heritage are promoted by the Governor General. National honours, decorations, & awards to recognize people who have demonstrated excellence, valour, bravery, or exceptional dedication to service are presented by the Governor General.

Governor General,Rt. Hon. David Johnston, C.C.
613-993-8200, Fax: 613-993-1967
Secretary to the Governor General, Sheila-Marie Cook
613-993-0259, Fax: 613-993-1967
Director General, Corporate Services, Dorothy M. Grandmaitre
613-993-8166, Fax: 613-954-4950
Superintendent, Associated Services - Security, Louis Lahaie
613-993-9332, Fax: 613-993-8641

The Chancellery of Honours / Chancellerie
1 Sussex Dr., Ottawa, ON K1A 0A1
613-998-8732, Fax: 613-991-1681

Deputy Secretary & Deputy Herald Chancellor, Office of the Secretary to the Governor General, The Chancellery of Honours, Emmanuelle Sajous
613-998-8731, Fax: 613-991-1681
Director, Honours, Office of the Secretary to the Governor General, Honours Directorate, Gabrielle Lappa
613-991-0894, Fax: 613-991-1681
Chief Herald of Canada & Director, Office of the Secretary to the Governor General, The Canadian Heraldic Authority, Claire Boudreau
613-991-2227, Fax: 613-990-5818

Policy, Program & Protocol Branch / Politique, programme et protocole
1 Sussex Dr., Ottawa, ON K1A 0A1

Director, Events & Visitor Services, Christine MacIntyre
613-993-1901, Fax: 613-991-5113
Director, Policy, Planning, & Correspondence, Duncan Mousseau
613-993-1934, Fax: 613-993-1552
Director, Security & Logistics, Jean-François Simard
613-993-0439, Fax: 613-993-4728
Director, Household Services, Philippe Wettel
613-990-7629, Fax: 613-998-5579
Chief, Information & Media Services, Public Affairs, Annabelle Cloutier
613-993-8158, Fax: 613-998-1664

Privy Council Office (PCO) / Bureau du Conseil privé (BCP)

#1000, 85 Sparks St., Ottawa, ON K1A 0A3
613-957-5153, Fax: 613-997-5043,
info@pco-bcp.gc.ca
www.pco-bcp.gc.ca

The Privy Council Office provides non-partisan advice & information from across the Public Service to the Prime Minister, the Cabinet, & its decision-making structures. The key roles of the Privy Council are as follows: advising the Prime Minister & supporting the Cabinet; managing the Cabinet's decision-making system & facilitating its efficient & effective functioning on a daily basis; & providing public service leadership, including the management of the appointments process for Crown corporations & agencies, & senior positions in federal departments. The Privy Council is led by the Clerk of the Privy Council. A member of the Privy Council is awarded the title, "Honourable", for life. The Governor General, the Prime Minister, & the Chief Justice of Canada area acoorded the title, "The Right Honourable", for life.

Acts Administered:
Canadian Transportation Accident Investigation & Safety Board Act
National Round Table on the Environment & the Economy Act
Oaths of Allegiance Act
Parliamentary Employment & Staff Relations Act
Public Service Staff Relations Act
Representation Act

President, Queen's Privy Council for Canada; Minister, Intergovernmental Affairs; Minister for La Francophonie (PCO Minister),Hon. Josée Verner
613-996-4151, Fax: 613-954-2269,VerneJ@parl.gc.ca
Leader of the Government in the House of Commons (PCO Minister),Hon. John Baird, B.A.(Hons.)
613-996-0984, Fax: 613-996-9880,BairdJ@parl.gc.ca; jhii@lghc-lgcc.gc.ca, Other Communications: Department Phone: 613-995-7226
Leader of the Government in the Senate (PCO Minister),Hon. Marjory LeBreton
613-943-0756, 800-267-7362,Fax: 613-943-1493,lebrem@sen.parl.gc.ca; Marjory.LeBreton@pco-bcp.gc.ca
Minister of State (Democratic Reform) (PCO Minister),Hon. Steven John Fletcher, B.Sc., M.B.A.
613-995-5609, Fax: 613-992-3199,FletcS@parl.gc.ca
Minister of State; Chief Government Whip (PCO Minister),Hon. Gordon O'Connor, B.A., B.Sc.
613-992-1119, Fax: 613-992-1043,OConnor.G@parl.gc.ca
Clerk of the Privy Council & Secretary to the Cabinet, Wayne Wouters
613-957-5400, Fax: 613-957-5729,info@clerk.gc.ca.
National Security Advisor to the Prime Minister; Associate Secretary to the Cabinet, Marie-Lucie Morin
613-957-5466, Fax: 613-957-5089
Deputy Minister, Afghanistan Task Force, Greta Bossenmaier
613-952-4900, Fax: 613-952-4924
Deputy Minister, Intergovernmental Affairs, Serge Dupont
613-947-5695, Fax: 613-943-1857
Deputy Minister, Administrative Services Review, Daniel Jean
613-996-6538, Fax: 613-995-3506
Deputy Secretary to the Cabinet; Foreign & Defence Policy Advisor to the Prime Minister, Claude Carrière
613-957-5476, Fax: 613-957-5365
Deputy Secretary to the Cabinet, Senior Personnel & Public Service Renewal, Patricia Hassard
613-957-5360, Fax: 613-957-5006
Deputy Secretary to the Cabinet, Plans & Consultation, Simon Kennedy
613-957-5462, Fax: 613-957-5487
Deputy Secretary to the Cabinet, Operations, Michael Martin
613-957-5417, Fax: 613-957-5637
Deputy Secretary to the Cabinet, Legislation & House Planning, & Machinery of Government;, Counsel to the Clerk of the Privy Council, Yvan Roy
613-957-5792, Fax: 613-952-4955

Privy Council Members & Date When Sworn In
Hon. Paul Theodore Hellyer, Apr. 26, 1957
H.R.H.Prince Philip, The Duke of Edinburg, Oct. 14, 1957
Hon. Paul Martineau, Aug. 9, 1962
Hon. J.H. Théogène Ricard, Mar. 18, 1963
Rt. Hon. Martial Asselin, Mar. 18, 1963
Hon. Allan Joseph MacEachen, Apr. 22, 1963
Hon. Yvon Dupuis, Feb. 3, 1964
Hon. Edgar John Benson, Jun. 29, 1964
Rt. Hon. John Napier Turner, Dec. 18, 1965
Rt. Hon. Joseph Jacques Jean Chrétien, Apr. 4, 1967
Hon. Alexander Bradshaw Campbell, Jul. 5, 1967
Hon. Donald Stovel Macdonald, Apr. 20, 1968
Hon. Jean-Eudes Dubé, Jul. 6, 1968
Hon. Otto Emil Lang, Jul. 6, 1968
Rt. Hon. Herbert Eser Gray, Oct. 20, 1969
Hon. Robert D. George Stanbury, Oct. 20, 1969
Hon. Jean-Pierre Goyer, Dec. 22, 1970
Hon. Alastair William Gillespie, Aug. 12, 1971
Hon. Patrick Morgan Mahoney, Jan. 28, 1972
Hon. Eugene Francis Whelan, Nov. 27, 1972
Hon. William Warren Allmand, Nov. 27, 1972
Hon. James Hugh Faulkner, Nov. 27, 1972
Hon. André Ouellet, Nov. 27, 1972
Hon. Marc Lalonde, Nov. 27, 1972
Hon. Barnett Jerome Danson, Aug. 8, 1974
Hon. J. Judd Buchanan, Aug. 8, 1974
Hon. Pierre Juneau, Aug. 29, 1975
Hon. Marcel Lessard, Sep. 26, 1975
Hon. Leonard Stephen Marchand, Sep. 15, 1976
Hon. John Roberts, Sep. 15, 1976
Hon. Monique Bégin, Sep. 15, 1976
Hon. Jean-Jacques Blais, Sep. 15, 1976
Hon. Francis Fox, Sep. 15, 1976
Hon. Anthony Chisholm Abbott, Sep. 15, 1976
Hon. Iona Campagnolo, Sep. 15, 1976
Hon. Norman A. Cafik, Sep. 16, 1977
Hon. J. Gilles Lamontagne, Jan. 19, 1978
Hon. John M. Reid, Nov. 24, 1978
Hon. Pierre De Bané, Nov. 24, 1978
Rt. Hon. Charles Joseph Clark, Jun. 4, 1979
Hon. Flora Isabel MacDonald, Jun. 4, 1979
Hon. James Aloysius McGrath, Jun. 4, 1979
Hon. Allan Frederick Lawrence, Jun. 4, 1979
Hon. John Carnell Crosbie, Jun. 4, 1979
Hon. David Samuel Horne MacDonald, Jun. 4, 1979
Hon. Lincoln MacCauley Alexander, Jun. 4, 1979
Hon. Roch La Salle, Jun. 4, 1979
Rt. Hon. Donald Frank Mazankowski, Jun. 4, 1979
Hon. Elmer MacIntosh MacKay, Jun. 4, 1979
Hon. Arthur Jacob Epp, Jun. 4, 1979
Hon. John Allen Fraser, Jun. 4, 1979
Hon. William H. Jarvis, Jun. 4, 1979
Hon. Sinclair McKnight Stevens, Jun. 4, 1979
Hon. John Wise, Jun. 4, 1979
Hon. Ronald George Atkey, Jun. 4, 1979
Hon. David Edward Crombie, Jun. 4, 1979
Hon. Henry Perrin Beatty, Jun. 4, 1979
Hon. J. Robert Howie, Jun. 4, 1979
Hon. Michael Holcombe Wilson, Jun. 4, 1979
Hon. Gerald Augustine Regan, Mar. 3, 1980
Hon. Robert Phillip Kaplan, Mar. 3, 1980
Hon. James Sydney Clark Fleming, Mar. 3, 1980
Hon. William H. Rompkey, Mar. 3, 1980
Hon. Pierre Bussières, Mar. 3, 1980
Hon. Charles Lapointe, Mar. 3, 1980
Hon. Edward C. Lumley, Mar. 3, 1980
Hon. Yvon Pinard, Mar. 3, 1980
Hon. Donald James Johnston, Mar. 3, 1980
Hon. Lloyd Axworthy, Mar. 3, 1980
Hon. Paul James Cosgrove, Mar. 3, 1980
Hon. Judith A. Erola, Mar. 3, 1980
Hon. Jacob Austin, Sep. 22, 1981
Hon. Serge Joyal, Sep. 22, 1981
Hon. W. Bennett Campbell, Sep. 22, 1981
Hon. Robert Gordon Robertson, Mar. 2, 1982
Hon. John Edward Broadbent, Apr. 17, 1982
Hon. William Grenville Davis, Apr. 17, 1982
Hon. Allan Emrys Blakeney, Apr. 17, 1982
Hon. E. Peter Lougheed, Apr. 17, 1982
Hon. William Richards Bennett, Apr. 17, 1982
Hon. John MacLennan Buchanan, Apr. 17, 1982
Hon. Alfred Brian Peckford, Apr. 17, 1982
Hon. James Matthew Lee, Apr. 17, 1982
Hon. Howard Russell Pawley, Apr. 17, 1982
Hon. Sterling Rufus Lyon, Apr. 17, 1982
Hon. David Michael Collenette, Aug. 12, 1983
Hon. Céline Hervieux-Payette, Aug. 12, 1983
Hon. Roger Simmons, Aug. 12, 1983
Hon. David Paul Smith, Aug. 12, 1983
Hon. Roy MacLaren, Aug. 17, 1983
Hon. Peter Michael Pitfield, Apr. 19, 1984
Rt. Hon. Martin Brian Mulroney, May 7, 1984
Rt. Hon. Edward Richard Schreyer, Jun. 3, 1984
Hon. Herb Breau, Jun. 30, 1984
Hon. Joseph Roger Rémi Bujold, Jun. 30, 1984
Hon. Jean-C. Lapierre, Jun. 30, 1984
Hon. Ralph Ferguson, Jun. 30, 1984
Hon. Robert Carman Coates, Sep. 17, 1984
Hon. Jack Burnett Murta, Sep. 17, 1984
Hon. Harvie Andre, Sep. 17, 1984
Hon. Otto John Jelinek, Sep. 17, 1984
Hon. Charles James Mayer, Sep. 17, 1984
Hon. Thomas Edward Siddon, Sep. 17, 1984
Hon. William Hunter McKnight, Sep. 17, 1984
Hon. Rev. Walter Franklin McLean, Sep. 17, 1984
Hon. Thomas Michael McMillan, Sep. 17, 1984
Hon. Patricia Carney, Sep. 17, 1984
Hon. André Bissonnette, Sep. 17, 1984
Hon. Suzanne Blais-Grenier, Sep. 17, 1984
Hon. Benoît Bouchard, Sep. 17, 1984
Hon. Andrée Champagne, Sep. 17, 1984
Hon. Michel Côté, Sep. 17, 1984

Hon. James Francis Kelleher, Sep. 17, 1984
Hon. Marcel Masse, Sep. 17, 1984
Hon. Barbara Jean McDougall, Sep. 17, 1984
Hon. Monique Vézina, Sep. 17, 1984
Hon. Saul Mark Cherniack, Nov. 30, 1984
Hon. Paule Gauthier, Nov. 30, 1984
Hon. Stewart Donald McInnes, Aug. 20, 1985
Hon. Frank Oberle, Nov. 20, 1985
Hon. Gordon F. Joseph Osbaldeston, Feb. 13, 1986
Hon. Lowell Murray, Jun. 30, 1986
Hon. Paul Wyatt Dick, Jun. 30, 1986
Hon. Pierre H. Cadieux, Jun. 30, 1986
Hon. Jean J. Charest, Jun. 30, 1986
Hon. Thomas Hockin, Jun. 30, 1986
Hon. Monique Landry, Jun. 30, 1986
Hon. Bernard Valcourt, Jun. 30, 1986
Hon. Gerry Weiner, Jun. 30, 1986
Hon. John William Bosley, Jun. 30, 1987
Hon. Douglas Grinslade Lewis, Aug. 27, 1987
Hon. Pierre Blais, Aug. 27, 1987
Hon. Lucien Bouchard, Mar. 31, 1988
Hon. Gerry St. Germain, Mar. 31, 1988
Hon. John Horton McDermid, Sep. 15, 1988
Hon. Shirley Martin, Sep. 15, 1988
Hon. Mary Collins, Jan. 30, 1989
Hon. Alan Redway, Jan. 30, 1989
Hon. William Charles Winegard, Jan. 30, 1989
Rt. Hon. A. Kim Campbell, Jan. 30, 1989
Hon. Gilles Loiselle, Jan. 30, 1989
Hon. Marcel Danis, Feb. 23, 1990
Hon. Audrey McLaughlin, Jan. 10, 1991
Hon. Pauline Browes, Apr. 21, 1991
Hon. J.J. Michel Robert, Dec. 5, 1991
Hon. Marcel Prud'homme, Jul. 1, 1992
Hon. Lorne Edmund Nystrom, Jul. 1, 1992
Hon. David Alexander Colville, Jul. 1, 1992
Hon. Paul Desmarais, Jul. 1, 1992
Hon. John Charles Polanyi, Jul. 1, 1992
Hon. Maurice F. Strong, Jul. 1, 1992
Hon. Antonine Maillet, Jul. 1, 1992
Hon. Richard Cashin, Jul. 1, 1992
Hon. Paul M. Tellier, Jul. 1, 1992
Hon. David Robert Peterson, Jul. 1, 1992
Hon. Conrad M. Black, Jul. 1, 1992
Hon. Charles Rosner Bronfman, Oct. 21, 1992
Hon. George W. Vari, Dec. 23, 1992
Hon. Pierre H. Vincent, Jan. 4, 1993
Hon. James Stewart Edwards, Jun. 25, 1993
Hon. Robert Douglas Nicholson, Jun. 25, 1993
Hon. Barbara Jane Sparrow, Jun. 25, 1993
Hon. Peter L. McCreath, Jun. 25, 1993
Hon. Ian Angus Ross Reid, Jun. 25, 1993
Hon. Larry Schneider, Jun. 25, 1993
Hon. Garth Turner, Jun. 25, 1993
Hon. David Anderson, Nov. 4, 1993
Hon. Ralph Edward Goodale, Nov. 4, 1993
Hon. David Charles Dingwall, Nov. 4, 1993
Hon. Ron Irwin, Nov. 4, 1993
Hon. Brian Tobin, Nov. 4, 1993
Hon. Joyce Fairbairn, Nov. 4, 1993
Hon. Sheila Maureen Copps, Nov. 4, 1993
Hon. Sergio Marchi, Nov. 4, 1993
Hon. John Manley, Nov. 4, 1993
Hon. Diane Marleau, Nov. 4, 1993
Rt. Hon. Paul Martin, Nov. 4, 1993
Hon. Douglas Young, Nov. 4, 1993
Hon. Michel Dupuy, Nov. 4, 1993
Hon. Arthur C. Eggleton, Nov. 4, 1993
Hon. Marcel Massé, Nov. 4, 1993
Hon. Anne McLellan, Nov. 4, 1993
Hon. Allan Rock, Nov. 4, 1993
Hon. Fernand Robichaud, Nov. 4, 1993
Hon. Ethel Blondin-Andrew, Nov. 4, 1993
Hon. Lawrence MacAulay, Nov. 4, 1993
Hon. Christine Stewart, Nov. 4, 1993
Hon. Raymond Chan, Nov. 4, 1993
Hon. Jon Gerrard, Nov. 4, 1993
Hon. Douglas Peters, Nov. 4, 1993
Hon. Alfonso Gagliano, Sep. 15, 1994
Hon. Lucienne Robillard, Feb. 22, 1995
Hon. Fred J. Mifflin, Jan. 25, 1996
Hon. Jane Stewart, Jan. 25, 1996
Hon. Stéphane Dion, Jan. 25, 1996
Hon. Pierre Pettigrew, Jan. 25, 1996
Hon. Martin Cauchon, Jan. 25, 1996
Hon. Hedy Fry, Jan. 25, 1996
Hon. James Andrew Grant, Sep. 30, 1996
Hon. Don Boudria, Oct. 4, 1996
Hon. Bernard Alasdair Graham, Jun. 11, 1997
Hon. Lyle Vanclief, Jun. 11, 1997
Hon. Herb Dhaliwal, Jun. 11, 1997
Hon. David Kilgour, Jun. 11, 1997
Hon. James Scott Peterson, Jun. 11, 1997
Hon. Andy Scott, Jun. 11, 1997
Hon. Andrew Mitchell, Jun. 11, 1997
Hon. Gilbert Normand, Jun. 18, 1997
Hon. Bob Rae, Apr. 30, 1998
Hon. Claudette Bradshaw, Nov. 23, 1998
Hon. Jocelyne Bourgon, Dec. 14, 1998
Hon. Raymond A. Speaker, Jun. 9, 1999
Hon. Frank Joseph McKenna, Jun. 9, 1999
Hon. George Baker, Aug. 3, 1999
Hon. Maria Minna, Aug. 3, 1999
Hon. Elinor Caplan, Aug. 3, 1999
Hon. Denis Coderre, Aug. 3, 1999
Hon. Robert Daniel Nault, Aug. 3, 1999
Hon. J. Bernard Boudreau, Oct. 4, 1999
Rt. Hon. Beverley M. McLachlin, Jan. 12, 2000
Hon. Sharon Carstairs, Jan. 9, 2001
Hon. Robert G. Thibault, Jan. 9, 2001
Hon. Rey Pagtakhan, Jan. 9, 2001
Hon. Gary Albert Filmon, Oct. 4, 2001
Hon. Susan Whelan, Jan. 15, 2002
Hon. Maurizio Bevilacqua, Jan. 15, 2002
Hon. Paul DeVillers, Jan. 15, 2002
Hon. Gar Knutson, Jan. 15, 2002
Hon. Denis Paradis, Jan. 15, 2002
Hon. Claude Drouin, Jan. 15, 2002
Hon. John McCallum, Jan. 15, 2002
Hon. Stephen Owen, Jan. 15, 2002
Hon. William Graham, Jan. 16, 2002
Hon. Gerry Byrne, Jan. 16, 2002
Hon. Jean Augustine, May 26, 2002
Hon. Wayne Easter, Oct. 22, 2002
Hon. Baljit Singh Chadha, Feb. 20, 2003
Hon. Steven W. Mahoney, Apr. 11, 2003
Hon. Roy J. Romanow, Nov. 13, 2003
Hon. Stan Kazmierczak Keyes, Dec. 12, 2003
Hon. Robert Speller, Dec. 12, 2003
Hon. Giuseppe (Joseph) Volpe, Dec. 12, 2003
Hon. Reginald B. Alcock, Dec. 12, 2003
Hon. Geoff Regan, Dec. 12, 2003
Hon. Tony Valeri, Dec. 12, 2003
Hon. David Pratt, Dec. 12, 2003
Hon. Jacques Saada, Dec. 12, 2003
Hon. Irwin Cotler, Dec. 12, 2003
Hon. Judy Sgro, Dec. 12, 2003
Hon. Hélène Chalifour Scherrer, Dec. 12, 2003
Hon. Ruben John Efford, Dec. 12, 2003
Hon. Liza Frulla, Dec. 12, 2003
Hon. Joseph Robert Comuzzi, Dec. 12, 2003
Hon. Albina Guarnieri, Dec. 12, 2003
Hon. Joseph McGuire, Dec. 12, 2003
Hon. Mauril Bélanger, Dec. 12, 2003
Hon. Carolyn Bennett, Dec. 12, 2003
Hon. M. Aileen Carroll, Dec. 12, 2003
Hon. André Harvey, Dec. 12, 2003
Hon. Susan Barnes, Dec. 12, 2003
Hon. David Price, Dec. 12, 2003
Hon. Jim Karygiannis, Dec. 12, 2003
Privy Council Mmeber,Hon. Shawn Murphy, Dec. 12, 2003
Hon. Joseph Louis Jordan, Dec. 12, 2003
Hon. Roger Gallaway, Dec. 12, 2003
Hon. Paul Bonwick, Dec. 12, 2003
Hon. Eleni Bakopanos, Dec. 12, 2003
Hon. Georges Farrah, Dec. 12, 2003
Hon. Mark Eyking, Dec. 12, 2003
Hon. Dan McTeague, Dec. 12, 2003
Hon. Walt Lastewka, Dec. 12, 2003
Hon. Brenda Kay Chamberlain, Dec. 12, 2003
Hon. Larry Bagnell, Dec. 12, 2003
Hon. John Harvard, Dec. 12, 2003
Hon. Gurbax Singh Malhi, Dec. 12, 2003
Hon. Yvon Charbonneau, Dec. 12, 2003
Hon. Joseph Frank Fontana, Dec. 12, 2003
Hon. Jerry Pickard, Dec. 12, 2003
Hon. John McKay, Dec. 12, 2003
Hon. Scott Brison, Dec. 12, 2003
Hon. John Ferguson Godfrey, Dec. 12, 2003
Hon. Andrew Telegdi, Jan. 30, 2004
Hon. Rev. William Alexander Blaikie, Feb. 19, 2004
Hon. Grant Hill, Feb. 19, 2004
Rt. Hon. Stephen Joseph Harper, May 4, 2004
Hon. Joseph Marin Jacques Olivier, May 5, 2004
Hon. Ujjal Dosanjh, Jul. 20, 2004
Hon. Ken Dryden, Jul. 20, 2004
Hon. David Emerson, Jul. 20, 2004
Hon. Tony Ianno, Jul. 20, 2004
Hon. Peter Adams, Jul. 20, 2004
Hon. Sarmite Bulte, Jul. 20, 2004
Hon. Roy Cullen, Jul. 20, 2004
Hon. Marlene Jennings, Jul. 20, 2004
Hon. Dominic LeBlanc, Jul. 20, 2004
Hon. Judi Longfield, Jul. 20, 2004
Hon. Paul Macklin, Jul. 20, 2004
Hon. Keith P. Martin, Jul. 20, 2004
Hon. Karen Redman, Jul. 20, 2004
Hon. Raymond Simard, Jul. 20, 2004
Hon. Patricia Ann Torsney, Jul. 20, 2004
Hon. Bryon Wilfert, Jul. 20, 2004
Hon. Jack Gilbert Layton, Mar. 21, 2005
Hon. Belinda Stronach, May 17, 2005
Hon. Aldéa Landry, Q.C., Jun. 24, 2005
Rt. Hon. Adrienne Clarkson, Oct. 3, 2005
Hon. Navdeep Bains, Oct. 7, 2005
Hon. Anita Neville, Oct. 7, 2005
Hon. Charles Hubbard, Oct. 7, 2005
Hon. Jean-Pierre Blackburn, Feb. 6, 2006
Hon. Greg Thompson, Feb. 6, 2006
Hon. Marjory LeBreton, Feb. 6, 2006
Hon. Monte Solberg, Feb. 6, 2006
Hon. Charles (Chuck) Strahl, Feb. 6, 2006
Hon. Gary Lunn, Feb. 6, 2006
Hon. Peter Gordon MacKay, Feb. 6, 2006
Hon. Loyola Hearn, Feb. 6, 2006
Hon. Stockwell Burt Day, Feb. 6, 2006
Hon. Carol Skelton, Feb. 6, 2006
Hon. Vic Toews, Feb. 6, 2006
Hon. Rona Ambrose, Feb. 6, 2006
Hon. Michael D. Chong, Feb. 6, 2006
Hon. Diane Finley, Feb. 6, 2006
Hon. Gordon O'Connor, Feb. 6, 2006
Hon. Beverley J. (Bev) Oda, Feb. 6, 2006
Hon. John Baird, Feb. 6, 2006
Hon. Maxime Bernier, Feb. 6, 2006
Hon. Lawrence Cannon, Feb. 6, 2006
Hon. Tony Clement, Feb. 6, 2006
Hon. James Michael (Jim) Flaherty, Feb. 6, 2006
Hon. Josée Verner, Feb. 6, 2006
Hon. Jim Prentice, Feb. 6, 2006
Hon. Michael Fortier, Feb. 6, 2006
Hon. John Reynolds, Feb. 6, 2006
Hon. Jay D. Hill, Feb. 16, 2006
Hon. Peter Van Loan, Nov. 27, 2006
Hon. Jason Kenney, Jan. 4, 2007
Hon. Gerry Ritz, Jan. 4, 2007
Hon. Helena Guergis, Jan. 4, 2007
Hon. Christian Paradis, Jan. 4, 2007
Hon. Daniel Philip Hays, Jan. 22, 2007
Hon. John Abbott, Oct. 15, 2007
Hon. Diane Ablonczy, Aug. 14, 2007
Hon. James Moore, Jun. 25, 2008
Hon. Denis Losier, Sep. 3, 2008
Hon. Arthur Thomas Porter, Sep. 3, 2008
Hon. Leona Aglukkaq, Oct. 30, 2008
Hon. Keith Ashfield, Oct. 30, 2008
Hon. Steven John Fletcher, Oct. 30, 2008
Hon. Gary Goodyear, Oct. 30, 2008
Hon. Peter Kent, Oct. 30, 2008
Hon. Denis Lebel, Oct. 30, 2008
Hon. Rob Merrifield, Oct. 30, 2008
Hon. Lisa Raitt, Oct. 30, 2008
Hon. Gail Shea, Oct. 30, 2008
Hon. Lynn Yelich, Oct. 30, 2008
Hon. Leonard Joseph Gustafson, Jan. 8, 2009
Hon. Frances Lankin, Jan. 22, 2009
Hon. Kevin Lynch, May 11, 2009
Hon. Rob Moore, Jan. 19, 2010
Hon. Michael Grant Ignatieff, May 7, 2010
Hon. John Duncan, Aug. 10, 2010

• Office of Intergovernmental Affairs/ Affaires intergouvernementales

Senate of Canada / Sénat du Canada

Ottawa, ON K1A 0A4

613-995-1900,
www.sen.parl.gc.ca

Senators are appointed by the Governor General, upon the recommendation of the Prime Minister of Canada. Senators hold their positions only until they attain the age of seventy-five years. To be eligible for appointment, a senatorial candidate must be a Canadian citizen, & be at least thirty years of age. The person must own $4,000 of equity in land in his or her province or territory, & have a personal net worth of at least $4,000. A senator must also be a resident of the province or territory for which he or she is appointed. The main tasks of the Senate are as follows: to examinine bills; to approve, reject, or amend legislation; to investigate policy matters & to present recommendations; & to examine the government's spending proposals. No bill may become law, unless it is passed by the Senate. The main thrust of the Senate's work is carried out in committees, where bills are interpreted & reviewed clause by clause, & evidence is heard from groups & individuals who may be affected by the particular bill under review. Senators' committees, or study groups, investigate key issues, such as poverty, terrorism, literacy, children's rights, Aboriginal peoples, constitutional affairs, & foreign affairs. The Senate reports produced from these investig ations have proved to be valuable, & have often led to changes in government policy or legislation. The Speaker of the Senate is appointed by the Governor General, upon the recommendation of the Prime Minister. The Senate, as originally constituted at Confederation, consisted of 72 members. Through the addition of new provinces & territories, & the general growth of Canada, the Senate now has 105 regular members. By provinces & territories, representation in the Senate of Canada is as follows (September 2010): Alberta 6; British Columbia 6; Manitoba 6; New Brunswick 10; Newfoundland & Labrador 6; Northwest Territories 1; Nova Scotia 10; Nunavut 1; Ontario 24: Prince Edward Island 4; Québec 24: Saskatchewan 6; & Yukon 1; Total 105. By party affiliation, representation is as follows (September 2010): Conservative 52; Liberal 49; Independent 2; Progressive Conservative 2; Total 105.

Speaker of the Senate,Hon. Noël Kinsella
613-992-4416, 800-267-7362,Fax:
613-992-9772,kinsen@sen.parl.gc.ca

Leader of the Government in the Senate,Hon. Marjory LeBreton
613-943-0756, 800-267-7362,Fax:
613-943-1493,lebrem@sen.parl.gc.ca

Leader of the Opposition,Hon. James S. Cowan
613-995-4268, 800-267-7362,Fax:
613-995-4287,cowanj@sen.parl.gc.ca

Deputy Leader of the Government,Hon. Gerald Comeau
613-943-1448, 800-267-7362,Fax:
613-943-1556,comeag@sen.parl.gc.ca,

Deputy Leader of the Opposition,Hon. Claudette Tardif
613-947-3589, 800-267-7362,Fax:
613-947-3609,tardic@sen.parl.gc.ca

Government Whip,Hon. Consiglio Di Nino
613-992-3756, 800-267-7362,Fax:
613-943-1883,dininc@sen.parl.gc.ca

Opposition Whip,Hon. Jim Munson
613-947-2504, 800-267-7362,Fax:
613-947-2506,munsoj@sen.parl.gc.ca

Chief, Public Information, Olivier Carré-Delisle
613-992-1889

Clerk of the Senate & Clerk of the Parliaments, Gary W. O'Brien
613-992-2493

Director General, Parliamentary Precinct Services, Gilles Duguay
613-992-4787

Director, Legislative Systems & Broadcasting, Diane Boucher
613-992-1222

Director, Information Services Directorate, Hélène Bouchard
613-993-5299

Director, Human Resources Directorate, Linda Dodd
613-996-1096

Director, Finance Directorate, Nicole Proulx
613-943-0197

Usher of the Black Rod, Kevin MacLeod
613-992-8483

Senators, with appointment year, political affiliation & contact information

Hon. Raynell Andreychuk,1993, Conservative Party
613-947-2239, 800-267-7362,Fax:
613-947-2241,andrer@sen.parl.gc.ca

Hon. W. David Angus,1993, Conservative Party
613-947-3193, 800-267-7362,Fax:
613-947-3195,anguswd@sen.parl.gc.ca

Hon. Salma Ataullahjan,2010, Conservative Party
613-947-5906, 800-267-7362,Fax: 613-947-5908

Hon. George S. Baker,2002, Liberal
613-947-2517, 800-267-7362,Fax:
613-947-1525,bakerg@sen.parl.gc.ca

Hon. Tommy Banks,2000, Liberal
613-995-1889, 800-267-7362,Fax:
613-995-1938,gautht@sen.parl.gc.ca (Thérèsa Gauthier, Executive Assistant)

Hon. Pierre-Hugues Boisvenu,2010, Conservative Party
613-943-4030, 800-267-7362,Fax:
613-943-4029,boisvp@sen.parl.gc.ca

Hon. David Braley,2010, Conservative Party
613-943-0040, 800-267-7362,Fax:
613-943-0083,braled@sen.parl.gc.ca

Hon. Patrick Brazeau,2008, Conservative Party
613-947-4231, 800-267-7362,Fax:
613-947-4228,brazep@sen.parl.gc.ca

Hon. Bert Brown,2007, Conservative Party
613-944-3434, 800-267-7362,Fax:
613-944-3438,brownb@sen.parl.gc.ca

Hon. Catherine S Callbeck,1997, Liberal
613-943-0686, 800-267-7362,Fax:
613-943-0693,callbc@sen.parl.gc.ca

Hon. Larry W. Campbell,2005, Liberal
613-995-4050, 800-267-7362,Fax:
613-995-4056,campbel@sen.parl.gc.ca

Hon. Claude Carignan,2009, Conservative Party
613-992-0240, 800-267-7362,Fax:
613-992-0246,carigc@sen.parl.gc.ca

Hon. Sharon Carstairs,1994, Liberal
613-947-7123, 800-267-7362,Fax:
613-947-7125,carsts@sen.parl.gc.ca

Hon. Andrée Champagne,2005, Conservative Party
613-995-3999, 800-267-7362,Fax:
613-995-4034,champa@sen.parl.gc.ca

Hon. Maria Chaput,2002, Liberal
613-943-2435, 800-267-7362,Fax:
613-943-2482,chapum@sen.parl.gc.ca

Hon. Ethel M. Cochrane,1986, Conservative Party
613-992-1577, 800-267-7362,Fax:
613-995-6691,cochre@sen.parl.gc.ca

Hon. Gerald J. Comeau,1990, Conservative Party
613-943-1448, 800-267-7362,Fax:
613-943-1556,comeag@sen.parl.gc.ca

Hon. Anne C. Cools,1984, Independent
613-992-2808, 800-267-7362,Fax:
613-992-8513,coolsa@sen.parl.gc.ca

Hon. Jane Marie Cordy,2000, Liberal
613-995-8409, 800-267-7362,Fax:
613-995-8432,cordyj@sen.parl.gc.ca

Hon. James S. Cowan,2005, Liberal
613-995-4268, 800-267-7362,Fax:
613-995-4287,cowanj@sen.parl.gc.ca

Hon. Roméo Dallaire,2005, Liberal
613-995-4191, 800-267-7362,Fax:
613-995-4219,dallar@sen.parl.gc.ca

Hon. Dennis Dawson,2005, Liberal
613-995-3978, 800-267-7362,Fax:
613-995-3998,dawsod@sen.parl.gc.ca

Hon. Joseph A. Day,2001, Liberal
613-992-0833, 800-267-7362,Fax:
613-992-1175,dayja@sen.parl.gc.ca

Hon. Pierre De Bané,1984, Liberal
613-992-8289, 800-267-7362,Fax:
613-995-6709,debanp@sen.parl.gc.ca

Hon. Jacques Demers,2009, Conservative Party
613-992-0151, 800-267-7362,Fax:
613-992-0128,tessil@sen.parl.gc.ca

Hon. Consiglio Di Nino,1990, Conservative Party
613-992-3756, 800-267-7362,Fax:
613-943-1883,dininc@sen.parl.gc.ca

Hon. Fred Dickson,2009, Conservative Party
613-947-4130, 800-267-7362,Fax:
613-947-4134,johnse@sen.parl.gc.ca

Hon. Percy E. Downe,2003, Liberal
613-943-8107, 800-267-7362,Fax:
613-943-8109,downep@sen.parl.gc.ca

Hon. Michael Duffy,2009, Conservative Party
613-947-4163, 800-267-7362,Fax:
613-947-4157,mikeduffy@sen.parl.gc.ca

Hon. Lillian Eva Dyck,2005, Liberal
613-995-4318, 800-267-7362,Fax:
613-995-4331,dyckli@sen.parl.gc.ca

Hon. Nicole Eaton,2009, Conservative Party
613-947-4047, 800-267-7362,Fax:
613-947-4044,eatonn@sen.parl.gc.ca

Hon. Art Eggleton,2005, Liberal
613-995-4230, 800-267-7362,Fax:
613-995-4237,egglea@sen.parl.gc.ca

Hon. Joyce Fairbairn,1984, Liberal
613-996-4382, 800-267-7362,Fax:
613-995-3223,fairbj@sen.parl.gc.ca

Hon. Doug Finley,2009, Conservative Party
613-992-0172, 800-267-7362,Fax:
613-992-0169,finled@sen.parl.gc.ca

Hon. Suzanne Fortin-Duplessis,2009, Conservative Party
613-947-4036, 800-267-7362,Fax:
613-947-4004,fortis@sen.parl.gc.ca

Hon. Francis Fox,2005, Liberal
613-943-3626, 800-267-7362,Fax:
613-943-3628,foxf@sen.parl.gc.ca

Hon. Joan Fraser,1998, Liberal
613-943-9556, 800-267-7362,Fax:
613-943-9558,frasej@sen.parl.gc.ca

Hon. Linda Frum,2009, Conservative Party
613-992-0310, 800-267-7362,Fax:
613-992-0316,fruml@sen.parl.gc.ca

Hon. George Furey,1999, Liberal
613-943-7805, 800-267-7362,Fax:
613-943-7807,fureyg@sen.parl.gc.ca

Hon. Irving R. Gerstein,2009, Conservative Party
613-947-4041, 800-267-7362,Fax: 613-947-4039

Hon. Stephen Greene,2009, Conservative Party
613-947-4210, 800-267-7362,Fax:
613-947-4224,greens@sen.parl.gc.ca

Hon. Mac Harb,2003, Liberal
613-996-2379, 800-267-7362,Fax:
613-996-2318,harbm@sen.parl.gc.ca

Hon. Céline Hervieux-Payette,1995, Liberal
613-947-8008, 800-267-7362,Fax:
613-947-8010,hervic@sen.parl.gc.ca

Hon. Leo Housakos,2009, Conservative Party
613-947-4237, 800-267-7362,Fax:
613-947-4239,lacomd@sen.parl.gc.ca

Hon. Elizabeth Hubley,2001, Liberal
613-992-1177, 800-267-7362,Fax:
613-992-1516,hublee@sen.parl.gc.ca

Hon. Mobina S.B. Jaffer,2001, Liberal
613-992-0189, 800-267-7362,Fax:
613-992-0673,jaffem@sen.parl.gc.ca

Hon. Janis G. Johnson,1990, Conservative Party
613-943-1430, 800-267-7362,Fax:
613-992-5029,johnsj@sen.parl.gc.ca

Hon. Serge Joyal,1997, Liberal
613-943-0434, 800-267-7362,Fax:
613-943-0441,joyals@sen.parl.gc.ca

Hon. Colin Kenny,1984, Liberal
613-996-2877, 800-267-7362,Fax:
613-996-3737,kennyco@sen.parl.gc.ca

Hon. Noël A. Kinsella,1990, Conservative Party
613-992-4416, 800-267-7362,Fax:
613-992-9772,kinsen@sen.parl.gc.ca

Hon. Vim Kochhar,2010, Conservative Party
613-943-4023, 800-267-7362,Fax:
613-943-4025,kochhv@sen.parl.gc.ca,

Hon. Daniel Lang,2009, Conservative Party
613-947-4050, 800-267-7362,Fax:
613-947-4049,langd@sen.parl.gc.ca

Hon. Jean Lapointe,2001, Liberal
613-992-0166, 800-267-7362,Fax:
613-992-0242,charrf@sen.parl.gc.ca

Hon. Raymond Lavigne,2002, Liberal
613-947-2547, 800-267-7362,Fax:
613-947-2569,lavigr@sen.parl.gc.ca

Hon. Marjory LeBreton,1993, Conservative Party
613-943-0756, 800-267-7362,Fax:
613-943-1493,lebrem@sen.parl.gc.ca;
Marjory.LeBreton@pco-bcp.gc.ca

Hon. Rose-Marie Losier-Cool,1995, Liberal
613-947-8011, 800-267-7362,Fax:
613-947-8013,losier@sen.parl.gc.ca

Hon. Sandra M. Lovelace Nicholas,2005, Liberal
613-943-3635, 800-267-7362,Fax:
613-943-3637,smithc@sen.parl.gc.ca

Hon. Michael L. MacDonald,2009, Conservative Party
613-995-1866, 800-267-7362,Fax: 613-995-1853

Hon. Frank W. Mahovlich,1998, Liberal
613-943-2065, 800-267-7362,Fax:
613-943-2067,mahovf@sen.parl.gc.ca

Hon. Fabian Manning,2009, Conservative Party
613-947-4203, 800-267-7362,Fax:
613-947-4170,mannif@sen.parl.gc.ca

Hon. Elizabeth (Beth) Marshall,2010, Conservative Party
613-943-4011, 800-267-7362,Fax:
613-943-4013,marshe@sen.parl.gc.ca

Hon. Yonah Martin,2009, Conservative Party
613-947-4078, 800-267-7362,Fax:
613-947-4082,martin@sen.parl.gc.ca

Hon. Paul Massicotte,2003, Liberal
613-943-8110, 800-267-7362,Fax:
613-943-8129,massip@sen.parl.gc.ca

Hon. Elaine McCoy,2005, PC
613-995-4293, 800-267-7362,Fax:
613-995-4304,mccoye@sen.parl.gc.ca

Hon. Michael A. Meighen,1990, Conservative Party
613-943-1421, 800-267-7362,Fax:
613-943-1565,meighen@sen.parl.gc.ca

Hon. Terry Mercer,2003, Liberal
613-996-2657, 800-267-7362,Fax:
613-947-2345,mercet@sen.parl.gc.ca

Hon. Pana Merchant,2002, Liberal
613-944-7777, 800-267-7362,Fax:
613-944-7778,merchp@sen.parl.gc.ca

Hon. Grant Mitchell,2005, Liberal
613-995-4254, 800-267-7362,Fax:
613-995-4265,mitchg@sen.parl.gc.ca

Hon. Percy Mockler,2009, Conservative Party
613-947-4225, 800-267-7362,Fax:
613-947-4227,mocklp@sen.parl.gc.ca

Hon. Wilfred P. Moore,1996, Liberal
613-947-1921, 800-267-7362,Fax:
613-943-1995,moorew@sen.parl.gc.ca

Hon. Jim Munson,2003, Liberal
613-947-2504, 800-267-7362,Fax:
613-947-2506,munsoj@sen.parl.gc.ca

Hon. Lowell Murray,1979, PC
613-995-2407, 800-267-7362,Fax:
613-947-4730,murral@sen.parl.gc.ca
Hon. Richard Neufeld,2009, Conservative Party
613-947-4055, 800-267-7362,Fax:
613-947-4065,neufer@sen.parl.gc.ca
Hon. Pierre Claude Nolin,1993, Conservative Party
613-943-1451, 800-267-7362,Fax:
613-943-1792,nolinp@sen.parl.gc.ca
Hon. Kelvin Kenneth Ogilvie,2009, Conservative Party
613-992-0331, 800-267-7362,Fax:
613-992-0334,nolinp@sen.parl.gc.ca
Hon. Donald H. Oliver,1990, Conservative Party
613-943-1445, 800-267-7362,Fax:
613-943-1502,olived@sen.parl.gc.ca
Hon. Dennis Glen Patterson,2009, Conservative Party
613-992-0480, 800-267-7362,Fax:
613-992-0495,patted@sen.parl.gc.ca
Hon. Lucie Pépin,1997, Liberal
613-996-1726, 800-267-7362,Fax:
613-996-8392,pepinl@sen.parl.gc.ca
Hon. Robert W. Peterson,2005, Liberal
613-995-4220, 800-267-7362,Fax:
613-995-4229,russem@sen.parl.gc.ca
Hon. Donald Neil Plett,2009, Conservative Party
613-992-0180, 800-267-7362,Fax:
613-992-0186,plettd@sen.parl.gc.ca
Hon. Rose-May Poirier,2010, Conservative Party
613-943-4027, 800-267-7362,Fax:
613-943-4026,poirir@sen.parl.gc.ca
Hon. Marie-P. Poulin (Charette),1995, Liberal
613-947-8005, 800-267-7362,Fax:
613-947-8007,poulim@sen.parl.gc.ca
Hon. Vivienne Poy,1998, Liberal
613-943-7854, 800-267-7362,Fax:
613-943-7856,poyv@sen.parl.gc.ca
Hon. Nancy Greene Raine,2009, Conservative Party
613-947-4052, 800-267-7362,Fax:
613-947-4054,rainen@sen.parl.gc.ca
Hon. Pierrette Ringuette,2002, Liberal
613-943-2248, 800-267-7362,Fax:
613-943-2245,ringup@sen.parl.gc.ca
Hon. Michel Rivard,2009, Conservative Party
613-947-4107, 800-267-7362,Fax:
613-947-4110,rivarm@sen.parl.gc.ca
Hon. Jean-Claude Rivest,1993, Independent
613-947-2236, 800-267-7362,Fax:
613-947-2238,jcrivest@sen.parl.gc.ca
Hon. Fernand Robichaud,1997, Liberal
613-943-0675, 800-267-7362,Fax: 613-943-0677
Hon. William Rompkey,1995, Liberal
613-947-9584, 800-267-7362,Fax:
613-947-9586,rompkw@sen.parl.gc.ca
Hon. Bob Runciman,2010, Conservative Party
613-943-4020, 800-267-7362,Fax:
613-943-4022,runcib@sen.parl.gc.ca
Hon. Nancy Ruth,2005, Conservative Party
613-995-4174, 800-267-7362,Fax:
613-995-4188,mcgeed@sen.parl.gc.ca
Hon. Gerry St. Germain,1993, Conservative Party
613-947-2242, 800-267-7362,Fax:
613-947-2244,stgerg@sen.parl.gc.ca
Hon. Hugh Segal,2005, Conservative Party
613-995-4059, 800-267-7362,Fax:
613-995-5259,kfl@sen.parl.gc.ca
Hon. Judith Seidman,2009, Conservative Party
613-992-0110, 800-267-7362,Fax:
613-992-0118,seidmj@sen.parl.gc.ca
Hon. Nick G. Sibbeston,1999, Liberal
613-943-7790, 800-267-7362,Fax:
613-943-7792,sibnic@sen.parl.gc.ca
Hon. David P. Smith, Q.C.,2002, Liberal
613-944-4079, 800-267-7362,Fax:
613-944-4083,smithd@sen.parl.gc.ca
Hon. Carolyn Stewart Olsen,2009, Conservative Party
613-992-0121, 800-267-7362,Fax:
613-992-0124,stewac@sen.parl.gc.ca
Hon. Peter A. Stollery,1981, Liberal
613-992-3012, 800-267-7362,Fax:
613-943-8737,stollp@sen.parl.gc.ca
Hon. Terry Stratton,1993, Conservative Party
613-947-2224, 800-267-7362,Fax:
613-943-1563,stratt@sen.parl.gc.ca
Hon. Claudette Tardif,2005, Liberal
613-947-3589, 800-267-7362,Fax:
613-947-3609,tardic@sen.parl.gc.ca
Hon. David Tkachuk,1993, Conservative Party
613-947-3196, 800-267-7362,Fax:
613-947-3198,tkachd@sen.parl.gc.ca
Hon. John D. Wallace,2009, Conservative Party
613-947-4240, 800-267-7362,Fax:
613-947-4252,wallaj@sen.parl.gc.ca
Hon. Pamela Wallin,2009, Conservative Party
613-947-4097, 800-267-7362,Fax:
613-947-4091,wallinp@sen.parl.gc.ca
Hon. Charlie Watt,1984, Liberal
613-992-2981, 800-267-7362,Fax:
613-990-5453,wattc@sen.parl.gc.ca
Hon. Rod A.A. Zimmer,2005, Liberal
613-995-4043, 800-267-7362,Fax:
613-995-4046,zimmer@sen.parl.gc.ca

House of Commons, Canada / Chambre des communes

House of Commons, Parliament Buildings, Ottawa, ON K1A 0A6

613-992-4793, 866-599-4999
info@parl.gc.ca
www.parl.gc.ca

The House of Commons is the major law-making unit in Canada. The 308 members of the House represent each constituency, or riding, across Canada. Members are elected in general elections, held at least once every five years. During general elections, one candidate per riding is elected, based on the largest number of votes, even if his or her vote is less than half the total. When a member resigns or dies between general elections, a by-election is held. The party that wins the largest number of seats in the general election usually forms the government. The party with the second largest number of votes becomes the Official Opposition. A minority government is created when one particular party holds no clear majority of seats in the House. In this case, the government is usually led by the party with the most seats in Parliament, providing it can sustain the support from other minor parties that enable it to pass legislation. Any bills within federal jurisdiction must be passed by a majority of House members to become law. Members usually vote on proposed legislation according to party affiliation. They may vote against their party. They may also leave their elected party to sit as an independent within the House. The Speaker of the House of Common s is a Member of Parliament, who is selected by fellow Members of Parliament through a secret ballot process. The Speaker's roles are to ensure that all procedures & rules are followed in the House, & to oversee administration in the House.

Speaker of the House,Hon. Peter Milliken
613-992-4793, 866-599-4999,Fax:
613-995-4253,SpkrOff@parl.gc.ca; Milliken.P@parl.gc.ca
Chair of Committees of the Whole of the House of Commons; Deputy Speaker, Andrew Scheer
613-992-4593, Fax: 613-996-3120,Scheer.A@parl.gc.ca
Deputy Chair of Committees of the Whole, Denise Savoie, B.A., M.A., M.Ed.
613-996-2358, Fax: 613-952-1458,Savoie.D@parl.gc.ca
Leader of the Government in the House of Commons; Conservative Party House Leader,Hon. John Baird, B.A.(Hons.)
613-996-0984, Fax: 613-996-9880,Baird.J@parl.gc.ca; bairdj1@parl.gc.ca
Official Opposition House Leader,Hon. Ralph Edward Goodale, B.A., LL.B.
613-947-1153, Fax: 613-996-9790,Goodale.R@parl.gc.ca
Bloc Québécois House Leader, Pierre A. Paquette, BSc, M.A.
613-992-2244, Fax: 613-995-2818,Paquette.P@parl.gc.ca; joliette@pierrepaquette.qc.ca
New Democratic Party House Leader, Libby Davies
613-992-6030, Fax: 613-995-7412,Davies.L@parl.gc.ca
Chief Government Whip; Whip of the Conservative Party of Canada; Minister of State,Hon. Gordon O'Connor, B.A., B.Sc.
613-992-1119, Fax: 613-992-1043,Oconnor.G@parl.gc.ca
Chief Opposition Whip; Whip of the Liberal Party, Rodger Cuzner, B.A.
613-992-6756, Fax: 613-992-4053,Cuzner.R@parl.gc.ca; cuzner1@parl.gc.ca
Whip of the Bloc Québécois, Claude DeBellefeuille, B.A.
613-946-0644, 866-561-0644,Fax:
613-941-3300,DeBellefeuille.C@parl.gc.ca; debelc1@parl.gc.ca
Whip of the New Democratic Party, Yvon Godin
613-992-2165, Fax: 613-992-4558,Godin.Y@parl.gc.ca
Conservative Party Caucus Chair, Guy Lauzon
613-992-2521, 888-805-2515,Fax:
613-996-2119,Lauzon.G@parl.gc.ca; info@guylauzon.ca
Liberal Party Caucus Chair, Anthony Rota, B.A., M.B.A.
613-995-6255, 800-461-1394,Fax:
613-996-7993,Rota.A@parl.gc.ca; rotaa2@parl.gc.ca; rotaa1@parl.gc.ca
Bloc Québécois Caucus Chair, Louis Plamondon, B.A.Ped., B.A.An.
613-995-9241, Fax: 613-995-6784,PlamoL@parl.gc.ca
New Democratic Party Caucus Chair, Jean Crowder, B.A.
613-943-2180, 866-609-9998,Fax:
613-993-5577,CrowdJ@parl.gc.ca
Clerk of the House of Commons, Audrey Elizabeth O'Brien
Sergeant-at-Arms, Kevin M. Vickers

Finance Services

House of Commons, 111 Wellington St., Ottawa, ON K1A 0A6

Chief Financial Officer, Claire Kennedy
613-996-0485, Fax: 613-995-4970
Director, Finance Operations Management, Jose Fernandez
613-947-2570
Director, Finance Operations Management, Allan Glenns
613-996-7558, Fax: 613-995-3072
Director, Policy & Financial Planning, Valle Gomez-Sims
613-996-3073, Fax: 613-947-3571
Director, Finance Operations Management, Mathieu Mainville
613-947-2368
Director, Policy & Financial Planning, Jane Princi
613-995-1618, Fax: 613-947-3571
Manager, Materiel Management & Warehousing, Stéphanie Charron
613-947-2485, Fax: 613-943-8353
Manager, Contracting Services, Ghislaine Parent
613-943-0838, Fax: 613-992-3037

Human Resources, Corporate Planning, & Communications Services

House of Commons, 111 Wellington St., Ottawa, ON K1A 0A6

Chief Human Resources Officer, Kathryn Butler Malette
613-992-0100, Fax: 613-947-0001
Director, Employee Relations & Human Resources Services, Renée de Bellefeuille
613-947-2413, Fax: 613-943-9772
Head, Corporate Communications, Léonie Bouvier
613-992-9216, Fax: 613-995-3052
Head, Corporate Planning, Kevin Whitehouse
613-947-6776, Fax: 613-996-1698
Manager, Learning & Organizational Development, Louise Chevrier
613-943-4516, Fax: 613-992-2599
Manager, Administration, Planning, IM, & HR Systems, Sylvie Farrell
613-992-2737, Fax: 613-947-0001
Senior Communications Officer, Kori Ghergari
613-947-4876, Fax: 613-995-3052

Information Services

House of Commons, 111 Wellington St., Ottawa, ON K1A 0A6

613-995-9631, Fax: 613-947-3547

Chief Information Officer, Louis Bard
613-995-8884, Fax: 613-947-3547
Chief, Application Architecture & Development, Soufiane Ben Moussa
613-943-1465, Fax: 613-943-1810
Chief, Information Management, Leslie Hamel
613-944-5227, Fax: 613-944-4118
Chief, Finance, Administration, & Planning, Stéphane Jacques
613-996-4994, Fax: 613-943-7890
Director, IT Operations, Stéphan Aubé
613-992-7449, Fax: 613-947-6292
Director, Multimedia Services & ISD Business Planning, Elaine Diguer
613-992-2217, Fax: 613-947-2329
Director, Printing Services, Benoit Giroux
613-992-7398, Fax: 613-992-7178
Director, Resource Information Management, Michelle Guay-Leblanc
613-992-3944, Fax: 613-943-1713
Director, Parliamentary Publications, Michel Roy
613-992-2420, Fax: 613-996-9496
Manager, IT Security, Kim Edwards
613-947-5272, Fax: 613-947-6292
Manager, IT Project Management Office, Jean Forgues
613-947-2397, Fax: 613-947-5356
Manager, IT Planning, Strategies, & Services Management, Caroline Riendeau
613-944-5072, Fax: 613-947-6292

Law Clerk & Parliamentary Counsel

House of Commons, 111 Wellington St., Ottawa, ON K1A 0A6

Law Clerk & Parliamentary Counsel, Robert Walsh
613-996-1057, Fax: 613-992-4441
Chief, Administrative Services, Suzanne Dupuis
613-947-1997, Fax: 613-947-5556
Deputy Law Clerk & Parliamentary Counsel, Richard Denis
613-943-2601, Fax: 613-947-5556

Office of the Clerk & Secretariat

Centre Block, House of Commons, Ottawa, ON K1A 0A6

Clerk of the House of Commons, Audrey O'Brien
613-992-2986, Fax: 613-995-6668
Director, Audit & Review, Brent Schwieg
613-947-0775, Fax: 613-996-0100

Parliamentary Precinct Services
Centre Block, House of Commons, Ottawa, ON K1A 0A6
613-995-7521, Fax: 613-995-4901,
Sergeant-at-Arms of the House of Commons, Kevin Vickers
613-992-2637, Fax: 613-995-4901
Executive Director to the Sergeant-At-Arms, Josée Knight
613-943-0473, Fax: 613-995-4901
Director General, Parliamentary Accommodation, Michel Séguin
613-996-7077, Fax: 613-995-7888
Chief, Security Operations, Pierre Beauchamp
613-943-9447, Fax: 613-996-0100
Chief, Postal, Distribution, Messenger, & Transportation Services, Robert Frenette
613-996-1021, Fax: 613-996-0221
Chief, Press Gallery, Terry Guillon
613-992-4511, Fax: 613-995-5795

Procedural Services
111 Wellington St., Ottawa, ON K1A 0A6
Deputy Clerk, Marc Bosc
613-992-3156, Fax: 613-995-1449
Deputy Principal Clerk, Ian McDonald
613-947-5584, Fax: 613-995-0212
Clerk Assistant & Director General, International & Interparliamentary Affairs, Eric Janse
613-992-6637, Fax: 613-992-3674

Committees of the House of Commons / Comités de la chambre des communes
Committees Directorate, House of Commons, 131 Queen St., 6th Fl., Ottawa, ON K1A 0A6
613-992-3150, Fax: 613-947-3089,
cmteweb@parl.gc.ca
www2.parl.gc.ca
The following are the House of Commons Committees: Aboriginal Affairs & Northern Development; Access to Information, Privacy, & Ethics; Agriculture & Agri-Food; Canadian Heritage; Citizenship & Immigration; Environment & Sustainable Development; Finance; Fisheries & Oceans; Foreign Affairs & International Development; Government Operations & Estimates; Health; Human Resources, Skills & Social Development, & the Status of Persons with Disabilities; Industry, Science, & Technology; International Trade; Justice & Human Rights; Liaison; National Defence; Natural Resources; Official Languages; Procedure & House Affairs; Public Accounts; Public Safety & National Security; Special Committee on the Canadian Mission in Afghanistan; Status of Women; Transport, Infrastructure, & Communities; & Veterans Affairs.
Principal Clerk, Committees Directorate & Legislative Services, Colette Labrecque-Riel
613-995-0516, Fax: 613-947-0309
Clerk, Aboriginal Affairs & Northern Development Committee, Graeme Truelove
613-996-1173, Fax: 613-943-0307,aano@parl.gc.ca
Clerk, Access to Information, Privacy, & Ethics Committee, Jacques Maziade
613-992-1240, Fax: 613-992-9069,ETHI@parl.gc.ca
Clerk, Agriculture & Agri-Food Committee, Isabelle Duford
613-947-6732, Fax: 613-995-2106,AGRI@parl.gc.ca
Clerk, Canadian Heritage Committee, Richard Dupuis
613-947-6729, Fax: 613-996-1626,chpc@parl.gc.ca
Clerk, Citizenship & Immigration Committee, Andrew Chaplin
613-995-8525, Fax: 613-996-1626,cimm@parl.gc.ca
Clerk, Environment & Sustainable Development Committee, Guyanne Desforges
613-992-5023, Fax: 613-996-1626,ENVI@parl.gc.ca
Clerk, Finance Committee, Jean-François Pagé
613-992-9753, Fax: 613-947-9670,FINA@parl.gc.ca
Clerk, Fisheries & Oceans Committee, Travis Ladouceur
613-996-3105, Fax: 613-992-9069,FOPO@parl.gc.ca
Clerk, Foreign Affairs & International Development Committee, Carmen DePape
613-996-1540, Fax: 613-992-7974,FAAE@parl.gc.ca
Clerk, Government Operations & Estimates Committee, Marc-Olivier Girard
613-995-9469, Fax: 613-992-9069,OGGO@parl.gc.ca
Clerk, Health Committee, Christine Holke
613-995-4108, Fax: 613-992-7974,HESA@parl.gc.ca
Clerk, Human Resources, Skills, & Social Development & the Status of Persons with Disabilities Committee, George Etoka
613-996-1542, Fax: 613-996-1626,HUMA@parl.gc.ca
Clerk, Industry, Science, & Technology Committee, Michelle Tittley
613-947-1971, Fax: 613-996-1626,INDU@parl.gc.ca
Clerk, International Trade Committee, Jean-Marie David
613-944-4364, Fax: 613-992-7974,CIIT@parl.gc.ca
Clerk, Justice & Human Rights Committee, Miriam Burke
613-996-1553, Fax: 613-992-1962,JUST@parl.gc.ca
Clerk, Liaison Committee, André Gagnon
613-947-5623, Fax: 613-947-0309,liai@parl.gc.ca
Clerk, National Defence Committee, André Gagnon
613-995-9461, Fax: 613-947-9670,NDDN@parl.gc.ca
Clerk, Natural Resources Committee, Carol Chafe
613-995-0047, Fax: 613-996-1626,rnnr@parl.gc.ca
Clerk, Official Languages Committee, Isabelle Dumas
613-947-8891, Fax: 613-996-1962,LANG@parl.gc.ca
Clerk, Procedure & House Affairs Committee, Angela Crandall
613-996-0506, Fax: 613-992-9069,PROC@parl.gc.ca
Clerk, Public Accounts Committeee, Joann Garbig
613-996-1664, Fax: 613-996-1962,PACP@parl.gc.ca
Clerk, Public Safety & National Security Committee, Roger Préfontaine
613-944-5635, SECU@parl.gc.ca
Clerk, Special Committee on the Canadian Mission in Afghanistan, Andrew Chaplin
613-995-8525, Fax: 613-996-1626,afgh@parl.gc.ca
Clerk, Status of Women Committee, Julia Lockhart
613-995-6119, FEWO@parl.gc.ca
Clerk, Transport, Infrastructure, & Communities Committee, Bonnie Charron
613-996-4663, Fax: 613-996-1626,TRAN@parl.gc.ca
Clerk, Veterans Affairs Committee, Jacques Lahaie
613-944-9354, Fax: 613-947-4177,acva@parl.gc.ca
Director, Marc Roy
613-957-5645
Deputy Director, Steven Hogue
613-957-5555
Senior Press Officer, Thoren Hudyma
613-957-5554
Senior Press Officer & Writer, Frédérique Tsai
613-957-5645
Media Advance Officer, Alphée Moreau
613-952-4959
Asst. Media Advance Officer, Tristan Cinq-Mars
613-957-5557

The Canadian Ministry / The Cabinet
Information Service, Parliament of Canada, Ottawa, ON K1A 0A9
613-992-4793, 866-599-4999
info@parl.gc.ca
www.parl.gc.ca
The Canadian Ministry, or Cabinet, is the most significant of all federal government committees or councils. Cabinet members are selected & led by the Prime Minister. They must also be or become members of the Queen's Privy Council. Cabinet ministers determine specific policies & are responsible for them in the House of Commons. The Cabinet is responsible for initiating all public bills in the House of Commons, & in some instances can create regulations that have the strength of law, termed decisions of the Governor-in-Council. Cabinet meetings are usually closed to the public, allowing members to discuss their opinions on particular policy in secret. Once decided, members usually support all policy uniformly. If a minister is unable to support the Ministry, he or she is obligated to resign. Ministers are responsible to Parliament for their actions & the actions of their department. The mailing address for all Cabinet members on Parliament Hill in Ottawa is as follows: Parliament Buildings, House of Commons, Ottawa, Ontario, K1A 0A6. Members of the The Canadian Ministry are presented in order of precedence.
Prime Minister,Rt. Hon. Stephen Harper
613-992-4211, Fax: 613-941-6900,Harper.S@parl.gc.ca; pm@pm.gc.ca
Minister, Justice; Attorney General of Canada,Hon. Robert Douglas Nicholson
613-995-1547, Fax: 613-992-7910,Nicholson.R@parl.gc.ca, Other Communications: Justice Canada, Phone: 613-992-4621
Minister, Veterans Affairs; Minister of State (Agriculture),Hon. Jean-Pierre Blackburn
613-947-9472, Fax: 613-947-2748,BlackJ@parl.gc.ca, Other Communications: Veterans Affairs, Phone: 613-996-4649
Leader of the Government in the Senate,Hon. Marjory LeBreton
613-943-0756, 800-267-7362,Fax: 613-943-1493,lebrem@sen.parl.gc.ca; Marjory.LeBreton@pco-bcp.gc.ca,
Minister, Transport, Infrastructure, & Communities,Hon. Charles (Chuck) Strahl
613-992-2940, Fax: 613-944-9376,Strahl.C@parl.gc.ca, Other Communications: Transport Canada, Phone: 613-991-0700
Minister, National Defence,Hon. Peter Gordon MacKay
613-992-6022, Fax: 613-992-2337,MacKay.P@parl.gc.ca; Mackay.P@forces.gc.ca, Other Communications: National Defence, Phone: 613-996-3100
Minister, Asia-Pacific Gateway; President, Treasury Board,Hon. Stockwell Burt Day
613-995-1702, Fax: 613-995-1154,DayS@parl.gc.ca; president@tbs-sct.gc.ca, Other Communications: Treasury Board of Canada, Phone: 613-957-2666
Minister, Public Safety,Hon. Vic Toews
613-992-3128, Fax: 613-995-1049,Toews.V@parl.gc.ca, Other Communications: Public Safety & Emergency Preparedness: 613-991-2924
Minister, Public Works & Government Services; Minister for Status of Women,Hon. Rona Ambrose
613-996-9778, Fax: 613-996-0785,Ambrose.R@parl.gc.ca; ministre@tpsgc-pwgsc.gc.ca, Other Communications: Public Works & Government Services:819-997-5421
Minister, Human Resources & Skills Development,Hon. Diane Finley
613-996-4974, Fax: 613-996-9749,Finley.D@parl.gc.ca; diane.finley@hrsdc-rhdsc.gc.ca, Other Communications: Human Resources & Skills Development: 819-994-2482
Minister, International Cooperation,Hon. Beverley J. (Bev) Oda
613-992-2792, Fax: 613-992-2794,Oda.B@parl.gc.ca; minister@acdi-cida.gc.ca, Other Communications: International Cooperation, Phone: 819-953-6238
Minister, Environment,Hon. Jim Prentice
613-992-4275, Fax: 613-947-9475,Prentice.J@parl.gc.ca; Jim.Prentice@ec.gc.ca, Other Communications: Environment Canada, Phone: 819-997-1441
Leader of the Government in the House of Commons,Hon. John Baird
613-996-0984, Fax: 613-996-9880,BairdJ@parl.gc.ca; jhii@lghc-lgcc.gc.ca, Other Communications: Department Phone: 613-995-7226
Minister, Foreign Affairs,Hon. Lawrence Cannon
613-992-5516, Fax: 613-992-6802,CannoL@parl.gc.ca; L.Cannon@international.gc.ca, Other Communications: Foreign Affairs, Phone: 613-995-1851
Minister, Industry; Minister Responsible, Canadian Space Agency,Hon. Tony Clement
613-944-7740, Fax: 613-992-5092,ClemeT@parl.gc.ca; ministre.industrie@ic.gc.ca, Other Communications: Industry Canada, Phone: 613-995-9001
Minister, Finance,Hon. James Michael (Jim) Flaherty
613-992-6344, Fax: 613-992-8320,FlaheJ@parl.gc.ca; jflaherty@fin.gc.ca, Other Communications: Finance Canada, Phone: 613-996-7861
Minister, Intergovernmental Affairs; Minister, La Francophonie; President, Queen's Privy Council for Canada,Hon. Josée Verner
613-996-4151, Fax: 613-954-2269,VerneJ@parl.gc.ca, Other Communications: Privy Council Office, Phone:613-943-1838
Minister, International Trade,Hon. Peter Van Loan
613-996-7752, Fax: 613-992-8351,VanLoan.P@parl.gc.ca, Other Communications: International Trade, Phone: 613-992-7332
Minister, Agriculture & Agri-Food; Minister, Canadian Wheat Board,Hon. Gerry Ritz
613-995-7080, Fax: 613-996-8472,Ritz.G@parl.gc.ca, Other Communications: Agriculture & Agri-Food, Phone: 613-773-1059
Minister, Citizenship, Immigration, & Multiculturalism,Hon. Jason Kenney
613-992-2235, Fax: 613-992-1920,kenneJ@parl.gc.ca; Minister@cic.gc.ca, Other Communications: Citizenship & Immigration, Phone: 613-954-1064
Minister, Natural Resources,Hon. Christian Paradis
613-995-1377, Fax: 613-943-1562,ParadC@parl.gc.ca, Other Communications: Natural Resources, Phone: 613-996-2007
Minister, Canadian Heritage & Official Languages,Hon. James Moore
613-992-9650, Fax: 613-992-9868,MooreJ@parl.gc.ca, Other Communications: Canadian Heritage, Phone: 819-997-7788
Minister, Health,Hon. Leona Aglukkaq
613-992-2848, Fax: 613-996-9764,Aglukkaq.L@parl.gc.ca; Minister_Ministre@hc-sc.gc.ca, Other Communications: Health Canada, Phone: 613-957-0200
Minister, Labour,Hon. Lisa Raitt
613-996-7046, Fax: 613-992-0851,Raitt.L@parl.gc.ca, Other Communications: Labour, Phone: 819-953-5646, Fax: 819-994-5168
Minister, Fisheries & Oceans,Hon. Gail Shea
613-992-9223, Fax: 613-992-1974,Shea.G@parl.gc.ca; Min@dfo-mpo.gc.ca, Other Communications: Fisheries & Oceans, Phone: 613-992-3474
Minister, National Revenue; Minister, Atlantic Canada Opportunities Agency; Minister, Atlantic Gateway,Hon. Keith Ashfield
613-992-1067, Fax: 613-996-9955,Ashfield.k@parl.gc.ca, Other Communications: National Revenue, Phone: 613-995-2960
Minister, Indian Affairs & Northern Development; Minister of the Canadian Northern Economic Development Agency;, Federal Interlocutor for Métis & Non-Status Indians,Hon. John Duncan
613-992-2503, Fax: 613-996-3306, Duncan.J@parl.gc.ca;Minister@ainc-inac.gc.ca, Other

Communications: Indian Affairs & Northern Development: 819-997-0002
Minister of State, Sport,Hon. Gary Lunn
613-996-1119, 866-811-0055,Fax: 613-996-0850,LunnG@parl.gc.ca, Other Communications: Canadian Heritage, Phone: 819-997-0055
Minister of State; Chief Government Whip,Hon. Gordon O'Connor
613-992-1119, Fax: 613-992-1043,OConnor.G@parl.gc.ca
Minister of State (Seniors),Hon. Diane Ablonczy
613-996-2756, Fax: 613-992-2537,Ablonczy.D@parl.gc.ca
Minister of State (Transport),Hon. Rob Merrifield
613-992-1653, Fax: 613-992-3459,Merrifield.R@parl.gc.ca, Other Communications: Transport Canada, Phone: 613-991-0700
Minister of State (Western Economic Diversification),Hon. Lynne Yelich
613-995-5653, Fax: 613-995-0126,Yelich.L@parl.gc.ca; lynne.yelich@wd.gc.ca, Other Communications: Western Economic Diversification, Phone: 613-952-2768
Minister of State (Democratic Reform),Hon. Steven John Fletcher
613-995-5609, Fax: 613-992-3199,FletcS@parl.gc.ca
Minister of State, Science & Technology; Minister of State, Federal Economic Development Agency for Southern Ontario,Hon. Gary Goodyear
613-996-1307, 800-328-6189,Fax: 613-996-8340,Goodyear.G@parl.gc.ca, Other Communications: Industry Canada, Phone: 613-947-2956
Minister of State, Economic Development Agency of Canada for the Regions of Québec,Hon. Denis Lebel
613-996-6236, Fax: 613-996-6252,Lebel.D@parl.gc.ca; denis.lebel@dec-ced.gc.ca, Other Communications: Economic Development Agency (QC):514-496-1282
Minister of State, Foreign Affairs (Americas),Hon. Peter Kent
613-992-0253, Fax: 613-992-0887,Kent.P@parl.gc.ca; Peter.Kent@international.gc.ca, Other Communications: Foreign Affairs, Phone: 613-944-2300
Minister of State, Small Business & Tourism,Hon. Rob Moore
613-996-2332, 800-328-6189,Fax: 613-995-4286,Moore.R@parl.gc.ca, Other Communications: Industry Canada, Phone: 613-947-2956

Fortieth Parliament - Canada

House of Commons, Parliament Buildings, Ottawa, ON K1A 0A9
www.parl.gc.ca

Members of the House of Commons are elected by the people. The Speaker is elected by the House. Last General Election: October 14, 2008. Political Party Leaders: Conservative Party - Rt. Hon. Stephen Joseph Harper; Liberal Party - Hon. Michael Grant Ignatieff; Bloc Québécois, Gilles Duceppe; New Democratic Party, Hon. Jack Gilbert Layton. Representation in the House of Commons by province is as follows (September 2010): Alberta - 28; British Columbia - 36; Manitoba - 14; New Brunswick - 10; Newfoundland & Labrador - 7; Northwest Territories - 1; Nova Scotia - 11; Nunavut - 1; Ontario - 106; Prince Edward Island - 4; Québec - 75; Saskatchewan - 14; Yukon - 1; Total 308. Representation in the House of Commons by party affiliation is as follows (September 2010): Conservative Party of Canada - 144; Liberal Party - 76; Bloc Québécois - 48; New Democratic Party - 36; Independent - 2; Vacant - 2; Total 308. Indemnities, Salaries & Allowances (2010): The basic sessional indemnity for each Member of the House of Commons is $157,731. In addition to the indemnity, members who occupy certain positions in the House of Commons receive additional remuneration. Prime Minister: $157,731, plus a car allowance of $2,122; Minister: $75,516, plus a car allowance of $2,122; Minister of State: $56,637; Secretary of State: $56,637; Parliamentary Secretary: $15,834; Speaker of the House of Commons: $75,516, plus a car allowance of $1,061, & a rent allowance of $3,000; Deputy Speaker of the House of Commons: $39,179, plus a rent allowance of $1,500; Leader of the Official Opposition: $75,516, plus a car allowance of $2,122; Leaders of Other Opposition Parties: $53,694; Opposition House Leader: $39,179; House Leader of Other Parties: $15,834; Deputy House Leaders of Government & Official Opposition: $15,834; Deputy House Leaders of Other Parties: $5,684; Chief Government Whip; $28,420; Chief Opposition Whip: $28,420; Whip of Other Parties: $11,165; Chief Government Whip's Assistant: $11,165; Deputy Whip of the Official Opposition: $11,165; Deputy Whip of Other Parties: $5,684; Caucus Chair of Government & Official Opposition: $11,165; Caucus Chair of Other Parties: $5,684; Deputy Chair, Committees of the Whole: $15,834; Assistant Deputy Chair, Committees of the Whole: $15,834; Chair of Standing & Standing Joint Committee: $11,165; Vice-Chair of Standing & Standing Joint Committee: $5,684. Mail may be sent postage-free to any Member of Parliamet at the following address: House of Commons, Parliament Buildings, Ottawa, Ontario, K1A 0A6. The following is a list of Members of Parliament, as of September 2010, with their constiuency, party affiliation, & contact information:

Members with Party Affiliation, Riding, & Contact Information

Hon. Jim Abbott, Kootenay - Columbia BC, Conservative Party
613-995-7246, Fax: 613-996-9923,Abbott.J@parl.gc.ca, Other Communications: Constituency Phone: 250-417-2250, Fax: 250-417-2253
Hon. Diane Ablonczy, Calgary - Nose Hill AB, Conservative Party
613-996-2756, Fax: 613-992-2537,Ablonczy.D@parl.gc.ca, Other Communications: Constituency Phone: 403-282-7980, Fax: 403-282-3587
Hon. Leona Aglukkaq, Nunavut NU, Conservative Party
613-992-2848, Fax: 613-996-9764,Aglukkaq.L@parl.gc.ca; Minister_Ministre@hc-sc.gc.ca, Other Communications: Constituency Phone: 867-979-4193, Fax: 867-979-4196
Harold Albrecht, Kitchener - Conestoga ON, Conservative Party
613-992-4633, Fax: 613-992-9932,Albrecht.H@parl.gc.ca, Other Communications: Constituency Phone: 519-578-3777, Fax: 519-578-0138
Malcolm Allen, Welland ON, New Democratic Party
613-995-0988, Fax: 613-995-5245,Allen.Ma@parl.gc.ca, Other Communications: Constituency Phone: 905-788-2204, Fax: 905-788-0071
Mike Allen, Tobique - Mactaquac NB, Conservative Party
613-947-4431, Fax: 613-947-4434,Allen.M@parl.gc.ca, Other Communications: Constituency Phone: 506-325-2224, Fax: 613-325-2786
Dean Allison, Niagara West - Glanbrook ON, Conservative Party
613-995-2772, Fax: 613-992-2727,Allison.D@parl.gc.ca, Other Communications: Constituency Phone: 905-563-7900, Fax: 905-563-7500
Hon. Rona Ambrose, Edmonton - Spruce Grove AB, Conservative Party
613-996-9778, Fax: 613-996-0785,Ambrose.R@parl.gc.ca; ministre@tpsgc-pwgsc.gc.ca, Other Communications: Constituency Phone: 780-495-7705, Fax:780-495-7741
Rob Anders, Calgary West AB, Conservative Party
613-992-3066, Fax: 613-992-3256,Anders.R@parl.gc.ca, Other Communications: Constituency Phone: 403-292-6666, Fax: 403-292-6670,
David Anderson, Cypress Hills -Grasslands SK, Conservative Party
613-992-0657, Fax: 613-992-5508,Anderson.Da@parl.gc.ca, Other Communications: Constituency Phone: 306-778-4480, Fax: 306-778-6981
Guy André, Berthier - Maskinongé QC, Bloc Quebecois
613-992-5681, Fax: 613-992-7276,Andre.G@parl.gc.ca, Other Communications: Constituency Phone: 819-228-1210, Fax: 819-228-1181
Scott Andrews, Avalon NL, Liberal
613-992-4133, Fax: 613-992-7277,Andrews.S@parl.gc.ca, Other Communications: Constituency Phone: 709-834-3424, Fax: 709-834-3628
Charlie Angus, Timmins - James Bay ON, New Democratic Party
613-992-2919, Fax: 613-995-0747,Angus.C@parl.gc.ca, Other Communications: Constituency Phone: 705-567-2747, Fax: 705-567-5232
Scott Armstrong, Cumberland - Colchester -Musquodoboit Valley NS, Conservative Party
613-992-3366, Fax: 613-992-7220,Armstrong.S@parl.gc.ca, Other Communications: Constituency Phone: 902-893-2455, Fax: 902-893-1959
André Arthur, Portneuf - Jacques-Cartier QC, Independent
613-992-2798, Fax: 613-995-1637,Arthur.A@parl.gc.ca, Other Communications: Constituency Phone: 418-285-0018, Fax: 418-285-0073
Hon. Keith Ashfield, Fredericton NB, Conservative Party
613-992-1067, Fax: 613-996-9955,Ashfield.k@parl.gc.ca, Other Communications: Constituency Phone: 506-452-4110, Fax: 506-452-4076
Niki Ashton, Churchill MB, New Democratic Party
613-992-3018, 866-785-0522,Fax: 613-996-5817,Ashton.N@parl.gc.ca, Other Communications: Constituency Phone: 866-669-7770, Fax: 204-677-1339
Gérard Asselin, Manicouagan QC, Bloc Quebecois
613-992-2363, Fax: 613-996-7954,Asselin.G@parl.gc.ca, Other Communications: Constituency Phone: 418-296-2780, Fax: 418-296-2476
Alex Atamanenko, British Columbia SouthernInterior BC, New Democratic Party
613-996-8036, Fax: 613-943-0922,Atamanenko.A@parl.gc.ca, Other Communications: Constituency Phone: 250-365-2792, Fax: 250-365-2793
Claude Bachand, Saint-Jean QC, Bloc Quebecois
613-992-5296, Fax: 613-992-9849,BachaC@parl.gc.ca, Other Communications: Constituency Phone: 450-357-9100, Fax: 450-357-9109
Hon. Larry Bagnell, Yukon YT, Liberal
613-995-9368, Fax: 613-995-0945,Bagnell.L@parl.gc.ca, Other Communications: Constituency Phone: 867-668-6565, Fax: 867-668-6570
Hon. Navdeep Bains, Mississauga - Brampton South ON, Liberal
613-995-7784, Fax: 613-996-9817,Bains.N@parl.gc.ca, Other Communications: Constituency Phone: 905-795-5220, 905-795-5252
Hon. John Baird, Ottawa West- Nepean ON, Conservative Party
613-996-0984, Fax: 613-996-9880,airdJ@parl.gc.ca; jhii@lghc-lgcc.gc.ca, Other Communications: Constituency Phone: 613-990-7720, Fax: 613-993-6501
Josée Beaudin, Saint-Lambert QC, Bloc Quebecois
613-998-5961, Fax: 613-954-0707,Beaudin.J@parl.gc.ca, Other Communications: Constituency Phone: 450-646-2423, Fax: 450-646-3018
Hon. Mauril Bélanger, Ottawa - Vanier ON, Liberal
613-992-4766, Fax: 613-992-6448,Belanger.M@parl.gc.ca, Other Communications: Constituency Phone: 613-947-7961, Fax: 613-947-7963
André Bellavance, Richmond -Arthabaska QC, Bloc Quebecois
613-995-1554, Fax: 613-995-2026,Bellavance.A@parl.gc.ca, Other Communications: Constituency Phone: 819-879-6161, Fax: 810-879-1166
Hon. Carolyn Bennett, St. Paul's ON, Liberal
613-995-9666, Fax: 613-947-4622,Bennett.C@parl.gc.ca, Other Communications: Constituency Phone: 416-952-3990, Fax: 416-952-3995
Leon Benoit, Vegreville - Wainwright AB, Conservative Party
613-992-4171, Fax: 613-996-9011,Benoit.L@parl.gc.ca, Other Communications: Constituency Phone: 780-763-6130, Fax: 780-763-6132
Hon. Maxime Bernier, Beauce QC, Conservative Party
613-992-8053, Fax: 613-995-0687,Bernier.M@parl.gc.ca, Other Communications: Constituency Phone: 418-227-2171, Fax: 418-227-3093
Dennis Bevington, Western Arctic NT, New Democratic Party
613-992-4587, Fax: 613-992-1586,Bevington.D@parl.gc.ca, Other Communications: Constituency Phone: 867-873-6995, Fax: 867-920-4233
James Bezan, Selkirk - Interlake MB, Conservative Party
613-992-2032, Fax: 613-992-6224,Bezan.J@parl.gc.ca, Other Communications: Constituency Phone: 204-785-6151, Fax: 204-785-6153
Bernard Bigras, Rosemont - LaPetite-Patrie QC, Bloc Quebecois
613-992-0423, Fax: 613-992-0878,Bigras.B@parl.gc.ca, Other Communications: Constituency Phone: 514-729-5342, Fax: 514-729-5875
Hon. Jean-Pierre Blackburn, Jonquière - Alma QC, Conservative Party
613-947-2744, Fax: 613-947-2748,BlackJ@parl.gc.ca
Raynald Blais, Gaspésie -Iles-de-la-Madeleine QC, Bloc Quebecois
613-992-6188, Fax: 613-992-6194,Blais.R@parl.gc.ca, Other Communications: Constituency Phone: 418-368-1855, Fax: 418-368-1924
Steven Blaney, Lévis - Bellechasse QC, Conservative Party
613-992-7434, Fax: 613-995-6856,Blaney.S@parl.gc.ca, Other Communications: Constituency Phone: 418-830-0500, Fax: 418-830-0504
Kelly Block, Saskatoon - Rosetown - Biggar SK, Conservative Party
613-995-1551, Fax: 613-943-2010,Block.K@parl.gc.ca, Other Communications: Constituency Phone: 306-975-6555, Fax: 306-975-5786
France Bonsant, Compton - Stanstead QC, Bloc Quebecois
613-995-2024, Fax: 613-992-1696,Bonsant.F@parl.gc.ca, Other Communications: Constituency Phone: 819-347-2598, Fax: 819-347-3583
Robert Bouchard, Chicoutimi - Le Fjord QC, Bloc Quebecois
613-992-7207, Fax: 613-992-0431,Bouchard.R@parl.gc.ca, Other Communications: Constituency Phone: 418-698-5648, Fax: 418-698-5611
Sylvie Boucher, Beauport - Limoilou QC, Conservative Party
613-992-4406, Fax: 613-992-4544,Boucher.S@parl.gc.ca, Other Communications: Constituency Phone: 418-663-2113, Fax: 418-663-2988
Ray Boughen, Palliser SK, Conservative Party
613-992-9115, Fax: 613-992-0131,Boughen.R@parl.gc.ca, Other Communications: Constituency Phone: 306-691-3577, Fax: 306-691-3579
Diane Bourgeois, Terrebonne -Blainville QC, Bloc Quebecois
613-947-4788, Fax: 613-947-4879,Bourgeois.D@parl.gc.ca, Other Communications: Constituency Phone: 450-965-9417, Fax: 450-965-7742
Peter Braid, Kitchener - Waterloo ON, Conservative Party
613-996-5928, Fax: 519-992-6251,Braid.P@parl.gc.ca, Other Communications: Constituency Phone: 519-746-1573, Fax: 519-746-6436
Garry Breitkreuz, Yorkton - Melville SK, Conservative Party
613-992-4394, Fax: 613-992-8676,Breitkreuz.G@parl.gc.ca,

Other Communications: Constituency Phone: 306-782-3309, Fax: 306-786-7207
Hon. Scott Brison, Kings - Hants NS, Liberal
613-995-8231, Fax: 613-996-9349,Brison.S@parl.gc.ca, Other Communications: Constituency Phone: 902-542-4010, Fax: 902-542-4184
Gord Brown, Leeds - Grenville ON, Conservative Party
613-992-8756, Fax: 613-996-9171,Brown.G@parl.gc.ca, Other Communications: Constituency Phone: 613-498-3096
Lois Brown, Newmarket - Aurora ON, Conservative Party
614-992-9310, Fax: 613-992-9407,Brown.L@parl.gc.ca, Other Communications: Constituency Phone: 905-953-7515, Fax: 905-953-7527
Patrick Brown, Barrie ON, Conservative Party
613-992-3394, Fax: 613-996-7923,Brown.P@parl.gc.ca, Other Communications: Constituency Phone: 705-726-5959, Fax: 705-726-3340
Rod Bruinooge, Winnipeg South MB, Conservative Party
613-995-7517, Fax: 613-943-1466,Bruinooge.R@parl.gc.ca, Other Communications: Constituency Phone: 204-984-6787, Fax: 204-984-6792
Paule Brunelle, Trois-Rivières QC, Bloc Quebecois
613-992-2349, Fax: 613-995-9498,BruneP@parl.gc.ca, Other Communications: Constituency Phone: 819-371-5901, Fax: 819-371-5912
Hon. Gerry Byrne, Humber - St. Barbe - BaieVerte NL, Liberal
613-996-5511, Fax: 613-996-9632,Byrne.G@parl.gc.ca, Other Communications: Constituency Phone: 709-637-4540, Fax: 709-637-4537
Dona Cadman, Surrey North BC, Conservative Party
613-992-2922, Fax: 613-992-0252,Cadman.D@parl.gc.ca, Other Communications: Constituency Phone: 604-586-2441, Fax: 604-586-2445
Paul Calandra, Oak Ridges - Markham ON, Conservative Party
613-992-3640, Fax: 613-992-3642,Calandra.P@parl.gc.ca, Other Communications: Constituency Phone: 905-833-3030, Fax: 905-833-3033
Blaine Calkins, Wetaskiwin AB, Conservative Party
613-995-8886, Fax: 613-996-9860,Calkins.B@parl.gc.ca, Other Communications: Constituency Phone: 403-783-5530, Fax: 403-783-5532
Ron Cannan, Kelowna - Lake Country BC, Conservative Party
613-992-7006, Fax: 613-992-7636,Cannan.R@parl.gc.ca, Other Communications: Constituency Phone: 250-470-5075, Fax: 250-470-5077
John Cannis, Scarborough Centre ON, Liberal
613-992-6823, Fax: 613-943-1045,Cannis.J@parl.gc.ca, Other Communications: Constituency Phone: 416-752-2358, Fax: 416-752-4624
Hon. Lawrence Cannon, Pontiac QC, Conservative Party
613-992-5516, Fax: 613-992-6802,CannoL@parl.gc.ca; L.Cannon@international.gc.ca, Other Communications: Constituency Phone: 819-281-2626, Fax:819-281-2755
Serge Cardin, Sherbrooke QC, Bloc Quebecois
613-943-7896, Fax: 613-943-7902,Cardin.S@parl.gc.ca, Other Communications: Constituency Phone: 819-564-4200, Fax: 819-564-3745
Colin Carrie, Oshawa ON, Conservative Party
613-996-4756, Fax: 613-992-1357,Carrie.C@parl.gc.ca, Other Communications: Constituency Phone: 905-440-4868, Fax: 905-440-4872
Robert Carrier, Alfred - Pellan QC, Bloc Quebecois
613-992-0611, Fax: 613-992-8556,Carrier.R@parl.gc.ca, Other Communications: Constituency Phone: 450-661-4117, Fax: 450-661-5623
Rick Casson, Lethbridge AB, Conservative Party
613-996-0633, Fax: 613-995-5752,Casson.R@parl.gc.ca, Other Communications: Constituency Phone: 403-320-0070, Fax: 403-380-4026
Chris Charlton, Hamilton Mountain ON, New Democratic Party
613-995-9389, Fax: 613-992-7802,Charlton.C@parl.gc.ca, Other Communications: Constituency Phone: 905-574-3331, Fax: 905-574-4980
Hon. Michael Chong, Wellington - HaltonHills ON, Conservative Party
613-992-4179, Fax: 613-996-4907,Chong.M@parl.gc.ca, Other Communications: Constituency Phone: 519-843-7344, Fax: 519-843-3760
Olivia Chow, Trinity - Spadina ON, New Democratic Party
613-992-2352, Fax: 613-992-6301,Chow.O@parl.gc.ca, Other Communications: Constituency Phone: 416-533-2710, Fax: 416-533-2236
David Christopherson, HamiltonCentre ON, New Democratic Party
613-995-1757, Fax: 613-992-8356,Christopherson.D@parl.gc.ca, Other Communications: Constituency Phone: 905-526-0770, Fax: 905-526-9943
Rob Clarke, Desnethé - Missinippi - ChurchillRiver SK, Conservative Party
613-995-8321, Fax: 613-995-7697,Clarke.R@parl.gc.ca, Other Communications: Constituency Phone: 306-425-2643, Fax: 306-425-2677
Hon. Tony Clement, Parry Sound - Muskoka ON, Conservative Party
613-944-7740, Fax: 613-992-5092,ClemeT@parl.gc.ca; ministre.industrie@ic.gc.ca, Other Communications: Constituency Phone: 705-746-9053, Fax: 705-789-8857
Siobhan Coady, St. John's South - MountPearl NL, Liberal
613-992-0927, Fax: 613-995-7858,Coady.S@parl.gc.ca, Other Communications: Constituency Phone: 709-772-4608, Fax; 709-772-4776
Hon. Denis Coderre, Bourassa QC, Liberal
613-995-6108, Fax: 613-995-9755,Coderre.D@parl.gc.ca, Other Communications: Constituency Phone: 514-323-1212, Fax: 514-323-2875
Joe Comartin, Windsor - Tecumseh ON, New Democratic Party
613-947-3445, Fax: 613-947-3448,Comartin.J@parl.gc.ca, Other Communications: Constituency Phone: 519-988-1826, Fax: 519-988-0152
Hon. Irwin Cotler, Mount Royal QC, Liberal
613-995-0121, Fax: 613-992-6762,cotler.I@parl.gc.ca, Other Communications: Constituency Phone: 514-283-0171, Fax: 514-283-2407
Bonnie Crombie, Mississauga—Streetsville ON, Liberal
613-943-1762, Fax: 613-943-1768,Crombie.B@parl.gc.ca, Other Communications: Constituency Phone: 905-812-1811, Fax: 905-812-8464
Jean Crowder, Nanaimo - Cowichan BC, New Democratic Party
613-943-2180, Fax: 613-993-5577,Crowder.J@parl.gc.ca, Other Communications: Constituency Phone: 250-746-4896, Fax: 250-746-2354,
Nathan Cullen, Skeena - Bulkley Valley BC, New Democratic Party
613-993-6654, Fax: 613-993-9007,Cullen.N@parl.gc.ca, Other Communications: Constituency Phone: 250-877-4140, Fax: 250-877-4141
John Cummins, Delta - Richmond East BC, Conservative Party
613-992-2957, Fax: 613-992-3589,Cummins.J@parl.gc.ca, Other Communications: Constituency Phone: 604-940-8040, Fax: 604-940-8041
Rodger Cuzner, Cape Breton - Canso NS, Liberal
613-992-6756, Fax: 613-992-4053,Cuzner.R@parl.gc.ca, Other Communications: Constituency Phone: 902-842-9763, Fax: 902-842-9025
Jean-Claude D'Amours, Madawaska -Restigouche NB, Liberal
613-995-0581, Fax: 613-996-9736,Damours.J@parl.gc.ca, Other Communications: Constituency Phone: 506-739-4600, Fax: 506-739-4607
Patricia Davidson, Sarnia - Lambton ON, Conservative Party
613-957-2649, Fax: 613-957-2655,Davidson.P@parl.gc.ca, Other Communications: Constituency Phone: 519-383-6600, Fax: 519-383-0609
Don Davies, Vancouver Kingsway BC, New Democratic Party
613-943-0267, Fax: 613-943-0219,Davies.D@parl.gc.ca, Other Communications: Constituency Phone: 604-775-6263, Fax: 604-775-6284
Libby Davies, Vancouver East BC, New Democratic Party
613-992-6030, Fax: 613-995-7412,Davies.L@parl.gc.ca, Other Communications: Constituency Phone: 604-775-5800, Fax: 604-775-5811
Hon. Stockwell Burt Day, Okanagan - Coquihalla BC, Conservative Party
613-995-1702, Fax: 613-995-1154,DayS@parl.gc.ca; president@tbs-sct.gc.ca, Other Communications: Constituency Phone: 250-770-4480, Fax: 250-770-4484
Claude DeBellefeuille, Beauharnois -Salaberry QC, Bloc Quebecois
613-946-0644, Fax: 613-941-3300,DeBellefeuille.C@parl.gc.ca, Other Communications: Constituency Phone: 450-371-0644, Fax: 450-371-3330
Bob Dechert, Mississauga - Erindale ON, Conservative Party
613-995-7321, Fax: 613-992-6708,Dechert.B@parl.gc.ca, Other Communications: Constituency Phone: 905-897-1952, Fax: 905-897-6117
Dean Del Mastro, Peterborough ON, Conservative Party
613-995-6411, Fax: 613-996-9800,DelMastro.D@parl.gc.ca, Other Communications: Constituency Phone: 705-745-2108, Fax: 705-741-4123
Nicole Demers, Laval QC, Bloc Quebecois
613-995-7398, Fax: 613-996-1195,Demers.N@parl.gc.ca, Other Communications: Constituency Phone: 450-686-2562, Fax: 450-686-0450
Johanne Deschamps, Laurentides -Labelle QC, Bloc Quebecois
613-992-2289, Fax: 613-992-6864,Deschamps.J@parl.gc.ca, Other Communications: Constituency Phone: 819-326-5098, Fax: 819-326-8262
Luc Desnoyers, Rivière-des-Mille-Iles QC, Bloc Quebecois
613-992-7330, Fax: 613-992-2602,Desnoyers.L@parl.gc.ca, Other Communications: Constituency Phone: 450-473-4864, Fax: 450-473-9043
Barry Devolin, Haliburton - Kawartha Lakes -Brock ON, Conservative Party
613-992-2474, Fax: 613-996-9656,Devolin.B@parl.gc.ca, Other Communications: Constituency Phone: 705-324-2400, Fax: 705-324-0880
Paul Dewar, Ottawa Centre ON, New Democratic Party
613-996-5322, Fax: 613-996-5323,Dewar.P@parl.gc.ca, Other Communications: Constituency Phone: 613-946-8682, Fax: 613-946-8680
Sukh Dhaliwal, Newton - North Delta BC, Liberal
613-992-0666, Fax: 613-992-1965,Dhaliwal.S@parl.gc.ca, Other Communications: Constituency Phone: 604-598-2200, Fax: 604-598-2212
Ruby Dhalla, Brampton - Springdale ON, Liberal
613-995-4843, Fax: 613-995-7003,Dhalla.R@parl.gc.ca, Other Communications: Constituency Phone: 905-874-6868, Fax: 905-874-1415
Hon. Stéphane Dion, Saint-Laurent -Cartierville QC, Liberal
613-996-5789, Fax: 613-996-6562,Dion.S@parl.gc.ca, Other Communications: Constituency Phone: 514-335-6655, Fax: 514-335-2712
Fin Donnelly, New Westminster -Coquitlam BC, New Democratic Party
613-947-4455, Fax: 613-947-4458,Donnelly.F@parl.gc.ca, Other Communications: Constituency Phone: 604-664-9229, Fax: 604-664-9231
Jean Dorion, Longueuil - Pierre-Boucher QC, Bloc Quebecois
613-992-8514, Fax: 613-992-2744,Dorion.J@parl.gc.ca, Other Communications: Constituency Phone: 450-928-4288, Fax: 450-928-4293
Hon. Ujjal Dosanjh, Vancouver South BC, Liberal
613-995-7052, Fax: 613-995-2962,Dosanjh.U@parl.gc.ca, Other Communications: Constituency Phone: 604-775-5323, Fax: 604-775-5420
Earl Dreeshen, Red Deer AB, Conservative Party
613-995-0590, Fax: 613-995-6831,Dreeshen.E@parl.gc.ca, Other Communications: Constituency Phone: 403-347-7426, Fax: 403-347-7423
Hon. Ken Dryden, York Centre ON, Liberal
613-941-6339, Fax: 613-941-2421,Dryden.K@parl.gc.ca, Other Communications: Constituency Phone: 416-638-3700, Fax: 416-638-1407
Gilles Duceppe, Laurier - Sainte-Marie QC, Bloc Quebecois
613-992-6779, Fax: 613-954-2121,Duceppe.G@parl.gc.ca, Other Communications: Constituency Phone: 514-522-1339, Fax: 514-522-9899
Nicolas Dufour, Repentigny QC, Bloc Quebecois
613-992-5257, Fax: 613-996-4338,Dufour.N@parl.gc.ca, Other Communications: Constituency Phone: 450-581-3896, Fax: 450-581-9958
Hon. John Duncan, Vancouver Island North BC, Conservative Party
613-992-2503, Fax: 613-996-3306,Duncan.J@parl.gc.ca; Minister@ainc-inac.gc.ca, Other Communications: Constituency Phone: 250-338-9381, Fax: 250-338-9361
Kirsty Duncan, Etobicoke North ON, Liberal
613-995-4702, Fax: 613-995-8359,Duncan.K@parl.gc.ca, Other Communications: Constituency Phone: 416-747-6003, Fax: 416-747-8295
Linda Duncan, Edmonton - Strathcona AB, New Democratic Party
613-995-7325, Fax: 613-995-5342,Duncan.L@parl.gc.ca, Other Communications: Constituency Phone: 780-495-8404, Fax: 790-495-8403
Richard Dykstra, St. Catharines ON, Conservative Party
613-992-3352, Fax: 613-947-4402,Dykstra.R@parl.gc.ca, Other Communications: Constituency Phone: 905-934-6767, Fax: 905-934-1577
Hon. Wayne Easter, Malpeque PE, Liberal
613-992-2406, Fax: 613-995-7408,Easter.W@parl.gc.ca, Other Communications: Constituency Phone: 902-964-2428, Fax: 902-964-3242
Hon. Mark Eyking, Sydney - Victoria NS, Liberal
613-995-6459, Fax: 613-995-2963,Eyking.M@parl.gc.ca, Other Communications: Constituency Phone: 902-567-6275, Fax: 902-564-2479
Meili Faille, B.B.A., Vaudreuil - Soulanges QC, Bloc Quebecois
613-957-3744, Fax: 613-952-0874,Faille.M@parl.gc.ca, Other Communications: Constituency Phone: 450-510-2305, Fax: 450-510-2383
Edward Fast, Abbotsford BC, Conservative Party
613-995-0183, Fax: 613-996-9795,Fast.E@parl.gc.ca, Other Communications: Constituency Phone: 604-557-7888, Fax: 604-557-9918
Hon. Diane Finley, Haldimand - Norfolk ON, Conservative Party
613-996-4974, Fax: 613-996-9749,Finley.D@parl.gc.ca; diane.finley@hrsdc-rhdsc.gc.ca, Other Communications: Constituency Phone: 519-426-3400, Fax: 519-426-0003
Hon. James Michael (Jim) Flaherty, B.A., LL.B., Whitby - Oshawa ON, Conservative Party
613-992-6344, Fax: 613-992-8320,Flaherty.J@parl.gc.ca;

jimflaherty@rogers.com, Other Communications: Constituency Phone: 905-665-8182, Fax:905-665-8124

Hon. Steven John Fletcher, Charleswood - St.James - Assiniboia MB, Conservative Party
613-995-5609, Fax: 613-992-3199,Fletcher.S@parl.gc.ca, Other Communications: Constituency Phone: 204-984-6432, Fax: 204-984-6451

Raymonde Folco, Laval - Les Iles QC, Liberal
613-992-2659, Fax: 613-992-9469,Folco.R@parl.gc.ca, Other Communications: Constituency Phone: 450-689-4594

Judy Foote, Random - Burin - St. George's NL, Liberal
613-992-8655, Fax: 613-992-5324,Foote.J@parl.gc.ca, Other Communications: Constituency Phone: 709-643-4189, Fax: 709-643-5171

Carole Freeman, Châteauguay -Saint-Constant QC, Bloc Quebecois
613-996-7265, Fax: 613-996-9287,Freeman.C@parl.gc.ca, Other Communications: Constituency Phone: 450-691-7044, Fax: 450-691-3114

Hon. Hedy Fry, Vancouver Centre BC, Liberal
613-992-3213, Fax: 613-995-0056,Fry.H@parl.gc.ca, Other Communications: Constituency Phone: 604-666-0135l, Fax: 604-666-0114

Christiane Gagnon, Québec QC, Bloc Quebecois
613-992-8865, Fax: 613-995-2805,Gagnon.C@parl.gc.ca, Other Communications: Constituency Phone: 418-523-6666; Fax, 418-523-6672

Royal Galipeau, Ottawa - Orléans ON, Conservative Party
613-995-1800, Fax: 613-995-6298,Galipeau.R@parl.gc.ca, Other Communications: Constituency Phone: 613-834-1800, Fax: 613-590-1201

Cheryl Gallant, Renfrew - Nipissing -Pembroke ON, Conservative Party
613-992-7712, Fax: 613-995-2561,Gallant.C@parl.gc.ca, Other Communications: Constituency Phone: 613-732-4404, Fax: 613-732-4697

Marc Garneau, Westmount - Ville-Marie QC, Liberal
613-996-7267, Fax: 613-995-8632,Garneau.M@parl.gc.ca, Other Communications: Constituency Phone: 514-283-2013, Fax: 514-283-9790

Roger Gaudet, Montcalm QC, Bloc Quebecois
613-992-0164, Fax: 613-992-5341,Gaudet.Ro@parl.gc.ca, Other Communications: Constituency Phone 450-439-8821, Fax: 450-474-1585

Bernard Généreux, Montmagny - L'Islet -Kamouraska - Rivière-du-Loup QC, Conservative Party
613-995-0265, Fax: 613-943-1229,Genereux.B@parl.gc.ca, Other Communications: Constituency Phone: 418-248-1211, Fax: 418-248-1244

Shelly Glover, Saint Boniface MB, Conservative Party
613-995-0579, Fax: 613-996-7571,Glover.S@parl.gc.ca, Other Communications: Constituency Phone: 204-983-3183, Fax: 204-983-4274

Yvon Godin, Acadie - Bathurst NB, New Democratic Party
613-992-2165, Fax: 613-992-4558,Godin.Y@parl.gc.ca, Other Communications: Constituency Phone: 504-548-7511, Fax: 506-548-7418

Peter Goldring, Edmonton East AB, Conservative Party
613-992-3821, Fax: 613-992-6898,Goldring.P@parl.gc.ca, Other Communications: Constituency Phone: 780-495-3261, Fax: 780-495-5142

Hon. Ralph Eward Goodale, Wascana SK, Liberal
613-947-1153, Fax: 613-996-9790,Goodale.R@parl.gc.ca, Other Communications: Constituency Phone: 306-585-2202, Fax: 306-585-2280

Hon. Gary Goodyear, Cambridge ON, Conservative Party
613-996-1307, Fax: 613-996-8340,Goodyear.G@parl.gc.ca, Other Communications: Constituency Phone: 519-624-7440, Fax: 519-624-3517

Jacques Gourde, Lotbinière -Chutes-de-la-Chaudière QC, Conservative Party
613-992-2639, Fax: 613-992-1018,Gourde.J@parl.gc.ca, Other Communications: Constituency Phone: 418-836-0970, Fax: 418-836-6177

Claude Gravelle, Nickel Belt ON, New Democratic Party
613-995-9107, Fax: 613-995-9109,Gravelle.C@parl.gc.ca, Other Communications: Constituency Phone: 705-897-2222, Fax: 705-897-2223

Nina Grewal, Fleetwood - Port Kells BC, Conservative Party
613-996-2205, Fax: 613-995-7139,Grewal.N@parl.gc.ca, Other Communications: Constituency Phone: 604-501-5900, Fax: 604-501-5901

Hon. Albina Guarnieri, Mississauga East -Cooksville ON, Liberal
613-996-0420, Fax: 613-996-0279,Guarnieri.A@parl.gc.ca, Other Communications: Constituency Phone: 905-566-0009, Fax: 905-566-0017

Monique Guay, Rivière-du-Nord QC, Bloc Quebecois
613-992-3257, Fax: 613-992-2156,Guay.M@parl.gc.ca, Other Communications: Constituency Phone: 450-565-0061, Fax: 450-565-0118

Hon. Helena Guergis, Simcoe -Grey ON, Independent
613-992-4224, 866-435-1809,Fax: 613-992-2164,Guergis.H@parl.gc.ca, Other Communications: Constituency Phone: 705-445-6762, Fax: 705-445-7157

Claude Guimond, Rimouski - Neigette -Témiscouata - Les Basques QC, Bloc Quebecois
613-992-5302, Fax: 613-996-8298,Guimond.C@parl.gc.ca, Other Communications: Constituency Phone: 418-725-2562, Fax: 418-725-3993

Michel Guimond, Montmorency - Charlevoix -Haute-Côte-Nord QC, Bloc Quebecois
613-995-9732, Fax: 613-996-2656,Guimond.M@parl.gc.ca, Other Communications: Constituency Phone: 418-660-6776, Fax: 418-660-6777

Martha Hall Findlay, Willowdale ON, Liberal
613-992-4964, Fax: 613-992-1158,HallFindlay.M@parl.gc.ca, Other Communications: Constituency Phone: 416-223-2858, Fax: 416-223-9715

Rt. Hon. Stephen Joseph Harper, Calgary Southwest AB, Conservative Party
613-992-4211, Fax: 613-941-6900,Harper.S@parl.gc.ca; pm@pm.gc.ca, Other Communications: Constituency Phone: 403-253-7990, Fax: 403-253-8203,

Jack Harris, St. John's East NL, New Democratic Party
613-996-7269, Fax: 613-992-2178,Harris.J@parl.gc.ca, Other Communications: Constituency Phone: 709-772-7171, Fax: 709-772-7175

Richard M. Harris, Cariboo - PrinceGeorge BC, Conservative Party
613-995-6704, 800-668-4282,Fax: 613-996-9850,Harris.R@parl.gc.ca, Other Communications: Constituency Phone: 250-564-7771, Fax: 250-564-6224

Laurie Hawn, Edmonton Centre AB, Conservative Party
613-992-4524, Fax: 613-943-0044,Hawn.L@parl.gc.ca, Other Communications: Constituency Phone: 780-442-1888, Fax: 780-442-1891

Russ Hiebert, South Surrey - White Rock -Cloverdale BC, Conservative Party
613-947-4497, Fax: 613-947-4500,Hiebert.R@parl.gc.ca, Other Communications: Constituency Phone: 604-561-7922, Fax: 604-564-2754

Hon. Jay Hill, Prince George - Peace River BC, Conservative Party
613-947-4524, Fax: 613-947-4527,Hill.J@parl.gc.ca, Other Communications: Constituency Phone: 250-787-1194, Fax: 250-787-1195

Randy Hoback, Prince Albert SK, Conservative Party
613-995-3295, Fax: 613-995-6819,Hoback.R@parl.gc.ca, Other Communications: Constituency Phone: 306-953-8622, Fax: 306-953-8625

Candice Hoeppner, Portage - Lisgar MB, Conservative Party
613-995-9511, Fax: 613-947-0313,Hoeppner.C@parl.gc.ca, Other Communications: Constituency Phone: 204-822-7440, Fax: 204-822-7445

Ed Holder, London West ON, Conservative Party
613-996-6674, Fax: 613-996-6772,Holder.E@parl.gc.ca, Other Communications: Constituency Phone: 519-473-5955, Fax: 519-473-7333

Mark Holland, Ajax - Pickering ON, Liberal
613-995-8042, Fax: 613-996-1289,Holland.M@parl.gc.ca, Other Communications: Constituency Phone: 905-426-6808, Fax: 905-426-9564

Carol Hughes, Algoma - Manitoulin -Kapuskasing ON, New Democratic Party
613-996-5376, Fax: 613-995-6661,Hughes.C@parl.gc.ca, Other Communications: Constituency Phone: 705-848-8080, Fax: 705-848-1818

Bruce Hyer, Thunder Bay - Superior North ON, New Democratic Party
613-996-4792, Fax: 613-996-9785,Hyer.B@parl.gc.ca, Other Communications: Constituency Phone: 807-345-1818, Fax: 807-345-4752

Hon. Michael Grant Ignatieff, Etobicoke -Lakeshore ON, Liberal
613-995-9364, Fax: 613-947-0310,Ignatieff.M@parl.gc.ca, Other Communications: Constituency Phone: 416-251-5510, Fax: 416-251-2845

Brian Jean, Fort McMurray - Athabasca AB, Conservative Party
613-992-1154, Fax: 613-992-4603,Jean.B@parl.gc.ca, Other Communications: Constituency Phone: 780-743-2201, Fax: 780-743-2287

Hon. Marlene Jennings, Notre-Dame-de-Grâce -Lachine QC, Liberal
613-995-2251, Fax: 613-996-1481,Jennings.M@parl.gc.ca, Other Communications: Constituency Phone: 514-489-8703, Fax: 514-489-2806

Peter Julian, Burnaby - New Westminster BC, New Democratic Party
613-992-4214, Fax: 613-947-9500,Julian.P@parl.gc.ca, Other Communications: Constituency Phone: 604-775-5707, Fax: 604-775-5743

Randy Kamp, Pitt Meadows - Maple Ridge -Mission BC, Conservative Party
613-947-4613, Fax: 613-947-4615,Kamp.R@parl.gc.ca, Other Communications: Constituency Phone: 604-466-2761, Fax: 604-466-7593

Andrew Kania, Brampton West ON, Liberal
613-995-5381, Fax: 613-995-6796,Kania.A@parl.gc.ca, Other Communications: Constituency Phone: 905-846-0076, Fax: 905-846-3901

Hon. Jim Karygiannis, Scarborough -Agincourt ON, Liberal
613-992-4501, Fax: 613-995-1612,Karygiannis.J@parl.gc.ca, Other Communications: Constituency Phone: 416-321-5454, Fax: 416-321-5456

Gerald Keddy, South Shore - St. Margaret's NS, Conservative Party
613-996-0877, Fax: 613-996-0878,Keddy.G@parl.gc.ca, Other Communications: Constituency Phone: 902-637-3945, Fax: 902-637-3946

Gerard Kennedy, Parkdale - High Park ON, Liberal
613-992-2936, Fax: 613-995-1629,Kennedy.G@parl.gc.ca, Other Communications: Constituency Phone: 416-769-5072, Fax: 416-769-8343

Hon. Jason Kenney, CalgarySoutheast AB, Conservative Party
613-992-2235, Fax: 613-992-1920,kenneJ@parl.gc.ca; Minister@cic.gc.ca, Other Communications: Constituency Phone: 403-225-3480, Fax: 403-225-3504

Hon. Peter Kent, Thornhill ON, Conservative Party
613-992-0253, Fax: 613-992-0887,Kent.P@parl.gc.ca; Peter.Kent@international.gc.ca, Other Communications: Constituency Phone: 905-886-9911, Fax: 905-886-5267

Greg Kerr, West Nova NS, Conservative Party
613-995-5711, Fax: 613-996-9857,Kerr.G@parl.gc.ca, Other Communications: Constituency Phone: 902-742-6808, Fax: 902-742-6815

Ed Komarnicki, Souris - Moose Mountain SK, Conservative Party
613-992-7685, Fax: 613-995-8908,Komarnicki.E@parl.gc.ca, Other Communications: Constituency Phone: 306-634-3000, Fax: 306-634-4835

Daryl Kramp, Prince Edward - Hastings ON, Conservative Party
613-992-5321, Fax: 613-996-8652,Kramp.D@parl.gc.ca, Other Communications: Constituency Phone: 613-969-3800, Fax: 613-969-3803

Jean-Yves Laforest, Saint-Maurice -Champlain QC, Bloc Quebecois
613-995-4895, Fax: 613-996-6883,LaforJ@parl.gc.ca, Other Communications: Constituency Phone: 819-538-5291, Fax: 819-538-7624

Mario Laframboise, Argenteuil - Papineau -Mirabel QC, Bloc Quebecois
613-992-0902, Fax: 613-992-2935,Laframboise.M@parl.gc.ca, Other Communications: Constituency Phone: 450-562-0737, Fax: 450-562-2527

Mike Lake, Edmonton - Mill Woods - Beaumont AB, Conservative Party
613-995-8695, Fax: 613-995-6465,Lake.M@parl.gc.ca, Other Communications: Constituency Phone: 780-495-2149, Fax: 780-495-2147

Francine Lalonde, La Pointe-de-l'Ile QC, Bloc Quebecois
613-995-6327, Fax: 613-996-5173,Lalonde.F@parl.gc.ca, Other Communications: Constituency Phone: 514-645-0101, Fax: 514-645-0032

Guy Lauzon, Stormont - Dundas - SouthGlengarry ON, Conservative Party
613-992-2521, Fax: 613-996-2119,Lauzon.G@parl.gc.ca, Other Communications: Constituency Phone: 613-937-3331, Fax: 613-937-3251

Carole Lavallée, Saint-Bruno -Saint-Hubert QC, Bloc Quebecois
613-996-2416, Fax: 613-995-6973,Lavallee.C@parl.gc.ca, Other Communications: Constituency Phone: 450-926-5979, Fax: 450-926-5985

Hon. Jack Gilbert Layton, Toronto -Danforth ON, New Democratic Party
613-995-7224, Fax: 613-995-4565,Layton.J@parl.gc.ca, Other Communications: Constituency Phone: 416-405-8914, Fax: 416-405-8918

Hon. Denis Lebel, Roberval - Lac-Saint-Jean QC, Conservative Party
613-996-6236, Fax: 613-996-6252,Lebel.D@parl.gc.ca; denis.lebel@dec-ced.gc.ca, Other Communications: Constituency Phone: 418-275-2768, Fax: 418-275-6535

Hon. Dominic LeBlanc, Beauséjour NB, Liberal
613-992-1020, Fax: 613-992-3053,Leblanc.D@parl.gc.ca, Other Communications: Constituency Phone: 506-533-5700, Fax: 506-533-5888

Derek Lee, Scarborough - Rouge River ON, Liberal
613-996-9681, Fax: 613-996-6643,Lee.D@parl.gc.ca, Other Communications: Constituency Phone: 416-298-4224, Fax: 416-298-6035

Marc Lemay, Abitibi - Témiscamingue QC, Bloc Quebecois
613-996-3250, Fax: 613-992-3672,Lemay.M@parl.gc.ca, Other Communications: Constituency Phone: 819-762-3733, Fax: 819-762-8732

Pierre Lemieux, Glengarry - Prescott -Russell ON, Conservative Party
613-992-0490, Fax: 613-996-9123,Lemieux.P@parl.gc.ca, Other Communications: Constituency Phone: 613-632-4162, Fax: 613-632-5668

Megan Leslie, Halifax NS, New Democratic Party
613-995-7614, Fax: 613-992-8569,Leslie.M@parl.gc.ca, Other Communications: Constituency Phone: 902-426-8691, Fax: 902-426-8693

Yves Lessard, Chambly - Borduas QC, Bloc Quebecois
613-992-6035, Fax: 613-995-6223,LessaY@parl.gc.ca, Other Communications: Constituency Phone: 450-441-7802, Fax: 450-441-3674

Yvon Lévesque, Abitibi - Baie-James - Nunavik -Eeyou QC, Bloc Quebecois
613-992-3030, Fax: 613-996-0828,LevesY@parl.gc.ca, Other Communications: Constituency Phone: 819-824-2942, Fax: 819-824-2958

Ben Lobb, Huron - Bruce ON, Conservative Party
613-992-8234, Fax: 613-995-6350,Lobb.B@parl.gc.ca, Other Communications: Constituency Phone: 519-524-6560, Fax: 519-612-1141

Tom Lukiwski, Regina - Lumsden - LakeCentre SK, Conservative Party
613-992-4573, Fax: 613-996-6885,Lukiwski.T@parl.gc.ca, Other Communications: Constituency Phone: 306-790-4747, Fax: 306-790-4746

Hon. Gary Lunn, Saanich - Gulf Islands BC, Conservative Party
613-996-1119, Fax: 613-996-0850,Lunn.G@parl.gc.ca, Other Communications: Constituency Phone: 250-656-2320, Fax: 250-656-1675

James Lunney, Nanaimo - Alberni BC, Conservative Party
613-992-5243, Fax: 613-992-9112,Lunney.J@parl.gc.ca, Other Communications: Constituency Phone: 250-390-7550, Fax: 250-390-7551

Hon. Lawrence MacAulay, Cardigan PE, Liberal
613-995-9325, Fax: 613-995-2754,MacAulay.L@parl.gc.ca, Other Communications: Constituency Phone: 902-838-4139, Fax: 902-838-3790

Hon. Peter Gordon MacKay, Central Nova NS, Conservative Party
613-992-6022, Fax: 613-992-2337,MacKay.P@parl.gc.ca; Mackay.P@forces.gc.ca, Other Communications: Constituency Phone: 902-863-7005, Fax:902-863-7006

Dave MacKenzie, Oxford ON, Conservative Party
613-995-4432, Fax: 613-995-4433,MacKenzie.D@parl.gc.ca, Other Communications: Constituency Phone: 519-421-7214, Fax: 519-421-9704

Hon. Gurbax Malhi, Bramalea - Gore - Malton ON, Liberal
613-992-9105, Fax: 613-947-0443,Malhi.G@parl.gc.ca, Other Communications: Constituency Phone: 905-790-9211, Fax: 905-790-9507

Luc Malo, Verchères-Les Patriotes QC, Bloc Quebecois
613-996-2998, Fax: 613-995-1062,Malo.L@parl.gc.ca, Other Communications: Constituency Phone: 450-652-4442, Fax: 450-652-4447

Jim Maloway, Elmwood - Transcona ON, New Democratic Party
613-995-6339, Fax: 613-995-6688,Maloway.J@parl.gc.ca, Other Communications: Constituency Phone: 204-984-2499, Fax: 204-984-2502

Inky Mark, Dauphin - Swan River - Marquette MB, Conservative Party
613-992-3176, Fax: 613-992-0930,Mark.I@parl.gc.ca, Other Communications: Constituency Phone: 204-622-4659, Fax: 204-622-4654

Wayne Marston, Hamilton East - StoneyCreek ON, New Democratic Party
613-992-6535, Fax: 613-992-7764,Marston.W@parl.gc.ca, Other Communications: Constituency Phone: 905-662-4763, Fax: 905-662-2285

Hon. Keith Martin, Esquimalt - Juan de Fuca BC, Liberal
613-996-2625, Fax: 613-996-9779,Martin.K@parl.gc.ca, Other Communications: Constituency Phone: 250-474-6505, Fax: 250-474-5322

Pat Martin, Winnipeg Centre MB, New Democratic Party
613-992-5308, Fax: 613-992-2890,Martin.Pd@parl.gc.ca, Other Communications: Constituency Phone: 204-984-1675, Fax: 204-984-1676

Tony Martin, Sault Ste. Marie ON, New Democratic Party
613-992-9723, Fax: 613-992-1954,Martin.T@parl.gc.ca, Other Communications: Constituency Phone: 705-941-2900, Fax: 705-941-2903

Brian Masse, Windsor West ON, New Democratic Party
613-996-1541, Fax: 613-992-5397,Masse.B@parl.gc.ca, Other Communications: Constituency Phone: 519-255-1631, Fax: 519-255-7913

Irene Mathyssen, London - Fanshawe ON, New Democratic Party
613-995-2901, Fax: 613-943-8717,Mathyssen.I@parl.gc.ca, Other Communications: Constituency Phone: 519-685-4745, Fax: 519-685-1462

Colin Mayes, Okanagan - Shuswap BC, Conservative Party
613-995-9095, Fax: 613-992-3195,Mayes.C@parl.gc.ca, Other Communications: Constituency Phone: 250-260-5020, Fax: 250-260-5025

Hon. John McCallum, Markham - Unionville ON, Liberal
613-996-3374, Fax: 613-992-3921,McCallum.J@parl.gc.ca, Other Communications: Constituency Phone: 905-479-8100, Fax: 905-479-3440

Phil McColeman, Brant ON, Conservative Party
613-992-3118, Fax: 613-992-6382,McColeman.P@parl.gc.ca, Other Communications: Constituency Phone: 519-754-4300, Fax: 519-751-8177

David McGuinty, Ottawa South ON, Liberal
613-992-3269, Fax: 613-995-1534,McGuinty.D@parl.gc.ca, Other Communications: Constituency Phone: 613-990-8640, Fax: 613-990-2592

Hon. John McKay, Scarborough - Guildwood ON, Liberal
613-992-1447, Fax: 613-992-8968,McKay.J@parl.gc.ca, Other Communications: Constituency Phone: 416-283-1226, Fax: 416-283-7935

Cathy McLeod, Kamloops - Thompson -Cariboo BC, Conservative Party
613-995-6931, Fax: 613-995-9897,McLeod.C@parl.gc.ca, Other Communications: Constituency Phone: 250-851-4991, Fax: 250-851-4994,

Hon. Dan McTeague, Pickering - ScarboroughEast ON, Liberal
613-995-8082, Fax: 613-993-6587,McTeague.D@parl.gc.ca, Other Communications: Constituency Phone: 416-287-0110, Fax: 416-287-6160

Serge Ménard, Marc-Aurèle - Fortin QC, Bloc Quebecois
613-992-2617, Fax: 613-992-6069,MenarSe@parl.gc.ca, Other Communications: Constituency Phone: 450-965-1188, Fax: 450-965-3221

Alexandra Mendes, Brossard - La Prairie QC, Liberal
613-995-9301, Fax: 613-992-7273,Mendes.A@parl.gc.ca, Other Communications: Constituency Phone: 450-466-6872, Fax: 450-466-9822

Ted Menzies, Macleod AB, Conservative Party
613-995-8471, Fax: 613-996-9770,Menzies.T@parl.gc.ca, Other Communications: Constituency Phone: 403-625-5532, Fax: 403-625-5592

Hon. Rob Merrifield, Yellowhead AB, Conservative Party
613-992-1653, Fax: 613-992-3459,Merrifield.R@parl.gc.ca, Other Communications: Constituency Phone: 780-723-6068, Fax: 780-723-5060

Larry Miller, Bruce - Grey - Owen Sound ON, Conservative Party
613-996-5191, Fax: 613-952-0979,Miller.L@parl.gc.ca, Other Communications: Constituency Phone: 519-371-1059, Fax: 519-371-1752

Hon. Peter Milliken, Kingston & the Islands ON, Liberal
613-996-1955, Fax: 613-996-1958,Milliken.P@parl.gc.ca; SpkrOff@parl.gc.ca, Other Communications: Constituency Phone: 613-542-3243, Fax: 613-542-5461

Hon. Maria Minna, Beaches - East York ON, Liberal
613-992-2115, Fax: 613-996-7942,Minna.M@parl.gc.ca, Other Communications: Constituency Phone: 416-467-0860, Fax: 416-467-0905

Hon. James Moore, Port Moody - Westwood - PortCoquitlam BC, Conservative Party
613-992-9650, Fax: 613-992-9868,Moore.J@parl.gc.ca, Other Communications: Constituency Phone: 604-937-5650, Fax: 604-937-5601

Hon. Rob Moore, Fundy Royal NB, Conservative Party
613-996-2332, Fax: 613-995-4286,Moore.R@parl.gc.ca, Other Communications: Constituency Phone: 506-832-4200, Fax: 506-832-4235

Maria Mourani, Ahuntsic QC, Bloc Quebecois
613-992-0983, Fax: 613-992-1932,Mourani.Ma@parl.gc.ca, Other Communications: Constituency Phone: 514-383-3709, Fax: 514-383-3589

Thomas Mulcair, Outremont QC, New Democratic Party
613-995-7691, Fax: 613-995-0114,Mulcair.T@parl.gc.ca, Other Communications: Constituency Phone: 514-736-2727, Fax: 514-736-2726

Brian Murphy, Moncton-Riverview-Dieppe NB, Liberal
613-992-8072, Fax: 613-992-8083,Murphy.B@parl.gc.ca, Other Communications: Constituency Phone: 506-851-3310, Fax: 506-851-3273

Hon. Shawn Murphy, Charlottetown PE, Liberal
613-996-4714, Fax: 613-995-7685,Murphy.S@parl.gc.ca, Other Communications: Constituency Phone: 902-566-7770, Fax: 902-566-7780

Joyce Murray, Vancouver Quadra BC, Liberal
613-992-2430, Fax: 613-995-0770,Murray.J@parl.gc.ca, Other Communications: Constituency Phone: 604-664-9220, Fax: 604-664-9221

Richard Nadeau, Gatineau QC, Bloc Quebecois
613-992-4351, Fax: 613-992-1037,Nadeau.R@parl.gc.ca, Other Communications: Constituency Phone: 819-561-5555, Fax: 819-561-0005

Hon. Anita Neville, Winnipeg South Centre MB, Liberal
613-992-9475, Fax: 613-992-9586,Neville.A@parl.gc.ca, Other Communications: Constituency Phone: 204-983-1355, Fax: 204-984-3979

Hon. Robert Douglas Nicholson, NiagaraFalls ON, Conservative Party
613-995-1547, Fax: 613-992-7910,Nicholson.R@parl.gc.ca, Other Communications: Constituency Phone: 905-353-9590, Fax: 905-353-9588

Rick Norlock, Northumberland - QuinteWest ON, Conservative Party
613-992-8585, Fax: 613-995-7536,Norlock.R@parl.gc.ca, Other Communications: Constituency Phone: 905-372-8757, Fax: 905-372-1500

Deepak Obhrai, Calgary East AB, Conservative Party
613-947-4566, Fax: 613-947-4569,Obhrai.D@parl.gc.ca, Other Communications: Constituency Phone: 403-207-3030, Fax: 403-207-3035

Hon. Gordon O'Connor, Carleton - MississippiMills ON, Conservative Party
613-992-1119, Fax: 613-992-1043,OConnor.G@parl.gc.ca, Other Communications: Constituency Phone: 613-592-3469, Fax: 613-592-4756

Hon. Beverley J. (Bev) Oda, Durham ON, Conservative Party
613-992-2792, Fax: 613-992-2794,Oda.B@parl.gc.ca; minister@acdi-cida.gc.ca, Other Communications: Constituency Phone: 905-697-1699, Fax: 905-697-1678

Robert Oliphant, Don Valley West ON, Liberal
613-992-2855, Fax: 613-995-1635,Oliphant.R@parl.gc.ca, Other Communications: Constituency Phone: 416-467-7275, Fax: 416-467-8550

Tilly O'Neill-Gordon, Miramichi NB, Conservative Party
613-992-5335, Fax: 613-996-8418,ONeill-Gordon.T@parl.gc.ca, Other Communications: Constituency Phone: 506-778-8448, Fax: 506-778-8150

Christian Ouellet, Brome - Missisquoi QC, Bloc Quebecois
613-947-8185, Fax: 613-947-8188,Ouellet.C@parl.gc.ca, Other Communications: Constituency Phone: 450-266-6062, Fax: 450-266-6064

Massimo Pacetti, Saint-Léonard -Saint-Michel QC, Liberal
613-995-9414, Fax: 613-992-8523,Pacetti.M@parl.gc.ca, Other Communications: Constituency Phone: 514-256-4548, Fax: 416-256-8828

Daniel Paillé, Hochelaga QC, Bloc Quebecois
613-947-4576, Fax: 613-947-4579,Paille.D@parl.gc.ca, Other Communications: Constituency Phone: 514-283-2655, Fax: 514-283-6485

Pascal-Pierre Paillé, Louis-Hébert QC, Bloc Quebecois
613-995-4995, Fax: 613-996-8292,Paille.P@parl.gc.ca, Other Communications: Constituency Phone: 418-648-3244, Fax: 418-648-3260

Pierre Paquette, Joliette QC, Bloc Quebecois
613-996-6910, Fax: 613-995-2818,Paquette.P@parl.gc.ca, Other Communications: Constituency Phone: 450-752-1940, Fax: 450-752-1719

Hon. Christian Paradis, Mégantic-L'Érable QC, Conservative Party
613-995-1377, Fax: 613-943-1562,Paradis.C@parl.gc.ca, Other Communications: Constituency Phone: 418-338-2903, Fax: 428-338-3631

Bernard Patry, Pierrefonds - Dollard QC, Liberal
613-992-2689, Fax: 613-996-8478,Patry.B@parl.gc.ca, Other Communications: Constituency Phone: 514-624-5725, Fax: 514-624-5728

LaVar Payne, Medicine Hat AB, Conservative Party
613-992-4516, Fax: 613-992-6181,Payne.L@parl.gc.ca, Other Communications: Constituency Phone: 403-528-4698, Fax: 403-528-4365

Glen Pearson, London North Centre ON, Liberal
613-992-0805, Fax: 613-992-9613,Pearson.G@parl.gc.ca, Other Communications: Constituency Phone: 519-663-9777, Fax: 519-663-2238

Daniel Petit, Charlesbourg -Haute-Saint-Charles QC, Conservative Party
613-995-8857, Fax: 613-995-1625,Petit.D@parl.gc.ca, Other Communications: Constituency Phone: 418-624-0022, Fax: 418-624-1095

Louis Plamondon, Bas-Richelieau - Nicolet -Bécancour QC, Bloc Quebecois
613-995-9241, Fax: 613-995-6784,PlamoL@parl.gc.ca, Other Communications: Constituency Phone: 450-742-0479, Fax: 450-742-1976

Pierre Poilievre, Nepean - Carleton ON, Conservative Party
613-992-2772, Fax: 613-992-1209,PoiliP@parl.gc.cagc.ca, Other Communications: Constituency Phone: 613-990-4300, Fax: 613-990-4333

Roger Pomerleau, Drummond QC, Bloc Quebecois
613-947-4550, Fax: 613-947-4551,Pomerleau.R@parl.gc.ca, Other Communications: Constituency Phone: 819-477-3611, Fax: 819-477-7116

Hon. Jim Prentice, Calgary Centre-North AB, Conservative Party
613-992-4275, Fax: 613-947-9475,Prentice.J@parl.gc.ca;

Jim.Prentice@ec.gc.ca, Other Communications: Constituency Phone: 403-216-7777, Fax: 403-230-4368
Joe Preston, Elgin - Middlesex - London ON, Conservative Party
613-990-7769, Fax: 613-996-0194,Preston.J@parl.gc.ca, Other Communications: Constituency Phone: 519-637-2255, Fax: 519-637-3358
Marcel Proulx, Hull - Aylmer QC, Liberal
613-992-7550, Fax: 613-992-7599,Proulx.M@parl.gc.ca, Other Communications: Constituency Phone: 819-994-8844, Fax: 819-994-8557
Hon. Bob Rae, Toronto Centre ON, Liberal
613-992-5234, Fax: 613-996-9607,Rae.B@parl.gc.ca, Other Communications: Constituency Phone: 416-954-2222, Fax: 416-954-9649
John Rafferty, Thunder Bay - Rainy River ON, New Democratic Party
613-992-3061, Fax: 613-995-3515,Rafferty.J@parl.gc.ca, Other Communications: Constituency Phone: 807-623-6000, Fax: 807-623-6001
Hon. Lisa Raitt, Halton ON, Conservative Party
613-996-7046, Fax: 613-992-0851,Raitt.L@parl.gc.ca, Other Communications: Constituency Phone: 905-693-0166, Fax: 905-693-0704
James Rajotte, Edmonton-Leduc AB, Conservative Party
613-992-3594, Fax: 613-992-3616,Rajotte.J@parl.gc.ca, Other Communications: Constituency Phone: 780-495-4351, Fax: 780-495-4485
Yasmin Ratansi, Don Valley East ON, Liberal
613-995-4988, Fax: 613-995-1686,Ratansi.Y@parl.gc.ca, Other Communications: Constituency Phone: 416-443-0623, Fax: 416-443-9819
Brent Rathgerber, Edmonton - St. Albert AB, Conservative Party
613-996-4722, Fax: 613-995-8880,Rathgeber.B@parl.gc.ca, Other Communications: Constituency Phone: 780-459-0809, Fax: 780-460-1246
Hon. Geoff Regan, Halifax West NS, Liberal
613-996-3085, Fax: 613-996-6988,Regan.G@parl.gc.ca, Other Communications: Constituency, Phone: 902-426-2217, Fax: 902-426-8339
Scott Reid, Lanark - Frontenac - Lennox -Addington ON, Conservative Party
613-947-2277, Fax: 613-947-2278,Reid.S@parl.gc.ca, Other Communications: Constituency Phone: 613-257-8130, Fax: 613-257-4371
Blake Richards, Wild Rose AB, Conservative Party
613-996-5152, Fax: 613-947-4601,Richards.B@parl.gc.ca, Other Communications: Constituency Phone: 403-948-5103, Fax: 403-948-0879
Lee Richardson, Calgary Centre AB, Conservative Party
613-995-1561, Fax: 613-995-1862,Richardson.L@parl.gc.ca, Other Communications: Constituency Phone: 403-244-1880, Fax: 403-245-3468
Greg Rickford, Kenora ON, Conservative Party
613-996-1161, Fax: 613-996-1759,Rickford.G@parl.gc.ca, Other Communications: Constituency Phone: 807-468-2170, Fax: 807-468-4896
Hon. Gerry Ritz, Battlefords - Lloydminster SK, Conservative Party
613-995-7080, Fax: 613-996-8472,Ritz.G@parl.gc.ca, Other Communications: Constituency Phone: 306-445-2004, Fax: 306-445-0207
Pablo Rodriguez, Honoré - Mercier QC, Liberal
613-995-0580, Fax: 613-992-1710,Rodriguez.P@parl.gc.ca, Other Communications: Constituency Phone: 514-353-5044, Fax: 514-353-3050
Anthony Rota, Nipissing - Timiskaming ON, Liberal
613-995-6255, Fax: 613-996-7993,Rota.A@parl.gc.ca, Other Communications: Constituency Phone: 705-474-3700, Fax: 705-474-6964
Jean-Yves Roy, Haute-Gaspesie - La Mitis - Matane- Matépédia QC, Bloc Quebecois
613-995-1013, Fax: 613-995-5184,Roy.J@parl.gc.ca, Other Communications: Constituency Phone: 418-629-2295, Fax: 418-629-2326
Todd Russell, Labrador NL, Liberal
613-996-4630, Fax: 613-996-7132,Russell.T@parl.gc.ca, Other Communications: Constituency Phone: 709-896-2483, Fax: 709-896-9425
Michael Savage, Dartmouth - Cole Harbour NS, Liberal
613-995-9378, Fax: 613-995-9379,Savage.M@parl.gc.ca, Other Communications: Constituency Phone: 902-462-6453, Fax: 902-462-6493
Denise Savoie, Victoria BC, New Democratic Party
613-996-2358, Fax: 613-952-1458,Savoie.D@parl.gc.ca, Other Communications: Constituency Phone: 250-363-3600, Fax: 250-363-8422
Andrew Saxton, North Vancouver BC, Conservative Party
613-995-1225, Fax: 613-992-7319,Saxton.A@parl.gc.ca, Other Communications: Constituency Phone: 604-775-6333, Fax: 604-775-6332
Francis Scarpaleggia, Lac-Saint-Louis QC, Liberal
613-995-8281, Fax: 613-995-0528,Scarpaleggia.F@parl.gc.ca, Other Communications: Constituency Phone: 514-695-6661, Fax:514-695-3708
Andrew Scheer, Regina - Qu'Appelle SK, Conservative Party
613-992-4593, Fax: 613-996-3120,Scheer.A@parl.gc.ca, Other Communications: Constituency Phone: 306-332-2575, Fax: 306-332-2576
Gary Schellenberger, Perth -Wellington ON, Conservative Party
613-992-6124, Fax: 613-998-7902,Schellenberger.G@parl.gc.ca, Other Communications: Constituency Phone: 519-273-1400, Fax: 519-273-9045
Hon. Judy Sgro, York West ON, Liberal
613-992-7774, Fax: 613-947-8319,Sgro.J@parl.gc.ca, Other Communications: Constituency Phone: 416-744-1882, Fax: 416-952-1696,
Hon. Gail Shea, Egmont PE, Conservative Party
613-992-9223, Fax: 613-992-1974,Shea.G@parl.gc.ca; Min@dfo-mpo.gc.ca, Other Communications: Constituency Phone: 902-432-6899, 902-882-4493
Bev Shipley, Lambton - Kent - Middlesex ON, Conservative Party
613-947-4581, Fax: 613-947-4584,Shipley.B@parl.gc.ca, Other Communications: Constituency Phone: 519-245-6561, Fax: 519-245-6736
Devinder Shory, Calgary Northeast AB, Conservative Party
613-947-4487, Fax: 613-947-4490,Shory.D@parl.gc.ca, Other Communications: Constituency Phone: 403-291-0018, Fax: 403-291-9516
Bill Siksay, Burnaby - Douglas BC, New Democratic Party
613-996-5597, Fax: 613-992-5501,Siksay.B@parl.gc.ca, Other Communications: Constituency Phone: 604-291-8863, Fax: 604-666-0727
Mario Silva, Davenport ON, Liberal
613-992-2576, Fax: 613-995-8202,Silva.M@parl.gc.ca, Other Communications: Constituency Phone: 416-654-8048, Fax: 416-654-5083
Scott Simms, Bonavista - Gander - GrandFalls-Windsor NL, Liberal
613-996-3935, Fax: 613-996-7622,Simms.S@parl.gc.ca, Other Communications: Constituency Phone: 709-256-3130, Fax: 709-256-3169
Michelle Simson, Scarborough Southwest ON, Liberal
613-995-0284, Fax: 613-996-6309,Simson.M@parl.gc.ca, Other Communications: Constituency Phone: 416-261-8613, Fax: 416-261-5268
Joy Smith, Kildonan - St. Paul MB, Conservative Party
613-992-7148, Fax: 613-996-9125,Smith.J@parl.gc.ca, Other Communications: Constituency Phone: 204-984-6322, Fax: 204-984-6415
Kevin Sorenson, Crowfoot AB, Conservative Party
613-947-4608, 800-665-4358,Fax: 613-947-4611,Sorenson.K@parl.gc.ca, Other Communications: Constituency Phone: 780-608-4600, Fax: 780-608-4603
Bruce Stanton, Simcoe North ON, Conservative Party
613-992-6582, Fax: 613-996-3128,Stanton.B@parl.gc.ca, Other Communications: Constituency Phone: 705-327-0513, Fax: 705-327-8310
Thierry St-Cyr, Jeanne - Le Ber QC, Bloc Quebecois
613-995-6403, Fax: 613-995-6404,St-Cyr.T@parl.gc.ca, Other Communications: Constituency Phone: 514-496-4885, Fax: 514-496-8097
Peter Stoffer, Sackville - Eastern Shore NS, New Democratic Party
613-995-5822, Fax: 613-996-9655,Stoffer.P@parl.gc.ca, Other Communications: Constituency Phone: 902-861-2311, Fax: 902-861-4620
Brian Storseth, Westlock - St. Paul AB, Conservative Party
613-996-1783, Fax: 613-995-1415,Storseth.B@parl.gc.ca, Other Communications: Constituency Phone: 780-349-8333, Fax: 780-349-8340
Hon. Charles (Chuck) Strahl, Chilliwack - FraserCanyon BC, Conservative Party
613-992-2940, Fax: 613-944-9376,Strahl.C@parl.gc.ca, Other Communications: Constituency Phone: 604-847-9711, Fax: 604-847-9744
David Sweet, Ancaster - Dundas - Flamborough -Westdale ON, Conservative Party
613-996-4984, Fax: 613-996-4986,Sweet.D@parl.gc.ca, Other Communications: Constituency Phone: 905-627-9169, Fax: 905-627-3803
Paul Szabo, Mississauga South ON, Liberal
613-992-4848, Fax: 613-996-3267,Szabo.P@parl.gc.ca, Other Communications: Constituency Phone: 905-822-2111, Fax: 905-822-2115
Eve-Mary Thaï Thi Lac, BA, Saint-Hyacinthe -Bagot QC, Bloc Quebecois
613-996-4585, Fax: 613-992-1815,ThiLac.E@parl.gc.ca, Other Communications: Constituency Phone: 450-771-0505, Fax: 450-771-0767
Glenn Thibeault, Sudbury ON, New Democratic Party
613-996-8962, Fax: 613-995-2569,Thibeault.G@parl.gc.ca, Other Communications: Constituency Phone: 705-673-7107, Fax: 705-673-0944
Hon. Greg Thompson, New BrunswickSouthwest NB, Conservative Party
613-995-5550, Fax: 613-995-5226,Thompson.G@parl.gc.ca, Other Communications: Constituency Phone: 506-466-3928, Fax: 506-466-2813
David Tilson, Dufferin - Caledon ON, Conservative Party
613-995-7813, Fax: 613-992-9789,Tilson.D@parl.gc.ca, Other Communications: Constituency Phone: 519-941-1832, Fax: 519-941-8660
Hon. Vic Toews, Provencher MB, Conservative Party
613-992-3128, Fax: 613-995-1049,Toews.V@parl.gc.ca, Other Communications: Constituency Phone: 204-326-9889, Fax: 204-346-9874
Alan Tonks, York South - Weston ON, Liberal
613-995-0777, Fax: 613-992-2949,Tonks.A@parl.gc.ca, Other Communications: Constituency Phone: 416-656-2526, Fax: 416-656-9908
Bradley Trost, Saskatoon - Humboldt SK, Conservative Party
613-992-8052, Fax: 613-996-9899,Trost.B@parl.gc.ca, Other Communications: Constituency Phone: 306-975-6133, 306-975-6670
Justin Trudeau, Papineau QC, Liberal
613-995-8872, Fax: 613-995-9926,Trudeau.J@parl.gc.ca; info@justin.ca, Other Communications: Constituency Phone: 514-277-6020, Fax: 514-277-3454
Mervin Tweed, Brandon - Souris MB, Conservative Party
613-995-9372, Fax: 613-992-1265,Tweed.M@parl.gc.ca, Other Communications: Constituency Phone: 204-726-7600, Fax: 204-726-7699
Tim Uppal, Edmonton - Sherwood Park AB, Conservative Party
613-995-3611, Fax: 613-995-3612,Uppal.T@parl.gc.ca, Other Communications: Constituency Phone: 780-467-4944, Fax: 780-449-1471
Frank Valeriote, Guelph ON, Liberal
613-996-4758, Fax: 613-996-9922,Valeriote.F@parl.gc.ca, Other Communications: Constituency Phone: 519-837-8276, Fax: 519-837-8443
David Van Kesteren, Chatham-Kent -Essex ON, Conservative Party
613-992-2612, Fax: 613-992-1852,VanKesteren.D@parl.gc.ca, Other Communications: Constituency Phone: 519-358-7555, Fax: 519-358-1428
Hon. Peter Van Loan, York - Simcoe ON, Conservative Party
613-996-7752, Fax: 613-997-8351,VanLoan.P@parl.gc.ca, Other Communications: Constituency Phone: 905-898-1600, Fax: 905-898-4600
Maurice Vellacott, Saskatoon -Wanuskewin SK, Conservative Party
613-992-1899, Fax: 613-992-3085,Vellacott.M@parl.gc.ca, Other Communications: Constituency Phone: 306-975-4725, Fax: 306-975-4728
Hon. Josée Verner, Louis - Saint-Laurent QC, Conservative Party
613-996-4151, Fax: 613-954-2269,Verner.J@parl.gc.ca, Other Communications: Constituency Phone: 418-626-5522, Fax: 418-626-5646
Robert Vincent, Shefford QC, Bloc Quebecois
613-992-5279, Fax: 613-992-7871,Vincent.R@parl.gc.ca, Other Communications: Constituency Phone: 450-378-3221, Fax: 450-378-3380
Hon. Giuseppe (Joseph) Volpe, Eglinton-Lawrence ON, Liberal
613-992-6361, Fax: 613-992-9791,Volpe.J@parl.gc.ca, Other Communications: Constituency Phone: 416-781-5583, Fax:416-781-5586
Mike Wallace, Burlington ON, Conservative Party
613-995-0881, Fax: 613-995-1091,Wallace.M@parl.gc.ca, Other Communications: Constituency Phone: 905-639-5757, Fax: 905-639-6031
Mark Warawa, Langley BC, Conservative Party
613-992-1157, Fax: 613-943-1823,warawm7@parl.gc.ca, Other Communications: Constituency Phone: 604-534-5955, Fax: 604-534-5970
Chris Warkentin, Peace River AB, Conservative Party
613-992-5685, Fax: 613-947-4782,Warkentin.C@parl.gc.ca, Other Communications: Constituency Phone: 780-538-1677, Fax: 780-538-9257
Jeff Watson, Essex ON, Conservative Party
613-992-1812, Fax: 613-995-0033,Watson.J@parl.gc.ca, Other Communications: Constituency Phone: 519-776-4700, Fax: 519-776-1383
John Weston, West Vancouver - Sunshine Coast -Sea to Sky Country BC, Conservative Party
613-947-4617, Fax: 613-947-4620,Weston.J@parl.gc.ca, Other Communications: Constituency Phone: 604-981-1790, Fax: 604-981-1794
Rodney Weston, Saint John NB, Conservative Party
613-947-2700, Fax: 613-947-4574,Weston.R@parl.gc.ca,

Other Communications: Constituency Phone: 506-657-2500, Fax: 506-657-2504
Hon. Bryon Wilfert, Richmond Hill ON, Liberal
613-992-3802, Fax: 613-996-1954,Wilfert.B@parl.gc.ca, Other Communications: Constituency Phone: 905-709-5905; Fax: 905-709-5908
Alice Wong, Richmond BC, Conservative Party
613-995-2021, Fax: 613-995-2174,Wong.A@parl.gc.ca, Other Communications: Constituency Phone: 604-775-5790; Fax: 604-775-6291
Stephen Woodworth, Kitchener Centre ON, Conservative Party
613-995-8913, Fax: 613-996-7329,Woodworth.S@parl.gc.ca, Other Communications: Constituency Phone: 519-741-2001, Fax: 519-579-2404
Borys Wrzesnewskyj, EtobicokeCentre ON, Liberal
613-947-5000, Fax: 613-947-4276,Wrzesnewskyj.B@parl.gc.ca, Other Communications: Constituency Phone: 416-249-7322; Fax: 416-249-6117
Hon. Lynne Yelich, Blackstrap SK, Conservative Party
613-995-5653, Fax: 613-995-0126,Yelich.L@parl.gc.ca, Other Communications: Constituency Phone: 306-252-6100, Fax: 306-693-2221
Terence Young, Oakville ON, Conservative Party
613-995-4014, Fax: 613-992-0520,Young.T@parl.gc.ca, Other Communications: Constituency Phone: 905-338-2008
Lise Zarac, LaSalle - Émard QC, Liberal
613-943-6636, Fax: 613-943-6637,Zarac.L@parl.gc.ca, Other Communications: Constituency Phone: 514-363-0954, Fax: 514-367-5533
Vacant, Vaughan ON
Vacant, Winnipeg North MB

Federal Government Departments & Agencies / Agences et departements du gouvernement fédéral

Editor's Note: The entries listed below are entered alphabetically, using applied titles as registered by the Federal Identity Program. Cross references are used to help you to locate the entry quickly. The two departments that incorporate Department of as part of their applied titles (Department of Finance Canada; Department of Justice Canada) are nevertheless listed alphabetically under Finance & Justice.

Agriculture & Agri-Food Canada / Agriculture et Agro-alimentaire Canada

1341 Baseline Rd., Ottawa, ON K1A 0C5
613-773-1000, Fax: 613-773-2772, 866-345-7972
info@agr.gc.ca
www.agr.ca

Other Communication: AgriInvest & AgriStability, Toll-Free Phone: 1-866-367-8506; Developing Innovative Agri-Products: 1-866-857-2287; Community Development Program: 1-877-295-7160

Agriculture & Agri-Food Canada is responsible for all matters related to agriculture. Examples of services provided by Agriculture & Agri-Food Canada include the following: research, development, & technology; policies & programs; the inspection & regulation of animals & plant-life forms; the coordination of rural development; the support of agricultural productivity & trade; the stabilization of farm incomes; & the provision of information. The goals of Agriculture & Agri-Food Canada are as follows: to achieve security of the food system; to ensure health of the environment; & to provide innovation for growth. Agriculture & Agri-Food Canada reports to Parliament & Canadians through the Minister of Agriculture & Agri-Food & the Minister for the Canadian Wheat Board.

Acts Administered:
Agricultural Marketing Programs Act
Agricultural Products Marketing Act
Animal Pedigree Act
Canada Grain Act
Canadian Agricultural Loans Act
Canadian Dairy Commission Act
Canadian Wheat Board Act
Department of Agriculture & Agri-Food Act
Experimental Farm Stations Act
Farm Debt Mediation Act
Farm Credit Canada Act
Farm Income Protection Act
Farm Products Agencies Act
Prairie Farm Rehabilitation Act

Minister, Agriculture & Agri-Food; Minister, Canadian Wheat Board,Hon. Gerry Ritz
613-773-1059, Fax: 613-773-1060,Ritz.G@parl.gc.ca
Parliamentary Secretary to the Minister of Agriculture, Pierre Lemieux
613-992-0490, Fax: 613-996-9123,Lemieux.P@parl.gc.ca
Director, Policy, Mindy Pearce
613-773-1059, Fax: 613-773-1081,mindy.pearce@agr.gc.ca
Director, Policy, Matthew Wolf
613-773-1059, Fax: 613-773-1081,matthew.wolf@agr.gc.ca

• Canadian Dairy Commission(CDC) / Commission canadienne du lait
Building 55, NCC Driveway, Central Experimental Farm
960 Carling Ave.
Ottawa, ON K1A 0Z2
613-792-2000 Fax: 613-792-2009 866-366-0676TDD: 613-792-2082
cdc-ccl@cdc-ccl.gc.ca; carole.cyr@cdc-ccl.gc.ca
www.cdc-ccl.gc.ca
Other Communication: Special Milk Class Permits, Phone: 613-792-2057; Dairy Imports & Exports, Phone: 613-792-2010

• Canadian Food Inspection Agency(CFIA) / Agence canadienne d'inspection des aliments
1400 Merivale Rd.
Ottawa, ON K1A 0Y9
613-225-2342 Fax: 613-228-6601 800-442-2342TDD: 800-465-7735
www.inspection.gc.ca
Other Communication: Atlantic Area, Phone: 506-851-7400; Ontario Area: 519-837-9400; Québec Area: 514-283-8888; Western Area: 403-292-4301

• Canadian Grain Commission(CGC) / Commission canadienne des grains
#603, 303 Main St.
Winnipeg
Winnipeg, MB R3C 3G8
204-983-2770 Fax: 204-983-2751 800-853-6705TDD: 866-317-4289
contact@grainscanada.gc.ca
www.grainscanada.gc.ca
Other Communication: Grain Sanitation & Infestation Control Industry Services, Fax: 204-984-7550; Licensing & Security Unit, Fax: 204-983-4654; Statistics Unit, Phone: 204-983-2739

• Farm Credit Canada(FCC) / Financement agricole Canada
1800 Hamilton St.
PO Box 4320
Regina, SK S4P 4L3
306-780-8100 Fax: 306-780-8919 888-332-3301TDD: 306-780-6974
csc@fcc-fac.ca
www.fcc-fac.ca
Other Communication: Careers, E-mail: hr-rh@fcc-fac.ca; Media & Publications: Communications@fcc-fac.ca; Legal Services: legal_services@fcc-fac.ca; FCC Learning: fcclearning@fcc-fac.ca

• Canadian Wheat Board(CWB)
423 Main St.
PO Box 816 Main
Winnipeg, MB R3C 2P5
204-983-0239 Fax: 204-983-3841 800-275-4292
questions@cwb.ca; farmers@cwb.ca
www.cwb.ca
Other Communication: Media relations, Phone: 204-983-3101; Government relations, Phone: 204-984-8167

• Canadian Pari-Mutuel Agency(CPMA)
800-268-8835
cpmawebacpm@agr.gc.ca
www4.agr.gc.ca/AAFC-AAC/display-afficher.do?id=1204043533186&lang
Other Communication: Toll-Free Phone, French: 1-800-326-3344; Equine Drug Control Program, Phone: 613-949-0745

Agri-Environment Services Branch (AESB)
Tower 4, 1341 Baseline Rd., Ottawa, ON K1A 0C5
613-759-1000, Fax: 613-773-1211,
www4.agr.gc.ca/AAFC-AAC/display-afficher.do?id=1187362338955&lang

Other Communication: Agroforestry Development Centre, Phone: 1-866-766-2284, Fax: 306-695-2568; Canada-Manitoba Crop Diversification Centre, Phone: 204-834-6000, Fax: 204-834-3777

The Agri-Environment Services Branch integrates the following components: Prairie Farm Rehabilitation Administration; National Land & Water Information Service; & Agri-Environmental Policy Bureau. The mission of the branch is to deliver innovative environmental solutions to the agriculture & agri-food sector. Applied Technology Development Centres of the Agri-Environment Services Branch include the following: Agroforestry Development Centre (formerly known as the Prairie Farm Rehabilitation Administration); Canada-Saskatchewan Irrigation Diversification Centre; & the Canada-Manitoba Crop Diversification Centre.

Assistant Deputy Minister, Jamshed Merchant
613-773-1200, Fax: 613-773-1211,jamshed.merchant@agr.gc.ca
Director General, Agri-Environmental Knowledge, Innovation, & Technology Directorate,Dr. Richard Butts
506-452-4802, Fax: 506-474-7533,richard.butts@agr.gc.ca
Director General, Agri-Environmental Adaptation & Practice Change Directorate, Alan Parkinson
306-780-5081, Fax: 306-780-6533,alan.parkinson@agr.gc.ca
Director, Achieving Excellence Secretariat, Christian Pilon
613-773-1225, Fax: 613-773-1222,christian.pilon@agr.gc.ca
Director General, Agri-Environmental Policy & Strategic Priorities Directorate, Greg Strain
613-773-1207, Fax: 613-773-1222,greg.strain@agr.gc.ca
Administrative Coordinator, Integrated Planning & Reporting Directorate, Shelley McEwen
306-780-8618, Fax: 306-780-7519,shelley.mcewen@agr.gc.ca

Communications & Consultations Branch
Tower 7, 1341 Baseline Rd., Ottawa, ON K1A 0C7
613-759-1000, Fax: 613-773-2772

Assistant Deputy Minister, Jodi Redmond
613-773-2922, Fax: 613-773-2772,jodi.redmond@agr.gc.ca
Director General, Communications Services, Jane Towley
613-773-2840, Fax: 613-773-2772,jane.taylor@agr.gc.ca
Director, E-Communications, Joan Anderson
613-773-2601, Fax: 613-773-2398,joan.anderson@agr.gc.ca
Director, Strategic Planning, Advice, & Coordination, Lori Harrop
613-773-2750, Fax: 613-773-2772,lori.harrop@agr.gc.ca
Director, Strategic & Ministerial Communications, Steven Jurgutis
613-773-2760, Fax: 613-773-2772,steven.jurgutis@agr.gc.ca
Director, Operations, Robert LeBlond
613-773-2630, Fax: 613-773-2398,robert.leblond@agr.gc.ca
Director, Media & Writing Services, & Special Projects, Darell M. Pack
613-773-2755, Fax: 613-773-2772,darell.pack@agr.gc.ca
Director, Translation & Revision Services, Caroline Rahal
613-773-0986, Fax: 613-773-2397,caroline.rahal@agr.gc.ca
Manager, Branch Planning & Resource Management, Penny O'Shaughnessy-Wallace
613-773-2746, Fax: 613-773-2727,penny.oshaughnessy@agr.gc.ca

Corporate Management
Tower 4, 1341 Baseline Rd., Ottawa, ON K1A 0C5
613-759-1000, Fax: 613-773-0911,

Assistant Deputy Minister, Pierre Corriveau
613-773-1330, Fax: 613-773-1233,pierre.corriveau@agr.gc.ca
Director General, Asset Management & Capital Planning, Lynden Hillier
613-773-0923, Fax: 613-773-0966,lynden.hillier@agr.gc.ca
Director General, Finance & Resource Management Services, Bev Levere
613-773-1332, Fax: 613-773-0777,bev.levere@agr.gc.ca
Director General, Strategic Management, Debbie Winker
613-773-1344, Fax: 613-773-0911,debbie.winker@agr.gc.ca
Executive General, Canadian Pari-Mutuel Agency, Sean Malone
613-949-0742, Fax: 613-949-0750,sean.malone@agr.gc.ca

Deputy Minister's Office / Bureau du sous-ministre
Tower 7, 1341 Baseline Rd., Ottawa, ON K1A 0C5
613-759-1011, Fax: 613-759-1040

The Deputy Minister's Office oversees the following organizations: Corporate Secretariat; Food Safety Review Secretariat; & Portfolio Coordination Secretariat.

Deputy Minister, Agriculture & Agri-Food Canada, John Knubley
613-773-1101, Fax: 613-773-1040,john.knubley@agr.gc.ca
Associate Deputy Minister, Agriculture & Agri-Food Canada, Andrea Lyon
613-773-1011, Fax: 613-773-1061,andrea.lyon@agr.gc.ca
Executive Director, Portfolio Coordination Secretariat, Todd F. Hunter
613-773-1062, Fax: 613-773-1051,todd.hunter@agr.gc.ca
Executive Director, Food Safety Review Secretariat, Anna Romano
613-773-2128, Fax: 613-773-2939,anna.romano@agr.gc.ca
Manager, Governance Committees Secretariat, Corporate Secretariat, Monique Deguire
613-773-1096, Fax: 613-773-1061,monique.deguire@agr.gc.ca
Manager, Finance & Administration, Corporate Secretariat, Jeanne Johnson
613-773-1057, Fax: 613-773-1061,jeanne.johnson@agr.gc.ca

Farm Financial Programs Branch / Direction générale des programmes de financement agricoles
Tower 7, 1341 Baseline Rd., Ottawa, ON K1A 0C5
613-759-1000, Fax: 613-773-2121

The Farm Financial Programs Branch of Agriculture & Agri-Food Canada oversees the following organizations: Agriculture Transformation Programs Directorate; Business Risk Management Program Development; Centre of Program Excellence (COPE); Farm Income Programs Directorate; Finance & Renewal Programs Directorate; & Service Policy & Transformation Directorate.

Assistant Deputy Minister, Farm Financial Programs Branch, Rita Moritz
613-773-2815, Fax: 613-773-2121,rita.moritz@agr.gc.ca
Director General, Finance & Renewal Programs Directorate, Jody Aylard
613-773-2005, Fax: 613-773-2099,jody.aylard@agr.gc.ca
Director General, Centre of Program Excellence (COPE), Ray Edwards
613-773-0612, Fax: 613-773-1911,ray.edwards@agr.gc.ca
Director General, Business Risk Management Program Development, Danny Foster
613-773-2100, Fax: 613-773-2198,danny.foster@agr.gc.ca
Director General, Service Policy & Transformation Directorate, Danny Foster
613-773-2144, Fax:
613-773-2121,michele.goshulak@agr.gc.ca
Director General, Farm Income Programs Directorate, Patti Miller
204-984-5645, Fax: 204-983-7557,patti.miller@agr.gc.ca
Director General, Agriculture Transformation Programs Directorate, Linda Parsons
613-773-1900, Fax: 613-773-1911,linda.parsons@agr.gc.ca

Human Resources Branch / Direction générale des ressources humaines
Tower 1, 560 Rochester St., Ottawa, ON K1A 0C5
613-759-1000, Fax: 613-759-7105
Assistant Deputy Minister, Human Resources Branch, Catherine MacQuarrie
613-759-1196, Fax:
613-759-7105,catherine.macquarrie@agr.gc.ca
Director General, Planning, Policy, & Workplace Programs, Consuelo Francolini
613-759-7469, Fax:
613-715-5150,consuelo.francolini@agr.gc.ca
Director General, Workplace Relations, Lisa Imbesi
613-715-5260, Fax: 613-759-6143,Lisa.Imbesi@agr.gc.ca
Director General, Agriculture & Agri-Food Canada Client Services, Tim Pettipas
613-759-6231, Fax: 613-759-6143,tim.pettipas@agr.gc.ca
Senior Director, Learning, Development, & Official Languages, Scott Aughey
613-759-6527, Fax: 613-792-3426,scott.aughey@agr.gc.ca
Director, Human Resources, Canadian Grain Commission, Marilyn Galliott
204-983-7781, Fax: 204-983-1681,marilyn.galliott@agr.gc.ca

Information Systems Branch
Tower 4, 1341 Baseline Rd., Ottawa, ON K1A 0C5
613-759-1000, Fax: 613-773-0676
The Information Systems Branch of Agriculture & Agri-Food Canada is reponsible for the following organizations: Applications Development Directorate; Information Management Services; IT Operations; & the Strategic Management Directorate.
Chief Information Officer, Peter Bruce
613-773-1395, Fax: 613-773-0676,peter.bruce@agr.gc.ca
Director General, IT Operations, Gail Eagen
613-773-0400, Fax: 613-773-0444,gail.eagen@agr.gc.ca
Director General, Applications Development Directorate, Angus Howieson
613-759-7735, Fax:
613-759-6045,angus.howieson@agr.gc.ca
Director General, Information Management Services, Jeff Lamirande
613-773-2916, Fax: 613-773-0666,jeff.lamirande@agr.gc.ca
Director General, Strategic Management Directorate, Rama Rai
613-773-0615, Fax: 613-773-0666,rama.rai@agr.gc.ca
Director, Canadian Agriculture Library, Danielle Jacques
613-773-1448, Fax:
613-773-1499,danielle.jacques@agr.gc.ca

Legal Services
Tower 7, 1341 Baseline Rd., Ottawa, ON K1A 0C5
613-759-1000, Fax: 613-773-2929
General Counsel & Executive Director, Legal Services, Louise Sénéchal
613-773-2901, Fax:
613-773-2929,louise.senechal@agr.gc.ca
Business Manager, Aysha Johnson
613-773-2915, Fax: 613-773-2929,aysha.johnson@agr.gc.ca
Information Specialist, Aurora Bravar
613-773-2920, Fax: 613-773-2929,aurora.bravara@agr.gc.ca

Market & Industry Services Branch (MISB) / Direction générale des services à l'industrie et aux marchés
Tower 5, 1341 Baseline Rd., Ottawa, ON K1A 0C5
613-759-1000, Fax: 613-773-1755,
Other Communication: Government of Canada Export Services Information, Toll-Free Phone: 1-888-576-4444
The Market & Industry Services Branch of Agriculture & Agri-Food Canada oversees the following organizations: Bilateral Relations & Technical Trade Policy Directorate; Food Value Chain Bureau; International Markets Bureau; Market Access Secretariat; Negotiations & Multilateral Trade Policy Directorate; & the Operations Directorate. The Operations Directorate operates regional offices throughout Canada, which provide access to market & trade programs & services. Marketing & trade officers offer the following information: statistics by country & product; market access advice; investment opportunities; regulatory issues; export counselling; & news about promotional events.
Assistant Deputy Minister, Steve Tierney
613-773-1790, Fax: 613-773-1755,steve.tierney@agr.gc.ca
Director General, Bilateral Relations & Technical Trade Policy Directorate, Blair Coomber
613-773-1600, Fax: 613-773-1616,blair.coomber@agr.gc.ca
Director General & Chief Agriculture Negotiator, Negotiations & Multilateral Trade Policy Directorate, Gilles Gauthier
613-773-0985, Fax: 613-773-1755,gilles.gauthier@agr.gc.ca
Director General, Market Access Secretariat, Fred Gorrell
613-773-1512, Fax: 613-773-0199,fred.gorrell@agr.gc.ca
Director General, Operations Directorate,Dr. Jaspinder Komal
613-773-1501, Fax:
613-773-1500,jaspinder.komal@agr.gc.ca,
Director General, Food Value Chain Bureau, Susie Miller
613-773-1750, Fax: 613-773-0300,susie.miller@agr.gc.ca
Director General, International Markets Bureau, Paul Murphy
613-773-1517, Fax: 613-773-1500,paul.murphy@agr.gc.ca

Market & Industry Services Branch Regional Offices:

Alberta & Territories Regional Office
#720, 9700 Jasper Ave., Edmonton, AB T5J 4G5
780-495-4141, Fax: 780-495-3324
Regional Director, Alberta & Territories Regional Office, Rodney Dlugos
780-495-5525, Fax: 780-495-3324,rodney.dlugos@agr.gc.ca
Deputy Director, Janet Dorey
780-495-5526, Fax: 780-495-3324,janet.dorey@agr.gc.ca

Atlantic Regional Office
#405, 1791 Barrington St., PO Box 248, Halifax, NS B3J 2N7
902-426-3198, Fax: 902-426-3439
The Atlantic Regional Office in Halifax, Nova Scotia, is the headquarters for the following operations: New Brunswick Operations (Phone: 506-452-3706, Fax: 506-452-3509); Newfoundland & Labrador Operations (Phone: 709-772-4063, Fax: 709-772-4803); Nova Scotia Operations (Phone: 902-896-0332, Fax: 902-896-0100); & Prince Edward Island Operations (Phone: 902-566-7300, Fax: 902-566-7316).
Regional Director, Atlantic Regional Office, Janet Steele
902-426-7171, Fax: 902-426-3439,janet.steele@agr.gc.ca
Deputy Director, Prince Edward Island Operations, Heath Coles
902-566-7305, Fax: 902-566-7316,heath.coles@agr.gc.ca
Deputy Director, Newfoundland & Labrador Operations, Brian Goldsworthy
709-772-4055, Fax:
709-772-4803,brian.goldsworthy@agr.gc.ca
Deputy Director, New Brunswick Operations, Bernard P. Mallet
506-452-3732, Fax: 506-452-3509,bernard.mallet@agr.gc.ca
Deputy Director, Nova Scotia Operations, Shelley Manning
902-896-0098, Fax:
902-896-0100,shelley.manning@agr.gc.ca

British Columbia Regional Office
#420, 4321 Stillcreek Dr., Burnaby, BC V5C 6S7
604-666-6344, Fax: 604-666-7235
Regional Director, British Columbia Regional Office, John Berry
604-666-6344, Fax: 604-666-7235,john.berry@agr.gc.ca
Deputy Director, Michelle Soucie
604-666-3054, Fax: 604-666-7235,michelle.soucie@agr.gc.ca

Manitoba Regional Office
303 Main St., Winnipeg, MB R3C 3G7
204-983-3032, Fax: 204-983-4583
Regional Director, Manitoba Regional Office, Brian Lemon
204-983-8622, Fax: 204-983-4583,brian.lemon@agr.gc.ca
Deputy Director, Bob Nawolsky
204-983-3891, Fax: 204-983-4583,bob.nawolsky@agr.gc.ca

Ontario Regional Office
174 Stone Rd. West, Guelph, ON N1G 4S9
519-837-9400, Fax: 519-837-9782
Regional Director, Ontario Regional Office, Ezio Di Emanuele
519-837-5825, Fax:
519-837-9782,ezio.diemanuele@agr.gc.ca
Deputy Director, Ezio Di Emanuele
519-837-5821, Fax: 519-837-9782,marg.bancroft@agr.gc.ca
Deputy Director, Bill Robinson
519-837-5822, Fax: 519-837-9782,bill.robinson@agr.gc.ca

Québec Regional Office
2001, rue Université, 7e étage, Montréal, QC H3A 3N2
514-283-8888, Fax: 514-496-3966
Regional Director, Québec Regional Office, Sandra Gagné
514-315-6170, Fax: 514-496-3966,sandra.gagne@agr.gc.ca
Regional Deputy Director, Scott Patterson
514-315-6171, Fax:
514-496-3966,scott.patterson2@agr.gc.ca

Saskatchewan Regional Office
1800 Hamilton St., Regina, SK S4P 4K7
306-780-5545, Fax: 306-780-7360
Regional Director, Saskatchewan Regional Office, Dean L. Vey
306-780-7065, Fax: 306-780-7360,dean.vey@agr.gc.ca
Deputy Director, Saskatchewan Regional Office, Wendy Collinge
306-780-5452, Fax: 306-780-7360,wendy.collinge@agr.gc.ca
Deputy Director, Markets & Trade, Gavin M. Conacher
306-780-5216, Fax: 306-780-7360,gavin.conacher@agr.gc.ca

Office of Audit & Evaluation
Tower 4, 1341 Baseline Rd., Ottawa, ON K1A 0C5
613-759-1000, Fax: 613-773-0660
Agriculture & Agri-Food Canada's Office of Audit & Evaluation is responsible for the following services: evaluation; governance & review; & internal audit & assurance.
Chief Audit & Evaluation Executive, Graham Barr
613-773-0650, Fax: 613-773-0660,graham.barr@agr.gc.ca
Director, Governance & Review Services, Jennifer Moher
613-773-1773, Fax: 613-773-0660,jennifer.moher@agr.gc.ca
Director, Evaluation Services, Sally Scott
613-773-0655, Fax: 613-773-0660,sally.scott@agr.gc.ca
Senior Audit Manager, Internal Audit & Assurance Services, Gene Marostica
613-773-0675, Fax: 613-773-0660,gene.marostica@agr.gc.ca

Canada-Saskatchewan Irrigation Diversification Centre
901 McKenzie St. South, PO Box 700, Outlook, SK S0L 2N0
306-867-5400, Fax: 306-867-9656, csidc@agr.gc.ca

Manitoba
#200, 303 Main St., Winnipeg, MB R3C 3G7
204-984-3695, Fax: 204-983-2178

Manitoba Crop Diversification Centre
PO Box 309, Carberry, MB R0K 0H0
204-834-6005, Fax: 204-834-3777

Northern Alberta & BC
Canada Place, #945, 9700 Jasper Ave. NW, Edmonton, AB T5J 4C3
780-495-3307, Fax: 780-495-4504,

Northern Saskatchewan
#1101, 11 Innovation Blvd., Saskatoon, SK S7N 3H5
306-975-4693, Fax: 306-975-4594

Shelterbelt Centre
PO Box 940, Indian Head, SK S0G 2K0
306-695-2284, Fax: 306-695-2568, pfratree@agr.gc.ca

Southern Alberta
Harry Hays Bldg., #600, 138 - 4 Ave. SE, Calgary, AB T2G 4Z2
403-292-5638, Fax: 403-292-5659

Southern Saskatchewan
#603, 1800 Hamilton St., Regina, SK S4P 4L2
306-780-5150, Fax: 306-780-6778

Research Branch / Direction générale de la recherche
Tower 5, 1341 Baseline Rd., Ottawa, ON K1A 0C5
613-759-1000, Fax: 613-773-1866
Agriculture & Agri-Food Canada's Research Branch consists of the following organizations: Innovation Directorate; International Scientific Cooperation Bureau; Land Resources; Science Centres Directorate, Science Partnerships Directorate; & Science Policy & Planning. Scientists from Agriculture & Agri-Food Canada work on projects to benefit the agricultural & agri-food sector at research centres located across Canada.
Assistant Deputy Minister,Dr. Marc Fortin, PhD
613-773-1860, Fax: 613-773-1866,marc.fortin@agr.gc.ca
Director General, Science Policy & Planning,Dr. Christiane Deslauriers, PhD
613-773-1870, Fax:
613-773-1877,christiane.deslauriers@agr.gc.ca
Director General, Science Partnerships Directorate,Dr. Stephen D. Morgan Jones, PhD
403-317-2200, Fax:
403-317-2197,steve.morganjones@agr.gc.ca
Director General, Science Centres Directorate,Dr. Gilles Saindon, PhD
613-773-1843, Fax: 613-773-1844,gilles.saindon@agr.gc.ca
Director General, Innovation Directorate, Michael J. Whittaker
613-773-2308, Fax:
613-773-1822,michael.j.whittaker@agr.gc.ca
Director, Multilateral Science Relations, International Scientific Cooperation Bureau, Brad Fraleigh
613-773-1838, Fax: 613-773-1822,brad.fraleigh@agr.gc.ca

Chief Scientist, International Scientific Cooperation Bureau,Dr. Yvon Martel, PhD
613-773-1830, Fax: 613-773-1833,yvon.martel@agr.gc.ca
Chief Officer for Scientific Relations, China, International Scientific Cooperation Bureau, Jianqiang (Joe) Zhou, PhD
613-759-1744, Fax: 613-773-1833,joe.zhou@agr.gc.ca
Senior Officer, Land Resources, Warren D. Eilers
306-975-4062, Fax: 306-966-4226,warren.eilers@agr.gc.ca

Research Centres:

Atlantic Food & Horticulture Research Centre
32 Main St., Kentville, NS B4N 1J5
902-679-5333, Fax: 902-679-2311
Manager, Research,Dr. D. Mark Hodges, PhD
902-679-5544, Fax: 902-679-5784,mark.hodges@agr.gc.ca
Manager, Facilities, Brian Wagner
902-679-5583, Fax: 902-679-2311,brian.wagner@agr.gc.ca
Manager, Farm, Innovation & Renewal, David L. Bowlby
902-679-5589, Fax: 902-670-0004,david.bowlby@agr.gc.ca
Science Director, Crop Production Systems, Peter Hicklenton
902-679-5760, Fax:
902-679-5344,peter.hicklenton@agr.gc.ca

Brandon Research Centre
RR#3, PO Box 1000A, Brandon, MB R7A 5Y3
204-726-7650, Fax: 204-728-3858
Manager, Research,Dr. Fernando Selles, PhD
204-578-3539, Fax: 204-578-3528,fernando.selles@agr.gc.ca
Manager, Building, Frank Thompson
204-578-3525, Fax:
204-728-3858,frank.thompson@agr.gc.ca
Manager, Farm, Clay Jackson
204-578-3610, Fax: 204-578-3522,clayton.jackson@agr.gc.ca

Cereal Research Centre
195 Dafoe Rd., Winnipeg, MB R3T 2M9
204-983-5533, Fax: 204-983-4604
Manager, Research,Dr. David Wall
204-983-0099, Fax: 204-984-6333,david.wall@agr.gc.ca
Manager, Integrated Services, Bill Atkinson
204-983-0293, Fax:
204-984-8053,william.atkinson@agr.gc.ca
Science Director, Water & Soil Resources,Dr. Johanne B. Boisvert, PhD
204-983-0466, Fax:
204-983-4604,johanne.boisvert@agr.gc.ca

Crops & Livestock Research Centre
440 University Ave., Charlottetown, PE C1A 4N6
902-566-6800, Fax: 902-566-6821
The Crops and Livestock Research Centre (CLRC) in Charlottetown, Prince Edward Island is one of Agriculture and Agri-Food Canada's network of 19 research centres. The Centre's mandate is to develop scientific knowledge and new technologies in agriculture with the prime focus on Prince Edward Island and Atlantic Canada.
Manager, Research,Dr. Maria Rodriguez
902-566-6817, Fax:
902-566-6821,maria.rodriguez@agr.gc.ca
Manager, Research Operations, Roddy C. Pratt
902-672-6426, Fax: 902-566-6821,roddy.pratt@agr.gc.ca
Manager, Facilities, Kenny J. MacInnis
902-566-7353, Fax:
902-566-6821,kenneth.macinnis@agr.gc.ca
Manager, Integrated Services, Jamie Coffin
902-566-6811, Fax: 902-566-6821,jamie.coffin@agr.gc.ca

Dairy & Swine Research & Development Centre
2000, rue College, CP 90 Lennoxville, Sherbrooke, QC J1M 1Z3
819-565-9171, Fax: 819-564-5507
The Dairy & Swine Research & Development Centre oversees the operations of the Beef Research Farm in Kapuskasing, Ontario, as well as the Office of Intellectual Property & Commercialization in Sherbrooke, Québec.
Manager, Research,Dr. Alain Giguère
819-565-9174, Fax:
819-564-5407,alain.giguere@agr.gc.cagc.ca
Science Director, Livestock Production Systems,Dr. Jacques Surprenant, PhD, MPA
819-565-9174, Fax:
819-564-4974,jacques.surprenant@agr.gc.ca
Commercialization Officer, Office of Intellectual Property & Commercialization, Denise Call
613-759-1708, Fax: 613-759-1765,calld@agr.gc.ca
Head Herdsman, Kapuskasing Beef Research Farm, Maurice Portelance
705-335-6148, Fax:
705-337-6000,maurice.portelance@agr.gc.ca,

Eastern Cereal & Oilseed Research Centre
960 Carling Ave., Ottawa, ON K1A 0C6
613-759-1858, Fax: 613-759-1970
Manager, Research,Dr. Marc Savard
613-759-1683, Fax: 613-759-1970,marc.savard@agr.gc.ca
Manager, Research Support, Ron Wheeler
613-759-1544, Fax: 613-952-6438,ron.wheeler@agr.gc.ca
Science Director, Food & Health,Dr. Michèle Marcotte, PhD, Eng
613-759-1525, Fax:
613-759-1970,michele.marcotte@agr.gc.ca
Director, System Architecture, National Science Programs, Peter Schut, PhD, Eng
613-759-1874, Fax: 613-759-1937,peter.schut@agr.gc.ca

Food Research & Development Centre
3600, boul Casavant ouest, Saint-Hyacinthe, QC J2S 8E3
450-773-1105, Fax: 450-773-8461
Manager, Research,Dr. Christian J. Toupin, PhD
450-768-3331, Fax: 450-773-2888,christian.toupin@agr.gc.ca
Manager, Integrated Services & Industry, Jean C. Gagnon
450-768-3260, Fax: 450-773-8461,jean.gagnon@agr.gc.ca
Science Director, Food Production, Safety, & Quality, Gabriel Piette
450-768-3304, Fax: 450-773-2888,gabriel.piette@agr.gc.ca

Greenhouse & Processing Crops Research Centre
2585 Country Rd. 20, Harrow, ON N0R 1G0
519-738-2251, Fax: 519-738-2929
Manager, Research, Ranjana Sharma
519-738-1208, Fax:
519-738-2929,ranjana.sharma@agr.gc.ca
Manager, Integrated Services, Adrian Lancop
519-738-1210, Fax: 519-738-2929,adrian.lancop@agr.gc.ca
Science Director, Integrated Pest Management, Environmental Health,Dr. Gary Whitfield
519-738-1218, Fax: 519-738-3756,gary.whitfield@agr.gc.ca

Guelph Food Research Centre
93 Stone Rd. West, Guelph, ON N1G 5C9
519-829-2400, Fax: 519-829-2600
Manager, Research,Dr. Punidadas Piyasena
519-780-8063, Fax: 519-829-2602,puni.piyasena@agr.gc.ca
Manager, Facility, Michael Kerr
519-780-8084, Fax: 519-829-2600,mike.kerr@agr.gc.ca
Manager, Integrated Services, Joan Leatherdale
519-780-8039, Fax:
519-829-2601,joan.leatherdale@agr.gc.ca

Horticulture Research & Development Centre
430, boul Gouin, Saint-Jean-sur-Richelieu, QC J3B 3E6
450-346-4494, Fax: 450-346-7740
Manager, Research, Roger Chagnon
450-515-2001, Fax: 450-346-7908,roger.chagnon@agr.gc.ca
Manager, Integrated Services, Sylvie Joncas
450-515-2111, Fax: 450-346-7740,sylvie.joncas@agr.gc.ca
Manager, Facilities, Guy Lahaie
450-515-2090, Fax: 450-346-7740,guy.lahaie@agr.gc.ca
Manager, Greenhouse, Guy Boulet
450-515-2016, Fax: 450-346-7740,guy.boulet@agr.gc.ca

Lacombe Research Centre
6000 C & E Trail, Lacombe, AB T4L 1W1
403-782-8100, Fax: 403-782-6120
The Lacombe Research Centre is responsible for the operations of research farms in Beaverlodge & Fort Vermilion in Alberta.
Manager, Research, Rick Lawrence
403-782-8110, Fax: 403-782-4308,rick.lawrence@agr.gc.ca
Manager, Integrated Services, Danielle Girard
403-782-8105, Fax: 403-782-6120,danielle.girard@agr.gc.ca
Manager, Farm, Ken B. Grimson
403-782-8139, Fax: 403-782-8186,ken.grimson@agr.gc.ca
Facilities Management Officer, Beaverlodge Research Farm, Mervin R. Hegland
780-354-5120, Fax: 780-354-5150,merv.hegland@agr.gc.ca
Foreman, Fort Vermilion Research Farm, Mervin R. Hegland
780-927-3253, Fax: 780-927-3330,joe.unruh@agr.gc.ca

Lethbridge Research Centre
5403 - 1st Ave. South, PO Box 3000, Lethbridge, AB T1J 4B1
403-327-4561, Fax: 403-382-3156
The Lethbridge Research Centre oversees the operations of the Onefour Research Substation, the Stavely Research Substation, & the Vauxhall Research Substation in Alberta.
Manager, Research,Dr. Brian Freeze, PhD
403-317-3445, Fax: 403-317-2211,brian.freeze@agr.gc.ca
Manager, Facility, Donavan T. Casson
403-317-2233, Fax:
403-317-3491,donavan.casson@agr.gc.ca
Manager, Feed Mill, Dave Dancoisne
403-317-3383, Fax:
403-382-3156,dave.dancoisne@agr.gc.ca
Manager, Stavely Research Substation Site, Albert J. Middleton
403-549-2152, Fax:
403-549-3744,albert.middleton@agr.gc.ca
Manager, Vauxhall Research Substation Site, Jim Sukeroff
403-654-2255, Fax: 403-654-4243,jim.sukeroff@agr.gc.ca
Manager, Onefour Research Substation Site, Ian Walker
403-868-2364, Fax: 403-868-2489,ian.walker@agr.gc.ca
Science Director, Crop Genetic Enhancement,Dr. Jeff Stewart
403-317-2208, Fax: 403-317-2197,jeff.stewart@agr.gc.ca

Pacific Agri-Food Research Centre (PARC)
4200 Hwy. 97, PO Box 5000, Summerland, BC V0H 1Z0
250-494-7711, Fax: 250-494-0755
The Pacific Agri-Food Research Centre oversees the following organizations: the Agassiz Site, the Kamloops Range Research Unit, & the Summerland Site.
Research Manager, Summerland Site, Kenna MacKenzie
250-494-6358, Fax:
250-494-6415,kenna.mackenzie@agr.gc.ca
Facility Manager, Agassiz Site, Lorne Primeau
604-796-1719, Fax: 604-796-0359,lorne.primeau@agr.gc.ca
Facility Manager, Kamloops Range Research Unit, Larry Maio
250-554-5227, Fax: 250-554-5229,larry.maio@agr.gc.ca
Integrated Services Manager, Summerland Site, Bruce Jensen
250-494-6357, Fax: 250-494-0755,bruce.jensen@agr.gc.ca
Field Services Manager, Summerland Site, Mark Neufield
250-494-6427, Fax: 250-494-0755,mark.neufield@agr.gc.ca
Grounds & Greenhouse Manager, Summerland Site, David Weir
250-494-6387, Fax: 250-494-0755,david.weir@agr.gc.ca

Potato Research Centre
850 Lincoln Rd., PO Box 20280, Fredericton, NB E3B 4Z7
506-452-3260, Fax: 506-452-3316
The Potato Research Centre is also responsible for the Senator Hervé J. Michaud Research Farm, located in Bouctouche, New Brunswick.
Manager, Research, Jacques Millette, PhD
506-452-4845, Fax:
506-452-3212,jacques.millette@agr.gc.ca
Manager, Facilities, Sean Brown
506-452-4839, Fax: 506-452-3316,sean.brown@agr.gc.ca
Manager, Integrated Services, Senator Hervé J Michaud Research Farm, Louise Boucher
506-743-1140, Fax: 506-743-8316,louise.boucher@agr.gc.ca
Manager, Integrated Services, Potato Research Centre, Jeanne Caissie
506-452-4951, Fax: 506-452-3316,jeanne.caissie@agr.gc.ca
Manager, Farm, Larry McMillan
506-452-4838, Fax: 506-452-3316,larry.mcmillan@agr.gc.ca

Saskatoon Research Centre
107 Science Pl., Saskatoon, SK S7N 0X2
306-956-7200, Fax: 306-956-7247
Manager, Research,Dr. Felicitas Katepa-Mupondwa
306-956-2489, Fax:
306-956-7248,felicitas.katepa-mupondwa@agr.gc.ca
Science Director, Bioproducts Platforms & Genomics,Dr. Paul McCaughey
306-956-7211, Fax:
306-956-7248,paul.mccaughey@agr.gc.ca

Semiarid Prairie Agricultural Research Centre
PO Box 1030, Swift Current, SK S9H 3X2
306-778-7200, Fax: 306-778-3188
The Semiarid Prairie Agricultural Research Centre is responsible for the operations of research farms in Indian Head & Regina, Saskatchewan.
Manager, Research,Dr. Campbell G. Davidson
306-778-7270, Fax:
306-778-3186,campbell.davidson@agr.gc.ca
Manager, Integrated Services, Debbie Biese
306-778-7223, Fax: 306-778-3188,debbie.biese@agr.gc.ca
Manager, Regina Research Farm, Myron Knelsen
306-780-7426, Fax: 306-780-5501,myron.knelsen@agr.gc.ca
Head, Facilities Management, Brad Olfert
306-778-7219, Fax: 306-778-3188,brad.olfert@agr.gc.ca
Supervisor, Indian Head Research Farm, Darren Pollock
306-695-5264, Fax: 306-695-3445,darren.pollock@agr.gc.ca

Soils & Crops Research & Development Centre
2560, boul Hochelaga, Québec, QC G1V 2J3
418-657-7980, Fax: 418-648-2402
The Soils & Crops Research & Development Centre is also responsible for a research farm in Normandin, Québec.
Manager, Research, Claude Lapierre, MSc
418-210-5002, Fax: 418-648-2402,claude.lapierre@agr.gc.ca
Manager, Facilities, Rémi Lafrenière
418-210-5029, Fax: 418-648-2402,remi.lafreniere@agr.gc.ca
Manager, Integrated Services, Normandin Research Farm, Mario Fortin
418-274-5881, Fax: 418-274-3386,mario.fortin@agr.gc.ca
Chief, Greenhouse, Normand Charest
418-210-5014, Fax:
418-648-2402,normand.charest@agr.gc.ca

Southern Crop Protection & Food Research Centre
1391 Sandford St., London, ON N5V 4T3
519-457-1470, Fax: 519-457-3997

The Southern Crop Protection & Food Research Centre oversees the operations of research farms in Delhi & Vineland, Ontario, as well as an Office of Intellectual Property & Commercialization in London, Ontario.
Manager, Research, Southern Crop Protection & Food Research Centre,Dr. Karl Volkmar
519-457-1470, Fax: 519-457-3503,karl.volkmar@agr.gc.ca
Manager, Research, Vineland Research Farm, Antonet Svircev
604-796-1709, Fax: 604-796-0359,antonet.svircev@agr.gc.ca
Manager, Facility, Joe Pratt
519-457-1470, Fax: 519-457-3997,joe.pratt@agr.gc.ca
Supervisor, Farm Services, Delhi Research Farm, Albert Asztalos
519-582-1950, Fax: 519-582-4223,albert.asztalos@agr.gc.ca

Rural & Co-operatives Secretariat
Tower 7, 1341 Baseline Rd., Ottawa, ON K1A 0C5
613-759-1000, Fax: 613-773-2727
Executive Director, Rural & Co-operatives Secretariat, Donna Mitchell
613-773-2946, Fax: 613-773-2727,donna.mitchell@agr.gc.ca
Associate Executive Director, Rural & Co-operatives Secretariat, Christine Burton
613-773-2955, Fax: 613-773-2727,christine.burton@agr.gc.ca
Director, Partnerships & Programs, Louise Boudreau
613-773-2988, Fax:
613-773-2198,louise.boudreau@agr.gc.ca
Manager, Program Development & Implementation, Rural Programs, Lawrence Euteneier
613-773-2943, Fax:
613-773-2198,lawrence.euteneier@agr.gc.ca
Manager, Financial Services, Theresa Hedquist
613-773-2947, Fax:
613-773-2727,theresa.hedquist@agr.gc.ca
Manager, Co-op Policy & Research Unit, Co-operatives Secretariat, Anne Marie McInnis
613-773-2971, Fax:
613-773-2199,anne-marie.mcinnis@agr.gc.ca
Manager, Partnership, Co-operatives Secretariat, Alain Roy
613-773-2925, Fax: 613-773-2198,alain.roy@agr.gc.ca
Officer, Rural Communications, Lauraine Watson
204-983-8376, Fax:
204-983-8357,lauraine.watson@agr.gc.ca

Strategic Policy Branch / Direction générale des politiques stratégiques
Tower 7, 1341 Baseline Rd., Ottawa, ON K1A 0C5
613-759-1000, Fax: 613-773-2111
The Strategic Policy Branch of Agriculture & Agri-Food Canada includes the following organizations: Policy Development & Analysis Directorate; Policy, Planning, & Integration Directorate; & the Research & Analysis Directorate.
Assistant Deputy Minister, Greg Meredith
613-773-2930, Fax: 613-773-2121,greg.meredith@agr.gc.ca
Director General, Policy Development & Analysis Directorate, Paul Martin
613-773-2700, Fax: 613-773-2111,paul.martin@agr.gc.ca
Director General, Research & Analysis Directorate, Thomas Shenstone
613-773-2400, Fax: 613-773-2499,tom.shenstone@agr.gc.ca
Director General, Policy, Planning, & Integration Directorate, Heather Smith
613-773-2305, Fax: 613-773-2332,heather.smith@agr.gc.ca
Manager, Branch Planning & Resource Management, Taryn Barone
613-773-2301, Fax: 613-773-2333,taryn.barone@agr.gc.ca

Atlantic Canada Opportunities Agency (ACOA) / Agence de promotion économique du Canada atlantique (APECA)

Blue Cross Centre, 644 Main St., 3rd Fl., PO Box 6051, Moncton, NB E1C 9J8
506-851-2271, Fax: 506-851-7403, 800-561-7862
information@acoa-apeca.gc.ca
www.acoa-apeca.gc.ca
The role of the Atlantic Canada Opportunities Agency is the development of opportunities for economic growth in Atlantic Canada. The agency achieves its mission in the following ways: assisting businesses to become more innovative, productive, & competitive; promoting the strengths of Atlantic Canada; & helping communities to develop more diversified local economies.
Minister, National Revenue; Minister, Atlantic Canada Opportunities Agency; Minister, Atlantic Gateway,Hon. Keith Ashfield
613-992-1067, Fax: 613-996-9955,Ashfield.K@parl.gc.ca, Other Communications: National Revenue, Phone: 613-995-2960
President, Monique Collette
506-851-6128, Fax:
506-851-7403,President-presidente@acoa-apeca.gc.ca,
Executive Vice-President, Paul J. LeBlanc
506-851-7075, Fax: 506-851-7403
Senior Vice-President, David Slade
506-851-6141
Vice-President, Finance & Corporate Services, Denise Frenette
506-851-6438
Director General, Human Resources, Charlene Sullivan
506-851-2141
Director General, Communications, Susan Wisking
506-851-7731, Fax: 613-952-6393
Director, Energy, Environment Policy, & Coordination, Daniel McCarthy
613-952-8216
Director, Regional Affairs, Raymond Vogan
506-444-6120

Regional Offices:

New Brunswick Regional Office
570 Queen St., PO Box 578, Fredericton, NB E3B 5A6
506-452-3285, Fax: 506-452-3296, 800-561-4030
The New Brunswick Regional Office oversees operations at the following offices: Campbellton (Phone: 506-789-4735); Edmundston (Phone: 506-735-4236); Fundy Region (Phone: 506-636-4485); Miramichi (506-778-1909); Northeast (Phone: 506-548-7420); Northwest (Phone: 506-473-5556); Southeast (Phone: 506-851-6432); Southwest (506-452-3135); & Tracadie-Sheila (506-395-1025).
Director General, New Brunswick Regional Operations, Janet Gagnon
506-452-3342
Executive Director, New Brunswick Federal Council, Raymond Gallant
506-452-4986
Director, Business Programs, André Charron
506-452-2413
Director, Communications, Patricia Field
506-452-4287
Director, Financial Management Services, David Hubbard
506-452-2423
Director, Policy, Advocacy, & Coordination, Gail Moser
506-452-3155

Newfoundland & Labrador Regional Office
John Cabot Building, 10 Barter's Hill, 11th Fl., PO Box 1060 C, St. John's, NL A1C 5M5
709-772-2751, Fax: 709-772-2712, 800-668-1010
The Atlantic Canada Opportunities Agency's Newfoundland & Labrador Regional Office oversees the following offices throughout the province: Clarenville (Phone: 709-466-5980); Corner Brook (Phone: 709-637-4477); Gander (Phone: 709-651-4457); Grand Bank (Phone: 709-832-2517); Grand Falls-Windsor (Phone: 709-489-6600); & Labrador (709-896-2648).
Vice-President, Newfoundland & Labrador, Paul Mills
709-772-4150
Director General, Newfoundland & Labrador Regional Operations, Richard Comerford
709-772-2453
Director General, Policy, Advocacy, & Coordination, David Collins
709-772-2334
Executive Director, Federal / Regional Council, Mark Butler
709-772-2781
Director, Communications, Julie Afonso
709-772-2984
Director, Community Development, John Kennedy
709-772-2741
Director, Financial Management Services, Francis Mackey
709-772-6286
Director, Enterprise Development, Kenneth Martin
709-772-0212

Nova Scotia Regional Office
#600, 1801 Hollis St., PO Box 2284 M, Halifax, NS B3J 3C8
902-426-6743, Fax: 902-426-2054, 800-565-1228
The Nova Scotia Regional Office of the Atlantic Canada Opportunities Agency oversees the following offices throughout Nova Scotia: Antigonish (Phone: 902-867-6075); Bridgewater (Phone: 902-541-5543); Digby (Phone: 902-245-7308); Kentville (902-679-5356); Pictou (Phone: 902-755-3746); Truro (902-895-2743), & Yarmouth (Phone: 902-742-0809).
Vice-President, Deborah Windsor
902-426-8364
Director General, Regional Operations, Peter Hogan
902-426-1288
Director, Finance & Management Services, Nancy Ives
902-426-5968
Director, Intergovernmental Affairs & Coordination, Lisa Muton
902-426-4820
Director, Communications, Alexander Smith
902-426-9417, Fax: 902-426-5843

Prince Edward Island Regional Office
Royal Bank Building, 100 Sydney St., 3rd Floor, PO Box 40, Charlottetown, PE C1A 7K2
902-566-7492, Fax: 902-566-7098, 800-871-2596
The Prince Edward Island Regional Office oversees the Summerside District Office (Phone: 902-888-4145).
Vice-President, Prince Edward Island & Tourism, Patrick Dorsey
902-368-0760
Director General, Enterprise Development & Policy, Wayne Hooper
902-626-2877, Fax: 902-566-7098
Director General, Atlantic Tourism, Robert McCloskey
902-626-2479, Fax: 902-566-7098
Executive Director, Prince Edward Island Federal Council, Catherine MacInnis
902-368-0889, Fax: 902-566-7489
Director, Corporate Programs & Services, Lynne Beairsto
902-566-7499
Director, Infrastructure Programs, Pat McAulay
902-626-2794
Director, Communicatons, Cindy Roy
902-566-7569, Fax: 902-566-7098
Director, Business Programs & Strategic Infrastructure, Brian Schmeisser
902-566-7422
Director, Trade & Business Programs, Douglas Smith
902-368-0890

Atlantic Pilotage Authority (APA) / Administration de pilotage de l'Atlantique

Cogswell Tower, #910, 2000 Barrington St., Halifax, NS B3J 3K1
902-426-2550, Fax: 902-426-4004, 877-272-3477
dispatch@atlanticpilotage.com
www.atlanticpilotage.com

Other Communication: Toll-Free Fax: 1-877-745-3477
The Federal Crown Corporation is responsible for the safe & efficient operation, maintenance, & administration of marine pilotage service to Atlantic Canada.
Chief Executive Officer, R.A. Anthony McGuinness
902-426-2553
Chief Financial Officer, Peter L. MacArthur
902-426-8657
Director, Operations, Patrick Gates
902-426-6389

Atomic Energy of Canada Limited (AECL) / Énergie atomique du Canada Ltée (EACL)

Head Office, Sheridan Science & Technology Park, 2251 Speakman Dr., Mississauga, ON L5K 1B2
905-823-9040, 866-886-2325
librarycr@aecl.ca (Library); speakers@aecl.ca (Community speakers)
www.aecl.ca

Other Communication: Community inquiries, Toll-Free: 1-800-364-6989
Established in 1952, Atomic Energy of Canada Limited is a nuclear technology & services company, which employs 4,300 employees. It provides services to utilities in Canada & throughout the world. Atomic Energy of Canada Limited's head office in Mississauga employs more than 1,500 people. The head office provides the following services: nuclear service initiatives; the development, manufacturing, & testing of commercial products; engineering; the management & support of nuclear projects; commercial operations; & international sales & marketing. Atomic Energy of Canada Limited is also responsible for the management & operation of laboratories. Laboratories include the Chalk River Laboratories (Phone: 613-584-3311), northwest of Ottawa, Ontario, the Whiteshell Laboratories (Phone: 204-753-2311), situated northeast of Winnipeg, Manitoba, & the Underground Research Laboratory, located northeast of Winnipeg, Manitoba. At the Chalk River Laboratories, many of the organization's major research & development efforts are conducted. Atomic Energy of Canada Limited is widely known as the designer & builder of CANDU technology, including the CANDU 6.
President & Chief Executive Officer, Hugh MacDiarmid
Senior Vice-President, External Relations & Communications, George Bothwell
Senior Vice-President & Chief Technology Officer,Dr. Anthony (Tony) De Vuono
Senior Vice-President, Operations, Ramzi Fawaz
Senior Vice-President & Chief Financial Officer, Kent Harris
Senior Vice-President, Strategic Contracting, Allan A. Hawryluk
Senior Vice-President, General Counsel & Corporate Secretary, Jonathan Lundy
Senior Vice-President, Human Resources, Beth Medhurst

Senior Vice-President & Chief Nuclear Officer, Bill Pilkington
Senior Vice-President, Restructuring, Michael Robins
Vice-President, Marketing & Business Development, Ala Alizadeh
Vice-President, Contracts, Bruce Ambeault
Vice-President, Commercial, Richard V. Coté
Vice-President & General Manager, Operations, Earnest (Hank) Drumhiller
Vice-President, Supply Chain, Tracy Greig
Vice-President, Product Development, Jerry Hopwood
Vice-President, Finance, Georgina Kossivas
Vice-President & General Manager, Research & Development, William Kupferschmidt
Vice-President, Engineering & Technical Delivery, Joseph Lau
Vice-President & General Manager, Waste Management & Decommissioning, Joan Miller
Vice-President, Life Extension Projects & Project Management, Ian Trotman

Auditor General of Canada / Vérificateur général du Canada

240 Sparks St., Ottawa, ON K1A 0G6
613-995-3708, Fax: 613-957-0474, 888-761-5953
communications@oag-bvg.gc.ca; infomedia@oag-bvg.gc.ca
www.oag-bvg.gc.ca

Other Communication: Media Relations, Phone: 613-952-0213, ext. 6292; Publications, Toll-Free Phone: 1-888-761-5953; Work Opportunities, E-mail: emplo@oag-bvg.gc.ca

The Office of the Auditor General of Canada was established in 1878. Today, the head office in Ottawa & regional offices in Halifax, Montréal, Edmonton, & Vancouver employ approximately 650 employees. The Office of the Auditor General of Canada provides objective, fact-based information required by Parliament to hold the federal government accountable for its stewardship of public funds. An Officer of Parliament, the Auditor General of Canada is responsible for auditing the following organizations: federal government departments; federal government agencies; most Crown corporations; many federal organizations; the government of the Yukon; the government of the Northwest Territories; & the government of Nunavut. The Auditor General, Sheila Fraser, reports publicly to the House of Commons about matters she believes should be brought to the attention of the House of Commons. stainable development matters that she believes should be brought to the attention of the House of Commons. The report can include chapters on audits & studies, sustainable development strategies, & environmental petitions

Auditor General, Sheila Fraser
613-992-2512
Deputy Auditor General, John Wiersema
613-952-0213
Chief Information Officer & Assistant Auditor General, Ira Greenblatt
613-952-0213
Assistant Auditor General, IC, Aboriginal Issues, HRMA, Nunavut, Industry, & NRC, Ronnie Campbell
613-952-0213
Assistant Auditor General, Crown Corporations Group, Nancy Cheng
613-952-0213, Fax: 613-941-8284
Assistant Auditor General, Yukon & the Northwest Territories, Andrew Lennox
613-952-0213
Assistant Auditor General, CBSA, CIDA, CSIS, CIC, CSC, IRB, Justice, Public Safety, & RCMP, Wendy Loschiuk
613-952-0213
Assistant Auditor General, CDIC, CMHC, OP, FI, EDC, FCC, IDRC, & PSPIB, Clyde MacLellan
613-952-0213
Assistant Auditor General, Health Canada, SC, CFIA, AAFC, & Fisheries & Oceans, Neil Maxwell
613-952-0213
Assistant Auditor General, CRA, AA, FS, Separate Opinions, Income Tax, GST, & Performance Reporting, Marian McMahon
613-952-0213
Assistant Auditor General, Office of the Senior Advisor on Performance Audit, Hugh McRoberts
613-952-0213
Assistant Auditor General, HRSDC, Small Entities, Crown Corporations, & Other Entities, Sylvain Ricard
613-952-0213
Assistant Auditor General, Canadian Heritage Arts & Culture, Museums, NAC, CBC, TC, CATSA, VIA Rail, NCC, NRTEE, & ILO, John Rossetti
613-952-0213
Assistant Auditor General, Corporate Services, Lyn Sachs
613-952-0213
Principal, National Defence, Veteran Affairs Canada, Foreign Affairs, & International Trade Canada, Jerome Berthelette
613-952-0213
Principal, Practice Review & Internal Audit, & Strategic Planning, Julie Charron
613-952-0213
Principal, Forensic Audit Section, Linda Drainville
613-952-0213
Principal, Parliamentary Liaison & International Relations, Jocelyne Therrien
613-952-0213
Principal, Communications, Susan Wheeler
613-952-0213
Commissioner, Environment & Sustainable Development, Scott Vaughan
613-952-0213
Principal, Sustainable Development Strategies, Audits, & Studies, Richard Arseneault
613-952-0213
Principal, Sustainable Development Strategies, Audits, & Studies, Andrew Ferguson
613-952-0213
Principal, Sustainable Development Strategies, Audits, & Studies, James McKenzie
613-952-0213

Regional Offices:

Regional Offices:

Edmonton
Manulife Place, #2460, 10180 - 101st St., Edmonton, AB T5J 3S4
780-495-2028, Fax: 780-495-2031
Principal, Guy LeGras
780-495-2029,
Director, David Irving
780-495-6338

Halifax
Centennial Building, #414, 1660 Hollis St., Halifax, NS B3J 1V7
902-426-7721, Fax: 902-426-8591
Principal, Kevin Potter
902-426-9371
Director, Glenn Doucette
902-426-2097
Director, Heather McManaman
902-426-7728

Montréal
#545, 1255, rue Peel, Montréal, QC H3B 2T9
514-283-6086, Fax: 514-283-1715
Principal, René Béliveau
514-283-8324
Director, Jean-Pierre Morin
514-283-8136
Director, Tina Swiderski
514-283-7793

Vancouver
#250, 351 Abbott St., Vancouver, BC V6B 0G6
604-666-3596, Fax: 604-666-6162
Principal, Eric Hellsten
604-666-7600

Bank of Canada / Banque du Canada

234 Wellington St., Ottawa, ON K1A 0G9
613-782-8111, Fax: 613-782-7713, 800-303-1282
info@bankofcanada.ca; communications@bankofcanada.ca (Media)
www.bankofcanada.ca

Other Communication: Access to information & privacy issues, E-mail: ATIP-AIPRP@bankofcanada.ca; Publications, E-mail: publications@bankofcanada.ca

Founded in 1934, the Bank of Canada was orignially a privately owned corporation. It became a Crown corporation, belonging to the federal government, in 1938. As Canada's central bank, the role of the Bank of Canada is the promotion of the economic & financial welfare of the nation. The following are the main responsibilities of the Bank of Canada: Canada's financial system; monetary policy; funds management; & bank notes. The Governor & Senior Deputy of the Bank of Canada are appointed by the Bank's Board of Directors, with the approval of the Cabinet. Regional offices of the Bank of Canada are located in the following cities: Halifax (Phone: 902-420-4600); Montréal (Phone: 514-496-4800); Toronto (Phone: 416-542-1251); Calgary (Phone: 403-215-6700); Vancouver (Phone: 604-643-6227); & New York (Phone: 212-596-1673).

Governor, Mark J. Carney
Senior Deputy Governor, Tiff Macklem
Deputy Governor, Jean Boivin
Deputy Governor, Agathe Côté
Deputy Governor, Timothy Lane
Deputy Governor, John Murray
Special Adviser to the Governor, Timothy Hodgson
General Counsel & Corporate Secretary, Executive & Legal Services, W. John Jussup
Chief, Information Technology Services, Carole Briard
Chief, Canadian Economic Analysis, Paul Fenton
Chief, Currency, Gerry T. Gaetz
Chief Librarian, Information Resource Centre, Beverly Graham
613-782-8466, Fax: 613-782-7387,ref1@bankofcanada.ca
Chief, Financial Markets, Donna Howard
Chief, Corporate Services, Colleen Leighton
Chief, Funds Management & Banking, George Pickering
Chief Internal Auditor, Carmen Prévost Vierula
Chief, International Economic Analysis, Lawrence L. Schembri
Chief, Communications, Jill Vardy
Chief, Financial Services; Chief Accountant, Sheila Vokey
Chief, Financial Stability, Mark Zelmer
Director, Data & Statistics Office, Dinah Maclean
Archivist, Jane Boyko
613-782-8673, Fax: 613-782-7387,archives@bankofcanada.ca
Chief Internal Auditor, Carmen Prévost Vierula
Chief, Gerry T. Gaetz
Deputy Chief, Lorna Thomas
Director, Nicole Poirier
Chief, Brigid Janssen
Deputy Chief, Jill Vardy
Chief, Colleen Leighton
Deputy Chief, Janice Gabie
General Counsel & Corporate Secretary, W. John Jussup
Deputy Corporate Secretary, Susan Chibuk
Asst. General Counsel, Robert Turnbull
Deputy Chief, Research & Risk Management, Carolyn Wilkins
Research Director, Scott Hendry
Director, Paul Chilcott
Director, Montréal Division, Miville Tremblay
Director, Toronto Division, Mark Caplan
Chief, Mark Zelmer
Deputy Chief, Toni Gravelle
Director, Research, Walter N. Engert
Director, Data and Statistics Office, Dinah Maclean
Director, Research, Graydon Paulin
Chief, Sheila Vokey
Deputy Chief, Rudy Wytenburg
Chief, Larry L. Schembri
Deputy Chief, Sharon Kozicki
Director, Research, Robert Lafrance
Director, Research, Eric Santor
Chief, Paul Fenton
Deputy Chief, Donald Coletti
Research Director, Robert Amano
Research Director, Stephen Murchison
Chair, Jim Thomson
Chief Executive Officer, Ron Baker
ceo@sidit-bc.ca
Senior Regional Representative, Economics, David Amirault
Senior Regional Representative, Currency, Monique LeBlanc
Senior Regional Representative, Economics, Farid Novin
Senior Regional Representative, Currency, Trevor Frers
Senior Regional Representative, Economics, Jane T. Voll
Senior Regional Representative, Currency, Manuel Parreira
Senior Regional Representative, Currency, Ted Mieszkalski
Senior Regional Representative, Economics, Thérèse Laflèche
Senior Regional Representative, Currency, Phuong Anh Ho Huu

Business Development Bank of Canada (BDC) / Banque de développement du Canada (BDC)

#400, 5, Place Ville-Marie, Montréal, QC H3B 5E7
514-283-5904, Fax: 514-283-2872, 877-232-2269
www.bdc.ca

Other Communication: Toll-Free Fax 1-877-329-9232; Corporate Financing (Québec & Atlantic Regions), Fax: 514-283-8410

The Business Development Bank of Canada is a financial institution which is wholly owned by the Government of Canada. It was created by an Act of Parliament in 1944. The Bank is governed by an independent Board of Directors, & reports to the Minister of Industry. The mission of the Business Development Bank of Canada is to assist in the establishment & development of Canadian businesses in all industries. The Bank focuses its efforts on small & medium-sized enterprises. The following services are carried out by the Business Development Bank of Canada: consulting services; flexible financing, such as long term business financing & subordinate financing; & venture capital. Branches of the Business Development Bank of Canada are located throughout Canada. Smaller communities are served

by satellite branches, consultants, & travelling account managers.
Chair, John A. MacNaughton
President & Chief Executive Officer, Jean-René Halde
Executive Vice-President & Chief Financial Officer, Paul Buron
Executive Vice-President, Financing & Consulting, Edmée Métivier
Executive Vice President, Investments, Jacques Simoneau
Senior Vice President, Operations, Québec, Patrice Bernard
Senior Vice President, Human Resources, Mary Karamanos
Senior Vice President, Operations, Ontario, Peter Lawler
Senior Vice President, Legal Affairs; Corporate Secretary, Louise Paradis
Senior Vice President, Operations, Atlantic, Terry Quinn
Senior Vice President, Credit Risk Management, André St-Pierre
National Vice President, Subordinate Financing, Roger Giraldeau
National Vice President, Subordinate Financing, Eastern Quebec, Montréal, North-Shore, & South-Shore, Danielle Landry
Vice President, Corporate Relations, Michel Bergeron
Vice President, Venture Capital, Charles Cazabon
Vice President, Securitization, Paula Cruickshank
Vice President, Information & Communication Technologies, Glen R. Egan
Vice President, Energy, Environment, Electronic, & Materials, Robert Inglese
Vice President, Consulting, Bruce McConnell
Vice President, Strategy, & Enterprise Risk Management, Jérôme Nycz
Vice President, Fund Investments, Frank Pho

Alberta Branches:

Calgary Area Branch
Barclay Centre, #110, 444 - 7 Ave. SW, Calgary, AB T2P 0X8
403-292-5600, Fax: 403-292-6616

Calgary North Branch
#100, 1935 - 32 Ave. NE, Calgary, AB T2E 7C8
403-292-5333, Fax: 403-292-6651

Calgary South Branch
#200, 6700 MacLeod Trail SE, Calgary, AB T2H 0L3
403-292-8882, Fax: 403-292-4345,

Edmonton Branch
#200, 10665 Jasper Ave., Edmonton, AB T5J 3S9
780-495-2277, Fax: 780-495-6616

Edmonton South Branch
#201, 4628 Calgary Trail NW, Edmonton, AB T6H 6A1
780-495-7200, Fax: 780-495-7198

Grande Prairie Branch
#203, 10625 West Side Dr., Grande Prairie, AB T8V 8E6
780-532-8875, Fax: 780-539-5130

Lethbridge Branch
520 - 5th Ave. South, Lethbridge, AB T1J 0T8
403-382-3000, Fax: 403-382-3162

Medicine Hat Branch
#101, 2248 - 13th Ave. SE, Medicine Hat, AB T1A 8G6
403-527-2601, Fax: 403-528-6899

Red Deer Branch
#107, 4815 - 50th Ave., Red Deer, AB T4N 4A5
403-340-4203, Fax: 403-340-4243

British Columbia Branches:

Cranbrook Branch
205B Cranbrook St. North, Cranbrook, BC V1C 3R1
250-417-2200, Fax: 250-417-2213

Fort St. John Branch
#7, 10230 - 100 St., Fort St. John, BC V1J 3Y9
250-787-0622, Fax: 250-787-9423

Kamloops Branch
205 Victoria St., Kamloops, BC V2C 2A1
250-851-4900, Fax: 250-851-4925

Kelowna Branch
313 Bernard Ave., Kelowna, BC V1Y 6N6
250-470-4802, Fax: 250-470-4832

Langley Branch
#101B, 6424 - 200th St., Langley, BC V2Y 2T3
250-532-5150, Fax: 250-532-5166

Nanaimo Branch
#500, 6581 Aulds Rd., Nanaimo, BC V9T 6J6
250-390-5757, Fax: 250-390-5753

North Vancouver Branch
#6, 221 West Esplanade, North Vancouver, BC V7M 3J3
604-666-7703, Fax: 604-666-1957
Branch Manager, Chris Boissevain
604-666-6007

Prince George Branch
#150, 177 Victoria St., Prince George, BC V2L 5R8
250-561-5323, Fax: 250-561-5512

Surrey Branch
#160, 10362 King George Blvd., Surrey, BC V3T 2W5
604-586-2400, Fax: 604-586-2430

Terrace Branch
3233 Emerson St., Terrace, BC V8G 5L2
250-615-5300, Fax: 250-615-5320

Vancouver Branch
One Bentall Centre, #2100, 505 Burrard St., PO Box 6, Vancouver, BC V7X 1M6
604-666-7850, Fax: 604-666-1068,
Other Communication: Subordinate Financing (British Columbia & Yukon), Phone: 604-666-7875

Victoria Branch
990 Fort St., Victoria, BC V8V 3K2
250-363-0161, Fax: 250-363-8029

Manitoba Branches:

Brandon Branch
#10, 940 Princess Ave., Brandon, MB R7A 0P6
204-726-7570, Fax: 204-726-7555

Winnipeg Branch
#1100, 155 Carlton St., Winnipeg, MB R3C 3H8
204-983-7900, Fax: 204-983-0870,

Winnipeg West Branch
#200, 1655 Kenaston Blvd., Winnipeg, MB R3P 2M4
204-983-6530, Fax: 204-983-6531

New Brunswick Branches:

Bathurst Branch
#205, 275 Main St., Bathurst, NB E2A 1A9
506-548-7360, Fax: 506-548-7381

Edmundston Branch
#407, 121, rue de l'Église, Edmundston, NB E3V 1J9
506-739-8311, Fax: 506-735-0019

Fredericton Branch
#504, 570 Queen St., PO Box 754, Fredericton, NB E3B 5B4
506-452-3030, Fax: 506-452-2416

Moncton Branch
766 Main St., Moncton, NB E1C 1E7
506-851-6120, Fax: 506-851-6033

Saint John Branch
53 King St., Saint John, NB E2L 1G5
506-636-4751, Fax: 506-636-3892

Newfoundland & Labrador Branches:

Corner Brook Branch
4 Herald Ave., 1st Fl., Corner Brook, NL A2H 4B4
709-637-4515, Fax: 709-637-4522

Grand Falls-Windsor Branch
42 High St., PO Box 744, Grand Falls-Windsor, NL A2A 2M4
709-489-2181, Fax: 709-489-6569

St. John's Branch
215 Water St., PO Box 520, St. John's, NL A1C 5K4
709-722-5505, Fax: 709-772-2516

Northwest Territories Branches:

Yellowknife Branch
4912 - 49th St., Yellowknife, NT X1A 1P3
867-873-3565, Fax: 867-873-3501

Nova Scotia Branches:

Halifax Branch
#1400, 2000 Barrington St., Halifax, NS B3J 2Z7
902-426-7850, Fax: 902-426-6783
Vice-President & Area Manager, Craig Levangie
902-426-7865, craig.levangie@bdc.ca

Sydney Branch
#117, 275 Charlotte St., Sydney, NS B1P 1C6
902-564-7700, Fax: 902-564-3975

Truro Branch
622 Prince St., PO Box 1378, Truro, NS B2N 5N2
902-895-6377, Fax: 902-893-7957
Senior Manager, Business Development, Matthew Fraser
902-895-6378, matthew.fraser@bdc.ca

Yarmouth Branch
103 Water St., PO Box 98, Yarmouth, NS B5A 4B1
902-742-7119, Fax: 902-742-8180

Ontario Branches:

Barrie Branch
#301, 151 Ferris Lane, PO Box 876, Barrie, ON L4M 4Y6
705-725-2533, Fax: 705-739-0467

Brampton Branch
#100, 24 Queen St. East, Brampton, ON L6V 1A3
905-450-9845, Fax: 905-450-7514

Burlington / Halton Branch
#401, 4145 North Service Rd., Burlington, ON L7L 6A3
905-315-9230, Fax: 905-315-9243

Durham (Whitby) Branch
400 Dundas St. West, Whitby, ON L1N 2M7
905-666-6694, Fax: 905-666-1059

Hamilton Branch
#1900, 25 Main St. West, Hamilton, ON L8P 1H1
905-572-2954, Fax: 905-572-4282,

Kenora Branch
227 - 2nd St. South, Kenora, ON P9N 1G1
807-467-3535, Fax: 807-467-3533

Kingston Branch
#201, 1000 Gardiners Rd., Kingston, ON K7L 3C4
613-389-0999, Fax: 613-389-2543

Kitchener-Waterloo Branch
#110, 50 Queen St. North, Kitchener, ON N2H 6P4
519-571-6676, Fax: 519-571-6685

London Branch
380 Wellington St., London, ON N6A 5B5
519-645-4229, Fax: 519-645-5450,
Other Communication: Subordinate Financing (Southwestern Ontario), Phone: 519-675-3114, Fax: 519-645-5989

Markham Branch
3130 Hwy. 7 East, Markham, ON L3R 5A1
905-305-6867, Fax: 905-305-1969

Mississauga Branch
#100, 4310 Sherwoodtowne Blvd., Mississauga, ON L4Z 4C4
905-566-6417, Fax: 905-566-6425,
Other Communication: Corporate Financing (Ontario), Fax: 905-566-5425

North Bay Branch
222 McIntyre St. West, North Bay, ON P1B 2Y8
705-495-5700, Fax: 705-495-5707

Ottawa Branch
55 Metcalfe St., Ground Fl., Ottawa, ON K1P 6L5
613-995-0234, Fax: 613-995-9045,
Other Communication: Subordinate Financing (Ottawa & Atlantic Regions), Phone: 613-995-4084, Fax: 613-943-9866

Peterborough Branch
340 George St. North, 4th Fl., PO Box 1419, Peterborough, ON K9J 7H6
705-750-4800, Fax: 705-750-4808

Sault Ste Marie Branch
153 Great Northern Rd., Sault Ste Marie, ON P6B 4Y9
705-941-3030, Fax: 705-941-3040

St Catharines Branch
#100, 39 Queen St., PO Box 1193, St Catharines, ON L2R 7A7
905-988-2874, Fax: 905-988-2890

Stratford Branch
516 Huron St., Stratford, ON N5A 5T7
519-271-5650, Fax: 519-271-8472

Sudbury Branch
#10, 233 Brady St., Sudbury, ON P3B 4H5
705-670-6482, Fax: 705-670-6387

Thunder Bay Branch
#102, 1136 Alloy Dr., Thunder Bay, ON P7B 6M9
807-346-1780, Fax: 807-346-1790

Timmins Branch
#214, 119 Pine St. South, Timmins, ON P4N 2K3
705-267-6416, Fax: 705-268-5437

Toronto (Finch Ave. West) Branch
#502, 1120 Finch Ave. West, Toronto, ON M3J 3H7
416-736-3420, Fax: 416-736-3425

Toronto (King St.) Branch
#1200, 121 King St. West, Toronto, ON M5H 3T9
416-973-0341, Fax: 416-954-5009,
Other Communication: Subordinate Financing (Greater Toronto Area), Phone: 416-952-9673, Fax: 416-954-2630
The King Street West branch offers corporate financing for the Greater Toronto Area.

Toronto (Milner Ave.) Branch
#112, 305 Milner Ave., Toronto, ON M1B 3V4
416-954-0709, Fax: 416-954-0716

Vaughan Branch
#600, 3901 Hwy. 7 West, Vaughan, ON L4L 8L5
905-264-2100, Fax: 905-264-2122

Windsor Branch
#200, 2485 Ouellette Ave., Windsor, ON N8X 1L5
519-257-6808, Fax: 519-257-6811

Prince Edward Island Branches

Charlottetown Branch
#230, 119 Kent St., PO Box 488, Charlottetown, PE C1A 7L1
902-566-7454, Fax: 902-566-7459,

Québec Branches:

Brossard Branch
#200, 4255, boul Lapinière, Brossard, QC J4Z 0C7
450-926-7220, Fax: 450 926 7221

Chaudière - Appalaches (Saint-Romuald) Regional Branch
#100, 1175, boul de la Rive sud, Saint-Romuald, QC G6W 5M6
418-834-5144, Fax: 418-834-1855

Des Moulins - Lanaudière (Terrebonne) Regional Branch
2785, boul des Plateaux, Terrebonne, QC J6X 4J9
450-964-8778, Fax: 450-964-8773

Drummondville Branch
1010, boul René-Lévesque, Drummondville, QC J2C 5W4
819-478-4951, Fax: 819-478-5864

Gatineau Branch
#104, 259, boul St-Joseph, Gatineau, QC J8Y 6T1
819-997-4434, Fax: 819-997-4435

Granby Branch
#302, 155, rue St-Jacques, Granby, QC J2G 9A7
450-372-5202, Fax: 450-372-2423

Laval Branch
#100, 2525, Daniel-Johnson, Laval, QC H7T 1S9
450-973-6868, Fax: 450-973-6860

Longueuil Branch
#100, 550, ch de Chambly, Longueuil, QC J4H 3L8
450-928-4120, Fax: 450-928-4127

Montréal Branch
#12525, 5, Place Ville-Marie, Montréal, QC H3B 2G2
514-496-7966, Fax: 514-496-7974,
Other Communication: Subordinate Financing (Montréal), Phone: 514-496-0626, Fax: 514-496-1020; Subordinate Financing (North-Shore & South-Shore), Phone: 514-283-8265, Fax: 514-496-1020

Pointe-Claire Branch
#110, 755, boul St-Jean, Pointe-Claire, QC H9R 5M9
514-697-8014, Fax: 514-697-3160

Québec (Grande Allée ouest) Branch
1134, Grande-Allée ouest, Québec, QC G1S 1E5
418-648-3972, Fax: 418-648-5525,
Other Communication: Subordinate Financing (Eastern Quebec), Phone: 418-648-5517, Fax: 418-649-6301

Québec (Lebourgneuf) Branch
#310, 1165, boul Lebourgneuf, Québec, QC G2K 2C9
418-648-4740, Fax: 418-648-4745

Rimouski Branch
391, boul Jessop, Rimouski, QC G5L 1M9
418-722-3304, Fax: 418-722-3362

Rouyn-Noranda Branch
#301, 139, boul Québec, Rouyn-Noranda, QC J9X 6M8
819-764-6701, Fax: 819-764-5472

Saint-Jérôme Branch
#102, 55, rue Castonguay, Saint-Jérôme, QC J7Y 2H9
450-432-7111, Fax: 450-432-8366

Saint-Laurent Branch
#160, 3100, boul de la Côte-Vertu, Saint-Laurent, QC H4R 2J8
514-496-7500, Fax: 514-496-7510

Saint-Léonard Branch
6347, rue Jean-Talon est, Saint-Léonard, QC H1S 3E7
514-251-2818, Fax: 514-251-2758

Sherbrooke Branch
2532, rue King ouest, Sherbrooke, QC J1J 2E8
819-564-5700, Fax: 819-564-4276

Thérèse-de-Blainville (Boisbriand) Regional Branch
3000, rue Cours le Corbusier, Boisbriand, QC J7G 3E8
450-420-4900, Fax: 450-420-4904

Trois-Rivières Branch
#150, 1500, rue Royale, Trois-Rivières, QC G9A 6E6
819-371-5215, Fax: 819-371-5220

Saskatchewan Branches:
Chair,Dr. David A. Chalack, DVM
President & CEO, Gordon Cove
780-638-6489, gordon.cove@almaltd.ca

Regina
#320, 2220 - 12th Ave., Regina, SK S4P 0M8
306-780-6478, Fax: 306-780-7516

Saskatoon
135 - 21st St. East, Main Fl., Saskatoon, SK S7K 0B4
306-975-4822, Fax: 306-975-5955

Yukon Branches:

Whitehorse
204 Lambert St., Whitehorse, YT Y1A 1Z4
867-633-7510, Fax: 867-667-4058

Canada Border Services Agency (CBSA) / Agence des services frontaliers du Canada (ASFC)

Headquarters, 191 Laurier Ave. West, Ottawa, ON K1A 0L8
800-461-9999
CBSA-ASFC@canada.gc.ca; communications@ps.gc.ca (Public Safety)
www.cbsa-asfc.gc.ca

Other Communication: Border Information Service, Service in French, Toll-Free Phone: 1-800-959-2036; Public Safety Canada, Phone: 613-944-4875, Toll-Free: 1-800-830-3118
Established in 2003, as a response to the need for increased border services, the Canada Border Services Agency ensures the security & prosperity of Canada. The agency is responsible for managing the access of people & goods to & from Canada. To carry out its mission, Canada Border Services Agency administers more than ninety pieces of legislation. Some of the agencies duties include the following: managing over 100 border crossings; offering services at points throughout Canada & internationally; operating detention centres across the nation; conducting marine operations at the ports of Prince Rupert, Vancouver, Montréal, & Halifax; managing postal services at major mail centres in Montréal, Toronto, & Vancouver; & forming part of more than twenty Integrated Border Enforcement Teams across Canada.

Acts Administered:
Access to Information Act
Act to Establish the Canada Border Services Agency
Aeronautics Act
Anti-Personnel Mines Convention Implementation Act (through EIPA)
Blue Water Bridge Authority Act
Bretton Woods & Related Agreements Act
Canada Agricultural Products Act
Canada Customs & Revenue Agency Act
Canada Grain Act
Canada Post Corporation Act
Canada Shipping Act
Canada-Chile Free Trade Agreement Implementation Act
Canada-Costa Rica Free Trade Agreement Implementation Act
Canada-Israel Free Trade Agreement Implementation Act
Canada-United States Free Trade Agreement Implementation Act
Canadian Dairy Commission Act
Canadian Environmental Protection Act, 1999
Canadian Food Inspection Agency Act
Canadian International Trade Tribunal Act
Canadian Wheat Board Act
Carriage by Air Act
Chemical Weapons Convention Implementation Act (through EIPA)
Civil International Space Station Agreement Implementation Act
Coastal Fisheries Protection Act
Coasting Trade Act
Consumer Packaging & Labelling Act
Controlled Drug & Substances Act
Convention on International Trade in Endangered Species of Wild Fauna & Flora
Copyright Act
Criminal Code
Cultural Property Export & Import Act
Customs Act
Customs & Excise Offshore Application Act
Customs Tariff Act
Defence Production Act
Department of Health Act
Department of Industry Act
Energy Administration Act
Energy Efficiency Act
Excise Act
Excise Act, 2001
Excise Tax Act
Explosives Act
Export Act
Export & Import of Rough Diamonds Act
Export & Import Permits Act
Federal-Provincial Fiscal Arrangements Act
Feeds Act
Fertilizers Act
Financial Administration Act
Firearms Act
Fish Inspection Act
Fisheries Act
Foods & Drugs Act
Foreign Missions & International Organizations Act
Freshwater Fish Marketing Act
Hazardous Products Act
Health of Animals Act
Immigration & Refugee Protection Act
Importation of Intoxicating Liquors Act
Integrated Circuit Topography Act
International Boundary Commission Act
Manganese-based Fuel Additives Act
Meat Inspection Act
Motor Vehicle Fuel Consumption Standards Act (not in force)
Motor Vehicle Safety Act
National Energy Board Act
Navigable Waters Protection Act
North American Free Trade Agreement Implementation Act
Nuclear Energy Act
Nuclear Safety & Control Act
Pest Control Products Act
Pilotage Act
Plant Breeders' Rights Act
Plant Protection Act
Precious Metals Marking Act
Preclearance Act
Privacy Act
Privileges & Immunities (North Atlantic Organization Act)
Proceeds of Crime (Money Laundering) & Terrorist Financing Act
Quarantine Act
Quebec Harbour, Port Warden Act
Radiation Emitting Devices Act
Radiocommunication Act
Seeds Act
Special Economic Measures Act
Special Import Measures Act
Statistics Act
Telecommunications Act
Textile Labelling Act
Trade-Marks Act
Transportation of Dangerous Goods Act, 1992
United Nations Act
United States Wreckers Act
Visiting Forces Act
Wild Animals & Plant Protection & Regulation of International & Interprovincial Trade Act

Minister, Public Safety,Hon. Vic Toews
613-992-3128, Fax: 613-995-1049,Toews.V@parl.gc.ca, Other Communications: Public Safety & Emergency Preparedness: 613-991-2924
President, Stephen Rigby
Executive Vice-President, Luc Portelance
Regional Director General, Québec Region, Martin Bolduc
514-283-8700, Fax: 514-496-5181
Regional Director General, Greater Toronto Area Region, Rick Comerford
905-803-5595
Regional Director General, Pacific Region, Blake Delgaty
604-666-0760, Other Communications: Executive Assistant, Phone: 604-666-3305
Regional Director General, Windsor - St. Clair Region, Pete Diponio
519-967-4010
Regional Director General, Niagara - Fort Erie Region, Tony Geoghegan
905-994-6011, Other Communications: Administrative Assistant, Phone: 905-994-6002
Regional Director General, Atlantic Region, Diane Giffin-Boudreau
902-426-2914, Other Communications: Administrative Assistant, Phone: 902-426-2914
Regional Director General, Northern Ontario Region, Denis R. Vinette
613-991-0566, Other Communications: Executive Assistant, Phone: 613-991-0565,
Director, Prairie Region, Edmonton District, Bill Axten
780-890-8040
Director, Prairie Region, Calgary District, Paul Dumouchel
403-292-5690, Fax: 403-292-4840

Director, Atlantic Region, Southern New Brunswick & Prince Edward Island District, Don Collins
506-636-4506, Other Communications: Administrative Assistant, Phone: 506-636-4501
Director, Atlantic Region, Northwestern New Brunswick District, John Dolimount
506-324-8663, Other Communications: Administrative Assistant, Phone: 506-324-8660
Director, Pacific Region, Metro Vancouver District, John Dyck
604-775-6790, Fax: 604-775-6792
Director, Atlantic Region, Newfoundland & Labrador Districtt, John Fagan
709-772-2719, Other Communications: Administrative Assistant, Phone: 709-772-4335
Director, Northern Ontario Region, Northwest Districtt, Gary Flanagan
705-941-3052, Fax: 705-941-3060
Director, Pacific Region, Vancouver Airport District, Sari Hellsten
604-666-1800, Fax: 604-666-1812,Other Communications: Executive Assistant, Phone: 604-666-9337
Director, Prairie Region, Southern Alberta District, Kevin Hewson
403-344-2061
Director, Québec Region, Montérégie District, Claire Jacques
450-246-2272
Director, Prairie Region, Southern Manitoba District, Darlene Klips
204-373-2352, Fax: 204-373-2007
Director, Pacific Region, Okanagan & Kootenay District, Glyn Lee
250-770-4512, Fax: 250-482-5983
Director, Atlantic Region, Nova Scotia District, Andrew LeFrank
902-426-1784
Director, Prairie Region, Winnipeg & Northwest Territories District, Barry Lutz
204-983-3770, Fax: 204-984-3106
Director, Northern Ontario Region, St. Lawrence District, Darko Nikolic
613-382-8495, Fax: 613-382-4366
Director, Pacific Region, West Coast & Yukon District, Ivan Peterson
250-363-3365, Fax: 250-363-8261
Director, Québec Region, St-Lawrence District, Danielle Petitclerc
514-350-6100, Fax: 514-283-8591,Other Communications: Executive Assistant, Phone: 514-350-6100
Director, Québec Region, Airports District, Pierre Provost
514-633-7702
Director, Pacific Region, Pacific Highway District, Kim Scoville
778-538-3602, Fax: 604-541-5968,Other Communications: Executive Assistant, Phone: 778-545-5559
Director, Prairie Region, Saskatchewan District, Mike Shoobert
306-780-7356, Fax: 306-780-8222
Director, Northern Ontario Region, Ottawa District, Debbie Zion
613-991-1214, Fax: 613-991-1407

Admissibility Branch / Admissibilité
191 Laurier Ave. West, Ottawa, ON K1A 0L8
The Admissibility Branch of the Canada Border Agency oversees the following organizations: Border & Compliance Programs Directorate; People Programs Directorate; Recourse Directorate; & the Trade Programs Directorate.
Vice-President, Admissibility Branch, Cathy Munroe
613-954-7220, Fax: 613-941-6577
Director General, Recourse Directorate, Candace Breakwell
613-960-5015, Fax: 613-960-5125
Director General, Border & Compliance Programs Directorate, Lorne Lawson
613-952-8655, Fax: 613-952-8670
Director General, People Programs Directorate, Sara Wiebe
613-954-7282, Fax: 613-941-2060
Program Advisor, Trade Programs Directorate, Manon Gilbert
613-954-7152, Fax: 613-957-9723

Comptrollership Branch
191 Laurier Ave. West, Ottawa, ON K1A 0L8
613-952-6278
Canada Border Services Agency's Comptrollership Branch consists of the following divisions & directorates: Contracting, Assets, & Telecommunications Division; Corporate Finance Directorate; Corporate Services Division; Infrastructure & Environmental Operations Directorate; & the Security & Professional Standards Directorate.
Vice-President, Comptrollership Branch, Sylvain St-Laurent
613-948-8604, Fax: 613-948-8825
Director General, Infrastructure & Environmental Operations Directorate, Claude Béland
613-941-7905, Other Communications: Alternate Phone:613-222-3035
Director General, Security & Professional Standards Directorate, Roger Lavergne
613-948-9376, Other Communications: Alternate Phone:613-290-9405
Director General, Corporate Finance Directorate, Terry Perkins
613-946-9337, Fax: 613-957-6652
Director, Corporate Services Division, Rachelle Laurin
613-941-6597
Director, Contracting, Assets, & Telecommunications Division, Barbara Roesch
613-941-6616

Enforcement Branch / Exécution de la loi
191 Laurier Ave. West, Ottawa, ON K1A 0L8
The Enforcement Branch consists of the following organizations: Enforcement Programs Directorate; Intelligence Directorate; NRAC Operations; & the Policy & Program Development Directorate.
Director General, Enforcement Programs Directorate, Peter D. Hill
613-948-9041, Fax: 613-990-2858
Director, Intelligence Directorate, National Security, Rick Herringer
613-957-6912, Fax: 613-952-6825
Director, Policy & Program Development Directorate, Horizontal Policy & Planning, Megan Imrie
613-952-2728, Fax: 613-952-2468
Director, Enforcement Branch, Management Services, Joanne Kennedy
613-952-2781
Manager, NRAC Intelligence Operations, Steve MacNaughton
613-957-8293
Manager, Policy & Program Development Directorate, Program Development, Steve Millman
613-948-5245

Human Resources Branch
100 Metcalfe St., Ottawa, ON K1A 0L8
Vice-President, Human Resources Branch, Camille Therriault-Power
613-948-3180, Fax: 613-952-1783,Other Communications: Alternate Telephone: 613-948-3186
Director General, Labour Relations & Compensation, Patti Bordeleau
613-948-9861, Fax: 613-948-9838
Director General, Training & Learning, Diane Massicotte
613-946-4280, Fax: 613-957-4298
Director General, Human Resources Programs & Business Strategies, Line Vallières
613-954-6815, Other Communications: Alternate Telephone: 613-952-0496

Innovation, Science, & Technology Branch
191 Laurier Ave. West, 8th Fl., Ottawa, ON K1A 0L8
The Canada Border Services Agency Innovation, Science, & Technology Branch oversees the following programs: strategic planning & integration; EDI reporting; eManifest; technology services; major projects & systems; the Laboratory & Scientific Services Directorate; & the Western Hemisphere Travel Initiative Directorate.
Vice-President, Innovation, Science, & Technology Branch, Deirdre Kerr-Perrott
613-946-4884, Fax: 613-941-6557,Other Communications: Executive Assistant, Phone: 613-941-3357
Director General, Technology Services, Anne Craig
613-952-1920, Fax: 613-952-0033
Director General, Strategic Planning & Integration, Mike Feniak
613-948-1838, Fax: 613-948-4568,Other Communications: Executive Assistant, Phone: 613-946-4002
Director General, Laboratory & Scientific Services Directorate, Diane Keller
613-954-2200,
Director General, Major Projects & Systems (People), Rachelle F. May
613-954-1909, Fax: 613-954-1931
Director General, Western Hemisphere Travel Initiative Directorate & eManifest, Bruna Rados
613-954-2157, Fax: 613-954-3439
Director, Major Projects & Systems (Commercial), Diane Billey
613-954-8599, Fax: 613-954-8241

Operations Branch
191 Laurier Ave. West, Ottawa, ON K1A 0L8
Fax: 613-941-9866
The Operations Branch of the Canada Border Services Agency is responsible for the Operational Performance & Readiness Directorate, & the Operational Programs Directorate.
Vice-President, Operations Branch, Pierre Sabourin
613-948-4445, Fax: 613-948-7130
Director General, Operational Programs Directorate, Maureen Tracy
613-954-6431, Fax: 613-990-2858
Director, Operational Programs Directorate, Goods Processing, Elizabeth Childers
613-952-3659, Fax: 613-954-7558
Director, Operational Performance & Readiness Directorate, Arming Task Force, Calvin Christiansen
613-941-6614
Director, Operational Programs Directorate, People Processing, Susan Kramer
613-941-5550
Director, Operational Performance & Readiness Directorate, Operational Preparedness, Stuart MacPherson
613-948-4447, Fax: 613-948-1273

Strategy & Coordination Branch
191 Laurier Ave. West, Ottawa, ON K1A 0L8
The Strategy & Coordination Branch of the Canada Border Services Agency oversees the following divisions & directorates: Communications & Consultation; Corporate Secretariat; Ethics & Conflict Resolution Division; Internal Audit Directorate; International Affairs Directorate; & the Strategic Policy & Governance Directorate.
Director General, Communications & Consultation, Benoît Chiquette
613-954-7075
Director General, Strategic Policy & Governance Directorate, Paul Haddow
613-941-4347, Fax: 613-952-2870
Director General, International Affairs Directorate, Chris Henderson
613-957-6623
Director General, Corporate Secretariat, Caroline Xavier
613-954-6900
Chief Audit Executive, Internal Audit Directorate, Richard Hill
613-941-7216, Fax: 613-957-6411
National Coordinator, Ethics & Conflict Resolution Division, Informal Conflict Management System, Mike Deveau
506-739-0360
Manager, Ethics & Conflict Resolution Division, Values & Ethics, Brenda Wiseman
613-941-5499

Canada Business (CBSC) / Entreprises Canada (CSEC)

235 Queen St., Ottawa, ON K1A 0H5
Fax: 888-417-0442, 888-576-4444
www.canadabusiness.ca
Canada Business provides a wide range of information on government services, programs & regulations to Canadian business people. The base framework is an organized network of centres across Canada, one in each province & territory. The network of Canada Business is expanding to include regional access partners in many other communities across Canada. The centres offer various products and services aimed at helping clients obtain quick, accurate & comprehensive business information. Each centre exists as a result of cooperative arrangements between federal & provincial governments, & the private sector in some cases. Administration & management of the CBSC varies depending on location between the following federal agencies: Western Economic Diversification (WD), Industry Canada, the Canada Economic Development for Quebec Regions (CEDQR) & the Atlantic Canada Opportunities Agency (ACOA). The Federal Business Information System (BIS) is a collection of information on business-related programs, services & selected regulations which are accessible through the CBSC & on the CBSC web site (www.cbsc.org). The Federal BIS acts as a single window for individuals or businesses to access relevant information from all federal departments
Executive Director, Marcie Girouard
613-954-3576, Fax: 613-954-5463
Executive Assistant, Diane Lepage
613-941-9275, Fax: 613-954-5463,lepage.diane@ic.gc.ca

Regional Offices:

Regional Offices:
Chief Develoment Officer, Livestock Genomics, Brian Rhiness
brian.rhiness@gov.ab.ca

The Business Link Business Service Centre
#100, 10237 - 104 St. NW, Edmonton, AB T5J 1B1
780-422-7722, Fax: 780-422-0055, 800-272-9675
buslink@cbsc.ic.gc.ca
www.cbsc.org/alberta

Other Communication: Info-Fax: 780/422-0055

Small Business BC
82 - 601 West Cordova St., Vancouver, BC V6B 1G1

604-775-5525, Fax: 604-775-5520, 800-667-2272
askus@smallbusinessbc.ca
www.smallbusinessbc.ca

Canada/Manitoba Business Service Centre
#250, 240 Graham Ave., PO Box 2609, Winnipeg, MB R3C 4B3
204-984-2272, Fax: 204-983-3852, 800-665-2019
manitoba@canadabusiness.ca
www.cbsc.org/manitoba

Canada/New Brunswick Business Service Centre
570 Queen St., Fredericton, NB E3B 6Z6
506-444-6140, Fax: 506-444-6172, 888-576-4444
infonb@canadabusiness.ca
www.cbsc.org/nb

Canada/Newfoundland & Labrador Business Service Centre
90 O'Leary Ave., PO Box 8687 A, St. John's, NL A1B 3T1
709-772-6022, Fax: 709-772-6090, 800-668-1010
info@cbsc.ic.gc.ca
www.cbsc.org/nf

Canada/NWT Business Service Centre
#701, 5201 - 50 Ave., PO Box 1320, Yellowknife, NT X1A 3S9
867-873-7958, Fax: 867-873-0573, 888-576-4444
yel@cbsc.ic.gc.ca
www.cbsc.org/nwt

Canada/Nova Scotia Business Service Centre (CNSBSC)
1575 Brunswick St., Halifax, NS B3J 2G1
902-426-8604, Fax: 902-426-6530, 888-576-4444
halifax@cbsc.ic.gc.ca
www.cbsc.org/ns

Canada/Nunavut Business Service Centre
Inuksugait Plaza, PO Box 1000 1198, Iqaluit, NU X0A 0H0
867-975-7860, Fax: 867-975-7885, 877-499-5199
cnbsc@gov.nu.ca
www.cbsc.org/nunavut

Other Communication: Toll Free Fax: 1-877-499-5299

Canada/Ontario Business Service Centre (COBSC)
151 Yonge St., 3rd Fl., Toronto, ON M5C 2W7
416-775-3456, Fax: 416-954-8597, 888-576-4444
ontario@cbsc.ic.gc.ca
www.cbsc.org/ontario

Canada/Prince Edward Island Business Service Centre (CPEIBSC)
Jean Canfield Building, 191 University Ave., 1st Fl., Charlottetown, PE C1A 4L2
902-368-0771, Fax: 902-566-7377, 888-576-4444
Info.cb.pei@acoa-apeca.gc.ca
www.cbsc.org/pe

Canada/Saskatchewan Business Service Centre (CSBSC)
#2, 345 Third Ave. South, Saskatoon, SK S7K 1M6
306-956-2323, Fax: 306-956-2328, 800-667-4374
saskatchewan@canadabusiness.ca
www.cbsc.org/sask/index.cfm

Canada/Yukon Business Service Centre
#101, 307 Jarvis St., Whitehorse, YT Y1A 2H3
867-633-6257, Fax: 867-667-2001, 888-576-4444
yukon@cbsc.ic.gc.ca
www.cbsc.org/yukon

Info entrepreneurs
380, rue St-Antoine ouest, local 6000, Montréal, QC H2Y 3X7
514-496-4636, Fax: 514-496-5934, 888-576-4444
infoentrepreneurs@cbsc.ic.gc.ca
http://infoentrepreneurs.org

Other Communication: Toll Free Fax: 1-888-417-0442

Canada Council for the Arts / Conseil des Arts du Canada

350 Albert St., PO Box 1047, Ottawa, ON K1P 5V8
613-566-4414, Fax: 613-566-4390, 800-263-5588
info@canadacouncil.ca
www.canadacouncil.ca

The Canada Council for the Arts is a national arm's-length agency created by an Act of Parliament in 1957. According to the Canada Council Act, the role of the Council is to foster & promote the study & enjoyment of, & the production of works in the arts. To fulfill this mandate, the Council offers a broad range of grants & services to professional Canadian artists & arts organizations in dance, interdisciplinary work & performance art, media arts, music, interdisciplinary work, theatre, visual arts, & writing & publishing. The Council awards more than 100 prizes every year. It administers the Killam Program of scholarly awards, the Governor General's Literary Awards & the Governor General's Awards in Visual & Media Arts. The Canadian Commission for UNESCO & the Public Lending Right Commission operate under its aegis.

Chair, Joseph L. Rotman
Vice-Chair, Simon Brault
Contact, Media Relations, Grace Thrasher
613-566-4414

Canada Deposit Insurance Corporation (CDIC) / Société d'assurance-dépôts du Canada (SADC)

50 O'Connor St., 17th Floor, PO Box 2340 D, Ottawa, ON K1P 5W5
613-996-2081, Fax: 613-996-6095, 800-461-2342
info@cdic.ca; info@sadc.ca
www.cdic.ca; www.sadc.ca

Other Communication: Toll Free: 1-800-461-2342 (English); 1-800-461-7232 (French)

CDIC, a Crown corporation established in 1967, ensures eligible deposits in member institutions (banks, trust companies, loan companies & cooperative credit associations) in case a member becomes insolvent. Funding is provided by its member institutions through premiums paid on insured deposits. Reports to government through the Minister of Finance. CDIC responsibilities include: providing deposit insurance in case of member failure; contributing to the stability of the Canadian financial system.

Chair, Bryan P. Davies
President/CEO, Guy Saint-Pierre
Vice-President, Insurance & Risk Assessment, Michèle Bourque
Vice-President, Corporate Affairs/General Counsel & Corporate Secretary, M. Claudia Morrow
Vice-President, Finance & Administration/CFO, Thomas J. Vice

Canada Economic Development for Québec Regions / Développement économique Canada pour les régions du Québec

Édifice Dominion Square, #900, 1255, rue Peel, Montréal, QC H3B 2T9
514-283-6412, Fax: 514-283-3302, 866-385-6412
www.dec-ced.gc.ca

Defines federal objectives relating to development opportunities & delivers business assistance programs for small- & medium-sized businesses in Qu,bec for innovation, entrepreneurial & market development purposes. Supports a series of programs for appropriate environmental initiatives in various regions of Québec. The agency fosters alliances among the various environmental industry stakeholders including small- & medium-sized enterprises & industrial associations. Goals include a strengthening of existing & new partnerships, & an improvement of access to government programs. The agency also provides a significant amount of support for research & development in areas of environmental technology, demonstration, marketing & transfer projects. Supports initiatives that contribute to making Montréal an industrial centre of excellence in the environment. Aids small- & medium-sized firms in gaining access to federal procurement process, & encourages training & education focusing on business management. Helps business develop export markets through cooperative efforts with Industry Canada & Foreign Affairs & International Trade Canada

Minister of State, Economic Development Agency of Canada for the Regions of Québec,Hon. Denis Lebel 613-996-6236, Fax: 613-996-6252,Lebel.D@parl.gc.ca; denis.lebel@dec-ced.gc.ca, Other Communications: Economic Development Agency (QC):514-496-1282
President, Suzanne Vinet
514-283-4843, Fax: 514-283-7778
Chief of Staff, Sonia Forget
514-283-8400, Fax: 514-283-7778
Director General, Communications, Jean-Pierre Thibault
514-283-8817, Fax: 514-283-7951
Acting Executif Director-General Counsel, Legal Services, Christine Calvé
514-283-2997, Fax: 514-283-1549
Director General, Corporate Services, Pierre Bordeleau
514-283-4565, Fax: 514-283-1549
Vice-President, Operations, Manon Brassard
514-283-3510, Fax: 514-283-4547
Vice-President, Policy & Planning, Rita Tremblay
514-283-1294, Fax: 514-283-5940

Operations
Vice-President, Manon Brassard
514-283-3510, Fax: 514-283-4547
Director General, Business Development & Infrastructure, Gilles Pelletier
514-283-2704, Fax: 514-283-4131
Director General, Regional Coordination, Jean-Pierre Thibault
514-283-3628, Fax: 514-283-7491

Regional Offices:

Abitibi-Témiscamingue
906, 5e av, Val-d'Or, QC J9P 1B9
819-825-5260, Fax: 819-825-3245, 800-567-6451
Director, Léo Couture

Bas St-Laurent
Édifice Trust général du Canada, #310, 2, rue Saint-Germain Est, Rimouski, QC G5L 8T7
418-722-3282, Fax: 418-722-3285, 800-463-9073
Director, Pierre Roberge

Centre-du-Québec
Place du Centre, #502, 150, rue Marchand, Drummondville, QC J2C 4N1
819-478-4664, Fax: 819-478-4666, 800-567-1418
Acting Director, Mariette Larochelle

Côte-Nord
#202B, 701, boul Laure, PO Box 698, Sept-Iles, QC G4R 4K9
418-968-3426, Fax: 418-968-0806, 800-463-1707
Acting Director, Pierre Lacoursière

Estrie
Place Andrew Paton, #240, 65, rue Belvédère nord, Sherbrooke, QC J1H 4A7
819-564-5904, Fax: 819-564-5912, 800-567-6084
Director, Marie-Andrée Katia Bertrand

Gaspésie—Iles-de-la-Madeleine
Place Jacques-Cartier, 120, rue de la Reine, 3e étage, Gaspé, QC G4X 2S1
418-368-5870, Fax: 418-368-6256, 866-368-0044
Director, France Simard

Ile-de-Montréal
3340, boul de l'Assomption, Montréal, QC H1N 3S4
514-283-2500, Fax: 514-496-8310, 800-322-4636
Director, Jacques Langelier

Laval - Laurentides - Lanaudière
#410, 2990, av Pierre-Péladeau, Laval, QC H7T 3B3
450-973-6844, Fax: 450-973-6851, 800-430-6844
Director, Carole Hart

Mauricie
Immeuble Bourg du Fleuve, #413, 25, rue des Forges, Trois-Rivières, QC G9A 2G4
819-371-5182, Fax: 819-371-5186, 800-567-8637
Director, Chantal Mimeault

Montérégie
Place Agropur, #400, 101, boul Roland-Therrien, Longueuil, QC J4H 4B9
450-928-4088, Fax: 450-928-4097, 800-284-0335
Director, Stéphane Dufour

Nord-du-Québec
Édifice Dominion Square, #900, 1255 rue Peel, Montréal, QC H3B 2T9
514-283-8131, Fax: 514-283-3637, 800-561-0633
Director, Daniel Ricard

Outaouais
#202, 259 boul Saint-Joseph, Gatineau, QC J8Y 6T1
819-994-7442, Fax: 819-994-7846, 800-561-4353
Director, Marc Boily

Québec - Chaudière - Appalaches
Place Iberville IV, #030, 2954, boul Laurier, Québec, QC G1V 4T2
418-648-4826, Fax: 418-648-7291, 800-463-5204
Director, Christian Audet

Policy & Planning / Politiques et planification
Vice-President, France Pégeot
514-283-1294, Fax: 514-283-5940
Acting Director General, Governmental Affairs, Alain Desruisseaux
819-997-7716, Fax: 819-997-8519
Director General, Policy & Programs, Johanne Béchard
514-283-2664, Fax: 514-283-8429
Director General, Departmental Performance, André Cliche
514-283-7982, Fax: 514-283-0041

Saguenay - Lac-Saint-Jean
#203, 170, rue Saint-Joseph sud, Alma, QC G8B 3E8
418-668-3084, Fax: 418-668-7584, 800-463-9808
Director, Donald Hudon
Director, François Yassa
514-283-8224, Fax: 514-283-4131
President/CEO, CSTM Corporation, Denise Amyot
613-993-0775
Director General, Canada Science & Technology Museum, Claude Faubert
613-991-0372
Curator, Agriculture, Franz Klingender
613-996-7822

Curator, Transportation, Garth Wilson
613-991-3087

Canada Industrial Relations Board (CIRB) / Conseil canadien des relations industrielles (CCRI)

240 Sparks St., 4th Floor West, Ottawa, ON K1A 0X8
613-947-5440, Fax: 613-995-9493, 800-575-9696
info@cirb-ccri.gc.ca
www.cirb-ccri.gc.ca

The Board is an independent, administrative, quasi-judicial tribunal which administers Part I & certain provisions of Part II of the Canada Labour Code. Its responsibilities include the granting or revoking of collective bargaining rights, the mediation & adjudication of unfair labour practice complaints, the determination of unlawful strikes & lockouts & other matters.

Chair, Elizabeth MacPherson
Vice-Chairperson, Graham J. Clarke
Vice-Chairperson, Louise Fecteau
Vice-Chairperson, Judith F. MacPherson
Vice-Chairperson, Claude Roy
Vice-Chairperson, Richard I. Hornung
Publications Officer, Marie-France Grenier
613-947-5391, mfgrenier@cirb-ccri.gc.ca

Canada Lands Company Ltd. (CLCL) / Société immobilière du Canada limitée (SICL)

#1200, 1 University Ave., Toronto, ON M5J 2P1
416-952-6111, Fax: 416-952-6115, 888-252-5263
www.clcl.ca

CLCL is a Crown corporation with a mandate to enhance the quality of life of the communities in which it conducts business, to generate best value for the taxpayer through the orderly disposal of strategic real estate properties no longer required by the federal government, as well as the management of certain other select properties. The agency reports to government through the Minister of Transport, Infrastructure & Communities.

President/CEO, Mark B. Laroche
Vice President, Strategic Acquisitions, Public & Government Affairs, Gordon McIvor
416-952-6111, gmcivor@clc.ca

Old Port of Montréal Corporation Inc. / Société du Vieux port de Montréal
333, rue de la Commune ouest, Montréal, QC H2Y 2E2
514-283-5256, Fax: 514-283-8423

Parc Downsview Park Inc.
#1, 35 Carl Hall Rd., Toronto, ON M3K 2B6
613-952-2222, Fax: 613-952-2225,
info@pdp.ca
www.pdp.ca

Canada Mortgage & Housing Corporation (CMHC) / Société canadienne d'hypothèques et de logement (SCHL)

700 Montreal Rd., Ottawa, ON K1A 0P7
613-748-2000, Fax: 613-748-2098, 800-668-2642
chic@cmhc-schl.gc.ca
www.cmhc.ca; www.schl.ca

Other Communication: Canadian Housing Information Centre: 613/748-2367

CMHC works closely with a network of professional associations, groups & institutions concerned with regional planning & the residential sector. It prepares various research projects for the examination of relationships between urban areas, housing & sustainable development issues. Involved in numerous technical research projects addressing interrelationships between housing, energy & resource use. Through its research & information transfer function, CMHC will undertake initiatives such as identifying approaches & solutions that lead to more sustainable & healthy communities, examining barriers to potential development of brownfield sites.CMHC will focus on ways to reduce residential energy consumption in multiple-unit housing, educate consumers on energy-saving changes to homes. The Net Zero Healthy Healthy Housing Initiative combines passive solar, energy-efficient design, construction & appliances, integrated with renewable energy systems, to achieve net zero energy consumption on an annual basis, significantly reducing environmental impacts & GHG emissions. Twenty demonstration projects across Canada are underway

Acts Administered:
CMHC Act
National Housing Act (NHA)

Chair, Dino Chiesa
President/CEO, Karen Kinsley
613-748-2186, Fax: 613-748-2067
Vice-President, Corporate Services & CFO, Marc Joyal
613-748-2958
Vice-President, Insurance Underwriting, Servicing & Policy, Mark McInnis
613-748-5124, Fax: 613-742-5337
Vice-President, Policy & Planning, Douglas A. Stewart
613-748-2553, Fax: 613-748-4793
Vice-President, Assisted Housing, Sharon Matthews
613-748-2251, Fax: 613-748-2189
Vice-President, Human Resources, Gail Tolley
613-748-2082, Fax: 613-742-5353
Vice-President, Insurance Product & Business Development, Pierre Serré
613-748-2818, Fax: 613-748-2189
Executive Director, CMHC International, André Asselin
613-748-2347, Fax: 613-748-2302
Executive Director, Communications, Anne Dawson
613-748-2520, Fax: 613-748-4072
Executive Director, Risk Management & Investments, Gilles Proulx
613-748-2012, Fax: 613-748-2067
Executive Director, Corporate Marketing, Charles Chenard
613-748-2505, Fax: 613-748-4097
Director, Audit & Evaluation Services, Serge Gaudet
613-748-4099

Atlantic Region
Barrington Tower, 9th Fl., 1894 Barrington St., Halifax, NS B3J 2A8
902-426-3530, Fax: 902-426-9991
General Manager, Carolyn Kavanaugh
902-426-1813, Fax: 902-426-9991
Principal, Marketing, Info and Communications, Emily Poitras-Benedict
902-426-8127

British Columbia
#200, 1111 West Georgia St., Vancouver, BC V6E 4S4
604-731-5733, Fax: 604-737-4139
Manager, Business Development and Marketing, Marcia Freeman
604-666-2529, Fax: 604-666-7376
Senior Consultant, Communications and Marketing, Tracy Wells
416-250-3247, Fax: 604-737-4073

Ontario
#300, 100 Sheppard Ave. East, Toronto, ON M2N 6Z1
416-221-2642, Fax: 416-218-3310
General Manager, Peter Friedmann
416-218-3300, Fax: 416-218-3310
Senior Consultant, Communications and Marketing, Sally Ritchie
416-250-2760

Prairie & Territories Region
#200, 1000 - 7 Ave. SW, Calgary, AB T2P 5L5
403-515-3000, Fax: 403-515-2930
General Manager, Trevor Gloyn
403-515-3001, Fax: 403-515-2928,
Senior Consultant, Communications & Marketing, Kimberlee Jones
403-515-3048, Fax: 403-575-2935

Québec
1100, boul René-Levesque ouest, 1er étage, Montréal, QC H3B 5J7
514-283-2222, 888-772-0772
General Manager, Sylvie Crispo
514-283-3023, Fax: 514-496-1302
Principal, Marketing, Info and Communications, Juliette Cohen
514-283-3679, Fax: 514-283-5739

Canada Pension Plan Investment Board / Office d'investissement du Régime de pensions du Canada

#2600, 1 Queen St. East, PO Box 101, Toronto, ON M5C 2W5
416-868-4075, Fax: 416-868-8689, 866-557-9510
csr@cppib.ca
www.cppib.ca

The CPP Investment Board is a Crown corporation created as part of 1997 reforms designed to ensure the soundness & sustainability of the CPP. The Board operates under similar investment rules as other pension plans in Canada, which require the prudent management of pension plan assets in the interests of plan contributors & beneficiaries.

President/CEO, David Denison
Senior Vice-President/General Counsel & Corporate Secretary, John H. Butler
Senior Vice-President/CFO, Nicholas Zelenczuk
Senior Vice-President, Communications & Stakeholder Relations, Ian Dale
Senior Vice-President, Real Estate Investments, Graeme Eadie
Senior Vice-President, Portfolio Design & Investment Research, John H. Ilkiw
Senior Vice-President, Human Resources, Saylor Millitz-Lee
Senior Vice-President, Public Market Investments, Donald M. Raymond
Senior Vice-President/COO, Benita M. Warmbold
Senior Vice-President, Private Investments, Mark Wiseman
Chair, Board of Directors, Robert Astley

Canada Place Corporation / Corporation Place du Canada

504 - 999 Canada Place, Vancouver, BC V6C 3E1
604-775-7200, Fax: 604-775-6251,
administration@canadaplace.ca
www.canadaplace.ca

The Corporation is the landlord & in charge of property management at Canada Place in Vancouver, which includes a cruise ship facility, a trade & convention centre, a hotel, an IMAX theatre, & a parking structure

Chair, Robin Wilson
President/CEO, Michael J. Shardlow

Canada Post Corporation / Société canadienne des postes

Corporate Secretariat, 2701 Riverside Dr., Ottawa, ON K1A 0B1
613-734-8440, Fax: 613-734-6084, 800-267-1177
service@mailposte.ca
www.canadapost.ca; www.postescanada.ca

Federal commercial Crown corporation responsible for Canada's postal system. Reports to government through the Minister of Transport, Infrastructure & Communities. For postal rates, codes, abbreviations & other general information; see Postal Information in the main Index.

President/CEO, Moya Greene
CFO, Wayne Cheeseman
Chief Operating Officer, Jacques Côté
Chief Sales & Marketing Officer, Stewart Bacon
Senior Vice-President, Enterprise Sales, Peter V. Melanson
Senior Vice-President, Direct Marketing, Advertising & Publishing Business, Laurene Cihosky
Senior Vice-President, Postal Transformation, Cal Hart
Senior Vice-President & Chief Information Officer, John D. Smith
Senior Vice-President, Operations, Mary Traversy
Senior Vice-President, Corporate Social Responsbility, Robert Waite
Senior Vice-President, Parcels, Louis O'Brien
Senior Vice-President, Transaction Mail, Cheryl A. Persad
Senior Vice-President, Strategy, Philip Ventura
Vice-President/General Counsel & Corporate Secretary, Bonnie Boretsky
Vice-President, Finance, Clary Ottman
Vice-President, Customer Service, Stephen Edmondson
Vice-President, Field Operations, Douglas Jones
Vice-President, General Business Sales, Serge Pitre
Vice-President, Marketing, Kathy Haley

ePost / Postel
393 University Ave., 13th Fl., Toronto, ON M5G 2P7
877-376-1212
service@to.epost.ca
Other Communication: Fax: 1-877-269-9711
President/CEO, Roger Couldrey

Office of the Ombudsman / Bureau de l'ombudsman
PO Box 90026, Ottawa, ON K1V 1J8
Fax: 800-204-4193, 800-204-4198
www.ombudsman.postescanadapost.ca
Ombudsman, Nicole Goodfellow

Canada Post Communications Offices:

Atlantic Division
6175 Almon St., Halifax, NS B3K 5N2
902-494-4076, Fax: 902-494-4767,

Huron Division
955 Highbury Ave., London, ON N5Y 1A3
519-457-5282, Fax: 519-457-5412

Pacific Division
1010 Howe St., PO Box 2110, Vancouver, BC V6B 4Z3
604-662-1592, Fax: 604-662-1710

Prairie Division
#1300, 10020 - 101A Ave., Edmonton, AB T5J 4J4
780-944-3137, Fax: 780-944-3140

Québec Division
#537, 300, rue St-Paul, Québec, QC G1K 3W0
418-694-3161, Fax: 418-694-6993

York Division
4567 Dixie Rd., Mississauga, ON L4W 1S2
905-214-9595, Fax: 905-214-9244

Canada Revenue Agency (CRA) / Agence du revenu du Canada

875 Heron Rd., Ottawa, ON K1A 0L5
613-952-0384, 800-267-6999
www.cra-arc.gc.ca

Other Communication: Individual Income Tax Enquiries: 1-800-959-8281; Telerefund: 1-800-959-1956; Business & Self-Employed Individuals: 1-800-959-5525; GST/HST Credit: 1-800-959-1953

The Canada Revenue Agency administers tax laws for the Canadian federal government & for most provincial & territorial governments. The Agency is also responisible for various social & economic benefit & incentive programs, which are delivered through the tax system.

Acts Administered:
Canada Pension Plan Act, Part I
Customs Act
Customs & Excise Offshore Application Act
Customs Tariff Act
Department of National Revenue Act
Excise Act
Excise Tax Act
Special Import Measures Act
Unemployment Insurance Act, Part III & VII

Minister, National Revenue; Minister, Atlantic Canada Opportunities Agency; Minister, Atlantic Gateway,Hon. Keith Ashfield
613-992-1067, Fax: 613-996-9955,Ashfield.K@parl.gc.ca, Other Communications: National Revenue, Phone: 613-995-2960
Commissioner & CEO, Linda Lizotte-MacPherson
613-957-3688
Assistant Commissioner, Human Resources, Cheryl Fraser
613-954-8200, Fax: 613-952-8557
Assistant Commissioner, Information Technology & Chief Information Officer, Peter Poulin
613-954-8983, Fax: 613-957-9058
Assistant Commissioner, Public Affairs, Sandra Lavigne
613-957-3508, Fax: 613-954-7955
Director General, Corporate Audit & Evaluation, Patricia A. MacDonald
613-957-7522
Director General, Communications, Michel Hébert
613-948-4847

Compliance Programs Branch / Programmes d'observation de la législation

Asst. Commissioner, Lyse Ricard
613-957-3709
Deputy Asst. Commissioner, John Kowalski
613-957-3585
Director General, Audit Professional Services, Mara Praulins
613-948-4744
Director General, International & Large Business, Jean-Jacques Lefebvre
613-952-7472
Director General, Enforcement & Disclosures, Denis Meunier
613-957-7780
Director General, Research, Risk & Business Management, Martin Leigh
613-954-5126
Director General, Scientific Research & Experimental Development, Hélène Dompierre
613-946-3447
Director General, Compliance Strategy, Claude St-Pierre
613-957-3648
Director General, Small & Medium Enterprises, Jim Gauvreau
613-941-6756

Corporate Strategies & Business Development / Stratégies d'entreprise et croissance des marchés

Asst. Commissioner, Susan Bowen
613-952-3660
Director General, Corporate Planning, Governance & Measurement, Normand Théberge
613-954-6082
Director General, Statistics & Information Management, Patricia Whitridge
613-957-8706
Director General, Strategic Policy, Victor Abele
613-954-6068
Director General, Client Relations, Sherry Moran
613-941-9964

Finance & Administration Branch / Finances et administration

Asst. Commissioner & Chief Financial Officer, James Ralston
613-946-1763
Director General, Administration, Judy Cosby
613-688-9270
Director General, Financial Administration, Michel Bernard
613-957-7343
Director General, Real Property & Service Integration, Gérald Doucet
613-954-8330
Director General, Resource Management, Filipe Dinis
613-957-7339
Director General, Security, Risk Management & Internal Affairs, Jocelyn Malo
613-948-2449
Acting Director General, Strategic Management & Program Support, Teresa Errett
613-957-7502

Legislative Policy & Regulatory Affairs / Politiques législatives et affaires réglementaires

Asst. Commissioner, Brian McCauley
613-957-3708
Deputy Asst. Commissioner, Tax & Regulatory Affairs, Ed Gauthier
613-952-9198
Director General, Charities, Terry de March
613-954-0931
Director General, Registered Plans, Danielle Laflèche
613-954-0933
Director General, Income Tax Rulings, Wayne Adams
613-957-2132
Director General, Legislative Policy, Richard Montroy
613-957-2061
Director General, Excise & GST/HST Rulings, Pierre Bertrand
613-948-4398

Taxpayer Services & Debt Management / Services aux contribuables et gestion des créances

Asst. Commissioner, Guy Proulx
613-954-1269
Deputy Asst. Commissioner, Danielle Morin
613-941-9801
Director General, Debt Management Research & Analytics, Fred Vivash
613-957-1863
Director General, Taxpaper Services, Marj Ogden
613-957-9362
Director General, Strategic Planning & Branch Services, EnikÖ Vermes
613-954-8291

Tax Services Offices

Atlantic Region

Bathurst
201 George St., PO Box 8888, Bathurst, NB E2A 4L8
Fax: 506-548-9905

Charlottetown
161 St. Peters Rd., PO Box 8500, Charlottetown, PE C1A 8L3
Fax: 902-566-7197

Halifax
1557 Hollis St., PO Box 638, Halifax, NS B3J 2T5
Fax: 902-426-7170

Moncton
50 King St., PO Box 1070, Moncton, NB E1C 4M2
Fax: 506-851-7018

Newfoundland & Labrador
Sir Humphrey Gilbert Building, 165 Duckworth St., PO Box 12075, St. John's, NL A1B 4R5
709-754-5928

Saint John
126 Prince William St., Saint John, NB E2L 4H9
Fax: 506-636-5200

St. John's Tax Centre
290 Empire Ave., St. John's, NL A1B 3Z1
Fax: 709-754-3416

Summerside Tax Centre
275 Pope Rd., Summerside, PE C1N 6A2
Fax: 902-432-6287

Sydney
47 Dorchester St., PO Box 1300, Sydney, NS B1P 6K3
Fax: 902-564-3095

Northern Ontario Region

Barrie
81 Mulcaster St., Barrie, ON L4M 6T7
Fax: 705-721-0056

Belleville
11 Station St., Belleville, ON K8N 2S3
Fax: 613-969-7845

Kingston
31 Hyperion Ct., PO Box 2600, Kingston, ON K7L 5P3
Fax: 613-545-3272

Ottawa & Nunavut
333 Laurier Ave. West, Ottawa, ON K1A 0L9
Fax: 613-238-7125

Peterborough
185 King St. West, 5th Fl., Peterborough, ON K9J 8M3
Fax: 705-876-6422

Sudbury Tax Centre
1050 Notre Dame Ave., Sudbury, ON P3A 5C1
Fax: 705-671-3994

Thunder Bay
130 South Syndicate Ave., Thunder Bay, ON P7E 1C7
Fax: 807-622-8512,

Pacific Region

Burnaby-Fraser
9737 King George Hwy., Surrey, BC V3T 5W6
Fax: 604-587-2010

Northern BC & Yukon
280 Victoria St., Prince George, BC V2L 5N8
Fax: 250-561-7869

Southern Interior
277 Winnipeg St., Penticton, BC V2A 1N6
Fax: 250-492-8346

Surrey Tax Centre
9755 King George Hwy., Surrey, BC V3T 5E1
Fax: 604-585-5769

Vancouver
1166 West Pender St., Vancouver, BC V6E 3H8
Fax: 604-689-7536

Vancouver Island
1415 Vancouver St., Victoria, BC V8V 3W4
Fax: 250-363-8188

Prairie Region

Edmonton & NWT
#10, 9700 Jasper Ave., Edmonton, AB T5J 4C8
Fax: 780-495-3533

Lethbridge
#200, 419 - 7 St. South, Lethbridge, AB T1J 4A9
Fax: 403-382-4765

Red Deer
4996 - 49 Ave., Red Deer, AB T4N 6X2
Fax: 403-341-7053

Regina
#260, 1783 Hamilton St., Regina, SK S4P 2B6
Fax: 306-757-1412

Saskatoon
340 - 3rd Ave. North, Saskatoon, SK S7K 0A8
Fax: 306-652-3211

Calgary
220 - 4 Ave. SE, Calgary, AB T2G 0L1
Fax: 403-264-5843

Winnipeg
325 Broadway, Winnipeg, MB R3C 4T4
Fax: 204-984-5164

Winnipeg Tax Centre
66 Stapon Rd., Winnipeg, MB R3C 3M2
Fax: 204-984-5164

Southern Ontario Region

Hamilton
55 Bay St., PO Box 2220, Hamilton, ON L8N 3E1
Fax: 905-546-1615

Kitchener-Waterloo
166 Frederick St., Kitchener, ON N2G 4N1
Fax: 519-579-4532

London
451 Talbot St., London, ON N6A 5E5
Fax: 519-645-4029

St Catharines
32 Church St., PO Box 3038, St Catharines, ON L2R 3B9
Fax: 905-688-5996

Toronto Centre
1 Front St. West, Toronto, ON M5J 2X6
Fax: 416-360-8908

Toronto East
Rm 427, 200 Town Centre Court, Toronto, ON M1P 4Y3

Fax: 416-973-5126,

Toronto North
#1000, 5001 Yonge St., Toronto, ON M2N 6R9
Fax: 416-512-2558

Toronto West
5800 Hurontario St., PO Box 6000, Mississauga, ON L5R 4B4
Fax: 905-566-6182

Windsor
185 Ouellette Ave., Windsor, ON N9A 5S8
Fax: 519-257-6558

Québec Region

Chicoutimi
#123, 100, rue Lafontaine, Chicoutimi, QC G7H 6X2
Fax: 418-698-6387

Jonquière Tax Centre
2251, boul René-Lévesque, Jonquière, QC G7S 5J1
Fax: 418-548-0846

Laval
3400, av Jean-Béraud, Laval, QC H7T 2Z2
Fax: 514-956-7071

Montérégie-Rive-Sud
3250, boul Lapinière, Brossard, QC J4Z 3T8
Fax: 450-926-7100

Montréal
305, boul René-Lévesque ouest, Montréal, QC H2Z 1A6
Fax: 514-496-1309

Outaouais
1100, boul Maloney ouest, Gatineau, ON K1A 1L4
Fax: 819-994-1103

Québec
165, rue de la Pointe-aux-Lièvres sud, Québec, QC G1K 7L3
Fax: 418-649-6478

Rimouski
#101, 180, av de la Cathédrale, Rimouski, QC G5L 5H9
Fax: 418-722-3027

Rouyn-Noranda
44, av du Lac, Rouyn-Noranda, QC J9X 6Z9
Fax: 819-797-8366

Shawinigan-Sud Tax Centre
4695, 12e av, Shawinigan-Sud, QC G9P 5H9
Fax: 819-536-7078

Sherbrooke
50, Place de la Cité, CP 1300, Sherbrooke, QC J1H 5L8
Fax: 819-821-8582

Trois-Rivières
#111, 25, rue des Forges, Trois-Rivières, QC G9A 2G4
Fax: 819-371-2744

Canada School of Public Service (CCMD) / École de la fonction publique du Canada (EEPC)

373 Sussex Dr., Ottawa, ON K1N 6Z2
819-953-5400, Fax: 819-953-7953, 866-703-9598
info@csps-efpc.gc.ca
www.csps-efpc.gc.ca

Learning provider for the Public Service of Canada. The School brings together three well-established federal public service learning organizations: the Canadian Centre for Management Development, & from the Public Service Commission, Training & Development Canada & Language Training Canada. Contributes to building & maintaining a modern, high-quality, professional public service that is at the leading-edge of knowledge in modern public administration & public sector management. Through up-to-date adult learning techniques, it provides public servants across the country with access to the common learning opportunities they require to effectively serve Canada & Canadians

Acts Administered:
Canadian Centre for Management Development Act

President/CEO,Dr. Ruth Dantzer,
Ruth.Dantzer@csps-efpc.gc.ca
613-992-8165, Fax: 613-943-1038
Senior Vice-President, Individual Learning, Denise Boudrias
613-953-0957
Vice-President & Registrar, David Waung
613-995-4035, Fax: 613-943-7873
Vice-President, Organizational Leadership & Innovation, Michael Keenan
613-943-6007
Vice-President, Planning, Governance & Communities, Christine Donoghue
613-943-0321
Director General, Human Resources, Pierre Richer de La Flèche
819-934-8202
Director General, Regional Operations & Learning Events, Richard Rochefort
613-934-8254
Ombudsman, Amanda Coderre
613-943-4330

Canadian Artists & Producers Professional Relations Tribunal / Tribunal canadien des relations professionnelles artistes-producteurs

C.D. Howe Bldg., 240 Sparks St., 1st Fl., West Tower, Ottawa, ON K1A 1A1
613-996-4052, Fax: 613-947-4125, 800-263-ARTS
info@capprt-tcrpap.gc.ca
www.capprt-tcrpap.gc.ca

The Tribunal administers legislation providing a framework for professional relations between self-employed artists & the producers in the federal jurisdiction who use their services.

Acts Administered:
The Status of the Artist Act

Executive Director & General Counsel, Diane Chartrand
613-947-4263, chartrand.diane@capprt-tcrpap.gc.
Administrative & Financial Officer, Sylvie Besner
613-947-4264

Canadian Broadcasting Corporation (CBC) / Société Radio-Canada (SRC)

181 Queen St., PO Box 3220 C, Ottawa, ON K1Y 1E4
613-288-6033,
liaison@radio-canada.ca
www.cbc.radio-canada.ca

Other Communication: Toll Free: 1-866-306-4636

The Canadian Broadcasting Corporation (CBC) is a Crown corporation governed by the 1991 Broadcasting Act & subject to regulations of the Canadian Radio-television & Telecommunications Commission (CRTC). The CBC operates four national radio networks, CBC Radio One & CBC Radio Two in English, & La Radio de Radio-Canada & Espace musique in French, featuring information & general interest programs as well as classical music & cultural programs; two self-supporting specialty cable television services, CBC Newsworld in English & Le Réseau de l'information (RDI) in French which feature news & information programs 24 hours a day, seven days a week; & radio & television services for Canada's North in English, French & eight aboriginal languages. CBC also provides, on behalf of the Government of Canada, an international shortwave radio service, Radio Canada International, which broadcasts in seven languages.

President/CEO, Hubert T. Lacroix
Vice President & Chief Financial Officer, Johanne Charbonneau
President, Real Estate Division, Michel Saint-Cyr
Senior Vice-President, Corporate Priorities & Implementation, George C.B. Smith
Executive Vice-President, English Services, Richard Stursberg
Executive Vice-President, French Services, Sylvain Lafrance
Vice-President, Communications & Corporate Affairs, William B. Chambers
Vice-President/Corporate Secretary/Chief Legal Officer, Pierre Nollet
Senior Vice-President, Corporate Strategy & Business Partnerships, Michel Tremblay
Vice-President & Chief Techology Officer, Raymond Carnovale

CBC Ombudsman
Ombudsman, English Services, Vincent A. Carlin
ombudsman@cbc.ca
Ombudsman, French Services, Julie Miville-Dechêne
ombudsman@radio-canada.ca

Galaxie
CP 3220 C, Ottawa, ON K1Y 1E4
Fax: 514-288-6205, 877-425-2943
information@galaxie.ca
www.galaxie.ca

Provides 52 channels of commercial-free music of all types 24 hours a day, seven days a week.
General Manager, Eric Albert
Director, Programming, Mike Giunta

Radio Canada International
1400, boul René-Lévesque est, CP 6000, Montréal, QC H2L 2M2
514-597-7500,
info@rcinet.ca
www.rcinet.ca

CBC/Radio-Canada - English Services
250 Front St. W., PO Box 500 A, Toronto, ON M5W 1E6
866-306-4636
cbcinput@cbc.ca
www.cbc.ca/contact/

CBC/Radio-Canada - French Services
1400, boul René-Lévesque est, CP 6000, Montréal, QC H3C 3A8
514-597-6000, 866-306-4636
auditoire@radio-canada.ca

CBC Regional Offices:

Alberta (English & French)
10062 - 102nd Ave., PO Box 555, Edmonton, AB T5J 2P4
780-468-7500

British Columbia (English & French)
PO Box 4600, Vancouver, BC V6B 4A2
604-662-6000

CBC North
5002 Forrest Dr., PO Box 160, Yellowknife, NT X1A 2N2
867-920-5400

Manitoba (English & French)
541 Portage Ave., PO Box 160, Winnipeg, MB R3C 2H1
204-888-3222

Maritimes (English)
PO Box 3000, Halifax, NS B3J 3E9
902-420-8311

Atlantic Provinces (French Services) / Radio-Canada Acadie
250, av Université, Moncton, NB E1C 5K3
506-853-6666, 800-561-7010

Newfoundland (English)
PO Box 12010 A, St. John's, NL A1B 3T8
709-576-5000

Canadian Broadcasting Centre
250 Front St. W., PO Box 500 A, Toronto, ON M5W 1E6
416-205-3311, 866-306-4636
cbcinput@cbc.ca

Ottawa Production Centre
181 Queen St., PO Box 3220 C, Ottawa, ON K1Y 1E4
613-288-6000,
liaison@cbc.ca

Québec (English) / Maison de Radio-Canada
1400, boul René-Lévesque est, CP 6000, Montréal, QC H3C 3A8
514-597-6000

Québec (French) / Société Radio-Canada
880, rue Saint-Jean, CP 18800, Québec, QC G1K 9L4
418-654-1341,
cbvt@radio-canada.ca

Saskatchewan (English & French)
2440 Broad St., Regina, SK S4P 4A1
306-347-9540

Canadian Centre for Occupational Health & Safety (CCOHS) / Centre canadien d'hygiène et de sécurité au travail (CCHST)

135 Hunter St. East, Hamilton, ON L8N 1M5
905-572-2981, Fax: 905-572-2206, 800-668-4284
clientservices@ccohs.ca
www.ccohs.ca

Provides occupational health & safety & environmental information in the form of publications, responses to inquiries & a computerized information service available in various formats. Topics include: environmental acts & regulations; occupational & environmental health data; toxic effects of chemical substances; transport of dangerous goods; chemical evaluation; hazardous substances; & domestic substances listed under the Canadian Environmental Protection Act; biological hazards; ergonomics

President/CEO, S. Len Hong
905-572-2981
Vice-President,Dr. Patabendi K. Abeytunga
905-572-2981
Controller, Bonnie Easterbrook
905-572-2981
Manager, Communications, Eleanor Westwood
905-572-2981
Manager, Computer Systems & Services, David Brophy
905-572-2981
Manager, General Health & Safety Services, Norma Gibson-MacDonald
905-572-2981
Manager, Inquiries & Client Services, Renzo Bertolini
905-572-2981

Canadian Centre on Substance Abuse (CCSA) / Centre canadien de lutte contre l'alcoolisme et les toxicomanies (CCLAT)

#300, 75 Albert St., Ottawa, ON K1P 5E7
613-235-4048, Fax: 613-235-8101,
www.ccsa.ca
CCSA is a non-profit organization working to minimize the harm associated with the use of alcohol, tobacco, & other drugs.
Chair, Barry V. King, O.O.M.
613-235-4048
CEO, Michel Perron
613-235-4048
Deputy CEO & Director, Research & Policy, Rita Notarandrea
613-235-4048
Director, Operations & CFO, Carol Ann Banks
613-235-4048
Director, Public Relations & Marketing, Enid Harrison
613-235-4048

Canadian Commercial Corporation (CCC) / Corporation commerciale canadienne

50 O'Connor St., 11th Fl., Ottawa, ON K1A 0S6
613-996-0034, Fax: 613-995-2121, 800-748-8191
www.ccc.ca
A Crown Corporation mandated to facilitate international trade, particularly in government markets.CCC specializes in international procurement markets for Canadian companies & provides services to help them win, negotiate & manage export contracts. As prime contractor, CCC offers a government-to-government agreement that simplifies customer access to Canadian technology & expertise. CCC contracts have a government guarantee for performance.
Chair, Robert C. Kay
President, Marc Whittingham
613-996-0042, Fax: 613-992-2134
Vice-President, Strategy & Organizational Development, Mariette Fyfe-Fortin
613-943-4360
Vice-President, Defence Procurement, Jacques Greffe
613-996-0161
Vice-President, Business Development & Sales, Pierre Alarie
613-943-0953
Vice-President/CFO, Risk & Finance, Martin Zablocki
613-992-9638
Vice-President/Legal General Counsel & Corporate Secretary, Legal Services, Tamara Parschin-Rybkin, Q.C.
613-992-4419, Fax: 613-947-3903

Canadian Dairy Commission (CDC) / Commission canadienne du lait (CCL)

Central Experimental Farm, NCC Driveway, Bldg. 55, 960 Carling Ave., Ottawa, ON K1A 0Z2
613-792-2000, Fax: 613-792-2009,
cdc-ccl@agr.gc.ca
www.cdc.ca
The federal Crown corporation serves the interests of all dairy stakeholders, including producers, processors, further processors, exporters, consumers & governments. The following are the key objectives of the CDC: providing efficient milk & cream producers with the opportunity to obtain a fair return for their labour & investment; & ensuring an adequate supply of high quality dairy products for consumers.
CEO, John Core
613-792-2060, jcore@agr.gc.ca
Chair, Randy Williamson
Commissioner, Gilles Martin
Senior Director, Policy & Corporate Affairs, Gilles Froment
613-792-2030, gfroment@agr.gc.ca
Senior Director, Finance & Operations, Gaëtan Paquette
613-792-2070, gpaquette@agr.gc.ca
Director, Audit, Robert Hansis

Canadian Environmental Assessment Agency (CEAA) / Agence canadienne d'évaluation environnementale (ACEE)

Place Bell Canada, 160 Elgin St., 22nd Fl., Ottawa, ON K1A 0H3
613-957-0700, Fax: 613-957-0862, 866-582-1884
info@ceaa-acee.gc.ca
www.ceaa-acee.gc.ca
The Canadian Environmental Assessment Agency (CEAA) was established to administer the Canadian Environmental Assessment Act (the Act). The environmental assessment process identifies the environmental effects of proposed projects & measures to address those effects, in support of sustainable development. CEAA promotes environmental assessment as a tool to protect & sustain a healthy environment in harmony with a growing economy. The CEAA advocates high-quality environmental assessments by assisting federal departments & agencies with training & guidance & by investing in the research & development of best practices. CEAA provides administrative support to mediators & review panels & ensures that the public has opportunities to participate effectively in the environmental assessment process. Public participation strengthens the quality & credibility of environmental assessments by providing local & traditional knowledge, & insight into possible environmental effects. A publicly accessible master index of environmental assessments carried out by federal departments is available in the Canadian Environmental Assessment Registry (projects beginning before November 2003 are available in the Federal Environmental Assessment Index) located on the CEAA we b site. In addition, CEAA's participant funding program provides limited funds to ensure that interested individuals & groups have the opportunity to participate in mediations & panel reviews.
Accountable to the Minister of the Environment
President, Peter Sylvester
613-948-2671, peter.sylvester@ceaa-acee.gc.ca
Vice-President, Operations, Thao Pham
613-948-2665, thao.pham@ceaa-acee.gc.ca
Vice-President, Policy Development, Yves Leboeuf
613-948-2662, yves.leboeuf@ceaa-acee.gc.ca
Executive Director, Project Reviews, Steve Burgess
613-948-2663, steve.burgess@ceaa-acee.gc.ca
Director General, Corporate Services, Richard Gagné
613-957-0467, richard.gagne@ceaa-acee.gc.ca
Director, Operational Support, Andrée Chevrier
613-957-0641, andree.chevrier@ceaa-acee.gc.ca
Director, Communications, Charlene Gaudet
613-957-0712, charlene.gaudet@ceaa-acee.gc.ca
Director, Finance & Administration, Daniel Nadeau
613-948-2677, daniel.nadeau@ceaa-acee.gc.ca
Director, Human Resources, Brigitte Schryer
613-954-2201, brigitte.schryer@ceaa-acee.gc.ca
Director, Legislative & Regulatory Affairs, John D. Smith
613-948-1942, john.smith@ceaa-acee.gc.ca
Director, Policy Analysis, Margaret Bailey
613-957-0065, Margaret.bailey@ceaa-acee.gc.ca
General Counsel, Legal Services, Irene V. Gendron
613-957-0735, irene.gendron@ceaa-acee.gc.ca

Regional Offices:

Alberta & Northwest Territories
61 Airport Rd. NW, Edmonton, AB T5G 0W6
780-495-2037, Fax: 780-495-2876,
ceaa.alberta@ceaa-acee.gc.ca
Director, Lanny Coulson
780-495-2388

Ontario
#907, 55 St. Clair Ave. East, Toronto, ON M4T 1M2
416-952-1576, Fax: 416-952-1573,
ceaa.ontario@ceaa-acee.gc.ca
Director, Louise Knox
416-952-1575

Pacific & Yukon
#320, 757 West Hastings St., Vancouver, BC V6C 1A1
604-666-2434, Fax: 604-666-6990,
ceaa.pacific@ceaa-acee.gc.ca
Director, Jason Quigley
604-666-6989

Prairie Region
#445, 123 Main St., Winnipeg, MB R3C 4W2
204-983-5127, Fax: 204-983-7174,
ceaa.prairies@ceaa-acee.gc.ca
Director, Dan McNaughton
204-984-2457

Québec
1141, rte de l'Église, 2e étage, CP 9514 Ste-Foy, Québec, QC G1V 4B8
418-649-6444, Fax: 418-649-6443,
ceaa.quebec@ceaa-acee.gc.ca
Director, François Boulanger
418-649-6438

Canadian Food Inspection Agency (CFIA) / Agence canadienne d'inspection des aliments (ACIA)

1400 Merivale Rd., Ottawa, ON K1A 0Y9
613-225-2342, Fax: 613-228-6629, 800-442-2342
www.inspection.gc.ca
The agency is responsible for all inspection services related to food safety, economic fraud, trade-related requirements, & animal & plant health programs.
Acts Administered:
Agriculture & Agri-Food Administration Monetary Penalties Act
Canada Agricultural Products Act
Canadian Food Inspection Agency Act
Feeds Act
Fertilizers Act
Fish Inspection Act
Health of Animals Act
Meat Inspection Act
Plant Breeders' Rights Act
Plant Protection Act
Seeds Act
Acts Administered in Part by the Canadian Food Inspection Agency
Consumer Packaging & Labelling Act
Food & Drugs Act
President, Carole Swan
613-773-6000, Fax:
613-773-6060,carole.swan@inspection.gc.ca
Executive Vice-President, Office of the President, Dr. Brian Evans
613-773-5763, brian.evans@inspection.gc.ca
Vice-President, Finance, Administration & Information Technology, Stephen Baker
613-773-5700, Fax:
613-773-5792,Stephen.Baker@inspection.gc.ca
Vice-President, Human Resources, Omer Boudreau
613-773-5725, Fax:
613-773-5795,Omer.Boudreau@inspection.gc.ca
Vice-President, Operations, Cameron Prince
613-773-5717, Fax:
613-773-5671,Cameron.Prince@inspection.gc.ca
Vice-President, Policy & Programs, Sandra Wing
613-773-5734, Fax:
613-773-5791,Sandra.Wing@inspection.gc.ca
Vice-President, Science, Martine Dubuc
613-773-5722, Fax:
613-773-5797,Martine.Dubuc@inspection.gc.ca
Assoc. Vice-President, Integration & Management Services, Jim Butcher
613-773-6298, Fax:
613-773-5791,Jim.Butcher@inspection.gc.ca
Executive Director, Audit, Evaluation & Risk Oversight, Peter Everson
613-773-5759, Fax:
613-773-5696,Peter.Everson@inspection.gc.ca
Executive Director, Corporate Secretariat, Veronica McGuire
613-773-5751, Fax:
613-773-5791,Veronica.McGuire@inspection.gc.ca,
Executive Director, Programs Communications, Laurel Herwig
613-773-5501, Fax:
613-773-5618,Laurel.Herwig@inspection.gc.ca
Director, Executive Support & Coordination, Cynthia Richardson
613-773-5542, Fax:
613-773-5606,Cynthia.Richardson@inspection.gc.ca
Director, Corporate Planning & Reporting, Dr. Raman Srivastava
613-773-5528, Fax:
613-773-5605,Raman.Srivastava@inspection.gc.ca

Canadian Forces Grievance Board / Comité des griefs des Forces canadiennes

60 Queen St., 10th Fl., Ottawa, ON K1P 5Y7
613-996-8529, Fax: 613-996-6491, 877-276-4193
www.cfgb-cgfc.gc.ca
An administrative tribunal with quasi-judicial powers, independent from the Department of National Defence (DND) & the Canadian Forces (CF). The Board was created on March 1, 2000, in accordance with legislation enacted in December 1998 that contained amendments to the National Defence Act. The Board conducts objective & transparent reviews of grievances with due respect to fairness & equity for each individual member of the CF, regardless of rank or position. It plays a unique role within the military grievance review process because it ensures that the rights of CF personnel are considered fairly & impartially in the best interests of both parties concerned, thus balancing the rights of the grievor against the legal & operational requirements of the CF.
Acts Administered:
National Defence Act, ch. N-5, sec. 29
Queen's Regulation & Orders for the Canadian Forces, Ch. 7
Chair, Bruno Hamel
613-996-6453, Fax: 613-995-8129
Vice-Chair, James Price
613-996-8628, Fax: 613-996-6491

Canadian Grain Commission (CGC) / Commission canadienne des grains (CCG)

#600, 303 Main St., Winnipeg, MB R3C 3G8
204-983-2770, Fax: 204-983-2751, 800-853-6705
contact@grainscanada.gc.ca
www.grainscanada.gc.ca
The CGC is Canada's official grain quality assurance agency. The CGC offers a wide range of programs & services. It

regulates grain handling in Canada & establishes & maintains quality standards for Canadian grains. Responsibilities are as follows: officially inspecting & grading grain; weighing grain at terminal & transfer elevators; licensing grain elevators & dealers; conducting & publishing statistical & economic studies; & performing basic & applied research on Canadian grain.

Acts Administered:
Canada Grain Act

Chief Commissioner, Elwin Mermanson
Commissioner, Cam Dahl
Asst. Chief Commissioner, Jim Smolik
Chief Operating Officer, Gordon Miles
Chief Financial Officer, Sharon McShane
Director, Corporate Services, Barbara Elias
Director, Grain Research Laboratory, Peter Burnett
Director, Industry Services, Jim Stuart
Coordinator, Communications, Louise Worster
204-983-2748, Fax: 204-983-6098,lworster@grainscanada.gc.ca
President/CEO, Joanne DiCosimo
613-566-4733, Fax: 613-364-4020,jdicosimo@mus-nature.ca
Director, Collection Services, Roger Baird
613-364-4138, Fax: 613-364-4022,rbaird@mus-nature.ca
Director, Research Services, Dr. Mark S. Graham
613-566-4743, Fax: 613-364-4022,mgraham@mus-nature.ca
Chief, Anne Breau
613-566-4795, Fax: 613-364-4022,abreau@mus-nature.ca
Environmental Specialist, Jean Lauriault
613-566-4217, Fax: 613-364-4022,jlauriault@mus-nature.ca

Canadian Heritage / Patrimoine canadien

15 Eddy St., Gatineau, QC K1A 0M5
819-997-0055, 866-811-0055
info@pch.gc.ca
www.pch.gc.ca

Canadian Heritage works to achieve a more cohesive & creative nation. Goals of the department are for Canadians to express & share their cultural experiences with others in their own country & globally & for Canadians to live in an inclusive society with intercultural understanding & citizen participation. Responsibilities are carried out by the following sectors: Citizenship & Heritage; Cultural Affairs; International & Intergovernmental Affairs & Sport; Planning & Corporate Affairs; & Public & Regional Affairs.

Acts Administered:
An Act to Incorporate the Jules & Paul-Émile Léger Foundation
Broadcasting Act
Canada Council Act
Canadian Film Development Corporation Act
Canadian Heritage Languages Institute Act
Canadian Multiculturalism Act
Canadian Race Relations Foundation Act
Canadian Radio-television & Telecommunications Commission
Cultural Property Export & Import Act
Department of Canadian Heritage Act
Fitness & Amateur Sport Act
Historic Sites & Monuments Act
Holidays Act
Library & Archives of Canada Act
Lieutenant Governors Superannuation Act
Museums Act
National Anthem Act
National Arts Centre Act
National Battlefields at Québec Act
National Capital Act
National Film Act
National Flag of Canada Manufacturing Standards Act
National Library Act
National Sports of Canada Act
National Symbol of Canada Act
Official Languages Act
Physical Activity & Sport Act
Public Service Employment Act
Salaries Act
Status of the Artist Act
Trademarks Act

Minister, Canadian Heritage & Official Languages,Hon. James Moore
819-997-7788, Fax: 613-992-9868,Moore.J@parl.gc.ca
Deputy Minister, Judith A. LaRocque
819-994-1132, Fax: 819-997-0979,Judith.A.LaRocque@pch.gc.ca
Associate Deputy Minister, Stephen Wallace
819-997-1356, Fax: 819-997-2978,Stephen.Wallace@pch.gc.ca
Parliamentary Secretary to the Minister of Canadian Heritage, Dean Del Mastro
613-995-6411, Fax: 613-996-9800,DelMastro.D@parl.gc.ca
Parliamentary Secretary for Official Languages, Greg Rickford
613-996-1161, Fax: 613-996-1759,Rickford.G@parl.gc.ca

• Canada Council for the Arts/ Conseil des Arts du Canada
350 Albert St.
PO Box 1047
Ottawa, ON K1P 5V8
613-566-4414 Fax: 613-566-4390 800-263-5588TDD: 613-565-5194
www.canadacouncil.ca
• Canada Science & Technology Museum Corporation/ Musée des sciences et de la technologie du Canada
• Canadian Broadcasting Corporation(CBC) / Société Radio-Canada (SRC)
• Canadian Museum of Civilization/ Musée canadien des civilisations
• Canadian Museum of Nature/ Musée canadien de la nature
• Canadian Museum of Civilization(CMC) / Musée canadien des civilisations
• Canadian Museum of Nature/ Musée canadien de la nature
• Canadian Radio-television & Telecommunications Commission(CRTC) / Conseil de la radiodiffusion et des télécommunications canadiennes
• Library & Archives Canada
• National Arts Centre(NAC) / Centre national des Arts (CNA)
• National Battlefields Commission/ Commission des champs de bataille nationaux
• National Film Board of Canada/ Office national du film du Canada
• National Gallery of Canada/ Musée des Beaux-Arts du Canada
• National Gallery of Canada/ Musée des beaux-arts du Canada
• Public Service Commission of Canada/ Commission de la fonction publique du Canada
• Status of Women Canada/ Condition féminine Canada
• Telefilm Canada/ Téléfilm Canada

Citizenship & Heritage Sector / Citoyenneté et patrimoine
Asst. Deputy Minister, Diane Fulford
819-997-2832, Fax: 819-994-5032
Director General, Official Languages Support Programs, Hubert Lussier
819-994-0943, Fax: 819-953-9353
Director General, Multiculturalism & Human Rights, Kristina Namiesniowski
819-994-2994, Fax: 819-953-8720
Director General, Citizenship Participation & Promotion, Marie Bédard
819-998-7115, Fax: 819-998-9230
Executive Director, Heritage Group, Lyn Elliot Sherwood
819-997-7774, Fax: 819-997-8392
Director General, Canadian Conservation Institute & Chief Operating Officer, Jeanne E. Inch
819-998-3721, Fax: 819-998-4721
Director General, Canadian Heritage Information Network (CHIN), Gabrielle Blais
819-997-0091, Fax: 819-994-9555
Director General, Aboriginal Affairs, Allan Clarke
819-994-6035, Fax: 819-953-2673
Director General, Strategic Policy & Management, Martha LaBarge
819-997-1588, Fax: 819-997-0329

Regional Offices:

Atlantic
#106, 1045 Main St., Moncton, NB E1C 1H1
506-851-7069, Fax: 506-851-7079
Regional Executive Director, Jean-Bernard Lafontaine

Ontario
#400, 150 John St., Toronto, ON M5V 3T6
416-954-0396, Fax: 416-954-2909
Executive Director, Marie Moliner

Prairies & Northern Region
275 Portage Ave., 2nd Fl., PO Box 2160, Winnipeg, MB R3C 3R5
204-983-2630, Fax: 204-984-6996
Regional Executive Director, Bill Balan

Québec
Complexe Guy-Favreau, Tour Ouest, 200, boul René-Lévesque ouest, 6e étage, Montréal, QC H2Z 1X4
514-283-5797, Fax: 514-283-8762
Regional Executive Director, Marc Lemay

Western
300 West Georgia St., 4th Fl., Vancouver, BC V6B 6C6
604-666-1893, Fax: 604-666-6040,
Regional Executive Director, Ella Smith

Canadian Human Rights Commission / Commission canadienne des droits de la personne

344 Slater St., 8th Fl., Ottawa, ON K1A 1E1
613-995-1151, Fax: 613-996-9661, 888-214-1090
info.com@chrc-ccdp.ca
www.chrc-ccdp.ca

Other Communication: Toll Free: 1-800-999-6899 (Regional Offices)

The Commission administers the Canadian Human Rights Act which applies to federal government departments & agencies, & businesses under federal jurisdiction. The Commission accepts complaints of discrimination based on race, national or ethnic origin, colour, religion, age, sex, marital & family status, pardoned offence, disability & sexual orientation.It also administers the Employment Equity Act to remove barriers for four designated groups: women, Aboriginal peoples, persons with disabilities & members of visible minorities. Collect calls accepted throughout Canada.

Chief Commissioner, Jennifer Lynch, QC
613-943-9144, Fax: 613-943-6810
Deputy Chief Commissioner, David Langtry
613-943-9148
Secretary General, Richard Burton
613-943-9134
Director General, Corporate Management Branch, Heather Throop
613-943-9033

Regional Offices:

Alberta & Northwest Territories
#308, 10010 - 106 St., Edmonton, AB T5J 3L8
780-495-4040, Fax: 780-495-4044

Atlantic
#504, 5475 Spring Garden Rd., Halifax, NS B3J 3T2
902-426-8380, Fax: 902-426-2685

British Columbia & Yukon
#301, 1095 West Pender St., Vancouver, BC V6E 2M6
604-666-2251, Fax: 604-666-2386

Ontario
#1002, 175 Bloor St. East, Toronto, ON M4W 3R8
416-973-5527, Fax: 416-973-6184

Prairies
#750, 175 Hargrave St., Winnipeg, MB R3C 3R8
204-983-2189, Fax: 204-983-6132

Québec
#903, 425, boul de Maisonneuve ouest, Montréal, QC H3A 3G5
514-283-5218, Fax: 514-283-5084

Canadian Human Rights Tribunal (CHRT) / Tribunal canadien des droits de la personne (TCDP)

160 Elgin St., 11th Fl., Ottawa, ON K1A 1J4
613-995-1707, Fax: 613-995-3484,
registrar@chrt-tcdp.gc.ca
www.chrt-tcdp.gc.ca

Quasi-judicial body that adjudicates complaints of discrimination referred to it by the Canadian Human Rights Commission & determines whether the activities violate the Canadian Human Rights Act.

Acts Administered:
Canadian Human Rights Act
Employment Equity Act

Chair, J. Grant Sinclair
613-995-1707
Vice-Chair, Athanasios Hadjis
Executive Directory & Registrar, Gregory Smith

Canadian Institutes of Health Research (CIHR) / Instituts de recherche en santé du Canada (IRSC)

160 Elgin St., 9th Fl., Ottawa, ON K1A 0W9
613-941-2672, Fax: 613-954-1800, 888-603-4178
info@cihr-irsc.gc.ca
www.cihr-irsc.gc.ca

Promotes health research excellence in Canada through training & funding programs in basic, clinical, health systems & services, & population health research. Research is carried out in universities, in the health sciences faculties, affiliated hospitals & institutions & other faculties where research projects are highly relevant to human health. University-Industry programs create the opportunity for collaboration between Canadian companies & researchers conducting research in Canadian universities or affiliated institutions. Also manages the health-related Networks of Centres of Excellence.

President, Alain Beaudet
613-954-1974
Executive Vice-President, Christine Fitzgerald
613-957-6134
Vice-President, Research, Dr. Pierre Chartrand
613-954-1805

Director, Human Resources, Sandra Cooper
613-957-8762
Executive Director, Secretariat on Research Ethics, Susan Zimmerman
613-947-7148
Director, Communications & Marketing, Karen Spierkel
613-954-1812
Director, Ethics Office, Geneviève Dubois-Flynn
613-954-1801

Canadian Intergovernmental Conference Secretariat (CICS) / Secrétariat des conférences intergouvernementales canadiennes

222 Queen St., 10th Fl., PO Box 488 A, Ottawa, ON K1N 8V5
613-995-2341, Fax: 613-996-6091,
info@scics.gc.ca
www.scics.gc.ca

CICS is a conference support body which provides the administrative services required for the planning & the conduct of federal-provincial-territorial & provincial-territorial conferences at the First Ministers, ministers & deputy ministers level. The agency is at the disposal of individual federal, provincial & territorial government departments which may be called upon to organize & chair such meetings.
Secretary, André M. McArdle

Canadian International Development Agency (CIDA) / Agence canadienne de développement international (ACDI)

200, Promenade du Portage, Gatineau, QC K1A 0G4
819-997-5006, Fax: 819-953-6088, 800-230-6349
info@acdi-cida.gc.ca
www.acdi-cida.gc.ca

Other Communication: Toll Free TDD: 1-800-331-5018; Public Inquiries: 819-997-5006

Major agency responsible for delivering most of Canada's foreign aid.CIDA is committed to supporting sustainable development in developing countries to meet the needs of current & future generations. The mission statement demands that criteria of sustainability be integrated into each project undertaken by the Agency in order to improve the economic, social, cultural, ecological & political condition of the world's developing nations. Many of the projects CIDA supports are aimed directly at the environment. Projects include reforestation & watershed rehabilitation, small scale fishing development (to increase output & food), water projects (to improve health), increased food production, improved rural quality, & supply & generation of electricity. Various other projects help nations develop the legal & administrative framework needed to promote environmentally sustainable development.In February, 2004, the Agency released its Sustainable Development Strategy 2004-2006: Enabling Change." This strategy sets out a number of key directions for the Agency to advance sustainable development. The $100-million five-year Canada Climate Change Development Fund was extended to 2005-2006
Minister, International Cooperation,Hon. Beverley J. (Bev) Oda
613-992-2792, Fax: 613-992-2794,Oda.B@parl.gc.ca; minister@acdi-cida.gc.ca
Parliamentary Secretary to the Minister of International Cooperation,Hon. Jim Abbott
613-995-7246, Fax: 613-996-9923,Abbott.J@parl.gc.ca
Chief of Staff, Amy Baker
819-997-0843
Administration & Information Officer, Claudine Taillefer
819-997-6912, Fax: 819-997-0866
Senior Vice-President, Geographic Programs Branch, Hau Sing Tse
819-997-1665
Acting Vice-President, Afghanistan & Pakistan Task Force, Francoise Ducros
819-997-1408
Acting Vice-President, Canadian Partnership Branch, Naresh Singh
819-956-8266, Fax: 819-934-3587
Vice-President, Multilateral & Global Programs Branch, Diane Jacovella
819-997-7537, Fax: 819-953-5348
Vice-President, Pan Geographic Programs, Allan Culham
819-997-1643, Fax: 819-994-6174
Vice-President, Strategic Policy & Performance Branch, Christine Hogan
819-997-6133, Fax: 819-953-6356
Acting Director General, Communications Branch, Bernard Etzinger
819-953-9574
Acting Director General, Human Resources Branch, Sheila Tenasco-Banerjee
819-994-4418
Director General, Strategic Policy Directorate, Paul Samson
819-953-3139, Fax: 819-953-5229
Acting Chief Information Officer, Jacques Mailloux
819-994-3855

Canadian International Trade Tribunal / Tribunal canadien du commerce extérieur

Standard Life Centre, 333 Laurier Ave. West, 17 Floor, Ottawa, ON K1A 0G7
613-990-2452, Fax: 613-990-2439,
www.citt-tcce.gc.ca

The Tribunal is an independent, quasi-judicial body, which carries out both judicial & advisory functions relating to trade remedies for the North American Free Trade Agreement. In this capacity, the Tribunal succeeds the Procurement Review Board of Canada. Reports to government through the Minister of Finance.
Acts Administered:
Canadian International Trade Tribunal Act
Customs Act
Excise Tax Act
Special Import Measures Act
Chair, André F. Scott
Vice-Chair, Serge Fréchette
613-990-2432, Fax: 613-990-9881
Vice-Chair, Diane Vincent
613-990-1476, Fax: 613-990-9881
Secretary, Dominique Laporte
613-993-3595
Director General, Research, Sandy Greig
613-990-8724, Fax: 613-990-2431
General Counsel, Reagan Walker
613-991-9247, Fax: 613-990-7132
Chief Librarian, Ursula Schultz
613-990-2418, Fax: 613-990-2439,uschultz@citt.gc.ca

Canadian Judicial Council / Conseil canadien de la magistrature

150 Metcalfe St., 15th Fl., Ottawa, ON K1A 0W8
613-288-1566, Fax: 613-288-1575

The members of the Council include the Chief Justice of Canada (who acts as Chair), the Chief Justices & Associate Chief Justices of each Superior Court or Branch or Division thereof, the senior judges of the Supreme Court of the Yukon Territory, the Supreme Court of the Northwest Territories & the Nunavut Court of Justice, the Chief Judge & Associate Chief Judge of the Tax Court of Canada, & the Chief Justice of the Court Martial Court of Canada.
Executive Director & General Counsel, Norman Sabourin
Administrative Services Officer, Mary Gill
613-288-1566

Canadian Nuclear Safety Commission (CNSC) / Commission canadienne de sûreté nucléaire (CCSN)

280 Slater St., PO Box 1046 B, Ottawa, ON K1P 5S9
613-995-5894, Fax: 613-995-5086, 800-668-5284
info@cnsc-ccsn.gc.ca
www.nuclearsafety.gc.ca

Federal agency which regulates activities involving nuclear energy & prescribed substances in the interests of health & safety for workers & the public. Areas covered under the AECB's licensing process include the nuclear fuel cycle (from mining to waste disposal), heavy water plants, research reactors & accelerators, & radioisotopes. Operations ensure that the use of nuclear energy in Canada does not pose undue risk to health, safety, security & the environment. The Research & Support Program (RSP) augments & extends the AECB's regulatory program beyond the capability of in-house resources. It produces pertinent & independent information that will assist the Board & its staff in making sound, timely & credible decisions on regulating nuclear facilities & materials. The nine sectors of the program include: safety of nuclear facilities; radioactive waste management; health physics; physical security; development of regulatory processes; & social services
President, Michael Binder
613-992-8828, Fax: 613-995-5086
Executive Vice-President/Chief Regulatory Operations Officer, Ramzi Jammal
613-947-8899, Fax: 613-995-5086
Vice-President, Corporate Services & CFO, Gordon White
Vice-President, Regulatory Affairs, Patricia McDowell
613-943-7662, Fax: 613-995-5086
Director General, Environmental & Radiation Protection & Assessment, Patsy Thompson
613-947-3352, Fax: 613-995-5086
Director General, Nuclear Cycle & Facilities Regulation, Peter H. Elder
613-943-8948, Fax: 613-995-5086
Director, Systems Engineering Division, Robert Lojk
613-947-3992, Fax: 613-995-5086

Canadian Museum of Civilization (CMC) / Musée canadien des civilisations

100 Laurier St., PO Box 3100 B, Gatineau, QC J8X 4H2
819-776-7000, Fax: 819-776-8300, 800-555-5621
www.civilization.ca

President/CEO,Dr. Victor Rabinovitch
819-776-7116
Chair,Dr. John R. English
819-776-7115
COO, David Loye
819-776-8258
Acting Coordinator, Board of Trustees, Maureen Currans-Grenier
819-776-7117

Canadian Polar Commission (CPC) / Commission canadienne des affaires polaires (CCAP)

Constitution Square, #1710, 360 Albert St., Ottawa, ON K1R 7X7
613-943-8605, Fax: 613-943-8607, 888-765-2701
mail@polarcom.gc.ca
www.polarcom.gc.ca

Mandated to enhance the public's awareness of polar regions & to foster both international & domestic liaison & cooperation in circumpolar research & technology development. One of the Commission's main objectives in the short term is focus on climate change & energy. Maintains the Canadian Polar Information System (CPIS) which, in addition to polar data & information, includes services such as the Polar Science Forum, Researcher's Directory, Researcher's Toolbox, & links to International Partners. In September 2005, the federal government announced it will provide $150 million in new funding over six years for International Polar Year 2007-2008, an international research program.
Chair, Peter Johnson
613-943-8605, Fax: 613-943-8607
Executive Director, Steven Bigras
613-943-8606, bigrass@polarcom.gc.ca
Financial Officer, Bill Ryan
613-943-0718, Fax: 613-943-8607
Manager, Communications & Information, John Bennett
613-943-0716, Fax: 613-943-8607,bennettj@polarcom.gc.ca
Manager, Polar Science, Jean-Marie Beaulieu
613-947-9108, Fax: 613-943-8607,beaulieuj@polarcom.gc.ca
Executive Secretary, Sandy Bianchini
613-943-8605
Research Assistant, Elaine Anderson
613-947-9107, andersone@polarcom.gc.ca

Canadian Museum of Nature / Musée Canadien de la Nature

PO Box 3443 D, Ottawa, ON K1P 6P4
613-566-4700, Fax: 613-364-4021, 800-263-4433
enquiries@mus-nature.ca
www.nature.ca

Complete listing in Section 6, see index.
President/CEO, Joanne DiCosimo
613-566-4733, Fax: 613-364-4020,jdicosimo@mus-nature.ca
Vice-President, Corporate Services & Chief Operating Officer, Maureen Dougan
613-566-4241, Fax: 613-364-4020,mdougan@mus-nature.ca
Director, Collections, Roger Baird
613-364-4066
Director, Financial Management Services, Lynne Ladouceur
613-566-4253, Fax: 613-364-4025,lladouceur@mus-nature.ca
Director, Human Resources Management Services, Denyse Jomphe
613-566-4294, Fax: 613-364-4028,djomphe@mus-nature.ca
Director, Research Services, Dr. Mark Graham
613-566-4743, Fax: 613-364-4021,mgraham@mus-nature.ca
Campaign Director, Karen Van Sacker
613-566-4203, Fax: 613-364-4021,kvansacker@mus-nature.ca
Manager, Community Services, Mary Ellen Herbert
613-566-4704, Fax: 613-566-4759,meherbert@mus-nature.ca
Manager, Communications Services, Elizabeth McCrea
613-566-4249, Fax: 613-364-4021,emccrea@mus-nature.ca
Manager, Development & Fundraising Services, Rise Paquette
613-566-4790, Fax: 613-364-4021,rpaquette@mus-nature.ca
Manager, Exhibition Services, Monty Reid
613-566-4252, Fax: 613-364-4023,mreid@mus-nature.ca
Manager, Facilities Management Services, Lucie Lanctôt
613-566-4238, Fax: 613-364-4025,llanctot@mus-nature.ca
Manager, Information Services, Bruce Williams
613-364-4034, Fax: 613-364-4023,bwilliams@mus-nature.ca

Manager, Information Technology & Library Services, Greg Smith
613-566-4219, Fax: 613-364-4021,gsmith@mus-nature.ca
Chief, Canadian Centre for Biodiversity, Anne Breau
613-566-4795, Fax: 613-364-4022,abreau@mus-nature.ca
Chief, Conservation, Robert Waller
613-566-4705, Fax: 613-364-4027,rwaller@mus-nature.ca
Chief, Registrar, Peter Frank
613-364-4089, Fax: 613-364-4021,pfrank@mus-nature.ca
Chief & Collection Manager, Botany Collections, Mike Shchepanek
613-364-4076, Fax: 613-364-4027,mshchepanek@mus-nature.ca
Chief & Collection Manager, Earth Science Collections, Kieran Shepherd
613-364-4054, Fax: 613-364-4027,kshepherd@mus-nature.ca
Chief & Collection Manager, Invertebrate Collections,Dr. Jean-Marc Gagnon
613-364-4066, Fax: 613-346-4027,jgagnon@mus-nature.ca
Chief & Collection Manager, Vertebrate Collections, Darlene Balkwill
613-364-4070, Fax: 613-364-4027,dbalkwill@mus-nature.ca
Project Leader, Issues in Biodiversity, Dr. Robert Anderson
613-364-4050, Fax: 613-364-4027,randerson@mus-nature.ca
Project Leader, Paleobiological Studies, Dr. Steve Cumbaa
613-364-4049, Fax: 613-364-4027,scumbaa@mus-nature.ca
Project Leader, Rare Elements, Dr. Scott Ercit
613-364-4058, Fax: 613-364-4027,sercit@mus-nature.ca
Head, Biological Survey of Canada, Dr. Hugh Danks
613-566-4787, Fax: 613-364-4027,hdanks@mus-nature.ca
Administrative Officer, Lucille Fourneau
613-566-4785, Fax: 613-364-4021

Canadian Race Relations Foundation (CRRF) / Fondation canadienne des relations raciales (TCRR)

#701, 4576 Yonge St., Toronto, ON M2N 6N4
416-952-3500, Fax: 416-952-3326, 888-240-4936
info@crr.ca
www.crr.ca

Other Communication: Toll Free Fax: 1-888-399-0333
Crown corporation operating at arms length from the federal government from which it receives no funding. The Foundation is committed to building a national framework for the fight against racism in Canadian society.
Acts Administered:
Canadian Race Relations Foundation Act
Executive Director, Ayman Al-Yassini
416-952-3500, Fax: 416-952-3326,ayassini@crr.ca
Director, Finance & Administration, Daniel Chong
416-952-5063
Program Director, Support & Knowledge Base, Anne Marrian
416-952-3501

Canadian Radio-Television & Telecommunications Commission (CRTC) / Conseil de la radiodiffusion et des télécommunications Canadiennes

Central Office, 1, Promenade du Portage, Les Terrasses de la Chaudière, Gatineau, QC J8X 4B1
819-997-0313, Fax: 819-994-0218, 877-249-2782
www.crtc.gc.ca
The CRTC is vested with the authority to regulate & supervise all aspects of the Canadian broadcasting system, as well as to regulate telecommunications common carriers & service providers that fall under federal jurisdiction. Reports to Parliament through the Minister of Canadian Heritage.
Acts Administered:
Bell Canada Act
Broadcasting Act
Canadian Radio-television & Telecommunications Commission Act
Telecommunications Act
Chair, Konrad W. von Finckenstein
819-997-3430, Fax: 819-953-1555
Vice-Chair, Broadcasting, Michel Arpin
819-994-0870, Fax: 819-994-0218
Vice-Chair, Telecommunications, Leonard Katz
819-997-4644, Fax: 819-997-4923
Commissioner, Michel Morin
819-953-4375
Commissioner, Marc Patrone
819-953-9958
Commissioner, Alberta/Northwest Territories Regions, Vacant
Commissioner, Atlantic Region, Elizabeth A. Duncan
819-997-4764,
Commissioner, British Columbia/Yukon Regions, Stephen B. Simpson
819-953-6026
Commissioner, Manitoba/Saskatchewan Regions, Candice J. Molnar
819-997-4485
Commissioner, Ontario Region, Rita Cugini
819-997-2431
Commissioner, Québec Region, Suzanne Lamarre
819-934-6347
Executive Director, Broadcasting, Scott Hutton
819-997-4573, Fax: 819-994-0218
Executive Director, Telecommunications, John Traversy
819-953-5889, Fax: 819-994-0218
Executive Director, Policy Development & Research, Namir Anani
819-997-4534, Fax: 819-994-0218
Director General, Strategic Communications & Parliamentary Affairs, Renée Fairweather
819-997-9372, Fax: 819-997-4245
Secretary General, Corporate & Operations, Robert A. Morin
819-994-0233, Fax: 819-994-0218
Senior General Counsel, John Keogh
819-953-3990, Fax: 819-953-0589
Director General, Finance & Administrative Service, Jim Stefanik
819-997-0108

Regional Offices:

Alberta
#520, 10405 Jasper Ave., Edmonton, AB T5J 3N4
780-495-3224
Information Officer, Helen Randolph

British Columbia
#530, 580 Hornby St., Vancouver, BC V6C 3B6
604-666-2111, Fax: 604-666-8322
Regional Officer, Robert Stark

Manitoba
#1810, 275 Portage Ave., Winnipeg, MB R3B 2B3
204-983-6306, Fax: 204-983-6317
Director, Gary Krushen
204-983-6306

Nova Scotia
Metropolitan Place, #1410, 99 Wyse Rd., Dartmouth, NS B3A 4S5
902-426-7997, Fax: 902-426-2721
Acting Director, Donna Shewfelt
902-426-7997

Ontario
#624, 55 St. Clair Ave. East, Toronto, ON M4T 1M2
416-952-9096
Information Officer, Margaret Kennedy
416-954-6271

Québec
#504, 205, av Viger ouest, Montréal, QC H2Z 1G2
514-283-6607
Information Officer, Monique Cyr
514-496-4077

Saskatchewan
Cornwall Professional Bldg., #103, 2125 - 11 Ave., Regina, SK S4P 3X3
306-780-3422
Information Officer, Nola Hardie
306-780-3422

Canadian Security Intelligence Service (CSIS) / Service canadien du renseignement de sécurité

PO Box 9732 T, Ottawa, ON K1G 4G4
613-993-9620,
www.csis.gc.ca

Acts Administered:
Canadian Security Intelligence Service Act
Charities Registration (Security Information) Act
Citizenship Act
Employment Equity Act
Immigration & Refugee Protection Act
Proceeds of Crime (Money Laundering) & Terrorist Financing Act
Director, Ward Elcock
613-231-0000
Director General, Communications, Phil Gibson
613-231-0100, Fax: 613-231-0612

Canadian Space Agency (CSA) / Agence spatiale canadienne (ASC)

6767, rte de l'Aéroport, Saint-Hubert, QC J3Y 8Y9
450-926-4800, Fax: 450-926-4352,
webmaster@space.gc.ca
www.space.gc.ca
Established in 1989, & responsible for coordinating all civil, space-related policies & programs on behalf of the Government of Canada. Scientific research & industrial development in earth observation, space science & exploration, satellite communications, & space awareness & learning. RADARSAT International (RSI) develops products & services demanded by world markets. RADARSAT-1, the first Canadian commercial Earth Observation (EO) satellite, is uniquely capable of responding to disasters around the world. The system can support the operational mapping & monitoring of natural disasters in four critical ways: prevention, preparedness, emergency response & recovery. Moreover, the development of the high performance RADARSAT-2 to be launched in 2007, will further enhance Canada's competitive position. RADARSAT-2 will offer improved quality of data images to meet the growing world demand of Earth observation information. The SCISAT satellite is used in ozone depletion research.
Acts Administered:
Canadian Space Agency Act
Minister, Industry; Minister Responsible, Canadian Space Agency,Hon. Tony Clement
613-944-7740, Fax: 613-992-5092,ClemeT@parl.gc.ca; ministre.industrie@ic.gc.ca,
President & Chief Astronaut, Steven MacLean
450-926-4301, Fax: 450-926-4315
Vice-President, Jean Paquette
450-926-4760, Fax: 450-926-4332
CFO, Jacques Côté
450-926-4407, Fax: 450-926-4424
Director, Operations Engineering/Program Manager CSSP, Pierre Jean
450-926-4515, Fax: 450-926-4722
Director, Satellite Operations, Surendra Parashar
450-926-4412, Fax: 450-926-4888
Director, Communications & Public Affairs, Paul Engel
450-926-4342, Fax: 450-926-4377,paul.engel@space.gc.ca
Director, Government Liaison, Manon Larocque
613-993-3771, Fax: 613-990-4994

Canadian Transportation Agency (CTA) / Office des transports du Canada (OTC)

Les Terrasses de la Chaudière, 15, rue Eddy, Gatineau, QC K1A 0N9
819-997-0344, Fax: 819-997-6727, 888-222-2592
info@otc-cta.gc.ca
www.cta-otc.gc.ca
Responsible for the economic regulation of transportation in Canada. The agency requires that all applications for new railway lines, modifications to existing railway lines, disputed railway crossings at grade, grade separation, utility crossings & private crossings be accompanied by an environment impact assessment
Chair/CEO, Geoffrey C. Hare
819-997-9233, Fax: 819-953-9979
Vice-Chair, John Scott
819-953-8915, Fax: 819-953-9979
Director General, Corporate Management Branch, Arun Thangaraj
819-997-6764, Fax: 819-953-9842
Director General, Industry Regulation & Determinations Branch, Ghislain Blanchard
819-953-4657, Fax: 819-994-8807
Director General, Dispute Resolution Branch, Joan MacDonald
819-953-5074, Fax: 819-953-5562
Director, Communications Directorate, Jacqueline Bannister
819-953-7666, Fax: 819-953-8353
Director, Rail, Air & Marine Disputes Directorate, Joseph Dion
819-953-0327, Fax: 819-953-8353
Investigation Officer, Regulatory Approvals & Compliance Directorate, Darryl Salmaso
819-953-9924, Fax: 819-934-0631

Regional Enforcement Officers:

Atlantic
#109, 1045 Main St., Moncton, NB E1C 1H1
506-851-6950, Fax: 506-851-2518
Enforcement Officer, Brian Mercer

Central
#702, 269 Main St., PO Box 27007 Winnipeg Square, Winnipeg, MB R3C 4T3
204-984-6092, Fax: 204-984-6093
Enforcement Officer, Richard J. Tardi

Ontario
#300, 4900 Yonge St., Toronto, ON M2N 6A5
416-952-7895, Fax: 416-952-7897

Enforcement Officer, Jeannette Anderson

Pacific
#560, 800 Burrard St., Vancouver, BC V6Z 2V8
604-666-0620, Fax: 604-666-1267
Enforcement Officer, Wayne Wooldridge

Québec
#510, 101, boul Roland-Therrien, Longueuil, QC J4H 4B9
450-928-4173, Fax: 450-928-4174
Enforcement Officer, Richard Laliberté

Western
#1100, 9700 Jasper Ave. NW, Edmonton, AB T5J 4C3
780-495-6618, Fax: 780-495-5639
Enforcement Officer, Linda Brooklyn

Canadian Wheat Board (CWB) / Commission canadienne du blé

423 Main St., PO Box 816 Main, Winnipeg, MB R3C 2P5
204-983-0239, Fax: 204-983-3841, 800-275-4292
questions@cwb.ca
www.cwb.ca

Other Communication: Farmers: farmers@cwb.ca
The market agency serves farmers in Western Canada who grow wheat, durum wheat, & barley. The Canadian Wheat Board's main function is to market these grains in Canada & abroad.
Minister, Agriculture & Agri-Food; Minister, Canadian Wheat Board,Hon. Gerry Ritz
613-995-7080, Fax: 613-996-8472,Ritz.G@parl.gc.ca
President/CEO, Ian White
Chair, Larry Hill
306-778-2359
Chief Operating Officer, Ward Weisensel
Chief Financial Officer, Brita Chell
Chief Information Officer, Information & Technology, Graham Paul
Vice-President, People & Organizational Services, Diane Wiesenthal
Vice-President, Farmer Services, E. Geddes
Parliamentary Secretary to the Minister of Natural Resources & for the Canadian Wheat Board, David Anderson
613-992-0657, Fax: 613-992-5508,Anderson.Da@parl.gc.ca

Regional & Overseas Offices:

Airdrie
#309, 800 Airdrie Rd., PO Box 3340, Airdrie, AB T4B 2B6
403-912-4180, Fax: 403-912-4181

British Columbia
Marine Bldg., #650, 355 Burrard St., Vancouver, BC V6C 2G8
604-666-2992, Fax: 604-666-0293,
Other Communication: Telex: 04-508862

China
Tower B, Beijing COFCO Plaza, #708, 8 Jianguomen Nei St., Beijing,100005 China
Other Communication: 86-10-6526-3908; Fax: 86-10-6526-3907

Japan
No. 11 Mori Bldg., 3rd Fl., 6-4, Toranomon 2-chome, Minato-ku, Tokyo,105-0001 Japan
Other Communication: 81-3-3519-2288; Fax: 81-3-3519-2287

Saskatchewan
#310, 15 Innovation Blvd., Saskatoon, SK S7N 2X8
306-975-6999, Fax: 306-975-6966

Citizenship & Immigration Canada / Citoyenneté et Immigration Canada

Jean Edmonds, South Tower, 365 Laurier Ave. West, Ottawa, ON K1A 1L1
613-954-9019, Fax: 613-954-2221, 888-242-2100
www.cic.gc.ca
The Department of Citizenship & Immigration administers Canada's citizenship & immigration policies, procedures & service. The department is responsible for the following: examining immigrants, visitors & people claiming refugee status at land borders, seaports & airports; processing applications for permanent residence, extensions of visitor status requests & sponsorships for relatives & refugees overseas; admitting students, temporary workers & qualified business immigrants; investigating & removing people who are in Canada illegally; working with & helping fund a network of settlement agencies & services to help immigrants adapt to & participate in day-to-day Canadian life; promoting the acceptance of immigrants by Canadians; cooperating with various levels of government on enforcement, program development & the delivery of services; accepting applications & verifying the eligibility &documentation of applicants; granting citizenship & administration of the Oath of numerous community facilities across Canada; confirming Canadian citizenship status &; issuing proofs of citizenship to Canadians. The Immigration & Refugee Board reports to Parliament through the minister.
Acts Administered:
Citizenship Act
Immigration Act
Immigration & Refugee Protection Act
Minister, Citizenship, Immigration, & Multiculturalism,Hon. Jason Kenney
613-992-2235, Fax: 613-992-1920,kenneJ@parl.gc.ca; Minister@cic.gc.ca
Parliamentary Secretary to the Minister of Citizenship & Immigration, Richard Dykstra
613-992-3352, Fax: 613-947-4402,Dykstra.R@parl.gc.ca
Parliamentary Secretary for Multiculturalism, Alice Wong
613-995-2021, Fax: 613-995-2174,Wong.A@parl.gc.ca
Deputy Minister, Neil Yeates
613-954-3501
Director General, Human Resources, Diane Mikaelsson
613-941-7788, Fax: 613-957-3882
Acting Director General, Internal Audit & Accountability, Jacques Marquis
613-946-5651, Fax: 613-952-6556

Canada Immigration Centres & Citizenship Offices / Centres d'immigration et de citoyenneté
Immigration visa offices are located in most Canadian Embassies & Consulates abroad. Immigration centres are located at most ports of entry in Canada, & citizenship & immigration offices in major cities throughout the country. For specific addresses & other information contact 1-888-242-2100.

Office of the Asst. Deputy Attorney General / Bureau du Sous-procureur général adjoint
Asst. Deputy Attorney General, Brian Saunders
613-952-4744
Senior General Counsel, Dawn Edlund
613-952-4766

Centralized Services Delivery & Corporate Services / Services centralisés et services de gestion
Asst. Deputy Minister, John McWhinnie
613-957-3338
Chief Financial Officer, Wayne Ganim
613-954-4443
Director General, Administration, Guy Bélisle
613-954-4223
Director General, Communications, Stewart Edison
613-941-7042
Director General, Information Management & Technology & Chief Information Officer, Charles MacLennan
613-954-2700
Director General, Operational Management & Coordination, Diane Mikaelsson
613-954-9004

Client Service Modernization
Asst. Deputy Minister, Lilianne Binette
613-948-5970
Acting Director General, Admissibility, Brigitte Diogo
613-954-6132
Director General, Integration, Rose Kattackal
613-957-3257
Director General, Refugees, Micheline Aucoin
613-957-5874
Director General, Selection, Les Linklater
613-941-8989, Fax: 613-953-4701

Operations
Acting Asst. Deputy Minister, Daniel Jean
613-954-5335
Director General, Case Management, Anne Arnott
613-957-3941
Acting Director General, International Region, Burke Thornton
613-957-5893
Director General, Medical Services, Lise Scott
613-946-5597
Director General, Planning, Reporting, Access & Ministerials, Helen Amundsen

Strategic Program Policy / Politiques stratégiques et de programmes
Asst. Deputy Minister, Malcolm Brown
613-954-7353
Director General, International & Intergovernmental Relations, Brian Grant
613-957-5878
Director General, Strategic Policy & Priorities, Rick Stewart
613-957-5948
Director, Accounting Operations, André Couture
613-957-8905
Director, Financial Planning, Analysis & Reporting, Betty Shang
613-954-0091, Fax: 613-957-9772
Director, Financial Policy & Systems, Martin Andison
613-957-4556
Director General & Chief Information Officer,Vacant
613-954-2700, Fax: 613-954-6209
Director, Information Management, Ginette Fillion
613-954-5866, Fax: 613-954-4441
Director, Computer Operations, Jill Finlin
613-941-4848
Acting Director, Corporate Architecture, Barry Brock
613-954-8047,
Acting Director, Project Relations, Ken Sosnoski
613-954-6016
Acting Director General, Raylene Baker
613-941-1550
Director, Case Processing Centre - Sydney, Ernest Smith
902-564-7852, Fax: 902-564-2421
Director, Case Processing Centre - Vegreville, Tony Brothers
780-632-8030
Acting Director, Citizenship& Immigration Services, Mariette Lachance
613-941-1550
Director, Service Delivery Division, Mary Angus
613-957-5964
Acting Director, Support Services, Terry Lepine
613-941-8800
Manager, Query Response Centre,Vacant
613-957-4418, Fax: 613-957-4660
Manager, Case Processing Centre - Mississauga, Frank Perriccioli
905-803-7371, Fax: 905-803-7398
Director, Operational Coordination & Policy Liaison Selection, David Manicom
613-957-6981, Fax: 613-957-6991
Director, Personnel, Trudy Kernighan
613-941-1372, Fax: 613-957-6909
Director, Resource Management, Caroline Guimond
613-957-6944, Fax: 613-957-6952
Director, Field Support, Melody Duncan
613-957-5806
Acting Director General, Patricia Birkett
613-957-3257
Senior Citizenship Judge, Michel Simard
613-954-4624, Fax: 613-954-4621
Acting Director, Citizenship & Registrar, Clark Goodman
613-952-7273, Fax: 613-957-2206
Director, Promotion, Katharine Cornfield
613-948-3061
Director, Service Line Support, Marcia Shaw
613-957-3433, Fax: 613-957-7673
Director, Settlement, Deborah Spurr
613-952-2301, Fax: 613-957-7673
Director General, Robert Orr
613-957-5874
Acting Director, Asylum, Dick Graham
613-957-5867
Director, Refugee Program Support, John Kent
613-957-5831
Director, Resettlement, Rick Herringer
613-957-9349, Fax: 613-957-5836
Director, Policy Development & International Protection, Bruce Scoffield
613-957-5838
Director General, Renald Dussault
613-941-8989
Acting Director, Business Immigration, Michael Bockhoven
613-957-0001, Fax: 613-941-9014
Director, Economic Immigration Policy & Programs, Renald Gilbert
613-954-4214
Director, Immigration Levels Management, Pierre Coulombe
613-941-8996
Director, Social Policy & Programs, Johanne DesLauriers
613-957-5864
Director, Service Line Support, Leslie Toope
613-954-2156

Copyright Board of Canada / Commission du droit d'auteur du Canada

#800, 56 Sparks St., Ottawa, ON K1A 0C9
613-952-8621, Fax: 613-952-8630,
secretariat@cb-cda.gc.ca
www.cb-cda.gc.ca
The Board is an economic regulatory body empowered to establish, either mandatorily or at the request of an interested party, the royalties to be paid for the use of copyrighted works, when the administration of such copyright is entrusted to a collective-administration society. The Board also has the right to supervise agreements between users & licensing bodies & issues licences when the copyright owner cannot be located.

Chair, William J. Vancise
Vice-Chair & CEO, Claude Majeau
613-952-8625
Acting Secretary General, Gilles McDougall
613-952-8624, claude.majeau@cb-cda.gc.ca
General Counsel, Mario Bouchard
613-954-6470, mario.bouchard@cb-cda.gc.ca
Director, Research & Analysis, Vacant
613-946-4457, gilles.mcdougall@cb-cda.gc.ca

Office of the Correctional Investigator / L'Enquêteur correctionnel Canada

PO Box 3421 D, Ottawa, ON K1P 6L4
Fax: 613-990-9091, 877-885-8848
org@oci-bec.gc.ca
www.oci-bec.gc.ca

Investigates complaints from inmates in Canadian institutions. Reports on problems inmates have that fall within the responsibility of the Department of Public Safety & Emergency Preparedness & meet certain conditions.

Correctional Investigator, Howard Sapers
613-990-2689
Executive Director,Dr. Ivan Zinger
613-990-2690, mcisaaced@oci-bec.gc.ca

Correctional Service Canada (CSC) / Service correctionnel Canada

340 Laurier Ave. West, Ottawa, ON K1A 0P9
613-992-5891, Fax: 613-943-1630,
www.csc-scc.gc.ca

An agency within Public Safety & Emergency Preparedness Canada responsible for the administration of sentences with respect to convicted offenders sentenced to two or more years as decided by the federal courts, & certain provincial inmates who have been transferred to a federal institution.CSC is also responsible for the supervision of inmates who have been granted conditional release by the authority of the National Parole Board.

Acts Administered:
Corrections & Conditional Release Act
Criminal Code
Extradition Act
Old Age Security Act
Prisons & Reformatories Act
Transfer of Offenders Act

Commissioner, Don Head
613-995-5781, Fax: 613-943-1630
Senior Deputy Commissioner, Marc-Arthur Hyppolite
613-947-0643, Fax: 613-943-1630
Deputy Commissioner, Women, Elizabeth Van Allen
613-992-6067, Fax: 613-992-4692
Asst. Commissioner, Public Affairs & Parliamentary Relations, Lori MacDonald
613-995-6867, Fax: 613-947-0091
Asst. Commissioner, Corporate Services, Louise Saint-Laurent
613-996-4242, Fax: 613-992-8443,
Asst. Commissioner, Correctional Operations & Programs, Chris Price
613-943-0499
Asst. Commissioner, Policy & Research, Ian McCowan
613-996-2180, Fax: 613-995-3603
Asst. Commissioner, Health Services, Leslie MacLean
613-995-8023, Fax: 613-995-6277
Asst. Commissioner, Human Resource Management, Cheryl Fraser
613-947-1753
Director & General Counsel, Legal Services, Carole Johnson
613-992-9009, Fax: 613-995-9971
CEO, CORCAN, John Sargent
613-996-4530, Fax: 613-947-8875

Regional Headquarters:

Atlantic
#102, 1045 Main St., Moncton, NB E1C 1H1
Fax: 506-851-6316
Acting Deputy Commissioner, Simon Coakeley
506-851-6313

Ontario
440 King St. West, PO Box 1174, Kingston, ON K7L 4Y8
613-536-4527, Fax: 613-545-8684
Deputy Commissioner, Nancy Stableforth

Pacific
32560 Simon Ave., PO Box 4500, Abbotsford, BC V2T 5L7
604-870-2506, Fax: 604-870-2430
Deputy Commissioner, Don Demers

Prairies
2313 Hanselman Pl., PO Box 9223, Saskatoon, SK S7K 3X5
306-975-4850, Fax: 306-975-4435
Deputy Commissioner, Marc-Arthur Hyppolite

Québec
3, pl Laval, 2e étage, Laval, QC H7N 1A2
450-967-3333, Fax: 450-967-3326
Deputy Commissioner, Denis Méthé

District Offices:

BC Interior Area
#200, 175 - 2 Ave., Kamloops, BC V2C 5W1
250-851-4800, Fax: 250-851-4809
Acting Area Director, D. Lorrie Kelsey

Central Ontario
180 Dundas St. West, 2nd Fl., Toronto, ON M5G 1Z8
416-973-2393, Fax: 416-973-1779
District Director, Dave Pisapio

East & West Québec
#300, 222, rue St-Georges, Saint-Jérôme, QC J7Z 4Z9
450-432-3737, Fax: 450-432-3221
Acting District Director, Lise Bouthillier

Eastern & Northern Ontario
City Place II, 1473 John Counter St., Kingston, ON K7M 8Z6
613-545-8733, Fax: 613-545-8664
District Director, Derek Orr

Fraser Valley
32544 George Ferguson Way, Abbotsford, BC V2T 4Y1
604-870-2730, Fax: 604-870-2731
Area Director, Erwin Berg

Hamilton & Niagara
55 Bay St. North, 2nd Fl., Hamilton, ON L8R 3T7
905-308-8893, Fax: 905-308-8895
District Director, Marg Harlang

Manitoba/Northwestern Ontario
#102, 123 Main St., Winnipeg, MB R3C 1A3
204-983-4306, Fax: 204-983-5869
District Director, Don Kynoch

Montréal-Métropolitan
#917, Tour Ouest, 200, boul René-Lévesque ouest, Montréal, QC H2Z 1X4
514-283-1776, Fax: 514-283-1783
District Director, Marie-Andrée Cyrenne

New Brunswick & PEI
1 Factory Lane, 1st Fl., Moncton, NB E1C 9M3
506-851-6350, Fax: 506-851-3305,
Acting District Director, Lynn Chaplin

Newfoundland & Labrador
531 Charter Ave., St. John's, NL A1A 1P7
709-772-5359, Fax: 709-772-6415
District Director, Clara Rendell

Northern Alberta, NWT
9530 - 101 Ave., 2nd Fl., Edmonton, AB T5H 0B3
780-495-4900, Fax: 780-495-4975
District Director, Jan Fox

Ottawa
191 Gilmour St., Ottawa, ON K2P 0N8
613-996-7011, Fax: 613-954-1687
District Director, Ana Paquete

Nova Scotia
1888 Brunswick St., 7th Fl., Halifax, NS B3J 3J8
902-426-3408, Fax: 902-426-8000
District Director, Ron Lawlor

Nunavut
Bldg. 1043, PO Box 2349, Iqaluit, NU X0A 0H0
867-979-8892, Fax: 867-979-7441
Area Director, Nikki Smith

Saskatchewan
#601, 230 - 22 St. East, Saskatoon, SK S7K 0E9
306-975-6602, Fax: 306-975-6611
Acting District Director, Lynn McMurtry

Southern Alberta
#311, 510 - 12 Ave. SW, Calgary, AB T2R 0X5
403-292-5505, Fax: 403-292-5510
District Director, Tim Fullerton

Vancouver Area
#401, 877 Expo Blvd., Vancouver, BC V6B 1K9
604-666-8004, Fax: 604-666-2000
Area Director, Wayne Oster

Vancouver Island
#323, 816 Government St., Victoria, BC V8W 1W9
250-363-3267, Fax: 250-363-3269
District Director, Dave Keating

Western Ontario
#177, 255 Woodlawn Rd. West, Guelph, ON N1H 8J1
519-826-2139, Fax: 519-826-2143
District Director, Craig Townson

Defence Construction Canada (DCC) / Construction de Défense Canada (CDC)

Constitution Square, 350 Albert St., 19th Fl., Ottawa, ON K1A 0K3
613-998-9548, Fax: 613-998-1061, 800-514-3555
info@dcc-cdc.gc.ca
www.dcc-cdc.gc.ca

Federal government crown corporation responsible for the contracting & supervising of major military construction & maintenance projects required by National Defence. Services include construction, project management, environmental services & operational support services. DCC provides environmental science & environmental engineering services to help fulfill the Department of National Defence's sustainable development strategy, including: environmental impact & site assessment; environmental site remediation; environmental support for project & program management; sustainable development strategy support services; policy, compliance & advisory services; site decommissioning services; facility deconstruction & demolition; firing range decommissioning; waste management auditing & planning; waste reduction planning; landfill inventories & investigations; hazardous waste management; UST removals; training & education; ISO 14000 environmental management systems; environmental CIS applications; environmental checklists for property transactions & decommissioning; environmental monitoring & compliance auditing; designated substances inventories; environmental disclosures reporting; treatment & disposal facilities conceptual designs; environmental contrac ting & contract management; energy conservation. Projects include: the DEW (Distant Early Warning) Line cleanup, a dismantling of the DEW sites, scheduled for completion in 2012, & a major environmental project in the Canadian Arctic; green demolition at CFB Comox; biodiesel pilot program at 4 Wing Cold Lake, launched in 2005

President/CEO, James S. Paul
613-998-9541, Fax: 613-998-1218
Senior Vice-President, Operations, Ron de Vries, P.Eng
613-998-9543, Fax: 613-998-1218
Vice-President, Operations, Steve Irwin, P.Eng
613-949-7721, Fax: 613-998-1218
Vice-President, Operations, Randy McGee, P.Eng., GSC
613-949-0052, Fax: 613-998-1218
Vice-President, Corporate Services & CFO, Angelo Ottoni, C.A.
613-998-1001
Manager, Business Operations - Atlantic Region, George Theoharopoulos
902-426-4040, Fax: 902-426-9655
Manager, Environmental Services - Ontario, Dennis Katic
613-384-1256, Fax: 613-384-7747
Manager, Environmental Services - Québec, Alain Dufresne
514-283-8165, Fax: 514-496-6934
Manager, Environmental Services - Western Region, Sabrina Rock
780-495-3979, Fax: 780-495-5959
Executive Administrative Assistant, Claire Péladeau
613-991-3475, Fax: 613-998-1218

Environmental Protection Review Canada / Révision de la protection de l'environnement Canada

240 Sparks St., 1st Fl. West, Ottawa, ON K1A 1A1
613-995-7599, Fax: 613-992-4918,
eprc-rpec@eprc-rpec.gc.ca
www.eprc-rpec.gc.ca

Environmental Protection Review Canada is a group of expert adjudicators, entirely separate from Environment Canada, that conducts reviews of Environmental Protection Compliance Orders (EPCOs). Under the Canadian Environmental Protection Act, 1999 (CEPA, 1999), enforcement officers have the power to issue EPCOs to prevent a violation, to stop an on-going violation or to require that violations be corrected. Any person who has been issued an EPCO may ask for an independent review conducted by a Review Officer. Review Officers have the authority to confirm or cancel an EPCO. They may also amend, suspend, add or delete a term or condition of the Order. The decisions of Review Officers may be appealed to the Federal Court, Trial Division.

Chief Review Officer, Margot Priest
613-947-4060, Fax: 613-992-4918
Review Officer, Louis LaPierre
506-858-4152, Fax: 506-863-2000

Defence Research & Development Canada / Recherche et développement pour la défense Canada

305 Rideau St., Ottawa, ON K1A 0K2
613-992-7237,
info@drdc-rddc.gc.ca
www.drdc-rddc.gc.ca

Provides research & development both nationally & internationally by providing the Canadian Forces with relevant & timely technologies, while at the same time offering attractive collaborative opportunities to other government departments, the private sector, academia & international allies.

CEO,Dr. Robert Walker
613-996-2020
Director General, Science & Technology Operations, Richard Williams
613-992-5776
Director General, Corporate Services, Lesley Ullyet
613-992-6105
Director General, Research & Development Programs, Dr. Malcolm R. Vant
613-998-2303, Fax: 613-993-6095

Elections Canada / Élections Canada

The Jackson Bldg., 257 Slater St., Ottawa, ON K1A 0M6
613-993-2975, Fax: 613-954-8584, 800-463-6868
www.elections.ca

The Chief Electoral Officer of Canada is responsible for the conduct of federal elections & referendums in Canada & for ensuring that all provisions of the Canada Elections Act are complied with & enforced. Major activities include the maintenance of the National Register of Electors, the production of lists of electors, the training of returning officers, the revisions of polling division boundaries & the acquisition of election materials & supplies. Elections Canada is also responsible for the compilation & publishing of statutory & statistical reports, & the provision of advice & assistance to Parliament, as required. The agency also implements public education & information programs. As well, its mandate includes the registration of political parties & third parties engaged in election advertising, & the certification of statutory payments to be made to auditors, political parties, & candidates under the election expenses provisions of the Act. Following each decennial census, the Chief Electoral Officer must calculate the number of electoral districts to be assigned to each province according to rules contained in s. 51 of the Constitution Act, prepare population distribution maps for use by the ten electoral boundaires commission s (one per province) that are directly responsible for readjusting federal electroal boundaries & publish their reports.

Chief Electoral Officer, Marc Mayrand
613-993-5755, Fax: 613-993-5380
Deputy Chief Information Officer, Pierre LaFrance
613-993-4121, Fax: 613-990-3662
Commissioner, Canada Elections, William Corbett
613-998-4051, Fax: 613-990-4877
Acting CFO, Finance, Internal Audit and Administration, Brian Berry
613-998-8440, Fax: 613-993-8517
Deputy Chief Electoral Officer, Electoral Events, Rennie Molnar
613-949-3125, Fax: 613-954-2874
Acting Director, Outreach, Communications & Research, Marc Lamontagne
613-990-2979, Fax: 613-954-8584
Director/General Counsel, Electoral Affairs, Michèle René de Cotret
613-990-7239, Fax: 613-993-5880
Chief Information Officer, Information Technology, Stéphane Cousineau
613-991-2401
Director, Carol Séguin
613-993-3636, Fax: 613-990-7561
Asst. Director, Administration, Daniel Doré
613-998-0379, Fax: 613-991-1926
Asst. Director, Human Resources, Pierrette Lacroix
613-998-5262, Fax: 613-990-9791
Director, Claudine Renauld
613-990-1269, Fax: 613-954-8584
Asst. Director, Public Affairs, Marc Lamontagne
613-990-2979
Asst. Director, Communication Services, Francine Dulphond
613-998-1040
Asst. Director, Electronic Communications, Jean Richer
613-998-9817
Assoc. Director, Public Affairs, Robert Snyder
613-998-6528
Senior Director, Janice Vézina
613-990-3747, Fax: 613-990-2530
Chief Accounting Officer, Financial Operations, Josée Prud'homme
613-998-7728
Chief, Financial Operations, Michel Thibaudeau
613-990-8991
Asst. Director, Financial Planning, Analysis & Accounting Operations, Gilles Gauthier
613-990-9419, Fax: 613-990-2530
Training & ROPay Officer, Karen Levesque
613-991-1917, Fax: 613-990-1855
Director, Garry Saunders
613-991-2401
Asst. Director, Technical Services, Ronald Beaulne
613-998-0482
Assoc. Asst. Director, Project Development, Pat Owen
613-998-6927
Chief, Systems Integration, Chris Spiess
613-998-9956
Director, Luc Dumont
613-990-0464, Fax: 613-954-2874
Chief, Distribution Centre, Daniel Fournier
613-990-8045, Fax: 613-990-8189
Asst. Director, Electoral Coordination, Diane Bruyère
613-993-4988, Fax: 613-954-2874
Asst. Director, Local Office Systems, Jean Roussel
613-990-4249, Fax: 613-990-3068
Acting Asst. Director, Operation Support Services, Marc Douville
613-998-5656, Fax: 613-954-2874
Asst. Director, Training & Evaluation, Sylvie Patry
613-998-5682
Director, Rennie Molnar
613-990-0729, Fax: 613-990-7583
Assoc. Director, Electoral Geography, Maurice Bastarache
613-991-6182, Fax: 613-998-9961

Environment Canada (EC) / Environnement Canada

10 Wellington St., Gatineau, QC K1A 0H3
819-997-2800, Fax: 819-994-1412, 800-668-6767
enviroinfo@ec.gc.ca
www.ec.gc.ca

Other Communication: Environmental Emergencies (24-hour):|819/997-3742; TTY: 819/994-0736

Fosters a national capacity for sustainable development in cooperation with other governments, departments of government & the private sector that will result in a safe & healthy environment & a sound & prosperous economy by:undertaking & promoting programs to augment understanding of the environment; supporting environmentally responsible public & private decision-making; warning Canadians of risks to & from the environment; engaging Canadians as partners in measurably beneficial action to conserve, protect & restore the integrity of Canada's environment for the benefit of present & future generations.

Acts Administered:
Antarctic Environmental Protection Act
Canada Emission Reduction Incentives Agency Act
Canada Water Act
Canada Wildlife Act
Canadian Environment Week Act
Canadian Environmental Assessment Act
Canadian Environmental Protection Act
Department of the Environment Act
Greenhouse Gas Technology Investment Fund Act
International River Improvements Act
Lac Seul Conservation Act
Lake of the Woods Control Board Act
Manganese-Based Fuel Additives Act
Migratory Birds Convention Act
National Wildlife Week Act
Species at Risk Act, 2002
Weather Modification Information Act
Wild Animal & Plant Protection & Regulation of International & Interprovincial Trade Act
Acts Administered in Part by Environment Canada
Auditor General Act (Treasury Board)
Energy Supplies Emergency Act (National Research)
Fisheries Act (Fisheries & Oceans)
James Bay & Northern Québec Native Claims Settlement Act
Motor Vehicle Safety Act (Transport)
Resources & Technical Surveys Act (Natural Resources/Fisheries & Oceans)
Acts in which Environment Canada Provides Assistance
Arctic Waters Pollution Prevention Act
Canada Agricultural Products Act
Canada Shipping Act
Canada-Chile Free Trade Agreement Implementation Act (International Trade)
Canada-Newfoundland Atlantic Accord Implementation Act
Canada-Nova Scotia Offshore Petroleum Resources Accord Implementation Act
Emergency Preparedness Act (National Defence)
Hazardous Products Act (Health Canada)
International Boundary Waters Treaty Act (Foreign Affairs)
North American Free Trade Agreement Implementation Act
Nuclear Energy Act (Natural Resources)
Pest Control Products Act & Regulations (Health Canada)
Transportation of Dangerous Goods Act & Regulations (Transport Canada)
Environment Canada Related Acts & Regulations
Alternative Fuels Act & Regulations (Treasury Board)
Canada Marine Act (Transport Canada)
Canada Oil & Gas Operations Act (Indian & Northern Affairs/Natural Resources)
Canada Petroleum Resources Act (Indian Affairs & Northern Development/Natural Resouces)
Canadian Transportation Accident Investigation & Safety Board Act (Privy Council)
Food & Drugs Act (Agriculture & Agri-Foods/Health Canada)
Mackenzie Valley Resource Management Act (Indian & Northern Affairs)
National Energy Board Act (Natural Resources/Transport Canada)
National Round Table on the Environment & the Economy Act (Prime Minister)
Northern Pipeline Act (Natural Resources)
Oceans Act (Fisheries & Oceans)

Minister, Environment,Hon. Jim Prentice
819-997-1441, Fax: 819-953-0279,Prentice.J@parl.gc.ca; Jim.Prentice@ec.gc.ca
Parliamentary Secretary to the Minister of the Environment, Mark Warawa
613-992-1157, Fax: 613-943-1823,warawm7@parl.gc.ca
Deputy Minister, Ian Shugart
819-997-4203, Fax: 819-953-6897
Associate Deputy Minister, Bob Hamilton
819-953-2832
Assistant Deputy Minister, Human Resources, Lynette Cox
819-997-1847, Fax: 819-953-2757
Director General, Audit & Evaluation, Carol Najm
819-953-4736
Director General, Communications Branch, Charles Slowey
819-997-6820, Fax: 819-953-1599
Director General, Corporate Secretariat, Pierre Bernier
819-953-2743, Fax: 819-953-0749
Chief Enforcement Officer, Albin Tremblay
819-997-2019, Fax: 819-997-0086
Chief Information Officer, Chuck Shawcross
819-994-3634, Fax: 819-934-7975

Environmental Stewardship Branch / Direction générale de l'intendance environnementale

351 boul St-Joseph, Gatineau, QC K1A 0H3
819-997-1575, Fax: 819-953-9452

Assessment & management of risk associated with domestic & international sources of pollution. The range of activity is broad, assessment of substances & practices that pose a risk to the environment, development & implementation of environmental protection measures including pollution prevention, regulations, permits & technology advancement & ensuring compliance with federal pollution & wildlife laws. These activities lead to improvements in environmental quality which helps to support the health of Canadians & their economic security.

Acting Asst. Deputy Minister, Cynthia Wright
819-953-1711, Fax: 819-953-9452
Acting Assoc. Asst. Deputy Minister, Mike Beale
819-956-9500
Director General, Canadian Wildlife Service, Virginia Poter
819-994-1360, Fax: 819-953-7177
Director General, Climate Change International, John Moffet
819-953-6830, Fax: 819-953-9333
Director General, Energy & Transportation, Steve McCauley
819-997-1298, Fax: 819-953-9547
Director General, Environmental Protection Operations, Sue Milburn-Hopwood
819-934-5666, Fax: 819-934-6531
Chief, GHG Reporting Section, Lo Chiang Cheng
819-994-6143, Fax: 819-953-3006
Director, Greenhouse Gas Division, Art Jaques
819-994-3098, Fax: 819-953-3006
Executive Director, Habitat & Ecosystem Conservation, Robert McLean
819-997-1303, Fax: 819-994-4445
Executive Director, Outreach, Pat Dolan
819-953-4950, Fax: 819-953-9748
Director General, Public and Resources Sectors, Randa Meades
819-934-4205
Asst. Deputy Minister, Lynette Cox
819-997-1847, Fax: 819-953-2757
Director General, National HR Services, Donna Richard
819-934-7215, Fax: 819-953-2675

Acting Director General, Performance Measurement & Monitoring Business Systems, Donald Bilodeau
819-994-0201
Director General, Strategic Planning & Corporate Programs, Deirdre Keane
819-953-0432, Fax: 819-953-6963
Asst. Deputy Minister & Chief Information Officer, Chuck Shawcross
819-994-3634, Fax: 819-934-7975
Director General, Business Applications & Solutions Directorate, Denis Benoit
819-934-1523
Director General, Infrastructure Operations Directorate, Connie MacDonald
819-953-1162, Fax: 819-994-4224
Director General, Major Projects & Supercomputing Directorate, Mike Minuk
514-421-4765, Fax: 514-421-4703
Acting Director, MSC Regional Operations, Lina Assad
819-997-8810, Fax: 819-953-4509

Finance & Corporate Branch / Finances et services corporatifs
819-953-7026, Fax: 819-953-4064
Asst. Deputy Minister & Chief Financial Officer, Basia Ruta
Director General, Assets, Contracting & Environmental Management, Karen Anderson
819-997-2991, Fax: 819-997-1781
Director General, Corporate Management, David Henley
819-953-4171, Fax: 819-953-3388
Director General, Finance Directorate, Robert D'Aoust
819-953-5471, Fax: 819-953-2459
Director General, Integrated Enterprise Services, Randy Larkin
819-953-9569, Fax: 819-953-4064

International Affairs / Direction générale des affaires internationales
819-997-4882, Fax: 819-953-5981
Asst. Deputy Minister, David McGovern
819-934-6020
Director General, Americas, Dean Knudson
819-994-1670, Fax: 819-997-0199
Director General, Climate Change International, John Moffet
819-953-6830, Fax: 819-953-9333
Director General, Multilateral & Bilateral Affairs, France Jacovella
819-956-5263, Fax: 819-994-6227
Executive Director, Strategic Engagement, Darren Goetze
819-953-9525, Fax: 819-953-9333

Meteorological Service of Canada (MSC) / Le service météorologique du Canada
4905 Dufferin St., Toronto, ON M3H 5T4
416-739-4770, Fax: 416-739-4232,
www.msc-smc.ec.gc.ca/index_e.cfm

Other Communication: Weather Office:
weatheroffice.ec.gc.ca/canada_e.html
The Meteorological Service of Canada monitors water quantities, provides information & conducts research on climate, atmospheric science, air quality, ice & other environmental issues.
Asst. Deputy Minister, David Grimes
613-943-5585, Fax: 613-943-5737
Director General, Business Policy, Danielle Lacasse
613-943-5532, Fax: 613-995-0389
Director General, Weather & Environmental Operations, Angèle Simard
514-421-4601
Director General, Weather & Environmental Monitoring, Jim Abraham
416-739-4965, Fax: 416-739-4261
Director General, Weather & Environmental Prediction & Services, Diane E. Campbell
613-947-9200, Fax: 613-943-6440
Coordinator, GEOSS Interdepartmental Secretariat, Kenneth D. Korporal
613-995-2466, Fax: 613-947-1261

Science & Technology Branch / Direction générale des sciences et de la technologie
819-994-4751, Fax: 819-997-1541
Asst. Deputy Minister, Brian Gray
819-934-6851
Director General, Atmospheric Science & Technology, Charles A. Lin
416-739-4995, Fax: 416-739-4265
Acting Director General, Science & Risk Assessment, George Enei
819-997-4977, Fax: 819-953-5371
Director General, Science & Technology Strategies,Dr. Javier A. Gracia-Garza
819-953-3090, Fax: 819-953-9029
Director General, Water Science & Technology,Dr. John H. Carey
905-336-4625
Director General, Wildlife & Landscape Science, Dan Wicklum
613-998-0329

Strategic Policy / Direction générale de la politique stratégique
819-953-4818, Fax: 819-953-5981
Asst. Deputy Minister, Michael Keenan
819-953-4818
Director General, Economic Analysis Directorate, Tony Young
819-953-7624, Fax: 819-953-5916
Director General, Strategic Information & Integration, Brenda McKelvey
819-934-6028, Fax: 819-994-8864
Director General, Strategic Policy Directorate, Lawrence Hanson
819-934-4149, Fax: 819-953-4679

Environment Canada Regional Directors General:

Atlantic
Queen Sq., 45 Alderney Dr., Dartmouth, NS B2Y 2N6
902-426-7231, Fax: 902-426-6348,
15th.reception@ec.gc.ca
Regional Director General, Daniel Lebel
902-426-6700, Fax: 902-426-5168,

Pacific & Yukon
401 Burrard St., Vancouver, BC V6C 3S5
604-664-9100, Fax: 604-713-9517,
greenlane.pyr@ec.gc.ca
Regional Director General, Paul Kluckner
604-664-9145, Fax: 604-664-9190

Ontario
4905 Dufferin St., Toronto, ON M3H 5T4
416-739-4826, Fax: 416-739-4776,
EnviroInfo.Ontario@ec.gc.ca
Regional Director General, Jim Vollmershausen
416-739-4666, Fax: 416-739-4691

Prairie & Northern
#200, 4999 - 98 Ave., Edmonton, AB T6B 2X3
780-951-8600, Fax: 780-495-2615
Regional Director General, Randal Cripps
780-951-8869, Fax: 780-495-3086

Québec
1141, rte de l'Église, 6e étage, CP 10100, Québec, QC G1V 4H5
Fax: 418-648-4613, 800-463-4311
quebec.lavoieverte@ec.gc.ca
Regional Director General, Philippe Morel
418-648-4077, Fax: 418-649-6213

Associates Agencies, Boards & Commissions:
Director General, Virginia Poter
819-994-1360, Fax: 819-953-7177
Executive Director, Habitat & Ecosystem Conservation, Robert McLean
819-997-1303, Fax: 819-994-4445
Director, Conservation Service Delivery & Permitting, Mary Taylor
819-953-9097, Fax: 819-953-6283
Director, Population Conservation & Management, Basile van Havre
819-997-2957, Fax: 819-964-3684
Director General, Gord Owen
819-998-1298, Fax: 819-953-9029
Director, Domestic Clean Air Program Operations, Vincenza Galatone
819-934-4533
Director, Electricity & Industrial Combustion, Shannon Glenn
819-956-5560
Director, Oil, Gas & Energy, Helen Ryan
819-997-1221
Director, Transboundary Air Issues, Peggy Farnsworth
819-994-9535
Director, Transportation, Steve McCauley
819-994-3706
Acting Director General, Peter Blackall
780-951-8862
Acting Director, Compliance Promotion & Operations, René Drolet
819-994-0738
Director, Environmental Assessment Program, Diane Campbell
819-953-1690
Director, Environmental Emergencies, Tom Foote
819-953-0607
Acting Director General, Mike Beale
819-996-1521, Fax: 819-995-3663
Director, GHG Operations, Louise Métivier
613-947-6602
Acting Director, Mining & Manufacturing, Carmelita Olivotto
613-995-4643
Manager, Energy, Geoff Browning
613-943-1695
Acting Director General, Robert McLean
819-997-1303
Director, Biodiversity Convention Office, John Karau
819-953-9669
Director, Sustainable Water Management, Kate Moir
819-953-1101
Director General, Suzanne Matheson
913-993-6730
Director, Offset Credit System Management, Dominic Demers
613-949-5530
Director, Quantification Methodologies & Protocol, Jane Owen
613-949-1290
Director, Regional Operations & Coordination, Judith Hull
613-949-1294
Director General, Anne O'Toole
819-934-4205
Director, Natural Resources, Caroline Ladanowski
819-994-4705
Director, Public Sector, Sheila Gariepy
819-994-3503
Director, Waste Management, France Jacovella
819-953-5263
Director, National Office of Pollution Prevention, James Riordan
819-953-3353, Fax: 819-953-7970,james.riordan@ec.gc.ca
Director General, Jim Abraham
Director, Atmospheric Monitoring, Dave Wartman
416-739-4121
Acting Director, Data Analysis & Archives, Diane C. Johnston
416-739-4128
Acting Director, Hydrometric Monitoring, Al Pietroniro
306-975-4394
Director General, Diane E. Campbell
613-947-9200, Fax: 613-943-6440
Director, National Service Operations, Bill Appleby
613-943-5788, Fax: 613-943-6440
Director, National Prediction Operations, Richard Hogue
514-421-4622, Fax: 514-421-4679
Acting Director, Aviation & Defence Services, Abdoulaye Harou
613-992-3917, Fax: 613-992-4288
Director General, Michel Béland
514-421-4771
Director, Adaptation & Impacts Research, Don McIver
416-739-4271
Director, Air Quality Research, Keith Puckett
416-739-4836
Director, Climate Research,Dr. Doug Whelpdale
416-739-4869
Acting Director, Prediction Development, Louis Lefaivre
514-421-4654
Director General, John Arseneau
819-953-1114, Fax: 819-953-5371
Director, Existing Substances, George Enei
819-997-4977
Director, Greenhouse Gas Division, Art Jaques
819-994-3098,
Acting Director, New Substances, Bernard Madé
819-997-4336
Director, Pollution Data, Alain Chung
819-994-3127
Acting Director General, Alex Bielak
905-336-4503
Director, Science Policy & Priorities, Phillip Enros
819-994-5434
Acting Director, Science & Technology Liaison, Karl Schaefer
905-336-4884
Director, Technology Strategies, Shirley Anne Scharf
819-953-9364, Fax: 819-997-8427
Director General,Dr. J.H. Carey
905-336-4625
Director, Aquatic Ecosystem Impacts Research, Fred J. Wrona
250-472-5134
Director, Aquatic Ecosystem Management Research, John Lawrence
905-336-4913
Director, Aquatic Ecosystem Protection Research, Jim Maguire
905-336-4927
Director, Water Quality Monitoring & Surveillance, Jacinthe Leclerc
514-283-5869, Fax: 514-283-1719
Acting Director General, Kevin Cash
306-975-4676
Acting Director, Wildlife Research, Robert Clark
613-306-9754
Acting Director, Wildlife Toxicology, Keith Marshall
613-998-0450

Commission for Environmental Cooperation (CEC) / Commission coopération environnementale

Secretariat, #200, 393, rue St-Jacques ouest, Montréal, QC H2Y 1N9
514-350-4300, Fax: 514-350-4314, info@cec.org
www.cec.org

The Commission for Environmental Cooperation (CEC) is an international organization created by Canada, Mexico & the United States under the North American Agreement on Environmental Cooperation (NAAEC). The CEC was established to address regional environmental concerns, help prevent potential trade & environmental conflicts & to promote the effective enforcement of environmental law. The Agreement complements the environmental provisions of the North American Free Trade Agreement (NAFTA).

Executive Director, Evan Lloyd
514-350-4318, mvulpescu@cec.org
Legal Officer, Submission on Enforcement Matters Unit, Marcelle Marion
514-350-4337, mmarion@cec.org
Legal Officer, Submission on Enforcement Matters Unit, Paolo Solano
514-350-4321, psolano@cec.org
Program Manager, Air Quality, Orlando Cabrera-Rivera
514-350-4323, ocabrera@cec.org
Program Manager, Biodiversity, Thomas Hammond
514-350-4336, thammond@cec.org
Program Manager, Environmental Information, Karen Richardson
514-350-4326, krichardson@cec.org
Program Manager, Environmental Law, Marco Antonio Heredia Fragoso
514-350-4302, maheredia@cec.org
Council Secretary, Nathalie Daoust
514-350-4310, ndaoust@cec.org

Export Development Canada (EDC) / Exportation et développement Canada (SEE)

151 O'Connor St., Ottawa, ON K1A 1K3
613-598-2500, Fax: 613-598-3811, 800-267-8510
www.edc.ca

A financial services corporation assisting Canadian business to succeed in foreign markets. EDC provides a wide range of financial solutions to exporters across Canada & their customers around the world. The corporation's risk management services include: export-credit insurance protecting exporters against losses due to non-payment relating to commercial & political risks; & flexible medium- or long-term financing & guarantees. As a financially self-sustaining Crown corporation, EDC operates on commercial principles, charging fees & premiums for its products & interest on its loans. EDC is governed by a board of directors composed of representatives from both the private & public sectors, & reports to Parliament through the minister for international trade. An Environmental Review Directive is used to assess the environmental impacts of projects EDC is asked to support. EDC pursues an international multilateral consensus on environmental review practices so that all exporters are subject to the same rules. EDC has adopted & implemented the OECD Recommendation on Common Approaches on Environment & Officially Supported Export Credits. EDC has signed the UNEP Statement of Financial Institutions. Through the EnviroExport initiative, EDC helps Canadia n environmental exporters succeed internationally through financing products. Where EDC is considering providing financing support, political risk insurance or equity to the sponsor of a Category A project under the Environmental Review Directive, EDC will seek consent to inform the public on its website that it is considering support to such a project. The Chief Environmental Advisor's annual report for 2005 reported that 20 project-related transactions were assessed as meeting the ERD's criteria, & EDC facilitated $1.24 billion in exports of environmental goods & services with 283 Canadian companies

President/CEO, Eric D. Siegel
Senior Vice-President, Business Development, Benoit Daignault
Senior Vice-President, Human Resources, Susanne Laperle
Senior Vice-President, Business Solutions & Technology, Sherry Noble
Senior Vice-President, Financing, Stephen Poloz
Senior Vice-President, Insurance, Pierre Gignac
Senior Vice-President, Legal Services & Secretary, Jim McArdle
Senior Vice-President/CFO, Finance, Ken Kember
Media Contact, Phil Taylor
613-598-2904, ptaylor@edc.ca

EDC Regional Offices:

Calgary
Home Oil Tower, #606, 3240 - 8 Ave. SW, Calgary, AB T2P 2Z2
403-537-9800, Fax: 403-537-9811

Edmonton
#1000, 10810 - 101 St., Edmonton, AB T5J 3S4
780-702-5233, Fax: 780-702-5235

Halifax
Purdy's Wharf Tower II, #1605, 1969 Upper Water St., Halifax, NS B3J 3R7
902-442-5205, Fax: 902-442-5204

London
#1512, 148 Fullarton St., London, ON N6A 5P3
519-963-5400, Fax: 519-963-5407

Moncton
#400, 735 Main St., Moncton, NB E1C 1E5
506-851-6066, Fax: 506-851-6406,

Montréal
Tour de la Bourse, #4520, 800, Victoria Square, CP 124, Montréal, QC H4Z 1C3
514-908-9200, Fax: 514-878-9891

Québec
#1340, 2875, boul Laurier, Québec, QC G1V 2M2
418-266-6130, Fax: 418-266-6131

St. John's
90 O'Leary Ave., St. John's, NL A1B 2C7
709-772-8808, Fax: 709-772-8693

Toronto
#810, 150 York St., PO Box 810, Toronto, ON M5H 3S5
416-640-7600, Fax: 416-862-1267

Vancouver
#1030, 505 Burrard St., PO Box 58, Vancouver, BC V7X 1M5
604-638-6950, Fax: 604-638-6955

Winnipeg
Commodity Exchange Tower, #2075, 360 Main St., Winnipeg, MB R3C 3Z3
204-975-5090, Fax: 204-975-5094

Farm Credit Canada / Financement agricole Canada

1800 Hamilton St., PO Box 4320, Regina, SK S4P 4L3
306-780-8100, Fax: 306-780-8919, 888-332-3301
csc@fcc-fac.ca
www.fcc-fac.com

Federal Crown corporation reporting to Parliament through the Minister of Agriculture & Agri-Food. Under the Farm Credit Canada Act FCC offers financing to primary producers & agribusiness through 100 offices in rural communities across Canada.

President/CEO, Greg Stewart, P.Ag.
Executive Vice-President/CFO, Moyez Somani, CMA, MBA, FCMA
Executive Vice-President/COO, Operations, Dan Bergen, P.Ag.
Senior Vice-President, Marketing, Lyndon Carlson, P.Ag.
Senior Vice-President, Strategy, Knowledge & Reputation, Kellie Garrett, ABC, MA
Senior Vice-President, Human Resources, Greg Honey
Senior Vice-President, Portfolio and Credit Risk, Rémi Lemoine, MBA, FCI
Senior Vice-President/CIO, Paul MacDonald

Office of the Commissioner for Federal Judicial Affairs / Bureau du Commissaire à la magistrature fédérale

99 Metcalfe St., 8th Fl., Ottawa, ON K1A 1E3
613-995-5140, Fax: 613-995-5615, 877-583-4266
info@fja.gc.ca
www.fja.gc.ca

Commissioner, Claude Provencher
613-992-9175, Fax: 613-995-5615
Deputy Commissioner, Marc A. Giroux
613-995-7438, mgiroux@cmf.gc.ca
Executive Editor, Federal Court Reports, Patricia Pritchard
613-992-2899, ppritchard@fja.gc.ca
Executive Director, Judicial Appointments Secretariat, Margaret-Rose Jamieson
613-992-9400, mjamieson@fja.gc.ca
Chief, Administrative Services, Anne Barnabé
613-995-2310

Finance Canada / Finances Canada

L'esplanade Laurier, 140 O'Connor St., Ottawa, ON K1A 0G5
613-992-1573, Fax: 613-943-0938,
finpub@fin.gc.ca
www.fin.gc.ca

Other Communication: Library Services: 613-995-5877; Human Resources: 613-992-1105

The Department of Finance Canada is responsible for providing the federal government with analysis & advice on financial & economic issues. It also monitors & researches the performance of the Canadian economy's major factors (output, growth, employment, income, price stability, monetary policy, & long-term change). Interacting with various other federal departments & agencies, the Department encourages coordination in all federal initiatives with an impact on the economy. Emphasis is placed on consulting with the public regarding policy directions & options.

Acts Administered:
Bank Act
Bank of Canada Act
Banks & Banking Law Revision Act
Bills of Exchange Act
Bretton Woods & Related Agreements Act
Canada Deposit Insurance Corporation Act
Canada Development Corporation Reorganization Act
Canada Mortgage & Housing Corporation Act
Canada-Newfoundland Atlantic Accord Implementation Act
Canada Pension Plan Act
Canadian International Trade Tribunal Act
Canadian National Railways Capital Revision Act
Canadian National Railways Refunding Act
Canadian National Steamship (West Indies Service) Act
Co-operative Credit Association Act
Currency Act
Customs & Excise Offshore Application Act
Customs Tariff, Debt Servicing & Reduction Account Act
Diplomatic Service (Special) Superannuation Act
Excise Tax Act
Export Credit Insurance Act
Federal Provincial Fiscal Arrangements & Federal Post-Secondary Education & Health Contributions Act
Financial Administration Act
Garnishment Attachment & Pension Diversion Act
Governor General's Retiring Annuity Act
Halifax Relief Commission Pension Continuation Act
Income Tax Act
Income Tax Conventions Interpretation Act
Insurance Companies Canadian & British Act
Insurance Companies Foreign Act
Interest Act
International Development (Financial Institutions) Assistance Act
Investment Companies Act
Loan Companies Act
Members of Parliament Retiring Allowances Act
Newfoundland Additional Finance Assistance Act
Nova Scotia Offshore Retail Sales Tax Act
Office of the Superintendent of Financial Institutions Act
Pension Benefits Standards Act
Prince Edward Island Subsidy Act
Provincial Subsidies Act
Public Service Superannuation Act
Québec Savings Bank Act
Residential Mortgage Financing Act
Small Business Loans Act
Special Import Measures Act
Tax Rental Agreements Act
Trust & Loans Companies Act
Winding Up Act

Minister, Finance,Hon. James Michael (Jim) Flaherty, B.A., LL.B.
613-992-6344, Fax: 513-992-8320,FlaheJ@parl.gc.ca; jflaherty@fin.gc.ca
Deputy Minister, Michael Horgan
613-992-4925, Fax: 613-952-9569
Associate Deputy Minister & G-7 Deputy for Canada, Tiff Macklem
613-943-2314, Fax: 613-952-9569
Associate Deputy Minister, Stephen Richardson
613-996-1963
Assistant Deputy Minister, Denis Gauthier
613-992-1527, Fax: 613-992-0387

- Auditor General of Canada/ Vérificateur Général du Canada
- Bank of Canada/ Banque du Canada
- Canada Deposit Insurance Corporation/ Société d'assurance-dépôts du Canada
- Canada Investment & Savings(CI&S) / Placements Épargne Canada (PEC)
#900, 110 Yonge St.
Toronto, ON M5C 1T4
416-952-1252 Fax: 416-952-1270 800-575-5151
csb@csb.gc.ca
www.csb.gc.ca

• Canada Revenue Agency
• Financial Consumer Agency of Canada/ Agence de la consommation en matière financière du Canada
• Financial Transactions & Reports Analysis Centre of Canada(FINTRAC) / Centre d'analyse des opérations et déclarations financières du Canada (CANAFE)
234 Laurier Ave. West, 24th Fl.
Ottawa, ON K1P 1H7
Fax: 613-943-7931 866-346-8722
guidelines-lignesdirectrices@fintrac-canafe.gc.ca
www.fintrac.gc.ca
Created in 2000, FINTRAC is Canada's financial intelligence unit, a specialized agency created to collect, analyze & disclose financial information & intelligence on suspected money laundering & terrorist activities financing.
• Office of the Superintendent of Financial Institutions/ Bureau du surintendant des institutions financières Canada

Consultations & Communications Branch / Direction des consultations et des communications
East Tower, 140 O'Connor St., 19th Fl., Ottawa, ON K1A 0G5
613-992-1573,
consltcomm@fin.gc.ca

General Director, Jean-Michel Catta
613-992-1369, Fax: 613-943-0938
Director, Communications Policy & Strategy, Lucian Blair
613-992-9195
Director, Public Affairs & Operations, David Gamble
613-992-7763

Corporate Services Branch / Direction des services ministériels
Provides joint services for the federal Treasury Board Secretariat & Finance Canada.
Asst. Deputy Minister, Linda Gobeil
613-995-8487, Fax: 613-952-3009
Executive Director/CIO, Information Management & Technology, Robert Aubé
613-996-0313, Fax: 613-943-2077
Executive Director, Human Resources Division, Edward Poznanski
613-992-1105, Fax: 613-943-2807

Tax Policy Branch / Direction de la politique de l'impôt
Asst. Deputy Minister, Clément Gignac
613-996-9903, Fax: 613-952-9569,
Director, Business Income Tax Division, Geoff Trueman
613-992-1008, Fax: 613-943-2486
Director, Tax Policy Evaluation & Research, Paul Berg-Dick
613-992-6846, Fax: 613-947-1677
Director, Sales Tax Division, Lise Potvin
613-992-6298, Fax: 613-995-8970
Director, Tax Legislation Division, Brian Ernewein
613-992-3045, Fax: 613-996-0660
Senior Chief, Personal Income Tax, Sean Keenan
613-992-6729, Fax: 613-943-5597

Financial Consumer Agency of Canada (FCAC) / Agence de la consommation en matière financière du Canada (ACFC)

427 Laurier Ave. West, 6th Fl., Ottawa, ON K1R 1B9
Fax: 613-941-1436,
info@fcac-acfc.gc.ca
www.fcac-acfc.gc.ca

Other Communication: TollFree: 1-866-461-FCAC (3222) for services in English; 1-866-461-ACFC (2232) for services in French

Created by Parliament in 2001, the Financial Consumer Agency of Canada (FCAC) exists to protect Canada's financial consumers; to make them aware oftheir rights & responsibilities; & to inform Canadians about the financial products & services available to them. The FCAC ensures that the nearly 500 federally regulated financial institutions respect the consumer provisions in the laws that govern them & monitors the voluntary codes of conduct financial institutions have adopted. As well as informing people about their rights as financial consumers, the FCAC provides user-friendly information & easy-to-use tools to help consumers shop around for the best financial product/service for their situation.

Acts Administered:
Bank Act
Co-operative Credit Associations Act
Financial Consumer Agency of Canada Act
Insurance Companies Act
Trust & Loan Companies Act

Commissioner, Ursula Menke
613-941-4300
Deputy Commissioner, Lucie Tedesco
613-941-4335
Director, Financial Literacy & Consumer Education, Jane Rooney
613-941-1528
Senior Counsel, Legal Services, Joseph de Pencier
613-941-1425
Team Leader, Consumer Education, Roger Dowdall
613-941-1527

Office of the Superintendent of Financial Institutions (OSFI) / Bureau du surintendant des institutions financières Canada

Kent Square, 255 Albert St., Ottawa, ON K1A 0H2
613-990-7788, Fax: 613-990-5591, 800-385-8647
information@osfi-bsif.gc.ca
www.osfi-bsif.gc.ca

Responsible for regulating & supervising financial institutions & pension plans under federal jurisdiction. Included under federal jurisdiction are: banks, some insurance companies, trust companies, loan companies, cooperative credit associations, & fraternal benefit societies. OSFI monitors & examines these institutions & pension plans for solvency, liquidity, & compliance with legislation, regulations & Office guidelines. Provides actuarial services & advice to the Government of Canada. Reports to government through the Minister of Finance.

Superintendent, Julie Dickson
613-990-3667, Fax:
613-993-6782,julie.dickson@osfi-bsif.gc.ca
Director, Security Services, Raymond Bullard
613-990-7781, Fax:
613-990-0081,raymond.bullard@osfi-bsif.gc.ca
Communications Officer, Christina Stefanski
613-949-8941, Fax:
613-660-5591,christina.stefanski@osfi-bsif.gc.ca

Audit & Consulting Services / Services de vérification et de consultation
Fax: 416-954-3169

Senior Director, Joanne Bagnall
416-973-8935, Fax:
416-954-3169,joanne.bagnall@osfi-bsif.gc.ca

Corporate Services Sector / Secteur des services intégrés
Fax: 613-949-3968,
Other Communication: Alt. Fax: 613-993-6782

Asst. Superintendent, Coleen Volk
613-990-7491, Fax:
613-954-6477,coleen.volk@osfi-bsif.gc.ca
Director, Communications & Public Affairs Division, Margaret Pearcy
613-993-0577, Fax:
613-990-5591,margaret.pearcy@osfi-bsif.gc.ca
Managing Director, Finance & Corporate Planning, Michele Bridges
613-991-4607, Fax:
613-990-6328,michele.bridges@osfi-bsif.gc.ca
Senior Director, Human Resources & Administration, Gary Walker
613-990-8761, Fax:
613-949-3968,gary.walker@osfi-bsif.gc.ca
Senior Director, Projects & IM/IT Services, Gordon J. Dunn
416-954-2141, Fax:
416-952-1663,gordon.dunn@osfi-bsif.gc.ca
Director, Human Resources & Administration, Denis L. Leroux
613-990-7774, Fax:
613-990-9017,denis.leroux@osfi-bsif.gc.ca
Manager, Regulatory Information Division, Debbie Smith
613-990-3591, Fax:
613-991-6248,debbie.smith@osfi-bsif.gc.ca

Office of the Chief Actuary / Bureau de l'actuaire en chef
Fax: 613-990-9900

Chief Actuary, Jean-Claude Ménard
613-990-7577, Fax:
613-990-9900,jean-claude.menard@osfi-bsif.gc.c

Regulation Sector / Secteur de la réglementation
Fax: 613-993-6525

Asst. Superintendent, Robert J. Hanna
613-990-7278, Fax: 613-993-6525,bob.hanna@osfi-bsif.gc.ca
Senior Director, Actuarial, Stuart Wason
416-973-2056, Fax:
416-952-0664,stuart.wason@osfi-bsif.gc.ca
Managing Director, Capital, Gilbert Ménard
613-990-8081, Fax:
613-991-6822,gilbert.menard@osfi-bsif.gc.ca
Senior Director, Compliance, Nicolas Burbridge
416-973-6117, Fax:
416-954-3169,nicolas.burbridge@osfi-bsif.gc.ca
Senior Director, Legislation & Approvals, Patricia A. Evanoff
613-990-9004, Fax:
613-998-6716,patty.evanoff@osfi-bsif.gc.ca
Managing Director, International Advisory Group, Arvind Baghel
416-973-6758, Fax:
416-952-1662,arvind.baghel@osfi-bsif.gc.ca
Managing Director, Accounting Policy, Karen F. Stothers
416-973-0744, Fax:
416-952-1662,karen.stothers@osfi-bsif.gc.ca
Director, Research, Gerald Goldstein
613-990-8911, Fax:
613-991-6822,gerald.goldstein@osfi-bsif.gc.ca
General Counsel, Legal Services, Alain Prévost
613-990-7787, Fax:
613-952-5031,alain.prevost@osfi-bsif.gc.ca

Supervision Sector / Secteur de la surveillance
Other Communication: Toronto Fax: 416/973-1168; Ottawa Fax: 613/993-6782

Asst. Superintendent, Ted F. Price
416-973-4385, Fax: 416-973-1168,ted.price@osfi-bsif.gc.ca
Senior Director, Financial Conglomerate Group, Kent D. Andrews
416-952-1469, Fax:
416-973-8994,kent.andrews@osfi-bsif.gc.ca
Senior Director, Financial Institutions Group, Karen Badgerow-Croteau
416-952-3909, Fax:
416-954-5015,karen.badgerow-croteau@osfi-bsif.gc.ca
Senior Director, Regulatory & Supervisory Practices Division, Bruce J. Rutherford
416-973-4378, Fax:
416-973-8994,bruce.rutherford@osfi-bsif.gc.ca,
Managing Director, Financial Institution Group, Penny M. Lee
416-952-0557, Fax: 416-954-6478,penny.lee@osfi-bsif.gc.ca
Managing Director, Operational Risk & Capital Assessment Services, Abhilash D. Bhachech
416-973-6654, Fax:
416-952-1663,abhilash.bhachech@osfi-bsif.gc.ca
Managing Director, Strategic Initiatives, Pamela H. Hopkins
416-973-6657, Fax:
416-973-1168,pamela.hopkins@osfi-bsif.gc.ca
Director, Supervision, Maria Moutafis
416-973-3699, Fax:
416-954-3167,maria.moutafis@osfi-bsif.gc.ca
Managing Director, Capital Markets/Risk Assessment, Chris R. Elgar
416-952-0555, Fax: 416-952-1663,chris.elgar@osfi-bsif.gc.ca

Fisheries & Oceans Canada (DFO) / Pêches et Océans Canada (MPO)

200 Kent St., Ottawa, ON K1A 0E6
613-993-0999, Fax: 613-996-1866,
info@dfo-mpo.gc.ca
www.dfo-mpo.gc.ca

The Department of Fisheries & Oceans (DFO), on behalf of the Government of Canada, is responsible for policies & programs in support of Canada's economic, ecological & scientific interests in the oceans & freshwater fish habitat; for the conservation & sustainable utilization of Canada's fisheries resources in marine & inland waters; & for safe, effective & environmentally soundmarine services responsive to the needs of Canadians in a global economy. The Department's mandate is extremely broad & covers management & protection of the marine & fisheries resources inside the 200-mile exclusive economic zone; management & protection of freshwater fisheries resources; marine safety along the world's longest coastline; facilitation of marine transportation; protection of the marine environment; support to other federal government institutions & objectives, as the government's civilian marine service; & research to support government priorities such as climate change & biodiversity. Because of its broad mandate, DFO does not operate alone. Federal & provincial governments share jurisdiction in a number of areas related to the Department's mandate. A $28-million investment over two years for the first phase of the Oceans Action Plan was announced in Feb ruary, 2005. The Plan is designed to develop ocean resources while protecting marine ecosystems, through sustainable development, integrated management plans, & marine protected areas.

Acts Administered:
Atlantic Fisheries Restructuring Act
Canada Shipping Act
Coastal Fisheries Protection Act
Department of Fisheries & Oceans Act
Fisheries Act
Fisheries Development Act
Fisheries Improvement Loans Act
Fishing & Recreational Harbours Act
Freshwater Fish Marketing Act
Great Lakes Fisheries Convention Act
Navigable Waters Protection Act
Oceans Act
Species at Risk Act

Minister, Fisheries & Oceans,Hon. Gail Shea
613-992-9223, Fax: 613-992-1974,Shea.G@parl.gc.ca; Min@dfo-mpo.gc.ca, Other Communications: Fisheries & Oceans, Phone: 613-992-3474
Deputy Minister, Claire Dansereau
613-993-2200, Fax: 613-993-2194
Executive Advisor to the Deputy Minister, Christine Lavergne
613-993-9226, Fax: 613-993-2194
Assistant Deputy Minister, Special Envoy for Asia-Pacific, Donna Petrachenko
604-666-8922, Fax: 604-666-8959
Director General, Communications, Susan Gardner-Barclay
613-990-0219, Fax: 613-993-8277
Acting Senior General Counsel, Lynn Lovett
613-993-0966
Parliamentary Secretary to the Minister of Fisheries and Oceans, Randy Kamp
613-947-4613, Fax: 613-947-4615,Kamp.R@parl.gc.ca

• Fisheries Resource Conservation Council(FRCC) / Le Conseil pour la conservation desressources halieutiques (CCRH)
PO Box 2001 D
Ottawa, ON K1P 5W3
613-998-0433 Fax: 613-998-1146
info@frcc-ccrh.ca
www.frcc.ca
Created in 1993 to form a partnership between scientific & academic expertise, & all sectors of the fishing industry.Council members make public recommendations to the Minister of Fisheries & Oceans on conservation measures for the Atlantic fishery.

• Freshwater Fish Marketing Corporation/ Office de commercialisation du poisson d'eau douce

Canadian Coast Guard (CCG) / Garde côtière canadienne
Centennial Towers, #6S018, 200 Kent St., Ottawa, ON K1A 0E6
613-998-1573, Fax: 613-990-2780, www.ccg-gcc.gc.ca

The Canadian Coast Guard provides the following maritime programs & services: search & rescue; marine communications & traffic services, including radio communications & radio navigational aids services; marine navigation services, a program which establishes & maintains navigational aids to assist vessels in safe navigation; enrvironmental response program, which works to minimize impacts of marine pollution incidents & to provide humanitarian aid in disasters; aids to navigation, such as the Differential Global Positioning System (DGPS) & Notices to Mariners (NOTMAR); icebreaking services; & client relations & international affairs.
Commissioner, George DaPont
613-998-1571, Fax: 613-990-2780
Acting Deputy Commissioner, Charles Gadula
613-998-1570, Fax: 613-990-2780
Director General, Fleet, Gary B. Sidock
613-990-9172
Director General, Integrated Business Management Directorate, Claudine Gagnon
613-998-1440
Director General, Integrated Technical Services, David G. Faulkner
613-998-1638, Fax: 613-993-5333
Director General, Maritime Services, Michel Vermette
613-990-5608
Director, Safety & Environmental Response Systems, Stevn Troy
613-990-3115, Fax: 613-996-8902

Human Resources & Corporate Services / Services généraux
200 Kent St., Ottawa, ON K1A 0E6
Assistant Deputy Minister, Cal Hegge
613-990-0023
Director General, Finance & Administration, Susan MacGowan
613-993-9372
Director General, Human Resource Strategies & Programs, Patti Kuntz
613-990-0013
Acting Director General & Chief Information Officer, Information Management & Technology Services Directorate, Robert Laframboise
613-990-6220
Director General, Real Property, Safety & Security, Krishna Sahay
613-993-9291
Director General, Small Craft Harbours Directorate, Robert Bergeron
613-993-1937

Fisheries & Aquaculture Management / Gestion des pêches et de l'aquaculture
200 Kent St., Ottawa, ON K1A 0E6
Responsible for the management & development of all federal fisheries & habitat in Canada. The division conserves, protects, develops & enhances fishery resources & habitats, encompassing the Atlantic & Pacific sectors, adjacent provinces, & the 200-mile offshore zone. Also manages Canadian parts of trans-boundary rivers.
Assistant Deputy Minister, David Bevan
613-990-9864, Fax: 613-990-9557
Director General, Aboriginal Policy & Governance, David Balfour
613-993-2574
Director General, Conservation & Protection, Paul Steele
613-998-9537
Director General, International Affairs Directorate, Guy Beaupré
613-993-1873, Fax: 613-993-5995
Director General, Resource Management, Kevin Stringer
613-990-6794

Oceans & Habitats / Océans et habitats
200 Kent St., Ottawa, ON K1A 0E6
Services include: oceans sciences (ocean's physical properties, behaviour of organic & inorganic materials & their impact on fish & ecosystems, pollutants); regulation, enforcement & management of fisheries resources & habitat that are exploited for aboriginal, commercial & recreational purposes. The Marine Protected Areas Policy & the National Framework for Establishing & Managing Marine Protected Areas represents DFO's approach to establishing & maintaining MPOs in Canada.
Assistant Deputy Minister, Mimi Breton
613-993-9850
Director General, Habitat Management Directorate, David McBain
613-991-1280
Director General, Oceans Directorate, Wayne Moore
613-990-0001

Policy / Politiques
200 Kent St., Ottawa, ON K1A 0E6
Provides leadership in recommending, developing & monitoring policy frameworks that advance DFO's initiatives, support DFO programs, & are responsive to the changing needs of DFO clients.Provides strategic advice on departmental programs, develops long-term planning priorities for the department & coordinates cross-sectoral activities in support of government goals & departmental objectives.
Assistant Deputy Minister, Michaela Huard
613-993-1808
Director General, International Policy & Integration, Lori Ridgeway
613-993-1914
Director General, Economic Analysis & Statistics, Bill Doubleday
613-991-6867
Director General, Policy Coordination & Liaison, Gilles Belzile
613-993-2507

Science Sector / Secteur des sciences
200 Kent St., Ottawa, ON K1A 0E6
Services provided by the science sector include the following: research & data gathering; provision of information & advice in the fields of fisheries sciences (fish, invertebrates, marine mammals & plants, & ecosystems), oceans sciences (ocean's physical properties, behaviour of organic & inorganic materials & their impact on fish & ecosystems, pollutants), & hydrography (bathymetric, tide & current systems); & regulation, enforcement & management of fisheries resources & habitat that are exploited for aboriginal, commercial & recreational purposes. The sector assesses major stocks of exploited species of anadromous & marine fish, invertebrates, mammals & plants in Canada's Atlantic, Pacific, Arctic & marine waters, as well as freshwater fish in the Yukon & Northwest Territories. Research is conducted in the following areas: the biology & population of fish stocks, in order to provide scientific information & advice to fishery managers; the effects of changes in the ocean environment on the recruitment & distribution of fish populations; & studies to improve the productivity of aquaculture.
Assistant Deputy Minister, Wendy M. Watson-Wright
613-990-5123, Fax: 613-990-5113
Senior Director General, Science Renewal, Serge Labonté
613-990-9082
Director General, Canadian Hydrography Service, Savithri Narayanan
613-995-4413
Director General, Ecosystem Science, Sylvain Paradis
613-990-0271
Director General, Integrated Business Management, Jacqueline Gonçalves
613-991-0475
Director General, Species at Risk Secretariat, Pardeep Ahluwalia
613-990-0417
Associate Director, Ocean Sciences - Canadian Hydrographic Service, Howard Freeland
613-991-6850
Executive Director, Strategic Directions & Science Outreach, Barbara Adams
613-993-1884

Regional Directors:

Central & Arctic
#703, 201 Front St., Sarnia, ON N7T 8B1
519-383-1810, Fax: 519-464-5128
Regional Director, Bob Lambe

Gulf
PO Box 5030, Moncton, NB E1C 9B6
506-851-7747, Fax: 506-851-2435
Regional Director General, Jim Jones
506-851-7750

Maritimes
176 Portland St., Halifax, NS B2Y 4T3
902-426-2581, Fax: 902-426-2479
Acting Regional Director, Faith Scattolon
902-426-2581

Newfoundland & Labrador
PO Box 5667 Whitehills, St. John's, NL A1C 5X1
709-772-4423, Fax: 709-772-4880
Regional Director General, Wayne Follett
709-772-4417, Fax: 709-772-6306

Pacific
#200, 401 Burrard St., Vancouver, BC V6C 3S4
604-666-0384, Fax: 604-666-8956
Regional Director General, Paul Sprout
604-666-6098, Fax: 604-666-8756

Québec
104, rue Dalhousie, Québec, QC G1K 7Y7
418-648-7747, Fax: 418-648-4758
Regional Director General, Marc Demonceaux

Research Facilities:

Bayfield Institute
867 Lakeshore Rd., PO Box 5050, Burlington, ON L7R 4A6
905-336-6240
Comprises fisheries research, habitat management, hydrographic surveys & chart production & ships support. Together with the Freshwater Institute in Winnipeg, it provides the federal Fisheries & Oceans science programs for the Central & Arctic Region. Multiple partnerships with a variety of external stakeholders allow the Institute to be recognized internationally as a site of leading research in freshwater science.
District Manager, Ron DesJardine
705-750-4017

Bedford Institute of Oceanography (BIO) / L'institut océanographique de Bedford
1 Challenger Dr., PO Box 1006, Dartmouth, NS B2Y 4A2
902-426-3492, Fax: 902-426-8484, www.bio.gc.ca
Administered by Fisheries & Oceans, Bedford Institute of Oceanography (BIO) is Canada's largest centre for ocean research. Scientists, engineers & technicians primarily from Fisheries & Oceans, & Natural Resources Canada, (smaller components are from National Defense & Environment Canada) perform targeted research & provide advice on Atlantic marine environments. Programs include: fisheries research, ocean sciences & management, habitat ecology, marine chemistry, Canadian Hydrographic Service (producing navigation charts for the Atlantic & Arctic areas), marine environmental regional & resources geoscience, & seabird research & management. BIO based staff also conduct joint projects, such as sea floor mapping & exploration, & provide scientific response to marine environmental emergencies. Also located at Bedford is the Canadian Shark Research Laboratory & the Otolith Research Laboratory.
Regional Science Director,Dr. Michael Sinclair
sinclairm@mar.dfo-mpo.gc.ca

Freshwater Institute / Institut des eaux douces
501 University Cres., Winnipeg, MB R3T 2N6
204-983-5000, Fax: 204-983-6285
Main areas of research are: fish habitats; limnology emphasizing mechanisms & processes of biological production & decomposition in lakes; studies related to energy development use, acidification, radionuclide & heavy metal pollution. Arctic research emphasizes commercially important fish & marine mammals & associated ecosystems, & the effects of hydroelectric developments & toxic chemical pollution on aquatic ecosystems. The Institute supports a major field camp at the Experimental Lakes Area. Activities include freshwater & arctic science, science oceans initiative, fish habitat management, fisheries management, small craft harbours, corporate services, communications & regional senior management. The federal fish inspection program, recently transferred to the new Canadian

Food Inspection Agency (CFIA), continues to operate out of the FWI.
Administrative Assistant, Judy Fredette
204-983-5118

Gulf Fisheries Centre / Centre de poissonerie du gulfe
343, av Université, 5th Fl., Moncton, NB E1C 9B6
506-851-3886, Fax: 506-851-7732
Regional Director General, James B. Jones
506-851-7750, Fax: 506-851-2224

Institut Maurice-Lamontagne / Maurice Lamontagne Institute
850, rte de le Mer, CP 1000, Mont-Joli, QC G5H 3Z4
418-775-0555, Fax: 418-775-0730,
www.qc.dfo.ca/iml/en/intro.htm
Provides extensive research on: fisheries, fish habitat, oceanography, hydrography; development of marine renewable resources in the fields of fisheries, ocean industry development, commercial shipping & recreational boating. Main area of focus centres on the Gulf of St. Lawrence & estuary, Saguenay Fjord, Canadian Arctic, & the James, Hudson & Ungava Bays. Also performs the following research: environmental chemistry research on the distribution, transport & fate of contaminants in sediments, water & the food chain; ecotoxicology research & field assessments for biomarkers, fish pathology & embryotoxicity; molecular toxicology research for biomarkers, fish reproduction & steroid hormones; bioremediation study on the microbial degradation of petroleum oil hydrocarbons & microbial bioassays. Projects include the temporal & spatial monitoring of organic & inorganic contaminants in fish, shellfish & sediments of the St. Lawrence gulf & estuary. Also studying the effects of pulp & paper effluents & mercury & municipal effluents on the reproduction of fish.
Regional Director, Regional Science Branch, Ariane Plourde

Centre for Aquaculture & Environmental Research
4160 Marine Dr., West Vancouver, BC V7V 1N6
604-666-7453, Fax: 604-666-3497
The Center for Aquaculture & Environmental Research (CAER) is a specialized centre for aquaculture and coastal research co-founded by Fisheries and Oceans Canada and the University of British Columbia.
Regional Director, Science Branch, Laura Richards
250-729-8369, Fax: 250-756-7053

Institute of Ocean Sciences (IOS) / Institut des sciences de la mer (ISM)
9860 West Saanich Rd., PO Box 6000, Sidney, BC V8L 4B2
250-363-6517, Fax: 250-363-6390
Science divisions at IOS include: Canadian Hydrographic Service, Marine Environment & Habitat Science, Ocean Science & Productivity. Other departments & organizations at the IOS facility include: GSC Pacific - Sidney Pacific Geoscience Centre, Canadian Wildlife Service, Canadian Coast Guard, North Pacific Marine Science Organization (PICES). Science Division also includes Pacific Biological Station, West Vancouver Laboratory. Cultus Lake Laboratory.
Director, Denis D'Amours
250-363-6347

Pacific Biological Station (PBS) / La station de biologie du Pacifique
3190 Hammond Bay Rd., Nanaimo, BC V9T 6N7
250-756-7000, Fax: 250-756-7053
Research at PBS responds to stock assessment, aquaculture, marine environment & habitat science, & ocean science & productivity priorities.
Regional Director, Science Branch, Laura Richards
250-729-8369

St. Andrews Biological Station / La Station biologique de St. Andrews
531 Brandy Cove Rd., St Andrews, NB E5B 2L9
506-529-8854, Fax: 506-529-5862,
XMARSABS@mar.dfo-mpo.gc.ca
www.mar.dfo-mpo.gc.ca/sabs
Chemical & ecological studies on the interaction between oceanography & fisheries/aquaculture & the aquatic environment. Stock assessments & associated research on commercially important groundfish, pelagic finfish, invertebrate species in the Bay of Fundy & other areas of Atlantic Canada. Research in support of the existing salmon aquaculture industry & research on other species with potential for aquaculture in Atlantic Canada.Major environmental research projects include: risk assessment of organic chemicals to fisheries; biochemical indicators of health of aquatic animals; aquatic toxicity of marine phytotoxins; molluscan toxins, techniques & improvements; phytotoxin research; aquaculture ecology research; effectiveness of acid rain control programs; effects of aquaculture in the coastal environment.
Head, Environmental Sciences & Research Scientist,Dr. Kats Haya
506-529-5916

Director General, Charles Gadula
613-993-1849
Director, Professional Staff Support, John Falardeau
613-998-1662
Director, Program & Operational Support, Peter Ballard
613-990-0341
Director, Safety, Trevor Whitehouse
613-998-1138, Fax: 613-991-4160
Director General, Denis Hains
613-998-1440
Director, Information Strategies, David Delcorde
613-998-5889
Director, Planning/Performance & Monitoring, Keith Cuddihy
613-998-1441
Director, Policy & Liaison, Melanie Tod
613-991-4596
Director General, David G. Faulkner
613-998-1638,
Director, Service Delivery, Réal Thibault
613-998-1505, Fax: 613-998-9258
Acting Director, Service Quality Review, David Waters
613-998-1509, Fax: 613-991-4879
Director, Technical Business, Suzanne Ewanovich
613-998-1616, Fax: 613-993-5333
Acting Director, Technical Services, John Boyachok
613-998-1551, Fax: 613-993-5333
Director General, Debra Normoyle
613-990-5608
Director, Navigation Systems, Jacques Lorquet
613-998-1384
Director, Planning & Performance Measurement, Stephen Lord
613-990-5619
Director, Policy & Legislation, Tim Meisner
613-993-6943, Fax: 613-990-4338
Director, Safety & Environmental Response Systems, Steve Troy
613-990-3115, Fax: 613-996-8902
Director General, Rosemarie Karnes
613-991-0181
Director General, Kevin Stringer
613-993-3460
Director, Resource Management Atlantic, Barry Rashotte
613-990-0087, Fax: 613-990-7051
Director, Resource Management Pacific, Arctic & Inland, Max Stanfield
613-993-1879, Fax: 613-990-9764
Director, Resource Management,Vacant
613-991-6651
Director, Accounting, Material & Administrative Services, Bill Lumsdon
613-993-2804, Fax: 613-991-4643
Director, Financial & Administrative Systems, Gerard Lacasse
613-993-7347, Fax: 613-991-4414
Director, Financial Management, Alain Corrivieau
613-990-8346
Director General, Scott Streiner
613-990-0023
Director, Corporate Competition, Sylvie Joseph
613-990-5860
Director, Human Resources Management Systems, Thomas Falardeau
613-990-9765
Director, Organization & Classification, Lise Sincennes
613-990-0050
Director, Application Services, Christopher Seifried
613-990-0427, Fax: 613-998-9859
Director, Planning & Information Management, Julia Goodman
613-993-7544
Acting Director, Technology Services, Christopher Seifried
613-990-0427
Director General, Richard Wex
613-991-1280
Chief, Environmental Assessments & Major Projects, Bruce Hood
613-993-4922
Director, Habitat Program Services Branch, Brian Torrie
613-993-7354
Director, Habitat Protection & Sustainable Development, Patrice Leblanc
613-990-5252
Director General, Céline Gaulin
613-990-0001
Oceans Policy Advisor, Oceans Action Plan Secretariat, Pamela J. Rizzo
613-990-0253
Director, Oceans Policy & Planning, Camille Mageau
613-991-1285
Director, Regional Oceans Operations, Michael Murphy
613-991-2283
Director, Economic Analysis,Vacant
613-993-1876, Fax: 613-991-3254
Acting Director, Restructuring & Adjustment, L. Anderson

Director, Horizontal Policy, André-Marc Lanteigne
613-993-7783
Director, Gilles Betzille
613-993-2507
Acting Director, Legislative & Regulatory Affairs, Mike Berthiaume
613-990-1297, Fax: 613-990-0120
Director, Intergovernmental Affairs,Vacant
613-993-2507
Director General, Danielle Labonté
613-990-0146
Director, Strategic Planning, Christine Loth
613-990-7153
Director, Strategic Priorities, James Gilbert
613-998-4973
Director General, Savithri Narayanan
613-995-4413, Fax: 613-947-4369
Acting Director, Hydrography, Steve Forbes
613-996-9163
Director General, Tony O'Connor
613-995-4413, Other Communications: Chart Distribution: 613/998-4931
Director, Hydrography Planning & Applied Research, Michel Poulin
613-995-4405, Fax: 613-996-9053
Acting Director, Marine Cartography, Michael Casey
613-995-4666, Fax: 613-996-9053
Director, Biodiversity Science Branch, Howard Powles
613-990-0280
Director General, Sylvain Paradis
613-990-0271
Assoc. Director General, Denis Rivard
613-990-0281
Senior Advisor, Aquaculture, Edward Black
613-990-0272
Acting Director, Environment & Biodiversity Science, Paul Keizer
613-990-0314
Acting Director, Policy & Planning, Helen Joseph
613-990-6930
Acting Director, Sector Program Management, Michael Gardiner
613-993-2708
Research Scientist & Senior Advisor, Jim Helbig
613-990-0314
Assoc. Director, Howard Freeland
613-991-6850
Senior Policy Advisor, Oceanography & Climate, Leah Braithwaite
613-991-1313
Chief, Data Management & Client Services Division, Jean J. Gagnon
Senior Technical & Policy Advisor, J. Robert Keeley

Foreign Affairs & International Trade Canada (FAIT) / Affaires étrangères et Commerce international Canada (AECT)

125 Sussex Dr., Ottawa, ON K1A 0G2
613-944-4000, Fax: 613-996-9709, 800-267-8376
enqserv@international.gc.ca
www.international.gc.ca

Other Communication: Media Relations: 613/995-1874
FAIT works to ensure that its policies, programmes & operations reflect sustainable development criteria & to make a difference in sustainable development terms in the international arena. The Department defines its intent in a 3-year SD strategy which is tabled in Parliament. Annual progress reports are also tabled in Parliament. The current strategy, Agenda 2006, covers the 2004-2006 period. FAIT strives to defend & advance Canada's international interests in environmental protection & sustainable development in bilateral, multilateral & regional fora including issues relating to climate change, trade & environment, sustainable forest management, hazardous & toxic substances, desertification, human settlements, biological diversity, biosafety, genetic resources for food & agriculture, air & marine pollution, whaling, & non-Canada-USA freshwater. To achieve progress in this area of responsibility, FAIT's Environmental & Sustainable Development Bureau works with the major international environmental & sustainable development organizations. It also recommends & oversees funding where appropriate. Domestically, the Bureau works toward agreement & productive partnerships with other government departments, agencies & non-governmental environmental, no n-nuclear energy, developmental & business organizations. It prepares & monitors implementation of the Department's Sustainable Development Strategy & provides advice & assistance in the areas of environmental assessment & the greening of departmental operations both in Canada & at the 157 missions abroad. FAIT established an environmental management system (EMS), based on the International Organization for Standardization's (ISO) 14000 series, in a commitment to incorporate best environmental management practices into its operations. A

database of international environmental agreements & arrangements to which Canada is a party may be searched at pubx.dfait-maeci.gc.ca/A_Branch/AES/Env_commitments.nsf/VE Welcome/Homepage

Acts Administered:
Asia-Pacific Foundation of Canada Act
Bretton Woods Agreements Act
Canadian Commercial Corporation Act
Canadian Institute for International Peace & Security Act
Comprehensive Nuclear Test-Ban Treaty Implementation Act
Cultural Property Export & Import Act
Department of Foreign Affairs & International Trade Act
Diplomatic & Consular Privileges & Immunities Act
Export Development Act
Export & Import Permits Act
Food & Agriculture Organization of the United Nations Act
Forgiveness of Certain Official Development Assistance Debts Act
Fort-Falls Bridge Authority Act
Geneva Conventions Act
High Commissioner of the United Kingdom Act
International Boundary Waters Treaty Act
International Development (Financial Institutions) Continuing Assistance Act
International Development Research Centre Act
Meat Import Act
North American Free Trade Agreement Implementation Act
Northern Pipeline Act
Privileges & Immunities (International Organizations) Act
Privileges & Immunities (North Atlantic Treaty Organization) Act
Prohibition of International Air Services Act
Rainy Lake Watershed Emergency Control Act
Roosevelt-Campobello International Park Commission Act
Skagit River Valley Treaty Implementation Act
State Immunity Act
United Nations Act

Minister, Foreign Affairs,Hon. Lawrence Cannon
613-992-5516, Fax: 613-992-6802,CannoL@parl.gc.ca; L.Cannon@international.gc.ca
Deputy Minister, Foreign Affairs, Morris Rosenberg
613-944-4911
Deputy Minister, International Trade, Louis Lévesque
613-944-5000, Fax: 613-944-8493
Parliamentary Secretary to the Minister of Foreign Affairs, Deepak Obhrai
613-947-4566, Fax: 613-947-4569,Obhrai.D@parl.gc.ca

Foreign Affairs / Affaires étrangères
Deputy Minister, Leonard Edwards
613-944-4911
Deputy Director, Angelica Liao-Moroz
613-995-7972, Fax: 613-944-0856
Assistant Deputy Minister, Human Resources, Michael D. Small
613-996-5369, Fax: 613-944-2411

Global Issues / Enjeux mondiaux
Assistant Deputy Minister, Keith Christie
613-944-2273
Director General, International Organizations Bureau, David J. Angell
613-944-0928, Fax: 613-944-0722
Director General, Human Security & Human Rights, Adèle Dion
613-944-0325, Fax: 613-944-1121
Director General, Environment, Energy & Sustainable Development Bureau, Sheila Riordon
613-944-0886
Director General, Economic Policy Bureau, John C. Sloan
613-992-7825

International Security Branch & Political Director / Sécurité international et directeur politique
Assistant Deputy Minister, Colleen Swords
613-944-4228, Fax: 613-944-1180
Senior Coordinator, International Crime & Terrorism, Mark Gwozdecky
613-944-2906, Fax: 613-944-4827
Director General, Secretariat for the Stabilization & Reconstruction Task Force, Robert Derouin
613-995-6689
Director, Global Partnership Program, Troy Lulashnyk
613-944-3311, Fax: 613-944-1130
Director General, Security & Intelligence, Paul Meyer
613-992-7400, Fax: 613-996-1724
Director General, International Security Bureau, Donald Sinclair
613-992-3402
Director, Non-Proliferation, Arms Control & Disarmament, André-François Giroux
613-944-0324, Fax: 613-944-1835
Director, Nuclear & Chemical Disarmament Implementation Agency, James A. Junke
613-996-6901, Fax: 613-944-3105
Director, Defence & Security Relations Division, Shelley Whiting
613-992-7921
Director, Global & Security Policy, Janice Attree-Smith
613-944-7646, Fax: 613-944-2104
Director, Peacekeeping & Peace Operations Group, Michael N. Kaduck
613-992-5457, Fax: 613-944-2128
Senior Coordinator, Mine Action & Small Arms Team, Earl Turcotte
613-995-9282, Fax: 613-944-2501

Office of Protocol / Bureau du Protocole
613-996-8683, Fax: 613-943-1075,
Chief of Protocol, Malcolm McKechnie
613-992-2344
Deputy Chief & Director, Diplomatic Corps Services, Haig Sarafian
613-995-5185
Deputy Chief & Director, Official Events Division, Jacinthe Lanthier
613-944-0674
Deputy Chief & Director, Official Visits Division, Roger Portelance
613-995-3166
Executive Assistant, Nicole Brien
613-992-8382, Fax: 613-943-1075

Strategic Policy & Planning
Assistant Deputy Minister, Drew Fagan
613-944-3022, Fax: 613-944-0285
Director General, Intergovernmental Affairs & Domestic Outreach, Don Costello
613-944-7162
Director General, Policy Planning Bureau, Robert McRae
613-944-3179
Director General, Public Policy Bureau, James Lambert
613-996-0232

• Canadian International Development Agency/ Agence canadienne de développement international
• Canadian International Grains Institute/ Institut international du Canada pour le grain
• International Joint Commission (Canadian Section)/ Commission mixte internationale

Passport Canada
Le 70 Crémazie, 70 Crémazie St., Gatineau, QC K1A 0G3
Fax: 819-953-5856, 800-567-6868
www.pptc.gc.ca

Other Communication: TTY: 1-866-255-7655
CEO, D. Steidle
819-994-3530, Fax: 819-994-7150
Information Officer, Dianne Belleau
819-934-3799, Fax: 819-934-3838,dbelleau@pptc.gc.ca

Passport Canada Offices:

Brampton
#401, 40 Gillingham Dr., Brampton, ON

Calgary
Harry Hays Bldg., #254, 220 - 4th Ave. SE, Calgary, AB

Calgary South
14331 Macleod Trail SW, Calgary, AB

Edmonton
Canada Place Building, #126, 9700 Jasper Ave., Edmonton, AB

Fredericton
Frederick Square, #430, 77 Westmorland St., Fredericton, NB

Gatineau
Place du Centre, Commercial Level 2, 200 Promenade du Portage, Gatineau, QC

Halifax
Maritime Centre, #1508, 1505 Barrington St., Halifax, NS

Hamilton
Standard Life Bldg., #330, 120 King St. West, Hamilton, ON

Kitchener
The Galleria, #630, 101 Frederick St., Kitchener, ON

Laval
#500, 3, place Laval, Laval, QC

London
#201, 400 York St., 2nd Fl., London, ON

Mississauga
Central Parkway Mall, #116, 377 Burnhamthorpe Rd. East, 2nd Fl., Mississauga, ON

Montréal
Complexe Guy Favreau, Tour Ouest, #803, 200, boul René-Lévesque ouest, Montréal, QC

North York
Joseph Shepard Bldg., #380, 4900 Yonge St., North York, ON

Ottawa
Level C, East Tower, C.D. Howe Bldg., 240 Sparks St., Ottawa, ON

Pointe Claire
Centre commercial Fairview, 6818, rte Transcanadienne, Pointe-Claire, QC

Québec
Tour Cominar, Place de la Cité, #200, 2640, boul Laurier, 2e étage, Québec, QC

Regina
#500, 1870 Albert St., Regina, SK

Richmond
#135, 8011 Saba Rd., Richmond, BC

Saguenay
Immeuble St-Michel, #408, 3885, boul Harvey, Saguenay, QC

St. Catharines
Landmark Bldg., #600, 43 Church St., St Catharines, ON

St. John's
TD Place, #802, 140 Water St., St. John's, NL

Saint-Laurent
#112, 3300, boul Côte Vertu, Saint-Laurent, QC

Saskatoon
Federal Bldg., #405, 101 - 22 St. East, Saskatoon, SK

Scarborough
#210, 200 Town Centre Crt., Scarborough, ON

Surrey
#900, 13401 - 108 Ave., Surrey, BC

Thunder Bay
979 Alloy Dr., 2nd Fl., Thunder Bay, ON

Toronto
#300, 74 Victoria St., Toronto, ON

Vancouver
Sinclair Centre, #200, 757 West Hastings St., Vancouver, BC

Victoria
747 Fort St., 5th Fl., Victoria, BC

Whitby
Whitby Mall, 1615 Dundas St. East, Whitby, ON

Windsor
CIBC Building, #503, 100 Ouellette Ave., Windsor, ON

Winnipeg
#400, 433 Main St., Winnipeg, MB

Canada Post Receiving Agents:

Acton
53 Bower St., Acton, ON L7J 1E0

Ancaster
27 Legend Court, Ancaster, ON L9K 1J0

Anjou
7200 rue Joseph-Renaud, Anjou, QC H1K 3W0

Aurora
20 Wellington St. East, Aurora, ON L4G 1H0

Barrie
150 Collier St., Barrie, ON L4M 1G0

Beaconsfield
186 Sutton Pl., Beaconsville, QC

Boucherville
131 rue Jacques-Ménard, Boucherville, QC J4B 5B0

Bracebridge
98 Manitoba St., Bracebridge, ON

Bradford
50 Barrie St., Bradford, ON

Brantford
38 Dalhousie St., Brantford, ON

Brossard
10 Place du Commerce, Brossard, QC

Cambridge
33 Water St. South, Cambridge, ON

Cap Rouge
#100, 1220 Provancher St., Cap-Rouge, QC

Charlottetown
135 Kent St., Charlottetown, PE

Chatham
120 Wellington St. West, Chatham, ON

Georgetown
112 Guelph St., Georgetown, ON

Guelph
88 Wyndham St. North, Guelph, ON

Kanata
145 Roland Michener Dr., Kanata, ON

Kelowna
190 Rutland Rd., Kelowna, BC

Kingston
120 Clarence St., Kingston, ON

Lasalle
7565 Newman Blvd., Lasalle, QC

Lévis
4870 de la Rive-Sud boul, Lévis, QC

Markham
21 Main St. North, Markham, ON

Midland
525 Dominion Ave., Midland, ON

Moncton
281 St. George St., Moncton, NB

North Bay
101 Worthington Ave., North Bay, ON

Oakville
193 Church St., Oakville, ON

Orangeville
216 Broadway Ave., Orangeville, ON

Orillia
25 Peter St. North, Orillia, ON

Oshawa
47 Simcoe St. South, Oshawa, ON

Ottawa - Caledon Pl.
1424 Caledon Pl., Ottawa, ON

Owen Sound
901 3rd Ave. East, Owen Sound, ON

Peterborough
150 King St., Peterborough, ON

Pickering
1740 Kingston Rd., Pickering, ON

Pierrefonds
14975 Pierrefonds Blvd., Pierrefonds, QC

Pointe-Claire
15 Donegani Ave., Pointe-Claire, QC

Prince George
1323 - 5th Ave., Prince George, BC

Québec - Galleries de la Capitale
#119, 5401, boul Des Galleries, Québec, QC

Québec - Haute-Ville
5, rue Dufort, Québec, QC

Québec - rue Saint-Paul
Terminus Station, 300, rue Saint-Paul, Québec, QC

Rimouski
136 St-Germain St. West, Rimouski, QC

Saint Bruno
50 de la Rabastalière St. West, Saint Bruno, QC

Saint John
125 Rothesay Ave., Saint John, NB

Sarnia
105 Christine St. South, Sarnia, ON

Sault-Sainte-Marie
451 Queen St. East, Sault Ste Marie, ON

Sherbrooke
50 Place de la Cité, Sherbrooke, QC

Stratford
75 Waterloo St. South, Stratford, ON

Sudbury - Lasalle Blvd.
1776 Lasalle Blvd., Sudbury, ON

Sudbury - Lisgar St.
1 Lisgar St., Sudbury, ON

Summerside
57 Central St., Summerside, PE

Sydney
269 Charlotte St., Sydney, NS

Toronto
2384 Yonge St., Toronto, ON

Trois-Rivières
1285 Notre Dame St., Trois-Rivières, QC

Uxbridge
67 Brock St. West, Uxbridge, ON

Woodstock
480 Peel St., Woodstock, ON

Yarmouth
15 Willow St., Yarmouth, NS

Ottawa - Riverside Dr.
2701 Riverside Dr., Ottawa, ON

Service Canada Receiving Agents:

Baie Comeau
235, boul Lasalle, 2e étage, Baie-Comeau, QC

Bridgewater
77 Dufferin St., Bridgewater, NS

Brandon
#100, 1039 Princess Ave., Brandon, MB

Cambridge Bay
PO Box 2010, Cambridge Bay, NU

Campbellton
157 Water St., Campbellton, NB

Chibougamau
623, 3e rue, Chibougamau, QC

Collingwood
44 Hurontario St., Collingwood, ON

Comox Valley
130 - 19th St., Comox Valley, BC

Corner Brook
1 Regent Sq., Corner Brook, NL

Drummondville
1525 Saint-Joseph Blvd., Drummondville, QC

Flin Flon
111 Main St., Flin Flon, MB

Fort McMurray
Provincial Bldg., Main Fl., 9915 Franklin Ave., Fort McMurray, AB

Fort Simpson
9606 - 100 St., Fort Simpson, NT

Fort Smith
136 McDougal Rd., Fort Smith, NT

Gander
1 Markham Pl., Gander, NL

Hay River
#204, 41 Capital Dr., Hay River, NT

Inuvik
170 McKenzie Rd., Inuvik, NT

Iqaluit
#300, Iqaluit House, Iqaluit, NU

Kamloops
235 Lansdowne St., Kamloops, BC

Kenora
308 Second St., Kenora, ON

La Tuque
290, rue St-Joseph, La Tuque, QC

Miramichi
150 Pleasant St., Miramichi, NB

Montague
541 Main St., Montague, PE

New Glasgow
340 East River Rd., New Glasgow, NS

North Battleford
9800 Territorial Dr., North Battleford, SK

Pembroke
141 Lake St., Pembroke, ON

Rankin Inlet
PO Box 97, Rankin Inlet, NU

Terrace
4630 Lazelle Ave., Terrace, BC

Thompson
#118, 3 Station Rd., Thompson, MB

Timmins
#300, 273 - 3 Ave., Timmins, ON

Val d'Or
400 Central Ave., Val-d'Or, QC

Whitehorse
#125, 300 Main St., Whitehorse, YT

Yellowknife
5020 - 48th St., Yellowknife, NT

Yorkton
214 Smith St. East, Yorkton, SK

International Trade Canada (ITCan) / Commerce international Canada
125 Sussex Dr., Ottawa, ON K1A 0G2
613-995-2901, Fax: 613-996-8924

International Trade Canada works to position Canada as a business leader for the 21st century. ITCan helps large & small Canadian companies expand & succeed internationally, promotes Canada as a dynamic place to do business, & negotiates & administers trade agreements.

Deputy Minister, Louis Lévesque
613-944-5000, Fax: 613-944-8493
Executive Director, Peter McGovern
613-944-0979, Fax: 613-947-8117
Director, Briefing & Correspondence Services, Noelle Grosse
613-944-6288
Director, Resource Management, Jean Guertin
613-996-2326, Fax: 613-943-2058

Global Operations & Chief Trade Commissioner
125 Sussex Dr,, Ottawa, ON K1A 0G2
613-944-2697, Fax: 613-996-1667

Assistant Deputy Minister & Chief Trade Commissioner, Ken Sunquist
613-944-2695, Fax: 613-944-3473
Director General, Bilateral Commercial Relations: Asia & Americas, Peter McGovern
613-944-0979, Fax: 613-947-8117
Director General, Bilateral Commercial Relations: Europe, Africa & Middle East, James K. Hill
613-944-0506, Fax: 613-944-0556
Director General, Trade Commissioner Service - Initiatives, Grant Manuge
613-944-1678, Fax: 613-947-8390
Director General, Trade Commissioner Service - Operations, Louise Leger
613-992-8785, Fax: 613-995-5773

International Business Development, Investment & Innovation
111 Sussex Dr., Ottawa, ON K1N 1J1
Fax: 613-944-3178

Assistant Deputy Minister, Stewart Beck
613-944-3122
Principal Advisor, Pacific Gateway International Marketing Group, Michael Fine
613-944-3146, Fax: 613-995-7832
Director General, Global Business Opportunities, Paul Thoppil
613-996-1745
Director General, Invest in Canada, Mario Ste-Marie
613-944-3125, Fax: 613-944-3178
Director General, Economic Policy Analysis & Consultations, Robert Clark
613-992-7979, Fax: 613-992-8727

Communications Bureau
125 Sussex Dr., Ottawa, ON K1A 0G2
613-944-0404, Fax: 613-944-0811

Director General, Communications Bureau, André-Marc Lanteigne
613-944-5400
Director, Communications Services, Kyle M. Nunas
613-995-0780, Fax: 613-944-0453
Director, Media Relations, Outreach & Ecommunications, Sophie Galarneau
961-394-3483, Fax: 613-996-9276
Director, Strategic Communications, Norm Ovenden
613-944-1714

Trade Law Bureau
125 Sussex Dr., Ottawa, ON K1A 0G2
613-943-2804, Fax: 613-944-0027

Senior General Counsel & Director General, Meg Kinnear
613-943-2803
Acting General Counsel, Trade Law Bureau, Matthew Kronby
613-944-3046
Director, Cynthia A. Westaway
613-944-3046

Trade Policy & Negotiations / Politique commercial et négociations
111 Sussex Dr., Ottawa, ON K1N 1J1
613-996-5677, Fax: 613-996-1667
Assistant Deputy Minister, Don Stephenson
613-992-0293, Fax: 613-996-1667
Director General, Bilateral & Regional Trade Policy, David Plunkett
613-944-9171
Director General, Export & Import Controls, Suzanne McKellips
613-995-2947
Director General, Multilateral Trade Policy, Gilles Gauthier
613-944-2002, Fax: 613-944-0757
Director General, North America Trade Policy, Paul Robertson
613-944-0462, Fax: 613-944-0231
Chief Trade Negotiator, Bilateral & Regional, Ian Burney
613-992-3386,

Americas Strategy
125 Sussex Dr., Ottawa, ON K1A 0G2
613-944-1903, Fax: 613-944-1910
Assistant Deputy Minister, Alex Bugailiskis
613-944-1909
Special Advisor, Randolph Harwood
613-944-1907

International Trade Centres:

BC & Yukon
#2000, 300 West Georgia St., Vancouver, BC V6B 6E1
604-666-0434, Fax: 604-666-0954,
itc-vancouver@ic.gc.ca
www.bctradeevents.com
Director & Senior Trade Commissioner, Bill Johnston
johnston.william@ic.gc.ca

Calgary
#400, 639 - 5 Ave. SW, Calgary, AB T2P 0M9
403-292-4575, Fax: 403-292-4578,
itc-calgary@ic.gc.ca
www.alberta-canada.com/tta/about/index.cfm
Trade Commissioner, Barry Schlinker
403-292-4509

Charlottetown
75 Fitzroy St., PO Box 1115, Charlottetown, PE C1A 7K2
902-566-7382, Fax: 902-566-7450,
itc-charlottetown@ic.gc.ca
www.tradeteampei.com
Acting Provincial Director & Sr. Trade Commissioner, Bernard Postma
902-566-7426

Edmonton
Canada Place, #725, 9700 Jasper Ave., Edmonton, AB T5J 4C3
780-495-2944, Fax: 780-495-4507
Acting Sr. Trade Commissioner, Dee Pannu
780-495-3329

Halifax
1800 Argyle St., 5th Fl., PO Box 940 M, Halifax, NS B3J 2V9
902-426-7540, Fax: 902-426-5218,
itc-halifax@ic.gc.ca
Acting Senior Trade Commissioner, Ron Rose
902-426-6660

Manitoba (NWT & Nunavut)
400 St. Mary Ave., 4th Fl., Winnipeg, MB R3C 4K5
204-983-5851, Fax: 204-983-3182,
itc-winnipeg@ic.gc.ca
www.gov.mb.ca/trade/index.html
Senior Trade Commissioner, Suzanne Cormie
cormie.suzanne@ic.gc.ca

New Brunswick
#103, 1045 Main St., Moncton, NB E1C 1H1
506-851-6452, Fax: 506-851-6429, 800-332-3801
itc-moncton@ic.gc.ca
www.ttnb.ca
Senior Trade Commissioner & Provincial Director, Michelyne Paulin
506-851-6440

Newfoundland & Labrador
John Cabot Bldg., Phase II, 10 Barter's HIll, 10th Fl., PO Box 8950, St. John's, NL A1B 3R9
709-772-5511, Fax: 709-772-5093,
itc-stjohns@ic.gc.ca
www.cbsc.org/nf/search/display.cfm?CODE=2438&coll=FE_FEDSBIS_E
Sr. Trade Commissioner, Anthony McLevey
709-772-4910

Québec
#800, 5, Place Ville Marie, Montréal, QC H3B 2G2
514-283-6328, Fax: 514-283-8794,
itc.montreal@ic.gc.ca
www.eciq.net/public/
Director, Michel Charland
charland.michel@ic.gc.ca

Regina
#320, 1801 Hamilton St., Regina, SK S4P 3N8
306-780-6124, Fax: 306-780-8797,
itc-regina@ic.gc.ca
www.cbsc.org/sask/trade_export.cfm

Saskatoon
Princeton Tower, 123 - 2nd Ave. South, 7th Fl., Saskatoon, SK S7K 7E6
306-975-5315, Fax: 306-975-5334,
itc-saskatoon@ic.gc.ca
www.cbsc.org/trade_export.cfm
Senior Trade Commissioner, Rod Johnson
johnson.rod@ic.gc.ca

Toronto
Yonge-Richmond Centre, 151 Yonge St., 4th Fl., Toronto, ON M5C 2W7
416-973-5053, Fax: 416-973-8161,
itc-toronto@ic.gc.ca
napoleon.ic.gc.ca/ontario_region/tcontario.nsf
Director, International Business & Senior Trade Commissioner, Randy Harwood
416-954-6326

Freshwater Fish Marketing Corporation / Office de commercialisation du poisson d'eau douce

1199 Plessis Rd., Winnipeg, MB R2C 3L4
204-983-6601, Fax: 204-983-6497,
sandi.cain@freshwaterfish.com
www.freshwaterfish.com

The Corporation is a buyer, processor & marketer of freshwater fish, harvested from over 400 lakes in Manitoba, Saskatchewan, Alberta, the Northwest Territories & Northwestern Ontario. Reports to the government through the Minister of Fisheries & Oceans.
President/CEO, John Wood
CFO, Stan Lazar

Great Lakes Pilotage Authority / Administration de pilotage des Grands Lacs

202 Pitt St., 2nd fl., PO Box 95, Cornwall, ON K6H 5R9
613-933-2991, Fax: 613-932-3793,
administration@glpa-apgl.com
www.glpa-apgl.com

The Authority provides pilotage services in the waters of the St. Lawrence River commencing at the northern entrance of St. Lambert Lock, the Great Lakes area & the Port of Churchill, Manitoba. Reports to government through the Minister of Transport.
CEO, Robert Lemire, C.A.
rlemire@glpa-apgl.com
Secretary-Treasurer, Réjean Ménard
rmenard@glpa-apgl.com
Administrative Asst., Nancy McAteer
nmcateer@glpa-apgl.com

Regional Offices:

Eastern
202 Pitt St., 2nd Fl., Cornwall, ON K6J 3P7
613-933-2991, Fax: 613-932-3793

Western
Upper Lock &, East Side, Welland Canal., Thorold, ON
905-688-3399, Fax: 905-688-5599

Health Canada / Santé Canada

Tunney's Pasture, Ottawa, ON K1A 0K9
613-957-2991, Fax: 613-941-5366,
Info@hc-sc.gc.ca
www.hc-sc.gc.ca

Other Communication: Media Relations: 613-957-2983; Office of the Access to Information: 613-954-8744; Public Services Health Medical Centre: 613-954-6582; Emergency Svs: 613-957-7711
In partnership with provincial & territorial governments, Health Canada (HC) develops health policy, enforces health regulations, promotes disease prevention, & enhances healthy living for all Canadians. HC ensures that health services are available & accessible to First Nations & Inuit communities. It works closely with other federal departments, agencies & health stakeholders to reduce health & safety risks to Canadians. Through its Health Intelligence Network, HC works with other levels of government & the health care system in the surveillance, prevention, control & research of disease outbreaks across Canada & around the world. It also monitors health & safety risks related to the sale & use of drugs, food, chemicals, pesticides, medical devices & certain consumer products. HC negotiates agreements regarding hazardous materials in the workplace, performs medical assessments for pilots & air traffic controllers, & conducts environmental health assessments.
Acts Administered:
Canada Health Act
Canada Medical Act
Canadian Centre on Substance Abuse Act
Canadian Institutes of Health Research Act
Controlled Drug Substances Act
Department of Health Act
Financial Administration Act
Fitness & Amateur Sport Act
Food & Drugs Act (Agriculture & Agri-Food Canada)
Hazardous Materials Information Review Act (Human Resources & Skills Development)
Hazardous Products Act
Health Resources Fund Act
Medical Research Council Act
Narcotic Control Act
Patent Act
Pest Control Products Act, 2002
Pesticide Residue Compensation Act
Quarantine Act
Queen Elizabeth II Canadian Research Fund Act
Radiation Emitting Devices Act
Tobacco Act
Minister, Health,Hon. Leona Aglukkaq
613-992-2848, Fax: 613-996-9764,Aglukkaq.L@parl.gc.ca; Minister_Ministre@hc-sc.gc.ca, Other Communications: Health Canada, Phone: 613-957-0200
Deputy Minister, Glenda Yeates
613-957-0212, Fax: 613-952-8422,glenda.yeates@hc-sc.gc.ca
Assistant Deputy Minister, Meena Ballantyne
613-957-1804, Fax: 613-957-3954,meena.ballantyne@hc-sc.gc.ca
Senior General Counsel, Irit Weiser
613-957-3766, Fax: 613-954-9485,irit.weiser@hc-sc.gc.ca
Director General, Jane Hazel
613-957-0215, Fax: 613-948-8092,jane.hazel@hc-sc.gc.ca
Director General, Michelle Kovacevic
613-957-3402, Fax: 613-952-5770,michelle_kovacevic@hc-sc.gc.ca
Chief Scientist, Wendy Sexsmith
613-941-3003, Fax: 613-941-3007,wendy.sexsmith@hc-sc.gc.ca

• Canadian Institutes of Health Research
• Hazardous Materials Information Review Commission(HMIRC) / Conseil de contrôle des renseignements relatifs aux matières dangereuses
427 Laurier Ave. West, 7th Fl.
Ottawa, ON K1A 1M3
613-993-4331 Fax: 613-993-4686
hmirc-ccrmd@hc-sc.gc.ca
www.hmirc-ccrmd.gc.ca
Independent agency that examines applications from suppliers & employers seeking exemptions from WHMIS disclosure requirements. Reviews the product labels & material safety data sheets related to claims &, if satisfied, keeps the actual ingredients on file & issues confidential numbers to safeguard the formulas. Fees are charged for the screening process & for administering appeals against the Commission's decisions.
• Pest Management Regulatory Agency(PMRA) / Agence de réglementation de la lutte antiparasitaire (ARLA)
2720 Riverside Dr.
Ottawa, ON K1A 0K9
613-736-3401 Fax: 613-736-3798
www.pmra-arla.gc.ca
Other Communication: Pesticides Information: 1-800-267-6315
The PMRA is responsible for protecting human health & the environment by minimizing the risks associated with pest control products. The Agency carries out its responsibility by evaluating pesticides to ensure they meet the latest human health & environmental safety standards before being registered for use in Canada; re-evaluating older pesticides to ensure they remain acceptable for use based on the latest standards; & setting the safe residue levels for pesticides in food. The Agency collaborates with Environment Canada, Agriculture & Agri-Food Canada, the Canadian Food Inspection Agency& other organizations in environmental pesticide research & monitoring, including sustainable pest management.
• Public Health Agency of Canada/ Agence de santé publique du Canada
130 Colonnade Rd.
Ottawa, ON K1A 0K9
www.phac-aspc.gc.ca/new_e.html
Promotes & protects the health & safety of all Canadians. Its activities focus on preventing chronic diseases, including cancer & heart disease, preventing injuries, & responding to public health emergencies & infectious disease outbreaks.

Corporate Services Branch / Direction générale aux services de gestion
Fax: 613-952-7580

Asst. Deputy Minister, Kin Choi
613-946-3209, Fax: 613-946-3236,kin.choi@hc-sc.gc.ca
Director General, Facilities & Security Directorate, Gary Lacey
613-692-6190, Fax: 613-946-0807,gary.lacey@hc-sc.gc.ca
Director General, Human Resources, Gerard Etienne
613-957-3236, Fax:
613-941-1814,gerard.etienne@hc-sc.gc.ca
Acting Director General, Planning, Integration & Management Services, Brenda Baxter
613-946-8132, Fax:
613-957-1587,brenda.baxter@hc-sc.gc.ca
Interim Chief Information Officer & Director General, Charles Henry
613-595-1307, charles.henry@hc-sc.gc.ca

First Nations & Inuit Health Branch / Direction générale de la santé des Premières nations et des Inuits
Fax: 613-957-1118

Assists First Nations & Inuit communities & people to address health inequalities & diseases threats through health surveillance & population health interventions. Ensures the availability of, or access to, health services for First Nations & Inuit people. Devolves control & management of community-based health services to First Nations & Inuit communities & organizations. The Environmental Health Division addresses conditions in the environment that could affect the health of community members, such as drinking water quality, mould, food safety, facilities inspections, transportation of dangerous goods. The Environmental Research Division conducts, coordinates & funds contaminants-related research, coordinates the replacement or upgrading of diesel-fuel tanks & remediation of fuel oil-contaminated sites, lab services for testing of PCBs & mercury, drinking water-related research & testing.
Acting Asst. Deputy Minister, Michelle Kovacevic
613-957-7700, michelle.kovacevic@hc-sc.gc.ca
Director General, Business Planning & Management Directorate, Stephane Hardy
613-946-8853, Fax:
613-948-4307,stephane.hardy@hc-sc.gc.ca
Director General, Community Programs, Kathy Langlois
613-952-9616, Fax:
613-941-3170,kathy.langlois@hc-sc.gc.ca
Director General, Non-Insured Health Benefits, Sony Perron
613-954-8825, Fax: 613-954-5265,sony.perron@hc-sc.gc.ca
Director General, Primary Health Care & Public Health, Shelagh Jane Woods
613-941-1956, Fax:
613-941-8904,shelagh.jane.woods@hc-sc.gc.ca
Director General, Strategic Policy, Planning & Analysis, David Baker
613-957-3402, Fax: 613-952-5770,david.baker@hc-sc.gc.ca
Director, Environmental Health, Ivy Chan
613-948-7773, Fax: 613-952-8639,ivy.chan@hc-sc.gc.ca
Director, Environmental Health Research, Roy Kwiatkowski
613-952-2828, Fax:
613-954-0692,roy.kwiatkowski@hc-sc.gc.ca
Manager, Drinking Water Program, Dominique Poulin
613-954-6655, Fax:
613-952-8639,dominique.poulin@hc-sc.gc.ca
Executive Director, Office of Community Medicine,Dr. RoseMarie Ramsingh
613-941-5358, Fax:
613-952-6407,rosemarie.ramsingh@hc-sc.gc.ca
Executive Director, Office of Nursing Services, Joyce Desjarlais
613-946-0442, Fax:
613-957-9986,joyce.desjarlais@hc-sc.gc.ca

Federal Hospitals (of twenty beds or more):

Fort Qu'Appelle Indian Hospital
Fort Qu'appelle, SK S0G 1S0
306-332-5611

Mayo General Hospital
Mayo, YT Y0B 1M0
867-996-2345

Moose Factory General Hospital
Moose Factory, ON P0L 1W0
705-658-4544

Percy E. Moore Hospital
Hodgson, MB R0C 1NO
204-372-8444

Sioux Lookout Zone Hospital
Sioux Lookout, ON P0V 2T0
807-737-3030

Whitehorse General Hospital
5 Hospital Rd., Whitehorse, YT Y1A 3H8
867-668-9444

Health Policy / Direction générale de la politique de la santé
Fax: 613-954-0336

Assoc. Asst. Deputy Minister, Abby Hoffman
613-946-1791, Fax:
613-954-0336,abby.hoffman@hc-sc.gc.ca
Director General, Applied Research & Analysis, Glenn Irwin
613-946-8030, Fax: 613-946-3166,glenn.irwin@hc-sc.gc.ca
Acting Director General, Health Care Policy, Gavin Brown
613-957-8994, Fax: 613-648-4663,gavin.brown@hc-sc.gc.ca
Director General, International Affairs, Bersabel Ephrem
613-941-3335, Fax:
613-952-7417,bersabel.ephrem@hc-sc.gc.ca
Director General, Policy Coordination & Planning Directorate, Marcel Saulnier
613-957-1940, marcel.saulnier@hc-sc.gc.ca
Executive Director, Nursing Policy Office, Sandra MacDonald-Rencz
613-941-4314, Fax:
613-946-3166,sandra.macdonald-rencz@hc-sc.gc.ca
Director, Federal-Provincial Relations, Barbara Moran
613-946-0345, Fax:
613-954-3580,barbara.moran@hc-sc.gc.ca

Health Products & Food Branch / Produits de santé et des aliments

HPFB's mandate is to take an integrated apporach to the management of risks & benefits related to health products & food by minimizing health factors to Canadians while maximizing the safety provided by the regulatory system for health products & food; & to promote conditions that enable Canadians to make healthy choices & provide information so that they can make informed decisions about their health. The Environmental Impact Initiative develops strategy & policy in response to the Canadian Environmental Protection Act requirement that all new substances for use in Canada must be assessed f or direct & indirect impact on human health & the environment.
Asst. Deputy Minister, Meena Ballantyne
613-957-1804, Fax:
613-957-3954,meena.ballantyne@hc-sc.gc.ca
Assoc. Asst. Deputy Minister, Catherine MacLeod
613-957-6817, Fax:
613-957-3954,catherine.macleod@hc-sc.gc.ca
Director General, Biologics & Genetic Therapies Directorate, Elwyn Griffiths
613-957-8065, Fax:
613-957-1679,elwyn.griffiths@hc-sc.gc.ca
Director General, Food Directorate,Dr. Samuel Godefroy
613-957-1821, Fax:
613-954-4674,samuel.godefroy@hc-sc.gc.ca
Director General, Marketed Health Products Directorate,Dr. Chris Turner
613-941-8889, Fax: 613-952-7738,chris.turner@hc-sc.gc.ca
Director General, Natural Health Products, Michelle Boudreau
613-952-2558, Fax:
613-948-6810,michelle.boudreau@hc-sc.gc.ca
Director General, Office of Nutrition Policy & Promotion,Dr. Hasan Hutchinson
613-957-8330, Fax:
613-946-8073,hasan.hutchinson@hc-sc.gc.ca,
Director General, Policy, Planning & International Affairs Directorate, Kendal Weber
613-952-8149, Fax:
613-954-9981,kendal.weber@hc-sc.gc.ca
Director General, Therapeutic Products Directorate,Dr. Supriya Sharma
613-957-6466, Fax:
613-952-7756,supriya.sharma@hc-sc.gc.ca
Director General, Veterinary Drugs Directorate,Dr. Ian Alexander
613-957-3859, Fax:
613-954-5694,ian.alexander@hc-sc.gc.ca
Director, Environmental Impact Initiative, Gordon Stringer
613-957-6682, Fax:
613-954-1556,gordon.stringer@hc-sc.gc.ca
Director, Litigation Support & Document Management Services, Mario Brillant
613-941-8256, mario.brillant@hc-sc.gc.ca

Healthy Environments & Consumer Safety Branch / Santé environnementale et sécurité des consommateurs
613-946-6700, Fax: 613-946-6666,
www.hc-sc.gc.ca/ahc-asc/branch-dirgen/hecs-dgsesc/index-eng.php

The Healthy Environments & Consumer Safety Branch promotes healthy & safe living, working & recreational environments with emphasis on health in the work environment & occupational health & safety. It assesses & reduces health risks posed by environmental factors & it regulates the safety of industrial & consumer goods. The branch also regulates tobacco & controlled substances, coordinates Canada's Drug Strategy, promotes initiatives that reduce or prevent the harm associated with tobacco, alcohol & other substances, & provides expert advice & drug analysis services to law enforcement agencies across the country. Finally, it is responsible for coordinating & monitoring Health Canada's Sustainable Development Strategy
Asst. Deputy Minister, Paul Glover
613-946-6701, paul.glover@hc-sc.gc.ca
Director General, Consumer Product Safety Directorate, Athana Mentzelopoulos
613-960-4725, Fax:
613-946-1100,athana.mentzelopoulos@hc-sc.gc.ca
Director General, Controlled Substances & Tobacco Directorate, Cathy A. Sabiston
613-941-1977, Fax:
613-946-6460,cathy.a.sabiston@hc-sc.gc.ca
Director General, Environmental & Radiation Health Sciences Directorate, Beth Pieterson
613-954-3859, beth.pieterson@hc-sc.gc.ca
Director General, Policy, Planning & Integration Directorate, Hilary Geller
613-946-6706, Fax: 613-954-5268,hilary.geller@hc-sc.gc.ca
Director General, Safe Environment Directorate, Karen Lloyd
613-954-0291, Fax: 613-952-2206,karen.lloyd@hc-sc.gc.ca
Director, Environmental Health Science & Research, David Blakey
613-957-3966, Fax: 613-957-3952,david.blakey@hc-sc.gc.ca
Director, Office of Controlled Substances, Diane Allan
613-952-2177, Fax: 613-946-4224,diane.allan@hc-sc.gc.ca
Director, Office of Workforce Initiatives, Debbie Holbrook
613-952-8773, Fax:
613-946-5692,debbie.holbrook@hc-sc.gc.ca
Director, Water, Air & Climate Change Bureau, John Cooper
613-948-2568, Fax: 613-952-2574,john.cooper@hc-sc.gc.ca

Regional Offices:

Alberta
9700 Jasper Ave., Edmonton, AB T5J 4C3
780-495-5147, Fax: 780-495-5551
Regional Director General, Arthur J. Murphy
780-495-6737, arthur.j.murphy@hc-sc.gc.ca

Atlantic
1505 Barrington St., Halifax, NS B3J 3Y6
902-426-6861, Fax: 902-426-3768
Regional Director General, Simon d'Entremont
902-426-4097, Fax:
902-426-6659,simon.dentremont@hc-sc.gc.ca

British Columbia
757 Hastings St. West, Vancouver, BC V6C 3E6
604-666-2396, Fax: 604-775-8716
Regional Director General, Catherine Lappe
604-775-7003, catherine.lappe@hc-sc.gc.ca

Manitoba/Saskatchewan Region
391 York Ave., Winnipeg, MB R3C 4W1
204-983-4764, Fax: 204-983-5325
Regional Director General, Laurette Burch
204-984-4363, laurette.burch@hc-sc.gc.ca

Northern Region
60 Queen St., Ottawa, ON K1A 0K9
613-954-2038, Fax: 613-948-2428
Acting Regional Director General, Cathy Praamsma
613-946-8104

Ontario
180 Queen St. West, Toronto, ON M5V 3L7
416-954-3593, Fax: 416-954-3599
Acting Regional Director General, Lucy Butts
416-954-3592, lucy.butts@hc-sc.gc.ca

Québec
Guy-Favreau Complexe, Tour Est, 200, boul René-Lévesque ouest, 2e étage, Montréal, QC H2Z 1X4
514-283-2569, Fax: 514-283-1364
Regional Director General, Marie-France Bérard
514-283-2856, Fax:
514-283-0910,marie-france.berard@hc-sc.gc.ca
Director General, Eric Russell
613-957-3375
Director, Environmental Management Systems Division, Elyse Routhier
613-952-2220
Executive Director, Facilities Management Division, Veronica Barnes
613-952-0936, Fax: 613-952-7389
Director, Health, Safety & Security Division, Sharon Savoie
613-957-1556, Fax: 613-941-2396
Executive Director, Material Management Division, Emmanuel Kitcher
613-941-3724, Fax: 613-941-2645
Acting Director General, Jamie Tibbetts
613-957-7762
Director, Financial Information & Accounting Services Division, Michelle Gleeson
613-957-7758

Director, Financial Services, Administration Program, Barry McBride
613-946-6477
Director, Planning, Analysis & Reporting Division, André Léger
613-957-3100, Fax: 613-952-7328
Acting Director, Revenue & Costing, Gregory Zubacz
613-957-2280
Director, Health Program Support,Vacant
613-957-3388, Fax: 613-954-8107
Director, Health Programs Analysis,Vacant
613-957-8367, Fax: 613-941-8904
Director, Research & Development Environmental Contaminants,Vacant
613-957-3428, Fax: 613-954-0692
Director, Benefit Management, Brenda Czich
613-954-9876,
Director, First Nations & Inuit Liaison/ Policy & Program Development,Vacant
613-941-5466
Director, Program Operations,Vacant
613-957-3294
Director, Program Analysis/Risk Management, Tom Bird
613-952-8580
Acting Director, Canada Health Act Division, Gigi Mandy
613-954-8685
Director, Federal-Provincial Relations Division, Aruna Sehgal
613-946-0345, Fax: 613-954-3580
Director, Health Human Resources Division, Robert Shearer
613-954-8608
Director, Health Care System Division, Mary Gregory
613-952-6717
Director, Primary Health Care, Nancy Swainson
613-954-0834
Director, International Health,Vacant
613-957-7288
Director General, Caroline Weber
613-957-1940
Director, Coordination Division, Gweneth Gowanlock
613-941-5494, Fax: 613-957-0154
Director, Horizontal Policy & Strategic Planning, Marian Campbell Jarvis
613-957-3084
Director, Policy Division, Phyllis Colvin
613-957-3085
Acting Director, Special Projects Division, Michael Vandergrift
613-957-8994
Director, Drug Analysis Service, Richard Viau
613-941-7290
Director, Office of Controlled Substances, Carole Bouchard
613-952-2177
Director, Office of Cannabis Medical Access,Vacant
613-941-2504
Director General,Vacant
613-941-1977
Director, Policy, Brenda Paine
613-941-9826
Director, Research Evaluation & Surveillance, Murray Kaiserman
613-954-5851
Director, Mass Media,Vacant
613-941-1564
Director, Consumer & Clinical Radiation Protection Bureau, Robert P. Bradley
613-954-6701
Director, Consumer Product Safety, Marta Caris
613-957-4469
Director, Product Safety Laboratory, Stephen Lee
613-952-0853
Acting Director, New Substances Assessment & Control, Jackie Sitwell
613-957-1501
Regional Manager, Barry Gordon
403-292-4106, gordonb@em.agr.ca
Regional Manager, Neil McTiernan
506-851-7876, mctiernann@em.agr.ca
Regional Manager, Ilze Rupners
613-666-0741, rupnersi@em.agr.ca
Regional Manager, Shannon Van Wallegham
204-983-8662, vanwalleghems@em.agr.ca
Regional Manager, Ross Pettigrew
519-837-9400, pettigrewr@em.agr.ca
Regional Manager, Johanne Lafortune
514-283-8888, lafortunej@em.agr.ca
Regional Manager, Bill Maksymetz
306-780-7123, bmaksymetz@em.agr.ca

Human Resources & Skills Development Canada (HRSDC) / Ressources humaines et Développement des compétences Canada (RHDCC)

140 Promenade du Portage, Ottawa, ON K1A 0J9
www.hrsdc.gc.ca
Other Communication: Employment Insurance: 1-800-206-7218; Income Security Programs: 1-800-277-9914
HRSDC works to build a competitive country & to support Canadians in making choices to live productively. The following are key responsibilities of the federal department: developing policies to assist Canadaians to use their talents, skills & resources to participate in learning, work, & their community; creating programs to support initiative to help citizens in life transitions; improving outcomes for people through services offered by Service Canada & other partners; & establishing a healthy work environment.
Acts Administered:
Canada Labour Code
Canada Pension Plan
Canada Student Financial Assistance Act
Canada Student Loans Act
Canadian Centre for Occupational Health & Safety Act
Corporations & Labour Unions Returns Act
Department of Human Resources Development Act
Employment Equity Act
Employment Insurance Act
Fair Wages & Hours of Labour Act
Family Orders & Agreements Enforcement Assistance Act
Federal-Provincial Fiscal Arrangements Act
Government Annuities Act
Government Employees Compensation Act
Labour Adjustment Benefits Act
Merchant Seamen Compensation Act
Non-smokers' Health Act (Transport Canada)
Old Age Security Act
Status of the Artist Act
Unemployment Assistance Act
Vocational Rehabilitation of Disabled Persons Act
Wages Liability Act
Minister, Human Resources & Skills Development,Hon. Diane Finley, B.A., M.B.A.
613-996-4974, Fax: 613-996-9749,Finley.D@parl.gc.ca; diane.finley@hrsdc-rhdsc.gc.ca
Minister, Labour,Hon. Lisa Raitt
613-996-7046, Fax: 613-992-0851,Raitt.L@parl.gc.ca, Other Communications: Labour, Phone: 819-953-5646, Fax: 819-994-5168,
Parliamentary Secretary to the Minister of Human Resources & Skills Development Canada & to the Minister of Labour, Ed Komarnicki
613-992-7685, Fax:
613-995-8908,Komarnicki.E@parl.gc.ca
Deputy Minister of Human Resources & Skills Development Canada, Ian Shugart
819-994-4514, Fax:
819-953-5603,ian.shugart@hrsdc-rhdcc.gc.ca
• Canada Employment Insurance Commission(CEIC) / Commission de l'assurance-emploi du Canada (CAEC)
140, Promenade du Portage, Phase IV
Gatineau, QC K1A 0J9
800-206-7218
www.ei-ae.gc.ca
Manages the Employment Insurance Program.
• Canada Industrial Relations Board/ Conseil canadien des relations industrielles
• Canadian Centre for Occupational Health & Safety/ Centre canadien d'hygiène et de sécurité au travail
• Canadian Council of Directors of Apprenticeship/ Conseil canadien des directeurs de l'apprentissage
140 Promenade du Portage, 5th Fl, Phase IV
Gatineau, QC K1A 0J9
819-953-7443 Fax: 819-994-0202
redseal-sceaurouge@hrsdc-rhdcc.gc.ca
www.red-seal.ca
A national body responsible for the certification of skilled workers, in the regulated trade, under the Interprovincial Standards (Red Seal) Program. This program is designed to facilitate the mobility of workers employed in the apprenticeable occupations in Canada through the establishment of common standards for certification. The apprenticeship program is generally administered by provincial & territorial departments responsible for education, labour & training (under the direction of the provincial & territorial Director of Apprenticeship) with authority delegated from the legislation in each province & territory. Through the program, apprentices who have completed their training & certified journeymen are able to obtain a Red Sealendorsement on their Certificate of Qualification by successfully completing an Interprovincial Standards Examination. The program encourages standardization of provincial & territorial apprenticeship training & certification programs. The Red Seal allows qualified trade persons to practice the trade in any province or territory in Canada where the trade is designated without having to write further examinations.
• Merchant Seamen Compensation Board/ Commission d'indemnisation des marins marchands du Canada
Secretary, Merchant Seamen Compensation Board
Phase II, Place du Portage, 10th Fl.
Gatineau, QC K1A 0J2
819-953-8001 Fax: 819-994-5368
• Office of the Commissioner of Review Tribunals/ Bureau du Commissaire des tribunaux de revision
PO Box 8250 T
Ottawa, ON K1G 5S5
613-954-1313 Fax: 613-946-1588 800-363-0076
info@ocrt-bctr.gc.ca
www.ocrt-bctr.gc.ca
Review Tribunals were created to provide a body independent from government to make determinations about eligibility for persons claiming CPP & OAS benefits that had previously been denied.
• Pension Appeals Board/ Commission d'appel des pensions
PO Box 8567 T
Ottawa, ON K1G 3H9
613-995-0612 Fax: 613-995-6834 888-640-8001
info@pab-cap.gc.ca
www.pab-cap.gc.ca
The Pension Appeals Board is the final opportunity for appeal under the Canada Pension Plan. Responsible for the hearing of appeals which arise from the decisions of the Review Tribunals of the Office of the Commissioner.

Citizen Service Branch / Direction générale de service aux citoyens

Asst. Deputy Minister, Charles Nixon
613-957-4500, Fax:
613-960-2489,charles.nixon@servicecanada.gc.ca
Program Officer, Josée Laperrière
613-957-9151, Fax:
613-960-2489,josee.laperriere@servicecanada.gc.ca

Corporate Stakeholder Relations / Relations avec les intervenants

Part II of the Canada Labour Code - Occupational Health & Safety - promotes & enforces federal occupational safety & health legislation & regulations. The Labour Program also uses its technical expertise in specialized fields such as industrial hygiene & industrial safety engineering to administer the legislation.
Director, Marie-Claude Pelletier
819-994-6309, Fax:
819-953-8136,marieclaude.pelletier@hrsdc-rhdcc.gc.ca
Assoc. Director, Kathy Kennedy
819-994-9658, kathy.kennedy@hrsdc-rhdcc.gc.ca

Homelessness Partnering Secretariat / Secrétariat des partenariats de lutte contre l'itinérance

165, rue Hôtel-de-Ville, Gatineau, QC K1A 0J2
Director General, Barbara Lawless
819-997-5464, Fax:
819-994-4211,barbara.lawless@hrsdc-rhdcc.gc.ca
Director, Communities & Partnerships Division, James Young
819-956-6857, Fax:
819-934-5309,james.young@hrsdc-rhdcc.gc.ca
Director, Planning & Coordination Division, Shirley Dyck
819-953-3701, Fax:
819-994-4211,shirley.dyck@hrsdc-rhdcc.gc.ca
Director, Properties, Results & Information Division, Myriam Paré
819-994-4748, Fax:
819-994-4211,myriam.pare@hrsdc-rhdcc.gc.ca

Labour / Travail

Deputy Minister, Hélène Gosselin
819-934-3320, Fax:
819-934-7066,gosselin.helene@labour-travail.gc.ca
Asst. Deputy Minister, Marie-Geneviève Mounier
819-997-1493, Fax:
819-953-5685,mg.mounier@labour-travail.gc.ca
Director General, Federal Mediation & Conciliation Service, Guy Baron
819-994-1118, Fax:
819-997-1693,guy.baron@labour-travail.gc.ca
Director General, International & Intergovernmental Labour Affairs, Debra Young
819-953-7405, Fax:
819-953-0227,debra.young@labour-travail.gc.ca
Director General, Program Development & Guidance Directorate, Caroline Cyr
819-934-3331, Fax:
819-953-8883,caroline.cyr@labour-travail.gc.ca
Director General, Regional Operations & Compliance Directorate, Danicae Shimbashi
819-997-0252, Fax:
613-956-7521,danica.shimbashi@labour-travail.gc.ca
Director General, Strategic Policy, Analysis & Workplace, Anthony J. Giles

819-997-4621, Fax:
819-994-0165,anthony.giles@labour-travail.gc.ca
Senior Director, Labour Standards & Workplace Equity, Jan Michaels
819-934-5745, Fax:
819-997-3701,jan.michaels@labour-travail.gc.ca
Director, Occupational Health & Safety Tribunal Canada, Pierre Rousseau
613-957-6344, Fax:
613-954-6404,pierre.rousseau@ohstc-tsstc.gc.ca

Learning Branch / Apprentissage
Asst. Deputy Minister, Kathryn McDade
819-953-3712, Fax:
819-953-7427,kathryn.mcdade@hrsdc-rhdcc.gc.ca
Director General, Canada Education Savings Program, David Swol
819-953-1530, Fax:
819-953-6500,david.swol@hrsdc-rhdcc.gc.ca
Director General, Canada Student Loans Directorate, Marc LeBrun
819-997-6684, Fax:
819-953-4226,marc.l.lebrun@hrsdc-rhdcc.gc.ca
Director General, Program Policy Planning, Danièle Besner
819-953-1966, Fax:
819-994-1868,daniele.besner@hrsdc-rhdcc.gc.ca

Service Canada
140, Promenade du Portage, Gatineau, QC K1A 0J9
800-622-6232
www.servicecanada.gc.ca
Service Canada was created in 2005 to improve the delivery of government programs and services to Canadians, by making access to them faster, easier, and more convenient. Service Canada offers single-window access to a wide range of Government of Canada programs and services for citizens through more than 600 points of service located across the country, call centres, and the Internet.
Senior Assist. Deputy Minister, Carolina Giliberti
819-934-1504, Fax:
819-934-1505,carolina.giliberti@servicecanada.gc.ca
Head, Service Delivery, Robin Flaherty
613-991-8061, Fax:
613-941-1827,robin.flaherty@servicecanada.gc.ca,
Director General, Citizen Service Strategy Directorate, Victor Abele
613-957-6727, Fax:
613-957-4400,victor.abele@servicecanada.gc.ca
Director General, Service Management, Mary O'Neill
819-956-7659, Fax:
819-953-1225,mary.o'neill@servicecanada.gc.ca
Director, Web Strategies & Product Management, Minh Doan
613-957-6220, Fax:
613-957-6767,minh.doan@servicecanada.gc.ca

Service Canada Centres:

Alberta, Northwest Territories & Nunavut:

Calgary Centre
#270, 220 - 4 Ave. SE, Calgary, AB T2G 4X3
Fax: 403-292-6561, 800-622-6232

Calgary East
#1502, 515 Marlborough Way NE, Calgary, AB T2A 7E7
Fax: 403-292-6845, 800-622-6232

Calgary North
1816 Crowchild Trail NW, PO Box 65037 North Hill, Calgary, AB T2N 4T6
Fax: 403-292-4076, 800-622-6232

Calgary South
Fisher Park Place II, #100, 6712 Fisher St. SE, Calgary, AB T2H 1X3
Fax: 403-292-5763, 800-622-6232

Cambridge Bay
15 Amogok, PO Box 2010, Cambridge Bay, NU X0C 0E0
867-983-4025, 800-622-6232

Camrose
4901 - 50 Ave., Camrose, AB T2H 1X3
780-672-1440, 800-622-6232

Canmore
Bldg. C, #113, 802 Bow Valley Trail, Canmore, AB T1W 1N6
403-609-6456, 800-622-6232

Edmonton Canada Place
Canada Place, #1440, 9700 Jasper Ave., Edmonton, AB T5J 4C1
800-829-6891
Other Communication: Toll Free Fax: 1-800-622-6232

Edmonton Meadowlark
#120, 15710 - 87 Ave. NW, Edmonton, AB T5R 5W9
Fax: 780-495-7717, 800-622-6232

Edmonton North
#2000, 9499 - 137 Ave. NW, Edmonton, AB T5E 5R8
780-495-3904, 800-622-6232

Edmonton South
6325 Gateway Blvd., Edmonton, AB T6H 5H6
Fax: 780-495-3902, 800-622-6232

Edson
#102, 111 - 54 St., Edson, AB T7E 1T2
780-723-3634, 800-622-6232

Fort McMurray
9915 Franklin Ave., Fort McMurray, AB T9H 2K4
800-622-6232

Fort Simpson
9606 - 100 St., PO Box 380, Fort Simpson, NT X0E 0P0
867-695-2238, Fax: 867-695-2229

Fort Smith
136 McDougal Rd., PO Box 1018, Fort Smith, NT X0E 0P0
867-872-2747, Fax: 867-872-2616

Hay River
#204, 41 Capital Dr., PO Box 204, Hay River, NT X0E 1G2
867-874-6739, Fax: 867-874-6100

Red Deer
4911 - 51 St., 2nd Fl., PO Box 5050, Lethbridge, AB T4N 6A1
Fax: 403-341-7105, 800-622-6232

Grande Prairie
#100, 9845 - 99 Ave., Grande Prairie, AB T8V 0R3
Fax: 780-532-3488, 800-622-6232

Inuvik
170 McKenzie Rd., PO Box 1678, Inuvik, NT X0E 0T0
867-777-2122, Fax: 867-777-4369

Iqaluit
#300, Iqaluit House, PO Box 639, Iqaluit, NU X0A 0H0
867-975-4700, Fax: 867-975-4711,

Lethbridge
200 - 5 Ave. South, Lethbridge, AB T1J 4L1
Fax: 403-381-5668, 800-622-6232

Lloydminster
5016 - 48 St., Lloydminster, AB T9V 0H8
780-871-7065, 800-622-6232

Medicine Hat
#4, 346 - 3 St. SE, Medicine Hat, AB T1A 0G7
403-529-1755, 800-622-6232

Rankin Inlet
PO Box 97, Rankin Inlet, NU X0C 0G0
867-645-4092, 800-260-0877

St Paul
5126 - 50 Ave., St Paul, AB T0A 3A0
780-645-777, 800-622-6232

Slave Lake
101 Main St. South, 2nd Fl., Slave Lake, AB T0G 2A0
780-849-3377, 800-622-6232

Yellowknife
5101 - 50 Ave., PO Box 1170, Yellowknife, NT X1A 3Z4
867-766-8300, Fax: 867-873-3621

British Columbia & Yukon:

BC/Yukon Regional Headquarters
#1400, 300 Georgia St. West, Vancouver, BC V6B 6G3
604-666-2282, Fax: 604-666-8222,
Other Communication: BC/Yukon Email:
bcytprograminquiry@servicecanada.gc.ca

Abbotsford
32525 Simon Ave., Abbotsford, BC V2T 6T6
604-854-5852, Fax: 604-870-2765

Burnaby
4729 Canada Way, Burnaby, BC V5G 4Y2
604-437-3761, Fax: 604-666-1015

Central & Northern Vancouver Island
#201, 60 Front St., Nanaimo, BC V9R 5H7
250-754-0222, Fax: 250-754-0319

Coquitlam
#100, 2963 Glen Dr., Coquitlam, BC V3B 2P7
604-464-7144, Fax: 604-945-1600

CPP/OAS BC/Yukon Processing Centre
PO Box 1177, Victoria, BC V8W 2V2
800-277-9914
bcytispinquiry@servicecanada.gc.c
Other Communication: Ligne sans frais: 1-800-277-9915

Kamloops
235 Lansdowne St., Kamloops, BC V2C 1X8
250-372-2515, Fax: 250-372-0761

Kelowna
471 Queensway Ave., Kelowna, BC V1Y 6S5
250-762-3018, Fax: 250-762-0357

Nelson
333 Victoria St., Nelson, BC V1L 4K3
250-352-3155, Fax: 250-352-5170

North Shore
#100, 221 West Esplanade, North Vancouver, BC V7M 3N7
604-988-1151, Fax: 604-666-6494

Prince George
1363 - 4 Ave., Prince George, BC V2L 3J6
250-561-5200, Fax: 250-561-5504

Southern Vancouver Island
595 Pandora Ave., Victoria, BC V8W 1N5
250-220-3200, Fax: 250-363-0553

Surrey
7404 King George Hwy., Surrey, BC V3W 0L4
604-590-3346, Fax: 604-590-5351

Terrace
4630 Lazelle Ave., Terrace, BC V8G 1S6
250-635-7134, Fax: 250-635-4073,

Vancouver
125 - 10 Ave. East, Vancouver, BC V5T 1Z3
604-872-7431, Fax: 604-666-1205

Whitehorse
#125, 300 Main St., Whitehorse, YT Y1A 2B5
867-667-5083, Fax: 867-668-6801

Manitoba:

Brandon
1039 Princess Ave., Brandon, MB R7A 6E2
204-726-7700, Fax: 204-726-7744

Dauphin
135 - 2 Ave. NE, Dauphin, MB R7N 0Z6
Fax: 204-622-4045, 800-622-6232

Flin Flon
111 Main St., Flin Flon, MB R8A 1J9
Fax: 204-687-4607

La Verendrye
#100, 614 Des Meurons St., Winnipeg, MB R2H 2P9
204-984-3438, Fax: 204-983-3719

Morden
158 Stephen St., Morden, MB R6M 1T3
204-822-7370, Fax: 204-822-7384

Notre-Dame-des-Lourdes
51 Rodgers St., PO Box 82, Notre Dame de Lourdes, QC R0G 1M0
204-248-7201, Fax: 204-248-7207

Portage la Prairie
1016 Saskatchewan Ave. East, Portage la Prairie, MB R1N 3V2
Fax: 204-239-8432, 800-622-6232

Saint-Pierre-Jolys
427 Sabourin St., PO Box 98, Saint-Pierre-Jolys, MB R0A 1V0
204-433-7373, Fax: 204-433-7356

Selkirk
237 Manitoba Ave., PO Box 7000, Selkirk, MB R1A 2M8
204-785-6200, Fax: 204-785-6222

Steinbach
321 Main St., Steinbach, MB R5G 1Z2
204-326-1371, Fax: 204-326-1275

Swan River
201 - 4 Ave. South, Swan River, MB R0L 1Z0
Fax: 204-734-5151, 800-206-7218

The Pas
305 - 4 Ave. SW, PO Box 660, The Pas, MB
Fax: 204-623-7205, 800-623-2

Thompson
#118, 3 Station Rd., Thompson, MB R8N 0N3
Fax: 204-677-7147, 800-622-6232

Winnipeg Centre
#201, 391 York Ave., PO Box 8850, Winnipeg, MB R3C 3E6
Fax: 204-984-8029, 800-206-7218

Winnipeg Northeast
1122 Henderson Hwy., Winnipeg, MB R2G 1L1

Fax: 204-983-4404, 800-622-6232

Winnipeg Southwest
3338 Portage Ave., Winnipeg, MB R3K 0Z1
Fax: 204-983-0319, 800-206-7218

Winnipeg St. Boniface
1031 Autumnwood Dr., Winnipeg, MB R2J 1C6
Fax: 204-983-0535, 800-206-7218

New Brunswick:

Bathurst
120 Harbourview Blvd., PO Box 4000, Bathurst, NB E2A 1R6
506-548-7998, Fax: 506-548-7186

Campbellton
157 Water St., PO Box 5002, Campbellton, NB E3N 3L3
Fax: 506-789-4547, 800-206-7218

Edmundston
22 Emmerson St., Edmundston, NB E3V 1R7
506-739-0222, Fax: 506-739-0220,
nb.inquiries@hrdc-drhc.gc.ca

Fredericton
633 Queen St., PO Box 12000, Fredericton, NB E3B 5G4
506-452-3823, Fax: 506-452-3303

Miramichi
150 Pleasant St., PO Box 1030, Miramichi, NB E1V 1Y1
506-627-2033, Fax: 506-627-2049,
nb.inquiries@hrdc-dhrc.gc.ca

Moncton
#310, 95 Foundry St., PO Box 5003, Moncton, NB E1C 8R5
506-851-6718, Fax: 506-851-6941

Saint John
1 Agar Place, PO Box 7000, Saint John, NB E2L 4V4
Fax: 506-636-3808, 800-206-7218

Newfoundland & Labrador:

Clarenville
50 Manitoba Dr., Clarenville, NL A5A 1K5
709-466-8200, Fax: 709-466-8210

Corner Brook
1 Regent Sq., PO Box 2004, Corner Brook, NL A2H 491
709-637-4243, Fax: 709-637-4224

Gander
1 Markham Place, PO Box 347, Gander, NL A1V 1W7
709-256-6519, Fax: 709-256-6506

Happy Valley-Goose Bay
23 Broomfield St., PO Box 3010 B, Happy Valley-Goose Bay, NL A0P 1E0
709-896-6270, Fax: 709-896-6268

Labrador West
500 Vanier Ave., Labrador City, NL A2V 2W7
709-944-3655, Fax: 709-944-3381

Placentia
61 Blockhouse Rd., PO Box 339, Placentia, NL A0B 2Y0
709-227-4001, Fax: 709-227-5588

Port Aux Basques
#4, 10 High St., PO Box 849, Port aux Basques, NL A0M 1C0
709-695-5002, Fax: 709-695-9671

St. John's
223 Churchill Ave., PO Box 8548, St. John's, NL A1B 3P3
709-772-2982, Fax: 709-772-0354

Nova Scotia:

Amherst
#202, 26-28 Prince Arthur St., Amherst, NS B4H 1V6
902-661-6619, Fax: 902-661-6637

Antigonish
325 Main St., 2nd Fl., Antigonish, NS B2G 2C3
902-863-7069, Fax: 902-863-7053

Bedford
1597 Bedford Hwy., PO Box 44176, Bedford, NS B4A 1E7
902-426-7698, Fax: 902-426-5552

Bridgewater
77 Dufferin St., PO Box 3100, Bridgewater, NS B4V 3J1
902-527-5524, Fax: 902-527-5570

Dartmouth
46 Portland St., PO Box 2400, Dartmouth, NS B2Y 1H3
902-426-5512, Fax: 902-426-7301

Digby
84 Warwick St., PO Box 1540, Digby, NS B0V 1A0
902-245-4784, Fax: 902-245-6226

Glace Bay
#201, 633 Main St., Glace Bay, NS B1A 6J3
902-842-2414, Fax: 902-842-2655

Halifax
7001 Mumford Rd., PO Box 1800, Halifax, NS B3J 3V1
902-426-9617, Fax: 902-426-7690,

Kentville
495 Main St., 2nd Fl., Kentville, NS B4N 3W5
902-679-5772, Fax: 902-679-5786

New Glasgow
340 East River Rd., New Glasgow, NS B2H 3P7
902-755-7826, Fax: 902-755-7869

North Sydney
105 King St., North Sydney, NS B2A 3S1
902-794-5715, Fax: 902-794-5724

Port Hawkesbury
#8, 811 Reeves St., Port Hawkesbury, NS B9A 2S4
902-625-4115, Fax: 902-625-4137

Shelburne
218 Water St., PO Box 819, Shelburne, NS B0T 1W0
902-875-3940, Fax: 902-875-3505

Sydney
15 Dorchester St., PO Box 850, Sydney, NS B1P 6J3
902-564-7249, Fax: 902-564-7104

Truro
#8, 60 Lorne St., Truro, NS B2N 3K3
902-893-0016, Fax: 902-893-0075

Windsor
90 Water St., PO Box 2760, Windsor, NS B0N 2T0
902-798-6518, Fax: 902-798-5816

Yarmouth
13 Willow St., PO Box 249, Yarmouth, NS B5A 4B2
902-742-6178, Fax: 902-742-0815

Ontario:

Ajax
320 Harwood Ave., Ajax, ON L1S 2J1
905-725-2001, Fax: 905-428-8410,
ontario.inquiry@hrsdc-rhdcc.gc.ca

Arnprior
#1 & 2, 75 Elgin St. West, Arnprior, ON K7S 3T9
613-623-3173, Fax: 613-623-2104,
ontario.inquiry@hrsdc-rhdcc.gc.ca

Bancroft
5 Fairway Blvd., Bancroft, ON K0L 1C0
Fax: 613-332-5517, 800-206-7218
ontario.inquiry@hrsdc-rhdcc.gc.ca

Barrie
#301, 48 Owen St., Barrie, ON L4M 3H1
705-728-2468, Fax: 705-725-2501,
ontario.inquiry@hrsdc-rhdcc.gc.ca

Belleville
1 North Front St., 2nd Fl., PO Box 4800, Belleville, ON K8N 5E2
613-969-3350, Fax: 613-969-3347,
ontario.inquiry@hrsdc-rhdcc.gc.ca

Bracebridge
98 Manitoba St., 2nd Fl., Bracebridge, ON P1L 1S1
705-645-2204, Fax: 705-645-7313,
ontario.inquiry@hrsdc-rhdcc.gc.ca

Brampton
18 Corporation Dr., Brampton, ON L6S 6B2
905-790-2525, Fax: 905-789-3885,
ontario.inquiry@hrsdc-rhdcc.gc.ca

Brantford
58 Dalhousie St., 2nd Fl., Brantford, ON N3T 2J2
519-751-6500, Fax: 519-751-6529,
ontario.inquiry@hrsdc-rhdcc.gc.ca

Brockville
153 King St. West, Brockville, ON K6V 3R4
613-342-4487, Fax: 613-342-7580,
ontario.inquiry@hrsdc-rhdcc.gc.ca

Burlington
440 Elizaebth St., Burlington, ON L7R 2M1
905-637-4525, Fax: 905-637-9585,
ontario.inquiry@hrsdc-rhdcc.gc.ca

Cambridge
73 Water St. North, Cambridge, ON N1R 7L6
519-579-1550, Fax: 519-571-5508,
ontario.inquiry@hrsdc-rhdcc.gc.ca

Carleton Place
46 Lansdowne Ave., Carleton Place, ON K7C 3S9
613-257-3344, Fax: 613-257-2505,
ontario.inquiry@hrsdc-rhdcc.gc.ca

Chatham-Kent
120 Wellington St. West, Chatham, ON N7M 4V9
519-380-6800, Fax: 519-380-6846,
ontario.inquiry@hrsdc-rhdcc.gc.ca

Cobourg
#103, 1005 Elgin St. West, Cobourg, ON K9A 5J4
905-372-3326, Fax: 905-372-1277,
ontario.inquiry@hrsdc-rhdcc.gc.ca

Collingwood
44 Huronontario St., Collingwood, ON L9Y 2L6
705-445-1010, Fax: 705-445-8643

Cornwall
111 Water St. East, Cornwall, ON K6H 6S4
613-938-5731, Fax: 613-938-9876,
ontario.inquiry@hrsdc-rhdcc.gc.ca

Dryden
41C Duke St., Dryden, ON P8N 1E6
807-223-2331, Fax: 807-223-6615,
ontario.inquiry@hrsdc-rhdcc.gc.ca

Elliot Lake
151 Ontario Ave., Elliot Lake, ON P5A 2T2
705-848-2231, Fax: 705-848-0971,
ontario.inquiry@hrsdc-rhdcc.gc.ca

Espanola
#200, 800 Centre St., Espanola, ON P5E 1J3
705-869-7030, Fax: 705-869-7035,
ontario.inquiry@hrsdc0rhdcc.gc.ca

Fort Frances
301 Scott St., Fort Frances, ON P9A 1H1
807-274-5307, Fax: 807-274-7858,
ontario.inquiry@hrsdc-rhdcc.gc.ca

Gananoque
5 Charles St. South, Gananoque, ON K7G 1V9
613-382-2124, Fax: 613-382-8942,
ontario.inquiry@hrsdc-rhdcc.gc.ca

Georgetown
232 Guelph St., Georgetown, ON L7G 4B1
905-877-6915, Fax: 905-877-4370,
ontario.inquiry@hrsdc-hrdcc.gc.ca

Geraldton
208 Beamish St., PO Box 640, Geraldton, ON P0T 1M0
807-854-0635, Fax: 807-854-0335,
ontario.inquiry@hrsdc-rhdcc.gc.ca

Goderich
52 East St., Goderich, ON N7A 1N3
519-524-8342, Fax: 519-524-6809,
ontario.inquiry@hrsdc-rhdcc.gc.ca

Guelph
259 Woodlawn Rd. West, Unit C, Guelph, ON N1H 8J1
Fax: 519-826-2257, 800-265-3595
ontario.inquiry@hrsdc-rhdcc.gc.ca

Hamilton Central/East
2255 Barton St. East, Hamilton, ON L8H 7T4
905-572-2211, Fax: 905-573-4117,
ontario.inquiry@hrsdc-rhdcc.gc.ca

Hamilton Mountain
1550 Upper James St., PO Box 2066 A, Hamilton, ON L9B 1K3
905-572-2211, Fax: 905-572-2563,
ontario.inquiry@hrsdc-rhdcc.gc.ca

Hawkesbury
134 Main St. East, Hawkesbury, ON K6A 1A3
613-632-2759, Fax: 613-632-6976

Kapuskasing
8 Queen St., Kapuskasing, ON P5N 1G7
705-335-2337, Fax: 705-337-1197,
ontario.inquiry@hrsdc-rhdcc.gc.ca

Kenora
308 Second St. South, 2nd Fl., PO Box 5170, Kenora, ON P9N 3X9
807-467-5700, Fax: 807-468-6209,
ontairo.inquiry@hrsdc-rhdcc.gc.ca

Kingston
299 Concession St., Kingston, ON K7L 5H5
613-545-8559, Fax: 613-545-8808

Kirkland Lake
10 Government Rd. East, PO Box 576, Kirkland Lake, ON P2N 1A2
705-567-9205, Fax: 705-568-8086, ontario.inquiry@hrsdc-rhdcc.gc.ca

Kitchener
409 Weber St. West, PO Box 9011, Kitchener, ON N2G 4L6
519-579-1550, Fax: 519-571-5508, ontario.inquiry@hrsdc-rhdcc.gc.ca

Leamington
215 Talbot St. East, Leamington, ON N8H 3X5
519-326-8695, Fax: 519-326-9203, ontario.inquiry@hrsdc-rhdcc.gc.ca

Lindsay
65 Kent St. West, Lindsay, ON K9V 2Y3
705-324-3562, Fax: 705-328-1202, ontario.inquiry@hrsdc-rhdcc.gc.ca

Listowel
210 Main St. East, Listowel, ON N4W 2B7
519-291-2920, Fax: 519-291-5848, ontario.inquiry@hrsdc-rhdcc.gc.ca

London
120 Queen's Ave., PO Box 5711, London, ON N6A 4S7
519-645-5944, Fax: 519-645-4613, ontario.inquiry@hrsdc-rhdcc.gc.ca

Malton
#5, 6877 Goreway Dr., Mississauga, ON L4V 1L9
905-608-7000, Fax: 905-677-3025, ontario.inquiry@hrsdc-rhdcc.gc.ca

Marathon
#105, 52 Peninsula Rd., PO Box 958, Marathon, ON P0T 2E0
807-229-0959, Fax: 807-229-1592

Midland
9225 Hwy. 93, Midland, ON L4R 4K4
705-526-2224, Fax: 705-526-0316

Milton
310 Main St. East, Milton, ON L9T 1P4
905-878-8418, Fax: 905-878-6861, ontario.inquiry@hrsdc-rhdcc.gc.ca

Mississauga East
2525 Dixie Rd., Mississauga, ON L4Y 2A1
905-608-7000, Fax: 905-803-7449, ontario.inquiry@hrsdc-rhdcc.gc.ca

Mississauga West
3085 Glen Erin Dr., Mississauga, ON L5L 1J3
905-608-7000, Fax: 905-608-7108, ontario.inquiry@hrsdc-rhdcc.gc.ca

Napanee
2 Dairy Ave., Napanee, ON K7R 3T1
Fax: 613-354-3728, 800-206-7218 ontario.inquiry@hrsdc-rhdcc.gc.ca

New Liskeard
290 Armstrong St. North, PO Box 6001, New Liskeard, ON P0J 1P0
705-647-6741, Fax: 705-647-3078, ontario.inquiry@hrsdc-rhdcc.gc.ca

Newmarket
#100, 465 David Dr., Newmarket, ON L3Y 7T9
905-953-4052, Fax: 905-895-5069, ontario.inquiry@hrsdc-rhdcc.gc.ca

Niagara Falls
5853 Peer St., Niagara Falls, ON L2G 1X4
905-988-2700, Fax: 905-354-2591, ontario.inquiry@hrsdc-rhdcc.gc.ca

North Bay
#102, 107 Shirreff Ave., North Bay, ON P1B 7K8
705-472-3700, Fax: 705-472-0870, ontario.inquiry@jrsdc-rhdcc.gc.ca

Oakville
1090 Speers Rd., Oakville, ON L6L 2X4
Fax: 905-845-4055, 800-959-9522

Orangeville
#102, 210 Broadway, Orangeville, ON L9W 5G4
519-941-4898, Fax: 519-941-2504, ontario.inquiry@hrsdc-rhdcc.gc.ca

Orillia
50 Andrew St. South, Orillia, ON L3V 7T5
705-326-7336, Fax: 705-326-6375

Oshawa
78 Richmond St. West, Oshawa, ON L1G 1E1
905-725-2001, Fax: 905-725-7001

Ottawa Centre
300 Laurier Ave. West, Level 2, Ottawa, ON K2P 1W5
613-990-5100, Fax: 613-990-5091

Ottawa East
2339 Ogilvie Rd., Gloucester, ON K1A 0J6
613-900-5100, Fax: 613-954-0676,

Ottawa Government Services Centre
110 Laurier Ave. West, Ottawa, ON K1P 1J1
613-990-5100, Fax: 613-990-5091

Ottawa West
2525 Carling Ave., Ottawa, ON K2B 7Z2
613-990-5100, Fax: 613-991-1447, ontario.inquiry@hrsdc-rhdcc.gc.ca

Owen Sound
#1, 1450 - 1 Ave. West, Owen Sound, ON N4K 6X7
519-376-4280, Fax: 519-376-4715

Parry Sound
74 James St., Parry Sound, ON P2A 1T8
705-746-9374, Fax: 705-746-5331

Pembroke
141 Lake St., Pembroke, ON K8A 5L8
613-735-0681, Fax: 613-735-0047, ontario.inquiry@hrsdc-rhdcc.gc.ca

Perth
13 Herriott St., PO Box 336, Perth, ON K7H 3E4
613-267-1921, Fax: 613-267-3947

Peterborough
185 King St., Peterborough, ON K9J 2R8
705-750-4500, Fax: 705-750-4520, ontario.inquiry@hrsdc-rhdcc.gc.ca

Picton
229 Main St., PO Box 970, Picton, ON K0K 2T0
Fax: 613-476-8569, 800-206-7218 ontario.inquiry@hrsdc-rhdcc.gc.ca

Prescott
292 Centre St., PO Box 1780, Prescott, ON K0E 1T0
613-925-2808, Fax: 613-925-3846, ontario.inquiry@hrsdc-rhdcc.gc.ca

Renfrew
39 Renfrew Ave. West, Renfrew, ON K7V 2Y2
613-432-4878, Fax: 613-432-4087, ontario.inquiry@hrsdc-rhdcc.gc.ca

Richmond Hill
35 Beresford Dr., Richmond Hill, ON L4B 4M3
905-886-7662, Fax: 905-707-6924, ontario.inquiry@hrsdc-rhdcc.gc.ca

St Catherines
43 Church St., PO Box 21, St Catharines, ON L2R 5C7
905-988-2700, Fax: 905-988-2722, ontario.inquiry@hrsdc-rhdcc.gc.ca

St Thomas
#400, 408 Talbot St., PO Box 515, St Thomas, ON N2P 3V6
519-631-5470, Fax: 519-631-3565, ontario.inquiry@hrsdc-rhdcc.gc.ca

Sarnia
150 Christina St. North, Sarnia, ON N7T 7W5
519-464-5025, Fax: 519-464-5040, ontario.inquiry@hrsdc-rhdcc.gc.ca

Sault Ste Marie
22 Bay St., PO Box 2400, Sault Ste Marie, ON P6A 5S2
705-941-4500, Fax: 705-941-4545, ontario.inquiry@hrsdc-rhdcc.gc.ca

Simcoe
5 Queensway Dr. East, Simcoe, ON N3Y 5K2
519-426-5270, Fax: 519-428-4096, ontario.inquiry@hrsdc-rhdcc.gc.ca

Smiths Falls
#115, 91 Cornelia St. West, Smiths Falls, ON K7A 5L3
613-283-4790, Fax: 613-283-9002

Stratford
100 Albert St., Stratford, ON N5A 3K4
519-271-4122, Fax: 519-271-7096, ontario.inquiry@hrsdc-rhdcc.gc.ca

Sudbury
19 Lisgar St., Sudbury, ON P3E 6L1
705-670-6600, Fax: 705-670-6669

Thunder Bay
975 Alloy Dr., Thunder Bay, ON P7B 6N5
807-346-2000, Fax: 807-346-2132, ontario.inquiry@hrsdc-rhdcc.gc.ca

Tillsonburg
96 Tillson Ave., Tillsonburg, ON N4G 3A1
519-842-9008, Fax: 519-688-3671, ontario.inquiry@hrsdc-rhdcc.gc.ca

Timmins
#300, 273 Third Ave., Timmins, ON P4N 1E2
705-267-6271, Fax: 705-267-7099, ontario.inquiry@hrsdc-rhdcc.gc.ca

Toronto Canada Quay
235 Queens Quay West, Toronto, ON M5J 2G8
416-954-6059, Fax: 416-954-6064, ontario.inquiry@hrsdc-rhdcc.gc.ca

Toronto Centre
25 St. Clair Ave. East, Toronto, ON M4T 3A4
416-973-6915, Fax: 416-973-6040, ontario.inquiry@hrsdc-rhdcc.gc.ca

Toronto East
811 Danforth Ave., Toronto, ON M4J 1L2
416-461-3511, Fax: 416-462-7373, ontario.inquiry@hrsdc-rhdcc.gc.ca

Toronto Etobicoke
Dundas-Kipling Centre, Phase II, #105, 5343 Dundas St. West, Toronto, ON M9B 6K6
416-954-1500, Fax: 416-954-1520, ontario.inquiry@hrsdc-rhdcc.gc.ca

Toronto Lakeside
Dufferin Mall, 900 Dufferin St., Toronto, ON M6H 4B1
416-583-4700, Fax: 416-583-4779, ontario.inquiry@hrsdc-rhdcc.gc.ca

Toronto Lawrence Square
Lawrence Square Mall, 700 Lawrence Ave. West, Toronto, ON M6B 4L4
416-780-4100, Fax: 416-954-8814, ontario.inquiry@hrsdc-rhdcc.gc.ca

Toronto North
373 Chesswood Dr., Toronto, ON M3J 2P6
416-954-8700, Fax: 416-954-8702, ontario.inquiry@hrsdc-rhdcc.gc.ca

Toronto Scarborough
200 Town Centre Ct., Toronto, ON M1P 4X9
416-973-4400, Fax: 416-973-3434, ontario.inqury@hrsdc-rhdcc.gc.ca

Toronto Willowdale
4900 Yonge St., Toronto, ON M2N 6B1
Fax: 416-954-2097, 800-277-9914 ontario.inquiry@hrsdc-rhdcc.gc.ca

Trenton
50 Dundas St. West, Trenton, ON K8V 6R5
Fax: 613-392-6148, 800-206-7218 ontario.inquiry@hrsdc-rhdcc.gc.ca

Walkerton
200 McNab St., PO Box 1139, Walkerton, ON N0G 2V0
519-881-2010, Fax: 519-881-0377, ontario.inquiry@hrsdc-rhdcc.gc.ca

Wallaceburg
786 Dufferin Ave., 2nd Fl., Wallaceburg, ON N8A 2V3
519-627-3348, Fax: 519-627-8885, ontario.inquiry@hrsdc-rhdcc.gc.ca

Welland
250 Thorold Rd. West, Welland, ON L3C 3W3
905-988-2700, Fax: 905-735-7036

Windsor
400 City Hall Sq., Windsor, ON N9A 7K6
519-560-2500, Fax: 519-560-2545, ontario.inquiry@hrsdc-rhdcc.gc.ca

Woodstock
#101, 959 Dundas St., Woodstock, ON N4S 1H2
519-421-7225, Fax: 519-421-1916, ontario.inquiry@hrsdc-rhdcc.gc.ca

Prince Edward Island:

Charlottetown
161 St. Peters Rd., PO Box 20105, Charlottetown, PE C1A 9E3
902-566-7723, Fax: 902-368-0178

Montague
541 Main St., Montague, PE C0A 1R0
902-838-5562, Fax: 902-838-3439

O'Leary
371 Main St., PO Box 700, O'Leary, PE C0B 1V0
902-859-1918, Fax: 902-859-1286

Souris
173 Main St., 2nd Fl., PO Box 40, Souris, PE C0A 2B0
902-687-7202, Fax: 902-687-3722

Summerside
120 Harbour Dr., PO Box 2000, Summerside, PE C1N 5P5
902-432-6804, Fax: 902-432-6808,

Wellington
48 Mill Rd., Wellington, PE C0B 2E0
902-854-2083, Fax: 902-854-2516

Quebec:

Abitibi-Témiscamingue
#300, 151, av du Lac, Rouyn-Noranda, QC J9X 6C3
819-764-6711, Fax: 819-762-4605

Bas-Saint-Laurent
140, av Belzile, Rimouski, QC G5L 8Y1
418-722-3200, Fax: 418-722-3369

Brossard
2501, boul Lapinière, Brossard, QC J4Z 3P1
450-445-0411, Fax: 450-445-3792

Centre-du-Québec
1525, boul St-Joseph, Drummondville, QC J2C 2E9
819-477-4150, Fax: 819-478-8137

Côte-Nord
701, boul Laure, 3e étage, Sept-Iles, QC G4R 1X8
418-962-5501, Fax: 418-962-8301

Est-de-Montréal
7141, rue Jean-Talon est, Anjou, QC H1M 3A4
514-355-3330, Fax: 514-514-3558

Gaspésie-Iles-de-la-Madeleine
98, rue de la Reine, 2e étage, Gaspé, QC G4X 2V4
418-368-3331, Fax: 418-368-2785

Laval
1575, boul Chomedey, Laval, QC H7V 2X2
450-682-8950, Fax: 450-682-3856

Longueuil
#114, 365, rue St-Jean, Longueuil, QC J4H 2X8
450-677-9471, Fax: 450-442-0708

Mauricie
#200, 444 - 5e rue, Shawinigan, QC G9N 1E6
819-536-5633, Fax: 819-536-7063

Montréal Centre-Ville/Sud-ouest-de-Montréal
1001, boul de Maisonneuve est, 2e étage, Montréal, QC H2L 5A1
514-522-4444, Fax: 514-283-6085

Nord-de-Montréal
#300, 1415, rue Jarry est, Montréal, QC H2E 3B2
514-723-7273, Fax: 514-723-6249

Ouest-de-Montréal
#3015, 6900, boul Decarie, Montréal, QC H3X 2T8
514-731-0060, Fax: 514-496-1335

Outaouais
920, boul St-Joseph, Gatineau, QC J8Z 1S9
819-953-2830, Fax: 819-953-0267

Québec
CP 10800 Ste-Foy, Québec, QC G1V 5B4
418-681-2599, Fax: 418-681-4810

Repentigny
#54, 155, rue Notre-Dame, Repentigny, QC J6A 7G5
450-585-2044, Fax: 450-585-2180

Richelieu-Yamaska
1225, rue Gauvin, 2e étage, Saint-Hyacinthe, QC J2S 8T8
450-773-7481, Fax: 450-773-8276

Rive-Sud-de-Québec
940, rte du Sault, Saint-Romuald, QC G6W 5M6
418-834-7697, Fax: 418-834-2551

Saguenay-Lac-Saint-Jean
3223, rue Ste-Émilie, Jonquière, QC G7S 5L1
418-699-5700, Fax: 418-699-5760

Saint-Jérôme
#1520, 500, boul Des Laurentides, Saint-Jérôme, QC J7Z 4M2
450-436-4230, Fax: 450-436-7886,

Sainte-Thérèse
100, boul Ducharme, Sainte-Thérèse, QC J7E 1X2
450-430-2800, Fax: 450-430-5885

Sherbrooke
124 Wellington St. North, PO Box 340, Sherbrooke, QC J1H 5X8
819-564-5864, Fax: 819-564-5769

Thetford Mines
#200, 222, boul Frontenac ouest, Thetford Mines, QC G6G 6N7
418-335-2972, Fax: 418-335-3715

Vaudreuil-Dorion
2555, av Dutrisac, local GR 23, Vaudreuil-Dorion, QC J7V 7E6
450-424-5717, Fax: 450-424-0506

Saskatchewan:

Assiniboia
110 - 4 Ave. West, Assiniboia, SK S0H 0B0
Fax: 306-642-3768, 800-622-6232

Carlyle
100 Main St., Carlyle, SK S0C 0R0
Fax: 306-453-2796, 800-622-6232

Estevan
1314 - 3 St., Estevan, SK S7K 0E2
Fax: 306-975-6426, 800-622-6232

La Ronge
1016 La Ronge Ave., La Ronge, SK S0J 1L0
Fax: 306-425-6515, 800-622-6232

Meadow Lake
106 - 1 St. East, Meadow Lake, SK S9X 1Y1
Fax: 306-236-7866, 800-622-6232

Melfort
104 McKendry Plaza, Melfort, SK S0E 1A0
Fax: 306-752-6640, 800-622-6232

Moose Jaw
111 Fairford St. East, Moose Jaw, SK S6H 7X5
Fax: 306-691-0048, 800-622-6232

Nipawin
435 Centre St., Nipawin, SK S0E 1E0
Fax: 306-862-1755, 800-622-6232

North Battleford
9800 Territorial Dr., North Battleford, SK S9A 3N6
Fax: 306-446-1812, 800-622-6232

Prince Albert
1288 Central Ave., Prince Albert, SK S6V 4V8
Fax: 306-953-8404, 800-622-6232

Regina
2045 Broad St., Regina, SK S4P 2N6
Fax: 306-780-5370, 800-622-6232

Regina North Central
2901 - 5 Ave., Regina, SK S4T 0L3
Fax: 306-780-6571, 800-622-6232

Saskatoon
101 - 22 St. East, Saskatoon, SK S7K 0E2
306-975-6426, 800-622-6232

Shaunavon
410 Centre St., Shaunavon, SK S0M 2M0
Fax: 306-297-3738, 800-622-6232

Swift Current
250 Central Ave. North, Swift Current, SK S9H 4G3
Fax: 306-778-4388, 800-622-6232

Weyburn
110 Souris Ave., Weyburn, SK S4H 2Z8
Fax: 306-848-4458, 800-622-6232

Wynyard
435 Bosworth St., Wynyard, SK S0A 4T0
800-622-6232

Yorkton
214 Smith St. East, Yorkton, SK S3N 3S6
Fax: 306-786-5249, 800-622-6232

Social Development / Développement social
L'esplanade Laurier, Level 2, 300 Laurier Ave. West, Ottawa, ON K1A 0J6
613-990-5100, Fax: 613-990-5091,
www.sdc.gc.ca

Helps to secure & strengthen Canada's social foundation. Does this by helping families with children, supporting people with disabilities & ensuring that seniors can fully participate in their communities. Also provides the policies, services & programs for Canadians who need assistance in overcoming challenges they encounter in their lives & their communities. This includes income security programs, such as the Canada Pension Plan.

Asst. Deputy Minister, Corporate Management & Public Affairs, Denise Amyot
613-941-2800
Asst. Deputy Minister, Income Security Programs, Susan Scotti
613-957-3111
Asst. Deputy Minister, Policy & Strategic Direction, Peter R. Hicks
613-957-4500
Director General, Community Development & Partnerships, Allen Zeesman
819-994-1021
Director General, Seniors, Mitch Bloom
613-957-1626

Strategic Policy & Planning / Politique stratégique
Fax: 819-997-7329

Asst. Deputy Minister, Andrew Treusch
819-953-3729, Fax: 819-997-7329
Director General, Audit & Evaluation, Elizabeth Murphy-Walsh
819-953-0821, Fax: 819-953-0831
Acting Director General, Corporate Planning & Accountability, Stephen E. Johnson
613-994-2098, Fax: 613-994-2374
Acting Director General, Labour Market Policy, Barbara Glover
819-997-1094, Fax: 819-997-5856
Director General, Learning Policy, Neil Bouwer
819-953-8005, Fax: 819-997-5433
Director General, Policy Research & Coordination, Cliff Halliwell
819-994-1825, Fax: 819-953-8868
Director General, Resource Management, Larry Gagne
819-953-2368, Fax: 819-953-4962

Workplace Skills / Compétences en milieu de travail

Asst. Deputy Minister, Karen Jackson
819-997-9236
Acting Director General, Program Policy Planning & Analysis, Martin Green
819-994-9949
Director General, Workplace Partnerships, Peter Larose
819-994-3713
Assoc. Director General, Planning & Resource Management, Catherine Cody
819-994-2332, Fax: 819-953-4102

Regional Offices:

Alberta-NWT-Nunavut
Canada Place, #1440, 9700 Jasper Ave. Northwest, Edmonton, AB T5J 4C1

British Columbia & Yukon
Library Sq. Tower, 300 West Georgia St., 15th Fl., Vancouver, BC V6B 6G3
604-666-2282

Manitoba
Canada Post Office Bldg., #750, 266 Graham Ave., Winnipeg, MB R3C 0K3
204-983-3781, Fax: 204-984-2113
Executive Head, George F. Skinner

New Brunswick
1081 Main St., PO Box 6044, Moncton, NB E1C 9G8

Newfoundland & Labrador
689 Topsail Rd., PO Box 12051, St. John's, NL A1B 3Z4
709-772-6204, Fax: 709-772-0815
Executive Head, Michael J. Alexander

Nova Scotia
Metropolitan Place, 99 Wyse Rd., PO Box 1350, Dartmouth, NS B2Y 4B9
902-426-5383, Fax: 902-426-1840

Ontario
#900, 4900 Yonge St., Toronto, ON M2N 6A8
416-954-7700, Fax: 416-954-7707

Prince Edward Island
85 Fitzroy St., PO Box 8000, Charlottetown, PE C1A 8K1

Québec
Complexe Guy-Favreau, Tour Ouest, 200, boul René-Levesque ouest, 5e étage, Montréal, QC H2Z 1X4
514-982-2384, Fax: 514-283-5549
Asst. Deputy Minister, Nicole Barbeau

Saskatchewan
2045 Broad St., 4th Fl., Regina, SK S4P 2N6

Immigration & Refugee Board of Canada (IRB) / Commission de l'immigration et du statut de réfugié du Canada (CISR)

Canada Bldg, 344 Slater St., 12th Fl., Ottawa, ON K1A 0K1
613-995-6486, Fax: 613-943-1550,
info@irb-cisr.gc.ca
www.irb-cisr.gc.ca

The IRB is an independent administrative tribunal that reports to Parliament through the Minister of Citizenship & Immigration Canada (CIC). The Board's mission, on behalf of Canadians, is to make well-reasoned decisions on immigration & refugee matters efficiently, fairly, & in accordance with the law. As Canada's largest federal tribunal, the IRB consists of three divisions. The Refugee Protection Division decides claims for refugee protection made by persons in Canada. The Immigration Division conducts detention reviews & immigration inquiries for certain categories of people believed to be inadmissable, or removable from, Canada. The Immigration Appeal Division hears appeals of sponsorship applications refused by officials of Citizenship & Immigration Canada; appeals from certain removal orders made against permanent residents, refugees & other protected persons, & holders of permanent resident visas; appeals by permanent residents who have been found outside Canada not to have fulfilled their residency obligation; & appeals by CIC from decisions of the Immigration Division at admissability hearings.

Chair, Brian Goodman
613-996-4752, Fax: 613-947-5338
Executive Director, Simon Coakeley
613-947-1040
Deputy Chairperson, Immigration Appeal Division, Shari Stein
613-995-7289
Deputy Chairperson, Refugee Protection Division, Ken Sandhu
613-947-6711
Director General, Corporate Planning & Services Branch, Serge Gascon
613-947-6679
Director General, Human Resources & Professional Development Branch, Diane Lacelle
613-995-0805
Director General, Immigration Division, Susan Bibeau
613-947-6922
Deputy Director General, Operations Branch, Thomas Vulpe
613-947-7184
Director General, Operations Branch, Gerry Deneault
613-996-0942
Director General, Strategic Communication & Partnerships Branch, Kevin White
613-995-3513
Senior General Counsel, Legal Services, Sylvia Cox-Duquette
613-943-2310, Fax: 613-947-2607
Director, Communications, Lori Simpson
613-996-1329
Communications Officer, Marie Gorman
613-992-7132

Indian & Northern Affairs Canada (INAC) / Affaires indiennes et du Nord Canada (AINC)

10 Wellington St., North Tower, Gatineau, QC K1A 0H4
819-997-0380, Fax: 819-953-3017, 866-817-3977
infopubs@ainc-inac.gc.ca
www.ainc-inac.gc.ca

Other Communication: Toll Free Fax: 1-800-567-9604

INAC is responsible for two separate mandates, Indian & Inuit Affairs, & Northern Affairs. This mandate is derived largely from the Department of Indian & Northern Development Act, the Indian Act, territorial acts & legal obligations arising from section 91(24) of the Constitution Act, 1867. The department administers over 50 statutes. INAC has responsibility to meet the government's responsibilities to First Nations, Inuit & Northerners & must work collaboratively with First Nations, Inuit, Northerners, departments, agencies, provinces & territories. The primary role is to support First Nations & Inuit in developing healthy, sustainable communities & assist in achieving their economic & social aspirations.

Acts Administered:

(An Act to confirm an) Agreement between the Governments of Canada & the province of New Brunswick respecting the Indian Reserves
(An Act to confirm an) Agreement between the Governments of Canada & the province of Nova Scotia respecting the Indian Reserves
Alberta Natural Resources Act
Arctic Waters Pollution Prevention Act (Transport Canada & Natural Resources)
Department of Indian & Northern Affairs Development Act
British Columbia Indian Cut-off Lands Settlement Act
British Columbia Indian Lands Settlement Act
British Columbia Treaty Commission Act
Canada Lands Surveys Act (Natural Resources)
Canada Oil & Gas Operations Act (Natural Resources)
Canada Petroleum Resources Act (Natural Resources)
Canada - Yukon Oil & Gas Accord Implementation Act
Canadian Polar Commission Act
Caughnawaga Indian Reserve Act
Claims Settlement (Alberta & Saskatchewan) Implementation Act
Condominium Ordinance Validation Act
Cree-Naskapi (of Québec) Act
Dominion Water Power Act
Fort Nelson Indian Reserve Minerals Revenue Sharing Act
Grassy Narrows & Islington Indian Band Mercury Pollution Claims Settlement Act
Gwich'in Land Claim Settlement Act
Indian Act (Health Canada)
Indian Lands Agreement Act
Indian Lands Settlement of Differences Act
Indian Oil & Gas Act
Indian (Soldier Settlement) Act
James Bay & Northern Quebec Native Claims Settlement Act
Land Titles Repeal Act
Mackenzie Valley Resource Management Act
Manitoba Natural Resources Act
Manitoba Supplementary Provisions Act
Natural Resources Transfer (School Lands) Amendments, Alberta, Manitoba & Saskatchewan
Nelson House First Nation Flooded Land Act
Northern Canada Power Commission (Share Issuance & Sale Authorization) Act
Northern Canada Power Commission Yukon Assets Disposal Authorization Act
Northwest Territories Act
Northwest Territories Waters Act
Nunavut Act
Nunavut Land Claims Agreement Act
Nunavut Waters & Nunavut Surface Rights Tribunal Act, 2002
Pictou Landing Indian Band Agreement Act
Railway Belt Act
Railway Belt & Peace River Block Act
Railway Belt Water Act
St. Peters Indian Reserve Act
St. Regis Islands Act
Sahtu Dene & Metis Land Claim Settlement Act
Saskatchewan Natural Resources Act
Saskatchewan Treaty Land Entitlement Act
Sechelt Indian Band Self-Government Act
(An Act for the) Settlement of Certain Questions Between the Governments of Canada & Ontario Respecting the Indian Reserve Lands Act
(An Act Respecting) Songhees Indian Reserve Act
Split Lake Cree First Nation Flooded Land Act
Territorial Lands Act
Western Arctic (Inuvialuit) Claims Settlement Act
York Factory First Nation Flooded Land Act
Yukon Act
Yukon Environmental & Socio-Economic Assessment Act, 2003
Yukon First Nations Land Claims Settlement Act
Yukon First Nations Self-Government Act
Yukon Placer Mining Act
Yukon Quartz Mining Act
Yukon Waters Act

Minister, Indian Affairs & Northern Development; Minister of the Canadian Northern Economic Development Agency;, Federal Interlocutor for Métis & Non-Status Indians, Hon. John Duncan, B.Sc.F.
613-992-2503, Fax: 613-996-3306, Duncan.J@parl.gc.ca; Minister@ainc-inac.gc.ca, Other Communications: Indian Affairs & Northern Development: 819-997-0002
Parliamentary Secretary to the Minister of Indian Affairs & Northern Development, Shelly Glover
613-995-0579, Fax: 613-996-7571,Glover.S@parl.gc.ca
Deputy Minister, Michael Wernick
819-997-0133, Fax: 819-953-2251
Associate Deputy Minister, Colleen Swords
819-934-0583, Fax: 819-953-2251
Acting Assistant Deputy Minister, Office of the Federal Interlocutor, Allan MacDonald
613-992-8186, Fax: 613-947-7580
Staff Ombudsman,VACANT
819-953-5965, Fax: 819-997-8206
Director General, Communications, Maryse Pesant
819-994-7526, Fax: 819-953-9465
Senior General Counsel, Legal Services, Andrew Saranchuk
819-994-4141, Fax: 819-953-7693

• Beverly & Qamanirjuaq Caribou Management Board Secretariat
PO Box 629
Stonewall, MB R0C 2Z0
204-467-2438
rossthompson@mymts.net
www.arctic-caribou.com
Group of hunters, biologists & wildlife managers working together to conserve Canada's vast Beverly & Qamanirjuaq caribou herds for the welfare of traditional caribou-using communities in northern Manitoba, Saskatchewan, Northwest Territories & Nunavut.

• First Nations Tax Commission(FNTC) / Commission de la fiscalité des premières nations (CFPN)
#200, 160 Grorge St.
Ottawa, ON K1N 9M2
613-789-5000 Fax: 613-789-5008
mail@fntc.ca
www.fntc.ca
The FNTC operates in the larger context of First Nation issues which goes beyond property tax. The FNTC is concerned with reducing the barriers to economic development on First Nation lands, increasing investor certainty, and enabling First Nations to be part of their regional economies. The FNTC is working to fill the institutional vacuum that has prevented First Nations from participating in the market economy and creating a national regulatory framework for First Nation tax systems that meets or beats the standards of provinces.

• Indian Oil & Gas Canada(IOGC) / Pétrole et gaz des Indiens du Canada
#100, 9911 Chula Blvd.
Tsuu T'ina (Sarcee), AB T2W 6H6
403-292-5625 Fax: 403-292-5618
ContactIOGC@inac-ainc.gc.ca
www.iogc-pgic.gc.ca
Indian Oil and Gas Canada (IOGC) is an organization committed to managing and regulating oil and gas resources on First Nation reserve lands. It is a special operating agency within Indian and Northern Affairs Canada.

• Mackenzie Valley Environmental Impact Review Board
200 Scotia Centre
5102 - 50th Ave.
PO Box 938
Yellowknife, NT X1A 2N7
867-766-7050 Fax: 867-766-7074 866-912-3472
tcharlo@reviewboard.ca
www.mveirb.nt.ca
In 1998, the Mackenzie Valley Environmental Impact Review Board was established, under the Mackenzie Valley Resources Management Act. The co-management Review Board is made up of members nominated by First Nations & federal & territorial governments. Board members represent the interests of all residents of the Mackenzie Valley.

• Nunavut Impact Review Board
PO Box 1360
Cambridge Bay, NU X0B 0C0
867-983-4600 Fax: 867-983-2594 866-233-3033
info@nirb.ca
www.nirb.ca
An institution of the government established under the Nunavut Land Claims Agreement to conduct environmental & socio-economic assessments. The NIRB process involves participation by members of the community, Inuit organizations, the Government of Nunavut & the Government of Canada through the entire environmental assessment. Under the Canadian Environmental Assessment Act, the federal departments with specific responsibilities for the project must ensure that the requirements of the Act are met throughout the assessment process. This open process facilitates sound environmental stewardship & promotes economic & sustainable development.

• Nunavut Planning Commission
PO Box 2101
Cambridge Bay, NU X0B 0C0
867-983-4625 Fax: 867-983-4626
staptuna@nunavut.ca
www.nunavut.ca
Responsible for land use planning & environmental reporting & management in Nunavut.

• Nunavut Water Board
PO Box 119
Gjoa Haven, NU X0B 1J0
867-360-6338 Fax: 867-360-6369
www.nunavutwaterboard.org
Responsible for the regulation, use & management of water in the Nunavut Settlement Area.

• Porcupine Caribou Management Board
PO Box 31723
Whitehorse, YT Y1A 6L3
867-633-4780 Fax: 867-393-3904
pcmb@taiga.net
http://taiga.net/pcmb
Works to manage the Porcupine Caribou herd, one of the largest herds of migratory caribou in North America, & to protect & maintain its habitat.

Chief Financial Officer Sector / Secteur du dirigeant principal des finances

819-953-1201, Fax: 819-953-4094

CFO, Susan MacGowan
819-953-4094, Fax: 819-956-8193
Acting Director, Continuous Business Process Improvements, Eva Jacobs
819-934-0564, Fax: 819-953-5410

Director General, Corporate Accounting & Materiel Management, Alain Gélinas
819-997-0640, Fax: 819-953-1093
CIO, Information Management Branch, Al McLarty
819-994-3334, Fax: 819-956-8739
Director General, Planning & Resource Management, Andrew Francis
819-994-6649, Fax: 819-953-8475

Lands & Trusts Services / Services fonciers et fiduciaires

Manages land-related statutory duties under the Indian Act & duties related to transferring land management services to First Nations. The Environment Directorate maintains an Inventory of Contaminated Sites on reserve land& coordinates remediation planning; responsible for the design & implementation of the Indian & Inuit Affairs Program Environmental Stewardship Strategy Action Plan; development of First Nations capacity, tools & enabling legislation inorder that first Nations undertake their own environmental protection initiatives; administers Indian Environmental Assistance Fund (IEAF). Environment Capacity Development Initiative (ECDI) supports First Nation, Innu & Inuit communities in efforts to promote environmental stewardship in a manner that is consistent with the principles of sustainable development.

Director General, Governance, Brenda Kustra
819-997-8154, Fax: 819-997-9541
Director General, Individual Affairs, Ray Hatfield
819-953-2605, Fax: 819-953-3371
Director General, Lands Branch, Andrew Beynon
819-953-0517, Fax: 819-953-0649
Director General, Policy, Planning & Coordination, Mary Donaghy
613-990-2666

Treaty Negotiation Offices:

Northern Affairs / Affaires du Nord

819-994-0044, Fax: 819-953-6121

Supports northern political & economic development through the management of federal interests; promotes sustainable development of the North's natural resources & northern communities. Works toward the devolution of all province-like responsibilities to northern governments of NWT, Nunavut & the Yukon. Develops & coordinates policies & programs related to northern environment & conservation, like the federal Northern Affairs Program Sustainable Development Strategy, the cleanup of northern hazardous waste sites, climate change & interdepartmental liaison with key policy departments like Environment Canada. Northern Contaminants Program is managed by INAC in partnership with the federal departments of Health, Environment & Fisheries & Oceans, the territorial governments, Aboriginal organizations & university researchers, & its aim is to work toward reducing & eliminating, where possible, contaminants in traditionally harvested foods. The Northern Information Network is designed to link users to information about the Yukon, the Northwest Territories & Nunavut for more effective decision making in the areas such as resource management & economic development. NIN supports various research initiatives about the North, including project impact assessme nts sustainable development strategies, wildlife management planning, land use planning & emergency preparedness. NIN has a directory of geo-referenced databases, provides a forum for discussion & has information & research documents pertaining to the North

Asst. Deputy Minister, Patrick Borbey
819-953-3760
Director General, Devolution & Territorial Relations, Jamie Tibbetts
819-997-0223, Fax: 819-953-9323
Director General, Natural Resources & Environment Branch, Paula Isaak
819-997-9381, Fax: 819-953-8766
Director General, Northern Oil & Gas Branch, Mimi Fortier
819-953-9393, Fax: 819-934-6375
Director General, Northern Policy & Science Integration Branch, Danielle Labonté
819-997-9449, Fax: 819-997-0552
Director, Circumpolar Liaison Directorate, Harald Finkler
819-997-8318, Fax: 819-953-0546

Vancouver
Comprehensive Claims Branch, #600, 1168 Melville St., Vancouver, BC V6E 4S3
604-775-7114, Fax: 604-666-2546

Victoria
#309, 1230 Government St., Victoria, BC V8W 2Z4
250-363-6910, Fax: 250-363-6911

Policy & Strategic Direction Sector / Politique et direction stratégique

Fax: 819-953-5082

Senior Asst. Deputy Minister, Jean-François Tremblay
819-994-7555
Director General, External Relations & Gender Issues Branch, Line Paré
819-997-8212, Fax: 819-934-7192
Director General, Federal Relations & Issues Management, Susan Anzolin
613-947-1716, Fax: 613-947-1732
Director General, Litigation Management & Resolution Branch, Daniel Ricard
819-953-4968, Fax: 819-997-1679
Director General, Policy Services Branch, Jill Wherrett
819-997-8359, Fax: 819-953-3320
Director General, Strategic Planning & Analysis Branch, Claudine Gagnon
819-994-7213, Fax: 819-953-0239
Director General, Strategic Policy & Research Branch, Céline Auclair
819-953-3088, Fax: 819-994-7860

Socio Policy & Programs Branch

Fax: 819-953-1974

Director General, Mary Quinn
613-947-6508, Fax: 613-947-9242
Director, Social Programs Reform Directorate, Odette Johnston
613-995-9074, Fax: 613-995-9410
Director, Social Services & Justice Directorate, Cassandra Lang
613-995-9103, Fax: 613-947-9242

Treaties & Aboriginal Government / Traités et gouvernement autochtone

Senior Asst. Deputy Minister, Michel Roy
819-953-3180, Fax: 819-953-3246
Director General, Financial Management & Strategic Services, Tony Richard
819-997-9757, Fax: 819-994-0273
Director General, Implementation Branch, Stephen Gagnon
819-994-3434, Fax: 819-953-6430
Director General, Negotiations - Central, Joëlle Montminy
819-953-4365, Fax: 819-956-7011
Director General, Negotiations - East, Lynn Bernard
819-994-7521, Fax: 819-953-6768
Director General, Negotiations - West, Anita Boscariol
604-775-7144, Fax: 604-775-7149,
Director General, Policy Development & Coordination Branch, Perry Billingsley
819-953-4315, Fax: 819-953-3855
Director General, Specific Claims Branch, Anik Dupont
819-994-2323, Fax: 819-994-4123

Regional Offices:

Alberta
#630, Canada Place, 9700 Jasper Ave., Edmonton, AB T5J 4G2
780-495-2834, Fax: 780-495-4354
Acting Regional Director General, Jim Sisson
780-495-2839

Atlantic
40 Havelock St., PO Box 160, Amherst, NS B4H 3Z3
902-661-6201, Fax: 902-661-6237
Regional Director General, Ian Gray
902-661-6262

British Columbia
#600, 1138 Melville St., Vancouver, BC V6E 4S3
604-666-5201, Fax: 604-666-2546
Regional Director General, George Arcand
Fax: 604-775-7149

Manitoba
#200, 365 Hargrave St., Winnipeg, MB R3B 3A3
204-983-7849, Fax: 204-983-2936
Regional Director General, Anna Fontaine
204-983-2474

Northwest Territories
PO Box 1500, Yellowknife, NT X1A 2R3
867-669-2507, Fax: 867-669-2709
Regional Director General, Trish Merrithew-Mercredi
867-669-2501, Fax: 867-669-2703
Director, Renewable Resources & Environment, Teresa Joudrie
867-669-2647, Fax: 867-669-2707
Acting Director, Contaminants & Remediation, Bill Mitchell
867-669-2434, Fax: 867-669-2439

Nunavut
PO Box 2200, Iqaluit, NU X0A 0H0
867-975-4500, Fax: 867-975-4560
Acting Regional Director General, Bernie MacIsaac
867-975-4501
Director, Contaminated Sites, Natalie Plato
867-975-4730

Ontario
25 St. Clair Ave. East, 8th Fl., Toronto, ON M4T 1M2
416-973-6599, Fax: 416-954-4326
Acting Regional Director General, Leigh Jessen
416-973-6201
Acting Director, Executive & Communications, Natalie Pennefather
416-973-6110, Fax: 416-973-3421

Québec
#400, 320, rue St-Joseph est, Québec, QC G1K 9J2
418-648-7551, Fax: 418-648-2266, 800-567-9604
Regional Director General, Pierre Nepton
418-648-3270
Director, Education & Social Development Programs, Céline Laverdière
418-648-4104, Fax: 418-648-7685
Director, Lands & Economic Development, Stéphane Greffard
418-648-7743, Fax: 418-648-3930

Saskatchewan
#200, 1 First Nations Way, Regina, SK S4S 7K5
306-780-6486, Fax: 306-780-5733
Regional Director General, Riel Bellegarde
306-780-6486, Fax: 306-780-7305
Director, Lands & Economic Development, Dwayne Johns
306-780-6420, Fax: 306-780-6128
Director, Strategic Initiatives & Innovations, Cherie Moreau
306-780-6442, Fax: 306-780-6897

Yukon
#415C, 300 Main St., Whitehorse, YT Y1A 2B5
867-667-3888, Fax: 867-667-6038
Regional Director General, Joanne Wilkinson
306-667-3300, Fax: 867-667-3801
Director, Environment, Michelle Edwards
867-393-7934, Fax: 867-667-3861
Director, Strategic Investments, Shari Borgford
867-667-3310, Fax: 867-667-3801
Director General, Terry Sewell
819-994-3434
Director, Implementation Management, Mavis Dellert
819-953-1732
Director, Implementation Planning & Negotiations, Pierre Goulet
819-997-3369
Director, James Bay Implementation Office, Michel Blondin
819-997-0881
Director, Special Implementation Projects Directorate, Michel Youssef
819-994-7222
Director, Fiscal Policy Directorate, Brian McCoy
819-994-3566
Director General, Ian McGregor
819-997-9381
Director, Environment & Renewable Resources Directorate, Leslie Whitby
819-994-6417
Director, Mineral Resources Directorate, Rick Meyers
819-997-9828
Acting Director, Northern Science & Contaminants Research Directorate, Russel Shearer
819-994-7484,
Director, Resource Policy & Transfers Directorate, Stephen Van Dine
819-953-8613

Indian Claims Commission / Commission des revendications des Indiens

Minto Enterprise Bldg., #400, 427 Laurier Ave. West, PO Box 1750 B, Ottawa, ON K1P 1A2
613-943-2737, Fax: 613-943-0157,
feedback@indianclaims.ca
http://24583.vws.magma.ca

Created by an Order in Council in 1991 as an independent & neutral commission of inquiry, operating at arm's length from government & First Nations.

Chief Commissioner, Renée Dupuis
Commissioner, Daniel J. Bellegarde
Commissioner, Jane Dickson-Gilmore
Commissioner, Alan C. Holman
Commissioner, Sheila G. Purdy

Industry Canada / Industrie Canada

235 Queen St., Ottawa, ON K1A 0H5
Fax: 613-954-6436, 800-328-6189
info@ic.gc.ca
www.ic.gc.ca

The mission of Industry Canada is to help make Canadians more productive & competitive in a global, knowledge-based economy. The department's policies, programs & services assists in the creation of an economy that offers the following: provides more & better-paying jobs for Canadians; supports stronger business growth through sustained improvements in productivity; & gives consumers, businesses & investors confidence that the marketplace is fair, efficient & competitive. To reach its clients, Industry Canada collaborates extensively with partners at all levels of government & the private sector.

Acts Administered:

Agreement on Internal Trade Implementation Act
Bankruptcy & Insolvency Act
Boards of Trade Act
Canada Business Corporations Act
Canada Co-operative Associations Act
Canada Corporations Act
Canada Small Business Financing Act
Canadian Space Agency Act
Canadian Tourism Commission Act
Companies' Creditors Arrangement Act
Department of Industry Act
Departmental Legislation
Electricity & Gas Inspection Act
Radiocommunication Act
Telecommunications Act
Teleglobe Canada Reorganization & Divestiture Act
Telesat Canada Reorganization & Divestiture Act
Marketplace & Trade Regulation
Competition Act
Consumer Packaging & Labelling Act
Government Corporations Operations Act
Telecommunications Legislation
Investment Canada Act
Lobbyists Registration Act
Small Business Loans Act
Winding-up & Restructuring Act
Canadian Intellectual Property Office (CIPO) Legislation
Copyright Act
Industrial Design Act
Integrated Circuit Topography Act
Patent Act
Public Servants Inventions Act
Trade-marks Act
Consumer Legislation
Bills of Exchange Act
Electricity & Gas Inspection Act
Precious Metals Marking Act
Textile Labelling Act
Timber Marking Act
Weights & Measures Act
Registrar General Functions
Public Documents Act
Public Officers Act
Seals Act
Trade Unions Act
Portfolio & Agency Legislation
Business Development Bank of Canada Act
Canada Foundation for Innovation Act (Part I & XI)
Competition Tribunal Act
Copyright Board: Sections 66ff of the Copyright Act
National Research Council Act
Natural Sciences & Engineering Research Council Act
Social Sciences & Humanities Research Council Act
Standards Council of Canada Act
Statistics Act
Largely Inactive or Minimal Involvement
Atlantic Fisheries Restructuring Act
Agricultural & Rural Development Act
Bell Canada Act
Corporations & Labour Unions Returns Act
Pension Fund Societies Act
Regional Development Incentives Act
Special Areas Act

Minister, Industry,Hon. Tony Clement
613-944-7740, Fax: 613-992-5092,ClemeT@parl.gc.ca; ministre.industrie@ic.gc.ca
Parliamentary Secretary to the Minister of Industry, Mike Lake
613-995-8695, Fax: 613-995-6465,Lake.M@parl.gc.ca
Deputy Minister, Richard Dicerni
613-992-4292, Fax: 613-954-3272,richard.dicerni@ic.gc.ca
Sr. Associate Deputy Minister, Simon Kennedy
613-943-7164, Fax: 613-954-2137
Sr. Assistant Deputy Minister, Industry Sectors, Ron Parker
613-954-3798, Fax: 613-941-1134
Director General, Information & Communications Technologies Branch, Alain Beaudoin
613-954-5598, Fax: 613-957-4076,alain.beaudoin@ic.gc.ca
Director General, Human Resources, Bill James
613-954-5474, Fax: 613-957-9709,mitch.davies@ic.gc.ca
Director General, Office of Consumer Affairs, Michael Jenkin
613-954-3277, Fax: 613-952-6927,michael.jenkin@ic.gc.ca
Director General, Corporations Canada, Richard Shaw
613-941-2837, Fax: 613-941-5783,richard.shaw@ic.gc.ca

• Canadian Tourism Commission(CTC) / Commission canadienne du Tourisme (CCT)
#1400, 1055 Dunsmuir St.
PO Box 49230
Vancouver, BC V7X 1L2
604-638-8300 Fax: 604-638-8425
ctc_feedback@businteractive.com
www.canadatourism.com
CTC is a unique partnership between tourism business & associations, provincial & territorial governments, & the Government of Canada. The CTC's Board of Directors is a decision-making body composed of 26 members with a wide variety of skills & knowledge, representing all regions of the country. The CTC's mission is to sustain a vibrant & profitable Canadian tourism industry.

• Cape Breton Development Fund Corporation/ Corporation Fonds d'investissement du Cap-Breton
Silicon Island
70 Crescent St.
PO Box 1264
Sydney, NS B1P 6T7
902-564-3600 Fax: 902-564-3825 800-705-3926
www.cbgf.ca
Responsible for the delivery of the economic adjustment fund established by the Governments of Canada & Nova Scotia in the wake of the federal government's decision to close the Cape Breton Development Corporation (Devco). The CBGF comprises a $86 million contribution from the Government of Canada, & a $12 million contribution from the Government of Nova Scotia.

• Chief Informatics Office/ Bureau principal de l'informatique
235 Queen St.
Ottawa, ON K1A 0H5
613-954-3570 Fax: 613-941-1938
Responsible for information management & information technology (IM/IT) activities for Industry Canada;provides strategic advice & leadership to assist the department in achieving its electronic information & service delivery strategy; champions Industry Canada's Government On-Line agenda; responsible for key leading information & service delivery channels, including Strategis, the National Secretariat for the Canada Business Service Centres &the Student Connection Program.

• Communications Research Centre Canada(CRC) / Centre de recherches sur les communications
3701 Carling Ave.
PO Box 11490 H
Ottawa, ON K2H 8S2
613-991-3313 Fax: 613-998-5355
info@crc.ca
www.crc.ca
Dedicated to advanced communications research & development for over 50 years. Key research areas include radio science, terrestrial wireless systems, satellite communications broadcasting, & broadband network technologies. CRC has a long history of technology transfer. CRC operates an Innovation Centre, a technology incubator for small & medium-sized high-tech start-ups, which provides increased access to CRC's technologies, research expertise & unique laboratories & facilities.

• Competition Tribunal/ Tribunal de la concurrence
Thomas D'Arcy McGee Bldg.
#600, 90 Sparks St.
Ottawa, ON K1P 5B4
613-957-3172 Fax: 613-957-3170
tribunal@ct-tc.gc.ca
www.ct-tc.gc.ca
Hears & decides all applications made under Parts V11.1 & VIII of the Competition Act.

• Electronic Commerce Branch/ Direction du commerce électronique
300 Slater St.
Ottawa, ON K1A 0C8
613-990-4268 Fax: 613-941-0178 800-328-6189
www.ic.gc.ca/eic/site/ecic-ceac.nsf/eng/home
Coordinates the development & implementation of a national electronic commerce strategy. It is responsible for both domestic & international aspects of electronic commerce. The Canadian Electronic Commerce Strategy was announced in September 1998. The Strategy, which was developed in collaboration with provincial & territorial governments, industry & consumer groups, among others, establishes a framework, goals, timetable, & implementation plan for electronic commerce domestically. The Strategy involves coordinating strategic elements that fall within the federal government's responsibilities, including the policy development areas of encryption & privacy.

• Enterprise Cape Breton Corporation(ECBC) / Société d'expansion du Cap-Breton
Silicon Island
70 Crescent St.
Sydney, NS B1S 2Z7
902-564-3600 Fax: 902-564-3825 800-705-3926
information@ecbc-secb.gc.ca
www.ecbc-secb.gc.ca
Crown corporation established pursuant to Part II of the Government Organization Act, Atlantic Canada, 1987 with a jurisdictional mandate which includes all of Cape Breton Island & a portion of mainland Nova Scotia in & around the Town of Mulgrave. The Corporation is charged with the responsibility for promoting & assisting the financing & development of industry in the region, providing employment outside the coal-producing sector & broadening the base of the local economy.

• Standards Council of Canada

Competition Bureau / Bureau de la concurrence
Place du Portage, Phase I, 50, rue Victoria, 21e étage, Ottawa, ON K1A 0C9
613-997-4282, Fax: 613-997-0324, 800-348-5358
compbureau@ic.gc.ca
www.competitionbureau.gc.ca
The Competition Bureau is the organization responsible for the enforcement of the Competition Act, the Consumer Packaging & Labelling Act except as it relates to food, the Precious Metals Marking Act & the Textile Labelling Act. The Competition Bureau ensures compliance by the business community with legislation administered by the Bureau, & oversees the development of policy & dissemination of information aimed at ensuring optimal compliance levels.
Commissioner of Competition, Melanie Aitken
819-997-3304, Fax: 819-953-5013
Acting Senior Deputy Commissioner, Mergers, Ann Wallwork
819-953-4308, Fax: 819-994-0998
Deputy Commissioner, Civil Matters, Richard Taylor
819-997-1209, Fax: 819-953-8546
Senior Deputy Commissioner, Criminal Matters, John Pecman
819-997-1208, Fax: 819-997-3835
Deputy Commissioner, Fair Business Practices, Andrea Rosen
819-997-1231, Fax: 819-953-4792

Industry Sector / Secteur de l'industrie
Industry Sector (IS) assists Canadian industry & businesses compete, expand & create jobs in the knowledge-based economy. IS contributes to Industry Canada's strategic objectives, trade, investment, innovation, connectedness & marketplace. It facilitates delivery of industrial, related policy analyses & strategies to promote global competitiveness of Canadian industry. IS provides a broad range of services, information resources, sector policies & strategies to support business growth. IS provides Canadian businesses with timely information products, business tools, research, strategic analyses, data & information resources. For more information about Industry Sector's products, visit the Business Information by Sector area on Strategis, Industry Canada's on-line business information source at
http://www.ic.gc.ca/eic/site/ic1.nsf/eng/h_00066.html
Senior Asst. Deputy Minister, Ron Parker
613-954-3798, Fax: 613-941-1134
Director General, Aerospace, Defence and Marine Branch, Brian Gear
613-941-8123, Fax: 613-998-6703
Director General, Policy and Sector Services Branch, Colette Jubinville
613-954-9633, Fax: 613-948-1230

Aerospace, Defence & Marine Branch / Aérospatiale, defense et la marine
Fax: 613-941-2379
Director General, Brian Gear
613-941-8123, Fax: 613-998-6703
Director, Aerospace, Sharon Harrison
613-954-3166, Fax: 613-998-6703
Acting Director, Defence & Marine Directorate, André Bernier
613-954-3774, Fax: 613-998-6703
Director, Industrial & Regional Benefit Directorate, Daniel Duguay
613-957-2651, Fax: 613-998-6703

Automotive & Industrial Materials Branch / Automobile et matériaux industriels
613-952-0441, Fax: 613-952-8088

Energy & Environment Industries Branch / Énergie et industries environnementales
Director General, Bruce Bowie
613-946-7317
Director, Energy Directorate, Glenn MacDonell
613-954-2703

Life Sciences Industries Branch / Sciences de la vie
Fax: 613-946-3144
Director General, Leah Clark
613-954-5258, Fax: 613-952-5822

Resource Processing Industries Branch / Industries de transformation des ressources naturelles
Director General, Tim Elliot
613-954-3394, Fax: 613-941-8048
Director, Energy Industries Directorate, Tim Karlsson
613-954-2991, Fax: 613-941-2463
Director, Forest Industries Directorate, Jyotsna Dalvi
613-941-2274, Fax: 613-952-8988

Director, Resource Manufacturing & Value-added Products Directorate, Simon Tuck
613-954-5609, Fax: 613-952-8988

Services Industries Branch / Industries de services
Deputy Director, Philippe Richer
613-941-3361, Fax: 613-952-9054
Director, Patrick Hurens
613-952-1710, Fax: 613-952-9054

Operations Sector / Secteur des opérations
Asst. Deputy Minister, Matthew King
613-957-4392, Fax: 613-995-2233
Assoc. Asst. Deputy Minister, Iain Stewart
613-960-1850
President, Measurement Canada, Alan E. Johnston
613-952-0655, Fax: 613-957-1265
Director General, Corporations Canada, Richard G. Shaw
613-941-2837, Fax: 613-941-5783
Director General, Sectorial Strategies & Services, Jeff Moore
613-941-2479, Fax: 613-952-9026
Director General, Small Business Financing Directorate, Nathalie Poirier-Mizon
613-946-3391, Fax: 613-952-0290

Office of the Superintendent of Bankruptcy / Bureau du surintendant des faillites
613-941-1000, Fax: 613-941-2862
Superintendent, James Callon
613-941-2690, Fax: 613-946-9205
Acting Asst./Deputy Superintendent, Programs, Standards & Regulatory Affairs, Isabelle Picard
613-941-9051, Fax: 613-946-2168

Canadian Intellectual Property Office / Office de la propriété intellectuelle du Canada
Place du Portage I, 50, rue Victoria, Gatineau, QC K1A 0C9
819-997-1936, Fax: 819-953-7620, 866-997-1936
www.cipo.ic.gc.ca
The Canadian Intellectual Property Office (CIPO), a Special Operating Agency (SOA) associated with Industry Canada, is responsible for the administration and processing of the greater part of intellectual property in Canada.

Spectrum, Information Technologies & Telecommunications / Spectre, technologies de l'information et télécommunications
Journal Tower North, 300 Slater St., 20th Fl., Ottawa, ON K1A 0C8
613-998-0368, Fax: 613-952-1203
Contributes to the Industry Canada mandate by fostering the early development & use of information & communications technologies, infrastructures & services. The sector uses its policy & regulatory rule-making powers, & marketplace & industry sectoral development services to: ensure Canada has a world-class telecommunications & information infrastructure; promote the international competitiveness of Canadian information technologies by all sectors of the Canadian economy; & ensure effective & efficient use of the radio frequency spectrum.
Asst. Deputy Minister, Helen McDonald
Director General, Electronic Commerce Branch, Janet DiFrancesco
613-990-2225, Fax: 613-941-1164
Director General, Engineering, Planning and Standards Branch, Marc Dupuis
613-990-4820, Fax: 613-954-6091
Acting Director General, Governance, Policy Coordination & Planning, Carol Bradley
613-946-9077, Fax: 613-946-9084
Director General, Information & Communications Technologies Branch, Alain Beaudoin
613-954-5598, Fax: 613-957-4076
Director General, Spectrum Management Operations Branch, Fiona Gilfillan
613-990-4817, Fax: 613-993-4433,

Infrastructure Canada / L'infrastructure Canada

90 Sparks St., 6th Fl., Ottawa, ON K1P 5B4
613-948-1148, Fax: 613-946-9888, 800-622-6232
info@infc.gc.ca
www.infrastructure.gc.ca
Infrastructure Canada consists of the following branches: Policy & Communications; Corporate Services, & Program Operations. The Program Operations sector undertakes the following functions: implentation of programs; management of infrastructure funding agreements; provision of risk management & analysis; promotion of environmental stewardship; management of the federal Gas Tax transfer to Canadian municipalities to support environmentally sustainable infrastructure; & program evaluation. In 2007, a team was established to develop a National Transit Strategy.

Minister, Transport, Infrastructure, & Communities,Hon. Charles (Chuck) Strahl
613-992-2940, Fax: 613-944-9376,Strahl.C@parl.gc.ca
Parliamentary Secretary, Brian Jean
613-992-1154, Fax: 613-992-4603,Jean.B@parl.gc.ca
Deputy Minister, Yaprak Baltacioglu
613-990-4507, Fax: 613-991-0851,yaprak.baltacioglu@infc.gc.ca
Assistant Deputy Minister, John Forster
613-948-8157, Fax: 613-948-6062,john.forster@infc.gc.ca
Assistant Deputy Minister, Corporate Services, David Miller
613-948-9161, Fax: 613-960-6348,david.miller@infc.gc.ca
Senior Counsel, Legal Services, Jean-Philippe Dallaire
613-952-2310, Fax: 613-954-5356,ouellet.richard@ic.gc.ca

Policy & Communications Branch
#605, 90 Sparks St., Ottawa, ON K1P 5B4
The branch conducts research, both independently & with partners, on infrastructure issues for potential federal action. Policy & Communications also shares knowledge to further understanding of infrastructure issues affecting cities & communities. Policy advice is also offered to the Minister.
Assistant Deputy Minister, John Forster
613-948-8157
Director General, Communications Directorate, Gerry Maffre
613-948-2940
Director General, Policy & Priorities Directorate, Taki Sarantakis
613-946-5188
Director General, Policy & Strategic Initiatives Directorate, Adam Ostry
613-952-9940

International Development Research Centre (IDRC) / Centre de recherches pour le développement international (CRDI)

150 Kent St., PO Box 8500, Ottawa, ON K1P 0B2
613-236-6163, Fax: 613-238-7230,
info@idrc.ca
www.idrc.ca
Helps scientists in developing countries identify long-term, practical solutions to pressing development problems. Support is given directly to scientists working in universities, private enterprise, government & non-profit-making organizations. Priority is given to research aimed at achieving equitable & sustainable development. One of the three program areas of focus is Environmental & Natural Resource Management. Initiatives in this area include a rural poverty & environment program initiative, an urban poverty & environment program, ecosystem approaches to human health, an international model forest network, biodiversity & regional water demand initiative
Chair, Barbara McDougall
613-236-6163, Fax: 613-565-8212,bmcdougall@idrc.ca
President, David M. Malone
613-236-6163, Fax: 613-235-6391,dmalone@idrc.ca
Vice-President, Resources & CFO, Denys Vermette
613-236-6163, Fax: 613-236-7293,dvermette@idrc.ca
Vice-President, Programs & Partnership Branch, Rohinton Medhora
613-236-6163, Fax: 613-567-7748,rmedhora@idrc.ca
Director, Communications Division, Angela Prokopiak
613-236-6163, Fax: 613-563-2476,aprokopiak@idrc.ca
Director, Environmental & Natural Resource Management, Jean Lebel
613-236-6163, Fax: 613-567-7748,jlebel@idrc.ca
Chief, Public Affairs & Parliamentary Relations, Jennifer Pepall
613-236-6163, Fax: 613-238-7230,jpepall@idrc.ca

Regional Offices:

Eastern & Southern Africa
IDRC, Liasion House, State House Avenue, PO Box 62084, Nairobi
vngugi@idrc.or.ke
www.idrc.ca/esaro

Other Communication: 254-20-2713160; Fax: 254-20-2711063

Latin America & the Caribbean
Avenida Brasil 2655, Montevideo,11300 Uruguay
lacroinf@idrc.org.uy
www.idrc.ca/lacro

Other Communication: 598-2-709-0042; Fax: 598-2-708-6776

Middle East & North Africa
8 Ahmed Niseem St., 8th fl., PO Box 14, Cairo
skamel@idrc.org.eg
www.idrc.ca/cairo

Other Communication: 20-2-336-7051; Fax: 20-2-336-7056

South Asia
IDRC, 208 Jor Bagh, New Delhi,110 003 India
saro@idrc.org.in
www.idrc.ca/saro

Other Communication: 91-11-461-9411; Fax: 91-11-462-2707

Southeast and East Asia
IDRC, Tanglin, #02-55 - 22 Cross St., Singapore,048421 Singapore
asro@idrc.org.sg
www.idrc.org.sg

Other Communication: 65-6438-7877; Fax: 65-6438-4844

West & Central Africa
CRDI, CD Annexe, BP 11007, Peytavin, Dakar
waro@idrc.ca
www.idrc.ca/waro

Other Communication: 221-33-864-0000; Fax: 221-33-825-3255

International Joint Commission (IJC) / Commission mixte internationale (CMI)

234 Laurier Ave. West, 22nd Fl., Ottawa, ON K1P 6K6
613-947-1420, Fax: 613-993-5583,
beckhoffb@ottawa.ijc.org
www.ijc.org

Other Communication: Great Lakes Water Quality Information: 519/257-6700
Established by the Boundary Waters Treaty of 1909 & is responsible for approving (by Order of Approval) certain works in boundary waters which affect levels & flows on both sides of the Canada-US border. The commission provides recommendations on matters along the common boundary which have been referred to the Commission by the governments. Also monitors & assesses theGreat Lakes Water Quality Agreement (GLWQA) & is responsible for reviewing & commenting on Remedial Action Plans (RAPs) in coordination with eight US States & the province of Ontario.
Chair & Commissioner,Rt. Hon. Herb Gray, P.C., C.C., Q.C.
613-992-2417, Fax: 613-947-9386
Secretary,Dr. Murray Clamen
613-995-0113
Administrative Assistant, Marie Lalonde
613-947-2527, Fax: 613-993-5583

Great Lakes Regional Office
100 Ouellette Ave., 8th fl., Windsor, ON N9A 6T3
Fax: 519-257-6740,
Other Communication: Information: 519/257-6700
Director, Great Lakes Regional Office, Karen E. Vigmostad
519-257-6715

United States Section / Section des États-Unis
#100, 1250 - 23 St. Northwest, Washington, DC 20440 USA
202-736-9000, Fax: 202-736-9015
Chair, Irene B. Brooks
Commissioner, Allen I. Olson
Commissioner, Sam Speck
Secretary,Dr. Charles A. Lawson
202-736-9008, lawsonc@washington.ijc.org

Justice Canada

East Memorial Bldg., 284 Wellington St., Ottawa, ON K1A 0H8
613-957-4222, Fax: 613-954-0811,
webadmin@justice.gc.ca
www.justice.gc.ca

Other Communication: Media Relations Phone: 613-957-4207; Access to Information and Privacy Phone: 613-952-8361
The Department ensures that the Canadian justice system is fair, accessible & efficient. Responsibilities are as follows: provision of policy & program advice & direction by the development of the legal content of bills, regulations, & guidelines; prosecution of federal offences throughout Canada; litigation of civil cases by or on behalf of the federal Crown; & provision of legal advice to federal law enforcement agencies & other government departments.
Acts Administered:
Annulment of Marriages (Ontario) Act
Anti-Terroism Act
Canada Evidence Act
Canada Prize Act
Canada-United Kingdom Civil & Commercial Judgments Convention Act
Canadian Bill of Rights
Canadian Human Rights Act
Commercial Arbitration Act
Contraventions Act
Controlled Drugs & Substance Act
Crown Liability & Proceedings Act

Department of Justice Act
Divorce Act
Escheats Act
Extradition Act
Family Orders Agreements Enforcement Assistance Act
Federal Courts Act
Firearms Act
Foreign Enlistment Act
Foreign Extraterritorial Measures Act
Fugitive Offenders Act
Identification of Criminals Act
International Sale of Goods Contracts Convention Act
Interpretation Act
Judges Act
Law Commission of Canada Act
Marriage (Prohibited Degrees) Act
Mutual Legal Assistance in Criminal Matters Act
Official Languages Act
Postal Services Interruption Relief Act
Revised Statutes of Canada, 1985 Act
Security Offences Act
State Immunity Act
Statute Revision Act
Statutory Instruments Act
Supreme Court Act
Tax Court of Canada Act
United Nations Foreign Arbitral Awards Convention Act
Youth Criminal Justice Act
Minister of Justice shares responsibility to Parliament for the following Acts:
Access to Information Act (President of the Treasury Board)
Bills of Lading Act (Minister of Transport)
Criminal Code (Solicitor General & Minister of Agriculture & Agri-Foods)
Garnishment, Attachment Pension Diversion Act (Minister of National Defense, Minister of Finance & Minister of Public Works & Government Services)
Privacy Act (President of the Treasury Board)

Minister, Justice; Attorney General of Canada,Hon. Robert Douglas Nicholson
613-992-4621, Fax: 613-992-7910,Nicholson.R@parl.gc.ca
Parliamentary Secretary to the Minister of Justice, Bob Dechert
613-995-7321, Fax: 613-992-6708,Dechert.B@parl.gc.ca
Deputy Minister & Deputy Attorney General, Miles J. Kirvan
613-957-4998
Associate Deputy Minister, Yves Côté
613-941-4073, Fax: 613-941-4074,
Associate Deputy Minister, Donna J. Miller
613-948-8990, Fax: 204-984-8649,Other Communications: Winnipeg: 204-983-6029
Assistant Deputy Attorney General, Donald J. Rennie
613-957-4840, Fax: 613-941-1972
Senior General Counsel, Gordon Bourgard
613-952-9810, Fax: 613-946-7449

Aboriginal Affairs Portfolio / Portfeuille des affaires autochtones
Fax: 613-954-4737

Asst. Deputy Attorney General, Pamela McCurry
613-946-6633, Fax: 613-954-4737
Deputy Asst. Deputy Attorney General, Michael Hudson
604-775-5173, Fax: 604-775-5152,Other Communications: Alt. Phone: 613-946-1385
Senior General Counsel, Indian & Northern Affairs Canada, Legal Services Unit, Andrew Saranchuk
819-994-4141
Senior Counsel, Aboriginal Law & Strategic Initiatives, Danielle Dussault
613-941-2240
General Counsel, Indian and Northern Affairs Canada - Legal Services Unit, Margaret McIntosh
819-953-0856
Counsel, Indian Residential Schools Resolution, Lisa Campbell
613-996-4214, Fax: 613-996-1810

Business & Regulatory Law Portfolio / Portefeuille du droit des affaires et du droit réglementaire
Fax: 613-946-9988

Asst. Deputy Minister, Pierre Legault
613-947-4944, Fax: 613-946-9988
General Counsel & Executive Director, Competition Bureau, Rhona Einbinder-Miller
819-997-9210, Fax: 819-953-9267
General Counsel, Transport Legal Services, Isabelle Jacques
613-993-4558, Fax: 613-990-5777

Central Agencies Group / Groupes centraux
Fax: 613-995-7223

Asst. Deputy Minister & Counsel to the Dept. of Finance, Valerie Hughes
613-996-4667, Fax: 613-995-7223
Senior General Counsel, Treasury Board, Michel LeFrançois
613-952-3379, Fax: 613-954-5806
Senior Counsel, Yvonne Milosevic
613-943-0418, Fax: 613-995-7223
General Counsel, Public Service Commission, Gaston Arseneault
613-995-0445, Fax: 613-995-0198
General Counsel, Office of the Superintendent of Financial Institutions, Alain Prévost
613-990-7787

Civil Litigation Division / Division du contentieux des affaires civiles
Asst. Deputy Attorney General, Donald J. Rennie
613-957-4840, Fax: 613-941-1972
Director General & Senior General Counsel, Alain Préfontaine
613-946-3815, Fax: 613-954-1920

Communications Branch
284 Wellington St., Ottawa, ON K1A 0H8
Fax: 613-941-2329

Director General, Suesan Saville
613-957-9596, Fax: 613-941-2329
Information Officer, Valerie Laforce
613-957-4223, Fax: 613-954-0811
Director, Creative Services & Outreach, Dorothy Love
613-954-6327, Fax: 613-948-2983
Director, Director, Strategic Communications, Steven Knight
613-941-4021, Fax: 613-941-2329

Corporate Services / Services à la gestion
Fax: 613-957-8382

Asst. Deputy Minister, Virginia McRae
613-941-7889, Fax: 613-957-6377
Director General, Human Resources & Professional Development, Camille Therriault-Power
613-941-1867, Fax: 613-954-3000
Chief Information Officer, Dave Adamson
613-941-3444, Fax: 613-941-5201

Federal Prosecution Service / Service fédéral des poursuites
Asst. Deputy Attorney General, Daniel Bellemare, Q.C.
613-957-4756, Fax: 613-954-2958
Senior General Counsel & Director, Strategic Operations Section, George Dolhai
613-941-2653
Senior General Counsel & Director, Criminal Law Section, Clare Barry
613-946-3822

Legislative Services Branch / Division des services législatifs
Chief Legislative Counsel, John Mark Keyes
613-954-5786, Fax: 613-952-4080
Chief Legislative Editor, Legislative Revising & Editing Services, Ingrid Ludchen
613-957-8497, Fax: 613-957-7866
Deputy Chief Legislative Counsel, Philippe Hallée
613-941-4178, Fax: 613-941-1193

Policy Sector / Secteur des politiques
Senior Asst. Deputy Minister, Donald K. Piragoff
613-957-4730, Fax: 613-957-9949
Senior General Counsel & Director General, Catherine Kane
613-957-4690, Fax: 613-952-1110
Senior General Counsel, Family, Children & Youth Section, Elissa Lieff
613-957-1200, Fax: 613-952-5740
General Counsel & Director General, Youth Justice, Catherine Latimer
613-957-9623, Fax: 613-954-3275
Director General, International Legal Programs, Mark Berlin
613-952-6595, Fax: 613-948-8910
Director General, Policy Integration & Coordination Section, Stan E. Lipinski
613-941-2267, Fax: 613-957-4019

Public Law Sector / Secteur du Droit public
Asst. Deputy Minister, Carolyn P. Kobernick
613-957-4939, Fax: 613-957-1403
Senior General Counsel, Constitutional & Administrative Law Section, Ann Chaplin
613-948-2992, Fax: 613-941-1937
General Counsel & Director, Official Languages Law Group, Marie Tremblay
613-941-4037, Fax: 613-952-0677
General Counsel & Director, Information Law & Privacy, Denis Kratchanov
613-957-4624, Fax: 613-941-2002
Deputy Director General & General Counsel, Human Rights Law Section, Jodie van Dieen
613-952-4131, Fax: 613-952-4137
Director & General Counsel, International Private Law Section, Kathryn Sabo
613-957-4967, Fax: 613-957-3854

Public Safety, Defence & Immigration Portfolio / Sécurité Publique, défense & immigration
Asst. Deputy Attorney General, Daniel Therrien
613-952-4774, Fax: 613-957-7840
Director & General Counsel, Crimes Against Humanity & War Crimes, Terry Beitner
613-954-2351, Fax: 613-952-7370,

Tax Law Services / Services du droit fiscal
Asst. Deputy Attorney General, Johanne D'Auray
613-957-4811, Fax: 613-941-1221
Senior General Counsel, Canada Revenue Agency, Charles McNab
613-957-2358
Senior General Counsel, Canada Revenue Agency, Jean-Marc Raymond
613-954-5881
Senior General Counsel, Tax Law Services, Gordon Bourgard
613-952-9810, Fax: 613-946-7449
Director General, Michelle Gosselin
613-952-8755, Fax: 613-957-4019
Deputy Director General, Intergovernmental & External Relations, Catherine MacLeod
613-946-9283
Director, Evaluation Division, Deborah McCorkell-Hoyle
613-957-7657
Acting Director, Priorities & Planning, Gail Bradshaw
613-941-6807
Director, Research & Statistics Division, Stan Lipinski
613-941-2267
Director, Strategic Planning, Joel Oliver
613-952-5619
Director General, Carolina Giliberti
613-957-4344, Fax: 613-954-4893
Acting Director, Innovations, Analysis & Integration Directorate, Karen Bron
613-954-2884
Director, Legal Aid Team, Barbara Merriam
613-952-5620
Director, Policy Planning Directorate, Michelle Adkins
613-952-5759
Senior Regional Director, Ted K. Tax
Senior Regional Director, Barbara Burns
604-666-0016
Senior Regional Director, Andy Watt
Senior Regional Director, Terance McAuley
Regional Director, Barbara Ritzen

Laurentian Pilotage Authority Canada / Administration de pilotage des Laurentides Canada

#1501, 555, boul René-Lévesque ouest, Montréal, QC H2Z 1B1
514-283-6320, Fax: 514-496-2409,
administration@apl.gc.ca
www.pilotagestlaurent.gc.ca

The Authority provides pilotage services in the province of Québec, north of St-Lambert Lock. Reports to government through the Minister of Transport.

CEO, Réjean Lanteigne
514-283-6320
Director, Administrative Services, Claude Lambert
514-283-6320
Director, Dispatch Services, Sylvia Masson
514-283-6320
Director, Operations, Denys Pouliot
514-283-6320
Secretary & Legal Advisor, Mario St-Pierre
514-283-6320

Library & Archives Canada / Bibliothèque et archives Canada

395 Wellington St., Ottawa, ON K1A 0N4
613-996-5115, Fax: 613-995-6274, 866-578-7777
reference@lac-bac.ca
www.collectionscanada.gc.ca

Other Communication: Genealogy Reference: 613/996-7458
The mandate of Library and Archives Canada is: To preserve the documentary heritage of Canada for the benefit of present and future generations; To be a source of enduring knowledge accessible to all, contributing to the cultural, social and economic advancement of Canada; To facilitate in Canada cooperation among communities involved in the acquisition, preservation and diffusion of knowledge; and To serve as the continuing memory of the government of Canada and its institutions.

Librarian & Archivist of Canada, Daniel J. Caron
819-934-5800, Fax:
819-934-5888,danielj.caron@lac-bac.gc.ca
Asst. Deputy Minister, Acquisitions Sector, Doug Rimmer
819-934-5790, Fax:
819-934-4422,doug.rimmer@lac-bac.gc.ca
Acting Asst. Deputy Minister, Collections Management Sector, Zahra Pourjafar-Ziaei
819-934-4618, Fax:
819-934-5262,zahra.pourjafar-ziaei@lac-bac.gc.ca
Acting Asst. Deputy Minister, Resource Discovery Sector, Jean-Stéphen Piché
613-992-7059, Fax:
613-992-5315,Jean-Stephen.Piche@lac-bac.gc.ca
Senior Director General, General Stakeholder Relations, Sean Berrigan
819-934-5858, Fax:
819-934-5839,sean.berrigan@lac-bac.gc.ca
Acting Director General, Government Records Branch, Geneviève Allard
819-934-7430, Fax:
819-934-7534,genevieve.allard@lac-bac.gc.ca
Assoc. Director General, Strategic Communications, Fabien Lengellé
819-934-5717, Fax:
819-934-5835,fabien.lengelle@lac-bac.gc.ca
Executive Director, Friends of Library & Archives Canada, Georgia Ellis
613-943-1544, Fax:
613-943-2343,georgia.ellis@lac-bac.gc.ca

Library of Parliament / Bibliothèque du Parlement

Parliamentary Bldgs., 111 Wellington St., Ottawa, ON K1A 0A9
613-992-4793, Fax: 613-943-6383, 866-599-4999
Other Communication: Visitors Information: 613/996-0896
The Library of Parliament provides Parliament with information, documentation, research & analysis; maintains collections to support parliamentarians in their work & provides information about Canada's Parliament to the public.
Parliamentary Librarian, William R. Young
613-992-3122, Fax: 613-943-6383
Asst. Parliamentary Librarian, Sonia L'Heureux
613-996-2391

Marine Atlantic Inc. / Marine Atlantique

Baine Johnston Centre, #302, 10 Fort William Place, St. John's, NL A1C 1K4
709-772-8957, Fax: 709-772-8956, 800-341-7981
info@marine-atlantic.ca
www.marine-atlantic.ca
A federal Crown corporation with a mandate to provide a passenger & commercial marine transportation ferry service between the Island of Newfoundland & the mainland of Canada.
Chair, Robert Crosbie
President/CEO, Wayne Follett
Communications Officer, Tara Laing
709-772-8974, tlaing@marine-atlantic.ca

National Advisory Council on Aging / Conseil consultatif national sur le troisième âge

Jeanne Mance Bldg., 8th Fl., Postal Locator 1908 A1, Ottawa, ON K1A 0K9
613-957-1968, Fax: 613-957-7627
The Council advises the Minister of Health on issues related to the aging of the Canadian population & the quality of life of seniors.It reviews the needs & problems of seniors & recommends remedial action, liaises with other groups interested in aging, encourages public discussion & publishes & disseminates information on aging.
Interim Chair, Robert Dorie
NACA Coordinator, Marjolaine Thompson
613-957-2872, Fax: 613-957-1176

National Arts Centre (NAC) / Centre national des Arts (CNA)

53 Elgin St., PO Box 1534 B, Ottawa, ON K1P 5W1
613-947-7000, Fax: 613-996-9578,
info@nac-cna.ca
www.nac-cna.ca
Dedicated to the development & promotion of the performing arts, the NAC co-produces & presents a wide range of theatre, music & dance productions. Reports to government through the Minister of Canadian Heritage.
Chair, Julia E. Foster
613-947-7000
President/CEO, Peter Herrndorf
613-947-7000, Fax: 613-238-4556,pherrndo@nac-cna.ca
Senior Director, Operations, Gilles Landry
613-947-7000, Fax: 613-947-4512,glandry@nac-cna.ca
CEO, NAC Foundation, Jayne Watson
613-947-7000, Fax: 613-947-8786,jwatson@nac-cna.ca
Chief Financial Officer, Daniel Senyk
613-947-7000, Fax: 613-943-1399,dsenyk@nac-cna.ca
Director, Communications, Rosemary Thompson
rthompson@nac-cna.ca
Music Director, NACO, Pinchas Zukerman
613-947-7000, Fax: 613-943-1400,pzukerman@nac-cna.ca
Artistic Director, English Theatre, Peter Hinton
613-947-7000, Fax: 613-943-1401,phinton@nac-cna.ca
Artistic Director, French Theatre, Wajdi Mouawad
613-947-7000, wmouawad@nac-cna.ca
Producer, Dance, Cathy Levy
613-947-7000, clevy@nac-cna.ca
Producer, Producer, Variety & Community Programming, Simone Deneau
613-947-7000, sdeneau@nac-cna.ca
Executive Assistant, Luce Courtemanche
613-947-7000, Fax: 613-238-4556

National Battlefields Commission / Commission des champs de bataille nationaux

390, av de Bernières, Québec, QC G1R 2L7
418-648-3506, Fax: 418-648-3638,
information@ccbn-nbc.gc.ca
www.ccbn-nbc.gc.ca
Established to preserve, administer & enhance the Plains of Abraham, the battlefields park in Québec City (Plains of Abraham & des Braves Park). Reports to government through the Minister of Canadian Heritage.
Communications Officer, Joanne Laurin
418-649-6251, Fax: 418-648-3809
Executive Secretary, Nathalie Marcotte

National Capital Commission (NCC) / Commission de la capitale nationale (CCN)

#202, 40 Elgin St., Ottawa, ON K1P 1C7
613-239-5555, Fax: 613-239-5063, 800-704-8227
info@ncc-ccn.ca
www.canadascapital.gc.ca
Responsible for the planning, development & preservation of the National Capital Region. Maintains a "greenbelt" which includes historical bogs & swamps & a 40-hectare farm circa 1875. Responsible for the operation of Gatineau Park.
CEO, Marie Lemay
613-239-5194, Fax: 613-239-5039
Director, Communications, Kathryn Keyes
613-239-5636, Fax: 613-239-5180

National Defence Canada / Défense nationale

Major-General George R. Pearkes Bldg., 101 Colonel By Dr., Ottawa, ON K1A 0K2
613-995-2534, Fax: 613-992-4739, 800-856-8488
www.forces.gc.ca

Other Communication: Access to Information: 613-992-0996; Media Inquiries: 613-996-2353
The Minister of National Defence is responsible for the Department of National Defence (DND), the Canadian Forces (CF), & related organizations. Canadian Forces members protect Canada, defend North America, & contribute to international peace & security. The work of DND & CF includes the following: assisting civil authorities to protect national interests, to handle national emergencies & to maintain an adequate level of emergency preparedness throughout Canada; protecting Canadian approaches to the continent; promoting Arctic security; pursuing opportunities for Canada-U.S.A. defence co-operation; participating in multilateral operations through international organizations, such as the United Nations (UN) & the North Atlantic Treaty Organization (NATO); supporting humanitarian relief efforts; assisting in the restoration of conflict-devastated places; & participating in confidence-building measures, like arms-control programs.
Acts Administered:
Aeronautics Act, with respect to any matter relating to defence
Army Benevolent Act
Canadian Forces Superannuation Act
Defence Services Pension Continuation Act
Emergencies Act
Emergency Preparedness Act
Garnishment, Attachment & Pension Diversion Act, with respect to members & former members of the Canadian Forces
National Defence Act
Pension Benefits Division Act, with respect to members & former members of the Canadian Forces
Visiting Forces Act
In addition, the DND administers, under the general direction of the Chief Electoral Officer, the Special Voting Rules (Schedule II to the Canada Elections Act) as they relate to Canadian Forces elect
Minister, National Defence,Hon. Peter Gordon MacKay
613-992-6022, Fax: 613-992-2337,MacKay.P@parl.gc.ca; Mackay.P@forces.gc.ca
Parliamentary Secretary to the Minister of National Defence, Laurie Hawn
613-992-4524, Fax: 613-943-0044,Hawn.L@parl.gc.ca
Deputy Minister, Robert Fonberg
613-992-4258, Fax: 613-995-2028
Chief of the Defence Staff,Gen. Walt Natynczyk
613-992-5054, Fax: 613-995-8578
Vice-Chief of Defence Staff,V.-Adm. Denis Rouleau
613-992-6052, Fax: 613-992-3945
Assistant Deputy Minister, Finance & Corporate Services, Bryn Weadon
613-992-5669, Fax: 613-992-9693
Assistant Deputy Minister, Information Management, John Turner
613-995-2017, Fax: 613-995-2189
Assistant Deputy Minister, Infrastructure & Environment, J. Scott Stevenson
613-945-7545, Fax: 613-995-6653
Assistant Deputy Minister, Human Resources - Civilian, Cynthia Binnington
613-992-7447, Fax: 613-995-8938
Assistant Deputy Minister, Materiel, Dan Ross
613-992-6622, Fax: 613-945-0949
Assistant Deputy Minister, Policy, Jill Sinclair
613-992-3458, Fax: 613-995-2876
Assistant Deputy Minister, Public Affairs, Josée Touchette
613-995-0383, Fax: 613-995-2610
Assistant Deputy Minister, Science & Technology; CEO, Defence R&D Canada, Dr. Robert S. Walker
613-996-2020, Fax: 613-995-3402
Associate Deputy Minister, National Defence, William F. Pentney
613-992-0275, Fax: 613-945-7011
Chief, Review Services, Greg Jarvis
613-992-7975, Fax: 613-992-0528
Associate Chief, Communications Security Establishment, Penny Reedie
613-991-7501, Fax: 613-991-8514
Judge Advocate General,B.Gen. Ken Watkin
613-992-3019, Fax: 613-992-5078
Ombudsman, Pierre Daigle
613-992-0787, Fax: 613-992-3167
• Communications Security Establishment/ Centre de la sécurité des telecommunications
PO Box 9703 Terminal
Ottawa, ON K1G 3Z4
613-991-7600
www.cse-cst.gc.ca
The Communications Security Establishment is Canada's national cryptologic agency, providing the Government of Canada with two key services: foreign signals intelligence in support of defence & foreign policy, & the protection of electronic information & communication.
• Office of the Communications Security Establishment Commissioner/ Bureau du Commissaire du Centre de la sécurité des télécommunications
PO Box 1984 B
Ottawa, ON K1P 5R5
613-992-3044
csec-ccst.gc.ca
The Commissioner reviews the activities of the Communications Security Establishment for compliance with the law; advises the Minister of National Defence & the Attorney General of Canada of any CSE activity not in compliance with the law; receives complaints about CSE activities; carries out specific duties under the public interest provisions of the Security of Information Act.
• Military Police Complaints Commission/ Commission d'examen des plaintes concernant la police militaire
270 Albert St., 10th Fl.
Ottawa, ON K1P 5G8
613-947-5625 Fax: 613-947-5713 800-632-0566
commission@mpcc-cppm.gc.ca
Other Communication: Toll Free Fax: 1-877-947-5713
Quasi-judicial, independent civilian agency examines complaints arising from either the conduct of military police members in the exercise of policing duties or functions or from interference in or obstruction of their police investigations.

Commands / Commandes
Chief of the Air Staff,L.Gen. Steve Lucas
Chief of the Land Staff,L.Gen. Andrew Leslie
Chief of the Marime Staff,V.Adm. Drew Robertson
Commander, Northern Area,Col. Normand Couturier

Operational Commands
Canada Command,L.Gen. Marc Dumais
Canadian Expeditionary Forces Command,L.Gen. Michel Gauthier
Canadian Special Forces Operations Command,Col. David Barr

Canadian Operational Support Command, M.Gen. Daniel Benjamin

Operations Groups:

Land Force Atlantic Area (Headquarters)
Halifax, NS
902-427-7580
Commander, B.Gen. Rick Parsons

Land Force Central Area (Headquarters)
Toronto, ON
416-633-6200
Commander, B.Gen. Guy Thibault

Land Force Western Area (Headquarters)
Edmonton, AB
780-973-4011
Commander, B.Gen Timothy Grant

Maritime Forces Atlantic (Headquarters)
Halifax, NS
902-427-6355
Commander, Comm. Dean McFadden

Maritime Forces Pacific (Headquarters)
Victoria, BC
250-363-2800
Commander, R.Adm. Roger Girourd

Secteur du Québec de la Force terrestre
Montréal, QC
514-252-2777
Commander, B.Gen. Christian Barabé

Canadian Forces Base (CFB) & Detachments:

BFC Bagotville
Alouette, QC G0C 1A0

CFB Borden
Borden, ON L0M 1C0

CFB Cold Lake
Cold Lake, AB T9M 2C6

CFB Comox
Lazo, BC V0R 2K0

CFB Edmonton
PO Box 10500, Edmonton, AB T5J 4J5

CFB Esquimalt
FMO, Victoria, BC V9A 7N2

CFB Gagetown
Oromocto, NB E2V 4J5

CFB Gander
PO Box 6000, Gander, NL A1V 1X1

CFB Goose Bay
Goose Airport, Happy Valley-Goose Bay, NL A0P 1S0

CFB Greenwood
Greenwood, NS B0P 1N0

CFB Halifax
Halifax, NS B3K 5X5

CFB Kingston
Vimy Post Office, Kingston, ON K7K 7B4

BFC Montréal
Richelain, QC J0J 1R0

CFB Moose Jaw
PO Box 5000, Moose Jaw, SK S6H 7Z8

CFB North Bay
Hornell Heights, ON P0H 1P0

CFB Petawawa
Petawawa, ON K8H 2X3

CFB Shilo
Shilo, MB R0K 2A0

CFB Suffield
PO Box 6000, Medicine Hat, AB T1A 8K8

CFB Trenton
Astra, ON K0K 3W0

BFC Valcartier
Courcelette, QC G0A 4Z0

CFB Winnipeg
Westwin, MB R3J 3Y5

Canadian Forces Stations:

CFS Alert
Belleville, ON K8N 5W6

CFS Leitrim
Ottawa, ON K1A 0K5

CFS Masset
PO Box 2000, Masset, BC V0T 1M0

CFS St. John's
PO Box 2028, St. John's, NL A1C 6B5

Canadian Defence Academy:

Canadian Forces College
Toronto, ON
416-482-6800
Commandant, B.Gen. Walter Semianiw

Canadian Land Forces Command & Staff College
Kingston, ON
613-451-5818
Commandant, Col. John Collin

Royal Military College
Kingston, ON
613-541-6000
Commandant, B.Gen. Jocelyn Lacroix

Regional Public Affairs Office (National Defense):

Calgary
#418, 100 - 4th Ave. SW, Calgary, AB T2P 3N2
403-974-2822

Moncton
#102, 95 Foundry St., Moncton, NB E1C 5H7
506-851-0556

Québec
Tour Ouest, Guy-Favreau Complex, #911, 200, boul Réné-Lévesque, Montréal, QC H2Z 1X4
514-283-5286

Toronto
4900 Yonge St., 6th Fl., Toronto, ON M2N 6B7
416-635-4406, 888-564-8625

Vancouver
#201, 1090 West Pender, Vancouver, BC V6E 2N7
604-666-0199

National Energy Board (NEB) / Office national de l'énergie (ONE)

444 - 7 Ave. SW, Calgary, AB T2P 0X8
403-292-4800, Fax: 403-292-5503, 800-899-1265
info@neb-one.gc.ca
www.neb-one.gc.ca

Other Communication: Toll free fax: 877-288-8803

Federal regulatory tribunal whose powers include: authorizing oil, natural gas & electricity exploration; certifying interprovincial & international pipelines & designated power lines; & setting tolls & tariffs for oil & gas pipelines under federal jurisdiction. The NEB reviews Canadian supply of all major commodities, with emphasis on electricity, oil, natural gas, & oil & natural gas by-products. It also reviews the demand for Canadian energy in Canada & in export markets. In addition to its regulatory role, the NEB is responsible for advising the government on the development & use of energy resources. Its responsibilities include regulating exploration, development & production of oil & gas on frontier lands in a manner that promotes worker safety, environmental protection & resource conservation. The NEB is responsible for environmental matters relating to the construction & operation of facilities & programs within its jurisdiction. Its environmental activities are carried out in three phases: The first phase involves evaluating the potential environmental effects of proposed projects. In the second phase, the environment is protected through monitoring & enforcement of terms & conditions attached to project approval. The third phase include s ongoing monitoring of operations to ensure that cleanup, restoration & maintenance of sites & rights of way are conducted to acceptable standards. The Board also verifies that emergency response plans are in place & that it or the operator can respond immediately to any incidents

Acts Administered:
Canada Oil & Gas Operations Act
Canada Petroleum Resources Act
Canada Transportation Act
Canadian Environmental Assessment Act
Energy Administration Act
National Energy Board Act
Northern Pipeline Act

Chair/CEO, Gaétan Caron
403-299-2724, Fax: 403-299-5503, gaetan.caron@neb-one.gc.ca

National Farm Products Council (NFPC) / Conseil national des produits agricoles (CNPA)

Canada Bldg., 344 Slater St., 10th Fl., Ottawa, ON K1R 7Y3
613-995-6752, Fax: 613-995-2097,
fpcc-cpac@agr.gc.ca
http://fpcc-cpac.gc.ca

Their mission is to oversee the national supply management agencies for poultry and eggs and national promotion research agencies to ensure an efficient system that works in the balanced interest of stakeholders, from producers to consumers. Reports to Government through the Minister of Agriculture & Agri-food.

Chair, Laurent Pellerin
Executive Director, Claude Janelle
613-995-0682, claude.janelle@agr.gc.ca
Director, Corporate & Regulatory Affairs, Marc Chamaillard
613-995-4116, marc.chamaillard@agr.gc.ca
Director, Policy & Program Operations, Christine Kwasse
613-995-5553, christine.kwasse@agr.gc.ca
Communication Officer, Chantal Lafontaine
613-995-9148, chantal.lafontaine@agr.gc.ca

National Film Board of Canada (NFB) / Office national du film du Canada

3155, rue Côte de Liesse, CP 1600 Centre-ville, Saint-Laurent, QC H4N 2N4
514-283-9000, Fax: 514-283-7564, 800-267-7710
www.nfb.ca

The Board is mandated to initiate & promote the production & distribution of films in the national interest, with the primary object of interpreting Canada to Canadians & to other nations. Reports to government through the Minister of Canadian Heritage.

Government Film Commissioner & Chair, Tom Perlmutter
514-283-9245
Director General, Accessibility & Digital Enterprises, Deborah Drisdell
514-283-9246
Director General, Marketing & Communications, Nathalie Courville
514-283-9246
Director General, English Program Branch, Cindy Witten
514-283-9501
Director General, Finance, Operations & Technology, Luisa Frate
514-283-9051
Director General, French Program Branch, Monique Simard
514-283-9285
Director, Human Resources, Robert Paquette
514-283-9108
Director, Technical Innovation & Resources, Joanne Carrière
514-283-9258
Director, Administration, Luisa Frate
514-283-9051

Regional Centres:

Edmonton
#100, 10815 - 104 Ave., Edmonton, AB T5J 4N6
780-495-3013, Fax: 780-495-6412
Executive Producer, David Christensen
780-495-3015

Halifax
#201 - 5475 Spring Garden Rd., Halifax, NS B3J 1G2
902-426-6000, Fax: 902-426-8901
Executive Producer, Kent Martin
902-426-7351

Moncton
#100, 95 Foundry St., Moncton, NB E1C 5H7
Fax: 506-851-2246, 866-663-8331
Executive Producer, Jacques Turgeon
506-851-6105

Montréal
1564, rue St-Denis, Montréal, QC H2X 3K2
514-496-6887, Fax: 514-283-2816,
cinerobotheque@nfb.ca

Québec
#368, 901 Cap Diamant, Québec, QC G1K 4K1
418-649-6377, Fax: 418-649-6379

Toronto
150 John St., Toronto, ON M5V 3C3
416-973-0904, Fax: 416-973-9640,
ontarioinfo@nfb.ca

Toronto (French Program)
150 John St., Toronto, ON M5V 3C3
416-973-5382, Fax: 416-973-2594,

Vancouver
#250, 351 Abbott St., Vancouver, BC V6B 0G6
604-666-3838, Fax: 604-666-1569
Executive Producer, Tracey Friesen
604-666-3411

Winnipeg
#300, 136 Market Ave., Winnipeg, MB R3B 0P4
204-983-3160, Fax: 204-983-0742
Executive Producer, Derek Mazur
204-983-7985

Offices Abroad:

France
5, rue de Constantine, Paris,75007 France
Other Communication: 33-1-44-18-35-40; Fax: 33-1-47-05-75-89

USA
#4820, 350 Fifth Ave., New York, NY 10118 USA
514-283-9700, Fax: 514-495-2573
Head, North American Sales, Heather Wyer

National Gallery of Canada (NGC) / Musée des Beaux-Arts du Canada (MBAC)

380 Sussex Dr., PO Box 427 A, Ottawa, ON K1N 9N4
613-990-1985, Fax: 613-993-4385, 800-319-2787
info@gallery.ca; info@beaux-arts.ca
www.national.gallery.ca

Other Communication: Bookstore: 613-990-1970
The permanent collection of the National Gallery comprises paintings, sculpture, prints & drawings, photographs, film & video art from the Canadian, European, American & Asian schools. Special exhibitions as well as permanent installations of the gallery's collections are on display. The gallery also sends its exhibitions on tour across the country & participates in international exhibitions. Services provided to the public include lectures, talks, tours, films, workshops, concerts & a bookstore.
Chair, Michael J. Audain
Vice-Chair, Michael J. Tims
Director/CEO, Marc Mayer
613-990-1927
Chief Curator & Deputy Director, David Franklin
613-990-0497, dfrankli@gallery.ca
Deputy Director, Administration & Finance, David Baxter
613-991-0040
Deputy Director, Exhibitions & Installations, Karen Colby-Stothart
613-998-4917
Director, Corporate Secretariat & Ministerial Liaison, Matthew Symonds
613-990-9232
Director, Human Resources Services, Michelle Miner
613-993-2856
Curator, Canadian Art, Charles Hill
613-990-0486, chill@gallery.ca
Curator, Contemporary Art, Josée Drouin-Brisebois
613-990-7645
Curator, European & American Art, Dr. Graham Larkin
613-990-8580
Curator, Indigenous Art, Greg Hill
613-949-0327
Curator, Photographs Collection, Ann Thomas
613-990-1961, athomas@gallery.ca
Senior Media & Public Relations Officer, Josée (Britanie) Mallet
613-990-6835

National Joint Council (NJC) / Conseil national mixte (CNM)

C.D. Howe Bldg., 240 Sparks St. West, 7th Fl., PO Box 1525 B, Ottawa, ON K1P 5V2
613-990-1805, Fax: 613-990-7071,
email.courrier@njc-cnm.gc.ca
www.njc-cnm.gc.ca
Provides a forum for consultation on labour issues between the Government of Canada & the bargaining agents for its employees.
General Secretary, Barry Fennessy
613-990-1807, Barry.Fennessy@njc-cnm.gc.ca
Committee Advisor, Karine Beauchamp
613-990-1725, Karine.Beauchamp@njc-cnm.gc.ca

National Parole Board / Commission nationale des libérations conditionnelles

410 Laurier Ave. West, Ottawa, ON K1A 0R1
613-954-7474, Fax: 613-995-4380, 800-874-2652
info@npb-cnlc.gc.ca
www.npb-cnlc.gc.ca

Other Communication: Communications Inquiries Phone: 613-954-6549; Pardons - Requests for Application Kit Toll Free: 1-800-874-2652; Victims Information Line Toll Free: 1-866-789-4636
Part of the criminal justice system, the National Parole Board makes independent, conditional release & pardon decisions & clemency recommendations. The Board also works to facilitate integration of offenders as law-abiding citizens.
Acts Administered:
Corrections & Conditional Release Act
Criminal Code
Criminal Records Act
Chair, Harvey Cenaiko
613-941-1154, Fax: 613-941-9426
Executive Vice-Chair, Marie-France Pelletier
613-954-6120
Executive Director, Shelley Trevethan
613-954-1153
Manager, Appeal Division, Denise Leblanc
613 954-5940
Director, Communications, Caroline Douglas
613-954-6547
Senior Counsel, Legal Services, Gertrude Lavigne
613-954-7451

Regional Offices:

Atlantic
1045 Main St., 1st Fl., Moncton, NB E1C 1H1
506-851-6345, Fax: 506-851-6926
Regional Director, Art Robson

Ontario
516 O'Connor Dr., Kingston, ON K7P 1N3
613-634-3857, Fax: 613-634-3861,
Regional Director, Simonne Ferguson

Pacific
#305, 32315 South Fraser Way, Abbotsford, BC V2T 1W6
604-870-2468, Fax: 604-870-2498
Regional Director, Dan Denis

Prairies
101 - 22 St. East, 6th Fl., Saskatoon, SK S7K 0E1
306-975-4228, Fax: 306-975-5892
Regional Director, Bernard Pitre

Québec
Complexe Guy-Favreau, Tour ouest, #1001, 200, boul René-Lévesque ouest, Montréal, QC H2Z 1X4
514-283-4584, Fax: 514-283-5484
Regional Director, Jean-Marc Trudeau

National Research Council Canada (NRC) / Conseil national de recherches Canada (CNRC)

Bldg. M-58, 1200 Montreal Rd., Ottawa, ON K1A 0R6
613-993-9101, Fax: 613-952-7928, 877-672-2672
info@nrc-cnrc.ca
www.nrc-cnrc.ca

Other Communication: IRAP Information: 613/993-1790; CISTI Information: 613/993-1600
NRC is Canada's principal public science & technology agency. It performs, supports & promotes scientific & industrial research for economic & social benefits, research & development in the national interest. Contributions are made to the national science & technology infrastructure & the development of a highly skilled workforce is fostered. Activities focus on strengthening industrial partnerships to bolster competitiveness in key information & telecommunications technologies. The Canada Institute for Scientific & Technical Information (CISTI), a component of NRC, provides access to hundreds of national/international databases, more than 50,000 journals, millions of books, technical reports & conference proceedings. Provides: customized literature searches; current awareness services; access to scientific, technical & medical databases; & referrals to experts.CISTI has an integrated online catalog accessible via the Internet. It publishes 14 international research journals including "Environmental Reviews". The NRC Industrial Research Assistance Program (IRAP) is Canada's national technology transfer & diffusion network helping Canadian firms develop world-class technology they cannot generate on their own. Advisory services involve assisting firms to: define technical needs; identify technical opportunities; obtain technical information & assistance; solve process & production problems; access or acquire technology & expertise from Canadian or foreign firms; & access financial assistance where appropriate. Technical & financial assistance is provided for R&D projects & for adapting existing technologies, with emphasis on advancing unproven technologies to the point of performance testing
President,Dr. John R. McDougall
613-993-2024, Fax: 613-957-8850
Vice-President, Research, Life Sciences, Dr. Roman Szumski
613-993-9244, Fax: 613-954-2066
Vice-President, Research, Physical Sciences, Dr. Danial D. Wayner
613-998-5404, Fax: 613-949-1314
Vice-President, Technology & Industry Support, Patricia Mortimer
613-998-3664, Fax: 613-998-3839
Acting Vice-President, Engineering, John M. Coleman
613-949-5955, Fax: 613-949-5987
Acting Vice-President, Corporate Management & CFO, Shane Brunas
613-991-3773, Fax: 613-991-3774
Acting Secretary General, Robert G. James
613-998-4579, Fax: 613-991-0398
Director General, Canada Institute for Scientific & Technical Information, Pam Bjornson
613-993-2341, Fax: 613-952-9112
Director General, Industrial Research Assistance Program (IRAP), Dr. Tony Rahilly
613-993-0695, Fax: 613-954-0501

Alberta & Northwest Territories
250 Karl Clark Rd., Edmonton, AB T6N 1E4
780-495-6509, Fax: 780-495-6510
Director,Dr. Kashmir Gill
780-495-2136, Fax:
780-495-6510,kashmir.gill@nrc-cnrc.gc.ca

IRAP Regional Offices:

Atlantic/Nunavut Region
1411 Oxford St., Halifax, NS B3H 3Z1
902-426-3138, Fax: 902-426-1624
Executive Director, Bradley C. Goodyear
902-426-1055, Fax: 902-426-1624

Pacific Region
#650 - 1185 West Georgia St., Vancouver, BC V6E 4E6
604-221-3100, Fax: 604-221-3101
Executive Director, Christopher Ryan
604-221-3163, Fax:
604-221-3101,christopher.ryan@nrc-cnrc.gc.ca

Newfoundland & Labrador
Kerwin Place & Arctic Ave., Memorial University, PO Box 12093, St. John's, NL A1B 3T5
709-772-5228, Fax: 709-772-5067
Director, David W. Rideout
709-772-2838, Fax:
709-772-5067,dave.rideout@nrc-cnrc.gc.ca

New Brunswick
PO Box 5678 W, Fredericton, NB E3B 5G4
506-452-3831, Fax: 506-452-3827, 877-994-4727
Executive Director, David Healey

Ontario
#903 55 St. Clair Ave. E, Toronto, ON M4T 1M2
416-973-4484, Fax: 416-973-4303
Executive Director,Dr. Sam Stevens
416-973-4483, Fax: 416-952-2996,r.stevens@nrc-cnrc.gc.ca

Québec
#P-101, 75, boul de Montagne, Boucherville, QC J4B 6Y4
450-641-5300, Fax: 450-641-5301
Executive Director, Bogdan Ciobanu
450-641-5305, Fax:
450-641-5301,bogdan.ciobanu@cnrc-nrc.gc.ca

Saskatchewan & Manitoba
435 Ellice Ave., Winnipeg, MB R3B 1X6
204-983-0092, Fax: 204-983-8835,
Director, Vivian Sullivan
204-984-6477, Fax:
204-983-8835,vivian.sullivan@nrc-cnrc.gc.ca

Biotechnology Research Institute (BRI) / Institut de recherche en biotechnologie (IRB)
6100, av Royalmount, Montréal, QC H4P 2R2
514-496-6100, Fax: 514-496-1928,
bri-info@cnrc-nrc.gc.ca
www.nrc-cnrc.gc.ca/eng/ibp/bri.html
Prevention & pollution control, including technology & process development, identification & behaviour of pollutants, monitoirng & ecotoxicological risk evaluation; green technologies & sustainable development. BRI scientists have unique expertise in the biotreatment of contaminated soils, groundwater, sediments, air, & industrial wastewater. The Sector works closely with industry on the R&D of innovative environmental technologies. BRI is also a founding member of the Montreal Centre of Excellence in Brownfields Rehabilitation (MCEBR), a joint initiative between government & industry to carry out research, development, & demonstration projects associated with soil decontamination & site rehabilitation.
Director General,Dr. Michel Desrochers
514-496-6101, Fax: 514-496-6388

Herzberg Institute of Astrophysics (HIA) / Institut Herzberg d'astrophysique (IHA)
5071 West Saanich Rd., Victoria, BC V9E 2E7
250-363-0001, Fax: 250-363-0045,
hia-www@nrc-cnrc.gc.ca
www.nrc-cnrc.gc.ca/eng/ibp/hia.html
Operation & maintenance of astronomical observatories as national facilities available to all interested scientists. Conducts research programs in the fields of astronomy, space science & studies solar activity measurements of trace elements in the atmosphere.
Director General,Dr. Greg Fahlman
250-363-0040, Fax:
250-363-8483,Gregory.Fahlman@nrc-cnrc.gc.ca
Director, Dominion Astrophysical Observatory, James E. Hesser
250-363-0007, Fax:
250-363-6970,James.Hesser@nrc-cnrc.gc.ca
Director, Operations, Susanna Gibson
250-363-0567, Fax:
250-363-0063,Susanna.Gibson@nrc-cnrc.gc.ca

Industrial Materials Institute (IMI) / Institut des matériaux industriels
75, boul de Mortagne, Boucherville, QC J4B 6Y4
450-641-5000, Fax: 450-641-5101,
Imi-Info@cnrc-nrc.gc.ca
www.nrc-cnrc.gc.ca/imi-imi
Materials processing technologies for the metal, polymer, aerospace & automotive sectors; virtual fabrication; advanced instrumentation & materials; envionmental technologies.
Director General,Dr. Blaise Champagne, Eng., Ph.D.
450-641-5050, Fax:
450-641-5101,Blaise.Champagne@cnrc-nrc.gc.ca
Acting Director, Aluminium Technology Centre, Bernard Arsenault
418-545-5546, Fax:
418-545-5543,Bernard.Arsenault@cnrc-nrc.gc.ca
Director, Modelling and Diagnostics, Jean F. Bussière
450-641-5252, Fax:
450-641-5106,Jean.Bussiere@cnrc-nrc.gc.ca
Director, London - Center for Automotive Materials & Manufacturing (CAMM), Sylvain Pelletier
450-641-5239, Fax:
450-641-5105,Sylvain.Pelletier@imi.cnrc-nrc.gc.ca

Institute for Aerospace Research (NRC) / Institut de recherche aérospatiale (IAR)
1200 Montreal Rd., Ottawa, ON K1A 0R6
613-990-0765, Fax: 613-952-7214,
www.nrc-cnrc.gc.ca/iar-ira
Development & use of national aeronautical facilities; advanced design & manufacture; transportation & safety; aerospace & the environment; international programs & strategic intelligence.
Director General, Jerzy P. Komorowski
613-993-0141, jerzy.komorowski@nrc-cnrc.gc.ca
Director, Aerodynamics Laboratory,Dr. Steven J. Zan
613-993-2423, Fax: 613-957-4309
Director, Aerospace Manufacturing Technology Centre, Pierre Dicaire
514-283-9139, Fax: 514-283-9484
Director, Flight Research Laboratory, Stewart W. Baillie
613-998-3071, Fax: 613-952-1704
Director, Gas Turbine Laboratory,Dr. Ibrahim A. Yimer
613-991-1139
Director, Operations, Andrew B. Sullivan
613-993-9447
Director, Structures, Materials and Performance Laboratory,Dr. Prakash Patnaik
613-991-6915, Fax: 613-990-7444
Communications Officer, Sheila Noble
613-991-5738, sheila.noble@nrc-cnrc.gc.ca

Institute for Biodiagnostics / Institut du biodiagnostic
435 Ellice Ave., Winnipeg, MB R3B 1Y6
204-983-7692, Fax: 204-984-7217,
Neela.Mitra@nrc-cnrc.gc.ca
www.nrc-cnrc.gc.ca/ibd-ibd
Director General,Dr. Ian Smith
204-983-7526, Fax: 204-984-6978,Ian.Smith@nrc-cnrc.gc.ca
Director, Business Development & Community Outreach, Paul Wiebe
204-984-6223, Fax:
204-983-3154,Paul.Wiebe@nrc-cnrc.gc.ca
Director, Research, Roxanne Deslauriers
204-984-5146, Fax:
204-984-6978,Roxanne.Deslauriers@nrc-cnrc.gc.ca
Communications Officer, Valerie McPherson
204-984-4890, Fax:
204-983-3154,Valerie.McPherson@nrc-cnrc.gc.ca

Institute for Biological Sciences (IBS) / Institut des sciences biologiques
Bldg. M-54, 1200 Montreal Rd., Ottawa, ON K1A 0R6
613-993-5812, Fax: 613-957-7867,
www.nrc-cnrc.gc.ca/ibs-isb
Research in molecular genetics, immunochemistry, microbiology, biochemistry, neurobiology including cell signaling, transduction, in vivo & in vitro models for therapeutics evaluation.
Director General,Dr. James Richards
613-993-7506, Fax:
613-957-7867,James.Richards@nrc-cnrc.gc.ca
Director, Business Development & Research Services, Scott Ferguson
613-990-5948, Fax:
613-952-5136,Scott.Ferguson@nrc-cnrc.gc.ca
Director, Immunobiology Program, Jean-Robert Brisson
613-990-3244, Fax:
613-941-1327,Jean-Robert.Brisson@nrc-cnrc.gc.ca

Institute for Chemical Process & Environmental Technology (ICPET) / Institut de technologie des procédés chimiques et de l'environnement
Bldg. M-12, 1200 Montreal Rd., Ottawa, ON K1A 0R6
613-993-4041, Fax: 613-957-8231,
www.nrc-cnrc.gc.ca/icpet-itpce
Focuses expertise in the areas of process & materials chemistry, process technology & related environmental technology. Supports environmentally responsible manufacturing in the fuel cell, oil sands & bioproducts sectors. Aids manufacturing & industrial clients in optimizing their process operations & reducing the impact of their operations on the environment. Promotes business opportunities in collaborative research, technology licensing & fee-for-service arrangements.
Director General,Dr. Janusz Lusztyk
Janusz.Lusztyk@nrc-cnrc.gc.ca
Director, Commercialization, Kanu Sikka
613-990-4624, Fax:
613-991-2384,Kanu.Sikka@nrc-cnrc.gc.ca
Director, Research, Kevin A. Jonasson
613-993-6570, Fax:
613-991-2384,kevin.jonasson@nrc-cnrc.gc.ca

Institute for Fuel Cell Innovation (IFCI) / Institut d'innovation en piles à combustible
4250 Wesbrook Mall, Vancouver, BC V6T 1W5
604-221-3000, Fax: 604-221-3001,
info.itci-iipac@nrc-cnrc.gc.ca
www.nrc-cnrc.gc.ca/ifci-iipc
Strategic research aimed at advancing fuel cell science & technology & facilitating the commercialization of hydrogen & fuel cell systems.

Institute for Information Technology (IIT) / Institut de technologie de l'information
Bldg. M-50, 1200 Montreal Rd., Ottawa, ON K1A 0R6
613-991-3373, Fax: 613-952-0074, 877-672-2672
www.nrc-cnrc.gc.ca/iit-iti
Director General, Christian Couturier
506-444-0555, Fax:
506-444-6187,christian.couturier@nrc-cnrc.gc.ca
Director, Business Development & Research Support, Marc-Alain Mallet
506-444-0375, Fax:
506-452-3859,Marc-Alain.Mallet@nrc-cnrc.gc.ca
Acting Director, Research Programs, NCR, Charles-Antoine Gauthier
613-993-8551, Fax:
613-952-7998,Charles-Antoine.Gauthier@nrc-cnrc.gc.ca
Director, Research Programs, New Brunswick, Andrew Reddick
506-444-0540, Fax:
506-452-3814,Andrew.Reddick@nrc-cnrc.gc.ca

Institute for Marine Biosciences (IMB) / Institut des biosciences marines (IBM)
1411 Oxford St., Halifax, NS B3H 3Z1
902-426-8332, Fax: 902-426-9413,
communications.imb@nrc-cnrc.gc.ca
www.nrc-cnrc.gc.ca/imb-ibm
Aquatic animal health & nutrition; natural toxins; mass spectrometry & proteomics; cell & molecular biology.
Director General,Dr. Joan C. Kean-Howie
902-426-8278, Fax:
902-426-8514,Joan.Kean-Howie@nrc-cnrc.gc.ca
Director, Corporate & Business Relations, Denise LeBlanc MacDonald
902-426-2496, Denise.LeBlancMacDonald@nrc-cnrc.gc.ca
Director, Research, Aleksander Patrzykat
902-426-4080, Aleksander.Patrzykat@nrc-cnrc.gc.ca

Institute for Microstructural Sciences (IMS) / Institut des sciences des microstructures
Bldg. M-50, 1200 Montreal Rd., Ottawa, ON K1A 0R6
613-949-9660, Fax: 613-957-8734,
ims.info@nrc-cnrc.gc.ca
www.nrc-cnrc.gc.ca/ims-ism
Director General, Marie D'Iorio
613-993-4597, Fax:
613-957-8734,Marie.D'iorio@nrc-cnrc.gc.ca
Director, Applications Technologies, Sylvain Charbonneau
613-998-9414, Sylvain.Charbonneau@nrc-cnrc.gc.ca
Director, Materials Technologies, Thomas E. Jackman
613-993-6711, Thomas.Jackman@nrc-cnrc.gc.ca
Director, Research Support Operations, Cheryl Lambert
613-991-4650, Cheryl.Lambert@nrc-cnrc.gc.ca

Institute for National Measurement Standards / Institut des étalons nationaux de mesure
Bldg. M-36, 1500 Montreal Rd., Ottawa, ON K1A 0R6
613-998-7018, Fax: 613-954-1473,
alexandra.shaw@nrc-cnrc.gc.ca
www.nrc-cnrc.gc.ca/inms-ienm
Canada's national metrology institute (NMI), charged with the responsibility to investigate & determine standards & methods of measurement.
Director General,Dr. James W. McLaren
613-993-7319, Fax:
613-952-5113,James.McLaren@nrc-cnrc.gc.ca

Institute for Nutrisciences & Health / Institut des sciences nutritionelles et de la santé
550 University Ave., Charlottetown, PE C1A 4P3
902-566-7000, Fax: 902-569-4289,
inh@nrc-cnrc.gc.ca
www.nrc-cnrc.gc.ca/inh-isns
Director, Research, Robert G. Chapman
902-566-7405, Fax:
902-566-7445,Bob.Chapman@nrc-cnrc.gc.ca

Institute for Ocean Technology (IOT) / Institut des technologies océaniques (ITO)
Kerwin Pl. & Arctic Ave., PO Box 12093, St. John's, NL A1B 3T5
709-772-4939, Fax: 709-772-2462,
Noel.Murphy@nrc-cnrc.gc.ca
www.nrc-cnrc.gc.ca/iot-ito
Ocean technology research in the areas of offshore engineering, marine vessel design, underwater vehicles, propulsion, electronic navigation, ice-vessel & ice structure interaction. Provides assistance to Canadian ocean technology companies & Canadian government departments. Research services performed in the following areas: tanker offloading & stationkeeping, offshore platform efficiency, navigation safety, all aspects of ocean technology. The Ocean Technology Enterprise Centre assists in the growth & development of new ventures in ocean technology. The centre helps new & established enterprises to develop their concepts & technologies in a supportive environment, with access to IOT facilities & expertise.
Director General,Dr. F. Mary Williams
709-772-2469, Fax: 709-772-3101,f.williams@nrc-cnrc.gc.ca
Director, Facilities, Carl J. Harris
709-772-2326, Fax:
709-772-2462,Carl.Harris@nrc-cnrc.gc.ca
Director, Research,Dr. Bruce Parsons
709-772-2326, Fax:
709-772-2462,bruce.parsons@nrc-cnrc.gc.ca
Communications Coordinator, Derek J. Yetman
709-772-6001, Fax:
709-772-2462,Derek.Yetman@nrc-cnrc.gc.ca

Institute for Research in Construction (IRC) / Institut de recherche en construction
Bldg. M-24, 1500 Montreal Rd., Ottawa, ON K1A 0R6
613-993-2607, Fax: 613-952-7673,
Irc.Client-Services@nrc-cnrc.gc.ca
www.nrc-cnrc.gc.ca/irc-irc
Research areas include building envelope & structure, indoor environment, urban infrastructure, fire research, sustainable built environment & climate change. A special initiative is the National Guide to Sustainable Municipal Infrastructure, in partnership with the Federation of Canadian Municipalities, Infrastructure Canada & the Canadian Public Works Association, a collection of best practices for core infrastructure.
Director General, Morad R. Atif
613-993-2443, Fax: 613-941-0822,Morad.Atif@nrc-cnrc.gc.ca

London - Centre for Automotive Materials and Manufacturing (CAMM) / Centre des matériaux et fabrication pour l'automobile
800 Collip Circle, London, ON N6G 4X8
519-430-7166, Fax: 519-430-7064,
John.Lyons@nrc-cnrc.gc.ca
www.nrc-cnrc.gc.ca/eng/facilities/imi/camm.html
The Centre for Automotive Materials and Manufacturing serves as the national headquarters for the National Research Council's automotive-related capabilities and facilities across Canada. Their purpose is to lead in the development of scalable, sustainable manufacturing technologies for green vehicles. CAMM research is focused on laser materials processing,

electrolytic, physical and chemical vapor deposition technologies and composites in manufacturing.
Director,Dr. Sylvain Pelletier
450-641-5239, Fax:
450-641-5105,Sylvain.Pelletier@imi.cnrc-nrc.gc.ca

National Institute of Nanotechnology / Institut national de nanotechnologie
Bldg. NINT, University of Alberta, 11421 Saskatchewan Dr., Edmonton, AB T6G 2M9
780-641-1600, Fax: 780-641-1601,
nintinfo@nrc.gc.ca
www.nrc-cnrc.gc.ca/nint-innt
Multi-disciplined research in physics, chemistry, engineering, biology, informatics, pharmacy & medicine, with applications in medicine & biotechnology, energy & environment, computing & telecommunications.
Director General,Dr. Nils O. Petersen
780-641-1610, Nils.Petersen@nrc-cnrc.gc.ca
Director, Business Development & External Relations, Richard Brommeland
780-641-1620, Richard.Brommeland@nrc-cnrc.gc.ca
Director, Research Programs,Dr. Christopher J. Haugen
780-641-1615, Chris.Haugen@nrc-cnrc.gc.ca
Research Officer, Nano Ethical, Environmental, Economic, Legal & Societal Issues (NEEELS), Michael D. Lounsbury
780-492-1684, Fax: 780-492-3325,ml37@ualberta.ca

Plant Biotechnology Institute (PBI) / Institut de biotechnologie des plantes (IBP)
110 Gymnasium Pl., Saskatoon, SK S7N 0W9
306-975-5248, Fax: 306-975-4839,
pbi-info@nrc-cnrc.gc.ca
www.nrc-cnrc.gc.ca/pbi-ibp
Canada's national laboratory for advanced research in new exploitable methods for genetic alteration of plants & for biochemical control of plant development in agriculture. Engineering projects include cell & molecular biology of higher plants. Technical services include: DNA synthesis & sequencing, bio-nuclear magnetic resonance spectroscopy, mass spectroscopy, advanced training services, & expert consultancy.
Director General, Jerome Konecsni
306-975-5575, Fax:
306-975-4191,Jerome.Konecsni@nrc-cnrc.gc.ca,
Director, Business & Corporate Services, Jeffrey P. Parker
306-975-5568, Fax:
306-975-4839,Jeff.Parker@nrc-cnrc.gc.ca
Director, Research, Suzanne R. Abrams
306-975-5569, Fax:
306-975-4191,Sue.Abrams@nrc-cnrc.gc.ca

Steacie Institute for Molecular Sciences / Institut Steacie des sciences moléculaires
100 Sussex Dr., Ottawa, ON K1A 0R6
613-993-1212, Fax: 613-954-5242,
Huguette.Morin-Dumais@nrc-cnrc.gc.ca
www.nrc-cnrc.gc.ca/sims-issm
NRC-SIMS conducts cutting-edge interdisciplinary research in selected areas of molecular sciences that have the potential to stimulate entirely new or emerging sectors of the Canadian economy. Strategic molecular sciences research fields for NRC-SIMS include: nanoscience, chemical biology, diagnostics, laser science, molecular interfaces, advanced materials, and their related technologies.
Acting Director General,Dr. James B. Webb
613-990-0915, James.Webb@nrc-cnrc.gc.ca

Technology Centres:

Canadian Hydraulics Centre (CHC) / Centre canadien d'hydraulique (CCH)
1200 Montreal Rd., Ottawa, ON K1A 0R6
613-993-9381, Fax: 613-952-7679,
info.chc@nrc-cnrc.gc.ca
www.nrc-cnrc.gc.ca/chc-chc
One of North America's largest hydraulic engineering laboratories, with expertise & experience in physical & numerical modeling, analysis & field studies to solve a wide range of hydraulic engineering problems. Specializations include: coastal engineering; marine structures; cold regions; environmental hydraulics; laboratory technologies; numerical models. Environmental hydraulics services include: coastal ecosystem management; river & watershed management; flood management & dam break; chemical & oil spill migration; water quality & pollutant transport; sediment transport, including shoreline erosion & dredged spoil disposal; aquaculture management; environmental information & simulation systems.
Acting General Manager,Dr. Garry W. Timco
613-993-6673, Garry.Timco@nrc-cnrc.gc.ca

Centre for Surface Transportation Technology (CSTT) / Centre de technologie des transports de surface (CTTS)
2320 Lester Rd., Ottawa, ON K1V 1S2
613-998-9639, Fax: 613-957-0831,
inquiries.cstt@nrc-cnrc.gc.ca
www.nrc-cnrc.gc.ca/cstt-ctts
Road & rail vehicle performance technology, studies & rail tribology; climatic engineering.
Director General, Paul Treboutat
613-998-9635, Paul.Treboutat@nrc-cnrc.gc.ca
Director, Rail Division, Harold M. Kohn
613-991-5522, Harold.Kohn@nrc-cnrc.gc.ca
Director, Road Vehicles & Military Systems Division, Michael S. Halasz
613-998-8015, Michael.Halasz@nrc-cnrc.gc.ca

National Round Table on the Environment & Economy (NRTEE) / Table ronde nationale sur l'environnement et l'économie (TRNEE)

#200, 344 Slater St., Ottawa, ON K1R 7Y3
613-992-7189, Fax: 613-992-7385,
admin@nrtee-trnee.ca
www.nrtee-trnee.ca
The National Round Table on the Environment & the Economy is an independent agency of the federal government committed to providing decision makers & opinion leaders with reliable information &objective views on the current state of the debate on the environment & the economy. Working with stakeholders across Canada, the NRTEE carries out its mandate by identifying key issues with both environmental &economic implications, fully exploring these implications, & suggesting action designed to balance economic prosperity with environmental preservation. A multistakeholder approach, combined with impartiality & neutrality, are the hallmarks of the NRTEE's activities. By creating an atmosphere in which all points of view can be expressed freely & debated openly, the NRTEE has established a process whereby stakeholders themselves define the environment/economy interface within issues, determine areas of consensus & identify the reasons for disagreement in other areas. The NRTEE's programs focus on the following areas: energy & climate change; capital markets & sustainability; climate change adaptation
President & CEO, David McLaughlin
613-943-0399, mclaughlind@nrtee-trnee.ca
Director, Communications & Public Affairs, Brian Laghi
613-943-2054, laghib@nrtee-trnee.ca
Director, Corporate Services, Jim McLachlan
613-947-4507, mclachlanj@nrtee-trnee.ca
Director, Policy & Research, René Drolet
613-996-4501, droletr@nrtee-trnee.ca

National Search & Rescue Secretariat / Secrétariat national de recherches et sauvetage

#400, 275 Slater St., Ottawa, ON K1A 0K2
613-992-0054, Fax: 613-996-3746, 800-727-9414
inquiry@nss.gc.ca
www.nss.gc.ca
Provides a central managerial role in the overall coordination of search & rescue. It addresses program & policy issues related to the National Search & Rescue Program, & advises the Lead Minister for search & rescue.
Executive Director, Géraldine Underdown
613-992-0054, Fax: 613-996-3746
Communications Officer, Kim Fauteux
613-992-3472, Fax: 613-996-3746

Natural Resources Canada (NRCan) / Ressources naturelles Canada (RNCan)

580 Booth St., Ottawa, ON K1A 0E4
613-995-0947, Fax: 613-992-7211,
www.nrcan-rncan.gc.ca/com/

Other Communication: Emergency Operations Centre: 613/995-5555, 943-0000
Advances development of Canada's economy by contributing to the development & use of Canada's mineral & energy resources in a manner consistent with federal environmental & social objectives; advances knowledge of the Canadian landmass through scientific & science-related activities.
Acts Administered:
Arctic Waters Pollution Prevention Act
Canada Foundation for Sustainable Development Technology Act
Canada-Newfoundland Atlantic Accord Implementation Act
Canada-Nova Scotia Offshore Petroleum Resources Accord Implementation Act
Canada Oil & Gas Operations Act (Indian Affairs & Northern Development)
Canada Petroleum Resources Act
Canadian Ownership & Control Determination Act
Co-operative Energy Act
Department of Natural Resources Act
Energy Administration Act
Energy Efficiency Act
Energy Monitoring Act
Energy Supplies Emergency Act
Explosives Act
Forestry Act
Hibernia Development Project Act
International Boundary Commission Act
Lands Surveys Act
Lands Surveyors Act
Motor Vehicle Fuel Consumption Standards Act
National Energy Board Act
Northern Pipeline Act
Nuclear Fuel Waste Act, 2002
Nuclear Liability Act
Nuclear Safety & Control Act
Oil Substitution & Conservation Act
Administration of Acts with respect to Changes in Provincial Boundaries
Alberta Act
Alberta/BC Boundary Act, 1974
Alberta/NWT Boundary Act, 1958
British Columbia 1857, 1866
BC-Yukon-NWT Boundary Act, 1967
Keewatin Act
Manitoba Boundaries Extension Act, 1912
Manitoba-NWT Boundary Act, 1966
Manitoba/Saskatchewan Boundary Act, 1966
New Brunswick, 1851
Newfoundland, 1949
Northwest Territories, 1905
Nova Scotia, 1851
Nunavut, 1993
Ontario, 1889
Ontario Boundaries Extension Act, 1912
Ontario-Manitoba Boundary Act
Prince Edward Island, 1873
Québec Boundaries Extension Act, 1912
Saskatchewan, 1905
Saskatchewan/NWT Boundary Act, 1966
Yukon, 1898
Acts Administered in Part by Natural Resources Canada
Arctic Waters Pollution Prevention Act (Transport Canada/Indian & Northern Affairs)
Canada Lands Survey Act (Indian & Northern Affairs)
Canada Petroleum Resources Act (Indian & Northern Affairs)
Cape Breton Development Corporation Act
National Energy Board Act (Transport Canada)
Resources & Technical Surveys Act (Fisheries & Oceans/Environment)
Minister, Natural Resources,Hon. Christian Paradis
613-996-2007, Fax: 613-943-1562,ParadC@parl.gc.ca
Parliamentary Secretary to the Minister of Natural Resources & for the Canadian Wheat Board, David Anderson
613-992-0657, Fax:
613-992-5508,Anderson.Da@parl.gc.ca
Deputy Minister, Cassie J. Doyle
613-992-3280, Fax:
613-992-3828,CassieJ.Doyle@NRCan-RNCan.gc.ca
Associate Deputy Minister, Malcolm Brown
613-996-9753, Fax:
613-992-3828,Malcolm.Brown@NRCan-RNCan.gc.ca
Assistant Deputy Minister, Energy Sector, Christine Donoghue
613-947-2751, Fax:
613-992-1405,Christine.Donoghue@NRCan-RNCan.gc.ca
Chief Scientist, Marian Chiu
613-947-9094, Fax:
613-944-4747,Marian.Chiu@NRCan-RNCan.gc.ca
Director General, External Relations, Mark Pearson
613-996-6055, Fax:
613-996-0478,Mark.Pearson@NRCan-RNCan.gc.ca
Chief Audit Executive, Joe Freamo
613-996-4940, Fax:
613-992-8799,Joe.Freamo@NRCan-RNCan.gc.ca
Director General, Corporate Renewal Office, Sylvie Letellier
613-947-7403, Fax:
613-992-8922,Sylvie.Letellier@NRCan-RNCan.gc.ca
• Atomic Energy of Canada Ltd.
• National Energy Board

Canadian Forest Service (CFS) / Service canadien des forêts
613-995-0947, Fax: 613-947-1208,
cfs-scf@nrcan.gc.ca
http://cfs.nrcan.gc.ca
Promotes the sustainable development of Canada's forests & competitiveness of the Canadian forest sector for the well-being of present & future generations of Canadians.It focuses on forest science & technology, & related national policy coordination.The CFS maintains five research centres across the country that share responsibility for research in the areas of biodiversity;

biotechnology; climate change; ecology & ecosytems; entomology; forest conditions, monitoring & reporting; forest fires; forest & landscape management; pathology; silviculture & regeneration; & socioeconomics.

CFS Regional Offices:

Atlantic Forestry Centre / Centre de foresterie de l'Atlantique
1350 Regent St. South, PO Box 4000, Fredericton, NB E3B 5P7
506-452-3500, Fax: 506-452-3525,
http://cfs.nrcan.gc.ca/regions/afc
Responsible for the overall Canadian Forest Service operations & programs in the Atlantic region. Liaises & negotiates with provincial government, industry officials, & other sector-related senior management on behalf of the CFS in the region.
Regional Director General, John E. Richards
506-452-3508, JohnE.Richards@NRCan-RNCan.gc.ca,
Director, Forest Production and Protection, Derek MacFarlane
506-452-3680, Derek.MacFarlane@NRCan-RNCan.gc.ca
Director, Science, Bruce Pendrel
506-452-3505, Bruce.Pendrel@NRCan-RNCan.gc.ca

Canadian Wood Fibre Centre (CWFC) / Centre canadien sur la fibre de bois (CCFB)
580 Booth Street, 8th Floor, Ottawa, ON K1A 0E4
613-947-9001, Fax: 613-947-8863,
http://cfs.nrcan.gc.ca/subsite/cwfc
The Canadian Wood Fibre Centre (CWFC) brings together forest sector researchers to develop solutions for the Canadian forest sector's wood fibre related industries in an environmentally responsible manner.Its mission is to create innovative knowledge to expand the economic opportunities for the forest sector to benefit from Canadian wood fibre.

Great Lakes Forestry Centre / Centre de foresterie des Grands Lacs
1219 Queen St. East, PO Box 490, Sault Ste Marie, ON P6A 2E5
705-949-9461, Fax: 705-541-5700,
http://cfs.nrcan.gc.ca/regions/glfc
Responsibilities include: forest research & regional forestry activities in Ontario; provides the primary federal focus for forestry in Ontario; emphasis on boreal mixed wood forest management & environmental impacts of pollutants & forestry practices; efforts also directed at the reduction of losses from insects, disease & fire; ecosystem dynamics & classification; nutrient problems & impacts from forestry practices; acid rain impacts (carbon dioxide/nitrogen oxide interactions).
Director General, Theodore Van Lunen
705-541-5555, Theodore.VanLunen@NRCan-RNCan.gc.ca

Laurentian Forestry Centre / Centre de foresterie des Laurentides
1055, rue du PEPS, CP 10380 Sainte-Foy, Québec, QC G1V 4C7
418-648-3335, Fax: 418-648-5849,
lucie.labrecque@RNCan-NRCan-gc.ca
http://scf.rncan.gc.ca/regions/cfl
Responsibilities include: increasing scientific & technical knowledge in the area of forest biology which includes biodiversity, tree biotechnology & advanced genetics, pest management methods, & in the area of forest ecosystem which cover forest ecosystem processes, effects of forestry practices, landscape management & climate change.
Director General, Jacinthe Leclerc
418-648-3957, Jacinthe.Leclerc@RNCan-NRCan.gc.ca
Director, Forest Biology Program, Lise Caron
418-648-7616, Fax:
418-649-6956,Lise.Caron@RNCan-NRCan.gc.ca
Research Director, Forest Ecosystems, Vincent Roy
418-648-3770, Fax:
418-649-6956,Vincent.Roy@NRCan-RNCan.gc.ca
Director, Planning & Development, Normand Laflamme
418-648-2528, Fax:
418-648-2529,Normand.Laflamme@RNCan-NRCan.gc.ca

Northern Forestry Centre / Centre de foresterie du Nord
5320 - 122 St., Edmonton, AB T6H 3S5
780-435-7210, Fax: 780-435-7359,
http://cfs.nrcan.gc.ca/regions/nofc
Responsibilities include: socio-economics & forest sociology; fire ecology, environment, & advanced fire management & prediction systems; climate change & forest interactions; carbon budget modeling; forest health, insect, & disease monitoring & management systems; remote sensing applications & landscape level classification systems; ecosystems productivity; biodiversity. Regional coordination of national programs relating to Model Forests & First Nation Forestry. Responsible for thedirection of forestry programs in the provinces of Alberta, Saskatchewan, Manitoba & the NWT, including R&D, & four federal-provincial partnership agreements in forestry.
Director General, Timothy Sheldan
780-435-7202, Fax:
780-435-7396,Timothy.Sheldan@NRCan-RNCan.gc.ca

Pacific Forestry Centre / Centre de foresterie du Pacifique
506 West Burnside Rd., Victoria, BC V8Z 1M5
250-363-0600, Fax: 250-363-0775,
http://cfs.nrcan.gc.ca/regions/pfc
Responsibilities include: forest management of federal lands; first nations programs; first nations land claims resource analysis; economic analysis of the regional forest sector (value-added, labour costs, & industrial sustainability); national strategic planning for the forestry practices & landscape management networks; science & technology programs in both forest biology (ecosystems processes, climate change, pest management, & tree biotechnology). Advises the CFS ADM on all forestry matters relating to the Pacific & Yukon region. The Mountain Pine Beetle Action Plan 2005-2010 set out strategies for confronting the infestation.

Corporate Management & Services Sector / Secteur de la gestion et des services intégrés
613-995-4243, Fax: 613-922-8922
Asst. Deputy Minister/CFO, Bill Merklinger
613-995-4252, Fax:
613-992-8922,Bill.Merklinger@NRCan-RNCan.gc.ca
Director General, Financial Management Branch, Thérèse Roy
613-943-8763, Fax:
613-996-2151,Therese.Roy@NRCan-RNCan.gc.ca
Director General, Human Resources & Security Management Branch, Monique Paquin
613-996-4008, Fax:
613-995-0025,Monique.Paquin@NRCan-RNCan.gc.ca
Executive Director, Real Property & Environmental Management Division, Anthony Thompson
613-957-7111, Fax:
613-957-7227,Anthony.Thompson@NRCan-RNCan.gc.ca

Earth Sciences Sector / Secteur des sciences de la Terre
http://ess.nrcan.gc.ca/index_e.php
Provides Canadians with timely & reliable geomatics & geoscience knowledge, products & services of the highest standards & in the most cost-effective manner possible. The Earth Sciences Sector is a predominantly science- and technology-based sector & includes the Geological Survey of Canada, Geomatics Canada, & the Polar Continental Shelf Project.These groups are major contributors to the comprehensive geoscience knowledge base of Canada & provide surveying, mapping, remote sensing, & digital information services describing the Canadian landmass.
Asst. Deputy Minister,Dr. David Boerner
613-992-9983, Fax:
613-995-1509,David.Boerner@NRCan-RNCan.gc.ca
Chief Geologist, Donald James
867-975-4412, Fax:
867-979-0708,Donald.James@NRCan-RNCan.gc.ca
Director General, Coordination & Strategic Issues Branch, Marian Campbell Jarvis
613-992-5032,
Marian.CampbellJarvis@NRCan-RNCan.gc.ca
Director General, Mapping Information Branch, Prashant Shukle
613-947-0467, Fax:
613-994-6749,Prashant.Shukle@NRCan-RNCan.gc.ca
Director, Planning & Operations Division, Fram Engineer
613-996-1169, Fax:
613-947-8768,Fram.Engineer@NRCan-RNCan.gc.ca

Geological Survey of Canada (GSC) / Commission géologique du Canada
601 Booth St., Ottawa, ON K1A 0E8
613-996-3919, Fax: 613-943-8742,
esic@nrcan.gc.ca
http://gsc.nrcan.gc.ca

Other Communication: Bookstore: 613-995-4342
Geoscientific information & research, geoscience surveys, sustainable development of Canada's resources, environmental protection, technology innovation.
Executive Manager, Atlantic & Western Branch, Laurie Lee McGuire
613-996-6574, Fax:
613-996-6575,LaurieLee.McGuire@NRCan-RNCan.gc.ca
Director General, Central & Northern Canada Branch,Dr. David Boerner
613-995-4314, Fax:
613-996-6575,David.Boerner@NRCan-RNCan.gc.ca

Energy Policy Sector / Secteur de la politique énergétique
613-996-7432, Fax: 613-992-1405,
www.nrcan-rncan.gc.ca/eneene/polpol/index-eng.php
Develops & promotes economic, regulatory& voluntary approaches to encourage sustainable development of energy resources to meet domestic needs & export markets. Advises the government on federal energy policies, strategies, emergency plans & activities; promotes efficient energy use.
Asst. Deputy Minister, Mark Corey
613-947-2751, Mark.Corey@NRCan-RNCan.gc.ca,
Director General, Energy Policy Branch, Nada Vrany
613-995-2821, Fax:
613-996-5943,Nada.Vrany@NRCan-RNCan.gc.ca
Director General, Petroleum Resources Branch, Jeff Labonte
613-992-8609, Fax:
613-992-8738,Jeff.Labonte@NRCan-RNCan.gc.ca
Senior Director, International Environment Policy Division, Margaret E. Martin
613-996-6474, Fax:
613-947-6799,Margaret.Martin@nrcan-rncan.gc.ca

Innovation and Energy Technology Sector / Secteur de l'innovation et de la technologie énergétique
Asst. Deputy Minister, Geoff Munro
613-947-1435, Fax:
613-944-4747,Geoff.Munro@NRCan-RNCan.gc.ca
Deputy Director General, Operations, Philippe Dauphin
613-943-4195, Fax:
613-995-7868,Philippe.Dauphin@NRCan-RNCan.gc.ca
Director General, Devon Research Centre,Dr. Hassan Hamza
780-987-8617, Fax:
780-987-8690,Hassan.Hamza@NRCan-RNCan.gc.ca
Director General, Ottawa Research Centre, John Marrone
613-996-8201, Fax:
613-947-2318,John.Marrone@NRCan-RNCan.gc.ca
Director General, Strategic Science-Technology Branch, Martin Aubé
613-996-8109, Fax:
613-947-1016,Martin.Aube@NRCan-RNCan.gc.ca
Director General, Varennes Research Centre, Gilles Jean
450-652-6639, Fax:
450-652-5994,Gilles.Jean@RNCan-NRCan.gc.ca
Acting Director General, Richard Davies
613-996-8115
Director General, CANMET Energy, Hassan Hamza
780-780-8617
Director General, CANMET Energy, Gilles Jean
450-652-6639
Director General, CANMET Energy, John Marrone
613-996-8201
Acting Deputy Director General, CANMET Energy, René Germain
780-987-8648

Minerals & Metals Sector (MMS) / Secteur des minéraux et des métaux
613-947-6580,
info-mms@nrcan-rncan.gc.ca
www.nrcan-rncan.gc.ca/mms-smm
MMS is the federal government's primary source of scientific & technological knowledge, & policy advice, on Canada's mineral & metal resources & on explosives regulation & technology. In addition to housing three scientific research institutions, MMS has the government lead in promoting sustainable development & responsible use of Canada's mineral & metal resources. The Sector is a leader in the generation & dissemination of knowledge on the Canadian minerals & metals industry, & collaborates with & provides research services to governmental, institutional & industrial clients for the development of new technology with economic, environmental & social benefits to Canadians.
Asst. Deputy Minister, Anil Arora
613-992-2490, Fax:
613-996-7425,Anil.Arora@NRCan-RNCan.gc.ca
Director General, CANMET Materials Technology Laboratory,Dr. Jennifer Jackman
613-995-8248, Fax:
613-992-8735,Jennifer.Jackman@NRCan-RNCan.gc.ca
Director General, Explosives Safety & Security Branch, Kiran Hanspal
613-948-5181, Fax:
613-948-5195,Kiran.Hanspal@NRCan-RNCan.gc.ca
Director General, Minerals, Metals and Materials Knowledge Branch, Christiane Villemure
613-996-5525, Fax:
613-943-8453,Christiane.Villemure@NRCan-RNCan.gc.ca
Director General, Minerals, Metals and Materials Policy Branch, Ginny Flood
613-996-5309, Fax:
613-952-7501,Ginny.Flood@NRCan-RNCan.gc.ca
Chief, Health & Safety, CANMET Mining and Mineral Sciences Laboratories, Katrina Nicholson
613-996-0826, Fax:
613-943-0575,Katrina.Nicholson@NRCan-RNCan.gc.ca

Canada Centre for Remote Sensing - Geomatics Canada (CCRSO) / Centre canadien de télédétection (CCT)
588 Booth St., Ottawa, ON K1A 0Y7

613-995-0947, Fax: 613-947-1382,
http://ccrs.nrcan.gc.ca

Remote sensing data for Canada; development of remote sensing technology & applications in conjunction with the private sector, & in support of environmental monitoring; development of the Canadian geospatial data infrastructure for distribution of remote sensing & other geographical databases, in partnership with other departments; development of GIS applications.

Director General, Douglas Bancroft
613-947-1358, Fax:
613-947-1382,Douglas.Bancroft@NRCan-RNCan.gc.ca

Director, Business, Policy & Planning, Gordon Deecker
613-947-1280, Fax:
613-947-1408,Gordon.Deecker@NRCan-RNCan.gc.ca

Director, Data Acquisition Division, Caroline Cloutier
613-995-0802, Fax:
613-947-1408,Caroline.Cloutier@NRCan-RNCan.gc.ca

Director, Earth Observation & GeoSolutions Divison, E. Paola de Rose
613-947-1350, Fax:
613-947-1385,E.Paola.deRose@NRCan-RNCan.gc.ca

Director, Geodetic Survey Division, Denis Hains
613-995-4282, Fax:
613-995-3215,Denis.Hains@NRCan-RNCan.gc.ca

Mapping Information Branch / Direction de l'information cartographique

615 Booth St., Ottawa, ON K1A 0E9
613-995-4945, Fax: 613-995-8737,
Other Communication: Canada Map Office: 1-800-465-6277 or 613/952-7009; Help Desk: 613/996-5916

Director General, Prashant Shukle
613-947-0467, Fax:
613-994-6749,Prashant.Shukle@NRCan-RNCan.gc.ca

Director, Centre for Topographic Information - Ottawa, Douglas O'Brien
613-947-1287, Fax:
613-947-7948,Douglas.O'Brien@NRCan-RNCan.gc.ca

Director, Centre for Topographic Information - Sherbrooke, Eric Loubier
819-564-5600, Fax:
819-564-5698,Eric.Loubier@RNCan-NRCan.gc.ca

Director, Data Dissemination Division, Ann Martin
613-947-5849, Fax:
613-944-6749,Ann.Martin@NRCan-RNCan.gc.ca

Director, GeoConnections Division, Sylvain Latour
613-996-1397, Sylvain.Latour@NRCan-RNCan.gc.ca

Chair, Geographical Names Board of Canada, Bruce Amos
Fax: 613-943-8282,geonames@nrcan.gc.ca, Other Communications: URL: geonames.nrcan.gc.ca

Director, Martin Bergmann
613-947-1601, Martin.Bergmann@NRCan-RNCan.gc.ca

General Counsel & Manager, Vella Mijal
613-992-0039

General Counsel, G. Trotman
613-992-0432

Director General, Tom Wallace
613-996-3027

Director, Nuclear Energy, Sylvana Guindon
613-995-2870

Director, Renewable & Electrical Energy, Christopher Padfield
613-947-5101

Director, Uranium & Radioactive Waste, P.A. Brown
613-996-2395

Director, David Burpee
613-995-7460

Director, Graham R. Campbell
613-995-8860

Director, PERD Program Operations, Mary Preville
613-995-3590

Director, Energy Infrastructure Protection Division, Felix Kwamena
613-995-3190

Director, Frontier Lands Management, Eric Landry
613-992-3794

Director, Oil Division, Kevin Cliffe
613-995-1525

Director, Natural Gas Division, J.S. Booth
613-992-9780

Acting Director General, Carol Buckley
613-944-7501

Director, Buildings Division, Anne Auger
613-996-4079

Director, Demand Policy & Analysis Division, Tim McIntosh
613-943-2396

Director, Housing & Equipment, Louis Marmen
613-996-7512,

Director, Outreach & Information, Colleen Paton
613-996-0765

Director, Transportation Energy Use Division,Vacant
613-995-7300

Director, CANMET Materials Technology Laboratory,Dr. Jennifer Jackman
613-995-8248

Natural Sciences & Engineering Research Council of Canada (NSERC) / Conseil des recherches en sciences naturelles et en génie du Canada (CRSNG)

Constitution Square, Tower II, 350 Albert St., Ottawa, ON K1A 1H5
613-995-4273, Fax: 613-943-1624,
marie-josee.duval@nserc-crsng.gc.ca
www.nserc.gc.ca

Science & Engineering Research Canada (NSERC) is a federal agency whose role is to make investments in people, discovery & innovation for the benefit of all Canadians. With an annual budget of more than $860 million, it supports more than 20,000 university students & postdoctoral fellows in their advanced studies. NSERC promotes discovery by funding more than 10,000 university professors every year & helps make innovation happen by encouraging more than 500 Canadian companies to participate & invest in university research projects.

President,Dr. Suzanne Fortier
613-995-5840, suzanne.fortier@nserc-crsng.gc.ca

Vice-President, Research Grants & Scholarships Directorate, Isabelle Blain
613-995-5833, isabelle.blain@nserc-crsng.gc.ca

Vice-President, Research Partnerships Programs Directorate, Janet Walden
616-139-9215, Fax:
613-947-6371,janet.walden@nserc-crsng.gc.ca

Director, Communications Division, Jacqueline Couture
613-995-5993, Jacqueline.Couture@nserc-crsng.gc.ca

North American Free Trade Agreement (NAFTA) Secretariat / Secrétariat de l'ALÉNA

Canadian Section, #705, 90 Sparks St., Ottawa, ON K1P 5B4
613-992-9388, Fax: 613-992-9392,
webmaster@nafta-alena.gc.ca
www.nafta-alena.gc.ca

The NAFTA Secretariat, comprised of a Canadian Section, a United States Section and a Mexican Section, is responsible for the administration of the dispute settlement provisions of the North American Free Trade Agreement. The Canadian Section also carries responsibility for similar provisions under the Canada-Chile, Canada-Israel and Canada-Costa Rica free trade agreements.

Canadian Secretary,Vacant
613-992-9382, Fax:
613-992-9392,webmaster@nafta-alena.gc.ca

Registrar/Acting Deputy Secretary, Feleke Bogale
613-992-9384, Fax:
613-992-9392,feleke.bogale@nafta-alena.gc.ca

Records & Information Management Officer, Marie-France Meunier
613-992-2303, Fax:
613-992-9392,mariefrance.meunier@nafta-alena.gc.ca

Northern Pipeline Agency Canada (NPAC) / Administration du pipe-line du Nord Canada (APNC)

580 Booth St., Ottawa, ON K1A 0E4
613-992-9612, Fax: 613-995-1913

Established to carry out federal responsibilities in relation to the planning & construction of the Canadian portion of the Alaska Natural Gas Transportation System.

Commissioner, Cassie J. Doyle
613-992-3280, Fax: 613-995-1913

Acting Assistant Commissioner & Comptroller, Jim Booth
613-992-9780, Fax: 613-995-1913

Administrator, Darlene Saikely
613-992-9612, Fax: 613-995-1913

Office of Intergovernmental Affairs (IGA) / Affaires intergouvernementales

c/o Privy Council Office, #1000, 85 Slater St., Ottawa, ON K1A 0A3
613-957-5153, Fax: 613-957-5043,
info@pco-bcp.gc.ca
www.pco-bcp.gc.ca/aia

The federal government office is responsible for the management of federal-provincial-territorial relations. The office supports & advises the Prime Minister & the Minister of Intergovernmental Affairs about issues related to federal-provincial-territorial relations, such as communications, policies, & parliamentary affairs. Fiscal federalism, the evolution of the federation, & Canadian unity are key areas for the IGA.

Minister, Intergovernmental Affairs; Minister, La Francophonie; President, Queen's Privy Council for Canada,Hon. Josée Verner
613-996-4151, Fax: 613-954-2269,VerneJ@parl.gc.ca

Deputy Minister, Serge Dupont
613-947-5695

Parliamentary Secretary to the Prime Minister & to the Minister of Intergovernmental Affairs, Pierre Poilievre
613-992-2772, Fax: 613-992-1209,PoiliP@parl.gc.cagc.ca

Office of the Commissioner of Official Languages / Commissariat aux langues officielles

344 Slater St., 3rd fl., Ottawa, ON K1A 0T8
613-996-6368, Fax: 613-993-5082, 877-996-6368
www.ocol-clo.gc.ca

Responsible for ensuring the equality of English & French in Parliament, within the Government of Canada, the federal administration, & the institutions subject to the Official Languages Act; the preservation & development of official language communities in Canada; & the equality of English & French in Canadian society.

Acts Administered:
Official Languages Act

Commissioner of Official Languages, Graham Fraser
613-995-7488, Fax: 613-943-2255

Director, Audits, Nycole Lafond
613-943-1159, Fax: 613-943-0451

Director, Finance & Procurement, Colette M. Lagacé
613-995-0412, Fax: 613-993-5082

Director, Human Resources, Mario Séguin
613-943-0390, Fax: 613-944-5477

Director, Information Management & Technology, JoHanne Verrier
613-943-0220, Fax: 613-947-4751

Director, Investigations, Carole Beauvais
613-943-1161, Fax: 613-943-0451

Director & General Counsel, Legal Affairs, Johane Tremblay
613-995-9069, Fax: 613-996-9671

Director, Operational Integration Initiative, Corita Harty
613-992-9874, Fax: 613-995-1161

Director, Policy & Research, Carsten Quell
613-943-0429, Fax: 613-995-1161

Director, Strategic Communications & Production, Robin Cantin
613-995-9356, Fax: 613-995-1161

Director, Strategic Performance Measurement, Pierre Coulombe
613-995-0815, Fax: 613-943-0451

Commissioner's Representative, Alberta, British Columbia, NWT, Yukon & Nunavut Region, Deni Lorieau
780-495-3111, Fax: 780-495-4094

Commissioner's Representative, Atlantic Region, Gilbert Taylor
506-851-6990, Fax: 506-851-7046

Commissioner's Representative, Manitoba & Saskatchewan Region, Michelle L. Freynet
204-983-6022, Fax: 204-983-7801

Commissioner's Representative, Ontario Region, Pascal Arseneau
416-973-1904, Fax: 416-973-1906

Commissioner's Representative, Québec Region, Eva Ludvig
514-283-1848, Fax: 514-283-6677

Office of the Ethics Commissioner / Bureau du commissaire en éthique

66 Slater St., 22nd Fl., Ottawa, ON K1A 0A6
613-995-0721, Fax: 613-995-7308,
ciec-ccie@parl.gc.ca
http://ciec-ccie.gc.ca

Administers the Conflict of Interest Code for Members of the House of Commons. Also administers the Prime Minister's Conflict of Interest & Post-Employment Code for Public Office Holders as it applies to federal ministers, secretaries of state, parliamentary secretaries, full-time Governor-in-Council appointees & ministerial staff.

Ethics Commissioner, Mary E. Dawson, C.M., Q.C.
613-995-0721, Fax: 613-995-7308

Executive Advisor, Sherry Perreault
613-996-4880, Fax: 613-995-7308

Office of the Information Commissioner of Canada / Commissariat à l'information du Canada

Place de Ville, Tower B, 112 Kent St., 7th Fl., Ottawa, ON K1A 1H3
613-995-2410, Fax: 613-947-7294, 800-267-0441
general@infocom.gc.ca
www.infocom.gc.ca

Investigates complaints from people who believe they have been denied rights under the Access of Information Act, Canada's freedom of information legislation. An independent ombudsman appointed by Parliament, the Information Commissioner has strong investigative powers. He mediates between dissatisfied applicants & government institutions.

Acts Administered:
Access to Information Act
Information Commissioner, Suzanne Legault
613-995-9976, Fax: 613-995-1501
Asst. Information Commissioner, Complaints Resolution & Compliance, Andrea J. Neill
613-995-2665, Fax: 613-947-7294
Ad Hoc Information Commissioner, Mario Dion
Interim Asst. Information Commissioner, Layla Michaud
613-995-2864, Fax: 613-995-1501

Office of the Leader, Bloc Québécois / Bureau du chef, Bloc Québécois

111 Wellington St., Ottawa, ON K1A 0A6
613-992-6779, Fax: 613-954-2121
Leader of the Bloc Québécois, Gilles Duceppe
613-992-6779, Fax: 613-954-2121,Duceppe.G@parl.gc.ca, Other Communications: Constituency Phone: 514-522-1339, Fax: 514-522-9899
Director, Communications, France Amyot
613-995-0531, Fax: 613-947-3373
Director, Administration, Josée Bergeron
613-943-0884, Fax: 613-995-1134
Director, Research, Benoît Cyr
613-995-7525, Fax: 613-996-3682
Coordinator, Bloc Québécois Caucus, Mireille Beaudin
613-947-4446, Fax: 613-947-4464

Office of the Leader, New Democratic Party (NDP) / Bureau du chef, Nouveau parti démocratique

111 Wellington St., Ottawa, ON K1A 0A6
613-995-7224, Fax: 613-995-4565,
www.npd.ca/jacklayton
Leader of the New Democratic Party,Hon. Jack Gilbert Layton
613-995-7224, Fax: 613-995-4565,Layton.J@parl.gc.ca
Chief of Staff, Anne McGrath
613-992-2888, Fax: 613-995-6426
Senior Press Secretary; Principal Secretary for Québec, Karl Bélanger
613-995-6767, Fax: 613-947-0868
Director, Strategic Communications, Rick Boychuk
613-995-0628, Fax: 613-995-4565
Director, Research & Policy, Peter Puxley
613-996-1420, Fax: 613-995-4565
Director, Operations, Jess Turk-Browne
613-995-8242, Fax: 613-996-7114
Coordinator, Leader's Tour, Rick Devereux
613-943-7882, Fax: 613-947-0868

Office of the Leader of the Opposition (Liberal Research Bureau) / Bureau de l'opposition officielle (Parti liberal du Canada)

131 Queen St., Ottawa, ON K1A 0A6
613-996-6740, Fax: 613-996-2551
Leader of the Opposition,Hon. Michael Grant Ignatieff, B.A., M.A., Ph.D.
613-995-9364, Fax: 613-947-0310,Ignatieff.M@parl.gc.ca, Other Communications: Constituency Phone: 416-251-5510; Fax: 416-251-2845
Chief of Staff, Peter Donolo
613-996-6740, Fax: 613-947-0310
Chief Operating Officer, Patricia Sorbara
613-995-0741, Fax: 613-996-2551
Principal Secretary, Jean-Marc Fournier
613-996-6740, Fax: 613-947-0310
Director, Policy & the Liberal Research Bureau, Brian Bohunicky
613-947-6720, Fax: 613-996-2551
Director, Legislative Affairs, Jeremy Broadhurst
613-996-3290, Fax: 613-996-2551
Team Lead, Communications, Sheamus Murphy
613-995-6715, Fax: 613-996-2551

Office of the Prime Minister (Conservative Party of Canada) / Cabinet du Premier ministre

Langevin Block, 80 Wellington St., Ottawa, ON K1A 0A2
613-992-4211, Fax: 613-941-6900,
pm@pm.gc.ca
www.pm.gc.ca

The Prime Minister is the Head of Government in Canada & usually the leader of the party in power in the House of Commons. The Prime Minister recommends the appointment of the Governor General to the monarchy, & is responsible for selecting a team of ministers, who are then appointed by the Governor General to the Queen's Privy Council. In addition, he or she also controls the appointment of senators, judges, & parliamentary secretaries. It is customary that the Prime Minister is also appointed to the Imperial Privy Council & is thus titled, "The Right Honourable". The Prime Minister has the right to dissolve parliament & can therefore control the timing of general elections. The Prime Minister's Office is a central agency which features the executive staff of the Prime Minister, such as partisan political advisors & administrators, who provide support to the Prime Minister exclusively.

Prime Minister,Rt. Hon. Stephen Harper, B.A., M.A.
613-992-4211, Fax: 613-941-6900,pm@pm.gc.ca; Harper.S@parl.gc.ca
Chief of Staff, Guy Giorno
613-992-4211
Parliamentary Secretary, Pierre Poilièvre
613-992-1209
Principal Secretary, Raymond Novak
613-992-4211
Director, Tour & Scheduling, Deborah Campbell
613-952-4959
Director, Personnel & Administration, Jay Dorey
613-957-5517
Director, Priorities & Planning, Jasmine Igneski
613-957-5507
Director, Communications, Dimitri Soudas
613-992-4211
Director, Issues Management; Senior Advisor to the Prime Minister, William Stairs
613-960-4051
Director, Appointments, Derek Vanstone
613-992-4211
Director, Policy & Stakeholder Relations, Paul Wilson
613-948-6406

Pacific Pilotage Authority Canada / Administration de pilotage du Pacifique Canada

#1000, 1130 Pender St. West, Vancouver, BC V6E 4A4
604-666-6771, Fax: 604-666-1647,
info@ppa.gc.ca
www.ppa.gc.ca

Other Communication: Vancouver Dispatch: 604-666-6776, Fax: 604-666-6093; Victoria Dispatch: 250-363-3878, Fax: 250-363-3293

Operates pilotage services in Canadian waters in & around British Columbia. Reports to government through the Minister of Transportation.

President/CEO,Capt. Kevin Obermeyer
Chair, David K. Gardiner
Director, Finance, Bruce Chadwick
Director, Operations, Capt. Brian Young

Parks Canada / Parcs Canada

25 Eddy St., Gatineau, QC K1A 0M5
613-860-1251, 888-773-8888
information@pc.gc.ca
www.pc.gc.ca

Responsible for the protection, management, operation & maintenance of national parks, historic sites, canals & other significant examples of Canada's natural & cultural heritage, for the benefit, understanding & enjoyment of Canadians. Administers one of the largest park systems in the world. Working towards establishing parks in each of 39 distinct natural regions. In addition to the national parks, national historic sites & national marine conservation areas, Parks Canada coordinates other heritage programs, including federal heritage buildings, heritage railway stations, grave sites of Canadian Prime Ministers, heritage rivers, archaeology programs, international programs.

CEO, Alan Latourelle
819-997-9525, Fax: 819-953-9745
Director General, National Parks, Ron Hallman
819-994-2657, Fax: 819-994-5140
Director General, National Historic Sites, Larry S. Ostola
819-994-1808, Fax: 819-934-1526
Chief Administrative Officer, Céline Gaulin
819-953-4013, Fax: 819-953-5632
Communications Advisor, Joanne Huppé
819-953-8699, Fax: 819-953-5523,joanne.huppe@pc.gc.ca, Other Communications: Alt. Phone: 613/799-6269

• Historic Sites & Monuments Board of Canada/ Commission des lieux et monuments historiques du Canada
Terrasses de la Chaudière
25 Eddy St.
Gatineau, QC K1A 0M5
819-997-4059 Fax: 819-934-1115
hsmbc-clmhc@pc.gc.ca
www.pc.gc.ca/clmhc-hsmbc/
A seventeen-member advisory board which reports to the Minister of Environment & recommends whether persons, places or events are of national historic &/or architectural significance, & therefore warrant commemoration. The board also makes recommendations concerning the designation of heritage railway stations.

Canal Offices:

Carillon
230, rue du Barrage, Carillon, QC J0V 1C0
450-447-4888, Fax: 450-658-2428, 888-773-8888
www.pc.gc.ca/canalcarillon

Chambly
1899, boul Périgny, Chambly, QC J3L 4C3
450-447-4888, Fax: 450-658-2428, 888-773-8888
www.pc.gc.ca/canalchambly

Lachine
200, boul René-Lévesque ouest, tour Ouest, 6e étage, Montréal, QC H2Z 1X4
514-283-6054, Fax: 514-496-1263, 888-773-8888
www.pc.gc.ca/canallachine

Rideau
34A Beckwith St. South, Smiths Falls, ON K7A 2A8
613-283-5170, Fax: 613-283-0677,
www.pc.gc.ca/lhn-nhs/on/rideau

Sainte-Anne-de-Bellevue
170, rue Sainte-Anne, Sainte-Anne-de-Bellevue, QC H9X 1N1
450-447-4888, Fax: 450-658-2428,
www.pc.gc.ca/canalsteanne

Saint-Ours
2930, ch des Patriotes, Saint-Ours, QC G1K 7R3
450-785-2212, Fax: 450-658-2428,
www.pc.gc.ca/canalstours

St. Peters
PO Box 8, St Peters, NS B0E 3B0
902-733-2280, Fax: 902-733-2362,
www.pc.gc.ca/stpeterscanal

Sault
1 Canal Dr., Sault Ste Marie, ON P6A 6W4
705-941-6262, Fax: 705-941-6206,
www.pc.gc.ca/lhn-nhs/on/ssmarie

Trent-Severn Waterway
PO Box 567, Peterborough, ON K9J 6Z6
705-750-4900, Fax: 705-742-9644,
www.pc.gc.ca/trentsevern

Atlantic National Parks/National Historic Sites:

Alexander Graham Bell Historic Site of Canada
PO Box 159, Baddeck, NS B0E 1B0
902-295-2069, Fax: 902-295-3496,
information@pc.gc.ca
www.pc.gc.ca/lhn-nhs/ns/grahambell/

Ardgowan National Historic Site of Canada
2 Palmer's Lane, Charlottetown, PE C1A 5V6
902-566-7050, Fax: 902-566-7226,
pc.gc.ca/lhn-nhs/pe/ardgowan/

Bank Fishery National Heritage Exhibit
PO Box 9080 A, Halifax, NS B3K 5M7
902-426-5080, Fax: 902-426-4228,
information@pc.gc.ca
www.pc.gc.ca/lhn-nhs/ns/bank/

Boishébert & Beaubears Shipbuilding National Historic Sites of Canada
186, route 117, Kouchibouguac National Park, NB E4X 2P1
506-876-2443, Fax: 506-876-4802,
kouch.info@pc.gc.ca
www.pc.gc.ca/lhn-nhs/nb/boishebert

Canso Islands National Historic Site of Canada
PO Box 159, Baddeck, NS B0E 1E0
902-295-2069, Fax: 902-295-3496,
pc.gc.ca/lhn-nhs/ns/canso/

Cape Breton Highlands National Park of Canada
Ingonish Beach, NS B0C 1L0
902-224-2306, Fax: 902-285-2866,
pc.gc.ca/pn-np/ns/cbreton/

Cape Spear National Historic Site of Canada
PO Box 1268, St. John's, NL A1C 5M9
709-772-5367, Fax: 709-772-6302,
cape.spear@pc.gc.ca
pc.gc.ca/lhn-nhs/nl/spear/

Carleton Martello Tower National Historic Site of Canada
454 Whipple St., Saint John, NB E2M 2R3
506-636-4011, Fax: 506-636-4574,
fundy.info@pc.gc.ca
pc.gc.ca/lhn-nhs/nb/carleton/

Castle Hill National Historic Site of Canada
PO Box 10, Jerseyside, Placentia Bay, NL A0B 2G0

709-227-2401, Fax: 709-227-2452,
castle.hill@pc.gc.ca
pc.gc.ca/lhn-nhs/nl/castlehill/

Other Communication: Off-season: 709/772-5367, Fax: 709/772-6302

Fort Amherst/Port-La-Joye National Historic Site of Canada
2 Palmer's Lane, Charlottetown, PE C1A 5V6
902-566-7626, Fax: 902-566-8295,
pc.gc.ca/lhn-nhs/pe/amherst/

Fort Anne National Historic Site of Canada
PO Box 9, Annapolis Royal, NS B0S 1A0
902-532-2397, Fax: 902-532-2232,
www.pc.gc.ca/lhn-nhs/ns/fortanne/

Other Communication: Off-season: 902/532-2321

Fort Beauséjour National Historic Site of Canada
111 Fort Beauséjour Rd., Aulac, NB E4L 2W5
506-364-5080, Fax: 506-536-4399,
fort.beausejour@pc.gc.ca
pc.gc.ca/lhn-nhs/nb/beausejour/

Fort Edward National Historic Site of Canada
PO Box 9, Annapolis Royal, NS B0S 1A0
902-532-2321, Fax: 902-532-2232,
pc.gc.ca/lhn-nhs/ns/edward/

Other Communication: July & August: 902/798-4706

Fort McNab National Historic Site of Canada
PO Box 9080 A, Halifax, NS B3K 5M7
902-426-5080, Fax: 902-426-4228,
halifax.citadel@pc.gc.ca
pc.gc.ca/lhn-nhs/ns/mcnab/

Fortress of Louisbourg National Historic Site
259 Park Service Rd., Louisbourg, NS B1C 2L2
902-733-2280, Fax: 902-733-2362,
pc.gc.ca/lhn-nhs/ns/louisbourg/

Fundy National Park of Canada
PO Box 1001, Alma, NB E4H 1B4
506-887-6000, Fax: 506-887-6008,
fundy.info@pc.gc.ca
pc.gc.ca/pn-np/nb/fundy/

Grand Pré National Historic Site of Canada
PO Box 150, Grand Pré, NS B0P 1M0
902-542-3631, Fax: 902-542-1691, 866-542-3631
grandpre.info@pc.gc.ca; contact@grand-pre.com
pc.gc.ca/lhn-nhs/ns/grandpre/; www.grand-pre.com

Georges Island National Historic Site of Canada
PO Box 9080 A, Halifax, NS B3K 5M7
902-426-5080, Fax: 902-426-4228,
halifax.citadel@pc.gc.ca
pc.gc.ca/lhn-nhs/ns/georges/

Green Gables Heritage Place
2 Palmer's Lane, Charlottetown, PE C1A 5V6
902-963-7874,
peinp-pnipe@pc.gc.ca
pc.gc.ca/lhn-nhs/pe/greengables/

Gros Morne National Park of Canada
PO Box 130, Rocky Harbour, NL A0K 4N0
709-458-2417, Fax: 709-458-2059,
grosmorne.info@pc.gc.ca
pc.gc.ca/pn-np/nl/grosmorne/

Halifax Citadel National Historic Site of Canada
PO Box 9080 A, Halifax, NS B3K 5M7
902-426-5080, Fax: 902-426-4228,
halifax.citadel@pc.gc.ca
pc.gc.ca/lhn-nhs/ns/halifax/

Hawthorne Cottage National Historic Site of Canada
PO Box 5542, St. John's, NL A1C 5W4
709-753-9262, Fax: 709-772-0879,
pc.gc.ca/lhn-nhs/nl/hawthorne/

Other Communication: Off-season: 709/528-4004

Kejimkujik National Park of Canada
PO Box 236, Maitland Bridge, NS B0T 1B0
902-682-2772, Fax: 902-682-3367,
kejimkujik.info@pc.gc.ca
pc.gc.ca/pn-np/ns/kejimkujik/index_e.asp

Kouchibouguac National Park of Canada
186, Route 117, Kouchibouguac National Park, NB E4X 2P1
506-876-2443, Fax: 506-876-4802,
kouch.info@pc.gc.ca
pc.gc.ca/pn-np/nb/kouchibouguac/

L'Anse aux Meadows National Historic Site of Canada
PO Box 70, St-Lunaire-Criquet, NL A0K 2X0
709-623-2608, Fax: 709-623-2028,
viking.lam@pc.gc.ca
www.pc.gc.ca/lhn-nhs/nl/meadows/

Marconi National Historic Site of Canada
PO Box 159, Baddeck, NS B0E 1B0
902-295-2069, Fax: 902-295-3496,
www.pc.gc.ca/lhn-nhs/ns/marconi/

Monument Lefebvre National Historic Site of Canada
480 rue Centrale, Memramcook, NB E4K 3S6
506-536-0720, Fax: 506-758-9813,
monument@nbnet.nb.ca
www.pc.gc.ca/lhn-nhs/nb/lefebvre/

Other Communication: Summer: 506/758-9808

Port-au-Choix National Historic Site of Canada
PO Box 140, Port au Choix, NL A0K 4C0
709-458-2417, Fax: 709-861-3827,
pc.gc.ca/lhn-nhs/nl/portauchoix/

Other Communication: Seasonal: 709/861-3522

Port Royal National Historic Site of Canada
PO Box 9, Annapolis Royal, NS B0S 1A0
902-532-2898, Fax: 902-532-2232,
www.pc.gc.ca/lhn-nhs/ns/portroyal/

Other Communication: Off-season: 902/532-2232

Prince Edward Island National Park of Canada
2 Palmers Lane, Charlottetown, PE C1A 5V6
902-672-6350, Fax: 902-672-6370,
pnipe.peinp@pc.gc.ca
http://pc.gc.ca/pn-np/pe/pei-ipe

Prince of Wales Tower National Historic Site
PO Box 9080 A, Halifax, NS B3K 5M7
902-426-5080, Fax: 902-426-4228,
halifax.citadel@pc.gc.ca
www.pc.gc.ca/lhn-nhs/ns/prince/

Province House National Historic Site of Canada
2 Palmer's Lane, Charlottetown, PE C1A 5V6
902-566-7626, Fax: 902-566-8295,
pc.gc.ca/lhn-nhs/pe/provincehouse/

Red Bay National Historic Site of Canada
PO Box 103, Red Bay, NL A0K 4K0
709-920-2142, Fax: 709-920-2144,
redbay.info@pc.gc.ca
pc.gc.ca/lhn-nhs/nl/redbay/

Ryan Premises National Historic Site
PO Box 1451, Bonavista, NL A0C 1B0
709-468-1600, Fax: 709-468-1604,
ryan.premises@pc.gc.ca
pc.gc.ca/lhn-nhs/nl/ryan/

St. Andrews Blockhouse National Historic Site of Canada
454 Whipple St., Saint John, NB E2M 2R3
506-636-4011, Fax: 506-636-4574,
fundy.info@pc.gc.ca
pc.gc.ca/lhn-nhs/nb/standrews/

Other Communication: Summer: 506/529-4270

St. Peters Canada National Historic Site of Canada
PO Box 8, St Peters, NS B0A 1M0
902-733-2280, Fax: 902-733-2362,
www.pc.gc.ca/lhn-nhs/ns/stpeters/

Signal Hill National Historic Site of Canada
PO Box 1268, St. John's, NL A1C 5M9
709-772-5367, Fax: 709-772-6302,
signal.hill@pc.gc.ca
pc.gc.ca/lhn-nhs/nl/signalhill/

Terra Nova National Park of Canada
General Delivery, Glovertown, NL A0G 2L0
709-533-2801, Fax: 709-533-2706,
info.tnnp@pc.gc.ca
pc.gc.ca/pn-np/nl/terranova/

York Redoubt National Historic Site of Canada
PO Box 9080 A, Halifax, NS B3K 5M7
902-426-5080, Fax: 902-426-4228,
halifax.citadel@pc.gc.ca
www.pc.gc.ca/lhn-nhs/ns/york/

Ontario National Parks/National Historic Sites:

Battle of the Windmill National Historic Site of Canada
370 Vankoughnet St., PO Box 479, Prescott, ON K0E 1T0
613-925-2896, Fax: 613-925-1536,
ont.wellington@pc.gc.ca
www.pc.gc.ca/lhn-nhs/on/windmill/

Bellevue House National Historic Site of Canada
35 Centre St., Kingston, ON K7L 4E5
613-545-8666, Fax: 613-545-8721,
bellevue.house@pc.gc.ca
www.pc.gc.ca/lhn-nhs/on/bellevue/

Bethune Memorial House National Historic Site of Canada
235 John St. North, Gravenhurst, ON P1P 1G4
705-687-4261, Fax: 705-687-4935,
ont-bethune@pc.gc.ca
pc.gc.ca/lhn-nhs/on/bethune/

Bois Blanc Island Lighthouse National Historic Site of Canada
c/o Fort Malden N.H.S., 100 Laird Ave., PO Box 38, Amherstburg, ON N9V 2Z2
519-736-5416, Fax: 519-736-6603,
ont.fort-malden@pc.gc.ca
pc.gc.ca/lhn-nhs/on/boisblanc/

Bruce Peninsula National Park
PO Box 189, Tobermory, ON N0H 2R0
519-596-2233, Fax: 519-596-2298,
bruce-fathomfive@pc.gc.ca
pc.gc.ca/pn-np/on/bruce/

Butler's Barracks c/o Fort George National Historic Site
26 Queen St., PO Box 787, Niagara on the Lake, ON L0S 1J0
905-468-4257, Fax: 905-468-4638,
www.pc.gc.ca/lhn-nhs/on/fortgeorge/

Fort George National Historic Site of Canada
26 Queen St., PO Box 787, Niagara on the Lake, ON L0S 1J0
905-468-4257, Fax: 905-468-4638,
ont-niagara@pc.gc.ca
pc.gc.ca/lhn-nhs/on/fortgeorge/

Fathom Five National Marine Park of Canada
PO Box 189, Tobermory, ON N0H 2R0
519-596-2233, Fax: 519-596-2298,
bruce-fathomfive@pc.gc.ca
www.pc.gc.ca/lhn-nhs/on/fathomfive

Fort Malden National Historic Site
100 Laird Ave., PO Box 38, Amherstburg, ON N9V 2Z2
519-736-5416, Fax: 519-736-6603,
ont.fort-malden@pc.gc.ca
www.pc.gc.ca/lhn-nhs/on/fortmalden/

Fort Mississauga National Historic Site of Canada
26 Queen St., PO Box 787, Niagara on the Lake, ON L0S 1J0
905-468-4257, Fax: 905-468-4638

Fort St. Joseph National Historic Site of Canada
PO Box 220, Richards Landing, ON P0R 1J0
705-246-2664, Fax: 705-246-1796,
fortstjoseph-info@pc.gc.ca
www.pc.gc.ca/lhn-nhs/on/fortstjoseph

Fort Wellington National Historic Site of Canada
PO Box 479, Prescott, ON K0E 1T0
613-925-2896, Fax: 613-925-1536,
ont-wellington@pc.gc.ca
www.pc.gc.ca/lhn-nhs/on/fortwellington/

Georgian Bay Islands National Park of Canada
901 Wye Valley Rd., PO Box 9, Midland, ON L4R 4K6
705-526-9804, Fax: 705-526-5939,
info.gbi@pc.gc.ca
www.pc.gc.ca/lhn-nhs/on/gbi/

Inverarden House National Historic Site of Canada
370 Vankoughnet St., PO Box 479, Prescott, ON K0E 1T0
613-925-2896, Fax: 613-925-1536,
www.pc.gc.ca/lhn-nhs/on/inverarden/

Kingston Martello Towers
35 Centre St., Kingston, ON K7L 4E5
613-545-8666, Fax: 613-545-8721,
www.pc.gc.ca/lhn-nhs/on/bellevue

Laurier House National Historic Site of Canada
335 Laurier Ave. East, Ottawa, ON K1A 6R4
613-992-8142, Fax: 613-947-4851,
laurier.house@pc.gc.ca
www.pc.gc.ca/lhn-nhs/on/laurierhouse/

Point Clark Lighthouse National Historic Site of Canada
c/o Woodside National Historic Site, 528 Wellington St. North, Kitchener, ON N2H 5L5
519-571-5684, Fax: 519-571-5286,
ont-woodside@pc.gc.ca
www.pc.gc.ca/lhn-nhs/on/pointclark/

Point Pelee National Park of Canada
407 Monarch Lane, RR#1, Leamington, ON N8H 3V4
519-322-2365, Fax: 519-322-1277,
pelee.info@pc.gc.ca
www.pc.gc.ca/lhn-nhs/on/pointpelee/

Pukaskwa National Park of Canada
Hwy. 627, Hattie Cove, PO Box 212, Heron Bay, ON P0T 1R0
807-229-0801, Fax: 807-229-2097,
ont-pukaskwa@pc.gc.ca
www.pc.gc.ca/lhn-nhs/on/pukaskwa/

Queenston Heights & Brock's Monument
Niagara Court House, 26 Queen St., PO Box 787, Niagara on the Lake, ON L0S 1J0
905-468-4257, Fax: 905-468-4638,
www.pc.gc.ca/lhn-nhs/on/queenston/

St. Lawrence Islands National Park of Canada
2 County Rd. 5, RR#3, Mallorytown Landing, ON K0E 1R0
613-923-5261, Fax: 613-923-1021,
ont-sli@pc.gc.ca
www.pc.gc.ca/pn-np/on/lawren/

Sir John Johnson National Historic Site of Canada
c/o Fort Wellington National Historic Site, 370 Vanhoughnet St., PO Box 479, Prescott, ON K0E 1T0
613-925-2896, Fax: 613-925-1536,
ont.wellington@pc.gc.ca
www.pc.gc.ca/lhn-nhs/on/johnjohnson/

Woodside National Historic Site of Canada
528 Wellington St. North, Kitchener, ON N2H 5L5
519-571-5684, Fax: 519-571-5686,
ont.woodside@pc.gc.ca
www.pc.gc.ca/lhn-nhs/on/woodside/

Quebec National Parks/National Historic Sites:

Artillery Park National Historic Site of Canada
2, rue d'Auteuil, CP 10 B, Québec, QC G1K 7A1
418-648-4205, Fax: 418-648-4825,
www.pc.gc.ca/lhn-nhs/qc/artillery/

Carillon Barracks National Historic Site of Canada
1899, boul. Périgny, Chambly, QC J3L 4C3
450-537-3861, Fax: 450-537-0975,
www.pc.gc.ca/lhn-nhs/qc/carillon/

Cartier-Brébeuf National Historic Site of Canada
175, rue de l'Espinay, CP 10 B, Québec, QC G1K 7R3
418-648-4038, Fax: 418-648-4367, 888-773-8888
www.pc.gc.ca/lhn-nhs/qc/brebeuf/

Battle of the Châteauguay National Historic Site of Canada
2371, ch de la Rivière Châteauguay nord, CP 250, Howick, QC J0S 1G0
450-829-2003, Fax: 450-829-3325,
www.pc.gc.ca/lhn-nhs/qc/chateauguay/

Battle of the Restigouche National Historic Site of Canada
Route 132, CP 359, Pointe-à-la-Croix, QC G0C 1L0
418-788-5676, Fax: 418-788-5895,
www.pc.gc.ca/lhn-nhs/qc/restigouche

Forges du Saint-Maurice National Historic Site of Canada
10000, boul des Forges, Trois-Rivières, QC G9C 1B1
819-378-5116, Fax: 819-378-0887,
www.pc.gc.ca/lhn-nhs/qc/forges/

Coteau-du-Lac National Historic Site of Canada
308 A, ch du Fleuve, Coteau-du-Lac, QC J0P 1B0
450-763-5631, Fax: 450-763-1654,
www.pc.gc.ca/lhn-nhs/qc/coteau/

Forillon National Park of Canada
122, boul Gaspé, Gaspé, QC G4X 1A9
418-368-5505, Fax: 418-368-6837,
www.pc.gc.ca/lhn-nhs/qc/forillon/

Fort Chambly National Historic Site of Canada
2, rue de Richelieu, Chambly, QC J3L 2B9
450-658-1585, Fax: 450-658-7216,
www.pc.gc.ca/lhn-nhs/qc/fortchambly/

Fort Lennox National Historic Site of Canada
1 - 61e av, St-Paul-de-l'Ile-aux-Noix, QC J0J 1G0
450-291-5700, Fax: 450-291-4389,
www.pc.gc.ca/lhn-nhs/qc/fortlennox/

Fort Témiscamingue National Historic Site of Canada
830, ch du Vieux-Fort, Duhamel ouest, QC J9V 1N7
819-629-3222, Fax: 819-629-2977,
fort.temiscamingue@pc.gc.ca
www.pc.gc.ca/lhn-nhs/qc/forttemiscamingue/

Fortifications of Québec National Historic Site of Canada
100, rue St-Louis, PO Box 10 B, Québec, QC G1K 7R3
418-648-7016, Fax: 418-648-9068,
www.pc.gc.ca/lhn-nhs/qc/fortifications/

Grosse Ile & the Irish Memorial National Historic Site of Canada
2 rue D'Auteuil, CP 10 B, Québec, QC G1K 7R3
418-248-8841, Fax: 866-790-8991,
www.pc.gc.ca/lhn-nhs/qc/grosseile/

La Mauricie National Park of Canada
702, 5e rue, CP 160 Bureau-Chef, Shawinigan, QC G9N 6T9
819-538-3232, Fax: 819-536-3661,
parkscanada-que @pc.gc.ca
www.pc.gc.ca/lhn-nhs/qc/mauricie

Lévis Forts National Historic Site of Canada
41, ch du Gouvernement, CP 10 B, Québec, QC G1K 7R3
418-835-5182, Fax: 418-948-9119,
www.pc.gc.ca/lhn-nhs/qc/levis/

Louis S. St-Laurent National Historic Site of Canada
6790, rte Louis-St-Laurent, Compton, QC J0B 1L0
819-835-5448, Fax: 819-835-9101,
www.pc.gc.ca/lhn-nhs/qc/st-laurent/

Manoir Papineau National Historic Site of Canada
500, rue Notre-Dame, Montebello, QC J0V 1L0
819-423-6965, Fax: 819-423-6455,
www.pc.gc.ca/lhn-nhs/qc/papineau/

Mingan Archipelago National Park Reserve of Canada
1340, rue de la Digue, CP 1180, Ha@vre-Saint-Pierre, QC G0G 1P0
418-538-3331, Fax: 418-538-3595,
www.pc.gc.ca/lhn-nhs/qc/mingan/

Old Port of Québec Interpretation Centre
100, rue Saint-André, CP 2474 Terminus postal, Québec, QC G1K 7R3
418-648-3300, Fax: 418-648-3678,
www.pc.gc.ca/lhn-nhs/qc/vieuxport/

Pointe-au-Père Lighthouse National Historic Site of Canada
1034, rue du Phare, Pointe-au-Père, QC G5M 1L8
418-724-6214, Fax: 418-721-0815, 888-773-8888
parkscanada-que@pc.gc.ca
www.pc.gc.ca/lhn-nhs/qc/pointaupere

Saguenay St. Lawrence Marine Park of Canada
182, rte de l'Église, CP 220, Tadoussac, QC G0T 2A0
418-235-4703, Fax: 418-235-4686,
parkscanada-que @pc.gc.ca
www.pc.gc.ca/lhn-nhs/qc/saguenay-saint-laurent

Sir George-Étienne Cartier National Historic Site of Canada
458, rue Notre-Dame est, Montréal, QC H2Y 1C8
514-283-2282, Fax: 514-283-5560, 888-773-8888
parkscanada-que @pc.gc.ca
www.pc.gc.ca/lhn-nhs/qc/cartier

Sir Wilfrid Laurier National Historic Site of Canada
#945, 12e av, St-Lin-Laurentides, QC J5M 2W4
450-439-3702, Fax: 450-439-5721, 888-773-8888
parkscanada-que @pc.gc.ca
www.pc.gc.ca/lhn-nhs/qc/laurier

The Fur Trade at Lachine National Historic Site of Canada
1255, boul Saint-Joseph, Lachine, QC H8S 2M2
514-637-7433, Fax: 514-637-5325, 888-773-8888
parkscanada-que @pc.gc.ca
www.pc.gc.ca/lhn-nhs/qc/lachine

Western & Northern Canada National Parks/National Historic Sites:

Aulavik National Park of Canada
PO Box 29, Sachs Harbour, NT X0E 0Z0
867-690-3904, Fax: 867-690-4808,
inuvik.info@pc.gc.ca
http://pc.gc.ca/pn-np/nt/aulavik/index_e.asp

Auyuittuq National Park of Canada
PO Box 353, Pangnirtung, NU X0A 0R0
867-473-2500, Fax: 867-473-8612,
nunavut.info@pc.gc.ca
http://pc.gc.ca/pn-np/nu/auyuittuq/index_e.asp

Banff National Park of Canada
PO Box 900, Banff, AB T1L 1K2
403-762-1550, Fax: 403-762-3380,
banff.vrc@pc.gc.ca
www.pc.gc.ca/pn-np/ab/banff/index_e.asp

Banff Park Museum National Historic Site of Canada
PO Box 900, Banff, AB T1L 1K2
403-762-1558, Fax: 403-762-1565,
banff.vrc@pch.gc.ca
www.pc.gc.ca/lhn-nhs/ab/banff/index_E.asp

Bar U Ranch National Historic Site of Canada
PO Box 168, Longview, AB T0L 1H0
403-395-2212, Fax: 403-395-2331, 888-773-8888
BarU.Info@pc.gc.ca
http://pc.gc.ca/lhn-nhs/ab/baru/index_e.asp

Batoche National Historic Site of Canada
RR#1 Box 1040, Wakaw, SK S0K 4P0
306-423-6227, Fax: 306-423-5400,
batoche@pc.gc.ca
pc.gc.ca/lhn-nhs/sk/batoche/imdex_e.asp

Cave & Basin National Historic Site of Canada
PO Box 900, Banff, AB T1L 1K2
403-762-1566, Fax: 403-762-1565,
banff.vrc@pc.gc.ca
http://pc.gc.ca/lhn-nhs/ab/caveandbasin/index_e.asp

Chilkoot Trail National Historic Site of Canada
#205, 300 Main St., Whitehorse, YT Y1A 2B5
867-667-3910, Fax: 867-393-6701, 800-661-0486
whitehorse.info@pc.gc.ca
http://pc.gc.ca/lhn-nhs/yt/chilkoot/index_e.asp

Dawson Historical Complex National Historic Site of Canada
PO Box 390, Dawson City, YT Y0B 1G0
867-993-7200, Fax: 867-993-7203,
dawson.info@pc.gc.ca
http://pc.gc.ca/lhn-nhs/yt/dawson/index_E.asp

Dredge No. 4 National Historic Site of Canada
PO Box 390, Dawson City, YT Y0B 1G0
867-993-7200, Fax: 867-993-7203,
dawson.info@pc.gc.ca
http://pc.gc.ca/lhn-nhs/yt/dn4/index_E.asp

Elk Island National Park of Canada
RR#1, Site 4, Fort Saskatchewan, AB T8L 2N7
780-992-5790, Fax: 780-992-2951,
elk.island@pc.gc.ca
http://pc.gc.ca/pn-np/ab/elkisland/index_e.asp

Fisgard Lighthouse National Historic Site of Canada
603 Fort Rodd Hill Rd., Victoria, BC V9C 2W8
250-478-5849, Fax: 250-478-2816,
fort.rodd@pc.gc.ca
http://pc.gc.ca/lhn-nhs/bc/fisgard/index_e.asp

Fort Battleford National Historic Site of Canada
PO Box 70, Battleford, SK S0M 0E0
306-937-2621, Fax: 306-937-3370,
battleford-info@pc.gc.ca
http://pc.gc.ca/lhn-nhs/sk/battleford/index_e.asp

Fort Langley National Historic Site of Canada
23433 Mavis Ave., PO Box 129, Fort Langley, BC V1M 2R5
604-513-4777, Fax: 604-513-4798,
fort.langley@pc.gc.ca
http://pc.gc.ca/lhn-nhs/bc/langley/index_e.asp

Fort Rodd Hill National Historic Site of Canada
603 Fort Rodd Hill Rd., Victoria, BC V9C 2W8
250-478-5849, Fax: 250-478-2816,
fort.rodd@pc.gc.ca
http://pc.gc.ca/lhn-nhs/bc/fortroddhill/index_e.asp

Fort St. James National Historic Site of Canada
PO Box 1148, Fort St James, BC V0J 1P0
250-996-7191, Fax: 250-996-8566,
http://pc.gc.ca/lhn-nhs/bc/stjames/index_e.asp

Fort Walsh National Historic Site of Canada
PO Box 278, Maple Creek, SK S0N 1N0
306-662-3590, Fax: 306-662-2711,
fort.walsh@pc.gc.ca
http://pc.gc.ca/lhn-nhs/sk/walsh/index_e.asp

Gitwangak Battle Hill National Historic Site of Canada
PO Box 37, Queen Charlotte, BC V0T 1S0
250-559-8818, Fax: 250-559-8366,
gwaii.haanas@pc.gc.ca
www.pc.gc.ca/lhn-nhs/bc/kitwanga/index_E.asp

Glacier National Park of Canada
PO Box 350, Revelstoke, BC V0E 2S0
250-837-7500, Fax: 250-837-7536,
revglacier.reception@pc.gc.ca
http://pc.gc.ca/pn-np/bc/glacier/index_e.asp

Grasslands National Park of Canada
PO Box 150, Val Marie, SK S0N 2T0
306-298-2257, Fax: 306-298-2042,
grasslands.info@pc.gc.ca
http://pc.gc.ca/pn-np/sk/grasslands/index_e.asp

Gulf Islands National Park Reserve of Canada
2220 Harbour Rd., Sidney, BC V8L 2P6

250-654-4000, Fax: 250-654-4014, 866-944-1744
gulf.islands@pc.gc.ca
http://pc.gc.ca/pn-np/bc/gulf/index_E.asp

Gulf of Georgia Cannery National Historic Site of Canada
12138 Fourth Ave., Richmond, BC V7E 3J1
604-664-9009, Fax: 604-664-9008,
gog.info@pc.gc.ca
http://pc.gc.ca/lhn-nhs/bc/georgia/index_e.asp

Gwaii Haanas National Park Reserve & Haida Heritage Site of Canada
60 Second Beach Rd., PO Box 37, Queen Charlotte, BC V0T 1S0
250-559-8818, Fax: 250-559-8366, 877-559-8818
gwaii.haanas@pc.gc.ca
http://pc.gc.ca/pn-np/bc/gwaiihaanas/index_e.asp

Ivvavik National Park of Canada
PO Box 1840, Inuvik, NT X0E 0T0
867-777-8800, Fax: 867-777-8820,
inuvik.info@pc.gc.ca
http://pc.gc.ca/pn-np/yt/ivvavik/index_e.asp

Jasper National Park of Canada
PO Box 10, Jasper, AB T0E 1E0
780-852-6176, Fax: 780-852-6152,
jnp_info@pc.gc.ca
http://pc.gc.ca/pn-np/ab/jasper/index_e.asp

Kluane National Park & Reserve of Canada
PO Box 5495, Haines Junction, YT Y0B 1L0
867-634-7250, Fax: 867-634-7208,
kluane.info@pc.gc.ca
http://pc.gc.ca/pn-np/yt/kluane/index_e.asp

Kootenay National Park of Canada
PO Box 220, Radium Hot Springs, BC V0A 1M0
250-347-9505, Fax: 250-347-9980,
kootenay.info@pc.gc.ca
http://pc.gc.ca/pn-np/bc/kootenay/index_e.asp

Lower Fort Garry National Historic Site of Canada
5925 Highway 9, St. Andrews, MB R1A 4A8
204-785-6050, Fax: 204-482-5887, 888-773-8888
LFGNHS_Info@pc.pc.gc.ca
http://pc.gc.ca/lhn-nhs/mb/fortgarry/index_e.asp

Motherwell Homestead National Historic Site of Canada
PO Box 70, Abernethy, SK S0A 0A0
306-333-2116, Fax: 306-333-2210,
Motherwell-Homestead@pc.gc.ca
http://pc.gc.ca/lhn-nhs/sk/motherwell/index_e.asp

Mount Revelstoke National Park of Canada
PO Box 350, Revelstoke, BC V0E 2S0
250-837-7500, Fax: 250-837-7536,
revglacier.reception@pc.gc.ca
http://pc.gc.ca/pn-np/bc/revelstoke/index_e.asp

Nahanni National Park Reserve of Canada
10002 - 100 Street, PO Box 348, Fort Simpson, NT X0E 0N0
867-695-3151, Fax: 867-695-2446,
nahanni.info@pc.gc.ca
http://pc.gc.ca/pn-np/nt/nahanni/index_e.asp

Pacific Rim National Park Reserve of Canada
2185 Ocean Terrace Rd., PO Box 280, Ucluelet, BC V0R 3A0
250-726-3500, Fax: 250-726-3520,
pacrim.info@pc.gc.ca
http://pc.gc.ca/pn-np/bc/pacificrim/index_e.asp

Prince Albert National Park of Canada
PO Box 100, Waskesiu Lake, SK S0J 2Y0
306-663-4522,
panp.info@pc.gc.ca
http://pc.gc.ca/pn-np/sk/princealbert/index_e.asp

Prince of Wales Fort National Historic Site of Canada
PO Box 127, Churchill, MB R0B 0E0
204-675-8863, Fax: 204-675-2026,
mannorth.nhs@pc.gc.ca
http://pc.gc.ca/lhn-nhs/mb/prince/index_e.asp

Quttinirpaaq National Park of Canada
PO Box 278, Iqaluit, NU X0A 0H0
867-975-4673, Fax: 867-975-4674,
nunavut.info@pc.gc.ca
http://pc.gc.ca/pn-np/nu/quttinirpaaq/index_e.asp

Riding Mountain National Park of Canada
Wasagaming, MB R0J 2H0
204-848-7275, Fax: 204-848-2596,
rmnp.info@pc.gc.ca
http://pc.gc.ca/pn-np/mb/riding/index_e.asp

Riel House National Historic Site of Canada
330 River Rd. (St. Vidal), PO Box 73, Winnipeg, MB R2N 3X9
204-257-1783, Fax: 204-983-2221,
FORKSNHS.Info@pc.gc.ca
http://pc.gc.ca/lhn-nhs/mb/riel/index_E.asp

Rocky Mountain House National Historic Site of Canada
Site 127, Comp 6, RR#4, Rocky Mountain House, AB T4T 2A4
403-845-2412, Fax: 403-845-5320,
rocky.info@pc.gc.ca
www.pc.gc.ca/lhn-nhs/ab/rockymountain/index_E.asp

Sirmilik National Park of Canada
PO Box 300, Pond Inlet, NU X0A 0S0
867-899-8092, Fax: 867-899-8104,
sirmilik.info@pc.gc.ca
http://pc.gc.ca/pn-np/nu/sirmilik/index_E.asp

SS Keno National Historic Site of Canada
PO Box 390, Dawson City, YT Y0B 1G0
867-993-7200, Fax: 867-993-7203,
dawson.info@pc.gc.ca
http://pc.gc.ca/lhn-nhs/yt/sskeno/index_e.asp

SS Klondike National Historic Site of Canada
#205, 300 Main St., Whitehorse, YT Y1A 2B5
Fax: 867-393-6701, 800-661-0486
whitehorse.info@pc.gc.ca
http://pc.gc.ca/lhn-nhs/yt/ssklondike/index_E.asp

St. Andrews Rectory National Historic Site of Canada
374, chemin River, St. Andrews, MB R1A 2Y1
204-334-6405, Fax: 204-338-3790, 888-773-8888
LFGNHS_Info@pc.gc.ca
http://pc.gc.ca/lhn-nhs/mb/standrews/contact_e.asp

The Forks National Historic Site of Canada
401-25 Forks Market Rd., Winnipeg, MB R3C 4S8
204-983-6757, Fax: 204-983-2221, 888-773-8888
FORKSNHS.Info@pc.gc.ca
http://pc.gc.ca/lhn-nhs/mb/forks/index_e.asp

Tuktut Nogait National Park of Canada
PO Box 91, Paulatuk, NT X0E 1N0
867-580-3233, Fax: 867-580-3234,
inuvik.info@pc.gc.ca
http://pc.gc.ca/pn-np/nt/tuktutnogait/index_e.asp

Ukkusiksalik National Park of Canada
PO Box 220, Repulse Bay, NU X0C 0H0
867-462-4500, Fax: 867-462-4095,
ukkusiksalik.info@ pc.gc.ca
www.pc.gc.ca/pn-np/nu/ukkusiksalik/index_E.asp

Wapusk National Park of Canada
Churchill Office, PO Box 127, Churchill, MB R0B 0E0
204-675-8863, Fax: 204-675-2026, 888-773-8888
wapusk.np@pc.gc.ca
pc.gc.ca/pn-np/mb/wapusk/index_e.asp

Vuntut National Park of Canada
c/o Yukon Field Unit - Parks Canada, #205, 300 Main St., Whitehorse, YT Y1A 2B5
867-667-3910, Fax: 867-393-6701,
whitehorse.info@pc.gc.ca
http://pc.gc.ca/pn-np/yt/vuntut/index_E.asp

Waterton Lakes National Park of Canada
PO Box 200, Waterton Park, AB T0K 2M0
403-859-2224, Fax: 403-859-5152,
waterton.info@pc.gc.ca
http://pc.gc.ca/pn-np/ab/waterton/index_E.asp

York Factory National Historic Site of Canada
PO Box 127, Churchill, MB R0B 0E0
204-675-8863, Fax: 204-675-2026, 888-773-8888
mannorth.nhs@pc.gc.ca
http://pc.gc.ca/lhn-nhs/mb/yorkfactory/index_E.asp

Wood Buffalo National Park of Canada
PO Box 750, Fort Smith, NT X0E 0P0
867-872-7900, Fax: 867-872-3910,
wbnp.info@pc.gc.ca
http://pc.gc.ca/pn-np/nt/woodbuffalo/index_e.asp

Yoho National Park of Canada
PO Box 99, Field, BC V0A 1G0
250-343-6783, Fax: 250-343-6012,
yoho.info@pc.gc.ca
http://pc.gc.ca/pn-np/bc/yoho/index_E.asp

Patented Medicine Prices Review Board / Conseil d'examen du prix des médicaments brevetés

Standard Life Centre, #1400, 333 Laurier Ave. West, PO Box L40, Ottawa, ON K1P 1C1
613-952-7360, Fax: 613-952-7626, 877-861-2350
pmprb@pmprb-cepmb.gc.ca
www.pmprb-cepmb.gc.ca

The Patented Medicine Prices Review Board (PMPRB) is an independent quasi-judicial body established by Parliament in 1987 under the Patent Act (Act). The PMPRB is responsible for regulating the prices that patentees charge, the "factory-gate" price, for prescription and non-prescription patented drugs sold in Canada, to wholesalers, hospitals or pharmacies, for human and veterinary use to ensure that they are not excessive. The PMPRB regulates the price of each patented drug product, including each strength of each dosage form of each patented medicine sold in Canada.

Chair,VACANT
Executive Director, Michelle Boudreau
613-957-3656
Director, Board Secretariat & Communications, Sylvie Dupont
613-954-8299, sdupont@pmprb-cepmb.gc.ca
Director, Corporate Services, Marian Eagen
613-952-3304
Director, Policy & Economic Analysis Branch, Gregory Gillespie
613-952-3305
Director, Regulatory Affairs & Outreach, Ginette Tognet
613-954-8297

Privacy Commissioner of Canada / Commissariat à la protection de la vie privée du Canada

Tower B, Place de Ville, 112 Kent St., 3rd Fl., Ottawa, ON K1A 1H3
613-995-8210, Fax: 613-947-6850, 800-282-1376
info@privcom.gc.ca
www.privcom.gc.ca

The Privacy Commissioner of Canada is an Officer of Parliament mandated to protect & promote privacy rights. She works independently from Government, reporting directly to the House of Commons & the Senate. The Privacy Commissioner oversees two federal privacy laws: the Privacy Act, which covers the federal government, & the new Personal Information Protection & Electronic Documents (PIPEDA) Act, which covers the collection use & disclosure of personal information in the course of commercial activities, except in provinces which have not, by then, enacted legislation that is deemed to be substantially similar to the federal law. The Privacy Commissioner's powers include: investigating complaints & conducting audits under both federal privacy laws; publishing information about personal information handling practices in the public & private sectors; conducting research into privacy issues; & promoting awareness & understanding of privacy issues in Canada.

Privacy Commissioner, Jennifer Stoddart
613-947-6000, Fax: 613-947-6850
Asst. Privacy Commissioner, PIDEDA, Elizabeth Denham
613-944-5599, Fax: 613-995-1139
Asst. Privacy Commissioner, Privacy Act, Chantal Bernier
613-995-6402, Fax: 613-995-1139

Public Safety Canada / Sécurité publique Canada

269 Laurier Ave. West, Ottawa, ON K1A 0P8
613-944-4875, Fax: 613-954-5186, 866-222-3006
communications@ps.gc.ca
www.publicsafety.gc.ca; www.securitepublique.gc.ca

Other Communication: National Crime Prevention Centre Toll Free: 1-877-302-6272; E-mail: prevention@ps.gc.ca; National Office for Victims Toll-Free: 866-525-0554; Media: 613-991-0657

Public Safety Canada works to keep Canadians safe in cases of natural disasters, crime, & terrorism. Policies are developed, & programs & services are delivered in the following areas: emergency management, including information about emergency preparedness; national security, which features the administration of the Government Operations Centre to monitor potential threats to the national interest; law enforcement, including the contribution of funds for policing services in First Nations & Inuit communities; federal corrections effectiveness, efficiency & accountability, with the development of federal policy & legislation; & crime prevention, such as work with other governments, businesses, & volunteer groups to support projects to reduce offences.

Acts Administered:
Canadian Security Intelligence Act
Corrections & Conditional Release Act
Criminal Records Act
Customs Act
Department of the Solicitor General Act
DNA Identification Act
Emergency Preparedness Act
Firearms Act
Prisons & Reformatories Act
Royal Canadian Mounted Police Act
Royal Canadian Mounted Police Pension Continuation Act

Transfer of Offenders Act
Witness Protection Program Act
Minister, Public Safety,Hon. Vic Toews
613-992-3128, Fax: 613-995-1049,ToewsV@parl.gc.ca, Other Communications: Public Safety & Emergency Preparedness: 613-991-2924,
Deputy Minister, William V. Baker
613-991-2895
Assistant Deputy Minister, Corporate Management, Elisabeth Nadeau
613-990-2615
Assistant Deputy Minister, Emergency Management, Lynda Clairmont
613-990-4976
Associate Assistant Deputy Minister, Emergency Management & National Security, Daniel Lavoie
613-990-2743
Inspector General, Canadian Security Intelligence Service (CSIS), Eva Plunkett
613-949-0675
Senior Counsel / Strategic Policy Advisor, Mary-Anne Kirvan
613-954-1067
Counsel, Legal Services, Caroline Fobes
613-949-9724
Parliamentary Secretary to the Minister of Public Safety, Dave MacKenzie
613-995-4432, Fax: 613-995-4433,MacKenzie.D@parl.gc.ca
• Canada Firearms Centre(CAFC) / Centre des armes à feu Canada
Ottawa, ON K1A 1M6
Fax: 613-825-0297 800-731-4000
cfp-pcaf@rcmp-grc.gc.ca
www.rcmp.gc.ca/cfp
The Canada Firearms Centre oversees the administration of the Firearms Act and the Canadian Firearms Program (CFP).
• Canadian Security Intelligence Service(CSIS) / Service canadien du renseignement de sécurité (SCRS)
• Commission for Public Complaints Against the Royal Canadian Mounted Police/ Commission des plaintes du public contre la Gendarmerie royale du Canada
#102, 7337 137 St.
Surrey, BC V3W 1A4
Fax: 613-952-8045 800-665-6878TDD: 866-432-5837
org@cpc-cpp.gc.ca
www.cpc-cpp.gc.ca
The Commission is responsible for the receipt of complaints from the public about the conduct of members of the RCMP. It is also responsible for the review of complaints when complainants are not satisfied with the disposition of their complaints by the RCMP. The Commission can inquire into complaints by means of public hearings & the chair of the Commission can investigate complaints. Annually, the chair reports to Parliament through the Minister of Public Safety & Emergency Preparedness Canada.
• Correctional Service of Canada/ Service correctionnel Canada
• National Parole Board
• Royal Canadian Mounted Police
• Royal Canadian Mounted Police External Review Committee/ Comité externe d'examen de la Gendarmerie royale du Canada
PO Box 1159 B
Ottawa, ON K1P 5R2
613-998-2134 Fax: 613-990-8969
org@erc-cee.gc.ca
www.erc-cee.gc.ca
The RCMP External Review Committee is an independent agency reporting to Parliament through the Minister of Public Safety Canada. It aims to independently and impartially promote fair and equitable labour relations within the RCMP, in accordance with applicable principles of law. To this end the Committee conducts an independent review of appeals in disciplinary and discharge and demotion matters, as well as certain categories of grievances that can be referred to it pursuant to s. 33 of the RCMP Act and s. 36 of the RCMP Regulations.

Regional Office:

Community Safety & Partnerships Branch / Sécurité de la population et des partenariats
340 Laurier Ave. West, Ottawa, ON K1A 0P8
The Community Safety & Partnerships Branch consist of the Aboriginal Policing Directorate, the Corrections & Criminal Justice Directorate, & the National Crime Prevention Centre.
Assistant Deputy Minister, Shawn Tupper
613-993-4325
Director General, Aboriginal Policing Directorate, Mary Donaghy
613-990-2666
Director General, Corrections Directorate, Mary Campbell
613-991-2952
Executive Director, National Crime Prevention Centre, Wayne Stryde
613-957-9639
Senior Director, Operations, Claude Turgeon
613-990-8434

Emergency Management & National Security Branch / Secteur de la gestion des urgences et de la sécurité nationale
340 Laurier Ave. West, Ottawa, ON K1A 0P8
The Emergency Management & National Security Branch consists of the following directorates & secretariat: Coordination Directorate; Emergency Management Policy Directorate; National Security Policy Directorate; Operations Directorate; Preparedness & Recovery Directorate; & the Cyber Security Strategy Secretariat.
Assistant Deputy Minister, Lynda Clairmont
613-990-4976
Associate Assistant Deputy Minister, Daniel Lavoie
613-990-2743
Director General, National Cyber Security, Robert Dick
613-990-2661
Director General, National Security Operations, Michael MacDonald
613-993-4595
Director General, National Security Policy, Paul MacKinnon
613-991-1970
Director General, Preparedness & Recovery, Serge C. Beaudoin
613-991-2944
Director General, Preparedness & Recovery, Robert Lesser
613-944-4853
Director General, Regional Operations Directorate, Jamie Deacon
613-991-1699
Senior Director, Public Service Renewal, Kevin Phillips
613-947-6492
Executive Director, Canadian Emergency Management College, Susan Daly
613-949-5000
Acting Associate Director General, Operations, Craig Oldham
613-991-7728
Senior Analyst, National Cyber Security, Tom Campbell
613-990-3577

Law Enforcement & Policing Branch / Secteur de la Police, et de l'application de la loi
340 Laurier Ave. West, Ottawa, ON K1A 0P8
The Policing, Law Enforcement & Interoperability Branch includes the following directorates: Law Enforcement & Border Strategies; Policing Policy; & Public Safety Interoperability.
Assistant Deputy Minister, Richard Wex
613-990-2703
Director General, Law Enforcement & Border Strategies Directorate, Barry MacKillop
613-991-4281
Director General, Policing Policy Directorate, Mark Potter
613-991-1632
Senior Policy Advisor, Interoperability Policy Division, Doug Carnegie
613-991-3759

Strategic Policy Branch
340 Laurier Ave. West, Ottawa, ON K1A 0P8
Assistant Deputy Minister, Kristina Namiesniowski
613-949-6435,
Director General, Cabinet, Parliamentary & Executive Services, Randall Koops
613-949-0477
Director General, Evaluation, Denis Gorman
613-990-2646
Director General, Intergovernmental Affairs & Citizen Engagement Directorate, Patrick Boucher
613-949-6553
Director General, International Affairs, Artur Wilczynski
613-949-7260
Director General, Strategic Policy, Planning & Research, Robert Mundie
613-991-2824

Public Service Commission (PSC) / Commission de la fonction publique (CFP)

West Tower, 300 Laurier Ave. West, Ottawa, ON K1A 0M7
613-992-9562, Fax: 613-992-9352,
infocom@psc-cfp.gc.ca
www.psc-cfp.gc.ca
An independent agency that reports directly to Parliament.For administrative purposes, the Minister of Canadian Heritage speaks on its behalf in the House of Commons, but has no jurisdiction over it.The commission is also responsible for safeguarding the values of a professional Public Service: competence, non-partisanship & representatives.
President, Maria Barrados
613-992-2788, Fax: 613-996-4337,maria.barrados@psc-cfp.gc.ca
Commissioner, Manon Vennat
613-943-8709, manon.vennat@psc-cfp.gc.ca
Commissioner, David Zussman
613-992-9864, david.zussman@psc-cfp.gc.ca
Senior Vice-President, Policy, Donald Lemaire
613-995-6135, Fax: 613-995-0221
Vice-President, Audit, Evaluation & Studies, Elizabeth Murphy-Walsh
613-947-0219, Fax: 613-995-6044
Vice-President, Corporate Management Branch, Richard Charlebois
613-992-2425, Fax: 613-992-7519
Vice-President, Staffing & Assessment Services, Gerry Thom
613-992-0894, Fax: 613-992-9905
Director General, Communications & Parliamentary Affairs, Andrew McGillivary
613-992-5428, Fax: 613-943-7723
Director General, Human Resources Management, Judith Flynn-Bédard
613-992-1225, Fax: 613-995-3795
Director General, Investigations, Denis Bilodeau
613-992-5418, Fax: 613-995-6985

Regional Offices:

Alberta & NWT
Canada Place, #830, 9700 Jasper Ave., Edmonton, AB T5J 4G3
780-495-6134, Fax: 780-495-3145

Atlantic
Maritime Centre, 1505 Barrington St., 17th Fl., Halifax, NS B3J 3Y6
Fax: 888-457-5333, 800-645-5605

BC & Yukon
#210, 757 West Hastings St., Vancouver, BC V6C 3M2
Fax: 866-280-6356

Central & Southern Ontario
Dominion Public Bldg., 1 Front St. West, 6th Fl., Toronto, ON M5J 2X5
416-973-3131, Fax: 888-515-4447

Central Prairies & Nunavut
320 Donald St., 1st Fl., Winnipeg, MB R3B 2H3
204-983-2486, Fax: 204-983-8188

National Capital & Eastern Ontario
66 Slater St., 4th Fl., Ottawa, ON K1A 0M7
Fax: 613-996-8048

Québec
Complexe Guy-Favreau, Tour Est, 200, boul René-Lévesque ouest, 8e étage, Montréal, QC H2Z 1X4
Fax: 866-667-4936

Senior Counsel, Gaston Arsenault
613-995-0445, Fax: 613-995-0198,gaston.arsenault@psc-cfp.gc.ca
Secretary General, Carole Theauvette
613-992-9879, Fax: 613-992-7519,carole.theauvette@psc-cfp.gc.ca
Vice-President, Doug Rimmer
613-995-6134, Fax: 613-995-0221,douglas.rimmer@psc-cfp.gc.ca
Director General, Communications & Outreach Directorate, Robert Desperrier
613-996-1208, robert.desperrier@psc-cfp.gc.ca
Director General, Research Directorate, Sally Luce
613-947-7690, Fax: 613-947-4725,sally.luce@psc-cfp.gc.ca
Acting Director General, Resourcing Policy & Legislation, Katie Fawkes
613-992-9788, Fax: 613-943-2481
Director, Strategic Policy, Planning & Coordination, Marc Grenier
613-996-4221, Fax: 613-995-0221,marc.grenier@psc-cfp.gc.ca
Vice-President, Yvette Mongeon
613-992-5418, Fax: 613-995-6985,yvette.mongeon@psc.cfp.gc.ca

Public Service Staffing Tribunal (PSSRB) / Tribunal de la dotation de la fonction publique

240 Sparks St., 6th Fl., Ottawa, ON K1A 0A5
613-949-6516, Fax: 613-949-6551, 866-637-4491
info@psst-tdfp.gc.ca
www.psst-tdfp.gc.ca
Established under the Public Service Employment Act, the Tribunal deals with complaints related to internal appointments & lay offs in the federal public service. The Tribunal conducts hearings & provides mediation services in order to resolve complaints.
Acts Administered:

Public Service Employment Act
Chair/CEO, Guy Giguère
613-949-5435, Fax: 613-949-5514
Executive Director & General Counsel, Josée Dubois
613-949-5511, Fax: 613-949-5514
Director, Planning & Communications, Elizabeth Holden
613-949-5513, Fax: 613-949-5514

Public Works & Government Services Canada (PWGSC) / Travaux publics et services gouvernementaux

Place du Portage, Phase III, 11, rue Laurier, Ottawa, ON K1A 0S5
819-997-6363, Fax: 819-956-9062, 800-622-6232
questions@tpsgc-pwgsc.gc.ca
www.tpsgc-pwgsc.gc.ca

Primary department responsible for purchasing goods & services for the Government of Canada. Purchases a variety of goods & services, construction, architectural, engineering & maintenance services & provides leasing services related to federal government works & facilities. Also maintains source lists of potential suppliers for some products. Ensures that the government's operational requirements are met in a cost-effective & timely manner, while taking into account the government's objectives including environmental considerations. As builders & caretakers of buildings, the department protects the environment by reducing solid waste, greening the construction & operation of buildings, conserving energy & water, improving fleet management, minimizing the effects of operations on climate change, & increasing environmental protection & conservation.

Acts Administered:
Anti-Personnel Mines Convention Implementation Act
Bridges Act
Canadian Arsenals Limited Divestiture Authorization Act
Defence Production Act
Dry Docks Subsidies Act
Expropriation Act
Federal District Commission to have acquired certain lands, An Act to Confirm the Authority of
Garnishment, Attachment & Pension Diversion Act
Government Property Traffic Act
Ottawa River, Act Respecting Certain Works
Pension Benefits Division Act
Public Works & Government Services Act
Seized Property Management Act
Statutes Act
Surplus Crown Assets Act
Translation Bureau Act

Minister, Public Works & Government Services; Minister for Status of Women,Hon. Rona Ambrose
613-996-9778, Fax: 613-996-0785,Ambrose.R@parl.gc.ca; ministre@tpsgc-pwgsc.gc.ca
Parliamentary Secretary, Jacques Gourde
613-992-2639, Fax: 613-992-1018,Gourdj@parl.gc.ca
Deputy Minister, François Guimont
819-956-1706, Fax:
819-956-8280,francois.guimont@tpsgc-pwgsc.gc.ca
Assoc. Deputy Minister, Andrew Treusch
819-956-4472, Fax:
819-956-8280,Andrew.Treusch@tpsgc-pwgsc.gc.ca
Asst. Deputy Minister, Human Resources, Diane Lorenzato
819-956-7548, Fax:
819-934-2523,diane.lorenzato@tpsgc-pwgsc.gc.ca
Asst. Deputy Minister, Departmental Oversight, Frank Brunetta
819-956-9096, Fax:
819-956-9949,frank.brunetta@tpsgc-pwgsc.gc.ca
Senior General Counsel, Sarah Paquet
819-956-0993, Fax:
819-953-3974,sarah.paquet@tpsgc-pwgsc.gc.ca
Chief Financial Officer, Finance Branch, Alex Lakroni
819-956-7226, Fax:
819-956-5060,alex.lakroni@tpsgc-pwgsc.gc.ca
• Canadian Wheat Board/ Commission canadienne du blé
• Defence Construction Canada/ Construction de Défense Canada

Acquisitions Branch / Direction générale des approvisionnements

Provides departments & agencies with expert assistance at each stage of the supply cycle & offers tools that simplify & accelerate the acquisition of goods & services. It ensures that the government exercises due diligence & maintains the integrity of the procurement process. It is a primary service provider offering client departments a broad base of procurement solutions aimed at securing best value for their procurement dollar.
Asst. Deputy Minister, Liliane Saint-Pierre
819-956-1711, Fax:
819-953-1058,liliane.saintpierre@tpsgc-pwgsc.gc.ca
Director General, Client Engagement Sector, Martin Edmondson
819-956-0901, Fax:
819-956-7475,martin.edmondson@tpsgc-pwgsc.gc.ca
Director General, Commercial Acquisitions & Supply Management Sector, Jacques Greffe
819-956-0472, Fax:
819-956-4491,jacques.greffe@tpsgc-pwgsc.gc.ca
Director General, Services & Technology Acquisition Management Sector, Jérôme Thauvette
819-956-1649, Fax:
819-956-2675,jerome.thauvette@tpsgc-pwgsc.gc.ca
Director General, Small & Medium Enterprises Sector, Shereen Miller
819-956-8416, Fax:
819-956-6859,shereen.miller@tpsgc-pwgsc.gc.ca
Director General, Land, Aerospace & Marine Systems & Major Projects Sector, Terry Williston
819-956-0010, Fax:
819-956-5750,terry.williston@tpsgc-pwgsc.gc.ca

Consulting & Audit Canada / Conseils et vérification Canada

Tower B, Place de Ville, 112 Kent St., Ottawa, ON K1A 0S5
613-996-0188
CEO, André Auger
613-996-2279, Fax:
613-947-2436,andre.auger@tpsgc-pwgsc.gc.ca
Director, NCR Operations, Daren Penteluke
613-992-6947, Fax:
613-947-2436,daren.penteluke@tpsgc-pwgsc.gc.ca

Finance, Accounting, Banking & Compensation Branch / Finances, comptabilité, gestion bancaire et rémunération

Responsible for managing the operations of the federal treasury, including issuing Receiver General payments for major government programs as well as maintaining the Accounts of Canada & producing the Government's financial statements. Responsible for providing government-wide accounting & reporting services. Directs the management & delivery of the administration of the public service pension & group insurance plans & maintains accounts for the various pension funds. Focuses in the financial management & control framework for the Department.
Asst. Deputy Minister, Accounting, Banking & Compensation, Renée Jolicoeur
819-934-0497, Fax:
819-934-0932,renee.jolicoeur@tpsgc-pwgsc.gc.ca
Acting CFO, Finance, Jean-Luc Caron
819-956-7226, jean-luc.caron@tpsgc-pwgsc.gc.ca
Director General, Central Accounting & Reporting, Kim Croucher
819-956-2875, Fax:
819-956-8400,kim.croucher@tpsgc-pwgsc.gc.ca
Director General, Compensation, Brigitte Fortin
819-956-1936, Fax:
819-956-3000,brigitte.fortin@tpsgc-pwgsc.gc.ca
Acting Director General, Superannuation, Pension Transition & Client Services, Jacques Laprise
516-533-5555, Fax:
516-533-5607,jacques.laprise@pwgsc-tpsgc.gc.ca
Director, Cheque Redemption Control Directorate, Gilles Pelletier
418-566-7222, Fax:
418-562-5183,gilles.pelletier@tpsgc-pwgsc.gc.ca

Information Technology Services Branch / Services d'infotechnologie

Provides common telecommunications & informatics services to government departments, agencies & organizations, to facilitate universal access to information throughout the federal government. Focussing on network & computer services, telecommunications, & application development, ITS is a key player in government-wide initiatives such as the Secure Channel, IM/IT community renewal, & Government-On-Line (GoL).
Acting CEO, Steven Poole
819-956-2632
Acting COO, Nancy Desormeau
819-934-0242
Acting Director General & Chief Technology Officer, Robert Maynard
819-956-8283
Director General, Application Management Services, Douglas Gauen
819-956-2354
Director General, Business Planning & Management Services, Christianne Poirier
819-956-9057
Director General, Government On-Line Initiative, Christine Desloges
613-941-4611, Fax: 613-952-7232
Director General, Government of Canada Marketplace, François Audet
819-956-4745,
Director General, Organizational Readiness Office, Nikolas Florakas
819-946-3049
Director General, Product Management, Jirka Danek
819-956-1166
Director General, Service Management & Delivery, Maurice Chenier
819-956-8510, Fax: 819-956-4986
Director General, Service Qualification & Transfer, Paul Hession
819-956-0226

MERX

Fax: 888-235-5800,
www.merx.com

Other Communication: Suppliers Support: 1-800-964-MERX (6379); Buyers Support: 1-888-738-3005 (Ottawa: 613/737-3796)

The federal government's Government Electronic Tendering Service (GETS) contracts MERX to advertise government procurement opportunities online. Architectural & engineering consulting services, or services related to real property above $84,000 are advertised on MERX; below $84,000, they are handled through SELECT. Construction opportunities above $100,000 are advertised through MERX; below are handled through SELECT. MERX is used for printing services valued at $10,000 or above, & most goods & services valued at $25,000 or above. Below this level PWGSC uses a variety of bid solicitation methods: T-buys (purchasing by telephone when the product or service is required quickly and can easily be identified over the phone); RFQ (Request for Quotation); an Invitation to Tender (ITT) is used for straightforward requirements above $25,000 & where the lowest price will determine the awarding of the contract; RFP (Request for Proposal) for more complex requirements above $25,000; RFSO (Request for Standing Offer); RFSA (Request for Supply Arrangement); Sole-sourcing, subject to trade agreements & government contracting regulations. For products, individual departments have authority to buy up to $5,000 directly from suppliers; above $5,000, the department must go to PWGSC. Departments have authority to purchase nearly all their services; for program delivery services, departments may buy directly from suppliers up to $400,000 competitively or up to $100,000 without competition; they may also buy competitively up to $2 million when they advertise their requirements through MERX. Subscribers to MERX have access to an opportunity matching service, may view historical opportunities, review contract awards & international opportunities

Real Property Branch / Biens immobiliers

Fax: 613-736-2789

Manages office space & other general-purpose property; acts as custodian for $7.6 billion of real property holdings; administers 2,000 lease contracts; provides working space for 241,000 public servants in 1,810 locations across Canada; provides professional & technical services to government departments & agencies. Government buildings are 34 per cent more energy efficient & 24 per cent more greenhouse gas efficient than in 1990. Green Leases address key environmental standards such as proper management of wastewater, indoor air quality, recycling, energy efficient lighting fixtures, greenhouse gas reduction. Works with other departments on the remediation of contaminated sites & is the federal lead in the cleanup of the Sydney Tar Ponds in Nova Scotia.
Asst. Deputy Minister, John McBain
819-956-3189, Fax:
819-956-7130,john.mcbain@tpsgc-pwgsc.gc.ca
Director General, Accelerated Infrastructure Program, Jean Vézina
819-956-7426, Fax:
819-934-0980,jean.vezina@tpsgc-pwgsc.gc.ca
Director General, Accommodation, Portfolio Management & Real Estate Services, Anne Auger
819-956-6304, Fax:
819-956-4347,anne.auger@tpsgc-pwgsc.gc.ca
Director General, Client Consultancy & Real Property Solutions, Daniel Leclair
613-960-6713, Fax:
613-960-6399,daniel.leclair@tpsgc-pwgsc.gc.ca
Director General, CRA Portfolio, Bill Doering
613-954-8330, Fax:
613-949-1284,bill.doering@tpsgc-pwgsc.gc.ca
Acting Director General, Major Crown Projects, Pierre Vaillancourt
819-956-4935, Fax:
819-956-7384,pierre.vaillancourt@tpsgc-pwgsc.gc.ca
Director General, National Capital Area Operations Sector, Mark Campbell
819-775-7217, Fax:
819-775-7279,mark.campbell@tpsgc-pwgsc.gc.ca
Acting Director General, NCA Portfolio Management, Claude Séguin

819-956-6363, Fax:
819-956-0603,claude.seguin@tpsgc-pwgsc.gc.ca
Director, NCA Real Estate Services, Denis Charette
819-956-7519, Fax:
819-956-5636,denis.charette@tpsgc-pwgsc.gc.ca
Director General, Professional & Technical Service Management, Anna Cullinan
819-956-2039, Anna.Cullinan@tpsgc-pwgsc.gc.ca
Director General, Program Management Sector, Stephen Twiss
819-956-6452, Fax:
819-934-0980,stephen.twiss@tpsgc-pwgsc.gc.ca
Director General, Special Initiatives Sector, Ralph Collins
819-775-6139, Fax:
613-947-9300,ralph.collins@tpsgc-pwgsc.gc.ca
Director General, Strategic Planning, Administration & Renewal Sector, Diane Orange
819-956-6443, Fax:
819-956-7154,Diane.Orange@tpsgc-pwgsc.gc.ca

Translation Bureau / Bureau de traduction
Richelieu Bldg., 975 St-Joseph Blvd., 5th Fl., Gatineau, QC K1A 0S5
819-934-0496, Fax: 819-997-9227
CEO, Francine Kennedy
819-997-8825, francine.kennedy@tpsgc-pwgsc.gc.ca
Vice-President, Client Services, Anne Nicholls
819-997-6339, anne.nicholls@tpsgc-pwgsc.gc.ca
Vice-President, Corporate Services, Gisèle Côté
819-994-5221, gisele.cote@tpsgc-pwgsc.gc.ca
Vice-President, Professional Services, Donald Barabé
819-994-1391, Fax:
819-934-0770,donald.barabe@tpsgc-pwgsc.gc.ca
Director, Parliamentary Translation & Interpretation, Alain Wood
613-992-0294, Fax: 613-996-8794,wooda@parl.gc.ca
Director, Terminology & Standardization, Gabriel Huard
819-997-6843, Fax:
819-953-8443,gabriel.huard@tpsgc-pwgsc.gc.ca
Director General, George Butts
819-956-0867
Senior Director, Major Projects Services, Monty Mukerji
819-934-0960

Royal Canadian Mint / Monnaie royale canadienne

320 Sussex Dr., Ottawa, ON K1A 0G8
613-993-3500, Fax: 613-993-4092, 800-267-1871
www.rcmint.ca
The RCM has two plants located in Ottawa & Winnipeg. Foreign & domestic circulating coinage is manufactured in Winnipeg.The Ottawa facility is responsible for the production of foreign & domestic numismatic products, precious metals & the refining of gold. Reports to government through Public Works & Government Services.
Vice-Chairman of the Board of Directors, James B. Love
President/CEO, Ian E. Bennett
613-993-1716
Vice-President, General Counsel & Corporate Secretary, Corporate and Legal Affairs, Marguerite F. Nadeau
613-993-1732
Vice-President/CFO, Finance & Administration, J. Marc Brûlé
613-993-5384
Chief Operating Officer, Beverley Lepine
613-993-0323
Vice-President, Human Resources & Lean Enterprise, Craig Szelestowski
613-993-2800
Vice-President, Marketing & Communications, Patrick Hadsipantelis
613-993-7746
Executive Director, Bullion and Refinery, John Moore
613-993-4689
Executive Director, Foreign Circulation, Peter J. Ho
613-993-9461

Royal Canadian Mounted Police (RCMP) / Gendarmerie royale du Canada (GRC)

1200 Vanier Pkwy., Ottawa, ON K1A 0R2
613-993-7267, Fax: 613-993-0260,
www.rcmp-grc.gc.ca
In 1873 the North West Mounted Police was constituted to provide Police protection in the unsettled portions of the North West. In 1904 the title Royal was given to the Force. In 1920 The Dominion Police was amalgamated with this Force & the name changed to Royal Canadian Mounted Police. The headquarters was moved from Regina to Ottawa & the Force may be called upon to perform duties in any portion of the Dominion. In 1928 the RCMP absorbed the Saskatchewan Provincial Police & in 1932 the Provincial Police Forces of Alberta, Manitoba, New Brunswick, Nova Scotia & PEI were absorbed in like manner.
Acts Administered:
Canadian Peacekeeping Service Medal Act
Controlled Drugs & Substances Act
Criminal Code
Criminal Records Act
DNA Identification Act
Employment Equity Act
Excise Act
Export & Import Permits Act
Firearms Act
Foreign Missions & International Organizations Act
National Defence Act
Royal Canadian Mounted Police Act
Royal Canadian Mounted Police Pension Continuation Act
Royal Canadian Mounted Police Superannuation Act
Security Offences Act
Witness Protection Program Act
Commissioner, William J.S. Elliott
613-993-0400
Honorary Commissioner,HerMajestyElizabeth II
Deputy Commissioner, Atlantic Region, Steve Graham
902-496-5042
Deputy Commissioner, Contract and Aboriginal Policing, H.D.M. (Darrell) Madill
Deputy Commissioner, North Western Region, Rod Knecht
306-780-6816
Deputy Commissioner, Pacific Region, Gary Bass
604-264-2003
CFAO, Alain Séguin
Deputy Commissioner, National Police Service, Joseph Buckle
613-993-1736
Deputy Commissioner, Operations & Integration, Tom Killam
613-993-3724
Acting Deputy Commissioner, Strategic Direction, Geoff Gruson
613-993-2323
Acting Commissioner, Public Affairs & Communication Services, Bernie Corrigan
613-993-3639, Fax: 613-993-1310

RCMP Divisions & Commanding Officers:

A Division
155 McArthur Ave., Ottawa, ON K1A 0R4
613-993-8860, Fax: 613-993-5870
Acting Commanding Officer, Allen Nause

B Division
PO Box 9700 B, St. John's, NL A1A 3T5
709-772-5465

C Division
4225, boul Dorchester ouest, Westmount, QC H3Z 1V5
514-939-8300, Fax: 514-283-2169, 800-771-5401

D Division
1091 Portage Ave., PO Box 5650, Winnipeg, MB R3C 3K2
204-983-5420

E Division
657 West 37 St., Vancouver, BC V5Z 1K6
604-264-3111, Fax: 604-264-3196

F Division
6101 Dewdney Ave. West, PO Box 2500, Regina, SK S4P 3K7
306-780-5477, Fax: 306-780-5410
Commanding Officer, D.N. (Dale) McGowan

G Division
Henry Larsen Bldg., 5010 - 49th Ave., PO Box 5010, Yellowknife, NT X1A 2R3
867-669-5100

H Division
3139 Oxford St., PO Box 2286, Halifax, NS B3J 3E1
902-426-3940, Fax: 902-426-2481
Commanding Officer, Steve Graham

J Division
1445 Regent St., PO Box 3900, Fredericton, NB E3B 4Z8
506-452-3400
Commanding Officer, Wayne Lang

K Division
11140 - 109 St., Edmonton, AB T5G 2T4
780-945-5444, Fax: 780-945-5601,
Commanding Officer, R.R. (Rod) Knecht

L Division
450 University Ave., PO Box 1360, Charlottetown, PE C1A 7N1
902-566-7112, Fax: 902-566-7235
Commanding Officer, Tracy Hardy

M Division
4100 - 4th Ave., Whitehorse, YT Y1A 1H5
867-667-5551, Fax: 867-393-6791
Commanding Officer, Peter Clark

O Division
130 Dufferin Ave., 5th Fl., PO Box 3240 B, London, ON N6A 4K3
519-640-7267, Fax: 519-640-7255
Commanding Officer, Norm Mazerolle

Training Facilities:

Canadian Police College / École de police canadienne
PO Box 8900, Ottawa, ON K1G 3J2
613-993-9500, Fax: 613-990-9738,
cpc-ccp@rcmp-grc.gc.ca
www.cpc.gc.ca
Director General & Chief Superintendent, Cal Corley
613-998-0883

RCMP Training Academy / Académie d'entrainement
6101 Dewdney Ave., Regina, SK S4P 3J7
306-780-5002, Fax: 306-780-7940
Officer in Charge, Centralized Training, Robert Castonguay

St. Lawrence Seaway Management Corporation (SLSMC) / Corporation de Gestion de la Voie Maritime du Saint-Laurent (CGVMSL)

202 Pitt St., Cornwall, ON K6J 3P7
613-932-5170, Fax: 613-932-7286,
marketing@seaway.ca
www.greatlakes-seaway.com
A not-for-profit corporation responsible for the safe & efficient movement of marine traffic through Canadian Seaway facilities.It shares operations with its American counterpart, the Saint Lawrence Seaway Development Corporation, in operating & maintaining 15 locks between Montr,al & Lake Erie.
President/CEO, Richard Corfe

Regional Offices:

Maisonneuve
151, rue Ecluse, Saint-Lambert, QC J4R 2V6
Vice-President, A. Juster

Niagara
508 Glendale Ave., St Catharines, ON L2R 6V8
Vice-President, M. Drolet

Security Intelligence Review Committee (SIRC) / Comité de Surveillance des activités de renseignement de sécurité (CSARS)

Jackson Bldg., 122 Bank St., 4th Fl., PO Box 2430 D, Ottawa, ON K1P 5W5
613-990-8441, Fax: 613-990-5230,
ellardm@sirc-csars.gc.ca
www.sirc-csars.gc.ca
Has as its mandate, under the Canadian Security Intelligence Service Act, to carry out the independent & external review of the Canadian Security Intelligence Service (CSIS) & to investigate complaints about CSIS activities. It is also required to investigate complaints from individuals who have had their employment prospects affected by the denial of a security clearance, & complaints referred to it by the Human Rights Commission. It is required to investigate reports made to it by the Minister of Citizenship & Immigration, & the Solicitor General of Canada, which relate to national security or to an individual's involvement in organized crime. The Committee is required to report annually to Parliament through the Minister of Public Safety & Emergency Preparedness on these matters.
Acts Administered:
Canadian Security Intelligence Service Act
Chair,Hon. Arthur Porter
613-990-8442, Fax: 613-990-5230
Executive Director, Susan Pollak
613-990-8442, Fax: 613-990-5230

Social Sciences & Humanities Research Council of Canada (SSHRC) / Conseil de recherches en sciences humaines du Canada (CRSH)

Constitution Sq., 350 Albert St., PO Box 1610 B, Ottawa, ON K1P 6G4
613-992-0691, Fax: 613-992-1787,
info@sshrc.ca
www.sshrc-crsh.gc.ca
The key national research agency investing in the knowledge & skills Canada needs to build the quality of its social, cultural & economic life. SSHRC supports university-based research & training in the human sciences. It funds basic, applied & collaborative research, student training, research partnerships, knowledge transfer & the communication of research findings in all disciplines of the social sciences & humanities. Grants &

fellowships are awarded through national competitions adjudicated by eminent researchers & scholars.
President, Chad Gaffield
613-995-5488, chad.gaffield@sshrc-crsh.gc.ca
Executive Vice-President, Carmen Charette
613-947-3275, carmen.charette@sshrc-crsh.gc.ca
Vice-President, Common Administrative Services, Jaime Pitfield
613-995-3914, Fax:
613-991-0969,Jaime.Pitfield@sshrc-crsh.gc.ca
Vice-President, Grants and Fellowships, Brent Herbert-Copley
613-995-5455, Brent.Herbert-Copley@sshrc-crsh.gc.ca
Vice-President, Partnerships, Gisèle Yasmeen
613-947-6938, gisele.yasmeen@sshrc-crsh.gc.ca

Standards Council of Canada (SCC) / Conseil canadien des normes (CCN)

#200, 270 Albert St., Ottawa, ON K1P 0N7
613-238-3222, Fax: 613-569-7808,
info@scc.ca
www.scc.ca

Federal Crown corporation with the mandate to promote efficient & effective standardization. The organization reports to Parliament through the Minister of Industry & oversees Canada's National Standards System. The National Standards System comprises organizations & individuals involved in voluntary standards development, promotion & implementation. In addition, more than 400 organizations have been accredited by the Standards Council, including environmental management systems (EMS) registration organizations that perform registrations to ISO 14000 series standards. The Council offers accreditation to registration bodies for specialized environmental management systems in industry-specific areas, including sustainable forestry management (CAN/CSZ809-02). Manages the Program for the Accreditation of Laboratories - Canada (PALCAN) which seeks to identify & accredit competent testing laboratories. Initial assessment is made & regular follow-up audits are performed; accredited organizations are included in the Standards Council directory of accredited testing organizations. Users of testing services can eliminate or reduce their need to establish the competence of a prospective lab. In cooperation with the Canadian Association of Environmental Analy tical Laboratories (CAEAL), SCC operates an accreditation program for environmental analytical laboratories. SCC's website provides free access to a wide variety of standards information, including searchable databases containing information on Canadian, foreign & international standards, regulations & SCC-accredited organizations. More speacialized information is available through SCC's information & Research Service. Other accreditation programs include ones for registrars of ISO 14000 environmental management systems; environmental auditor certifiers & auditor training course providers.
Chair, Hugh Krentz
613-238-3222, Fax: 613-569-7808
Executive Director, John Walter
613-238-3222, Fax: 613-569-7808,gclarke@scc.ca
Manager, Communications, Pilar Castro
613-238-3222, Fax: 613-569-7808,pcastro@scc.ca

Statistics Canada / Statistique Canada

R.H. Coats Bldg., Tunney's Pasture, 100 Tunney's Pasture Driveway, Ottawa, ON K1A 0T6
613-951-8116, Fax: 877-287-4369, 800-263-1136
infostats@statcan.ca
www.statscan.ca

Agency of the federal government, headed by the Chief Statistician of Canada which reports to Parliament through the Minister of Industry. As Canada's central statistical agency, it has a mandate to collect, compile, analyse, abstract & publish statistical information relating to the commercial, industrial, financial, social, economic & general activities & condition of the people of Canada; coordinates activities with its federal & provincial partners in the national statistical system to avoid duplication of effort & to ensure the consistency & usefulness of statistics. The agency profiles & measures both social & economic changes in Canada. It presents a comprehensive picture of the national economy through statistics on manufacturing, agriculture, retail sales, services, prices, productivity changes, trade, transportation, employment & unemployment, & aggregate measures such as gross domestic product. It also presents a comprehensive picture of social conditions through statistics on demography, health, areas.
Acts Administered:
Corporations Returns Act
Statistics Act
Chief Statistician of Canada,VACANT
613-951-9757, Fax: 613-951-4842
Director, Communications & Information Services, Lynn Barr-Telford
613-951-1518, Lynn.Barr-Telford@statcan.gc.ca

Business & Trade Statistics / Statistique du commerce et des entreprises
Includes: distributive trades; enterprise statistics; manufacturing, construction & energy; service industries
Asst. Chief Statistician, Philip Smith
613-951-9493, Fax:
613-951-3231,Philip.Smith@statcan.gc.ca
Director General, Economy-Wide Statistics, Louis Marc Ducharme
613-951-0688, Fax:
613-951-0411,LouisMarc.Ducharme@statcan.gc.ca
Director General, Industry Statistics, Peter Lys
613-951-4071, Fax: 613-951-0411,Peter.Lys@statcan.gc.ca
Director General, Agriculture, Technology & Transportation Statistics Branch, Marcelle Dion
613-951-3528, Fax:
613-951-0411,Marcelle.Dion@statcan.gc.ca

Statistics Canada Client Services/Services a la clientele:

Edmonton
Pacific Plaza, #900, 10909 Jasper Ave. NW, Edmonton, AB T5J 4J3
780-495-3027, Fax: 780-495-5318

Halifax
1888 Brunswick St., 1st Fl., Halifax, NS B3J 2G7

Montréal
Tour Est, Complexe Guy-Favreau, 200, boul René-Lévesque ouest, 4e étage, Montréal, QC H2Z 1X4

Ottawa
R.H. Coats Bldg., Lobby, West Wing, 100 Tunney's Pasture Driveway, Ottawa, ON K1A 0T6

Regina
Park Plaza, #440, 2365 Albert St., Regina, SK S4P 4K1

Toronto
Arthur Meighen Bldg., 25 St. Clair Ave. East, 10th Fl., Toronto, ON M4T 1M4

Vancouver
Library Square Tower, #600, 300 West Georgia St., Vancouver, BC V6B 6C7

Winnipeg
Via Rail Bldg., #200, 123 Main St., Winnipeg, MB R3C 4V9

Status of Women Canada (SWC) / Condition féminine Canada

123 Slater St., 10th Fl., Ottawa, ON K1P 1H9
613-995-7835, Fax: 613-947-0761, 866-902-2719
infonational@swc-cfc.gc.ca
www.swc-cfc.gc.ca

The federal government agency promotes gender equality, & the participation of women in the economic, social, cultural, & political life in Canada. Status of Women Canada focuses its work in the following areas: improvement of women's economic autonomy & well-being; elimination of systemic violence against women & children; & the advancement of women's human rights. To achieve results, SWC works with & supports research organizations, equality-seeking organizations, the non-governmental, voluntary & private sectors, & international organizations.
Minister, Public Works & Government Services; Minister for Status of Women,Hon. Rona Ambrose
613-996-9778, Fax: 613-996-0785,Ambrose.R@parl.gc.ca
Parliamentary Secretary for Status of Women, Sylvie Boucher
613-992-4406, Fax: 613-992-4544,Boucher.S@parl.gc.ca
Coordinator/Deputy Head, Clare Beckton
613-995-7838, Fax:
613-943-0449,clare.beckton@swc-cfc.gc.ca
Director General, Policy, Kathryn Bruce
613-992-7094, Fax:
613-947-0530,kathryn.bruce@swc-cfc.gc.ca
Director, Communications, Philippe Mailhot
819-956-4000, Fax:
819-956-4100,Philippe_Mailhot@pch.gc.ca
Director, Women's Program, Havelin Anand
613-947-0355, Fax:
613-947-0761,havelin.anand@swc-cfc.gc.ca
Director, Corporate Services Directorate, Cindy Paquette
613-947-1453, Fax:
613-947-6113,cindy.paquette@swc-cfc.gc.ca
Director General, Communications & Strategic Planning Directorate, Nanci-Jean Waugh
613-995-7839, Fax:
613-943-2386,nanci-jean.waugh@swc-cfc.gc.ca

Telefilm Canada / Téléfilm Canada

#500, 360, rue Saint-Jacques, Montréal, QC H2Y 1P5
514-283-6363, Fax: 514-283-2365, 800-567-0890
info@telefilm.gc.ca
www.telefilm.gc.ca

Telefilm Canada is a Crown corporation reporting to Parliament through the Department of Canadian Heritage. Headquartered in Montréal, Telefilm provides services to the Canadian audiovisual industry by means of four regional offices located in Vancouver, Toronto, Montréal and Halifax. Dedicated to the development and promotion of the Canadian audiovisual industry.
Chair, Michel Roy
Executive Director, Carolle Brabant
Director, Communications, Denise Arab
Director, Public & Government Affairs, Jean-Claude Mahé

Offices in Canada:

Halifax
1684 Barrington St., 3rd Fl., Halifax, NS B3J 2A2
902-426-8425, Fax: 902-426-4445

Toronto
2 Bloor St. West, 22nd Fl., Toronto, ON M4W 3E2
416-973-6436, Fax: 416-973-8606

Vancouver
#310, 440 Cambie St., Vancouver, BC V6B 2N5
604-666-1566, Fax: 604-666-7754

Transport Canada (TC) / Transports Canada

Place de Ville, 330 Sparks St., Tower C, Ottawa, ON K1A 0N5
613-990-2309, Fax: 613-954-4731,
minTC@tc.gc.ca
www.tc.gc.ca

Other Communication: TTY: 1-888-675-6863

Using EMS 14000 standards, Transport Canada incorporates environmental considerations in all decision-making to fulfill the department's sustainable development strategy. Working with airports & airlines to minimize environmental effects of de-icing fluids; working with Environment Canada & industry to more effectively manage road salt; participating with ICAO's Committee on Aviation Environmental Protection (CAEP) concerning aircraft emissions, noise & land use planning. Ongoing contaminated sites management program. The Moving on Sustainable Transportation (MOST) Program supports projects that educate, raise awareness & provide tools to understand, promote & encourage sustainable transportation, such as neighbourhood transit passes, idle-free workplaces, school walking routes. Development of strategies to reduce greenhouse gas emissions from freight transportation; information on fuel consumption. Urban Transportation Showcase Program aims to reduce greenhouse gas emissions through showcasing demonstrations in communities across Canada (www.tc.gc.ca/ programs/environment/utsp/menu.htm).
Acts Administered:
Aeronautics Act
(Act respecting regulations made pursuant to section 5 of the) Aeronautics Act
Air Canada Public Participation Act
Airport Transfer (Miscellaneous Matters) Act
Arctic Waters Pollution Prevention Act (Indian & Northern Affairs)
Bills of Landing Act
Blue Water Bridge Authority Act
Buffalo & Fort Erie Public Bridge Company Act
Canada Marine Act
Canada Post Corporation Act
Canada Shipping Act
Canada Shipping Act, 2001 (Fisheries & Oceans)
Canada Strategic Infrastructure Fund Act
Canada Transportation Act
Canadian Air Transport Security Authority Act
Canadian National Montréal Terminals Act
Canadian National Toronto Terminals Act
Carriage by Air Act
Civil Air Navigation Services Commercialization Act
CN Commercialization Act
Coasting Trade Act
Department of Transport Act
Government Property Traffic Act
Harbour Commissions Act
Harbour of Québec Act, The Corporation of Pilots for & below the
Intercolonial & PEI Railways Employees' Provident Fund Act
International Interests in Mobile Equipment (aircraft equipment) Act
International Rapids Power Development Act
Marine & Aviation War Risks Act
Marine Atlantic Inc. Acquisition Authorization Act
Marine Insurance Act

Marine Liability Act
Marine Transportation Security Act
Maritime Code Act
Meaford Harbour Act
Montréal Port Wardens Act
Motor Vehicle Fuel Consumption Standards Act
Motor Vehicle Safety Act
Motor Vehicle Transport Act, 1987
National Capital Act
National Transcontinental Railway Act
Navigable Waters Projection Act
Northern Transportation Company Ltd. Disposal Authorization Act
Northumberland Strait Crossing Act
Ontario Harbours Agreement Act
Pilotage Act
Pre-clearance Act
Québec Port Wardens Act
Railway Relocation & Crossing Act
Railway Safety Act
Royal Canadian Mint Act
Safe Containers Convention Act
Transportation Appeal Tribunal of Canada Act
Transportation of Dangerous Goods Act, 1992
Shipping Conferences Exemption Act, 1987
United States Wreckers Act
Winnipeg Terminals Act

Minister, Transport, Infrastructure, & Communities,Hon. Charles (Chuck) Strahl
613-992-2940, Fax: 613-944-9376,Strahl.C@parl.gc.ca
Deputy Minister, Yaprak Baltacioglu
613-990-4507, Fax: 613-991-0851,yaprak.baltacioglu@tc.gc.ca
Director General, Communications & Marketing, Jean Valin
613-990-6138, Fax: 613-991-6719,jean.valin@tc.gc.ca
Parliamentary Secretary to the Minister of Transport, Infrastructure, & Communities, Brian Jean
613-992-1154, Fax: 613-992-4603,Jean.B@parl.gc.ca
Senior General Counsel & Head, Legal Services, Henry K. Schultz
613-990-5768, Fax: 613-990-5777,henry.schultz@tc.gc.ca

- Atlantic Pilotage Authority Canada/ Administration de pilotage de l'Atlantique Canada
- Canada Lands Company/ Société Immobilière du Canada
- Canada Mortgage & Housing Corporation/ Société canadienne d'hypothèques et de logement
- Canada Post Corporation/ Société canadienne des postes
- Canadian Air Transport Security Authority(CATSA) / Administration canadienne de la sûreté du transport aérien (ACSTA)
99 Bank St., 13th Fl.
Ottawa, ON K1P 6B9
Fax: 613-991-6726 888-294-2202
www.catsa-acsta.gc.ca
- Canadian Transportation Agency/ Office des transports du Canada
- Federal Bridge Corporation Limited/ Société des ponts fédéraux Limitée
#1210, 55 Metcalfe St.
Ottawa, ON K1P 6L5
613-993-6880 Fax: 613-993-6945
info@federalbridge.ca
www.federalbridge.ca
The Federal Bridge Corporation Limited (FBCL) was incorporated in 1998 to assume the non-navigational management responsibilities of the St. Lawrence Seaway Authority, including the Jacques Cartier & Champlain Bridges Incorporated, & in a joint venture with its U.S. partner, the Seaway International Bridge Corporation, Ltd. At the same time, the FBCL assumed responsibility for the management of the Canadian portion of the Thousand Islands International Bridge. In 2000, the FBCL acquired the Canadian half of the Sault Ste. Marie International Bridge.
- Great Lakes Pilotage Authority/ Administration de pilotage des Grands Lacs
- Laurentian Pilotage Authority/ Administration de pilotage des Laurentides Canada
- Marine Atlantic Inc./ Marine Atlantique
- Pacific Pilotage Authority/ Administration de Pilotage du Pacifique Canada
- Royal Canadian Mint/ Monnaie royale canadienne
- Transportation Appeal Tribunal of Canada/ Anciennement le Tribunal de l'aviation civile
333 Laurier Ave. West, 12th Fl.
Ottawa, ON K1A 0N5
613-990-6906 Fax: 613-990-9153
info@tatc.gc.ca
- Transportation Safety Board of Canada/ Bureau de la sécurité des transports du Canada
- VIA Rail Canada Inc.

Corporate Services Group / Services généraux

Corporate Services is part of the Department's administration business line & is responsible for providing services & functional expertise in the areas of finance & administration, technology & information management, human resources & access to information, Crown corporation portfolio coordination, internal audit & evaluation services.

Director General, Executive Services, William McCullough
613-991-7412, Fax: 613-998-6609
Director General, Finance & Administration, William Carrothers
613-993-4307, Fax: 613-991-4410
Director General, Human Resources, Linda Brouillette
613-991-6317, Fax: 613-990-1880
Director General, Technology & Information Management Services, Chris Molinski
613-998-6465, Fax: 613-990-2469
Acting Director General, Crown Corporation Secretariat, April Nakatsu
613-991-2998, Fax: 613-991-4277
Director, Audit & Advisory Services, Duncan James
613-998-6469, Fax: 613-993-3746
Director, Departmental Evaluation Services, Gail Young
613-990-0117

Policy Group / Groupe de politiques

Responsible for setting policies relating to rail, marine, highways & borders, motor carrier, air, airports & accessible transportation, as well as setting departmental strategic policy & coordinating intergovernmental relations; assessing the performance of the overall transportation systems & its components, & developing supporting databases, forecasts & economic analysis; administering the management agreement with the St. Lawrence Seaway Management Corporation; & supporting rail passenger services through payments to VIA Rail & three regional railways, & ferry services through payments to Marine Atlantic & to provincial & private operators & border infrastructure improvements.

Asst. Deputy Minister, Kristine Burr
613-998-1880, Fax: 613-991-1440
Senior Advisor to the Asst. Deputy Minister, Policy, Valerie Dufour
613-991-6435, Fax: 613-991-1440
Director General, Air Policy, Brigita Gravitis-Beck
613-993-0054
Director General, International & Intergovernmental Relations, Arlene Turner
613-991-6500, Fax: 613-991-6422
Director General, Economic Analysis, Roger Roy
613-998-0684, Fax: 613-957-3280,
Director General, Marine Policy, Emile Di Sanza
613-991-3536, Fax: 613-998-1845
Acting Director General, Surface Transportation Policy, Helena Borges
613-998-2689, Fax: 613-998-2686
Director General, Strategic Policy, Brian Bohunicky
613-991-6503, Fax: 613-990-1719

Programs Group / Groupe des programmes
www.tc.gc.ca/programs/menu.htm

Responsible for the transfer of ports, harbours & airports to communities & other interests; the oversight & lease management of divested facilities; the operation of facilities not yet divested; &real property management. Responsible for environmental programs & policies, including environmental management system, sustainable development strategies, environmental assessment & national environmental issues in transportation, such as climate change.

Asst. Deputy Minister, Ronald Sully
613-990-3001, Fax: 613-998-5008
Director General, Airport & Port Programs, Rod Dean
613-990-0510, Fax: 613-990-8889
Director General, Environmental Affairs, Robert Lyman
613-991-5995, Fax: 613-993-8674
Director General, Surface Infrastructure Programs, Evelyn Marcoux
613-990-0624, Fax: 613-990-9639
Director, Strategic Planning & Communications, Helen Hutcheson
613-998-5153, Fax: 613-990-1427

Safety & Security Group / Groupe de sécurité et sûreté

The ADM, Safety & Security, directs the development of transportation safety & security legislation, regulations & national standards; is responsible for the uniform implementation of monitoring, testing, inspection, research & development, & subsidy programs in the aviation, marine, rail & road modes of transport; oversees the delivery of aircraft services to government & other transportation bodies; & is responsible for development & enforcement of regulations & standards under federal jurisdiction, to protect public safety in the transportation of dangerous goods, & to prevent unlawful interference in the aviation, marine & railways modes of transport, as well as ensuring that the department is prepared to respond to transportation & transportation-related emergencies.

Asst. Deputy Minister, Marc Grégoire
613-990-3838, Fax: 613-990-2947
Assoc. Asst. Deputy Minister, John Forster
613-949-2394
Director General, Aircraft Services, Michel Gaudreau
613-998-3316, Fax: 613-991-0365
Director General, Civil Aviation, Merlin Preuss
613-990-1322
Director General, Marine Safety, William Nash
613-998-0610
Director General, Marine Security, Laureen Kinney
613-991-4173
Executive Director, Rail & Mass Transit Task Force, Tony Ritchie
613-990-3885
Director General, Rail Safety, Luc Bourdon
613-998-2984, Fax: 613-990-7767
Director General, Road Safety & Motor Vehicle Regulation, Kash Ram
613-993-6735
Director General, Security & Emergency Preparedness, Debra Normoyle
613-990-3651, Fax: 613-996-6381
Director General, Transportation of Dangerous Goods, John Read
613-990-1147, Fax: 613-993-5925
Acting Director General, Strategies & Integration, Sheila K. Smith
613-990-1115
Executive Director, CATSA Act Review Secretariat, Tim Meisner
613-990-5437

Atlantic
95 Foundry St., 6th Fl., Moncton, NB E1C 5H7
800-387-4999

Ontario
#300, 4900 Yonge St., Toronto, ON M2N 6A5
416-952-0230, Fax: 416-952-0159, 888-231-2330

Pacific
#620, 800 Burrard St., Vancouver, BC V6Z 2J8
604-666-3518, Fax: 604-666-7255,
pacific-pacifique@tc.gc.ca

Prairie & Northern
344 Edmonton St., Winnipeg, MB R3C 0P6
204-983-3152, 888-463-0521
pnrweb@tc.gc.ca

Québec
700, Leigh Capreol, Zone 3A, Dorval, QC H4Y 1G7
514-633-2714, Fax: 514-633-2751

Transportation Safety Board of Canada / Bureau de la sécurité des transports du Canada

200 Promenade du Portage, 4th Fl., Ottawa, ON K1A 1K8
819-994-3741, Fax: 819-997-2239, 800-387-3557
www.tsb.gc.ca

The Board is an independent agency reporting to Parliament through the President of the Queen's Privy Council. The formal name for the Board is the Canadian Transportation Accident Investigation & Safety Board.Its sole aim is the advancement of transportation safety in the marine, rail, pipeline & air modes of transport. The TSB conducts independent investigations into selected transportation occurences in order to make findings as to their causes & contributing factors; identifies safety deficiences, & makes recommendations designed to prevent further occurences. Because the Board is independent, its transportation accident investigations are completely separate from the regulatory agencies responsible for transportation. In making findings & recommendations it is not the function of the Board to assign fault or determine civil liability.

Chair, Wendy A. Tadros
819-994-8000, Fax: 819-994-9759,Wendy.Tadros@tsb.gc.ca
COO, Jean L. Laporte
819-994-8004, Fax: 819-994-9759,Jean.Laporte@bst-tsb.gc.ca
Director, Communications, Aarin Masson
819-994-8051, Fax: 819-953-1733,aarin.bronson@bst-tsb.gc.ca

Treasury Board of Canada / Conseil du Trésor du Canada

300 Laurier Ave. West, 10th Fl., Ottawa, ON K1A 0R5

613-957-2400, Fax: 613-941-4000, 877-636-0656
info@tbs-sct.gc.ca
www.tbs-sct.gc.ca

The Treasury Board is a Cabinet Committee of government headed by the President of the Treasury Board.The committee constituting the Treasury Board includes, in addition to the President, the Minister of Finance & four other ministers appointed by the Governor-in-Council. The main role of the Treasury Board is the management of the government's financial, personnel & administrative responsibilities.The Treasury Board derives its authority primarily from the Financial Administration Act & is supported by the Treasury Board Secretariat.

Acts Administered:
Alternative Fuels Act
Federal Real Property & Federal Immovables Act

Minister, Asia-Pacific Gateway; President, Treasury Board,Hon. Stockwell Burt Day
613-995-1702, Fax: 613-995-1154,DayS@parl.gc.ca; president@tbs-sct.gc.ca
Parliamentary Secretary to the President of the Treasury Board, Andrew Saxton
613-995-1225, Fax: 613-992-7319,Saxton.A@parl.gc.ca
Secretary, Michelle d'Auray
613-952-1777, Fax: 613-952-6596
Comptroller General, James Ralston
613-957-7820, Fax: 613-952-0354
Associate Secretary, Anita Biguzs
613-941-1843, Fax: 613-952-6596
Assistant Deputy Minister, Corporate Services, Linda Gobeil
613-995-8487, Fax: 613-952-3009
Assistant Secretary, Economic Sector, Nada Semaan
613-957-0556, Fax: 613-957-0557
Assistant Secretary, Management Policy & Labour Relations, Hélène Laurendeau
613-952-3000, Fax: 613-952-3009
Correspondence Officer, Office of the Asst. Deputy Minister, Sonia Hust
613-992-1483, Fax: 613-947-3643

• Public Sector Pension Investment Board/ Office d'investissement des régimes de pensions du secteur public
#200, 440 Laurier Ave. West
Ottawa, ON K1R 7X6
613-782-3095 Fax: 613-782-6864
info@investpsp.ca
www.investpsp.ca
Crown corporation established by Parliament by the Public Sector Pension Investment Board Act (September 1999). The mandate of PSP Investments is to manage employer & employee contributions made after April 1, 2000 to the federal Public Service, the Canadian Forces & the Royal Canadian Mounted Police pension funds.

• Canada Public Service Agency(CPSA) / Agence de la fonction publique du Canada (AFPC)
269 Laurier Ave. West, 10th Fl.
Ottawa, ON K1A 0R3
613-946-5015 Fax: 613-948-4758
www.infosource.gc.ca/inst/hrh/fed00-eng.asp
Created in 2003 to put in place a new human resources management regime in the public service of Canada. Formerly the Public Service Human Resources Management Agency of Canada (PSHRMAC).

• Public Service Labour Relations Board/ Commission des relations de travail dans la fonction publique
CD Howe Building
240 Sparks St., 6th Fl.
PO Box 1525 B
Ottawa, ON K1P 5V2
613-990-1800 Fax: 613-990-1849 866-931-3454
mail.courrier@pslrb-crtfp.gc.ca
www.pslrb-crtfp.gc.ca
Independent, quasi-judicial statutory tribunal responsible for administering the collective bargaining & grievance adjudication systems in the federal Public & Parliamentary Service. Also provides mediation & conflict resolution services, compensation analysis & research services.

Office of the Registrar of Lobbyists
255 Albert St., 10th Fl., Ottawa, ON K1A 0R5
613-957-2760, Fax: 613-957-3078
Registrar, Michael Nelson
Commissioner of Lobbying, Karen E. Shepherd
613-941-9873, Fax: 613-957-3078

Veterans Affairs Canada / Anciens combattants Canada

161 Grafton St., PO Box 7700, Charlottetown, PE C1A 8M9
902-566-8888,
information@vac-acc.gc.ca
www.vac-acc.gc.ca

Provides pensions for disability or death, economic support in the form of allowances, and health care benefits and services to veterans and members of the Canadian Armed Forces, members and ex-members of the RCMP, and their dependents.

Acts Administered:
Army Benevolent Fund Act
Canadian Forces Members & Veterans Re-establishment & Compensation Act
Children of Deceased Veterans Education Assistance Act
Department of Veterans Affairs Act
Merchant Navy Veterans & Civilian War-related Benefits Act
Pension Act
The Returned Soldiers' Insurance Act
Soldier Settlement Act
Special Operators War Service Benefits Act
Supervisors War Service Benefits Act
Veterans Review & Appeal Board Act
Veterans Benefit Act
Veterans Insurance Act
Veterans' Land Act
War Service Grants Act
War Veterans Allowance Act
Women's Royal Naval Services & the South African Military Nursing Service (Benefits) Act
Related Acts
Aeronautics Act, section 9
Halifax Relief Commission Pension Continuation Act
Indian Soldier Settlement Act
Royal Canadian Mounted Police Pension Continuation Act (in Part)
Royal Canadian Mounted Police Superannuation Act (in Part)

Minister, Veterans Affairs; Minister of State (Agriculture),Hon. Jean-Pierre Blackburn
613-996-4649, Fax: 613-996-0287,Blackburn.J@parl.gc.ca
Parliamentary Secretary to the Minister of Veterans Affairs, Greg Kerr
613-995-5711, Fax: 613-996-9857,Kerr.G@parl.gc.ca
Deputy Minister, Suzanne Tining
613-996-6881, Fax: 613-952-7709
Assoc. Deputy Minister, Ron Herbert
902-566-8047, Fax: 902-566-8521
Asst. Deputy Minister, Service Delivery & Commemoration, Keith Hillier
902-626-2723, Fax: 902-566-8172
Director General, Audit & Evaluation, Orlanda Drebit
902-566-8018, Fax: 902-566-8343,
Director, Cabinet and Legislative Affairs, Suzanne Levesque
613-992-3801, Fax: 613-941-5434

• Veterans Review & Appeal Board/ Tribunal des anciens combattants (révision et appel)
Daniel J. MacDonald Bldg.
161 Grafton St.
PO Box 9900
Charlottetown, PE C1A 8V7
902-566-8751 Fax: 902-566-7850 800-450-8006
vrab_tacra@vac-acc.gc.ca
www.vrab-tacra.gc.ca
Other Communication: Ligne sans frais: 1-877-368-0859
The Board is an independent Board with full and exclusive jurisdiction to hear appeals from the decisions of the Minister of Veterans Affairs. The Board may affirm, vary or reverse the Minister's decisions, or refer decisions back to the Minister for reconsideration.The Board is completely independent from the Department of Veterans Affairs.

Bureau of Pension Advocates / Bureau de services juridiques des pensions
Chief Pensions Advocate, Brian McKenna
902-566-8916, Fax: 902-566-7804

Corporate Services / Coordination des politiques
Asst. Deputy Minister, Ron Herbert
902-566-8047, Fax: 902-566-8521
Director General, Finance, André Joannette
902-566-8320, Fax: 902-368-0411
Director General, Human Resources, Heather Parry
902-566-8408, Fax: 902-566-8425
Director General, Information Technology & Telecommunications Division, John Walker
902-566-8236, Fax: 902-566-8351
Director, Information Management Services, Anne Murtha
902-566-7060, Fax: 902-368-0496

Veterans Services / Service aux anciens combattants
Sr. Asst. Deputy Minister, Brian Ferguson
902-566-8100, Fax: 902-566-8780
Director General, Policy & Research Division, Darragh W. Mogan
902-566-8302, Fax: 902-566-8826
Director General, Program Management Division, Bernard Butler
902-566-7438, Fax: 902-370-4727
Executive Director, Ste. Annes Hospital, Rachel Corneille-Gravel
514-457-8400, Fax: 514-457-5741

Regional Offices:

Atlantic Region
40 Alderney Dr., PO Box 1002, Dartmouth, NS B2Y 2N5
902-426-6305, Fax: 902-426-0555
Director General, Krista Locke

Ontario Region
Bag Service 4000, 145 Government Rd. West, Kirkland Lake, ON P2N 3P4
705-568-4132, Fax: 705-567-7971
Acting Director General, Dan Fenety

Québec Region
#6505, 800, rue de la Gauchetière Ouest, Montréal, QC H5W 1L8
514-496-6412, Fax: 514-496-7303
Director General, Charlotte Bastien

Western Region (Vancouver)
#400, 900 - 605 Robson St., PO Box 5600, Vancouver, BC V6B 5G4
604-666-2675, Fax: 604-666-8839
Director General, Gisèle Toupin

Western Region (Winnipeg)
#610, 234 Donald St., PO Box 6050, Winnipeg, MB R3C 4G5
204-983-5316, Fax: 204-983-6286
Director General, Gisèle Toupin
District Pensions Advocate, Marilyn MacKinnon
Regional Director, Pensions Advcacy, Anthony Sweet
Pensions Advocate, Daniele Hart
Pensions Advocate, Barb LeGay
District Pensions Advocate, Aidan Murphy
District Pensions Advocate, Susan O'Keefe
District Pensions Advocate, Claudette Richer
Pensions Advocate, Lina Laverdière
Pensions Advocate, Gaetan Paquette
Regional Director, Pensions Advocacy, Eric Marinacci
Pensions Advocate, Walter Mutz
Pensions Advocate, Barbara Cowal
Pensions Advocate, Patricia Rodrique
District Pensions Advocate, Marie France Dubois
Pensions Advocate, Raynald Dion
District Pensions Advocate, Glenn Pruden
District Pensions Advocate, Lois Kit
Pensions Advocate, Catherine Lawson
Regional District Pensions Advocate, Sylvia Kissin
Pensions Advocate, Jennifer Kim
Regional Director, Pensions Advocacy, Nancy Hobson
District Pensions Advocate, Daniel Assh
Pensions Advocate, Brian Murphy
District Pensions Advocate, Nancy Kao
District Pensions Advocate, Kurt Clyde
District Pensions Advocate, Jim Beckett
Regional Director, Pensions Advocacy, Evan Elkin
Pensions Advocate, Janet Ellis
District Pensions Advocate, Susan Ruttan
Pensions Advocate, Marv Bisal

Via Rail Canada Inc.

#500, 3, Place Ville-Marie, Montréal, QC H3B 2C9
514-871-6000, Fax: 514-871-6768,
www.viarail.ca

The Corporation manages Canada's national passenger rail network. Reports to government through the Minister of Transport.

Chair, Donald A. Wright
President/CEO, Marc Laliberté
COO, John Marginson
Chief Customer Experience Officer, Denis Pinsonneault
Chief Financial & Administration Officer, Robert St-Jean
Chief People Officer, Laurent F. Caron
Chief Marketing & Sales Officer, Steve Del Bosco
Chief Information Officer, Yves Bourbonnais
Senior Director, Safety, Security & Risk Management, Jean Tierney
General Counsel & Secretary, Yves Desjardins-Siciliano

Western Economic Diversification Canada (WD) / Diversification de l'économie de l'Ouest Canada (DEO)

Canada Place, #1500, 9700 Jasper Ave. NW, Edmonton, AB T5J 4H7
780-495-4164, Fax: 780-495-4557, 888-338-9378
www.wd-deo.gc.ca

Responsible for promoting economic growth & diversification in the West.By investing in innovation, fostering entrepreneurship & using partnerships to enhance community sustainability, WD is helping to create a more prosperous future for western Canadians.Invests in R&D & commercialization in environmental technologies as a focus area for innovation strategies.

Minister of State (Western Economic Diversification),Hon. Lynne Yelich
613-952-2768, Fax: 613-952-9384,Yelich.L@parl.gc.ca; lynne.yelich@wd.gc.ca
Deputy Minister, Daniel Watson
780-495-5772, Fax: 780-495-6222,Other Communications: Ottawa: 613/952-9382; Fax: 613/954-1044
Executive Director, Finance & Corporate Management, Jim Saunderson
780-495-4301, Fax: 780-495-7618

Regional Offices:
Co-Chair, Wendy Ladner-Beaudry
Co-Chair, Frank Lento
President/CEO, Kelly Mann
kellym@bcgames.org

Regional Offices:

Edmonton
Canada Place, #1500, 9700 Jasper Ave. Northwest, Edmonton, AB T5J 4H7
780-495-4164, Fax: 780-495-4557, 888-338-9378
Asst. Deputy Minister, Doug Maley
780-495-4168, Fax: 780-495-6222

Vancouver
Price Waterhouse Bldg., #700, 333 Seymour St., Vancouver, BC V6B 5G9
604-666-6256, Fax: 604-666-2353, 888-338-9378
Asst. Deputy Minister, Gerry Salembier
604-666-6366, Fax: 604-666-1510

Calgary
#400, 639 - 5 Ave. SW, Calgary, AB T2P 0M9
403-292-5458, Fax: 403-292-5487, 888-338-9378

Winnipeg
The Cargill Bldg., #620, 240 Graham Ave., Winnipeg, MB R3C 0J7
204-983-4472, Fax: 204-983-3852, 888-338-9378
Asst. Deputy Minister, Marilyn Kapitany
204-983-5715, Fax: 204-983-0966

Ottawa
#500, 141 Laurier Ave. West, Ottawa, ON K1P 5J3
613-952-2768, Fax: 613-952-9384
Asst. Deputy Minister, Janet King
613-952-7096, Fax: 613-954-1044

Saskatoon
S.J. Cohen Bldg., #601, 119 - 4 Ave. South, PO Box 2025, Saskatoon, SK S7K 3S7
306-975-4373, Fax: 306-975-5484, 888-338-9378
Asst. Deputy Minister, Sharon Lee Smith
306-975-5858, Fax: 306-975-5484

Government of Alberta

Seat of Government:9718 - 107 St., Edmonton, AB T5K 1E4
www.alberta.ca

The Province of Alberta entered Confederation September 1, 1905.It has an area of 640,044.57 km2, & the StatsCan census population in 2009 was 3,687,700.

Office of the Lieutenant Governor

Legislature Bldg., 10800 - 97 Ave., 3rd Fl., Edmonton, AB T5K 2B6
780-427-7243, Fax: 780-422-5134,
ltgov@gov.ab.ca
www.lieutenantgovernor.ab.ca

Lieutenant Governor,The Hon. Donald S. Ethell, Colonel (Ret'd)
Secretary, Mary Hunt
780-427-7243, mary.hunt@gov.ab.ca

Office of the Premier

Legislature Bldg., #307, 10800 - 97 Ave., Edmonton, AB T5K 2B6
780-427-2251, Fax: 780-427-1349,
www.premier.alberta.ca

The Premier carries out the following responsibilities as the head of decision-making in the provincial government: appointment of Cabinet members; organization of goverment; provision of overall direction for the government; determination of government priorities; provision of direction for legislative debate; & contact with the Lieutenant Governor on the need and date for a general election. The Office of the Premier is comprised of the Chief of Staff, Deputy Chief of Staff, the Director of Communications, the Director of Scheduling, & the Executive Director, Southern Alberta Office of the Premier.

Premier,The Hon. Ed Stelmach
780-427-2251, Fax: 780-427-1349,premier@gov.ab.ca
Chief of Staff, Ron Glen
ron.glen@gov.ab.ca
Deputy Chief of Staff, Policy & Strategy, Elan MacDonald
elan.macdonald@gov.ab.ca
Deputy Chief of Staff, Operations & Legislative Affairs, George Samoil
Fax: 780-427-1349,george.samoil@gov.ab.ca
Director, Scheduling, Raeanne Peers
raeanne.peers@gov.ab.ca
Director, Communications, Cam Hantiuk
Fax: 780-422-3669,cam.hantiuk@gov.ab.ca
Executive Director, Southern Alberta Office, Ken Faulkner
403-297-6464, Fax: 403-297-4276,ken.faulkner@gov.ab.ca

Executive Council

Legislature Bldg., 10800 - 97 Ave., Edmonton, AB T5K 2B6
780-427-2251, Fax: 780-427-1349

The Executive Council Office is led by the Deputy Minister of the Executive Council. The Deputy Minister is also the Clerk of the Executive Council & Secretary to Cabinet. The Office consists of the Cabinet Secretariat, the Policy Coordination Office, the Protocol Office, & the Public Affairs Bureau. Its responsibilities are as follows: supporting the Premier & members of the Executive Council in administrative & decision making procedures, business planning, & policy coordination; providing protocol advice; communicating & communications support through the Public Affairs Bureau; & providing leadership to the Alberta Public Service.

Acts Administered:
Alberta Bill of Rights
Family Day Act
Queen's Printer Act

Premier & President, Executive Council,Hon. Ed Stelmach
780-427-2251, Fax: 780-427-1349,premier@gov.ab.ca
Deputy Premier; Minister, Advanced Education & Technology, Hon. Doug Horner
780-427-2025, Fax: 780-427-5582
Solicitor General; Minister, Public Security, Hon. Franke Oberle
780-415-9406, Fax: 780-415-9566
Government House Leader; Minister, Education, Hon. Dave Hancock
780-427-5010, Fax: 780-427-5018
President, Treasury Board, Hon. Lloyd Snelgrove
780-415-4855, Fax: 780-415-4853
Minister, International & Intergovernmental Relations, Hon. Iris Evans
780-427-2585, Fax: 780-422-9023
Minister, Energy, Hon. Ron Liepert
780-427-3740, Fax: 780-422-0195
Minister, Transportation, Hon. Luke Ouellette
780-427-2080, Fax: 780-422-2722
Minister, Sustainable Resource Development, Hon. Mel Knight
780-415-4815, Fax: 780-415-4818
Minister, Justice; Attorney General, Hon. Alison Redford
780-427-2339, Fax: 780-422-6621
Minister, Environment, Hon. Rob Renner
780-427-2391, Fax:
780-422-6259,rob.renner@gov.ab.ca
Minister, Health & Wellness, Hon. Gene Zwozdesky
780-427-3665, Fax: 780-415-0961
Minister, Children & Youth Services, Hon. Yvonne Fritz
780-415-4890, Fax: 780-415-4859
Minister, Agriculture & Rural Development, Hon. Jack Hayden
780-427-2137, Fax: 780-422-6035
Minister, Infrastructure, Hon. Ray Danyluk
780-427-5041, Fax: 780-422-2002
Minister, Seniors & Community Supports, Hon. Mary Anne Jablonski
780-415-9550, Fax: 780-415-9411
Minister, Culture & Community Spirit, Hon. Lindsay Blackett
780-422-3559, Fax: 780-427-7729
Minister, Tourism, Parks & Recreation, Hon. Cindy Ady
780-427-4928, Fax: 780-427-0188
Minister, Municipal Affairs, Hon. Hector Goudreau
780-427-3744, Fax: 780-422-9550
Minister, Aboriginal Relations, Hon. Len Webber
780-422-4144, Fax: 780-644-8389
Minister, Housing & Urban Affairs, Hon. Jonathan Denis
780-644-8954, Fax: 780-644-8959
Minister, Employment & Immigration, Hon. Thomas Lukaszuk
780-415-4800, Fax: 780-422-9556
Minister, Finance & Enterprise, Hon. Ted Morton
780-427-8809, Fax: 780-427-5543

Executive Council Office
Deputy Minister; Secretary to Cabinet, Brian Manning
780-422-4910, Fax: 780-422-1882,brian.manning@gov.ab.ca
Deputy Secretary to the Cabinet, Dwight Dibben
780-420-2251, Fax: 780-422-1917
Deputy Chief, Policy Coordination, Roxanna Benoit
780-427-9229, Fax: 780-427-0305,roxanna.benoit@gov.ab.ca
Assistant Deputy Minister, Strategic Policy Coordination, Christine Couture
780-644-5286, Fax:
780-427-0305,christine.couture@gov.ab.ca
Director, Planning & Policy Coordination, Gary Braeuer
780-422-0561, Fax: 780-644-4682,gary.braeuer@gov.ab.ca
Chief, Protocol, Betty Anne Spinks
780-422-2236, Fax:
780-422-0786,bettyanne.spinks@gov.ab.ca
Deputy Chief, Protocol, Norm Davies
780-422-1845, Fax: 780-422-0786,norm.davies@gov.ab.ca
Managing Director, Public Affairs Bureau, Lee Funke
780-644-5655, Fax: 780-427-1010,lee.funke@gov.ab.ca

Cabinet Policy Committees
Community Services: Chair, Art Johnston, 780-415-9526; Economy: Chair, Kyle Fawcett, 780-427-7984; Health: Chair, Tony Vandermeer, 780-422-5468; Resources & the Environment: Chair, George VanderBurg, 780-415-9473

Legislative Assembly

Legislature Annex Bldg., 9718 - 107 St., Edmonton, AB T5K 1E4
780-427-2826, Fax: 780-427-1623,
laocommunications@assembly.ab.ca
www.assembly.ab.ca

Other Communication: Reference information:
library@assembly.ab.ca

The Legislative Assembly Office provides nonpartisan services to Members of the Legislative Assembly and the public.

Acts Administered:
Auditor General Act
Conflict of Interest Act
Election Act
Election Finances & Contributions Disclosure Act
Electoral Boundaries Commission Act
Electoral Divisions Act
Legislative Assembly Act
Ombudsman Act

Speaker,Hon. Ken Kowalski
780-427-2464, Fax:
780-422-9553,ken.kowalski@assembly.ab.ca
Clerk,Dr. David McNeil
780-427-2478, Fax:
780-427-5688,david.mcneil@assembly.ab.ca
Sergeant-at-Arms & Director, Visitor, Ceremonial and Security Services, Brian Hodgson
780-427-6048, Fax:
780-415-5829,brian.hodgson@assembly.ab.ca
Senior Financial Officer & Director, Financial Management & Administrative Services, Scott Ellis
780-427-1566, Fax:
780-415-1714,scott.ellis@assembly.ab.ca
Director, House Services, Louise Kamuchik
780-427-2480, Fax:
780-427-5688,louise.kamuchik@assembly.ab.ca
Director, Human Resources, Information Technology & Broadcast Services, Cheryl Scarlett
780-427-1368, Fax:
780-427-6436,cheryl.scarlett@assembly.ab.ca
Senior Parliamentary Counsel, Legal Services, Shannon Dean
780-427-1345, Fax:
780-427-0744,shannon.dean@assembly.ab.ca
Senior Parliamentary Counsel, Legal Services, Robert Reynolds, Q.C.
780-427-1346, Fax:
780-427-0744,rob.reynolds@assembly.ab.ca
Legislature Librarian, Valerie Footz
780-427-0202, Fax:
780-427-6016,val.footz@assembly.ab.ca
Managing Editor, Hansard, Liz Sim
780-427-1875, Fax: 780-427-1623,liz.sim@assembly.ab.ca

Alberta Wildrose Alliance Office
Legislature Annex, #502A, 9718 - 107 St., Edmonton, AB T5K 1E4
780-415-0975, Fax: 780-638-3506,
www.wildrosealliance.ca

Leader, Rob Anderson
780-415-0975, Fax:
780-638-3506,rob.anderson@assembly.ab.ca
Opposition Whip, Heather Forsyth
heather.forsyth@assembly.ab.ca

Government Members' Office
Legislature Bldg., #132, 10800 - 97 Ave., Edmonton, AB T5K 2B6
780-427-1198, Fax: 780-415-0968

Director, Caucus, Paul Bajcer
paul.bajcer@assembly.ab.ca

Official Opposition Caucus Office (Liberal Party)
Legislature Annex, 9718 - 107 St., 2nd Fl., Edmonton, AB T5K 1E4
780-427-2292, Fax: 780-427-3697,
liberal.communications@assembly.ab.ca
www.liberalopposition.com

Other Communication: Media contact information:
liberal.communications@assembly.ab.ca

Leader, David Swann
Chief of Staff, Rick Miller
780-427-1227, rick.miller@assembly.ab.ca
Director, Southern Alberta Liberal Caucus Office, Denis Lapointe
403-233-8250
Director, Communications, Neil Mackie
neil.mackie@assembly.ab.ca
Director, Research, Jann Lynn-George
jann.lynngeorge@assembly.ab.ca

New Democratic Party Caucus Office
#501, 9718 - 107 St., Edmonton, AB T5K 1E4
780-415-1800, Fax: 780-415-0701,
nd@assembly.ab.ca
www.ndpopposition.ab.ca

Leader, Brian Mason
brian.mason@assembly.ab.ca
Chief of Staff, Jim Gurnett
780-415-4634, jim.gurnett@assembly.ab.ca
Director, Communications, Brookes Merritt
780-644-8669, brookes.merritt@assembly.ab.ca
Director, Communications, Brookes Merritt
780-644-8669, brookes.merritt@assembly.ab.ca
Director, Research, Sarah Hoffman
780-415-2028, sarah.hoffman@assembly.ab.ca

Committees of the Legislative Assemby of Alberta
• Legislative Offices
780-415-9590 Fax: 780-422-0351
Other Communication: Leonard Mitzel, Chair
• Private Bills
780-415-8368 Fax: 780-422-1234
Other Communication: Dr. Neil Brown, Chair
• Privileges & Elections, Standing Orders & Printing
780-422-3353 Fax: 780-422-0351
Other Communication: Raymond Prins, Chair
• Public Accounts
780-427-2292 Fax: 780-427-3697
Other Communication: Hugh MacDonald, Chair
• Alberta Heritage Savings Trust Fund
780-415-0993 Fax: 780-427-1835
Other Communication: Janis Tarchuk, Chair
• Members' Services
780-427-2464 Fax: 780-422-9553
Other Communication: Hon. Ken Kowalski, Chair
• Community Services
780-415-6125 Fax: 780-415-0951
Other Communication: Arno Doerksen, Chair
• Health
780-427-0879 Fax: 780-422-0351
Other Communication: Barry McFarland, Chair
• Public Safety & Services
780-415-0107 Fax: 780-422-1671
Other Communication: Wayne Drysdale, Chair
• Resources & the Environment
780-422-3353 Fax: 780-422-0351
Other Communication: Raymond Prins, Chair
• Economy
780-644-3845 Fax: 780-422-1671
Other Communication: Naresh Bhardwaj, Chair

Twenty-seventh Legislature - Alberta

Legislature Bldg., 10800 - 97 Ave., Edmonton, AB T5K 2B6
780-427-2826, Fax: 780-427-1623,
laocommunications@assembly.ab.ca
www.assembly.ab.ca

Other Communication: Reference Information:
library@assembly.ab.ca

Last General Election, March 3, 2008. Maximum Duration, 5 Years. Party Standings: Progressive Conservative (PC) 72; Liberal (Lib.) 9; New Democrat (NDP) 2; Total 83. However, since the election, as of Sept./10, some members have crossed parties, leaving the standings as: PC 68; Lib. 8; NDP 2; Wildrose Allisance (WA) 3; Independent (I) 2. Salaries, Indemnities & Allowances: Effective April 1, 2010 - MLA indemnity $52,092, plus $24,046 MLA tax free allowance. In addition to this are the following indemnities & allowances: Premier $81,312; Ministers with portfolio $63,912; Ministers without portfolio $28,392; Leader of the Official Opposition $63,912; Speaker $61,140; Deputy Speaker $31,968; Chair of Committees $31,968;Deputy Chair of Committees $15,984; Leader of a recognized opposition party $28,392.

Members
Diana McQueen, Drayton Valley-Calmar T7, P
780-415-9496, 800-542-7307,Fax:
780-415-0951,draytonvalley.calmar@assembly.ab.ca
Hon. Cindy Ady, Calgary-Shaw AB, P
780-427-4928, Fax:
780-427-0188,calgary.shaw@assembly.ab.ca
Naresh Bhardwaj, Edmonton-Ellerslie AB, P
780-644-3845, Fax:
780-422-1671,edmonton.ellerslie@assembly.ab.ca
Moe Amery, Calgary-East AB, P
780-422-5382, Fax:
780-427-1835,calgary.east@assembly.ab.ca
Peter Sandhu, Edmonton-Manning AB, P
780-427-2729, Fax:
780-415-0951,edmonton.manning@assembly.ab.ca
Laurie Blakeman, Edmonton-Centre AB, Liberal
780-427-2292, Fax:
780-427-3697,edmonton.centre@assembly.ab.ca
Janice Sarich, Edmonton-Decore AB, P
780-415-9462, Fax:
780-415-0951,edmonton.decore@assembly.ab.ca
Hon. Guy Boutilier, Fort McMurray-WoodBuffalo AB, Independent
780-427-1865, Fax:
780-638-3277,fortmcmurray.woodbuffalo@assembly.ab.ca, Other Communications: gboutilier@assembly.ab.ca
Dr. Neil Brown, Q.C., Calgary-Nose Hill AB, P
780-415-8368, Fax:
780-427-1234,calgary.nosehill@assembly.ab.ca
Pearl Calahasen, Lesser Slave Lake AB, P
780-427-5285, 866-625-0648,Fax:
780-415-0951,lesser.slavelake@assembly.ab.ca
Wayne Cao, Calgary-Fort AB, P
780-415-0984, Fax:
780-427-1835,calgary.fort@assembly.ab.ca
Jeff Johnson, Athabasca-Redwater AB, P
780-422-0057, Fax:
780-422-0951,athabasca.redwater@assembly.ab.ca
Kent Hehr, Calgary-Buffalo AB, Liberal
780-427-2292, Fax:
780-427-3697,calgary.buffalo@assembly.ab.ca
Harry B. Chase, Calgary-Varsity AB, Liberal
780-427-2292, Fax:
780-427-3697,calgary.varsity@assembly.ab.ca
Hon. Alison Redford, Calgary-Elbow AB, P
780-427-2339, Fax:
780-422-6621,calgary.elbow@assembly.ab.ca
Evan Berger, Livingstone-Macleod AB, P
780-427-3001, 800-565-0962,Fax:
780-415-0951,livingstone.macleod@assembly.ab.ca
Hon. Ray Danyluk, Lac La Biche-St. Paul AB, P
780-427-5041, 866-674-6999,Fax:
780-422-2002,laclabiche.stpaul@assembly.ab.ca
Alana DeLong, Calgary-Bow AB, P
780-415-9459, Fax:
780-427-1835,calgary.bow@assembly.ab.ca
Cal Dallas, Red Deer-South AB, P
780-415-8673, Fax:
780-422-1671,reddeer.south@assembly.ab.ca
Genia Leskiw, Bonnyville-Cold Lake AB, P
780-415-0995, Fax:
780-415-0951,bonnyville.coldlake@assembly.ab.ca
Greg Weadick, Lethbridge-West AB, P
780-427-5157, Fax:
780-422-1671,lethbridge.west@assembly.ab.ca
Doug Elniski, Edmonton-Calder AB, P
780-427-0858, Fax:
780-415-0951,edmonton.calder@assembly.ab.ca
David H. Xiao, Edmonton-McClung AB, P
780-422-1992, Fax:
780-415-0951,edmonton.mcclung@assembly.ab.ca
Hon. Iris Evans, Sherwood Park AB, P
780-427-2585, Fax:
780-422-9023,sherwood.park@assembly.ab.ca
Ken Allred, St. Albert AB, P
780-427-1148, Fax: 780-415-0951,st.albert@assembly.ab.ca
Heather Forsyth, Calgary-Fish Creek AB, WA
780-415-0058, Fax:
780-638-3506,calgary.fishcreek@assembly.ab.ca
Hon. Yvonne Fritz, Calgary-Cross AB, P
780-415-4890, Fax:
780-415-4859,calgary.cross@assembly.ab.ca
Hon. Hector Goudreau, Dunvegan-Central Peace AB, P
780-427-3744, 866-835-4988,Fax:
780-422-9550,dunvegan.centralpeace@assembly.ab.ca
Wayne Drysdale, Grande Prairie-Wapiti AB, P
780-415-0107, Fax:
780-427-1671,grandeprairie.wapiti@assembly.ab.ca
Doug Griffiths, Battle River-Wainwright AB, P
780-422-5369, Fax:
780-422-0351,battleriver.wainwright@assembly.ab.ca
Hon. George Groeneveld, Highwood AB, P
780-422-7199, Fax:
780-427-1835,highwood@assembly.ab.ca, Other Communications: george.groeneveld@assembly.ab.ca
Rob Anderson, Airdrie-Chestermere AB, WA
780-415-0975, 888-948-8741,Fax:
780-368-3506,airdrie.chestermere@assembly.ab.ca
Hon. Dave Hancock, Edmonton-Whitemud AB, P
780-427-5010, Fax:
780-427-5018,edmonton.whitemud@assembly.ab.ca
Hon. Jack Hayden, Drumheller-Stettler AB, P
780-427-2137, Fax:
780-422-6035,drumheller.stettler@assembly.ab.ca
Jonathan Denis, Calgary-Egmont AB, P
780-644-8954, Fax:
780-644-8959,calgary.egmont@assembly.ab.ca
Broyce Jacobs, Cardston-Taber-Warner AB, P
780-422-0685, Fax:
780-427-1835,cardston.taberwarner@assembly.ab.ca
Hon. Doug Horner, Spruce Grove-Sturgeon-St. Albert AB, P
780-427-2025, Fax:
780-427-5582,sprucegrovesturgeon.stalbert@assembly.ab.ca
Hon. Mary Anne Jablonski, Red Deer-North AB, P
780-415-9550, Fax:
780-415-9411,reddeer.north@assembly.ab.ca
Verlyn Olson, Wetaskiwin-Camrose AB, P
780-415-0977, Fax:
780-422-1671,wetaskiwin.camrose@assembly.ab.ca
Art Johnston, Calgary-Hays AB, P
780-415-9526, Fax:
780-427-1234,calgary.hays@assembly.ab.ca
Hon. Mel Knight, Grande Prairie-Smoky AB, P
780-415-4815, Fax:
780-415-4818,grandeprairie.smoky@assembly.ab.ca
Hon. Ken Kowalski, Barrhead-Morinville-Westlock AB, P
780-427-2464, Fax:
780-427-9553,barrheadmorinvillewestlock@assembly.ab.ca
Hon. Ronald Liepert, Calgary-West AB, P
780-427-3740, Fax:
780-422-0195,calgary.west@assembly.ab.ca
Hon. Fred Lindsay, Stony Plain AB, P
780-422-2140, Fax:
780-427-1835,stony.plain@assembly.ab.ca
Dave Quest, Strathcona AB, P
780-415-0990, Fax:
780-422-0351,strathcona@assembly.ab.ca
Thomas Lukaszuk, Edmonton-Castle Downs AB, P
780-415-4800, Fax:
780-422-9556,edmonton.castledowns@assembly.ab.ca
Ty Lund, Rocky Mountain House AB, P
780-422-5012, Fax:
780-427-1835,rocky.mountainhouse@assembly.ab.ca
Hugh MacDonald, Edmonton-Gold Bar AB, Liberal
780-427-2292, Fax:
780-427-3697,edmonton.goldbar@assembly.ab.ca, Other Communications: hugh.macdonald@assembly.ab.ca
Kyle Fawcett, Calgary-North Hill AB, P
780-427-7984, Fax:
780-427-5441,calgary.northhill@assembly.ab.ca
Teresa Woo-Paw, Calgary-Mackay AB, P
780-415-9479, Fax:
780-415-0951,calgary.mackay@assembly.ab.ca
Tony Vandermeer, Edmonton-Beverly-Clareview AB, P
780-422-5468, Fax:
780-427-4974,edmonton.beverlyclareview@assembly.ab.ca,
Richard Marz, Olds-Didsbury-Three Hills AB, P
780-415-0994, Fax:
780-415-0951,oldsdidsbury.threehills@assembly.ab.ca
Brian Mason, Edmonton-Highlands-Norwood AB, New Democratic Party
780-415-1800, Fax:
780-415-0701,edmonton.highlandsnorwood@assembly.ab.ca
Carl Benito, Edmonton-Mill Woods AB, P
780-422-9299, Fax:
780-422-1671,edmonton.millwoods@assembly.ab.ca
Barry McFarland, Little Bow AB, P
780-427-0879, 800-563-0917,Fax:
780-422-0351,little.bow@assembly.ab.ca
Hon. Lindsay Blackett, Calgary-North West AB, P
780-422-3559, Fax:
780-427-7729,calgary.northwest@assembly.ab.ca
Hon. Heather Klimchuk, Edmonton-Glenora AB, P
780-422-6880, Fax:
780-422-2496,edmonton.glenora@assembly.ab.ca
Fred Horne, Edmonton-Rutherford AB, P
780-427-2235, Fax:
780-422-1671,edmonton.rutherford@assembly.ab.ca
Leonard Mitzel, Cypress-Medicine Hat AB, P
780-415-9590, Fax:
780-422-0351,cypress.medicinehat@assembly.ab.ca

Hon. Ted Morton, Foothills-Rockyview AB, P
780-427-8809, 866-843-4314,Fax:
780-427-5543,foothills.rockyview@assembly.ab.ca
Arno Doerksen, Strathmore-Brooks AB, P
780-415-6125, Fax:
780-415-0951,strathmore.brooks@assembly.ab.ca
Hon. Frank Oberle, Peace River AB, P
780-415-9406, Fax:
780-415-9566,peace.river@assembly.ab.ca
Hon. Luke Ouellette, Innisfail-Sylvan Lake AB, P
780-427-2080, Fax:
780-422-2722,innisfail.sylvanlake@assembly.ab.ca
Rachel Notley, Edmonton-Strathcona AB, New Democratic Party
780-415-1800, Fax:
780-415-0701,edmonton.strathcona@assembly.ab.ca
Bridget A. Pastoor, Lethbridge-East AB, Liberal
780-427-2292, Fax:
780-427-3697,lethbridge.east@assembly.ab.ca
Manmeet Singh Bhullar, Calgary-Montrose AB, P
780-427-2877, Fax:
780-415-0951,calgary.montrose@assembly.ab.ca
Raymond Prins, Lacombe-Pomoka AB, P
780-422-3353, 800-565-6432,Fax:
780-422-0351,lacombe.ponoka@assembly.ab.ca
Hon. Rob Renner, Medicine Hat AB, P
780-427-2391, Fax:
780-422-6259,medicine.hat@assembly.ab.ca, Other Communications: rob.renner@assembly.ab.ca
Dave Rodney, Calgary-Lougheed AB, P
780-415-1325, Fax:
780-422-1671,calgary.lougheed@assembly.ab.ca
George Rogers, Leduc-Beaumont-Devon AB, P
780-422-2229, Fax:
780-422-0351,leduc.beaumontdevon@assembly.ab.ca
Darshan Kang, Calgary-McCall AB, Liberal
780-427-2292, Fax:
780-427-3697,calgary.mccall@assembly.ab.ca
Hon. Lloyd Snelgrove, Vermillion-Lloydminster AB, P
780-415-4855, 800-567-7644,Fax:
780-415-4853,vermilion.lloydminster@assembly.ab.ca
Premier Ed Stelmach, Fort Saskatchewan-Vegreville AB, P
780-427-2251, Fax:
780-427-1349,fortsaskatchewan.vegreville@assembly.ab.ca
Paul Hinman, Calgary-Glenmore AB, WA
780-638-3504, Fax:
780-638-3506,calgary.glenmore@assembly.ab.ca
Mr. Robin Campbell, West Yellowhead AB, P
780-427-1879, 800-661-6517,Fax:
780-415-0968,west.yellowhead@assembly.ab.ca
Dr. David Swann, Calgary-Mountain View AB, Liberal
780-427-2292, Fax:
780-427-3697,calgary.mountainview@assembly.ab.ca
Dr. Kevin Taft, Edmonton-Riverview AB, Liberal
780-427-2292, Fax:
780-427-3697,edmonton.riverview@assembly.ab.ca
Hon. Janis Tarchuk, Banff-Cochrane AB, P
780-415-0993, 866-760-8281,Fax:
780-427-1835,banff.cochrane@assembly.ab.ca
Dave Taylor, Calgary-Currie AB, Independent
780-427-2298, Fax:
403-638-3958,calgary.currie@assembly.ab.ca
Dr. Raj Sherman, Edmonton-Meadowlark AB, P
780-415-0976, Fax:
780-422-1671,edmonton.meadowlark@assembly.ab.ca
George VanderBurg, Whitecourt-Ste. Anne AB, P
780-415-9473, 800-786-7136,Fax:
780-427-5441,whitecourt.steanne@assembly.ab.ca
Hon. Len Webber, Calgary-Foothills AB, P
780-422-4144, Fax:
780-644-8389,calgary.foothills@assembly.ab.ca
Hon. Gene Zwozdesky, Edmonton-Mill Creek AB, P
780-427-3665, Fax:
780-415-0961,edmonton.millcreek@assembly.ab.ca

Alberta Government Departments & Agencies

Alberta Advanced Education & Technology

Legislature Bldg., #324, 10800 - 97 Ave., Edmonton, AB T5K 2B6

780-422-5400, Fax: 780-422-1263,-310-0000
aet.info@gov.ab.ca
www.advancededandtech.gov.ab.ca

In 2006-2007, the Ministry of Advanced Education & Technology was created to combine the responsibilities of the ministries of Advanced Education & Innovation & Science. The mission of the Ministry of Advanced Education & Technology is to assist Alberta to be a learning & innovative society. The goals of the ministry are to ensure that advanced learning is a lifelong pursuit that is accessible & affordable to Albertans. The province's advanced learning & innovation system continues work to respect a diversity of communities, learner aspirations & abilities. In order to ensure an adaptable learning system & to create value through innovation, partnerships, coalitions & networks are sought & built. Investments in Alberta's advanced learning system & innovation framework focus upon sustainability. The aim is for the province's advanced learning system's research, technology & knowledge transfer to be competitive & to achieve global excellence.

Acts Administered:
Access to the Future Act
Alberta Enterprise Corporation Act
Alberta Research & Innovation Act
Apprenticeship & Industry Training Act
Post-secondary Learning Act (PSLA)
Private Vocational Training Act
Student Support Legislation (various)
Advanced Education & Technology Grants Regulation

Minister,Hon. Doug Horner
780-427-2025, Fax: 780-427-5582
Deputy Minister, Annette Trimbee
780-415-4744, Fax:
780-422-1801,annette.trimbee@gov.ab.ca
Executive Director & Senior Financial Officer, Corporate Services, Blake Bartlett
780-427-1897, Fax: 780-415-9823,blake.bartlett@gov.ab.ca
Director, Communications, Kim Capstick
780-422-1562, Fax: 780-427-0821,kim.capstick@gov.ab.ca
Director, Human Resources, Dianna Wilk
780-422-5324, Fax: 780-427-3316,dianna.wilk@gov.ab.ca

• Alberta Agricultural Research Institute(AARI)
Phipps-McKinnon Bldg.
#500, 10020 - 101A Ave.
Edmonton, AB T5J 3G2
780-427-1956 Fax: 780-427-3252
aarimail@gov.ab.ca
www.aari.ab.ca
The Alberta Agricultural Research Institute (AARI) is the primary agency in Alberta for funding, coordinating & promoting strategic agricultural initiatives in research, development & technology transfer of the agriculture & agri-food sector. Its mission is to enhance the economic contributions of the Alberta agricultural & food industry through support for research, development & technology transfer, with a strategic emphasis on life sciences. This institute falls under the Alberta Innovates - Bio Solutions banner: www.albertainnovates.ca/bio.

• Alberta Prion Research Institute(APRI)
Scotia Place, Tower 2
#2001, 10060 Jasper Ave.
Edmonton, AB T5J 3R8
780-638-3790 Fax: 780-643-1432
www.prioninstitute.ca
APRI was established in response to the devastion that BSE brought to the province's beef industry in 2003. The institute is a research hub to challenge the economic and social threat posed by BSE and other prion-related diseases. In 2010, APRI became part of Alberta Innovates - Bio Solutions, an umbrella corporation that supports the growth and development of Alberta's agricultural, forestry and associated industries: www.albertainnovates.ca/bio.

• Alberta Innovates - Health Solutions
#1500, 10104 - 103 Ave
Edmonton, AB T5J 4A7
780-423-5727 Fax: 780-429-3509 877-423-5727
health@albertainnovates.ca
www.albertainnovates.ca/health

• Alberta Science & Research Authority(ASRA)
Phipps-McKinnon Bldg.
#500, 10020 - 101A Ave.
Edmonton, AB T5J 3G2
780-427-1488 Fax: 780-427-0979
asra@gov.ab.ca
www.asra.gov.ab.ca
Created in 1994, the Alberta Science & Research Authority (ASRA) is an independent board of members from Alberta's academic, business & research communities, appointed by provincial Cabinet.ASRA functions as the senior science & research body of the Government.It works collaboratively with government departments & agencies & stakeholders to stimulate & develop research & related scientific activities, policies & priorities compatible with economic & social priorities of the government.ASRA conducts annual reviews & evaluations of government science & research policies, priorities & programs, promotes communication on matters related to science & research & encourages Alberta's science & research sector to attain international competitiveness & recognition. In Jan., 2010, ASRA was placed under the umbrella of Alberta Innovates - Alberta Research and Innovation Authority: www.albertainnovates.ca/research.

• Informatics Circle of Research Excellence(iCORE)
3608 - 33 St. NW
Calgary, AB T2L 2A6
780-450-5111 Fax: 403-210-5337
techfutures@albertainnovates.ca
www.icore.ca
iCORE operates grant programs to develop chairs at Alberta universities. It invests in research scientists who work on fundamental and applied problems in informatics, in areas such as computer science, electrical and computer engineering, physics, mathematics and other disciplines related to information and communications technology (ICT). iCORE has been placed under the umbrella of Alberta Innovates - Technology Futures, a research and innovation system that helps technical industries find solutions, develop products and move technologies to market, building on Alberta's platform technologies, like nanotechnology, information communications technologies, and genomics: www.albertainnovates.ca/technology.

• Alberta Learning Information Service(ALIS)
City Centre
10242 - 105 St.
Edmonton, AB T5J 3L5
780-427-9674-310-0000
info@alis.gov.ab.ca
www.alis.gov.ab.ca
Other Communication: Alberta Career Information Hotline: 780-422-4266; Toll Free: 1-800-661-3753
ALIS is the provincial gateway in Alberta for career, learning & employment information & services. The service is a provincial government partnership between the Alberta Employment, Immigration and Industry, Alberta Education, & Alberta Advanced Education & Technology.

• Alberta Council on Admissions & Transfer(ACAT)
Commerce Place
10155 - 102 St., 11th Fl.
Edmonton, AB T5J 4L5
780-422-9021 Fax: 780-422-3688 800-232-7215TDD: 780-427-9999
acat@gov.ab.ca
www.acat.gov.ab.ca
ACAT serves as an independent body through which stakeholders work co-operatively to ensure effective transferability of courses & programs, national and international, for the benefit of students. It develops policies, guidelines, and procedures to facilitate transfer agreements among post-secondary institutions.

• Campus Alberta Quality Council
Commerce Place
10155 - 102 St., 11th Fl.
Edmonton, AB T5J 4L5
780-427-8921 Fax: 780-427-0423
caqc@gov.ab.ca
www.caqc.gov.ab.ca
The Campus Alberta Quality Council makes recommendations to the Minister of Advanced Education & Technology on applications from post-secondary institutions that want to offer new degree programs in the province.

• Alberta Apprenticeship & Industry Training Board
South Tower
10030 - 107 St., 7th Fl.
Edmonton, AB T5J 4X7
780-427-8517 Fax: 780-422-3734 800-232-7215TDD: 780-427-9999

• Private Vocational Schools Advisory Council
Commerce Place
10155 - 102 St., 10th Fl.
Edmonton, AB T5J 4L5
780-427-5609 Fax: 780-427-5920
Established in July 2006, this is a 9-member council appointed to provide strategic advice and recommendations to the Minister of Advanced Education and Technology, regarding the objectives, operation and reporting of the Access to the Future Fund, a reserve that is targeted to reach $3 billion and which serves to enhance and expand accessible, affordable and high quality learning opportunities for Albertans.

Research & Innovation Division

Phipps-McKinnon Bldg., 10020 - 101A Ave., 5th Fl., Edmonton, AB T5J 3G2

780-427-1488, Fax: 780-427-0979

Some of the branches, units & services include: Cross Ministry Initiatives; Innovation Planning & Accountability (Reporting & Accountability, Research Capacity Planning, Strategic Integration); Alberta Research & Innovation Authority - ARIA; Innovation Policy; Alberta Innovates (Bio Solutions, Energy & Environment Solutions, Health Solutions, Technology Futures).
Assistant Deputy Minister,Dr. Ronald Dyck
780-427-4497, Fax: 780-427-0979,ron.dyck@gov.ab.ca
Executive Director, Cross Ministry Initiatives, Daphne Cheel
780-422-0054, Fax: 780-427-3252,daphne.cheel@gov.ab.ca
Executive Director, Innovation Planning & Accountability, Michele Kirchner
780-427-5634, michele.kirchner@gov.ab.ca

Executive Director, Alberta Research & Innovation Authority, Lee Kruszewski
780-638-3795, Fax: 780-427-0979,lee.kruszewski@gov.ab.ca
Director, Innovation Policy, Sandra Duxbury
780-427-4498, Fax:
780-415-9823,sandra.duxbury@gov.ab.ca

Advanced Technology Industries Division
Phipps-McKinnon Bldg., 10020 - 101A Ave., 5th Fl., Edmonton, AB T5J 3G2
Branches, units & services in this division include: Emerging Technology Industries; Information & Technology Management (Client Service Delivery, External Client Liaison, Information & Applicatin Services, Strategic Technology Planning); Innovation Client Services; Technology Industry Development (Business Development, ICT Industries, Strategic Iniatives, Life Sciences Industries).
Assistant Deputy Minister, Mel Wong
780-427-2084, Fax: 780-427-5924,mel.wong@gov.ab.ca
Executive Director & CIO, Information and Technology Management Section, Leslie Sim-Kaiser
780-415-0813, Fax:
780-422-0880,leslie.sim-kaiser@gov.ab.ca
Executive Director, Technology Industry Development Section, Robert Lai
780-427-7722, Fax: 780-427-5924,robert.lai@gov.ab.ca
Branch Head, Emerging Technology Industries Branch, Ken Langhorn
780-415-8751, Fax: 780-427-5924,ken.langhorn@gov.ab.ca
Branch Head, Life Sciences Industries Branch, Brad Guthrie
780-427-6618, Fax: 780-427-5924,brad.guthrie@gov.ab.ca

Post Secondary Excellence Division
Commerce Place, 7th Fl., 10155 - 102 St., Edmonton, AB T5J 4L5
Some of the branches, units and services included in this division are: Campus Alberta Partnerships (Alberta Council on Admissions and Transfer - ACAT, Community Partnerships and Literacy, Inspiring Excellence, International Education); Investments and Quality (Campus Alberta Quality Council, Financial Planning, Post-Secondary Planning and Investment, Post-Secondary Programs, Private Vocational Training); System Capacity and Development (Business Integration & Consultation, Policy Development and Intergovernmental, Policy Research and Analysis, Business Operations & Reporting)
Assistant Deputy Minister, Connie Harrison
780-427-5607, Fax:
780-427-9430,connie.harrison@gov.ab.ca,
Acting Executive Director, Campus Alberta Partnerships, Dan Rizzoli
780-415-2966, Fax: 780-427-4185,dan.rizzoli@gov.ab.ca
Executive Director, Investments & Quality, Gerry Waisman
780-427-9667, Fax: 780-427-4185,gerry.waisman@gov.ab.ca
Executive Director, System Capacity & Development, Bruce McDonald
780-427-9635, Fax:
780-427-0266,bruce.mcdonald@gov.ab.ca
Director, Connie Harrison
780-415-9667, Fax:
780-415-8872,connie.harrison@gov.ab.ca
Director, Business Policy & Analysis, Bruce McDonald
780-427-9635, Fax:
780-422-3688,bruce.mcdonald@gov.ab.ca
Executive Director, Archie Clark
780-422-1347, archie.clark@gov.ab.ca
Director, Private Institutions, Jean Sprague
780-427-5609, Fax: 780-427-5920,jean.sprague@gov.ab.ca
Director, Institutional Planning & Coordination, Robert Lee
780-722-1209, Fax: 780-422-3688,robert.lee@gov.ab.ca
Executive Director, Gerry Waisman
780-422-4498, gerry.waisman@gov.ab.ca
Director, Learner Funding, Schubert Kwan
780-422-1208, schubert.kwan@gov.ab.ca
Director, Learner Services, Janice Park
780-427-9697, janice.park@gov.ab.ca

Community, Learner & Industry Connections Division
Phipps-McKinnon Bldg., 5th Fl., 10020 - 101A Ave., Edmonton, AB T5J 3G2
780-427-8517
Some of the branches, units and services offered are: Apprenticeship & Industry Training (International & Provincial Assessment Services, Technical Solutions & Support, Apprenticeship Technical Training & Certification); Learner Funding (Loans Administration, Assessing & Processing); Financial Operations & Control Services (Program & Awards Support, Program Compliance & Investigations); Program, Policy & Systems Support (Policy & Planning, Business & Systems Support, Program Services & Delivery, Student Funding Contact Centre).
Assistant Deputy Minister, Shirley Dul
780-422-1185, Fax: 780-422-2420,shirley.dul@gov.ab.ca
Executive Director, Apprenticeship & Industry Training, Darlene Bouwsema
780-643-1466, Fax:
780-422-7376,darlene.bouwsema@gov.ab.ca
Director, International & Provincial Assessment Services, Olie Schell
780-427-5770, Fax: 780-422-7376,olie.schell@gov.ab.ca
Director, Apprenticeship Policy & Legislation, Susan Johnston
780-422-1183, Fax:
780-422-2420,susan.johnston@gov.ab.ca
Director, Board Planning & Support, Carla Corbett
780-422-1193, Fax: 780-422-7376,carla.corbett@gov.ab.ca
Director, Apprenticeship Technical Training & Certification, James Tyler
780-638-3329, Fax: 780-422-7376,tyler.james@gov.ab.ca
Director, Learner Assistance, Schubert Kwan
780-422-4498, Fax: 780-422-4517,schubert.kwan@gov.ab.ca
Director, Technical Solutions & Support, Richard Wosnack
780-427-6976, Fax: 780-422-7376

Alberta Aboriginal Relations

Commerce Place, 19th Fl., 10155 - 102 St., Edmonton, AB T5J 4G8
780-422-4144, Fax: 780-644-8389,
www.aboriginal.alberta.ca
Alberta Aboriginal Relations works with Aboriginal communities and other partners to enhance social and economic opportunities for Aboriginal people in Alberta.
Acts Administered:
Constitution of Alberta Amendment Act, 1990
Metis Settlements Accord Implementation Act
Metis Settlements Amendment Act, 2004
Metis Settlements Act
Metis Settlements Land Protection Act
Minister,Hon. Len Webber
780-422-4144, Fax: 780-644-8389
Deputy Minister, Maria David-Evans
780-415-0900, Fax:
780-415-6144,maria.david-evans@gov.ab.ca
Assistant Deputy Minister, First Nations and Métis Relations, Donavon Young
780-422-5925, Fax:
780-427-4019,donavon.young@gov.ab.ca
Assistant Deputy Minister, Consultation and Land Claims, Stan Rutwind
780-643-1731, Fax: 780-427-0401,stan.rutwind@gov.ab.ca
Assistant Deputy Minister, Corporate Services, Lorne Harvey
780-422-2429, Fax: 780-427-0939,lorne.harvey@gov.ab.ca
Executive Director, Policy and Planning, Cameron Henry
780-427-2008, Fax:
780-427-1760,cameron.henry@gov.ab.ca
• Métis Settlements Appeal Tribunal
14605 - 134 St.
Edmonton, AB T5L 4S9
780-422-1541 Fax: 780-422-0019 800-661-8864
www.msat.gov.ab.ca
Quasi-judicial body set up to hear evidence & make decisions to settle disputes about membership, land dealings, surface rights & any other matters where the parties involved agree to let the Tribunal resolve the issue.

First Nations & Métis Relations
Commerce Place, 10155 - 102 St., 13th Fl., Edmonton, AB T5J 4G8
780-422-9526, Fax: 780-427-4019
Assistant Deputy Minister, Donavon Young
780-422-5925, Fax:
780-427-4019,donavon.young@gov.ab.ca
Executive Director, Métis Relations, Thomas Droege
780-427-9431, Fax:
780-427-1760,thomas.droege@gov.ab.ca
Director, First Nations Relations, Cynthia Dunnigan
780-415-6141, Fax:
780-427-4019,cynthia.dunnigan@gov.ab.ca
Director, Aboriginal Justice Initiatives, Aboriginal Community Initiatives, Bronwyn Shoush
780-427-3060, Fax:
780-227-1760,bronwyn.shoush@gov.ab.ca
Acting Director, Aboriginal Economic Partnerships, Lanny Der
780-644-1057, Fax: 780-427-1760,lanny.der@gov.ab.ca
Director, First Nations Development Fund, Peter Crossen
780-415-6142, Fax: 780-427-0401,peter.crossen@gov.ab.ca
Director, Land Claims, Steven Andres
780-427-6084, Fax: 780-427-0401,steven.andres@gov.ab.ca
Registrar, Métis Settlements Land Registry, Lisa Chartrand
780-415-0168, Fax: 780-427-3656,lisa.chartrand@gov.ab.ca

Métis Settlements Ombudsman Office
#203, 10525 - 170 St., Edmonton, AB T5P 4W2
780-427-9828, Fax: 780-427-9962, 866-427-6813
Ombudsman, John Brosseau
780-427-9463, Fax: 780-427-9962,john.brosseau@gov.ab.ca

Alberta Agriculture & Rural Development

J.G. O'Donoghue Bldg., 7000 - 113 St., 1st Fl., Edmonton, AB T6H 5T6
780-427-2727, Fax: 780-427-2861, 866-882-7677
www.agric.gov.ab.ca

Other Communication: Publications Office: 780/427-0391, Toll Free: 1-800-292-5697
The Ministry of Agriculture & Food provides a variety of services to Alberta's agricultural industry. Programs are aimed towards farmers & production, & to ag & food processing industries.
Acts Administered:
Agricultural Operations Practices Act
Agricultural Pests Act
Agricultural Service Board Act
Agricultural Societies Act
Agriculture Financial Services Act
Alberta Wheat and Barley Test Market Act
Animal Health Act
Animal Keepers Act
Animal Protection Act
Bee Act
Brand Act
Crop Liens Priorities Act
Crop Payments Act
Dairy Industry Act
Farm Implement Act
Farm Implement Dealerships Act
Federal-Provincial Farm Assistance Act
Feeder Associations Guarantee Act
Fuel Tax Act
Fur Farms Act
Gas Distribution Act
Government Accountability Act
Government Organization Act, Sched 2
Heating Oil & Propane Rebate Act
Irrigation Districts Act
Line Fence Act
Livestock Diseases Act
Livestock Identification and Brand Inspection Act
Livestock Identification and Commerce Act
Livestock Industry Diversification Act
Livestock and Livestock Products Act
Marketing of Agricultural Products Act
Meat Inspection Act
Rural Electrification Loan Act
Rural Electrification Long-term Financing Act
Rural Utilities Act
Soil Conservation Act
St. Mary and Milk Rivers Water Agreements (Termination) Act
Stray Animals Act
Weed Control Act
Wheat Board Money Trust Act
Women's Institute Act
Minister,Hon. Jack Hayden
780-427-2137, Fax: 780-422-6035
Deputy Minister, John Knapp
780-427-2145, Fax: 780-415-6002,john.knapp@gov.ab.ca
Executive Director, Human Resource Services & Facilities Management Services, Heather K.M. Behman
780-427-2430, Fax:
780-427-3398,heather.behman@gov.ab.ca
Director, Communications Branch, Cathy Housdorff
780-422-7683, Fax:
780-427-2861,cathy.housdorff@gov.ab.ca
Senior Financial Officer, Financial & Business Planning Services Division, Jim Carter
780-427-2162, Fax: 780-422-6529
• Agriculture Financial Services Corporation(AFSC)
5718 - 56 Ave.
Lacombe, AB T4L 1B1
403-782-8200 Fax: 403-782-4226 800-396-0215
www.afsc.ca
The provincial crown corporation provides farmers, agribusinesses, & other small businesses loans, crop insurance, & farm income disaster assistance.
• Alberta Grain Commission
7000 - 113 St., 3rd Fl.
Edmonton, AB T6H 5T6
780-427-7329 Fax: 780-422-9690
www1.agric.gov.ab.ca/$department/deptdocs.nsf/all/agc2620
• Farmers' Advocate of Alberta
7000 - 113 St., 3rd Fl.
Edmonton, AB T6H 5T6
780-427-2433 Fax: 780-427-3913
farmers.advocate@gov.ab.ca

• Irrigation Council
Provincial Bldg.
200 - 5 Ave. South, 3rd Fl., PO Bag 3014
Lethbridge, AB T1J 4L1
403-381-5176 Fax: 403-382-4406
• Alberta Livestock & Meat Agency(ALMA)
Ellwood Office Park South
1003 Ellwood Rd. SW
Edmonton, AB T6X 0B3
780-638-1699 Fax: 780-638-6496
info@almaltd.ca
www.alma.alberta.ca
• Alberta Centre for Livestock Genomics
College Plaza
8215 - 112 St., 14th Fl.
Edmonton, AB T6G 2C8
780-427-2442 Fax: 780-428-1900

Industry Development & Food Safety Sector
JG O'Donoghue, 7000 - 113 Street, 3rd fl., Edmonton, AB T6H 5T6

Asst. Deputy Minister, Jason Krips
780-427-2439, Fax: 780-422-6317,jason.krips@gov.ab.ca
Executive Director, Food Safety & Animal Health Division, Greg Orriss
780-427-6159, Fax: 780-427-1437,greg.orriss@gov.ab.ca
Branch Head, Animal Health Branch, Ken Manninen
780-422-0808, Fax: 780-427-1437,ken.manninen@gov.ab.ca
Branch Head, Agri-Food Laboratories Branch,Dr. Ole Sorensen
780-427-8307, Fax: 780-415-4527,ole.sorensen@gov.ab.ca
Chief Provincial Veterinarian, Office of the Chief Provincial Veterinarian,Dr. Gerald Hauer
780-415-9503, Fax: 780-415-0810,gerald.hauer@gov.ab.ca
Program Administrator, Safe Food Branch, Sandra Clarke
780-422-4744, Fax: 780-427-1437,sandra.clarke@gov.ab.ca
Director, Agriculture Research Division,vacant
780-427-5341, Fax: 780-427-1057,crystal.moore@gov.ab.ca
Branch Head, Feed Crops Branch, John Brown
403-782-8033, Fax: 403-782-5514,john.brown@gov.ab.ca
Centre Administrator, Field Crop Development Centre, Elaine Lacroix
403-782-8020, Fax: 403-782-5514,elaine.lacroix@gov.ab.ca
Acting Branch Head, Food & Bio-Industrial Crops Branch, Kirsty Piquette
780-644-2410, Fax: 780-638-3586,kirsty.piquette@gov.ab.ca
Centre Administrator, Crop Diversification Centre, Anna Moeller
403-362-1302, Fax: 403-362-1306,anna.moeller@gov.ab.ca
Branch Head, Pest Surveillance Branch, Paul Laflamme
780-422-4911, Fax: 780-427-1057,paul.laflamme@gov.ab.ca
Provincial Apiculturist, Pest Surveillance Branch, Medhat Nasr
780-415-2314, Fax: 780-422-6096,medhat.nasr@gov.ab.ca
Branch Head, Livestock Research Branch, Wesley Johnson
780-415-0828, Fax:
780-427-1057,wesley.johnson@gov.ab.ca
Director, Food Processing Division, Ken Gossen
780-980-4860, Fax: 780-986-5138,ken.gossen@gov.ab.ca
Senior Programs Manager, Food Processing Development Centre, Programs Branch, Karen Erin
780-980-4864, Fax: 780-986-5138,karen.erin@gov.ab.ca
Senior Operations Manager, Operations Branch, Robert Gibson
780-980-4866, Fax: 780-980-4250,robert.gibson@gov.ab.ca
Director, Bio-Industrial Technologies Division, Connie Phillips
780-644-8124, Fax: 780-638-3586,connie.phillips@gov.ab.ca
Branch Head, Bio-Industrial Technology Branch, Hong Qi
780-644-8128, Fax: 780-638-3586,hong.qi@gov.ab.ca
Branch Head, Bio-Industrial Development Branch, Kirsty Piquette
780-644-2410, Fax: 780-638-3586,kirsty.piquette.ab.ca
Director, Rural Extension & Industry Development Division, Jo-Ann Hall
780-968-3512, Fax: 780-963-4709,jo-ann.hall@gov.ab.ca
Acting Branch Head, Local/Domestic Market Expansion Branch, Shauna Johnston
780-968-3553, Fax:
780-968-3554,shauna.johnston@gov.ab.ca
Branch Head, Alberta Ag-Info Centre, Ross Hutchison
403-742-7542, Fax: 403-742-7527,ross.hutchison@gov.ab.ca
Branch Head, Processing Industry Business Development Branch, Lynn Stegman
403-340-7010, Fax: 403-340-4896,lynn.stegman@gov.ab.ca
Branch Head, Agriculture Grant Programs Branch, Murray Greer
780-980-4722, Fax: 780-980-4737,murray.greer@gov.ab.ca
Branch Head, Livestock Business Development Branch, Rod Carlyon
780-349-4466, Fax: 780-349-5240,rod.carlyon@gov.ab.ca
Branch Head, Crop Business Development Branch, James Calpas
403-340-5329, Fax: 403-340-4896,james.calpas@gov.ab.ca
Branch Head, Ag-Industry Extension Branch, Barb Shackel-Hardman
780-968-3550, Fax:
780-968-3554,barb.shackel.hardman@gov.ab.ca
Branch Head, 4-H & Agriculture Education Branch, Marguerite Stark
403-948-8510, Fax:
403-948-2069,marguerite.stark@gov.ab.ca
Executive Director, Traceability Division, Brent McEwan
780-427-2799, Fax: 780-422-3655,brent.mcewan@gov.ab.ca

Policy & Environment Sector

Same address as above sector.
Asst. Deputy Minister, Colin Jeffares
780-427-1957, Fax: 780-422-6317,colin.jeffares@gov.ab.ca
Acting Director, Economics & Competititveness Division, Don Brown
780-644-5634, Fax: 780-427-5220,don.brown@gov.ab.ca
Branch Head, Competitiveness & Market Analysis Branch, Darren Chase
780-422-4056, Fax: 780-427-5220,darren.chase@gov.ab.ca
Branch Head, Economics Branch, Richard Stadlwieser
780-422-3945, Fax:
780-427-5220,richard.stadlwieser@gov.ab.ca
Branch Head, Statistics & Data Development Branch, Reynold Jaipaul
780-427-5376, Fax: 780-427-5220,reynold.jaipaul@gov.ab.ca
Director, Environmental Stewardship Division, Brenda Brindle
780-427-0674, Fax: 780-422-9745,brenda.brindle@gov.ab.ca
Branch Head, Technology & Innovation Branch, Rick Atkins
403-329-1212, Fax: 403-328-5562,rick.atkins@gov.ab.ca
Branch Head, Agri-Environmental Management Branch, Sandi Jones
403-340-7609, Fax: 403-340-4896,sandi.jones@gov.ab.ca
Director, Irrigation & Farm Water Division, Brent Paterson
780-381-5143, Fax: 780-381-5903,brent.paterson@gov.ab.ca
Branch Head, Rural Water Branch, Marshall Eliason
780-427-4615, Fax:
780-422-9745,marshall.eliason@gov.ab.ca
Branch Head, Water Resources Branch,vacant
403-381-5140, Fax: 403-381-5903,arliss.boschee@gov.ab.ca
Branch Head, Irrigation Secretariat, Roger Hohm
403-381-5176, Fax:
403-382-4406,roger.hohm@gov.ab.ca.ab.ca
Director, Policy, Strategy & Intergovernmental Affairs Division, Andre Tremblay
780-422-9167, Fax:
780-427-5921,andre.tremblay@gov.ab.ca
Branch Head, International Relations & Marketing Branch, Annalisa Baer
780-427-4148, Fax: 780-427-5921,annalisa.baer@gov.ab.ca
Acting Branch Head, Growing Forward Coordination & Program Policy Branch, Wendy McCormick
780-427-3315, Fax:
780-427-5921,wendy.mccormick@gov.ab.ca
Branch Head, Policy Coordination & Research Branch, Shiferaw Adilu
780-422-7196, Fax: 780-427-5921,shiferaw.adilu@gov.ab.ca
Branch Head, Strategy & Program Delivery Branch, Linda Hawk
780-422-4463, Fax: 780-427-5921,linda.hawk@gov.ab.ca
Branch Head, Domestic & International Trade Policy Branch, Peter Kuperis
780-415-8608, Fax: 780-427-5921,peter.kuperis@gov.ab.ca

Business Service & Rural Utilities Sector

Executive Director, Jamie curran
780-422-6166, Fax: 780-422-6317,jamie.curran@gov.ab.ca
Executive Director, Regulatory Services Division, Cliff Munroe
780-422-7249, Fax: 780-422-4513,cliff.munroe@gov.ab.ca
Branch Head, Inspection & Investigation Branch, Floyd Mullaney
403-340-5320, Fax: 403-340-5870,floyd.mullaney@gov.ab.ca
Branch Head, Meat Inspection Branch, Bob Holowaychuk
780-422-2198, Fax:
780-422-4513,bob.holowaychuk@gov.ab.ca
Director, Rural Utilities Division, Terry Holmes
403-427-0134, Fax: 403-422-1613,terry.holmes@gov.ab.ca
Easement Supervisor, Business Services Branch, Marie Chornohus
780-427-0131, Fax:
780-422-1613,marie.chornohus@gov.ab.ca
Branch Head, Rural Electric & Information Systems Branch, Tom Kee
780-427-0944, Fax: 780-422-1613,tom.kee@gov.ab.ca,
Branch Head, Safety & Technical Services Branch, Bruce Partington
780-427-0111, Fax:
780-422-1613,bruce.partington@gov.ab.ca
Executive Director, Rural Development Division, Ron Popek
780-422-1858, Fax: 780-427-4227,ron.popek@gov.ab.ca
Senior Manager, Rural Initiatives & Research Unit, Robert Hornbrook
780-427-4218, Fax:
780-427-4227,robert.hornbrook@gov.ab.ca
Acting Director, Information Management Division, Gerard Vaillancourt
780-422-6796, Fax:
780-427-2861,gerard.vaillancourt@gov.ab.ca
Acting Director, Information Technology Division, Rob Pungor
780-422-6660, Fax: 780-422-4004,rob.pungor@gov.ab.ca
Director, Greg Orriss
780-427-6159, Fax: 780-427-1437
Head, Agri-Food Laboratories, Ken Manninen
780-422-0808, Fax: 780-415-4527,ken.manninen@gov.ab.ca
Head, Agri-Food Systems,Dr. Sandra Honour
780-427-4054, Fax: 780-427-7535,sandra.honour@gov.ab.ca
Head, Safe Food Systems Section, Kim Whitehead
780-415-4522, Fax: 780-427-7535,kim.whitehead@gov.ab.ca
Director, John Tackaberry
780-422-4596, john.tackaberry@gov.ab.ca
Head, Conservation & Development, John Hermans
780-427-3908, Fax: 780-422-0474,john.hermans@gov.ab.ca
Head, Irrigation, Brent Paterson
403-381-5143, Fax: 403-381-5903,brent.paterson@gov.ab.ca
Director, Carol Bettac
780-427-0674, Fax: 780-422-9745,carol.bettac@gov.ab.ca
Head, Agricultural Engineering, Rick Atkins
403-329-1212, Fax: 403-328-5562,rick.atkins@gov.ab.ca
Head, Environmental Practices & Livestock Welfare, Barb Shackel-Hardman
780-427-9801, Fax:
780-422-9745,barb.shackel.hardman@gov.ab.ca
Unit Leader, Environmental Practices, Sandi Jones
403-340-7609, Fax: 403-340-4896,sandi.jones@gov.ab.ca
Provincial Livestock Welfare Specialist,Dr. Derek Haley
403-340-5524, Fax: 403-340-4896,derek.haley@gov.ab.ca
Director,Dr. Cornelia Kreplin
780-427-5341, Fax:
780-427-1057,cornelia.kreplin@gov.ab.ca
Branch Head, Aquaculture,Vacant
403-381-5171, Fax: 403-381-5903
Branch Head, Crop Development - Food, Henry Nadja
403-362-1346, Fax: 403-362-1306,henry.nadja@gov.ab.ca
Branch Head, Crop Development - Non-Food,Dr. Christine Murray
403-644-1986, Fax:
403-427-1057,christine.murray@gov.ab.ca
Branch Head, Feeds & Feeding, Dave Dyson
403-782-8697, Fax: 403-782-5514,dave.dyson@gov.ab.ca
Branch Head, Livestock Production & Meat Quality, Michelle Follensbee
780-415-0828, Fax:
780-427-1057,michelle.follensbee@gov.ab.ca
Team Leader, Meat Quality Unit, Jake Kotowich
780-644-1741
Director, Jo-Ann Hall
780-968-3557, jo-ann.hall@gov.ab.ca
Head, Agri-preneur Feasability Team, Heather Loeppky
780-963-6101, heather.loeppky@gov.ab.ca
Director, Business Expansion and Commercialization Division, Marilynn Boehm
780-422-1851, Fax: 780-644-2400,marilyn.boehm@gov.ab.ca
Branch Head, Beef, Forage & Horse, Kirsty Piquette
780-427-7366
Branch Head, Livestock Products, Gordon Cover
403-340-5323, Fax: 403-340-4896,gordon.cove@gov.ab.ca
Branch Head, Pork, Poultry & Dairy, Gordon Cove
403-340-5322
Acting Manager, Bilateral Relations & Strategic Initiatives, Annalisa Baer
780-427-4242, Fax:
780-422-9746,annalisa@baer@gov.ab.ca
Unit Leader, Economics,Vacant
780-427-0364
Unit Leader, Statistics & Data Development, Bob Prather
780-427-4011, bob.prather@gov.ab.ca
Unit Leader, Strategic Information Services,Vacant
780-427-7196
Director, Lloyd Andruchow
780-427-3338, Fax:
780-422-7755,lloyd.andruchow@gov.ab.ca
Head, Program Policy Development & Coordination, Marcia Hewitt-Fisher
780-427-3315, Fax:
780-427-5921,marcia.hewitt.fisher@gov.ab.ca
Head, Strategic Planning, Cam Swan
780-427-4463, Fax: 780-427-5921,cam.swan@gov.ab.ca

Alberta Office of the Auditor General

9925 - 109 St., 8th Fl., Edmonton, AB T5K 2J8
780-427-4222, Fax: 780-422-9555,
info@oag.ab.ca
www.oag.ab.ca

The mission of the Auditor General of Alberta is to identify opportunities and propose solutions for the improved use of public resources, and to improve and add credibility to performance reporting, including financial reporting, to Albertans.

Auditor General, Merwan Saher, CA
780-422-6195, msaher@oag.ab.ca
Asst. Auditor General & CFO, Jeff Olson, CMA, MBA
780-422-6617, Fax: 780-427-5080,jolson@oag.ab.ca ca
Asst. Auditor General, Vinayak Dharap, CA, CISA
dvinayak@oag.ab.ca
Asst. Auditor General, Ed Ryan, B.Comm, CFE, DIFA, CMA
eryan@oag.ab.ca
Asst. Auditor General, Brad Ireland, CA
bireland@oag.ab.ca
Asst. Auditor General, Doug Wylie, CMA
dwylie@oag.ab.ca
Asst. Auditor General, Jeff Dumont, CA
jdumont@oag.ab.ca
Communications Manager, Lori Trudgeon
780-422-6655, Fax: 780-422-9555,ltrudgeon@oag.ab.ca

Alberta Children and Youth Services

Sterling Place, 9940 - 106 St., 12th Fl., Edmonton, AB T5K 2N2
780-422-3004, Fax: 780-422-3071, 866-714-5437
cs.communications@gov.ab.ca
www.child.alberta.ca

Other Communication: Child Abuse Hotline: 1-800-387-5437; Bullying Help Line: 1-888-456-2323; Child Disability Resource Link: 1-866-346-4661; Media inquiries :780-427-4801

The Ministry of Alberta Children's Services supports families & communities by working to break the cycles of family violence, abuse & poverty. The Ministry's wide range of programs & services for children & families are offered through the local offices in the Child and Family Services Authorities (CFSA), & through eighteen Delegated First Nations Agencies (DFNA).

Acts Administered:
Aboriginal Policy Initiative
Adult Adoption Act
Alberta Children & Youth Initiative
Child Care Licensing Act
Child and Family Services Authorities Act
Child, Youth and Family Enhancement Act
Drug-endangered Children Act
Family and Community Support Services Act
Family Support for Children with Disabilities Act
Premier's Council on Alberta's Promise Act
Protection Against Family Violence Act
Protection of Children Involved in Prostitution Act
Protection of Sexually Exploited Children Act
Social Care Facilities Licensing Act
Social Care Facilities Review Committee Act

Minister,Hon. Yvonne Fritz
780-415-4890, Fax: 780-415-4859
Deputy Minister, Steve MacDonald
780-427-6448, Fax:
780-422-9044,steve.macdonald@gov.ab.ca
Chair, Youth Secretariat, Alberta's Promise Secretariat, Kyle Fawcett
403-297-7500, Fax: 403-297-6664
Acting Executive Director, Prevention of Family Violence & Bullying, Susan Taylor
780-415-8907, Fax: 780-427-2039,susan.taylor@gov.ab.ca
Asst. Director, Communications, Stuart Elson
780-644-7018, Fax: 780-422-3071,stuart.elson@gov.ab.ca ca
Alberta Child & Youth Advocate, John Mould
780-644-8281, Fax: 780-644-8833,john.mould@gov.ab.ca

Community Strategies & Support Division

Asst. Deputy Minister, Karen Ferguson
780-427-6428, Fax:
780-422-9045,karen.ferguson@gov.ab.ca
Director, Child Development, Lynn Jerchel
780-427-4538, Fax: 780-427-1258,lynn.jerchel@gov.ab.ca
Director, Community Partnerships & Youth Strategies, Ken Dropko
780-644-2485, Fax: 780-644-2671,ken.dropko@gov.ab.ca
Director, Research Innovation, Tim Moorhouse
780-422-3305, Fax: 780-415-5841,tim.moorhouse@gov.ab.ca
Director, Youth Strategies, Darren Joslin
780-422-5680, Fax: 780-422-5036,darren.joslin@gov.ab.ca

Program Quality & Standards Division

Asst. Deputy Minister, Mark Hattori
780-415-1548, Fax: 780-422-5415,mark.hattori@gov.ab.ca
Director, Service Analysis, Maureen Mooney
780-422-5674, Fax:
780-422-5415,maureen.mooney@gov.ab.ca
Director, Aboriginal Initiatives, Fred Anderson
780-644-5386, Fax: 780-422-5415,fred.anderson@gov.ab.ca
Director, Child Intervention, David Wilson
780-422-4441, Fax: 780-422-5415,david.wilson@gov.ab.ca
Director, Family Support for Children with Disabilities (FSCD), Laura Alcock
780-427-5869, Fax: 780-415-0651,laura.alcock@gov.ab.ca

Ministry Support Services Division

Asst. Deputy Minister, Gord Johnston
780-415-6594, Fax: 780-422-6642,gord.johnston@gov.ab.ca
Manager, Administrative & Facility Services, Frances Cearns
780-427-7639, Fax: 780-644-4884,frances.cearns@gov.ab.ca
Director, Business Strategies, Stephen Gauk
780-422-7960, Fax: 780-644-2646,stephen.gauk@gov.ab.ca
Executive Director, Financial Strategies, Shehnaz Hutchinson
780-415-8911, Fax:
780-427-4067,shehnaz.hutchinson@gov.ab.ca
Director, Governance Services, Mary Jane Graham
780-422-5873, Fax:
780-644-6880,maryjane.graham@gov.ab.ca
Executive Director, Information Strategies, Lorie Baddock
780-643-1727, Fax: 780-422-2562,lorie.baddock@gov.ab.ca
Director, Intergovernmental Initiatives, Mary Berube
780-422-4781, Fax: 780-422-2562,mary.berube@gov.ab.ca a

Culture & Community Development Division

Standard Life Centre, 10405 Jasper Ave., 9th Fl., Edmonton, AB T5J 4R7
780-415-1167, Fax: 780-422-2891,
Other Communication: Board Development Information: 780-427-2001; Lottery Funding Programs Information: 780-447-8600

The Culture & Community Development Division oversees the following areas: Community Spirit Program; Arts; Human Rights & Citizenship; Alberta Foundation for the Arts; Alberta Sport, Recreation, Parks & Wildlife Foundation; Strategic Information; Board Development; Lottery Funding Programs; Voluntary Sector Services & Initiatives; Financial Services; & the Wild Rose Foundation.

Acting Assistant Deputy Minister, Sue Bohaichuk
780-415-4874, Fax: 780-422-2891,sue.bohaichuk@gov.ab.ca
Executive Director, Arts, Jeffrey Anderson
780-415-0283, jeffrey.anderson@gov.ab.ca
Director, Human Rights & Citizenship, Marie Riddle
780-427-3116, Fax: 780-422-3563,marie.riddle@gov.ab.ca
Director, Voluntary Sector Services, Pat Blakney
780-422-1724

Parks, Conservation, Recreation & Sport Division

Oxbridge Place, 9820 - 106 St., 2nd Fl., Edmonton, AB T5K 2J6
780-427-3582, Fax: 780-427-5980, 866-427-3582

The Division is responsible for the following program & branches: Parks & Protected Areas Program; Sport & Recreation Branch; & Historic Resources Management Branch.

Assistant Deputy Minister, Bill Werry
780-427-7896, bill.werry@gov.ab.ca b.ca
Executive Director, Field Operations, Fred Moffatt
780-427-8441, fred.moffatt@gov.ab.ca
Director, Policy & Program Coordination, Brian Kelly
780-427-9382, brian.kelly@gov.ab.ca
Director, Heritage Protection & Recreation Management Branch, Archie Landals
780-427-9470, archie.landals@gov.ab.ca
Director, Visitor Services Branch, June Markwart
780-427-9383, june.markwart@gov.ab.ca
Director, Sport and Recreation Branch, Lloyd Bentz
780-415-0263, Fax: 780-415-0308,lloyd.bentz@gov.ab.ca
Director, Historic Resources Management Branch, David Link
780-431-2313, david.link@gov.ab.ca

Client & Corporate Services Division

Bowker Building, 9833 - 109 St., 2nd fl., Edmonton, AB T5K 2E8
Asst. Deputy Minister, Bruce M. Perry
780-427-3301, Fax: 780-422-9639,bruce.m.perry@gov.ab.ca
Executive Director, JIMS Project Office, Stephen Bull
780-644-8411, Fax: 780-644-8424,stephen.bull@gov.ab.ca
Acting Executive Director, Client Services - Maintenance Enforcement Program, Esther de Vos
780-401-7500, Fax: 780-644-3678,esther.devos@gov.ab.ca
Executive Director, Client Services - Claims & Recoveries, Steve Jackson
780-427-8255, Fax: 780-415-2200,steve.jackson@gov.ab.ca

Regional Offices:

Calgary
Standard Life Bldg., 639 - 5 Ave. SW, 3rd Fl., Calgary, AB T2P 0M9
Fax: 403-297-6168,
Director, Walter Valentini
403-297-8920, walter.valentini@gov.ab.ca

Camrose
5005 - 49 St., Camrose, AB T4V 1N5
780-679-1235, Fax: 780-679-1250
Director, Al Walkey
780-679-1235, Fax: 780-679-1250,al.walkey@gov.ab.ca

Edmonton
Commerce Place, 10155 - 102 St., 5th Fl., Edmonton, AB T5J 4L6
780-427-6656, Fax: 780-422-5804
Executive Director, Rick Siddle
780-427-6656, Fax: 780-422-5804,rick.siddle@gov.ab.ca
Senior Director, Defence Industry Development, Bill Werny
780-427-5299
Director, Regional Alliance Development, George Brosseau
780-427-0802, Fax:
780-422-5804,george.brosseau@gov.ab.ca
Director, Aerospace Industry and Regional Development, Larry Pana
780-427-6764, Fax: 780-422-5804
Director, North Central Region, Garry Krause
780-415-8745, Fax: 780-422-5804,garry.krause@gov.ab.ca
Director, Transportation & Logistics, Gary Haynes
780-427-6643, Fax: 780-422-2091,gary.haynes@gov.ab.ca

Edmonton - Provincial Nominee Program
North Tower, Telus Plaza, 10025 Jasper Ave., 9th Fl., Edmonton, AB T5J 1S6
780-427-6496, Fax: 780-427-6560
Senior Director, Brad Trefan
brad.trefan@gov.ab.ca

Edson
Provincial Bldg., 111 - 54 St., Edson, AB T7E 1T2
780-723-8229, Fax: 780-723-8240
Director, Tammy Powell
780-723-8229, Fax: 780-723-8240,tammy.powell@gov.ab.ca

Grande Prairie
Provincial Bldg., 10320 - 99 St., 3rd Fl., PO Box 20, Grande Prairie, AB T8V 6J4
780-538-5636, Fax: 780-538-5332
Director, Bob Hall
780-538-5636, Fax: 780-538-5332,bob.hall@gov.ab.ca

Lethbridge
Provincial Bldg., #105, 200 - 5 Ave. South, Lethbridge, AB T1J 4L1
403-381-5414, Fax: 403-381-5741
Director, Linda Erickson
403-381-5741, Fax: 403-381-5741,linda.erickson@gov.ab.ca

Medicine Hat
Provincial Bldg., 346 - 3 St. SE, 1st Fl., Medicine Hat, AB T1A 0G7
403-529-3633, Fax: 403-529-3564
Senior Advisor, Alberta Economic Development Authority, Elvira Smid
403-529-3633, Fax: 403-529-3564,elvira.smid@gov.ab.ca

Pincher Creek
Provincial Bldg., 782 Main St., 2nd Fl., PO Box 2813, Pincher Creek, AB T0K 1W0
403-627-1165, Fax: 403-627-1169
Director, Beverley Thornton
403-627-1165, Fax: 403-627-1169,bev.thornton@gov.ab.ca

Red Deer
Provincial Bldg., 4920 - 51 St., 2nd Fl., Red Deer, AB T4N 6K8
403-340-5302, Fax: 403-340-5231
Regional Manager, Dawna Allard
403-340-5302, Fax: 403-340-5231,dawna.allard@gov.ab.ca

St. Paul
Provincial Bldg., 5025 - 49 Ave., 3rd Fl., St Paul, AB T0A 3A4
780-645-6358, Fax: 780-645-6241
Regional Manager, Cathy Goulet
780-645-6358, Fax: 780-645-6241,cathy.goulet@gov.ab.ca

Beijing

c/o Canadian Embassy, 19 Dongzhimenwai Dajie, Chaoyang District, Beijing,100600 China
Other Communication: International Number: 86-10-5139-4272; International Fax: 86-10-5139-4465
Managing Director, Alberta China Office (Beijing), David Wong
david.wong@international.gc.ca

Hong Kong

Alberta Government Office, Admiralty Centre, Tower Two, #1004, 18 Harcourt Rd., Hong Kong
www.alberta.org.hk

Other Communication: International Number: 011-852-2528-4729; International Fax: 011-852-2529-8115
Trade Director, Alberta Hong Kong Office, Chris Liu
chris.liu@alberta.org.hk
Trade Director, Christopher Liu
chris.liu@alberta.org.hk, Other Communications: International Number: 011-852-2528-4729

Mexico

Calle Schiller No. 529, Colonia Palanco, Del. Miguel Hidalgo, Mexico,11560 Mexico
www.alberta-canada.com/mexico

Other Communication: International Number: 011-52-555-387-9302; International Fax: 011-52-555-724-7913
Managing Director, David Nygaard
david.nygaard@international.gc.ca

Munich
Canadian Consulate, Tal 29, Munich,80331 Germany
Other Communication: International Number: 011-49-(0)89-2199-5740; International Fax: 011-49-(0)89-2199-5745
Consul - Alberta, Alberta Germany Office, Wes Sawatzky
wes.sawatzky@international.gc.ca,

London
Canadian High Commission, Macdonald House, 1 Grosvenor Sq., London,W1K 4AB United Kingdom
Other Communication: International Number: 011-44-20-7258-6472; International Fax: 011-44-20-7258-6309
Business Development Officer, Alberta United Kingdom Office, Lesley Cairns
lesley.cairns@international.gc.ca

Seoul
c/o Alberta Government Office, Canadian Embassy, 16-1 Jeong-dong, Jung-gu, Seoul,100-120 South Korea
www.albertakorea.com

Other Communication: International Number: 011-82-2-3783-6142; International Fax: 011-82-2-3783-6147
Commercial Director, Alberta Korea Office, Won-il Chung
Director, Trade & Investment, Ha-Kyun Yoon
ha-kyun.yoon@dfait-maeci.gc.ca, Other Communications: International Number: 011-82-2-3783-6142

Taipei
Canadian Trade Office, 365 Fu Hsing North Rd., 13th Fl., Taipei 105
Other Communication: International Number: 011-866-2-2715-3637; International Fax: 011-886-22-715-1717
Trade Representative, Alberta Taiwan Office, Li-an Chen
lian.chen@dfait-maeci.gc.ca

Tokyo
Alberta Government Office, Place Canada, 3-37 Akasaka 7-chome, 3rd Fl., Minato-Ku, Tokyo,107-0052 Japan
www.altanet.or.jp

Other Communication: International Number: 011-81-3-3475-1298; International Fax: 011-81-3-3470-3939
Managing Director, Alberta Japan Office, Sean Crockett
sean.crockett@altanet.or.jp

Tourism Marketing & Heritage Division
Commerce Place, 10155 - 102 St., 6th Fl., Edmonton, AB T5J 4L6
Fax: 780-427-6454
The Tourism Marketing & Heritage Division oversees the following areas: Divisional Services; Historic Sites & Museums; Royal Alberta Museum; Royal Tyrrell Museum of Palaeontology; Provincial Archives of Alberta; & the Tourism Development & Services Branch.
Assistant Deputy Minister, Bob Scott
780-415-0892, Fax: 780-427-6454,bob.scott@gov.ab.ca
Executive Director, Tourism Development Branch, Louise McGillivray
780-427-6638, Fax: 780-427-0778,louise.mcgillivray@gov.ab.ca
Director, Divisional Services, Marilyn Kimura
780-644-8394, Fax: 780-427-0778,marilyn.kimura@gov.ab.ca
Director, Historic Sites & Museums, Catherine Whalley
780-431-2306, Fax: 780-427-5598,catherine.whalley@gov.ab.ca
Executive Director, Royal Alberta Museum, Bruce McGillivray
780-453-9172, Fax: 780-453-9172,bruce.mcgillivray@gov.ab.ca
Director, Royal Tyrrell Museum of Palaeontology, Andy Neuman
403-820-6203, 888-440-4240,Fax: 403-823-7131,andrew.neuman@gov.ab.ca
Director & Provincial Archivist, Provincial Archives of Alberta, Leslie Latta-Guthrie
780-427-0058, Fax: 780-427-4646,leslie.latta-guthrie@gov.ab.ca
Director, Tourism Business Development, Research& Investment, Moe Rehemtulla
780-427-6689, Fax: 780-427-6454,moe.rehemtulla@gov.ab.ca

Alberta Education

Commerce Place, 10155 - 102 St., 7th Fl., Edmonton, AB T5J 4L5
780-427-7219, Fax: 780-427-0591, www.education.alberta.ca
From Early Childhood Services (ECS) to Grade 12, Alberta Education supports students, parents, teachers & administrators. The Ministry is engaged in the following activities: developing & evaluating curriculum; setting standards; assessing outcomes; supporting the education of special needs, aboriginal & francophone students; developing & certifying teachers; funding & supporting school boards; overseeing educational policies & regulations; & managing the Alberta Initiative for School Improvement (AISI).
Acts Administered:
Alberta School Boards Association Act
Government Organization Act, Schedules 4
Northland School Division Act
Private Vocational Schools Act
Remembrance Day Act
School Act
Teaching Profession Act
Teachers' Pension Plans Act
Government Accountability Act
Financial Administration Act
Freedom of Information & Protection of Privacy Act
Minister,Hon. Dave Hancock
780-427-5010, Fax: 780-427-5018,education.minister@gov.ab.ca
Deputy Minister, Keray Henke
780-427-3659, Fax: 780-427-7733,keray.henke@gov.ab.ca
Director, Communications, Kathy Telfer
780-427-5423, Fax: 780-427-0591,kathy.telfer@gov.ab.ca
• Council on Alberta Teaching Standards(COATS)
10044 - 108 St.
Edmonton, AB T5J 5E6
780-427-2045 Fax: 780-422-4199
www.teachingquality.ab.ca
The Council on Alberta Teaching Standards (COATS) was established in 1985 by Ministerial Order. Its mandate has since been reaffirmed, and COATS continues to provide advice and recommendations to the Minister on matters related to teaching.

Education Program Standards & Assessment Division
Asst. Deputy Minister, Ellen Hambrook
780-427-7484, Fax: 780-422-1400,ellen.hambrook@gov.ab.ca
Director, Curriculum Sector, Wesley Oginski
780-422-5256, Fax: 780-422-3745,wesley.oginski@gov.ab.ca
Executive Director, Division Planning & Standards Sector, Paul Lamoureux
780-422-3183, Fax: 780-422-9735,paul.lamoureux@gov.ab.ca
Acting Executive Director, French & International Education Services Sector, Gilbert Guimont
780-422-7793, Fax: 780-422-1947,gilbert.guimont@gov.ab.ca
Executive Director, Learner Assessment Sector, John Rymer
780-427-0010, Fax: 780-422-4200,john.rymer@gov.ab.ca

Learning Supports & Information Management Division
Asst. Deputy Minister, Wilma Haas
780-415-6092, Fax: 780-415-8938,wilma.haas@gov.ab.ca
Executive Director, Capital Planning Sector, Laura Cameron
780-427-0289, Fax: 780-644-2284,laura.cameron@gov.ab.ca
Executive Director, FNMI & Field Services Sector, Rick Hayes
780-427-5378, Fax: 780-422-9682,rick.hayes@gov.ab.ca
Executive Director, Information & Technology Management Sector, Aziza Jivraj
780-427-3880, Fax: 780-422-0880,aziza.jivraj@gov.ab.ca
Executive Director, Learning & Program Resources Sector, Rick Baker
780-427-5277, Fax: 780-422-0130,rick.baker@gov.ab.ca
Executive Director, Program Delivery Sector, Lorraine Stewart
780-422-6554, Fax: 780-643-1188,lorraine.stewart@gov.ab.ca
Director, School Technology Branch, Bette Gray
780-427-1509, Fax: 780-415-1091,bette.gray@gov.ab.ca

Strategic Services Division
Asst. Deputy Minister, Michael Walter
780-427-3663, Fax: 780-422-0408,michael.walter@gov.ab.ca
Acting Director, Legislative Services Branch, Chelsea Evans-Rymes
780-427-5446, Fax: 780-415-6546,chelsea.evans-rymes@gov.ab.ca
Executive Director, Policy & Planning, Don Napier
780-427-9998, Fax: 780-422-0880,don.napier@gov.ab.ca b.ca
Director, School Act Review, Maureen Towns
780-415-8525, Fax: 780-415-6546,maureen.towns@gov.ab.ca
Director, Strategic Business Services Sector, Hank Koning
780-422-3279, Fax: 780-415-6546,hank.koning@gov.ab.ca
Executive Director, Strategic Financial Services Sector, Gene Williams
780-415-1489, Fax: 780-422-6996,gene.williams@gov.ab.ca

People and Research Division
Executive Director, Carol McLean
780-644-3578, Fax: 780-638-3272,carol.mclean@gov.ab.ca
Director, Human Resources Branch, Doug German
780-644-7503, Fax: 780-422-5362,doug.german@gov.ab.ca
Director & Registrar, Professional Standards Branch, Marc Prefontaine
780-427-2045, Fax: 780-422-4199,marc.prefontaine@gov.ab.ca
Director, School Research & Improvement Branch,Dr. Dianna Millard
780-427-7882, Fax: 780-415-2481,dianna.millard@gov.ab.ca
Director, Workforce Planning & Development Branch, Randy Clarke
780-644-3774, Fax: 780-644-3591,randy.clarke@gov.ab.ca

Alberta Office of the Chief Electoral Officer/Elections Alberta

#100, 11510 Kingsway Ave., Edmonton, AB T5G 2Y5
780-427-7191, Fax: 780-422-2900, info@electionsalberta.ab.ca
www.electionsalberta.ab.ca
Provides administrative, logistic & financial support for the register of electors, general elections & by-elections, & plebiscites in support of the Election Act & the Senatorial Selection Act; monitors & records the financial activities of registered parties, constituency associations & candidates to ensure compliance with the Election Finances & Contributions Disclosure Act.
Acts Administered:
Election Act
Election Finances & Contributions Disclosure Act
Senatorial Selection Act
Chief Electoral Officer, O. Brian Fjeldheim
780-427-1035, Fax: 780-422-2900,brian.fjeldheim@elections.ab.ca
Deputy Chief Electoral Officer, Lori McKee-Jeske
780-427-6860, Fax: 780-422-2900,lori.mckeejeske@elections.ab.ca
Director, Election Finances, CJ Rhamey
780-427-1036, Fax: 780-422-2900,cj.rhamey@elections.ab.ca
Director, Election Operations & Communications, Drew Westwater
780-427-1038, Fax: 780-422-2900,drew.westwater@elections.ab.ca
Administrative Services Coordinator, Andrea Villetard
780-427-7191, Fax: 780-422-2900,andrea.villetard@elections.ab.ca

Alberta Employment & Immigration

Minister's Office, Legislature Bldg., #208, 10800 - 97 Ave., Edmonton, AB T5K 2B6
780-644-5135, Fax: 780-422-9556, 866-644-5135
eii.communications@gov.ab.ca
www.employment.alberta.ca
The Ministry's major responsibilities are: developing and delivering policies, programs and services to promote labour force development; helping Albertans train for, find and keep employment; providing financial and health benefits, child support services and employment training support to Albertans in need; ensuring Alberta's workplaces are safe, healthy, fair, and productive for employees and employers; providing leadership for immigration and interprovincial labour mobility policy for the Government of Alberta; coordinating resources to support the settlement and integration of new Albertans.
Acts Administered:
Agrology Profession Act
Architects Act
Blind Workers' Compensation Act
Consulting Engineers of Alberta Act
Employment Standards Code
Engineering, Geological & Geophysical Professions Act
Government Organization Act, Sched 3, 8, 10
Income & Employment Supports Act
Labour Relations Code
Land Agents Licensing Act
Land Surveyors Act
Managerial Exclusion Act
M.L.A. Compensation Act
Occupational Health and Safety Act
Police Officers Collective Bargaining Act
Professional and Occupational Associations Registration Act
Public Service Employee Relations Act
Radiation Protection Act
Regulated Accounting Profession Act
Regulated Forestry Profession Act
Special Payment Act
Office of Statistics & Information Act
Veterinary Profession Act
Widows' Pension Act
Workers' Compensation Act
Minister,Hon. Thomas A. Lukaszuk
780-415-4800, Fax: 780-422-9556
Deputy Minister, Shirley Howe
780-427-8305, Fax: 780-422-9205,shirley.howe@gov.ab.ca

Director, Communications, Janice Schroeder
780-427-5649, Fax:
780-427-5988,janice.schroeder@gov.ab.ca
• Alberta Economic Development Authority(AEDA)
McDougall Centre
455 - 6 St. SW
Calgary, AB T2P 4E8
403-297-3022 Fax: 403-297-6435
aeda.alberta.ca
AEDA is a partnership between Alberta's private and public sectors. It brings together 65 private sector volunteers from across the province — a network of business, academic and municipal leaders — to study issues, consult with experts, debate ideas and make recommendations to the Alberta government on ways to strengthen the province's economic performance.
• Alberta Workers' Compensation Board
9912 - 107 St.
PO Box 2415
Edmonton, AB T5J 2S5
780-498-3999 866-922-9221TDD: 780-498-7895
www.wcb.ab.ca
Other Communication: Calgary: 403-517-6000; Toll free outside Alberta: 1-800-661-9608 (in Canada)
• Appeals Commission for Alberta Workers' Compensation
Energy Square Bldg.
#901, 10109 - 106th St.
Edmonton, AB T5J 3L7
780-412-8700 Fax: 780-412-8701
www.appealscommission.ab.ca
• Labour Relations Board
#503, 10808 - 99 Ave.
Edmonton, AB T5K 0G5
780-422-5926 Fax: 780-422-0970 800-463-2572
alrbinfo@lab.gov.ab.ca
www3.gov.ab.ca/alrb
• Northern Alberta Development Council(NADC)
Provincial Bldg
#206, 9621 - 96 Ave.
PO Box 900-14
Peace River, AB T8S 1T4
780-624-6274 Fax: 780-624-6184
nadc.council@gov.ab.ca
www.nadc.gov.ab.ca
The Northern Alberta Development Council's (NADC) mandate is outlined in the Alberta Act of legislature. NADC objectives are to identify & implement measures that will advance northern development & advise government on opportunities & issues. Focus is on advancing development of the northern economy. Northern Alberta includes 60% of Alberta's landmass & has 10% of the province's population. It is resource rich, with 90% of alberta's forests, all of Canada's oil sands development, nearly 40% of Alberta's conventional oil & gas activity & 20% of Alberta's agricultural land. The NADC is involved with projects and initiatives in transportation, value-added agriculture, tourism, educational initiatives and inter-jurisdictional projects.
• Occupational Health & Safety Council
Labour Bldg
10808 - 99 Ave., 9th Fl.
Edmonton, AB T5K 0G5
780-415-0599 Fax: 780-422-8944
employment.alberta.ca/SFW/6446.html
The Occupational Health & Safety Council (the Council) is a group appointed by the Minister of Alberta Human Resources & Employment to hear appeals. The Council deals with matters that come under the Occupational Health & Safety Act & associated legislation. The issues that can be appealed before the Council are orders issued by Occupational Health & Safety Officers.

Immigration Division
Labour Bldg., 10808 - 99 Ave., 9th Fl., Edmonton, AB T5K 0G5
780-638-3531
Assistant Deputy Minister, Maryann Everett
780-422-9493, Fax:
780-422-2889,maryann.everett@gov.ab.ca
Executive Director, Immigration Policy & Programs, Percy Cummings
780-415-8945, Fax:
780-643-0905,percy.cummings@gov.ab.ca
Director, Alberta Immigrant Nominee Program, Brad Trefan
780-427-6496, Fax: 780-427-6560,brad.trefan@gov.ab.ca
Executive Director, Labour Attraction, Wendy Blackwell
780-427-1637, Fax:
780-644-3329,wendy.blackwell@gov.ab.ca
Director, Strategic Marketing, Danielle Comeau
780-427-0528, Fax:
780-422-2889,danielle.comeau@gov.ab.ca

Delivery Services Division
Labour Bldg., 10808 - 99 Ave., 10th Fl., Edmonton, AB T5K 0G5
Assistant Deputy Minister, Neil Irvine
780-415-2946, Fax: 780-427-7548,neil.irvine@gov.ab.ca
Director, Aboriginal Development, Clay Buchanan
780-427-5922, Fax: 780-638-3332,clay.buchanan@gov.ab.ca
Regional Director, Northwest Region - McLennan, Barb Hendry
780-324-3239, Fax: 780-324-3235,barb.hendry@gov.ab.ca
Regional Director, Northeast Region - Lac La Biche, Ken Shewchuk
780-623-5102, Fax: 780-623-5355,ken.shewchuk@gov.ab.ca
Regional Director, Edmonton Region, Elvin Collins
780-422-6993, Fax: 780-422-5125,elvin.collins@gov.ab.ca
Regional Director, Central Region - Red Deer, Donna Stewart-Wood
403-340-7001, Fax:
403-340-7057,donna.stewart-wood@gov.ab.ca
Regional Director, Calgary Region, Caroline Fairbrother
403-297-5334, Fax:
403-297-5988,caroline.fairbrother@gov.ab.ca
Regional Director, South Region - Coaldale, Noelle Becker
403-345-7979, Fax: 403-345-4915,noelle.becker@gov.ab.ca
Executive Director, Centrally Delivered Services, Chuck Conroy
780-644-1911, Fax: 780-415-1667,chuck.conroy@gov.ab.ca

Workplace Standards Division
Labour Bldg., 10808 - 99 Ave., 8th Fl., Edmonton, AB T5K 0G5
780-415-9057, Fax: 780-644-2100
The Division includes Mediation Services, Professions & Occupations & Land Agent Licensing, Workplace Innovation & Continuous Improvement, Workplace Partnerships Director's Office, Workplace Policy & Standards Development, & Workplace Health & Safety & Employment Standards Compliance.
Assistant Deputy Minister, Dan Kennedy
780-415-0458, Fax: 780-644-2100,dan.kennedy@gov.ab.ca
Director, Mediation Services (Labour Mediation), Bertha Greenstein
780-415-0530, Fax:
780-427-6327,bertha.greenstein@gov.ab.ca
Executive Director, Workplace Policy & Legislation, Tim Thompson
780-415-0527, Fax: 780-422-0014,tim.thompson@gov.ab.ca
Executive Director, Occupational Health & Safety,Vacant
780-415-0603, Fax: 780-644-1508
Executive Director, Employment Standards, Eric Reitsma
780-422-5932, Fax: 780-644-5424,eric.reitsma@gov.ab.ca

Strategic Corporate Services Division
Labour Building, 10808 - 99 Ave., Edmonton, AB T5K 0G5
780-427-6765
The Strategic Services & Information Division consists of Data Development & Evaluation, Intergovernmental Relations, Legislative Services, Organizational Planning & Effectiveness, & People, Skills & Workplace Resources.
Assistant Deputy Minister, Alex Stewart
780-427-6765, Fax: 780-427-5971,alex.stewart@gov.ab.ca a
Executive Director, Data Development & Evaluation, Yvonne McFadzen
780-427-9644, Fax:
780-422-5070,yvonne.mcfadzen@gov.ab.ca
Director, Intergovernmental Relations, John Vallacott
780-422-5996, Fax: 780-422-0274,john.vellacott@gov.ab.ca
Director, Legislative Services, Suzanne Harbottle
780-422-7325, Fax:
780-415-0070,suzanne.harbottle@gov.ab.ca
Director, Career & Workplace Resources, Judy Hutchinson
780-422-5312, Fax:
780-422-5319,judy.hutchinson@gov.ab.ca
Executive Director, Human Resources, Rick Nisbet
780-427-7274, Fax: 780-427-3937,rick.nisbet@gov.ab.ca
Executive Director & Senior Financial Officer, Finance, Organizational Planning & Administration, Shelley Engstrom
780-427-0034, Fax:
780-422-2861,shelley.engstrom@gov.ab.ca
Chief Information Officer, Information Management & Application Support, Marlene Casper
780-427-2815, Fax:
780-427-4310,marlene.casper@gov.ab.ca
Director, Information & Privacy Office (FOIP), George Alvarez
780-422-6481, Fax: 780-422-3204,george.alvarez@gov.ab.ca
Director, Appeals Secretariat, Kevin Young
780-422-9079, Fax: 780-422-1088,kevin.young@gov.ab.ca

Workforce Supports Division
Labour Building, 10808 - 99 Ave., 10th Fl., Edmonton, AB T5K 0G5
780-722-0010
The Workforce Supports Division features the following components: Income & Child Support; Strategic Policy & Supports; Business Innovations; Employment & Training Services; & Labour Force Development.
Assistant Deputy Minister, Shannon Marchand
780-422-0194, Fax:
780-422-1651,shannon.marchand@gov.ab.ca
Executive Director, Income & Child Support, Mic Farrell
780-427-0158, Fax: 780-422-0032,mic.farrell@gov.ab.ca
Director, Strategic Policy & Supports, Laurette Morris
780-644-4881, Fax:
780-422-6324,laurette.m.morris@gov.ab.ca
Director, Business Innovations, Brian Payne
780-427-6678, Fax: 780-422-6768,brian.payne@gov.ab.ca
Director, Employment & Training Services, D'arcy claypool
780-422-4293, Fax: 780-427-0354,d'arcy.claypool@gov.ab.ca
Executive Director, Labour Force Development, Marilynn Boehm
780-422-1851, Fax:
780-422-6400,marilynn.boehm@gov.ab.ca
Manager, Program & Business Support, Gordon Okamura
780-427-7445, Fax:
780-422-6324,gordon.okamura@gov.ab.ca

Alberta Energy

North Petroleum Plaza, 9945 - 108 St., 10th Fl., Edmonton, AB T5K 2G6
780-427-8050, Fax: 780-422-0698, 780-310-0000
www.energy.gov.ab.ca

Other Communication: Calgary: 403-297-8955; Public Information Centre: 780-427-0265; TTY Toll Free: 1-800-232-7215
The Alberta Department of Energy's mission is to guide the development of the province's non-renewable resources. The sustained development of these resources is managed by the Department, with the goal of maximizing long-term benefits to Alberta. Alberta Energy is organzied around ten business units: aboriginal relations; bioenergy; coal, electricty; environment and resource services; minerals; natural gas; oil; oil sands; and tenure. Tenure is the process of leasing and administering petroleum and natural gas (P&NG) rights owned by the Province of Alberta.
Acts Administered:
Alberta Corporate Tax Act
Alberta Utilities Commission Act
Coal Conservation Act
Coal Sales Act
Electric Utilities Act
Energy Resources Conservation Act
Energy Statutes Amendment Act, 2009
Freehold Mineral Rights Tax Act
Gas Resources Preservation Act
Gas Utilities Act
Hydro & Electric Energy Act
The Mineral Titles Redemption Act
Mines & Minerals Act
Natural Gas Marketing Act
Natural Gas Price Protection Act
Oil & Gas Conservation Act
Oil Sands Conservation Act
Petroleum Marketing Act
Pipeline Act
Public Utilities Act
Small Power Research & Development Act
Turner Valley Unit Operations Act
Water, Gas & Electric Companies Act
Minister,Hon. Ron Liepert
780-427-3740, Fax:
780-422-0195,minister.energy@gov.ab.ca
Deputy Minister, Peter Watson
780-415-8434, Fax: 780-644-3103,peter.watson@gov.ab.ca
Director, Communications, Jay O'Neill
780-422-3667, Fax: 780-422-0698,jay.o'neill@gov.ab.ca
Executive Director, Human Resources, Dave Prince
780-427-6294, Fax: 780-422-4299,david.prince@gov.ab.ca
• Energy Resources Conservation Board(ERCB)
#1000, 250 - 5 Ave. SW
Calgary, AB T2P 0R4
403-297-8311 Fax: 403-297-7336
inquiries@ercb.ca
www.ercb.ca
The ERCB is an independent, quasi-judicial agency of the Government of Alberta that regulates the safe, responsible, and efficient development of Alberta's energy resources: oil, natural gas, oil sands, coal, and pipelines.
• Alberta Utilities Commission(AUC)
Fifth Avenue Place
425 - 1 St. SW
Calgary, AB T2P 3L8
403-592-8845 Fax: 403-592-4406
www.auc.ab.ca

The AUC regulates the utilities sector, natural gas and electricity markets to protect social, economic and environmental interests of Alberta where competitive market forces do not.

Energy Future Division
Petroleum Plaza NT, 9945 - 108 St., 10th Fl., Edmonton, AB T5K 2G6
Executive Lead, Jeff Kucharski
780-638-3136, Fax: 780-427-7737,jeff.kucharski@gov.ab.ca
Project Coordinator Manager, Regulatory Enhancement Project, Anoushka Fernandes
780-427-2364, Fax:
780-427-7737,anoushka.m.fernandes@gov.ab.ca
Director, Business Planning & Performance, Sandra Stemmer
780-643-1438, Fax:
780-422-0800,sandra.stemmer@gov.ab.ca
Director, Strategic Energy Secretariat, Katherine Braun
780-427-7738, Fax:
780-427-7737,katherine.braun@gov.ab.ca

Resource Development Policy Division
Petroleum Plaza NT, 9945 - 108 St., Edmonton, AB T5K 2G6
Asst. Deputy Minister, Jennifer Steber
780-427-6370, Fax: 780-427-7737,jennifer.steber@gov.ab.ca
Executive Director, Resource Development, Sharla Rauschning
780-427-6230, Fax:
780-644-3604,sharla.rauschning@gov.ab.ca
Acting Branch Head, Economics & Markets, Matthew Foss
780-422-5059, Fax: 780-422-9677,matthew.foss@gov.ab.ca
Branch Head, Environmental & Resource Services, Audrey Murray
780-427-6383, Fax: 780-422-3044,audrey.murray@gov.ab.ca
Branch Head, Research & Technology, Chris Holly
780-422-9206, Fax: 780-427-0865,chris.holly@gov.ab.ca
Director, Regulatory Affairs, Jill Page
403-297-5574, Fax: 403-297-5499,jill.page@gov.ab.ca
Branch Head, Aboriginal Relations, Rand Smith
780-427-8957, Fax: 780-644-1271,rand.smith@gov.ab.ca

Strategic Initiatives Division
Petroleum Plaza NT, 9945 - 108 St., 10th Fl., Edmonton, AB T5K 2G6
Asst. Deputy Minister, Mike Ekelund
780-422-0813, Fax: 780-427-7737,mike.ekelund@gov.ab.ca

Electricity, Alternative Energy, & Carbon Capture & Storage Division
Petroleum Plaza NT, 9945 - 108 St., 10th Fl., Edmonton, AB T5K 2G6
Asst. Deputy Minister, Tim Grant
780-644-2384, Fax: 780-427-7737,tim.grant@gov.ab.ca
Executive Director, Electricity Markets Branch, Kathryn Wood
780-644-1232, Fax: 780-427-8065,kathryn.wood@gov.ab.ca
Director, Infrastructure & Alternative Energy Branch, Ian McKay
780-422-8726, Fax: 780-427-8065,ian.mckay@gov.ab.ca
Executive Director, Carbon Capture & Storage (CCS) Development / Energy Efficiency & Conservation Branch, Sandra Locke
780-644-7126, Fax: 780-638-3031,sandra.locke@gov.ab.ca

Resource Revenue & Operations Division
Petroleum Plaza NT, 9945 - 108 St., 10th Fl., Edmonton, AB T5K 2G6
Asst. Deputy Minister, Rhonda Wehrhahn
780-422-9430, Fax:
780-422-1123,rhonda.wehrhahn@gov.ab.ca
Acting Branch Head, Coal & Mineral Development, Gary V. White
780-415-0349, Fax: 780-422-5447,gary.v.white@gov.ab.ca
Branch Head, Tenure, Brenda Allbright
780-422-9393, Fax:
780-422-1123,brenda.allbright@gov.ab.ca
Branch Head, Compliance & Assurance, Larry McGuinness
403-297-6742, Fax:
403-297-5199,larry.mcguinness@gov.ab.ca
Executive Director, Petroleum Registry of Alberta (PRA), Wally Goeres
780-415-2079, Fax: 780-422-0229,wally.goeres@gov.ab.ca
Branch Head, Royalty Operations, Salim Merali
780-422-9124, Fax: 780-427-0865,salim.merali@gov.ab.ca
Branch Head, Petroleum Marketing & Valuation, & Site Services, Gale Robins
403-297-5460, gale.robins@gov.ab.ca

Oil Sands Strategy & Operations
Petroleum Plaza NT, 9945 - 108 St., 14th Fl., Edmonton, AB T5K 2G6
Asst. Deputy Minister, Matthew Machielse
780-644-8030, Fax:
780-427-7737,matthew.machielse@gov.ab.ca
Executive Director, Strategic Integration & Development, Anne Denman
780-422-9212, Fax: 780-427-8065,anne.denman@gov.ab.ca
Branch Head, Operations, Steve Tkalcic
780-422-9121, Fax: 780-422-0692,steve.tkalcic@gov.ab.ca
Branch Head, Business Design & Evaluation, Larry Ziegenhagel
780-427-6384, Fax:
780-422-0692,larry.ziegenhagel@gov.ab.ca
Branch Head, External Relations & Advocacy, Charlotte Moran
780-415-6187, Fax:
780-422-0800,charlotte.moran@gov.ab.ca
Branch Head, Value Added Development, Matthew Machielse
780-644-8030, Fax:
780-427-8065,matthew.machielse@gov.ab.ca

• Alberta Environmental Appeals Board
Peace Hills Trust Tower
#306, 10011 - 109 St. NW
Edmonton, AB T5J 3S8
780-427-6207 Fax: 780-427-4693
www.eab.gov.ab.ca

• Alberta Recycling Management Authority(ARMA)
Scotia Tower 1
#1310, 10060 Jasper Ave.
PO Box 189
Edmonton, AB T5J 2J1
780-990-1111 Fax: 780-990-1122 888-999-8762
info@albertarecycling.ca
www.albertarecycling.ca
Other Communication: Toll Free Fax: 1-866-990-1122; Electronics Recycling: electronics@albertarecycling.ca; Tire Recycling: tires@albertarecycling.ca
The not-for-profit association administers the electronics & tire recycling programs in Alberta. It reports to the Minister of Environment.

• Alberta Used Oil Management Association(AUMA)
Scotia One, Scotia Place
#1050, 10060 Jasper Ave.
Edmonton, AB T5J 3R8
780-414-1510 Fax: 780-414-1519
reception@usedoilrecycling.ca
www.usedoilrecycling.com
Other Communication: Info Line: 1-888-922-2298
With the approval by the provincial government of the LubricatingOil Material Recycling & Management in 1997, AUOMA was established as the Delegated Administrative Organization. AUOMA manages programs to facilitate the collection & recycling of used oil materials in Alberta.

• Beverage Container Management Board(BCMB)
#750, 10707 - 100 Ave.
Edmonton, AB T5J 3M1
780-424-3193 Fax: 780-428-4620 888-424-7671
info@bcmb.ab.ca
www.bcmb.ab.ca
The non-profit management board was established under Alberta's Environmental Protection & Enhancement Act. BCMB regulates the recycling system of beverage containers in Alberta.

• Clean Air Strategic Alliance(CASA)
Centre West Bldg
10035 - 108 St., 10th Fl.
Edmonton, AB T5J 3E1
780-427-9793 Fax: 780-422-3127
casa@casahome.org
www.casahome.org

• Environmental Response Centre
Twin Atria Bldg.
4999 - 98 Ave., 1st Fl.
Edmonton, AB T6B 2X3
780-422-4505 Fax: 780-427-3178 800-222-6514

Alberta Environment (AE)

South Tower, Petroleum Plaza, 9915 - 108 St., 10th Fl., Edmonton, AB T5K 2G8
780-427-2700, Fax: 780-422-4086,
env.infocent@gov.ab.ca
environment.alberta.ca

Other Communication: 24-hour Environment Hotline (to report an environmental emergency or file a complaint): 1-800-222-6514

To assure the effective stewardship of Alberta's environmental systems to sustain a high quality of life is the mission of Alberta Environment. In order to accomplish this mission, the department has staff in over 120 communities in Alberta. Alberta Environment consists of the following four business divisions: Environmental Stewardship, Environmental Assurance, Environmental Management, & Strategic Support and Integration.

Acts Administered:
Climate Change & Emissions Management Act, 2003
Drainage District Act, 2000
Environmental Protection & Enhancement Act (Community Development & Sustainable Resource Development)
Environmental Protection & Enhancement (Clean-Up) Instructions Amendment Act, 2002, (Unproclaimed)
Mines & Minerals Act (Energy & Sustainable Resource Development)
Natural Resources Conservation Board Act (Sustainable Resource Development)
North Red Deer Water Authorization Act
Stettler Regional Water Authorization Act
Water Act

Minister,Hon. Rob Renner
780-427-2391, Fax: 780-422-6259
Deputy Minister, Jim Ellis
780-427-6236, Fax: 780-427-0923,jim.ellis@gov.ab.ca
Executive Director, Finance & Administration, Mike Dalrymple
780-427-9148, Fax:
780-427-0923,mike.dalrymple@gov.ab.ca
Director, CEMS Transformation Secretariat, Tom Davis
780-644-3205, Fax: 780-427-2278,tom.davis@gov.ab.ca
Director, Communications, Mark Cooper
780-427-2848, Fax: 780-427-1874,mark.cooper@gov.ab.ca
Director, Environmental Law Section, Darin Stepaniuk
780-427-6121, Fax:
780-427-4343,darin.stepaniuk@gov.ab.ca
Leader, People Services, Mary Jefferies
780-422-7699, Fax: 780-644-7832,mary.jefferies@gov.ab.ca

Corporate Services
Petroleum Plaza NT, 9945 - 108 St., 10th Fl., Edmonton, AB T5K 2G6
Asst. Deputy Minister, John Buie
780-427-2159, Fax: 780-427-7737,john.buie@gov.ab.ca
Branch Head, Business & Facility Services, Mike G. Boyd
780-427-6382, Fax: 780-422-0800,mike.g.boyd@gov.ab.ca
Branch Head, Finance, Douglas Borland
780-427-6223, Fax:
780-422-4281,douglas.borland@gov.ab.ca
Branch Head, FOIP & Records Management Branch, Marlene Bruyere
780-644-3778, Fax:
780-644-3786,marlene.bruyere@gov.ab.ca
Branch Head, Information Technology, Carolanne Pasutto
780-415-2083, Fax:
780-427-5696,carolanne.pasutto@gov.ab.ca

Legal Services
Petroleum Plaza NT, 9945 - 108 St., 11th Fl., Edmonton, AB T5K 2G6
Branch Head, Bruce Laycock
780-422-8085, Fax: 780-427-1871,bruce.laycock@gov.ab.ca

Environmental Assurance Division
Petroleum Plaza ST, 9915 - 108 St., 10th Fl., Edmonton, AB T5K 2G8
Asst. Deputy Minister, Ernie Hui
780-415-8183, Fax: 780-415-6492,ernie.hui@gov.ab.ca
Director, Climate Change Secretariat, Andy Ridge
780-644-7970, Fax: 780-415-1718,andy.ridge@gov.ab.ca
Director, Monitoring Reporting & Innovation Branch, Bob Stone
780-415-9356, Fax: 780-422-8606,bob.stone@gov.ab.ca
Director, Integrated Monitoring, Evaluation & Reporting Framework (IMERF) Project, Albert Poulette
780-644-3771, Fax: 780-427-6334,albert.poulette@gov.ab.ca
Director, Water Policy Branch, Bob Barraclough
780-427-0029, Fax:
780-422-4192,bob.barraclough@gov.ab.ca
Director, Air, Land & Strategic Policy Branch, Keith Leggat
780-427-2234, Fax: 780-422-4192,keith.leggat@gov.ab.ca
Project Director, NE Plan, Chris Hunt
780-644-1259, Fax: 780-415-1718,chris.hunt@gov.ab.ca
Director, Oil Sands & Clean Energy Policy Branch, Roger Ramcharita
780-644-5290, Fax:
780-415-1718,roger.ramcharita@gov.ab.ca

Environmental Stewardship Division
Petroleum Plaza ST, 9915 - 108 St., 10th Fl., Edmonton, AB T5K 2G8
Asst. Deputy Minister, Bev Yee
780-427-6247, Fax: 780-427-1014,bev.yee@gov.ab.ca
Director, Environmental Relations, Bill Calder
780-427-1447, Fax: 780-421-0028,bill.calder@gov.ab.ca
Director, Conservation & Education, George Murphy
780-427-8472, Fax:
780-422-4086,george.murphy@gov.ab.ca
Director, Environmental Strategies,Vacant
780-422-8464, Fax: 780-638-3187
Director, Transboundary Water Policy, Robert Harrison
780-427-9288, Fax: 780-638-3187,robert.harrison@gov.ab.ca

Environmental Management Division
Petroleum Plaza ST, 9915 - 108 St., 10th Fl., Edmonton, AB T5K 2G8
Asst. Deputy Minister, Rick Brown
780-427-1335, Fax: 780-422-4715,rick.brown@gov.ab.ca

Director, Regional Integration, Luke Pantin
780-427-2010, Fax: 780-427-2278,luke.pantin@gov.ab.ca
Regional Director, Central Region - Red Deer, Andy Lamb
403-340-4326, Fax: 403-340-5022,andy.lamb@gov.ab.ca
Regional Director, Northern Region - Edmonton, Shannon Flint
780-422-8463, Fax: 780-427-7824,shannon.flint@gov.ab.ca
Regional Director, Southern Region, Jay Litke
403-297-6070, Fax: 403-297-6069
Director, Water Management Operations, Dave Ardell
403-297-5892, Fax: 403-297-6389,dave.ardell@gov.ab.ca

Strategic Support & Integration Division
Petroleum Plaza ST, 9915 - 108 St., 10th Fl., Edmonton, AB T5K 2G8
Asst. Deputy Minister, Al Sanderson
780-643-0890, Fax: 780-644-8469,al.sanderson@gov.ab.ca
Section Head, Geographic Information Office, Lana Robinson
403-382-4106, Fax: 403-381-5969,lana.robinson@gov.ab.ca
Chief Information Officer, Office of the CIO & Integrated Information Solutions, Roger Burns
780-644-5065, roger.burns@gov.ab.ca
Director, Performance Leadership Branch, Larry Williams
780-644-1094, Fax: 780-644-8946,larry.williams@gov.ab.ca,

Alberta Office of the Ethics Commissioner

#1250, 9925 - 109 St., Edmonton, AB T5K 2J8
780-422-2273, Fax: 780-422-2261,
generalinfo@ethicscommissioner.ab.ca
www.ethicscommissioner.ab.ca

Acts Administered:
Alberta Conflicts of Interest Act
Code of Conduct & Ethics for the Public Service of Alberta
Alberta Ethics Commissioner, Neil R. Wilkinson
Chief Administrative Officer, Glen Resler
780-422-4974, Fax:
780-422-2261,gresler@ethicscommissioner.ab.ca
Registrar, Lobbyists Act & General Counsel, Brad Odsen, Q.C.
780-644-3879, Fax:
780-422-2261,bodsen@ethicscommissioner.ab.ca

Alberta Finance & Enterprise

Terrace Building, #426, 9515 - 107 St., Edmonton, AB T5K 2C3
780-427-3035, Fax: 780-427-1147,
tra.revenue@gov.ab.ca
www.finance.alberta.ca

Other Communication: Tax & Revenue Administration: 780-427-3044 (Edmonton); 403-297-5200 (Calgary
Alberta Finance provides corporate financial services & manages Alberta's financial policies & affairs. The following are responsibilities of the Ministry: management of financial assets, risk related to loss of public assets & liability exposure, investment policy, long-term revenue & revenue programs & debt; provincial economic forecasts; analysis of financial trends; development of policies; coordination of the budget; maintenance of fair & competitive taxes; investment of financial assets; fostering the capital market in the province; & regulation of financial institutions, insurance, pensions & Alberta's capital market.
Acts Administered:
Alberta Corporate Tax Act
Alberta Heritage Savings Trust Fund Act
Alberta Income Tax Act
Alberta Personal Income Tax Act
Alberta Capital Finance Authority Act
Alberta Stock Exchange Restructuring Act
Alberta Taxpayer Protection Act
Alberta Treasury Branches Act
Appropriation Acts
Balanced Budget & Debt Retirement Act
Civil Services Garnishee Act
Credit Union Act
Employment Pensions Plan Act
Farm Credit Stability Fund Act
Financial Administration Act
Financial Consumers Act
Fiscal Responsibility Act
Government Accountability Act
Government Organization Act
Government Fees & Charges Review Act
Insurance Act
Loan & Trust Corporations Act
Lottery Fund Transfer Act
Members of the Legislative Assembly Pension Plan Act
Municipal Debentures Act
Pension Fund Act
Provincial Court Judges Act
Public Sector Pension Plans Act
Securities Act
Statistics Bureau Act
Telecommunications Act
Alberta Economic Development Authority Act
Northern Alberta Development Council Act
Income Trusts Liability Act
Securities Transfer Act
Statistics Bureau Amendment Act, 2008
Tobacco Tax Act
Tourism Levy Act
Alberta Capital Finance Authority Act
Minister,Hon. Ted Morton
780-427-8809, Fax: 780-427-5543,min.finance@gov.ab.ca
Deputy Minister, Finance, Tim Wiles
780-427-4106, Fax: 780-427-0178,tim.wiles@gov.ab.ca
Director, Communications, Bart Johnson
780-422-2126, Fax: 780-427-1147,bart.johnson@gov.ab.ca
Executive Director, Human Resource Services, Vacant
780-415-9113, Fax: 780-422-0421
• Alberta Capital Finance Authority(ACFA)
Canadian Western Bank Place
#2450, 10303 Jasper Ave.
Edmonton, AB T5J 3N6
780-427-9711 Fax: 780-422-2175
webacfa@gov.ab.ca
www.acfa.gov.ab.ca
This authority provides local authorities within the Province of Alberta with funding for capital projects at the lowest possible cost, consistent with the viability of the Alberta Capital Finance Authority. ACFA makes loans to Alberta municipalities, school boards and other local entities at interest rates based on the cost of its borrowings. It is a non-profit corporation established in 1956 under the authority of the Alberta Capital Finance Authority Act, Chapter A-14.5, Revised Statutes of Alberta 2000, as amended.
• Alberta Ingenuity Fund
250 Karl Clark Rd.
Edmonton, AB T6N 1E4
780-450-5111 Fax: 780-450-5333
info@albertaingenuity.ca
www.albertaingenuity.ca
The Alberta Ingenuity Fund was established to develop internationally competitive science and engineering expertise and build greater capacity for innovation, particularly in areas with lasting social and economic impact. Alberta Ingenuity has become part of Alberta Innovates - Technology Futures, www.albertainnovates.ca/technology.
• Alberta Pensions Services Corporation(APS)
5103 Windermere Blvd. SW
Edmonton, AB T6W 0S9
780-427-5101 Fax: 780-421-1652 800-358-0840
apa.info@gov.ab.ca; memberservices@apsc.ca
www.apaco.ab.ca
Responsible for the administration of the Public Sector Pension Plans Act; administering eight statutory pension plans under the direction of five pension boards & the Government of Alberta. The APA provides services to about 500 employees, 50,500 pensioners & 130,400 members.
• Alberta Local Authorities Pension Plan Corporation(ALAPP Corp.)
PO Box 1315
Edmonton, AB T5J 2M8
780-427-5447
www.lapp.ca/plan/corp.htm
ALAPP Corp. provides strategic support to the Board of Trustees of the Local Authorities Pension Plan, and guidance to LAPP's primary service providers which include Alberta Pensions Services Corporation (APS) who manage all benefit administration duties for LAPP, and Alberta Investment Management Corporation (AIMCo) who implement the Board's investment policies.
• ATB Financial
9888 Jasper Ave.
Edmonton, AB T5J 1P1
780-408-7000 800-332-8383
www.atb.com
Offers Albertans financial services on a commercial, non-subsidized basis; provides a wide range of deposit & loan products, including mutual funds, online transactions, ABMs; an arms-length organization that reports to the Minister of Finance.
• Automobile Insurance Rate Board
Terrace Bldg.
#200, 9515 - 107 St. NW
Edmonton, AB T5K 2C3
780-415-1126 Fax: 780-644-7771
airb@gov.ab.ca
www.airb.alberta.ca
The mandate of the board is to set premiums for basic coverage, monitor premiums for optional coverage and review and approve rating programs for new insurers entering the Alberta market. Its mission is to maintain long-term stability of automobile insurance rates.
• Credit Union Deposit Guarantee Corporation
10130 - 103 St., 18th Fl.
Edmonton, AB T5J 3N9
780-428-6680 Fax: 780-428-7571 800-661-0351
mail@cudgc.ab.ca
www.cudgc.ab.ca
Monitors & regulates the performance of credit unions in Alberta & the compliance of Alberta credit unions with the Credit Union Act. The primary role of the Corporation is to guarantee deposit protection to deposit holders with credit unions in Alberta.
• Northern Alberta Development Council(NADC)
Provincial Building
#206, 9621 - 96 Ave.
PO Box 900-14
Peace River, AB T8S 1T4
780-624-6274 Fax: 780-624-6184
nadc.council@gov.ab.ca
www.nadc.gov.ab.ca
The mission of the NADC is to identify and implement measures that will advance northern development, as well as advise government on opportunities and issues. It is involved with projects and initiatives in transportation, value-added agriculture, tourism, educational initiatives and inter-jurisdictional projects.
• Alberta Investment Management Corporation(AIMCo)
1100 - 10830 Jasper Ave.
Edmonton, AB T5J 2B3
780-392-3600
inquiries@aimco.alberta.ca
www.aimco.alberta.ca
AIMCo's $39 billion in balanced assets are invested globally across diverse asset classes. Operating within a crown corporation structure, AIMCo competes in a competitive global marketplace.
• Alberta Securities Commission
300 - 5 Ave. SW, 4th Fl.
Calgary, AB T2P 3C4
403-297-6454 Fax: 403-297-6156 877-355-0585
inquiries@asc.ca
www.albertasecurities.com
An industry-funded provincial corporation responsible for regulating Alberta's capital market. The Commission performs its responsibilities under the Securities Act.

Enterprise Division
Commerce Place, 10155 - 102 St., 6th Fl., Edmonton, AB T5J 4L6
Asst. Deputy Minister, Rick Sloan
780-427-6987, Fax: 780-422-0626,rick.sloan@gov.ab.ca
Executive Director, Regional Development, Diane Simsovic
780-427-6656, Fax: 780-422-5804,diane.simsovic@gov.ab.ca
Executive Director, Alberta Economic Development Authority, James Cleland
780-297-3161, Fax: 780-297-6435,james.cleland@gov.ab.ca, Other Communications: aeda.alberta.ca
Executive Director, Industry Development, Justin Riemer
780-297-6302, Fax: 780-422-2091,justin.riemer@gov.ab.ca
Executive Director, Economic Development Policy & Analysis, Duane Pyear
780-427-0850, Fax: 780-422-0061,duane.pyear@gov.ab.ca

Treasury Management
Terrace Building, 9515 - 107 St., 3rd Fl., Edmonton, AB T5K 2C3
Asst. Deputy Minister, Rod Matheson
780-415-0752, Fax: 780-427-2435,rod.matheson@gov.ab.ca
Director, Risk Management & Insurance, Mark Day
780-644-4045, Fax: 780-422-5271,mark.day@gov.ab.ca

Office of Budget & Fiscal Planning
Terrace Building, 9515 - 107 St., 4th Fl., Edmonton, AB T5K 2C3
Asst. Deputy Minister, Stephen LeClair
780-427-8417, Fax: 780-427-1296,stephen.leclair@gov.ab.ca
Executive Director & Chief Economist, Economics, Demography & Public Finance, Mary MAcGregor
780-427-8790, Fax:
780-426-3951,mary.macgregor@gov.ab.ca
Executive Director, Tax Policy, Nancy Cuelenaere
780-427-8893, Fax:
780-426-4564,nancy.cuelenaere@gov.ab.ca
Executive Director, Budget Planning & Integration, James Forrest
780-427-8752, Fax: 780-426-4564,james.forrest@gov.ab.ca

Tax & Revenue Administration
Sir Frederick W. Haultain Building, 9811 - 109 St., 2nd Fl., Edmonton, AB T5K 2L5
780-427-3044,
Asst. Deputy Minister, Jane Clerk
780-427-9403, Fax: 780-422-0899,jane.clerk@gov.ab.ca
Executive Director, Audit, Ian Ayton
780-644-4075, Fax: 780-422-2090,ian.ayton@gov.ab.ca

Director, Corporate Tax Audit, Tracy Teng
780-644-4248, Fax: 780-422-2090,tracy.teng@gov.ab.ca
Director, Aggressive Tax Planning, Kent Heine
780-644-4257, Fax: 780-422-2090,kent.heine@gov.ab.ca
Director, Revenue Operations, Melissa Banks
780-644-4212, Fax: 780-644-4921,melissa.banks@gov.ab.ca
Director, Business Technology Management, Rick Callaway
780-644-4164, Fax: 780-644-5016,rick.callaway@gov.ab.ca
Executive Director, Tax Services, Angelina Leung
780-644-4064, Fax: 780-427-5074,angelina.leung@gov.ab.ca
Director, Strategic & Client Services (SCS), Jason Waywood
780-644-1090, Fax:
780-422-0899,jason.waywood@gov.ab.ca

Regulatory Review Secretariat
780-422-1736, Fax: 780-415-4860
Director, Angela Prokopetz
angela.prokopetz@gov.ab.ca

Strategic & Business Services
Terrace Building, 9515 - 107 St., 4th Fl., Edmonton, AB T5K 2C3
Asst. Deputy Minister, Darwin Bozek
780-415-9718, Fax: 780-427-1296,darwin.bozek@gov.ab.ca
Executive Director, Bonnie Lovelace
780-427-3052, Fax:
780-427-0178,bonnie.lovelace@gov.ab.ca
Director & FOIP Coordinator, Administrative & Information Services, Roger Mariner
780-415-9180, Fax: 780-422-7235,roger.mariner@gov.ab.ca
Director, Corporate Planning Services, Dave Olson
780-644-2614, Fax: 780-638-3128,dave.olson@gov.ab.ca
Director, Corporate Technology Services, Glen Sustrik
780-427-5741, Fax: 780-415-6416,glen.sustrik@gov.ab.ca
Executive Director, Financial Services, Richard Isaak
780-415-9149, Fax: 780-422-2163,richard.isaak@gov.ab.ca

Financial Sector Regulation & Policy (FSRP)
Terrace Building, 9515 - 107 St., 4th Fl., Edmonton, AB T5K 2C3
Asst. Deputy Minister, Dennis Gartner
780-427-9722, Fax: 780-427-1636,dennis.gartner@gov.ab.ca
Senior Policy Advisor, Capital Markets Policy, Marsha Manolescu
780-415-9243, Fax:
780-644-7759,marsha.manolescu@gov.ab.ca
Superintendent of Insurance, Financial Institutions & Pensions, Alberta Superintendent of Financial Institutions, Dennis Gartner
780-427-8322, Fax: 780-420-0752,dennis.gartner@gov.ab.ca
FHU Administrator, Financial Hardship Unlocking Program (FHU), Sonia McAdam
780-644-5078, Fax:
780-644-7279,sonya.mcadam@gov.ab.ca
Executive Director, Public Sector Pension Policy, Ellen Nygard
780-415-0513, Fax: 780-644-7771,ellen.nygaard@gov.ab.ca

Alberta Health & Wellness

Telus Plaza NT, 10025 Jasper Ave., 22nd Fl., PO Box 1360 Main, Edmonton, AB T5J 2N3
780-427-7164,
health.ahinform@gov.ab.ca
www.health.alberta.ca

The Government has endorsed broad health goals for Albertans which support Alberta's vision for health.These health goals reflect the range of factors which determine health, families, communities & environments, public policy, information, behaviour, coping skills, heredity & health services. The goals of Alberta Health & Wellness reflect the interrelationship of health, prosperity & the environment. It's mandate is to work to improve the health by providing leadership & encouraging actions to address health concerns, protect & promote good health, & prevent disease & injury. The government also works to ensure that Albertans are well informed & able to make decisions about their health & health services.

Acts Administered:
ABC Benefits Corporation Act
Alberta Evidence Act (Section 9)
Alberta Health Care Insurance Act
Charitable Donation of Food Act
Emergency Health Services Act
Emergency Medical Aid Act
Government Organization Act, Schedule 7.1
Health Disciplines Act
Health Facilities Review Committee Act
Health Information Act
Health Insurance Premiums Act
Health Professions Act
Hospitals Act
Human Tissue & Organ Donation Act
Mandatory Testing & Disclosure Act
Mental Health Act
M.S.I. Foundation Act
Nursing Homes Act
Opticians Act
Pharmacy & Drug Act
Physical Therapy Profession Act
Podiatry Act
Prevention of Youth Tobacco Use Act
Protection of Children Abusing Drugs Act
Provincial Health Authorities of Alberta Act
Public Health Act
Regional Health Authorities Act
Tobacco Reduction Act
Alberta Cancer Prevention Legacy Act
Health Care Protection Act
Health Governance Transition Act

Minister,Hon. Gene Zwozdesky
780-427-3665, Fax:
780-415-0961,health.minister@gov.ab.ca
Deputy Minister, Jay Ramotar
780-422-0747, Fax: 780-427-1016,jay.ramotar@gov.ab.ca
Chief Medical Officer of Health,Dr. André Corriveau
780-415-2809, Fax:
780-427-7683,andre.corriveau@gov.ab.ca
Mental Health Patient Advocate, Fay Orr
780-422-1812, Fax: 780-422-0695,fay.orr@gov.ab.ca v.ab.ca
Director, Communications, Andy Weiler
780-427-5344, Fax: 780-427-1171,andy.weiler@gov.ab.ca .ca
Director, Human Resources, Rick Brick
780-427-1060, Fax: 780-422-1700,rick.brick@gov.ab.ca

• Alberta Health Services(AHS)
Manulife Place
10180 - 101 St.
Edmonton, AB T5J 3S4
780-342-2000 Fax: 780-342-2060 888-342-2471
www.albertahealthservices.ca
In 2008, The Minister of Health & Wellness announced the launch of Canada's first province-wide, fully integrated health system, bringing together 12 formerly separate health entities, including 9 geographically based health authorities, the Alberta Alcohol & Drug Abuse Commission (AADAC), Alberta Mental Health Board & the Alberta Cancer Board. Wholly owned subsidiaries include Carewest, Capital Care Group and Calgary Laboratory Services. Programs and services are offered at 400 facilities throughout the province, including hospitals, clinics, continuing care facilities, mental health facilities and community health sites.

• Health Disciplines Board
Telus Plaza NT, Health Professions Branch
10025 Jasper Ave., 17th Fl.
Edmonton, AB T5J 2N3
780-415-0486 Fax: 780-422-2880
Oversees the regulation of those health disciplines under the Health Disciplines Act & investigates the application of those disciplines for designation under the Act.

• Health Facilities Review Committee(HFRC)
First Edmonton Place
#590, 10665 Jasper Ave.
Edmonton, AB T5J 3S9
780-427-2791 Fax: 780-427-0806
The HFRC has the following principle responsibilities: to review & inspect health care facilities; & to investigate complaints about the care, treatment, & standards of accommodation.

Corporate Support Division
Telus Plaza NT, 10025 Jasper Ave., 19th Fl., Edmonton, AB T5J 1S6
Asst. Deputy Minister, Martin Chamberlain
780-422-1045, Fax:
780-422-3674,martin.chamberlain@gov.ab.ca
Executive Director, Compliance Monitoring & Risk Management Branch, Lorraine McKay
780-415-1424, Fax: 780-643-1527,lorraine.mckay@gov.ab.ca
Director, Corporate Services, Stephen Arthur
780-415-0201, Fax: 780-427-1643,stephen.arthur@gov.ab.ca
Executive Director, Health Care Insurance Plan Administration,Vacant
780-644-3149, Fax: 780-644-1445
Director & Corporate Counsel, Legal & Legislative Services, Denise Perret
780-422-8989, Fax: 780-422-2512,denise.perret@gov.ab.ca

Health Workforce Division
Telus Plaza NT, 10025 Jasper Ave., 10th Fl., Edmonton, AB T5J 1S6
Asst. Deputy Minister, Glenn Monteith
780-415-2745, Fax: 780-415-8455,glenn.monteith@gov.ab.ca
Executive Director, Innovative Compensation, Yolanda Lackie
780-427-0380, Fax: 780-422-5208,yolanda.lackie@gov.ab.ca
Executive Director, Labour Relations Branch, Deb Kaweski
780-415-0212, Fax: 780-415-1094,deb.kaweski@gov.ab.ca
Executive Director, Workforce Policy & Planning Branch, Linda Mattern
780-422-2720, Fax: 780-415-1094,linda.mattern@gov.ab.ca
Executive Director, Workforce Policy & Planning, Linda Mattern
780-422-2720, Fax: 780-415-1094,linda.mattern@gov.ab.ca
Provincial Medical Care Consultant, Joan Berezanski
780-422-9325, Fax:
780-415-1094,joan.bereznaski@gov.ab.ca
Director, Telehealth, Sharlene Stayberg
780-415-2609, Fax:
780-415-1094,sharlene.stayberg@gov.ab.ca

Community & Population Health Division
Telus Plaza NT, 10025 Jasper Ave., 24th Fl., Edmonton, AB T5J 1S6
Asst. Deputy Minister, Margaret King
780-415-2783, Fax: 780-422-3671,margaret.king@gov.ab.ca
Executive Director, Community Health, Silvia Vajushi
780-422-1344, Fax: 780-422-6663,silvia.vajushi@gov.ab.ca
Executive Director, Health Protection, Alex MacKenzie
780-422-4549, Fax:
780-427-1470,alex.mackenzie@gov.ab.ca
Acting Executive Director, Surveillance & Assessment, Kathy Ness
780-422-2561, Fax: 780-427-1470,kathy.ness@gov.ab.ca
Executive Director, Public Health Strategic Policy and Planning Branch, Neil MacDonald
780-415-2759, Fax:
780-422-5474,neil.macdonald@gov.ab.ca

Financial Accountability Division
Telus Plaza NT, 10025 Jasper Ave., 16th Fl., Edmonton, AB T5J 1S6
Asst. Deputy Minister, David Breakwell
780-415-1599, Fax:
780-422-3672,david.breakwell@gov.ab.ca
Senior Project Manager, Alternative Capital Financing Office, Robert Fernandez
780-427-1310, Fax:
780-422-3672,robert.fernandez@gov.ab.ca
Executive Director, Financial Planning Branch, Charlene Wong
780-427-7100, Fax: 780-422-3672,charlene.wong@gov.ab.ca
Acting Executive Director, Financial Reporting Branch, Charlene Wong
780-427-7100, Fax: 780-422-3672,charlene.wong@gov.ab.ca
Executive Director, Health Facilities Planning, Wayne Campbell
780-638-3546, Fax:
780-427-0738,wayne.campbell@gov.ab.ca

Financial Accountability Division
Telus Plaza NT, 10025 Jasper Ave., 21st Fl., Edmonton, AB T5J 1S6
Asst. Deputy Minister & CIO, Mark Brisson
780-427-1572, Fax: 780-422-5176,mark.brisson@gov.ab.ca
Executive Director, Performance Measurement, John Quince
780-415-1505, Fax: 780-422-2880,john.quince@gov.ab.ca
Executive Director, Information & Analysis, Tapan Chowdhury
780-427-4938, Fax:
780-427-1577,tapan.chowdhury@gov.ab.ca

Health Policy & Service Standards Division
Telus Plaza NT, 10025 Jasper Ave., 18th Fl., Edmonton, AB T5J 1S6
Asst. Deputy Minister, Susan Williams
780-644-3086, Fax: 780-415-0570,susan.williams@gov.ab.ca
Executive Director, Clinical Advisory & Research Branch, Joan Berezanski
780-422-9325, Fax:
780-422-4482,joan.berezanski@gov.ab.ca
Executive Director, Health Policy & Service Standards Development, Pearl Morrison
780-422-9678, Fax: 780-422-1515,pearl.morrison@gov.ab.ca
Executive Director, Pharmaceutical Funding & Guidance, Steve Long
780-427-8019, Fax: 780-422-3646,steve.long@gov.ab.ca
Acting Executive Director, Intergovernmental & Integrated Strategic Policy, Line Porfon
780-415-2762, Fax: 780-422-1515,line.porfon@gov.ab.ca,

Alberta Housing & Urban Affairs

44 Capital Blvd., 10044 - 108 St., 3rd fl., Edmonton, AB T5J 5E6
780-422-0122, Fax: 780-422-8462,-310-0000
housing@gov.ab.ca
www.housing.alberta.ca

The Ministry promotes the independence of lower-income Albertans through safe, sustainable and affordable housing, and assists urban communities with their unique needs.

Acts Administered:
Alberta Housing Act
Social Care Facilities Licensing Act
Government Organization Act

Minister,Hon. Jonathan Denis, Q.C.
780-644-8954, Fax: 780-644-8959
Deputy Minister, Marcia Nelson
780-644-5253, Fax:
780-644-5240,marcia.nelson@gov.ab.ca
Director, Communications, Vacant
780-644-6838, Fax: 780-644-5796
Director, Human Resource Services, Sandra Kraatz
780-422-8681, Fax: 780-422-0214,sandra.kraatz@gov.ab.ca
• Gunn Centre
PO Box 130
Gunn, AB T0E 1Ao
780-967-2221 Fax: 780-967-3494
The Centre has provided services for disadvantaged men to a capacity of 115 since 1941. It offers temporary accommodation to men who are homeless, or at risk of homelessness. It aims to establish links to affordable housing and services within the community meeting the special needs of each individual.

Homeless Support & Land Development
44 Capital Boulevard, 10044 - 108 St. 3rd Fl., Edmonton, AB T5J 5E6
780-422-3188
Asst. Deputy Minister, Robin Wigston
780-427-4093, Fax: 780-422-8462,robin.wigston@gov.ab.ca
Director, Homeless Cross Ministry Initiatives, Barry Bezuko
780-643-0757, Fax: 780-415-9345,barry.bezuko@gov.ab.ca
Executive Director, Homeless Support, Stephen Manley
403-297-7461, Fax:
403-297-6138,stephen.manley@gov.ab.ca
Director, Land & Special Projects, John Martin
780-422-8547, Fax: 780-415-9345,john.martin@gov.ab.ca
Director, Land Management, Larry Laverty
780-644-5780, Fax: 780-415-9345,larry.laverty@gov.ab.ca
Acting Executive Director, Alberta Secretariat for Action on Homelessness, Colin Penman
403-297-3196, Fax: 403-297-3358,colin.penman@gov.ab.ca

Housing Development & Operations
44 Capital Boulevard, 10044 - 108 St. 3rd Fl., Edmonton, AB T5J 5E6
Asst. Deputy Minister, Mike Leathwood
780-643-1020, Fax:
780-422-8462,mike.leathwood@gov.ab.ca
Executive Director, Corporate Projects, Rai Batra
780-427-2925, Fax: 780-422-8462,rai.batra@gov.ab.ca
Executive Director, Housing Development, Don Squire
780-427-5786, Fax: 780-422-5124,don.squire@gov.ab.ca
Executive Director, Housing Operations, Clarence Bereska
780-427-5784, Fax:
780-422-8551,clarence.bereska@gov.ab.ca

Strategic Services
44 Capital Boulevard, 10044 - 108 St. 3rd Fl., Edmonton, AB T5J 5E6
780-638-3736
Asst. Deputy Minister, Lana Lougheed
780-643-0766, Fax: 780-422-5124,lana.lougheed@gov.ab.ca
Executive Director & Senior Financial Officer, Finance & Administrative Services, Bev Walkner
780-643-1324, Fax: 780-427-0418,bev.walkner@gov.ab.ca
Director & CIO, Information Management & Technology, Dean Lussier
780-427-1751, Fax: 780-427-0418,dean.lussier@gov.ab.ca
Acting Executive Director, Policy & Urban Affairs, Lora Pillipow
780-422-2816, Fax: 780-422-5124,lora.pillipow@gov.ab.ca
Calgary
Cantury Park Place, 855 - 8 Ave. SWt, 11th Fl., Calgary, AB T2P 3P1
403-297-4575, Fax: 403-297-5988
Regional Director, Caroline Fairbrother
403-297-5334, Fax:
403-297-5988,caroline.fairbrother@gov.ab.ca
Central
Provincial Bldg., 4920 - 51 St., 5th Fl., Red Deer, AB T4N 6K8
403-340-7022, Fax: 403-340-7057
Regional Director, Donna Stewart-Wood
403-340-7001, Fax:
403-340-7057,donna.stewart-wood@gov.ab.ca
Edmonton
South Tower, 10030 - 107 St., 8th Fl., Edmonton, AB T5J 4X7
780-427-0003, Fax: 780-422-5125
Regional Director, Elvin Collins
780-422-6993, Fax: 780-422-5125,elvin.collins@gov.ab.ca
Northeast
Lakeview Bldg., 15 Nipewan Rd., PO Box 1410, Lac La Biche, AB T0A 2C0
780-623-5283, Fax: 780-623-5355
Regional Director, Ken Shewchuk
780-623-5102, Fax: 780-623-5355,ken.shewchuk@gov.ab.ca
Northwest
205 - 1 St. East, McLennan, AB T0H 2L0
780-324-3200, Fax: 780-324-3235
Regional Director, Barb Hendry
780-324-3239
South
2105 - 20 Ave., Coaldale, AB T1M 1M2
403-345-2277, Fax: 403-345-4915
Regional Director, Noelle Becker
403-345-7979, Fax: 403-345-4915,noelle.becker@gov.ab.ca,

Alberta Office of the Information & Privacy Commissioner

#410, 9925 - 109 St., Edmonton, AB T5K 2J8
780-422-6860, Fax: 780-422-5682, 888-878-4044
generalinfo@oipc.ab.ca
www.oipc.ab.ca
The Information and Privacy Commissioner has offices in Edmonton and Calgary. The Edmonton office deals with issues under the Freedom of Information and Protection of Privacy Act (FOIP) and the Health Information Act (HIA). The Calgary office deals exclusively with issues relating to the Personal Information Protection Act (PIPA).
Information & Privacy Commissioner, Frank Work, Q.C.
780-422-6860, Fax: 780-422-5682,fwork@oipc.ab.ca
Asst. Commissioner, Freedom of Information & Protection of Privacy Act Team (FOIP), Marilyn Mun
780-422-7617, Fax: 780-422-5682,mmun@oipc.ab.ca
Director, Health Information Act Team (HIA), LeRoy Brower
780-427-1919, Fax: 780-422-5682,lbrower@oipc.ab.ca
Director, Personal Information Protection Act Team (PIPA) - Calgary, Jill clayton
403-297-6452, Fax: 403-297-2711,jclayton@oipc.ab.ca
Director, Adjudication Team, Christina Gauk
780-422-6860, Fax: 780-422-5682,cgauk@oipc.ab.ca
Director, Legal Services, Sharon Ashmore
780-422-6860, Fax: 780-422-5682,sashmore@oipc.ab.ca
Director, Communications, Wayne Wood
780-644-4015, Fax: 780-422-5682,wwood@oipc.ab.ca
Director, Human Resources & Finance, Donna Check
780-422-9037, Fax: 780-422-5682,dcheck@oipc.ab.ca

Alberta Infrastructure

Infrastructure Building, 6950 - 101 St., 3rd Fl., Edmonton, AB T6H 5V7
780-415-0507, Fax: 780-427-2187,-310-0000
www.infrastructure.alberta.ca
The Ministry anticipates the growth of the province, and takes the necessary actions to build essential roads and highways, schools and hospitals, utilities and facilities to accommodate the changing Alberta.
Acts Administered:
Government Organization Act, Sched 1, 5, 11, 14
Highways Development and Protection Act
Hospitals Act
Mental Health Act
Nursing Homes Act
Post-secondary Learning Act
School Act
Water, Gas and Electric Companies Act
Minister,Hon. Ray Danyluk
780-427-5041, Fax: 780-422-2002
Deputy Minister, Barry Day
780-427-3835, Fax: 780-422-6565,barry.day@gov.ab.ca
Director, Communications, Cam Traynor
780-644-8596, Fax: 780-427-2187,cam.traynor@gov.ab.ca
Executive Director, Human Resources Branch, Lynn Cook
780-415-8711, Fax: 780-422-5138,lynn.cook@gov.ab.ca
• Alberta Research Council(ARC)
250 Karl Clark Rd.
Edmonton, AB T6N 1E4
780-450-5111 Fax: 780-450-5333
www.arc.ab.ca
ARC is an R&D corporation with a mandate to develop and commercialize technology. It aims to convert early stage ideas into marketable products and services. It is a not-for-profit corporation, wholly-owned by the province of Alberta and now operates under the umbrella of Alberta Innovates — Technology Futures: www.albertainnovates.ca/technology.

Capital Projects Division
Infrastructure Building, 6950 - 113 St., 2nd Fl., Edmonton, AB T6H 5V7
Asst. Deputy Minister, Diane Dagleish
780-422-7436, Fax:
780-422-7599,diane.dalgleish@gov.ab.ca
Executive Director, Project Delivery Branch, Kent Phillips
780-422-0770, Fax: 780-422-9749,kent.phillips@gov.ab.ca
Director, Divisional Coordination Branch, Roberta Killips
780-415-0678, Fax: 780-422-7599,roberta.killips@gov.ab.ca
Executive Director, Capital Programs Branch, Mike Irving
780-422-7224, Fax: 780-427-5816,mike.irving@gov.ab.ca
Executive Director, Program Management Branch, Brian Soutar
780-422-7461, Fax: 780-422-9594,brian.soutar@gov.ab.ca
Executive Director, Technical Services Branch, Tom O'Neill
780-422-7447, Fax: 780-422-7479,tom.o'neill@gov.ab.ca

Policy & Corporate Services Division
Twin Atria Building, 4999 - 98 Ave., 3rd Fl., Edmonton, AB T6B 2X3
Asst. Deputy Minister, Alan Humphries
780-415-1386, Fax:
780-422-1070,alan.humphries@gov.ab.ca
Executive Director, Strategic Policy Branch, Rod Thompson
780-415-0685, Fax: 780-422-1070,rod.thompson@gov.ab.ca
Executive Director & CIO, Information Management, Ken Bainey
780-644-5114, Fax: 780-644-7028,ken.bainey@gov.ab.ca
Director, Legislative Planning & FOIP, Jim H. Leitch
780-415-6489, Fax: 780-638-3497,jim.h.leitch@gov.ab.ca
Executive Director & Senior Financial Officer, Finance Branch, Rod Skura
780-644-1713, Fax: 780-643-0803,rod.skura@gov.ab.ca

Properties Division
Infrastructure Building, 6950 - 113 St., 3rd Fl., Edmonton, AB T6H 5V7
Asst. Deputy Minister, Bob Smith
780-427-3875, Fax: 780-422-1389,bob.smith@gov.ab.ca
Acting Executive Director, Property Management Branch - North Region, Dave Bentley
780-427-9225, Fax: 780-422-0284,dave.bentley@gov.ab.ca
Executive Director, Property Management Branch - South Region, John Enns
780-427-2710, Fax: 780-422-0284,john.enns@gov.ab.ca

Southern
Administration Bldg., 909 - 3 Ave. North, Lethbridge, AB T1H 0H5
Fax: 403-382-4412
Director, Terry Wallace
780-427-7508, terry.wallace@gov.ab.ca
Manager, Rail Safety, Bob Clyne
780-415-6147, Fax: 780-422-9193,bob.clyne@gov.ab.ca
Executive Director, Jeanette Espie
780-427-6588
Manager, Collison Research & Analysis, Liz Owens
780-427-6775, liz.owens@gov.ab.ca
Director, Vehicle Safety, Dennis Bell
780-427-7629, Fax: 780-422-3682,

Alberta International & Intergovernmental Relations

Commerce Place, 10155 - 102 St., 12th Fl., Edmonton, AB T5J 4G8
780-422-1510, Fax: 780-427-0699,
www.international.aberta.ca
Alberta's International & Intergovernmental Relations (IIR) Ministry coordinates the province's relationships with different levels of government both nationally & internationally. The IIR works in areas such as export, trade & govermental relations to enhance & develop Alberta's presence.
Acts Administered:
Constitutional Referendum Act
Government Organization Act
International Interests in Mobile Aircraft Equipment Act (unproclaimed)
International Trade and Investment Agreements Implementation Act
Senatorial Selection Act
Minister,Hon. Iris Evans
780-427-2585, Fax: 780-422-9023
Deputy Minister, Paul Whittaker
780-427-6644, Fax:
780-423-6654,paul.whittaker@gov.ab.ca
Director, Communications, Mike Deising
780-422-2524, Fax: 780-422-2635,mike.deising@gov.ab.ca

Corporate Services
Commerce Place, 10155 - 102 St., 12th Fl., Edmonton, AB T5J 4L8
Intergovernmental Relations works with other Alberta government ministries & the federal government to ensure that Alberta's interests are represented in the Canadian federation by reviewing policies, programs & legislation; participating in the negotiation of intergovernmental agreements; providing stragic advice & making recommendations on the intergovernmental implications of issues & policy initiatives advanced by the Alberta government, & coordinating & providing logistical support for intergovernmental meetings, including meetings of the Council of the Federation & Western Premiers' Conferences.
Asst. Deputy Minister, Lorne Harvey
780-422-2429, Fax: 780-427-0939,lorne.harvey@gov.ab.ca
Executive Director, Human Resource Services, Georgina Riddell
780-422-1341, Fax:
780-427-1272,georgina.riddell@gov.ab.ca
Executive Director, Finance & Administration, Howard Wong
780-427-0793, Fax: 780-427-0939,howard.wong@gov.ab.ca

Director, Corporate Planning, Carol Mayers
780-644-1160, Fax: 780-644-4939,carol.mayers@gov.ab.ca
Director, IMIT, Carol Lawrence
780-427-0269, Fax: 780-427-4625,carol.lawrence@gov.ab.ca
Director, FOIP, Gerry Kushlyk
780-427-9658, Fax: 780-644-4939,gerry.kushlyk@gov.ab.ca

Intergovernmental Relations
Commerce Place, 10155 - 102 St., 12th Fl., Edmonton, AB T5J 4L8

Intergovernmental Relations works with other Alberta government ministries & the federal government to ensure that Alberta's interests are represented in the Canadian federation by reviewing policies, programs & legislation; participating in the negotiation of intergovernmental agreements; providing stragic advice & making recommendations on the intergovernmental implications of issues & policy initiatives advanced by the Alberta government, & coordinating & providing logistical support for intergovernmental meetings, including meetings of the Council of the Federation & Western Premiers' Conferences.

Assistant Deputy Minister, Intergovernmental Relations, Garry Pocock
780-422-0453, Fax: 780-427-0939,garry.pocock@gov.ab.ca
Intergovernmental Officer, Intergovernmental Coordination, David Liles
780-422-0098, Fax: 780-427-0939,david.liles@gov.ab.ca
Executive Director, Federal/Provincial Relations, Bruce Tait
780-422-1127, Fax: 780-427-0939,bruce.tait@gov.ab.ca
Executive Director, Social and Economic Policy, Gordon Vincent
780-415-6548, Fax: 780-427-0939,gordon.vincent@gov.ab.ca

International Relations
Commerce Place, 10155 - 102 St., 12th Fl., Edmonton, AB T5J 4G8
780-427-6543

Assistant Deputy Minister, John Cotton
780-422-2789, Fax: 780-427-0392,john.cotton@gov.ab.ca ca
Executive Director, Energy Issues Advisor, Joe Miller
780-427-8397, Fax: 780-427-0392,joe.miller@gov.ab.ca
Executive Director, Advocacy, US Relations & Mission Planning, Marvin Schneider
780-422-2332, Fax:
780-422-5486,marvin.schneider@gov.ab.ca
Executive Director, Europe & US Branch, Chris Heseltine
403-297-6377, Fax: 403-297-6168,chris.heseltine@gov.ab.ca
Senior Director, US Trade & Investment, Doug Cameron
780-427-6702, Fax: 780-422-5486,doug.cameron@gov.ab.ca
Executive Director, North Asia & Business Planning, Yvette Ng
780-422-2305, Fax: 780-427-0699,yvette.ng@gov.ab.ca
Executive Director, Southern Hemisphere & Showcase, Greg Jardine
780-427-6368, Fax: 780-422-9127,greg.jardine@gov.ab.ca
Minister-Counsellor (Alberta), Alberta Washington DC Office, Gary Mar
202-448-6476, Fax: 202-448-6477,gary.mar@gov.ab.ca b.ca

Alberta Justice & Attorney General

Communications, Bowker Bldg., 9833 - 109 St., 3rd Fl., Edmonton, AB T5K 2E8
780-427-2745, Fax: 780-427-6821,-310-0000
justice.alberta.ca

Other Communication: Maintenance Enforcement Program Fax: 780-401-7575

The Ministry protects the rights of all Albertans by ensuring a trusted justice system, which includes the following initiatives: promoting safe communities; improving the understanding of the justice system; ensuring respect for the law; providing fair access to civil & criminal justice; improving confidence in the justice system; providing the legal foundation for societal cohesion & economic well-being; & assisting ministries by providing supportive legal & related strategic services.

Acts Administered:
Administration of Estates Act
Administrative Procedures & Jurisdiction Act
Adult Interdependent Relationships Act
Age of Majority Act
Alberta Evidence Act, except Section 9
Alberta Personal Property Bill of Rights
Arbitration Act
Civil Enforcement Act
Class Proceedings Act
Commissioners for Oaths Act
Conflicts of Interest Act
Contributory Negligence Act
Court of Appeal Act
Court of Queen's Bench Act
Criminal Notoriety Act
Dangerous Dogs Act
Daylight Saving Time Act
Defamation Act
Dependants Relief Act
Devolution of Real Property Act
Expropriation Act (Sustainable Resource Development)
Extra-provincial Enforcement of Custody Orders Act
Factors Act
Family Law Act
Fatal Accidents Act
Fatality Inquiries Act
Fraudulent Preferences Act
Frustrated Contracts Act
Government Organization Act, Schedule 9
Guarantees Acknowledgment Act
Innkeepers Act
International Child Abduction Act
International Commercial Arbitration Act
International Conventions Implementation Act
Interpretation Act
Interprovincial Subpoena Act
Intestate Succession Act
Judgement Interest Act
Judicature Act
Jury Act
Justice of the Peace Act
Landlord's Rights on Bankruptcy Act
Languages Act/Loi Linguistique
Legal Profession Act
Legitimacy Act
Limitations Act
Maintenance Enforcement Act
Married Women's Act
Masters & Servants Act
Maternal Tort Liability Act
Matrimonial Property Act
Minors' Property Act
Motor Vehicle Accident Claims Act
Notaries Public Act
Oaths of Office Act
Occupiers' Liability Act
Perpetuities Act
Personal Property Security Act, part 5
Petty Trespass Act
Powers of Attorney Act
Proceedings Against the Crown Act
Provincial Court Act
Provincial Offences Procedure Act
Public Inquiries Act
Public Trustee Act
Queen's Counsel Act
Reciprocal Enforcement of Judgements Act
Recording of Evidence Act
Regulations Act
Road Building Machinery Equipment Act
Rules of Court Statutes Amendment Act, 2009
Sale of Goods Act
Statute Revision Act
Survival of Actions Act
Survivorship Act
Tort-Feasors Act
Trespass to Premises Act
Trustee Act
Unconscionable Transactions Act
Victims Restitution & Compensation Payment Act
Warehouse Receipts Act
Wills Act
Young Justice Act
Financial Administration Act
Interjurisdictional Support Orders Act
Lobbyists Act

Minister & Attorney General,Hon. Alison Redford
780-427-2339, Fax: 780-422-6621
Deputy Minister & Deputy Attorney General, Ray Bodnarek, Q.C.
780-427-5032, Fax:
780-422-9639,ray.bodnarek@gov.ab.ca
Acting Executive Director, Human Resource Services, Denis Starnaud
780-427-0441, Fax: 780-422-1330,denis.starnaud@gov.ab.ca
Director, Communications, Jody Korchinski
780-427-6154, Fax: 780-422-7363,jody.korchinski@gov.ab.ca

• Alberta Review Board
Oxford Tower
10235 - 101 St., 11th Fl.
Edmonton, AB T5J 3E9
780-422-5994 Fax: 780-427-1762

• Fatality Review Board - Edmonton
Medical Examiner's Office
7007 - 116 St. NW
Edmonton, AB T6H 5R8
780-427-4987 Fax: 780-422-1265

• Fatality Review Board - Calgary
Medical Examiner's Office
4070 Bowness Rd. NW
Calgary, AB T3B 3R7
403-297-8123 Fax: 403-297-3429

Court Services Division
Bowker Building, 9833 - 109 St., 2nd Fl., Edmonton, AB T5K 2E8
780-427-4992, Fax: 780-422-6613

Asst. Deputy Minister, Vicki Brandt
780-427-9620, Fax: 780-422-9638,vicki.brandt@gov.ab.ca
Executive Director, Planning & Business Services, Lynn Varty
780-644-8105, Fax: 780-422-6613,lynn.varty@gov.ab.ca
Registrar, Court of Appeal, Sue Stushnoff
780-422-7710, Fax: 780-427-5507,sue.stushnoff@gov.ab.ca
Director, Alberta Law Society Libraries/Alberta Court Libraries, Sonia Poulin
780-422-1011, Fax: 780-427-0397,sonia.poulin@gov.ab.ca

Regional Offices:

Calgary Regional Office
Court House, 601 - 5 St. SW, Calgary, AB T2P 1P7
403-297-2313, Fax: 403-297-7152
Executive Director, Court Operations, Sharon Lepetich
sharon.lepetich@gov.ab.ca

Edmonton Regional Office
Law Courts Bldg., Mezzanine Fl., 1A Sir Winston Churchill Sq., Edmonton, AB T5J 0R2
780-422-2426, Fax: 780-422-9585
Executive Director, Court Operations, Lorna Ross
lorna.ross@gov.ab.ca

Central Regional Office - Leduc
Court House, 4612 - 50 St., Leduc, AB T9E 6L1
780-986-6903, Fax: 780-986-2429
Executive Director, Court Operations, Ed Towers
ed.towers@gov.ab.ca
District Manager, Ursula Owre
780-980-3550, Fax: 780-980-3551,ursula.owe@gov.ab.ca

North Regional Office - Grande Prairie
Court House, 10260 - 99 St., Grande Prairie, AB T8V 2H4
780-538-5360, Fax: 780-538-5454
District Manager, Court Operations, Wendy Smith
wendy.smith@gov.ab.ca

South Regional Office - Lethbridge
Court House, 320 - 4 St., 1st Fl., Lethbridge, AB T1J 1Z8
780-381-5453, Fax: 780-381-5762
District Manager, Court Operations, Clara Finan
clara.finan@gov.ab.ca

Criminal Justice Division
Bowker Building, 9833 - 109 St., 2nd Fl., Edmonton, AB T5K 2E8

Asst. Deputy Minister, Gregory Lepp, Q.C.
780-427-5046, Fax: 780-422-9639,greg.lepp@gov.ab.ca
Executive Director, Appeals & Prosecution Policy Branch, Richard Taylor, Q.C.
780-422-5402, Fax: 780-422-1106,richard.taylor@gov.ab.ca
Executive Director, Special Prosecutions - Edmonton, Sheila Brown, Q.C.
780-422-0640, Fax: 780-422-1217,sheila.brown@gov.ab.ca a
Acting Chief Crown Prosecutor, Regulatory Posecutions, Brian Caruk
780-644-2016, Fax: 780-644-2034,brian.caruk@gov.ab.ca

Legal Services Division
Bowker Building, 9833 - 109 St., 2nd Fl., Edmonton, AB T5K 2E8
780-422-0500,

Asst. Deputy Minister, Grant Sprague, Q.C.
780-415-2388, Fax: 780-422-9639,grant.sprague@gov.ab.ca
Chief Legislative Counsel, Peter J. Pagano, Q.C.
780-427-0303, Fax: 780-422-7366,peter.pagano@gov.ab.ca
Chief Medical Examiner,Dr. Graeme P. Dowling
780-427-4987, Fax:
780-422-1265,graeme.dowling@gov.ab.ca
Public Trustee, Office of the Public Trustee, Cindy Bentz
780-422-3141, Fax: 780-422-9136,cindy.bentz@gov.ab.ca
Executive Director, Legal Aid & Corporate Legal Services, Civil Law Branch, R. Neil Dunne, Q.C.
780-422-8787, Fax: 780-425-0307,r.neil.dunne@gov.ab.ca
Executive Director, Legislative Reform, Nolan Steed, Q.C.
780-422-9653, Fax: 780-425-0307,nolan.steed@gov.ab.ca
Executive Director, Departmental Legal Services Delivery, Constitutional & Aboriginal Law, Rita Sumka
780-422-3715, Fax: 780-643-0852,rita.sumka@gov.ab.ca

Safe Communities & Strategic Policy
Bowker Building, 9833 - 109 St., 2nd Fl., Edmonton, AB T5K 2E8
780-644-5595

Asst. Deputy Minister, Kurt Sandstrom
780-422-4160, Fax: 780-422-6613,kurt.sandstrom@gov.ab.ca
Manager, Safe Communities Innovation Fund, Doug Darwish
780-643-1346, Fax: 780-638-2870,doug.darwish@gov.ab.ca

Executive Director, Strategic Policy, Jeanette Fedorak
780-422-9760, Fax:
780-644-5609,jeanette.fedorak@gov.ab.ca

Alberta Municipal Affairs

Communications Branch, Commerce Place, 10155 - 102 St., 18th Fl., Edmonton, AB T5J 4L4
780-427-2732, Fax: 780-422-1419,
comments@gov.ab.ca
www.municipalaffairs.alberta.ca

The Ministry works to provide well-managed, accountable local governments. It aims to ensure safety standards in construction and maintenance of buildings & equipment and it manages the municipal & library system boards.

Acts Administered:
City of Lloydminster Act
Emergency Management Act
Government Organization Act, Sched 10, 13
Libraries Act
Local Authorities Election Admendment Act, 2009
Municipal Government Amendment Act
Parks Towns Act
Public Highways Development Act
Safety Codes Act
Special Areas Act

Minister,Hon. Hector Goudreau
780-427-3744, Fax: 780-422-9550
Deputy Minister, Ray Gilmour
780-427-4826, Fax: 780-422-9561,ray.gilmour@gov.ab.ca
Director, Communications, Donna Babchishin
780-415-4758, Fax:
780-422-1419,donna.babchishin@gov.ab.ca
Director, Human Resource Services, Sandra Kraatz
780-422-8681, Fax: 780-422-0214,sandra.kraatz@gov.ab.ca
Director & Solicitor, Legal Services, Bill Nugent
780-422-8795, Fax: 780-427-0996,bill.nugent@gov.ab.ca

• Alberta Municipal Government Board
Commerce Place
10155 - 102 St., 15th Fl.
Edmonton, AB T5J 4L4
780-427-4864 Fax: 780-427-0986
The Municipal Government Board is an independent & impartial body set up to make decisions on certain appeals & disputes stemming from the Municipal Government Act, including appeals on property assessment, equalized assessment, linear property assessment & subdivisions including provincial interest, intermunicipal disputes, conflicts between municipalities & housing authorities, annexation matters & any other matters referred by the Minister or Lieutenant Governor.

• Alberta Special Areas Board
212 - 2nd Ave. West
PO Box 820
Hanna, AB T0J 1P0
403-854-5600 Fax: 403-854-5527
specarea@telusplanet.net
www.specialareas.ab.ca
The Special Areas Board reports directly to the Assistant Deputy Minister of the Local Government Services Division. The Special Areas Board was set up under the Special Areas Act (1938) to administer this area where municipal services could not be provided due to financial hardship resulting from the Depression & drought of the 1930s.The board provides cost-effective, responsive municipal services & effective, long-term land resource management for the Special Areas.Special Areas is made up of a unique rural municipal area covering approximately 2.1 million hectares in southeastern Alberta. The Special Areas Board is made up of three members appointed by the Lieutenant Governor in Council, who also designates one member as Chairman.

• Alberta Emergency Management Agency(AEMA)
c/o Alberta Municipal Affairs, Communications Br.
10155 - 102 St., 18th Fl.
Edmonton, AB T5J 4L4
780-422-9000 Fax: 780-644-1044 866-618-2362
aema@gov.ab.ca
www.aema.alberta.ca
AEMA heads the co-ordination of all organizations involved in the prevention, preparedness and response to disasters and emergencies, aiming to enure delivery of vital services. Organizations include governmental, industrial & first responders.

• Safety Codes Council(SCC)
#1000, 10665 Jasper Ave. NW
Edmonton, AB T5J 3S9
780-413-0099 Fax: 780-424-5134 888-413-0099
sccinfo@safetycodes.ab.ca
www.safetycodes.ab.ca
The Council recommends codes and standards to the Ministry under the authority of the Safety Codes Act. It administers a system to accredit municipalities, corporations and agencies to pursue activities under the Act. It aims to promote uniform standards and barrier-free designs & access on behalf of the Ministry.

Corporate Strategic Services Division
Commerce Place, 10155 - 102 St., 18th Fl., Edmonton, AB T5J 4L4
Asst. Deputy Minister, Anthony Lemphers
780-427-8099, Fax:
780-422-4923,anthony.lemphers@gov.ab.ca
Executive Director, Corporate Planning & Policy, Indira Breitkreuz
780-422-7317, Fax:
780-422-4923,indira.breitkreuz@gov.ab.ca
Director, Information Management, Legislative & Administrative Services, Wilma Sisk
780-422-8834, Fax: 780-643-1090,wilma.sisk@gov.ab.ca
Executive Director & Senior Financial Officer, Financial Services, Dan Balderston
780-644-8098, Fax: 780-422-5840,dan.balderston@gov.ab.ca
Director, Information Technology, Heather Cox
780-427-6097, Fax: 780-422-0776,heather.cox@gov.ab.ca
Director, Public Library Services, Diana Davidson
780-415-0284, Fax:
780-415-8594,diana.davidson@gov.ab.ca,

Local Government Services Division
Commerce Place, 10155 - 102 St., 17th Fl., Edmonton, AB T5J 4L4
The Local Government Services Division provides support services & advice to municipalities to assist them in developing sustainable & effective local government.Services focus on innovation & cooperation, municipal viability, & assessment & tax policy. The division is divided into three branches, Municipal Services, Assessment Services & the Special Areas Board. Municipal Services provides policy, planning, & analytical support for municipal legislation, property taxation, land-use planning, intermunicipal & regional cooperation & municipal status changes. The branch also provides advisory & financial support to assist municipalities to operate efficiently.Assessment Services creates & develops the assessment standards & guidelines & audits municipal assessments to ensure standards are met. The Special Areas Board falls under this Division.
Asst. Deputy Minister, Michael Merritt
780-427-9660, Fax: 780-427-0453,michael.merritt@gov.ab.ca
Executive Director, Municipal Services Branch, Gary Sandberg
780-422-8034, Fax: 780-420-1016,gary.sandberg@gov.ab.ca
Executive Director, Assessment Services Branch, Steve White
780-422-1377, Fax: 780-422-3110,steve.white@gov.ab.ca
Director, Legislative Projects, Ronald Cust
780-422-8322, Fax: 780-644-4941,ron.cust@gov.ab.ca

Public Safety Division
Commerce Place, 10155 - 102 St., 16th Fl., Edmonton, AB T5J 4L4
866-421-6929
The Public Safety Division consists of three branches designed to help ensure safe buildings, equipment & facilities, & effective emergency response, Emergency Management Alberta, Safety Services & the Fire Commissioner's Office.The division works in partnership with Alberta's municipalities, other government departments, local authorities & various local organizations.
Asst. Deputy Minister, Ivan Moore
780-638-3245, Fax: 780-427-2538,ivan.moore@gov.ab.ca
Director, Legislation & Strategic Projects, Joan Armstrong
780-427-2279, Fax:
780-427-2538,joan.armstrong@gov.ab.ca
Executive Director, Safety Services, Chris Tye
780-644-5691, Fax: 780-427-8686,safety.services@gov.ab.ca
Manager, Operational Support Services, Don Rebus
780-644-1010, Fax: 780-427-8686,safety.services@gov.ab.ca
Director, Codes and Standards, James Orr
780-644-1010, Fax: 780-427-8686,safety.services@gov.ab.ca
Director, Field Technical Services, Randy Paulson
780-644-1010, Fax: 780-427-8686,safety.services@gov.ab.ca
Director, Safety Assurance Services, Alex Morrison
780-644-1010, Fax: 780-297-4174,safety.services@gov.ab.ca
Director, Risk Management & Finance, Diane McLean
780-427-6133, Fax: 780-427-2538,diane.mclean@gov.ab.ca
Program Coordinator, Tank Site Remediation Program, Stephen Hoare
780-415-8665, Fax: 780-415-8664,stephen.hoare@gov.ab.ca

Alberta Office of the Ombudsman

Canadian Western Bank Bldg., #2800, 10303 Jasper Ave., Edmonton, AB T5J 5C3
780-427-2756, Fax: 780-427-2759,
info@ombudsman.ab.ca
www.ombudsman.ab.ca

The Alberta Ombudsman determines administrative fairness, responding to complaints of unfair treatment by provincial government authorities & a number of professional organizations. The Ombudsman is independent from government, impartial, approachable & responsive, provides services free of charge, & is not an advocacy service.

Ombudsman, G.B. (Gord) Button
Deputy Ombudsman, Pamela McHugh
780-427-2756, Fax: 780-427-2759

Alberta Public Affairs Bureau

Park Plaza, 10611 - 98 Ave., 6th Fl., Edmonton, AB T5K 2P7
403-427-9261, Fax: 403-422-4168,
www.pab.gov.ab.ca

The PAB gives communication support to government ministries and coordinates cross-gervernmental initiatives. It is also a means by which the public can ask questions about the government's programs & services.

Managing Director, Lee Funke
780-644-5655, Fax: 780-427-1010,lee.funke@gov.ab.ca
Executive Director, Corporate Communications, Terry Willock
780-422-2787, Fax: 780-415-9485,terry.willock@gov.ab.ca
Director, Marketing Services, Marvin Luethe
780-427-2698, Fax: 780-422-4650,marvin.luethe@gov.ab.ca
Executive Director, Corporate Services, Elaine Dougan
780-422-4097, Fax: 780-422-4168,elaine.dougan@gov.ab.ca

Alberta Seniors & Community Supports

Standard Life Centre, 10405 Jasper Ave., Main Fl., Edmonton, AB T5J 4R7
780-427-7876, Fax: 780-422-6301, 800-642-3853
www.seniors.alberta.ca

Alberta Seniors and Community Supports is organized into four areas: seniors services; community support programs & strategic planning; disability supports; & strategic corporate services. Key responsibilities of the ministry are as follows: planning & delivering financial support programs for seniors; planning & researching policies, & analyzing issues relevant to seniors; working with government & community stakeholders to ensure seniors' issues are considered in government initiatives; planning & delivering the Assured Income for the Severely Handicapped (AISH) program; administering the Alberta Aids to Daily Living (AADL) Program; advancing the quality of life for persons with disabilities; & addressing the needs of adults with acquired brain injury.

Acts Administered:
Adult Guardianship and Trusteeship Act
Alberta Housing Act
Assured Income for the Severely Handicapped Act
Blind Persons' Rights Act
Nursing Homes Act
Persons with Developmental Disabilities Foundation Act
Personal Directives Act
Persons with Developmental Disabilities Community Governance Act
Premier's Council on the Status of Persons with Disabilities Act
Protection for Persons in Care Act
Seniors Advisory Council for Alberta Act
Seniors Benefit Act
Administered by other ministries
Administrative Procedure Act
Adult Interdependent Relationship Act
Financial Administration Act
Freedom of Information & Protection of Privacy Act
Government Accountability Act
Government Organization Act
Residental Tenancies Act
Social Care Facilities Licensing Act

Minister,Hon. Mary Anne Jablonski
780-415-9550, Fax: 780-415-9411
Deputy Minister, Tim Wiles
780-415-1357, Fax: 780-415-1686,tim.wiles@gov.ab.ca
Senior Financial Officer, Corporate Finance, Susan McCulloch
780-422-8550, Fax:
780-422-8550,susan.mcculloch@gov.ab.ca
Assistant Director, Communications, Marilyn Carlyle-Helms
780-644-5509, Fax:
780-644-1227,marilyn.carlyle-helms@gov.ab.ca
Director, Human Resources Services, Rita Cooper
780-415-8964, Fax: 780-415-2003,rita.cooper@gov.ab.ca

• Persons with Developmental Disabilities Boards
c/o PDD Program Branch, Peace Hills Trust Tower
#404, 10011 - 109 St.
Edmonton, AB T5J 3S8
780-427-1177 Fax: 780-427-1220 800-310-0000
PDD community boards have been estbalished to fund, monitor and evaluate specific services for adult Albertans with developmental disabilities. The aim is to support individuals in their home, work, and social environments based on individual need. Boards service 6 regions throughout the province: northeast, northwest, Edmonton, Central, Calgary and South.

• Premier's Council on the Status of Persons with Disabilities
HSBC Bldg.
#1110, 10055 - 106 St.
Edmonton, AB T5J 2Y2
780-422-1095 800-272-8841
pcspd@gov.ab.ca
www.seniors.gov.ab.ca/CSS/premiers_council/index.asp
• Seniors Advisory Council for Alberta
Standard Life Centre
#600, 10405 Jasper Ave.
Edmonton, AB T5J 4R7
780-422-2321 Fax: 780-422-8762
www.seniors.gov.ab.ca/services_resources/advisory_council/index.a

Alberta Service Alberta

John E. Brownlee Bldg., 10365 - 97 St., Mezzanine Fl., Edmonton, AB T5J 3W7
780-427-2711, 877-427-4088
government.services@gov.ab.ca
www.servicealberta.gov.ab.ca

Service Alberta is engaged in the following major areas: providing licensing & registry services for consumers & businesses; regulating & enforcing standards of consumer protection & business practices; providing secure & accessible services to Albertans; leveraging Alberta SuperNet, a high-speed network to connect Albertans with government; administering the Freedom of Information & Protection of Privacy legislation; delivering shared services to ministries; promoting a streamlined regulatory environment; working with ministries to achieve cost savings in information technology & business processes; ensuring computer systems operate in the same way across government; & managing government vehicles & air transportation.

Acts Administered:
Agricultural & Recreational Land Ownership Act
Business Corporations Act
Cemeteries Act
Cemetery Companies Act
Change of Name Act
Charitable Fund-Raising Act
Companies Act
Condominium Property Act
Cooperatives Act
Debtors' Assistance Act
Dower Act
Electronic Transactions Act
Fair Trading Act
Franchises Act
Freedom of Information & Protection of Privacy Act
Funeral Services Act
Garage Keepers' Lien Act
Government Organization Act, Sched 11, 12, 13
Land Titles Act
Law of Property Act
Marriage Act
Mobile Home Sites Tenancies Act
Motor Vehicle Accident Claims Act
Partnership Act
Personal Information Protection Act
Personal Property Security Act
Possessory Liens Act
Public Service Act
Queen's Printer Act
Real Estate Act
Religious Societies' Land Act
Residential Tenancies Act
Surveys Act
Traffic Safety Act
Vital Statistics Act
Warehousemen's Lien Act
Woodmen's Lien Act
Builders' Lien Act

Minister,Hon. Heather Klimchuk
780-422-6880, Fax: 780-422-2496
Deputy Minister, Paul Pellis
780-427-1990, Fax: 780-427-4999,paul.pellis@gov.ab.ca
Acting Executive Director, Human Resource Services, Gerry Jacubo
780-427-8352, Fax: 780-644-2630,gerry.jacubo@gov.ab.ca
Director, Communications, Cameron Traynor
780-422-8049, Fax:
780-422-9816,cameron.traynor@gov.ab.ca

Business Services
John E Brownlee Bldg., 10365 - 97 St., 9th Fl., Edmonton, AB T5J 3W7
Fax: 780-644-2630,
Other Communication: Consumer Contact Centre Information: 780-427-4088; Residential Tenancy Dispute Resolution Service Information: 780-644-3000; Alberta Queen's Printer: 780-427-4952

Assistant Deputy Minister, Business Services, Cathryn Landreth
780-415-8761, cathryn.landreth@gov.ab.ca
Executive Director, Procurement Services, Lorne Dennis
780-644-1746, lorne.dennis@gov.ab.ca
Executive Director, Consumer Services & UCA, David Gray
780-644-5204, david.gray@gov.ab.ca
Executive Director, Service Delivery, Rob Phillips
780-422-8177, rob.phillips@gov.ab.ca
Director, Trade & Vendor Development, Paul Abrol
780-427-4638, paul.abrol@gov.ab.ca
Director, Contracted Services, Bill Moulton
780-427-4120, bill.moulton@gov.ab.ca
Director, Corporate Purchasing, Michael G. Fleming
780-415-9738, michael.g.fleming@gov.ab.ca
Director, Consumer Programs, George Yates
780-422-8179, george.yates@gov.ab.ca
Director, Consumer Contact Centre, Gary Peckham
780-401-4012, gary.peckham@gov.ab.ca
Director, Field Services - North, Dian Kuhtey
780-427-4032, dian.kuhtey@gov.ab.ca
Manager, Field Services - South, Mike Areshenko
780-297-8387, mike.areshenko@gov.ab.ca
Director, Print, Production & Distribution Services, Neil Johnson
780-427-0254, neil.johnson@gov.ab.ca
Director, Library Services, Robert Bateman
780-415-8344, robert.a.bateman@gov.ab.ca
Manager, Office Services, Tina Hilbrecht
780-422-7905, tina.hilbrecht@gov.ab.ca

Corporate Human Resources
Peace Hills Trust Tower, 10011 - 109 St., 6th Fl., Edmonton, AB T5J 3S8
780-408-8400, Fax: 780-420-1997, 800-696-6427
www.chr.alberta.ca

Other Communication: Alberta Government Employment Line: 780-427-7640

Corporate Human Resources was formerly known as the Personnel Administration Office. It is the central human resources department of the provincial government. Corporate Human Resources supports the Alberta Public Service by providing human resource strategies & frameworks.

Public Service Commissioner, Dale Silver
780-408-8450, Fax: 780-422-5428,dale.silver@gov.ab.ca
Acting Assistant Commissioner, Labour & Employment Practices, Jan Loree Symon
780-408-8447, jan.loree@gov.ab.ca
Assistant Commissioner, Workforce Development & Engagement, Mary Anne Wilkinson
780-408-8478, maryanne.wilkinson@gov.ab.ca
Executive Director, Labour Relations, Don Windsor
780-408-8466, don.windsor@gov.ab.ca
Director, Health Practices, Tim Royer
780-408-8428, tim.royer@gov.ab.ca
Director, Physical Sector, Tim Hajar
780-408-8371, tim.hajar@gov.ab.ca
Director, Corporate Development, Chantal MacLean
780-427-1438, chantal.maclean@gov.ab.ca
Director, Management Development, Marina Christopherson
780-408-8415, marina.christopherson@gov.ab.ca
Executive Director, Workforce Development, John Kelly
780-644-5083, john.kelly@gov.ab.ca
Acting Director, Human Resource Information Systems Technology, Raymond Chow
780-644-1783, raymond.chow@gov.ab.ca
Director, Executive Search, Alayne Stewart
780-408-8471, alayne.stewart@gov.ab.ca

Enterprise Services
John E Brownlee Bldg., 10365 - 97 St., Edmonton, AB T5J 3W7
Fax: 780-427-0238

Assistant Deputy Minister, Kate Rozmahel
780-644-4529, kate.rozmahel@gov.ab.ca
Executive Director, Enterprise Infrastructure Projects, Andrew Mak
780-644-2014, andrew.mak@gov.ab.ca
Executive Director, ICT Directions & Coordination, Kim Wieringa
780-644-3284, kim.wieringa@gov.ab.ca
Director, Program Delivery, ICT Directions & Coordination, Doug Bewick
780-422-0734, doug.bewick@gov.ab.ca

Financial Services
John E. Brownlee Bldg., 10365 - 97 St., 9th Fl., Edmonton, AB T5J 3W7
Fax: 780-644-1015

Assistant Deputy Minister, Brian Fischer
780-427-2214, brian.fischer@gov.ab.ca
Acting Executive Director, Client Services, Lynne Tetzlaff
780-427-7150, lynne.tetzlaff@gov.ab.ca
Director, Planning & Performance Measurement, Carol Moerth
780-644-2113, carol.moerth@gov.ab.ca
Director, Air Transportation, Rob Madden
780-427-7341, rob.madden@gov.ab.ca

Information Services
Commerce Place, 10155 - 102 St., 3rd Fl., Edmonton, AB T5J 4L4
780-422-2657

Assistant Deputy Minister, Tom Thackeray
780-415-5852, tom.thackeray@gov.ab.ca
Executive Director, Governance & Program Integrity, Laura Cameron
780-427-0289, laura.cameron@gov.ab.ca
Acting Executive Director, Records & Information Management, Uli Will
780-427-5672, uli.will@gov.ab.ca
Director, Legislation & FOIP Services, Di Nugent
780-422-7840, di.nugent@gov.ab.ca
Director, Regulatory Review, Angela Prokopetz
780-422-1736, angela.prokopetz@gov.ab.ca,

Registries Services
John E. Brownlee Bldg., 10365 - 97 St., 3rd Fl., Edmonton, AB T5J 3W7
Services include the following: Land Titles & Personal Properties Registry; Divisional Support; Motor Vehicles & Agent Support; & Vital Statistics & Corporate Registry

Assistant Deputy Minister, Laurie Beveridge
780-427-4095, Fax:
780-422-8151,laurie.beveridge@gov.ab.ca
Executive Director, Land Titles & Personal Properties Registry, Doug Morrison
780-415-2847, Fax: 780-422-4225,doug.morrison@gov.ab.ca
Executive Director, Motor Vehicles & Agent Support, Les Speakman
780-427-0108, Fax: 780-422-3096,les.speakman@gov.ab.ca
Executive Director, Vital Statistics & Corporate Registry, Rae Runge
780-422-8079, Fax: 780-422-4225,rae.runge@gov.ab.ca

Technology Services
John E. Brownlee Bldg., 10365 - 97 St., 8th Fl., Edmonton, AB T5J 3W7
780-422-8545

Assistant Deputy Minister, Dennis Mudryk
780-427-6005, Fax: 780-422-0956,dennis.mudryk@gov.ab.ca
Director, Operations - Planning & Support, Ian Phimester
780-427-6326, ian.phimester@gov.ab.ca
Executive Director, Operations - Service Delivery, Darcy Wiltse
780-644-4532, darcy.wiltse@gov.ab.ca
Executive Director, Operations- Infrastructure Support, Ron Boehm
780-644-2536, ron.boehm@gov.ab.ca

Community Support Programs & Strategic Planning Division
Standard Life Centre, 10405 Jasper Ave. 3rd Fl., Edmonton, AB T5J 4R7
780-415-2466

Asst. Deputy Minister, Dave Arsenault
780-427-2593, Fax: 780-427-1689,dave.arsenault@gov.ab.ca

Seniors Financial Assistance Branch
Standard Life Centre, 10405 Jasper Ave., 6th Fl., Edmonton, AB T5J 4R7
Director, John Cabral
780-422-7270, Fax: 780-644-1602,john.cabral@gov.ab.ca

Seniors Services Division
Standard Life Centre, 10405 Jasper Ave., 6th Fl., Edmonton, AB T5J 4R7
780-427-7876

Asst. Deputy Minister, Chi Loo
780-422-3179, Fax: 780-644-7602,chi.loo@gov.ab.ca
Director, Client & Information Services Branch, Denine Ritchie
780-415-0845, Fax: 780-422-8762,denine.ritchie@gov.ab.ca
Director, Seniors Financial Assistance Branch, John Cabral
780-422-7270, Fax: 780-422-5954,john.cabral@gov.ab.ca
Director, Special Needs Assistance for Seniors, Heather King
780-422-7257, Fax: 780-422-5954,heather.king@gov.ab.ca
Director, Seniors Policy & Planning, Sarah Carr
780-644-2975, Fax: 780-644-7602,sarah.carr@gov.ab.ca
Acting Director, Dental, Optical & Property Tax Assistance, Kindy Joseph
780-644-8613, Fax: 780-415-2744,kindy.joseph@gov.ab.ca

Disability Supports Division
Milner Building, 10040 - 104 St., 12 Fl., Edmonton, AB T5J 0Z2
Asst. Deputy Minister, Donna Ludvigsen
780-644-4555, Fax:
780-427-5148,donna.ludvigsen@gov.ab.ca
Executive Director, Policy, Innovation & Partnerships, Helen Stacey
780-644-9910, Fax: 780-644-2315,helen.stacey@gov.ab.ca

Director, Health Related Supports, Marianne Baird
780-422-6985, Fax:
780-422-0968,marianne.baird@gov.ab.ca
Executive Director, Delivery Services, Dale Beesley
780-644-4731, Fax: 780-644-3299,dale.beesley@gov.ab.ca

Social Based Assistance Review Initiative (SBAR Initiative)
Standard Life Centre, 10405 Jasper Ave., 4th Fl., Edmonton, AB T5J 4R7
Asst. Deputy Minister, Reegan McCullough
780-638-2808, Fax:
780-638-2813,reegan.mccullough@gov.ab.ca
Committee Secretariat & Project Coordinator, Barbara Reid
780-638-2807, Fax: 780-638-2821,barbara.reid@gov.ab.ca

Alberta Solicitor General & Public Security

John E. Browntree Bldg, 10365 - 97 St., 10th Fl., Edmonton, AB T5J 3W7
780-427-3441, Fax: 780-427-2789,-310-0000
www.solgen.gov.ab.ca
The Solicitor General & Public Security Ministry promotes safe communities through effective law enforcement & correctional & victim services. The ministry is also responsible for ensuring integrity, accountability & social responsibility in gaming and liquor industries in Alberta. Key businesses within the ministry are as follows: law enforcement & crime prevention; custody, supervision & facilitation of rehabilitative opportunities for offenders; protection services for officials, facilities & infrastructure; victim programs & services; & socially responsible operation of liquor & gaming industries.
Acts Administered:
Corrections Act
Gaming and Liquor Act
Government Organization Act, Sched 15
Horse Racing Alberta Act
Peace Officer Act
Police Act
Private Investigators and Security Guards Act
Victims of Crime Act
Minister & Solicitor General,Hon. Fred Lindsay
780-415-9406, Fax: 780-415-9566
Deputy Minister & Deputy Solicitor General, Brad Pickering
780-427-3841, Fax:
780-427-0727,brad.pickering@gov.ab.ca
Director, Aboriginal Justice Initiatives, Bronwyn Shoush
780-422-2779, Fax:
780-427-4670,bronwyn.shoush@gov.ab.ca
Director, Communications, Andy Weiler
780-427-6153, Fax: 780-427-0771,andy.weiler@gov.ab.ca
• Alberta Gaming & Liquor Commission(AGLC)
50 Corriveau Ave.
St Albert, AB T8N 3T5
780-447-8600 Fax: 780-447-8911 800-272-8876
www.aglc.gov.ab.ca
• Criminal Injuries Review Board
J.E. Brownlee Bldg.
10365 - 97 St., 5th Fl.
Edmonton, AB T5J 3W7
780-427-7330 Fax: 780-427-7347
ciab@just.gov.ab.ca
www.gov.ab.ca/just/victims/benefit2.htm
• Law Enforcement Review Board
John E. Brownlee Bldg.
10365 - 97th St.
Edmonton, AB T5J 3W7
780-422-9376 Fax: 780-422-4782
lerb@gov.ab.ca

Correctional Services Division
780-427-3441, Fax: 780-427-5905
Asst. Deputy Minister, Bruce V. Anderson
780-427-3440, Fax:
780-427-5905,bruce.v.anderson@gov.ab.ca
Executive Director, Adult Centre Operations Branch, Mike Tholenaer
780-427-4703, Fax: 780-427-1904,mike.tholenaer@gov.ab.ca
Executive Director, Community Corrections & Release Program, Brent Doney
780-422-5757, Fax: 780-422-3098,brent.doney@gov.ab.ca
Executive Director, Young Offender Branch, Judith Barlown
780-644-8080, Fax: 780-422-0732,judith.barlow@gov.ab.ca
Director, Correctional Services Intelligence, Terry Garnett
780-422-3341, Fax: 780-422-0732,terry.garnett@gov.ab.ca
Director, Division Support Services, Jim Cook
780-427-3441, Fax: 780-427-1903,jim.cook@gov.ab.ca

Public Security Division
10365 - 97 St., Edmonton, AB T5J 3W7
Fax: 780-427-1194
Asst. Deputy Minister, Brian Skeet
780-427-3457, Fax: 780-427-1194,brian.skeet@gov.ab.ca
Senior Manager, Policing Standards & Evaluation, Joe Rodgers
780-427-6920, Fax: 780-427-5916,joe.rodgers@gov.ab.ca
Executive Director, Victim Services, Cal Wrathall
780-427-3457, Fax: 780-422-4213,cal.wrathall@gov.ab.ca
Executive Director, Security Services, Doug Fulford
780-422-3500

Alberta Sustainable Resource Development

Information Centre, 9920 - 108 St., Main Fl., Edmonton, AB T5K 2M4
780-944-0313, Fax: 780-427-4407, 877-944-0313
srd.infocent@gov.ab.ca
www.srd.alberta.ca
Sustainable Resource Development works with Albertans to manage fish & wildlife, to oversee the development of the province's forests, to fight forest fires, & to manage the use of public lands. Programs & services are provided in the following areas: hunting & fishing, including species, news, licenses, regulations & management programs; wildlife, including diseases, species at risk, status reports, & watchable wildlife; Alberta species, such as bears & bighorn sheep; forests & wildfires, including forest health, meanagement & fire reports; public lands, featuring information about management, access & use, & photographs; & information about Alberta, such as areas & maps.
Acts Administered:
Boundary Surveys Act
Environmental Protection & Enhancement Act (jointly with Environment & Community Development)
Expropriation Act (sections 25 to 28 & 72)
Fisheries (Alberta) Act
Forest & Prairie Protection Act
Forest Reserves Act
Forests Act
Government Organization Act (jointly with Alberta Environment & Infrastructure)
Mines & Minerals Act (jointly with Alberta Energy)
Natural Resources Conservation Board Act (jointly with Alberta Environment)
Public Lands Act
Surface Rights Act
Surveys Act (jointly with Alberta Government Services)
Wildlife Act
Minister,Hon. Ted Morton
780-415-4815, Fax: 780-415-4818
Deputy Minister, Eric McGhan
780-427-1799, Fax: 780-415-9669,eric.mcghan@gov.ab.ca
Executive Director, Corporate Business Support, Joyce Ingram
780-415-2634, Fax: 780-415-9669,joyce.ingram@gov.ab.ca
Executive Director, Human Resources Services, Diane Dunn
780-422-5779, Fax: 780-427-2513,diane.dunn@gov.ab.ca
Director, Communications, Carol Chawrun
780-427-8122, Fax: 780-422-6339,carol.chawrun@gov.ab.ca
Manager, Issues Management, Denine Westman
780-415-0845, Fax:
780-422-8762,denine.westman@gov.ab.ca
Director, Strategic Projects, Mike Poscente
780-427-6350, Fax: 780-427-7434,mike.poscente@gov.ab.ca
• Land Compensation/Surface Rights Board
Phipps-McKinnon Bldg.
10020 - 101A Ave., 18th Fl.
Edmonton, AB T5J 3G2
780-427-2444 Fax: 780-427-5798
• Natural Resources Conservation Board(NRCB)
Sterling Place
9940 - 106 St., 4th Fl.
Edmonton, AB T5K 2N2
780-422-1977 Fax: 780-427-0607 866-383-6722
www.nrcb.gov.ab.ca

Fish & Wildlife Division
Fish & Wildlife Management ensures Albertans benefit economically, environmentally & socially from the province's fish & wildlife resources.Goals are to provide a balanced approach to fish & wildlife management through a fish & wildlife policy, legislative & regulatory framework that maximizes the benefits received from these resources, sustains the recreational enjoyment of fish & wildlife resources with appropriate allocation & licensing decisions, mitigates & reduces negative interactions between wildlife & humans & partner with Aboriginal communities to sustain traditional uses of fish & wildlife resources.Management plans are up-to-date for all game species & species at risk.Sustainable fishing has improved the viability of the commercial fishing industry, along with habitat maintenance, restoration, the system of stocking fish & appropriate management information.
Asst. Deputy Minister, Ken Ambrock
780-427-6749, Fax: 780-427-8884,ken.ambrock@gov.ab.ca
Executive Director, Fisheries Management, Ken Crutchfield
780-427-7763, Fax: 780-422-9559,ken.crutchfield@gov.ab.ca
Executive Director, Wildlife Management, Ron Bjorge
780-427-9503, Fax: 780-422-9557,ron.bjorge@gov.ab.ca
Director, Enforcement Field Services, Deryl Empson
780-422-0044, Fax: 780-422-9560,deryl.empson@gov.ab.ca

Forestry Division
Forest Protection protects the multiple values received from forests within the Forest Protection Area of the province by working co-operatively with municipalities, industry & other stakeholders to prevent & suppress wildfires.
Asst. Deputy Minister, Don Harrison
780-427-3542, Fax: 780-422-6068,don.harrison@gov.ab.ca
Director, Wildfire Prevention, Hugh Boyd
780-427-7811, Fax: 780-427-0292,hugh.boyd@gov.ab.ca
Director, Wildfire Operations, John Brewer
780-427-7925, Fax: 780-422-7230,john.brewer@gov.ab.ca
Section Head, Business Planning & Information, Deanna McCullough
780-427-4293, Fax:
780-415-1831,deanna.mccullough@gov.ab.ca
Director, Wildfire Service,Vacant
780-427-2545

Public Lands & Forests Division
Approximately 60 per cent of the province's land base is public land. It is managed under an integrated resource management philosophy that supports forest production, watershed protection, wildlife habitat, recreation, oil & gas well sites, agricultural production & industrial development, to mention only a few of the uses. Public land management focuses on establishing & sustaining an optimum balance of use, conservation & development of resources, in harmony with the values & needs of Albertans. Historically, public land management was directed at homesteading & agricultural development in the White (settled) area of the province, & timber management in the Green (forested) area. Today, land management practices & policies addressesa greater variety of competing demands including recreation, watershed management, agricultural uses, industrial uses, commercial uses & conservation.
Asst. Deputy Minister, Craig Quintillo
780-422-4415, Fax: 780-422-6068,craig.quintillo@gov.ab.ca
Executive Director, Forest Management Branch, Doug Sklar
780-422-4590, Fax: 780-427-0085,doug.sklar@gov.ab.ca
Acting Executive Director, Forest Operations Branch, Ken McCrae
780-644-5497, Fax: 780-427-0085,ken.mccrae@gov.ab.ca
Executive Director, Land Management Branch, Glenn Selland
780-427-3570, Fax: 780-724-1185,glenn.selland@gov.ab.ca
Executive Director, Rangeland Management Branch, Keith Lyseng
780-427-3595, Fax: 780-422-0454,keith.lyseng@gov.ab.ca

Strategic Forestry Initiative Division
Senior Manager, Economics & Trade,Ron, Dunnigan
780-422-4799, Fax: 780-644-5728,ron.dunnigan@gov.ab.ca
Executive Director, Forest Business and Bio-economy Initiatives, Pat Guidera
780-427-4351, Fax: 780-644-5728,pat.guidera@gov.ab.ca
Senior Manager, Value Added Section, Paul Short
780-427-6571, Fax: 780-644-5728,paul.short@gov.ab.ca

Sustainable Resource & Environmental Management
Asst. Deputy Minister, Morris Seiferling
780-644-7978, Fax:
780-644-1034,morris.seiferling@gov.ab.ca

Alberta Tourism, Parks, Recreation & Culture

Communications Branch, Standard Life Centre, 10405 Jasper Ave., 7th Fl., Edmonton, AB T5J 4R7
780-427-6530, Fax: 780-427-1496,
Comdev.Communications@gov.ab.ca
www.tprc.alberta.ca
Committed to the development & preservation of Alberta's tourism, culture & heritage, the Ministry of Tourism, Parks, Recreation & Culture provides programs & services to support active & inclusive communities. Tourist destinations are developed & marketed. Community enhancement is provided through financial support. Support is also given to the non-profit sector, including the arts, film, sport & recreation. The province's natural heritage is preserved, through a network of parks & protected areas. Preservation of Alberta's historical resources is realized, through Provincial Archives of Alberta, as well as museums & historic sites. The natural heritage & historical resources of the province are promoted to tourists.
Acts Administered:
Alberta Centennial Medal Act
Alberta Sport, Recreation, Parks and Wildlife Foundation Act
Amusements Act
Emblems of Alberta Act
First Nations Sacred Ceremonial Objects Repatriation Act
Foreign Cultural Property Immunity Act
Glenbow-Alberta Institute Act
Government House Act

Historical Resources Act
Holocaust Memorial Day & Genocide Remembrance Act
Human Rights, Citizenship & Multiculturalism Act
Provincial Parks Act
Queen Elizabeth II Golden Jubilee Recognition Act
Recreation Development Act
Wild Rose Foundation Act
Wilderness Areas, Ecological Reserves, Natural Areas and Heritage Rangelands Act
Willmore Wilderness Park Act
Minister,Hon. Hector Goudreau
780-427-4928, Fax: 780-427-0188,TPRC.minister@gov.ab.ca
Associate Minister, Tourism Promotion, Hon. Cindy Ady
Fax: 780-644-8960
Deputy Minister, Fay Orr
780-427-2921
Director, Communications, Anne Douglas
780-427-2395
• Alberta Film Commission
10155 - 102 St., 5th Fl.
Edmonton, AB T5J 4L6
780-422-8584 Fax: 780-422-8582 888-813-1738
• Alberta Foundation for the Arts
Standard Life Centre
#901, 10405 Jasper Ave.
Edmonton, AB T5J 4R7
780-427-9968 Fax: 780-422-1162
www.affta.ab.ca
• Alberta Historical Resources Foundation
Old St. Stephen's College
8820 - 112 St.
Edmonton, AB T6G 2P8
780-431-2300
Assists in the preservation & interpretation of Alberta's historical resources, & acts as the single window for Alberta Lottery Fund support to heritage in Alberta.
• Alberta Human Rights & Citizenship Commission
Northern Regional Office, Standard Life Centre
#800, 10405 Jasper Ave.
Edmonton, AB T5J 4R7
780-427-7661 Fax: 780-427-6013-310-0000TDD: 780-297-5639
humanrights@gov.ab.ca.
www.albertahumanrights.ab.ca
Other Communication: Southern Regional Office (Calgary): 403-297-6571; Fax: 403-297-6567; TTY: 403-297-5639; Toll Free TTY: 1-800-232-7215
• Alberta Sport, Recreation, Parks & Wildlife Foundation
Standard Life Centre
10405 Jasper Ave., 9th Fl.
Edmonton, AB T5J 4R7
780-415-1167 Fax: 780-415-0308
www.cd.gov.ab.ca/asrpwf
To enhance the quality of life in Alberta, the Alberta Sport, Recreation, Parks & Wildlife Foundation provides financial support to eligible sport & recreation organizations.The Development Initiatives Program provides support to those working in the areas of sport, recreation, parks & wildlife for project & program related endeavors.The Hosting Program encourages the development of youth in sport, recreation, parks & wildlife & promotes economic growth.
• Government House Foundation
12845 - 102 Ave.
Edmonton, AB T5N 0M6
780-427-2281 Fax: 780-422-6508
www.cd.gov.ab.ca/all_about_us/commissions/government_house/index.
• Wild Rose Foundation
#901, 10405 Jasper Ave.
Edmonton, AB T5J 4R7
780-422-9305
Lottery-funded agency provides funding to non-profit organizations.

Alberta Transportation

Twin Atria Building, 4999 - 98 Jasper Ave., 2nd Fl., Edmonton, AB T6B 2X3
780-427-2731

Minister,Hon. Luke Ouellette
780-427-2080, Fax: 780-422-2722
Deputy Minister, Gary Boddez
780-427-6912, Fax: 780-422-6515,gary.boddez@gov.ab.ca
Director, Communications, Tammy Forbes
780-415-1841, Fax: 780-466-3166,tammy.forbes@gov.ab.ca
Executive Director, Human Resources Branch, Lynn Cook
780-415-1811, Fax: 780-422-5138,lynn.cook@gov.ab.ca
• Transportation Safety Board
Twin Atria Bldg.
4999 - 98 Ave., Main Fl.
Edmonton, AB T6B 2X3
780-427-7178 Fax: 780-422-9739
The Board was established under the Traffic Safety Act. It functions as the final administrative authority charged with making operator licence determinations, and it holds hearings in relation to driver conduct, reinstatement of licences for suspended drivers through the Alberta Administrative Licence Suspension Program & the Alberta Zero Tolerance Program, impaired driving convictions through the Ignition Interlock Program, & early release of vehicles under the Vehicle Seizure Program. In addition, the Board functions as the appeal body for decisions of the Registrar, relating to driver training schools, driver instructors, driver examiners, vehicle inspection stations & technicians, operating authority certificates, safety fitness certificates, carrier safety ratings, exemption permits, & assessed administrative penalties. It is responsible for appeals surronding decisions & actions taken under the Railway (Alberta) Act.
• Transportation Safety Board - Calgary
Willowglen Business Park
803 Manning Rd. NE, Main Fl.
Calgary, AB T2E 7M8
The Board was established under the Traffic Safety Act. It functions as the final administrative authority charged with making operator licence determinations, and it holds hearings in relation to driver conduct, reinstatement of licences for suspended drivers through the Alberta Administrative Licence Suspension Program & the Alberta Zero Tolerance Program, impaired driving convictions through the Ignition Interlock Program, & early release of vehicles under the Vehicle Seizure Program. In addition, the Board functions as the appeal body for decisions of the Registrar, relating to driver training schools, driver instructors, driver examiners, vehicle inspection stations & technicians, operating authority certificates, safety fitness certificates, carrier safety ratings, exemption permits, & assessed administrative penalties. It is responsible for appeals surronding decisions & actions taken under the Railway (Alberta) Act.

Francophone Secretariat
HSBC Bldg., 10055 - 106 St., 5th Fl., Edmonton, AB T5J 1G3
Fax: 780-422-7533
Executive Director, Denis Tardif
780-415-3348, denis.tardif@gov.ab.ca

Policy & Corporate Services Division
Twin Atria Building, 4999 - 98 Ave., 3rd Fl., Edmonton, AB T6B 2X3
Asst. Deputy Minister, Alan Humphries
780-415-1386, Fax: 780-422-1070,alan.humphries@gov.ab.ca
Executive Director, Strategic Policy Branch, Rod Thompson
780-415-0685, Fax: 780-422-1070,rod.thompson@gov.ab.ca
Executive Director & CIO, Information Management Branch, Ken Bainey
780-644-5114, Fax: 780-644-7028,ken.bainey@gov.ab.ca
Director, Legislative Planning & FOIP, Jim H. Leitch
780-415-6489, Fax: 780-638-3497,jim.h.leitch@gov.ab.ca
Executive Director & Senior Financial Officer, Finance Branch, Winnie Yiu-Young
780-427-1440, Fax: 780-415-1219,winnie.yiu-young@gov.ab.ca

Strategic Transportation Initiatives
Twin Atria Building, 4999 - 98 Ave., 3rd Fl., Edmonton, AB T6B 2X3
Asst. Deputy Minister, Tim Hawnt
780-427-3642, Fax: 780-415-0475,tim.hawnt@gov.ab.ca

Transportation Safety Services
Twin Atria Building, 4999 - 98 Ave., Main Fl., Edmonton, AB T6B 2X3
Transportation Safety Services is responsible for vehicle/driver safety, driver licensing & drivers license enforcement, impaired driving intervention programs, road safety programs, dangerous goods control, & monitoring the motor carrier industry & provincial railways.
Asst. Deputy Minister, Shaun Hammond
780-415-1146, Fax: 780-415-0782,shaun.hammond@gov.ab.ca
Chief Transport Officer, Commercial Vehicle Enforcement Branch, Steve Callahan
403-340-5225, Fax: 403-340-5074,steve.callahan@gov.ab.ca
Executive Director, Vehicle Safety & Carrier Services, Roger Clarke
403-340-5033, Fax: 403-340-4811,roger.clarke@gov.ab.ca
Manager, Divisional Coordination, Danielle Paradis
780-427-2090, Fax: 780-415-0782,danielle.paradis@gov.ab.ca
Executive Director, Office of Traffic Safety, Jeanette Espie
780-427-6588, Fax: 780-422-3682,jeanette.espie@gov.ab.ca
Director, Transport Engineering, Kim Durdle
403-340-5189, Fax: 403-340-5092,kim.durdle@gov.ab.ca
Director, Dangerous Goods & Rail Safety Branch, Terry Wallace
780-427-7508, Fax: 780-422-9193,terry.wallace@gov.ab.ca
Executive Director, Driver Programs, Mitch Fuhr
780-644-4576, Fax: 780-427-0833,mitch.fuhr@gov.ab.ca

Transportation & Civil Engineering
Twin Atria Building, 4999 - 98 Ave., 2nd Fl., Edmonton, AB T6B 2X3
Asst. Deputy Minister, Bruno Zutautas
780-422-2184, Fax: 780-415-1268,bruno.zutautas@gov.ab.ca
Executive Director, Major Capital Projects Branch, Tom Loo
780-415-4876, Fax: 780-415-0475,tom.loo@gov.ab.ca
Executive Director, Program Management Branch, John Engleder
780-644-4004, Fax: 780-427-0783,john.engleder@gov.ab.ca,
Executive Director, Divisional Services, Gordon Zack
780-427-4548, Fax: 780-415-1268,gordon.zack@gov.ab.ca
Executive Director, Technical Standards Branch, Moh Lali
780-415-1083, Fax: 780-422-2027,moh.lali@gov.ab.ca
Executive Director, Planning Branch, Jim Der
780-415-1300, Fax: 780-422-2027,jim.der@gov.ab.ca
Regional Director, Southern Region, Darrell Camplin
403-382-4060, Fax: 403-382-4412,darrell.camplin@gov.ab.ca
Regional Director, Central Region, Stu Becker
403-340-4325, Fax: 403-340-4810,stu.becker@gov.ab.ca
Regional Director, North Central Region,Vacant
780-674-8221, Fax: 780-674-8383
Regional Director, Peace Region, Wayne Franklin
780-674-6280, Fax: 780-674-2440,wayne.franklin@gov.ab.ca
Regional Director, Northeast Alberta Transportation Corridor (NATC) - Fort McMurray, Ranjit Tharmalingam
780-422-7672, Fax: 780-427-0369,ranjit.tharmalingam@gov.ab.ca

Alberta Treasury Board

Legislature Bldg., #204, 10800 - 97 Ave., Edmonton, AB T5K 2B6
780-415-4855, Fax: 780-422-4853,
www.treasuryboard.gov.ab.ca
The Treasury Board is organized into the following units: Strategic Capital Planning; Alternative Capital Financing Office; Spending Management & Planning; Office of the Controller; Corporate Internal Audit Services; Treasury Board Secretariat; & Oil Sands Sustainable Development Secretariat.
President,Hon. Lloyd Snelgrove
780-415-4855, Fax: 780-415-4853
Deputy Minister, Grant Robertson
780-415-4515, Fax: 780-427-6596
Director, Communications, Gerald Kastendieck
780-427-6699, Fax: 780-427-6596,gerald.kastendieck@gov.ab.ca

Strategic Corporate Services Division
Standard Life Centre, 10405 Jasper Ave., 7th Fl., Edmonton, AB T5J 4R7
780-415-0257,
Other Communication: Information Management & Technology Services Help Desk: 780-427-2450
Acting Assistant Deputy Minister, Wilma Haas
780-415-6092, Fax: 780-422-3142,wilma.haas@gov.ab.ca
Executive Director, Policy, Planning & Legislative Services Branch, Susan Cribbs
780-422-1290, susan.cribbs@gov.ab.ca
Executive Director, Financial Services Branch, Pam Arnston
780-427-0120, pam.arnston@gov.ab.ca
Executive Director & Chief Information Officer, Marsha Capell
780-427-1075, Fax: 780-644-1286,marsha.capell@gov.ab.ca

Travel Alberta
PO Box 2500, Edmonton, AB T5J 2Z4
780-427-4321, Fax: 780-427-0867, 800-252-3782
travelinfo@TravelAlberta.com
www.travelalberta.com
Managing Director, Travel Alberta, Derek Coke-Kerr
403-297-2849, Fax: 403-297-5068,derek.coke-kerr@travelalberta.com
Director, Communications, Don Boynton
403-297-8753, don.boynton@travelalberta.com

Corporate Internal Audit Services
Legislature Annex, #1101, 9718 - 107 St., Edmonton, AB T5K 1E4
780-644-7185
Chief Internal Auditor, Heather Zomar
780-427-4228, Fax: 780-644-4761,heather.zomar@gov.ab.ca
Executive Director, Kathleen Gora
780-644-5271, Fax: 780-644-5271,kathleen.gora@gov.ab.ca
Executive Director, Internal Audit Operations, Dan Stadlwieser
780-644-4736, Fax: 780-644-4761,dan.stadlwieser@gov.ab.ca

Office of the Controller
Oxbridge Place, 9820 - 106 St., 4th Fl., Edmonton, AB T5K 2J6

Controller, Doug Lynkowski
780-427-3076, Fax:
780-422-2164,doug.lynkowski@gov.ab.ca
Executive Director, Financial & Accounting Standards, Gisele Simard
780-415-9253, Fax: 780-422-2164,gisele.simard@gov.ab.ca
Executive Director, Performance Planning & Reporting, Murray Lyle
780-427-7784, Fax: 780-422-2164,murray.lyle@gov.ab.ca

Oil Sands Sustainable Development Secretariat
Commerce Place, 10155 - 102 St., 6th Fl., Edmonton, AB T5J 4L6
Assistant Deputy Minister, Heather Kennedy
780-422-4919, Fax:
780-427-2852,heather.kennedy@gov.ab.ca

Secretariat to Treasury Board
J.G. O'Donoghue Bldg., 7000 - 113 St., Main Fl., Edmonton, AB T6H 5T6
Assistant Deputy Minister, Kathleen LeClair
780-644-5642, Fax:
780-644-7474,kathleen.leclair@gov.ab.ca

Spending Management & Planning
Oxbridge Place, 9820 - 106 St., 5th Fl., Edmonton, AB T5K 2J6
Assistant Deputy Minister, Aaron Neumeyer
780-644-8078, Fax:
780-644-3907,aaron.neumeyer@gov.ab.ca
Executive Director, SMP 1, Larry Bailer
780-427-8701, Fax: 780-644-3907,larry.bailer@gov.ab.ca
Executive Director, SMP 2, Darren Hedley
780-415-4733, Fax: 780-644-3907,darren.hedley@gov.ab.ca
Executive Director, SMP 3, Greg Findlay
780-415-9258, Fax: 780-644-3907,greg.findlay@gov.ab.ca
Executive Director, SMP 4, Dale Fulford
780-427-8736, Fax: 780-644-3907,dale.fulford@gov.ab.ca

Strategic Capital Planning
Oxbridge Place, 9820 - 106 St., 5th Fl., Edmonton, AB T5K 2J6
Assistant Deputy Minister, Neill McQuay
780-415-1076, Fax: 780-440-8719,neill.mcquay@gov.ab.ca
Executive Director, Alternative Capital Financing, Faye McCann
780-644-8774, Fax: 780-644-3906,faye.mccann@gov.ab.ca
Executive Director, Capital Spending, Rod Skura
780-427-8898, Fax: 780-644-3906,rodney.skura@gov.ab.ca
Director, Capital Planning, Roberta Malysh
780-644-3856, Fax: 780-644-3906,roberta.malysh@gov.ab.ca
Director, Alternative Capital Financial Services, Guy A. Smith
780-422-7459, Fax: 780-644-3906,guy.smith@gov.ab.ca

Alberta Utilities Consumer Advocate

TD Tower, 10088 - 102 Ave., Edmonton, AB T5J 2Z1
780-644-5130, Fax: 780-644-5129, 866-714-4455
UtilitiesConsumerAdvocate@gov.ab.
www.utilitiesconsumeradvocate.gov.ab.ca

The Office of the Utilities Consumer Advocate was created in October 2003 to provide a voice for electricity & natural gas consumers in Alberta's restructured utilities market. The Office of the Utilities Consumer Advocate works closely with other consumer advocacy agencies to ensure that retail utility consumers in Alberta; homeowners & tenants, farmers & small businesses, are represented fairly in their dealings with electricity & natural gas companies, regulatory agencies such as the Alberta Energy & Utilities Board (EUB) & the provincial government.

Acting Utilities Consumer Advocate, Cathryn Landreth
780-415-8761, Fax:
780-422-8191,cathryn.landreth@gov.ab.ca

Northern Development Branch
780-624-6274, Fax: 780-624-6184
Director, Projects & Research, Allen Geary
780-624-6337, Fax: 780-624-6184,allen.geary@gov.ab.ca
Senior Northern Development Officer, Audrey DeWit
780-624-6342, audrey.dewit@gov.ab.ca
Senior Northern Development Officer, Kim Pinnock
780-624-6432, kim.pinnock@gov.ab.ca
Senior Northern Development Officer, Kris Rollheiser
780-624-6336, kris.rollheiser@gov.ab.ca
Research Officer, Natalie Butler
780-624-6350, natalie.butler@gov.ab.ca
Research Officer, Sam Warrior
780-624-6433, sam.warrior@gov.ab.ca

Government of British Columbia

Seat of Government: Parliament Bldgs., Victoria, BC V8V 1X4
EnquiryBC@gov.bc.ca
www.gov.bc.ca

The Province of British Columbia entered Confederation on July 20, 1871. It has an area of 924,815.43 km2. According to Statistics Canada, the population of the province in 2007 was 4,380,300.

Office of the Lieutenant Governor

Government House, 1401 Rockland Ave., Victoria, BC V8S 1V9
250-387-2080, Fax: 250-387-2078,
ghinfo@gov.bc.ca
www.ltgov.bc.ca

Lieutenant Governor, British Columbia, Hon. Steven L. Point, OBC
Private Secretary to the Lieutenant Governor & Executive Director, Government House, Herb A. LeRoy
250-387-2083, Fax: 250-387-2078
Director, Operations & Management Services, Jerymy Brownridge
250-387-2087

Office of the Premier

West Annex, Parliament Bldgs., PO Box 9041 Prov Govt, Victoria, BC V8W 9E1
250-387-1715, Fax: 250-387-0087,
premier@gov.bc.ca
www.gov.bc.ca/premier

Premier,Hon. Gordon Campbell
Chief of Staff, Martyn Brown
Deputy Chief of Staff & Executive Assistant to the Premier, Lara Dauphinee
Deputy Chief of Staff, Policy Coordination & Issues Management, Jeff Hanman
Director, Communications, Dale Steeves
Press Secretary, Bridgitte Anderson

Executive Council

Parliament Bldgs., Victoria, BC V8V 1X4
www.gov.bc.ca/premier/cabinet_ministers

Premier,Hon. Gordon Campbell
250-387-1715, Fax: 250-387-0087,premier@gov.bc.ca, Other Communications: URL: www.gordoncampbellmla.bc.ca
Minister of State, Intergovernmental Relations, Hon. Naomi Yamamoto
250-356-7562, Fax: 250-356-8545
Minister, Aboriginal Relations & Reconciliation, Hon. George Abbott
250-953-4844, Fax: 250-953-4856
Minister, Advanced Education & Labour Market Development, Hon. Moira Stilwell
250-356-2771, Fax: 250-356-3000,ALMD.Minister@gov.bc.ca
Minister, Agriculture & Lands, Hon. Steve Thomson
250-387-1023, Fax: 250-387-1522
Attorney General,Hon. Michael de Jong
250-387-1866, Fax: 250-387-6411
Minister, Children & Family Development; Minister responsible for Child Care, Hon. Mary Polak
250-387-9699, Fax: 250-387-9722
Minister, Citizens' Services, Hon. Ben Stewart
250-952-7623, Fax: 250-952-7628
Minister, Community & Rural Development, Hon. Bill Bennett
250-387-2283, Fax: 250-387-4312
Minister, Education & Minister responsible for Early Learning & Literacy, Hon. Margaret MacDiarmid
250-387-1977, Fax: 250-387-3200,minister.educ@gov.bc.ca
Minister, Energy, Mines & Petroleum Resources, Hon. Blair Lekstrom
250-387-5896, Fax: 250-356-2965
Minister of State, Mining, Hon. Randy Hawes
250-953-4100, Fax: 250-387-1803
Minister, Environment, Hon. Barry Penner
250-387-1187, Fax: 250-387-1356
Minister of State, Climate Action, Hon. John Yap
250-952-7609, Fax:
250-952-7621,Minister.ClimateAction@gov.bc.ca
Minister, Finance & Deputy Premier, Hon. Colin Hansen
250-387-3751, Fax: 250-387-5594
Minister, Forests & Range & Minister responsible for Integrated Land Management Bureau, Hon. Patrick Bell
250-387-6240, Fax: 250-387-1040
Minister, Health Services, Hon. Kevin Falcon
250-953-3547, Fax: 250-356-9587
Minister, Healthy Living & Sports, Hon. Ida Chong
250-387-3504, Fax: 251-387-3420
Minister of State, Olympics and ActNow BC, Hon. Mary McNeil
250-952-7634, Fax: 250-952-7641
Minister, Housing & Social Development, Hon. Rich Coleman
250-356-7750, Fax: 250-356-7292,eia.minister@gov.bc.ca; rich.coleman.mla@leg.bc.ca, Other Communications: URL: www.richcolemanmla.bc.ca
Minister, Labour, Hon. Murray Coell
250-356-6348, Fax: 250-356-6595
Minister, Small Business, Technology and Economic Development, Hon. Iain Black
250-356-7411, Fax: 250-356-6376
Minister, Tourism, Culture & the Arts, Hon. Kevin Krueger
250-953-4246, Fax: 250-953-4250,TCA.Minister@gov.bc.ca
Minister, Transportation & Infrastructure, Hon. Shirley Bond
250-387-1978, Fax: 250-356-2290

Cabinet Operations
PO Box 9487 Prov Govt, Victoria, BC V8W 9W6
Fax: 250-387-7392
Associate Deputy Minister & Deputy Cabinet Secretary, Robert Lapper
250-387-1042, Fax: 250-387-7392
Assistant Deputy Minister, Kevin Jardine
250-387-7686, Fax: 250-387-7392
Executive Coordinator, Cabinet Operations, Vanessa R. Ginger
250-952-6748

Legislative Assembly

Clerk's Office, #221, Parliament Bldgs., Victoria, BC V8V 1X4
250-387-3785, Fax: 250-387-0942,
ClerkHouse@leg.bc.ca
www.leg.bc.ca

Clerk, E. George MacMinn, Q.C.
250-387-3785, Fax: 250-387-0942
Speaker, Legislative Assembly, Hon. Bill Barisoff
250-387-3952, Fax: 250-387-2813
Sergeant-at-Arms, Vacant
250-356-6966
Deputy Sergeant-At-Arms, David V. Adamthwaite
250-387-0953
Director, Hansard Services, Jo-Anne Kern
250-387-0944, Fax:
250-356-5681,Hansard.Services@leg.bc.ca;
Director, Legislative Library Administration Office, Jane Taylor
250-387-6508, LLBC.Ref@leg.bc.ca, Other Communications: URL: www.llbc.leg.bc.ca
Auditor General, John Doyle
250-387-6803, Fax: 250-387-1230,info@bcauditor.com, Other Communications: URL: www.bcauditor.com
Deputy Auditor General, Errol S. Price
250-356-2628, Fax: 250-387-1230,info@bcauditor.com; eprice@bcauditor.com

Government Caucus Office (Liberal)
East Annex, Parliament Bldgs., Victoria, BC V8V 1X4
250-356-6171, Fax: 250-356-6176,
premier@gov.bc.ca
www.governmentcaucus.bc.ca
Leader,Hon. Gordon Campbell, Liberal
250-387-1715, Fax: 250-387-0087
Executive Director, Michael Morton
250-387-2950, Fax: 250-387-9066
Director, Research, Lisa Braman
250-387-8943, Fax: 250-356-0329
Director, Communications, Shane Mills
250-356-0393, Fax: 250-387-7957
Senior Manager, Administration & Project Development, Nicole Hamilton
250-356-6134, Fax: 250-387-9066

Office of the Opposition (New Democrat)
#201, Parliament Bldgs., Victoria, BC V8V 1X4
250-387-3655, Fax: 250-387-4680,
ndp@leg.bc.ca
www.bc.ndp.ca
Leader, Carole James
carole.james.mla@leg.bc.ca
Executive Director, Mary O'Donoghue
Director, Research, AnneMarie Delorey
Director, Communications, Chris Gainor

Legislative Committees
#224, Parliament Bldgs., Victoria, BC V8V 1X4
250-356-2933, Fax: 250-356-8172,
ClerkComm@leg.bc.ca

At the beginning of each session, Select Standing Committees are established by the Legislative Assembly in British Columbia. The following nine Select Standing Committees have been established: Aboriginal Affairs; Children & Youth; Crown Corporations; Education; Finance & Government Services; Health; Legislative Initiatives; Parliamentary Reform, Ethical Conduct, Standing Orders, & Private Bills; & Public Accounts.
Clerk of Committees, Craig James

Thirty-Eighth Legislature - British Columbia

Parliament Bldgs., Victoria, BC V8V 1X4

250-387-3785, Fax: 250-387-0942, ClerkHouse@leg.bc.ca
www.leg.bc.ca

Last General Election: May 17, 2005. Next General Election: May 12, 2009. Party Standings (July 2008): Liberal (Lib.) 46; New Democratic Party (NDP) 32; Vacant 1; Total 79. Salaries, Indemnities & Allowances: (April 1, 2007):Basic Compensation $98,100 for members. Each person who holds a salaried position receives an annual salary, determined as the amount of basic compensation for that year multiplied by the following values: Premier .90; Member of the Executive Council with portfolio .50; Member of the Executive Council without portfolio .35; Parliamentary Secretary .15; Speaker .50; Deputy Speaker .35; Leader of the Official Opposition .50; Leader of a recognized political party other than the government or the Official Opposition .25; Government Whip .20; Official Opposition Whip .20; Party Whip of a recognized political party other than the government or the Official Opposition .10; Official Opposition House Leader .20; House Leader of a recognized political party other than the government or the Official Opposition .10; Government Caucus Chair .20; Official Opposition Caucus Chair .20; Caucus Chair of a recognized political party other than the government or the Official Opposition .10; Chair of Select Standing or Special Committees .15. The following is a list of each MLA, the MLA's constitueny, party affiliation, & contact information:

Members

Hon. George Abbott, Shuswap BC, Liberal
250-953-3547, 877-771-7557,Fax: 250-356-9587,hlth.health@gov.bc.ca; george.abbott.mla@leg.bc.ca, Other Communications: Constituency Phone: 250-833-7414

Robin Austin, Skeena BC, New Democratic Party
250-387-3655, Fax: 250-387-4680,robin.austin.mla@leg.bc.ca, Other Communications: Terrace Constituency Phone: 250-638-7906

Harry Bains, Surrey-Newton BC, New Democratic Party
250-387-3655, Fax: 250-387-4680,harry.bains.mla@leg.bc.ca, Other Communications: Constituency Phone: 604-597-8248

Hon. Bill Barisoff, Penticton-OkanaganValley BC, Liberal
250-387-3952, 866-387-3952,Fax: 250-387-2813,bill.barisoff.mla@leg.bc.ca, Other Communications: Penticton Constituency Phone: 250-487-4400

Hon. Patrick Bell, Prince George North BC, Liberal
250-387-6240, Fax: 250-387-1040,pat.bell.mla@leg.bc.ca, Other Communications: Prince George Constituency Phone: 250-612-4194

Hon. Bill Bennett, EastKootenay BC, Liberal
250-953-4246, 866-417-6022,Fax: 250-953-4250,TCA.Minister@gov.bc.ca; bill.bennett.mla@leg.bc.ca, Other Communications: Constituency Phone: 250-417-6022

Hon. Iain Black, Port Moody-Westwood BC, Liberal
250-356-6348, Fax: 250-356-6595,LCS.Minister@gov.bc.ca; iain.black.mla@leg.bc.ca, Other Communications: Constituency Phone: 604-933-2312

Harry Bloy, Burquitlam BC, Liberal
250-387-2765, Fax: 250-387-9103,harry.bloy.mla@leg.bc.ca, Other Communications: Constituency Phone: 604-933-2077

Hon. Shirley Bond, Prince George-MountRobson BC, Liberal
250-387-1977, Fax: 250-387-3200,Minister.Educ@gov.bc.ca; shirley.bond.mla@leg.bc.ca, Other Communications: Constituency Phone: 250-612-4181

Jagrup Brar, Surrey-Panorama Ridge BC, New Democratic Party
250-387-3655, Fax: 250-387-4680,jagrup.brar.mla@leg.bc.ca, Other Communications: Constituency Phone: 604-501-8227

Hon. Gordon Campbell, Vancouver-Point Grey BC, Liberal
250-387-1715, Fax: 250-387-0087,gordon.campbell.mla@leg.bc.ca, Other Communications: Constituency Phone: 604-660-3202

Ron Cantelon, Nanaimo-Parksville BC, Liberal
250-953-4866, 800-663-7867,Fax: 250-387-9103,ron.cantelon.mla@leg.bc.ca, Other Communications: Nanaimo Constituency Phone: 250-729-7041

Hon. Ida Chong, Oak Bay-Gordon Head BC, Liberal
250-356-7411, Fax: 250-356-6376,ida.chong.mla@leg.bc.ca, Other Communications: Gordon Head Constituency Phone: 250-472-8528

Raj Chouhan, Burnaby-Edmonds BC, New Democratic Party
250-387-3655, Fax: 250-387-4680,raj.chouhan.mla@leg.bc.ca, Other Communications: Constituency Phone: 604-520-2756

Hon. Tom Christensen, Okanagan-Vernon BC, Liberal
250-387-9699, 866-870-4189,Fax: 250-387-9722,minister.mcf@gems1.gov.bc.ca; tom.christensen.mla@leg.bc.ca, Other Communications: Constituency Phone: 250-503-3600

David Chudnovsky, Vancouver-Kensington BC, New Democratic Party
250-387-3655, Fax: 250-387-4680,david.chudnovsky.mla@leg.bc.ca, Other Communications: Constituency Phone: 604-775-1033

Hon. Murray Coell, Saanich North &the Islands BC, Liberal
250-387-2771, 866-655-5711,Fax: 250-356-3000,aved.minister@gov.bc.ca; murray.coell.mla@leg.bc.ca, Other Communications: Constituency Phone: 250-655-5711

Hon. Rich Coleman, FortLangley-Aldergrove BC, Liberal
250-356-7750, Fax: 250-356-7292,eia.minister@gov.bc.ca; rich.coleman.mla@leg.bc.ca, Other Communications: Constituency Phone: 604-607-6200

Katrine Conroy, West Kootenay-Boundary BC, New Democratic Party
250-387-3655, 888-755-0556,Fax: 250-387-4680,katrine.conroy.mla@leg.bc.ca, Other Communications: Constituency Phone: 250-304-2783

Gary Earl Coons, North Coast BC, New Democratic Party
250-387-3655, 866-624-7734,Fax: 250-387-4680,gary.coons.mla@leg.bc.ca, Other Communications: Constituency Phone: 250-624-7734

David Cubberley, Saanich South BC, New Democratic Party
250-387-3655, Fax: 250-387-4680,david.cubberley.mla@leg.bc.ca, Other Communications: Constituency Phone: 25-952-4418

Hon. Michael de Jong, Abbotsford-Mount Lehman BC, Liberal
250-953-4844, Fax: 250-953-4856,mike.dejong.mla@leg.bc.ca, Other Communications: Constituency Phone: 604-870-5486

Adrian Dix, Vancouver-Kingsway BC, New Democratic Party
250-387-3655, Fax: 250-387-4680,adrian.dix.mla@leg.bc.ca, Other Communications: Constituency Phone: 604-660-0314

Corky Evans, Nelson-Creston BC, New Democratic Party
250-387-3655, Fax: 250-387-4680,corky.evans.mla@leg.bc.ca, Other Communications: Constituency Phone: 250-354-5944,

Hon. Kevin Falcon, Surrey-Cloverdale BC, Liberal
250-387-1978, Fax: 250-356-2290,kevin.falcon.mla@leg.bc.ca, Other Communications: Constituency Phone: 604-576-3792

Mike Farnworth, Port Coquitlam-Burke Mountain BC, New Democratic Party
250-387-3655, mike.farnworth.mla@leg.bc.ca

Rob Fleming, Victoria-Hillside BC, New Democratic Party
250-387-3655, Fax: 250-387-4680,rob.fleming.mla@leg.bc.ca, Other Communications: Constituency Phone: 250-360-2023

Scott Fraser, Alberni-Qualicum BC, New Democratic Party
250-387-3655, Fax: 250-387-4650,scott.fraser.mla@leg.bc.ca, Other Communications: Port Alberni Constituency Phone: 250-720-4515

Guy Gentner, Delta North BC, New Democratic Party
250-387-3655, Fax: 250-387-4680,guy.gentner.mla@leg.bc.ca, Other Communications: Constituency Phone: 604-597-1488

Hon. Stan Hagen, Comox Valley BC, Liberal
250-387-1023, 877-603-2422,Fax: 250-387-1522,stan.hagen.mla@leg.bc.ca, Other Communications: Constituency Phone: 250-703-2422

Sue Hammell, Surrey-Green Timbers BC, New Democratic Party
250-387-3655, Fax: 250-387-4680,sue.hammell.mla@leg.bc.ca, Other Communications: Constituency Phone: 604-586-2791

Hon. Colin Hansen, Vancouver-Quilchena BC, Liberal
250-387-3751, Fax: 250-387-5594,Fin.Minister@gov.bc.ca; colin.hansen.mla@leg.bc.ca, Other Communications: Constituency Phone: 604-664-0748

Randy Hawes, Maple Ridge-Mission BC, Liberal
250-387-8950, 866-370-6203,Fax: 250-356-0596,randy.hawes.mla@leg.bc.ca, Other Communications: Constituency Phone: 604-820-6203

Sindi Hawkins, Kelowna-Mission BC, Liberal
250-953-4887, 866-870-4182,Fax: 250-356-0596,sindi.hawkins.mla@leg.bc.ca, Other Communications: Constituency Phone: 250-712-3620

Dave Hayer, Surrey-Tynehead BC, Liberal
250-387-8076, Fax: 250-387-9091,dave.hayer.mla@leg.bc.ca, Other Communications: Constituency Phone: 604-501-3201

Hon. Gordon Hogg, Surrey-White Rock BC, Liberal
250-953-4100, Fax: 250-387-1803,gordon.hogg.mla@leg.bc.ca, Other Communications: Constituency Phone: 604-542-3930

John Horgan, Malahat-Juan de Fuca BC, New Democratic Party
250-387-3655, Fax: 250-387-4680,john.horgan.mla@leg.bc.ca, Other Communications: West Shore Constituency Phone: 250-391-2801

Al Horning, Kelowna-Lake Country BC, Liberal
250-953-4869, 866-765-8516,Fax: 250-387-9091,al.horning.mla@leg.bc.ca, Other Communications: Constituency Phone: 250-765-8516

Olga Ilich, Richmond Centre BC, Liberal
250-356-6171, Fax: 250-356-6176,olga.ilich.mla@leg.bc.ca, Other Communications: Constituency Phone: 604-775-0754

Carole James, Victoria-Beacon Hill BC, New Democratic Party
250-387-3655, Fax: 250-387-4680,carole.james.mla@leg.bc.ca, Other Communications: Constituency Phone: 250-952-4211

Daniel Jarvis, North Vancouver-Seymour BC, Liberal
250-356-3078, Fax: 250-952-0222,daniel.jarvis.mla@leg.bc.ca, Other Communications: Constituency Phone: 604-775-0803

Maurine Karagianis, Esquimalt-Metchoskin BC, New Democratic Party
250-387-3655, Fax: 250-387-4680,maurine.karagianis.mla@leg.bc.ca, Other Communications: Constituency Phone: 250-479-8326

Leonard Krog, Nanaimo, New Democratic Party
250-387-3655, Fax: 250-387-4680,leonard.krog.mla@leg.bc.ca, Other Communications: Constituency Phone: 250-714-0630

Hon. Kevin Krueger, Kamloops-North Thompson BC, Liberal
250-356-6611, Fax: 250-356-8294,sbr.minister@gov.bc.ca; kevin.krueger.mla@leg.bc.ca, Other Communications: Constituency Phone: 250-314-6031

Jenny Wai Ching Kwan, Vancouver-Mount Pleasant BC, New Democratic Party
250-387-3655, Fax: 250-387-4680,jenny.kwan.mla@leg.bc.ca, Other Communications: Constituency Phone: 604-775-0790

Harry Lali, Yale-Lillooet BC, New Democratic Party
250-387-3655, 877-378-4802,Fax: 250-384-4680,harry.lali.mla@leg.bc.ca, Other Communications: Constituency Phone: 250-378-4802

Richard T. Lee, Burnaby North BC, Liberal
250-356-3052, Fax: 250-387-9103,richard.lee.mla@leg.bc.ca, Other Communications: Constituency Phone: 604 775-0778

Hon. Blair Lekstrom, Peace RiverSouth BC, Liberal
250-387-2283, 877-784-1330,Fax: 250-387-4312,CS.minister@gov.bc.ca; blair.lekstrom.mla@leg.bc.ca, Other Communications: Constituency Phone: 250-784-1330

John Les, Chilliwack-Sumas BC, Liberal
250-356-6171, 866-424-8350,Fax: 250-356-6176,john.les.mla@leg.bc.ca, Other Communications: Constituency Phone: 604-702-5214

Norm Macdonald, Columbia River-Revelstoke BC, New Democratic Party
250-387-3655, 866-870-4188,Fax: 250-387-4680,norm.macdonald.mla@leg.bc.ca, Other Communications: Golden Constituency Phone: 250-344-4816

Dennis MacKay, Bulkley Valley-Stikine BC, Liberal
250-356-9574, 866-877-4500,Fax: 250-356-0596,dennis.mackay.mla@leg.bc.ca, Other Communications: Constituency Phone: 250-877-4500

Lorne Mayencourt, Vancouver-Burrard BC, Liberal
250-387-2796, Fax: 250-356-7652,lorne.mayencourt.mla@leg.bc.ca, Other Communications: Constituency Phone: 604-775-2484

Hon. Joan McIntyre, West-Vancouver-Garibaldi BC, Liberal
250-356-7562, Fax: 250-356-8545,joan.mcintyre.mla@leg.bc.ca, Other Communications: Constituency Phone: 604-981-0045

Hon. Richard Neufeld, Peace RiverNorth BC, Liberal
250-387-5896, 866-263-0101,Fax: 250-356-2965,empr.minister@gov.bc.ca; richard.neufeld.mla@leg.bc.ca, Other Communications: Constituency Phone: 250-263-0101

John Nuraney, Burnaby-Willingdon BC, Liberal
250-952-6784, Fax: 250-387-9091,john.nuraney.mla@leg.bc.ca, Other Communications: Constituency Phone: 604-775-2414

Hon. Wally Oppal, Q.C., Vancouver-Fraserview BC, Liberal
250-387-1866, Fax: 250-387-6411,ag.minister@gov.bc.ca; wally.oppal.mla@leg.bc.ca, Other Communications: Constituency Phone: 604-775-2246

Hon. Barry Penner, Chilliwack-Kent BC, Liberal
250-387-1187, 866-553-5537,Fax: 250-387-1356,env.minister@gov.bc.ca; barry.penner.mla@leg.bc.ca, Other Communications: Constituency Phone: 604-858-6202

Hon. Mary Polak, Langley BC, Liberal
250-387-3504, Fax: 250-387-3420,mary.polak.mla@leg.bc.ca, Other Communications: Constituency Phone: 604-514-8206

Chuck Puchmayr, New Westminster BC, New Democratic Party
250-387-3655, Fax: 250-387-4680,chuck.puchmayr.mla@leg.bc.ca, Other Communications: Constituency Phone: 604-775-2101

Bruce Ralston, Surrey-Whalley BC, New Democratic Party
250-387-3655, Fax:
250-387-4680,bruce.ralston.mla@leg.bc.ca, Other Communications: Constituency Phone: 604-586-2740
Hon. Linda Reid, Richmond East BC, Liberal
250-356-7662, Fax: 250-356-8337,linda.reid.mla@leg.bc.ca
Claude Richmond, Kamloops BC, Liberal
250-356-6171, 866-470-4187,Fax:
250-356-6176,claude.richmond.mla@leg.bc.ca, Other Communications: Constituency Phone: 250-314-6027
Valerie Roddick, Delta South BC, Liberal
250-387-3820, Fax: 250-952-0222,val.roddick.mla@leg.bc.ca, Other Communications: Constituency Phone: 604-940-7924
Doug Routley, Cowichan-Ladysmith BC, New Democratic Party
250-387-3655, Fax:
250-387-4680,douglas.routley.mla@leg.bc.ca, Other Communications: Duncan Constituency Phone: 250-746-8770
John Rustad, Prince George-Omineca BC, Liberal
250-953-4892, Fax:
250-356-5471,john.rustad.mla@leg.bc.ca, Other Communications: Prince George Constituency Phone: 250-964-5650
Michael Sather, Maple Ridge-Pitt Meadows BC, New Democratic Party
250-387-3655, Fax:
250-387-4680,michael.sather.mla@leg.bc.ca, Other Communications: Constituency Phone: 604-476-9823
Nicholas Simons, PowellRiver-Sunshine Coast BC, New Democratic Party
250-387-3655, 866-373-0792,Fax:
250-387-4680,nicholas.simons.mla@leg.bc.ca, Other Communications: Powell River Constituency Office Phone: 604-485-1249
Bob Simpson, Cariboo North BC, New Democratic Party
250-387-3655, 866-991-0296,Fax:
250-387-4680,bob.simpson.mla@leg.bc.ca, Other Communications: Quesnel Constituency Phone: 250-991-0296
Shane Simpson, Vancouver-Hastings BC, New Democratic Party
250-387-3655, Fax:
250-387-4680,shane.simpson.mla@leg.bc.ca, Other Communications: Constituency Phone: 604-775-2277
Ralph Sultan, West Vancouver-Capilano BC, Liberal
250-356-9495, Fax:
250-356-5471,ralph.sultan.mla@leg.bc.ca, Other Communications: Constituency Phone: 604-981-0050
Carole Taylor, Vancouver-Langara BC, Liberal
250-356-6171, Fax:
250-356-6176,carole.taylor.mla@leg.bc.ca, Other Communications: Constituency Phone: 604 664-0115
Diane Thorne, Coquitlam-Maillardville BC, New Democratic Party
250-387-3655, Fax:
250-387-4680,diane.thorne.mla@leg.bc.ca, Other Communications: Constituency Phone: 604-933-2001
Rick Thorpe, Okanagan-Westside BC, Liberal
250-356-6171, 866-404-3008,Fax:
250-356-6176,rick.thorpe.mla@leg.bc.ca, Other Communications: Summerland Constituency Phone: 250 404-3008
Claire Trevena, North Island BC, New Democratic Party
250-387-3655, 866-387-5100,Fax:
250-387-4680,claire.trevena.mla@leg.bc.ca, Other Communications: Campbell River Constituency Phone: 250-287-5100
Hon. John van Dongen, Abbotsford-Clayburn BC, Liberal
250-356-7717, Fax: 250-356-8270,SG.Minister@gov.bc.ca; john.vandongen.mla@leg.bc.ca, Other Communications: Constituency Phone: 604-870-5945
Katherine Whittred, North Vancouver-Lonsdale BC, Liberal
250-953-5144, Fax:
250-387-9106,katherine.whittred.mla@leg.bc.ca, Other Communications: Constituency Phone: 604-981-0033
Charlie Wyse, Cariboo South BC, New Democratic Party
250-387-3655, 866-305-3804,Fax:
250-387-4680,charlie.wyse.mla@leg.bc.ca, Other Communications: Constituency Phone: 250-305-3800
John Yap, Richmond-Steveston BC, Liberal
250-387-2203, Fax: 250-387-9066,john.yap.mla@leg.bc.ca, Other Communications: Constituency Phone: 604-241-8452
Vacant, Vancouver-Fairview

British Columbia Government Departments & Agencies

Ministry of Aboriginal Relations & Reconciliation

2957 Jutland Rd., PO Box 9100 Prov Govt, Victoria, BC V8W 9B1

250-387-6121, 800-663-7867
abrinfo@gov.bc.ca
www.gov.bc.ca/arr

Other Communication: Vancouver Phone: 604-660-2421; Toll Free Phone Treaty Information: 1-800-880-1022
The Ministry's activities include negotiating treaties & other agreements & improving the lives of Aboriginal people.
Minister, Aboriginal Relations & Reconciliation, Hon. Michael de Jong
250-953-4844, Fax:
250-953-4856,mike.dejong.mla@leg.bc.ca
Deputy Minister, Lorne Brownsey
250-356-1394
Director, Communications, Maria Wilkie
250-953-3211, maria.wilkie@gov.bc.ca,
• British Columbia Treaty Commission(BCTC)
#203, 1155 West Pender St.
Vancouver, BC V6E 2P4
604-482-9200 Fax: 604-482-9222 800-665-8330
info@bctreaty.net
www.bctreaty.net
The independent & neutral body facilitates treaty negotiations among the governments of Canada, British Columbia, & First Nations in BC.
• Native Economic Development Advisory Board
c/o Director, Economic Initiatives
2955 Jutland Rd.
PO Box 9100 Prov Govt
Victoria, BC V8W 9B1
250-387-2536 Fax: 250-356-9467
www.gov.bc.ca/arr/economic/fcf/nedab.html
Supporting sustainable Aboriginal economic development throughout British Columbia is the role of the Native Economic Development Advisory Board.

Ministry of Advanced Education & Labour Market Development

PO Box 9059 Prov Govt, Victoria, BC V8W 9E2

250-356-2771, Fax: 250-356-3000,
ALMD.WEBMASTER@gov.bc.ca
www.gov.bc.ca/aved

Other Communication: Public Affairs Bureau Phone: 250-952-6508; Fax: 250-356-6942
The Ministry of Advanced Education & Labour Market Development strives to lead & support an excellent & accessible post-secondary education system, & to ensure an integrated approach to research & innovation.
Acts Administered:
Accountants (Certified General) Act
Accountants (Chartered) Act
Accountants (Management) Act
Applied Science Technologists & Technicians Act
Architects Act
Architects (Landscape) Act
College & Institute Act
Degree Authorization Act
Engineers & Geoscientists Act
Industry Training Authority Act
Institute of Technology Act
Knowledge Nework Corporation Act
Ministry of International Business & Immigration Act
Music Teachers (Registered) Act
Open Learning Agency Act
Private Career Training Institutions Act
Public Education Flexibility & Choice Act, Part I
Public Education Labour Relations Act
Public Sector Employers Act
Public Sector Pension Plans Act (except as it relates to the Investment Management Corporation)
Public Service Act
Public Service Benefit Plan Act
Public Service Labour Relations Act
Royal Roads University Act
Thompson Rivers University Act
University Act
University Foundations Act
Workers Compensation Act, Section 3 (6)
Minister, Advanced Education & Labour Market Development, Hon. Moira Stilwell
250-356-2771, Fax: 250-356-3000,ALMD.Minister@gov.bc.ca
Deputy Minister, Lorne Brownsey
250-356-5170, Fax:
250-356-5468,ALMD.DeputyMinister@gov.bc.ca
• British Columbia Pension Corporation
2995 Jutland Rd.
PO Box 9460
Victoria, BC V8W 9V8
250-387-1002 Fax: 250-953-0429 800-663-8823
PensionCorp@pensionsbc.ca;
Retired.Members@pensionsbc.ca
www.pensionsbc.ca
Other Communication: College Pension Plan: 250-953-4324; Municipal Pension Plan: 250-953-3000; Public Service Pension Plan: 250-953-3033; Teachers' Pension Plan: 250-953-3022
The British Columbia Pension Corporation is a Crown corporation, which was established by The Public Sector Pension Plans Act. The Pension Corporation serves as the plan administrator for the following pension plans: College (CPP@pensionsbc.ca); Municipal (MPP@pensionsbc.ca); Public Service (PSPP@pensionsbc.ca); Teachers' (TPP@pensionsbc.ca); & the Workers' Compensation Board (WCB@pensionsbc.ca). The Corporation also continues to administer the Members of the Legislative Assembly Pension Plan.
• Degree Quality Assessment Board
Degree Quality Assessment Board Secretariat
835 Humboldt St., 1st Fl.
PO Box 9177 Prov Govt
Victoria, BC V8V 4W8
250-387-5163
aved.dqabsecretariat@gov.bc.ca
www.aved.gov.bc.ca/degree-authorization/board/welcome.htm
The Degree Quality Assessment Board reviews applications from British Columbia public post-secondary institutions, & private & out-of-province public post-secondary institutions. Applications concern new degree programs & exempt status, & the use of the word "university". Recommendations are then made to the Minister of Advanced Education & Labour Market Development.
• Industry Training Authority(ITA)
#1223, 13351 Commerce Pkwy.
Richmond, BC V6V 2X7
604-214-8700 Fax: 604-214-8701 866-660-6011
info@itabc.ca; customerservice@itabc.ca
www.itabc.ca
Other Communication: Customer Service: 778-328-8700
British Columbia's Industry Training Authority is a provincial government agency which oversees the province's training & apprenticeship system. The ITA works with industry, employers, training providers, trainees, & apprentices.
• Leading Edge Endowment Fund Board(LEEF)
1188 West Georgia St., 9th Fl.
Vancouver, BC V6E 4A2
604-438-3220 Fax: 604-438-6564
contact@leefbc.ca
www.leefbc.ca
To encourage social & economic development in British Columbia, the provincial government established the Leading Edge Endowment Fund in 2002. The Fund establishes Leadership Research Chairs at the province's public, post-secondary institutions, & Regional Innovation Chairs through colleges, university-colleges, & institutes.
• Private Career Training Institutions Agency
#300, 5172 Kingsway
Burnaby, BC V5H 2E8
604-660-4400 Fax: 604-660-3312 800-661-7441
info@pctia.bc.ca
www.pctia.bc.ca
The Private Career Training Institutions Agency is the regulatory agency for private training institutions in British Columbia. The Agency works in accordance with the Private Career Training Institutions Act, Regulations & Bylaws.
• Public Sector Employers' Council Secretariat(PSEC)
#210, 880 Douglas St.
PO Box 9400 Prov Govt
Victoria, BC V8V 9V1
250-387-0842 Fax: 250-387-6258
www.aved.gov.bc.ca/psec
The coordination of the management of labour relations policies & practices in the public sector is the principal responsibility of the Public Sector Employers' Council. The Council consists of the following members: Eight Ministers or Deputy Ministers; Commissioner of the BC Public Service Agency; & Representatives from six public sector employers' associations. The Public Sector Employers' Council Secretariat carries out the work of the Council.

Management Services Division

620 Superior St., 5th Fl., PO Box 9879 Prov Govt, Victoria, BC V8W 9T6

250-953-3536, Fax: 250-356-8322,
EDUC.ADMManagementServices@gov.bc.ca

Assistant Deputy Minister, Neil Matheson
Executive Director & Senior Financial Officer, Finance & Administration Servies, Pat Brown
250-356-2470, Fax:
250-387-9695,EDUC.FinanceAdministrativeServices@gov.bc.ca
Director, Ministry Strategic Human Resources, Allan Pollock
250-356-2495, Fax:
250-356-1520,EDUC.HumanResources@gov.bc.ca

Director, Privacy & Records Management, Alex Bjelica
250-356-8985, Fax:
250-387-6315,EDUC.InformationPrivacy@gov.bc.ca

Post-Secondary Education Division
835 Humboldt St., 3rd Fl., PO Box 9880 Prov Govt, Victoria, BC V8W 9T6
250-953-3585, Fax: 250-356-5468,
AVED.ADMPostSecondaryEducation@gov.bc.ca

Assistant Deputy Minister, Ruth Wittenberg
250-356-2498
Executive Director, Funding & Analysis, Joseph Thompson
250-387-8820, Fax: 250-356-7922,AVED.FAB@gov.bc.ca
Director, Colleges & University Colleges, Dawn Minty
250-387-8871, Fax:
250-952-6110,AVED.Colleges&UnivColleges@gov.bc.ca
Director, Policy & System Quality, Susan Brown
250-387-6166, Fax: 250-356-8851,PSQ@gov.bc.ca
Director, Universities & Institutes, Deborah Hull
250-356-8382, Fax:
250-356-5962,AVED.UniversitiesInstitutes@gov.bc.ca

Research, Technology, & Innovation Division
835 Humboldt St., 3rd Fl., PO Box 9164 Prov Govt, Victoria, BC V8W 9H4
250-356-2496, Fax: 250-356-5468

Assistant Deputy Minister, Brent Sauder

Students & Learning Division
835 Humboldt St., 3rd Fl., PO Box 9145 Prov Govt, Victoria, BC V8W 9H1
250-356-0075, Fax: 250-356-5468,
www.aved.gov.bc.ca/studentaidbc (Student Aid BC)

Other Communication: StudentAid BC TTY line for deaf & hearing impaired: 250-952-6832; StudentAid BC Toll Free: 1-800-561-1818

Assistant Deputy Minister, Tom Vincent
250-356-1777
Director, Learning Programs, Janice Nakamura
250-952-6567, Fax:
250-387-0878,AVED.LearningPrograms@gov.bc.ca
Director, Governance, Tony Loughran
250-356-7254, Fax:
250-387-3750,AVED.Governance@gov.bc.ca
Director, Information & Data Management, Jacqui Stewart
250-356-1779, Fax: 250-387-1377
Director, StudentAid BC, Victoria Thibeau
250-387-3605, 800-561-1818,Fax: 250-356-9455

Ministry of Agriculture & Lands

PO Box 9120 Prov Govt, Victoria, BC V8W 9E2
250-387-5121, Fax: 250-387-1522,
www.gov.bc.ca/al

The mission of the Ministry is to provide a business climate for a competitive & profitable industry that supplies safe, high quality food for consumers & the export market.

Acts Administered:
Agri-Food Choice & Quality Act
Agricultural Lands Commission
Agricultural Produce Grading Act
Animal Disease Control Act
Bee Act
Boundary Act
British Columbia Wine Act
Cattle (Horned) Act
Environment & Land Use Act
Farm Income Insurance Act
Farm Practices Protection (Right to Farm) Act
Farmers & Womens Institutes Act
Farming & Fishing Industries Development Act
Fisheries Act
Food Products Standards Act
Fur Farm Act
Game Farm Act
Greenbelt Act
Insurance for Crops Act
Land Act
Land Survey Act
Land Surveyors Act
Land Title & Survey Authority
Libby Dam Reservoir Act
Livestock Act
Livestock Identification Act
Livestock Lien Act
Livestock Protection Act
Livestock Public Sale Act
Local Government Act (in part)
Ministry of Agriculture & Food Act
Muskwa-Kechika Management Area Act
Natural Products Marketing (BC) Act
Pharmacists, Pharmacy Operations & Drug Scheduling Act (in part)
Plant Protection Act
Prevention of Cruelty to Animals Act
Private Managed Forest Land Act
Veterinarians Act
Weed Control Act
Wine Act

Minister, Agriculture & Lands, Hon. Steve Thompson
250-387-1023, Fax: 250-387-1522
Deputy Minister, Larry Pedersen
250-356-1800, Larry.Pedersen@gov.bc.ca

• Agricultural Land Commission(ALC)
#133, 4940 Canada Way
Burnaby, BC V5G 4K6
604-660-7000 Fax: 604-660-7033
www.alc.gov.bc.ca
The independent Crown agency strives to preserve agricultural land in British Columbia. The Provincial Agricultural Land Commission also works to encourage & enable farm businesses throughout the province. The Commission's chief responsibility is the administration of the Agricultural Land Commission Act.

• British Columbia Farm Industry Review Board(BCFIRB)
1007 Fort St., 3rd Fl.
PO Box 9129 Prov Govt
Victoria, BC V8W 9B5
250-356-8945 Fax: 250-356-5131
firb@gov.bc.ca
www.firb.gov.bc.ca
The British Columbia Farm Industry Review Board is a statutory appeal body. It is engaged in the general supervision of marketing boards & commodity boards which operate in the agricultural & aquaculture sectors.

Agriculture Operations
808 Douglas St., 5th Fl, PO Box 9120 Prov Govt, Victoria, BC V8W 9B4
250-356-7279

Assistant Deputy Minister, Lindsay Kislock
250-356-1815
Director, Food Safety & Plant Health, Marney K. James
604-556-3058, Fax: 604-556-3117
Acting Director, Regional Operations, Wray McDonnell
250-861-7201
Director, Animal Health,Dr. Ron Lewis
604-556-3038, Fax: 604-556-3010
Director, Sustainable Agriculture Management, Ken Nickel
604-556-3103, Fax: 604-556-3099

Corporate Services
2975 Jutland Rd., 5th Fl., PO Box 9339 Prov Govt, Victoria, BC V8W 9M1
250-387-9878, Fax: 250-953-3414

Assistant Deputy Minister, Denise Bragg
250-387-9878
Acting Chief Information Officer & Executive Director, Information Management, Doug Say
250-387-1348, Fax: 250-387-1085
Executive Director, People Strategies, Duff McCaghey
250-356-6243, Fax: 250-387-3522
Executive Director, Finance & Administration, Anne Minnings
250-356-9220
Director, Corporate Services Delivery, Trish Dohan
250-356-9221

Crown Land Administration
808 Douglas St., 5th Fl., PO Box 9120 Prov Govt, Victoria, BC V8W 9B4
250-356-3076, Fax: 250-356-7279

Assistant Deputy Minister, Grant Parnell
Director, Crown Land Opportunities, Randy Wenger
604-586-2889, Fax: 604-586-2900
Director, Crown Contaminated Sites, Brian D. Clarke
250-387-9659, Fax: 250-356-6791
Director, Land Program Services, Ward Trotter
250-356-2166, Fax: 250-356-5450
Director, Strategic Initiatives, Jane Spackman
250-356-0911, Fax: 250-356-7830
Acting Director, Strategic Land Policy & Legislation, Allan Lidstone
250-356-1659, Fax: 250-356-7830

Strategic Industry Development
808 Douglas St., 5th Fl., PO Box 9120 Prov Govt, Victoria, BC V8W 9B4
250-356-1821, Fax: 250-356-7279

Assistant Deputy Minister, Harvey Sasaki
250-356-1122
Director, Governance & Legislation, Mark Parsons
250-387-3195
Director, Strategic Policy & Planning, Daphne Sidaway-Wolf
250-356-2945, Fax: 250-387-0357
Director, Business Risk Management, Gary Falk
250-861-7232
Director, Investment & Innovation, Grant Thompson
250-356-8299, Fax: 250-356-2949
Director, Aquaculture Policy, Al Castledine
250-387-9574, Fax: 250-356-0358,
Acting Director, Aquaculture Operations, Jim Russell
250-897-7561, Fax: 250-334-1410

Ministry of the Attorney General

PO Box 9044 Prov Govt, Victoria, BC V8W 9E2
250-387-1866, Fax: 250-387-6411,
www.gov.bc.ca/ag

The Ministry of the Attorney General strives to improve British Columbia's justice system, so that citizens have access to quality justice services.

Acts Administered:
Adult Guardianship Act
Age of Majority Act
Attorney General Act
Civil Rights Protection Act
Class Proceedings Act
Commercial Arbitration Act
Commissioner on Resources & Environment Act
Company Act
Conflict of Laws Rules for Trusts Act
Constitution Act
Constitutional Amendment Approval Act
Constitutional Question Act
County Boundary Act
Court Agent Act
Court of Appeal Act
Court Order Enforcement Act
Court Order Interest Act
Court Rules Act
Crown Counsel Act
Crown Franchise Act
Crown Proceeding Act
Debtor Assistance Act
Disciplinary Authority Protection Act
Election Act
Electoral Boundaries Commission Act
Electoral Districts Act
Enforcement of Canadian Judgments Act
Escheat Act
Estate Administration Act
Estates of Missing Persons Act
Evidence Act
Expropriation Act
Family Compensation Act
Family Maintenance Enforcement Act
Family Relations Act
Federal Courts Jurisdiction Act
Financial Disclosure Act
Foreign Arbitral Awards Act
Foreign Money Claims Act
Foresters Act s. 9(2)
Fraudulent Conveyance Act
Fraudulent Preference Act
Frustrated Contract Act
Good Samaritan Act
Holocaust Memorial Day Act
Human Rights Code
Indian Cut-off Lands Dispute
Infants Act
Inquiry Act
Insurance Corporation Divisions 1 & 2 Act
Interjurisdictional Support Order Act
International Commerical Arbitration Act
International Sale of Goods Act
International Trusts Act
Interpretation Act
Judicial Review Procedure Act
Jury Act
Justice Administration Act
Law & Equity Act
Law Reform Commission Act
Legal Profession Act
Legal Services Society Act
Libel & Slander Act
Limitation Act
Lobbyists Registration Act
Members' Conflict of Interest Act
Ministry of Consumer & Corporate Affairs Act
Ministry of Provincial Secretary & Government Services Act
Negligence Act
Nisga'a Final Agreement
Notaries Act
Occupiers Liability Act
Offence Act
Office for Children & Youth Act

Ombudsman Act
Partition of Property Act
Patients Property Act
Perpetuity Act
Power of Appointment Act
Power of Attorney Act
Privacy Act
Probate Recognition Act
Property Law Act
Provincial Court Act
Public Guardian & Trustee Act
Queen's Counsel Act
Recall & Initiative Act
Referendum Act
Regulations Act
Representation Agreement Act
Representative for Children & Youth Act
Sechelt Indian Government District Enabling Act
Sheriff Act
Small Claims Act
Statute Revision Act
Statute Uniformity Act
Subpoena (Interprovincial) Act
Supreme Court Act
Survivorship & Presumption of Death Act
Treaty Commission Act
Trespass Act
Trust & Settlement Variation Act
Trustee Act
Trustee (Church Property) Act
Wills Act
Wills Variation Act
Young Offenders (British Columbia) Act

Attorney General,Hon. Michael de Jong
250-387-1866, Fax: 250-387-6411,ag.minister@gov.bc.ca
Deputy Attorney General, David Loukidelis
250-356-0149, Fax: 250-387-6224
Assistant Deputy Attorney General, Legal Services, Richard Fyfe
250-356-8800, richard.fyfe@gov.bc.ca
Assistant Deputy Attorney General, Criminal Justice, Robert Gillen, Q.C.
250-387-5174
Assistant Deputy Minister, Management Services, Deborah Fayad
250-387-5258, deborah.fayad@gov.bc.ca
Assistant Deputy Minister, Justice Services, Jerry McHale
250-356-6582
Assistant Deputy Minister, Court Services, Rob Wood
250-356-1527
Assistant Deputy Minister, Multiculturalism Services, Barbara Walman
Executive Director, Strategic Human Resource Services, Cathy Fulton
Executive Director, Strategic Planning & Legislation, Carol Anne Rolf

• British Columbia Ferry Commission
PO Box 1497
Comox, BC V9M 8A2
250-339-2714
info@bcferrycommission.com
www.bcferrycommission.com
The British Columbia Ferry Commission was established under the Coastal Ferry Act. The fares & service levels of the province's ferry operator, British Columbia Ferry Services Inc., are regulated by the Commission.

• British Columbia Human Rights Tribunal
#1170, 605 Robson St.
Vancouver, BC V6B 5J3
604-775-2000 Fax: 604-775-2020 888-440-8844TDD: 604-775-2021
BCHumanRightsTribunal@gov.bc.ca
www.bchrt.bc.ca
The independent, quasi-judicial body was established by the British Columbia Human Rights Code. The British Columbia Human Rights Tribunal is engaged in accepting, screening, mediating, & adjudicating human rights complaints.

• British Columbia Review Board
#1020, 510 Burrard St.
Vancouver, BC V6C 3A8
604-660-8789 Fax: 604-660-8809 877-305-2277
www.bcrb.bc.ca
The British Columbia Review Board was created in accordance with the Criminal Code of Canada. The Board is an independent tribunal, with responsibility for holding hearings to establish & review dispositions. The dispositions involve persons who have been charged with criminal offenses & received verdicts of not criminally responsible on account of mental disorder, or unfit to stand trial on account of mental disorder.

• Elections British Columbia

• Judicial Council of British Columbia
Pacific Centre
#602, 700 West Georgia St.
PO Box 10287
Vancouver, BC V7Y 1E8
604-660-2864 Fax: 604-660-1108
www.provincialcourt.bc.ca/judicialcouncil
As designated by the Provincial Court Act, the Judicial Council of British Columbia consists of nine members. The process of the Judicial Council is governed by a Procedure Bylaw. The overall goal of the Council is the improvement of the quality of judicial service in the province.

• Legal Services Society(LSS)
#400, 510 Burrard St.
Vancouver, BC V6C 3A8
604-601-6000
communications@lss.bc.ca
www.lss.bc.ca
Other Communication: Call Centre: 1-866-577-2525; LawLINE: 604-408-2172 (Lower Mainland), 1-866-577-2525 (Outside Lower Mainland); Media inquiries: 604-601-6004
The Legal Services Society was established by the Legal Services Society Act. The non-profit Society provides legal information, advice, & representation services to assist British Columbians in the resolution of their legal issues. Regional centres & local agents' offices are located throughout the province.

• Office of the Representative for Children & Youth(RCY)
1019 Wharf St.
PO Box 9207 Prov Govt
Victoria, BC V8W 9J1
250-356-6710 Fax: 250-356-0837 800-476-3933
rcy@rcybc.ca
www.rcybc.ca
Other Communication: Northern Office - Prince George: 1-800-476-3933; Lower Mainland Office - Burnaby: 1-800-476-3933
Acting in accordance with British Columbia's Representative for Children and Youth Act, the Representative for Children & Youth is responsible for advocacy, monitoring, & investigation.

• Public Guardian & Trustee of British Columbia(PGT)
#700, 808 West Hastings St.
Vancouver, BC V6C 3L3
604-660-4444 Fax: 604-660-0374
mail@trustee.bc.ca
www.trustee.bc.ca
Other Communication: Communications & Media Relations: 604-660-4474; Child & Youth Svs.: 604-775-3480; Health Care Decisions: 1-877-511-4111; Estate & Personal Trust Svs.: 604-660-4444
The Public Guardian & Trustee of British Columbia was established under the Public Guardian and Trustee Act. The corporation offers the following programs: Child & Youth Services; Services to Adults; & Estate & Personal Trust Services.

Court Services Branch
850 Burdett Ave., 6th Fl., PO Box 9249 Prov Govt, Victoria, BC V8W 9J2
250-356-1550, Fax: 250-356-8152
Executive Director, Court Services Strategic Priorities, Jan Rossley
250-356-1525
Executive Director, Court Administration, William Grandage
604-660-9823, Fax: 604-660-9580
Executive Director, Sheriff Services, Dave Maedel
250-387-0096

Criminal Justice Branch
1001 Douglas St., 9th Fl., PO Box 9276 Prov Govt, Victoria, BC V8V 1X4
250-387-3840, Fax: 250-387-0090
Director, Legal Services, Geoffrey Gaul
250-953-4798
Director, Policy & Legislation, Richard de Boer
250-356-0284
Director, Management Services, Jenny Manton
250-387-1184

Justice Service Branch
1001 Douglas St., 8th Fl., PO Box 9222 Prov Govt, Victoria, BC V8W 9J1
250-356-6582, Fax: 250-356-2721
Provincial Director, Family Justice Services, Irene Robertson
250-387-5903, Fax: 250-356-1279
Executive Director, Administrative Justice, Dianne Flood
250-387-0116, Fax: 250-387-0079
Director, Civil / Family Law Policy, Nancy Carter
250-356-6182, Fax: 250-387-1189
Director, Legal Access Policy, George Faddis
250-387-5003
Director, Dispute Resolution, David Merner
250-387-5257, Fax: 250-387-1189
Director, Maintenance Enforcement & Locate Services, Chris Beresford
604-660-2528, Fax: 604-660-1346,agjuserv@gov.bc.ca

Legal Services Branch
1001 Douglas St., PO Box 9280 Prov Govt, Victoria, BC V8W 9J7
250-356-8800
Chief Legislative Counsel, Janet Erasmus
250-356-8123, Fax: 250-356-5758
Director, Corporate Services, Aaron Plater
250-356-8941
Senior Counsel, Barristers Division - Civil Litigation, Gordon Houston
250-356-6175, Fax: 250-953-4348
Senior Counsel, Barristers Division - Constitutional & Administrative Law, George Copley, Q.C.
250-356-8875
Senior Solicitor, Solicitors Division - Aboriginal Law Group, Geoff Moyse
250-356-8937, Fax: 250-356-8939
Senior Solicitor, Solicitors Division - Health & Social Services, Fiona St. Clair
250-356-8444, Fax: 250-356-8444
Senior Solicitor, Solicitors Division - Resource, Environmental & Land Law, Paul Jarman
250-356-8899

Multiculturalism & Immigration Branch
1019 Wharf St., 6th Fl., PO Box 9213 Prov Govt, Victoria, BC V8W 9J1
250-356-8481, Fax: 250-387-0271,
Director, Immigration Policy & Intergovernmental Relations, Deb Zehr
250-356-1125, Fax: 250-387-0271
Director, Anti-racism & Multiculturalism, Meharoona Ghani
604-660-5140

Office of the Auditor General

8 Bastion Sq., Victoria, BC V8V 1X4
250-387-6803, Fax: 250-387-1230,
info@bcauditor.com
www.bcauditor.com
The chief responsibility of the Office of the Auditor General is auditing most of the British Columbia provincial government, with its ministries, Crown corporations, & other organizations.
Auditor General, John Doyle, MBA, CA
250-387-6803
Assistant Auditor General, Bill Gilhooly
250-356-2637
Assistant Auditor General, Malcolm Gaston
250-356-2660
Assistant Auditor General, Russ Jones
250-356-1416
Assistant Auditor General, Morris Sydor
250-356-2612

Ministry of Children & Family Development

PO Box 9770 Prov Govt, Victoria, BC V8W 9S5
250-387-7027, 877-387-7027
MCF.CorrespondenceManagement@gov.bc.ca
www.mcf.gov.bc.ca

Other Communication: Helpline for Children: 310-1234; Emergencies outside office hours: 604-660-4927 (Vancouver); 604-660-8180 (Lower Mainland); 1-800-663-9122 (remainder of province)
The Ministry works toward the goal of healthy children & families living in safe & inclusive communities.
Acts Administered:
Adoption Act
Child Care BC Act
Child Care Subsidy Act
Child, Family & Community Service Act
Community Living Authority Act
Community Services Interim Authorities Act
Health & Social Services Delivery Act
Human Resource Facility Act
Social Workers Act
Youth Justice Act
Minister,Hon. Tom Christensen
250-387-9699, Fax: 250-387-9722,minister.mcf@gems1.gov.bc.ca; tom.christensen.mla@leg.bc.ca
Minister of State for Child Care,Hon. Linda Reid
250-356-7662, Fax: 250-356-8337,linda.reid.mla@leg.bc.ca
Deputy Minister, Children & Family Development, Lesley du Toit
250-387-1541, MCF.DeputyMinistersOffice@gov.bc.ca

• Board of Registration for Social Workers in BC(BRSW)
#302, 1765 West 8th Ave.
Vancouver, BC V6J 5C6
604-737-4916 Fax: 604-737-6809
brsw@brsw.bc.ca
www.brsw.bc.ca
The regulatory body for the practice of social work in British Columbia is the Board of Registration for Social Workers in BC. The Board's responsibility is establishing & supporting high standards for Registered Social Workers in the province.

Ministry of Citizens' Services

PO Box 9068 Prov Govt, Victoria, BC V8W 9E2
250-952-7623, Fax: 250-952-7628, 800-663-7867
Feedback@gov.bc.ca
www.gov.bc.ca/citz
The Ministry of Community Development supports healthier, greener, & more inclusive communities in British Columbia.

Aboriginal Regional Support Services
#4, 765 Broughton St., PO Box 9721 Prov Govt, Victoria, BC V8W 9S2
250-387-5275, Fax: 250-356-6534
Assistant Deputy Minister, Debra Foxcroft
250-387-3810
Director, Operations, Aboriginal Services, Rob Parenteau
250-387-7073
Director, Policy & Legislation & Implementation Planning & Coordination, Dena Carroll
250-356-5581
Manager, Quality Assurance, Denise Connell
250-953-3261
Acting Manager, Delegation Negotiations & Implementation, Michael Kennedy
250-387-7653
Manager, Branch Operations & Finance, David Kostman
250-387-1433

Corporate Services
765 Broughton St., 3rd Fl., PO Box 9738 Prov Govt, Victoria, BC V8W 9S2
250-387-5954, Fax: 250-387-2481
Assistant Deputy Minister & Executive Financial Officer, Sarf Ahmed
250-953-4432
Executive Director, Financial Services, Craig Wilkinson
250-356-2954
Director, Capital & Administrative Services, Dwayne Quesnel
250-387-7697
Director, Jordan's Principle Implementation Project, Lorna Pritchard
250-953-3449
Director, Procurement Governance & Policy, Delmer Samson
250-387-3380
Director, Regional Devolution, Sreeni Keshava
250-356-2792

Regional Offices:

Information Services
716 Courtney St., 4th Fl., PO Box 9702 Prov Govt, Victoria, BC V8W 9S1
250-356-1181, Fax: 250-356-7346
Chief Information Officer, Karen Dellert
250-356-5507
Senior Director, Information System Transformation, CJ Ritchie
250-387-0833,
Senior Director, Strategic Planning, Client Services & Governance, Gina Pala
250-356-0463
Director, Information & Infrastructure Services, Errol Nadeau
250-387-7039

Integrated Policy & Legislation
765 Broughton St., 5th Fl., PO Box 9766 Prov Govt, Victoria, BC V8W 9S5
250-387-3006, Fax: 250-356-6534
Assistant Deputy Minister, Mark Seiben
250-387-3006
Acting Senior Director, Integrated Planning & Analysis, Karen Wallace
250-387-7418
Director, Child Welfare Policy, Karen Wallace
250-356-5201, Fax: 250-356-2995

Integrated Quality Assurance
765 Broughton St., 4th Fl., PO Box 9721 Prov Govt, Victoria, BC V8W 9S2
250-356-9808, Fax: 250-356-6534
Assistant Deputy Minister, Sandra Griffin
Director, Advocacy, Kathy Berggren-Clive
604-660-4951, Fax: 604-660-4005
Director, Adoption, Anne Clayton
250-387-2281, Fax: 250-387-8000

Provincial Services
#203, 940 Blanshard St., PO Box 9717 Prov Govt, Victoria, BC V8W 9S1
250-387-0978, Fax: 250-356-2079
Assistant Deputy Minister, Alan Markwart
Executive Director, Children & Youth with Special Needs, Randi Mjolsness
250-387-7090, Fax: 250-356-0399
Executive Director, Child Care Programs & Services, Lenora Angel
250-952-6089, Fax: 250-953-3327
Acting Executive Director, Child & Youth Mental Health Policy & Program Support, Karen Wallace
250-356-6003, Fax: 250-356-0580
Assistant Executive Director, Youth Custody Service, Rick Faoro
604-660-5578
Director, Child Care Subsidy Service, Doug Bull
888-338-6622, Fax: 877-544-0699
Director, Early Years, Loreen O'Byrne
250-387-2002, Fax: 250-356-2528
Acting Director, Provincial Services for Deaf & Hard of Hearing, Monte Hardy
604-660-1800, 800-667-4770,Fax:
604-660-1859,psdhh@gov.bc.ca, TDD: 604-660-1807
Director, Youth Justice Policy & Program Support, Phil Hawley
250-387-1335, Fax: 250-356-2079
Director, Provincial Youth Forensic Psychiatric Services, André Picard
778-452-2202, Fax: 778-452-2201
Director, Maples Adolescent Treatment Centre, Ken Moore
604-660-5811, Fax: 604-660-5814

Strategic Human Resource & Sectoral Relations
765 Broughton St., 2nd Fl., PO Box 9757 Prov Govt, Victoria, BC V8W 9S3
250-356-6883, Fax: 250-952-6880
Assistant Deputy Minister, Patrick Doyle
250-356-7103
Director, Strategic Human Resources Projects & Recruitment, Cheryl Howarth
250-387-7659
Director, Human Resources Strategies & Sectoral Relations, Brian Scofield
250-953-3833
Acting Director, Learning & Development, Annemarie Travers
250-387-7665

Columbia Power Corporation (CPC)

#200, 445 - 13th Ave., Castlegar, BC V1N 1G1
250-365-8585, Fax: 250-365-8537,
cpc.info@columbiapower.org
www.columbiapower.org
Columbia Power Corporation was established under the Company Act in 1994. A Crown corporation, it is wholly owned & controlled by the Province of British Columbia. On a joint venture basis with the Columbia Basin Trust, Columbia Power Corporation undertakes power project investments as the agent of the Province of British Columbia. Some power projects include the following: Arrow Lakes Generating Station, Brilliant Expansion Project, & Waneta Expansion Project.
President/CEO, Barry Chuddy
250-365-8529
Vice-President, Human Resources & Corporate Services, Debbie Martin
250-365-8595
Vice-President, Sales & Development, Victor Jmaeff
250-304-6023
Vice-President, Project Implementation, Giulio Ambrosone
250-365-9930
Vice-President, Operations & Environment, Health & Safety Affairs, Amy Stevenson
250-359-6738
Chief Financial Officer & Vice-President, Finance & Stakeholder Relations, Robert Krysac
250-365-9331
General Counsel & Corporate Secretary, Don Rose
604-267-1945, don.rose@columbiapower.org

Ministry of Community & Rural Development

800 Johnson St., 6th Fl., PO Box 9490 Prov Govt, Victoria, BC V8W 9N7
250-387-2283, Fax: 250-387-4312,
Feedback@gov.bc.ca
www.gov.bc.ca/cd

Other Communication: Public Affairs Bureau Phone: 250-387-4089; Fax: 250-356-1070
The Ministry of Community Development supports healthier, greener, & more inclusive communities in British Columbia.
Acts Administered:
Capital Region Water Supply & Sooke Hills Protection
Community Charter Act
Community Charter Council Act
Islands Trust Act
Land Title Act (in part)
Local Government Act
Local Government Grants Act
Local Services Act
Manufactured Home Tax Act
Ministry of Municipal Affairs Act
Mountain Resort Associations act
Municipal Aid Act
Municipal Finance Authority Act
Nanaimo & Southwest Water Supply Act
Ports Property Tax Act
Resort Municipality of Whistler Act
Sechelt Indian Government District Enabling Act
University Endowment Land Act
Vancouver Charter Act
Minister, Community & Rural Development, Hon. Bill Bennett
Deputy Minister, Dale Wall
250-387-4104, Fax: 250-387-7973
• Columbia Basin Trust(CBT)
Southwest Basin
5400, 445 - 13 Ave.
Castlegar, BC V1N 1G1
250-365-6633 Fax: 250-365-6670 800-505-8998
cbt@cbt.org
www.cbt.org
Other Communication: Northwest Basin: 250-265-9936; Southeast Basin: 250-426-8810; Northeast Basin: 250-344-7065
The Columbia Basin Trust manages its assets to benefit the economy, environment, & social well-being of the region. The Trust works to establish collaborative partnerships to achieve improved self-sufficiency.
• Islands Trust
#200, 1627 Fort St.
Victoria, BC V8R 1H8
250-405-5151 Fax: 250-405-5155
information@islandstrust.bc.ca
www.islandstrust.bc.ca
Other Communication: Northern Office: 250-247-2063; Salt Spring Office: 250-537-9144
The Islands Trust area covers the following islands & waters between the British Columbia mainland & southern Vancouver Island: Bowen, Denman, Gabriola, Galiano, Gambier, Hornby, Lasqueti, Mayne, North Pender, Salt Spring, Saturna, South Pender, & Thetis. The Trust is a federation of independent local governments. The federation plans land use & regulates development to preserve & protect the area and its environment.
• Northern Development Initiative Trust
#301, 1268 Fifth Ave.
Prince George, BC V2L 3L2
250-561-2525 Fax: 250-561-2563
admin@nditrust.ca
www.nditrust.ca
The Northern Trust consists of a Board of Directors which makes funding decisions for programs of the Trust. According to provincial legislation, investments can be made in the following areas: agriculture, economic development, energy, forestry, mining, Olympic opportunities; pine beetle recovery, small business, tourism, & transportation.
• Southern Interior Development Initiative Trust
#103, 2903 - 35th Ave.
Vernon, BC V1T 2S7
250-545-6829 Fax: 250-545-6896
admin@sidit-bc.ca
www.sidit-bc.ca
The government of British Columbia enacted legislation in 2006 to establish the Southern Interior Development Initiative Trust. The mission of the Trust is to grow & diversify the economy of the Southern Interior of British Columbia through investments in economic development projects that will benefit the area.

Community Development Trust
634 Humboldt St., 2nd Fl., PO Box 9595 Prov Govt, Victoria, BC V8W 9K4
877-238-8882, Fax: 250-387-4425
Executive Director, Community Development Trust, Tracey Thompson
250-387-3130
Program Manager, Donna Brand
250-387-4491

Local Government Department
800 Johnson St., 6th Fl., PO Box 9490 Prov Govt, Victoria, BC V8W 9N7
lgd_feedback@gov.bc.ca
www.cd.gov.bc.ca/lgd
Working with a great range of partners, the Local Government Department develops communities that can manage change & offer affordable services to residents of British Columbia. The Department's programs include the following: developing local

government legislation; facilitating partnerships with local governments & First Nations; fostering positive inter-governmental relations to facilitate community & regional planning; offering financial support; & providing information & advice.
Assistant Deputy Minister, Mike Furey
250-356-6575, Fax: 250-387-7973
Executive Director, Governance & Structure, Gary Paget
250-953-4129, Fax: 250-387-7972
Executive Director, Intergovernmental Relations & Planning, Alan Osborne
250-387-0089, Fax: 250-387-6212
Executive Director, Local Government Policy & Research, Nicola Marotz
250-356-6257, Fax: 250-387-6212
Director, Local Government Infrastructure & Finance, Julia Duff
250-387-4069, Fax: 250-356-1873,lgsi@gov.bc.ca

Management Services
800 Johnson St., 6th Fl., PO Box 9842 Prov Govt, Victoria, BC V8W 9T2
250-387-8705, Fax: 250-387-7973
Assistant Deputy Minister, Shauna Brouwer
250-387-9180, Fax: 250-387-7973
Executive Director, Strategic Human Resources & Corporate Policy & Planning, Kim Russell
250-387-8976, Fax: 250-356-5395
Director, Financial & Administrative Services, Jim MacAulay
250-387-9179, Fax: 250-387-8772
Director, Information Systems, Debbie Fritz
250-356-0803, Fax: 250-387-1590
Director, Information, Privacy, & Records, Danine Leduc
250-387-7917, Fax: 250-387-8038

Rural Development
800 Johnson St., 6th Fl., PO Box 9824 Prov Govt, Victoria, BC V8W 9W4
250-953-3005, Fax: 250-387-7935
Assistant Deputy Minister, Rural Development, Tom Jensen
250-953-4126, Fax: 250-387-7935
Executive Director, Special Projects & Strategic Initiatives, Greg Goodwin
250-953-3008, Fax: 250-387-7972
Executive Director, Community Partnerships, Sarah Fraser
250-387-5440, Fax: 250-387-1407
Director, Regional Economic Development, Jim Cameron
250-751-7259, Fax: 250-751-3245

Pine Beetle Epidemic Response
#390, 546 St. Paul St., Kamloops, BC V2C 5T1
250-371-3725, Fax: 250-371-3735
Assistant Deputy Minister, Pine Beetle Epidemic Response, Ray Schultz
250-371-3725, Fax: 250-371-3735,Ray.Schultz@gov.bc.ca,
Director, Community Economic Development, Kamloops, Gordon Borgstrom
250-371-3741
Director, Community Economic Development, Victoria, Doug Macfarlane
250-896-6882
Director, Policy & Innovation, Colene Wood
250-356-5538

Office of the Conflict of Interest Commissioner

#101, 431 Menzies St., Victoria, BC V8V 1X4
250-356-0750, Fax: 250-356-6580,
ConflictofInterest@gov.bc.ca
www.gov.bc.ca/oci
The Conflict of Interest Commissioner is an independent Officer of the Legislative Assembly. The following roles are carried out by the Commissioner: Advising Members of the Legislative Assembly; Meeting with Members of the Legislative Assembly for review of disclosure of Members' interests, & obligations imposed by the Members' Conflict of Interest Act; & Undertaking investigations into alleged contraventions of the Act or the Constitution Act, section 25.
Acts Administered:
Members' Conflict of Interest Act
Commissioner, Paul D. K. Fraser, Q.C.
Officer, Research, Betsi Curdie
250-387-8677

Ministry of Small Business, Technology & Economic Development

1810 Blanshard St., PO Box 9324 Prov Govt, Victoria, BC V8W 9N3
250-356-7411, Fax: 250-356-6376,
Feedback.CSE@gov.bc.ca
www.gov.bc.ca/tted
The Ministry of Technology, Trade, & Economic Development works to establish a strong & diverse economy in British Columbia by carrying out the following responsibilities: Innovation & technology; Innovative Clean Energy Fund; Low carbon economy; International & internal trade policy; Export market development; Trade, Investment, & Labour Mobility Agreement; BC Trade Commission, Education & Skills Development; Economic development policy; Business climate; Business immigration programs; & BC Venture Capital Program.
Acts Administered:
British Columbia Enterprise Corporation Act
British Columbia Innovation Council Act
Builders Lien Act
Business Paper Reduction Act
Employee Investment Act
International Financial Activity Act (except Parts 3, 4, & 5, & Part 6, as it pertains to Parts 3, 4, & 5)
Ministry of International Business & Immigration Act (except as the act relates to immigrant recruitment & labour market development, & programs respecting immigrant & refugee settlement)
Small Business Venture Capital Act
Special Accounts Appropriation & Control Act (s. 9.5)
Trade, Investment, & Labour Mobility Agreement Implementation Act
Minister, Small Business, Technology & Economic Development, Hon. Iain Black
Deputy Minister, Don Fast
250-952-0102, Fax: 250-952-0600
Executive Director, Corporate Affairs, Lisa Nye
250-387-2809, Fax: 250-952-0600
Manager, Communications, Public Affairs Bureau, Joanne Whittier
250-356-9428, Fax:
250-952-0627,Joanne.Whittier@gov.bc.ca
• Asia Pacific Foundation of Canada/ Fondation Asie Pacifique du Canada
#666, 999 Canada Pl.
Vancouver, BC V6C 3E1
604-684-5986
info@asiapacific.ca; researchgrants@asiapacific.ca
www.asiapacific.ca
Other Communication: Research Grants Program, Address: #220, 890 West Pender St., Vancouver, BC V6C 1J9
The Asia Pacific Foundation of Canada is an independent think tank on Canadian-Asian relations. The Foundation's research grants program supports research & discussion on Canada's relations with Asia. The grants fund research, graduate & media fellowships, conferences, & special initiatives.
• Asia Pacific Trade Council
#730, 999 Canada Pl.
Vancouver, BC V6C 3E1
604-775-2100 Fax: 604-775-2070
www.asiapacifictradecouncil.ca
The Asia Pacific Trade Council advises the Premier of British Columbia on investment & trade opportunities with the Asia Pacific Region.
• British Columbia Innovation Council(BCIC)
1188 West Georgia St., 9th Fl.
Vancouver, BC V6E 4A2
604-683-2724 Fax: 604-683-6567 800-665-7222
info@bcic.ca
www.bcic.ca
The British Columbia Innovation Council strives to advance innovation & commercialization by focusing on the following strategies: developing, recruiting & retaining science & technology professionals; fostering innovation & entrepreneurship; & bringing innovation to commercial success by establishing partnerships.
• British Columbia Progress Board
#730, 999 Canada Pl.
Vancouver, BC V6C 3E1
604-775-1664 Fax: 604-775-2129
ideas@bcprogressboard.com
www.bcprogressboard.com
The BC Progress Board has the following responsibilities: Determining if the province is improving its competitiveness & quality of life; & Making recommendations to the Premier to enhance the province's economy & social well-being.
• International Financial Centre British Columbia(IFC BC)
Park Place
#1170, 666 Burrard St.
Vancouver, BC V6C 2X8
604-683-6626 Fax: 604-683-6646
info@ifcvancouver.com
www.ifcbc.com
The International Financial Centre British Columbia is a non-profit society which was established by the Federal Government. IFC BC promotes investment in British Columbia & the advantageous tax treatment available to corporations through the International Financial Activity Act (IFAA).
• Premier's Technology Council
#730, 999 Canada Pl.
Vancouver, BC V6C 3E1
604-775-2122 Fax: 604-775-2129
premiers.technologycouncil@gov.bc.ca
www.gov.bc.ca/premier/technology_council
The 23 member Premier's Technology Council advises the Premier on all technology-related issues that affect British Columbia & its residents.

Asia Pacific, Trade, & Investment Division
#730, 999 Canada Pl., Vancouver, BC V6E 3C1
604-775-2251, Fax: 604-775-2070,
Assistant Deputy Minister, Mike Carter
Michael.Carter@gov.bc.ca
Executive Director, International Business Development, Marcus Ewert-Johns
604-775-2145
Acting Executive Director, International Operations & Logistics, Rob Pysden
604-660-5897
Acting Executive Director, International Partnerships & Programs, Chris Carter
604-660-5896, Fax: 604-660-6833
Team Manager, Investor Services, Michael Track
604-775-2202, Fax: 604-775-2070

Economic Competitiveness Division
1810 Blanshard St., 7th Fl., PO Box 9327 Prov Govt, Victoria, BC V8W 9N3
250-952-0367, Fax: 250-952-0137
Assistant Deputy Minister, Shannon Baskerville
Executive Director, Economic & Trade Initiatives, Don D. White
250-952-0708, Fax: 250-952-0716
Director, Labour Market Development, Mark Gillis
250-952-0678, Fax: 250-952-0705

Management Services Division
1810 Blanshard St., 8th Fl., PO Box 9324 Prov Govt, Victoria, BC V8W 9N3
250-952-0126, Fax: 250-952-0101
Assistant Deputy Minister, Doug Callbeck
Acting Director, Finance & Administration, Terry Gelinas
250-952-0174, Fax: 250-952-0171
Director, Strategic Human Resources, Elizabeth Vickery
250-952-0601, Fax: 250-952-0171
Chief Information Officer & Director, Information Management, Stewart Symmers
250-952-0729, Fax: 250-952-0739

Technology, Research & Innovation Division
#730, 999 Canada Place, Vancouver, BC V6C 3E1
Fax: 604-775-2070
Director, Economic Immigration, Provincial Nominee Program, Ian Mellor
604-775-2183, Fax: 604-660-4092,pnpinfo@gov.bc.ca
Director, Research & Innovation, Glen Scobie
250-387-6189, Fax: 250-952-6110
Director, Investment Capital Branch & BC Renaissance Capital Fund Ltd., Todd Tessier
250-952-0612, Fax: 250-952-0371

Ministry of Education

PO Box 9146 Prov Govt, Victoria, BC V8W 9H1
250-387-1977, Fax: 250-387-3200, 888-879-1166
www.bced.gov.bc.ca
Other Communication: Public Affairs Bureau Phone: 250-356-8156; Fax: 250-356-5945
The Ministry's mission is the provision of high quality education for students in British Columbia from kindergarten to grade 12.
Acts Administered:
Independent School Act
School Act
Teaching Profession Act
Minister,Hon. Shirley Bond
Minister.Educ@gov.bc.ca; shirley.bond.mla@leg.bc.ca
Deputy Minister, James Gorman
250-387-2026, Fax:
250-356-2011,dm.Education@gov.bc.ca
Superintendent, Liaison, Sherri Mohoruk
250-514-2543, Fax: 250-356-6007,Other Communications: URL: www.bced.gov.bc.ca/departments/liaison

Governance & Accountability Division
620 Superior St., 5th Fl., PO Box 9146 Prov Govt, Victoria, BC V8W 9H1
250-356-8981, Fax: 250-356-7923,
EDUC.GovernanceDepartment@gov.bc.ca
Responsibilities include legislation for & governance of the public school system, homeschooling, independent schools, & offshore schools.
Assistant Deputy Minister, Scott D. MacDonald
Executive Director & Inspector, International Programs, Ed Vanderboom
250-387-3711, Fax:

250-953-4908,EDUC.IndependentSchoolsOffice@gov.bc.ca, Other Communications: URL: www.bced.gov.bc.ca/independentschools
Executive Director, Diversity & Equity, Susan E. Kennedy
250-356-2337, Fax: 250-356-6161,EDUC.DiversityandEquity@gov.bc.ca
Director, Governance & Legislation, Dave Duerksen
250-356-1404, Fax: 250-356-7541,Other Communications: URL: www.bced.gov.bc.ca/legislation
Director, Aboriginal Education Enhancements, Trish Rosborough
250-356-1891, Fax: 250-356-1742,educ.aboriginaleducation@gov.bc.ca, Other Communications: URL: www.bced.gov.bc.ca/abed
Provincial Coordinator, French Programs, Gilbert Verrier
250-387-6296, Fax: 250-387-1470,EDUCAFP@Victoria1.gov.bc.ca, Other Communications: URL: www.bced.gov.bc.ca/frenchprograms

Achievement Division
620 Superior St., 5th Fl., PO Box 9187 Prov Govt, Victoria, BC V8W 9H3
250-356-2332, Fax: 250-356-6007
Superintendent, Achievement, Rod Allen
250-356-2305
Superintendent, Achievement, Rick Davis
250-356-2335
Superintendent, Achievement, Marion Turner
250-387-1939

Partnerships & Planning Division
620 Superior St., 5th Fl., PO Box 9161 Prov Govt, Victoria, BC V8W 9H3
250-387-6399, Fax: 250-387-0044, EDUCADMO@Victoria1.gov.bc.ca
www.bced.gov.bc.ca/departments/partnerships_plan
Assistant Deputy Minister, Paige MacFarlane
250-387-6399
Director, Corporate Planning, Caroline Ponsford
250-387-6282, Fax: 250-387-0044,IGR.Education@gov.bc.ca
Director, Intergovernmental Relations, Jane Gardiner
250-356-7685, Fax: 250-356-2011,IGR.Education@gov.bc.ca
Director, Internal Communications & Partner Relations, Talya Cohen
250-356-6616, Fax: 250-387-0044,IGR.Education@gov.bc.ca
Director, Provincial Literacy Planning & Performance,
250-356-9913, Fax: 250-356-6033,Other Communications: URL: www.bced.gov.bc.ca/literacy
Director, Public Library Services, Jacqueline van Dyk
604-660-7346, 800-663-7051,PLSB@gov.bc.ca, Other Communications: URL: www.bced.gov.bc.ca/pls

Knowledge Management Division
620 Superior St., 5th Fl., PO Box 9132 Prov Govt, Victoria, BC V8W 9B5
250-356-6068, Fax: 250-387-0044, EDUC.ADMO.Knowledge.Management@gov.bc.ca
Assistant Deputy Minister & Education Sector Chief Information Officer, Renate Butterfield
250-356-6068
Director, Common Business Initiatives, Andrew Macauley
250-387-0170, Fax: 250-356-0033
Director, Business Integration, Beverley Shaw
250-356-9546, Bev.Shaw@gov.bc.ca
Director, Information, Gerald Morton
250-356-2558, Fax: 250-356-0407,EDUC.ReportingUnit@gov.bc.ca, Other Communications: URL: www.bced.gov.bc.ca/reporting
Director, Provincial Learning Network, Peter Goldberg
250-387-5439, Fax: 250-356-0033,Peter.Goldberg@gov.bc.ca

Resource Management Division
620 Superior St., 4th Fl, PO Box 9151 Prov Govt, Victoria, BC V8W 9H1
250-356-2588, Fax: 250-356-8003,
www.bced.gov.bc.ca/departments/resource_man
Assistant Deputy Minister, Resource Management, Keith F. Miller
250-356-2588
Director, School District Financial Reporting, Ian Aaron
250-356-2585, Fax: 250-387-1451
Director, Capital Management, Tom Smith
250-356-1240, Fax: 250-953-4985
Acting Director, Funding & Compliance, Ian Aaron
250-356-2585, Fax: 250-387-1451

Elections British Columbia

PO Box 9275 Prov Govt, Victoria, BC V8W 9J6
250-387-5305, Fax: 250-387-3578, 800-661-8683
electionsbc@elections.bc.ca
www.elections.bc.ca

Other Communication: Toll-free Fax: 1-866-466-0665

Elections British Columbia is a non-partisan, independent Office of the Legislature. Its responsibility is the administration of the electoral process in the province, including provincial general elections, by-elections, provincial referendums, & recall & initiative petitions & votes.
Chief Electoral Officer, Harry Neufeld
250-387-5305
Deputy Chief Electoral Officer, Linda M. Johnson
Director, Corporate Planning & Event Management, Anton Boegman
250-356-2713
Director, Electoral Finance, M. Nola Western
250-387-4141
Director, Information Technology, Bob Jasperse
250-387-4139
Acting Director, Voter Registration & Boundaries, Peter Gzowski
250-387-7258

Ministry of Housing & Social Development

PO Box 9058 Prov Govt, Victoria, BC V8W 9E2
250-356-7750, Fax: 250-356-7292,
EIA.Minister@gov.bc.ca; EnquiryBC@gov.bc.ca
www.gov.bc.ca/hsd

Other Communication: Senior's Supplement Call Centre: 1-866-866-0800; Persons with Disabilities: 1-800-337-3531; Service BC: 387-6121 (Victoria), 604-660-2421 (Vancouver), 1-800-663-7867

Major responsibilities of the Ministry of Housing & Social Development include the following: Housing & homeless policy; Building policy; Safety standards & inspections; Landlord-tenant dispute resolution; Adult Community Living Services; Transition houses; Disability assistance; Mental health & addictions services coordination; Community access grants & volunteer support; Employment assistance programs; Income assistance programs; Gaming policy; Responsible Gaming Strategy; & Liquor control & licensing.
Acts Administered:
Building Officials' Association Act
Commercial Tenancy Act
Community Living Authority Act
Employment & Assistance Act (ss. 17(3) & (4), 18-20, 21(1), 22(1)-(3), (4) (b), (5) & (6), 23(1) (a) (ii) & (iii) & (b) (ii) & (iii), 23(2), 24(1), (2) (a) & (3) (7) & 29; all other provisions except
Employment & Assistance for Persons with Disabilities Act
Fire Services Act (as it relates to the portfolio of the minister)
Gaming Control Act
Homeowner Protection Act
Liquor Control & Licensing Act
Liquor Distribution Act
Local Government Act (ss. 692 & 693)
Manufactured Home Park Tenancy Act
Ministry of Lands, Parks & Housing Act (ss. 5 (c), 8.1 & 10)
Rent Distress Act
Residential Tenancy Act
Safety Authority Act
Safety Standards Act
Shelter Aid for Elderly Renters Act
Special Accounts Appropriation & Control Act (s. 9.3)
Minister,Hon. Rich Coleman
250-356-7750, Fax: 250-356-7292,eia.minister@gov.bc.ca; rich.coleman.mla@leg.bc.ca
Deputy Minister, Cairine MacDonald
250-387-2325, Fax: 250-387-5775
Associate Deputy Minister, Mary Freeman
Assistant Deputy Minister, Employee Transition & Service Delivery, Allison Bond
250-953-3924, Fax: 250-953-3928
Assistant Deputy Minister, Gaming Policy & Enforcement, Derek Sturko
250-953-4482, Fax: 250-387-1818,derek.sturko@gov.bc.ca; Gaming.branch@gov.bc.ca
Assistant Deputy Minister & General Manager, Liquor Control & Licensing, Karen Ayers
250-387-9131, Fax: 250-387-9184
Assistant Deputy Minister, Program Management & Development, Heather Dickson
250-356-0050, Fax: 250-953-3928
Executive Director, Government, Non-Profit, & Volunteer Secretariat, Mark Medgyesi
Director, Communications, Paul Woolley
250-387-1412, Fax: 250-356-7801
• British Columbia Lottery Corporation
74 West Seymour St.
Kamloops, BC V2C 1E2
250-828-5500 Fax: 250-828-5631 866-815-0222
www.bclc.com
Other Communication: Lottery Player Complaint Centre Toll-Free Phone: 1-866-601-1818; BCLC Marketing & Sales Phone: 604-270-0649
• Community Living British Columbia(CLBC)
Airport Square
#700, 1200 West 73rd Ave.
Vancouver, BC V6P 6G5
604-664-0101 Fax: 604-664-0765 877-660-2522
info@communitylivingbc.ca
www.communitylivingbc.ca

Corporate Planning & Operations Division
614 Humboldt St., 7th Fl., PO Box 9944 Prov Govt, Victoria, BC V8W 9R2
250-356-1635, Fax: 250-387-2364
Executive Director, Robert O'Neill
Director, Corporate Planning & Performance, Jacob Teng
250-387-6318, Fax: 250-387-2364

Employment Division
614 Humboldt St., 7th Fl., PO Box 9176 Prov Govt, Victoria, BC V8W 9H8
250-387-1074, Fax: 250-387-3296
Assistant Deputy Minister, Sharon Moysey
Sharon.Moysey@gov.bc.ca
Executive Director, Employment Programs Management, Gloria Back
250-356-8128
Director, Disabilities & Employment Supports, Mark Creighton
250-387-3651, Fax: 250-356-2734

Management Services Division
614 Humboldt St., 7th Fl., PO Box 9940 Prov Govt, Victoria, BC V8W 1A4
250-387-3159, Fax: 250-387-2418,
Other Communication: Financial & Administrative Services General Enquiries: 604-660-1440 (Vancouver)
Assistant Deputy Minister, Sharon Moysey
Sharon.Moysey@gov.bc.ca
Executive Director, Financial & Administrative Services, Brad Grundy
250-356-7047, Fax: 250-356-5994,Brad.Grundy@gov.bc.ca
Chief Information Officer & Executive Director, Information Management, Jeff Gauthier
250-387-3112, Fax: 250-356-1612
Executive Director, Strategic Human Resources Operations, David Glockzin
250-387-7667, Fax: 250-387-4264,David.Glockzin@gov.bc.ca

Policy & Research Division
614 Humboldt St., 7th Fl., PO Box 9936 Prov Govt, Victoria, BC V8W 9R2
250-356-5065, Fax: 250-387-5775
Assistant Deputy Minister, Molly Harrington
Executive Director, Strategic Policy & Research, Rob Bruce
250-387-1488, Fax: 250-387-8164
Executive Director, Provincial Services, Debi Moreland
250-356-9728, Fax: 250-356-8261
Director, Legislation & Legal Services, Judy D'Gal
250-387-6434, judy.dgal@gov.bc.ca

Regional Services Division
614 Humboldt St., 7th Fl., PO Box 9937 Prov Govt, Victoria, BC V8W 9R2
250-387-6905, Fax: 250-387-6905
Assistant Deputy Minister, Heather Davidson
Executive Director, Regional Operations, Effie Henry
250-356-6493
Executive Director, Simplifcation, Robert O'Neill
250-356-9253, Fax: 250-387-2418
Executive Director, Prevention & Loss Management Services, Kim Saastad
250-387-0397, Fax: 250-356-1615

Regional Human Resources Offices & Employment & Assistance Centres:

Fraser
#1800, 13450 - 102 Ave., Surrey, BC V3T 5X3
604-586-2992, Fax: 604-586-2681, Off300@gems9.gov.bc.ca
Executive Director, Pat Gilchrist
304-576-2959

Interior
#300, 619 Victoria St., Kamloops, BC V2C 6W7
888-939-9278, Fax: 250-828-4614, OFF400@gems3.gov.bc.ca
Executive Director, Bruce Smith
Bruce.Smith@gov.bc..ca

North
#404, 299 Victoria St., Prince George, BC V2L 5B8
250-565-6220, Fax: 250-565-6366
Director, Service Delivery, Roberta Smith
250-565-6220
Director, Performance & Risk Management, Matthew Treger

Vancouver Island
908 Pandora Ave., 4th Fl., PO Box 9956 Prov Govt, Victoria, BC V8W 9R4
250-387-9606, Fax: 250-387-9566, OFF100@gov.bc.ca
Director, Service Delivery, Tami Currie

Vancouver Coastal
#910, 360 West Georgia St., Vancouver, BC V6B 6B2
604-660-3224, Fax: 604-660-2503, off200@.gov.bc.ca
Executive Director, Lynda Cavanaugh
Director, Service Delivery, Nancy Shewchuk

Ministry of Energy, Mines & Petroleum Resources

PO Box 9318 Prov Govt, Victoria, BC V8W 9N3
250-952-0241, www.gov.bc.ca/empr
The development of sustainable & competitive energy & mineral resource sectors in British Columbia is the focus of the Ministry.
Acts Administered:
BC Hydro Public Power Legacy & Heritage Contract
Coal Act
Coalbed Gas Act, 2003
Columbia Basin Trust Act
Energy Efficiency Act
Gas Utility Act
Geothermal Resources Act
Hydro & Power Authority Act
Hydro Power Measures Act
Mineral Land Tax Act
Mineral Tax Act
Mineral Tenure Act
Mines Act
Mining Right of Way Act
Mining Tax Act
Ministry of Energy & Mines Act
Natural Gas Price Act
Oil & Gas Commission Act
Petroleum & Natural Gas Act
Petroleum & Natural Gas (Vancouver Island Railway Lands) Act
Pipeline Act
Transmission Corporation Act
Utilities Commission Act
Vancouver Island Natural Gas Pipeline Act
West Kootenay Power & Light Company, Ltd. Act
Minister,Hon. Richard Neufeld
250-387-5896, Fax: 250-356-2965,empr.minister@gov.bc.ca; richard.neufeld.mla@leg.bc.ca
Minister of State, Mining, Hon. Gordon Hogg
250-953-4100, Fax: 250-387-1803,gordon.hogg.mla@leg.bc.ca
Deputy Minister, Greg Reimer
250-952-0504, Fax: 250-952-0269
Officer, Public Affairs, Jake Jacobs
250-952-0628, Fax: 250-952-0627,Jake.Jacobs@gov.bc.ca
• Mediation & Arbitration Board
#310, 9900 - 100 Ave.
Fort St John, BC V1J 5S7
250-787-3403 Fax: 250-787-3228
mab.office@gov.bc.ca
www.empr.gov.bc.ca/OG/mab
The Mediation & Arbitration Board is an independent, quasi-judicial organization which was established under the authority of the Petroleum & Natural Gas Act. The Board functions under the following acts: the Geothermal Resources Act, the Mineral Tenure Act, the Mining Right of Way Act, & the Coal Act. It assists in resolving disputes between companies & landowners concerning petroleum or natural gas resources.
• Oil & Gas Commission(OGC)
#100, 10003 - 110 Ave.
Fort St John, BC V1J 6M7
250-261-5700 800-663-7867
www.ogc.gov.bc.ca
Other Communication: Incident Reporting: 1-800-663-3456
The Oil & Gas Commission was enacted under the Oil & Gas Commission Act, The Commission regulates British Columbia's oil & gas activities & pipelines.

Electricity & Alternative Energy
1810 Blanshard St., 4th Fl., PO Box 9314 Prov Govt, Victoria, BC V8W 9N1
250-952-0204, Fax: 250-952-0258
Assistant Deputy Minister, Les MacLaren
Fax: 250-952-0926
Acting Executive Director, Alternative Energy Policy, Dan Green
250-952-0279
Director, Bioenergy & Renewable, Janice Larson
250-952-0706
Director, Electricity Policy, Shelley Murphy
250-952-0264
Director, Independent Power Producers, Neil Banera
250-952-0655

Management Services
1810 Blanshard St., 8th Fl., PO Box 9324 Prov Govt, Victoria, BC V8W 9N3
250-952-0606, Fax: 250-952-0101
Assistant Deputy Minister, Doug Callbeck
250-952-0126
Chief Information Officer & Director, Information Management, Stewart Symmers
250-952-0229, Fax: 250-952-0739
Director, Strategic Human Resources, Brenda Vachon
250-952-0601
Acting Director, Finance & Administration, Terry Gelinas
250-952-0174

Marketing, Aboriginal & Community Relations
1810 Blanshard St., 4th Fl., PO Box 9396 Prov Govt, Victoria, BC V8W 9M3
250-356-9569, Fax: 250-356-5092
Assistant Deputy Minister, Jody Shimkus
Executive Director, Marketing & Community Relations, Ellen Frisch
250-952-0651, Fax: 250-356-5092
Acting Executive Director, Aboriginal Relations, Giovanni Puggioni
250-952-0530, Fax: 250-952-0111
Executive Director, Corporate Policy, Planning & Legislation, Karen Koncohrada
250-952-0274, Fax: 250-952-0637

Mining & Minerals
1675 Douglas St., 7th Fl., PO Box 9320 Prov Govt, Victoria, BC V8W 9N3
250-952-0596, Fax: 250-952-0491
Assistant Deputy Minister, John Cavanagh
Chief Inspector, Mines, Douglas Sweeney
250-952-0793
Chief Geologist & Director, British Columbia Geological Survey, Dave Lefebvre
250-952-0374, Fax: 250-952-0381,
Executive Director, Policy & Sustainability, Karina Brino
250-952-0868

Oil & Gas
1810 Blanshard St., 5th Fl., PO Box 9323 Prov Govt, Victoria, BC V8W 9N3
250-952-0115, Fax: 250-952-0926
Assistant Deputy Minister, Gordon Goodman
Executive Director, Innovation & Investment, Alex McMIllan
250-952-6277
Acting Executive Director, Business Development, Ines Piccinino
250-356-9825
Executive Director, Major Initiatives, Linda Beltrano
250-356-1183, Fax: 250-952-0255
Acting Executive Director, Oil & Gas Policy, Paula Barrett
250-953-3766, Fax: 250-953-3770
Executive Director, Resource Development & Geoscience, Vic Levson
250-952-0391, Fax: 250-952-0922

Titles & Offshore
1675 Douglas St., 2nd Fl., PO Box 9312 Prov Govt, Victoria, BC V8W 9N2
250-356-0510, Fax: 250-356-0582
Assistant Deputy Minister, Bill Phelan
250-356-0552
Acting Executive Director, Offshore Oil & Gas, Susan Kelly
250-356-7512, Fax: 250-952-0541
Director, Land Use Coordination, Norman Marcy
250-387-1780
Director, Compliance & Administration, Debbie Fischer
250-952-0336, Fax: 250-952-0331
Director, Oil & Gas Titles, Laurel Nash
250-952-0335, Fax: 250-952-0331
Director, Mineral Titles, Rick Conte
604-660-2814, Fax: 604-660-2653,Mineral.Titles@gov.bc.ca

Ministry of Environment

PO Box 9339 Prov Govt, Victoria, BC V8W 9M1
250-387-1161, Fax: 250-387-5669, www.envmail@gov.bc.ca www.gov.bc.ca/env
Other Communication: Environmental Emergencies: 1-800-663-3456; Conservation Officer Svs.: 1-877-952-7277; Recycling Hotline: 1-800-667-4321; Dangerous Wildlife Conflicts: 1-800-663-9453
The Ministry provides sustainable environmental management to work towards a healthy, clean, & naturally diverse environment.
Acts Administered:
Agriculture Land Commission Act
Assessment Act
Assessment Authority Act
Boundary Act
Budget Measures Implementation Act
Commercial Rafting Safety Act
Creston Valley Wildlife Act
Dike Maintenance Act
Drainage, Ditch & Dike Act
Ecological Reserve Act
Emergency Program Act
Environment & Land Use Act (Sustainable Resource Management)
Environmental Assessment Act
Environmental Management Act
Environmental Protection Act
Fish Protection Act
Financial Administration Act
Flood Hazard Statutes Amendment Act, 2003
Forest & Range Practices Act
Forest Land Reserve Act
Hunting & Fishing Heritage Act
Industrial Operation Compensation Act
Integrated Pest Management Act, 2003
Land Act
Ministry of Environment Act
Okanagan River Boundaries Settlement
Park Act
Parks & Protected Areas Statutes Amendment Act, 2004
Pesticide Control Act
Protected Areas of British Columbia Act
Skagit Environmental Enhancement Act
Sustainable Environment Fund Act
Waste Management Act
Water, Land & Air Protection Statutes Amendment Act, 2003
Water Act
Water Protection Act
Water Utility Act
Wildlife Act
Wildlife Amendment Act
Minister,Hon. Barry Penner
250-387-1187, Fax: 250-387-1356,env.minister@gov.bc.ca; barry.penner.mla@leg.bc.ca
Deputy Minister, Doug Konkin
250-387-5429
• British Columbia Environmental Assessment Office
• Environmental Appeal Board
747 Fort St., 4th Fl.
PO Box 9425 Prov Govt
Victoria, BC V8W 9V1
250-387-3464 Fax: 250-356-9923
eabinfo@gov.bc.ca
www.eab.gov.bc.ca
The Environmental Appeal Board is an independent agency which was created under the Environment Management Act. The Board hears appeals from administrative decisions under the following acts: the Environmental Management Act, the Health Act, the Integrated Pest Management Act, the Water Act, & the Wildlife Act. Notices of appeal are reviewed & evaluated to determine if an alternative dispute resolution is possible.
• Fraser Basin Council(FBC)
Central Office
470 Granville St., 1st Fl.
Vancouver, BC V6C 1V5
604-488-5350 Fax: 604-488-5351
info@fraserbasin.bc.ca
www.fraserbasin.bc.ca
Other Communication: Thompson: 250-314-9660; Upper Fraser: 250-612-0252; Fraser Valley: 604-826-1661; Cariboo-Chilcotin: 250-392-1400; Greater Vancouver Sea to Sky: 604-488-5365
The Fraser Basin Council is a not-for-profit, non-partisan organization. The Council works to advance sustainability throughout the Fraser River Basin.

Compliance Division
2975 Jutland Rd., 5th Fl., PO Box 9339 Prov Govt, Victoria, BC V8W 9M1
250-387-9997, Fax: 250-387-5669
Executive Director, Compliance, Brian W. Rendell
Director, Compliance Policy & Planning, Gwenda Laughland
250-387-9641, Fax: 250-387-8433
Chief Conservation Officer & Director, Enforcement Program & Conservation Officer Services, Mark Hayden
250-952-4635, Fax: 250-952-4628,Mark.Hayden@gov.bc.ca

Corporate Services Division
2975 Jutland Rd., 5th Fl., PO Box 9339 Prov Govt, Victoria, BC V8W 9M1
250-387-9878, Fax: 250-953-3414
Assistant Deputy Minister, Denise Bragg
Chief Information Officer & Executive Director, Information Management, Doug Say
250-387-1348, Fax: 250-387-1085

Executive Director, Finance & Administration, Anne Minnings
250-356-9220, Fax: 250-356-9239
Executive Director, People Strategies, Duff McCaghey
250-356-6243, Fax: 250-356-7286
Director, Corporate Services Delivery, Trish Dohan
250-356-9221, Fax: 250-356-9836

Environmental Protection Division
2975 Jutland Rd., 5th Fl., PO Box 9339, Victoria, BC V8W 9M1
250-387-1288, Fax: 250-387-5669
Assistant Deputy Minister, Lynn Bailey
Acting Director, Environmental Quality, Glen Okrainetz
250-387-9933, Fax: 250-356-7197
Director, Environmental Management, Jim Hofweber
250-387-9971, Fax: 250-387-8897
Director, Regional Operations, Jim Standen
250-397-9990, Fax: 250-356-5496
Regional Manager, Kootenay & Okanagan Regional Office, Robyn Roome
250-354-6362, Fax: 250-354-6332
Regional Manager, Lower Mainland Regional Office, Steffanie Warriner
604-582-5284, Fax: 604-584-9791
Regional Manager, Omineca Regional Office, Sean Sharpe
250-565-6443, Fax: 250-565-6629
Regional Manager, Skeena Regional Office, Ian Sharpe
250-847-7251, Fax: 250-847-7591
Regional Manager, Thompson Regional Office, Rick Adams
250-371-6225, Fax: 250-371-6234
Regional Manager, Vancouver Island Regional Office, Randy Alexander
250-751-3176, Fax: 250-751-3103
Section Head, Cariboo Regional Office, Douglas Hill
250-398-4542, Fax: 250-398-4214

Environmental Stewardship Division
2975 Jutland Rd., 5th Fl., PO Box 9339 Prov Govt, Victoria, BC V8T 5J9
250-356-0121, Fax: 250-953-3414
Assistant Deputy Minister, Ralph Archibald
Executive Director, Protected Areas, Scott Benton
250-387-3637, Fax: 250-387-5757
Director, Protected Areas Visitor Services, Christine Houghton
250-356-9241, Fax: 250-387-5757
Director, Parks Planning & Management, Brian Bawtinheimer
250-387-4355, Fax: 250-387-5757
Director, Ecosystems, Kaaren Lewis
250-387-9731, Fax: 250-356-9145
Director, Fish & Wildlife, Tom Ethier
250-387-5657, Fax: 250-387-9568
Director, Regional Operations, Brian J. Clark
250-356-0874, Fax: 250-356-9299
Regional Manager, Cariboo Regional Office, Rodger Stewart
250-398-4214, Fax: 250-398-4214
Regional Manager, Kootenay Regional Office, Wayne Stetski
250-489-8523, Fax: 250-489-8506
Regional Manager, Lower Mainland Regional Office, Jennifer McGuire
604-582-5370, Fax: 604-930-7119
Regional Manager, Okanagan Regional Office, Drew Carmichael
250-490-8262, Fax: 250-490-2231
Regional Manager, Omineca Regional Office, Don Cadden
250-614-9915, Fax: 250-565-6940
Regional Manager, Peace Regional Office, Maurice Lirette
250-787-3426, Fax: 250-787-3490
Regional Manager, Thompson Regional Office, John Metcalfe
250-371-6304, Fax: 250-828-4000
Regional Manager, Vancouver Island Regional Office, Dick Heath
250-751-3211, Fax: 250-751-3208
Section Head, Skeena Regional Office, Peter Levy
250-847-7303, Fax: 250-847-7728

Oceans & Marine Fisheries Division (OMFD)
2975 Jutland Rd., 3rd Fl., PO Box 9309, Victoria, BC V8W 9N1
250-387-0389, Fax: 250-953-3401, fishstats@gov.bc.ca; fishinfo@gov.bc.ca
Director, Jamie Alley
250-953-3417
Manager, Operations, Barron Carswell
Manager, Seafood Development, Lorraine Saunders
Manager, Sustainablility, Bob Williams
Manager, Marine Fisheries, Martin Paish

Strategic Policy Division
2975 Jutland Rd., 5th Fl., PO Box 9335 Prov Govt, Victoria, BC V8W 9M1
250-387-9666, Fax: 250-387-8894
Executive Director, Anthony J. Danks
250-387-8483
Director, Intergovernmental & External Relations, Lisa Paquin
250-387-9661, Fax: 250-387-8894
Director, Policy & Legislation, Peter Trotzki
250-953-5147, Fax: 250-387-8894
Manager, Planning & Performance Management, Rozlynne Mitchell
250-387-7980, Fax: 250-387-8894
Manager, Science Policy & Economics, Jennifer A. Maxwell
250-387-9642, Fax: 250-387-8894

Water Stewardship Division
2975 Jutland Rd., 5th Fl., PO Box 9339 Prov Govt, Victoria, BC V8W 9M1
250-356-9443, Fax: 250-953-3414
Assistant Deputy Minister, Jim Mattison
Director, Innovation & Planning, Lynn Kriwoken
250-387-9481, Fax: 250-356-1202
Director, Management & Standards, Glen Davidson
250-387-6949, Fax: 250-356-0605
Director, Science & Information, Fern Schultz
250-387-6722, Fax: 250-356-1202
Director, Regional Operations, Brian Symonds
250-490-8255
Regional Manager, Thompson Regional Office, Valerie Cameron
250-371-6270, Fax: 250-828-4000
Regional Manager, Vancouver Island Regional Office, Larry Barr
250-751-7105, Fax: 250-751-7079
Regional Manager, Lower Mainland Regional Office, Julia Berardinucci
604-582-5353, Fax: 604-582-5235
Regional Manager, Okanagan / Kootenay Regional Offices, Ken Cunningham
250-490-8232, Fax: 250-490-2231
Regional Manager, Omineca, Peace, & Skeena Regional Offices, Norm Bilodeau
250-565-6424

British Columbia Environmental Assessment Office

836 Yates St., 1st Fl., PO Box 9426 Prov Govt, Victoria, BC V8W 9V1
250-356-7441, Fax: 250-356-7440, eaoinfo@gov.bc.ca
www.eao.gov.bc.ca

Operating independently, the Environmental Assessment Office (EAO) coordinates the assessment of proposed projects in British Columbia. The Office acts under the requirements of the Environmental Assessment Act. Working with the public, government agencies, & First Nations, the Environmental Assessment Office ensures that projects are developed in a sustainable manner.

Associate Deputy Minister & Executive Director, Robin Junger
250-356-7475
Director, Strategic Policy & Planning, Alan Moyes
250-387-2307, Fax: 250-356-6448
Director, Communications, Sarah Harrison
250-387-9973, Fax: 250-387-4966
Project Assessment Director, Shoreline Modification Projects, Garry Alexander
Acting Project Assessment Director, Mining, Joe Truscott
Project Assessment Director, Climate Change, Kathy Eichenberger
Project Assessment Director, Water Projects, Paul Finkel
Project Assessment Director, Industrial & Waste Disposal Projects, Derek Griffin
Project Assessment Director, Oil & Gas (Pipeline), & Food Processing Projects, Graeme McLaren
Project Assessment Director, Energy (Power) & General Water Projects (Dams), Brian Murphy
Project Assessment Director, Destination Resorts, & Groundwater Projects, Archie Riddell

British Columbia Ferry Services Inc.

1112 Fort St., Victoria, BC V8V 4V2
250-381-1401, 888-223-3779
www.bcferries.com

Other Communication: Outside North America Phone: 250-386-3431

BC Ferries operates as the primary provider of coastal ferry service in British Columbia. The fleet covers 25 routes.

President/CEO, David Hahn
Executive Vice-President & Chief Financial Officer, Rob Clarke
Executive Vice-President & Chief Operating Officer, Mike Corrigan
Executive Vice-President, Human Resources & Corporate Development, Glen N. Schwartz
Executive Vice-President, New Vessel Construction & Industry Affairs, Captain Trafford Taylor
General Counsel & Executive Vice-President, Corporate Affairs, Bill Cottick
Vice-President, Safety, Security, & Environment, Captain Jamie Marshall

Ministry of Finance

PO Box 9048 Prov Govt, Victoria, BC V8W 9E2
250-387-3751, Fax: 250-387-5594, Fin.Minister@gov.bc.ca
www.gov.bc.ca/fin

Other Communication: Corporate & Personal Property Registries Phone: 250-387-7848 or 604-775-1041; Fax: 250-356-0206; Media Phone: 250-356-9872; Fax: 250-356-2822

The goal of the Ministry of Finance is the provision of strong fiscal management & a balanced budget. It develops fiscal policies & regulatory frameworks to maintain a vibrant provincial economy.

Acts Administered:
Auditor General Act
Balanced Budget & Ministerial Accountability Act
BC Railway Act
BC University Loan Act
Bonding Act
Budget Transparency & Accountability Act
Business Corporations Act
Business Number Act
Capital Financing Authority Repeal & Debt Restructuring Act
Community Services Labour Relations Act
Constitution Act, ss. 25-27
Cooperative Association Act
Credit Union Incorporation Act
Creditor Assistance Act
Financial Administration Act
Financial Information Act
Financial Institutions Act
Industrial Development Act
Insurance Act
Insurance (Captive Company) Act
Insurance (Marine) Act
International Financial Business Act
Manufactured Home Act
Medical & Health Care Services Special Account Act
Ministerial Accountability Bases (2004, 2004-2005) Acts
Ministry of Consumer & Corporate Affairs Act, ss. 3-4
Ministry of Intergovernmental Relations Act, s. 3
Miscellaneous Registrations Act, 1992
Mortgage Brokers Act
Mutual Fire Insurance Companies Act
Pacific North Coast Native Cooperative Act
Partnership Act
Pension Agreement Act
Pension Benefits Standards Act
Pension Fund Societies Act
Personal Property Security Act
Ports Property Tax Act
Probate Fee Act
Public Education Support Staff Collective Bargaining Assistance Act
Public Works Agreement Act
Real Estate Development Marketing Act
Real Estate Services Act
Repairers Lien Act
Securities (Forged Transfer) Act
Society Act
Strata Property Act
Tugboat Worker's Lien Act
Unclaimed Property Act
Warehouse Lien Act
Warehouse Receipt Act
Woodworker Lien Act

Minister, Finance, Hon. Colin Hansen
Fin.Minister@gov.bc.ca; colin.hansen.mla@leg.bc.ca
Deputy Minister, Graham Whitmarsh
250-387-3184, Fax: 250-387-1655
Director, Strategic Initiatives, Doug Foster
250-387-9022, Fax: 250-387-1655,Doug.Foster@gov.bc.ca
Deputy Secretary, Treasury Board, Nick Paul
250-356-5427, Fax: 250-356-9054

• Auditor Certification Board
940 Blanshard St., 2nd Fl.
PO Box 9431 Prov Govt
Victoria, BC V8W 9V3
250-356-8658 Fax: 250-356-9422
sherrilyn.johnson@gov.bc.ca
www.fin.gov.bc.ca/registries/corppg/acb.htm
The Auditor Certification Board is authorized under the Business Corporations Act. The Board receives applications from individuals who apply to becertified as auditors. Persons with the necessary qualifications are then certified.

• British Columbia 2010 Olympic & Paralympic Games Secretariat
3585 Graveley St., 7th Fl.
Vancouver, BC V5K 5J5
604-660-2010 Fax: 604-660-3437 877-604-2010
bcsecretariat@gov.bc.ca
www.2010bcsecretariat.ca
To be certain that British Columbia's Olympic hosting goals are met, the provincial agency oversees the financial commitments of the 2010 Winter Games. A major objective of the BC Secretariat is the delivery of the Games on time, within the approved budget. BC Secretariat is also responsible for ensuring that the economic, sporting, cultural, & social opportunities associated with the 2010 Winter Games evolve into legacies which benefit communities & businesses throughout the province.
• British Columbia Securities Commission
Pacific Centre
701 West Georgia St., 12th Fl.
PO Box 10142
Vancouver, BC V7Y 1L2
604-899-6500 Fax: 604-899-6506 800-373-6393
inquiries@bcsc.bc.ca
www.bcsc.bc.ca
The British Columbia Securities Commission is an independent provincial government agency. Through administration of the Securities Act, the Commission regulates securities trading in British Columbia.
• Crown Agencies Secretariat(CAS)
#400, 1675 Douglas St,
PO Box 9300 Prov Govt
Victoria, BC V8W 9N2
250-952-0750 Fax: 250-952-0777 800-663-7867
Trena.Huson@gov.bc.ca
www.gov.bc.ca/cas
Implementation of the governance framework for British Columbia's Crown agencies is the role of the Crown Agencies Secretariat. The Secretariat advises Ministries & Crown agencies on the requirements of the Crown Agency Accountability System. It also maintains the Crown Agency Registry.
• Financial Institutions Commission(FICOM)
#1200, 13450 - 102 Ave.
Surrey, BC V3T 5X3
604-953-5300 Fax: 604-953-5301 866-206-3030
FICOM@ficombc.ca; HR@ficombc.ca
www.fic.gov.bc.ca
Other Communication: Complaints & inquiries: 604-953-5200
The Financial Institutions Commission is a regulatory agency of British Columbia's Ministry of Finance. The Commission's responsibility is the administration of statutes that regulate the financial services, pension, & real estate sectors in the province.
• Insurance Council of British Columbia
#300, 1040 West Georgia St.
PO Box 7
Vancouver, BC V6E 4H1
604-688-0321 Fax: 604-662-7767 877-688-0321
www.insurancecouncilofbc.com
The Insurance Council of British Columbia reports to the province's Minister of Finance. The Council has the following responsibilities: Licensing insurance agents, salespersons, & adjusters; Regulating insurance licensees; & Investigating & disciplining licensees.
• Real Estate Council of British Columbia
#900, 750 West Pender St.
Vancouver, BC V6C 2T8
604-683-9664 Fax: 604-683-9017 877-683-9664
info@recbc.ca
www.recbc.ca
The Real Estate Council of British Columbia is a regulatory agency with the following responsibilities under the requirements of the Real Estate Services Act: Licensing individuals & brokerages involved in real estate sales, rental & strata property management; Enforcing licensing qualifications & licensee conduct; & Investigating complaints against licensees & imposing discipline.

Office of the Comptroller General
617 Government St., 2nd Fl., PO Box 9413 Prov Govt, Victoria, BC V8W 9V1
250-387-6692, Fax: 250-356-2001
Comptroller General, Cheryl Wenezenki-Yolland
Chief Procurement Officer, Procurement Governance, Anne Kirkaldy
250-356-8331, Fax: 250-356-6164,procurementgovernance@gov.bc.ca
Executive Director, Corporate Compliance & Controls Monitoring & Legal Encumbrance, Shyrl Kennedy
250-356-7434, Fax: 250-953-0462,corporatecompliance@gov.bc.ca
Executive Director, Internal Audit & Advisory Services, Stuart Newton
250-387-8198, Fax: 250-356-2001
Executive Director, Financial Management, Sheila Dodds
250-387-0279, Fax: 250-356-6164,ocgmanuals@gov.bc.ca
Director, Financial Reporting & Advisory Services, Carl Fischer
250-356-9272, Fax: 250-356-8388
Director, Activity Based Management & Advisory Services, Dan Ho
250-356-6999, Fax: 250-356-2001
Director, Corporate Operations, Ron Tannhauser
250-387-8551, Fax: 250-356-0560

Corporate & Ministry Support Services
617 Government St., 3rd Fl., PO Box 9415 Prov Govt, Victoria, BC V8W 9V1
250-356-1787, Fax: 250-356-7326
Assistant Deputy Minister, Tara Faganello
250-387-8139, Fax: 250-356-7326
Chief Information Officer & Executive Director, Information Management, Beau Choo
250-387-8962, Fax: 250-356-1494
Executive Director & Senior Financial Officer, Financial Services & Administration, Greg Gudgeon
250-387-3867, Fax: 250-356-7326
Executive Director, Strategic Human Resources, Melissa Thickens
250-387-5071, Fax: 250-387-0694
Director, Divisional Operations, Belinda Lucoe
250-356-0403, Fax: 250-356-7326

Provincial Treasury
620 Superior St., PO Box 9414 Prov Govt, Victoria, BC V8V 9V1
250-387-4541, Fax: 250-356-3041, Jim.Hopkings@gov.bc.ca
www.fin.gov.bc.ca/pt.htm
The Provincial Treasury consist of the following branches: Banking / Cash Management; Corporate Operations; Corporate & Project Finance; Debt Management; Information Systems; Risk Management; & BC Registry Services.
Assistant Deputy Minister, Jim Hopkins
250-387-5729
Acting Executive Director, Debt Management, Darshi Klear
250-387-8815, Fax: 250-387-3024
Executive Director, Risk Management, Phil Grewar
250-387-0521, Fax: 250-356-6222
Director, Banking / Cash Management, Nicholas Krischanowsky
250-387-7105
Director, Corporate & Project Finance, Matthew O'Rae
250-356-9370, Fax: 250-387-3024
Director, Information Systems, Tom Caldwell
250-356-5473, Fax: 250-387-6577
Manager, Corporate Operations, Ida Stephenson
250-387-7124
Registrar, BC Registry Services, Ron Townshend
250-356-8658

Strategic & Corporate Policy
#109, 617 Government St., PO Box 9417 Prov Govt, Victoria, BC V8W 9V1
Fax: 250-387-9093
Assistant Deputy Minister, Strategic & Corporate Policy, Andy Robinson
250-387-9011
Executive Director, Pacific Carbon Trust, Su-Lin Shum
250-356-5068, Fax: 250-356-9061
Director, Intergovernmental Fiscal Relations, Rory Molnar
250-356-5033
Acting Director, Financial & Corporate Sector Policy, Andrew Alley
250-387-7364
Director, Tax Policy, Glen Armstrong
250-387-4196

Ministry of Forests & Range

PO Box 9529 Prov Govt, Victoria, BC V8W 9C3
250-387-4809, Fax: 250-953-3687, www.gov.bc.ca/for
Other Communication: Report Wildfires Toll Free: 1-800-663-5555
Revitalization of British Columbia's forest sector is the mission of the Ministry. Through strategic innovation, the Ministry strives to maintain high environmental standards, which will ensure long-term jobs & renewed prosperity.
Acts Administered:
Forest Act
Forest Practices Code of British Columbia Act
Forest & Range Practices Act
Forest Stand Management Fund Act
Foresters Act
Forestry Revitalization Act, 2003
Manufactured Forest Products Regulation
Ministry of Forests Act
Protected Areas Forests Compensation Act
Range Act
Safety Authority Act
Safety Standards Act
South Moresby Implementation Account Act
Timber Licences Settlement Act
Timber Sale Licence Replacement (Sliammon First Nation) Act
Wildfire Act, 2004
Minister, Forests & Range, Hon. Patrick Bell
250-387-6240, Fax: 250-387-1040,pat.bell.mla@leg.bc.ca
Deputy Minister, Dana Hayden
250-387-4809, Forests.DeputyMinistersOffice@gov.bc.ca
• Forest Appeals Commission
747 Fort St., 4th Fl.
PO Box 9425 Prov Govt
Victoria, BC V8W 9V1
250-387-3464 Fax: 250-356-9923
facinfo@gov.bc.ca
www.fac.gov.bc.ca
Established in 1996 under the Forest Practices Code of British Columbia Act, the Forest Appeals Commission is an independent agency which now continues under the Forest & Range Practices Act. The Commission hears appeals from administrative decisions made under the following statutes: Forest Act, Forest & Range Practices Act, Forest Practices Code of British Columbia Act, Private Managed Forest Land Act, Range Act, & the Wildfire Act.
• Forest Practices Board
1675 Douglas St., 3rd Fl.
PO Box 9905 Prov Govt
Victoria, BC V8W 9R1
250-387-7964 Fax: 250-387-7009 800-994-5899
fpboard@gov.bc.ca
www.fpb.gov.bc.ca
British Columbia's Forest Practices Board is responsible for reporting to the government & public about compliance with the Forest & Range Practices Act. The Board engages in the following activities: Investigation of public complaints; Undertaking special investigations; Auditing forest practices of government, government enforcement of the Forest & Range Practices Act, & licence holders on public lands; Participation in appeals; & Provision of reports & recommendations.
• Forestry Innovation Investments(FII)
#1200, 1130 West Pender St.
Vancouver, BC V6E 4A4
604-685-7507 Fax: 604-685-5373
info@bcfii.ca
www.bcfii.ca
British Columbia's Forestry Innovation Investment strives to support a prosperous & environmentally sustainable forest economy in the province. The role of the organization includes the following activities: Promotion of British Columbia's forest practices & wood products to international markets; Working in partnership with the forestry sector, the Government of British Columbia, & the Government of Canada; & Assisting the forestry sector with issues such as Mountain Pine Beetle outbreak.
• Timber Export Advisory Committee
1520 Blanshard St., 2nd Fl.
PO Box 9514 Prov Govt
Victoria, BC V8W 9C2
250-387-8916 Fax: 250-387-5050

British Columbia Timber Sales
727 Fisgard St., 3rd Fl., PO Box 9510 Prov Govt, Victoria, BC V8W 9C2
250-387-1261, Fax: 250-356-6209, Forests.BCTimberSalesHQOffice@gov.bc.ca
www.for.gov.bc.ca/bcts/
Assistant Deputy Minister, BC Timber Sales, Dave Peterson
Director, Operations, Mike Falkiner
250-387-8309
Acting Director, Business Operations, Jerry Kennah
250-387-8643
Director, Forestry, Jim Sutherland
250-356-1473

Corporate Services
1520 Blanshard St., 3rd Fl., PO Box 9525 Prov Govt, Victoria, BC V8W 9C3
250-387-1300, Fax: 250-953-3687, Forests.CorporateServicesExecutiveOffice@gov.bc.ca
Assistant Deputy Minister, Joan Elangovan
Chief Information Officer, Information Management, Guy Gondor
250-387-8400, Fax: 250-387-5132,Forests.InformationManagementGroup@gov.bc.ca
Executive Director, Organizational Development, Shelagh Ryan-McNee
250-387-9016, Fax: 250-387-9086

Acting Director, Finance & Management Services, Mary Myers
250-356-6624, Fax:
250-387-8818,Forests.FinanceandManagementServicesBranch@gov.bc.ca
Acting Director, Strategic Policy & Planning, Rick Brand
250-356-6675, Fax:
250-356-7903,Forests.StrategicPolicyAndPlanningBranchOffice@gov.bc.ca
Director, Strategic Corporate Initiatives, Sue Stephen
250-387-2248, Fax: 250-356-7903

Forest Stewardship
1520 Blanshard St., 3rd Fl., PO Box 9525 Prov Govt, Victoria, BC V8W 9C3
250-387-1296, Fax: 250-953-3687,
Forests.ForestStewardshipExecutiveOffice@gov.bc.ca
Chief Forester, Jim Snetsinger
Deputy Chief Forester, Craig Sutherland
Acting Director, Climate Change & Forest Carbon, Dale Draper
250-217-7735, Fax:
250-356-8124,Forests.ClimateChangeandForestCarbon@gov.bc.ca
Director, Forest Analysis & Inventory, Melanie Boyce
250-356-5958, Fax:
250-387-5999,Forests.ForestAnalysisBranchOffice@gov.bc.ca
Acting Director, Forest Practices, Lorne Bedford
250-387-8901, Fax:
250-387-1467,Forests.ForestPracticesBranchOffice@gov.bc.ca
Director, Research, Gerry Still
250-387-6579, Fax:
250-387-0046,Forests.ResearchBranchOffice@gov.bc.ca,
Director, Tree Improvement, Brian Barber
250-356-0888, Fax:
250-356-8124,Forests.TreeImprovementBranchOffice@gov.bc.ca
Ministry Librarian, BC Ministry of Forests & Range Library, Pamela Wilkins
250-387-2169, Fax: 250-953-3079,Forests.Library@gov.bc.ca
Coordinator, Future Forests Ecosystems Initiative, Silvia Lac
250-387-8902
Coordinator, Provincial Bark Beetle, Rod DeBoice
250-371-3734

Operations
1520 Blanshard St., 3rd Fl., PO Box 9525 Prov Govt, Victoria, BC V8W 9C3
250-387-1236, Fax: 250-953-3687,
Forests.OperationsDivisionExecutiveOffice@gov.bc.ca
Assistant Deputy Minister, Tim R. Sheldan
Executive Director, Operations, Peter Fuglem
250-387-1236
Director, Forest Worker Safety, Mark Vieweg
250-356-9287
Director, Compliance & Enforcement, Dan Graham
250-356-9785, Fax:
250-387-2539,Forests.ComplianceAndEnforcementBranchOffice@gov.bc.ca
Director, Protection Program, Brian Simpson
250-356-1068, Fax:
250-387-5685,Forests.ProtectionBranchOffice@gov.bc.ca
Director, Range, David Borth
250-371-3827, Fax: 250-828-4987

Regional Forestry Offices:

Coast
2100 Labieux Rd., Nanaimo, BC V9T 6E9
250-751-7001, Fax: 250-751-7190,
Forests.CoastRegionOffice@gov.bc.ca
www.for.gov.bc.ca/rco
Regional Executive Director, Jim Gowriluk
250-751-7163

Northern Interior
1011 - 4 Ave., 5th Fl., Prince George, BC V2L 3H9
250-565-6100, Fax: 250-565-6671,
www.for.gov.bc.ca/rni
Forests.NorthernInteriorRegionOffice@gov.bc.ca
Regional Executive Director, Bill I. Warner
250-565-6102

Southern Interior
515 Columbia St., Kamloops, BC V2C 2T7
250-828-4131, Fax: 250-828-4154,
Forests.SouthernInteriorRegionOffice@gov.bc.ca
www.for.gov.bc.ca/rsi
Regional Executive Director, T.P. (Phil) Zacharatos
250-828-4120

Tenure & Revenue
1520 Blanshard St., 3rd Fl., PO Box 9525 Prov Govt, Victoria, BC V8W 9C3
250-387-3656, Fax: 250-953-3687,
Forests.TenureRevenueExecutiveOffice@gov.bc.ca
Assistant Deputy Minister, Bob S. Friesen
Director, Aboriginal Affairs, Darrell A. Robb
250-387-6719, Fax:
250-356-6076,Forests.AboriginalAffairsBranchOffice@gov.bc.ca
Director, Economics & Trade, Lois McNabb
250-387-8374, Fax:
250-387-5050,Forests.EconomicsAndTradeBranchOffice@gov.bc.ca
Director, Resource Tenures & Engineering, Jim Langridge
250-387-8300, Fax:
250-387-6445,Forests.ResourceTenuresAndEngineeringBranchOffice@gov.bc.ca
Director, Revenue, Murray Stech
250-356-9807, Fax:
250-387-5670,Forests.RevenueBranchOffice@gov.bc.ca

Ministry of Health Services

1515 Blanshard St., Victoria, BC V8W 3C8
250-952-1742, Fax: 250-356-9587, 800-465-4911
hlth.health@gems1.gov.bc.ca
www.gov.bc.ca/healthservices

Other Communication: Media Relations Phone: 250-952-1887; Fax: 250-952-1883

The Ministry of Health Services is responsible for guiding & enhancing British Columbia's health system. The goal of the Ministry is to improve health care & ensure that citizens of the province have access to the care they require, when they need it.

Acts Administered:
Access to Abortion Services Act
Anatomy Act
BC Benefits (Income Assistance) Act
Community Care Facility Act
Continuing Care Act
Drinking Water Protection Act
Forensic Psychiatry Act
Health Act
Health Authorities Act
Health Care (Consent) & Care Facility (Admission) Act (not in force)
Health Emergency Act
Health Special Account Act
Hearing Aid Act
Hospital Act
Hospital District Act
Hospital Insurance Act
Human Tissue Gift Act
Marriage Act
Meat Inspection Act
Mental Health Act
Milk Industry Act
Ministry of Health Act
Name Act
Tobacco Sales Act
Vital Statistics Act
Wills Act (Part II)

Minister,Hon. George Abbott
250-953-3547, Fax: 250-356-9587,hlth.health@gov.bc.ca; george.abbott.mla@leg.bc.ca
Deputy Minister, Gordon Macatee
250-952-1911, Fax:
250-952-1909,hlth.dmoffice@gov.bc.ca
Executive Director, Program Integration, Jan Wheeler
250-952-1410
Chief Administrative Officer, Stephen Brown
250-952-1164
Chief Operating Officer, Michael MacDougall
250-952-1764

• Hospital Appeal Board(HAB)
747 Fort St., 4th Fl.
PO Box 9425 Prov Govt
Victoria, BC V8W 9V1
250-387-3464 Fax: 250-356-9923 800-663-7867
hab@gov.bc.ca
www.hab.gov.bc.ca
The Hospital Appeal Board of British Columbia is an independent, quasi-judicial administrative appeal tribunal, which was created by the Hospital Act. The Board provides an appeal process for medical practitioners. The role of the Board is to review hospital board of management decisions concerning hospital privileges. Board members are appointed by British Columbia's Minister of Health.

• Medical Services Commission(MSC)
1515 Blanshard St., 3rd Fl.
Victoria, BC V8W 3C8
250-952-3073 Fax: 250-952-3131
www.health.gov.bc.ca/msp/legislation/msc.html
The Medical Services Commission is a statutory body made up of nine members. In accordance with the Medicare Protection Act & Regulations, the Commission acts on behalf of the Government of British Columbia to manage the Medical Services Plan. The Commission works to ensure British Columbia residents have access to medical care, & to manage the provision & payment of medical services.

Corporate Policy, Legislation, & Intergovernmental Relations
1515 Blanshard St., 5th Fl., Victoria, BC V8W 3C8
250-952-2165, Fax: 250-952-2109
Assistant Deputy Minister, Craig Knight
250-952-2159
Executive Director, Legislation & Professional Regulation, Linda Gee
250-952-2281, Fax:
250-952-2205,HLTH.LPRAdmin@gov.bc.ca, Other Communications: URL: www.healthservices.gov.bc.ca/leg
Executive Director, Intergovernmental Relations, Mariana Diacu
250-952-1304, Fax: 250-952-2516
Executive Director, Strategic Policy & Research, Elisabeth Wagner
250-952-2282, Fax: 250-952-2516
Registrar, Emergency Medical Assistants Licensing Board, Dale Broemeling
250-952-1203, Fax: 250-952-1222

Financial & Corporate Services
1515 Blanshard St., 4th Fl., Victoria, BC V8W 3C8
250-952-2067, Fax: 250-952-1573
Assistant Deputy Minister, Manjit Sidhu
250-952-2066, Fax: 250-952-1573
Executive Director, Capital Services, Kevin Brewster
250-952-1102, Fax: 250-952-1851
Executive Director & SFO, Finance & Decision Support, George Day
250-952-2016, Fax: 250-952-1573
Executive Director, Regional Grants - Decision Support, Gordon Cross
250-952-1120, Fax: 250-952-1420

Health Authorities
1515 Blanshard St., 6th Fl., Victoria, BC V8W 3C8
250-952-1049, Fax: 250-952-1052
Assistant Deputy Minister, Wendy Hill
250-952-1297, Fax: 250-952-1052
Executive Director, Acute Care & Performance Accountability, Rebecca Harvey
250-952-1514, Fax: 250-952-1052
Executive Director, Home & Community Care & Performance Accountabiity, Leigh Ann Seller
250-952-1274, Fax: 250-952-1282
Executive Director, Mental Health & Addictions & Performance Accountability, Ann Marr
250-952-3519, Fax: 250-952-1689
Acting Executive Director, Patient Safety & Clinical Innovation, Ted Patterson
250-952-1543, Fax: 250-952-1034
Director, Strategic Management, Teri Collins
250-952-2871, Fax: 250-952-1689

Vital Statistics
818 Fort St., Victoria, BC V8W 1H8
250-952-2681, Fax: 250-952-2587,
www.vs.gov.bc.ca
For a certificate of a registration or record: $25 per copy. For each search for one registration or record for each three-year period or fraction thereof over which the search is conducted: $25.
Chief Executive Officer, Andrew McBride

Health Sector Information Management / Information Technology
1515 Blanshard St., 7th Fl., Victoria, BC V8W 3C8
250-952-2563, Fax: 250-952-1827
Assistant Deputy Minister, Elaine McKnight
250-952-2563, Fax: 250-952-1827
Acting Chief Executive Officer, British Columbia Vital Statistics Agency, Jack Shewchuk
250-952-1310, Fax: 250-952-2587,Other Communications: Information Line: 250-952-2681
Executive Director, Business Management Office, Carolyn Bell
250-952-6202, Fax: 250-952-6084
Executive Director, Corporate Management & Operations, Darcy Goodwin
250-952-3664, Fax: 250-952-3676
Executive Director, eHealth Privacy, Security, & Legislation, John Cheung
250-387-1718, Fax: 250-387-1730
Director, Data Access, Research, & Stewardship, Bob Hart
250-952-1166, Fax: 250-952-0979

Health System Planning
1515 Blanshard St., 3rd Fl., Victoria, BC V8W 3C8
250-952-3465, Fax: 250-952-3131
Assistant Deputy Minister, Stephen Brown
250-952-2404, Fax: 250-952-3131
Executive Director, Health System Planning Analysis, Ian Rongve
250-952-1343, Fax: 250-952-2235
Executive Director, Management Information, Nick Grant
250-952-1116
Director, Strategic & Corporate Services, Debbie Godfrey
250-952-1798, Fax: 250-952-3131,

Medical Services
1515 Blanshard St., 3rd Fl., Victoria, BC V8W 3C8
250-952-3465, Fax: 250-952-3131
Executive Director, Medical Services, Phyllis Chuly
250-952-1706, Fax: 250-952-3133
Executive Director, Physician Human Resource Management, Rod Frechette
250-952-3146, Fax: 250-952-3486
Executive Director, Primary Health Care, Valerie Tregillus
250-952-2961, Fax: 250-952-1417
Director, Medical Services Operations & Policy, Stephanie Power
250-952-1169, Fax: 250-952-3133
Director, Guidelines & Priority Projects, Nichola Manning
250-952-1323, Fax: 250-952-3133,hlth.guidelines@gov.bc.ca; Nichola.Manning@gov.bc.ca, Other Communications: URL: www.bcguidelines.ca
Director, Supplementary Benefits, Blood, & Lab Services, Jane Crickmore
250-952-2878, Fax: 250-952-3133

Pharmaceutical Services
1515 Blanshard St., 3rd Fl., Victoria, BC V8W 3C8
250-952-1859, Fax: 250-952-1584
Assistant Deputy Minister, Bob Nakagawa
250-952-1464, Fax: 250-952-1584
Executive Director, Business Management & Supplier Relations, Paul Mochrie
604-660-1303, Fax: 604-660-2108
Executive Director, Drug Intelligence, Eric Lun
250-952-2988, Fax: 250-952-2790
Executive Director, Drug Use Optimization, Suzanne Taylor
604-660-1217, Fax: 604-660-2108
Executive Director, Policy Outcomes, Evaluation, & Research, Darlene Therrien
250-952-1187, Fax: 250-952-1584
Executive Director, Stakeholder & Partner Relations, Paul Gudaitis
250-952-3017, Fax: 250-952-1391

Social Development Policy Office
1515 Blanshard St., 2nd Fl., Victoria, BC V8W 3C8
250-952-1112, Fax: 250-952-1186
Coordinator, Climate Action Project, Crystal Oberg
250-952-1240

System Evaluation & Accountability Office
1483 Douglas St., 5th Fl., Victoria, BC V8W 3K4
250-952-1109, Fax: 250-356-6221
Executive Director, System Evaluation & Accountability, Anne Sandbu
250-387-4159, Fax: 250-356-6221
Director, Ken Champoux
250-387-4108

British Columbia Hydro

333 Dunsmuir St., 18th Fl., Vancouver, BC V6B 5R3
604-224-9376, Fax: 604-623-4467, 800-224-9376
www.bchydro.com
BC Hydro is a provincial Crown corporation. It reports to the Minister of Energy & Mines, & is regulated by the British Columbia Utilities Commission. BC Hydro is engaged in the generation & distribution of electricity throughout British Columbia. It strives to provide these services in an environmentally & socially responsible manner. On behalf of BC Hydro, BC Transmission Corporation facilitates the transmission of electricity.
Chair, Mossadiq S. Umedaly
President/CEO, Robert G. Elton
Executive Vice-President, Customer Care & Conservation, Bev Van Ruyven
Senior Vice-President, Engineering, Aboriginal Relations & Generation, Chris O'Riley
Senior Vice-President, Corporate Affairs, Susan Yurkovich
Chief Officer, Safety, Health, & Environment, Ray Stewart
Chief Officer, Human Resources, Debbie Nagle
• Powerex Corp.
#1400, 666 Burrard St.
Vancouver, BC V6C 2X8
604-891-5000 Fax: 604-891-6060 800-220-4907
customer.service@bchydro.com
www.powerex.com
Other Communication: Toronto Location, Phone: 416-345-8854
A wholly-owned subsidiary of BC Hydro, Powerex Corp. markets wholesale energy products & services to utilities, power pools, industrials, & power marketers in North America, particularly western Canada, the western United States.
• Powertech Labs Inc.
12388 - 88 Ave.
Surrey, BC V8W 7R7
604-590-7500 Fax: 604-590-5347
info@powertechlans.com
www.powertechlabs.com
A wholly owned subsidiary of BC Hydro, Powertech Labs offers environmental, mechanical, electrical, metallurgical, civil, chemical, gas technologies, & structural engineering to deal with technical problems with power equipment & systems.

Office of the Information & Privacy Commissioner for British Columbia (OIPC)

756 Fort St., 3rd Fl., PO Box 9038 Prov Govt, Victoria, BC V8W 9A4
250-387-5629, Fax: 250-387-1696, 800-663-7867
info@oipc.bc.ca
www.oipc.bc.ca

Other Communication: Vancouver Phone: 604-660-2421; Elsewhere in B.C. Toll Free: 1-800-663-7867
Operating independently from the government, the Office of the Information & Privacy Commissioner is responsible for monitoring & enforcing the following acts in British Columbia: Freedom of Information & Protection of Privacy Act; & Personal Information Protection Act.
Commissioner, David Loukidelis
Executive Director, Mary Carlson
Coordinator, Customer Service & Communications, Maria Dupuis
Manager, Investigations & Mediation, Catherine Tully

Insurance Corporation of British Columbia (ICBC)

151 West Esplanade, North Vancouver, BC V7M 3H9
604-661-2800, 800-663-3051
www.icbc.com

Other Communication: New Claims, Lower Mainland Phone: 604-520-8222; Elsewhere in BC, Toll Free: 1-800-910-4222; TIPS Lower Mainland, Phone: 604-661-6844; TIPS BC Line: 1-800-661-6844
A provincial Crown corporation, The Insurance Corporation of British Columbia was established in 1973. The main responsibilities of the Insurance Corporation of British Columbia are as follows: Provision of universal auto insurance to motorists in British Columbia; Registration & licensing of vehicles; & Driver licensing.
Chair, T. Richard Turner
President/CEO, Jon Schubert
Chief Financial Officer, Geri Prior
Chief Information Officer, Dave Govett
Senior Vice-President, Claims, Craig Horton
Senior Vice-President, Insurance, Donnie Wing
Vice-President, Human Resources & Corporate Law, Len Posyniak
Vice-President, Driver Licensing, Fred Hess

Intergovernmental Relations Secretariat (IGRS)

548 Michigan St., 1st Fl., PO Box 9433 Prov Govt, Victoria, BC V8W 9V3
250-387-0783, Fax: 250-387-1920,
igrs@gov.bc.ca
www.igrs.gov.bc.ca
The mission of IGRS is to ensure that the province's relations with provincial governments, the federal government, & international governments advance British Columbia's interests.
Minister of State, Intergovernmental Relations, Hon. Joan McIntyre
250-356-7562, Fax:
250-356-8545,joan.mcintyre.mla@leg.bc.ca
Associate Deputy Minister, Robert Lapper
250-387-0752
Assistant Deputy Minister, Pierrette Maranda
250-387-1875
Executive Director, Social Policy & Operations Support, Cathy Stigant
250-387-0793
Executive Director, Intergovernmental Relations, Pacific Coast Collaborative Commission, Bryant Fairley
250-387-1134
Executive Director, Economic Initiatives & Asia Pacific, Robert Musgrave
250-387-1174
Director, International Relations, Sukumar Periwal
250-387-0761
Director, Federalism & Constitutional Policy, Paul Craven
250-356-2272

Ministry of Labour

PO Box 9052 Prov Govt, Victoria, BC V8W 9E2
250-356-6348, Fax: 250-356-6595,
LCS.Minister@gov.bc.ca
www.gov.bc.ca/lbr

Other Communication: Employment Standards Inquiries: 1-800-663-3316, 250-612-4100 (Prince George area)
Responsibilities of the Ministry of Labour include the following: Labour relations; Employment standards; Workers' Compensation Act; Occupational health & safety; Chief Information Officer; Information & privacy; Alternative Service Delivery Secretariat; Queen's Printer; Solutions BC; BC Stats; BC Internet Services; BC Online; Enquiry BC; BC Bid; Enquiry BC; & Canada-BC Business Service Centre.
Acts Administered:
BC Online Act
Business Number Act (s. 10.1)
Coastal Forest Industry Dispute Settlement Act
Community Services Labour Relations Act
Document Disposal Act
Education Services Collective Agreement Act
Electronic Transactions Act
Employment Standards Act
Fire & Police Services Collective Bargaining Act
Fire Department Act
Fishing Collective Bargaining Act
Freedom of Information and Protection of Privacy Act
Labour Relations Code
Legislative Assembly Management Committee Act
Legislative Assembly Privilege Act
Legislative Library Act
Legislative Procedure Review Act
Members' Remuneration & Pensions Act
Ministry of Labour Act (except in relation to gas safety, electrical safety, elevating devices, boiler & pressure vessel safety)
Ministry of Provincial Secretary & Government Services Act (ss. 1, 2 (4) & 4)
Personal Information Protection Act
Procurement Services Act
Public Agency Accommodation Act
Queen's Printer Act
Statistics Act
Workers' Compensation Act
Minister, Labour, Hon. Murray Coell
Murray.Coell@gov.bc.ca
Deputy Minister, Robert Lapper
250-387-3123, Fax:
250-356-5186,SDL.DeputyMinister@gems3.gov.bc.ca
Associate Deputy Minister, Labour, Paul Straszak
250-387-3914, Fax:
250-356-5186,SDL.DeputyMinister@gems3.gov.bc.ca
Managing Director, Board Resourcing & Development, Ann Wicks
604-775-1668, Fax: 604-775-0158,Ann.Wicks@gov.bc.ca
• British Columbia Labour Relations Board
Oceanic Plaza
#600, 1066 West Hastings St.
Vancouver, BC V6E 3X1
604-660-1300 Fax: 604-660-1892
information@lrb.bc.ca
www.lrb.bc.ca
The British Columbia Labour Relations Board is an independent, administrative tribunal. The Board is responsible for mediating & adjudicating employment & labour relations matters related to unionized workplaces.
• Employment Standards Tribunal
Oceanic Plaza
#650, 1066 West Hastings St.
Vancouver, BC V6E 3X1
604-775-3512 Fax: 604-775-3372
registrar.est@bcest.bc.ca
www.bcest.bc.ca
Established under the Employment Standards Act, the Employment Standards Tribunal operates as an administrative tribunal. The responsibility of the Tribunal is to provide an independent appeal of Determinations made by the Director of Employment Standards.
• Workers' Compensation Appeal Tribunal(WCAT)
#150, 4600 Jacombs Rd.
Richmond, BC V6V 3B1
604-664-7800 Fax: 604-664-7898 800-663-2782
www.wcat.bc.ca

The Workers' Compensation Appeal Tribunal of British Columbia is an independent appeal tribunal, which was established by the Workers Compensation Amendment Act (No. 2), 2002. The Tribunal decides appeals from workers & employers from decisions of the Workers' Compensation Board (WorkSafeBC).
• Workers' Compensation Board

Alternative Service Delivery Secretariat
548 Michigan St., PO Box 9438 Prov Govt, Victoria, BC V8W 9V3
250-387-1911, Fax: 250-356-2805

Assistant Deputy Minister, John Bethel
250-387-4503, Fax: 250-952-8299
Executive Director, New Business Development & Acting Executive Director, Alliance Support, Wayne Powell
250-387-1911
Executive Director, Solutions Development, Dave Bacharach
250-217-4788
Executive Director, Project Management Centre of Excellence, Dale Christenson
250-356-5390

Chief Information Office
4000 Seymour Pl., PO Box 9412 Prov Govt, Victoria, BC V8W 9V1
250-356-7970, Fax: 250-387-1940, www.cio.gov.bc.ca

Chief Information Officer, Dave Nikolejsin
250-387-8509
Executive Director, Advanced Communication & Collaboration Services, Gary Cooney
250-387-5975
Executive Director, Architecture & Standards, Bob Duggan
250-387-8583
Executive Director, Community & External Initiatives, Wilf R. Bangert
250-387-9637
Executive Director, Cross Government Information Management / Information Technology Initiatives, Peter Watkins
250-387-2184
Executive Director, Cross Government Research, Policy & Practice, Wendy Taylor
250-952-6161, Fax: 250-356-1182
Executive Director, Finance, Matt Mannix
250-356-8321
Executive Director, Information Management / Information Governance, Bruce Cuthbert
250-387-2194, Fax: 250-952-6250
Acting Executive Director, Information Security, Rob Todd
250-387-8823
Executive Director, Intergration Infrastructure Program, Don Henkelman
604-660-6442
Executive Project Director, Social Sector Integrated Information Management Project, Bobbi Sadler
250-387-1349, Fax: 250-952-6627

Client Services
525 Superior St., 2nd Fl., PO Box 9472 Prov Govt, Victoria, BC V8W 9W6
250-952-6861, Fax: 250-952-6803

Assistant Deputy Minister, Trish Shwart
Executive Director, Coordinated Client Relationship Management Program, Bobbi Plecas
250-952-6952, Fax: 250-387-0380
Executive Director, Strategic Planning, Operations, & Development, Gary Swift
250-952-6841
Lead, Client Services Integration, Ron Colquhoun
250-387-3890, Fax: 250-387-4722,WTS.ClientServices@gov.bc.ca; Ron.Colquhoun@gov.bc.ca

Common Business Services
548 Michigan St, 2nd Fl., PO Box 9451 Prov Govt, Victoria, BC V8W 9V7
250-356-5846, Fax: 250-387-1399

Assistant Deputy Minister, Richard Poutney
Executive Director, Strategic Acquisitions & Intellectual Property, Frank Hudson
250-356-0843, Fax: 250-356-0846,SATP@gov.bc.ca; Frank.Hudson@gov.bc.ca
Executive Director, Corporate Accounting Services, Nashater Sanghera
250-356-9116, Fax: 250-953-3352
Queen's Printer for British Columbia & Executive Director, Procurement & Supply Services (P&SS), Vern Burkhardt
250-356-9969, Fax: 250-387-0388,Vern.Burkhardt@gov.bc.ca, Other Communications: URL:www.pss.gov.bc.ca; Customer Service: 250-387-3309

Service BC
548 Michigan St., 2nd Fl., PO Box 9804 Prov Govt, Victoria, BC V8W 9W1
604-660-2421, Fax: 250-387-5633, 800-663-7867
EnquiryBC@gov.bc.ca
www.servicebc.gov.bc.ca

Other Communication: Service BC Contact Centre - Enquiry BC, Victoria Phone: 387-6121; Outside B.C. Phone: 604-660-2421; Metro Vancouver TTY: 604-775-0303

Service BC provides frontline government services & information. Citizens in British Columbia are assisted in accessing services they need. These programs & services are available in person, by phone, & online. Service BC Centres are located in 59 places throughout British Columbia. The following are examples of services offered by Service BC: Doing business in B.C.; Education; Employment & labour standards; Exploring B.C.; Fees & payments; Health; Land & property; Legal services; License & registration; Life events; Living in B.C.; Reports & publications; & Taxation.

Assistant Deputy Minister, Service BC, Lois Fraser
250-387-4823
Executive Director, Online Channel Office, Laurie Barker
250-953-3679, Fax: 250-387-2144
Executive Director, Service Solutions & Planning, Deborah Ainsworth
250-387-8574, Fax: 250-387-9843
Executive Director, BC Stats, Don McRae
250-356-2119, Fax: 250-387-0380,BC.Stats@gov.bc.ca; Don.McRae@gov.bc.ca, Other Communications: URL: www.bcstats.gov.bc.ca
Executive Director, Service Delivery Operations, Bette-Jo Hughes
250-356-2031, Fax: 250-387-5633,Other Communications: URL: www.governmentagents.gov.bc.ca
Regional Director, Service Delivery Operations, Interior Northeast Service BC Centre, Deborah Lipscombe
250-828-4545, Fax: 250-828-4542
Regional Director, Service Delivery Operations, Northwest Service BC Centre, Perry Slump
250-565-6001, Fax: 250-992-4314
Regional Director, Service Delivery Operations, Southeast Service BC Centre, Vacant
250-426-1249, Fax: 250-426-1253
Customer Service Representative, Service Delivery Operations, Vancouver Island / South Coast Service BC Centre, Jason Bell
250-741-3636, Fax: 250-741-3663

Strategic Infrastructure
548 Michigan St, 2nd Fl., PO Box 9438 Prov Govt, Victoria, BC V8W 9V3
250-387-4632, Fax: 250-356-2805

Assistant Deputy Minister, Strategic Infrastructure, Wayne Jensen
250-387-4524, Fax: 250-387-9332
Executive Director, Business Planning & Development Services, Gary Lakusta
250-387-7849, Fax: 250-387-9332,
Executive Director, Strategic Telecommunications Services, Roman Mateyko
250-387-7915, Fax: 250-387-3623

Workplace Technology Services
4000 Seymour Pl., PO Box 9412 Prov Govt, Victoria, BC V8W 9V1
250-387-0672, Fax: 250-387-5693

Assistant Deputy Minister, Workplace Technology Services, Jill Kot
Jill.Kot@gov.bc.ca
Executive Director, Business Strategy & Planning Services, Brian Bowman
250-387-9533, Fax: 250-387-5693
Executive Director, Client Services, Sue Goldsmith
250-387-4821, Fax: 250-387-5693
Executive Director, Workplace Application Services, Randy Fehr
250-387-8083
Acting Executive Director, Workplace Communication Services, Workstations, Steve Banks
250-953-3637, Fax: 250-387-8419
Acting Executive Director, Workplace Communication Services, Communications,
250-387-9322, Fax: 250-387-8419
Executive Director, Workplace Hosting Services, Nelson Lah
250-356-5600

Office of the Ombudsman

756 Fort St., 2nd Fl., PO Box 9039 Prov Govt, Victoria, BC V8W 9A5
250-387-5855, Fax: 250-387-0198, 800-567-3247
systems@ombudsman.bc.ca (Information technology inquiries)
www.ombudsman.bc.ca

Complaints about the services of public agencies are submitted to the Office of the Ombudsman. The responsibility of the Office of the Ombudsman is to investigate impartially these inquiries about the practices of public agencies within its jurisdiction. The Office determines if public agencies acted fairly in accordance with relevant legislation & policies.

Ombudsman, Kim Carter
250-356-1559
Director, Corporate Services, Lanny Hubbard
250-387-0177
Acting Director, Investigations, Linda Carlson
250-387-0189
Acting Director, Outreach, Intake, Early Resolution & Systemic Investigations, Bruce Ronayne
250-387-0196
Librarian, David Gagnon
250-356-7563, librarian@ombudsman.bc.ca

British Columbia Provincial Emergency Program (PEP)

PO Box 9201 Prov Govt, Victoria, BC V8W 9J1
250-952-4913, Fax: 250-952-4888, 888-257-4777
www.pep.gov.bc.ca

Other Communication: Emergency Coordination Centre: 1-800-663-3456; Recovery & Funding Programs Phone: 250-952-5505

The Provincial Emergency Program (PEP) is a division of the Ministry of Public Safety & Solicitor General, Emergency Management BC. PEP works with local governments to provide the following training & support services for emergencies: Awareness & education to lessen the effects of emergencies; Promotion of preparedness for disasters, through planning & exercises; Coordination & assistance in response to emergencies; & Development & implementation of recovery measures.

Minister, Public Safety & Solicitor General, Hon. John van Dongen
250-356-7717, Fax: 250-356-8270,SG.Minister@gov.bc.ca; john.vandongen.mla@leg.bc.ca
Executive Director, Cam Filmer
Cam.Filmer@gov.bc.ca
Director, Management Services & Programs, Steve Bachop
250-952-4892
Director, Operations, Chris Duffy
250-952-4544
Director, Integrated Planning, Aja Norgaard
250-952-4854
Coordinator, Recovery & Funding Programs, Teresa Ferguson
250-952-5525

Ministry of Public Safety & Solicitor General

PO Box 9282 Prov Govt, Victoria, BC V8W 9J7
250-387-6121, 800-663-7867
pssgwebfeedback@gov.bc.ca
www.gov.bc.ca/pssg

Other Communication: Public Affairs Bureau Phone: 250-356-6961, Fax: 250-387-1753; B.C. Coroners Service: 604-660-7745; Provincial Emergency Program: 250-952-4846

The goal of the Ministry of Public Safety & Solicitor General is the maintenance & enhancement of public safety in communities across British Columbia. The following are the key responsibilities of the Ministry: Crime prevention programs; Police & correctional services; Criminal record check & protection order registry; Victim assistance; Provincial emergency management; Emergency social services; Consumer services; & Gaming enforcement.

Acts Administered:
Attorney General Act (ss. 2(e), 5 & 6, as they relate to the powers, duties, & functions of the Minister of Public Safety & the Solicitor General)
BC Neurotrauma Fund Contribution Act
Business Practices & Consumer Protection Act
Business Practices & Consumer Protection Authority Act
Civil Forfeiture Act
Commercial Transport Act (ss. 2, 6, 7, 10, 13; & ss. 1, 4, 5, 8, 9, 11, 12 & 14, as they relate to affairs of the Insurance Corporation of British Columbia)
Coroners Act
Correction Act
Cremation, Interment & Funeral Services Act
Crime Victim Assistance Act
Criminal Injury Compensation Act
Criminal Records Review Act
Emergency Communications Corporations Act
Emergency Program Act
Fire Services Act (as it relates to the portfolio of the minister)
Firearm Act
Fireworks Act

Flood Relief Act
Food Donor Encouragement Act
Guide Animal Act
Insurance Corporation Act (Part 1)
Insurance (Vehicle) Act
Ministry of Consumer & Corporate Affairs Act (ss. 3 & 4(a), in relation to consumer affairs; s. 4(b)-(d))
Motion Picture Act
Motor Dealer Act
Motor Vehicle Act
Parental Responsibility Act
Police Act
Sale of Goods Act
Senior Citizen Automobile Insurance Grant Act
Sex Offender Registry Act
Special Accounts Appropriation & Control Act (ss. 7 & 10 (2) (a) & (b))
Victims of Crime Act

Minister, Public Safety & Solicitor General, Hon. Kash Heed
250-356-7717, Fax: 250-356-8270,SG.Minister@gov.bc.ca
Deputy Solicitor General, David Morhart
250-356-0149, Fax:
250-387-6224,David.Morhart@gov.bc.ca
Deputy Minister, Public Safety, Wes Shoemaker
250-953-4083, Fax: 250-387-4872
Executive Director, Civil Forfeiture Office, Rob Kroeker
250-387-5091, Fax: 250-356-1092,Rob.Kroeker@gov.bc.ca
Director, Corporate Policy & Planning Office, Toby Louie
250-356-6389, Fax: 250-387-2631,Toby.Louie@gov.bc.ca

• British Columbia Office of the Police Complaint Commissioner
756 Fort St., 3rd Fl.
PO Box 9895 Prov Govt
Victoria, BC V8W 9T8
250-356-7458 Fax: 250-356-6503 800-663-7867
info@opcc.bc.ca
www.opcc.bc.ca
Other Communication: Vancouver Phone: 604-660-2385
Established under the Police Act, the British Columbia Office of the Police Complaint Commissioner is an independent agency. The responsibility of the agency is overseeing complaints against municipal police & ensuring that these complaints are dealt with in a fair & impartial manner. The Office reports directly to the Legislature.

• Coroners Service of British Columbia
Metrotower II
#800, 4720 Kingsway
Burnaby, BC V5H 4N2
604-660-7745 Fax: 604-660-7766
BC.CorSer@gov.bc.ca
www.pssg.gov.bc.ca/coroners
Governed by the Coroners Act, the Coroners Service of British Columbia investigates all unnatural, unexplained, unattended, or sudden & unexpected deaths. Based on its fact-finding, the agency recommends public safety improvements in order to prevent similar deaths.

Corrections Branch
1001 Douglas St., 7th Fl., PO Box 9278 Prov Govt, Victoria, BC V8W 9J7
250-387-5059, Fax: 250-387-5698,
www.pssg.gov.bc.ca/corrections

Other Communication: Adult Custody Phone: 250-387-5098; Community Corrections & Corporate Programs Phone: 250-356-7930
The Corrections Branch consists of the Adult Custody Division & the Community Corrections & Corporate Programs Division. The Adult Custody Division operates correctional centres for persons awaiting trial or serving a provincial custody sentence. The Community Corrections & Corporate Programs Division operates over fifty community corrections offices throughout British Columbia.
Assistant Deputy Minister, Corrections, A.O. (Bert) Phipps
250-387-5363
Provincial Director, Adult Custody Division, Brent Merchant
250-387-5959
Provincial Director, Community Corrections & Corporate Programs Division, Rob Watts
250-387-5936
Director, Health Services,Dr. Diane A. Rothon
250-995-0009, Fax: 250-995-0010
Director, Mental Health Services,Dr. Maureen Olley
250-387-5098, Fax: 250-952-6883

Emergency Management BC
525 Fort St., 2nd Fl., PO Box 9223 Prov Govt, Victoria, BC V8W 9J1
250-953-4002, Fax: 250-953-4081,
BC.CorSer@gov.bc.ca (Coroner); OFC@gov.bc.ca (Fire Commissioner)
www.pssg.gov.bc.ca/coroners; www.pssg.gov.bc.ca/firecom

Other Communication: Office of the Chief Coroner: 604-660-7745; Office of the Fire Commissioner Phone: 250-356-9000, Toll Free: 1-888-988-9488; Provincial Emergency Program: 250-952-4913
Emergency Management BC oversees the Coroners Service of British Columbia, the Office of the Fire Commissioner, & the Provincial Emergency Program (www.pep.bc.ca). B.C. Coroners Service investigates all unexpected, unnatural, unexplained, & unattended deaths in the province. Improvements to public safety & recommendations to prevent similar deaths are made by the Coroners Service. The Office of the Fire Commissioner administers & enforces fire safety legislation, trains local assistants to the fire commissioner, certifies fire fighters, provides public fire safety education, advises local governments, responds to major fires, & investigates fires. The Provincial Emergency Program provides training & support to local governments.
Chief Coroner, Chief Coroner's Office, Terry P. Smith
604-660-7745, Fax: 604-660-7766,BC.CorSer@gov.bc.ca; Terry.Smith@gov.bc.ca
Fire Commissioner, Becky Denlinger
250-387-5536, 888-988-9488,Fax: 250-356-9019,OFC@gov.bc.ca
Executive Director, Provincial Emergency Program, Cam Filmer
250-952-4913, Fax: 250-952-4888
Executive Director, Finance & Administration Division, Brian Price
250-953-3099, Fax: 250-356-8739
Director, Director, Accounting, Budgeting & Reporting,
250-356-7077, Fax: 250-356-9185

Information Technology Services Division
910 Government St., 4th Fl., PO Box 9262 Prov Govt, Victoria, BC V8W 9J4
250-356-8787, Fax: 250-356-7699
Acting Executive Director & Chief Information Officer, Robert McDonald
250-356-8787
Acting Director, Strategic Planning & Development Services, Steve Rossander
250-387-1620
Acting Director, Technical & Operational Support Services, Peteyl Provan
250-356-6061
Director, Application Management, James Tepoorten
250-356-2202
Director, Privacy, Risk, & Information Security Management, Mark Scherling
250-953-3371, Fax: 250-953-3559

Liquor Distribution Branch
2625 Rupert St., Vancouver, BC V5M 3T5
604-252-3000, Fax: 604-252-3026
General Manager, Jay Chambers
250-252-3021
Executive Director, Retail Services, Kelly Wilson
604-252-3103
Executive Director, Human Resources, Gordon Zelenika
604-252-3241
Executive Director, Finance, Roger Bissoondatt
604-252-3151
Director, Corporate Policy, Gord Hall
604-252-3035,
Director, Information Services, Don Farley
604-252-3264
Director, Corporate Security, Donna Morse
604-252-3051

Management Services Branch
910 Government St., 5th Fl., PO Box 9256 Prov Govt, Victoria, BC V8W 9J4
250-387-5258, Fax: 250-387-0081
Assistant Deputy Minister, Management Services, Deborah Fayed
250-387-5258, Deborah.Fayad@gov.bc.ca
Director, Risk Management, Anne McKeachie
250-356-8921, Fax: 250-356-8736

Office of the Superintendent of Motor Vehicles (OSMV)
940 Blanshard St., PO Box 9254 Prov Govt, Victoria, BC V8W 9J2
250-387-7747, Fax: 250-387-4891,
OSMV.Mailbox@gov.bc.ca
www.pssg.gov.bc.ca/osmv
The Office of the Superintendent of Motor Vehicles is responsible for regulating drivers in British Columbia. The following services are provided: Establishment & maintenance of standards for driving behaviour & medical fitness; Provision of an independent method of appeal of certain Insurance Corporation of British Columbia decisions; Scheduling & hearing evidence related to proposals by the Insurance Corporation of British Columbia concerning licences, driving training schools, & AirCare Certified repair facilities; & Reviewing driving prohibitions & vehicle impoundments imposed by police.
Superintendent, Motor Vehicles, Steve Martin
250-387-5692
Deputy Superintendent, Lisa Howie
250-387-5371
Director, Hearings & Fair Practices, Sydney Swift
250-387-5371
Director, Policy & Business Reform, Wendy Trotter
250-953-3330

Policing & Community Safety Branch
1001 Douglas St., 10th Fl., PO Box 9285, Victoria, BC V8W 9J7
250-387-1100, Fax: 250-356-7747,
sgpcsb@gov.bc.ca; vsdvistimservices@gov.bc.ca
www.pssg.gov.bc.ca/victim_services

Other Communication: Victim Services Phone: 604-660-5199; VictimLINK: 1-800-563-0808
Assistant Deputy Minister, Policing & Community Safety Branch & Director, Police Services, Kevin Begg
Executive Director, Police Services Division, Sandra Sajko
250-387-6943
Executive Director, Security Programs & Police Technology, Sam MacLeod
250-356-1501, Fax: 250-387-5367,SGSPDSEC@gov.bc.ca
Executive Director, Strategic Justice Partnerships, Provincial Congress on Public Safety & Crystal Meth Secretariat, Mark Tatchell
250-387-2036
Deputy Director, Protective Services, Dennis Verge
250-356-1512, Fax: 250-387-5367
Deputy Director, Private Investigators & Security Agencies ACT, Greg Langham
250-356-1509, Fax: 250-387-5367
Director, Policy & Legislation, Police Services, Kathy Kirby
250-387-6950
Senior Program Manager, Governance & First Nations, Bob Cole
250-356-6676
Senior Program Manager, Terrorism & Critical Infrastructure, Michael Thompson
250-387-0076
Senior Program Manager, Contract Policing Team, Kimberley McLean
250-387-2787

BC Public Service Agency
#4, 810 Blanshard St., PO Box 9404 Prov Govt, Victoria, BC V8W 9V1
250-356-6830, Fax: 250-356-7074,
www.bcpublicservice.ca
The provision of human resource management services is the responsibility of the British Columbia Service Agency. The services are provided to persons & organizations working in the provinces's public sector.
Associate Deputy Minister, British Columbia Public Service Agency, Dave Byng
250-356-8371
Assistant Deputy Minister, Labour Relations, Doug Caul
250-387-0497
Assistant Deputy Minister & Executive Financial Officer, Tara Faganello
250-387-8139, tara.faganello@gov.bc.ca
Assistant Deputy Minister, Talent Management, Lynda Tarras
250-952-6296
Assistant Deputy Minister, Client Services, Barry Wilton
250-356-6830

Ministry of Small Business & Revenue
1810 Blanshard St., 3rd Fl., PO Box 9432 Prov Govt, Victoria, BC V8W 9N6
250-387-6206, Fax: 250-952-0712,
MSBROffice@gov.bc.ca
www.gov.bc.ca/sbr

Other Communication: Tax inquiries email: CTBTaxQuestions@gov.bc.ca
The responsibilities of the Ministry of Small Business & Revenue (Minister Responsible for Deregulation) are as follows: Small Business Roundtable; Property, income, & consumer tax collection; Collection & loan management; Student loan debt administration; Homeowner grants; Forestry, mines, oil, & gas revenue; & Smart regulation.
Acts Administered:
Assessment Act
Assessment Authority Act
Carbon Tax Act (except Part 2)
Corporation Capital Tax Act

Esquimalt & Nanaimo Railway Belt Tax Act
Forest Act (as the act relates to the collection of public money, as defined in section 1 of the Financial Administration Act, other than a fine, or to the administration of deposits & securities paya
Forest & Range Practices Act (as the act relates to the collection of public money, other than a fine, or to the administration of deposits & securities payable)
Forest Practices Code of British Columbia Act (as the act relates to the collection of public money, other than a fine, or to the administration of deposits & securities payable)
Forest Stand Management Fund Act (as the act relates to the collection of public money, other than a fine, or to the administration of deposits & securities payable)
Home Owner Grant Act
Hotel Room Tax Act
Income Tax Act
Indian Self Government Enabling Act
Insurance Premium Tax Act
International Financial Activity Act (Parts 3, 4, & 5; & Part 6, as it pertains to Parts 3, 4, & 5)
Land Tax Deferment Act
Logging Tax Act
Medicare Protection Act (ss. 5 (1) (b), 7 (5), 8 (4), 8.1, 8.2, & 32)
Mineral Land Tax Act (as the act relates to the collection of public money, other than a fine, or to the administration of deposits & securities payable)
Mineral Tax Act (as the act relates to the collection of public money, other than a fine, or to the administration of deposits & securities payable)
Ministry of Forests & Range Act (as the act relates to the collection of public money, other than a fine, or to the administration of deposits & securities payable)
Motor Fuel Tax Act
Petroleum & Natural Gas Act (as the act relates to the collection of public money, other than a fine, or to the administration of deposits & securities payable; & ss. 74-77)
Property Transfer Tax Act
Range Act (as the act relates to the collection of public money, other than fines, & to the administration of deposits & securities payable)
School Act (as the act relates to the collection of public money, other than a fine, or to the administration of deposits & securities payable)
Sechelt Indian Government District Home Owner Grant Act
Social Service Tax Act
South Moresby Implementation Account Act (as the act relates to the collection of public money, other than a fine, or to the administration of deposits & securities payable)
Taxation (Rural Area) Act
Tobacco Tax Act
Tourist Accommodation (Assessment Relief) Act
Wildfire Act (as the act relates to the collection of public money, other than a fine, or to the administration of deposits & securities payable)

Minister, Small Business & Revenue & Minister Responsible for Deregulation, Hon. Kevin Krueger
250-356-6611, Fax: 250-356-8294,sbr.minister@gov.bc.ca; kevin.krueger.mla@leg.bc.ca
Deputy Minister, Bob de Faye
SBR.DeputyMinister@gov.bc.ca
Executive Director, Appeals & Litigation Branch, Julie Gagnon
250-387-5883
Executive Director, Property Assessment Services, Rob Fraser
250-356-7835

• British Columbia Assessment Authority(BCAA)
1537 Hillside Ave.
Victoria, BC V8T 4Y2
250-595-6211 Fax: 250-595-6222
info@bcassessment.ca
www.bcassessment.bc.ca
The British Columbia Assessment Authority is an independent, provincial Crown corporation. Governed by a Board of Directors, the role of BC Assessment is the production of annual property assessments for each property owner in British Columbia. Area offices are located across the province.

• Property Assessment Appeal Board(PAAB)
#10, 10551 Shellbridge Way
Richmond, BC V6X 2W9
604-775-1740 Fax: 604-775-1742 888-775-1740
office@paab.bc.ca
www.assessmentappeal.bc.ca
The Property Assessment Appeal Board is responsible for resolving appeals of assessments throughout British Columbia. The Board deals with appeal submissions from those who disagree with the Property Assessment Review Panel's decision on property assessment.

• Small Business BC
#82, 601 West Cordova St.
Vancouver, BC V6B 1G1
800-775-5525 Fax: 604-775-5520 800-667-2272TDD: 800-457-8466
askus@smallbusinessbc.ca
www.smallbusinessbc.ca
Small Business BC is a not-for-profit society, which was founded by British Columbia's Ministry of Small Business & Revenue & Western Economic Diversification Canada. The organization is a resource centre for business information & services in the province. The following are some of the services offered by Small Business BC: Business Bookstore, Library, & Information Services; Business Registration; Business Plan Advisory Services; Seminars; eBusiness Connection, Market Research Services; & Export Coaching.

Revenue Programs Division
Asst. Deputy Minister, Elan Symes
250-387-0664, Fax: 250-387-6218
Acting Executive Director, Consumer Taxation Programs, Pat Parkinson
604-660-6024
Executive Director, Income Taxation Branch, Ian Forman
250-387-3320
Executive Director, Property Taxation Branch, Neilane Mayhew
250-387-0532
Director, Mineral, Oil & Gas Revenue, Doug Stangeland
250-952-0194

Revenue Services Division
Asst. Deputy Minister, Karen Dellert
250-387-1158
Executive Director, Alliance Management Office, Shannon Lundquist
250-387-1510
Director, Receivables Management Branch, Dennis Forbes
250-356-8031
Director, Forest Revenue Branch, Pat Plunkett
250-356-7400

Strategic Initiatives & Administration Branch
Asst. Deputy Minister, John Powell
250-387-3693, Fax: 250-356-1333
Acting CIO & Executive Director, Michael Carpenter
250-356-1165
Acting Executive Director, Customer Service & Information Branch, Wayne Sparanese
250-356-0670
Director, Employee Development & Leadership, Elaine Jones
250-387-0595
Director, Special Investigations Branch, Walt Charlton
604-775-0733
Director, Strategic Planning & Performance Reporting Branch, Donna Selbee
250-356-0044

Small Business & Regulatory Reform
Acting Asst. Deputy Minister, Lindsay Kislock
250-356-1993
Executive Director, PST Review & Small Business Roundtable, Simone Decosse
250-387-0661
Executive Director, Regulatory Reform, Gail Greenwood
250-387-8709

Ministry of Tourism, Culture, & the Arts

PO Box 9071 Prov Govt, Victoria, BC V8W 9E9
250-953-4246, Fax: 250-953-4250, www.gov.bc.ca/tca

The following are the main responsibilities of the Ministry of Tourism, Culture, & the Arts: Aboriginal tourism; Archaeology; Arts & culture programs; Commercial & public back-country recreation; Film policy & classification; Forest recreation sites & trails; Heritage conservation; Recreational fish & wildlife recreation promotion; Resorts & alpine ski developments; & Tourism strategy.

Acts Administered:
Arts Council Act
Capital Commission Act
Forest & Range Practices Act (ss. 56, 57, 118 (2) (d), & 148; s. 58, except as it relates to the protection of a recreation resource & management of a public recreation use on Crown land, & except as
Heritage Conservation Act
Hotel Guest Registration Act
Hotel Keepers Act
Motor Vehicle (All Terrain) Act
Museum Act
Recreational Facility Act
Resort Timber Administration Act
Special Accounts Appropriation & Control Act (s. 9)
Tourism Act
Tourism British Columbia Act
Vancouver Tourism Levy Enabling Act

Minister, Tourism, Culture & the Arts, Hon. Kevin Krueger
TCA.Minister@gov.bc.ca
Deputy Minister, Lori Wanamaker
250-356-6981, Fax: 250-356-1195,Lori.Wanamaker@gov.bc.ca
Manager, Communications, David Greer
250-387-2799, Fax: 250-356-9829,david.greer@gov.bc.ca

• British Columbia Film Commission
#201, 865 Hornby St.
Vancouver, BC V6Z 2G3
604-660-2732 Fax: 604-660-4790
info@bcfilmcommission.com
www.bcfilmcommission.com
The British Columbia Film Commission's mission is to ensure that film & television production thrives for Canadian & international clients. As one of the largest production centres in North America, the province offers film producers & production companies a great range of services.

• BC Pavilion Corporation (PavCo)
777 Pacific Blvd.
Vancouver, BC V6B 4Y8
604-482-2200 Fax: 604-681-9017
info@bcpavco.com
www.bcpavco.com
A Provincial Crown Corporation of the Ministry of Tourism, Culture & The Arts, the BC Pavilion Corporation provides leadership in the meetings & events industry. It operates BC Place & The Vancouver Convention & Exhibition Centre.

• Provincial Capital Commission(PCC)
613 Pandora Ave.
Victoria, BC V8W 1N8
250-953-8800 Fax: 250-386-1303
info.pcc@bcpcc.com
www.bcpcc.com
A Crown agency, the Provincial Capital Commission works to raise awareness of the Capital's history & character. The Commission's operations are funded through commercial revenues from provincially-owned properties & heritage buildings in the Capital region.

• Royal BC Museum Corporation
675 Belleville St.
Victoria, BC V8W 9W2
250-356-7226 Fax: 250-387-5674 888-447-7977
reception@royalbcmuseum.bc.ca
www.royalbcmuseum.bc.ca
The Royal BC Museum Corporation was created through the proclamation of the Museum Act. It is British Columbia's provincial museum & archives.

• Tourism British Columbia
1803 Douglas St., 3rd Fl.
Victoria, BC V8W 9W5
250-356-6363
research@tourismbc.com; superhost@tourismbc.com
www.tourismbc.com
Other Communication: Vancouver Phone: 604-660-2861; Research & Planning Phone: 250-387-1567; SuperHost Programs Phone: 250-387-1711
Tourism British Columbia is a Crown corporation which provides information for industry & the media. Its goals are increases in revenue, economic benefits, & employment in British Columbia, through the promotion of development & growth in the tourism industry. The organization is accountable to the Minister of Tourism, Culture & The Arts.

Art & Culture Division
#1, 800 Johnson St., PO Box 9819 Prov Govt, Victoria, BC V8W 9W3
250-387-4484, Fax: 250-387-4099
Assistant Deputy Minister, Jane Milner
250-356-6967
Executive Director, BC Arts Council, Jeremy Long
250-356-1730, Fax: 250-387-4099,BCArtsCouncil@gov.bc.ca

Management Services Division
800 Johnson St., 6th Fl., PO Box 9842 Prov Govt, Victoria, BC V8W 9T2
250-387-8705, Fax: 250-387-7973
Assistant Deputy Minister, Shauna Brouwer
250-387-9180
Executive Director, Strategic Human Resources & Corporate Policy & Planning, Kim Russell
250-387-8976, Fax: 250-356-5395
Director, Information Systems, Debbie Fritz
250-356-0803, Fax: 250-387-1590
Director, Finance & Administrative Services, Jim MacAulay
250-387-9179, Fax: 250-387-8772
Director, Information, Privacy, & Records, Danine Leduc
250-387-7917, Fax: 250-387-8038

Tourism Division
800 Johnson St., 5th Fl., PO Box 9846, Victoria, BC V8W 9T2
250-952-6204, Fax: 250-356-1195
Assistant Deputy Minister, Peter Walters

Executive Director, Tourism Development, John Willow
250-952-0891, Fax: 250-952-0151
Director, Archaeology, Justine Batten
250-953-3355, Fax: 250-953-3340
Director, Recreation, Sites, & Trails, Bill Marshall
250-387-8382, Fax: 250-356-2842
Director, Heritage,
250-356-1431, Fax: 250-356-7796,Heritage@gov.bc.ca
Manager, Aboriginal Tourism & Resort Development, Drew Frymire
250-371-3905
Acting Manager, Tenure Administration, Barb Duncan
250-371-3938, Fax: 250-377-2383

Ministry of Healthy Living & Sport

PO Box 9067 Prov Govt, Victoria, BC V8W 9E2
250-387-3504, Fax: 250-387-3420,
Feedback@gov.bc.ca
www.gov.bc.ca/hls

Other Communication: Public Affairs Bureau Phone: 250-812-4012

The main responsibilities of the Ministry of Healthy Living & Sport are as follows: Aboriginal health promotion; ActNow BC; Addictions services promotion; Chronic disease prevention; Communicable diseases prevention; Dial-a-Dietician; Health promotion & protection; Healthy living; Provincial Health Officer; Provincial Nutritionist; Public health planning; Sports & recreation; Water & air monitoring & reporting; & Women & seniors.

Acts Administered:
Drinking Water Protection Act
Food Safety Act
Milk Industry Act (s. 12, except in respect of tank milk receiver licences)
Public Toilet Act
Special Accounts Appropriation & Control Act
Tobacco Control Act
Tobacco Damages & Health Care Costs Recovery Act
Venereal Disease Act

Minister, Healthy Living & Sport, Hon. Mary Polak
mary.polak.mla@leg.bc.ca
Deputy Minister, Grant Main
250-952-1164, Fax: 250-952-1390
Acting Director, Program Integration & Strategic Human Resources, Amanda Morris
250-952-1854

• BC Games Society
990 Fort St.
Victoria, BC V8V 3K2
250-387-1375 Fax: 250-387-4489
info@bcgames.org
www.bcgames.org
The BC Games Society is incorporated under the Societies Act. With responsibility to British Columbia's Minister of Healthy Living & Sport, the Crown Agency works with its partners to provide event management leadership. The Society strives to create development opportunities for athletes, coaches, & officials, sport organizations, & host communities.

ActNow BC

800 Johnson St., 1st Fl., PO Box 9898 Prov Govt, Victoria, BC V8W 1N3
Fax: 250-387-8720

Assistant Deputy Minister, ActNow BC, David Galbraith
250-356-7139, David.Galbraith@gov.bc.ca
Executive Director, Nancy Bain
250-387-6922
Director, Del Nyberg
250-356-9002
Director, Performance Management, Marilyn Shinto
250-356-6995
Director, Marketing, Lisa Stevens
250-952-6731

Office of the Assisted Registrar

#300, 1275 West 6th Ave., Vancouver, BC V6H 1A6
604-714-3378, Fax: 604-733-5996, 866-714-3378
info@alregistrar.bc.ca
www.health.gov.bc.ca/assisted

Assisted Living Registrar, Susan Adams
604-714-3378

Office of the Provincial Health Officer

1515 Blanshard St., 4th Fl., Victoria, BC V8W 3C8
250-952-1330, Fax: 250-952-1362

Provincial Health Officer,Dr. Perry Kendall
Perry.Kendall@gov.bc.ca
Deputy Provincial Health Officer,Dr. Eric Young
250-952-1329
Physician Advisor, Aboriginal Health,Dr. Evan Adams
Provincial Drinking Water Officer, Barry Boettger
250-952-1572

Population & Public Health

1515 Blanshard St., 4th Fl., Victoria, BC V8W 3C8

Assistant Deputy Minister, Andrew G. Hazlewood
Executive Director, Aboriginal Health, Deborah Schwartz
250-952-3151, Fax: 250-952-3151
Executive Director, Business Operations & Surveillance, Tom Gregory
250-952-1467, Fax: 250-952-1713
Executive Director, Communicable Disease & Addictions Prevention, Warren O'Briain
250-952-2481, Fax: 250-952-1570
Executive Director, Health Protection, Tim Lambert
250-952-1987, Fax: 250-952-1713
Acting Executive Director, Healthy Children, Women & Seniors, Joan Geber
250-952-3678, Fax: 250-952-1570
Executive Director, Healthy Living / Chronic Disease Prevention, Laurie Woodland
250-952-2847, Fax: 250-952-1713
Acting Director, Women's, Maternal & Children's Health, Carla Springinotic
250-952-1364, Fax: 250-952-1570

Sport Branch

800 Johnson St., 1st Fl., PO Box 9820 Prov Govt, Victoria, BC V8W 9W3
Fax: 250-387-8720

Director,Margo, Ross
250-356-7168
Assistant Director, Graham McKay
250-356-0364

Women's, Seniors' & Community Services

800 Johnson St., 6th Fl., PO Box 9824, Victoria, BC V8W 9W4
250-953-3005, Fax: 250-387-7935

Executive Director, Seniors' & Women's Partnership & Information,Anne, Horan
250-387-2268, Fax: 250-356-0542
Manager, Aging Well in BC, Silas Brownsey
250-356-0461, Fax: 250-387-1407

British Columbia Transmission Corporation

Four Bentall Centre, #1100, 1055 Dunsmuir St., PO Box 49260, Vancouver, BC V7X 1V5
604-699-7300, Fax: 604-699-7333, 866-647-3334
contact.us@bctc.com
www.bctc.com

Other Communication: Media inquiries: 604-699-7445; Customer Services: 604-699-7391; Settlements & Billing: 604-699-7383; Emergencies: 1-888-769-3766; Before Digging: 1-800-474-6886

The British Columbia Transmission Corporation is a provincial Crown corporation. In accordance with the Transmission Corporation Act, the Minister for the Crown holds 100 percent of the shares of the Corporation. Its main activities include the planning, operation, & maintenance of British Columbia's publicly-owned electrical transmission system.

President/CEO, Jane Peverett
Chief Financial Officer & Vice-President, Corporate Services, Janet P. Woodruff
Vice-President, System Operations, Martin Huang
Vice-President & General Counsel, John Irving
Vice-President, Customer & Strategy Development, Doug Little
Vice-President, Major Projects, Bruce Barrett
Vice-President, System Planning & Asset Management, Julius Pataky
Director, Human Resources, Scott oogemans
Corporate Controller, Elizabeth Hong

Ministry of Transportation & Infrastructure

940 Blanshard St., PO Box 9850 Prov Govt, Victoria, BC V8W 9T5
250-387-3198, Fax: 250-356-7706,
tran.webmaster@gov.bc.ca
www.gov.bc.ca/tran

In carrying out its mission to move people & goods safely in British Columbia, the Ministry of Transportation & Infrastructure is responsible for the following: Transportation planning & policy; Highway construction & maintenance; Commercial vehicle safety & inspections; Infrastructure grants; & Port & airport development.

Acts Administered:
British Columbia Rail Benefits (First Nations) Trust Act
British Columbia Railway Act
British Columbia Transit Act
Coastal Ferry Act (Parts 1-3; & ss. 71, & 74-77)
Commercial Transport Act (s. 3; ss. 1, 4, 5, 8, 9, 11, & 12, as they relate to highway infrastructure & weigh scales; & ss. 1, 4, 5, 8, 9, 11, 12, & 14, as they relate to Commercial Vehicle Safety & E
Industrial Roads Act
Land Title Act (s. 77.2)
Motor Vehicle Act (ss. 116.1, 118.94-118.992, 119-125.1, 126-135.1, 136-148.1, 149-169.1, 170-182, 185-209, 212-212.2, 213, 214, 216-218, 219, 223, 237, 239-240; ss. 1, 75-76, 78, 83, 83.1, 183 & 210;
Passenger Transportation Act
Public Works Agreement Act
Railway Act (ss. 1-5, 14-27, 30, 32, 34-63, 135, 136, 138, 161, 180, 183, 185 (1), (2) & (5)-(10), 186, 187, 197 (1)-(6), 198, 204-207, 225, 229-232, 253, 255-257, & 282)
Railway Safety Act
Significant Projects Streamlining Act
South Coast British Columbia Transportation Authority Act
Transport of Dangerous Goods Act
Transportation Act
Transportation Investment Act

Minister,Hon. Kevin Falcon
250-387-1978, Fax:
250-356-2290,Minister.Transportation@gov.bc.ca; kevin.falcon.mla@leg.bc.ca
Deputy Minister, John Dyble
250-387-3280, Fax:
250-387-6431,DeputyMinister.Transportation.gov.bc.ca
Director, Human Resources, Marilyn Wargo
250-387-7823, Fax: 250-387-5334
Project Director, Climate Action Program, Dave Duncan
250-387-6742, Fax: 250-387-6431

• British Columbia Ferry Services Inc.

• British Columbia Transit
520 Gorge Rd. East
PO Box 610
Victoria, BC V8W 2P3
250-385-2551 Fax: 250-995-5639
www.bctransit.com
A provincial crown agency, BC Transit coordinates the delivery of public transportation in British Columbia, outside the Greater Vancouver Regional District. The corporation's specific role, in accordance with the BC Transit Act, is the planning, acquisition, construction, operation, & maintenance of public passenger transportation systems & rail systems.

• Passenger Transportation Board
#202, 940 Blanshard St.
PO Box 9850 Prov Govt
Victoria, BC V8W 9T5
250-953-3777 Fax: 250-953-3788
ptboard@gov.bc.ca
www.ptboard.bc.ca
The Passenger Transportation Board carries out its responsibilities in accordance with the Passenger Transportation Act. The independent tribunal makes decisions regarding the operation of passenger directed vehicles and inter-city buses in British Columbia.

Finance & Management Services Department

#5B, 940 Blanshard St., PO Box 9850, Victoria, BC V8W 9T5
250-387-3100, Fax: 250-387-5012

Assistant Deputy Minister, Finance & Management Services, Sheila A. Taylor
Director, Transit, Jim Hester
250-387-6024, Fax: 250-387-3059
Chief Information Officer & Director, Information Management, Bob Buckingham
250-953-3111, Fax: 250-356-7184

Highways Department

940 Blanshard St., PO Box 9850, Victoria, BC V8W 9T5
250-387-3260, Fax: 250-387-6431

Assistant Deputy Minister, Mike Proudfoot
Executive Director, Properties & Business Management, John Dowler
250-387-7767, Fax: 250-356-8767
Director, Construction & Maintenance, Rodney Chapman
250-387-7626, Fax: 250-356-8143
Director, Rehabilitation & Maintenance, Reg Fredrickson
250-387-7627, Fax: 250-356-7276
Director, Commercial Vehicle Safety & Enforcement, Greg Gilks
250-953-4024, Fax: 250-952-0578
Regional Director, South Coast Regional Office, Tracy Cooper
604-660-8205, 877-660-8218,Fax:
604-660-0350,Tracy.Cooper@gov.bc.ca
Regional Director, Southern Interior Regional Office, Kevin Richter
250-828-4220, Fax: 250-828-4204,Kevin.Richter@gov.bc.ca,
Regional Director, Northern Regional Office, Shanna Mason
250-565-6479, Fax: 250-565-6065

Deputy Director, Commercial Vehicle Safety & Enforcement, Dawn Major
250-953-4024, Fax: 250-952-0578
Chief Engineer, Dirk Nyland
250-387-2310, Fax: 250-387-7735

Partnerships Department
#5A, 940 Blanshard St., PO Box 9850 Prov Govt, Victoria, BC V8W 9T5
250-356-0517, Fax: 250-387-6431
Assistant Deputy Minister, Frank Blasetti
250-356-1403, Frank.Blasetti@gov.bc.ca
Executive Director, Gateway Program, Geoff Freer
604-775-0489, Fax: 604-775-0348
Executive Project Director, Sea to Sky Highway Improvement Project, Peter Milburn
604-775-1152, Fax: 604-775-1144
Acting Director, Partnership & Project Development, Bob Steele
250-356-2051, Fax: 250-356-2112
Director, Operations Transitions & Procurement, Bruce McAllister
250-356-7108, Fax: 250-356-2112

Transportation Planning & Policy Department
#5C, 940 Blanshard St., PO Box 9850 Prov Govt, Victoria, BC V8W 9T5
250-387-5062, Fax: 250-387-6431
Assistant Deputy Minister, Sandra Carroll
Sandra.Carroll@gov.bc.ca
Executive Director, Infrastructure Development, Kirk Handrahan
250-952-0678, Fax: 250-952-0688
Executive Director, Pacific Gateway, Lisa Gow
250-387-2672, Fax: 250-387-5812
Executive Director, Planning & Programming, David Marr
250-356-2100, Fax: 250-953-4974
Director, Highway Planning, Jim Hester
250-387-6024
Director, Marine, Nancy Merston
250-356-0297, Fax: 250-356-0897
Director, Project Management Support Services, Svein Haugen
250-356-0515, Fax: 250-953-4974
Director, Transportation Policy, Kirsten Pedersen
250-387-0882, Fax: 250-356-0897
Director, Project Delivery, Border Infrastructure Program, John Bodnarchuk
250-751-3287, Fax: 250-953-4975
Director & Registrar, Passenger Transportation, Tom Greene
604-453-4278, 888-453-4280,Fax: 604-453-4253,passengertransportationbr@gov.bc.ca; Tom.Greene@gov.bc.ca, Other Communications: URL: www.th.gov.bc.ca/rpt
Deputy Registrar & Manager, Business Standards & Planning, Passenger Transportation, Doris Sundquist
604-453-4235, 888-453-4280,Fax: 604-453-4253,passengertransportationbr@gov.bc.ca

British Columbia Utilities Commission

900 Howe St., 6th Fl., PO Box 250, Vancouver, BC V6Z 2N3
604-660-4700, Fax: 604-660-1102, 800-663-1385
commission.secretary@bcuc.com
www.bcuc.com

The British Columbia Utilities Commission is an independent regulatory agency of the Provincial Government of British Columbia. The Commission's regulates the province's natural gas & electricity utilities. Other activities of the Utilities Commission include the regulation of universal compulsory automobile insurance & intra-provincial pipelines.

Acts Administered:
Utilities Commission Act

Chair/CEO, Len Kelsey
604-660-4757
Commission Secretary, Erica Hamilton
604-660-4727, commission.secretary@bcuc.com; Erica.Hamilton@bcuc.com
Director, Strategic Services, James W. Fraser
604-660-4740
Director, Rates & Finance, Philip W. Nakoneshny
604-660-4736
Director, Engineering & Energy Markets, J. Brian Williston
604-660-4773

Workers' Compensation Board of British Columbia

PO Box 5350 Terminal, Vancouver, BC V6B 5L5
604-276-3100, Fax: 604-244-6490, 888-621-7233
www.worksafebc.com

Other Communication: Head Office Physical Address: 6951 Westminster Hwy., Richmond; Health care benefits: 604-276-3085; Employer Service Centre: 604-244-6181; Compensation: 604-231-8888

The Workers' Compensation Board of British Columbia, or WorkSafeBC, assists workers & employers in British Columbia by promoting health & safety in workplaces. WorkSafeBC's key repsonsiblities are as follows: Consultation with & education of employers & workers; Monitoring compliance with the Occupational Health & Safety Regulation; & Provision of return-to-work compensation, rehabilitation, health care benefits, & other services for parties affected by work-related injuries or diseases.

Chair, Roslyn Kunin
President/CEO, David Anderson
Chief Financial Officer, Finance Division, Steve Barnett
Vice-President, Human Resources & Facilities, Pamela Cohen
Vice-President, Policy, Investigations & Review, Roberta Ellis
Vice-President, Worker & Employer Services, Diana Miles
General Counsel & Secretary, Ed Bates

Government of Manitoba

Seat of Government: Legislative Building, Rm. 237, Winnipeg, MB R3C 0V8
204-945-3636, Fax: 204-948-2507,
clerkla@leg.gov.mb.ca
www.gov.mb.ca

The Province of Manitoba entered Confederation July 15, 1870. It has an area of 647,797 km2, & the StatsCan census population in 2008 was 1,196,291.

Office of the Lieutenant Governor

Legislative Building, #235, 450 Broadway Ave., Winnipeg, MB R3C 0V8
204-945-2753, Fax: 204-945-4329,
ltgov@leg.gov.mb.ca
www.lg.gov.mb.ca

Lieutenant Governor,Hon. Philip S. Lee, C.M., O.M.

Office of the Premier

Legislative Building, #204, 450 Broadway Ave., Winnipeg, MB R3C 0V8
204-945-3714, Fax: 204-949-1484,
premier@leg.gov.mb.ca
www.gov.mb.ca

Premier,Hon. Greg Selinger
204-945-3714, Fax: 204-949-1484,
Deputy Premier,Hon. Rosann Wowchuk
204-945-3952, Fax: 204-945-6057
Clerk of the Executive Council & Cabinet Secretary, Paul Vogt
204-945-5640, Fax: 204-945-8390
Chief of Staff, Michael Balagus
204-945-8753
Administrative Officer, Sonia Stubler
204-945-1494
Press Secretary to Cabinet, Rachel Morgan
204-945-1494

Manitoba Government Office - Ottawa
#908, 130 Albert St., Ottawa, ON K1P 5G4
613-233-4228, Fax: 613-233-3509
Reports to the Clerk of the Executive Council on Federal-Provincial issues & to the Minister of Intergovernmental Affairs & Trade on business & procurement issues.
Senior Representative, Jim Stewart

Executive Council

Legislative Building, 450 Broadway Ave., Winnipeg, MB R3C 0V8
www.gov.mb.ca/minister

Premier & President, Executive Council; Minister, Federal-Provincial Relations; Minister responsible for Francophone affairs,Hon. Greg Selinger
204-945-3714, Fax: 204-949-1484,premier@leg.gov.mb.ca
Minister, Infrastructure & Transportation; Minister responsible for Emergency Measures, Hon. Steve Ashton
204-945-3723, Fax: 204-945-7610,minmit@leg.gov.mb.ca
Minister, Innovation, Energy & Mines, Hon. David Walter Chomiak
204-945-5356, Fax: 204-948-2692,miniem@leg.gov.mb.ca
Deputy Premier; Minister, Finance; Minister responsible for the Civil Service; Minister responsible for the Manitoba Securities Commission, Hon. Rosann Wowchuk
204-945-3952, Fax: 204-945-6057,minfin@leg.gov.mb.ca
Minister, Family Services & Consumer Affairs, Hon. Gord Mackintosh
204-945-4173, Fax: 204-945-5149,minfam@leg.gov.mb.ca
Deputy Premier; Minister, Aboriginal & Northern Affairs; Minister responsible for sport, Aboriginal Education & East Side Road Authority, Hon. Eric Robinson
204-945-3719, Fax: 204-945-8374,minna@leg.gov.mb.ca
Minister, Advanced Education & Literacy; Minister responsible for International Education, Hon. Diane McGifford
204-945-0825, Fax: 204-948-2216,minaed@leg.gov.mb.ca
Minister, Local Government, Hon. Ron Lemieux
204-945-3788, Fax: 204-945-1383,minlg@leg.gov.mb.ca
Minister, Agriculture, Food & Rural Initiatives, Hon. Stan Struthers
204-945-3722, Fax: 204-945-3470,minagr@leg.gov.mb.ca
Minister, Education, Hon. Nancy Allan
204-945-3720, Fax: 204-945-1291,minedu@leg.gov.mb.ca
Minister, Healthy Living, Youth & Seniors; Minister responsible for Healthy Child Manitoba, Mental Health & Recreation, Hon. Jim Rondeau
204-945-1373, Fax: 204-945-2703,Minhliv@leg.gov.mb.ca
Minister, Entrepreneurship, Training & Trade, Hon. Peter Bjornson
204-945-0067, Fax: 204-945-4882,minett@leg.gov.mb.ca
Minister, Water Stewardship, Hon. Christine Melnick
204-945-1133, Fax: 204-948-2684,minwsd@leg.gov.mb.ca
Minister, Health, Hon. Theresa Oswald
204-945-3731, Fax: 204-945-0441,minhlt@leg.gov.mb.ca
Minister, Housing & Community Development; Minister responsible, Neighbourhoods Alive!, Community Places & Co-operative Development, Hon. Kerri Irvin-Ross
204-945-6190, Fax: 204-945-1491,minhcd@leg.gov.mb.ca
Attorney General; Minister, Justice; Minister responsible for Constitutional Affairs, Hon. Andrew Swan
204-945-3728, Fax: 204-945-2517,minjus@leg.gov.mb.ca
Minister, Labour & Immigration; Minister responsible for the Status of Women & Persons with Disabilities, Hon. Jennifer Howard
204-945-4079, Fax: 204-945-8312,minlab@leg.gov.mb.ca
Minister, Culture, Heritage & Tourism, Hon. Flor Marcelino
204-945-3729, Fax: 204-945-5223,mincht@leg.gov.mb.ca
Government House Leader; Minister, Conservation; Minister responsible for Recycling and Environmental Education, Climate change & GreenInitiatives, Hon. Bill Blaikie
204-945-3730, Fax: 204-945-3586,mincon@leg.gov.mb.ca

Cabinet Office
Legislative Assistant to the Premier, Bidhu Jha
204-945-6021, bjha@leg.gov.mb.ca
Legislative Assistant, Agriculture, Food & Rural Initiatives, Thomas Nevakshonoff
204-945-4966, tnevakshonoff@leg.gov.mb.ca
Legislative Assistant, Brandon & Western Manitoba, Drew Caldwell
Legislative Assistant, Culture, Heritage, Tourism & Sport, Flor Marcelino
Legislative Assistant, Family Services & Housing, Doug Martindale
204-945-2645, dmartindale@leg.gov.mb.ca
Legislative Assistant, Labour & Immigration, Justice, Marilyn Brick

Cabinet Committees
Community & Economic Development Committee Treasury Board Committee

Legislative Assembly

c/o Clerk's Office, Legislative Bldg., #237, 450 Broadway, Winnipeg, MB R3C 0V8
204-945-3636, Fax: 204-948-2507,
clerkla@leg.gov.mb.ca
www.gov.mb.ca/legislature

Clerk of the Legislative Assembly, Patricia Chaychuk
Speaker of the House,Hon. George Hickes
Chief Electoral Officer, Michael T. Green
204-945-3225, 866-628-6837,Fax: 204-945-6011,election@elections.mb.ca
Ombudsman, Irene Hamilton
204-982-9130, 800-665-0531,Fax: 204-942-7803,ombudsma@ombudsman.mb.ca
Commissioner, Conflict of Interest, Ron Perozzo
204-948-1018, Fax: 204-945-4585
Children's Advocate,Ms. Billie Schibler
204-988-7440, 800-263-7146,Fax: 204-988-7472,bschibler@childrensadvocate.mb.ca
Law Clerk, Valerie Perry
204-945-1727, Fax: 204-945-1940,valerie.perry@gov.mb.ca

Government Caucus Office (New Democratic Party)
Legislative Bldg., #234, 450 Broadway Ave., Winnipeg, MB R3C 0V8
204-945-3710, Fax: 204-948-2005,
www.ndpcaucus.mb.ca

Premier & Leader,Hon. Greg Selinger
204-945-3714, Fax: 204-949-1484,premier@leg.gov.mb.ca
Deputy Premier,Hon. Rosann Wowchuk
204-945-3722, Fax: 204-945-3470
Government House Leader,Hon. David Walter Chomiak
204-945-3728, Fax: 204-945-2517

Progressive Conservative Caucus Office
Legislative Building, #227, 450 Broadway Ave., Winnipeg, MB R3C 0V8
204-945-3709, Fax: 204-945-1284, 800-282-8069
pccaucus@leg.gov.mb.ca
www.manpc.mb.ca
Leader of the Opposition, Hugh McFadyen
204-945-3593, Fax:
204-945-1299,hugh.mcfadyen@leg.gov.mb.ca
Communications Officer, Liz Peters
204-945-5519, Fax: 204-945-5921,liz.peters@leg.gov.mb.ca

Office of the Liberal Party of Canada in Manitoba
635 Broadway Ave., Winnipeg, MB R3C 0X1
204-988-9380, Fax: 204-284-1492,
manager@manitobaliberals.ca
mlp.manitobaliberals.ca
Leader,Hon. Jon Gerrard
204-945-5194, Fax:
204-948-3220,jon.gerrard@leg.gov.mb.ca

Legislative Committees
Legislative Building, #249, 450 Broadway Ave., Winnipeg, MB R3C 0V8
Fax: 204-945-0038
Contact, Committee Clerks, Rick Yarish
204-945-4729, rick.yarish@leg.gov.mb.ca

Thirty-ninth Legislature - Manitoba

Legislative Building, 450 Broadway Ave., Winnipeg, MB R3C 0V8
204-945-3636, Fax: 204-948-2507,
clerkla@leg.gov.mb.ca
www.gov.mb.ca/legislature
Last General Election: May 22, 2007. Legal Duration: 5 Years. Party Standings (December 2007): New Democratic Party (NDP) - 36; Progressive Conservative (PC) - 19; Liberal (Lib.) - 1; Vacant - 1; Total - 57.Salaries, Indemnities & Allowances (April 2008): Members' basic annual indemnity - $83,722. In addition to this annual indemnity are the following annual salaries: Premier - $68,425; Cabinet Ministers (with portfolio) - $44,942; Cabiniet Ministers (without portfolio) - $39,837; Leader of the Official Opposition - $44,942; Leader of a Recognized Opposition Party - $39,837; Speaker - $44,942; Deputy Speaker - $8,852; Government House Leader - $8,852; House Leader of the Official Opposition - $6,323; House Leader of a Recognized Opposition Party - $5,060; Government Whip - $6,323; Whip of the Official Opposition - $5,060; Whip of a Recognized Opposition Party - $3,796; Caucus Chair - $5,450; Permanent Chairperson, Standing or Special Committees - $3,796. The following is a list of members of the legislative assembly, with their constituency, party affiliation, & contact information
Members
Hon. Nancy Allan, MLA, St. Vital MB, New Democratic Party
204-945-3720, Fax: 204-945-1291,minedu@leg.gov.mb.ca
Rob Altemeyer, MLA, Wolseley MB, New Democratic Party
204-945-5985, Fax:
204-948-2005,rob.altemeyer@leg.gov.mb.ca
Hon. Steve Ashton, Thompson MB, New Democratic Party
204-945-3723, Fax: 204-945-7610,minmit@leg.gov.mb.ca
Hon. Peter Bjornson, Gimli MB, New Democratic Party
204-945-3720, Fax: 204-945-1291,minett@leg.gov.mb.ca
Sharon Blady, Kirkfield Park MB, New Democratic Party
204-945-0932, Fax:
204-948-2005,sharon.blady@leg.gov.mb.ca
Hon. Bill Blaikie, Elmwood MB, New Democratic Party
204-945-3730, Fax: 204-945-3586,mincon@leg.gov.mb.ca
Rick Borotsik, Brandon West MB, PC
204-945-8165, Fax:
204-948-2092,rick.borotsik@leg.gov.mb.ca
Erna Braun, Rossmere MB, New Democratic Party
204-945-7349, Fax:
204-948-2005,erna.braun@leg.gov.mb.ca
Marilyn Brick, St. Norbert MB, New Democratic Party
204-945-5479, Fax:
204-948-2005,marilyn.brick@leg.gov.mb.ca
Stuart Briese, Ste. Rose MB, PC
204-945-4698, Fax:
204-948-2092,stuart.briese@leg.gov.mb.ca
Drew Caldwell, Brandon East MB, New Democratic Party
204-945-3081, Fax:
204-948-2005,drew.caldwell@leg.gov.mb.ca
Hon. David Walter Chomiak, Kildonan MB, New Democratic Party
204-945-5356, Fax: 204-945-2692,miniem@leg.gov.mb.ca
Cliff Cullen, Turtle Mountain MB, PC
204-945-5083, Fax: 204-945-5921,cliff.cullen@leg.gov.mb.ca
Len Derkach, Russell MB, PC
204-945-4812, Fax:
204-948-2092,len.derkach@leg.gov.mb.ca
Gregory Dewar, Selkirk MB, New Democratic Party
204-945-0143, Fax:
204-948-2005,greg.dewar@leg.gov.mb.ca
Myrna Driedger, Charleswood MB, PC
204-945-3280, Fax:
204-945-5921,myrna.driedger@leg.gov.mb.ca
Peter George Dyck, Pembina MB, PC
204-945-4469, Fax: 204-948-2092,peter.dyck@leg.gov.mb.ca
Ralph Eichler, Lakeside MB, PC
204-945-0541, Fax:
204-948-2092,ralph.eichler@leg.gov.mb.ca
David Faurschou, Portage la Prairie MB, PC
204-945-8088, Fax:
204-942-6613,david.faurschou@leg.gov.mb.ca
Hon. Jon Gerrard, River Heights MB, Liberal
204-945-5194, Fax:
204-948-3220,jon.gerrard@leg.gov.mb.ca
Kelvin Goertzen, Steinbach MB, PC
204-945-0231, Fax:
204-942-6613,kelvin.goertzen@leg.gov.mb.ca
Cliff Graydon, Emerson MB, PC
204-945-5639, Fax:
204-942-6613,cliff.graydon@leg.gov.mb.ca
Gerald Hawranik, Lac du Bonnet MB, PC
204-945-2190, Fax:
204-945-5921,gerald.hawranik@leg.gov.mb.ca
Hon. George Hickes, Point Douglas MB, New Democratic Party
204-945-3706, Fax:
204-945-1443,george.hickes@leg.gov.mb.ca
Hon. Jennifer Howard, Fort Rouge MB, New Democratic Party
204-945-4079, Fax: 204-945-8312,minlab@leg.gov.mb.ca
Hon. Kerri Irvin-Ross, Fort Garry MB, New Democratic Party
204-945-6190, Fax: 204-945-1491,minhcd@leg.gov.mb.ca
Gerard Jennissen, Flin Flon MB, New Democratic Party
204-945-2936, Fax:
204-948-2005,gerard.jennissen@leg.gov.mb.ca
Bidhu Jha, Radisson MB, New Democratic Party
204-945-6021, Fax: 204-948-2005,bidhu.jha@leg.gov.mb.ca
Bonnie Korzeniowski, St. James MB, New Democratic Party
204-945-7510, Fax:
204-948-2005,bonnie.korzeniowski@leg.gov.mb.ca
Kevin Lamourex, Inkster MB, Liberal
204-945-5194, Fax:
204-948-3220,kevin.lamoureux@leg.gov.mb.ca
Hon. Ron Lemieux, La Verendrye MB, New Democratic Party
204-945-3788, Fax: 204-945-1383,minlg@leg.gov.mb.ca
Hon. Gord Mackintosh, St. Johns MB, New Democratic Party
204-945-4173, Fax: 204-945-5149,minfam@leg.gov.mb.ca
Larry Maguire, Arthur-Virden MB, PC
204-945-4975, Fax:
204-948-2092,larry.maguire@leg.gov.mb.ca
Hon. Flor Marcelino, Wellington MB, New Democratic Party
204-945-3729, Fax: 204-945-5229,mincht@leg.gov.mb.ca
Doug Martindale, Burrows MB, New Democratic Party
204-945-2645, Fax:
204-948-2005,doug.martindale@leg.gov.mb.ca
Hugh McFadyen, Fort Whyte MB, PC
204-945-3593, Fax:
204-945-1299,hugh.mcfadyen@leg.gov.mb.ca
Hon. Diane McGifford, Lord Roberts MB, New Democratic Party
204-945-0825, Fax: 204-948-2216,minaed@leg.gov.mb.ca
Hon. Christine Melnick, Riel MB, New Democratic Party
204-945-1133, Fax: 204-948-2684,minwsd@leg.gov.mb.ca
Bonnie Mitchelson, River East MB, PC
204-945-0008, Fax:
204-942-6613,bonnie.mitchelson@leg.gov.mb.ca
Thomas G. Nevakshonoff, Interlake MB, New Democratic Party
204-945-4966, Fax:
204-948-2005,tom.nevakshonoff@leg.gov.mb.ca
Hon. Theresa Oswald, Seine River Mb, New Democratic Party
204-945-3731, Fax: 204-945-0441,minhlt@leg.gov.mb.ca
Blaine Pedersen, Carman MB, PC
204-945-7909, Fax:
204-948-2092,blaine.pedersen@leg.gov.mb.ca
Daryl Gary Reid, Transcona MB, New Democratic Party
204-945-0774, Fax: 204-948-2005,daryl.reid@leg.gov.mb.ca
Hon. Eric Robinson, Rupertsland MB, New Democratic Party
204-945-3719, Fax: 204-945-8374,minna@leg.gov.mb.ca
Hon. Jim Rondeau, Assiniboia MB, New Democratic Party
204-945-1373, Fax: 204-948-2703,minhliv@leg.gov.mb.ca
Leanne Rowat, Minnedosa MB, PC
204-945-0258, Fax:
204-942-6613,leanne.rowat@leg.gov.mb.ca
Mohinder Saran, The Maples MB, New Democratic Party
204-945-3153, Fax:
204-948-2005,mohinder.saran@leg.gov.mb.ca
Ron Schuler, Springfield MB, PC
204-945-4321, Fax:
204-942-6613,ron.schuler@leg.gov.mb.ca
Erin Selby, Southdale MB, New Democratic Party
204-945-1190, Fax: 204-948-2005,erin.selby@leg.gov.mb.ca,
Hon. Gregory F. Selinger, St. Boniface MB, New Democratic Party
204-945-3417, Fax: 204-949-1484,premier@leg.gov.mb.ca
Heather Stefanson, Tuxedo MB, PC
204-945-0827, Fax:
204-945-5921,heather.stefanson@leg.gov.mb.ca
Hon. Stan Struthers, Dauphin-Roblin MB, New Democratic Party
204-945-3722, Fax: 204-945-3470,minagr@leg.gov.mb.ca
Hon. Andrew Swan, Minto MB, New Democratic Party
204-945-3728, Fax: 204-945-2517,minjus@leg.gov.mb.ca
Mavis Taillieu, Morris MB, PC
204-945-3525, Fax:
204-942-6613,mavis.taillieu@leg.gov.mb.ca
Frank Whitehead, The Pas MB, New Democratic Party
204-945-1696, Fax:
204-945-2005,frank.whitehead@leg.gov.mb.ca
Matt Wiebe, Concordia MB, New Democratic Party
204-945-6244, Fax:
204-948-2005,matt.wiebe@leg.gov.mb.ca
Hon. Rosann Wowchuk, Swan River MB, New Democratic Party
204-945-3952, Fax: 204-945-6057,minfin@leg.gov.mb.ca

Manitoba Government Departments & Agencies

Manitoba Aboriginal & Northern Affairs

59 Elizabeth Dr., PO Box 37, Thompson, MB R8N 1X4
204-677-6607, Fax: 204-677-6753,
amartin@gov.mb.ca
www.gov.mb.ca/ana/
To improve the quality of life & opportunities for Aboriginal & Northern people. To facilitate better services, opportunities & results for Manitoba's Aboriginal & northern people. Goals are: to support the mental, emotional, physical & spiritual health of northern communities & Aboriginal people; to resolve outstanding provincial obligations to Aboriginal/northern communities; to foster self-determination, accountability & sustainable growth; to strengthen the participation of Aboriginal & northern people in Manitoba's economy
Acts Administered:
Northern Affairs Act
Planning Act
Minister,Hon. Oscar Lathlin
204-945-3719, Fax: 204-954-8374,minna@leg.gov.mb.ca
Deputy Minister, Harvey Bostrom
204-945-0565, Fax: 204-945-1256,dmna@leg.gov.mb.ca
Director, Finance & Administrative Services, Rene Gagnon
204-677-6609, Fax: 204-677-6753,rgagnon@gov.mb.ca
Executive Director, Local Government Development Division, Freda Albert
• Communities Economic Development Fund
#100, 23 Station Rd.
Thompson, MB R8N 0N6
204-778-4138 Fax: 204-778-4313 800-561-4315
www.cedf.mb.ca

Aboriginal Affairs Secretariat
#200, 500 Portage Ave., Winnipeg, MB R3C 3X1
204-945-2510, Fax: 204-945-3689
Executive Director, Joe Morriseau
204-945-3689, Fax: 204-945-3689,jmorrissea@gov.mb.ca

Agreements Management
#200, 500 Portage Ave., Winnipeg, MB R3C 3X1
204-945-8337, Fax: 204-945-3689
Director, David Hicks
204-945-2506, Fax: 204-945-3689,dhicks@gov.mb.ca

Local Government Development Division
59 Elizabeth Dr., PO Box 33, Thompson, MB R8N 1X4
204-677-6794, Fax: 204-677-6525
Provides support to 50 northern & remote communities, including public works, environmental services, infrastructure development. Promotes cooperative, community-driven sustainable development
Executive Director, Freda Albert
204-677-6795, falbert@gov.mb.ca
Director, Program Planning & Development, Jeff Gordon
204-945-1713, jgordon@gov.mb.ca

Regional Offices:

Dauphin
Provincial Bldg., 27 Second Ave. SW, PO Box 15, Dauphin, MB R7N 3E5
204-622-2152, Fax: 204-622-2305
Regional Director, Karen Barker
kbarker@gov.mb.ca

Thompson
59 Elizabeth Dr., PO Box 27, Thompson, MB R8N 1X4
204-677-6786, Fax: 204-677-6525
Regional Director, Harold Smith
hsmith@gov.mb.ca

Manitoba Advanced Education & Literacy

Legislative Building, #162, 450 Broadway Ave., Winnipeg, MB R3C 0V8
204-945-0825, Fax: 204-948-2216,
minaed@leg.gov.mb.ca
www.edu.gov.mb.ca

Acts Administered:
Brandon University Act
Colleges Act
Council on Post-Secondary Education Act
University of Manitoba Act
University of Winnipeg Act
Minister,Hon. Diane McGifford
204-945-0825, Fax: 204-948-2216,minaed@leg.gov.mb.ca
Deputy Minister, Heather Reichert
204-945-1648, Fax: 204-945-8330,dmedu@leg.gov.mb.ca
• Council on Post-Secondary Education
#410, 330 Portage Ave.
Winnipeg, MB R3C 0C4
204-945-1833 Fax: 204-945-1841
info@copse.mb.ca
www.copse.mb.ca

Council on Post-Secondary Education
204-945-1833, Fax: 204-945-1841,
info@copse.mb.ca
Manager, Policy, Dan Smith
204-945-4720
Manager, Institutional Relations, Ray Karasevich
204-945-5452
Financial Officer, Margaret McDonald

College Expansion Initiative Branch
#401, 1181 Portage Ave., Winnipeg, MB R3G 0T3
204-945-5150, Fax: 204-948-2676,
www.copse.mb.ca/en/cei/
Manager, College Relations, COPSE, Ray Karasevich
ray.karasevich@gov.mb.ca

Aboriginal Education Directorate
Director, Helen Robinson-Settee
204-945-4763
Program Manager & Evaluation Consultant, Dino Altieri
204-945-6181

Manitoba Agriculture, Food & Rural Initiatives

Norquay Bldg., 401 York Ave., Winnipeg, MB R3C 0P8
www.gov.mb.ca/agriculture/

Acts Administered:
Agricultural Credit Corporation Act
Agricultural Productivity Council Act
Agricultural Producers' Organization Funding Act
Animal Care Act
Animal Diseases Act
Crop Insurance Act
Crown Lands Act, (in part) Sections 6, 7, 10, 12(1), 14, 16, 17, 18, 21, 23, 24 to 28 both inclusive
Dairy Act
Department of Agriculture, Food & Rural Initiatives Act
Family Farm Protection Act
Farm Income Assurance Plans Act
Farm Lands Ownership Act
Farm Machinery & Equipment Act
Farm Practices Protection Act
Fruit & Vegetable Sales Act
Horse Racing Regulation Act
Land Rehabilitation Act
Livestock Industry Diversification Act
Livestock & Livestock Products Act
Margarine Act
Milk Prices Review Act
Natural Products Marketing Act
Noxious Weeds Act
Pesticides & Fertilizers Control Act
Plant Pests & Diseases Act
Seed & Fodder Relief Act
Veterinary Medical Act
Veterinary Science Scholarship Fund Act
Veterinary Services Act
Wildlife Act, (in part) Section 89(e)
Women's Institute Act
Minister,Hon. Rosann Wowchuk
204-945-3722, Fax: 204-945-3470,minagr@leg.gov.mb.ca
Deputy Minister, Barry Todd
204-945-3734, Fax: 204-948-2095,dmagr@leg.gov.mb.ca
Executive Director, Strategic Planning, Maurice Bouvier
204-792-5406
• Agricultural Societies
1129 Queens Ave.
Brandon, MB R7A 1L9
204-726-6195 Fax: 204-726-6260
Promotes improvement in agriculture & development of Manitoba agricultural products. Provide organizational assistance to rural & urban people.
• Farm Lands Ownership Board
#812, Norquay Bldg.
401 York Ave.
Winnipeg, MB R3C 0P8
204-945-3149 Fax: 204-945-1489 800-282-8069
robert.mckenzie@gov.mb.ca
www.web2gov.mb.ca/agriculture/programs/
• Farm Machinery Board
Norquay Bldg.
#812, 401 York Ave.
Winnipeg, MB R3C 0P8
204-945-3856 Fax: 204-948-2844
randy.ozunko@gov.mb.ca
www.web2.gov.mb.ca/agriculture/programs/
• Food Development Centre
810 Phillips St.
PO Box 1240
Portage la Prairie, MB R1N 3J9
204-239-3150 Fax: 204-239-3180 800-870-1044
www.gov.mb.ca/agriculture/fdc
The Food Development Centre (FDC) is a Special Operating Agency of Manitoba Agriculture, Food and Rural Initiatives (MAFRI). Its mandate is to assist the agri-food industry in the development and commercialization of conventional and functional foods and natural health products.
• Manitoba Agricultural Services Corporation(MASC)
#100, 1525 First St. South
Brandon, MB R7A 7A1
204-726-6850 Fax: 204-726-6849
mailbox@masc.mb.ca
www.masc.mb.ca
Formerly the Manitoba Agricultural Credit Corporation & the Manitoba Crop Insurance Corporation. Manitoba Agricultural Services Corporation (MASC) fully supports the province's producers and rural communities, through innovative and targeted risk management and financial programs. MASC is represented across Manitoba by 19 insurance offices and 16 lending offices, with corporate offices located in Portage la Prairie and Brandon.
• Manitoba Farm Mediation Board
c/o Boards, Commissions & Legislation Branch
#812, 401 York Ave.
Winnipeg, MB R3C 0P8
204-945-0357 Fax: 204-945-1489
robert.mckenzie@gov.mb.ca
www.web2.gov.mb.ca/agriculture/programs/
Mediates options to legal action by creditors when farmers cannot meet their obligations.
• Farm Practices Protection Board
c/o Boards, Commissions & Legislation Branch
#812, 401 York Ave.
Winnipeg, MB R3C 0P8
204-945-0630 Fax: 204-948-2844
www.web2.gov.mb.ca/agriculture/programs/
• Farm Products Marketing Council
c/o Boards, Commissions & Legislation Branch
#812, 401 York Ave.
Winnipeg, MB R3C 0P8
204-945-4495 Fax: 204-948-2844
gordon.mackenzie@gov.mb.ca
www.web2.gov.mb.ca/agriculture/programs/
• Manitoba Horse Racing Commission
c/o Boards, Commissions & Legislation Branch
#812, 401 York Ave.
Winnipeg, MB R3C 0P8
204-945-4495 Fax: 204-948-2844
gordon.mackenzie@gov.mb.ca
www.web2.gov.mb.ca/agriculture/programs/
Governs, directs, controls, & regulates horse racing & the operation of all race tracks in Manitoba.
• Manitoba Milk Prices Review Commission
c/o Boards, Commissions & Legislation Branch
#812, 401 York Ave.
Winnipeg, MB R3C 0P8
204-945-3854 Fax: 204-948-2844
randy.ozunko@gov.mb.ca
www.web2.gov.mb.ca/agriculture/programs/

Agri-Food & Rural Development Division
Asst. Deputy Minister, Dori Gingera-Beauchemin
204-945-3735
Director, Economy & Rural Development Knowledge Centre, Mona Cornock
204-726-6410
Director, Food Commercialization & Marketing Knowledge Centre, Randy Stoyko
204-795-2437
Director, GO Teams, Gerald Huebner
204-797-4522, Fax: 204-886-3657

Growing Opportunities (GO) Offices:

North Interlake
317 River Rd., PO Box 2000, Arborg, MB R0C 0A0
Fax: 204-376-3311
GO Team Manager, Susan Nicoll
204-641-1454

South Interlake
77 Main St., PO Box 70, Teulon, MB R0C 3B0
Fax: 204-886-3657
GO Team Manager, Wray Whitmore

Red River
67 - 2 St. NE, PO Box 969, Altona, MB R0G 0B0
Fax: 204-324-2803
GO Team Leader, Jacquie Cherewayko

Central Plains
Morris Ave., PO Box 532, Gladstone, MB R0J 0T0
204-871-4219
GO Team Leader, Dennis Beernaert

Pembina
279 Carlton St., PO Box 189, Somerset, MB R0G 2L0
GO Team Leader, Shane Dobson

Southwest
247 Wellington St., PO Box 850, Virden, MB R0M 2C0
Fax: 204-748-4775
GO Team Manager, John Corbey
204-851-2442

South Parkland
221 Elm St., Hwy 21 N, PO Box 50, Hamiota, MB R0M 0T0
GO Team Manager, Gwenda Skayman

Valleys North
120 - 6th Ave. North, PO Box 370, Swan River, MB R0L 1Z0
Fax: 204-734-5271
GO Team Manager, Allen Muggaberg

Eastman
20 First St. South, PO Box 50, Beausejour, MB R0E 0C0
204-268-6099, Fax: 204-268-6060
GO Team Manager, Shaunda Rossington

North Parkland
27 - Second Ave. SW, Dauphin, MB R7N 3E5
Fax: 204-734-5271,
GO Team Manager, Debra Watson

Agri-Industry Development & Innovation Division
Asst. Deputy Minister, Allan Preston
204-945-3736
Acting Director, Agri-Environment, Leloni Scott
204-745-5658
Director, Agri-Food Innovation & Adaptation, Daryl Domitruk
204-745-0214
Director, Crops, Mike Kagan
204-745-5653
Director, Food Safety & Chief Veterinary Office,Dr. John Taylor
204-945-7690, Fax: 204-945-4327
Acting Director, Land Use Planning & Manager, Agricultural Crown Lands, Robert Fleming
204-867-6551
Director, Livestock Knowledge Centre, Brent McCannell
204-945-7650

Regional Agricultural Services Division
Acting Asst. Deputy Minister, Dory Gingera-Beauchemin
204-945-3735
Director, Agricultural Crown Lands Branch, Dennis Hodgson
204-867-3419, Fax: 204-867-5696

Office of the Auditor General

#500, 330 Portage Ave., Winnipeg, MB R3C 0C4
204-945-3790, Fax: 204-945-2169,
contact@oag.mb.ca
www.oag.mb.ca
Established under The Auditor General Act, the Office of the Auditor General is an independent office of the Legislative Assembly. Through audit of management practices & accountability reports, the Office contributes to effective governance & public trust
Auditor General, Carol Bellringer, FCA, MBA
cbellringer@aog.mb.ca
Deputy Auditor General, Mala Sachdeva, CA
204-945-2686
Executive Director, Strategic Initiatives, Norman Ricard, CA
204-945-2782
Executive Director, Quality Assurance & Professional Practice, Greg MacBeth, CA
204-945-6883

Manitoba Civil Service Commission

#935, 155 Carlton St., Winnipeg, MB R3C 3H8
204-945-2332, Fax: 204-945-1486, 800-282-8069
cschrp@gov.mb.ca
www.gov.mb.ca/csc/

Acts Administered:
The Civil Service Act
Employment Standards Code
Freedom of Information & Protection of Privacy Act
Labour Relations Act
Manitoba Act
Personal Health Information Act
Minister responsible,Hon. Gregory F. Selinger
204-945-3952, Fax: 204-945-6057,minfin@leg.gov.mb.ca
Deputy Minister & Commissioner, Debra Woodgate
• Civil Service Commission Board
#935, 155 Carlton St.
Winnipeg, MB R3C 3H8
204-945-1435 Fax: 204-945-1486

Manitoba Competitiveness, Training & Trade

International Business Centre, The Paris Building, 259 Portage Ave., Winnipeg, MB R3B 3P4
204-945-2475, Fax: 204-945-3977,
minctt@leg.gov.mb.ca
www.gov.mb.ca/ctt/

Mission is to support the growth of business in the province, meet provincial labour demands, increase training opportunities, and expand global trade relations
Acts Administered:
Biofuels Act
Crocus Investment Fund
Design Institute Act
Development Corporations Act
Economic Innovation & Technology Council Act
Electronic Commerce & Information Act (except part 5)
Energy Act
Gas Allocation Act
Gas Pipe Line Act
Greater Winnipeg Gas Distribution Act (S.M. 1988-89, C.40)
Income Tax Act (S. 7.5 & 7.10)
Labour-Sponsored Venture Capital Corporations Act
Manitoba Health Research Council Act
Mines & Minerals Act
Mining & Metallurgy Compensation Act
Oil & Gas Act
Oil & Gas Production Tax Act
Statistics Act
Surface Rights Act
Sustainable Development Act
Minister,Hon. Andrew Swan
204-945-0067, Fax: 204-945-4882,minctt@leg.gov.mb.ca
Deputy Minister, Hugh Eliasson
204-945-4076, Fax: 204-945-1561,
Director, Policy, Planning & Coordination, Alan Barber
204-945-8714, abarber@gov.mb.ca
Director, Financial & Administration Services, Craig Halwachs
204-945-3675, chalwachs@gov.mb.ca
Director, Industry Development Financial Services, Jim Kilgour
204-945-7626, jkilgour@gov.mb.ca
Senior Manager, Industry Consulting & Marketing Support, David Sprange
204-945-7938, dsprange@gov.mb.ca
Executive Director, Industry & Workforce Development, B. Knight

Community & Economic Development Committee of Cabinet Secretariat
#648, 155 Carlton St., Winnipeg, MB R3C 3H8
204-945-8221, Fax: 204-945-8229
Director, Anna Rothney
204-945-3036
Administrative Officer, Colleen Davies
204-945-4346, codavies@gov.mb.ca

Business Services Division - Financial Services
To encourage & facilitate entrepreneurial & employment opportunities within the Province through the establishment of new businesses or the expansion/retention of existing Manitoba businesses.The Branch promotes increased access to capital for industry by serving as a principal source of financial advice & assistance for businesses to expand or locate in Manitoba. The Branch develops & administers a number of third party delivered pools of risk capital
Executive Director, Jim Kilgour
204-945-7626

Manitoba Bureau of Statistics
#824, 155 Carlton St., Winnipeg, MB R3C 3H9
204-945-2406, Fax: 204-945-0695
Chief Statistician, Wilf Falk
204-945-2988, wfalk@mbs.gov.mb.ca

Premier's Economic Advisory Council
#648, 155 Carlton St., Winnipeg, MB R3C 3N8
204-945-6133, Fax: 204-945-8229
Executive Coordinator, Alissa Brandt
204-945-5297

Small Business Development
#250, 240 Graham Ave., PO Box 2609, Winnipeg, MB R3C 4B3
204-984-2272, Fax: 204-983-3852,
manitoba@cbsc.ic.gc.ca
www.cbsc.org/manitoba
Director, Tony Romeo
204-945-2019
Manager, Western Regional Office, Bonnie Nay
204-726-6253

Manitoba Conservation

200 Saulteaux Cres., Winnipeg, MB R3J 3W3
204-945-6784, 800-214-6497
mincon@leg.gov.mb.ca
www.gov.mb.ca/conservation

Manitoba Conservation protects, conserves, manages & sustains development of forest, fisheries, wildlife, water, energy & Crown & Park land resources, protects environmental integrity & ensures a high level of environmental quality.The department is the lead agency for providing outdoor recreational opportunities for Manitobans & visitors.The department is a contributor to the economic development & wellbeing of the province, through resource-based harvesting operations & in co-operation with other departments responsible for agriculture & tourism.Providing for domestic use & protecting people & property from floods, wildfires & adverse effects of other natural occurrences, are also major roles. The department administers legislation & regulations protecting the environment & public health, participates in approval, licensing & appeals for industrial development activities, administers waste reduction & pollution prevention activities & monitors environmental quality
Acts Administered:
Contaminated Sites Remediation Act
Crown Lands Act
Dangerous Goods Handling & Transportation Act
Dutch Elm Disease Act
Ecological Reserves Act
Endangered Species Act
Environment Act
Forest Act
Ground Water & Water Well Act
High Level Radioactive Waste Act
Homeowners Tax & Insulation Assistance Act
International Peace Garden Act
Manitoba Hazardous Waste Management Corporation Act
Manitoba Natural Resources Transfer Act
Manitoba Natural Resources Transfer Act, Amendment Act
Manitoba Natural Resources Transfer Act, Amendment Act, 1963
Ozone Depleting Substances Act
Provincial Parks Act
Plant Pests & Diseases Act
Polar Bear Protection Act, 2003
Public Health Act
Resource Tourism Operators Act
Surveys Act (Part II)
Sustainable Development Act
Waste Reduction & Prevention Act
Water Commission Act
Wildlife Act
Water Resources Conservation & Protection Act
Water Rights Act
Wild Rice Act
Minister,Hon. Bill Blaikie
204-945-3730, Fax: 204-945-3586,mincon@leg.gov.mb.ca
Deputy Minister, Fred Meier
204-945-3785, Fax: 204-948-2403,dmcon@leg.gov.mb.ca
• Clean Environment Commission
#305, 155 Carlton St.
Winnipeg, MB R3C 3H8
204-945-0594 Fax: 204-945-0090
www.cecmanitoba.ca/
Arm's-length provincial agency that holds public hearings on the subject of the regulation of a broad range of private industry, municipal or provincial government operations. Investigates environmental matters or considers proposed abatement projects with public hearings. Reports to the Minister with advice & recommendations & acts as a mediator between two or more parties to an environmental dispute.
• Ecological Reserves Advisory Committee
c/o Manitoba Conservation, Parks & Natural Areas Branch
200 Saulteaux Cres.
Winnipeg, MB R3J 3W3
204-945-4148 Fax: 204-945-0012
hhernandez@gov.mb.ca
• Endangered Species Advisory Committee
200 Saulteaux Cres.
PO Box 24
Winnipeg, MB R3J 3W3
204-945-7465 Fax: 204-945-3077
• Lake of the Woods Control Board
c/o Executive Engineer
Ottawa, ON K1A 0H3
Fax: 819-953-4666 800-661-5922
secretariat@lwcb.ca
www.lwcb.ca

Conservation Programs Division
Manages Manitoba's natural resources, parks, lands, forests, fish, wildlife, & the environment. Implements the principles of sustainable development.
Asst. Deputy Minister, Fred Meier
204-945-7008, Fax: 204-945-3125
Director, Forestry, John Dojack
204-945-7998
Director, Lands & Geomatics, Harley Jonasson
204-945-8288
Director, Parks & Natural Areas, Barry J. Bentham
204-945-4413
Director, Survey Services, Wayne Leeman
204-945-0011
Director, Wildlife & Ecosystem Protection, Jack Dubois
204-945-7761
Director, Pollution Prevention, Laurie Streich
204-945-7482
Manager, Habitat Management & Ecosystem Monitoring, Floyd Phillips
204-945-7003

Environmental Stewardship Division
The Branch co-ordinates & integrates departmental policy, natural resource allocation & crown land-use planning, environmental impact assessment, legislative interpretation & co-management in accordance with principles of sustainable development.The Branch monitors cross-boundary water projects, administers licensing of resource-based tourism facilities, represents the department in issues related to internal & international trade agreements, co-ordinates settlements & litigation arising out of hydro-electric & water-control projects & Treaty Land Entitlement.
Asst. Deputy Minister, Serge Scrafield
204-945-7107, Fax: 204-945-5229
Director, Environmental Assessment & Licensing, Tracey Braun
204-945-7071
Director, Aboriginal Relations, Ron Missyabit
204-945-7088, Fax: 204-945-5229
Director, Sustainable Resource & Policy Management, Tammy Gibson
204-945-6658

Manitoba Round Table for Sustainable Development (MRTSD)
#160, 123 Main St., Winnipeg, MB R3C 1A5
204-945-1671, Fax: 204-948-2357,
mrtsd@gov.mb.ca
Advisory body to the provincial government that provides advice & support to decision makers toward making responsible resource, land use, environment, social & economic development decisions for the province
Chair,Hon. Stan Struthers

Regional Operations Division
Operates six regional offices in rural Manitoba & co-ordinated from Headquarters operations in Winnipeg. The Division co-ordinates the delivery of programs & services at the community level
Asst. Deputy Minister, Bruce Bremner
204-945-4842

Regional Offices:

Eastern
Provincial Hwy #502, CP 4000, Lac du Bonnet, MB R0E 1A0
204-345-1431, Fax: 204-345-1440
Regional Director, Bruce Bremner

Central (Gimli)
75 - 7th Ave., PO Box 6000, Gimli, MB R0C 1B0
204-642-6070, Fax: 204-642-6108
Regional Director, Brian Gillespie

Northeastern
59 Elizabeth Dr., PO Box 28, Thompson, MB R8N 1X4
204-677-6648, Fax: 204-677-6359

Regional Director, Steve Kearney

Northwestern
3rd St. & Ross Ave., PO Box 2550, The Pas, MB R9A 1M4
204-627-8215, Fax: 204-623-1773

Central (Winnipeg)
#160, 123 Main St., Winnipeg, MB R3C 1A5
204-945-7100, Fax: 204-948-2338,

Western
1129 Queens Ave., Brandon, MB R7A 1L9
204-726-6441, Fax: 204-726-6567
Regional Director, Bruce Wright

Manitoba Culture, Heritage, Tourism & Sport

Legislative Building, #118, 450 Broadway Ave., Winnipeg, MB R3C 0V8
204-945-3729, Fax: 204-945-5223,
minchth@leg.gov.mb.ca
www.gov.mb.ca/chc

Committed to the development & implementation of programs & services which promote & enhance the well-being, identity & creativity of Manitobans & which contribute to Manitoba's continued economic growth & steadily rising quality of life. Working with its partners in the community & with government, the Department raises the national & international profile of the talents & abilities of our people, encourages healthy active living, promotes pride of place, creates jobs & attracts & maintains investment in our province

Acts Administered:
Amusements Act (except Part II)
Arts Council Act
Boxing Commission Act
Centennial Centre Corporation Act
Le Centre Culturel Franco-Manitobain Act
Coat of Arms, Emblems & The Manitoba Tartan Act
Convention Centre Corporation Act
Foreign Cultural Objects Immunity from Seizure Act
Freedom of Information & Protection of Privacy Act
Heritage Manitoba Act
Heritage Resources Act
Legislative Library Act
Manitoba Film & Sound Recording Development Corporation Act
Museums & Miscellaneous Grants Act
Public Libraries Act
Public Printing Act
Travel Manitoba Act

Minister,Hon. Eric Robinson
204-945-3729, Fax: 204-945-5223,mincht@leg.gov.mb.ca
Deputy Minister, Sandra Hardy
204-945-4136, Fax: 204-948-3102,dmcht@leg.gov.mb.ca
Executive Director, Administration & Finance Division,
David Paton
204-945-2233, Fax: 204-945-5760,dpaton@chc.gov.mb.ca

• Le Centre Culturel franco-manitobain/Franco-Manitoban Cultural Centre
340, boul Provencher
St Boniface, MB R2H 0G7
204-233-8972 Fax: 204-233-3324
ccfm@ccfm.mb.ca
www.ccfm.mb.ca

• Heritage Grants Advisory Council
213 Notre Dame Ave., 3rd Fl.
Winnipeg, MB R3B 1N3
204-945-2213 Fax: 204-948-2086

• Manitoba Arts Council
#525, 93 Lombard Ave.
Winnipeg, MB R3B 3B1
204-945-2237 Fax: 204-945-5925 866-994-2787
info@artscouncil.mb.ca
www.artscouncil.mb.ca
An arms-length agency of the provincial government dedicated to artistic excellence. It offers a broad-based granting program for professional artists & arts organizations. It promotes, preserves, supports & advocates for the arts as essential to the quality of life of all the people of Manitoba.

• Manitoba Centennial Centre Corporation
555 Main St.
Winnipeg, MB R3B 1C3
204-956-1360 Fax: 204-944-1390

• Manitoba Film Classification Board
#216, 301 Weston St.
Winnipeg, MB R3E 3H4
204-945-8962 Fax: 204-945-0890 866-612-2399
mfcb@gov.mb.ca
www.gov.mb.ca/filmclassification

• Manitoba Heritage Council
213 Notre Dame Ave., Main Fl.
Winnipeg, MB R3B 1N3
204-945-2118 Fax: 204-948-2384
hrb@gov.mb.ca
Protects, interprets & promotes the heritage resources of the province; offers advice & recommendations on places & events which should be protected by the department; protection of significant buildings & sites.

• Manitoba Museum/ Musée du Manitoba
190 Rupert Ave.
Winnipeg, MB R3B 0N2
204-956-2830 Fax: 204-942-3679
info@manitobamuseum.mb.ca
www.manitobamuseum.mb.ca
Other Communication: Info Line:|204/943-3139

• Manitoba Film & Sound Recording Development Corporation
#410, 93 Lombard Ave.
Winnipeg, MB R3B 3B1
204-947-2040 Fax: 204-956-5261
carole@mbfilmsound.mb.ca
www.mbfilmsound.mb.ca
Pomotes the province's film & sound recording artists & industries.

Administration & Finance Division
Fax: 204-945-5760

Executive Director, David Paton
204-945-2233
Acting Director & Facilities Consultant, Community Places Program, Mark Ranson
204-945-1374,
Director, Amalgamated Human Resources, Melanie Schade
204-945-3001
Manager, Grants Administration, Pauline Belanger
204-945-4580
Acting Manager, Information Systems, Lori Constant
204-945-4356
Management Analyst, Management Services, Lou Remillard
204-945-2598

Communications Services Manitoba
155 Carlton St., 10th Fl., Winnipeg, MB R3C 3H8
204-945-3765, Fax: 204-948-2147

Asst. Deputy Minister, Cindy Stevens
204-945-4271, Fax: 204-948-2219
Director, Advertising & Program Promotion, Michelle Wallace
204-945-5164, Fax: 204-948-2147
Director, Public Affairs, Debbie MacKenzie
204-945-4971, Fax: 204-948-2147
Director, Creative Services, Cam McCullough
204-945-8830, Fax: 204-948-2147
Manager, Internet & Business Services, Mike Baudic
204-945-4392, Fax: 204-948-2219
Director, News Media Services, Stu Fawcett
204-945-3746
Manager, Production & Media Procurement, Heather A. Coleman
204-945-7121, Fax: 204-945-1366
Manager, Manitoba Government Inquiry, Aggie Hasselfield
204-945-3744, Fax: 204-945-4261
Supervisor, Statutory Publications, Keith Holness
204-945-3101, Fax: 204-945-7172,statpub@gov.mb.ca

Culture, Heritage & Recreation Programs Division
Acting Asst. Deputy Minister, Ann Hultgren-Ryan
204-945-4078, Fax: 204-948-2739
Director, Arts Branch, Craig Walls
204-945-4579, Fax: 204-945-1684
Director, Historic Resources, Donna Dul
204-945-4389, Fax: 204-948-2384
Acting Director, Public Library Services, Trevor Surgenor
204-726-6864, Fax: 204-726-6868
Director, Recreation & Regional Services, Annette Willborn
204-945-4396, Fax: 204-945-1684
Manager, Agency Relations, Pat A. Tooth
204-945-4509, Fax: 204-948-2739

Provincial Services Division
#100, 200 Vaughan St., Winnipeg, MB R3C 1T5
Executive Director & Legislative Librarian, Legislative Library, Sue Bishop
204-945-4245
Director, Translation Services, Melanie Cwikla
204-945-3096

Sport Secretariat
213 Notre Dame Ave., Winnipeg, MB R3B 1N3
204-945-0216, Fax: 204-945-1675,
diane.meldrum@gov.mb.ca
www.gov.mb.ca/chc/sport/

Acting Executive Director, Terry Welsh
204-945-2449

Tourism Secretariat & Travel Manitoba
155 Carlton St., 7th Fl., Winnipeg, MB R3C 3H8
800-665-0040
www.travelmanitoba.com

Acting Executive Director, Tourism Manitoba, Terry Welsh
204-945-2449

Manitoba Development Corporation (MDC)

#555, 155 Carlton St., Winnipeg, MB R3C 3H8
204-945-7626, Fax: 204-945-1193

General Manager, Jim Kilgour

Manitoba Education, Citizenship & Youth

#168, Legislative Bldg., 450 Broadway, Winnipeg, MB R3C 0V8
204-945-3720, Fax: 204-945-1291,
minedu@leg.gov.mb.ca
www.edu.gov.mb.ca

Acts Administered:
Blind & Deaf Persons' Maintenance & Education Act
Education Administration Act
Public Schools Act
Public Schools Finance Board Act
Teachers' Pension Act
Teachers' Society Act

Minister,Hon. Peter Bjornson
204-945-3720, Fax: 204-945-1291,minedu@leg.gov.mb.ca
Deputy Minister, Gerald Farthing
204-945-1648, Fax: 204-945-8330,dmedu@leg.gov.mb.ca

• Public Schools Finance Board
#506, 1181 Portage Ave.
Winnipeg, MB R3G 0T3
204-945-6628 Fax: 204-948-2001

• Teachers' Retirement Allowances Fund Board
#330 Johnston Terminal
35 Forks Market Rd.
Winnipeg, MB R3C 4S8
204-949-0048 Fax: 204-944-0361

Division du Bureau de l'éducation française / French Language Education Office
#509, 1181 av Portage, Winnipeg, MB R3C 0T3
204-945-6916, Fax: 204-945-1625

Sous-ministre adjoint, Jean-Vianney Auclair
204-945-6928, Fax: 204-948-2994
Directeur (par intérim), Programmes, Jacques Dorge
204-945-6022, Fax: 204-945-1625
Directrice, Services de soutien en éducation, Florence Girouard
204-945-8797,
Directeur, Programmes de langues officielles et services administratifs, Kassy Assie
204-945-6029, Fax: 204-945-1625
Directrice, Ressources éducatives française, Huguette Dandeneau
204-945-1342

MB4Youth Division
#310, 800 Portage Ave., Winnipeg, MB R3G 0N4
204-945-3556, Fax: 204-945-5726,
mb4youth@gov.mb.ca
www.edu.gov.mb.ca/youth/

Executive Director, Veronica Dyck
204-945-0371
Executive Director, Partners for Careers, Roberta Hewson
204-945-0447
Manager, Youth Citizenship, Leadership & Career Development, Nancy Buchanan
204-945-0884
Manager, Finance & Administration, Elizabeth Lawrie
204-945-5117
Program Manager, Youth Services, Greg Kristalovich
204-945-3755
Provincial Coordinator, Manitoba Youth Job Centres, Krista Hiebert
204-945-8115

School Programs Division
#307, 1181 Portage Ave., Winnipeg, MB R3G 0T3
Fax: 204-945-8303

Asst. Deputy Minister, Anne Longston
204-945-7935
Director, Instruction, Curriculum & Assessment, Aileen Najduch
204-945-2138
Director, Program & Student Services, Joanna Blais
204-945-7911, Fax: 204-945-7914
Financial Coordinator, Yvonne Pennings
204-945-3546

Shared Services
510 Selkirk Ave., Winnipeg, MB R2W 2M7
Director, Aboriginal Education Directorate, Helen Robinson-Settee
204-945-4763, Fax: 204-948-2010
Executive Financal Officer, Claude Fortier
204-945-1117, Fax: 204-948-2851

Director, Amalgamated Human Resources, Robert (Butch) Berube
204-945-6892, Fax: 204-948-2193
Director, Systems & Technology Services, John Frazer
204-945-5843, Fax: 204-948-2542

Elections Manitoba

#120, 200 Vaughan St., Winnipeg, MB R3C 1T5
204-945-3225, Fax: 204-945-6011, 866-628-6837
election@elections.mb.ca
www.electionsmanitoba.ca

Independent from government, Elections Manitoba conducts fair elections. It ensures that political financing laws are followed, & increases public awareness of the electoral process

Chief Electoral Officer, Richard D. Balasko
204-945-3225
Deputy Chief Electoral Officer, Scott Gordon
204-945-7156
Manager, Elections Finances, Shipra Verma, CA
204-945-1283
Analyst, Financial Compliance, Maggie Anderson
416-945-7559
Officer, Communications & Community Relations, Amanda Jeninga
204-945-3804

Manitoba Family Services & Housing

#219, 114 Garry St., Winnipeg, MB R3C 4V6
204-945-3242, Fax: 204-945-2156,
minfam@leg.gov.mb.ca
www.gov.mb.ca/fs

Supports citizens in need to achieve fuller participation in society & greater self-suffiency & independence. Helps keep children, families & communities safe & secure & promotes healthy citizen development & well-being. Mission is accomplished through: provision of financial support; provision of services & supports that assist individuals improve their attachment to the labour market; provision of supports & services for adults & children with disabilities; provision of child protection & related services; assistance to people facing family violence or family disruption; provision of services & supports to promote the healthy development & well-being of children & families; assistance to Manitobans to access safe, appropriate & affordable housing; fostering community capacity & engaging the broader community to participate in & contribute to decision-making; & respectful & appropriate delivery of programs & services

Acts Administered:
The Adoption Act
The Authorities Act
The Child & Family Services Act
The Community Child Day Care Standards Act
The Elderly & Infirm Persons' Housing Act
The Employment & Income Assistance Act
The Housing & Renewal Corporation Act
The Intercountry Adoption (Hague Convention) Act
The Parents' Maintenance Act (s. 10)
The Social Services Administration Act
The Social Services Appeal Board Act
The Vulnerable Persons Living with a Mental Disability Act

Minister,Hon. Gord Mackintosh
204-945-4173, Fax: 204-945-5149,minfam@leg.gov.mb.ca
Deputy Minister, Martin Billinkoff
204-945-6700, Fax: 204-948-1896,dmfam@leg.gov.mb.ca
Executive Director, Policy & Planning, Jan Forster
204-945-3231, Fax: 204-945-2156
Administrative Assistant, Financial & Administrative Services, Lana Harrison
204-945-8119, Fax: 204-945-2760

• Disabilities Issues Office
#630, 240 Graham Ave.
Winnipeg, MB R3C 0J7
204-945-7613 Fax: 204-948-2896TDD: 204-948-2901
dio@gov.mb.ca

• Manitoba Housing Authority - Public Housing
#2100, 185 Smith St.
Winnipeg, MB R3C 3G4
204-945-4663 Fax: 204-948-2013 800-661-4663
www.gov.mb.ca/fs/housing/mha.html

• Manitoba Housing & Renewal Corporation
280 Broadway
Winnipeg, MB R3C 0R8
204-945-4895 Fax: 204-945-5710
www.gov.mb.ca/fs/org/eih/mhrc.html

• Social Services Appeal Board
175 Hargrave St., 7th Fl.
Winnipeg, MB R3C 3R8
204-945-3003 Fax: 204-945-1736 800-282-8069TDD: 204-948-2037
www.gov.mb.ca/fs/ssab/index.html

Administration & Finance Division

Acting Asst. Deputy Minister, Sheila Lebredt
204-945-5943
Acting Director, Information Technology, Munna Zaman
204-945-4807, Fax: 204-948-2394
Director, Integrated Service Delivery, Debbie Besant
204-945-4998, Fax: 204-948-4656
Director & Chief Negotiator, Agency Accountability & Support Unit, Gord Greasley
204-945-7927, Fax: 204-948-4656
Acting Manager, Financial & Administrative Services, Paul Cormier
204-945-1990, Fax: 204-945-2760
Acting Director & Manager, Financial Planning & Review, Wayne Pestun
204-945-4005, Fax: 204-945-2760

Child & Family Services Division

Acting Asst. Deputy Minister, Carolyn Loeppky
204-945-3257, Fax: 204-948-2669
Acting Executive Director, Child Protection, Josie Hill
204-945-4575, Fax: 204-945-6717
Acting Executive Director, Strategic Initiatives & Program Support, Tammy Mattern
204-945-8300
Acting Director, Child Care, Lois Speirs
204-945-2668, Fax: 204-948-2630
Acting Director, Family Violence Prevention, Paulette Fortier
204-945-7245

Community Service Delivery Division

Asst. Deputy Minister, Peter Dubienski
204-945-2204
Executive Director, Rural & Northern Services, Debbie Besant
204-945-4998
Executive Director, Winnipeg Services, Gerry Schmidt
204-945-2685, Fax: 204-945-0082
Executive Director, Service Delivery Support, Janet Wikstrom
204-945-1268, Fax: 204-948-3267
Director, Provincial Services, Pat Sanderson
204-945-6554, Fax: 204-945-3930
Acting CEO, Winnipeg Child & Family Services, Darlene MacDonald
204-944-4570, Fax: 204-944-4395

Employment, Income & Housing Division

#201, 280 Broadway Ave., Winnipeg, MB R3C 0R8
Asst. Deputy Minister, Joy Cramer
204-945-5600, Fax: 204-948-2736
Executive Director, Employment & Income Assistance Programs, Charlene Paquin
204-945-6374
Director, Corporate Services, Henry Bos
204-945-4703, Fax: 204-945-4710

Services for Persons with Disabilities

Asst. Deputy Minister, Gisela Rempel
204-945-2692, Fax: 204-948-2153
Executive Director, Disability Programs & EIA, Wes Henderson
204-945-6541, Fax: 204-945-5668
Acting Director, Children's Programs, Tracy Moore
204-945-3255, Fax: 204-945-5668
Acting Director, Strategic Initiatives & Program Support, Joy Goertzen
204-945-2326, Fax: 204-945-5668
Acting Director, Supported Living, Ralf Margraf
204-945-3589, Fax: 204-945-5668
Acting Vulnerable Persons' Commissioner, JoAnne Reinsch
204-945-0564, Fax: 204-948-2603
Director, Kathy Reid
204-945-2668
Asst. Director, Financial & Administrative Services, Annette Enns
204-945-4893
Asst. Director, Program Operations, Lynda Rosenstock
204-945-2677
CEO, Donna Bjore
204-856-4237
Manager, Financial Services, Alan Dell
204-856-4200

Manitoba Finance

#109, Legislative Bldg., Winnipeg, MB R3C 0V8
204-945-3754, Fax: 204-945-8316,
minfin@leg.gov.mb.ca
www.gov.mb.ca/finance/

Established in 1969 under authority of the Financial Administration Act. Responsible for central accounting, payroll & financial reporting services for the government, consumer & corporate affairs & central financial control of cost-shared agreements. The ministry manages government borrowing programs & is responsible for federal-provincial relations.

Acts Administered:
Business Names Registration Act
Business Practices Act
Cemeteries Act
The title to Certain Lands Act (R.S.M. 1990, c.259).
Change of Name Act
Charities Endorsement Act
Commodity Futures Act
Condominium Act
Consumer Protection Act
Cooperatives Act
Corporations Act
Corporation Capital Tax Act
Credit Unions & Caisses Populaires Act
Electronic Commerce & Information Act
Embalmers & Funeral Directors Act
Energy Rate Stabilization Act
Financial Administration Act
Fire Insurance Reserve Fund Act
Fiscal Stabilization Fund Act
Gasoline Tax Act
Health & Post Secondary Education Tax Levy Act
Hospital Capital Financing Authority Act
Housing & Renewal Corporation Act
Hudson's Bay Company Land Register Act
Income Tax Act
Insurance Act
Insurance Corporations Tax Act
Landlord & Tenant Act
Life Leases Act
Manitoba Investment Pool Authority Act
Manitoba Evidence Act (Part II & III)
Manitoba Investment Pool Authority Act
Marriage Act
Mining Claim Tax Act
Mining Tax Act
Mortgage Act (Part III)
Mortgage Dealers Act
Motive Fuel Tax Act
Pari-Mutuel Levy Act
Partnership Act
Personal Investigations Act
Personal Property Security Act
Prearranged Funeral Services Act
Professional Home Economists Act
Property Tax & Insulation Assistance Act
Public Health Act
Bedding, Upholstered & Stuffed Articles Regulation
Public Officers Act
Public Utilities Board Act
Real Estate Brokers Act
Real Property Act
Registry Act
Religious Societies' Lands Act
Residential Tenancies Act
Retail Sales Tax Act
Revenue Act
Succession Duty Act
Securities Act
Special Survey Act
Suitors' Moneys Act
Surveys Act (Part I)
Provincial-Municipal Tax Sharing Act
Tobacco Tax Act
Trade Practises Inquiry Act
Vital Statistics Act

Minister,Hon. Gregory F. Selinger
204-945-3952, Fax: 204-945-6057,minfin@leg.gov.mb.ca
Deputy Minister,Diane, Gray
204-945-5343, dmfin@leg.gov.mb.ca
Secretary, Treasury Board Secretariat, Tannis Mindell
204-945-1100
Assoc. Secretary, Treasury Board, David Woodbury
204-945-1524

• Automobile Injury Compensation Appeal Commission
#301, 428 Portage Ave..
Winnipeg, MB R3C 0E2
204-945-4155 Fax: 204-948-2402
autoinjury@gov.mb.ca
www.gov.mb.ca/cca/autom

• Claimant Adviser Office
#200, 330 Portage Ave.
Winnipeg, MB R3C 0C4
204-945-7413 Fax: 204-948-3157

• Credit Union Deposit Guarantee Corporation
#390, 200 Graham Ave.
Winnipeg, MB R3C 4L5
204-942-8480 Fax: 204-947-1723 800-697-4447
mail@cudgc.com
www.cudgc.com

• Crown Corporations Council/ Conseil des corporations de la Couronne
#1130, 444 St. Mary Ave.
Winnipeg, MB R3C 3T1
204-949-5270 Fax: 204-949-5283
crowncc@mts.net
www.crowncc.mb.ca
• Manitoba Securities Commission
#500, 400 St. Mary Ave.
Winnipeg, MB R3C 4K5
204-945-2548 Fax: 204-945-0330 800-655-5244
securities@gov.mb.ca
www.msc.gov.mb.ca
The Manitoba Securities Commission is an independent agency of the Government of Manitoba that protects investors and promotes fair and efficient capital markets throughout the province.
• Public Utilities Board
#400, 330 Portage Ave.
Winnipeg, MB R3C 0C4
204-945-2638 Fax: 204-945-2643 866-854-3698
publicutilities@gov.mb.ca
www.pub.gov.mb.ca
Regulate the rates charged by Manitoba Hydro (electrical utility), Manitoba Public Insurance (auto insurance), some gas or propane utilities (Centra Gas, Stittco, Swan Valley Gas Corp.) and all water and sewer utilities outside Winnipeg.
• Residential Tenancies Commission
#1650, 155 Carlton St.
Winnipeg, MB R3C 3H8
204-945-2028 Fax: 204-945-5453 800-782-8403
rtc@gov.mb.ca
www.gov.mb.ca/finance/cca/residtc
Landlords and tenants may appeal orders and decisions issued by the Residential Tenancies Branch. The commission hears these appeals. Appeals are heard by a panel of three consisting of one landlord and one tenant representative and either the chief commissioner or a deputy commissioner as the neutral chairperson.

Administration & Finance Division
Executive Financial Officer, Erroll Kavanagh
204-945-4319
Director, Amalgamated Human Resources, Melanie Schade
204-945-3001
Director, Insurance & Risk Management, John Rislahti
204-945-2482

Comptroller Division
#715, 401 York Ave., Winnipeg, MB R3C 0P8
204-945-4920, Fax: 204-945-2394
Provides central accounting, payroll & financial reporting services, & central financial control of cost-shared agreements for the government. The division develops government-wide financial systems, policies & procedures, & provides policy advice for financial & management systems. The division coordinates, develops & maintains departmental data processing systems, & provides direction to the government on the effective use of information systems technology
Provincial Comptroller, Betty-Anne Pratt
204-945-4919
Director, Internal Audit & Consulting Services, Jane Holatko
204-945-8110
Director, Disbursements & Accounting, Terry Patrick
204-945-1343

Consumer & Corporate Affairs Division
Asst. Deputy Minister, Alexandra Morton, Q.C.
204-945-3742, Fax: 204-945-4009
Director, Research & Planning, Ian Anderson
204-945-7892
Director, Consumers' Bureau, Nancy Anderson
204-945-4062
Acting Director, Residential Tenancies Branch, Laura Gowerluk
204-945-0377, Fax: 204-945-6273
Director, Claimant Advisor Office, Bob Sample
204-945-8171

Federal-Provincial Relations & Research Division
#910, 386 Broadway, Winnipeg, MB R3C 3R6
204-945-3757, Fax: 204-945-5051
Provides research & analytical support for national/provincial fiscal & economic matters & inter-governmental financial relations. Also administers fiscal arrangements & tax collection agreements with the federal government & tax credit programs with federal & municipal governments
Asst. Deputy Minister, Heather Wood
204-945-4120, Fax: 204-945-5051
Director, Economic & Fiscal Analysis, Jim Hrichishen
204-945-1468
Acting Director, Intergovernmental Finance, René Perreault
204-945-1478

Director, Taxation Analysis Branch, Stephen Watson
204-945-1473

Taxation Division
#101, 401 York Ave., Winnipeg, MB R3C 0P8
204-945-6444, Fax: 204-948-2360

Treasury Division
Created as a separate entity in 1976, to address the need for placing greater emphasis on the management of substantial amounts of money, debt & investments. Currency & interest rate risk management programs have been developed due to the increase in volumes & dollar values. The division assists with the arrangement of financing for municipalities, schools & hospitals
Asst. Deputy Minister, Gary Gibson
204-945-1184
Director, Capital Markets, Deborah Deen
204-945-6637
Director, Treasury & Banking Operations, Scott Wiebe
204-945-6677

Companies Office
#1010, 405 Broadway, Winnipeg, MB R3C 3L6
204-945-2500, Fax: 204-945-1459,
companies@gov.mb.ca
companiesoffice.gov.mb.ca
Chief Operating Officer, Myron Pawlowsky
204-945-4206

Financial Institutions Regulation Branch
#1115, 405 Broadway, Winnipeg, MB R3C 3L6
204-945-2542, Fax: 204-948-2268
Superintendent, Financial Institutions, Jim Scalena
204-945-3911
Deputy Superintendent, Lofgren Ken
204-945-6111
Deputy Superintendent, Insurance, Scott Moore
204-945-1150

Property Registry
Acting Director, Grant Kernested
204-945-1946

Vital Statistics
254 Portage Ave., Winnipeg, MB R3C 0B8
204-945-3701, Fax: 204-948-3128, 800-282-8063
vitalstats@gov.mb.ca
www.gov.mb.ca/cca/vital

Other Communication: Fax Certificate Requests: 204/948-3128
Provincial agency responsible for the issuance of birth, death, change of name & marriage certificates.Written or faxed requests must be submitted.

Manitoba Health & Healthy Living

#100, 300 Carlton St., Winnipeg, MB R3B 3M9
204-786-7191,
minhlt@leg.gov.mb.ca
www.gov.mb.ca/health/index.html
Responsible for the overall quality of the health system in the province, for maintaining the health system, & for ensuring that the health needs of Manitobans are met. Services are provided through regional delivery systems, hospitals & other health care facilities. The Department also makes insured benefits claims payments for residents of Manitoba related to the cost of medical, hospital, personal care, pharmacare & other health services. To lead the way to quality health care, built with creativity, compassion, confidence, trust & respect; empower Manitobans through knowledge, choices & access to the best possible health resources; & build partnerships & alliances for healthy & supportive communities. To foster innovation in the health care system. This is accomplished through: developing mechanisms to assess & monitor quality of care, utilization & cost effectiveness; fostering behaviours & environments which promote health; & promoting responsiveness & flexibility of delivery systems, & alternative & less expensive services.
Acts Administered:
Ambulance Services Act
Anatomy Act
Cancer Care Manitoba Act
Dental Association Act
Dental Health Services Act
Dental Health Workers Act
Denturists Act
Department of Health Act
District Health & Social Services Act
Elderly & Infirm Persons' Housing Act (with respect to elderly persons housing units as defined in the Act)
(Manitoba) Health Research Council Act
Health Sciences Centre Act, 1988-89
Health Services Act
Health Services Insurance Act
Hearing Aid Act
Hospitals Act
Human Tissue Act
Licensed Practical Nurses Act
Medical Act
Manitoba Medical Association Dues Act
Mental Health Act (except parts 9 & 10 & clauses 125 (1)(i) & (j)
Midwifery Act
Occupational Therapists Act
Personal Health Information Act
Pharmaceutical Act
Physiotherapists Act
Podiatrists Act
Prescription Drugs Cost Assistance Act
Private Hospitals Act
Protection for Persons in Care Act
Public Health Act
Regional Health Authorities Act
Registered Dieticians Act
Registered Nurses Act
Registered Psychiatric Nurses Act
Registered Respiratory Therapists Act
Sanitorium Board of Manitoba Act
Minister,Hon. Theresa Oswald
204-945-3731, Fax: 204-945-0441,minhlt@leg.gov.mb.ca
Deputy Minister, Arlene Wilgosh
204-945-3771, Fax: 204-945-4564,dmhlt@leg.gov.mb.ca
Chief Medical Officer of Health,Dr. Joel Kettner
204-788-6766, Fax: 204-948-2204
Provincial Director, Patient Access, Dr. Luis Oppenheimer
Administrative Secretary, Betty Rubin
204-786-7191, Fax: 204-774-1325,brubin@gov.mb.ca
• Appeal Panel for Home Care
#4012, 300 Carlton St.
Winnipeg, MB R3B 3M9
204-788-6788 Fax: 204-948-2024 800-491-4993
appeals@gov.mb.ca
• Manitoba Drug Standards & Therapeutics Committee
#1014, 300 Carlton St.
Winnipeg, MB R3B 3M9
204-786-7317 Fax: 204-942-2030
• Manitoba Health Appeal Board
#4011, 300 Carlton St.
Winnipeg, MB R3B 3M9
204-788-6704 Fax: 204-948-2024 866-744-3257
Quasi-judicial body responsible for making decisions on appeals under The Health Services Insurance Act, The Ambulance Services Act & The Mental Health Act.
• Addictions Foundation of Manitoba(AFM) / Fondation manitobaine de lutte contre les dépendances
1031 Portage Ave.
Winnipeg, MB R3G 0R8
204-944-6200 Fax: 204-786-7768
library@afm.mb.ca
www.afm.mb.ca
• Manitoba Seniors & Health Aging Secretariat

Corporate & Provincial Program Support
Fax: 204-775-3712
Asst. Deputy Minister, Kim Sharman
204-788-6439
Acting Director, Operations, Provincial Drug Programs, Jeannine Ste. Marie
204-786-7333, Fax: 204-786-6634
Director, Corporate Services, Valdine Berry
204-788-6749, Fax: 204-945-4559
Manager, Protection for Persons in Care, Paul Lamoureux
204-788-6347
Director, Information Systems - Technical Services & Operations, Cliff Greenhalgh
204-786-7234
Coordinator, French Language Services, Robert V. Loiselle
204-788-6698, Fax: 204-772-2943

Finance
Chief Financial Officer & Asst. Deputy Minister, Karen Herd
204-788-2525, Fax: 204-775-3412
Acting Executive Director, Nardia Maharaj
204-786-7138
Executive Director, Accountability Support, Lorraine E. Dacombe Dewar
204-786-7266
Acting Director, Health Information Management, Deborah Malazdrewicz
204-786-7149, Fax: 204-944-1911
Acting Director, Regional Financial Support, Rhonda Hogg
204-786-7140
Controller, Tony Messner
204-786-7135, Fax: 204-774-1325

Primary Care & Healthy Living
300 Carlton St., 2nd Floor, Winnipeg, MB R3B 3M9
Mission is to encourage the prevention of illness & injury, coordinate access to health care, & strengthen existing primary health care services with new initiatives

Asst. Deputy Minister, Marie O'Neill
204-786-6656, Fax: 204-948-2366
Acting Director, Chronic Disease Management, Kristin Anderson
204-788-6746
Executive Director, Mental Health & Addictions, Yvonne Block
204-786-7281
Executive Director, Aboriginal Health & Northern Nursing Stations, Rose Neufeld
204-788-6649, Fax: 204-945-4559
Executive Director, Primary Health Care, Barbara Wasilewski
204-786-7176
Acting Director, Emergency Medical Services, Brenda Gregory
204-945-0711

Public Health
300 Carlton St., 4th Fl., Winnipeg, MB R3B 3M9
204-788-6701, Fax: 204-948-2040
Mission is to assure conditions in which people can be healthy, by applying scientific & medical knowledge to systematically identify & analyze the health of groups & populations, & by assisting communities to organize, implement & monitor efforts aimed at the prevention & control of disease & promotion of health.The Environmental Health Unit of the Public Health Branch responds to biological, chemical or social health threats to the public. The Unit manages several programs including Environmental Health, Food Protection, Tobacco Reduction & Dental/Oral Health
Chief Provincial Public Health Officer,Dr. Joel Kettner
204-788-6766

Manitoba Healthy Child Office

#219, 114 Garry St., Winnipeg, MB R3C 1G1
204-945-2266, 888-848-0140
healthychild@gov.mb.ca
Office provides leadership & encourages actions that address health concerns & reduces the need for medical care for children
Acts Administered:
The Addictions Foundation Act
The Non-Smokers Health Protection Act
Manitoba Prenatal Benefit Regulation
Minister,Hon. Kerri Irvin-Ross
204-945-1373, Fax: 204-948-2703
Chief Executive Officer, Healthy Child Manitoba, Jan Sanderson
204-945-6707, Fax: 204-948-2585
Director, Programs, Susan Tessler
204-945-1275

Manitoba Human Rights Commission

175 Hargrave St., 7th Fl., Winnipeg, MB R3C 3R8
204-945-3007, Fax: 204-945-1292, 888-884-8681
hrc@gov.mb.ca
www.gov.mb.ca/hrc/

Executive Director, Dianna Scarth
204-945-3020

Manitoba Hydro

PO Box 815 Main, Winnipeg, MB R3C 2P4
204-474-3311, Fax: 204-475-0069,
publicaffairs@hydro.mb.ca
www.hydro.mb.ca
Manitoba Hydro (MH) is a major energy utility. One of the largest electricity & natural gas utilities in Canada, it serves 521,600 electric customers throughout Manitoba & 261,150 gas customers in various communities throughout southern Manitoba. Virtually all electricity generated by the provincial Crown Corporation is from self-renewing water power. MH is the major distributor of natural gas in the province. Developing & implementing an environmental management system consistent with ISO standards. Actively pursuing a vairety or projects & programs aimed at reducing GHG & vehicle emissions, recycling, conserving energy, digging out contaminated soils, partnering with NGOs
Minister responsible,Hon. Gregory F. Selinger
204-945-3952, Fax: 204-945-6057,minfin@leg.gov.mb.ca
President/CEO, Bob B. Brennan
204-474-3600
Chair, Victor H. Schroeder, Q.C.
Vice-President, Customer Service & Marketing, Gerry W. Rose
Vice-President, Finance & Administration & CFO, Vince A. Warden
Vice-President, Power Supply, Ken R. Adams
Vice-President, Transmission & Distribution, Al M. Snyder
General Counsel & Corporate Secretary, Ken M. Tennenhouse
Vice President, Corporate Relations, Ruth Kristjanson

Manitoba Infrastructure & Transportation

Legislative Building, #203, 450 Broadway Ave., Winnipeg, MB R3C 0V8
204-945-3723, Fax: 204-945-7610,
www.gov.mb.ca/mit/

Acts Administered:
Crown Lands Act
Drivers & Vehicles Act
Government Air Services Act
Government House Act
Government Purchases Act
Highway Traffic Act
Highways Protection Act
Highways & Transportation Act
Highways & Transportation Construction Contracts Disbursement Act
Land Acquisition Act
Manitoba Floodway Authority Act
Manitoba Water Services Board Act
Off-Road Vehicles Act
Provincial Parks Act
Provincial Railways Act
Public Works Act
Taxicab Act
Trans-Canada Highway Act
Wild Rice Act
Minister,Hon. Ron Lemieux
204-945-3723, Fax:
204-945-7610,mininfratran@leg.gov.mb.ca
Deputy Minister, Andrew Horosko
204-945-3768, Fax:
204-945-4766,dminfratran@leg.gov.mb.ca
• Lake Winnipeg Stewardship Board
PO Box 305
Gimli, MB R0C 1B0
204-642-4899
www.lakewinnipeg.org
Established in 2003 to assist the government of Manitoba to achieve the main commitments in the Lake Winnipeg Action Plan of reducing phosphorus & nitrogen in the lake to pre-1970 levels. The Lake Winnipeg Stewardship Board's Interim Report (Jan. 2005), contained 32 sets of recommendations & was followed by public discussions.
• Highway Traffic Board/Motor Transport Board
#200, 301 Weston St.
Winnipeg, MB R3E 3H4
204-945-8912 Fax: 204-783-6529
• Manitoba Floodway Authority(MFA)
#200, 155 Carlton St.
Winnipeg, MB R3C 3H8
204-945-4900 Fax: 204-948-2462 866-356-6355
floodway@gov.mb.ca
Separate, independent, publicly accountable provincial agency that will manage the expansion & maintenance of the Red River Floodway on behalf of Manitobans.
• Manitoba Habitat Heritage Corporation
#200, 1555 St. James St.
Winnipeg, MB R3H 1B5
204-784-4350 Fax: 204-784-7359
mhhc@mhhc.mb.ca
www.mhhc.mb.ca
• License Suspension Appeal Board/Medical Review Committee
#200, 301 Weston St.
Winnipeg, MB R3E 3H4
204-945-7350 Fax: 204-948-2682
• Manitoba Water Services Board
PO Box 22080
Brandon, MB R7A 6Y9
204-726-6076 Fax: 204-726-6290
www.gov.mb.ca/waterstewardship/mwsb/
Assists rural residents outside Winnipeg in developing safe & sustainable water &/or sewerage facilities.
• Manitoba Land Value Appraisal Commission
800 Portage Ave.
Winnipeg, MB R3G 0N4
204-945-2941 Fax: 204-948-2235
• Taxicab Board
#200, 301 Weston St.
Winnipeg, MB R3E 3H4
Fax: 204-948-2315

Canada-Manitoba Infrastructure Secretariat
204-945-4074, Fax: 204-945-2035, 800-268-4883
infra@gov.mb.ca

Government Services
Legislative Bldg., #332, 450 Broadway, Winnipeg, MB R3C 0V8

Accommodation Services
1700 Portage Ave., Winnipeg, MB R3J 0E1
Asst. Deputy Minister, Chris Hauch
204-945-7535, Fax: 204-945-2546
Director, Corporate Accommodation Planning, Hilary Oakman
204-945-7965,
Director, Project Services, Pat Landry
204-945-6615
Director, Operations, Rod Berscheid
204-945-7528
Director, Security Branch, Gary Walker
204-945-7608

Supply & Services Division
270 Osborne St. North, Winnipeg, MB R3C 1V7
Asst. Deputy Minister, Tracey Danowski
204-945-6340, Fax: 204-948-2509
COO, Fleet Vehicles Agency, Al Franchuk
204-945-0275
Director, Procurement Services, David Ash
204-945-6380, Fax: 204-945-1455
COO, Materials Distribution Agency, David Bishop
204-945-6043, Fax: 204-948-3273

Transportation
Legislative Bldg., #209, 450 Broadway, Winnipeg, MB R3C 0V8
Deputy Minister, Andrew Horosko
204-945-3768, Fax: 204-945-4766

Construction & Maintenance Branch
#1610, 215 Garry St., Winnipeg, MB R3C 3Z1
Fax: 204-945-3841,
Other Communication: Highway Condition Information:
204/945-3705, 1-877-627-6237
Executive Director, Ron Weatherburn
204-945-3775
Director, Mechanical Equipment Services, Mike Knight
204-945-8567, Fax: 204-948-3274

Administrative Services Division
215 Garry St., 17th Fl., Winnipeg, MB R3C 3Z1
Fax: 204-945-5115
Asst. Deputy Minister, Paul Rochon
204-945-3887
Acting Director, Financial Services, Ian Hasanally
204-945-3883
Director, Information Technology Services, Dan Buhler
204-945-4512
Director, Amalgamated Human Resources, Jennifer Morris
204-945-5846, Fax: 204-948-3382

Engineering & Operations Division
215 Garry St., 16th Fl., Winnipeg, MB R3C 3Z1
Fax: 204-945-3841
Asst. Deputy Minister, Lance Vigfusson
204-945-3733
Director, Northern Airports & Marine, Mary Bartman
204-945-3421
Northern
11 Nelson Rd., Thompson, MB R8N 0B3
204-677-6540, Fax: 204-677-6354
Director, Doug McMahon

Highway Engineering Branch
Executive Director, Walter Burdz
204-945-3772
Director, Highway Planning & Design, Eric Christiansen
204-945-0236
Director, Materials Engineering, Said Kass
204-945-2279
Director, Traffic Engineering, Glenn Cuthbertson
204-945-0329

Transportation Policy Division
215 Garry St., 15th Fl., Winnipeg, MB R3C 3Z1
Fax: 204-945-5539
Asst. Deputy Minister, John Spacek
204-945-1025
Director, Corporate Policy & Legislation Branch, Lawrence Mercer
204-945-1894
Director, Transportation Policy & Service Development, Richard Danis
204-945-0800
Director, Transportation Systems Planning & Development, Amar Chadha
204-945-2269

Manitoba Intergovernmental Affairs

#301, 450 Broadway Ave., Winnipeg, MB R3C 0V8
Fax: 204-945-1383,
mnia@leg.gov.mb.ca
www.gov.mb.ca/ia/
Mission is to improve the economic, social & environmental wellbeing of Manitoba communities & citizens.The Department serves individuals, local governments, community organizations

& businesses; & establishes a legislative, financial, planning & policy framework that supports democratic, accountable, effective & financially efficient local government, & the sustainable development of our communities. Programs are aimed at meeting particular needs for training, on-going advice, technical analysis & funding related to community revitalization & development, infrastructure development, land management, business support & local governance. The Department functions as an advocate of community needs, a catalyst & co-ordinator of action, promotes & participates in partnerships with private sector & non-government organizations & intergovernmental alliances

Acts Administered:
Capital Region Partnership Act
City of Winnipeg Charter
Convention Centre Corporation Act
An Act respecting Debts Owing by Municipalities to School Districts
Emergency Measures Act
Emergency 911 Public Safety Answering Point Act
Liquor Control Act
Local Authorities Election Act
Local Government Districts Act
Manitoba Lotteries Corporation Act
Manitoba Trade & Investment Corporation Act
Municipal Act
Municipal Affairs Administration Act
Municipal Assessment Act
Municipal Board Act
Municipal Councils & School Boards Elections Act
Municipal Revenue (Grants & Taxation) (Part 2)
Official Time Act
Planning Act (in part)
Soldiers' Taxation Relief Act
Regional Waste Management Authorities Act
Unconditional Grants Act

Minister,Hon. Steve Ashton
204-945-3788, Fax: 204-945-1383,minia@leg.gov.mb.ca
Deputy Minister, Intergovernmental Affairs, Linda McFadyen
204-945-4309, Fax: 204-945-5255,dmnia@leg.gov.mb.ca
Director, Administration & Finance, Craig Halwachs
Director, Amalgamated Human Resources, Craig McGregor

• Manitoba Liquor Control Commission
1555 Buffalo Pl.
PO Box 1023
Winnipeg, MB R3C 2X1
204-284-2501 Fax: 204-475-7666
info@mlcc.mb.ca
www.mlcc.mb.ca

• Manitoba Municipal Board
#1144, 363 Broadway
Winnipeg, MB R3C 3N9
204-945-2941 Fax: 204-948-2235

Provincial-Municipal Support Services
#508, 800 Portage Ave., Winnipeg, MB R3G 0N4
Asst. Deputy Minister, Laurie Davidson
204-945-2565, Fax: 204-948-2107
Acting Director, Municipal Finance & Advisory Services, Denise Carlyle
204-945-1944, Fax: 204-948-2780
Provincial Municipal Assessor, Assessment Branch, Mark Boreskie
204-945-2604, Fax: 204-945-1994
Director, Information Systems, Larry Phillips
204-945-2585, Fax: 204-945-1994

Community Land Use Planning Services
#604, 800 Portage Ave., Winnipeg, MB R3G 0N4
Asst. Deputy Minister,Vacant
Director, Community Planning Services, David Neufeld
204-945-2192, Fax: 204-945-5059
Director, Provincial Planning Services, Michael Teillet
204-945-2592, Fax: 204-945-5059

Emergency Measures Organization (EMO)
405 Broadway Ave., 15th Floor, Winnipeg, MB R3C 3L6
204-945-4772, Fax: 204-945-4929, 888-267-8298
emo@gov.mb.ca
www.manitobaemo.ca
Coordinates emergency response, municipal emergency planning & training, & disaster recovery programs
Executive Director, Chuck Sanderson
204-945-5228, Fax: 204-945-4929

Urban Strategic Initiatives
#607, 800 Portage Ave., Winnipeg, MB R3G 0N4
Fax: 204-948-3512
Asst. Deputy Minister,Vacant
Director, Programs & Policy, Jon Gunn
204-945-3864
Director, Winnipeg Partnership Agreement,Vacant
204-984-1806, Fax: 204-983-3844
Coordinator, Neighbourhoods Alive!, Bob Dilay
204-945-3379, Fax: 204-945-5059

Manitoba Justice

Legislative Building, #104, 405 Broadway Ave., Winnipeg, MB R3C 3L6
204-945-3728, Fax: 204-945-2517,
minjus@gov.mb.ca
www.gov.mb.ca/justice/index.html

Promotes a safe, just & peaceful society supported by a justice system that is fair, effective, trusted & understood by: providing a fair & effective prosecution service; managing offenders in an environment that promotes public safety & rehabilitation; providing mechanisms for timely & peaceful resolution of civil & criminal matters; providing legal advice & services to government; providing programs which assist in protecting & enforcing individual & collective rights; providing support & assistance to victims of crime; & promoting effective policing & crime prevention initiatives

Acts Administered:
Canada-United Kingdom Judgements Enforcement Act
Constitutional Questions Act
Correctional Services Act
Court of Appeal Act
Court of Queens' Bench Act
Court Security Act
Crime Prevention Foundation Act
Crown Attorneys Act
Child Custody Enforcement Act
Department of Justice Act
Discriminatory Business Practices Act
Domestic Violence & Stalking Prevention, Protection & Compensation Act
Enforcement of Judgements Conventions Act
Escheats Act
Executive Government Organization Act (subsection 12(2), only, as Keeper of the Great Seal)
Expropriation Act
Fatality Inquiries Act
Fortified Buildings Act
Helen Betty Osborne Memorial Foundation Act
Human Rights Code
Inter-jurisdictional Support Orders Act
International Commercial Arbitration Act
International Sale of Goods Act
Interprovincial Subpoena Act
Intoxicated Persons Detention Act
Jury Act
Law Enforcement Review Act
Law Fees & Probate Charge Act
Law Reform Commission Act
Legal Aid Services Society of Manitoba Act
Mental Health Act Part 10 & clauses 125(1)(i) & (j)
Minors Intoxicating Substances Control Act
Privacy Act
Private Investigators & Security Guards Act
Proceedings Against the Crown Act
Provincial Police Act
Public Trustee Act
Reciprocal Enforcement of Judgement Act
Regulations Act
Safer Communities & Neighbourhood Act
Sheriffs Act
Summary Convictions Act
Transboundary Pollution Reciprocal Access Act
Uniform Law Conference Commissioners Act
Vacant Property Act
Victims' Bill of Rights

Minister & Attorney General,Hon. David Walter Chomiak
204-945-3728, Fax: 204-945-2517,minjus@leg.gov.mb.ca
Deputy Minister & Deputy Attorney General, Ron Perozzo, Q.C.
204-945-3739, Fax: 204-945-4133,dmjus@leg.gov.mb.ca

• Compensation for Victims of Crime
1410 - 405 Broadway
Winnipeg, MB R3C 3L6
204-945-0899 Fax: 204-948-3071 800-262-9344
www.gov.mb.ca/justice/victims/index.html
The Compensation for Victims of Crime Program provides compensation for personal injury or death resulting from certain crimes occurring within Manitoba.

• Law Enforcement Review Agency(LERA)
#420, 155 Carlton St.
Winnipeg, MB R3C 3H8
204-945-8667 Fax: 204-948-1014 800-282-8069
lera@gov.mb.ca
www.gov.mb.ca/justice/lera
The mission of the Law Enforcement Review Agency (LERA) is to deliver a judicious, timely, impartial, client-oriented service to the public and to the police services and police officers within its jurisdiction.

• Law Reform Commission
#432, 405 Broadway
Winnipeg, MB R3C 3L6
204-945-2896 Fax: 204-948-2184
lawreform@gov.mb.ca
www.gov.mb.ca/justice/mlrc
The Manitoba Law Reform Commission is an independent agency of the Government of Manitoba established by The Law Reform Commission Act, C.C.S.M. c. L95. The Commission's duties are to inquire into and consider any matter relating to law in Manitoba with a view to making recommendations for the improvement, modernization and reform of law.

• Legal Aid Manitoba
402 - 294 Portage Ave.
Winnipeg, MB R3C 0B9
204-985-8500 Fax: 204-944-8582 800-261-2960
info@legalaid.mb.ca
www.legalaid.mb.ca
Legal Aid Manitoba works to ensure people with low incomes have the protections guaranteed in Canada by the The Charter of Rights and Freedoms, enacted as part of The Constitution Act in 1982.

• Manitoba Gaming Control Commission
#800, 215 Garry St.
Winnipeg, MB R3C 3P3
204-954-9400 Fax: 204-954-9450 800-782-0363
information@mgcc.mb.ca
www.mgcc.mb.ca
Other Communication: Toll Free Fax: 1-866-999-6688
To regulate and control gaming activity in Manitoba by protecting the public interest, being proactive and responsive to Manitoba's evolving gaming environment and working in consultation with our clients, stakeholders and partners to establish fair, balanced and responsible gaming practices.

• Manitoba Human Rights Commission

• Office of the Chief Medical Examiner
#210, 1 Wesley Ave.
Winnipeg, MB R3C 4C6
204-945-2088 Fax: 204-945-2442 800-282-9069
www.gov.mb.ca/justice/about/chief.html
The Chief Medical Examiner's Office investigates deaths where the cause is not readily known or when the death is a result of violence.

• Office of the Public Trustee
#500, 155 Carlton St.
Winnipeg, MB R3C 5R9
204-945-2700 Fax: 204-948-2251
publictrustee@gov.mb.ca
www.gov.mb.ca/publictrustee/index.html
The Public Trustee of Manitoba is a provincial government Special Operating Agency that manages and protects the affairs of Manitobans who are unable to do so themselves and have no one else willing or able to act. This includes mentally incompetent and vulnerable adults, deceased estates, and children.

• Manitoba Review Board
408 York Ave., 2nd Fl.
Winnipeg, MB R3C 0P9
204-945-4438 Fax: 204-945-5751

Civil Justice Division
Acting Director, Civil Legal Services, Lynn Romeo
204-945-2846
Director, Constitutional Law, Heather Leonoff
204-945-0679
Director, Family Law, Joan A. MacPhail, Q.C.
204-945-0268, Fax: 204-948-2004

Corrections Division
#810, 405 Broadway Ave., Winnipeg, MB R3C 3L6
204-945-7291
Asst. Deputy Minister, Greg Graceffo
204-945-7291, Fax: 204-945-5537
Executive Director, Adult Custody, Reg Forester
204-945-7283, Fax: 204-945-5537
Acting Executive Director, Youth Correctional Services, Carolyn Brock
204-945-6063, Fax: 204-948-2166
Acting Director, Adult Probation Services, Bob Dojack
204-945-4639, Fax: 204-948-2166
Manager, Fine Option Program, Tom Jennings
204-945-7894, Fax: 204-948-2299

Courts Division
405 Broadway, 2nd Fl., Winnipeg, MB R3C 3L6
Asst. Deputy Minister, Jeff Schnoor
204-945-3027
Acting Executive Director, Judicial Services, Lavonne Ross
204-945-0413
Executive Director, Regional Courts,Vacant
204-726-6561
Executive Director, Winnipeg Courts & Acting Director, Court Services, Debra Baker

204-945-5883, Other Communications: Court Services: 204/945-1579

Criminal Justice Division
Asst. Deputy Minister, Mike Horn
204-945-2887
Director, Aboriginal & Community Law Enforcement, Al Brolly
204-945-5556
Director, Victim Services,Vacant
204-945-4589

Legislative Counsel Division
#410, 405 Broadway Ave., Winnipeg, MB R3C 3L6
204-945-5758
Legislative Counsel & Asst. Deputy Minister, Valerie Perry
204-945-1727
Director, Legal Translation, Michel Nantel
204-945-4597

Prosecutions Division
#510, 405 Broadway Ave., Winnipeg, MB R3C 3L6
204-945-2852
Asst. Deputy Attorney General,Vacant
204-945-2873
Director, Regional Prosecutions & Legal Education, Brian Kaplan
204-945-2860
Director, Specialized Prosecutions & Appeals, Don Slough
204-945-2868
Director, Winnipeg Prosecutions, Jacqueline St.Hill
204-945-3228
Director, Policy Development & Analysis, Jeff Schnoor
204-945-2900
Director, Business Operations, Carol Abbott
204-945-3417

Manitoba Labour & Immigration

Legislative Building, 317, 450 Broadway Ave., Winnipeg, MB R3C 0V8
204-945-4079, Fax: 204-945-8312,
minlab@leg.gov.mb.ca
www.gov.mb.ca/labour

Acts Administered:
Amusements Act (Part II)
Architects Act
Architects & Engineers Scope of Practice Dispute Settlement Act
Buildings & Mobile Homes Act
Construction Industry Wages Act
Department of Labour & Immigration Act
Electricians' Licence Act
Elevator Act
Employment Services Act
Employment Standards Code
Engineering & Geoscientific Professions Act
Firefighters & Paramedics Arbitration Act
Fires Prevention & Emergency Response Act
Gas & Oil Burner Act
Holocaust Memorial Day Act
Labour Relations Act
Manitoba Ethnocultural Advisory & Advocacy Council Act
Manitoba Immigration Council Act
Manitoba Multiculturalism Act
Manitoba Women's Advisory Council Act
Pay Equity Act
Pension Benefits Act
Power Engineers Act
Remembrance Day Act
Retail Business Holiday Closing Act
Steam & Pressure Plants Act
Workplace Safety & Health Act
Minister,Hon. Nancy Allan
204-945-4079, Fax: 204-945-8312,minlab@leg.gov.mb.ca
Deputy Minister, Jeff Parr
204-945-3782, Fax: 204-948-2203,dmlab@leg.gov.mb.ca
Director, Amalgamated Human Resources, Robert (Butch) Berube
204-945-6892
• Advisory Council on Workplace Safety & Health
#200, 401 York Ave.
Winnipeg, MB R3C 0P8
204-945-3446 Fax: 204-945-4556
www.gov.mb.ca/labour/safety/council.html
The Advisory Council on Workplace Safety & Health was established in 1977 under the authority of the Workplace Safety & Health Act. The council reports directly to the Minister of Labour & Immigration.The council advises & makes recommendations to the Minister of Labour & Immigration concerning general workplace safety & health issues, protection of workers in specific situations & appointment of consultants & advisors.
• Manitoba Civil Service Commission
#935, 155 Carlton St.
Winnipeg, MB R3C 3H8
204-945-2332 Fax: 204-945-1486
cschrp@gov.mb.ca
www.gov.mb.ca/csc/
• Manitoba Ethnocultural Advisory & Advocacy Council
215 Notre Dame Ave. 4th Fl.
Winnipeg, MB R3B 1N3
204-945-2339 Fax: 204-948-2323 800-665-8332
meaac@gov.mb.ca
www.gov.mb.ca/labour/immigrate/multiculturalism/5.html
• Manitoba Labour Board
A.A. Heaps Bldg.
#402, 258 Portage Ave.
Winnipeg, MB R3C 0B6
204-945-3783 Fax: 204-945-1296
mlb@gov.mb.ca
www.gov.mb.ca/labour/labbrd
• Manitoba Minimum Wage Board
614 - 401 York Ave.
Winnipeg, MB R3C 0P8
204-945-4889 Fax: 204-948-2085
mw@gov.mb.ca
www.gov.mb.ca/labour/labmgt/resbr/wages/minwagbd.html
• Manitoba Women's Advisory Council
#301, 155 Carlton St.
Winnipeg, MB R3C 3H8
204-945-6281 Fax: 204-945-6511 800-282-8069
001women@gov.mb.ca
• Multiculturalism Secretariat
213 Notre Dame Ave., 4th Fl.
Winnipeg, MB R3B 1N3
204-945-1156 Fax: 204-948-2323
• Office of the Fire Commissioner
#508, 401 York Ave.
Winnipeg, MB R3C 0P8
204-945-3322 Fax: 204-948-2089 800-282-8069
firecomm@gov.mb.ca
www.firecomm.gov.mb.ca/
• Pension Commission of Manitoba
#1004, 401 York Ave.
Winnipeg, MB R3C 0P8
204-945-2740 Fax: 204-948-2375
pensions@gov.mb.ca
www.gov.mb.ca/labour/pension/index.html

Employment Standards Division
204-945-3352, Fax: 204-948-3046, 800-821-4307
employmentstandards@gov.mb.ca
Executive Director, Dave Dyson
204-945-3354, Fax: 204-948-3046
Manager, Worker Advisor Office, Terry Hampson
204-945-4211, Fax: 204-948-2020

Immigration & Multiculturalism Division
213 Notre Dame Ave., 5th Floor, Winnipeg, MB R3B 1N3
204-945-6300, Fax: 204-948-2148,
immigratemanitoba@gov.mb.ca
www.immigrationmanitoba.com
Asst. Deputy Minister, Gerald L. Clement
204-945-8174, Fax: 204-948-2882
Director, Adult Language Training Branch, Margaret Pidlaski
204-945-7415, Fax: 204-948-2148
Acting Director, Immigration Promotion & Recruitment, Ben Rempel
204-945-4984, Fax: 204-948-2256
Director, Settlement & Labour Market Services Branch, Ximena Munoz
204-945-5978, Fax: 204-948-2148

Status of Women
#409, 401 York Ave., Winnipeg, MB R3C 0P8
204-945-3476, Fax: 204-945-0013, 800-263-0234
mwd@gov.mb.ca
Executive Director, Yvonne Spyropoulos
204-945-5812

Workplace Safety & Health Division
#200, 401 York Ave., Winnipeg, MB R3C 0P8
204-945-3446, Fax: 204-948-2209,
wshcompl@gov.mb.ca
www.gov.mb.ca/labour/safety/index.html
Operates a 24-hour response service to accidents & complaints; monitors & evaluates workplace areas for chemical, physical, biological & ergonomic factors; participates in worker education & training programs for workers, employers & other interested parties on matters relating to maintaining a safe & healthy workplace
Asst. Deputy Minister, Don Hurst
204-945-3605
Director, Inspection Services, Bryan Zirk
204-945-8429, bzirk@gov.mb.ca
Acting Director, Mining Safety Unit, Bill Comaskey
204-677-6821, bcomaskey@gov.mb.ca
Chief Occupational Medical Officer,Dr. Ted Redekop
204-945-3608, tredekop@gov.mb.ca

Manitoba Lotteries Corporation

830 Empress St., Winnipeg, MB R3G 3H3
204-957-2500, Fax: 204-957-3991,
communications@casinosofwinnipeg.com
www.mlc.mb.ca
President/CEO, Winston Hodgins
Communications Coordinator, Lindsay Sprange
204-957-3930

Manitoba Public Insurance

#820, 234 Donald St., PO Box 6300, Winnipeg, MB R3C 4A4
204-985-7000, Fax: 204-943-9851, 800-665-2410
www.mpi.mb.ca
Administers Manitoba's Public Automobile Insurance Program & sells extension auto coverage on a competitive basis.
Minister responsible,Hon. David Chomiak
President/CEO, Marilyn McLaren
Vice-President, Claims Operations & Service Delivery, Wilf Bedard
Vice-President, Corporate Information Technology & Chief Information Officer, Wayne Wedge
Vice-President, Human Resources, MaryAnn Kempe
Vice-President, Finance & CFO, Don Palmer
Vice-President, Business Innovation & Insurance Operations, Dan Guimond
Vice-President, Corporate Legal,General Counsel & Corporate Secretary, Kevin McCulloch

Manitoba News Media Services

#29, Legislative Bldg., 450 Broadway, Winnipeg, MB R3C 0V8
204-945-3746, Fax: 204-945-3988,
nmservices@leg.gov.mb.ca
Provides news releases, television & radio news items.
Supervisor, Stu Fawcett
204-945-4097, Fax: 204-945-3988,sfawcett@leg.gov.mb.ca

Manitoba Government Inquiry
204-945-3744, Fax: 204-945-4261, 866-626-4862
mgi@gov.mb.ca
Answers queries regarding Manitoba's provincial government departments & agencies.
Supervisor, Aggie Hasselfield
204-945-2424, ahasselfield@gov.mb.ca

Statutory Publications
#20, 200 Vaughan St., Winnipeg, MB R3C 1T5
204-945-3101, Fax: 204-945-7172, 800-321-1203
statpub@gov.mb.ca
www.gov.mb.ca/chc/statpub/
Sale & distribution of Manitoba statutes, regulations & a wide variety of other government publications & forms
Supervisor, Keith Holness
204-945-3101, Fax: 204-945-7172,kholness@gov.mb.ca

Manitoba Office of the Ombudsman

750 - 500 Portage Ave., Winnipeg, MB R3C 3X1
204-982-9130, Fax: 204-942-7803, 800-665-0531
ombudsma@ombudsman.mb.ca
www.ombudsman.mb.ca
The Ombudsman, an independent & non-partisan Officer of the Legislative Assembly, investigates complaints from persons who feel they have been unfairly dealt with by government departments or agencies
Manitoba Ombudsman, Irene Hamilton

Manitoba Science, Technology, Energy & Mines

#333, 450 Broadway, Winnipeg, MB R3C 0V8
www.gov.mb.ca/stem/index.html
Acts Administered:
Gaming Control Act
Manitoba Hydro Act
Minister, Jim Rondeau
204-945-5356, Fax: 204-948-2692,minstem@leg.gov.mb.ca
Deputy Minister, John Clarkson
204-945-2771, Fax: 204-948-2747,dmstem@leg.gov.mb.ca
• Industrial Technology Centre
#200, 78 Innovation Dr.
Winnipeg, MB R3T 6C2
www.itc.mb.ca
• Mining Board
#360, 1395 Ellice Ave.
Winnipeg, MB R3G 3P2
204-489-0018
Arbitration of disputes between surface rights holders & mineral rights holders with respect to accessing of minerals other than oil & gas.

• Surface Rights Board
#360, 1395 Ellice Ave.
Winnipeg, MB R3G 3P2
204-945-0731 Fax: 204-948-2578 800-282-8069
bmiskimmin@gov.mb.ca
Arbitrates disputes relating to right of entry or compensation for surface rights used by holders of oil & gas rights.
• Manitoba Education, Research & Learning Information Networks(MERLIN)
#100 - 135 Innovation Dr., University of Manitoba
Winnipeg, MB R3T 6A8
204-474-7800 Fax: 204-474-7830 800-430-6404
www.merlin.mb.ca
• Manitoba Health Research Council
#P216, 770 Bannatyne Ave.
Winnipeg, MB R3E 0W3
204-775-1096 Fax: 204-786-5401
info@mhrc.mb.ca
mhrc.mb.ca

Energy Development Initiative
The Initiative's focus is on: Agri-Energy, Biofuels, Geothermal systems, Wind Energy, Green Building & Energy Efficiency, Hydrogen, as well as hybrid-electric vehicles, solar energy, ethanol fuels
Asst. Deputy Minister, Energy Development Initiative, Garry Hastings
204-945-1454, Fax: 204-943-0031
Director, Energy Economic Development, Jim Crone
204-945-1874, Fax: 204-943-0031,jcrone@gov.mb.ca
Director, Energy Policy, Shaun Loney
204-945-5804, Fax: 204-943-0031,sloney@gov.mb.ca

Energy Climate Change & Green Strategy Initiatives Branch
#1202 - 155 Carlton St., Winnipeg, MB R3C 3H8
204-945-7382, Fax: 204-948-3739,
ccinfo@gov.mb.ca
www.manitoba.ca
The Branch promotes awareness, programs & funding for climate change initiatives, facilitates partnerships between government & community to develop green initiatives that result in environmental, economic & social benefits, advances climate change mitigation & adaptation research, & develops regional partnerships for climate change action
Acting Executive Director, Andrea Merredew
204-945-2245
Director, Communications, Colin Lemoine
204-945-1494

Mineral Resources Division
#360, 1395 Ellice Ave., Winnipeg, MB R3G 3P2
Fax: 204-945-8427
Promotes wise land management & environmentally sustainable economic development in the province based on Manitoba's mineral & petroleum resources; fosters & enhances business development opportunities in mineral & petroleum economic development through promotion & marketing activities; provides authoritative documentation of the province's mineral & petroleum endowment & development potential; administers the delivery of mineral & petroleum industry support programs; administers legislation governing the disposition of mineral rights, oil & gas rights, exploration, development & production of Manitoba's mineral & petroleum resources
Assistant Deputy Minister, John Fox
204-945-4317, Fax: 204-945-1406,jfox@gov.mb.ca

Manitoba Geological Survey
#360, 1394 Ellice Ave., Winnipeg, MB R3G 3P2
Fax: 204-945-1406, 800-223-5215
minesinfo@gov.mb.ca
Generates technical information on the geology of Manitoba in order to encourage & guide mineral exploration in the province & to provide a database for developing mineral policy & for determining effective land-use policies.
Director, Ric Syme
204-945-6556, rsyme@gov.mb.ca

Mineral Policy & Business Development
Manager, Gary Ostry
204-945-6564, Fax: 204-945-8427,gostry@gov.mb.ca
MEAP Coordinator, Minerals Policy & Business Development, Linda Rogoski
204-945-6586, Fax: 204-945-8427,lrogoski@gov.mb.ca

Regional Geological Survey Offices:

Mines Branch
#360, 1395 Ellice Ave., Winnipeg, MB R3G 3P2
Fax: 204-948-2578
The Mines Branch administers legislation governing the disposition of mineral rights (permits, claims & leases), exploration, development, & production of the province's non-fuel mineral resources & the rehabilitation of mines & quarries.
Director, Ernie Armitt
204-945-6505, earmitt@gov.mb.ca

Regional Office:

Petroleum
#360, 1395 Ellice Ave., Winnipeg, MB R3G 3P2
204-945-6577, Fax: 204-945-0586
Administers provisions under The Oil & Gas Act & The Oil & Gas Production Tax Act relating to exploration, development, production & transportation of oil & gas. The Branch develops, recommends, implements & administers policies & legislation, to provide for the sustainable development of Manitoba's oil & gas resources. The Branch deals with matters relating to well spacing, production allowables, pool designations, salt water disposal, enhanced recovery projects & unitization. The Branch publishes several reports each year, providing the public, industry & government with information on the petroleum industry in Manitoba
Director, Keith Lowdon
klowdon@gov.mb.ca

District Offices:

Virden
Petroleum Inspection, 227 King St., Virden, MB R0M 2C0
204-748-4260, Fax: 204-748-2208

Waskada
Petroleum Inspection, 23 Railway Ave., Waskada, MB R0M 2E0
204-673-2472, Fax: 204-673-2767

ICT Services Manitoba
#300 - 259 Portage Ave., Winnipeg, MB R3B 2A9
800-665-0204
www.gov.mb.ca/est/KnowledgeEnterprises
Project Manager, ICT, Geoff King
204-945-6298

Knowledge Enterprises Branch
259 Portage Ave., Winnipeg, MB R3B 3P4
204-945-6298, Fax: 204-945-3977
Director, Doug McCartney
204-945-6298, Fax: 204-945-3977,Douglas.McCartney@gov.mb.ca
Project Manager, ICT/Investment Promotion/Branch Communications, Cindy Hodges
204-945-6657, Cindy.Hodges@gov.mb.ca
Program Manager, Interactive Digital Media, Linda English
204-945-3307, Linda.English@gove.mb.ca
Program Manager, Interactive Digital Media, Rod Higgins
204-945-0723, Rod.Higgins@gove.mb.ca
Program Manager, Interactive Digital Media, Wayne Clark
204-945-0589, Wayne.Clark@gov.mb.ca

Manitoba Seniors & Healthy Aging Secretariat

#822, 155 Carlton St., Winnipeg, MB R3C 3H8
204-945-6565, Fax: 204-948-2514, 800-665-6565
seniors@gov.mb.ca
www.gov.mb.ca/shas

Minister responsible,Hon. Kerri Irvin-Ross
204-945-1373
Acting Executive Director, Patti Chiappetta
204-945-1825
• Manitoba Council on Aging
#822, 155 Carlton St.
Winnipeg, MB R3C 3H8
204-945-6565 Fax: 204-948-2514 800-665-6565

Manitoba Telecom Services Inc. (MTS)

333 Main St., PO Box 6666, Winnipeg, MB R3C 3V6
204-941-4111, Fax: 204-772-6391,
www.mts.mb.ca/

Chair, Thomas E. Stefanson
CEO, Pierre Blouin
President, Enterprise Solutions, John A. MacDonald
President, Consumer Markets, Kelvin Shepherd, P.Eng.
CFO, Wayne S. Demkey, CA

Manitoba Treasury Board Secretariat

#200, 386 Broadway, Winnipeg, MB R3C 3R6
204-945-4150, Fax: 204-948-4878
Minister responsible,Hon. Gregory F. Selinger
204-945-3952
Secretary to the Treasury Board, Tannis Mindell
204-945-1100
Executive Director, Expenditure Management/Continuous Improvement, Chris Roed
204-945-8835
Asst. Deputy Minister, Labour Relations, Richard (Rick) Stevenson
204-945-2136
Asst. Deputy Minister, Fiscal Management & Capital Planning, Barb Dryden
204-945-1096

Manitoba Water Stewardship

200 Saulteaux Cres., PO Box 11, Winnipeg, MB R3J 3W3
204-945-6398, 800-282-8069
wsd@gov.mb.ca
www.gov.mb.ca/waterstewardship/index.html
Provides leadership in environmental stewardship for the benefit of current & future generations of Manitobans, so that the social, economic & inherent environmental value of water is protected & realized, Manitoba's water & fish resources are managed sustainably, & people are safe from water hazards. Comprised of the former Water Branch, Fisheries Branch, & Office of Drinking Water from Manitoba Conservation, the Manitoba Water Services Board, & the Conservation Districts Program from the Department of Intergovernmental Affairs
Acts Administered:
Conservation Agreements Act
Conservation Districts Act
Drinking Water Safety Act, 2004
Dyking Authority Act
Fisheries Act
Fishermen's Assistance & Polluter's Liability Act
Ground Water & Water Well Act
Lake of the Woods Control Board Act
Manitoba Habitat Heritage Act
Manitoba Natural Resources Transfer Act
Natural Resources Agreement Act
Red River Floodway Act
Water Power Act
Water Protection Act
Water Resources Administration Act
Water Resources Conservation Act
Water Rights Act
Water Supply Commissions Act
Minister,Hon. Christine Melnick
204-945-1133, Fax: 204-948-2684,minwsd@leg.gov.mb.ca
Deputy Minister, Don Norquay
204-945-0982, Fax: 204-948-2519,dmwsd@leg.gov.mb.ca
Executive Director, Regulatory & Operational Services, Steven Topping
204-945-7488, Fax: 204-945-7419
• Manitoba Conservation Districts Commission
Secretariat c/o Planning & Coordination Branch
123 Main St.
PO Box 20000
Neepawa, MB R0J 1H0
204-476-7033 Fax: 204-476-7539
whildebran@gov.mb.ca
The Conservation Districts Program has been delivering a comprehensive, sustainable approach to water & soil management for over 25 years. Conservation Districts are established under the authority of The Conservation District Act. There are 16 Conservation Districts covering approximately 60% of Agro-Manitoba.Individual district boundaries may vary depending on the needs of the people.Districts are usually based on the drainage basin or watershed of the major river in the area.

Ecological Services Division
Asst. Deputy Minister, Dwight Williamson
204-945-7030
Director, Fisheries Branch, Joe O'Connor
204-945-7814, Fax: 204-945-2308
Director, Planning & Coordination, Rhonda McDougal
204-945-8271
Director, Water Science & Management Branch, Nicole Armstrong
204-945-3991

Office of Drinking Water
1007 Century St., Winnipeg, MB R3H 0W4
204-945-5762, Fax: 204-945-1365
Coordinates the activities of the province's drinking water program; provides guidance, technical expertise, information & education materials; ensures water suppliers provide safe, adequate & aesthetically pleasing water
Manager,P.Eng. Don Rocan
204-945-7010

Regulatory & Operational Services

Manitoba Workers' Compensation Board

333 Broadway Ave., Winnipeg, MB R3C 4W3
204-954-4321, Fax: 204-954-4999, 800-362-3340
wcb@wcb.mb.ca
www.wcb.mb.ca

President/CEO, Doug Sexsmith
CFO, Harold Dueck

Vice President, Prevention, Assessments & Customer Service, Alice Sayant
Vice President, Rehabilitation & Compensation Services, Dave Scott
General Counsel & Corporate Secretary, Lori Ferguson Sain
Associate Vice President, Human Resources & Administration, Rob Campbell
Director, Communications/SAFE Work, Warren Preece

Government of New Brunswick

Seat of Government:PO Box 6000, Fredericton, NB E3B 5H1
www.gnb.ca
The Province of New Brunswick entered Confederation July 1, 1867.It has an area of 71,355.12 km2. The Statistics Canada census population in 2006 was 730,000.

Office of the Lieutenant-Governor / Bureau du Lieutenant gouverneur

Old Government House, 51 Woodstock Rd., PO Box 6000, Fredericton, NB E3B 5H1
506-453-2505, Fax: 506-444-5280, www.gnb.ca/lg
Lieutenant-Governor,Hon. Herménégilde Chiasson Hermenegilde.Chiasson@gnb.ca
Principal Secretary, Office of the Lieutenant-Governor, Tim Richardson
tim.richardson@gnb.ca

Office of the Premier / Cabinet du Premier ministre

Centennial Bldg., 670 King St., PO Box 6000, Fredericton, NB E3B 5H1
506-453-2144, Fax: 506-453-7407, premier@gnb.ca
www.gnb.ca/0089/index-e.asp
Premier; President, Executive Council; Minister, Intergovernmental Affairs; Minister Responsible, Premier's Council on the Status of Disabled Persons; Minister Responsible, Office of Self-Sufficiency, Hon. Shawn M. Graham
Shawn.Graham@gnb.ca; Premier@gnb.ca
Chief of Staff, Bernard Thériault
Bernard.Theriault@gnb.ca
Director, Operations, Linda Haché
lindahache@gnb.ca
Director, Writing & Research, Heather Allaby
Heather.Allaby@gnb.ca
Director, Communications, Nicole Picot
Nicole.Picot@gnb.ca

Population Growth Secretariat

Centennial Bldg., 670 King St., PO Box 6000, Fredericton, NB E3B 5H1
506-453-3981, Fax: 506-444-6729, immigration@gnb.ca
www.gnb.ca/3100/index-e.asp
The Population Growth Secretariat consists of the Immigration Division & the Population Support Division. Issues such as settlement & multiculturalism, retention, & repatriation are handled by the Secretariat.
Minister, Business New Brunswick; Minister Responsible, Service New Brunswick; Minister Responsible, Population Growth Secretariat; Minister Responsible, Communications New Brunswick, Minister Responsible, Red Tape Reduction, Hon. Greg Byrne
506-453-5898, Fax: 506-453-5893,greg.byrne@gnb.ca
Chief Executive Officer, Humphrey Sheehan
506-457-7640, Fax:
506-453-3899,humphrey.sheehan@gnb.ca
Executive Director, Immigration, Tony Lampart
506-453-3455, Fax: 506-444-6729,tony.lampart@gnb.ca
Executive Director, Population Support, Monique Drapeau-Miles
506-453-8786, Fax:
506-453-3899,Monique.Drapeau-Miles@gnb.ca
Officer, Marketing & Communications, Karen Vessey
506-444-2483, Fax: 506-453-5329,karen.vessey@gnb.ca

Executive Council / Conseil exécutif

Centennial Bldg., 670 King St., PO Box 6000, Fredericton, NB E3B 5H1
506-453-2144, Fax: 506-453-7407, Shawn.Graham@gnb.ca
Premier; President, Executive Council; Minister, Intergovernmental Affairs; Minister Responsible, Premier's Council on the Status of Disabled Persons; Minister Responsible, Office of Self-Sufficiency, Hon. Shawn M. Graham
506-453-2144, Fax: 506-453-7407,Premier@gnb.ca; Shawn.Graham@gnb.ca
Minister, Justice & Consumer Affairs & Attorney General, Hon. Thomas J. Burke, Q.C.
506-462-5100, Fax: 506-453-3651,t.j.burke@gnb.ca
Minister, Public Safety & Solicitor General, Hon. John W. Foran
506-453-7414, Fax: 506-453-3870,John.Foran@gnb.ca
Minister, Finance; Minister Responsible, NB Liquor Corporation; Minister Responsible, NB Investment Management Corporation, Minister Responsible, NB Lotteries & Gaming Corporation; Minister Responsible, Regional DevelopmentCorporation, Hon. Victor E. Boudreau
506-444-2627, Fax: 506-457-4989,Victor.Boudreau2@gnb.ca
Minister, Transportation, Hon. Denis Landry
506-457-7345, Fax: 506-453-7987,Denis.Landry2@gnb.ca
Minister, Natural Resources, Hon. Donald Arseneault
506-453-2510, Fax: 506-444-5839,donald.arseneault@gnb.ca
Minister, Energy; Minister, Supply & Services; Minister Responsible, Efficiency NB,Hon. Jack Keir
506-658-3177, Fax: 506-658-3191,Jack.Keir2@gnb.ca
Minister, Agriculture & Aquaculture, Hon. Ronald Ouellette
506-453-2662, Fax: 506-453-3402,ronald.ouellette@gnb.ca
Minister, Fisheries, Hon. Rick Doucet
506-444-6734, Rick.Doucet@gnb.ca
Minister, Health, Hon. Michael B. Murphy
506-457-4800, Fax: 506-453-5442,MichaelB.Murphy@gnb.ca
Minister, Wellness, Culture, & Sport; Minister Responsible, Francophonie,Hon. Hédard Albert
506-444-2517, Fax: 506-453-6668,Hedard.Albert2@gnb.ca
Minister, Social Development; Minister Responsible, Advisory Council on the Status of Women,Hon. Mary Schryer
506-457-7866, Fax: 506-453-2164,mary.schryer@gnb.ca
Minister, Office of Human Resources, Hon. Wally Stiles
506-462-5092, Fax: 506-453-7195,wally.stiles@gnb.ca
Minister, Post-Secondary Education, Training, & Labour; Minister Responsible, Aboriginal Affairs Secretariat,Hon. Edward Doherty
506-453-2342, Fax: 506-453-3038,ed.doherty@gnb.ca
Minister, Education; Minister Responsible, New Brunswick Advisory Council on Youth; Minister Responsible, New Brunswick Provincial Capital Commission, Hon. Kelly Lamrock
506-453-2523, Fax: 506-457-4960,kelly.lamrock@gnb.ca
Minister, Environment; Minister Responsible, Northern New Brunswick Initiative,Hon. Roland Haché
506-444-5136, Fax: 506-453-3377,roland.hache@gnb.ca
Minister, Local Government; Minister Responsible, Community Non-Profit Organizations Secretariat,Hon. Carmel Robichaud
506-453-2807, Fax:
506-453-3988,carmel.robichaud@gnb.ca
Minister, Business New Brunswick; Minister Responsible, Service New Brunswick; Minister Responsible, Population Growth Secretariat; Minister Responsible, Communications New Brunswick, Minister Responsible, Red Tape Reduction, Hon. Greg Byrne
506-453-5898, Fax: 506-453-5893,greg.byrne@gnb.ca,
Minister, Tourism & Parks, Hon. Stuart Jamieson
506-453-3009, Fax: 506-457-4984,Stuart.jamieson@gnb.ca
Minister of State, Seniors & Housing, Hon. Eugene McGinley, Q.C.
506-453-2057, Fax: 506-453-2164,eugene.mcginley@gnb.ca

Executive Council Office
Centennial Bldg, #273, 670 King St., PO Box 6000, Fredericton, NB E3B 5H1
506-444-4417, Fax: 506-453-2266, www.gnb.ca/0012/index-e.asp
The Executive Council Office is responsible for the provision of secretariat & administrative services to the following: the Executive Council; Ministers with policy coordination responsibilities; & the Priorities Committee.
Premier; President, Executive Council; Minister, Intergovernmental Affairs; Minister Responsible, Premier's Council on the Status of Disabled Persons; Minister Responsble, Office of Self-Sufficiency,Hon. Shawn M. Graham
506-453-2144, Fax: 506-453-7407,Shawn.Graham@gnb.ca; Premier@gnb.ca
Deputy Minister; Clerk of the Executive Council; Secretary to Cabinet, W. David Ferguson
506-453-2718, David.Ferguson@gnb.ca
Deputy Minister, Policy & Priorities, Chris Baker
506-462-5003, Chris.Baker@gnb.ca
Assistant Deputy Minister, Women's Issues, Norma Dubé
506-453-2975, Fax: 506-453-7977,Norma.Dube@gnb.ca
Manager, Records Management, Line Michaud-Little
506-444-5553, line.michaud-little@gnb.ca

Legislative Assembly of New Brunswick / Assemblée législative

Centre Block, Legislative Bldg., 706 Queen St., PO Box 6000, Fredericton, NB E3B 5H1
506-453-2506, Fax: 506-453-7154, wwwleg@gnb.ca
www.gnb.ca/legis/index-e.asp
The Office of the Legislative Assembly is responsible for the following services: Assisting Members of the Legislative Assembly, their staff, & the public; Recording the proceedings of the Legislative Assembly; Maintaining the records of the Legislative Assembly; & Providing information services on behalf of the Legislative Assembly.
Speaker of the Legislative Assembly,Hon. Roy Boudreau
506-453-2907, roy.boudreau@gnb.ca
Deputy Speaker, Bill Fraser
506-453-2548, Fax: 506-453-3956,bill.fraser@gnb.ca
Deputy Speaker, Brian Kenny
506-453-2548, Fax: 506-453-3956,brian.kenny@gnb.ca
Clerk of the Legislative Assembly, Loredana Catalli Sonier
l.catalli.sonier@gnb.ca
Sergeant-at-Arms, Daniel Bussières
506-453-2527, dan.bussieres@gnb.ca
Commissioner, Office of the Conflict of Interest, Hon. Patrick A.A. Ryan, Q.C.
506-457-7890, Fax: 506-444-5224,coi@gnb.ca
Official Reporter, Hansard Office, Linda Fahey
506-453-8352, Fax: 506-453-3199,linda.fahey@gnb.ca
Legislative Librarian, Kenda Clark-Gorey
506-453-8346, Fax:
506-444-5889,kenda.clark.gorey@gnb.ca
Manager, Debates Translation, Aurella Losier-Vienneau
506-453-6270, Fax:
506-453-3126,aurella.losier.vienneau@gnb.ca
Officer, Special Projects, Valmond LeBlanc
506-472-0214, Fax: 506-472-4724,vall2@rogers.com

Government Caucus Office (Liberal)
West Block, Departmental Bldg., 96 Saint John St., PO Box 6000, Fredericton, NB E3B 5H1
506-453-2548, Fax: 506-453-3956, denise.scott@gnb.ca
Leader of the Government (Premier); President, Executive Council; Minister, Intergovernmental Affairs; Minister Responsible, Premier's Council on the Status of Disabled Persons; Minister Responsible, Office of Self-Sufficiency,Hon. Shawn M. Graham
506-453-2144, Fax: 506-453-7407,Premier@gnb.ca; Shawn.Graham@gnb.ca
House Leader (Government),Hon. Michael B. Murphy
MichaelB.Murphy@gnb.ca
Whip (Government), Rick Brewer
rick.brewer@gnb.ca
Caucus Chair (Government), Rick Miles
rick.miles@gnb.ca
Chief of Staff (Office of the Government Members), Leopold Mallet
leopold.mallet@gnb.ca
Director, Communications (Office of the Government Members), Carl Davies
carl.davies@gnb.ca

Office of the Official Opposition (Progressive Conservative) / Bureau de l'opposition officielle
East Block, Old Education Bldg., 710 Queen St., PO Box 6000, Fredericton, NB E3B 5H1
506-453-7494, Fax: 506-453-3461, pcmemb@gnb.ca@gnb.ca
Leader of the Official Opposition, Jeannot Volpé
House Leader (Official Opposition), Bev Harrison
bev.harrison@gnb.ca
Whip (Official Opposition), Cy LeBlanc
cy.leblanc@gnb.ca
Caucus Chair (Official Opposition), Madeleine Dubé
madeleine.dube@gnb.ca
Director, Communications (Official Opposition), Tyler Campbell
tyler.campbell@gnb.ca

Standing Committees of the House / Comites se pertenant de la chambre
The following are the Standing Committees of the Legislative Assembly of New Brunswick: Crown Corporations; Estimates; Law Amendments; Legislative Administration; Legislative Officers; Private Bills; Privileges; Procedure; & Public Accounts.

Fifty-sixth Legislature - New Brunswick

Legislative Assembly of New Brunswick, 706 Queen St., PO Box 6000, Fredericton, NB E3B 5H1
506-453-2506, Fax: 506-453-7154, www.gnb.ca/legis/index-e.asp
Last General Election, September 18, 2006. Maximum Duration, 5 years. Party Standings (September 2008): Liberal (Lib.) 32;

Progressive Conservatives (PC) 22; Vacant: 1; Total 55. Members' Salaries, Indemnities, & Allowances (January 2008): Members' annual indemnity $46,934.45, plus $18,772.78 for non-taxable expense allowance. Additional Members' Salaries, Indemnities, & Allowances: Premier $62,860.76; Ministers with portfolio $41,908.04; Ministers without portfolio $31,432.34; Leader of the Opposition $41,908.04; Leader of Registered Political Party $12,000.00; Speaker $31,432.34, plus $1,000.00 non-taxable allowance; Deputy Speaker $9,744.02, plus non-taxable allowance; Government Whip $9,744.02; Official Opposition Whip $4,872.01; Third Party Whip $500.00. The following list of Members of the Legislative Assembly includes the following information: Constituency & population; Party affiliation; & Contact information.

Members

Hon. Hédard Albert, Caraquet,Electoral District 6 NB, Liberal
506-444-2517, Fax: 506-453-6668,hedard.albert@gnb.ca, Other Communications: Constituency Phone: 506-726-2929; Fax: 506-726-2966

David Alward, Woodstock, ElectoralDistrict 49 NB, P
506-453-7494, Fax: 506-453-3461,david.alward@gnb.ca, Other Communications: Constituency Phone: 506-325-4990; Fax: 506-325-4991

Hon. Donald Arseneault, Dalhousie-Restigouche East, Electoral District 2 NB, Liberal
506-453-2510, Fax: 506-444-5839,donald.arseneault@gnb.ca, Other Communications: Constituency Phone: 506-685-5252; Fax: 506-685-5255

John W. Betts, Moncton-Crescent, ElectoralDistrict 24 NB, P
506-453-7494, Fax: 506-453-3461,johnw.betts@gnb.ca, Other Communications: Constituency Phone: 506-869-6579; Fax: 506-869-6614

Member

Margaret-Ann Blaney, Rothesay,Electoral District 32 NB, P
506-453-7494, Fax: 506-453-3461,margaret-ann.blaney@gnb.ca, Other Communications: Constituency Phone: 506-848-6646; Fax: 506-848-6648

Hon. Roy Boudreau, Campbellton-Restigouche Centre, Electoral District 1 NB, Liberal
506-453-2907, Fax: 506-453-7154,roy.boudreau@gnb.ca, Other Communications: Constituency Phone: 506-789-2426; Fax: 506-789-4855,

Hon. Victor E. Boudreau, Shediac-Cap-Pelé,Electoral District 17 NB, Liberal
506-444-2627, Fax: 506-457-4989,victor.boudreau@gnb.ca, Other Communications: Constituency Phone: 506-533-3450; Fax: 506-533-3452

Rick Brewer, Southwest-Miramichi, ElectoralDistrict 13 NB, Liberal
506-453-2548, Fax: 506-453-3956,rick.brewer@gnb.ca, Other Communications: Constituency Phone: 506-843-2600; Fax: 506-843-2601

Hon. Thomas J. Burke, Fredericton-Nashwaaksis, Electoral District 42 NB, Liberal
506-453-2583, Fax: 506-453-3651,tjbconstituency@hotmail.com, Other Communications: Constituency Phone: 506-453-3365; 506-453-5469

Hon. Greg Byrne, Fredericton-Lincoln, ElectoralDistrict 44 NB, Liberal
506-453-5898, Fax: 506-453-5893,greg.byrne@gnb.ca, Other Communications: Constituency Phone: 506-457-7668; Fax: 506-444-2004

Jody Carr, Oromocto, Electoral District 40 NB, P
506-453-7494, Fax: 506-453-3461,jody.carr@gnb.ca, Other Communications: Constituency Phone: 506-357-4141; Fax: 506-357-4147

Chris Collins, Moncton East, Electoral District21 NB, Liberal
506-453-2548, Fax: 506-453-3956,chris.collins@gnb.ca, Other Communications: Constituency Phone: 506-453-2548; Fax: 506-856-2596

Hon. Dr. Ed Doherty, Saint John Harbour, ElectoralDistrict 34 NB, Liberal
506-453-2342, Fax: 506-453-3038,ed.doherty@gnb.ca, Other Communications: Constituency Phone: 506-643-7102; 506-643-7502

Hon. Rick Doucet, Charlotte-The Isles,Electoral District 38 NB, Liberal
506-444-6734, Fax: 506-444-5477,rick.doucet@gnb.ca, Other Communications: Constituency Phone: 506-755-4200; Fax: 506-755-4207

Madeleine Dubé, Edmundston-Saint-Basile,Electoral District 54 NB, P
506-453-7494, Fax: 506-453-3461,madeleine.dube@gnb.ca, Other Communications: Constituency Phone: 506-735-2528; Fax: 506-735-2583

Bruce Fitch, Riverview, ElectoralDistrict 26 NB, P
506-453-7494, Fax: 506-453-3461,bruce.fitch@gnb.ca, Other Communications: Constituency Phone: 506-869-6117; Fax: 506-869-6114

Hon. John W. Foran, Miramichi Centre,Electoral District 12 NB, Liberal
506-453-7414, Fax: 506-453-3870,johnforan.mla@nb.aibn.com, Other Communications: Constituency Phone: 506-624-2131; Fax: 506-624-2140

Bill Fraser, Miramichi-Bay du Vin,Electoral District 11 NB, Liberal
506-453-2548, Fax: 506-453-3956,bill.fraser@gnb.ca, Other Communications: Constituency Phone: 506-624-5516; Fax: 506-624-5517

Dale Graham, Carleton, Electoral District50 NB, P
506-453-7494, Fax: 506-453-3461,dale.graham@gnb.ca, Other Communications: Constituency Phone: 506-276-4016; Fax: 506-276-4020

Hon. Shawn M. Graham, Kent,Electoral District 15 NB, Liberal
506-453-2144, Fax: 506-453-7407,Premier@gnb.ca; Shawn.Graham@gnb.ca, Other Communications: Constituency Phone: 506-523-7980; Fax: 506-523-7982

Hon. Roland Haché, Nigadoo-Chaleur, ElectoralDistrict 3 NB, Liberal
506-444-5136, Fax: 506-453-3377,roland.hache@gnb.ca, Other Communications: Constituency Phone: 506-542-2424; Fax: 506-542-2425

Bev Harrison, Hampton-Kings, ElectoralDistrict 29 NB, P
506-453-7494, Fax: 506-453-3461,bev.harrison@gnb.ca, Other Communications: Constituency Phone: 506-832-6464; Fax: 506-832-6466

Trevor Holder, Saint JohnPortland, Electoral District 35 NB, P
506-453-7494, Fax: 506-453-3461,trevor.holder@gnb.ca, Other Communications: ConstituencyPhone: 506-657-2335; Fax: 506-642-2588

Antoon (Tony) Huntjens, Charlotte-Campobello, Electoral District 39 NB, P
506-453-7494, Fax: 506-453-3461,tony.huntjens@gnb.ca, Other Communications: Constituency Phone: 506-466-7434; 506-466-7420

Hon. Stuart Jamieson, SaintJohn-Fundy, Electoral District 31 NB, Liberal
506-453-3009, Fax: 506-453-4984,saintjohnfundy@hotmail.com, Other Communications: Constituency Phone: 506-658-6333; Fax: 506-658-6330

Hon. Jack Keir, Fundy-RiverValley, Electoral District 37 NB, Liberal
506-658-3180, Fax: 506-444-5405,jack.keir@gnb.ca, Other Communications: Constituency Phone: 506-738-8696; Fax: 506-738-6559

Dr. Larry Kennedy, Victoria-Tobique, ElectoralDistrict 51 NB, Liberal
506-453-2548, Fax: 506-453-3956,Other Communications: Constituency Phone: 506-273-9522; Fax: 506-273-6331

Brian Kenny, Bathurst, Electoral District4 NB, Liberal
506-453-2548, Fax: 506-453-3956,brian.kenny@gnb.ca, Other Communications: Constituency Phone: 506-549-5355; Fax: 506-549-5261

Hon. Kelly Lamrock, Fredericton-FortNashwaak, Electoral District 43 NB, Liberal
506-453-2523, Fax: 506-453-4960,kelly.lamrock@gnb.ca, Other Communications: Constituency Phone: 506-444-4648; Fax: 506-444-4515

Claude Landry, Tracadie-Sheila,Electoral District 9 NB, P
506-453-7494, Fax: 506-453-3461,claude.landry@gnb.ca, Other Communications: Constituency Phone: 506-395-9162; Fax: 506-393-7794

Hon. Denis Landry, Centre-Péninsule-Saint-Saveur, Electoral District 8 NB, Liberal
506-457-7345, Fax: 506-453-7987,dlandry@nbnet.nb.ca, Other Communications: Constituency Phone: 506-764-2530; Fax: 506-764-2535

Cheryl Lavoie, Nepisiguit, Electoral District5 NB, Liberal
506-453-2548, Fax: 506-453-3956,cheryl.lavoie@gnb.ca, Other Communications: Constituency Phone: 506-549-5644; Fax: 506-549-5638

Abel LeBlanc, Saint John Lancaster,Electoral District 36 NB, Liberal
506-453-2548, Fax: 506-453-3956,aleblanc.mla@nb.aibn.com, Other Communications: Constituency Phone: 506-658-6324; Fax: 506-658-6328

Bernard LeBlanc, Memramcook-Lakeville-Dieppe, Electoral District 19 NB, Liberal
506-453-2548, Fax: 506-453-3956,bernard.leblanc@gnb.ca, Other Communications: Constituency Phone: 506-758-4088; Fax: 506-758-4089

Cy (Richard) LeBlanc, Dieppe Centre-Lewisville,Electoral District 20 NB, P
506-453-7494, Fax: 506-453-3461,cy.leblanc@gnb.ca, Other Communications: Constituency Phone: 506-869-6580; Fax: 506-869-6581

L. Joan MacAlpine-Stiles, Moncton West,Electoral District 22 NB, Liberal
506-453-2548, Fax: 506-453-3956,monctonwest@hotmail.com, Other Communications: Constituency Phone: 506-869-6360; Fax: 506-869-6572

Kirk MacDonald, YorkNorth, Electoral District 48 NB, P
506-453-7494, Fax: 506-453-3461,kirk.macdonald@gnb.ca, Other Communications: Constituency Phone: 506-363-4949; Fax: 506-363-4998

Roly MacIntyre, Saint John East, ElectoralDistrict 33 NB, Liberal
506-453-2548, Fax: 506-453-3956,roly.macintyre@gnb.ca, Other Communications: Constituency Phone: 506-643-6000; 506-643-6005

Hon. Eugene McGinley, Q.C., Grand Lake-Gagetown,Electoral District 41 NB, Liberal
506-453-2057, Fax: 506-453-2164,eugene.mcginley2@gnb.ca, Other Communications: Constituency Phone: 506-339-7065; 506-339-7064

Richard (Rick) Miles, Fredericton-Silverwood,Electoral District 45 NB, Liberal
506-453-2548, Fax: 506-453-3956,rick.miles@gnb.ca, Other Communications: Constituency Phone: 506-457-7668; Fax: 506-444-2004

Percy Mockler, Restigouche-La-Vallée,Electoral District 53 NB, P
506-453-7494, Fax: 506-453-3461,percy.mockler@gnb.ca, Other Communications: Constituency Phone: 506-423-3130; Fax: 506-423-3133

Hon. Michael B. Murphy, Moncton North,Electoral District 23 NB, Liberal
506-453-2548, Fax: 506-453-3956,michaelb.murphy@gnb.ca, Other Communications: Constituency Phone: 506-869-6115; Fax: 869-6118

Bruce Northrup, Kings East, Electoral District 28 NB, P
506-453-7494, Fax: 506-453-3461,bruce.northrup@gnb.ca, Other Communications: Constituency Phone: 506-432-2686; Fax: 506-432-2647

Mike Olscamp, Tantramar, Electoral District18 NB, P
506-453-7494, Fax: 506-453-3461,mike.olscamp@gnb.ca, Other Communications: Constituency Phone: 506-364-4774; Fax: 506-364-4775

Hon. Ronald Ouellette, GrandFalls-Drummond-Saint-André, Electoral District 52 NB, Liberal
506-453-2662, Fax: 506-453-3402,ronald.ouellette@gnb.ca, Other Communications: Constituency Phone: 506-475-4380; 506-475-4385

Rose-May Poirier, Rogersville-Kouchibouguac, Electoral District 14 NB, P
506-453-7494, Fax: 506-453-3461,rose-may.poirier@gnb.ca, Other Communications: Constituency Phone: 506-876-3530; Fax: 506-876-3549

Hon. Carmel Robichaud, MiramichiBay-Neguac, Electoral District 10 NB, Liberal
506-453-2807, Fax: 506-453-3988,carmel.robichaud@gnb.ca, Other Communications: Constituency Phone: 506-776-3949; Fax: 506-776-3956

Paul Robichaud, Lamèque-Shippagan-Miscou, Electoral District 7 NB, P
506-453-7494, Fax: 506-453-3461,paul.robichaud@gnb.ca, Other Communications: Constituency Phone: 506-336-3388; Fax: 506-336-3387

Hon. Mary Schryer, Quispamsis, ElectoralDistrict 30 NB, Liberal
506-457-7866, Fax: 506-453-2164,mary.schryer@gnb.ca, Other Communications: Constituency Phone: 506-848-6676; Fax: 506-848-6678

Wayne Steeves, Albert, ElectoralDistrict 27 NB, P
506-453-7494, Fax: 506-453-3461,wayne.steeves@gnb.ca, Other Communications: Constituency Phone: 506-856-3006; Fax: 506-856-3000

Hon. Wally Stiles, Petitcodiac, ElectoralDistrict 25 NB, Liberal
506-462-5092, Fax: 506-453-7195,wally.stiles@gnb.ca, Other Communications: Constituency Phone: 506-756-3137; Fax: 506-756-3138

Carl Urquhart, York, Electoral District47 NB, P
506-453-7494, Fax: 506-453-3461,carl.urquhart@gnb.ca, Other Communications: Constituency Phone: 506-457-7878; Fax: 506-457-7865

Jeannot Volpé, Madawaska-les-Lacs,Electoral District 55 NB, P
506-444-2324, Fax: 506-453-3461,jeannot.volpe@gnb.ca, Other Communications: Constituency Phone: 506-737-4420; Fax: 506-737-4436

Claude Williams, Kent South, ElectoralDistrict 16 NB, P
506-453-7494, Fax: 506-453-3461,claude.williams@gnb.ca, Other Communications: Constituency Phone: 506-525-4025; 506-525-4034

Vacant, New Maryland-Sunbury West, Electoral District 46

New Brunswick Government Departments & Agencies / Ministères et organismes du gouvernement du Nouveau-Brunswick

Aboriginal Affairs Secretariat / Secrétariat des affaires autochtones

Kings Place, #237, 440 King St., PO Box 6000, Fredericton, NB E3B 5H1
506-462-5177, Fax: 506-444-5142, www.gnb.ca/0016/index-e.asp

The Aboriginal Affairs Secretariat strives to enhance the Government of New Brunswick's relationship with Mi'kmaq & Maliseet communities & Aboriginal organizations. The Secretariat works with provincial departments in the areas of policies & intergovernmental processes related to Aboriginal people, dialogue between Aboriginal representatives & the government, the provision of information on programs & services, & increasing cross-cultural awareness.

Minister, Post-Secondary Education, Training, & Labour; Minister Responsible, Aboriginal Affairs Secretariat,Hon. Edward Doherty
506-453-2342, Fax: 506-453-3038,ed.doherty@gnb.ca
Deputy Minister, Aboriginal Affairs Secretariat, Patrick Francis
506-462-5177, Patrick.Francis@gnb.ca
Director, Corporate Services, Maryanne Bourgeois
506-462-5177, Maryanne.Bourgeois@gnb.ca
Director, Bilateral / Community Relations, Brian G. Harquail
506-462-5177, Brian.Harquail@gnb.ca
Officer, Communications, Nichole Bowman
506-462-5177, Nichole.Bowman@gnb.ca

Department of Agriculture & Aquaculture / Agriculture et Aquaculture

PO Box 6000, Fredericton, NB E3B 5H1
506-453-2666, Fax: 506-453-7170, DAA-MAA@gnb.ca
www.gnb.ca/0027/Index-e.asp

This Department is to be split into the Department of Agriculture & Aquauculture & the Department of Fisheries, as announced by Premier Graham in October 2006.

Acts Administered:
Agricultural Commodity Price Stabilization Act
Agricultural Land Protection & Development Act
Agricultural Operation Practices Act
Apiary Inspection Act
Aquaculture Act
Crop Insurance Act
Diseases of Animals Act
Farm Income Assurance Act
Fish Processing Act
Fish & Wildlife Act (in part)
Injurious Insect & Pest Act
Inshore Fisheries Representation Act
Livestock Operations Act
Livestock Yard Sales Act
Marshland Reclamation Act
Natural Products Act
New Brunswick Grain Act
Pipeline Act
Plant Health Act
Potato Disease Eradication Act
Poultry Health Protection Act
Sheep Protection Act
Weed Control Act
Women's Institute & Institut féminin Act

Minister, Agriculture & Aquaculture, Hon. Ronald Ouellette
506-453-2662, Fax: 506-453-3402,ronald.ouellette@gnb.ca
Deputy Minister, Jim McKay
506-453-2450, Fax: 506-444-5022,Jim.McKay@gnb.ca
Director, Communications, Paul Harpelle
506-444-4218, Paul.Harpelle@gnb.ca

• New Brunswick Crop Insurance Commission/ Commission de l'assurance récolte du Nouveau-Brunswick
PO Box 6000
Fredericton, NB E3B 5H1
506-453-2185 Fax: 506-453-7406
To provide farmers with insurance protection against crop production losses caused by natural hazards beyond their control through the Canada / New Brunswick Crop Insurance Program.

• New Brunswick Farm Products Commission/ Commission des produits de ferme du Nouveau-Brunswick
c/o Department of Agriculture & Aquaculture
PO Box 6000
Fredericton, NB E3B 5H1
506-453-3647 Fax: 506-444-5969
Products Act. ment/administrative support to the Commission in the monitoring of commodity boards under the provisions of the Natural Products Act.

Agriculture & Bio-Economy Division / Agriculture et Bioéconomie

To encourage the development of a prosperous, globally competitive & sustainable agriculture & agri-food business using the latest technologies to produce & market innovative & safe food as well as other bio-products.

Asst. Deputy Minister, Kevin McKendy
506-453-2366, Fax: 506-444-5022,kevin.mckendy@gnb.ca
Executive Director, Livestock Development, Michael Maloney
506-453-5443
Director, Crop Development, Kevin McCully
506-453-3481
Director, Business Risk Management, Cathy Larochelle
506-444-2728
Director, Land & Environment, Lynn Moore
506-453-2109
Director, Regional Agri-Business Development, Gerry Chevrier
506-453-2172

Regional Offices:

Central
Miramichi, NB
506-778-6030, Fax: 506-778-6679
Regional Manager, Vernon Taylor

East
Bathurst, NB
506-547-2088, Fax: 506-547-2064
Regional Manager,Dr. Michel Beaulieu

Northwest
Grand Falls, NB
506-473-7755, Fax: 506-473-6641
Regional Manager, Bertrand Cyr

South
Sussex, NB
506-432-2000, Fax: 506-432-2044
Regional Manager, Phil Parlee

Southeast
Moncton, NB
506-856-2277, Fax: 506-856-2092,
Regional Manager,Dr. André Saindon

West
Wicklow, NB
Regional Manager, Brian DuPlessis
506-392-5100, Fax: 506-392-5089,brian.duplessis@gnb.ca

Fisheries Division / Pêches

To foster the continued development of & innovation within the commercial fisheries & aquaculture sectors & to provide policy & planning support for all departmental programs.

Asst. Deputy Minister, Roland Cormier
506-457-6964, Fax: 506-444-5022,roland.cormier@gnb.ca
Executive Director, Resource Management & Operations, Yvon Chiasson
506-453-8432, Fax: 506-462-5929,yvon.chiasson@gnb.ca
Director, Business Development, Louis Arsenault
506-444-4218, Fax: 506-444-5022,louis.rsenault@gnb.ca
Director, Licensing & Technical Services, Ghislain Chiasson
506-453-5229, Fax: 506-453-5210,ghislain.chiasson@gnb.ca

St. George
506-755-4000, Fax: 506-755-4001
Regional Director, Marc Johnston

Bouctouche
506-743-7222, Fax: 506-743-7229
Regional Director, Louis Arsenault

Caraquet
506-726-2400, Fax: 506-726-2419
Regional Director, Mario Gaudet

Department of the Attorney General / Procureur général

Centennial Bldg., #412, 670 King St., PO Box 6000, Fredericton, NB E3B 5H1
506-453-3132, Fax: 506-453-3651, justice.comments@gnb.ca
www.gnb.ca/0227/index-e.asp

The Attorney General carries out responsibilities regarding criminal law enforcement, the provision of legal advice & representation to the Government, & the preparation of legislation & regulations.

Minister, Justice & Consumer Affairs & Attorney General, Hon. Thomas J. Burke, Q.C.
506-462-5100, Fax: 506-453-3651,t.j.burke@gnb.ca
Deputy Attorney General, Yvon LeBlanc
yvon.leblanc3@gnb.ca

Legal Services

Centennial Bldg., #445, 670 King St., PO Box 6000, Fredericton, NB E3B 5H1
506-453-2222, Fax: 506-453-3275

Assistant Deputy Attorney General, Legal Services, C. Clyde Spinney, Q.C.
clyde.spinney@gnb.ca
Coordinator, Commercial, Corporate, & Property Law Group, Guy Daigle
Guy.Daigle@gnb.ca
Coordinator, Employment & Administrative Law Group, Andrea M. Folster
andrea.folster@gnb.ca
Coordinator, Government Services Group, Richard Duke
Richard.Duke@gnb.ca
Coordinator, Litigation Group, Nancy E. Forbes
nancy.forbes@gnb.ca

Legislative Services

Centennial Bldg., #418, 670 King St., PO Box 6000, Fredericton, NB E3B 5H1
506-453-2855, Fax: 506-457-7342

Assistant Deputy Attorney General, Legislative Services, Judith Keating, Q.C.
506-453-2544, Judith.Keating@gnb.ca
Registrar of Regulations, Legislative Drafting, Susan Burns
506-453-2569, Susan.Burns@gnb.ca
Solicitor, Law Reform, Tim Rattenbury
506-453-2569, Tim.Rattenbury@gnb.ca
Solicitor, Statute Revision, Francoise M. Belanger
francoise.belanger@gnb.ca
Solicitor & Queen's Printer, Queen's Printer, Elizabeth Strange
506-453-2520, Fax: 506-457-7899,Elizabeth.Strange@gnb.ca

Public Prosecutions

HSBC Place, 520 King St., 6th Fl., PO Box 6000, Fredericton, NB E3B 5H1
506-453-2784, Fax: 506-453-5364

Assistant Deputy Attorney General, Public Prosecutions, Glen Abbott, Q.C.
Coordinator, Specialized Prosecutions, Bill Wister
Coordinator, Family & Youth Justice, Catherine A. Berryman
506-856-2310, Fax: 506-856-2625

Support Services

Centennial Bldg., #412, 670 King St., PO Box 6000, Fredericton, NB E3B 5H1
506-453-3132, Fax: 506-453-3651, general.comments@gnb.ca

Executive Director, Administrative Services, Neil E. Foreman
506-453-6503, Fax: 506-453-8718,neil.foreman@gnb.ca
Director, Policy & Planning, Debbie Hackett
506-453-3693, debbie.hackett@gnb.ca
Director, Communications, Valerie Kilfoil
506-453-6543, Fax: 506-444-2661,valerie.kilfoil@gnb.ca

Office of the Auditor General / Bureau du Vérificateur général

HSBC Place, 520 King St., 6th Fl., Fredericton, NB E3B 6G3
506-453-2243, Fax: 506-453-3067,
www.gnb.ca/OAG-BVG/Index-e.asp

The role of the Office of the Auditor General is the promotion of accountability. On behalf of the Legislative Assembly, the Office of the Auditor General audits the accounts of the province & certain Crown agencies. Objective information is provided to the citizens of New Brunswick through the Legislative Assembly.

Auditor General, Michael Ferguson, C.A.
mike.ferguson@gnb.ca
Deputy Auditor General, Kenneth Robinson, C.A.
506-453-6751, ken.robinson@gnb.ca
Director, Value-for-money Audit, Brent White, C.A.
506-453-6752, brent.white@gnb.ca
Director, Financial Audit, Paul Jewett, C.A.
506-453-6754, paul.jewett@gnb.ca

Department of Business New Brunswick / Entreprises Nouveau-Brunswick

Centennial Bldg., 670 King St., PO Box 6000, Fredericton, NB E3B 5H1
506-444-5228, Fax: 506-453-5428,
www.gnb.ca/0398/index-e.asp

The Department of Business New Brunswick provides the following serices: Business expansion & innovation; Export development; Investment, for the establishment of new business in the province; & Services & support to the film & television industry in New Brunswick.

Acts Administered:
Agricultural Associations Act
Economic Development Act
Farm Credit Corporation Assistance Act
Farm Improvement Assistance Loans Act
Farm Machinary Loans Act
Fisheries Development Act
Industrial Relations Act
Livestock Incentives Act

Youth Assistance Act
Minister, Business New Brunswick; Minister Responsible, Service New Brunswick; Minister Responsible, Population Growth Secretariat; Minister Responsible, Communications New Brunswick, Minister Responsible, Red Tape Reduction, Hon. Greg Byrne
506-453-5898, Fax: 506-453-5893,greg.byrne@gnb.ca
Deputy Minister, Brian Dick
506-453-5897, Fax: 506-453-6389,brian.dick@gnb.ca
Director, Human Resource Services, Shannon Ferris
506-462-5053, Fax: 506-453-8508,shannon.ferris@gnb.ca
Officer, Communications, Ryan Donaghy
506-453-2694, Fax: 506-453-3993,ryan.donaghy@gnb.ca
• New Brunswick Film/ Film Nouveau-Brunswick
Assumption Pl.
770 Main St., 16th Fl.
PO Box 5001
Moncton, NB E1C 8R3
506-869-6868 Fax: 506-869-6840
nbfilm@gnb.ca
www.nbfilm.ca
Responsible for fostering New Brunswick's film, television & new media industry.
• New Brunswick Industrial Development Board/ Conseil de développement industriel du Nouveau-Brunswick
Business New Brunswick, Centennial Bldg.
670 King St.
PO Box 6000
Fredericton, NB E3B 5H1
506-453-4200 Fax: 506-444-4182

Business Development / Développement des entreprises
Centennial Bldg., 670 King St., 5th Fl., PO Box 6000, Fredericton, NB E3B 5H1
506-453-2111, Fax: 506-444-4182
Assistant Deputy Minister, Business Development, Phil LePage
Phil.Lepage@gnb.ca
Executive Director, Innovation / Regional Development, Yvon Belliveau
506-453-3799, Fax: 506-457-7282,yvon.belliveau@gnb.ca
Director, Industry Services, Michel Albert
506-444-5053, Fax: 506-457-7282,michel.albert@gnb.ca
Acting Director, Planning, Shannon D. Sanford
506-444-5854, shannon.sanford@gnb.ca

Business Financial Support
Centennial Bldg., #571, 670 King St., PO Box 6000, Fredericton, NB E3B 5H1
506-453-2794, Fax: 506-444-4182
Assistant Deputy Minister, Business Financial Support, Richard Burgess
506-453-2461, dick.burgess@gnb.ca
Executive Director, Business Financial Support, John Rosengren
506-453-3929, john.rosengren@gnb.ca
Manager, Financial Programs, Ron Harriot
506-444-5809, Fax: 506-453-7904,ron.harriott@gnb.ca

Corporate Services
Centennial Bldg., 670 King St., 5th Fl., PO Box 6000, Fredericton, NB E3B 5H1
506-453-3707, Fax: 506-453-3993
Executive Director, Corporate Services, Gary Jochelman
506-444-4238, Fax: 506-453-5428,gary.jochelman@gnb.ca
Director, Financial Administration, Barbara Yerxa
506-444-5197, Fax: 506-453-5428,Barbara.Yerxa@gnb.ca
Director, Office of Red Tape Reduction, Wendy L. Betts
506-444-4167, Fax: 506-453-5428,Wendy.Betts@gnb.ca
Manager, Information Technology, Doug Waugh
506-457-7324, Fax: 506-453-5428,doug.waugh@gnb.ca

Investment & Export Development
Centennial Bldg., 670 King St., 5th F., PO Box 6000, Fredericton, NB E3B 5H1
506-453-2875, Fax: 506-444-4277
Assistant Deputy Minister, Investment & Export Development, Jeff Trail
jeff.trail@gnb.ca
Executive Director, Export Development, Joanne Walker
506-453-3412, Fax: 506-453-3783,joanne.walker@gnb.ca
Manager, Investment - Knowledge Industry, Jonathan Downey
506-444-6758, Fax: 506-444-4277,Jon.downey@gnb.ca
Manager, Investment - Manufacturing & Research, Joel Richardson
506-457-7545, Fax: 506-444-4277,joel.richardson@gnb.ca
Manager, New Brunswick Film, Joe Richard
joe.richard@gnb.ca
Manager, Marketing, Suzanne Turmel
506-444-5107, Fax: 506-444-4586,Suzanne.turmel@gnb.ca

Communications New Brunswick / Communications Nouveau-Brunswick

Wilcom Bldg., 225 King St., 2nd Fl., PO Box 6000, Fredericton, NB E3B 5H1
506-453-2240, Fax: 506-453-5329,
www.gnb.ca/cnb
Communications New Brunswick provides a great range of communications services to government departments & agencies.
Minister, Business New Brunswick; Minister Responsible, Service New Brunswick; Minister Responsible, Population Growth Secretariat; Minister Responsible, Communications New Brunswick, Minister Responsible, Red Tape Reduction, Hon. Greg Byrne
506-453-5898, Fax: 506-453-5893,greg.byrne@gnb.ca
Deputy Minister, Maurice Robichaud
506-444-2381, Maurice_Robichaud@gnb.ca
General Manager, Tim Porter
506-444-2548, Tim.Porter@gnb.ca
Director, Design & Advertising Services, Michael Côté
Michael.Cote@gnb.ca
Director, Corporate Writing, Craig Chouinard
Craig.Chouinard@gnb.ca
Director, Web Services, Bonnie Buckingham Land
Bonnie.Buckingham@gnb.ca,

Office of the Comptroller / Bureau du Contrôleur

Centennial Bldg., 670 King St., Fredericton, NB E3B 1G1
506-453-2565, Fax: 506-453-2917,
wwwooc@gnb.ca
www.gnb.ca/0087/index-e.asp
Provide leadership in accounting and internal auditing services to their clients and encourage the effective management of the resources of the Province.
Comptroller, Kim MacPherson, C.A.
506-453-2565, Kim.MacPherson@gnb.ca
Director, Accounting Services, Karen Cunningham
506-453-8975, Fax:
506-444-5220,karen.cunningham@gnb.ca
Director, Audit & Consulting Services, Stephen Thompson, C.M.A.
506-444-4560, Fax: 506-453-2917,steve.t.thompson@gnb.ca
Executive Secretary, Jocelyne Macfarlane
506-453-2565, jocelyne.macfarlane@gnb.ca

Premier's Council on the Status of Disabled Persons / Conseil du Premier ministre sur la condition des personnes handicapées

Kings Place, #648, 440 King St., Fredericton, NB E3B 5H8
506-444-3000, Fax: 506-444-3001, 800-442-4412
pcsdp@gnb.ca
www.gnb.ca/0048
The role of the Premier's Council on the Status of Disabled Persons is to provide advice to the provincial government of New Brunswick & the public about issues of interest & concern that affect the status of persons with disabilities.
Premier; President, Executive Council; Minister, Intergovernmental Affairs; Minister Responsible, Premier's Council on the Status of Disabled Persons; Minister Responsible, Office of Self-Sufficiency, Hon. Shawn M. Graham
506-453-2144, Fax: 506-453-7407,Premier@gnb.ca; Shawn.Graham@gnb.ca
Chair, Laura Peters
Fax: 506-444-3001,TDD: 506-444-3000
Executive Director, Randy Dickinson
randy.dickinson@gnb.ca

Department of Education / Éducation

Place 2000, 250 King St., PO Box 6000, Fredericton, NB E3B 5H1
506-453-3678, Fax: 506-453-3325,
www.gnb.ca/0000/index-e.asp
The Department of Education, which oversees public schools in New Brunswick, consists of an Anglophone Sector & a Francophone Sector. The English Educational Services Division is responsible for curriculum development, student services, e-learning, & student evaluation & assessment. The Francophone Educational Services Division oversees curriculum development & implementation, special education, psychology, guidance counselling, professional development, & assessment & evaluation.
Acts Administered:
Education Act
Minister, Education; Minister Responsible, New Brunswick Advisory Council on Youth; Minister Responsible, New Brunswick Provincial CapitalCommission, Hon. Kelly Lamrock
506-453-2523, Fax: 506-457-4960,kelly.lamrock@gnb.ca
Deputy Minister, John D. Kershaw
506-453-2529, Fax: 506-457-4810,John.Kershaw@gnb.ca
Sous-ministre, Roger Doucet
506-453-2409, Fax: 506-457-4810,Roger.Doucet@gnb.ca
Agent, Communications, Angélique Binet
506-444-4714, angelique.binet@gnb.ca

Administration & Finance / Administration et Finances
Place 2000, 250 King St., 4th Fl., PO Box 6000, Fredericton, NB E3B 5H1
506-453-2085, Fax: 506-457-4810
Assistant Deputy Minister, Elizabeth Abraham
506-453-2085, Liz.Abraham@gnb.ca
Director, Educational Facilities & Pupil Transportation, Ron J. White
506-453-2242, Fax: 506-444-5529,mailto:ron.white@gnb.ca
Director, Finance & Services, Luc Paulin
506-444-4963, Fax: 506-453-3325,luc.paulin@gnb.ca
Director, Human Resources, Valmond Guimond
506-444-4914, Fax:
506-444-4761,Valmond.Guimond@gnb.ca
Director, Information System Services, Louise Ouellette
506-453-7158, Louise.Ouellette@gnb.ca

Educational Services (Anglophone) / Division des services éducatifs
Place 2000, 250 King St., PO Box 6000, Fredericton, NB E3B 5H1
506-453-3326, Fax: 506-457-4810
Assistant Deputy Minister, David Roberts
506-453-3326, david.roberts@gnb.ca
Executive Director, Educational Programs & Services, Dawn Weatherbie
506-453-2155, Fax: 506-457-7835,dawn.weatherbie@gnb.ca
Executive Director, Strategic Initiatives, Amanda Harpelle
506-453-7441, Fax: 506-444-5523,Amanda.Harpelle@gnb.ca
Acting Director, Improvement Planning, Inga Boehler
506-453-3696, Fax: 506-457-7835,inga.boehler@gnb.ca
Manager, District Education Councils, Nancy Whyte
506-453-2618, Nancy.Whyte@gnb.ca
Project Manager, Future to Discover Pilot Project, Margie Layden-Oreto
506-462-5127, Fax:
506-444-4447,margie.layden-oreto@gnb.ca

Policy & Planning
Place 2000, 250 King St., 4th Fl., PO Box 6000, Fredericton, NB E3B 5H1
506-453-3090, Fax: 506-453-3111
Executive Director, Policy & Planning, Margaret Smith
Margaret.Smith@gnb.ca
Director, Policy & Legislative Affairs, Andree Guy
andree.guy@gnb.ca
Manager, Corporate Data Analysis, Monica LeBlanc
monica.leblanc@gnb.ca

Secteur des services Éducatifs francophones / Educational Services Section
Place 2000, 250 King St., 4th Fl., Fredericton, NB E3B 9M9
506-453-2086, Fax: 506-457-4810
Assistant Deputy Minister, Guy Léveillé
guy.leveille@gnb.ca
Executive Director, Transformation et Innovation stratégique, Rino Levesque
506-444-2906, Fax: 506-444-2969,rino.levesque@gnb.ca
Executive Director, Services pédagogiques, Marcel Lavoie
506-453-2743, Fax: 506-457-7835,Marcel.Lavoie@gnb.ca
Manager, Conseils d'éducation de district, Rachel Dion
506-453-3037, Fax: 506-453-7942,rachel.dion@gnb.ca

Teacher Certification
Huttle Bldg., 125 Hilton Rd., 3rd Fl., PO Box 6000, Fredericton, NB E3B 5H1
506-453-2785, Fax: 506-453-5349
Registrar, Teacher Certification, Yves King
Yves.King@gnb.ca
Deputy Registrar, Teacher Certification, Joseph Arseneault
506-453-5349, Joseph.Arseneault@gnb.ca

Office of the Chief Electoral Officer / Bureau de la directrice générale des élections

PO Box 6000, Fredericton, NB E3B 5H1
506-453-2218, Fax: 506-457-4926, 800-308-2922
www.gnb.ca/elections
Chief Electoral Officer, Annise Hollies
Elections Coordinator, Ann McIntosh
ann.mcintosh@gnb.ca

Department of Energy / Énergie

Brunswick Square, #100M, 1 Germain St., PO Box 5001, Saint John, NB E2L 4Y9
506-658-3180, Fax: 506-658-3191,
www.gnb.ca/0085/index-e.asp
The New Brunswick Department of Energy is responsible for the following: Ensuring a reliable & cost effective energy supply; Promoting economic efficiency in energy systems; Encouraging

economic development opportunities; Protecting & improving the environment; & Ensuring an effective regulatory regime.
Acts Administered:
Electricity Act
Energy Efficiency Act
Energy Efficiency & Conservation Agency of New Brunswick Act
Gas Distribution, 1999 Act
Petroleum Products Pricing Act
Pipeline, 2005 Act
Minister, Energy; Minister, Supply & Services; Minister Responsible, Efficiency NB,Hon. Jack Keir
506-658-3177, Fax: 506-658-3191,Jack.Keir2@gnb.ca
Deputy Minster, Claire Lepage
506-658-3179, Claire.Lepage@gnb.ca
• Efficiency NB/ Efficacité NB
#101, 33 Charlotte St.
Saint John, NB E2L 2H3
506-643-7826 Fax: 506-643-7835 866-643-8833
www.efficiencynb.ca
Efficiency NB is engaged in the following activities: Promoting energy efficiency measures throughout New Brunswick; Encouraging the development of an energy efficiency services industry; Implementing & offering programs related to energy efficiency; & Increasing awareness of the relation between energy efficiency measures & a reliable energy supply for the province.

Alternative Energy & Market Development
Brunswick Square, #M100, 1 Germain St., Saint John, NB E2L 4V1
506-658-3180, Fax: 506-658-3191
Assistant Deputy Minister, Alternative Energy & Market Development, Neil Jacobsen
506-658-3132, Fax: 506-658-3191
Director, Science & Technology, Bill Breckenridge
506-658-3144, bill.breckenridge@gnb.ca
Director, Pipeline, Petroleum, & Natural Gas, Patrick Ervin
506-658-3124, patrick.ervin@gnb.ca
Director, Electricity, Stephen Waycott
506-658-3126, Stephen.Waycott@gnb.ca
Coordinator, Corporate Services, Education & Awareness, Bonnie Doyle
506-658-2410, bonnie.doyle@gnb.ca
Senior Consultant, Corporate Services, Education & Awareness, David Duplisea
506-658-3158, David.Duplisea@gnb.ca

Policy Development & Planning
Brunswick Square, #100M, 1 Germain St., Saint John, NB E2L 4V1
506-658-3180, Fax: 506-658-3191
Executive Director, Policy Development & Planning, Shelley Rinehart
506-658-3180, shelley.rinehart@gnb.ca
Policy Advisor, Laura Delong
506-658-3184
• New Brunswick Round Table on Environment & Economy/ Table Ronde sur Environnement & Economie
20 McGloin St.
PO Box 6000
Fredericton, NB E3B 5H1
506-453-3703 Fax: 506-453-3876
Mandate is to monitor/report on New Brunswick's progress towards implementing the elements of its Plan for Action & to act as a catalyst for change towards sustainable development within the Province.

Department of the Environment / Environnement

Marysville Place, 20 McGloin St., PO Box 6000, Fredericton, NB E3B 5H1
506-453-2690, Fax: 506-457-4991,
env-info@gnb.ca
www.gnb.ca/0009/index-e.asp

Other Communication: To report oil, pesticide, chemical spills, & other environmental emergencies, Toll-Free: 1-800-565-1633.
The Department of the Environment carries out the following responsibilities: Provision of integrated stewardship; Ensuring enforcement of environmental legislation & regulations; & Consultation with municipal governments & Local Service Districts.
Acts Administered:
Beverage Containers Act
Clean Air Act
Clean Environment Act
Clean Water Act
Community Planning Act
Environmental Trust Fund Act (except administration of fund)
Gas Distribution, 1999 Act (subsection 18(2), paragraph 32(1)(a), & subsection 39(1))
Mining Act (subsection 68(2))
Pesticides Control Act
Topsoil Preservation Act
Minister,Hon. Richard Miles
506-444-5136, Fax: 506-453-3377,rick.miles@gnb.ca
Deputy Minister, Bonny Hoyt-Hallett
506-453-3256, Fax: 506-453-3377,Bonny.Hoyt-Hallett@gnb.ca
Executive Director, Corporate Initiatives, K. Bradford Marshall
506-453-3700, Fax: 506-453-3676,Brad.Marshall@gnb.ca
Director, Strategic Planning & Policy Development, Kim Hughes
506-453-3700, Kim.HUGHES@gnb.ca
Director, Public Affairs, Vicky Deschênes
506-453-3700, Fax: 506-453-3843,Vicky.Deschenes@gnb.ca

Environmental Management / Gestion de l'environnement
Marysville Place, 20 McGloin St., PO Box 6000, Fredericton, NB E3B 5H1
506-444-5119, Fax: 506-457-7333
The main responsibility of the Environmental Management Division is initiatives to control pollutants, promote pollution prevention. & protect the environment. The Division acts as a major regulatory arm of the Department.
Assistant Deputy Minister, Perry Haines
Perry.Haines@gnb.ca
Executive Director, Regional Services, Kirk M. Gordon
Kirk.Gordon@gnb.ca
Director, Environmental Technologies & Innovation, Michael R. Sprague
506-444-5416, mike.sprague@gnb.ca
Director, Stewardship, Gregory Shanks
506-453-7945, Fax: 506-453-2390,greg.shanks@gnb.ca
Director, Project Assessment & Approvals, Paul Vanderlaan
506-444-4599, Fax: 506-457-7805,Paul.Vanderlaan@gnb.ca
Director, Greg Shanks
506-453-7945, greg.shanks@gnb.ca

Regional Environmental Services

Bathurst Regional Office
#202, 159 Main St., Bathurst, NB E2A 1A6
506-547-2092, Fax: 506-547-7655,
elg,egl-region1@gnb.ca
Regional Director, Paul Fournier
Paul.Fournier@gnb.ca

Fredericton Regional Office
Priestman Centre, 565 Priestman St., PO Box 6000, Fredericton, NB E3B 5H1
506-444-5149, Fax: 506-453-2893,
elg.egl-region5@gnb.ca
Regional Director, Serge Gagnon
Serge.Gagnon@gnb.ca

Grand Falls Regional Office
#200, 65 Broadway Blvd., PO Box 5001, Grand Falls, NB E3Z 1G1
506-473-7744, Fax: 506-475-2510,
elg.egl-region6@gnb.ca
Regional Director, Richard Keeley
Richard.Keeley@gnb.ca

Miramichi Regional Office
Industrial Park, 316 Dalton Ave., Miramichi, NB E1V 3N9
506-778-6032, Fax: 506-778-6796,
elg.egl-region2@gnb.ca
Regional Director, Denis Daigle
Denis.Daigle@gnb.ca

Moncton Regional Office
Provincial Bldg., 428 Collishaw St., PO Box 5001, Moncton, NB E1C 8R3
506-856-2374, Fax: 506-856-2370,
elg.egl-region3@gnb.ca
Regional Director, Laurie Collette
Laurie.Collette@gnb.ca

Saint John Regional Office
8 Castle St., PO Box 5001, Saint John, NB E2L 4Y9
506-658-2558, Fax: 506-658-3046,
elg.egl-region4@gnb.ca
Regional Director, Susan M. Atkinson

Sciences & Planning / Science et planification
Marysville Place, 20 McGloin St., 2nd Fl., PO Box 6000, Fredericton, NB E3B 5H1
506-453-2862, Fax: 506-453-2265
Scientific assessment, monitoring functions, & planning for sustainability are the major activities of the Sciences & Planning Division.
Assistant Deputy Minister, Sciences & Planning, Diane Kent Gillis
diane.kentgillis@gnb.ca
Executive Director, Environmental Services, David Schellenberg
506-444-2654, Fax: 506-444-2734,dave.schellenberg@gnb.ca
Director, Science & Reporting, Daryl Pupek
506-457-4844, Darryl.Pupek@gnb.ca
Director, Sustainable Planning, Kim Hughes
506-457-4846, Fax: 506-457-7823,Kim.Hughes@gnb.ca
Director, Climate Change Secretariat, Dean Mundee
506-457-4844, Dean.Mundee@gnb.ca

Department of Finance / Finances

670 King St., PO Box 6000, Fredericton, NB E3B 5H1
506-453-2451, Fax: 506-444-4724,
www.gnb.ca/0024/index-e.asp
The Department of Finance manages the public finances of New Brunswick.
Acts Administered:
Appropriation Act
Arts Development Trust Fund
Balanced Budget Act
Beaverbrook Art Gallery Act (Section 9)
Beaverbrook Auditorium Act (Section 7)
Environmental Trust Fund (administration of fund)
Equity Tax Credit Act
Financial Administration Act (expect provisions assigned to the Office of the Comptroller or to the Board of Management)
Financial Corporation Capital Tax Act
Fiscal Stabilization Fund
Fishermen's Disaster Fund Act (functions vested in Provincial Secretary-Treasurer)
Fredericton-Moncton Highway Financing Act
Gasoline & Motive Fuel Tax Act
Harmonized Sales Tax Act
Health Care Funding Guarantee Act
Income Tax Act
Loan Act
Municipal Assistance Act (except Section 5, 9 & 10)
Municipalities Act (subsection 19(8) & paragraphs 87.1(b) & (2)(b)
New Brunswick Income Tax Act
Northumberland Strait Crossing Act
Pari-Mutuel Tax Act
Pay Equity Act
Provincial Loans Act
Real Property Tax Act (except Sections 4 & subsection 5 (10))
Real Property Transfer Tax Act
Retirement Plan Benificiaries Act
Revenue Administration Act
Small Business Investment Tax Credit Act
Social Services & Education Tax Act
Special Appropriations Act
Special Retirement Program Act
Sport Development Trust Fund Act (administration of fund)
Statistics Act
Taxpayers Protection Act
Teachers' Pension Act
Tobacco Tax Act
Statutes under the Jurisdiction of the Minister of Finance in the Minister's Capacity as Chairman of the Board of Management
Auditor General Act (subsections 4(3) & 16(1) & Section 17
Crown Construction Contracts Act
Expenditure Management Act, 1991
Expenditure Management Act, 1992
Financial Administration Act (responsibilties pursuant to subsection 2(2) & Section 6
Member's Pension Act
Members Superannuation Act
Ombudsman Act (pension provision, subsection 2(4))
Provincial Court Act (pension provisions)
Public Service Labour Relations Act (61)
Public Service Superannuation Act
Special Retirement Program Act
Teachers' Pension Act
Statutes under the Jurisdiction of the Minister of Finance & Administered by the Office of the Comptroller
Financial Administration Act (responsibilities pursuant to subsection 2(1))
Statutes under the Jurisdiction of the Minister of Finance & Administered by a Board, Commission or Corporation
Lotteries Act (except provisions related to enforcement by inspectors)
Maritime Provinces Harness Racing Commission Act
New Brunswick Investment Management Corporation Act
New Brunswick Liquor Corporation Act
New Brunswick Municipal Finance Corporation Act
Pay Equity Act
Minister, Finance; Minister Responsible, NB Liquor Corporation; Minister Responsible, NB Investment Management Corporation, Minister Responsible, NB Lotteries & Gaming Corporation; Minister Responsible, Regional DevelopmentCorporation, Hon. Victor E. Boudreau
506-444-2627, Fax: 506-457-4989,victor.boudreau2@gnb.ca

Deputy Minister, John Mallory
506-453-2534, Fax: 506-457-4989,John.Mallory@gnb.ca
Director, Communications Services, Marc Belliveau
506-453-2451, Fax: 506-457-4989,Marc.Belliveau@gnb.ca
• New Brunswick Lotteries & Gaming Corporation
Centennial Bldg.
670 King St.
PO Box 6000
Fredericton, NB E3B 5H1
506-453-2451 Fax: 506-457-4989
www.gnb.ca/0162/gaming/Gaming_policy-e.asp
The name of the Lotteries Commission of New Brunswick, which was established as a Crown corporation under the Lotteries Act, was changed to the New Brunswick Lotteries & Gaming Corporation.
• New Brunswick Electric Finance Corporation/ Corporation financière de l'électricité du N.-B.
#376, 670 King St.
PO Box 6000
Fredericton, NB E3B 5H1
506-453-3952 Fax: 506-453-2053
• New Brunswick Investment Management Corporation(NBIMC) / Société de gestion des placements du Nouveau-Brunswick
York Tower
#581, 440 King St.
Fredericton, NB E3B 5H8
506-444-5800 Fax: 506-444-5025
comments@nbimc.com
www.nbimc.com
The New Brunswick Investment Management Corporation assists in the development of the financial services industry & capital markets in the province of New Brunswick.
• New Brunswick Municipal Finance Corporation/ Corporation de Financement des municipalités du Nouveau-Brunswick
#376, 670 King St.
PO Box 6000
Fredericton, NB E3B 5H1
506-453-3952 Fax: 506-453-2053

Budget & Financial Management / Gestion financière et budgétaire
Centennial Bldg., #250, 670 King St., PO Box 6000, Fredericton, NB E3B 5H1
506-453-2808, Fax: 506-444-4499
The Budget & Financial Management Division has the following responsibilities: Implementation of multi-year expenditure plans; Development & monitoring of budgets; & Offering options for the government to consider.
Assistant Secretary, Board of Management, Keith MacNevin
Keith.MacNevin@gnb.ca
Director, Board of Management Operations, Kelly Barr
506-453-6006, Kelly.barr@gnb.ca
Director, Budget & Expenditure Monitoring, Troy Mann
506-444-3621, Troy.Mann@gnb.ca

Finance & Administration / Finances et administration
Centennial Bldg., #373, 670 King St., PO Box 6000, Fredericton, NB E3B 5H1
506-457-6863, Fax: 506-444-4724
Director, Finance & Administration, Nicholas Guitard
506-457-6863, Nicholas.Guitard@gnb.ca
Director, Policy & Planning, Ann Deveau
506-444-4498, Ann.Deveau@gnb.ca
Director, Human Resources Services, Cécile Guérette
506-444-5099, Cecile.Guerette@gnb.ca
Director, Information Management & Technology, Pam Gagnon
506-453-3310, Fax: 506-444-3471,Pam.Gagnon@gnb.ca
Director, Financial Services, Rick Phillips
506-453-2286, Fax: 506-462-5056,Rick.Phillips@gnb.ca

Fiscal Policy / Politiques fiscales
Centennial Bldg., #245, 670 King St., PO Box 6000, Fredericton, NB E3B 5H1
506-453-2096, Fax: 506-453-2281
The Fiscal Policy Division provides the following services: Advice & analysis in the areas of fiscal & budget policy, federal-provincial fiscal relations, & the economy; Statistical services for the government; & Forecasting & monitoring of government revenues & the economy.
Assistant Deputy Minister, Fiscal Policy, Peter Kieley
506-453-6921, Fax: 506-453-2281,Peter.Kieley@gnb.ca
Director, Federal-Provincial Fiscal & Statistical Relations, Lucy St-Jean
506-444-5640, lucy.St-Jean@gnb.ca
Director, Fiscal Policy & Economics, George Richardson
506-453-6917, George.Richardson@gnb.ca

Revenue & Taxation / Revenu et Impôt
Centennial Bldg., #671, 670 King St., PO Box 3000, Fredericton, NB E3B 5G5
506-444-2826, Fax: 506-444-4920
Provincial Tax Commissioner, Revenue Administration, Richard McCullough
506-444-2826, Rick.McCullough@gnb.ca
Acting Director, Strategic Business Initiatives, Gary McCarville
506-457-4887, Fax: 506-444-5818,gary.Mccarville@gnb.ca
Director, Tax Policy, George McAllister
506-444-4065, Fax: 506-444-5818,George.Mcallister@gnb.ca
Director, First Nations / Gaming Policy, Patricia Steeves
506-444-4065, Fax: 506-444-5818,Pat.Steeves@gnb.ca

Treasury / Trésorerie
Centennial Bldg., #376, 670 King St., PO Box 6000, Fredericton, NB E3B 5H1
506-453-3952, Fax: 506-453-2053
The Treasury Division is engaged in the following activities: Evaluating & advising concerning the financial position of New Brunswick; Performing trustee functions for certain trust funds; Providing cash management & receipt of revenues; Funding borrowing requirements of the provincial & crown agencies; Providing advice on pension management & other liabilities.
Assistant Deputy Minister, Leonard Lee-White
leonard.lee-white@gnb.ca
Managing Director, Capital Markets, Richard Luton
506-444-4161, Richard.Luton@gnb.ca
Managing Director, Banking & Cash Management, Roger Jones
Roger.Jones@gnb.ca

Department of Fisheries / Pêches

Research Station, 850 Lincoln Rd., Fredericton, NB E3B 9H8
506-453-3966, Fax: 506-444-5477,
MDP-DOF@gnb.ca
www.gnb.ca/9999/index-e.asp
A strategically focused team, promoting sustainable growth of the fisheries sector from the ocean to the plate, as well as the aquaculture processing sector, through innovative partnerships and targeted policies and programs resulting in greater prosperity for New Brunswickers.
Minister,Hon. Rick Doucet
506-444-6734, Rick.Doucet@gnb.ca
Deputy Minister, Jim McKay
506-453-2450, Fax: 506-444-5022,Jim.McKay@gnb.ca
Director, Communications, Paul Harpelle
506-444-4218, Fax: 506-444-5022,Paul.Harpelle@gnb.ca

Department of Health / Santé

PO Box 5100, Fredericton, NB E3B 5G8
506-457-4800, Fax: 506-453-5243,
dh-ms@dh-ms.ca
www.gnb.ca/0051/index-e.asp
To work with New Brunswickers in achieving well-being by promoting self-sufficiency & personal responsibility, & providing approved services as required. The development & delivery of health programs & services to New Brunswick residents is supported by a range of internal department functions such as administration, planning & evaluation, & program support. Provides the continuum of services to prevent illness & disability. The department's education & awareness raising initiatives promote the health & well-being of New Brunswickers of all ages so that they can achieve their best potential while enjoying an independent & healthy lifestyle for as long as possible.
Acts Administered:
Ambulance Services Act
Anatomy Act
Cemetery Companies Act
Change of Name Act
Clean Air (Paragraph 8(2a) & Subsection 4)
Clean Water Act (in part)
Fish Inspection Act
Health Act
Hospital Act
Hospital Services Act
Human Tissues Act
Human Tissues Gift Act
Insurance Act
Liquor Control Act
Marriage Act
Medical Consent of Minors Act
Medical Services Payment Act
Mental Health Act
Mental Health Services Act
Motor Vehicle Act (in part)
Municipalities Act
Pesticides Control Act (in part)
Prescription Drug Payment Act
Public Health
Radiological Health Protection Act
Regional Health Authorities Act
Smoke-Free Places Act, 2004
Tobacco Sales Act
Venereal Disease Act
Vital Statistics Act
Minister,Hon. Michael B. Murphy
MichaelB.Murphy@gnb.ca
Deputy Minister, Donald Ferguson
don.j.ferguson@gnb.ca
Director, Communications, Tracey Burkhardt
506-453-2536, tracey.burkhardt@gnb.ca
Administrative Support, Kathy Densmore
506-453-2536, Fax:
506-444-4697,kathy.densmore@gnb.ca

Addiction & Mental Health Services Division / Services de traitement des dépendances et de santé mentale
506-444-4442
Asst. Deputy Minister, Ken Ross
506-453-4238
Acting Executive Director, Programs, Jean-Louis Bouchard
Director, Acute Services, Andrée Guy
Acting Director, Child & Adolescent Programs, Barbara Whitenect
Acting Director, Quality Management & Executive Support, John Estey

Public Health & Medical Services / Santé publique et services médicaux
Public Health services are delivered through the province's seven health regions, under the management of Regional Directors.A Chief Medical Officer of Health & a Deputy Chief Medical Officer of Health oversee the development of policy & regulations, & provide medical operational support to the regional Medical Officers of Health. Public Health Services support healthy growth & development, foster healthy lifestyles, control communicable diseases, & protect the public from adverse health consequences of exposure to chemical, physical & biological agents.
Chief Medical Officer,Dr. Wayne MacDonald
506-453-2323
Provincial Epidemologist,Dr. B. Christofer Balram
506-453-3092
Director, Medicare Services, Linda M. Lingley
506-453-6851

Office of Human Resources / Bureaux des ressources humaines

Centennial Bldg, #345, 670 King St., PO Box 6000, Fredericton, NB E3B 5H1
506-453-2264, Fax: 506-453-7195,
www.gnb.ca/0163/index-e.asp
The Office of Human Resources has responsibility for the policies which govern the following human resources issues: Recruitment; Compensation; & Staff development for the provision of quality public services.
Acts Administered:
Civil Services Act (staffing responsibilities)
Public Interest Disclosure Act
Minister, Office of Human Resources, Hon. Wally Stiles
506-462-5092, Fax: 506-453-7195,wally.stiles@gnb.ca
Deputy Minister, Carolyn MacKay
506-453-3036, Fax: 506-453-7195,Carolyn.Mackay@gnb.ca
Director, Communications, Christina Winsor
506-453-8014, Fax: 506-453-4225,christina.winsor@gnb.ca
Legislative Coordinator, Management Services, Doris Doucet
506-462-5098, Fax: 506-453-2124,doris.doucet2@gnb.ca

Compensation & Employee Benefits
York Tower, Kings Place, #680, 440 King St., PO Box 6000, Fredericton, NB E3B 5H8
506-453-2296, Fax: 506-457-7388, 800-561-4012
www.gnb.ca/0163/pension/pension-e.asp
Assistant Deputy Minister, Compensation & Employee Benefits, Brian Durelle
506-453-5359, Fax: 506-444-5311,Brian.Durelle@gnb.ca
Director, Employee Benefits & Client Services, Lynn Noel
506-453-2296, Fax: 506-457-7388,Lynn.Noel@gnb.ca
Director, Employee Benefits & Divisional Services, Don Harrington
506-453-2296, Fax: 506-457-7388,don.harrington@gnb.ca
Director, Corporate Strategic Services & Employee Benefit Policy, Mark J. Gaudet
506-453-2296, Fax: 506-457-7388,Mark.Gaudet@gnb.ca
Director, Compensation & Classification, Lori Anne McCracken
506-457-7216, Fax:
506-444-5311,LoriAnne.Mccracken@gnb.ca

Labour Relations Services
Centennial Bldg., #360, 670 King St., PO Box 6000, Fredericton, NB E3B 5H1
506-453-2115, Fax: 506-444-5786
Assistant Deputy Minister, Labour Relations Services, Dorine Taylor
506-453-2699, Fax: 506-444-5786,Dorine.Taylor@gnb.ca
Researcher, Gloria Dean
506-453-6184, Fax: 506-444-5786,Gloria.Dean@gnb.ca

Official Languages, Workplace Equity, & HRIS
Centennial Bldg., #344, 670 King St., PO Box 6000, Fredericton, NB E3B 5H1
506-453-2264, Fax: 506-453-2124
Executive Director, Official Languages, Workplace Equity, & HRIS, Hubert Cormier
506-453-2264, Fax: 506-453-2124,Hubert.Cormier@gnb.ca
Director, Human Resource Information Services, Darren Caterini
506-457-4964, Fax: 506-457-4964,Darren.Caterini@gnb.ca,
Manager, Official Languages & Workplace Equity, Michelle Anne Duguay
506-453-2264, Fax:
506-453-2264,MichelleAnne.Duguay@gnb.ca

Staffing, Development & Human Resources Policy
Centennial Bldg., #348, 670 King St., PO Box 6000, Fredericton, NB E3B 5H1
506-453-2141, Fax: 506-453-4225
Assistant Deputy Minister, Staffing, Development & Human Resources Policy, Lisa M. Doucette
506-453-2141, Fax: 506-453-4225,Lisa.Doucette@gnb.ca
Director, Michael Murray
506-444-3666, Fax: 506-453-4225,michael.murray@gnb.ca
Registrar, Lisa Hennessy-Adams
506-453-5596, Fax:
506-453-4225,lisa.hennessy-adams@gnb.ca

New Brunswick Human Rights Commission / Commission des droits de la personne

PO Box 6000, Fredericton, NB E3B 5H1
506-453-2301, Fax: 506-453-2653, 888-471-2233
hrc.cdp@gnb.ca
Chair, Gordon Porter
Director, Susan Butterfield

Department of Intergovernmental Affairs / Affaires intergouvernementales et relations internationales

Centennial Bldg., #274, 670 King St., PO Box 6000, Fredericton, NB E3B 5H1
506-444-5418, Fax: 506-453-2995,
iga@gnb.ca
www.gnb.ca/0056/index-e.asp
New Brunswick's Department of Intergovernmental Affairs manages relations withgovernments, communities, & organizations. The North American Division, the International Relations & Francophonie Division, & the Trade Policy Division conduct operations with a strategic & corporate approach.
Acts Administered:
Council of Maritime Premiers Act
Executive Council Act
Maritime Economic Cooperation Act
Order of New Brunswick Act
Premier; President, Executive Council; Minister, Intergovernmental Affairs; Minister Responsible, Premier's Council on the Status of Disabled Persons; Minister Responsible, Office of Self-Sufficiency, Hon. Shawn M. Graham
506-453-2144, Fax: 506-453-7407,Premier@gnb.ca; Shawn.Graham@gnb.ca
Minister, Wellness, Culture, & Sport; Minister Responsible, Francophonie,Hon. Hédard Albert
506-444-5418, Fax: 506-444-5612,Hedard.Albert@gnb.ca
Deputy Minister, Edith Doucet
506-457-7275, Fax: 506-457-6507,Edith.Doucet@gnb.ca
Director, Communications, Gisele Regimbal
506-444-4594, Fax: 506-457-6507,Gisele.Regimbal@gnb.ca

International Relations & la Francophonie / Relations internationales et La Francophonie
Centennial Bldg., #118, 670 King St., PO Box 6000, Fredericton, NB E3B 5H1
506-453-3078, Fax: 506-453-2995
Assistant Deputy Minister, Mirelle Cyr
Mirelle.Cyr@gnb.ca
Director, Official Languages, Line Pinet
506-444-4948, Fax: 506-444-5612,line.pinet@gnb.ca
Director, International Relations & Francophonie, Danielle Mingay
506-444-4948, Fax: 506-444-5612,danielle.mingay@gnb.ca
Chief of Protocol, Office of the Protocol, Anne Reynolds
506-453-2671, Anne.Reynolds@gnb.ca

North American Division / Division des relations nord-américaines
Centennial Bldg., #274, 670 King St., PO Box 6000, Fredericton, NB E3B 5H1
506-444-6775, Fax: 506-453-2995
Assistant Deputy Minister, Jocelyne Mills
Jocelyne.Mills@gnb.ca
Director, Arnold Kearney
Arnold.Kearney@gnb.ca

Trade Policy
Centennial Bldg., #175, 670 King St., PO Box 6000, Fredericton, NB E3B 5H1
506-444-5094, Fax: 506-444-5299
Executive Director, Elaine Campbell
506-444-5788, elaine.campbell@gnb.ca
Senior Policy Advisor, Andrew David Hashey
506-444-4250, Andrew.Hashey@gnb.ca

Department of Justice & Consumer Affairs / Justice et la consommation

Centennial Bldg., 670 King St., PO Box 6000, Fredericton, NB E3B 5H1
506-462-5100, Fax: 506-453-3651,
justice.comments@gnb.ca
www.gnb.ca/0062/index-e.asp
Promoting the impartial administration of justice, & ensuring protection of the public interest are the chief responsibilities of New Brunswick's Department of Justice & Consumer Affairs. The province's Public Legal Education & Information Service is funded by Justice Canada.
Acts Administered:
Absconding Debtors Act
Age of Majority Act
Arbitration Act
Arrest & Examinations Act
Assignments & Preferences Act
Auctioneers Licence Act
Canadian Judgments Act
Charter Compliance Acts
Collection Agencies Act
Commissioners for Taking Affidavits Act
Conflict of Laws Rules for Trusts Act
Consumer Product Warranty & Liability Act
Contributory Negligence Act
Controverted Elections Act
Co-operative Associations Act
Corrupt Practices Inquiries Act
Cost of Credit Disclosure Act
Court Reporters Act
Credit Unions Act
Creditors Relief Act
Criminal Prosecution Expenses Act
Crown Debts Act
Crown Prosecutors Act
Defamation Act
Demise of the Crown Act
Devolution of Estates Act
Direct Sellers Act
Divorce Court Act
Easements Act
Electronic Transactions Act
Entry Warrants Act
Escheats & Forfeitures Act
Evidence Act
Executors & Trustees Act
Expropriation Act
Factors & Agents Act
Family Services Act (Part VII)
Fatal Accidents Act
Federal Courts Jurisdiction Act
Foreign Judgments Act
Frustrated Contracts Act
Garnishee Act
Great Seal Act
Guardianship of Children Act
Habeas Corpus Act
Infirm Persons Act
Innkeepers Act
Inquiries Act
Insurance Act
Interjurisdicational Support Orders Act
International Child Abduction Act
International Commercial Arbitration Act
International Sale of Goods Act
International Trusts Act
International Wills Act
Interpretation Act
Interprovincial Subpoena Act
Judges Disqualification Removal Act
Judicature Act
Jury Act
Landlord & Tenant Act
Law Reform Act
Legal Aid Act
Liens on Goods & Chattels Act
Limitation of Actions Act
Loan & Trust Companies Act
Marital Property Act
Married Woman's Property Act
Mechanics' Lien Act
Memorials & Executions Act
Merger of Supreme & County Courts of New Brunswick Act
Notaries Public Act
Nova Scotia Grants Act
Postal Services Interruption Act
Pre-arranged Funeral Services Act
Premium Tax Act
Presumption of Death Act
Probate Court Act
Proceedings Against the Crown Act
Property Act
Protection of Persons Acting Under Statute Act
Provincial Court Act
Provincial Offences Procedure Act
Provincial Offences Procedure for Young Persons Act
Provision for Dependants Act
Public Records Act
Queen's Counsel & Precedence Act
Queen's Printer Act
Quieting of Titles Act
Real Estate Agents Act
Reciprocal Enforcement of Judgments Act
Reciprocal Recognition & Enforcement of Judgements in Civil & Commerical Matters Act
(An Act Respecting the Convention Between Canada & the United Kingdom of Great Britain & Northern Ireland Providing For the Reciprocal Recognition & Enforcement of Judgments in Civil & Commercial Matt
Recording of Evidence by Sound Recording Machine Act
Regulations Act
(An Act Respecting the) Removal of Archaic Terminology from the Acts of New Brunswick
Residential Tenancies Act
Sale of Goods Act
Sale of Lands Publication Act
Sheriffs Act
Small Claims Act
Special Insurance Companies Act
Statute Law Amendment Acts
Statute of Frauds Act
Statute Revision Act
Succession Law Amendment Acts
Support Enforcement Act
Surety Bonds Act
Survival of Actions Act
Survivorship Act
Tortfeasors Act
Trespass Act
Trustees Act
Unconscionable Transactions Relief Act
Wage-Earners Protection Act
Warehouse Receipts Act
Warehouseman's Lien Act
Wills Act
Woodmen's Lien Act
Minister, Justice & Consumer Affairs & Attorney General, Hon. Thomas J. Burke, Q.C.
506-462-5100, Fax: 506-453-365,t.j.burke@gnb.ca
Deputy Minister, Justice & Consumer Affairs, Yvon G. LeBlanc, Q.C.
yvon.leblanc3@gnb.ca
Executive Director, Administrative Services, Neil E. Foreman
506-453-6503, Fax: 506-453-8718,neil.foreman@gnb.ca
Executive Director, Public Legal Education & Information Service, Deborah Doherty
506-453-5369, Fax: 506-462-5193
Director, Policy & Planning, Debbie Hackett
506-453-3693, debbie.hackett@gnb.ca
Director, Communications, Valerie Kilfoil
Fax: 506-444-2661
• New Brunswick Credit Union Deposit Insurance Corp./ Société d'assurance-dépôts des caisses populaires du Nouveau-Brunswick
PO Box 6000
Fredericton, NB E3B 5H1
506-457-4852 Fax: 506-453-7474
www.assurance-nb.ca/index-e.asp
The New Brunswick Credit Union Deposit Insurance Corporation is a Crown corporation that provides deposit insurance to members of New Brunswick's credit unions and caisses populaires.
• New Brunswick Expropriations Advisory Office/ Bureau sur l'expropriation
Phoenix Square Bldg.
371 Queen St.
Fredericton, NB E3B 1B1
506-453-7771 Fax: 506-453-9600

• New Brunswick Insurance Board/ Commission des assurances du N.-B.
Saint John Mercantile Centre
#600, 55 Union St.
Saint John, NB E2L 5B7
506-643-7710 Fax: 506-652-5011
info@nbib-canb.org
www.nbib-canb.org
The New Brunswick Insurance Board regulates automobile insurance rates. The Board is also responsible for approving rates for all products being sold in New Brunswick as of January 2005.
• New Brunswick Real Estate Association/ Association des agents immobiliers du Nouveau-Brunswick
#1, 22 Durelle St.
Fredericton, NB E3C 1N8
506-459-8055 Fax: 506-459-8057 800-762-1677
info@nbrea.ca
www.nbrea.ca
The New Brunswick Real Estate Association serves and regulates its members through education, professional and ethical standards, and promotion of public awareness for the benefit of REALTORS and the public they serve.
• New Brunswick Securities Commission/ Commission des valeurs mobilières du N.-B.
#300, 85 Charlotte St.
Saint John, NB E2L 2J2
506-658-3060 Fax: 506-658-3059 866-933-2222
information@nbsc-cvmnb.ca
www.nbsc-cvmnb.ca/nbsc
The New Brunswick Securities Commission (NBSC) is the Crown Corporation established by the Province of New Brunswick in 2004 to regulate the securities industry and ensure the efficiency and integrity of capital markets in New Brunswick.

Court Services / Services à la court
Asst. Deputy Minister, Michael Comeau
506-462-5100, Fax: 506-444-2661,michael.comeau@gnb.ca
Director, Program Support Branch, Anne McKay
506-462-5100, Anne.Mckay@gnb.ca
Director, Sheriff Services, Jack MacKay
506-457-6499, Jack.E.MacKay@gnb.ca

Regional Court Services/Services aux tribunal regionaux:

Bathurst
Regional Director, Grégoire Boudreau
506-547-2150, Fax: 506-547-2966

Fredericton
Regional Director, Dominique Laundry
506-453-2015, Fax: 506-453-7921

Miramichi
Regional Director, Matthew Cripps
506-627-4023, Fax: 506-627-4069

Moncton
Regional Director, David Léger
506-856-2415, Fax: 506-869-6168

Saint John
Regional Director, Tom Bishop
506-658-2400, Fax: 506-658-3762

Justice Services / Services judiciaires
Fax: 506-444-2661
Asst. Deputy Minister, Suzanne Bonnell-Burley
506-462-5100, suzanne.bonnell-burley@gnb.ca
Director, Credit Unions, Cooperatives & Trust Companies Branch & Director, Examinations, Robert Penney
506-453-2315, Fax: 506-453-7474
Director, Insurance, Roderick Mackenzie, Q.C.
506-453-5100, Fax:
506-453-7435,Roderick.Mackenzie@gnb.ca
Director, Office of the Rentalsman & Consumer Affairs Branch, Marilyn Evans-Born
506-462-5100, Fax: 506-453-2613,marilyn.born@gnb.ca

New Brunswick Liquor Corporation (Alcool NB Liquor) / Société des alcools du Nouveau-Brunswick

170 Wilsey Rd., PO Box 20787, Fredericton, NB E3B 5B8
506-452-6826, Fax: 506-462-2024,
info@anbl.com
www.nbliquor.com

Other Communication: Public Affairs Phone: 506-452-6453
The Crown corporation manufactures, buys, imports, & sells liquor of every kind.
Minister, Finance; Minister Responsible, NB Liquor Corporation; Minister Responsible, NB Investment Management Corporation, Minister Responsible, NB Lotteries & Gaming Corporation; Minister Responsible, Regional DevelopmentCorporation, Hon. Victor E. Boudreau
506-444-2627, Fax: 506-457-4989,Victor.Boudreau2@gnb.ca
Chair, Larry Jackson
506-452-6510
President/CEO, Dana Clendenning
506-452-6522
Senior Vice-President, Richard A. Smith
506-452-6501
Vice-President/CFO, Chris Evans
506-452-6460
Vice-President, Human Resources & Communications, Jane Washburn
506-452-6500
Vice-President, Customer Service & Retail Operations, Brad Cameron
506-452-6826
Vice-President, Supply Chain & Facilities, Michael G. O'Brien
506-452-6505

Department of Local Government / Gouvernementaux locales

Marysville Place, 20 McGloin St., PO Box 6000, Fredericton, NB E3B 5H1
506-453-2807, Fax: 506-453-3988,
www.gnb.ca/0370/index-e.asp
The Department of Local Government oversees the following areas: Assessment & planning appeals; Local governance & regional collaboration for New Brunswick; Local Service Districts; Municipalities (cities, towns, & villages) & rural communities, including municipal capital borrowing, orientation, & restructuring; Registration of dogs & dog kennels in unincorporated areas; Resource manuals for local government in New Brunswick; & grants.
Acts Administered:
Agricultural Land Protection & Development Act (subsection 10(2) & section 11)
Assessment & Planning Appeal Board Act
Business Improvement Areas Act
Cemetery Companies Act (paragraph 5(1)(c))
Control of Municipalities Act
Days of Rest Act
Edmundston, 1998 Act
Evidence Act (sections 88, 89, & 90)
Highway Act (sections 58 - 62.1)
Metric Conversion Act
Municipal Assistance Act
Municipal Capital Borrowing Act
Municipal Debentures Act
Municipalities Act (except subsection 19(8), 125(1), & 188(3))
Municipal Thoroughfare Easements Act
New Brunswick Municipal Finance Corporation Act (section 14 & subsection 16(4))
Police Act (paragraph 17.05(2)(b), subsections 17.06(3), & (4), paragraph 17.2(3)(b), & subsections 17.4(3) & (4))
Real Property Tax (section 4 & subsection 5(10))
Service New Brunswick Act (paragraph 15.1(3)(b))
Society for the Prevention of Cruelty to Animals Act
Unsightly Premises Act
Minister, Local Government, Hon. Carmel Robichaud
carmel.robichaud@gnb.ca
Deputy Minister, Bonny Hoyt-Hallett
506-453-3256, Fax:
506-453-3988,Bonny.Hoyt-Hallett@gnb.ca
• Assessment & Planning Appeal Board/ Commission d'appel en matière d'évaluation et d'urbanisme
#201, 435 King St.
PO Box 6000
Fredericton, NB E3B 5H1
506-453-2126 Fax: 506-444-4881

Corporate & Community Finance
Marysville Place, 20 McGloin St., PO Box 6000, Fredericton, NB E3B 5H1
506-453-2154, Fax: 506-457-4933
Executive Director, Community Finance, Dan Rae
506-453-2154, Fax: 506-453-7128,Dan.Rae@gnb.ca
Director, Community Finance, Sandra Jessop-Roach
506-453-2154, Fax: 506-453-7128,Sandra.Roach@gnb.ca
Director, Corporate Finance, Yvonne Samson
Yvonne.Samson@gnb.ca

Corporate Services / Services généraux
Marysville Place, 20 McGloin St., PO Box 6000, Fredericton, NB E3B 5H1
506-453-2020, Fax: 506-457-7800
Executive Director, Corporate Services, Alan J. Roy
506-453-2020, Fax: 506-457-7800,alan.roy@gnb.ca
Director, Information & Technology Management, Laurie Robichaud
506-453-2020, Fax: 506-453-7128,Laurie.Robichaud@gnb.ca

Local Governance & Community Infrastructure
Marysville Place, 20 McGloin St., 2nd Fl., PO Box 6000, Fredericton, NB E3B 5H1
506-444-4423, Fax: 506-457-4933
Executive Director, Community Infrastructure, Stephen Battah
506-444-4423, Fax: 506-457-4933,stephen.battah@gnb.ca
Director, Community Restructuring, Johnny St. Onge
506-444-4423, Fax: 506-457-4933,Johnny.St-Onge@gnb.ca
Director, Capacity Building, Thierry Arseneau
506-444-4423, Fax: 506-457-4933,Thierry.arseneau@gnb.ca

Local Service District
Marysville Place, 20 McGloin St., 2nd Fl., PO Box 6000, Fredericton, NB E3B 5H1
506-453-2434, Fax: 506-457-4933
Offices of the Local Service District Division are located in the following places: Bathurst, Edmundston, Richibucto, Tracadie-Sheila, Miramichi, St, Stephen, & Woodstock.
Director, Local Service District, Colleen Mullin
506-453-2434, Fax: 506-457-4933,Colleen.Mullin@gnb.ca

Policy, Planning & Public Affairs
Marysville Place, 20 McGloin St., 2nd Fl., PO Box 6000, Fredericton, NB E3B 5H1
506-453-2434, Fax: 506-457-4933
Executive Director, Policy, Planning & Public Affairs, Elizabeth Hayward
506-453-2434, Fax: 506-457-4933,bebo.hayward@gnb.ca
Director, Policy & Legislative Affairs, Christy Shaw
506-453-2434, Fax: 506-453-7128,Christy.Shaw@gnb.ca
Manager, Strategic Initiatives Development, Martin Corbett
506-453-2434, Fax: 506-457-4933,martin.corbett@gnb.ca

Department of Natural Resources / Ressources naturelles

PO Box 6000, Fredericton, NB E3B 5H1
506-453-2510, Fax: 506-444-5839,
dnrweb@gnb.ca
www.gnb.ca/0078/index-e.asp
Manages all natural resources within the province including fish & wildlife, timber, minerals, Crown lands & water resources. Responsible for the development, protection, allocation & utilization of resources in a way that is considered economically, environmentally & socially acceptable.
Acts Administered:
Act Respecting Angling Lease Number 7
Bituminous Shale Act
Conservation Easements Act
Crown Grant Restrictions Act
Crown Lands & Forests Act
Endangered Species Act
Fish & Wildlife Act
Forest Fires Act
Grants Act
Kouchibouguac National Park, An Act to Implement Recommendation 16 of the Report of the Special Inquiry on
Mining Act (in part)
National Parks Act
Natural Products Act (in part)
Off-Road Vehicle Act
Oil & Natural Gas Act
Ownership of Minerals Act
Parks Act
Pipe Line Act
Protected Natural Areas Act, 2003
Quarriable Substances Act
Scalers Act
Territorial Divisions Act
Transportation of Primary Forest Products Act
Underground Storage Act
Acts administered by an Associated Agency, Board, Commission or Corporation
Forest Products Act
Maritime Forestry Complex Coporation Act
Roosevelt Campobello International Park Act
St. Croix International Waterway Commission Act
Minister,Hon. Wally Stiles
wally.stiles@gnb.ca
Deputy Minister, Tom Reid
506-453-2501, Fax: 506-453-2930,Tom.REID@gnb.ca
Director, Communications, Steven Benteau
506-453-2614, Fax: 506-457-4881,Steve.Benteau@gnb.ca
Office Manager, Geoff Payne
506-453-2614, Fax: 506-457-4881,Geoff. Payne@gnb.ca
• Board of Examiners under the Scaler's Act/ Bureau des examinateurs (Loi sur les mesureurs)
1350 Regent St. South
PO Box 6000
Fredericton, NB E3B 5H1
506-453-2441 Fax: 506-453-6689

• Forest Protection Limited/ Protection des Forêts
2502 Hwy. 102
Lincoln, NB E3B 7E6
506-446-6930 Fax: 506-446-6934
info@forestprotectionlimited.com
www.forestprotectionlimited.com
Forest Protection Limited (FPL) is a non-profit aerial forest protection company whose mandate is to protect forests through assistance to the Forest Management Branch, for fire protection, fire fighting assistance & aerial surveys.
• New Brunswick Forest Products Commission/ Commission des produits forestiers du Nouveau-Brunswick
PO Box 6000
Fredericton, NB E3B 5H1
506-453-2196 Fax: 506-457-4966
www.gnb.ca/0078/fpc/index.asp
The New Brunswick Forest Products Commission is an independent Commission overseeing the marketing relationships involving forest industries (pulp mills & sawmills), forest products marketing boards (private woodlot owners & producers) & the provincial government.

Minerals, Policy & Planning Division / Ressources minières, politique et planification
506-453-2206, Fax: 506-457-6762
Asst. Deputy Minister, Ellen Barry
506-453-2684
Director, Mineral & Petroleum Development Branch, Samuel K. McEwan
506-444-5005, Fax: 506-453-3671
Director, Geological Surveys Branch, Les Fyffe
506-453-2206, Fax: 506-453-3671

Renewable Resources / Ressources renouvelables
Asst. Deputy Minister, Tom Reid
506-453-3063, Fax: 506-453-2930
Director, Fish & Wildlife, Mike Sullivan
506-453-2433, Fax: 506-453-6699
Director, Forest Management, Daniel Murphy
506-453-2432, Fax: 506-453-6689
Executive Director, Regional Operations, Julius Tarjan
506-453-3063, Fax: 506-453-2930

Office of the Ombudsman / Bureau de l'ombudsman

767 Brunswick St., PO Box 6000, Fredericton, NB E3B 5H1
506-453-2789, Fax: 506-453-5599, 800-465-1100
nbombud@gnb.ca
Ombudsman, Bernard Richard
Legal Counsel, Claire Pitre
Executive Secretary, Julie Dickison
506-453-2789, Fax: 506-453-5599

New Brunswick Police Commission (NBPC) / Commission de police du Nouveau-Brunswick

Fredericton City Centre, #202, 435 King St., Fredericton, NB E3B 1E5
506-453-2069, Fax: 506-457-3542
The Commission investigates & determines complaints alleging misconduct by municipal & regional police officers; investigates any matter relating to any aspect of policing in any area of the province; determines the adequacy of municipal, regional & RCMP police forces within the province.
Chair, Grant S. Garneau
Executive Director, Clem Bolduc
506-453-2069, Fax: 506-457-3542

Department of Post-Secondary Education, Training & Labour / Éducation postsecondaire, Formation et Travail

470 York St., PO Box 6000, Fredericton, NB E3B 5H1
506-453-2597, Fax: 506-453-3618,
dpetlinfo@gnb.ca
www.gnb.ca/0105/index.htm
Formerly the Department of Training & Employment.
Acts Administered:
Adult Education & Training Act
Apprenticeship & Occupational Certification Act
Blind Workmen's Compensation Act
Degree Granting Act
Employment Development Act
Employment Standards Act
Fisheries Bargaining Act
Higher Education Foundation Act
Human Rights Act
Industrial Relations Act
Labour & Employment Board Act
Labour Market Research Act
Maritime Provinces Higher Education Commission Act
New Brunswick Public Libraries Act
New Brunswick Public Libraries Foundation Act
Occupational Health & Safety Act
Pension Benefits Act
Private Occupational Training Act
Public Service Labour Relations Act
Silicosis Compensation Act
Special Payment to Certain Dependent Spouses of Deceased Workers Act
Workers' Compensation Act (administered by Workplace Health, Safety & Compensation Commission)
Workplace Health, Safety & Compensation Commission Act
Youth Assistance Act
Minister,Hon. Donald Arseneault
506-453-2342, Fax: 506-453-3038,donald.arseneault@gnb.ca
Deputy Minister, Byron James
506-453-2343, Fax: 506-453-3038,Byron.James@gnb.ca
Director, Communications, Marie-Josée Groulx
506-444-3465, Fax: 506-444-4314,marie-josee.groulx@gnb.ca
Media Relations Coordinator, Sheri Strickland
506-453-8617, Fax: 506-444-4314,sheri.strickland@gnb.ca
• Apprenticeship & Occupational Certification Board/ Direction de l'apprentissage et de la certification professionnelle
PO Box 6000
Fredericton, NB E3B 5H1
506-453-2260 Fax: 506-453-5317
• Ministerial Advisory Committee on Multiculturalism/ Comité consultatif ministériel sur le multiculturalisme
PO Box 6000
Fredericton, NB E3B 5H1
• New Brunswick Human Rights Commission/ Commission des droits de la personne
• Workplace Health, Safety & Compensation Commission(WHSCC) / Commission de la santé, de la sécurité et de l'indemnisation des accidents au travail
• Workplace Health, Safety & Compensation Commission of New Brunswick(WHSC) / Commission de la santé, de la sécurité et de l'indemnisation des accidents au travail

Labour & Legislative Development / Travail et Élaboration des législations
Asst. Deputy Minister, Paul G. Blackmore
506-453-8202, Fax: 506-444-4314
Director, Industrial Relations, David Moore
506-453-2261, Fax: 506-453-2678
Director, Legislative Review & Development, Kelli Simmonds
506-453-2525, Fax: 506-453-2148
Director, Labour Market Analysis, Kelly Rodgers-Sturgeon
506-457-7891

NBCC / CCNB
Asst. Deputy Minister/CEO, Michel Thériault
506-444-5732, Fax: 506-444-4314
Executive Director, NBCC (Anglophone), Richard Corey
506-453-8258, Fax: 506-444-4960
Executive Director, NBCC (Francophone), Yves Chouinard
506-789-4957, Fax: 506-789-2430
Acting Director, NBCC-Operations, Dan Fraser
506-453-2291, Fax: 506-444-4960
Director, NBCC-Programs,Vacant
506-453-8230
Director, Student Services & Marketing, Robert Chouinard
506-444-4412

New Brunswick Power Group of Companies (NBPC) / Énergie NB

515 King St., PO Box 2000, Fredericton, NB E3B 4X1
506-458-4444, Fax: 506-458-4000,
questions@nbpower.com
www.nbpower.com
NB Power will be restructured to form a holding company with four subsidiary companies, NB Power Generation, NB Power Nuclear, NB Power Transmission & NB Power Distribution & Customer Service. NB Power is legislated to provide electric power to the province of NB. It is the largest electric utility in Atlantic Canada.Economic generation is from hydro, oil, nuclear, coal & Orimulsion powered facilities.NB Power is developing a comprehensive station environmental management system & is moving towards ISO 14001 certification.The Corporate Environmental Policy applies to all aspects of NB Power's activities. These include the generation of electricity from various energy sources, including nuclear, oil, coal, Orimulsion(193), & hydro, the transmission & distribution of electricity to customers. It also includes those activities that support the generation, transmission & distribution of electricity, including management of land, raw materials, & by-products.
Acts Administered:
Electric Power Act
Chair, Derek Burney
President/CEO, David Hay
Vice-President, Shared Services, Andrew Cormier
Vice-President, Finance, Sharon MacFarlane
Vice-President, Generation (Conventional), Darrell Bishop
Vice-President, Human Resources, Paul Thériault
Vice-President, Nuclear, Gaëtan Thomas
Vice-President, Transmission, Wayne Snowdon
Vice-President, Distribution & Customer Service, Rock Marois
Director, Environmental Affairs, Glen Wilson
Director, Corporate Communication, Brian Duplessis
Manager, Environmental Assessment & Assurance, Charles Hickman

Department of Public Safety / Sécurité publique

364 Argyle St., PO Box 6000, Fredericton, NB E3B 5H1
506-453-3992, Fax: 506-453-3870,
DPS-MSP.Information@gnb.ca
www.gnb.ca/0276/index-e.asp
Provides leadership in the areas of public order & community safety. Provides fair, accessible, community-focused, & coordinated public safety programs & services. Ensures effective inspection & enforcement of designated public safety programs & services. Acts in partnership with communities to prevent crime, assist victims, & create opportunities for offenders to change. Coordinates & cooperates with the federal government in the administration of correctional services & law enforcement in New Brunswick.
Acts Administered:
All Terrain Vehicle Act
Boiler & Pressure Vessel Act
Coroners Act
Corrections Act
Custody & Detention of Young Persons Act
Electrical Installation & Inspection Act
Elevators & Lifts Act
Emergency 911 Act
Emergency Measures Act
Film & Video Act
Fire Prevention Act
Intoxicated Persons Detention Act
Liquor Control Act
Lotteries Act
Motor Vehicle Act
Plumbing Installation & Inspection Act
Police Act
Private Investigators & Security Services Act
Restricted Beverage Act
Salvage Dealers Licensing Act
Sheriffs Act
Transportation of Dangerous Goods Act
Victim Services Act
Minister,Hon. John W. Foran
506-453-7414, John.Foran@gnb.ca
Deputy Minister, Marc Leger
506-453-7412, Marc.Leger@gnb.ca
Director, Communications & Public Awareness, Lisa Harrity
506-444-3425, Lisa.Harrity@gnb.ca
Director, Financial Services, Brian Wilkins
506-453-5446, Fax: 506-444-4743,Brian.Wilkins@gnb.ca
Director, Human Resources, John Smith
506-453-3903, Fax: 506-453-7481
Director, Information Technology, Virender Ambwani
506-444-4433, Fax: 506-453-3321,vic.ambwani@gnb.ca
Executive Assistant, Penné Buckley
506-453-7414, Penne.Buckley@gnb.ca
• New Brunswick Emergency Measures Organization(EMO) / Organisation des mesures d'urgence (OMU)
Victoria Health Centre
65 Brunswick Ave.
Fredericton, NB E3B 1G5
506-453-2133 Fax: 506-453-5513 800-561-4034
emo@gnb.ca
www.gnb.ca/cnb/emo-omu/index-e.asp
Coordinates preparedness for emergencies by provincial government departments & municipal governments. NB EMO works at both provincial & municipal levels to ensure that communities are protcted by emergency plans. Coordinates provincial response operations during emergencies & administers disaster financial assistance programs.

Safety Services / Direction des services de sécurité
Provides leadership in the areas of law enforcement & community safety in order to preserve & enhance the quality of life in New Brunswick.
Asst. Deputy Minister, Marc Léger
506-453-7142, Fax: 506-453-3870
Executive Director, Police, Fire & Emergency Services, Dick Isabelle
506-453-3603
Chief Coroner, Dianne Kelly
506-453-3604
Director, Compliance & Regulatory Services, Eric Howatt
506-457-7822
Director, Emergency Services, Ernest MacGillivray
506-453-5507, ernest.macgillivray@gnb.ca

Director, Provincial Firearms Office, Brian Doyle
506-453-3775
Director, Security & Emergencies, Andrew Easton
506-457-7535
Director, Technical Inspections Services, Arnie Wilkins
506-453-2336, arnie.wilkins@gnb.ca
Registrar, Motor Vehicle, Charles O'Donnell
506-453-2410
Deputy Fire Marshal, Benoit Laroche

Regional Development Corporation (RDC) / Société d'aménagement régional (SAR)

RDC Bldg., 836 Churchill Row, PO Box 428, Fredericton, NB E3B 5R4
506-453-2277, Fax: 506-453-7988,
www.gnb.ca/0096/index-e.asp

The Regional Development Corporation is a Crown corporation which carries out its mandate in accordance with the Regional Development Corporation Act. The following are responsibilities of the Corporation; Administration & management of development agreements between the Province of New Brunswick & the federal government; Assistance in the establishment & development of enterprises & institutions; Assistance to municipalities in the planning & development of projects to benefit the public; Assistance in the development of tourism & recreational facilities; Planning, coordinating, & guiding regional development; & Performing duties assigned by the Lieutenant-Governor-in-Council.

Minister, Finance; Minister Responsible, NB Liquor Corporation; Minister Responsible, NB Investment Management Corporation, Minister Responsible, NB Lotteries & Gaming Corporation; Minister Responsible, Regional DevelopmentCorporation, Hon. Victor E. Boudreau
victor.boudreau@gnb.ca
President, Bill Levesque
bill.levesque@gnb.ca
Senior Vice-President, Corporate Services & Programs, Douglas Holt
506-444-5804, doug.holt@gnb.ca
Vice-President, Development & Special Initiatives, Denis Caron
506-457-4912, denis.caron@gnb.caa
Corporate Secretary, Bruce Macfarlane
506-444-4606, bruce.macfarlane@gnb.ca

New Brunswick Research & Productivity Council (RPC) / Conseil de la recherche et de la productivité du Nouveau-Brunswick (RPC)

921 College Hill Rd., Fredericton, NB E3B 6Z9
506-452-1212, Fax: 506-452-1395,
info@rpc.ca
www.rpc.ca

RPC's vision is to excel in technological innovation, enabling its partners in business & industry to create wealth & high quality employment opportunities in New Brunswick;to steadily improve its capacity to develop & apply new technology in partnership with firms in the private sector, & to provide an expanding range of high quality technical services to clients in the global marketplace. RPC is registered to the ISO 9001:2000 International Standard.

Executive Director, Eric Cook, P.Eng.
506-452-0585, eric.cook@rpc.ca
CFO, Stephen A. Fox
506-452-1380, stephen.fox@rpc.ca
Head, Physical Metallurgy, John Aikens
506-460-5766, john.aikens@rpc.ca
Head, Food, Fisheries & Aquaculture, Dr. Rachael Ritchie
506-452-1365, rachael.ritchie@rpc.ca
Head, Inorganic Analytical Services, Ross Kean
506-452-1399, ross.kean@rpc.ca
Head, Mechanical Systems & Diagnostics, John Aikens
506-460-5766, john.aikens@rpc.ca
Manager, Organic Analytical Services, Bruce Phillips
506-452-1369, bruce.phillips@rpc.ca
Manager, High Res Section, Dr. John Macaulay
506-452-1369, john.macaulay@rpc.ca
Manager, Process Technology, Ross Gilders
506-460-5672, ross.gilders@rpc.ca
Manager, Air Quality Services, Thelma Green
506-452-0586, thelma.green@rpc.ca
Coordinator, Susi Chamberlain
506-452-1244, susi.chamberlain@rpc.ca
Executive Assistant, Linda Horsman
506-452-1363, Fax: 506-452-1386,linda.horsman@rpc.ca

Service New Brunswick (SNB) / Services Nouveau-Brunswick (SNB)

Westmorland Place, #200, 82 Westmorland St., PO Box 1998, Fredericton, NB E3B 5G4
506-457-3581, Fax: 506-457-7520, 888-762-8600
snb@snb.ca
www.snb.ca

Other Communication: Technical Assistance: 1-888-832-2762; SNB TeleServices outside the province: 506-684-7901

Service New Brunswick provides authoritative information to the public about federal, provincial, & municipal government services. The Crown corporation, which is owned by the Province of New Brunswick, operates the following services: New Brunswick's Land Registry; New Brunswick's Personal Property Registry; New Brunswick's Corporate Affairs Registry; & New Brunswick's Property Assessment & Taxation System.

Acts Administered:
Air Space Act
Assessment Act
Boundaries Confirmation Act
Business Corporation Act
Common Business Identifier Act
Companies Act
Condominium Property Act
Corporations Act
Foreign Resident Corporations Act
Land Titles Act
Limited Partnership Act
Partnership Act
Partnerships & Business Names Registration Act
Personal Property Security Act
Registry Act
Residential Property Tax Relief Act
Service New Brunswick Act
Special Corporate Continuance Act
Standard Forms of Conveyances Act
Surveys Act
Winding-Up Act

Minister, Business New Brunswick; Minister Responsible, Service New Brunswick; Minister Responsible, Population Growth Secretariat; Minister Responsible, Communications New Brunswick, Minister Responsible, Red Tape Reduction, Hon. Greg Byrne
506-453-5898, Fax: 506-453-5893,greg.byrne@gnb.ca
Chair, Derek Pleadwell
506-444-2897, Fax: 506-457-7520,derek.pleadwell@snb.ca
President, Sylvie Levesque-Finn
506-444-2897, sylvie.levesque-finn@snb.ca
Corporate Legal Counsel, Corporate Counsel Directorate, Claude Poirier
506-869-6389, Fax: 506-869-6523,claude.poirier@snb.ca
Vice-President, Technology & Business Innovation, Carol MacDonald
506-444-2322, Fax: 506-453-5384,carol.macdonald@snb.ca
Acting Vice-President, Corporate Services, Linda J. Corbett
506-457-4805, Fax: 506-444-5239,linda.corbett@snb.ca
Vice-President, Operations, Bernard Arseneau
506-457-3582, Fax: 506-457-7520,bernard.arseneau@snb.ca
Executive Director, Corporate Strategy, Judy Ross, C.A.
506-444-4103, Fax: 506-453-5384,judy.ross@snb.ca
Director, Marketing & Communications, Brent Staeben
506-453-6775, Fax: 506-453-5384,brent.staeben@snb.ca
Director, Human Resources Directorate, Donat Theriault
506-453-3912, Fax: 506-453-3043,donat.theriault@snb.ca

New Brunswick Advisory Council on the Status of Women / Conseil consultatif sur la condition de la femme au Nouveau-Brunswick

236 King St., Fredericton, NB E3B 1E2
506-444-4101, Fax: 506-444-4318, 800-332-3087
acswcccf@gnb.ca
www.acswcccf.nb.ca

Chair, Ginette Petitpas-Taylor
Executive Director, Rosella Melanson

Department of Social Development / Développement social

Sartain MacDonald Bldg., 551 King St., PO Box 6000, Fredericton, NB E3B 5H1
506-453-2001, Fax: 506-453-7478,
www.gnb.ca/0017/index-e.asp

The Department of Social Development oversees services to the following citizens of New Brunswick: Seniors & persons with disabilities who need long-term care & nursing home services; Children who require assistance to prepare for school; Abused & neglected children & adults; Families in need of affordable day care; & Persons in need of affordable housing & social assistance.

Acts Administered:
Change of Name Act (paragraphs 5(1)(b) & (2)(b))
Charitable Donation of Food Act
Education Act (section 19)
Employment Standards Act (subsection 44.02(6))
Family Income Security Act
Family Services Act (except Part VII)
Health Services Act
Hospital Act (section 21)
Intercountry Adoption Act
Reciprocal Enforcement of Maintenance Orders Act (section 10)
Vocational Rehabilitation of Disabled Persons Act

Minister, Social Development; Minister Responsible, Advisory Council on the Status of Women,Hon. Mary Schryer
506-457-7866, Fax: 506-453-2164,mary.schryer@gnb.ca
Minister of State, Seniors & Housing, Hon. Eugene McGinley, Q.C.
506-453-2057, Fax: 506-453-2164,eugene.mcginley@gnb.ca
Deputy Minister, James Hughes
506-453-2590, Fax: 506-453-2164,james.hughes@gnb.ca
Acting Director, Communications, Shannon Hagerman
506-444-2416, Fax:
506-453-6555,shannon.hagerman@gnb.ca
Director, Human Resources Services, Sharon Hallett
506-453-2940, Fax: 250-453-6555,Sharon.Hallett@gnb.ca

• Family Income Security Appeal Board/ Commission d'appel sur la sécurité du revenu familial
PO Box 6000
Fredericton, NB E3B 5H1
506-525-4007 Fax: 506-525-4008

• New Brunswick Advisory Council on Seniors/ Conseil consultatif des ainés du N.-B.
#620, 440 King St.
Fredericton, NB E3B 5H8
506-444-5757 Fax: 506-446-784 888-762-5411

Planning & Corporate Services / Planification et services corporatif

Sartain MacDonald Bldg., 551 King St., 4th Fl., PO Box 6000, Fredericton, NB E3B 5H1
506-453-2181, Fax: 506-453-3829

Assistant Deputy Minister, Jack Brown
506-453-2181, Fax: 506-453-3829,Jack.Brown@gnb.ca
Director, Finance & Administration, Paulette Boudreau-Clark
506-457-6735, Fax:
506-453-2128,paulette.boudreau-clark@gnb.ca
Director, Information Technology Services, Carol LaChapelle
506-453-2033, Fax: 506-453-2841,carol.lachapelle@gnb.ca
Director, Policy & Federal / Provincial Relations, Bill MacKenzie
506-457-4803, Fax: 506-462-5150,Bill.MacKenzie@gnb.ca
Director, Planning, Research, & Evaluation, Janet P. Thomas
506-444-3380, Fax: 506-462-5150,Janet.Thomas@gnb.ca

Program Delivery / Délivrance des programmes

Sartain MacDonald Bldg., 551 King St., 4th Fl., PO Box 6000, Fredericton, NB E3B 5H1
506-453-2379, Fax: 506-453-2164

Assistant Deputy Minister, Geraldine Poirier Baiani
506-453-2379, Fax:
506-453-2164,geraldine.poirier-baiani@gnb.ca
Director, Central Office Program Delivery, Luc J. Sirois
506-453-7450, Fax: 506-462-5150,Luc.Sirois@gnb.ca
Director, Operational Support, Charles Boulay
506-444-4828, Fax: 506-453-2152,Charles.Boulay@gnb.ca

Program Development & Monitoring / Développement des programmes et surveillance

Sartain MacDonald Bldg., #4007, 551 King St., PO Box 6000, Fredericton, NB E3B 5H1
506-453-2181, Fax: 506-453-3829

Acting Assistant Deputy Minister, Wendy McLeod-MacKnight
506-453-2181, Fax:
506-453-2164,Wendy.Mcleod-Macknight@gnb.ca
Acting Director, Adults with Disabilities & Long Term Care Services, Joan M. McCarthy
416-462-5155, Fax: 506-453-2869,Joan.Mccarthy@gnb.ca
Director, Child Welfare & Youth Services, Joan L. Mix
506-444-5970, Fax: 506-453-2082,Joan.Mix@gnb.ca
Director, Early Childhood & School-based Services, Nicole Gervais
506-457-7893, Fax: 506-453-2082,nicole.gervais@gnb.ca
Director, Housing & Income Support, Jean Rioux
506-453-7466, Fax: 506-444-5768,Jean.Rioux@gnb.ca
Director, Nursing Home Services, Barbara J. Burnett
506-453-2376, Fax: 506-457-4909,Barb.Burnett@gnb.ca
Director, Senior & Healthy Aging Secretariat, André Lepine
506-457-6856, Fax: 506-453-2869
Project Manager, Community & Individual Development, Pierrette Dupuis
506-444-3601, Fax: 506-453-2869,pierrette.dupuis@gnb.ca

Department of Supply & Services / Approvisionnement et services

PO Box 6000, Fredericton, NB E3B 5H1

506-453-3742, Fax: 506-444-4400, Reception.Marysville@gnb.ca
www.gnb.ca/0099/index-e.asp
Provides effective & efficient services within government. Among the varied & diverse services the department provides are: the procurement of goods & services; printing & postal services; translation services; records management; the construction & operation of government-owned buildings; & information technology management.
Acts Administered:
Archives Act
Public Purchasing Act
Public Works Act
Minister,Hon. Edward Doherty
506-453-6100, Fax: 506-462-5049,ed.doherty@gnb.ca
Deputy Minister, Louise Lemon
506-453-2504, Louise.LEMON@gnb.ca
Executive Director, Corporate Services, Byard A. Smith
506-444-2808, byard.smith@gnb.ca
Director, Technology Support, Christine Colborne
506-457-7279, Christine.Colborne@gnb.ca
Director, Human Resources & Administration, Ray Butler
506-453-3742, ray.butler@gnb.ca
Chief Information Officer, Corporate Information Management Services, Danny Keizer
506-453-3742, Fax: 506-462-2006,Danny.KEIZER@gnb.ca

Buildings Group / Direction générale des bâtiments
Asst. Deputy Minister, Ashley Cummings
506-453-2228
Executive Director, Design & Construction, Barb Nicholson
506-453-2228,
Executive Director, Facilities Management, Greg Cook
506-444-4527
Director, Property Management, Gary Lenehan
506-453-2221

Services / Direction générale des services
www.gov.nb.ca/supply/sgs/index.htm (Purchasing)
Asst. Deputy Minister, Dick Burgess
506-453-2245
Director, Central Purchasing, Joanne Lynch
506-453-2245
Director, Provincial Archives of New Brunswick, Marion Beyea
506-453-3811, Fax: 506-453-3288
Director, Translation Bureau, Joanne Kearney
506-453-2920, Fax: 506-459-7911
Manager, Publications & Distribution, Gary Norcott
506-453-2545

Department of Tourism & Parks / Tourisme et Parcs

Centennial Bldg., 670 King St., Fredericton, NB E3B 1G1
506-444-5205, Fax: 506-457-4984, taponlinedirectory@gnb.ca
www.gnb.ca/0397/index-e.asp
To increase the profile and performance of the tourism industry in New Brunswick and to ensure that provincial parks are an integral part of this effort.
Acts Administered:
Kings Landing Corporation Act
Municipalities Act (subsection 188 (3))
Parks Act
Tourism Development Act
Minister,Hon. Stuart Jamieson
506-453-3009, Stuart.jamieson@gnb.ca
Deputy Minister, Ellen Barry
506-453-3261, Ellen.Barry@gnb.ca
Asst. Deputy Minister, Clarence Lebreton
506-726-2600, Fax: 506-726-2601,clarence.lebreton@gnb.ca
Director, Communications, Alison Aiton
506-444-4454, alison.aiton@gnb.ca
Coordinator, Human Resources Services, Maryse McFarlane
506-444-2757, Fax: 506-462-2202,maryse.mcfarlane@gnb.ca

Planning & Product Branch / Planification et production
506-453-2170, Fax: 506-453-2854
Executive Director, Jane Garbutt
Executive Director, Kings Landing, Robert Moreau
506-363-4957, Fax: 506-363-4989,office.kingsland@gnb.ca
Director, Planning & Research, Janet Cameron
506-444-4521, Fax: 506-453-2854,Janet.Cameron@gnb.ca
Director, Product Development, Kara Sutherland
506- -, Fax: 506-444-2323,kara.sutherland@gnb.ca
Manager, Village Historique Corporation, Gabriel Lebreton
506-726-2600, Fax: 506-726-2601,gabriel.lebreton@gnb.ca

Regional Operations Branch:

The Anchorage
506-453-4283, Fax: 506-662-7035

La République
Manager, Jocelyne Michaud
506-735-2525, Fax: 506-735-4445,jocelyne.michaud@gnb.ca

Herring Cove
506-752-7012

Parlee Beach
506-533-3363, Fax: 506-533-3312
Manager, Marcel Richard

Sugarloaf
506-759-2365, Fax: 506-789-2099
Manager, Paul Ferguson

Department of Transportation / Transports

Kings Pl., 440 KingSt., PO Box 6000, Fredericton, NB E3B 5H8
506-453-3939, Fax: 506-453-2900, Transportation.Web@gnb.ca
www.gnb.ca/0113/index-e.asp
To ensure the effective development & implementation of an integrated transportation approach for New Brunswick (roads, airports, ports & other infrastructure), to support New Brunswick's economic & social goals; develop & maintain safe & efficient network of highways & roads; & maintain the long-term integrity of our transportation infrastructure including roads, ports & airports through effective planning, maintenance & oversight.
Acts Administered:
Highway Act
Motor Carrier Act
New Brunswick Highway Corporation Act
New Brunswick Transportation Authority Act
Public Landings Act
Shortline Railways Act
Minister,Hon. Denis Landry
506-457-7345, Fax: 506-453-7987,Denis.Landry2@gnb.ca
Deputy Minister, David J. Johnstone
506-453-2549, Fax: 506-453-7987,David.JOHNSTONE@gnb.ca
Director, Communications, Andrew Holland
506-453-5634, Fax: 506-457-4968,andrew.holland@gnb.ca
• NB Board of Commissioners of Public Utilities/ Commission des entreprises de service public du N.-B.
#1400, 15 Market Sq.
PO Box 5001
Saint John, NB E2L 4Y9
506-658-2504 Fax: 506-643-7300 866-766-2782
general@pub.nb.ca
www.pub.nb.ca
• New Brunswick Transportation Authority/ Régie des transports du Nouveau-Brunswick
Kings Place
440 King St.
PO Box 6000
Fredericton, NB E3B 5H1
506-453-3939 Fax: 506-453-2900
Crown corporation responsible for the promotion, operation & development of transportation terminals in New Brunswick. Encourages the development of transport terminal-related services.

Assistant Deputy Minister & Chief Engineer Office / Sous-ministre adjoint et ingénieur en chef
Asst. Deputy Minister, Michael Trites
506-453-2351
Executive Director, Operations, Henri Allain
506-453-2849
Executive Director, Engineering Services, Neil Gilbert
506-453-2849
Director, Trans Canada Highway Project, Denis LaChapelle
506-444-2007
Director, Planning & Land Management, Brian McEwing
506-453-2754

Corporate Services & Fleet Management / Services généraux et gestion de flotte
Asst. Deputy Minister, Dale Wilson
506-453-2552, dale.wilson@gnb.ca
Director, Vehicle Management Agency, Andrew Aiton
506-453-2601, Andy.AITON@gnb.ca
Director, Information Management & Technology, Ken Fitzpatrick
506-453-2990, ken.fitzpatrick@gnb.ca
Director, Financial & Administrative Services, Pierre LeBlanc
506-444-4464
Director, Human Resources, Marguerite Levesque
506-453-2332, marguerite.levesque@gnb.ca

Policy, Strategic Development & Intergovernmental Relations / Politiques, développement et relations intergouvernementales
Asst. Deputy Minister, Doug L. Johnson
506-453-5818
Director, Transportation Policy, Susan Andrews-Caron
506-453-2802, susan.andrews-caron@gnb.ca
Director, Strategic Development, Margaret Grant-McGivney
506-453-5818
Manager, Passenger Services, Don Mason

Department of Wellness, Culture & Sport / Mieux-être, Culture et Sport

Place 2000, 250 King St., 4th Fl., PO Box 6000, Fredericton, NB E3B 5H1
506-453-2909, Fax: 506-453-6548,
www.gnb.ca/0131/index-e.asp
The Department of Wellness, Culture, & Sport is repsonsible for arts development, heritage, wellness, & sport, recreation, & active living.
Acts Administered:
Arts Development Trust Fund Act (except administration of fund)
Assessment Act (s. 15.3)
Historic Sites Protection Act
Municipal Heritage Preservation Act
Sport Development Trust Fund Act (except administration of fund)
Youth Assistance Act (section 11)
Minister, Wellness, Culture, & Sport; Minister Responsible, Francophonie,Hon. Hédard Albert
506-444-2517, Fax: 506-453-6668,Hedard.Albert2@gnb.ca
Deputy Minister, Ellen Barry
506-453-2909, Fax: 506-453-6668,ellen.barry@gnb.ca
Director, Communications, Vicky Deschênes
506-457-6445, Fax: 506-453-6668,Vicky.Deschenes@gnb.ca
• New Brunswick Arts Board/ Conseil des arts Nouveau-Brunswick
#300, 634 Queen St.
Fredericton, NB E3B 1C2
506-444-4444 Fax: 506-444-5543
1-866-460-2787
www.artsnb.ca

Arts Development
Place 2000, 250 King St., Fredericton, NB E3B 9M9
506-453-2555, Fax: 506-453-2416
Director, Arts Development, Nathalie Dubois
506-453-2729, Fax: 506-453-2416,nathalie.dubois@gnb.ca
Coordinator, Art Bank Services, Caroline Walker
506-444-5303, Fax: 506-453-2416,Caroline.Walker@gnb.ca
Manager, Programs, Alain Boisvert
506-453-2166, Fax: 506-453-2416,alain.boisvert@gnb.ca

Heritage
Place 2000, 250 King St., 4th Fl., PO Box 6000, Fredericton, NB E3B 5H1
506-453-2324, Fax: 506-453-2416
Director, Heritage, Wayne Burley
506-453-8774, Fax: 506-453-2416,Wayne.Burley@gnb.ca
Manager, Archaeological Services, Albert M. Ferguson
506-453-2756, Fax: 506-457-4880,albert.ferguson@gnb.ca
Manager, Historic Places, William Hicks
506-444-5320, Fax: 506-453-2416,Bill.Hicks@gnb.ca
Manager, Museum Services, Guy Tremblay
506-444-5892, Fax: 506-453-2416,Guy.Tremblay@gnb.ca
Manager, Toponymy, Gilles Bourque
506-453-8125, Fax: 506-453-2416,Gilles.Bourque@gnb.ca
Project Manager, Heritage Education, Cynthia Wallace-Casey
506-453-2915, Fax: 506-453-2416,Cynthia.Wallace-Casey@gnb.ca

New Brunswick Museum
277 Douglas Ave., Saint John, NB E2K 1E5
506-643-2300, Fax: 506-643-2360, nbmuseum@nbm-mnb.ca
www.nbm-mnb.ca
Director, New Brunswick Museum, Jane Fullerton
Jane.Fullerton@nbm-mnb.ca
Manager, Natural Science, Randall Miller
506-643-2361, Fax: 506-643-2360,Randall.Miller@nbm-mnb.ca
Manager, Library & Archives, Felicity Osepchook
506-643-2324, Fax: 506-643-2360,Felicity.Osepchook@nbm-mnb.ca
Manager, Interpretation Services, Wendy Martindale
506-643-2338, Fax: 506-643-6081,wmrdale@nb.aibn.com
Manager, Temporary Exhibitions, Regina Mantin
506-643-2330, Fax: 506-643-6081,rmantin@nb.aibn.com
Controller, Judith Brown
506-643-2356, Fax: 506-643-6081,jbrown@nb.aibn.com

Wellness, Sport, & Community Development
Place 2000, 250 King St., 4th Fl., PO Box 6000, Fredericton, NB E3B 5H1
506-444-2451, Fax: 506-453-6548
Assistant Deputy Minister, Wellness, Sport, & Community Development, Jane Garbutt
506-444-2451, Fax: 506-453-6548,jane.garbutt@gnb.ca
Acting Director, Sport & Recreation, Roger H. Duval
506-457-4950, Fax: 506-453-6548,roger.duval@gnb.ca,
Acting Director, Regional Operations & Community Development, Allen Bard
506-453-3193, Fax: 506-453-6548,Allen.Bard@gnb.ca
Director, Wellness, Michelle Bourgoin
506-453-4217, Fax: 506-444-5722,michelle.bourgoin@gnb.ca

Workplace Health, Safety & Compensation Commission of New Brunswick (WHSCC) / La commission de la santé, de la sécurité et de l'indemnisation des accidents au travail du Nouveau-Brunswick

1 Portland St., PO Box 160, Saint John, NB E2L 3X9
506-632-2200, 800-222-9775
communications@ws-ts.nb.ca
www.whscc.nb.ca

The Workplace Health, Safety & Compensation Commission (WHSCC) of New Brunswick is a crown corporation charged with overseeing the implementation & application of the New Brunswick Occupational Health & Safety Act, the Workers' Compensation Act of New Brunswick, & the Workplace Health, Safety & Compensation Commission Act of New Brunswick on behalf of the workers & employers of this province. The Commission administers no-fault workplace accident & disability insurance & comprehensive accident prevention health & safety initiatives for employers & their workers, funded solely through premiums paid by employers.

Acts Administered:
Occupational Health & Safety Act
Workers' Compensation Act
Workplace Health, Safety & Compensation Commission Act
Chair, Roberta Dugas
President/CEO, Douglas C. Stanley
Chair, Appeals Tribunal, Paul M. LeBreton
Corporate Secretary & General Counsel, Richard Tingley
506-632-2837
Vice-President, Corporate Services, Peter Murphy
506-632-2204
Vice-President, Worksafe Services, David Greason
506-632-2816
Manager, Communications, Mary Tucker
506-632-2828

New Brunswick Advisory Council on Youth (NBACY) / Conseil consultatif de la jeunesse du Nouveau-Brunswick (CCJNB)

Frederick Square, #130, 77 Westmorland St., PO Box 6000, Fredericton, NB E3B 5H1
506-453-3271, Fax: 506-444-4413, 888-830-5588
nbacy-ccjnb@gnb.ca
www.gnb.ca/0049/index-e.asp

The Lieutenant Governor in Council appoints thirteen young people from all regions of New Brunswick, & from both official language groups, to a two-year term on the New Brunswick Advisory Council on Youth. Representative of youth, the Council on Youth voices the concerns, interests, needs, & perspectives of persons between fifteen & twenty-four years of age. The provincial body presents its recommendations to government.

Minister, Education; Minister Responsible, New Brunswick Advisory Council on Youth; Minister Responsible, New Brunswick Provincial CapitalCommission, Hon. Kelly Lamrock
506-453-2523, Fax: 506-457-4960,kelly.lamrock@gnb.ca
Chair, Kara Hachey
Kara.Hachey@gnb.ca
Executive Director, Ivan Corbett
Ivan.Corbett@gnb.ca

Government of Newfoundland & Labrador

Seat of Government: Confederation Bldg., St. John's, NL A1B 4J6
info@gov.nl.ca
www.gov.nl.ca

The Province of Newfoundland & Labrador entered Confederation March 31, 1949.It has an area of 370,494.89 km2, & the StatsCan census population in 2006 was 505,469.

Office of the Lieutenant Governor

Government House, Military Rd., PO Box 5517, St. John's, NL A1C 5W4
709-729-4494, Fax: 709-729-2234,
governmenthouse@gov.nl.ca
www.mun.ca/govhouse/
Lieutenant Governor,The Hon. John C. Crosbie
709-729-4494, Fax: 709-729-2234
Private Secretary, Doug Smith
709-729-4494, Fax: 709-729-2234

Office of the Premier

East Block, Confederation Bldg., 8th F., PO Box 8700, St. John's, NL A1B 4J6
709-729-3570, Fax: 709-729-5875,
premier@gov.nl.ca
www.gov.nl.ca/premier

Premier,Hon. Danny Williams
709-729-3570, Fax: 709-729-5875,premier@gov.nl.ca
Chief of Staff, Brian Crawley
709-729-3558, Fax: 709-729-5875
Personal Assistant to the Premier, Christine Ings
709-729-3565, Fax: 709-729-5875
Director, Communications, Elizabeth Matthews
709-729-3960, Fax:
709-729-5875,elizabethmatthews@gov.nl.ca

Executive Council

c/o Communications Branch, East Block, Confederation Bldg., 10th Fl., St. John's, NL A1B 4J6
709-729-5645,
info@gov.nl.ca
www.exec.gov.nl.ca/exec/

Premier,Hon. Danny Williams
709-729-3570, Fax: 709-729-5875,premier@gov.nl.ca
Minister, Natural Resources, Hon. Kathy Dunderdale
709-729-2920, Fax:
709-729-0059,KathyDunderdale@gov.nl.ca
Minister, Education & Minister Responsible, Status of Women, Hon. Joan Burke
709-729-5040, Fax: 709-729-0414,Joanburke@gov.nl.ca, Other Communications: Toll Free: 1-866-838-5620
Minister, Health & Community Services, Hon. Ross Wiseman
709-729-3124, 800-514-9073,Fax:
709-729-0121,rosswiseman@gov.nl.ca
Minister, Tourism, Culture & Recreation, Hon. Clyde Jackman
709-729-0657, 877-787-0707,Fax:
709-729-0662,clydejackman@gov.nl.ca
Minister, Government Services, Hon. Kevin O'Brien
709-729-4712, Fax: 709-729-4754,kevinobrien@gov.nl.ca
Minister, Municipal Affairs, Hon. Dave Denine
709-729-3048, Fax: 709-729-0943,davedenine@gov.nl.ca
Minister, Fisheries & Aquaculture; Deputy Premier; Attorney General; Government House Leader; Minister Responsible, Aboriginal Affairs, Hon. Tom Rideout
709-729-3705, 877-585-0515,Fax:
709-729-0360,hynesa@gov.nl.ca
Minister, Human Resources, Labour & Employment; Minister Responsible, Newfoundland & Labrador Housing, Hon. Shawn Skinner
709-729-3580, Fax: 709-729-6996,ShawnSkinner@gov.nl.ca
Minister, Innovation, Trade & Rural Development & Minister Responsible, Rural Secretariat, Hon. Trevor Taylor
709-729-4728, Fax: 709-729-0654,trevortaylor@gov.nl.ca
Minister, Finance & President, Treasury Board, Hon. Tom Marshall
709-729-3775, Fax: 709-729-6791,tommarshall@gov.nl.ca
Minister, Justice, Hon. Jerome P. Kennedy
709-729-2869, Fax: 709-729-0469
Minister, Intergovernmental Affairs, Hon. Thomas J. Hedderson
Minister, Environment & Conservation, Hon. Charlene Johnson
709-729-2574, Fax:
709-729-0112,charlenejohnson@gov.nl.ca, Other Communications: Toll Free: 1-800-423-3301
Minister, Transportation & Works, Hon. Dianne C. Whalen
709-729-3678, 866-996-5670,Fax: 709-729-4285
Minister, Business, Hon. Paul Oram
709-729-7895, Fax: 709-729-3306,pauloram@gov.nl.ca, Other Communications: Toll free: 1-800-813-6850,
Document Control Officer, Jeanette Fleming
709-729-2921, Fax: 709-729-5218,jfleming@cab.gov.nf.ca

Rural Secretatariat
PO Box 8700, St. John's, NL A1B 4J6
709-729-0168, Fax: 709-729-1673,
ruralinfo@gov.nl.ca
www.exec.gov.nl.ca/rural/
Minister Responsible,Hon. Trevor Taylor
709-729-4728, Fax: 709-729-0654,TrevorTaylor@gov.nl.ca
Asst. Deputy Minister,Dr. Bruce Gilbert
709-729-1611, brucegilbert@gov.nl.ca

Cabinet Secretariat
Fax: 709-729-5218
Clerk, Executive Council & Secretary to the Cabinet, Robert Thompson
709-729-4092, Fax: 709-729-5435,rthompson@gov.nl.ca
Deputy Clerk, Executive Council & Associate Secretary to the Cabinet, Sandra Barnes
709-729-2844, Fax: 709-729-5218,sbarnes@gov.nl.ca
Assistant Secretary, Communications, Josephine Cheeseman
709-729-4782, Fax:
709-729-5645,josephinecheeseman@gov.nl.ca
Assistant Secretary, Economic Policy, Jamie Chippett
709-729-2845, Fax: 709-729-5218,jamiechippett@gov.nl.ca
Assistant Secretary, Social Policy, Gary Cake
709-729-2850, Fax: 709-729-5218
Acting Director, Financial & General Operations, Linda Vaughan
709-729-7337, Fax: 709-729-0435,lvaughan@gov.nl.ca
Director, Protocol, David Dempster
709-729-2911

Cabinet Committees
Cabinet Committee on Routine Matters & Appointments; Economic Policy Committee Planning & Priorities Committee; Social Policy Committee; Treasury Board Committee

Office of the Chief Information Officer
PO Box 8700, St. John's, NL A1B 4J6
709-729-4000, Fax: 709-729-6767,
ocio@gov.nl.ca
Chief Information Officer, Peter Shea
709-729-2617, Fax: 709-729-6767

Women's Policy Office
Asst. Deputy Minister, Heather MacLellan
709-729-5098, Fax: 709-729-2331,hmaclellan@gov.nl.ca

House of Assembly

c/o Clerk's Office, Confederation Bldg., PO Box 8700, St. John's, NL A1B 4J6
709-729-3405, Fax: 709-729-4820,
www.gov.nl.ca/hoa

Other Communication: Legislative Library: 709/729-3604
Clerk, William MacKenzie
709-729-3405, Fax: 709-729-0654,ClerkHOA@gov.nl.ca
Speaker,Hon. Roger Fitzgerald
709-729-3404, Fax: 709-729-4820,rfitzgerald@gov.nl.ca
Clerk Assistant, Elizabeth Murphy
709-729-3434
Sergeant-at-Arms, Elizabeth Gallagher
709-729-3630
Manager, Hansard, Irene Tapper
709-729-3413, Fax: 709-729-6547,itapper@gov.nl.ca
Director, Information Management (Legislative Library), Kimberley Hammond
709-729-5646, Fax:
709-729-0234,Kimberleyhammond@gov.nl.ca
Information & Privacy Commissioner, Ed Ring
709-729-6309, 877-729-6309,Fax:
709-729-6500,oipc@gov.nl.ca
Child & Youth Advocate, James Igloliorte
709-753-3888, 877-753-3888,Fax:
709-753-3988,office@childandyouthadvicate.nl.ca

Government Caucus Office (PC)
PO Box 8700, St. John's, NL A1B 4J6

Office of the Official Opposition (Lib.)
Confederation Building, East Block, 5th fl., PO Box 8700, St. John's, NL A1B 4J6
Leader, Yvonne Jones
709-729-6925, 800-286-9118,Fax:
709-729-5202,yvonnejones@gov.nl.ca
Opposition House Leader, Kelvin Parsons
709-729-0434, 800-518-9479,Fax:
709-729-5202,kparsons@gov.nl.ca

Office of the New Democratic Party (NDP)
PO Box 8700, St. John's, NL A1B 4J6
709-729-0270, Fax: 709-576-1443
Leader, Lorraine Michael
709-729-0270

House Committees
Clerk of Committees, Elizabeth Murphy
709-729-3434

Forty-sixth House of Assembly - Newfoundland & Labrador

PO Box 8700, St. John's, NL A1B 4J6
709-729-3405,
ClerkHOA@gov.nl.ca
Other Communication: Tours: 709-729-3630

Last General Election, October 9, 2007. Maximum Duration, 4 years Party Standings (October 2007): Progressive Conservative (PC) 43 Liberal (Lib.) 3 New Democratic Party (NDP) 1 Total 48; Salaries, Indemnities & Allowances (December 2005): Members' sessional indemnity $47,240.In addition to this are the following: Premier $68,252; Ministers; Speaker; Leader of the Opposition $49,480; Government Whip & Opposition Whip $12,370; Chair of Committees (Deputy Speaker) $24,740; Deputy Chair of Committees $12,370; Opposition House Leader $24,740 Following is: constituency (population of constituency at 2007 election) member, party affiliation, telephone & fax number & email address. (Address for all is Confederation Bldg., PO Box 8700, St. John's NL A1B 4J6.)

Members

Jim Baker, Labrador West, PC
709-729-0510, Fax: 709-729-1082,jimcbaker@gov.nl.ca,
Other Communications: Toll Free: 1-800-729-0510
Ed Buckingham, St. John's East, PC
709-729-3651, Fax: 709-729-1503,EdBuckingham@gov.nl.ca
Hon. Joan Burke, St. George's-Stephenville East, PC
709-729-5040, 866-838-5620,Fax:
709-729-0414,Joanburke@gov.nl.ca
Roland Butler, Port De Grave, Liberal
709-729-1594, 866-729-1594,Fax:
709-729-5202,RolandButler@gov.nl.ca
Kevin Parsons, Cape St. Francis, PC
KevinParsons@gov.nl.ca
Felix Collins, Placentia & St. Mary's, PC
709-729-6926, 877-898-0898,Fax:
709-729-2076,felixcollins@gov.nl.ca
Tony Cornect, Port au Port, PC
709-729-3138, 800-809-0360,Fax:
709-729-1082,tonycornect@gov.nl.ca
Derrick Dalley, The Isles of Notre Dame, PC
709-729-1191, Fax: 709-729-5774,DerrickDalley@gov.nl.ca
Dave Denine, Mount Pearl South, PC
709-729-3048, Fax: 709-729-0943,davedenine@gov.nl.ca,
John Dinn, Kilbride, PC
709-729-3758, Fax: 709-729-1082,johndinn@gov.nl.ca
Hon. Kathy Dunderdale, Virginia Waters, PC
709-729-4715, Fax:
709-729-2076,KathyDunderdale@gov.nl.ca
Roger Fitzgerald, Bonavista South, PC
709-729-6131, 800-600-4875,Fax:
709-729-5774,RFitzgerald@gov.nl.ca
Clayton Forsey, Exploits, PC
709-729-6594, 888-554-7799,Fax:
709-729-1503,ClaytonForsey@gov.nl.ca
Terry French, Conception Bay South, PC
709-729-5907, Fax: 709-729-6996,Terryfrench@gov.nl.ca
Harry Harding, Bonavista North, PC
709-729-0032, 866-929-0032,Fax:
709-729-0360,HarryHarding@gov.nl.ca
Hon. Tom Hedderson, Harbour Main, PC
709-729-7032, 877-787-0707,Fax:
709-729-3686,THedderson@gov.nl.ca
Hon. John Hickey, Lake Melville, PC
709-729-3678, 866-996-5670,Fax:
709-729-4285,JHickey@gov.nl.ca
Ray Hunter, Grand Falls-Windsor-Green Bay South, PC
709-729-6932, 877-585-0505,Fax:
709-729-1082,RHunter@gov.nl.ca
Keith Hutchings, Ferryland, PC
709-729-1390, Fax: 709-729-5774,keithhutchings@gov.nl.ca
Hon. Clyde Jackman, Burin-Placentia West, PC
709-729-0657, 800-423-3301,Fax:
709-729-0662,clydejackman@gov.nl.ca
Hon. Charlene Johnson, Trinity-Bay De Verde, PC
709-729-2574, Fax:
709-729-0112,CharleneJohnson@gov.nl.ca
Yvonne Jones, Cartwright-L'Anse au Clair, Liberal
709-729-6925, 800-286-9118,Fax:
709-729-5202,yvonnejones@gov.nl.ca
Darryl Kelly, Humber Valley, PC
709-729-1577, 877-635-0132,Fax:
709-729-1503,DarrylKelly@gov.nl.ca
Hon. Jerome Kennedy, Q.C., Carbonear-Harbour Grace, PC
709-729-2869, Fax:
709-729-0469,JeromeKennedy@gov.nl.ca
Steve Kent, Mount Pearl North, PC
709-729-1526, Fax: 709-729-1503,SteveKent@gov.nl.ca
Darin T. King, Ph.D, Grand Bank, PC
709-729-0340, Fax: 709-729-0414,DarinKing@gov.nl.ca
Terry Loder, Bay of Islands, PC
709-729-1573, Fax: 709-729-1503,TerryLoder@gov.nl.ca
Elizabeth Marshall, Topsail, PC
709-729-6670, Fax: 709-729-5774,BethMarshall@gov.nl.ca
Hon. Tom Marshall, Humber East, PC
709-729-2858, Fax: 709-729-6791,tommarshall@gov.nl.ca,
Other Communications: URL: www.tommarshall.ca
Lorraine Michael, Signal Hill-Quidi Vidi, New Democratic Party
709-729-0270, Fax: 709-576-1443,lorrainemichael@gov.nl.ca
Hon. Kevin O'Brien, Gander, PC
709-729-4712, 800-813-6850,Fax:
709-729-4754,Kevinobrien@gov.nl.ca
Paul Oram, Terra Nova, PC
709-729-7895, Fax: 709-729-3306,pauloram@gov.nl.ca
Hon. Tom Osborne, St. John's South, PC
709-729-4882, Fax: 709-729-0469,TOsborne@gov.nl.ca
Sheila Osborne, St. John's West, PC
709-729-5869, Fax: 709-729-1082,sosborne@gov.nl.ca
Kelvin Parsons, Burgeo & La Poile, Liberal
709-729-0434, 800-518-9479,Fax:
709-729-5202,kparsons@gov.nl.ca
Calvin Peach, Bellevue, PC
709-729-1546, Fax: 709-729-1503,CalvinPeach@gov.nl.ca
Tracy Perry, Fortune Bay-Cape La Hune, PC
709-538-3112, Fax: 709-538-3079,TraceyPerry@gov.nl.ca
Hon. Patty Pottle, Torngat Mountains, PC
709-729-1069, 877-788-8822,Fax:
709-729-4000,PattyPottle@gov.nl.ca
Kevin Pollard, Baie Verte-Springdale, Liberal
KevinPollard@gov.nl.ca
Bob Ridgley, St. John's North, PC
709-729-6921, Fax: 709-729-1082,BobRidgley@gov.nl.ca
Hon. Shawn Skinner, St. John's Centre, PC
709-729-3580, Fax: 709-729-6996,ShawnSkinner@gov.nl.ca
Hon. Trevor Taylor, The Straits & White Bay North, PC
709-729-4729, Fax: 709-729-0654,trevortaylor@gov.nl.ca
Wade Verge, Lewisporte, PC
709-729-3399, 877-585-0515,Fax:
709-729-1082,WadeVerge@gov.nl.ca
Hon. Dianne Whalen, Conception Bay East & Bell Island, PC
709-729-3678, Fax: 709-729-4285,dianne.whalen@gov.nl.ca
Hon. Danny Williams, Humber West, PC
709-729-3570, Fax: 709-729-5875,DannyWilliams@gov.nl.ca,
Other Communications: URL: www.gov.nl.ca/premier
Hon. Ross Wiseman, Trinity North, PC
709-729-3124, 800-514-9073,Fax:
709-729-0121,rosswiseman@gov.nl.ca
Wallace Young Jr., St. Barbe, PC
709-729-1731, 866-729-1677,Fax:
709-729-5774,WallyYoung@gov.nl.ca
Clerk, William MacKenzie
709-729-3405

Newfoundland & Labrador Government Departments & Agencies

Office of the Auditor General

Viking Bldg., 3rd Fl., PO Box 8700, St. John's, NL A1B 4J6
709-729-2700, Fax: 709-729-5970,
oag@gov.nl.ca
www.ag.gov.nl.ca

Auditor General, John L. Noseworthy, C.A.
709-729-2700, jnoseworthy@gov.nl.ca
Dpeuty Auditor General, Wayne Loveys
709-729-4999, Fax: 709-729-5970

Department of Business

Confederation Bldg., East Block, 6th Fl., PO Box 8700, St. John's, NL A1B 4J6
709-729-3254, Fax: 709-729-3306,
business@gov.nl.ca
www.nlbusiness.ca

New department announced Spring 2006.
Minister,Hon. Paul Oram
709-729-7895, Fax: 709-729-3306,pauloram@gov.nl.ca
Deputy Minister, Ray Dillon
709-729-3451, Fax: 709-729-3306,raydillon@gov.nl.ca
Acting Director, Brand Development, Vanessa McBay
709-729-0075, Fax: 709-729-3306,vanessamcbay@gov.nl.ca
Acting Director, Strategic Policy & Planning, William Griffin
709-729-2302, griffinw@gov.nl.ca
Director, Communications, Mark King
709-729-7628, Fax: 709-729-3306,markking@gov.nl.ca

Department of Education

West Block, Confederation Bldg., 100 Prince Philip Dr., 3rd Fl., PO Box 8700, St. John's, NL A1B 4J6
709-729-5097, Fax: 709-729-5896,
education@gov.nl.ca
www.ed.gov.nl.ca

Responsible for the K-12 & post-secondary school system, literacy & library services; comprises four executive branches: Primary, Elementary & Secondary Education, Corporate Services Branch; Post-Secondary Branch; International Education & Planning Branch; Literacy School Services; reporting to the department through their various boards are the Provincial Information & Library Resources Board, the Literacy Development Council, 4 geographical school boards & a francophone school board.

Acts Administered:
Literacy Development Council Act
Public Libraries Act
School Boards' Association Act
Schools Act, 1997
Teacher Training Act
Teachers' Association Act
Minister,Hon. Joan Burke
709-729-5040, 866-838-5620,Fax:
709-729-0414,Joanburke@gov.nl.ca
Deputy Minister, Rebecca Roome
709-729-5086, rebeccaroome@gov.nl.ca
Assistant Deputy Minister, Corporate Services, Rick Hayward
709-729-3025, rhayward@gov.nl.ca
Assistant Deputy Minister, Primary, Elementary & Secondary Education, Marian Fushell
709-729-5720, marianfushell@gov.nl.ca
Assistant Deputy Minister, Advanced Studies, Rachelle Cochrane
709-729-3026, rachellecochrane@gov.nl.ca
Director, Communications, Jacquelyn Howard
709-729-0048, jacquelynhoward@gov.nl.ca
• Provincial Information & Library Resources Board
48 St. George's Ave
Stephenville, NL A2H 1K9
709-643-0900 Fax: 709-643-0925
www.nlpubliclibraries.ca
To establish & operate those public libraries in the province that it considers necessary & provide support to ensure that library materials, information & programs are available to meet the needs of the public.

Advanced Studies Branch
Asst. Deputy Minister, Rachelle Cochrane
709-729-3026, rachellecochrane@gov.nl.ca
Director, Adult Learning & Literacy, Candice Ennis-Williams
709-729-2087, CandiceEnnis-Williams@gov.nl.ca
Director, Institutional & Industrial Education, Denise Hanrahan
709-729-2350, hanrahand@gov.nl.ca
Director, Student Financial Services, Hayward Harris
709-729-3576, hayward.harris@gov.nl.ca
Director, Student Loan Corporation of Newfoundland & Labrador, Julie Moore
709-729-3036, juliemoore@gov.nl.ca

Corporate Services Branch
Asst. Deputy Minister, Jim Strong
709-729-0580, jstrong@gov.nl.ca
Director, Program Support Centre, Harry T. Hutchings
709-729-0444, hhutchings@gov.nl.ca
Director, Federal & Provincial Agreements, Brian Evans
709-729-1841
Director, Financial Services, Karen Legge
709-729-5287, Fax: 709-729-3151
Clerk, Human Resources, Joy Colbert
709-729-3067, Fax: 709-729-6737

Primary, Elementary & Secondary Education
Asst. Deputy Minister, Marian Fushell
709-729-5720, marianfushell@gov.nl.ca
Director, School Services, Brian Miller
709-729-5129, brianmiller@gov.nl.ca
Director, Centre for Distance Learning & Innovation, Jim Tuff
709-729-7614, 866-836-3559,jimtuff@gov.nl.ca
Director, Early Childhood Learning, Charlotte Strong
709-729-5128, charlottestrong@gov.nl.ca
Director, Program Development, Eldred Barnes
709-729-3004, eldredbarnes@gov.nl.ca
Director, Student Support Services, Dan Goodyear
709-729-3023, dangoodyear@gov.nl.ca

Office of the Chief Electoral Officer

39 Hallett Cr., St. John's, NL A1B 4C4
709-729-0712, Fax: 709-729-0679, 877-729-7987
oceo@gov.nl.ca
www.gov.nl.ca/elections

Chief Electoral Officer, Paul Reynolds
Administrative Officer, Elizabeth Furlong
709-729-0714, Fax: 709-729-0679

Newfoundland & Labrador Emergency Measures Organization

PO Box 8700, St. John's, NL A1B 4J6
709-729-3703, Fax: 709-729-3857,
www.ma.gov.nl.ca/ma/fes/emo

Other Communication: 24 hr. Emergencies: 709/729-3703
The Provincial Emergency Measures Program is responsible for the development & maintenance of provincial emergency

preparedness, response & recovery measures with a view to mitigating the human suffering & loss of property caused by actual or imminent emergencies & disasters.Using its legislative support, The Emergency Measures Act, it has the responsibility to co-ordinate &/or manage an emergency situation. It is the only agency that is authorized to control & coordinate the activities of all Police, Fire, Health, Social Services, & other services in the area, either municipal or provincial, & to engage civilian personnel to assist in these services.Programs & Services provided include Emergency Response, Planning & Operations, Training & Education, Joint Emergency Preparedness, Disaster Financial Assistance Arrangements, Emergency Air Services & Emergency Response.

Director, Fred Hollett
709-729-3703
Clerk Typist, Ryan Hurley
709-729-3703, Fax: 709-729-3857,rhurley@gov.nl.ca

Department of Environment & Conservation

Confederation Bldg., West Block, 4th Fl., PO Box 8700, St. John's, NL A1B 4J6
709-729-2664, Fax: 709-729-6639, 800-563-6181
info@gov.nl.ca
www.env.gov.nl.ca

To protect, conserve & enhance the Province's environment through the management of water resources, the environmental assessment of undertakings & the control & management of substances & activities that may pollute the environment. The Department is actively working towards reducing the number of landfill sites & implementing the Provincial Waste Management Strategy.The strategy will divert 50 percent of materials from landfill sites,phase out municipal solid waste incinerators by 2008 & prohibit such facilities from being built in the future.

Acts Administered:
Endangered Species Act
Environmental Protection Act
Geographical Name Act
Land Surveyors Act
Lands Act
National Parks Lands Act
Provincial Parks Act
Smoke-Free Environment Act
Water Resources Act

Minister,Hon. Charlene Johnson
709-729-2577, Fax: 709-729-0112,charlenejohnson@gov.nl.ca
Deputy Minister, William Parrott
709-729-2572
Director, Communications, Melony O'Neil
709-729-2575
Director, Environmental Assessment, Bas Cleary
709-729-2562
Director, Policy & Planning, John Drover
709-729-0027, jdrover@gov.nl.ca
Director, Pollution Prevention, Derrick Maddocks
709-729-2556
Acting Director, Water Resources, Haseen Khan
709-729-2563

• Multi-Materials Stewardship Board(MMSB)
PO Box 8131 A
St. John's, NL A1B 3M9
709-753-0948 Fax: 709-753-0974
www.mmsb.nf.ca

Environment Branch

Other Communication: Spill Reporting (24 hours): 709/772-2083; Environmental Assessment: 1-800-563-6181
Director, Bas Cleary
709-729-0673, Fax: 709-729-5518,clearyb@gov.nl.ca
Director, Environmental Assessment, Phil Graham
709-729-5752
Director, Policy & Planning, John Drover, P. Eng
709-729-1090, jdrover@gov.nl.ca
Director, Pollution Prevention, Derrick Maddocks
709-729-5782
Director, Water Resources, Martin Goebel
709-729-2563, Fax: 709-729-0320,mgoebel@gov.nl.ca

Natural Heritage

Asst. Deputy Minister, Robert Warren
709-637-2135, Fax: 709-637-2180,rwarren@gov.nl.ca
Executive Director, Science, Shane Mahoney
709-729-2542, Fax: 729-729-7677,shanemahoney@gov.nl.ca
Acting Director, Parks & Natural Areas, Calvin C. Yates
709-635-3849, CYates@gov.nl.ca
Director, Science, Wildlife & Natural Heritage, Robert D. Otto
709-729-2970, Fax: 709-637-2036
Director, Wildlife Division, Jim Hancock
709-637-2008

Department of Finance

Confederation Bldg., PO Box 8700, St. John's, NL A1B 4J6
709-729-6310,
finance@gov.nl.ca
www.fin.gov.nl.ca

Acts Administered:
Department of Finance Act
Financial Administration Act
Financial Corporations Capital Tax Act
Gasoline Tax Act
Government Money Purchase Pension Plan Act
Health & Post-Secondary Education Tax Act
Horse Racing Regulation & Tax Act
Industrial Development Corporation Act
Insurance Companies Tax Act
Liquor Corporation Act
The Loan Act
The Loan & Guarantee Act, 1957
The Local Authority Guarantee Act, 1957
Members of the House of Assembly Pensions Act
Mining & Mineral Rights Tax Act
Municipal Financing Corporation Act
Pension Benefits Act, 1997
Pensions Funding Act
Public Service Pensions Act, 1991
Retail Sales Tax Act
School Tax Authorities Winding Up Act
Statistics Agency Act
Tax Agreement Act
Taxation of Utilities & Cable Television Companies Act
Teachers' Pensions Act
Tobacco Tax Act
Uniformed Services Pensions Act

Minister & President, Treasury Board,Hon. Tom Marshall
709-729-3775, Fax: 709-729-6791,tommarshall@gov.nl.ca
Deputy Minister, Terry Paddon
709-729-2946
Comptroller General, Finance, Ron Williams
709-729-4866
Director, Communications, Billy Hickey
709-729-6830, Fax: 709-729-6390,billyhickey@gov.nl.ca

• C.A. Pippy Park Commission
Mount Scio House
15 Mount Scio Rd.
St. John's, NL A1B 3T2
709-737-3655 Fax: 709-737-3303 877-477-3655
pippyparkinfo@nf.aibn.com
www.pippypark.com
C.A. Pippy Park was established by an Act of the Newfoundland Legislature in 1968. The Act created the C.A. Pippy Park Commission, a semi-autonomous Crown Corporation under the laws of the Province of Newfoundland and Labrador. The Commission currently reports to the Minister of Finance.

• Newfoundland & Labrador Municipal Financing Corporation(NMFC)
Confederation Bldg.
PO Box 8700
St. John's, NL A1B 4J6
709-729-6686 Fax: 709-729-2095
Newfoundland and Labrador Municipal Financing Corporation is a Crown Corporation established to consolidate the long-term borrowing programs of all municipalities in one central agency.

• Newfoundland Labrador Liquor Corporation
90 Kenmount Rd.
PO Box 8750 A
St. John's, NL A1B 3V1
709-724-1100 Fax: 709-754-0321
info@nfliquor.com
www.nfliquor.com
The Newfoundland Labrador Liquor Corporation (NLC) is a provincial crown corporation responsible for managing the importation, sale and distribution of beverage alcohol within the province.

Economics & Statistics

Asst. Deputy Minister, Alton Hollett
709-729-3255, Fax: 709-729-0393
Director, Economic Research & Analysis, Rod Forsey
709-729-0864, rforsey@gov.nl.ca
Director, Newfoundland Statistics Agency, Alton Hollett
709-729-0158, Fax: 709-729-0393

Financial Planning & Benefits Administration

Asst. Deputy Minister, Donna Brewer
709-729-4581, Fax: 709-729-1746,dbrewer@gov.nl.ca
Director, Budgeting, Wendy O'Keefe
709-729-1054, Fax: 709-729-7627,wendyo'keefe@gov.nl.ca
Director, Insurance, Anthony Lannon
709-729-0502, Fax: 709-729-2156
Director, Debt Management, Paul Myrden
709-729-6848, Fax: 709-729-2095
Director, Pensions Administration, Maureen McCarthy
709-729-5983

Office of the Comptroller General

Comptroller General, Ronald Williams
709-729-5926, Fax: 709-729-7627
Director, Government Accounting, Paul Smith
709-729-2341, Fax: 709-729-7627,smithp@gov.nl.ca
Director, Professional Services & Internal Audit, David Hill
709-729-0702, Fax: 709-729-2098,davehill@gov.nl.ca

Department of Fisheries & Aquaculture

Petten Bldg., 30 Strawberry Marsh Rd., PO Box 8700, St. John's, NL A1B 4J6
709-729-3723, Fax: 709-729-6082,
fishaqwebmaster@gov.nl.ca
www.fishaq.gov.nl.ca

Contributes to economic & community growth in the province by encouraging sustainable growth & development of the harvesting, processing, & distribution sectors; includes providing support for the marketing of fish & aquaculture products produced in Newfoundland & Labrador for domestic & export markets. Responsible for: setting & enforcing standards for the processing & sale of fish products in the province; licensing fish processing establishments; undertaking developmental initiatives in the harvesting, processing, & marketing sectors of the fishing industry; developing, promoting & licensing of aquaculture facilities; developing & maintaining strategic fisheries infrastructure; articulating policies & providing advice for the management & development of fisheries & aquaculture; providing statistical information.

Acts Administered:
Aquaculture Act
Fish Inspection Act
Fish Processing Licensing Board Act
Fisheries Act
Fisheries Products International Limited Act
Fisheries Restructuring Act
Fishing Industry Collective Bargaining Act
Professional Fish Harvesters Act

Acting Minister,Hon. Trevor Taylor
trevortaylor@gov.nl.ca
Deputy Minister, Alastair O'Rielly
709-729-3707, Fax: 790-729-4219,aorielly@gov.nl.ca
Director, Communications, Lori Lee Oates
709-729-3733, oatesll@gov.nl.ca
Manager, Financial Operations, Duane Winsor
709-729-3525, Fax: 709-729-2092,duanewinsor@gov.nl.ca
Manager, Human Resources, Len Croke
709-729-7900, Fax: 709-729-1860

• Professional Fish Harvesters Certification Board(PFHCB)
15 Hallett Cres.
PO Box 8541
St. John's, NL A1B 3P2
709-722-8170 Fax: 709-722-8201
pfh@pfhcb.com
www.pfhcb.com

Aquaculture Branch

Fax: 709-729-0360
The Branch is responsible for licensing & aquaculture development.
Asst. Deputy Minister, Brian Meaney
709-729-3710, Fax: 709-729-1882,bmeaney@gov.nl.ca
Director, Aquaculture Development, Shawn Robinson
709-292-4111, Fax: 709-292-4113,srobinson@gov.nl.ca

Fisheries Branch

Fax: 709-729-6082
Asst. Deputy Minister, David Lewis
709-729-3713
Director, Ian Burford
709-729-3736
Director, Processing & Marketing Development, Mike Handrigan
709-729-3749

Policy Development & Planning Branch

Provides policy & program planning services to the Department. Through the Sustainable Fisheries & Oceans Policy Division participates in oceans policy & governance issues, in addition to the resource assessment & management process of the federal Department of Fisheries & Oceans, including local, national, & international bodies responsible for fisheries conservation & management.
Executive Director, Mike Warren
709-729-3708, Fax: 709-729-6082,mikewarren@gov.nl.ca
Director, Fishing Industry Renewal, Brian Delaney
709-729-3712, Fax: 709-729-6082
Director, Sustainable Fisheries & Oceans Policy, Tom Dooley
709-729-0335

Regional Offices:

Gander
709-292-4102, Fax: 709-292-4113

Regional Director, Nelson Higdon
709-292-4109, Fax: 709-292-4113,nhigdon@gov.nl.ca

Avalon & Eastern
709-832-2860, Fax: 709-832-1669
Regional Director, Rex Matthews
709-832-2860

Labrador
709-896-3412, Fax: 709-896-3483
Regional Director, Craig Taylor
709-896-3412, Fax: 709-896-3483,craigtaylor@gov.nl.ca

Western
709-861-3537, Fax: 709-861-3556
Clerk, Vivian Hynes
709-861-3537, vivianhynes@gov.nl.ca

Department of Government Services

PO Box 8700, St. John's, NL A1B 4J6
709-729-4860,
www.gs.gov.nl.ca
Departmental responsibilities include: motor vehicle registration, government service centres, consumer protection, trade practices, vital statistics, lotteries, registries, building accessibility, residential tenancies services, regulation of financial institutions, occupational health & safety, Office of the Queen's Printer, Government Purchasing Agency, permits, licences, approvals & inspections for public health & safety.
Acts Administered:
Accident & Sickness Insurance Act
Architects Act
Automobile Insurance Act
Bank of Nova Scotia Trust Company Act, 1997
Buildings Accessibility Act
Bulk Sales Act
Business Electronic Filing Act
Certified General Accountants Act
Certified Public Accountants Act
Change of Name Act
Chartered Accountants Act
Chartered Accountants & Certified Public Accountants Merger Act
Collections Act
Consumer Protection Act
Condominium Act
Consumer Reporting Agencies Act
Co-operatives Act
Conveyancing Act
Corporations Act
Corporations Guarantee Act
Credit Union Act
Criminal Code
Direct Sellers Act
Electronic Commerce Act
Embalmers & Funeral Director Act
Engineers & Geoscientists Act
Fire Insurance Act
Income Tax Savings Plan Act
Insurance Adjusters, Agents & Brokers Act
Insurance Companies Act
Insurance Contracts Act
Intergovernmental Joint Purchasing Act
Investment Contracts Act
Judgement Recovery (Nfld) Ltd. Act
Life Insurance Act
Limited Partnership Act
Lodgers' Goods Protection Act
Management Accountants Act
Maritime Hospital Service Association Re-Incorporation Act
Mechanics Lien Act
Mortgage Brokers Act
Occupational Health & Safety Act
Pension Benefits Act, 1997
Pension Plans Designation of Beneficiaries Act
Perpetuities & Accumulations Act
Personal Property Security Act
Petroleum Products Act
Prepaid Funeral Services Act
Printing Services Act
Private Investigation & Security Services Act
Public Accountancy Act
Public Safety Act
Public Tender Act
Radiation Health & Safety Act
Real Estate Trading Act
Registration of Deeds Act
Residential Tenancies Act, 2000
Sale of Goods Act
Securities Act
Security Interest Registration Act
Solemnization of Marriage Act
Trade Practices Act
Trust & Loan Corporations Licensing Act
Trustee Act
Unconscionable Transactions Relief Act
Unsolicited Goods & Credit Cards Act
Vital Statistics Act
Warehouse Receipts Act
Warehouse's Lien Act
Workplace Health, Safety & Compensation Act
Acts Shared in Part with Other Ministries
Adoptions Act (Health & Community Services)
Building Standards Act (Municipal Affairs)
Child Care Services Act (Health & Community Services)
Child, Youth & Family Services Act (Health & Community Services)
Children's Law Act (Justice)
Communicable Diseases Act (Health & Community Services)
Dangerous Goods Transportation Act (Justice)
Employers' Liability Act (Justice)
Environmental Protection Act (Environment & Conservation)
Fire Prevention Act, 1991 (Municipal Affairs)
Food & Drug Act (Health & Community Services)
Fraudulent Conveyance Act (Justice)
Health & Community Services Act (Health & Community Services)
Highway Traffic Act (Transportation & Works)
Meat Inspection Act (Natural Resources)
Motor Carrier Act (Transportation & Works)
Motorized Snow Vehicles & All-Terrain Vehicles Act (Natural Resources)
Tobacco Act (Federal) (Health & Community Services)
Urban & Rural Planning Act (Municipal Affairs)
Water Resources Act (Environment & Conservation)
Minister,Hon. Kevin O'Brien
709-729-4712, Fax: 709-729-4754,kevinobrien@gov.nl.ca
Deputy Minister, Sheree MacDonald
709-729-4752, Fax: 709-729-4754
Director, Communications, Vanessa Colman-Sadd
709-729-4860, Fax: 709-729-4754,vanessacolmansadd@gov.nl.ca
Director, Audit, Information & Training, Joseph Day
709-729-5429, dayj@gov.nl.ca
Director, Procurement & Development, Patricia Hearn
709-729-3344, hearnp@gov.nl.ca
Director, Government Purchasing, Policy & Administration, Wayne Hendry
709-729-3347, Fax: 709-729-5817,hendryw@gov.nl.ca
Director, Policy & Planning, Wanda Lundrigan
709-729-6470, Fax: 709-729-3205,wlundrigan@gov.nl.ca
Manager, Registration & Enforcement, Craig Whalen
709-729-5661, Fax: 709-729-6187,cwhalen@gov.nl.ca
Manager, Organization & Development, Shaunna Reid
709-729-0683, Fax: 709-729-6661,shaunnareid@gov.nl.ca
• Credit Union Deposit Guarantee Corporation
PO Box 340
Marystown, NL A0E 2M0
709-279-0170 Fax: 709-279-0177 877-279-0170
www.cudgc.nf.net
The Credit Union Deposit Guarantee Corporation guarantees deposits up to $250,000 per account type: demand accounts, registered retirement savings plans, registered retirement income fund, trust accounts, and joint accounts. Established in 1991 under the Co-operative Societies Act, replacing the Newfoundland and Labrador Stabilization fund, which was enacted in 1983.

Consumer & Commercial Affairs Branch
Promotes economic development by assisting businesses & protecting consumers. The branch is responsible for regulating the insurance industry, the securities industries, the trust & loan industry, the credit union industry, the real estate industry, collection agencies, mortgage brokers, automobile dealers, charitable gaming, private investigation agencies, & landlord-tenant relations.
Asst. Deputy Minister, Winston Morris
709-729-2570, Fax: 709-729-4151
Director, Commercial Registrations, Doug Laing
709-729-3300
Deputy Registrar, Deeds & Personal Property Securities Act, Lorraine Vokey
709-729-5724, Fax: 709-729-0232,lvokey@gov.nl.ca
Deputy Registrar, Lobbyists & Companies, Dean Doyle
709-729-4043, Fax: 709-729-0232
Director, Financial Services Regulation, Doug Connolly, C.A.
709-729-4909, Fax: 709-729-3205,connolly@gov.nl.ca
Director, Trade Practices, Gerard Burke
709-729-2618, Fax: 709-729-6998

Government Services Branch
Provides a one-stop service to the public & business community for a wide range of government regulatory & information functions. The Branch processes various permits, licences, & approvals, carries out inspections & investigations on behalf of various departments & conducts highway enforcement of the motor carrier industry. Also administers the Highway Traffic Act & registers vital events such as births, marriages, deaths & name changes. Through the Office of the Queen's Printer publishes, distributes & sells the Newfoundland & Labrador Consolidated Statutes, Regulations, the Newfoundland & Labrador Gazette & selected publications. Operates printing & micrographic services for all government departments.

GSC Area Offices:

Office of the Queen's Printer
Queen's Printer-Earl Tucker, Ground Fl., Confederation Blg., PO Box 8700, St. John's, NL A1B 4J6
709-729-3649, Fax: 709-729-1900,
queensprinter@gov.nl.ca
Provides a retail outlet for purchase of government legislation & various government reports. Publishes Hansard, Bills, Statutes & Regulations for the House of Assembly. Publishes weekly The Newfoundland & Labrador Gazette which contains government & public legal notices as well as subordinate legislation. Provides subscription & mail-out services for some of these publications. Provides ISBN numbers for government publications.

Vital Statistics Division
5 Mews Pl., PO Box 8700, St. John's, NL A1B 4J6
709-729-3308, Fax: 709-729-0946,
vstats@gov.nl.ca
Registers births, marriages & deaths in the province. In addition, the division registers adoptions & legal name changes & certifies clergy who are authorized to solemnize marriages. From this division, the public may obtain a birth, marriage, death, or change of name certificate, or a marriage licence. Vital Statistics services are also available from GSC offices.
Registrar, Brenda Andrews
709-729-3311
Manager, Operations, Ken Mullaly
709-729-3313, Fax: 709-729-0946,kmullaly@gov.nl.ca

Regional Offices:

Eastern Office
15 Dundee Ave., Mount Pearl, NL A1N 4R6
709-729-2706, Fax: 709-729-3445

Occupational Health & Safety Branch
Other Communication: Accident Reporting Line: 709/729-4444 (24 hours); Toll Free for Occupational Health & Safety: 1-800-563-5471 (in Nfld. & Lab.)
Maintains & improves health & safety standards in the workplace through the administration of the Occupational Health & Safety Act & Regulations, The Mines Safety of Workers Regulations, the Radiation Health & Safety Act & Regulations &, other associated regulations, codes of practice & specified standards. The Division is supported by inspections officers, industrial hygienists, engineers & radiation specialists to per form various multi-disciplinary activities such as: investigating workplace accidents & statistics; conducting compliance inspections & detailed audits of workplaces; hygiene assessments of various physical, chemical, biological& ergonomic agents in the workplace in order to protect worker health; evaluating & inspecting radiation control measures in workplaces & enforcing occupational health & safety Legislation.
Asst. Deputy Minister, Kim Dunphy
709-729-5548, Fax: 709-729-4151
Director, Reg Bennett
709-729-7454, Fax: 709-729-3445,regbennett@gov.nl.ca

Corner Brook
Fortis Towers, 4 Herald Ave., 2nd fl., Corner Brook, NL
709-637-2946, Fax: 709-637-2928

Grand Falls-Windsor
7 High St., Grand Falls-Windsor, NL
709-292-4400, Fax: 709-292-4430

Labrador City
Provincial Court Bldg., Wabush, NL
709-282-2680, Fax: 709-282-2688

Department of Health & Community Services (HCS)

West Block, Confederation Bldg., PO Box 8700, St. John's, NL A1B 4J6
709-729-5021, Fax: 709-729-5824,
www.health.gov.nl.ca/
Provides a leadership role in health & community service programs & policy development for the Province. This involves working in partnership with a number of key stakeholders including regional boards, community organizations, professional associations, post-secondary educational institutions, unions, consumer & other government departments.
Acts Administered:
Adoption Act
Cancer Treatment & Research Foundation Act
Centre for Health Information Act

Child Care Services Act
Child, Youth & Family Services Act
Chiropractors Act
Communicable Diseases Act
Dental Act
Denturists Act
Dieticians Act
Dispensing Opticians Act
Emergency Medical Aid Act
Food & Drug Act
Health & Community Services Act
Health Care Association Act
Homes for Special Care Act
Hearing Aid Dealers Act
Hospital Insurance Agreement Act
Hospitals Act
Human Tissue Act
Licensed Practical Nurses Act
Massage Therapy Act
Medical Act
Medical Care Insurance Act, 1999
Mental Health Act
Midwifery Act
Neglected Adults Welfare Act
Occupational Therapists Act
Optometry Act
Pharmacy Act
Physiotherapy Act
Private Homes for Special Care Allowances Act
Psychologists Act
Registered Nurses Act
Self-managed Home Support Services Act
Smoke-free Environment Act
Social Workers Association Act
Tobacco Control Act
Venereal Disease Prevention Act
Young Persons Offences Act
Youth Criminal Justice Act (Canada)
Minister,Hon. Ross Wiseman
709-729-3124, 800-514-9073,Fax: 709-729-0121,rosswiseman@gov.nl.ca
Deputy Minister, Don Keats
709-729-3125, Fax: 709-729-0121
Director, Communications, Glenda Power
709-729-1377, Fax: 709-729-0121
• Newfoundland & Labrador Health Boards Associations
Board of Trade Bldg.
#202, 66 Kenmount Rd.
St. John's, NL A1B 3V7
709-364-7701 Fax: 709-364-6460
nlhba@nlhba.nf.ca
www.nlhba.nf.ca

Public Health, Wellness, & Children & Youth Services
Asst. Deputy Minister, Jennifer Jeans
709-729-5864
Chief Medical Officer of Health, Public Health Division,Dr. Faith Stratton
709-729-3430
Director, Children & Youth Services, Ivy Burt
709-729-6721
Director, Health Emergency Management,Vacant
Director, Environmental Public Health, Darryl Johnson
709-729-3422, Fax: 709-729-0730,djohnson@gov.nl.ca
Director, Public Health Labs,Dr. Sam Ratnam
709-777-7235
Director, Health Promotion & Wellness, Eleanor Swanson
709-729-5023

Newfoundland & Labrador Housing Corporation (NLHC)

Sir Brian Dunfield Bldg., 2 Canada Dr., PO Box 220, St. John's, NL A1C 5J2
709-724-3000, Fax: 709-724-3250,
jmbowering@nsmail.nlhc.nl.ca
www.nlhc.nl.ca

Minister Responsible,Hon. Shawn Skinner
709-729-3580, Fax: 709-729-6996,shawnskinner@gov.nl.ca
Chair, Len Simms
709-724-3054, lensimms@nlhc.nl.ca
Manager, Communications, Jenny Bowring
709-724-3055, jmbowring@nlhc.nl.ca

Department of Human Resources, Labour & Employment

Confederation Bldg., PO Box 8700, St. John's, NL A1B 4J6
709-729-2478, Fax: 709-729-6996,
hreweb@gov.nl.ca
www.hrle.gov.nl.ca/hrle

Acts Administered:
Income & Employment Support Act
Minister,Hon. Shawn Skinner
709-729-3580, Fax: 709-729-6996,ShawnSkinner@gov.nl.ca
Deputy Minister, Brenda Caule
709-729-3582
Director, Communications, Ronalda Walsh
709-729-0753, Fax: 709-729-3996,ronaldawalsh@gov.nl.ca
Acting Director, Policy, Planning & Evaluation, Rob Boychuk
709-729-0494, rboychuk@gov.nl.ca
• Income & Employment Support Appeal Board
Confederation Bldg.
PO Box 8700
St. John's, NL A1B 4J6
709-729-2479 Fax: 709-729-5139
• Labour Relations Board
Beothuck Bldg.
20 Crosbie Pl., 5th Fl.
PO Box 8700
St. John's, NL A1B 4J6
709-729-2707 Fax: 709-729-5738
www.hrle.gov.nl.ca/lrb
• Workplace Health, Safety & Compensation Commission

Corporate Services
Asst. Deputy Minister, Denise Tubrett
709-729-3594, Fax: 709-729-5139,dtubrett@@gov.nl.ca
Director, Finance & General Operations, Brendan Hanlon
709-729-3530, Fax: 709-729-4379,brenhanlon@gov.nl.ca
Director, Human Resources,Vacant

Income, Employment & Youth Services
Asst. Deputy Minister, Lynn Vivian-Book
709-729-5151, Fax: 709-729-5139,lbook@gov.nl.ca
Director, Career, Employment & Youth Services, Sharon Knott
709-729-2084, sharonknott@gov.nl.ca
Director, Income Support, Brendan Mullaly
709-729-2665, brendanmullaly@gov.nl.ca
Director, Poverty Reduction Strategy, Aisling Gogan
709-729-6053, Fax: 709-729-5139,AislingGogan@gov.nl.ca
Regional Director, Central, Carson Saunders
709-292-4509, Fax: 709-292-4383,carsonsaunders@gov.nl.ca
Regional Director, Western, Wayne Fillier
709-637-2308, waynefillier@gov.nl.ca
Regional Director, Labrador, Agnes Rumbolt
709-896-3306, agnesrumbolt@gov.nl.ca
Regional Director, Avalon, Donna O'Brien
709-729-7884, Fax: 709-729-3018,donnaobrien@gov.nl.ca

Labour Market Development & Client Services
Asst. Deputy Minister, Wayne Penney
709-729-0217, waynepenney@gov.nl.ca
Executive Director, Immigration & Multiculturalism, Nellie Burke
709-729-6967, nellieburke@gov.nl.ca

Labour Relations Agency
Other Communication: Labour Standards: 1-877-563-1063
Asst. Deputy Minister, Policy & Planning, Bruce Cooper
709-729-1760, Fax: 709-729-5905,brucecooper@gov.nl.ca
CEO, Wayne Fowler
709-729-2715, Fax: 709-729-1759,WFowler@gov.nl.ca
Director, Labour Relations, Yvonne Scott
709-729-0707, Fax: 709-729-5905,YScott@gov.nl.ca
Director, Labour Standards, Ken Clements
709-729-2743, Fax: 709-729-3528,kclements@gov.nl.ca
Manager, Employment Programs, Clayton Johnson
709-729-5751
Manager, Career Services, David Smyth
709-729-1071
Manager, Support Employment Program, Ken O'Brien
709-729-5184

Newfoundland & Labrador Human Rights Commission

PO Box 8700, St. John's, NL A1B 4J6
709-729-2709, Fax: 709-729-0790, 800-563-5808
humanrights@mail.gov.nl.ca
www.justice.gov.nl.ca/hrc

Executive Director, Jane Fitzpatrick
709-729-4184, Fax: 709-729-0790,janefitzpatrick@gov.nl.ca

Newfoundland & Labrador Hydro

Hydro Place, Columbus Dr., PO Box 12400, St. John's, NL A1B 4K7
709-737-1400, Fax: 709-737-1800

Crown corporation, owned by the Province of Newfoundland & Labrador. Hydro generates, transmits & distributes electrical power & energy to utility, residential & industrial customers throughout the province. Hydro is the parent company of the Hydro Group of Companies (Hydro Group), comprising Newfoundland & Labrador Hydro, Churchill Falls (Labrador) Corporation Limited (CF(L)Co), Lower Churchill Development Corporation Limited (LCDC), Gull Island Power Company Limited (GIPCo), & Twin Falls Power Corporation Limited (TwinCo).The Hydro Group's installed generating capacity is the fourth largest of all utility companies in Canada, consisting of ten hydroelectric plants, including the Churchill Falls hydraulic plant, which is the largest underground powerhouse in the world with a rated capacity of 5,428 megawatts (MW) of power, one oil-fired plant, four gas turbines & 26 diesel plants.
President/CEO, Ed Martin
Vice-President, Business Development, Jim Keating
Vice-President, Engineering, John Mallam
Vice-President, Finance & CFO, Derrick Sturge
Vice-President, Human Resources, Gerard McDonald
Vice-President, Regulated Operations, Jim Haynes

Churchill Falls (Labrador) Corporation Limited
Hydro Place, 500 Columbus Dr., PO Box 12500, St. John's, NL A1B 4K7
709-737-1859, Fax: 709-737-1816
Churchill Falls (Labrador) Corporation operates a hydroelectric generating plant & transmission facilities.
President/CEO, Ed Martin
Vice-President, Finance & CFO, John C. Roberts
General Manager, Andrew MacNeill
709-925-8227
Manager, Corporate Affairs & Risk Management, Donald J. Barrett
709-737-1370, Fax: 709-737-1816

Gull Island Power Co. Ltd.
President/CEO, Ed Martin
Vice-President, Regulated Operations, Jim Haynes
CFO & Vice-President, Finance, Derrick Sturge

Lower Churchill Development Corporation Ltd.
Vice-President, Gilbert Bennett

Twin Falls Power Corporation
PO Box 12500, St. John's, NL A1B 3T5
Twin Falls Power Corporation has developed a hydroelectric generating plant on the Unknown River in Labrador.The plant has been inoperative since 1974.
President, Jim Haynes
709-737-1400
General Manager, Andrew MacNeill
Vice-President, Finance & CFO, Derrick Sturge

Department of Innovation, Trade & Rural Development

West Block, Confederation Bldg., PO Box 8700, St. John's, NL A1B 4J6
709-729-7000, Fax: 709-729-0654, 800-563-2299
itrd@gov.nl.ca
www.intrd.gov.nl.ca

The department has a number of initiatives to assist businesses in the province or to open in the province.
Acts Administered:
Business Investment Corporation Act
Economic Diversification & Growth Enterprises (EDGE) Act
Industries Act
Research Council Act
Minister,Hon. Trevor Taylor
709-729-4728, Fax: 709-729-0654,trevortaylor@gov.nl.ca
Deputy Minister, Cathy Duke
709-729-4731, Fax: 709-729-0654,cathyduke@gov.nl.ca
Director, Communications, Scott Barfoot
709-729-4570, Fax: 709-729-4880,ScottBarfoot@gov.nl.ca
Director, Policy & Strategic Planning, Andrea Dicks
709-729-4868, Fax: 709-729-4869,adicks@gov.nl.ca
Director, Trade & Investment, Paul Morris
709-729-2781, Fax: 709-729-3208,pmorris@gov.nl.ca
• Ireland Business Partnership
PO Box 8700
St. John's, NL A1B 4J6
709-729-1684 Fax: 709-729-2236
A joint public-private partnership with the Government of Ireland to promote business opportunities & educational & cultural exchanges with Newfoundland & Labrador.
• Nearshore Atlantic
84 Elizabeth Ave., 1st Fl.
St. John's, NL A1A 1W7
709-772-8324 Fax: 709-757-6284
info@nearshoreatlantic.com
www.nearshoreatlantic.com
A public-private partnership between the Government of Newfoundland & Labrador, Aliant & the Newfoundland & Labrador Association of Technical Industries (Nati). The initiative has been developed to promote the Province as a premier destination for nearshore services in the expanding global IT service delivery model. Nearshore Atlantic is governed by a

Steering Committee consisting of representatives of both private & public sectors.

Innovation, Research & Advanced Technologies Branch
Asst. Deputy Minister, Dennis Hogan
709-729-7101, Fax: 709-729-7234,dhoghan@gov.nl.ca
Director, Diane Hooper

Regional Development
Asst. Deputy Minister, Rita Malone
709-637-2977, Fax: 709-639-7713,rmalone@gov.nl.ca
Director, Regional Development & Planning, John Wickham
709-729-7260, Fax: 709-729-5124,jwickham@gov.nl.ca

Regional Offices:

Avalon
28 Pippy Place, St. John's, NL A1B 3X4
Fax: 709-729-7135
Acting Regional Director, Jim Antsey
709-729-7124, Fax: 709-729-7135,jkantsey@gov.nl.ca

Central
McCurdy Complex, Markham Place, PO Box 2222, Gander, NL A1V 2N9
Fax: 709-256-1490
Regional Director, Percy Farwell
709-256-1483, pfarwell@gov.nl.ca

Eastern
211B Memorial Drive, Clarenville, NL A5A 1R3
Fax: 709-466-1306
Acting Regional Director, Denis Sullivan
709-466-4171, Fax: 709-466-1306,sullivan@gov.nl.ca

Labrador
2 Hillcrest Rd., PO Box 3014 B, Happy Valley-Goose Bay, NL A0P 1E0
709-896-2400, Fax: 709-896-0234
Regional Director, Reg Kean
709-896-0306

Western
PO Box 2006, Corner Brook, NL A2H 6J8
Fax: 709-639-7713
Acting Regional Director, John Davis
709-637-2981, jdavis@gov.nl.ca

Strategic Industries & Business Development Branch
Asst. Deputy Minister, Philip McCarthy
709-729-4711, Fax: 709-729-4858,pmccarth@gov.nl.ca
Director, Strategic Industries Development, Kirk Tilley
709-729-7080, Fax: 709-729-6853,ktilley@gov.nl.ca
Director, Business Analysis, Don Kavanagh
709-729-5622, Fax: 709-729-7609,dkavanagh@gov.nl.ca

Trade & Investment Branch
Specializes in assisting provincial businesses develop an export plan to enter new markets, find export business partners & research national & international market opportunities.
Director, Paul Morris
709-729-2781, Fax: 709-729-3208,pmorris@gov.nl.ca
Director, Strategic Partnerships Initiative, Derek Staubitzer
709-729-6137, Fax: 709-729-4858,dstaubit@gov.nl.ca

Intergovernmental Affairs Secretariat

Confederation Bldg., East Block, 7th Fl., PO Box 8700, St. John's, NL A1B 4J6
709-729-3164, Fax: 709-729-5038, iga@gov.nl.ca

Minister,Hon. Thomas J. Hedderson
thedderson@gov.nl.ca
Deputy Minister, Sean Dutton
709-729-2131, sdutton@gov.nl.ca,
Asst. Deputy Minister, Douglas Smith
709-729-3164
Asst. Deputy Minister, Special Initiatives, Karen McCarthy
709-729-7630
Acting Director, Intergovernmental Policy, Jamie Chippett
709-729-2852
Acting Director, Resource & Economic Policy, Tom Graham
709-729-3954
Director, Social & Fiscal Policy, Jacqueline Power
709-729-1341, Fax: 709-729-5038,jpower@gov.nl.ca

Department of Justice

Confederation Bldg., East Block, 4th Fl., PO Box 8700, St. John's, NL A1B 4J6
709-729-5942, Fax: 709-729-2129, justice@gov.nl.ca
www.justice.gov.nl.ca

Acts Administered:
Adult Corrections Act
Advance Health Care Directives Act
Age of Majority Act
Agreement for Policing the Province Act
American Bases Act, 1941
Apportionment Act
Arbitration Act
Bankers' Books Act
Blind Persons' Rights Act
Canada & United Kingdom Reciprocal Recognition & Enforcement of Judgments Act
Change of Name Act (with Government Services & Lands)
Chattels Real Act
Children's Law Act (with Government Services & Lands)
Commissioners for Oaths Act
Contributory Negligence Act
Criminal Code
Defamation Act
Detention of Intoxicated Persons Act
Divorce Act, 1985 (Canada)
Electoral Boundaries Act
Enduring Powers of Attorney Act
Evidence Act
Exhumation Act
Family Law Act
Family Relief Act
Fatal Accidents Act
Fatalities Investigations Act
Federal Courts Jurisdiction Act
Fraudulent Conveyances Act (with Government Services & Lands)
Freedom of Information Act
Frustrated Contracts Act
Human Rights Code
International Commercial Arbitration Act
International Sale of Goods Act
International Trusts Act
Interpretation Act
Interprovincial Subpoena Act
Intestate Succession Act
Judgement Enforcement Act
Judgment Interest Act
Judicature Act
Jury Act, 1991
Justices Act
Justices & Other Public Authorities Protection Act
Law Reform Commission Act
Law Society Act (1999)
Leaseholds in St. John's Act
Legal Aid Act
Limitations Act
Mentally Disabled Persons' Estates Act
Notaries Public Act
Oaths Act
Oaths of Office Act
Partnership Act
Penitentiary Act (Canada)
Petty Trespass Act
Presumption of Death Act
Prisons Act
Prisons & Reformatories Act (Canada)
Privacy Act
Proceedings Against the Crown Act
Proof of Death Members of Armed Forces Act
Provincial Court Act (1991)
Provincial Offences Act
Public Inquiries Act
Public Investigations Evidence Act
Public Trustee Act
Public Utilities Acquisition of Lands Act
Public Utilities Act
Queen's Counsel Act
Quieting of Titles Act
Reciprocal Enforcement of Judgments Act
Reciprocal Enforcement of Support Orders Act
Recording of Evidence Act
Revised Statutes, 1990 Act
Royal Newfoundland Constabulary Act, 1992
Sheriff's Act, 1991
Small Claims Act
Statutes Act
Statutes Amendment Act
Statutes & Subordinate Legislation Act
Subordinate Legislation Revision & Consolidation Act
Support Orders Enforcement Act (with Social Services)
Survival of Actions Act
Survivorship Act
Unified Family Court Act
Victims of Crime Services Act
Wills Act
Young Offenders Act (Canada - with Social Services)
Young Persons Offences Act(with Social Services)

Minister,Hon. Tom Osborne
709-729-2869, Fax: 709-729-0469,TOsborne@gov.nl.ca
Deputy Minister, Christopher Curran, Q.C.
709-729-2872, Fax: 709-729-0469
Assistant Deputy Minister, Deborah Paquette, Q.C.
709-729-0288, Fax: 709-729-2129,debbiep@gov.nl.ca
Director, Strategic Human Resource Management, Karen Bartlett
709-729-4256, Fax: 709-729-6344,karenbartlett@gov.nl.ca
Acting Director, Finance & General Operations, Debbie Dunphy
709-729-2890, Fax: 709-729-5100,ddunphy@gov.nl.ca
Director, Access to Information & Protection of Privacy, Jennifer Berlin
709-729-7939, Fax: 709-729-5466,jenniferberlin@gov.nl.ca
Acting Director, Public Prosecutions, Pam Goulding
709-729-2868, Fax: 709-729-2129
Director, Policy & Strategic Planning, Jackie Lake-Kavanagh
709-729-0543, Fax: 709-729-2129,jackiekavanagh@gov.nl.ca
Director, Communications, Deborah Pennell
709-729-6985, Fax: 709-729-0469,deborahpennell@gov.nl.ca
Director, Civil Law, Dianne Smith, Q.C.
709-729-3402, Fax: 709-729-2129

• Human Rights Commission
• Newfoundland & Labrador Board of Commissioners of Public Utilities
• Newfoundland & Labrador Legal Aid Commission
Cormack Bldg.
2 Steers Cove
PO Box 399 C
St. John's, NL A1C 5J9
709-753-7860 Fax: 709-753-6226 800-563-9911
www.gov.nf.ca/just/Other/otherx/legalaid.htm
The Legal Aid Commission ensures that persons with limited financial means have access to legal counsel.
• Royal Newfoundland Constabulary Public Complaints Commission
Bally Rou Place
#E-160, 280 Torbay Rd.
St. John's, NL A1A 3W8
709-729-0950 Fax: 709-729-1302
www.gov.nl.ca/rncpcc

Civil Law & Related Services
Asst. Deputy Minister, Heather Jacobs
709-729-2371, Fax: 709-729-2129
Director, Legal Services, Dianne Smith, Q.C.
709-729-3402, Fax: 709-729-2129
Director, Legal Information Services, Sean Dawe
709-729-2861, Fax: 709-729-1370,seand@gov.nl.ca

Public Protection & Support Services
Asst. Deputy Minister, Ralph Alcock
709-729-4896, Fax: 709-729-2129
Superintendent, Prisons, John Scoville
709-729-2978
Chief, Royal Newfoundland Constabulary, Joseph Browne
709-729-8151, Fax: 709-729-8214,
Director, Adult Corrections Division, Marvin McNutt
709-729-3880, Fax: 709-729-2129
Manager, Victim Services, Ada Emberly
709-729-0900, Fax: 709-729-0053,adaemberley@gov.nl.ca

Senior Legislative Counsel
Asst. Deputy Minister, Calvin Lake
709-729-2881, Fax: 709-729-2129

Department of Labrador & Aboriginal Affairs

Confederation Bldg., East Block, 6th Fl., PO Box 8700, St. John's, NL A1B 4J6
709-729-4776, Fax: 709-729-4900, 877-788-8822
laa@gov.nl.ca
www.laa.gov.nl.ca

Responsible for coordinating government's activities related to Labrador Affairs & Aboriginal Affairs, including developing policy & programs, managing federal-provincial agreements, negotiating land claims, public information & all matters of significant public interest in Labrador.The principal tasks of the Department in the field of Aboriginal Affairs are policy development for Aboriginal issues, negotiating land claims treaties & self-government agreements, implementing & managing land claims agreements once achieved & providing public information & education in matters related to land claims.The principal tasks of the Department in the field of Labrador Affairs are developing policies & programs related to significant issues of Government interest in Labrador, managing Federal-Provincial Agreements related to the development of Labrador & managing Federal-Provincial Agreements for the Innu & Inuit communities of Labrador.

Minister Responsible, Labrador Affairs, Hon. John Hickey
709-896-3099, Fax: 709-896-4285,JHickey@gov.nl.ca
Minister Responsible, Aboriginal Affairs, Hon. Patty Pottle
709-729-1069, 877-788-8822,Fax:
709-729-4900,pattypottle@gov.nl.ca

Deputy Minister, Robert Coombs
709-896-1711, Fax: 709-896-4648
Assistant Deputy Minister, Resource Planning & Development, Ron Bowles
709-896-4449, Fax: 709-896-0045,rabowles@gov.nl.ca
Director, Communications, Lori Lee Oates
709-729-3733, Fax: 709-729-0360,oatesll@gov.nl.ca
Director, Resource Planning & Development, Michelle Watkins
709-896-1780, Fax:
709-896-0045,michellewatkins@gov.nl.ca
Senior Negotiator, Innu Land Claims, Robert Pelley
709-729-0166, Fax: 709-729-4900,bpelley@gov.nl.ca
Senior Negotiator, Inuit Land Claims, Ruby Carter
709-729-0137, Fax: 709-729-4900,rcarter@gov.nl.ca
Acting Administrator, Policy & Planning, David Hughes
709-729-4665, Fax: 709-729-4900,dhughes@gov.nl.ca

Department of Municipal Affairs

West Block, Main Fl., Confederation Bldg., PO Box 8700, St. John's, NL A1B 4J6
709-729-3053,
www.ma.gov.nl.ca

Works with municipalities to ensure communities are properly managed & planned to ensure residents have a high standard of living in a clean, healthy & safe environment.The department is responsible for community-related activities such as the Office of the Fire Commissioner, the Emergency Measures Organization, Engineering & Land Use Planning.

Acts Administered:
Assessment Act
Avian Emblem Act
Building Standards Act
City of Corner Brook Act
City of Mount Pearl Act
City of St. John's Act
Coat of Arms Act
Commemoration Day Act
Crown Corporations Local Taxation Act
Emergency Measures Act
Evacuated Communities Act
Family Homes Expropriation Act
Fire Prevention Act
Floral Emblem Act
Housing Act
Labrador Act
Mineral Emblem Act
Municipal Affairs Act
Municipal Elections Act
Municipalities Act
Provincial Anthem Act
Provincial Flag Act
Remembrance Day Act
Regional Service Boards Act
St. John's Assessment Act
St. John's Centennial Foundation Act
St. John's Municipal Council Parks Act
St. John's Municipal Elections Act
Standard Time Act
Taxation of Utilities & Cable Television Companies Act
Urban & Rural Planning Act, 2000

Minister,Hon. Dave Denine
709-729-3048, Fax: 709-729-0943,davedenine@gov.nl.ca
Deputy Minister, Rose Baxter
709-729-3052, Fax: 709-729-0943,brose@gov.nl.ca
Assistant Deputy Minister, Municipal Support & Policy, Lori Anne Companion
709-729-3066, Fax:
709-729-4475,loriannecompanion@gov.nl.ca
Director, Fire & Emergency Services, Fred Hollett
709-729-1608, Fax: 709-729-2524
Director, Communications, Jennifer Collingwood
709-729-1983, Fax:
709-729-0943,jennifercollingwood@gov.nl.ca

• Office of the Fire Commissioner
2 Wellon Dr.
Deer Lake, NL A8A 2G5
709-635-4153 Fax: 709-635-4163

Department of Natural Resources

Natural Resources Bldg., 50 Elizabeth Ave., 7th Fl., PO Box 8700, St. John's, NL A1B 4J6
709-729-2920, Fax: 709-729-0059,
www.nr.gov.nl.ca

Responsible for the management of the province's mineral, energy, land, forest & wildlife resources in a manner that will ensure optimum benefits for the people of the province.

Acts Administered:
Animal Protection Act
Canada-Newfoundland Atlantic Accord Implementation (Newfoundland) Act, 1986
Dog Act
Electrical Power Control Act
Food & Drug Act
Forest Protection Act
Forestry Act
Heritage Animals Act
Hydro Corporation Act
Livestock Act
Livestock Health Act
Livestock Insurance Act
Lower Churchill Development Act
Meat Inspection Act
Mineral Act
Mineral Holdings Impost Act
Mining Act
Motorized Snow Vehicles & All-Terrain Vehicles Act (Shared with Government Services)
Natural Products Marketing Act
Petroleum & Natural Gas Act
Plant Protection Act
Poultry & Poultry Products Act
Quarry Materials Act
Undeveloped Minerals Areas Act
Vegetable Grading Act
Veterinary Medical Act
Wildlife Act

Minister,Hon. Kathy Dunderdale
709-729-2920, Fax:
709-729-0059,KathyDunderdale@gov.nl.ca
Deputy Minister, Chris Kieley
709-729-2766, Fax: 709-729-0059,chriskieley@gov.nl.ca
Assistant Deputy Minister, Keith Deering
709-729-2269, Fax: 709-637-2461,keithdeering@gov.nl.ca
Director, Communications, Tracy Barron
709-729-5282, Fax: 709-729-0059,tracybarron@gov.nl.ca
Director, Financial Operations, Leonard Clarke
709-729-5054
Director, Mineral Lands, Kenneth Andrews
709-729-6425, Fax: 709-729-6782,kenandrews@gov.nl.ca
Director, Animal Health & Provincial Veterinarian, Dr. Hugh Whitney
709-729-6879, Fax: 709-729-0055,hughwhitney@gov.nl.ca

• Canada-Newfoundland Offshore Petroleum Board
TD Place
140 Water St., 5th Fl.
St. John's, NL A1C 6H6
709-778-1400 Fax: 709-778-1473
postmaster@cnlopb.nl.ca
www.cnlopb.nl.ca

The Canada-Newfoundland Offshore Petroleum Board manages the petroleum resources in the Newfoundland offshore area on behalf of the Government of Canada & the Government of Newfoundland & Labrador. The Board's authority is derived from the legislation implementing the 1985 Atlantic Accord between the two governments.The Environmental Affairs department ensures that offshore oil & gas industrial activities proceed in an environmentally acceptable manner & evaluates the effect of the offshore environment upon the safety of offshore activities & by ensuring protection of the environment during the conduct of these activities. Working in close consultation with the Operations & Safety department, Environmental Affairs assesses the effects of environmental conditions, such as winds, waves & ice conditions, in the Newfoundland offshore area upon the safety of operations. Environmental Affairs reviews operators' plans for collecting the weather, oceanographic & ice data that they are required to measure at offshore

Agrifoods Branch

Provincial Agriculture Bldg., Brookfield Rd., PO Box 8700, St. John's, NL A1B 4J6
709-729-6588, Fax: 709-729-2674

To contribute to economic & rural development throughout the province by promoting the continued development, expansion & diversification of competitive & sustainable primary & value-added agrifood businesses.

Asst. Deputy Minister, Jeffrey Whalen
709-729-3787, Fax: 709-729-0973,jeffwhalen@gov.nl.ca
Director, Animal Health Division & Provincial Veterinarian,Dr. Hugh Whitney
709-729-6879, Fax: 709-729-0055,hughwhitney@gov.nl.ca
Director, Agriculture Business Development Division, Cindy MacDonald
709-637-2077
Director, Production & Marketing Division, Dave Mackey
709-729-6758
Director, Land Resource Stewardship, Jeff Whalen
709-637-2081, Fax: 709-637-2586

Energy Branch

Acting Deputy Minister, Pierre Tobin
709-729-2349, Fax: 709-729-2871,ptobin@gov.nl.ca
Director, Electricity Industry Development, David Bazeley
709-729-6760, Fax: 709-729-2508,dbazeley@gov.nl.ca
Assistant Deputy Minister, Petroleum Resources Development, Wes Foote
709-729-2206, Fax: 709-729-2508,wesfoote@gov.nl.ca
Director, Regulatory Affairs/Energy Policy, Fred Allen
709-729-2778, Fax: 709-729-2508,fredallen@gov.nl.ca

Forest Resources

Fortis Bldg., PO Box 2006, Corner Brook, NL A2H 6J8
709-637-2284, Fax: 709-634-4378

Manages & conserves the Province's ecosystems, under the principles of sustainable development, using an ecologically based management philosophy, & sound environmental practices. This is achieved through the implementation of forest management programs, such as silviculture, access road construction, forest fire suppression, insect control, management planning, tree nursery operations, inventory, dealing with wildlife in residential areas, collisions or similar situations, & public relations. In addition the Department is responsible for issuing permits under various legislation as well as the enforcement of forestry & wildlife regulations in such areas as hunting & timber harvesting.

Forestry Branch (Newfoundland Forest Service) (NFS)

Fortis Bldg., PO Box 2006, Corner Brook, NL A2H 6J8
709-637-2349, Fax: 709-637-2403

CEO, Len Moores
709-637-2339, Fax: 709-637-2461
Director, Forest Engineering & Industry Services, Gerald Fleming
709-637-2349, Fax: 709-637-2403,gfleming@gov.nl.ca
Director, Forest Ecosystem Management, Ivan Downton
709-634-2284, idownton@gov.nl.ca
Director, Legislation & Compliance, Tony Porter
709-535-0102, Fax: 709-535-0102,tonyporter@gov.nl.ca

Mines Branch

Promotes & facilitates the sustainable development of the province's mineral & energy resources through its resource assessment, management & development activities for the overall benefit of the citizens of Newfoundland & Labrador.

Asst. Deputy Minister, Richard Wardle
709-729-2768, Fax: 709-729-2871,richardwardle@gov.nl.ca
Director, Mineral Lands Division, Kenneth Andrews
709-729-6425, Fax: 709-729-6782,kenandrews@gov.nl.ca
Acting Director, Mineral Development, John D. Davis
709-729-6449, Fax: 709-729-3493,johnddavis@gov.nl.ca
Asst. Deputy Minister, Industrial Benefits, Brian Condon
709-729-1644, Fax: 709-729-0868,bcondon@gov.nl.ca

Geological Survey

709-729-4014, Fax: 709-729-4270

Director, Dave Liverman
709-729-4014, Fax: 709-729-4270,dliverman@gov.nl.ca

Eastern

PO Box 2222, Gander, NL A1V 5T4
709-256-1450, Fax: 709-256-1459

Regional Ecosystem Director, David Fong
709-256-1451

Labrador

PO Box 3014 B, Happy Valley-Goose Bay, NL A0P 1E0
709-896-3405,
Other Communication: Fax: 709-896-3747 (Forestry); 896-0188 (Wildlife)

Regional Manager, Mildred Johnson
709-896-2732, Fax: 709-896-3747,mildredjohnson@gov.nl.ca

Western

Massey Drive Bldg., PO Box 2006, Corner Brook, NL A2H 6J8
709-637-2409, Fax: 709-639-1377

Regional Ecosystem Director, Perry Benoit
709-637-2692
District Manager, Ed Stewart
District Manager, William Clarke
District Manager, George Gibbons
District Manager, Hubert Smith

Newfoundland & Labrador Public Service Commission

2 Canada Dr., 3rd Fl., PO Box 8700, St. John's, NL A1B 4J6
709-729-5810, Fax: 709-729-6234,
www.gov.nl.ca/psc

Chair/CEO, Ed Walsh
709-729-2650, Fax: 709-729-3178,ewalsh@gov.nl.ca
Vice-Chair, Keith Barry
709-729-2651, Fax: 709-729-3178,keithbarry@gov.nl.ca
Commissioner, Ann Chafe
709-729-2659, Fax: 709-729-3178,annchafe@gov.nl.ca

Public Service Secretariat

Confederation Bldg., Main Fl., East Block, PO Box 8700, St. John's, NL A1B 4J6
709-729-6479, Fax: 709-729-2156

Deputy Minister, David Gale
709-729-2633, Fax: 709-729-1746
Asst. Deputy Minister, Human Resources, Marilyn Field
709-729-3106, Fax: 709-729-1746
Asst. Deputy Minister, Labour Relations & Classifications, David Norman
709-729-3559, Fax: 709-729-1746
Director, Classification, Organization & Management, Marilyn Thompson
709-729-3387, Fax: 709-729-2156,marilynthompson@gov.nl.ca
Director, Collective Bargaining, Geoff Williams
709-729-1585, Fax: 709-729-2156
Officer, Human Resources Development & Services, Renee Tinkov
709-729-5201, Fax: 709-729-5421,rtinkov@gov.nl.ca

Newfoundland & Labrador Board of Commissioners of Public Utilities

PO Box 21040, St. John's, NL A1A 5B2
709-726-8600, Fax: 709-726-9604, 866-782-0006
ito@pub.nf.ca
www.pub.nf.ca

Regulates electrical utilities in Newfoundland & Labrador.
Acts Administered:
Act to Amend the Electric Power Control Act
Automobile Insurance Act
Electric Power Control Act
Expropriation Act
Motor Carrier Act
Motor Vehicle Act
Petroleum Products Act
Public Utilities Act
Public Utilities Acquisition of Lands Act
Chair & CEO, Andy Wells
709-726-1133, awells@pub.nl.ca,
Vice-Chair, Darlene Whalen
709-726-0955, dwhalen@pub.nl.ca
Director, Corporate Services & Board Secretary, G. Cheryl Blundon
709-726-8600, Fax: 709-726-9604,cblundon@pub.nl.ca
Director, Regulatory & Advisory Services, Robert Byrne
709-726-0742, rbyrne@pub.nl.ca

Provincial Advisory Council on the Status of Women

#103, 15 Hallett Cres., St. John's, NL A1B 4C4
709-753-7270, Fax: 709-753-2606, 877-753-7270
info@pacsw.ca
www.pacsw.com

Minister Responsible,Hon. Joan Burke
709-729-5040, Fax: 709-729-0414
President, Leslie MacLeod
lesliemacleod@pacsw.ca
Policy Analyst, Elaine Wychreschuk
elainewychreschuk@pacsw.ca
Director, Communications, Danielle Finney
daniellefinney@pacsw.ca
Office Manager, Sandy Abbott
709-753-7270, Fax: 709-753-2606,sandyabbot@pacsw.ca

Department of Tourism, Culture & Recreation

Confederation Bldg., West Block, 2nd Fl., PO Box 8700, St. John's, NL A1B 4J6
709-729-0862, Fax: 709-729-0870,
tcrinfo@gov.nl.ca
www.tcr.gov.nl.ca

Ensures the development of provincial vacation & business travel markets.The department conserves, preserves & protects natural & cultural resources & promotes the resources for economic benefit, sport & recreation in the province. It also protects, preserves & develops the historic resources of the province.Programs promote the development of travel & tourism & assist in transforming the province's natural & cultural attractions into opportunities for employment & revenue generation.
Acts Administered:
Arts Council Act
Books Preservation of Copies Act
Boxing Authority Act
Colonial Buildings Act
Cruiseship Authority Act
Grand Concourse Authority Act
Historic Resources Act
Newspapers & Books Act
Rooms Act
Tourist Establishments Act
Minister,Hon. Clyde Jackman
709-729-0659, 877-787-0707,Fax: 709-729-0662,clydejackman@gov.nl.ca
Deputy Minister, Brent Meade
709-729-3555, Fax: 709-729-0662,bmeade@gov.nl.ca
Director, Communications, Heather May
709-729-0928, Fax: 709-729-0662,heathermay@gov.nl.ca
Director, Human Resources, Gerry Crocker
709-729-5292, gcrocker@gov.nl.ca
Director, Tourism Marketing, Carmela Murphy
709-729-2831, Fax: 709-729-0057,carmelamurphy@gov.nl.ca
Director, Strategic Planning & Policy, Janet Miller-Pitt
709-729-5623, Fax: 709-729-0870,jpitt@gov.nl.ca
Director, Arts & Culture Centers, Doreen McCarthy
709-729-3453, Fax: 709-729-5444
Director, Recreation & Sport, Jim Tee
709-729-5241, Fax: 709-729-5293
• Newfoundland & Labrador Film Development Corporation
12 King's Bridge Rd.
St. John's, NL A1C 3K3
709-738-3456 Fax: 709-739-1680 877-738-3456
info@nlfdc.ca
www.nlfdc.ca

Culture & Heritage

The department administers archeology permits, the Art Procurement Program, the Heritage Foundation of Newfoundland & Labrador, provides grants to artists, arts organizations, museums & archives through the Newfoundland & Labrador Arts Council, provides grants to assists the Newfoundland & Labrador Film Development Corporation & administers provincial historic sites.
Asst. Deputy Minister,Vacant
709-729-3609
Director, Culture, Recreation & Sport, Jim Tee
709-729-5241, Fax: 709-729-5293
Director, Art Gallery of Newfoundland & Labrador, Shauna McCabe
709-757-8042, Fax: 709-757-8041
Director, Arts & Culture Centres, Doreen McCarthy
709-729-3453
Manager, Cultural Affairs, Elizabeth A. Channing
709-729-3905, Fax: 709-729-5952
Director, Newfoundland Museum, Penney Houlden
709-757-8022, Fax: 709-757-8021
CEO, The Rooms, Dean Brinton
709-757-8012, Fax: 709-757-8017
Director, Heritage, Jerry Dick
709-729-7393, Fax: 709-729-0870,jerrydick@gov.nl.ca

Tourism

Asst. Deputy Minister, Mary Taylor-Ash
709-729-2821, Fax: 709-729-5293,mtaylorash@gov.nl.ca
Director, Tourism Product Development, Juanita Keel-Ryan
709-729-1708, Fax: 709-729-0474,jkeelryan@gov.nl.ca
Director, Tourism Marketing Division, Carmela Murphy
709-729-2831, Fax: 709-729-0057
Manager, Labrador Regional Office, Rose Dyson
709-896-8480
Manager, Education & Promotion, Sharon Porter
709-729-2418, Fax: 709-729-1100
Officer, Historic Sites, Frank Browne
709-729-7957
Manager, Advertising & Communications, Andrea Peddle
709-729-0559, Fax: 709-729-0057,apeddle@gov.nl.ca
Manager, Provincial Training Centre, David Garland
709-729-2792
Manager, Visitor Services, Glen Ryan
709-729-2427, Fax: 709-729-0474,gryan@gov.nl.ca
Manager, Travel Trade, Charlotte Jewczyk
709-729-0992, Fax: 709-729-0057,cjewczyk@gov.nl.ca

Department of Transportation & Works

Confederation Bldg., West Block, 6th Fl., PO Box 8700, St. John's, NL A1B 4J6
709-729-3679, Fax: 709-729-4285,
twminister@gov.nl.ca
www.tw.gov.nl.ca

To provide a safe, efficient & sustainable transportation system & to provide landlord services & support services such as leasing & mail services for all government departments. The department liaises with other agencies & the federal government to ensure the overall public works & transportation needs & interest of the province are fully provided & protected.
Acts Administered:
Expropriation Act
Local Road Boards Act
Motor Carrier Act
Pippy Park Commission Act
Rail Services Act
Transportation & Works Act
Minister,Hon. Dianne C. Whalen
709-729-3679, 866-996-5670,Fax: 709-729-4285,twminister@gov.nl.ca
Deputy Minister, Robert Smart
709-729-3676, Fax: 709-729-4285
Director, Communications, David Salter
709-729-3015, Fax: 709-729-4285,davidsalter@gov.nl.ca
Solicitor, George Horan
709-729-1966, Fax: 709-729-6934,georgehoran@gov.nl.ca
Director, Financial Operations, Kevin Antle
709-729-5356, Fax: 709-729-0703

Transportation Services

Asst. Deputy Minister, Cluney Mercer
709-729-3796, Fax: 709-729-0283,mercerc@gov.nl.ca
Director, Highway Design & Construction, Gary Gosse
709-729-5483, Fax: 709-729-0283
Senior Engineer, Highway Design, Garry Spencer
709-729-7293, Fax: 709-729-0283
Chief Operating Officer, Marine Services, Tom Prim
709-429-3278, Fax: 709-729-6934

Works Branch

709-729-3019, Fax: 709-729-4658

Asst. Deputy Minister, Weldon Moores
709-729-6882, Fax: 709-729-3418,wmoores@gov.nl.ca
Director, Design & Construction, Gunar Leja
709-729-1969, Fax: 709-729-0646,lejag@gov.nl.ca
Director, Engineering Support Services, Keith Noel
709-729-5786, Fax: 709-729-5934,noelka@gov.nl.ca
Director, Realty Services, Martin Balodis
709-729-3690, Fax: 709-729-0984
Regional Director, Works - Avalon, Dave Roberts
709-729-1355, Fax: 709-729-0036,robertsd@gov.nl.ca
Regional Director, Works - Central, Barry Day
709-256-1000, Fax: 709-256-1013,daybc@gov.nl.ca

Newfoundland & Labrador Workplace Health, Safety & Compensation Commission

146 - 148 Forest Rd., PO Box 9000, St. John's, NL A1A 3B8
709-778-1000, Fax: 709-738-1714, 800-563-9000
general.inquiries@whscc.nl.ca
www.whscc.nf.ca

Other Communication: Grand Falls toll-free: 800/563-3448; Corner Brook toll-free: 800/563-2772

Utilizing skilled, professional employees, in partnership with workplace parties, the commission facilitates safe & healthy workplaces by assisting employers & workers to prevent accidents, & manage workplace injuries/illnesses & return-to-work processes. Operating as the administrator of the workers' compensation insurance program, the commission provides a reasonable level of benefits to injured workers & their dependents based on reasonable assessment rates for employers, while maintaining or exceeding service level performance when compared to other jurisdictions in Canada.
Chair, Ralph Tucker
CEO, Leslie Galway

Government of the Northwest Territories

Seat of Government:PO Box 1320, Yellowknife, NT X1A 2L9
www.gov.nt.ca

The Northwest Territories was reconstituted September 1, 1905.It has an area of 1,140,834.90 km2, & the StatsCan population in 2006 was 41,464. On April 1, 1999, the Northwest Territories was divided into two new territories: Nunavut Territories and the as yet unnamed territory (known as the Northwest Territories). The Northwest Territories is governed by a fully elected Legislative Assembly of 19 members elected for a four-year term. Government is by consensus rather than party politics. The Legislature elects the Premier & a seven-member Executive Council, which is charged with the operation of government & the establishment of program & spending priorities. The Commissioner of the Northwest Territories is appointed by the Federal Government, & serves a role similar to that of a Lieutenant Governor in provincial jurisdictions.

Department of the Executive

PO Box 1320, Yellowknife, NT X1A 2L9
executive@gov.nt.ca

Minister,Hon. Floyd Roland
867-669-2311, floyd_roland@gov.nt.ca

Cabinet Secretariat

867-873-7817, Fax: 867-873-0279

Secretary to Cabinet, Dave Ramsden
867-873-7100, dave_ramsden@gov.nt.ca
Deputy Secretary to Cabinet, Alan Cash
867-873-7652, Fax: 867-873-0279,alan_cash@gov.nt.ca
Asst. Deputy Minister, Executive Operations, David Stewart
867-873-7823, david_stewart@gov.nt.ca

Director, Corporate Services, Cathy Myres
867-873-7148, cathy_myres@gov.nt.ca
Advisor, Status of Women, Gail Cyr
867-920-3106, gail_cyr@gov.nt.ca
Chief of Protocol, Carmen Moore
867-873-7167, carmen_moore@gov.nt.ca
Territorial Statistician, Bureau of Statistics, Angelo Cocco
867-873-7147, angelo_cocco@gov.nt.ca

Office of the Commissioner

#803 Northwest Tower, PO Box 1320, Yellowknife, NT X1A 2L9
867-873-7400, Fax: 867-873-0223, 888-270-3318
commissioner@gov.nt.ca
www.commissioner.gov.nt.ca

Commissioner,Hon. Anthony W.J. Whitford
867-873-7400, Fax: 867-873-0223
Asst. to the Commissioner, Phila Fyten
867-873-7332, phila_fyten@gov.nt.ca

Office of the Premier

Legislative Assembly Bldg., PO Box 1320, Yellowknife, NT X1A 2L9
867-669-2311, Fax: 867-873-0385,
premier@gov.nt.ca
www.premier.gov.nt.ca

Premier,Hon. Floyd Roland
867-669-2311, 800-661-0784,Fax:
867-873-0385,floyd_roland@gov.nt.ca
Communications Coordinator, Julia Mott
867-669-2304, julia_mott@gov.nt.ca,

Executive Council

PO Box 1320, Yellowknife, NT X1A 2L9
executive@gov.nt.ca
www.executive.gov.nt.ca

Other Communication: Protocol: executive_protocol@gov.nt.ca; Corporate Communications: executive_communications@gov.nt.ca; Corporate Services:executive_services@gov.nt.ca

Coordination & advisory functions are performed for the Government of the Northwest Territories.

Premier & Minister, Finance; Minister, Executive; Minister, Aboriginal Affairs & Intergovernmental Relations,Hon. Floyd Roland
867-669-2311, 800-661-0784,Fax:
867-873-0385,floyd_roland@gov.nt.ca
Deputy Premier & Minister, Environment & Natural Resources; Government House Leader; Minister Responsible for the Workers Com,Hon. J.Michael Miltenberger
867-669-2355, Fax:
867-873-0169,michael_miltenberger@gov.nt.ca
Minister, Justice; Minister, Education, Culture & Employment; Minister Responsible, Homeless, Hon. Jackson Lafferty
867-669-2399, Fax:
867-873-0169,jackson_lafferty@gov.nt.ca
Minister, Human Resources; Minister, Industry, Tourism & Investment; Minister Responsible, Public Utilities Board, Hon. Bob McLeod
867-669-2388, Fax: 867-873-0169,bob_mcleod@gov.nt.ca
Minister, Public Works & Services;Minister, Municipal & Community Affairs; Minister Responsible, Youth; Minister Responsible,Transportation, Hon. Michael McLeod
867-669-2377, Fax:
867-873-0169,michael_mcleod@gov.nt.ca
Minister, Health & Social Services; Minister Responsible, Status of Women; Minister Responsible, Persons with Disabilities, Hon. Sandy Lee
867-669-2344, Fax: 867-873-0169,sandy_lee@gov.nt.ca

Intergovernmental Affairs - Ottawa

613-234-6525, Fax: 613-234-9667

Legislation & House Planning

Legislative Coordinator, Kevin O'Keefe
867-669-2239, Fax: 867-873-0139,kevin_o'keefe@gov.nt.ca

Legislative Assembly

c/o Clerk's Office, PO Box 1320, Yellowknife, NT X1A 2L9
867-669-2299, Fax: 867-920-4735, 800-661-0784
www.assembly.gov.nt.ca

Clerk, Tim Mercer
867-669-2299, tim_mercer@gov.nt.ca
Speaker, Paul Delorey
867-669-2233, Fax: 867-873-0273,paul_delorey@gov.nt.ca
Deputy Clerk, Doug Schauerte
867-669-2277, doug_schauerte@gov.nt.ca
Director, Library Services, Vera Raschke
867-669-2203, Fax: 867-873-0207,vera_raschke@gov.nt.ca
Director, Corporate Services, Olin Lovely
867-669-2334, Fax: 867-920-4735,olin_lovely@gov.nt.ca
Director, Research Services, Colette Langlois
867-669-2212, colette_langlois@gov.nt.ca
Public Affairs & Communications Advisor, Danielle O'Neill
867-669-2230, danielle_o'neill@gov.nt.ca.ca

Elections NWT/Plebiscite Office

PO Box 1320, Yellowknife, NT X1A 2L9
867-920-6999, Fax: 867-873-0366, 800-661-0796
www.electionsnwt.com

Chief Electoral Officer, Saundra Arberry
867-920-6999, saundra_arberry@gov.nt.ca

Office of the Languages Commissioner

PO Box 1320, Yellowknife, NT X1A 2L9
867-873-7034, Fax: 888-305-7353, 800-661-0889

Languages Commissioner, Shannon Gullberg
876-873-7034, shannon_gullberg@gov.nt.ca
Information & Privacy Commissioner, Elaine Keenan-Bengts
867-669-0976, Fax: 867-920-2511,atippcom@theedge.ca
Conflict of Interest Commissioner, Gerald Gerrand
867-669-2298, Fax: 867-873-0276

Standing Committees of the Legislature

www.assembly.gov.nt.ca/_live/pages/wpPages/Committees.aspx
Priorities & Planning; Economic Development & Infrastructure; Rules & Procedures; Government Operations; Social Programs

Sixteenth Legislature - Northwest Territories

PO Box 1320, Yellowknife, NT X1A 2L9
867-669-2200, Fax: 867-920-4735, 800-661-0784

Last General Election: October 17, 2007. Maximum Duration: Four years. Salaries, Indemnities & Allowances (April 1, 2007): Members of the Legislative Assembly are entitled to a basic indemnity of $90,199. Members are entitled to a non-taxable annual expense allowance of $6,988 for a Ministers or fors Members living within commuting distance of the capital. Members, who are not Ministers, & who do not live within commuting distance of the capital, are entitled to $10,797 annually. Up to $27,840 annually is paid to Members for accommodation, when their residence is not within 80 km of Yellowknife, & when they are attending sittings of the Legislature & performing constituency duties in Yellowknife. Members will be deducted $127 for each morning or afternoon that they fail to attend the sitting of the Legislature. Members are also provided with a set operating budget to defray the expenses of working on behalf of their constituents. In addition are the following remunerations: Premier $68,602; Minister $48,275; Speaker $39,260; Deputy Speaker $6,352; Deputy Chairperson of Committee of the Whole $3,812; Chairperson of a Standing Committee $5,628. The following is a list of members of the Legislative Assembly. The address in Yellowknife to reach all ML As is as follows: PO Box 1320, Yellowknife, NT, X1A 2L9.

Members

Glen Abernethy, Yellowknife - Great Slave
867-669-2290, Fax: 867-873-0276,glen_abernethy@gov.nt.ca
Tom Beaulieu, Tu Nedhe
867-669-2287, Fax: 867-873-0276,tom_beaulieu@gov.nt.ca, Other Communications: Additional Phone: 867-444-8463
Wendy Bisaro, Yellowknife - Frame Lake
867-669-2274, Fax: 867-873-0276,wendy_bisaro@gov.nt.ca
Bob Bromley, Yellowknife - Weledeh
867-669-2272, Fax: 867-873-0276,bob_bromley@gov.nt.ca
Hon. Paul Delorey, Hay River North NT
867-874-6301, Fax: 867-874-6079,paul_delorey@gov.nt.ca, Other Communications: Speaker's Office: 867-669-2234; Fax: 867-873-0273
Jane Groenewegen, Hay River South NT
867-874-6141, Fax:
867-874-6143,jane_groenewegen@gov.nt.ca, Other Communications: Yellowknife Phone: 867-669-2292; Fax: 867-873-0276
Robert Hawkins, Yellowknife Centre
867-669-2265, Fax: 867-873-0276,robert_hawkins@gov.nt.ca
Jackie Jacobson, Nunakput
867-669-2276, Fax:
867-873-0276,jackie_jacobson@gov.nt.ca
Hon. David Krutko, Mackenzie Delta NT
867-952-2652, david_m_krutko@gov.nt.ca, Other Communications: Yellowknife Phone: 867-669-2285; Fax: 867-873-0274
Hon. Jackson Lafferty, Monfwi
867-669-2399, Fax:
867-873-0169,jackson_lafferty@gov.nt.ca
Hon. Sandy Lee, Yellowknife - Range Lake
867-669-2344, Fax: 867-873-0169,sandy_lee@gov.nt.ca
Hon. Bob McLeod, Yellowknife South
867-669-2388, Fax: 867-873-0169,bob_mcleod@gov.nt.ca
Hon. Michael McLeod, Deh Cho NT
867-874-5967, Fax:
867-874-5968,michael_mcleod@gov.nt.ca, Other Communications: Minister's Office: 867-669-2377; Fax: 867-873-0169
Robert C. McLeod, Inuvik Twin Lakes
867-669-2279, Fax: 867-873-0276,robert_mcleod@gov.nt.ca, Other Communications: Additional Phone: 867-678-0319
Kevin A. Menicoche, Nahendeh NT
867-695-3780, Fax:
867-695-3781,kevin_menicoche@gov.nt.ca, Other Communications: Yellowknife Phone: 867-669-2294; Fax: 867-873-0276
Hon. J. Michael Miltenberger, Thebacha NT
867-872-5511, Fax:
867-872-5642,michael_miltenberger@gov.nt.ca, Other Communications: Minister's Office: 867-669-2355; Fax: 867-873-0169,
David Ramsay, Kam Lake
867-669-2296, Fax: 867-873-0276,david_ramsay@gov.nt.ca
Hon. Floyd K. Roland, Inuvik BootLake NT
867-777-4693, 800-661-0784,Fax:
867-777-4694,floyd_roland@gov.nt.ca, Other Communications: Premier's Office: 867-669-2311; Fax: 867-873-0385
Hon. Norman Yakeleya, Sahtu
867-669-2366, Fax:
867-873-0169,norman_yakeleya@gov.nt.ca

Northwest Territories Government Departments & Agencies

Department of Aboriginal Affairs & Intergovernmental Relations

4910 - 52nd St., PO Box 1320, Yellowknife, NT X1A 2L9
867-873-7143, Fax: 867-873-0233, 877-838-8194
nancy_gardiner @gov.nt.ca
www.daair.gov.nt.ca

The Department of Aboriginal Affairs & Intergovernmental Relations is charged with the following responsibilities: to negotiate, implement, & monitor land, resource & self-government agreements; to manage governmental relationships with Aboriginal, federal, provincial, & territorial governments, & with circumpolar countries; to provide advice on federal-provincial-territorial-Aboriginal relations; & to contribute to the political & constitutional development of the Northwest Territories.

Minister,Hon. Floyd Roland
867-669-2311, Fax: 867-873-0385,floyd_roland@gov.nt.ca
Deputy Minister, Gabriela Sparling
867-873-7143, Fax:
867-873-0233,gabriela_sparling@gov.nt.ca
Director, Intergovernmental Relations, Andy Bevan
867-920-8701, andy_bevan@gov.nt.ca
Director, Policy, Legislation & Communications, Vacant
867-920-3141, Fax: 867-873-0540
Director, Implementation, Scott Alexander
867-873-7149, Fax:
867-873-0540,scott_alexander@gov.nt.ca
Director, Negotiations, Fred Talen
867-873-7388, Fax: 867-873-0593,fred_talen@gov.nt.ca

Aurora Research Institute (ARI)

191 MacKenzie Rd., PO Box 1450, Inuvik, NT X0E 0T0
867-777-3298, Fax: 867-777-4264,
webmaster@nwtresearch.com
www.nwtresearch.com

A division of Aurora College that is dedicated to excellence, leadership & innovations in Northern education & research. Administers the research licencing provisions of the Northwest Territories Scientists Act & provides year round logistical assistance for researchers.

Director, Andrew Applejohn
867-777-3298, director@nwtresearch.com
Manager, Fort Smith, Ruthann Gal
867-872-4909, rgal@auroracollege.nt.ca
Manager, Scientific Services, Paulo Flieg
867-777-3298, licence@nwtresearch.com
Manager, Research & Technology, Sharon Katz
867-777-3298, skatz@auroracollege.nt.ca

Department of Education, Culture & Employment (ECE)

PO Box 1320, Yellowknife, NT X1A 2L9
867-669-2399, Fax: 867-873-0431, 866-606-5627
www.ece.gov.nt.ca

Other Communication: Jobs North Phone: 867-873-7690; Fax: 867-873-0636; Email: jobsnorth@gov.nt.ca

The Ministry's responsibilities cover the following areas: Early Childhood; Kindergarten to Grade 12; Adult & Post-Secondary Education; Career Development & Employment; Apprenticeship & Occupational Certification; Culture, Heritage & Languages; Income Security; & Labour Services.
Acts Administered:
Apprenticeship, Trade & Occupations Certification Act
Archives Act
Child Day Care Act
Education Act
Library Act
Occupational Training Agreements Act
Official Languages Act
Public Colleges Act
Scientists Act
Senior Citizens Benefits Act
Social Assistance Act
Student Financial Assistance Act
Minister,Hon. Jackson Lafferty
867-669-2399, Fax:
867-873-0274,jackson_lafferty@gov.nt.ca
Deputy Minister, Dan Daniels
867-920-6240, Fax: 867-873-0338,dan_daniels@gov.nt.ca
Director, Strategic & Business Services, Paul Devitt
867-873-7739, Fax: 867-873-0338,paul_devitt@gov.nt.ca
Acting Director, Income Security, Aranka Raffai
867-920-8921, Fax: 867-873-0443,aranka_raffai@gov.nt.ca
Director, Official Languages, Albert Canadien
867-920-6484, Fax:
867-873-0185,albert_canadien@gov.nt.ca
Director, Education Operations & Development, Janet Grinsted
867-873-7673, Fax: 867-873-0338,janet_grinsted@gov.nt.ca
Directeur General, Commission scolaire francophone, Paul Theriault
867-873-6555, Fax: 867-873-5644,paul_theriault@gov.nt.ca
Supervisor, Student Financial Assistance, Nicole Beauchamp
867-920-6236, Fax:
867-873-0336,nicole_beauchamp@gov.nt.ca
• Northwest Territories Apprenticeship, Trade & Occupations Certification Board
PO Box 1320
Yellowknife, NT X1A 2L9
867-873-7357 Fax: 867-873-0200
• NWT Arts Council
PO Box 1320 Main
Yellowknife, NT X1A 2L9
867-920-6370 Fax: 867-873-0205
pwnhc.learnnet.nt.ca/artscouncil/

College & Careers Development Branch
867-873-7252, Fax: 867-873-0155
Asst. Deputy Minister, Advanced Education & Careers, Gloria Iatridis
867-873-7252, Fax: 867-873-0338,gloria_iatridis@gov.nt.ca
Director, College & Career Development, Laurie Clarke
867-873-7552, Fax: 867-873-0200,laurie_clarke@gov.nt.ca
Manager, Income Security Programs, Lois Walbourne
867-873-7746, Fax: 867-873-0443,lois_walbourne@gov.nt.ca

Education & Culture
867-920-8061, Fax: 867-873-0155,
Asst. Deputy Minister, Roy Erasmus
867-920-8061, Fax: 867-873-0338,roy_erasmus@gov.nt.ca
Director, Culture & Heritage, Charles Arnold
867-873-7551, charles_arnold@gov.nt.ca
Director, Early Childhood & School Services, Rita Mueller
867-920-3491, Fax: 867-873-0109,rita_mueller@gov.nt.ca
Territorial Archaeologist, Tom Andrews
867-873-7688, tom_andrews@gov.nt.ca
Territorial Archivist, Richard Valpy
867-873-7657, richard_valpy@gov.nt.ca
Territorial Librarian, Alison Hopkins
867-874-6531, Fax: 867-874-3321,alison_hopkins@gov.nt.ca

Department of Environment & Natural Resources (ENR)

PO Box 1320, Yellowknife, NT X1A 2L9
www.enr.gov.nt.ca
Operations cover a broad spectrum of activities directed at promoting a healthy environment that supports traditional lifestyles within a modern economy. The wise use & protection of natural resources are encouraged. The Department's activities are carried out through the following divisions: Environmental Protection, Forest Management, Policy, Legislation & Communications, Protected Areas Strategy, Informatics, & Wildlife.
Acts Administered:
Environmental Protection Act
Environmental Rights Act
Forest Management Act
Forest Protection Act
Natural Resources Conservation Trust Act
Pesticide Act
Waste Reduction & Recovery Act
Water Resources Agreement Act
Wildlife Act
Minister,Hon. J. Michael Miltenberger
867-669-2355, Fax:
867-873-0596,michael_miltenberger@gov.nt.ca
Deputy Minister, Gary Bohnet
867-873-7401, gary_bohnet@gov.nt.ca
Director, Policy & Strategic Planning, Doris Eggers
867-920-8046, Fax: 867-873-0114,doris_eggers@gov.nt.ca
Director, Shared Services, Finance & Administration, Nancy Magrum
867-920-8649, Fax:
867-873-0551,NANCY_MAGRUM@gov.nt.ca
Director, Shared Services & Informatics, Rick Wind
867-920-3327, Fax: 867-873-0293,rick_wind@gov.nt.ca
Director, Environment, Ray Case
867-873-7654, Fax: 867-873-0221,ray_case@gov.nt.ca
Director, Wildlife, Susan Fleck
867-920-8043, Fax: 867-873-0293,susan_fleck@gov.nt.ca
Director, Forest Management, William Mawdsley
867-872-7725, WILLIAM_MAWDSLEY@gov.nt.ca

Regional Offices:

Deh Cho
Milton Bldg., 2nd Fl., PO Box 240, Fort Simpson, NT X0E 0N0
867-695-7451, Fax: 867-695-2381
Regional Superintendent, Stephen Charlie
867-695-7451

Inuvik
Semmler Bldg., 2nd Fl., Bag Service #1, Inuvik, NT X0E 0T0
867-678-6651, Fax: 867-678-6659
Regional Superintendent, Ron Morrison
867-678-6651, ron_morrison@gov.nt.ca

North Slave
PO Box 2668, Yellowknife, NT X1A 2P9
867-920-6134, Fax: 867-873-6230
Acting Regional Superintendent, Lance Schmidt
867-920-6134, Fax: 867-873-6230,lance_schmidt@gov.nt.ca

Sahtu
PO Box 130, Norman Wells, NT X0E 0V0
867-587-3508
Regional Superintendent, Keith Hickling
867-587-3508, keith_hickling@gov.nt.ca

Fort Smith
Sweetgrass Bldg., PO Box 390, Fort Smith, NT X0E 0P0
867-872-6401, Fax: 867-872-4250
Regional Superintendent, Jack Bird
867-872-6401, jack_bird@gov.nt.ca

Department of Finance

YK Center, 3rd Fl., PO Box 1320, Yellowknife, NT X1A 2L9
867-669-2311, Fax: 867-873-0385,
www.fin.gov.nt.ca
The government of the Northwest Territories has a budget of over $700,000,000 (including federal government transfers of over $500,000,000). The Department of Finance obtains the financial resources to carry on the functions of government & for intergovernmental fiscal negotiations & arrangements.
Acts Administered:
Borrowing Authorization Act
Central Trust Company Act
Certified General Accountants' Association Act
Financial Agreement Act
Income Tax Act
Income Tax Collection Agreement Questions Act
Institute of Chartered Accountants Act
Insurance Act
Liquor Act
Loan Authorization Act
Northwest Territories Energy Corporation Ltd. Loan Guarantee Act
Payroll Tax Act, 1993
Petroleum Products Tax Act
Property & Assessment Taxation Act
Public Utilities Income Tax Rebates Act
Risk Capital Investment Tax Credit Act
Society of Management Accountants Act
Tobacco Tax Act
Minister,Hon. J. Michael Miltenberger
867-669-2355, Fax:
867-873-0169,michael_miltenberger@gov.nt.ca
Deputy Minister, Margaret M. Melhorn
867-873-7117, Fax:
867-873-0414,margaret_melhorn@gov.nt.ca
Director, Policy & Planning, Joseph LaFerla
867-920-6364, Fax: 867-873-0414,joseph_laferla@gov.nt.ca
• Northwest Territories Liquor Commission
#201, 31 Capital Dr.
Hay River, NT X0E 1G2
867-874-2100 Fax: 867-874-2180
• Northwest Territories Liquor Licensing Board
#210, 31 Capital Dr.
Hay River, NT X0E 1G2
867-874-2906 Fax: 867-874-6011
delilah_st-arneault@gov.nt.ca
• Northwest Territories Liquor Licensing & Enforcement
#210, 31 Capital Dr.
Hay River, NT X0E 1G2
867-874-2906 Fax: 867-874-6011

Finance & Administration
Fax: 867-873-0325
Director, Mel Enge
867-873-7158, mel_enge@gov.nt.ca

Fiscal Policy
Fax: 867-873-0381
Responsible for developing policies & providing research, analysis & recommendations on the fiscal policies of government. The Division also administers the Formula Financing Agreement with Canada & is responsible for intergovernmental fiscal relations.
Director, John Monroe
867-920-6436, john_monroe@gov.nt.ca
Manager, Tax Policy, Kim Vu
867-920-8891, kim_vu@gov.nt.ca
Manager, Fiscal Relations & Economic Policy, Kelly Bluck
867-873-7171, kelly_bluck@gov.nt.ca

Treasury
Fax: 867-873-0325, 800-661-0820
Treasury is responsible for managing the government's cash position; conducting banking, borrowing & investment activities; protecting the government's activities & assets from risk of loss by means of appropriate insurance coverage & risk management activities; & regulating insurance companies, agents, brokers & adjusters operating in the NWT.
Director, Doug Doak
867-920-3423, doug_doak@gov.nt.ca

Financial Management Board Secretariat (FMBS)

c/o Secretary of the FMB / Comptroller General, 5003 - 49 St., PO Box 1320, Yellowknife, NT X1A 2L9
867-873-7211, Fax: 867-873-0112,
www.fmbs.gov.nt.ca
Coordinating & promoting the efficient use of the Government's financial & information resources are the chief responsibilities of the Financial Management Board Secretariat. The central agency, that supports the Minister of Finance, provides leadership in functions related to governmental business planning, information management, & program & service evaluation. The FMBS also supports sustainable resource development, self-government development, & the improvement of programs & services.
Minister Responsible,Hon. J. Michael Miltenberger
867-669-2355, Fax:
867-873-0385,michael_miltenberger@gov.nt.ca
Secretary & Comptroller General, Margaret Melhorn
867-873-7117, Fax:
867-873-0414,margaret_melhorn@gov.nt.ca
Chief Information Officer, Fred Ruthven
867-920-8963, Fax: 867-873-0128,fred_ruthven@gov.nt.ca
Director, Policy & Planning, Robert Taggart
867-873-7127, Fax: 877-873-0128,robert_taggart@gov.nt.ca
Deputy Secretary, Budgeting & Evaluation, Sandy Kalgutkar
867-920-8689, Fax:
867-873-0258,sandy_kalgutkar@gov.nt.ca
Director, Audit Bureau, Bob Shahi
867-873-7700, Fax: 867-873-0209,bob_shahi@gov.nt.ca
Assistant Comptroller General, Louise Lavoie
867-920-3254, Fax: 867-873-0296,louise_lavoie@gov.nt.ca

Vital Statistics
Bag #9, Inuvik, NT X0E 0T0
867-777-7400, Fax: 867-777-3197, 800-661-0830
hsa@gov.nt.ca
Birth certificates: $10
Registrar General, Donna Manuel
867-777-7400, donna_manuel@gov.nt.ca

Regional & Community Boards:

Deh Cho
PO Box 246, Fort Simpson, NT X0E 0N0
867-695-3815, Fax: 867-695-2920

Tlicho
Bag #5, Behchoko, NT X0E 0Y0

867-392-3000, Fax: 867-392-3001,

Fort Smith
PO Box 1080, Fort Smith, NT X0E 0P0
867-872-6200, Fax: 867-872-6275

Hay River
3 Gaetz Dr., Hay River, NT X0E 0R8
867-874-7100, Fax: 867-874-7118

Beaufort-Delta
Bag #2, 285 Mackenzie Rd., Inuvik, NT X0E 0T0
867-777-8000, Fax: 867-777-8062

Sahtu
PO Box 340, Norman Wells, NT X0E 0V0
867-587-3652, Fax: 867-587-3436

Stanton
PO Box 10, Yellowknife, NT X1A 2N1
867-669-4224, Fax: 867-669-4128,
www.srhb.org

Yellowknife
Jan Stirling Bldg., 4702 Franklin Ave., PO Box 608, Yellowknife, NT X1A 2N5
867-873-7276, Fax: 867-920-7025,
yhssa@gov.nt.ca
www.yhssa.org

Department of Health & Social Services

Centre Square Tower, PO Box 1320, Yellowknife, NT X1A 2L9
Fax: 867-873-0266,
www.hlthss.gov.nt.ca

The Department of Health & Social Services is mandated to provide a broad range of health & social programs & services to the residents of the NWT.Seven regional Health & Social Services Authorities plan, manage & deliver a full spectrum of community & facility-based services for health care & social services. Community health programs include daily sick clinics, public health clinics, home care, school health programs & educational programs. Visiting physicians & specialists routinely visit the communities.

Acts Administered:
Aboriginal Custom Adoption Recognition Act
Adoption Act
Change of Name Act
Child & Family Services Act
Child Welfare Act
Dental Auxiliaries Act
Dental Mechanics Act
Dental Professions Act
Disease Registries Act
Emergency Medical Aid Act
Guardianship & Trusteeship Act (jointly with Dept. of Justice)
Hospital Insurance & Health & Social Services Administration Act
Human Tissue Act
Intercountry Adoption (Hague Convention) Act
Licensed Practical Nurses Act
Marriage Act (jointly with Dept. of Justice)
Medical Care Act
Medical Profession Act
Mental Health Act
Midwifery Profession Act
Nursing Profession Act
Ophthalmic Medical Assistants Act
Optometry Act
Personal Directives Act
Pharmacy Act
Psychologists Act
Public Health Act
Veterinary Profession Act
Vital Statistics Act

Minister,Hon. Sandy Lee
867-669-2344, Fax: 867-873-0481,sandy_lee@gov.nt.ca
Deputy Minister, Greb Cummings
867-920-6173, Fax:
867-873-0266,greg_cummings@gov.nt.ca
Asst. Deputy Minister, Operational Support Branch, Dana Heide
867-873-7737, Fax: 867-873-0266,dana_heide@gov.nt.ca
Director, Children & Family Services, Dean Soenen
867-873-7046, Fax: 867-873-7706,dean_soenen@gov.nt.ca
Director, Financial Services, Derek Elkin
867-873-7367, Fax: 867-920-4969,derek_elkin@gov.nt.ca
Director, Health Services Administration, Donna Manuel
867-777-7400, 800-661-0830,Fax:
867-777-3197,donna_manuel@gov.nt.ca
Director, Policy, Planning & Evaluation, Lisa Cardinal
867-873-7908, Fax: 867-873-0484,lisa_cardinal@gov.nt.ca
Manager, Policy & Legislation, Denise Canuel
867-920-3283, Fax: 867-873-0484,denise_canuel@gov.nt.ca
Director, Population Health & Chief Medical Officer, Andre Corriveau
867-920-3231, Fax:
867-873-0122,andre_corriveau@gov.nt.ca,
Director, Territorial/Integrated Services, Vacant
867-873-7715
Chief Information Officer, Information Services, Michele Hancsicsak
867-873-7223, Fax:
867-873-0280,michele_hanscicsak@gov.nt.ca
Public Guardian, Ron MacLellan
867-920-8025, Fax:
867-873-0248,ron_maclellan@gov.nt.ca
Comptroller, Financial Processing & Management, Kim Weir
867-920-3003, kim_weir@gov.nt.ca
Communications Specialist, Umesh Sutendra
867-920-3368, Fax:
867-873-0204,umesh_sutendra@gov.nt.ca
Manager, Children & Family Services, Carolyn Mandrusiak
867-873-7047, carolyn_mandrusiak@gov.nt.ca
Manager, Community Wellness Programs, Mary-Jane Stewart
867-873-7403, mary-jane_stewart@gov.nt.ca
Director, Warren St. Germaine
867-930-8931, warren_st.germaine@gov.nt.ca
Manager, Financial Processing & Management, Brian Puskas
867-920-3003, Fax: 867-873-0280,brian_puskas@gov.nt.ca
Chief Information Officer, Information Systems, Kees Hamming
867-873-7429, kees.hamming@gov.nt.ca
Director, Bronwyn Watters
867-873-7703, bronwyn_watters@gov.nt.ca
Manager, Human Resources, Jim Myres
867-920-3060, Fax: 867-873-0281,jim.myres@gov.nt.ca
Manager, Planning & Communications, Laura Seddon
867-920-8927, laura_seddon@gov.nt.ca
Manager, Policy & Legislation, Doug Ritchie
867-920-3275, doug_ritchie@gov.nt.ca
Director, Andre Corriveau
867-920-3231, andre_corriveau@gov.nt.ca
Manager, Health Promotion, Gillian Burles
867-873-7371, Fax: 867-873-0202,gillian_burles@gov.nt.ca
Manager, Health Protection, Jack MacKinnon
867-920-3241, jack_mackinnon@gov.nt.ca
Manager, Health Services Administration & Vital Statistics, Carol McKie
867-777-7412, Fax: 867-777-3197,carol_mckie@gov.nt.ca
Manager, Research & Analysis, Andrew Langford
867-873-7054, Fax:
867-873-0204,andrew_langford@gov.nt.ca

Northwest Territories Housing Corporation

Scotia Centre, 5102 50th Ave., PO Box 2100, Yellowknife, NT X1A 2P6
867-873-7853, Fax: 867-873-9426,
www.nwthc.gov.nt.ca

Other Communication: Official Languages Coordination Phone: 867-873-7899; Fax: 867-669-7901

The mandate of the Northwest Territories Housing Corporation is to ensure, where necessary, a sufficient supply of affordable, adequate & suitable housing to meet the needs of residents. To accomplish this mandate, the corporation works with citizens, communities, Local Housing Organizations, aboriginal organizations, the business community, non-government organizations, & other governments. Through Housing Choices, the following four programs are available: Providing Assistance for Territorial Homeownership (PATH); Contributing Assistance for Repairs and Enhancements (CARE); Homeowner Entry Level Program (HELP); & Solutions to Educate People (STEP).

Minister Responsible,Hon. Michael McLeod
867-669-2377, Fax:
867-873-0596,michael_mcleod@gov.nt.ca
President, Jeff Polakoff
867-873-7853, Fax: 867-873-9426,jeff_polakoff@gov.nt.ca
Vice Presiden, Finance & Infrastructure Services, Jeff Anderson
867-873-7873, Fax: 867-920-8024,jeff_anderson@gov.nt.ca
Director, Programs & District Operations, Franklin Carpenter
867-873-7858, Fax:
867-669-7901,franklin_carpenter@gov.nt.ca
Director, Infrastructure Services, Scott Reid
867-873-7875, Fax: 867-669-7010,scott_reid@gov.nt.ca

Department of Industry, Tourism & Investment (ITI)

PO Box 1320, Yellowknife, NT X1A 2L9
Fax: 867-873-0306,
info@iti.ca
www.iti.gov.nt.ca

The Department of Industry, Tourism & Investment promotes & supports economic prosperity & community self-reliance in the Northwest Territories by providing programs & services. Programs & services are available through the following departmental divisions: Diamonds; Energy Planning; Industrial Initiatives; Informatics; Investment & Economic Analysis; Mackenzie Valley Pipeline Office; Minerals, Oil & Gas; Policy, Legislation & Communications; & Tourism & Parks.

Acts Administered:
Agricultural Products Marketing Act
Business Development & Investment Corporation Act
Co-operative Associations Act
Credit Union Act
Freshwater Fish Marketing Act
Herd & Fencing Act
Industry, Tourism & Investment Act
Territorial Parks Act

Minister,Hon. Bob McLeod
867-669-2388, Fax: 867-873-0306,bob_mcleod@gov.nt.ca
Deputy Minister, Peter Vician
867-920-8048, Fax: 867-873-0563,peter_vician@gov.nt.ca
Assistant Deputy Minister, Programs & Operations, Doug Doan
867-873-7115, doug_doan@gov.nt.ca
Director, Minerals, Oil & Gas, Tim Coleman
867-920-3222, tim_cokleman@gov.nt.ca
Director, Mackenzie Valley Pipeline Office, Tim Coleman
867-874-5405, tim_coleman@gov.nt.ca
Director, Shared Services, Finance & Administration, Jeffrey Dalley
867-920-8649, Fax: 867-873-0551,jeffrey_dalley@gov.nt.ca
Director, Energy Planning, Dave Nightingale
867-920-3274, dave_nightingale@gov.nt.ca
Director, Policy, Legislation & Communications, Deborah Saunders
867-873-7005, Fax:
867-873-0645,deborah_archibald@gov.nt.ca
Director, Investment & Economic Analysis, Garry Singer
867-873-7361, Fax: 867-873-0101,garry_singer@gov.nt.ca
Director, Shared Services Informatics, Rick Wind
867-920-3327, rick_wind@gov.nt.ca
Director, Tourism & Parks, Richard Zieba
867-873-7902, richard_zieba@gov.nt.ca
Chief Geologist, Scott Cairns
867-669-2479, scott_cairns@gov.nt.ca

• Northwest Territories Business Development & Investment Corporation(BDIC)
#701, 5201 - 50 Ave.
Yellowknife, NT X1A 3S9
867-920-6455 Fax: 867-765-0652
bdicinfo@gov.nt.ca
www.bdic.ca
Formerly the Northwest Territories Development Corporation (DEVCORP). The BDIC is a recognized leader in the NWT's regional economic development and the growth of a dynamic small and mid-sized business sector.

Department of Human Resources

PO Box 1320, Yellowknife, NT X1A 2L9
867-920-3409, Fax: 867-873-0306, 866-475-8162
HRHelpDesk@gov.nt.ca
www.hr.gov.nt.ca

Other Communication: Yellowknife Recruitment Office Phone: 867-920-8900; Fax: 867-873-0282; Email: jobsyk@gov.nt.ca; Current Employment Opportunites: www.hr.gov.nt.ca/employment/#current

The Department services the people of the Northwest Territories & supports the development of employees in the northern public service. Services are provided through the following divisions: Management & Recruitment Services; Corporate Human Resource Services; Human Resource Strategy & Policy; & Employee Services.

Minister,Hon. Bob McLeod
867-669-2388, Fax: 867-873-0306,bob_mcleod@gov.nt.ca
Deputy Minister, Debbie DeLancey
867-873-7187, Fax:
867-873-0667,debbie_delancey@gov.nt.ca
Director, Corporate Human Resources, Sharilyn Alexander
867-873-7852, sharilyn_alexander@gov.nt.ca
Director, Employee Services, Alison Welch
867-873-7906, Fax: 867-873-0167,alison_welch@gov.nt.ca
Director, Strategy & Policy, Shaleen Woodward
867-873-7786, Fax:
867-873-0634,shaleen_woodward@gov.nt.ca

Department of Justice

Courthouse, 4903 - 49th St., 6th Fl., PO Box 1320, Yellowknife, NT X1A 2L9
867-920-6197,
www.justice.gov.nt.ca

Other Communication: Access to Information and Protection of Privacy Phone: 867-920-6418

The following are some of the services offered by the Department of Justice: Aboriginal Rights Court Challenges Program; Access to Information & Protection of Privacy; Commissioner for Oaths/Notary Public; Coroner; Corporate Registries; Land Titles Office; Legal Aid; Maintenance Enforcement; Mental Disorder Review Board; Personal Property Registry; Public Trustee; Rental Office; Securities Registry; Victim Services; Witness Expense Assistance Program; & Youth Justice.

Minister,Hon. Jackson Lafferty
867-669-2399, Fax:
867-873-0274,jackson_lafferty@gov.nt.ca
Deputy Minister, Bronwyn Watters
867-920-6197, Fax:
867-873-0307,brownyn_watters@gov.nt.ca
Assistant Deputy Minister & Attorney General, Karan Shaner
867-920-6197, karan_shaner@gov.nt.ca
Assistant Deputy Minister & Solicitor General,Vacant
867-873-7772
Administrator & Deputy Chief Coroner, Coroner's Office, Cathy Menard
867-920-8713, Fax: 867-873-0426,cathy_menard@gov.nt.ca
Chief Information Officer, Norm Embleton
867-920-6100, Fax:
867-873-0197,norm_embleton@gov.nt.ca
Public Trustee, Public Trustee's Office, Larry Pontus
867-873-7464, 866-535-0423,Fax:
867-873-0184,larry_pontus@gov.nt.ca
Executive Director, Legal Services Board, Lucy Austin
867-873-7450, Fax: 867-873-5320,lucy_austin@gov.nt.ca
Director, Legislation Division, Mark Aitken
867-873-7462, Fax: 867-873-0234,mark_aitken@gov.nt.ca
Director, Corrections Services, Colin G. Gordon
867-920-8922, Fax: 867-873-0299,colin_g_gordon@gov.nt.ca
Director, Court Services, Anne Mould
867-920-8852, Fax: 867-873-0307,anne_mould@gov.nt.ca
Director, Community Justice & Community Policing, Shirley KemeysJones
867-873-7002, Fax:
867-873-0199,shirley_kemeysjones@gov.nt.ca
Director, Legal Registries, Gary MacDougall
867-873-7490, Fax:
867-873-0243,gary.macdougall@gov.nt.ca
Director, Finance, Kim Schofield
867-873-7641, Fax: 867-873-0173,kim_schofield@gov.nt.ca
Director, Policy & Planning, Laura Seddon
867-920-3225, Fax: 867-873-0659,laura_seddon@gov.nt.ca
Director, Legal Division, Clarence Hudson
867-873-7787, Fax:
867-873-0234,clarence_hudson@gov.nt.ca
Registrar, Land Titles & Registrar, Personal Property Registry, Tom Hall
867-920-8986, Fax: 867-873-0243,tom_hall@gov.nt.ca
Registrar, Corporate Registries & Deputy Registrar, Securities Registry (Legal & Enforcement), Donald MacDougall
867-920-8984, Fax:
867-873-0243,donald_macdougall@gov.nt.ca
Administrator, Commissioner for Oaths / Notary Public, Samantha VanGenne
867-920-8985, Fax:
867-873-0243,samantha_vangenne@gov.nt.ca

• Judicial Council
PO Box 188
Yellowknife, NT X1A 2N2
867-873-7105 Fax: 867-873-0287

• Legal Services Board of the Northwest Territories
PO Box 1320
Yellowknife, NT X1A 2L9
867-873-7450 Fax: 867-873-5320 www-jus-tice
www.justice.gov.nt.ca

• Victims Assistance Committee
c/o Community Justice Division
PO Box 1320
Yellowknife, NT X1A 2L9
867-920-6911 Fax: 867-873-0299

• Assessment Appeal Tribunal of the Northwest Territories
#500, 5201 - 50th Ave.
PO Box 1320
Yellowknife, NT X1A 2L9
867-873-7125 Fax: 867-873-0609

• Territorial Board of Revision
PO Box 1320
Yellowknife, NT X1A 2L9
867-873-7125 Fax: 867-873-0609

Department of Municipal & Community Affairs

PO Box 1320, Yellowknife, NT X1A 2L9
867-873-7118, Fax: 867-873-0309,
www.maca.gov.nt.ca

Supports capable, accountable & self-directed community governments providing a safe, sustainable & healthy environment for community residents. Works with community governments & other partners in supporting community residents as they organize & manage democratic, responsible & accountable community governments. The Department assists municipalities with administrative services & infrastructure project management, provides expertise in engineering to communities & arranges for debentures on behalf of communities which are undertaking public works programs.Advisory services are supplied to community councils for the planning, development & administration of public lands within municipal boundaries.Technical expertise is provided for mapping, surveying & air photography & zoning by-law administration.

Acts Administered:
Area Development Act
Civil Emergency Measures Act
Commissioner's Land Act
Community Employees Benefits Act
Consumer Protection Act
Curfew Act
Dog Act
Film Classification Act
Fire Prevention Act
Flood Damage Reduction Agreements Act
Hamlets Act
Home Owner's Property Tax Rebate Act
Local Authorities Elections Act
Lotteries Act
Municipal Employees Benefits Act
Municipal Statutes Replacement Act
Pawnbrokers & Second-Hand Dealers Act
Planning Act
Property Assessment & Taxation Act
Real Estate Agent's Licensing Act
Religious Societies Land Act
Senior Citizens' & Disabled Persons' Property Tax Relief Act
Settlements Act
Western Canada Lotteries Act

Minister,Hon. Sandy Lee
867-669-2344, Fax: 867-873-0431,sandy_lee@gov.nt.ca
Deputy Minister, Jeff Polakoff
867-873-7118, Fax: 867-873-0309,heff_polakoff@gov.nt.ca
Asst. Deputy Minister, Regional Operations, Sheila Bassi Kellett
867-920-6146, Fax:
867-873-0309,sheila_bassi-kellett@gov.nt.ca
Director, Community Relations, Eleanor Young
867-873-7671, Fax: 867-873-0609,eleanor_young@gov.nt.ca
Director, Corporate Affairs, Laura Gareau
867-873-7613, Fax: 867-873-0152,laura_gareau@gov.nt.ca
Director, Sport, Recreation & Youth, Ian Legaree
867-873-7245, Fax: 867-920-6467,ian_legaree@gov.nt.ca
Territorial Emergency Management Coordinator, Eric Bussey
867-920-6133, Fax: 867-873-8134,eric_busset@gov.nt.ca
Fire Marshal, Stephen Moss
867-873-7469, Fax:
867-873-0260,stephen_moss@gov.nt.ca
Administrative Assistant, Terry Kungl
867-920-6286, Fax: 867-873-0152,terry_kung@gov.nt.ca

Lands Administration

867-873-7569, Fax: 867-920-6156

Responsible for the administration of Commissioner's lands in & around the communities of the Northwest Territories. Commissioner's lands make up about 2 percent of all land in the North. The Federal Government administers about 97 percent & municipal corporations administer the remaining 1 percent.Under the Lands Program, MACA is in the process of transferring certain lands from the Commissioner to municipalities. Land administration is being decentralized from MACA headquarters to regional offices or to the communities.As authority for land devolves, MACA will take on a training & advisory role, teaching & advising communities how to look after their own lands. The division supplies information & advice regarding land leases, surrenders, transfers, & mortgage registration for Commissioner's land & notifications.

Director, Andy Tereposky
867-873-7569, andy_tereposky@gov.nt.ca
Manager, Lands Policy, Beverly Chamberlin
867-920-6284, beverly_chamberlin@gov.nt.ca
Manager, Lands Program, Robert Marchiori
867-920-8919, robert_marchiori@gov.nt.ca

School of Community Government

#400, 5201 - 50th Ave., Yellowknife, NT X1A 3S9
867-920-3159, Fax: 867-873-0584, 877-531-9194

Director, Dan Schofield
867-873-7755, Fax: 867-873-0584,dan_schofield@gov.nt.ca
Director, Ian Legaree
867-873-7245, ian_legaree@gov.nt.ca
Manager, Community Technical Services, Linda Hayden
867-920-6205
Manager, Sport & Recreation, Chris Szabo
867-873-7757

Northwest Territories Power Corporation

4 Capital Dr., Hay River, NT X0E 1G2
867-874-5200, Fax: 867-874-5229,
info@ntpc.com
www.ntpc.com

Other Communication: Fort Simpson: 800/288-4784; Fort Smith: 800/661-0855; Inuvik: 800/661-0856; Yellowknife: 800/661-0854

Made up of 28 separate power systems, the NWT Power Corporation serves approximately 42,000 people in communities across the Northwest Territories. Facilities include hydro-electric, diesel & natural gas generation plants, transmission systems, & several isolated electrical distribution systems. The Corporation works to provide environmentally sound, safe, reliable, cost-effective energy & related services in the territories.

Minister Responsible,Hon. Floyd K. Roland
867-669-2311, Fax: 867-873-0169,floyd_roland@gov.nt.ca
Chair, Lew Voytilla
President/CEO, Leon Courneya
Director, Engineering, Stephen Kerr
Director/CFO, Finance, Judith Goucher

Public Utilities Board of the Northwest Territories (PUB)

#203, 62 Woodland Dr., PO Box 4211, Hay River, NT X0E 1G1
867-874-3944, Fax: 867-874-3639,
www.nwtpublicutilitiesboard.ca

The independent, quasi-judicial agency of the Government of the Northwest Territories is responsible for the regulation of public utilities in the territory. Its authority is from the Public Utilities Act. Issues are handled by an application & decision process.

Minister Responsible,Hon. Bob McLeod
867-669-2388, Fax: 867-873-0431,bob_mcleod@gov.nt.ca
Chair, Joe Acorn
Board Secretary, Louise-Ann Larocque
louise-ann_larocque@gov.nt.ca

Department of Public Works & Services

PO Box 1320, Yellowknife, NT X1A 2L9
867-873-7114, Fax: 867-873-0226,
www.pws.gov.nt.ca

Designs, constructs, maintains & operates territorial buildings; implements energy efficiency projects; provides essential petroleum products to the public where they are not available from the private sector; provides data systems & communication services to government departments.

Acts Administered:
Boilers & Pressure Vessels Act
Electrical Protection Act
Gas Protection Act
Public Utilities Act

Minister,Hon. Michael McLeod
867-669-2377, Fax:
867-873-0169,michael_mclwod@gov.nt.ca
Deputy Minister, Mike Aumond
867-873-7114, Fax:
867-873-0226,mike_aumond@gov.nt.ca
Director, Technology Service Centre (TSC), John Gabel
867-873-7836, Fax: 867-873-0135,john_gabel@gov.nt.ca
Director, Petroleum Products Division, John Vandenberg
867-920-3447, Fax:
867-873-0100,john_vandenberg@gov.nt.ca
Director, Asset Management Division, Paul Guy
867-920-6142, Fax: 867-873-0226,paul_guy@gov.nt.ca
Director, Corporate Services, Steve Lewis
867-920-8672, Fax: 867-873-0100,steve_lewis@gov.nt.ca
Executive Secretary, Marvia Rivet
867-873-7114, Fax: 867-873-0226,marvia_rivet@gov.nt.ca

Status of Women Council of the Northwest Territories

PO Box 1320, Yellowknife, NT X1A 2L9
867-920-6177, Fax: 867-873-0285, 888-234-4485
council@statusofwomen.nt.ca
www.statusofwomen.nt.ca

To work towards the equality of women through advice to the government; research; public education; advocacy on behalf of women; & workshops & other support for the development of women's groups, & other groups working on issues of concern to women.

Minister Responsible,Hon. Sandy Lee
867-669-2344, Fax: 867-873-0481,sandy_lee@gov.nt.ca

Executive Director, Sharon Thomas
sharon@statusofwomen.nt.ca

Department of Transportation

Lahm Ridge Bldg., 4501 50 Ave., PO Box 1320, Yellowknife, NT X1A 2L9
867-920-3460, Fax: 867-873-0363, www.dot.gov.nt.can

Acts Administered:
All-Terrain Vehicles Act
Motor Vehicles Act
Public Highways Act
Public Service Vehicles Act
Transportation of Dangerous Goods Act, 1990

Minister,Hon. Michael McLeod
867-669-2377, Fax: 867-873-0388,michael_mcleod@gov.nt.ca
Deputy Minister, Russell Neudorf
867-920-3460, Fax: 867-873-0363,russell_neudorf@gov.nt.ca
Asst. Deputy Minister, Daniel Auger
867-920-3461, Fax: 867-873-0363,daniel_auger@gov.nt.ca
Director, Corporate Services, Jim Martin
867-920-3459, Fax: 867-873-0283,jim_martin@gov.nt.ca
Director, Planning & Policy, Jim Stevens
867-920-3366, Fax: 867-920-2565,jim_stevens@gov.nt.ca

Airports
YK Centre, 4922 - 28th St., 4th fl., PO Box 1320, Yellowknife, NT X1A 2L9
867-873-7725, Fax: 867-873-0297

Director, Alex Home
867-873-7725, alex_home@gov.nt.ca
Asst. Director, Airport Facilities, Delia Chesworth
867-873-7845, delia_chesworth@gov.nt.ca
Asst. Director, Programs & Standards, Ben Webber
867-873-7822, Fax: 867-873-0297,ben_webber@gov.nt.ca
Manager, Finance & Systems, Nigel Moorhouse
867-873-7702, nigel_moorhouse@gov.nt.ca

Highways
4510 - 50 Ave., 2nd fl., PO Box 1320, Yellowknife, NT X1A 2L9
867-920-8771, Fax: 867-873-0288

Director, Kevin McLeod
867-873-7800, Fax: 867-920-3085,kevin_mcleod@gov.nt.ca
Head, Structures, Ann Lanteigne
867-920-8010, ann_lanteigne@gov.nt.ca
Manager, Contracts, Martina Simons
867-920-8080, martina_simons@gov.nt.ca
Manager, Technical Services, Larry Purcka
867-873-7647, larry_purcka@gov.nt.ca
Strategic Highways & Marine Planner, Blair Chapman
867-920-8023, Fax: 867-873-0288,blair_chapman@gov.nt.ca

Road Licensing & Safety
4510 - 50 Ave., 1st fl., PO Box 1320, Yellowknife, NT X1A 2L9
867-873-7972, Fax: 867-873-0120

Director, Al Kaylo
867-920-8633, Fax: 867-873-0120,al_kaylo@gov.nt.ca

Northwest Territories Water Board

5114 - 49th St., PO Box 1326, Yellowknife, NT X1A 1N9
867-765-0106, Fax: 867-765-0114, info@nwtwb.com
www.nwtwb.com

Responsible for the development, maintenance & conservation of water resources; administers licences for utilizing water or disposing of wastes into water under the Northwest Territories Waters Act; has federal/territorial jurisdiction.

Chair, Eddie Dillon

Northwest Territories & Nunavut Workers' Compensation Board (WCB)

Centre Square Tower, 5022 - 49th St., 5th Fl., PO Box 8888, Yellowknife, NT X1A 2R3
867-920-3888, Fax: 867-873-4596, 800-661-0792
wcb@wcb.nt.ca
www.wcb.nt.ca; www.wcbnunavut.ca

Other Communication: Toll Free Fax: 1-866-277-3677; Incident/Accident Line: 1-800-661-0792

The Workers' Compensation Board of the Northwest Territories & Nunavut is engaged in the following activities: ensuring compensation & pensions are awarded to injured workers or their dependents; assessubg enokiters sufficiently & fairly to meet obligations; maintaining balance in providing benefits to injured workers, while keeping costs to employers as low as possible; & promoting safe workplaces through education & enforcement.

Acts Administered:
Explosives Use Act
Mine Health & Safety Act
Safety Act
Workers' Compensation Act

Minister Responsible, Northwest Territories, Hon. J. Michael Miltenberger
867-669-2355, Fax: 867-873-0596,michael_miltenberger@gov.nt.ca
President/CEO, Anne Clark
867-920-3887, AnneC@wcb.nt.ca
Vice-President, Northwest Territories Operations, Marie Wilson
867-920-3815, MarieW@wcb.nt.ca
Vice-President, Nunavut Operations, Derek Dinham
902-979-8507, DerekD@wcb.nt.ca
Vice-President, Prevention Services, Sylvester Wong
867-669-4408, SylvesterW@wcb.nt.ca
Director, Corporate Services, John Doyle
867-920-3840, JohnD@wcb.nt.ca
Director, Communications & Information, Dave Grundy
867-669-4442, DaveGru@wcb.nt.ca
Director, Human Resources, Kim Collins Riffel
867-920-3821, KimCR@wcb.nt.ca
Director, Legal Services, Mike Triggs
867-920-3895, MikeT@wcb.nt.ca

Council of Atlantic Premiers (CAP)

Council Secretariat, #1006, 5161 George St., PO Box 2044, Halifax, NS B3J 2Z1
902-424-7590, Fax: 902-424-8976, info@cap-cpma.ca
www.cap-cpma.ca

The Premiers of New Brunswick, Newfoundland & Labrador, Nova Scotia & Prince Edward Island constitute the Council. It was established by memorandum of understanding to: promote unity of purpose among their respective Governments; ensure maximum coordination of the activities of the Governments & their agencies &; establish a framework for joint action & undertakings.The Council meets up to four times annually to discuss matters of mutual interest or concern to the four Atlantic governments.A Secretariat acts as the focal point for coordinating the efforts of the four Governments in identifying potential benefits that could result from a regional approach to policy formulation & program development.

Acting Secretary to Council, Rhéal Poirier
902-424-7600
Administrative Assistant, Janice Henderson
902-424-7601, Fax: 902-424-1976,info@cap-cpma.ca

• Council of Ministers of Education & Training
PO Box 2044
Halifax, NS B3J 2Z1
902-424-5352 Fax: 902-424-8976
camet_camef@cap-cpma.ca
www.camet-camef.ca

• Maritime Provinces Harness Racing Commission
5 Gerald McCarville Dr.
PO Box 128
Kensington, PE C0B 1M0
902-836-5500 Fax: 902-836-5390
dwalsh@mphrc.ca
www.mphrc.ca
To govern & regulate harness racing in the Maritime provinces.

Government of Nova Scotia

Seat of Government: Province House, Halifax, NS B3J 2T3
www.gov.ns.ca

The Province of Nova Scotia entered Confederation July 1, 1867.It has an area of 52,917,46 km2, & the StatsCan census population in 2006 was 913,462.

Office of the Lieutenant Governor

Government House, 1451 Barrington St., Halifax, NS B3J 1Z2
902-424-7001, Fax: 902-424-0537

Lieutenant Governor,Hon. Mayann Francis

Office of the Premier

One Government Place, 1700 Granville St., PO Box 726, Halifax, NS B3J 2T3
902-424-6600, Fax: 902-424-7648, 800-267-1993
premier@gov.ns.ca
www.gov.ns.ca/premier

Premier,Hon. Darrell Dexter
premier@gov.ns.ca
Deputy Minister, Angus MacIsaac
902-424-8910, Fax: 902-424-7638,macisaaa@gov.ns.ca
Chief of Staff, Bob Chisholm
902-424-6600, chishobj@gov.ns.ca
Director, Communications, Wade Keller
902-424-4092, kellerwm@gov.ns.ca
Principal Assistant to the Premier & Director, Community Relations, Stephen Greene

Executive Council

One Government Place, PO Box 2125, Halifax, NS B3J 3B7
902-424-5970, Fax: 902-424-0667

Premier & President, Executive Council;, Minister, Policy and Priorities; Minister, Intergovernmental Affairs; Minister, Aboriginal Affairs; Min. responsible for MilitaryRelations, Hon. Darrell Dexter
902-424-6600, Fax: 902-424-7648,premier@gov.ns.ca
Deputy Premier, Minister, Public Service Commission; Minister, Communications Nova Scotia; Minister, Information Management; Chair of TreasuryBoard, Hon. Frank Corbett
902-424-5465, Fax: 902-424-0555,min_psc@gov.ns.ca
Minister, Health & Minister, Health Promotion and Protection; Minister, Gaelic Affairs, Hon. Maureen MacDonald
902-424-3377, Fax: 902-424-0559,health.minister@gov.ns.ca
Minister, Agriculture & Minister, Natural Resources; Minister responsible for the Maritime Provinces Harness Racing Commission Act, Hon. John MacDonell
902-424-4388, Fax: 902-424-0699,min_dag@gov.ns.ca
Minister, Transportation and Infrastructure Renewal & Minister, Energy; Minister responsible for Conserve Nova Scotia, Gateway Initiative, Hon. Bill Estabrooks
902-424-5875, Fax: 902-424-0171,tirmin@gov.ns.ca
Minister, Finance & Minister, Acadian Affairs; Minister responsible for the Securities Act, Insurance Act, Credit Union Act, Gaming Contol Act (Pt.1), Hon. Graham Steele
902-424-5720, Fax: 902-424-0635,finamin@gov.ns.ca
Minister, Education & Minister, Labour and Workforce Development; Minister, Volunteerism, Hon. Marilyn More
902-424-6647, Fax: 902-424-0575,min_lwd@gov.ns.ca
Minister, Fisheries & Aquaculture & Minister, Environment, Hon. Sterling Belliveaut
902-424-3736, Fax: 902-424-1599,min_env@gov.ns.ca
Minister, Economic and Rural Development & Minister Tourism, Culture & Heritage; Minister, African Nova Scotian Affairs, Hon. Percy Paris
902-424-5790, Fax: 902-424-0514,econmin@gov.ns.ca
Minister, Community Services & Minister, Seniors; Minister responsible, Advisory Council on the Status of Women Act & Disabled Persons' CommissionAct, Hon. Denise Peterson-Rafuse
902-424-4304, Fax: 902-428-0618, petersdj@gov.ns.ca
Minister, Service Nova Scotia & Municipal Relations; Minister, Emergency Management; Minister, Immigration; Min. responsible Residential TenanciesAct, Hon. Ramona Jennex
902-424-5550, Fax: 902-424-0581,snsmrmin@gov.ns.ca
Attorney General & Minister, Justice;, Minister responsible for Human Rights Act, Regulations Act, Workers' Compensation Act (Pt. 2) & Retail Business Uniform Closing Day Act, Hon. Ross Landry
902-424-4044, Fax: 902-424-0510, justmin@gov.ns.ca
Council Order Clerk, Ann T. Broughm
902-424-5152

Cabinet Office
Secretary to the Executive Council & Clerk of the Executive Council, Paul LaFleche
902-424-6611, Fax: 902-424-0667,
Deputy Minister, Intergovernmental Affairs,Vacant
Executive Director, Intergovernmental Affairs,Dr. Alastair Saunders
902-424-4899, Fax: 902-424-0728

Legislative House of Assembly

c/o Clerk's Office, Province House, 1st Fl., PO Box 1617, Halifax, NS B3J 2Y3
902-424-5978, Fax: 902-424-0632, www.gov.ns.ca/legi/house.htm

Clerk of Assembly, R.K. MacArthur, Q.C.
Speaker, Cecil Clarke
Sergeant-at-Arms, Kenneth Greenham
Legislative Librarian, Margaret Murphy
902-424-5932
Manager, Hansard, Robert Kinsman
902-424-7990
Asst. Clerk, Arthur Fordham, Q.C.
Asst. Clerk, Neil Ferguson
Director, Administration, Jocelyn Scallion
902-424-4479
Director, Legislative TV, Jim MacInnes
902-424-3875
Chief Legislative Counsel, Gordon D. Hebb
902-424-8941
Secretary to the Chief Clerk, Ginelle MacKinnon
902-424-5978, Fax: 902-424-0632,mackingl@gov.ns.ca

Government Caucus Office (PC)
Centennial Bldg., #805, 1645 Granville St., Halifax, NS B3J 1X3
902-424-2731, Fax: 902-424-7484, 800-363-1998
pcmlas@gov.ns.ca
Caucus Chair,Hon. Ron Chisholm
Principal Assistant, David Hovell

Office of the Official Opposition (NDP)
Centennial Bldg., #1001, 1660 Hollis St., Halifax, NS B3J 2Y3
902-424-4134, Fax: 902-424-0504,
ndpcaucus@gov.ns.ca
Leader, Darrell Dexter
Caucus Chair, Frank Corbett
Chief of Staff & Director, Communications, Dan O'Connor
Administrative Assistant, Susan Wells

Office of the Liberal Party (Lib.)
Bank of Montreal Bldg., 5151 George St., Halifax, NS B3J 2X8
902-424-8637, Fax: 902-424-0539
Leader, Francis Mackenzie
Caucus Chair, Keith Colwell

Standing Committees of the House
Committees Office, 1740 Granville St., 3rd Fl., PO Box 2630 M, Halifax, NS B3J 3N5
902-424-4432, Fax: 902-424-0513
Chief Clerk, Legislative Committees, Mora Stevens
902-424-4494
Clerk, Legislative Committees, Darlene Henry
902-424-4432

Sixtieth Assembly - Nova Scotia

Province House, PO Box 1617, Halifax, NS B3J 2Y3
902-424-5978, Fax: 902-424-0632
Last General Election, June 13, 2006.Maximum Duration, 5 years. Party Standings (June 2006): Progressive Conservatives (PC) 23 New Democratic Party (NDP) 20 Liberal (Lib.) 9 Total, 52; Salaries, Indemnities & Allowances: Members' sessional indemnity $30,130 plus a $15,065 expense allowance.In addition to this are the following: Premier $52,012 Ministers $37,055 Leader of the Opposition $37,055 Leader of a recognized Party $17,650 Speaker $37,055 Deputy Speaker $18,533. Following is: constituency (number of eligible voters at 2006 election) member, party affiliation.(Address for all is c/o House of Assembly, Province House, Halifax NS B3J 2Y3.) Refer to Cabinet List, Government Caucus Office, the Offices of the Official Opposition & of the New Democratic Party, for phone & Fax numbers.
Members
Keith Bain, Victoria-The Lakes, PC
Hon. Michael Baker, Q.C., Lunenburg, PC
Hon. Barry Barnet, Hammonds Plains Upper Sackville, PC
Sterling Belliveau, Shelburne, New Democratic Party
Hon. Carolyn Bolivar-Getson, Lunenburg West, PC
Hon. Karen Casey, Colchester North, PC
Hon. Ron Chisholm, Guysborough-Port Hawkesbury, PC
Cecil Clarke, Cape Breton North, PC
Keith Colwell, Preston, Liberal
Vicki Conrad, Queens, New Democratic Party
Frank Corbett, Cape Breton Centre, New Democratic Party
Hon. Chris A. d'Entremont, Argyle, PC
Kevin Deveaux, Cole Harbour-Eastern Passage, New Democratic Party
Darrell Dexter, Cole Harbour, New Democratic Party
Hon. Bill Dooks, Eastern Shore, PC
Pat Dunn, Pictou Centre, PC
Howard Epstein, Halifax Chebucto, New Democratic Party
Bill Estabrooks, Timberlea-Prospect, New Democratic Party
Hon. Ernest Fage, Cumberland North, PC
Wayne J. Gaudet, Clare, Liberal
Leo Glavine, Kings West, Liberal
Gordie Gosse, Cape Breton Nova, New Democratic Party
Hon. Len Goucher, Bedford, PC
Hon. Richard Hurlburt, Yarmouth, PC
Manning MacDonald, Cape Breton South, Liberal
Maureen MacDonald, Halifax Needham, New Democratic Party
Hon. Rodney MacDonald, Inverness, PC
John MacDonell, Hants East, New Democratic Party
Hon. Angus MacIsaac, Antigonish, PC
Clarrie MacKinnon, Pictou East, New Democratic Party
Alfie MacLeod, Cape Breton West, PC
Joan Massey, Dartmouth East, New Democratic Party
Stephen McNeil, Annapolis, Liberal
Marilyn More, Dartmouth South-Portland Valley, New Democratic Party
Hon. David Morse, Kings South, PC
Hon. Jamie Muir, Truro-Bible Hill, PC
Hon. Mark Parent, Kings North, PC
Percy Paris, Waverley-Fall River-Beaverbank, New Democratic Party
C.L. (Charlie) Parker, Pictou West, New Democratic Party
Chuck Porter, Hants West, PC
Leonard Preyra, Halifax Citadel, New Democratic Party
Michele Raymond, Halifax Atlantic, New Democratic Party
Michael Samson, Richmond, Liberal
Hon. Murray K. Scott, Cumberland South, PC
Graham Steele, Halifax Fairview, New Democratic Party
Hon. Judy Streatch, Chester-St. Margaret's, PC
Hon. Brooke Taylor, Colchester Musquodoboit Valley, PC
Harold Theriault, Jr., Digby-Annapolis, Liberal
Diana Whalen, Halifax Clayton Park, Liberal
Dave Wilson, Glace Bay, Liberal
Dave Wilson, Sackville-Cobequid, New Democratic Party
Trevor Zinck, Dartmouth North, New Democratic Party
Secretary to the Chief Clerk, Ginelle MacKinnon
902-424-5978, Fax: 902-424-0632,mackingl@gov.ns.ca

Nova Scotia Government Departments & Agencies

Department of Agriculture

1741 Brunswick St., 3rd Fl., PO Box 2223, Halifax, NS B3J 3C4
902-424-4560, Fax: 902-424-4671,
www.gov.ns.ca/nsaf
The Department of Agriculture has a legislated mandate to support & develop the agriculture & food industries, recognizing that these sectors are economic engines of Nova Scotia's rural communities. Fosters prosperous & sustainable agriculture & food industries through the delivery of quality public services for the betterment of rural communities in Nova Scotia.
Acts Administered:
Agriculture & Marketing Act
Agriculture & Rural Credit Act
Agriculture Marshland Conservation Act
Agrologists Act
Animal Cruelty Prevention Act
Animal Health & Protection Act
Animal Health & Protection Regulations
Baby Chick Protection Act
Bee Industry Act
Cattle Pest Control Act
Crop & Livestock Insurance Act
Dairy Industry Act
Farm Practices Act
Farm Registration Act
Federations & Agriculture Act
Fences & Detention of Stray Livestock Act
Health Act (Food Safety, Inspection & Regulations)
Imitation Dairy Products Act
Livestock Brands Act
Livestock Health Services Act
Margarine Act
Maritime Provinces Harness Racing Commission Act
Meat Inspection Act
Natural Products Act
Potato Industry Act
Provincial Berry Act
Sheep Protection Act
Veterinary Medical Act
Weed Control Act
Wildlife Act
Women's Institute of Nova Scotia Act
Minister,Hon. Mark Parent
902-424-4388, min_dag@gov.ns.ca
Deputy Minister, Paul LaFleche
902-424-0300, laflecpt@gov.ns.ca
Executive Director, Agriculture Services, Alan Grant
902-893-6591, grantac@gov.ns.ca
Executive Director, Industry Development & Business Services, Linda MacDonald
902-424-8870, macdonald@gov.ns.ca
Executive Director, Policy & Planning, Diane Kenny
902-424-0308, kennyd@gov.ns.ca
Acting President, Nova Scotia Agricultural College, Dr. Leslie MacLaren
902-893-2773, lmaclaren@nsac.ca
Director, Communications, Celeste Sulliman
902-424-0192, Fax: 902-424-3948,sullimcc@gov.ns.ca
Executive Secretary, Yvelle Poirier
902-424-4388, ypoirier@gov.ns.ca
• Nova Scotia Crop & Livestock Insurance Commission
MacRae Library Bldg.
#2, 137 College Rd.
PO Box 1092
Truro, NS B2N 5G9
902-893-7755 Fax: 902-895-4622 800-565-6371
nsclic@gov.ns.ca
www.gov.ns.ca/nsaf/ci
• Nova Scotia Farm Loan Board
PO Box 550
Truro, NS B2N 5E3
902-893-6506 Fax: 902-895-7693
flb@gov.ns.ca
www.gov.ns.ca/nsaf/loanboards/farmlb/
• Nova Scotia Farm Practices Board
PO Box 550
Truro, NS B2N 5E3
902-893-7314
• Nova Scotia Natural Products Marketing Council
550
Truro, NS B2N 5E3
902-893-6306
www.gov.ns.ca/nsaf/npmc
Executive Director, G. Brian Smith
902-893-6591, Fax: 902-895-4460,smithgb@gov.ns.ca
Manager, 4-H & Rural Organization, Elizabeth Anne Crouse
902-893-6587, crouseea@gov.ns.ca
Manager, Programs & Risk Management, Michael Johnson
902-893-7534

Agriculture Services
Manager, Programs & Risk Management, Michael Johnson
902-893-7534
Acting Director Resource Stewardship

Legislation & Compliance Services
Licenses meat processing, retail food outlets & restaurants, fur & game farms, oversees activities related to food & consumer safety, as well as on-farm quality evaluation. Responsible for monitoring & enforcing compliance with departmental regulations.
Executive Director, Leo Muise
902-424-0337, muiselj@gov.ns.ca
Director, Quality Evaluation, George Smith
902-893-6363, smithgc@gov.ns.ca
Manager, Legislation Services, Susan Horne
902-424-8860, Fax: 902-424-3948,shorne@gov.ns.ca
Manager, Fisheries Licensing & Investigation Services, Nadene MacAulay
902-424-0335

Office of the Auditor General

#302, 1888 Brunswick St., Halifax, NS B3J 3J8
902-424-5907, Fax: 902-424-4350,
http://oag-ns.ca
Auditor General, Jacques R. Lapointe, B.A., C.A., C.I.A.
902-424-4046, lapoinjr@gov.ns.ca
Deputy Auditor General, Alan D. Horgan, C.A.
902-424-3945, horganad@gov.ns.ca
Asst. Auditor General, Evangeline Colman-Sadd, C.A.
902-424-4347, colmansa@gov.ns.ca
Asst. Auditor General, Ann T. McDonald, C.A.
902-424-4970, mcdonaat@gov.ns.ca
Asst. Auditor General, Terry M. Spicer, C.M.A.
902-424-8565, spicert@gov.ns.ca

Department of Fisheries & Aquaculture

1741 Brunswick St., 3rd Fl., PO Box 2223, Halifax, NS B3J 3C4
902-424-4560, Fax: 902-424-4671,
www.gov.ns.ca/fish
The Department of Fisheries & Aquaculture's mission is to foster prosperous and sustainable fisheries, aquaculture and food industries through the delivery of quality public services for the betterment of coastal communities and of all Nova Scotians.
Acts Administered:
Fisheries & Coastal Resources Act
Fisheries Organizations Support Act
Minister,Hon. Ronald Chisholm
902-424-8953, Fax: 902-428-3145,min_dfa@gov.ns.ca
Deputy Minister / CEO, Paul LaFleche
902-424-0300, laflecpt@gov.ns.ca
Asst. Deputy Minister, Gregory Roach
902-424-0348, roachg@gov.ns.ca,
Director, Aquaculture, Marshall Giles
902-424-3664, gilesm@gov.ns.ca
Director, Inland Fisheries, Murray Hill
902-485-7021, hillm@gov.ns.ca
Manager, Innovations in Fisheries & Aquaculture, Bruce Osborne
902-424-0352, osbornbd@gov.ns.ca
Admin. Assistant, Jo-Anne Sutherland
902-424-3735
• Fisheries & Aquaculture Loan Board
PO Box 2223
Halifax, NS B3J 3C4
902-424-4560 Fax: 902-424-1766
www.gov.ns.ca/nsaf/loanboards/fishlb/

Communications Nova Scotia

1723 Hollis St., PO Box 608, Halifax, NS B3J 2R7

902-424-7690, Fax: 902-424-0515, www.gov.ns.ca/cmns/

Other Communication: Queen's Printer: 902/424-4481
Minister Responsible,Hon. Barry Barnet
Deputy Minister, Robert Fowler
Asst. Deputy Minister, Laura Lee Langley
902-424-4886, langleyl@gov.ns.ca
Director, Publication Services, Dan Sargeant
902-424-2974

Department of Community Services

Nelson Place, 5675 Spring Garden Rd., 3rd Fl., PO Box 696, Halifax, NS B3J 2T7
902-424-4304, Fax: 902-428-0618, www.gov.ns.ca/coms

The Department of Community Services is committed to a sustainable social service system that promotes the independence, self-reliance, and security of the people it serves.
Acts Administered:
Adoption Information Act
Children & Family Services Act
Day Care Act
Disabled Persons' Commission Act
Employment Support & Income Assistance Act
Homes for Special Care Act
Housing Act
Housing Development Corporation Act
Senior Citizens' Financial Aid Act
Senior Citizens' Secretariat Act
Senior Citizens' Social Services Act
Social Assistance Act
Minister,Hon. Chris A. d'Entremont
902-424-8296, dentreca@gov.ns.ca
Deputy Minister, Judith Ferguson
902-424-1628, fergusjf@gov.ns.ca
Executive Director, Finance & Administration, George Hudson
902-424-2750
Director, Communications, Linda Laffin
902-424-6283, Fax: 902-424-3287,llaffin@gov.ns.ca
Director, Human Resources, Kate Martin
902-424-2751
Director, Program & Operations Support, Dave Ryan
902-424-7776
• Nova Scotia Disabled Persons Commission
PO Box 222 CRO
Halifax, NS B3J 2M4
902-424-8280 Fax: 902-424-0592 800-565-8280
www.gov.ns.ca/disa

Employment Support, Income Assistance & Housing Services
Fax: 902-424-0721

Senior Director, Harold Dillon
902-424-6729
Director, Employment Support Services, Mike Townsend
902-424-4329
Director, Housing Services, Kathleen Spicer
902-424-6683
Director, Income Assistance, Janet Rathbun
902-424-4262

Family & Children's Services
Fax: 902-424-0708

Senior Director, George Savoury
902-424-8256
Director, Child Welfare, Vicki Wood
902-424-5653
Director, Early Childhood Development Services, Virginia O'Connell
902-424-3204
Director, Services for Persons with Disabilities, Greg Gammon
902-424-3387
Senior Advisor, Shulamith Medjuck
902-424-4039

Policy & Information Management
Fax: 902-424-0502

Executive Director, Susan Logue
902-424-3914
Acting Director, Policy Support & Evaluation, Brenda Murray
902-424-7900, Fax: 902-945-8303
Director, IT Services, Kevin Hall
902-424-7907

Regional Offices:

Eastern
#38, 360 Prince St., Sydney, NS B1P 5L1
902-563-3302

Regional Administrator, Frank Capstick

Eastern
295 Charlotte St., Sydney, NS B1P 1C6
902-563-2093, Fax: 902-563-1648
Controller, Winston Musgrave

Central
664 Prince St., 2nd Fl., Truro, NS B2N 1G6
902-893-5896, Fax: 902-893-1648
Controller, Dominic Fewer

Western
151 Exhibition St., Kentville, NS B4N 4E5
902-679-6100, Fax: 902-679-6322
Controller, Vern Fraser

Central
McDonald Bldg., 2131 Gottingen St., PO Box 2623, Halifax, NS B3J 3P7
902-424-4755, Fax: 902-424-5115
Regional Administrator, Gary Porter

Northern
#255, 610 East River Rd., New Glasgow, NS B2H 3S2
902-755-7023, Fax: 902-752-5088
Regional Administrator, Cathy Berliner

Western
#202, 10 Webster St., Kentville, NS B4N 1H7
902-679-6716, Fax: 902-679-6127
Regional Administrator, Phil Warren

Maritime Provinces Higher Education Commission (MPHEC)
PO Box 6000, Fredericton, NB E3B 5H1
506-453-2844, Fax: 506-453-2106, info@mphec.ca
www.mphec.ca

CEO, Mireille Duguay

Department of Economic & Rural Development

Centennial Building, #600, 1660 Hollis St., PO Box 2311, Halifax, NS B3J 1V7
902-424-0377, Fax: 902-424-7008, comm@gov.ns.ca
www.gov.ns.ca/econ/

The office assists with knowledge management, trade policy, special projects, government relations regarding economic development issues, labour advice, regarding the work force of the future, information on the business climate & assistance on strategic infrastructure.The Office provides assistance withstrategic management & rural development regarding the business climate, & services such as the Rural Development Branch, Rural Development Service Locations & Co-operatives Branch, dealing with trade policy negotiations & agreements.
Acts Administered:
Business Development Corporation Act
Cooperation Associations Act
Economic Renewal Agency Act
Industrial Development Act
Industrial Estates Limited Act
Industrial Loan Act
Industrial Property Act
Industry Closing Act
Innovation Corporation Act
Nova Scotia Business Incorporated Act
Nova Scotia Film Development Corporation Act
Regional Community Development Act
Research Foundation Corporation Act
Small Business Development Act
Sydney Steel Corporation Act
Trade Development Authority Act
Venture Corporation Act
Venture Corporation Act - Regulations
Voluntary Planning Act
Minister,Hon. Percy Paris
902-424-5790, Fax: 902-424-0514,econmin@gov.ns.ca
Deputy Minister, Ian Thompson
902-424-2901, Fax: 902-424-0619,thompsia@gov.ns.ca
Director, Decision Support, Chris Bryant
902-424-3545, cbryant@gov.ns.ca
Director, Communications, Heather Spidell
902-424-4998, Fax: 902-424-7008,spidelhd@gov.ns.ca
Director, Corporate Information Strategies, Holly Fancy
902-424-2863, fancyh@gov.ns.ca
Director, Economic Strategies and Initiatives, Bruce Hennebury
902-424-5757, hennebub@gov.ns.ca
• Canada-Nova Scotia Offshore Petroleum Board
TD Centre
1791 Barrington St., 6th Fl.
Halifax, NS B3J 3K9
902-422-5588 Fax: 902-422-1799
postmaster@cnsopb.ns.ca
www.cnsopb.ns.ca
The Canada-Nova Scotia Offshore Petroleum Board (CNSOPB) is responsible for protection of the environment during all phases of offshore petroleum activities, from initial exploration to abandonment.The Board is a Federal Authority under the Canadian Environmental Assessment Act. The environmental assessment process starts at the Call for Bids stage. At this stage, a strategic or broad environmental assessment is conducted which identifies environmental concerns or issues. All subsequent projects, including seismic programs & exploratory wells, must undergo an environmental assessment prior to approval by the CNSOPB.The Board also uses class screenings or generic assessments to streamline the regulatory process.These more in-depth environmental assessments, usually jointly funded by a number of petroleum companies, provide more detailed overviews of potential environmental effects, research priorities & mitigation measure than can be accomplished in a single project-specific environmental assessment.
• InNOVACorp
#1400, 1801 Hollis St.
Halifax, NS B3J 3N4
902-424-8670 Fax: 902-424-4679 800-565-7051
communications@innovacorp.ca
www.innovacorp.ns.ca
A network of critical business resources for the early stage technology entrepreneur. Key services include research & development support, business advice, investment & partnership advice. Focuses on two main growth sectors: life sciences & information technology.
• Nova Scotia Business Inc.(NSBI)
World Trade & Convention Centre
#701, 1800 Argyle St.
PO Box 2374
Halifax, NS B3J 3E4
902-424-6650 Fax: 902-424-5739 800-260-6682
info@nsbi.ca
www.novascotiabusiness.com
NSBI is the first point of contact for local companies that want to grow in Nova Scotia, and for international companies that have heard about the province and want to know more.
• Film Nova Scotia
Collins Bank Bldg.
1869 Upper Water St., 3rd Fl.
Halifax, NS B3J 1S9
902-424-7177 Fax: 902-424-0617 888-360-2111
connorkm@gov.ns.ca
www.film.ns.ca
Created in 1990 under the Film Development Corporation Act, Film Nova Scotia is a Provincial Crown Corporation reporting to the Minister of Economic and Rural Development. A Board of Directors, appointed by the Governor in Council, directs the Corporation's activities.
• Trade Centre Limited
1800 Argyle St.
PO Box 955
Halifax, NS B3J 2V9
902-421-8686 Fax: 902-422-2922
www.tradecentrelimited.com
Trade Centre Limited creates economic benefits by bringing people together in Halifax and Nova Scotia.
• Waterfront Development Corporation Ltd.
1751 Lower Water St., 2nd Fl.
Halifax, NS B3J 1S5
902-422-6591 Fax: 902-422-7582
info@wdcl.ca
www.wdcl.ca
Coordinates the commercial & recreational development of the downtown waterfront of Halifax & Dartmouth.

Regional/Service Offices:

Antigonish
#4, 149 Church St., Antigonish, NS B2G 2E2
902-863-7539, Fax: 902-863-7477

Amherst
35 Church St., Amherst, NS B4H 4A1
902-667-3233, Fax: 902-667-2270

Bridgewater
220 North St., Bridgewater, NS B4V 2V6
902-530-3117, Fax: 902-543-1156

Cape Breton
#207, 275 Charlotte St., Sydney, NS B1P 1C6
902-563-2070, Fax: 902-563-0500

Capital Region
Centennial Building, #600, 1660 Hollis St., Halifax, NS B3J 1V7
902-424-4319, Fax: 902-424-1263, 800-565-2009

Kentville
#103, 35 Webster St., Kentville, NS B4N 1H4
902-679-6116, Fax: 902-679-6094

Northeastern Region
#101, 35 Commercial St., Truro, NS B2N 3H9
902-893-6212, Fax: 902-893-6108

Southwestern Shore/Valley
Pier One Complex, 103 Water St., Yarmouth, NS B5A 4P4
902-742-8404, Fax: 902-742-0019

Department of Education

Trade Mart Bldg., 2021 Brunswick St., 4th Fl., PO Box 578, Halifax, NS B3J 2S9
902-424-5168, Fax: 902-424-0680, www.ednet.ns.ca

Acts Administered:
Acadia University Act
Agriculture & Marketing Act, as it pertains to the Agreements of the Nova Scotia Agricultural College Regulations
Apprenticeship & Trades Qualifications Act
Atlantic Institute of Education Act
Atlantic School of Theology Act
Barbers Act
Community Colleges Act
Cosmetology Act
Dalhousie College & University Act
Dalhousie-Technical University Amalgamation Act
Degree Granting Act
Education Act
Education Amendments Act
Education Assistance Act
Educational Communications Agency Act
Handicapped Persons' Education Act
Hospital Education Assistance Act
Libraries Act
Maritime Provinces Higher Education (Nova Scotia) Act
Mi'kmaq Education Act
Mount Saint Vincent University Act
Nova Scotia College of Art & Design Act
Nova Scotia School Boards Association Act
Nova Scotia Teachers College Foundation Act
Private Career Colleges Regulations Act
Registered Barbers Act
Saint Mary's University Act
School Loan Fund Act
Southwestern Nova Scotia Community College Act
St. Francis Xavier University Act
Student Aid Act
Teachers' Collective Bargaining Act
Teaching Profession Act
Universities Assistance Act
Université Saint-Anne Act
University Foundations Act
University College of Cape Breton Act
University Kings College Act
Youth Secretariat Act
Minister,Hon. Judy Streatch
902-424-4236, streatjl@gov.ns.ca
Deputy Minister, Dennis Cochrane
902-424-5643, Fax: 902-424-0680,cochrand@gov.ns.ca
Director, Communications, Nancy Watson
902-424-8286, Fax: 902-424-0680,watsonnm@gov.ns.ca
• Nova Scotia Advisory Board on Colleges & Universities
2021 Brunswick St.
PO Box 2086 M
Halifax, NS B3J 3B7
902-424-6992 Fax: 902-424-0651
nsabcu.ednet.ns.ca
• Nova Scotia Apprenticeship Board
2021 Brunswick St.
PO Box 578
Halifax, NS B3J 2S9
902-424-0872 Fax: 902-428-0605
apprenticeboard@ednet.ns.ca
apprenticeboard.ednet.ns.ca

Acadian & French Language Services Branch
Executive Director, Margelaine Holding
902-424-3927, Fax: 902-424-3937,holdinms@gov.ns.ca
Director, French First Language Programs, Ronald Boudreau
902-424-0538, Fax: 902-424-6546,boudrere@gov.ns.ca
Director, French Second Language Programs, Andrée Green
902-424-0057, Fax: 902-424-3937,greenan@gov.ns.ca

Corporate Policy
Director, Shannon Delbridge
902-424-4740, Fax: 902-424-0626,delbrisd@gov.ns.ca
Director, Statistics & Data Management, Ted Vaughan
902-424-3577, Fax: 902-424-0626,vaughatj@gov.ns.ca

Corporate Services
Sr. Executive Director, Darrell Youden
902-424-7366, Fax: 902-424-1866,youdendb@gov.ns.ca
Executive Director, Finance, Ken Moors
902-424-4728, Fax: 902-424-1866,moorsk@gov.ns.ca
Director, Financial Management, Ben McIntyre
902-424-5698, Fax: 902-424-1866,mcintybr@gov.ns.ca
Director, Grants & Audits, Joe MacEachern
902-424-3956, Fax: 902-424-1866,maceacj@gov.ns.ca
Executive Director, Facilities Management, Charles Clattenburg
902-424-3646, Fax: 902-424-0732,clattecd@gov.ns.ca
Regional Director, Project Management, Don Lohnes
902-424-6957, Fax: 902-424-0732,lohnesdr@gov.ns.ca
Regional Director, Project Management, Paul MacLellan
902-424-4582, Fax: 902-424-0732,maclelpj@gov.ns.ca
Asst. Director, Facilities Management, Charles Ritchey
902-424-4799, Fax: 902-424-0732,ritcheyc@gov.ns.ca
Director, Information Technology Services, John Fahie
902-424-2823, Fax: 902-424-0874,fahiejw@gov.ns.ca
Coordinator, Environmental Health & Safety, Gerald Muise
902-424-7669, Fax: 902-424-0732,muisege@gov.ns.ca

Higher Education
Sr. Executive Director, Wayne Doggett
902-424-4377, Fax: 902-424-0626,doggetws@gov.ns.ca
Director, Kevin Chapman
902-424-8427, Fax: 902-424-0540,chapmank@gov.ns.ca
Director, Universities & Colleges, N.S. Advisory on Colleges & Universities, Greg Ells
902-424-3758, Fax: 902-424-0651,ellsgr@gov.ns.ca
Director, Private Career Colleges, Carol Lowthers
902-424-5189, Fax: 902-424-0666,lowthecm@gov.ns.ca
Director, Provincial Library, Jennifer Evans
902-424-2455, Fax: 902-424-2455,evansje@gov.ns.ca
Registrar, Teacher Certification, D. Brett Woodbury
902-424-6620, Fax: 902-424-3814,woodbudb@gov.ns.ca,

Human Resources & Legal Services
Senior Executive Director, Paula Wedge
902-424-6688, Fax: 902-424-0657,wedgepm@gov.ns.ca
Director, Human Resources, David Allen
902-424-7659, Fax: 902-424-0657,allenda@gov.ns.ca
Solicitor, Judith Begley
902-424-5284, Fax: 902-424-0657,belgleyik@gov.ns.ca

Public Schools
Senior Executive Director, Mike Sweeney
902-424-5829, Fax: 902-424-0680,sweenemd@gov.ns.ca
Director, African Canadian Services, Patrick Kakembo
902-424-2586, Fax: 902-424-7210,kakembpn@gov.ns.ca
Director, English Program Services, Ann Blackwood
902-424-5745, Fax: 902-424-0613,blackwaa@gov.ns.ca
Director, Learning Resources & Technology, Michael Jeffrey
902-424-2462, Fax: 902-424-0633,jeffremg@gov.ns.ca
Director, Mi'kmaq Services, Lorraine Smith-Collins
902-424-3551, Fax: 902-424-1877,smithcla@gov.ns.ca
Director, Student Services, Ann Power
902-424-7454, Fax: 902-424-0749,powerda@gov.ns.ca
Director, Evaluation Services, Vince Warner
902-424-7764, Fax: 902-424-0614,warnerhv@gov.ns.ca

Skills & Learning Branch
Senior Executive Director, Stuart Gourley
902-424-8880, Fax: 902-424-0489,goulems@gov.ns.ca
Director, Adult Education Division,Vacant
902-424-6503, Fax: 902-424-1171,dentrect@gov.ns.ca
Director, Apprenticeship Training & Skill Development Division,Vacant
902-424-8903, Fax: 902-424-0488,davisome@gov.ns.ca
Executive Director, Youth Services Division,Vacant
902-424-3780, Fax: 902-424-0874,gilberrf@gov.ns.ca

Elections Nova Scotia

3667 Strawberry Hill St., PO Box 2246, Halifax, NS B3J 3C8
902-424-8584, Fax: 902-424-6622, 800-565-1504
elections@gov.ns.ca
www.gov.ns.ca/elo/elections
Chief Electoral Officer, Christine McCulloch

Nova Scotia Emergency Management Office (EMO)

PO Box 2581, Halifax, NS B3J 3N5
902-424-5620, Fax: 902-424-5376, 866-424-5620
emo@gov.ns.ca
www.gov.ns.ca/emo
Coordinating agency of the Nova Scotia Government with the responsibility of assisting municipalities to plan & prepare for emergencies; responsible for the implementation of the province-wide 911 service. Coordinates emergency efforts of provincial & federal departments & agencies, as well as private health & social services, to provide assistance to disaster areas; sponsors the Ground Search & Rescue Program; maintains a professional planner at all offices. Coordinates all emergency preparedness training for municipal staff at the Emergency Preparedness College (Arnprior, ON) & through the Joint Emergency Preparedness Program (JEPP) which provides a federal government cost-sharing formula for emergency equipment for first-response agencies.

Acts Administered:
Emergency Management Act
Emergency 911 Act
Minister Responsible,Hon. Ernest Fage
CEO/Deputy Head, Craig D. MacLaughlan
Director, Emergency Programs, Andy S. Lathem
Director, Emergency Services, Michael Myette
Director, Training & Strategic Planning, Dennis P. Kelly
Communications/Public Education Officer, Sheliah Tulloch
Civic Addressing Coordinator, Darrell Marsh
Federal/Provincial Liaison Officer, Adam Rostis
Exec. Assistant/Office Manager, Dianne Caswell

Department of Energy

Bank of Montreal Bldg., #400, 5151 George St., PO Box 2664, Halifax, NS B3J 3P7
902-424-4575, Fax: 902-424-0528,
energyinfo@gov.ns.ca
www.gov.ns.ca/energy
To serve as the government's focal point in the development of the province's energy resources, as outlined in the Energy Strategy. Responsible for a wide range of initiatives in the following areas: energy Transportation & utilization policy & analysis; resource assessment & royalties; climate change; business & technology; communications & public education.
Acts Administered:
Canada-Nova Scotia Offshore Petroleum Resources Accord Implementation (Nova Scotia) Act
Electricity Act
Energy-Efficient Appliances Act
Energy Resources Conservation Act
Gas Distribution Act
Offshore Petroleum Royalty Act
Petroleum Resources Act
Petroleum Resources Removal Permit Act
Pipeline Act
Underground Hydrocarbons Storage Act
Minister,Hon. Barry Barnet
902-424-7793, barnetbe@gov.ns.ca
Deputy Minister, Alison Scott
902-424-1710, Fax: 902-424-3265,scottal@gov.ns.ca
Solicitor, J.Marshall Burgess, Q.C.
902-424-8131, burgesmx@gov.ns.ca
Director, Business & Technology, Bernie MacDonald
902-424-2704, macdonbwn@gov.ns.ca
Director, Communications, Ross McLaren
902-424-4536, Fax: 902-424-0528,mclarenr@gov.ns.ca
Director, Policy & Analysis, Bruce Cameron
902-424-2288, Fax: 902-499-8849
Director, Resource Assessment & Royalties Division, Sandy MacMullin
902-424-8129, macmulsa@gov.ns.ca,
Manager, Energy Transportation & Utilization, Allan Crandlemire
902-424-6229
Executive Secretary to the Minister, Diane Bernard
902-424-7793, Fax: 902-424-3265,bernardm@gov.ns.ca

Department of Environment

5151 Terminal Rd., 5th Fl., PO Box 442, Halifax, NS B3J 2T8
902-424-3600, Fax: 902-424-0503, 877-936-8476
www.gov.ns.ca/nse
Major program responsibilities for Nova Scotia Environment are environmental and natural areas management, environmental monitoring and compliance, and climate change. Pollution prevention, the NS Youth Conservation Corps., solid waste reduction and recycling, and environmental trade and innovation are all part of the new Nova Scotia Environment.
Acts Administered:
Amusement Device Safety Act
Building Code Act (Shared with Service Nova Scotia)
Court & Administrative Reform Act
Crane Operators & Power Engineers Act
Credit Union Act
Electrical Installation & Inspection Act
Elevators & Lifts Act
Environment Act
Fire Safety Act
Gaming Control Act
Health Act (in part)
Insurance Act
Insurance Premiums Tax Act
Labour Standards Code
Liquor Control Act
Mutual Insurance Companies Act
Occupational Health & Safety Act
Remembrance Day Act
Securities Act
Smoke-free Places Act
Special Places Protection Act (Shared with Tourism, Culture & Heritage)

Steam Boiler & Pressure Vessel Act
Teachers' Collective Bargaining Act
Theaters & Amusements Act
Trade Union Act
Trust & Loan Companies Act
Water Resources Protection Act
Wilderness Areas Protection Act
Workers' Compensation Act
Minister,Hon. Sterling Belliveau
902-424-3736, Fax: 902-424-1599,min_env@gov.ns.ca
Deputy Minister, Nancy Vanstone
902-424-8150, nvanston@gov.ns.ca
Director, Communications, Penny McCormick
902-424-2575, mccormpl@gov.ns.ca
Executive Secretary, Virginia Messervey
902-424-3736, messerv@gov.ns.ca
• Crane Operators Appeal Board
5151 Terminal Rd., 7th Fl.
PO Box 697
Halifax, NS B3J 2T8
902-424-8595 Fax: 902-424-0217
fraserej@gov.ns.ca
www.gov.ns.ca/lwd/coab
The Crane Operators Appeal Board is one of the newest tribunals in Nova Scotia Labour and Workforce Development, created pursuant to the Crane Operators and Power Engineers Act which came into force on September 1, 2001. It is an independent adjudicative tribunal charged with considering appeals filed under Part I of the Act.
• Labour Relations Board & Construction Industry Panel
5151 Terminal Rd.,7th Fl.
PO Box 697
Halifax, NS B3J 2T8
902-424-6730 Fax: 902-424-1744
www.gov.ns.ca/lwd/lrb
The Labour Relations Board and Construction Industry Panel help to resolve disputes between labour and management that relate to the Trade Union Act.
• Labour Standards Tribunal
5151 Terminal Rd., 7th Fl.
PO Box 697
Halifax, NS B3J 2T8
902-424-6730 Fax: 902-424-1744
noeljl@gov.ns.ca
www.gov.ns.ca/lwd/lst
The Labour Standards Tribunal is a body that hears complaints of failure to comply with the Labour Standards Code. This Code came into effect by proclamation on February 1, 1973.
• Nova Scotia Securities Commission
Joseph Howe Bldg.
1690 Hollis St., 2nd Fl.
PO Box 458
Halifax, NS B3J 2P8
902-424-7768 Fax: 902-424-4625
www.gov.ns.ca/nssc
Their mission is to protect investors in Nova Scotia from practices and activities that tend to undermine their confidence in the fairness and efficiency of securities markets and to foster the process of capital formation, where it would not be inconsistent with an adequate level of investor protection.
• Occupational Health & Safety Advisory Council
PO Box 697
Halifax, NS B3J 2T8
902-424-2484 Fax: 902-424-5640
www.gov.ns.ca/lwd/abct/ohsadvisory.asp
The Occupational Health and Safety Advisory Council advises the Minister of Labour and Workforce Development on occupational health and safety matters.
• Occupational Health & Safety Appeal Panel
5151 Terminal Rd., 7th Fl.
PO Box 697
Halifax, NS B3J 2T8
902-424-6730
www.gov.ns.ca/lwd/ohsapo
The Occupational Health & Safety Appeal Panel adjudicates disputes relating to both the technical aspects of health & safety & the protection of individual employees from union & employer reprisals when they have discharged their responsibilities under the Occupational Health & Safety Act. The OHS Appeal Panel Office administers & coordinates the process of appeals of orders or decisions made by the executive director of the OHS Division. The OHS Appeal Panel is separate from & independent from the OHS Division.
• Pay Equity Commission
5151 Terminal Rd., 7th Fl.
PO Box 697
Halifax, NS B3J 2T8
902-424-2385 Fax: 902-424-0575
www.gov.ns.ca/lwd/payequity
The Pay Equity Commission is responsible for administrating the Pay Equity Act. In addition to monitoring the pay equity process, the Commission has the power to resolve disputes when employers and employees cannot agree, conducts research, maintains statistics, and advises the Minister of Labour on matters relating to pay equity.
• Workers' Advisers Program
#502, 5670 Spring Garden Rd.
PO Box 1063
Halifax, NS B3J 2X1
902-424-5050 Fax: 902-424-0530 800-774-4712
www.gov.ns.ca/lwd/wap
The Workers' Advisers Program is a legal clinic that is funded by the provincial government offering services to injured workers. Our purpose is to provide legal assistance when an injured worker has been denied Workers' Compensation Board benefits.
• Workers' Compensation Board of Nova Scotia

Alcohol & Gaming Division
Alderney Gate, 40 Alderney Dr., 5th Fl., PO Box 545, Dartmouth, NS B2Y 3Y8
902-424-6160, Fax: 902-424-6313, 877-565-0556
www.gov.ns.ca/lwd/agd
Responsible for licensing & regulating gaming activity, liquor activity, & film classification in Nova Scotia.
Executive Director, Dennis Kerr
902-424-4884, kerrdw@gov.ns.ca
Financial Services Manager, Bruce Marsh
902-424-3326, marshbg@gov.ns.ca
Director, Licensing & Registration Division, Terry Kelly
902-424-6023, kellytb@gov.ns.ca
Director, Investigation & Enforcement, John MacDonald
902-424-6092, macdonjr@gov.ns.ca
Manager, Policy & Research, Joel Baltzer
902-424-4096, baltzeji@gov.ns.ca

Environmental & Natural Areas Management
PO Box 697, Halifax, NS B3J 3T8
902-424-3571
Promotes sustainable management & protection of the environment through both regulatory & non-regulatory means, including developing & implementing plans, standards, guidelines, & policies for the management & protection of Nova Scotia's air, water & terrestrial resources including protected areas, & by providing regionally-based regulatory approval, inspection, monitoring & enforcement.
Executive Director, Robert Langdon, P.Eng.
902-424-2386, langdobe@gov.ns.ca
Manager, Education, Training & Youth Corps, Paul Schwartz
902-424-5206
Manager, Environmental Assessment, Chris Daly
902-424-4936
Manager, Air Quality, Andrew Murphy
902-424-2177
Manager, Environmental Innovations, Craig Morrison
902-424-2541, morriscp@gov.ns.ca
Manager, Water & Wastewater, David Briggins
902-424-2571

Environmental Monitoring & Compliance
Responsible for the majority of field operations relating to environmental protection. Activities in this Division include processing applications, inspection & monitoring of approvals, enforcement activities & response to public issues & complaints. Services of Environmental Monitoring & Compliance include the Regional & District Offices Network & Solid Waste Resource Management.
Executive Director, Regional & District Offices, Gerard MacLellan
902-424-2547, Fax: 902-424-0569,maclelgj@gov.ns.ca

Regional Offices:

Central
Sunnyside Mall, #224, 1595 Bedford Hwy., Bedford, NS B4A 3Y4
902-424-2382, Fax: 902-424-0597
Regional Manager, Darlene Fenton

Eastern
#125, 400 Reeves St., Port Hawkesbury, NS B9A 2R5
902-625-0791, Fax: 902-625-3722
District Manager, Terry MacPherson

Northern
32 Church St., Amherst, NS B2H 3A8
902-667-6205, Fax: 902-667-6214
District Manager, Brad Skinner

Western
60 Logan Rd., Briwdewater, NS B4V 3J8
902-543-4685, Fax: 902-527-5480
Acting District Manager, Adrian Fuller

Financial Institutions
902-424-6331, Fax: 902-424-1298
The Financial Institutions Division regulates the operations of credit unions, trust & loan companies & insurance companies, agents, brokers & adjusters in the Province. The Division also provides a complaint & enquiry service to the public relating to financial institutions & the insurance industry & collects & verifies the insurance premiums tax.
Acting Superintendent, Doug Murphy
902-424-7552,
Acting Deputy Superintendent, William Ngu
902-424-2787
Insurance Officer, Jennifer Calder
902-424-4987

Information & Business Services
5151 Terminal Rd., 5th Fl., PO Box 697, Halifax, NS B3J 2T8
902-424-4313, Fax: 902-424-6925
Is responsible for providing a focus within the department for the development, use, and access to our information holdings, including operational records and published material; providing consistency in the department's business practices; and developing and implementing the department's Occupational Health and Safety program.
Director, Scott Nicholson
902-424-4313, nicholsw@gov.ns.ca
Librarian, Natalie MacPherson
902-424-8474, macphend@gov.ns.ca
Air Quality Specialist, Kamila Tomcik
902-424-2324
Inspector Specialist, John McPherson
902-424-2566
Manager, Chris Daly
902-424-4936
Environmental Assessment Officer, Helen MacPhail
902-424-3960

Labour Services
902-424-4156
Executive Director, Laurie Rantala
Chief Industrial Relations Officer, Conciliation Services, Kenneth Zwicker
902-424-5977

Labour Standards Division
902-424-4311, Fax: 902-424-0648, labrstd@gov.ns.ca
Deals with enquiries & complaints from the public about how the provincial Labour Standards Code applies to specific employment situations.Labour Standards staff help to facilitate settlements of complaints through a self-help process. If this process fails, staff investigate & work to achieve compliance in areas where the Labour Standards Code has not been adhered to. The Labour Standards Division also promotes an understanding of the Labour Standards Code & respective legislation, through continuing education.
Director, Mary Belliveau
902-424-5404, bellivma@gov.ns.ca

Occupational Health & Safety Division
902-424-5400, Fax: 902-424-5640, 800-952-2687
Executive Director, Jim LeBlanc
leblajim@gov.ns.ca
Provincial Manager, Inspection & Compliance Services, Ray O'Neil
902-424-8478, oneilrx@gov.ns.ca
Provincial Manager, Professional Services, Stewart Sampson
902-424-8055, sampsons@gov.ns.ca

Public Safety
The Office of the Fire Marshal, through the Fire Prevention Act, has the authority & responsibility for the provision of fire safety in buildings & for safe storage of flammable & combustible materials. The Office advises various levels of government on fire-related matters, including fire protection, & is also responsible for the safe installation of propane & electricity.
Director & Fire Marshall, Robert Cormier
902-424-4553, cormierr@gov.ns.ca

Pension Regulation Division
PO Box 2531, Halifax, NS B3J 3N5
902-424-8915, Fax: 902-424-0662
The Pension Regulation Division administers & enforces the Pension Benefits Act to safeguard benefits promised under pension plans. The Division supervises over 470 registered pension plans to ensure the plans are well managed & adequately funded in order to meet their obligations to pension plan members.
Superintendent, Pensions, Nancy MacNeil Smith
902-424-4444, macneiln@gov.ns.ca

Department of Finance

Provincial Bldg., 1723 Hollis St., 7th Fl., PO Box 187, Halifax, NS B3J 2N3
902-424-5554, Fax: 902-424-0635, FinanceWeb@gov.ns.ca
www.gov.ns.ca/fina
The Nova Scotia Department of Finance's vision is to provide financial leadership that strengthens Nova Scotia; and their

mission is to provide corporate financial services and manage the province's financial affairs and policies in the interests of Nova Scotians.

Acts Administered:
Corporation Capital Tax Act
Equity Tax Credit Act
Halifax-Dartmouth Bridge Commission Act
Home Ownership Savings Plan (Nova Scotia) Act
Homeowners' Incentive Act
Income Tax Act
Members' Retiring Allowances Act
Provincial Finance Act
Public Sector Unpaid Leave Act
Public Service Superannuation Act
Revenue Act
Sales Tax Act
Securities Act
Sydney Steel Corporation Sale Act
Teachers' Pension Act

Minister,Hon. Jamie Muir
902-424-5720, Fax: 902-424-0635,finamin@gov.ns.ca
Deputy Minister, Vicki Harnish
902-424-5773, harnisvl@gov.ns.ca
Asst. Deputy Minister, Elizabeth Cody
902-424-4168, Fax: 902-424-0635,codye@gov.ns.ca
Controller, Byron Rafuse
rafuseb@gov.ns.ca,
Director, Communications, Cathy Shaw
902-424-8787, Fax: 902-424-0635,shawcn@gov.ns.ca
Manager, Community Counts, Malcolm Shookner
shooknmr@gov.ns.ca
Executive Secretary to the Deputy Minister, Alison MacIsaac
902-424-5553, macisaab@gov.ns.ca
• Nova Scotia Utility and Review Board(NSUARB)
Summit Place
1601 Lower Water St., 3rd Fl.
Halifax, NS B3J 3P6
902-424-4448
uarb.board@gov.ns.ca
www.nsuarb.ca
The Nova Scotia Utility and Review Board (NSUARB) is an independent quasi-judicial body which has both regulatory and adjudicative jurisdiction flowing from the Utility and Review Board Act. It reports to the Legislature through the Minister of Finance.

Controller's Branch
Controller, Byron Rafuse
902-424-2424, rafusebg@gov.ns.ca
Director, Corporate Internal Audit, Pamela Muir
902-424-6102, Fax: 902-424-3191,muirpg@gov.ns.ca
Director, Government Accounting Division, Suzanne Wile
902-424-6543, Fax: 902-424-2777,wilesm@gov.ns.ca
Director, Corporate Information Systems, Steve Feindel
902-424-2939, feindesj@gov.ns.ca
Director, Payroll Services Division, Shirley Carras
902-424-5567, Fax: 902-424-0590,scarras@gov.ns.ca

Fiscal & Economic Policy Branch
Executive Director, Nancy McInnis-Leek
902-424-4160, Fax: 902-424-0590,nrmsinni@gov.ns.ca
Director, Economic & Statistics Division, Fred Bergman
902-424-6129, Fax: 902-424-0714,bergmanf@gov.ns.ca
Director, Taxation & Fiscal Policy, Rod MacDougall
902-424-4118, Fax: 902-424-0590,macdourx@gov.ns.ca

Nova Scotia Pension Agency
CEO, John Traves
902-424-5557, travesj@gov.ns.ca
Director, Investments, Elizabeth Vandenburg
902-424-1170, Fax: 902-424-4539,vandenbe@gov.ns.ca
Director, Pensions, Kim Blinn
902-424-4539, blinnkm@gov.ns.ca

Department of Health

Joseph Howe Bldg., 1690 Hollis St., 4th Fl., PO Box 488, Halifax, NS B3J 2R8
902-424-5818, Fax: 902-424-0730, 800-387-6665
DoHweb@gov.ns.ca
www.gov.ns.ca/health

Other Communication: TeleHealth Network: 1-800-889-5949
Mission: Working together to empower individuals, families, partners, and communities to promote, improve, and maintain the health of Nova Scotians through a proactive and sustainable health care system.

Acts Administered:
Chiropractic Act
Cobequid Multi-Service Centre Act
Dental Act
Dental Technicians Act
Denturist Act
Department of Health Promotion & Protection Act
Disabled Persons' Commission Act
Dispensing Opticians Act
Drug Dependency Act
Health Act
Health Authorities Act
Health Research Foundation Act
Health Services & Insurance Act
Homemakers' Services Act
Homes for Special Care Act
Hospitals Act
Municipal Hospitals Loan Act
Nursing Assistants Act
Occupational Therapists Act
Optometry Act
Pharmacy Act
Physiotherapy Act
Psychologists Act
Registered Nurses Association Act
Smoke Free Places Act
Tobacco Access Act

Minister,Hon. Karen Casey
902-424-3377, Fax: 902-424-0559,caseykl@gov.ns.ca
Deputy Minister, Cheryl A. Doiron
902-424-7570, Fax: 902-424-4570,doironca@gov.ns.ca
CFO, Allan Horsborough
Director, NS TeleHealth Network, Ron MacFarlane
902-424-2152, Fax: 902-424-0270,macfarr@gov.ns.ca
• Nova Scotia Advisory Commission on AIDS
Dennis Bldg.
1740 Granville St., 6th Fl.
Halifax, NS B3J 1X5
902-424-5730 Fax: 902-424-4727
• Seniors' Secretariat
Dennis Bldg.
1740 Granville St., 4th Fl.
PO Box 2065
Halifax, NS B3J 2Z1
902-424-0065 Fax: 902-424-0561 800-670-0065
scs@gov.ns.ca
www.gov.ns.ca/scs

Emergency Health Services
Fax: 902-424-0155
Emergency Health Services Nova Scotia (EHS) is a division of the Nova Scotia Department of Health. It is responsible for the development, implementation, monitoring & evaluation of pre-hospital emergency health services.
Senior Director, Marilyn Pike
902-424-8902
Director, EHS Oversight, Ed Cain
902-424-3781
Director, EHS Provincial Programs, Paula Poirier
902-424-3928
Director, EHS Technical Operations, Tony Eden
902-424-4429

Mental Health & Addiction Services
Fax: 902-424-0647
Acting Executive Director & Director, Child & Youth Mental Health Services, Linda Smith
902-424-0830
Director, Addiction Services, Brian Wilbur
902-424-7220
Director, Adult Mental Health Services, John Campbell
902-424-7933

Continuing Care
Fax: 902-424-0506
Executive Director, Kevin Menzies
902-424-3221
Provincial Coordinator, Adult Protection Services, Robert Turnbull
902-424-8257
Director, Monitoring & Evaluation, Donna Dill
902-424-4982
Director, Service & Business Support, Kathy Greenwood
902-424-6985
Director, Standards & Policy Development, Susan Weagle
902-424-6857

Department of Health Promotion & Protection

Summit Place, 1601 Lower Water St., 5th Fl., PO Box 487, Halifax, NS B3J 2R7
902-424-4807, Fax: 902-424-4716, 866-231-3882
healthpromotion@gov.ns.ca
www.gov.ns.ca/hpp
Dedicated to helping Nova Scotians live healthier and safer lives.
Minister,Hon. Pat Dunn
902-424-5627, Fax: 902-424-7983,dunnpr@gov.ns.ca
Deputy Minister, Duff Montgomerie
902-424-3095, montgodm@gov.ns.ca
Chief Public Health Officer,Dr. Robert Strang
902-424-2358, Fax: 902-424-4716,robert.strang@gov.ns.ca
Director, Addiction Services, Carolyn Davison
902-424-7218, davisocj@gov.ns.ca
Senior Director, Sport & Recreation, Farida Gabanni
902-424-7554, gabbanfg@gov.ns.ca
Director, Communications, Sue McKeage
902-424-0913, Fax: 902-428-3148,mckeagsm@gov.ns.ca

Nova Scotia Human Rights Commission

Joseph Howe Bldg., 1690 Hollis St., 6th Fl., Halifax, NS B3J 3C4
902-424-4111, Fax: 902-424-0596,
www.gov.ns.ca/humanrights

Acts Administered:
Human Rights Act
President/CEO,Vacant
Chair, Ernest Bolivar
Librarian, Corinne Reffer

Regional Offices:

Digby
84 Warwick St., PO Box 1029, Digby, NS B0V 1A0
902-245-4791, Fax: 902-245-7103

New Glasgow
2561 Westville Rd., RR#3, PO Box 728, New Glasgow, NS B2H 5C6
902-752-3086, Fax: 902-755-7239

Sydney
Provincial Bldg., 360 Prince St., Sydney, NS B1P 5L1
902-563-2140, Fax: 902-563-5613

Department of Intergovernmental Affairs

Joseph Howe Bldg., 1690 Hollis St., 7th Fl., PO Box 1617, Halifax, NS B3J 2Y3
902-424-5153, Fax: 902-424-0728,
iga@gov.ns.ca
http://gov.ns.ca/iga
Provides leadership in the development of corporate strategies for Nova Scotia's relations with governments & organizations.
Minister,Hon. Rodney MacDonald
902-424-6600, Fax: 902-424-7648,premier@gov.ns.ca
Deputy Minister, Judith Sullivan-Corney
902-424-3219, corneyjm@gov.ns.ca
General Counsel, Pat Clahane
902-424-4894, clahanpg@gov.ns.ca
Director, Strategic Policy, Norma MacIsaac
902-424-7662, macisanj@gov.ns.ca
Sr. Trade Policy Analyst, John Hoar
902-424-7108, hoarj@gov.ns.ca
Director, Environmental & Social Affairs, Albert Walzak
902-424-7748, walzakag@gov.ns.ca
Director, Regional Relations, Darryl C. Eisan
902-424-4535, dceisan@gov.ns.ca
Director, Economic Policy & Analysis, André Moore
902-424-7728, mooreac@gov.ns.ca
Research Assistant, Federal-Provincial, Cathy Richard
902-424-1198, richarcl@gov.ns.ca

Department of Justice

5151 Terminal Rd., 4th Fl., PO Box 7, Halifax, NS B3J 2L6
902-424-4030, Fax: 902-424-0510,
webbermj@gov.ns.ca
www.gov.ns.ca/just/

Acts Administered:
Accountant General of the Supreme Court Act
Age of Majority Act
Alimony Act
Alternative Penalty Act
Apportionment Act
Arbitration Act
Architects Act
Assignments & Preferences Act
Barristers & Solicitors Act
Beneficiaries Designation Act
Bills of Lading Act
Canada & the United Kingdom Reciprocal Recognition & Enforcement of Judgments Act
Cape Breton Barristers' Society Act
Change of Name Act
Child Abduction Act
Collection Act
Compensation for Victims of Crime Act
Constables Act
Constables' Protection Act
Constitutional Questions Act
Contributory Negligence Act
Controverted Elections Act

Conveyancing Act
Corporations Miscellaneous Provisions Act
Corrections Act
Costs & Fees Act
Court for Divorce & Matrimonial Causes Act
Court Houses & Lockup Houses Act
Court Officials Act
Court Security Act
Creditors' Relief Act
Defamation Act
Demise of the Crown Act
Descent of Property Act
Elections Act
Engineering Profession Act
Escheats Act
Estate Actions Act
Estreats Act
Evidence Act
Expropriation Act, 1973
Family Court Act
Family Maintenance Act
Family Orders Information Release Act
Fatal Injuries Act
Fatality Inquiries Act
Federal/Provincial Power Act
Floral Emblem Act
Forcible Entry & Detainer Act
Freedom of Information & Protection of Privacy Act
Guardianship Act
House of Assembly Act
Human Rights Act
Incompetent Persons Act
Indigent Debtors Act
Inebriates' Guardianship Act
Interest on Judgements Act
International Commercial Arbitration Act
Interpretation Act
Interprovincial Subpoena Act
Intestate Succession Act
Judicature Act
Judicial Disqualifications Removal Act
Juries Act
Justices of the Peace Act
Land Actions Venue Act
Law Reform Commission Act
Legal Aid Act
Liberty of the Subject Act
Lieutenant Governor & Great Seal Act
Limitation of Actions Act
Maintenance Enforcement Act
Maintenance Orders Enforcement Act
Married Women's Deed Act
Married Women's Property Act
Matrimonial Property Act
Mechanics' Lien Act
Members & Public Employees Disclosure Act
Municipal Conflict of Interest Act
Night Courts Act
Notaries & Commissioners Act
Nova Scotia Tartan Act
Occupiers Liability Act
Official Tree Act
Overholding Tenants Act
Partition Act
Payment into Court Act
Pledging of Service Emblems Act
Police Act
Police Services Act
Powers of Attorney Act
Presumption of Death Act
Private Investigators & Private Guards Act
Probate Act
Proceedings Against the Crown Act
Protection of Property Act
Provincial Bird Act
Provincial Dog Act
Public Inquiries Act
Public Prosecutions Act
Public Service Act
Public Subscriptions Act
Public Trustee Act
Quieting Titles Act
Real Property Act
Real Property Transfer Validation Act
Reciprocal Enforcement of Custody Orders Act
Reciprocal Enforcement of Judgments Orders
Regulations Act
Religious & Charitable Corporations Property Act
Religious Congregations & Societies Act
Remembrance Day Act
Remission of Penalties Act
Residential Tenancies Act
Retail Business Uniform Closing Day Act
Sale of Goods Act
Sale of Land under Execution Act
Salvage Yards Licensing Act
Securities Act
Small Claims Court Act
Solemnization of Marriage Act
Statute Revision Act
Summary Proceedings Act
Supreme & Exchequer Courts of Canada Act
Sureties Act
Survival of Actions Act
Survivorship Act
Taxing Masters Act
Tenancies & Distress for Rent Act
Testators' Family Maintenance Act
Ticket of Leave Act
Time Definition Act
Tortfeasors Act
Trustee Act
Unclaimed Articles Act
Uniform Law Act
Utility & Review Board Act
Variation of Trusts Act
Vendors & Purchasers Act
Victims Rights & Services Act
Volunteer Services Act
Warehouse Receipts Act
Warehousemen's Lien Act
Wills Act
Woodmen's Lien Act
Young Persons Summary Proceedings Act

Minister & Attorney General,Hon. Ross Landry
902-424-4044, Fax: 902-424-0510,justmin@gov.ns.ca
Deputy Minister, Marian F. Tyson, Q.C.
902-424-4223, tysonmf@gov.ns.ca
Director, Communications, Sherri Aikenhead
902-424-3313, aikenhsl@gov.ns.ca
Director, Public Safety, Fred Sanford
902-424-0069, sanforfg@gov.ns.ca

• Human Rights Commission
• Nova Scotia Legal Aid Commission
#102, 137 Chain Lake Dr.
Halifax, NS B3S 1B3
902-420-6573 Fax: 902-420-3471
nsla.exec@ns.sympatico.ca
www.gov.ns.ca/just/legad.htm
• Nova Scotia Medical Examiner Service
Halifax Insurance Bldg.
#701, 5670 Spring Garden Rd.
Halifax, NS B3J 1H7
902-424-2722 Fax: 902-424-0607 888-424-4336
• Nova Scotia Police Commission
#300, 1601 Lower Water St.
PO Box 1573
Halifax, NS B3J 2Y3
902-424-3246 Fax: 902-424-3919
uarb.polcom@gov.ns.ca
www.gov.ns.ca/just/polcomm.htm
• Public Trustee Office
#201, 5151 Terminal Rd.
PO Box 385
Halifax, NS B3J 2T3
902-424-7760 Fax: 902-424-0616
• Workers' Compensation Appeals Tribunal
#1002, 5670 Spring Garden Rd.
Halifax, NS B3J 1H6
902-424-2250 Fax: 902-424-2321 800-274-8281
www.gov.ns.ca/wcat/

Department of Labour & Workforce Development

5151 Terminal Rd., 6th Fl., PO Box 697, Halifax, NS B3J 2T8
902-424-5301, Fax: 902-424-0575,
www.gov.ns.ca/lwd

The Department of Labour and Workforce Development focuses on labour issues, employment rights and responsibilities, adult learning, apprenticeship training and trade qualification, skill development, public and workplace safety, industry regulation, licensing and pensions.

Minister,Hon. Mark Parent
902-424-6647, min_lwd@gov.ns.ca
Deputy Minister, Margaret F. MacDonald
902-424-6632, macdonmf@gov.ns.ca
Director, Communications, Karen Stone
902-424-2107, Fax: 902-424-0644,stonekk@gov.ns.ca
Executive Secretary, Lorna Kennedy
902-424-6647, kennedlj@gov.ns.ca

Correctional Services Division

902-424-7640, Fax: 902-424-0692

Executive Director, Fred Honsberger
Director, Community Corrections, Gary W. Dupuis
902-424-7641
Director, Program Services, Diana McKinnon
902-424-5661

Court Services

Fax: 902-424-7596

Executive Director, Christine Mosher
902-424-4389
Director, Court Services, Bill Clancey
902-424-6414
Director, Court Services, Nancy MacLellan
902-424-5181
Director, Court Services, Judith McPhee
902-424-2691
Director, Sheriff Services, David Horner
902-424-2838

Legal Services Division

Fax: 902-424-1730,

Executive Director, Bill Wilson
902-424-3236
Director, Solicitor Services & Registrar, Regulations, Jonathan Davies
902-424-5476

Policing & Victim Services

Fax: 902-424-0700

Executive Director, Alex Steeves
902-424-7795
Acting Director, Policing Services, Ingrid Brodie
902-424-6437
Director, Support Services, Weldon Myers
902-442-4778
Chief Firearms Officer, Martin Kramers
902-424-1712
Director, Victim Services, Joanne Marriott-Thorne
902-424-4858
Executive Director, Finance CSU, Clarence Guest
902-424-4593
Acting Director, Human Resources, Mary Jane Wortman
902-424-3930

Nova Scotia Liquor Corporation

Bayers Lake Business Park, 93 Chain Lake Dr., Halifax, NS B3S 1A3
902-450-6752, 800-567-5874
www.nsliquor.ca

Minister Responsible,Hon. Carolyn Bolivar-Getson
Chair, Peter McCreath
President/CEO, Bret Mitchell

Department of Natural Resources

Founder's Square, 1701 Hollis St., 3rd Fl., PO Box 698, Halifax, NS B3J 2T9
902-424-5935, Fax: 902-424-0594, 800-565-2224
www.gov.ns.ca/natr

Responsible for the administration & management of provincial Crown lands, development of mineral & energy resources, protection & sustainable development of forest resources & operation & maintenance of parks system, & promoting the conservation & sustainable use of wildlife populations, habitat & ecosystems.Initiatives include: a State of the Forest report; working with other departments on State of the Environment report; leading the development of a provincial climate change strategy; implementing recovery plans for endangered & threatened wildlife species; & developing strategic land use plans for Crown lands using an integrated resource management planning process.

Acts Administered:
Act to Confer Certain Powers upon the Lieutenant Governor in Council & to amend the Mines Act
Angling Act
Beaches Act
Blueberry Association Act
Bowater Mersey Agreement Act
Conservation Easements Act
Endangered Species Act
Expropriation Act
Forests Act
Gypsum Mining Income Tax Act
Indian Lands Act
Halifax Power & Pulp Company Limited Agreement Act, 1962
Land Holdings Disclosure Act
Land Surveyors Act
Mineral Resources Act
Mines Act
Nova Scotia Federation of Anglers & Hunters Act
Off Highway Vehicles Act
Primary Forest Products Marketing Act
Provincial Parks Act
Private Ways Act

Scalers Act
Scott Maritimes Limited Agreement (1965) Act
Special Places Protection Act (Shared with Tourism, Culture & Heritage)
Stora Forest Industries Agreement Act
Trails Act
Treasure Trove Act
Wildlife Act

Minister,Hon. Carolyn Bolivar-Getson
902-424-4037, Fax: 902-424-0594,bolivargetson@gov.ns.ca
Deputy Minister, Peter Underwood
902-424-4121, Fax: 902-424-0594,underwpc@gov.ns.ca
Secretary to the Deputy Minister, Nancy Parsons
902-424-4121, parsonn@gov.ns.ca

• Crown Lands Record Centre
Founders Square
#501, 1701 Hollis St.
PO Box 698
Halifax, NS B3J 2T9
902-424-8681

• NS Primary Forest Products Marketing Board
#804, 45 Alderney Dr.
Dartmouth, NS B2Y 2N6
902-424-7598 Fax: 902-424-6965

Land Services Branch

The Land Services Branch management oversees, coordinates & approves all activities within the Branch relating to the administration of Crown land. The Branch provides advice on legislative revisions & advises & drafts policies relating to the administration of Crown land & provides on all matters respecting Crown land administration.

Executive Director, Jo-Anne Himmelman
902-424-4267, himmelgj@gov.ns.ca
Director, Land Administration Division, Dave Steeves
902-424-3160, steeveda@gov.ns.ca
Acting Director, Surveys Division, Sandy Cameron
902-424-3144
Manager, Crown Lands Disposals, Harry Ashcroft
902-424-3159

Minerals Resources Branch

Fax: 902-424-7735, www.gov.ns.ca/natr/meb/

Implements policies & programs dealing with the exploration, development, management & efficient use of energy & mineral resources, promotes scientific studies of the geology of the province for use by government, industry & the public, provides a mineral rights tenure system to establish legal rights to minerals for exploration & development. Promotes concepts of environmental responsibility & sustainable, stewardship or the mineral & energy resource sector & integrated resource planning.

Executive Director, Scott Swinden
902-424-7943, hsswinde@gov.ns.ca
Director, Mineral Development & Management, Don Jones, Ph.D., P.Eng.
902-424-5618, jonesds@gov.ns.ca

Planning Secretariat

Provides planning & policy coordination support to the Department, ensures that policies & plans developed in the Department are coordinated, support the integrated management of our natural resources & are compatible with & support the strategic direction of the government.Also provides a range of administrative, planning, research, information management, information distribution, graphics, cartographic, communication, & occupational health & safety-related services.

Executive Director, Patricia MacNeil
902-424-4988, macneipb@gov.ns.ca

Regional Services Branch

Delivers departmental programs & services through a field office network, responsible for forest protection & planning, forest nurseries, research & development, enforcement, coordination of the hunter safety program, regional geological services, Crown land surveys, operation & maintenance of provincial parks, resource conservation, forest fire prevention & monitoring of forest insects & diseases.

Executive Director, Brian Gilbert
902-424-3949, giberbs@gov.ns.ca
Director, Enforcement Division, John Mombourquette
902-424-5254, jamombou@gov.ns.ca
Director, Fleet Management, Ross Wickwire
902-758-7019, Fax: 902-758-3355,wickwire@gov.ns.ca

Regional Offices:

Central
626 College Rd., Bible Hill, NS B2N 2R2
902-893-5620, Fax: 902-893-5613
Regional Director, Roger Aggas
aggasr@gov.ns.ca

Eastern
300 Mountain Rd., Sydney, NS B1L 1A9
902-563-3370, Fax: 902-567-2535
Regional Director, Dave Harris
harrisdl@gov.ns.ca

Western
Provincial Bldg., 99 High St., Bridgewater, NS B4V 1V8
902-543-8167, Fax: 902-543-6157
Regional Director, Gerald Joudrey
gtjoudre@gov.ns.ca

Renewable Resources Branch

The Renewable Resources Branch provides coordination & leadership on policy, planning & program development including industry development & resource promotion, marketing, resource inventories & research, & the preparation of strategies & plans for the integrated development, management & conservation of the province's forests, parks & wildlife resources.

Executive Director, Ed MacAulay
902-424-4103, emmacaul@gov.ns.ca
Director, Forestry, Jorg Beyeler
902-893-5749, Fax: 902-893-6102
Director, Parks & Recreation, Harold Carroll
902-662-5062, Fax: 902-662-2190
Director, Program Development, G. Peter MacQuarrie
902-424-7708, gpmacqua@gov.ns.ca.
Director, Wildlife, Barry Sabean
902-678-6091, Fax: 902-679-6176,sabeane@gov.ns.ca
Manager, Forest Protection, Walter Fanning
902-758-3210
Director, Ross Wickwire
902-758-7019, Fax: 902-758-3355,wickwira@gov.ns.ca

Office of the Ombudsman

#700, 5670 Spring Garden Rd., PO Box 2152, Halifax, NS B3J 3B7
902-424-6780, Fax: 902-424-6675, 800-670-1111
www.gov.ns.ca/ombu

Ombudsman, Dwight Bishop
Office Manager, Lois Smith
902-424-5401, Fax: 902-424-6675

Nova Scotia Public Service Commission

One Government Place, 1700 Granville St., PO Box 943, Halifax, NS B3J 2V9
902-424-7660, www.gov.ns.ca/psc

Minister Responsible,Hon. Ernest Fage
Commissioner, Rick Nurse
902-424-6617

• Advisory Council on the Status of Women

Department of Service Nova Scotia & Municipal Relations

1505 Barrington St., PO Box 216, Halifax, NS B3J 2M4
902-424-4141, Fax: 902-424-0581, public-enquiries@gov.ns.ca
www.gov.ns.ca/snsmr

Other Communication: Nova Scotia Business Registry: 1-800-670-4357

Provides leadership in the achievement of effective local government, assessment services, business licensing & registration, vehicle registration & driver licensing, taxation & revenue collection, vital statistics & an integrated land information management system to meet the needs of local & provincial agencies & residents of Nova Scotia.

Acts Administered:
Assessment Act
Building Access Act
Business Electronic Filing Act
Cemetery & Funeral Services Act
Change of Name Act
Collection Agencies Act
Communications & Information Act
Companies Act
Condominium Act
Consumer Creditors' Conduct Act
Consumer Protection Act
Consumer Reporting Act
Consumer Services Act
Corporations Registration Act
Direct Sellers' Regulation Act
Embalmers & Funeral Directors Act
Land Registration Act
Limited Partnerships Act
Marketable Titles Act
Mortgage Brokers' & Lenders' Registration Act
Motor Vehicle Act
Municipal Conflict of Interest Act
Municipal Elections Act
Municipal Finance Corporation Act
Municipal Fiscal Year Act
Municipal Government Act
Municipal Grants Act
Municipal Housing Corporations Act
Municipal Loan & Building Fund Act
Off-Highway Vehicles Act
Part X of the Bankruptcy & Insolvency Act
Part IV of the Revenue Act for administrative purposes
Partnerships & Business Names Registration Act
Personal Property Security Act
Private Investment Holding Companies Act
Public Accountants Act
Real Estate Trading Act
Registry Act
Rental Property Conversion Act
Residential Tenancies Act
Rural Fire District Act
Sales Tax Act
Shopping Centre Development Act
Societies Act
Solemnization of Marriage Act
Unconscionable Transactions Relief Act
Vital Statistics Act

Minister,Hon. Richard Hurlburt
902-424-5550, Fax: 902-424-0581,snsmrmin@gov.ns.ca
Deputy Minister, Kevin Malloy
902-424-4100, keefeg@gov.ns.ca
Asst. Deputy Minister, Kevin Malloy
902-424-4559
Director, Communications, Donna Chislett
902-424-6336, Fax: 902-424-0581,chisledp@gov.ns.ca

• Nova Scotia Municipal Finance Corporation
Maritime Centre
1505 Barrington St., 10th Fl. South
PO Box 850 M
Halifax, NS B3J 2V2
902-424-4590 Fax: 902-424-0525
www.gov.ns.ca/nsmfc

NSMFC issues pooled debentures that provide low-cost, long-term capital financing for municipal capital projects. The NSMFC issues in capital markets twice a year, generally in the spring and fall. On occasion the NSMFC will do a single issue, provided the size is large enough.

Assessment Services

Fax: 902-424-0587

Acting Director, Kathy Gillis
902-424-3955, gilliska@gov.ns.ca
Acting Director, Operations, Debi Karrel
902-424-4131
Director, Assessment Technology, Rick MacLeod
902-424-3962

Program Management & Corporate Services

Acting Executive Director, Cameron MacNeil
902-424-4417
Director, Consumer & Business Policy, Richard Shaffner
902-424-0676
Acting Director, Corporate Development, Mike Duda
902-424-4580,
Director, Human Resources, Janet Lee
902-424-7840

Co-operative Branch

902-893-6190, Fax: 902-893-6108

Inspector, Ron Skibbens

Tax Commission
Maritime Centre, 1505 Barrington St., Halifax, NS B3J 3K5
902-424-5200, Fax: 902-424-0720, 800-670-4357
www.gov.ns.ca/snsmr/taxcomm/

Integrated Service Delivery

Fax: 902-424-5510

Asst. Deputy Director, Kevin Malloy
902-424-4559, kdmalloy@gov.ns.ca
Executive Director, Alternative Program Delivery, John C. MacKay
902-424-4241
Acting Executive Director, Registry & Information Management, Gretchen Pohlkamp
902-424-7136
Director, Business & Consumer Registration, Anne James
902-424-4794

Nova Scotia Geomatics Centre
160 Willow St., Amherst, NS B4H 3W3
902-667-7231, Fax: 902-667-6008, 800-798-0706
info@nsgc.gov.ns.ca
www.gov.ns.ca/snsmr/land/

Director, Geographic Information Services, Danny Gray
902-424-4966
Manager, Client Services, Curt Speight

Registry of Deeds
PO Box 2205, Halifax, NS B3J 3C4
Fax: 902-424-5872
Director, Peter Kittilsen
902-424-6335
Registrar General, Mark Coffin
902-424-7228

Registry of Joint Stock Companies
Martime Centre, 1505 Barrington St., 9th Fl., Halifax, NS B3J 3K5
902-424-7770, Fax: 902-424-4633, 800-225-8227
joint-stock@gov.ns.ca
www.gov.ns.ca/snsmr/rjsc
Registrar, Hayley Clarke
902-424-0639, clarkehe@gov.ns.ca

Registry of Motor Vehicles
902-424-7801, Fax: 902-424-0772
Registrar, Paul Arsenault
902-424-7801

Vital Statistics
Joseph Howe Bldg., 1690 Hollis St., Ground Floor, PO Box 157, Halifax, NS B3J 2M9
902-424-4071, Fax: 902-424-0678, 877-848-2578
vstat@gov.ns.ca
Manager, E. Crowley Meagher
902-424-2599

Service Delivery
Maritime Centre, 1505 Barrington St., 8th Fl. North, PO Box 2734, Halifax, NS B3J 3P7
Executive Director, Graham Poole
902-424-4597

Antigonish
20 St. Andrew's St., Antigonish, NS B2G 2L4

Access Nova Scotia Centres:

Bridgewater
80 Logan Rd., Bridgewater, NS B4V 3J8

Dartmouth
Super Store Mall, 650 Portland St., Dartmouth, NS B2W 6A3

Halifax
West End Mall, 6960 Mumford Rd., Halifax, NS B3L 4P1

Kentville
28 Aberdeen St., Kentville, NS B4N 2N1

Municipal Services Division
Fax: 902-424-0821
Executive Director, Nathan Gorall
902-424-2499
Director, Grants & Programs, Marvin MacDonald
902-424-3858
Director, Planning & Advisory Services, Brant Wishart
902-424-7418

Sydney
Moxam Centre, 380 King's Rd., Sydney, NS B1S 1A8

Truro
#3, 80 Walker St., Truro, NS B2N 4A7

Yarmouth
Provincial Bldg., #127, 10 Starrs Rd., Yarmouth, NS B5A 2T1

Nova Scotia Advisory Council on the Status of Women

PO Box 745, Halifax, NS B3J 2T3
902-424-8662, Fax: 902-424-0573, 800-565-8663
nsacsw@gov.ns.ca
www.gov.ns.ca/staw/
The agency advocates for improved legislation, policies & programs for women, & provides research & policy advice to government on ways in which public policies & programs could better serve women. Minister Responsible Hon. Carolyn Bolivar-Getson Executive Director, Brigitte Neumann, 902/474-7548
Minister Responsible,Hon. Carolyn Bolivar-Getson
Executive Director, Brigitte Neumann
902-424-7548

Department of Tourism, Culture & Heritage

World Trade & Convention Centre, 1800 Argyle St., 6th Fl., PO Box 456, Halifax, NS B3J 2R5
902-424-5000, Fax: 902-424-4872, 800-565-0000
tns@gov.ns.ca
www.gov.ns.ca/tch
Acts Administered:
Art Council Act
Art Gallery of Nova Scotia Act
Cemeteries Protection Act
Cultural Foundation Act
Government Records Act
Heritage Property Act
Multiculturalism Act
Nova Scotia Museum Act
Nova Scotia Tartan Act
Peggy's Cove Commission Act
Public Archives Act
Schooner Bluenose Foundation Act
Sherbrooke Restoration Commission Act
Special Places Protection Act (Ecological Site Designations: Abraham Lake, Bornish Hill, Duncans Cove, Great Barren & Quinan Lakes, Indian Man Lake, MacFarlane Woods, Panuke Lake, Ponhook Lake, Quinns
Tourist Accommodations Act
Minister,Hon. William Dooks
902-424-4889, Fax: 902-424-4872,dooksbf@gov.ns.ca
Deputy Minister, Kelliann Dean
902-424-4869, deankm@gov.ns.ca
Secretary to the Deputy Minister, Renata Aube
902-424-4869, Fax: 902-424-4872,auberg@gov.ns.ca
• Nova Scotia Tourism Partnership Council
World Trade & Convention Centre
#603, 1800 Argyle St.
Halifax, NS B3J 3N8
902-424-0048 Fax: 902-424-0723
pashermc@gov.ns.ca
www.nstpc.com

NS Archives & Records Management
Fax: 902-424-0628
Provincial Archivist, Brian Speirs
902-424-6051

Culture Division
#601, 1800 Argyle St., PO Box 456, Halifax, NS B3J 2R5
Fax: 902-424-0710
Responsible for Nova Scotia museums which administer the Special Places Protection Act; preserves ecological sites in the province.
Executive Director, Dianne Coish
902-424-6471, Fax: 902-424-0710,coishdm@gov.ns.ca

Heritage Division
1747 Summer St., Halifax, NS B3H 3A6
902-424-7344, Fax: 902-424-0560, 800-632-1114
heritage@gov.ns.ca
The mission of Heritage Division is to protect, enhance, & celebrate heritage for all Nova Scotians & for future generations.
Executive Director, Bill Greenlaw
902-424-7344, greenlbe@gov.ns.ca

Tourism Division
Fax: 902-424-2668
Director, Tourism Development, Robert Book
902-424-3141
Manager, Enquiries & Research, Robert Boyd
902-424-2906

Department of Transportation & Infrastructure Renewal

Johnston Bldg., 1672 Granville St., 2nd Fl., PO Box 186, Halifax, NS B3J 2N2
902-424-2297, Fax: 902-424-0171, 888-432-3233
tpwpaff@gov.ns.ca
http://gov.ns.ca/tran
Provides a transportation network for the safe & efficient movement of people & goods; serves the building, property & accommodation needs of government departments & agencies; employs professional, dedicated people & offers a high level of customer service.
Acts Administered:
Dangerous Goods Transportation Act
Ferries Act
Highway 104: Western Alignment Act
Highway Workers Collective Bargaining Act
Motor Vehicle Act
Off-Highway Vehicles Act
Public Highways Act
Railways Act
Surplus Crown Property Disposal Act
Unsightly Premises Act
Minister,Hon. Brooke D. Taylor
902-424-5875, Fax: 902-424-0171,tirmin@gov.ns.ca
Deputy Minister, David Darrow
902-424-4036, Fax: 902-424-2014,ddarrow@gov.ns.ca
Executive Director, Maintenance & Operations, Kevin Caines
Director, Public Affairs & Communications, Cathy MacIsaac
902-424-8978, Fax: 902-424-0532,macisacl@gov.ns.ca
• Sydney Tar Ponds Agency
1 Inglis St.
PO Box 1028 A
Sydney, NS B1P 6J7
902-567-1035 Fax: 902-567-1032
www.tarpondscleanup.ca

Public Works
This division provides technical expertise & services required by the Department's highway, building & property divisions. The Highway Engineering Services section provides delivery of highway planning, geometric & structural design, traffic engineering, capital program maintenance & asset management business functions.The Engineering & Design section provides engineering, architectural, environmental & technical services & project management services for projects that are related to maintaining & constructing highway & building infrastructure.The Building Services & Operations section oversees the management, operation, maintenance & renovation of government buildings, infrastructure & properties, as well as the provision of trade & contract services in both leased & owned premises.
Executive Director, Al MacRae
902-424-5687
Acting Director, Building Services & Operations, Neil Whyte
902-424-2281
Director, Engineering & Design, John O'Connor
902-424-2756
Director, Highway Engineering Services, Ralph Hessian
902-424-4268, hessiara@gov.ns.ca
Manager, Asset Management, Kenton Sperien
902-424-3510
Manager, Building Design, Donald Beaton
902-424-7026
Manager, Environmental Services, Denis Rushton
902-424-4082
Manager, Highway Planning & Design, Phil Corkum
902-424-3508
Acting Manager, Project Management, Lee Stark
902-424-8124
Manager, Structural Engineering, Mark Pertus
902-424-6777
Manager, Technical Services, Tom Gouthro
902-860-5600
Manager, Traffic Engineering, David Smith
902-424-7778
Manager, Traffic Signals & Lighting, David Hamilton
902-861-4102

Nova Scotia Treasury & Policy Board

1700 Granville St., 5th Fl., PO Box 1617, Halifax, NS B3J 2Y3
902-424-8910, Fax: 902-424-7638,
tpbenquiries@gov.ns.ca
www.gov.ns.ca/tpb
Advances the priorities of government, aligns government policies & plans with these priorities, & promotes accountability.
Chair,Hon. Frank Corbett
902-424-5465, Fax: 902-424-0555,min_psc@gov.ns.ca
Deputy Minister, Gregory P. Keefe
keefeg@gov.ns.ca

Nova Scotia Utility & Review Board

1601 Lower Water St., 3rd Fl., PO Box 1692 M, Halifax, NS B3J 3S3
902-424-4448, Fax: 902-424-3919,
uarb.board@gov.ns.ca
The Board has a very broad mandate encompassing a number of acts.Operations fall into two categories, regulatory & adjudicative. The regulatory category includes the regulation of public utilities, licensing of public passenger carriers, monitoring of automobile insurance rates, the approval of Halifax-Dartmouth bridge fares, & the regulation of natural gas distribution & pipelines. The Board conducts hearings relating to gaming control, liquor control & film classification. The adjudicative category includes appeals or applications relating to property assessments, expropriation compensation claims, planning & subdivisions, heritage properties, criminal injury compensation claims, municipal boundaries, municipal & school board electoral boundaries, as well as gasoline, diesel oil & tobacco taxes.The Board receives its authority from the Public Inquiries Act & the Utility & Review Board Act.
Acts Administered:
Assessment Act
Electrical Installation & Inspection Act
Education Act
Energy & Mineral Resources Conservation Act
Expropriation Act
Fire Safety Act
Gaming Control Act (Part II)
Gas Distribution Act
Halifax-Dartmouth Bridge Commission Act
Liquor Control Act
Motor Carrier Act (public passenger only)
Motor Vehicle Transport Act of Canada, 1987 (Federal)
Municipal Government Act

Nova Scotia Power Finance Corporation Act
Nova Scotia Power Privatization Act
Petroleum Resources Removal Permit Act
Pipeline Act
Public Utilities Act
Railways Act
Revenue Act
Theatres & Amusement Act
Underground Hydrocarbons Storage Act
Utility & Review Board Act
Victims' Rights & Services Act
Minister Responsible,Hon. Michael Baker, Q.C.
Chair, Peter W. Gurnham, Q.C.
uarb.board@gov.ns.ca
Administrator, Paul G. Allen
902-424-4448, uarb.paul@gov.ns.ca,

Workers' Compensation Board of Nova Scotia

5668 South St., PO Box 1150, Halifax, NS B3J 2Y2
902-491-8999, Fax: 902-491-8002, 800-870-3331
info@wcb.gov.ns.ca
www.wcb.gov.ns.ca

Coordinates the workers' compensation system to assist injured workers & their employers by providing timely medical & rehabilitative support to help injured workers return to work.Also, to provide appropriate compensation for work-related injuries & illnesses.

Acting Chair, Chris Power
902-491-8382
CEO, Nancy MacCready-Williams
902-491-8300
Director, Communications, Mary Kingston
902-491-8101
Administrative Assistant, Dianne Barnes
902-491-8317, dianne.barnes@wcb.gov.ns.ca

Government of the Nunavut Territory

Seat of Government:PO Box 1200, Iqaluit, NU X0A 0H0
888-252-9869
www.gov.nu.ca

On April 1, 1999, Nunavut Territory was created as part of the Nunavut Land Claims Agreement signed in 1993. It has area of 1,932,254.97 km2, & the StatsCan population in 2006 was 29,474. Nunavut Territory is governed by a fully elected Legislative Assembly of 19 members elected for a five-year term. Government is by consensus rather than party politics. The Legislature elects the Premier & a seven-member Executive Council, which is charged with the operation of government & the establishment of program & spending priorities. Nunavut Territory acts under the same conditions as other territories in Canada. For an explanation of the difference between provinces & territories please see the Yukon Territory listing. The Commissioner of Nunavut Territory is appointed by the Federal Government, & serves a role similar to that of the Lieutenant Governor in provincial jurisdictions.

Office of the Commissioner

PO Box 2379, Iqaluit, NU X0A 0H0
867-975-5120, Fax: 867-975-5123,
nunavutcommissioner@gov.nu.ca
www.commissioner.gov.nu.ca

Commissioner,Hon. Ann Heekitjuk Hanson
Asst. to the Commissioner, Marie Fortier
867-975-5120, Fax: 867-975-5123,mfortier@gov.nu.ca

Office of the Premier

Legislative Assembly Bldg., 2nd Fl., PO Box 2410, Iqaluit, NU X0A 0H0
867-975-5050, Fax: 867-975-5051,
www.gov.nu.ca

Premier,Hon. Paul Okalik
867-975-5050, Fax: 867-975-5051,premier@gov.nu.ca
Principal Secretary, Bill Clay
867-975-5053, Fax: 867-975-5051
Executive Assistant, Maili-Elise Coley

Executive Council

Legislative Bldg., 2nd Fl., Box 2410, Iqaluit, NU X0A 0H0
867-975-5090, Fax: 867-975-5095

Premier & Minister, Executive & Intergovernmental Affairs; Minister, Justice,Hon. Paul Okalik
867-975-5050, Fax: 867-975-5051,premier@gov.nu.ca
Deputy Premier & Minister, Community & Government Services; Minister Responsible, Status of Women,Hon. Levinia Brown
Minister, Health & Social Services & Minister, Environment, Hon. Olayuk Akesuk
Minister, Economic Development & Transportation & Minister Responsible, Nunavut Housing Corporation; Minister Responsible, Mines, Hon. Patterk Netser
Minister, Education & Minister, Energy; Government House Leader; Minister Responsible, Nunavut Arctic College; Minister Responsible, Homeless, Hon. Ed Picco
Minister, Finance & Administration; Minister, Culture, Language, Elders & Youth, Hon Louis Tapardjuk
Minister, Human Resources & Minister Responsible, Workers' Compensation Board, Hon. Levi Barnabus
Executive Secretary, Leah Inutiq
867-975-5050, Fax: 867-975-5051

Legislative Assembly

Legislative Assembly Bldg., 3rd Fl., PO Box 1200, Iqaluit, NU X0A 0H0
867-975-5000, Fax: 867-975-5190, 877-334-7266
leginfo@assembly.nu.ca
www.assembly.nu.ca

Clerk of the Assembly, John Quirke
867-975-5100, jquirke@assembly.nu.ca
Speaker, Peter Kilabuk
867-975-5148, Fax: 867-975-5049
Deputy Clerk, Nancy Tupik
867-975-5115, ntupik@assembly.nu.ca
Legislative Librarian, Yvonne Earle
867-975-5132, Fax: 867-975-5190

Second Legislature - Nunavut

PO Box 1200, Iqaluit, NU X0A 0H0
www.assembly.nu.ca

Last General Election: Feb. 16, 2004. Maximum Duration, five years. Following is: constituency, member, phone & fax number. Address for all is care of the Legislative Assembly of Nunavut, PO Box 1200, Iqaluit NU X0A 0H0.

Hon. Olayuk Akesuk, South Baffin (Cape Dorset & Kimmirut)
867-897-8753, Fax: 867-897-8645,Other Communications: Legislature Phone: 867/975-5026
David Alagalak, Arviat
867-857-4485, Fax: 867-857-4486,Other Communications: Legislature Phone: 867/975-5032
James Arreak, Uqqumiut (Clyde River-Qikiqtarjuaq)
867-924-6423, Fax: 867-924-6429,Other Communications: Legislature Phone: 867/975-5019
Hon. Levi Barnabas, Quttiktuq (Grise Fiord-Resolute-Nanisivik-Arc
867-439-8050, Fax: 867-439-8051,Other Communications: Legislature Phone: 867/975-5023
Hon. Levinia Brown, Rankin Inlet South (Whale Cove)
867-645-4866, Fax: 867-645-4865,Other Communications: Legislature Phone: 867/975-5075
Tagak Curley, Rankin Inlet North
867-645-4900, Fax: 867-645-4981,Other Communications: Legislature Phone: 867/975-5027
Vacant, Kugluktuk
867-982-4232, Fax: 867-982-5733,Other Communications: Legislature Phone: 867/975-5017
Peter Kattuk, Hudson Bay (Sanikiluaq)
867-266-8518, Fax: 867-266-8315,Other Communications: Legislature Phone: 867/975-5030
Hon. Peter Kilabuk, Pangnirtung
867-473-8220, Fax: 867-473-8227,Other Communications: Legislature Phone: 867/975-5148
Steve Mapsalak, Akulliq (Kugaaruk, Repuse Bay)
867-462-4363, Fax: 867-462-4364,Other Communications: Legislature Phone: 867/975-5014
Hon. Patterk Netser, Nanulik
867-925-9890, Fax: 867-925-9891,Other Communications: Legislature Phone: 867/975-5024
Hon. Paul Okalik, Iqaluit West
867-979-5807, Fax: 867-979-2226,Other Communications: Legislature Phone: 867/975-5050
Keith Peterson, Cambridge Bay
867-983-3777, Fax: 867-983-3778,Other Communications: Legislature Phone: 867/975-5015
Hon. Ed Picco, Iqaluit East
867-979-3954, Fax: 867-979-0507,Other Communications: Legislature Phone: 867/975-5020,
David Simailak, Baker Lake
867-793-4949, Fax: 867-793-4950,Other Communications: Legislature Phone: 867/975-5047
Hon. Louis Taparjuk, Amittuq (Hall Beach-Igloolik)
867-934-4070, Fax: 867-934-4071,Other Communications: Legislature Phone: 867/975-5070
Hunter Tootoo, Iqaluit Centre
867-979-2210, Fax: 867-979-2211,Other Communications: Legislature Phone: 867/975-5021
James Arvaluk, Tunnuniq (Pond Inlet
867-899-8999, Fax: 867-899-8713,Other Communications: Legislature Phone: 867/975-5035

Deputy Clerk, Nancy Tupik
867-975-5115, Fax: 867-975-5190,ntupik@assembly.nu.ca

Nunavut Territory Government Departments & Agencies

Department of Community & Government Services

J.G. Brown Bldg., PO Box 1000 700, Iqaluit, NU X0A 0H0
867-975-5400, Fax: 867-975-5305

To support the development, provision & maintenance of programs & services which affect the communities in all areas of municipal responsibility & transportation.

Acts Administered:
Area Development Act
Boilers & Pressure Vessels Act
Business Licenses Act
Cities, Towns & Villages Act
Civil Emergency Measures Act
Commissioner's Land Act
Community Employees' Benefits Program Transfer Act
Conflict of Interest Act
Consumer Protection Act
Dog Act
Electrical Protection Act
Film Classification Act
Fire Prevention Act
Gas Protection Act
Hamlets Act
Home Owners Property Tax Rebate Act
Local Authorities Elections Act
Lotteries Act
Pawnbrokers & Second-Hand Dealers Act
Planning Act
Property Assessment & Taxation Act
Real Estate Agents Licencing Act
Religious Societies Lands Act
Residential Tenancies Act
Senior Citizens & Disabled Persons Property Tax Relief Act
Settlements Act
Technical Standards & Safety Act
Minister,Hon. Levinia Brown
867-975-5075, Fax: 867-975-5095
Deputy Minister, David Akeeagok
867-975-5306, Fax: 867-975-5305
Asst. Deputy Minister, Shawn Maley
867-645-8101, Fax: 867-645-8141,smaley@gov.nu.ca
Asst. Deputy Minister, Brent Boddy
867-975-5409, Fax: 867-975-5457
Director, Policy, Lucy Magee
867-975-5309, Fax: 867-975-5305,lmagee@gov.nu.ca
Director, Finance, Mike Rafter
867-979-5333, Fax: 867-979-5330,mrafter@gov.nu.ca
Director, Protection Services, Ed Zebedee
867-975-5319, Fax: 867-975-5453,ezebedee@gov.nu.ca
Manager, Procurement, Logistics & Contract Support, Mark McCulloch
867-975-5427, Fax: 867-975-5450
Senior Consumer Affairs Officer, Leah Aupaluktuq
867-793-3303, Fax: 867-793-3321
Administrative Officer, Caroline Nutata
867-975-5306, Fax: 867-975-5305

Regional Offices:

Cambridge
PO Box 200, Cambridge Bay, NU X0B 0C0
Fax: 867-983-4123
Regional Director, Kevin Niptanatiak
867-983-4138, Fax: 867-983-4026

Cape Dorset
PO Box 330, Cape Dorset, NU X0A 0C0
Regional Director, Timoon Toonoo
867-897-3601, Fax: 867-897-3633,ttoonoo@gov.nu.ca

Pond Inlet
PO Box 379, Pond Inlet, NU X0A 0S0
Asst. Regional Director, Johnathan Palluq
867-899-7301, Fax: 867-899-7330,jpalluq@gov.nu.ca

Rankin Inlet
PO Box 490, Rankin Inlet, NU X0C 0G0
Fax: 867-645-8197
Regional Director, Ralph Ruediger
867-645-8153, Fax: 867-645-8197,

Department of Culture, Language, Elders & Youth (CLEY)

PO Box 1000 800, Iqaluit, NU X0A 0H0
867-975-5500, Fax: 867-975-5504, 866-934-2035
www.gov.nu.ca/cley

Responsible for the protection, preservation & promotion of Inuit languages. Cultural initiatives & departmental goals are reached in coordination with & in support of elder & youth groups.CLEY acts in respect to issues concerning women & people with disabilities.The government is dedicated to preserving & promoting elements that make up the Inuit identity.

Acts Administered:
Archives Act
Historical Resources Act
Official Languages Act
Minister,Hon. Louis Tapardjuk
867-975-5070, Fax: 867-975-5095
Deputy Minister, Phoebe Hainnu
867-975-5501, Fax: 867-975-5504
Asst. Deputy Minister, Naullaq Arnaquq
867-975-5532, Fax: 867-975-5504,narnaquq@gov.nu.ca
Director, Community Programs, Thoretta Iyerak
867-934-2032, Fax: 867-934-2047
Director, Heritage, Douglas Stenton
867-975-5524, Fax: 867-975-5523,dstenton1@gov.nu.ca
Director, Finance & Administration, David Kolot
867-975-5510, Fax: 867-975-5504,dkolot@gov.nu.ca
Director, Inuit Quajimajatuqangit, Shuvinai Mike
867-975-5525, Fax: 867-975-5504
Director, Official Languages & Services, Stephane Cloutier
867-975-5507, Fax: 867-975-5523
Director, Policy & Planning, Jodi Durdie
867-975-5505, Fax: 867-975-5504
Director, Sport Nunavut, Frank Tootoo
867-793-3316, Fax: 867-793-3321,ftootoo@gov.nu.ca
Manager, Communications, Vacant
867-975-5531, Fax: 867-975-5523
Communications Officer,Vacant
867-975-5512, Fax: 867-975-5523

Department of Economic Development & Transportation

#1104 Inuksugait Plaza, PO Box 1000 1500, Iqaluit, NU X0A 0H0
867-975-7800, Fax: 867-975-7870, 888-975-5999
edt@gov.nu.ca
www.edt.gov.nu.ca

Acts Administered:
Agricultural Products Marketing Act
All-Terrain Vehicles Act
Economic Development Agreements Act
Motor Vehicles Act
Exemption of Motor Vehicles Act Regulations
Nunavut Development Corporation
Public Highways Act
Transportation of Dangerous Goods Act
Travel & Tourism Act
Minister,Hon. Patterk Netser
867-975-5024, Fax: 867-975-5095
Deputy Minister, Rosemary Keenainak
867-975-7829, Fax: 867-975-7880
Director, Fisheries & Sealing, Wayne Lynch
867-975-7734, Fax: 867-975-7739
Director, Policy, Planning& Communications, Ed McKenna
867-975-7817, Fax: 867-975-7870,emckenna@gov.nu.ca
Director, Finance & Administration, Sherri Rowe
867-975-7801, Fax: 867-975-7870
Communications Manager, Matthew Illaszewicz
867-975-7818, Fax: 867-975-7870
• Nunavut Business Credit Corporation
PO Box 224
Cape Dorset, NU X0A 0C0
867-897-3647 800-758-0038
www.nbcc.nu.ca

Economic Development
Asst. Deputy Minister, Jane Cooper
867-975-7832, Fax: 867-975-7880
Director, Community Economic Development, Steve Hannah
867-473-2661, Fax: 867-473-2663
Director, Minerals & Petroleum, Gordon MacKay
867-975-7822, Fax: 867-975-7870

Transportation
Asst. Deputy Minister, Methusalah Kunuk
867-975-7832, Fax: 867-975-7880
Director, Iqaluit Airports, John Graham
867-979-5224, Fax: 867-979-6985
Director, Motor Vehicles, Lorna Gee
867-360-4614, Fax: 867-360-4619
Director, Nunavut Airports, Neal Carmichael
867-645-8203, Fax: 867-645-8246
Director, Transportation Policy & Planning, John Hawkins
867-975-7826, Fax: 867-795-7870

Community Operations:

Kitikmeot
PO Box 316, Kugluktuk, NU X0B 0E0
Director, Beatrice Bernhardt
867-982-7459, Fax: 867-982-3204

Kivalliq
PO Box 2, Rankin Inlet, NU X0C 0G0
Acting Director, Robert Connely
867-645-8458, Fax: 867-645-8455

Qikiqtaaluk
#1045, PO Box 389, Pond Inlet, NU X0A 0S0
Director, Rhoda Katsak
867-899-7339, Fax: 867-899-7348,

Department of Education

PO Box 1000 910, Iqaluit, NU X0A 0H0
867-975-5600, Fax: 867-975-5605, 888-531-1456
www.gov.nu.ca/education/

Acts Administered:
Apprenticeship, Trade & Occupation Certification Act
Child Care Act
Divisional Education Councils Dissolution Act
Education Act
Federation of Nunavut Teachers Act
Library Act (CLEY)
Occupational Training Agreement Act
Official Languages Act (CLEY)
Public Colleges Act
Scientists & Education Act (CLEY)
Senior Citizens Benefits Act
Social Assistance Act
Student Financial Assistance Act
Minister,Hon. Ed Picco
867-975-5020, Fax: 867-979-5095
Deputy Minister, Kathy Okpik
867-975-5601, Fax: 867-975-5635
Director, Corporate Services, Murray Horn
867-975-5616, Fax: 867-975-5605,mhorn@gov.nu.ca
Director, Policy & Planning, Brad Chambers
867-975-5659, Fax: 867-975-5605
Director, Education & Services in French, André Corbeil
867-975-5627, Fax: 867-975-5613
Manager, Human Resources & Career Planning, Elizabeth Qulaut
867-975-5622, Fax: 867-975-5605
Manager, Information Systems Planning, Malcolm Campbell
867-975-5638, Fax: 867-975-5605

Adult Learning, Career & Early Childhood Services
Fax: 867-857-3090
Asst. Deputy Minister, Irene Tanuyak
867-975-5604, Fax: 867-975-5635,itanuyak@gov.nu.ca
Director, Income Support, Sandy Teiman
867-975-5685, Fax: 867-975-5690,STeiman@gov.nu.ca
Director, Adult Learning & Post-Secondary Services, Mark Mackay
867-857-3062, Fax: 867-857-3090
Manager, Early Childhood & School Services, Leslie Leafloor
867-975-5607, Fax: 867-975-5610
Supervisor, Apprenticeship & Occupation, Zsolt Munkacsy
867-975-5658, Fax: 867-975-5610

Curriculum & School Services
Asst. Deputy Minister, Peter Geikie
867-975-5604, Fax: 867-975-5635
Director, Curriculum & School Services, Cathy McGregor
867-975-5641, Fax: 867-975-5635,cmcgregor@gov.nu.ca
Director, French Education, Suzanne Lefebvre
867-975-5602, Fax: 867-975-5605,SLefebvre@gov.nu.ca

Regional Offices:
867-983-7214, Fax: 867-983-2004

Cambridge Bay
867-983-4031, Fax: 867-983-7309
Superintendent, Brenda Jancke
867-983-4030, Fax: 867-983-4191

Kivalliq
867-645-5040, Fax: 867-645-2148

Nunavut Emergency Management

PO Box 1000 700, Iqaluit, NU X0A 0H0
867-975-5403, Fax: 867-979-4221, 800-693-1666
cgs.gov.nu.ca/en/nunavut-emergency-management

Other Communication: Emergency Services Response Centre: 867/979-6262

Manager, Emergency Services, Glen Higgins
867-975-5403, Fax: 867-979-4221,ghiggins@gov.nu.ca
Acting Fire Marshall, Robert Prima
867-975-5310, Fax: 867-975-5315

Department of Environment

PO Box 1000 1300, Iqaluit, NU X0A 0H0
867-975-7700, Fax: 867-975-7742, 866-222-9063
environment@gov.nu.ca

Acts Administered:
Environmental Protection Act
Environmental Rights Act
Flood Damage Reduction Agreements Act
Forest Management Act
Forest Protection Act
Freshwater Fish Marketing Act
Herd & Fencing Act
Natural Resource Conservation Trust Act
Pesticides Act
Territorial Park Act
Travel & Tourism Act
Waste Reduction & Recovery Act
Water Resources Agreements Act
Wildlife Act
Minister,Hon. Olayuk Akesuk
867-975-5026, Fax: 867-975-0595
Deputy Minister, Alukie Rojas
867-975-7705, Fax: 867-975-7740
Asst. Deputy Minister,Vacant
867-975-7705, Fax: 867-975-7740
Director, Corporate Services, Camilius Egeni
867-975-7708, Fax: 867-975-7740
Director, Environmental Protection, Earle Baddaloo
867-975-7729, Fax: 867-975-7739
Director, Parks & Conservation Areas, David Monteith
867-975-7723, Fax: 867-975-7739,dmonteith@gov.nu.ca
Director, Policy, Planning & Legislation, Steve Pinksen
867-975-7718, Fax: 867-975-7740,spinksen@gov.nu.ca
Director, Fisheries & Sealing, Wayne Lynch
867-975-7821
Executive Secretary, Lena Hughes
867-975-7705, Fax: 867-975-7740

Regional Offices:

Baffin
PO Box 569, Pond Inlet, NU X0A 0S0
Regional Wildlife Manager, Dirkus Gissing
867-899-8034, Fax: 867-889-8004

Kitikmeot
PO Box 377, Kugluktuk, NU X0B 0E0
Regional Wildlife Manager, Dustin Fredlund
867-982-7441, Fax: 867-982-3701

Kivalliq
PO Box 120, Arviat, NU X0C 0E0
Fax: 867-857-2986
Regional Wildlife Manager, Dan Shewchuk
867-857-2828, Fax: 867-857-2986

Department of Executive & Intergovernmental Affairs

1084 Aeroplex bldg., PO Box 1000 200, Iqaluit, NU X0A 0H0
867-975-6000, Fax: 867-975-6090

The department provides advice & administrative support to Cabinet & the government, works to ensure that the Nunavut Land Claims Agreement & Nunavut's relationships with other governments in Canada & the circumpolar world are used to support common goals. The department compiles & communicates information & evaluates government programs & data.The Intergovernmental Affairs Division is responsible for the management & development of government strategies, policies & initiatives relating to federal, provincial, territorial, circumpolar & aboriginal affairs. This office participates in preparations for Intergovernmental activities such as the Western & Annual Premiers Conferences, First Ministers meetings & the Social Union Framework Agreement, the Arctic Council, the Nunavut Implementation Panel & the Clyde River Protocol.

Acts Administered:
Nunavut Power Corporation Assets Transfer Confirmation Act
Public Utilities Act
Minister,Hon. Paul Okalik
867-975-5050, Fax: 867-975-5051
Deputy Minister & Secretary to Cabinet, David Omilgoitok
867-975-6010, Fax: 867-975-6095
Deputy Minister, Intervovernmental Affairs, Simon Awa
867-975-6034, Fax: 867-975-6091
Asst. Deputy Minister, Intergovernmental Affairs - Ottawa Liason, Robert Carson
613-233-9890, Fax: 613-233-2543
Asst. Deputy Minister, Policy, Planning & Evaluation, Paul Suvega
867-975-6009, Fax: 867-975-6089
Director, Aboriginal & Circumpolar Affairs, Letia Obed
867-975-6036, Fax: 867-975-6091

Director, Policy, Planning & Evaluation, Rachel Mark
867-975-6029, Fax: 867-975-6029
Director, Corporate Services, Vacant
Acting Director, Communications, Lena Kilabuk
867-975-6048, Fax: 867-975-6099
Director, Statistics, Ron McMahon
867-473-2693, Fax: 867-473-2626

Department of Finance

Bldg. 1079, 1st Fl., PO Box 1000 Stn 330, Iqaluit, NU X0A 0H0
867-975-5800, Fax: 867-975-5805,
www.gov.nu.ca/finance

The Department of Finance is committed to provide direction and leadership to ensure fiscal responsibility and to create a secure base for Nunavut's economic growth, while promoting and maintaining public confidence in the prudence, propriety and integrity of government financial operations and respecting the principles of Inuit Qaujimajatuqangit (IQ).

Acts Administered:
Explosives Use Act
Mine Health & Safety Act
Safety Act
Environmental Tobacco Smoke Work Site Reguations
Technical Standards & Safety Act
Worker's Compensation Act
Minister,Hon. Keith Peterson
867-983-3777, Fax: 867-983-3778
Deputy Minister, Peter Ma
867-975-5803, Fax: 867-975-5805,pma@gov.nu.ca
Comptroller General, Gerry O'Donnell
867-975-5833, Fax: 867-975-5896
Acting Asst. Deputy Minister, Chris D'Arcy
867-975-6865, Fax: 867-975-5805
Director, Fiscal Policy, Peter Tumilty
867-975-5893, Fax: 867-975-5845
Director, Corporate Services, Scott Mariott
867-975-6803, Fax: 867-975-6868
Director, Accounting Policy, Jeff Chown
867-975-5894, Fax: 867-975-5844,Other Communications: Alternate Fax: 867/975-6833
Acting Director, Expenditure Management, Dianne Moebis
867-975-5813, Fax: 867-975-6825,
Manager, Taxation, Belinda Mack
867-975-6851, Fax: 867-975-5845
Director, Compensation & Benefits, Nasim Bhanji
867-975-5847, Fax: 867-975-5863
Asst. Comptroller General, Shirley Allder
867-975-5866, Fax: 867-975-5896
Acting Chief Internal Auditor, Grace Wilk
867-975-6848, Fax: 867-975-6842
• Nunavut Liquor Licensing Board
Bag 002
Rankin Inlet, NU X0C 0G0
Fax: 867-645-3327

Regional Offices:
867-983-4043, Fax: 867-983-4041

Kitikmeot
867-983-4043, Fax: 867-983-4041
Director, Regional Financial Services, Sandra Peterson
867-983-4042, speterson@gov.nu.ca

Kivalliq
867-645-8009, Fax: 867-645-8093
Director, Regional Financial Services, Kerry Angidlik
kangidlik@gov.nu.ca

Qikiqtaaluk
867-934-2056, Fax: 867-934-8677
Director, Regional Financial Services,Vacant

Department of Health & Social Services

Sivummut bldg., PO Box 1007 1000, Iqaluit, NU X0A 0H0
867-975-5700, Fax: 867-975-5705,
health@gov.nu.ca
www.gov.nu.ca/hsssite/hssmain.shtml

The Environmental Health Specialist provides recommendations & direction, consultation, development of standards, monitoring, maintenance & evaluation of all environmental health programs within Nunavut. Reviews the Public Health Act & Regulations & environmental health standards & policies & makes recommendations for revisions. Guides the regional environmental health officers in development & implementation of programs & policies in prevention of diseases caused by environmental factors, including food, water, waste disposal, housing & the sanitation of public places, including schools, day cares & other institutional facilities. Guides the Regional Environmental Health Officers in water & food-borne related illness investigations & food recalls. Guides the regions in the monitoring of drinking water supplies. Assists with development of health education & promotional materials & activities related to environmental health.

Acts Administered:
Boards of Management Dissolution Act
Disease Registries Act
Public Health Act
Tobacco Control Act
Minister,Hon. Olayuk Akesuk
867-975-5026, Fax: 867-975-5095
Deputy Minister, Alex Campbell
867-975-5702, Fax: 867-975-5705
Chief Medical Officer of Health,Dr. Isaac Sobol
867-975-5744, Fax: 867-975-5755
Director, Finance, Vacant
867-975-5741, Fax: 867-975-5799
Asst. Deputy Minister, Operations, Vacant
867-983-4581, Fax: 867-983-4116
Executive Director, Corporate Services, Kevin Compton
867-975-5704, Fax: 867-975-5799
Acting Executive Director, Population Health, Janet Brewster
867-975-5703, Fax: 867-975-8648
Acting Director, Communications, Yasmine Pepa
867-975-5714, Fax: 867-975-5705
Director, Health & Social Services, Virginia Turner
867-473-2629, Fax: 867-473-2657
Acting Director, Medical Affairs, Dr. Wm (Sandy) MacDonald
867-979-7601, Fax: 876-979-7346
Acting Manager, Health Information & Research, Paul Tchouaffi
867-975-5916, Fax: 867-975-5940
Manager, Public Health, Kristine Hutchinson
867-975-4813, Fax: 867-975-4830
Home Care Coordinator, Shona Barkley
867-975-5936, Fax: 867-975-5945
Environmental Health Consultant, Peter Workman
867-975-5764, Fax: 867-975-5755

Nunavut Housing Corporation

PO Box 1000, Arviat, NU X0C 0E0
867-857-3000, Fax: 867-857-3040,
www.nunavuthousing.ca

Minister Responsible,Hon. Patterk Netser
867-975-5024, Fax: 867-975-5095
President, Peter Scott
867-975-7201, Fax: 867-975-7222,pscott@gov.nu.ca
Vice-President, Patsy Owlijoot
867-857-3001, Fax: 867-857-3040,powlijoot@gov.nu.ca
Director, Operations, Alain Barriault
867-857-3006, Fax: 867-857-3040,abarriault@gov.nu.ca
Executive Director, Corporate Services & CFO, Eric Whitworth
867-975-7202, Fax: 867-975-7222,ewhitworth@gov.nu.ca

Department of Human Resources

PO Box 1000 400, Iqaluit, NU X0A 1H0
867-975-6200, Fax: 867-975-6216, 888-668-9993
gnhr@gov.nu.ca

Minister,Hon. Levi Barnabas
867-975-5023, Fax: 867-975-5095
Deputy Minister, Koovian Flanagan
867-975-6213, Fax: 867-975-6216
Asst. Deputy Minister, Community Operations, Vacant
867-975-6213
Senior Advisor, Human Resources, Laulit Raut
Director, Corporate Services, Bob Loehr
867-975-6207, Fax: 867-975-6266,bloehr@gov.nu.ca
Director, Employee Relations Division, Louise Wasson
867-975-6211, Fax: 867-975-6241,gpinto@gov.nu.ca
Director, Inuit Employee Planning, Richard Paton
867-975-6272, Fax: 867-975-6280
Director, Job Evaluation & Organization Design, Melinda Jones
867-975-6208, Fax: 867-975-6215,
Director, Policy & Planning Division, David Kolot
867-975-6203, Fax: 867-975-6216,mwacyk@gov.nu.ca
Director, Training & Development Division, Sheyla Kolola
867-975-6283, Fax: 867-975-6245
Acting Director, Staffing, Terri Ross
867-975-6221, Fax: 867-975-6220

Regional Offices:

Cambridge Bay
PO Box 2375, Cambridge Bay, NU X0B 0C0
867-983-4058, Fax: 867-983-4061, 866-667-6624
Director, Community Operations, Alice Lafrance
867-983-4060, Fax: 867-983-4061

Qikigtaaluk
Fax: 867-934-2027, 800-682-9033
Regional Director, Solomon Allurut
867-934-2024

Rankin Inlet
Bag 002, Rankin Inlet, NU X0C 0G0
Fax: 867-645-2870, 800-933-3072
Director, Community Operations, Jacqueline Curley
867-645-2954, jcurley@gov.nu.ca

Department of Justice

Sivummut, 1st Fl., PO Box 1000 500, Iqaluit, NU X0A 0H0
867-975-6170, Fax: 867-975-6195

Acts Administered:
Engineers, Geologists & Geophysicists Act
Expropriation Act
Land Titles Act
Minister,Hon. Paul Okalik
867-975-5050, Fax: 867-975-5051
Deputy Minister, Markus Weber
867-975-6180, Fax: 867-975-6195
Asst. Deputy Minister, Rebekah Williams
867-975-6180, Fax: 867-975-6195
Director, Policy & Planning, Alysa d'Argencourt
867-975-6335, Fax: 867-975-6151
Director, Corporate Services, Edward Dingle
867-975-6181, Fax: 867-975-6188
• Baffin Correctional Centre
1550 Federal Rd.
PO Box 368
Iqaluit, NU X0A 0H0
867-979-8100 Fax: 867-979-4646
• Office of the Chief Coroner
PO Box 1000 590
Iqaluit, NU X0A 0H0
• Legal Services Board of Nunavut
PO Box 125
Gjoa Haven, NU X0A 0H0
Fax: 867-360-6112
• Young Offenders
1548 Federal Rd.
PO Box 1439
Iqaluit, NU X0A 0H0
867-979-4452 Fax: 867-979-5506

Corrections & Community Justice
867-975-6311, Fax: 867-975-6347
Director, Corrections, Alan Hartley
867-975-6501, Fax: 867-975-6515
Director, Community Justice, Judy Anilniliak
867-975-6176, Fax: 867-975-6160
Manager, Community Corrections, Doug Strader
867-975-6505, Fax: 867-975-6515,dstrader@gov.nu.ca

Court Services
Fax: 867-979-6168, 866-286-0546
Director, Heather Daley
867-975-6131, Fax: 867-975-6151,hdaley@gov.nu.ca
Sheriff, Chris Kennedy
867-975-6119, Fax: 867-975-6168
Rentals Officer, Bill Riddell
867-975-7291, Fax: 867-975-7294,briddell@gov.nu.ca
Head of Labour Services, Richard Gillis
867-975-7293, Fax: 867-975-7294,rgillis@gov.nu.ca
Manager, Maintenance Enforcement Office, Lou Hall
867-975-6137, Fax: 867-975-6148
Administrator, Judicial Services, Cyndi Weir
867-975-6121, Fax: 867-975-6169

Legal & Constitutional Division
867-975-6321, Fax: 867-975-6349
Director, Doug Garson
867-975-6316, Fax: 867-975-6349
Legal Counsel, Norman Tarnow
867-975-6332
Legal Counsel, Juan Estable
867-975-6325
Legal Counsel, David Savoie
867-975-6157
Legal Counsel, Barth Curley
867-975-6346
Legal Counsel, Lorraine Land
867-975-6323
Legal Counsel, Lauren Bowman
867-975-6365
Public Trustee Administrator, Martha Gibbons
867-975-6344, Fax: 867-975-6343

Legislation Division
867-975-6330, Fax: 867-975-6189,
Director & Registrar, Regulations, Diane Buckland
867-975-6329, dbuckland@gov.nu.ca

Manager, Legal Translation - Inuktitut & Inuinnaqtun, Betty Brewster
867-975-6164
Manager, Legal Translation - French, Andre Samson
867-975-6336
Publications Editor, Sue Ann Gibbons
867-975-6305

Nunavut Legal Registries Division
Brown Bldg., 1st Fl., PO Box 1000 570, Iqaluit, NU X0A 0H0
867-975-6190, Fax: 867-975-6194
Director, Louis Arki
867-975-6586
Registrar of Legal Registries,Vacant
Deputy Registrar, Securities & Corporate Registry, Jeff Mason
867-975-6591

Policy & Planning Division
867-975-6170, Fax: 867-975-6151
Director, Alysa d'Argencourt
867-975-6335, Fax: 867-975-6151
Policy Counsel, Andre Thorsen
867-975-6185
Policy Analyst, Gary Pon
867-975-6174
Grants & Programs Contribution Analyst, Joanne Laronde
867-975-6153, Fax: 867-975-6188
Policy Analyst, Siobhan Arnatsiaq-Murphy
867-975-6158

Ottawa Office

#1209, 350 Sparks St., Ottawa, ON K1R 7S8
613-233-9890, Fax: 613-233-2543,
lcooper@gov.nu.ca

Minister,Hon. Paul Okalik
867-975-5050, Fax: 867-975-5051
Asst. Deputy Minister, Intergovernmental Affairs, Robert Carson
613-233-9890, Fax: 613-233-2543,rcarson@gov.nu.ca
Senior Legal Advisor, William MacKay
613-233-9890, wmackay@gov.nu.ca
Acting Office Manager, Carmel Murphy
613-233-9890

Northwest Territories & Nunavut Workers Compensation Board

Other Communication: For a detailed listing please see Northwest Territories

Government of Ontario

Seat of Government: Queen's Park, Toronto, ON M7A 1A2
416-326-1234, 800-267-8097
www.gov.on.ca
The Province of Ontario entered Confederation July 1, 1867.It has an area of 907,573.82 km2, & the StatsCan census population in 2006 was 12,160,282.

Office of the Lieutenant Governor

Room 131, Legislative Bldg., Queen's Park, Toronto, ON M7A 1A1
416-325-7780, Fax: 416-325-7787,
ltgov@gov.on.ca
www.lt.gov.on.ca
Represents Her Majesty The Queen in Ontario. The Office coordinates, supports & promotes the activities of the Lieutenant Governor. In his constitutional role, the Lieutenant Governor swears-in the Executive Council, outlines the Government's plans in the Speech from the Throne, provides the Royal Assent needed for bills to become laws, approves orders-in-council & appointments recommended by Cabinet, & prorogues or dissolves each session of Parliament. In his community role, he represents the people of Ontario & acts as the Province's official host, welcoming world leaders & diplomats. He hosts or attends hundreds of community events throughout Ontario & presents honours & awards to outstanding Ontarians. His Honour has focused on three themes: reducing the stigma of mental illness, fighting racism, & supporting aboriginal youth.His Honour is also a champion for people living with disabilities.
Lieutenant Governor,Hon. David C. Onley, O.Ont.
416-325-7780, Fax: 416-325-7787,ltgov@gov.on.ca
Chief of Staff, Nanda Casucci-Bryne
416-325-7781, nanda.casuccibyrne@ontario.ca
Chief Aide-de-Camp, A. Cameron
416-325-7780, ltgov@gov.on.ca

Office of the Premier

Legislative Bldg., #281, 1 Queen's Park Cres. South, Toronto, ON M7A 1A1
416-325-1941, Fax: 416-325-3745,
webprem@gov.on.ca
www.premier.gov.on.ca
Premier,Hon. Dalton McGuinty
416-325-1941, Fax: 416-325-3745,dmcguinty.mpp.co@liberal.ola.org
Chief of Staff, Chris Morley
416-325-2228, Fax: 416-325-9895
Press Secretary, Jane Almeida
416-314-8975, Fax: 416-325-0803
Director & Executive Assistant, Tracey Sobers
416-325-2228, Fax: 416-325-9895
Executive Director, Communications, Aaron Lazarus
416-325-5972, Fax: 416-325-0803
Director, Caucus Relations, Rod MacDonald
416-325-2491, Fax: 416-314-5189
Director, Issues Management & Legislative Affairs, Karman Wong
416-325-8510, Fax: 416-325-0246
Deputy Chief of Staff, Operations, Dave Gene
416-325-2486, Fax: 416-325-6749
Director, Policy & Research, Alex Johnston
416-314-2598, Fax: 416-314-3853
Special Assistant to the Chief of Staff, Wendy Wai
416-325-1619, Fax: 416-325-9895

Executive Council

Whitney Block, Queen's Park, 99 Wellesley St. West, 6th Fl., Toronto, ON M7A 1A1
416-325-5721, Fax: 416-314-1551
Premier,Hon. Dalton McGuinty
416-325-1941, Fax: 416-325-3745,premier@gov.on.ca; dmcguinty.mpp.co@liberal.ola.org
Minister, Revenue; Minister Responsible, Seniors, Hon. Sophia Aggelonitis
416-327-8300, Fax:
416-326-1947,saggelonitis.mpp@liberal.ola.org
Minister, Municipal Affairs & Housing, Hon. Rick Bartolucci
416-585-7507, Fax:
416-585-6470,rbartolucci.mpp@liberal.ola.org
Attornet General; Minister, Aboriginal Affairs, Hon. Chris Bentley
416-314-2617, Fax:
416-326-4007,cbentley.mpp@liberal.ola.org
Minister, Health Promotion & Sport, Hon. Margarett R. Best
416-326-8500, Fax: 416-326-8520,mbest.mpp@liberal.ola.org
Minister, Community Safety & Correctional Services, Hon. James J. Bradley
416-585-7000, Fax:
416-585-6470,jbradley.mpp@liberal.ola.org
Minister, Children & Youth Services; Minister Responsible, Women's Issues, Hon. Laurel C. Broten
416-212-7432, Fax:
416-212-7431,lbroten.mpp.co@liberal.ola.org,
Minister, Tourism & Culture, Hon. Michael Chan
416-326-9326, Fax:
416-326-9338,mchan.mpp.co@liberal.ola.org
Minister, Infrastructure, Hon. Bob Chiarelli
416-325-8841, Fax:
416-325-8860,bchiarelli.mpp.co@liberal.ola.org
Minister, Education, Hon. Leona Dombrowsky
416-325-2600, Fax:
416-325-2608,ldombrowsky.mpp@liberal.ola.org
Minister, Energy, Hon. Brad Duguid
416-327-6758, Fax:
416-327-6754,bduguid.mpp@liberal.ola.org
Minister, Finance; Chair, Management Board of Cabinet, Hon. Dwight Duncan
416-325-0400, Fax:
416-325-0374,dduncan.mpp@liberal.ola.org
Minister, Labour, Hon. Peter Fonseca
416-326-7600, Fax:
416-326-1449,pfonseca.mpp.co@liberal.ola.org
Minister, Consumer Services, Hon. John Gerretsen
416-327-8300, Fax:
416-326-1947,jgerretsen.mpp@liberal.ola.org
Minister, Nothern Development, Mines & Forestry, Hon. Michael Gravelle
416-327-0633, Fax:
416-327-0665,mgravelle.mpp@liberal.ola.org
Minister, Citizenship & Immigration, Hon. Eric Hoskins
416-325-6200, Fax:
416-325-6195,ehoskins.mpp.co@liberal.ola.org
Minister, Natural Resources, Hon. Linda Jeffrey
416-314-2301, Fax:
416-325-5316,ljeffrey.mpp.co@liberal.ola.org
Minister, Health & Long-Term Care, Hon. Deborah Matthews
416-327-4300, Fax:
416-327-3679,dmatthews.mpp.co@liberal.ola.org
Minister, Community & Social Services; Minister Responsible, Francophone Affairs, Hon. Madeleine Meilleur
416-325-5225, Fax:
416-325-5191,mmeilleur.mpp@liberal.ola.org
Minister, Training, Colleges & Universities, Hon. John Milloy
416-326-1600, Fax:
416-326-1656,jmilloy.mpp@liberal.ola.org
Minister, Agriculture, Food & Rural Affairs, Hon. Carol Mitchell
416-326-3074, Fax:
416-326-3083,cmitchell.mpp.co@liberal.ola.org
Minister, Research and Innovation, Hon. Glen R. Murray
416-325-5744, Fax:
416-325-5754,gmurray.mpp@liberal.ola.org
Minister, Without Portfolio; Deputy Government House Leader; Chair of Cabinet, Hon. Gerry Phillips
416-325-3628, Fax:
416-314-7421,gphillips.mpp@liberal.ola.org
Minister, Economic Development & Trade, Hon. Sandra Pupatello
416-325-6900, Fax:
416-325-6918,spupatello.mpp@liberal.ola.org
Minister, Intergovernmental Affairs; Government House Leader, Hon. Monique M. Smith
416-325-7754, Fax:
416-325-7755,msmith.mpp.co@liberal.ola.org
Minister, Environment, Hon. John Wilkinson
416-314-6729, Fax:
416-314-6748,jwilkinson.mpp.co@liberal.ola.org
Minister, Transportation, Hon. Kathleen O. Wynne
416-327-9200, Fax:
416-327-9188,kwynne.mpp@liberal.ola.org

Cabinet Office
Whitney Block, 99 Wellesley St. West, 6th Fl., Toronto, ON M7A 1A1
416-325-1941, Fax: 416-314-1551
Secretary to the Cabinet & Clerk of the Executive Council, Shelly Jamieson
416-325-7641, Fax:
416-314-8980,shelly.jamieson@ontario.ca
Deputy Minister, Communications & Special Projects & Associate Secretary of Cabinet, Lynn Betzner
416-325-9698, Fax: 416-325-1979,lynn.betzner@ontario.ca
Deputy Minister, Policy & Associate Secretary of Cabinet, Giles Gherson
416-325-3759, Fax: 416-325-7631,giles.gherson@ontario.ca
Director, Corporate Planning & Services, Kevin Owens
416-212-0786, Fax: 416-325-2388,kevin.owens@ontario.ca
Deputy Minister & Assoc. Secretary of Cabinet, Ross Peebles
416-325-1607
Deputy Minister, Administration, Darlene Winter
416-325-1611, Fax: 416-325-1612
Vice-President, Executive Development Branch, Linda Clifford
416-325-4996
Manager, Executive Information Services, Gayle Herrington
416-325-1736
Deputy Minister & Assoc. Secretary of Cabinet, Colin Andersen
416-325-3759
Asst. Deputy Minister, Health, Social & Education Policy, Leah Myers
416-325-4732, Fax: 416-325-6747
Asst. Deputy Minister, Policy & Strategic Planning, Don Black
416-325-5836, Fax: 416-325-7135
Acting Executive Coordinator, Executive Council Office, Karen Tilford
416-325-7693, Fax: 416-325-7690

Legislative Assembly

c/o Clerk's Office, #104, Legislative Bldg., Queen's Park, Toronto, ON M7A 1A2
416-325-7340, Fax: 416-325-7344,
assembly@ontla.ola.org
www.ontla.on.ca

Acts Administered:
Election Act
Election Finances Act
Fewer Politicians Act, 1996
Freedom of Information & Protection of Privacy Act
Legislative Assembly Act
Legislative Assembly Retirement Allowances Act
Members' Integrity Act
Ombudsman Act
Speaker,Hon. Steve Peters
416-325-7435, Fax: 416-325-7483
Clerk, Deborah Deller
416-325-7340, Fax:
416-325-7344,debbie_deller@ontla.ola.org
Executive Director, Administrative Services, Sylvia Nemanic
416-325-3568, Fax:
416-314-5995,sylvia_nemanic@ontla.ola.org
Deputy Clerk & Executive Director, Legislative Services, Todd Decker

416-325-3502, Fax:
416-325-5848,todd_decker@ontla.ola.org
Executive Director, Legislative Library, Vicki Whitmell
416-325-3939, Fax:
416-325-3909,vicki_whitmell@ontla.ola.org, Other Communications: Reference Inquiries: 416/325-3900
Sergeant-at-Arms & Executive Director, Precinct Properties Division, Dennis M. Clark
416-325-7446, Fax:
416-325-7154,dennis_clark@ontla.ola.org, Other Communications: Emergency: 416/325-1111
Executive Assistant to the Clerk, Zina Decker
416-325-7343, Fax:
416-325-7344,zina_decker@ontla.ola.org

Government Members Services
#124, North Wing, Legislative Bldg., Queen's Park, 111 Wellesley St. West, Toronto, ON M7A 1A8
416-325-7200, Fax: 416-325-3810, www.ontariopc.on.ca

Government House Leader,Hon. Michael Bryant
416-325-7754, Fax:
416-325-7755,mbryant.mpp@liberal.ola.org
Chief Government Whip, Mike Colle
416-325-4091, Fax:
416-325-4136,mcolle.mpp@liberal.ola.org
Chair, Management Board of Cabinet,Hon. Dwight Duncan
416-325-0400, Fax:
416-325-0374,dduncan.mpp@liberal.ola.org; dduncan.mpp.co@liberal.ola.org

Office of the Opposition (PC)
Legis. Bldg., North Wing, #381, Queen's Park, Toronto, ON M7A 1A8
416-325-0445, Fax: 416-325-0491, www.ontariopc.com

Leader, Robert W. Runciman
416-325-0445, Fax: 416-325-0491
Deputy Leader, Elizabeth Witmer
416-325-1306, Fax: 416-325-1329
Opposition House Leader, Elizabeth Witmer
416-325-1306, Fax: 416-325-1329
Deputy House Leader, Ernie Hardeman
416-325-1239, Fax: 416-325-1259
Chief Opposition Whip, Norm Miller
416-325-7736, Fax: 416-325-7739

New Democratic Party
Legislative Bldg., #114, Queen's Park, Toronto, ON M7A 1A4
416-325-8300, Fax: 416-325-8222, 866-909-9952 www.ontariondp.com

Leader, Andrea Horwath
416-325-2777, Fax: 416-325-2770,ahorwath-qp@ndp.on.ca

Standing Committees of the Legislative Assembly:

Estimates Committee
Clerk, Sylwia Przezdzieki
416-325-3515, sylwia_przezdziecki@ontla.ola.org

Finance & Economic Affairs Committee
Clerk, William Short
416-325-3883, william_short@ontla.ola.org

General Government Committee
Clerk, Trevor Day
416-325-3509, trevor_day@ontla.ola.org

Government Agencies
Clerk, Douglas Arnott
416-325-3506, douglas_arnott@ontla.ola.org

Justice Policy Committee
Clerk, Susan Sourial
416-325-7352, susan_sourial@ontla.ola.org

Legislative Assembly Committee
Clerk, Tonia Grannum
416-325-3519, tonia_grannum@ontla.ola.org

Public Accounts Committee
Clerk, Katch Koch
416-325-3526, katch_koch@ontla.ola.org

Regulations & Private Bills Committee
Clerk, Sylwia Przezdziecki
416-325-3515, sylwia_przezdziecki@ontla.ola.org

Social Policy
Clerk, Katch Koch
416-325-3526, katch_koch@ontla.ola.org

Thirty-ninth Parliament - Ontario

Clerk's Office, Legislative Bldg., Queen's Park, Toronto, ON M7A 1A2
416-325-7500, Fax: 416-325-7489, www.ontla.on.ca

Last General Election, October 10, 2007.Maximum Duration, 5 years. Party Standings (October 2007): Liberal (Lib.) 72 Progressive Conservative (PC) 25 New Democratic Party (NDP) 10 Total 107; Salaries, Indemnities & Allowances (April 1, 2005): Each Member is entitled to an annual base salary of $86,860. Additional salary is paid to the following office holders: Premier $68,880; Cabinet Ministers $36,742 (with portfolio); Cabinet Ministers $16,677 (without portfolio); Leader of the Official Opposition $47,947; Leaders of Parties with recognized membership of 8 or more in the Assembly $31,009; Speaker $27,100; Parliamentary Assistants $12,421; Deputy Speaker & Chair of the Committee of the Whole House $12,855. The following is: member, constituency, population, total eligible voters, party affiliation & contact information:

Members

Hon. Sophia Aggelonitis, Hamilton Mountain ON, Liberal
905-388-9734, Fax:
905-388-7862,saggelonitis.mpp.co@liberal.ola.org, Other Communications: Queen's Park Phone: 416-327-0300; Fax: 416-326-1947
Laura Albanese, York South-Weston ON, Liberal
416-243-7984, Fax: 416-243-0327,Other Communications: Queen's Park Phone: 416-325-1800; Fax: 416-325-1802
Ted Arnott, Wellington-Halton Hills ON, PC
519-787-5247, 800-265-2366,Fax:
519-787-5249,ted.arnottco@pc.ola.org; ted.arnott@pc.ola.org, Other Communications: Queen's Park Phone: 416-325-3880; Fax: 416-325-6649
Wayne Arthurs, Pickering-Scarborough East ON, Liberal
905-509-0336, Fax:
905-509-0334,warthurs.mpp.co@liberal.ola.org; warthurs.mpp@liberal.ola.org, Other Communications: Queen's Park Phone: 416-325-3581; Fax: 416-325-3453
Robert Bailey, Sarnia-Lambton ON, PC
519-337-0051, Fax: 519-337-3246,bob.bailey@pc.ola.org; bob.baileyco@pc.ola.org, Other Communications: Queen's Park Phone: 416-325-1715; Fax: 416-325-1852
Bas Balkissoon, Scarborough-Rouge River ON, Liberal
416-297-5040, Fax:
416-297-6767,bbalkissoon.mpp.co@liberal.ola.org, Other Communications: Queen's Park Phone: 416-212-3066; Fax: 416-325-3862
Toby Barrett, Haldimand-Norfolk ON, PC
519-428-0446, Fax: 519-428-0835,toby.barrett@pc.ola.org, Other Communications: Queen's Park Phone: 416-325-8404; Fax: 416-325-8408
Hon. Rick Bartolucci, Sudbury ON, Liberal
705-675-1914, Fax:
705-675-1456,rbartolucci.mpp.co@liberal.ola.org, Other Communications: Queen's Park Phone: 416-585-7000; Fax: 416-585-6470
Hon. Christopher Bentley, London West ON, Liberal
519-657-3120, 800-518-7901,Fax:
519-657-0368,cbentley.mpp@liberal.ola.org; cbentley.mpp.co@liberal.ola.org, Other Communications: Queen's Park Phone: 416-326-2220; Fax: 416-326-4007, TDD: 416-326-4012
Lorenzo Berardinetti, Scarborough Southwest ON, Liberal
416-261-9525, Fax:
416-261-0381,lberardinetti.mpp@liberal.ola.org, Other Communications: Queen's Park Phone: 416-325-1008; Fax: 416-325-1219
Hon. Margarett Best, Scarborough-Guildwood ON, Liberal
416-281-2787, Fax:
416-281-2360,mbest.mpp.co@liberal.ola.org; mbest.mpp@liberal.ola.org, Other Communications: Queen's Park Phone: 416-326-8500; Fax: 416-326-8520
Gilles Bisson, Timmins-JamesBay ON, New Democratic Party
705-268-6400, 800-461-9878,Fax:
705-266-9125,gbisson@ndp.on.ca, Other Communications: Queen's Park Phone: 416-325-7122; Fax: 416-325-7111
Hon. James J. Bradley, St. Catharines ON, Liberal
905-935-0018, Fax:
905-935-0191,jbradley.mpp.co@liberal.ola.org; jbradley.mpp@liberal.ola.org, Other Communications: Queen's Park Phone: 416-585-7000; Fax: 416-585-6470
Hon. Laurel C. Broten, Etobicoke-Lakeshore ON, Liberal
416-259-2249, Fax:
416-259-3704,lbroten.mpp@liberal.ola.org; lbroten.mpp.co@liberal.ola.org, Other Communications: Queen's Park Phone: 416-212-7432; Fax: 416-212-7431
Michael A. Brown, Algoma-Manitoulin ON, Liberal
705-461-9710, 800-831-1899,Fax:
705-461-9720,mbrown.mpp.co@liberal.ola.org, Other Communications: Queen's Park Phone: 416-325-3601; Fax: 416-325-3713
Jim Brownell, Stormont-Dundas-South Glengarry ON, Liberal
613-933-6513, 800-514-9660,Fax:
613-933-6449,jbrownell.mpp@liberal.ola.org; jbrownell.mpp.co@liberal.ola.org, Other Communications: Queen's Park Phone: 416-325-5300; Fax: 416-326-3112
Hon. Donna H. Cansfield, Etobicoke Centre ON, Liberal
416-234-2800, Fax:
416-234-2276,dcansfield.mpp@liberal.ola.org; dcansfield.mpp.co@liberal.ola.org, Other Communications: Queen's Park Phone: 416-585-7007; Fax: 416-585-4035
Hon. David Caplan, Don Valley East ON, Liberal
416-494-6856, Fax:
416-494-9937,dcaplan.mpp@liberal.ola.org; dcaplan.mpp.co@liberal.ola.org, Other Communications: Queen's Park Phone: 416-325-3290; Fax: 416-325-3204
Hon. Aileen Carroll, Barrie ON, Liberal
705-726-5538, Fax:
705-726-2880,acarroll.mpp@liberal.ola.org; acarroll.mpp.co@liberal.ola.org, Other Communications: Queen's Park Phone: 416-325-4366; Fax: 416-325-4843
Hon. Michael Chan, Markham-Unionville ON, Liberal
905-305-1935, Fax:
905-305-1938,mchan.mpp@liberal.ola.org; mchan.mpp.co@liberal.ola.org, Other Communications: Queen's Park Phone: 416-326-9326; Fax: 416-326-9338
Hon. Bob Chiarelli, OttawaWest-Nepean ON, Liberal
613-721-8075, Fax:
613-721-5756,bchiarelli.mpp.co@liberal.ola.org, Other Communications: Queen's Park Phone: 416-325-8841; Fax: 416-325-8860
Ted Chudleigh, Halton ON, PC
905-878-1729, Fax: 905-878-5144,ted.chudleigh@pc.ola.org, Other Communications: Queen's Park Phone: 416-325-5747; Fax: 416-325-5750
Steve Clark, Leeds-Grenville ON, PC
613-342-9522, 800-267-4408,Fax:
613-342-2501,steve.clark@pc.ola.org, Other Communications: Queen's Park Phone: 416-325-1522; Fax: 416-325-1493
Mike Colle, Eglinton-Lawrence ON, Liberal
416-781-2395, Fax:
416-781-4116,mcolle.mpp@liberal.ola.org; mcolle.mpp.co@liberal.ola.org, Other Communications: Queen's Park Phone: 416-325-4091; Fax: 416-325-4136
Kim Craitor, Niagara Falls ON, Liberal
905-357-0681, Fax:
905-357-9456,kcraitor.mpp@liberal.ola.org; kcraitor.mpp.co@liberal.ola.org, Other Communications: Queen's Park Phone: 416-325-3715; Fax: 416-212-7155,
Bruce Crozier, Essex ON, Liberal
519-776-6420, 800-265-3909,Fax:
519-776-5763,bcrozier.mpp@liberal.ola.org; bcrozier.mpp.co@liberal.ola.org, Other Communications: Queen's Park Phone: 416-325-7298; Fax: 416-325-9003
Bob Delaney, Mississauga-Streetsville ON, Liberal
905-569-1643, Fax:
905-569-6416,bdelaney.mpp@liberal.ola.org; bdelaney.mpp.co@liberal.ola.org, Other Communications: Queen's Park Phone: 416-325-0161; Fax: 416-325-0186
Vic Dhillon, Brampton West ON, Liberal
905-796-8669, Fax:
905-796-8069,vdhillon.mpp@liberal.ola.org; vdhillon.mpp.co@liberal.ola.org, Other Communications: Queen's Park Phone: 416-325-0241; Fax: 416-325-0272
Cheri DiNovo, Parkdale-High Park ON, New Democratic Party
416-763-5630, Fax: 416-763-5640,dinovoc-qp@ndp.on.ca; dinovoc-co@ndp.on.ca, Other Communications: Queen's Park phone: 416-325-0244; Fax: 416-325-0305
Joe Dickson, Ajax-Pickering ON, Liberal
905-427-2060, Fax:
905-427-6976,jdickson.mpp@liberal.ola.org, Other Communications: Queen's Park Phone: 416-325-1182; Fax:416-325-1191
Hon. Leona Dombrowsky, Prince Edward-Hastings ON, Liberal
613-962-1144, 877-536-6248,Fax:
613-969-6381,ldombrowsky.mpp.co@liberal.ola.org, Other Communications: Queen's Park Phone: 416-325-2600; Fax: 416-325-2608
Hon. Brad Duguid, Scarborough Centre ON, Liberal
416-615-2183, Fax:
416-615-2011,bduguid.mpp@liberal.ola.org; bduguid.mpp.co@liberal.ola.org, Other Communications: Queen's Park Phone: 416-327-6758; Fax: 416-327-6754
Hon. Dwight Duncan, Windsor-Tecumseh ON, Liberal
519-251-5199, Fax:
519-251-5299,dduncan.mpp@liberal.ola.org; dduncan.mpp.co@liberal.ola.org, Other Communications: Queen's Park Phone: 416-325-0400; Fax: 416-325-0374
Garfield Dunlop, Simcoe North ON, PC
705-326-3246, 800-304-7341,Fax:
705-326-9579,garfield.dunlop@pc.ola.org; garfield.dunlopco@pc.ola.org, Other Communications: Queen's Park Phone: 416-325-3855; Fax: 416-325-9035
Christine Elliott, Whitby-Oshawa ON, PC
905-430-1141, Fax:

905-430-1840,christine.elliott@pc.ola.org, Other Communications: Queen's Park Phone: 416-325-1331; Fax: 416-325-1423
Kevin Daniel Flynn, Oakville ON, Liberal
905-827-5141, Fax:
905-827-3786,kflynn.mpp@liberal.ola.org; kflynn.mpp.co@liberal.ola.org, Other Communications: Queen's Park Phone: 416-325-7215; Fax: 416-325-9295
Hon. Peter Fonseca, Mississauga East-Cooksville ON, Liberal
905-238-1751, Fax:
905-238-4918,pfonseca.mpp@liberal.ola.org; pfonseca.mpp.co@liberal.ola.org, Other Communications: Queen's Park Phone: 416-326-7600; Fax: 416-326-1449
Hon. John Gerretsen, Kingston & the Islands ON, Liberal
613-547-2385, Fax:
613-547-5001,jgerretsen.mpp@liberal.ola.org; jgerretsen.mpp.co@liberal.ola.org, Other Communications: Queen's Park Phone: 416-327-8300; Fax: 416-326-1947
Hon. Michael Gravelle, Thunder Bay-Superior North ON, Liberal
807-345-3647, 888-516-5555,Fax:
807-345-2922,mgravelle.mpp@liberal.ola.org, Other Communications: Queen's Park Phone: 416-327-0633; Fax: 416-327-0665
France Gélinas, Nickel Belt ON, New Democratic Party
705-969-3621, Fax: 705-969-3538,fgelinas-co@ndp.on.ca; fgelinas-qp@ndp.on.ca, Other Communications: Queen's Park Phone: 416-325-9203; Fax: 416-325-9185
Howard Hampton, Kenora-Rainy River ON, New Democratic Party
807-467-2415, 800-465-8501,Fax:
807-467-2641,hhampton-qp@ndp.on.ca, Other Communications: Queen's Park Phone: 416-325-2750; Fax: 416-325-1645
Ernie Hardeman, Oxford ON, PC
519-537-5222, 800-265-4046,Fax:
519-537-3577,ernie.hardeman@pc.ola.org; ernie.hardemanco@pc.ola.org, Other Communications: Queen's Park Phone: 416-325-1239; Fax: 416-325-1259
Randy Hillier, Lanark-Frontenac-Lennox& Addington ON, PC
613-267-8293, Fax: 613-267-7398,randy.hillierco@pc.ola.org, Other Communications: Queen's Park Phone: 416-325-2244; Fax: 416-325-2166
Andrea Horwath, Hamilton Centre ON, New Democratic Party
905-544-9644, Fax: 905-544-5152,ahorwath-qp@ndp.on.ca; ahorwath-co@ndp.on.ca, Other Communications: Queen's Park Phone: 416-325-2777; Fax: 416-325-2770
Hon. Eric Hoskins, St.Paul's ON, Liberal
416-656-0943, Fax:
416-656-0875,ehoskins.mpp.co@liberal.ola.org, Other Communications: Queen's Park Phone: 416-325-6200; Fax: 416-325-6195
Pat Hoy, Chatham-Kent-Essex ON, Liberal
519-351-0510, 800-265-3992,Fax:
519-351-7714,phoy.mpp@liberal.ola.org; phoy.mpp.co@liberal.ola.org, Other Communications: Queen's Park Phone: 416-325-9099; Fax: 416-325-9000
Tim Hudak, NiagaraWest-Glanbrook ON, PC
905-563-1755, 800-665-3697,Fax:
905-563-1317,tim.hudakco@pc.ola.org, Other Communications: Queen's Park Phone: 416-325-8454; Fax: 416-325-0998
Helena Jaczek, OakRidges-Markham ON, Liberal
905-294-4931, 866-531-9551,Fax:
905-294-0014,hjaczek.mpp@liberal.ola.org, Other Communications: Queen's Park Phone: 416-325-0737; Fax: 416-325-4112
Hon. Linda Jeffrey, Brampton-Springdale ON, Liberal
905-495-8030, Fax:
905-495-1041,ljeffrey.mpp@liberal.ola.org; ljeffrey.mpp.co@liberal.ola.org, Other Communications: Queen's Park Phone: 416-314-2301; Fax: 416-325-5316
Rick Johnson, Haliburton-Kawartha Lakes-Brock ON, Liberal
705-324-6654, 800-424-2490,Fax:
705-324-6938,rjohnson.mpp.co@liberal.ola.org, Other Communications: Queen's Park Phone: 416-326-3061; Fax: 416-325-6640
Sylvia Jones, Dufferin-Caledon ON, PC
519-941-7751, Fax: 519-941-3246,sylvia.jones@pc.ola.org; sylvia.jonesco@pc.ola.org, Other Communications: Queen's Park Phone: 416-325-1898; Fax: 416-325-1936
Frank Klees, Newmarket-Aurora ON, PC
905-750-0019, Fax: 905-750-0050,frank.klees@pc.ola.org; frank.kleesco@pc.ola.org, Other Communications: Queen's Park Phone: 416-325-7316; Fax: 416-325-1573
Peter Kormos, Welland ON, New Democratic Party
905-732-6884, Fax: 905-732-9782,pkormos-qp@ndp.on.ca, Other Communications: Queen's Park Phone: 416-325-7106
Kuldip Kular, Bramalea-Gore-Malton ON, Liberal
905-799-3939, Fax:
905-799-9505,kkular.mpp@liberal.ola.org; kkular.mpp.co@liberal.ola.org, Other Communications: Queen's Park Phone: 416-325-0235; Fax: 416-325-0378
Monte Kwinter, York Centre ON, Liberal
416-630-0080, Fax:
416-630-8828,mkwinter.mpp@liberal.ola.org; mkwinter.mpp.co@liberal.ola.org, Other Communications: Queen's Park Phone: 416-325-0036; Fax: 416-325-0316
Jean-Marc Lalonde, Glengarry-Prescott-Russell ON, Liberal
613-446-4010, 800-355-9666,Fax:
613-446-6605,jmlalonde.mpp@liberal.ola.org, Other Communications: Queen's Park Phone: 416-325-7289; Fax: 416-325-2827
Jeff Leal, Peterborough ON, Liberal
705-742-3777, Fax: 705-742-1822,jleal.mpp@liberal.ola.org; jleal.mpp.co@liberal.ola.org, Other Communications: Queen's Park Phone: 416-325-0534; Fax: 416-325-0570
Dave Levac, Brant ON, Liberal
519-759-0361, Fax:
519-759-6439,dlevac.mpp@liberal.ola.org; dlevac.mpp.co@liberal.ola.org, Other Communications: Queen's Park Phone: 416-325-4140
Lisa MacLeod, Nepean-Carleton ON, PC
613-823-2116, Fax: 613-823-8284,lisa.macleod@pc.ola.org, Other Communications: Queen's Park Phone: 416-325-6351; Fax: 416-325-6364
Amrit Mangat, Mississauga-Brampton South ON, Liberal
905-696-0367, Fax:
905-696-7545,amangat.mpp.co@liberal.ola.org, Other Communications: Queen's Park Phone: 416-325-1050; Fax: 416-325-1138
Rosario Marchese, Trinity-Spadina ON, New Democratic Party
416-603-9664, Fax: 416-603-1241,rmarchese-co@ndp.on.ca, Other Communications: Queen's Park Phone: 416-325-9092; Fax: 416-325-4976
Gerry Martiniuk, Cambridge ON, PC
519-623-5852, Fax:
519-623-3250,gerry.martiniuk@pc.ola.org; gerry.martiniukco@pc.ola.org, Other Communications: Queen's Park Phone: 416-325-8451; Fax: 416-325-8413
Hon. Deborah Matthews, London North Centre ON, Liberal
519-432-7339, Fax:
519-432-0613,dmatthews.mpp@liberal.ola.org; dmatthews.mpp.co@liberal.ola.org, Other Communications: Queen's Park Phone: 416-327-4300; Fax: 416-327-3679
Bill Mauro, ThunderBay-Atikokan ON, Liberal
807-623-9237, Fax:
807-623-4983,bmauro.mpp.co@liberal.ola.org, Other Communications: Queen's Park Phone: 416-327-6611; Fax: 416-327-6618
Hon. Dalton McGuinty, OttawaSouth ON, Liberal
613-736-9573, Fax:
613-736-7374,dmcguinty.mpp.co@liberal.ola.org, Other Communications: Queen's Park Phone: 416-325-1941; Fax: 416-325-3745
Hon. Ted McMeekin, Ancaster-Dundas-Flamborough-Westdale ON, Liberal
905-690-6552, 888-566-6614,Fax:
905-690-6562,tmcmeekin.mpp@liberal.ola.org; tmcmeekin.mpp.co@liberal.ola.org, Other Communications: Queen's Park Phone: 416-326-1600; Fax: 416-326-2807
Phil McNeely, Ottawa-Orléans ON, Liberal
613-834-8679, Fax:
613-834-7647,pmcneely.mpp@liberal.ola.org; pmcneely.mpp.co@liberal.ola.org, Other Communications: Queen's Park Phone: 416-325-0505; Fax: 416-325-0532
Hon. Madeleine Meilleur, Ottawa-Vanier ON, Liberal
613-744-4484, 800-628-7507,Fax:
613-744-0889,mmeilleur.mpp.co@liberal.ola.org; ofa@ofa.gov.on.ca, Other Communications: Queen's Park Phone: 416-325-5225; Fax: 416-325-5191
Norm Miller, ParrySound-Muskoka ON, PC
705-746-4266, 888-701-1176,Fax:
705-746-1578,norm.millerco@pc.ola.org, Other Communications: Queen's Park Phone: 416-325-1012; Fax: 416-325-1153
Paul Miller, HamiltonEast-Stoney Creek ON, New Democratic Party
905-545-0114, Fax: 905-545-9024,pmiller-co@ndp.on.ca; pmiller-qp@ndp.on.ca, Other Communications: Queen's Park Phone: 416-325-0707; Fax: 416-325-0853
Hon. John Milloy, Kitchener Centre ON, Liberal
519-579-5460, Fax:
519-579-2121,jmilloy.mpp@liberal.ola.org; jmilloy.mpp.co@liberal.ola.org, Other Communications: Queen's Park Phone: 416-326-1600; Fax: 416-326-1656
Carol Mitchell, Huron-Bruce ON, Liberal
519-396-3007, 866-396-3007,Fax:
519-396-3011,cmitchell.mpp@liberal.ola.org, Other Communications: Queen's Park Phone: 416-585-6768; Fax: 416-585-6777
Reza Moridi, Richmond Hill ON, Liberal
905-884-8080, Fax:
905-884-1040,rmoridi.mpp@liberal.ola.org, Other Communications: Queen's Park Phone: 416-326-5968; Fax: 416-326-5834
Julia Munro, York-Simcoe ON, PC
905-478-2572, 866-206-1373,Fax:
905-478-8470,julia.munro@pc.ola.org; julia.munroco@pc.ola.org, Other Communications: Queen's Park Phone: 416-325-3392; Fax: 416-325-3466
Bill Murdoch, Bruce-Grey-Owen Sound ON, PC
519-371-2421, 800-461-2664,Fax:
519-371-0953,bill.murdoch@pc.ola.org; bill.murdochco@pc.ola.org, Other Communications: Queen's Park Phone: 416-325-6242; Fax: 416-325-6248

Members

Hon. Glen R. Murray, TorontoCentre ON, Liberal
416-972-7683, Fax:
416-972-7686,gmurray.mpp.co@liberal.ola.org, Other Communications: Queen's Park Phone: 416-325-5744; Fax: 416-325-5754
Yasir Naqvi, Ottawa Centre ON, Liberal
613-722-6414, Fax:
613-722-6703,ynaqvi.mpp@liberal.ola.org, Other Communications: Queen's Park Phone: 416-327-4394; Fax: 416-314-9369
John O'Toole, Durham ON, PC
905-697-1501, 800-661-2433,Fax:
905-697-1506,john.otoole@pc.ola.org; john.otooleco@pc.ola.org, Other Communications: Queen's Park Phone: 416-325-6745; Fax: 416-325-6255
David Orazietti, Sault Ste. Marie ON, Liberal
705-949-6959, Fax:
705-946-6269,dorazietti.mpp@liberal.ola.org; dorazietti.mpp.co@liberal.ola.org, Other Communications: Queen's Park Phone: 416-314-6467; Fax: 416-314-6470
Jerry J. Ouellette, Oshawa ON, PC
905-723-2411, Fax: 905-723-1054,jerry.ouellette@pc.ola.org; jerry.ouelletteco@pc.ola.org, Other Communications: Queen's Park Phone: 416-325-2147; Fax: 416-325-2169
Leeanna Pendergast, Kitchener-Conestoga ON, Liberal
519-571-3276, Fax:
519-571-8660,lpendergast.mpp@liberal.ola.org, Other Communications: Queen's Park Phone: 519-571-3276; Fax: 416-212-3720
Hon. Steve Peters, Elgin-Middlesex-London ON, Liberal
519-631-0666, 800-265-7638,Fax:
519-631-9478,speters.mpp@liberal.ola.org; speters.mpp.co@liberal.ola.org, Other Communications: Queen's Park Phone: 416-325-7435 Fax: 416-325-7483
Hon. Gerry Phillips, Scarborough-Agincourt ON, Liberal
416-297-6568, Fax:
416-297-4962,gphillips.mpp.co@liberal.ola.org; gphillips.mpp@liberal.ola.org, Other Communications: Queen's Park Phone: 416-325-3628; Fax: 416-314-7421
Michael Prue, Beaches-EastYork ON, New Democratic Party
416-690-1032, Fax: 416-690-8420,mprue-qp@ndp.on.ca; mprue-co@ndp.on.ca, Other Communications: Queen's Park Phone: 416-325-1303; Fax: 416-325-1367
Hon. Sandra Pupatello, Windsor West ON, Liberal
519-977-7191, Fax:
519-977-7029,spupatello.mpp@liberal.ola.org, Other Communications: Queen's Park Phone: 416-325-6900; Fax: 416-325-6918,
Shafiq Qaadri, Etobicoke North ON, Liberal
416-745-2859, Fax:
416-745-4601,sqaadri.mpp@liberal.ola.org; sqaadri.mpp.co@liberal.ola.org, Other Communications: Queen's Park Phone: 416-325-6679; Fax: 416-325-6691
Khalil Ramal, London-Fanshawe ON, Liberal
519-668-1104, Fax:
519-668-1941,kramal.mpp.co@liberal.ola.org; kramal.mpp@liberal.ola.org, Other Communications: Queen's Park Phone: 416-325-6002; Fax: 416-212-1812
David J. Ramsay, Timiskaming-Cochrane ON, Liberal
705-567-4650, 800-461-2186,Fax:
705-567-4208,dramsay.mpp@liberal.ola.org, Other Communications: New Liskeard Phone: 1-888-701-1105
Lou Rinaldi, Northumberland-Quinte West ON, Liberal
613-392-3038, Fax:
613-392-2241,lrinaldi.mpp@liberal.ola.org;, Other Communications: Queen's Park Phone: 416-585-6768; Fax: 416-585-6777
Tony Ruprecht, Davenport ON, Liberal
416-535-3158, Fax:
416-325-9961,truprecht.mpp@liberal.ola.org; truprecht.mpp.co@liberal.ola.org, Other Communications: Queen's Park Phone: 416-325-7777; Fax: 416-325-9961
Liz Sandals, Guelph ON, Liberal
519-836-4190, Fax:
519-836-4191,lsandals.mpp@liberal.ola.org; lsandals.mpp.co@liberal.ola.org, Other Communications: Queen's Park Phone: 416-327-1322; Fax: 416-325-3862
Joyce Savoline, Burlington ON, PC
905-639-7924, Fax: 905-639-3284,joyce.savoline@pc.ola.org,

Other Communications: Queen's Park Phone: 416-325-5362; Fax: 416-325-5357
Mario Sergio, York West ON, Liberal
416-743-7272, Fax:
416-743-3292,msergio.mpp@liberal.ola.org, Other Communications: Queen's Park Phone: 416-325-4925; Fax: 416-325-4926
Peter Shurman, Thornhill ON, PC
905-731-8462, Fax:
905-731-2984,peter.shurman@pc.ola.org; peter.shurmanco@pc.ola.org, Other Communications: Queen's Park Phone: 416-325-1415; Fax: 416-325-3810
Hon. Monique M. Smith, Nipissing ON, Liberal
705-474-8340, Fax:
705-474-9747,msmith.mpp@liberal.ola.org; msmith.mpp.co@liberal.ola.org, Other Communications: Queen's Park Phone: 416-325-7754; Fax: 416-325-7755
Greg Sorbara, Vaughan ON, Liberal
905-851-0440, Fax:
905-851-0210,gsorbara.mpp@liberal.ola.org; gsorbara.mpp.co@liberal.ola.org, Other Communications: Queen's Park Phone: 416-212-1022; Fax: 416-212-1025
Charles Sousa, Mississauga South ON, Liberal
905-274-8228, Fax:
905-274-8552,csousa.mpp@liberal.ola.org; csousa.mpp.co@liberal.ola.org, Other Communications: Queen's Park Phone: 416-327-6611; Fax: 416-327-6618
Norman W. Sterling, Carleton-Mississippi Mills ON, PC
613-599-3000, 800-267-1020,Fax:
613-599-8183,norm.sterling@pc.ola.org; norm.sterlingco@pc.ola.org, Other Communications: Queen's Park Phone: 416-314-7900; Fax: 416-314-7966
Peter Tabuns, Toronto-Danforth ON, New Democratic Party
416-461-0223, Fax: 416-461-9542,tabunsp-qp@ndp.on.ca; tabunsp-co@ndp.on.ca, Other Communications: Queen's Park Phone: 416-325-3250; Fax: 416-325-3252
Hon. Harinder S. Takhar, Mississauga-Erindale ON, Liberal
905-828-8989, Fax:
905-828-8670,htakhar.mpp@liberal.ola.org; htakhar.mpp.co@liberal.ola.org, Other Communications: Queen's Park Phone: 416-327-2333; Fax: 416-327-3790
Maria Van Bommel, Lambton-Kent-Middlesex ON, Liberal
519-245-8696, Fax:
519-245-8697,mvanbommel.mpp@liberal.ola.org; mvanbommel.mpp.co@liberal.ola.org, Other Communications: Queen's Park Phone: 416-326-6160; Fax: 416-326-3951
Hon. John Wilkinson, Perth-Wellington ON, Liberal
519-272-0660, Fax:
519-272-1064,jwilkinson.mpp.co@liberal.ola.org, Other Communications: Queen's Park Phone: 416-314-6729; Fax: 416-314-6748
Jim Wilson, Simcoe-Grey ON, PC
705-446-1090, 800-268-7542,Fax:
705-446-3397,jim.wilson@pc.ola.org; jim.wilsonco@pc.ola.org, Other Communications: Queen's Park Phone: 416-325-2069; Fax: 416-325-2079
Elizabeth Witmer, Kitchener-Waterloo ON, PC
519-725-3477, Fax:
519-725-3667,elizabeth.witmer@pc.ola.org; elizabeth.witmerco@pc.ola.org, Other Communications: Queen's Park Phone: 416-325-1306; Fax: 416-325-1329
Hon. Kathleen O. Wynne, Don Valley West ON, Liberal
416-425-6777, Fax:
416-425-0350,kwynne.mpp@liberal.ola.org; kwynne.mpp.co@liberal.ola.org, Other Communications: Queen's Park Phone: 416-327-9200; Fax: 416-327-9188
John Yakabuski, Renfrew-Nipissing-Pembroke ON, PC
613-735-6627, Fax:
613-735-6692,john.yakabuski@pc.ola.org; john.yakabuskico@pc.ola.org1, Other Communications: Queen's Park Phone: 416-325-2170; Fax: 416-325-2196
David Zimmer, Willowdale ON, Liberal
416-733-7878, Fax:
416-733-7709,dzimmer.mpp@liberal.ola.org; dzimmer.mpp.co@liberal.ola.org, Other Communications: Queen's Park Phone: 416-327-4516; Fax: 416-325-4175

Ontario Government Departments & Agencies

Ministry of Aboriginal Affairs / Ministère des Affaires autochtones

720 Bay St., 4th Fl., Toronto, ON M5G 2K1
416-326-4740, Fax: 416-326-4017,
www.nativeaffairs.jus.gov.on.ca; www.aboriginalaffairs.gov.on.ca
The Ministry operates with the following units: Office of the Deputy Minister of Aboriginal Affairs; Office of the Assistant Deputy Minister of Aboriginal Affairs; Policy & Relationships Branch; Ipperwash Response Team; Negotiations Branch; Legal Services Branch; Communications Branch; & the Business Services Unit.

Minister,Hon. Brad Duguid
416-314-8693, Fax:
416-314-2701,bduguid.mpp.co@liberal.ola.org
Deputy Minister, Lori Sterling
416-314-1141, Fax: 416-314-1165,lori.sterling@ontario.ca
Acting Chief Administrative Officer, David Lynch
416-314-1939, Fax: 416-326-4017,david.lynch@ontario.ca

Business Services Branch
416-326-4740, Fax: 416-212-1644
Corporate functions are provided by the branch. Functions include the following: business planning; financial control & budgeting; & facilities & assets management
Manager, Brian Hamilton
416-326-4748, Brian.Hamilton@ontario.ca

Communications Branch
416-326-4740, Fax: 416-314-2102
Acting Director, Rosemary Sampson
416-326-4780, Rosemary.Sampson@ontario.ca

Ipperwash Response Team
LuCliff Bldg., #2108, 700 Bay St., Toronto, ON M7A 2H4
416-327-9518, Fax: 416-327-3903
The team facitlitate coordination of response to the Ipperwash Inquiry Report & researches & analyzes the implementation of the inquiry recommendations.
Director, Hanita Tiefenbach
416-327-9632, Hanita.Tiefenbach@ontario.ca

Legal Services Branch
416-326-4740, Fax: 416-326-4017
Director, Grant Wedge
416-326-2372, Grant.Wedge@ontario.ca

Negotiations Branch
416-326-4740, Fax: 416-326-2361
The branch carries out the following responsibilities: researching & conducting land claim negotiations; managing & coordinating negotiations; representing the province for federally-led governance negotiations; & implementing settlements.
Assistant Deputy Minister, Negotiations & Land Claims, doug.carr@ontario.ca
Didluck, David Didluck
416-326-2839, Fax: 416-326-4017

Policy & Relationships Branch
416-326-4743
The branch is engaged in the following key activities: developing & coordinating government-wide Aboriginal policy; providing corporate planning & policy advice on Aboriginal matters; & developing & maintaining positive relationships with Aboriginal leaders.
Assistant Deputy Minister, Alison Pilla
416-212-2302, Alison.Pilla@ontario.ca
Director, Pam Wheaton
416-326-4053, Fax: 416-326-4017,pam.wheaton@ontario.ca

Ministry of Agriculture, Food & Rural Affairs (OMAF)

1 Stone Rd. West, Guelph, ON N1G 4Y2
519-826-3100, 888-466-2372
www.omafra.gov.on.ca
The ministry works in partnership with an industry that employs over 640,000 people & contributes over $25 billion annually to the provincial economy. The ministry plays a key role in bringing a strong agricultural & rural perspective to provincial policies. The ministry works with other ministries to resolve local economic issues & assists rural communities in retaining & attracting business. Staff at the ministry's Guelph headquarters & across the province provide a wide range of agri-food & rural economic development programs & services to clients.
Acts Administered:
Agricorp Act
Agricultural Employees Protection Act 2002
Agricultural & Horticultural Organizations Act
Agricultural Rehabilitation & Development Act (Ontario)
Agricultural Research Institute of Ontario Act
Agricultural Lands Regulations
Agricultural Tile Drainage Installation Act
Animals for Research Act
Beef Cattle Marketing Act
Bees Act
Crop Insurance Act
Dead Animal Disposal Act
Drainage Act
Edible Oil Products Act
Farm Products Container Act
Farm Products Marketing Act
Farm Implements Act
Farm Products Grades & Sales Act
Farm Products Payments Act
Farm Registration & Farm Organizations Funding Act
Farming & Food Production Protection Act
Food Safety & Quality Act, 2001
Grain Corn Marketing Act
Grains Act
Livestock & Livestock Products Act
Livestock Community Sales Act
Livestock Identification Act
Livestock Medicines Act
Livestock, Poultry & Honey Bee Protection Act
Meat Inspection Act (Ontario)
Milk Act
Ministry of Agriculture, Food & Rural Affairs Act
Nutrient Management Act, 2002
Ontario Agricultural Museum Act
Ontario Agricultural Week Act, 1998
Ontario Food Terminal Act
Plant Diseases Act
Pounds Act
Tile Drainage Act
Veterinarians Act
Weed Control Act
Minister,Hon. Leona Dombrowsky
416-326-3074, Fax:
416-326-3083,minister.omafra@ontario.ca
Deputy Minister, Bruce Archibald
416-326-3101, bruce.archibald@ontario.ca
Director, Communications, Tom Rekstis
519-826-3174, tom.rekstis@ontario.ca
Director, Legal Services, Michael Brady
519-826-3378, Fax:
519-826-3385,michael.p.brady@ontario.ca
Admin. Asst., Maureen Boyd
416-326-3101, Fax:
416-326-3106,maureen.boyd@ontario.ca

• AGRICORP
1 Stone Rd. West
PO Box 3660 Central
Guelph, ON N1H 8M4
Fax: 519-826-4118 888-247-4999
cac@agricorp.com
Responsible for delivering government & non-government priority products & services that assist Ontario's agri-food industry in managing risks. Since its inception, AGRICORP has developed a reputation for innovation, excellent customer service & reliable, cost-effective delivery

• Agricultural Research Institute of Ontario
1 Stone Rd. West, 2nd Fl. NW
Guelph, ON N1G 4Y2
519-826-4199 Fax: 519-826-4211
The role of ARIO is to enquire into programs of research with respect to agriculture, veterinary medicine & consumer studies, select & recommend areas of research for the betterment of agriculture, veterinary medicine & consumer studies, & stimulate interest in research as a means of developing a high degree of efficiency in the production & marketing of agricultural products in Ontario.

• Agriculture, Food & Rural Affairs Tribunal
1 Stone Rd. West, 1st Fl.
Guelph, ON N1G 4Y2
519-826-3433 Fax: 519-826-4232
appeals.tribunal@omafra.gov.on.ca
www.omafra.gov.on.ca/english/index.html

• College of Veterinarians of Ontario
2106 Gordon St.
Guelph, ON N1L 1G6
519-824-5600 Fax: 519-824-6497 800-424-2856

• Grain Financial Protection Board
1 Stone Rd. West
PO Box 3660
Guelph, ON N1H 8M4
519-826-3949 Fax: 519-826-3367

• Livestock Financial Protection Board
1 Stone Rd. West, 5th Fl. NW
Guelph, ON N1G 4Y2
519-826-3886 Fax: 519-826-4375
jim.wideman@omaf.gov.on.ca

• Livestock Medicines Advisory Committee
1 Stone Rd. West, 3rd Fl. NE
Guelph, ON N1G 4Y2
519-826-4110 Fax: 519-826-3254

• Normal Farm Practices Protection Board
1 Stone Rd. West, 3rd Fl., Northeast
Guelph, ON N1G 4Y2
519-826-3549 Fax: 519-826-6611
www.gov.on.ca/OMAFA/english/engineer/nfppb/nfppb.htm

• Ontario Farm Products Marketing Commission
1 Stone Rd. West, 5th Fl.
Guelph, ON N1G 4Y2
519-826-4220 Fax: 519-826-3400

• Ontario Food Terminal Board
165 The Queensway
Toronto, ON M8Y 1H8
416-259-5479 Fax: 416-259-4303
www.oftb.com

Food Safety & Environment Division
519-826-4304, Fax: 519-826-4416
Asst. Deputy Minister,Dr. Deb Stark
519-826-4301, Fax: 519-826-4416,deb.stark@ontario.ca
Director, Animal Health & Welfare,Dr. Tom Baker
519-826-3577, Fax: 519-826-4375,tom.baker@ontario.ca
Director, Food Inspection Branch, Rena Hubers
519-826-4366, Fax: 519-826-4375,rena.hubers@ontario.ca
Acting Director, Food Safety Programs, Martin Bohl
519-826-3112, Fax: 519-826-4466,martin.bohl2@ontario.ca
Director, Nutrient Management, Earl Pollock
519-826-4975, Fax: 519-826-6611,earl.pollock@ontario.ca

Innovation & Competitiveness Division
Asst. Deputy Minister, Bonnie Winchester
519-826-3528, Fax: 519-826-3259,bonnie.winchester@ontario.ca
Director, Regulatory Modernization, Michael Toombs
519-826-3781, Fax: 519-826-3259,michael.toombs@ontario.ca
Director, Transition, Bill Ingratta
519-826-3151, Fax: 519-826-3267,bill.ingratta@ontario.ca
Director, Food Industry Competitiveness Branch, George Borovilos
519-826-4452, Fax: 519-826-4333,george.borovilos@ontario.ca
Director, Livestock Technology, Aileen MacNeil
519-826-6588, Fax: 519-826-3254,aileen.macneil@ontario.ca

Policy & Programs Division
519-826-4020, Fax: 519-826-3492
Responsible for the ministry's policy processes, the administration & delivery of several farm business risk management programs & the management of the ministry's strategic partnership with AGRICORP.
Asst. Deputy Minister, Dave Antle
519-826-4151, Fax: 519-826-3492,dave.antle@ontario.ca
Director, Farm Finance, Christine Kuepfer
519-826-3244, Fax: 519-826-3170,christine.kuepfer@ontario.ca
Director, Food Safety & Environmental Policy Branch, Peter Meerveld
519-826-6800, Fax: 519-826-3492,peter.meerveld@ontario.ca
Director, Strategic Policy, Phil Malcolmson
416-326-3207, phil.malcolmson@ontario.ca

Research & Corporate Services Division
NW, 1 Stone Road W., 2nd fl., Guelph, ON N1G 4Y2
519-826-4551, Fax: 519-826-3390
Asst. Deputy Minister, Karen D. Chan
519-826-6599, Fax: 519-826-3390,karen.chan@ontario.ca
Director, Financial Management, Madeleine Davidson
519-826-3336, Fax: 519-826-4130,madeleine.davidson@ontario.ca
Director, Human Resources Branch, Jim Felker
519-826-3739, Fax: 519-826-3160,jim.felker@ontario.ca
Director, Research & Innovation,Dr. Gwen Zellen
519-826-4172, Fax: 519-826-4211,gwen.zellen@ontario.ca
Director, Service Management Branch, Shelley Gibson
519-826-4698, Fax: 519-826-4543,shelley.gibson@ontario.ca
Chief Information Officer, Land & Resources Cluster, Robert Hollis
705-755-1528, Fax: 705-755-1599,robert.hollis@ontario.ca

Economic Development Division
1 Stone Road W., 2nd Fl., Guelph, ON N1G 4Y2
519-826-6636, Fax: 519-826-4328
Asst Deputy Minister, Christine Dukelow
416-326-6707
Director, Economic Development Policy, Thom Hagerty
519-826-3918, Fax: 519-826-4328,thom.hagerty@ontario.ca
Manager, Rural Investments, Dino Radacchia
519-826-3787, Fax: 519-826-4336,dino.radocchia@ontario.ca
Director, Rural Community Development, Brian Cardy
519-826-3419, Fax: 519-826-4336,brian.cardy@ontario.ca
Director, Tom Baker
519-826-4366
Acting Manager, Dairy Food Safety Program, Brenda Mitchell
519-826-4378
Program Manager, Beef Cattle Financial Protection Program, Jim Wideman
519-826-3886
Manager, Foods of Plant Origin, Robert Forrest
519-826-4379
Manager, Meat Inspection Policy & Audit Services, Robert Vanderwoude
519-826-4361
Manager, Science & Advisory Unit, Patricia Johnson
519-826-3667
Field Inspection Manager, Meat Inspection Operations, Ralph Rangai
519-826-4364

Deputy Minister, Frank Ingratta
416-326-3101
Director, Legal Services Branch, Stephen Stepinac
519-826-3378,
Director, Kirk Smith
519-826-3169
Manager, Creative Services, Marilyn Harris
519-826-3142
Manager, Strategic Communications, Tom Rekstis
519-826-3174
Director, Michael Toombs
519-826-3781
Director, Thom Hagerty
519-826-4533
Manager, Agriculture & Rural Business Development, Clarence Haverson
519-826-3285
Manager, Community Economic Development, Irene Sullivan
519-826-3189
Manager, Regional Economic Development, East, Luigia Cistera
613-258-8257
Manager, Regional Economic Development, West, Art Lawson
519-826-4093
Manager, Rural Development, Lera Ryan
519-826-6690
Officer, Marketing & Communications, Susan Powell
519-826-4042
Director, Bill Ingratta
519-826-3151
Acting Manager, Field Crops, John Finlay
519-826-6941
Manager, Greenhouse, Agroforestry & Specialty Crops, Annette Anderson
519-826-3286
Acting Manager, Horticultural Crops, Kelly Ward
519-826-3257
Director, Doug Chapman
519-826-4452
Director, Aileen MacNeil
519-826-6588
Chief Veterinary Inspector, Bill Holley
705-324-5854
Manager, Veterinary Science,Dr. David Alves
519-826-3127
Manager, Dairy Cattle & Swine, John Forsyth
519-826-3107
Manager, Beef Cattle & Sheep, Ralph Macartney
519-826-3291
Manager, Multi-Sectoral Issues, Aquaculture, Poultry & Alternative Livestock Pr, Dawn Pate
Officer, Marketing & Communications, Brita Ball
519-826-4847
Director, Christine Dukelow
519-826-3419
Acting Director, Andy Rankine
519-826-3510
Director, George McCaw
519-826-3336
Controller, Phyllis Taggart
519-826-3346
Manager, Planning & Analysis Unit, Robert Cunnington
519-826-3449

Ministry of the Attorney General

McMurtry-Scott Bldg., 720 Bay St., 11th Fl., Toronto, ON M5G 2K1
416-326-2220, Fax: 416-326-4007, 800-518-7901
www.attorneygeneral.jus.gov.on.ca
Justice services are delivered to Ontarians by the Ministry of the Attorney General. The Ministry is engaged in the following activities: supporting victims of crime; providing justice support services to vulnerable people in the province; ensuring the availability of effective & efficient criminal, civil & family courts, plus related justice services; prosecuting crime; & giving legal advice & services to government.
Acts Administered:
Absconding Debtors Act
Absentees Act
Accumulations Act
Administration of Justice Act
Age of Majority & Accountability Act
Aliens' Real Property Act
Arbitrations Act
Architects Act
Assessment Review Board Act
Bail Act
Barristers Act
Blind Persons' Rights Act
Bulk Sales Act
Business Records Protection Act
Charitable Gifts Act
Chartered Accountants Act
Charities Accounting Act
Children's Law Reform Act
Class Proceedings Act
Commercial Tenancies Act
Commissioners for Taking Affidavits Act
Compensation for Victims of Crime Act
Construction Lien Act
Conveyance & Law of Property Act
Costs of Distress Act
Courts of Justice Act
Creditors' Relief Act
Crown Administration of Estates Act
Crown Agency Act
Crown Attorneys Act
Crown Witnesses Act
Declarations of Death Act
Disorderly Houses Act
Dog Owners' Liability Act
Electronic Commerce Act
Employers & Employees Act
Enforcement of Judgement Conventions Act
Escheats Act
Estates Act
Estates Administration Act
Evidence Act
Execution Act
Expropriation Act
Family Law Act
Fines & Forfeitures Act
Fraudulent Conveyances Act
Frustrated Contracts Act
Habeas Corpus Act
Hospitals & Charitable Institutions Inquiries Act
Hotel Registration of Guests Act
Innkeepers Act
International Commercial Arbitration Act
International Sale of Goods Act
Interpretation Act
Inter-Provincial Summonses Act
Judicial Review Procedure Act
Juries Act
Justices of the Peace Act
Law Society Act
Legal Aid Services Act
Libel & Slander Act
Limitations Act
Mercantile Law Amendment Act
Ministry of the Attorney General Act
Mortgages Act
Negligence Act
Notaries Act
Occupiers' Liability Act
Ombudsman Act
Ontario Law Reform Commission Act
Ontario Lottery & Gaming Corporation Act
Parental Responsibility Act
Partition Act
Pawnbrokers Act
Perpetuities Act
Police Services Act (s. 113)
Powers of Attorney Act
Proceedings Against the Crown Act
Professional Engineers Act
Property & Civil Rights Act
Provincial Offences Act
Public Accountancy Act
Public Authorities' Protection Act
Public Guardian & Trustee Act
Public Inquiries Act
Public Officers Act
Reciprocal Enforcement of Judgements Act
Reciprocal Enforcement of Judgements (U.K.) Act
Regulations Act
Religious Freedom Act
Religious Organizations' Lands Act
Remedies for Organized Crime & Other Unlawful Activities Act
Safe Streets Act
Sale of Goods Act
Settled Estates Act
Short Forms of Leases Act
Solicitors Act
Statute & Regulation Revision Act
Statute of Frauds
Statutes Act
Statutory Powers Procedure Act
Substitute Decisions Act
Succession Law Reform Act
Ticket Speculation Act
Time Act
Transboundary Pollution Reciprocal Access Act
Trespass to Property Act

Trustee Act
Unconscionable Transactions Relief Act
University Expropriation Powers Act
Variation of Trusts Act
Vendors & Purchasers Act
Victims Bill of Rights Act
Victims Right to Proceeds of Crime Act
Wages Act
Warehouse Receipts Act
Attorney General,Hon. Christopher Bentley
416-326-2220, 800-518-7901,Fax:
416-326-4007,cbentley.mpp@liberal.ola.org, TDD:
416-326-4012
Deputy Attorney General, Murray Segal
416-326-2640, Fax:
416-326-4018,Murray.Segal@ontario.ca
Acting Director, Communications, Marianne Summers
416-326-2604, Fax:
416-326-4007,marianne.summers@ontario.ca
Parliamentary Assistant, David Zimmer
416-327-4516, Fax:
416-325-4175,dzimmer.mpp@liberal.ola.org;
dzimmer.mpp.co@liberal.ola.org
• Assessment Review Board
Eaton Tower
250 Yonge St., 29th Fl.
Toronto, ON M5B 2L7
416-314-6900 Fax: 416-314-3717
www.arb.gov.on.ca
• Chief Inquiry Officer - Expropriations Act
720 Bay St., 8th Fl.
Toronto, ON M5G 2K1
416-326-4093
• Criminal Injuries Compensation Board
439 University Ave., 4th Fl.
Toronto, ON M5G 1Y8
416-326-2900 Fax: 416-326-2883 800-372-7463
www.attorneygeneral.jus.gov.on.ca/english/about/vw/cicb.asp
• Human Rights Tribunal of Ontario(ARB)
400 University Ave., 7th Fl.
Toronto, ON M7A 1T7
416-314-8419 Fax: 416-314-8743 800-668-3946TDD:
416-314-2379
hrto.registrar@jus.gov.on.ca
www.hrto.ca
• Judicial Appointments Advisory Committee
720 Bay St., 3rd Fl.
Toronto, ON M5G 2K1
416-326-4060 Fax: 416-212-7316
• Legal Aid Ontario
#404, 375 University Ave.
Toronto, ON M5G 2G1
416-979-1446 Fax: 416-979-8669 800-668-8258
info@lao.on.ca
www.legalaid.on.ca
• Office for Victims of Crime
700 Bay St., 3rd Fl.
Toronto, ON M5G 1Z6
416-326-1682 Fax: 416-326-2343 887-435-7661
• Ontario Human Rights Commission
• Ontario Municipal Board & Board of Negotiation
655 Bay St., 15th Fl.
Toronto, ON M5G 1E5
416-326-6800 Fax: 416-326-5370
www.omb.gov.on.ca

Special Investigations Unit
5090 Commerce Blvd., Mississauga, ON L4W 5M4
416-622-0748, Fax: 416-622-2455, 800-787-8529
www.siu.on.ca
Director, James L. Cornish
416-622-2381, Fax: 416-622-2455,james.cornish@ontario.ca

Corporate Services Management Division
Asst. Deputy Attorney General & Chief Admin. Officer, Stephen Rhodes
416-326-4432, Fax:
416-326-4441,stephen.rhodes@ontario.ca
Director, Business & Fiscal Planning, Paula Reid
416-326-4020, Fax: 416-326-4019,paula.reid@ontario.ca
Director, Human Resources Branch, Karen Pashleigh
416-326-3283, Fax:
416-326-2298,karen.pashleigh@ontario.ca
Director, Facilities Management, Judy Stamp
416-326-4033, Fax: 416-326-4029,judy.stamp@ontario.ca
Project Coordinator, Courthouse Development, Sandra Hornung
416-212-2084, sandra.hornung@ontario.ca,

Court Services Division
Asst. Deputy Attorney General, Ann Merritt
416-326-2609, Fax: 416-326-2652,ann.merritt@ontario.ca
Acting Director, Business Solutions, Chris Walpole
416-326-4267, Fax: 416-212-4981,chris.walpole@ontario.ca
Director, Family Policy & Programs, Anne Marie Predko
416-326-7867, annemarie.predko@ontario.ca
Acting Director, Corporate Planning, Lynn Norris
416-326-2534, Fax: 416-326-1011,lynn.norris@ontario.ca
Director, Criminal/POA Policy & Programs Branch, Diana Hunt
416-326-2531, Fax: 416-326-1869,diana.hunt@ontario.ca

Regional Court Services Offices:

Regional Court Services Offices:

Central East
#201, 1091 Gorham St., Newmarket, ON L3Y 8X7
905-836-5621, Fax: 905-836-5620
Director, Court Operations, Lynne Wagner
905-836-5484, Fax: 905-836-5620,lynne.wagner@ontario.ca

Central West
#518B, 45 Main St. East, Hamilton, ON L8N 2B7
905-645-5333, Fax: 905-645-5375
Director, Court Operations, Joanne Spriet
905-645-5333, Fax: 905-645-5375,joanne.spriet@ontario.ca

East
#100 - 343 Preston St., Ottawa, ON K1S 1N4
613-239-1551, Fax: 613-239-1273
Director, Court Operations, Thomas Fagan
613-239-1174, Fax: 613-239-1273,thomas.fagan@ontario.ca

Northeast
501, 159 Cedar St., Sudbury, ON P3E 6A5
705-564-7675, Fax: 705-564-7664
Director, Court Operations, Paul Langlois
705-564-7667, Fax: 705-564-7664,paul.langlois@ontario.ca

Northwest
277 Camelot St., Thunder Bay, ON P7A 4B3
807-343-2747, Fax: 807-345-6383
Director, Court Operations, Robert Gordon
807-343-2701, Fax: 807-345-6383,robert.gordon@ontario.ca

Toronto
#1601, 700 Bay St., Toronto, ON M5G 1Z6
416-326-4249, Fax: 416-326-2073
Regional Director, Lou Bartucci
416-326-4250, Fax: 416-326-2073,lou.bartucci@ontario.ca

West
80 Dundas St., Unit D, London, ON N6A 6A4
519-660-3090, Fax: 519-660-3098
Director, Court Operations, Len Griffiths
519-660-3094, len.griffiths@ontario.ca

Criminal Law Division
McMurty-Scott Bldg., 720 Bay St., 6th fl., Toronto, ON M5G 2K1
416-326-4656, Fax: 416-326-2063
Asst. Deputy Attorney General, Criminal Law, Paul Lindsay
416-326-2616, Fax: 416-326-2063,paul.lindsay@ontario.ca
Co-Director, Criminal Law Policy Branch, Laura Aplett
416-314-3563, Fax: 416-314-6646,laura.eplett@ontario.ca
Director, Crown Law Office - Criminal, Kenneth Campbell
416-326-4600, kenneth.campbell@ontario.ca
Director, Divisional Planning & Administration, Margaret Dwyer
416-326-2099, Fax:
416-326-2423,margaret.dwyer@ontario.ca
Acting Director, Law & Technology, Thomas Fitzgerald
416-326-3060, Fax: 416-326-8431,tom.fitzgerald@ontario.ca

Family Justice Services Division
Atrium on Bay, 595 Bay St, 8th Fl., Toronto, ON M5G 2M6
416-314-2504, Fax: 416-314-2500
Asst. Deputy Attorney General, Mark Leach
416-314-2502, Fax: 416-314-2500,mark.leach@ontario.ca
Children's Lawyer, Clare Burns
416-314-8011, Fax: 416-314-8050,clare.burns@ontario.ca
Public Guardian & Trustee, Louise Stratford
416-314-2791, Fax: 416-326-1366,louise.stratford@ontario.ca
Counsel, Legal Aid Policy & Liaison, Nolasco DeSousa
416-326-2996, Fax:
416-326-3214,nolasco.desousa@ontario.ca

Legal Services Division
McMurty-Scott Bldg., 720 Bay St., 6th fl., Toronto, ON M5G 2K1
416-326-0891, Fax: 416-326-6996
Acting Asst. Deputy Attorney General, Malliha Wilson
416-326-2505, Fax: 416-326-6996,malliha.wilson@ontario.ca
Director, Constitutional Law, Michel Y. Hélie
416-326-4454, Fax: 416-326-4015,michel.helie@ontario.ca
Acting Director, Crown Law Office-Civil, Denise Dwyer
416-326-4108, Fax: 416-326-4181,denise.dwyer@ontario.ca
Director, Legal Services Program Support Branch, Wendy Eastaugh
416-326-4173, Fax:
416-314-7926,wendy.eastaugh@ontario.ca

Civil Remedies for Illicit Activities
77 Wellesley St. West, PO Box 333, Toronto, ON M7A 1N3
416-212-0556, Fax: 416-314-3714
Legal Director, Jeff Simser
416-326-4188, Fax: 416-314-3714,jeff.simser@ontario.ca

Legislative Counsel
Whitney Block, #3600, 99 Wellesley St. West, Toronto, ON M7A 1A2
416-326-2841, Fax: 416-326-2806,
Chief Legislative Counsel, Alison M. Fraser
416-326-2770, Fax: 416-326-2806,alison.m.fraser@ontario.ca
Assoc. Chief Legislative Counsel, Mariam Leitman
416-326-2740, mariam.leitman@ontario.ca
Director, French Legislative Services, Michel Moisan
416-326-2786, michel.moisan1@ontario.ca

Ontario Victim Services Secretariat
18 King St. E, 7th Fl., Toronto, ON M5C 1C4
416-325-3265, Fax: 416-212-1091
Asst. Deputy Minister, Elizabeth Patterson
416-325-5549
Director, Programs & Community Development, Sonia Faryna
416-326-2428, Fax: 416-212-1091,sonia.faryna@ontario.ca
Director, Policy & Program Development, Rachele Dabraio
416-325-3695, Fax:
416-212-1091,rachele.dabnaio@ontario.ca

Office of the Provincial Auditor

20 Dundas St. West, 15th Fl., PO Box 105, Toronto, ON M5G 2C2
416-327-2381, Fax: 416-327-9862,
comments@auditor.on.ca
www.auditor.on.ca
Provincial Auditor, Jim R. McCarter
416-327-1326, jim.mccarter@auditor.on.ca
Deputy Auditor General, Gary Peall
416-327-1658, gary.peall@auditor.on.ca
Director, Public Accounts, Finance & Information Technology Portfolio, Paul Amodeo
416-327-1659, paul.amodeo@auditor.on.ca
Director, Community, Social Services & Revenue Portfolio, Walter Bordne
416-327-1329, walter.bordne@auditor.on.ca
Director, Justice & Regulatory Portfolio, Vince Mazzone
416-327-1669, vince.mazzone@auditor.on.ca
Director, Economic Development, Environment & Natural Resources Portfolio, Gerard Fitzmaurice
416-327-1371, gerard.fitzmaurice@auditor.on.ca
Director, Health & Long-term Care Facilities Portfolio, Susan Klein
416-327-1668, susan.klein@auditor.on.ca
Director, Crown Agencies Portfolio, John McDowell
416-327-1656, john.mcdowell@auditor.on.ca
Director, Education and Training Portfolio, Nick Mishchenko
416-327-1657, nick.mishchenko@auditor.on.ca
Manager, Corporate Communications, Christine Pedias
416-327-2336, christine.pedias@auditor.on.ca

Ministry of Children & Youth Services

56 Wellesley St. West, 14th Fl., Toronto, ON M5S 2G3
Fax: 416-325-5191, 866-821-7770
www.gov.on.ca/children
Working collaboratively with community partners, as well as the Ministries of Education, Health & Long-Term Care, Community & Social Services, Citizenship & Immigration, Culture, & Tourism & Recreation to integrate a number of Ontario's children & youth programs & services. By bringing these programs under one roof, this government is making children a top priority to give them the best start in life, to prepare youth to become productive adults, & to make it easier for families to get the services they need at all stages of a child's development.
Acts Administered:
Child & Family Services Act
Day Nurseries Act
French Language Services Act
Intercountry Adoption Act, 1998
Youth Criminal Justice Act
Minister,Hon. Deborah Matthews
416-212-7432, Fax:
416-212-7431,dmatthews.mpp@liberal.ola.org;
dmatthews.mpp.co@liberal.ola.org
Deputy Minister, Judith Wright
416-212-2280, Fax: 416-325-5332,judith.wright@ontario.ca
Acting Provincial Advocate, Office of The Provincial Advocate for Children & Youth, Irwin Elman
416-325-5989, Fax:
416-325-5681,irwin.elman@provincialadvocate.on.ca
Director, Communications & Marketing Branch, Jean-Claude Camus
416-326-3512, Fax: 416-325-5191

Director, Legal Services Branch, John Calcott
416-327-4936, Fax: 416-327-0568,john.calcott@ontario.ca
Chief Information Officer, Children, Youth & Social Services, Corbin Kerr
416-326-4330, Fax: 416-325-0266,corbin.kerr@ontario.ca

Business Planning & Corporate Services
Asst. Deputy Minister, Bohodar Rubashewsky
416-325-5588
Director, Capital & Accommodation Services, Valerie Beckett
416-325-7160
Director, Corporate Policy & Intergovernmental Affairs, Sharon Weller
416-325-5627
Director, Financial Planning & Business Management, Robert Rupnik
416-325-5739
Director, Human Resources, Colette Kent
416-327-4753
Director, Internal Audit Services, Pam Gould

Policy Development & Program Design
56 Wellesley St. W, 14th Fl., Toronto, ON M5S 2S3
416-327-4865, Fax: 416-314-1862
Senior Adviser, Pamela Loring
416-314-5857, Fax: 416-314-1862,pamela.loring@ontario.ca
Director, Specialized Services & Supports Branch, Louise Paul
416-325-5331, Fax: 416-325-8330,louise.paul@ontario.ca
Director, Children & Youth at Risk, Marian Mlakar
416-212-5205, Fax: 416-212-2021,marian.mlakar@ontario.ca
Director, Child Welfare Secretariat, Cathy Paul
416-325-3560, Fax: 416-326-8098,cathy.paul@ontario.ca

Program Management
Asst. Deputy Minister, Alexander Bezzina
Director, Management Support, Lauro Monteiro
416-325-5446
Director, Performance Management, Alex Sarchuk
416-325-5510
Director, Social Assistance & Municipal Operations, Martin Thumm

Strategic Policy & Planning Division
56 Wellesley St., 14th Fl., Toronto, ON M5S 2S3
416-327-9460, Fax: 416-314-1862
Asst. Deputy Minister, Darryl Sturtevant
416-327-9481, Fax:
416-314-1862,darryl.sturtevant@ontario.ca,
Director, Early Learning & Child Development Branch, Julie Mathien
416-325-5874, Fax: 416-326-0478
Director, Research & Outcome Measurement, Jeff Wright
416-326-3567, Fax: 416-327-0570,jeff.wright@ontario.ca
Director, Strategic Planning, Holly Big Canoe
416-314-1489, Fax: 416-326-3140,holly.bigcanoe@ontario.ca

Youth Justice Services
56 Wellesley St. W, 14th fl., Toronto, ON M5S 2S3
416-314-3502, Fax: 416-327-0478
Asst. Deputy Minister, Gilbert Tayles
416-327-9914, Fax: 416-327-0478,gilbert.tayles@ontario.ca
Director, Operational Support, JoAnn Miller-Reid
416-212-7609, Fax:
416-327-2418,joann.millerreid@ontario.ca
Director, Integration, Angela James
416-314-6576, Fax: 416-327-2418,angela.james@ontario.ca
Director, Community Development & Partnerships, Trish Moloughney
416-212-7610, Fax:
416-212-2021,trish.moloughney@ontario.ca

Regional Offices:

Regional Offices:

Toronto
477 Mount Pleasant Rd., 3rd Fl., Toronto, ON M7A 1G1
416-325-0500, Fax: 416-325-0565

Central East
465 Davis Dr., Newmarket, ON L3Y 8T2
905-868-8900

Central West
#200, 6733 Mississauga Rd., Mississauga, ON L5N 6J5
905-567-7177, Fax: 905-567-3215, 877-832-2818

Eastern
10 Rideau St., 7th Fl., Ottawa, ON K1N 9J1
613-234-1188, Fax: 613-787-5252, 800-267-5111

Hamilton Niagara
Ellen Fairclough Bldg., #600, 119 King St., Hamilton, ON L8P 4Y7
905-521-7280, Fax: 905-546-8277

North East
621 Main St., North Bay, ON P1B 2V6
705-474-3540, Fax: 705-474-5815, 800-461-6977

Northern
#1002, 199 Larch St., Sudbury, ON P3E 5P9
705-564-6699, Fax: 705-564-3099, 800-461-1167

South East
11 Beechgrove Lane, Kingston, ON K7M 9A6
613-545-0539, Fax: 613-536-7272, 800-646-3209

South West
#203, 217 York St., PO Box 5217, London, ON N6A 5R1
519-438-5111, Fax: 519-672-9510, 800-265-4197

Ministry of Citizenship & Immigration

400 University Ave., 6th Fl., Toronto, ON M7A 2R9
416-327-2422, Fax: 416-314-4965, 800-267-7329
www.citizenship.gov.on.ca

Other Communication: Information URL: OntarioImmigration.ca
Acts Administered:
Historical Parks Act
Ontario Human Rights Code
Minister,Hon. Michael Chan
416-325-6200, Fax:
416-325-6195,mchan.mpp@liberal.ola.org, TDD:
888-335-6611
Deputy Minister, Joan C. Andrew
416-325-6220, Fax: 416-325-6196,joan.andrew@ontario.ca
Director, Communications, Diane Gumbs
416-314-7606, Fax: 416-314-4965,diane.gumbs@ontario.ca

Citizenship & Immigration Division
400 University Ave., 3rd Fl., Toronto, ON M7A 2R9
416-314-7541, Fax: 416-314-7599
Asst. Deputy Minister, Katherine Hewson
416-314-6278, Fax:
416-314-7599,katherine.hewson@ontario.ca
Acting Director, Citizenship, Brian Beattie
416-314-7523, brian.beattie@ontario.ca
Director, Immigration, Riet Verheggen
416-314-6989, Fax: 416-314-7307,riet.verheggen@ontario.ca

Ontario Seniors' Secretariat
Ferguson Block, #601C, 777 Bay St., Toronto, ON M7A 2J4
416-326-7076, Fax: 416-326-7078, 888-910-1999
infoseniors@ontario.ca
www.ontarioseniors.ca

Other Communication: Seniors' InfoLine, TTY: 1-800-387-5559
Minister,Hon. Aileen M. Carroll
416-325-1660, 888-910-1999,Fax:
416-325-1726,acarroll.mpp.co@liberal.ola.org, TDD:
800-387-5559
Assistant Deputy Minister, Geoffrey Quirt
416-326-7069, Fax: 416-326-7079,geoff.quirt@ontario.ca

Ontario Women's Directorate
777 Bay Street, 6th Fl., Toronto, ON M7A 2J4
416-314-0300, Fax: 416-314-0247, 866-510-5902
info.mci@ontario.ca
www.citizenship.gov.on.ca/owd

Regional & Corporate Services Division
400 University Ave., 2nd fl., Toronto, ON M7A 2R9
416-314-7311, Fax: 416-314-7313,
Asst. Deputy Minister & Chief Administration Officer, Robert Montgomery
416-314-7311, Fax:
416-314-7313,robert.m.montgomery@ontario.ca
Chief Information Officer, Community Services & Information Technology Cluster, Jim Hamilton
416-325-4727, jim.hamilton@ontario.ca
Director, Human Resources, Cindy Lam
416-212-2783, Fax: 416-325-6371,cindy.lam@ontario.ca
Director, Regional Services, Brian Lemiere
416-314-6680, Fax: 416-314-6686,brian.lemire@ontario.ca

Central Area Regional Offices:

Central Area Regional Offices:

Bracebridge
15 Dominion St., Bracebridge, ON P1L 2E7
705-646-0641, Fax: 705-646-0544

Durham
300 Water St., 2nd Fl., Peterborough, ON K9J 8M5
705-755-2624, Fax: 705-755-2631, 800-461-7629

Hamilton
119 King St. West, 14th Fl., Hamilton, ON L8P 4Y7
905-521-7459, Fax: 905-521-7398, 877-998-9927

Huntsville
207 Main St. West, Huntsville, ON P1H 1Z9
705-789-4448, Fax: 705-789-9533

Midhurst
2284 Nursery Rd., Midhurst, ON L0L 1X0
Fax: 705-739-6697, 877-395-4105

St Catharines
301 St. Paul St., 9th Fl., St Catharines, ON L2R 7R4
Fax: 905-704-3955, 800-263-2441

Toronto
180 Dundas St. West, 5th Fl., Toronto, ON
416-314-6044, Fax: 416-314-2024, 877-395-4105
Regional Adviser, Tricia Hong
416-325-6542, Fax: 416-314-2024,tricia.hong@ontario.ca

Northern Area Regional Offices:

Dryden
Ontario Government Bldg., 479 Government Rd., PO Box 3000, Dryden, ON P8N 3B3
Fax: 807-223-8502, 800-525-8785

Kenora
810 Robertson St., Kenora, ON P9N 4J4
807-468-2540, Fax: 807-468-2788, 800-465-1108

North Bay
447 McKeown Ave., North Bay, ON P1B 9S9
705-494-4182, Fax: 705-494-4069, 800-461-9563

Sault Ste. Marie
Roberta Bondar Place, #200, 70 Foster Dr., Sault Ste Marie, ON P6A 6V8
705-945-5885, Fax: 705-945-5931, 800-461-7284

Sioux Lookout
62 Queen St., PO Box 267, Sioux Lookout, ON P8T 1A3
807-737-1018, Fax: 807-737-3379, 800-529-6619

Sudbury
Ontario Government Bldg., #401, 199 Larch St., Sudbury, ON P3E 5P9
705-564-3035, Fax: 705-564-3043, 800-461-4004

Thunder Bay
#334, 435 James St. South, Thunder Bay, ON P7E 6S7
807-475-1683, Fax: 807-475-1297, 800-465-6861
Manager, Elaine Lynch
807-475-1635, Fax: 807-475-1297,elaine.lynch@ontario.ca

Timmins
Ontario Government Complex, Hwy. 101 East, PO Box 3085, South Porcupine, ON P0N 1H0
705-235-1550, Fax: 705-235-1553, 800-305-4442

Southeast Area Regional Offices:

Kingston
Ontario Government Bldg., Beechgrove Complex, 51 Heakes Lane, Kingston, ON K7M 9B1
613-531-5580, Fax: 613-531-5585, 800-293-7543

Ottawa
347 Preston St., 2sndFl., Ottawa, ON K1S 3J4
613-742-3360, Fax: 613-742-5300, 800-267-9340
Regional Adviser, Carmen Goold
613-742-3372, Fax: 613-742-5300,carmen.goold@ontario.ca

Southwest Area Regional Offices:
Executive Director, Dan Dibbelt
780-624-6277, dan.dibbelt@gov.ab.ca
Manager, Projects & Research, Allen Geary
780-624-6337, allen.geary@gov.ab.ca
Manager, Programs & Coordination, Audrey DeWitt
780-624-6342, audrey.dewit@gov.ab.ca
Manager, Finance & Administration, Kathy Miller
780-422-9176, kathy.miller@gov.ab.ca

Peterborough
South Tower, 300 Water St., 2nd Fl., Peterborough, ON K9J 8M5
705-755-2624, Fax: 705-755-2631, 800-461-7629

Kitchener
#405, 30 Duke St. West, Kitchener, ON N2H 3W5
Fax: 519-578-1632, 800-265-2189
Regional Adviser, Laura-Lee Dam
519-571-6118, Fax: 519-578-1632,laura-lee.dam@ontario.ca

London
659 Exeter Rd., 2nd Fl., London, ON N6A 1L3
Fax: 519-873-4061, 800-265-4730

Markdale
181 Toronto St. South, PO Box 496, Markdale, ON N0C 1H0
Fax: 519-986-3014, 800-265-5520

Windsor
221 Mill St., Windsor, ON N9C 2R1
Fax: 519-973-1414, 800-265-1330
Manager, Immigration & Settlement, Luby Carr
416-314-7306
Manager, Corporate Policy, Brian Beattie
416-314-6562
Director, Human Resources, Nancy Navkar
416-325-6085, Fax: 416-325-6371
Director, David Clifford
416-325-6137
Manager, Facilities, Information & Records Management, Nelson Janicas
416-314-7094
Acting Manager, Ontario Honours & Awards Unit, Rick Brewer

Ministry of Community & Social Services (MCSS)

Hepburn Block, 80 Grosvenor St., 6th Fl., Toronto, ON M7A 1E9
416-325-5666, Fax: 416-325-5172, 888-789-4199
www.mcss.gov.on.ca

Other Communication: Welfare Fraud Hotline:|1-800-394-7867
Acts Administered:
Charitable Institutions Act
Child & Family Services Act
Day Nurseries Act
Developmental Services Act
District Social Services Administration Boards Act
Family Benefits Act
General Welfare Assistance Act
Homes for Retarded Persons Act
Indian Welfare Services Act
Intercountry Adoption Act, 1998
Ministry of Community & Social Services Act
Ontario Disability Support Program Act, 1997
Ontario Work Act, 1997
Social Assistance Reform Act, 1997
Social Work & Social Service Work Act, 1998
Soldiers' Aid Commission Act
Minister,Hon. Madeleine Meilleur
416-325-5225, Fax:
416-325-3347,madeleine.meilleur@ontario.ca
Deputy Minister, Lucille Roch
416-325-5225, Fax: 416-325-5240,lucille.roch@ontario.ca
Director, Communications & Marketing, Karin Dillabough
416-325-5203, karin.dillabough@ontario.ca
Director, Legal Services, Barbara Nawrocki
416-240-2480, barbara.nawrocki@ontario.ca
Chief Information Officer, Children, Youth & Social Services Cluster, Corbin Kerr
416-326-4330, Fax: 416-325-0266,corbin.kerr@ontario.ca
Asst. Deputy Minister, Family Responsibility Office, Lois Bain
416-240-2477, Fax: 416-240-2401
• Social Benefits Tribunal
1075 Bay St., 7th Fl.
Toronto, ON M5S 2B1
416-326-0978 Fax: 416-325-5135 800-753-3895

Accessibility Directorate of Ontario
#601, 777 Bay St., Toronto, ON M7A 2J4
416-326-0207, Fax: 416-325-5615, 866-515-2025
Asst. Deputy Minister, Ellen Waxman
416-325-5247, Fax: 416-326-9725
Director, Education & Partnerships, Nadia Temple
416-314-7289, Fax: 416-326-9725,nadia.temple@ontario.ca
Director, Standards, Development & Compliance, Scot Weeres
416-325-5586, Fax: 416-327-9725,scot.weeres@ontario.ca

Business Planning & Corporate Services Division
Hepburn Block, 80 Grosvenor St., 6th Fl., Toronto, ON M7A 1E9
416-325-5595, Fax: 416-325-5615,
Asst. Deputy Minister, Trinela Cane
416-325-5588, Fax: 416-325-5615,trinela.cane@ontario.ca
Director, Corporate Policy & Intergovernmental Affairs, Pearl Ing
416-325-5550, Fax: 416-325-5397,pearl.ing1@ontario.ca
Acting Director, Financial Planning & Business Management Branch, Betty Sanders
416-325-5135, Fax: 416-325-5125,betty.sanders@ontario.ca
Director, Human Resources, Frank Caccia
416-327-4753, Fax: 416-325-0561,frank.caccia@ontario.ca

Program Management Division
Hepburn Block, 80 Grosvenor St., 6th Fl., Toronto, ON M7A 1E9
416-325-5581, Fax: 416-325-5432,
Other Communication: Client Information & Support Services: 416/325-5766; 1-800-665-6129
Asst. Deputy Minister, Alexander Bezzina
416-325-5579, Fax:
416-325-5432,alexander.bezzina@ontario.ca
Director, Operational Support Branch, Nancy Francis
416-325-5446, Fax: 416-212-1499,nancy.francis@ontario.ca
Director, Business Innovations Branch, Alex Sarchuk
416-325-5510, Fax: 416-325-9631,alex.sarchuk@ontario.ca
Director, Social Assistance & Municipal Operations, Antonietta DiNiro
416-212-1246, antonietta.diniro@ontario.ca

Regional Offices:
Chair, A. Charles Baillie, Q.C.
Chief Investment Officer & CEO, Leo de Bever
Chief Operating Officer, Jagdeep Singh Bachher
Chief Financial Officer, Warren Cabral
Controller, Chris Mochulski
Chief Legal Counsel & Corporate Secretary, Carole Hunt

Central East
465 Davis Dr., Newmarket, ON L3Y 8T2
905-868-8900, Fax: 905-895-4330, 877-669-6658
Regional Director, Claudine Cousins
905-868-8900, claudine.cousins@ontario.ca

Central West
#200, 6733 Mississauga Rd., Mississauga, ON L5N 6J5
905-567-7177, Fax: 905-567-3215, 877-832-2818
Regional Director, Vince Tedesco
905-567-7177, vince.tedesco@ontario.ca

Eastern
347 Preston St., 2nd & 3rd fl., Ottawa, ON K1S 3H8
613-234-1188, Fax: 613-787-3990, 800-267-5111
Regional Director, Susan Bihun
613-787-3962, susan.bihun@ontario.ca

Hamilton Niagara
Ellen Fairclough bldg., 119 King St. West, 7th fl., Hamilton, ON L8P 4Y7
905-521-7280, Fax: 905-546-8277
Regional Director, Lorraine Graham-Watson
905-521-7844

Northern
#1002, 199 Larch St., Sudbury, ON P3E 5P9
705-564-6699, Fax: 705-564-3099, 800-265-1222
Regional Director, Dave Zuccato
705-541-2111, Fax: 705-564-3099

North East
621 Main St. West, North Bay, ON P1B 2V6
705-474-3540, Fax: 705-474-5815, 800-461-6977
Regional Director, Monique Legault
705-474-3540, monique.legault@ontario.ca

South East
11 Beechgrove Lane, Kingston, ON K7M 9A6
613-545-0539, Fax: 613-536-7272, 800-646-3209
Acting Regional Director, Maxine Daley
613-536-7260, Fax: 613-536-7272,maxine.daley@ontario.ca

South West
#203, 217 York St., PO Box 5217, London, ON N6A 5R1
519-483-5111, Fax: 519-672-9510, 800-265-4197
Regional Director, Peter Steckenreiter
519-438-5111, Fax:
519-672-9510,peter.steckenreiter2@ontario.ca

Toronto
477 Mount Pleasant Rd., 3rd Fl., Toronto, ON M7A 1G1
416-325-0500, Fax: 416-325-0541
Regional Director, Margaret Renwick
416-325-0536, Fax:
416-325-0541,marilyn.renwick@ontario.ca

Social Policy Development Division
Hepburn Block, 80 Grosvenor St, 6th fl., Toronto, ON M7A 1E9
416-325-5421, Fax: 416-325-9408
Asst. Deputy Minister, David Carter-Whitney
416-325-3592, Fax:
416-325-9408,david.carter-whitney@ontario.ca
Director, Community Services, Carol Latimer
416-325-5359, Fax: 416-325-8865,carol.latimer@ontario.ca
Director, Developmental Services, Kent Colette
416-327-4986, Fax: 416-325-5554,colette.kent@ontario.ca
Director, Ontario Disabilities Support Program, Norman Helfand
416-314-1122, Fax:
416-326-1735,norman.helfand@ontario.ca
Acting Director, Ontario Works, Erin Hannah
416-325-6203, Fax: 416-326-9777,erin.hannah@ontario.ca
Director, Policy Research & Analysis, Peter Amenta
416-212-6274, Fax: 416-325-8764,peter.amenta@ontario.ca,

Ministry of Community Safety & Correctional Services

George Drew Bldg., 25 Grosvenor St., 18th Fl., Toronto, ON M7A 1Y6
416-326-5000, Fax: 416-325-6067, 866-517-0571
jus.g.sgcs.webmaster@jus.gov.on.ca
www.mpss.jus.gov.on.ca

Other Communication: TTY Toll Free: 1-866-517-0572
The Ministry ensures that communities across the province are protected by safe, effective & accountable law enforcement and public safety systems. General responsibilities of the ministry are as follows: correctional services; public safety & security; & policing services.
Acts Administered:
Ammunition Regulation Act, 1994
Anatomy Act
Christopher's Law (Sex Offender Registry), 2000
Coroners Act
Emergency Management Act
Fire Protection & Prevention Act, 1997
Firefighters' Memorial Day Act
Imitation Firearms Regulation Act
Lightning Rod Act
Ministry of Correctional Services Act
Ministry of the Solicitor General Act
Ontario Society for the Prevention of Cruelty to Animals Act
Police Services Act
Private Investigators & Security Guards Act
Public Works Protection Act
Minister,Hon. Rick Bartolucci
416-325-0408, Fax:
416-325-6067,rbartolucci.mpp@liberal.ola.org
Deputy Minister, Community Safety, Deborah Newman
416-326-5060, Fax:
416-327-0469,deborah.newman@ontario.ca
Commissioner of Corrections, Arnold Galet
416-326-3648, Fax: 416-325-4576
Acting Director, Communications, Laurie LeBlanc
416-326-5004, Fax: 416-326-3200,laurie.leblanc@ontario.ca
Parliamentary Assistant, Correctional and Emergency Services, Dave Levac
416-325-6261, Fax: 416-325-0818,dave.levac@ontario.ca
• Animal Care Review Board
77 Grenville St., 8th Fl.
Toronto, ON M5S 1B3
416-314-3509 Fax: 416-314-3518
• Fire Safety Commission
Place Nouveau Bldg.
5775 Yonge St., 7th Fl.
Toronto, ON M2M 4J1
416-325-3100 Fax: 416-314-1217
• Ontario Civilian Commission on Police Services(OCCPS)
25 Grosvenor St., 1st Fl.
Toronto, ON M7A 1Y6
416-326-1189 Fax: 416-314-2036 888-515-5005
Other Communication: Toll Free Fax: 1-888-311-7555
• Ontario Parole & Earned Release Board
415 Yonge St.
Toronto, ON M5B 2E7
416-325-4480 Fax: 416-325-4485
• Ontario Police Arbitration Commission
George Drew Bldg.
25 Grosvenor St., 1st Fl.
Toronto, ON M7A 1Y6
416-314-3520 Fax: 416-314-3522
www.policearbitration.on.ca

Community Safety
416-314-3000, Fax: 416-314-4037
Director, Legal Services Branch, Anne McChesney
416-314-3515, anne.mcchesney@ontario.ca

Emergency Management Ontario
77 Wellesley St. W, PO Box 222, Toronto, ON M7A 1N3
416-314-3723, Fax: 416-314-3758
Chief, Dan Hefkey
416-314-6186, Fax: 416-314-3758,dan.hefkey@ontario.ca
Deputy Chief, Program Development, Michael Morton
416-212-3472, Fax:
416-314-3758,michael.j.morton@ontario.ca
Asst. Chief, Provincial Prevention/Mitigation & Preparedness, Maureen Griffiths
416-212-3459, maureen.griffiths@jus.gov.on.ca
Deputy Chief, Program Support, Randy Reid
416-314-8608, Fax: 416-314-3758,randy.r.reid@ontario.ca
Asst. Chief, Training & Education, Michael Morton
416-212-3472

Ontario Provincial Police (OPP)
Lincoln M. Alexander Bldg., 777 Memorial Ave., Orillia, ON L3V 7V3

705-329-6111, 888-310-1122
www.opp.ca

Other Communication: Crime Stoppers: 1-800-222-8477
Commissioner, Julian Fantino
705-329-6199, Fax: 705-329-6195,julian.fantino@ontario.ca
Deputy Commissioner & Provincial Commander, Traffic Safety and Operational Support, Larry Beechey
705-329-7500, Fax: 705-329-6317,larry.beechey@ontario.ca
Provincial Commander, Corporate Services, Gwen M. Strachan
705-329-7500, Fax: 705-329-6317

Public Safety Division
George Drew bldg, 25 Grosvenor St., 12th fl., Toronto, ON M7A 2H3
416-314-3000, Fax: 416-314-4037
Asst. Deputy Minister, Glen Murray
416-325-3454, Fax: 416-314-4037,glenn.murray@ontario.ca
Chief Coroner,Dr. Andrew McCallum
416-314-4009, Fax:
416-314-4030,andrew.mccallum@ontario.ca,
Director, Centre of Forensic Sciences,Dr. Ray Prime
416-314-3224, Fax: 416-314-3225,ray.prime@ontario.ca
Director, Strategic Planning & Research Branch, Renu Kulendran
416-325-3457, renu.kulendran@ontario.ca
Fire Marshal, Patrick R. Burke
416-325-3101, Fax: 416-325-3119,patr.burke@ontario.ca

Corporate Planning & Services Division
George Drew bldg., 25 Grosvenor St., 13th fl., Toronto, ON M7A 1Y6
416-325-3445, Fax: 416-325-3465
Asst. Deputy Minister & Chief Administration Officer, Allan Gunn
416-325-9208, Fax: 416-326-3149,allan.gunn@ontario.ca
Director, Business & Financial Planning, Melanie Fraser
416-326-1016, Fax: 416-325-3465,melanie.fraser@ontario.ca
Acting Director, Facilities, Emergency Management & Security, Robert Burns
416-314-6683, Fax: 416-327-1470,robert.burns@ontario.ca
Director, Human Resources, David Walker
416-212-3555, Fax: 416-314-5559,david.n.walker@ontario.ca

Correctional Services
Acting Asst. Deputy Minister, Adult Community Corrections, Peter Lesperance
416-327-2387, Fax:
416-314-9255,peter.lesperance@ontario.ca
Acting Asst. Deputy Minister, Adult Institutional Services, Kevin Cowie
416-327-9992, Fax: 416-314-6669,kevin.cowie@ontario.ca
Director, Management & Operational Support, Mike Conry
416-327-9918, Fax: 416-314-5987,mike.conry@ontario.ca
Director, Strategic & Operational Initiatives, Loretta Ely
416-327-2329, Fax: 416-314-5987,loretta.eley@ontario.ca

Justice Technology Services Division
#300, 21 College St, Toronto, ON M5G 2B3
416-326-6950, Fax: 416-326-1104
Asst. Deputy Minister & Chief Information Officer, John DiMarco
416-326-6954, Fax: 416-326-1104,john.dimarco@ontario.ca
Manager, IT Services & Support Management, Tim Bondett
416-326-6636, Fax: 416-326-6628,tim.bondett@ontario.ca
Manager, Finance & Administration, Cathy Noble
416-314-0178, Fax: 416-314-0216,cathy.noble@ontario.ca
Acting Head, Technology Solutions, Rick Looy
416-326-7637, Fax: 705-494-3217,rick.looy@ontario.ca
Director, Jim Cowan
416-326-5004
Acting Senior Manager, Strategic Communications, MariAnne Kazmer
416-314-7779
Manager, Corporate Issues, Cheryl Mahyr
416-325-4004
Manager, Correspondence, Pierrette Thibault
416-314-3369
Director, Anne McChesney
416-314-3515
Senior Member, Gary Leadston
gary.leadston@jus.gov.on.ca
Senior Member,Vacant
Senior Member, Dennis Murphy
dennis.murphy@jus.gov.on.ca
Senior Member,Vacant

Ministry of Culture

Mowat Block, 900 Bay St., 5th Fl., Toronto, ON M7A 1L2
416-325-1660, Fax: 416-325-1726, 866-454-0049
www.culture.gov.on.ca

The Ministry is responsible for the following: encouraging the arts & cultural industries; protecting the province's heritage; advancing the public library system; implementing strategies to promote cultural & heritage attractions; & working with communities & agencies to preserve Ontario's culture & heritage.

Acts Administered:
AGO Act
Arts Council Act
George R. Gardiner Museum of Ceramic Art Act
Hummingbird Performing Arts Centre Corporation Act
McMichael Canadian Art Collection Act
Metropolitan Toronto Convention Centre Act
Ontario Heritage Act
Public Libraries Act
Royal Ontario Museum Act
Science North Act
Minister,Hon. Aileen M. Carroll
416-325-1600, 866-454-0049,Fax:
416-325-1726,acarroll.mpp.co@liberal.ola.org, TDD:
416-325-5170
Deputy Minister, Marg Rappolt
416-212-0646, Fax:
416-212-0641,marg.rappolt@ontario.ca
Director, Communications, Mary E. Ferguson
416-212-3929, Fax:
416-325-5968,mary.e.ferguson@ontario.ca
Director, Culture & Innovation Audit Service Team, Charles Meehan
416-325-5983, Fax:
416-314-3467,charles.meehan@ontario.ca
Parliamentary Assistant, Laura Albanese
416-325-1800, Fax:
416-325-1802,lalbanese.mpp.co@liberal.ola.org

• Art Gallery of Ontario
317 Dundas St. West
Toronto, ON M5T 1G4
416-977-0414 Fax: 416-979-6646
www.ago.net
• Conservation Review Board
400 University Ave. 4th Fl.
Toronto, ON M7A 2R9
416-314-7137 Fax: 416-314-7175
• McMichael Canadian Art Collection
10365 Islington Ave.
Kleinburg, ON L0J 1C0
905-893-1121 Fax: 905-893-0692 888-213-1121
info@mcmichael.com
www.mcmichael.com/
• Minister's Advisory Council for Arts & Culture
400 University Ave., 5th Fl.
Toronto, ON M7A 2R9
416-314-8321 Fax: 416-314-7091 866-888-5829
www.culture.gov.on.ca./english/about/macac.htm
• Ontario Arts Council
151 Bloor St. West, 5th Fl.
Toronto, ON M5S 1T6
416-961-1660 Fax: 416-961-7796
www.arts.on.ca
• Ontario Heritage Trust(OHT)
10 Adelaide St. East
Toronto, ON M5C 1J3
416-325-5000 Fax: 416-325-5071
marketing@heritagefdn.on.ca
www.heritagetrust.on.ca; www.doorsopenontario.on.ca
For more than three decades, the Ontario Heritage Trust has preserved, protected & promoted Ontario's rich & varied heritage.The Trust celebrates the people, places & events that have influenced & continue to shape our culture.As Ontario's lead heritage agency, the Trust's work extends to every corner of the province.
• Ontario Library Service - North/ Service des bibliothèques de l'Ontario - Nord
334 Regent St.
Sudbury, ON P3C 4E2
705-675-6467 Fax: 705-675-2285 800-461-6348
www.olsn.ca
• Ontario Media Development Corporation(OMDC)
South Tower
#501, 175 Bloor St. East
Toronto, ON M4W 3R8
416-314-6858 Fax: 416-314-6876
mail@omdc.on.ca
www.omdc.on.ca
Formerly the Ontario Film Development Corporation (OFDC).
• Ontario Science Centre
770 Don Mills Rd.
Toronto, ON M3C 1T3
416-696-1000 Fax: 416-696-3124
www.OntarioScienceCentre.ca
• Ontario Trillium Foundation
45 Charles St. East, 5th Fl.
Toronto, ON M4Y 1S2
416-963-4927 Fax: 416-963-8781 800-263-2887
trillium@trilliumfoundation.org
www.trilliumfoundation.org
The Ontario Trillium Foundation is an agency of the Ministry of Culture.Grants are provided to eligible not-for-profit & charitable organizations in the areas of arts & culture, sports and recreation, human & social services, & the environment.
• Royal Botanical Gardens
680 Plains Rd. West
Burlington, ON L7T 4H4
905-527-1158 Fax: 905-577-0375 800-694-4769
www.rbg.ca
• Royal Ontario Museum(ROM)
100 Queen's Park Cres.
Toronto, ON M5S 2C6
416-586-5549 Fax: 416-586-5685
info@rom.on.ca
www.rom.on.ca/
• Science North
100 Ramsey Lake Rd.
Sudbury, ON P3E 5S9
705-522-3701 Fax: 705-522-4954 800-461-4898
www.sciencenorth.ca
• Southern Ontario Library Service
#902, 111 Peter St.
Toronto, ON M5V 2H1
416-961-1669 Fax: 416-961-5122 800-387-5765

Culture Policy, Programs & Services Division
400 University Ave., 5th Fl., Toronto, ON M7A 2R9
416-314-7265, Fax: 416-314-7461
Assistant Deputy Minister, Steven Davidson
416-314-7265, Fax:
416-314-7461,steven.davidson@ontario.ca
Acting Director, Policy, Donna Ratchford
416-314-7122, Fax:
416-314-7091,donna.ratchford@ontario.ca
Manager, Strategic Policy & Planning, Dawn Landry
416-327-2059, Fax: 416-314-7460,dawn.landry@ontario.ca

Office of the Chief Information Officer & Community Services I&IT Cluster
Mowat Block, 900 Bay St., 3rd Fl., Toronto, ON M7A 1L2
Chief Information Officer & Assistant Deputy Minister, Jim Hamilton
416-325-4727, Jim.Hamilton@ontario.ca
Corporate Chief Information, Information Technology Officer & Chief Strategist, Service Delivery, Ron McKerlie
416-327-9696, Fax: 416-327-3264,ron.mckerlie@ontario.ca
Director, Technology & Business Solutions, Tricia Ireland
416-314-4954, Fax: 416-325-6388,Tricia.Ireland@ontario.ca
Director, IT Negotiations & Coordination, Rick Morasch
416-326-9571, Fax: 416-325-2262,Rick.Morasch@ontario.ca

Regional & Corporate Services Division
400 University Ave., 2nd Fl., Toronto, ON M7A 2R9
416-314-7311, Fax: 416-314-7313
Assistant Deputy Minister & Chief Administrative Officer, Robert Montgomery
416-314-7311, Fax:
416-314-7313,robert.m.montgomery@ontario.ca
Director, Corporate Resources, Todd Kilpatrick
416-325-6135, Fax: 416-314-4968,todd.kilpatrick@ontario.ca
Director, Human Resources, Cindy Lam
416-212-2783, Fax: 416-325-6371,cindy.lam@ontario.ca
Director, Legal Services, Andrea Baston
416-314-7022, Fax: 416-314-7038,andrea.baston@ontario.ca
Director, Regional Services, Brian Lemire
416-314-6680, Fax: 416-314-6686,brian.lemire@ontario.ca
Coordinator, French Language Services, Guylaine Rheault-Oliver
416-212-2159, Fax:
416-314-9729,guylaine.rheault-oliver@Ontario.ca

Regional Offices:
Chair, Larry Murray
President & CEO, Meryl Whittaker
VP, Policy and Research, Beth Spark
VP, Investments, Laurence Waring

Central
180 Dundas St. West, 5th Fl., Toronto, ON M7A 2R9
416-314-6044, Fax: 416-314-2024, 877-395-4105
Manager, Tom Chrzan
416-314-6682, Fax: 416-314-2024,tom.chrzan@ontario.ca

Northern
#334, 435 James St. South, Thunder Bay, ON P7E 6S7
807-475-1683, Fax: 807-475-1297, 800-465-6861
Manager, Elaine Lynch
807-475-1635, Fax: 807-475-1297,elaine.lynch@ontario.ca

Southeast
347 Preston St., 4th Fl., Ottawa, ON K1S 3J4
613-742-3360, Fax: 613-742-5300, 800-267-9340
Manager, Mary Beach
613-742-3366, Fax: 613-742-5300,mary.beach@ontario.ca

Southwest
#405, 30 Duke St. West, Kitchener, ON N2H 3W5
Fax: 519-578-1632, 800-265-2189
Manager, George Potter
519-571-6050, Fax: 519-578-1632,george.potter@ontario.ca

Ministry of Economic Development & Trade

Hearst Block, 900 Bay St., 8th Fl., Toronto, ON M7A 2E1
416-325-6666, Fax: 416-325-6688, 866-668-4249
info@edt.gov.on.ca
www.ontariocanada.com

Promotes economic development & job creation in Ontario by creating a climate for business to prosper & eliminate red tape as well as stimulating trade. This Ministry markets the province as a desirable place to live, work, invest & raise a family. It works with its private sector partners to ensure that its core responsibilities of employment & business development, investment & trade continue to help Ontario businesses compete globally; contribute to a highly-skilled, well-educated workforce; & generate prosperity for all Ontarians. In Northern Ontario, the Ministry is represented by the Northern Development Division of the Ministry of Northern Development & Mines.

Acts Administered:
Development Corporations Act
Idea Corporation Act
Ministry of Industry, Trade & Technology Act
Research Foundation Act
Telephone Act

Minister,Hon. Sandra Pupatello
416-325-6900, Fax:
416-325-6918,spupatello.mpp@liberal.ola.org
Deputy Minister, Wendy Tilford
416-325-6927, wendy.tilford@ontario.ca
Parliamentary Asst., Charles Sousa
905-274-8228, csousa.mpp.co@liberal.ola.org
Director, Communications Branch, Dino Rocca
416-325-8058, dino.rocca@ontario.ca

Industry Division
Hearst Block, 900 Bay St., 7th fl., Toronto, ON M7A 2E1
416-325-6964, Fax: 416-325-2102
Asst. Deputy Minister, Bob Seguin
416-325-3668, Fax: 416-325-2102,bob.seguin@ontario.ca
Director, Automotive Strategy Branch, Ken Albright
416-314-2126, Fax: 416-325-2102,ken.albright@ontario.ca
Director, Economic Development Policy, Steve Harlow
416-212-7397, Fax: 416-325-6825,steve.harlow@ontario.ca
Director, Sector Competitiveness, Reed Barrett
416-325-9897, reed.barrett@ontario.ca
Director, Trade & International Policy, Katherine McGuire
416-325-6930, Fax:
416-325-6949,katherine.mcguire@ontario.ca

Investment & Trade Division
Hearst Block, 900 Bay St., 5th fl., Toronto, ON M7A 2E1
416-325-9802, Fax: 416-325-5617
Asst. Deputy Minister, William Forward
416-325-9801, Fax:
416-325-5617,william.forward@ontario.ca
Director, International Representation & Research, John Monahan
416-314-7274, Fax: 416-212-1101,john.monahan@ontario.ca
Director, Investment Branch, John Langley
416-325-6758, Fax: 416-325-6799,john.langley@ontario.ca
Administrative Assistant, Marketing Branch, Asha Amin
416-325-0423, Fax: 416-325-6375,asha.amin@ontario.ca

Ministry of Education

Mowat Block, 900 Bay St., 22nd. Fl., Toronto, ON M7A 1L2
416-325-2929, Fax: 416-325-2934, 800-387-5514
info@edu.gov.on.ca
www.edu.gov.on.ca

Acts Administered:
Education Accountability Act, 2000
Education Act
Education Quality & Accountability Office Act, 1996
Fairness for Parents & Employees Act (Teachers' Withdrawal of Services), 1997
Instructional Time: Minimum Standards Act, 1998
Ontario College of Teachers Act, 1996
Ontario Institute for Studies in Education Repeal Act, 1996
Ontario School Trustees' Council Act
Ottawa-Carleton French Language School Board Transferred Employees Act
Provincial Schools Negotiations Act
School Trust Conveyances Act
Teachers Pension Act
Teachers Pension Act, 1989
Teaching Profession Act

Minister,Hon. Kathleen O. Wynne
416-325-2600, Fax:
416-325-2608,kwynne.mpp@liberal.ola.org;
kwynne.mpp.co@liberal.ola.org,
Deputy Minister, Steve Marshall
416-325-2600, Fax:
416-327-9063,steve.marshall@ontario.ca
Chief Information Officer, Jim Hamilton
416-325-4727, Fax: 416-325-8371,jim.hamilton@ontario.ca
Manager, Correspondence Unit, Victoria Pensa
416-325-2444, Fax: 416-325-6348,victoria.pensa@ontario.ca

Corporate Management & Services Division
416-325-2772, Fax: 416-325-2778
Asst. Deputy Minister, David Fulford
416-325-2773, Fax: 416-325-2778,david.fulford@ontario.ca
Director, Internal Audit Services, Warren McCay
416-212-4814, Fax: 416-325-1120,warren.mccay@ontario.ca
Director, Corporate Finance & Services Branch, Noah Morris
416-325-7677, Fax: 416-325-1835,noah.morris@ontario.ca
Director, Human Resources, Lisa Sherin
416-325-4511, Fax: 416-327-9043,lisa.sherin@ontario.ca

Elementary/Secondary Business & Finance Division
Mowat Block, 900 Bay St., 20th fl., Toronto, ON M7A 1L2
416-325-6127, Fax: 416-327-1182
Acting Asst. Deputy Minister, Nancy Naylor
416-325-6127, Fax: 416-325-9560,nancy.naylor@ontario.ca
Director, Capital Programs Branch, Nancy Whynot
416-325-4030, Fax: 416-325-4024,nancy.whynot@ontario.ca
Director, Labour Relations & Governance Branch, Margot Trevelyan
416-325-2836, Fax:
416-325-7247,margot.trevelyan@ontario.ca
Director, Transfer Payments & Financial Reporting, Andrew Davis
416-327-9356, Fax: 416-325-2007,andrew.davis@ontario.ca

French Language Education & Educational Operations Division
Mowat Block, 900 Bay St., 22nd fl., Toronto, ON M7A 1L2
416-325-2132, Fax: 416-327-1182
Asst. Deputy Minister, Dominic Giroux
416-325-2132, Fax: 416-327-1182,dominic.giroux@ontario.ca
Coordinator, Operational Issues, Field Services, Rebecca Beausejour
416-325-7676, rebecca.beausejour@ontario.ca
Director, French Language Education Policy & Programs, Ginette Plourde
416-327-9072, Fax:
416-325-2156,ginette.plourde@ontario.ca
Director, Provincial Schools Branch, Beth Davies
905-878-2851

Instruction Leadership Development Division
Mowat Block, 900 Bay St., 13th fl., Toronto, ON M7A 1L2
416-314-3664, Fax: 416-325-7019
Acting Asst. Deputy Minister, Barry Pervin
416-325-2411, Fax: 416-325-7019,barry.pervin@ontario.ca
Director, Information Management, Don Young
416-325-2720, Fax: 416-325-2373,don.young@ontario.ca
Director, Policy & Program Branch, Elizabeth Harding
416-325-7645, Fax: 416-325-2664,liz.harding@ontario.ca
Director, Teaching Policy & Standards, Paul Anthony
416-325-7744, Fax: 416-325-7019

Strategic Planning & Elementary/Secondary Programs Division
Mowat Block, 900 Bay st., 22nd fl., Toronto, ON M7A 1L2
416-325-2135, Fax: 416-327-1182
Asst Deputy Minister, George Zegarac
416-314-5788, Fax:
416-327-1182,george.zegarac@ontario.ca
Director, Curriculum & Assessment Policy, Sue Durst
416-325-2576, Fax: 416-325-2575,sue.durst@ontario.ca
Acting Director, Special Education Policy & Programs, Barry Finlay
416-325-2889, Fax: 416-314-0637,barry.finlay@ontario.ca

Elections Ontario

51 Rolark Dr., Toronto, ON M1R 3B1
416-326-6300, Fax: 416-326-6200, 888-668-8683
info@elections.on.ca
www.elections.on.ca

Other Communication: Election Finances 416/325-9401 or 866/566-9066; Fax: 416/325-9466

Acts Administered:
Election Act
Elections Finance Act

Chief Electoral Officer, Greg Essensa
416-326-6383, Fax:
416-326-6201,greg.essensa@elections.on.ca
Deputy Chief Electoral Officer, Loren A. Wells
416-326-6387, Fax:
416-326-6201,loren.wells@elections.on.ca
Manager, Planning & Policy, Lisa Forte
416-326-4394, Fax: 416-326-6201,lisa.forte@elections.on.ca

Ministry of Energy and Infrastructure

Hearst Block, 900 Bay St., 4th Fl., Toronto, ON M7A 2E1
416-327-6758, Fax: 416-327-6754, 888-668-4636
www.mei.gov.on.ca

The Ministry of Energy's responsibility is to ensure that Ontario's electricity system functions at the highest level of reliability & productivity. The electricity system lies at the heart of the economy & way of life & by ensuring the system remains reliable, efficient & secure, the ministry is making sure Ontario remains one of the best places in the world in which to live, work, invest & raise a family. The Ministry of Energy is also focused on promoting ingenuity & innovation in the energy sector. By encouraging the development of new ideas & technologies it is helping to make Ontario a world leader in the global energy market. Protecting the environment is also a top priority for the Ministry. Developing renewable sources of energy, cleaner forms of fuel, as well as fostering a conservation culture, are all cornerstones of the Ministry's vision for Ontario's electricity future.

Acts Administered:
Energy Efficiency Act
Hydro One Directors & Officers Act, 2002
Ministry of Energy Act
Ontario Energy Board Act
Power Corporation Act
Toronto District Heating Corporation Act

Minister,Hon. Brad Duguid
416-327-6758, Fax:
416-327-6754,bduguid.mpp@liberal.ola.org
Deputy Minister, Fareed Amin
416-327-6734, Fareed.Amin@ontario.ca
Director, Communications Branch, Kevin Powers
416-327-6541, Fax: 416-326-3947,kevin.powers@ontario.ca
Manager, Media Relations, Sylvia Kovesfalvi
416-327-4334, Fax:
416-326-3947,sylvia.kovesfalvi@ontario.ca,

- Hydro One
- Independent Electricity System Operator
- Ontario Energy Board

#2700, 2300 Yonge St.
Toronto, ON M4P 1E4
416-481-1967 Fax: 416-440-7656 888-632-6273
www.oeb.gov.on.ca

- Ontario Power Authority

#1600, 120 Adelaide St. West
Toronto, ON M5H 1T1
416-967-7474 Fax: 416-967-1947
info@powerauthority.on.ca
www.powerauthority.on.ca

- Ontario Power Generation

Office of Conservation & Strategic Policy
416-314-6246, Fax: 416-325-3438
Provides strategic policy coordination & development for the ministry as well as policy analysis & advice related to energy conservation & efficiency, demand management, & conservation.
Asst. Deputy Minister, Tony Rockingham
416-327-8552, Fax:
416-325-3438,tony.rockingham@ontario.ca
Director, Strategic Policy, Kaili Sermat-Harding
416-327-5555, kaili.sermat-harding@ontario.ca
Director, Conservation & Distributed Energy, Barry Beale
416-326-4551, Fax: 416-325-6972,barry.beale@ontario.ca

Office of Consumer & Regulatory Affairs
416-325-6559, Fax: 416-325-7041
Asst. Deputy Minister, Rosalyn Lawrence
416-325-6544, Fax:
416-325-7041,rosalyn.lawrence@ontario.ca

Office of Corporate Services
416-327-7106, Fax: 416-314-3354
Provides a structure to identify strategic issues, to coordinate policy & program development; & to coordinate & integrate action by the Ministry & other governments.
Asst. Deputy Minister, Jeanette Dias D'Souza
416-327-3682, Fax:
416-314-3354,jeanette.diasdsouza@ontario.ca
Director, Business & Resource Planning, Gary Wuschnakowski
416-314-3298, Fax:
416-314-3354,gary.wuschnakowski@ontario.ca
Acting Chief Information Officer, Business Cluster, Jon Junkin
416-326-1660, Fax: 705-755-1599,jon.junkin@ontario.ca
Director, Government Services Audit Service Team, Stuart Campbell

416-326-1702, Fax:
416-326-1712,stuart.campbell@ontario.ca
Acting Director, Service Management, Jane Albright
416-314-3309, Fax: 416-314-3554,jane.albright@ontario.ca

Office of Energy Supply
416-327-7353, Fax: 416-314-6224
Asst. Deputy Minister, Rick Jennings
416-314-6190, Fax: 416-314-6224,rick.jennings@ontario.ca
Director, Energy Supply & Competition, Garry McKeever
416-325-8627, Fax:
416-325-7023,garry.mckeever@ontario.ca
Manager, Energy Economics, Tom Chapman
416-325-6869, Fax:
416-325-7023,tom.c.chapman@ontario.ca

Ministry of Environment (MOE)

135 St. Clair Ave. West, Toronto, ON M4V 1P5
416-325-4000, Fax: 416-325-3159, 800-565-4923
www.ene.gov.on.ca

Other Communication: Pollution Hotline: 1-866-MOE-TIPS(1-866-663-8477); Spills or Emergencies: 1-800-268-6060; Public Information: 1-800-565-4923

The ministry is responsible for protecting clean & safe air, land & water to ensure healthy communities, ecological protection & sustainable development for present & future generations of Ontarians. Using stringent regulations, targeted enforcement & a variety of innovative programs & initiatives, the ministry continues to address environmental issues that have local, regional &/or global effects. The ministry has built a strong foundation of clear laws, stringent regulations, tough standards & rigorous permits & approvals. The ministry monitors pollution & restoration trends in an effort to determine the effectiveness of its activities & to assess risks to human health & the environment. This information is used to develop & implement environmental legislation, regulations, standards, policies, guidelines & programs to enhance environmental protection.

Acts Administered:
Adams Mine Lake Act, 2004
Environmental Bill of Rights Act
Environmental Protection Act
Environmental Review Tribunal, 2000
Ontario Water Resources Act
Pesticides Act
Safe Drinking Water Act, 2002
Sustainable Water & Sewage Systems Act, 2002
Waste Diversion Act, 2002
Waste Management Act

Minister,Hon. John Gerretsen
416-314-6790, Fax:
416-314-7337,jgerretsen.mpp.co@liberal.ola.org
Deputy Minister, Gail Beggs
416-314-6753, Fax: 416-314-6791
Director, Communications Branch, Garth Cramer
416-314-6677, Fax: 416-314-6711,Garth.Cramer@ontario.ca

• Office of Consolidated Hearings
#1700, 2300 Yonge St.
Toronto, ON M4P 1E4
416-314-4600 Fax: 416-314-4506
Under the Consolidated Hearings Act, the Environmental Assessment Board holds public hearings in conjunction with the Ontario Municipal Board. This occurs when a proposal requires more than one tribunal hearing under more than one of the acts set out in the schedule to the Consolidated Hearings Act, 1981. The hearings registrar must receive written notice from the person proposing the undertaking, specifying the nature of the undertaking, required hearings & governing acts. The matter is then referred to the chairs of the two boards, who establish a joint board for the hearing. The board's decision can be varied or rescinded only by the Lieutenant-Governor-in-Council or, on a question of law, may be appealed to the Divisional Court.

• Advisory Council on Drinking Water Quality & Testing Standards
40 St. Clair Ave. West, 3rd Fl.
Toronto, ON M4V 1M2
416-212-7779 Fax: 416-212-7595

• Environmental Review Tribunal
#1700, 2300 Yonge St.
PO Box 2382
Toronto, ON M4P 1E4
416-314-4600 Fax: 416-314-4506
www.ert.gov.on.ca
The Environmental Review Tribunal's primary role is adjudicating applications & appeals under various environmental & planning statutes. The Tribunal hears applications & appeals under the Environmental Assessment Act, the Environmental Protection Act, the Ontario Water Resources Act, & the Pesticides Act, & leave to appeal applications under the Environmental Bill of Rights, 1993. The Environmental Review Tribunal also functions as the Office of Consolidated Hearings to hear applications made under the Consolidated Hearings Act & as the Niagara Escarpment Hearing Office to hear development permit appeals & Niagara Escarpment Plan amendment applications under the Niagara Escarpment Planning & Development Act.

• Ontario Clean Water Agency(OCWA)
1 Yonge St., 17th Fl.
Toronto, ON M5E 1E5
416-314-5600 Fax: 416-314-8300 800-667-6292
www.ocwa.com
The Ontario Clean Water Agency (OCWA) was established as a Provincial Crown Agency in November 1993 & is committed to providing safe & reliable clean water services. The Agency is an established leader in the operation, maintenance & management of water & wastewater treatment facilities & their associated distribution & collection systems. OCWA operates hundreds of water & wastewater facilities, ranging in size from small wells & pumping stations to large-scale urban water & wastewater systems.

• Pesticides Advisory Committee
#1203, 2300 Yonge St., 12th Fl.
Toronto, ON M4P 1E4
416-314-9230 Fax: 416-314-9237
www.opac.gov.on.ca
This committee advises the Minister of the Environment on matters pertaining to pesticides. It annually reviews the Pesticides Act & regulations, & government publications respecting pesticides & control of pests. The committee also recommends classifications for all new pesticide products prior to their marketing & use in Ontario, & publishes an annual report, which is available upon request. For other ministry publications on pests & pest control & information on pesticide licensing, contact the Standards Development Branch, Pesticides Section.

• Walkerton Clean Water Centre
PO Box 160
Walkerton, ON N0G 2V0
519-881-2003 Fax: 519-881-4947
inquiry@wcwc.ca
www.wcwc.ca
The vision of the Walkerton Clean Water Centre is to create a world-class intitute dedicated to safe & secure drinking water for the people of Ontario. Established by Ontario Regulation 304/04 as a crown agency of the Ministry of the Environment in October 2004, & governed by a 12-member board of directors, the Centre's work will complement & support that of the Ministry with a focus on ensuring that training, education & information is available & accessible to owners, operators & operating authorities of Ontario's drinking water systems, particularly in rural & remote communities.
Director, Legal Services, Rand Roszell
416-212-0853
Manager, Internal Audit Services,Vacant
416-314-9210, Fax: 416-314-9220

Corporate Management Division
416-314-6426, Fax: 416-314-6425
Asst. Deputy Minister, Debra Sikora
416-314-6424, Fax: 416-314-6425,debra.sikora@ontario.ca
Director, Business & Fiscal Planning, Rob W. Campbell
416-314-7370, Fax:
416-314-7858,rob.w.campbell@ontario.ca
Director, Information Management & Access Branch, Jim Lewis
416-314-3856, Fax: 416-314-6872,jim.d.lewis@ontario.ca
Director, Human Resources Branch, Jacques LeGris
416-314-9305, Fax: 416-314-9313,jacques.legris@ontario.ca
Director, Janet O'Grady
416-314-9305
Manager, Organizational Effectiveness & Learning, Michael Maddock
416-314-9246
Manager, Human Resources Consulting Services, Dave Cook
416-314-7888
Manager, Performance Improvement Unit, Michael Burger
416-314-7402
Acting Manager, Results Based Planning Unit, Carol MacLellan
416-314-7304

Drinking Water Management Division
Director, John Mayes
416-235-6160, john.mayes@ontario.ca
Manager, Air Monitoring, Gary DeBrou
416-235-6157, Fax: 416-235-6037,gary.debrou@ontario.ca
Manager, Water Monitoring, Wolfgang Scheider
416-235-5701, wolfgang.scheider@ontario.ca
Manager, Biomonitoring & Dorset Environmental Science Centre Section, Wolfgang Scheider
705-766-2418, wolfgang.scheider@ontario.ca
Manager, Hazardous Waste Information Systems, Anna Gortva
416-235-6264, Fax: 416-235-5818,anna.gortva@ontario.ca
Manager, Business Monitoring and Reporting, Cynthia Carr
416-235-6262, cynthia.carr@ontario.ca
Issues Management Coordinator, Stephanie DeSousa
416-235-5768, stephanie.desousa@ontario.ca

Drinking Water Management Division
416-314-4475, Fax: 416-314-6935
The Drinking Water Management Division, led by the Chief Drinking Water Inspector, has lead responsibility for program & operational activities related to the protection & provision of safe drinking water in Ontario.
Asst. Deputy Minister & Inspector, Keith West
416-314-4463, Fax: 416-314-6935,keith.west@ontario.ca
Director, Drinking Water Programs Branch, Orna Salamon
416-212-2355, Fax: 416-314-9477,orna.salamon@ontario.ca
Director, Safe Drinking Water, Paul Neiweglowski
416-314-1977, Fax:
416-212-7576,paul.nieweglowski@ontario.ca

Environmental Sciences & Standards Division
416-314-6357, Fax: 416-314-6358
The Environmental Sciences & Standards Division (ESSD) provides the best available science & technology to support decisions about the natural environment, & implements those decisions by developing & managing programs & partnerships, setting scientifically credible standards, monitoring the environment & providing valuable analytical & scientific expertise. Programs such as Drive Clean, that improve the environment & increase public awareness, are central to the ministry's efforts to strengthen environmental protection.
Asst. Deputy Minister, Carl Griffith
416-314-6310, Fax: 416-314-6358,carl.griffith@ontario.ca
Director, Drive Clean Office, Michael Burger
416-314-3920, Fax:
416-314-4160,michael.burger@ontario.ca
Director, Environmental Monitoring & Reporting Branch, John Mayes
416-235-6160, john.mayes@ontario.ca
Director, Environmental Innovations & Emerging Sciences, Anne Buntic
416-314-5888, Fax: 416-314-0251,anne.buntic@ontario.ca
Director, Laboratory Services,Dr. P.K. Misra
416-235-5747, Fax: 416-235-5744,pk.misra@ontario.ca
Director, Standards Development, Dale Henry
416-327-5543, Fax: 416-327-2936,dale.henry@ontario.ca
Policy Adviser, Strategy and Policy, Don Macleod
416-327-1457, don.macleod@ontario.ca
Manager, Global Air Issues, Terrance P. Stopps
416-314-4194
Manager, Regional Air Issues, Eric Loi
416-314-1700
Director, Brian Nixon
416-314-7020, Fax: 416-314-7200
Manager, Program Development & Support, Stephen Carty
416-314-7201,
Manager, Policy & Analysis, David Neufeld
416-314-7049
Asst Director, Non-Hazardous Waste Policy & Manager, John Taylor
416-212-7097
Director, Brian Nixon
416-314-7020
Manager, Strategic Analysis Section, David Neufeld
416-314-7049
Manager, Drinking Water, Matt Uza
416-314-7286
Supervisor, Kevin Hosler
613-933-7402

Central District Offices:
District Manager, J. Budz
905-319-1389
Area Supervisor, Dick Worthington
416-326-5603
District Manager, Dave Fumerton
905-427-5626

Eastern District Offices:
Acting Supervisor, John Romard
ActingDistrict Manager, John Allen
District Manager, Steve Burns
613-521-3450
District Manager, Bruce Hancock
705-755-4315

Northern District Offices:
Area Supervisor, Tom Brown
705-564-3214
District Manager, Arnie Laine
807-475-1690
District Manager, Dennis Durocher
705-235-1505

Southwestern District Offices:
District Manager, Phil Bye
705-739-6436
District Manager, Lee Orphan
519-873-5031

Acting District Supervisor, Phil Bye
519-381-6022
District Manager, Mike Moroney
519-383-3780
Area Supervisor, Kim Ferguson
519-254-7098

West Central District Offices:
District Manager, Dolly Goyette
519-826-4258
District Manager, Rich Vickers
905-704-3904

Integrated Environmental Planning Division
416-314-6338, Fax: 416-314-6346
Integrated Environmental Planning Division is responsible for integrating the overall policy development & planning functions of the Ministry. This involves integrating & synthesizing all information, data & perspectives on the many aspects of the Ministry's mandate. The division consults extensively on developing policies, strategies & programs that support the Ministry's core business of conservation & environmental protection.
Asst. Deputy Minister, John Lieou
416-314-6352, Fax: 416-314-6346,john.lieou@ontario.ca
Director, Air Policy & Climate Change, Jim Whitestone
416-314-8562, Fax: 416-314-4128,jim.whitestone@ontario.ca
Director, Land & Water Policy, Sharon Bailey
416-314-7020, Fax: 416-314-7200,sharon.bailey@ontario.ca
Acting Director, Strategic Policy, Mary Anne Covelli
416-314-1501, Fax:
416-314-2976,maryanne.covelli@ontario.ca
Director, Transformation Office,Vacant
416-325-8785
Director, Waste Management Policy, John Vidan
416-314-4157, Fax: 416-325-4437,john.vidan@ontario.ca

Operations Division
416-314-6378, Fax: 416-314-6396
The Operations Division is the operations & program delivery arm of the ministry. It is responsible for delivering programs to protect air quality, to protect surface & ground water quality & quantity, to ensure appropriate management of wastes, to ensure an adequate quality of drinking water & to control the use of pesticides. In addition, the division is responsible for administering the ministry's approvals & licensing programs as well as an investigative & enforcement program to ensure compliance with environmental laws. The division has a province-wide network of regional, district & area offices.
Asst. Deputy Minister, Michael Williams
416-314-6366, Fax:
416-314-6396,michael.williams@ontario.ca
Director, Investigations & Enforcement Branch, Greg Sones
416-326-3444, Fax: 416-326-5256,greg.sones@ontario.ca
Senior Manager, Spills Action Centre, Jan Woelfle
416-314-6370, Fax: 416-325-3011,jan.woelfle@ontario.ca
Director, Sector Compliance, Andy Dominski
416-314-4241, Fax: 416-314-4464,andy.dominski@ontario.ca
Director, Eastern Regional Office, Gayla Campney
613-548-6901, Fax:
613-548-6911,gayla.campney@ontario.ca
Director, Northern Regional Office, Franca Dignem
705-564-3305, Fax: 807-475-1754,franca.dignem@ontario.ca
Director, Southwestern Regional Office, Jim Richardson
519-873-5001, 800-265-7672,Fax:
519-873-5020,jim.richardson@ontario.ca
Director, West Central Regional Office, Bill Bardswick
905-521-7652, 800-668-4557,Fax:
905-521-7820,bill.bardswick@ontario.ca

Environmental Commissioner of Ontario (ECO)

#605, 1075 Bay St., Toronto, ON M5S 2B1
416-325-3377, Fax: 416-325-3370, 800-701-6454
commissioner@eco.on.ca
www.eco.on.ca
An independent officer of the Legislative Assembly of Ontario, the Environmental Commissioner of Ontario promotes the values, goals & purposes of the Environmental Bill of Rights (EBR) to improve the quality of Ontario's natural environment. The ECO monitors & reports on the application of the EBR, provides public education to facilitate Ontario residents' participation in the EBR & reviews government accountability for environmental decision-making.
Commissioner, Gord Miller
416-325-3377, Fax:
416-325-3370,commissioner@eco.on.ca

Ministry of Finance

Frost Bldg. South, 7 Queen's Park Cres., 7th Fl., Toronto, ON M7A 1Y7
416-325-0333, Fax: 905-433-6777, 800-263-7965
financecommunications.fin@ontario.ca
www.fin.gov.on.ca
Other Communication: Toll Free (French): 1-800-668-5821
The Ministry of Finance recommends taxation, fiscal & economic policies. Other responsibilities include the management of provincial finances & the development & allocation of Ontario's budget.
Acts Administered:
Assessment Act
Auditor General Act
Automobile Insurance Rate Stabilization Act, 2003
Capital Investment Plan Act, 1993
Commercial Concentration Tax Act
Community Small Business Investment Funds Act
Compulsory Automobile Insurance Act
Co-operative Corporations Act
Corporations Tax Act
Credit Unions and Caisses Populaires Act, 1994
Crown Foundations Act, 1996
Education Act (joint)
Electricity Act, 1998 (only specific provisions)
Employer Health Tax Act
Estate Administration Tax Act, 1998
Financial Administration Act
Financial Services Commission of Ontario Act, 1997
Fiscal Transparency and Accountability Act, 2004
Fuel Tax Act
Gasoline Tax Act
Highway Traffic Act (only specific provisions)
Income Tax Act (Ontario)
Insurance Act
Land Transfer Tax Act
Loan & Trust Corporations Act
Management Board of Cabinet Act
Marine Insurance Act
Mining Tax Act
Ministry of Revenue Act
Ministry of Treasury and Economics Act
Mortgage Brokerages, Lenders and Administrators Act, 2006
Mortgage Brokers Act
Motor Vehicle Accident Claims Act
MPPs Pension Act, 1996
Municipal Property Assessment Corporation Act, 1997
Ontario Credit Union League Limited Act, 1972 (unconsolidated and unrepealed)
Ontario Guaranteed Annual Income Act 1996
Ontario Home Ownership Savings Plan Act
Ontario Loan Act, 2005, S.O. 2005, c. 28, Sched. K
Ontario Loan Act, 2006, S.O. 2006, c. 9, Sched. J
Pension Benefits Act 1990
Prepaid Hospital and Medical Services Act
Province of Ontario Savings Office Act
Province of Ontario Savings Office Privatization Act, 2002
Provincial Land Tax Act, 1990
Provincial Land Tax Act, 2006
Public Sector Salary Disclosure Act, 1996
Race Tracks Tax Act
Registered Insurance Brokers Act
Retail Sales Tax Act
SkyDome Act (Bus Parking), 2002
Small Business Development Corporations Act
Social Contract Act, 1993
Statistics Act
Succession Duty Act Supplementary Provisions Act, 1980
Supply Act, 2007
Tax Incentive Zone Act (Pilot Projects), 2002
Tax Increment Financing Act, 2006
Taxpayer Protection Act, 1999
Tobacco Tax Act
Treasury Board Act, 1991
Unclaimed Intangible Property Act (unproclaimed)
Minister,Hon. Dwight Duncan
416-325-0400, Fax:
416-325-0374,dduncan.mpp@liberal.ola.org; dduncan.mpp.co@liberal.ola.org
Deputy Minister, Peter Wallace
416-325-1592, Fax:
416-325-1595,peter.wallace@ontario.ca,
Acting Director, Legal Services, Malle Hanslep
416-325-1457, Fax: 416-325-1460,malle.hanslep@ontario.ca
Director, Communications, Dianne Lone
416-212-1440, Fax: 416-325-0339,dianne.lone@ontario.ca
• Deposit Insurance Corporation of Ontario
#700, 4711 Yonge St.
Toronto, ON M2N 6K8
416-325-9444 Fax: 416-325-9722 800-268-6653
www.dico.com
The Deposit Insurance Corporation of Ontario provides deposit insurance, to the extent provided under the Credit Unions and Caisses Populaires Act, on deposits of members of credit unions and caisses populaires.
• Financial Services Commission of Ontario(FSCO)
5160 Yonge St.
PO Box 85
Toronto, ON M2N 6L9
416-250-7250 Fax: 416-590-7070 800-668-0128TDD: 800-387-0584
www.fsco.gov.on.ca
Regulates insurance, pensions plans, credit unions, caisses populaires, mortgage brokers, cooperative corporations & loan & trust companies in Ontario. FSCO provides regulatory services that protect financial services consumers & pension plan beneficiaries & support a healthy & competitive financial services industry.
• Ontario Electricity Financial Corporation(OEFC)
#1400, 1 Dundas St. West
Toronto, ON M7A 1Y7
416-325-8000 Fax: 416-325-8005
www.oefc.on.ca
• Ontario Financing Authority(OFA)
#1400, 1 Dundas St. West
Toronto, ON M7A 1Y7
416-325-8000 Fax: 416-325-8005
www.ofina.on.ca
The Ontario Financing Authority (OFA) is an agency of the Province of Ontario that manages the Province's debt and borrowing program. The OFA is governed by a Board of Directors that reports to the Minister of Finance.
• Ontario Securities Commission(OSC) / Commission des valeurs mobilières de l'Ontario
#1903, 20 Queen St. West
PO Box 55
Toronto, ON M5H 3S8
416-597-0681 Fax: 416-593-8122
www.osc.gov.on.ca
The mandate of the Ontario Securities Commission (OSC) is to protect investors while fostering capital formation and the efficiency and integrity of Ontario's and Canada's capital markets.
• Stadium Corporation of Ontario Ltd.
33 King St. West, 6th Fl.
Oshawa, ON L1H 8H5
416-314-5158 Fax: 905-433-6688
The corporation continues to exist to comply with legal commitments by the Province of Ontario as part of the sale of SkyDome. The agency is currently commercially active as it addresses obligations to provide a permanent solution to SkyDome bus parking. The agency has real estate assets in the form of a bus parking facility.

Office of the Budget & Taxation
416-314-0700, Fax: 416-326-0046
Asst. Deputy Minister, Steve Orsini
416-327-0223, Fax: 416-326-0046,steve.orsini@ontario.ca
Director, Corporate & Commodity Taxation Branch, Ann Langleben
416-327-0222, Fax: 416-314-8635,ann.langleben@ontario.ca
Director, Pension & Income Security Branch, Bruce MacNaughton
416-327-0140, Fax:
416-327-0160,bruce.macnaughton@ontario.ca
Acting Director, Personal Tax Policy & Design, Kostas Plainos
416-327-0246, Fax: 416-327-0260,kostas.plainos@ontario.ca

Corporate & Quality Service Division
905-433-6844, Fax: 905-433-6688,
Other Communication: Freedom of Information & Protection of Privacy: 416/325-8370, Toll Free: 1-800-263-7965, Ligne sans frais: 1-800-668-5821
Asst. Deputy Minister & CAO, Helmut Zisser
416-314-5158, Fax: 905-433-6688,helmut.zisser@ontario.ca
Director, Human Resources Branch, Esther Wade
416-325-8281, esther.wade@ontario.ca
Director, Revenue Operations & Client Services Branch, Jennette Frost
905-433-5880, Fax: 905-433-6288,jennette.frost2@ontario.ca
Director, Corporate Planning & Finance Branch, Linda Gibney
905-433-5637, Fax: 905-433-5124,linda.gibney@ontario.ca

Office of Economic Policy
416-325-0840, Fax: 416-325-9224
Asst. Deputy Minister & Chief Economist, Patrick Deutscher
416-325-0850, Fax: 416-325-9224,pat.deutscher@ontario.ca
Director, Economic & Revenue Forecasting & Analysis, Brian Lewis
416-325-0754, Fax: 416-325-0796,brian.Lewis@ontario.ca
Director, Industrial & Financial Policy Branch, Helen Graham
416-325-0928, Fax: 416-325-1187,helen.graham@ontario.ca
Director, Labour & Demographic Analysis Branch, Anne Martin
416-325-0801, Fax: 416-325-0841,anne.martin@ontario.ca

Fiscal Strategy and Coordination Division
416-327-2020, Fax: 416-212-7767

Asst. Deputy Minister, John Whitehead
416-325-4569, Fax:
416-212-7767,john.whitehead@ontario.ca
Director, Resources, Economic Development & Justice, Helen Harper
416-327-2060
Acting Director, Education & Planning Branch, Steve Romanyshyn
416-327-0171, Fax:
416-327-9115,steve.romanyshyn@ontario.ca
Director, Business Planning & Expenditure Management, Karen Hughes
416-212-0553
Asst. Deputy Minister & Provincial Controller, Office of the Provincial Controller, Bruce L. Bennett
416-325-8017, Fax: 416-325-2029,bruce.bennett@ontario.ca
Director, Health, Social & Education,Vacant
416-327-0169

Treasury Board Office
416-325-0400, Fax: 416-325-0290

Assoc. Deputy Minister,Vacant
416-327-2177, Fax: 416-325-1595
Asst. Deputy Minister, BPS Supply Chain Secretariat, Dan Wright
416-325-2627, Fax: 416-327-8197,dan.wright@ontario.ca,
Other Communications: URL: www.fin.gov.on.ca/ontariobuys
Asst. Deputy Minister & Chief Internal Audito, Richard Kennedy
416-327-9319, Fax:
416-327-9486,richard.kennedy@ontario.ca
Executive Lead, Audit Centre for Excellence, Paul Wallis
416-325-1135, Fax: 416-314-3467,paul.wallis@ontario.ca
Director, Enterprise-Wide Audit Service Team, Sanjeev Batra
416-325-8273, Fax: 416-314-3467,sanjeev.batra@ontario.ca
Director, Finance & Revenue Audit Service Team - Toronto, Larry Yarmolinksy
416-325-8323, Fax:
416-325-5096,larry.yarmolinsky@ontario.ca
Acting Director, Enterprise-Wide I&IT Audit & Quality Assurance, Laura Koo
416-314-1312, Fax: 416-314-3467,laura.koo@ontario.ca

Provincial-Local Financial Secretariat
416-325-8796,

Asst. Deputy Minister, Sriram Subrahmanyan
416-327-0240, Fax:
416-325-7644,sriram.subrahmanyan@ontario.ca
Director, Property Tax Analysis & Municipal Funding Policy, Allan Doheny
416-327-9592, Fax: 416-314-3853,allan.doheny@ontario.ca
Director, Property Tax Legislation & Assessment Policy, Diane Ross
416-327-0266, Fax: 416-314-7670,diane.ross@ontario.ca
Director, Provincial Local Initiatives, Helen Harper
416-314-2286, Fax: 416-314-3853,helen.harper@ontario.ca

Tax Revenue Division
Fax: 905-433-6686, 800-263-7965
www.rev.gov.on.ca

Asst. Deputy Minister, Terry Hewak
905-433-5614, Fax: 905-433-6686,terry.hewak@ontario.ca
Director, Strategic Management Services Branch, Nancy Crabbe
905-433-6307, Fax: 905-433-6303,nancy.crabbe@ontario.ca
Director, Special Investigations Branch, Peter Deschamps
905-433-6905, Fax:
905-436-4493,peter.deschamps@ontario.ca
Director, Client Accounts & Services Branch, Mark Grimsditch
905-433-6556, Fax:
905-433-6998,mark.grimsditch@ontario.ca
Acting Senior Manager, Income Tax Related Programs Section, Ian Hubling
905-433-6197, Fax: 905-436-4471,ian.hubling@ontario.ca
Executive Director, Tax Compliance, Pauline Goral
905-837-5200, pauline.goral@ontario.ca
Senior Manager, Motor Fuels & Tobacco Tax Section, Bruce Mitchell
905-433-6380, bruce.mitchell@ontario.ca
Director, Revenue Collections, Christine Primeau
905-433-5640, Fax:
605-433-6266,christine.primeau@ontario.ca
Director, Tax Appeals Branch, Tom Abi-Rashed
905-435-2040, Fax:
905-435-2000,tom.abi-rashed@ontario.ca

Office of Francophone Affairs

777 Bay St., 6th Fl., Toronto, ON M7A 2J4
416-325-4949, Fax: 416-325-4980, 800-268-7507
ofa@ontario.ca
www.ofa.gov.on.ca

A central agency that assists the Government of Ontario in its delivery of services in French, & in the development of policies & programs that meet the needs of the province's francophones.

Acts Administered:
French Language Services Act

Minister Responsible,Hon. Madeleine Meilleur
416-325-4949, 800-628-7507,Fax:
416-325-4980,ofa@ontario.ca;
mmeilleur.mpp.co@liberal.ola.org
Deputy Minister, Lucille Roch
416-325-5225, Fax: 416-325-5240,lucille.roch@ontario.ca
Asst. Deputy Minister, Daniel Cayen
416-325-4936, daniel.cayen@ontario.ca
Acting Director, Policy & Ministry Services, Éric Mézin
416-325-4943, eric.mezin@ontario.ca
Senior Manager, Strategic Communications & Community Relations Branch, Charles Jean Sucsan
416-325-4968, charlesjean.sucsan@ontario.ca

Ministry of Government Services (MGS)

Whitney Block, #4320, 99 Wellesley St. West, 4th Fl., Toronto, ON M7A 1W3
416-326-1234, Fax: 416-327-3790, 800-268-1142
www.mgs.gov.on.ca

Other Communication: Consumer Protection, Phone: 416-326-8800; Toll Free: 1-800-889-9768

MGS is responsible for the delivery of government services, the government workforce, procurement & technology resources. The ministry is engaged in the following main activities: providing government information to individuals & businesses, including distribution through Publications Ontario; protecting consumers through information about frauds & scams & mediating complaints about businesses; & issuing birth, death & marriage certificates, & managing Land Registry Offices throughout the province.

Acts Administered:
Alcohol & Gaming Regulation & Public Protection Act
Apportionment Act
Archives Act
Assignments & Preferences Act
Bailiffs Act
Boundaries Act
Bread Sales Act
Business Corporations Act
Business Names Act
Business Practices Act
Business Regulation Reform Act
Cemeteries Act
Certification of Titles Act
Change of Name Act
Collection Agencies Act
Condominium Act
Consumer Protection Act
Consumer Protection Bureau Act
Consumer Reporting Act
Corporations Act
Corporations Information Act
Debt Collectors Act
Discriminatory Business Practices Act
Electricity Act
Electronic Registration Act
Extra-Provincial Corporations Act
Factors Act
Funeral Directors & Establishments Act
Gaming Control Act
Land Registration Reform Act
Land Titles Act
Limited Partnerships Act
Liquor Licence Act
Management Board of Cabinet Act
Loan Brokers Act
Marriage Act
Ministry of Consumer & Commercial Relations Act
Ministry of Consumer & Commercial Relations Red Tape Reduction Act
Motor Vehicle Dealers Act
Motor Vehicle Repair Act
Ontario New Home Warranties Plan Act
Paperback & Periodical Distributors Act
Partnerships Act
Partnerships Registration Act
Personal Property Security Act
Petroleum Products Price Freeze Act
Prearranged Funeral Services Act
Prepaid Services Act
Public Service Act
Racing Commission Act
Real Estate & Business Brokers Act
Repair & Storage Liens Act
Residential Complex Sales Representation Act
Retail Business Holidays Act
Safety & Consumer Statutes Administration Act
Technical Standards & Safety Act, 2000
Travel Industry Act
Vintners Quality Alliance Act
Vital Statistics Act
Wine Content Act
Criminal Code (Canada), s. 207 (administration dealing with lottery licences issued to charitable & religious organizations to raise money for charitable or religious purposes)

Minister,Hon. Harinder S. Takhar
416-327-2333, Fax:
416-327-3790,htakhar.mpp@liberal.ola.org
Parliamentary Assistant, Bill Mauro
416-327-6611, Fax:
416-325-4136,bmauro.mpp.co@liberal.ola.org
Parliamentary Assistant, Bill Mauro
416-327-6611, Fax:
416-325-4136,bmauro.mpp.co@liberal.ola.org

• Advertising Review Board
Macdonald Block
#M2-56, 900 Bay St., 2nd Fl.
Toronto, ON M7A 1N3
416-327-2183 Fax: 416-327-2179

• Alcohol & Gaming Commission of Ontario
20 Dundas St. West
Toronto, ON M5G 2N6
416-326-8700 Fax: 416-326-5555 800-522-2876
www.agco.on.ca

• Licence Appeal Tribunal (LAT)
1 St. Clair Ave. West, 12th Fl.
Toronto, ON M4V 1K6
416-314-4260 Fax: 416-314-4270 800-255-2214
www.lat.gov.on.ca
Other Communication: Toll Free Fax: 1-800-720-5292
The LAT hears appeals when a decision or order to suspend or a proposal is made to cancel or to refuse to grant or renew a registration, certificate or a licence, or when a claim for compensation has been denied.

• Ontario Film Review Board
1075 Millwood Rd.
Toronto, ON M4G 1X6
416-314-3626 Fax: 416-314-3632

• Ontario Pension Board
#1100, 1 Adelaide St. East
Toronto, ON M5C 2X6
416-364-8558 Fax: 416-364-7578 800-668-6203
office.services@opb.on.ca
www.opb.on.ca

• Ontario Racing Commission
20 Dundas St. West, 9th Fl.
Toronto, ON M5G 2C2
416-327-0520 Fax: 416-325-3478
orcinqry@cbs.gov.on.ca

• OPSEU Pension Trust
#1200, 1 Adelaide St. East
Toronto, ON M5C 3A7
416-681-6161 Fax: 416-681-6175
www.optrust.com

Deputy Minister, MGS, Associate Secretary of the Cabinet & Secretary of Mgmt Board of Cabinet
416-325-1630, Fax: 416-325-1612,
www.mgs.gov.on.ca

Deputy Minister, Ron McKerlie
416-325-1607, Fax: 416-325-1612,ron.mckerlie@ontario.ca
Director, Operations, Kelly Burke
416-325-3620
Director, Communications, Jennifer Lang
416-325-1376, Fax: 416-327-2817,jennifer.lang@ontario.ca

Archives of Ontario
77 Grenville St., 3rd Fl., Toronto, ON M5S 1B3
416-327-1600, Fax: 416-327-1999, 800-668-9933

Archivist of Ontario, Miriam McTiernan
416-327-1602, Fax:
416-327-1992,miriam.mctiernan@ontario.ca

Office of the Corporate Chief Information Officer (OCCIO)
416-327-3442, Fax: 416-327-3264

Corporate Chief Information & Information Technology Officer, David Nicholl
416-327-9696, Fax: 416-327-3264,david.nicholl@ontario.ca
Asst. Deputy Minister, E-Ontario Program Management Office, Angela Forest
416-212-6654
Corporate Chief, Infrastructure Technology Services, Marty Gallas
416-326-7224, marty.gallas@ontario.ca
Corporate Chief Strategist, Rob Dowler
416-212-1624, Fax: 416-314-7710,rob.dowler@ontario.ca
Corporate Chief Technology Officer, Ron Huxter
416-327-1476, Fax: 416-327-3347,ron.huxter@ontario.ca
Chief Information & Privacy Officer, Mark Vale
416-327-1450, Fax: 416-327-1449,mark.vale@ontario.ca

Head, Corporate Security, Peter Macaulay
416-327-0413, Fax:
416-327-3262,peter.macaulay@ontario.ca

Policy & Consumer Protection Services Division
416-326-8578, Fax: 416-325-6192
Asst. Deputy Minister, Frank Denton
416-326-2826, Fax: 416-325-6192,frank.denton@ontario.ca
Director, Consumer Protection, Chris Ferguson
416-326-8598, Fax: 416-326-8665,chris.ferguson@ontario.ca
Director, Policy Branch, John Mitsopulos
416-326-8877, Fax:
416-326-8885,john.mitsopulos@ontario.ca

ServiceOntario
College Park, 777 Bay St., 15th fl., Toronto, ON M7A 2J3
416-326-6205, Fax: 416-326-5106
CEO, Bob Stark
416-326-7102, Fax: 416-326-5106,bob.stark@ontario.ca
Acting Asst. Deputy Minister, Business Improvement, Richard Steele
416-325-8804, Fax: 416-326-5106,richard.steele@ontario.ca
Director, Companies & Personal Property Security, Michelle Kalsbeek
416-314-4832, michelle.kalsbeek@ontario.ca
Business Manager, Business Support, Richard Holland
416-326-4733, richard.holland@ontario.ca
Asst. Deputy Minister, Customer Care, Frank D'Onofrio
416-314-3709, Fax: 416-326-5106,frank.d'onofrio@ontario.ca
Director, Real Property Registration Branch, John Dalgliesh
416-314-4879, Fax: 416-314-4899,john.dalgliesh@ontario.ca
Director, Retail Offices Branch, Jane Lee
416-326-1895, Fax: 416-326-3229,jane.lee@ontario.ca
Director, Business & Services Development Branch, Debbie Farr
416-326-5459, Fax: 416-326-1313,debbie.farr@ontario.ca
Director, Policy & Ragulatory Services Branch, Kate Murray
416-314-4881, kate.murray@ontario.ca

Registrar General Branch
189 Red River Rd., PO Box 4600, Thunder Bay, ON P7B 6L8
807-343-7414, Fax: 807-343-7411, 800-461-2156
Other Communication: Toronto: 416/325-8305
Fees are: Birth Certificate, $11; Marriage Certificate, $11; Death Certificate, $11; Certified Copies, $22; Genealogical Extracts, $22.
Deputy Registrar General & Director, Judi Hartman
807-343-7408, judi.hartman@ontario.ca

Land Registrars:

Algoma
420 Queen St. E, Sault Ste Marie, ON P6A 1Z7
705-253-8887, Fax: 705-253-9245

Brant
Court House, 80 Wellington St., Brantford, ON N3T 2L9
519-752-8321, Fax: 519-752-8321

Bruce
203 Cayley St., PO Box 1690, Walkerton, ON N0G 2V0
519-881-2259, Fax: 519-881-2322

Cochrane
143 4th Ave., PO Box 580, Cochrane, ON P0L 1C0
705-272-5791, Fax: 705-272-2951

Dufferin
#7 - 41 Briadway Ave., Orangeville, ON L9W 1J7
519-941-1481, Fax: 519-941-6444

Dundas
8 Fifth St., PO Box 645, Morrisburg, ON K0C 1X0
613-543-2583, Fax: 613-543-4541

Durham
590 Rossland Rd. East, Whitby, ON L1N 9G5
416-665-4007, Fax: 416-666-9806

Elgin
Courthouse Block, 4 Wellington St., St Thomas, ON N5R 2P2
519-631-3015, Fax: 519-631-8182

Essex
#100 - 949 McDougall St., Windsor, ON N9A 1L9
519-971-9980, Fax: 519-971-9937

Frontenac
1 Court St., Kingston, ON K7L 2N4
613-548-6767, Fax: 613-548-6766,

Glengarry
63 Kenyon St. W., Alexandria, ON K0C 1A0
613-525-1315, Fax: 613-525-0509

Grenville
499 Centre St., PO Box 1660, Prescott, ON K0E 1T0
613-925-3177, Fax: 613-925-0302

Grey
East Court Plaza, #1-2 - 1555 16th St. E., Owen Sound, ON N4K 5N3
519-376-1637, Fax: 519-376-1639

Haldimand
10 Echo St. W., PO Box 310, Cayuga, ON N0A 1E0
905-772-3531

Haliburton
12 Newcastle St., PO Box 270, Minden, ON K0M 2K0
705-286-1391, Fax: 705-286-4324

Halton
491 Steeles Ave. East, Milton, ON L9T 1Y7
905-878-7287, Fax: 905-876-8806

Hastings
#109 - 199 Front St., Belleville, ON K8N 5H5
613-968-4597, Fax: 613-968-3606
Land Registrar, David Faires
613-968-4597

Huron
38 North St., Goderich, ON N7A 2T4
519-524-9562, Fax: 519-524-2482

Kenora
220 Main St. South, Kenora, ON P9N 1T2
807-468-2794, Fax: 807-468-2796

Kent
40 William St. North, Chatham, ON N7M 5L8
519-352-5520, Fax: 519-352-3222

Lambton
#102 - 700 North Christina St., Sarnia, ON N7Y 7N5
519-337-2393, Fax: 519-337-8371

Lanark
2 Industrial Dr., PO Box 1180, Almonte, ON K0A 1A0
613-256-1456, Fax: 613-256-0940

Leeds
7 King St. West, Brockville, ON K6V 3P7
613-345-5751, Fax: 613-345-7390

Lennox
Unit 2, 7 Snow Rd., Napanee, ON K7R 0A2
613-354-3751, Fax: 613-354-1474
Land Registrar, Vicki Bourbonnais
613-354-3751, Fax:
613-354-1474,vicki.bourbonnais@ontario.ca

Manitoulin
Courthouse, 27 Phipps St., PO Box 619, Gore Bay, ON P0P 1H0
705-282-2442, Fax: 705-282-2131

Middlesex East
100 Dundas St., London, ON N6A 5B6
519-675-7600, Fax: 519-675-7611

Muskoka
15 Dominion St. N., Bracebridge, ON P1L 2E7
705-645-4415, Fax: 705-645-7826

Niagara North
59 Church St., St Catharines, ON L2R 3C3
905-684-6351, Fax: 905-684-5874

Niagara South
59 Church St., St. Catherines, ON L2R 3C3
905-684-6351, Fax: 905-684-5874

Nipissing
360 Plouffe St., North Bay, ON P1B 9L5
705-474-2270, Fax: 705-495-8511

Norfolk
Court House, 530 Queensway W., 2nd Fl., Simcoe, ON N3Y 4K8
519-426-2216, Fax: 519-426-9627,

Northumberland
Fleming Bldg., #105, 1005 Elgin St. W., Cobourg, ON K9A 5J4
705-372-3813, Fax: 905-372-4758

Ottawa-Carleton
Court House, 161 Elgin St., 4th Fl., Ottawa, ON K2P 2K1
613-239-1230, Fax: 613-239-1422

Oxford
75 Graham St., Woodstock, ON N4S 6J8
519-537-6287, Fax: 519-537-3107

Parry Sound
28 Miller St., Parry Sound, ON P2A 1T1
705-746-5816, Fax: 705-746-6517

Peel
7765 Hurontario St., 1st Fl., Brampton, ON L6W 4S8
905-874-4008, Fax: 905-874-4012

Perth
5 Huron St., Stratford, ON N5A 5S4
519-271-3343, Fax: 519-271-2550

Peterborough
Robinson Pl. South Tower, 300 Water St., 2nd Fl., Peterborough, ON K9J 8M5
705-755-1342, Fax: 705-755-1343

Prescott
499 Centre St., PO Box 1660, Prescott, ON K0E 1T0
613-925-3177, Fax: 613-925-0302

Prince Edward
1 Pitt St., PO Box 1310, Picton, ON K0K 2T0
613-476-3219, Fax: 613-476-7908

Rainy River
353 Church St., Fort Frances, ON P9A 1C9
807-274-5451, Fax: 807-274-1704

Renfrew
400 Pembroke St. E., Pembroke, ON K8A 3K8
613-732-8331, Fax: 613-732-0297

Russell
1122 Concession St., PO Box 10, Russell, ON K4R 1C8
613-445-2138, Fax: 613-445-0614

Simcoe
Court House, 114 Worsley St., Barrie, ON L4M 1M1
705-734-2722, Fax: 705-725-7246

Stormont
127 Sydney St., Cornwall, ON K6H 3H1
613-932-4522, Fax: 613-932-4524

Sudbury
199 Larch St., 3rd Fl., Sudbury, ON P3E 5P9
705-675-4300, Fax: 705-675-4148

Thunder Bay
189 Red River Rd., 2nd Fl., Thunder Bay, ON P7B 1A2
807-343-7436, Fax: 807-343-7439

Timiskaming
375 Main St., PO Box 159, Haileybury, ON P0J 1K0
705-672-3332, Fax: 705-672-3906

Toronto (Metropolitan Registry)
#420, 20 Dundas St. West, PO Box 117, Toronto, ON M5G 2C2
416-314-4400, Fax: 416-314-4453

Toronto (Metropolitan Land Titles)
#420, 20 Dundas St. West, PO Box 117, Toronto, ON M5G 2C2
416-314-4430, Fax: 416-314-4453

Victoria
440 Kent St. West, Lindsay, ON K9V 6G8
705-324-4912, Fax: 705-324-6290

Waterloo
30 Duke St., 2nd Fl., Kitchener, ON N2H 3W5
519-571-6043, Fax: 519-571-6067,

Wellington
1 Stone Rd. W., Guelph, ON N1G 4Y2
519-826-3372, Fax: 519-826-3373
Land Registrar, Donna Trevors
519-826-3372, Fax: 519-826-3373,donna.trevors@ontario.ca

Wentworth
119 King St. West, 4th Fl., Hamilton, ON L8P 4Y7
905-521-7561, Fax: 905-521-7505

York Region
50 Bloomington Rd. W., 2nd Fl., Aurora, ON L4G 3G8
905-713-7798, Fax: 905-713-7799

Ontario Shared Services
416-326-9300, 866-979-9300
Assoc. Deputy Minister, David Hallett
416-212-7550, Fax: 416-212-7551,david.hallett@ontario.ca
Asst. Deputy Minister, Strategy & Enterprise Services, Glen Medeiros
416-212-6569, Fax: 416-327-4246
Asst. Deputy Minister, Integrated Financial Information System, David Fulford
416-327-2022
Asst. Deputy Minister, HR Transactional Services, Dave Slater
416-212-6731, dave.slater@ontario.ca
Asst. Deputy Minister, Enterprise Financial Services, Roman Zydownyk
416-212-3713, Fax:
416-212-3715,roman.zydownyk@ontario.ca

Supply Chain Management
413-212-0967, Fax: 416-327-3573,
www.ppitpb.gov.on.ca/mbs/psb/psb.nsf/english/index.html
Develops & implements an integrated corporate procurement strategy to: leverage & optimize government procurement of

goods & services; identify and implement procurement process improvements; enhance procurement controllership; provide strategic advice on large scale procurements; develop innovative policy frameworks to support service delivery through third party service providers.
Asst. Deputy Minister, Neil Sentance
416-327-3536, Fax: 416-327-3573,neil.sentance@ontario.ca
Director, Corporate Procurement Policy & Planning Branch, Marian Macdonald
416-327-7508, Fax:
416-327-3573,marian.macdonald@ontario.ca
Director, Goods & Services Procurement, Diane Horvath
416-325-7553, Fax: 416-314-3960,diane.horvath@ontario.ca

Ministry of Health & Long-Term Care

Hepburn Block, 80 Grosvenor St., 10th Fl, Toronto, ON M7A 2C4
416-327-4327, 800-268-1153
www.health.gov.on.ca

Other Communication: TTY: 1-800-387-5559
The ministry is responsible for administering the health care system & providing services to the Ontario public through such programs as health insurance, drug benefits, assistive devices, care for the mentally ill, long-term care, home care, community & public health, & health promotion & disease prevention. It also regulates hospitals & nursing homes, operates psychiatric hospitals & medical laboratories, & co-ordinates emergency health services.

Acts Administered:
Alcoholism & Drug Addiction Research Foundation Act
Ambulance Act
Audiology & Speech Pathology Act
Cancer Act
Cancer Remedies Act
Charitable Institutions Act
Chiropody Act
Chiropractic Act
Community Psychiatric Hospitals Act
Dental Hygiene Act, 1991
Dental Technology Act, 1991
Dentistry Act, 1991
Denturism Act, 1991
Developmental Services Act (long-term care programs & services)
Dietetics Act, 1991
Drug & Pharmacies Regulation Act
Drug Interchangeability & Dispensing Fee Act
Drugless Practitioners Act
Elderly Persons Centres Act
General Welfare Assistance Act (long-term care programs & services only)
Health Cards & Numbers Control Act, 1991
Health Care Accessibility Act
Health Care Consent Act
Health Facilities Special Orders Act
Health Insurance Act
Health Protection & Promotion Act
Homemakers & Nurses Services Act
Homes for Retarded Persons Act (long-term care programs & services)
Homes for Special Care Act
Homes for the Aged & Rest Homes Act
Human Tissue Gift Act
Hypnosis Act
Immunization of School Pupils Act
Independent Health Facilities Act
Laboratory & Specimen Collection Centres Licensing Act
Long Term Care Act, 1994
Massage Therapy Act
Mental Health Act
Mental Hospitals Act
Midwifery Act, 1991
Ministry of Community & Social Services Act (sections 11.1 & 12 re: long-term care programs & services only)
Ministry of Health & Long-Term Care Act
Nursing Homes Act
Occupational Therapy Act
Ontario Drug Benefit Act
Ontario Medical Association Dues Act, 1991
Ontario Mental Health Foundation Act
Opticianry Act, 1991
Optometry Act, 1991
Pharmacy Act, 1991
Physician Services Delivery Management Act, 1995
Physiotherapy Act, 1991
Private Hospitals Act
Psychology Act, 1991
Public Hospitals Act
Regulated Health Professions Act, 1991
Respiratory Therapy Act, 1991
Tobacco Control Act, 1994
War Veterans Burial Act

Minister,Hon. David Caplan
416-327-4300, Fax:
416-326-1571,dcaplan.mpp@liberal.ola.org
Deputy Minister, Ron Sapsford
416-327-4496, Fax:
416-326-1570,ron.sapsford@ontario.ca
Parliamentary Assistant, Laurel C. Broten
416-326-3981, Fax:
416-326-1571,laurel.broten@ontario.ca;lbroten.mpp.co@liberal.ola.org
Acting Chief Medical Officer of Health,Dr. David Williams
416-212-3831, Fax:
416-325-8412,david.williams@ontario.ca

• Cancer Care Ontario
620 University Ave., 15th Fl.
Toronto, ON M5G 2L7
416-971-9800 Fax: 416-971-6888
www.cancercare.on.ca

• Consent & Capacity Board
151 Bloor St. West, 10th Fl.
Toronto, ON M5S 2T5
416-327-4142 Fax: 416-327-4207
Hears appeals relating to involuntary placement in a psychiatric facility, capacity to make personal care & financial decisions & access to personal records from a psychiatric facility.

• Healing Arts Radiation Protection Commission(HARP)
5700 Yonge St., 3rd Fl.
Toronto, ON M2M 4K5
416-327-7952 Fax: 416-327-8805

• Health Boards Secretariat
151 Bloor St. West, 9th Fl.
Toronto, ON M5S 2T5
416-327-8512 Fax: 416-327-8524

• Medical Eligibility Committee
370 Select Dr.
PO Box 168
Kingston, ON K7M 8T4
613-548-6405
Deals with the eligibility of insured services as well as other matters assigned to it by the act or the regulation or by the minister; makes recommendations to the general manager with respect to these decisions.

• Ontario Mental Health Foundation
#508, 489 College St.
Toronto, ON M6G 1A5
416-920-7721 Fax: 416-920-0026
grants@omhf.on.ca
www.omhf.on.ca

• Ontario Review Board
151 Bloor St. West, 10th Fl.
Toronto, ON M5S 2T5
416-327-8866 Fax: 416-327-8867

• Smart Systems for Health
#1900, 415 Yonge St.
Toronto, ON M5B 2E7
416-586-6500 Fax: 416-586-4363
www.ssha.com

• Trillium Gift of Life Network
#1440, 155 University Ave.
Toronto, ON M5H 3B7
416-363-4001 Fax: 416-363-4002
www.giftoflife.on.ca

Corporate Services & Direct Services Division
416-327-4266, Fax: 416-314-5915
Asst. Deputy Minister, Dawn Ogram
416-327-4266, Fax: 416-314-5915,dawn.ogram@ontario.ca
Director, Financial Management Branch, Pier Faltico
416-212-0723, pier.falotico@ontario.ca,
Acting Director, Corporate Management Branch, Michele Sanborn
416-326-5725, Fax:
416-327-2714,michele.sanborn@ontario.ca
Acting Director, Human Resources Branch, Janis Bartley
416-327-8747, Fax: 416-327-4482,janis.bartley@ontario.ca
Director, Capital Planning & Strategies Branch, Meryl Hodnett
416-327-7051, Fax: 416-327-3489,meryl.hodnett@ontario.ca
Director, Health Reform Implementation Team, David Stolte
416-326-1276, david.stolte@ontario.ca
Director, Hospital Alternative Financing & Procurement Branch, David W. Clarke
416-314-0402, Fax: 416-326-5533,david.clarke@ontario.ca

Health Human Resources Strategy Division
416-212-6115, Fax: 416-314-3751
Asst. Deputy Minister,Dr. Joshua Tepper
416-212-6115, Fax: 416-314-3751,joshua.tepper@ontario.ca
Director, Health Human Resource Policy, Jeff Goodyear
416-327-7482, Fax: 416-327-9429,jeff.goodyear@ontario.ca
Director, Health Professionals Regulatory Policy & Programs, Marilyn Wang
416-327-8888, Fax: 416-327-8879,marilyn.wang@ontario.ca
Director, Health Sector Labour Market Policy, John Amodeo
416-212-0873, Fax: 416-325-9827,john.amodeo@ontario.ca

Health Services
Acting Asst. Deputy Minister, Dawn Ogram
416-327-4266
Acting Executive Director, Physician Services, Susan Fitzpatrick
416-326-2492
Director, Drug Programs Branch, Susan Paetkau
416-327-8095
Assistant Director, Fraud Programs, Ali Ebrahim
416-327-7674, Fax: 416-327-4439,ali.ebrahim@ontario.ca
Director, Operational Support Branch, Gordon Aue
416-327-4490
Acting Director, Registration & Claims Branch, Susan Pinney
613-548-6454, Fax: 613-548-6320,susan.pinney@ontario.ca
Medical Director, Public Health Laboratories Branch,Dr. Donald Low
416-235-5944, Fax: 416-235-6063,don.low@ontario.ca

Health System Strategy Division
416-327-8295, Fax: 416-327-5109
Asst. Deputy Minister, Adalsteinn Brown
416-327-8295, Fax:
416-327-5109,adalsteinn.brown@ontario.ca
Acting Manager, Intergovernmental Relations Unit, Tasneem Essaji
416-327-8850, tasneem.essaji@Ontario.ca
Acting Director, Population Health Policy & Planning & Women's Health,Dr. Vasanthi Srinivasan
613-327-0951
Acting Director, Resources Management Policy & Legislative Support, Juanita Dobson
416-212-4790
Director, Health System Strategy Branch, Sheree Davis
416-327-8319

Public Health Division
416-325-8412
Acting Chief Medical Officer of Health,Dr. David C. Williams
416-314-5487, Fax: 416-325-8412,david.williams@ontario.ca
Director, Infectious Diseases Branch, Marie Muir
416-314-5487, Fax: 416-327-7438,marie.muir@ontario.ca
Executive Lead,Vacant
416-325-7672, Fax: 416-325-8412
Director, Chronic Disease Prevention & Health Promotion, Pegeen Walsh
416-327-7445, Fax: 416-314-5497,pegeen.walsh@ontario.ca
Acting Director, Emergency Management, Tiffany Jay
416-212-5229, Fax: 416-212-4466,tiffany.jay@ontario.ca
Director, Operational Effectiveness, Becky Taylor
416-326-2783, Fax: 416-314-7078,becky.taylor@ontario.ca

Ministry of Health Promotion

777 Bay Street, 18th Fl., Toronto, ON M7A 1S5
416-326-8475, Fax: 416-326-4864,
info@mhp.gov.on.ca
www.mhp.gov.on.ca

Other Communication: Sport & Recreation Inquiries: 416-314-7440; Chronic Disease Inquiries: 416-327-7384; Smoke-Free Ontario Cessation & Prevention Inquiries: 416-327-7384
Formed in 2005, the Ministry assists people in Ontario to lead healthier lives. To accomplish this goal, the Ministry works with partners, stakeholders & all levels of government to deliver programs which promote healthy choices & lifestyles.

Minister,Hon. Margarett R. Best
416-326-8500, Fax:
416-326-8520,mbest.mpp@liberal.ola.org
Deputy Minister, Cynthia Morton
416-326-8475, Fax:
416-326-8409,cynthia.morton@ontario.ca
Chief Information Officer, Health Services I&IT Cluster, Alice Keung
416-314-1279, Fax: 416-314-0289,alice.keung@ontario.ca
Director, Legal Services, Janice B. Crawford
416-327-8565, Fax:
416-327-8605,janice.b.crawford@ontario.ca
Director, Communications, Shirley Paquette
416-326-4863, Fax:
416-326-4864,shirley.paquette@ontario.ca
Parliamentary Assistant, Helena Jaczek
416-325-7200, Fax:
416-325-2827,helena.jaczek@ontario.ca

Public Health Division
Hepburn Block, 80 Grosvenor St., 11th Fl., Toronto, ON M7A 1R3
416-212-3831, Fax: 416-325-8412

Acting Assistant Deputy Minister, Allison Stuart
416-325-7672, Fax: 416-325-8412,allison.j.stuart@ontario.ca
Acting Chief Medical Officer of Health,Dr. David Williams
416-314-5487, Fax: 416-325-8412,david.williams@ontario.ca
Associate Chief Medical Officer of Health,Dr. David Williams
416-212-3831, Fax: 416-327-7438,david.williams@ontario.ca

Health Promotion
416-326-4371, Fax: 416-326-4366
Acting Assistant Deputy Minister, Mary Beth Valentine
416-326-4790, marybeth.valentine@ontario.ca
Director, Chronic Desease Prevention & Health Promotion Branch, Pegeen Walsh
416-327-7445, Fax: 416-314-5497,pegeen.walsh@ontario.ca
Director, Sport & Recreation Branch, Janie Romoff
416-314-7185, janie.romoff@ontario.ca
Travel Promotion Officer, Jack Lynch
705-725-7276
Acting Team Leader, Gema Kochovski
416-314-5900
Region Team Leader, Debra Baker
613-933-2150
Region Team Leader, Jane Johnstone
807-274-7566
General Counsel, Vella Mijal
819-953-1380, Fax: 819-953-9110
Travel Consultant, Rosa Afonso
Travel Consultant, Jackie Radomski
Team Leader, Lorraine Duncan
705-945-7640
Travel Consultant, Pam Beaton
Travel Consultant, Kelly Garneau
Travel Consultant, Denise Tickner

Ontario Human Rights Commission

180 Dundas St. West, 7th Fl., Toronto, ON M7A 2R9
416-314-4500, Fax: 416-326-9520, 800-387-9080
info@ohrc.on.ca
www.ohrc.on.ca

Chief Commissioner, Barbara Hall
416-314-4536, Fax: 416-314-7752
Executive Director, Nancy Austin
416-314-4562, Fax:
416-325-2004,nancy.austin@ohrc.on.ca
Director, Policy & Education, François Larsen
416-314-4532, Fax:
416-314-4533,francois.larsen@ohrc.on.ca
Director, Legal Services, Hart Schwartz
416-326-9858, Fax: 416-326-9867,hart.schwartz@ohrc.on.ca
Acting Director, Mediation & Investigation, Michael Harris
416-326-9501, Fax: 416-314-4515,michael.harris@ohrc.on.ca

Hydro One Inc.

North Tower, 483 Bay St., Toronto, ON M5G 2P5
416-345-5000, 877-955-1155
webmaster@HydroOne.com
www.HydroOne.com

President/CEO, Laura Formusa
CFO & Executive VP, Beth Summers
General Counsel, Joe Agostino
Vice-President, External Relations, Steve Dorey
Vice-President, Internal Audit & Chief Risk Officer, John Fraser
Vice-President, Network Services, Rick Kellestine
Vice-President, Corporate Communications, Peter Gregg
Vice-President, Corporate Services, Tom Goldie
Vice-President, Labour Relations, Steve Strome
Vice-President, Asset Management, Geoff Ogram
Vice-President, Business Transformation, Les McKay
Vice-President, Facilities & Real Estate, Mike Sheehan
Vice-President, Customer Operations & President/CEO, Remote Communities, Myles D'Arcey
Vice-President, Grid Operations, Wayne Smith
Vice-President, Engineering & Construction Services, Nairn McQueen
Vice-President, Health, Safety & Environment, Michelle Morrissey O'Ryan
President/CEO, Hydro One Telecom, Paul Marchant
President/CEO, Hydro One Brampton, Roger Albert
Hydro One Networks, Bonnie Lennie
416-345-6786

Independent Electricity System Operator (IESO)

PO Box 4474 A, Toronto, ON M5W 4E5
905-403-6900, Fax: 905-403-6921, 888-448-7777
customer.relations@ieso.ca
www.ieso.ca

President/CEO, Paul Murphy
paul.murphy@ieso.ca
Vice-President, Corporate Relations & Market Development, Bruce Campbell
416-506-2829, bruce.campbell@ieso.ca
Vice-President, Corporate Services, Gary Sherkey
gary.sherkey@ieso.ca
Vice-President, Information Technology & Infrastructure, Bill Limbrick
Vice-President, Market & System Operations, Ken Kozlik
ken.kozlik@ieso.ca
Vice-President, Market Services, Derek Cowbourne
905-855-6211, Fax: 905-855-6471,derek.cowbourne@ieso.ca
Director, Human Resources, Norm Thomas
Director, Market Assessment & Compliance, Harry Chandler
905-855-6170, Fax: 905-855-6408,harry.chandler@ieso.ca

Information & Privacy Commissioner of Ontario

#1400, 2 Bloor St. East, Toronto, ON M4W 1A8
416-326-3333, Fax: 416-325-9195, 800-387-0073
info@ipc.on.ca
www.ipc.on.ca

The IPC is the oversight body for Ontario's three provincial freedom of information & protection of privacy statues, & is responsible for resolving appeals when government organizations refuse to grant access to information; investigating privacy complaints related to government-held information; ensuring government compliance with the acts; conducting research on access & privacy issues & providing advice on proposed government legislation & programs; educating the public on Ontario's access, privacy & personal health information laws & access & privacy issues; investigating complaints related to personal health information; reviewing policies & procedures, & ensuring compliance with the Personal Health Information Protection Act.

Acts Administered:
Freedom of Information & Protection of Privacy Act
Municipal Freedom of Information & Protection of Privacy Act
Personal Health Information Protection Act
Commissioner,Dr. Ann Cavoukian
416-326-3333, commissioner@ipc.on.ca
Asst Commissioner, Privacy, Ken Anderson
416-326-3942, ken.anderson@ipc.on.ca
Asst. Commissioner, Access, Brian Beamish
416-326-3333, brian.beamish@ipc.on.ca
Director, Corporate Services, Janet Geisberger
416-326-3937, janet.geisberger@ipc.on.ca
Registrar, Tribunal Services, Robert Binstock
416-326-0008, robert.binstock@ipc.on.ca
Director, Policy, Michelle Chibba
416-326-3966, michelle.chibba@ipc.on.ca,
Secretary, Policy, Olga Toscano
416-326-0080, olga.toscano@ibc.on.ca

Office of the Integrity Commissioner

#2101, 2 Bloor St. East, Toronto, ON M4W 1A8
416-314-8983, Fax: 416-314-8987,
integrity.mail@oico.on.ca
www.oico.on.ca

The Commissioner administers the Member's Integrity Act, 1994 as it applies to members of the Legislative Assembly & Executive Council in Ontario, including the filing of Public Disclosure Statements, & the right to conduct an inquiry if there are reasonable & probable grounds to believe that the Act has been contravened. The Commissioner also has responsiblity under the MPP Compensation Reform Act (Arm's Length Process), 2001 & the Accountability for Expenses Act (Cabinet Ministers & Opposition Leaders), 2002

Acting Commissioner, Lynn Morrison
416-314-8983, Fax:
416-314-8987,lynn.morrison@oico.on.ca
Administrative Assistant, Claire Allen
416-314-8983, Fax: 416-314-8987,claire.allen@oico.on.ca

Lobbyists Registration Office
#2101 - 2 Bloor St. E., Toronto, ON M4W 1A8
416-327-4053, Fax: 416-327-4017,
lobbyist.mail@oico.on.ca
lobbyist.oico.on.ca

Under the Lobbyists Registration Act, 1998, the Registrar is responsible for administering the lobbyist registration process, ensuring paid lobbyists report their lobbying of public office holders by filing a return; & ensuring public accessibility to the information contained in the lobbyist's registry.

Registrar, Lynn Morrison
416-327-4053, Fax:
416-327-4017,lobbyist.registrar@oico.on.ca;
lynn.morrison@oico.on.ca

Ministry of Intergovernmental Affairs

77 Wellesley St. West, Toronto, ON M7A 1N3
416-325-4800, Fax: 416-325-4787,
www.ontario.ca/en/your_government/ONT06_023584

Acts Administered:
Ministry of Intergovernmental Affairs Act
Minister,Hon. Monique M. Smith
416-325-7754, Fax:
416-325-7755,msmith.mpp.co@liberal.ola.org
Deputy Minister, Paul Genest
416-314-9710, paul.genest@ontario.ca

Ministry of Labour

400 University Ave., 14th Fl., Toronto, ON M7A 1T7
416-326-7770, 800-268-8013
www.labour.gov.on.ca

Advances safe, fair & harmonious workplace practices that are essential to the social & economic well-being of the people of Ontario. Through the ministry's key areas of occupational health & safety, employment rights & responsibilities, labour relations & internal administration, the ministry's mandate is to set, communicate & enforce workplace standards while encouraging greater workplace self-reliance. A range of specialized agencies, boards & commissions assist the ministry in its work.

Acts Administered:
Ambulance Services Collective Bargaining Act
Crown Employees Collective Bargaining Act
Employment Standards Act
Fire Protection & Prevention Act
Hospital Labour Disputes Arbitration Act
Labour Relations Act
Ministry of Labour Act
Occupational Health & Safety Act
Pay Equity Act
Public Sector Dispute Resolution Act
Public Sector Labour Relations Transitions Act
Public Sector Transition Stability Act
Rights of Labour Act
Workplace Safety & Insurance Act
Minister,Hon. Peter Fonseca
416-326-7600, Fax:
416-726-1449,pfonseca.mpp@liberal.ola.org;
pfonseca.mpp.co@liberal.ola.org
Deputy Minister, Virginia M. West
416-326-7576, Fax: 416-326-0507,virginia.west@ontario.ca
Asst. Deputy Minister, Inspections, Investigations & Enforcement Secretariat, John Stager
416-326-5441, Fax: 416-326-9624,john.stager@ontario.ca
Director, Legal Services, Ken Lung
416-326-7953, Fax: 416-326-7985,ken.lung@ontario.ca
Director, Communications & Marketing, Tom Zach
416-326-7404, Fax: 416-314-5809,tom.zach@ontario.ca
Chief Information Officer, Ken Kawall
416-327-1955, Fax: 416-327-3755,ken.kawall@ontario.ca
Contact, Bruce Stewart

- Office of the Employer Advisor
#704, 151 Bloor St. West.
Toronto, ON M5S 1S4
416-327-0020 Fax: 416-327-0726 800-387-0774
Advise & represent employers with fewer than 100 employees in relation to worker's compensation issues at no cost to the employer.
- Office of the Worker Advisor
#1300, 123 Edward St.
Toronto, ON M5G 1E2
416-325-8570 Fax: 416-325-4830 800-435-8980
Other Communication: 1-800-661-6365 (French)
- Ontario Labour Relations Board
505 University Ave., 2nd Fl.
Toronto, ON M5G 2P1
416-326-7500 Fax: 416-326-7531 877-339-3335
www.gov.on.ca/lab/olrb/home.htm
- Pay Equity Commission
400 University Ave., 11th Fl.
Toronto, ON M7A 1T7
416-314-1896 Fax: 416-314-8741 800-387-8813
www.payequity.gov.on.ca
- Workplace Safety & Insurance Board

Internal Administrative Services Division
416-326-7586, Fax: 416-326-7599
Chief Administrative Officer, Len Marino
416-326-7305, Fax: 416-326-7599,len.marino@ontario.ca
Acting Director, Finance & Administration, Ray Boyce
416-326-7271, Fax: 416-326-9069,ray.boyce@ontario.ca
Director, Human Resources, Stephanie McCleave
416-326-7215, stephanie.mccleave@ontario.ca

Operations Division
416-326-7606, Fax: 416-212-4455
Asst. Deputy Minister, Sophie Dennis
416-326-7665, Fax: 416-212-4455,sophie.dennis@ontario.ca
Director, Occupational Health & Safety,Dr. Maurice Bitran
416-326-7866, Fax: 416-326-7242,maurice.bitran@ontario.ca
Director, Employment Practices, Tracey Mill
416-326-7004, Fax: 416-326-7061,tracey.mill@ontario.ca

Regional Offices:
Office Administrator, Judith Esmail
403-297-3466, Fax: 403-297-4139,judith.esmail@gov.ab.ca

Central
West Bldg., 1201 Wilson Ave., 2nd Fl., Toronto, ON M3M 1J8
416-235-5330, Fax: 416-235-5355
Regional Director, Filomena Savoia
412-235-5217, filomena.savoia@ontario.ca

Eastern
#200, 1111 Prince of Wales Dr., Ottawa, ON K2C 3T2
613-228-8050, Fax: 613-727-2900
Regional Director, Sandra Lawson
613-727-2844, Fax: 613-727-2900,sandra.lawson@ontario.ca

Northern
#301, 159 Cedar St., Sudbury, ON P3E 6A5
705-564-7400, Fax: 705-670-7435, 800-461-6325
Regional Director, Candys Ballanger-Michaud
705-564-7433, Fax:
705-564-7435,candys.ballanger-michaud@ontario.ca

Western
1 Jarvis St., Main Fl., Hamilton, ON L8R 3J2
905-577-6221, Fax: 905-577-1200, 800-263-6906
Acting Regional Director, Dino Mozzon
905-577-1275, dino.mozzon@ontario.ca

Policy, Program Development & Dispute Resolution Services
416-326-7558, Fax: 416-326-7599
The Division provides the Minister & senior officials with information, analysis & advice to assist in the development, adoption & implementation of policies, programs & legislation related to the workplace. The division includes policy & information co-ordination.
Asst. Deputy Minister, Susanna Zagar
416-326-7555, Fax: 416-326-7599,susanna.zagar@ontario.ca
Director, Dispute Resolution Services, Reg Pearson
416-326-7322, Fax: 416-314-8755,reg.pearson@ontario.ca
Acting Director, Jobs Protection Office, Bob Onyschuk
613-260-8363, Fax: 613-260-8369,bob.onyschuk@ontario.ca
Director, Health & Safety Policy & Program Development Branch, John Vander Doelen
416-326-7628, Fax:
416-314-7650,john.vanderdoelen@ontario.ca
Acting Director, Employment & Labour Policy & Program Development Branch, Marcelle Crouse
416-326-7631, Fax:
416-314-5855,marcelle.crouse@ontario.ca
Acting Director, Ray Bouce
416-326-7271
Acting Manager, Business Planning, Susan Flanagan
416-326-7292
Coordinator, Agency Relations, Donna Johanson
416-326-7311
Chief Accountant, Financial Control, Harvey Lim
416-314-8750
Manager, Service Management & Coordination, David Sheffe
416-326-7310
Manager, Chris Berzins
416-326-7785
Director, Tony Day
416-326-7215
Manager, Staff Relations, Carolyn Truman
416-326-7259
Acting Team Leader, Human Resources Services, Jim Snedden
416-326-7077
Manager, Corporate Services, Lisa Cwyk
416-326-7017
Acting Provincial Coordinator, Employment Standards, Len May
416-326-6419
Manager, Financial & Information Services, Adam Plackett
416-314-7959
Director, Ed McCloskey
416-326-7866
Chief, Radiation Protection Service & Provincial Coordinator, Professional & Specialized Services, Ken Gilmer
416-235-5913, Fax: 416-235-5926
Manager, Information & Administrative Services, Marg Fraser
416-326-7732, Fax: 416-326-7745
Provincial Coordinator, Construction Health & Safety Program, Fil Savoia
416-326-7776
Provincial Coordinator, Industrial Health & Safety Program, Nax Nagalingam
416-326-7904
Acting Provincial Coordinator, Mining, Bernie Deck
705-670-5714
Director, Reg Pearson
416-326-7322
Acting Asst. Director, Office of Mediation, J. Mather
416-326-7326, Fax: 416-326-7367
Manager, Office of Arbitration, Ursula Hardman
416-326-1303, Fax: 416-326-1329
Acting Program Manager, Office of Collective Bargaining Information, Kathie Waterhouse
416-326-1293, Fax: 416-326-1277

Ministry of Municipal Affairs & Housing

777 Bay St., 17th Fl., Toronto, ON M5G 2E5
416-585-7041, Fax: 416-585-6227, 866-220-2290
mininfo.mah@ontario.ca
www.mah.gov.on.ca

Other Communication: TDD/TTY: 416-585-6991
Responsible for providing provincial leadership in defining the framework for governance, finances & management for the local government systems; as well as leadership in the development & administration of the legislative & policy framework for land use planning. It is also responsible for providing the operational, policy & accountability framework for local government to fund & administer social housing; policy & program instruments to create a competitive marketplace for rental housing; & the regulatory framework for buildings.
Acts Administered:
Barrie Innisfil Annexation Act
Barrie-Vespra Annexation Act
Brantford-Brant Annexation Act
Building Code Act
City of Cornwall Annexation Act
City of Gloucester Act
City of Greater Sudbury Act
City of Hamilton Act
City of Hazeldean-March Act
City of Kawartha Lakes Act
City of London Act
City of Nepean Act
City of Ottawa Act
City of Ottawa Road Closing & Conveyance Validation Act
City of Port Colborne Act
City of Sudbury Hydro-Electric Service Act
City of Thunder Bay Act
City of Thorold Act
City of Timmins-Porcupine Act
City of Toronto Act
City of Toronto Act (No. 2)
Commercial Tenancies Act
Community Economic Development Act
County of Haliburton Act
County of Oxford Act
County of Simcoe Act
Development Charges Act
District Municipality of Muskoka Act
District of Parry Sound Local Government Act
Elderly Person's Housing Aid Act
Geographic Township of Hansen Act
Greater Toronto Services Board Act
Greenbelt Act
Housing Development Act
Local Government Disclosure of Interest Act
London-Middlesex Act
Ministry of Municipal Affairs & Housing Act
Municipal Act
Municipal Affairs Act
Municipal Arbitrations Act
Municipal Conflict of Interest Act
Municipal Corporations Quieting Orders Act
Municipal Elderly Residents' Assistance Act
Municipal Elections Act
Municipal Extra - Territorial Tax Act
Municipal Franchises Act
Municipal Interest & Discount Rates Act
Municipal Private Acts Repeal Act
Municipal & School Tax Credit Assistance Acts
Municipal Subsidies Adjustment Repeal Act
Municipal Tax Assistance Act
Municipal Tax Sales Act
Municipal Unemployment Relief Act
Municipal Water & Sewage Transfer Act
Municipal Works Assistance Act
Municipality of Metropolitan Toronto Act
Municipality of Shuniah Act
North Pickering Development Corporation Act
Oak Ridges Moraine Conservation Act
Oak Ridges Moraine Protection Act, 2001
Ontario Housing Corporation Act
Ontario Municipal Employees Retirement System Act
Ontario Municipal Support Grants Act
Ontario Planning & Development Act
Ottawa-Carleton Amalgamations & Elections Act
Planning Act
Police Village of St. George Act
Public Utilities Act
Public Utilities Corporations Act
Regional Municipalities Act
Regional Municipality of Durham Act
Regional Municipality of Halton Act
Regional Municipality of Hamilton-Wentworth Act
Regional Municipality of Niagara Act
Regional Municipality of Ottawa-Carleton Act
Regional Municipality of Ottawa-Carleton Land Acquisition Act
Regional Municipality of Peel Act
Regional Municipality of Waterloo Act
Regional Municipality of York Act
Road Access Act
Rural Housing Assistance Act
Sarnia-Lambton Act
Shoreline Property Assistance Act
Snow Roads & Fences Act
Social Housing Reform Act
Statute Labour Act
Tax Sales Confirmation Act
Tenant Protection Act
Territorial Division Act
Tom Longboat Act
Toronto Islands Residential Community Stewardship Act
Town of Haldimand Act
Town of Moosonee Act
Town of Norfolk Act
Town of Wasaga Beach Act
Township of North Plantagenet Act
Township of South Dumfries Act
Wharfs & Harbours Act
Minister,Hon. James J. Bradley
416-585-7000, Fax:
416-585-6470,jbradley.mpp.co@liberal.ola.org
Interim Deputy Minister, Dana Richardson
416-585-7100, Fax:
416-585-7211,Dana.Richardson@ontario.ca
Acting Director, Communications, Jodi Melnychuk
416-585-6900, Jodi.Melnychuk@ontario.ca
Chief Information Officer, Jim Hamilton
416-325-4727, Fax: 416-325-8371,jim.hamilton@ontario.ca
Executive Assistant, Communications Branch, Lina Minniti
416-585-7105, Fax: 416-585-6227,lina.minniti@ontario.ca
• Building Code Commission
777 Bay St., 2nd Fl.
Toronto, ON M5G 2E5
416-585-6503 Fax: 416-585-7531
www.obc.mah.gov.on.ca
Works with the municipal & building sectors & consumer groups to improve & streamline the building regulatory system. This leads to efficient development & more construction jobs, while protecting public safety.The Branch administers the Building Code Act (BCA) & the Ontario Building Code (OBC), which govern the construction of new buildings & the renovation & maintenance of existing buildings.It provides enforcement officials & other building code users with advice & information so that they can apply building code requirements more consistently.
• Building Materials Evaluation Commission
777 Bay St., 2nd Fl.
Toronto, ON M5G 2E5
416-585-4234 Fax: 416-585-7531
• Ontario Housing Corporation
777 Bay St., 2nd Fl.
Toronto, ON M5G 2E5
• Ontario Rental Housing Tribunal
777 Bay St., 12th Fl.
Toronto, ON M5G 2E5
416-585-7295 Fax: 416-585-6363 888-332-3234
www.orht.gov.on.ca

Business Management Division
416-585-7209, Fax: 416-585-6191
Asst. Deputy Minister, Pam Skinner
416-585-6670, Fax: 416-585-6191,pam.skinner@ontario.ca
Director, Controllership & Financial Planning, Jim Cassimatis
416-585-7693, Fax: 416-585-7328,jim.cassimatis@ontario.ca
Director, Information Technology Service Management, Joanne Hiscock
416-327-1087, Fax:
416-327-1093,joanne.hiscock@ontario.ca
Director, Organizational Effectiveness, Diane Phillipson
416-585-6742, Fax:
416-585-7259,diane.phillipson@ontario.ca
Director, Corporate Planning, Karen Rodman
416-585-7321, Fax: 416-585-7643,karen.rodman@ontario.ca

Housing Division
416-585-6277, Fax: 416-585-6800,
Asst. Deputy Minister, Kathleen Blinkhorn
416-585-6755, Fax:
416-585-6800,kathleen.blinkhorn@ontario.ca

Director, Housing Programs Branch, Keith Extance
416-585-7021, keith.extance@ontario.ca
Director, Community Partnerships & Projects, Randy Hodge
416-585-6566, Fax: 416-585-6588,randy.hodge@ontario.ca
Director, Housing Policy, Craig Brown
416-585-6400, Fax: 416-585-7607,craig.brown@ontario.ca

Local Government & Planning Policy Division
416-585-6320, Fax: 416-585-6463
Asst. Deputy Minister, Dana Richardson
416-585-6320, Fax:
416-585-6463,dana.richardson@ontario.ca
Director, Municipal Finance, Janet Hope
416-585-6951, Fax: 416-585-6315,janet.hope@ontario.ca
Director, Intergovernmental Relations & Partnerships, Andrew Posluns
416-585-6177, Fax:
416-585-7695,andrew.posluns@ontario.ca
Director, Local Government Policy, Ralph Walton
416-585-7260, Fax: 416-585-7638,ralph.walton@ontario.ca

Municipal Services Division
Fax: 416-585-6445
Asst. Deputy Minister, Robert Taylor
416-585-6427, Fax: 416-585-6445,robert.taylor3@ontario.ca
Director, Municipal Programs & Education, Diana Jardine
416-585-7251, Fax: 416-585-7292,diana.jardine@ontario.ca

Municipal Services Offices:

Central
777 Bay St., 2nd Fl., Toronto, ON M5G 2E5
416-585-6226, Fax: 416-585-6882, 800-668-0230
Regional Director, Larry Clay
416-585-7264, Fax: 416-585-6882,larry.clay@ontario.ca

Eastern
Rockwood House, 8 Estate Lane, Postal Bag 2500, Kingston, ON K7M 9A8
613-548-4304, Fax: 613-548-6822, 800-267-9438
Regional Director, Vincent Fabilli
613-545-2133, Fax: 613-548-6822,vincent.fabiilli@ontario.ca

Northeastern
#401, 159 Cedar St., Sudbury, ON P3E 6A5
705-564-0120, Fax: 705-564-6863, 800-461-1193
Regional Director, Lynn Buckham
705-564-6858, Fax: 705-564-6863,lynn.buckham@ontario.ca

Northwestern
#223, 435 James St. South, Thunder Bay, ON P7E 6S7
807-475-1651, Fax: 807-475-1196, 800-465-5027
Regional Director, Ian Smith
807-475-1187, Fax: 807-475-1196,ian.smith@ontario.ca

Western
659 Exeter Rd., 2nd Fl., London, ON N6E 1L3
519-873-4020, Fax: 519-873-4018, 800-265-4736
Regional Director, Michelle Riopelle
519-873-4037, Fax:
519-873-4018,micheline.riopelle@ontario.ca

Planning & Development Division
Asst. Deputy Minister, Elizabeth McLaren
416-585-6427
Director, Building & Development, David Brezer
416-585-6656, Fax: 416-585-7531,david.brezer@ontario.ca
Director, Provincial Planning Policy, Audrey Bennett
416-585-6072, Fax:
416-585-4245,audrey.bennett@ontario.ca
Manager, Cabinet Liaison, Susan Wang
416-585-7308
Manager, Information Access & Facilities Management, Elizabeth Mason
416-585-7232
Manager, Strategic Business Services, Nilam Bedi
416-585-4288
Manager, Business Improvement Services, Geoffrey Gladdy
416-585-6916, Fax: 416-585-7242
Manager, Infrastructure Support Serviceds, Brian Savard
416-585-7198
Manager, Application Services, Jocelyn Kohlmaier
416-585-7228
Supervisor, Client Support Centre, Shannon Boyd
416-325-6389
Manager, Capital & Grants Policy, Frances Johnston
416-585-6296
Manager, Tax & Revenue Policy, Michael Ptolemy
416-585-6460

Ministry of Natural Resources (MNR)

Whitney Block, #6630, 99 Wellesley St. West, 6th Fl., Toronto, ON M7A 1W3
800-667-1940
www.mnr.gov.on.ca

The MNR manages & protects natural resources in the province for wise use. Working with environmental organizations, private industries, fish & game associations, researchers, & other government agencies, the MNR is responsible for the following areas: science & information resources; forest management; fish & wildlife management; land & waters management; Ontario Parks; aviation & forest fire management; & geographic information.

Acts Administered:
Aggregate Resources Act
Algonquin Forestry Authority Act
An Act for the Settlement of certain Questions between the Governments of Canada & Ontario respecting Indian Reserve Lands
An Act to Confirm the title of the Government of Canada to certain Lands & Indian Lands
Arboreal Emblem Act
Beds of Navigable Waters Act
Conservation Authorities Act
Conservation Land Act
Crown Forest Sustainability Act
Endangered Species Act
Fish Inspection Act
Fish & Wildlife Conservation Act
Forest Fires Prevention Act
Forestry Act
Forestry Workers Lien for Wages Act
Freshwater Fish Marketing Act (Ontario)
Gas & Oil Leases Act
Heritage Hunting & Fishing Act, 2002
Indian Lands Act
Indian Lands Agreement Confirmation Act
Industrial & Mining Lands Compensation Act
Kawartha Highlands Signature Park Act
Lac Seul Conservation Act
Lake of the Woods Control Board Act
Lakes & Rivers Improvement Act
Manitoba-Ontario Lake St. Joseph Diversion Agreement Authorization Act
Mineral Emblem Act
Mining Act
Ministry of Natural Resources Act
Niagara Escarpment Planning & Development Act
North Georgian Bay Recreational Reserve Act
Northern Ontario Heritage Fund Act
Northern Services Boards Act
Oil, Gas & Salt Resources Act
Ontario Geographic Names Board Act
Ottawa River Water Powers Act
Provincial Parks Act
Public Lands Act
Surveys Act
Water Transfer Control Act
Wild Rice Harvesting Act
Wilderness Areas Act

Minister,Hon. Donna H. Cansfield
416-314-2301, Fax:
416-325-5316,dcansfield.mpp@liberal.ola.org
Deputy Minister, David L. Lindsay
416-314-2150, Fax: 416-314-2159
Commissioner, Mining & Lands, Linda Kamerman
416-314-2322, Fax:
416-314-2327,linda.kamerman@ontario.ca
Director, Legal Services, Anne Marie Gutierrez
416-314-2025, Fax:
416-314-2030,annemarie.gutierrez@ontario.ca
Director, Communications, John Whytock
416-314-2119, Fax: 416-314-2102,john.whytock@ontario.ca
Director, Resources & Labour Audit Service Team, Ray Masse
416-314-9208, Fax: 416-314-9220,ray.masse2@ontario.ca
Parliamentary Assistant, Bill Mauro
416-314-6467, Fax:
416-314-6470,bmauro.mpp.co@liberal.ola.org

• Academic & Experience Requirements Committee of the Association of Ontario Land Surveyors(AERC)
1043 McNicoll Ave.
Toronto, ON M1W 3W6
416-491-9020 Fax: 416-491-2576 800-268-0718
admin@aols.org

• Algonquin Forestry Authority - Huntsville
222 Main St. West
Huntsville, ON P1H 1Y1
705-789-9647 Fax: 705-789-3353
www.algonquinforestry.on.ca
Other Communication: Email:
huntsville.office@algonquinforestry.on.ca
Ensures the viability of the local forest industry while preserving the soil & water resources, fish & wildlife habitat & recreational areas in the park.

• Algonquin Forestry Authority - Pembroke
Victoria Centre
84 Isabella St., 2nd Fl.
Pembroke, ON K8A 5S5
613-735-0173 Fax: 613-735-4192
www.algonquinforestry.on.ca
Other Communication: EMail:
pembroke.office@algonquinforestry.on.ca

• Association of Ontario Land Surveyors
1043 McNicoll Ave.
Toronto, ON M1W 3W6
416-491-9020 Fax: 416-491-2576
admin@aols.org

• Crown Timber Board of Examiners
Roberta Bondar Place
#400, 70 Foster Dr.
Sault Ste Marie, ON P6A 6V5
705-945-6643

• Fish & Wildlife Heritage Commission
Robinson Pl.
300 Water St.
PO Box 7000
Peterborough, ON K9J 8M5
Fax: 705-755-5093

• Ontario Geographic Names Board
Robinson Place
300 Water St., 2nd Fl.
PO Box 7000
Peterborough, ON K9J 8M5
705-755-2134 Fax: 705-755-2131
The Board investigates the background of geographic names & recommends names to be used on maps.

• Ontario Moose & Bear Allocation Advisory Committee
PO Box 964
Sioux Lookout, ON P8T 1B3
807-737-2615 Fax: 807-737-4173
An independent advisory committee to allocate moose & bear hunting opportunities provided by the Ministry of Natural Resources within the tourism industry in a manner which is ecologically sustainable & supports the economic viability of the industry in general & specific tourist establishments.

• Ottawa River Regulation Planning Board/ Commission de planification de la régularisation de la rivière des Outaouais
351 St Joseph Blvd.
Gatineau, QC J8Y 3Z5
613-997-1735 800-778-1246
secretariat@ottawariver.ca
www.ottawariver.ca
Established under the terms of a Canada-Ontario-Québec Agreement, it is responsible for the preparation & continuing review of policies, guidelines & criteria for the integrated management of the principal reservoirs of the Ottawa River Basin in order to reduce flood damages along the river, its tributaries & in the Montréal area; it is also responsible for the operation & coordination of inflow forecasting, flow routing & optimization models that will reduce flood damages while having the least possible impact on users of the basin.

• Rabies Advisory Committee
Trent University Science Complex
PO Box 4840
Peterborough, ON K9J 8N8
705-755-2270
Established in 1979 it advises the Minister on the development of suitable vaccines against rabies & an effective system for vaccinating wild animals.

• Shibogama Interim Planning Board
PO Box 105
Wunnumin, ON P0V 2Z0
807-442-2559 Fax: 807-442-2627
Advises the province on land use & resource development in an 11,131-square-kilometre area south of Big Trout Lake in northwestern Ontario.

• Windigo Interim Planning Board
PO Box 299
Sioux Lookout, ON P8T 1A3
807-737-1585 Fax: 807-737-3133
Advises the province on land use & resource development in two areas totalling 15,959 square kilometres south of Big Trout Lake.

Niagara Escarpment Commission (NEC)
232 Guelph St., Georgetown, ON L7G 4B1
905-877-5191, Fax: 905-873-7452,
Other Communication: Toronto: 905/453-2468
Responsible for implementing the Niagara Escarpment Planning & Development Act, which is designed to maintain the escarpment & surrounding area as a continuous natural environment & to ensure that all new development in the escarpment area is compatible with provincial goals of environmental protection & conservation. The commission is also the main source of information on the Niagara Escarpment & the Niagara Escarpment Plan.

Chair, Don Scott
905-877-5594, Fax: 905-873-7452,don.scott@ontario.ca
Director, Mark Frawley
905-877-4810, Fax: 905-873-7452,mark.frawley@ontario.ca

Corporate Management Division
416-314-1900, Fax: 416-314-1901
Asst. Deputy Minister, David Lynch
416-314-1939, Fax: 416-314-1901,david.lynch@ontario.ca
Director, Finance & Business Services, Larry Davis
705-755-2532, Fax: 705-755-2508,larry.davis@ontario.ca
Acting Director, Human Resources, Steve Boyd
705-755-3131, steve.boyd@ontario.ca
Director, Policy & Planning Coordination, Ray Pichette
416-314-1923, Fax: 416-314-1948,ray.pichette@ontario.ca

Field Services Division
Fax: 416-314-2629, 800-667-1940
Field Services Division is the ministry's local presence in communities across the province, delivering integrated programs on resource management through 3 regions & 25 districts. The division delivers programs on provincial enforcement, native affairs, fisheries, forests & provincial lands, in addition to resources such as finance, facilities & engineering infrastructure, equipment & vehicles.
Asst. Deputy Minister, Charlie Lauer
416-314-2621, charlie.lauer@ontario.ca
Director, Aviation & Forest Fire Management, Ralph Wheeler
705-945-5937, ralph.wheeler@ontario.ca
Director, Enforcement, Lois Deacon
705-755-1750, Fax: 705-755-1757,lois.deacon@ontario.ca
Director, Natural Spaces, Lynne Peterson
705-755-1748, Fax: 705-755-3289
Director, David Lynch
705-755-3131
Manager, Corporate Advisory Section, Robert Kennedy
705-755-3160, Fax: 705-755-1330
Manager, Client Services, Ila Watson
705-945-5802
Manager, Learning & Revitalization, Andrew Rothfischer
705-755-1574
Team Leader, Planning & Development, Joyce Minielly
705-755-1459
Manager, Corporate & Editorial Services Section, Charity Haines
416-314-2132
Manager, Multi-Media Communication Services, Helen Ambrose
705-755-1360
Manager, Financial Analysis, Controllership, Services & Quality Management, Jorg Peterson
705-755-1852
Manager, Financial Planning, Accounting & Control Section, Mike Lesurf
705-755-1857, Fax: 705-755-2506
Director, Ralph Wheeler
705-945-5937
Manager, Aviation Services, Barry O'Brien
705-779-4030
Acting Manager, Forest Fire Management, Al Tithecott
705-945-5782
Manager, East Fire Region, Ken Gibbons
705-564-6030
Fire Program Manager, Northwest Region Fire Management Centre, Terry Popowich
807-937-7210

Regional Offices:
Managing Director,Vacant
780-422-6592, Fax: 780-644-1044

Northeast Region
Ontario Government Complex, Hwy. 101 East, PO Box 3020, South Porcupine, ON P0N 1H0
705-235-1157, Fax: 705-235-1246,
Regional Director, Eric Doidge
705-235-1153, eric.doidge@ontario.ca
Acting District Manager, Paul Bernier
705-864-3122, paul.bernier@ontario.ca
Fire Management Supervisor, Wes Woods
705-864-3126, wesley.woods@ontario.ca
District Manager, Marty Blake
705-272-7137, marty.blake@ontario.ca
Supervisor, Fred Welch
705-272-7141, Fred.Welch@ontario.ca
District Manager, Martha Heidenheim
705-273-2204, martha.heidenheim@ontario.ca
District Manager, Corrinne Nelson
705-568-3201, corrinne.nelson@ontario.ca
District Manager, Dave Payne
705-457-5599, dave.payne@ontario.ca
District Manager, Bob Johnston
705-941-5120, bob.johnston1@ontario.ca
Fire Management Supervisor, Daryl Curran
705-946-7855, daryl.curran@ontario.ca
District Manager, Ed Tear
705-564-7872, ed.tear@ontario.ca
Fire Management Supervisor, Ted Shannon
705-564-6003, ted.shannon@ontario.ca
Acting District Manager, Jim Duncan
705-235-1325, jim.duncan@ontario.ca
Fire Management Supervisor, Anne-Marie Larivee
705-235-1362, marie.larivee@ontario.ca
District Manager, John Peluch
705-856-2396, john.peluch@ontario.ca
Fire Management Supervisor,Vacant

Northwest Region
Ontario Government Bldg., #221A, 435 James St. South, Thunder Bay, ON P7E 6S8
807-475-1261, Fax: 807-473-3023
Acting District Manager, Matt Myers
807-223-7515, matt.myers@ontario.ca
Fire Management Supervisor, Rod Kellar
807-937-7321, rod.kellar@ontario.ca
District Manager, Bill Darby
807-274-8633, bill.darby@ontario.ca
Acting Fire Management Supervisor, Harrold Boven
807-274-8647, harrold.boven@ontario.ca
District Manager, Fred Hall
807-468-2528, fred.hall@ontario.ca
Fire Management Supervisor, Walt Lesenke
807-548-8416
District Manager, Kim Groenendyk
807-887-5013, kim.groenendyk@ontario.ca
District Manager, Graeme Swanwick
807-727-1333, graeme.swanwick@ontario.ca
Acting Fire Management Supervisor, Randy Crampton
807-727-2041
District Manager, Bob David
807-737-5026, bob.david@ontario.ca
Fire Management Supervisor, Darren McLarty
807-737-5005, darren.mclarty@ontario.ca
District Manager, Bill Baker
807-475-1174, bill.baker@ontario.ca
Fire Management Supervisor, Dave Manol
807-476-2230, Dave.Manol@ontario.vc

Southern Region
Robinson Place, South Tower, 300 Water St., 4th Fl. South, PO Box 7000, Peterborough, ON K9J 8M5
705-755-2000, Fax: 705-755-3233
Regional Director, Ray Bonenberg
705-753-3235, ray.bonenberg@ontario.ca
District Manager, Tracey Smith
905-713-7372, tracy.c.smith@ontario.ca
District Manager, Mitch Wilson
519-773-4710, mitch.wilson@ontario.ca
District Manager, Vince Ewing
613-332-3940, vince.ewing@ontario.ca
District Manager, Ian Hagman
519-826-4931, ian.hagman@ontario.ca
District Manager, Alex Gardner
613-258-8201, Alex.Gardner@ontario.ca
District Manager, Mark Shoreman
705-725-7504, mark.shoreman@ontario.ca
District Manager, Andy Heerschap
705-773-4236, andy.heerschap@ontario.ca
District Manager, Paul V. Moreau
613-732-5520, paul.v.moreau@ontario.ca
District Manager, Jane Ireland
705-755-3363, jane.ireland@ontario.ca
Manager, Central Agency Liaison, Tom Coape-Arnold
416-314-1929
Manager, Corporate Planning Section, John Kerr
416-314-1806, Fax: 416-314-2262

Forests Division
Roberta Bondar Place, #400, 70 Foster Dr., Sault Ste Marie, ON P6A 6V5
Fax: 705-945-5977, 800-667-1940
Provides assistance, advice & direction to ministry staff at all levels, on a variety of compliance & law enforcement matters. The branch is responsible for the development, coordination & delivery of an Integrated Provincial Compliance Program which focuses on the promotion, monitoring & enforcement aspects of compliance.
Asst. Deputy Minister, Bill Thornton
705-945-6660, Fax: 705-945-5977,bill.thornton@ontario.ca
Director, Forest Management, Rich Greenwood
705-945-6653, Fax: 705-945-6667,rich.greenwood@ontario.ca
Director, Industry Relations, Mark Speers
705-945-6636, Fax: 705-945-6667,mark.speers@ontario.ca
Manager, Forest Fire Management Section, Eric Doidge
705-945-5790, Fax: 705-945-5785
General Manager, Aviation Services, Barry O'Brien
705-779-4030
Manager, Forest Evaluation & Standards Section, Chris Walsh
705-945-5748
Manager, Forest Health & Silviculture Section, Albert King
705-945-6718
Manager, Forest Management Planning Section, Dan Pyke
705-945-6708
Manager, Forest Policy Section, Brian Hillier
705-945-6601, Fax: 705-945-6711
Director, Bill Thornton
705-945-6660
Manager, Forest Business & Economics Section, Bill Kissick
705-945-6675,
Manager, Conservation & Planning Section, Pat Freistatter
705-755-5705
Acting Manager, Land Management Section, Eric Boysen
705-755-5999
Manager, Aggregate & Petroleum Resources, Brian Messerschmidt
705-755-1949, Fax: 705-755-1206
Manager, Water Resources, Rob Messervey
705-755-1278
Managing Director, Adair Ireland-Smith
705-755-1702
Manager, Marketing & Communications Section, Greg Maude
705-755-1732, Fax: 705-755-1732
Manager, Park Operations & Development Section, Bruce van Staalduinen
705-755-1712, Fax: 705-755-1735
Manager, Planning & Research Section, Barton Feilders
705-755-1730
Manager, Species at Risk Section, Steve Bowcott
705-755-1754

Natural Resources Management Division
Whitney Block, #6540, 99 Wellesley St. West, Toronto, ON M7A 1W3
416-314-2000, Fax: 416-314-1994
The division provides leadership & direction for the ministry's resource management programs. The division leads programs for the province's fish, wildlife, parks, Crown lands & waters & is responsible for the delivery of natural resource management programs, including fish hatcheries, the provincial parks system & the management of the Great Lakes.
Asst. Deputy Minister, Kevin J. Wilson
416-314-6131, Fax: 416-314-1994,kevin.j.wilson@ontario.ca
Director, Fish & Wildlife, Cameron Mack
705-755-1909, cameron.mack@ontario.ca
Director, Great Lakes, Eric Boysen
705-755-5999, Fax: 705-755-2901,eric.boysen@ontario.ca
Director, Lands & Waters, Dan Marinigh
705-755-1620, Fax: 705-755-1201,dan.marinigh@ontario.ca
Managing Director, Ontario Parks, Adair Ireland-Smith
705-755-1702, 880-667-1940,adair.ireland-smith@ontario.ca

Science & Information Resources Division
Robinson Place, North Tower, 300 Water St., 2nd Fl., Peterborough, ON K9J 8M5
705-755-2000, Fax: 705-755-2802, 800-667-1940
The division leads the development & application of scientific knowledge, information management systems & information technologies in support of the Ministry mandate.The division is responsible for ensuring operational decision-making requirements of the Ministry are supported by sound science & reliable data, by providing accurate, relevant & timely information to manage resources in an ecologically sustainable manner.
Asst. Deputy Minister, David de Launay
705-755-2800, Fax: 705-755-2802,david.delaunay@ontario.ca
Director, Applied Research & Development, Cheryl Lewis
705-755-2807, Fax: 705-755-2802,cheryl.lewis@ontario.ca
Director, Geographic Information, Brian Maloney
705-755-2204, Fax: 705-755-1640,brian.j.maloney@ontario.ca
Acting Director, Science & Information Branch, Frank Kennedy
705-945-6703, Fax: 705-945-6527,frank.kennedy@ontario.ca
Manager, Aquatic Research & Development Section, Cheryl Lewis
705-755-1561, Fax: 705-755-1559
Manager, Forest Research & Development, Wayne Fiset
705-946-7400
Manager, Southcentral Science Section, Alex Gardner
705-755-3275, Fax: 705-755-3289
Manager, Wildlife & Natural Heritage, Chris Davies
705-755-1560, Fax: 705-755-1559
Manager, Geosmart, Derek Landry
416-314-3396
Manager, Information Access Services Section, Anne Halverson
705-755-1693, Fax: 705-755-1677
Manager, Information Infrastructure Systems, John deLagran
705-755-5548
Manager, Land & Resources Data Administration, Rob Parry
705-755-2158

Acting Director, Frank Kennedy
705-945-6703

Niagara Falls Bridge Commission

PO Box 395, Niagara Falls, ON L2E 6T8
905-354-5641, Fax: 905-353-6644
General Manager & Secretary-Treasurer, Thomas E. Garlock
Executive Assistant, Sandra Phillips
sphillip@niagarafallsbridges.com

Ministry of Northern Development, Mines & Forestry

99 Wellesley St. West, Toronto, ON M7A 1W3
416-327-0633, Fax: 416-327-0665,
www.mndm.gov.on.ca

The Ministry of Northern Development & Mines is the only regional ministry within the government & plays a central role in northern affairs. MNDM supports the mineral industry by providing it with valuable information about the province's goology. It also delivers & administers Ontario's Mining Act to improve the investment climate for mineral development. The ministry has a two-fold mandate, to promote northern economic development & support mineral sector competitiveness.The ministry is developing an initiative to help Ontario's Far North communities attract environmentally sound development, work with First Nation communities, partner ministries, the federal government, the mineral sector & private sector stakeholders to create opportunities for residents to help First Nation communities become more self-reliant.The ministry works with the Northern Ontario Heritage Fund Corporation & with the Ontario Northland Transportation Commission to bring much-needed service improvements to the northeast.

Acts Administered:
Mining Act
Ministry of Northern Development & Mines Act
Northern Services Boards Act
Ontario Mineral Exploration Projects Act
Ontario Northland Transportation Commission Act
Tourism Act

Minister,Hon. Michael Gravelle
807-345-3647, Fax:
807-345-2922,mgravelle.mpp@liberal.ola.org
Deputy Minister, David Lindsay
416-212-2701, david.lindsay@ontario.ca
Director, Legal Services, Andrew Macdonald
416-327-0640, Fax:
416-327-0646,andrew.macdonald@ontario.ca

• Ontario Northland
555 Oak St. East
North Bay, ON P1B 8L3
705-472-4500 Fax: 705-476-5598 800-363-7512
info@ontc.on.ca
www.ontc.on.ca

• Owen Sound Transportation Company Ltd.
RR#5, Hwy 6 & 21
Owen Sound, ON N4K 5N7
519-376-8740
www.chicheemaun.com

Corporate Management Division

#704, 159 Cedar St., Sudbury, ON P3E 6A5
705-564-7443, Fax: 705-564-7447
Asst. Deputy Minister, Don Ignacy
705-564-7448, Fax: 705-564-7447,don.ignacy@ontario.ca
Director, Executive Projects, Indira Singh
807-475-1687, Fax: 807-475-1120,indira.singh1@ontario.ca
Director, Business Planning, Scott Mantle
705-564-7949, Fax: 705-564-7747,scott.mantle@ontario.ca
Director, Human Resources, Cleo Degagne
705-564-7931, Fax: 705-564-7942,cleo.degagne@ontario.ca

Mines & Minerals Division

Willet Green Miller Centre, 933 Ramsey Lake Rd., 6th Fl., Sudbury, ON P3E 6B5
705-670-5755, Fax: 705-670-5818

The Mines & Minerals Division works to generate new wealth & benefits for the residents of Ontario by providing basic geological information gathering & interpretation in support of Ontario's exploration, mine development & mining sectors & the administration of Ontario's Mining Act in a fair & consistent fashion. Collects, analyzes & publishes valuable information about the state of the mining & mineral industries, as well as specific information about the location & quality of mineral deposits. The field staff throughout the province provide consultative services to the industry through all phases of the mining sequence, & include resident geologists, mining recorders & mineral development officers.

Asst. Deputy Minister, Christine Kaszycki
705-670-5877, Fax:
705-670-5818,christine.kaszycki@ontario.ca
Senior Manager, Geoscience Laboratories, Ed Debicki
705-670-5643, Fax: 705-670-3047,ed.debicki@ontario.ca
Manager, Business Solutions Services, Carol Smith
705-564-7083, Fax: 705-564-7919,carol.smith@lrc.gov.on.ca
Manager, Administration & Operational Services, Jeannie Barty
705-670-5831, Fax: 705-670-5818,jeannie.barty@ontario.ca
Manager, Information & Marketing, Marc Leroux
705-670-5869, Fax: 705-670-5807,marc.leroux@ontario.ca

Northern Development Division

Roberta Bondar Place, #200, 70 Foster Dr., Sault Ste Marie, ON P6A 6V8
705-945-5900, Fax: 705-945-5931, 800-461-2287
Other Communication: Delivery of Government Services: 705/945-5904

Responsible for promoting business, industrial, community & regional economic development & diversification; improving access to social & health services for northerners; planning & coordinating an integrated transportation system to meet private & commercial transportation needs at local, regional & provincial levels; coordinating the policies & programs of other ministries to ensure the special needs of northerners are addressed by government.

Asst. Deputy Minister, Cal McDonald
705-945-5901, Fax: 705-945-5932,cal.mcdonald@ontario.ca
Executive Director, Northern Ontario Heritage Fund Corporation, Aime Dimatteo
705-945-6734, aime.dimatteo@ontario.ca
Director, Programs & Transportation Branch, Tom Marcolini
705-945-5836, tom.marcolini@ontario.ca
Director, Regional Economic Development, Hial Newsome
705-564-7134, hial.newsome@ontario.ca
Acting Manager, Northern Ontario Grow Bonds Corp., Sharon Tansley
705-564-7115, Fax: 705-564-7220,sharon.tansley@ontario.ca

Area Offices:

Kenora
#104, 810 Robertson St., Kenora, ON P9N 4J2
807-468-2937, Fax: 807-468-2930
Manager, Christine Hansen
807-468-2938, christine.hansen@ontario.ca

North Bay
#203, 447 McKeown Ave., North Bay, ON P1B 9S9
705-494-4045, Fax: 705-494-4069
Manager, Louise Brinkmann
705-494-4176, louise.brinkmann@ontario.ca

Sault Ste. Marie
Roberta Bondar Place, #200, 70 Foster Dr., Sault Ste Marie, ON P6A 6V8
705-945-5914, Fax: 705-945-5931
Manager, Eileen Forestell
705-945-5839, eileen.forestell@ontario.ca

Sudbury
#601, 159 Cedar St., Sudbury, ON P3E 6A5
705-564-7517, Fax: 705-564-7583
Manager, Murray Morello
705-564-7519, murray.morello@ontario.ca

Thunder Bay
#332, 435 James St. South, Thunder Bay, ON P7E 6L3
807-475-1648, Fax: 807-475-1589
Manager, Dave Laderoute
807-475-1573, dave.laderoute@ontario.ca

Timmins
Hwy. 101 East, Bag 3060, South Porcupine, ON P0N 1H0
705-235-1664, Fax: 705-235-1660
Manager, Brian Pountney
705-235-1654, brian.pountney@ontario.ca

Office of the Ombudsman

483 Bay St., 10th Fl., Toronto, ON M5G 2C9
416-586-3300, Fax: 416-586-3485, 800-263-1830
info@ombudsman.on.ca
www.ombudsman.on.ca

Other Communication: Ligne sans frais: 1-800-387-2620 (Français)

An impartial body independent of government that investigates & resolves complaints about the administrative actions & decisions of provincial government organizations such as ministries, boards, agencies, commissions & tribunals.The Ombudsman is an Officer of the provincial Legislature & has jurisdiction over all provinical government organizations as an office of last resort. All available complaint & appeal procedures whenever possible should be used before the Ombudsman conducts an investigation.The Ombudsman decides cases based on independent investigations & works to find solutions that are acceptable to everyone involved.Services are free & confidential & are available in English, French or any other language.

Acts Administered:
Ombudsman Act

Ombudsman, André Marin
416-586-3409
Manager, Communications & Media Relations, Linda Williamson
416-586-3426, Fax: 416-586-3485

Ontario Power Generation

700 University Ave., Toronto, ON M5G 1X6
416-592-2555, 877-592-2555
www.opg.com

Mandate is to meet Ontario's requirements for electricity so as to result in the greatest overall benefit to the community & the lowest cost to the consumer, while operating in a safe & environmentally responsible manner. Assets include 3 nuclear generating stations, 5 fossil generating stations, 64 hydroelectric stations, 3 wind generating stations.

Chair,Hon. Jake Epp
416-592-2115, Fax: 416-971-3691
President/CEO, James F. Hankinson
Executive Vice-President & Chief Operating Officer, Pierre Charlebois
Executive Vice-President, Corporate Development, Jim Burpee
Executive Vice-President, Hydro, John Murphy
Executive Vice-President, Fossil, Jim Twomey
Senior Vice-President & CFO, Donn Hanbridge
Senior Vice-President, Corporate Affairs, Bruce Boland
Senior Vice-President, Human Resources & Chief Ethics Officer, Janice Dunlop
Senior Vice-President, Law & General Counsel, David Brennan
Vice-President & Corporate Secretary, Catriona King
Manager, Media Relations,
416-592-4008, media@opg.com, Other Communications: Toll-free Ontario: 877/592-4008

Agencies Division

Asst. Deputy Minister, Joyce Barretto
416-325-2070
Director, Realty Relations, David Cope
416-326-4857
Director, Gaming & Alcohol Policy, Barbara Hewett
416-314-2736
Director, Transmission Corridor Program, Barbara Ko
416-327-2840
Director, Project Development & Agency Liaison, Pat McClellan
416-325-4824

Ontario Growth Secretariat

#425 - 777 Bay St., 4th Fl., Toronto, ON M5G 2E5
416-325-1210, Fax: 416-325-7405, 866-479-9781

Provides leadership in the development of a growth management agenda. Smart Growth will result in integrated decision-making that brings together all levels of government & to their stakeholders on issues such as transportation, infrastructure, land-use, the environment, housing & public investment to create a higher quality of life.

Asst. Deputy Minister, Brad Graham
416-325-5803, Fax: 416-325-7405,brad.graham@ontario.ca

Infrasutucture Ontario

777 Bay St., 9th Fl., Toronto, ON M5G 2C8
416-212-7289, Fax: 416-325-4646,
info@infrastructureontario.ca
www.infrastructureontario.ca
President & CEO, J. David Livingston
Vice-President, Community Finance & CFO, Gregg Smyth
416-212-6439
Vice-President, Community Relations & Communications, Susan McGovern
416-212-6453

Ministry of Research & Innovation

Ferguson Block, 77 Wellesley St. West, 12th Fl., Toronto, ON M7A 1N3
416-325-5181, Fax: 416-325-3877, 866-446-5216
www.mri.gov.on.ca

The Ministry of Research & Innovation works collaboratively across all government ministries to ensure improved coordination & alignment of research, commercialization & innovation activities & to foster a culture of innovation. The Ministry of Research & Innovation is also committed to engaging all external partners, including the private sector, education & research communities in supporting & delivering on the research & innovation agenda.

Minister,Hon. John Milloy
416-326-1600, Fax:
416-326-1656,jmilloy.mpp@liberal.ola.org
Deputy Minister, George Ross
416-325-7517, Fax: 416-325-5927,george.ross@ontario.ca

Corporate Services Division
416-325-6486, Fax: 416-325-6392
Chief Administrative Officer, David Clifford
416-325-6600, Fax: 416-325-6392,david.clifford@ontario.ca
OCC Chair, Development Corporations of Ontario, David Clifford
416-325-6600, Fax: 416-326-1113,david.clifford@ontario.ca
Director, Business Transformation & Organizational Development, Angela Faienza
416-325-7150
Acting Director, Human Resources, Dan Keating
416-325-6598, Fax: 416-325-6715,dan.keating@ontario.ca
Acting Director, Business Planning & Finance, Sheila McGrory
416-327-1137, Fax: 416-327-4239,sheila.mcgrory@ontario.ca

Research & Commercialization Division
416-314-1163, Fax: 416-314-4344
Acting Asst. Deputy Minister, Robert Taylor
416-314-8219, robert.taylor@ontario.ca
Director, Commercialization Branch, Bill Mantel
416-314-0670, Fax: 416-314-0680,bill.mantel@ontario.ca
Director, Infrastructure & Innovation Partnerships Branch, Ian Bromley
416-925-0544
Acting Director, Research Branch, Allison Barr
416-212-6990, Fax: 416-314-8224,allison.barr@ontario.ca

Ministry of Revenue

Frost Bldg. South, 7 Queen's Park Cres., 6th Fl., Toronto, ON M7A 1Y7
Fax: 866-888-3850, 866-668-8297
www.rev.gov.on.ca
The Ministry of Revenue administers Ontario's major tax statutes & tax assistance programs. Taxpayer education & customer service are provided, as well as enforcement activities for non-compliance.
Acts Administered:
Commercial Concentration Tax Act
Community Small Business Investment Funds Act
Corporations Tax Act
Electricity Act, 1998 (only specific provisions)
Employer Health Tax Act
Fuel Tax Act
Gasoline Tax Act
Highway Traffic Act (only specific provisions)
Income Tax Act (Ontario)
Land Transfer Tax Act
Mining Tax Act
Ontario Guaranteed Annual Income Act
Ontario Home Ownership Savings Plan Act
Provincial Land Tax Act
Provincial Land Tax Act, 2006
Race Tracks Tax Act
Retail Sales Tax Act
Small Business Development Corporations Act
Succession Duty Act Supplementary Provisions Act, 1980
Tobacco Tax Act
Minister,Hon. John Wilkinson
416-325-0702, Fax:
416-327-4493,jwilkinson.mpp.co@liberal.ola.org
Deputy Minister, Carol Layton
905-436-4674, carol.layton@ontario.ca
Director, Communications & Corporate Affairs, Dianne Lone
416-212-1440, Fax: 416-325-0339,Dianne.Lone@ontario.ca
Director, Legal Services, James D. Sinclair
416-325-1450, Fax: 416-325-1460,James.Sinclair@ontario.ca
Director, Finance & Revenue Autdit Service Team, Larry Yarmolinsky
416-325-8323, Fax:
416-325-5096,Larry.Yarmolinsky@ontario.ca

Central Agencies Information & Information Technology Cluster
33 King St. West, Oshawa, ON L1H 8H5
905-433-6797, Fax: 905-433-5708
The Central Agencies Information and Information Technology Cluster (CA) supports the Ministry of Finance, Ministry of Revenue, Cabinet Office, and Ministry of Energy and Infrastructure.
Assistant Deputy Minister & Chief Information Officer, Marty Gallas
905-433-6890, Fax: 905-433-5708,marty.gallas@ontario.ca

Corporate & Quality Service Division
Michael Starr Bldg., 33 King St. West, 6th Fl., Oshawa, ON L1H 8H5
905-433-6844, Fax: 905-433-6688
Assistant Deputy Minister & Chief Administrative Officer, Helmut Zisser
416-314-5158, Fax: 905-433-6688,helmut.zisser@ontario.ca
Director, Revenue Operations & Client Services, Jennette Frost
905-433-5880, Fax: 905-433-6288,jennette.frost2@ontario.ca
Director, Corporate Planning & Finance, Linda Gibney
905-433-5637, Fax: 905-433-5124,linda.gibney@ontario.ca
Support Clerk, Human Resources, Esther Wade
416-325-8281, esthter.wade@ontario.ca

Office of the Commissioner of Revenue
Michael Starr Bldg, 33 King St. West, Oshawa, ON L1H 8H5
905-433-6000, Fax: 905-433-6777
Assistant Deputy Minister, Tax Revenue, Terry Hewak
905-433-5614, Fax: 905-433-6686,Terry.hewak@ontario.ca
Commissioner of Revenue, Angela Longo
905-433-5602, Angela.Longo@ontario.ca
Asst. Deputy Minister, Tax Compliance & Regional Operations, Bob Laramy
905-837-5200, Bob.Laramy@ontario.ca

Ministry of Small Business & Customer Services

Whitney Block, #1306 - 99 Wellesley St. W., Toronto, ON M7A 1W2
416-325-6000, Fax: 416-326-1947, 866-668-4249
info.sbe@ontario.ca
www.sbe.gov.on.ca

Other Communication: Canada-Ontario Business Service Centre Toll-free: 1-800-567-2345
The Ministry enables the development of firms by engaging in the following activities: promoting entrepreneurial skills & opportunities to youth; encouraging entrepreneurship & assisting new entrepreneurs in the start-up process; providing information, advice & services; promoting e-business & new technologies; & offering policy analysis & advice to the Ontario government.
Minister,Hon. Harinder S. Takhar
416-325-6000, Fax:
416-326-1947,htakhar.mpp@liberal.ola.org; htakhar.mpp.co@liberal.ola.org
Deputy Minister, Angela Longo
416-327-8342, Fax:
416-314-7167,angela.longo@ontario.ca
Acting Director, Communications, Dino Rocca
416-325-8058, Fax: 416-325-6688,dino.rocca@ontario.ca
Director, Internal Audit, Culture & Innovation Audit Service, Charles Meehan
416-325-5983, Fax:
416-314-3467,charles.meehan@ontario.ca
Parliamentary Assistant, Sophia Aggelonitis
416-314-7882, Fax:
416-314-7906,sophia.aggelonitis@ontario.ca

Small & Medium Enterprise Division
416-325-9585, Fax: 416-326-5154
Asst. Deputy Minister, Neil Smith
416-212-7793, Fax: 416-326-5154,neil.h.smith@ontario.ca
Director, Entrepreneurship, Ann Hoy
416-314-3809, Fax: 416-325-6538,ann.hoy@ontario.ca
Director, Business & Advisory Services, Bob Marrs
416-325-6522, Fax: 416-325-6757,bob.marrs@ontario.ca
Director, Small & Medium Enterprise Policy & Outreach, Rob Swaffield
416-325-4595, Fax: 416-325-3732,rob.swaffield@ontario.ca

Ministry of Tourism

Hearst Block, 900 Bay St., 9th Fl., Toronto, ON M7A 2E1
416-326-9326, Fax: 416-314-7854, 800-668-2746
www.tourism.gov.on.ca

Other Communication: Ontario Travel Information: 1-800-668-2746

Acts Administered:
Historical Parks Act
Ontario Place Corporation Act
St. Clair Parks Commission Act
St. Lawrence Parks Commission Act
Tourism Act
Minister,Hon. Monique M. Smith
416-326-9326, Fax:
416-314-7854,msmith.mpp.co@liberal.ola.org
Deputy Minister, Philip Howell
416-314-7846, Fax: 416-314-7854,phil.howell@ontario.ca
Director, Communications, Mary E. Ferguson
416-212-3929, Fax:
416-325-5968,mary.e.ferguson@ontario.ca
• St. Clair Parks Commission
ACPC Administrative Office
264 Paget St.
Corunna, ON N0N 4G0
519-862-2291 Fax: 519-862-2294
info@stclairparkway.com
www.stclairparkway.com
The St. Clair Parks Commission is committed to creating, maintaining & operating, in cooperation with other agencies, regional parks for people of the region & tourists; people-oriented outdoor recreation facilities; fiscal accountability; environmental accountability by action, example & education.
• Metro Toronto Convention Centre Corporation
255 Front St. West
Toronto, ON M5V 2W6
416-585-8000 Fax: 416-585-8270
info@mtcc.com
www.mtcc.com
• Niagara Parks Commission
7400 Portage Rd. South
PO Box 150
Niagara Falls, ON L2E 6T2
905-356-2241 Fax: 905-354-6041 877-642-7275
www.niagaraparks.com
• Ontario Place Corporation
955 Lake Shore Blvd. West
Toronto, ON M6K 3B9
416-314-9900 Fax: 416-314-9992
www.ontarioplace.com
• Ontario Tourism Marketing Partnership Corporation
Hearst Block
900 Bay St., 10th Fl.
Toronto, ON M7A 2E1
416-212-0757 Fax: 416-325-6004 800-668-2746
www.ontariotravel.net
• Ottawa Congress Centre
55 Colonel By Dr.
Ottawa, ON K1N 9J2
613-563-1984 Fax: 613-563-7646
www.ottawacongresscentre.com
• St. Lawrence Parks Commission
RR#1
Morrisburg, ON K0C 1X0
613-543-3704 Fax: 613-543-2847 800-437-2233TDD: 613-543-4181
The St. Lawrence Parks Commission is an Ontario provincial agency established in 1955 to provide recreation, tourism, cultural & educational opportunities for residents of Ontario & visitors to the province through the presentation & interpretation of historical attractions & the development & operation of parks, campgrounds, scenic parkways & recreational areas.

Deputy Minister's Office
416-326-9326, Fax: 416-314-7854
Deputy Minister, Philip Howell
416-314-7846, Fax: 416-314-7854,phil.howell@ontario.ca
Director, Communications Branch, Mary E. Ferguson
416-212-3929, Fax:
416-325-5968,mary.e.ferguson@ontario.ca
Director, Investment & Development, Michael Langford
416-314-7105, Fax:
416-327-2506,michael.langford@ontario.ca
Director, Resources & Culture Audit Service Team, Charles Meehan
416-325-5983, Fax:
416-314-3467,charles.meehan@ontario.ca

Regional & Corporate Services Division
416-314-7311, Fax: 416-314-7313
Asst. Deputy Minister & Chief Administrative Officer, Robert Montgomery
416-314-7311, Fax:
416-314-7313,robert.m.montgomery@ontario.ca
Chief Information Officer, Community Services Cluster, Jim Hamilton
416-325-4727, jim.hamilton@ontario.ca
Director, Human Resources, Cindy Lam
416-212-2783, Fax: 416-325-6371,cindy.lam@ontario.ca
Director, Legal Services, Andrea Baston
416-314-7022, Fax: 416-314-7038,andrea.baston@ontario.ca
Director, Regional Services Branch, Brian Lemir
416-314-6680, Fax: 416-314-6686,brian.lemire@ontario.ca

Tourism Policy & Development Division
416-326-9326, Fax: 416-325-6985
Acting Asst. Deputy Minister, Michael Kurts
416-325-6961, Fax: 416-325-6985,michael.kurts@ontario.ca
Acting Director, Sport & Recreation, Anita Comella
416-314-7696, anita.comella@ontario.ca
Director, Tourism Agencies Unit, Susan Patterson
416-326-9579, Fax:
416-314-7003,susan.patterson@ontario.ca
Director, Tourism Policy & Research, Joan MacDonald
416-325-6055, Fax:
416-314-7341,joan.macdonald@ontario.ca

Associated Agencies, Boards & Commissions:

Ministry of Training, Colleges & Universities

Mowat Block, 900 Bay St., 3rd Fl., Toronto, ON M7A 1L2
416-325-1600, Fax: 416-325-2934,
www.edu.gov.on.ca/eng/tcu
Acts Administered:

Apprenticeship & Certification Act, 1998
Colleges Collective Bargaining Act
Ministry of Training, Colleges & Universities Act
Ontario Colleges of Applied Arts & Technology Act, 2002
Ontario Educational Communications Authority Act
Ontario Youth Employment Act
Post-secondary Education Choice & Excellence Act, 2000
Private Career Colleges Act
Private Vocational Schools Act
Trades Qualification & Apprenticeship Act
University Foundations Act, 1992

Minister,Hon. John Milloy
416-326-1600, Fax: 416-326-1656,jmilloy.mpp@liberal.ola.org; jmilloy.mpp.co@liberal.ola.org
Deputy Minister, Philip Steenkamp
416-314-9244, Fax: 416-314-7117,philip.steenkamp@ontario.ca
Director, Change Management Office, Anthony Brenders
416-212-3560, anthony.brenders@ontario.ca
Chief Information Officer, Jim Hamilton
416-325-4727, Fax: 416-325-8371,jim.hamilton@ontario.ca
Director, Communications, Adrian Mann
416-325-2944, Fax: 416-325-2934,adrian.mann@ontario.ca
Manager, Brian Fleming Library, Simon Loban
416-325-2654, Fax: 416-325-4235,simon.loban@edu.gov.on.ca

• College Compensation & Appointments Council
#1102, 2 Carlton St.
Toronto, ON M5B 1J3
416-325-2914 Fax: 416-325-2917

• Ontario Graduate Scholarship Program Selection Board
189 Red River Rd., 4thFl.
PO Box 4500
Thunder Bay, ON P7B 6G9
807-343-7257 Fax: 807-343-7278 800-465-3957
www.osap.gov.on.ca
Provides advice & recommendations to the minister concerning the policies & administration of the Ontario Graduate Scholarship program & selects successful candidates for funding under the program.

• Ontario Student Assistance Appeal Board
Mowat Block
900 Bay St., 7th Fl.
Toronto, ON M7A 1L2
416-314-0714 Fax: 416-325-3096

• Postsecondary Education Quality Assessment Board
#1511, 2 Carlton St.
Toronto, ON M5B 1J3
416-325-1686 Fax: 416-325-1711
peqab.edu.gov.on.ca

Corporate Management & Services Division
Mowat Block, #342 - 900 Bay St., Toronto, ON M7A 1L2
416-325-2772, Fax: 416-325-2778
Asst. Deputy Minister, David Fulford
416-325-2773, Fax: 416-325-2778,david.fulford@ontario.ca
Acting Director, Corporate Coordination, Russell Riddell
416-326-6662, Fax: 416-327-1912,russell.riddell@ontario.ca
Director, Human Resources, Lisa Sherin
416-325-4511, Fax: 416-327-9043,lisa.sherin@ontario.ca
Director, Legal Services, David Costen
416-325-2399, Fax: 416-325-2410,david.costen@ontario.ca

Employment & Training Division
Fax: 416-325-2995, 888-562-4769
Asst. Deputy Minister, Kevin French
416-325-2989, Fax: 416-325-2995,kevin.french@ontario.ca
Director, Business & Systems Management Branch, Robert Lowry
416-325-4056, Fax: 416-314-0499,robert.lowry@ontario.ca
Director, Programs Branch, Patti Redmond
416-326-5849, Fax: 416-326-5505,patti.redmond@ontario.ca
Director, Workplace Training, Sandie Birkhead-Kirk
416-326-5456

Post-secondary Education Division
416-325-2199, Fax: 416-326-3256
Asst. Deputy Minister, Janet Mason
416-325-2116, Fax: 416-326-3256
Manager, Colleges Unit, Joanne Brown
416-325-4081, joanne.brown@ontario.ca
Manager, Private Institutions Unit, Charlotte McCloskey
416-325-5958, charlotte.mccloskey@ontario.ca
Director, Student Support, Richard Jackson
416-325-2853, Fax: 416-325-3096,richard.jackson@ontario.ca
Director, Research & Planning Branch, Chris Monahan
416-325-4034, Fax: 416-326-0601,chris.monahan@ontario.ca
Manager, Universities Branch, Frances Lamb
416-325-2876, frances.lamb@ontario.ca

Ministry of Transportation (MTO)

Ferguson Block, 77 Wellesley St. West, 3rd Fl., Toronto, ON M7A 1Z8
416-235-4686, Fax: 416-327-9185, 800-268-4686
www.mto.gov.on.ca

Other Communication: TTY Toll Free: 1-866-471-8929; Driver and Vehicle Licensing: 1-800-387-3445; Road Test Booking: 1-888-570-6110

The Ministry performs the following functions: planning, designing & building highways; performing environmental assessments; rehabilitating existing highways to increase their efficiency & safety; performing ongoing highway maintenance; developing standards, operational guidelines & policies relating to highways; & researching & introducing new technologies for more effective highway management. MTO commits to providing & promoting transportation services in a way that sustains a healthful environment through the Ministry's Statement of Environmental Values. The Ministry applies & integrates environmental concerns, along with prevailing social, economic, scientific & other considerations when conducting its business activities.

Acts Administered:
Airports Act
Bluewater Bridge Act
Bridges Act
Commuter Services Act
Dangerous Goods Transportation Act
Ferries Act
Freedom of Information Act
Go Transit Act
Highway Traffic Act
Local Roads Boards Act
Ministry of Transportation Act
Motorized Snow Vehicles Act
Northern Transportation Commission Act
Off-Road Vehicles Act
Ontario Highway Transport Board Act
Ontario Transportation Development Corporation Act
Public Service Works on Highways Act
Public Transportation & Highway Improvement Act
Public Vehicles Act
Railways Act
Rainbow Bridge Act
Statute Labour Act (part)
Toll Bridges Act
Toronto Area Transit Operating Authority Act
Township of Pelee Act
Truck Transportation Act
Urban Transportation Development Corporation Ltd. Act

Minister,Hon. James J. Bradley
416-327-9200, 800-268-4686,Fax: 416-327-9188,jbradley.mpp@liberal.ola.org, TDD: 866-471-8929
Deputy Minister, Bruce McCuaig
416-327-9162, Fax: 416-327-9185,bruce.mccuaig@ontario.ca
Acting Director, Transportation & Agriculture Audit Service Team, Tracy Dallaire
905-704-2881, Fax: 905-704-2333,tracy.dallaire@ontario.ca
Director, Communications, Kimberley Bates
416-327-2117, Fax: 416-327-2591,kimberley.bates@ontario.ca
Director, Legal Services, Mary Gersht
416-235-4406, Fax: 416-235-4924,mary.gersht@ontario.ca
Parliamentary Assistant, Michael A. Brown
416-325-3601, Fax: 416-325-3713,mbrown.mpp.co@liberal.ola.org

• GO Transit
#600, 20 Bay St.
Toronto, ON M5J 2W3
416-869-3600 Fax: 416-869-1755 888-438-6646
www.gotransit.com

• Ontario Highway Transport Board
151 Bloor St. West, 10th Fl.
Toronto, ON M5S 2T5
416-326-6732 Fax: 416-326-6738
ohtb@mto.gov.on.ca
www.ohtb.gov.on.ca

Corporate Services Division
Garden City Tower, 301 St. Paul St., 6th Fl., St Catharines, ON L2R 7R4
905-704-2693, Fax: 905-704-2445
Asst. Deputy Minister, Rob Fleming
905-704-2701, Fax: 905-704-2445,rob.fleming@ontario.ca
Director, Facilities & Business Services, Lesley Spinney
905-704-2727, Fax: 905-704-2833,lesley.spinney@ontario.ca
Director, Finance, Steve M. Naylor
905-704-2702, Fax: 905-704-2525,steve.m.naylor@ontario.ca
Director, Human Resources, Alan Hogan
905-704-2688, Fax: 905-704-2747,alan.hogan@ontario.ca
Manager, Priority Initiatives Office, Ather Shabbar
905-704-3242, Fax: 905-704-2445,ather.shabbar@ontario.ca
Manager, Employee Relations Office (ERO) Downsview, Frank Caccia
416-235-3878, Fax: 416-235-3892
Manager, Equal Opportunity Program, Marsha Smith
416-235-5143
Manager, Human Resources Client Services (HRCS), Jean Stewart
905-704-2585, Fax: 905-704-2590
Manager, Strategic Human Resources Office, Allan Hogan
905-704-2671
Manager, French Language Services, Rachel Baril
905-704-2045

Economics & Transportation I&IT Cluster
416-327-3754, Fax: 416-327-3755
Chief Information Officer, Ken Kawall
416-327-1955, Fax: 416-327-3755,ken.kawall@ontario.ca
Director, Highways & Economics Solutions Branch, Howard Bertrand
905-704-2488, howard.bertrand@ontario.ca
Acting Director, Road User Safety Solutions Branch, Harjeet Kaur
416-235-5315, Fax: 416-235-5658,harjeet.kaur@ontario.ca
Senior Manager, IT Service Management, Candys Ballanger-Michaud
905-704-2834, candys.ballanger-michaud@ontario.ca

Policy & Planning Division
Ferguson Block, 77 Wellesley St. West, 3rd Fl., Toronto, ON M7A 1Z8
416-327-8521, Fax: 416-327-8746
Asst. Deputy Minister, Scott Thompson
416-327-8521, Fax: 416-327-8746,scott.thompson@ontario.ca
Chief Engineer, Highway Standards Branch, Gerry Chaput
905-704-2194, Fax: 905-704-2055,gerry.chaput@ontario.ca
Director, Modal Policy & Partnerships, Kim Lambert
416-235-3664
Director, Strategic Policy & Transportation Economics Branch, David Ward
416-212-1893, Fax: 416-212-1897,david.ward@ontario.ca
Manager, Regional Transit Policy Office, Chris Burke
416-585-7352, Fax: 416-585-7343,chris.burke@ontario.ca

Provincial Highways Management
Ferguson Block, 77 Wellesley St. West, 3rd Fl., Toronto, ON M7A 1Z8
416-327-9044, Fax: 416-327-9226
Asst. Deputy Minister, Brian Gaston
416-327-9044, Fax: 416-327-9226,brian.gaston@ontario.ca
Manager, Construction & Operations Branch,Vacant
905-704-2618
Director, Contract Management & Operations Branch, Mike Goodale
905-704-2601, Fax: 905-704-2626,

Regional Offices:

Central
Atrium Tower, 1201 Wilson Ave., 2nd Fl., Toronto, ON M3M 1J8
416-235-5412, Fax: 416-235-5266
Regional Director, Roger Hamner
416-235-5400, Fax: 416-235-5266,roger.hanmer@ontario.ca

Eastern
1355 John Counter Blvd., PO Box 4000, Kingston, ON K7L 5A3
613-545-4711, Fax: 613-545-4786, 800-267-0295
Regional Director, Kathryn Moore
613-545-4600, kathryn.moore@ontario.ca

Northeastern
Ontario Government Bldg., #301, 447 McKeown Ave., North Bay, ON P1B 9S9
705-472-7900, Fax: 705-497-5422, 800-461-9547
Regional Director, Keith Bryer
705-497-5500, keith.bryer@ontario.ca

Northwestern
615 James St. South, Thunder Bay, ON P7E 6P6
807-473-2000, Fax: 807-473-2157, 800-465-5034
Regional Director, Larry Lambert
807-473-2050, Fax: 807-473-2165,larry.lambert@ontario.ca

Southwestern
659 Exeter Rd., London, ON N6A 1L3
519-873-4335, Fax: 519-873-4236, 800-265-6072
Acting Regional Director, Kevin Bentley
519-873-4333, Fax: 519-873-4236,kevin.bentley@ontario.ca
Director & Chief Engineer, Gerry Chaput
905-704-2940, Fax: 905-704-2055

Manager, Bridge Office, Bala Tharmabala
905-704-2341, Fax: 905-704-2060
Chief Surveyor & Manager, Geomatics Office, Russ Hogan
905-704-2328, Fax: 905-704-2051
Manager, Highway Design Office, Joe Bucik
905-704-2284, Fax: 905-704-2050
Senior Manager, Materials Engineering & Research Office, Guy Cautillo
416-235-3732, Fax: 416-235-3487
Director, David Ward
416-212-1893, Fax: 416-212-1897
Manager, Policy Coordination Office, Gabija Petrauskas
416-235-4556
Acting Manager, Strategic Intelligence Office, Donna Connelly
416-212-1903
Manager, Strategic Policy & Planning Office, Ansar Ahmed
416-235-3718
Manager, Inter-Regional Transit Office, Peter Chackeris
416-235-5468
Manager, Freight Office, Rod Taylor
416-235-3636
Manager, Municipal Office, Bill Paterson
416-235-4060
Director, Malcolm MacLean
905-704-2033
Manager, Claims Office, Clare Riepma
905-704-2997, Fax: 905-704-2777
Manager, Construction Office, Gary Todd
905-704-2199, Fax: 905-704-2040
Manager, Maintenance Office, Shael Gwartz
905-704-2622, Fax: 905-904-2848
Manager, Property Office, Rob Parker
905-704-2233
Director, Mike Goodale
905-704-2601
Manager, Program & Resources Management, Noris Bot
905-704-2463
Manager, Program Development & Evaluation Office, Jelena Markovic
905-704-2630
Manager, Resources Planning Office, Paul Botelho
905-704-2633

Road User Safety Division
#191, Bldg A, 1201 Wilson Ave., Toronto, ON M3M 1J8
416-235-2999, Fax: 416-235-4153

The division sets safety standards, develops policies, legislation & regulation, & educates road users about road user safety. Responsibilities include evaluating the effectiveness of safety measures, inspecting, monitoring & enforcing compliance with standards, testing, licenses & drivers, & registering vehicles. Through public education, legislation & enforcement, the government strives to ensure all motorists take responsibility for their driving behaviour. The Assistant Deputy Minister, Road User Safety, is responsible for the co-ordination of all Road User Safety activities for the province & acts as the Registrar of Motor Vehicles for Ontario.

Asst. Deputy Minister, Bohodar Rubashewsky
416-235-4454, Fax:
416-235-4153,bohodar.rubashewsky@ontario.ca
Acting Director, Business Services, Shelley Unterlander
416-235-4769, shelley.unterlander@ontario.ca
Director, Projects & Change Management, Paul Harbottle
416-235-4199, Fax: 416-235-4111,paul.harbottle@ontario.ca
Director, Safety Policy & Education, Susan Lo
416-235-4050, Fax: 416-235-5139,sue.lo@ontario.ca
Acting Executive Director, Road User Safety, Brian Gaston
416-235-4827, Fax: 416-235-5672

Service Development & Implementation Office
416-235-4396, Fax: 416-235-4111

Ontario Women's Directorate (OWD)

777 Bay St., 6th Fl., Toronto, ON M7A 2J4
416-314-0300, Fax: 416-314-0247, 866-510-5902
info.mci@ontario.ca
www.citizenship.gov.on.ca/owd

A division of the Ministry of Citizenship and Immigration, the OWD focuses upon the following issues related to women: social, economic & justice-related concerns. The main activities of the OWD are preventing violence against women & promoting women's economic independence.

Minister Responsible,Hon. Deborah Matthews
416-212-2278, Fax:
416-212-7431,dmatthews.mpp@liberal.ola.org; dmatthews.mpp.co@liberal.ola.org
Executive Director, Susan Seaby
416-314-1850, Fax: 416-314-0247,susan.seaby@ontario.ca
Manager, Education, Awareness & Outreach, Christine Gardner
416-314-0312, Fax:
416-314-0256,christine.gardner@ontario.ca,
Manager, Stakeholder Relations & Policy Development, Suzanne Hastie
416-314-1783, Fax:
416-314-0255,suzanne.hastie@ontario.ca
Parliamentary Assistant, Leeanna Pendergast
416-325-1270, Fax:
416-326-3951,lpendergast.mpp@liberal.ola.org

Workplace Safety & Insurance Board

200 Front St. West, Ground Fl., Toronto, ON M5V 3J1
416-344-1000, Fax: 416-344-4684, 800-387-0750
www.wsib.on.ca

Other Communication: Information Centre: 416/344-4078

Chair,Hon. Steven W. Mahoney, P.C.
416-344-4451
President & CEO, Jill Hutcheon
416-344-4009
Vice-President, Business Technology Services & Chief Information Officer, Valerie Adamo
416-344-4024, valerie_adamo@wsib.on.ca
Acting Vice-President, Prevention, Wayne Thompson
416-344-2664, wayne_thompson@wsib.on.ca
Board Auditor, Internal Audit & ERM, Roman W. Kosmyna
416-344-4537, roman_kosmyna@wsib.on.ca
General Counsel & Vice-President, Legal Services & Secretary to the Board, Brenda Abrams
416-344-4880, brenda_abrams@wsib.on.ca
Chief Operating Officer, John Slinger
416-344-4450, john_slinger@wsib.on.ca
Vice-President & Chief Actuary, Actuarial Services, Rob Hinrichs
416-344-5300, rob_hinrichs@wsib.on.ca
Vice-President, Strategic Communications, Policy & Research, Moira McIntyre
416-344-4374, Fax:
416-344-4366,moira_mcintyre@wsib.on.ca
Chief Financial Officer, Malen Ng
416-344-4505, malen_ng@wsib.on.ca
Vice-President, Health Services, Jane McCarthy
416-344-4334, jane_mccarthy@wsib.on.ca
Vice-President, Human Resources, Steve Jackson
416-344-4320, steve_jackson@wsib.on.ca
Vice-President, Investments, John Denham
416-344-4095, john_denham@wsib.on.ca
Chief Corporate Services Officer, John Slinger
416-344-5671
Chief Prevention Officer, Tom Beegan
416-344-4446, tom_beegan@wsib.on.ca
Project Assistant, External Relations, Christine Munro
416-344-4185, christine_munro@wsib.on.ca
Vice-President, Moira McIntyre
Director, Corporate Communications & Language Services, Cheryl Tucker
416-344-4768
Acting Director, External Relations, Sharon Gilchrist
416-344-6886
Executive Director, Roy Thomas
416-344-4750
Chief Financial Officer, Malen Ng
416-344-6669
Director, Accounting, Bob Lau
416-203-4900
Director, Corporate Services (Administration), Kathy Shewell
416-344-3683
Acting Director, Financial Services, Rob McMurtrie
416-203-4901
Director, Revenue Audit, Bobbie McAdam
416-344-3612
Director, Systems & Collections, Gord Petrie
905-521-4468
Manager, Treasury, Wayne Jeanes
416-203-4965
Vice-President, Jane McCarthy
416-344-4433
Executive Director, Health Services Management, Donna Bain
416-344-1000
Director, Clinical Services, Catherine Painvin
416-344-2992
Director, Corporate Health Centre, Alice Dong
416-344-3864
Director, Professional Practice & Chief Nursing Officer, Claire Mallette
416-344-4891
Vice-President, Steve Jackson
416-344-4375
Director, Labour Relations/Security, Sandy Douglas
416-344-4505
Director, Human Resources Development, Mark Goodale
416-344-4453
Director, Organizational Effectiveness, Lynne Barone
416-344-4894
Senior Vice-President, Brock Horseman
416-344-4450
Director, Administrative Services, Nadia Fahmy
416-344-2880
Director, Appeals, John Slinger
416-344-4755
Director, Quality Improvement, Joe Sgro
416-344-2727
General Manager, Industry Sectors, Garry Thomson
416-344-2468
General Manager, Small Business Services, Wayne Weatherbee
416-344-2845
General Manager, Specialized Claims Services, Judy Geary
416-344-2323
Vice-President, Moira McIntyre
Director, Benefits Policy, Slavica Todorovic
416-344-4327
Director, Medical & Occupational Policy, Claire-Marie Fortin
416-344-6915
Director, Research & Evaluation, Richard Allingham
416-344-4210
Director, Revenue Policy, Ian Welton
416-344-4146
Chief Prevention & Corporate Strategy Officer, Roy Mould
416-344-6869
Director, Best Practices, Marianne Levitsky
416-344-4932
Director, Prevention Services, Ron Lovelock
416-344-3452
Director, Provider Relations, David Frame
416-344-6644

Government of Prince Edward Island

Seat of Government:PO Box 2000, Charlottetown, PE C1A 7N8
902-368-4000, Fax: 902-368-5544,
island@gov.pe.ca
www.gov.pe.ca

The Province of Prince Edward Island entered Confederation July 1, 1873. It has an area of 5,683.91 km2, & the StatsCan census population in 2006 was 135,851.

Office of the Lieutenant Governor

Government House, PO Box 846, Charlottetown, PE C1A 7L9
902-368-5480, Fax: 902-368-5481,
www.gov.pe.ca/olg

Lieutenant Governor,Hon. Barbara A. Hagerman
902-368-5480, Fax: 902-368-5481,bahagerman@gov.pe.ca
Executive Assistant, Cindy Cheverie
ccheverie@gov.pe.ca

Office of the Premier

Shaw Bldg., 95 Rochford St., 5th Fl. South, PO Box 2000, Charlottetown, PE C1A 7N8
902-368-4400, Fax: 902-368-4416,
www.gov.pe.ca/premier

Premier; President, Executive Council; Minister Responsible, Intergovernmental Affairs; Leader, Liberal Party of PEI,Hon. Robert W.J. Ghiz
902-368-4400, Fax: 902-386-4416,premier@gov.pe.ca
Deputy Minister & Chief of Staff, Chris LeClair
902-368-4400, Fax: 902-368-4416,cleclair@gov.pe.ca
Director, Communications & Legislative Affairs, Geoff Townsend
902-368-4400, gatownsend@gov.pe.ca
Executive Assistant, Ian "Tex" MacDonald
902-368-4400, Fax: 902-368-4416,ilmacdonald@gov.pe.ca
Private Secretary, Brenda Kelly
902-368-4400, Fax: 902-368-4416,bmkelly@gov.pe.ca

Executive Council

Shaw Bldg., 5th Fl., PO Box 2000, Charlottetown, PE C1A 7N8
902-368-4502, Fax: 902-368-6118,
www.gov.pe.ca/ec

Premier; President, Executive Council; Minister Responsible, Intergovernmental Affairs; Leader, Liberal Party of PEI,Hon. Robert W.J. Ghiz
902-368-4400, Fax: 902-368-4416,rwjghiz@gov.pe.ca
Deputy Premier; Minister, Agriculture, Hon. George T. Webster
902-368-4820, Fax: 902-368-4846,gtwebster@gov.pe.ca
Minister, Transportation & Infrastructure Renewal, Hon. Ron W. MacKinley
902-368-5120, Fax: 902-368-5385,rwmackinley@gov.pe.ca
Minister, Environment, Energy & Forestry, Hon. Richard Brown
902-368-6410, Fax: 902-368-6488,rebrown@gov.pe.ca

Minister, Health and Wellness; Aboriginal Affairs, Hon. Carolyn I. Bertram
902-368-5250, Fax: 902-368-4121,cibertram@gov.pe.ca
Minister, Innovation & Advanced Learning, Hon. Allan V. Campbell
902-368-4230, Fax: 902-368-4242,avcampbell@gov.pe.ca
Minister, Education & Early Childhood Development; Attorney General, Hon. Doug W. Currie
902-438-4876, Fax: 902-438-4150,dwcurrie@edu.pe.ca
Minister, Fisheries, Aquaculture & Rural Development, Hon. Neil J. LeClair
902-620-3646, Fax: 902-368-5542,njleclair@gov.pe.ca
Minister, Finance & Municipal Affairs, Hon. Wesley J. Sheridan
902-368-4050, Fax: 902-368-6575,wjsheridan@gov.pe.ca
Minister, Community Services, Seniors & Labour, Hon. Janice Sherry
902-368-4930, Fax: 902-368-4974,jasherry@gov.pe.ca
Minister, Tourism & Culture, Hon. Robert Vassey
902-368-4801, Fax: 902-368-5277,rsvessey@gov.pe.ca

Executive Council Office
Shaw Bldg., 5th Fl. Centre, PO Box 2000, Charlottetown, PE C1A 7N8
902-368-4502, Fax: 902-368-6118
The Executive Council Office advises the Executive Council, & provides administrative services. The Office is made up of the Intergovernmental Affairs & the Acadian & Francophone Affairs divisions. Research, analysis, & advice are given on intergovernmental affairs & social & economic policies. The Office also supports the Minister Responsible for Acadian & Francophone Affairs.
Premier; President, Executive Council; Minister Responsible, Intergovernmental Affairs; Leader, Liberal Party of PEI,Hon. Robert W.J. Ghiz
902-368-4400, Fax: 902-386-4416,rwjghiz@gov.pe.ca
Clerk of the Executive Council & Secretary to Cabinet, Allan Rankin
902-368-4300, Fax: 902-368-6118,arrankin@gov.pe.ca
Senior Policy Advisor, Matt McGuire
902-368-4400, Fax: 902-368-4416,mdmcguire@gov.pe.ca
Policy Advisor, Legislative Planning & Communications, Geoff Townsend
902-368-4313, gatownsend@gov.pe.ca
Administrative Officer, Karen Cheverie
902-368-4300, Fax: 902-368-6118,kacheverie@gov.pe.ca
Records Secretary, Rose Long
902-368-4301, Fax: 902-368-6118,rmlong@gov.pe.ca

Acadian & Francophone Affairs
PO Box 58, Wellington, PE C0B 2E0
902-854-7250, Fax: 902-854-7255
To increase the Provincial Government's capacity to provide French services to the Acadian & Francophone communities, the Division offers advice on plannning & implementating measures. Acadian & Francophone Affairs also supports departments & agencies on related issues.
Minister, Communities, Cultural Affairs & Labour,Hon. Carolyn I. Bertram
902-368-5250, Fax: 902-368-4121,cibertram@gov.pe.ca
Director, Acadian & Francophone Affairs, Donald DesRoches
902-368-4872, Fax: 902-368-4224
Officer, Communications & Planning, Dominique Chouinard
902-368-4828, Fax: 902-368-4224
Advisor, Interdepartmental French Language Services, Ricky Hitchcock
902-569-7592, Fax: 902-368-4224

Intergovernmental Affairs
Shaw Bldg., 5th Fl. Centre, PO Box 2000, Charlottetown, PE C1A 7N8
902-368-4502, Fax: 902-368-6118
Ensuring that Prince Edward Island's interests are represented in regional & national policy discussions is the role of Intergovernmental Affairs. It is involved in the following programs: Canadian Intergovernmental Conference Secretariat; Council of Atlantic Premiers; Council of the Federation; & Working Together for Atlantic Canada.
Premier; President, Executive Council; Minister Responsible, Intergovernmental Affairs; Leader, Liberal Party of PEI,Hon. Robert W.J. Ghiz
902-368-4400, Fax: 902-368-4416,rwjghiz@gov.pe.ca
Deputy Minister, Intergovernmental Affairs, Sandy Stewart
swstewart@gov.pe.ca
Deputy Minister, Strategic Initiatives, Rory Beck
902-620-3799, rbeck@gov.pe.ca
Director, Intergovernmental Affairs, Rochelle Gallant
902-368-4415, ragallant@gov.pe.ca

Committees of the Executive Council
Chair, Alberta Innovates - Technology Futures, Ron Triffo
President & CEO, Alberta Innovates - Technology Futures,Dr. Gary Albach
techfutures@albertainnovates.ca
Facilities Manager, Alberta Research Council, Property Management - Edmonton South, Rick Kostyshen
780-450-5008, Fax: 780-461-2921,rick.kostyshen@gov.ab.ca

Legislative Review Committee
Shaw Bldg., 5th Fl. Centre, PO Box 2000, Charlottetown, PE C1A 7N8
902-368-4305, Fax: 902-368-6118
The Committee has the following responsibilities: coordination of the legislative development process for reviewing & analyzing all proposed legislation; review & analysis of regulations or amendments before they are submitted for approval to Executive Council.
Chair, Robert Vessey
902-368-4330, Fax: 902-368-4348,rsvessey@gov.pe.ca,
Vice-Chair,Hon. Neil J. LeClair
902-620-3646, Fax: 902-368-5542,njleclair@gov.pe.ca
Committee Secretary & Clerk of the Executive Council, Allan Rankin
902-368-4300, Fax: 902-368-6118,arrankin@gov.pe.ca
Committee Secretary, Legal, Shawn Flynn
902-368-5284, Fax: 902-368-5176,sbflynn@gov.pe.ca

Strategic Planning Committee
Shaw Bldg., 5th Fl. Centre, PO Box 2000, Charlottetown, PE C1A 7N8
902-368-4502, Fax: 902-368-6118,
www.gov.pe.ca/ec/stratplan/index.php3
Chair,Hon. George T. Webster
902-368-4820, Fax: 902-368-4846,gtwebster@gov.pe.ca
Vice-Chair,Hon. Carolyn I. Bertram
902-368-5250, Fax: 902-368-4121,cibertram@gov.pe.ca
Committee Secretary & Clerk of the Executive Council, Allan Rankin
902-368-4300, Fax: 902-368-6118,arrankin@gov.pe.ca
Coordinator, Corporate Policy, Christine MacKinnon
902-368-4605, Fax: 902-368-6118,cgmackinnon@gov.pe.ca

Legislative Assembly

c/o Clerk's Office, Province House, Richmond St., PO Box 2000, Charlottetown, PE C1A 7K7
902-368-5970, Fax: 902-368-5175,
www.assembly.pe.ca/index.php3?number=1012313
The Clerk has the following responsibilities: to ensure the implementation of the expressed wills of the Speaker & the Standing Committee on Legislative Management; to guarantee the availability of support services for Members; to be certain records of the House are maintained; & to ensure that independent advice about House proceedings are received by the Speaker & Members.
Clerk of the Legislative Assembly, Charles H. MacKay
902-368-5970, Fax: 902-368-5175,chmackay@gov.pe.ca
Speaker of the Legislative Assembly, Kathleen Casey
902-368-4310, Fax: 902-368-4473,kmcasey@gov.pe.ca
Deputy Speaker, Paula Biggar
902-368-4330, Fax: 902-368-4348,pjbiggar@gov.pe.ca
Sergeant-at-Arms & Director, Security, Al J. McDonald
902-368-5976, Fax: 902-368-5175,ajmcdonald@gov.pe.ca
Auditor General, Colin P. Younker
902-368-4520, Fax: 902-368-4598,cpyounker@gov.pe.ca
Editor, Hansard, Jeff Bursey
902-368-5371, Fax: 902-368-5175,jrbursey@gov.pe.ca
Provincial Librarian, Provincial Librarian, Kathleen Eaton
902-961-7316, Fax: 902-961-7322,keeaton@gov.pe.ca
Commissioner, Information & Privacy, M. Rebecca Wellner
902-368-4099, Fax: 902-368-5947,rmwellner@gov.pe.ca
Commissioner, Conflict of Interest, Neil Robinson
902-566-8992, Fax: 902-566-8793
Clerk Assistant & Clerk of Committees, Marian Johnston
902-368-5972, Fax: 902-368-5175,majohnston@gov.pe.ca

Government Members' Office (Liberal)
Coles Bldg., 175 Richmond St., 2nd Fl., PO Box 2890, Charlottetown, PE C1A 8C5
902-368-4330, Fax: 902-368-4348
Premier; President, Executive Council; Minister Responsible, Intergovernmental Affairs; Leader, Liberal Party of PEI,Hon. Robert W.J. Ghiz
902-368-4400, Fax: 902-368-4416,rwjghiz@gov.pe.ca
Government House Leader, Robert Vessey
rvessey@gov.pe.ca
Office Manager, Hazel Gallant
hggallant@gov.pe.ca
Researcher, Kathy Paugh
kjpaugh@gov.pe.ca
Special Assistant, Lori A. Richard
larichard@gov.pe.ca

Office of the Official Opposition (Progressive Conservative)
Coles Bldg., 175 Richmond St., 3rd Fl., PO Box 338, Charlottetown, PE C1A 7K7
902-368-4360, Fax: 902-368-4377,
www.assembly.pe.ca/index.php3?number=1025010&lang=E
Leader of the Official Opposition,Hon. Olive Crane
902-368-4360, Fax: 902-368-4377,omcrane@gov.pe.ca
Opposition House Leader, Jim Bagnall
902-368-4360, Fax: 902-368-4377,jdbagnall@gov.pe.ca
Director, Research & Policy, Mary McQuaid
902-368-4363, mcmcquaid@gov.pe.ca

Sixty-third General Assembly - Prince Edward Island

Province House, 165 Richmond St., 1st Fl., PO Box 2000, Charlottetown, PE C1A 7N8
902-368-5970, Fax: 902-368-5175, 877-315-5518
www.assembly.pe.ca
Last General Election: May 28, 2007. Legal Duration: 5 Years. Party Standings (October 2008): Progressive Conservative 3; Liberal 24; Total 27. Salaries, Indemnities & Allowances (April 2008): MLA's salary $63,750. In addition to this basic salary for each Member of the Legislative Assembly are the following additional salaries: Premier $69,360 (total $133,110); Ministers $44,574 (total $108,324); Speaker $37,536 (total $101,286); Deputy Speaker $18,768 (total $82,518); Leader of the Opposition $44,574 (total $101,324); Government House Leader $12,036 (total $75,786); Opposition House Leader $4,233 (total $67,983); Government & Opposition Whip $3,570 (total $67,320); Non-Ministerial Members of Executive Council Committees $5,850 (total $69,600); Leader of a Third Party $16,355 (total $80,105). The following is a list of Members of the Legislative Assembly, with their district number & name, the number of electors in their district, party affiliation, & contact information. The Charlottetown address for all MLAs is as follows: PO Box 2000, Charlottetown PE, C1A 7N8.
Hon. Jim Bagnall, District #3 - Montague - Kilmuir PE, PC
902-368-4360, Fax: 902-368-4377,jdbagnall@gov.pe.ca
Hon. Carolyn Bertram, District #18 - Rustico - Emerald PE, Liberal
902-368-5250, Fax: 902-368-4121,cibertram@gov.pe.ca
Paula Biggar, District #23 - Tyne Valley - Linkletter PE, Liberal
902-368-4330, Fax: 902-368-4348,pjbiggar@gov.pe.ca
Hon. Richard Brown, District #12 - Charlottetown - Victoria Park PE, Liberal
902-368-6410, Fax: 902-368-6488,rebrown@gov.pe.ca
Hon. Allan V. Campbell, District #1 - Souris - Elmira PE, Liberal
902-368-4230, Fax: 902-368-4242,avcampbell@gov.pe.ca
Hon. Kathleen Casey, District #14 - Charlottetown - LewisPoint PE, Liberal
902-368-4310, Fax: 902-368-4473,kmcasey@gov.pe.ca
Hon. Olive Crane, District #7 - Morell - Mermaid PE, PC
902-368-4360, Fax: 902-368-4377,omcrane@gov.pe.ca
Hon. Doug W. Currie, District #11 - Charlottetown - Parkdale PE, Liberal
902-368-5152, Fax: 902-368-4910,dwcurrie@gov.pe.ca
Michael F. Currie, District #2 - Georgetown - St. Peters PE, PC
902-368-4360, Fax: 902-368-4377,mfcurrie@gov.pe.ca
Hon. Valerie E. Docherty, District #17 - Kellys Cross - Cumberland PE, Liberal
902-368-4330, Fax: 902-368-4348,vedocherty@gov.pe.ca
Bush Dumville, District #15 - West Royalty - Springvale PE, Liberal
902-368-4330, Fax: 902-368-4348,sfdumville@gob.pe.ca
Cynthia Dunsford, District #6 - Stratford - Kinlock PE, Liberal
902-368-4330, Fax: 902-368-4348,cldunsford@gov.pe.ca
Sonny Gallant, District #24 - Evangeline - Miscoucheh PE, Liberal
902-368-4330, Fax: 902-368-4348,sjgallant@gov.pe.ca
Hon. Robert W.J. Ghiz, District #13 - Charlottetown - Brighton PE, Liberal
902-368-4400, Fax: 902-386-4416,rwjghiz@gov.pe.ca
Hon. Gerard Greenan, District #22 - Summerside - St. Eleanors PE, Liberal
902-368-4610, Fax: 902-368-4699,glgreenan@gov.pe.ca
Robert Henderson, District #25 - O'Leary - Inverness PE, Liberal
902-368-4330, Fax: 902-368-4348,rlhenderson@gov.pe.ca,
Hon. Neil J. LeClair, District #27 - Tignish - Palmer Road PE, Liberal
902-620-3646, Fax: 902-368-5542,njleclair@gov.pe.ca
Hon. Ron MacKinley, District #16 - Cornwall - Meadowbank PE, Liberal
902-368-5120, Fax: 902-368-5385,rmmackinley@gov.pe.ca
Charles McGeoghegan, District #4 - Belfast - Murray River PE, Liberal
902-368-4330, Fax:
902-368-4348,cemcgeoghegan@gov.pe.ca
Alan McIsaac, District #5 - Vernon River - Stratford PE, Liberal
902-368-4330, Fax: 902-368-4348,jamcisaac@gov.pe.ca
Robert Mitchell, District #10 - Charlottetown - Sherwood PE, Liberal
902-368-4330, Fax: 902-368-4348,rjmitchell@gov.pe.ca
Pat Murphy, District #26 - Alberton - Roseville PE, Liberal
902-368-4330, Fax: 902-368-4348,pwmurphy@gov.pe.ca
Hon. Wesley J. Sheridan, District #20 - Kensington - Malpeque PE, Liberal
902-368-4050, Fax: 902-368-6575,wjsheridan@gov.pe.ca

Hon. Janice Sherry, District #21 - Summerside - Wilmot PE, Liberal
902-368-4930, Fax: 902-368-4974,jasherry@gov.pe.ca
Hon. Robert Vessey, District #9 - York - Oyster Bed PE, Liberal
902-368-4801, Fax: 902-368-5277,rsvessey@gov.pe.ca
Buck Watts, District #8 - Tracadie - Hillsborough Park PE, Liberal
902-368-4330, Fax: 902-368-4348,fdwatts@gov.pe.ca
Hon. George T. Webster, District #19 - Borden - Kinkora PE, Liberal
902-368-4820, Fax: 902-368-4846,gtwebster@gov.pe.ca

Prince Edward Island Government Departments & Agencies

Department of Agriculture

Jones Bldg., 11 Kent St., PO Box 2000, Charlottetown, PE C1A 7N8
902-368-4880, Fax: 902-368-4857,
www.gov.pe.ca/af/agweb/index.php3

Other Communication: Pest Information Line:|902/368-5658
Promotes the sustainable growth & development of Prince Edward Island's primary industries & improvement of the quality of products, co-administering projects demonstrating practical, cost-effective soil conservation practices, operates a potato composting program, instituted a pest information hotline to provide information of environmental significance.Financial & technical assistance is being offered to farmers & owners of agricultural & wood land to implement practices to protect the quality of the Island's soil, water & forest resources & to reduce the risk & use of pesticides. Projects include manure storage, structural soil erosion control, strip cropping, fuel & pesticide storage, deadstock composting, milkhouse waste storage, developing nutrient management plans & planting trees.Details are also being finalized for a forestry component, which would provide financial & technical assistance to woodlot owners in preparing forest management plans & carry out work identified in the plans.

Acts Administered:
Agricultural Crop Rotation Act
Agricultural Insurance Act
Agricultural Products Standards Act
Agrologists Act
Animal Health & Protection Act
Artificial Insemination Act
Companion Animal Protection Act
Dairy Industry Act
Dairy Producers Act
Dog Act
Environmental Protection Act (in part)
Farm Machinery Dealers & Vendors Act
Farm Practices Act
Fences & Detention of Stray Livestock Act
Fire Prevention Act
Fish Inspection Act
Fisheries Act
Gasoline Tax Act
Grain Elevators Corporation Act
Livestock Community Auction Sales Act
Natural Products Marketing Act
Occupational Health & Safety Act
Planning Act
Plant Health Act
Poultry & Poultry Products Act
Real Property Assessment Act
Real Property Tax Act
Revenue Tax Axt
Veterinary Profession Act
Weed Control Act
Women's Institute Act

Minister,Hon. George T. Webster
902-368-4880, Fax: 902-368-4846,gtwebster@gov.pe.ca
Deputy Minister, Brian Douglas
902-368-4830, Fax: 902-368-4846,bwdouglas@gov.pe.ca
Director, Corporate & Financial Services, Jerry Gavin
902-368-5741, Fax: 902-368-4857,jpgavin@gov.pe.ca
Communications Officer, Communications Section, Wayne S. MacKinnon
902-368-4888, Fax: 902-368-4857,wemackinnon@gov.pe.ca

• Agricultural Insurance Corporation
29 Indigo Cres.
PO Box 1600
Charlottetown, PE C1A 7N3
902-368-4842 Fax: 902-368-6677
peiaic@gov.pe.ca
www.gov.pe.ca/af/agweb/index.php3?number=1000214
In Prince Edward Island, production insurance is administered by the Prince Edward Island Agricultural Insurance Corporation. The province delivers the Production Insurance Program by sharing costs with the federal government through the Canada-Prince Edward Island Agricultural Policy Framework Agreement on Agricultural Business Risk Management.

• Grain Elevators Corporation(PEIGEC)
PO Box 250
Kensington, PE C0B 1M0
902-836-8929
www.peigec.com
The Prince Edward Island Grain Elevators Corporation will, in accordance with its mandate continue to play a leadership role in the cereal and protein sector of Prince Edward Island.

• Aquaculture & Fisheries Research Initiative Inc.
902-368-5790 Fax: 902-368-5542
Established to provide industry associations, private businesses, public institutions &/or individual fishers & aquaculturists with increased access to applied & developmental research to address priorities & opportunities in the industry.

Agriculture Policy & Regulatory Division
Works in partnership with general agriculture & agrifood organizations, provincial commodity organizations & education institutions in the development & implementation of industry led strategies that address short & long term critical issues & create wealth for the agri-food sector.
Director, Robert Morrison
902-368-5087, Fax: 902-368-4857,wrmorrison@gov.pe.ca
Acting Manager, Farm Practices Review Board, Michael Delaney
902-836-8929
Manager, Legislative & Regulatory Section,Vacant
Manager, Plant Health Regulatory Program, Brian Craig
902-368-4044

Agriculture Resource Division
Research Station, University Avenue, PO Box 1600, Charlottetown, PE C1A 7N3
902-368-5600, Fax: 902-368-5661
Director, Brian Douglas
902-368-5645
Manager, Agriculture & Agri-Food Development, Shane Murphy
902-368-5611
Manager, Laboratory, Tracey Wood
902-368-4190
Acting Manager, Sustainable Agriculture Resources, Ron DeHaan
902-368-5642, Fax: 902-368-5661
Lab Supervisor, Soil & Feed Testing Laboratory, Lori C. Connolly
902-368-6294, Fax: 902-368-6299,hhcairns@gov.pe.ca

District Agricultural Offices:

Charlottetown
Research Station, 440 University Ave., Charlottetown, PE C1A 4N6
902-368-5600, Fax: 902-368-5661, 800-236-5214
Agriculture Innovation Manager, Linda MacSwain
902-368-4815, Fax: 902-368-5729,lemacswain@gov.pe.ca

Montague/Souris
Access PEI Montague, PO Box 1500, Montague, PE C0A 1R0
902-838-0600, Fax: 902-838-0610,
ACCESSPEIMONTAGUE@gov.pe.ca

Summerside
Access PEI Summerside, PO Box 2063, Summerside, PE C1N 5L2
902-888-8000, Fax: 902-888-8306,
accesspeisummerside@gov.pe.ca

West Prince
Access PEI O'Leary, West Prince Regional Services Centre, PO Box 8, O'Leary, PE C0B 1V0
902-859-8800, Fax: 902-859-8709,
accesspeioleary@gov.pe.ca

PEI Public Archives & Records Office

PO Box 1000, Charlottetown, PE C1A 7M4
902-368-4290, Fax: 902-368-6327,
archives@gov.pe.ca
www.gov.pe.ca/cca/index.php3?number=1004626&lang=E
Provincial Archivist, Jill MacMicken-Wilson
902-368-4351, Fax: 902-368-6327,jswilson@gov.pe.ca

Office of the Attorney General

Shaw Building, North, 105 Rochford St., 4th Fl., PO Box 2000, Charlottetown, PE C1A 7N8
902-368-5152, Fax: 902-368-4910,
www.gov.pe.ca/attorneygeneral
The Attorney General is also responsible for the Coroners Office.

Acts Administered:
Affidavits Act
Age of Majority Act
Ancient Burial Grounds Act
Appeals Act
Apportionment Act
Arbitration Act
Auctioneers Act
Bailable Proceedings Act
Business Practices Act
Canada-United Kingdom Judgements Recognition Act
Canadian Judgements (Enforcement) Act
Cemeteries Act
Charities Act
Child Status Act
Collection Agencies Act
Commorientes Act
Companies Act
Condominium Act
Consumer Protection Act
Consumer Reporting Act
Contributory Negligence Act
Controverted Elections (Provincial) Act
Cooperative Associations Act
Coroners Act
Correctional Services Act
Court Security Act
Credit Unions Act
Crown Proceedings Act
Custody Jurisdiction & Enforcement Act
Defamation Act
Dependents of a Deceased Person Relief Act
Designation of Beneficiaries under Benefit Plans Act
Direct Sellers Act
Electronic Commerce Act
Electronic Evidence Act
Escheats Act, (jointly with Dept. of Transportation & Public Works)
Evidence Act
Factors Act
Family Law Act
Fatal Accidents Act
Films Act
Foreign Resident Corporations Act
Frauds on Creditors Act
Freedom of Information & Protection of Privacy Act
Frustrated Contracts Act
Garage Keepers' Lien Act
Garnishee Act
Gulf Trust Corporations Act
Habeas Corpus Act
Human Rights Act
Insurance Act
Intercountry Adoption (Hague Convention) Act
Interjurisdictional Support Orders Act
International Commercial Arbitration Act
International Sale of Goods Act
International Trusts Act
Interpretation Act
Investigation of Titles Act
Judgement & Execution Act
Judicial Review Act
Jury Act
Landlord & Tenant Act
Legal Profession Act
Licencing Act
Limited Partnerships Act
Maintenance Enforcement Act
Mechanics' Lien Act
Occupiers' Liability Act
Partnership Act
Perpetuities Act
Personal Property Security Act
Police Act
Powers of Attorney Act
Prearranged Funeral Services Act
Premium Tax Act
Private Investigators & Security Guards Act
Probate Act
Probation Act
Provincial Administrator of Estates Act
Provincial Court Act
Public Accounting & Auditing Act
Public Trustee Act
Quieting Titles Act
Real Estate Trading Act
Real Property Act
Reciprocal Enforcement of Judgements Act
Reciprocal Enforcement of Maintenance Orders Act
Retail Business Holidays Act
Sale of Goods Act
Securities Act
Sheriffs Act
Statute of Frauds
Statute of Limitations
Store Hours Act

Summary Proceedings Act
Supreme Court Act
Supreme Court Reporters Act
Survival of Actions Act
Transboundary Pollution (Reciprocal Access) Act
Trespass to Property Act
Truck Operators' Remuneration Act
Trust & Fiduciary Companies Act
Trustee Act
Unclaimed Articles Act
Unconscionable Transactions Relief Act
Uniformity Commissioners Act
Variation of Trusts Act
Vendors & Purchasers Act
Victims of Crime Act
Victims of Family Violence Act
Volunteers Liability Act
Warehousemen's Liens Act
Winding Up Act
Youth Employment Act
Youth Justice Act

Attorney General,Hon. Gerard Greenan
902-368-5152, Fax: 902-368-4910,glgreenan@edu.pe.ca
Deputy Attorney General, Edison J. Shea
902-368-5152, Fax: 902-368-4910,ejshea@gov.pe.ca
Director, Justice Policy, Ellie Reddin
902-368-6619, Fax: 902-368-5335,eereddin@gov.pe.ca
Director, Policy & Administration, Kevin Barnes
902-368-4865, Fax: 902-368-4224,kcbarnes@gov.pe.ca

Community & Correctional Services
902-432-2847, Fax: 902-432-2851
Director, John Picketts
902-432-2850, Fax: 902-432-2851,jrpicketts@gov.pe.ca
Provincial Manager, Community Services, Alan St. Paquet
902-432-2849, aspaquet@gov.pe.ca
Provincial Manager, Correctional Programs, Donna Myers
902-838-0611, Fax: 902-838-0616
Provincial Manager, Victim Services, Susan Maynard
902-368-4584, Fax: 902-368-4514

Consumer, Corporate & Insurance Division
Shaw Building, 95 Rochford St., 4th Fl., PO Box 2000, Charlottetown, PE C1A 7N8
902-368-4580, Fax: 902-368-5283, 800-658-1799
mww.gov.pe.ca/attorneygeneral/index.php3?number=1002799&lang=E

The Consumer Affairs section is responsible for administering Orderly Payment of Debts (OPD), lottery schemes, gun control & film classification, & for handling consumer complaints & inquiries. The Corporations section is responsible for registering business names, incorporating companies, cooperatives & credit unions, & licensing out-of-province companies, brokers, security sales people & securities sold to the public. The insurance, real estate & public trustee section operates under the supervision of the Superintendent of Insurance & is responsible for real estate licenses, insurance legislation, insurance complaints, & collecting premium & fire prevention taxes.

Director, Edison Shea, FCA
902-368-4551, ejshea@gov.pe.ca
Public Trustee, Mark Gallant
902-368-4552
Manager, Consumer Affairs,Vacant
Chief Firearms Officer, Consumer Affairs, Vivian Haywood
902-368-4585, Fax: 902-368-9189
Superintendent, Insurance, Robert Bradley
902-368-6478, rabradley@gov.pe.ca

Securities Office
Registrar, Edison Shea, FCA
902-368-4551
Deputy Registrar, Mark Gallant
902-368-4552

Crown Attorneys Division
Director, Cyndria L. Wedge
902-368-5073, Fax: 902-368-5812

Legal & Judicial Services
Director, Barrie L. Grandy, Q.C.
902-368-4554, Fax: 902-368-4563
Manager, Legal Aid, Kent Brown
902-368-6015, Fax: 902-368-6122,wkbrown@gov.pe.ca
Manager, Family Law Section, Loretta Coady MacAulay
Officer, Maintenance Enforcement, Deborah Conway
902-368-6010, Fax: 902-368-0266,djconway@gov.pe.ca
Legislative Counsel & Law Clerk, Shawn B. Flynn
902-368-5284, Fax: 902-368-5176,

Office of the Auditor General

Shaw Bldg., 105 Rochford St, 2nd Fl., PO Box 2000, Charlottetown, PE C1A 7N8
902-368-4520, Fax: 902-368-4598

Conducting independent audits & examinations with objective information, the Office of the Auditor General advises & assures the Legislative Assembly.

Auditor General, Colin P. Younker, CA
902-368-4520, Fax: 902-368-4598,cpyounker@gov.pe.ca
Audit Director, Allan Moore
902-368-4518, anmoore@gov.pe.ca
Audit Director, Jane MacAdam, CA
902-368-4524, bjmacadam@gov.pe.ca

Department of Communities, Cultural Affairs & Labour

Shaw Bldg., 95 Rochford St., 4th Fl., PO Box 2000, Charlottetown, PE C1A 7N8
902-368-5250, Fax: 902-368-4121,
www.gov.pe.ca/cca

The role of this department is to strengthen the communities by preserving the foundations of social development and public safety while setting new directions that encourage Islanders to maintain and enhance the province's unique physical and cultural characteristics.

Acts Administered:
Amusement Devices Act
Archaeological Sites Protection Act
Archives & Records Act
Blind Workers' Compensation Act
Boilers & Pressure Vessels Act
Charlottetown Area Municipalities Act
City of Summerside Act
Electrical Inspection Act
Elevators & Lifts Act
Emergency 911 Act
Emergency Measures Act
Employment Standards Act
Fathers of Confederation Buildings Act
Fire Prevention Act
Heritage Places Protection Act
Labour Act
Lands Protection Act, PEI
Lightning Rod Act
Lucy Maud Montgomery Foundation Act
Municipal Boundaries Act
Municipal Debenture Guarantee Act
Municipalities Act
Museum Act
North American Labour Cooperation Agreement Implementation Act
Pay Equity Act
P.E.I. Firefighters Long Service Medal Act
Planning Act
Power Engineers Act
Provincial Building Code Act
Public Libraries Act
Rural Community Fire Companies Act

Minister,Hon. Carolyn Bertram
902-368-5250, Fax: 902-368-4121,cibertram@gov.pe.ca
Deputy Minister, Tracey Cutcliffe
902-368-5290, Fax: 902-368-4121,tdcutcliffe@gov.pe.ca
Admin. Assistant, Gayle Roberts
902-368-5250, Fax: 902-368-4121,gfroberts@gov.pe.ca

• Employment Standards Board
161 St. Peters Rd.
PO Box 2000
Charlottetown, PE C1A 7N8
902-368-5550 Fax: 902-368-5476
www.gov.pe.ca/commcul/lair-info/index.php3
The primary role of the Employment Standards Board is to hear appeal presentations from employers who have a complaint filed against them for alleged violations of the Employment Standards Act and also to make recommendations to the Lieutenant Governor in Council with regard to changes in the Minimum Wage Order.

• Labour Relations Board
PO Box 2000
Charlottetown, PE C1A 7N8
902-368-5550 Fax: 902-368-5476
www.gov.pe.ca/commcul/lair-info/index.php3
The Labour Relations Board provides a quasi-judicial process to resolve applications that either management or labour may bring before it. The board attempts to provide a speedy resolution for all matters while at the same time trying to provide for and maintain harmonious labour relations in the province.

• PEI Museum & Heritage Foundation
2 Kent St.
PO Box 2000
Charlottetown, PE C1A 1M6
902-368-6600 Fax: 902-368-6608
mhpei@gov.pe.ca
www.peimuseum.com
The PEI Museum and Heritage Foundation is an integral part of the Island's community. Museum and Heritage Prince Edward Island operates the seven provincial museums and heritage sites in Prince Edward Island, providing Islanders and visitors alike with an opportunity to discover our Island heritage and culture. The PEI Museum and Heritage Foundation is a Schedule B Provincial Crown Corporation governed by the Museum Act. It is a registered charitable corporation whose purpose is "to study, collect, preserve, interpret, and protect the human and natural heritage of Prince Edward Island for the use, benefit and enjoyment of the people of the province."

• Prince Edward Island Emergency Measures Organization

Culture, Heritage & Libraries
Fax: 902-368-4663
Director, Harry Holman
902-368-4784, hthoIman@gov.pe.ca
Manager, Sport & Recreation, John Morrison
902-894-0283, jwmorris@gov.pe.ca
Provincial Librarian, Allan J. Groen
902-961-7316, Fax: 902-961-7322,ajgroen@gov.pe.ca
Acting Manager, John Chisholm
902-368-4744

Planning & Inspection Services
902-368-5490, Fax: 902-368-5526
Provides an integrated delivery of various Acts & regulations pertinent to land use planning for sustainable provincial growth as well as building & development control standards & central delivery of programs in the areas of fire prevention.
Director, Albert MacDonald
902-368-5582, afmacdonald@gov.pe.ca
Chief Fire Marshal, Office of the Fire Marshal, David Blacquiere
902-368-4869, djblacquiere@gov.pe.ca
Chief Officer, Boiler & Pressure Vessel, Plumbing & Propane Inspection, Ken Hynes
902-368-5567, ckhynes@gov.pe.ca
Chief Officer, Building & Development Services, Don Walters
902-368-4874, dewalters@gov.pe.ca
Manager, Administration & Customer Services, Marjorie Ramsay
902-368-5490, mrramsay@gov.pe.ca

Policy & Administration
902-368-4865, Fax: 902-368-5335
Director, Kevin Barnes
902-368-4865, Fax: 902-368-5335,kcbarnes@gov.pe.ca
Manager, Finance & Administration, Barry Gosby
902-368-4897, bbgosby@gov.pe.ca
Manager, Information Technology, Murray Brownell
902-368-4233, Fax: 902-368-5335,jmbrownell@gov.pe.ca
Manager, Gerry MacDonald
902-368-4884
Manager, Jack Saunders

Department of Education & Early Childhood Development

Sullivan Bldg., 16 Fitzroy St., 2nd Fl., PO Box 2000, Charlottetown, PE C1A 7N8
902-368-4600, Fax: 902-368-4663,
www.gov.pe.ca/educ

Prince Edward Island's Department of Education & Early Childhood Development works with individuals, communities, & its partners to ensure equitable opportunities for learning. The Department also strives to ensure quality learning experiences & healthy child development for young children from birth to age eight.

Acts Administered:
Child Care Facilities Act
Island Regulatory & Appeals Commission Act
School Act
Teachers' Superannuation Act

Minister, Education & Early Childhood Development; Attorney General, Hon. L. Gerard Greenan
902-368-4610, Fax: 902-368-4699,glgreenan@edu.pe.ca
Deputy Minister, Education & Early Childhood Development, Shauna Sullivan Curley, Q.C.
902-368-4662, Fax: 902-368-4699,sscurley@edu.pe.ca
Communications Officer, Jean Doherty
902-368-6449, Fax: 902-368-4663,jmdoherty@edu.pe.ca

Administration & Corporate Services
Sullivan Bldg., 16 Fitzroy St., 2nd Fl., PO Box 2000, Charlottetown, PE C1A 7N8
902-368-4620, Fax: 902-368-4663
The Administration & Corporate Services Branch oversees the following services: Finance & school board operations; Policy, planning, evaluation, & assessment; Research; Technology in learning; & Human resources.
Director, Finance & School Board Operations, John Cummings
902-368-4456
Manager, Human Resources, Yvette Blanchard
902-368-4672
Manager, Program Evaluation & Student Assessment, Cindy Wood
902-368-4084

Manager, Research & Corporate Services, Robin Phillips
902-620-3045
Registrar & Coordinator, International Education, Debbie Pineau
902-368-5556, Fax: 902-368-6144
Coordinator, Education Technology, Guy Albert
902-368-4681, Fax: 902-368-4622

Public Education
Sullivan Bldg,, 16 Fitzroy St., Charlottetown, PE C1A 7N8
902-368-4690, Fax: 902-368-4663
The Public Education Branch is responsible for the following services: English & French programs; Student support services; & Kindergarten.
Senior Director, Public Education, Linda Lowther
902-368-4282
Director, English Programs & School Development, Frank Hennessey
902-894-0262, Fax: 902-368-6144
Director, French Programs, Imelda Arsenault
902-368-4477, Fax: 902-368-4622
Director, Student Support Services, Glenn Edison
902-620-3486, Fax: 902-368-4622
Administrator, Provincial Kindergarten Program, Carolyn Simpson
902-569-7526, Fax: 902-368-4622

Elections Prince Edward Island

J. Angus MacLean Bldg., 94 Great George St., PO Box 774, Charlottetown, PE C1A 7L3
902-368-5895, Fax: 902-368-6500, www.electionspei.ca
The principal mandate of Elections PEI is to inform and enable all qualified electors and candidates to exercise their democratic right and ensure their constitutional entitlement in elections as entrenched in the Canadian Charter of Rights and Freedoms.
Chief Electoral Officer, Lowell Croken
902-368-5898, Fax: 902-368-6500,ljcroken@gov.pe.ca
Deputy Chief Electoral Officer, Norma E. Palmer-Bowers
902-368-5895
Elections Officer, Norma E. Palmer

Prince Edward Island Emergency Measures Organization

National Bank Tower, #600, 134 Kent St., PO Box 2000, Charlottetown, PE C1A 7N8
902-894-0385, Fax: 902-368-6362, www.gov.pe.ca/cca/index.php3?number=1002518
Prepares, approves & implements plans, programs, or procedures that are intended to mitigate the effects of an emergency or disaster; provides for the safety, health or welfare of the civil population & the protection of property & the environment in the event of such an occurrence. Conducts public information programs relating to the prevention & mitigation of damage due to disasters, & conducts training exercises for the effective implementation of emergency plans; procures emergency equipment & goods; coordinates emergency preparedness with federal authorities.
Emergency Measures Officer, Cindy MacDougall
902-368-6325, Fax: 902-368-6362,cdmacdougall@gov.pe.ca
Emergency Measures Officer, Barry Folland
902-368-6629, bffolland@gov.pe.ca

Department of Environment, Energy & Forestry

Jones Bldg., 11 Kent St., 4th & 5th Fl., PO Box 2000, Charlottetown, PE C1A 7N8
902-368-5000, Fax: 902-368-5830, www.gov.pe.ca/enveng/index.php3
Ensures the quality of the Island's natural environment for the benefit of all residents; encourages Islanders to become stewards of natural resources in order to sustain the resources for the future. Operates & maintains the Bunbury/Stratford Pollution Control Commission, Charlottetown Area Pollution Control Commission, Summerside Area Water Commission & Natural Areas Advisory Committee. Joint enforcement of fish & wildlife regulations with Fisheries & Oceans Canada & the Canadian Wildlife Service.
Acts Administered:
Agriculture Crop Rotation Act
Automobile Junk Yards Act
Energy Corporation Act
Environmental Protection Act
Fish Inspection Act (related)
Fisheries Act (related)
Forest Management Act
Mineral Resources Act
Natural Areas Protection Act
Oil & Natural Gas Act
Pesticides Control Act
Public Forest Council Act
Renewable Energy Act
Unsightly Property Act
Wildlife Conservation Act
Minister,Hon. Richard Brown
902-368-6410, Fax: 902-368-6488,rebrown@gov.pe.ca
Deputy Minister, John MacQuarrie
902-368-5340, Fax: 902-368-6488,jamacquarrie@gov.pe.ca
Director, Administrative Services, Mary Kinsman
902-368-5032, Fax: 902-368-5830,makinsman@gov.pe.ca
Director, Energy & Minerals, Wayne MacQuarrie
902-894-0289, Fax: 902-894-0290,dwmacquarrie@gov.pe.ca
Head, Investigation & Enforcement, John Clements
902-368-4808, Fax: 902-368-5830,jkclements@gov.pe.ca
Communications Officer, Kim Devine
902-368-5286, Fax: 902-368-5830,kmdevine@gov.pe.ca
• Public Forest Council
Forestry Division
PO Box 2000
Charlottetown, PE C1A 7N8
Fax: 902-368-4713
publicforest@gov.pe.ca
The main purpose of the Public Forest Council is to stimulate & foster public discussions on the wealth creation potential of Provincial Woodlands primarily in the areas of non-consumptive & non-traditional uses of the forest resource.
• PEI Energy Corporation
Jones Bldg.
11 Kent St., 4th Fl.
PO Box 2000
Charlottetown, PE C1A 7N8
902-894-0288 Fax: 902-368-0290
www.gov.pe.ca/enveng/pec-info/index.php3
Responsible for pursuing & promoting the development of energy systems & the generation, production, transmission & distribution of energy, in all its forms, on an economic & efficient basis.
• Environmental Advisory Council
11 Kent St.
PO Box 2000
Charlottetown, PE C1A 7N8
Advises the Minister of Environment on environmental issues of concern.
Energy Officer, Mike Proud
902-368-5019, mpproud@gov.pe.ca

Pollution Prevention Division
Administers a wide range of programs, legislation & activities which are designed to protect the environment in the province.These include: air quality, protection of the ozone layer, management of hazardous wastes, litter, beverage containers, petroleum storage tanks, used oil, tires, lead-acid batteries, derelict vehicles, excavation pits, unsightly properties, & special projects.
Director, Don Jardine
902-368-5035, dejardine@gov.pe.ca
Climate Change Coordinator, Erin Swansburg
902-368-6111, Fax: 902-894-0290

Water Management Division
902-368-5028, Fax: 902-368-5830, 866-368-5044
Responsible for sustainable management, protection & enhancement of the Province's drinking water, groundwater, inland surface water & coastal estuaries; regulates water & sewer infrastructure & assists in the administration of funding that supports this infrastructure; division provides water testing services (microbiological & chemical) & engineering advisory services to the general public, other provincial departments & agencies, industry & municipalities; also responsible for conducting baseline monitoring & assessment of the Province's water resources.
Director, Jim Young, P.Eng.
902-368-5034, jyyoung@gov.pe.ca
Manager, Drinking Water Management Section, George Somers
902-368-5046, ghsomers@gov.pe.ca
Manager, Watershed Management Section, Bruce Raymond
902-368-5054, bgraymond@gov.pe.ca

Department of Fisheries, Aquaculture & Rural Development

Jones Bldg., 11 Kent St., 5th Fl., PO Box 2000, Charlottetown, PE C1A 7N8
902-368-6330, Fax: 902-368-5542, www.gov.pe.ca/fa/faweb
This Department provides an advocacy role in the area of marine fisheries management and supports development of the marine fishery and the aquaculture sector. It also provides support to the processing sector, professional and technical services and fish inspection services.
Minister,Hon. Neil J. LeClair
902-620-3646, Fax: 902-368-5542,njleclair@gov.pe.ca
Deputy Minister, Richard Gallant
902-620-3675, Fax: 902-368-5542,rkgallant@gov.pe.ca

Aquaculture
Jones Bldg., 11 Kent St., 5th Fl., Charlottetown, PE C1A 7N8
902-368-5524, Fax: 902-368-5542
The Aquaculture Division delivers the following services: Advice & information to the provinces's aquaculture industry; Financial programs to assist in aquaculture development; & Biological & technical services to the shellfish & finfish sectors on the Island.
Director, Aquaculture, Neil MacNair
902-368-5615
Aquaculture Biologist, Kim Gill
902-368-5252

Community Development
PO Box 2000, Charlottetown, PE C1A 7N8
902-368-4467, www.gov.pe.ca/communitydevelopment/index.php3
Prince Edward Island has been divided into six regions. Each region is represented by a Community Development Officer. The Officer helps communities in each region identify their needs, & encourages residents to assist community growth & prosperity.
Chief, Community Development Bureau, Bill Buell
902-368-6360
Community Development Officer, West Prince Region, Brenda Profit
902-859-8839, Fax: 902-859-8709,bfprofit@gov.pe.ca
Community Development Officer, Evangeline Region, Marcel Bernard
902-854-7250, Fax: 902-854-7255,mjbernard@gov.pe.ca
Community Development Officer, East Prince Region, Kellie Mulligan
902-432-2705, Fax: 902-432-2634,kamulligan@gov.pe.ca
Community Development Officer, Central Queens Region, Nancy Murphy
902-894-0347, Fax: 902-368-4224,nkmurphy@gov.pe.ca
Community Development Officer, Eastern Kings Region, Chris Blaisdale
902-687-7083, Fax: 902-687-7091,cwblaisdell@gov.pe.ca
Community Development Officer, Southern Kings & Queens, Stephen Lewis
902-838-0618, Fax: 902-838-0610,sjlewis@gov.pe.ca

Marine Fisheries & Seafood Services
Jones Bldg., 11 Kent St. 5th Fl., Charlottetown, PE C1A 7N8
902-368-5251, Fax: 902-368-5542
The Marine Fisheries & Seafood Services Division is engaged in the following activities: Advocating for Prince Edward Island's fishing industry; Offering programs to support new technology, & value-added processing of seafood;Supporting development of emerging species; & Undertaking biological research in support of major fish species.
Director, Marine Fisheries & Seafood Services, Barry MacPhee
902-569-7710, Fax: 902-368-5542,jbmacphee@gov.pe.ca
Manager, Seafood Services, Lloyd Murphy
902-368-5259, lgmurphy@gov.pe.ca
Officer, Program Statistics, Parnell Trainor
902-368-5248, patrainor@gov.pe.ca
Manager, Marine Fisheries, Dave MacEwen
902-368-5244, dgmacewen@gov.pe.ca
Lobster Biologist, Robert MacMillan
902-368-5593, rjmacmillan@gov.pe.ca

Single Window Service
105 Rochford St., PO Box 2000, Charlottetown, PE C1A 7N8
902-368-4136, Fax: 902-368-4224, www.gov.pe.ca/accesspei/index.php3
Programs & services include government service centres, known as Access PEI. At the eight Access PEI centres across Prince Edward Island, citizens obtain information about the Provincial Government & its programs & services. The Access PEI Centres are situated in the following places: Tignish (902-882-7351); Alberton (902-853-8622); O'Leary (902-859-8800); Wellington (902-854-7250); Summerside (902-888-8000); Charlottetown (902-368-5200); Montague (902-838-0600); & Souris (902-687-7000). Bilingual services are available at all locations, except Montague & Souris.
Director, Single Window Service, Carol A. Mayne
902-368-4264, Fax: 902-368-5542
Manager, Access PEI Summerside & Access PEI Wellington, Amand Arsenault
902-888-8001, Fax: 902-888-8306,accesspeisummerside@gov.pe.ca; accesspeiwellington@gov.pe.ca, Other Communications: Access PEI Wellington Address: 48 Mill Rd.
Manager, Access PEI Souris & Access PEI Montague, Eleanor Avery
902-687-7050, Fax: 902-687-7091,accesspeisouris@gov.pe.ca; accesspeimontague@gov.pe.ca, Other Communications: Access PEI Montague Address: 41 Wood Islands Hill
Manager, Access PEI O'Leary, Access PEI Tignish, & Access PEI Alberton, Martha Dawson
902-859-8801, Fax: 902-859-8709,accesspeioleary@gov.pe.ca;

accesspeitignish@gov.pe.ca, Other Communications: Access PEI Alberton Email accesspeialberton@gov.pe.ca
Manager, Access PEI Charlottetown, Mary Lynn Arsenault
902-368-6847, Fax:
902-569-7560,accesspeicharlottetown@gov.pe.ca, Other Communications: Access PEI Charlottetown Phone:
902-368-5200

Department of Health

Jones Bldg., 11 Kent St., 2nd Fl., PO Box 2000, Charlottetown, PE C1A 7N8
902-368-4900, Fax: 902-368-4974,
www.gov.pe.ca/health/index.php3

Provides public health services, primary care, acute care, community hospital and continuing care services to Islanders to help ensure their optimal health.

Acts Administered:
Adoption Act
Adult Protection Act
Change of Name Act
Chiropractic Act
Community Care Facilities & Nursing Homes Act
Consent to Treatment & Health Care Directives Act
Dental Profession Act
Dental Technicians Association Act
Dietitians Act
Dispensing Opticians Act
Donation of Food Act
Drug Cost Assistance Act
Family & Child Services Act
Funeral Directors & Embalmers Association Act
Health & Community Services Act
Health Services Payment Act
Hospital & Diagnostic Services Insurance Act
Hospitals Act
Housing Corporation Act
Human Tissue Donation Act
Licensed Practical Nurses Act
Marriage Act
Medical Act
Mental Health Act
Nurses Act
Occupational Therapists Act
Optometry Act
Pharmacy Act
Physiotherapy Act
Premarital Health Examination Act
Provincial Health Number Act
Psychologists Act
Public Health Act
Rehabilitation of Disabled Persons Act
Smoke-Free Places Act
Social Work Act
Tobacco Sales to Minors Act
Vital Statistics Act
Welfare Assistance Act
White Cane Act

Minister,Hon. Doug W. Currie
902-368-4930, Fax: 902-368-4974,dwcurrie@gov.pe.ca
Deputy Minister, Keith Dewar
902-368-4935, Fax: 902-368-4974,kdewar@gov.pe.ca
Director, Community Hospitals & Continuing Care, Cecil Villard
902-894-0337, Fax: 902-894-0363,cfvillard@gov.pe.ca
Acting Director, Corporate Services, Glen Doyle
902-368-6142, Fax: 902-368-4969,grdoyle@gov.pe.ca
Director, Finance, Terry Keefe
902-368-6125, Fax: 902-368-6136,tekeefe@gov.pe.ca
Director, Medical Programs, Dr. Richard Wedge
902-368-6261, Fax: 902-620-3072,rhwedge@gov.pe.ca
Director, Primary Care, Leanne Sayle
902-368-6157, Fax: 902-368-6136,ilsayle@gov.pe.ca
Chief Health Officer,Dr. Heather G. Morrison
902-368-4996, Fax: 902-620-3354,hgmorrison@gov.pe.ca

Department of Innovation & Advanced Learning

Shaw Bldg., 105 Rochford St., 5th Fl., PO Box 2000, Charlottetown, PE C1A 7N8
902-368-4240, Fax: 902-368-4242,
www.gov.pe.ca/ial/index.php3

Acts Administered:
Apprenticeship & Trades Qualification Act
Area Industrial Commission Act
Business Development Inc. Act, P.E.I.
Employment Development Agency Act
Hairdressers Act
Holland College Act
Island Investment Development Act
Lending Agency Act
Liquor Control Act
Maritime Economic Cooperation Act
Maritime Provinces Higher Education Commission Act
Prince Edward Island Science & Technology Corporation Act
Private Training Schools Act
University Act

Minister,Hon. Allan V. Campbell
902-368-4230, Fax: 902-368-4242,avcampbell@gov.pe.ca
Deputy Minister,Dr. Michael Mayne
902-368-4250, Fax: 902-368-4242,mbmayne@gov.pe.ca
Director, Communications, Kim Devine
902-620-3774, Fax: 902-368-4242,kmdevine@gov.pe.ca

• Employment Development Agency
Sullivan Bldg., 1st Fl.
PO Box 2000
Charlottetown, PE C1A 7N8
902-368-5805 Fax: 902-368-5909
In Prince Edward Island, the Employment Development Agency strives to provide employment opportunities & training incentives.

• Food Technology Centre(FTC)
101 Belvedere Ave.
PO Box 2000
Charlottetown, PE C1A 7N8
902-368-5548 Fax: 902-368-5549 877-368-5548
ftcweb@gov.pe.ca
www.gov.pe.ca/ftc
The Food Technology Centre provides technical support to the food processing industry. It is an ISO 9001:2000 registered company.

• Island Investment Development Inc.(IIDI)
94 Euston St., 2nd Fl.
Charlottetown, PE C1A 1W4
902-894-0351 Fax: 902-368-5886
The goal of the Island Investment Development Inc. is the encouragement & facilitation of immigration of experienced business persons. Through the Federal Government's Immigrant Investor Program, the crown corporation administers the Prince Edward Island Century 2000 Fund & the Island Funds.

• Prince Edward Island Business Development Inc.
94 Euston St., 1st & 2nd Fl.
PO Box 910
Charlottetown, PE C1A 7L9
902-368-6300 Fax: 902-368-6301 800-563-3734
business@gov.pe.ca
www.peibusinessdevelopment.com
Prince Edward Island Business Development leads business development efforts in the province. Information is provided about investment opportunities, business services, finances, trade & marketing, & government services.

• Prince Edward Island Lending Agency
Confederation Court Office Tower
#201, 134 Kent St.
PO Box 1420
Charlottetown, PE C1A 7N1
902-368-6200 Fax: 902-368-6201
Assistance is provided by the Lending Agency to new & growing businesses. Loans are available for organizations with export potential in the following industries: agriculture, fisheries & aquaculture, tourism, manufacturing & processing, information technology, & small business.

• Technology PEI Inc.
94 Euston St., 2nd Fl.
PO Box 340
Charlottetown, PE C1A 7K7
902-368-6300 Fax: 902-368-6301
techpei@gov.pe.ca
www.techpei.com
The Agency works to create an economic development environment which is supportive of information technology companies, & to ensure effective use of information technology.

Community & Labour Development

Shaw Bldg., 105 Rochford St., 5th Fl., PO Box 2000, Charlottetown, PE C1A 7N8
902-368-4244, Fax: 902-368-4242

Working with economic development partners, the Community & Labour Development Division facilitates development of the rural areas of the provincial economy.
Director, Community & Labour Development, Birt MacKinnon
902-368-4244, bwmackinnon@gov.pe.ca
Manager, Federal Provincial Relations, Mary Hunter
902-620-3488, mehunter@gov.pe.ca

Finance & Administration

105 Rochford St., Charlottetown, PE C1A 7N8
902-368-5878, Fax: 902-368-7087

Responsibilities include financial management, administration, the Prince Edward Island Business Development Inc., & human resource management.
Chief Financial Officer, Reagh Hicken
902-368-5875
Manager, Human Resources, Leah Eldershaw
902-368-5876

Higher Education

Sullivan Bldg., 16 Fitzroy St., 3rd Fl., Charlottetown, PE C1A 7N8
902-368-4615, Fax: 902-368-6144

Acting Director, Higher Education & Corporate Services, Susan A. MacKenzie
samackenzie@edu.pe.ca
Manager, Student Financial Services, Susan Graham
902-368-4603
Manager, Literacy Initiatives Secretariat; GED Chief Examiner & Chief Administrator, Barbara MacNutt
902-368-6286
Manager, Apprenticeship, Karen Redmond
902-368-4625

Population Secretariat

94 Euston St., PO Box 910, Charlottetown, PE C1A 7L9
902-368-6300, Fax: 902-368-6255,
Populationsecretariat@gov.pe.ca
www.gov.pe.ca/popsec

The Population Secretariat promotes Prince Edward Island as a welcoming place to live. The Secretariat works to attract immigrants & former Islanders, & to retain youth & immigrants.
Director, Jane Mallard
902-569-7556, jmallard@gov.pe.ca
Settlement & Retention Officer, Kate Flanagan
902-368-5018, kgflanagan@gov.pe.ca
Recruitment Officer, Carson Birch
902-368-4861, cfbirch@gov.pe.ca
Policy & Repatriation Officer, Erin Docherty
902-368-5127, ecdocherty@gov.pe.ca

Prince Edward Island Human Rights Commission

53 Water St., PO Box 2000, Charlottetown, PE C1A 7N8
902-368-4180, Fax: 902-368-4236, 800-237-5031
lbuell@peihumanrights.ca
www.peihumanrights.ca

The Prince Edward Island Human Rights Commission administers and enforces the Prince Edward Island Human Rights Act. The Act establishes a complaint process under which the Commission has the authority to receive, investigate, attempt to settle and make rulings on complaints. The Commission also develops programs of public information and education about human rights through seminars, publications, responses to general inquiries and a resource centre. The Commission also advises the government on human rights issues.

Chair, Richard Montigny
902-368-4180, Fax: 902-368-4236
Commissioner, Anne Nicholson
Commissioner, Maurice H.J. Rio
Commissioner, John Rogers
Commissioner, Ann Sherman
Commissioner, Lou Ann Thomson
Executive Director, David Larter
Fax: 902-368-4134,dlarter@peihumanrights.ca
Human Rights Officer, Maria E. McQuaid
mmcquaid@peihumanrights.ca
Administrative/Intake Officer, B. Lorraine Buell
902-368-4180, Fax:
902-368-4236,lbuell@peihumanrights.ca

Prince Edward Island Liquor Control Commission

3 Garfield St., PO Box 967, Charlottetown, PE C1A 7M4
902-368-5710, Fax: 902-368-5735,
www.peilcc.ca

The Prince Edward Island Liquor Control Commission (PEILCC) is a crown corporation responsible for the administration of the PEI Liquor Control Act and Regulations, along with the purchase, control, and sale of all beverage alcohol in the province.

Chair, Gordon Coles
CEO, Brooke MacMillan
902-368-5720, jbmacmillan@gov.pe.ca,
Director, Finance, Wendy L. MacDonald
902-368-5718, wlmacdonald@gov.pe.ca
Director, Licensing & Security, James C. MacLeod
902-368-5714, jcmacleod@gov.pe.ca
Director, Marketing, Fred MacDonald
902-368-5715, fjmacdonald@gov.pe.ca
Acting Director, Purchasing & Distribution, David Stewart
902-368-5721, dlstewart@gov.pe.ca
Admin. Assistant, Pam Campbell
902-368-5720, Fax: 902-368-5735,pjcampbell@gov.pe.ca

Prince Edward Island Public Service Commission

Shaw Bldg., 105 Rochford St., 1st Fl., PO Box 2000, Charlottetown, PE C1A 7N8
902-368-4080, Fax: 902-368-4383,
www.gov.pe.ca/pt/psc-info

To maintain a professional & independent civil service, to foster the development of a public service that is representative of the province's diversity; to provide the public with a service which is responsive & flexible to their needs; to foster a constructive working relationship among the Government, its employees & their representatives.

Acts Administered:

Civil Service Act

Civil Service Superannuation Act

CEO, Jim Ferguson
902-368-4207, Fax: 902-368-4383,jhferguson@gov.pe.ca

Director, Corporate Services, Classification & Employee Relations, Allan O'Keefe
902-368-4188, Fax: 902-368-4383,awokeefe@gov.pe.ca

Director, Staffing & Human Resources Planning, Susan MacLeod
902-368-6900, Fax: 902-368-4383,sfmacleod@gov.pe.ca

Admin. Assistant, Judy Morrison
902-368-4207, jmmorrison@gov.pe.ca

Island Regulatory & Appeals Commission

National Bank Tower, #501, 134 Kent St., PO Box 577, Charlottetown, PE C1A 7L1

902-892-3501, Fax: 902-566-4076, 800-501-6268
irac@irac.pe.ca
www.irac.pe.ca

The Commission is an independent tribunal that hears appeals on issues relating to land use, property & revenue (sales) tax & unsightly premises. It administers land ownership legislation in Prince Edward Island & regulates the petroleum industry & automobile insurance rates. The Commission also regulates electric utilities & certain water & wastewater utilities in Prince Edward Island & hears & considers appeals from decisions or orders of the Director of Residential Rental Property (Rentalsman).

Acts Administered:

Insurance Act

Electric Power Act

Petroleum Products Act

Rental of Residential Property Act

Water & Sewerage Act

Chair & CEO, Maurice (Moe) Rodgerson
902-892-3501, Fax: 902-566-4076,mrodgerson@irac.pe.ca

Vice-Chair, Brian J. McKenna
bmckenna@irac.pe.ca

Director, Rental Division, Cathy Flanagan
cflanagan@irac.pe.ca

Director, Technical & Regulatory Services Division, Donald G. Sutherland
dgsutherland@irac.pe.ca

Director, Corporate Services Division, Eileen Callaghan
mecallaghan@irac.pe.ca

Commission Administrator, Susan D. Jefferson
sdjefferson@irac.pe.ca

Department of Social Services & Seniors

Jones Bldg., 11 Kent St., 2nd Fl., PO Box 2000, Charlottetown, PE C1A 7N8

902-620-3777, Fax: 902-894-0242,
www.gov.pe.ca/sss/index.php3

Responsible for pharmacy & dental programs, child & family services, social programs, seniors issues.

Minister,Hon. Doug W. Currie
902-368-4930, Fax: 902-368-4974,dwcurrie@gov.pe.ca

Deputy Minister, Sharon Cameron
902-368-6520, Fax: 902-368-4740,secameron@gov.pe.ca

Director, Child & Family Services, Rona M. Brown
902-368-5396, Fax: 902-368-4258,rmbrown@gov.pe.ca

Director, Corporate & Finance Services, W. Lorne Clow
902-368-6109, Fax: 902-894-0242,wlclow@gov.pe.ca

Director, Pharmacy & Dental Services, Faye M. Martin
902-569-0545, Fax: 902-894-0242,fmmartin@gov.pe.ca

Acting Director, Social Programs & Seniors, Bob D. Creed
902-368-6446, Fax: 902-368-6443,bdcreed@ihis.org

Department of Tourism

PO Box 2000, Charlottetown, PE C1A 7N8

800-463-4734
www.tourismpei.com/index.php3

The Tourism PEI mandate is to promote continued growth in the tourism sector; aggressively market PEI as a premier destination; proactively facilitate product and plant development; aggressively promote special events; provide continued emphasis on customer service; manage provincial infrastructure projects (i.e. golf courses and parks); and facilitate community development through tourism.

Acts Administered:

Highway Signage Act

National Park Act

Recreation Development Act

Tourism Industry Act

Tourism PEI Act

Trails Act

Minister,Hon. Valerie E. Docherty
902-368-4801, Fax: 902-368-5277,vedocherty@gov.pe.ca

Deputy Minister, Melissa MacEachern
902-368-5956, Fax:
902-368-5277,mamaceachern@gov.pe.ca

Director, Policy, Planning & Research, Chris K. Jones
902-368-6342, Fax: 902-368-6155,ckjones@gov.pe.ca

Administrative Assistant, Janice Walters
902-368-4801, Fax: 902-368-5277,jwalters@gov.pe.ca

• Advisory Council on the Status of Women
Sherwood Business Centre
161 St. Peter's Rd.
PO Box 2000
Charlottetown, PE C1A 7N8
902-368-4510 Fax: 902-368-4516
peistatusofwomen@eastlink.ca
www.gov.pe.ca/acsw

The advisory agency consists of nine members who are appointed by government. Issues addressed by the Council include equality & support for women's participation in the social, cultural, economic, legal, & political spheres.

Tourism Development

The Tourism Development Branch is responsible for delivering programs to assist the Island's travel industry, including the development of new tourism products. The Branch co-ordinates the development of major events & infrastructure through the Province. It has both an operational & a developmental role. It manages provincial parks & through Golf Links PEI, provincial golf courses.

Director, Ron MacNeill
902-368-5505, Fax: 902-368-4438,rnmacnei@gov.pe.ca

Manager, Provincial Parks, Shane Arbing
902-368-4404, Fax: 902-368-5922,sdarbing@gov.pe.ca

Supervisor, Visitor Services, Heather Pollard
902-368-4441, Fax: 902-368-4438,hlpollard@gov.pe.ca

Tourism Marketing

Fax: 902-368-4438

Director, Greg Arsenault
902-368-5513, gjarsenault@gov.pe.ca

Manager, Advertising & Publicity, Carol Horne
902-368-6332, cahorne@gov.pe.ca

Manager, Trade & Sales, Robert Ferguson
902-368-5522, rnfergus@gov.pe.ca

Fulfillment Coordinator, Harold McGuigan
902-368-4452, hjmcguig@gov.pe.ca

Department of Transportation & Public Works

Jones Bldg., 11 Kent St., PO Box 2000, Charlottetown, PE C1A 7N8

902-368-5100, Fax: 902-368-5395,
www.gov.pe.ca/tpwpei

Responsible for provincial coordination of the transportation of dangerous goods; holding discussions with the Environmental Advisory Council aimed at introducing environmental protection guidelines during construction & maintenance activities.

Acts Administered:

Architects Act

Crown Building Corporation Act

Dangerous Goods (Transportation) Act

Engineering Profession Act

Expropriation Act

Highway Traffic Act

Judgement Recovery (PEI) Ltd., An Act to Incorporate

Land Survey Act

Off Highway Vehicle Act

Public Works Act

Roads Act

Minister,Hon. Ron W. MacKinley
902-368-5120, Fax: 902-368-5385,rwmackinley@gov.pe.ca

Deputy Minister, Steve MacLean, P. Eng
902-368-5130, Fax: 902-368-5385,scmaclean@gov.pe.ca

Director, Finance, Human Resources & Operations, Bob S. Clow
902-368-5126, Fax: 902-368-5395,bsclow@gov.pe.ca

Director, Highway Maintenance, Alan Maynard, P.Eng
902-368-5103, Fax: 902-368-6244,aemaynard@gov.pe.ca

Director, Highway Safety, John B. MacDonald
902-368-5225, Fax: 902-368-5236,jbmacdonald@gov.pe.ca

Communications Officer, Andrew Sprague
902-368-5112, Fax: 902-368-5385,asgsprague@gov.pe.ca

• Island Waste Management Corporation(IWMC)
110 Watts Ave.
Charlottetown, PE C1E 2C1
902-894-0330 Fax: 902-894-0331 888-280-8111
reception@iwmc.pe.ca; info@iwmc.pe.ca
www.iwmc.pe.ca

Management, administration, & provision of solid waste management services throughout Prince Edward Island is the role of the Island Waste Management Corporation. The Crown Agency operates or oversees the following facilities: the Central Compost Facility, the East Prince Waste Management Facility, the Energy from Waste Facility, & the Waste Watch Drop-Off Centers.

Capital Projects Division

902-368-5180

The Capital Projects Division is responsible for the design & construction of Government's highway & building infrastructure. The Division consists of four sections: Highway Construction, Planning & Design, Engineering Services & Materials Lab.

Acting Chief Engineer & Director, Stephen J. Yeo, P.Eng.
902-368-5105, Fax: 902-368-5425,sjyeo@gov.pe.ca

Manager, Materials Testing, Terry Kelly
902-696-7979

Engineer, East Region, Matt Collins
902-368-5183

Engineer, Western Region, Stephen Yeo
902-368-5182

Engineer, Central Region, Alan Aitken
902-368-5006

Land & Environment

The Land & Environment Division provides a wide range of environmental services for both public works & transportation related projects. The Division also oversees highway construction & maintenance activities to ensure compliance with Federal & Provincial environmental legislation & regulations. Division staff develop & provide training to staff & the construction industry on policies, programs & guidelines to be followed on highway construction & maintenance projects. This division is also responsible for provincial lands.

Director, Brian Thompson, P.Eng.
902-368-5185, Fax: 902-368-5395,bfthompson@gov.pe.ca

Public Works & Planning Division

The Public Works & Planning Division is responsible for assessment & analysis of long term transportation requirements within the Province, combined with the planning & implementation of major projects required to meet the initiatives of various government departments, agencies & corporations. In addition, the Division is responsible for the planning, design & construction associated with building construction projects, including major repair & renovation, for Department building facilities required by Department clients. This division is also responsible for building maintenance & accommodations.

Director, Foster P. Millar
902-368-5147, jfmillar@gov.pe.ca

Department of the Provincial Treasury

Shaw Bldg., 95 Rochford St., 2nd Fl. South, PO Box 2000, Charlottetown, PE C1A 7N8

902-368-4050, Fax: 902-368-6575,
www.gov.pe.ca/pt/index.php3

The Department of the Provincial Treasury facilitates the effective & efficient management of government's human & financial resources. The Office of the Comptroller administers the Corporate Procurement Service.

Acts Administered:

Appropriation Act

Civil Service Act

Civil Service Superannuation Act

Deposit Receipt (Winding up) Act

Environment Tax Act

Financial Administration Act

Financial Corporation Capital Tax Act

Gasoline Tax Act

Health Tax Act

Income Tax Act

Lending Agency Act

Loan Act

Lotteries Commission Act

Maritime Province Harness Racing Commission Act

Northumberland Strait Crossing Act

Public Purchasing Act

Public Sector Pay Reduction Act

Queen's Printer Act

Real Property Assessment Act

Real Property Tax Act

Registry Act

Revenue Administration Act

Revenue Tax Act

Supplementary Appropriation Act

Provincial Treasurer,Hon. Wesley J. Sheridan
902-368-4050, Fax: 902-368-6575,wjsheridan@gov.pe.ca

Deputy Provincial Treasurer, Paul R. Jelley
902-368-4053, Fax: 902-368-6575,prjelley@gov.pe.ca

Communications Officer, Jennifer MacDonald-Donovan
902-620-3679, Fax:
902-368-6575,jwmacdonald@gov.pe.ca

• Prince Edward Island Lotteries Commission
Office of the Deputy Provincial Treasurer
95 Rochford St.
PO Box 2000
Charlottetown, PE C1A 7N8
902-368-4053 Fax: 902-368-6575
• Prince Edward Island Public Service Commission

Office of the Comptroller
902-368-4020, Fax: 902-368-6661
Comptroller, Scott K. Stevens
902-368-4001, Fax: 902-368-6661,ksstevens@gov.pe.ca
Manager, Procurement, Ian K. Burge
902-368-4041, Fax: 902-368-5171,ikburge@gov.pe.ca

Fiscal Management
902-368-5802, Fax: 902-368-4077,
Other Communication: Investments: 902/368-4167; Fax: 902/368-4077
Director, Doug Clow
dmclow@gov.pe.ca

Information Technology Shared Services
902-368-4100, Fax: 902-368-5444
Acting Director, Information Systems Delivery, Carol A. Mayne
902-368-4126, Fax: 902-368-5444,camayne@gov.pe.ca
Manager, IT Operations, Edmund Malone
902-368-4111, Fax: 902-368-4716,emmalone@gov.pe.ca

Program Evaluation & Fiscal Relations
902-368-4178, Fax: 902-569-7632
Director, Rick Adams
radams@gov.pe.ca

Prince Edward Island Workers Compensation Board

14 Weymouth St., PO Box 757, Charlottetown, PE C1A 7L7
902-368-5680, Fax: 902-368-5705, 800-237-5049
www.wcb.pe.ca

Other Communication: Customer Liaison Service: 866-460-3074
WCB exists to promote safe workplaces & to protect employers & injured workers through a sustainable accident insurance program.
Acts Administered:
Occupational Health & Safety Act
Workers Compensation Act
Chair, Nancy Guptill
902-368-5688, Fax: 902-368-6359
CEO, Carol Anne Duffy
902-368-5688, caduffy@wcb.pe.ca
Director, Client Services, Mary Hughes Power
902-368-5687, Fax: 902-368-5705,mhpower@wcb.pe.ca
Director, Corporate Services, Tammy Turner
902-368-4102, teturner@wcb.pe.ca
Director, Occupational Health & Safety Council, George Stewart
902-368-5562, Fax: 902-368-5696,gwstewart@wcb.pe.ca
Officer, Communications, Mark Barrett
902-894-0362, Fax: 902-620-3885,mabarretta@wcb.pe.ca
Manager, Employer Services, Greg MacCallum
902-368-5679, ggmaccallum@wcb.pe.ca
Finance Officer, Annette Johnson
902-368-5708, aljohnson@wcb.pe.ca
Manager, Information Technology Services, Darren MacDonald
902-368-5669, Fax: 902-368-5696,dpmacdonald@wcb.pe.ca

Gouvernement du Québec / Government of Québec

Siege du gouvernement:Hôtel du Parlement, 1045, rue des Parlementaires, Québec, QC G1A 1A4
418-643-7239, Fax: 418-646-4271, 866-337-8837
www.gouv.qc.ca; www.asnat.qc.ca
La Province de Québec est entrée dans la Confédération le 1ère juillet, 1867.Terre: 1,356,366.78 km2. Population: 7,866,108 (2010)

Cabinet du Lieutenant-gouverneur / Office of the Lieutenant Governor

Édifice André-Laurendeau, 1050, rue des Parlementaires R.C., Québec, QC G1A 1A1
418-643-5385, Fax: 418-644-4677, 866-791-0766
www.lieutenant-gouverneur.qc.ca
Rôles constitutionnels et cérémoniels: le lieutenant-gouverneur a des pouvoirs constitutionnels d'un chef d'État et est le fonctionnaire exécutif en chef de la province; il/elle donne une suite légale à la politique déterminée par le gouvernement en ce qui concerne la nomination du premier ministre, et les membres du Conseil exécutif, la convocation, la prorogation et la dissolution de l'Assemblée nationale, la ratification des décrets du gouvernement, et la nomination des juges des cours de la province; il/elle occupe le plus haut rang protocolaire du Québec et il/elle a préséance sur tous les membres de la famille royale, à l'exception de Sa Majesté qu'il/elle représente
Lieutenant-gouverneur,L'hon. Pierre Duschesne
Administrateur, Paul-Arthur Gendreau
418-649-3431, pagendreau@judex.qc.ca

Cabinet du premier ministre / Office of the Premier

Édifice Honoré-Mercier, 835, boul René-Lévesque est, 3e étage, Québec, QC G1A 1B4
418-643-5321, Fax: 418-643-3924,
www.premier-ministre.gouv.qc.ca
Premier ministre/Premier,L'hon. Jean J. Charest
Secrétaire général/Secretary General, Gérard Bibeau
418-643-7355
Attaché de presse, Hugo D'Amours
418-643-5321, communications-pm@mce.gouv.qc.ca

Ministère du Conseil exécutif / Executive Council

875, Grande Allée est, Québec, QC G1R 4Y8
418-646-3021, Fax: 418-528-9242,
www.mce.gouv.qc.ca
Premier ministre &, Ministre responsable des dossiers jeunesse, L'hon. Jean J. Charest
418-643-5321, Fax: 418-643-3924
Vice-première ministre & Ministre, Ressources naturelles et de la Faune; Ministre responsable du Plan Nord, L'hon. Nathalie Normandeau
418-643-7295, Fax: 418-643-4318,ministre@mrnf.gouv.qc.ca
Ministre des Relations internationales;, Ministre responsable de la Francophonie, L'hon. Monique Gagnon-Tremblay
418-649-2319, Fax: 418-643-4804,cabinet@mri.gouv.qc.ca
Ministre, Justice; Ministre responsable de la Réforme des institutions démcratiques; Ministre responsable de l'Accès à l'information, L'hon. Jean-Marc Fournier
jfournier@assnat.qc.ca
Ministre, Éducation, Loisir et Sport, L'hon. Line Beauchamp
418-644-0664, Fax: 418-646-7551,ministre@mels.gouv.qc.ca
Présidente, Conseil du trésor; Ministre respsonable de l'Administration gouvernementale; Ministre des Services gouvernementaux, L'hon. Michelle Courchesne
418-643-5926, Fax: 418-643-7824,cabinet@sct.gouv.qc.ca
Ministre, Agriculture, Pêcheries & Alimentation; Ministre resp. Affaires intergouvernementales canadiennes & Francophonie canadienne, VACANTE
418-380-2525, Fax:
418-380-2184,ministre.mapaq@mapaq.gouv.qc.ca
Ministre, Finances; Ministre du Revenu, L'hon. Raymond Bachand
418-643-5270, Fax:
418-646-1574,ministre@finances.gouv.qc.ca
Ministre, Santé et Services Sociaux, L'hon. Dr Yves Bolduc
418-266-7171, Fax: 418-266-7197,ministre@msss.gouv.qc.ca
Ministre, Emploi et Solidarité sociale, L'hon. Julie Boulet
418-643-4810, Fax:
418-643-2802,ministre@mess.gouv.qc.ca
Ministre, Transports, L'hon. Sam Hamad
418-643-6980, Fax: 418-643-2011,ministre@mtq.gouv.qc.ca
Ministre, Affaires municipales, Régions & Occupation du territoire, L'hon. Laurent Lessard
418-691-2050, Fax:
418-643-1795,ministre@mamrot.gouv.qc.ca
Ministre, Développement économique, Innovation & Exportation, L'hon. Clément Gignac
418-691-5650, Fax:
418-643-8553,ministre@mdeie.gouv.qc.ca
Ministre, Sécurité publique; Leader parlementaire adjoint du gouvernment, L'hon. Robert Dutil
418-643-2112, Fax: 418-646-6168,ministre@msp.gouv.qc.ca
Ministre, Développement durable, Environnement et Parcs, L'hon. Pierre Arcand
418-521-3911, Fax: 418-643-4143
Ministre, Culture, Communications et Condition féminine, L'hon. Christine St-Pierre
418-380-2310, Fax:
418-380-2311,ministre@mcccf.gouv.qc.ca
Ministre, Famille et Aînés, L'hon. Yolande James
418-643-2181, Fax:
418-643-2640,ministre.famille@mfa.gouv.qc.ca
Ministre, Immigration et Communautés culturelles, L'hon. Kathleen Weil
418-644-2128, Fax: 418-528-0829
Ministre, Travail, L'hon. Lise Thériault
418-643-5297, Fax:
418-644-0003,ministre@travail.gouv.qc.ca
Ministre, Tourisme, L'hon. Nicole Ménard
418-528-8063, Fax:
418-528-8066,ministre@tourisme.gouv.qc.ca
Ministre responsable des, Aînés, L'hon. Marguerite Blais
418-646-7757, Fax: 418-646-7769,m.blais@aines.gouv.qc.ca
Ministre responsable des, Affaires autochtones, L'hon. Pierre Corbeil
418-646-9131, Fax:
418-646-9487,pieere.corbeil@mce.gouv.qc.ca
Ministre délégué aux, Transports, L'hon. Norman MacMillan
418-643-6980, Fax:
418-643-2033,ministredelegue@mtq.gouv.qc.ca
Ministre déléguée aux, Services sociaux, L'hon. Dominique Vien
418-266-7181, Fax:
418-266-7199,ministre.deleguee@msss.gouv.qc.ca
Ministre délégué aux, Ressources naturelles & Faune, L'hon. Serge Simard
418-643-7295, Fax:
418-643-4318,ministredelegue@mrnf.gouv.qc.ca
Whip en chef,L'hon. Pierre Moreau
418-643-6018, Fax:
418-643-5462,pierre.moreau@assnat.qc.ca
Président du, Caucus du gouvernement, L'hon. Lawrence S. Bergman
418-528-1960, Fax:
418-643-0183,lbergman-dmg@assnat.qc.ca

Cabinet du Conseil exécutif / Cabinet Office
Édifice Honoré-Mercier, #2.12A, 835, boul René-Lévesque est, Québec, QC G1A 1B4
418-643-7355, Fax: 418-528-9552
Secrétaire général, Gérard Bibeau
gerard.bibeau@mce.gouv.qc.ca

Comités ministériels / Cabinet Committees
Secrétariat général, Édifice Honoré-Mercier, #2.12A, 835, boul René-Lévesque est, Québec, QC G1A 1B4
418-643-7355, Fax: 418-528-9552
Répondante, Sylvie Banville

L'Assemblée nationale / National Assembly

Hôtel du Parlement, 1045, rue des Parlementaires, Québec, QC G1A 1A4
418-643-7239, Fax: 418-646-4271, 866-337-8837
responsable.contenu@assnat.qc.ca
www.assnat.qc.ca
Président de l'Assemblée nationale/Speaker of the National Assembly, Président de la Commission de l'Assemblée nationale, et la Sous-commission de la réforme parlementaire, Yvon Vallières
418-643-2820, Fax: 418-643-3423,
presidentcabinet@assnat.qc.ca
Première vice-présidente/First Vice-President, Fatima Houda-Pepin
418-643-2750, Fax:
418-643-2942,fhoudapepin@assnat.qc.ca
Deuxième vice-président/Second Vice-President, Jacques Chagnon
418-643-2810, Fax: 418-643-3688,jchagnon@assnat.qc.ca
Troisième vice-président/Third Vice-President, François Gendron
418-644-1007, Fax: 418-644-1368,fgendron@assnat.qc.ca
Secrétaire général/Secretary General, François Côté
418-643-2724, Fax:
418-643-5062,sec.general@assnat.qc.ca
Whip en chef du gouvernement, Pierre Moreau
418-643-6018, Fax:
418-643-5462,pierre.moreau@assnat.qc.ca
Whip adjoint du gouvernement, Vincent Auclair
418-644-0877, Fax:
418-528-0421,vauclair-vimo@assnat.qc.ca,
Whip adjointe du gouvernement, Lucie Charlebois
418-644-0953, Fax:
418-644-1581,lcharlebois-soul@assnat.qc.ca
Leader parlementaire du gouvernement, Jean-Marc Fournier
jfournier@assnat.qc.ca
Leader parlementaire adjoint du gouvernement, Robert Dutil
418-643-2112, Fax:
418-646-6168,ministre@msp.gouv.qc.ca
Leader parlementaire adjoint du gouvernement, Henri-François Gautrin
418-646-7497, Fax:
418-643-0241,hfgautrin-verd@assnat.qc.ca

Cabinet du chef de l'opposition officielle / Office of the Official Opposition (ADQ)
Hôtel du Parlement, #2.89, 1045, rue des Parlementaires, Québec, QC G1A 1A4
Chef de l'opposition officielle/Leader of the Official Opposition, Mario Dumont
418-643-2743, Fax: 418-528-9479,mdumont@assnat.qc.ca
Leader parlementaire de l'opposition officielle, Sébastien Proulx
418-643-1275, Fax: 418-644-2721,sproulx@assnat.qc.ca
Whip en chef de l'opposition officielle, François Bonnardel
418-643-2301, Fax:
418-643-1905,fbonnardel-shef@assnat.qc.ca

Whip adjointe de l'opposition officielle, Linda Lapointe
418-644-0958, Fax:
418-643-1905,linda.lapointe-grou@assnat.qc.ca

Direction de l'Assemblée nationale du Québec / Directorate of the National Assembly of Québec

Directeur, Secrétariat du Bureau, Gilles Gauthier
418-643-2724, Fax: 418-644-7124
Secrétaire générale adjointe, Affaires administratives, Cécilia Tremblay
Directrice, Secrétariat des commissions, Hélène Galarneau
Directeur, Ressources matérielles et des restaurants, Denis Leclerc
Directeur, Recherche et procédure parlementaire, Michel Bonsaint
418-528-0020, Fax: 418-641-2634
Directeur, Protocole et accueil, Denis Desrosiers
Directeur, Affaires juridiques et législatives, René Chrétien
418-528-0727, Fax: 418-641-2642
Directrice, Diffusion des débats, Lise Grondin
Directrice, Communications, Patricia Rousseau
Directeur, Relations interparlementaires et internationales, Marcel Lacharité
Directrice, Secrétariat de l'Assemblée, Doris Arsenault
Directeur, Gestion immobilière, Guy L. Huot
418-643-1828, Fax: 418-641-2624
Directeur, Ressources humaines, Normand Légaré
Directeur, Ressources financières et services de l'approvisionnement, Daniel Cloutier
Directeur, Sécurité, Pierre Paquet
418-643-2244, Fax: 418-641-2620
Directeur, Informatique, Jean-Louis Parent
418-643-2725, Fax: 418-641-2626
Directeur, Études documentaires, Gaston Deschênes
Directeur, Bibliothèque, Philippe Sauvageau
418-643-4032, Fax: 418-641-2635
Directeur, Programmes pédagogiques, Robert Tremblay
418-643-4101, Fax: 418-643-4150

Les Régions administratives au Québec - Les ministres responsables / Regional Parliamentary Assistants

Abitibi-Témiscamingue,L'hon. Pierre Corbeil
Bas-Saint-Laurent,VACANTE
Capitale-Nationale,L'hon. Sam Hamad
Centre-du-Québec,L'hon. Laurent Lessard
Chaudière-Appalaches,L'hon. Laurent Lessard
Côte-Nord,L'hon. Serge Simard
Estrie,L'hon. Monique Gagnon-Tremblay
Gaspésie-Iles-de-la-Madeleine,L'hon. Nathalie Normandeau
Laurentides,L'hon. Michelle Courchesne
Lanaudière,L'hon. Michelle Courchesne
Laval,L'hon. Michelle Courchesne
Mauricie,L'hon. Julie Boulet
Montérégie,L'hon. Nicole Ménard
Montréal,L'hon. Raymond Bachand
Nord-du-Québec,L'hon. Pierre Corbeil
Outaouais,L'hon. Norman MacMillan
Saguenay-Lac-Saint-Jean,L'hon. Serge Simard

Trente-huitième législature / Thirty-eigth Legislature - Québec

Hôtel du Parlement, 1045, rue des Parlementaires, Québec, QC G1A 1A4

418-643-7239, Fax: 418-646-4271, 866-337-8837
www.assnat.qc.ca

La dernière élection générale: le 26 mars, 2007.Résultats:Parti Libéral du Québec (PLQ): 48; Action démocratique du Québec (ADQ): 41; Parti québécois (PQ): 36;Total: 125. Élections partielles: le 24 septembre, 2007 (Charlevoix); le 12 mai, 2008 (Bourget, Hull, Pointe-aux-Trembles); et le 29 septembre, 2008 (Jean-Talon).Salaires, indemnités, allocations: indemnité annuelle: $83,714 et une allocation de dépenses de $14,811. En plus, le Premier ministre reçot $87,900, les ministres $62,786, le Leader parlementaire du gouvernement et le Président $62,786, le Chef de l'Opposition officielle $62,786. Par la suite: membre, circonscription, allégeance politique, téléphone & télécopieur, courriel,(Adresse:Hôtel du Parlement, Québec, QC G1A 1A4)

Members

L'hon. Pierre Arcand, Mont-Royal, Liberal
418-521-3911, Fax: 418-643-4143
Vincent Auclair, Vimont, Liberal
418-644-0877, Fax:
418-528-0421,vauclair-vimo@assnat.qc.ca
Jean-Martin Aussant, Nicolet-Yamaska, 2008-09-10, Parti Quebecois
418-646-7505, Fax:
418-528-7114,jmaussant-niya@assnat.qc.ca
Claude Bachand, Arthabaska, Liberal
418-644-1470, Fax:
418-646-7791,cbachand-arth@assnat.qc.ca
L'hon. Raymond Bachand, Outremont, Liberal
418-643-5270, Fax:
418-646-1574,ministre@finances.gouv.qc.ca
L'hon. Line Beauchamp, Bourassa-Sauvé, Liberal
418-644-0664, Fax: 418-646-7551,ministre@mels.gouv.qc.ca
Denise Beaudoin, Mirabel, Parti Quebecois
418-644-1543, Fax:
418-644-9697,denise.beaudoin-mira@assnat.qc.ca,
Louise Beaudoin, Rosemont, Parti Quebecois
418-644-1667, Fax:
418-643-8924,lbeaudoin-rose@assnat.qc.ca
VACANTE, Kamouraska-Témiscouata, Liberal
Stéphane Bédard, Chicoutimi, Parti Quebecois
418-643-1275, Fax: 418-643-1906,sbedard@assnat.qc.ca
Stéphane Bergeron, Verchères, Parti Quebecois
418-644-9368, Fax:
418-646-6640,sbergeron-verc@assnat.qc.ca
L'hon. Lawrence S. Bergman, D'Arcy-McGee, Liberal
418-528-1960, Fax:
418-643-0183,lbergman-dmg@assnat.qc.ca
Daniel Bernard, Rouyn-Noranda—Témiscamingue, 2008-09-11, Liberal
418-644-0588, Fax:
418-528-0416,dbernard-rnt@assnat.qc.ca
Raymond Bernier, Montmorency, Liberal
418-644-9600, Fax:
418-646-7795,rbernier-mont@assnat.qc.ca
Pascal Bérubé, Matane, 2008-09-10, Parti Quebecois
418-644-0054, pberube@assnat.qc.ca
Stéphane Billette, Huntingdon, Liberal
418-644-5992, Fax:
418-646-8169,sbillette-hunt@assnat.qc.ca
L'hon. Marguerite Blais, Saint-Henri—Sainte-Anne, 2008-09-10, Liberal
418-646-7757, Fax: 418-646-7769,m.blais@aines.gouv.qc.ca
Yves-François Blanchet, Drummond, 2008-09-11, Parti Quebecois
418-644-1052, Fax:
418-643-1216,yfblanchet-drum@assnat.qc.ca
L'hon. Yves Bolduc, Jean-Talon, Liberal
418-266-7171, Fax: 418-266-7197,ministre@msss.gouv.qc.ca
François Bonnardel, Shefford, 2008-09-10, Action Democratique du Qc
418-528-0407, Fax:
418-528-9479,fbonnardel-shef@assnat.qc.ca
Etienne-Alexis Boucher, Johnson, 2008-09-10, Parti Quebecois
418-644-1541, Fax:
418-646-4098,eaboucher-john@assnat.qc.ca
Marie Bouillé, Iberville, 2008-09-11, Parti Quebecois
418-644-1475, Fax:
418-644-1085,mbouille-iber@assnat.qc.ca
L'hon. Julie Boulet, Laviolette, Liberal
418-643-4810, Fax:
418-643-2802,ministre@mess.gouv.qc.ca
Éric Caire, La Peltrie, 2008-09-10, Independent
418-644-0185, Fax: 418-528-6935,ecaire-lape@assnat.qc.ca
Marc Carrière, Chapleau, Liberal
418-528-0390, Fax:
418-528-5668,mcarriere-chap@assnat.qc.ca
Jacques Chagnon, Westmount—Saint-Louis, Liberal
418-643-2810, Fax: 418-643-3688,rchagnon@assnat.qc.ca
Noëlla Champagne, Champlain, Parti Quebecois
418-644-2499, Fax:
418-528-0427,nchampagne-chmp@assnat.qc.ca
Francine Charbonneau, Mille-Iles, Liberal
418-644-0866, Fax:
418-644-5990,fcharbonneau-miil@assnat.qc.ca
L'hon. Jean J. Charest, Sherbrooke, Liberal
418-643-5321, Fax:
418-646-1854,www.premier-ministre.gouv.qc.ca/premier-ministre/nous-joindre/
Benoit Charette, Deux-Montagnes, 2008-09-11, Parti Quebecois
418-528-0765, Fax:
418-646-7800,bcharette-demo@assnat.qc.ca
Lucie Charlebois, Soulanges, Liberal
418-644-0953, Fax:
418-644-1581,lcharlebois-soul@assnat.qc.ca
Germain Chevarie, Iles-de-la-Madeleine, Liberal
418-644-1454, Fax:
418-644-5990,gchevarie-idlm@assnat.qc.ca
Alexandre Cloutier, Lac-Saint-Jean, 2008-09-10, Parti Quebecois
418-644-0901, Fax: 418-644-2062,acloutier-lsj@assnat.qc.ca
L'hon. Pierre Corbeil, Abitibi-Est, 2008-09-11, Liberal
418-646-9131, Fax:
418-646-9487,pierre.corbeil@mce.gouv.qc.ca
L'hon. Michelle Courchesne, Fabre, Liberal
418-643-5926, Fax: 418-643-7824,cabinet@sct.gouv.qc.ca
Claude Cousineau, Bertrand, Parti Quebecois
418-643-2769, Fax:
418-644-2121,ccousineau-berr@assnat.qc.ca
Pierre Curzi, Borduas, 2008-09-10, Parti Quebecois
418-644-0752, Fax: 418-644-3712,pcurzi-bord@assnat.qc.ca
Jean D'Amour, Rivière-du-Loup, Liberal
418-528-2914, Fax: 418-644-5990,jdamour-rdl@assnat.qc.ca
Gérard Deltell, Chauveau, Action Democratique du Qc
418-644-9318, Fax: 418-528-9479,gdeltell@assnat.qc.ca
Jean-Paul Diamond, Maskinongé, 2008-09-10, Liberal
418-644-0617, Fax:
418-646-8169,jpdiamond-mask@assnat.qc.ca
Danielle Doyer, Matapédia, Parti Quebecois
418-646-6147, Fax:
418-644-7851,ddoyer-matp@assnat.qc.ca
Bernard Drainville, Marie-Victorin, 2008-09-10, Parti Quebecois
418-643-5611, Fax:
418-646-7812,bdrainville-mavi@assnat.qc.ca
André Drolet, Jean-Lesage, 2008-09-11, Liberal
418-646-7635, Fax: 418-528-0425,adrolet-jele@assnat.qc.ca
Emmanuel Dubourg, Viau, 2008-09-10, Liberal
418-646-7648, Fax:
514-728-2759,edubourg-viau@assnat.qc.ca
Marjolain Dufour, René-Lévesque, Parti Quebecois
418-644-0809, Fax:
418-646-7811,marjolaindufour-rele@assnat.qc.ca
L'hon. Robert Dutil, Beauce-Sud, 2008-09-11, Liberal
418-643-2112, Fax: 418-646-6168,ministre@msp.gouv.qc.ca
Luc Ferland, Ungava, 2008-09-10, Parti Quebecois
418-644-1363, Fax:
418-528-0439,lferland-unga@assnat.qc.ca
Jean-Marc Fournier, Liberal
jfournier@assnat.qc.ca
L'hon. Monique Gagnon-Tremblay, Saint-François, Liberal
418-649-2319, Fax: 418-643-4804,cabinet@mri.gouv.qc.ca
Maryse Gaudreault, Hull, 2008-09-10, Liberal
418-644-9954, Fax:
418-643-0595,mgaudreault-hull.assnat.qc.ca
Sylvain Gaudreault, Jonquière, 2008-09-10, Parti Quebecois
418-646-7647, Fax:
418-646-7801,sgaudreault-jonq@assnat.qc.ca
Henri-François Gautrin, Verdun, Liberal
418-646-7497, Fax:
418-643-0241,hfgautrin-verd@assnat.qc.ca
René Gauvreau, Groulx, 2008-09-11, Parti Quebecois
418-644-0958, Fax:
418-646-7800,rgauvreau-grou@assnat.qc.ca
François Gendron, Abitibi-Ouest, Parti Quebecois
418-644-1007, Fax: 418-644-1368,fgendron@assnat.qc.ca
L'hon. Clément Gignac, Marguerite-Bourgeoys, Liberal
418-691-5650, Fax:
418-643-8553,ministre@mdeie.gouv.qc.ca
Nicolas Girard, Gouin, Parti Quebecois
418-644-1367, Fax: 418-644-6828,ngirard-goui@assnat.qc.ca
Johanne Gonthier, Mégantic-Compton, 2008-09-11, Liberal
418-644-0711, Fax:
418-646-0516,jgonthier-meco@assnat.qc.ca
Janvier Grondin, Beauce-Nord, Action Democratique du Qc
418-643-5016, Fax: 418-528-9479,jgrondin@assnat.qc.ca
L'hon. Sam Hamad, Louis-Hébert, Liberal
418-643-6980, Fax: 418-643-2033,ministre@mtq.gouv.qc.ca
Véronique Hivon, Joliette, 2008-09-10, Parti Quebecois
418-644-1598, Fax: 418-644-9697,vhivon-joli@assnat.qc.ca
Fatima Houda-Pepin, La Pinière, Liberal
418-643-2750, Fax:
418-643-2942,fhoudapepin@assnat.qc.ca
Patrick Huot, Vanier, Liberal
418-643-7719, Fax: 418-643-9164,phuot-vani@assnat.qc.ca
L'hon. Yolande James, Nelligan, Liberal
418-643-2181, Fax:
418-643-2640,ministre.famille@mfa.gouv.qc.ca
Geoffrey Kelley, Jacques-Cartier, Liberal
418-646-7627, Fax: 418-643-0595,gkelley@assnat.qc.ca
Amir Khadir, Mercier, QS
418-644-1430, Fax:
418-643-0624,akhadir-merc@assnat.qc.ca
Maka Kotto, Bourget, 2008-09-11, Parti Quebecois
418-646-2128, Fax: 418-646-8166,mkotto-bour@assnat.qc.ca
Lisette Lapointe, Crémazie, 2008-09-11, Parti Quebecois
418-643-2152, Fax:
418-646-8166,lisette.lapointe-crem@assnat.qc.ca
Charlotte L'Écuyer, Pontiac, Liberal
418-644-0679, Fax:
418-528-5668,clecuyer-pont@assnat.qc.ca
Guy Leclair, Beauharnois, Parti Quebecois
418-644-7844, Fax:
418-528-7410,guy.leclair-beau@assnat.qc.ca
Nicole Léger, Pointe-aux-Trembles, Parti Quebecois
418-643-2301, Fax: 418-643-3325,nleger-pat@assnat.qc.ca,
Gilles Lehouillier, Lévis, 2008-09-11, Liberal
418-646-7673, Fax: 418-528-7447,glehouillier@assnat.qc.ca
Martin Lemay, Sainte-Marie—Saint-Jacques, Parti Quebecois
418-644-1632, Fax:
418-528-9534,mlemay-smsj@assnat.qc.ca

L'hon. Laurent Lessard, Frontenac, Liberal
418-691-2050, Fax:
418-643-1795,ministre@mamrot.gouv.qc.ca
L'hon. Norman MacMillan, Papineau, Liberal
418-643-6980, Fax:
418-643-2033,ministredelegue@mtq.gouv.qc.ca
Marie Malavoy, Taillon, Parti Quebecois
418-646-4283, Fax:
418-644-9697,mmalavoy-tail@assnat.qc.ca
Agnès Maltais, Taschereau, Parti Quebecois
418-644-1042, Fax:
418-646-4991,amaltais-tasc@assnat.qc.ca
Georges Mamelonet, Gaspé, Liberal
418-528-5818, Fax:
418-646-8169,gmamelonet-gasp@assnat.qc.ca
Nicolas Marceau, Rousseau, 2008-09-11, Parti Quebecois
418-644-1417, Fax:
418-646-7804,nmarceau-rous@assnat.qc.ca
Yvon Marcoux, Vaudreuil, Liberal
418-646-7623, Fax:
418-643-0595,ymarcoux-vaud@assnat.qc.ca
Pauline Marois, Charlevoix, Parti Quebecois
418-643-2743, Fax:
418-643-2957,pauline.marois@assnat.qc.ca
Pierre Marsan, Robert-Baldwin, Liberal
418-646-5554, Fax:
418-643-9127,pmarsan-roba@assnat.qc.ca
Michel Matte, Portneuf, 2008-09-10, Liberal
418-644-1473, Fax: 418-268-4348,mmatte@assnat.qc.ca
Scott McKay, L'Assomption, 2008-09-11, Parti Quebecois
418-528-5974, Fax:
418-528-0439,smckay-asso@assnat.qc.ca
L'hon. Nicole Ménard, Laporte, 2008-09-11, Liberal
418-528-8063, Fax:
418-528-8066,ministre@tourisme.gouv.qc.ca
L'hon. Pierre Moreau, Châteauguay, 2008-09-11, Liberal
418-643-6018, Fax:
418-643-5462,pierre.moreau@assnat.qc.ca
Norbert Morin, Montmagney-L'Islet, 2008-09-11, Liberal
418-644-0513, Fax:
418-644-8589,nmorin-mois@assnat.qc.ca
L'hon. Nathalie Normandeau, Bonaventure, Liberal
418-643-7295, Fax: 418-643-4318,ministre@mrnf.gouv.qc.ca
Martine Ouellet, Vachon, Parti Quebecois
418-644-0751, Fax:
418-646-7810,martineouellet@assnat.qc.ca
Guy Ouellette, Chomedey, 2008-09-11, Liberal
418-644-4050, Fax:
418-646-7385,gouellette-chom@assnat.qc.ca
François Ouimet, Marquette, Liberal
418-646-3202, Fax:
418-643-9127,fouimet-marq@assnat.qc.ca
Sylvain Pagé, Labelle, Parti Quebecois
418-528-1349, Fax: 418-528-7185,spage@assnat.qc.ca
Alain Paquet, Laval-des-Rapides, Liberal
418-644-0672, Fax: 418-646-0707,apaquet-ldr@assnat.qc.ca
Pierre Paradis, Brome-Missisquoi, Liberal
418-644-0551, Fax:
418-646-6684,pparadis-brmi@assnat.qc.ca
Émilien Pelletier, Saint-Hyacinthe, 2008-09-11, Parti Quebecois
418-644-5283, Fax:
418-646-7815,epelletier-sahy@assnat.qc.ca
Irvin Pelletier, Rimouski, 2008-09-11, Parti Quebecois
418-644-1386, Fax:
418-644-7851,ipelletier-rimo@assnat.qc.ca
Marc Picard, Chutes-de-la-Chaudière, Independent
418-528-1694, Fax:
418-528-6935,mpicard-cdlc@assnat.qc.ca
Michel Pigeon, Charlesbourg, 2008-09-11, Liberal
418-644-9506, Fax:
418-646-7796,mpigeon-chlb@assnat.qc.ca
Claude Pinard, Saint-Maurice, 2008-09-10, Parti Quebecois
418-528-1277, Fax:
418-528-0427,cpinard-sama@assnat.qc.ca
Carole Poirier, Hochelaga-Maisonneuve, Parti Quebecois
418-644-1629, Fax: 418-646-7810,cpoirier@assnat.qc.ca
Daniel Ratthé, Blainville, 2008-09-11, Parti Quebecois
418-644-1444, Fax: 418-646-7804,dratthe-blai@assnat.qc.ca
François Rebello, La Prairie, 2008-09-11, Parti Quebecois
418-644-1489, Fax:
418-644-2062,frebelloe-lapr@assnat.qc.ca
Pierre Reid, Orford, Liberal
418-644-3944, Fax: 418-646-0516,preid-orfo@assnat.qc.ca
Lorraine Richard, Duplessis, Parti Quebecois
418-643-2446, Fax:
418-644-3219,lorrainerichard-dupl@assnat.qc.ca
Monique Richard, Margeurite-D'Youville, 2008-09-10, Parti Quebecois
418-644-0655, Fax:
418-644-3712,mrichard-mayo@assnat.qc.ca
Gilles Robert, Prévost, 2008-09-10, Parti Quebecois
418-644-1504, Fax:
418-646-7804,grobert-prev@assnat.qc.ca
Filomena Rotiroti, Jeanne-Mance-Viger, 2008-09-11, Liberal
418-646-5743, Fax: 418-644-5990,frotiroti-jmv@assnat.qc.ca
Sylvie Roy, Lotbinière, Action Democratique du Qc
418-644-1467, Fax: 418-528-9479,sylvieroy@assnat.qc.ca
L'hon. Serge Simard, Dubuc, Liberal
418-643-7295, Fax:
418-643-4318,ministredelegue@mrnf.gouv.qc.ca
Sylvain Simard, Richelieu, Parti Quebecois
418-644-1587, Fax: 418-644-1085,ssimard-ricl@assnat.qc.ca
Gerry Sklavounos, Laurier-Dorion, 2008-09-11, Liberal
418-644-5987, Fax:
418-644-5977,gsklavounos-lado@assnat.qc.ca
Danielle St-Amand, Trois-Rivières, 2008-09-11, Liberal
418-528-0413, Fax:
418-646-8169,dstamand-trri@assnat.qc.ca
Bertrand St-Arnaud, Chambly, 2008-09-11, Parti Quebecois
418-646-7508, Fax:
418-643-0924,bstarnaud-chmb@assnat.qc.ca
L'hon. Christine St-Pierre, Acadie, 2008-09-11, Liberal
418-380-2310, Fax:
418-380-2311,ministre@mcccf.gouv.qc.ca
L'hon. Lise Thériault, Anjou, Liberal
418-643-5297, Fax:
418-644-0003,ministre@travail.gouv.qc.ca
Tony Tomassi, LaFontaine, Independent
418-528-7413, Fax:
418-528-7415,ttomassi-lafo@assnat.qc.ca
Mathieu Traversy, Terrebonne, 2008-09-11, Parti Quebecois
418-644-1616, Fax:
418-644-5976,mtraversy-terr@assnat.qc.ca
Guillaume Tremblay, Masson, 2008-09-11, Parti Quebecois
418-643-5771, Fax:
418-528-2960,gtremblay-mass@assnat.qc.ca
Denis Trottier, Roberval, Parti Quebecois
418-644-0707, Fax:
418-646-7801,dtrottier-robe@assnat.qc.ca
Dave Turcotte, Saint-Jean, 2008-09-11, Parti Quebecois
418-644-1463, Fax:
418-646-7798,dave.turcotte-saje@assnat.qc.ca
Stéphanie Vallée, Gatineau, 2008-09-11, Liberal
418-644-5980, Fax: 418-643-0595,svallee-gati@assnat.qc.ca
Yvon Vallières, Richmond, Liberal
418-643-2820, Fax:
418-643-3423,yvallieres-ricm@assnat.qc.ca
L'hon. Dominique Vien, Bellechasse, 2008-09-10, Liberal
418-266-7181, Fax:
418-266-7199,ministre.deleguee@msss.gouv.qc.ca
André Villeneuve, Berthier, 2008-09-10, Parti Quebecois
418-644-1399, Fax:
418-646-7801,avilleneuve-berh@assnat.qc.ca
L'hon. Kathleen Weil, Notre-Dame-de-Grâce, Liberal
418-644-2128, Fax: 418-528-0829
David Whissell, Argenteuil, Liberal
418-528-6379, Fax:
418-643-5462,dwhissell-arge@assnat.qc.ca
VACANTE, Saint-Laurent
Directeur, Direction des communications, Jean Dumas
communications@assnat.qc.ca

Ministères et organismes du gouvernement du Québec / Québec Government Departments & Agencies

• Commission municipale du Québec/ Québec Municipal Commission
Mezzanine, aile Chaveau
10, rue Pierre-Olivier-Chauveau, Tour 5e etage
Québec, QC G1R 4J3
418-691-2014 Fax: 418-644-4676 866-353-6767
cmq@mamr.gouv.qc.ca
www.cmq.gouv.qc.ca
CMQ est un tribunal et un organisme administratif, d'enquête et de conseil, spécialisé en matière municipale.
• Régie du logement du Québec/ Québec Rental Board
Pyramide Ouest
#2360, 5199, rue Sherbrooke est
Montréal, QC H1T 3X1
514-873-6575 Fax: 514-873-6805 800-683-2245
www.rdl.gouv.qc.ca
• Société d'habitation du Québec/ Housing Québec
Aile St-Amable
1054, rue Louis-Alexandre-Taschereau, 3e étage
Québec, QC G1R 5E7
418-643-4035 Fax: 418-643-4560 800-463-4315
www.habitation.gouv.qc.ca

Secrétariat aux affaires autochtones / Aboriginal Affairs

905, av Honoré-Mercier, 1er étage, Québec, QC G1R 5M6
418-643-3166, Fax: 418-646-4918,
www.autochtones.gouv.qc.ca
Ministre responsable,L'hon. Pierre Corbeil
418-646-9131, Fax:
418-646-9487,pierre.corbeil@mce.gouv.qc.ca

Secrétariat aux Affaires intergouvernementales canadiennes / Canadian Intergovernmental Affairs Secretariat

875, Grande Allée est, 3e étage, Québec, QC G1R 4Y8
418-643-4011, Fax: 418-528-0052,
www.saic.gouv.qc.ca
Ministre responsable,VACANTE
418-646-5950, Fax:
418-528-0981,ministre.saic@mce.gouv.qc.ca
Secrétaire général associé, aux Affaires intergouvernementales canadiennes, Yves Castonguay
Secrétaire adjointe, Suzanne Levesque
Secrétaire adjointe, à la Francophonie canadienne, Sylvie Lachance
Directeur, des Affaires économiques, culturelles et sociales, Artur J. Pires
Directeur, des Politiques institutionnelles et constitutionnelles, Michel Frédérick, 2008-09-12
Directeur, de la Francophonie et des Bureaux du Québec au Canada, Yves Robertson
Directeur, de la Réflexion stratégique, Marc-Antoine Adam
Responsable, Bureau du Secrétaire général associé/Responsable de l'accès à l'information, Mario Plamondon, 2008-09-12

Bureaux du Quebec au Canada/Regional Offices:

Moncton
Bureau du Québec dans les Provinces atlantiques, #510, 777, rue Main, 5e étage, Moncton, NB E1C 1E9
506-857-9851, Fax: 506-857-9883,
bqmoncton@mce.gouv.qc.ca
Chef de poste, Richard Barrette

Ottawa
Bureau du Québec à Ottawa, #300, 81 rue Metcalfe, Ottawa, ON K1P 6K7
613-238-5322, Fax: 613-563-9137,
bqottawa@mce.gouv.qc.ca
Chef de poste, Roch Cholette

Toronto
Bureau du Québec à Toronto, #1504, 20 rue Queen ouest, CP 13, Toronto, ON M5H 3S3
416-977-6713, Fax: 416-596-1407,
bqtoronto@mce.gouv.qc.ca
Chef de poste, Paul-Arthur Huot

Vancouver
Antenne de Vancouver, #780, 789 rue Pender ouest, Vancouver, BC V6C 1H2
604-682-3500, Fax: 604-682-6670,
vancouver@mce.gouv.qc.ca
Sous la responsabilité du Bureau du Québec à Toronto
Responsable, Paul-Arthur Huot

Ministère des Affaires municipales et Occupation du territoire / Municipal Affairs

Aile Chaveau, 10, rue Pierre-Olivier-Chauveau, 3e étage, Québec, QC G1R 4J3
418-691-2019, Fax: 418-643-7385,
communications@mamrot.gouv.qc.ca
www.mamrot.gouv.qc.ca
A la charge de conseiller le gouvernement & d'assurer la coordination interministérielle dans ces domaines; a pour mission de favoriser la mise en place & le maintien d'un cadre de vie & de services municipaux de qualité pour des citoyens/citoyennes; le développement des régions & des milieux ruraux; & le progrès & le rayonnement de la métropole; intervient auprès des municipalités locales, régionales de comté, des communautés métropolitaines de Montréal & de Québec, & de l'administration régionale Kativik
Acts Administered:
Code municipal du Québec
Loi concernant la consultation des citoyens sur la réorganisation territoriale
Loi concernant la négociation d'ententes relatives à la réduction des coûts de main-d'oeuvre dans le secteur municipal
Loi concernant la réglementation municipale des édifices publics
Loi concernant la Ville de Schefferville
Loi concernant les droits sur les mutations immobilières
Loi instituant le fonds spécial de financement des activités locales

Loi modifiant de nouveau diverses dispositions législatives concernant le domaine municipal
Loi portant réforme de l'organisation territoriale municipale des régions métropolitaines de Montréal, de Québec et de l'Outaouais
Loi sur Immobilière SHQ
Loi sur l'aide municipale à la protection du public aux traverses de chemin de fer
Loi sur l'aménagement et l'urbanisme
Loi sur l'exercice de certaines compétences municipales dan certaines agglomérations
Loi sur l'expropriation
Loi sur l'instruction publique
Loi sur l'instruction publique pour les autochtones cris, inuits et naskapis
Loi sur l'interdiction de subventions municipales
Loi sur l'organisation territoriale municipale
Loi sur la Commission municipale
Loi sur la Communauté métropolitaine de Montréal
Loi sur la Communauté métropolitaine de Québec
Loi sur la conservation du patrimoine naturel
Loi sur la conservation et la mise en valeur de la faune
Loi sur la fiscalité municipale
Loi sur la police
Loi sur la qualité de l'environnement
Loi sur la Régie du logement
Loi sur la Société d'habitation du Québec
Loi sur la Société du Parc industriel et portuaire de Bécancour
Loi sur la Société Innovatech du grand Montréal
Loi sur la Société québécoise d'assainissement des eaux
Loi sur la vente des services publics municipaux
Loi sur le développement de la région de la Baie-James
Loi sur le Ministère de l'Agriculture, des Pêcheries et de l'Alimentation
Loi sur le Ministère du Développement durable, de l'Environnement et des Parcs
Loi sur le régime de retraite des élus municipaux
Loi sur les abus préjudiciables à l'agriculture
Loi sur les compétences municipales
Loi sur les cités et villes
Loi sur les conseils intermunicipaux de transport dans la région de Montréal
Loi sur les cours municipales
Loi sur les dettes et les emprunts municipaux
Loi sur les élections et les référendums dans les municipalités
Loi sur les espèces menacées ou vulnérables
Loi sur les immeubles industriels municipaux
Loi sur les impôts
Loi sur les régimes de retraite des maires et des conseillers des municipalités
Loi sur les sociétés de transport en commun
Loi sur les sociétés d'économie mixte dans le secteur municipal
Loi sur le traitement des élus municipaux
Loi sur les travaux municipaux
Loi sur les villages cris et le village Naskapi
Loi sur les villages Nordiques et l'Administration régionale Kativik

Ministre,L'hon. Laurent Lessard
418-691-2050, Fax: 418-643-1795,ministre@mamrot.gouv.qc.ca
Sous-ministre, Marc Lacoix
418-691-2040, Fax: 418-643-7708
Sous-ministre adjoint, (Politiques), Sylvain Boucher
Sous-ministre adjoint, (Infrastructures & finances municipales), Jacques A. Tremblay
Sous-ministre adjoint, (Métropole), Jean Séguin

Territoires / Regions
Sous-ministre adjointe, Linda Morin
418-691-2040
Directeur, Bureau municipal de la géomatique & de la statistique, Gilles W. Boivin
418-691-2088
Directrice (par intérim), Développement rural, Danielle Leduc
418-691-2078
Directeur, Affaires régionales/Direction de la Capitale-Nationale, Stéphane Bouchard
418-691-2016
Directeur du projet, Occupation des territoires, Yannick Routhier
418-691-2038

Directions régionales/Regional Offices:

Abitibi-Témiscamingue
#105, 170, av Principale, 1er étage, Rouyn-Noranda, QC J9X 4P7
819-763-3582, Fax: 819-763-3803, Dr.Abitibi-Temis@mamrot.gouv.qc.ca
Directeur, Denis Moffet

Bas-Saint-Laurent
337, rue Moreault, 2e étage, Rimouski, QC G5L 1P4
418-727-3629, Fax: 418-727-3537, Dr.Bas-St-Laur@mamrot.gouv.qc.ca
Directeur, Gilles Julien

Capitale-Nationale
8, rue Cook, 5e étage, Québec, QC G1R 5J8
418-643-1343, Fax: 418-643-4086, Dr.CapNat@mamrot.gouv.qc.a
Directeur, Paul Arsenault

Centre-du-Québec
#S-05, 62, rue Saint-Jean-Baptiste, Victoriaville, QC G6P 4E3
819-752-2453, Fax: 819-795-3673, Dr.Centre-Quebec@mamrot.gouv.qc.ca
Directeur, Gaétan Désilets

Chaudière-Appalaches
#102, 1100, boul Frontenac est, Thetford Mines, QC G6G 6H1
418-338-4624, Fax: 418-338-1908, Dr.Chaud-App@mamrot.gouv.qc.ca
Directrice, Danie Croteau

Côte-Nord
#RC-708, 625, boul Laflèche, Baie-Comeau, QC G5C 1C5
418-295-4241, Fax: 418-295-4955, Dr.CoteNord@mamrot.gouv.qc.ca
Directeur, Jacques Tremblay

Estrie
#4.04, 200, rue Belvédère nord, Sherbrooke, QC J1H 4A9
819-820-3244, Fax: 819-820-3979, Dr.Estrie@mamrot.gouv.qc.ca
Directeur, Pierre Poulin

Gaspésie-Iles-de-la-Madeleine
#10B, 500, av Daigneault, CP 310, Chandler, QC G0C 1K0
418-689-5024, Fax: 418-689-4823, Dr.Gaspe-IlesMad@mamrot.gouv.qc.ca
Directeur, Michel Gionest

Lanaudière
#3200, 40, rue Gauthier sud, Joliette, QC J6E 4J4
450-752-8050, Fax: 450-752-8064, Dr.Lanaudiere@mamrot.gouv.qc.ca
Directeur, Jean Ouellet

Laurentides
#210, 161, rue de la Gare, Saint-Jérôme, QC J7Z 2B9
450-569-7646, Fax: 450-569-3131, Dr.Laurentides@mamrot.gouv.qc.ca
Directeur (par intérim), Jean Ouellet

Mauricie
#321, 100, rue Laviolette, Trois-Rivières, QC G9A 5S9
819-371-6653, Fax: 819-371-6953, Dr.Mauricie@mamrot.gouv.qc.
Directeur, Pierre Robert

Montérégie
#403, 201, place Charles-Le Moyne, Longueuil, QC J4K 2T5
450-928-5670, Fax: 450-928-5673, Dr.Monteregie@mamrot.gouv.qc.c
Directeur, Robert Sabourin

Métropole
Tour de la Bourse, #2.17, 800, rue du Square-Victoria, CP 83, Montréal, QC H4Z 1B7
514-873-8246, Fax: 514-864-5912, courrier.ddrm@mamrot.gouv.qc.ca
Directrice, Johanne Dumont

Nord-du-Québec
#1, 215, 3e Rue, Chibougamau, QC G8P 1N3
418-748-7737, Fax: 418-748-7841, Nord-du-Quebec@mamrot.gouv.qc.ca
Directeur, Richard Leclerc

Outaouais
#9.300, 170, rue de l'Hôtel-de-Ville, Gatineau, QC J8X 4C2
819-772-3006, Fax: 819-772-3989, Dr.Outaouais@mamrot.gouv.qc.ca
Directeur, Pierre Ricard

Saguenay-Lac-Saint-Jean
#RC-03, 227, rue Racine est, Chicoutimi, QC G7H 7B4
418-698-3523, Fax: 418-698-3526, Dr.Sag-Lac@mamrot.gouv.qc.ca
Directrice, Lison Rhéaume

Infrastructures et finances municipales / Infrastructures & Municipal Financing
Sous-ministre adjoint, Jacques A. Tremblay
418-691-2040
Directeur général, Finances municipales, Jean Monfet
418-691-2007
Directeur général, Infrastructures, Jean-Pierre Beaumont
418-691-2005

Métropole / Metropolitan Regions
Sous-ministre adjoint, Jean Séguin
514-873-8395
Directrice, Développement régional & métropolitain, Johanne Dumont
514-873-6992
Directrice métropolitaine, Aménagement et des affaires municipales, Lucie Tremblay
514-873-8246

Politiques / Policy
Sous-ministre adjoint, Sylvain Boucher
418-691-2040
Directrice générale, Urbanisme/Aménagement du territoire, Marie-Lise Côté
418-691-2015
Directeur, Évaluation foncière, Luc Sauvageau
418-691-2044
Directeur général, Fiscalité, Bernard Guay
418-691-2035
Directrice générale, Politiques, Sylvie Desaulniers
418-691-2039

Services à la gestion / Administrative Services
Directeur général, Raymond Sarrazin, 2010-09-07
418-691-2015
Directrice, Ressources humaines/Performance organisationnelle, Marie-Claude Samuel, 2010-09-07
418-691-2025
Directrice, Ressources financières et matérielles, Sylvie Plante, 2010-09-07
418-691-2001,

Gaspésie—Iles-de-la-Madeleine
195, boul Perron est, Caplan, QC G0C 1H0
418-388-2125, Fax: 418-388-2444, gaspesie-iles-de-la-madeleine@mrnf.gouv.qc.ca

Nord-du-Québec
1121, boul Industriel, CP 159, Lebel-sur-Quévillon, QC J0Y 1X0
819-755-4838, Fax: 819-755-3541, nord-du-quebec@mrnf.gouv.qc.ca

Nord-du-Québec
1121, boul Industriel, CP 159, Lebel-sur-Quévillon, QC J0Y 1X0
819-755-4838, Fax: 819-755-3541, nord-du-quebec@mrnf.gouv.qc.ca
Directeur général, Guy Hétu

Planification, performance et qualité / Planning, Performance and Quality
Sous-ministre adjoint, Denis Lalumière, 2010-09-13
418-266-5990
Directrice, Qualité, Danielle St-Louis, 2010-09-13
418-266-7505
Directrice, Évaluation, Monique Savoie, 2010-09-13
418-266-7030
Directrice, Affaires intergouvernementales & coopération internationale/Études et analyses, Patricia Caris, 2010-09-13
418-266-8740
Directrice, Planification et orientations stratégiques, Andrée Quenneville, 2010-09-13
418-266-7088
Directrice, Recherche, innovation et transfert des connaissances, Manon St-Pierre, 2010-09-13
418-266-7056

Services de santé et médecine universitaire / Health Services & Academic Medicine
Directeur général, Services de santé et médecine universitaire, Michel A. Bureau, 2010-09-13
418-266-6930
Directeur, Main d'oeuvre médicale, Daniel Poirier, 2010-09-13
418-266-6975
Directrice, Organisation des services médicaux et technologiques, Sylvie Bernier, 2010-09-13
418-266-6946
Directrice, Services médicaux généraux et préhospitaliers et traumatologie, Jeannine Auger, 2010-09-13
418-266-5827
Directeur, Affaires universitaires, Louis Dufresne, 2010-09-13
418-266-7500
Directeur, Lutte contre le cancer, Antoine Loutfi, 2010-09-13
418-266-6940
Directrice, Organisation des services de première ligne intégrés, Yolaine Galarneau, 2010-09-13
418-266-6976
Directeur, Santé mentale, André Delorme, 2010-09-13
418-266-6835
Directeur nationale, Urgences, Daniel Lefrançois, 2010-09-13
418-266-5811
Directeur, Biovigilance, Yves Jalbert, 2010-09-13
418-266-6710

Sous-ministre adjoint, Sylvain Gagnon, 2010-09-13
418-266-6800
Directrice, Secrétariat à l'adoption internationale, Luce de Bellefeuille, 2010-09-13
514-873-4747
Directeur, Personnes âgées en perte d'autonomie, Christian Gagné, 2010-09-13
418-266-6818
Directrice, Personnes handicapées/Programme dépendances, Rachel Ruest, 2010-09-13
418-266-6852
Directeur, Services sociaux généraux/Activités communautaires, Mario Frechette, 2010-09-13
418-266-6936
Directrice, Projet pour la mise en oeuvre de la Loi sur la représentation des RI-RTF, Diane Lapointe, 2010-09-13
418-663-5226
Directrice, Jeunes et des familles, Chantal Maltais, 2010-09-13
418-226-6840

Services administratifs / Administrative Services
Sous-ministre associée, Services à la gestion, Liette Larrivée
418-643-3500, Fax: 418-643-0275
Directeur, Gestion immobilière, Jean Leclerc
418-646-6777, Fax: 418-646-1869
Directeur, Planification et politiques, Louis Métiver
418-646-6777, Fax: 418-643-1713
Directrice, Ressources financières et matérielles, Lucie Picard
418-646-6777, Fax: 418-643-1713
Directeur, Ressources humaines, René Boulanger
418-646-6777, Fax: 418-528-6878
Directeur, Technologies de l'information, Abdelaziz Younsi
418-646-6777, Fax: 418-644-4593

Services à la gestion / Administrative Services
Directeur, Ressources financières, Francis Mathieu
Directrice, Ressources humaines, Nicole Lévesque
Directeur, Ressources informationnelles, Guy Leclerc

Services à la gestion / Administrative Services
Directrice (par intérim), Josée Dupont
418-528-0808
Directrice, Ressources humaines, Hélène Verret
418-646-4157
Directrice, Ressources financières, Danièle Cantin
418-646-9934
Directeur, Contrats et ressources matérielles, Marcel Carpentier
418-643-5473
Directrice, Technologies de l'information, Odile Béland
418-643-4431

Politiques et recherche / Policy & Research
Sous-ministre adjoint, Normand Pelletier
Directeur, Politiques du travail, Steeve Audet
Directeur, Information sur le travail, Gilles Fleury
Directeur, Recherche et innovation en milieu de travail, Dalil Maschino

Relations du travail / Labour Relations
Sous-ministre adjointe, Suzanne Thérien
Directeur générale, Daniel Cholette
Directeur, Médiation-conciliation & prévention (Montréal), Julien Perron
Directeur, Médiation-conciliation, prévention & arbitrage (Québec), Jean Poirier
Directeur, Bureau d'évaluation médicale,Dr André Perron

Ministère de la Culture, des Communications & de la Condition féminine / Culture, Communications & the Status of Women

225, Grande Allée est, Québec, QC G1R 5G5
Fax: 418-380-2364, 888-380-8882
infos@mcccf.gouv.qc.ca
www.mcccf.gouv.qc.ca

Acts Administered:
Charte de la langue française
Loi sur Bibliothèque et archives nationales du Québec
Loi sur la programmation éducative
Loi sur la Société de développement des entreprises culturelles
Loi sur la Société de la Place des Arts de Montréal
Loi sur la Société de télédiffusion du Québec
Loi sur la Société du Grand Théâtre de Québec
Loi sur le cinéma
Loi sur le Conseil des arts et des lettres du Québec
Loi sur le Conservatoire
Loi sur le Conservatoire de musique et d'art dramatique du Québec
Loi sur le développement des entreprises québécoises dans le domaine du livre
Loi sur le ministère de la Culture et des Communications
Loi sur le Musée des beaux-arts de Montréal
Loi sur le statut professionnel des artistes des arts visuels, des métiers d'art et de la littérature et sur leurs contrats avec les diffuseurs
Loi sur le statut professionnel et les conditions d'engagement des artistes de la scène, du disque et du cinéma
Loi sur les archives
Loi sur les biens culturels
Loi sur les concours artistiques, littéraires et scientifiques
Loi sur les musées nationaux

Ministre,L'hon. Christine St-Pierre
418-380-2310, Fax: 418-380-2311
Sous-ministre, Sylvie Barcelo
418-380-2330, Fax: 418-380-2391
Sous-ministre adjointe, Action territoriale, Danielle-Claude Chartré
418-380-2330, Fax: 418-380-2392
Sous-ministre adjointe, Secrétariat à la condition féminine, Thérèse Mailloux
418-646-8395, Fax: 418-643-4991
Responsable, Planification stratégique, Jacques Laflamme
418-380-2362, Fax: 418-380-2345
Responsable, Secrétariat à la diversité culturelle, Dave Atkinson
418-380-2372, Fax: 418-380-2340
Directrice, Relations publiques, Nathalie Pitre
418-380-2363, Fax: 418-380-2364
Directeur, Affaires juridiques, Yves D. Dussault
418-643-3747, Fax: 418-646-6849
Directeur général, Administration, François Bérubé
418-380-2355, Fax: 418-380-2394
Directeur, Ressources financières et matérielles, Marc Gagné
418-380-2301, Fax: 418-380-2302
Directeur, Ressources humaines/Gestion immobilière, Marc Tremblay
418-380-2329, Fax: 418-380-2332
Directeur, Technologies de l'information, Pierre Bonneau
418-380-2312, Fax: 418-380-2314

Directions régionales/Regional Offices:

Abitibi-Témiscamingue et Nord-du-Québec
#450, 19, rue Perreault ouest, Rouyn-Noranda, QC J9X 6N5
819-763-3517, Fax: 819-763-3382,
dratnq@mcccf.gouv.qc.ca
Directrice, Monik Duhaime

Bas-St-Laurent
337, rue Moreault, Rimouski, QC G5L 1P4
418-727-3650, Fax: 418-727-3824,
drbsl@mcccf.gouv.qc.ca
Directrice (par intérim), Danielle Dubé

Capitale-Nationale
Bloc C, RC, 225, Grande-Allée est, Québec, QC G1R 5G5
418-380-2346, Fax: 418-380-2347,
dcn@mcccf.gouv.qc.ca
Directeur, René Bouchard

Chaudière-Appalaches
6210, rue St-Laurent, Lévis, QC G6V 3P4
418-838-9886, Fax: 418-838-1485,
drca@mcccf.gouv.qc.ca
Directeur, Richard Saint-Pierre

Côte-Nord
#1.806, 625, boul Laflèche, Baie-Comeau, QC G5C 1C5
418-295-4979, Fax: 418-295-4070,
drcn@mcccf.gouv.qc.ca
Directeur, Luc Bourassa

Estrie
#410, 225, rue Frontenac, Sherbrooke, QC J1H 1K1
819-820-3007, Fax: 819-820-3930,
dre@mcccf.gouv.qc.ca
Directrice, Lucette Bouchard

Gaspésie/Iles-de-la-Madeleine
146, av de Grand-Pré, CP 370, Bonaventure, QC G0C 1E0
418-534-4431, Fax: 418-534-4564,
drgim@mcccf.gouv.qc.ca
Directrice, Suzanne Provost

Laval, Lanaudière et les Laurentides
#200, 300, rue Sicard, Sainte-Thérèse, QC J7E 3X5
450-430-3737, Fax: 450-430-2475,
drlll@mcccf.gouv.qc.ca
Directeur, Gilbert Lepage

Mauricie et Centre-du-Québec
#315, 100, rue Laviolette, Trois-Rivières, QC G9A 5S9
819-387-6001, Fax: 819-371-6984,
drmcq@mcccf.gouv.qc.ca
Directrice, Hélène McGee

Montérégie
#500, 2, boul Desaulniers, Saint-Lambert, QC J4P 1L2
450-671-1231, Fax: 450-671-3884,
drmonter@mcccf.gouv.qc.ca
Directrice (par intérim), Diane Dupré

Montréal
#600, 480, boul St-Laurent, Montréal, QC H2Y 3Y7
514-873-2255, Fax: 514-864-2448,
dm@mcccf.gouv.qc.ca
Directrice, Brigitte Jacques

Outaouais
#4.140, 170, rue de l'Hôtel-de-Ville, 4e étage, Gatineau, QC J8X 4C2
819-772-3002, Fax: 819-772-3950,
dro@mcccf.gouv.qc.ca
Directrice, Danielle Dubé

Saguenay—Lac-Saint-Jean
202, rue Jacques-Cartier est, Chicoutimi, QC G7H 6R8
418-698-3500, Fax: 418-698-3522,
drslstj@mcccf.gouv.qc.ca
Directeur, Michel Bonneau

Directions régionales/Regional Offices:

Bas-Saint-Laurent - Gaspésie - Iles-de-la-Madeleine - Saguenay - Lac Saint Jean
#2, 1600, rue Bersimis, Chicoutimi, QC G7K 1H9
418-698-3530, Fax: 418-698-3533
Directrice régionale, Johanne Martel

Laurentides - Outaouais - Abitibi-Témiscamingue
Galeries de Buckingham, 999, rue Dollard, Gatineau, QC J8L 3E6
819-986-8985, Fax: 819-986-9793
Directrice régionale, Joanne Twigg

Mauricie - Centre-du-Québec - Estrie
#55, 5195, boul des Forges, Trois-Rivières, QC G8Y 4Z3
819-475-8506, Fax: 819-371-4907
Directeur régional, Guy Caron

Montérégie - Secteur Est
#3300, 1355, rue Gauvin, Saint-Hyacinthe, QC J2S 8W7
450-778-6530, Fax: 450-778-6540
Directeur régional, Claude Rivard

Montréal - Laval - Lanaudière
201, boul Crémazie est, 2e étage, Montréal, QC H2M 1L4
514-873-8101, Fax: 514-873-9994
Directeur régional (par intérim), Guy Caron

Québec - Chaudière-Appalaches
#C RC.245, 2700, rue Einstein, Québec, QC G1P 3W8
418-643-6140, Fax: 418-644-6327
Directeur régional, Laurent Bolduc

Pêches et aquaculture commerciales / Commercial Fishing & Aquaculture
Sous-ministre adjoint, Louis Vallée
418-380-2136, Fax: 418-380-2171
Directeur, Analyses et politiques, Abdoul Aziz Niang
418-380-2100, Fax: 418-380-2182
Directeur, Centre de coordination des projects spéciaux, Denis Lacerte
418-380-2100, Fax: 418-380-2182
Directeur, Innovation et technologies, Lucien Poirier
418-368-7637, Fax: 418-360-8400

Directions régionales/Regional Offices:

Côte-Nord
466, av Arnaud, Sept-Iles, QC G4R 3B1
418-964-8521, Fax: 418-964-8744,
drcn@mapag.gouv.qc.ca
Directeur régional, Alain Côté

Estuaire et Eaux intérieures
460, boul Louis-Fréchette, RC, Nicolet, QC J3T 1Y2
819-293-5677, Fax: 819-293-8519,
dreei@mapaq.gouv.qc.ca
Directeur régional, Paul Morin

Gaspésie
#206, 96, montée de Sandy Beach, Gaspé, QC G4X 2V6
418-368-7631, Fax: 418-360-8851,
drg@mapaq.gouv.qc.ca
Directeur régional, Marcel Roussy

Iles-de-la-Madeleine
Édifice Réjean-Richard, 101-125, ch du Parc, Cap-aux-Meules, QC G4T 1B3
418-986-2098, Fax: 418-986-4421,
drim@mapaq.gouv.qc.ca
Directeur régional, Donald Arseneau

Transformation Alimentaire Québec
Sous-ministre associé, Jean-Yves Lavoie
418-380-2136, Fax: 418-380-2171
Directeur, Daniel Chez
418-380-2100, Fax: 418-380-2189

Directeur, Appui à l'investissement, Gilles Hains
418-380-2202, Fax: 418-380-2164
Directeur, Coordination et analyses stratégiques, Gilles Bourget
418-380-2120, Fax: 418-380-2164
Directeur, Développement des exportations, Jean-Paul Lussiaà-Berdou
514-873-4147, Fax: 514-873-2364
Directrice (par intérim), Développement régional, Lyne Fournier
418-380-2202
Directeur, Institut de technologie agroalimentaire, André Simard
Directrice (par intérim), Développement régional, Lyne Fournier
514-873-4147, Fax: 514-873-2364

Action territoriale
Sous-ministre adjointe, Danielle-Claude Chartré
418-380-2330, Fax: 418-380-2392
Directrice générale, Relations multilatérales, diffusion & formation artistique, Sylvie Lemieux
418-380-2339, Fax: 418-380-2340
Directrice générale, Interventions régionales, Monique Barriault
418-380-2348, Fax: 418-380-2349

Bibliothèque et Archives nationales du Québec (BAnQ) / National Library & Archives of Québec
475, boul De Maisonneuve est, Montréal, QC H2L 5C4
514-873-1100, Fax: 514-873-9312, 800-363-9028
www.banq.qc.ca
Présidente-directrice générale, Lise Bissonnette

Commission de reconnaissance des associations d'artistes et des associations de producteurs / Commission for Recognition of Artists & Production Associations
#14.60, 500, boul René-Lévesque ouest, Montréal, QC H2Z 1W7
514-873-6012, Fax: 514-873-6267,
tribunal@craaap.gouv.qc.ca
www.craaap.gouv.qc.ca
Présidente (par intérim), Andrée St-Georges

Commission des biens culturels du Québec / Québec Cultural Property Commission
Bloc A-RC, 225, Grande Allée est, Québec, QC G1R 5G5
418-643-8378, Fax: 418-643-8591,
info@cbcq.gouv.qc.ca
www.cbcq.gouv.qc.ca
Président, Mario Dufour
Vice-présidente, Suzel Brunel

Conseil des arts et des lettres du Québec
#320, 79, boul René-Lévesque est, Québec, QC G1R 5N5
418-643-1707, Fax: 418-643-4558, 800-897-1707
info@calq.gouv.qc.ca
www.calq.gouv.qc.ca
Président et Directeur général, Yvan Gauthier

Institution nationale & sociétés d'État / Crown Corporations
Chargé de mission, Pierre Lafleur
418-380-2330, Fax: 418-380-2391
Directrice générale, Centre de conservation du Québec, Christiane Lévesque
418-643-7001, Fax: 418-646-5419
Directrice, Opérations, Francine Lalonde
418-380-2333, Fax: 418-380-2324
Directeur, Sociétés d'État, Yves Laliberté
418-380-2339, Fax: 418-380-2340

Musée d'art contemporain de Montréal (MACM) / Montréal Museum of Contemporary Art
185, rue Ste-Catherine ouest, Montréal, QC H2X 3X5
514-847-6226, Fax: 514-847-6290,
www.macm.org
Président, Marc De Serres

Musée de la civilisation / Museum of Civilisation
85, rue Dalhousie, CP 155 B, Québec, QC G1K 7A6
418-643-2158, Fax: 418-646-9705, 866-710-8031
mcqweb@mcq.org
www.mcq.org
Directrice générale, Claire Simard
csimard@mcq.org
Président, Henri Grondin

Musée national des beaux-arts du Québec
Parc des Champs-de-Bataille, 1, av Wolfe-Montcalm, Québec, QC G1R 5H3
418-643-2150, Fax: 418-646-3330, 866-220-2150
webmestre@mnba.qc.ca
www.mnba.qc.ca
Directeur général,Dr. John R. Porter
Président, Pierre Lassonde

Politiques, patrimoine, muséologie & communications / Policy, Heritage, Museology & Communication
Sous-ministre adjoint, Louis Vallée
418-380-2330, Fax: 418-380-2331
Directeur général, Patrimoine, muséologie & immobilisations, Denis Delangie
418-380-2352, Fax: 418-380-2336
Directeur (par intérim), Politiques de culture & de communications, Daniel Cloutier
418-380-2350, Fax: 418-380-2336,
Directeur (par intérim), Patriomoine & muséologie, Jean Bissonnette
418-380-2352, Fax: 418-380-2336
Directeur, Immobilisations, André Couture
418-380-2343, Fax: 418-380-2349

Régie du cinéma / Film Board
#100, 390, rue Notre-Dame ouest, Montréal, QC H2Y 1T9
514-873-2371, Fax: 514-873-2142, 800-463-2463
regieducinema@rcq.gouv.qc.ca
www.rcq.gouv.qc.ca
Président, Charles Bélanger
Directeur, Opérations, Robert Arthur
Directeur, Administration, Jean-Pierre Gagnon

Secrétariat à la Condition féminine / Status of Women Secretariat
Sous-ministre adjointe, Thérèse Mailloux
418-646-8395, Fax: 418-643-4991
Directrice, Coordination, Gina Morency
418-644-4417, Fax: 418-643-4991

Directions régionales/Regional Offices:

Secrétariat à la politique linguistique / French Language Board
225 Grande-Allée est, 4e étage, Québec, QC G1R 5G5
418-643-4248, Fax: 418-646-7832,
info@spl.gouv.qc.ca
www.spl.gouv.qc.ca
Sous-ministre associé responsable de l'application de la politique linguistique, Guy Dumas
Directeur, Jacques Gosselin

Société de développement des entreprises culturelles (SODEC) / Arts & Cultural Enterprise Development Commission
#800, 215, rue Saint-Jacques, Montréal, QC H2Y 1M6
514-841-2200, Fax: 514-841-8606, 800-363-0401
info@sodec.gouv.qc.ca
www.sodec.gouv.qc.ca
Président, Jean-Guy Chaput
Directeur des affaires juridiques & Secrétaire, Jean Valois
Directrice générale, Administration, Carole Hamelin

Société de la Place des Arts de Montréal / Montréal Place des Arts Corporation
260, boul de Maisonneuve ouest, Montréal, QC H2X 1Y9
514-285-4200, Fax: 514-285-1968,
info@pda.qc.ca
www.pda.qc.ca
Directrice générale, Marie Lavigne

Société de télédiffusion du Québec (Télé-Québec) / Radio-Québec
1000, rue Fullum, Montréal, QC H2K 3L7
514-521-2424, Fax: 514-873-7739, 800-361-4301
info@telequebec.tv
www.telequebec.tv
Présidente-directrice générale, Michèle Fortin
Directeur général, Programmes & nouveaux médias, Martin Roy
Directrice générale, Administration et finances, Michèle Parent

Société du Grand Théâtre de Québec / Grand Theatre of Québec
269, boul René-Lévesque est, Québec, QC G1R 2B3
418-644-8921, Fax: 418-646-7670,
www.grandtheatre.qc.ca
Présidente-directrice générale, Ann Mundy

Ministère de l'Agriculture, des Pêcheries et de l'Alimentation (MAPAQ) / Agriculture, Fisheries & Food

200, ch Sainte-Foy, Québec, QC G1R 4X6
418-380-2110, 888-222-6272
www.mapaq.gouv.qc.ca

Le Ministère influence et appuie l'essor de l'industrie bioalimentaire québécoise dans une perspective de développement durable; réalise des interventions en production, transformation, commercialisation & consommation des produits agricoles, marins & alimentaires; & joue un rôle important en matière de recherche & de développement, d'enseignement & de formation

Acts Administered:
Code municipal du Québec/Municipal Code of Québec (certain sections)
Loi assurant la reprise des activités de Madelipêche inc.
Loi sur l'acquisition de terres agricoles par des non-résidants/An Act governing the acquisition of farm land by non-residents
Loi sur les appellations réservées
Loi sur l'aquaculture commerciale/ An Act respecting commercial aquaculture
Loi sur l'assurance-prêts agricoles et forestiers/An Act respecting farm-loan insurance & forestry-loan insurance
Loi sur l'assurance-récolte/Crop Insurance Act
Loi sur l'assurance-stabilisation des revenus agricoles/An Act respecting farm income stabilization insurance
Loi sur l'école de laiterie et lesécoles moyennes d'agriculture/An Act respecting the École de laiterie & intermediate agricultural schools
Loi sur la commercialisation des produits marins/An Act respecting the marketing of marine products
Loi sur la conservation et la mise en valeur de la faune/An Act respecting the conservation & development of wildlife
Loi sur la prévention des maladies de la pomme de terre/An Act respecting prevention of disease in potatoes
Loi sur la protection des animaux pur sang/Thoroughbred Cattle Act
Loi sur la protection des plantes/Plant Protection Act
Loi sur la protection sanitaire des animaux/Animal Health Protection Act
Loi sur la transformation des produits marins/The Marine Products Processing Act
Loi sur le financement de la pêche commerciale/Maritime Fisheries Credit Act
Loi sur le mérite national de la pêche et de l'aquaculture/Fishermen's Merit Act
Loi sur le Mérite national de la restauration et de l'alimentation/Restaurant Merit Act
Loi sur le ministère de l'Agriculture, des Pêcheries et de l'Alimentation/An Act respecting the Ministère de l'Agriculture, des Pêcheries et de l'Alimentation
Loi sur les abus préjudiciables à l'agriculture/Agricultural Abuses Act
Loi sur les cités et villes/Cities & Towns Act (certain sections)
Loi sur les pêcheries commerciales et la récolte commerciale de végétaux aquatiques
Loi sur les produits agricoles, les produits marins et les aliments/Farm, Food & Fishery Products Act
Loi sur les producteurs agricoles/Farm Producers Act
Loi sur les produits alimentaires/Food Products Act
Loi sur les races animales du Patrimoine agricole du Qu ébec
Loi sur les sociétés agricoles et laitières/An Act respecting farmers' & dairymen's associations
Loi sur les sociétés d'horticulture/Horticultural Societies Act
Loi sur les terres agricoles du domaine de l'État/An Act respecting agricultural lands in the domain of the state
Ordre national du mérite agricole/Agricultural Merit Act
La Charte de la ville de Québec/The Charter of the City of Québec (certain sections)
La Charte de la Ville de Sherbrooke/The Charter of the City of Sherbrooke (certain sections)
La Charte de la Ville de Trois-Rivières/The Charter of the City of Trois-Rivières (certain sections)

Ministre,VACANTE
418-380-2525, Fax: 418-380-2184,ministre.mapaq@mapaq.gouv.qc.ca
Sous-ministre, Marc Dion
418-380-2136, Fax: 418-380-2171
Sous-ministre associée, Transformation Alimentaire Québec, Dominique Fortin
418-380-2136, Fax: 418-380-2171
Sous-ministre adjoint & Directeur général, Politiques agroalimentaires, Norman Johnston
418-380-2136, Fax: 418-380-2171
Sous-ministre adjoint & Directeur général, Développement régional & développement durable, Michel Bonneau
418-380-2136, Fax: 418-380-2171
Sous-ministre adjointe & Directrice générale, Alimentation, Madeleine Fortin
418-380-2136, Fax: 418-380-2171
Sous-ministre adjoint & Directeur général, Pêches & aquaculture commerciales, Yvan Savoie
418-380-2136, Fax: 418-380-2171
Sous-ministre adjointe & Directrice générale, Innovation & formation, Hélène Vincent
418-380-2136, Fax: 418-380-2171

• Commission de protection du territoire agricole du Québec/ Agricultural Land Preservation Commission
200, ch Ste-Foy, 2e étage
Québec, QC G1R 4X6
418-643-3314 Fax: 418-643-2261 800-667-5294
info@cptaq.gouv.qc.ca
www.cptaq.gouv.qc.ca
• La financière agricole de Québec
1400, boul de la Rive-Sud
Saint-Romuald, QC G6W 8K7

418-838-5602 Fax: 418-833-3871 800-749-3646
dir.comm@fadq.qc.ca
www.financiereagricole.qc.ca

• Régie des marchés agricoles et alimentaires du Québec/ Québec Agriculture & Food Marketing Board
201, boul Crémazie est, 5e étage
Montréal, QC H2M 1L3
514-873-4024 Fax: 514-873-3984
rmaaqc@rmaaq.gouv.qc.ca
www.rmaaq.gouv.qc.ca

Directions régionales/Regional Offices:

Abitibi-Témiscamingue - Nord-du-Québec
#2.01, 180, boul Rideau, Rouyn-Noranda, QC J9X 1N9
819-763-3287, Fax: 819-763-3359
Directrice régionale, Line Charland

Québec
Édifice 2, #RC22, 1685, boul Hamel ouest, Québec, QC G1N 3Y7
418-643-0033, Fax: 418-644-8263
Directrice régionale, Suzanne Pilote

Saguenay - Lac-Saint-Jean - Côte-Nord
801, ch du Pont-Taché nord, Alma, QC G8B 5W2
418-662-6457, Fax: 418-668-8694
Directeur régional, Alain Dessureault

Développement régional et développement durable / Regional Development/Sustainable Development
Sous-ministre adjoint, Michel Bonneau
Coordinateur, Opérations régionales, Sylvain Tremblay
Directeur, Soutien à l'enregistrement & remboursement des taxes, François Michaud
Directrice, Appui au développement des entreprises et de l'aménagement du territoire, Hélène Doddridge
Directeur (par intérim), Agroenvironnement et développement durable, Michel Riendeau

Alimentation / Food
dga@mapaq.gouv.qc.ca
Other Communication: Centre québécois d'inspection des aliments et de santé animale: 1-800-463-5023
Sous-ministre adjointe, Madeleine Fortin
418-380-2136, Fax: 418-380-2171
Directrice (par intérim), Institut national de santé animale, Martine Bouchard
418-380-2100, Fax: 418-380-2169
Directeur, Centre ministériel de sécurité civile, Guy Auclair
418-380-2100, Fax: 418-380-2169
Directrice, Coordination administrative et Services à la clientèle, Michèle Lavoie
418-380-2100, Fax: 418-380-2169
Directeur, Laboratoire d'expertises et d'analyses alimentaires, Jacques Ménard
418-266-4440, Fax: 418-266-4438
Directeur, Inspection des viandes, Claude Rivard
418-380-2100, Fax: 418-380-2169

Ministère du Développement durable, de l'Environnement et des Parcs / Sustainable Development, Environment & Parks

Édifice Marie-Guyart, 675, boul René-Lévesque est, 29e étage, Québec, QC G1R 5V7
418-521-3830, Fax: 418-646-5974, 800-561-1616
info@mddep.gouv.qc.ca
www.mddep.gouv.qc.ca

A pour mission d'assurer la protection de l'environnement & des écosystèmes naturels; de promouvoir le développement durable & d'assurer à la population un environnement sain en harmonie avec le développement économique & le progrès social du Québec

Acts Administered:
Loi instituant le Fonds national de l'eau
Loi portant restrictions à l'élevage de porcs/Act to Impose Restrictions on Pig Farming, 2002
Loi portant sur la délimitation de la ligne des hautes eaux du Fleuve Saint-Laurent sur le territoire de la municipalité régionale de comté de la Côte-de-Beaupré/An Act to delimit the high water mark
Loi sur la conservation du patrimoine naturel/Natural Heritage Conservation Act
Loi sur la conservation et la mise en valeur de la faune/Act respecting the Conservation & Development of Wildlife (in part)
Loi sur la protection des arbres/Tree Protection Act
Loi sur la provocation artificielle de la pluie/Act respecting the artificial inducement of rain
Loi sur la qualité de l'environnement/Environment Quality Act
Loi sur la sécurité des barrages/Dam Safety Act
Loi sur la Société des établissements de plein air du Québec
Loi sur la Société québécoise de récupération et de recyclage
Loi sur la vente et la distribution de bière et de boissons gazeuses dans des contenants à remplissage unique/Act respecting the Sale & Distribution of Beer & Soft Drinks in Non-returnable Containers
Loi sur le développement durable
Loi sur le ministère du Développement durable, de l'Environnement et des Parcs
Loi sur le parc de la Mauricie et ses environs
Loi sur le Parc Forillon et des environs
Loi sur le parc marin du Saguenay-Saint-Laurent
Loi sur le régime des eaux/Watercourses Act
Loi sur les espèces menacées ou vulnérables/Act respecting Threatened or Vulnerable Species
Loi sur les pesticides/Pesticides Act
Loi sur les parcs
Loi sur les villages cris et le village naskapi/The Cree Villages and the Naskapi Village Act
Loi visant la préservation des ressources en eau/Water Resources Preservation Act

Ministre,L'hon. Pierre Arcand
418-521-3911, Fax: 418-643-4143
Sous-ministre, Diane Jean
418-521-3860, Fax: 418-643-3619
Directeur (par intérim), Affaires juridiques, Pierre Normandin
418-521-3816, Fax: 418-646-0908
Secrétaire générale et Directrice, Vérification interne, Caroline Drouin
418-521-3810, Fax: 418-646-4762
Directeur, Communications, Jérôme Thibaudeau
418-521-3823, Fax: 418-646-4852
Directeur du Cabinet, François Émond
418-521-3911
Sous-ministre adjoint, Services à la gestion & au milieu terrestre, Frédéric Guay
Sous-ministre adjoint, Changements climatiques, à l'air & à l'eau, Charles Larochelle
Sous-ministre adjoint, Développement durable, Léopold Gaudreau
Sous-ministre adjoint, Expertise hydrique, analyse et évaluations environnementales, Jacques Dupoint
Sous-ministre adjoint, Analyse & expertise régionales/Centre de contrôle environnemental du Québec, Michel Rousseau

• Bureau d'audiences publiques sur l'environnement(BAPE) / Environmental Public Hearing Board
Édifice Lomer-Gouin
#2.10, 575, rue Saint-Amable, 2e étage
Québec, QC G1R 6A6
418-643-7447 Fax: 418-643-9474 800-463-4732
communication@bape.gouv.qc.ca
www.bape.gouv.qc.ca

• Comité consultatif de l'environnement Kativik(CCEK) / Kativik Environmental Advisory Committee
CP 930
Kuujjuaq, QC J0M 1C0
819-964-2961 Fax: 819-964-0694
ndea@krg.ca

• Société des établissements en plein air du Québec(SÉPAQ)
Place de la Cité
#250, 2640, boul Laurier
Sainte-Foy, QC G1V 5C2
418-890-6527 Fax: 418-528-6025 800-665-6527
inforeservation@sepaq.com
www.sepaq.com

• Société québécoise de récupération et de recyclage(RECYC-QUÉBEC)
Siège social
#200, 420, boul Charest est
Québec, QC G1K 8M4
418-643-0394 Fax: 418-643-6507 866-523-8290
info@recyc-quebec.gouv.qc.ca
www.recyc-quebec.gouv.qc.ca
Other Communication: Infoline: 1-800-807-0678; Montréal: 514/351-7835

Analyse et expertise régionales / Regional Analysis & Expertise
Édifice Marie-Guyart, 675, boul René-Lévesque est, 30e étage, Québec, QC G1R 5V7
418-521-3861, Fax: 418-646-1800
La mission est d'assurer l'analyse & la délivrance d'autorisations environnementales & d'offrir une expertise professionnelle en matière d'environnement
Sous-ministre adjoint, Michel Rousseau
418-521-3861, Fax: 418-646-1800

Changements climatiques / Climate Change
Sous-ministre adjoint, Charles Larochelle, 2008-09-16
418-521-3813, Fax: 418-646-4920
Directeur, Bureau des changements climatiques, Marcel Gaucher, 2008-09-16
Directrice, Relations intergouvernementales, Danielle Pronovost, 2008-09-16
Directeur (par intérim), Politiques de l'eau, Normand Boulianne, 2008-09-16
Directeur, Politiques de la qualité de l'atmosphère, Michel Goulet, 2008-09-16

Directions régionales/Regional Offices:

Baie-Comeau
20, boul Comeau, Baie-Comeau, QC G4Z 3A8
418-294-8888, Fax: 418-294-8018, cote-nord@mddep.gouv.qc.ca
Directeur, Alain Gaudreault

Gatineau
98, rue Lois, Gatineau, QC J8Y 3R7
819-772-3434, Fax: 819-772-3952, outaouais@mddep.gouv.qc.ca
Directeur, Marc Dubreuil

Laval
850, boul Vanier, Laval, QC H7C 2M7
450-661-2008, Fax: 450-661-2217, laval@mddep.gouv.qc.ca
Directeur, Pierre Robert

Longueuil
201, Place Charles-Le Moyne, 2e étage, Longueuil, QC J4K 2T5
450-928-7607, Fax: 450-928-7625, monteregie@mddep.gouv.qc.ca
Directeur, Pierre Paquin

Montréal
#3860, 5199, rue Sherbrooke est, Montréal, QC H1T 3X9
514-873-3636, Fax: 514-873-5662, montreal@mddep.gouv.qc.ca
Directeur, Pierre Robert

Nicolet
1579, boul Louis-Fréchette, Nicolet, QC J3T 2A5
819-293-4122, Fax: 819-293-8322, centre-du-quebec@mddep.gouv.qc.ca
Directeur, Luc St-Martin

Québec
365, 55e, rue Ouest, Québec, QC G1H 7M7
418-644-8844, Fax: 418-646-1214, capitale-nationale@mddep.gouv.qc.ca
Directeur, Jean-Marc Lachance

Repentigny
100, boul Industriel, Repentigny, QC J6A 4X6
450-654-4355, Fax: 450-654-6131, lanaudiere@mddep.gouv.qc.ca
Directeur, Pierre Robert

Rimouski
212, rue Belzile, Rimouski, QC G5L 3C3
418-727-3511, Fax: 418-727-3849, bas-saint-laurent@mddep.gouv.qc.ca
Directeur, Jean-Marie Dionne

Rouyn-Noranda
180, boul Rideau, 1er étage, Rouyn-Noranda, QC J9X 1N9
819-763-3333, Fax: 819-763-3202, abitibi-temiscamingue@mddep.gouv.qc.ca
Directrice, Edith van de Walle

Saguenay
3950, boul Harvey, 4e étage, Saguenay, QC G7X 8L6
418-695-7883, Fax: 418-695-7897, saguenay-lac-saint-jean@mddep.gouv.qc.ca
Directrice, Édith Tremblay

Sainte-Anne-des-Monts
124, 1e av ouest, Sainte-Anne-des-Monts, QC G4V 1C5
418-763-3301, Fax: 418-763-7810, gaspesie-iles-de-la-madeleine@mddep.gouv.qc.ca
Directeur, Jean-Marie Dionne

Sainte-Marie
#200, 675, rte Cameron, Sainte-Marie, QC G6E 3V7
418-386-8000, Fax: 418-386-8080, chaudiere-appalaches@mddep.gouv.qc.ca
Directeur, Jean-Marc Lachance

Sainte-Thérèse
#80, 300, rue Sicard, Sainte-Thérèse, QC J7E 3X5
450-433-2220, Fax: 450-433-1315, laurentides@mddep.gouv.qc.ca
Directeur, Pierre Robert

Sept-Iles
818, boul Laure, RC, Sept-Iles, QC G4R 1Y8
418-964-8888, Fax: 418-964-8023, cote-nord@mddep.gouv.qc.ca
Directeur, Alain Gaudreault

Sherbrooke
770, rue Goretti, Sherbrooke, QC J1E 3H4
819-820-3882, Fax: 819-820-3958, estrie@mddep.gouv.qc.ca
Directeur, Pierre Paquin

Trois-Rivières
100, rue Laviolette, 1er étage, Trois-Rivières, QC G9A 5S9
819-371-6581, Fax: 819-371-6987, mauricie@mddep.gouv.qc.ca
Directeur, Luc St-Martin

Expertise hydrique, analyse & évaluations environnementales / Water Systems, Analysis & Environmental Assessment
Sous-ministre adjoint, Jacques Dupont
418-521-3860, Fax: 418-643-7812
Directrice, Évaluations environnementales, Marie-Josée Lizotte
Directeur général, Centre d'expertise en analyse environnementale du Québec, Guy Chouinard
Directeur général, Centre d'expertise hydrique du Québec, Yvon Gosselin
Directeur, Accréditation et Relations externes, Julien Moreault

Directions régionales/Regional Offices:

Baie-Comeau
20, boulevard Comeau, Baie-Comeau, QC G4Z 3A8
418-294-8888, Fax: 418-294-8018, cote-nord@mddep.gouv.qc.ca
Directrice, Nadine Bégin

Gatineau
98, rue Lois, Gatineau, QC J8Y 3R7
819-772-3434, Fax: 819-772-3952, outaouais@mddep.gouv.qc.ca
Directeur, Léon Martin

Nicolet
1579, boulevard Louis-Fréchette, Nicolet, QC J3T 2A5
819-293-4122, Fax: 819-293-8322, centre-du-quebec@mddep.gouv.qc.ca
Directrice, Isabelle Olivier

Rimouski
212, avenue Belzile, Rimouski, QC G5L 3C3
418-727-3511, Fax: 418-727-3849, bas-saint-laurent@mddep.gouv.qc.ca
Directeur, Jules Boulanger

Rouyn-Noranda
180, boul Rideau, 1er étage, Rouyn-Noranda, QC J9X 1N9
819-763-3333, Fax: 819-763-3202, abitibi-temiscamingue@mddep.gouv.qc.ca
Directrice (par intérim), Édith van de Walle

Saguenay
3950, boul Harvey, 4e étage, Saguenay, QC G7X 8L6
418-695-7883, Fax: 418-695-7897, saguenay-lac-saint-jean@mddep.gouv.qc.ca
Directeur, Daniel Labrecque

Sainte-Marie
#200, 675, rte Cameron, Sainte-Marie, QC G6E 3V7
418-386-8000, Fax: 418-386-8080, chaudiere-appalaches@mddep.gouv.qc.ca
Directeur,VACANTE

Sherbrooke
770, rue Goretti, Sherbrooke, QC J1E 3H4
819-820-3882, Fax: 819-820-3958, estrie@mddep.gouv.qc.ca
Directeur, Émile Grieco

Montréal
#3860, 5199, rue Sherbrooke est, Montréal, QC H1T 3X9
514-873-3636, Fax: 514-873-5662, montreal@mddep.gouv.qc.ca
Directrice (par intérim), Hélène Proteau

Développement durable / Sustainable Development
418-521-3860, Fax: 418-646-5883
Sous-ministre adjoint, Léopold Gaudreau
418-521-3860, Fax: 418-646-5883
Directeur, Suivi de l'état de l'environnement, Luc Berthiaume
418-521-3820, Fax: 418-646-8483
Directeur, Bureau de Coordination du développement durable, Luc Vézina
418-521-3848
Directeur, Patrimoine écologique et des parcs, Patrick Beauchesne
418-521-3907, Fax: 418-646-6169

Services à la gestion & au milieu terrestre / Administrative Services & Earth Environment
418-521-3860, Fax: 418-643-9990
Sous-ministre adjoint (par intérim), Frédéric Guay
418-521-3860, Fax: 418-643-9990

Directeur, Matières résiduelles & lieux contaminés, Mario Bérubé
Directeur, Secteur agricole & pesticides, Didier Bicchi
Directeur, Ressources informationnelles & matérielles, Yvan Déry

Ministère du Développement économique, de l'Innovation et de l'Exportation / Economic Development, Innovation & Export Trade

710, place D'Youville, 3e étage, Québec, QC G1R 4Y4
418-691-5950, Fax: 418-644-0118, 866-680-1884
www.mdeie.gouv.qc.ca

A pour mission de soutenir le développement économique, l'innovation & l'exportation; d'offrir des services-conseils; de promouvoir l'image du Québec à l'étranger auprès des investisseurs

Acts Administered:
Loi favorisant l'augmentation du capital des petites et moyennes entreprises/An Act to promote the capitalization of small and medium-sized businesses
Loi sur Investissement Québec et sur la Financière du Québec/An Act respecting Investissement Québec and La Financière du Québec
Loi sur l'aide au développement des coopérative et des personnes morales sans but lucratif/An Act respecting assistance for the development of cooperatives and non-profit legal persons
Loi sur la Régie des installations olympiques
Loi sur la Société des alcools du Québec/An Act respecting the Société des alcools du Québec
Loi sur la Société du Centre des congrès de Québec
Loi sur la Société du Palais de Congrès de Montréal
Loi sur la Société du parc industriel et portuaire de Bécancour/ An Act respecting the Société du parc industriel et portuaire de Bécancour
Loi sur la Société générale de financement du Québec/ An Act respecting the Société générale de financement du Québec
Loi sur la Société Innovatech du Grand Montréal/An Act respecting the Société Innovatech du Grand Montréal
Loi sur la Société Innovatech du sud du Québec/An Act respecting the Société Innovatech du sud du Québec
Loi sur la Société Innovatech Québec et Chaudière-Appalaches/An Act respecting Société Innovatech Québec et Chaudière-Appalaches
Loi sur la Société Innovatech Régions ressources/An Act respecting Société Innovatech Régions ressources
Loi sur le Centre de recherche industriel du Québec/An Act respecting the Centre de recherche industrielle du Québec
Loi sur le ministère des Relations internationales/An Act respecting the Ministère des Relations internationales
Loi sur le ministère du Développement économique et régional et de la Recherche/An Act respecting the Ministère du Développement économique et régional et de la Recherche
Loi sur les concours artistiques, littéraires et scientifiques/An Act respecting artistic, literary and scientific competitions
Loi sur les coopératives/Cooperatives Act
Loi sur les heures et les jours d'admission dans les établissements commerciaux/An Act respecting hours and days of admission to commercial establishments
Loi sur les matériaux de rembourrage et les articles rembourrés/An Act respecting stuffing and upholstered and stuffed articles
Loi sur les sociétés de placement dans l'entreprise québécoise

Ministre,L'hon. Clément Gignac
418-691-5650
Sous-ministre, Christyne Tremblay
418-691-5656, Fax: 418-646-6497
Directeur général, Communications et services à la clientèle, Pierre Tessier
418-691-5653
Directeur (par intérim), Services à la gestion, Jean-Marc Sauvé
418-691-5963
Directeur, Vérification interne, Jacques St-Pierre
418-691-5698
Secrétaire général (par intérim), Linda Landry
418-691-5656, Fax: 418-646-6497

• Centre de recherche industrielle du Québec(CRIQ) / Industrial Research Centre of Québec
333, rue Franquet
Québec, QC G1P 4C7
418-659-1550 Fax: 418-652-2251 800-667-2386
infocriq@criq.qc.ca
www.criq.qc.ca
Recherche industrielle appliquée; services de RD pour des entreprises

• Conseil de la science et de la technologie/ Science & Technology Council
1150, Grande Allée ouest, RC
Québec, QC G1S 4Y9
418-691-5986
cst@cst.gouv.qc.ca
www.cst.gouv.qc.ca

• Fonds québécois de la recherche sur la nature et les technologies/ Québec Fund for Research on Nature and Technologies
#450, 140, Grande Allée est
Québec, QC G1R 5M8
418-643-8560 Fax: 418-643-1451
info@fqrnt.gouv.qc.ca
www.fqrnt.gouv.qc.ca

• Fonds québécois de la recherche sur la société et la culture/ Québec Fund for Research on Society and Culture
#470, 140, Grande Allée est
Québec, QC G1R 5M8
418-643-7582 Fax: 418-644-5248
fqrsc@fqrsc.gouv.qc.ca
www.fqrsc.gouv.qc.ca

• Fonds de la recherche en santé du Québec/ Québec Health Research Fund
#800, 500, rue Sherbrooke ouest
Montréal, QC H3A 3C6
514-873-2114 Fax: 514-873-8768
www.frsq.gouv.qc.ca

• Investissement Québec/ Investment Québec
#500, 1200, rte de l'Église
Québec, QC G1V 5A3
418-643-5172 866-870-0437
www.investquebec.com

• Société générale de financement du Québec/ Québec Financial Corporation
#1500, 600, rue de La Gauchetière ouest
Montréal, QC H3B 4L8
514-876-9290 Fax: 514-395-8055
info@sgfqc.com
www.sgfqc.com

• Innovatech Québec
#120, 925, Grande Allée ouest
Québec, QC G1S 1C1
418-528-9770 Fax: 418-528-9783 866-605-1676
info@innovatech-regions.qc.ca
www.innovatechquebec.com

Affaires économiques régionales / Regional Economic Affairs
Sous-ministre adjoint, Jean-Marc Sauvé
Directrice, Coordination régionale, Michèle Robert
418-528-0930, Fax: 418-528-8428
Directeur, Projet ACCORD, Xavier Fonteneau
Directrice, Programmes et mesures, Lise Mathieu
418-643-0060, Fax: 418-646-3609

Affaires économiques internationales / International Economic Affairs
Sous-ministre adjoint, Jean Séguin
514-499-2188, Fax: 514-873-4230
Directeur de la coordination (par intérim), Herman Vyncke
Directeur (par intérim), Amérique latine et Antilles, Rafaël Sanchez
418-691-5698, Fax: 418-643-0825
Directrice, Amérique du Nord, Chantal Castonguay
Directeur, Asie-Pacifique, Afrique et Moyen-Orient, Daniel Gagné
Directeur, Europe, Yves Lafortune
514-499-2185, Fax: 514-873-1540
Directeur, Promotion des investissements, Alain Proulx

Secteurs stratégiques et des projets économiques / Strategic Sectors and Economic Projects
Directrice, Biens de consommation, Marie-Annick Drouin
Directeur, Chimie, plasturgie, métallurgie et équipements, Clément Drolet
418-691-5976, Fax: 418-644-0519
Directrice, Coordination, Lisette Seyer
Directrice, Développement des industries, Diane Hastie
418-691-5698
Directeur, Environnement et services aux entreprises, Gaétan Poiré
418-691-5815, Fax: 418-644-1687
Directeur (par intérim), Équipements de transport, Bernard Strauss
514-499-6535, Fax: 514-864-3755
Directrice (par intérim), Santé et biotechnologies, Michèle Houpert
514-499-6534, Fax: 514-864-3755
Directrice, Technologies de l'information et des communications, Guylaine Leblanc
418-691-5957, Fax: 418-643-6947
Directeur, Commerce et construction, Pierre A. Forgues, 2008-09-16

Politiques et sociétés d'État / Policy & Crown Corporations
Sous-ministre adjoint, Brian Girard
418-691-5698, Fax: 418-644-3109
Directeur, Analyse économique, Christian Desbiens
Directrice (par intérim), Politiques économiques, Sylvie Miguel
Directeur, Politique commerciale pour les accords internationaux, Jocelyn Savoie
Directrice, Coopératives, Lise Jacob
418-646-6145, Fax: 418-646-6145
Directeur, Sociétés d'État & entrepreneuriat, Richard Carbonneau
Directeur, Coordination, planification et évaluation, François-Maxime Langlois
Directeur (par intérim), Politique commerciale/Politique commercial pour l'Amérique du Nord, Patrick Muzzi
418-643-4347, Fax: 418-691-5995
Directeur, Développement des entreprises, Bertrand Verbruggen

Recherche, innovation, science et société / Research, Innovation, Science & Society
Sous-ministre adjointe, Geneviève Tanguay
418-528-2515, Fax: 418-528-0234
Directrice, Collaborations internationales, Marie-Josée Blais
Directeur, Recherche universitaire & collégiale, Luc Castonguay
418-646-1447, Fax: 418-646-6888
Directeur, Financement des infrastructures de recherche, Gaston Beaudoin
Directrice (par intérim), Innovation & transfert, Frédérique-Myriam Villemure
Directrice, Science & société, Monique La Rue
Directeur (par intérim), Politiques & analyses, Mawana Pongo, 2008-09-16
Directrice (par intérim), Coordination & concertation, Marie-Odile Koch, 2008-09-16

Directions régionales/Regional Offices:

Abitibi-Témiscamingue
#202, 170, av Principale, Rouyn-Noranda, QC J9X 4P7
819-763-3561, Fax: 819-763-3462
Directeur, Gilles Quintal

Bas-St-Laurent
#RC 04, 337, rue Moreault, Rimouski, QC G5L 1P4
418-727-3577, Fax: 418-727-3640
Directeur, Roger Cyr

Capitale-Nationale
900, Place d'Youville, 3e étage, Québec, QC G1R 3P7
418-691-5824, Fax: 418-643-4099
Directeur (par intérim), Jean-François Talbot

Centre-du-Québec
Édifice provincial, #1.03, 62, rue Saint-Jean-Baptiste, Victoriaville, QC G6P 4E3
819-752-9781, Fax: 819-758-4306
Directeur, Vincent Bourassa

Chaudière-Appalaches
#1, 1055, boul Vachon nord, Sainte-Marie, QC G6E 1M4
418-386-8677, Fax: 418-386-8037
Directeur, Normand Giguère

Côte-Nord
#RC 711, 625, boul Laflèche, Baie-Comeau, QC G5C 1C5
418-589-4349, Fax: 418-295-4199
Directeur, Jacques Chiasson

Estrie
#4.05, 200, rue Belvédère nord, Sherbrooke, QC J1H 4A9
819-820-3731, Fax: 819-820-3929
Directeur, Robert Fortin

Gaspésie/Iles-de-la-Madeleine
#10A, 500, av Daigneault, CP 1360, Chandler, QC G0C 1K0
418-689-2019, Fax: 418-689-4108
Directeur (par intérim), Denis Goulet

Lanaudière
#3300, 40, rue Gauthier sud, Joliette, QC J6E 4J4
450-752-8050, Fax: 450-752-8064,
Directeur, Daniel Boutin

Laurentides
#C3.35, 85, rue de Martigny, Saint-Jérôme, QC J7Y 3R8
450-569-3031, Fax: 450-569-3039
Directeur (par intérim), Serge Thériault

Laval
#RC-30, 705, ch de Trait-Carré, Laval, QC H7N 1B3
450-680-6175, Fax: 450-972-3090
Directrice, Diane F. Bélanger

Mauricie
Édifice Capitanal, #114, 100, rue Laviolette, Trois-Rivières, QC G9A 5S9
819-371-6617, Fax: 819-371-6960
Directeur (par intérim), Denis Hébert

Montérégie
#101, 201, Place Charles-Lemoyne, Longueuil, QC J4K 2T5
450-928-7645, Fax: 450-928-7465
Directeur, Yves Lafortune

Montréal
380, rue Saint-Antoine ouest, 5e étage, Montréal, QC H2Y 3X7
514-499-2550, Fax: 514-873-9913
Directeur, Pierre Hébert

Nord-du-Québec
333, 3e rue, Chibougamau, QC G8P 1N4
418-748-6681, Fax: 418-748-6698
Directeur, Denis Darveau

Outaouais
#7.200, 170, rue de l'Hôtel-de-Ville, Gatineau, QC J8X 4C2
819-772-3038, Fax: 819-772-3968
Directeur, Jeffrey MacHan

Saguenay/Lac-Saint-Jean
3950, boul Harvey, 2e étage, Jonquière, QC G7X 8L6
418-695-7971, Fax: 418-695-7870
Directeur, Denis Darveau

Commission des droits de la personne et des droits de la jeunesse / Commission for Human Rights & the Rights of Youth

360, rue St-Jacques, 2e étage, Montréal, QC H2Y 1P5
514-873-5146, Fax: 514-873-6032, 800-361-6477
webmestre@cdpdj.qc.ca
www.cdpdj.qc.ca

A pour mission d'assurer la promotion et la respect des droits et libertés affirmés par la Charte des droits et libertés de la personne, par la Loi sur la protection de la jeunesse, et par la Loi sur les jeunes contrevenants
Président, Gaétan Cousineau
Vice-présidente, Sylvie Godin

Ministère de l'Éducation, du Loisir et du Sport / Education, Leisure & Sports

1035, rue De La Chevrotière, 28e étage, Québec, QC G1R 5A5
418-643-7095, Fax: 418-646-6561, 866-747-6626
www.mels.gouv.qc.ca

Acts Administered:
Charte de la langue française/Charter of the French language
Loi concernant le transfert de la propriété d'un immeuble à la Commission scolaire de Montréal et modifiant la Loi sur l'instruction publique/Act respecting the transfer of the ownership of an immovab
Loi concernant les conditions d'utilisation d'immeubles de la Commission des écoles protestantes du Grand Montréal par la Commission des écoles catholiques de Montréal/Act respecting conditions govern
Loi du mérite scolaire/Scholastic Merit Act
Loi favorisant la conclusion d'ententes dans le secteur de l'éducation/Act to foster labour agreements in the education sector
Loi modifiant diverses dispositions législatives dans le secteur de l'éducation concernant la confessionnalité/Act to amend various legislative provisions respecting education as regards confessional
Loi sur l'accréditation et le financement des associations d'élèves ou d'étudiants/Act respecting the accreditation and financing of students' associations
Loi sur l'aide financière aux études/Act respecting financial assistance for education expenses
Loi sur l'École de laiterie et les écoles moyennes d'agriculture/Act respecting the École de laiterie and intermediate agricultural schools
Loi sur l'élection des premiers commissaires des commissions scolaires nouvelles et modifiant diverses dispositions législatives/Act respecting the election of the first commissioners of the new schoo
Loi sur l'enseignement privé/Act respecting private education
Loi sur l'Institut de tourisme et d'hôtellerie du Québec/Act respecting the Institut de tourisme et d'hôtellerie du Québec
Loi sur l'instruction publique/Education Act
Loi sur l'instruction publique pour les autochtones cris, inuits et naskapis/Education Act for Cree, Inuit and Naskapi Native Persons
Loi sur l'Université du Québec/Act respecting the Université du Québec
Loi sur la Commission d'évaluation de l'enseignement collégial/Act respecting the Commission d'évaluation de l'enseignement collégial
Loi sur le Conseil supérieur de l'éducation/Act respecting the Institut de tourisme et d'hôtellerie du Québec
Loi sur le ministère de l'Éducation/Act respecting the Ministère de l'Éducation
Loi sur les collèges d'enseignement général et professionnel/General and Vocational Colleges Act
Loi sur les élections scolaires/Act respecting school elections
Loi sur les établissements d'enseignement de niveau universitaire/Act respecting educational institutions at the university level
Loi sur les fondations universitaires/Act respecting university foundations
Loi sur les investissements universitaires/Univeristy Investments Act
Ministre,L'hon. Line Beauchamp
418-644-0664, Fax: 418-646-7551
Sous-ministre, Christiane Barbe
418-643-3810, Fax: 418-644-4591
Directeur, Secrétariat aux affaires religieuses, Roger Boisvert
418-643-7070, Fax: 418-644-7142
Directeur, Accès à l'information et plaintes, Paul Rémillard
Directeur (par intérim), Affaires juridiques, Jean Emond
418-643-3747, Fax: 418-646-6849
Directrice, Secrétariat général, Anne Moore
Directrice, Condition féminine, Raymonde Villemure
Directeur, Vérification interne, Christian Boivin
Directrice, Communications, Marie Lavoie
Sous-ministre adjoint, Services à la communauté anglophone & Affaires autochtones, Leo La France
Sous-ministre adjoint, Éducation préscolaire, enseignement primaire & secondaire/Régions, Alain Veilleux
Sous-ministre adjointe, Réseaux, Manuelle Oudar
Sous-ministre adjointe, Formation professionnelle, technique & continue, Mimi Pontbriand
Sous-ministre adjoint (par intérim), Enseignement supérieur, Pierre Boutet
Sous-ministre adjoint, Rémunération globale dans le réseau universitaire, Gilles Charland
Sous-ministre adjointe, Services en soutien à la mission & aide financière aux études, Brigitte Guay
Sous-ministre adjoint, Secrétariat au loisir & au sport, Jean-Guy Ouellette
Directeur général, Politiques, recherche & planification stratégique, Jean Tremblay

• Commission consultative de l'enseignement privé/ Advisory Committee on Private Education
1035, rue De La Chevrotière, 14e étage
Québec, QC G1R 5A5
418-646-1249 Fax: 418-643-7752
Other Communication: EMail: commission.consultative@mels.gouv.qc.ca

• Commission de l'éducation en langue anglaise/ Advisory Board on English Education
600, rue Fullum, 9e étage
Montréal, QC H2K 4L1
514-873-5656 Fax: 514-864-4181
cela-abee@mels.gouv.qc.ca
www.mels.gouv.qc.ca/cela/anglais.htm

• Commission d'évaluation de l'enseignement collégial/ College Teachers Assessment Commission
800, place d'Youville, 18e étage
Québec, QC G1R 5P4
418-643-9938 Fax: 418-643-9019
info@ceec.gouv.qc.ca
www.ceec.gouv.qc.ca

• Commission des programmes d'études/ Study Program Commission
#1.85, 525, boul René-Lévesque est
Québec, QC G1R 5Z4
418-646-0133 Fax: 418-643-5431
cpe@mels.gouv.qc.ca
www.cpe.gouv.qc.ca

• Conseil supérieur de l'éducation/ Superior Council of Education
#180, 1175, av Lavigerie
Sainte-Foy, QC G1V 5B2
418-643-3850 Fax: 418-644-2530
panorama@cse.gouv.qc.ca
www.cse.gouv.qc.ca

Direction générale des politiques, recherche et planification stratégique / Policy, Research & Strategic Planning
Directeur général, Jean Tremblay
Directrice, Politiques, Josée Bourdages
Directrice, Recherche, statistiques et information, Myriam Proulx
Directrice (par intérim), Service de la recherche et évaluation, Valérie Saysset
Directrice, Service de l'information décisionnelle et de la géomatique, Anne-Marie Carpentier

Secteur du Soutien à la mission et l'Aide financière aux études / Student Financial Aid
1035, rue De La Chevrotière, Québec, QC G1R 5A5
418-643-3750, 877-643-3750
www.afe.gouv.qc.ca
Sous-ministre adjointe, Brigitte Guay
418-646-5313, Fax: 418-528-0779
Directrice, Services administratifs, Nicole Martel
Directrice, Service de planification & programmes, Sonia Léveillé
Directrice, Gestion des prêts, Suzanne Gingras

Secteur de l'Éducation préscolaire, enseignement primaire et secondaire, et régions / Preschool, Elementary & Secondary School Education
Sous-ministre adjoint, Alain Veilleux
418-643-3810, Fax: 418-644-2131
Directrice, Services de soutien aux élèves, Denise Gosselin
Directeur, Services à l'enseignement, Guy Dumais
Directrice, Service aux communautés culturelles, Claire Chamberland
514-873-3458, Fax: 514-873-8793
Directrice, Programmes, Catherine Dupont
418-644-5213, Fax: 418-528-8023
Directrice, Adaptation scolaire, Anne Robitaille
418-646-7000, Fax: 418-644-5914
Directeur, Sanction des études, Jean-Guy Hamel
418-644-0905, Fax: 418-644-6909
Directrice, Évaluation, Linda Drouin
514-864-1896, Fax: 514-873-2571
Directeur (par intérim), Ressources didactiques, Guy Dumais

Secteur de l'Enseignement supérieur / Higher Education
Sous-ministre adjointe, Christiane Piché
418-643-3810, Fax: 418-646-1526
Directeur, Affaires universitaires et collégiales, Robert Poulin
Directrice, Affaires étudiantes, Ginette Dion
418-646-4133, Fax: 418-643-0622,
Directeur, Enseignement collégial, Christian Ragusich
418-644-8976, Fax: 418-646-7447
Directrice, Équipement, Hélène Guenette
418-643-6524, Fax: 418-644-3090
Directeur, Financement et équipement, Pierre Boutet
418-646-4533, Fax: 418-644-3090
Directeur, Programmation budgétaire et financement, Jean Leroux
418-528-0074, Fax: 418-644-3090
Directeur (par intérim), Soutien aux établissements, Michel-André Roy
418-646-1534, Fax: 418-643-7100
Directeur, Systèmes et contrôle, Pierre Larochelle
418-643-2999, Fax: 418-643-8456

Régions / Regions
Directeur général, Régions, Alain Veilleux
418-643-7498, Fax: 418-646-8419
Abitibi-Témiscamingue/Nord-du-Québec
215, boul Rideau, Rouyn-Noranda, QC J9X 5Y6
819-763-3001, Fax: 819-763-3017,
dr-08@meq.gouv.qc.ca
Directrice régionale par intérim, Louise Bilodeau
Bas-Saint-Laurent/Gaspésie/Iles-de-la-Madeleine
355, boul Saint-Germain ouest, 2e étage, Rimouski, QC G5L 3N2
418-727-3600, Fax: 418-727-3557,
dr-01@meq.gouv.qc.ca
Directeur régional, Gérard Bédard
Capitale-Nationale/Chaudière-Appalaches
1020, rte de l'Église, 3e étage, Québec, QC G1V 3V9
418-643-7934, Fax: 418-643-0972,
dr-03@meq.gouv.qc.ca
Directrice régionale, Marie-Sylvie Descôteaux
Côte-Nord (Services adm. et gen.)
Édifice Paul-Provencher, #1.812, RC, 625, boul Laflèche, Baie-Comeau, QC G5C 1C5
418-295-4400, Fax: 418-295-4467,
dr09-bc@meq.gouv.qc.ca
Directrice régionale, Lucy de Mendonça
Côte-Nord (Services éducatifs)
106, rue Napoléon, 2e étage, Sept-Iles, QC G4R 3L7
418-964-8420, Fax: 418-964-8504,
dr09-si@meq.gouv.qc.ca
Directrice régionale, Lucy de Mendonça
Estrie
#3.05, 200, rue du Belvédère nord, Sherbrooke, QC J1H 4A9
819-820-3382, Fax: 819-820-3947,
dr-05@meq.gouv.qc.ca
Directrice régionale, Diane Lamothe
Laval/Laurentides/Lanaudière
#200, 300, rue Sicard, Sainte-Thérèse, QC J7E 3X5
450-430-3611, Fax: 450-430-4005,
dr-061@meq.gouv.qc.ca
Directrice régionale, Lauraine Langlois
Mauricie/Centre-du-Québec
Édifice Capitanal, #213, 100, rue Laviolette, Trois-Rivières, QC G9A 5S9
819-371-6711, Fax: 819-971-6075,
dr-04@meq.gouv.qc.ca
Other Communication: Email: dr-17@meq.gouv.qc.ca
Directeur régional, Claude Lamarre
Montérégie
Édifice Montval, 201, Place Charles-Le Moyne, 6e étage, Longueuil, QC J4K 2T5
450-928-7438, Fax: 450-928-7451,
dr-062@meq.gouv.qc.ca
Directeur régionale, Francis Culée
Montréal
600, rue Fullum, 10e étage, Montréal, QC H2K 4L1
514-873-4630, Fax: 514-873-7281,
dr-063@meq.gouv.qc.ca
Directeur régional, Gilles Lamirande
Outaouais
170, rue de l'Hôtel-de-Ville, 4e étage, Gatineau, QC J8X 4C2
819-772-3382, Fax: 819-772-3955,
dr-07@meq.gouv.qc.ca
Directrice régionale (par intérim), Hélène Audet

Directions régionales/Regional Offices:
Saguenay/Lac-Saint-Jean
Édifice Marguerite-Belley, 3950, boul Harvey, 2e étage, Jonquière, QC G7X 8L6
418-695-7982, Fax: 418-695-7990,
dr-02@meq.gouv.qc.ca
Directeur régionale, François Paquette

Secteur de la Formation professionnelle et technique et formation continue / Professional & Technical Training & Continuing Education
Sous-ministre adjointe, Mimi Pontbriand
418-643-3810, Fax: 418-644-4591
Directrice, Éducation des adultes & action communautaire, Geneviève Moisan
Directrice, Formation continue et soutien, Jocelyne Hallé
Directeur, Gestion sectorielle des ressources, Yves Bourassa
Directrice, Planification et coordination sectorielles, Julie Lévesque
Directrice, Programmes et la veille sectorielle, Nora Desrochers

Secteur des Réseaux / Networks
Sous-ministre adjointe, Manuelle Oudar
418-643-3810, Fax: 418-646-9220
Directeur, Financement et équipement, René Lepage
Directrice, Enseignement privé, Lise Briand
418-646-3935, Fax: 418-643-7752
Directeur, Relations du travail-personnel professionnel & soutien, Mario Doyon
Directeur, Relations du travail, Jean Beauchesne
Directeur, Relations du travail-personnel enseignant, Éric Bergeron
Directeur, Politiques et opérations budgétaires, Serge Dupéré
Directeur, Équipement scolaire, Gilles Marchand
418-644-2525, Fax: 418-643-9224
Directrice, Conditions de travail du personnel d'encadrement, Françoise Dion
Directrice, Opérations financières aux réseaux, Catherine Tremblay
Responsable, Greffe des tribunaux d'arbitrage, Marc Pelletier

Secrétariat au loisir et au sport / Sport & Recreation Secretariat
Sous-ministre adjoint, Jean-Guy Ouellette
418-646-6018, Fax: 418-644-9474
Directeur, Sport et activité physique, Robert Bédard
Directeur (par intérim), Loisir, Robert Bédard, 2008-09-17

Secteur des Services à la communauté anglophone et Affaires autochtones / Anglophone Services & Aboriginal Affairs
Sous-ministre adjoint, Directeur, Politiques & projets, & Directeur par intérim, Affaires autochtones, Léo La France
Directrice, Production en langue anglaise, Liette Michaud
514-873-6073, Fax: 514-873-2687

Directeur général des Élections du Québec / Chief Electoral Officer of Québec

Édifice René-Lévesque, 3460, rue de La Pérade, Québec, QC G1X 3Y5
418-528-0422, Fax: 418-643-7291, 888-353-2846
info@electionsquebec.qc.ca
www.dgeq.qc.ca

Acts Administered:
Loi électorale du Québec/Election Act
Loi sur la consultation populaire/Referendum Act
Loi sur les élections et les référendums dans les municipalités/An Act respecting Elections & Referendums in Municipalities
Loi sur les élections scolaires
Directeur général, Élections du Québec & Président de la Commission de la représentation électorale, Marcel Blanchet
Commissaire, Serge Courville
Commissaire, John Zacharias

Ministère de l'Emploi et de la Solidarité sociale / Employment & Social Solidarity

425, rue St-Amable, 4e étage, Québec, QC G1R 4Z1
418-643-4721, 888-643-4721
www.mess.gouv.qc.ca

Acts Administered:
Loi favorisant le développement de la formation de la main-d'ouvre/An Act to foster the development of manpower training
Loi instituant le Fonds de lutte contre la pauvreté par la réinsertion au travail/An Act to establish a fund to combat poverty through reintegration into the labour market
Loi sur l'Office de la sécurité du revenu des chasseurs et piégeurs cris/An Act respecting income security for Cree hunters and trappers who are beneficiaries under the Agreement concerning James Bay
Loi sur la formation et la qualification professionnelles de la main-d'ouvre/An Act respecting manpower vocational training and qualification
Loi sur le ministère de l'Emploi et de la Solidarité sociale et instituant la Commission des partenaires du marché du travail/An Act respecting the Ministère de l'Emploi et de la Solidarité and establ
Loi sur le ministère du Conseil exécutif/An Act respecting the Ministère du Conseil exécutif
Loi sur le régime de rentes du Québec/An Act respecting the Québec Pension Plan
Loi sur le soutien du revenu et favorisant l'emploi et la solidarité sociale/An Act respecting income support, employment assistance and social solidarity
Loi sur les régimes complémentaires de retraite/Supplemental Pension Plans Act
Loi sur les villages nordiques et l'Administration régionale Kativik/An Act respecting Northern villages and the Kativik Regional Government
Loi visant à lutter contre la pauvreté et l'exclusion sociale/An Act to combat poverty and social exclusion
Ministre,L'hon. Julie Boulet
418-643-6980, Fax: 418-643-2033
Sous-ministre, Dominique Savoie
418-643-4820, Fax: 418-643-1226
Directeur, Bureau du sous-ministre, Laval Tremblay
418-643-4820, Fax: 418-643-1226
Directeur, Affaires juridiques, Daniel Morin
418-643-4998, Fax: 418-646-8559
Directrice, Direction de la vérification interne et des enquêtes administratives, Annie Tremblay
418-643-1356, Fax: 418-644-3641
Directrice (par intérim), Ressources humaines, Sylvie Grenier
418-643-4960
• Commission des partenaires du marché du travail/ Labour Market Partnerships Commission
#2800, 800, rue du Square-Victoria
CP 100
Montréal, QC H4Z 1B7
514-873-5252 Fax: 514-864-8005
partenaires@messf.gouv.qc.ca
• Office de la sécurité du revenu des chasseurs et piègeurs cris/ Cree Hunters & Trappers Income Security Board
Édifice Champlain
#1110, 2700, boul Laurier
Sainte-Foy, QC G1V 4K5
418-643-7300 Fax: 418-643-6803
courrier@osrcpc.ca
• Régie des rentes du Québec/ Québec Pension Board
CP 5200
Sainte-Foy, QC G1K 7S9
418-643-5185
rrq@rrq.gouv.qc.ca
www.rrq.gouv.qc.ca

Affaires gouvernementales et relations avec les citoyens / Governmental Affairs & Citizen Relations
Sous-ministre adjoint, Jacques Duguay
418-644-6430, Fax: 418-646-5426,
Directrice, Communications, Josée Tremblay
Directrice, Bureau des renseignements et plaintes, Louise Proulx
Directrice, Affaires canadiennes et internationales, Ginette Galarneau
514-864-6058, Fax: 514-873-1087
Directeur, Révision et recours administratifs, Bertrand Olivier
418-528-8004, Fax: 418-528-7803

Centre de communication avec la clientèle / Client Call Centre
514-873-4000, 877-767-8773
Centre d'appels dont la mission est de répondre rapidement aux questions sur les services de solidarité sociale

Emploi-Québec / Employment Québec
#2800, 800, rue du Square-Victoria, Montréal, QC H4Z 1B7
514-873-1892, 888-367-5647
www.emploiquebec.net
Sous-ministre associé, Bernard Matte

Opérations Emploi-Québec / Emploi-Québec Operations Directorate
Sous-ministre associée, Dominique Savoie
Directeur général adjoint, Planification, performance & information sur le marché du travail, Michel Cournoyer
Directrice générale adjointe, Mesures & services, Johanne Bourassa
Directrice, Mesures & services de solidarité sociale, Monique Delisle
Directeur, Planification, stratégies & information de gestion, Richard St-Pierre
Directrice, Mesures & services d'emploi, Odette Corneau

Politiques & l'analyse stratégique / Policy & Strategic Analysis
Sous-ministre adjointe, Marie-Renée Roy
418-643-7006, Fax: 418-644-1299
Directeur général adjoint, Recherche, évaluation & statistique, Serge Hamel
Directeur général adjoint, Politiques & prospective, Éric Théroux
Directeur, Politiques d'emploi & de main-d'oeuvre, Daniel Doyon

Opérations / Operations
Sous-ministre adjoint, Claude Blouin
418-646-2876, Fax: 418-643-6329
Directeur général adjoint (par intérim), Administration & projets corporatifs, Michel Lalande
Directeur, Coordination du développement des systèmes d'information, Beniamino Colombo
Directrice, Modernisation des modes de prestation de services, Claudine Bouchard
Directeur, Soutien & qualité des applications informatiques, Mario Godin
Directeur, Budget & services administratifs, Michel Lalande

Ministère de la Famille et des Aînés / Family & Seniors

425, rue Saint-Amable, 1er étage, Québec, QC G1R 4Z1
877-216-6202
www.mfa.gouv.qc.ca

Acts Administered:
Loi favorisant l'établissement d'un régime de retraite à l'intention d'employés oeuvrant dans le domaine des services de garde à l'enfance/An Act to facilitate the establishment of a Pension Plan for
Loi sur le Conseil de la famille et de l'enfance/An Act respecting the Conseil de la Famille et de l'Enfance
Loi sur le ministère de la Famille et de l'Enfance/An Act respecting the Ministère de la Famille et de l'Enfance
Loi sur les centres de la petite enfance et autres services de garde à l'enfance/An Act respecting Childcare Centres and Childcare Services
Loi sur les prestations familiales/An Act respecting Family Benefits
Ministre, Famille, L'hon. Yolande James
418-643-2181, Fax: 418-643-2640,ministre.famille@mfa.gouv.qc.ca
Ministre responsable, Aînés, L'hon. Marguerite Blais
418-646-7757, Fax: 418-646-7769
Sous-ministre, Louise Pagé
418-646-4680, Fax: 418-646-4903
Secretaire générale, Carmen Bellemare
• Conseil de la famille et de l'enfance/ Family & Childhood Council
#800, 900, boul René-Lévesque est
Montréal, QC G1R 6B5
514-646-7678 Fax: 514-643-9832 877-221-7024
www.cfe.gouv.qc.ca/
Other Communication: Email: conseil.famille.enfance@cfe.gouv.qc.ca
• Conseil des aînés/ Seniors Council
#810, 900, boul René-Lévesque est, 8e étage
Québec, QC G1R 2B5
418-643-0071 Fax: 418-643-1916 877-657-2463
aines@conseil-des-aines.qc.ca
www.conseil-des-aines.qc.ca
• Conseil du statut de la femme/ Status of Women Council
800, place D'Youville, 3e étage
Québec, QC G1R 6E2
418-643-4326 Fax: 418-643-8926 800-463-2851
csf@csf.gouv.qc.ca
www.csf.gouv.qc.ca
• Curateur public du Québec/ Québec Public Trustee
600, boul René-Lévesque ouest, 10e étage
Montréal, QC H3B 4W9
514-873-4074 Fax: 514-873-5033 800-363-9020
information@curateur.gouv.qc.ca
www.curateur.gouv.qc.ca

Agences, conseils et commissions/associes/Associated Agencies, Boards & Commissions:

Ministère des Finances / Finance

Édifice Gérard-D.-Lévesque, 12, rue Saint-Louis, Québec, QC G1R 5L3
418-528-9323, Fax: 418-646-1631,
info@finances.gouv.qc.ca
www.finances.gouv.qc.ca

Acts Administered:
Loi sur l'administration financière/Financial Administration Act
Loi sur l'assurance automobile
Loi sur l'assurance-dépôts
Loi sur les assurances
Loi sur l'Autorité des marchés financiers
Loi sur la Caisse de dépôt et placement du Québec
Loi sur les caisses d'entraide économique
Loi concernant certaines caisses d'entraide économique
Loi sur les caisses d'épargne et de crédit
Loi constituant Capital régional et coopératif Desjardins
Loi sur les centres financiers internationaux
Loi sur les compagnies
Loi sur les compagnies de télégraphe et de téléphone
Loi sur les compagnies minières
Loi sur les coopératives de services financiers
Loi sur le courtage immobilier
Loi sur les dépôts et consignations
Loi sur la distribution de produits et services financiers
Loi sur l'équilibre budgétaire
Loi sur l'exercice des activités de bourse au Québec par Nasdaq
Loi sur Financement-Québec
Loi constituant Fondaction, le Fonds de développement de la Confédération des syndicats nationaux pour la coopération et l'emploi
Loi constituant le Fonds de solidarité des travailleurs du Québec
Loi sur les frais de garantie relatifs aux emprunts des organismes gouvernementaux
Loi sur l'information concernant la rémunération des dirigeants de certaines personnes morales
Loi sur l'Institut de la statistique du Québec
Loi sur le ministère de l'Agriculture, des Pêcheries et de l'Alimentation
Loi sur le ministère des Finances/Act respecting the ministère des Finances
Loi sur le Mouvement Desjardins
Loi sur les pouvoirs spéciaux des personnes morales
Loi sur la réduction du capital-actions de personnes morales de droit public et leurs filiales
Loi sur la Régie de l'assurance maladie du Québec
Loi sur le remplacement de programmes conjoints par un abattement fiscal
Loi sur la Société de financement des infrastructures locales du Québec et modifiant le Code de la Sécurité routière
Loi sur la Société des alcools du Québec
Loi sur la Société des loteries du Québec
Loi concernant la Société nationale du cheval de course
Loi sur les sociétés d'entraide économique
Loi sur les sociétés fiducie et les sociétés d'épargne
Loi concernant les subventions relatives au paiement en capital et intérêts des emprunts des organismes publics ou municipaux
Loi sur les valeurs mobilières
Ministre, Raymond Bachand
418-643-5270, Fax: 418-646-1574
Sous-ministre, Gilles Paquin
418-643-5738, Fax: 418-528-5546
Sous-ministre ajoint, Politiques féd.-prov., financement, gestion de la dette & opérations financières, Bernard Turgeon
418-643-5738, Fax: 418-646-8611
Sous-ministre adjoint, Politiques économiques & fiscales, Carl Gauthier
418-691-2214, Fax: 418-646-6688
Sous-ministre adjoint, Politiques relatives aux Institutions financières & Encadrement des personnes morales, Richard Boivin
418-646-7563, Fax: 418-646-7610
Sous-ministre adjointe, Sociétés d'État & Projets économiques, Suzanne Lévesque
418-643-5704, Fax: 416-646-9810
Sous-ministre adjointe, Droit fiscal & la fiscalité, Josée Morin
418-691-2261, Fax: 418-644-1666
Sous-ministre adjoint, Politiques fédérales-provinciales et financières, Patrick Déry
Sous-ministre adjoint, Politique budgétaire et à l'économique, Luc Monty
Contrôleur, Finances et comptabilité gouvernementale, Simon-Pierre Falardeau
• Autorité des marchés financiers
Tour de la Bourse
800, Square Victoria, 22e étage
Montréal, QC H4Z 1G3
514-395-0337 Fax: 514-873-3090 877-525-0337
www.lautorite.qc.ca
• Caisse de dépôt et placement du Québec
1000, place Jean-Paul-Riopelle
Montréal, QC H2Z 2B3
514-842-3261 Fax: 514-842-4833 866-330-3936TDD: 514-847-2190
info@lacaisse.com
www.lacaisse.com
• Institut de la statistique du Québec(BSQ) / Québec Statistics Office
200, ch Ste-Foy, 3e étage
Québec, QC G1R 5T4
418-691-2401 Fax: 418-643-4129 800-463-4090
direction@stat.gouv.qc.ca
www.stat.gouv.qc.ca
• Loto-Québec/ Québec Lotteries
500, rue Sherbrooke ouest
Montréal, QC H3A 3G6
514-282-8000 Fax: 514-873-8999
www.loto-quebec.com
• Société des alcools du Québec(SAQ) / Québec Liquor Corporation
905, av De Lorimier
Montréal, QC H2K 3V9
514-873-2020 Fax: 514-873-6788 866-873-2020
info@saq.com
www.saq.com
• Société générale de financement du Québec/ General Investment Corporation
#1500, 600, rue de La Gauchetière ouest
Montréal, QC H3B 4L8
514-876-9290 Fax: 514-395-8055
info@sgfqc.com
www.sgfqc.com

Droit fiscal et la fiscalité / Fiscal Law & Taxation
Sous-ministre adjointe, Josée Morin
418-691-2236, Fax: 418-644-5262
Directeur, Impôts des entreprises, P.-J. Bergeron
Directrice, Impôts des particuliers, Lyse Gauthier
Directrice, Taxes, Lyne Dussault

Politiques fédérales-provinciales, financement, gestion de dette et opérations financières / Federal-Provincial Policy, Financing, Debt Management & Financial Transactions
Sous-ministre adjoint, Bernard Turgeon
Directeur général, Opérations bancaires et financières, François Tardif
Directeur général, Financement et gestion de la dette, Alain Bélanger
Directeur, Contrôle des risques et évaluation de la performance, Carl Lessard
Directrice, Documentation financière et Fonds de financement, Nathalie Parenteau
Directrice, Financement à long terme, Marie-Claude Desroches
Directeur, Gestion de l'encaisse, Renaud Raymond
Directeur, Gestion de la dette et del'ingénierie financière, Éric Deschênes
Directeur, Opérations de trésorie, Michel Beaudet
Directrice générale, Prévisions financières et relations avec les agences de crédit, Odette Hamelin
Directeur, Prévisions du service de la dette, Jean-Charles Doucet
Directeur, Prévision de la dette et relations avec les agences de crédit, Gino Ouellet
Directeur, Relations fédérales-provinciales, Patrick Déry
Directeur, Services post-marchés, Pierre Larochelle

Politique budgétaire et économique / Budgetary & Economic Policy
Sous-ministre adjoint, Luc Monty
Directeur général, Brian Girard
Directeur (par intérim), Planification et analyse budgetaire, Richard Massé
Directeur, Politiques et organisation financière, Jacques Caron
Directeur, Politiques de tarification et finances publiques, Charles Duclos
Directeur, Politiques locales et autochtones, Marc Grandisson
Directeur, Suivi budgetaire et régimes de retraite, Robert Poirier

Politiques économiques et fiscales / Economic & Fiscal Policy
Sous-ministre adjoint, Carl Gauthier
Directeur général, Politiques aux entreprises, Carl Gauthier
Directeur général, Politiques aux particuliers,Vacant
Directeur, Développement économique, Bernard Cayouette
Directeur, Évaluations fiscales et taxe de vente,Vacant
Directeur, Mesures structurantes, Luc Bilodeau
Directeur, Politique sociale, Jean-Pierre Simard
Directeur, Taxation des particuliers, Gérald Tremblay
Directeur, Taxation des entreprises, Éric Ducharme

Politiques relatives aux institutions financières et l'encadrement des personnes morales / Policy Regarding Financial Institutions & Corporations
Sous-ministre adjoint, Richard Boivin
Directeur général, Maurice Lalancette
Directeur (par intérim), Encadrement des personnes morales et développment du secteur financier, Martin Landry
Directeur, Encadrement du secteur financier, Pierre Rhéaume

Sociétés d'État et projets économiques / Crown Corporations & Economic Projects
Sous-ministre adjointe, Suzanne Lévesque
Directeur général,Vacant
Directeur, Projets économiques, Denis Dufresne
Directeur, Sociétés d'État,Vacant

Commission de la fonction publique / Public Service Commission

800, Place D'Youville, 7e étage, Québec, QC G1R 3P4
418-643-1425, Fax: 418-643-7264, 800-432-0432
cfp@cfp.gouv.qc.ca
www.cfp.gouv.qc.ca

Présidente, Doris Paradis

Hydro-Québec

75, boul René-Lévesque ouest, 20e étage, Montréal, QC H2Z 1A4
514-289-2211,
www.hydroquebec.com
Président, Conseil d'administration, Michael Louis Turcotte
Président-directeur général, Thierry Vandal
Vice-présidente exécutive, Affaires corporatives & Secrétaire générale, Marie-José Nadeau
Vice-président exécutif, Technologie, Élie Saheb
Présidente, Hydro-Québec TransÉnergie, Isabelle Courville
Président, Hydro-Québec Production, Richard Cacchione
Président, Hydro-Québec Équipement & services partagés, Réal Laporte
Protectrice de la personne, Justine Sentenne
Vérificateur interne, Élie Rabbat
Vice-président, Ressources humaines, Michel Martinez
Vice-président, Financement, trésorerie et caisse de retraite, Jean-Hugues Lafleur
Vice-présidente, Comptabilité et contrôle, Lise Croteau
Président-directeur général, Thierry Vandal

Subsidiaries/Filiales:

Hydro-Québec CapiTech
#1600, 1000, rue Sherbrooke ouest, Montréal, QC H3A 3G4
hqcapitech@hydro.qc.ca
www.hydroquebec.com/technologie/capitech/index.html
Une société de capitale de risque corporatif dont la mission est de fournir une meilleure connaissance des produits & des services liés au domaine de l'énergie. Elle favorise les investissements dans des entreprises québécoises
Président, Conseil d'administration & Chef de la direction, Élie Saheb
Président et chef de l'exploitation, Serge Y. Piotte

Hydro-Québec International
75, boul René-Lévesque ouest, 20e étage, Montréal, QC H2Z 1A4
514-289-4020

Société d'énergie de la Baie-James (SEBJ) / James Bay Energy
888, de Maisonneuve est, 2e étage, Montréal, QC H2L 5B2
514-286-2020,
www.hydroquebec.com/sebj
Président-directeur général, Réal Laporte

Ministère de l' Immigration et des Communautés culturelles / Immigration & Cultural Communities

360, rue McGill, 4e étage, Montréal, QC H2Y 2E9
514-864-9191, Fax: 514-864-2899,
www.immigration-quebec.gouv.qc.ca

Other Communication: Téléscripteur: 1-866-227-5968
Acts Administered:
Loi sur l'immigration au Québec/An act respecting immigration to Québec
Loi sur le ministèrede l'Immigration et des Communautés culturelles/An act respecting the ministère de l'Immigration et des Communautés culturelles
Ministre, Kathleen Weil
514-873-9940
Sous-ministre, Marie-Claude Champoux
514-873-9450
Directeur, Affaires juridiques, Daniel Morin
514-873-7484
Directrice, Affaires publiques et communications, Hélène Saint-Pierre
514-873-8624, Fax: 514-873-7349
Secrétaire général & Directeur, Vérification interne, Younes Mihoubi
514-873-3464
• Conseil des relations interculturelles(CRI)
#10.04, 500, boul René-Lévesque ouest
Montréal, QC H2Z 1W7
514-873-8501 Fax: 514-873-3469
www.conseilinterculturel.gouv.qc.ca
Other Communication: Email:
info@conseilinterculturel.gouv.qc.ca

Francisation, performance, partenariats & la promotion
Sous-ministre adjoint, Yvan Turcotte
514-864-2691
Directeur, Ressources financières, Denis Lazure
514-864-1565, Fax: 514-873-4611
Directeur, Ressources matérielles, Jacques Bordeleau
514-873-9646, Fax: 514-873-7794
Directeur, Systèmes & technologies de l'information, François Mongrain
514-873-2396, Fax: 514-873-8180
Directrice, Soutien aux opérations, Dominique Laniel
514-873-1565

Immigration / Immigration
Sous-ministre adjoint, Robert Baril
514-873-0706, Fax: 514-873-0453
Directrice générale, Joane Boyer
514-873-2446
Directrice, Politiques, programmes & promotion de l'immigration, Louise Fontaine
514-873-5914
Directrice, Immigration économique, Sylvie Proulx
514-873-2812
Directrice, Promotion & prospection, Marie KronstrÖm
514-873-5914
Directeur, Immigration temporaire, Giovanni Carboni
514-864-1165
Directrice, Immigration familiale & humanitaire, Lyn Fleury
514-864-9305
Directeur, Sélection, Owen-John Peate
514-873-5657

Intégration / Integration
Sous-ministre adjointe, Claire Deronzier
514-864-3404
Directeur, Politiques et programmes d'intégration, régionalisation & relations interculturelles, Martin Faille
514-873-6440, Fax: 514-864-4695
Directeur, Accès aux professions & métiers réglementés, Marc Lafrance
514-864-8352, Fax: 514-864-7726
Directrice, Promotion & gestion de la diversité, Johanne Côté-Galarneau
514-864-3576, Fax: 514-864-3123

Immigration-Québec - Capitale-Nationale/Est-de-Québec
Édifice Bois-Fontaine, 930, ch Sainte-Foy, RC, Québec, QC G1S 2L4
418-643-1435, Fax: 418-646-0783, 888-643-1435
direction.quebec@micc.gouv.qc.ca
www.immigration-quebec.gouv.qc.ca
Directrice régionale, Louise Boucher
418-646-1605

Immigration-Québec - Estrie/Mauricie/Centre-du-Québec
202, rue Wellington nord, Sherbrooke, QC J1H 5C6
819-820-3606, Fax: 819-820-3213, 888-879-4288
direction.estrie@micc.gouv.qc.ca
www.immigration-quebec.gouv.qc.ca
Directrice régionale, Chantal Lussier
819-820-3600

Immigration-Québec - Laval, Laurentides et Lanaudière
705, ch de Trait-Carré, RC, Laval, QC H7N 1B3
450-972-3225, Fax: 450-972-3250, 800-375-7426
direction.drlll@micc.gouv.qc.ca
www.immigration-quebec.gouv.qc.ca
Directeur régional, Serge Tétreault

Immigration-Québec - Montérégie
2, boul Desaulniers, 3e étage, Saint-Lambert, QC J4P 1L2
450-466-4461, Fax: 450-466-4481, 888-287-5819
direction.monteregie@micc.gouv.qc.ca
www.immigration-quebec.gouv.qc.ca
Directeur régional, Guy Gagnon

Immigration-Québec - Sud de Montréal
800, boul de Maisonneuve est, RC, Montréal, QC H2L 4L8
514-864-9191,
Renseignements@micc.gouv.qc.ca
www.immigration-quebec.gouv.qc.ca
Directrice régionale, Johanne Côté-Galarneau
514-873-4696
Directrice, Est de Montréal, Majida El Mrabet
514-321-3457, Fax: 514-321-6656
Directrice, Nord de Montréal, Jacinthe Michaud
514-873-5165, Fax: 514-873-7118
Directrice, Ouest de Montréal, Françoise Bouchard
514-426-1307
Directrice, Sud de Montréal, Lucie Rodrigue
514-873-4696

Immigration-Québec - Outaouais/Abitibi-Témiscamingue/Nord-du-Québec
#100, 227, rue Montcalm, Gatineau, QC J8Y 3B9
819-246-3212, Fax: 819-246-3314,
direction.outaouais@micc.gouv.qc.ca
www.immigration-quebec.gouv.qc.ca
Directrice régionale, Suzanne Ménard
819-246-3212

Agences, conseils et commissions associes/Associated Agencies, Boards & Commissions:

Ministère de la Justice / Justice

Édifice Louis-Philippe-Pigeon, 1200, rte de l'Église, Québec, QC G1V 4M1
418-643-5140, 866-536-5140
informations@justice.gouv.qc.ca
www.justice.gouv.qc.ca
Acts Administered:
Charte des droits et libertés de la personne/Charter of Human Rights & Freedoms (in part)
Code civil du Québec/Civil Code of Québec
Code de la sécurité routière/Highway Safety Code (in part)
Code de procédure civile/Code of Civil Procedure
Code de procédure pénale/Code of Penal Procedure
Code des professions/Professional Code
Code du travail/Labour Code
Convention des Nations Unies sur les contrats de vente internationale de marchandises/An Act respecting the United Nations Convention on Contracts for the International Sale of Goods
Jugements rendus par la Cour suprême du Canada sur la langue des lois et d'autres actes de nature législative/An Act respecting the Judgements rendered in the Supreme Court of Canada on the language o
Loi assurant l'application de l'entente sur l'entraide judiciaire entre la France et le Québec/An Act to secure the carrying out of the Entente between France & Québec respecting mutual aid in judicia
Loi concernant la loi constitutionnelle de 1982/An Act respecting Constitution Act, 1982
Loi concernant le cadre juridique des technologies de l'information/An Act to establish a Legal framework for information technology
Loi d'interprétation/Interpretation Act
Loi médicale/Medical Act
Loi sur l'acupuncture/An Act respecting Acupuncture
Loi sur l'adoption d'enfants domiciliés en République populaire de Chine/An Act respecting Adoptions of children domiciled in the People's Republic of China
Loi sur l'aide aux victimes d'actes criminels/An Act respecting Assistance for victims of crime
Loi sur l'aide juridique/Legal Aid Act
Loi sur l'exécution réciproque d'ordonnances alimentaires/An Act respecting Reciprocal enforcement of maintenance orders
Loi sur l'indemnisation des victimes d'actes criminels/Crime Victims Compensation Act
Loi sur l'optométrie/Optometry Act
Loi sur la chiropratique/Chiropractic Act
Loi sur la denturologie/Denturologists Act
Loi sur la division territoriale/Territorial Division Act (in part)
Loi sur la justice administrative/An Act respecting Administrative Justice
Loi sur la liberté des cultes/Freedom of Worship Act
Loi sur la pharmacie/Pharmacy Act
Loi sur la podiatrie/Podiatry Act
Loi sur la presse/Press Act
Loi sur la protection de la jeunesse/Youth Protection Act (in part)
Loi sur la protection du consommateur/Consumer Protection Act

Loi sur la réforme du cadastre québécois/An Act to promote the Reform of the cadastre in Québec
Loi sur la refonte des lois et des règlements/An Act respecting the Consolidation of the statutes & regulations
Loi sur la Société québécoise d'information juridique/An Act respecting the Société québécoise d'information juridique
Loi sur la transparence et l'éthique en matière de lobbyisme/Lobbying transparency and Ethics Act
Loi sur le barreau/An Act respecting the Barreau
Loi sur le drapeau et les emblèmes du Québec/An Act respecting the Flag and emblems of Québec
Loi sur le ministère de la Justice/An Act respecting the Ministère de la Justice
Loi sur le notariat/Notarial Act
Loi sur le paiement de certaines amendes/An Act respecting the Payment of certain fines
Loi sur le paiement de certains témoins/An Act respecting Payment of certain Crown witnesses
Loi sur le recours collectif/An Act respecting the Class Action
Loi sur le recouvrement de certaines créances/An Act respecting the collection of certaln debts
Loi sur le temps réglementaire/Official Time Act
Loi sur les agences des voyages/Travel Agents Act
Loi sur les agronomes/Agrologists Act
Loi sur les architectes/Architects Act
Loi sur les arpenteurs-géomètres/Land Surveyors Act
Loi sur les arrangements préalables de services funéraires et de sépulture/An Act respecting Prearranged funeral services and sepultures
Loi sur les aspects civils de l'enlèvement internaional et interprovincial d'enfants/An Act respecting Civil aspects of international and interprovincial child abduction
Loi sur les audioprothésistes/Hearing-aid Acousticians Act
Loi sur les chimistes professionnels/Professional Chemists Act
Loi sur les commissions d'enquête/An Act respecting Public inquiry commissions
Loi sur les comptables agréés/Chartered Accountants Act
Loi sur les cours municipales/An Act respecting the Municipal courts
Loi sur les dentistes/Dental Act
Loi sur les employés publics/Public Officers Act
Loi sur les huissiers de justice/Court Bailiffs Act
Loi sur les infirmières et infirmiers/Nurses Act
Loi sur les ingénieurs/Engineers Act
Loi sur les ingénieurs forestiers/Forest Engineers Act
Loi sur les journaux et autres publications/Newspaper Declaration Act
Loi sur les jurés/Jurors Act
Loi sur les maisons de désordre/Disorderly Houses Act
Loi sur les médecins vétérinaires/Veterinary Surgeons Act
Loi sur les opticiens d'ordonnance/Dispensing Opticians Act
Loi sur les privilèges des magistrats/Magistrate's Privileges Act
Loi sur les règlements/Regulations Act (in part)
Loi sur les renvois à la Cour d'appel/Court of Appeal Reference Act
Loi sur les sages-femmes/Midwives Act
Loi sur les salaires d'officiers de justice/An Act respecting the Salaries of officers of Justice
Loi sur les shérifs/Sheriffs' Act
Loi sur les sténographes/Stenographers' Act
Loi sur les substituts du procureur général/An Act respecting Attorney General's Prosecutors
Loi sur les technologues en radiologie/Radiology Technologists Act
Loi sur les tribunaux judiciaires/Courts of Justice Act
Loi visant à favoriser le civisme/An Act to promote Good citizenship

Ministre,L'hon. Jean-Marc Fournier
418-643-4210, Fax: 418-646-0027,ministre@justice.gouv.qc.ca
Sous-ministre, Michel Bouchard
418-643-4090, Fax: 418-644-7680
Directrice, Bureau du sous-ministre, Andrée Giguère
418-643-4090
Directeur, Communications, Jean Guay
Directrice, Vérification interne, Francine Asselin
418-643-8372

• Commission des services juridiques/ Legal Services Commission
Tour de l'Est
#1404, 2, Complexe Desjardins
Montréal, QC H5B 1B3
514-873-3562 Fax: 514-873-8762
info@csj.qc.ca
www.csj.qc.ca/

• Conseil de la justice administrative/ Administrative Justice Council
#RC-01, 575, rue Saint-Amable
Québec, QC G1R 2G4
418-644-6279 Fax: 418-528-8471 888-848-2581
courrier@cja.gouv.qc.ca
www.cja.gouv.qc.ca

• Conseil de la magistrature
#5.12, 300, boul Jean-Lesage
Québec, QC G1K 8K6
418-644-2196 Fax: 418-528-1581
information@cm.gouv.qc.ca
www.cm.gouv.qc.ca

• Directeur de l'état civil/ Vital Statistics
2535, boul Laurier
Québec, QC G1V 5C5
418-643-3900 Fax: 418-646-3255 800-567-3900
etatcivil@gouv.qc.ca
www.etatcivil.gouv.qc.ca
Other Communication: Montréal: 514/864-3900, Fax: 514/864-4563

• Fonds d'aide aux recours collectifs
#10.30, 1, rue Notre-Dame est
Montréal, QC H2Y 1B6
514-393-2087 Fax: 514-864-2998
farc@justice.gouv.qc.ca

• Office des professions du Québec/ Occupations Board

• Société québécoise d'information juridique/ Judicial Information Society of Québec
715, carré Victoria, 8e étage
Montréal, QC H2Y 2H7
514-842-8741 Fax: 514-844-8984 800-363-6718
info@soquij.qc.ca
www.soquij.qc.ca

• Tribunal administratif du Québec/ Administrative Tribunal of Québec
575, rue Saint-Amable
Québec, QC G1R 5R4
418-643-3418 Fax: 418-643-5335
www.taq.gouv.qc.ca
Other Communication: EMail: tribunal.administratif@taq.gouv.qc.ca

Affaires juridiques et législatives / Judicial & Legislative Affairs
Sous-ministre associée, Dominique Langis
418-643-4228, Fax: 418-644-0420
Directrice générale adjointe, Anne Trotier
Directeur général adjoint, Jean-Paul Dupré
Directeur général associé, Affaires contentieuses, Jean-Yves Bernard
Directeur, Droit administratif, Michel Fortin
Directrice, Droit autochtone et constitutionnel, Monique Rousseau
Directeur, Direction des services professionnels, Serge Massicotte
Directrice, Législation, Solange Ferron

Services à l'organisation / Administrative Services
Sous-ministre associé, Fernand Archambault
Directeur, Personnel & administration, Gaëtan Tremblay
Directeur, Ressources informationnelles, Louis Potvin

Services de justice & Registres / Judicial Services & Registries
Sous-ministre associé, Denis Marsolais
418-643-8654, Fax: 418-528-9539
Directrice générale associée, Services judiciaires de la Métropole, Marcelle Beaulieu
Directeur général associé, Services judiciaires de l'Est du Québec, Kevin Walsh
Directeur régional associé, Services judiciaires de l'Ouest du Québec, Marc Lyrette
Directeur, Gestion immobilière, Onil Larrivée, 2008-09-18
Directrice, Ressources budgétaires, financières, matérielles & informationnelles, Danielle Martineau, 2008-09-18
Directrice générale associée, Registres & la certification, Suzanne Potvin Plamondon, 2008-09-18
Directrice, Soutien aux activités judiciaires, France Lynch

Office des professions du Québec / Occupations Board

800, place D'Youville, 10e étage, Québec, QC G1R 5Z3
418-643-6912, Fax: 418-643-0973, 800-643-6912
courrier@opq.gouv.qc.ca
www.opq.gouv.qc.ca

Acts Administered:
Code des professions/Professional Code
Loi médicale/Medical Act
Loi sur l'acupuncture/An Act respecting Acupuncture
Loi sur l'optométrie/Optometry Act
Loi sur la chiropratique/Chiropractic Act
Loi sur la denturologie/Denturologists Act
Loi sur la pharmacie/Pharmacy Act
Loi sur la podiatrie/Podiatry Act
Loi sur le Barreau/An Act respecting the Barreau de Québec
Loi sur le notariat/Notarial Act
Loi sur les agronomes/Agrologists Act
Loi sur les architectes/Architects Act
Loi sur les arpenteurs-géomètres/Land Surveyors Act
Loi sur les audioprothésistes/Hearing-aid Acousticians Act
Loi sur les chimistes professionnels/Professional Chemists Act
Loi sur les comptables agrées/Chartered Accountants Act
Loi sur les dentistes/Dental Act
Loi sur les géologues/Geologists Act
Loi sur les infirmières et les infirmiers/Nurses Act
Loi sur les ingénieurs/Engineers Act
Loi sur les ingénieurs forestiers/Forest Engineers Act
Loi sur les médecins vétérinaires/Veterinary Surgeons Act
Loi sur les opticiens d'ordonnances/Dispensing Opticians Act
Loi sur les sages-femmes/Midwives Act
Loi sur les technologues en radiologie/Radiology Technologists Act

Président, Jean Paul Dutrisac
Vice-présidente, Christiane Gagnon
Directeur, Affaires juridiques, Jean-François Paquet
Directrice, Recherche & analyse, Hélène Dubois
Directrice (par intérim), Services-conseils à la gestion, Marielle Audet

Le Protecteur du Citoyen / Ombudsman

#1.25, 525, boul René-Lévesque est, Québec, QC G1R 5Y4
418-643-2688, Fax: 418-643-8759, 800-463-5070
www.protecteurducitoyen.qc.ca

Other Communication: Email: protecteur@protecteurducitoyen.qc.ca

Protectrice du citoyen, Raymonde Saint-Germain
Vice-protecteur, Services aux citoyens & aux usagers, Pierre-Paul Veilleux
Vice-protectrice, Prévention & innovation, Micheline McNicoll
Directeur (par intérim), Ressources humaines & l'administration, Serge Hébert

Registraire des entreprises

787, boul. Lebourgneuf, Québec, QC G2J 1C3
418-644-4545, Fax: 418-528-5703, 877-644-4545
registre@servicesquebec.gouv.qc.ca
www.registreentreprises.gouv.qc.ca

Depuis le 1er avril, 2007, en partenariat avec Services Québec, Revenu Québec a pris en charge les activités anciennement sous la responsabilité du Registraire des entreprises

Acts Administered:
Charte de la Ville de Québec/Charter of Ville de Québec
Code civil du Québec/Civil Code of Québec
Code de procédure civile/Civil Code of Québec
Code du travail/Labour Code
Code municipal du Québec/Municipal Code of Québec
Loi concernant les services de transport par taxi
Loi constituant Capital régional et cooperatif Desjardins
Loi constituant Fondaction, le Fonds de développement de la Confédération des syndicats nationaux pour la coopération et l'emploi
Loi constituant le Fonds de solidarité des travailleurs du Québec
Loi sur la constitution de certaines Églises/Québec Church Incorporation Act
Loi sur la liquidation des compagnies/Winding Up Act
Loi sur la publicité légale des entreprises individuelles, des sociétés et des personnes morales/An Act respecting the Legal Publicity of Sole Proprietors, Partnerships & Legal Persons
Loi sur le courtage immobilier
Loi sur le ministère de la Culture et des Communications
Loi sur le registraire des entreprises/An Act respecting the Entreprise registrar
Loi sur les assurances/Québec Act respecting insurance
Loi sur les cités et villes/Cities & Towns Act
Loi sur les clubs de chasse et de pêche/Québec Fish and Game Clubs Act
Loi sur les clubs de récréation/Québec Amusement Clubs Act
Loi sur les compagnies/Québec Companies Act
Loi sur les compagnies de cimetière/Québec Cemetery Companies Act
Loi sur les compagnies de cimetière catholiques romains/Québec Act respecting Roman Catholic cemetery corporations
Loi sur les compagnies de flottage/Québec Timber-Driving Companies Act
Loi sur les compagnies de gaz, d'eau et d'électricité/Québec Gas, Water and Electricity Companies Act
Loi sur les compagnies de télégraphe et de téléphone/Québec Telegraph and Telephone Companies Act
Loi sur les compagnies minières Québec/Québec Mining Companies Act
Loi sur les coopératives/Québec Cooperatives Act
Loi sur les coopératives de services financiers/Québec Act respecting financial services cooperatives
Loi sur les corporations religieuses/Québec Religious Corporations Act

Loi sur les évêques catholiques romains/Québec Roman Catholic Bishops Act
Loi sur les fabriques/Québec Act respecting fabriques
Loi sur les pouvoirs spéciaux des personnes morales
Loi sur les services de santé et les services sociaux/Québec Act respecting health services & social services
Loi sur les services de santé et les services sociaux pour les autochtones cris/Act respecting health services & social services for Native persons
Loi sur les sociétés agricoles et laitières/Québec Act respecting farmers' and dairymen's associations
Loi sur les sociétés d'horticulture/Québec Horticultural Societies Act
Loi sur les sociétés de fiducie et les sociétés d'épargne/Québec Act respecting trust companies and savings companies
Loi sur les sociétés de transport en commun
Loi sur les sociétés préventives de cruauté envers les animaux/Québec Act respecting societies for the prevention of cruelty to animals
Loi sur les sociétés nationales de bienfaisance/Qué National Benefit Societies Act
Loi sur les syndicats professionnels/Québec Professional Syndicates Act

Ministre responsable,L'hon. Robert Dutil
418-652-6835, Fax: 418-643-7379

Ministère des Relations internationales / International Relations

Édifice Hector-Fabre, 525, boul Réne-Lévesque est, Québec, QC G1R 5R9
418-649-2300, Fax: 418-649-2656,
communications@mri.gouv.qc.ca
www.mri.gouv.qc.ca

Acts Administered:
Loi sur l'immigration au Québec/An act respecting immigration to Québec
Loi sur le Conseil des relations interculturelles/An act respecting the Conseil des relations interculturelles
Loi sur le ministère de l'Immigration et des Communautés culturelles/An act respecting the ministère de l'Immigration et des Communautés culturelles

Ministre & Ministre responsable de la Francophonie,L'hon. Monique Gagnon-Tremblay
418-649-2319, Fax: 418-643-4804,Other Communications: Montréal: 514/864-2252, Fax: 514/873-7257
Sous-ministre, François Turenne
418-649-2335, Fax: 418-649-2667
Directeur, Communications & affaires publiques, Jacques Villemure
418-649-2333
Directeur, Affaires bilatérales, Robert Keating
Directrice, Politiques & affaires francophones & multilatérales, Marie-Claude Francoeur
Directeur, Protocole & missions, Denis Turcotte
418-649-2346, Fax: 418-649-2657,
Directeur, Administration, Bernard Dubois
418-649-2666

Administration / Administration
Directeur général, Bernard Dubois
418-649-2666
Directrice, Information & diplomatie publique, Nicole McKinnon
418-649-2345
Directeur, Ressources matérielles, Jean Lefebvre
418-649-2337

Amériques et Asie-Pacifique / Americas & Asia-Pacific
Directeur général, Affaires bilatérales, Robert Keating
Directeur, Amérique du Nord, Jean Saintonge
418-649-2310, Fax: 418-649-2418
Directeur, Asie-Pacifique & Amérique latine et Antilles, Éric Marquis
418-649-2662

Beijing, Chine
Ambassade du Canada en République populaire de Chine, 19, Dongzhimenwai Dajie,Dist. de Chaoyang, Beijing,100600 China
qc.beijing@mri.gouv.qc.ca
Other Communication: Tél: 86 10 5139 4445 poste 3600; Téléc:86 10 6532 1304
Chef de poste, René Milot

Boston, MA, USA
One Boston Place, #1920, 201 Washington St., Boston, MA 2108 USA
617-482-1193, Fax: 617-482-1195,
qc.boston@mri.gouv.qc.ca
Chef de poste, France Dionne

Buenos Aires, Argentina
Édifice Laminar Plaza, Ing. Butty 240, 3e étage, Buenos Aires,C1001AFB Argentina
qc.buenosaires@mri.gouv.qc.ca
Other Communication: 54-11- 4343-2033; Fax 54-11-4343-2122

Chicago, IL, USA
#1900, 444 N Michigan Ave., Chicago, IL 60611-3977 USA
312-645-0932, Fax: 312-645-0542,
qc.chicago@mri.gouv.qc.ca
Chef de poste, Marc T. Boucher

Los Angeles, CA, USA
#720, 10940 Wilshire Blvd., Los Angeles, CA 90024 USA
310-824-4173, Fax: 310-824-7759,
qc.losangeles@mri.gouv.qc.ca
Chef de poste, Denis Turcotte

Mexico City, Mexico
Délégation générale du Québec, Avenida Taine 411, Colonia Bosques de Chapultepec, Mexico,DF 11580 Mexico
qc.mexico@mri.gouv.qc.ca
Other Communication: 525-55-250-8222; Fax: 525-55-250-2396

New York, NY, USA
Délégation générale du Québec, One Rockefeller Plaza, 26e étage, New York, NY 10020-2102 USA
212-843-0950, Fax: 212-376-8983,
qc.newyork@mri.gouv.qc.ca
Chef de poste, Robert Keating

Shanghai, Chine
a/s Consulat général du Canada, Shanghai Centre, #604, West Tower, 1376 Nanjing Xi Rd., Shanghai,200040 Chine
shanghai@mri.gouv.qc.ca
Other Communication: Tél: 86 21 6279 8400, poste 8943; Téléc.: 86 21 6279 8401
Chef de poste, Franççois Gaudreau

Tokyo, Japon
Délégation générale du Québec, Shiroyama JT Trust Tower, 32e étage, 4-3-1 Toranomon, Minato-Ku, Tokyo,105-6032 Japan
qc.tokyo@mri.gouv.qc.ca
Other Communication: Tél: 81 3 5733 4001; Téléc.: 81 3 5472 6721
Chef de poste, Suzanne Éthier

Washington, DC, USA
Bureau du Québec à Washington, #450, 805 15th St. NW, Washington, DC 20005 USA
202-659-8990, Fax: 202-659-5654,
qc.washington@mri.gouv.qc.ca
Chef de poste, Jean-Stéphane Bernard

Europe, Afrique et Moyen-Orient / Europe, Africa & the Middle East
Directeur général, Affaires bilatérales, Robert Keating
418-649-2335
Directeur, France, Christian Leslauriers
418-649-2329, Fax: 418-649-2654
Directrice, Europe ouest & nord/Institutions européennes, Rita Poulin
418-649-2669, Fax: 418-649-2421
Directrice, Solidarité internationale/Haïti et Afrique subsaharienne, Marjolaine Ricard
418-649-2341
Directeur, Europe méditerranéenne et est/Maghreb et Moyen-Orient, Bernard Denault
418-649-2343

Bureaux à l'étranger/Offices Abroad:

Barcelona, Spain
Bureau du Québec, Avinguda Diagonal, 420,3er 1a, Barcelona,8037 Spain
qc.barcelone@mri.gouv.qc.ca
Other Communication: 34-93-476-4258; Fax: 34-93-476-4774

Damascus, Syria
a/s Ambassade du Canada, 38, Autostrade Mezzeh, CP 3394, Mezzeh-Est
Other Communication: Tel: 963-11 611-6692; Fax: 963-11 613-1600

Brussels, Belgium
Délégation générale du Québec, 46, av des Arts, 7e étage, Brussels,1000 Belgium
qc.bruxelles@mri.gouv.qc.ca
Other Communication: 322-512-0036; Fax: 322-514-2641

London, England
Délégation générale du Québec, 59 Pall Mall, London,SW1Y 5JH United Kingdom
qc.londres@mri.gouv.qc.ca
Other Communication: 020 7766-5900; Fax: 020 7930-7938

Munich, Germany
Bureau du Québec, Dienerstrasse 20, Munich,D-80331 Germany
qc.munich@mri.gouv.qc.ca
Other Communication: 49-89-2420-870; Fax: 49-89-2420-8737

Paris, France
Délégation générale du Québec, 66, rue Pergolèse, Paris
qc.paris@mri.gouv.qc.ca
Other Communication: 33 0 1-4067-8500; Fax: 33 0 1-4067-8519

Vienna, Austria
Service d'immigation, a/s Ambassade du Canada, Laurenzerberg 2, Vienna,A-1010 Austria
Other Communication: Tel: 0043-1053-138-3005; Fax: 0043-1 53-138-3443

Affaires bilatérales / Bilateral Affairs
Directeur, Robert Keating
418-649-2335

Politiques et affaires francophones et multilatérales / Policy and Francophone and Multilateral Affairs
Directrice générale, Marie-Claude Francoeur
418-649-2335
Directeur, Planification et politiques, Roger Ménard
418-649-2305
Directeur adjoint, Analyses, Claude Trudelle
418-649-2428
Directeur, Organisations internationales, Daniel Lacroix
418-649-2320, Fax: 418-649-2403
Directeur, Engagements internationaux, Patrice Bachand
418-649-2411
Directrice, Francophonie, Régine Lavoie
418-649-2411
Directeur, Ententes de reconnaissance des qualifications professionnelles, Luc Bergeron
418-649-2321

Ministère des Ressources naturelles et de la Faune / Natural Resources & Wildlife

880, ch Sainte-Foy, Québec, QC G1S 4X4
418-627-8600, Fax: 418-644-6513, 866-248-6936
services.clientele@mrnf.gouv.qc.ca
www.mrnf.gouv.qc.ca

Acts Administered:
Loi approuvant la convention de la Baie-James et du nord québécois/An Act approving the Agreement concerning James Bay and Northern Québec
Loi approuvant la convention du nord-est québécois/An Act approving the Northeastern Québec Agreement
Loi assurant la mise en oeuvre de l'entente concernant une nouvelle relation entre le gouvernement du Québec et les Cris du Québec/An Act to ensure the implementation of the Agreement Concerning a New
Loi concernant la construction par Hydro-Québec d'infrastructures et d'équipements par suite de la tempête de verglas survenue du 5 au 9 janvier 1998
Loi concernant les droits sur les mines/Mining Duties Act
Loi de 1994 sur la convention concernant les oiseaux migrateurs
Loi favorisant la réforme du cadastre québécois/An Act to promote the reform of the cadastre in Québec
Loi favorisant le crédit forestier par les institutions privées/An Act to promote forest credit by private institutions
Loi sur les forêts/Forest Act
Loi régissant les activités d'aménagement forestier de bénéficiaires de contrats d'approvisionnement et d'aménagement forestier pour les années 2000-2001 et 2001-2002
Loi sur Hydro-Québec/Hydro-Québec Act
Loi sur l'agence de l'efficacité énergétique
Loi sur l'efficacité énergétique d'appareils fonctionnant à l'électricité ou aux hydrocarbures/An Act respecting the energy efficiency of electrical or hydrocarbon-fuelled appliances
Loi sur la conservation et la mise en valeur de la faune/Act respecting the conservation and development of wildlife
Loi sur la division territoriale/Territorial Division Act
Loi sur la Régie de l'énergie/An Act respecting the Régie de l'énergie
Loi sur la société de développement autochtone de la Baie James/An Act respecting the James Bay Native Development Corporation
Loi sur la société Eeyou de la Baie-James/An Act respecting the James Bay Eeyou Corporation
Loi sur la société nationale de l'amiante/An Act respecting the Société nationale de l'amiante
Loi sur le cadastre/Cadastre Act
Loi sur le crédit forestier/Forestry Credit Act
Loi sur le développement et l'organisation municipale de la région de la Baie-James/James Bay Region Development and Municipal Organization Act
Loi sur le ministère des ressources naturelles, de la faune et des parcs/An Act respecting the Ministère des Ressources naturelles, de la Faune et des Parcs

Loi sur le mode de paiement des services d'électricité et de gaz dans certains immeubles/An Act respecting the mode of payment for electric and gas service in certain buildings
Loi sur le programme d'aide aux Inuits bénéficiaires de la convention de la Baie-James et du nord québécois pour leurs activités de chasse, de pêche et de piégeage/An Act respecting the support progra
Loi sur le régime des eaux/Watercourses Act
Loi sur le régime des terres dans les territoires de la Baie-James et du Nouveau-Québec/An Act respecting the land regime in the James Bay and New Québec territories
Loi sur les arpentages/An Act respecting land survey
Loi sur les bureaux de la publicité des droits/An Act respecting registry offices
Loi sur les clubs de chasse et de pêche/Fish and Game Clubs Act
Loi sur les compagnies de flottage/Timber-Driving Companies Act
Loi sur les droits de chasse et de pêche dans les territoires de la Baie James et du Nouveau-Québec/An Act respecting hunting and fishing rights in the James Bay and New Québec territories
Loi sur les espèces menacées ou vulnérables/An Act respecting threatened or vulnerable species
Loi sur les mesurers de bois/Cullers Act
Loi sur les mines/Mining Act
Loi sur les Pêches
Loi sur les produits et les équipements pétroliers/An Act respecting petroleum products and equipment
Loi sur les systèmes municipaux et les systèmes privés d'électricité/An Act respecting municipal and private electric power systems
Loi sur les terres du domaine de l'état/An Act respecting the lands in the domain of the State
Loi sur les titres de propriété dans certains districts électoraux/An Act respecting land titles in certain electoral districts
Loi sur l'exportation de l'électricité/An Act respecting the exportation of electric power

Ministre,L'hon. Serge Simard
418-643-7295, Fax: 418-643-4318
Sous-ministre, Robert Sauvé
418-627-6370, Fax: 418-643-1443
Directeur général, Administration/Services partagés, Guy Mercier
418-627-6260, Fax: 418-646-2614
Sous-ministre associé, Opérations régionales, Pierre Grenier, 2008-09-18
418-627-6354, Fax: 418-646-0042

• Agence de l'efficacité énergétique/ Energy Efficiencies Agency
#B-405, 5700, 4e av ouest
Québec, QC G1H 6R1
418-627-6379 Fax: 418-643-5828 877-727-6655
aee@aee.gouv.qc.ca
www.aee.gouv.qc.ca
Promotes the efficient use of all forms of energy, in all sectors of activity, for the benefit of the people of Québec. The Agency achieves this through demonstration projects, which highlight new technologies, new approaches or new applications that save energy; design, management & evaluation of energy efficient programs; information, training & educational materials; technical & organizational support for export of products & services; review, commentary on proposed amendments to applicable laws & regulations.

• Comité conjoint de chasse, de pêche et de piégeage/ Hunting, Fishing & Trapping Joint Committee
#C220, 383 rue Saint-Jacques
Montréal, QC H2Y 1N9
514-284-2151 Fax: 514-284-0039
hftcc@bellnet.ca
www.cccpp-hftcc.com

• Fondation de la faune du Québec/ Québec Wildlife Foundation
Place Iberville II
#420, 1175, av Lavigerie
Québec, QC G1V 4P1
418-644-7926 Fax: 418-643-7655 877-639-0742
ffq@riq.qc.ca
www.fondationdelafaune.qc.ca
Non-profit organization whose mission is to enhance the value & promote the conservation of wildlife & its habitats.

• Hydro Québec
75, boul René-Lévesque ouest
Montréal, QC H2Z 1A4
514-385-7252 800-790-2424
www.hydroquebec.com
Other Communication: Residential Customer Service: 1-888-385-7252; TTY: 711; Persons with a visual impairment: 1-888-385-7252

• Régie de l'énergie/ Energy Regulation Board
Tour de la Bourse
#255, 800, Place Victoria
CP 1
Montréal, QC H4Z 1A2
514-873-2452 Fax: 514-873-2070 888-873-2452
secretariat@regie-energie.qc.ca
www.regie-energie.qc.ca
An economic regulation agency, its mission is to reconcile the public interest, consumer protection, & fair treatment of the electricity carrier & distributors.

• Société de développement de la Baie James(SDBJ) / James Bay Development Society
110, boul Matagami
CP 970
Matagami, QC J0Y 2A0
819-739-4717 Fax: 819-739-4329
www.sdbj.gouv.qc.ca
Developed in 1971, this organization uses its resources & vast knowledge of the territory, contributors, & development projects to promote & maintain activities in the James Bay area, with a perspective of integrated economic development & harmonious cohabitation with territorial residents.

Bureaux de la protection de la faune/Regional Wildlife Proection Offices:

Énergie / Energy
#B401, 5700, 4e av ouest, Québec, QC G1H 6R1
418-627-6377, Fax: 418-643-0701
Le gouvernement québécois prévoit le lancement des projets hydoélectriques représentant 4,500 MW, qui susciteront des investissements de l'ordre de 25m de dollars, et la création d'environ 70,000 emplois sur six ans. Il mise sur le développement du potential existant d'énergie éolienne, avec l'objectif de 4,000 MW d'ici 2015, et prend plusieurs moyens afin de renforcer la sécurité des approvisionnements en pétrole et gaz naturel
Sous-ministre associé, Mario Gosselin
Directeur général, Électricité, René Paquette
Directeur général, Hydrocarbures et Bioarburants, Alain Lefebvre
Directrice générale (par intérim), Politiques, coordination et analyse économique, Julie Grignon

Faune Québec / Wildlife Québec
RC-80, 880, ch Sainte-Foy, Québec, QC G1S 4X4
418-627-8688, Fax: 418-646-4223
Sous-ministre associée, Nathalie Camden

Foncier Québec
#E306, 5700, 4e av ouest, Québec, QC G1H 6R1
418-643-3582, Fax: 418-528-8721, 866-226-0977
assistance.clientele@mrnf.registrefoncier.gouv.qc.ca
Sous-ministre associée, Louise Ouellet
418-627-6252, Fax: 418-643-3954
Directeur général, Arpentage et cadastre, Julien Arsenault
418-627-6267, Fax: 418-646-7405
Directrice générale, Registre Foncier, Marie-Claude Rioux
418-643-3155

Forêt Québec / Québec Forests
880, ch Ste-Foy, 10e étage, Québec, QC G1S 4X4
418-627-8652, Fax: 418-528-1278,
foretquebec@mrnf.gouv.qc.ca
Sous-ministre associé, Richard Savard
Sous-ministre associé/Forestier en chef, Pierre Levac
Directeur général, Connaissance et gestion de l'information forestière, Francis Forcier
Directeur général, Gestion du milieu forestier/Développement, Mario Gibeault
Directeur général, Attribution des bois et développement industriel, Pierre Marineau
Directrice, Inventaires forestiers, Élisabeth Bossert
Directeur, Aménagement des forêts publiques et privées, Ronald Brizard
Directeur, Recherche forestière, Robert Jobidon
Directeur, Gestion de l'information forestière, Denis Robitaille
Directeur, Développement de l'industrie et des produits forestiers, André Denis
Directeur, Environnement et Protection des forêts, Paul Lamirande
Directeur, Gestion des stocks ligneux, Réal Paris
Directrice, Développement et Coordination, Cécile Tremblay

Bureaux à l'étranger/Offices Abroad:

Mines
RC, 880, ch Ste-Foy, Québec, QC G1S 4X4
418-627-6278, Fax: 418-418-6432, 800-363-7233
service.mines@mrnf.gouv.qc.ca
Sous-ministre associé, Mines, Jean-Sylvain Lebel
418-627-8652
Directeur général, Géologie Québec, Robert Marquis
Directeur général, Développement de l'industrie minérale, Pierre Verpaelst
Directrice générale, Gestion du milieu minier, Lucie Ste-Croix

Territoire / Lands
#A313, 5700, 4e av ouest, Québec, QC G1H 6R1
418-627-6256, Fax: 418-528-2075,
territoire@mrnf.gouv.qc.ca
Le Ministère favorise une utilisation du territoire qui rejoint les préoccupations économiques, sociales & environnementales des Québécois
Sous-ministre associé, Plan Nord et Territoire, Christian Dubois
418-627-6260
Directeur général, Affaires stratégiques et territoire, André Auclair
Directrice, Coordination du Plan Nord, Andrée Bélanger
Directeur, Environnement et Coordination, Marcel Grenier
Directeur, Affaires autochtones, François Dupuis
Directeur, Politiques et Intégité du territoire, Mario Perron

Centre de service des Mines (Capitale-Nationale)
RC, 880, ch Sainte-Foy, Québec, QC G1S 4X4
418-627-6278, Fax: 418-643-2816, 800-363-7233
service.mines@mrnf.gouv.qc.ca

Bureaux de la protection de la faune/Regional Wildlife Protection Offices:

Abitibi-Témiscamingue
70, av Québec, Rouyn-Noranda, QC J9X 6R1
819-763-3388, Fax: 819-763-3186

Bas-Saint-Laurent
#207, 92, 2e Rue ouest, Rimouski, QC G5L 8B3
418-727-3710, Fax: 418-727-3735

Capitale-Nationale
#1.14, 1685, boul Hamel, Québec, QC G1N 3Y7
418-643-4680, Fax: 418-644-8960

Mauricie—Centre-du-Québec
#207, 100, rue Laviolette, Trois-Rivières, QC G9A 5S9
819-371-6151, Fax: 819-371-6978

Chaudière-Appalaches
8400, av Sous-le-Vent, Charny, QC G6X 3S9
418-832-7222, Fax: 418-832-1827

Côte-Nord
818, boul Laure, Sept-Iles, QC G4R 1Y8
418-964-8889, Fax: 418-964-8021

Estrie
770, rue Goretti, Sherbrooke, QC J1E 3H4
819-820-3883, Fax: 819-820-3747

Gaspésie—Iles-de-la-Madeleine
124, 1re av ouest, Sainte-Anne-des-Monts, QC G4V 1C5
418-763-3302, Fax: 418-764-2378

Laval—Lanaudière—Laurentides
#1.50B, 999, rue Nobel, Saint-Jérôme, QC J7Z 7A3
450-569-3113, Fax: 450-569-7568

Montérégie et Montréal
Bureau local de Granby, 329, rue Racine, Granby, QC J2G 3B6
450-776-7131, Fax: 450-776-7133
Autres bureau dans la région: Saint-Jean-sur-Richelieu, Salaberry-de-Valleyfield, et Sorel-Tracy. S.O.S. Braconnage: 1-800-463-2191 ou courriel: centralesos@mrnf.gouv.qc.ca

Nord-du-Québec
951, boul Hamel, Chibougamau, QC G8P 2Z3
418-748-7701, Fax: 418-748-3338

Outaouais
#RC-100, 16, impasse de la Gare-Talon, Gatineau, QC J8T 0B1
819-246-4827, Fax: 819-246-5049,

Saguenay—Lac-Saint-Jean
3950, boul Harvey, 4e étage, Jonquière, QC G7X 8L6
418-695-8125, Fax: 418-695-8436,
saguenay-lac-saint-jean@mrnf.gouv.qc.ca

Sous-ministre associé & Forestier en chef / Chief Forester
845, boul Saint-Joseph, Roberval, QC G8H 2L4
418-275-7770, Fax: 418-275-8884,
bureau@forestierenchef.gouv.qc.ca
www.forestierenchef.gouv.qc.ca
Forestier en chef, Pierre Levac

Opérations régionales/Regional Operations:

Abitibi-Témiscamingue
70, av Québec, Rouyn-Noranda, QC J9X 6R1
819-763-3388, Fax: 819-763-3216,
abitibi-temiscamingue@mrnf.gouv.qc.ca
Directeur général, Martin Gingras

Bas-Saint-Laurent
#207, 92, 2e Rue ouest, Rimouski, QC G5L 8B3
418-727-3710, Fax: 418-727-3735,
bas-saint-laurent@mrnf.gouv.qc.ca
Directeur général (par intérim), Alain Lachapelle

Capitale-Nationale—Chaudières-Appalaches
#1.14, 1665, boul Hamel, Québec, QC G1N 3Y7
418-643-4680, Fax: 418-644-8960,
capitale-nationale@mrnf.gouv.qc.ca
Directrice générale, Line Drouin

Côte-Nord
#RC702, 625, boul Laflèche, Baie-Comeau, QC G5C 1C5
418-295-4676, Fax: 418-295-4682,
cote-nord.@mrnf.gouv.qc.ca
Directeur général, Normand Laprise

Gaspésie—Iles-de-la-Madeleine
195, boul Perron est, Caplan, QC G0C 1H0
418-388-2125, Fax: 418-388-2444,
gaspesie-iles-de-la-madeleine@mrnf.gouv.qc.ca
Directeur général, Bernard Landry

Mauricie—Centre-du-Québec
#207, 100, rue Laviolette, Trois-Rivières, QC G9A 5S9
418-371-6151, Fax: 418-371-6978,
mauricie@mrnf.gouv.qc.ca
Directeur général, Alain Simard

Estrie—Montréal—Montérégie et Laval—Lanaudière—Laurentides
545, boul Crémazie est, 8e étage, Montréal, QC H2M 2V1
514-873-2140, Fax: 514-873-8983,
montreal@mrnf.gouv.qc.ca; laval@mrnf.gouv.qc.ca
Directeur général, André B. Lemay

Outaouais
#RC-100, 16, impasse de la Gare-Talon, Gatineau, QC J8T 0B1
819-246-4827, Fax: 819-246-5049,
outaouais@mrnf.gouv.qc.ca
Directeur général, Jean Benoît

Saguenay—Lac-Saint-Jean
3950, boul Harvey, 3e étage, Jonquière, QC G7X 8L6
418-695-8125, Fax: 418-695-8133,
saguenay-lac-saint-jean@mrnf.gouv.qc.ca
Directeur général, Alain Thibeault

Directions régionales Territoire/Lands Regional Offices:

Abitibi-Témiscamingue
70, av Québec, Rouyn-Noranda, QC J9X 6R1
819-763-3388, Fax: 819-763-3216,
abitibi-temiscamingue@mrnf.gouv.qc.ca

Bas-Saint-Laurent
#207, 92, 2e rue ouest, Rimouski, QC G5L 8B3
418-727-3710, Fax: 418-727-3735,
bas-saint-laurent@mrnf.gouv.qc.ca

Capitale-Nationale et Chaudière-Appalaches
#1.14, 1685, boul. Hamel, Québec, QC G1N 3Y7
418-643-4680, Fax: 418-644-8960,
capitale-nationale@mrnf.gouv.qc.ca

Côte-Nord
#RC702, 625, boul Laflèche, Baie-Comeau,G5C 1C5
418-295-4676, Fax: 418-295-4682,
cote-nord@mrnf.gouv.qc.ca

Estrie—Montréal—Montérégie et Laval—Lanaudière—Laurentides
545, boul Crémazie est, 8e étage, Montréal, QC H2M 2V1
514-873-2140, Fax: 514-873-8983,
estrie@mrnf.gouv.qc.ca; lanaudiere@mrnf.gouv.qc.ca

Mauricie—Centre-du-Québec
#207, 100, rue Laviolette, Trois-Rivières, QC G9A 5S9
819-371-6151, Fax: 819-371-6978, 866-821-4625
mauricie@mrnf.gouv.qc.ca

Outaouais
#RC100, 16, impasse de la Gare-Talon, Gatineau, QC J8T 0B1
819-246-4827, Fax: 819-246-5049,
outaouais@mrnf.gouv.qc.ca

Saguenay—Lac-Saint-Jean
3950, boul Harvey, 3e étage, Jonquière, QC G7X 8L6
418-695-8125, Fax: 418-695-8133,
saguenay-lac-saint-jean@mrnf.gouv.qc.ca

Revenu Québec / Revenue Québec

Direction des relations publiques/Communications, 3800, rue de Marly, Québec, QC G1X 4A5
418-652-6831, Fax: 418-646-0167,
www.revenu.gouv.qc.ca

Acts Administered:
Loi concernant l'application de la Loi sur les impôts/Act respecting the application of the Taxation Act
Loi concernant l'impôt sur le tabac/Tobacco Tax Act
Loi concernant la taxe sur les carburants/Fuel Tax Act
Loi favorisant le développement de la formation de la main-d'ouvre (partiellement)/Act to foster the development of manpower training (in part)
Loi facilitant le paiement des pensions alimentaires/Act to facilitate the payment of support
Loi sur la fiscalité municipale/Act respecting municipal taxation (in part)
Loi sur la Régie de l'assurance maladie du Québec (partiellement)/Act respecting the Régie de l'assurance-maladie du Québec (in part)
Loi sur la Société d'habitation du Québec (partiellement)/Act respecting the Société d'habitation du Québec (in part)
Loi sur la taxe d'accise (partiellement)/Excise Tax Act (in part)
Loi sur la taxe de vente du Québec/Act respecting the Québec Sales Tax
Loi sur le ministère du Revenu/Act respecting the Ministère du Revenu
Loi sur le Régime de rentes du Québec (partiellement)/Act respecting the Québec Pension Plan (in part)
Loi sur le remboursement d'impôts fonciers/Act respecting real estate tax refund
Loi sur le soutien du revenu et favorisant l'emploi et la solidarité sociale (partiellement)/Act respecting income support, employment assistance and social solidarity (in part)
Loi sur les centres financiers internationaux (partiellement)/Act respecting international financial centres (in part)
Loi sur les impôts/Taxation Act
Loi sur les licences/Licenses Act
Loi sur les normes du travail (partiellement)/Act respecting labour standards (in part)
Ministre,L'hon. Raymond Bachand
514-482-0199, Fax: 514-482-9985,cabinet@mrq.gouv.qc.ca
Sous-ministre, Francine Martel-Vaillancourt
418-652-6835

Bureau de la sous-ministre / Office of the Deputy Minister
Sous-ministre, Francine Martel-Vaillancourt
418-652-6835, Fax: 418-643-4962
Directeur du Bureau & Secrétaire général, Marc Samson
418-652-6834
Directeur, Registre des entreprises, Yves Bannon
Directeur, Traitement des plaintes, Daniel Bourassa
418-652-6159, Fax: 418-652-4036
Directeur, Vérification interne, enquêtes et évaluation, Pierre Gagné
418-652-6808, Fax: 418-652-4913
Directrice, Communications administratives, Mary-Andrée Jobin
418-652-6831, Fax: 418-646-0167
Directrice, Relations publiques et Communications, Michelle Rompré

Centre de perception fiscale / Tax Collection
3800, rue de Marly, Secteur 6-4-3, Québec, QC G1X 4A5
Le rôle du Centre est de recouvrer les créances de la clientèle de Revenu Québec
Sous-ministre adjoint & Directeur général, Centre de perception fiscale et Biens non réclamés, Claude Provencher
418-577-0011, Fax: 418-646-8269
Directeur régional, Capitale-Nationale et autres régions, Marcel Turgeon
418-577-0313, Fax: 418-646-7057
Directrice régionale, Montérégie, Claire Garceau
450-466-6210, Fax: 450-928-8606
Directeur régional, Montréal, Lucien Larrivée
514-415-5012, Fax: 514-285-3820
Directeur régional, Outaouais, Alain Gamache
819-779-7321, Fax: 819-779-6085
Directeur régional, Laval-Laurentides-Lanaudière, Jacques Hébert
450-967-6466, Fax: 450-967-4761
Directeur, Services administratifs et techniques, Richard Demers
418-577-0033, Fax: 418-646-8269

Législation & enquêtes / Legislation & Investigations
418-652-6844, Fax: 418-643-9381
Sous-ministre adjoint & Directeur général, Législation, enquêtes & Registraire des entreprises, François T. Tremblay
Directeur (par intérim), Lois sur les impôts, Gaétan Lépine
418-652-6836, Fax: 418-643-2699
Directrice, Accès à l'information et protection des renseignements confidentiels, Danielle Corriveau
418-652-5772, Fax: 418-577-5233
Directrice, Services administratifs & informatiques, Ginette St-Laurent
418-652-6840, Fax: 418-652-6237
Directeur, Oppositions de Québec, Denis Morin
418-652-6268, Fax: 418-643-5025
Directrice, Oppositions de Montréal, Louise Haspect
514-287-8322, Fax: 514-873-9253
Directeur, Enquêtes, Pierre Bouchard
418-652-5195, Fax: 418-528-2049
Directeur, Enquêtes et inspections de Québec, Pierre Montminy
Directrice, Enquêtes, Guylaine Isabelle
514-287-4146, Fax: 514-864-3669
Chef, Service des enquêtes informatiques, Luc Boulanger
514-287-4146, Fax: 514-285-5388
Directeur, Enquêtes et projets spéciaux, Daniel Caumartin
514-287-4146, Fax: 514-864-3669

Planification, administration et recherche / Planning, Administration & Research
Sous-ministre adjoint & Directeur général, Daniel Prud'homme
418-652-4152, Fax: 418-528-6882,
Directeur, Systèmes administratifs et soutien à l'organisation, Alain Gagnon
418-652-4764, Fax: 418-528-6882
Directrice, Ressources matérielles et immobilières, Renée Delisle
418-652-5549, Fax: 418-643-1347
Directeur, Planification stratégique & gestion des revenus, Éric Maranda
418-652-4839, Fax: 418-577-5015
Chef, Service de planification et suivis stratégiques, Valérie Dran
Directeur général adjoint, Recherche fiscale, Gilles Bernard
514-287-6707, Fax: 514-873-0758
Directrice, Études économiques, fiscales et statistiques, Sylvie Thomas
418-652-4556, Fax: 418-652-5730
Directrice (par intérim), Gestion de l'information, Sylvie Thomas
Directeur, Bureau de la lutte contre l'évasion fiscale, Sami Jabbour
514-287-6707, Fax: 514-873-0758
Directeur général, Ressources humaines, Alain Blouin
418-652-5348, Fax: 418-646-1827
Directeur, Paie et avantages sociaux, Claude Hogue
418-652-4222, Fax: 418-652-0240
Directrice, Santé et mieux-être au travail, Danielle Rheault
418-652-6433, Fax: 418-646-9546

Traitement et des Technologies / Data Processing & Technologies
Sous-ministre adjoint & directeur général, Jean-Marie Lévesque
418-652-4959, Fax: 418-577-5041
Directeur, Solutions informatiques pour les entreprises, Marco Beaulieu
418-652-5425, Fax: 418-577-5223
Directeur, Traitement massif, Hajib Amachi
Directeur, Solutions informatiques pour les particuliers, Denis Légaré
418-652-6738, Fax: 418-646-3461
Directeur, Solutions informatiques pour les mandataires, René Hébert
418-652-6868, Fax: 418-577-518

Particuliers / Individuals Directorate
Sous-ministre adjointe & Directrice générale, Particuliers, Carole Imbeault
418-652-6807, Fax: 418-652-5049
Directrice, Services à la clientèle des particuliers, Christianne Lebleu
418-689-1400, Fax: 418-689-1420
Directeur régional, Services à la clientèle des particuliers - Centre et Sud du Québec, Normand Bilodeau
819-694-4811, Fax: 819-577-5069
Directrice régionale, Services à la clientèle des particuliers - Montréal, Michelle Page-Melançon
514-215-3719, Fax: 514-215-3575
Directeur régional (par intérim), Services à la clientèle des particuliers - Nord et Ouest du Québec, France Richard
819-779-6035, Fax: 819-772-3377
Directeur régional, Contrôle fiscal des particuliers - Capitale-Nationale et autres régions, Michel Lepage
418-725-6900, Fax: 418-727-3922
Directeur, Comptabilisation et non-production des déclarations de particuliers, Magdi Abdel-Malak
418-652-4726, Fax: 418-577-5047
Directrice, Cotisation des particuliers, Céline Goyette
418-652-5126, Fax: 418-646-1649
Directeur, Pensions alimentaires, Michel Stewart
418-652-6704, Fax: 418-646-8270

Registre des Entreprises / Businesses Directorate
Sous-ministre adjointe & Directrice générale des entreprises, Johanne L. Bergeron
514-287-3700, Fax: 514-864-7242
Directeur, Soutien opérationnel et Développement des compétences, Danny Pagé
514-287-2020, Fax: 514-864-7242
Directeur régional, Vérification des entreprises de Montréal, Pierre Leclerc
514-287-4187, Fax: 514-285-3875
Directrice régionale, Vérification des entreprises - Nord et Ouest du Québec, Camelia Attya
514-215-3600, Fax: 514-215-3670,Other Communications: Nord et Ouest: 450/972-2356, Fax: 450/972-2354

Directeur, Cotisation des entreprises, Gilbert Caccia
514-287-8126, Fax: 514-285-5374
Directrice régionale, Vérification des entreprises - Capitale-Nationale, Sud et Est du Québec, Sylvie Bégin
418-652-6811, Fax: 418-643-5050
Directeur principal, Services à la clientèle des entreprises, Denis Gendron
514-287-8055, Fax: 514-864-4364
Directeur, Bureau de Toronto, Jocelyn Hamel
416-977-6713, Fax: 416-977-9748

Biens non réclamés / Unclaimed Property Directorate
Sous-ministre adjoint & Directeur général, Centre de perception fiscale et des biens non réclamés, Claude Provencher

Ministère de la Santé et des Services sociaux / Health & Social Services

Direction des communications et Renseignements généraux, 1075, ch Sainte-Foy, Québec, QC G1S 2M1
418-266-8900, 800-707-3380
regisseur.web@msss.gouv.qc.ca
www.msss.gouv.qc.ca

Acts Administered:
Loi assurant l'exercice des droits des personnes handicapées/An Act to secure the handicapped in the exercise of their rights
Loi assurant la mise en oeuvre de la Convention sur la protection des enfants et la coopération en matière d'adoption internationale et modifiant diverses dispositions législatives en matière d'adopti
Loi assurant le maintien des services essentiels dans le secteur de la santé et des services sociaux/An Act to ensure that essential services are maintained in the health and social services sector
Loi concernant les unités de négociation dans le secteur des affaires sociales/An Act respecting bargaining units in the social affairs sector
Loi sur Héma-Québec et sur le Comité d'hémovigilance/An Act respecting Héma-Québec and the haemovigilance committee
Loi sur l'administration publique/Public Administration Act
Loi sur l'assurance-hospitalisation/Hospital Insurance Act
Loi sur l'assurance-maladie/Health Insurance Act
Loi sur l'assurance-médicaments/An Act respecting prescription drug insurance
Loi sur l'équilibre budgétaire du réseau public de la santé et des services sociaux/An Act to provide for balanced budgets in the public health and social services network
Loi sur l'Institut national de Santé publique du Québec/An Act respecting the Institut national de Santé publique du Québec
Loi sur la Corporation d'hébergement du Québec/An Act respecting the Corporation d'hébergement du Québec
Loi sur la protection de la jeunesse/Youth Protection Act
Loi sur la protection de la santé publique/Public Health Protection Act
Loi sur la protection des personnes dont l'état mental présente un danger pour elles-mêmes ou pour autrui/An Act respecting the protection of persons whose mental state presents a danger to themselves
Loi sur la Régie de l'assurance-maladie du Québec/An Act respecting the Régie de l'assurance-maladie du Québec
Loi sur la santé publique/Public Health Act
Loi sur le Commissaire à la santé et au bien-être/An Act respecting the Health and Welfare Commissioner
Loi sur le Conseil de la santé et du bien-être/An Act respection g the Conseil de la santé et du bien-être
Loi sur le Conseil médical du Québec/An Act respecting the Conseil médical du Québec
Loi sur le ministère de la Santé et des Services Sociaux/An Act respecting the Ministède la Santé des Services sociaux
Loi sur le Protecteur des usagers en matière de santé et de services sociaux/An Act respecting the Health and Social Services Ombudsman
Loi sur le tabac/Tobacco Act
Loi sur les activités cliniques et de recherche en matière de procréation assistée et modifiant d'autres dispositions législatives
Loi sur les agences de développement de réseaux locaux de services de santé et de services sociaux/An Act respecting local health and social services network development agencies
Loi sur les cimetières non-Catholiques/Non-Catholic Cemeteries Act
Loi sur les inhumations et les exhumations/Burial Act
Loi sur les laboratoires médicaux, la conservation des organes, des tissus, des gamètes et des embryons, les services ambulanciers et la disposition des cadavres/An Act respecting medical laboratories
Loi sur les sages-femmes/Midwives Act
Loi sur les services de santé et les services sociaux/An Act respecting health services and social services
Loi sur les services de santé et les services sociaux pour les autochtones cris/An Act respecting health services and social services for Cree Native persons

Ministre,L'hon. Dr Yves Bolduc
418-266-7171
Ministre déléguée, Services sociaux, L'hon. Dominique Vien
418-266-7181
Sous-ministre, Jacques Cotton
418-266-8989, Fax: 418-266-8990
Sous-ministre adjoint, Planification, performance & qualité, Denis Lalumière
418-266-5990
Sous-ministre adjoint, Santé publique, Alain Poirier
418-266-6700
Sous-ministre adjoint, Services sociaux, Sylvain Gagnon
418-266-6800
Sous-ministre adjoint, Personnel réseau et ministériel, Michel Delamarre
418-266-8400
Sous-ministre adjolnte, Coordination, financement, immobilisations et budget, Lise Verreault
418-266-8850
Directeur général, Technologies de l'information, Marc Vézina
418-266-5865
Directeur général, Services de santé et médecine universitaire, Michel A. Bureau
418-266-6930

• Agence d'évaluation des technologies et des modes d'intervention en santé(AETMIS) / Technology Assessment & Health Solutions Agency
#10.083, 2021, av Union
Montréal, QC H3A 2S9
514-873-2563 Fax: 514-873-1369
www.aetmis.gouv.qc.ca

• Bureau des projets Centres hospitaliers universitaires de Montréal, CHUM, CUSM et CHU Sainte-Justine/ Project Office for the Modernization of Montréal's University Health Centres CHUM, MUHC and Sainte-Justine UHC
#10.049, 2021, rue Union
Montréal, QC H3A 2S9
514-864-9883 Fax: 514-873-7362
www.construction3chu.msss.gouv.qc.ca

• Secrétariat à l'accès aux services en langue anglaise et aux communautés ethnoculturelles/ English Language & Ethnocultural Communities Services Secretariat
#840, 2021, av Union
Montréal, QC H3A 2S9
514-873-5130 Fax: 514-873-9876
www.msss.gouv.qc.ca/ministere/saslacc

• Conseil du médicament/ Medication Council
#100, 1195, av Lavigerie
Sainte-Foy, QC G1V 4N3
418-644-8103 Fax: 418-644-8120
cdm@cdm.gouv.qc.ca
www.cdm.gouv.qc.ca

• Commissaire à la santé et du bien-être/ Health & Welfare Commission
#700, 1020, rte de l'Église
Québec, QC G1V 3V9
418-643-3040 Fax: 418-644-0654
csbe@csbe.gouv.qc.ca
www.csbe.gouv.qc.ca

• Corporation d'hébergement du Québec/ Long Term Care Facilities Corporation of Québec
2535, boul Laurier, 5e étage
Québec, QC G1V 4M3
418-644-3600 Fax: 418-644-3609
danielle.dussault@chq.gouv.qc.ca
www.chq.gouv.qc.ca

• Institut national de santé publique du Québec/ National Public Health Institute of Québec
945, av Wolfe
Québec, QC G1V 5B3
418-650-5115 Fax: 418-646-9328
info@inspq.qc.ca
www.inspq.qc.ca

• Office des personnes handicapées du Québec/ Office for Handicapped Persons
309, rue Brock
Drummondville, QC J2B 1C5
819-475-8585 Fax: 819-475-8767 800-567-1465
www.ophq.gouv.qc.ca
Other Communication: Téléscripteur: 1-800-567-1477

• Urgences-santé Québec/ Emergency Health Services Québec
3232, rue Bélanger
Montréal, QC H1Y 3H5
514-723-5600
info@urgences-sante.qc.ca
www.urgences-sante.qc.ca

• Régie de l'assurance maladie du Québec/ Québec Health Insurance Board
1125, Grande Allée ouest
Québec, QC G1S 1E7
418-646-4636
www.ramq.gouv.qc.ca

Santé publique / Public Health
Sous-ministre adjoint, Alain Poirier
418-266-6700, Fax: 418-266-6707
Directrice, Planification, évaluation et développement en santé publique/Surveillance de l'état de santé, Lyne Jobin
418-266-6780
Directeur, Développement des individus de l'environnement, André Dontigny
418-266-6714
Directrice, Prévention des maladies chroniques et des traumatismes, Marie Rochette
418-266-6750
Directeur, Protection de la santé publique, Horacio Arruda
418-266-6720

Agences, conseils et commissions associes/Associated Agencies, Boards & Commissions:

Commission de la santé et de la sécurité du travail du Québec (CSST) / Québec Occupational Health & Safety Commission

524, rue Bourdages, CP 1200 Terminus postal, Québec, QC G1K 7E2
418-266-4850, Fax: 418-266-4398, 866-302-2778
www.csst.qc.ca

A pour mission de soutenir aux travailleurs & aux employeurs dans leurs démarches pour éliminer les dangers présents dans leur milieu de travail, inspecter des lieux de travail, & promouvoir la santé & sécurité du travail

Président & Chef de la direction, Luc Meunier
Vice-présidente, Partenariat et l'expertise-conseil, Guylaine Rioux
Vice-présidente, Administration, communications & relations publiques, Carole Théberge
Vice-président, Finances, André Beauchemin
Vice-président, Opérations, Paul Marceau
Directeur, Affaires juridiques, Pierre Vigneault
Directeur, Affaires corporatives/Secrétariat général, Paul Gendron
Directrice, Bureau du président du Conseil d'administration & Chef de la direction, Louise Lambert

Ministère de la Sécurité publique / Ministry of Public Security

Tour des Laurentides, 2525, boul Laurier, 5e étage, Québec, QC G1V 2L2
418-643-2112, Fax: 418-646-6168, 866-644-6826
www.securitepublique.gouv.qc.ca

A pour mission d'assurer la sécurité publique au Québec

Acts Administered:
Loi de tempérance/Temperance Act
Loi favorisant la libération conditionnelle des détenus/An Act to promote the parole of inmates
Loi sur la police/Police Act
Loi sur la propriété des bicyclettes/Bicycle Ownership Act
Loi sur la recherche des causes et des circonstances des décès/An Act respecting the determination of the causes & circumstances of death
Loi sur la sécurité civile/Civil Protection Act
Loi sur la sécurité dans les sports/An Act respecting safety in sports
Loi sur la sécurité incendie/Fire Safety Act
Loi sur la Société des alcools du Québec/An Act respecting the Société des alcools du Québec (partially administered by MSP)
Loi sur la Société des loteries du Québec/An Act respecting the Société des loteries du Québec (partially administered by the MSP)
Loi sur le ministère de la Sécurité publique/An Act respecting the Ministère de la Sécurité publique
Loi sur le régime syndical applicable à la Sûreté du Québec/An Act respecting the Syndical Plan of the Sûreté du Québec
Loi sur le système correctionnel du Québec/An Act respecting the Québec correctional system
Loi sur les agences d'investigation ou de sécurité/An Act respecting detectives or security agencies
Loi sur les bombes lacrymogènes/Act respecting tear bombs
Loi sur les coffrets de sûreté/Safe-Deposit Boxes Act
Loi sur les courses/An Act respecting racing
Loi sur les explosifs/An Act respecting explosives
Loi sur les infractions en matière de boissons alcooliques/An Act respecting offences relating to Alcoholic Beverages

Loi sur les loteries, les concours publicitaires et les appareils d'amusement/An Act respecting lotteries, publicity, contests & amusement machines
Loi sur les permis d'alcool/An Act respecting liquor permits
Loi sur les services correctionnels/An Act respecting correctional services
Loi sur les villages nordiques et l'Administration régionale Kativik/An Act respecting Northern Villages & the Kativik Regional Government (partially administered by the MSP)
Ministre,L'hon. Robert Dutil
418-643-2112, Fax: 418-646-6168,ministre@msp.gouv.qc.ca
Sous-ministre, Robert Lafrenière
418-643-3500, Fax: 418-643-0275
Directrice de cabinet, Isabelle Lessard
418-643-2112, Fax: 418-646-6168
Directeur, Vérification interne, enquêtes & inspection, Sylvain Ayotte
418-644-6777
• Bureau du coroner/ Office of the Coroner
#390, 2875, boul Laurier
Sainte-Foy, QC G1V 5B1
418-643-1845 Fax: 418-643-6174
clientele.coroner@msp.gouv.qc.ca
• Comité de déontologie policière/ Police Ethics Committee
Tour du Saint-Laurent
#A-200, 2525, boul Laurier, 2e étage
Québec, QC G1V 4Z6
418-646-1936 Fax: 418-528-0987
comite.deontologie@msp.gouv.qc.ca
www.deontologie-policiere.gouv.qc.ca
• Commissaire à la déontologie policière/ Police Ethics Commissioner
1200, rte de l'Église, R-C20
Sainte-Foy, QC G1V 4Y9
418-643-7897 Fax: 418-528-9473 877-237-7897
www.deontologie-policiere.gouv.qc.ca
Other Communication:
deontologie-policiere.quebec@msp.gouv.qc.ca
• Commissariat des incendies/ Fire Commissioner
455, rue Dupont
Québec, QC G1K 6N2
418-529-5706 Fax: 418-529-9922
• Commission québecoise des libérations conditionnelles/ Parole Board
#1.32A, 300, boul Jean-Lesage
Québec, QC G1K 8K6
418-646-8300 Fax: 418-643-7217
liberation.conditionnel@msp.gouv.
www.msp.gouv.qc.ca
• Direction générale de la Sûreté du Québec/ Provincial Police
1701, rue Parthenais
Montréal, QC H2K 3S7
514-598-4488 Fax: 514-598-4957
info@surete.qc.ca
www.surete.qc.ca
• École nationale de police du Québec/ National Police School of Québec
350, rue Marguerite-d'Youville
Nicolet, QC J3T 1X4
819-293-8631 Fax: 819-293-4018
courriel@enpq.qc.ca
www.enpq.qc.ca
• École nationale des pompiers du Québec/ Québec National Fire Fighters School
#3.08, 2800, boul Saint-Martin ouest
Laval, QC H7T 2S9
450-680-6800 Fax: 450-680-6818 866-680-3677
enpq@enpq.gouv.qc.ca
www.enpq.gouv.qc.ca
• Régie des alcools, des courses et des jeux/ Liquor, Gaming & Racing Board
560, boul Charest est
Québec, QC G1K 3J3
418-643-7667 Fax: 418-643-5971 800-363-0320
racj.quebec@racj.gouv.qc.ca

Affaires policières / Police Services
418-643-3500, Fax: 418-643-0275
Sous-ministre associé & directeur général, Martin Prud'homme
Directrice générale adjointe, Sylvie Tousignant
418-646-6777, Fax: 418-644-0132

Sécurité civile et Sécurité incendie / Public Safety & Fire Services
Sous-ministre associé & directeur général, Michel C. Doré
418-643-3500, Fax: 418-643-0275
Directeur général adjoint/Directeur (par intérim), Opérations, Éric Houde
418-646-6777, Fax: 418-646-5426
Directrice, Mobilisation, Hélène Chagnon
418-646-6777, Fax: 418-646-5427
Directeur, Gestion des risques, Martin Simard
418-643-3821, Fax: 418-644-4547
Directeur, Rétablissement, Denis Landry, 2008-09-19
418-646-6638, Fax: 418-646-6628

Directions régionales/Regional Offices:

Bas-Saint-Laurent, Gaspésie et Iles-de-la-Madeleine
#110, 70, rue Saint-Germain est, Rimouski, QC G5L 7J9
418-727-3589, Fax: 418-727-3643, securite.civile01@msp.gouv.qc.ca
Directrice, France-Sylvie Loisel

Capitale-Nationale, Chaudière Appalaches et Nunavik
#200, 1122, Grande-Allée ouest, Québec, QC G1S 1E5
418-643-3244, Fax: 418-644-2080, securite.civile03@msp.gouv.qc.ca
Directrice, Hélène Chagnon

Estrie et Montérégie
165, rue Jacques-Cartier nord, Saint-Jean-sur-Richelieu, QC J3B 6S9
450-346-3200, Fax: 450-346-5856, securite.civile16@msp.gouv.qc.ca
Directrice, Diane Migneault

Mauricie et Centre-du-Québec
4000, rue Louis-Pinard, Trois-Rivières, QC G8Y 4L9
819-371-6703, Fax: 819-371-6983, securite.civile04@msp.gouv.qc.ca
Directeur, Jacques Raymond

Montréal, Laval, Lanaudière et Laurentides
RC #23, 5100, rue Sherbrooke est, Montréal, QC H1V 3R9
514-873-1300, Fax: 514-864-8654, securite.civile06@msp.gouv.qc.ca
Directeur (par intérim), Yvan Leroux

Outaouais, Abitibi-Témiscamingue et Nord-du-Québec
817, boul St-René ouest, Gatineau, QC J8T 8M3
819-772-3737, Fax: 819-772-3954, securite.civile07@msp.gouv.qc.ca
Directeur, Jacques Viger

Saguenay-Lac-Saint-Jean et Côte-Nord
RC-01, 3950, boul Harvey, Jonquière, QC G7X 8L6
418-695-7872, Fax: 418-695-7875, securite.civile02@msp.gouv.qc.ca
Directeur, Réal Delisle

Services correctionnels / Correctional Services
Directrice générale adjointe (par intérim), Programmes et sécurité, Johanne Beausoleil
418-644-7887, Fax: 418-644-5645
Directrice, Administration, Sophie Boisvert
418-646-6777, Fax: 418-643-3426
Directrice, Recherche, Johanne Levesque
418-646-6767, Fax: 418-646-6228
Directrice, Conseil à l'organisation, Marlène Langlois, 2010-09-13
418-646-6777, Fax: 418-644-5645

Directions régionales/Regional Offices:

Abitibi-Témiscamingue, Nord-du-Québec
#203, 170, av Principale, Rouyn-Noranda, QC J9X 4P7
819-763-3790, Fax: 819-763-3882
Directeur, Daniel Guénard
daniel.guenard@mps.gouv.qc.ca

Bas-Saint-Laurent
Place Saint-Laurent, #101, 70, rue Saint-Germain est, Rimouski, QC G5L 7J9
418-727-3687, Fax: 418-727-3531
Directrice (par intérim), Linda Hudon
linda.hudon@msp.gouv.qc.ca

Capitale-Nationale, Chaudière-Appalaches
#3.05, 1200, rte de l'Église, 3e étage, Québec, QC G1V 4K9
418-646-0570, Fax: 418-646-9254
Directeur, Michel Roberge
michel.roberge@msp.gouv.qc.ca

Côte-Nord
1191, boul Laflèche, 2e étage, Baie-Comeau, QC G5C 1E1
418-295-1333, Fax: 418-295-4819, 866-640-3026
Directeur (par intérim), Georges Blais
georges.blais@msp.gouv.qc.ca

Estrie, Centre-du-Québec
#1.10, 200, Belvedère nord, Sherbrooke, QC J1H 4A9
819-820-3017, Fax: 819-820-3074, hebert@msp.gouv.qc.ca
Directeur (par intérim), Michel Gagnon
michel.gagnon2@msp.gouv.qc.ca

Gaspésie-Iles-de-la-Madeleine
#101, 484, rue Hôtel-de-Ville, 1er étage, Chandler, QC G0C 1K0
418-689-4947, Fax: 418-689-5549
Directrice, Suzanne Bourget
suzanne.bourget@msp.gouv.qc.ca

Laval, Lanaudière, Laurentides
#3.02, 2800, boul Saint-Martin ouest, Laval, QC H7T 2S9
450-680-6040, Fax: 450-680-6035
Directrice, Nicole Quesnel
nicole.quesnel@msp.gouv.qc.ca

Mauricie, Centre-du-Québec
#212, 100, rue Laviolette, Trois-Rivières, QC G9A 5S9
819-371-6124, Fax: 819-371-6176
Directeur, Roger Deschamps
roger.deschamps@msp.gouv.qc.ca

Montérégie
#3300, 5245, boul Cousineau, Saint-Hubert, QC J3Y 6Y8
450-656-3822, Fax: 450-656-7633, 866-337-0184
Directeur, Robert Jacques
robert.jacques@msp.gouv.qc.ca

Montréal
#11.87, 10, rue Saint-Antoine est, Montréal, QC H2Y 1A2
514-864-1800, Fax: 514-873-9362
Directeur, Gilles Soucy
gilles.soucy@msp.gouv.qc.ca

Outaouais
#2.230, 17, rue Laurier, Gatineau, QC J9A 1B4
819-772-3929, Fax: 819-772-3025, 866-466-7603
Directrice (par intérim), Johanne Beausoleil
johanne.beausoleil@msp.gouv.qc.ca

Saguenay-Lac-Saint-Jean
#4.09, 227, rue Racine est, Chicoutimi, QC G7H 7B4
418-698-3779, Fax: 418-690-8560, alain.dastous@msp.gouv.qc.ca
Directeur (par intérim), René St-Pierre
rene.st-pierre@msp.gouv.qc.ca

Sûreté du Québec / Québec Provincial Police
info@surete.qc.ca
Directeur général, Richard Deschesnes, 2008-09-19
514-598-4488

Ministère des Services gouvernementaux / Government Services

4e étage, Secteur 500, 875, Grande Allée est, Québec, QC G1R 5R8
418-643-8383, Fax: 418-528-6153, communication@msg.gouv.qc.ca
www.msg.gouv.qc.ca
A pour mission de faire progresser la modernisation de l'État, simplifier l'accès aux services gouvernementaux, regrouper des services pour l'Administration, et développer le gouvernement en ligne
Acts Administered:
Loi concernant le cadre juridique des technologies de l'information
Loi sur la Société immobilière du Québec
Loi sur le Centre de services partagés du Québec
Loi sur le ministère des Services gouvernementaux
Loi sur le Service des achats du gouvernement
Loi sur les services gouvernementaux aux ministères et organismes publics
Loi sur Services Québec
Ministre,L'hon. Michelle Courchesne
418-643-5926, Fax: 418-643-7824,cabinet@sct.gouv.qc.ca
Sous-ministre & dirigeante principale de l'information (par intérim), Denis Garon
Sous-ministre associé, Bureau de la recherche et de l'innovation, Sylvie Grondin
Directeur général, Service aérien gouvernemental, Lucien Tremblay
Directeur (par intérim), Affaires publiques et Communications, Jean Talbot
• Services Québec
800, place D'Youville, 20e étage
Québec, QC G1R 3P4
418-644-4545 Fax: 418-528-9341 877-644-4545TDD: 800-361-9596
www.gouv.qc.ca/portail/quebec/pgs/commun
Other Communication: Montréal Citizens: 514-644-4545; Address: Place Dupuis, RC#2, 800, boul Maisonneuve est, Montréal, QC H2L 4L8
Services Québec est un guichet multiservices chargé d'offrir des services intégrés aux citoyens et aux entreprises
• Société immobilière du Québec(SIQ) / Québec Buildings Corp.
1075, rue de l'Amérique-Française
Québec, QC G1R 5P8
418-646-1766 Fax: 418-646-6911 877-747-9911
courrier@siq.gouv.qc.ca
www.siq.gouv.qc.ca
La Société immobilière du Québec (SIQ) a pour mission de mettre à la disposition des ministères et organismes publics des

immeubles et de leur fournir des services de construction, d'exploitation et de gestion immobilière

Centre de services partagés / Shared Services Centre
Présidente-directrice générale, Diane Jean
418-643-0578, Fax: 418-643-9735
Vice-président, Ressources humaines, Claude Sicard
418-528-6296, Fax: 418-644-0405
Vice-président, Opérations & services, Gordon Smith
Vice-président, Technologies de l'information, Raymond Sarrazin
Directeur général, Services en ressources matérielles & documentaires, Pierre-A. Thibaudeau
Directrice générale, Information gouvernementale, Céline Roy
Directeur général, Solutions d'affaires en gestion intégrée des ressources, Guy St-Onge
Directeur général, Acquisitions, André Brindamour
Directeur général, Services aux utilisateurs & opérations, Patrick Amiot
Directeur général, Réseaux de télécommunications, Guy Chouinard
Responsable, Centre de gestion de la dotation & Services en région, Nicolas Vérilli
Responsable, Centre de gestion de la rémunération, François Bérubé

Société immobilière du Québec
1075, rue de l'Amérique-Française, 1er étage, Québec, QC G1R 5P8
418-646-1766, Fax: 418-646-6911,
courrier@siq.gouv.qc.ca
A pour mission à loger les ministères & organismes publics au meilleur rapport qualité & prix. Créée en 1984, la SIQ a remplacé le Ministère des Travaux publics et de l'Approvisionnement
Président & Chef de la direction, Richard Verreault
Vice-président (par intérim), Exploitation-Est, Claude Dubé
Vice-président, Administration & finances, Jacques Vaillancourt
Vice-président, Exécutif, Pierre Babineau
Vice-président, Exploitation-Ouest, Jules Chevrier

Services Québec
877-644-4545
www.gouv.qc.ca/portail/quebec/
Créé en 2004 pour améliorer la façon d'offrir des services publics aux citoyens et aux entreprises

Services Québec

Bureau de la qualité, 800, place D'Youville, 20e étage, Québec, QC G1R 3P4
418-646-4011, Fax: 418-528-9341,
www.gouv.qc.ca/portail/quebec/servicesquebec/
Président-Directeur général (par-intérim) & Vice-président, Services à la clientèle, Jocelyn Girard
418-528-9328
Directrice, Planification, recherche et coordination intergouvernementale, Réjeanne Lachance
Directrice générale, Services à l'organisation et communications, Carole Lafond
Directeur, État civil, Pierre E. Rodrigue
Directrice (par intérim), Services juridiques, Manon Godin

Les Publications du Québec
#500, 1000 rte de l'Eglise, Québec, QC G1V 3V9
418-643-5150, Fax: 418-643-6177, 800-463-2100
publicationsduquebec@cspq.gouv.qc.ca
www.publicationsduquebec.gouv.qc.ca

Directions régionales/Regional Offices:

Abitibi-Témiscamingue-Nord-du-Québec
RC #01, 255, av Principale, Rouyn-Noranda, QC J9X 7G9
Fax: 819-763-3040, 877-644-4545

Bas-Saint-Laurent
RC #01, 337, rue Moreault, Rimouski, QC G5L 1P4
Fax: 418-727-3900, 877-644-4545

Capitale-Nationale
787, boul Lebourneuf, Québec, QC G2J 1C3
418-644-4545, 877-644-4545

Chaudière-Appalaches
44, rte du Président-Kennedy, Lévis, QC G6V 6C5
877-644-4545

Côte-Nord
280, av Arnaud, Sept-Iles, QC G4R 3A7

Estrie
#120, 3425, rue King ouest, Sherbrooke, QC J1L 1P8
877-644-4545

Gaspésie-Iles-de-la-Madeleine
#1.02A, 96, montée Sandy Beach, Gaspé, QC G4X 2W4
877-644-4545

Lanaudière
RC #20, 450, rue Saint-Louis, Joliette, QC J6E 2Y8
877-644-4545

Laurentides
Galeries des Laurentides, #1503C, 500, boul des Laurentides, Saint-Jérôme, QC J7Z 4M2
877-644-4545

Laval
1796, boul des Laurentides, Laval, QC H7M 2P6
877-644-4545

Mauricie
RC #26, 100, rue Laviolette, Trois-Rivières, QC G9A 5S9
877-644-4545

Montérégie
125, boul Sainte-Foy, RC, Longueuil, QC J4J 1W7
877-644-4545

Montréal
Place Dupuis, #RC 2, 800, boul Maisonneuve est, Montréal, QC H2L 4L8
514-644-4545, Fax: 514-873-3511, 877-644-4545

Outaouais
RC #120, 170, rue de l'Hôtel-de-Ville, Gatineau, QC J8X 4C2
877-644-4545

Centre-du-Québec
RC #16, 270, rue Lindsay, Drummondville, QC J2B 1G3
877-644-4545

Saguenay-Lac-Saint-Jean
2655, boul du Royaume, Jonquière, QC G7S 4S9
877-644-4545

Ministère du Tourisme / Tourism Québec

#400, 900, boul René-Lévesque est, Québec, QC G1R 2B5
418-643-5959, Fax: 418-646-8723, 800-482-2433
www.tourisme.gouv.qc.ca
Acts Administered:
Loi sur l'aide au développement touristique
Loi sur le ministère du Tourisme
Loi sur l'Institut de tourisme et d'hôtellerie du Québec
Loi sur les établissements d'hébergement touristique
Ministre,L'hon. Nicole Ménard
418-528-8063, Fax: 418-528-8066
Sous-ministre, Suzanne Giguère
418-643-9141, Fax: 418-643-2268
Directrice (par intérim), Communications, Dominique Lavoie
Directrice, Affaires juridiques, Maryse Beaumont
Sous-ministre adjoint, Marketing & clientèles touristiques, Georges Vacher
• Palais des congrès de Montréal
159, rue Saint-Antoine ouest, 9é étage
Montréal, QC H2Z 1H2
514-871-8122 Fax: 514-871-3188 800-268-8122
pcmcomm@congresmtl.com
congresmtl.com
• Société du Centre des congrès de Québec/ Québec City Convention Centre
900, boul René-Lévesque est, 2e étage
Québec, QC G1R 2B5
418-644-4000 Fax: 418-644-6455 888-679-4000
www.convention.qc.ca

Administration / Administration
Directrice générale, Clémence Verret
Directeur (par intérim), Ressources humaines, Charles Bélanger
Directeur, Ressources financières & matérielles, Sylvain Bergeron
Directeur (par intérim), Ressources informationelles, Rémy Cadorette

Développement / Development
Directeur général, Développement, François Diguer
Directrice, Partenariat et intervention régionale, Geneviève Moisan
Directeur général adjoint & Coordonnateur, Stratégie des croisières internationales, François Belzile
Directeur, Stratégies & développement des entreprises touristiques, Marc Leduc

Marketing et clientèles touristiques / Marketing & Tourism Consumers
Sous-ministre adjoint, Georges Vacher
514-864-1016, Fax: 514-864-6152
Directrice générale, Marketing, Sylvie Quenneville
Directeur général, Services à la clientèle touristique, Sylvain Lacombe
Directrice, Centre d'affaires électroniques, Michèle Morel
Directrice, Renseignements par téléphone et Internet, Nicole Desrochers

Ministère des Transports (MTQ) / Transportation

700, boul René-Lévesque est, 27e étage, Québec, QC G1R 5H1
418-643-6980, Fax: 418-643-2011, 888-355-0511
communications@mtq.gouv.qc.ca
www.mtq.gouv.qc.ca

Other Communication: Au Québec: 5-1-1
Acts Administered:
Code de la sécurité routière/Highway Safety Code
Loi concernant la Compagnie de gestion de Matane inc./Act respecting the Compagnie de gestion de Matane Inc.
Loi concernant les partenariats en matière d'infrastructures de transport/Act respecting transport infrastructure partnerships
Loi concernant les propriétaires et exploitants de véhicules lourds/Act respecting owners and operators of heavy vehicles
Loi concernant les services de transport par taxi/Act respecting transportation services by taxi
Loi interdisant l'affichage publicitaire le long de certaines voies de circulation/Act to prohibit commercial advertising along certain thoroughfares
Loi modifiant la Loi sur les transports en matière de camionnage en vrac/Act to amend the Transport Act as regards bulk trucking
Loi sur l'Agence métropolitaine de transport/Act respecting the Agence métropolitaine de transport
Loi sur l'assurance automobile/Automobile Insurance Act
Loi sur l'expropriation/Expropriation Act
Loi sur la publicité au long des routes/Roadside Advertising Act
Loi sur la sécurité du transport terrestre guidé/Act to ensure safety in guided land transportation
Loi sur la Société de l'assurance automobile du Québec/Act respecting the Société de l'assurance automobile du Québec
Loi sur la Société des traversiers du Québec/Act respecting the Société des Traversiers du Québec
Loi sur la Société du port ferroviaire de Baie-Comeau-Hauterive/Act respecting the Société du port ferroviaire de Baie-Comeau-Hauterive
Loi sur la voirie/Act respecting roads
Loi sur le Ministère des Transports/Act respecting the Ministère des Transports
Loi sur les chemins de fer/Railway Act
Loi sur les conseils intermunicipaux de transport dans la région de Montréal/Act respecting intermunicipal boards of transport in the area of Montréal
Loi sur les sociétés de transport en commun/Act respecting public transit authorities
Loi sur les transports/Transport Act
Loi sur les transports instituant la Commission des transports du Québec/Transport Act established by the Commission des transports du Québec
Loi sur les véhicules hors route/Act respecting off-highway vehicles
Ministre,L'hon. Sam Hamad
418-643-6980, Fax: 418-643-2033
Ministre délégué, Norman MacMillan
418-643-6980, Fax: 418-643-2033
Sous-ministre, Michel Boivin
418-643-6740, Fax: 418-643-9836
Directeur général de Montréal & de l'Ouest,VACANTE
Directeur général de Québec & de l'Est, André Caron, s.m.a.
418-528-0808
Directrice générale, Infrastructures & Technologies, Anne-Marie Leclerc
418-528-0808
Directrice générale (par intérim), Services à la gestion, Josée Dupont
418-528-0808
Directeur, Politiques & sécurité en transport, André Meloche, s.m.a.
418-528-0808
• Commission des transports du Québec/ Québec Transport Commission
200, ch Sainte-Foy, 7e étage
Québec, QC G1R 5V5
Fax: 418-644-8034 888-461-2433
courrier@ctq.gouv.qc.ca
www.ctq.gouv.qc.ca
• Société de l'assurance automobile du Québec
333, boul Jean-Lesage
CP 19600 Terminus
Québec, QC G1K 8J6
418-643-7620 Fax: 418-644-0339 800-361-7620
courrier@saaq.gouv.qc.ca
www.saaq.gouv.qc.ca

• Société du port ferroviaire Baie-Comeau-Hauterive/ Baie-Comeau-Hauterive Railway Station
18, rte Maritime
Baie-Comeau, QC G4Z 2L6
418-296-6785 Fax: 418-296-2377
soport@globetrotter.qc.ca
• Société des traversiers du Québec/ Ferries Québec
250, rue Saint-Paul
Québec, QC G1K 9K9
418-643-2019 Fax: 418-643-7308
stq@traversiers.gouv.qc.ca
www.traversiers.gouv.qc.ca

Infrastructures et technologies / Infrastructure & Technologies
Directrice générale, Anne-Marie Leclerc, s.m.a.
418-528-0808
Directeur, Laboratoire des chaussées, Claude Tremblay
418-643-6618
Directeur, Structures, Daniel Bouchard
418-643-6906
Directeur, Soutien aux opérations, Éric Breton
418-643-9298
Directeur, Environnement et recherche, Christian Therrien
418-643-8326

Montréal et de l'Ouest / Montreal & the West
Directeur (par intérim), Planification & coordination des ressources, Pierre Fernandez Galvan
514-864-1730

Directions régionales/Regional Offices:

Abitibi-Témiscamingue-Nord-du-Québec
80, av Québec, Rouyn-Noranda, QC J9X 6R1
819-763-3271, Fax: 819-763-3493,
datnq@mtq.gouv.qc.ca

Est-de-la-Montérégie
201, place Charles-Lemoyne, 5e étage, Longueuil, QC J4K 2T5
450-677-3413, Fax: 450-442-1317,
dtem@mtq.gouv.qc.ca

Estrie
#2.02, 200, rue Belvédère nord, Sherbrooke, QC J1H 4A9
819-820-3280, Fax: 819-820-3118,
dte@mtq.gouv.qc.ca

Ile-de-Montréal
440, boul René-Lévesque ouest, 10e étage, Montréal, QC H2Z 2A6
514-873-7781, Fax: 514-864-3867,
dtim@mtq.gouv.qc.ca

Laurentides-Lanaudière
222, rue Saint-Georges, 2e étage, Saint-Jérôme, QC J7Z 4Z9
450-569-3057, Fax: 450-569-3072,
dll@mtq.gouv.qc.ca

Laval-Mille-Iles
1725, boul Le Corbusier, Laval, QC H7S 2K7
450-680-6330, Fax: 450-973-4959,
dtlmi@mtq.gouv.qc.ca

Ouest-de-la-Montérégie
#200, 180, boulevard d'Anjou, Châteauguay, QC J6K 1C4
450-698-3400, Fax: 450-698-3452,
dtom@mtq.gouv.qc.ca

Outaouais
#5.110, 170, rue de l'Hôtel-de-Ville, Gatineau, QC J8X 4C2
819-772-3849, Fax: 819-772-3338,
dto@mtq.gouv.qc.ca

Politiques et sécurité en transport / Transportation Policy & Security
Directeur général, André Meloche, s.m.a.
418-528-0808
Directeur, Transport routier des marchandises, Claude Larose
418-528-0631
Directeur, Sécurité en transport, Claude Morin
418-643-1564
Directrice, Transport terrestre des personnes, France Dompierre
418-644-0324
Directeur (par intérim), Transport maritime, aérien et ferroviaire, André Meloche
418-643-1864

Québec et de l'Est / Québec & the East
Directeur, Coordination, planification & ressources, Robert Beaulieu
418-643-7726

Directions régionales/Regional Offices:

Bas-Saint-Laurent-Gaspésie-Iles-de-la-Madeleine
#101, 92, 2e rue ouest, Rimouski, QC G5L 8E6
418-727-3674, Fax: 418-727-3673,
dtbgi@mtq.gouv.qc.ca

Chaudière-Appalaches
1156, boul de la Rive-Sud, Saint-Romuald, QC G6W 5M6
418-839-5581, Fax: 418-834-7338,
dtca@mtq.gouv.qc.ca

Côte-Nord
#110, 625, boul Laflèche, Baie-Comeau, QC G5C 1C5
418-295-4765, Fax: 418-295-4766,
dtcn@mtq.gouv.qc.ca

Mauricie-Centre-du-Québec
100, rue Laviolette, 4e étage, Trois-Rivières, QC G9A 5S9
819-371-6896, Fax: 819-371-6136,
dmcq@mtq.gouv.qc.ca

Capitale-Nationale
475, boul de l'Atrium, 2e étage, Québec, QC G1H 7H9
418-643-1911, Fax: 418-646-0003,
dcnat@mtq.gouv.qc.ca

Saguenay-Lac-Saint-Jean-Chibougamau
3950, boul Harvey, Jonquière, QC G7X 8L6
418-695-7916, Fax: 418-695-7926,
dt.slsjc@mtq.gouv.qc.ca

Agencies, conseils et commissions associes/Associated Agencies, Boards & Commissions:

Ministère du Travail / Labour

200, ch Sainte-Foy, 6e étage, Québec, QC G1R 5S1
418-643-4817, Fax: 418-528-0559, 800-643-4817
service_clientele@travail.gouv.qc.ca
www.travail.gouv.qc.ca

Acts Administered:
Code du travail/Labour Code
Loi assurant l'exercice des droits des personnes handicapées/Act to secure the handicapped in the exercise of their rights
Loi sur le ministère du Travail/Act respecting the Ministère du travail
Loi sur le régime de négociation des conventions collectives dans les secteurs public et parapublic/Act respecting the process of negotiating of the collective agreements in the public & parapublic se
Loi sur les décrets de convention collective/Act respecting Collective Agreement Decrees
Loi sur les relations du travail, la formation professionnelle et la gestion de la main-d'ouvre dans l'industrie de la construction/Act Respecting Labour Relations, Vocational Training, and Manpower M
Loi sur les syndicats professionnels/Professional Syndicates Act
Acts administered by Labour Agencies
Commission de l'équité salariale
Loi sur l'équité salariale/Pay Equity Act
Commission de la construction du Québec
Loi sur les relations du travail, la formation professionnelle et la gestion de la main-d'ouvre dans l'industrie de la construction/Act respecting labour relations vocational training & manpower manag
Commission de la santé et de la sécurité du travail
Loi sur les accidents du travail et les maladies professionnelles/Act respecting accidents at work & professional illness or sickness
Loi sur l'indemnisation des victimes d'amiantose ou de silicose dans les mines et les carrières/Act respecting compensation - victims of asbestos or silicosis in mines & quarries
Loi sur la santé et la sécurité du travail/Occupational Health & Safety Act
Commission des lésions professionelles
Commission des normes du travail
Loi sur la fête nationale/National Holiday Act
Loi sur les normes du travail/Act respecting Labour Standards
Conseil consultatif du travail et de la main-d'oeuvre
Loi sur le bâtiment /Building Act
Loi sur le Conseil consultatif du travail et de la main-d'ouvre/Act respecting the Conseil consultatif du travail et de la main d'oeuvre
Loi sur les appareils sous pression/Act respecting pressure vessels
Régie du bâtiment du Québec
Loi sur l'économie de l'énergie dans le bâtiment/Act respecting the conservation of energy in buildings
Loi sur la distribution du gaz/Gas distribution Act
Loi sur la sécurité dans les édifices publics/Public Buildings Safety Act
Loi sur les mécaniciens de machines fixes/Master Pipe Mechanics Act

Ministre,L'hon. Lise Thériault
418-643-5297, Fax: 418-644-0003,ministre@travail.gouv.qc.ca
Sous-ministre, Jocelin Dumas
418-643-2902, Fax: 418-643-0735
Directeur, Communications, Gilles Beaulé
418-643-4508
Directrice, Cabinet du ministre, Louise Bédard
418-643-5297
• Commissaire de l'industrie de la construction/ Construction & Industry Commission
150, boul René-Lévesque est, 18e étage,
Québec, QC G1R 5B1
418-646-7200 Fax: 418-644-9977
www.cic.gouv.qc.ca
• Commission de la construction du Québec/ Québec Construction Commission
3530, rue Jean-Talon ouest
Montréal, QC H3R 2G3
514-341-7740 Fax: 514-341-6354 888-842-8222
www.ccq.org
• Commission de l'équité salariale/ Pay Equity Commission
200, ch Ste-Foy, 4e étage
Québec, QC G1R 6A1
418-528-8765 Fax: 418-528-6999 888-528-8765
equite.salariale@ces.gouv.qc.ca
www.ces.gouv.qc.ca
• Commission des lésions professionnelles/ Work-Related Injuries Commission
#700, 900, Place d'Youville
Québec, QC G1R 3P7
418-644-7777 Fax: 418-644-6443 800-463-1591
www.clp.gouv.qc.ca
Other Communication: Montréal: 1-800-361-9593
Administrative tribunal that is the last recourse for employers or workers who contest a decision made by the Commission de la sant, et de la s,curit, du travail.
• Commission des normes du travail/ Labour Standards Commission
Hall Est
400, boul Jean-Lesage, 7e étage
Québec, QC G1K 8W1
418-644-0817 Fax: 418-643-5132 800-563-9058
www.cnt.gouv.qc.ca
• Commission des relations du travail/ Labour Relations Commission
35, rue de Port-Royal est, 2e étage
Montréal,H3L 3T1
514-864-3646 Fax: 514-873-3112 866-864-3646
crtm@crt.gouv.qc.ca
www.crt.gouv.qc.ca
• Commission de la santé et de la sécurité du travail(CSST) / Occupational Health & Safety Commission
425, rue du Pont
CP 4900 Terminus
Québec, QC G1K 7S6
418-266-4000 Fax: 418-266-4015 800-668-6811
www.csst.qc.ca
Other Communication: Ile-de-Montréal: 514-906-3000; Address: Tour Sud, 1, complexe Desjardins, 31e étage, CP 3, Succursale Place-Desjardins, Montréal, QC, H5B 1H1
• Conseil consultatif du travail et de la main d'oeuvre/ Advisory Council on Labour & Manpower
#9.400, 500, boul René-Lévesque ouest
Montréal, QC H2Z 1W7
514-873-2880 Fax: 514-873-1129
cctm@cctm.gouv.qc.ca
www.cctm.gouv.qc.ca
• Conseil des services essentiels du Québec/ Essential Services Council
800, tour de la place-Victoria, 25e étage
CP 365
Montréal, QC H4Z 1H9
514-873-7246 Fax: 514-873-3839 800-337-7246
info@cses.gouv.qc.ca
www.cses.gouv.qc.ca
• Régie du bâtiment du Québec/ Québec Construction Companies Board
545, boul Crémazie est, 4e étage
Montréal, QC H2M 2V2
514-873-0976 Fax: 514-864-2903 800-361-0761
crc@rbq.gouv.qc.ca
www.rbq.gouv.qc.ca

Agences, conseils et commissions associes/Associated Agencies, Boards & Commissions:

Secrétariat du Conseil du trésor / Treasury Board

875, Grande Allée est, 3e étage, secteur 100, Québec, QC G1R 5R8
418-643-1529, Fax: 418-643-9226, 866-552-5158
communication@sct.gouv.qc.ca
www.tresor.gouv.qc.ca
Ministre responsable de l'Administration gouvernementale & Présidente du Conseil du trésor,L'hon. Michelle

Courchesne
418-643-5926, Fax: 418-643-7824,cabinet@sct.gouv.qc.ca
Secrétaire, Denys Jean
418-643-1977, Fax: 418-643-6494,communication@sct.gouv.qc.ca
Directrice-générale, Vérification interne, l'accès à l'information & la gestion documentaire, Hélène Caouette
418-646-6833, Fax: 418-528-6271
Greffière adjointe, Guylaine Bérubé
418-528-6108, Fax: 418-643-4877
Directrice, Affaires juridiques, Josée De Bellefeuille
418-528-6666
Directeur général (par intérim), Administration, Yvan Bouchard
418-644-2541
Directrice, Communications, Francine Tremblay
418-644-9067

• Agence des partenariats publics-privés du Québec/ Public-Private Partnerships
888, rue Saint-Jean, 4e étage
Québec, QC G1R 5H6
418-646-6097 Fax: 418-528-7155

• Commission administrative des régimes de retraite et d'assurances (Québec)/ Retirement & Insurance Planning Commission
475, rue Saint-Amable
Québec, QC G1R 5X3
418-643-4881 Fax: 418-644-3839 800-463-5533
www.carra.gouv.qc.ca

• Commission de la fonction publique (Québec)/ Public Service Commission
800, Place d'Youville, 7e étage
Québec, QC G1R 3P4
418-643-1425 800-432-0432
cfp@cfp.gouv.qc.ca
www.cfp.gouv.qc.ca
The Commission works towards the following goals: to ensure equal access for all citizens to the public service; to ensure the competence of persons recruited & promoted; & to guarantee the fairness of decisions in human resources management.

Agences, conseils et commissions associes/Associated Agencies, Boards & Commissions:

Sous-secrétariat au personnel de la fonction publique
Secrétaire associé, Normand Légaré
418-528-6180
Directrice générale, Relations de travail, Dominique Gauthier, 2010-09-17
418-528-0202
Directeur, Relations professionnelles, Rhéal St-Pierre
418-528-6227,
Directrice, Planification de la main-d'oeuvre & de l'information de gestion, Yola Dubé
418-528-6397
Directrice, Politiques de main-d'oeuvre, Elisabeth Allard
418-528-6462
Directeur, Classification & rémunération, secteur fonction publique, Jean-Olivier Ferron
418-528-6479
Direction, Assurance traitement de la santé & sécurité du travail,VACANTE
Directrice, Développement des persones et des organisations, Jocelyne Tremblay
418-528-6461

Sous-secrétariat aux marchés publics / Public Markets
418-643-1529, Fax: 418-643-9226, marches.publics@sct.gouv.qc.ca
Secrétaire associé, Alain Parenteau
418-643-9383, Fax: 418-528-6877
Directeur général, Bureau de gouvernance des grandes infrastructures publiques, Bernard Buteau, 2010-09-17
418-528-1098
Directeur général, Politiques de marchés publics, Jacques Darveau
418-528-6055
Directrice générale, Services à la gestion contractuelle, Julie Blackburn
418-528-6166
Directeur, Analyse & vérification aux contrats, Étienne Sabourin
418-528-2861
Directeur, Réglementation & politiques de gestion contractuelle, Lucien Turcotte
418-644-3421, Fax: 418-643-2987
Directrice, Formation sur les marchés publics, Pauline Larouche, 2010-09-17
418-646-6171
Directeur, Tarification & accords sur les marchés publics, Marc Sarra-Bournet, 2010-09-17
418-643-5838
Directrice, Services d'information à la gestion contractuelle, Doris Blanchet, 2010-09-17
418-528-6114

Sous-secrétariat aux politiques budgétaires et programmes / Budget Policies & Programs
Secrétaire associée, Michèle Bourget
418-528-6210
Directeur général (par intérim), Politiques & opérations budgétaires, Jacques Fortin
418-528-6301, Fax: 418-643-4974
Directeur général (par intérim), Programmes administratifs, sociaux & de santé, Jean-François Lachaine
418-528-6512
Directeur général, Programmes économiques, éducatifs & culturels, Yves Lessard
418-528-6252, Fax: 418-643-7288
Directeur (par intérim), Programmes administratifs, Claude Lamonde
418-528-6314, Fax: 418-643-6569
Directeur, Programmes économiques, Mario Deschamps
418-528-6254, Fax: 418-643-7288
Directrice (par intérim), Programmes éducatifs & culturels, Anne Boucher
418-528-6260
Directeur (par intérim), Programmes sociaux & de santé, Jean-François Lachaine
418-528-6258, Fax: 418-643-6569
Directrice (par intérim), Opérations de prévisions & de suivi des dépenses, Claire Rainville
418-528-6303, Fax: 418-643-4974
Directeur, Études & analyses en dépenses publiques, Carl Lessard, 2010-09-17
418-646-5333
Directeur, Analyses des investissements en infrastructures & technologies de l'information, Stéphane Tousignant, 2010-09-17
418-528-6256

Sous-secrétariat aux politiques de rémunération & coordination intersectorielle des négociations
Secrétaire associé, Clément D'Astous
418-643-7628, Fax: 418-643-7682
Directeur général, Régimes collectifs & actuariat, Jean-Marc Tardif, 2010-09-17
418-528-6431
Directeur général, Politiques de rémunération, Charles Duclos, 2010-09-17
418-528-6424
Directeur, Actuariat, Michel Groulx, 2010-09-17
418-644-3682
Directeur, Politiques de rémunération & conditions de travail, Bruno Côté, 2010-09-17
418-528-6411
Directeur, Coordination intersectorielle des négociations & organismes publics, Robert Lessard, 2010-09-17
418-644-2145
Directrice, Analyse & comparaison de marché en rémunération, Brigitte Dufort, 2010-09-17
418-528-6406

Vérificateur général du Québec / Auditor General

750, boulevard Charest est, 3e étage, Québec, QC G1K 9J6
418-691-5900, Fax: 418-644-4460, verificateur.general@vgq.gouv.qc. www.vgq.gouv.qc.ca
Vérificateur général, Renaud Lachance

Government of Saskatchewan

Seat of Government: Regina, SK S4S 0B3
www.gov.sk.ca
The Province of Saskatchewan entered Confederation on September 1, 1905.It has an area of 588,276.09 km2, & the StatsCan census population in 2006 was 968,157.

Office of the Lieutenant Governor

Government House, 4607 Dewdney Ave., Regina, SK S4P 1B7
306-787-4070, Fax: 306-787-7716, lgo@ltgov.sk.ca
www.ltgov.sk.ca
Lieutenant Governor,Hon. Dr. Gordon L. Barnhart
306-787-4070, Fax: 306-787-7716
Private Secretary, Heather Salloum
hsalloum@ltgov.sk.ca

Office of the Premier

Legislative Bldg., #226, 2405 Legislative Dr., Regina, SK S4S 0B3
306-787-9433, Fax: 306-787-0885, premier@gov.sk.ca
www.gov.sk.ca/premier
Premier,Hon. Brad Wall
306-787-9433, Fax: 306-787-0885,premier@gov.sk.ca; bradw@bradwall.com, Other Communications: Website: www.bradwall.com
Deputy Minister to the Premier & Cabinet Secretary, Doug Moen
306-787-6338, Fax: 306-787-8338,doug.moen@gov.sk.ca
Chief of Staff to the Premier, Joe Donlevy
306-787-0064, Fax: 306-787-0883,joe.donlevy@gov.sk.ca
Executive Secretary to the Premier, Ruth Gaura
306-787-9433, Fax: 306-787-0885,ruth.gaura@gov.sk.ca

Executive Council

Legislative Bldg., 2405 Legislative Dr., Regina, SK S4S 0B3
306-787-7448, www.gov.sk.ca/executive-council

Other Communication: Corporate Services Phone: 306-787-7448; Email: admin.ec@gov.sk.ca
Led by the Premier, the Cabinet, or Executive Council of Saskatchewan is a decision-making body. The Premier appoints each cabinet minister. Each minister has responsibility for a department or portfolio.
Premier & President, Executive Council,Hon. Brad Wall
306-787-9433, Fax: 306-787-0885,premier@gov.sk.ca; bradw@bradwall.com, Other Communications: Website: www.bradwall.com
Minister, Finance; Deputy Premier, Hon. Ken Krawetz
306-787-6060, Fax: 306-798-0263,minister.fin@gov.sk.ca
Minister, Energy & Resources, Hon. Bill Boyd
306-787-9124, Fax: 306-787-0395,minister.er@gov.sk.ca,
Minister, Social Services; Minister Responsible for the Status of Women, Hon. June Draude
306-787-7339, Fax: 306-798-3140,minister.cc@gov.sk.ca
Minister, Agriculture; Minister Responsible, Saskatchewan Crop Insurance Corporation, Hon. Bob Bjornerud
306-787-0338, Fax: 306-787-0630,minister.ag@gov.sk.ca
Minister, Health, Hon. Don McMorris
306-787-7345, Fax: 306-787-0237,minister.he@gov.sk.ca
Minister, Education; Provincial Secretary, Hon. Donna Harpauer
306-787-7360, Fax: 306-787-0656,minister.edu@gov.sk.ca
Minister, Justice; Attorney General, Hon. Don Morgan, Q.C.
306-787-5353, Fax: 306-787-1232,minister.ju@gov.sk.ca
Minister, First Nations and Métis Relations, Hon. Ken Cheveldayoff
306-787-0804, Fax: 306-798-2009,minister.fnmr@gov.sk.ca
Minister, Advanced Education, Employment & Labour; Minister Responsible, Immigration; Minister Responsible, Workers Compensation Board, Hon. Rob Norris
306-787-0341, Fax: 306-787-6946,minister.aeel@gov.sk.ca
Minister, Municipal Affairs, Hon. Darryl Hickie
306-787-6100, minister.ma@gov.sk.ca
Minister, Tourism, Parks, Culture and Sport; Minister Responsible for the Provincial Capital Commission, Hon. Bill Hutchinson
306-787-0354, Fax: 306-798-8050,minister.tpcs@gov.sk.ca
Minister, Corrections, Public Safety & Policing, Hon. D.F. (Yogi) Huyghebaert
306-787-4377, Fax: 306-787-5331,minister.cpsp@gov.sk.ca
Minister, Environment, Hon. Dustin Duncan
306-787-0393, Fax: 306-798-0264,minister.env@gov.sk.ca
Deputy Government House Leader; Minister, Enterprise; Minister Responsible for Trade, Hon. Jeremy Harrison
306-787-6100, Fax: 306-787-0399,minister.ent@gov.sk.ca
Minister, Highways and Infrastructure, Hon. Jim Reiter
306-787-6447, Fax: 306-787-1736,minister.hi@gov.sk.ca
Minister Responsible, Crown Investments Corporation, Information Technology Office, Information Services Corporation, Saskatchewan Government Insurance, Hon. Tim McMillan
306-787-7339, minister.cic@gov.sk.ca
Minister, Government Services, Hon. Laura Ross
306-787-0942, Fax: 306-787-8677,minister.gs@gov.sk.ca
Clerk of the Executive Council; Deputy Cabinet Secretary; Deputy Provincial Secretary, Rick Mantey
306-787-9630, Fax: 306-787-8299,rick.mantey@gov.sk.ca

Deputy Minister's Office
Legislative Bldg., #135, 2405 Legislative Dr., Regina, SK S4S 0B3
306-787-6337, Fax: 306-787-8338, dmo.ec@gov.sk.ca
www.executive.gov.sk.ca/branch_info/dmo.htm
The Office of the Deputy Minister to the Premier has the following functions: to support the Premier; to provide executive leadership; to overseefinancial & human resource needs of the department; to provide coordination between government departments, agencies, Crown corporations & Cabinet; & to

coordinate appointments of senior executives for departments & certain agencies.
Deputy Minister to the Premier & Cabinet Secretary, Garnet Garven
Associate Deputy Minister, Executive Resourcing, Ron Dedman

Cabinet Secretariat
Legislative Bldg., #145, 2405 Legislative Dr., Regina, SK S4S 0B3
306-787-9636, Fax: 306-787-8299, cabsec.ec@gov.sk.ca
www.gov.sk.ca/executive-council/cabinet-secretariat
The Cabinet Secretariat is charged with the following responsibilities: to support the Premier in his role as President of Executive Council; to provide administrative support to the Cabinet & cabinet committees; to maintain public records of all orders in council & regulations; to give secretariat support for the Legislative Instruments Committee; & to maintain employment contracts of senior executives pursuant to The Crown Employment Contracts Act.
Cabinet Secretary & Deputy Minister to the Premier, Garnet Garven
306-787-6338, Fax: 306-787-8338,garnet.garven@gov.sk.ca
Deputy Cabinet Secretary; Clerk of the Executive Council; Deputy Provincial Secretary, Rick Mantey
306-787-9630, Fax: 306-787-8299,rick.mantey@gov.sk.ca

Cabinet Planning Unit
Legislative Bldg., #37, 2405 Legislative Dr., Regina, SK S4S 0B3
306-787-7162, Fax: 306-787-0012, cpu@ec.gov.sk.ca
www.gov.sk.ca/executive-council/cabinet-planning
The Cabinet Planning Unit gives secretariat support & policy analysis to the Committee on Planning & Priorities, & to the Premier & members of Executive Council.
Associate Deputy Minister, Cabinet Planning, Marian Zerr
306-787-6339, Fax: 306-787-0012,marian.zerr@gov.sk.ca
Senior Policy Advisor, Marc Boucher
306-787-6308, Fax: 306-787-0012,marc.boucher@gov.sk.ca
Senior Policy Advisor, Nancy Martin
306-787-9727, Fax: 306-787-0012,nancy.martin@gov.sk.ca
Senior Policy Advisor, Greg Elliott
306-787-0187, Fax: 306-787-0012,greg.elliott@gov.sk.ca
Senior Policy Advisor, Wolfgang Langenbacher
306-787-1301, Fax:
306-787-0012,wolfgang.langenbacher@gov.sk.ca

Cabinet Standing Committees
Legislative Instruments Committee, Secretary, Bev Cardinal, Committee on Public Sector Compensation, Secretary, Alan Barss, Treasury Board, Secretary, Doug Mathies Committee on Planning & Priorities, Secretary, Marianne Weston

Legislative Assembly

c/o Clerk's Office, Legislative Bldg., #123, 2405 Legislative Dr., Regina, SK S4S 0B3
306-787-2376, Fax: 306-787-1558, info@legassembly.sk.ca
www.legassembly.sk.ca

Other Communication: Visitor Services: visitorserv@legassembly.sk.ca; Library Reference Questions: reference@legassembly.sk.ca
Clerk, Greg Putz
306-787-2335, Fax:
306-787-0408,gputz@legassembly.sk.ca
Speaker,Hon. Don Toth
306-787-2282, Fax:
306-787-2283,speaker@legassembly.sk.ca
Sergeant-at-Arms, Patrick Shaw
306-787-8798
Chief Technology Officer, Communication & Information Technology Systems, Darcy Hislop
306-787-8071, Fax: 306-789-4278,darcy@gov.sk.ca; dhislop@legassembly.sk.ca
Director, Hansard, Lenni Frohman
306-787-1924, Fax:
306-787-1556,lfrohman@legassembly.sk.ca
Director, Financial & Administrative Services, Marilyn Borowski
306-787-2384, Fax:
306-798-0040,mborowski@legassembly.sk.ca
Director, Human Resource & Payroll Services, Linda Kaminski
306-787-2338, Fax:
306-787-1558,lkaminski@legassembly.sk.ca
Director, Visitor Services, Lorraine deMontigny
306-787-5357, Fax:
306-787-8217,ldemontigny@legassembly.sk.ca
Journals Clerk, Allison Gartner
306-787-3992, Fax:
306-787-1558,agartner@legassembly.sk.ca
Journals Clerk, Traci Willis
306-787-0421, Fax:
306-787-1558,twillis@legassembly.sk.ca

Office of the Official Opposition (New Democratic Party)
#203, Legislative Bldg., 2405 Legislative Dr., Regina, SK S4S 0B3
306-787-7388, Fax: 306-787-6247, caucus@sk.ndpcaucus.sk.ca
www.ndpcaucus.sk.ca
Leader, Lorne Calvert
306-651-1211, Fax: 306-244-3602,lcalvertmla@sasktel.net
Deputy Leader, Pat Atkinson
306-664-6101, Fax: 306-665-5633,patatkinson@sasktel.net
Director, Administration, Gail Fehr
306-787-7389, Fax: 306-787-6247

Government Caucus Office (Saskatchewan Party)
Legislative Bldg., #265, 2405 Legislative Dr., Regina, SK S4S 0B3
306-787-4300, Fax: 306-787-3174, info@skcaucus.com
www.skcaucus.com

Premier & Leader,Hon. Brad Wall
306-778-2429, Fax: 306-778-3614,bradw@bradwall.com, Other Communications: Website: www.bradwall.com
Deputy Premier & Deputy Leader,Hon. Ken Krawetz
306-563-4425, 800-213-4279,Fax:
306-563-5752,krawetz@sasktel.net, Other Communications: Website: www.kenkrawetz.ca
Deputy Minister to the Premier & Cabinet Secretary, Garnet Garven
306-787-6338, Fax: 306-787-8338,garnet.garven@gov.sk.ca
Chief of Staff, Reg Downs
306-787-0908, Fax: 306-787-0883,reg.downs@gov.sk.ca
Communications Advisor to the Premier, Ian Hanna
306-787-2127, Fax: 306-787-0175,ian.hanna@gov.sk.ca
Government Whip, Randy Weekes
rweekes@mla.legassembly.sk.ca
Deputy Government Whip, Greg Brkich
306-567-2843, Fax:
306-567-3259,gbrkich@mla.legassembly.sk.ca

Crown Investments Corporation of Saskatchewan (CIC)

#400, 2400 College Ave., Regina, SK S4P 1C8
306-787-6851, Fax: 306-787-8125, www.cicorp.sk.ca
Acting as a financially self-sufficient holding company, Crown Investments Corporation of Saskatchewan oversees the operations of commercial Crown corporations. The main functions of the CIC are as follows: establishing the strategic direction for subsidiary Crown corporations; & through the Crown corporations, enhancing the province's long term economic growth & diversification.
Minister, Crown Corporations, Hon. June Draude
306-787-7339, Fax: 306-798-3140,minister.cc@gov.sk.ca
President/CEO, Ron Styles
306-787-4553, Fax: 306-787-8125,rstyles@cicorp.sk.ca
Senior Vice-President & CFO, Blair Swystun
306-787-9085, Fax: 306-787-8030,bswystun@cicorp.sk.ca
Vice-President, Crown Sector Initiatives, Iain Harry
306-787-8647, iharry@cicorp.sk.ca
Vice-President/General Counsel, Human Resources, Policy and Governance Division, Doug Kosloski
306-787-5892, Fax: 306-787-0294,dkosloski@cicorp.sk.ca
Executive Director, Capital Pension & Benefits Administration, Ken Klein
306-787-5948, Fax:
306-787-5798,ken.klein@capitalpension.com
Executive Director, Communications, Mike Woods
306-787-5889, Fax: 306-787-8125,mwoods@cicorp.sk.ca
Director, Special Projects, Loree MacPherson
306-787-0381, Fax:
306-787-8125,lmacpherson@cicorp.sk.ca

Provincial Auditor Saskatchewan

#1500, 1920 Broad St., Regina, SK S4P 3V2
306-787-6398, Fax: 306-787-6383, info@auditor.sk.ca
www.auditor.sk.ca
The Provincial Auditor is the auditor of public money managed by the Government of Saskatchewan. The Provincial Auditor Act gives the Provincial Auditor the responsibility, authority, and independence to audit and publicly report on all government organizations.
Provincial Auditor, Fred Wendel
306-787-6366, Fax: 306-787-6383,fwendel@auditor.sk.ca
Asst. Provincial Auditor, Brian Atkinson
306-787-6384, Fax: 306-787-6383,atkinson@auditor.sk.ca
Deputy Provincial Auditor, Education, Ed Montgomery
306-787-6389, Fax:
306-787-6383,montgomery@auditor.sk.ca
Deputy Provincial Auditor, Finance & Crown Corporations, Judy Ferguson
306-787-6372, Fax: 306-787-6383,ferguson@auditor.sk.ca
Deputy Provincial Auditor, Gaming & Insurance, Mike Heffernan
306-787-6364, Fax: 306-787-6383,heffernan@auditor.sk.ca
Deputy Provincial Auditor, Health, Mobashar Ahmad
306-787-6387, Fax: 306-787-6383,ahmad@auditor.sk.ca
Administrative Assistant, Dawn Watkins
306-787-6398, Fax: 306-787-6383,watkins@auditor.sk.ca

Standing Committees of the Legislature
The following are the four Standing Policy Committees of the Saskatchewan Legislature: Standing Committee on Crown & Central Agencies; Standing Committee on Human Services; Standing Committee on the Economy; & Standing Committee on Intergovernmental Affairs & Infrastructure.
Chair, Standing Committee on Crown & Central Agencies, Dustin Duncan
Chair, Standing Committee on Human Services, Glen Hart
Chair, Standing Committee on the Economy, Yogi Huyghebaert
Chair, Standing Committee on Intergovernmental Affairs & Infrastructure, Delbert Kirsch

Twenty-sixth Legislature - Saskatchewan

#123, Legislative Bldg., 2405 Legislative Dr., Regina, SK S4S 0B3
306-787-2376, Fax: 306-787-1558, info@legassembly.sk.ca
www.legassembly.sk.ca

Other Communication: Library Reference Questions: reference@legassembly.sk.ca; Visitor Services: visitorserv@legassembly.sk.ca
Last General Election: Nov. 7, 2007; Maximum Duration: 4 Years; Next General Election: Nov. 7, 2011; Party Standings (Nov. 2007): Saskatchewan Party (SP): 37 seats, New Democratic Party (NDP): 20 seats, Indepndent (I): 1 seat, Total 58; Salaries, Indemnities & Allowances (April 2008): Member's indemnity: $84,409, Member's expense allowance: $0. In addition to this, are the following amounts: Premier $61,390, Deputy Premier: $49,114, Ministers: $42,975, Leader of the Opposition: $42,975, Leader of the Third Party: $21,487, Speaker $42,975, Deputy Speaker $12,560. The following is a list of members, with their constituency, the population of the constituency, party affiliation, & contact information.
Members
Denis Allchurch, Rosthern-Shellbrook SK, Saskatchewan Party
306-883-3003, 877-580-8988,Fax:
306-883-3012,dallchurch@mla.legassembly.sk.ca, Other Communications: Website: www.denisallchurch.ca
Pat Atkinson, Saskatoon Nutana SK, New Democratic Party
306-664-6101, Fax:
306-665-5633,patkinson@mla.legassembly.sk.ca
Buckley Belanger, Athabasca SK, New Democratic Party
306-833-3200, 800-239-9820,Fax:
306-833-2622,bbelanger@mla.legassembly.sk.ca
Hon. Bob Bjornerud, Melville-Saltcoats SK, Saskatchewan Party
306-728-3882, Fax:
306-728-3883,bbjornerud@mla.legassembly.sk.ca, Other Communications: Website: www.bobbjornerud.ca; Saltcoats: 306-744-2519
Hon. Bill Boyd, Kindersley SK, Saskatchewan Party
306-463-4480, Fax:
306-463-6873,bboyd@mla.legassembly.sk.ca, minister.er@gov.sk.ca, Other Communications: Website: www.billboyd.ca
Fred Bradshaw, Carrot RiverValley SK, Saskatchewan Party
306-768-3977, Fax:
306-768-3979,fbradshaw@mla.legassembly.sk.ca, Other Communications: Website: www.fredbradshaw.ca
Greg P. Brkich, Arm River-Watrous SK, Saskatchewan Party
306-567-2843, 800-539-3979,Fax:
306-567-3259,gbrkich@mla.legassembly.sk.ca, Other Communications: Website:www.gregbrkich.ca
Cam Broten, Saskatoon Massey Place SK, New Democratic Party
306-384-7200, Fax:
306-384-4280,cbroten@mla.legassembly.sk.ca
Danielle Chartier, Saskatoon Riversdale SK, New Democratic Party
306-244-5167, Fax:
306-244-6070,dchartier@mla.legassembly.sk.ca
Hon. Ken Cheveldayoff, Saskatoon Silver Springs SK, Saskatchewan Party
306-651-7100, Fax:
306-651-6008,kcheveldayoff@mla.legassembly.sk.ca; minister.cc@gov.sk.ca, Other Communications: Website: www.cheveldayoff.com

Michael Chisholm, CutKnife-Turtleford SK, Saskatchewan Party
306-893-2619, Fax:
306-893-2660,mchisholm@mla.legassembly.sk.ca, Other Communications: Website: www.michaelchisholm.ca
Hon. Dan D'Autremont, Cannington SK, Saskatchewan Party
306-443-2420, Fax:
306-443-2269,ddautremont@mla.legassembly.sk.ca, Other Communications: Website: www.dandautremont.ca
Hon. June Draude, Kelvington-Wadena SK, Saskatchewan Party
306-338-3973, 800-234-4134,Fax:
306-338-3977,jdraude@mla.legassembly.sk.ca, Other Communications: Website: www.junedraude.ca
Hon. Dustin Duncan, Weyburn-Big Muddy SK, Saskatchewan Party
306-842-4810, Fax:
306-842-4811,dduncan@mla.legassembly.sk.ca, Other Communications: Website: www.dduncan.ca
Doreen Eagles, Estevan SK, Saskatchewan Party
306-634-7311, Fax:
306-634-7332,deagles@mla.legassembly.sk.ca
Hon. Wayne Elhard, Cypress Hills SK, Saskatchewan Party
306-295-3688, 877-703-3374,Fax:
306-295-3699,welhard@mla.legassembly.sk.ca; minister.hi@gov.sk.ca, Other Communications: Website: www.wayneelhard.ca
David Forbes, Saskatoon Centre SK, New Democratic Party
306-244-3555, Fax:
306-244-3602,dforbes@mla.legassembly.sk.ca, Other Communications: Website: dforbes.sasktelwebhosting.com,
Darcy Furber, Prince Albert Northcote SK, New Democratic Party
306-763-4400, Fax:
306-763-1827,dfurber@mla.legassembly.sk.ca
Hon. Rod Gantefoer, Melfort SK, Saskatchewan Party
306-752-9500, 800-242-6796,Fax:
306-752-9005,rgantefoer@mla.legassembly.sk.ca; minister.fin@gov.sk.ca, Other Communications: Website: www.melfortconstituency.ca
Hon. Donna Harpauer, Humboldt SK, Saskatchewan Party
306-682-5141, 800-682-9909,Fax:
306-682-5144,dharpauer@mla.legassembly.sk.ca, Other Communications: Website: www.donnaharpauer.ca
Ron Harper, Regina Northeast SK, New Democratic Party
306-569-2233, Fax:
306-569-2303,rharper@mla.legassembly.sk.ca, Other Communications: Website: www.ronharper.ca
Jeremy Harrison, Meadow Lake SK, Saskatchewan Party
306-236-6669, Fax:
306-236-6744,jharrison@mla.legassembly.sk.ca
Glen Hart, Last Mountain-Touchwood SK, Saskatchewan Party
306-723-4421, 877-723-4488,Fax:
306-723-4654,ghart@mla.legassembly.sk.ca, Other Communications: Website: www.glenhart.ca
Hon. Nancy Heppner, Martensville SK, Saskatchewan Party
306-975-0284, 866-639-4377,Fax:
306-975-0283,nheppner@mla.legassembly.sk.ca; minister.env@gov.sk.ca, Other Communications: Website: www.nancyheppner.com
Hon. Darryl Hickie, Prince Albert Carlton SK, Saskatchewan Party
306-922-4676, Fax:
306-922-4674,dhickie@mla.legassembly.sk.ca; minister.cpsp@gov.sk.ca, Other Communications: Website: www.darrylhickie.ca
Deb Higgins, Moose Jaw Wakamow SK, New Democratic Party
306-694-1001, Fax:
306-691-0486,dhiggins@mla.legassembly.sk.ca
Hon. Bill Hutchinson, Regina South SK, Saskatchewan Party
306-205-2067, Fax:
306-205-2069,bhutchinson@mla.legassembly.sk.ca
Hon. D.F. (Yogi) Huyghebaert, Wood River SK, Saskatchewan Party
306-642-4744, Fax:
306-642-4515,yhuyghebaert@mla.legassembly.sk.ca, Other Communications: Website: www.mlawoodriver.ca
Andy Iwanchuk, Saskatoon Fairview SK, New Democratic Party
306-651-3801, Fax:
306-651-3804,aiwanchuk@mla.legassembly.sk.ca
Judy Junor, Saskatoon Eastview SK, New Democratic Party
306-477-4233, Fax:
306-477-4236,jjunor@mla.legassembly.sk.ca, Other Communications: Website: www.judyjunor.ca
Delbert Kirsch, Batoche SK, Saskatchewan Party
306-256-3930, Fax:
306-256-3924,dkirsch@mla.legassembly.sk.ca
Hon. Ken Krawetz, Canora-Pelly SK, Saskatchewan Party
306-563-4425, 800-213-4279,Fax:
306-563-5752,kkrawetz@mla.legassembly.sk.ca, Other Communications: Website: www.kenkrawetz.ca
Serge LeClerc, Saskatoon Northwest SK, Independent
306-934-2847, Fax:
306-934-2867,sleclerc@mla.legassembly.sk.ca
Dwain Lingenfelter, Regina Douglas Park SK, New Democratic Party
306-525-4155, Fax:
306-525-4470,dlingenfelter@mla.legassembly.sk.ca
Warren McCall, Regina Elphinstone-Centre SK, New Democratic Party
306-352-2002, Fax:
306-825-4473,wmccall@mla.legassembly.sk.ca
Hon. Tim McMillan, Lloydminster SK, Saskatchewan Party
306-825-4477, Fax:
306-825-4473,tmcmillan@mla.legassembly.sk.ca
Hon. Don McMorris, Indian Head-Milestone SK, Saskatchewan Party
306-771-2733, 877-337-3366,Fax:
306-771-2574,dmcmorris@mla.legassembly.sk.ca; minister.he@gov.sk.ca, Other Communications: Website: www.donmcmorris.ca
Warren Michelson, Moose Jaw North SK, Saskatchewan Party
306-692-8884, Fax:
306-692-8872,wmichelson@mla.legassembly.sk.ca
Hon. Don Morgan, Saskatoon Southeast SK, Saskatchewan Party
306-955-4755, Fax:
306-955-4765,dmorgan@mla.legassembly.sk.ca; minister.jus@gov.sk.ca, Other Communications: Website: www.donmorgan.ca
Sandra Morin, Regina Walsh Acres SK, New Democratic Party
306-781-9102, Fax:
306-781-4227,smorin@mla.legassembly.sk.ca, Other Communications: Website: www.sandramorin.ca
John Nilson, Q.C., Regina Lakeview SK, New Democratic Party
306-751-7740, Fax:
306-585-2030,jnilson@mla.legassembly.sk.ca
Hon. Rob Norris, Saskatoon Greystone SK, Saskatchewan Party
306-933-7852, Fax:
306-933-7869,rnorris@mla.legassembly.sk.ca
Greg Ottenbreit, Yorkton SK, Saskatchewan Party
306-783-7275, Fax:
306-783-7273,gottenbreit@mla.legassembly.sk.ca, Other Communications: Website: www.gregottenbreit.ca
Frank Quennell, Q.C., Saskatoon Meewasin SK, New Democratic Party
306-651-3581, Fax:
306-651-4670,fquennell@mla.legassembly.sk.ca, Other Communications: Website: www.frankquennell.ca
Hon. Jim Reiter, Rosetown-Elrose SK, Saskatchewan Party
306-882-4105, Fax:
306-882-4108,jreiter@mla.legassembly.sk.ca, Other Communications: Website: www.jimreiter.ca
Laura Ross, Regina Qu'Appelle Valley SK, Saskatchewan Party
306-545-6333, Fax:
306-545-6112,lross@mla.legassembly.sk.ca
Joceline Schriemer, Saskatoon Sutherland SK, Saskatchewan Party
306-244-5623, Fax:
306-244-5626,jschriemer@mla.legassembly.sk.ca, Other Communications: Website: www.jocelinemla.ca
Hon. Lyle Stewart, Thunder Creek SK, Saskatchewan Party
306-693-3229, Fax:
306-693-3251,lstewart@mla.legassembly.sk.ca, Other Communications: Website: www.lylestewart.ca
Len Taylor, The Battlefords SK, New Democratic Party
306-445-5454, Fax:
306-445-5617,ltaylor@mla.legassembly.sk.ca
Hon. Christine Tell, Regina Wascana Plains SK, Saskatchewan Party
306-205-2126, Fax:
306-205-2127,ctell@mla.legassembly.sk.ca
Donald J. Toth, Moosomin SK, Saskatchewan Party
306-435-3329, 888-255-8684,Fax:
306-435-3921,dtoth@mla.legassembly.sk.ca, Other Communications: Website: www.dontoth.ca
Kim Trew, Regina Coronation Park SK, New Democratic Party
306-775-2444, Fax:
306-352-4999,ktrew@mla.legassembly.sk.ca
Doyle Vermette, Cumberland SK, New Democratic Party
306-425-2525, Fax:
306-425-2885,dvermette@mla.legassembly.sk.ca
Hon. Brad Wall, Swift Current SK, Saskatchewan Party
306-778-2429, Fax: 306-778-3614,bradw@bradwall.com; premier@gov.sk.ca, Other Communications: Website: www.bradwall.com
Randy Weekes, Biggar SK, Saskatchewan Party
306-948-4880, 877-948-4880,Fax:
306-948-4882,rweekes@mla.legassembly.sk.ca, Other Communications: Website: www.randyweekes.ca
Nadine Wilson, Saskatchewan Rivers SK, Saskatchewan Party
306-763-0615, Fax:
306-763-2503,nwilson@mla.legassembly.sk.ca
Trent Wotherspoon, Regina Rosemont SK, New Democratic Party
306-565-2444, Fax:
306-565-2952,twotherspoon@mla.legassembly.sk.ca
Kevin Yates, Regina Dewdney SK, New Democratic Party
306-569-0247, Fax:
306-569-0805,kyates@mla.legassembly.sk.ca, Other Communications: Website: www.kevinyates.ca

Saskatchewan Government Departments & Agencies

Saskatchewan Advanced Education & Employment (AEE)

2220 College Ave., Regina, SK S4P 4V9
306-787-9478,
aeeinquiry@gov.sk.ca
www.aee.gov.sk.ca

Other Communication: JobStart: jobstart@sasked.gov.sk.ca; General Educational Development: GED@sasked.gov.sk.ca; SK Immigrant Nominee Program: immigration@gov.sk.ca

The Ministry strives to create a vital, educated & skilled workforce by focussing on the following areas: retaining educated & skilled workers in Saskatchewan; providing educational & training programs to develop a skilled workforce; & promoting the province's opportunities to attract educated & skilled workers from outside Saskatchewan & Canada. In November 2007, a new provincial government resulted in the reorganization of provincial government ministries. An expanded Ministry of Advanced Education, Employment & Labour was formed. Rob Norris was named the Minister of Advanced Education, Employment & Labour.

Acts Administered:
Apprenticeship & Trade Certification Act
Post-Secondary Education & Skills Training Act
Post-Secondary Graduate Tax Credit Act
Private Vocational Schools Regulation Act
Regional Colleges Act
Saskatchewan Indian Institute of Technologies Act
Saskatchewan Institute of Applied Science & Technology Act
Student Assistance & Student Aid Fund Act
University of Regina Act
University of Saskatchewan Act

Minister, Advanced Education, Employment & Labour; Minister Responsible, Immigration; Minister Responsible, Workers Compensation Board, Hon. Rob Norris
306-787-0341, minister.aeel@gov.sk.ca
Deputy Minister, Advanced Education, Employment & Labour, Wynne Young
Assistant Deputy Minister, Rob Cunningham
306-787-0952, Fax: 306-798-0975
Assistant Deputy Minister, Immigration, Rick Pawliw
306-787-6846, Fax: 306-798-0975,
Assistant Deputy Minister, International Education, Larry Symes
306-787-7017, Fax: 306-798-0975
Executive Director, Can-Sask Career & Employment Services, Jan Morgan
306-787-1626, Fax: 306-798-5022
Executive Director, Corporate Services, Trina Vicq Fallows
306-787-3501, Fax: 306-787-7392
Executive Director, Facilities, Nancy Inglis
306-798-0445, Fax: 306-798-3159
Executive Director, Human Resources, Gwen Mowbray
306-787-7985, 800-597-8278,Fax: 306-787-7149
Executive Director, Training Institutions, Raman Visvanathan
306-787-5739, Fax: 306-787-7182
Executive Director, Programs, Tammy Bloor Cavers
306-787-5984, Fax: 306-787-7182
Executive Director, Universities & Adult Learning,
306-787-5900, Fax: 306-798-2616
Executive Director, Policy & Evaluation, Linda Smith
306-787-2984, Fax: 306-787-5870
Executive Director, Student Financial Assistance, Brady Salloum
306-787-0106, 800-597-8278,Fax: 306-787-1608

Saskatchewan Agriculture

Walter Scott Bldg., 3085 Albert St., Regina, SK S4S 0B1
306-787-5140, 866-457-2377
aginfo@gov.sk.ca
www.agriculture.gov.sk.ca

The Ministry's mandate is to foster, in partnership with individuals, communities, industry, & government, a commercially viable, self-sufficient, & sustainable agricultural sector in Saskatchewan. The Ministry addresses needs of individual farmers & ranchers, encourages & develops higher value production & processing, & promotes sustainable economic development in rural areas of the province. Some responsibilities are as follows: agri-business development through provision of agriculture-based business experts & technical support; agricultural research to promote development & diversification; corporate services to support the Information Technology Office & the Rural Economic Co-operative Development; crop development; financial programs; inspection & administration of regulations for food & crop protection, animal disease surveillance, environmental reviews, licenses, registrations, & complaint resolution; irrigation development; promotion of sustainable use of Crown land; livestock development; provision of food safety, quality, policy, regulatory, market & business development programs; policy analysis, strategies, & agricultural information services; & delivery of Saskatchewan Crop Insurance Corporation programs & services.

Acts Administered:
Agri-Food Act, 2004
Agri-Food Innovation Act
Agricultural Credit Corporation of Saskatchewan Act
Agricultural Equipment Dealerships Act
Agricultural Implements Act
Agricultural Operations Act
Agricultural Safety Net Act
Agricultural Societies Act
Agrologists Act, 1994
Animal Identification Act
Animal Products Act
Animal Protection Act, 1999
Apiaries Act
Cattle Marketing Deductions Act, 1998
Crop Insurance Act
Crop Payments Act
Department of Agriculture, Food & Rural Revitilization Act
Disease of Animal Act
Expropriation (Rehabilitation Projects) Act
Farm Financial Stability Act
Farmers' Counselling & Assistance Act
Farming Communities Land Act
Government Organization Act
Grain Charges Limitation Act
Horned Cattle Purchases Act
Irrigation Act
Land Bank Repeal & Temporary Provisions Act
Leafcutting Beekeepers Registration Act
Line Fence Act
Milk Control Act, 1992
Noxious Weeds Act, 1984
On-farm Quality Assurance Programs Act
Pastures Act
Pest Control Act
Pest Control Products (Saskatchewan) Act
Prairie Agricultural Machinery Institute Act, 1999
Provincial Lands Act
Sale or Lease of Certain Lands Act
Saskatchewan 4-H Foundation Act
Saskatchewan Farm Security Act
Saskatchewan Wetland Conservation Corporation Land Regulation
Soil Drifting Control Act
Stray Animals Act
Vegetable, Fruit & Honey Sales Act
Veterinarians Act, 1987
Veterinary Services Act

Minister,Hon. Bob Bjornerud
306-787-0338, Fax: 306-787-0630,minister.ag@gov.sk.ca
Deputy Minister, Alanna Koch
306-787-5170, Fax: 306-787-2393,alanna.koch@gov.sk.ca
Assistant Deputy Minister, Rick Burton
306-787-8077, Fax: 306-787-2393,rick.burton@gov.sk.ca
Assistant Deputy Minister, Nithi Govindasamy
306-787-5247, Fax:
306-787-2393,nithi.govindasamy@gov.sk.ca
Director, Regional Services, Lee Giroux
306-787-5018, Fax: 306-787-9623,lee.giroux@gov.sk.ca
Director, Agriculture Research, Abdul Jalil
306-787-5960, Fax: 306-787-2654,abdul.jalil@gov.sk.ca
Acting Director, Communications, Donna Rehirchuk
306-787-5389, Fax: 306-787-0216
Director, Corporate Services, Laurier Donais
306-787-5211, Fax: 306-787-0600,laurier.donais@gov.sk.ca
Director, Crop Development, Doug Billett
306-787-8061, Fax: 306-787-0428,doug.billett@gov.sk.ca
Director, Financial Programs, Tom Schwartz
306-787-6395, Fax: 306-798-3042,tom.schwartz@gov.sk.ca
Director, Lands Administration, Gloria Parisien
306-787-5154, Fax: 306-787-5180,gloria.parisien@gov.sk.ca
Director, Livestock Development, Paul Johnson
306-787-6423, Fax: 306-787-1315,paul.johnson@gov.sk.ca
Director, Policy, Scott Brown
306-787-5961, Fax: 306-787-5134,scott.brown@gov.sk.ca
Director, Irrigation Development, John Babcock
306-787-8711, Fax: 306-787-9623,john.babcock@gov.sk.ca

• Agri-Food Council
#302, 3085 Albert St.
Regina, SK S4S 0B1
306-787-5139 Fax: 306-787-5134
james.kettel@gov.sk.ca
www.agr.gov.sk.ca/agrifood
The Agri-Food Council is an independent board appointed by the provincial government. The Council is accountable to the Minister of Agriculture for the supervision of all agencies established under The Agri-Food Act, 2004.

• Agricultural Implements Board
#202, 3085 Albert St.
Regina, SK S4S 0B1
306-787-4693 Fax: 306-787-1315

• Farm Stress Unit
#329, 3085 Albert St.
Regina, SK S4S 0B1
306-787-5196 Fax: 306-798-3042 800-667-4442
ken.imhoff@gov.sk.ca

• Prairie Agricultural Machinery Institute(PAMI)
Hwy#5 West
PO Box 1900
Humboldt, SK S0K 2A0
306-682-2555 Fax: 306-682-5080 800-567-7264
humboldt@pami.ca
www.pami.ca
PAMI works for the advancement of technology in agriculture through research and development.

• Saskatchewan Crop Insurance Corporation
484 Prince William Dr.
PO Box 3000
Melville, SK S0A 2P0
306-728-7200 Fax: 306-728-7268 888-935-0000
customer.service@scic.gov.sk.ca
www.saskcropinsurance.com
The provincial Crown Corporation provides responsive & flexible risk management tools. Crop insurance programs are as follows: Multi-Peril Insurance; Organic Insurance; Forage Insurance; & Weather Based Insurance.

• Saskatchewan Lands Appeal Board
#202, 3085 Albert St.
Regina, SK S4S 0B1
306-787-4693 Fax: 306-787-1315
dbrooks@agr.gov.sk.ca

Saskatchewan Archives Board

University of Regina, 3303 Hillsdale St., Regina, SK S4S 0A2
306-787-4068, Fax: 306-787-1197,
info.regina@archives.gov.sk.ca
www.saskarchives.com

The Saskatchewan Archives is a joint university-government agency, which was established under legislation. The Archives collects official records of the Government of Saskatchewan, as well as documentary material from local government & private sources.

Chair, Merrilee Rasmussen, Q.C.
306-525-8911, Fax: 306-787-1197
Provincial Archivist, Don Herperger
306-787-4066, Fax:
306-787-1197,dherperger@archives.gov.sk.ca
Acting Chief Archivist, Information Management, Adrienne Cottrell
306-787-0733, Fax:
306-787-0708,acottrell@archives.gov.sk.ca
Chief Archivist, Reference & Outreach, Regina, Nadine Charabin
306-933-8321, Fax:
306-787-1197,ncharabin@archives.gov.sk.ca
Chief Archivist, Records Processing, Linda Putz
306-798-4018, Fax: 306-798-0333,lputz@archives.gov.sk.ca
Acting Chief Archivist, Appraisal & Acquisition, Trina Gillis
306-787-0452, Fax: 306-798-0708,tgillis@archives.gov.sk.ca
Chief Archivist, Collection Preservation & Management, Ivan Saunders
306-787-8124, Fax:
306-787-1197,isaunders@archives.gov.sk.ca

Saskatchewan Assessment Management Agency (SAMA)

#200, 2201 - 11th Ave., Regina, SK S4P 0J8
306-924-8000, Fax: 306-924-8070, 800-667-7262
info.request@sama.sk.ca
www.sama.sk.ca

SAMA is an independent agency with responsibility to develop & maintain the province's assessment policies, standards & procedures, audit assessments, & review & confirm municipal assessment rolls & provide property valuation services to local governments (municipalities & school boards).

Chair, Neal Hardy
CEO, Irwin Blank
306-924-8046, 800-667-7262,Fax:
306-924-8060,irwin.blank@sama.sk.ca
Managing Director, Finance, George Dobni
306-924-8025, Fax: 306-928-8060,george.dobni@sama.sk.ca

Saskatchewan Communications Network (SCN)

#313E, 2440 Broad St., Regina, SK S4P 0A5
306-787-0490, Fax: 306-787-0496, 800-667-5055
inquiries@scn.ca
www.scn.ca

The regional, public broadcaster delivers cultural, informational & educational programming through the following services: Broadcast Network, E Learning Network, & Technology Services. SCN also acts as an enabler for the regional film & television industry.

Minister Responsible,Hon. Christine Tell
306-787-0354, Fax: 306-798-0264,minister.tpcs@gov.sk.ca
President/CEO, Twyla MacDougall
306-787-0490, Fax: 306-787-0496,tmacdougall@scn.ca
Executive Director, Programming, Richard Gustin
306-787-0490, Fax: 306-787-0496,rgustin@scn.ca
Manager, Finance and Administration, Jody Wise
306-787-0490, Fax: 306-787-0496,jwise@scn.ca
Director, Marketing & Communications, Ranjan Thakre
306-787-0490, Fax: 306-787-0496,rthakre@scn.ca
Director, Business Development Technology, David Stanchuk
306-787-0490, Fax: 306-787-0496,dstanchuk@scn.ca

Saskatchewan Social Services

1920 Broad St., Regina, SK S4P 3V6
306-787-3700,
www.cr.gov.sk.ca

The Ministry works with citizens in the following areas: income support; child & family services; supports for persons with disabilities; affordable housing; economic independence; & active involvement in the labour market & the community. In November 2007, a new provincial government resulted in the reorganization of provincial government ministries. The work of Saskatchewan Community Resources was merged into a newly named ministry. Donna Harpauer was named the Minister of Social Services.

Acts Administered:
Adoption Act
Child Care Act
Child & Family Services Act
Department of Social Services Act
Donation of Food Act
Emergency Protection for Victims of Child Sexual Abuse & Exploitation Act
Intercountry Adoption (Hague Convention) Implementation Act
Rehabilitation Act
Residential Services Act
Saskatchewan Assistance Act
Saskatchewan Housing Corporation Act
Saskatchewan Income Plan Act
Social Workers Act

Minister, Social Services, Hon. Donna Harpauer
306-787-3661, Fax: 306-787-0656,minister.ss@gov.sk.ca, Other Communications: 74
Deputy Minister, Allan Hansen
306-787-3491, Fax: 306-787-1032,allan.hansen@gov.sk.ca
Assistant Deputy Minister, Policy, Shelley Whitehead
306-787-4909, Fax:
306-787-1032,shelley.whitehead@gov.sk.ca
Executive Director, Service Management, Arlene Mongovius
306-787-0158, Fax:
306-798-2118,arlene.mongovius@gov.sk.ca
Executive Coordinator, Office of Disability Issues, Daryl Stubel
306-787-3670, 877-915-7468,Fax:
306-787-3650,daryl.stubel@gov.sk.ca, TDD: 306-787-7283
Administrative Assistant, Human Resources Services, Karen Varin
306-787-2216, Fax: 306-787-3441,karen.varin@gov.sk.ca
Assistant Executive Director, Strategic Policy, Janet Mitchell
306-787-1533, Fax: 306-787-3650,janet.mitchell@gov.sk.ca
Director, Communications & Public Education, Trish Alcorn
306-787-0916, Fax: 306-787-8669,trish.alcorn@gov.sk.ca
Director, Research & Evaluation, David Rosenbluth
306-787-7354, Fax:
306-787-3650,david.rosenbluth@gov.sk.ca
Legislative Secretary to the Minister of Social Services, Community Based Organizations Initiative, Greg Ottenbreit

Child & Family Services Division
306-787-7010, Fax: 306-787-0925
Executive Director, Andrea Brittin
306-787-3652, Fax: 306-787-0925,andrea.brittin@gov.sk.ca
Assoc. Executive Director, Child Welfare,Vacant
306-787-3647
Director, Program Support Services, Jennifer Colin
306-787-3648, Fax: 306-787-0925,jennifer.colin@gov.sk.ca

Community Living Division
1920 Broad St., 10th fl., Regina, SK S4P 3V6
306-787-7803, Fax: 306-798-4450
Executive Director, Jeff Redekop
306-787-9013, Fax: 306-798-4450,jeff.redekop@gov.sk.ca
Assoc. Executive Director, Bob Neufeldt
306-933-6301, Fax: 306-798-4450,bob.neufeldt@gov.sk.ca
Director, Regional & Community Programs, Jim Wallace
Director, Management & Information Services, Barb Clarke
306-694-3504

Income Assistance Division
306-787-7469, Fax: 306-787-2134
Executive Director, Lynn Tullach
306-787-1967, Fax: 306-787-2134,lynn.tulloch@gov.sk.ca
Assoc. Executive Director, Program Policy and Services, Gord Tweed
306-787-0015, Fax: 306-787-2134,gord.tweed@gov.sk.ca

Financial Planning Branch
306-787-8667, Fax: 306-787-6825
Director, Miriam Myers
306-787-1911, Fax: 306-787-6825,miriam.myers@gov.sk.ca
Director, Financial Services, Brent Bogard
306-787-3575, Fax: 306-787-1600,brent.bogard@gov.sk.ca

Housing Division
306-787-4177, 800-667-7567
http://www.cr.gov.sk.ca/housing
Asst. Deputy Minister, Craig Marchinko
306-787-7288, Fax: 306-787-1081
Executive Director, Housing Program Operations Division, Larry Chaykowski
306-787-1008, Fax:
306-787-5166,larry.chaykowski@gov.sk.ca
Director, Housing Financial Operations, Rachel Ratch
306-787-4961, Fax: 306-787-8571,rachel.ratch@gov.sk.ca
Assoc. Executive Director, Affordable Housing Branch, Tim Gross
306-787-7311, Fax: 306-787-0137,tim.gross@gov.sk.ca
Assoc. Executive Director, Social Housing Branch, Dianne Baird
306-787-8569, Fax: 306-787-5166,dianne.baird@gov.sk.ca,
Director, Technical Services Branch, Bob Trafananko
306-787-4208, Fax: 306-787-0137,bob.trafananko@gov.sk.ca
Executive Director, Housing Policy & Program Services, Craig Marchinko
306-787-7288, Fax:
306-787-1081,craig.marchinko@gov.sk.ca

Regional Operations
Asst. Deputy Minister, Bob Wihlidal
306-787-7357, Fax: 306-787-1032,bob.wihlidal@gov.sk.ca

Regional Offices:

Central Region
Regional Director, Gerry Prediger
306-933-6075, Fax: 306-933-6005,garry.prediger@gov.sk.ca

Northeast Region
800 Central Ave., PO Box 3003, Prince Albert, SK S6V 6G1
306-953-2575, Fax: 306-953-2589
Regional Director, Alan Jones
306-953-3345, Fax: 306-935-2589,alan.jones@gov.sk.ca

Northwest Region
Royal Bank Tower, 1101 - 101 St., 3rd fl., North Battleford, SK S9A 1E9
306-446-7721, Fax: 306-446-7525, 877-993-9911
Regional Director, Ruth Seime
306-446-7721, Fax: 306-446-7525,ruth.seime@gov.sk.ca

Southeast Region
72 Smith St. East, Yorkton, SK S3N 2Y4
306-786-1310, Fax: 306-786-1305, 877-786-3288
Regional Director, Wayne Phaneuf
306-786-1310, Fax:
306-786-1469,wayne.phaneuf@gov.sk.ca

Southwest Region
2045 Broad St., Regina, SK S4P 3V7
306-787-3416, Fax: 306-787-4940
Regional Director, Lynn Allan
306-787-3416, Fax: 306-787-4940,lynn.allan@gov.sk.ca

Saskatchewan Corrections, Public Safety & Policing

1874 Scarth St., Regina, SK S4P 4B3
306-787-7872, Fax: 306-787-8747,
www.cpsp.gov.sk.ca
The Ministry of Corrections, Public Safety & Policing promotes safe communities in Saskatchewan. Adult correction & young offender programs & services are delivered that serve individuals in conflict with the law. Public safety is also addressed through the following programs & services: protection & emergency planning & communication; monitoring of building standards; fire prevention & disaster assistance programs; & licensing & inspections services.
Acts Administered:
Amusement Ride Safety Act
Boiler & Pressure Vessel Act
Correctional Services Act
Electrical Licensing Act
Emergency 911 System Act
Emergency Planning Act
Fire Prevention Act, 1992
Gas Licensing Act
Passenger & Freight Elevator Act
Uniform Building & Accessibility Standards Act
Youth Justice Administration Act
Minister,Hon. Darryl Hickie
306-787-4377, Fax:
306-787-5331,minister.cpsp@gov.sk.ca
Deputy Minister, Terry Coleman
306-787-8065, Fax:
306-798-0270,terry.coleman@gov.sk.ca
Executive Director, Strategic Policy, Karen Lautsch
306-787-7344, Fax: 306-798-0270,karen.lautsch@gov.sk.ca
Executive Director, Corporate Services, Mae Boa
306-787-8081, Fax: 306-798-0270,mae.boa@gov.sk.ca
Co-Director, Communications, Judy Orthner
306-787-5883, Fax: 306-787-3874,judy.orthner@gov.sk.ca
Co-Director, Communications, Laur'Lei Silzer
306-787-0775, Fax: 306-787-3874,laurlei.silzer@gov.sk.ca
Director, Corporate Services, Gord Sisson
306-787-5472, Fax: 306-787-5830,gord.sisson@gov.sk.ca
Director, Human Resources, Marlys Tafelmeyer
306-787-5475, Fax:
306-798-2084,marlys.tafelmeyer@gov.sk.ca
Director, Information Management, Jim Bingaman
306-787-9512, Fax: 306-787-6979,jim.bingaman@gov.sk.ca
Legislative Secretary to the Minister of Corrections, Public Safety & Policing, Corrections Facilities Initiative, Serge LeClerc
306-934-2847, Fax:
306-934-2867,sleclerc@mla.legassembly.sk.ca

Adult Corrections
306-787-3490, Fax: 306-787-0676
Asst. Deputy Minister, Maureen Lloyd
306-787-3573, Fax: 306-787-0676,maureen.lloyd@gov.sk.ca
Director, Community Corrections, Carol Fiedelleck
306-787-3572, Fax: 306-787-0676,carol.fiedelleck@gov.sk.ca
Director, Institutional Operations, Heather Scriver
306-787-3571, Fax: 306-787-0676,heather.scriver@gov.sk.ca
Project Manager, Regina Provincial Correctional Centre, Nick Surtees
306-787-9076, Fax: 306-787-0676,nick.surtees@gov.sk.ca
Manager, Corrections Offender Programs, Doris Schnell
306-787-5467, Fax: 306-787-0676,doris.schnell@gov.sk.ca
Manager, Corrections Information Systems, Rick Davis
306-787-3640, Fax: 306-787-0676,rick.davis@gov.sk.ca
Manager, Prism Industries,Vacant
306-787-3631, Fax: 306-787-0676

Licensing & Inspections
306-787-1443, Fax: 306-787-9273, 866-530-8599
Administers a wide range of regulatory, enforcement, & advisory services which provide safety standards to industry & the general public in the areas of boiler, pressure vessel, elevators, amusement rides, gas & electrical equipment installations.
Acting Executive Director, Brian Krasiun
306-787-4509, Fax: 306-787-9273,brian.krasiun@gov.sk.ca

Protection & Emergency Services
306-787-8568, Fax: 306-787-1694,
www.cpsp.gov.sk.ca/ProtectionandEmergencyServices
Delivers emergency planning & preparedness services, including Sask 911 emergency calling, the Provincial Disaster Assistance Program (PDAP), building standards & the Office of the Fire Commissioner.
Executive Director, Tom Young
306-787-3316, Fax: 306-787-1694,tom.young@gov.sk.ca

Office of the Fire Commissioner
The Office of the Fire Commissioner provides communities, fire departments & emergency service organizations with information, education & leadership to enhance their capabilities to protect people, property & the environment from the devastation of fire. The Office includes the Fire Commissioner, Fire Prevention Officer supervisors in charge of regional services, technical services, programs & standards & Fire Prevention Officers who deliver programs to regions.
Fire Commissioner, Duane McKay
306-787-4516, Fax: 306-787-9273,duane.mckay@gov.sk.ca

Saskatchewan Emergency Management Organization (SaskEMO)
#100, 1855 Victoria Ave., Regina, SK S4P 3V7
306-787-9563, Fax: 306-787-1694,
infosafety@cps.gov.sk.ca
www.cpsp.gov.sk.ca/saskemo
Saskatchewan Emergency Management Organization (SaskEMO) maintains the Provincial Emergency Plan & related contingencies as part of their provincial preparedness program to deal with events that may affect government operations. SaskEMO also offers training & education for emergency measures officials, volunteer organizations & public service groups &, to support community preparedness, has municipal emergency measures advisors available 24 hours per day to advise & assist municipalities during local emergencies.
Director, Kevin Roche
306-787-9567, Fax: 306-787-1694,kevin.roche@gov.sk.ca

Young Offender Programs
306-787-5699, Fax: 306-787-0676,
www.cpsp.gov.sk.ca/yo
Executive Director, Bob Kary
306-787-4701, Fax: 306-787-0676,bob.kary@gov.sk.ca
Director, Program Development & Therapeutic Services, Brian Rector
306-787-3892, Fax: 306-787-0676,brian.rector@gov.sk.ca
Director, Custody Programs, Kim Gurnsey
306-787-9237, Fax: 306-787-0676,kim.gurnsey@gov.sk.ca
Director, Community Youth Services, Constance Hourie
306-787-1394, Fax:
306-787-0676,constance.hourie@gov.sk.ca

Saskatchewan Tourism, Parks, Culture, & Sport

1919 Saskatchewan Dr., 4th Fl., Regina, SK S4P 4H2
306-787-5729, Fax: 306-787-8560,
www.tpcs.gov.sk.ca
The Ministry enhances the province's cultural, artistic, recreational & social life by working cooperatively with diverse groups & communities as it strives to promote leadership, recognize accomplishments, & sustain excellence in the arts, culture & sport. It is dedicated to ensuring that Saskatchewan people, especially the young people, reach their fullest potential in provincial, national, & international communities. In November 2007, a new provincial government resulted in the reorganization of provincial government ministries. The work of Saskatchewan Culture, Youth & Recreation was merged into an expanded ministry. Christine Tell was named the Minister of Tourism, Parks, Culture & Sport.
Minister, Tourism, Parks, Culture & Sport, Hon. Christine Tell
306-787-0354, Fax: 306-798-0264,minister.tpcs@gov.sk.ca
Deputy Minister, Tourism, Parks, Culture & Sport, Van Isman
306-787-5050, Fax: 306-798-0033,van.isman@gov.sk.ca
Executive Director, Culture & Heritage, Susan Hetu
306-787-0730, Fax: 306-787-3177,susan.hetu@gov.sk.ca
Director, Strategic Policy, Planning & Partnerships, Nevin Danielson
306-787-0619, Fax:
306-798-0033,nevin.danielson@gov.sk.ca
Director, Communications, Janet Peters
306-787-4967, Fax: 306-798-0033,janet.peters@gov.sk.ca
Director, Corporate Services, Melinda Gorrill
306-787-5896, Fax: 306-798-0033,melinda.gorrill@gov.sk.ca
• Saskatchewan Communications Network(SCN)
#313E, 2440 Broad St.
Regina, SK S4P 0A5
306-787-0490 Fax: 306-787-0496 800-667-5055
inquiries@scn.ca
www.scn.ca
• Royal Saskatchewan Museum
2445 Albert St.
Regina, SK S4P 4W7
306-787-2815 Fax: 306-787-2820
info@royalsaskmuseum.ca
www.royalsaskmuseum.ca
• Saskatchewan Archives Board
University of Regina
3303 Hillsdale St.
Regina, SK S4S 0A2
306-787-4068 Fax: 306-787-1197
info.regina@archives.gov.sk.ca
www.saskarchives.com
• Sask Film
1831 College Ave.
Regina, SK S4P 3V7
306-798-3456 Fax: 306-798-7768 800-561-9933
www.saskfilm.com

Provides support, financial assistance & equity financing to the Saskatchewan film, television & new media industries through a variety of programs & services. Saskfilm administers the Saskatchewan Film Employment Tax Credit Program, & manages the Saskatchewan Production Studios.
• Sask Heritage Foundation
1919 Saskatchewan Dr., 9th Fl.
Regina, SK S4P 3V7
306-787-4188 Fax: 306-787-0069
• Saskatchewan Arts Board
2135 Broad St.
Regina, SK S4P 3V7
306-787-4056 Fax: 306-787-4199 800-667-7526
sab@artsboard.sk.ca
www.artsboard.sk.ca
• Saskatchewan Science Centre
2903 Powerhouse Dr.
Regina, SK S4N 0A1
306-522-4629 Fax: 306-525-0194 800-667-6300
info@sasksciencecentre.com
www.sasksciencecentre.com
• Wanuskewin Heritage Park
RR#4
Saskatoon, SK S7K 3J7
306-931-6767 Fax: 306-931-4522
wanuskewin@wanuskewin.com
www.wanuskewin.com
• Western Development Museum
2935 Melville St.
Saskatoon, SK S7J 5A6
306-934-1400 Fax: 306-934-4467 800-363-6345
info@wdm.ca
www.wdm.ca

Elections Saskatchewan

1702 Park St., Regina, SK S4N 6B2
306-787-4000, Fax: 306-787-4052, 877-958-VOTE
info@elections.sk.ca
www.elections.sk.ca

Chief Electoral Officer, Jean Ouellet
306-787-4000, Fax: 306-787-4052,jouellet@elections.sk.ca
Asst. Chief Electoral Officer, Dave Wilkie
306-787-4061, Fax: 306-787-4052,dwilkie@elections.sk.ca
Admin. Coordinator, Debra Dorsch
306-787-4000, Fax:
306-787-4052,ddorsch@elections.sk.ca

Saskatchewan Environment

3211 Albert St., 2nd Fl., Regina, SK S4S 5W6
306-953-3750, Fax: 306-787-9544, 800-567-4224
inquiry@serm.gov.sk.ca
www.environment.gov.sk.ca

Other Communication: Provincial Parks Information Toll Free: 1-800-205-7070; Firewatch Line: 1-800-667-9660; Spill Control Centre: 1-800-667-7525; TIPS (Turn in Poachers: 1-800-667-7561

Saskatchewan Environment protects & mananges the province's environmental & natural resources by offering the following programs & services: compliance & enforcement to protect the public's interests in the management of air, land, water & natural resources; protection & management of forest ecosystems; wildfire management; Green Strategy; environmental assessment; legislation, & policies to ensure that Crown land is used in ways that respect environmental, economic & social values; fishing & fisheries management; hunting management; licensing & guiding the trapping industry; protection of wildlife; recycling; waste management; & water resource & treatment plant operations management.

Acts Administered:
Clean Air Act
Conservation Development Act
Conservation Easements Act
Ecological Reserves Act
Environmental Assessment Act
Environmental Management & Protection Act, 2002
Fisheries Act
Forest Resources Management Act
Grasslands National Park Act
Litter Control Act
Natural Resources Act
Parks Act
Prairie & Forest Fires Act, 1982
Provincial Lands Act
Regional Parks Act, 1979
Sale or Lease of Certain Lands Act
Saskatchewan Watershed Authority Act 2005
State of the Environment Report Act
Water Appeal Board Act
Water Regulations Act, 2002
Water Power Act
Watershed Associations Act
Wildlife Act, 1998
Wildlife Habitat Protection Act

Minister,Hon. Nancy Heppner
306-787-0393, Fax: 306-787-1669,minister.env@gov.sk.ca
Deputy Minister, Liz Quarshie
306-787-2930, Fax: 306-787-2947,liz.quarshie@gov.sk.ca
Associate Deputy Minister, Bob Ruggles
306-787-5122, Fax: 306-798-0599,bob.ruggles@gov.sk.ca
Acting Executive Director, Finance & Administration, Laurel Welsh
306-787-2484, Fax: 306-787-8441,laurel.welsh@gov.sk.ca
Director, Communications, Greg Leake
306-787-5511, Fax: 306-787-3941,greg.leake@gov.sk.ca
• Saskatchewan Conservation Data Centre
3211 Albert St.
Regina, SK S4S 5W6
306-787-9038 Fax: 306-787-9544
www.biodiversity.sk.ca
The SKCDC was formed as a co-operative venture between the province, The Nature Conservancy USA & The Nature Conservancy of Canada.The SKCDC gathers, interprets & distributes scientific information on the ecological status of provincial wild species & communities. The SKCDC is committed to conserving biological diversity; producing scientific reports & being the provincial clearinghouse for threatened & endangered species information.
• Saskatchewan Watershed Authority
111 Fairford St. East
Moose Jaw, SK S6H 7X9
306-694-3900 Fax: 306-694-3465
comm@swa.ca
www.swa.ca
The Saskatchewan Watershed Authority administers the following legislation and regulations: Conservation & Development Act; Saskatchewan Watershed Authority Act, 2005; Water Power Act; Watershed Associations Act; Conservation & Development Regulations; Drainage Control Regulations; Ground Water Regulations; & Reservoir Development Area Regulations.

Lands & Forests Division
3211 Albert St., 5th fl., Regina, SK S4S 5W6
306-787-5407, Fax: 306-787-2947
Provides delivery of integrated resource management & environmental protection programs.
Executive Director, Compliance & Field Services, Kevin Callele
306-787-3388, Fax: 306-787-9313,kevin.callele@gov.sk.ca
Executive Director, Fire Management & Forest Protection, Steve Roberts
306-953-2206, Fax: 306-953-3575,steve.roberts@gov.sk.ca
Executive Administrative Assistant, Forest Service, Carole Buyan
306-953-2437, Fax: 306-953-2360,carole.buyan@gov.sk.ca

Conservation Division
3211 Albert St., 5th fl., Regina, SK S4S 5W6
306-787-9075, Fax: 306-787-2947,
Assistant Deputy Minister, Dave Phillips
306-787-9079, Fax: 306-787-2947,dave.phillips@gov.sk.ca
Director, Environmental Protection,Dr. Paul James
306-787-9058, Fax: 306-787-0024,paul.james@gov.sk.ca
Executive Director, Human Resources, Ray Deck
306-787-8311, Fax: 306-787-4292,ray.deck@gov.sk.ca
Executive Director, Parks, Syd Barber
306-787-2846, Fax: 306-787-7000,syd.barber@gov.sk.ca
Executive Director, Fish and Wildlife Branch, Hugh Hunt
306-787-2309, Fax: 306-787-9544,hugh.hunt@gov.sk.ca

Northern Field Services
McIntosh Mall, 800 Central Ave., PO Box 3003, Prince Albert, SK S6V 6G1
306-953-2896, Fax: 306-953-2502
Director, Ron Erickson
306-953-2899, Fax: 306-953-2502,ron.erickson@gov.sk.ca

Swift Current Compliance Area
350 Chedle St. West, PO Box 5000, Swift Current, SK S9H 4G3
306-778-8205, Fax: 306-778-8212
Compliance Manager, Bob Roberts
306-778-8644, Fax: 306-778-8212,bob.roberts@gov.sk.ca

Saskatoon Compliance Area
112 Research Dr., Saskatoon, SK S7K 2H6
306-933-6240, Fax: 306-933-5773
Compliance Manager, Doug Robinson
306-933-7929, Fax: 306-933-5773,doug.robinson@gov.sk.ca

La Ronge Compliance Area
#1100 - 1328 La Ronge Ave., PO Box 5000, La Ronge, SK S0J 1L0
306-425-4234, Fax: 306-425-2580
Compliance Manager, Lyle Galloway
306-425-4234, Fax: 306-425-2580,lyle.galloway@gov.sk.ca

Meadow Lake Compliance Area
#1, 101 - Railway Place, Meadow Lake, SK S9X 1X6
306-236-7557, Fax: 306-236-7677
Compliance Manager, Rob Tether
306-236-9818, Fax: 306-236-7677,rob.tether@gov.sk.ca

Saskatchewan Finance

2350 Albert St., Regina, SK S4P 4A6
306-787-6768, Fax: 306-787-0241,
www.finance.gov.sk.ca

Other Communication: General Tax Inquiries: 1-800-667-6102
The Ministry of Finance manages the financing, revenue, & expenses of the provincial government. The following are some of the duties performed by the department: administering provincial taxes, grant, & refund programs; managing banking, investment, & public debt functions; providing financial & policy analysis; offering economic forecasting & economic & social statistics; producing the provincial budget; assisting the government in the management of public monies; & managing governmental pension & benefit plans.

Acts Administered:
Balanced Budget Act
Certified General Accountants Act, 1994
Certified Management Accountants Act
Certified Management Consultants Act
Chartered Accountants Act, 1986
Corporation Capital Tax Act
Federal-Provincial Agreements Act
Financial Administration Act, 1993
Fiscal Stabilization Fund Act
Fuel Tax Act, 2000
Home Energy Loan Act
Income Tax Act
Income Tax Act, 2000
Insurance Premiums Tax Act
Liquor Board Superannuation Act
Liquor Consumption Tax Act
Management Accountants Act
Members of the Legislative Assembly Benefits Act
Motor Vehicle Insurance Premiums Tax Act
Municipal Employees' Pension Act
Municipal Financing Corporation Act
Provincial Auditor Act
Provincial Sales Tax Act
Public Employees Pension Plan Act
Public Service Superannuation Act
Revenue & Financial Services Act
Saskatchewan Development Fund Act
Saskatchewan Pension Annuity Fund Act
Saskatchewan Pension Plan Act
Statistics Act
Superannuation (Supplementary Provisions) Act
Tabling of Documents Act, 1991
Tobacco Tax Act
Workers' Compensation Board Superannuation Act

Minister,Hon. Rod Gantefoer
306-787-6060, Fax: 306-787-6055,minister.fin@gov.sk.ca
Deputy Minister, Doug Matthies
306-787-6621, Fax:
306-787-7155,doug.matthies@gov.sk.ca
Provincial Comptroller, Terry Paton
306-787-9254, Fax: 306-787-9720,terry.paton@gov.sk.ca
Assistant Deputy Minister, Public Employees Benefits Agency, Brian L. Smith
306-787-6757, Fax:
306-798-0065,brian.smith@peba.gov.sk.ca
Executive Director, Personnel Policy Secretariat, Tor Veltheim
306-787-3101, Fax: 306-798-0386,tor.veltheim@gov.sk.ca
Executive Director, Communications, Randy Burton
306-787-6578, Fax: 306-787-7155,Randy.Burton@gov.sk.ca
Director, Human Resources, Jim Graham
306-787-6535, Fax: 306-787-0138,jim.graham2@gov.sk.ca
Director, Financial Services, Larry Jacobson
306-787-6530, Fax:
306-787-6544,Larry.Jacobson@gov.sk.ca
• Board of Revenue Commissioners
#480, 2151 Scarth St.
Regina, SK S4P 2H8
306-787-6221 Fax: 306-787-1610
www.gov.sk.ca/BRC/
Any write-off or cancellation of monies owing to the Crown is subject to prior approval of the Board of Revenue Commissioners as delegated by the Treasury Board. The Board has the power to hear & determine appeals respecting taxes imposed or assessed pursuant to & by virtue of any taxing enactment & respecting other monies claimed to be due & payable to the Crown where the right of taking appeal to the Board is given by any statute.

• Saskatchewan Development Fund Corporation
#300, 2400 College Ave.
Regina, SK S4P 1C8
306-787-1645 800-667-7543
www.gov.sk.ca/SDF
The Saskatchewan Development Fund is a low risk investment fund that provides income & long-term investment growth to Saskatchewan residents. The Fund is administered by the Saskatchewan Development Fund Corporation. Since 1983, the Fund no longer sells new shares to the public.

Budget Analysis Division
306-787-6742
Asst. Deputy Minister, Taxation & Intergovernmental Affairs Branch, Kirk McGregor
306-787-6731, Fax: 306-787-7003,kirk.mcgregor@gov.sk.ca
Asst. Deputy Minister, Treasury Board, Karen Layng
306-787-6780, Fax: 306-787-3982,karen.layng@gov.sk.ca
Executive Director, Economic & Fiscal Policy Branch, Joanne Brockman
306-787-6743, Fax:
306-787-1426,joanne.brockman@gov.sk.ca
Director, Performance Management, Raelynn Douglas
306-787-7762, Fax:
306-787-3982,raelynn.douglas@gov.sk.ca
Provincial Comptroller, Terry Paton
306-787-9254, Fax: 306-787-9720,Terry.Paton@gov.sk.ca
Executive Director, Financial Management, Chris Bayda
306-787-6848, Fax: 306-787-9720,Chris.Bayda@gov.sk.ca
Director, Financial Systems, Reg Ronyk
306-787-6709, Fax: 306-787-7227,Reg.Ronyk@gov.sk.ca
Director, Internal Audit, Ken Gabora
306-787-6956, Fax: 306-787-9720,Ken.Gabora@gov.sk.ca
Asst. Deputy Minister, Brian L. Smith
306-787-6757, Fax: 306-787-0244
Director, Benefits Program, Perry Bahr
306-787-3745, perry.bahr@peba.gov.sk.ca
Director, Communications, John Charlton
306-787-3265, john.charlton@peba.gov.sk.ca
Director, Financial Services, Kathy Morgan
306-787-6818, kathy.morgan@peba.gov.sk.ca
Director, Pension Programs, Ann Mackrill
306-787-3239, ann.mackrill@peba.gov.sk.ca

Revenue Division
Fax: 306-787-0241, 800-667-6102
Asst. Deputy Minister, Margaret Johannsson
306-787-6685, Fax:
306-787-0241,margaret.johannsson@gov.sk.ca
Director, Provincial Sales Tax (PST) Branch, Rob Dobson
306-787-7785, Fax: 306-798-3045,rob.dobson@gov.sk.ca
Director, Revenue Programs Branch, Doug Lambert
306-787-4600, Fax:
306-787-0241,dlambert@finance.gov.sk.ca
Supervisor, Fuel & Tobacco Taxes, Craig Lyon
306-787-9658, Fax: 306-787-0241,craig.lyon@gov.sk.ca
Director, Audit Branch, Scott Giroux
306-787-7784, Fax: 306-798-3045,scott.giroux@gov.sk.ca
Director, Revenue Operations Branch, Kelly Laurans
306-787-7788, Fax: 306-787-6653,kelly.laurans@gov.sk.ca

Treasury & Debt Management Division
306-787-6752
Asst. Deputy Minister, Dennis Polowyk
306-787-6753, Fax:
306-787-8493,dennis.polowyk@gov.sk.ca
Executive Director, Cash & Debt Management Branch, Jim Fallows
306-787-3923, Fax: 306-787-8493,jim.fallows@gov.sk.ca
Executive Director, Capital Markets Branch,Vacant
306-787-6753, Fax: 306-787-8493

Saskatchewan First Nations & Métis Relations

#210, 1855 Victoria Ave., Regina, SK S4P 3T2
306-787-6250, Fax: 306-787-5832,
www.fnmr.gov.sk.ca
Working with First Nations and Métis people, the Ministry carries out the following responsibilities: providing overall direction to the government's approach to issues concerning First Nations & Métis people; coordinating programs in other government departments; ensuring that Saskatchewan's commitments regarding lands & resources are fulfilled; & working in partnership with First Nations & Métis people on issues of education & economic participation.
Acts Administered:
Indian & Native Affairs Act
Métis Act
Saskatchewan Gaming Corporation Act, Part III
Treaty Land Entitlement Implementation Act
Government Organization Act (Dept. of First Nations & Métis Relations Regulations)

Minister,Hon. June Draude
306-787-0605, Fax:
306-798-8050,minister.fnmr@gov.sk.ca
Acting Deputy Minister & Assistant Deputy Minister, Ron Crowe
306-787-6253, Fax: 306-787-5832,ron.crowe@gov.sk.ca
Executive Director, Seonaid MacPherson
306-787-8142, Fax:
306-798-0083,seonaid.macpherson@gov.sk.ca,
Director, Communications, Alethea Foster
306-787-5701, Fax: 306-787-6336,alethea.foster@gov.sk.ca
Director, Finance, Accountability & Corporate Services, Kerry Gray
306-787-2123, Fax: 306-798-0004,kerry.gray@gov.sk.ca
Director, Gaming Trusts & Grants, Kerry Gray
306-787-2123, Fax: 306-798-0004,kerry.gray@gov.sk.ca
Director, Aboriginal Employment Development Program, Victoria Gubbels
306-798-0341, Fax:
306-798-0004,victoria.gubbels@gov.sk.ca

Aboriginal Policy & Operations
306-787-9709, Fax: 306-787-5832
Acting Executive Director, Giselle Marcotte
306-787-0998, Fax:
306-787-5832,giselle.marcotte@gov.sk.ca
Acting Senior Director, Aboriginal Urban Issues, Mark La Rocque
306-787-6400, mlarocque@fnmr/gov.sk.ca

Lands & Resources Branch
306-787-5722, Fax: 306-787-6336
Manages & coordinates Saskatchewan's obligations under Treaty Land Entitlement. The Branch also performs a similar function with respect to Specific Claims.
Executive Director, Trisha Delormier-Hill
306-787-6681, Fax:
306-787-6336,trisha.delormier-hill@gov.sk.ca
Director, Susan Carani
306-787-9706, Fax: 306-787-6336,susan.carani@gov.sk.ca

Saskatchewan Government Insurance (SGI)

2260 - 11th Ave., Regina, SK S4P 0J9
306-751-1200, Fax: 306-787-7477, 800-667-8015
sgiinquiries@sgi.sk.ca
www.sgi.sk.ca

Other Communication: Customer Support Unit: 1-888-558-5559
Operating in twenty claims centres in Saskatchewan communities, SGI sells property & casualty insurance products. One of SGI's operations is The Saskatchewan Auto Fund, the province's compulsory auto insurance program. The Auto Fund administers the driver's licensing & vehicle registration system.
Minister, Crown Corporations, Hon. June Draude
306-787-7339, Fax: 306-798-3140,minister.cc@gov.sk.ca
Chair, Board of Directors, Warren Sproule
President/CEO, Andrew Cartmell
306-751-1717, Fax: 306-525-6040,acartmell@sgi.sk.ca
Chief Financial Officer, Don Thompson
306-751-1585, dthompson@sgi.sk.ca
Chief Internal Auditor, Kevin Taylor
306-751-1781, ktaylor@sgi.sk.ca
Vice-President, Auto Fund, Sherry Wolf
306-751-1646, swolf@sgi.sk.ca
Vice-President, Canadian Operations, John Dobie
306-751-1597, jdobie@sgi.sk.ca
Vice-President, Claims & Salvage, Earl Cameron
306-751-1705, ecameron@sgi.sk.ca
Assistant Vice-President, Human Resources & Corporate Services, Tamara Erhardt
306-775-6994, Fax: 306-347-0089,terhardt@sgi.sk.ca
Vice-President, Systems & Facilities, Dwain Wells
306-775-6093, dwells@sgi.sk.ca
Vice-President, Underwriting, Randy Heise
306-751-1653, rheise@sgicanada.ca

Saskatchewan Government Relations

1855 Victoria Ave., Regina, SK S4P 3T2
306-787-2635,
www.gr.gov.sk.ca
The Ministry has the following main duties: to create & maintain effective partnerships with governments in Saskatchewan, Canada, & abroad; to promote the province's interests with other governments; to support local governance to meet the needs of municipal governments; to coordinate & manage matters related to Government House, French language services, official protocol, & provincial honours; & to provide administrative services to the Office of the Lieutenant Governor. In November 2007, a new provincial government resulted in the reorganization of provincial government ministries. Saskatchewan Government Relations established separate roles for the Provincial Secretary, Municipal Affairs, & Intergovernmental Affairs. Bill Hutchinson was named Minister of Municipal Affairs.
Acts Administered:
Assessment Appraisers Act
Assessment Management Agency Act
Border Areas Act
Cities Act
City of Lloydminster Act
Community Planning Profession Act
Controverted Municipal Elections Act
Cut Knife Reference Act
Department of Rural Development Act
Department of Urban Affairs Act
Flin Flon Extension of Boundaries Act, 1952
Lloydminster Municipal Amalgamation Act, 1930
Local Government Election Act
Local Improvements Act, 1993
Municipal Board Act
Municipal Debentures Repayment Act
Municipal Development & Loan (Saskatchewan) Act
Municipal Expropriation Act
Municipal Industrial Development Corporations Act
Municipal Revenue Sharing Act
Municipal Tax Sharing (Potash) Act
Municipalities Act
Municipality Improvements Assistance (Saskatchewan) Act
Northern Municipalities Act
Planning & Development Act, 1983
Provincial Emblems & Honours Act
Provincial Secretary's Act
Rural Development Act
Rural Municipal Administrators Act
Rural Municipality Act, 1989
Subdivisions Act
Tax Enforcement Act
Time Act
Urban Municipal Administrators Act
Urban Municipality Act, 1984
Minister, Municipal Affairs, Hon. Bill Hutchinson
306-787-6100, Fax: 306-787-0399,minister.ma@gov.sk.ca
Minister Responsible, Intergovernmental Affairs, Hon. Bill Boyd
306-787-9124, Fax: 306-787-0395,minister.er@gov.sk.ca
Deputy Minister, Intergovernmental Affairs, Al Hilton
306-787-4220, Fax: 306-787-7317,alan.hilton@gov.sk.ca
Provincial Secretary,Hon. Wayne Elhard
306-787-6447, Fax: 306-787-1736,minister.hi@gov.sk.ca
Deputy Provincial Secretary; Clerk of the Executive Council; Deputy Cabinet Secretary, Rick Mantey
306-787-9630, Fax: 306-787-8299,rick.mantey@gov.sk.ca
Chief of Protocol, Office of Protocol & Honours, Deborah Johnson
306-787-3109, 877-427-5505,Fax:
306-787-1269,deborah.johnson7@gov.sk.ca
Executive Director, Communications, Jeff Welke
306-787-6156, Fax: 306-787-4181,jeff.welke@gov.sk.ca
Executive Director, Government House, Deborah Johnson
306-787-3109, Fax:
306-787-5714,deborah.johnson7@gov.sk.ca
Director, Office of Francophone Affairs Branch/Direction des affaires francophones (DAF), René Boudreau
306-787-8035, Fax: 306-787-6352,rboudreau@gr.gov.sk.ca

Municipal Affairs
www.municipal.gov.sk.ca
The Municipal Relations Division strengthens Saskatchewan communities by providing the legal framework, organizational support, financial assistance & other services for the operation of municipalities. Working in partnership with municipal organizations & other communities, the Division encourages cooperation, understanding & self-reliance.
Asst. Deputy Minister, Maryellen Carlson
306-787-5765, Fax:
306-787-1987,maryellen.carlson@gov.sk.ca
Director, Community Planning, Ralph Leibel
306-787-7672, Fax: 306-798-0194,ralph.leibel@gov.sk.ca
Executive Director, Grants Administration & Financial Management, Russ Krywulak
306-787-8887, Fax: 306-787-3641,russ.krywulak@gov.sk.ca
Director, Northern Municipal Services Branch, Randy Braaten
306-425-4322, Fax: 306-425-2401,randy.braaten@gov.sk.ca
Executive Director, Policy Development, John Edwards
306-787-2665, Fax: 306-787-5822,john.edwards2@gov.sk.ca

Canadian Intergovernmental Relations
#800, 1919 Saskatchewan Dr., Regina, SK S4P 4H2
Fax: 306-787-7317
Asst. Deputy Minister, Canadian Intergovernmental Relations, Dylan Jones
306-787-0306, Fax: 306-787-7317,dylan.jones@gov.sk.ca

Central Management Services
#1410, 1855 Victoria Ave., Regina, SK S4P 3T2

306-787-2136, Fax: 306-787-4161
Executive Director, Wanda Lamberti
306-787-1640, Fax:
306-787-4161,wanda.lamberti@gov.sk.ca
Director, Finance & Administration, Marj Abel
306-787-4172, Fax: 306-787-4161,marj.abel@gov.sk.ca

Trade & International Relations
#800, 1919 Saskatchewan Dr., Regina, SK S4P 4H2
306-787-6445, Fax: 306-787-7317
Asst. Deputy Minister, Paul Osborne
306-787-6322
Acting Director, International Relations, Dave Christopherson
306-787-6881, Fax:
306-787-7317,david.christopherson@gov.sk.ca
Director, Trade Policy, Robert Donald
306-787-8910, Fax: 306-787-7317,robert.donald@gov.sk.ca

Saskatchewan Health

T.C. Douglas Bldg., 3475 Albert St., Regina, SK S4S 6X6
306-787-0146, 800-667-7766
info@health.gov.sk.ca
www.health.gov.sk.ca

Other Communication: Family Health Benefits: 1-800-266-0695; HealthLine: 1-877-800-0002; Health Registration / Health Card: 1-800-667-7551; Prescription Drug Plan: 1-800-667-7581
Saskatchewan Health offers the following programs & services: continuing care to help people live independently; e-health & information systems for access to medical information; emergency services; health benefits; recruitment & retention of healthcare providers; promotion of mental health & treatment for mental illness & addictions; personal health services; prescription drug coverage; public health programs; privacy of health information; services for people with long term disabilities or illnesses; surgery & diagnostics initiatives; & vital statistics.
Acts Administered:
Ambulance Act
Cancer Foundation Act
Change of Name Act
Chiropody Profession Act
Chiropractic Act, 1994
Dental Care Act
Dental Disciplines Act
Department of Health Act
Dietitians Act
Emergency Medical Aid Act
Health Districts Act
Health Facilities Licensing Act
Health Information Protection Act
Health Quality Control Act
Hearing Aid Act
Hearing Aid Sales & Services Act
Hospital Standards Act
Housing & Special-care Homes Act
Human Tissue Gift Act
Licensed Practical Nurses Act
Medical & Hospitalization Tax Repeal Act
Medical Laboratory Licensing Act
Medical Laboratory Technologists Act
Medical Profession Act, 1981
Medical Radiation Technologists Act
Medical Scholarships & Bursaries Act
Mental Health Services Act
Midwifery Act
Mutual Medical & Hospital Benefit Associations Act
Naturopathy Act
Occupational Therapists Act
Opthalmic Dispensers Act
Optometry Act, 1985
Personal Care Homes Act
Pharmacy Act
Physical Therapists Act, 1988
Prescription Drugs Act
Psychologists Act
Public Health Act
Regional Health Services Act
Registered Nurses Act, 1988
Registered Psychiatric Nurses Act
Saskatchewan Health Research Foundation Act
Saskatchewan Medical Care Insurance Act
Speech Language Pathologists & Audiologists Act
Tobacco Control Act
Vital Statistics Act
White Cane Act
Youth Detoxification & Stabilization Act
Minister,Hon. Don McMorris
306-787-7345, Fax: 306-787-0237,minister.he@gov.sk.ca
Deputy Minister, Dan Florizone
306-787-3041, Fax:
306-787-4533,dflorizone@health.gov.sk.ca
Associate Deputy Minister,Dr. Louise Greenberg
306-787-4595, Fax:
306-787-4533,lgreenberg@health.gov.sk.ca
Associate Deputy Minister, Mike Shaw
306-787-3160, Fax:
306-787-4533,mshaw@health.gov.sk.ca
Legislative Secretary to the Minister of Health, Nurse Recruitment & Retention, Laura Ross
306-545-6333, Fax:
306-545-6112,lross@mla.legassembly.sk.ca
Legislative Secretary to the Minister of Health, Addictions, Joceline Schriemer
306-244-5623, Fax:
306-244-5626,jschriemer@mla.legassembly.sk.ca
Executive Director, Communications, Marg Moran McQuinn
306-787-8433, Fax:
306-787-8310,mmoranmc@health.gov.sk.ca
Executive Director, Finance & Administration, Ted Warawa
306-787-5006, Fax: 306-787-0218,twarawa@health.gov.sk.ca
Executive Director, Health Information Solutions Centre, Scott Livingstone
306-787-0234, Fax:
306-798-0337,slivingstone@health.gov.sk.ca
Executive Director, Human Resources Branch, Donna Gelsinger
306-787-7118, Fax: 306-787-3950
Executive Director, Northern Health Services, Kathy Chisholm
306-425-4517
Executive Director, Primary Health Services, Donna Magnusson
306-787-0875, Fax:
306-787-0890,dmagnusson@health.gov.sk.ca
Executive Director, Saskatchewan Disease Control Laboratory, Bob Firnesz
306-787-3129, Fax: 306-787-1525,bfirnesz@health.gov.sk.ca
Executive Director, Regional Accountability, Bert Linklater
306-787-6679, Fax: 306-787-4534
Director, Policy & Regional Programs, Shaylene Salazar
306-787-8938, Fax: 306-787-3761,ssalazar@health.gov.sk.ca
Director, Budget & Financial Planning, Jeannette Lowe
306-787-0050, Fax: 306-787-0218,jlowe@health.gov.sk.ca
• Health Quality Council
241, 111 Research Dr.
Saskatoon, SK S7N 3R2
306-668-8810 Fax: 306-668-8820
www.hqc.sk.ca

Acute & Emergency Services
Fax: 306-787-6113
Executive Director, Deborah Jordan
306-787-7854, Fax: 306-787-6113,djordan@health.gov.sk.ca
Director, Central Support, Valerie Phillips
306-787-1101, Fax: 306-787-6113,vphillips@health.gov.sk.ca
Director, Community Hospitals & Emergency Services, Patrick O'Byrne
306-787-3219, Fax: 306-787-6113,pobyrne@health.gov.sk.ca

Community Care Branch
306-787-7239, Fax: 306-787-7095
Executive Director, Roger Carriere
306-787-6092, Fax:
306-787-7095,rcarriere@health.gov.sk.ca,
Director, Program Support Unit A, Linda Restau
306-787-7901, Fax: 306-787-7095,lrestau@health.gov.sk.ca
Director, Program Support Unit B, Rick Kilarski
306-787-3236, Fax: 306-787-7095,rkilarski@health.gov.sk.ca
Director, Program Support Unit C, Kathy Willerth
306-787-5020, Fax: 306-787-7095,kwillerth@health.gov.sk.ca

Drug Plan & Extended Benefits
306-787-3317
Executive Director, Kevin Wilson
306-787-3301, kwilson@health.gov.sk.ca
Director, Extended Benefits, Mark Herzog
306-787-6970, mherzog@health.gov.sk.ca
Director, Pharmaceutical Services, Margaret Baker
306-787-3305, Fax: 306-787-8679,tsmith@health.gov.sk.ca
Director, System & Client Support Services, Clarence Woloshyn
306-787-3308, Fax:
306-787-8679,cwoloshy@health.gov.sk.ca

Health Registration & Vital Statistics
306-787-3251, Fax: 306-787-8951, 800-667-7551
Vital Statistics Unit is responsible for the issuance of provincial birth, marriage & death certificates. Fee for each certificate is $20.00.
Director, Ronn Wallace
306-787-1167, Fax: 306-787-8951,rwallace@health.gov.sk.ca

Medical Services
306-787-3475, Fax: 306-787-3761, 800-667-7523
Executive Director, Brad Havervold
306-787-3423, Fax:
306-787-3761,bhavervold@health.gov.sk.ca
Director, Operations and Client Services, Lori St. Dennis
306-787-3425, Fax:
306-787-3761,lstdennis@health.gov.sk.ca
Manager, Claims Analysis, Lori Hutchison Hunter
306-787-3465, Fax:
306-798-1124,lhutchison@health.gov.sk.ca
Director, Professional Review and Quality Management, Perry Behl
306-787-3442, Fax: 306-787-3761,pbehl@health.gov.sk.ca
Director, Management Services, June Schultz
306-787-2655, Fax: 306-787-3761,jschultz@health.gov.sk.ca
Director, Medical Policy & Compensation, John-Paul Cullen
306-787-8938
Director, Operations and Client Services, Dietmar Bartel
306-787-3473, Fax: 306-787-3761,dbartel@health.gov.sk.ca

Policy & Planning Branch
Fax: 306-787-2974
Executive Director, Pauline Rousseau
306-787-3951, Fax:
306-787-2974,prousseau@health.gov.sk.ca
Director, Health System Planning, Policy and Legislation Services, Dorothea Warren
306-787-8197, Fax: 306-787-2974,dwarren@health.gov.sk.ca
Director, Intergovernmental & Aboriginal Health Policy, Mark Wyatt
306-787-3153, Fax: 306-787-2974,mwyatt@health.gov.sk.ca

Population Health Branch
Fax: 306-787-3112
Coordinates & encourages initiatives that promote & protect health & prevent disease & injury. The branch actively supports research & evaluation into health status, health trends & the risks to & determinants of health. Population Health Branch also supports food Ssfety programs which work at reducing the risk of the public contracting a food-borne illness. It is a leader in the development of food safety legislation, regulations & guidelines.
Executive Director, Rick Trimp
306-787-8847, Fax: 306-787-3237,rtrimp@health.gov.sk.ca
Chief Medical Officer of Health,Dr. Ross Findlater
306-787-8847, Fax: 306-787-3237
Director, Disease Prevention & Health Protection,Vacant
306-787-7129, Fax: 306-787-3237
Director, Health Promotion, Mary Martin-Smith
306-787-7110, Fax:
306-787-3823,mmartin-smith@health.gov.sk.ca
Acting Provincial Epidemiologist, Epidemiology, Research & Evaluation,Dr. Drona Rasali
306-787-7219, Fax: 306-787-3237,drasali@health.gov.sk.ca

Workforce Planning Branch
Fax: 306-798-0023
Executive Director, Ron Knaus
306-787-6672, Fax: 306-798-0023,rknaus@health.gov.sk.ca
Chief Nursing Officer, Lynn Digney Davis
306-787-7195, Fax:
306-798-0023,ldigneydavis@health.gov.sk.ca
Director, Labour Policy & Research, Stephen Eger
306-787-3072, Fax: 306-798-0023,seger@health.gov.sk.ca
Director, Planning and Provincial Recruitment Projects, Dawn Martin
306-787-3070, Fax: 306-798-0023,dmartin@health.gov.sk.ca
Director, Programs & Resource Development, Sandra Cripps
306-787-5693, Fax: 306-798-0023,scripps@health.gov.sk.ca

Saskatchewan Highways & Infrastructure

1855 Victoria Ave., Regina, SK S4P 3T2
306-787-4800,
www.highways.gov.sk.ca

Other Communication: Hotline for Road Information: 306-933-8333 (North SK); 306-787-7623 (South SK); Toll Free: 888-335-7623; Website: roadinfo.telenium.ca/shwyw.html
The Ministry operates, preserves, & guides the development of the transportation system in Saskatchewan.
Acts Administered:
Dangerous Goods Transportation Act
Engineering & Geoscience Professions Act
Highway Traffic Act
Highways & Transportation Act
Railway Act
Sand & Gravel Act
Minister,Hon. Wayne Elhard
306-787-6447, Fax: 306-787-1736,minister.hi@gov.sk.ca
Deputy Minister, John Law
306-787-4949, Fax: 306-787-9777,john.law@gov.sk.ca
Director, Communications, Doug Wakabayashi
306-787-4804, Fax:
306-798-0438,doug.wakabayashi@gov.sk.ca

Director, Human Resources, Curtis Goodfellow
306-787-4757, Fax:
306-787-0608,curtis.goodfellow@gov.sk.ca
• Saskatchewan Highway Traffic Board
1550 Saskatchewan Dr.
Regina, SK S4P 0E4
306-775-6674
The Highway Traffic Board's mandate is to establish & to administer legislation relating to the safe & legal operations of private vehicles, the bus-truck industry & the short line rail industry in Saskatchewan, where specifically legislated to do so.

Corporate Services Division
306-787-4904
Asst. Deputy Minister, Ted Stobbs
306-787-9287, Fax: 306-787-9777,ted.stobbs@gov.sk.ca
Director, Finance & Administration, Gary Diebel
306-787-4794, Fax: 306-787-8700,gary.diebel@gov.sk.ca
Director, Corporate Support, Tim Kealey
306-787-4781, Fax: 306-787-8700,tim.kealey@gov.sk.ca

Operations Division
306-787-4901
Asst. Deputy Minister, Terry Schmidt
306-787-4859, terry.schmidt@gov.sk.ca
Executive Director, Engineering Standards, Ron Gerbrandt
306-787-4858, Fax: 306-787-4836,ron.gerbrandt@gov.sk.ca

Policy & Programs Division
306-787-4904
Asst. Deputy Minister, George Stamatinos
306-787-5028, Fax:
306-787-9777,george.stamatinos@gov.sk.ca
Executive Director, Transportation Programs and Services, Les Bell
306-787-0825, Fax: 306-787-3963,les.bell@gov.sk.ca
Director, Transport Compliance, Blair Wagar
306-787-4072, Fax: 306-787-6697,blair.wagar@gov.sk.ca
Director, Land Branch, Jeff Grigg
306-787-4885, Fax: 306-787-4100,jeff.grigg@gov.sk.ca
Director, Trade & Logistics, Michael Makowsky
306-787-7664, Fax:
306-787-3963,michael.makowsky@gov.sk.ca
Executive Director, Transportation Policy, Harold Hugg
306-787-5311, Fax: 306-787-3963,harold.hugg@gov.sk.ca

Saskatchewan Human Rights Commission (SHRC)

Saskatoon Office, Sturdy Stone Bdg., #816, 122 - 3 Ave. North, 8th Fl., Saskatoon, SK S7K 2H6
306-933-5952, Fax: 306-933-7863, 800-667-9249
shrc@shrc.gov.sk.ca
www.shrc.gov.sk.ca
The Saskatchewan Human Rights Commission promotes & protects individual dignity & equal rights by discouraging & eliminating discrimination. The Commission's guide is The Saskatchewan Human Rights Code. The following are the principle functions of the Commission: approving equity programs; educating people & promoting human rights laws in Saskatchewan; & investigating complaints of discrimination.
Minister Responsible,Hon. Don Morgan, Q.C.
306-787-5353, Fax: 306-787-1232,minister.ju@gov.sk.ca
Acting Chief Commissioner, John C. Hill
306-933-5952, Fax: 306-933-7863,john.hill@gov.sk.ca
Coordinator, Budget, Lois Henderson
306-933-8286, Fax: 306-933-7863
Coordinator, Human Resources, Brenda Rorke
306-933-8285, Fax: 306-933-7863,brenda.rorke@gov.sk.ca

Saskatchewan Energy & Resources (SIR)

#300, 2103 - 11th Ave., Regina, SK S4P 3Z8
306-787-2528, Fax: 306-787-0395, 866-727-5427
www.er.gov.sk.ca
The Ministry encourages the growth & development of the provincial resource sector. The Ministry's two main roles are as follows: offering programs & services to individuals & businesses; & coordinating economic development activities with other departments & agencies. In November 2007, a new provincial government resulted in the reorganization of provincial government ministries. The work of Saskatchewan Industry & Resources was merged into a newly named ministry. Bill Boyd was named the Minister of Energy & Resources.
Acts Administered:
Crown Minerals Act
Department of Economic Development Act, 1993
Department of Energy & Mines Act
Ethanol Fuel Act, 2002
Mineral Resources Act
Oil & Gas Conservation Act
Pipelines Act
Minister, Energy & Resources, Hon. Bill Boyd
306-787-9124, Fax: 306-787-0395,minister.er@gov.sk.ca
Deputy Minister, Energy & Resources, Kent Campbell
306-787-9580, Fax: 306-787-2159,kent.campbell@gov.sk.ca
Director, Public Affairs, Bob Ellis
306-787-8983, Fax: 306-787-2198,robert.ellis@gov.sk.ca
• Saskatchewan Trade & Export Partnership(STEP)
#320, 1801 Hamilton St.
PO Box 1787
Regina, SK S4P 3C6
306-787-9210 Fax: 306-787-6666 877-313-7244
inquire@sasktrade.sk.ca
www.sasktrade.sk.ca
Works in partnership with provincial export companies & emerging export companies to maximize commercial success in foreign ventures. STEP provides marketing services using a team of trade professionals, innovative approaches & world-wide networks. By promoting & developing sales, contracts, projects & referrals, STEP increases exports to existing foreign markets & taps into new markets.
• Tourism Saskatchewan
1922 Park St.
Regina, SK S4N 7M4
306-787-9600 877-237-2273
www.sasktourism.com
Tourism Saskatchewan is a market-driven, industry-led partnership responsible for developing and promoting tourism in Saskatchewan.

Corporate & Financial Services
306-787-2188, Fax: 306-787-3872
Executive Director, Hal Sanders
306-787-3524, Fax: 306-787-3872,hal.sanders@gov.sk.ca
Director, Administration & Financial Services, Doreen Yurkoski
306-787-1612, Fax:
306-787-3872,doreen.yurkoski@gov.sk.ca
Director, Revenue Operations and Audit Services, Dale Amundson
306-787-5343, Fax:
306-798-2158,dale.amundson@gov.sk.ca
Director, Human Resources, Debbie Brotheridge
306-787-0798
Director, Lands and Development Services, Doug MacKnight
306-787-2082, Fax:
306-787-7338,doug.macknight@gov.sk.ca
Director, Planning & Evaluation, Jeff Ritter
306-787-0999, Fax: 306-787-3872,jeff.ritter@gov.sk.ca
Director, Research & Infrastructure Program, Dale Amundson
306-787-7006
Assistant Director, Revenue Operations, Glen Downton
306-787-2830, Fax: 306-787-0083,glen.downton@gov.sk.ca

Exploration & Geological Services
306-787-2585, Fax: 306-787-1284,
Executive Director, George Patterson
306-787-2560, Fax:
306-787-1284,george.patterson@gov.sk.ca
Director, Mines, Mike Detharet
306-787-2139, Fax: 306 798 0047,mike.detharet@gov.sk.ca
Director, Northern Geological Survey,Dr. Gary Delaney
306-787-1160, Fax: 306-787-1284,gary.delaney@gov.sk.ca
Director, Sedimentary Geodata & Director, Petroleum Geology, Chris Gilboy
306-787-2573, Fax: 306-787-2488,chris.gilboy@gov.sk.ca

Petroleum & Natural Gas
306-787-2592, Fax: 306-787-2478
Director, Geology & Petroleum Lands, Ed Dancsok
306-787-2602, Fax: 306-787-0620,ed.dancsok@gov.sk.ca
Acting Director, Petroleum Development, Todd Han
306-787-2221, Fax: 306-787-2478,todd.han@gov.sk.ca
Director, Petroleum Royalties, Mike Ferguson
306-787-2605, Fax: 306-787-2478,mike.ferguson@gov.sk.ca
Director, Petroleum Statistics, Darwin Roske
306-787-2607, Fax: 306-787-8236,darwin.roske@gov.sk.ca

Resource & Economic Policy
306-787-0900, Fax: 306-787-2198
Executive Director, Energy Policy, Floyd Wist
306-787-2477, Fax: 306-787-2198,floyd.wist@gov.sk.ca
Director, Economic Analysis, David McQuinn
306-787-7983, Fax: 306-787-2198,david.mcquinn@gov.sk.ca
Director, Industrial Policy, Cam Pelzer
306-787-2378, Fax: 306-787-2198,cam.pelzer@gov.sk.ca
Director, Mineral Policy,Vacant
306-787-3377, Fax: 306-787-2198

Information & Privacy Commissioner of Saskatchewan

#503, 1801 Hamilton St., Regina, SK S4P 4B4
306-787-8350, Fax: 306-798-1603, 877-748-2298
info@oipc.sk.ca
www.oipc.sk.ca
Commissioner, R. Gary Dickson, Q.C.
306-787-8350, Fax: 306-798-1603,gdickson@oipc.sk.ca

Saskatchewan Justice

1874 Scarth St., Regina, SK S4P 4B3
306-787-7872, Fax: 306-787-3874,
www.justice.gov.sk.ca
Acts Administered:
Aboriginal Courtworkers Commission Act
Absconding Debtors Act
Absentee Act
Administration of Estates Act
Adult Guardianship & Co-decision-making Act
Age of Majority Act
Agreements of Sale Cancellation Act
Agricultural Leaseholds Act
Alberta-Saskatchewan Boundary Act, 1939
Arbitration Act, 1992
Assignment of Wages Act
Attachments of Debts Act
Auctioneers Act
Builders' Lien Act
Business Corporations Act
Business Names Registration Act
Canada-United Kingdom Judgements Enforcement Act
Canadian Institute of Management (Saskatchewan Division) Act
Cemeteries Act, 1999
Charitable Fundraising Businesses Act
Children's Law Act, 1997
Choses in Action Act
Class Actions Act
Closing-out Sales Act
Collection Agents Act
Commercial Liens Act
Commissioners for Oaths Act
Companies Act
Companies Winding Up Act
Condominium Property Act, 1993
Constituency Boundaries Act, 1993
Constitutional Questions Act
Consumer & Commercial Affairs Act
Consumer Protection Act
Contributory Negligence Act
Co-operatives Act, 1996
Coroners Act, 1999
Cost of Credit Disclosure Act 2002 (NYP)
Court Jurisdiction & Proceedings Transfer Act
Court of Appeal Act, 2000
Court Officials Act, 1984
Court Reporting Act
Credit Reporting Act
Credit Union Act, 1985
Credit Union Act, 1998
Creditors' Relief Act
Criminal Enterprise Suppression Act
Crown Administration of Estates Act
Crown Employment Contracts Act
Crown Suits (Costs) Act
Department of Justice Act
Dependants' Relief Act, 1996
Devolution of Real Property Act
Direct Sellers Act
Distress Act
Electronic Information & Documents Act, 2000
Enforcement of Canadian Judgements Act, 2002
Enforcement of Foreign Judgements Act
Enforcement of Foreign Arbitral Awards Act, 1996
Enforcement of Judgements Conventions Act (NYP)
Enforcement of Maintenance Orders Act, 1997
Equality of Status of Married Persons Act
Escheats Act
Executions Act
Exemptions Act
Expropriation Act
Expropriation Procedure Act
Factors Act
Family Farm Credit Act
Family Maintenance Act, 1997
Family Property Act
Fatal Accidents Act
Federal Courts Act
Film & Video Classification Act
Foreign Judgments Act
Fraudulent Preferences Act
Freedom of Information & Protection of Privacy Act
Frustrated Contracts Act
Funeral & Cremation Services Act
Guarantee Companies Securities Act
Health Care Directives & Substitute Health Care Decision Makers Act
Home Owners' Protection Act
Homesteads Act, 1989
Hotel Keepers Act
Improvements under Mistake of Title Act

Interjurisdictional Support Orders Act
International Child Abduction Act, 1996
International Commercial Arbitration Act
International Protection of Adults Act (NYP)
International Sale of Goods Act
Interpretation Act, 1995
Interprovincial Subpoena Act
Intestate Succession Act, 1996
Judges' Orders Enforcement Act
Judgments Extension Act
Jury Act, 1998
Justice of the Peace Act, 1988
Land Contracts (Actions) Act
Land Information Services Facilitation Act
Land Titles Act, 2000
Land Surveyors & Professional Surveyors Act
Land Surveys Act, 2000
Landlord & Tenant Act
Language Act
Law Reform Commission Act
Laws Declaratory Act
Legal Aid Act
Legal Profession Act, 1990
Libel & Slander Act
Limitations Act
Limitation of Actions Act
Limitation of Civil Rights Act
Local Authority Freedom of Information & Protection of Privacy Act
Lord's Day (Saskatchewan) Act
Mandatory Testing & Disclosure (Bodily Substances) Act
Manitoba-Saskatchewan Boundary Act, 1937
Manitoba-Saskatchewan Boundary Act, 1942
Manitoba-Saskatchewan Boundary Act, 1966
Manitoba-Saskatchewan Boundary Act, 1978
Marriage Act, 1995
Marriage Settlement Act
Members' Conflict of Interest Act
Mentally Disordered Persons Act
Mortgage Brokers Act
Motor Dealers Act
Municipal Hail Insurance Act
Names of Homes Act
New Generation Co-operatives Act
Non-profit Corporations Act, 1995
Notaries Public Act
Ombudsman & Children's Advocate Act
Parents' Maintenance Act
Partnership Act
Pawned Property (Recording) Act
Penalties & Forfeitures Act
Pension Benefits Act, 1992
Personal Property Security Act, 1993
Police Act, 1990
Powers of Attorney Act, 2002
Pre-judgement Interest Act
Privacy Act
Private Investigators & Security Guards Act, 1997
Proceedings Against the Crown Act
Professional Corporations Act
Provincial Court Act, 1998
Provincial Mediation Board Act
Public Disclosure Act
Public Guardian & Trustee Act
Public Inquiries Act
Public Officers' Protection Act
Public Utilities Easements Act
Queen's Bench Act, 1998
Queen's Counsel Act
Queen's Printer Act
Real Estate Act
Reciprocal Enforcement of Judgments Act, 1996
Recording of Evidence by Sound Recording Machine Act
Recovery of Possession of Land Act
Referendum & Plebiscite Act
Registered Plan (Retirement Income) Exemption Act
Regulations Act, 1995
Religious Societies Land Act
Residential Tenancies Act
Revised Statutes Act, 1979
Safer Communities & Neighbourhoods Act
Sale of Goods Act
Sale of Training Courses Act
Sales on Consignment Act
Saskatchewan Evidence Act
Saskatchewan Farm Security Act
Saskatchewan Financial Services Commission Act
Saskatchewan Human Rights Code
Saskatchewan Insurance Act
Saskatchewan Northwest Territories Boundary Act, 1966
Securities Act, 1988
Seizure of Criminal Property Act
Slot Machine Act
Small Claims Act, 1997
Summary Offences Procedure Act, 1990
Surface Rights Acquisition & Compensation Act
Survival of Actions Act
Survivorship Act, 1993
Thresher Employees Act
Threshers' Lien Act
Trading Stamp Act
Traffic Safety Court of Saskatchewan Act, 1988
Trust & Loan Corporations Act, 1997
Trustee Act
Trusts Convention Implementation Act
Unconscionable Transactions Relief Act
Variation of Trusts Act
Victims of Crime Act, 1995
Victims of Domestic Violence Act
Wills Act, 1996
Woodmen's Lien Act

Minister & Attorney General,Hon. Don Morgan, Q.C.
306-787-5353, Fax: 306-787-1232,minister.ju@gov.sk.ca
Deputy Minister & Deputy Attorney General, Gerald Tegart
306-787-5351, Fax: 306-787-3874,gerald.tegart@gov.sk.ca
Executive Director, Policy, Planning & Evaluation, Betty Ann Pottruff, Q.C.
306-787-8954, Fax:
306-787-9008,bettyann.pottruff@gov.sk.ca
Director, Corporate Services, Dave Tulloch
306-787-5472, Fax: 306-787-5830,dave.tulloch@gov.sk.ca
Director, Communications, Laur'Lei Silzer
306-787-0775, Fax: 306-787-3874,laurlei.silzer@gov.sk.ca

• Law Reform Commission of Saskatchewan
410 26th St. West
Saskatoon, SK S7L 0H9
306-665-6428
mjfinley@shaw.ca
www.lawreformcommission.sk.ca
The Law Reform Commission of Saskatchewan was established by An Act to Establish a Law Reform Commission, proclaimed in force in November, 1973, and began functioning in February of 1974.

• Provincial Mediation Board
#120, 2151 Scarth St.
Regina, SK S4P 2H8
306-787-5387 Fax: 306-787-5574 888-215-2222
www.justice.gov.sk.ca/provincialmediationboard
The Provincial Mediation Board provides budgeting advice and counselling to individuals with personal debt problems.It may be able to arrange repayment plans with creditors.The Board also deals with problems of debtors related to property tax arrears, eviction of commercial tenants and residential mortgage foreclosures.

• Public & Private Rights Board
23-3085 Albert St.
Regina, SK S4S 0B1
306-787-4071 Fax: 306-787-0088

• Saskatchewan Farm Land Security Board
#207, 3988 Albert St.
Regina, SK S4S 3R1
306-787-5047 Fax: 306-787-8599
inquiries@farmland.gov.sk.ca
www.farmland.gov.sk.ca
The Farm Land Security Board is a Board of three members appointed by Order-in-Council to oversee the Farm Foreclosure process, Home Quarter Protection mechanisms and Farm Ownership regulations that are part of The Saskatchewan Farm Security Act.

• Saskatchewan Farm Security Programs
#207, 3988 Albert St.
Regina, SK S4S 3R1
306-787-5047 Fax: 306-787-8599

• Saskatchewan Film & Video Classification Board
#500, 1919 Saskatchewan Dr.
Regina, SK S4P 4H2
306-787-5550 Fax: 306-787-9779 888-374-4636
adwyer@justice.gov.sk.ca
On October 1, 1997, an agreement between the province of British Columbia and Saskatchewan came into effect, under which the British Columbia Film Classification Office will classify all new theatrical releases and adult videos on behalf of the Saskatchewan Film and Video Classification Board.

• Saskatchewan Financial Services Commission(SFSC)
#601, 1919 Saskatchewan Dr.
Regina, SK S4P 4H2
306-787-5645 Fax: 306-787-5899
www.sfsc.gov.sk.ca
The Saskatchewan Financial Services Commission (SFSC) protects consumer and public interests and supports economic well-being through responsive financial marketplace regulation. The SFSC enhances consumer protection through licensing, registration, audit, complaint handling and enforcement activities pursuant to various provincial statutes.

• Saskatchewan Human Rights Commission(SHRC)
#301, 1942 Hamilton St.
Regina, SK S4P 3V7
306-787-2530 Fax: 306-787-0454 800-667-8577TDD: 306-787-8550
shrc@shrc.gov.sk.ca
www.shrc.gov.sk.ca

• Saskatchewan Legal Aid Commission
#502, 201 - 21 St. East
Saskatoon, SK S7K 2H6
306-933-5300 Fax: 306-933-6764 800-667-3764
central@legalaid.gov.sk.ca
www.legalaid.sk.ca
The Saskatchewan Legal Aid Commission provides legal services to persons and organizations for criminal and civil matters where those persons and organizations are financially unable to secure these services from their own resources. The organization has been in existence since 1974.

• Saskatchewan Police Commission
600 - 1874 Scarth St.
Regina, SK S4P 4B3
306-787-6518 Fax: 306-787-0136
www.cpsp.gov.sk.ca/Saskatchewan-Police-Commission
The Saskatchewan Police Commission promotes adequate and effective policing throughout the province. The Commission also promotes the preservation of peace, prevention of crime, efficiency of police services and the improvement of police relationships with Saskatchewan communities.

• Saskatchewan Public Complaints Commission
#300, 1919 Saskatchewan Dr.
Regina, SK S4P 4H2
306-787-6519 Fax: 306-787-6528 866-256-6194
www.justice.gov.sk.ca/publiccomplaintscommission
The Public Complaints Commission (PCC) is a five-person, non-police body appointed by the government. It is responsible for ensuring that both the public and police receive a fair and thorough investigation of a complaint against the police or an investigation of a possible criminal offence by a police officer.

• Surface Rights Board of Arbitration
113 - 2nd Ave. East
PO Box 1597
Kindersley, SK S0L 1S0
306-463-5447 Fax: 306-463-5449
SurfaceRightsBoard@gov.sk.ca
www.er.gov.sk.ca/SurfaceRights
Governed by The Surface Rights Acquisition and Compensation Act, the Surface Rights Board of Arbitration is a last resort when an occupant or landowner & an oil, gas or potash operator are unable to reach an agreement.

Civil Law Division
306-787-5224, Fax: 306-787-0581, www.justice.gov.sk.ca/civillaw
Executive Director, Gerald Tegart, Q.C.
306-787-5495, Fax: 306-787-0581,gerald.tegart@gov.sk.ca

Community Justice Division
306-787-5096, Fax: 306-787-0078
Executive Director & Executive Director, Community Services, Jan Turner
306-787-5112, Fax: 306-787-0078,jturner@justice.gov.sk.ca
Chief Coroner, R. Kent Stewart
306-787-5541, Fax: 306-787-5503,kent.stewart@gov.sk.ca
Executive Director, Law Enforcement Services & Director, Saskatchewan Police Commission, Murray Sawatsky
306-787-6534, Fax:
306-787-0136,murray.sawatsky@gov.sk.ca
Director, Law Enforcement Operations, Rick Peach
306-787-9292, Fax: 306-787-0136
Director, Victims Services, Pat Thiele
306-787-6707, Fax: 306-787-0081,patrick.thiele@gov.sk.ca
Director, Aboriginal & Northern Justice Initiations Branch, Maxine Hodgson
306-787-3684, Fax:
306-787-0078,maxine.hodgson@gov.sk.ca

Courts & Civil Justice Division
306-787-5359, Fax: 306-787-8737
Asst. Deputy Minister, Ken Acton
306-787-0991, Fax: 306-787-8737,ken.acton@gov.sk.ca
Executive Director, Court Services, Linda Bogard
306-787-5680, Fax: 306-787-8737,linda.bogard@gov.sk.ca
Public Guardian & Trustee, Public Trustees' Office, Ron Kruzeniski, Q.C.
306-787-5427, Fax: 306-787-5065
Director, Corporations, Philip Flory
306-787-2970, Fax: 306-787-8999,phil.flory@gov.sk.ca
Director, Family Justice Services, Lionel McNabb
306-787-1650, Fax: 306-787-1420,lionel.mcnabb@gov.sk.ca
Director, Dispute Resolution Office, Glen Gardner
306-787-5749, Fax: 306-787-0088,glen.gardner@gov.sk.ca

Public Law Division
306-787-8389, Fax: 306-787-9111
Executive Director & Director, Legislative Services, Susan Amrud, Q.C.
306-787-8990, susan.amrud@gov.sk.ca
Chief Crown Counsel, Legislative Drafting, Ian Brown, Q.C.
306-787-9346, Fax: 306-787-9111,ian.brown@gov.sk.ca
Director, Constitutional Law Branch, Graeme G. Mitchell, Q.C.
306-787-8385, Fax:
306-787-9111,graeme.mitchell@gov.sk.ca
Manager, Queen's Printer, Marilyn Lustig-McEwen
306-787-9345, 800-226-7302,Fax:
306-798-0835,marilyn.lustig-mcewen@gov.sk.ca

Public Prosecutions Division
306-787-5490, Fax: 306-787-8878,
www.justice.gov.sk.ca/publicprosecutionsdivision
Executive Director, Daryl Rayner, Q.C.
306-787-5490, Fax: 306-787-8878

Saskatchewan Advanced Education, Employment & Labour

1945 Hamilton St., Regina, SK S4P 2C8
306-787-9478, Fax: 306-787-2315,
www.aeel.gov.sk.ca

The Ministry is responsible for labour standards, labour support services, labour relations, mediation, occupational health & safety, workers' advocacy, & the Status of Women Office. In November 2007, a new provincial government resulted in the reorganization of provincial government ministries. An expanded Ministry of Advanced Education, Employment & Labour was formed. Rob Norris was named the Minister of Advanced Education, Employment & Labour.

Acts Administered:
Building Trades Protection Act
Construction Industry Labour Relations Act, 1992
Employment Agencies Act
Labour Standards Act
Occupational Health & Safety Act, 1993
Radiation Health & Safety Act, 1985
Trade Union Act
Worker's Compensation Act

Minister, Advanced Education, Employment & Labour; Minister Responsible, Immigration; Minister Responsible for the Workers Compensation Board, Hon. Rob Norris
306-787-0341, Fax: 306-787-6946,minister.aeel@gov.sk.ca
Deputy Minister, Advanced Education, Employment & Labour, Wynne Young
306-787-7071, Fax: 306-798-0975,wynne.young@gov.sk.ca
Executive Director, Policy & Evaluation, Linda Smith
306-787-2984, Fax: 306-787-5870,linda.smith@gov.sk.ca
Executive Assistant, Work & Family Unit, Gayl Basler
306-933-7983, Fax: 306-933-5444
Director, Marketing & Communications, Herman Hulshof
306-787-9715, Fax:
306-798-5021,herman.hulshof@gov.sk.ca
Executive Director, HR Services, Greg Tuer
306-787-3292, Fax: 306-787-7149,gtuer@psc.gov.sk.ca

• Labour Relations Board
#1600, 1920 Broad St.
Regina, SK S4P 3V2
306-787-2406 Fax: 306-787-2664
mbaldwin@lrb.gov.sk.ca
An independent, quasi-judicial tribunal charged with the responsibility of adjudicating disputes that arise under The Trade Union Act, The Construction Industry Labour Relations Act, 1992 & The Health Labour Relations Reorganization Act

• Minimum Wage Board
#400, 1870 Albert St.
Regina, SK S4P 4W1
306-787-2391 Fax: 306-787-7229
webmaster@lab.gov.sk.ca
www.labour.gov.sk.ca
Makes recommendations respecting minimum employment standards including: the minimum wage, minimum age, maximum work periods, maximum rates for room & board & minimum rest periods.

• Office of the Worker's Advocate
#400, 1870 Albert St.
Regina, SK S4P 4W1
306-787-2456 Fax: 306-787-0249 877-787-2456
www.labour.gov.sk.ca
The Office of the Worker's Advocate provides free assistance to workers who are experiencing difficulties with workers' compensation claims. The Office offers information about the following programs & services: wage loss, benefits, survivor's benefits, medical aid, rehabilitation, & retraining. Working with advocacy groups & unions, The Office of the Worker's Advocate strives to improve service to injured workers. Workers' Compensation Board (WCB) decisions about claims can be reviewed & appealed.

• Saskatchewan Workers' Compensation Board
#200, 1881 Scarth St.
Regina, SK S4P 4L1
306-787-4370 Fax: 306-787-7582 800-667-7590TDD: 888-844-7773
internet_clientsvc@wcbsask.com
www.wcbsask.com
Other Communication: Injury Reports: 1-800-787-9288; Employer Inquiries: reainquiry@wcbsask.com; Health Care Provider Inquiries: internet_healthcare@wcbsask.com; Appeal Fax: 306-787-1116

• Status of Women
#400, 1870 Albert St.
Regina, SK S4P 4W1
306-787-7401 Fax: 306-787-2058

Finance & Administration Branch
306-787-2413, Fax: 306-787-4038
Actign Director, Kevin Kuntzt
306-787-4527
Director, Public Affairs,Vacant
306-787-4156, Fax: 306-798-5021

Labour Relations & Mediation Division
306-787-0817, Fax: 306-787-1064
Executive Director, Doug Forseth
306-787-9106, Fax: 306-787-1064,doug.forseth@gov.sk.ca

Labour Standards
306-787-2438, Fax: 306-787-4780, 800-667-1783
Acting Executive Director, Glen McRorie
306-933-5087, Fax: 306-787-4780,glen.mcrorie@gov.sk.ca, Other Communications: Alt. phone: 306/787-2432

Occupational Health & Safety Division
306-787-4496, Fax: 306-787-2208, 800-567-7233
www.labour.gov.sk.ca/ohs
The division protects employee's health & safety at work.Its goal is to prevent & reduce the number of accidents, injuries, illnesses & deaths on the job.OH&S staff work with Occupational Health Committees or representatives to ensure the workplace fulfils health & safety responsibilities, creates & trains Occupational Health Committees, enforces workplace health & safety laws, inspects workplaces, investigates workplace accidents, hazards, concerns & complaints, provides health & safety training, information & advice, provides lab & technical services on chemical, biological & radiological hazards, ensures hazardous substances are properly managed & provides health & safety resources.
Executive Director, Glennis Bihun
306-787-4481, Fax: 306-787-2208,glennis.bihun@gov.sk.ca
Chief Mine Inspector, Mines Safety Unit, Neil Crocker
306-933-5106, Fax: 306-933-7339
Manager, Occupational Hygiene Unit, Herb Wooley
306-787-4506, Fax: 306-787-2208,herb.wooley@gov.sk.ca

Saskatchewan Education

2220 College Ave., Regina, SK S4P 4V9
306-787-6030, 888-775-3276
learninginquiry@sasked.gov.sk.ca
www.education.gov.sk.ca

The Ministry provides programs & services in the following key areas: early learning & child care, the prekindergarten to grade 12 education system, & the Provincial Library. In November 2007, a new provincial government resulted in the reorganization of provincial government ministries. The work of Saskatchewan Learning was merged into a newly named ministry. Ken Krawetz was named the Minister of Education.

Acts Administered:
Education Act
Education Property Tax Act
League of Educational Administrators, Directors & Superintendents Act
Public Libraries Act
Registered Music Teachers Act
Saskatchewan Association of School Business Officials Act
Teachers' Dental Plan Act
Teachers' Federation Act
Teachers' Life Insurance (Government Contributory) Act
Teachers' Superannuation & Disability Benefits Act

Minister, Education, Hon. Ken Krawetz
306-787-7360, Fax: 306-787-0263,minister.edu@gov.sk.ca,
Legislative Secretary to the Minister of Education, Jim Reiter
Deputy Minister, Education, Audrey Roadhouse
306-787-2471, Fax:
306-787-1300,audrey.roadhouse@gov.sk.ca
Asst. Deputy Minister, Darren McKee
306-787-3222, Fax:
306-787-1300,darren.mckee@gov.sk.ca
Asst. Deputy Minister, Helen Horsman
306-787-6056, Fax:
306-787-1300,helen.horsman@gov.sk.ca
Executive Director, Communications, Jacquie McLean
306-787-5609, Fax: 306-798-2045,jacquie.mclean@gov.sk.ca
Executive Director, Accountability, Assessment & Records, Darryl Hunter
306-787-6053, Fax: 306-787-9178,darryl.hunter@gov.sk.ca
Executive Director, Corporate Services, Trina Vicq Fallows
306-787-3501, Fax:
306-787-7392,trina.vicqfallows@gov.sk.ca
Executive Director, Curriculum & E-Learning, Jane Thurgood Sagal
306-787-6842, Fax:
306-787-2223,jane.thurgoodsagal@gov.sk.ca
Executive Director, Early Learning & Child Care, Lois Zelmer
306-787-0765, Fax: 306-787-0277,lois.zelmer@gov.sk.ca
Executive Director, Education Finance & Facilities, Rhonda Smysnuik
306-787-6634, Fax: 306-787-5059
Executive Director, First Nations & Métis Education, Maureen Johns Simpson
306-787-6215, Fax:
306-787-0277,maureen.johnssimpson@gov.sk.ca
Executive Director, French Education, Simone Gareau
306-787-5632, Fax: 306-787-3164,simone.gareau@gov.sk.ca
Human Resources Consultant, Human Resources Services - Education, Clarence Yam
306-787-7228, Fax: 306-787-7149,clarence.yam@gov.sk.ca
Executive Director, Human Services Integration Forum, Vacant
306-787-5679, Fax: 306-787-0277
Executive Director, Policy, Evaluation & Legislative Services, Rosanne Glass
306-787-3897, Fax: 306-787-0277,rosanne.glass@gov.sk.ca
Provincial Librarian, Provincial Library, Joylene Campbell
306-787-2972, Fax:
306-787-2029,joylene.campbell@gov.sk.ca

Regional Offices:

Region 1
J. Auburn Bldg., 110 Souris Ave., PO Box 2003, Weyburn, SK S4H 2Z9
306-848-2428, Fax: 306-848-2325
Regional Director, Tom Chell

Region 2
350 Cheadle St. West, PO Box 5000, Swift Current, SK S9H 4G3
306-778-8247, Fax: 306-778-8583
Regional Director, Wanda Biffart

Region 3
4635 Wascana Pkwy., Regina, SK S4P 3A3
306-787-1195, Fax: 306-787-6139
Regional Director, Wayne Back

Region 4
Sturdy Stone Bldg., 122 - 3 Ave. North, 8th Fl., Saskatoon, SK S7K 2H6
306-933-5027, Fax: 306-933-7469
Regional Director, Crandall Hrynkiw

Region 5
107 Crawford Ave. East, PO Box 6500, Melfort, SK S0E 1A0
306-752-6166, Fax: 306-752-6168
Regional Director, Darlene Thompson

Region 6
1146 - 102 St., North Battleford, SK S9A 1E9
306-446-7439, Fax: 306-446-7586
Regional Director,Dr. Lois Duffee

Northern
PO Box 5000, La Ronge, SK S0J 1L0
306-425-4380, Fax: 306-425-4383
Regional Director, Kevin Greschner

Saskatchewan Liquor & Gaming Authority (SLGA)

2500 Victoria Ave., PO Box 5054, Regina, SK S4P 3M3
306-787-4213, Fax: 306-787-8468,
www.slga.gov.sk.ca

The Treasury Board Crown Corporation is responsible for the distribution, control, & regulation of liquor & most gaming across Saskatchewan.

Minister Responsible,Hon. Dan D'Autremont
306-787-0942, Fax: 306-787-8677,minister.gs@gov.sk.ca
President/CEO, Barry Lacey
306-787-1737, Fax: 306-787-8439,blacey@slga.gov.sk.ca
Chief Financial Officer & Vice-President, Corporate Services, Rod Wiley
306-787-2606, Fax: 306-787-7336,rwiley@slga.gov.sk.ca

Saskatchewan Northern Affairs

Mistasinihk Place, 1328 La Ronge Ave., PO Box 5000, La Ronge, SK S0J 1L0

306-425-4207, Fax: 306-425-4349, 866-663-4065
admin@sna.gov.sk.ca
www.northern.gov.sk.ca

Northern Affairs has the following responsibilities: to stimulate & support business & employment development in northern Saskatchewan; to promote benefits & opportunities for northerners from development; to provide leadership & support for regional economic planning & sector development in northern Saskatchewan by working with agencies & northerners; & to advance northern perspectives & interests within government.

Minister Responsible,Hon. June Draude
306-787-0605, Fax:
306-798-8050,minister.fnmr@gov.sk.ca

Executive Director, Resource & Industry Development, Richard Turkheim
306-787-2143, Fax:
306-787-6014,richard.turkheim@gov.sk.ca

Executive Director, Planning & Financial Management, Anita Jones
306-787-0174, Fax: 306-787-6014,anita.jones@gov.sk.ca

Director, Communications, Scott Boyes
306-425-6669, Fax: 306-425-4349,scott.boyes@gov.sk.ca

Budget & Administration Officer, Finance & Administration, Tammy Watt
306-425-4284, Fax: 306-425-4613,tammy.watt@gov.sk.ca

Saskatchewan Ombudsman

#150, 2401 Saskatchewan Dr., Regina, SK S4P 4H8
306-787-6211, Fax: 306-787-9090, 800-667-7180
www.ombudsman.sk.ca

The Ombudsman is an Officer of the Legislative Assembly with the authority to investigate complaints received from members of the public who believe the government administration has dealt with them unfairly. Government administration includes any department, branch, board, agency or commission responsible to the Crown & any public servant in Saskatchewan. The Ombudsman was established by the Ombudsman & Children's Advocate Act.

Ombudsman, Kevin Fenwick, Q.C.
306-787-6211, Fax:
306-787-9090,kfenwick@ombudsman.sk.ca

Deputy Ombudsman, Regina Office, Janet Mirwaldt
306-787-6142, Fax:
306-787-9090,jmirwaldt@ombudsman.sk.ca

Deputy Ombudsman, Saskatoon Office, Joni Sereda
306-933-8165, Fax:
306-933-8406,jsereda@ombudsman.sk.ca

Saskatchewan Power Corporation (SaskPower)

2025 Victoria Ave., Regina, SK S4P 0S1
306-566-2121, Fax: 306-566-2330, 800-667-4749
www.saskpower.com

A Crown Corporation which provides services to over 439,000 customers over 652,000 square kilometres of diverse terrain in Saskatchewan; operates 15 generating facilities including, four base-load thermal stations, seven hydroelectric stations, three gas-fired peaking stations, & the Cypress Wind Power facility; capacity of 3,655 megawatts. The SaskPower Environmental policy maintains a commitment to environmental responsibility. The policy includes compliance with relevant environmental legislation, regulations & corporate environmental committees; continual improvement of environmental management systems & prevention of pollution. SaskPower's management system is ISO 14001 registered.

Minister, Crown Corporations, Hon. Ken Cheveldayoff
306-787-7339, Fax: 306-798-3140,minister.cc@gov.sk.ca

President/CEO, Pat Youzwa
306-566-3103

Chief Information Officer, Corporate Information & Technology, Ken Hoff
306-566-2097

Acting President & CEO, SaskPower International, Garner Mitchell
306-566-2667

Acting Vice-President, Corporate & Financial Services & CFO, Grant Ring
306-566-2620, Fax: 306-566-2115

Vice-President, Customer Services, Judy May
306-566-2161

Vice-President, Planning, Environment and Regulatory Affairs, Gary L. Wilkinson

Vice-President, Power Production, Garner Mitchell
306-566-2067

Vice-President, Transmission & Distribution, Mike Marsh
306-566-3271

Acting Vice-President, General Counsel and Assistant Secretary, Rachelle Verret Morphy
306-566-3139

Manager, Communications & Public Affairs, Keith Moen
306-566-3421

Exec. Assistant, Cecile Matysio
306-566-3103

Saskatchewan Government Services (SPM)

Century Plaza, 1920 Rose St., Regina, SK S4P 0A9
306-787-6911, Fax: 306-787-1061,
www.gs.gov.sk.ca

Responsibilities of the Ministry include the following: management, operation, & maintenance of accommodation; administration of commercial services such as relocation services, information services, & distribution; & coordination of corporate support services, including protective services, planning, & policy. In November 2007, a new provincial government resulted in the reorganization of provincial government ministries. The work of Saskatchewan Property Management was merged into a newly named ministry. Dan D'Autremont was named Minister of Government Services.

Acts Administered:
Architects Act
Interior Designers Act
Purchasing Act
Saskatchewan Property Management Corporation Act

Minister, Government Services; Minister Responsible, Information Technology Office, Hon. Dan D'Autremont
306-787-0942, Fax: 306-787-8677,minister.gs@gov.sk.ca

Acting Deputy Minister, Phil Lambert
306-787-6520, Fax: 306-787-6547,phil.lambert@gov.sk.ca

Assistant Deputy Minister, Accommodation Services, Donald Koop
306-787-9909, Fax: 306-798-0370,donald.koop@gov.sk.ca

Assistant Deputy Minister, Commercial Services, Phil Lambert
306-787-8202, Fax: 306-787-8582,phil.lambert@gov.sk.ca

Assistant Deputy Minister, Corporate Support Services, Debbie Koshman
306-787-1071, Fax:
306-787-0700,debbie.koshman@gov.sk.ca

Director, Communications, Maureen Boyle
306-787-5959, Fax: 306-787-8582,maureen.boyle@gov.sk.ca

Saskatchewan Public Service Commission (PSC)

2100 Broad St., Regina, SK S4P 1Y5
306-787-7575, Fax: 306-787-7578, 866-319-5999
webmaster@psc.gov.sk.ca
www.psc.gov.sk.ca

The independent agency provides leadership & policy direction for the human resource function in the public service. The PSC works with departments to deliverhuman resource services.

Minister Responsible,Hon. Wayne Elhard
306-787-6447, Fax: 306-787-1736,minister.hi@gov.sk.ca

Chair, Clare Isman
306-787-7552, Fax: 306-787-5045,cisman@psc.gov.sk.ca

Assistant Chair, Corporate HR Management and Employee Relations, Rick McKillop
306-787-7606, Fax: 306-787-4074,rmckillop@psc.gov.sk.ca

Director, Communications, Shelley Banks
306-787-6479, Fax: 306-787-4074,sbanks@psc.gov.sk.ca

Director, Corporate Services, Mike Mestill
306-787-8278, Fax: 306-787-4074,mike.pestill@gov.sk.ca

Enterprise Saskatchewan

#200, 3085 Albert St., Regina, SK S4S 0B1
Fax: 306-798-0629, 800-265-2001
Webmaster@enterprisesask.ca
www.enterprisesaskatchewan.ca

Enterprise Saskatchewan (ES) is a bold and innovative approach to creating sustainable economic growth in Saskatchewan. It is a special agency for co-ordinating the province's growth agenda, led by key economic development and community stakeholders with one ultimate goal: to ensure Saskatchewan has a competitive environment that will attract investment at every level. Enterprise Saskatchewan provides leadership as the central co-ordinating agency of the Government of Saskatchewan for economic development. In partnership with key stakeholders, Enterprise Saskatchewan advances a transformative sustainable economic growth agenda and develops a culture of innovation and entrepreneurship that encourages investment and population growth, creating prosperity for all Saskatchewan residents.

Acts Administered:
Economic & Co-operative Development Act
Regional Economic & Co-operative Development Act

Minister, Enterprise, Hon. Ken Cheveldayoff
306-787-0804, Fax: 306-798-2009,minister.ei@gov.sk.ca

Interim Chief Executive Officer, Chris Dekker
306-933-6744, Fax:
306-933-8244,chris.dekker@enterprisesask.ca

Chief Financial Officer, Denise Haas
306-787-2756, Fax:
306-798-0629,denise.haas@enterprisesask.ca

Vice President, Regional Enterprise, Ernest Heapy
306-787-2561, Fax:
306-787-7559,ernest.heapy@enterprisesask.ca

Acting Director, Investment Programs, Marv Weismiller
306-787-5014, Fax:
306-787-8702,marv.weismiller@enterprisesask.ca,

Regional Offices:

Estevan
1133 - 4 St., Estevan, SK S0A 0W6
306-637-4505, Fax: 306-637-4510, 800-265-2001

Moose Jaw
88 Saskatchewan St. East, Moose Jaw, SK S6H 0V4
306-694-3623, Fax: 306-694-3500, 800-265-2001

North Battleford
1202 - 101 St., North Battleford, SK S9A 1E9
306-446-7444, Fax: 306-446-7442, 800-265-2001

Prince Albert
City Hall, 1084 Central Ave., 3rd fl., PO Box 3003, Prince Albert, SK S9H 4G3
306-953-2280, Fax: 306-922-6499, 800-265-2001

Regina
1925 Rose St., Regina, SK S4P 3P1
Fax: 306-787-1620

Saskatoon
345 - 3 Ave. South, Saskatoon, SK S7K 2H6
Fax: 306-933-7692

Swift Current
885 - 6 Ave. NE, PO Box 5000, Swift Current, SK S9H 4G3
306-778-8415, Fax: 306-778-8526, 800-265-2001

Yorkton
23 Smith St. West, Yorkton, SK S3N 0H9
306-786-1415, Fax: 306-786-1417, 800-265-2001

Saskatchewan Research Council (SRC)

#125, 15 Innovation Blvd., Saskatoon, SK S7N 2X8
306-933-5400, Fax: 306-933-7446,
info@src.sk.ca
www.src.sk.ca

Research activities include: gas emissions testing; indoor environment testing; groundwater pesticides testing; indoor air quality & source testing for rayon & asbestos; spray drift research; vegetation studies for range, forestry, conservation; aquatic monitoring & assessment methods; climate impact assessment for environmental economic & urban stormwater management; development of plant bioassays for assessing the effects of hazardous materials in aquatic ecosystems; radiochemistry, chromatographic analysis, water analysis; parenting verification centre for the Canadian livestock industry; develops the optimum engine & fuel system for natural gas operation; bioprocessing technology; emulsions research; studies to support mineral exploration; analyses various sample material used in mineral exploration; geoenvironmental research. SRC's Biofuels Test Centre opened in September, 2006.

President/CEO,Dr. Laurier Schramm
306-933-5402, Fax: 306-933-7519,schramm@src.sk.ca

CFO, Crystal Smudy
306-933-8111, Fax: 306-933-7519,smudy@src.sk.ca

Vice-President, Agriculture, Biotechnology & Food, Dale Kelly
306-933-8136, Fax: 306-933-7662,kelly@src.sk.ca

Vice-President, Energy, Ernie S. Pappas
306-787-9351, Fax: 306-787-8811,pappas@src.sk.ca

Vice President, Environment & Forestry, Joe Muldoon
306-933-5439, Fax: 306-933-7299,muldoon@src.sk.ca

Vice-President, Alternative Energy & Manufacturing, Craig Murray
306-933-5482, Fax: 306-933-7446,murray@src.sk.ca

Acting Vice-President, Mining & Minerals, Craig Murray
306-933-5482, Fax: 306-933-7446,murray@src.sk.ca

Director, Business Ventures & Communications, Wanda Nyirfa
306-933-6666, Fax: 306-933-7519,nyirfa@src.sk.ca

Director, Business Intelligence, Dave Grier
306-933-8131, Fax: 306-933-7299,grier@src.sk.ca

Director, Corporate Services, Ken Owens
306-933-5422, owens@src.sk.ca

Vice-President, Organizational Effectiveness, Toby Arnold
306-933-5479, Fax: 306-933-7896,arnold@src.sk.ca

Corporate Relations Officer, Judy Peters
306-933-5429, Fax: 306-933-7896,petersj@src.sk.ca

Vice-President, Michael E. Weekes
306-933-5439, Fax: 306-933-7299,weekes@src.sk.ca

Business Unit Manager, Air & Climate, Keith Wallace
306-933-8120, wallace@src.sk.ca

Business Unit Manager, Climatology, Elaine Wheaton
306-933-8179, wheaton@src.sk.ca

Business Unit Manager, Ecosystems, Mark Johnston
306-933-8175, johnston@src.sk.ca
Business Unit Manager, Hydrogeology, Harm Maathuis
306-993-5496, maathuis@src.sk.ca
Director, Grant McIvor
306-787-6033, mcvicar@src.sk.ca

Saskatchewan Telecommunications (SaskTel)

2121 Saskatchewan Dr., 7th Fl., Regina, SK S4P 3Y2
306-777-3737, Fax: 306-359-7854, 800-727-5835
www.sasktel.com

The provincial Crown Corporation delivers full service telecommunications to the people of Saskatchewan. Services are as follows: competitive voice, data, dial-up, & high speed internet; entertainment & multimedia services; security; web hosting; text & messaging services; & cellular & wireless data services.

Minister, Crown Corporations, Hon. Ken Cheveldayoff
306-787-7339, Fax: 306-798-3140,minister.cc@gov.sk.ca
President/CEO, Robert Watson
306-777-2200
Vice-President, Marketing, Stacey Sandison
306-777-3670
Vice-President, Corporate Counsel & Regulatory Affairs, John Meldrum
306-777-2223
Vice-President, Human Resources & Corporate Services, Doug Burnett
306-777-2283
Vice-President, Customer Service - Sales, Ken Keesey
CFO, Mike Anderson
306-777-3185
Chief Technology Officer, Kym Wittal
306-777-4504,
Senior Director, Corporate Communications, Darcee MacFarlane
306-777-4441

SaskEnergy Incorporated

1777 Victoria Ave., Regina, SK S4P 4K5
306-777-9225, Fax: 306-777-9200, 800-567-8899
www.saskenergy.com

Other Communication: Natural Gas Emergency: 1-888-700-0427; Line Locates: 1-866-828-4888; Emergency & Safety Line: 1-888-700-0427

The provincial Crown corporation provides natural gas to residential, farm, commercial, & industrial customers in 92% of Saskatchewan's communities.

Acts Administered:
SaskEnergy Act

Minister, Crown Corporations, Hon. Ken Cheveldayoff
306-787-7339, Fax: 306-798-3140,minister.cc@gov.sk.ca
President/CEO, Doug Kelln
306-777-9568, Fax: 306-777-9889,dkelln@saskenergy.com
Executive Vice-President, Dean Reeve
306-777-9402, Fax:
306-522-2217,dreeve@saskenergy.com
Executive Director, Corporate Affairs, Ron Podbielski
306-777-9432, Fax:
306-352-4438,rpodbielski@saskenergy.com
Sr. Vice-President, Gas Supply & Business Development, Daryl Posehn
306-777-9567, Fax: 306-569-3522
Vice-President, TransGas, Phil Sandham
306-777-9603, Fax: 306-352-8892
Vice-President, Corporate Support, Colleen Huber
306-777-9660, Fax: 306-777-9191,chuber@saskenergy.com
Vice-President, Finance & CFO, Greg Mrazek
306-777-9417, Fax:
306-777-9070,gmrazek@saskenergy.com
Vice-President, General Counsel & Corporate Secretary, Mark Guillet
306-777-9427, Fax: 306-565-3332
Vice-President, Human Resources, Robert Haynes
306-777-9405, Fax: 306-781-7050,rhaynes@saskenergy.com
Sr. Admin. Coordinator, Legal Dept., Candace LeBlanc
306-777-9403, Fax: 306-565-3332

TransGas Limited

1777 Victoria Ave, Regina, SK S4P 4K5
Fax: 306-352-8892

TransGas & its affiliates, Many Islands Pipelines Canada Limited, MIPCL, & Swan Valley Gas Corporation, SVGC, own & operate over 13,800 kilometres of gathering & transmission pipeline in Saskatchewan, operates storage facilities to ensure safe & reliable operationduring the winter.TransGas transports natural gas for over 280 customers, producers & industrial & commercial customers. The TransGas pipeline system is connected to TransCanada pipelines, ATCO pipelines, & Havre pipeline, providing the Saskatchewan market access to Alberta & Montana gas supplies. TransGas' & MIPCL'sinterconnections with other transmission systems, Foothills Pipelines Ltd., TransCanada Pipelines Ltd., Swan Valley Gas & Williston Basin Interstate, provide access to Manitoba, eastern Canadian & United States markets for Saskatchewan, Alberta & United States-sourced gas supplies

President/CEO, Doug Kelln
306-777-9568, Fax: 306-777-9889,dkelln@saskenergy.com
Sr. Vice-President, Daryl Posehn
306-777-9567, Fax: 306-569-3522
Vice-President, General Counsel & Corporate Secretar, Mark Guillet
306-777-9427, Fax: 306-565-3332

Saskatchewan Water Corporation (SaskWater)

#200, 111 Fairford St. East, Moose Jaw, SK S6H 1C8
306-694-3098, Fax: 306-694-3207, 888-230-1111
comm@saskwater.com
www.saskwater.com

Other Communication: SaskWater Customer Emergencies: 1-800-667-5799

SaskWater, a provincial Crown corporation, is Saskatchewan's water utility service provider. Lines of business are as follows: supply of potable & non-potable water; treatment & management of wastewater; & certified operations & maintenance. SaskWater is responsible for designing, building, & operating transmission, regional, & stand-alone water supply & wastewater systems. All systems must meet regulatory requirements.

Acts Administered:
Saskatchewan Water Corporation Act, 2002

Minister, Crown Corporations, Hon. Ken Cheveldayoff
306-787-7339, Fax: 306-787-3140,minister.cc@gov.sk.ca
President, Stuart Kramer
306-694-3903, Fax:
306-694-7722,stuart.kramer@saskwater.com
Vice-President, Corporate & Human Services, Denise Soar
306-694-3687, Fax:
306-694-3207,denise.soar@saskwater.com
Acting Vice-President, Engineering & Business Development, Eric Light
306-694-3920, Fax: 306-694-3207,eric.light@saskwater.com
Vice-President, Operations, Mart Cram
306-694-3909, Fax:
306-694-3207,mart.cram@saskwater.com

Saskatchewan Workers' Compensation Board

#200, 1881 Scarth St., Regina, SK S4P 4L1
306-787-4370, Fax: 306-787-7582, 800-667-7590
internet_clientsvc@wcbsask.com
www.wcbsask.com

Other Communication: Injury Reports: 1-800-787-9288; Employer Inquiries: reainquiry@wcbsask.com; Health Care Provider Inquiries: internet_healthcare@wcbsask.com; Appeal Fax: 306-787-1116

The Saskatchewan's Workers' Compensation Board was created by the following provincial legislation in Saskatchewan: the Workers' Compensation Act 1979, General Regulations, & Exclusion Regulations. The Board is an independent body that administers a no-fault compensation system to protect employers and workers against the result of work injuries. The WCB provides financial protection, medical benefits. & rehabilitation services to injured workers & their dependents in cases of injury or death arising from, & in the course of, employment.

Minister Responsible,Hon. Rob Norris
306-787-0341, Fax: 306-787-6946,minister.aeel@gov.sk.ca
Chairman, David Eberle
306-787-4379, Fax: 306-787-0213
CEO, Peter Federko
306-787-7398, Fax: 306-787-0213,pfederko@wcbsask.com
Vice President, Prevention, Finance & Information Technology, Gail Kruger
306-787-2475, Fax: 306-787-4311,gkruger@wcbsask.com
Vice President, Human Resources & Team Support, Donna Kane
306-787-4440, Fax: 306-787-3915,dkane@wcbsask.com
Vice President, Operations, Graham Topp
306-787-4371, Fax: 306-787-7582,gtopp@wcbsask.com

Government of the Yukon Territory

Seat of Government:PO Box 2703, Whitehorse, YT Y1A 2C6
867-667-5811, 800-661-0408
www.gov.yk.ca

The Yukon was created as a separate territory June 13, 1898.It has an area of 474,711.02 km2, & the StatsCan census population in 2006 was 30,372. A federally appointed commissioner (similar to a provincial lieutenant-governor) oversees federal interests in the territory, but the day-to-day operation of the government rests with the wholly elected executive council (cabinet).The territorial legislature has power to make acts on generally all matters of a local nature in the territory, including the imposition of local taxes, property & civil rights & the administration of justice, education & health & social services. Legislative powers vested in the provinces but not available to the territory include control of unoccupied Crown land, renewable & non-renewable resources (except wildlife & sport fisheries) & the power to amend the Yukon Act, a federal statute.

Office of the Commissioner

1098 First Ave., Whitehorse, YT Y1A 0C1
867-667-5121, Fax: 867-393-6201,
commissioner@gov.yk.ca
www.commissioner.yk.ca

The Yukon Territory is governed by a commissioner appointed for a 5-year term by the federal government, a government leader, an executive council which functions as a cabinet, & a legislative assembly. The Yukon Act provides for the establishment of a commissioner & the elected legislative assembly.

Commissioner,Hon. Geraldine Van Bibber
Executive Assistant, Cathy Cheeseman
cathy.cheeseman@gov.yk.ca

Office of the Premier

2071 Second Ave., PO Box 2703, Whitehorse, YT Y1A 1B2
867-667-8660, Fax: 867-393-6252,
premier@gov.yk.ca
www.yukonpremier.ca

Premier,Hon. Dennis Fentie
867-393-7053, Fax: 867-393-6252,dennis.fente@gov.yk.ca
Chief of Staff, Dale Drown
867-667-8507, dale.drown@gov.yk.ca
Principal Secretary, Gordon Steele
867-667-5842, gordon.steele@gov.yk.ca
Sr. Communications Advisor, Roxanne Vallevand
867-633-7949, roxanne.vallevand@gov.yk.ca

Executive Council

PO Box 2703, Whitehorse, YT Y1A 2C6
867-667-5800, Fax: 867-393-6202, 800-040-8 ex
eco@gov.yk.ca

Acts Administered:
Cabinet & Caucus Employees Act
Conflict of Interest Act
Corporate Governance Act
Environmental Assessment Act, 2003
First Nations (Yukon) Self-Government Act
Flag Act
Floral Emblem Act
Government Organisation Act
Intergovernmental Agreements Act
Official Tree Act
Plebiscite Act
Public Inquiries Act
Raven Act
Statistics Act
Waters Act, (shared with Environment & Energy, Mines & Resources)
Yukon Act (Canada)
Yukon Environmental & Socio-Economic Assessment Act
Yukon Land Claim Final Agreements, An Act Approving
Yukon Tartan Act

Premier & Minister, Finance,Hon. Dennis Fentie
867-393-7053
Minister, Tourism & Culture; Minister, Environment; Deputy Premier, Hon. Elaine Taylor
867-667-8641, Fax: 867-393-6252
Minister, Justice, Hon. Marian Horne
867-633-7973, Fax: 867-393-7400
Minister, Community Services; Minister, Highways & Public Works, Hon. Archibald Lang
867-667-8643, Fax: 867-393-7400
Minister, Health & Social Services; Minister Responsible, Yukon Workers Compensation Health and Safety Board & French Language Services, Hon. Glenn Hart
867-667-8629, Fax: 867-393-6252
Minister, Economic Development; Minister Responsible, Yukon Energy Corporatiom,Yukon Housing Corporation & Yukon Development Corporation, Hon. James Kenyon
867-668-8628, Fax: 867-393-7400
Minister, Energy, Mines & Resources; Minister Responsible, Yukon Liquor Corporation & Yukon Lottery Corporation, Hon. Brad Cathers
867-667-5806, Fax: 867-393-6252
Minister, Education; Minister Responsible, Public Service Commission, Hon. Patrick Rouble
867-667-8644, Fax: 867-393-7400

Executive Council Office
Deputy Minister & Cabinet Secretary, Janet Moodie
867-667-5866
Asst. Deputy Minister, Corporate Services, Janet Mann
867-667-5866
Asst. Deputy Minister, Land Claims & Implementation Secretariat/First Nations Relations, Karyn Armour
867-667-8566
Director, Policy & Planning, Karen Hougen-Bell
867-667-8201
Director, First Nation Relations, Cheryl McLean
867-456-6131, Fax: 867-667-3599
Director, Bureau of Statistics, Gren Finnegan
867-667-5463, Fax: 867-393-6203
Senior Government Representative, Intergovernmental Relations Office, Harley Trudeau
613-234-3206, Fax: 613-563-9602
Protocol Officer, Pamela Bangart
867-667-5875, Fax:
867-563-9602,pamela.bangart@gov.yk.ca
Manager, Youth Directorate, Gord Kurzynski
867-667-8213, Fax: 867-393-6341

Government Inquiry Office
Yukon Government Administration Building, 2071 Second Ave., PO Box 2703, Whitehorse, YT Y1A 2C6
867-667-5811,
information@gov.yk.ca
Other Communication: Alternate Phone: 867/667-5812

Legislative Assembly

c/o Clerk's Office, PO Box 2703, Whitehorse, YT Y1A 2C6
867-667-5498, Fax: 867-393-6280

Acts Administered:
Cabinet & Caucus Employees Act
Elections Act
Electoral District Boundaries Act
Legislative Assembly Act
Legislative Assembly Retirement Allowances Act
Clerk, Floyd McCormick
867-667-5494, Fax: 867-393-6280,
Speaker, Ted Staffen
867-667-5662
Sergeant-at-Arms, Rudy Couture
Deputy Speaker & Chair, Committee of the Whole, Steve Nordick
Deputy Clerk, Linda Kolody
867-667-5499
Receptionist/Finance Clerk, Dawn-Alena Brown
867-667-5498

Office of the Official Opposition (Liberal)
Leader, Arthur Mitchell
867-667-8828, Fax:
867-393-7444,arthur.mitchell@yla.gov.yk.ca

Office of the Leader of the Third Party (NDP)
Fax: 867-393-6499
Leader, Todd Hardy
867-393-7050, Fax: 867-393-6499,todd.hardy@yla.gov.yk.ca

Standing Committees of the Legislature
Members' Services Board; Rules, Elections and Privileges; Public Accounts; Statuatory Instruments; Appointments to Major Government Boards and Committees

Thirty-Second Legislature - Yukon Territory

PO Box 2703, Whitehorse, YT Y1A 2C6
867-667-5498

Last General Election, October 10, 2006.Maximum Duration, 4 years. Party Standings (October 2006): Liberal (Lib.) 5 New Democratic Party (NDP) 3 Yukon Party (YP) 10 Total 18; Salaries, Indemnities & Allowances (April 2006): Members' indemnity $38,183 plus a $19,091 expense allowance for Rural Members (Whitehorse members receive $16,669). In addition to this are the following: Premier $28,971(includes Minister's pay) Ministers $21,147 Leader of the Official Opposition $21,147 Leader of the Third Party $4,229 Speaker $7,049 Deputy Speaker $5,287. Following is: constituency (number of votes cast at 2006 election) member, party affiliation, phone number.(Address for all is PO Box 2703, Whitehorse YT Y1A 2C6.)

Acts Administered:
Cabinet & Caucus Employees Act, (shared with Executive Council Office)
Conflict of Interest (Members & Ministers) Act, (shared with Executive Council Office)
Elections Act
Electoral District Boundaries Act, 2002
Legislative Assembly Act
Legislative Assembly Retirement Allowances Act
Ombudsman Act
Yukon Day Act

Members
Steve Cardiff, Mount Lorne, New Democratic Party
867-393-7050, Fax:
867-393-6499,steve.cardiff@yla.gov.yk.ca
Hon. Brad Cathers, Lake Laberge, Yukon Party
867-667-5806, Fax: 867-393-6252,brad.cathers@gov.yk.ca
John Edzerza, McIntyre-Takhini, New Democratic Party
867-456-6730, Fax:
867-393-6280,john.edzerza@yla.gov.yk.ca
Darius Elias, Vuntut Gwitchin, Liberal
867-456-6710, Fax: 867-393-7444,darius.elias@yla.gov.yk.ca
Eric Fairclough, Mayo-Tatchun, Liberal
867-393-7054, Fax:
867-393-7444,eric.fairclough@yla.gov.yk.ca
Hon. Dennis Fentie, Watson Lake, Yukon Party
867-393-7053, Fax: 867-393-6252,dennis.fentie@gov.yk.ca
Todd Hardy, Whitehorse Centre, New Democratic Party
867-393-7050, Fax: 867-393-6499,todd.hardy@yla.gov.yk.ca
Hon. Glenn Hart, Riverdale South, Yukon Party
867-667-8629, Fax: 867-393-6252,glenn.hart@gov.yk.ca
Hon. Marian Horne, Pelly-Nisutlin, Yukon Party
867-633-7973, Fax: 867-393-7400,marian.horne@gov.yk.ca
Don Inverarity, Porter Creek South, Liberal
867-667-8879, Fax:
867-393-7444,don.inverarity@yla.gov.yk.ca
Hon. James Kenyon, Porter Creek North, Yukon Party
867-667-8628, Fax: 867-393-7400,jim.kenyon@gov.yk.ca
Hon. Archie Lang, Porter Creek Centre, Yukon Party
867-667-8643, Fax: 867-393-6252,archie.lang@gov.yk.ca
Gary McRobb, Kluane, Liberal
867-393-7057, Fax:
867-393-7444,gary.mcrobb@yla.gov.yk.ca
Arthur Mitchell, Copperbelt, Liberal
867-667-8828, Fax:
867-393-7444,arthur.mitchell@yla.gov.yk.ca
Steve Nordick, Klondike, Yukon Party
867-633-7947, Fax: 867-393-7400,steve.nordick@gov.yk.ca
Hon. Patrick Rouble, Southern Lakes, Yukon Party
867-667-8661, Fax: 867-393-7400,patrick.rouble@gov.yk.ca
Hon. Ted Staffen, Riverdale North, Yukon Party
867-667-8661, Fax: 867-393-7400,ted.staffen@gov.yk.ca
Hon. Elaine Taylor, Whitehorse West, Yukon Party
867-667-8641, Fax: 867-939-2652,elaine.taylor@gov.yk.ca
Receptionist/Finance Clerk, Dawn-Alena Brown
867-667-5498, Fax: 867-393-6280

Yukon Territory Government Departments & Agencies

Yukon Community Services

PO Box 2703, Whitehorse, YT Y1A 2C6
867-667-5811, Fax: 867-393-6295, 800-661-0408
inquiry@gov.yk.ca
www.community.gov.yk.ca

The main purpose of the department is to serve Yukoners & their communities by providing access to services to strengthen communities.The department focuses on community affairs & municipal relations within government on behalf of Yukon communities & acts as a liaison between community groups & government departments.

Acts Administered:
Animal Protection Act (shared with Energy, Mines & Resources)
Area Development Act
Assessment & Taxation Act
Boiler & Pressure Vessels Act
Builder's Lien Act
Building Standards Act
Business Corporation Act
Cemeteries & Burial Sites Act
Certified General Accountants Act
Certified Management Accountants Act
Chartered Accountants Act
Chiropractors Act
Choses in Action Act shared with Department of Justice
Civil Emergency Measures Act
Consumer Protection Act
Cooperative Associations Act
Dental Professions Act
Denture Technicians Act
Dog Act
Electrical Protection Act
Elevator & Fixed Conveyances Act
Emergency Medical Aid Act
Employment Agencies Act
Employment Standards Act
Engineering Profession Act
Factors Act
Fire Prevention Act
First Nation Indemnification (Fire Management) Act
Forest Protection Act shared with Department of Energy, Mines & Resources
Funeral Directors Act
Garage Keepers Lien Act
Gas Burning Devices Act
Gasoline Handling Act
Health Professions Act
Home Owner's Grant Act
Insurance Act
International Commercial Arbitration Act
International Sale of Goods Act
Landlord & Tenant Act
Licensed Practical Nurses Act
Lottery Licensing Act
Medical Profession Act
Miner's Lien Act
Motor Vehicles Act (shared with Highways & Public Works)
Municipal Act
Municipal Finance & Community Grants Act
Municipal Loans Act
Noise Prevention Act
Optometrists Act
Partnership & Business Name Act
Pawnbrokers & Second-Hand Dealers Act
Personal Property Security Act
Pharmacists Act
Private Investigators & Security Guards Act
Public Libraries Act
Real Estate Agents Act
Recreation Act
Registered Nurses Profession Act
Sales of Goods Act
Securities Act
Seniors Property Tax Deferment Act
Societies Act
Subdivision Act
Trustee Act (shared with Economic Development)
Warehouse Keepers Lien Act
Warehouse Receipts Act
Whitehorse Streets & Lanes Ordinance
Yukon Foundation Act
Minister,Hon. Archie Lang
867-667-8643
Deputy Minister, Ron Macmillan
867-667-5155, Fax: 867-393-6274
Director, Corporate Policy & Communications, Janet Lecamp
867-667-5865, Fax: 867-393-6404
Director, Finance, Systems & Administration, Christine Mahar
867-667-5311, Fax: 867-393-6264,
Director, Human Resources, Ellen Zimmerman
867-667-5667, Fax: 867-393-6933
Secretary, Shiela Baker
867-667-5155, Fax: 867-393-6274
• Assessment Appeal Board
867-668-6598 Fax: 867-633-2640
• Driver Control Board
308 Steele St.
PO Box 2703
Whitehorse, YT Y1A 2C6
867-667-3774 Fax: 867-393-6483
dcb@gov.yk.ca
• Yukon Lottery Commission
312 Wood St.
Whitehorse, YT Y1A 2E6
867-633-7890 Fax: 867-668-7561
lotteriesyukon@gov.yk.ca

Community Development
The branch assists, advises & organizes municipal & unincorporated communities, provides funding by administering the comprehensive municipal grants & grants in lieu of taxes, assesses properties, collects property taxes & administers the Rural Electrification & Telecommunication program & the Home Owner Grant program.The branch collaborates with communities for the planning, design, & construction of land development projects & includes residential, rural residential, commercial, industrial, & cottage lots.The branch is responsible for regulatory approvals & design, managing construction capital works projects, such as upgrading roads, water & sewage treatment facilities & solid waste disposal sites & assists communities in developing land use plans, working closely with the Yukon Municipal Board & the Association of Yukon Communities.The branch is responsible for the operation of Yukon Government owned facilities for water supply & distribution, sewage treatment & solid waste disposal.
Acting Asst. Deputy Minister, Pat Molloy
867-667-5707, Fax: 867-393-6216
Acting Director, Community Affairs, Matt King
867-667-5154, Fax: 867-393-6258

Acting Director, Community Infrastructure, Kriss Sarson
867-667-5425, Fax: 867-393-6216
Director, Community Land Planning, George Stetkiewicz
867-667-8945, Fax: 867-393-6258
Director, Property Assessment & Taxation, Kelly Eby
867-667-5234, Fax: 867-667-8276
Director, Sport & Recreation, Karen Thomson
867-667-5254, Fax: 867-393-6416
Director, Yukon Public Libraries, Julie Ourom
867-667-5447, Fax: 867-393-6333

Consumer & Safety Services

Acting Director, Dale Kozmen
867-667-8290
Registrar, Corporate Affairs, Rhonda Horte
867-667-5005, Fax: 867-393-6251
Director, Consumer Services, Fiona Charbonneau
867-667-5257, Fax: 867-667-3609
Manager, Corporate Affairs, Frederik Pretorius
867-667-5225, Fax: 867-393-6251
Manager, Labour Services, Bill Wilcox
867-667-5259, Fax: 867-393-6317
Manager, Building Safety, Stan Dueck
867-456-6596, Fax: 867-393-6249
Manager, Motor Vehicles, Walter Brennan
867-667-5313, Fax: 867-393-6220

Protective Services

Asst. Deputy Minister, Dan Boyd
867-667-5486, Fax: 867-393-6251
Director, Wildland Fire Management, Ken Colbert
867-456-3904, Fax: 867-667-3165

Emergency Measures Organization (EMO)
PO Box 2703, Whitehorse, YT Y1A 2C6
867-667-5220, Fax: 867-393-6266, 800-661-0408
emo.yukon@gov.yk.ca
www.community.gov.yk.ca/emo/index.html

Responsible for coordinating the Territory's preparedness for, response to, & recovery from, major emergencies & disasters. EMO provides authority to ensure that contingency plans are in place to deal with foreseeable risks & hazards. The Yukon EMO is divided into 13 geographical preparedness areas, mirroring the RCMP detachment boundaries.Eight of these areas have incorporated Municipalities that have appointed a Municipal EMO Coordinator to chair the local Emergency Planning Committee. In the remaining areas, the Emergency Measures Branch appoints a co-ordinator.

Manager, Michael Templeton
867-667-5220, Fax: 867-393-6266
Finance/Admin. Assistant, Bridget Wondga
867-667-8894, Fax: 867-456-6589

Fire Marshal's Office
PO Box 2703, Whitehorse, YT Y1A 2C6
867-667-5811, Fax: 867-393-6295,
inquiry@gov.yk.ca
www.community.gov.yk.ca/fireprotection/index.html

The Fire Marshal's Office works to reduce the loss of life & property due to fire &is responsible for public education & fire fighter training, as well as for funding & administering volunteer fire departments in Yukon unincorporated communities. Staff carry out fire & life safety inspections on hotels, motels, public assembly buildings, schools, day care centers, homes for special care, restaurants, etc. throughout Yukon. The Office inspects & permits underground fuel storage tank installations.

Fire Marshal, Marty Dobbin
867-667-5217, Fax: 867-667-3165

Yukon Development Corporation (YDC)

PO Box 2703 D-1, Whitehorse, YT Y1A 2C6
867-393-5337, Fax: 867-393-5401

The Yukon Development Corporation (YDC) assists with implementation of energy policies from the Department of Energy, Mines & Resources, by designing & delivering related energy programs.YDC facilitates the generation, production, transmission & distribution of energy in a manner consistent with sustainable development.YDC has investments in electricity & related energy infrastructure & acts as the primary vehicle for delivery of territorial energy programs & services.YDC owns two subsidiary corporations, Yukon Energy Corporation, YEC, & the Energy Solutions Centre Inc., ESC.YEC is the primary producer & transmitter of electrical energy in the territory & operates under the Yukon Utilities Board & the Public Utilities Act.ESC provides technical services, promotes efficiency & renewable energy technologies, co-ordinates & delivers federal & territorial energy programs to households, businesses, institutions, First Nation & public governments.

Acts Administered:
Yukon Development Corporation Act

Minister Responsible,Hon. Jim Kenyon
867-667-8628, Fax: 867-393-4700
CEO, David Morrison
867-393-5400, Fax: 867-393-5401

Yukon Economic Development

PO Box 2703, Whitehorse, YT Y1A 2C6
867-393-7191, Fax: 867-395-7199, 800-661-0408
www.economicdevelopment.gov.yk.ca

The Department works with the Yukon business community & with other governments to support business development, trade & investment opportunities, & partnerships for the development of the Yukon economy.It co-ordinates & facilitates the Yukon Government's economic development agenda. The Department is focused on creating a positive business climate in Yukon & is committed to First Nation business development in the territory. Economic Development markets Yukon as a great place to do business.

Minister,Hon. Jim Kenyon
867-667-8628, Fax: 867-393-7400
Deputy Minister, Harvey Brooks
867-393-7191, Fax: 867-667-3159
Asst. Deputy Minister, Operations, Terry Hayden
867-456-3912
Director, Finance & Information Services, Karen Mason
867-667-5933, Fax: 867-393-7199
Acting Director, Strategic Industries, Kim Cholette
867-667-5633, Fax: 867-456-6818
Director, Policy, Planning & Research, Stephen Rose
867-667-8416, Fax: 867-393-6412
Director, Business & Trade, Luke Pantin
867-667-8075, Fax: 867-393-6944
Director, Regional Economic Development, Sharon Hickey
867-456-3929, Fax: 867-393-6228
Assistant to the ADM, Judith Voswinkel
867-667-3180, Fax:
867-667-3159,judith.voswinkel@gov.uk.ca

Film & Sound Commission
PO Box 2703, Whitehorse, YT Y1A 2C6
867-667-5400, Fax: 867-393-7040,
info@reelyukon.com
www.reelyukon.com

Film & Sound Commissioner, Barbara Dunlop
867-667-8285, Fax: 867-393-7040

Yukon Education

PO Box 2703, Whitehorse, YT Y1A 2C6
867-667-5141, Fax: 867-393-6254

The Yukon has 28 public schools (14 in Whitehorse, 14 in other communities) & two private schools. The public schools are administered directly by the Department of Education, although elected school council officials are gradually assuming more powers under the 1990 Education Act, & may evolve into school boards in the near future. In 1996, the Yukon Francophone School Board was created, becoming Yukon's first school board. Curriculum is largely based on that of British Columbia, with flexibility for locally developed courses, particularly from a First Nations perspective (one quarter of the Yukon's 5977 students are of native ancestry). Seven different native languages are taught in various Yukon schools, as well as French immersion.

Acts Administered:
Apprentice Training Act
Canada Student Loans Act (federal)
Education Act
Education Staff Relations Act, (shared with Public Services Commission)
Occupational Training Act
School Trespass Act
Students' Financial Assistance Act
Teaching Profession Act
Trade Schools Regulation Act
Yukon College Act

Minister,Hon. Patrick Rouble
867-667-8644, Fax: 867-393-7400
Deputy Minister, Pamela Hine
867-667-5126, Fax: 867-393-6254

Advanced Education Branch
Fax: 867-667-8555

Acting Asst. Deputy Minister, Brent Slobodin
867-667-5129, brent.slobodin@gov.yk.ca
Director, Apprenticeship, Trades Certification & Training Programs, John Gryba
867-667-5133
Director, Labour Market Programs & Services, Shawn Kitchen
867-667-5727

Education Support Services
Fax: 867-393-6254

Acting Director, Finance & Administration, Cyndy Dekuysscher
867-667-5701
Director, Human Resources, Val Stehelin
867-667-5808, Fax: 867-667-5435,val.stehelin@gov.yk.ca
Director, Policy, Planning & Evaluation, Ann MacDonald
867-667-8181, Fax: 867-456-6788
Facilities Project Manager, Gordon deBruyn
867-667-3741, Fax: 867-393-6254,gord.debruyn@gov.yk.ca

Public Schools Branch
Fax: 867-393-6339

Asst. Deputy Minister, Christie Whitley
867-667-5127
Executive Director, Yukon Francophone School Board, Lorraine Taillefer
867-667-8680, Fax: 867-393-6946
Director, First Nations Programs & Partnerships, Tina Jules
867-393-6905, Fax: 867-456-6766
Director, Native Language Centre, John Ritter
867-668-8820, Fax: 867-668-8825
Director, Programs & Services, Elizabeth Lemay
867-667-8238, Fax: 867-393-6339

Yukon Energy, Mines & Resources

PO Box 2703, Whitehorse, YT Y1A 2C6
867-667-5466, Fax: 867-667-8601, 800-661-0408
emr@gov.yk.ca
www.emr.gov.yk.ca

The territory has extensive mineral deposits, oil & gas potential, with two producing gas wells, which rank among the top producing wells in Canada, forest reserves & local manufacturing of wood products, such as furniture, wood laminate stock & lumber. The territory has abundant & diverse energy resources due to the presence of fossil fuel reserves, numerous lakes & rivers, windy & mountainous terrain, broad forest cover & sunny conditions. The Yukon is one of the few places left in Canada where Crown land can be obtained for agricultural purposes.

Acts Administered:
Agricultural Products Acts
Agriculture Development Act
Animal Health Act, (shared with Environment)
Animal Protection Act, (shared with Community Services)
Brands Act
Economic Development Act, (shared with Economic Development)
Energy Conservation Assistance Act
Forest Protection Act, (shared with Community Services)
Lands Act
Oil & Gas Act
Pounds Act
Placer Mining Act
Quartz Mining Act
Territorial Lands (Yukon) Act
Waters Act, (shared with Environment & the Executive Council Office)

Minister,Hon. Brad Cathers
867-667-5806, Fax: 867-393-6252
Deputy Minister, Angus Robertson
867-667-5417, Fax:
867-393-7167,angus.robertson@gov.yk.ca
Executive Director, Yukon Placer Secretariat, Robert Thomson
867-667-5802, Fax: 867-667-3632
Director, Client Services & Inspections, Mark Zrum
867-667-3136, Fax: 867-667-3199,mark.zrum@gov.yk.ca
Director, Communications, Mark Roberts
867-667-5307, Fax: 867-393-7421
Acting Director, Corporate Services, Ross McLachlan
867-456-3960, Fax: 867-456-3965
Director, Energy Solutions Centre, Colin McDowell
867-393-7070, Fax: 867-393-7061
Director, Human Resources, Ingrid Fawcus
867-667-3549, Fax: 867-393-7422
Asst. to the Deputy Minister, Vicki Bailie
867-456-3837, Fax: 867-393-7167

Energy Corporate Policy
Fax: 867-667-8601

Asst. Deputy Minister, Shirley Abercrombie
867-667-5496, Fax: 867-393-7421
Director, Corporate Policy & Planning, John Spicer
867-393-7126, Fax: 867-393-7421
Director, Energy & Resource Policy,Vacant
867-667-5032, Fax: 867-667-8601

Oil & Gas Mineral Resources
Fax: 867-393-6262

Asst. Deputy Minister, Greg Komaromi
867-667-3011, Fax: 867-667-8601
Director, Assessment & Abandoned Mines, Marg Crombie
867-393-7098, Fax: 867-456-6780,marg.crombie@gov.yk.ca
Senior Manager, Faro Project Management Team, Stephen Mead
867-393-6904

Director, Mineral Resources, Bob Holmes
867-667-3126, Fax: 867-456-3899
Executive Director, Oil & Gas Resources, Brian Love
867-667-3566, Fax: 867-393-7046,brian.love@gov.yk.ca
Manager, Oil & Gas Business Development, Ron Sumanik
867-667-5026
Director, Yukon Geological Survey, Carolyn Relf
867-667-8892, Fax: 867-393-6232

Sustainable Resources
Fax: 867-667-8601

Asst. Deputy Minister, Jeff O'Farrell
867-456-3827, Fax: 867-393-6340
Director, Agriculture, Tony Hill
867-667-5838, Fax: 867-939-6222
Director, Forest Management, Diane Reed
867-456-3838, Fax: 867-667-3138
Director, Lands, Lyle Henderson
867-667-5218, Fax: 867-393-6340,lyle.henderson@gov.yk.ca
Director, Dave Beckman
david.beckman@gov.yk.ca

Yukon Environment

PO Box 2703, Whitehorse, YT Y1A 2C6
867-667-5652, Fax: 867-393-7197, 800-661-0408
environmentyukon@gov.yk.ca
www.environmentyukon.gov.yk.ca

The department is responsible for legislation, regulations licensing, management, policies, programs, services, education & information regarding the natural environment in three program areas: fish & wildlife, environmental protection & assessment & parks & protection areas.The department's branches educate resource users & the general public, develop & enforce policies, regulations, & legislation & assist other departments in the sustainable use & management of the territory's natural resources. The department supports land claims negotiations & assists in implementing land claims agreements.The department represents the Yukon government at national & global environmental forums on issues such as climate change & biodiversity conservation.Through the Environmental Awareness Fund the government provides funding to assist registered non-government organizations to promote environmental education or awareness, resource planning & sustainable development in the Yukon.

Acts Administered:
Animal Health Act, (shared with Energy, Mines & Resources)
Environment Act
Environmental Assessment Act
Fresh Water Fisheries Agreement Act
Mackenzie River Basin Agreement Act
Parks & Land Certainty Act
Waters Act, (shared with Energy, Mines & Resources & the Executive Council Office)
Waters Regulation
Wilderness Tourism Licensing Act
Wildlife Act
Yukon River Basin & Alsek River Basin Agreements Act
Minister,Hon. John Edzerza
867-667-5806, Fax: 867-393-6252,john.edzerza@gov.yk.ca
Deputy Minister, Kelvin Leary
867-667-5460, Fax: 867-393-6213,kelvin.leary@gov.yk.ca
Director, Human Resources, Mindy Crayford
867-667-8486, Fax:
867-393-7012,mindy.crayford@gov.yk.ca,
Director, Policy & Planning, Ed Van Randen
867-667-3028, Fax: 867-393-6213,ed.vanranden@gov.yk.ca
Manager, Client Services, Dee Balsam
867-667-5797, Fax: 867-393-7197,dee.balsam@gov.yk.ca

• Alsek Renewable Resource Council
PO Box 2077
Haines Junction, YT Y0B 1L0
867-634-2524 Fax: 867-634-2527
• Carmacks Renewable Resource Council
PO Box 122
Carmacks, YT Y0B 1C0
867-863-6838 Fax: 867-863-6429
carmacksrrc@lscfn.ca
• Dawson District Renewable Resource Council
PO Box 1380
Dawson City, YT Y0B 1G0
867-993-6976 Fax: 867-993-6093
dawsonrrc@yknet.yk.ca
• Mayo District Renewable Resources Council
PO Box 249
Mayo, YT Y0B 1M0
867-996-2942 Fax: 867-996-2948
mayorrc@yknet.yk.ca
• North Yukon Renewable Resources Council
PO Box 80
Old Crow, YT Y0B 1N0
vgrrc@yknet.yk.ca
• Selkirk Renewable Resources Council
PO Box 32
Pelly Crossing, YT Y0B 1P0
867-537-3937 Fax: 867-537-3939
selkirkrre@yknet.yk.ca
• Teslin Renewable Resource Council
PO Box 186
Teslin, YT Y0A 1B0
867-390-2323 Fax: 867-390-2919
teslinrrc@yknet.yk.ca
• Yukon Fish & Wildlife Management Board
106 Main St.
Whitehorse, YT Y1A 5P7
867-667-3754 Fax: 867-393-6947
yfwmbadmin@yknet.yk.ca
www.yfwmb.yk.ca
The Board was established as an independent advisory body under the Umbrella Final Agreement to make recommendations on fish & wildlife management.
• Yukon Land Use Planning Council
#201, 307 Jarvis St.
Whitehorse, YT Y1A 2H3
867-667-7397 Fax: 867-667-4624
ylupc@planyukon.ca
www.planyukon.ca/
The Yukon Land Use Planning Council assists government & Yukon First Nationsto co-ordinate efforts to conduct community based regional land use planning. This planning is necessary to resolve land use & resource conflicts. The plans ensure that use of lands & resources is consistent with social, cultural, economic & environmental values. These plans build upon traditional knowledge & experience of the residents of each region.

Conservation Officer Services
867-667-8005, Fax: 867-393-6206, 800-661-0408
Ronalane.Anderson@gov.yk.ca

The Branch provides environmental education, environmental youth camps & projects, provides hunting, fishing & trapping licences, provides hunter & trapper education, resource management support, wildlife safety for the public & provides enforcement & compliance.
Director, John Russell
867-667-5786, Fax: 867-393-6206
Manager, Enforcement & Compliance, Tony Grabowski
867-667-5115, Fax: 867-393-6206
Manager, Field Operations, Torrie Hunter
867-993-5492

Environmental Programs
867-667-5683, Fax: 867-393-6205, 800-661-0408
envprot@gov.yk.ca

Formed in 1994, the Branch is responsible for development of regulations & standards under the Environment Act & programs associated with everyday waste management, contaminated sites, air quality & pesticides. The Branch is also responsible for monitoring & inspection of permits, spill cleanup & environmental assessments of development project, recycling education & promotion, public education & awareness.
Director, Jon Bowen
867-667-8177, Fax: 867-393-6213
Chief, Water Resources, Kevin McDonnell
867-667-3145, Fax: 867-667-3195
Manager, Environmental Affairs, Randy Lamb
867-667-5409, Fax: 867-667-3641
Manager, Hydrology, Richard Janowicz
867-667-3223
Manager, Monitoring & Inspections, Bryan Levia
867-667-3436, Fax: 867-393-6205,bryan.levia@gov.yk.ca
Manager, Standards & Approvals, Shannon Jensen
867-667-8787, Fax: 867-393-6205
Manager, Water Inspections, Rob Savard
867-667-3227
Manager, Water Quality, Bob Truelson
867-667-3217
Climate Change Coordinator, Johanna Martin
867-633-7971, Fax: 867-456-6124

Fish & Wildlife Branch
867-667-5715, Fax: 867-393-6405,
fish.wildlife@gov.yk.ca

The Branch maintains the ecosystem based on sound management of fish, wildlife & their habitats, preserves the sustainability of fish & wildlife populations, works with First Nations & community relations to preserve & enhance the ecosystem, develops management plans, provides policy & planning, collects, assesses & disseminates natural resource data & provides public education for resource users.
Director, Harvey Jessup
867-667-5715, Fax: 867-393-6405
Biologist, Fisheries Management, Nathan Millar
867-667-5117
Acting Manager, Habitat Programs, Karen Clyde
867-667-5464, Fax: 867-393-6405
Manager, Species Programs, Rob Florkiewicz
867-667-5177, Fax: 867-393-6263
Manager, Habitat Protection, Bruce McLean
867-667-5803, Fax: 867-393-6405

Parks Yukon
867-667-5639, Fax: 867-393-7003, 800-661-0408
yukonparks@gov.yk.ca
www.environmentyukon.gov.yk.ca/parks/parks.html

Director, Erik Val
867-667-5639, Fax: 867-393-6223
Regional Superintendent, Klondike Region, Gordon MacRae
867-993-6850, Fax: 867-993-6548
Regional Superintendent, Kluane Region, George Nassiopoulos
867-634-2026, Fax:
867-634-2435,george.nassiopoulos@gov.yk.ca
Regional Superintendent, Liard Region, Gary Vantell
867-667-5282, Fax: 867-393-6223

Yukon Finance

PO Box 2703, Whitehorse, YT Y1A 2C6
867-667-5343, Fax: 867-393-6217

Acts Administered:
Appropriation Acts
Banking Agency Guarantee Act
Faro Mine Loan Act
Financial Administration Act
Fireweed Fund Act
Fuel Oil Tax Act
Income Tax Act
Insurance Premium Tax Act
Interim Supply Appropriation Acts
Liquor Tax Act
Taxpayer Protection Act
Tobacco Tax Act
Yukon Development Corporation Loan Guarantee Act
Minister,Hon. Dennis Fentie
867-393-7053, Fax: 867-393-6252
Deputy Minister, David Hrycan
867-667-3571, Fax: 867-393-6217
Director, Finance & Administration, Bill Curtis
867-667-5276, Fax: 867-393-6217

Financial Operations & Revenue Services
Fax: 867-393-6217

Acting Asst. Deputy Minister, Clarke Laprarie
867-667-5355, Fax: 867-393-6217
Comptroller, Miko Miyahara
867-667-5375
Acting Director, Financial Systems, Anne-Marie Smith
867-667-5278, Fax: 867-393-6217
Director, Investments & Debt Services, Lisa Pan
867-667-5346
Director, Revenue Services, Gerald Gagnon
867-667-3074, Fax: 867-456-6709

Fiscal Relations & Management Board Secretariat
Fax: 867-393-6355

Director, Budgets,Vacant
867-667-5344, Fax: 867-393-6355
Director, Fiscal Relations, Tim Shoniker
867-667-5303, Fax: 867-393-6355
Director, Management Board Secretariat, Mary Rae Cafferty
867-667-3542

Yukon Health & Social Services

PO Box 2703, Whitehorse, YT Y1A 2C6
867-667-3673, Fax: 867-667-3096, 800-661-0408
hss@gov.yk.ca
www.hss.gov.yk.ca/

Committed to quality health & social services for Yukoners. This is achieved by helping individuals acquire the skills to live responsible, healthy & independent lives; & providing a range of accessible, affordable services that assist individuals, families & communities to reach their full potential.

Acts Administered:
Canadian Blood Agency/Canadian Blood Services Indemnification Act
Canadian Council for Donation & Transplantation Indemnifiction Act
Change of Name Act
Child Care Act
Children's Act
Decision Making, Support & Protection to Adults Act
Health Act
Health Care Insurance Plan Act
Hospital Act
Hospital Insurance Services Act
Intercounty Adoption (Hague Convention) Act
Marriage Act
Mental Health Act

Pioneer Utility Grant Act
Public Health & Safety Act
Rehabilitation Services Act
Seniors' Income Supplement Act
Social Assistance Act
Travel for Medical Treatment Act
Vital Statistics Act
Young Persons Offences Act
Youth Criminal Justice Act (Canada), (shared with Justice)
Yukon Family Services Association Rent Guarantee Act
Minister,Hon. Glenn Hart
867-667-8629, Fax: 867-393-6252
Deputy Minister, Stuart Whitley
867-667-5770, Fax: 867-667-3096
Director, Finance, Systems & Administration, Vacant
867-667-8309, Fax: 867-393-6457
Director, Policy & Program Development, Brian Kitchen
867-667-5688, Fax: 867-667-3096
Director, Human Resources, Bonnie Donnelly
867-667-3031, Fax: 867-393-6900
Director, Communications & Social Marketing, Pat Living
867-667-3673, Fax: 867-667-3096,patricia.living@gov.yk.ca

Yukon Highways & Public Works

PO Box 2703, Whitehorse, YT Y1A 2C6
867-393-7193, Fax: 867-393-6218, 800-661-0408
hpw-info@gov.yk.ca
www.hpw.gov.yk.ca
The Department of Highways & Public Works is responsible for ensuring safe & efficient public highways, airstrips, buildings & information systems.
Acts Administered:
Access to Information & Protection Act
Dangerous Goods Transportation Act
Highways Act
Languages Act
Motor Transport Act
Motor Vehicles Act (shared with Community Services)
Public Printing Act
Minister,Hon. Archie Lang
867-667-8643, Fax: 867-393-7400
Deputy Minister, Mike Johnson
867-667-3732, Fax: 867-393-6218
Asst. Deputy Minister, Corporate Services Branch, Leslie Anderson
867-667-5128, Fax: 867-393-6218
Director, Finance, Jacqueline McBride-Dickson
867-667-5410, Fax: 867-667-8231
Director, Human Resources, Carolyn MacDonald
867-667-5156, Fax: 867-667-3685
Director, Information & Communications Technology, Siegfried Fuchbichler
867-667-3712, Fax: 867-667-5304
Director, Office of French Language Services, Carol Genest
867-667-3735
Director, Policy & Communications, Tim Hierlihy
867-667-5436, Fax: 867-393-6218
• Yukon Motor Transport Board
PO Box 2703
Whitehorse, YT Y1A 2C6
867-667-5782 Fax: 867-393-6408
Laurie.Hrynuik@gov.yk.ca

Property Management Agency

Asst. Deputy Minister, Steven Gasser
867-667-8191, Fax: 867-667-5349
Chief Financial Officer, Faye Doiron
867-667-3706
Director, Facilities Management & Regional Services, Lynn Standing
867-667-3589, Fax: 867-393-7039
Director, Space Planning & Development, Pat Hogan
867-667-3064, Fax: 867-667-5349

Supply Services

Director, Carl Rumscheidt
867-667-5289, Fax: 867-667-2958
Senior Purchasing Officer, Procurement Services, David Knight
867-393-6387, Fax: 867-667-2958
Manager, Fleet Vehicle Agency, Stefan Voswinkel
867-667-5793, Fax: 867-393-6463
Manager, Materiel Management,Vacant
867-667-5459
Manager, Queen's Printer, Jo Pond
867-667-3585, Fax: 867-393-6210

Transportation

Asst. Deputy Minister, Robert Magnuson
867-667-5196, Fax: 867-393-6218
Director, Aviation & Marine Branch, Bill Blahitka
867-634-2440, Fax: 867-634-2131
Acting Director, Transportation Maintenance Branch, Catherine Harwood
867-667-5761, Fax: 867-667-3648
Director, Transportation Engineering, Robin Walsh
867-633-7928, Fax: 867-393-6447
Director, Transport Services Branch, Vern Janz
867-667-5833, Fax: 867-667-5799
Manager, Transportation Planning & Programming, Wally Hidinger
867-633-7930
Acting Manager, Finance & Administration, Allan Campbell
867-667-5902, Fax: 867-667-3648
Acting Manager, Environmental Affairs, Toos Omtzigt
867-633-7929
Manager, Mechanical Operations, Jack Schneider
867-667-5157, Fax: 867-667-3648

Yukon Housing Corporation

410H Jarvis St., Whitehorse, YT Y1A 2H5
867-667-5759, Fax: 867-667-3664, 800-661-0408
ykhouse@housing.yk.ca
www.housing.yk.ca/
Acts Administered:
Government Employee Housing Plan Act
Housing Corporation Act
Housing Development Act
Minister Responsible,Hon. Jim Kenyon
867-667-8628, Fax: 867-393-7400
President & Deputy Minister, Ron Macmillan
867-667-5155, Fax: 867-393-6274
Director, Corporate Policy & Communications, Janet Lecamp
867-667-5865, Fax: 867-393-6404

Yukon Justice

PO Box 2703, Whitehorse, YT Y1A 2C6
867-667-8655, Fax: 867-393-5790,
www.justice.gov.yk.ca
Acts Administered:
Age of Majority Act
Arbitration Act
Auxiliary Police Act
Canadian Charter of Rights & Freedoms (Canada) Act
Choices in Action Act
Collection Act
Condominium Act
Conflict of Laws (Traffic Accidents) Act
Constitutional Questions Act
Consumers Protection Act
Continuing Consolidation of Statutes Act
Contributory Negligence Act
Coroners Act
Corrections Act
Court of Appeal Act
Creditor's Relief Act
Crime Prevention & Victim Services Trust Act
Decision Making, Support & Protection to Adults Act, (shared with Health & Social Services
Defamation Act
Department of Justice Act
Dependant's Relief Act
Devolution of Real Property Act
Distress Act
Electronic Evidence Act
Electronic Registration (Dept. of Public Statutes) Act
Enactment Republication Act
Enduring Power of Attorney Act
Estate Administration Act
Evidence Act
Executions Act
Exemptions Act
Expropriation Act
Family Property & Support Act
Family Violence Prevention Act
Fatal Accidents Act
Fine Option Act
Foreign Arbitral Awards Act
Fraudulent Preferences & Conveyances Act
Frustrated Contracts Act
Garnishee Act
Human Rights Act
Human Tissue Gift Act
Interpretation Act
Interprovincial Subpoena Act
Jails Act
Judicature Act
Jury Act
Land Titles Act
Legal Profession Act
Legal Services Society Act
Limitation of Actions Act
Lord's Day Act
Maintenance Enforcement Act
Married Women's Property Act
Mediation Board Act
Notaries Act
Perpetuities Act
Presumption of Death Act
Public Utilities Act
Reciprocal Enforcement of Judgements Act
Reciprocal Enforcement of Judgements UK Act
Reciprocal Enforcement of Maintenance Orders Act
Recording of Evidence Act
Regulations Act
Small Claims Court Act
Spousal Tort Immunity Abolition Act
Summary Convictions Act
Supreme Court Act
Survival of Actions Act
Survivorship Act
Tenants in Common Act
Territorial Court Act
Territorial Court Judiciary Pension Plan
Torture Prohibition Act
Variation of Trusts Act
Wills Act
Youth Criminal Justice Act (Canada), (shared with Health & Social Services)
Minister,Hon. Marian Horne
867-633-7973, Fax: 867-393-7400
Deputy Minister, Dennis Cooley
867-667-5959, Fax: 867-393-5790
Director, Finance, Systems & Administration, Brigitte Hunter
867-667-5615, Fax: 867-667-5790
Director, Policy, Dan Cable
867-667-3508
Acting Executive Assistant to the Deputy Minister, Charmaine Hall
867-667-5959, Fax: 867-667-5790
• Law Society of Yukon - Executive
#202, 302 Steele St.
Whitehorse, YT Y1A 2C5
867-668-4231 Fax: 867-667-7556
lsy@yknet.yk.ca
www.lawsocietyyukon.com
• Law Society of Yukon - Discipline Committee
#201, 302 Steele St.
Whitehorse, YT Y1A 2C5
867-668-4231 Fax: 867-667-7556
lsy@yknet.yk.ca
www.lawsocietyyukon.com
• Yukon Human Rights Commission
#201, 211 Hawkins St.
Whitehorse, YT Y1A 1X3
867-667-6226 Fax: 867-667-2662 800-661-0535
humanrights@yhrc.yk.ca
www.yhrc.yk.ca
• Yukon Human Rights Panel of Adjudication
#202, 407 Black St.
Whitehorse, YT Y1A 2N2
867-667-5412 Fax: 867-633-6952
• Yukon Judicial Council
PO Box 31222
Whitehorse, YT Y1A 5PT
867-667-5438 Fax: 867-393-6400
• Yukon Law Foundation
#202, 302 Steele St.
Whitehorse, YT Y1A 2C5
867-668-4231 Fax: 867-667-7556
lsy@yknet.yk.ca
www.lawsocietyyukon.com
• Yukon Legal Services Society/Legal Aid
#203, 2131 - 2nd Ave.
Whitehorse, YT Y1A 1C3
867-667-5210 Fax: 867-667-8649
legalaid@yknet.yk.ca
www.legalaid.yk.net
Other Communication: 1-800-661-0408, extension 5210 (Yukon only)
• Yukon Utilities Board
#19, 1114 - 1st Ave.
PO Box 31728
Whitehorse, YT Y1A 6L3
867-667-5058

Community Justice & Public Safety Branch

Asst. Deputy Minister, Robert Riches
867-393-7077, Fax: 867-393-6326
Chief Coroner, Coroner's Service, Sharon Hanley
867-667-5317, Fax: 867-456-6826
Manager, Consumer Services & Registrar, Medical Practitioners; Superintendent, Insurance, Elsie Bagan
867-667-5111

Manager, Corporate Affairs & Registrar, Securities, Richard Roberts
867-667-5225
Acting Manager, Labour Services, Bill Wilcox
867-667-5944

Court Services Branch
Director, Shauna Curtin
867-667-5942, Fax: 867-393-6212
Trial Coordinator, Iris Proctor
867-667-3442, Fax: 867-393-6212
Sheriff, Linda Balcaen
867-667-5365, Fax: 867-393-6212
Registrar, Land Titles, Denise Dollin
867-667-5611, Fax: 867-393-6358
Acting Public Guardian & Trustee, Sue Christianson
867-667-5807, Fax: 867-393-6246

Legal Services Branch
Asst. Deputy Minister, Thomas Ullyett
867-667-3469, Fax: 867-393-6379

Yukon Liquor Corporation

9031 Quartz Rd., Whitehorse, YT Y1A 4P9
867-667-5245, Fax: 867-393-6306,
yukon.liquor@gov.yk.ca
www.ylc.yk.ca

Acts Administered:
Liquor Act
Minister Responsible,Hon. Jim Kenyon
867-667-8628, Fax: 867-393-7400
President, Marc Tremblay
867-667-5155
Vice-President, Virginia Labelle
867-667-5708, Fax: 867-393-6306,virginia.labelle@gov.yk.ca

Yukon Public Service Commission

PO Box 2703, Whitehorse, YT Y1A 2C6
867-667-5252, Fax: 867-667-6705,
www.psc.gov.yk.ca

Acts Administered:
Education Staff Relations Act, (shared with Education)
Public Sector Compensaion Restraint Act
Public Servants Superannuation Act
Public Service Act
Public Service Group Insurance Benefits Plan Act
Public Service Staff Relations Act
Retirement Plan Beneficiaries Act
Minister Responsible,Hon. Patrick Rouble
867-667-8644, Fax: 867-393-7400
Commissioner, Patricia Daws
867-667-5252, Fax: 867-393-6919
Director, Corporate Human Resource Services, Martha Kenney
867-667-5250, Fax: 867-667-5755
Director, Employee Compensation, Terry Kinney
867-667-5251, Fax: 867-667-6705
Director, Finance & Administration, Bonnie Love
867-667-5861, Fax: 867-667-6705
Director, Human Resources Management Systems, Felix Vogt
867-667-8222, Fax: 867-667-6705
Director, Policy, Planning & Communication, Liz McKee
867-667-3537, Fax: 867-667-6705
Director, Staff Development, Cheryl Van Blaricom
867-667-8267, Fax: 867-393-6920
Director, Staff Relations, Megan Slobodin
867-667-5201, Fax: 867-393-6919
Information Analyst, Policy, Planning & Communication, Mary Martin
867-667-8160, Fax: 867-667-6705

Yukon Tourism & Culture

PO Box 2703, Whitehorse, YT Y1A 2C6
867-667-5036, Fax: 867-667-3546,
www.tc.gov.yk.ca/

The department focuses on business, tourism, cultural industries & technology/telecommunications to develop & promote economic capacity & entrepreneurial skills to stimulate economy. The department works with the Yukon's diverse arts communities to foster creativity & quality of life & with heritage interests to preserve & interpret heritage resources.
Acts Administered:
Archives Act
Arts Act
Arts Centre Act
Historical Resources Act
Hotel & Tourist Establishments Act
Scientists & Explorers Act

Minister,Hon. Elaine Taylor
867-667-8641, Fax: 867-393-6252
Deputy Minister, Sally Sheppard
867-667-5430, Fax: 867-667-8844
Acting Director, Cultural Services, Ian Burnett
867-667-8592, Fax: 867-393-6456
Director, Corporate Services, Lucy Coulthard
867-667-3009, Fax: 867-667-8844
Director, Policy & Communications, Jonathan Parker
867-667-3016, Fax: 867-667-8844
Director, Tourism Branch, Pierre Germain
867-667-3087, Fax: 867-667-3546
Yukon Archaeologist, Ruth Gotthardt
867-667-5983, Fax: 867-667-5377
Yukon Paleontologist, Grant Zazula
867-667-8089
Territorial Archivist, Lesley Buchan
867-667-5275, Fax: 867-393-6253
Executive Assistant, Shannon Van Bibber
867-667-5430, Fax: 867-667-8844

Yukon Women's Directorate

PO Box 2703, Whitehorse, YT Y1A 2C6
867-667-3030, Fax: 867-393-6270,
www.womensdirectorate.gov.yk.ca

Acts Administered:
Yukon Advisory Council on Women's Issues Act
Minister Responsible,Hon. Marian Horne
867-633-7973, Fax: 867-393-7400
Director, Jennifer England
867-667-5182, jennifer.england@gov.yk.ca
Manager, Administration & Finance, Lorie Larose
867-667-3030, Fax: 867-393-6270,lorie.larose@gov.yk.ca

Yukon Workers' Compensation Health & Safety Board (YWCHSB)

401 Strickland St., Whitehorse, YT Y1A 5N8
867-667-5645, Fax: 867-393-6279, 800-661-0443
worksafe@gov.yk.ca
wcb.yk.ca/

The Yukon Workers' Compensation Health and Safety Board (YWCHSB) administers workers' compensation and occupational health and safety in the Yukon.
Acts Administered:
Day of Mourning for Victims of Workplace Injuries Act
Occupational Health & Safety Act
Spousal Compensation Act
Worker's Compensation Act
Minister Responsible,Hon. Glenn Hart
867-667-8629, Fax: 867-393-6252,glenn.hart@gov.yk.ca
President/CEO, Valerie Royle
867-667-5975, Fax: 867-393-6419,valerie.royle@gov.yk.ca
Vice-President, Operations & CFO, Jim Stephens
867-667-8210, Fax: 867-393-6279,jim.stephens@gov.yk.ca
Director, Social Marketing & Communications, Mark Hill
867-667-8695, Fax: 867-393-6279,mark.hill@gov.yk.ca

The Queen & Royal Family

The House of Windsor

In 1917 the late King George V, by Proclamation, changed the House name of the Royal Family from Saxe-Coburg-Gotha to the House of Windsor.

THE QUEEN. - Elizabeth the Second, (Elizabeth Alexandra Mary, of Windsor) by the Grace of God, of the United Kingdom, Canada and Her other Realms and Territories Queen; Head of the Commonwealth, Defender of the Faith, Succeeded to the throne February 6th, 1952 , and was crowned June 2nd, 1953, at Westminster Abbey. Her Majesty, the elder daughter of the late King George VI and Queen Elizabeth The Queen Mother, was born at 17 Bruton St., London, W.1, on April 21st, 1926, married November 20th, 1947, H.R.H. The Prince Philip, Duke of Edinburgh, K.G., K.T., O.M., G.B.E., A.C., Q.S.O.

THE CHILDREN of Queen Elizabeth and H.R.H. The Prince Philip, Duke of Edinburgh are:

H.R.H. Prince Charles Philip Arthur George, Prince of Wales and Earl of Chester, Duke of Cornwall and Duke of Rothesay, Earl of Carrick and Baron Renfrew, Lord of the Isles, and Great Steward of Scotland, K.G., K.T., G.C.B., O.M., A.K., Q.S.O., A.D.C., born November 14th, 1948. Married July 29th, 1981. Marriage dissolved 1996. The Lady Diana Spencer (died August 31st, 1997) and has issue. Prince William of Wales, born June 21st, 1982 and Prince Henry of Wales, born September 15th, 1984. Married April 9th, 2005 Mrs. Camilla Parker Bowles (H.R.H. The Duchess of Cornwall).

H.R.H. The Princess Royal, Anne Elizabeth Alice Louise, K.G., K.T., G.C.V.O., Q.S.O., born August 15th, 1950. Married 1st November 14th, 1973 Captain Mark Anthony Peter Phillips, C.V.O., A.D.C. and has issue. Peter Phillips born November 15th, 1977 and Zara Phillips born May 15th, 1981. Marriage dissolved 1992. Married 2nd December 12th, 1993 Commodore Timothy James Hamilton Laurence, M.V.O., R.N.

H.R.H. The Prince Andrew Albert Christian Edward, K.C.V.O., A.D.C., Duke of York, Earl of Inverness and Baron Killyleagh, born February 19th, 1960, married July 23rd, 1986 Miss Sarah Margaret Ferguson and has issue, Princess Beatrice of York, born August 8th, 1988, and Princess Eugenie of York, born March 23rd, 1990. Marriage dissolved 1996.

H.R.H. The Prince Edward Antony Richard Louis, K.C.V.O., Earl of Wessex, and Viscount Severn, born March 10th, 1964, married June 19, 1999 Miss Sophie Rhys-Jones.

THE LATE GEORGE VI. - George VI succeeded to the Throne December 11th, 1936; and was crowned at Westminster Abbey, May 12th, 1937. Second son of King George V and Queen Mary, he was born at York Cottage, Sandringham, on December 14th, 1895, married, April 26th, 1923, Lady Elizabeth Bowes-Lyon, daughter of the Earl and Countess of Strathmore and Kinghorne. As Heir Presumptive succeeded to the Throne on the abdication of Edward VIII.

QUEEN ELIZABETH, THE QUEEN MOTHER - born August 4th, 1900, daughter of the 14th Earl of Strathmore and Kinghorne; married, April 26th, 1923. Died March 30th, 2002.

THE ISSUE of the late King George VI and Queen Elizabeth are:

The reigning Sovereign, Elizabeth the Second (elder daughter).

The Princess Margaret (Rose), Countess of Snowdon, C.I., G.C.V.O., born August 21st, 1930, married Antony Charles Robert Armstrong-Jones, G.C.V.O., (since created Earl of Snowdon) May 6th, 1960, and has issue, Viscount Linley, born November 3rd, 1961 and the Lady Sarah Frances Elizabeth Armstrong-Jones, born May 1st, 1964. Marriage dissolved 1978. Died February 9th, 2002.

SUCCESSION-The order stands:

The Prince of Wales
Prince William of Wales
Prince Henry of Wales
The Duke of York
Princess Beatrice of York
Princess Eugenie of York
The Earl of Wessex
The Lady Louise Mountbatten-Windsor
The Princess Royal
Mr. Peter Phillips
Miss Zara Phillips
Viscount Linley
The Hon. Charles Armstrong-Jones
The Hon. Margarita Armstrong-Jones
The Lady Sarah Chatto
Master Samuel Chatto
Master Arthur Chatto
The Duke of Gloucester
Earl of Ulster
The Lady Davina Windsor
The Lady Rose Windsor
The Duke of Kent
The Lady Marina Charlotte Windsor
The Lady Amelia Windsor
The Lady Helen Taylor
Master Columbus Taylor
Master Cassius Taylor
Miss Eloise Taylor
The Lord Frederick Windsor
The Lady Gabriella Windsor
Princess Alexandra, The Hon. Lady Ogilvy
Mr. James Ogilvy
Master Alexander Ogilvy
Miss Flora Ogilvy
Mrs. Paul Mowatt
Master Christian Mowatt
Miss Zenouska Mowatt
The Earl of Harewood

NOTES

1. The Sucession is governed by the Act of Settlement 1701 (12 & 13 Will 3 c 2) which limits the succession to the Throne to the heirs, being Protestants, of Princess Sophia of Hanover, granddaughter of King James I. Section 6 (4) of the Legitimacy Act of 1959 (ôNothing in this Act affects the succession to the Throneö) is also relevant.
2. Earl of St. Andrews & Prince Michael of Kent were excluded from the succession to the Throne on marriage to Roman Catholics, & Lord Downpatrick & the Lord Nicholas Windsor on conversion to Roman Catholicism.

HER MAJESTY'S HOUSEHOLD

Lord Chamberlain, The Lord Luce, G.C.V.O.
Private Secretary to The Queen, The Rt. Hon. Sir Robin Janvrin, K.C.V.O., K.C.B.
The Lord Chamberlain has the general supervision of the Royal Household.

The Commonwealth

The Commonwealth is a voluntary association of 53 independent member countries representing 1.8 billion people around the world - in Africa, the Americas, Asia, the Caribbean, Europe & the Pacific. It promotes good governance, democracy, sustainable economic & social development, the rule of law & human rights. These & other principles are enshrined in the Harare Commonwealth Declaration of 1991.

There are three principal international organizations of the Commonwealth:

THE COMMONWEALTH SECRETARIAT

Marlborough House, Pall Mall, London SW1Y 5HX, +44 (0)20 7747 6500; Fax: +44 (0)20 7930 0827, Email: info@commonwealth.int, URL: www.thecommonwealth.org
Rt. Hon. Donald C. McKinnon (New Zealand), Commonwealth Secretary-General
Florence Mugasha, Commonwealth Deputy Secretary-General
Ransford Smith, Commonwealth Deputy Secretary-General
Winston Cox, Commonwealth Deputy Secretary-General (Development Co-operation)
Joel Kibazo, Official Spokesperson, Director, Communicaitons & Public Affairs
For information pertaining to the Commonwealth write to: The Director, Information Public Affairs Division, Commonwealth Secretariat, Marlborough House, Pall Mall, London SW1Y 5HX, U.K.

THE COMMONWEALTH FOUNDATION

Marlborough House, Pall Mall, London SW1Y 5HY, +44 (0)20 7830 3783; Fax: +44 (0)20 7839 8157, Email: geninfo@commonwealth.int, URL: www.commonwealthfoundation.com

THE COMMONWEALTH OF LEARNING (COL)

#1200-1055 West Hastings, Vancouver BC V6E 2E9, 604/775-8200; Fax: 604/775-8210, Email: info@ col.org, URL: www.col.org
The Commonwealth of Learning's focus is in strengthening institutions in developing Commonwealth countries that are striving to provide affordable education to larger numbers of their citizens.

Member States

(showing capital, population (2003) & date of membership. Dates for Australia, Canada & New Zealand are those on which Dominion Status was acquired):

Antigua & Barbuda - St. John's; 73,000; Nov. 1, 1981
Australia - Canberra; 19,731,000; Jan. 1, 1901
- External territories: Norfolk Island, Coral Sea Islands Territory, Australian Antarctic Territory, Heard Island & McDonald Islands, Cocos (Keeling) Islands, Christmas Island, Territory of Ashmore & Cartier Islands

The Bahamas - Nassau; 340,000; July 10, 1973
Bangladesh - Dhaka; 143,736,000; Mar. 26, 1972
Barbados - Bridgetown; 270,000; Nov. 30, 1966
Belize - Belmopan; 256,000; Sept. 21, 1981
Botswana - Gaborone; 1,785,000; Sept. 30, 1966
Brunei Darussalam - Bandar Seri Begawan; 358,000; Feb. 23, 1984
Cameroon - Yaoundé; 16,018,000; May 20, 1995
Canada - Ottawa; 31,510,000; July 1, 1867
Cyprus - Nicosia; 802,000; Oct. 1, 1961
Dominica - Roseau; 79,000; Nov. 3, 1978
Fiji Islands - Suva; 839,000; Oct. 10, 1997 N.B. Fiji Islands was suspended from the councils of the Commonwealth in May 2000 following the overthrow of its democratically elected government.
The Gambia - Banjul; 1,426,000; Feb. 18, 1965
Ghana - Accra; 20,922,000; Mar. 6, 1957
Grenada - St. George's; 80,000; Feb. 7, 1974
Guyana - Georgetown; 765,000; Feb. 23, 1966
India - New Delhi; 1,065,426,000; Jan. 26, 1947
Jamaica - Kingston; 2,651,000; Aug. 6, 1962
Kenya - Nairobi; 31,987,000; Dec. 12, 1963
Kiribati - Tarawa; 88,000; July 12, 1979
Lesotho - Maseru; 1,802,000; Oct. 4, 1966
Malawi - Lilongwe; 12,105,000; July 6, 1964
Malaysia - Kuala Lumpur; 24,425,000; Aug. 31, 1957
Maldives - Malé; 318,000; July 26, 1982
Malta - Valletta; 394,000; Mar. 31, 1964
Mauritius - Port Louis; 1,221,000; Mar. 12, 1968
Mozambique - Maputo; 18,863,000; June 25, 1995
Namibia - Windhoek; 1,987,000; Mar. 21, 1990
Nauru - Nauru; 13,000; Jan. 31, 1968 [Special Member as of July 1, 2005]
New Zealand - Wellington; 3,875,000; Sept. 26, 1907 - Includes the territories of Tokelau & the Ross Dependency (Antarctic). Self-governing countries in free association with New Zealand: Cook Islands & Niue.
Nigeria - Abuja; 124,009,000; Oct. 1, 1960
Pakistan - Islamabad; 153,578,000; Mar. 23, 1989 (previously member 1947-1972; rejoined in 1989) N.B. Pakistan was suspended from participation in the councils of the Commonwealth in October1999 following a military coup.
Papua New Guinea - Port Moresby; 5,711,000; Sept. 16, 1975
St. Kitts & Nevis - Basseterre; 42,000; Sept. 19, 1983
St. Lucia - Castries; 149,000; Feb. 22, 1979
St. Vincent & The Grenadines - Kingstown; 120,000; Oct. 27, 1979
Samoa - Apia; 178,000; June 1, 1970
Seychelles - Victoria; 81,000; June 18, 1976
Sierra Leone - Freetown; 4,971,000; Apr. 27, 1961
Singapore - Singapore; 4,253,000; Aug. 9, 1965
Solomon Islands - Honiara; 477,000 (2001); July 7, 1978
South Africa - Pretoria; 45,026,000; 1931 - Left Commonwealth 1961, rejoined 1994
Sri Lanka - Colombo; 19,065,000; Feb. 4, 1948
Swaziland - Mbabane; 1,077,000; Sept. 6, 1968
Tonga - Nuku'alofa; 104,000; June 4, 1970
Trinidad & Tobago - Port of Spain; 1,303,000; Aug. 31, 1962
Tuvalu - Funafuti; 11,000; Oct. 1, 1978
Uganda - Kampala; 25,827,000; Oct. 9, 1962
United Kingdom- London; 59,251,000
- Overseas territories: Anguilla, Bermuda, British Antarctic Territory, British Indian Ocean Territory, British Virgin Islands, Cayman Islands, Falkland Islands, Gibraltar, Montserrat, Pitcairn, Henderson, Ducie & Oeno Islands, St. Helena & St. Helena Dependencies (Ascension & Tristan da Cunha), South Georgia & the South Sandwich Islands, & Turks & Caicos Islands

United Republic of Tanzania - Dar es Salaam; 36,977,000; Dec. 9, 1961
Vanuatu - Port Vila; 212,000; July 30, 1980
Zambia - Lusaka; 10,812,000; Oct. 24, 1964

La Francophonie

ORGANISATION INTERNATIONALE DE LA FRANCOPHONIE

Secrétariat général, 28, rue de Bourgogne, 75007 Paris, France 1- 44-11-12-50; Téléc: 1-44-11-12-80; URL: www.francophonie.org

Member States

(showing member name, population, national holiday):

Albanie (République d'), 3,100 M, 11 janvier et 28 novembre
Andorre (Principauté), 0,078 M, 8 septembre
Belgique (Royaume de), 10,400 M, 21 juillet
Bénin (République du), 8,400 M, 1er août
Bulgarie (République de), 7,700 M, 3 mars
Burkina Faso, 13,200 M, 11 décembre
Burundi (République du), 7,500 M, 1er juillet
Cambodge (Royaume du), 14,100 M, 7 janvier - 17 avril
Cameroun (République du), 16,300 M, 20 mai
Canada, 32,300 M, 1er juillet
Canada - Nouveau-Brunswick (Province du), 0,730 M, 15 août
Canada - Québec (Province du), 7,500 M, 24 juin
Cap-Vert (République du), 0,400 M, 5 juillet

Centrafricaine (République), 4 M, 1er décembre
Communauté française de Belgique (Wallonie-Bruxelles), 4 M, 27 septembre
Comores (Union des), 0,558 M, 6 juillet
Congo (République du), 4 M, 15 août
Congo (République démocratique du Congo), 57,500 M, 30 juin
Côte d'Ivoire (République de), 18,200 M, 7 août
Djibouti (République de), 0,632 M, 27 juin
Dominique (Commonwealth de la), 0,730 M, 3 novembre
Égypte (République arabe d'), 74,000 M, 23 juillet
France (République française), 62 M, 14 juillet
Gabon (République gabonaise), 1,400 M, 17 août
Grèce, 11,100 M, 25 mars
Guinée (République de), 9,400 M, 2 octobre
Guinée-Bissau (République de), 1,600 M, 24 septembre
Guinée-équatoriale (République de), 0,457 M, 12 octobre
Haïti (République d'), 8,500 M, 1er janvier
Laos (République démocratique populaire Lao), 5,900 M, 2 décembre
Liban (République libanaise), 3,600 M, 22 novembre
Luxembourg (Grand-Duché de), 0,438 M, 23 juin
Macédonie (ARY), 2 M, 8 septembre
Madagascar (République de), 18,600 M, 26 juin
Mali (République du), 13,500 M, 22 septembre
Maroc (Royaume du), 31,500 M, 30 juillet
Maurice (République de), 1,200 M, 12 mars
Mauritanie (République islamique de), 3,100 M, 28 novembre
Moldavie, 4,200 M, 27 août
Monaco (Principauté de), 0,032 M, 19 novembre
Niger (République du), 14 M, 18 décembre
Roumanie, 21,700 M, 1er décembre
Rwanda (République rwandaise), 9 M, 1er juillet
Sainte-Lucie, 0,156 M, 22 février
Sao Tomé et Principe (République démocratique de), 0,148 M, 12 juillet
Sénégal (République du), 11,700 M, 4 avril
Seychelles (République des), 0,081 M, 18 juin
Suisse (Confédération), 7,300 M, 1er août
Tchad (République du), 9,700 M, 11 janvier
Togo (République du), 6,100 M, 13 janvier et 27 avril
Tunisie (République tunisienne), 10,100 M, 20 mars
Vanuatu (République de), 0,197 M, 30 juillet
Vietnam (République socialiste du), 84,200 M, 2 septembre

Canadian Permanent Missions Abroad

Canadian Joint Delegation to NATO (North Atlantic Treaty Organization)
Léopold III Blvd., Brussels, 1110 Belgium
322-707-5041, Fax: 322-707-5057
natocanada@dfait-maeci.gc.ca
www.dfaitmaeci.gc.ca/foreign _policy/nato/canada_natoen.asp
Jean-Pierre Juneau, Ambassador & Permanent Representative of Canada
Vice-Admiral Glenn Davidson, Military Representative of Canada CMM, CD

Mission of Canada to the European Union, Brussels
2, av de Tervuren, Brussels, 1040 Belgium
322-741-06-60, Fax: 322-741-06-29
annie.bollaert@international.gc.ca
www.dfait-maeci.gc.ca/canada-europa/E U
Jeremy K.B. Kinsman, Ambassador
Kevin D. O'Shea, Deputy Head of Mission
Denis Robert, Counsellor & Sec. Head, Pol. Affairs, Foreign & Sec. Policy

NORAD (North American Aerospace Defense Command)
NORAD Public Affairs, Peterson AFB, #B-016, 250 Vandenberg, Colorado Springs, 80914-3808 USA
719-554-6889
noradpa@norad.mil
www.norad.mil
Timothy J. Keating, Commander, Adm. USN
Eric A. Findley, Deputy Commander-in-Chief, Lt. Gen. Cdn. Forces CMM, CD, Ph.D.

Organization for Economic Cooperation & Development
2, rue André Pascal, Paris, F-75775 France
331-45-24-82-00, Fax: 331-45-24-85-00
webmaster@oecd.org
www.oecd.org
Angel Gurria, Secretary-General

Permanent Mission of Canada to the Organization of American States
501 Pennsylvania Ave. NW, Washington, DC 20001 USA
202-682-1768, Fax: 202-682-7264
wshdc-prmoas@dfait-maeci.gc.ca
www.dfaitmaeci.gc.ca/latin-america/latina merica
Paul Durand, Permanent Representative of Canada

UN: Permanent Delegation of Canada to the UN Educational, Scientific & Cultural Organization
UNESCO, 1, rue Mollis, Paris, 75732 France
331-45-68-35-17, Fax: 331-43-06-87-27
pesco@international.gc.ca
www.dfait-maeci.gc.ca/canada_un/paris/
Yvon Charbonneau, Ambassador & Permanent Delegate

UN: Permanent Mission of Canada to the Food & Agriculture Organization (FAO)
FAO, Via Zara 30, Rome, 00198 Italy
39-06-854-441, Fax: 39-06-85444-2930
fao-hq@fao.org
www.fao.org
Robert R. Fowler, Permanent Representative
J. Melanson, Deputy Permanent Representative
K. McKinley, Alternate Permanent Representative

UN: Permanent Mission of Canada to the International Civil Aviation Organization
ICAO, #1535, 999, rue Université, Montréal, QC H3C 5J9 Canada
514-954-5800, Fax: 514-954-5809
icaohq@icao.int
www.icao.int

UN: Permanent Mission of Canada to the International Organizations in Vienna
Laurenzerberg 2, Vienna, A-1010 Austria
431-531-38-3000, Fax: 431-531-38-3915
vosce@international.gc.ca
www.international.gc.ca/world/embassies/mission-en.asp?MID=239
Ingrid Hall, Permanent Representative & Ambassador
LCol. A. Sevigny, Military Adviser

UN: Permanent Mission of Canada to the Office of the UN, The Conference on Disarmement
5, av de l'Ariana, Geneva, 1202 Switzerland
41-22-919-9200, Fax: 41-22-919-9233
genev@dfait-maeci.gc.ca
www.dfait-maeci.gc.ca/geneva
Hon. Don Stephenson, Permanent Representative & Ambassador
Paul Meyer, Alternate Permanent Representative & Ambassador

UN: Permanent Mission of Canada to the United Nations
One Dag Hammarskjold Plaza, 885 Second Ave., 14th Fl., New York, NY 10017 USA
212-848-1100, Fax: 212-848-1195
prmny@international.gc.ca
www.dfait-maeci.gc.ca/canada_un/new_york/about/
John McNee, Permanent Representative, Ambassador

UN: Permanent Mission of Canada to the United Nations Centre for Human Settlements (Habitat)
PO Box, Nairobi, 00621 Kenya
254-20-366-3000, Fax: 254-20-366-3900
nrobi@international.gc.ca
www.dfait-maeci.gc.ca/world/embassies/mission-en.asp?MID=92
James Wall, Permanent Representative
B. Liddar, Deputy Permanent Representative
L. Hindle, Second Secretary

UN: Permanent Mission of Canada to the United Nations Environment Program
PO Box, Nairobi, 00621 Kenya
254-20-366-3000, Fax: 254-20-366-3900
nrobi@international.gc.ca
www.unep.org
James Wall, Permanent Representative
B. Liddar, Deputy Permanent Representative

Diplomatic & Consular Representatives in Canada

Islamic State of Afghanistan
240 Argyle Ave., Ottawa, ON K2P 1B9
613-563-4223, Fax: 613-563-4962,
Seddiqullah Habibi, Second Secretary
His Excellency Jawed Ludin, Ambassador
Mehrabodin Masstan, Counsellor
Mirwais Salehi, Third Secretary

Republic of Albania
Embassy of Albania (to Canada), #302, 130 Albert St., Ottawa, ON K1P 5G4
613-236-4114, Fax: 613-236-0804,
embassyrepublicofalbania@on.aibn.com
His Excellency Besnik Konci, Ambassador
Fatbardha Kola, First Secretary

People's Democratic Republic of Algeria
Embassy of Algeria, 500 Wilbrod St., Ottawa, ON K1N 6N2
613-789-8505, Fax: 613-789-1406,
www.ambalgott.com
Redhouane Malek, Counsellor
Nadia Lamrani, First Secretary
Mohamed Reza Louzouaz, Attaché
Abbesed Benoussat, Minister-Counsellor
Alil Alaoui, Counsellor
His Excellency Smail Benamara, Ambassador

Argentina
Embassy of the Argentine Republic, 81 Metcalfe St., 7th Fl., Ottawa, ON K1P 6K7
613-236-2351, Fax: 613-235-2659,
embargentina@argentina-canada.net
www.argentina-canada.net
Maria Cristina Tosonotti, Counsellor
His Excellency Arturo G. Bothamley, Ambassador
Ricardo Fernando Fernandez, Minister
Luis Fernando Del Solar Dorrego, Counsellor

Commonwealth of Australia
Australian High Commission, #710, 50 O'Connor St., Ottawa, ON K1P 6L2
613-236-0841, Fax: 613-236-4376,
Lt.Col. Lyndon Anderson, Defence Advisor
Wendy Walsh, First Secretary
Caroline Jane Linke, First Secretary
Glenda Price, Second Secretary
Christine Florence Franço Pearce, First Secretary, Immigration
Jo-Anne Lorraine Hardie, First Secretary & Consul
His Excellency Justin Hugh Brown, High Commissioner
Martin Anthony Huber, Counsellor & Deputy High Commissioner

Republic of Austria
Embassy of Austria, 445 Wilbrod St., Ottawa, ON K1N 6M7
613-789-1444, Fax: 613-789-3431,
ottawa-ob@bmaa.gv.at
www.austro.org
Maria Unger, Third Secretary & Vice-Consul, Administrative Affairs
Sigurd Pacher, Minister-Counsellor
His Excellency Werner Brandstetter, Ambassador

Republic of Azerbaijan
Embassy of Azerbaijan (to Canada), #904, 275 Slater St., Ottawa, ON K1P 5H9
613-288-0497, Fax: 613-230-8089,
azerbaijan@azembassy.ca
www.azembassy.ca
Farid Shafiyev, Counsellor
Orkhan Hajiyev, Third Secretary & Consul, Legal Affairs
Jeyhun Shahverdiyev, Third Secretary, Economic & Political Affairs
His Excellency Fakhraddin Gurbanov, Ambassador

Commonwealth of The Bahamas
High Commission for the Commonwealth of The Bahamas, #1313, 50 O'Connor St., Ottawa, ON K1P 6L2
613-232-1724, Fax: 613-232-0097,
ottawa-mission@bahighco.com
www.bahamas.gov.bs
Donald M. McCartney, Counsellor & Consul
Kerry Bonamy, Second Secretary & Vice-Consul
His Excellency Michael Douglas Smith, High Commissioner

Kingdom of Bahrain
Embassy of Bahrain (to Canada), 3502 International Dr. NW, Washington, DC 20008 USA
202-342-0741, Fax: 202-362-2192,
Her Excellency Huda Ezra Ebrahim Nonoo, Ambassador

People's Republic of Bangladesh
Bangladesh High Commission, #1250, 340 Albert St., Ottawa, ON K1R 7Y6
613-236-0138, Fax: 613-567-3213,
bang@bellnet.ca
www.bdhc.org
Abu Saleb Md. Mamunur R. Khalili, Ckounsellor, Commercial
Syed Masud Mahmood Khundoker, Counsellor
Fawzia Nahar Islam, First Secretary
Mohammed Erfan Sharif, First Secretary
His Excellency A.M. Yakub Ali, High Commissioner

Barbados
High Commission for Barbados, #470, 55 Metcalfe St., Ottawa, ON K1P 6L5
613-236-9517, Fax: 613-230-4362, ottawa@foreign.gov.bb
Estuko Anderson, Counsellor
His Excellency Edward E. Greaves, High Commissioner
Natalie Cox, First Secretary

Kingdom of Belgium
#820, 360 Albert St., Ottawa, ON K1R 7X7
613-236-7267, Fax: 613-236-7882, ottawa@diplobel.org
www.diplomatie.be/ottawa
Robert S.J.G. Gernay, Minister-Counsellor
His Excellency Jean L.A. Lint, Ambassador

Belize
High Commission for Belize, 2535 Massachusetts Ave. NW, Washington, DC 20008 USA
202-332-9636, Fax: 202-332-6888, hcbelize@bellnet.ca
Vacant, High Commissioner

Republic of Benin
Embassy of Benin, 58 Glebe Ave., Ottawa, ON K1S 2C3
613-233-4429, Fax: 613-233-8952, ambaben2@on.aira.com
www.benin.ca
Awahou Labouda, Minister-Counsellor & Chargé d'Affaires
Laure Regina Vignon Codo, Second Counsellor
His Excellency Honoré Théodore Ahimakin, Ambassador

Bhutan
Royal Bhutanese Embassy, 763 United Nations Plaza, 1st Ave., New York, NY 10017 USA
212-682-2268, Fax: 212-661-0551,
His Excellency Lhatu Wangchuk, Ambassador
Tshering Gyaltshen Penjor, First Secretary

Republic of Bolivia
Embassy of Bolivia, #416, 130 Albert St., Ottawa, ON K1P 5G4
613-236-5730, Fax: 613-236-8237, bolivianembassy@bellnet.ca
Virginia de la Quintana, Counsellor
Juan Garrett Kent, First Secretary
His Excellency Edgar Jose Torrez Mosqueira, Ambassador

Bosnia & Herzegovina
#805, 130 Albert St., Ottawa, ON K1P 5G4
613-236-0028, Fax: 613-236-1139, embassyofbih@bellnet.ca
www.bhembassy.ca
His Excellency Mithat Pasic, Ambassador

Republic of Botswana
High Commission for Botswana (to Canada): c/o Republic of Botswana, 1531 - 1533 New Hampshire Ave. NW, Washington, DC 20036 USA
202-244-4990, Fax: 202-244-4164,
www.botswanaembassy.org
Herold Caspar Luke, Second Secretary
His Excellency Lapologang Lekoa, High Commissioner
Lt.Col. Jeremiah Therego, Defence Attaché

Federative Republic of Brazil
Embassy of Brazil, 450 Wilbrod St., Ottawa, ON K1N 6M8
613-237-1090, Fax: 613-237-6144, mailbox@brasembottawa.org
www.brasembottawa.org
Ivanise de Melo Maciel, First Secretary
Celso de Tarso Pereira, First Secretary
Norberto Moretti, First Secretary
His Excellency Paolo Corderio de Andrade Pinto, Ambassador
Pedro Murilo Ortega Terra, Counsellor

Brunei Darussalam
High Commission of Brunei Darussalam, 395 Laurier Ave. East, Ottawa, ON K1N 6R4
613-234-5656, Fax: 613-234-4397, bhco@bellnet.ca
Faizal Bahrin Haji Bakri, Second Secretary
Haji Mursidi Bin Haji Setia, Third Secretary
Her Excellency Rakiah Hj Abd Lamit, High Commissioner

Republic of Bulgaria
Embassy of the Republic of Bulgaria, 325 Stewart St., Ottawa, ON K1N 6K5
613-789-3215, Fax: 613-789-3524, mailmn@storm.ca
Dimiter Dimitrov, Minister & Chargé d'Affaires
Galina Genova Bachvarova, Third Secretary
His Excellency Evgueni Stefanov Stoytchev, Ambassador

Burkina-Faso
Embassy of Burkina-Faso, 48 Range Rd., Ottawa, ON K1N 8J4
613-238-4796, Fax: 613-238-3812, burkina.faso@sympatico.ca
Fatimata Diallo, Counsellor, Economic & Commercial Affairs
Charles Karosy Bamouni, First Counsellor
Her Excellency Juliette Bonkoungou Yameogo, Ambassador

Republic of Burundi
Embassy of Burundi, #815, 325 Dalhousie St., Ottawa, ON K1N 7G2
613-789-0414, Fax: 613-789-9537, ambabucanada@infonet.ca
Pascal Kamo, First Counsellor
Her Excellency Appolonie Simbizi, Ambassador

Republic of Cameroon
Cameroon High Commission, 170 Clemow Ave., Ottawa, ON K1S 2B4
613-236-1522, Fax: 613-236-3885, cameroun@rogers.com
His Excellency Solomon Azoh-Mbi Anu'A-Gheyle, High Commissioner
Jean Bosco Etoa Etoa, Counsellor, Cultural Affairs
Labarang Abdoullahi, First Secretary
Joseph Pipimae Ayafor, First Secretary, Administration & Consular Affairs

Republic of Cape Verde
Embassy of Cape Verde (to Canada), 3415 Massachusetts Ave. NW, Washington, DC 20007 USA
202-965-6820, Fax: 202-965-1207, cveisabel@caboverdeus.net
www.virtualcapeverde.net
Maria Semedo, Second Secretary
Emanuel Duarte, Chargé d'Affaires
Her Excellency Maria de Fátima Lima de Veiga, Ambassador

Central African Republic
Embassy of Central African Republic (to Canada), 1618 - 22nd St. NW, Washington, DC 20008 USA
202-483-7800, Fax: 202-332-9893,
Vacant, Ambassador

Republic of Chad
Embassy of Chad (to Canada), 2002 R St. NW, Washington, DC 20009 USA
202-462-4009, Fax: 202-265-1937, info@chadembassy.org
www.chadembassy-usa.org
His Excellency Adam Bechir Mahamoud, Ambassador

Republic of Chile
Embassy of Chile, #1413, 50 O'Connor St., Ottawa, ON K1P 6L2
613-235-4402, Fax: 613-235-1176, echileca@chile.ca
www.chile.ca
Fidel Coloma Grimberg, First Secretary
Annemarie Duncker, Third Secretary & Consul
His Excellency Eugenio Luis Ortega Riquelme, Ambassador
Eduardo Tapia, Minister-Counsellor

People's Republic of China
Embassy of China, 515 St. Patrick St., Ottawa, ON K1N 5H3
613-789-3434, Fax: 613-789-1911,
www.chinaembassycanada.org
Yuansong Jiang, Counsellor & Consul General
Huikang Huang, Minister-Counsellor & Deputy Head of Mission
Shuyun Shi, Minister-Counsellor
Xuelun Yang, Counsellor
Lushan Sun, Counsellor
Yongyue Hyang, Counsellor
Weidong Zhang, Minister-Counsellor
Guosheng Liu, Minister-Counsellor
His Excellency Lijun Lan, Ambassador

Republic of Colombia
Embassy of Colombia, #1002, 360 Albert St., Ottawa, ON K1R 7X7
613-230-3760, Fax: 613-230-4416, embajada@embajadacolombia.ca
www.embajadacolombia.ca
Rafael Arismendy, First Secretary, Consular Affairs
His Excellency Jaime Giron Duarte, Ambassador
Guillermo Mejia, Minister-Counsellor

Commonwealth of Dominica
See: Organization of the Eastern Caribbean Stat

Republic of the Congo
Embassy of the Congo (to Canada), 4891 Colorado Ave. NW, Washington, DC 20011 USA
202-726-5500, Fax: 202-726-1860,
Jean-Christophe Lingoua, First Secretary
Henri Blaise Gotienne, Minister-Counsellor
Albert Ondongo, Second Secretary
His Excellency Serge Mombouli, Ambassador

Republic of Costa Rica
Embassy of Costa Rica, #407, 325 Dalhousie St., Ottawa, ON K1N 7G2
613-562-2855, Fax: 613-562-2582,
Ana Matilde Rivera Figueroa, Counsellor
Lina Eugenia Ajoy Rojas, Minister-Counsellor & Consul General
Her Excellency Emilia Maria Alvarez Navarro, Ambassador

Republic of Côte d'Ivoire
Embassy of Côte d'Ivoire, 9 Marlborough Ave., Ottawa, ON K1N 8E6
613-236-9919, Fax: 613-563-8287, info@canada.diplomatie.gouv.ci
www.canada.diplomatie.gouv.ci
Ibrahim Cissoko, Counsellor
Georges Aboua, First Counsellor, Economic Affairs
His Excellency Louis Leon Boguy Bony, Ambassador

Republic of Croatia / Hrvatska
Embassy of Croatia, 229 Chapel St., Ottawa, ON K1N 7Y6
613-562-7820, Fax: 613-562-7821, croemb.ottawa@mvpei.hr
ca.mfa.hr
Vesela Mrden Korac, Ambassador

Republic of Cuba
Embassy of Cuba, 388 Main St., Ottawa, ON K1S 1E3
613-563-0141, Fax: 613-563-0068, cuba@embacuba.ca
http://embacu.cubaminrex.cu/Default.aspx?tabid=73
Denia Bada Gonzalez, Counsellor
Ceferino H. Hernandez Palenzuela, Counsellor
Mary Carmen Arencibia Vazquez, Counsellor, Commercial
Antonio G. Castanon Perez, Counsellor, Economic Affairs
Her Excellency Teresita De Jesus Vicente Sotolongo, Ambassador

Republic of Cyprus
High Commission of the Repulic of Cyprus, 2211 R St. NW, Washington, DC 20008 USA
202-462-5772, Fax: 202-483-6710, info@cyprusembassy.net
www.cyprusembassy.net
Other information: Phone, Press Office: 202-232-8993; Fax, Press Room: 202-234-1936
His Excellency Andreas S. Kakouris, High Commissioner
Mr. Solon Savva, Deputy High Commissioner
Mr. Nicholaos Manolis, First Secretary

Czech Republic
Embassy of the Czech Republic, 251 Cooper St., Ottawa, ON K2P 0G2
613-562-3875, Fax: 613-562-3878, ottawa@embassy.mzv.cz
www.czechembassy.org
Stanislav Benes, Counsellor, Commercial
His Excellency Karel Zebrakovsky, Ambassador
Jan Buben, Third Secretary
Tomas Vacek, Councellor
Karel Hejc, First Secretary

Democratic Republic of Congo
18 Range Rd., Ottawa, ON K1N 8J3
613-230-6391, Fax: 613-230-1945,
Vacant, Ambassador
Louise Nzanga Ramazani, First Counsellor & Chargé d'Affaires

Kingdom of Denmark
Royal Danish Embassy, #450, 47 Clarence St., Ottawa, ON K1N 9K1
613-562-1811, Fax: 613-562-1812, ottamb@um.dk
www.ambottawa.um.dk/en
Vacant, Ambassador
Jakob Henningsen, First Secretary & Chargé d'Affaires

Republic of Djibouti
c/o Embassy of the Republic of Djibouti, #515, 1156 - 15th St. NW, Washington, DC 20005 USA

202-331-0270, Fax: 202-331-0302,
usdjibouti@aol.com
Issa Bouraleh, First Secretary
His Excellency Roble Olhaye, Ambassador

Dominican Republic
#418, 130 Albert St., Ottawa, ON K1P 5G4
613-569-9893, Fax: 613-569-8673,
info@drembassy.org
www.drembassy.org
Angelica M. Florentino Morel, Counsellor
Luis Maria Kalaff Sanchez, Minister-Counsellor
Iris Joseline Pujol Rodriguez, First Secretary
His Excellency Jose Del Carmen Urena Almonte, Ambassador
Renso Antonio Herrera Franco, Minister-Counsellor

Republic of Ecuador
Embassy of Ecuador, #316, 50 O'Connor St., Ottawa, ON K1P 6L2
613-563-8206, Fax: 613-235-5776,
mecuacan@rogers.com
Oscar Filipe Izquierdo Arboleda, First Secretary
Ruth Maria Duenas Monteeroa, Counsellor & Deputy Head of Mission
His Excellency Franklin Gustavo Chavez Pareja, Ambassador

Egypt
Embassy of the Arab Republic of Egypt, 454 Laurier Ave. East, Ottawa, ON K1N 6R3
613-234-4931, Fax: 613-234-9347,
egyptemb@sympatico.ca
Amr Mahmoud Abbas Abdel Hadi, Minister & Deputy Head of Mission
Maha Gamil Ali Hamdy, First Secretary
His Excellency Shalem Elsayed Nasser, Ambassador
Hoda Aly Sayed El Mazriky, Counsellor, Press & Information

Republic of El Salvador
Embassy of El Salvador, 209 Kent St., Ottawa, ON K2P 1Z8
613-238-2939, Fax: 613-238-6940,
embajada@elsalvador-ca.org
His Excellency Rafael Angel Alfaro Pineda, Ambassador
Mireya Carolina Calderon Tovar, Minister-Counsellor

Equatorial Guinea
242 East 51st St., New York, NY 10022 USA
212-223-2324, Fax: 212-223-2366,
His Excellency Lino-Sima Ekua Avomo, Ambassador

Eritrea
Embassy of Eritrea (to Canada), #610, 75 Albert St., Ottawa, ON K1P 5E7
613-234-3989, Fax: 613-234-6213,
Vacant, Ambassador

Embassy of the Republic of Estonia
Embassy of Estonia, #210, 260 Dalhousie St., Ottawa, ON K1N 7E4
613-789-4222, Fax: 613-789-9555,
embassy.ottawa@mfa.ee
www.estemb.ca
Rasmus Lumi, Counsellor ja Chargé d'Affaires
His Excellency Jüri Luik, Ambassador (Washington)

Democratic Republic of Ethiopia
Embassy of Federal Democratic Republic of Ethiopia, #210, 151 Slater St., Ottawa, ON K1P 5H3
613-235-6637, Fax: 613-235-4638,
infoethi@magi.com
Tebege Berhe Shook, Counsellor
Birtukan Ayano Dadi, First Secretary
His Excellency Getachew Hamussa Hailemariam, Ambassador
Almaz Amaha Tesfay, Minister-Counsellor

European Union
Delegation of the European Commission to Canada, #1900, 45 O'Connor St., Ottawa, ON K1P 1A4
613-238-6464, Fax: 613-238-5191,
Delegation-Canada@ec.europa.eu
www.delcan.ec.europa.eu
Christopher John Otto Kendall, Counsellor
Eric Hayes, Ambassador & Head of Delegation
Anya Irmgard Oram, Counsellor

Federal Republic of Nigeria
Nigeria High Commission, 295 Metcalfe St., Ottawa, ON K2P 1R9
613-236-0521, Fax: 613-236-0529,
chancery@nigeriahcottawa.com
www.nigeriahcottawa.com
Walter Iteky Ajogbor, Minister
Zhiri James Gana, Minister
Ahmed Adams, Minister
Sola Enikanolaiye, Minister
Eniola Otepola, Minister
Iyorwuese Hagher, High Commissioner

Fiji
Embassy of Fiji (to Canada), 200 M St. NW #240, Washington, DC 20036 USA
202-337-8320, Fax: 202-466-8325,
info@fijiembassy.com
www.fijiembassydc.com
Sakiusa Rabuka, Counsellor
Penijamini R.T. Lomaloma, Acting High Commissioner

Republic of Finland
Embassy of Finland, #850, 55 Metcalfe St., Ottawa, ON K1P 6L5
613-288-2233, Fax: 613-288-2244,
embassy@finland.ca
www.finland.ca
His Excellency Risto Piipponen, Ambassador
Matti Toumas Juhani Aaltola, Counsellor

French Republic
Embassy of France, 42 Sussex Dr., Ottawa, ON K1M 2C9
613-789-1795, Fax: 613-562-3735,
politique@ambafrance-ca.org
www.ambafrance-ca.org
Xavier Barès, Counsellor, Cultural Affairs
Gilles Baudouin, Counsellor, Commerical & Economics
Jean-Baptiste Lesecq, Second Secretary, Economic & Commercial Affairs
His Excellency François Marie Delattre, Ambassador
Phillippe Henri Albert Meunier, Minister-Counsellor

Gabonese Republic
Embassy of Gabon, PO Box 368 , 4 Range Rd., Ottawa, ON K1N 8J5
613-232-5301, Fax: 613-232-6916,
ambgabon@sprint.ca
François Ebibi Mba, First Counsellor
Venance Mbingt Abdoulaye, Counsellor, Economic Affairs
His Excellency Andre William Anguile, Ambassador
Lucien Moubouyi, First Counsellor, Economic, Commercial & Consular Affaires

Republic of the Gambia
High Commission for Gambia (to Canada): c/o Gambia Embassy, #600, 1424 K St. NW, Washington, DC 20005 USA
202-785-1399, Fax: 202-785-1430,
info@gambiaembassy.us
www.gambiaembassy.us
Pa Njagga Mendy, First Secretary
Tijan Masanneh Ceesay, First Secretary
His Excellency Dodou Bammy Jagne, High Commissioner

Embassy of the Federal Republic of Germany
Embassy of Germany, 1 Waverley St., Ottawa, ON K2P 0T8
613-232-1101, Fax: 613-594-9330,
info@ottawa.diplo.de
www.ottawa.diplo.de
Embassy wants people excluded for the Embassy and Consulates General due to constant changes.
His Excellency Johann Georg Witschel, Ambassador

Republic of Ghana
High Commission for Ghana, 1 Clemow Ave., Ottawa, ON K1S 2A9
613-236-0871, Fax: 613-236-0874,
ghanacom@ghanahighcommission-canada.com
www.ghc-ca.com
Kwadwo Tuntum Addo, Counsellor
Yaw Odei Osei, Deputy High Commissioner
Yaw Asa Yirenkyi, First Secretary
Francis Danti Kotia, Acting High Commissioner
Susan Hagan Annobil, Minister

Hellenic Republic
Embassy of Greece, 80 MacLaren St., Ottawa, ON K2P 0K6
613-238-6271, Fax: 613-238-5676,
embassy@greekembassy.ca
www.greekembassy.ca
Theodosios Dimitrakopoulos, Press Counsellor, Press
His Excellency Nikolaos Matsis, Ambassador
Michael Votsis, First Secretary
Kostas Dikaros, Commercial Attaché

Grenada
See: Organization of the Eastern Caribbean Stat

Republic of Guatemala
Embassy of Guatemala, #1010, 130 Albert St., Ottawa, ON K1P 5G4
613-233-7237, Fax: 613-233-0135,
embassy1@embaguate-canada.com
Sandra Refugio Cruz Ordonez, Third Secretary, Cultural & Tourism Affairs
Martha Aida Rogelia Argueta Molina, First Secretary
His Excellency Georges de la Roche Plihal, Ambassador

Republic of Guinea
Embassy of Guinea, 483 Wilbrod St., Ottawa, ON K1N 6N1
613-789-8444, Fax: 613-789-7560,
ambaguineaott@sympatico.ca
Hawa Diakité, Counsellor & Chargé d'Affaires
Frederick Bangoura, Counsellor (Finance & Consular Affairs), Financial & Consular Affairs
Vacant, Ambassador
Aïssata Sow, Counsellor (Cultural Affairs), Cultural Affairs

Republic of Guinea-Bissau
Embassy of Guinea-Bissau (to Canada), 15929 Yukon Lane, Washington, DC 20855 USA
301-947-3958, Fax: 301-947-3958,
Vacant, Ambassador
Henrique Da Silva, Minister-Counsellor & Chargé d'Affaires

Republic of Guyana
Burnside Bldg., #309, 151 Slater St., Ottawa, ON K1P 5H3
613-235-7249, Fax: 613-235-1447,
guyanahcott@rogers.com
His Excellency Rajnarine Singh, High Commissioner

Republic of Haiti
Embassy of Haiti, #1500, 130 Albert St., Ottawa, ON K1P 5G4
613-238-1628, Fax: 613-238-2986,
bohio@sympatico.ca
Joseph Pierre Daniel Charles, Counsellor
Marie-Jose Justinvil, Counsellor
Marjorie Auguste, First Secretary
Margarete Lemaire, Counsellor
Marie Menos-Gissel, Minister-Counsellor & Chargé d'Affaires
Vacant, Ambassador

Republic of Honduras
Embassy of Honduras, #805, 151 Slater St., Ottawa, ON K1P 5H3
613-233-8900, Fax: 613-232-0193,
embhonca@magma.ca
www.embassyhonduras.ca
Guillermo J. Vallagares Lainez, Counsellor & Chargé d'Affaires
Erich Roberto Bondy Reyes, First Secretary
Delia Beatriz Valle Marichal, Ambassador

Republic of Hungary
Embassy of the Republic Hungary, 299 Waverley St., Ottawa, ON K2P 0V9
613-230-2717, Fax: 613-230-7560,
sysadmin@huembott.org
www.mfa.gov.hu/emb/ottawa
Laszlo Bakos, Attaché & Consul, Cultural Affairs
His Excellency Pal Vastagh, Ambassador
Ferenc Banyai, Counsellor

Republic of Iceland
Embassy of Iceland, #710, 360 Albert St., Ottawa, ON K1R 7X7
613-482-1944, Fax: 613-482-1945,
www.iceland.org/ca
Her Excellency Sigridur Anna Thordardottir, Ambassador

Republic of India
High Commission of India, 10 Springfield Rd., Ottawa, ON K1M 1C9
613-744-3751, Fax: 613-744-0913,
hicomind@hciottawa.ca
www.hciottawa.ca
Niraj Srivastava, Deputy High Commissioner
Narendra Kumar Sharma, Counsellor
Vinod Kumar Sachdeva, Minister
Chandra Ballabh Thapliyal, First Secretary
Ajay Kumar Sharma, First Secretary
Rani Malick, Second Secretary
Rakesh Kumar Malhotra, Second Secretary
R.R.P.N. Sahi, Minister, Consular Affairs
His Excellency Shashishekhar Madhukar Gavai, High Commissioner

Republic of Indonesia / Republik Indonesia
55 Parkdale Ave., Ottawa, ON K1Y 1E5
613-724-1100, Fax: 613-724-1105,
info@indonesia-ottawa.org
www.indonesia-ottawa.org
Sadewo Joedo, Minister & Deputy Head of Mission
XXX Iswayudha, Minister-Counsellor, Public Affairs
His Excellency Djoko Hardono, Ambassador
Ronald Yosef Pariaman Manik, Minister-Counsellor, Economic Affairs

Islamic Republic of Iran
Embassy of the Islamic Republic of Iran, 245 Metcalfe St., Ottawa, ON K2P 2K2
613-235-4726, Fax: 613-238-5712,
iranemb@salamiran.org
www.salamiran.org
Ataollah Mobarhani, First Counsellor
Seyed Mohammad Kazem Naeimi, First Counsellor
Seyed Javad Azhari, Counsellor, Science
Vacant, Ambassador
Bahram Ghasemi, Chargé d'Affaires

Republic of Iraq
Embassy of Iraq, 215 McLeod St., Ottawa, ON K2P 0Z8
613-236-9177, Fax: 613-236-9641,
media@iraqembassy.ca
www.iraqembassy.ca
His Excellency Howar M. Ziad, Ambassador

Republic of Ireland
Embassy of Ireland, #1105, 130 Albert St., Ottawa, ON K1P 5G4
613-233-6281, Fax: 613-233-5835,
embassyofireland@rogers.com
Karl Gardner, First Secretary
His Excellency Declan Michael Kelly, Ambassador

Islamic Federal Republic of the Comoros
c/o Permanent Mission of the Comoros to the UN, #418, 866 UN Plaza, New York, NY 10017 USA
212-750-1637, Fax: 212-750-1657,
comoros@un.int
www.un.int/comoros
Vacant, Ambassador

State of Israel
Embassy of Israel, #1005, 50 O'Connor St., Ottawa, ON K1P 6L2
613-567-6450, Fax: 613-567-8978,
info@ottawa.mfa.gov.il
www.ottawa.mfa.gov.il
Ofir Gendelman, Second Secretary
Amit Gil-Bayaz, Counsellor & Deputy Head of Mission
Her Excellency Miriam Ziv, Ambassador

Italian Republic
Embassy of Italy, 275 Slater St., 21st Fl., Ottawa, ON K1P 5H9
613-232-2401, Fax: 613-233-1484,
ambital@italyincanada.com
www.ambottawa.esteri.it/ambasciata_ottawa
Giulio Alaimo, Counsellor, Social Affairs
Spartaco Caldararo, First Secretary, Commercial Affairs
His Excellency Gabriele Sardo, Ambassador
Alessandro Cortese, Deputy Head of Mission & Minister Counsellor

Ivory Coast
See: Republic of Côte d'Ivoire

Jamaica
Jamaican High Commission, #800, 275 Slater St., Ottawa, ON K1P 5H9
613-233-9311, Fax: 613-233-0611,
hc@jhcottawa.ca
www.jhcottawa.ca
Her Excellency Ruby Violet Evadne Coye, High Commissioner
Lola Patrica Rodney Evering, Counsellor

Japan
Embassy of Japan, 255 Sussex Dr., Ottawa, ON K1N 9E6
613-241-8541, Fax: 613-241-2232,
www.ca.emb-japan.go.jp
Masataka Tarahara, Minister & Deputy Head of Mission
His Excellency Tsuneo Nishida, Ambassador
Yasushi Misawa, Minister

Hashemite Kingdom of Jordan
Embassy of Jordan, #701, 100 Bronson Ave., Ottawa, ON K1R 6G8
613-238-8090, Fax: 613-232-3341,
Jordon@on.aibn.com
www.embassyofjordan.ca
Ma'en A. Al-Khreasat, Third Secretary
His Excellency Nabil Ali Mohamed Barto, Ambassador

Republic of Kazakhstan
Embassy of the Republic of Kazakhstan, 56 Hawthorne Ave., Ottawa, ON K1S 0B1
613-788-3704, Fax: 613-788-3702,
kazak@intr.net
His Excellency Yerlan Ablidayev, Ambassador
Samat Zhanabay, Second Secretary
Aigul Moldabekova, Second Secretary
Talgat Kaliyev, Counsellor & Deputy Chief of Mission
Mainyura Murzamadiyeva, Counsellor
Roman Vassilenko, First Secretary
Aibek Nurbalin, Third Secretary

Republic of Kenya
High Commission for Kenya, 415 Laurier Ave. East, Ottawa, ON K1N 6R4
613-563-1773, Fax: 613-233-6599,
kenyahighcommission@rogers.com
www.kenyahighcommission.ca
Michael Aor Oloo, First Secretary
His Excellency Simon Waynonyi Nabukwesi, High Commissioner
Christine Martha Wanjiru Mwangi, Counsellor & Deputy High Commissioner

Kingdom of Cambodia
327 East 58 St., New York, NY 10022 USA
212-336-0777, Fax: 212-759-7672,
cambodia@un.int
www.un.int/cambodia
His Excellency Kosal Sea, Ambassador

Kingdom of Tonga
High Commission for the Kingdom of Tonga, 250 East 51st St., New York, NY 10022 USA
917-369-1025, Fax: 917-369-1024,
Her Excellency Fekitamoeloa T.M. Utoikamanu, High Commissioner

Republic of Korea
Embassy of Korea, 150 Boteler St., Ottawa, ON K1N 5A6
613-244-5010, Fax: 613-244-5034,
Gi Soo Ryu, Minister-Counsellor
His Excellency Chan Ho Ha, Ambassador
Soontaik Hwang, Minister

Democratic People's Republic of Korea
Permanent Mission of Democratic People's Republic of Korea to the UN, 820 Second Ave., 13th Fl., New York, NY 10017 USA
212-972-3105, Fax: 212-972-3154,
His Excellency Son Ho Sin, Ambassador
Song Chol Sin, First Secretary

State of Kuwait
Embassy of Kuwait, 333 Sussex Dr., Ottawa, ON K1N 1J9
613-780-9999, Fax: 613-780-9905,
info@embassyofkuwait.com
www.embassyofkuwait.ca
Mohammad S.R.B. Al-Mutairi, Second Secretary
Mesaid Al-Kulaib, Third Secretary
His Excellency Musaed Rashed A. Al-Haroun, Ambassador
Yaqoub Yousef Eid Khalaf Al-Sanad, First Secretary

Kyrgyz Republic
Embassy of the Kyrgyz Republic, 2360 Masachussets. Ave. NW, Washington, DC 20008 USA
202-449-9822, Fax: 202-386-7550,
consul@kgembassy.org
www.kyrgyzembassy.org
Her Excellency Zamira Sydykova, Ambassador

Laos
The Embassy of the Lao People's Democratic Republic (to Canada), 2222 S St. NW, Washington, DC 20008 USA
202-332-6416, Fax: 202-332-4923,
laoemb@erols.com
www.laoembassy.com
Amphayvanh Chanthavong, Third Secretary
Khamphanthong Soutsady, Third Secretary
Chansamone Thonpraseuth, Second Secretary
Bounneme Chouanghom, First Secretary
Inphachanh Sisavath, First Secretary
Vanhtha Sengmeuang, Second Secretary
His Excellency Phiane Philakone, Ambassador
Phomma Sidsena, Counsellor & Deputy Chief of Mission

Embassy of the Republic of Latvia
Embassy of Latvia, #1200, 350 Sparks St., Ottawa, ON K1R 7S8
613-238-6014, Fax: 613-238-7044,
embassy.canada@mfa.gov.lv
www.ottawa.mfa.gov.lv
His Excellency Margers Krams, Ambassador

Lebanese Republic
Embassy of Lebanon, 640 Lyon St., Ottawa, ON K1S 3Z5
613-236-5825, Fax: 613-232-1609,
info@lebanonembassy.ca
www.lebanonembassy.ca
His Excellency Massoud Maalouf, Ambassador
Oussama Khachab, First Secretary

Kingdom of Lesotho
#1820, 130 Albert St., Ottawa, ON K1P 5G4
613-234-0770, Fax: 636-234-5665,
Lesotho.Ottawa@bellnet.ca
Her Excellency Motseoa Philadel Senyane, High Commissioner
Tumelo Ephraim Raboletsi, First Secretary
Lerato Makoele Agnes Khutlnag, Third Secretary

Republic of Liberia
Embassy of the Republic of Liberia, 5201, 16th St. NW, Washington, DC 20011 USA
202-723-0437, Fax: 202-723-0436,
His Excellency Charles A. Minor, Ambassador

Libya
Embassy of the Great Socialist People's Libyan Arab Jamahiriya, #1000, 81 Metcalfe, Ottawa, ON K1P 6K7
613-230-0919, Fax: 613-230-0683,
info@libya-canada.org
www.libya-canada.org/index-eng.html
Al Hussein A.M. Elzawawi, Counsellor & Chargé d'Affaires
Hasan M.A. Eilabidi, Counsellor, Finance
Sadegh M.O Bensadegh, Counsellor
Maatoug A.M. Embarak, Counsellor, Cultural Affairs
Vacant, Ambassador

Liechtenstein
See: Swiss Confederation

Embassy of the Republic of Lithuania
Embassy of Lithuania, #1600, 150 Metcalfe St., Ottawa, ON K2P 1P1
613-567-5458, Fax: 613-567-5315,
ottawa@lithuanianembassy.ca
www.lithuanianembassy.ca
Migle Jurgita Jankauskiene, Counsellor, 613-567-5458 ext.22, migle.jankuskiene@lithuanianembassy.ca
Ramune Zitikiene, First Secretary, 613-567-5458 ext.25, ramune.zitikiene@lithuanianembassy.ca
Her Excellency Ginte Damusis, Ambassador

Grand Duchy of Luxembourg
Embassy of Luxembourg (to Canada), 2200 Massachusetts Ave. NW, Washington, DC 20008 USA
202-265-4171, Fax: 202-328-8270,
Washington.Amb@mae.etat.lu
His Excellency Jean-Paul Ernest Senninger, Ambassador
Paul Schmidt, Deputy Head of Mission

Republic of Macedonia
Embassy of the Republic of Macedonia, #1006, 130 Albert St., Ottawa, ON K1P 5G4
613-234-3882, Fax: 613-233-1852,
emb.macedonia.ottawa@sympatico.ca
www3.sympatico.ca/emb.macedonia.ottawa /
His Excellency Sasko Nasevt, Ambassador
Slavica Dimovska, First Secretary & Chargé d'Affaires

Republic of Madagascar
Embassy of Madagascar, 3 Raymond St., Ottawa, ON K1R 1A3
613-537-0505, Fax: 613-537-2882,
ambamadcanada@bellnet.ca
www.madagascar-embassy.ca
His Excellency Simon Constant Horace, Ambassador

Republic of Malawi
High Commission for Malawi, #1000, 1029 Vermont Ave., Washington, DC 20005 USA
202-721-0270, Fax: 202-721-0288,
malawi.highcommission@bellnet.ca
Her Excellency Hawa Olga Ndilowe, High Commissioner

Malaysia
High Commission of Malaysia, 60 Boteler St., Ottawa, ON K1N 8Y7

613-241-5182, Fax: 613-241-5214,
mwottawa@kln.gov.my
His Excellency Selwyn Vijayarajan Das, High Commissioner
Mohamad Nizan bin Mohamed, Counsellor

Republic of Mali
Embassy of Mali, 50 Goulburn Ave., Ottawa, ON K1N 8C8
613-232-1501, Fax: 613-232-7429,
ambassadedumali@rogers.com
www.ambamalicanada.org
Mamadou Mandjou Berthe, Second Counsellor
Nene Fofana Kebe, First Secretary
His Excellency Mamadou Bandiougoi Diawara, Ambassador
Macki N'Diaye, First Counsellor

Republic of the Marshall Islands
2433 Massachusetts Ave. NW, Washington, DC 20008 USA
202-234-5414, Fax: 202-232-3236,
His Excellency Banny De Brum, Ambassador

Islamic Republic of Mauritania
Permanent Mission of the Islamic Republic of Mauritania, 116 East 38th St., New York, NY 10016 USA
212-252-0113, Fax: 212-252-0175,
Aicha Mint Mohamed Saleck, First Counsellor
Jiddou Ould Abderrahmane, First Counsellor
Youssouf Ould Mohamed Mahmoud, First Counsellor
His Excellency Abderrahim Oluld Hadrami, Ambassador

Republic of Mauritius
High Commission for Mauritius (to Canada): c/o Embassy of Mauritius, #441, 4301 Connecticut Ave. NW, Washington, DC 20008 USA
202-244-1491, Fax: 202-966-0983,
mauritius.embassy@prodigy.net
His Excellency Keerteecoomar Ruhee, High Commissioner

United Mexican States
Embassy of Mexico, #1000 & #1030, 45 O'Connor St., Ottawa, ON K1P 1A4
613-233-8988, Fax: 613-235-9123,
www.sre.gob.mx/canada
Carlos Jesus Pinera Gonzalez, Minister, Trade
His Excellency Francisco Javier Barrio Terrazas, Ambassador
Jose Ignacio Madrazo Bolivar, Minister & Deputy Head of Mission

Mongolia
Embassy of Mongolia, #503, 151 Slater St., Ottawa, ON K1P 5H3
613-569-3830, Fax: 613-569-3916,
mail@mongolembassy.org
www.mongolembassy.org
Khaliun Dalantai, First Secretary & Consul
Narangua Puntsagnorov, First Secretary
His Excellency Gotov Dugerjav, Ambassador

Montenegro
Embassy of the Republic of Montenegro, 1610 New Hampshire Ave., Washington, DC
202-234-6108, Fax: 202-234-6109,
His Excellency Miodrag Vlahovic, Ambassador

Montserrat
See: Organization of the Eastern Caribbean Stat

Kingdom of Morocco
Embassy of Morocco, 38 Range Rd., Ottawa, ON K1N 8J4
613-236-7391, Fax: 613-236-6164,
info@ambamaroc.ca
www.ambamaroc.ca
Salim Lhjomri, Counsellor
Mohamed Aziz Mouline, Counsellor
Fatima Bouziani, Counsellor
Mohamed Taieb Ben Faida, Counsellor
Her Excellency Nouzha Chekrouni, Ambassador
El Mostafa Benmegdoul, Minister

Republic of Mozambique
High Commission of the Republic of Mozambique to Canada, 1525 New Hampshire Ave. NW, Washington, DC 20036 USA
202-293-7146, Fax: 202-835-0245,
mozambvisa@aol.com
www.embamoc-usa.org
His Excellency Armando A. Panguene, High Commissioner

Myanmar
Embassy of the Union of Myanmar, #902/903, 85 Range Rd., Ottawa, ON K1N 8J6
613-232-9990, Fax: 613-232-6999,
meottawa@rogers.com
Aung Ba Kyu, Counsellor & Chargé d'Affaires
Wai Zin Tun, Second Secretary
Daw Ni Ni Shein, Second Secretary
Vacant, Ambassador

Republic of Namibia
High Commission for Namibia (to Canada), 1605 New Hampshire Ave. NW, Washington, DC 200092503 USA
202-986-0540, Fax: 202-986-0443,
info@namibianembassyusa.org
www.namibianembassyusa.org
Selma Ashipala-Musavyi, Minister-Counsellor & Deputy Head of Mission
His Excellency Patrick Nandago, High Commissioner

Kingdom of Nepal
Royal Nepalese Embassy (to Canada): c/o Embassy of Nepal, 2131 Leroy Place NW, Washington, DC 20008 USA
202-667-4550, Fax: 202-667-5534,
nepali@erols.com
Netra Bahadur Tandan, Third Secretary
Krishna C. Aryal, First Secretary
His Excellency Kedar Bhakta Shyestha, Ambassador

Kingdom of the Netherlands
Royal Netherlands Embassy, #2020, 350 Albert St., Ottawa, ON K1R 1A4
613-237-5031, Fax: 613-237-6471,
nlgovott@netcom.ca
www.netherlandsembassy.ca
Saskia Elisabeth De Lang, Minister & Deputy Head of Mission
Hillebrand Dirk Knook, Counsellor, Commercial
His Excellency Wilhelm Julius Petrus Geerts, Ambassador

New Zealand
New Zealand High Commission, Clarica Centre, #727, 99 Bank St., Ottawa, ON K1P 6G3
613-238-5991, Fax: 613-238-5707,
info@nzhcottawa.org
www.nzembassy.com/canada
Elizabeth Dixon, Second Secretary
Her Excellency Kathleen Janet Lackey, High Commissioner
Andrew Needs, Deputy High Commissioner
Barry Prior, Counsellor

Republic of Nicaragua
Embassy of Nicaragua, 1627 New Hamphire Ave. NW, Washington, DC 20009 USA
202-939-6570, Fax: 202-939-6545,
Vacant, Ambassador

Republic of Niger
Embassy of Niger, 38 Blackburn Ave., Ottawa, ON K1N 8A3
613-232-4291, Fax: 613-230-9808,
ambanigeracanada@rogers.com
www.ambanigeracanada.ca
Fifi Mahamane Bachir, Counsellor
Her Excellency Nana Aicha Mouctari Foumakoye, Ambassador
Moumouni Saley Brah, Second Secretary, Financial Affairs

Kingdom of Norway
Royal Norwegian Embassy, #1300, 130 Albert St., Ottawa, ON K2P 1P1
613-238-6571, Fax: 613-238-2765,
emb.ottawa@mfa.no
www.emb-norway.ca
Kristin Melsom, First Secretary
Vacant, Ambassador
Mr. Jo Sletbak, Minister-Counsellor & Chargé d'Affaires

Sultanate of Oman
Embassy of Oman (to Canada), 2535 Belmont Rd. NW, Washington, DC 20008 USA
202-387-1980, Fax: 202-745-4933,
www.omani.info
Talib Issa Zahran Al Salmi, Attaché, Cultural Affairs & Education
Her Excellency Hunaina Sultan Ahmed Al Mughairy, Ambassador

Organization of the Eastern Caribbean States (OECS)
High Commission for the Countries of the Eastern Caribbean States, #700, 130 Albert St., Ottawa, ON K1P 5G4
613-236-8952, Fax: 613-236-3042,
oesec@oecs.org
www.oecs.org
Includes: Antigua & Barbuda, Commonwealth of Dominica, Grenada, Montserrat, Saint Christopher (Saint Kitts) & Nevis, Saint Lucia, Saint Vincent & the Grenadines
Darius Pope, Third Secretary
Anita Joseph, First Secretary
His Excellency Brendon Browne, High Commissioner

Islamic Republic of Pakistan
High Commission for Pakistan, Burnside Bldg., 10 Range Rd., Ottawa, ON K1N 8J3
613-238-7881, Fax: 613-238-7296,
parepottawa@rogers.com
Saqlain Asad, First Secretary
His Excellency Akbar Zeb, High Commissioner
Najm us Saqib, Counsellor

Republic of Panama
Embassy of Panama, #300, 130 Albert St., Ottawa, ON K1P 5G4
613-236-7177, Fax: 613-236-5775,
info@embassyofpanama.ca
www.embassyofpanama.ca
Jorge E. Constantino Gonzalez, Minister-Counsellor
Carlos Diaz Vallarino, Counsellor, Economic Affairs
Vacant, Ambassador

Papua New Guinea
High Commission of Papua New Guinea (to Canada), #805, 1779 Massachusetts Ave. NW, Washington, DC 20036 USA
202-745-3680, Fax: 202-745-3679,
info@pngembassy.org
www.pngembassy.org
His Excellency Evan Jeremy Paki, High Commissioner

Republic of Paraguay
Embassy of Paraguay, #501, 151 Slater St., Ottawa, ON K1P 5H3
613-567-1283, Fax: 613-567-1679,
consularsection@embassyofparaguay.ca
www.embassyofparaguay.ca
Helena Concepci¢n Felip-Salazar, Counsellor
His Excellency Juan Esteban O. Aguirre Martinez, Ambassador
Victor Hugo Rondan Samaniego, First Secretary

Republic of Peru
Embassy of Peru, #1901, 130 Albert St., Ottawa, ON K1P 5G4
613-238-1777, Fax: 613-232-3062,
emperuca@bellnet.ca
www.embassyofperu.ca
Pedro Buitron, Minister
His Excellency Jorge Juan Castaneda Mendez, Ambassador

Republic of the Philippines
Embassy of the Philippines, #606, 130 Albert St., Ottawa, ON K1P 5G4
613-233-1121, Fax: 613-233-4165,
embassyofphilippines@rogers.com
Rhenita Rodriguez, Second Secretary & Vice-Consul
Shirley E. Banquicio, First Secretary & Consul
Eloy Luis Bello, Second Secretary & Vice-Consul
His Excellency Jose S. Brillantes, Ambassador
Joseph Gerard B. Angeles, Minister & Consul General

Republic of Poland
Embassy of Poland, 443 Daly Ave., Ottawa, ON K1N 6H3
613-789-0468, Fax: 613-789-1218,
ottawa@ottawa.polemb.net
www.ottawa.polemb.net
Artur Antoni Michalski, Counsellor, Political Affairs
Grazyna Sosnowska-Sikorska, First Counsellor
His Excellency Piotr Ogrodzinski, Ambassador

Portuguese Republic
Embassy of Portugal, 645 Island Park Dr., Ottawa, ON K1Y 0B8
613-729-0883, Fax: 613-729-4236,
embportugal@embportugal-ottawa.org
www.embportugal-ottawa.org
Other information: Consular Section: Tel: 613/729-2270
Carlos Alberto Gomes da Silva, Counsellor, Social & Cultural Affairs
Luis Miguel Santos Moura, Counsellor, Economic Affairs
His Excellency Pedro Luis Baptista Moitinho de Almeida, Ambassador
Maria Joao Boavida Urbano, Counsellor

Principality of Andorra
Two United Nations Plaza, 25th Fl., New York, NY 10017 USA
212-750-8064, Fax: 212-750-6630,
Jelena Pia Comella, Minister & Chargé d'Affaires
Vacant, Ambassador

State of Qatar
Embassy of Qatar (to Canada), 2555 M Street NW, Washington, DC 20037-1305 USA
202-274-1600, Fax: 202-237-0061,
ingo@qatarembassy.net
www.qatarembassy.net

His Excellency Ali Fahad F.A. Al-Hajri, Ambassador

Republic of Angola
189 Laurier Ave. East, Ottawa, ON K1N 6P1
613-234-1152, Fax: 613-234-1179, info@embangola-can.org
www.embangola-can.org
Mayuma T. Afonso Do Nascimento, Attaché
Manuel Espirito Santo, Attaché
Mario Augusto, Attaché, Press
Sofia Silvério Pegado da Silva, Minister Counselor & Chargé d'Affairs
Emanuel Fontes Pereira, Third Secretary, Consular Affairs
Eliseu Prata Silas Nunulo, First Secretary, Economic Affairs
Vacant, Ambassador

Republic of Armenia
7 Delaware Ave., Ottawa, ON K2P 0Z2
613-234-3710, Fax: 613-234-3444, embottawa@rogers.com
www.armembassycanada.ca
Arman Akopian, Minister-Counsellor & Chargé d'Affaires
Mikhayil Vardanian, Counsellor
Lilit Davtyan, Second Secretary & Consul
Vacant, Ambassador

Republic of Belarus
#600, 130 Albert St., Ottawa, ON K1P 5G4
613-233-9994, Fax: 613-233-8500, belamb@igs.net
Pavel Pustovoy, Counsellor & Chargé d'Affaires
Uladzimir Matusevich, First Secretary & Consul
Vacant, Ambassador

Republic of Georgia
Embassy of Georgia, 2209 Massachusetts Ave., NW, Washington, DC 20008 USA
202-387-2390, Fax: 202-387-0864, embgeorgiausa@yahoo.com
Malkhaz Mikeladze, Minister & Chargé d'Affaires
Beka Dvali, Senior Counsellor & Consul
His Excellency Vasil Sikharulidze, Ambassador

Republic of Malta
High Commission for Malta (to Canada); c/o Embassy of Malta, 2017 Connecticut Ave. NW, Washington, DC 20008 USA
202-462-3611, Fax: 202-387-5470, maltaembassy.washington@gov.mt
www.gov.mt
Christine Pace, First Secretary & Chargé d'Affaires
His Excellency Mark Amthony Miceli-Farrugia, High Commissioner

Republic of Moldova
2101 S St. NW, Washington, DC 20008 USA
202-667-1130, Fax: 202-667-1204, moldova@dgsys.com
His Excellency Nicolae Chirtoaca, Ambassador

Republic of Turkmenistan
2207 Massachussets Ave. NW, Washington, DC 20008 USA
202-588-1500, Fax: 202-588-0697,
Vacant, Ambassador

Republic of Uzbekistan
1746 Massachusetts Ave. NW, Washington, DC 20036 USA
202-887-5300, Fax: 202-293-6804, uzbekembassy@covad.net
www.uzbekistan.org
Bakhtiyorkhon Abdullakhanov, Counsellor, Trade & Economic Affairs
Iamatulla Fayzullaev, First Secretary
His Excellency Abdulaziz Kamilov, Ambassador

Romania
Embassy of Romania, 655 Rideau St., Ottawa, ON K1N 6A3
613-789-3709, Fax: 613-789-4365, romania@romanian-embassy.com
www.ampli2de.com/embassy/ottawa_en.php
Aurelian Cretu, Minister-Counsellor, Consular Affairs
Dragos Viorel Radu Tigau, Counsellor & Deputy Head of Mission, Political Affairs
Petre Andrei, Counsellor, Economic Affairs
George Sorin Zaharia, First Secretary, Political Affairs
Danut Cristian Matei, Counsellor, Press & Cultural Affairs
Col. Marius Gabriel Safta, Defence, Military, Naval & Air Attaché
Her Excellency Elena Stefoi, Ambassador

Russian Federation
Embassy of the Russian Federation, 285 Charlotte St., Ottawa, ON K1N 8L5
613-235-4341, Fax: 613-236-6342, rusemb@intranet.ca
www.russianembassy.net
Alexander Komarov, Counsellor
Valery Chumakov, Counsellor
His Excellency Georgy Mamedov, Ambassador
Sergey Petrov, Minister-Counsellor
Nikolay Orekhov, Counsellor

Republic of Rwanda
121 Sherwood Dr., Ottawa, ON K1Y 3V1
613-569-5420, Fax: 613-569-5421, generalinfo@ambarwaottawa.ca
www.ambarwaottawa.ca
Déo Nkusi, First Counsellor
Her Excellency Edda Mukabagwiza, Ambassador

Saint Kitts & Nevis
See: Organization of the Eastern Caribbean Stat

Saint Lucia
See: Organization of the Eastern Caribbean Stat

Saint Vincent & the Grenadines
See: Organization of the Eastern Caribbean Stat

Samoa
#400J, 800 Second Ave., New York, NY 10017 USA
212-599-6196, Fax: 212-599-0797, samoa@un.int
His Excellency Ali'ioaiga Feturi Elisaia, High Commissioner

Democratic Republic of Sao Tomé & Principe
1211 Conneticut Ave., NW Suite 300, Washington, DC 20036 USA
202-775-2075, Fax: 202-775-2077,
Ovidio Manuel Barbosa Pequeno, Ambassador
Domingos Ferreira, First Secretary

Kingdom of Saudi Arabia
Royal Embassy of Saudi Arabia, 201 Sussex Dr., Ottawa, ON K1N 1K6
613-237-4100, Fax: 613-237-0567,
Fouad M.F. Shukrey, First Secretary
Abdullah Saleh Al Awwad, Counsellor & Chargé d'Affaires
Vacant, Ambassador

Republic of Senegal
Embassy of Senegal, 57 Marlborough Ave., Ottawa, ON K1N 8E8
613-238-6392, Fax: 613-238-2695, ambassn@sympatico.ca
Lamine Lo, Second Counsellor
Daouda Ba, First Counsellor
His Excellency Issakha Mbacke, Ambassador
Mamadou Saliou Diouf, Minister-Counsellor

Serbia
See: Serbia & Montenegro 17 Blackburn Ave., Ottawa, ON K1N 8A2 Canada 613-233-6289, Fax: 613-233-7850,
Mr. Djordje Ciklovan, Minister-Counsellor & Chargé d'Affaires
Vacant, Ambassador

Republic of Seychelles
High Commission for Seychelles (to Canada), #400C, 800 Second Ave., New York, NY 10017 USA
212-972-1785, Fax: 212-972-1786, seychelles@un.int
His Excellency Roland Jean Jumeau, High Commissioner

Republic of Sierra Leone
High Commission for Sierra Leone (to Canada), 1701 - 19th St. NW, Washington, DC 20009 USA
202-939-9261, Fax: 202-483-1793, slehoc@starpower.net
Hassan Mohamed Conteh, Minister-Counsellor
Sheku Mesali, First Secretary
His Excellency Bockari Kortu Stevens, High Commissioner

Republic of Singapore
c/o Permanent Mission of the Republic of Singapore to the UN, 231 East 51st St., New York, NY 10022 USA
212-826-0840, Fax: 212-826-2964,
His Excellency Yong Guan Koh, High Commissioner
Syed Muhammad Raziff Aljunied, Counsellor

Slovak Republic / Slovenská Republika
Embassy of the Slovak Republic, 50 Rideau Terrace, Ottawa, ON K1M 2A1
613-749-4442, Fax: 613-749-4989, slovakemb@sprint.ca
www.ottawa.mfa.sk
Viera Ruzekova, Counsellor
Ladislav Babcan, Third Secretary
Rastislav Puchala, Third Secretary, Consular Affairs
His Excellency Stanislav Opiela, Ambassador

Republic of Slovenia
Embassy of Slovenia, #2200, 150 Metcalfe St., Ottawa, ON K2P 1P1
613-565-5781, Fax: 613-565-5783, vot@gov.si
www.gov.si/mzz/dkp/vot/eng
His Excellency Tomaz Kunstelj, Ambassador
Boris Jelovsek, Counsellor
Barbara Susnik, First Secretary

Solomon Islands
High Commission c/o Permanent Mission to the U.N., #400L, 800 - 2 Ave., New York, NY 10017 USA
212-599-6192, Fax: 212-661-8925,
His Excellency Collin David Beck, High Commissioner

Republic of South Africa
High Commission for South Africa, 15 Sussex Dr., Ottawa, ON K1M 1M8
613-744-0330, Fax: 613-741-1639, rsafrica@sympatico.ca
www.southafrica-canada.ca
Christina Louisa Britz, First Secretary, Administration & Consular Affairs
Nowetu Ethel Luti, Counsellor & Chargé d'Affaires
Abraham Sokhaya Nkomo, High Commissioner

Kingdom of Spain
Embassy of Spain, 74 Stanley Ave., Ottawa, ON K1M 1P4
613-747-2252, 613-236-0409, Fax: 613-744-1224, Fax: 613-563-2849, embespca@mail.mae.es
Enrique Fanjul Martin, Counsellor, Economic & Commercial Affairs
Antonio Torres-Dulce Ruiz, Minister-Counsellor
His Excellency Eudaldo Mirapeix, Ambassador Baron of Abella

Democratic Socialist Republic of Sri Lanka
High Commission of the Democratic Socialist Republic of Sri Lanka, #1204, 333 Laurier Ave. West, Ottawa, ON K1P 1C1
613-233-8449, Fax: 613-238-8448, slhcit@rogers.com
www.srilankahcottawa.org
Susiri Kumararatne Raigala D.L., Minister, Commercial & Economics
His Excellency Dayananda Rupasoma Perera, High Commissioner

Republic of The Sudan
Embassy of The Sudan, 354 Stewart St., Ottawa, ON K1N 6K8
613-235-4000, Fax: 613-235-6880, sudanembassy-canada@rogers.com
www.sudanembassy.ca
Asim Mohamed Ali Mukhtar Ibrahim, Minister
His Excellency Dr. Faiza Hassan Taha Armousa, Ambassador
Adil Yousif Omer Banaga, Minister

Republic of Suriname
Embassy of Suriname (to Canada), Van Ness Center, #460, 4301 Connecticut Ave. NW, Washington, DC 20008 USA
202-244-7488, Fax: 202-244-5878, embsur@erols.com
His Excellency Jacques Ruben Constantijn Kross, Ambassador

Kingdom of Swaziland
High Commission for Swaziland, 1712 New Hampshire, Washington, DC 20009 USA
202-234-5002, Fax: 202-234-8254, www.magma.ca/~mali/swaziland
His Excellency Ephraim Mandlenkosi M. Hlophe, High Commissioner

Embassy of Sweden
Embassy of Sweden, 377 Dalhousie St., Ottawa, ON K1N 9N8
613-244-8200, Fax: 613-241-2277, sweden.ottawa@foreign.ministry.se
www.swedishembassy.ca
Her Excellency Ingrid Iremark, Ambassador
Pontus Melander, Counsellor

Switzerland
Embassy of Switzerland, 5 Marlborough Ave., Ottawa, ON K1N 8E6
613-235-1837, Fax: 613-563-1394, vertretung@ott.rep.admin.ch
www.eda.admin.ch/canada
Claude Charles Wild, Minister
Jean Philippe Praz, First Secretary
His Excellency Werner Baumann, Ambassador

Syrian Arab Republic
Embassy of Syria (to Canada), 46 Cartier St., Ottawa, ON K2P 1J3
613-569-5556, Fax: 613-569-3800, syrianembassy@on.aibn.com
www.syrianembassy.ca
Bashar Safiey, Second Secretary
Mounzer Ahmad, Third Secretary
His Excellency Jamil Sakr, Ambassador

Tanzania
High Commission of the United Republic of Tanzania, 50 Range Rd., Ottawa, ON K1N 8J4
613-232-1500, Fax: 613-232-5184, tzottawa@synapse.net
Dora Msechu, Minister
Richard Tibandebage, Minister
His Excellency Peter Allan Kallaghe, High Commissioner

Kingdom of Thailand
Royal Thai Embassy, 180 Island Park Dr., Ottawa, ON K1Y 0A2
613-722-4444, Fax: 613-722-6624, thaiott@magma.ca
www.magma.ca/~thaiott/mainpage.htm
Ruengdej Mahasaranond, Minister & Chargé d'Affaires
Chatchai Viriyavejakul, First Secretary
Montri Kittiwangchai, Minister-Counsellor
Walaiporn Pitawanik, Second Secretary
Vacant, Ambassador

Republic of Togo
Embassy of Togo, 12 Range Rd., Ottawa, ON K1N 8J3
613-238-5916, Fax: 613-235-6425,
His Ecxellency Bawoumondom Amelete, Ambassador

Republic of Trinidad & Tobago
High Commission for Trinidad & Tobago, 200 First Ave., 3rd Fl., Ottawa, ON K1S 2G6
613-232-2418, Fax: 613-232-4349, ottawa@ttmissions.com
www.ttmissions.com
Her Excellency Camille Rosemarie Robinson-Regis, High Commissioner
Garth Andrew Lamsee, First Secretary

Republic of Tunisia
Embassy of Tunisia, 515 O'Connor St., Ottawa, ON K1S 3P8
613-237-0330, Fax: 613-237-7939, aottawa@comnet.ca
Slaheddine Ben Mahmoud, Minister-Counsellor
Mohamed Elloumi, Counsellor
His Excellency Mouldi Sakri, Ambassador

Republic of Turkey
Embassy of Turkey, 197 Wurtemburg St., Ottawa, ON K1N 8L9
613-789-4044, Fax: 613-789-3442, turkishottawa@mfa.gov.tr
turkishembassy.com
Other information: Commercial Section: 613/789-2090; Fax: 613/789-2306
Turgul Biltekin, First Secretary
Yonet Can Tezel, Counsellor
Gulcan Akoguz Karagoz, Counsellor, Commercial Affairs
His Excellency Merih Rafet Akgunay, Ambassador

Republic of Uganda
High Commission for Uganda, 231 Cobourg St., Ottawa, ON K1N 8J2
613-789-7797, Fax: 613-789-8909, uhc@ugandahighcommission.com
www.ugandahighcommission.com
Joseph Kiiza Kahigwa, Deputy High Commissioner
Berti Kawooya, Counsellor
His Excellency George Marino Abola, High Commissioner

Republic of Ukraine
Embassy of Ukraine, 310 Somerset St. West, Ottawa, ON K2P 0J9
613-230-2961, 613/230-8015, Fax: 613-230-2400, Fax: 613/230-2655, emb_ca@ukremb.ca
www.ukremb.ca
Mykola Kryzhanovskyi, Counsellor, Trade & Economic Affairs
Vadym Prystaiko, Counsellor & Chargé d'Affaires
His Excellency Ihor Ostash, Ambassador

United Arab Emirates
Embassy of the United Arab Emirates, World Exhange Plaza, #1800, 45 O'Connor St., Ottawa, ON K1P 1A4
613-565-7272, Fax: 613-565-8007, safara@uae-embassy.com
www.uae-embassy.com
His Excellency Mohamed Abdulla Alghafli, Ambassador

United Kingdom of Great Britain
British High Commission, 80 Elgin St., Ottawa, ON K1P 5K7
613-237-1530, Fax: 613-237-7980, generalenquiries@britainincanada.org
www.britishhighcommission.gov.uk
His Excellency Anthony Joyce Cary, High Commissioner
Julian Evans, Deputy High Commissioner
Martin Hill, Counsellor, Economic, Science & Trade
Clive Newell, Counsellor, Political Affairs

United States of America
Embassy of USA, PO Box 866 B, 490 Sussex Dr., Ottawa, ON K1P 5T1
613-238-5335, 613/238-5335, Fax: 613-688-3088, Fax: 613/688-3032,
Ambassador pending confirmation as of September 2009
Brian Flora, Minister-Counsellor, Political Affairs
Brian Jeffery Mohler, Minister-Counsellor, Economic Affairs
Thomas Lee Boam, Minister-Counsellor, Foreign Commercial Affairs
Timothy Edward Roddy, Minister-Counsellor
His Excellency David Jacobson, Ambassador
John S. Dickson, Minister

Oriental Republic of Uruguay
Embassy of Uruguay, #1905, 130 Albert St., Ottawa, ON K1P 5G4
613-234-2727, Fax: 613-233-4670, embassy@embassyofuruguay.ca
www.embassyofuruguay.ca
Eduardo Bouzout Vignoli, Minister-Counsellor
His Excellency Enrique Juanlo Delgado Genta, Ambassador

Holy See
Apostolic Nunciature, 724 Manor Ave., Rockcliffe Park, Ottawa, ON K1M 0E3
613-746-4914, Fax: 613-746-4786, apostolic.nunciature@rogers.com
Monsignor Michael F. Crotty, First Secretary
His Excellency The Most Re Luigi Ventura, Apostolic Nuncio

Republic of Venezuela
Embassy of Venezuela, 32 Range Rd., Ottawa, ON K1N 8J4
613-235-5151, Fax: 613-235-3205, info.canada@misionvenezuela.org
www.misionvenezuela.org
Vacant, Ambassador

Socialist Republic of Vietnam
Embassy of Vietnam, 470 Wilbrod St., Ottawa, ON K1N 6M8
613-236-0772, Fax: 613-236-2704, vietem@istar.ca
Ngoc Canh Pham, Counsellor, Commercial
Hoang Le Huy, Minister-Counsellor & Deputy Head of Mission
His Excellency Duc Hung Nguyen, Ambassador

Republic of Yemen
Embassy of the Republic of Yemen, 54 Chamberlain Ave., Ottawa, ON K1S 1V9
613-729-6627, Fax: 613-729-8915,
Farook Mohamed Saeed Shibani, Minister
His Excellency Khaled Mahfoudh Bahah, Ambassador

Republic of Zambia
High Commission for Zambia (to Canada), #205, 151 Slater St., Ottawa, ON K1B 5H3
613-232-4400, Fax: 613-232-4410, embzambia@aol.com
Lubasi Nyambe, First Secretary, Economic Affairs
His Excellency David Clifford Saviye, High Commissioner

Republic of Zimbabwe
Embassy for the Republic of Zimbabwe, 332 Somerset St. West, Ottawa, ON K2P 0J9
613-421-2824, Fax: 613-422-7403, zimembassy@bellnet.ca
www.zimbabweembassy.ca
Bornway Mwanyara Chiripanhura, Counsellor
Her Excellency Florence Zano Chideya, Ambassador
Makumbe Makambwa, Counsellor

Canadian Diplomatic & Consular Representatives Abroad

Islamic State of Afghanistan
Canadian Embassy, House 256, Street 15, Wazir-Akbar-Khan, Kabul, Afghanistan
93-0-799-742-800, Fax: 93-0-799-742-805, Kabul@international.gc.ca
www.canada-afghanistan.gc.ca
J. Goodings, First Secretary, Development
E. Baldwin-Jones, Counsellor, Political
K. Ursu, Consul
William Crosbie, Ambassador

Republic of Albania
See: Italian Republic

People's Democratic Republic of Algeria
Canadian Embassy, PO Box 48 , Alger-Gare, 16035 Algeria
011-213-7008-3000, Fax: 011-213-7008-3070, alger@international.gc.ca
www.international.gc.ca/world/embassies/algeri a/
E. Mercier, First Secretary & Consul
Kristine Randall, Second Secretary (Commercial & Development), Trade Commissio, Environmental Industries
P. Parisot, Ambassador
A. Dubois, Counsellor, Commercial

Principality of Andorra
See: Kingdom of Spain

People's Republic of Angola
See: Republic of Zimbabwe

Anguilla
See: Barbados

Antigua & Barbuda
See: Barbados

Argentine Republic
Canadian Embassy, Casilla de Correo 1598, Correa Central, Buenos Aires, C1000WAP Argentine
011-54-11-4808-1000, Fax: 011-54-11-4808-111, bairs-webmail@international.gc.ca
www.buenosaires.gc.ca
R. Miller, Counsellor, Commercial
T. Toung, Counsellor, Development
Paula Solari, Trade Commissioner, Environmental Industries
T. Martin, Ambassador
D. Graham, Counsellor

Republic of Armenia
See: Russian Federation

Aruba
See: Republic of Venezuela

Commonwealth of Australia
Canadian High Commission, Commonwealth Ave., Canberra, ACT 2600 Australia
61-2-6270-4000, Fax: 61-2-6270-3585, cnbra@international.gc.ca
www.canada.org.au
K. Madan, Counsellor, Commercial
Sarah Powles, Trade Commissioner
Ilsa Stuart-Muirk, Trade Commissioner
Michael Leir, High Commissioner
R. Cremonese, Deputy High Commissioner
D. Menzies-McVey, Counsellor, Political

Republic of Austria
Canadian Embassy, Laurenzerberg 2, Vienna, A-1010 Austria
43-1-531-38-3321, Fax: 43-1-531-38-3910, vienn@international.gc.ca
www.dfait-maeci.gc.ca/canadaeurope/austria
Roland Rossi, Trade Commissioner, Environmental Industries, roland.rossi@international.gc.ca
P. Hay, Counsellor, Commercial
Marie Gervais-Vidricaire, Ambassador
S. Coutts, Counsellor, Political
N. Smolynec, Counsellor, Immigration

Republic of Azerbaijan
See: Republic of Turkey

Commonwealth of the Bahamas
See: Jamaica

State of Bahrain
See: Kingdom of Saudi Arabia

People's Republic of Bangladesh
Canadian High Commission, GPO Box 569, Dhaka, 1212 Bangladesh
88-2-988-7091, Fax: 88-2-882-3043,
dhaka@international.gc.ca
www.bangladesh.gc.ca
Mortoza Tarafder, Sr. Trade Commissioner, Environmental Industries, mortoza.tarafder@international.gc.ca
Robert McDougall, High Commissioner
J. Sebhatu, First Secretary, Development

Barbados
Canadian High Commission, PO Box 404 , Bridgetown, Barbados
246-429-3550, Fax: 246-429-3780,
bdgtn@international.gc.ca
D. Holland, Counsellor
Tammy Griffith, Trade Commissioner, Environmental Industries
D. Smyl, Second Secretary, Administration
J. Desjardins, Counsellor, Commercial
Ruth Archibald, High Commissioner

Republic of Belarus
See: Republic of Poland

Kingdom of Belgium
Canadian Embassy, 2, av de Tervuren, Brussels, 1040 Belgium
32-2-741-0611, Fax: 32-2-741-0643,
bru@international.gc.ca
www.ambassade-canada.be
A. Vary, Counsellor, Commercial
Fabienne De Kimpe, Trade Commissioner, Environmental Industries, fabienne.de-kimpe@international.gc.ca
F. LaRochelle, Counsellor
L. de Lorimier, Ambassador
L. Sustersich, Counsellor (Administration) & Consul

Belize
See: Republic of Guatemala

Republic of Benin
See: Republic of Ivory Coast

Bermuda
See: United States of America c/o New York City Office,

Republic of Bolivia
See: Republic of Peru

Bosnia & Herzegovina
See: Hungary
P. Paproski, Counsellor, Technical Assistance
B. Steen, First Secretary, Development
D. Kelly, Second Secretary & Consul
David Hutchings, Ambassador

Republic of Botswana
See: Republic of Zimbabwe

Federative Republic of Brazil
Canadian Embassy, SES-Av. das Naçes - Qd. 803 - Lote 16, Brasilia, D.F., 70410-900 Brazil
55-61-424-5400, Fax: 55-61-424-5490,
brsla@international.gc.ca
www.canadainternational.gc.ca/brazil/
Jillian Senkiw, Third Secretary & Trade Commissioner, Environmental Industries, jillian.senkiw@international.gc.ca
K. McDonald, Minister-Counseller, Political
F. Lafond, Counsellor, Commercial
R. Beaulieu, Counsellor, Development
P. Hunt, Ambassador
R. Siwak, Counsellor (Administration) & Consul

British Virgin Islands
See: Barbados

Brunei Darussalam
Canadian High Commission, PO Box 2808 , Bandar Seri Begawan, BS8675 Brunei Darussalam
673-2-220-043, Fax: 673-2-220-040,
bsbgn@international.gc.ca
www.dfait-maeci.gc.ca/brunei
Celestina Leong, Trade Commissioner, celestina.leong@international.gc.ca
Wendell Sanford, High Commissioner
Peter Chen, Trade Commissioner, peter.chen@international.gc.ca

Republic of Bulgaria
See: Republic of Romania c/o Republic of Romania, Consulate of Canada, 9, Moskovska str., Sofia, Bulgaria (011-359-2)969-9719, Fax: (011-359-2)981-6081, bucst-td@international.gc.ca
Magdalena Goranova, Trade Commissioner, Environmental Industries

Burkina-Faso
Canadian Embassy, PO Box 548, Ouagadugou 01, Kadiogo, Burkina-Faso
226-50-31-18-94, Fax: 226-50-31-19-00,
ouaga@international.gc.ca
Jules Savaria, Ambassador

Republic of Burundi
See: Republic of Kenya

Kingdom of Cambodia
See: Thailand

Republic of Cameroon
Canadian High Commission, Immeuble SCI-TOM (formerly Stamatiades), PO Box 572 , Yaoundé, Cameroon
011-237-2223-2311, Fax: 011-237-2222-1090,
yunde@international.gc.ca
Gillian Goodwin, Management Consular Officer
Jude Bijingsi, Trade Commissioner, Environmental Industries, jude.bijingsi@international.gc.ca
Jean Pierre Lavoie, High Commissioner
G. Mercier, Counsellor, Development

Republic of Cape Verde
See: Republic of Senegal

Cayman Islands
See: Jamaica

Central African Republic
See: Republic of Cameroon

Republic of Chad
See: Republic of Cameroon

Republic of Chile
Canadian Embassy, Cassilla 139, Correo 10, Santiago, Chile
56-2-652-3800, Fax: 56-2-652-3912,
stago@international.gc.ca
www.chile.gc.ca
Margot Edwards, Trade Commissioner, Environmental Industries
J. Kimmell, Counsellor (Admimistration) & Consul
P. Furesz, Counsellor, Commercial
S. Fountain Smith, Ambassador
H. Laverdiere, Counsellor, Political/Economic
J. Jonk, Counsellor, Immigration

People's Republic of China
Canadian Embassy, 19 Dong Zhi Men Wai St., Chao Yang Dist., Beijing, 100600 China
011-86-10-5139-4000, Fax: 011-86-10-5139-4454,
bejing@international.gc.ca
www.beijing.gc.ca
T. Khan, Counsellor, Development
S. Frank, Minister-Counsellor
K. Lewis, Minister, Commercial
Owen Teo, Senior Trade Commissioner, Environmental Industries
David Mulroney, Ambassador
J. Nankivell, Minister
M. Kruger, Minister-Counsellor

Republic of Colombia
Canadian Embassy, Apartado Aereo 110067, Bogota, Colombia
57-1-657-9800, Fax: 57-1-657-9912,
bgota@international.gc.ca
www.bogota.gc.ca
G. Salesse, Counsellor
Claudia Paola Gutierrez Chaves, Trade Commissioner
J. Tabah, Counsellor, Development
G. des Rivières, Ambassador
W. Farrell, Counsellor, Immigration
David Smarth, Counsellor (Adminitration) & Consul

Islamic Federal Republic of the Comoros
See: United Republic of Tanzania

Democratic Republic of Congo
Canadian Embassy to the Democratic Republic of Congo, PO Box 8341 , Kinshasa, Democratic Republic of Congo
243-89895-0310, Fax: 243-81301-6515,
knsha@international.gc.ca
www.dfait-maeci.gc.ca/world/embassies/drc/
J.C. Mailhot, Counsellor, Development
J. Crôteau, Counsellor & Consul
G. Goodwin, Counsellor (Administration) & Consul
S.A. Johnson, Ambassador

Republic of Costa Rica
Canadian Embassy, Apartado Postal 351-1007 Centro Colon, San José, Costa Rica
506-2242-4400, Fax: 506-2242-4410,
sjcra@international.gc.ca
www.costarica.gc.ca
Adolfo Quesada, Trade Commissioner, Environmental Industries, adolfo.quesada@international.gc.ca
S. Veilleux, First Secretary, Commercial
Julia McNeill, Counsellor (Administration) & Consul
N. Reeder, Ambassador
S. Hughes, Counsellor

Republic of Croatia
Prilaz Gjure Dezelica #4, Zagreb, 10 000 Croatia
385-1-488-1200, Fax: 385-1-488-1230,
zagrb@international.gc.ca
Synthia Dodig, Trade Commissioner, Environmental Industries, synthia.dodig@international.gc.ca
Claude Demers, First Secretary
Thomas Marr, Ambassador

Republic of Cuba
Canadian Embassy, Calle 30, No. 518, Esquina 7a, Miramar, Havana, Cuba
53-7-204-2516, Fax: 53-7-204-9772,
havan@international.gc.ca
www.dfait-maeci.gc.ca/cuba
Francisco Rodriguez, Trade Commissioner, Environmental Industries
M. Schroeter, Second Secretary, Commercial
J.P. Juneau, Ambassador
S. Cridland, First Secretary

Republic of Cyprus
See: Republic of Romania c/o Republic of Romania, PO Box 22125 , Consulate of Canada c/o The Canadian Embassy, Nicosia, 1517 Cyprus (00-357-22 775-508, Fax: (00-357-22) 779-905, info@consulcanada.com.cy
Rhea Pelides, Trade Commissioner, Environmental Industries

Czech Republic
Canadian Embassy, Muchova 6, 160 00, Prague, 6 Czech Republic
420 272 101 800, Fax: 420 272 101 898,
prgue@dfait-maeci.gc.ca
www.canada.cz
M. Kahle, First Secretary (Administration) & Consul
Lyne-Marie Tremblay, Counsellor, Trade Policy
Jitka Hoskova, Trade Commissioner, Environmental Industries, jitka.hoskova@international.gc.ca
Y. Saint-Hilaire, Counsellor, Political/Economic
Michael Calcott, Ambassador

Kingdom of Denmark
Canadian Embassy, Kr. Bernikows Gade 1, Copenhagen, DK-1105 Denmark
45-33-48-32-00, Fax: 45-33-48-32-20,
copen@international.gc.ca
www.denmark.gc.ca
His Excellency P. Lundy, Ambassador
Suzanne Steensen, Trade Commissioner, Environmental Industries

Republic of Djibouti
The Embassy of Canada, Place Lagarde, Djibouti, 1188 Djibouti

Commonwealth of Dominica
See: Barbados

Dominican Republic
Canadian Embassy, PO Box 2054 , Santo Domingo, Dominican Republic

809-685-1136, Fax: 809-682-2691,
sdmgo@international.gc.ca
www.santodomingo.gc.ca

Vacant, Ambassador
Regis Batista-Lemaire, Trade Commissioner, Environmental Industries, regis.barista@international.gc.ca
N. Larocque, First Secretary (Administration) & Consul
H. Guillot, Counsellor, Commercial

Republic of Ecuador
PO Box 17-11-6512 , Quito, Ecuador
593-2-2455-499, Fax: 593-2-2277-672,
quito@international.gc.ca
www.ecuador.gc.ca

Ryan Kuffner, Trade Commissioner, Environmental Industries
A. Shisko, Ambassador
A.M. Alvarez Tello, First Secretary (Administration) & Consul

Arab Republic of Egypt
Canadian Embassy, PO Box 1667 , Cairo, Egypt
(011 20 2) 2791-8700, Fax: (011 20 2) 2791-8860,
cairo@international.gc.ca
www.dfait-maeci.gc.ca/cairo

F. de Kerckhove, Ambassador
Christopher Hull, Counsellor, Political
J. Broadbent, Counsellor, Commercial
P. Paproski, Counsellor, Development
J. Loo, Counsellor & Consul, Administration

Republic of El Salvador
Canadian Embassy, Edificio Centro Financiero Gigante, Alameda Roosevelt y 63 Avenida Sur, Nivel Lobby 2, Loca, San Salvador, El Salvador
503-2279-4655, Fax: 503-2279-0765,
ssal@international.gc.ca
www.sansalvador.gc.ca

Romeo Calderon, Trade Commissioner, Environmental Industries, romeo.calderon@international.gc.ca
Claire A. Poulin, Ambassador

England
See: United Kingdom of Great Britain & Northern

Republic of Equatorial Guinea
See: Gabonese Republic

Eritrea
See: Republic of Kenya

Republic of Estonia
Office of the Canadian Embassy, Toom Kooli 13, 2nd Fl., Tallinn, 0100 Estonia
372-627-3311, Fax: 372-627-3312,
tallinn@canada.ee
www.canada.ee

S. Heatherington, Ambassador (located in Riga, Latvia)

Federal Democratic Republic of Ethiopia
Canadian Embassy, PO Box 1130 , Addis Ababa, Ethiopia
251-1-71-30-22, Fax: 251-1-71-30-33,
addis@international.gc.ca

I. Hentic, First Secretary, Development
Richard Le Bars, Second Secretary & Vice-Consul & Sr. Trade Commissioner, Environmental Industries, richard.lebars@international.gc.ca
Vacant, Ambassador

European Union
The Mission of Canada to the European Union, 2, av de Tervuren, Brussels, 1040 Belgium
322-741-0660, Fax: 322-741-0629,
breu@international.gc.ca
www.canadainternational.gc.ca/eu-ue

Jean Saint-Jacques, Minister-Counsellor & Deputy Head of Mission
Y. Mondy, First Secretary, Trade Policy
Ross Hornby, Ambassador & Head of Mission
T. Milanetti, Counsellor, Agriculture

Faroe Islands
See: Kingdom of Denmark

Fiji
See: New Zealand

Republic of Finland
Canadian Embassy, PO Box 779 , Helsinki, FIN-00101 Finland
358-9-228-530, Fax: 358-9-601-060,
hsnki@international.gc.ca
www.canada.fi

Aline Lemieux-Lewin, Attaché & Vice-Consul
Seppo Vihersaari, Trade Commissioner, Environmental Industries, seppo.vihersaari@international.gc.ca
Scott Fraser, Ambassador

French Republic
Canadian Embassy, 35 - 37, av Montaigne, Paris, 75008 France
33-1-44-43-29-00, Fax: 33-1-44-43-29-99,
paris@international.gc.ca
www.international.gc.ca/canada-europa/france

S. Scrimshaw, Minister
Michel Charland, Counsellor, Commercial
Musto Mitha, Trade Commissioner, Environmental Industries
M. Lortie, Ambassador
Richard Têtu, Minister-Counsellor, Political
André Dubois, Minister-Counsellor

Gabonese Republic
Canadian Embassy, PO Box 4037 , Libreville, Gabon
241-73-73-54, Fax: 241-73-73-88,
lbrve@international.gc.ca

François Coté, Trade Commissioner, Environmental Industries, francois.cote@international.gc.ca
Louis Guay, Ambassador

Republic of the Gambia
See: Republic of Senegal

Republic of Georgia
See: Republic of Turkey

Federal Republic of Germany
Canadian Embassy, Leipziger Platz 17, Berlin, 10117 Germany
41-30-20-312-0, Fax: 49-30-20-312-590,
brlin@international.gc.ca
www.dfait-maeci.gc.ca/canada-europa/germany

Dr. Steffen Preusser, Trade Commissioner, Environmental Industries, steffen.preusser@international.gc.ca
J. Kur, Minister-Counsellor, Commecial/Economic
P. Boehm, Ambassador
H. Childs-Adams, Minister

Republic of Ghana
Canadian High Commission, PO Box 1639 , 42 Independence Ave., Accra, Ghana
233-21-211521, Fax: 233-21-211523,
accra@international.gc.ca
www.dfait-maeci.gc.ca/accra

Joseph Abanyin, Commercial Officer
W. McKenzie, Counsellor, Commercial
J. Tieman, Second Secretary, Immigration
D. Schemmer, Ambassador

Hellenic Republic
Canadian Embassy, 4 Ioannou Ghennadiou St., Athens, 115 21 Greece
30-210-727-3400, Fax: 30-210-727-3480,
athns@international.gc.ca
www.dfait-maeci.gc.ca/canadaeuropa/greece/

Marguerita Niada, Trade Commissioner, Environmental Industries, marguerita.niada@international.gc.ca
D. Tessier, Counsellor, Political
G. Ptolemy, First Secretary (Administration) & Consul
C. Rego, Second Secretary (Administration) & Vice-Consul
B. Young, Counsellor, Commercial
R. Wielgosz, Ambassador

Greenland
See: Kingdom of Denmark

Grenada
See: Barbados

Saint Vincent & the Grenadines
See: Barbados

Republic of Guatemala
Canadian Embassy, PO Box 400 , Guatemala City, 1001 Guatemala
502-2363-4348, Fax: 502-2365-1210,
gtmla@international.gc.ca
www.guatemala.gc.ca

D. Carriere, Counsellor, Immigration
M. Guibeault, Counsellor, Political
M. Veilleux, First Secretary, Development
L. McKechnie, Ambassador
Christine Luttmann, Trade Commissioner, Environmental Industries

Republic of Guinea-Bissau
See: Republic of Senegal

Republic of Guyana
Canadian High Commission, PO Box 10880 , Georgetown, Guyana
592-227-2081, Fax: 592-225-8380,
grgtn@international.gc.ca
www.guyana.gc.ca

A. Gibbons, Second Secretary, Development
C. Munante, First Secretary (Administration) & Consul
Vacant, High Commissioner
Lyris Primo, Commercial Officer, lyris.primo@international.gc.ca

Republic of Haiti
PO Box 826 , Port-au-Prince, Haiti
509-2249-9000, Fax: 509-2249-9920,
prnce@international.gc.ca
www.port-au-prince.gc.ca

F. Montour, Counsellor, Development
G. Rivard, Ambassador
Svend Holm, Counsellor (Administration) & Consul

Republic of Honduras
Canadian Embassy, PO Box 3552 , Tegucigalpa, Honduras
504-232-4551, Fax: 504-239-7769,
tglpa@international.gc.ca
www.canadainternational.gc.ca/costa_rica

N. Reeder, Ambassador

Republic of Hungary
Canadian Embassy, Ganz U. 12-14, Budapest, 10 1027 Hungary
36-1-392-3360, Fax: 36-1-392-3390,
bpest@international.gc.ca
www.canadaeuropa.gc.ca/hungary

Zsuzsanna Matyus, Trade Commissioner, Environmental Industries, zsuzsanna.matyus@international.gc.ca
R. Martin-Nielsen, Counsellor
E. Yu, Counsellor & Consul, Administration
Micheal Danagher, Counsellor, Commercial
P. Guimond, Ambassador

Republic of Iceland
PO Box 1510 , Reykjavik, 121 Iceland
354-575-6500, Fax: 354-575-6501,
rkjvk@international.gc.ca
www.canada.is

Alan Bones, Ambassador
Kristbjorg Agustsdottir, Trade Commissioner, Environmental Industries, kristbjorg.agustsdottir@international.gc

Republic of India
Canadian High Commission, PO Box 5208 , New Delhi, 110021 India
91-11-4178-2000, Fax: 91-11-4178-2020,
delhi@international.gc.ca
www.india.gc.ca

Viney Gupta, Trade Commissioner, Environmental Industries, delhi.commerce@international.gc.ca
K. Macartney, Deputy High Commissioner
S. Tuckey, Counsellor
P. Beaudoin, Minister-Counsellor
Joseph Caron, High Commissioner
T. Kernighan, Counsellor

Republic of Indonesia
Canadian Embassy, PO Box 8324/JKS.MP, Jakarta, 12083 Indonesia
62-21-2550-7800, Fax: 62-21-2550-7811,
jkrta@international.gc.ca
www.jakarta.gc.ca

Dian Martosoebroto, Trade Commissioner, Environmental Industries
P. McCullagh, Counsellor
G. Shantz, Counsellor, Commercial/Economic
Mackenzie Clugston, Ambassador

Islamic Republic of Iran
Canadian Embassy, 57 Shahid Sarafraz St., Dr. Beheshti Ave., Tehran, 15868 Iran
98-21-8873-2623, Fax: 98-21-8873-3202,
teran@international.gc.ca
www.dfait-maeci.gc.ca/world/embassies/iran/

R. Cooper, Counsellor, Political
D. Horak, First Secretary
D. Horak, Counsellor
Vacant, Ambassador

Republic of Iraq
See: Hashemite Kingdom of Jordan Iraq
Vacant, Ambassador

Republic of Ireland
Canadian Embassy, 7-8 Wilton Terrace, Dublin 2, Ireland
353-1-234-4000, Fax: 353-1-234-4101,
dubln@international.gc.ca
www.canada.ie
Gerry Mongey, Trade Commissioner, Environmental Industries, gerry.mongey@international.gc.ca
M. Leroux, Counsellor & Consul
Aslin Unlusoy, Trade Commissioner
Richard Philippe, First Secretary, Commercial
P. Binns, Ambassador

State of Israel
Canadian Embassy, PO Box 9442 , 3 Nirim St., 4th Fl., Tel Aviv, 67060 Israel
011-972-3-636-3300, Fax: 011-972-3-636-3380,
taviv@international.gc.ca
www.dfait-maeci.gc.ca/telaviv/
Mona Ashkar, Trade Commissioner, Environmental Industries
L. Helfand, Minister-Counsellor
W. Bazette, Counsellor, Immigration
R. Wassill, Counsellor, Communications & Culture
Jon Allen, Ambassador

Italian Republic
Canadian Embassy, Villa Grazioli, Via Salaria 243, Rome, 00199 Italy
39-06-85444-1, Fax: 39-06-85444-3947,
rome@international.gc.ca
www.canada.it
Patrizia Giuliotti, Trade Commissioner, Environmental Industries
T. Guttman, Minister-Counsellor
Khawar Nasim, Senior Trade Commissioner
J. Fox, Ambassador

Republic of Ivory Coast
Canadian Embassy, Immeuble Trade Centre, 23, av Nogues, 6th & 7th Fls., Le Plateau, Abidjan, 01 Ivory Coast
225-20 30 07 00, Fax: 225-20 30 07 20,
abdjn@international.gc.ca
www.dfait-maeci.gc.ca/abidjan
Jean-Claude Diplo, Trade Commissioner, Environmental Services, jean-claude.diplo@international.gc.ca
L. Jouvarne, Counsellor & Consul
Marie-Isabelle Massip, Ambassador

Jamaica
Canadian High Commission, PO Box 1500 , Kingston, 10 Jamaica
876/926-1500-7, Fax: 876/511-3494,
kngtn-cs@international.gc.ca
www.kingston.gc.ca
Yasmin Chong, Trade Commissioner, Environmental Industries, yasmin.chong@international.gc.ca
C. Duggan, Counsellor, Political/Economic
R. Merifield, Counsellor, Commercial
Vacant, High Commissioner

Hashemite Kingdom of Jordan
Canadian Embassy, PO Box 815403 , Amman, 11180 Jordan
962-6-520-3300, Fax: 962-6-520-3390,
amman@international.gc.ca
www.amman.gc.ca
Wafa Herzallah, Trade Commissioner, Environmental Industries, wafa.herzallah@international.gc.ca
E. Madueno, First Secretary, Development
M. Huber, Ambassador
S. Pomel, Counsellor

Republic of Kazakhstan
Canadian Embassy, 34 Karasai Batir St., Almaty, 050010 Kazakhstan
73-27-250-11-51, Fax: 73-27-258-24-93,
almat@international.tc.ca
www.infoexport.gc.ca/kz
David Mallette, Trade Commissioner
Mark Opgenorth, First Secretary
Maxim Berdichevsky, First Secretary & Vice-Consul
Guillaume Legros, First Secretary, Development
Jan Sheltinga, Counsellor, Development
Margaret Skok, Ambassador

Republic of Kenya
Canadian High Commission, PO Box 1013, Nairobi, 00621 Kenya
254-20-366-3000, Fax: 254-20-366-3900,
nrobi@international.gc.ca
www.nairobi.gc.ca
Dominique Collinge, Counsellor, Immigration
Stephen Weaver, Counsellor, Development
Ross Hynes, High Commissioner
D. Burns, Counsellor

Republic of Kiribati
See: New Zealand

Republic of Korea
Canadian Embassy, 16-1 Jeong-dong, Jung-gu, Seoul, Korea
82-2-3783-6000, Fax: 82-2-3783-6239,
seoul@international.gc.ca
www.korea.gc.ca
Yon-Ho Choi, Trade Commissioner, Environmental Industries, yon-ho.cho@international.gc.ca
Duane McMullen, Minister-Counsellor, Commercial
Ted Lipman, Ambassador

State of Kuwait
Canadian Embassy, PO Box 25281, Safat, Kuwait City, 13113 Kuwait
965-2256-3025, Fax: 965-2256-0173,
kwait@international.gc.ca
www.infoexport.gc.ca/kw
Martin Barratt, Sr. Trade Commissioner, martin.barratt@international.gc.ca
Reif Henry, Ambassador
G. Sanderson, Counsellor (Commercial) & Consul)

Kyrgyz Republic
See: Republic of Kazakhstan

Republic of Latvia
Canadian Embassy, 20/22 Baznicas St., 6th Fl., Riga, LV-1010 Latvia
371-6781-3945, Fax: 371-6781-3960,
riga@international.gc.ca
www.balticstates.gc.ca
Irena Cirpuse, Trade Commissioner, Environmental Industries, irena.cirpuse@international.gc.ca
Scott Heatherington, Ambassador

Lebanese Republic
Canadian Embassy, 43 Autostrade Jal El Dib, Beirut, Lebanon
961-4-713-900, Fax: 961-4-710-595,
berut@international.gc.ca
www.dfait-maeci.gc.ca/beirut/
G. Menard, Counsellor, Immigration
Grace Dib, Trade Commissioner, Environmental Industries, grace.dib@international.gc.ca
Vacant, Ambassador
C. Miranda, First Secretary, Commercial
D. Joly, Counsellor

Kingdom of Lesotho
See: Republic of South Africa

Republic of Liberia
See: Republic of Ivory Coast

Socialist People's Libyan Arab Jamahiriya
PO Box 93392 , Al-Fateh Tower, 7th Fl., Tripoli, Libya
218-21-335-1633, Fax: 218-21-335-1630,
trpli@international.gc.ca
www.dfait-maeci.gc.ca/world/embassies/libya/
Hesham Ganem, Trade Commissioner, Environmental Industries, hesham.ganem@international.gc.ca
S. McCardell, Ambassador
M.A. Jacques, Second Secretary (Administration) & Consul

Principality Liechtenstein
See: Swiss Confederation

Republic of Lithuania
Office of the Canadian Embassy, Business Center 2000, Jogailos St. 4, 7th Fl., Vilnius, LT-01116 Lithuania
370-5249-0950, Fax: 370-5249-7865,
vilnius@canada.lt
www.balticstates.gc.ca
Scott Heatherington, Ambassador (located in Riga)
H. Massoud, Chargé d'Affaires

Grand Duchy of Luxembourg
See: Kingdom of Belgium

Macao
See: People's Republic of China

Democratic Republic of Madagascar
Embassy of Canada, PO Box 1022 , Dar es Salaam, Tanzania

Republic of Malawi
See: Republic of Zambia

Federation of Malaysia
Canadian High Commission, PO Box 10990 , Kuala Lumpur, Malaysia
60-3-2718-3333, Fax: 60-3-2718-3399,
klmpr@international.gc.ca
http://www.international.gc.ca/missions/malays ia-malaisie/
Mia Yen, Second Secretary (Commercial) & Trade Commissioner, Environmental Industries, mia.yen@international.gc.ca
René-François Désamoré, Counsellor, Commercial
David Collins, High Commissioner

Republic of Maldives
See: Democratic Socialist Republic of Sri Lanka

Republic of Mali
Canadian Embassy, PO Box 198 , Route de Koulikoro, Immeuble séméga, Bamako, Mali
223-2021-2236, Fax: 223-2021-4362,
bmako@international.gc.ca
www.bamako.gc.ca
S. Tremblay, First Secretary & Consul
Ernest Akpoue, Trade Commissioner, Environmental Industries, ernest.akpoue@international.gc.ca
S. Marchand, First Secretary, Cooperation
Virginie Saint-Louis, Ambassador

Republic of Malta
See: Italian Republic

Marshall Islands
See: Republic of the Philippines

Islamic Republic of Mauritania
See: Kingdom of Morocco

Republic of Mauritius
See: Republic of South Africa

United Mexican States
Canadian Embassy, Apartado Postal 105-05, Mexico City, 11580 Mexico
52-57-24-7900, Fax: 52-57-24-7980,
mxico@international.gc.ca
www.mexico.gc.ca
Other information: Emergency: 1-800-703-2900
Paula Caldwell, Senior Trade Commissioner, mexico.commerce@international.gc.ca
Rosalba Cruz, Trade Commissioner, Environmental Industries, mexico.commerce@international.gc.ca
G. Manuge, Minister-Counsellor, Commercial
Guillermo Rishchynski, Ambassador
J. Herran-Lima, Deputy Head of Mission & Minister-Counsellor

Federated States of Micronesia
See: Republic of The Philippines

Republic of Moldova
See: Republic of Romania

Principality of Monaco
See: French Republic

Mongolian People's Republic
The Canadian Embassy, 2nd Fl., 8 Zovkhis building, Seoul St., Ulaanbaatar, 210628 Mongolia

A. Biolik, Ambassador

Montenegro
See: Serbia & Montenegro

Montserrat
See: Barbados

Kingdom of Morocco
Canadian Embassy, PO Box 709 , Rabat-Agdal, Morocco
212-37-68-74-00, Fax: 212-37-68-74-30,
rabat@international.gc.ca
www.rabat.gc.ca
V. Saint-Louis, Counsellor, Political & Consul
G. Tassé, Counsellor, Commercial
R. Gaulin, First Secretary & Consul
Asmae Amrouche, Trade Commissioner, Environmental Industries
Vacant, Ambassador
M. Floyd, Counsellor, Immigration

Republic of Mozambique
Canadian High Commission, PO Box 1578 , 1138, Kenneth Kaunda Ave., Maputo, Mozambique
258-21-492-623, Fax: 258-21-492-667,
mputo@international.gc.ca
R. Kerr, First Secretary & Consul
Lurdes Magneli, Trade Commissioner, Environmental Industries
Philip Baker, High Commissioner
K. Neufeld, Counsellor, Development

Union of Myanmar
See: Kingdom of Thailand

Republic of Namibia
See: Republic of South Africa

Nauru
See: Commonwealth of Australia c/o Canberra,

Kingdom of Nepal
Canadian Embassy to Nepal, c/o Canadian Cooperation Office, PO Box 4574 , Kathmandu, Nepal
977-1-441-5193, Fax: 977-1-441-0422,
cco@canadanepal.org
Joseph Caron, Ambassador (located in New Delhi, India)

Kingdom of the Netherlands
Canadian Embassy, Sophialaan 7, The Hague, 2514 JP The Netherlands
31-70-311-1600, Fax: 31-70-311-1620,
hague@international.gc.ca
www.canada.nl
G. Martindale, Counsellor
Judith Baguley, Trade Commissioner, Environmental Industries
Y. Saint-Hilaire, Counsellor, Economic
Ann Adcock-Hart, Counsellor (Administration) & Consul
J. Wall, Ambassador
P. Leduc, Counsellor

Netherlands Antilles
See: Republic of Venezuela

New Caledonia
See: Commonwealth of Australia

New Zealand
Canadian High Commission, PO Box 8047 , 125 The Terrace, Wellington, 6143 New Zealand
64-4-473-9577, Fax: 64-4-471-2082,
wlgtn@international.gc.ca
www.wellington.gc.ca
P. Deacon, Counsellor
Caroline Chrétien, High Commissioner

Republic of Nicaragua
c/o Canadian Embassy, Apartado Postal 25, Managua, Nicaragua
505-268-0433, Fax: 505-268-0437,
mngua@international.gc.ca
www.nicaragua.gc.ca
N. Reeder, Ambassador (located in Costa Rica)

Republic of Niger
Canadian Embassy, PO Box 362 , Niamey, Niger
227-753-686, Fax: 227-753-107,
niamy@international.gc.ca
Michèle Lévesque, Ambassador (located in Côte d'Ivoire)

Federal Republic of Nigeria
Canadian High Commission, 15 Bobo St., Maitama, Abuja, Nigeria
234-9-413-9910, Fax: 234-9-413-9911,
abuja@international.gc.ca
www.dfait-maeci.gc.ca/nigeria/
K. Garner, First Secretary, Political
Sylvia Koleva, Trade Commissioner, Environmental Industries, sylvia.koleva@international.gc.ca
Denis Kingsley, High Commissioner
M.E. Havlik, Counsellor & Consul
J. Bracken, Counsellor, Development

Northern Ireland
See: United Kingdom of Great Britain & Northern

Northern Marianas
See: Commonwealth of Australia

Kingdom of Norway
Canadian Embassy, Wergelandsveien 7, Oslo, 0244 Norway
47-2299-5300, Fax: 47-2299-5301,
oslo@international.gc.ca
www.canada.no
John Winterbourne, Trade Commissioner, Environmental Industries, john.winterbourne@international.gc.ca
Georges Lemieux, Councellor, Commercial
John Hannaford, Ambassador
G. Norman, Councellor, Political

Sultanate of Oman
See: Kingdom of Saudi Arabia c/o The Canadian Embassy, PO Box 94321 , Riyad, 11693 Saudi Arabia

Islamic Republic of Pakistan
Canadian High Commission, PO Box 1042 , Islamabad, 44000 Pakistan
92-51-208-6000, Fax: 92-51-227-9188,
isbad@internationl.gc.ca
M. Samper, Counsellor, Development
M. Denton, Counsellor, Commercial
B. Marshall, First Secretary, Immigration
Randolph Mank, High Commissioner
K. Roberts, Counsellor

Republic of Panama
Apartado Postal 0832-2446, Estafata World Trade Centre, Panama City, Panama
011-507-264-9731, Fax: 011-507-263-8083,
panam@international.gc.ca
www.panama.gc.ca
J. Herran-Lima, Ambassador Designate
Luis Cedeno, Trade Commissioner, Environmental Industries, luis.cedeno@international.gc.ca

Papua New Guinea
See: Commonwealth of Australia Australia

Republic of Paraguay

Republic of Peru
Canadian Embassy, Calle Bolognesi 228, Miraflores, Lima, Peru
511-319-3200, Fax: 511-446-4912,
lima@international.gc.ca
E. Jager, First Secretary, Commercial
Alexandra Laverdure, Trade Commissioner, Environmental Industries, lima.commerce@international.gc.ca
M. Friesen, First Secretary
S. Roy, Counsellor (Administration) & Consul
J.B. Parenteau, First Secretary, Cooperation
Richard Lecoq, Ambassador

Republic of the Philippines
PO Box 2098, Makati Central Post Office, Makati City, 1200 Philippines
63-2-857-9000, Fax: 63-2-843-1082,
manil@international.gc.ca
www.dfait-maeci.gc.ca/manila/
Ramon Yazon, Trade Commissioner, Environmental Industries, ramon.yazon@international.gc.ca
A. Dugas, Counsellor (Administration) & Consul
E.R. Zeisler, Counsellor, Commercial
T. Carroll, Counsellor, Development
S. Rheault Kihara, Counsellor, Political/Economic
R. Desjardins, Ambassador

Republic of Poland
Canadian Embassy, ul. Jana Matejiki 1/5, Warsaw, 00-481 Poland
48-22-584-3100, Fax: 48-22-584-3192,
wsaw@international.gc.ca
www.canada.pl
B. St-Jean, Counsellor, Political, Cultural & Academic Relations
S. Flamand-Hubert, Counsellor (Administration) & Consul
Ewa Gawron-Dobroczynska, Trade Commissioner, Environmental Industries
David Preston, Ambassador
Roger Bélanger, Counsellor, Trade
C. Bailey, Counsellor, Immigration

Portuguese Republic
Canadian Embassy, Avenida da Liberdade, 196-200, 3rd Fl., Lisbon, 1269-121 Portugal
351-21-316-4600, Fax: 351-21-316-4691,
lsbon@international.gc.ca
www.portugal.gc.ca
Lyne Boulet, First Secretary (Administration) & Consul
L. Levasseur, First Secretary, Commercial
Carlos Lindo da Silva, Trade Commissioner, Environmental Industries
Anne-Marie Bourcier, Ambassador
C. Sheck, Counsellor, Political

Principe
See: Gabonese Republic

Puerto Rico
See: United States of America

State of Qatar
See: State of Kuwait

Republic of Palau
See: Republic of the Philippines

Republic of Romania
Canadian Embassy, 1-3 Tuberozelor Str., Bucharest, 011411 Romania
40-21-307-5000, Fax: 40-21-307-5010,
bucst@international.gc.ca
www.dfait-maeci.gc.ca/bucharest
Octavian Bonea, Trade Commissioner, Environmental Industries
C. Lord, Counsellor, Immigration
P. Beaulne, Ambassador
D. McGregor, Counsellor, Commercial

Russian Federation
Canadian Embassy, 23 Starokonyushenny Pereulok, Moscow, 119002 Russian Federation
7-495-925-6000, Fax: 7-495-925-6025,
mosco@international.gc.ca
Lilya Panova, Trade Commissioner, Environmental Industries, lilya.panova@international.gc.ca
Ralph Lysyshyn, Ambassador
J. Kur, Minister-Counsellor, Commercial
J. Morrison, Minister-Counsellor

Rwandese Republic
Canadian Embassy, PO Box 1117 , Kigali, Rwanda
250-573-210, Fax: 250-572-719,
kgali@international.gc.ca
J. Fournier, Second Secretary, Development & Vice-Consul
Jim Wall, Ambassador (located in Kenya)

Saint Kitts & Nevis
See: Barbados

Saint Lucia
See: Barbados

Samoa
See: New Zealand

Republic of San Marino
See: Italian Republic Italy

Kingdom of Saudi Arabia
Canadian Embassy, PO Box 94321 , Riyadh, 11693 Saudi Arabia
966-1-488-2288, Fax: 966-1-488-1997,
ryadh@international.gc.ca
Ursula Holland, Counsellor, Political
Mazen El-Khatib, Trade Commissioner, Environmental Industries, mazen.el-khatib@international.gc.ca
C. Andeel, Counsellor (Administration) & Consul
P. MacKinnon, Ambassador
Andreas Weichert, Minister-Counsellor, Commercial

Scotland
See: United Kingdom of Great Britain & Northern

Republic of Senegal
Canadian Embassy, PO Box 3373 , Dakar, Senegal
221-33-889-4700, Fax: 221-33-889-4720,
dakar@international.gc.ca
www.dakar.gc.ca
Aminata Ly Faye, Trade Commissioner, Environmental Industries, aminata.ly@international.gc.ca
L. Minville, First Secretary, Development
J.P. Bolduc, Ambassador

Serbia
See: Serbia & Montenegro

Serbia & Montenegro
Canadian Embassy, Kneza Milosa 75, Belgrade, 11000 Serbia & Montenegro
381-11-306-3000, Fax: 381-11-306-3042,
bgrad@international.gc.ca
www.serbia.gc.ca
K. Sooley, Counsellor (Administration) & Consul
B. Steen, Counsellor, Development
John Morrison, Ambassador

Republic of Seychelles
See: United Republic of Tanzania

Republic of Sierra Leone
See: Republic of Ivory Coast

Republic of Singapore
Canadian High Commission, PO Box 845 , Singapore, 901645 Singapore
65 68545900, Fax: 65 68545930,
spore@international.gc.ca
www.dfait-maeci.gc.ca/singapore/
Fumiko Kitano, Second Secretary (Commercial) & Trade Commissioner
R. Borowyk, Counsellor, Commercial
J. Gobeil, Counsellor, Administration
David Sevigny, High Commissioner

Slovak Republic
Embassy of Canada, Mostova 2, Bratislava, 811 02 Slovak Republic
421-259-204-031, Fax: 421-254-434-227,
brtsv@international.gc.ca
www.ocanada.sk
Ambassador resides in Prague, Czech Republic
M. Calcott, Ambassador

Republic of Slovenia
See: Republic of Hungary

Solomon Islands
See: Commonwealth of Australia

Somali Democratic Republic
See: Republic of Kenya

Republic of South Africa
Canadian High Commission, Private Bag X13, Hatfield, Pretoria, 0028 South Africa
27-12-422-3000, Fax: 27-12-422-3052,
pret@international.gc.ca
www.canada.co.za
G. Rent, Second Secretary
Col. R. Hatton, Counsellor
Adèle Dion, High Commissioner
P. Jamieson, First Secretary, Immigration

Kingdom of Spain
Canadian Embassy, Apartado 587, Madrid, 28080 Spain
34-9-423-3250, Fax: 34-9-423-3251,
mdrid@international.gc.ca
www.spain.gc.ca
S. Savage, Minister-Counsellor
M. Lebleu, Counsellor, Commercial
C. Munante, Counsellor (Administration) & Consul
Amaya Jauregui, Trade Commissioner, Environmental Industries
Graham Shantz, Ambassador

Democratic Socialist Republic of Sri Lanka
Canadian High Commission, PO Box 1006 , Colombo, 7 Sri Lanka
94-11-522-6232, Fax: 94-11-522-6299,
clmbo@international.gc.ca
Sanjeeva Sellahewe, Trade Commissioner, Environmental Industries, sanjeeva.sellahewe@international.gc.ca
R. Bedlington, Chargé d'Affaires
Angela Bogdan, High Commissioner
C. Parker, Counsellor, Development

Republic of The Sudan
Canadian Embassy, 29 Africa Rd., Block 56, Khartouom, 10503 Sudan
249-156-550-500, Fax: 249-156-550-501,
KHRM@international.gc.ca
S. Hanson, Chargé d'Affaires

Republic of Suriname
See: Republic of Guyana

Kingdom of Swaziland
See: Republic of South Africa

Kingdom of Sweden
Canadian Embassy, PO Box 16129, Stockholm, 103 23 Sweden
46-8-453-3000, Fax: 46-8-453-3016,
stkhm@international.gc.ca
www.canadaeuropa.gc.ca/sweden
M.A. Jacques, First Secretary & Consul
M. Siewecke, Counsellor, Commercial
Inga-Lill Olsson, Trade Commissioner, Environmental Industries
A. Volkoff, Ambassador
P. Low-Bédard, Counsellor

Swiss Confederation
Canadian Embassy, Kirchenfeldstrasse 88, Bern, CH-3005 Switzerland
41-31-357-3200, Fax: 41-31-357-3210,
bern@international.gc.ca
www.switzerland.gc.ca
Werner Naef, Trade Commissioner, Environmental Industries, werner.naef@international.gc.ca
C. Schwenger, Counsellor & Consul
Roberta Santi, Ambassador

Syrian Arab Republic
Canadian Embassy, PO Box 3394 , Damascus, Syria
963-11-611-6692, Fax: 963-11-611-4000,
dmcus@international.gc.ca
www.international.gc.ca/syria
Nidal Bitar, Trade Commissioner, Environmental Industries, nidal.bitar@international.gc.ca
M. Dupuis, Counsellor, Immigration
Glenn Davidson, Ambassador
C. Hull, Counsellor
Stéphane Beaulieu, Counsellor (Commercial) & Sr. Trade Commissioner, stephane.beaulieu@international.gc.ca

Taiwan
Canadian Trade Office, 365 Fu Hsing North Rd., 13th Fl., Taipei, 10483 Taiwan
886-2-2544-3000, Fax: 886-2-2544-3592,
taipei@international.gc.ca
www.canada.org.tw
Karen Huang, Sr. Commercial Officer, Trade
Francis Huot, Deputy Director
Ron MacIntosh, Executive Director
Stephanie Berlet, Deputy Director, Investment Promotion
J. Reeve, Director, General Relations
Vanessa Chen, Commercial Officer, Environmental Industries, vanessa.chen@international.gc.ca
S. McLuckie, Director, Visa

Republic of Tajikistan
See: Republic of Kazakhstan

United Republic of Tanzania
Canadian High Commission, PO Box 1022 , Dar-es-Salaam, Tanzania
255-22-216-3300, Fax: 255-22-211-6897,
dslam@international.gc.ca
www.dfait-maeci.gc.ca/tanzania
Noel Amos, Trade Commissioner, Environmental Industries, noel.amos@international.gc.ca
J. Moore, Counsellor, Development
R. Orr, Counsellor, Development
Janet Sidall, High Commissioner
S. Potter, Counsellor, Development

Kingdom of Thailand
Canadian Embassy, PO Box 2090 , Bangkok, 10501 Thailand
66-2-636-0540, Fax: 66-2-636-0566,
bngkk@international.gc.ca
www.thailand.gc.ca
Orawan Chandrangsu, Trade Commissioner, Environmental Industries
D. Yasui, Counsellor, Development
D. Danch, Counsellor (Administration) & Consul
R. Hoffmann, Ambassador
G. Goldhawk, Counsellor, Commercial

Republic of Togo
See: Republic of Ghana

Kingdom of Tonga
See: New Zealand

Republic of Trinidad & Tobago
Canadian High Commission, PO Box 1246 , Port of Spain, Trinidad
868-622-6232, Fax: 868-628-2581,
pspan@international.gc.ca
www.trinidadandtobago.gc.ca
Michaeline Narcisse, Trade Commissioner, Environmental Industries, michaeline.narcisse@international.gc.ca
F. Fournier, Counsellor, Commercial
C. Guimond, Counsellor, Immigration
Karen L. McDonald, High Commissioner

Republic of Tunisia
Canadian Embassy, PO Box 31, Tunis, 1002 Tunisia
216-71-104-000, Fax: 216-71-104-191,
tunis@international.gc.ca
www.dfait-maeci.gc.ca/tunisia
Lassaad Bourguiba, Trade Commissioner, Environmental Industries, lassaad.bourguiba@international.gc.ca
Peter Stulken, Counsellor, Commercial, peter.stulken@international.gc.ca
Jean Se@nécal, Management/Consular Officer, jean.senedal@international.gc.ca
Ariel Delouya, Ambassador

Republic of Turkey
Canadian Embassy, Cinnah Caddesi 58, Cankaya, Ankara, 06690 Turkey
90-312-409-2700, Fax: 90-312-312-409-2810,
ankra@international.gc.ca
www.dfait-maeci.gc.ca/canadaeuropa/turkey/menu -en.asp
Akin Kosetorunu, Trade Commissioner, Environmental Industries, akin.kosetorunu@international.gc.ca
J. Davison, Counsellor
M. Ward, First Secretary, Commercial
M. Bailey, Ambassador
D. Vaughan, Counsellor, Immigration

Turkmenistan
See: Republic of Turkey

Turks & Caicos Islands
See: Jamaica

Republic of Tuvalu
See: New Zealand

Republic of Uganda
See: Republic of Kenya

Ukraine
Canadian Embassy, 31 Yaroslaviv Val, Kyiv, 1901 Ukraine
380-44-590-3100, Fax: 380-44-590-3109,
kyiv@international.gc.ca
www.kyiv.gc.ca
George Grushchenko, Trade Commissioner
Valerie Sorel, Mission Consular Officer
Doris Wong, Counsellor, CIDA/Development
Yury Mardak, Trade Commissioner, Environmental Industries, yury.mardak@international.gc.ca
Daniel Caron, Ambassador
Michael Bates, Counsellor, Political/Economic

United Arab Emirates
The Canadian Embassy, PO Box 6970 , Abu Dhabi, United Arab Emirates
971-2-694-0300, Fax: 971-2-694-0399,
abdbi@international.gc.ca
www.uae.gc.ca
Sara Hradecky, Ambassador
P. Bedard, Counsellor (Administration) & Consul
Imad Arafat, Trade Commissioner, Environmental Industries, imad.arafat@international.gc.ca
M. Lazaruk, Counsellor, Commercial

United Kingdom of Great Britain & Northern Ireland
Canadian High Commission, MacDonald House, One Grosvenor Sq., London, W1K 4AB United Kingdom
44-20-7258-6600, Fax: 44-20-7258-6384,
ldn@international.gc.ca
www.london.gc.ca
C. Boucher, Deputy High Commissioner
J. St-George, Minister, Commercial/Economic
A. Arnott, Minister-Counsellor, Immigration
Sushma Gera, Trade Commissioner, Environmental Industries
James Wright, High Commissioner
R. Fry, Minister-Counsellor, Political/Public Affairs

United States of America
Canadian Embassy, 501 Pennsylvannia Ave. NW, Washington, DC 20001 USA
202-682-1740, Fax: 202-682-7726,
wshdc@international.gc.ca
www.canadianembassy.org
His Excellency Gary Doer, Ambassador

Eastern Republic of Uruguay
Canadian Embassy, #102, Plaza Independencia 749, C.P. 11100, Montevideo, Uruguay
598-2-902-2030, Fax: 598-2-902-2029,
mvdeo@international.gc.ca
www.montevideo.gc.ca
C. Hardman, Second Secretary & Consul
Patricia Wilson, Trade Commissioner, Environmental Industries
A. Latulippe, Ambassador

Republic of Uzbekistan
See: Russian Federation

Republic of Vanuatu
See: Commonwealth of Australia

Holy See
Canadian Embassy, Via della Conciliazione 4/D, Rome, 00193 Italy
39-06-6830-7316, Fax: 39-06-6880-6283,
vatcn@international.gc.ca
www.dfait-maeci.gc.ca/canadaeuropa/holysee/
Jean Bourassa, Counsellor
Anne Leahy, Ambassador

Republic of Venezuela
Canadian Embassy, Apartado Postal 62302, Caracas, 1060A Venezuela
58-212-600-3000, Fax: 58-212-263-8326,
crcas@international.gc.ca
www.caracas.gc.ca
Guy Salesse, Trade Commissioner
Denise Keating, Counsellor (Administration) & Consul
Daniela Oyague, Trade Commissioner, Environmental Industries
Perry Calderwood, Ambassador
N. Morgan, First Secretary

Socialist Republic of Vietnam
Canadian Embassy, 31 Huong Vuong St., Hanoi, Vietnam
84-4-3734-5000, Fax: 84-4-3734-5049,
hanoi@international.gc.ca
www.vietnam.gc.ca
Dang-Anh Thu, Trade Commissioner, Environmental Industries, dang-anh.thu@international.gc.ca
M. Perras, Counsellor (Administration) & Consul
D. Horton, Ambassador
Pierre Delorme, Counsellor, Trade

Wales
See: United Kingdom of Great Britain & Northern

Republic of Yemen
See: Kingdom of Saudi Arabia

Republic of Zambia
Canadian High Commission, PO Box 31313 , Lusaka, 10101 Zambia
260-1-25-08-33, Fax: 260-1-25-41-76,
lsaka@international.gc.ca
www.international.gc.ca/world/embassies/zambia /
S. Landry, First Secretary & Consul
Solomon Milimbo, Trade Commissioner, Environmental Industries, solomon.milimbo@international.gc.ca
P.P. Perron, Acting High Commissioner
L. Rogers, First Secretary, Development

Republic of Zimbabwe
Canadian Embassy, PO Box 1430 , Harare, Zimbabwe
263-425-2181, Fax: 263-425-2186,
hrare@international.gc.ca
www.zimbabwe.gc.ca
N. Forfar, Second Secretary
M. Nyiramana, Counsellor, Development
Barbara Richardson, Ambassador
D. Langlois, Counsellor

SECTION 8
GOVERNMENT/MUNICIPAL

Listings in this Section are arranged by Province. Each Provincial section includes a district map, notes concerning local government structure and elections. Each Province includes the following categories.

Counties & Municipal Districts

Major Municipalities

Other Municipalities

MUNICIPAL GOVERNMENT

The Municipal Section of the almanac is a list of local municipalities in Canada, arranged by provinces, and including population and electoral districts. Each provincial list is preceded by notes about local municipal organization and elections.

Regional Governments, Major Cities, Cities, Towns, Villages, Other Municipalities, etc., with Officials, listed by Province

ALBERTA

The major legislation concerning municipal government in Alberta is the Municipal Government Act.

Municipal government in Alberta is rural, urban or specialized. Rural municipal governments are organized into Municipal Districts, with Specialized Municipalities created to meet the unique needs of a specific municipality. Elected councils are responsible for the welfare & interests of the municipalities. Two other rural categories are Improvement Districts and Special Areas, which are geographically large, sparsely populated areas for which the provincial government levies and collects all taxes and provides services.

Urban municipalities include Summer Villages, Villages, Towns and Cities. These are fully autonomous municipal units, each with an elected council. They are responsible for providing all municipal services within their corporate limits and for levying taxes and rates.

In addition to the above forms of municipal government there are eight Metis Settlements established under the Metis Settlements Act.

Types of Municipalities that may be formed:

- Municipal District: A majority of the buildings used as dwellings are on parcels of land with an area of at least 1,850 square metres and there is a population of 1,000 or more.
- Village: A majority of the buildings are on parcels of land smaller than 1,850 square metres and there is a population of 300 or more.
- Town: A majority of the buildings are on parcels of land smaller than 1,850 square metres and there is a population of 1,000 or more.
- City: A majority of the buildings are on parcels of land smaller than 1,850 square metres and there is a population of 10,000 or more.

Specialized Municipality: An area in which the Minister is satisfied that a type of municipality (as listed above) does not meet the needs of the proposed municipality; to provide for a form of local government that, in the opinion of the Minister, will provide for the orderly development of the municipality to a type of municipality (as listed above), or to another form of specialized municipality; an area in which the Minister is satisfied for any other reason that it is appropriate in the circumstances to form a specialized municipality.

Incorporation and changes in status are determined by the Lieutenant Governor in Council (Provincial Cabinet) on the recommendation of the Minister of Municipal Affairs. It is not necessary to change status by reason of population change. Elections are held in October. Terms of office are three years (2007, 2010, etc.).

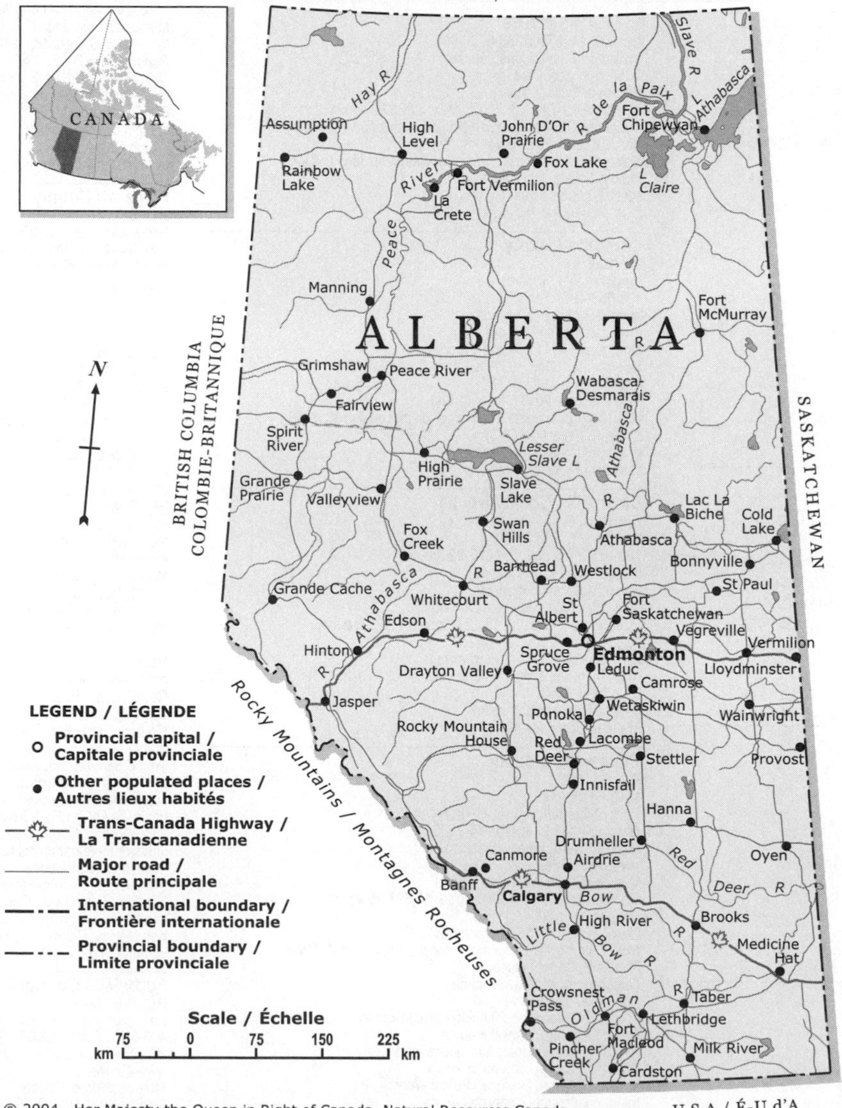

Alberta

Counties & Municipal Districts in Alberta

Acadia No. 34
P.O. Box 30
Acadia Valley, AB T0J 0A0
403-972-3808 Fax: 403-972-3833
admin@mdacadia.ab.ca
www.mdacadia.ab.ca
Municipal Type: Municipal District
Incorporated: Dec. 9, 1913; *Area:* 1,076.26 sq km
Population in 2006: 545
Next Election: 2013 (3 year terms)
Gary E. Peers, Municipal Administrator
Larry Heeg, Reeve
reeve.heeg@mdacadia.ab.ca

Athabasca County No. 12
3602 - 48 Ave.
Athabasca, AB T9S 1M8
780-675-2273 Fax: 780-675-5512
info@athabascacounty.com
www.athabascacounty.com
Municipal Type: Municipal District
Incorporated: Dec. 18, 1913; *Area:* 6,126.43 sq km
Population in 2006: 7,587
Next Election: 2013 (3 year terms)
Note: Incorporated as a municipal district on Dec. 14, 1914.
Jim Woodward, Manager
jwoodward@athabascacounty.com
Charlie Ashbey, Reeve

Barrhead County No. 11
5306 - 49 St.
Barrhead, AB T7N 1N5
780-674-3331 Fax: 780-674-2777
duhrbach@phrd.ab.ca
www.countybarrhead.ab.ca
Municipal Type: Municipal District
Incorporated: Dec. 18, 1913; *Area:* 2,404.55 sq km
Population in 2006: 5,845
Next Election: 2013 (3 year terms)
Note: Incorporated as a municipal district on Dec. 14, 1914.
Dale Uhrbach, County Manager
duhrbach@phrd.ab.ca
Lawrence Miller, Reeve

Beaver County
P.O. Box 140
Ryley, AB T0B 4A0
780-663-3730 Fax: 780-663-3602
administration@beaver.ab.ca
www.beaver.ab.ca
Municipal Type: Municipal District
Incorporated: Feb. 1, 1943; *Area:* 3,319.1 sq km
Population in 2006: 5,676
Next Election: 2013 (3 year terms)
Margaret Jones, CAO
mjones@beaver.ab.ca
James Kallal, Reeve
beavco2@telus.net

Big Lakes
P.O. Box 239
High Prairie, AB T0G 1E0
780-523-5955 Fax: 780-523-4227
biglakes@mdbiglakes.ca
www.mdbiglakes.ca
Municipal Type: Municipal District
Incorporated: Dec. 18, 1913; *Area:* 13,892.91 sq km
Population in 2006: 5,805
Next Election: 2013 (3 year terms)
Note: Incorporated as a municipal district on Jan. 1, 1995.
Gilles Lussier, CAO
cao@mdbiglakes.ca
Alvin Billings, Reeve

Bighorn No. 8
P.O. Box 310
Exshaw, AB T0L 2C0
403-673-3611 Fax: 403-673-3895
bighorn@mdbighorn.ca
www.mdbighorn.ca
Municipal Type: Municipal District
Incorporated: April 1, 1945; *Area:* 2,767.94 sq km
Population in 2006: 1,264
Next Election: 2013 (3 year terms)
Note: Incorporated as a municipal district on Jan. 1, 1988.
Martin Buckley, CAO
martin.buckley@mdbighorn.ca
Dene Cooper, Reeve

Birch Hills
P.O. Box 157
Wanham, AB T0H 3P0
780-694-3793 Fax: 780-694-3788
irenec@birchhillscounty.com
www.birchhillscounty.com
Municipal Type: Municipal District
Incorporated: Dec. 18, 1913; *Area:* 2,856.69 sq km
Population in 2006: 1,470
Next Election: 2013 (3 year terms)
Irene Cooper, CAO
Shirley Emerson, Reeve
rushirl@telus.net

Bonnyville No. 87
P.O. Box 1010
4905 - 50 Ave.
Bonnyville, AB T9N 2J7
780-826-3171 Fax: 780-826-4524
kkalinski@md.bonnyville.ab.ca
www.md.bonnyville.ab.ca
Municipal Type: Municipal District
Incorporated: Dec. 14, 1914; *Area:* 6,057.44 sq km
Population in 2006: 10,194
Next Election: 2013 (3 year terms)
Ryan Poole, CAO
rpoole@md.bonnyville.ab.ca
Ed Rondeau, Reeve

Brazeau County
P.O. Box 77
5516 Industrial Rd.
Drayton Valley, AB T7A 1R1
780-542-7777 Fax: 780-542-7770
krobinson@brazeau.ab.ca
www.brazeau.ab.ca
Municipal Type: Municipal District
Incorporated: Dec. 18, 1913; *Area:* 3,015.83 sq km
Population in 2006: 7,040
Next Election: 2013 (3 year terms)
Note: Incorporated as a municipal district on Dec. 13, 1915.
Ron McCullough, CAO
rmccullough@brazeau.ab.ca
Wes Tweedle, Reeve

Camrose County No. 22
3755 - 43 Ave.
Camrose, AB T4V 3S8
780-672-4446 Fax: 780-672-1008
county@county.camrose.ab.ca
www.county.camrose.ab.ca
Municipal Type: County
Incorporated: Dec. 23, 1912; *Area:* 3,331.98 sq km
County or District: Camrose No. 22; *Population in 2008:* 7,577
Next Election: 2013 (3 year terms)
Note: Incorporated as a municipal district on Jan. 1, 1944.
Steven Gerlitz, Administrator
sgerlitz@county.camrose.ab.ca
Don L. Gregorwich, Reeve

Cardston County
P.O. Box 580
Cardston, AB T0K 0K0
403-653-4977 Fax: 403-653-1126
office@cardstoncounty.com
www.cardstoncounty.com
Municipal Type: Municipal District
Incorporated: Dec. 18, 1913; *Area:* 3,414.87 sq km
Population in 2006: 4,037
Next Election: 2013 (3 year terms)
Note: Incorporated as a municipal district on Jan. 1, 1946.
Murray Millward, CAO
murray@cardstoncounty.com
Cameron Francis, Reeve

Clear Hills County No. 21
P.O. Box 240
Worsley, AB T0H 3W0
780-685-3925 Fax: 780-685-3960
info@clearhillscounty.ab.ca
www.clearhillscounty.ab.ca
Municipal Type: Municipal District
Incorporated: Dec. 18, 1913; *Area:* 15,112.69 sq km
Population in 2006: 2,714
Next Election: 2013 (3 year terms)
Note: Incorporated as a municipal district on Jan. 1, 1995.
Ray Coad, CAO
cao@clearhillscounty.ab.ca
Frances Davis, Reeve

Clearwater County
P.O. Box 550
4340 - 47th Ave.
Rocky Mountain House, AB T4T 1A4
403-845-4444 Fax: 403-845-7330
admin@county.clearwater.ab.ca
www.county.clearwater.ab.ca
Municipal Type: Municipal District
Incorporated: April 1, 1945; *Area:* 18,691.65 sq km
Population in 2006: 11,826
Next Election: 2013 (3 year terms)
Note: Incorporated as a municipal district on Jan. 1, 1985.
Ron Leaf, County Manager
rleaf@county.clearwater.ab.ca
Pat Alexander, Reeve
Joe Baker, Manager, Planning / West Country
jbaker@county.clearwater.ab.ca
Kim Nielsen, Manager, Agricultural Services
knielsen@county.clearwater.ab.ca
Marshall Morton, Manager, Public Works
mmorton@county.clearwater.ab.ca

Crowsnest Pass
P.O. Box 600
Blairmore, AB T0K 0E0
403-562-8833 Fax: 403-563-5474
cao@crowsnestpass.com
www.town.crowsnestpass.ab.ca
Municipal Type: Regional Municipality
Incorporated: Jan. 1, 1979; *Area:* 373.07 sq km
Population in 2006: 5,749
Provincial Electoral District(s): Livingstone-Macleod
Federal Electoral District(s): Macleod
Next Election: 2013 (3 year terms)
Gordon Lundy, CAO
John Irwin, MD, Mayor
execass@crowsnestpass.com

Cypress County
816 - 2nd Ave.
Dunmore, AB T1B 0K3
403-526-2888 Fax: 403-526-8958
cypress@cypress.ab.ca
www.cypress.ab.ca
Municipal Type: Municipal District
Incorporated: Dec. 18, 1913; *Area:* 13,166.13 sq km
Population in 2006: 6,729
Next Election: 2013 (3 year terms)
Note: Incorporated as a municipal district on Jan. 1, 1985.
Lutz Perschon, County Manager
lutz@cypress.ab.ca
Darcy Geigle, Reeve
403-834-2244, Fax: 403-834-2270
dgeigle@xplornet.com

Fairview No. 136
P.O. Box 189
Fairview, AB T0H 1L0
780-835-4903 Fax: 780-835-3131
mdinfo@mdfairview.ab.ca
www.albertafirst.com/profiles/community
Municipal Type: Municipal District
Incorporated: Dec. 18, 1913; *Area:* 1,390.66 sq km
Population in 2006: 1,432
Next Election: 2013 (3 year terms)
Note: Incorporated as a municipal district on Dec. 9, 1914.
Ben Boettcher, CAO
ben@mdfairview.ab.ca
Walter Doll, Reeve
ben@mdfairview.ab.ca

Flagstaff County
P.O. Box 358
Sedgewick, AB T0B 4C0
780-384-4100 Fax: 780-384-3635 Toll Free: 1-877-387-4100
county@flagstaff.ab.ca
www.flagstaff.ab.ca
Municipal Type: County
Incorporated: Dec. 9, 1912; *Area:* 4,066.92 sq km
Population in 2006: 3,506
Next Election: 2013 (3 year terms)
Shelly Armstrong, CAO
sarmstrong@flagstaff.ab.ca
Gerald Kuefler, Reeve
780-583-2208, Fax: 780-583-2437

Foothills No. 31
P.O. Box 5605
309 Macleod Trail
High River, AB T1V 1M7
403-652-2341 Fax: 403-652-7880 Emergencies: 1-888-808-3722
mdfthlls@mdfoothills.com
www.mdfoothills.com
Municipal Type: Municipal District
Incorporated: Dec. 23, 1912; *Area:* 3,643.6 sq km
Population in 2006: 19,736
Next Election: 2013 (3 year terms)
Note: Incorporated as a municipal district on Jan. 1, 1944.
Harry Riva Cambrin, Municipal Manager
hrc@mdfoothills.com
Roy McLean, Reeve
council@mdfoothills.com
Graham Clark, Fire Chief, Protective Services
graham.clark@mdfoothills.com
Tom Gillis, Director, Public Works & Engineering
tom.gillis@mdfoothills.com
Nasir Sheikh, Municipal Engineer
nasir.sheikh@mdfoothills.com
Judy Gordon, Coordinator, Planning & Development
judy.gordon@mdfoothills.com
Marilyn Gordon-Cooper, Contact, Property Tax & Utilities Department
marilyn.gordon-cooper@mdfoothills.com
Heather Hemingway, Contact, Environment Committee
heather.hemingway@mdfoothills.com
Ken McKay, Contact, Building Safety Codes & Bylaw Enforcement
ken.mckay@mdfoothills.com

Forty Mile County No. 8
P.O. Box 160
Foremost, AB T0K 0X0
403-867-3530 Fax: 403-867-2242
info@fortymile.ab.ca
www.40mile.ca
Municipal Type: County
Incorporated: Dec. 9, 1912; *Area:* 7,229.84 sq km
Population in 2006: 3,414
Next Election: 2013 (3 year terms)

Dale Brown, Administrator
dale@fortymile.ab.ca
Lynden Hutchinson, Reeve
403-867-2190
reeve@fortymile.ab.ca

Grande Prairie No. 1
10001 - 84 Ave.
Clairmont, AB T0H 0W0
780-532-9722 Fax: 780-539-9880
info@countygp.ab.ca
www.countygp.ab.ca
Municipal Type: County
Incorporated: Dec. 9, 1912; *Area:* 5,883.92 sq km
Population in 2006: 17,970
Next Election: 2013 (3 year terms)
Note: Incorporated as a county on Jan. 1, 1951.
W.A. Rogan, County Administrator
brogan1@countygp.ab.ca
Everett McDonald, Reeve
John Simpson, Director, Planning
780-513-3950
plan@countygp.ab.ca
Everett Cooke, Fire Chief
780-567-5590
fire@countygp.ab.ca
Steve Madden, Manager, Environment
780-532-7393
Herb Pfau, Superintendent, Public Works
780-532-7393
pubwks@countygp.ab.ca

Greenview No. 16
P.O. Box 1079
Valleyview, AB T0H 3N0
780-524-7600 Fax: 780-524-4307
mdg1@mdgreenview.ab.ca
www.mdgreenview.ab.ca
Municipal Type: Municipal District
Incorporated: Jan. 1, 1969; *Area:* 32,994.14 sq km
Population in 2006: 5,464
Next Election: 2013 (3 year terms)
Note: Incorporated as a municipal district on Jan. 1, 1994.
Jim Squire, CAO
Jim@mdgreenview.ab.ca
Tony Yelenik, Reeve
780-524-2269
Esecretary@mdgreenview.ab.ca

Jasper
P.O. Box 520
Jasper, AB T0E 1E0
780-852-3356 Fax: 780-852-4019
j.cooper@town.jasper.ab.ca
www.jasper-alberta.com
Municipal Type: Regional Municipality
Incorporated: Aug. 31, 1995; *Area:* 925.52 sq km
Population in 2006: 4,265
Next Election: 2013 (3 year terms)
Note: Incorporated as a specialized municipality on July 20, 2001.
George Krefting, Municipal Manager
gkrefting@town.jasper.ab.ca
Richard Ireland, Mayor
rireland@town.jasper.ab.ca

Kneehill County
P.O. Box 400
Three Hills, AB T0M 2A0
403-443-5541 Fax: 403-443-5115
office@kneehillcounty.com
www.kneehillcounty.com
Municipal Type: Municipal District
Incorporated: Dec. 9, 1912; *Area:* 3,380.04 sq km
Population in 2006: 5,218
Next Election: 2013 (3 year terms)
Kevin Miner, CAO
kevincao@kneehillcounty.com
Carol Calhoun, Reeve

Lac La Biche County
P.O. Box 1679
Lac La Biche, AB T0A 2C0
780-623-1747 Fax: 780-623-2039 Toll Free: 1-877-806-5632
main.office@laclabichecounty.com
www.laclabichecounty.com
Municipal Type: County
Incorporated: Aug. 1, 2007;
Provincial Electoral District(s): Lac La Biche-St. Paul
Federal Electoral District(s): Fort McMurray-Athabasca
Next Election: 2013 (3 year terms)
Note: The Town of Lac La Biche & Lakeland County amalgamated on August 1, 2007 to create Lac La Biche County.
Lucien Cloutier, County Clerk
lucien.cloutier@laclabichecounty.com
Peter Kirylchuk, Mayor
780-623-7732, Fax: 780-623-7720

Lac Ste. Anne County
P.O. Box 219
Sangudo, AB T0E 2A0
780-785-3411 Fax: 780-785-2359 Toll Free: 1-866-880-5722
lsac@gov.lacsteanne.ab.ca
www.gov.lacsteanne.ab.ca
Municipal Type: Municipal District
Incorporated: Jan. 1, 1944; *Area:* 2,842.46 sq km
Population in 2006: 9,516
Next Election: 2013 (3 year terms)
Len Szybunka, Municipal Administrator
lszybunka@gov.lacsteanne.ab.ca
Derril C. Butler, Reeve

Lacombe County
RR#3
Lacombe, AB T4L 2N3
403-782-6601 Fax: 403-782-3820
info@lacombecounty.com
www.lacombecounty.com
Municipal Type: County
Incorporated: Jan. 1, 1944; *Area:* 2,777.26 sq km
County or District: Lacombe No. 14; *Population in 2008:* 10,507
Next Election: 2013 (3 year terms)
Note: Incorporated as a county on Jan. 1, 1961.
Terry Hager, County Commissioner
thager@lacombecounty.com
Terry Engen, Reeve
Keith Boras, Manager, Agriculture Services
kboras@lacombecounty.com
Dale Freitaq, Manager, Planning Services
dfreitag@lacombecounty.com
Julian Veuger, County Constable, Disaster Services
jveuger@lacombecounty.com
Dale Freitaq, Planner & Development Officer
dfreitaq@lacombecounty.com
Dale Kary, Project Coordinator, Public Works
dkary@lacombecounty.com
Phil Lodermeier, Supervisor, Public Works
plodermeier@lacombecounty.com

Lamont County
Administration Bldg.
5303 - 50 Ave.
Lamont, AB T0B 2R0
780-895-2233 Fax: 780-895-7404 Toll Free: 1-877-895-2233
countyinfo@lamontcounty.ca
www.lamontcounty.ca
Municipal Type: County
Incorporated: Dec. 23, 1912; *Area:* 2,400.78 sq km
County or District: Lamont No. 30; *Population in 2006:* 3,925
Next Election: 2013 (3 year terms)
Note: Incorporated as a county on Jan. 1, 1968.
Allan Harvey, CAO
allan.h@tclamont.ca
Wayne Woldanski, Reeve
wayne.w@lamontcounty.ca

Leduc County
#101, 1101 - 5 St.
Nisku, AB T9E 2X3
780-955-3555 Fax: 780-955-3444 Toll free: 1-800-379-9052
shaunaf@leduc-county.com
www.leduc-county.com
Municipal Type: County
Incorporated: Jan. 1, 1944; *Area:* 2,610.25 sq km
County or District: Leduc No. 25; *Population in 2006:* 12,730
Next Election: 2013 (3 year terms)
Note: Incorporated as a county on Jan. 1, 1964.
Doug Wright, County Manager
780-955-6400
dougw@leduc-county.com
John Whaley, Reeve
Michael MacLean, Director, Public Works & Engineering
780-955-6416
michael@leduc-county.com
Phil Newman, Director, Planning & Development
780-955-6413
phil@leduc-county.com
Dean Ohnysty, Director, Parks & Recreation
780-955-4535
dean@leduc-county.com
Garett Broadbent, Director, Agricultural Services
780-955-6404
garett@leduc-county.com
Bob Galloway, Chief, Fire
780-955-7099
bobg@leduc-county.com
Deryld Dublanko, Manager, Maintenance & Materials Supply
780-955-2469
deryld@leduc-county.com
Janis Fong, Manager, Public Works & Infrastructure
Des Mryglod, Manager, Engineering
Dave McPhee, Officer, Utilities
780-955-4541
dave@leduc-county.com

Lesser Slave River No. 124
P.O. Box 722
Slave Lake, AB T0G 2A0
780-849-4888 Fax: 780-849-4939
md124@md124.ca
www.md124.ca
Municipal Type: Municipal District
Incorporated: Jan. 1, 1969; *Area:* 10,075.88 sq km
Population in 2006: 2,820
Next Election: 2013 (3 year terms)
Note: Incorporated as a municipal district on Jan. 1, 1995.
Allan Winarski, CAO
allan.winarski@md124.ca
Denny Garratt, Reeve
denny1@telusplanet.net

Lethbridge County
#100, 905 - 4 Ave. South
Lethbridge, AB T1J 4E4
403-328-5525 Fax: 403-328-5602
mailbox@county.lethbridge.ab.ca
www.county.lethbridge.ab.ca
Municipal Type: County
Incorporated: Jan. 1, 1954; *Area:* 2,839.28 sq km
County or District: Lethbridge No. 26; *Population in 2006:* 10,302
Next Election: 2013 (3 year terms)
Note: Incorporated as a county on Jan 1, 1964.
Dennis Shigematsu, County Manager
dshigematsu@county.lethbridge.ab.ca
Lorne Hickey, Reeve
lhickey@county.lethbridge.ab.ca

Mackenzie County
P.O. Box 640
4511 - 46 Ave.
Fort Vermilion, AB T0H 1N0
780-927-3718 Fax: 780-927-4266 Toll Free: 1-877-927-0677
office@mackenziecounty.com
www.mackenziecounty.com
Municipal Type: Regional Municipality
Incorporated: Jan. 1, 1995; *Area:* 80,484.42 sq km
Population in 2006: 10,002
Next Election: 2013 (3 year terms)
Note: Incorporated as a specialized municipality on June 23, 1999. Name changed from The Municipal District of Mackenzie No. 23 to Mackenzie County in 2007.
William (Bill) Kostiw, CAO
780-841-1801
bkostiw@mackenziecounty.com
Gregory Alan Newman, Reeve
780-927-3807
greg@mackenziecounty.com

Minburn County No. 27
P.O. Box 550
Vegreville, AB T9C 1R6
780-632-2082 Fax: 780-632-6296
info@minburncounty.ab.ca
www.minburncounty.ab.ca
Municipal Type: County
Incorporated: Jan. 30, 1942; *Area:* 2,911.14 sq km
County or District: Minburn No. 27; *Population in 2006:* 3,319
Next Election: 2013 (3 year terms)
Note: Incorporated as a county on Jan. 1, 1965.
David Marynowich, Manager
Albert Melnyk, Reeve

Mountain View County
P.O. Box 100
1408 Twp Rd. 320
Didsbury, AB T0M 0W0
403-335-3311 Fax: 403-335-9207 Toll Free Phone: 1-877-264-9754
info@mountainviewcounty.com
www.mountainviewcounty.com
Municipal Type: County
Incorporated: Dec. 9, 1912; *Area:* 3,804.43 sq km
Population in 2007: 12,570
Next Election: 2013 (3 year terms)
Note: Incorporated as a county on Jan. 1, 1961.
Doug Plamping, CAO
doug.plamping@mountainviewcounty.com
Albert Kemmere, Reeve
Steve McInnis, Director, Operational Services
steve.mcinnis@mountainviewcounty.com
Tony Martens, Director, Legislative & Community Services
tony.martens@mountainviewcounty.com
Jeff Holmes, Manager, Agriculture & Parks Services
jeff.holmes@mountainviewcounty.com

Newell County No. 4
P.O. Box 130
707 - 2nd Ave. East
Brooks, AB T1R 1B2
403-362-3266 Fax: 403-362-8681
administration@countyofnewell.ab.ca
www.countyofnewell.ab.ca
Municipal Type: County
Incorporated: Feb. 10, 1948; *Area:* 5,903.47 sq km
Population in 2009: 7,101
Next Election: 2013 (3 year terms)
Note: Incorporated as a county on Jan. 1, 1953.
Kevin Stephenson, CAO
stephensonk@countyofnewell.ab.ca
Molly Douglass, Reeve

Northern Lights No. 22
P.O. Box 10
#600, 7th Ave. NW
Manning, AB T0H 2M0
780-836-3348 Fax: 780-836-3663
info@mdnorth22.ab.ca, mdnorth22@mdnorth22.ab.ca
www.mdnorth22.ab.ca
Municipal Type: Municipal District
Incorporated: Dec. 18, 1913; *Area:* 20,745.45 sq km
Population in 2006: 3,772
Next Election: 2013 (3 year terms)
Note: Incorporated as a municipal district on April 1, 1995.
Theresa Van Oort, CAO
cao@mdnorth22.ab.ca
Edward Kamieniecki, Reeve

Northern Sunrise County
P.O. Box 1300
Peace River, AB T8S 1Y9
780-624-0013 Fax: 780-624-0023
general@northernsunrise.net
www.northernsunrise.net
Municipal Type: Municipal District
Incorporated: Dec. 18, 1913; *Area:* 21,141.25 sq km
Population in 2006: 1,747
Next Election: 2013 (3 year terms)
Note: Incorporated as a municipal district on April 1, 1994.
Bob Miles, CAO
ramiles@northernsunrise.net
Agnes Knudsen, Reeve

Opportunity No. 17
P.O. Box 60
Wabasca, AB T0G 2K0
780-891-3778 Fax: 780-891-3772
general_inquiries@mdopportunity.ab.ca
www.mdopportunity.ab.ca
Municipal Type: Municipal District
Incorporated: Dec. 18, 1913; *Area:* 29,140.78 sq km
Population in 2006: 2,847
Next Election: 2013 (3 year terms)
Note: Incorporated as a municipal district on Aug. 1, 1995.
Harvey Prockiw, Manager
harvey@mdopportunity.ab.ca
Paul Sinclair, Reeve

Paintearth County No. 18
P.O. Box 509
Castor, AB T0C 0X0
403-882-3211 Fax: 403-882-3560
info@countypaintearth.ca
www.countypaintearth.ca
Municipal Type: County
Incorporated: Dec. 8, 1913; *Area:* 3,287.24 sq km
County or District: Paintearth No. 18; *Population in 2006:* 2,126
Next Election: 2013 (3 year terms)
Note: Incorporated as a county on Jan. 1, 1962.
Julie Falkenberg, County Administrator
julie@countypaintearth.ca
George Glazier, Reeve
gglazier@countypaintearth.ca

Parkland County
53109A Sec Hwy. 779
Parkland County, AB T7Z 1R1
780-968-8888 Fax: 780-968-8413 Toll Free: 1-888-880-0858
inquiries@parklandcounty.com
www.parklandcounty.com
Municipal Type: County
Incorporated: March 1, 1918; *Area:* 2,392.61 sq km
Population in 2009: 30,089
Next Election: 2013 (3 year terms)
Note: Incorporated as a county on Jan. 1, 1969.
Pat Vincent, CAO
780-968-8411
pvincent@parklandcounty.com
Rodney Shaigec, Mayor
rshaigec@parklandcounty.com
Mark Cardinal, Manager, Agricultural Services
mcardinal@parklandcounty.com
Andy Haden, Manager, Planning & Development Services
ahaden@parklandcounty.com
Rob McGowan, Manager, Engineering Services
rmcgowan@parklandcounty.com
Daryl Phillips, Manager, Public Works
dphillips@parklandcounty.com
Ken Sault, Manager, Protective Services
ksault@parklandcounty.com
Ken Van Buul, Manager, Recreation & Parks Services
kvanbuul@parklandcounty.com
Janette Szucs, Coordinator, Purchasing
jszucs@parklandcounty.com
Trent Tompkins, Coordinator, Solid Waste
ttompkins@parklandcounty.com
Kevin Bryant, Supervisor, Utilities & Waste Services
kbryant@parklandcounty.com
Brian Rimmer, Supervisor, Environmental Services
brimmer@parklandcounty.com
Grace Horsfield, Officer, Development
ghorsfield@parklandcounty.com

Peace No. 135
P.O. Box 34
Berwyn, AB T0H 0E0
780-338-3845 Fax: 780-338-2222
mdpeace@wispernet.ca
www.albertafirst.com/profiles/community
Municipal Type: Municipal District
Incorporated: Dec. 11, 1916; *Area:* 851.92 sq km
Population in 2006: 1,487
Next Election: 2013 (3 year terms)
Lyle McKen, CAO
Veronica Bliska, Reeve

Pincher Creek No. 9
P.O. Box 279
Pincher Creek, AB T0K 1W0
403-627-3130 Fax: 403-627-5070
info@mdpinchercreek.ab.ca
www.mdpinchercreek.ab.ca
Municipal Type: Municipal District
Incorporated: Jan. 1, 1944; *Area:* 3,482.26 sq km
Population in 2006: 3,309
Next Election: 2013 (3 year terms)
Loretta Thompson, CAO
lthompson@mdpinchercreek.ab.ca
Rodney Cyr, Reeve
bhammond@mdpinchercreek.ab.ca

Ponoka County
4205 Hwy. 2A
Ponoka, AB T4J 1V9
403-783-3333 Fax: 403-783-6965
ponokacounty@ponokacounty.com
www.ponokacounty.com
Municipal Type: County
Incorporated: Jan. 1, 1944; *Area:* 2,807.94 sq km
County or District: Ponoka No. 3; *Population in 2006:* 8,640
Next Election: 2013 (3 year terms)
Note: Incorporated as a county on July 1, 1999.
Charlie Cutforth, CAO
charliecutforth@ponokacounty.com
Gordon Svenningsen, Reeve

Provost No. 52
P.O. Box 300
Provost, AB T0B 3S0
780-753-2434 Fax: 780-753-6432
mdprovost@mdprovost.ca
www.mdprovost.ca
Municipal Type: Municipal District
Incorporated: Dec. 9, 1912; *Area:* 3,625.2 sq km
Population in 2006: 2,547
Next Election: 2013 (3 year terms)
Iris Larson, Administrator
ilarson@mdprovost.ca
Allan Murray, Reeve

Ranchland No. 66
P.O. Box 1060
Nanton, AB T0L 1R0
403-646-3131 Fax: 403-646-3141
cao@ranchland66.com
Municipal Type: Municipal District
Incorporated: Jan. 1, 1969; *Area:* 2,639.16 sq km
Population in 2006: 86
Next Election: 2013 (3 year terms)
Note: Incorporated as a municipal district on Jan. 1, 1995.
Gregory Brkich, Acting Municipal Administrator
Harry Streeter, Reeve

Red Deer County
Red Deer County Centre
38106 Range Rd. 275
Red Deer County, AB T4S 2L9
403-350-2150 Fax: 403-346-9840
info@rdcounty.ca
http://rdcounty.ca
Municipal Type: County
Incorporated: Jan. 1, 1944; *Area:* 4,002.58 sq km
Population in 2006: 19,108
Next Election: 2013 (3 year terms)
Note: Incorporated as a county on Jan. 1, 1963.
Curtis Herzberg, County Manager
cherzberg@reddeercounty.ab.ca
Jim Wood, Mayor
403-350-2152
Harry Harker, Director, Planning & Development
hharker@reddeercounty.ab.ca
Ric Henderson, Director, Community & Protective Services
rhenderson@reddeercounty.ab.ca
Frank Peck, Director, Operations Services
fpeck@reddeercounty.ab.ca
Cliff Fuller, Fire Chief
cfuller@reddeercounty.ab.ca
Don Bardonnex, Manager, Fire Services
dbardonnex@reddeercounty.ab.ca
Joe D'Onofrio, Manager, Land
jd'onofrio@reddeercounty.ab.ca
Linda Henrickson, Manager, Rural Planning
lhenrickson@reddeercounty.ab.ca
Johan van der Bank, Manager, Urban Planning
jvanderbank@reddeercounty.ab.ca
Marty Campbell, Coordinator, Engineering
mcampbell@reddeercounty.ab.ca
Jo-Ann Symington, Coordinator, Community Services
jsymington@reddeercounty.ab.ca
Andrew Treu, Coordinator, Environmental Services
atreu@reddeercounty.ab.ca
Donna Trottier, Coordinator, Conservation
Dawna Barnes, Specialist, Community Development
dbarnes@reddeercounty.ab.ca
Art Preachuk, Fieldman, Agricultural Services
apreachuk@reddeercounty.ab.ca

Rocky View No. 44
911 - 32 Ave. NE
Calgary, AB T2E 6X6
403-230-1401 Fax: 403-277-5977
comments@rockyview.ca
www.rockyview.ca
Municipal Type: Municipal District
Incorporated: Feb. 1, 1943; *Area:* 4,014.89 sq km
Population in 2006: 34,171
Next Election: 2013 (3 year terms)
Robert Coon, CAO
rcoon@rockyview.ca
Lois Habberfield, Reeve
council@rockyview.ca
Brian Jobson, Director, Transportation Services
bjobson@gov.mdrockyview.ab.ca
Frank Misura, Manager, Development/Utility Services
Linda Ratzlaff, Coordinator, Policy Planning
403-520-8166
Tim Dietzler, Fieldman, Agriculture
403-520-1271

Saddle Hills County
P.O. Box 69
Spirit River, AB T0H 3G0
780-864-3760 Fax: 780-864-3904
admin@saddlehills.ab.ca
www.saddlehills.ab.ca
Municipal Type: Municipal District
Incorporated: April 1, 1945; *Area:* 5,836.94 sq km
Population in 2006: 2,458
Next Election: 2013 (3 year terms)
Note: Incorporated as a municipal district on Jan. 1, 1995.
Tarolyn Peach, CAO
tpeach@saddlehills.ab.ca
Tim Stone, Reeve
council@saddlehills.ab.ca

St. Paul County No. 19
5015 - 49 Ave.
St Paul, AB T0A 3A4
780-645-3301 Fax: 780-645-3104
countysp@county.stpaul.ab.ca
www.county.stpaul.ab.ca
Municipal Type: Municipal District
Incorporated: Jan. 30, 1942; *Area:* 3,297.74 sq km
Population in 2006: 5,925
Next Election: 2013 (3 year terms)
Kim Heyman, County Administrator
kheyman@county.stpaul.ab.ca
Robert Bouchard, Reeve

Smoky Lake County
P.O. Box 310
Smoky Lake, AB T0A 3C0
780-656-3730 Fax: 780-656-3768
county@smokylakecounty.ab.ca
www.smokylakecounty.ab.ca
Municipal Type: Municipal District
Incorporated: May 3, 1922; *Area:* 3,412.81 sq km
Population in 2006: 3,357
Next Election: 2013 (3 year terms)
Cary Smigerowsky, CAO
csmigerowsky@smokylakecounty.ab.ca
Cory Ollikka, Reeve
collikka@smokylakecounty.ab.ca

Smoky River No. 130
P.O. Box 210
Falher, AB T0H 1M0
780-837-2221 Fax: 780-837-2453
lturcotte@mdsmokyriver.com
www.mdsmokyriver.com
Municipal Type: Municipal District
Incorporated: Dec. 18, 1913; *Area:* 2,842.82 sq km
Population in 2006: 2,442
Next Election: 2013 (3 year terms)
Note: Incorporated as a municipal district on Jan. 1, 1952.
Lucien G. Turcotte, Municipal Administrator
Donald Dumont, Reeve

Spirit River No. 133
P.O. Box 389
Spirit River, AB T0H 3G0
780-864-3500 Fax: 780-864-4303
mdsr133@mdspiritriver.ab.ca
www.mdspiritriver.ab.ca
Municipal Type: Municipal District
Incorporated: Dec. 18, 1913; *Area:* 684.14 sq km
Population in 2006: 662
Next Election: 2013 (3 year terms)
Note: Incorporated as a municipal district on Dec. 11, 1916.
Monique Jeffrey, Municipal Administrator
mjeffrey@mdspiritriver.ab.ca
Kelly Hudson, Reeve

Starland County
P.O. Box 249
Morrin, AB T0J 2B0
403-772-3793 Fax: 403-772-3807
info@starlandcounty.com
www.starlandcounty.com
Municipal Type: Municipal District
Incorporated: Dec. 9, 1912; *Area:* 2,557.7 sq km
Population in 2006: 2,371
Next Election: 2013 (3 year terms)
Ross D. Rawlusyk, Administrator
ross@starlandcounty.com
J. Barrie Hoover, Reeve
bhoover@starlandcounty.com

Stettler County No. 6
P.O. Box 1270
Stettler, AB T0C 2L0

403-742-4441 Fax: 403-742-1277
info@stettlercounty.ca
www.stettler.net
Municipal Type: Municipal District
Incorporated: Dec. 9, 1912; *Area:* 4,008.72 sq km
Population in 2006: 5,216
Next Election: 2013 (3 year terms)
Tim Fox, CAO
tfox@stettlercounty.ca
Victor Carey, Reeve

Strathcona County

2001 Sherwood Dr.
Sherwood Park, AB T8A 3W7
780-464-8111 Fax: 780-464-8050
info@strathcona.ab.ca
www.strathcona.ab.ca
Municipal Type: Regional Municipality
Incorporated: Jan. 1, 1962; *Area:* 1,179.43 sq km
Population in 2009: 87,998
Next Election: 2013 (3 year terms)
Note: Incorporated as a specialized municipality on Jan. 1, 1996.
Robyn W. Singleton, Q.C., Chief Commissioner
780-464-8100
singleton@strathcona.ab.ca
Linda Osinchuk, Mayor
Peter Vana, Associate Commissioner, Infrastructure & Planning Services
780-464-8188
vana@strathcona.ab.ca
Denise Exton, Associate Commissioner, Community Services
780-464-8291
exton@strathcona.ab.ca

Sturgeon County

9613 - 100 St.
Morinville, AB T8R 1L9
780-939-4321 Fax: 780-939-3003 Toll free: 1-866-939-9303
sturgeonmail@sturgeoncounty.ab.ca
www.sturgeoncounty.ab.ca
Municipal Type: Municipal District
Incorporated: Feb. 1, 1943; *Area:* 2,108.9 sq km
Population in 2008: 19,165
Next Election: 2013 (3 year terms)
Case Van Herk, County Commissioner
780-939-8345
cvanherk@sturgeoncounty.ab.ca
Donald Rigney, B.Sc., MBA, Mayor
780-921-3041, Fax: 780-921-3041
drigney@sturgeoncounty.ab.ca
Ian McKay, General Manager, Infrastructure Services
780-939-8337
imckay@sturgeoncounty.ab.ca
Peter Tarnawsky, General Manager, Public Services
780-939-8344
ptarnawsky@sturgeoncounty.ab.ca
Bart Clark, Manager, Protective Services
780-939-0600
bclark@sturgeoncounty.ab.ca
Collin Steffes, Manager, Planning & Development
780-939-8275
csteffes@sturgeoncounty.ab.ca
Roy Lidgren, Manager, Transportation Services
780-939-8250
rlidgern@sturgeoncounty.ab.ca
Quentin Bochar, Manager, Agriculture Services
780-939-8325
qbochar@sturgeoncounty.ab.ca
Mike Hittinger, Coordinator, Municipal Conservation
780-939-8339
nwaci@sturgeoncounty.ab.ca

Taber

4900B - 50 St.
Taber, AB T1G 1T2
403-223-3541 Fax: 403-223-1799
dkrizsan@mdtaber.ab.ca
www.mdtaber.ab.ca
Municipal Type: Municipal District
Incorporated: April 1, 1945; *Area:* 4,204.38 sq km
Population in 2006: 6,280
Next Election: 2013 (3 year terms)
Derrick Krizsan, Municipal Administrator
Hank Van Beers, Reeve
hvanbeers@mdtaber.ab.ca

Thorhild County No. 7

P.O. Box 10
Thorhild, AB T0A 3J0
780-398-3741 Fax: 780-398-3748
dan@thorhildcounty.com
www.thorhildcounty.com
Municipal Type: County
Incorporated: Jan. 1, 1955; *Area:* 1,998.38 sq km
County or District: Thorhild No. 7; *Population in 2006:* 3,042
Next Election: 2013 (3 year terms)
Dan Small, County Manager
dan@thorhildcounty.com
Henry Zolkewski, Reeve
div31@telus.net

Two Hills County No. 21

P.O. Box 490
Two Hills, AB T0B 4K0
780-657-3358 Fax: 780-657-3504
rjorgensen@thcounty.ab.ca
www.thcounty.ab.ca
Municipal Type: County
Incorporated: Jan. 1, 1944; *Area:* 2,630.95 sq km
County or District: Two Hills No. 21; *Population in 2006:* 2,801
Next Election: 2013 (3 year terms)
Note: Incorporated as a county on Jan. 1, 1963.
Robert Jorgensen, CAO
rjorgensen@thcounty.ab.ca
Allen Sayler, Reeve
asayler@thcounty.ab.ca

Vermilion River County

P.O. Box 69
4912 - 50 Ave.
Kitscoty, AB T0B 2P0
780-846-2244 Fax: 780-846-2716
county24@telusplanet.net
www.vermilion-river.com
Municipal Type: Municipal District
Incorporated: Jan. 1, 1944; *Area:* 5,518.71 sq km
Population in 2008: 7,900
Next Election: 2013 (3 year terms)
Note: Name changed from Vermilion River No. 24 County on Sept. 13, 2006.
Rhonda King, County Administrator
780-846-3303
rking@county24.com
Richard Van Ee, Reeve
780-853-2730

Vulcan County

P.O. Box 180
Vulcan, AB T0L 2B0
403-485-2241 Fax: 403-485-2920
administration@vulcancounty.ab.ca
www.vulcancounty.ab.ca
Municipal Type: County
Incorporated: April 1, 1945; *Area:* 5,430.06 sq km
County or District: Vulcan County; *Population in 2006:* 3,718
Next Election: 2013 (3 year terms)
Note: Incorporated as a county on Jan. 1, 1951.
Gary Buchanan, CAO
countyadmin@vulcancounty.ab.ca
Ian A. Donovan, Reeve

Wainwright No. 61

717 - 14 Ave.
Wainwright, AB T9W 1B3
780-842-4454 Fax: 780-842-2463
mdwain@mdwainwright.ca
www.mdwainwright.ca
Municipal Type: Municipal District
Incorporated: Jan. 30, 1942; *Area:* 4,154.74 sq km
Population in 2006: 3,558
Next Election: 2013 (3 year terms)
Kelly Buchinski, Municipal Administrator
admin@mdwainwright.ca
Bob Barss, Reeve

Warner County No. 5

P.O. Box 90
Warner, AB T0K 2L0
403-642-3635 Fax: 403-642-3631
county5@countyofwarner5.ab.ca
www.countyofwarner5.ab.ca
Municipal Type: Municipal District
Incorporated: Dec. 9, 1912; *Area:* 4,519.77 sq km
Population in 2006: 3,674
Next Election: 2013 (3 year terms)
Allan K. Romeril, Administrator
administrator@countyofwarner5.ab.ca
Robert Jones, Reeve
div5_wa@countyofwarner5.ab.ca

Westlock County

10336 - 106 St.
Westlock, AB T7P 2G1
780-349-3346 Fax: 780-349-2012
info@westlockcounty.com
www.westlockcounty.com
Municipal Type: Municipal District
Incorporated: Feb. 1, 1943; *Area:* 3,174.6 sq km
Population in 2006: 6,910
Next Election: 2013 (3 year terms)
Edward LeBlanc, Municipal Administrator
eleblanc@westlockcounty.com
Charles Navratil, Reeve
780-349-2818

Wetaskiwin County No. 10

P.O. Box 6960
Wetaskiwin, AB T9A 2G5
780-352-3321 Fax: 780-352-3486 Toll Free: 1-800-661-4125
fcoutney@county.wetaskiwin.ab.ca
www.county.wetaskiwin.ab.ca
Municipal Type: County
Incorporated: Dec. 13, 1915; *Area:* 3,130.9 sq km
County or District: Wetaskiwin No. 10; *Population in 2006:* 10,535
Next Election: 2013 (3 year terms)
Note: Incorporated as a county on Jan. 1, 1958.
Frank Coutney, County Administrator
fcoutney@county.wetaskiwin.ab.ca
Garry Dearing, Reeve
Ken Carlson, Director, Disaster Services
780-361-6340
kcarlson@county.wetaskiwin.ab.ca
Dave Dextraze, Director, Public Works
780-361-6230
ddextraze@county.wetaskiwin.ab.ca
Steve Majek, Director, Agricultural Services
780-361-6226
smajek@county.wetaskiwin.ab.ca

Wheatland County

Hwy. 1, RR#1
Strathmore, AB T1P 1J6
403-934-3321 Fax: 403-934-4889
admin@wheatlandcounty.ca
www.wheatlandcounty.ca
Municipal Type: County
Incorporated: April 1, 1945; *Area:* 4,550.92 sq km
Population in 2006: 8,164
Next Election: 2013 (3 year terms)
Note: Incorporated as a county on Jan. 1, 1961.
Jennifer Deak, County Manager
jennifer.deak@wheatlandcounty.ca
Ben Armstrong, Reeve

Willow Creek No. 26

P.O. Box 550
Claresholm, AB T0L 0T0
403-625-3351 Fax: 403-625-3886
cindy@mdwillowcreek.com
www.mdwillowcreek.com
Municipal Type: Municipal District
Incorporated: Jan. 1, 1944; *Area:* 4,560.22 sq km
Population in 2006: 5,337
Next Election: 2013 (3 year terms)
Cynthia Vizzutti, Administrator
Henry Van Hierden, Reeve

Wood Buffalo

9909 Franklin Ave.
Fort McMurray, AB T9H 2K4
780-743-7000 Fax: 780-743-7028 Toll Free: 1-800-973-9663
communications@woodbuffalo.ab.ca
www.woodbuffalo.ab.ca
Municipal Type: Regional Municipality
Incorporated: April 1, 1995; *Area:* 63,342.89 sq km
Population in 2006: 51,496
Next Election: 2013 (3 year terms)
Kelly Kloss, Acting CAO
780-743-7023
kelly.kloss@woodbuffalo.ab.ca
Melissa Blake, Mayor
Wes Holodniuk, Manager, Operations & Maintenance
780-743-7931, Fax: 780-799-5909
wes.holodniuk@woodbuffalo.ab.ca
Salem Abushawashi, Superintendent, Fort Chipewyan
780-697-3600
salem.abushawashi@woodbuffalo.ab.ca
Guy Jette, Acting Superintendent, Operations & Facilities Maintenance
780-799-7486
guy.jette@woodbuffalo.ab.ca
Darcy Elder, Superintendent, Infrastructure
780-799-7475
darcy.elder@woodbuffalo.ab.ca
Michel Savard, Superintendent, Environment
780-799-7490
michel.savard@woodbuffalo.ab.ca
Dwayne Harvie, Project Engineer
780-743-7855
dwayne.harvie@woodbuffalo.ab.ca

Woodlands County

P.O. Box 60
Whitecourt, AB T7S 1N3
780-778-8400 Fax: 780-778-8402
admin@woodlands.ab.ca
www.woodlands.ab.ca
Municipal Type: Municipal District
Incorporated: Jan. 1, 1969; *Area:* 7,668.11 sq km
Population in 2006: 4,158
Next Election: 2013 (3 year terms)
Note: Incorporated as a municipal district on Jan. 1, 1994.
Luc Mercier, CAO
luc.mercier@woodlands.ab.ca
Jim Rennie, Reeve
dynamic@telusplanet.net

Yellowhead County

2716 - 1st Ave.
Edson, AB T7E 1N9
780-723-4800 Fax: 780-723-5066 Toll Free Phone: 1-800-665-6030
info@yellowheadcounty.ab.ca
www.yellowheadcounty.ab.ca
Municipal Type: Municipal District
Incorporated: Jan. 1, 1994; *Area:* 22,303.82 sq km
Population in 2006: 10,045
Next Election: 2013 (3 year terms)
Jack Ramme, CAO
jack.ramme@yellowheadcounty.ab.ca
Gerald Soroka, Mayor
gsoroka@yellowheadcounty.ab.ca

Major Municipalities in Alberta

Airdrie
400 Main St. SE
Airdrie, AB T4B 3C3
403-948-8800 Fax: 403-948-6567
information.systems@airdrie.ca
www.airdrie.ca
Municipal Type: City
Incorporated: Sept. 10, 1909; *Area:* 33.10 sq km
Population in 2010: 39,822
Provincial Electoral District(s): Airdrie-Chestermere
Federal Electoral District(s): Wild Rose
Next Election: 2013 (3 year terms)
Note: Incorporated as a city on Jan. 1, 1985.

Council
Peter Brown, Mayor
mayor@airdrie.ca

Administration
George Keene, City Manager
george.keen@airdrie.ca
Mark Locking, Director, Engineering & Public Works
Jeff Greene, City Planner & Team Leader
403-948-8848
planning.development@airdrie.ca
Dave Rimes, Leader, Parks
403-948-8402
parks@airdrie.ca
Mary Grace Curtis, Coordinator, Recycling & Composting
780-948-0246
environmental.services@airdrie.ca
Darryl Wolski, Coordinator, Solid Waste
403-948-0246
pubwrks@airdrie.ca

Beaumont
5600 - 49 St.
Beaumont, AB T4X 1A1
780-929-8782 Fax: 780-929-8729
admin@town.beaumont.ab.ca
www.town.beaumont.ab.ca
Municipal Type: City
Incorporated: Jan. 1, 1973; *Area:* 10.5 sq km
Population in 2010: 12,586
Provincial Electoral District(s): Leduc-Beaumont-Devon
Federal Electoral District(s): Edmonton-Mill Woods-Beaumont
Next Election: 2013 (3 year terms)
Note: Incorporated as a town on Jan 1, 1980.

Council
Camille Bérubé, Mayor

Administration
Marc Landry, General Manager
marc.landry@town.beaumont.ab.ca

Brooks
P.O. Box 880
201 - 1 Ave. West
Brooks, AB T1R 0Z6
403-362-3333 Fax: 403-362-4787
admin@brooks.ca
www.brooks.ca
Municipal Type: City
Incorporated: July 14, 1910; *Area:* 17.7 sq km
Population in 2007: 13,581
Provincial Electoral District(s): Strathmore-Brooks
Federal Electoral District(s): Medicine Hat
Next Election: 2013 (3 year terms)
Note: Incorporated as a city on Sept. 1, 2005.

Council
Martin Shields, Mayor
mshields@brooks.ca

Administration
Kevin Stephenson, City Manager
kstephenson@brooks.ca
Neil Hollands, Director, Engineering & Property Services
nhollands@brooks.ca
Kevin Swanson, Director, Protective Services
403-362-2331
Terry Walsh, Director, Parks & Recreation
twalsh@brooks.ca
Maurice Landry, Manager, Development Services
mlandry@brooks.ca
Bill Prentice, Manager, Public Works
403-362-3146
bprentice@brooks.ca
Gord Shaw, Manager, Planning Services
gshaw@brooks.ca

Calgary
P.O. Box 2100 M
800 Macleod Trail SE
Calgary, AB T2P 2M5
403-268-2489 Fax: 403-538-6111 TTY: 403-268-4889
www.calgary.ca
Municipal Type: City
Incorporated: Nov. 7, 1884; *Area:* 726.5 sq km
Population in 2009: 1,230,248
Provincial Electoral District(s): Cal.-Bow; Cal.-Buffalo; Cal.-Cross; Cal.-Currie; Cal.-Egmont; Cal.-East; Cal.-Elbow; Cal.-Fish Creek; Cal.-Foothills; Cal.-Fort; Cal.-Glenmore; Cal.-Hays; Cal.-Lougheed; Cal.-McCall; Cal.-Mackay; Cal.-Montrose; Cal.-Mountain View; Cal.-North Hill; Cal.-Nose Hill; Cal.-Shaw; Cal.-Varsity; Cal.-West
Federal Electoral District(s): Calgary Centre; Calgary Centre-North; Calgary East; Calgary Northeast; Calgary-Nose Hill; Calgary Southeast; Calgary Southwest; Calgary West; Macleod; Wild Rose
Next Election: 2013 (3 year terms)
Note: Incorporated as a city on Jan. 1, 1894.

Council
Naheed K. Nenshi, Mayor
403-268-5622, Fax: 403-268-8130
themayor@calgary.ca
Dale Hodges, Aldermen, Ward(s): 1
403-268-2445, Fax: 403-268-8091
Frederick Gordon Lowe, Aldermen, Ward(s): 2
403-268-2430, Fax: 403-268-3823
Jim Stevenson, Aldermen, Ward(s): 3
403-268-2430, Fax: 403-268-8091
Gael MacLeod, Aldermen, Ward(s): 4
403-268-2430, Fax: 403-268-8091
Ray Jones, Aldermen, Ward(s): 5
403-268-2430, Fax: 403-268-3823
Richard Pootmans, Aldermen, Ward(s): 6
403-268-2430, Fax: 403-268-8091
Druh Farrell, Aldermen, Ward(s): 7
403-268-2475, Fax: 403-268-3823
John Mar, Aldermen, Ward(s): 8
403-268-2430, Fax: 403-268-3823
Gian-Carlo Carra, Aldermen, Ward(s): 9
403-268-2430, Fax: 403-268-8091
Andre Chabot, Aldermen, Ward(s): 10
403-268-2430, Fax: 403-268-3823
Brian Pincott, Aldermen, Ward(s): 11
403-268-2430, Fax: 403-268-8091
Shane A. Keating, Aldermen, Ward(s): 12
403-268-2430, Fax: 403-268-4673
Diane Colley-Urquhart, Aldermen, Ward(s): 13
403-268-2430, Fax: 403-268-8091
Linda Fox-Mellway, Aldermen, Ward(s): 14
403-268-2430, Fax: 403-268-3823

Administration
Diana L. Garner, City Clerk
403-268-5861, Fax: 403-268-2362
cityclerk@calgary.ca
George McLauchlan, Director, Human Resources
403-268-2201, Fax: 403-268-4680
Stuart Dalgleish, Director & City Assessor
403-268-4609, Fax: 403-268-8278
J. Bernie Trahan, Director, Fleet Services
403-268-1122, Fax: 403-266-2496
btrahan@calgary.ca
Anne Charlton, Director, Parks
403-268-3888
John Hubbell, General Manager, Transportation
Mary Axworthy, Director, Land Use Planning & Policy
David L. Day, Director, Environmental & Safety Management
403-268-3668
Dave Griffiths, Director, Waste & Recycling Services
Allyn Humber, Director, Water Services
403-268-2702
waterworks@calgary.ca
Ian Norris, Director, Transportation Infrastructure
403-974-4876
Wolf Keller, Director, Water Resources
403-268-6752
Jack Beaton, Chief of Police
403-206-5900
W. Bruce Burrell, Fire Chief
403-287-4255, Fax: 403-243-1490
Tom Sampson, Deputy Chief, Calgary Emergency Management Agency
tom.sampson@calgary.ca
Owen Tobert, P.Eng., City Manager
owens.tobert@calgary.ca
David Watson, General Manager, Planning Development & Assessment
403-268-2601
david.watson@calgary.ca
Rob Pritchard, General Manager, Utilities & Environmental Protection
403-268-2042, Fax: 403-537-3023
Erika Hargesheimer, General Manager, Community & Protective Services
403-268-5636
Kathy Strong-Duffin, Manager, Environmental Policy & Strategic Initiatives
403-268-4699
kstrongd@calgary.ca
Kevan van Velzen, M.Sc., P.Biol., Manager, Environmental Assessment & Liabilities
403-250-6448
Richard Binder, Manager, Infrastructure & Program Development
richard.binder@calgary.ca

Camrose
City Hall
5204 - 50 Ave.
Camrose, AB T4V 0S8
780-672-4426 Fax: 780-672-2469
admin@camrose.ca
www.camrose.ca
Municipal Type: City
Incorporated: May 4, 1905; *Area:* 31.14 sq km
Population in 2008: 16,543
Provincial Electoral District(s): Wetaskiwin-Camrose
Federal Electoral District(s): Crowfoot
Next Election: 2013 (3 year terms)
Note: Incorporated as a city on Jan. 1, 1955.

Council
Marshall Chalmers, Mayor
admin@camrose.ca

Administration
Brian Hamblin, P.Eng., City Manager
bhamblin@camrose.ca
Damian Herle, Manager, Corporate & Protective Services
Diane Urkow, Manager, Financial Services
Jeremy Enarson, Acting City Engineer, Engineering Services
Chris Clarkson, Director, Parks
780-672-9195
Jim Kupka, Director, Public Works
780-672-5513
Darrell Kambeitz, Police Chief
Peter Krich, Fire Chief/Deputy Director, Emergency Management
Brenda Hisey, Director, Planning & Development
780-672-4428
Doug Delmage, Chief Building Inspector
780-672-4428

Canmore
902 - 7 Ave.
Canmore, AB T1W 3K1
403-678-1500 Fax: 403-678-1524
info@canmore.ca
www.canmore.ca
Municipal Type: City
Incorporated: Jan. 1, 1965; *Area:* 68.9 sq km
Population in 2006: 12,039
Provincial Electoral District(s): Banff-Cochrane
Federal Electoral District(s): Wild Rose
Next Election: 2013 (3 year terms)
Note: Incorporated as a town on June 1, 1966.

Council
Ron Casey, Mayor
mayor@canmore.ca

Administration
Don Kochan, CAO
donkochan@canmore.ca
Don Kochan, Director, Environmental Services
donkochan@canmore.ca
Doug Townsend, Manager, Facilities
403-678-1586
Kevin Van Vliet, Manager, Engineering
403-678-1545, Fax: 403-678-1534

Chestermere
105 Marina Rd.
Chestermere, AB T1X 1V7
403-207-7050 Fax: 403-569-0512
town@chestermere.ca
www.chestermere.ca
Municipal Type: City
Incorporated: April 1, 1977; *Area:* 8.91 sq km
Population in 2010: 14,285
Provincial Electoral District(s): Airdrie-Chestermere
Federal Electoral District(s): Crowfoot
Next Election: 2013 (3 year terms)
Note: Incorporated as a town on March 1, 1993.

Council
Patricia Matthews, Mayor
403-207-7073
pmatthews@chestermere.ca
Patrick Bergen, Councillor
Heather Davies, Councillor
Stewart Hutchinson, Councillor
Kelsey Johnson, Councillor
Terry Leighton, Councillor
Christopher Steeves, Councillor

Administration
Terry Hurlbut, CAO
403-207-7070
thurlbut@chestermere.ca

Cochrane
P.O. Box 10
101 Ranche House Rd.
Cochrane, AB T4C 2K8
403-851-2505 Fax: 403-851-2581
cochrane@cochrane.ca
www.cochrane.ca
Municipal Type: City
Incorporated: June 17, 1903; *Area:* 30.03 sq km
Population in 2006: 13,760
Provincial Electoral District(s): Banff-Cochrane
Federal Electoral District(s): Wild Rose
Next Election: 2013 (3 year terms)
Note: Incorporated as a town on Feb. 15, 1971.

Council
Truper McBride, Mayor
truper.mcbride@cochrane.ca

Administration
Julian deCocq, Clerk
julian.decocq@cochrane.ca
Jim Anderson, Director, Operational Services
403-851-2560
jim.anderson@cochrane.ca
Lori Leipnitz, Director, Corporate Services
403-851-2510
lori.leipnitz@cochrane.ca
Ian Smith, Director, Community & Protective Services
403-851-2530
ian.smith@cochrane.ca
Frank Wesseling, Director, Planning & Engineering
403-851-2570
frank.wesseling@cochrane.ca
Elise Harnick, Engineer, Subdivision & Development
403-851-2575
elise.harnick@cochrane.ca

Cold Lake
5513 - 40 Ave.
Cold Lake, AB T9M 1A1
780-594-4494 Fax: 780-594-3480
city@coldlake.com
www.coldlake.com
Municipal Type: City
Incorporated: Dec. 31, 1953; *Area:* 59.3 sq km
Population in 2009: 13,924
Provincial Electoral District(s): Bonnyville-Cold Lake
Federal Electoral District(s): Westlock-St. Paul
Next Election: 2013 (3 year terms)
Note: Incorporated as a city on Oct. 1, 2000.

Council
Craig Copeland, Mayor

Administration
Gordon Frank, CAO
gfrank@coldlake.com
Allan Weiss, Chief, Fire
780-594-4494
Carry Grant, Manager, Operations
780-594-3776
cgrant@coldlake.com
George McIntosh, Foreman, Utilities
780-639-3604
wtp@coldlake.com
John McLean, Foreman, Parks & Facilities
780-594-3776
parks@coldlake.com

Edmonton
City Hall
1 Sir Winston Churchill Sq., 3rd Fl.
Edmonton, AB T5J 2R7
Fax: 780-496-8210 Telephone: 311 in Edmonton; or 780-442-5311
311@edmonton.ca
www.edmonton.ca
Municipal Type: City
Incorporated: Jan. 9, 1892; *Area:* 684.37 sq km
Population in 2009: 782,439
Provincial Electoral District(s): Ed.-Beverly-Clareview; Ed.-Calder; Ed.-Castle Downs; Ed.-Centre; Ed.-Decore; Ed.-Ellerslie; Ed.-Glenora; Ed.-Gold Bar; Ed.-Highlands-Norwood; Ed.-Manning; Ed.-McClung; Ed.-Meadowlark; Ed.-Mill Creek; Ed.-Mill Woods; Ed.-Riverview; Ed.-Rutherford; Ed.-Strathcona; Ed.-Whitemud
Federal Electoral District(s): Edmonton Centre; Edmonton East; Edmonton-Leduc; Edmonton-Mill Woods-Beaumont; Edmonton-Sherwood Park; Edmonton-Spruce Grove; Edmonton-St. Albert; Edmonton-Strathcona
Next Election: 2013 (3 year terms)
Note: Incorporated as a city on Oct. 08, 1904.

Council
Stephen Mandel, Mayor
780-496-8100, Fax: 780-496-8292
Linda Sloan, Councillor, Ward(s): 1
780-496-8122, Fax: 780-496-8113
linda.sloan@edmonton.ca
Kim Krushell, Councillor, Ward(s): 2
780-496-8128, Fax: 780-496-8113
kim.krushell@edmonton.ca
Dave Loken, Councillor, Ward(s): 3
dave.loken@edmonton.ca
Ed Gibbons, Councillor, Ward(s): 4
ed.gibbons@edmonton.ca
Karen Leibovici, Councillor, Ward(s): 5
780-496-8120, Fax: 780-496-8113
karen.leibovici@edmonton.ca
Jane Batty, Councillor, Ward(s): 6, Fax: 780-496-8113
jane.batty@edmonton.ca
Tony Caterina, Councillor, Ward(s): 7
780-496-8333, Fax: 780-496-8113
tony.caterina@edmonton.ca
Ben Henderson, Councillor, Ward(s): 8
780-496-8146, Fax: 780-496-8113
ben.henderson@edmonton.ca
Bryan Anderson, Councillor, Ward(s): 9
780-496-8130, Fax: 780-496-8113
bryan.anderson@edmonton.ca
Don Iveson, Councillor, Ward(s): 10
780-496-8132, Fax: 780-496-8113
don.iveson@edmonton.ca
Kerry Diotte, Councillor, Ward(s): 11, Fax: 780-496-8113
kerry.diotte@edmonton.ca
Amarjeet Sohi, Councillor, Ward(s): 12
780-496-8148, Fax: 780-496-8113
amarjeet.sohi@edmonton.ca

Administration
Simon Farbrother, City Manager
780-496-8231, Fax: 780-496-8220
simon.farbrother@edmonton.ca
David Edey, General Manager, Corporate Services
780-496-7201, Fax: 780-496-8854
david.edey@edmonton.ca
David Wiun, City Auditor
780-496-8315, Fax: 780-496-8062
david.wiun@edmonton.ca
Mike Boyd, Police Chief
780-421-3333
Dave Galea, Director, Office of Emergency Preparedness
780-944-6420, Fax: 780-496-3062
david.galea@edmonton.ca
Doug Costigan, Director, Asset Management & Public Works, Parks Branch
780-496-4956, Fax: 780-496-4978
doug.costigan@edmonton.ca
John Hodgson, Manager, Drainage Services
780-496-5658, Fax: 780-496-3629
Gerald W. Goodall, Consultant, Corporate Services, Materials Management Branch
780-496-3729, Fax: 780-496-5015
gerry.goodall@edmonton.ca
Audra Jones, Director, Transportation Planning
780-496-1790, Fax: 780-496-4287
Gary Klassen, General Manager, Planning & Development
780-496-6050, Fax: 780-496-6916
gary.klassen@edmonton.ca
Bob Boutilier, General Manager, Transportation
780-496-2808, Fax: 780-496-2803
transportation@edmonton.ca
Linda Cochrane, General Manager, Community Services
780-496-5804, Fax: 780-577-3525
linda.cochrane@edmonton.ca
Joyce Tustian, General Manager, Deputy City Manager's Office
780-442-6356, Fax: 780-496-8220
joyce.tustian@edmonton.ca
Mary Pat Barry, Manager, Deputy City Manager's Office, Communications Branch
780-496-8191, Fax: 780-496-4877
marypat.barry@edmonton.ca
Peter Muller, EMT-P, ABCP, Emergency Management Officer (Planning), Office of Emergency Preparedness
780-496-1530, Fax: 780-496-3062
peter.muller@edmonton.ca
Grant Pearsell, Director, Asset Management & Public Works, Parks Branch
780-496-6080, Fax: 780-496-5636
grant.pearsell@edmonton.ca
Garth Clyburn, Planner II, Planning & Development, Planning & Policy Branch
780-496-6209, Fax: 780-496-6299
garth.clyburn@edmonton.ca
Roy Neehall, Manager, Waste Management
780-496-5405, Fax: 780-496-5657

Fort Saskatchewan
10005 - 102 St.
Fort Saskatchewan, AB T8L 2C5
780-992-6200 Fax: 780-998-4774
lrosen@fortsask.ca
www.fortsask.ca
Municipal Type: City
Incorporated: March 1, 1899; *Area:* 48.12 sq km
Population in 2009: 17,469
Provincial Electoral District(s): Fort Saskatchewan-Vegreville
Federal Electoral District(s): Edmonton-Sherwood Park
Next Election: 2013 (3 year terms)
Note: Incorporated as a city on July 1, 1985.

Council
Gale Katchur, Mayor

Administration
Lorna Rosen, City Manager
John Rop, Treasurer
Scott Mack, Director, Planning
780-992-6573
smack@fortsask.ca
Todd Burge, Manager, Corporate Services
780-992-6255
tburge@fortsask.ca
Richard Hobson, Manager, Community & Protective Services
780-992-6205, Fax: 780-992-0192
rhobson@fortsask.ca
Dave Worman, Manager, Planning & Public Works
780-992-6207
dworman@fortsask.ca
Ken Lura, Superintendent, Public Works
780-992-6247
klura@fortsask.ca
Gale Katchur, Contact, Environmental Awareness Committee
gkatchur@fortsask.ca

Grande Prairie
P.O. Box 4000
10205 - 98 St.
Grande Prairie, AB T8V 6V3
780-538-0300 Fax: 780-538-0746
www.cityofgp.com
Municipal Type: City
Incorporated: April 30, 1914; *Area:* 61.08 sq km
Population in 2006: 47,076
Provincial Electoral District(s): Grande Prairie-Smoky; Grande Prairie-Wapiti
Federal Electoral District(s): Peace River
Next Election: 2013 (3 year terms)
Note: Incorporated as a city on Jan. 1, 1958.

Council
Bill Given, Mayor
bgiven@cityofgp.com

Administration
Greg Scerbak, City Manager
780-538-0312, Fax: 780-814-7560
gscerbak@cityofgp.com
Janette Ferguson, City Clerk
780-538-0314, Fax: 780-539-1056
jferguson@cityofgp.com
Frank Daskewech, Director, Public Works
780-538-0350, Fax: 780-538-4667
fdaskewech@cityofgp.com
Ken Anderson, Director, Financial Services
780-538-0302, Fax: 780-539-1056
kanderson@cityofgp.com
Josy Burrough, Manager, Parks
780-538-0476, Fax: 780-532-7588
jburrough@cityofgp.com
Michael MacIntyre, Planning Manager, Development Services
780-538-0440, Fax: 780-538-0746
mmacintyre@cityofgp.com
Valerie Norris-Kirk, Development Coordinator, Development Services
780-513-5236, Fax: 780-538-0746
vnorrisk@cityofgp.com
Uli Wolf, Solid Waste Services Supervisor, Aquatera Utilities Inc.
780-538-0360, Fax: 780-830-7060
uwolf@aquatera.ca
Amy Horne, Recycling Coordinator, Aquatera Utilities Inc.
780-538-0452, Fax: 780-830-7060
ahorne@aquatera.ca
Mark Simpson, Operations Coordinator, Aquatera Utilities Inc.
780-538-0442, Fax: 780-830-7430
msimpson@aquatera.ca
Dan Lemieux, Sr. Deputy Fire Chief
780-538-0398, Fax: 780-538-0395
dlemieux@cityofgp.com

High River
309B MacLeod Trail SW
High River, AB T1V 1Z5
403-652-2110 Fax: 403-652-2396
info@highriver.ca
www.highriver.ca
Municipal Type: City
Incorporated: Dec. 5, 1901; *Area:* 14.27 sq km
Population in 2010: 11,788
Provincial Electoral District(s): Highwood
Federal Electoral District(s): Macleod
Next Election: 2013 (3 year terms)
Note: Incorporated as a town on Feb. 12, 1906.

Council
Emile Blokland, Mayor

Administration
Harry Harker, Town Manager

Lacombe
5432 - 56 Ave.
Lacombe, AB T4L 1E9
403-782-6666 Fax: 403-782-5655
webmaster@lacombe.ca
www.lacombe.ca
Municipal Type: City
Incorporated: July 28, 1896; *Area:* 18.24 sq km
Population in 2009: 11,733
Provincial Electoral District(s): Lacombe-Ponoka
Federal Electoral District(s): Wetaskiwin
Next Election: 2013 (3 year terms)
Note: Incorporated as a town on May 5, 1902.

Council
Steve Christie, Mayor

Administration
Ken Kendall, CAO
kkendall@town.lacombe.ab.ca

Leduc
1 Alexandra Park
Leduc, AB T9E 4C4
780-980-7177 Fax: 780-980-7127
info@leduc.ca
www.leduc.ca
Municipal Type: City
Incorporated: Dec. 15, 1899; *Area:* 36.97 sq km
Population in 2010: 23,293
Provincial Electoral District(s): Leduc-Beaumont-Devon

Federal Electoral District(s): Edmonton-Leduc
Next Election: 2013 (3 year terms)
Note: Incorporated as a city on Sept. 01, 1983.

Council
Greg Krischke, Mayor
mayor@leduc.ca

Administration
Laura Knoblock, City Clerk
lknoblock@leduc.ca
Linda Kyluik, Treasurer
Paul Benedetto, City Manager
pbenedetto@leduc.ca
Kevin Cole, Director, Public Services
Doug Parrish, Director, Planning & Development
780-980-7124
dparrish@leduc.ca
Rick Sereda, Fire Chief & Director, Protective Services
Allan Yamashita, City Engineer & General Manager, Operations

Lethbridge
City Hall
910 - 4 Ave. South
Lethbridge, AB T1J 0P6
403-329-7355 Fax: 403-320-7575
info@lethbridge.ca
www.lethbridge.ca
Municipal Type: City
Incorporated: Nov. 29, 1890; *Area:* 121.97 sq km
Population in 2010: 86,659
Provincial Electoral District(s): Lethbridge-East; Lethbridge-West
Federal Electoral District(s): Lethbridge
Next Election: 2013 (3 year terms)
Note: Incorporated as a city on May 9, 1906.

Council
Rajko Dodic, Mayor
403-320-3823, Fax: 403-320-7575
mayor@lethbridge.ca
Bob Babki, Aldermen, Fax: 403-320-7575
Jeff Carlson, Aldermen
403-360-7550, Fax: 403-320-7575
aldermancarlson@gmail.com
Faron Ellis, Aldermen, Fax: 403-320-7575
Liz Iwaskiw, Aldermen, Fax: 403-320-7575
Joe Mauro, Aldermen, Fax: 403-320-7575
Bridget Mearns, Aldermen, Fax: 403-320-7575
Ryan Parker, Aldermen
403-380-4848, Fax: 403-320-7575
aldermanryanparker@gmail.com
Tom Wickersham, Aldermen
403-381-1521, Fax: 403-381-1571
thwicker@gmail.com

Administration
Dianne Nemeth, City Clerk
403-320-3821, Fax: 403-320-7575
dnemeth@lethbridge.ca
Garth Sherwin, B.Comm., CA, City Manager
gsherwin@lethbridge.ca
Douglas Hudson, Q.C., City Solicitor
dhudson@lethbridge.ca
Brian Cornforth, Fire Chief
403-320-3800, Fax: 403-327-3503
astrandlund@lethbridge.ca
Tom McKenzie, Police Chief
403-327-2210, Fax: 403-328-6999
Byron Buzunis, M.Eng., PMP, P.Eng., Urban Construction Manager
403-320-3975
Kathy Hopkins, Director, Community Services
403-320-3015, Fax: 403-380-2512
khopkins@lethbridge.ca
Warren Andrews, Manager, Public Operations
wandrews@lethbridge.ca
Kevin Viergutz, Manager, Transportation Operations
kviergutz@lethbridge.ab.ca
Bary Beck, Director, Corporate Initiatives
Jody Meli, Manager, Corporate & Community Relations
jmeli@lethbridge.ca
John King, Manager, Transit
403-320-3884, Fax: 403-380-3876
jking@lethbridge.ca
Craig Milley, Manager, Purchasing
403-320-3961
cmilley@lethbridge.ca
Kevin Theodore, Manager, Waste & Recycling
403-320-3088
ktheodore@lethbridge.ab.ca
Don Bulpitt, Manager, Water & Wastewater Operations
dbulpitt@lethbridge.ca
Kevin Jensen, Coordinator, Parks
403-330-5108
kjensen@lethbridge.ab.ca
George Kuhl, Senior Planner, Development Services
403-327-3926, Fax: 403-327-6571
gkuhl@lethbridge.ca

Lloydminster
City Hall
4420 - 50 Ave.
Lloydminster, AB T9V 0W2
780-875-6184 Fax: 780-871-8345
jkeeley@lloydminster.ca
www.lloydminster.ca
Municipal Type: City
Incorporated: Nov. 25, 1903; *Area:* 24.19 sq km
Population in 2009: 26,502
Provincial Electoral District(s): Vermilion-Lloydminster
Federal Electoral District(s): Vegreville-Wainwright
Next Election: 2012 (3 year terms)
Note: Population figure represents both the Alberta & Saskatchewan populations. Incorporated as a city on Jan. 1, 1958.

Council
Jeff Mulligan, Mayor
mayor@lloydminster.ca

Administration
Beth Kembel, City Clerk
780-871-8328
bkembel@lloydminster.ca
Diane Beecroft, Treasurer
780-875-6184
dbeecroft@lloydminster.ca
Adam Homes, Director, Planning & Public Works
780-875-8332
ahomes@lloydminster.ca
Corwin McCullagh, Director, Parks & Recreation
780-871-8340
cmccullagh@lloydminster.ca
Richard Power, Chief Development Officer
780-871-8335
rpower@lloydminster.ca
Kirk Morrison, Engineer, Transportation & Works
kmorrison@lloydminster.ca
Lindsay Parnwell, Engineer, Utilities
lparnwell@lloydminster.ca
Trisha Le, Urban Planner
tle@lloydminster.ca

Medicine Hat
City Hall
580 - 1 St. SE
Medicine Hat, AB T1A 8E6
403-529-8115 Fax: 403-529-8182
clerk@medicinehat.ca
www.medicinehat.ca
Municipal Type: City
Incorporated: May 31, 1894; *Area:* 112.01 sq km
Population in 2009: 61,097
Provincial Electoral District(s): Cypress-Medicine Hat; Medicine Hat
Federal Electoral District(s): Medicine Hat
Next Election: 2013 (3 year terms)
Note: Incorporated as a city on May 9, 1906.

Council
Normand Boucher, Mayor
403-529-8181, Fax: 403-529-8182
mayor@medicinehat.ca; norbou@medicinehat.ca
Ted Clugston, Aldermen
403-526-8760
tedclu@medicinehat.ca
Wayne Craven, Aldermen, Fax: 403-529-8182
waycra@medicinehat.ca
Robert C. Dumanowski, Aldermen
John Hamill, Aldermen
403-526-7196, Fax: 403-529-8282
johham@medicinehat.ca
Graham Kelly, Aldermen
403-527-1891, Fax: 403-528-2453
gldarops@shaw.ca
Les Pearson, Aldermen
lespea@medicinehat.ca
Jeremy Thompson, Aldermen
403-504-5647, Fax: 403-526-1422
jertho@medicinehat.ca
Phil Turnbull, Aldermen

Administration
Dave Leflar, City Clerk
403-529-8234, Fax: 403-529-8182
davlef@medicinehat.ca
Gerry Labas, COO
403-529-8222
gerlab@medicinehat.ca
John Hughes, City Solicitor
403-529-8350
johhug@medicinehat.ca
Andy McGrogan, Police Chief
403-529-8410, Fax: 403-529-8444
Ron Robinson, Fire Chief
403-502-8006, Fax: 403-526-1352
Albert Bizio, Commissioner, Public Services
403-529-8229
albbiz@medicinehat.ca
Don Knutson, Acting Commissioner, Corporate Services
403-529-8231
onknu@medicinehat.ca
John Komanchuk, Commissioner, Development & Infrastructure
403-529-8354
johjo@medicinehat.ca
Dwight Brown, General Manager, Planning, Building & Development Services
Dale Descoteau, General Manager, Information & Computer Services
403-529-8108
daldes@medicinehat.ca
John Fedoruk, General Manager, Environmental Utilities
403-529-8176, Fax: 403-528-4955
eu@medicinehat.ca
Tony Klauwers, General Manager, Municipal Works
Grant MacKay, General Manager, Human Resources
403-529-8239
gramac@medicinehat.ca
Dave Panabaker, General Manager, Gas Utility
403-529-8288
davepan@medicinehat.ca
Ron Webb, General Manager, Community Development
403-529-8310
ronweb@medicinehat.ca
Les Wickenheiser, General Manager, Corporate Asset Management
403-529-8327
leswic@medicinehat.ca
Kendall Woodacre, General Manager, Electric Utility
403-502-8081
kenwoo@medicinehat.ca
R. Vizbar, General Manager, Parks & Outdoor Recreation
403-529-8312, Fax: 403-527-4798
parks@medicinehat.ca
Russ Smith, Manager, Environment Management
403-529-8188
russmi@medicinhat.ca
Frank Wetsch, Manager, Water & WasteWater Treatment
403-529-8227
S. Schentag, Coordinator, Recycling Development
403-502-8593
Ron Davis, Officer, Health & Safety
403-529-8359
rondav@medicine-hat.ca

Okotoks
P.O. Box 20 Main
5 Elizabeth St.
Okotoks, AB T1S 1K1
403-938-4404 Fax: 403-938-7387
info@okotoks.ca
www.okotoks.ca
Municipal Type: City
Incorporated: Oct. 25, 1899; *Area:* 18.55 sq km
Population in 2010: 23,201
Provincial Electoral District(s): Highwood
Federal Electoral District(s): Macleod
Next Election: 2013 (3 year terms)
Note: Incorporated as a town on June 1, 1904.

Council
Bill Robertson, Mayor
mayor@okotoks.ca

Administration
Rick Quail, Municipal Manager
403-938-8900
municipalmanager@okotoks.ca
Marley Oness, Municipal Engineer
403-938-8930
municipalengineer@okotoks.ca
Dave Robertson, Manager, Operations
403-938-8952
operations@okotoks.ca
Ken Thevenot, Fire Chief
403-938-4066
fire@okotoks.ca

Red Deer
City Hall
P.O. Box 5008
4914 - 48th Ave.
Red Deer, AB T4N 3T4
403-342-8111 Fax: 403-346-6195
feedback@reddeer.ca
www.reddeer.ca
Municipal Type: City
Incorporated: May 31, 1894; *Area:* 69.23 sq km
Population in 2010: 90,084
Provincial Electoral District(s): Red Deer-North; Red Deer-South
Federal Electoral District(s): Red Deer
Next Election: 2013 (3 year terms)
Note: Incorporated as a city on March 25, 1913.

Council
Morris Flewwelling, Mayor
403-342-8154, Fax: 403-342-8365
mayor@reddeer.ca
Buck Buchanan, Councillor
403-343-6550, Fax: 403-346-6195
buck.buchanan@reddeer.ca
Paul Harris, Councillor
Cindy Jefferies, Councillor
403-302-3706, Fax: 403-346-6195
cindy.jefferies@reddeer.ca
Lynne Mulder, Councillor
403-341-6418, Fax: 403-346-6195
lynne.mulder@reddeer.ca
Chris Stephan, Councillor
Tara Veer, Councillor
403-358-3568, Fax: 403-340-7466
tara.veer@reddeer.ca
Frank Wong, Councillor
403-347-6514, Fax: 403-346-6195
frank.wong@reddeer.ca
Dianne Wyntjes, Councillor

Administration
Craig Curtis, City Manager

403-342-8156, Fax: 403-342-8365
craig.curtis@reddeer.ca
Lorraine Poth, Director, Corporate Services
lorraine.poth@reddeer.ca
Don Simpson, City Solicitor
Brian Simpson, Superintendent, RCMP
rcmp@reddeer.ca
Paul Goranson, Director, Development Services
403-342-8162, Fax: 403-342-8211
paul.goranson@reddeer.ca
Colleen Jensen, Director, Community Services
403-342-8323, Fax: 403-342-8222
communityservices@reddeer.ca
Scott Cameron, Manager, Social Planning
403-342-8100
communityservices@reddeer.ca
Frank Colosimo, Manager, Public Works
403-342-8238, Fax: 403-343-7074
publicworks@reddeer.ca
Kevin Joll, Manager, Transit
403-342-8225, Fax: 403-342-8116
transit@reddeer.ca
Paul Meyette, Director, Planning Division
Rod Risling, Manager, Assessment & Taxation
assessment@reddeer.ca
Greg Scott, Manager, Recreation, Parks & Culture
403-342-8159, Fax: 403-342-8222
Dave Matthews, Supervisor, Planning & Technical Services
Tom Marstaller, Superintendent, Environmental Services
403-342-8238, Fax: 403-343-7074
publicworks@reddeer.ca

St. Albert
5 St. Anne St.
St. Albert, AB T8N 3Z9
780-459-1500 Fax: 780-460-2394
stalbert@st-albert.net
www.stalbert.ca
Municipal Type: City
Incorporated: Dec. 7, 1899; *Area:* 35.04 sq km
Population in 2010: 60,138
Provincial Electoral District(s): Spruce Grove-Sturgeon-St. Albert; St. Albert
Federal Electoral District(s): Edmonton-St. Albert
Next Election: 2013 (3 year terms)
Note: Incorporated as a city on Jan. 1, 1977.

Council
Nolan Crouse, Mayor
780-459-1606, Fax: 780-459-1591
mayor@st-albert.net
Len Bracko, Councillor
780-458-6478, Fax: 780-418-2961
len@bracko.ca
Wes Broadhead, Councillor
Cathy Heron, Councillor
Roger Lemieux, Councillor
780-460-7223, Fax: 780-651-6147
jrcl@shaw.ca
Cam MacKay, Councillor
Malcolm Parker, Councillor

Administration
Bill Holtby, City Manager
780-459-1607, Fax: 780-459-1591
bholtby@st-albert.net
Gail Barrington-Moss, General Manager, Community & Protective Services
N. Jamieson, General Manager, Planning & Engineering Services
D. Screpnek, General Manager, Corporate Services
B. Treidler, General Manager, Business & Strategic Services
C. Cundy, Director, Planning & Development
D. Irving, Manager, Planning
S. Laarhuis, Chief Legislative Officer
Tracy Young, Administrative Resources Coordinator, Fire & Emergency Medical Services
780-458-2020, Fax: 780-459-7636

Spruce Grove
315 Jespersen Ave.
Spruce Grove, AB T7X 3E8
780-962-2611 Fax: 780-962-2526
info@sprucegrove.org
www.sprucegrove.org
Municipal Type: City
Incorporated: March 14, 1907; *Area:* 26.4 sq km
Population in 2010: 24,646
Provincial Electoral District(s): Spruce Grove-Sturgeon-St. Albert
Federal Electoral District(s): Edmonton-Spruce Grove
Next Election: 2013 (3 year terms)
Note: Incorporated as a city on March 1, 1986.

Council
Stuart Houston, Mayor
shouston@sprucegrove.org

Administration
Doug Lagore, City Manager
dlagore@sprucegrove.org
Kathy Chan, Treasurer
Ken Luck, Director, FCSS & Recreation
Jackie Araujo, General Manager, Community Services
780-962-7617
David Hales, General Manager, Planning & Infrastructure
780-962-7622
Robert Kosterman, Chief, Fire
780-962-4496
Jeff Mustard, Superintendent, Engineering
780-962-7624
Paul Hanlan, Supervisor, Planning & Development
Jane Holmes, Coordinator, Sustainable Development

Stony Plain
4905 - 51 Ave.
Stony Plain, AB T7Z 1Y1
780-963-2151 Fax: 780-963-2197
info@stonyplain.com
www.stonyplain.com
Municipal Type: City
Incorporated: March 14, 1907; *Area:* 35.61 sq km
Population in 2010: 14,177
Provincial Electoral District(s): Stony Plain
Federal Electoral District(s): Edmonton-Spruce Grove
Next Election: 2013 (3 year terms)
Note: Incorporated as a town on Dec. 10, 1908

Council
Ken Lemke, Mayor
780-963-6310
k.lemke@stonyplain.com

Administration
Thomas Goulden, Manager
780-963-8584, Fax: 780-963-2197
t.goulden@stonyplain.com

Strathmore
680 Westchester Rd.
Strathmore, AB T1P 1J1
403-934-3133 Fax: 403-934-4713
Lindan@strathmore.ca
www.strathmore.ca
Municipal Type: City
Incorporated: March 20, 1908; *Area:* 15.59 sq km
Population in 2010: 12,139
Provincial Electoral District(s): Strathmore-Brooks
Federal Electoral District(s): Crowfoot
Next Election: 2013 (3 year terms)
Note: Incorporated as a town on July 6, 1911.

Council
Steve Grajczyk, Mayor
council@strathmore.ca

Administration
Dwight Stanford, CAO
dwights@strathmore.ca

Sylvan Lake
4926 - 50th Ave.
Sylvan Lake, AB T4S 1A1
403-887-2141 Fax: 403-887-3660
tsl@sylvanlake.ca
www.sylvanlake.ca
Municipal Type: City
Incorporated: Dec. 30, 1912; *Area:* 10.83 sq km
Population in 2008: 11,115
Provincial Electoral District(s): Innisfail-Sylvan Lake
Federal Electoral District(s): Red Deer
Next Election: 2013 (3 year terms)
Note: Incorporated as a town on May 20, 1946.

Council
Susan Samson, Mayor
ssamson@sylvanlake.ca

Administration
Archie Grover, Acting CAO
403-887-2141

Wetaskiwin
P.O. Box 6210
4705 - 50th Ave.
Wetaskiwin, AB T9A 2E9
780-361-4400 Fax: 780-352-0930 Toll Free Phone: 1-800-989-6899
reception@wetaskiwin.ca
www.wetaskiwin.ca
Municipal Type: City
Incorporated: Dec. 4, 1899; *Area:* 16.74 sq km
Population in 2009: 12,285
Provincial Electoral District(s): Wetaskiwin-Camrose
Federal Electoral District(s): Wetaskiwin
Next Election: 2013 (3 year terms)
Note: Incorporated as a city on May 9, 1906.

Council
Bill Elliot, Mayor
mayor@wetaskiwin.ca

Administration
Ted Gillespie, City Manager
Merlin Klassen, Fire Chief
780-361-4429, Fax: 780-352-6261
fireservices@wetaskiwin.ca

Other Municipalities in Alberta

Acme
P.O. Box 299
Acme, AB T0M 0A0
403-546-3783 Fax: 403-546-3014
caoacme@airenet.com
www.albertafirst.com/profiles/statspack/20490.html
Municipal Type: Village
Incorporated: July 7, 1910; *Area:* 2.47 sq km
Population in 2006: 656
Provincial Electoral District(s): Olds-Didsbury-Three Hills
Federal Electoral District(s): Crowfoot
Next Election: 2013 (3 year terms)
Sue Schmidt, Municipal Clerk
acme@airenet.com
Dennis Kuiken, Mayor

Alberta Beach
P.O. Box 278
Alberta Beach, AB T0E 0A0
780-924-3181 Fax: 780-924-3313
aboffice@3web.com
www.albertabeach.com
Municipal Type: Village
Incorporated: Aug. 23, 1920; *Area:* 1.98 sq km
Population in 2006: 339
Provincial Electoral District(s): Whitecourt-Ste. Anne
Federal Electoral District(s): Yellowhead
Next Election: 2013 (3 year terms)
Note: Status changed to a village on Nov. 25, 1998.
Kathy Skwarchuk, CAO
Bill Love, Mayor

Alberta Capital Region Wastewater Commission
23262 Township Rd. 540
Fort Saskatchewan, AB T8L 4A2
780-467-8655 Fax: 780-467-5398
Municipal Type: Water Commission
Gordon Thompson, General Manager
gthompson@acrwc.ab.ca

Alix
P.O. Box 87
4849 - 50 St.
Alix, AB T0C 0B0
403-747-2495 Fax: 403-747-3663
info@villageofalix.ca; cao@villageofalix.ca
www.villageofalix.ca
Municipal Type: Village
Incorporated: June 3, 1907; *Area:* 3.15 sq km
Population in 2006: 851
Provincial Electoral District(s): Lacombe-Ponoka
Federal Electoral District(s): Wetaskiwin
Next Election: 2013 (3 year terms)
Wendy Menage, Municipal Clerk
wmanage@villageofalix.ca
Curtis Peterson, Mayor
403-747-2414

Alliance
P.O. Box 149
Alliance, AB T0B 0A0
780-879-3911 Fax: 780-879-2235
allivil@wildroseinternet.ca
www.albertafirst.com/profiles/statspack/20493.html
Municipal Type: Village
Incorporated: Aug. 26, 1918; *Area:* 0.64 sq km
Population in 2006: 158
Provincial Electoral District(s): Battle River-Wainwright
Federal Electoral District(s): Vegreville-Wainwright
Next Election: 2013 (3 year terms)
Laura Towers, Administrator
Muriel Fankhanel, Mayor

Amisk
P.O. Box 72
Amisk, AB T0B 0B0
780-856-3980 Fax: 780-856-3980
amiskvil@telusplanet.net
Municipal Type: Village
Incorporated: Jan. 1, 1956; *Area:* 0.76 sq km
Population in 2006: 172
Provincial Electoral District(s): Battle River-Wainwright
Federal Electoral District(s): Vegreville-Wainwright
Next Election: 2013 (3 year terms)
Kathy Ferguson, Municipal Administrator
Arnold Nordin, Mayor

Andrew
P.O. Box 180
5021 - 50 St.
Andrew, AB T0B 0C0
780-365-3687 Fax: 780-365-2061
vandway@mcsnet.ca
www.albertafirst.com/profiles/statspack/20495.html
Municipal Type: Village
Incorporated: June 24, 1930; *Area:* 1.23 sq km
Population in 2006: 465
Provincial Electoral District(s): Fort Saskatchewan-Vegreville
Federal Electoral District(s): Vegreville-Wainwright
Next Election: 2013 (3 year terms)
Pat Skoreyko, CAO

Tina M. Warawa, Mayor

Argentia Beach
P.O. Box 100
Ma-Me-O Beach, AB T0C 1X0
780-586-2494 Fax: 780-586-3567
svadminoffice@xplornet.com
Municipal Type: Summer Village
Incorporated: Jan. 1, 1967; *Area:* 0.69 sq km
Population in 2006: 52
Provincial Electoral District(s): Drayton Valley-Calmar
Federal Electoral District(s): Wetaskiwin
Next Election: 2013 (3 year terms)
Peter Irwin, Administrator
Ernie Elko, Mayor

Arrowwood
P.O. Box 36
22 Center St.
Arrowwood, AB T0L 0B0
403-534-3821 Fax: 403-534-3821
vlgarrw@telusplanet.net
www.villageofarrowwood.ca/
Municipal Type: Village
Incorporated: May 13, 1926; *Area:* 0.66 sq km
Population in 2006: 221
Provincial Electoral District(s): Little Bow
Federal Electoral District(s): Macleod
Next Election: 2013 (3 year terms)
George F.E. (Ted) Oakes, Village Administrator
Roger Montgomery, Mayor

Athabasca
4705 - 49 Ave.
Athabasca, AB T9S 1B7
780-675-2063 Fax: 780-675-4242
town@town.athabasca.ab.ca
www.town.athabasca.ab.ca
Municipal Type: Town
Incorporated: May 18, 1905; *Area:* 16.98 sq km
Population in 2006: 2,575
Provincial Electoral District(s): Athabasca-Redwater
Federal Electoral District(s): Fort McMurray-Athabasca
Next Election: 2013 (3 year terms)
Note: Incorporated as a town on Aug. 4, 1913.
Doug Topinka, CAO
Colleen Powell, Mayor

Athabasca Regional Waste Management Services Commission
P.O. Box 90
Athabasca, AB T9S 2A2
780-675-1117 Fax: 780-675-8881
arwmsc@telusplanet.net
Municipal Type: Water Commission
Robert Smith, Manager

Banff
P.O. Box 1260
Banff, AB T1L 1A1
403-762-1200 Fax: 403-762-1260
comments@banff.ca
www.banff.ca
Municipal Type: Town
Incorporated: Jan. 1, 1990; *Area:* 4.85 sq km
Population in 2007: 7,437
Provincial Electoral District(s): Banff-Cochrane
Federal Electoral District(s): Wild Rose
Next Election: 2013 (3 year terms)
Robert Earl, Town Manager
403-762-1203
robert.earl@banff.ca
Karen Sorensen, Mayor

Barnwell
P.O. Box 159
Barnwell, AB T0K 0B0
403-223-4018 Fax: 403-223-2373
barnwell@platinum.ca
Municipal Type: Village
Incorporated: Jan. 1, 1980; *Area:* 0.9 sq km
Population in 2006: 613
Provincial Electoral District(s): Cardston-Taber-Warner
Federal Electoral District(s): Medicine Hat
Next Election: 2013 (3 year terms)
Wendy Bateman, Administrator
Delbert Bodnarek, Mayor

Barons
P.O. Box 129
Barons, AB T0L 0G0
403-757-3633 Fax: 403-757-2599
barons@figment.ca
Municipal Type: Village
Incorporated: May 6, 1910; *Area:* 0.68 sq km
Population in 2006: 276
Provincial Electoral District(s): Little Bow
Federal Electoral District(s): Lethbridge
Next Election: 2013 (3 year terms)
Laurie Beck, CAO
Ronald Gorzitza, Mayor

Barrhead
P.O. Box 4189
Barrhead, AB T7N 1A2
780-674-3301 Fax: 780-674-5648
town@barrhead.ca
www.barrhead.ca
Municipal Type: Town
Incorporated: Nov. 14, 1927; *Area:* 8.1 sq km
Population in 2006: 4,209
Provincial Electoral District(s): Barrhead-Morinville-Westlock
Federal Electoral District(s): Yellowhead
Next Election: 2013 (3 year terms)
Note: Proclaimed as a town on Nov. 26, 1946.
Farrell O'Malley, Municipal Manager
fomalley@barrhead.ca
Brian Schulz, Mayor
bdshulz@barrhead.ca

Bashaw
P.O. Box 510
Bashaw, AB T0B 0H0
780-372-3911 Fax: 780-372-2335
admin@townofbashaw.com
www.townofbashaw.com
Municipal Type: Town
Incorporated: Aug. 18, 1911; *Area:* 2.84 sq km
Population in 2006: 796
Provincial Electoral District(s): Lacombe-Ponoka
Federal Electoral District(s): Crowfoot
Next Election: 2013 (3 year terms)
Note: Incorporated as a town on May 1, 1964.
Rosemary Wittevrongel, CAO
rwittevrongel@townofbashaw.com
Robert (Bob) Cammidge, Mayor

Bassano
P.O. Box 299
Bassano, AB T0J 0B0
403-641-3788 Fax: 403-641-2585
townbass@eidnet.org
www.bassano.ca
Municipal Type: Town
Incorporated: Dec. 28, 1909; *Area:* 5.16 sq km
Population in 2006: 1,345
Provincial Electoral District(s): Strathmore-Brooks
Federal Electoral District(s): Medicine Hat
Next Election: 2013 (3 year terms)
Note: Incorporated as a town on Jan. 16, 1911.
Jerry Neighbour, CAO
Audrey Wilcox, Mayor

Bawlf
P.O. Box 40
Bawlf, AB T0B 0J0
780-373-3797 Fax: 780-373-3797
vilbawlf@syban.net
www.bawlf.com
Municipal Type: Village
Incorporated: Oct. 12, 1906; *Area:* 0.96 sq km
Population in 2006: 367
Provincial Electoral District(s): Battle River-Wainwright
Federal Electoral District(s): Crowfoot
Next Election: 2013 (3 year terms)
Lynn Horbasenko, Village Manager
LHorbasenko@bawlf.com
Jerry Iwanus, Mayor
780-373-2263
jiwanus@bawlf.com

Beaver Regional Waste Management Services Commission
P.O. Box 322
Ryley, AB T0B 4A0
780-663-2038 Fax: 780-663-2006
brwmsccc@telusplanet.net
www.brwmsc.com
Municipal Type: Waste Commission
Forrest Wright, CAO
Owen Ligard, Director, Operations
owen.ligard@brwmsc.com

Beaver River Regional Waste Management Commission
Bag 1010
Bonnyville, AB T9N 2J7
780-826-3951 Fax: 780-826-5064
Municipal Type: Water Commission
Marco Schroeninger, Manager
marco@md.bonnyville.ab.ca

Beaverlodge
P.O. Box 30
Beaverlodge, AB T0H 0C0
780-354-2201 Fax: 780-354-2207
ivan@beaverlodge.ca
www.beaverlodge.ca
Municipal Type: Town
Incorporated: July 31, 1929; *Area:* 5.58 sq km
Population in 2006: 2,264
Provincial Electoral District(s): Grande Prairie-Wapiti
Federal Electoral District(s): Peace River
Next Election: 2013 (3 year terms)
Note: Incorporated as a town on Jan. 24, 1956.
Ivan Hegland, Town Manager
ivan@beaverlodge.ca
Leona Hanson, Mayor
leona@coaction.ca

Beiseker
P.O. Box 349
Beiseker, AB T0M 0G0
403-947-3774 Fax: 403-947-2146
beiseker@beiseker.com
www.beiseker.com
Municipal Type: Village
Incorporated: Feb. 23, 1921; *Area:* 2.84 sq km
Population in 2006: 804
Provincial Electoral District(s): Airdrie-Chestermere
Federal Electoral District(s): Crowfoot
Next Election: 2013 (3 year terms)
Jo-Anne Lambert, CAO
gpeckham@beiseker.com
Bruce T. Rowe, Mayor

Bentley
P.O. Box 179
Bentley, AB T0C 0J0
403-748-4044 Fax: 403-748-3213
vlgben@telusplanet.net
www.town.bentley.ab.ca
Municipal Type: Town
Incorporated: March 17, 1915; *Area:* 2.3 sq km
Population in 2006: 1,083
Provincial Electoral District(s): Rocky Mountain House
Federal Electoral District(s): Wetaskiwin
Next Election: 2013 (3 year terms)
Note: Incorporated as a town on Jan. 1, 2001.
Elizabeth Smart, CAO
liz.bentley@telus.net
Joan Dickau, Mayor

Berwyn
P.O. Box 250
Berwyn, AB T0H 0E0
780-338-3922 Fax: 780-338-2224
vberwyn@wispernet.ca
www.berwyn.govoffice.com
Municipal Type: Village
Incorporated: Nov. 28, 1936; *Area:* 1.66 sq km
Population in 2006: 516
Provincial Electoral District(s): Dunvegan-Central Peace
Federal Electoral District(s): Peace River
Next Election: 2013 (3 year terms)
Harry Aspin, Municipal Administrator
Ron Longtin, Mayor
RonLongtin@wispernet.ca

Betula Beach
P.O. Box 161
Seba Beach, AB T0E 2B0
780-797-2455
svbetula@telusplanet.net
Municipal Type: Summer Village
Incorporated: Jan. 1, 1960; *Area:* 0.18 sq km
Population in 2006: 15
Provincial Electoral District(s): Stony Plain
Federal Electoral District(s): Yellowhead
Next Election: 2013 (3 year terms)
Linda Bolton, Administrator
Marlene Hobart-Stratton, Mayor

Big Country Waste Management Commission
P.O. Box 1906
Hanna, AB T0J 1P0
403-854-5600 Fax: 403-854-5527
Municipal Type: Waste Commission
Greg R. Sheppard, Operations Manager

Big Valley
P.O. Box 236
29 - 1 Ave. South
Big Valley, AB T0J 0G0
403-876-2269 Fax: 403-876-2223
villagebigvalley@libs.prl.ab.ca; info@villagebigvalley.ca
www.villagebigvalley.ca
Municipal Type: Village
Incorporated: July 28, 1914; *Area:* 1.84 sq km
Population in 2006: 351
Provincial Electoral District(s): Drumheller-Stettler
Federal Electoral District(s): Crowfoot
Next Election: 2013 (3 year terms)
Corinne Feusi, CAO
Walter Stefanik, Mayor

Birch Cove
#16, 26213 Township Rd. 512
Spruce Grove, AB T7Y 1C6
780-702-3204 Fax: 780-702-6743
birch.cove@tbwifi.ca
Municipal Type: Summer Village
Incorporated: Dec. 31, 1988; *Area:* 0.29 sq km
Population in 2006: 38
Provincial Electoral District(s): Whitecourt-Ste. Anne
Federal Electoral District(s): Yellowhead
Next Election: 2013 (3 year terms)
Dennis Evans, Administrator
Ron Gray, Mayor

Birchcliff
#104, 4505 - 50 Ave.
Sylvan Lake, AB T4S 1W2
403-887-2822 Fax: 403-887-2897
fivesv@telusplanet.net

Municipal Type: Summer Village
Incorporated: Jan. 1, 1972; *Area:* 0.98 sq km
Population in 2006: 125
Provincial Electoral District(s): Rocky Mountain House
Federal Electoral District(s): Wetaskiwin
Next Election: 2013 (3 year terms)
Myra Reiter, Administrator
Wayne Carey, Mayor

Bittern Lake
P.O. Box 5
300 Rail Way Ave.
Bittern Lake, AB T0C 0L0
780-672-7373 Fax: 780-672-7380
vobl@syban.net
Municipal Type: Village
Incorporated: Nov. 21, 1904; *Area:* 6.64 sq km
Population in 2006: 225
Provincial Electoral District(s): Wetaskiwin-Camrose
Federal Electoral District(s): Crowfoot
Next Election: 2013 (3 year terms)
Angie Burwash, CAO
Sheldon Grettum, Sendecki

Black Diamond
P.O. Box 10
Black Diamond, AB T0L 0H0
403-933-4348 Fax: 403-933-5865
info@town.blackdiamond.ab.ca
www.town.blackdiamond.ab.ca
Municipal Type: Town
Incorporated: May 8, 1929; *Area:* 3.21 sq km
Population in 2006: 1,900
Provincial Electoral District(s): Foothills-Rocky View
Federal Electoral District(s): Macleod
Next Election: 2013 (3 year terms)
Note: Incorporated as a town on Jan 1, 1956.
Dianne Kreh, Town Manager
Rolly Magee, Mayor

Blackfalds
P.O. Box 220
Blackfalds, AB T0M 0J0
403-885-4677 Fax: 403-885-4610
info@blackfalds.com
www.blackfalds.com
Municipal Type: Town
Incorporated: June 17, 1904; *Area:* 8.4 sq km
Population in 2006: 4,571
Provincial Electoral District(s): Lacombe-Ponoka
Federal Electoral District(s): Wetaskiwin
Next Election: 2013 (3 year terms)
Note: Incorporated as a town on April 1, 1980.
Corinne Newman, CAO
corinne@blackfalds.com
Melodie Stol, Mayor
melodie@blackfalds.com

Bon Accord
P.O. Box 100
Bon Accord, AB T0A 0K0
780-921-3550 Fax: 780-921-3585
townoffice@town.bonaccord.ab.ca
www.town.bonaccord.ab.ca
Municipal Type: Town
Incorporated: Jan. 1, 1964; *Area:* 2.11 sq km
Population in 2006: 1,534
Provincial Electoral District(s): Athabasca-Redwater
Federal Electoral District(s): Westlock-St. Paul
Next Election: 2013 (3 year terms)
Note: Incorporated as a town on Nov. 20, 1979.
Linda Zacharias, CAO
lzacharias@town.bonaccord.ab.ca
Lin VanDusen, Mayor
mayor@town.bonaccord.ab.ca

Bondiss
724 Baptiste Dr.
West Baptiste, AB T9S 1R8
780-675-9270 Fax: 780-675-9526
tomaszyk@mcsnet.ca
Municipal Type: Summer Village
Incorporated: Jan. 1, 1983; *Area:* 1.33 sq km
Population in 2006: 131
Provincial Electoral District(s): Athabasca-Redwater
Federal Electoral District(s): Fort McMurray-Athabasca
Next Election: 2013 (3 year terms)
Edwin Tomaszyk, CAO
Wilfred Tiedemann, Mayor

Bonnyville
P.O. Box 1006
4917 - 49 Ave.
Bonnyville, AB T9N 2J7
780-826-3496 Fax: 780-826-4806 Toll free: 1-866-826-3496
admin@town.bonnyville.ab.ca
www.town.bonnyville.ab.ca
Municipal Type: Town
Incorporated: Sept. 19, 1929; *Area:* 14.1 sq km
Population in 2009: 6,470
Provincial Electoral District(s): Bonnyville-Cold Lake
Federal Electoral District(s): Westlock-St. Paul
Next Election: 2013 (3 year terms)
Note: Proclaimed as a town on Feb. 3, 1948.
Mark Power, CAO
mpower@town.bonnyville.ab.ca
Ernie Isley, Mayor

Bonnyville Beach
P.O. Box 6439
Bonnyville, AB T9N 2G9
780-826-2925 Fax: 780-812-2904
svbbeach@mcsnet.ca
Municipal Type: Summer Village
Incorporated: Jan 1, 1958; *Area:* 0.38 sq km
Population in 2006: 97
Provincial Electoral District(s): Bonnyville-Cold Lake
Federal Electoral District(s): Westlock-St. Paul
Next Election: 2013 (3 year terms)
Lionel P. Tercier, Administrator
Chuck Dechene, Mayor

Botha
P.O. Box 160
Botha, AB T0C 0N0
403-742-5079 Fax: 403-742-6586
vlbotha@xplornet.com
Municipal Type: Village
Incorporated: Sept. 5, 1911; *Area:* 1.09 sq km
Population in 2006: 185
Provincial Electoral District(s): Drumheller-Stettler
Federal Electoral District(s): Crowfoot
Next Election: 2013 (3 year terms)
Michelle Renschler, CAO
Jean S. Jackson, Mayor

Bow Island
P.O. Box 100
Bow Island, AB T0K 0G0
403-545-2522 Fax: 403-545-6642
townoffice@bowisland.com
www.bowisland.com
Municipal Type: Town
Incorporated: June 14, 1910; *Area:* 5.92 sq km
Population in 2006: 1,790
Provincial Electoral District(s): Cypress-Medicine Hat
Federal Electoral District(s): Medicine Hat
Next Election: 2013 (3 year terms)
Note: Incorporated as a town on Feb. 1, 1912.
Anna-Marie Bridge, Town Manager
anna-marie@bowisland.com
Alan Hyland, Mayor
mayor@bowisland.com

Bow Valley Waste Management Commission
Wild Earth Associates Inc.
185 Carey
Canmore, AB T1W 2R7
403-609-7229 Fax: 403-609-0320
bvwmc@wildearth.ab.ca
Municipal Type: Water Commission
John Stutz, Chair
jstutz@telusplanet.net

Bowden
P.O. Box 338
Bowden, AB T0M 0K0
403-224-3395 Fax: 403-224-2244
admin@town.bowden.ab.ca
www.town.bowden.ab.ca
Municipal Type: Town
Incorporated: June 17, 1904; *Area:* 1.9 sq km
Population in 2006: 1,205
Provincial Electoral District(s): Innisfail-Sylvan Lake
Federal Electoral District(s): Red Deer
Next Election: 2013 (3 year terms)
Note: Incorporated as a town on Sept. 1, 1981.
Lori Conkin, CAO
cao@town.bowden.ab.ca
Cody Berggren, Mayor

Boyle
P.O. Box 9
Boyle, AB T0A 0M0
780-689-3643 Fax: 780-689-3998
admin@villageofboyle.com
www.villageofboyle.com
Municipal Type: Village
Incorporated: Dec. 31, 1953; *Area:* 4.1 sq km
Population in 2006: 844
Provincial Electoral District(s): Athabasca-Redwater
Federal Electoral District(s): Fort McMurray-Athabasca
Next Election: 2013 (3 year terms)
Ken Gwozdz, CAO
ken@villageofboyle.com
Bob Clark, Mayor

Breton
P.O. Box 480
4916 - 50 Ave.
Breton, AB T0C 0P0
780-696-3636 Fax: 780-696-3590
vbreton@telusplanet.net
www.village.breton.ab.ca
Municipal Type: Village
Incorporated: Jan. 1, 1957; *Area:* 1.73 sq km
Population in 2006: 550
Provincial Electoral District(s): Drayton Valley-Calmar
Federal Electoral District(s): Wetaskiwin
Next Election: 2013 (3 year terms)
Eileen Simmers, Municipal Administrator
esimmers@telusplanet.net
Darren Aldous, Mayor

Bruderheim
P.O. Box 280
Bruderheim, AB T0B 0S0
780-796-3731 Fax: 780-796-3037
info@bruderheim.ca
www.bruderheim.ca
Municipal Type: Town
Incorporated: May 29, 1908; *Area:* 4.23 sq km
Population in 2006: 1,215
Provincial Electoral District(s): Fort Saskatchewan-Vegreville
Federal Electoral District(s): Vegreville-Wainwright
Next Election: 2013 (3 year terms)
Note: Incorporated as a town on Sept. 17, 1980.
David K. Dubauskas, CAO
dubauska@strathcona.ab.ca
Jack Lambert, Mayor

Burnstick Lake
P.O. Box 1555
Cochrane, AB T4C 1B5
403-932-3866 Fax: 403-932-6652
rickbutler@pathcom.ca
Municipal Type: Summer Village
Incorporated: Dec. 31, 1991; *Area:* 0.18 sq km
Population in 2006: 43
Provincial Electoral District(s): Rocky Mountain House
Federal Electoral District(s): Wild Rose
Next Election: 2013 (3 year terms)
Rick Butler, Administrator
Diane Auld, Mayor

Calmar
P.O. Box 750
Calmar, AB T0C 0V0
780-985-3604 Fax: 780-985-3039
jdonovan@town.calmar.ab.ca
www.town.calmar.ab.ca
Municipal Type: Town
Incorporated: Jan. 1, 1949; *Area:* 4.34 sq km
Population in 2006: 1,959
Provincial Electoral District(s): Drayton Valley-Calmar
Federal Electoral District(s): Wetaskiwin
Next Election: 2013 (3 year terms)
Note: Incorporated as a town on Jan. 19, 1954.
Jeanette Donovan, Town Manager
jdonovan@town.calmar.ab.ca
Kirk Popik, Mayor
kpopik@town.calmar.ab.ca

Capital Region Northeast Water Services Commission
10005 - 102 St.
Fort Saskatchewan, AB T8L 2C5
780-992-6207 Fax: 780-992-1375
Municipal Type: Water Commission
Dave Worman, Manager
dworman@fortsask.ca

Capital Region Parkland Water Services
c/o 315 Jesperson Ave.
Spruce Grove, AB T7X 3E8
780-962-2611
Municipal Type: Water Commission

Capital Region Southwest Water Services Commission
#101, 1101 - 5 St.
Nisku, AB T9E 2X3
780-955-3555 Fax: 780-955-3444
Municipal Type: Water Commission
Darryl Rubis, Manager
darryl@leduc-county.com

Capital Region Vegreville Corridor Water Services Commission
P.O. Box 176
Chipman, AB T0B 0W0
780-363-3982 Fax: 780-363-2386
chipmanab@primus.ca
Municipal Type: Waste Commission
Pat Tomkow, Manager

Carbon
P.O. Box 249
Carbon, AB T0M 0L0
403-572-3244 Fax: 403-572-3778
admincarbon@wildroseinternet.ca
www.albertafirst.com/profiles/statspack/20509.html
Municipal Type: Village
Incorporated: Nov. 18, 1912; *Area:* 2 sq km
Population in 2006: 570
Provincial Electoral District(s): Olds-Didsbury-Three Hills
Federal Electoral District(s): Crowfoot
Next Election: 2013 (3 year terms)
Debra Grosfield, Municipal Administrator
caocarbon@wildroseinternet.ca
Shirley D. Buyer, Mayor

Cardston
P.O. Box 280
Cardston, AB T0K 0K0
403-653-3366 Fax: 403-653-2499
info@cardston.ca
www.cardston.ca
Municipal Type: Town
Incorporated: Dec. 29, 1898; *Area:* 8.64 sq km
Population in 2006: 3,452
Provincial Electoral District(s): Cardston-Taber-Warner
Federal Electoral District(s): Lethbridge
Next Election: 2013 (3 year terms)
Note: Incorporated as a town on July 2, 1901.
Marian Carlson, Administrator
marian@cardston.ca
Rick Schow, Mayor

Carmangay
P.O. Box 130
Carmangay, AB T0L 0N0
403-643-3595 Fax: 403-643-2007
villagec@telusplanet.net
www.albertafirst.com/profiles/statspack/20510.html
Municipal Type: Village
Incorporated: Jan. 20, 1910; *Area:* 1.86 sq km
Population in 2006: 336
Provincial Electoral District(s): Little Bow
Federal Electoral District(s): Macleod
Next Election: 2013 (3 year terms)
Anne Kirby, Administrator
Art Cogdale, Mayor

Caroline
P.O. Box 148
Caroline, AB T0M 0M0
403-722-3781 Fax: 403-722-4050
administration@caroline.ca
www.caroline.ca
Municipal Type: Village
Incorporated: Dec. 31, 1951; *Area:* 1.98 sq km
Population in 2006: 515
Provincial Electoral District(s): Rocky Mountain House
Federal Electoral District(s): Wild Rose
Next Election: 2013 (3 year terms)
Michael Haugen, CAO
Laura Cudmore, Mayor
Mary Hughes, Technician, Solid Wastes Recycling
403-329-7367
mhughes@lethbridge.ca

Carstairs
P.O. Box 370
Carstairs, AB T0M 0N0
403-337-3341 Fax: 403-337-3343
admin@town.carstairs.ab.ca
www.town.carstairs.ab.ca
Municipal Type: Town
Incorporated: May 15, 1903; *Area:* 5 sq km
Population in 2006: 2,656
Provincial Electoral District(s): Olds-Didsbury-Three Hills
Federal Electoral District(s): Wild Rose
Next Election: 2013 (3 year terms)
Note: Incorporated as a town on Sept. 1, 1966.
Carl McDonnell, CAO
carl@town.carstairs.ab.ca
Lance Colby, Mayor

Castle Island
11318 - 10th Ave.
Edmonton, AB T6J 6S9
780-431-9712 Fax: 780-431-0882
svoffice@telusplanet.net
Municipal Type: Summer Village
Incorporated: Jan. 1, 1955; *Area:* 0.05 sq km
Population in 2006: 22
Provincial Electoral District(s): Whitecourt-Ste. Anne
Federal Electoral District(s): Yellowhead
Next Election: 2013 (3 year terms)
Anita Blais, Administrator
Katherine Hunter, Mayor

Castor
P.O. Box 479
Castor, AB T0C 0X0
403-882-3215 Fax: 403-882-2700
castor@telusplanet.net
www.castor.ca
Municipal Type: Town
Incorporated: Nov. 26, 1909; *Area:* 2.72 sq km
Population in 2006: 931
Provincial Electoral District(s): Battle River-Wainwright
Federal Electoral District(s): Crowfoot
Next Election: 2013 (3 year terms)
Note: Incorporated as a town on June 27, 1910.
Michael Yakielashek, CAO
Gerry DeVloo, Mayor

Central Peace Regional Waste Management Commission
c/o Saddle Hills County
P.O. Box 69
Spirit River, AB T0H 3G0
780-864-3760 Fax: 780-864-3904
Municipal Type: Water Commission
Cliff Travis, Chair

Cereal
P.O. Box 160
Cereal, AB T0J 0N0
403-326-3823 Fax: 403-326-382g
vofc@telusplanet.net
Municipal Type: Village
Incorporated: Aug. 19, 1914; *Area:* 0.95 sq km
Population in 2006: 126
Provincial Electoral District(s): Drumheller-Stettler
Federal Electoral District(s): Crowfoot
Next Election: 2013 (3 year terms)
Mary Ann Salik, Administrator
Betty Cooper, Mayor

Champion
P.O. Box 367
Champion, AB T0L 0R0
403-897-3833 Fax: 403-897-2250
champvil@telus.net
www.albertafirst.com/profiles/statspack/20513.html
Municipal Type: Village
Incorporated: May 27, 1911; *Area:* 0.88 sq km
Population in 2006: 364
Provincial Electoral District(s): Little Bow
Federal Electoral District(s): Macleod
Next Election: 2013 (3 year terms)
Melissa Rhodes, Administrator
Trevor Wagenvoort, Mayor

Chauvin
P.O. Box 160
Chauvin, AB T0B 0V0
780-858-3881 Fax: 780-858-2125
vchauvin@telusplanet.net
www.villagechauvin.ca
Municipal Type: Village
Incorporated: Dec. 30, 1912; *Area:* 2.32 sq km
Population in 2006: 308
Provincial Electoral District(s): Battle River-Wainwright
Federal Electoral District(s): Vegreville-Wainwright
Next Election: 2013 (3 year terms)
Shelly McMann, Municipal Administrator
vchauvin@wy-com.ca
Velda Nutbrown, Mayor

Chipman
P.O. Box 176
Chipman, AB T0B 0W0
780-363-3982 Fax: 780-363-2386
chipmanab@mcsnet.ca
www.chipmanab.ca
Municipal Type: Village
Incorporated: Oct. 21, 1913; *Area:* 0.62 sq km
Population in 2006: 238
Provincial Electoral District(s): Fort Saskatchewan-Vegreville
Federal Electoral District(s): Vegreville-Wainwright
Next Election: 2013 (3 year terms)
Pat Tomkow, Administrator
Jim Palmer, Mayor
jvpalmer@mcsnet.ca

Claresholm
P.O. Box 1000
Claresholm, AB T0L 0T0
403-625-3381 Fax: 403-625-3869
clares@telusplanet.net
www.townofclaresholm.com
Municipal Type: Town
Incorporated: May 30, 1903; *Area:* 8.3 sq km
Population in 2006: 3,700
Provincial Electoral District(s): Livingstone-Macleod
Federal Electoral District(s): Macleod
Next Election: 2013 (3 year terms)
Note: Incorporated as a town on Aug. 31, 1905.
Kris Holbeck, CAO
kris.holbeck@townofclaresholm.com
Rob Steel, Mayor
rob.steel@townofclaresholm.com

Clive
P.O. Box 90
Clive, AB T0C 0Y0
403-784-3366 Fax: 403-784-2012
cliveab@platinum.ca
www.clive.ca
Municipal Type: Village
Incorporated: Jan. 9, 1912; *Area:* 2.12 sq km
Population in 2006: 562
Provincial Electoral District(s): Lacombe-Ponoka
Federal Electoral District(s): Wetaskiwin
Next Election: 2013 (3 year terms)
Val Rowland, Municipal Clerk
Anita Gillard, Mayor

Clyde
P.O. Box 190
Clyde, AB T0G 0P0
780-348-5356 Fax: 780-348-5699
admin@villageofclyde.ca
www.albertafirst.com/profiles/community
Municipal Type: Village
Incorporated: Jan. 28, 1914; *Area:* 1.36 sq km
Population in 2006: 470
Provincial Electoral District(s): Barrhead-Morinville-Westlock
Federal Electoral District(s): Westlock-St. Paul
Next Election: 2013 (3 year terms)
Darlene Gross, CAO
cao@villageofclyde.ca
Douglas Paul Nyal, Mayor
mayor@villageofclyde.ca

Coaldale
1920 - 17 St.
Coaldale, AB T1M 1M1
403-345-1300 Fax: 403-345-1311
admin@coaldale.ca
www.coaldale.ca
Municipal Type: Town
Incorporated: Dec. 27, 1919; *Area:* 7.95 sq km
Population in 2009: 6,943
Provincial Electoral District(s): Little Bow
Federal Electoral District(s): Lethbridge
Next Election: 2013 (3 year terms)
Note: Incorporated as a town on Jan. 7, 1952.
Leo Ludwig, Town Manager
lludwig@coaldale.ca
Kim Craig, Mayor

Coalhurst
P.O. Box 456
Coalhurst, AB T0L 0V0
403-381-3033 Fax: 403-381-2924
main@town.coalhurst.ab.ca
www.town.coalhurst.ab.ca
Municipal Type: Town
Incorporated: Dec. 17, 1913; *Area:* 1.64 sq km
Population in 2006: 1,523
Provincial Electoral District(s): Little Bow
Federal Electoral District(s): Lethbridge
Next Election: 2013 (3 year terms)
Note: Incorporated as a town on June 1, 1995.
R. Kim Hauta, CAO
rkhauta@town.coalhurst.ab.ca
Dennis Cassie, Mayor
cassiefamily@shaw.ca

Cold Lake Regional Utility
5513 - 48 Ave.
Cold Lake, AB T9M 1A1
780-594-4494 Fax: 780-594-3480
Municipal Type: Water Commission

Consort
P.O. Box 490
Consort, AB T0C 1B0
403-577-3623 Fax: 403-577-2024
consort@xplornet.com
www.village.consort.ab.ca
Municipal Type: Village
Incorporated: Sept. 23, 1912; *Area:* 2.63 sq km
Population in 2006: 739
Provincial Electoral District(s): Drumheller-Stettler
Federal Electoral District(s): Crowfoot
Next Election: 2013 (3 year terms)
Sandra King, CAO
Terry McMahon, Mayor

Coronation
P.O. Box 219
Coronation, AB T0C 1C0
403-578-3679 Fax: 403-578-3020
admin@town.coronation.ab.ca
www.town.coronation.ab.ca
Municipal Type: Town
Incorporated: Dec. 16, 1911; *Area:* 3.73 sq km
Population in 2006: 1,015
Provincial Electoral District(s): Battle River-Wainwright
Federal Electoral District(s): Crowfoot
Next Election: 2013 (3 year terms)
Note: Incorporated as a town on April 29, 1912.
David Connauton, Town Manager
davidc@town.coronation.ab.ca
Herb Rock, Mayor

Coutts
P.O. Box 236
Coutts, AB T0K 0N0
403-344-3848 Fax: 403-344-4360
vilcoutt@telus.net
www.villagecoutts.ab.ca
Municipal Type: Village
Incorporated: Jan. 1, 1960; *Area:* 0.98 sq km
Population in 2006: 305
Provincial Electoral District(s): Cardston-Taber-Warner
Federal Electoral District(s): Lethbridge
Next Election: 2013 (3 year terms)
Lori Rolfe, CAO
Jamie Woodcock, Mayor

Cowley
P.O. Box 40
Cowley, AB T0K 0P0
403-628-3808 Fax: 403-628-2807
vilocow@shaw.ca
Municipal Type: Village
Incorporated: Aug. 16, 1906; *Area:* 1.4 sq km
Population in 2006: 219

Provincial Electoral District(s): Livingstone-Macleod
Federal Electoral District(s): Macleod
Next Election: 2013 (3 year terms)
Laurie Wilgosh, Administrator
wilgosh@shaw.ca
Wyatt Martin, Mayor

Cremona
P.O. Box 10
Cremona, AB T0M 0R0
403-637-3762 Fax: 403-637-2101
admin@village.cremona.ab.ca
www.village.cremona.ab.ca
Municipal Type: Village
Incorporated: Jan. 1, 1955; *Area:* 0.68 sq km
Population in 2006: 463
Provincial Electoral District(s): Olds-Didsbury-Three Hills
Federal Electoral District(s): Wild Rose
Next Election: 2013 (3 year terms)
Terry Lofstrom, CAO
Elizabeth Bell, Mayor

Crossfield
P.O. Box 500
Crossfield, AB T0M 0S0
403-946-5565 Fax: 403-946-4523
town@crossfieldalberta.com
www.crossfieldalberta.com
Municipal Type: Town
Incorporated: June 3, 1907; *Area:* 4.8 sq km
Population in 2006: 2,648
Provincial Electoral District(s): Foothills-Rocky View
Federal Electoral District(s): Wild Rose
Next Election: 2013 (3 year terms)
Note: Incorporated as a town on Aug. 1, 1980.
Cheryl Skelly, CAO
cheryls@crossfieldalberta.com
Phil McCracken, Mayor

Crystal Springs
256 Grandview, RR#1
Westerose, AB T0C 2V0
780-586-3522 Fax: 780-586-2037
crystalsprings@xplornet.com
www.svcrystalsprings.ca
Municipal Type: Summer Village
Incorporated: Jan. 1, 1957; *Area:* 0.58 sq km
Population in 2006: 112
Provincial Electoral District(s): Drayton Valley-Calmar
Federal Electoral District(s): Wetaskiwin
Next Election: 2013 (3 year terms)
Bev Schneider, Administrator
N. Roger MacEachern, Mayor
780-586-2423
nrmac@shaw.ca

Czar
P.O. Box 30
Czar, AB T0B 0Z0
780-857-3740 Fax: 780-857-2353
villczar@xplornet.com
Municipal Type: Village
Incorporated: Nov. 12, 1917; *Area:* 1.18 sq km
Population in 2006: 175
Provincial Electoral District(s): Battle River-Wainwright
Federal Electoral District(s): Vegreville-Wainwright
Next Election: 2013 (3 year terms)
Tricia Strang, Administrator
Mary Dambrowsky, Mayor

Daysland
P.O. Box 610
Daysland, AB T0B 1A0
780-374-3767 Fax: 780-374-2455
daystown@telusplanet.net
www.daysland.com
Municipal Type: Town
Incorporated: April 23, 1906; *Area:* 1.75 sq km
Population in 2006: 818
Provincial Electoral District(s): Battle River-Wainwright
Federal Electoral District(s): Vegreville-Wainwright
Next Election: 2013 (3 year terms)
Note: Incorporated as a town on April 2, 1907.
Shelley Munro, CAO
smunro@daysland.com
Lenard A. Calon, Mayor

Delburne
P.O. Box 341
Delburne, AB T0M 0V0
403-749-3606 Fax: 403-749-2800
village@delburne.ca
www.delburne.ca
Municipal Type: Village
Incorporated: Jan. 17, 1913; *Area:* 1.32 sq km
Population in 2006: 765
Provincial Electoral District(s): Innisfail-Sylvan Lake
Federal Electoral District(s): Red Deer
Next Election: 2013 (3 year terms)
Karen Fegan, CAO
karen.fegan@delburne.ca
Robert M. Manning, Mayor
bob.manning@delburne.ca

Delia
P.O. Box 206
Delia, AB T0J 0W0
403-364-3787 Fax: 403-364-2089
delia@netago.ca
Municipal Type: Village
Incorporated: July 20, 1914; *Area:* 1.31 sq km
Population in 2006: 207
Provincial Electoral District(s): Drumheller-Stettler
Federal Electoral District(s): Crowfoot
Next Election: 2013 (3 year terms)
Kristy Isaac, CAO
Gordon Isaac, Mayor

Derwent
P.O. Box 102
Derwent, AB T0B 1C0
780-741-3792 Fax: 780-741-3792
admincf@telus.net
Municipal Type: Village
Incorporated: June 25, 1930; *Area:* 0.38 sq km
Population in 2006: 117
Provincial Electoral District(s): Lac la Biche-St. Paul
Federal Electoral District(s): Vegreville-Wainwright
Next Election: 2013 (3 year terms)
Michelle Wright, CAO
Shawn Cousins, Mayor

Devon
1 Columbia Ave. West
Devon, AB T9G 1A1
780-987-8300 Fax: 780-987-4778
www.town.devon.ab.ca
Municipal Type: Town
Incorporated: Dec. 31, 1949; *Area:* 8.63 sq km
Population in 2009: 6,534
Provincial Electoral District(s): Leduc-Beaumont-Devon
Federal Electoral District(s): Edmonton-Leduc
Next Election: 2013 (3 year terms)
Note: Incorporated as a town on Feb. 24, 1950.
Tony Kulbisky, CAO
780-987-8301
Anita Marie Fisher, Mayor

Dewberry
P.O. Box 30
Dewberry, AB T0B 1G0
780-847-3053 Fax: 780-847-3053
dewberry@hmsinet.ca
Municipal Type: Village
Incorporated: Jan. 1, 1957; *Area:* 0.84 sq km
Population in 2006: 196
Provincial Electoral District(s): Vermilion-Lloydminster
Federal Electoral District(s): Vegreville-Wainwright
Next Election: 2013 (3 year terms)
Sherry Johnson, Acting Sec.-Treas.
Headley Dennill, Mayor

Didsbury
P.O. Box 790
Didsbury, AB T0M 0W0
403-335-3391 Fax: 403-335-9794
webmaster@didsbury.ca
www.didsbury.ca
Municipal Type: Town
Incorporated: Dec. 24, 1901; *Area:* 5.47 sq km
Population in 2006: 4,275
Provincial Electoral District(s): Olds-Didsbury-Three Hills
Federal Electoral District(s): Wild Rose
Next Election: 2013 (3 year terms)
Note: Incorporated as a town on Sept. 27, 1906.
Roy R. Brown, CAO
rbrown@didsbury.ca
Brian Wittal, Mayor
bwittal@didsbury.ca

Donalda
P.O. Box 160
Donalda, AB T0B 1H0
403-883-2345 Fax: 403-883-2022
vdonalda@telusplanet.net
www.village.donalda.ab.ca
Municipal Type: Village
Incorporated: Dec. 30, 1912; *Area:* 0.99 sq km
Population in 2006: 224
Provincial Electoral District(s): Drumheller-Stettler
Federal Electoral District(s): Crowfoot
Next Election: 2013 (3 year terms)
Peter Simons, CAO
Terry Nordahl, Mayor
403-883-2259
kurbits2@gmail.com

Donnelly
P.O. Box 200
Donnelly, AB T0H 1G0
780-925-3835 Fax: 780-925-2100
vilofdon@serbernet.com
www.albertafirst.com/profiles/statspack/20528.html
Municipal Type: Village
Incorporated: Jan. 1, 1956; *Area:* 1.04 sq km
Population in 2006: 293
Provincial Electoral District(s): Dunvegan-Central Peace
Federal Electoral District(s): Peace River
Next Election: 2013 (3 year terms)

Rita Therriault, Administrator
Charles Doyle, Mayor

Drayton Valley
P.O. Box 6837
5120 - 52nd St.
Drayton Valley, AB T7A 1A1
780-514-2200 Fax: 780-542-5753
info@town.draytonvalley.ab.ca
www.town.draytonvalley.ab.ca
Municipal Type: Town
Incorporated: Jan. 1, 1956; *Area:* 12.27 sq km
Population in 2006: 6,893
Provincial Electoral District(s): Drayton Valley-Calmar
Federal Electoral District(s): Yellowhead
Next Election: 2013 (3 year terms)
Note: Incorporated as a town on June 1, 1956.
Manny Deol, Town Manager
mdeol@town.draytonvalley.ab.ca
Mohammed (Moe) Hamdon, Mayor
mayor@town.draytonvalley.ab.ca

Drumheller
703 - 2nd Ave. West
Drumheller, AB T0J 0Y3
403-823-6300 Fax: 403-823-7739
rmroman@dinosaurvalley.com
www.dinosaurvalley.com
Municipal Type: Town
Incorporated: May 15, 1913; *Area:* 107.93 sq km
Population in 2006: 7,932
Provincial Electoral District(s): Drumheller-Stettler
Federal Electoral District(s): Crowfoot
Next Election: 2013 (3 year terms)
Note: Incorporated as a town on March 2, 1916.
Ray Romanetz, CAO
rmroman@dinosaurvalley.com
Terry Yemen, Mayor

Duchess
P.O. Box 158
Duchess, AB T0J 0Z0
403-378-4452 Fax: 403-378-3860
administration@villageofduchess.com
Municipal Type: Village
Incorporated: May 12, 1921; *Area:* 1.89 sq km
Population in 2006: 978
Provincial Electoral District(s): Strathmore-Brooks
Federal Electoral District(s): Medicine Hat
Next Election: 2013 (3 year terms)
Yvonne Cosh, Joint CAO
Shelley Thomas, Joint CAO
Anthony Steidel, Mayor

Eckville
P.O. Box 578
Eckville, AB T0M 0X0
403-746-2171 Fax: 403-746-2900
info@eckville.com
www.eckville.com
Municipal Type: Town
Incorporated: Nov. 3, 1921; *Area:* 1.58 sq km
Population in 2006: 951
Provincial Electoral District(s): Rocky Mountain House
Federal Electoral District(s): Wetaskiwin
Next Election: 2013 (3 year terms)
Note: Incorporated as a town on July 1, 1966.
Therese Kleeberger, Administrator
admin@eckville.com
Helen Posti, Mayor

Edberg
P.O. Box 160
Edberg, AB T0B 1J0
780-877-3999 Fax: 780-877-2562
vledberg@syban.net
www.villageofedberg.com
Municipal Type: Village
Incorporated: Feb. 4, 1930; *Area:* 0.36 sq km
Population in 2006: 155
Provincial Electoral District(s): Lacombe-Ponoka
Federal Electoral District(s): Crowfoot
Next Election: 2013 (3 year terms)
Patrick Risk, CAO
Lorne Klevgaard, Mayor

Edgerton
P.O. Box 57
Edgerton, AB T0B 1K0
780-755-3933 Fax: 780-755-3750
info@edgerton-oasis.ca
www.edgerton-oasis.ca
Municipal Type: Village
Incorporated: Sept. 11, 1917; *Area:* 1.22 sq km
Population in 2006: 373
Provincial Electoral District(s): Battle River-Wainwright
Federal Electoral District(s): Vegreville-Wainwright
Next Election: 2013 (3 year terms)
Terry Tiffen, CAO
Barbara L. Sjoquist, Mayor

Edson
P.O. Box 6300
605 - 50th St.
Edson, AB T7E 1T7

780-723-4401 Fax: 780-723-8617
civiccentre@townofedson.ca
www.townofedson.ca
Municipal Type: Town
Incorporated: Jan. 9, 1911; *Area:* 29.54 sq km
Population in 2006: 8,098
Provincial Electoral District(s): West Yellowhead
Federal Electoral District(s): Yellowhead
Next Election: 2013 (3 year terms)
Note: Incorporated as a town on Sept. 21, 1911.
Clarence Joly, CAO
clarencej@townofedson.ca
Greg Pasychny, Mayor

Elk Point

P.O. Box 448
Elk Point, AB T0A 1A0
780-724-3810 Fax: 780-724-2762
town@elkpoint.ca
www.elkpoint.ca
Municipal Type: Town
Incorporated: May 31, 1938; *Area:* 4.88 sq km
Population in 2006: 1,487
Provincial Electoral District(s): Lac La Biche-St. Paul
Federal Electoral District(s): Westlock-St. Paul
Next Election: 2013 (3 year terms)
Note: Incorporated as a town on Jan. 1, 1962.
Myron J. Goyan, Manager
mjgoyan@elkpoint.ca
Parrish Tung, Mayor

Elnora

P.O. Box 629
Elnora, AB T0M 0Y0
403-773-3922 Fax: 403-773-3173
elnoravl@platinum.ca
www.villageofelnora.com
Municipal Type: Village
Incorporated: July 22, 1929; *Area:* 0.69 sq km
Population in 2006: 275
Provincial Electoral District(s): Innisfail-Sylvan Lake
Federal Electoral District(s): Red Deer
Next Election: 2013 (3 year terms)
Michelle Smith, Administrator
Dale Brown, Mayor

Empress

P.O. Box 159
Empress, AB T0J 1E0
403-565-3938 Fax: 403-565-2010
voe14@telus.net
www.villageofempress.com
Municipal Type: Village
Incorporated: Feb. 5, 1914; *Area:* 1.75 sq km
Population in 2006: 136
Provincial Electoral District(s): Drumheller-Stettler
Federal Electoral District(s): Medicine Hat
Next Election: 2013 (3 year terms)
Darren Dick, CAO
darran.dick@gov.ab.ca
Roderick L. Briggs, Mayor

Evergreen Regional Waste Management Services Commission

5015 - 49 Ave.
St Paul, AB T0A 3A4
780-645-3301 Fax: 780-645-3104
Municipal Type: Water Commission
Dennis Bergheim, Manager

Fairview

P.O. Box 730
10209 - 109 St.
Fairview, AB T0H 1L0
780-835-5461 Fax: 780-835-3576
municipalsecretary@fairview.ca
www.fairview.ca
Municipal Type: Town
Incorporated: March 28, 1929; *Area:* 9.65 sq km
Population in 2006: 3,297
Provincial Electoral District(s): Dunvegan-Central Peace
Federal Electoral District(s): Peace River
Next Election: 2013 (3 year terms)
Note: Incorporated as a town on April 25, 1949.
Martin Taylor, CAO
cao@fairview.ca
Gordon MacLeod, Mayor
mayor@fairview.ca

Falher

P.O. Box 155
Falher, AB T0H 1M0
780-837-2247 Fax: 780-837-2647
info@town.falher.ab.ca
www.town.falher.ab.ca
Municipal Type: Town
Incorporated: Sept. 05, 1923; *Area:* 2.87 sq km
Population in 2006: 941
Provincial Electoral District(s): Dunvegan-Central Peace
Federal Electoral District(s): Peace River
Next Election: 2013 (3 year terms)
Note: Incorporated as a town on Jan. 1, 1955.
Adele Parker, CAO
aparker@town.falher.ab.ca
Margaret Tardif, Mayor
mtardif@town.falher.ab.ca

Ferintosh

P.O. Box 160
Ferintosh, AB T0B 1M0
780-877-3767 Fax: 780-877-2338
villfer@telus.net
Municipal Type: Village
Incorporated: Jan. 9, 1911; *Area:* 0.62 sq km
Population in 2006: 153
Provincial Electoral District(s): Lacombe-Ponoka
Federal Electoral District(s): Crowfoot
Next Election: 2013 (3 year terms)
Grant Johnson, CAO
Marvin Jassman, Mayor

Foothills Regional Services

P.O. Box 5605
High River, AB T1V 1M7
403-652-2341 Fax: 403-652-7880
Municipal Type: Waste Commission
Bill Robinson, Sec.-Treas.
wrobins@mdfoothills.com
Irv Cherneski, Chair

Foremost

P.O. Box 159
Foremost, AB T0K 0X0
403-867-3733 Fax: 403-867-2031
vlg4most@telusplanet.net
www.foremostalberta.com
Municipal Type: Village
Incorporated: Dec. 31, 1950; *Area:* 1.74 sq km
Population in 2006: 524
Provincial Electoral District(s): Cypress-Medicine Hat
Federal Electoral District(s): Medicine Hat
Next Election: 2013 (3 year terms)
Kelly Calhoun, Municipal Administrator
Kenneth R. Kultgen, Mayor

Forestburg

P.O. Box 210
Forestburg, AB T0B 1N0
780-582-3668 Fax: 780-582-2233
forestburg@persona.ca
www.forestburg.ca
Municipal Type: Village
Incorporated: Aug. 21, 1919; *Area:* 2.19 sq km
Population in 2006: 895
Provincial Electoral District(s): Battle River-Wainwright
Federal Electoral District(s): Vegreville-Wainwright
Next Election: 2013 (3 year terms)
Monica Northey, CAO
Bob Coutts, Mayor

Fort Macleod

P.O. Box 1420
Fort MacLeod, AB T0L 0Z0
403-553-4425 Fax: 403-553-2426
edo@fortmacleod.com
www.fortmacleod.com
Municipal Type: Town
Incorporated: Dec. 31, 1892; *Area:* 23.34 sq km
Population in 2006: 3,072
Provincial Electoral District(s): Livingstone-Macleod
Federal Electoral District(s): Macleod
Next Election: 2013 (3 year terms)
Barry Elliott, Municipal Manager
manager@fortmacleod.com
R. Shawn Patience, Mayor
mayor@fortmacleod.com

Fox Creek

P.O. Box 149
Fox Creek, AB T0H 1P0
780-622-3896 Fax: 780-622-4247
info@town.fox-creek.ab.ca
www.town.fox-creek.ab.ca
Municipal Type: Town
Incorporated: July 19, 1967; *Area:* 11.54 sq km
Population in 2006: 2,278
Provincial Electoral District(s): Grande Prairie-Smoky
Federal Electoral District(s): Yellowhead
Next Election: 2013 (3 year terms)
Dennis Egyedy, Town Manager
dennis@foxcreek.ca
Leora MacKinnon, Mayor
lole@telusplanet.net

Gadsby

P.O. Box 80
Gadsby, AB T0C 1K0
403-574-3793 Fax: 403-574-2369
vgadsby@telusplanet.net
Municipal Type: Village
Incorporated: May 6, 1910; *Area:* 0.82 sq km
Population in 2006: 35
Provincial Electoral District(s): Drumheller-Stettler
Federal Electoral District(s): Crowfoot
Next Election: 2013 (3 year terms)
Lavonne Smith, CAO
Mareena O'Brien, Mayor

Galahad

P.O. Box 66
Galahad, AB T0B 1R0
780-583-3741 Fax: 780-583-2230
galahad@telus.net
www.albertafirst.com/profiles/statspack/20538.html
Municipal Type: Village
Incorporated: March 5, 1918; *Area:* 0.6 sq km
Population in 2006: 134
Provincial Electoral District(s): Battle River-Wainwright
Federal Electoral District(s): Vegreville-Wainwright
Next Election: 2013 (3 year terms)
Shelly Armstrong, CAO
sarmstrong@flagstaff.ab.ca
Frank Herle, Mayor

Ghost Lake

P.O. Box 5754
High River, AB T1V 1P3
403-652-4636 Fax: 403-206-7209
admin@ghostlake.ca
www.ghostlake.ca
Municipal Type: Summer Village
Incorporated: Dec. 31, 1953; *Area:* 0.63 sq km
Population in 2006: 78
Provincial Electoral District(s): Banff-Cochrane
Federal Electoral District(s): Wild Rose
Next Election: 2013 (3 year terms)
Sharon Plett, CAO
Ron Kennard, Mayor
403-881-2276
rkennard@Xplornet.com

Gibbons

P.O. Box 68
4807 - 50 Ave.
Gibbons, AB T0A 1N0
780-923-3331 Fax: 780-923-3691
town@gibbons.ca
www.gibbons.ca
Municipal Type: Town
Incorporated: Jan. 1, 1959; *Area:* 6.46 sq km
Population in 2007: 2,848
Provincial Electoral District(s): Athabasca-Redwater
Federal Electoral District(s): Westlock-St. Paul
Next Election: 2013 (3 year terms)
Note: Incorporated as a town on April 1, 1977.
Maisie Metrunec, Town Manager
mmetrunec@gibbons.ca
William H. Nimmo, Mayor
gov@gibbons.ca

Girouxville

P.O. Box 276
Girouxville, AB T0H 1S0
780-323-4270 Fax: 780-323-4110
girouxvl@telusplanet.net
www.albertafirst.com/profiles/statspack/20539.html
Municipal Type: Village
Incorporated: Dec. 31, 1951; *Area:* 0.58 sq km
Population in 2006: 282
Provincial Electoral District(s): Dunvegan-Central Peace
Federal Electoral District(s): Peace River
Next Election: 2013 (3 year terms)
Estelle Girard, Municipal Administrator
Carmen Ewing, Mayor

Glendon

P.O. Box 177
Glendon, AB T0A 1P0
780-635-3807 Fax: 780-635-2100
glendon@mcsnet.ca
Municipal Type: Village
Incorporated: Jan. 1, 1956; *Area:* 1.98 sq km
Population in 2006: 421
Provincial Electoral District(s): Bonnyville-Cold Lake
Federal Electoral District(s): Westlock-St. Paul
Next Election: 2013 (3 year terms)
Tammy Hellum, CAO
Johnnie Doonanco, Mayor

Glenwood

P.O. Box 1084
Glenwood, AB T0K 2R0
403-626-3233 Fax: 403-626-3234
admin@glenwood.ca
www.glenwood.ca
Municipal Type: Village
Incorporated: Jan. 1, 1961; *Area:* 1.46 sq km
Population in 2006: 280
Provincial Electoral District(s): Cardston-Taber-Warner
Federal Electoral District(s): Macleod
Next Election: 2013 (3 year terms)
Brad Salmon, CAO
Doral LaMar Lybbert, Mayor

Golden Days

11318 - 10th Ave.
Edmonton, AB T6J 6S9
780-431-9712 Fax: 780-431-0882
svoffice@telusplanet.net
Municipal Type: Summer Village
Incorporated: Jan. 1, 1965; *Area:* 2.27 sq km
Population in 2006: 207
Provincial Electoral District(s): Drayton Valley-Calmar

Federal Electoral District(s): Wetaskiwin
Next Election: 2013 (3 year terms)
Anita Blais, Administrator
Jerry Korchinski, Mayor

Grande Cache
P.O. Box 300
Grande Cache, AB T0E 0Y0
780-827-3362 Fax: 780-827-2406
admin@grandecache.ca
www.grandecache.ca
Municipal Type: Town
Incorporated: Sept. 1, 1966; *Area:* 35.48 sq km
Population in 2006: 3,783
Provincial Electoral District(s): West Yellowhead
Federal Electoral District(s): Yellowhead
Next Election: 2013 (3 year terms)
Darren Ottaway, CAO
darren.ottaway@grandecache.ca
Louise Krewusik, Mayor

Grandview
P.O. Box 100
603 - 2nd Ave.
Ma-Me-O Beach, AB T0C 1X0
780-586-2494 Fax: 780-586-3567
svadminoffice@xplornet.com
www.svgrandview.com
Municipal Type: Summer Village
Incorporated: Jan. 1, 1967; *Area:* 0.8 sq km
Population in 2006: 127
Provincial Electoral District(s): Drayton Valley-Calmar
Federal Electoral District(s): Wetaskiwin
Next Election: 2013 (3 year terms)
Peter Irwin, Administrator
Leslie Ellis, Mayor

Granum
P.O. Box 88
Granum, AB T0L 1A0
403-687-3822 Fax: 403-687-2285
cao@townofgranum.ca
www.townofgranum.ca
Municipal Type: Town
Incorporated: July 12, 1904; *Area:* 1.87 sq km
Population in 2006: 415
Provincial Electoral District(s): Livingstone-Macleod
Federal Electoral District(s): Macleod
Next Election: 2013 (3 year terms)
Note: Incorporated as a town on Nov. 7, 1910.
Larry Flexhaug, Municipal Administrator
Melva Stinson, Mayor
Interim Mayor

Greenview Regional Waste Management Commission
P.O. Box 115
Valleyview, AB T0H 3N0
780-524-7601 Fax: 780-524-4432
Municipal Type: Water Commission
Gordon Frank, Acting Administrator

Grimshaw
P.O. Box 377
Grimshaw, AB T0H 1W0
780-332-4626 Fax: 780-332-1250
wjohnson@grimshaw.ca
www.grimshaw.ca
Municipal Type: Town
Incorporated: Feb. 18, 1930; *Area:* 7.21 sq km
Population in 2006: 2,537
Provincial Electoral District(s): Dunvegan-Central Peace
Federal Electoral District(s): Peace River
Next Election: 2013 (3 year terms)
Note: Incorporated as a town on Feb. 2, 1953.
Wendy Johnson, CAO
Brian Allen, Mayor

Gull Lake
RR#1
Tees, AB T0C 2N0
403-784-3267 Fax: 403-784-3267
mckenney@platinum.ca
www.summervillageofgulllake.com
Municipal Type: Summer Village
Incorporated: Sept. 1, 1993; *Area:* 0.7 sq km
Population in 2006: 204
Provincial Electoral District(s): Rocky Mountain House
Federal Electoral District(s): Wetaskiwin
Next Election: 2013 (3 year terms)
J. Carla Kenney, CAO
Trevor H. Wannop, Mayor
twannop@telusplanet.net

Half Moon Bay
#104, 4505 - 50 Ave.
Sylvan Lake, AB T4S 1W2
403-887-2822 Fax: 403-887-2897
fivesv@telusplanet.net
Municipal Type: Summer Village
Incorporated: Jan. 1, 1978; *Area:* 0.17 sq km
Population in 2006: 32
Provincial Electoral District(s): Rocky Mountain House
Federal Electoral District(s): Wetaskiwin
Next Election: 2013 (3 year terms)
Myra Reiter, Administrator
Edward (Ted) Hiscock, Mayor

Halkirk
P.O. Box 126
Halkirk, AB T0C 1M0
403-884-2464 Fax: 403-884-2113
halkirk@wildroseinternet.ca
Municipal Type: Village
Incorporated: Feb. 10, 1912; *Area:* 0.65 sq km
Population in 2006: 113
Provincial Electoral District(s): Battle River-Wainwright
Federal Electoral District(s): Crowfoot
Next Election: 2013 (3 year terms)
Doris Cordel, Village Administrator
Ross Elsasser, Mayor

Hanna
P.O. Box 430
Hanna, AB T0J 1P0
403-854-4433 Fax: 403-854-2772
admin@hanna.ca
www.hanna.ca
Municipal Type: Town
Incorporated: Dec. 31, 1912; *Area:* 8.39 sq km
Population in 2006: 2,847
Provincial Electoral District(s): Drumheller-Stettler
Federal Electoral District(s): Crowfoot
Next Election: 2013 (3 year terms)
Note: Incorporated as a town on April 14, 1914.
Geraldine Gervais, CAO
ggervais.cao@hanna.ca
Mary Collins, Mayor

Hardisty
P.O. Box 10
Hardisty, AB T0B 1V0
780-888-3623 Fax: 780-888-2200
town.office@hardisty.ca
www.hardisty.ca
Municipal Type: Town
Incorporated: Dec. 11, 1906; *Area:* 5.48 sq km
Population in 2006: 760
Provincial Electoral District(s): Battle River-Wainwright
Federal Electoral District(s): Vegreville-Wainwright
Next Election: 2013 (3 year terms)
Note: Incorporated as a town on Nov. 9, 1910.
Tony Kulbisky, CAO
tonykcao@hardisty.ca
Anita Miller, Mayor

Hay Lakes
P.O. Box 40
Hay Lakes, AB T0B 1W0
780-878-3200 Fax: 780-878-3200
haylakes@syban.net
Municipal Type: Village
Incorporated: April 17, 1928; *Area:* 0.58 sq km
Population in 2006: 362
Provincial Electoral District(s): Leduc-Beaumont-Devon
Federal Electoral District(s): Crowfoot
Next Election: 2013 (3 year terms)
Heather Nadeau, Municipal Administrator
Glenn Harke, Mayor

Heisler
P.O. Box 60
Heisler, AB T0B 2A0
780-889-3774 Fax: 780-889-2280
vheisler@telusplanet.net
www.premiervillage.ca
Municipal Type: Village
Incorporated: July 27, 1920; *Area:* 0.75 sq km
Population in 2006: 153
Provincial Electoral District(s): Battle River-Wainwright
Federal Electoral District(s): Vegreville-Wainwright
Next Election: 2013 (3 year terms)
Shari-Anne Doolaege, Interim CAO
Sheldon Steil, Mayor

Henry Kroeger Regional Water Services Commission
P.O. Box 25
Youngstown, AB T0J 3P0
403-779-3904 Fax: 403-779-2279
Municipal Type: Waste Commission
Evelyn Manion, Manager

High Level
10511 - 103 St.
High Level, AB T0H 1Z0
780-926-2201 Fax: 780-926-2899
town@highlevel.ca
www.highlevel.ca
Municipal Type: Town
Incorporated: June 1, 1965; *Area:* 31.99 sq km
Population in 2006: 3,887
Provincial Electoral District(s): Peace River
Federal Electoral District(s): Peace River
Next Election: 2013 (3 year terms)
Dean Krause, CAO
780-821-4001
dkrause@highlevel.ca
Peter Ernst, Mayor
780-926-4878
mayor@highlevel.ca

High Prairie
P.O. Box 179
High Prairie, AB T0G 1E0
780-523-3388 Fax: 780-523-5930
admin@highprairie.ca
www.highprairie.ca
Municipal Type: Town
Incorporated: April 6, 1945; *Area:* 6.39 sq km
Population in 2006: 2,750
Provincial Electoral District(s): Lesser Slave Lake
Federal Electoral District(s): Fort McMurray-Athabasca
Next Election: 2013 (3 year terms)
Note: Incorporated as a town on Jan. 10, 1950.
Larry Baran, Town Manager
cao@highprairie.ca
Rick Dumont, Mayor

Highway 14 Regional Water Services
P.O. Box 322
Ryley, AB T0B 4A0
780-663-2039 Fax: 780-663-2006
brwmsccc@telusplanet.net
Municipal Type: Water Commission
Forrest Wright, CAO
brwmscfw@telusplanet.net

Highway 43 East Waste Commission Services
P.O. Box 219
Sangudo, AB T0E 2A0
780-785-3411 Fax: 780-785-2359
bweldon@vennercs.com
Municipal Type: Waste Commission
Ron Kidd, Chair
Mark Anker, Manager
780-454-9414

Hill Spring
P.O. Box 40
Hill Spring, AB T0K 1E0
403-626-3876 Fax: 403-626-2333
office@hillspring.ca
www.hillspring.ca
Municipal Type: Village
Incorporated: Jan. 1, 1961; *Area:* 1.11 sq km
Population in 2006: 192
Provincial Electoral District(s): Cardston-Taber-Warner
Federal Electoral District(s): Macleod
Next Election: 2013 (3 year terms)
Boyd Campbell, CAO
Peter Griffiths, Mayor

Hines Creek
P.O. Box 421
Hines Creek, AB T0H 2A0
780-494-3690 Fax: 780-494-3605 Other Phone: 780-494-3690
admin@hinescreek.com
www.hinescreek.com
Municipal Type: Village
Incorporated: Dec. 31, 1951; *Area:* 4.37 sq km
Population in 2006: 430
Provincial Electoral District(s): Dunvegan-Central Peace
Federal Electoral District(s): Peace River
Next Election: 2013 (3 year terms)
Leanne Walmsley, Municipal Manager
lwalmsley@hinescreek.com
Susan Hansen, Mayor
shansen@hinescreek.com

Hinton
131 Civic Centre Rd., 2nd Fl.
Hinton, AB T7V 2E5
780-865-6000 Fax: 780-865-5706
bkreiner@town.hinton.ab.ca
www.hinton.ca
Municipal Type: Town
Incorporated: Nov. 1, 1956; *Area:* 25.76 sq km
Population in 2009: 9,825
Provincial Electoral District(s): West Yellowhead
Federal Electoral District(s): Yellowhead
Next Election: 2013 (3 year terms)
Bernie Kreiner, Town Manager
bkreiner@hinton.ca
Glenn Taylor, Mayor
mayor@hinton.ca

Holden
P.O. Box 357
Holden, AB T0B 2C0
780-688-3928 Fax: 780-688-2091
vholden@telusplanet.net
www.village.holden.ab.ca
Municipal Type: Village
Incorporated: April 14, 1909; *Area:* 1.7 sq km
Population in 2006: 398
Provincial Electoral District(s): Fort Saskatchewan-Vegreville
Federal Electoral District(s): Vegreville-Wainwright
Next Election: 2013 (3 year terms)
Katherine Whiteside, CAO
Ivan Hrabec, Mayor

Horseshoe Bay
P.O. Box 1053
5837 - 44 Ave.
St Paul, AB T0A 3A0
780-724-4422 Fax: 780-724-4422
d_smereka@telus.net
www.svhorseshoebay.ca
Municipal Type: Summer Village
Incorporated: Jan. 1, 1985; *Area:* 1.04 sq km
Population in 2006: 214
Provincial Electoral District(s): Lac La Biche-St. Paul
Federal Electoral District(s): Westlock-St. Paul
Next Election: 2013 (3 year terms)
Darlene Smereka, Administrator
Gary Burns, Mayor
780-645-4609
g_burns@telus.net

Hughenden
P.O. Box 26
Hughenden, AB T0B 2E0
780-856-3830 Fax: 780-856-2034
vofhugh@telusplanet.net
Municipal Type: Village
Incorporated: Dec. 27, 1917; *Area:* 0.78 sq km
Population in 2006: 231
Provincial Electoral District(s): Battle River-Wainwright
Federal Electoral District(s): Vegreville-Wainwright
Next Election: 2013 (3 year terms)
Trudy Martineau, CAO
Doug Chambers, Mayor

Hussar
P.O. Box 100
Hussar, AB T0J 1S0
403-787-3766 Fax: 403-787-2560
hussar@myipplus.net
Municipal Type: Village
Incorporated: April 20, 1928; *Area:* 1.05 sq km
Population in 2006: 187
Provincial Electoral District(s): Strathmore-Brooks
Federal Electoral District(s): Crowfoot
Next Election: 2013 (3 year terms)
Tracy Anderson, CAO
Michelle Brown, Mayor

Hythe
P.O. Box 219
Hythe, AB T0H 2C0
780-356-3888 Fax: 780-356-2009
admin@hythe.ca
www.hythe.ca
Municipal Type: Village
Incorporated: Aug. 31, 1929; *Area:* 4.12 sq km
Population in 2006: 821
Provincial Electoral District(s): Grande Prairie-Wapiti
Federal Electoral District(s): Peace River
Next Election: 2013 (3 year terms)
Christene Livingstone, Administrator
Rhonda Tofteland, Mayor
mayor@hythe.ca

Innisfail
4943 - 53 St.
Innisfail, AB T4G 1A1
403-227-3376 Fax: 403-227-4045
townhall@innisfail.ca
www.townofinnisfail.com
Municipal Type: Town
Incorporated: Dec. 15, 1899; *Area:* 13.02 sq km
Population in 2009: 7,883
Provincial Electoral District(s): Innisfail-Sylvan Lake
Federal Electoral District(s): Red Deer
Next Election: 2013 (3 year terms)
Note: Incorporated as a town on Nov. 20, 1903.
Helen Dietz, Town Manager
helen.dietz@innisfail.ca
Jim Romane, Mayor
mayor@innisfail.ca

Innisfree
P.O. Box 69
Innisfree, AB T0B 2G0
780-592-3886 Fax: 780-592-3729
inisfree@telus.net
www3.telus.net/public/inisfree
Municipal Type: Village
Incorporated: March 11, 1911; *Area:* 1.27 sq km
Population in 2006: 233
Provincial Electoral District(s): Vermilion-Lloydminster
Federal Electoral District(s): Vegreville-Wainwright
Next Election: 2013 (3 year terms)
Lori Leibel, Municipal Administrator
lorileibel@telus.net
Dean Lindballe, Mayor

Irma
P.O. Box 419
Irma, AB T0B 2H0
780-754-3665 Fax: 780-754-3668
info@villageofirma.ca
www.villageofirma.ca
Municipal Type: Village
Incorporated: May 30, 1912; *Area:* 1.11 sq km
Population in 2006: 444
Provincial Electoral District(s): Battle River-Wainwright
Federal Electoral District(s): Vegreville-Wainwright
Next Election: 2013 (3 year terms)
Jackie Fenton, CAO
780-754-2160
Jackie@villageofirma.ca
Douglas Coubrough, Mayor
780-754-3077

Irricana
P.O. Box 100
Irricana, AB T0M 1B0
403-935-4672 Fax: 403-935-4270
irricana@irricana.com
www.irricana.com
Municipal Type: Town
Incorporated: June 9, 1911; *Area:* 3.18 sq km
Population in 2006: 1,243
Provincial Electoral District(s): Airdrie-Chestermere
Federal Electoral District(s): Crowfoot
Next Election: 2013 (3 year terms)
Note: Incorporated as a town on June 9, 2005.
Carol White, CAO
cao@irricana.com
Frank Dusome, Mayor

Island Lake
724 Baptiste Dr.
West Baptiste, AB T9S 1R8
780-675-9270
tomaszyk@mcsnet.ca
Municipal Type: Summer Village
Incorporated: Jan. 1, 1958; *Area:* 1.45 sq km
Population in 2006: 351
Provincial Electoral District(s): Athabasca-Redwater
Federal Electoral District(s): Fort McMurray-Athabasca
Next Election: 2013 (3 year terms)
Edwin Tomaszyk, CAO
Bruce McIntosh, Mayor

Island Lake South
10511 - 109th St.
Westlock, AB T7P 1A9
780-349-3651 Fax: 780-349-3651
mbancrof@telusplanet.net
Municipal Type: Summer Village
Incorporated: Jan. 1, 1983; *Area:* 0.63 sq km
Population in 2006: 105
Provincial Electoral District(s): Athabasca-Redwater
Federal Electoral District(s): Fort McMurray-Athabasca
Next Election: 2013 (3 year terms)
Garth Bancroft, Administrator
Gary Tym, Mayor

Itaska Beach
5515 - 44 Ave., #A
Wetaskiwin, AB T9A 0C8
780-312-0928
svoffice@telusplanet.net
www.itaska.ca
Municipal Type: Summer Village
Incorporated: June 30, 1953; *Area:* 0.28 sq km
Population in 2006: 35
Provincial Electoral District(s): Drayton Valley-Calmar
Federal Electoral District(s): Wetaskiwin
Next Election: 2013 (3 year terms)
June Boyda, CAO
cao@extremesolutions.org
Jerry Rudnisky, Mayor

Jarvis Bay
#104, 4505 - 50 Ave.
Sylvan Lake, AB T4S 1W2
403-887-2822 Fax: 403-887-2897
fivesv@telusplanet.net
Municipal Type: Summer Village
Incorporated: Jan. 1, 1986; *Area:* 0.55 sq km
Population in 2006: 183
Provincial Electoral District(s): Innisfail-Sylvan Lake
Federal Electoral District(s): Red Deer
Next Election: 2013 (3 year terms)
Myra Reiter, Administrator
Annabelle Wiseman, Mayor

Kapasiwin
P.O. Box 9
Kapasiwin, AB T0E 2Y0
780-892-2684
gckapa@cruzinternet.com
Municipal Type: Summer Village
Incorporated: Oct. 25, 1913; *Area:* 0.31 sq km
Population in 2006: 39
Provincial Electoral District(s): Stony Plain
Federal Electoral District(s): Yellowhead
Next Election: 2013 (3 year terms)
Note: Incorporated as a summer village on Sept. 01, 1993.
George Jones, Administrator
John Dewart, Mayor

Killam
P.O. Box 189
Killam, AB T0B 2L0
780-385-3977 Fax: 780-385-2120
tkillam@telusplanet.net
www.town.killam.ab.ca
Municipal Type: Town
Incorporated: Dec. 29, 1906; *Area:* 4.53 sq km
Population in 2006: 1,019
Provincial Electoral District(s): Battle River-Wainwright
Federal Electoral District(s): Vegreville-Wainwright
Next Election: 2013 (3 year terms)
Note: Incorporated as a town on May 1, 1965.
Wendy Ramberg, CAO
cao@town.killam.ab.ca
H.L. (Bud) James, Mayor
bjames@town.killam.ab.ca

Kinuso
P.O. Box 57
Kinuso, AB T0G 1K0
780-775-3570 Fax: 780-775-3571
kinuso@gmail.com; villageofkinuso@telusplanet.net
www.kinuso.ca
Municipal Type: Village
Incorporated: Dec. 31, 1949; *Area:* 0.61 sq km
Population in 2006: 219
Provincial Electoral District(s): Lesser Slave Lake
Federal Electoral District(s): Fort McMurray-Athabasca
Next Election: 2013 (3 year terms)
Brad Watson, Administrator
Darcy Hunt, Mayor

Kitscoty
P.O. Box 128
Kitscoty, AB T0B 2P0
780-846-2221 Fax: 780-846-2213
kitscoty@ruralsurf.net
www.albertafirst.com/profiles/statspack/20555.html
Municipal Type: Village
Incorporated: March 22, 1911; *Area:* 1.54 sq km
Population in 2006: 709
Provincial Electoral District(s): Vermilion-Lloydminster
Federal Electoral District(s): Vegreville-Wainwright
Next Election: 2013 (3 year terms)
Harold Trew, CAO
Daryl Frank, Mayor

Kneehill Regional Water Services Commission
P.O. Box 592
Acme, AB T0M 2A0
403-546-3783 Fax: 403-546-3014
vacme@telus.net
Municipal Type: Water Commission
John Van Doesburg, Manager

Lakeland Regional Waste Management Services Commission
P.O. Box 387
Lac La Biche, AB T0A 2C0
780-623-4323 Fax: 780-623-3510
townlib@telusplanet.net
Municipal Type: Water Commission
Gordon Elliott, Chair

Lakeview
P.O. Box 190
Seba Beach, AB T0E 2B0
780-797-3863 Fax: 780-797-3800
svseba@telusplanet.net
Municipal Type: Summer Village
Incorporated: Oct. 25, 1913; *Area:* 0.33 sq km
Population in 2006: 36
Provincial Electoral District(s): Stony Plain
Federal Electoral District(s): Yellowhead
Next Election: 2013 (3 year terms)
Susan H. Evans, CAO
Earle Robertson, Mayor

Lamont
P.O. Box 330
Lamont, AB T0B 2R0
780-895-2010 Fax: 780-895-2595
tom.m@tclamont.ca
www.lamont.ca
Municipal Type: Town
Incorporated: June 14, 1910; *Area:* 4.59 sq km
Population in 2006: 1,664
Provincial Electoral District(s): Fort Saskatchewan-Vegreville
Federal Electoral District(s): Vegreville-Wainwright
Next Election: 2013 (3 year terms)
Note: Incorporated as a town on May 31, 1968.
Tom Miller, CAO
Rick Koroluk, Mayor

Lamont County Regional Solid Waste Commission
General Delivery
Lamont, AB T0B 2R0
780-895-2233 Fax: 780-895-7404
Municipal Type: Water Commission
John Stribling, Chair

Larkspur
PO Box 16, Site 1, RR#2
Carvel, AB T0E 0H0
780-963-6049 Fax: 780-963-6434
ldonner@cruzinternet.com
Municipal Type: Summer Village
Incorporated: Jan. 1, 1985; *Area:* 0.22 sq km
Population in 2006: 56
Provincial Electoral District(s): Barrhead-Morinville-Westlock

Federal Electoral District(s): Westlock-St. Paul
Next Election: 2013 (3 year terms)
Lori Donner, CAO
John Deshoux, Mayor

Legal
P.O. Box 390
Legal, AB T0G 1L0
780-961-3773 Fax: 780-961-4133
main@town.legal.ab.ca
www.town.legal.ab.ca
Municipal Type: Town
Incorporated: Feb. 20, 1914; *Area:* 2.55 sq km
Population in 2006: 1,192
Provincial Electoral District(s): Barrhead-Morinville-Westlock
Federal Electoral District(s): Westlock-St. Paul
Next Election: 2013 (3 year terms)
Note: Incorporated as a town on Jan. 1, 1998.
Wilma Weiss, Administrator
wweiss@town.legal.ab.ca
Albert St. Jean, Mayor
council@town.legal.ab.ca

Lesser Slave Lake Regional Waste Management Services Commission
P.O. Box 722
Slave Lake, AB T0G 2A0
780-369-2590 Fax: 780-369-2599
md124@md124.ca
www.md124.ca
Municipal Type: Water Commission
George Snider, Interim Manager

Lethbridge Regional Waste Management Services
P.O. Box 1594
Lethbridge, AB T1J 4K3
403-732-4722 Fax: 403-732-4328
rsnowdon@county.lethbridge.ab.ca
Municipal Type: Waste Commission
Eugene Wauters, Chair
Larry Thomson, Vice-Chair
Sandy Trocakstad, Sec.-Treas.

Lethbridge Regional Water Services Commission
c/o County of Lethbridge
#100, 905 - 4 Ave. South
Lethbridge, AB T1J 4E4
403-328-5525 Fax: 403-328-5602
rrobinson@county.lethbridge.ab.ca
Municipal Type: Water Commission
Rick Robinson, Commission Manager
Duncan Lloyd, Chair

Linden
P.O. Box 213
Linden, AB T0M 1J0
403-546-3888 Fax: 403-546-2112
voladmin@telus.net
www.linden.ca
Municipal Type: Village
Incorporated: Jan. 1, 1964; *Area:* 2.56 sq km
Population in 2006: 660
Provincial Electoral District(s): Olds-Didsbury-Three Hills
Federal Electoral District(s): Crowfoot
Next Election: 2013 (3 year terms)
Amy Beattie, Municipal Administrator
volclerk@telus.net
Annon John Hovde, Mayor
volinden@telus.net

Lomond
P.O. Box 268
Lomond, AB T0L 1G0
403-792-3611 Fax: 403-792-3300
voflom@wildroseinternet.ca
www.albertafirst.com/profiles/statspack/20557.html
Municipal Type: Village
Incorporated: Feb. 16, 1916; *Area:* 1.28 sq km
Population in 2006: 175
Provincial Electoral District(s): Little Bow
Federal Electoral District(s): Macleod
Next Election: 2013 (3 year terms)
Tracy Doram, CAO
Brad Koch, Mayor

Long Lake Regional Waste Management Commission
P.O. Box 178
Grimshaw, AB T0H 1W0
780-971-2200 Fax: 780-971-2200
llrwmsc@telusplanet.net
Municipal Type: Waste Commission
Elzina Vance, Acting Manager
May Rowe, Chair

Longview
P.O. Box 147
Longview, AB T0L 1H0
403-558-3922 Fax: 403-558-3743 Other Email:
office-manager@village.longview.ab.ca
info@village.longview.ab.ca
www.village.longview.ab.ca
Municipal Type: Village
Incorporated: Jan. 1, 1964; *Area:* 1.09 sq km
Population in 2006: 300
Provincial Electoral District(s): Highwood
Federal Electoral District(s): Macleod
Next Election: 2013 (3 year terms)
Alana Healy-Newton, CAO
cao@village.longview.ab.ca
Ivor McCorquindale, Mayor
mayor@village.longview.ab.ca

Lougheed
P.O. Box 5
Lougheed, AB T0B 2V0
780-386-3970 Fax: 780-386-2136
stowers@telusplanet.net
Municipal Type: Village
Incorporated: Nov. 7, 1911; *Area:* 1.13 sq km
Population in 2006: 217
Provincial Electoral District(s): Battle River-Wainwright
Federal Electoral District(s): Vegreville-Wainwright
Next Election: 2013 (3 year terms)
Stan Towers, Sec.-Treas.
John Larson, Mayor

Ma-Me-O Beach
P.O. Box 100
603 - 2 Ave.
Ma-Me-O Beach, AB T0C 1X0
780-586-2494 Fax: 780-586-3567
svadminoffice@xplornet.com
www.mameobeach.ca
Municipal Type: Summer Village
Incorporated: Dec. 31, 1948; *Area:* 0.65 sq km
Population in 2006: 155
Provincial Electoral District(s): Drayton Valley-Calmar
Federal Electoral District(s): Wetaskiwin
Next Election: 2013 (3 year terms)
Peter Irwin, Administrator
Don Fleming, Mayor
780-437-4101

Mackenzie Regional Waste Management Commission
9813 - 102 St.
High Level, AB T0H 1Z0
780-926-2201 Fax: 780-926-2899
landfill@highlevel.ca
Municipal Type: Water Commission
Ron Pelensky, Manager
Pat Kulscar, Chair

Magrath
P.O. Box 520
Magrath, AB T0K 1J0
403-758-3212 Fax: 403-758-6333
info@magrath.ca
www.magrath.ca
Municipal Type: Town
Incorporated: Aug. 20, 1901; *Area:* 4.97 sq km
Population in 2006: 2,081
Provincial Electoral District(s): Cardston-Taber-Warner
Federal Electoral District(s): Lethbridge
Next Election: 2013 (3 year terms)
Note: Incorporated as a town on July 24, 1907.
Wade Alston, CAO
wade@magrath.ca
James Murphy, Mayor

Manning
P.O. Box 125
Manning, AB T0H 2M0
780-836-3606 Fax: 780-836-3570
info@manning.ca
www.manning.ca
Municipal Type: Town
Incorporated: Dec. 31, 1951; *Area:* 3.42 sq km
Population in 2006: 1,493
Provincial Electoral District(s): Peace River
Federal Electoral District(s): Peace River
Next Election: 2013 (3 year terms)
Note: Incorporated as a town on Jan. 1, 1957.
John Brodrick, CAO
jbrodrick@manning.ca
Sunni-Jeanne Walker, Mayor
sonnij@telus.net

Mannville
P.O. Box 180
5127 - 50th St.
Mannville, AB T0B 2W0
780-763-3500 Fax: 780-763-3643
info@mannville.com; cao@mannville.com
www.mannville.com
Municipal Type: Village
Incorporated: Dec. 29, 1906; *Area:* 2.15 sq km
Population in 2006: 782
Provincial Electoral District(s): Vermilion-Lloydminster
Federal Electoral District(s): Vegreville-Wainwright
Next Election: 2013 (3 year terms)
Candace Dueck, CAO
cdueck@mannville.com
Chanse Hinton, Mayor
council@mannville.com

Marwayne
P.O. Box 113
Marwayne, AB T0B 2X0
780-847-3962 Fax: 780-847-3324
marwayne@hmsinet.ca
www.village.marwayne.ab.ca
Municipal Type: Village
Incorporated: Dec. 31, 1952; *Area:* 1.15 sq km
Population in 2006: 516
Provincial Electoral District(s): Vermilion-Lloydminster
Federal Electoral District(s): Vegreville-Wainwright
Next Election: 2013 (3 year terms)
Joanne Horton, Administrative Officer
cao.marwayne@hmsinet.ca
Roger Parkyn, Mayor
vilmar@telusplanet.net

Mayerthorpe
P.O. Box 420
Mayerthorpe, AB T0E 1N0
780-786-2416 Fax: 780-786-4590
admin@mayerthorpe.ca
www.mayerthorpe.ca
Municipal Type: Town
Incorporated: March 5, 1927; *Area:* 4.78 sq km
Population in 2006: 1,474
Provincial Electoral District(s): Whitecourt-Ste. Anne
Federal Electoral District(s): Yellowhead
Next Election: 2013 (3 year terms)
Note: Incorporated as a town on March 20, 1961.
Karen St. Martin, CAO
cao@mayerthorpe.ca
Doug McDermid, Mayor

McLennan
P.O. Box 356
19 - 1st Ave. NW
McLennan, AB T0H 2L0
780-324-3065 Fax: 780-324-2288
twnmcl@serbernet.com
www.townofmclennan.com
Municipal Type: Town
Incorporated: Feb. 1, 1944; *Area:* 3.58 sq km
Population in 2006: 824
Provincial Electoral District(s): Dunvegan-Central Peace
Federal Electoral District(s): Peace River
Next Election: 2013 (3 year terms)
Note: Incorporated as a town on Feb. 11, 1948.
Tammy Stout, CAO
Donald Regier, Mayor

Mewatha Beach
10511 - 109th St.
Westlock, AB T7P 1A9
780-349-3651 Fax: 780-349-3651
Municipal Type: Summer Village
Incorporated: Jan. 1, 1978; *Area:* 0.78 sq km
Population in 2006: 167
Provincial Electoral District(s): Athabasca-Redwater
Federal Electoral District(s): Fort McMurray-Athabasca
Next Election: 2013 (3 year terms)
Garth Bancroft, Administrator
mbancrof@telusplanet.net
Ronald Whitson, Mayor

Milk River
P.O. Box 270
Milk River, AB T0K 1M0
403-647-3773 Fax: 403-647-3772
main@milkriver.ca
www.milkriver.ca
Municipal Type: Town
Incorporated: July 11, 1916; *Area:* 2.39 sq km
Population in 2006: 816
Provincial Electoral District(s): Cardston-Taber-Warner
Federal Electoral District(s): Lethbridge
Next Election: 2013 (3 year terms)
Note: Incorporated as a town on Feb. 7, 1956.
Shawn Hathaway, CAO
cao@milkriver.ca
Terry Michaelis, Mayor

Millet
P.O. Box 270
Millet, AB T0C 1Z0
780-387-4554 Fax: 780-387-4459
millet@millet.ca
www.millet.ca
Municipal Type: Town
Incorporated: June 17, 1903; *Area:* 3.74 sq km
Population in 2006: 2,068
Provincial Electoral District(s): Wetaskiwin-Camrose
Federal Electoral District(s): Wetaskiwin
Next Election: 2013 (3 year terms)
Note: Incorporated as a town on Sept. 1, 1983.
Ted Tymchuk, Interim CAO
cao-storey@millet.ca
David W. Gursky, Mayor

Milo
P.O. Box 65
Milo, AB T0L 1L0
403-599-3883 Fax: 403-599-2201
vilmilo@wildroseinternet.ca
www.telusplanet.net/public/vilmilo

Municipal Type: Village
Incorporated: May 7, 1931; *Area:* 0.48 sq km
Population in 2006: 100
Provincial Electoral District(s): Little Bow
Federal Electoral District(s): Macleod
Next Election: 2013 (3 year terms)
Virginia (Ginger) Deitz, Municipal Administrator
Steve Edwards, Mayor
scuba@wildroseinternet.ca

Minburn
P.O. Box 65
Minburn, AB T0B 3B0
780-593-3939 Fax: 780-593-3939
vminburn@telus.net
Municipal Type: Village
Incorporated: June 24, 1919; *Area:* 0.73 sq km
Population in 2006: 65
Provincial Electoral District(s): Vermilion-Lloydminster
Federal Electoral District(s): Vegreville-Wainwright
Next Election: 2013 (3 year terms)
Nicolette Elgie, CAO
Donald Drury, Mayor

Morinville
10125 - 100 Ave.
Morinville, AB T8R 1L6
780-939-4361 Fax: 780-939-5633
treaume@morinville.ca
www.morinville.ca
Municipal Type: Town
Incorporated: Aug. 24, 1901; *Area:* 11.34 sq km
Population in 2009: 7,636
Provincial Electoral District(s): Barrhead-Morinville-Westlock
Federal Electoral District(s): Westlock-St. Paul
Next Election: 2013 (3 year terms)
Note: Incorporated as a town on April 21, 1911.
Edie Doepker, CAO
R. Lloyd Bertschi, Mayor
lbertschi@morinville.ca

Morrin
P.O. Box 149
Morrin, AB T0J 2B0
403-772-3870 Fax: 403-772-2123
morrin@netago.ca
Municipal Type: Village
Incorporated: April 16, 1920; *Area:* 0.82 sq km
Population in 2006: 253
Provincial Electoral District(s): Drumheller-Stettler
Federal Electoral District(s): Crowfoot
Next Election: 2013 (3 year terms)
Annette Plachner, CAO
Suzanne Lacher, Mayor

Mountain View Regional Waste Management Commission
1230
Didsbury, AB T0M 0W0
403-335-2005 Fax: 403-335-8132
nrkivell@telusplanet.net
Municipal Type: Water Commission
Dave Derksen, Chair

Mountain View Regional Water Services
Site 22, Box 1, RR#1
Innisfail, AB T4G 1T6
403-227-5828 Fax: 403-227-5831
mtnwater@telusplanet.net
Municipal Type: Water Commission
John Van Doesburg, Administrator

Mundare
P.O. Box 348
5128 - 50 St.
Mundare, AB T0B 3H0
780-764-3929 Fax: 780-764-2003
reception@mundare.ca
www.mundare.ca
Municipal Type: Town
Incorporated: March 6, 1907; *Area:* 3 sq km
Population in 2006: 712
Provincial Electoral District(s): Fort Saskatchewan-Vegreville
Federal Electoral District(s): Vegreville-Wainwright
Next Election: 2013 (3 year terms)
Note: Incorporated as a town on Jan. 4, 1951.
Colin Zyla, CAO
cao@mundare.ca
Michael Saric, Mayor
msaric@mundare.ca

Munson
P.O. Box 10
Munson, AB T0J 2C0
403-823-6987 Fax: 403-823-9883
munson@netago.ca
Municipal Type: Village
Incorporated: May 5, 1911; *Area:* 2.6 sq km
Population in 2006: 217
Provincial Electoral District(s): Drumheller-Stettler
Federal Electoral District(s): Crowfoot
Next Election: 2013 (3 year terms)
Lyle Cawiezel, Administrator
Dave Vanderkolk, Mayor

Myrnam
P.O. Box 278
5007 - 50th St.
Myrnam, AB T0B 3K0
780-366-3910 Fax: 780-366-2246
vmyrnam@mcsnet.ca
www.myrnam.info
Municipal Type: Village
Incorporated: Aug. 22, 1930; *Area:* 2.76 sq km
Population in 2006: 362
Provincial Electoral District(s): Lac la Biche-St. Paul
Federal Electoral District(s): Vegreville-Wainwright
Next Election: 2013 (3 year terms)
Elsie Howanyk, Administrator
Edward Sosnowski, Mayor

Nakamun Park
13 Grandin Rd.
St Albert, AB T8N 3B2
780-460-7226 Fax: 780-419-2476
hmarsh@telusplanet.net
www.svnakamun.com
Municipal Type: Summer Village
Incorporated: Jan. 1, 1966; *Area:* 0.41 sq km
Population in 2006: 88
Provincial Electoral District(s): Whitecourt-Ste. Anne
Federal Electoral District(s): Yellowhead
Next Election: 2013 (3 year terms)
Hilda Marsh, CAO
William (Bill) Burrell, Mayor
780-482-2728
cabinvil@telusplanet.net

Nampa
P.O. Box 69
Nampa, AB T0H 2R0
780-322-3852 Fax: 780-322-2100
office@nampa.ca
www.nampa.ca
Municipal Type: Village
Incorporated: Jan. 1, 1958; *Area:* 1.86 sq km
Population in 2006: 360
Provincial Electoral District(s): Peace River
Federal Electoral District(s): Peace River
Next Election: 2013 (3 year terms)
Dale Harrison, CAO
dharrison@nampa.ca
Bernadette Hebert, Mayor

Nanton
P.O. Box 609
Nanton, AB T0L 1R0
403-646-2029 Fax: 403-646-2653
admin@town.nanton.ab.ca
www.town.nanton.ab.ca
Municipal Type: Town
Incorporated: June 22, 1903; *Area:* 4.25 sq km
Population in 2006: 2,055
Provincial Electoral District(s): Livingstone-Macleod
Federal Electoral District(s): Macleod
Next Election: 2013 (3 year terms)
Note: Incorporated as a town on Aug. 9, 1907.
Mary Robley, CAO
cao@town.nanton.ab.ca
John J. Blake, Mayor

New Norway
P.O. Box 60
New Norway, AB T0B 3L0
780-855-3915 Fax: 780-855-3916
nnorway@cable-lynx.net
www.cable-lynx.net/~nnorway
Municipal Type: Village
Incorporated: May 6, 1910; *Area:* 1.12 sq km
Population in 2006: 323
Provincial Electoral District(s): Lacombe-Ponoka
Federal Electoral District(s): Crowfoot
Next Election: 2013 (3 year terms)
Marguerite Jensen, Village Clerk
Sharon Haselwood, Mayor

New Sarepta
P.O. Box 278
New Sarepta, AB T0B 3M0
780-941-3929 Fax: 780-941-3890
srptownoffice@airsurfer.ca
www.newsarepta.com
Municipal Type: Village
Incorporated: Jan. 1, 1960; *Area:* 2.28 sq km
Population in 2006: 410
Provincial Electoral District(s): Leduc-Beaumont-Devon
Federal Electoral District(s): Vegreville-Wainwright
Next Election: 2013 (3 year terms)
Gerrylyn Wrubleski, CAO
sarepta@telusplanet.net
Carmen Fedirko, Mayor
admin@safety1stalbertacorp.com

Nobleford
P.O. Box 67
906 Highway Ave.
Nobleford, AB T0L 1S0
403-824-3555 Fax: 403-824-3553
admin@village.nobleford.ab.ca
www.village.nobleford.ab.ca
Municipal Type: Village
Incorporated: Feb. 28, 1918; *Area:* 1.17 sq km
Population in 2006: 689
Provincial Electoral District(s): Little Bow
Federal Electoral District(s): Lethbridge
Next Election: 2013 (3 year terms)
Kirk Hofman, CAO
Paul Goldade, Mayor
403-824-3857
pmagoldade@platinum.ca

Norglenwold
#104, 4505 - 50 Av.
Sylvan Lake, AB T4S 1W2
403-887-2822 Fax: 403-887-2897
fivesv@telusplanet.net
Municipal Type: Summer Village
Incorporated: Jan. 1, 1965; *Area:* 0.67 sq km
Population in 2006: 270
Provincial Electoral District(s): Innisfail-Sylvan Lake
Federal Electoral District(s): Red Deer
Next Election: 2013 (3 year terms)
Myra Reiter, Administrator
Toby Lampard, Mayor

Norris Beach
P.O. Box 100
Ma-Me-O Beach, AB T0C 1X0
780-586-2494 Fax: 780-586-3657
svadminoffice@xplornet.com
Municipal Type: Summer Village
Incorporated: Dec. 31, 1988; *Area:* 0.16 sq km
Population in 2006: 40
Provincial Electoral District(s): Drayton Valley-Calmar
Federal Electoral District(s): Wetaskiwin
Next Election: 2013 (3 year terms)
Peter Irwin, Administrator
Brian Keeler, Mayor

North 43 Lagoon Commission
14403 - 110 Ave.
Edmonton, AB T5N 1J7
780-454-9414 Fax: 780-452-2322
Municipal Type: Water Commission
Mark Anker, Manager

North Forty Mile Regional Waste Management Services Commission
P.O. Box 276
Bow Island, AB T0K 0G0
403-833-3805
Municipal Type: Waste Commission
Bill Ressler, Chair
Ron Lane, Vice-Chair
Roselyn Pahl, Sec.-Treas.

North Peace Regional Landfill Commission
P.O. Box 2654
Fairview, AB T0H 1L0
780-835-2576 Fax: 780-835-2579
info@nprlandfill.com
www.nprlandfill.com
Municipal Type: Water Commission
Darren Lubeck, Manager
Brent Dechant, Chair

North Red Deer River Water Services Commission
5432 - 56 Ave.
Lacombe, AB T4L 1E9
403-391-0270
Municipal Type: Water Commission
Judy Gordon, Chair

Northeast Pigeon Lake Regional Services Commission
P.O. Box 6960
Wetaskiwin, AB T9A 2G5
780-352-3321 Fax: 780-352-3486
fcoutney@telusplanet.net
Municipal Type: Water Commission
Frank Coutney, Manager
Ralph B. Johnston, Chair

Olds
4512 - 46 St.
Olds, AB T4H 1R5
403-556-6981 Fax: 403-556-6537
admin@olds.ca
www.olds.ca
Municipal Type: Town
Incorporated: May 26, 1896; *Area:* 11.05 sq km
Population in 2006: 7,248
Provincial Electoral District(s): Olds-Didsbury-Three Hills
Federal Electoral District(s): Wild Rose
Next Election: 2013 (3 year terms)
Note: Incorporated as a town on July 01, 1905.
Norman McInnis, CAO
mcInnis@olds.ca
Judy Dahl, Mayor
403-507-4114
mayor@olds.ca

Onoway
P.O. Box 540
Onoway, AB T0E 1V0
780-967-5338 Fax: 780-967-3226
info@onoway.com
www.onoway.com
Municipal Type: Town
Incorporated: June 25, 1923; *Area:* 3.34 sq km
Population in 2006: 875
Provincial Electoral District(s): Whitecourt-Ste. Anne
Federal Electoral District(s): Yellowhead
Next Election: 2013 (3 year terms)
Note: Incorporated as a town on Sept. 1, 2005.
Ryan Bard, Town Manager
ryan@onoway.com
George Jendyk, Mayor

Oyen
P.O. Box 360
Oyen, AB T0J 2J0
403-664-3511 Fax: 403-664-3712
townoyen@telusplanet.net
www.townofoyen.com
Municipal Type: Town
Incorporated: Jan. 17, 1913; *Area:* 4.93 sq km
Population in 2006: 1,015
Provincial Electoral District(s): Drumheller-Stettler
Federal Electoral District(s): Crowfoot
Next Election: 2013 (3 year terms)
Note: Incorporated as a town on Sept. 1, 1965.
Debbie Kovitch, Administrator
Wayne Wilson, Mayor

Paradise Valley
P.O. Box 24
Paradise Valley, AB T0B 3R0
780-745-2287 Fax: 780-745-2287
villpv@mwwireless.ca
Municipal Type: Village
Incorporated: Jan. 1, 1964; *Area:* 0.57 sq km
Population in 2006: 183
Provincial Electoral District(s): Vermilion-Lloydminster
Federal Electoral District(s): Vegreville-Wainwright
Next Election: 2013 (3 year terms)
Connie Wilkinson, Municipal Administrator
Curtis Schneider, Mayor

Parkland Beach
P.O. Box 130
Rimbey, AB T0C 2J0
403-843-2055 Fax: 888-470-2762
admin@parklandbeachsv.ca
Municipal Type: Summer Village
Incorporated: Jan. 1, 1984; *Area:* 0.93 sq km
Population in 2006: 135
Provincial Electoral District(s): Lacombe-Ponoka
Federal Electoral District(s): Wetaskiwin
Next Election: 2013 (3 year terms)
Marilee Yakunin, CAO
Larry Scheible, Mayor

Peace River
P.O. Box 6600
9911 - 100 St.
Peace River, AB T8S 1S4
780-624-2574 Fax: 780-624-4664
info@peaceriver.net
http://peaceriver.net
Municipal Type: Town
Incorporated: June 2, 1914; *Area:* 24.87 sq km
Population in 2006: 6,315
Provincial Electoral District(s): Peace River
Federal Electoral District(s): Peace River
Next Election: 2013 (3 year terms)
Note: Incorporated as a town on Dec. 1, 1919.
Norma MacQuarrie, CAO
nmacquarrie@peaceriver.net
Lorne Mann, Mayor
780-624-8384

Pelican Narrows
P.O. Box 7878
Bonnyville, AB T9N 2J2
780-826-5907 Fax: 780-826-2804
plapointe@mcsnet.ca
Municipal Type: Summer Village
Incorporated: July 1, 1979; *Area:* 0.7 sq km
Population in 2006: 141
Provincial Electoral District(s): Bonnyville-Cold Lake
Federal Electoral District(s): Westlock-St.Paul
Next Election: 2013 (3 year terms)
Padey Lapointe, Administrator
Bob Hornseth, Mayor

Penhold
P.O. Box 10
Penhold, AB T0M 1R0
403-886-4567 Fax: 403-886-4039
community1@townofpenhold.ca
www.townofpenhold.ca
Municipal Type: Town
Incorporated: May 4, 1904; *Area:* 2.35 sq km
Population in 2006: 1,961
Provincial Electoral District(s): Innisfail-Sylvan Lake
Federal Electoral District(s): Red Deer
Next Election: 2013 (3 year terms)
Note: Incorporated as a town on Sept. 1, 1980.
Rick Binnendyk, CAO
cao@townofpenhold.ca
Julia King, Mayor
mayorking@townofpenhold.ca

Picture Butte
P.O. Box 670
Picture Butte, AB T0K 1V0
403-732-4555 Fax: 403-732-4334
info@picturebutte.ca
www.picturebutte.ca
Municipal Type: Town
Incorporated: Feb. 4, 1943; *Area:* 2.9 sq km
Population in 2006: 1,592
Provincial Electoral District(s): Little Bow
Federal Electoral District(s): Lethbridge
Next Election: 2013 (3 year terms)
Note: Incorporated as a town on Jan. 1, 1960.
Audrey Mortensen, CAO
audrey@picturebutte.ca
Terry Kerkhoff, Mayor
tkerkhoff@picturebutte.ca

Pincher Creek
P.O. Box 159
Pincher Creek, AB T0K 1W0
403-627-3156 Fax: 403-627-4784
townhall@pinchercreek.ca
www.pinchercreek.ca
Municipal Type: Town
Incorporated: Aug. 18, 1898; *Area:* 8.84 sq km
Population in 2006: 3,625
Provincial Electoral District(s): Livingstone-Macleod
Federal Electoral District(s): Macleod
Next Election: 2013 (3 year terms)
Note: Incorporated as a town on May 12, 1906.
Fran Kornfeld, CAO
cao@pinchercreek.ca
Gary Mills, Mayor
reception@pinchercreek.ca

Point Alison
4323 - 49A St.
Edmonton, AB T6L 6J5
780-462-6372
point_alison@hughes.net
Municipal Type: Summer Village
Incorporated: Dec. 31, 1950; *Area:* 0.16 sq km
Population in 2006: 15
Provincial Electoral District(s): Stony Plain
Federal Electoral District(s): Yellowhead
Next Election: 2013 (3 year terms)
Tom Thompson, Municipal Administrator
thomtom@telus.net
C. Gordon Wilson, Mayor

Ponoka
5102 - 48 Ave.
Ponoka, AB T4J 1P7
403-783-4431 Fax: 403-783-6745
town@ponoka.org
www.ponoka.org
Municipal Type: Town
Incorporated: Oct. 19, 1900; *Area:* 13.05 sq km
Population in 2006: 6,576
Provincial Electoral District(s): Lacombe-Ponoka
Federal Electoral District(s): Wetaskiwin
Next Election: 2013 (3 year terms)
Note: Incorporated as a town on Oct. 15, 1904.
Brad Watson, CAO
bwatson@ponoka.org
Larry L. Henkelman, Mayor

Poplar Bay
P.O. Box 100
Ma-Me-O Beach, AB T0C 1X0
780-586-2494 Fax: 780-586-3567
svadminoffice@xplornet.com
Municipal Type: Summer Village
Incorporated: Jan. 1, 1967; *Area:* 0.76 sq km
Population in 2006: 84
Provincial Electoral District(s): Drayton Valley-Calmar
Federal Electoral District(s): Wetaskiwin
Next Election: 2013 (3 year terms)
Peter Irwin, Administrator
Kevin D. Davies, Mayor

Provost
P.O. Box 449
Provost, AB T0B 3S0
780-753-2261 Fax: 780-753-6889
info@provost.ca
www.provost.ca
Municipal Type: Town
Incorporated: Jan. 20, 1910; *Area:* 4.93 sq km
Population in 2006: 2,072
Provincial Electoral District(s): Battle River-Wainwright
Federal Electoral District(s): Vegreville-Wainwright
Next Election: 2013 (3 year terms)
Note: Incorporated as a town on Dec. 29, 1952.
Judy Larson, Town Administrator
Kenneth E. (Ken) Knox, Mayor

Rainbow Lake
P.O. Box 149
Rainbow Lake, AB T0H 2Y0
780-956-3934 Fax: 780-956-3570
admin@rainbowlake.ca
www.rainbowlake.ca
Municipal Type: Town
Incorporated: Sept. 1, 1966; *Area:* 11.04 sq km
Population in 2006: 965
Provincial Electoral District(s): Peace River
Federal Electoral District(s): Peace River
Next Election: 2013 (3 year terms)
Terry Broome, CAO
tbroome@rainbowlake.ca
Jeff Savage, Acting Mayor

Raymond
P.O. Box 629
15 Broadway St.
Raymond, AB T0K 2S0
403-752-3322 Fax: 403-752-4379
contact@raymond.ca
www.raymond.ca
Municipal Type: Town
Incorporated: May 30, 1902; *Area:* 4.75 sq km
Population in 2006: 3,205
Provincial Electoral District(s): Cardston-Taber-Warner
Federal Electoral District(s): Lethbridge
Next Election: 2013 (3 year terms)
Note: Incorporated as a town on July 1, 1903.
Scott Barton, CAO
scottbarton@raymond.ca
L. George Bohne, Mayor
bohne@raymond.ca

Redcliff
P.O. Box 40
Redcliff, AB T0J 2P0
403-548-3618 Fax: 403-548-6623
redcliff@town.redcliff.ab.ca
www.town.redcliff.ab.ca
Municipal Type: Town
Incorporated: Oct. 29, 1910; *Area:* 10.51 sq km
Population in 2006: 5,096
Provincial Electoral District(s): Cypress-Medicine Hat
Federal Electoral District(s): Medicine Hat
Next Election: 2013 (3 year terms)
Note: Incorporated as a town on Aug. 5, 1912.
Randy Giesbrecht, Municipal Manager
randyg@town.redcliff.ab.ca
Robert Hazelaar, Mayor

Redwater
P.O. Box 397
Redwater, AB T0A 2W0
780-942-3519 Fax: 780-942-4321
cao@town.redwater.ab.ca
www.town.redwater.ab.ca
Municipal Type: Town
Incorporated: Dec. 31, 1949; *Area:* 7.95 sq km
Population in 2006: 2,192
Provincial Electoral District(s): Athabasca-Redwater
Federal Electoral District(s): Westlock-St. Paul
Next Election: 2013 (3 year terms)
Note: Incorporated as a town on Dec. 31, 1950.
Ray Reid, CAO
Mel Smith, Mayor
melsophie@telus.net

Rimbey
P.O. Box 350
4938 - 50th Ave.
Rimbey, AB T0C 2J0
403-843-2113 Fax: 403-843-6599
generalinfo@rimbey.com
www.rimbey.com
Municipal Type: Town
Incorporated: June 13, 1919; *Area:* 11.34 sq km
Population in 2006: 2,252
Provincial Electoral District(s): Lacombe-Ponoka
Federal Electoral District(s): Wetaskiwin
Next Election: 2013 (3 year terms)
Note: Incorporated as a town on Dec. 13, 1948.
Russell Wardrope, Town Manager
russwardrope@rimbey.com
Dale L. Barr, Mayor
dale@rimbey.com

Rochon Sands
1 Hall St.
Rochon Sands, AB T0C 3B0
403-742-4717 Fax: 403-742-4771 Cell Phone: 403-742-7690
info@rochonsands.net
www.rochonsands.net
Municipal Type: Summer Village
Incorporated: May 17, 1929; *Area:* 2.32 sq km
Population in 2006: 66
Provincial Electoral District(s): Drumheller-Stettler
Federal Electoral District(s): Crowfoot
Next Election: 2013 (3 year terms)
Alan Willis, Village Administrator
Wayne Miller, Mayor

Rocky Mountain House
P.O. Box 1509
Rocky Mountain House, AB T4T 1B2
403-845-2866 Fax: 403-845-3230
town@rockymtnhouse.com
www.rockymtnhouse.com
Municipal Type: Town
Incorporated: May 15, 1913; *Area:* 12.44 sq km
Population in 2006: 6,874
Provincial Electoral District(s): Rocky Mountain House
Federal Electoral District(s): Wetaskiwin
Next Election: 2013 (3 year terms)
Note: Incorporated as a town on Aug. 31, 1939.
Larry Holstead, Town Manager
lholstead@rockymtnhouse.com
Jim Bague, Mayor
mayor@rockymtnhouse.com

Rockyford
P.O. Box 294
Rockyford, AB T0J 2R0
403-533-3950 Fax: 403-533-3744
loism_village@rockyford.ca
www.albertafirst.com/profiles/statspack/20575.html
Municipal Type: Village
Incorporated: March 28, 1919; *Area:* 1.05 sq km
Population in 2006: 349
Provincial Electoral District(s): Strathmore-Brooks
Federal Electoral District(s): Crowfoot
Next Election: 2013 (3 year terms)
Lois Mountjoy, Administrator
Darcy J. Burke, Mayor

Rosalind
P.O. Box 181
Rosalind, AB T0B 3Y0
780-375-3996 Fax: 780-375-3997
rosalindvillage@xplornet.com
www.villageofrosalind.ca
Municipal Type: Village
Incorporated: Jan. 1, 1966; *Area:* 0.59 sq km
Population in 2006: 190
Provincial Electoral District(s): Battle River-Wainwright
Federal Electoral District(s): Crowfoot
Next Election: 2013 (3 year terms)
Nancy Friend, Municipal Administrator
James McTavish, Mayor

Rosemary
P.O. Box 128
Rosemary, AB T0J 2W0
403-378-4246 Fax: 403-378-3144
rosemary.admin@eidnet.org
Municipal Type: Village
Incorporated: Dec. 31, 1951; *Area:* 0.56 sq km
Population in 2006: 388
Provincial Electoral District(s): Strathmore-Brooks
Federal Electoral District(s): Medicine Hat
Next Election: 2013 (3 year terms)
Margaret Loewen, CAO
Yoko Fujimoto, Mayor

Roseridge Waste Management Services Commission
P.O. Box 19
Site 1, RR#1
Morinville, AB T8R 1P4
780-939-5678 Fax: 780-939-4788
sbberry@sturgeoncounty.ab.ca
Municipal Type: Water Commission
Susan Berry, Manager
Vic Pasay, Chair

Ross Haven
#16, 26213 Township Rd. 512
Spruce Grove, AB T7Y 1C6
780-987-3204 Fax: 780-702-6743
ross.haven@tbwifi.ca
Municipal Type: Summer Village
Incorporated: Jan. 1, 1962; *Area:* 0.7 sq km
Population in 2006: 198
Provincial Electoral District(s): Whitecourt-Ste. Anne
Federal Electoral District(s): Yellowhead
Next Election: 2013 (3 year terms)
Dennis Evans, Municipal Administrator
Debra Oakley, Mayor

Rycroft
P.O. Box 360
Rycroft, AB T0H 3A0
780-765-3652 Fax: 780-765-2002
rycroft@telusplanet.net
Municipal Type: Village
Incorporated: March 15, 1944; *Area:* 1.69 sq km
Population in 2006: 638
Provincial Electoral District(s): Dunvegan-Central Peace
Federal Electoral District(s): Peace River
Next Election: 2013 (3 year terms)
Julene Isaac, Clerk
Matt Dika, Mayor

Ryley
P.O. Box 230
Ryley, AB T0B 4A0
780-663-3653 Fax: 780-663-3541
info@ryley.ca
www.ryley.ca
Municipal Type: Village
Incorporated: April 2, 1910; *Area:* 1.97 sq km
Population in 2006: 458
Provincial Electoral District(s): Fort Saskatchewan-Vegreville
Federal Electoral District(s): Vegreville-Wainwright
Next Election: 2013 (3 year terms)
Ross Good, CAO
Elisabeth Kuz, Mayor
e.kuz@ryley.ca

St. Paul
P.O. Box 1480
St Paul, AB T0A 3A0
780-645-4481 Fax: 780-645-5076
townhall@town.stpaul.ab.ca
www.town.stpaul.ab.ca
Municipal Type: Town
Incorporated: June 14, 1912; *Area:* 6.86 sq km
Population in 2006: 5,106
Provincial Electoral District(s): Lac La Biche-St. Paul
Federal Electoral District(s): Westlock-St. Paul
Next Election: 2013 (3 year terms)
Note: Incorporated as a town on Dec. 15, 1936.
Ronald O. Boisvert, CAO
rboisvert@town.stpaul.ab.ca
Glenn Andersen, Mayor

Sandy Beach
PO Box 63, Site 1, RR#1
Onoway, AB T0E 1V0
780-967-2873 Fax: 780-967-2813
svsandyb@telusplanet.net
Municipal Type: Summer Village
Incorporated: Jan. 1, 1956; *Area:* 2.43 sq km
Population in 2006: 239
Provincial Electoral District(s): Whitecourt-Ste. Anne
Federal Electoral District(s): Yellowhead
Next Election: 2013 (3 year terms)
Wendy Wildman, CAO
Thea McDougall, Mayor

Seba Beach
P.O. Box 190
Seba Beach, AB T0E 2B0
780-797-3863 Fax: 780-797-3800
svseba@telusplanet.net
Municipal Type: Summer Village
Incorporated: Aug. 2, 1920; *Area:* 0.66 sq km
Population in 2006: 203
Provincial Electoral District(s): Stony Plain
Federal Electoral District(s): Yellowhead
Next Election: 2013 (3 year terms)
Susan H. Evans, CAO
Gary E. Schultz, Mayor

Sedgewick
P.O. Box 129
Sedgewick, AB T0B 4C0
780-384-3504 Fax: 780-384-3545
sedgewick@persona.ca
www.sedgewick.ca
Municipal Type: Town
Incorporated: March 6, 1907; *Area:* 2.6 sq km
Population in 2006: 891
Provincial Electoral District(s): Battle River-Wainwright
Federal Electoral District(s): Vegreville-Wainwright
Next Election: 2013 (3 year terms)
Note: Incorporated as town on May 1, 1966.
Thelma Rogers, CAO
Helen Marie Whitten, Mayor

Sexsmith
9927 - 100 St.
Sexsmith, AB T0H 3C0
780-568-3681 Fax: 780-568-2200
www.sexsmith.ca
Municipal Type: Town
Incorporated: April 12, 1929; *Area:* 3.43 sq km
Population in 2007: 2,255
Provincial Electoral District(s): Grande Prairie-Smoky
Federal Electoral District(s): Peace River
Next Election: 2013 (3 year terms)
Note: Incorporated as a town on Oct. 15, 1979.
Carolyn Gaunt, Town Manager
cagaunt@sexsmith.ca
Claude Lagace, Mayor

Silver Beach
P.O. Box 60631 U of Alberta
Edmonton, AB T6G 2S9
780-454-4775 Fax: 780-454-4787
info@sbalberta.ca
www.sbalberta.ca
Municipal Type: Summer Village
Incorporated: Dec. 31, 1953; *Area:* 0.66 sq km
Population in 2006: 47
Provincial Electoral District(s): Drayton Valley-Calmar
Federal Electoral District(s): Wetaskiwin
Next Election: 2013 (3 year terms)
Wendy Nickel, Municipal Administrator
Allan Watt, Mayor

Silver Sands
P.O. Box 540
Onoway, AB T0E 1V0
780-967-0008 Fax: 780-967-3226
cdunn@onoway.com
Municipal Type: Summer Village
Incorporated: Jan. 1, 1969; *Area:* 2.35 sq km
Population in 2006: 173
Provincial Electoral District(s): Whitecourt-Ste. Anne
Federal Electoral District(s): Yellowhead
Next Election: 2013 (3 year terms)
Catherine Dunn, Municipal Administrator
Liz Turnbull, Mayor

Slave Lake
P.O. Box 1030
Slave Lake, AB T0G 2A0
780-849-8000 Fax: 780-849-2633
town@slavelake.ca
www.slavelake.ca
Municipal Type: Town
Incorporated: Jan. 1, 1961; *Area:* 14.18 sq km
Population in 2006: 6,703
Provincial Electoral District(s): Lesser Slave Lake
Federal Electoral District(s): Fort McMurray-Athabasca
Next Election: 2013 (3 year terms)
Note: Incorporated as a town on Aug. 2, 1965.
Betty Osmond, CAO
betty@slavelake.ca
Karina Pillay-Kinnee, Mayor

Smoky Lake
P.O. Box 460
Smoky Lake, AB T0A 3C0
780-656-3674 Fax: 780-656-3675
town@town.smokylake.ab.ca
www.town.smokylake.ab.ca
Municipal Type: Town
Incorporated: arch 26, 1923; *Area:* 4.2 sq km
Population in 2006: 1,010
Provincial Electoral District(s): Athabasca-Redwater
Federal Electoral District(s): Westlock-St. Paul
Next Election: 2013 (3 year terms)
Note: Incorporated as a town on Feb. 1, 1962.
Tom Carney, CAO
TCarney@town.smokylake.ab.ca
Dave Franchuk, Mayor

Smoky River Regional Waste Management Commission
P.O. Box 155
Falher, AB T0H 1M0
780-837-2247 Fax: 780-837-2647
tnfalher@telusplanet.net
Municipal Type: Water Commission
Carmen Ewing, Chair

Smoky River Regional Water Management Commission
P.O. Box 155
Falher, AB T0H 1M0
780-837-2247 Fax: 780-837-2647
Municipal Type: Water Commission
Margaret Tardif, Chair

South Baptiste
724 Baptiste Dr.
West Baptiste, AB T9S 1R8
780-675-9270 Fax: 780-675-9526
tomaszyk@mcsnet.ca
www.southbaptiste.com
Municipal Type: Summer Village
Incorporated: Jan. 1, 1983; *Area:* 1.05 sq km
Population in 2006: 69
Provincial Electoral District(s): Athabasca-Redwater
Federal Electoral District(s): Fort McMurray-Athabaska
Next Election: 2013 (3 year terms)
Edwin Tomaszyk, CAO
Tom Dolan, Mayor

South Forty Waste Services Commission
P.O. Box 307
Foremost, AB T0K 0X0
403-867-3530 Fax: 403-867-2242
Municipal Type: Water Commission
Lynden Hutchinson, Chair
lhutch@telusplanet.net

South View
P.O. Box 540
Onoway, AB T0E 1V0
780-967-0008 Fax: 780-967-3226
cdunn@onoway.com
Municipal Type: Summer Village
Incorporated: Jan. 1, 1970; *Area:* 0.69 sq km
Population in 2006: 115
Provincial Electoral District(s): Whitecourt-Ste. Anne
Federal Electoral District(s): Yellowhead
Next Election: 2013 (3 year terms)
Catherine Dunn, Municipal Administrator
Sandra Benford, Mayor

Spirit River
P.O. Box 130
Spirit River, AB T0H 3G0
780-864-3998 Fax: 780-864-3433
clerk@townsofspiritriver.ca
www.townofspiritriver.ca
Municipal Type: Town
Incorporated: June 13, 1916; *Area:* 2.81 sq km
Population in 2006: 1,148
Provincial Electoral District(s): Dunvegan-Central Peace
Federal Electoral District(s): Peace River
Next Election: 2013 (3 year terms)
Note: Incorporated as a town on Sept. 18, 1951.
Linda Hannah, CAO
manager@townofspiritriver.ca
Theresa Sandul, Mayor

Spring Lake
990 Bauer Ave.
Spring Lake, AB T7Z 2S9
780-963-4211 Fax: 780-963-4260
springlake@cruzinternet.com
www.springlakealberta.com
Municipal Type: Village
Incorporated: Jan. 1, 1959; *Area:* 2.12 sq km
Population in 2006: 501
Provincial Electoral District(s): Stoney Plain
Federal Electoral District(s): Edmonton-Spruce Grove
Next Election: 2013 (3 year terms)
Note: Incorporated as a village on Jan. 1, 1999.
Emily House, Acting CAO
emily@springlakealberta.com
Sandra Ledwon, Mayor
sandi@springlakealberta.com

Standard
P.O. Box 249
Standard, AB T0J 3G0
403-644-3968 Fax: 403-644-2284
cao@standardab.ca
www.standardab.ca
Municipal Type: Village
Incorporated: April 29, 1922; *Area:* 2.34 sq km
Population in 2006: 380
Provincial Electoral District(s): Strathmore-Brooks
Federal Electoral District(s): Crowfoot
Next Election: 2013 (3 year terms)
Leah Jensen, CAO
Allan Bragg, Mayor
allanbragg@hotmail.com

Stavely
P.O. Box 249
Stavely, AB T0L 1Z0
403-549-3761 Fax: 403-549-3743
stavely@platinum.ca
www.stavely.ca
Municipal Type: Town
Incorporated: Oct. 16, 1903; *Area:* 1.62 sq km
Population in 2006: 435
Provincial Electoral District(s): Livingstone-Macleod
Federal Electoral District(s): Macleod
Next Election: 2013 (3 year terms)
Note: Incorporated as a town on May 25, 1912.
Sheryl Fath, Municipal Administrator
Barry Johnson, Mayor

Stettler
P.O. Box 280
Stettler, AB T0C 2L0
403-742-8305 Fax: 403-742-1404
townoffice@stettler.net
www.stettler.net
Municipal Type: Town
Incorporated: June 30, 1906; *Area:* 9.5 sq km
Population in 2006: 5,418
Provincial Electoral District(s): Drumheller-Stettler
Federal Electoral District(s): Crowfoot
Next Election: 2013 (3 year terms)
Note: Incorporated as a town on Nov. 23, 1906.
Robert Stoutenberg, Town Manager
robs@stettler.net
James Hunter, Mayor
hunterja@telusplanet.net

Stirling
P.O. Box 360
229 Fourth Ave.
Stirling, AB T0K 2E0
403-756-3379 Fax: 403-756-2262
stirl_ng@telus.net
www.villageofstirling.com
Municipal Type: Village
Incorporated: Sept. 3, 1901; *Area:* 2.64 sq km
Population in 2006: 921
Provincial Electoral District(s): Cardston-Taber-Warner
Federal Electoral District(s): Lethbridge
Next Election: 2013 (3 year terms)
Scott Barton, CAO
scottbarton@raymond.ca
Larry Nilsson, Mayor

Strome
P.O. Box 179
5025 - 50th St.
Strome, AB T0B 4H0
780-376-3558 Fax: 780-376-3557
strome@telusplanet.net
www.villageofstrome.com
Municipal Type: Village
Incorporated: Feb. 3, 1910; *Area:* 0.92 sq km
Population in 2006: 252
Provincial Electoral District(s): Battle River-Wainwright
Federal Electoral District(s): Vegreville-Wainwright
Next Election: 2013 (3 year terms)
Connie Prendergast, Clerk
Brian McGaffigan, Mayor

Sunbreaker Cove
#104, 4505 - 50 Ave.
Sylvan Lake, AB T4S 1W2
403-887-2822 Fax: 403-887-2897
fivesv@telusplanet.net
Municipal Type: Summer Village
Incorporated: Dec. 31, 1990; *Area:* 0.49 sq km
Population in 2006: 137
Provincial Electoral District(s): Rocky Mountain House
Federal Electoral District(s): Wetaskiwin
Next Election: 2013 (3 year terms)
Myra Reiter, Administrator
Gilbert (Gib) Clark, Mayor

Sundance Beach
11318 - 10th Ave.
Edmonton, AB T6J 6S9
780-431-9712 Fax: 780-431-0882
svoffice@telusplanet.net
Municipal Type: Summer Village
Incorporated: Jan. 1, 1970; *Area:* 0.42 sq km
Population in 2006: 102
Provincial Electoral District(s): Drayton Valley-Calmar
Federal Electoral District(s): Wetaskiwin
Next Election: 2013 (3 year terms)
Anita Blais, Administrator
Peter Pellatt, Mayor

Sundre
P.O. Box 420
Sundre, AB T0M 1X0
403-638-3551 Fax: 403-638-2100
townmail@sundre.com
www.sundre.com
Municipal Type: Town
Incorporated: Dec. 31, 1949; *Area:* 7.65 sq km
Population in 2006: 2,518
Provincial Electoral District(s): Rocky Mountain House
Federal Electoral District(s): Wild Rose
Next Election: 2013 (3 year terms)
Note: Incorporated as a town on Jan. 1, 1956.
Nita Bartholow, CAO
nita.b@sundre.com
Roy Cummings, Mayor
san1roy@telus.net

Sunrise Beach
Box 540
Onoway, AB T0E 1V0
780-967-0008 Fax: 780-967-3226
cdunn@onoway.com
Municipal Type: Summer Village
Incorporated: Dec. 31, 1988; *Area:* 1.72 sq km
Population in 2006: 170
Provincial Electoral District(s): Whitecourt-Ste. Anne
Federal Electoral District(s): Yellowhead
Next Election: 2013 (3 year terms)
Catherine Dunn, Municipal Administrator
Everett Steenbergen, Mayor

Sunset Beach
PO Box 83001, RPO Belmead
Edmonton, AB T5T 6S1
780-487-5357 Fax: 780-487-1313
sunsetbeach@shaw.ca
Municipal Type: Summer Village
Incorporated: May 1, 1977; *Area:* 0.99 sq km
Population in 2006: 88
Provincial Electoral District(s): Athabasca-Redwater
Federal Electoral District(s): Fort McMurray-Athabasca
Next Election: 2013 (3 year terms)
Don McCallum, Municipal Administrator
Mark Lindskoog, Mayor

Sunset Point
13 Grandin Rd.
St Albert, AB T8N 3B2
780-460-7226
hmarsh@telusplanet.net
Municipal Type: Summer Village
Incorporated: Jan. 1, 1959; *Area:* 1.11 sq km
Population in 2006: 242
Provincial Electoral District(s): Whitecourt-Ste. Anne
Federal Electoral District(s): Yellowhead
Next Election: 2013 (3 year terms)
Hilda Marsh, CAO
Elizabeth Morrison, Mayor

Swan Hills
P.O. Box 149
Swan Hills, AB T0G 2C0
780-333-4477 Fax: 780-333-4547
town@townofswanhills.com
www.townofswanhills.com
Municipal Type: Town
Incorporated: Sept. 1, 1959; *Area:* 25.44 sq km
Population in 2006: 1,645
Provincial Electoral District(s): Barrhead-Morinville-Westlock
Federal Electoral District(s): Yellowhead
Next Election: 2013 (3 year terms)
Hilda Price, CAO
hprice@townofswanhills.com
Pamela Marriott, Mayor

Taber
4900A - 50 St.
Taber, AB T1G 1T1
403-223-5500 Fax: 403-223-5530
town@taber.ca
www.taber.ca
Municipal Type: Town
Incorporated: March 15, 1905; *Area:* 15.09 sq km
Population in 2008: 7,821
Provincial Electoral District(s): Cardston-Taber-Warner
Federal Electoral District(s): Medicine Hat
Next Election: 2013 (3 year terms)
Note: Incorporated as a town on July 1, 1907.
Gordon Frank, CAO
town@taber.ca
Ray Bryant, Mayor
mayor@taber.ca

Thorhild
P.O. Box 310
Thorhild, AB T0A 3J0
780-398-3688 Fax: 780-398-2100
village@thorhild.com
www.thorhild.com
Municipal Type: Village
Incorporated: Dec. 31, 1949; *Area:* 1.67 sq km
Population in 2006: 505
Provincial Electoral District(s): Athabasca-Redwater
Federal Electoral District(s): Westlock-St. Paul
Next Election: 2013 (3 year terms)
Darlene Gross, CAO
cao@thorhild.com
Stanley Olchowy, Mayor

Thorhild Regional Waste Management Services Commission
P.O. Box 10
Thorhild, AB T0A 3J0
780-398-3741 Fax: 780-398-3748
Municipal Type: Water Commission
Debbie Hamilton, Acting Commission Manager
debbie@thorhild.com

Thorhild Regional Water Services Commission
P.O. Box 310
Thorhild, AB T0A 3J0
780-398-3688 Fax: 780-398-2100
dhamilton@telusplanet.net
Municipal Type: Water Commission
Debbie Hamilton, Manager

Thorsby
P.O. Box 297
Thorsby, AB T0C 2P0
780-789-3935 Fax: 780-789-3779
municlerk@village.thorsby.ab.ca
www.village.thorsby.ab.ca
Municipal Type: Village
Incorporated: Dec. 31, 1949; *Area:* 2.92 sq km
Population in 2006: 945
Provincial Electoral District(s): Drayton Valley-Calmar
Federal Electoral District(s): Wetaskiwin
Next Election: 2013 (3 year terms)
Martin Taylor, CAO
mtaylor@village.thorsby.ab.ca
Allan Gee, Mayor

Three Hills
P.O. Box 610
Three Hills, AB T0M 2A0
403-443-5822 Fax: 403-443-2616
info@threehills.ca
www.threehills.ca
Municipal Type: Town
Incorporated: June 14, 1912; *Area:* 5.63 sq km
Population in 2006: 3,089
Provincial Electoral District(s): Olds-Didsbury-Three Hills
Federal Electoral District(s): Crowfoot
Next Election: 2013 (3 year terms)
Note: Incorporated as a town on Jan. 1, 1929.
Jack Ramsden, Town Manager
jramsden@threehills.ca
Kevin Edwards, Mayor
kedwards@threehills.ca

Tilley
P.O. Box 155
Tilley, AB T0J 3K0

403-377-2203 Fax: 403-377-2234
village.tilley@eidnet.org
www.albertafirst.com/profiles/statspack/20587.html
Municipal Type: Village
Incorporated: May 9, 1940; *Area:* 0.62 sq km
Population in 2006: 381
Provincial Electoral District(s): Strathmore-Brooks
Federal Electoral District(s): Medicine Hat
Next Election: 2013 (3 year terms)
Jeannette Zahn, CAO
John Timko, Mayor
john.timko@tyson.com

Tofield
P.O. Box 30
Tofield, AB T0B 4J0
780-662-3269 Fax: 780-662-3929
tofield@supernet.ab.ca
www.tofieldalberta.ca
Municipal Type: Town
Incorporated: Sept. 9, 1907; *Area:* 6.01 sq km
Population in 2006: 1,876
Provincial Electoral District(s): Fort Saskatchewan-Vegreville
Federal Electoral District(s): Vegreville-Wainwright
Next Election: 2013 (3 year terms)
Note: Incorporated as a town on Sept. 10, 1909.
Cindy Neufeld, CAO
cneufeld@tofieldalberta.ca
Nabil Chehayeb, Mayor

Tri Village Regional Sewage Services
Box 16, Site 1, RR#2
Carvel, AB T0E 0H0
780-963-4211 Fax: 780-963-4260
Municipal Type: Water Commission
Don Boudreaux, Chair

Trochu
P.O. Box 340
Trochu, AB T0M 2C0
403-442-3085 Fax: 403-442-2528
chiefadmin@town.trochu.ab.ca
www.town.trochu.ab.ca
Municipal Type: Town
Incorporated: May 5, 1911; *Area:* 2.82 sq km
Population in 2006: 1,005
Provincial Electoral District(s): Olds-Didsbury-Three Hills
Federal Electoral District(s): Crowfoot
Next Election: 2013 (3 year terms)
Note: Incorporated as a town on Aug. 1, 1962.
Maureen Malaka, CAO
Barry Kletke, Mayor
bkletke@xplornet.com

Turner Valley
P.O. Box 330
Turner Valley, AB T0L 2A0
403-933-4944 Fax: 403-933-5377
admin@turnervalley.ca
www.turnervalley.ca
Municipal Type: Town
Incorporated: Feb. 25, 1930; *Area:* 5.45 sq km
Population in 2006: 1,908
Provincial Electoral District(s): Foothills-Rocky View
Federal Electoral District(s): Macleod
Next Election: 2013 (3 year terms)
Note: Incorporated as a town on Sept.1, 1977.
Stan Ogrodniczuk, CAO
stano@turnervalley.ca
Dona Fluter, Mayor

Two Hills
P.O. Box 630
Two Hills, AB T0B 4K0
780-657-3395 Fax: 780-657-2158
info@townoftwohills.com
www.townofhills.com
Municipal Type: Town
Incorporated: June 4, 1929; *Area:* 3.31 sq km
Population in 2006: 1,047
Provincial Electoral District(s): Lac La Biche-St. Paul
Federal Electoral District(s): Vegreville-Wainwright
Next Election: 2013 (3 year terms)
Note: Incorporated as a town on Jan. 1, 1955.
Sheila Kitz, CAO
cao@townoftwohills.com
Mark H. Kussmann, Mayor

Two Hills Regional Waste Management Commission
P.O. Box 8
Two Hills, AB T0B 4K0
780-567-2016
Municipal Type: Water Commission
Darren Banack, Operations Manager

Val Quentin
13 Grandin Rd.
St Albert, AB T8N 3B2
780-460-7226 Fax: 780-419-2476
hmarsh@telusplanet.net
Municipal Type: Summer Village
Incorporated: Jan. 1, 1966; *Area:* 0.3 sq km
Population in 2006: 181
Provincial Electoral District(s): Whitecourt-Ste. Anne
Federal Electoral District(s): Yellowhead
Next Election: 2013 (3 year terms)
Hilda R. Marsh, CAO
Bob Lehman, Mayor

Valleyview
P.O. Box 270
Valleyview, AB T0H 3N0
780-524-5150 Fax: 780-524-2727
valvadmn@telusplanet.net
http://valleyview.govoffice.com
Municipal Type: Town
Incorporated: Jan. 1, 1955; *Area:* 4.57 sq km
Population in 2007: 1,884
Provincial Electoral District(s): Grande Prairie-Smoky
Federal Electoral District(s): Peace River
Next Election: 2013 (3 year terms)
Note: Incorporated as a town on Feb. 5, 1957.
Frank Besinger, Twon Manager
Vern Lymburner, Mayor

Vauxhall
P.O. Box 509
Vauxhall, AB T0K 2K0
403-654-2174 Fax: 403-654-4110
cao@town.vauxhall.ab.ca
www.town.vauxhall.ab.ca
Municipal Type: Town
Incorporated: Dec. 31, 1949; *Area:* 2.88 sq km
Population in 2006: 1,069
Provincial Electoral District(s): Little Bow
Federal Electoral District(s): Medicine Hat
Next Election: 2013 (3 year terms)
Note: Incorporated as a town on Jan. 1, 1961.
Troy Ormann, CAO
tormann@town.vauxhall.ab.ca
Lois Maloney, Mayor
mayor@town.vauxhall.ab.ca

Vegreville
P.O. Box 640
Vegreville, AB T9C 1R7
780-632-2606 Fax: 780-632-3088
vegtown@vegreville.com
www.vegreville.com
Municipal Type: Town
Incorporated: April 4, 1906; *Area:* 13.49 sq km
Population in 2006: 5,519
Provincial Electoral District(s): Fort Saskatchewan-Vegreville
Federal Electoral District(s): Vegreville-Wainwright
Next Election: 2013 (3 year terms)
Note: Incorporated as a town on Aug 15, 1906.
Jody Quickstad, Town Manager
jquickstad@vegreville.com
Richard N. Coleman, Mayor

Vermilion
5021 - 49th Ave.
Vermilion, AB T9X 1X1
780-853-5358 Fax: 780-853-4910
townofvermilion@vermilion.ca
www.vermilion.ca
Municipal Type: Town
Incorporated: Feb. 17, 1906; *Area:* 13.69 sq km
Population in 2006: 4,036
Provincial Electoral District(s): Vermilion-Lloydminster
Federal Electoral District(s): Vegreville-Wainwright
Next Election: 2013 (3 year terms)
Note: Incorporated as a town on Aug. 27, 1906.
Robert Watt, Town Manager
rwatt@vermilion.ca
Bruce Marriott, Mayor
bgmarr@telusmail.net

Veteran
P.O. Box 439
Veteran, AB T0C 2S0
403-575-3954 Fax: 403-575-3954
veteran@veterancable.net
Municipal Type: Village
Incorporated: June 30, 1914; *Area:* 0.84 sq km
Population in 2006: 293
Provincial Electoral District(s): Drumheller-Stettler
Federal Electoral District(s): Crowfoot
Next Election: 2013 (3 year terms)
Debbie Johnstone, CAO
Pat Gorcak, Mayor

Viking
P.O. Box 369
Viking, AB T0B 4N0
780-336-3466 Fax: 780-336-2660
laura.arndt@town.viking.ab.ca
www.town.viking.ab.ca
Municipal Type: Town
Incorporated: Feb. 5, 1909; *Area:* 3.76 sq km
Population in 2006: 1,085
Provincial Electoral District(s): Vermilion-Lloydminster
Federal Electoral District(s): Vegreville-Wainwright
Next Election: 2013 (3 year terms)
Note: Incorporated as a town on Nov. 10, 1952.
Rod Krips, Town Manager
rod.krips@town.viking.ab.ca
Cindy Lefsrud, Mayor
clefsrud@telus.net

Vilna
P.O. Box 10
5103 - 50th St.
Vilna, AB T0A 3L0
780-636-3620 Fax: 780-636-3022
info@historicvilna.ca
www.historicvilna.ca
Municipal Type: Village
Incorporated: June 23, 1923; *Area:* 0.9 sq km
Population in 2006: 274
Provincial Electoral District(s): Lac La Biche-St. Paul
Federal Electoral District(s): Westlock-St. Paul
Next Election: 2013 (3 year terms)
Twila Bauman, CAO
780-650-5207
Carol Trider, Mayor
780-636-3666

Vulcan
P.O. Box 360
Vulcan, AB T0L 2B0
403-485-2417 Fax: 403-485-2914
vulcan@townofvulcan.ca
www.town.vulcan.ab.ca
Municipal Type: Town
Incorporated: Dec. 23, 1912; *Area:* 6.58 sq km
Population in 2006: 1,940
Provincial Electoral District(s): Little Bow
Federal Electoral District(s): Macleod
Next Election: 2013 (3 year terms)
Note: Incorporated as a town on Jun 15, 1921.
Alcide Cloutier, CAO
acloutier@townofvulcan.ca
Thomas Grant, Mayor

Vulcan District Waste Commission
P.O. Box 180
Vulcan, AB T0L 2B0
403-485-2241 Fax: 403-482-2920
countyadmin@vulcancounty.ab.ca
www.vulcancounty.ab.ca
Municipal Type: Water Commission
Merle Wyatt, Chair

Wabamun
P.O. Box 240
5217 - 52 St.
Wabamun, AB T0E 2K0
780-892-2699 Fax: 780-892-2669
admin@wabamun.ca
www.wabamun.ca
Municipal Type: Village
Incorporated: July 18, 1912; *Area:* 3.24 sq km
Population in 2006: 601
Provincial Electoral District(s): Stony Plain
Federal Electoral District(s): Yellowhead
Next Election: 2013 (3 year terms)
Leagh Randle, Administrator
lrandle@wabamun.ca
Larry Burton, Mayor

Wainwright
1018 - 2 Ave.
Wainwright, AB T9W 1R1
780-842-3381 Fax: 780-842-2898
tofwain@town.wainwright.ab.ca
www.town.wainwright.ab.ca
Municipal Type: Town
Incorporated: March 25, 1909; *Area:* 8.55 sq km
Population in 2006: 5,426
Provincial Electoral District(s): Battle River-Wainwright
Federal Electoral District(s): Vegreville-Wainwright
Next Election: 2013 (3 year terms)
Note: Incorporated as town on July 14, 1910.
Ray Poulin, Administrator
rpoulin@town.wainwright.ab.ca
Norm Coleman, Mayor

Waiparous
P.O. Box 5754
High River, AB T1V 1P3
403-652-4636 Fax: 403-206-7209
admin@waiparous.ca
www.waiparous.ca
Municipal Type: Summer Village
Incorporated: Jan. 1, 1986; *Area:* 0.41 sq km
Population in 2006: 49
Provincial Electoral District(s): Banff-Cochrane
Federal Electoral District(s): Wild Rose
Next Election: 2013 (3 year terms)
Sharon Plett, Administrator
Shirley Begg, Mayor
403-932-3381

Warburg
P.O. Box 29
5212 - 50 Ave.
Warburg, AB T0C 2T0
780-848-2841 Fax: 780-848-2296
warburg@telusplanet.net
www.villageofwarburg.ab.ca
Municipal Type: Village
Incorporated: Dec. 31, 1953; *Area:* 2.08 sq km
Population in 2006: 621
Provincial Electoral District(s): Drayton Valley-Calmar

Federal Electoral District(s): Wetaskiwin
Next Election: 2013 (3 year terms)
Christine Pankewitz, Municipal Administrator
May Metke, Mayor

Warner
P.O. Box 88
Warner, AB T0K 2L0
403-642-3877 Fax: 403-642-2011
vowarner@shockware.com
www.warner.ca
Municipal Type: Village
Incorporated: Nov. 12, 1908; *Area:* 1.15 sq km
Population in 2006: 307
Provincial Electoral District(s): Cardston-Taber-Warner
Federal Electoral District(s): Lethbridge
Next Election: 2013 (3 year terms)
Kim Dalton, CAO
Verne Strain, Mayor

Waskatenau
P.O. Box 99
5008 - 51st St.
Waskatenau, AB T0A 3P0
780-358-2208 Fax: 780-358-2208
info@waskatenau.ca
www.waskatenau.ca
Municipal Type: Village
Incorporated: May 19, 1932; *Area:* 0.6 sq km
Population in 2006: 278
Provincial Electoral District(s): Athabasca-Redwater
Federal Electoral District(s): Westlock-St. Paul
Next Election: 2013 (3 year terms)
Bernice Macyk, CAO
780-358-2612
Gail Zaplotinsky, Mayor
780-358-2282

Wembley
P.O. Box 89
Wembley, AB T0H 3S0
780-766-2269 Fax: 780-766-2868
office@wembley.ca
www.wembley.ca
Municipal Type: Town
Incorporated: Jan. 3, 1928; *Area:* 3.63 sq km
Population in 2006: 1,443
Provincial Electoral District(s): Grande Prairie-Wapiti
Federal Electoral District(s): Peace River
Next Election: 2013 (3 year terms)
Note: Incorporated as a town on Aug. 1, 1980.
Lori Parker, CAO
Owen Smith, Mayor

West Baptiste
945 Baptiste Dr.
West Baptiste, AB T9S 1R8
780-675-3900 Fax: 780-675-4174
viviandriver@mcsnet.ca
Municipal Type: Summer Village
Incorporated: Jan. 1, 1983; *Area:* 0.6 sq km
Population in 2006: 104
Provincial Electoral District(s): Athabasca-Redwater
Federal Electoral District(s): Fort McMurray-Athabasca
Next Election: 2013 (3 year terms)
Vivian Driver, Administrator
Keith Wilson, Mayor
wilsonkd@shaw.ca

West Cove
#16, 26213 Township Rd. 512
Spruce Grove, AB T7Y 1C6
780-702-3204 Fax: 780-702-6743
west.cove@tbwifi.ca
Municipal Type: Summer Village
Incorporated: Jan. 1, 1963; *Area:* 1.21 sq km
Population in 2006: 169
Provincial Electoral District(s): Whitecourt-Ste. Anne
Federal Electoral District(s): Yellowhead
Next Election: 2013 (3 year terms)
Dennis Evans, Municipal Administrator
Gordon Harris, Mayor
shirleyj@look.ca

Westend Regional Sewage Services
P.O. Box 330
Turner Valley, AB T0L 2A0
403-933-4744 Fax: 403-933-5377
Municipal Type: Water Commission
Sharlene Brown, Chair

Westlock
10003 - 106 St.
Westlock, AB T7P 2K3
780-349-4444 Fax: 780-349-4436 Toll Free Phone: 1-866-349-4445
info@westlock.ca
www.westlock.ca
Municipal Type: Town
Incorporated: March 13, 1916; *Area:* 9.64 sq km
Population in 2006: 5,008
Provincial Electoral District(s): Barrhead-Morinville-Westlock
Federal Electoral District(s): Westlock-St. Paul
Next Election: 2013 (3 year terms)
Note: Incorporated as a town on Jan. 7, 1947.
Norman McInnis, Town Manager
nmcinnis@westlock.ca
Bruce Lennon, Mayor
blennon@westlock.ca

Westlock Regional Waste Management Commission
10336 - 106 St.
Westlock, AB T7P 2G1
780-349-3346 Fax: 780-349-2012
Municipal Type: Water Commission
Vacant, Manager

Whispering Hills
10511 - 109 St.
Westlock, AB T7P 1A9
780-349-3651
mbancrof@telusplanet.net
Municipal Type: Summer Village
Incorporated: Jan. 1, 1983; *Area:* 1.73 sq km
Population in 2006: 125
Provincial Electoral District(s): Athabasca-Redwater
Federal Electoral District(s): Fort McMurray-Athabasca
Next Election: 2013 (3 year terms)
Garth Bancroft, Administrator
Dennis Irving, Mayor

White Sands
P.O. Box 119
Stettler, AB T0C 2L0
403-742-8305 Fax: 403-742-1404
townoffice@stettler.net
www.summervillageofwhitesands.ca
Municipal Type: Summer Village
Incorporated: Jan. 1, 1980; *Area:* 1.6 sq km
Population in 2006: 120
Provincial Electoral District(s): Drumheller-Stettler
Federal Electoral District(s): Crowfoot
Next Election: 2013 (3 year terms)
Greg Switenky, CAO
gswitenky@stettler.net
Colin Adair, Mayor

Whitecourt
P.O. Box 509
5004 - 52 Ave.
Whitecourt, AB T7S 1N6
780-778-2273 Fax: 780-778-2062
administration@whitecourt.ca
www.whitecourt.ca
Municipal Type: Town
Incorporated: Jan. 1, 1959; *Area:* 26.14 sq km
Population in 2008: 9,202
Provincial Electoral District(s): Whitecourt-Ste. Anne
Federal Electoral District(s): Yellowhead
Next Election: 2013 (3 year terms)
Note: Incorporated as a town on Aug. 15, 1961.
Peter Smyl, CAO
petersmyl@whitecourt.ca
Trevor Thain, Mayor
780-778-0909
trevorthain@whitecourt.ca

Willingdon
P.O. Box 210
Willingdon, AB T0B 4R0
780-367-2337 Fax: 780-367-2167
vilwil@telusplanet.net
Municipal Type: Village
Incorporated: Aug. 31, 1928; *Area:* 0.97 sq km
Population in 2006: 295
Provincial Electoral District(s): Lac La Biche-St. Paul
Federal Electoral District(s): Vegreville-Wainwright
Next Election: 2013 (3 year terms)
Sharon Van Sickle, CAO
Bill Albers, Mayor
billalbers@diditialweb.net

Willow Creek Regional Waste Management Services Commission
P.O. Box 2820
Claresholm, AB T0L 0T0
403-687-2603 Fax: 403-287-2602
wcrwmsc@telusplanet.net
Municipal Type: Water Commission
Gerry McGueire, Chair

Yellowstone
P.O. Box 278
Alberta Beach, AB T0E 0A0
780-924-3181 Fax: 780-924-3313
aboffice@3web.com
Municipal Type: Summer Village
Incorporated: Jan. 1, 1965; *Area:* 0.28 sq km
Population in 2006: 170
Provincial Electoral District(s): Whitecourt-Ste. Anne
Federal Electoral District(s): Yellowhead
Next Election: 2013 (3 year terms)
Kathy Skwarchuk, CAO
Alice Solesbury, Mayor

Youngstown
P.O. Box 99
Youngstown, AB T0J 3P0
403-779-3873 Fax: 403-779-3873
ytown@xplornet.com
Municipal Type: Village
Incorporated: March 8, 1913; *Area:* 1 sq km
Population in 2006: 170
Provincial Electoral District(s): Drumheller-Stettler
Federal Electoral District(s): Crowfoot
Next Election: 2013 (3 year terms)
Emma Garlock, Administrator
Robert Allen, Mayor

Improvement Districts

Improvement District No. 12 (Jasper National Park)
Municipal Services Branch
10155 - 102 St., 17th Fl.
Edmonton, AB T5J 4L4
780-422-8098 Fax: 780-420-1016
rick.grimson@gov.ab.ca
Municipal Type: Improvement Districts
Incorporated: April 1, 1945; *Area:* 10,181.58 sq. km
Population in 2006: 24

Improvement District No. 13 (Elk Island)
Municipal Services Branch
10155 - 102 St., 17th Fl.
Edmonton, AB T5J 4L4
780-422-8098 Fax: 780-420-1016
rick.grimson@gov.ab.ca
Municipal Type: Improvement Districts
Incorporated: April 1, 1958; *Area:* 165.28 sq. km
Population in 2006: 21
Rick Grimson, ID Manager
Ian Mackie, Chair

Improvement District No. 24 (Wood Buffalo)
Municipal Services Branch
10155 - 102 St.
Edmonton, AB T5J 4L4
780-422-8098 Fax: 780-420-1016
rick.grimson@gov.ab.ca
Municipal Type: Improvement Districts
Incorporated: Jan. 1, 1967; *Area:* 165.28 sq km.
Population in 2006: 422
Rick Grimson, ID Manager

Improvement District No. 25 (Willmore Wilderness)
Municipal Services Branch
10155 - 102 St.
Edmonton, AB T5J 4L4
780-422-8098 Fax: 780-420-1016
rick.grimson@gov.ab.ca
Municipal Type: Improvement Districts
Incorporated: Jan. 2, 1994; *Area:* 4,604.97 sq. km
Rick Grimson, ID Manager

Improvement District No. 4 (Waterton)
Municipal Services Branch
10155 - 102 St., 17th Fl.
Edmonton, AB T5J 4L4
780-422-8098 Fax: 780-420-1016
rick.grimson@gov.ab.ca
Municipal Type: Improvement Districts
Incorporated: Jan. 1, 1944; *Area:* 480.58 sq. km
Population in 2006: 160
Rick Grimson, ID Manager
Brian Reeves, Chair
Brian Reeves, Chair

Improvement District No. 9 (Banff)
Municipal Services Branch
10155 - 102 St., 17th Fl.
Edmonton, AB T5J 4L4
780-422-8098 Fax: 780-420-1016
rick.grimson@gov.ab.ca
Municipal Type: Improvement Districts
Incorporated: April 1, 1945; *Area:* 6,782.26 sq. km
Population in 2006: 938

Kananaskis Improvement District
P.O. Box 70
Kananaskis, AB T0L 2H0
403-591-7774 Fax: 403-591-7123
cheryl.dubuc@gov.ab.ca
www.kananaskisid.ca
Municipal Type: Improvement Districts
Incorporated: April 1, 1945; *Area:* 4,210.72 sq km
Population in 2006: 429
Mike Benny, CAO
mike.benny@gov.ab.ca
Dan DeSantis, Chair
ddesantis@deltahotels.com

Metis Settlement in Alberta

Buffalo Lake
P.O. Box 16
Caslan, AB T0A 0R0
780-689-2170 Fax: 780-689-2024
buffalolakemetis@buffalolakemetis.com
Municipal Type: Metis Settlement
Margaret Daniels, Administrator
mdaniels@buffalolakemetis.com
Bruce Gordon, Chair

East Prairie
P.O. Box 1289
High Prairie, AB T0G 1E0
780-523-2594 Fax: 780-523-2777
joanh@telus.net
Municipal Type: Metis Settlement
Harry Supernault, Administrator
Louis Haggerty, Chair

Elizabeth
P.O. Box 420
Cold Lake, AB T9M 1P1
780-594-5026 Fax: 780-594-5452
ems@jetnet.ab.ca
Municipal Type: Metis Settlement
Ambrose Lepine, Administrator
emsadmin@jetnet.ab.ca
Archie Collins, Chair
emscouncil@jetnet.ab.ca

Fishing Lake
General Delivery
Sputinow, AB T0A 3G0
780-943-2202 Fax: 780-943-2575
www.fishinglake.ca
Municipal Type: Metis Settlement
Brenda Anderson, Interim Administrator
Ryck Chalifoux, Chair, M

Gift Lake
P.O. Box 60
Gift Lake, AB T0G 1B0
780-767-3794 Fax: 780-767-3888
Municipal Type: Metis Settlement
Randy Anderson, Acting Administrator
Hector Lamouche, Chair

Kikino
General Delivery
Kikino, AB T0A 2B0
780-623-7868 Fax: 780-623-7080
kikino01@telus.net
Municipal Type: Metis Settlement
Roger Littlechilds, Administrator
Floyd Thompson, Chair

Paddle Prairie
P.O. Box 58
Paddle Prairie, AB T0H 2W0
780-981-2227 Fax: 780-981-3737
reception@paddleprairie.com
Municipal Type: Metis Settlement
Tina St. Germain, Acting Administrator
Greg Calliou

Peavine
P.O. Box 238
High Prairie, AB T0G 1E0
780-523-2557 Fax: 780-523-2626
Municipal Type: Metis Settlement
Dale LeClair, Settlement Administrator
Raymond Carifelle

BRITISH COLUMBIA

Incorporated municipalities in British Columbia include Villages, Towns, Cities, and District Municipalities as well as one Indian Government District, a Resort Municipality, and an Island Municipality. Twenty-seven regional districts provide services to unincorporated areas and member municipalities.

Municipal elections in all municipalities are held on the third Saturday of November. Terms of office are three years (2008, 2011, etc.).

Legislation: The Local Government Act, excluding the City of Vancouver, which is regulated under the provisions of the Vancouver Charter.

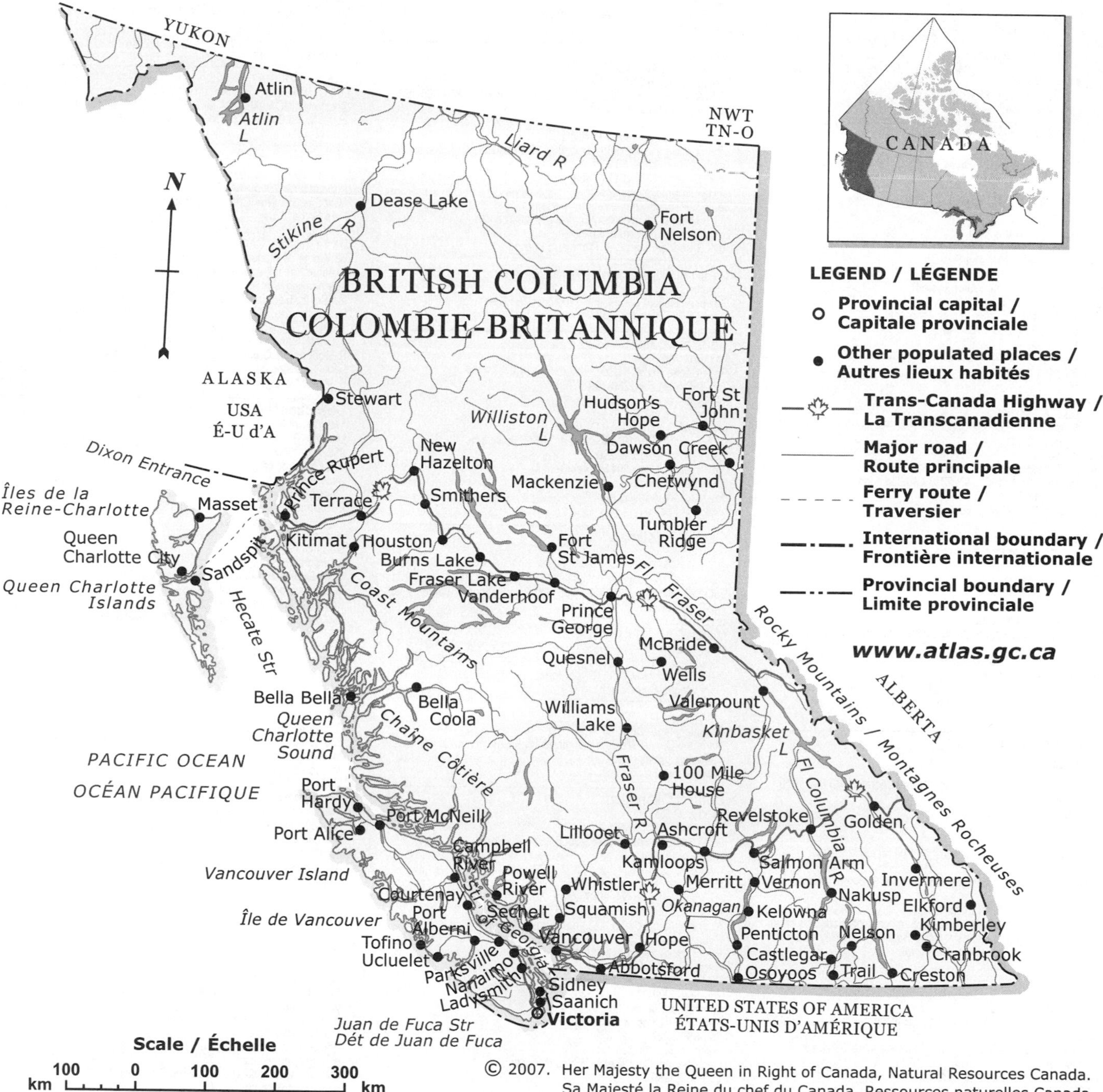

British Columbia

Counties & Municipal Districts in British Columbia

Alberni-Clayoquot

3008 - 5 Ave.
Port Alberni, BC V9Y 2E3
250-720-2700 Fax: 250-723-1327
mailbox@acrd.bc.ca
www.acrd.bc.ca
Municipal Type: Regional Districts
Incorporated: April 21, 1966; *Area:* 6,596.58 sq km
Population in 2006: 28,601
Next Election: Nov. 2011 (3 year terms)
Hira Chopra, Chair
250-723-2146, Fax: 250-723-1003
citypa@portalberni.ca
Wendy Thompson, Deputy Secretary
250-720-2706, Fax: 250-723-1327
wendy.thomson@acrd.bc.ca
Sean McGinn, Coordinator, Public Works
250-720-2714
smcginn@acrd.bc.ca
Riley Varns, West Coast Landfill
250-726-7176
Robert A. Harper, Administrator
rharper@acrd.bc.ca
Richard Zoet, Bamfield Water System
250-728-1237
Cyril Johnson, Millstream Water System
250-726-7088
Mike Irg, Manager, Planning & Development
250-720-2710, Fax: 250-723-1327
mirg@acrd.bc.ca

Bulkley-Nechako

P.O. Box 820
37, 3rd Ave.
Burns Lake, BC V0J 1E0
250-692-3195 Fax: 250-692-3305 Toll Free Phone: 1-800-320-3339
inquiries@rdbn.bc.ca
www.rdbn.bc.ca
Municipal Type: Regional Districts
Incorporated: Feb. 1, 1966; *Area:* 73,440.95 sq km
Population in 2006: 38,243
Next Election: Nov. 2011 (3 year terms)
Eileen Benedict, Chair
250-692-3195, Fax: 250-692-3305
Jason Llewellyn, Director, Planning
250-692-3195, Fax: 250-692-3305
jason.llewellyn@rdbn.bc.ca
Janine Dougall, Director, Environmental Services
250-692-3195
janine.dougall@rdbn.bc.ca
Rory McKenzie, Supervisor, Field Operations, Environmental Services
250-692-3195, Fax: 250-692-3305
rory.mckenzie@rdbn.bc.ca
Gail Chapman, CAO
250-692-3195, Fax: 250-692-3305
gail.chapman@rdbn.bc.ca

Capital Regional District

625 Fisgard St.
Victoria, BC V8W 1R7
250-360-3000 Fax: 250-360-3234 Mailing address: PO Box 1000, Victoria, BC V8W 2S6
corporatecommunications@crd.bc.ca
www.crd.bc.ca
Municipal Type: Regional Districts
Incorporated: Feb. 1, 1966; *Area:* 2,341.02 sq km
Population in 2006: 345,164
Provincial Electoral District(s): Juan de Fuca; Southern Gulf Islands; Salt Spring Island.
Next Election: Nov. 2011 (3 year terms)
Note: Member municipalities: Central Saanich; Colwood; Esquimalt; Highlands; Langford; Metchosin; North Saanich; Oak Bay; Saanich; Sidney; Sooke; Victoria; and View Royal.
Geoff Young, Board Chair
250-385-5711
Diana Lokken, General Manager, Corporate Services
250-360-3010
Larissa Hutcheson, General Manager, Environmental Sustainability
250-360-3000
Tracy Corbett, Senior Manager, Regional Planning Services
250-360-3244
Dan Telford, Senior Manager, Environmental Engineering
250-360-3064
Glenn Harris, Senior Manager, Environmental Protection
250-360-3090
Alan Summers, Senior Manager, Environmental Resource Management
250-260-3080
Tom Watkins, Manager, Solid Waste Operations
250-360-3030
Malcolm MacPhail, Senior Manager, Transportation Planning
250-360-3052
Jack Hull, General Manager, Integrated Water Services
250-474-9604
Ted Robbins, Senior Manager, Water Management
250-360-3061
Jan van Niekerk, Senior Manager, Integrated Water Services - Customer & Technical Services
250-474-9655
Tim Tanton, Senior Manager, Infrastructure Engineering
250-474-9611
Gordon Joyce, Senior Manager, Watershed Protection
250-474-9621
John Craveiro, Manager, Environmental Resource Management Policy & Planning
250-360-3164
Chris Neilson, Senior Manager, Human Resources
250-360-3282
Rita Estock, Senior Manager, Financial Services
250-360-3011

Cariboo

180 North 3rd Ave., #D
Williams Lake, BC V2G 2A4
250-392-3351 Fax: 250-392-2812 Toll Free Phone: 1-800-665-1636
mailbox@cariboord.bc.ca
www.cariboord.bc.ca
Municipal Type: Regional Districts
Incorporated: July 9, 1968; *Area:* 80,629.34 sq km
Population in 2006: 58,920
Next Election: Nov. 2011 (3 year terms)
Al Richmond, Chairperson
Janis Bell, CAO
Mitch Minchau, Supervisor, Environmental Services
mminchae@cariboord.bc.ca
Rick Brundrige, Manager, Planning Services
rbrundrige@cariboord.bc.ca
Gordon Gillette, Manager, 108 Greenbelt
ggillette@cariboord.bc.ca
Rowena Bastien, Supervisor, Protective Services
rbastien@cariboord.bc.ca

Central Coast

P.O. Box 186
Bella Coola, BC V0T 1C0
250-799-5291 Fax: 250-799-5750
info@ccrd-bc.ca
www.ccrd-bc.ca
Municipal Type: Regional Districts
Incorporated: July 16, 1968; *Area:* 24,556.35 sq km
Population in 2006: 1,250
Next Election: Nov. 2011 (3 year terms)
Brian Lande, Chair
Joy MacKay, Administrator
cao@ccrd-bc.ca

Central Kootenay

P.O. Box 590
202 Lakeside Dr.
Nelson, BC V1L 5R4
250-352-6665 Fax: 250-352-9300 Toll Free Phone: 1-800-268-7325
info@rdck.bc.ca
www.rdck.bc.ca
Municipal Type: Regional Districts
Incorporated: Nov. 30, 1965; *Area:* 22,130.72 sq km
Population in 2006: 55,883
Next Election: Nov. 2011 (3 year terms)
Gary Wright, Board Chair
office@newdenver.ca
Jim Gustafson, CAO
Grant Roeland, CFO
Marianne Crowe, Manager, Engineering & Environmental Services
wastedept@rdck.bc.ca
Dave Wahn, Sr. Planner

Central Okanagan

1450 KLO Rd.
Kelowna, BC V1W 3Z4
250-763-4918 Fax: 250-763-0606
info@cord.bc.ca
www.cord.bc.ca
Municipal Type: Regional Districts
Incorporated: Aug. 24, 1967; *Area:* 2,904.01 sq km
Population in 2006: 162,276
Next Election: Nov. 2011 (3 year terms)
Robert Hobson, Chair
Robert.Hobson@cord.bc.ca
Harold Reay, Administrator
Bill Vos, Director, Parks & Recreation
250-868-5232
parks@cord.bc.ca
Ken Arcuri, Director, Planning
250-868-5227
planning@cord.bc.ca
Carol Suhan, Coordinator, Waste Reduction
250-469-6259
csuhan@cord.bc.ca
Hilary Hettinga, Director, Engineering Services
250-868-5241
engineer@cord.bc.ca

Columbia-Shuswap

P.O. Box 978
781 Marine Park Dr. NE
Salmon Arm, BC V1E 4P1
250-832-8194 Fax: 250-832-3375 Toll Free Phone: 1-888-248-2773
enquiries@csrd.bc.ca
www.csrd.bc.ca
Municipal Type: Regional Districts
Incorporated: Nov. 30, 1965; *Area:* 29,003.97 sq km
Population in 2006: 50,141
Next Election: Nov. 2011 (3 year terms)
Marty Bootsma, Chair
mbootsma@salmonarm.ca
Charles Hamilton, Administrator
admin@csrd.bc.ca, chamilton@csrd.bc.ca
Doug Dymond, Manager, Works Services
ddymond@csrd.bc.ca
Geoff Power, Manager, Development Services
gpower@csrd.bc.ca
Rhona Martin, Chair, Shuswap Emergency Management Program
semp@csrd.bc.ca
Darcy Mooney, Coordinator, Waste Management
dmooney@csrd.bc.ca
Hamish Kassa, Coordinator, Environmental Services
hkassa@csrd.bc.ca

Comox Valley

600 Comox Rd.
Courtenay, BC V9N 3P6
250-334-6000 Fax: 250-334-4358 Toll Free Phone: 1-800-331-6007
administration@comoxvalleyrd.ca
www.comoxvalleyrd.ca
Municipal Type: Regional Districts
Incorporated: Aug. 19, 1965; *Area:* 20,013.48 sq km
Population in 2006: 101,595
Next Election: Nov. 2011 (3 year terms)
Fred Bates, Chair
fbates@cumberlandbc.net
Debra Oakman, CAO
W. Whyte, Manager, Water Utilities & Services
Graeme Faris, General Manager, Operational Services
operations@rdcs.bc.ca
Ian Smith, General Manager, Community Services
Marci Crossan, Manager, Operational Communications
T. Knight, Manager, Planning Operations
J. Elliott, Manager, Wastewater Operations
R. Boogaards, General Manager, Park Services
parks@rdcs.bc.ca
B. Rees, Manager, Parks

Cowichan Valley

175 Ingram St.
Duncan, BC V9L 1N8
250-746-2500 Fax: 250-746-2513
cvrd@cvrd.bc.ca
www.cvrd.bc.ca
Municipal Type: Regional Districts
Incorporated: Sept. 26, 1967; *Area:* 3,473.12 sq km
Population in 2006: 73,338
Next Election: Nov. 2011 (3 year terms)
Gerry Giles, Chair
chairperson@cvrd.bc.ca
Brian Dennison, Manager, Engineering
Frank Raimondo, Administrator
Bob McDonald, Program Coordinator, Solid Waste Reduction
Tom Anderson, Manager, Development Services
Brian Farquhar, Manager, Parks
Dave Leitch, Manager, Utilities
Warren Jones, CAO
wjones@cvrd.bc.ca

East Kootenay

19 - 24 Ave. South
Cranbrook, BC V1C 3H8
250-489-2791 Fax: 250-489-3498 Toll Free Phone: 1-888-478-7335
rdek@rdek.bc.ca
www.rdek.bc.ca
Municipal Type: Regional Districts
Incorporated: Nov. 30, 1965; *Area:* 27,560.49 sq km
Population in 2006: 54,932
Next Election: Nov. 2011 (3 year terms)
Norman Walter, Chair
norm.walter@gmail.com
Andrew McLeod, Manager, Planning & Development Services
amcleod@rdek.bc.ca
Eric Sharpe, Manager, Environmental Services
esharpe@rdek.bc.ca
Dan McNeill, Manager, Building & Protective Services
dmcneill@rdek.bc.ca
Loree Duczek, Public Education Coordinator, Engineering & Environmental Services
lduczek@rdek.bc.ca
Carol Lind, Coordinator, Emergency Services
clind@rdek.bc.ca
Brian Funke, Superintendent, Utilities
bfunke@rdek.bc.ca
Eric Sharpe, Superintendent, Solid Waste
esharpe@rdek.bc.ca
Lee-Ann Crane, CAO & Manager, Administration
lcrane@rdek.bc.ca

Fraser Valley

#1, 45950 Cheam Ave.
Chilliwack, BC V2P 1N6
604-702-5000 Fax: 604-792-9684 Toll Free Phone: 1-800-528-0061
info@fvrd.bc.ca
www.fvrd.com
Municipal Type: Regional Districts
Incorporated: Dec. 12, 1995; *Area:* 13,361.74 sq km
Population in 2006: 257,031
Next Election: Nov. 2011 (3 year terms)
Patricia Ross, Chair
pross@fvrd.bc.ca

Gerald H. Kingston, CAO
gkingston@fvrd.bc.ca
Gale McMahon, Assistant, Administration
Doug Wilson, Manager, Parks
dwilson@fvrd.bc.ca
Tareq Islam, Director, Engineering
tislam@fvrd.bc.ca
Siri Bertelsen, Planner, Regional Growth
Hugh Sloan, Director, Planning
hsloan@fvrd.bc.ca
Mike Hofer, Coordinator, Environmental Services & Operations
mhofer@fvrd.bc.ca
Lance Lilley, Planner, Watershed
llilley@fvrd.bc.ca
Mike Hofer, Manager, Environmental Services & Operations
mhofer@fvrd.bc.ca

Fraser-Fort George

155 George St.
Prince George, BC V2L 1P8
250-960-4400 Fax: 250-563-7520 Toll Free Phone: 1-800-667-1959
district@rdffg.bc.ca
www.rdffg.bc.ca
Municipal Type: Regional Districts
Incorporated: March 8, 1967; *Area:* 50,705.84 sq km
Population in 2006: 92,063
Next Election: Nov. 2011 (3 year terms)
Art Kaehn, Chair
akaehn@rdffg.bc.ca
Tom Yates, General Manager, Corporate Services
tyates@rdffg.bc.ca
Terry McEachen, General Manager, Development & Community Services
tmceachen@rdffg.bc.ca
Diane Hiscock, General Manager, Financial Services
dhiscock@rdffg.bc.ca
Jim Martin, General Manager, Environmental Services
jmartin@rdffg.bc.ca

Kitimat-Stikine

#300, 4545 Lazelle Ave.
Terrace, BC V8G 4E1
250-615-6100 Fax: 250-635-9222 Toll Free Phone: 1-800-663-3208
info@rdks.bc.ca
www.rdks.bc.ca
Municipal Type: Regional Districts
Incorporated: Sept. 14, 1967; *Area:* 91,917.88 sq km
Population in 2006: 30,307
Next Election: Nov. 2011 (3 year terms)
Harry Nyce, Board Chair
Robert Marcellin, Administrator
Roger Tooms, Manager, Works & Services
250-615-6100
rtooms@rdks.bc.ca
Andrew Webber, Manager, Planning & Economic Development
awebber@rdks.bc.ca
Ted Pellegrino, Planner
tpellegrino@rdks.bc.ca

Kootenay Boundary

#202, 843 Rossland Ave.
Trail, BC V1R 4S8
250-368-9148 Fax: 250-368-3990 Toll Free Phone: 1-800-355-7352 (BC only)
ekumar@rdkb.com
www.rdkb.com
Municipal Type: Regional Districts
Incorporated: Feb. 22, 1966; *Area:* 8,095.63 sq km
Population in 2006: 30,742
Next Election: Nov. 2011 (3 year terms)
Marguerite Rotvold, Chair
250-449-2222
John MacLean, CAO
jmaclean@rdkb.com
Raymond Gaudart, Coordinator, Resource Recovery
zerowaste@rdkb.com
Marten Kruysse, Officer, Economic Development
Mark Andison, Director, Planning

Metro Vancouver

4330 Kingsway
Burnaby, BC V5H 4G8
604-432-6200 Fax: 604-436-6901
icentre@metrovancouver.org
www.metrovancouver.org
Municipal Type: Regional Districts
Incorporated: June 29, 1967; *Area:* 2,877.36 sq km
Population in 2006: 2,109,031
Next Election: Nov. 2011 (3 year terms)
Lois Jackson, Chair
mayor@corp.delta.bc.ca
George Peary, Directors, Ward(s): Abbotsford
Moe Gill, Directors, Ward(s): Abbotsford
Hal Weinberg, Directors, Ward(s): Anmore
Ralph Drew, Directors, Ward(s): Belcarra
Peter Frinton, Directors, Ward(s): Bowen Island
Derek Corrigan, Directors, Ward(s): Burnaby
Sav Dhaliwal, Directors, Ward(s): Burnaby
Colleen Jordan, Directors, Ward(s): Burnaby
Mae Reid, Directors, Ward(s): Coquitlam
Richard Stewart, Directors, Ward(s): Coquitlam
Lois Jackson, Directors, Ward(s): Delta
Maria Harris, Directors, Ward(s): Electoral Area A
Gayle Martin, Directors, Ward(s): Langley City
Rick Green, Directors, Ward(s): Langley Township
Brenda Boughton, Directors, Ward(s): Lions Bay
Judy Dueck, Directors, Ward(s): Maple Ridge
Wayne Wright, Directors, Ward(s): New Westminster
Darrell Mussatto, Directors, Ward(s): North Vancouver City
Richard Walton, Director, Ward(s): North Vancouver District
Don MacLean, Directors, Ward(s): Pitt Meadows
Greg Moore, Directors, Ward(s): Port Coquitlam
Joe Trasolini, Directors, Ward(s): Port Moody
Malcolm Brodie, Directors, Ward(s): Richmond
Harold Steves, Directors, Ward(s): Richmond
Linda Hepner, Directors, Ward(s): Surrey
Marvin Hunt, Directors, Ward(s): Surrey
Judy Villeneuve, Directors, Ward(s): Surrey
Dianne Watts, Directors, Ward(s): Surrey
George Chow, Directors, Ward(s): Vancouver
Heather Deal, Directors, Ward(s): Vancouver
Raymond Louie, Directors, Ward(s): Vancouver
Andrea Reimer, Directors, Ward(s): Vancouver
Gregor Robertson, Directors, Ward(s): Vancouver
Pamela Goldsmith-Jones, Directors, Ward(s): West Vancouver
Catherine Ferguson, Directors, Ward(s): White Rock
Johnny Carline, CAO
Jim Rusnak, CFO
Linda Shore, Manager, Human Resources
Hugh Kellas, Manager, Policy & Planning
Heather Shoemaker, Manager, Corporate Relations
Tracy Husoy, Manager, Purchasing & Risk
Tim Jervis, P.Eng., Manager, Engineering & Construction
Ed Andrusiak, Manager, Regional Parks
Toivo Allas, Manager, Policy & Planning
Malcolm Graham, Manager, Labour Relations
Doug Humphris, P.Eng., Manager, Operations & Maintenance
Delia Laglagaron, Deputy CAO

Mount Waddington

P.O. Box 729
Port McNeill, BC V0N 2R0
250-956-3161 Fax: 250-956-3232
info@rdmw.bc.ca
www.rdmw.bc.ca
Municipal Type: Regional Districts
Incorporated: June 13, 1966; *Area:* 20,288.19 sq km
Population in 2006: 11,651
Next Election: Nov. 2011 (3 year terms)
Al Huddlestan, Chair
Greg Fletcher, Administrator
gfletcher@rdmw.bc.ca
Neil Smith, Manager, Economic Development
Paddy Hinton, Coordinator, Parks
Karl Digby, Supervisor, Salvage
Madeline McDonald, Manager, Local Services
250-956-3301
mmcdonald@rdmw.bc.ca
Joe MacKenzie, Treasurer

Nanaimo

6300 Hammond Bay Rd.
Nanaimo, BC V9T 6N2
250-390-4111 Fax: 250-390-4163 Toll Free Phone: 1-877-607-4111
corpsrv@rdn.bc.ca
www.rdn.bc.ca
Municipal Type: Regional Districts
Incorporated: Aug. 24, 1967; *Area:* 2,034.93 sq km
Population in 2006: 138,631
Next Election: Nov. 2011 (3 year terms)
Joseph Stanhope, Chair
jstanhope@shaw.ca
Carol Mason, CAO
Neil Connelly, General Manager, Community Services
Wayne Moorman, P.Eng., Manager, Engineering Services
Dennis Trudeau, Manager, Transportation & Solid Waste
John Finnie, Manager, Water & Wastewater
250-390-6560, Fax: 250-390-1542
envsrv@rdn.bc.ca
Alan Stanley, Coordinator, Solid Waste Program
John Finnie, General Manager, Environmental Services
250-390-6560, Fax: 250-390-1542
envsrv@rdn.bc.ca
Pam Shaw, Deputy Manager, Community Planning
250-390-6510, Fax: 250-390-7511
planning@rdn.bc.ca
Tom Osborne, General Manager, Parks & Recreation
Mike Donnelly, Manager, Utilities

North Okanagan

9848 Aberdeen Rd.
Coldstream, BC V1B 2K9
250-550-3700 Fax: 250-550-3701
info@nord.ca
www.nord.ca
Municipal Type: Regional Districts
Incorporated: Nov. 9, 1965; *Area:* 7,511.94 sq km
Population in 2006: 77,301
Next Election: Nov. 2011 (3 year terms)
Herman Halvorson, Chair
Greg Betts, Administrator
250-550-3714
greg.betts@rdno.ca
Nicole Kohnert, Manager, Solid Waste
nicole.kohnert@rdno.ca
Al McNiven, Director, Greater Vernon Parks & Recreation District
250-550-3664
Rob Smailes, Manager, Development Services
rob.smailes@rdno.ca
Doug Buchholz, Officer, Protective Services
doug.buchholz@rdno.ca
John Slater, Chair, Okanagan Basin Water Board
Maggie Knox, Manager, Infrastructure Services
maggie.knox@rdno.ca
Steve Noakes, Planner
steve.noakes@rdno.ca
Joseph Kennedy, Coordinator, Solid Waste & Noxious Weeds
joseph.kennedy@rdno.ca
Greg Armour, Field Supervisor, Okanagan Basin Water Board
Nicole Marzinzik, Coordinator, Waste Reduction
nicole.marzinzik@rdno.ca

Northern Rockies

P.O. Box 399
Fort Nelson, BC V0C 1R0
250-774-2541 Fax: 250-774-6794
admin@northernrockies.org
www.northernrockies.org
Municipal Type: Regional Districts
Incorporated: Oct. 31, 1987; *Area:* 85,148.87 sq km
Population in 2006: 6,147
Next Election: Nov. 2011 (3 year terms)
Chris Morey, Chair
mayor@northernrockies.org
Randy McLean, CAO

Okanagan-Similkameen

101 Martin St.
Penticton, BC V2A 5J9
250-492-0237 Fax: 250-492-0063 Toll Free Phone: 1-877-610-3737
info@rdos.bc.ca
www.rdos.bc.ca
Municipal Type: Regional Districts
Incorporated: March 4, 1966; *Area:* 10,412.64 sq km
Population in 2006: 79,475
Next Election: Nov. 2011 (3 year terms)
Dan Ashton, Chair
Bill Newell, CAO
D. Hamilton, Superintendent, Solid Waste Management
Susanne Theurer, Director, Planning & Building Inspection
stheurer@rdos.bc.ca
D. Vaykovich, Coordinator, Special Projects
Andrew Reeder, Manager, Engineering Services

Peace River

P.O. Box 810
1981 Alaska Ave.
Dawson Creek, BC V1G 4H8
250-784-3200 Fax: 250-784-3201
prrd.dc@prrd.bc.ca
www.peaceriverrd.bc.ca
Municipal Type: Regional Districts
Incorporated: Oct. 31, 1987; *Area:* 117,761.07 sq km
Population in 2006: 58,264
Next Election: Nov. 2011 (3 year terms)
Karen Goodings, Chair
Fred Banham, CAO
250-784-3208
George Kunz, Supervisor, Public Works
Jeff Rahn, Manager, Regional Solid Waste Management
Bruce General Manager, Director, Development Services
Shannon Anderson, General Manager, Environmental Services
Paul Solmes, Coordinator, Parks & Recreation

Powell River

5776 Marine Ave.
Powell River, BC V8A 2M4
604-483-3231 Fax: 604-483-2229
administration@powellriverrd.bc.ca
www.powellriverrd.bc.ca
Municipal Type: Regional Districts
Incorporated: Dec. 19, 1967; *Area:* 5,092.05 sq km
Population in 2006: 19,599
Next Election: Nov. 2011 (3 year terms)
Colin Palmer, Chair
Frances Ladret, CAO
Don Turner, Regional Planner
Mike Bolch, Manager, Community & Infrastructure Services

Skeena-Queen Charlotte

100 - 1st Ave. East
Prince Rupert, BC V8J 1A6
250-624-2002 Fax: 250-627-8493 Toll Free Phone: 1-888-301-2002
sqcrd@sqcrd.bc.ca
www.sqcrd.bc.ca
Municipal Type: Regional Districts
Incorporated: Aug. 17, 1967; *Area:* 19,871.85 sq km
Population in 2006: 19,664
Next Election: Nov. 2011 (3 year terms)
Barry Pages, Chair
John Farrell, Interim Administrator
Bob Thompson, Chair, Mainland Solid Waste Advisory Committee
Janet Brown, Chair, Islands Solid Waste Advisory Committee
iswac@islands.net
Tim DesChamp, Operations Supervisor, Regional Recycling
Janet Beil, Director, Planning
jbeil@sqcrd.ca
Thor Collison, Contact, Islands Landfill
Barry Pages, Chair, Skeena-Queen Charlotte Regional District Board of Directors

Squamish-Lillooet

P.O. Box 219
Pemberton, BC V0N 2L0

604-894-6371 Fax: 604-894-6526 Toll Free Phone: 1-800-298-7753
info@slrd.bc.ca
www.slrd.bc.ca
Municipal Type: Regional Districts
Incorporated: Oct. 3, 1968; *Area:* 16,353.66 sq km
Population in 2006: 35,225
Next Election: Nov. 2011 (3 year terms)
Russ Oakley, Chair
Paul Edgington, CAO
pedgington@slrd.bc.ca
Rudy D'Souza, Manager, Utilities & Environmental Services
rdsouza@slrd.bc.ca
Steven Olmstead, Manager, Planning & Development
Wendy Horan, Coordinator, Waste Reduction
zerowaste@slrd.bc.ca

Sunshine Coast
1975 Field Rd.
Sechelt, BC V0N 3A1
604-885-6800 Fax: 604-885-7909
info@scrd.bc.ca
www.scrd.bc.ca
Municipal Type: Regional Districts
Incorporated: Jan. 4, 1967; *Area:* 3,778.08 sq km
Population in 2006: 27,759
Next Election: Nov. 2011 (3 year terms)
Donna Shugar, Chair
John France, CAO
604-885-6800
Paul Fenwick, General Manager, Community Services
Bryan Shoji, General Manager, Infrastructure Services

Thompson-Nicola
#300, 465 Victoria St.
Kamloops, BC V2C 2A9
250-377-8673 Fax: 250-372-5048
admin@tnrd.bc.ca
www.tnrd.bc.ca
Municipal Type: Regional Districts
Incorporated: Nov. 24, 1967; *Area:* 44,475.73 sq km
Population in 2006: 122,286
Next Election: Nov. 2011 (3 year terms)
Peter Milobar, Chair
mayor@kamloops.ca
Greg Toma, CAO
Andy Swetlishoff, Director, Development Services
Don May, P.Eng., Manager, Environmental Health Services
dmay@tnrd.bc.ca

Major Municipalities in British Columbia

Abbotsford
32315 South Fraser Way
Abbotsford, BC V2T 1W7
604-853-2281 Fax: 604-853-1934 Toll Free Phone: 1-866-853-2281
info@abbotsford.ca
www.abbotsford.ca; twitter.com/City_Abbotsford
Municipal Type: City
Incorporated: Jan. 1, 1995; *Area:* 359.36 sq km
County or District: Fraser Valley; *Population in 2006:* 123,864
Provincial Electoral District(s): Abbotsford-Mission; Abbotsford South; Abbotsford West
Federal Electoral District(s): Abbotsford
Next Election: Nov. 2011 (3 year terms)

Council
George Peary, Mayor
Les Barkman, Councillor
Simon Gibson, Councillor
Mohindar (Moe) Gill, Councillor
Lynne Harris, Councillor
Dave Loewen, Councillor
Bill MacGregor, Councillor
Patricia Ross, Councillor
John Smith, Councillor

Administration
Bill Flitton, City Clerk
604-864-5603
bflitton@abbotsford.ca
Judy Lewis, General Manager, Finance & Corporate Services
604-864-5532, Fax: 604-853-1934
jlewis@abbotsford.ca
Jay Teichroeb, General Manager, Economic Development/Development Services
604-864-5525
jteichroeb@abbotsford.ca
Jim Gordon, P.Eng., General Manager, Engineering & Regional Utilities
604-864-5556
jgordon@abbotsford.ca
Mark Taylor, General Manager, Parks, Recreation & Culture
604-859-3134, Fax: 604-853-1934
mtaylor@abbotsford.ca
Don Beer, Fire Chief
604-853-2281
dbeer@abbotsford.ca
Bob Rich, Chief Constable, Abbotsford Police Department
604-864-4724, Fax: 604-864-4809
Karen Sinclair, Manager, Strategic & Community Planning
604-557-4416
ksinclair@abbotsford.ca
Mike Pastro, General Manager, Airport
604-864-5651
mpastro@abbotsford.ca
Frank Pizzuto, City Manager
604-864-5501
fpizzuto@abbotsford.ca

Burnaby
4949 Canada Way
Burnaby, BC V5G 1M2
604-294-7944 Fax: 604-294-7537
postmaster@burnaby.ca
www.city.burnaby.bc.ca
Municipal Type: City
Incorporated: Sept. 22, 1892; *Area:* 89.12 sq km
County or District: Greater Vancouver; *Population in 2006:* 202,799
Provincial Electoral District(s): Burnaby-Edmonds; Burnaby North; Burnaby-Willingdon
Federal Electoral District(s): Burnaby-Douglas; Burnaby-New Westminster
Next Election: Nov. 2011 (3 year terms)

Council
Derek Corrigan, Mayor
Pietro Calendino, Councillor
Richard Chang, Councillor
Sav Dhaliwal, Councillor
Dan Johnston, Councillor
Colleen Jordan, Councillor
Anne Kang, Councillor
Paul McDonell, Councillor
Nick Volkow, Councillor

Administration
Debbie R. Comis, City Clerk
604-294-7290, Fax: 604-294-7537
Rick Earle, Director, Finance
604-294-7360, Fax: 604-294-7544
rick.earle@burnaby.ca
Basil Luksun, Director, Planning & Building
604-294-7432
D. Ellenwood, Director, Parks, Recreation & Cultural Services
604-294-7450, Fax: 604-294-7201
Lambert Chu, Director, Engineering
604-294-7460, Fax: 604-294-7425
Vacant, Deputy Director, Engineering
604-294-7466, Fax: 604-294-7425
Robert H. Moncur, City Manager
604-294-7110, Fax: 604-294-7733
Chad Turpin, Deputy City Manager
604-294-7110, Fax: 604-294-7733
B.R. Rose, City Solicitor
604-294-7382, Fax: 604-294-7985
Patrick Shek, P.Eng, Chief Building Inspector
Bob Cook, Fire Chief
604-294-7195, Fax: 604-294-0490
K. Basi, Coordinator, Emergency Program, Fax: 604-294-7733
Dipak Dattani, Supervisor, Environmental Services
604-294-7771, Fax: 604-294-7425
Robyn Wark, Planner, Ecosystem
604-294-7297, Fax: 604-570-3680
Gisele Caron, Agent, Purchasing, Fax: 604-294-7529

Campbell River
301 St. Ann's Rd.
Campbell River, BC V9W 4C7
250-286-5700 Fax: 250-286-5760
info@campbellriver.ca
www.campbellriver.ca
Municipal Type: City
Incorporated: June 24, 1947; *Area:* 143.48 sq km
County or District: Comox-Strathcona; *Population in 2006:* 29,572
Provincial Electoral District(s): North Island
Federal Electoral District(s): Vancouver Island North
Next Election: Nov. 2011 (3 year terms)

Council
Charlie Cornfield, Mayor
mayor.cornfield@campbellriver.ca

Administration
Tom Stevens, City Manager
tom.stevens@campbellriver.ca
Rob Harley, By-law Enforcement Officer & Manager, Property Services
Larry Samson, Coordinator, Provincial Emergency
Paul Stanton, Manager, Planning Services
Dave Morris, Manager, Materials
William Halstead, GM, Corporate Services
Rob Neufeld, GM, Operations Services
Ross Milnthrop, GM, Parks, Recreation & Culture
Debra Law, Manager, Finance
Ron Neufeld, Manager, Engineering Services
Gordon Brown, Manager, Public Works
Mary Ellen Callaghan, Manager, Information Services
Pat Mulcahy, Manager, Human Resources
Tyler Massee, Manager, Airport
Larry Stright, RCMP Inspector
Rob Owens, Fire Chief

Chilliwack
8550 Young Rd
Chilliwack, BC V2P 8A4
604-792-9311 Fax: 604-795-8443
info@chilliwack.com
www.chilliwack.com
Municipal Type: City
Incorporated: Jan. 1, 1980; *Area:* 260.19 sq km
County or District: Fraser Valley; *Population in 2006:* 69,217
Provincial Electoral District(s): Chilliwack-Kent, Chilliwack-Sumas
Federal Electoral District(s): Chilliwack-Fraser Canyon
Next Election: Nov. 2011 (3 year terms)

Council
Sharon Gaetz, Mayor
Sue Attrill, Councillor
Pat Clark, Councillor
Ken Huttema, Councillor
Diane Janzen, Councillor
Stewart McLean, Councillor
Chuck Stam, Councillor

Administration
Robert Carnegie, Clerk & Director, Corporate Services
604-793-2910
rcarnegie@chilliwack.com
Kathleen Fraser, Director, Finance
604-792-9311, Fax: 604-795-8443
David Blain, Director, Engineering
604-793-2841, Fax: 604-795-8443
Ian Crane, Director, Municipal Development
604-793-2906, Fax: 604-793-8443
Glen MacPherson, Director, Public Works
604-792-9311, Fax: 604-795-8443
Gordon Pederson, Director, Parks, Recreation & Culture
604-792-9311, Fax: 604-795-8443
Peter Monteith, CAO
604-793-2903, Fax: 604-792-2561
pmonteith@chilliwack.com
Rick Ryall, Fire Chief
604-792-9311, Fax: 604-795-8443
Janet Demarcke, Manager, Environmental Services
604-792-9311, Fax: 604-795-8443
Paul Whitehouse, Manager, Purchasing
604-792-9311, Fax: 604-795-8443
whitehouse@chilliwack.com
Keith Robinson, Superintendent, RCMP
604-702-4086, Fax: 604-702-4045
keith.robinson@rcmp-grc.gc.ca
Tara Friesen, Sr. Specialist, Environmental Services
604-792-9311, Fax: 604-795-8443

Colwood
3300 Wishart Rd.
Victoria, BC V9C 1R1
250-478-5541 Fax: 250-478-7516
generalinquiry@colwood.ca
www.colwood.bc.ca
Municipal Type: City
Incorporated: June 24, 1985; *Area:* 17.76 sq km
County or District: Capital; *Population in 2006:* 14,687
Provincial Electoral District(s): Esquimalt-Metchosin
Federal Electoral District(s): Esquimalt-Juan de Fuca
Next Election: Nov. 2011 (3 year terms)

Council
David Saunders, Mayor
mayor@colwood.bc.ca

Administration
Chris Pease, CAO
cpease@colwood.ca
Adia Mavrikos, Director, Finance
amavrikos@colwood.ca
Simon Lawrence, Director, Planning
250-478-5541
slawrence@colwood.bc.ca
Dan Brazier, Manager, Public Works
250-474-4133
dbrazier@colwood.bc.ca
Russ Cameron, Fire Chief
rcameron@colwood.bc.ca

Comox
Town Hall
1809 Beaufort Ave.
Comox, BC V9M 1R9
250-339-2202 Fax: 250-339-7110
town@comox.ca
www.comox.ca
Municipal Type: City
Incorporated: Jan. 14, 1946; *Area:* 15.16 sq km
County or District: Comox-Strathcona; *Population in 2006:* 12,136
Provincial Electoral District(s): Comox Valley
Federal Electoral District(s): Vancouver Island North
Next Election: Nov. 2011 (3 year terms)

Council
Paul Ives, Mayor
town@comox.ca

Administration
Gord Schreiner, Fire Chief
250-339-2432, Fax: 250-339-1988
gschreiner@comox.ca
Allan Fraser, Superintendent, Parks
250-339-2421
afraser@comox.ca

Marvin Kamenz, Municipal Planner
250-339-1118
mkamenz@comox.ca
Glenn Westendorp, Superintendent, Public Works
250-339-2485, Fax: 250-890-0698
gwestendorp@comox.ca
Richard Kanigan, Administrator
rkanigan@comox.ca

Coquitlam

3000 Guildford Way
Coquitlam, BC V3B 7N2
604-927-3000 Fax: 604-927-3015
feedback@coquitlam.ca
www.coquitlam.ca
Municipal Type: City
Incorporated: July 25, 1891; *Area:* 121.69 sq km
County or District: Greater Vancouver; *Population in 2006:* 114,565
Provincial Electoral District(s): Coquitlam-Maillardville
Federal Electoral District(s): New Westminster-Coquitlam; Port Moody-Westwood-Port Coquitlam
Next Election: Nov. 2011 (3 year terms)

Council
Richard Stewart, Mayor
rstewart@coquitlam.ca
Brent Asmundson, Councillor
Fin Donnelly, Councillor
Barrie Lynch, Councillor
Doug Macdonell, Councillor
Mae Reid, Councillor
Linda Reimer, Councillor
Selina Robinson, Councillor
Lou Sekora, Councillor

Administration
Jay Gilbert, City Clerk
jgilbert@coquitlam.ca
Sheena Macleod, Treasurer & Manager, Financial Services
Peter Steblin, City Manager
managersoffice@coquitlam.ca
Lori MacKay, General Manager, Leisure & Parks Services
604-927-3000
leisureandparks@coquitlam.ca
Jim McIntyre, General Manager, Planning & Development
604-927-3000, Fax: 604-927-3405
jmcintyre@coquitlam.ca
Bill Susak, General Manager, Engineering & Public Works
604-927-3000, Fax: 604-927-3015
bsusak@coquitlam.ca
Trevor Wingrove, General Manager, Corporate Services
twingrove@coquitlam.ca
Ron Price, Manager, Human Resources
humanresources@coquitlam.ca
Tony Delmonico, Fire Chief
firerescue@coquitlam.ca
Peter A. Lepine, Superintendent, RCMP Coquitlam Detachment
604-945-1550

Courtenay

830 Cliffe Ave.
Courtenay, BC V9N 2J7
250-334-4441 Fax: 250-334-4241
info@courtenay.ca
www.courtenay.ca
Municipal Type: City
Incorporated: Jan. 1, 1915; *Area:* 26.68 sq km
County or District: Comox-Strathcona; *Population in 2006:* 21,940
Provincial Electoral District(s): Comox Valley
Federal Electoral District(s): Vancouver Island North
Next Election: Nov. 2011 (3 year terms)

Council
Greg Phelps, Mayor
gphelps@courtenay.ca

Administration
Sandy Gray, City Administrator
sgray@courtenay.ca
D. Slobodan, Director, Regulatory & Property Services
Peter Crawford, Director, Planning Services
pcrawford@courtenay.ca
Randy Wiwchar, Director, Community Services
Kevin Lagan, Director, Operational Services
250-703-4860
klagan@courtenay.ca

Cranbrook

40 - 10 Ave. South
Cranbrook, BC V1C 2M8
250-426-4211 Fax: 250-426-4026 Toll Free Phone: 1-800-728-2726
hales@cranbrook.ca
www.cranbrook.ca
Municipal Type: City
Incorporated: Nov. 1, 1905; *Area:* 25.14 sq km
County or District: East Kootenay; *Population in 2006:* 18,267
Provincial Electoral District(s): East Kootenay
Federal Electoral District(s): Kootenay-Columbia
Next Election: Nov. 2011 (3 year terms)

Council
Scott Manjak, Mayor
mayor@cranbrook.ca

Administration
Roy Hales, Director, Corporate Services
hales@cranbrook.ca
Jamie Hodge, City Engineer
Joe McGowan, Director, Public Works
250-489-0240, Fax: 250-489-1828
mcgowan@cranbrook.ca
Wayne Price, Coordinator, Emergency Program
price@cranbrook.ca
Will Pearce, CAO
pearce@cranbrook.ca
Marnie Dueck, Municipal Clerk
dueck@cranbrook.ca
Wayne Staudt, Director, Finance
staudt@crankbook.ca

Dawson Creek

P.O. Box 150
10105 - 12A St.
Dawson Creek, BC V1G 4G4
250-784-3600 Fax: 250-782-3203
admin@dawsoncreek.ca
www.dawsoncreek.ca
Municipal Type: City
Incorporated: May 26, 1936; *Area:* 22.32 sq km
County or District: Peace River; *Population in 2006:* 10,994
Provincial Electoral District(s): Peace River South
Federal Electoral District(s): Prince George-Peace River
Next Election: Nov. 2011 (3 year terms)

Council
Mike Bernier, Mayor

Administration
Jim Chute, CAO
jchute@dawsoncreek.ca
Greg Dobrowolski, Manager, Special Projects
250-784-3619
gdobrowolski@dawsoncreek.ca
Rod Harmon, Manager, Water Resource
250-782-3114
rharmon@dawsoncreek.ca
Gordon (Shorty) Smith, Fire Chief
250-784-3635
shorty@dawsoncreek.ca
Kevin Henderson, Director, Operations
250-784-3622
khenderson@dawsoncreek.ca
Barry Reynard, Director, Parks & Recreation
250-784-3605
breynard@dawsoncreek.ca

Fort St. John

10631 - 100 St.
Fort St John, BC V1J 3Z5
250-787-8150 Fax: 250-787-8181
info@fortstjohn.ca
www.fortstjohn.ca
Municipal Type: City
Incorporated: Dec. 31, 1947; *Area:* 22.74 sq km
County or District: Peace River; *Population in 2006:* 17,402
Provincial Electoral District(s): Peace River North
Federal Electoral District(s): Prince George-Peace River
Next Election: Nov. 2011 (3 year terms)

Council
Bruce Lantz, Mayor

Administration
Janet Prestley, Director, Corporate Administration
jprestley@fortstjohn.ca
Fred Burrows, Fire Chief
250-785-4333, Fax: 250-785-0080
fburrows@fortstjohn.ca
Don Demers, Director, Public Works & Utilities
ddemers@fortstjohn.ca
Sarah Cockerill, Director, Community Services
scockerill@fortstjohn.ca
Horacio Galanti, Director, Engineering Services
hgalanti@fortstjohn.ca
Jeremy Garner, Superintendent, Utilities
jgarner@fortstjohn.ca

Kamloops

City Hall
7 Victoria St. West
Kamloops, BC V2C 1A2
250-828-3311 Fax: 250-828-3578
info@kamloops.ca
www.kamloops.ca
Municipal Type: City
Incorporated: Oct. 17, 1967; *Area:* 297.3 sq km
County or District: Thompson-Nicola; *Population in 2006:* 80,376
Provincial Electoral District(s): Kamloops; Kamloops-North Thompson
Federal Electoral District(s): Kamloops-Thompson-Cariboo
Next Election: Nov. 2011 (3 year terms)

Council
Peter Milobar, Mayor
mayor@kamloops.ca
Nancy Bepple, Councillor
John De Cicco, Councillor
Jim Harker, Councillor
Tina Lange, Councillor
John O'Fee, Councillor
Marg Spina, Councillor
Patricia Wallace, Councillor
Denis Walsh, Councillor

Administration
Len Hrycan, Director, Community & Corporate Affairs
Sally Edwards, Director, Finance & Information Technology
250-828-3413, Fax: 250-828-0845
Solange Belleforte, Manager, Human Resources
David Duckworth, Director, Public Works & Utilities
Byron McCorkell, Director, Parks, Recreation & Culture Services
250-828-3850, Fax: 250-372-7529
David A. Trawin, Director, Development & Engineering Services
250-828-3473
Randy H. Diehl, CAO
250-828-3498
cao@kamloops.ca
Kundan Bubbar, Chief Building Inspector
Neill Moroz, Fire Chief, Fire & Rescue Services
250-372-3311, Fax: 250-372-3578
Maurice J. Gravelle, Manager, Asset Management & Capital Projects
250-828-3463, Fax: 250-828-0952
D.C. Hilton, Manager, Parks
Randy Lambright, Manager, Planning & Development
J.B. McNeely, Manager, Streets & Environmental Services
250-828-3463
Errol Wild, Agent, Purchasing
Mike Warren, Manager, Engineering
Sharon E. Frissell, Chair, Water Treatment Committee

Kelowna

City Hall
1435 Water St.
Kelowna, BC V1Y 1J4
250-469-8500 Fax: 250-862-3399
ask@kelowna.ca
www.kelowna.ca
Municipal Type: City
Incorporated: May 4, 1905; *Area:* 211.69 sq km
County or District: Central Okanagan; *Population in 2006:* 106,707
Provincial Electoral District(s): Kelowna-Mission; Kelowna-Lake Country; Westside-Kelowna
Federal Electoral District(s): Kelowna-Lake Country; Okanagan-Coquihalla
Next Election: Nov. 2011 (3 year terms)

Council
Sharon Shepherd, Mayor
mayorandcouncil@kelowna.ca
Andre F. Blanleil, Councillor
Kevin Craig, Councillor
Robert Douglas Hobson, Councillor
Charlie Hodge, Councillor
Graeme James, Councillor
Angela Reid, Councillor
Michele Rule, Councillor
Luke Stack, Councillor

Administration
Ronald Mattiussi, City Manager
Stephen Fleming, Clerk
250-469-8500
cityclerk@kelowna.ca
John Vos, General Manager, Community Services
Jim Paterson, General Manager, Community Sustainability
Paul Macklem, General Manager, Corporate Sustainability
David Graham, Director, Strategic Initiatives
Joe Creron, Director, Civic Operations
William J. Berry, Director, Design & Construction Services
Ron Dickinson, Director, Development Services
Doug Gilchrist, Director, Real Estate & Building Services
Randy Cleveland, Director, Infrastructure Planning
Shelley Gambacort, Director, Land Use Management
Signe Bagh, Director, Policy & Planning
Ron W. Westlake, Director, Regional Services
Carla Stephens, Director, Community & Media Relations
Charlene Covington, Director, Human Resources
Rob Mayne, Director, Corporate Services
Rene M. Blanleil, Fire Chief

Langford

877 Goldstream Ave., 2nd Fl.
Victoria, BC V9B 2X8
250-478-7882 Fax: 250-391-3437
adminassist@cityoflangford.ca
www.cityoflangford.ca
Municipal Type: City
Incorporated: Dec. 8, 1992; *Area:* 39.55 sq km
County or District: Capital; *Population in 2006:* 22,459
Provincial Electoral District(s): Malahat-Juan de Fuca
Federal Electoral District(s): Esquimalt-Juan de Fuca
Next Election: Nov. 2011 (3 year terms)

Council
Stewart Young, Mayor
council@cityoflangford.ca

Administration
Jim Bowden, Acting Clerk Administrator
jbowden@cityoflangford.ca
Steve Ternent, Treasurer
sternent@cityoflangford.ca
Bob Beckett, Fire Chief
250-478-9555
firechief@cityoflangford.ca

John Manson, City Engineer
engineering@cityoflangford.ca
Matthew Baldwin, City Planner
mbaldwin@cityoflangford.ca
Trevor Auger, Chief Engineering Technologist
tauger@cityoflangford.ca

Langley

20399 Douglas Cres.
Langley, BC V3A 4B3
604-514-2800 Fax: 604-530-4371
council@city.langley.bc.ca
www.city.langley.bc.ca
Municipal Type: City
Incorporated: March 15, 1955; *Area:* 10.22 sq km
County or District: Greater Vancouver; *Population in 2006:* 23,606
Provincial Electoral District(s): Langley
Federal Electoral District(s): Langley
Next Election: Nov. 2011 (3 year terms)

Council
Peter Fassbender, Mayor
mayor@langleycity.ca
Jack Arnold, Councillor
Dave Hall, Councillor
Teri James, Councillor
Gayle Martin, Councillor
Rudy Storteboom, Councillor
Rosemary Wallace, Councillor

Administration
Tracey Arthur, Acting City Clerk
604-514-2803
Darrin W. Leite, Director, Corporate Services
604-514-2806
dleite@langleycity.ca
Gerald Minchuk, Director, Development Services & Economic Development
604-514-2815
gminchuk@langleycity.ca
Gary Vlieg, Director, Engineering, Parks & Environment
gvlieg@langleycity.ca
F. Cheung, CAO
604-514-2805
fcheung@langleycity.ca
Bruce Dundas, Fire Chief
604-514-2881
Kim Hilton, Manager, Recreation, Culture & Community Services
Len Walters, Manager, Park Operations
604-514-2912

Nanaimo

455 Wallace St.
Nanaimo, BC V9R 5J6
250-754-4251 Fax: 250-755-4440
mayor&council@nanaimo.ca
www.nanaimo.ca
Municipal Type: City
Incorporated: Dec. 24, 1874; *Area:* 89.3 sq km
County or District: Nanaimo; *Population in 2006:* 78,692
Provincial Electoral District(s): Nanaimo-Parksville; Nanaimo
Federal Electoral District(s): Nanaimo-Cowichan; Nanaimo-Alberni
Next Election: Nov. 2011 (3 year terms)

Council
John Ruttan, Mayor
250-754-4251
john.ruttan@nanaimo.ca
William Leslie (Bill) Bestwick, Councillor
bill.bestwick@nanaimo.ca
Bill Holdom, Councillor
bill.holdom@nanaimo.ca
Diana Johnstone, Councillor
diana.johnstone@nanaimo.ca
Jim Kipp, Councillor
jim.kipp@nanaimo.ca
Larry McNabb, Councillor
larry.mcnabb@nanaimo.ca
Fred Pattje, Councillor
fred.pattje@nanaimo.ca
Loyd Sherry, Councillor
loyd.sherry@nanaimo.ca
Mervin Wayne (Merv) Unger, Councillor
merv.unger@nanaimo.ca

Administration
Doug Holmes, General Manager, Corporate Services
250-755-4488
Doug.Holmes@nanaimo.ca
Brian Clemens, Director, Finance
250-755-4431
brian.clemens@nanaimo.ca
Richard Harding, Director, Parks, Recreation & Culture
250-755-7516
Richard.Harding@nanaimo.ca
Tom Hickey, Director, Engineering & Public Works
Tom.Hickey@nanaimo.ca
Ian Howat, Director, Legislative Services
506-755-4405
Terry Hartley, Director, Human Resources
250-755-4427
terry.hartley@nanaimo.ca
Andrew Tucker, Director, Planning & Development
250-754-4251
Andrew.Tucker@nanaimo.ca
Gerald (Jerry) Berry, City Manager
250-755-4401
gerry.berry@nanaimo.ca
Ron Lambert, Fire Chief
250-755-7550
Ron.Lambert@nanaimo.ca
Andy Laidlaw, General Manager, Community Services
250-756-5346
andy.laidlaw@nanaimo.ca
Ted Swabey, General Manager, Development Services
250-755-4429
Ted.Swabey@nanaimo.ca
Jim Bowden, Manager, Occupational Health & Rehabilitation
Brian Denbigh, Manager, Roads & Traffic Services
Kurtis Felker, Manager, Purchasing & Stores
250-756-5317
gino.dimenna@nanaimo.ca
John Elliot, Manager, Utilities
Gary Franssen, Manager, Sanitation, Recycling & Cemeteries
Bob Prokopenko, Manager, Engineering Services
Jeff Ritchie, Senior Manager, Parks
Jeff.Ritchie@nanaimo.ca
Graham Savage, Manager, Engineering & Environment Services
Andrew Tucker, Director, Community Planning
250-754-4251
andrew.tucker@nanaimo.ca
Kevin Brydges, Environmental Coordinator
250-755-4460
kevin.brydges@nanaimo.ca
Jim Kipp, Coordinator, Emergency Management
250-753-4572
jim.kipp@nanaimo.ca
Jeff Lott, Superintendent & Officer-in-Charge, Nanaimo RCMP Detachment
250-754-2345
Jeff.Lott@nanaimo.ca
Marilyn Hutchinson, Officer, Economic Development
250-755-4465
Marilyn.Hutchinson@nanaimo.ca
Rob Lawrance, Environmental Planner
250-755-4483
rob.lawrance@nanaimo.ca

New Westminster

511 Royal Ave.
New Westminster, BC V3L 1H9
604-521-3711 Fax: 604-521-3895
postmaster@newwestcity.ca
www.city.new-westminster.bc.ca
Municipal Type: City
Incorporated: July 16, 1860; *Area:* 15.41 sq km
County or District: Greater Vancouver; *Population in 2006:* 58,549
Provincial Electoral District(s): New Westminster
Federal Electoral District(s): Burnaby-New Westminster; New Westminster-Coquitlam
Next Election: Nov. 2011 (3 year terms)

Council
Wayne Wright, Mayor
604-527-4522
wwright@newwestcity.ca
Jonathan Cote, Councillor
jcote@newwestcity.ca
Bill Harper, Councillor
Jamie McEvoy, Councillor
jmcevoy@newwestcity.ca
Betty McIntosh, Councillor
bmcintosh@newwestcity.ca
Bob Osterman, Councillor
bosterman@newwestcity.ca
Lorrie Williams, Councillor
lwilliams@newwestcity.ca

Administration
Rick Page, Director, Legislative Services
rpage@newwestcity.ca
Gary Holowatiuk, Director, Finance & Information Technology
gholowatiuk@newwestcity.ca
Paul Daminato, CAO
pdaminato@newwestcity.ca
Dean Gibson, Director, Parks, Recreation & Culture
dgibson@newwestcity.ca
Jim Lowrie, Director, Engineering Services
jlowrie@newwestcity.ca
Carl Nepstad, Fire Chief, Fire & Rescue Services
cnepstad@newwestcity.ca
Lisa Spitale, Director, Development Services
lspitale@newwestcity.ca
Joan Burgess, Director, Human Resources
jburgess@newwestcity.ca
Lorne Zapotichny, Police Chief, Police Services
lzapotichny@newwestcity.ca
Rod Carle, General Manager, Electric Utility
rcarle@newwestcity.ca
Jon McDonald, Manager, Engineering Operations
604-521-6594
jmcdonald@newwestcity.ca
Roger Emanuels, Coordinator, Transportation & Infrastructure
604-527-4540
Roy Moulder, Manager, Purchasing
604-527-4632
rmoulder@newwestcity.ca
Bob Jack, Supervisor, Waste Management
604-526-4691
bjack@newwestcity.ca
Sheldon Rigby, Supervisor, Sewer & Drainage Branch
604-517-5416
srigby@newwestcity.ca

North Vancouver

141 - 14 St. West
North Vancouver, BC V7M 1H9
604-985-7761 Fax: 604-985-9417
info@cnv.org
www.cnv.org
Municipal Type: City
Incorporated: May 13, 1907; *Area:* 11.85 sq km
County or District: Greater Vancouver; *Population in 2006:* 45,165
Provincial Electoral District(s): N. Vancouver-Lonsdale; N. Vancouver-Seymour; W. Vancouver-Capilano; W. Vancouver-Garibaldi
Federal Electoral District(s): North Vancouver
Next Election: Nov. 2011 (3 year terms)

Council
Darrell R. Mussatto, Mayor
dmussatto@cnv.org

Administration
Sandra Dowey, City Clerk
sdowey@cnv.org
Isabel Gordon, Director, Finance
Barrie Penman, Fire Chief
604-980-5021, Fax: 604-980-8544
bpenman@cnv.org
Steven Ono, City Engineer
sono@cnv.org
Fred A. Smith, Director, Community Development
604-990-4206
Heather Turner, Director, Recreation
604-983-6305, Fax: 604-984-4294
Wolfgang Beier, Manager, Purchasing
604-983-7392
Allen Lynch, Manager, North Shore Recycling Program
604-984-9730, Fax: 604-984-3563
Nikii Hoglund, Manager, Public Works & Operations
604-983-7388
Doug Pope, Manager, Environment & Parks
604-983-7337
Michael Hunter, Environmental Coordinator
604-990-4224
John Guenther, Building Inspector
604-985-7761, Fax: 604-985-0576

Parksville

P.O. Box 1390
100 Jensen Ave. East
Parksville, BC V9P 2H3
250-248-6144 Fax: 250-248-6650
citypark@parksville.ca
www.parksville.ca
Municipal Type: City
Incorporated: June 19, 1945; *Area:* 14.6 sq km
County or District: Nanaimo; *Population in 2006:* 10,993
Provincial Electoral District(s): Nanaimo-Parksville
Federal Electoral District(s): Nanaimo-Alberni
Next Election: Nov. 2011 (3 year terms)

Council
Ed Mayne, Mayor

Administration
Fred Manson, CAO
250-954-4666
fmanson@city.parksville.bc.ca
Doug Banks, Fire Chief
250-954-4671
dbanks@parksville.ca
Gayle Jackson, Director, Community Planning
250-954-4660
gjackson@city.parksville.bc.ca
Mike Squire, Manager, Engineering
250-954-4698
msquire@parksville.ca
Alan Metcalf, Manager, Operations
250-954-4667
ametcalf@parksville.ca
Lynn Kitchen, Deputy Corporate Administrator, Administrative Services
lkitchen@parksville.ca

Penticton

171 Main St.
Penticton, BC V2A 5A9
250-490-2400 Fax: 250-490-2402
ask@penticton.ca
www.penticton.ca
Municipal Type: City
Incorporated: Jan. 1, 1909; *Area:* 42.02 sq km
County or District: Okanagan-Similkameen; *Population in 2006:* 31,909
Provincial Electoral District(s): Penticton-Okanagan Valley
Federal Electoral District(s): Okanagan-Coquihalla
Next Election: Nov. 2011 (3 year terms)

Council
Dan Ashton, Mayor
mayor@penticton.ca

Administration

Cathy Ingram, Manager, Legislative Services
250-490-2412
cathy.ingram@penticton.ca
Michael Ummenhofer, Agent, Purchasing
250-490-2555, Fax: 250-490-2557
purch-agent@city.penticton.bc.ca
Berne Udala, Supervisor, Water Quality
250-490-2550, Fax: 250-490-2552
berne.udala@penticton.ca
Douglas Leahy, Treasurer
John Kirbyson, Director, Parks, Recreation & Culture
250-490-2426, Fax: 250-490-2427
john.kirbyson@penticton.ca
Wayne Williams, Fire Chief
250-492-4209, Fax: 250-490-4288
wayne.williams@penticton.ca
Mitch Moroziuk, Director, Development & Engineering Services
mitch.moroziuk@penticton.ca
Brent Edge, Supervisor, Water
brent.edge@penticton.ca
Carolyn Stewart, Coordinator, Water Conservation Program
carolyn.stewart@penticton.ca

Pitt Meadows

Municipal Hall
12007 Harris Rd.
Pitt Meadows, BC V3Y 2B5
604-465-5454 Fax: 604-465-2404
info@pittmeadows.bc.ca
www.pittmeadows.bc.ca
Municipal Type: City
Incorporated: April 25, 1914; *Area:* 85.38 sq km
County or District: Greater Vancouver; *Population in 2006:* 15,623
Provincial Electoral District(s): Maple Ridge-Pitt Meadows
Federal Electoral District(s): Pitt Meadows-Maple Ridge-Mission
Next Election: Nov. 2011 (3 year terms)
Note: Effective Jan. 1, 2007, Pitt Meadows' designation was changed from a district to a city.

Council
Don MacLean, Mayor
604-465-2416
dmaclean@pittmeadows.bc.ca

Administration
Dean Rear, Director, Corporate Services
604-465-2449
drear@pittmeadows.bc.ca
Jake Rudolph, CAO
604-465-2413
jrudolph@pittmeadows.bc.ca
Don Jolley, Fire Chief, Protective Services
djolley@pittmeadows.bc.ca
Kelly Swift, Director, Recreation
kswift@mapleridge.org
Kim Grout, Director, Operations & Development Services
604-465-2420
kgrout@pittmeadows.bc.ca
Adrian Kopystynski, General Manager, Development Services
604-467-2432
akopystynski@pittmeadows.bc.ca
Y. (Ike) de Boer, Coordinator, Engineering Services
604-465-2425
ideboer@pittmeadows.bc.ca
Randy Evans, Superintendent, Operations
604-465-2435
revans@pittmeadows.bc.ca
Dana Parr, Planner
604-465-2497
dparr@pittmeadows.bc.ca

Port Alberni

4850 Argyle St.
Port Alberni, BC V9Y 1V8
250-723-2146 Fax: 250-723-1003
citypa@portalberni.ca
www.portalberni.ca
Municipal Type: City
Incorporated: Oct. 28, 1967; *Area:* 19.92 sq km
County or District: Alberni-Clayoquot; *Population in 2006:* 17,548
Provincial Electoral District(s): Alberni-Qualicum
Federal Electoral District(s): Nanaimo-Alberni
Next Election: Nov. 2011 (3 year terms)

Council
Ken McRae, Mayor
ken_mcrae@portalberni.ca

Administration
Russell Dyson, City Clerk
russell_dyson@portalberni.ca
Ann Hopkins, Director, Finance
ann_hopkins@portalberni.ca
Guy Cicon, Director/City Engineer, Public Works
guy_cicon@port-alberni.ca
Ken Watson, City Manager
ken_watson@port-alberni.ca
Scott Smith, Planner
scott_smith@port-alberni.ca
Scott Kenny, Director, Parks & Recreation
scott_kenny@portalberni.ca
Brian Mousley, Superintendent, Utilities
brian_mousley@portalberni.ca
Tim Pley, Fire Chief
250-724-1351
tim_pley@portalberni.ca

Port Coquitlam

2580 Shaughnessy St.
Port Coquitlam, BC V3C 2A8
604-927-5411 Fax: 604-927-5360
info@portcoquitlam.ca
www.portcoquitlam.ca
Municipal Type: City
Incorporated: March 7, 1913; *Area:* 28.85 sq km
County or District: Greater Vancouver; *Population in 2006:* 52,687
Provincial Electoral District(s): Port Coquitlam-Burke Mountain
Federal Electoral District(s): Port Moody-Westwood-Port Coquitlam
Next Election: Nov. 2011 (3 year terms)

Council
Greg Moore, Mayor
604-927-5498
mooreg@portcoquitlam.ca
Sherry Carroll, Councillor
Mike Forrest, Councillor
Darrell Penner, Councillor
Glenn Pollock, Councillor
Brad West, Councillor
Michael Wright, Councillor

Administration
Tony Chong, P. Eng., CAO
chongt@portcoquitlam.ca
Susan Rauh, CMC, Corporate Officer
rauhs@portcoquitlam.ca
Jim Maitland, Officer, Finance
maitlandj@portcoquitlam.ca
S. Gamble, Fire Chief
Barry Becker, Director, Parks & Recreation
Laura Lee Richard, Director, Development Services
Mindy Smith, Director, Corporate Services
smithm@portcoquitlam.ca
I. Zahynacz, Director, Engineering & Operations
engineering@portcoquitlam.ca
A. Jensen, Manager, Evironmental Services
Karen Laustrup, Manager, Purchasing
604-927-5430, Fax: 604-927-5408
L. Richard, Manager, Planning
Gordon Voncina, Manager, Operations
Robin Wishart, Manager, Information Services

Port Moody

P.O. Box 36
100 Newport Dr.
Port Moody, BC V3H 3E1
604-469-4500 Fax: 604-469-4550
info@cityofportmoody.com
www.cityofportmoody.com
Municipal Type: City
Incorporated: March 11, 1913; *Area:* 25.62 sq km
County or District: Greater Vancouver; *Population in 2006:* 27,512
Provincial Electoral District(s): Port Moody-Westwood
Federal Electoral District(s): Port Moody-Westwood-Port Coquitlam; New Westminster-Coquitlam
Next Election: Nov. 2011 (3 year terms)

Council
Joe Trasolini, Mayor
604-469-4501
joe.trasolini@cityofportmoody.com

Administration
Colleen Rohde, City Clerk
604-469-4505
colleen.rohde@cityofportmoody.com
Paul Rockwood, Director, Corporate Services
paul.rockwood@cityofportmoody.com
Tim Savoie, Director, Planning & Development Services
604-469-4545
planning@cityofportmoody.com
Gaetan Royer, City Manager
gaetan.royer@cityofportmoody.com
Jeff Lambert, Fire Chief
pmfd.info@cityofportmoody.com
Ron Higo, Director, Community Services
604-469-4542
Bob Parsons, Acting Director, Engineering & Operations

Powell River

6910 Duncan St.
Powell River, BC V8A 1V4
604-485-6291 Fax: 604-485-2913
info@cdpr.bc.ca
www.powellriver.ca
Municipal Type: City
Incorporated: Oct. 15, 1955; *Area:* 29.77 sq km
County or District: Powell River; *Population in 2006:* 12,957
Provincial Electoral District(s): Powell River-Sunshine Coast
Federal Electoral District(s): West Vancouver-Sunshine Coast-Sea to Sky Country
Next Election: Nov. 2011 (3 year terms)

Council
Stewart Alsgard, Mayor

Administration
Stan Westby, CAO
swestby@cdpr.bc.ca
Dave Douglas, Director, Financial Services
ddouglas@cdpr.bc.ca
Richard Stogre, Manager, Engineering Services
Barry Jantz, Director, Public Works
Dan Ouellette, Director, Fire & Emergency Services
Regina Sadilkova, Manager, Development Services
rsadilkova@cdpr.bc.ca
Vacant, City Engineer

Prince George

City Hall
1100 Patricia Blvd.
Prince George, BC V2L 3V9
250-561-7600 Fax: 250-561-0183
cityclerk@city.pg.bc.ca
www.city.pg.bc.ca
Municipal Type: City
Incorporated: March 6, 1915; *Area:* 316 sq km
County or District: Fraser-Fort George; *Population in 2006:* 70,981
Provincial Electoral District(s): Pr. George-Mt. Robson; Pr. George N.; Pr. George-Omineca
Federal Electoral District(s): Prince George-Peace River; Cariboo Prince George
Next Election: Nov. 2011 (3 year terms)

Council
Dan Rogers, Mayor
Don Bassermann, Councillor
Garth Frizzell, Councillor
Shari Green, Councillor
Murry Krause, Councillor
Debora Munoz, Councillor
Brian Skakun, Councillor
Cameron Stolz, Councillor
Dave Wilbur, Councillor

Administration
Walter Babicz, Corporate Officer
250-561-7605
wbabicz@city.pg.bc.ca
Sandra Stibrany, Manager, Financial Services
250-561-7677, Fax: 250-561-7759
Derek Bates, City Manager
250-561-7607, Fax: 250-561-0183
Dave Dyer, Chief Engineer
250-561-7663
ddyer@city.pg.bc.ca
Jeff Rowland, Fire Chief
250-561-7670, Fax: 250-561-7670
Tom Madden, Director, Community Services
250-561-7644, Fax: 250-561-7718
Grant Bain, Director, Development Services
250-561-7616, Fax: 250-561-0183
Kathleen Soltis, Director, Corporate Services
Rob Whitwham, Director, Administrative Services
250-561-7608, Fax: 250-561-0183
Dan Milburn, Manager, Long Range Planning
250-561-7614, Fax: 250-561-7721
Scott Bone, Manager, Supply & Fleet Services
250-561-7511, Fax: 250-612-5603
Frank Blues, Manager, Transportation
250-561-7503
fblues@city.pg.bc.ca
Mark Fercho, Manager, Environment
250-561-7698
Marco Fornari, Manager, Utilities
250-561-7509
mfornari@city.pg.bc.ca
Bill Gaal, Manager, Parks & Solid Waste Services
250-561-7691, Fax: 250-564-5809
Dan Milburn, Manager, Current Planning
250-561-7614, Fax: 250-561-7721
Gina Layte-Liston, Environmental Coordinator
250-614-7824
glayte@city.pg.bc.ca
Ann Bailey, Supervisor, RCMP Support Services
Tom Kadla, Supervisor, Solid Waste
250-561-7575
Tony Pirillo, Supervisor, Utility Plant (Pump Stations)
250-614-7830, Fax: 250-561-7519
Alan Clark, Engineer, Development & Projects
250-561-7617
Glenn Stanker, Engineer, Transportation
250-561-7757
Norm Gobbi, Chief Operator, Wastewater Treatment Plant
250-562-4578
ngobbi@city.pg.bc.ca

Prince Rupert

424 - 3rd Ave. West
Prince Rupert, BC V8J 1L7
250-627-0934 Fax: 250-627-0999
cityhall@princerupert.ca
www.princerupert.ca
Municipal Type: City
Incorporated: March 10, 1910; *Area:* 54.9 sq km
County or District: Skeena-Queen Charlotte; *Population in 2006:* 12,815
Provincial Electoral District(s): North Coast
Federal Electoral District(s): Skeena-Bulkley Valley
Next Election: Nov. 2011 (3 year terms)

Council

Jack Mussallem, Mayor
jmussallem@princerupert.ca

Administration
Gord Howie, City Manager
gord.howie@princerupert.ca
Dan Rodin, Chief Financial Officer
dan.rodin@princerupert.ca
Robert M. Thompson, General Manager, Engineering & Public Works
250-627-0954
bob.thompson@princerupert.ca
Ron Miller, Fire Chief
250-624-5115, Fax: 250-624-3407
ron.miller@princerupert.ca
T.J. Ireland, City Administrator & Planner

Richmond
6911 No. 3 Rd.
Richmond, BC V6Y 2C1
604-276-4000 Fax: 604-278-5139
cityclerk@richmond.ca
www.richmond.ca
Municipal Type: City
Incorporated: Nov. 10, 1879; *Area:* 128.76 sq km
County or District: Greater Vancouver; *Population in 2006:* 174,461
Provincial Electoral District(s): Richmond-Centre; Richmond E.; Richmond-Steveston
Federal Electoral District(s): Richmond; Delta-Richmond East
Next Election: Nov. 2011 (3 year terms)

Council
Malcolm D. Brodie, Mayor
mayorandcouncillors@richmond.ca
Linda Barnes, Councillor
Derek Dang, Councillor
Evelina Halsey-Brandt, Councillor
Sue Halsey-Brandt, Councillor
Greg Halsey-Brandt, Councillor
Ken Johnston, Councillor
Bill McNulty, Councillor
Harold Steves, Councillor

Administration
David Weber, Director, City Clerk's Office
604-276-4007
Andrew Nazareth, General Manager, Business & Finance Services
604-276-4095
finance@richmond.ca
George Duncan, CAO
604-276-4336, Fax: 604-276-4222
administratorsoffice@richmond.ca
Jim Hancock, Fire Chief
604-303-2700
fire@richmond.ca
Ward Clapham, RCMP Officer-in-Charge
604-207-4741
Jerry Chong, Director, Finance
604-276-4064
Allan Cameron, Director, Information Technology
604-276-4096
Robert Gonzalez, P. Eng., General Manager, Engineering & Public Works
604-276-4000
robert.gonzalez@richmond.ca
Mike Pellant, Director, Human Resources
604-276-4092
humanresources@richmond.ca
Dave Semple, Director, Operations
604-244-1206
dave.semple@richmond.ca
Cathryn Carlile, General Manager, Parks, Recreation & Cultural Services
604-276-4068
ccarlile@richmond.ca
Phyllis Carlyle, General Manager, Law & Community Safety
604-276-4104
pcarlyle@richmond.ca
Joe Erceg, General Manager, Planning & Development
604-276-4083
planningdevelopment@richmond.ca
Mike Kirk, General Manager, Corporate Services
604-276-4142
corporateservices@richmond.ca
Suzanne Bycraft, Manager, Fleet & Environmental Programs
604-233-3338
sbycraft@richmond.ca
Terry Crowe, Manager, Policy Planning
604-276-4139
tcrowe@richmond.ca
Margot Daykin, Asst. Manager, Environmental Programs
604-276-4130
mdaykin@richmond.ca

Salmon Arm
P.O. Box 40
500 - 2nd Ave. NE
Salmon Arm, BC V1E 4N2
250-832-6021 Fax: 250-832-5584
cityhall@salmonarm.ca
www.salmonarm.ca
Municipal Type: City
Incorporated: May 15, 1905; *Area:* 155.36 sq km
County or District: Columbia-Shuswap; *Population in 2006:* 16,012
Provincial Electoral District(s): Shuswap
Federal Electoral District(s): Okanagan-Shuswap
Next Election: Nov. 2011 (3 year terms)

Council
Marty Bootsma, Mayor
mbootsma@salmonarm.ca

Administration
Carl Bannister, CAO
cbannistser@salmonarm.ca
Charles Ward, Director, Operations
cward@salmonarm.ca
Brad Shirley, Fire Chief
250-803-4064
bshirley@salmonarm.ca
Dale McTaggart, Municipal Engineer
dmctaggart@salmonarm.ca
Monica Dennis, Treasurer
Corey Paiement, Director, Development Services
cpaiement@salmonarm.ca
John Rosenberg, Manager, Public Works, Utilities & Parks
Monica Dalziel, Director, Corporate Services
mdalziel@salmonarm.ca

Sidney
Municipal Hall
2440 Sidney Ave.
Sidney, BC V8L 1Y7
250-656-1184 Fax: 250-655-4508
townhall@sidney.ca
www.sidney.ca
Municipal Type: City
Incorporated: Sept. 30, 1952; *Area:* 5.04 sq km
County or District: Capital; *Population in 2006:* 11,315
Provincial Electoral District(s): Saanich N. & the Islands
Federal Electoral District(s): Saanich-Gulf Islands
Next Election: Nov. 2011 (3 year terms)
Alison Myerscough, Municipal Planner
250-655-5419
amyerscough@sidney.ca

Council
Larry Cross, Mayor

Administration
Murray Clarke, CAO/Corporate Administrator
250-656-1139
mclarke@sidney.ca
Andrew Hicik, Manager, Finance
ahicik@sidney.ca
Rob Hall, P.Eng., Director, Engineering & Works
250-656-4502
rhall@sidney.ca
Dan Holder, Fire Chief
250-656-2121
dholder@sidney.ca
Randy Humble, Director, Development Services
250-655-5418
rhumble@sidney.ca
Mike van der Linden, Manager, Engineering
mvanderlinden@sidney.ca

Surrey
14245 - 56 Ave.
Surrey, BC V3X 3A2
604-591-4011 Fax: 604-591-8731
www.surrey.ca
Municipal Type: City
Incorporated: Nov. 10, 1879; *Area:* 317.19 sq km
County or District: Greater Vancouver; *Population in 2006:* 394,976
Provincial Electoral District(s): Surrey-Cloverdale; Surrey-Green Timbers; Surrey-Newton; Surrey-Panorama Ridge; Surrey-Tynehead; Surrey-Whalley; Surrey-White Rock
Federal Electoral District(s): Surrey North; South Surrey-White Rock-Cloverdale; Newton-North Delta; Fleetwood-Port Kells
Next Election: Nov. 2011 (3 year terms)

Council
Dianne L. Watts, Mayor
604-591-4126, Fax: 604-591-4481
Robert Bose, Councillor
604-591-4624
Tom Gill, Councillor
604-591-4634
Linda Hepner, Councillor
604-591-4626
Marvin Hunt, Councillor
604-591-4635
Mary Martin, Councillor
604-591-4622
Barinder Rasode, Councillor
604-591-4011
H. Barbara Steele, Councillor
604-591-4623
Judy Villeneuve, Councillor
604-591-4625

Administration
Jane Sowik, City Clerk
604-591-4113, Fax: 604-591-8731
Vivienne Wilke, General Manager, Finance & Technology
604-591-4011, Fax: 604-591-8731
Murray Dinwoodie, City Manager
604-591-4441
Craig MacFarlane, City Solicitor
Len Garis, Fire Chief
604-541-4011
Laurie Cavan, General Manager, Parks, Recreation & Culture
604-598-5765
parksrecculture@surrey.ca
Vincent Lalonde, General Manager, Engineering
604-591-4011, Fax: 604-591-8731
Jean Lamontagne, General Manager, Planning & Development
604-591-4441, Fax: 604-591-2507
Nicola Webb, General Manager, Human Resources
Vincent Lalonde, P. Eng., Manager, Utilities & Transportation
604-591-4146
Violet McGregor, CMA, C.P.P., Manager, Purchasing & Payments
604-591-4011
Gerry McKinnon, Manager, Operations
604-590-4011
Rob Wilson, P. Eng., Manager, Land Development
604-591-4276
Erin Desautels, Coordinator, Environmental Stewardship
604-501-5158

Terrace
3215 Eby St.
Terrace, BC V8G 2X8
250-635-6311 Fax: 250-638-4777
cityhall@terrace.ca
www.city.terrace.bc.ca
Municipal Type: City
Incorporated: Dec. 31, 1927; *Area:* 41.52 sq km
County or District: Kitimat-Stikine; *Population in 2006:* 11,320
Provincial Electoral District(s): Skeena
Federal Electoral District(s): Skeena-Bulkley Valley
Next Election: Nov. 2011 (3 year terms)

Council
David Pernarowski, Mayor
dpernarowski@terrace.ca

Administration
Denise Fisher, Corporate Administrator
250-638-4722
dfisher@terrace.ca
Ron Bowles, Director, Finance
205-638-4725
rbowles@terrace.ca
Ron Poole, CAO
rpoole@terrace.ca
Lisa Teggarty, Deputy Treasurer
rbowles@terrace.ca
Ross Bretherick, Agent, Purchasing
250-615-4036
rbretherick@terrace.ca
David Block, City Planner
250-615-4028
dblock@terrace.ca
Brad North, Contact, Solid Waste Management
250-615-4032
bnorth@terrace.ca
Peter Weeber, Fire Chief
Herb Dusdal, Director, Public Works
250-615-4030
hdusdal@terrace.ca
Marvin Kwiatkowski, Director, Development Services
250-615-4041
mkwiatkowski@terrace.ca
Lyle Marleau, Contact, Environmental Health
250-635-6871
lmarleau@terrace.ca

Vancouver
453 West 12th Ave.
Vancouver, BC V5Y 1V4
604-873-7000 Fax: 604-873-7419 Telephone locally: 311
info@vancouver.ca
www.vancouver.ca
Municipal Type: City
Incorporated: November 15, 2008; *Area:* 114.71 sq km
County or District: Greater Vancouver; *Population in 2006:* 578,041
Provincial Electoral District(s): Vancouver Burrard; Vanc.-Fraserview; Vanc.-Hastings; Vanc.-Kensington; Vanc.-Kingsway; Vanc.-Langara; Vanc.-Mt. Pleasant; Vanc.-Point Grey; Vanc.-Quilchena; Vanc.-Fairview
Federal Electoral District(s): Vancouver Centre; Vancouver East; Vancouver-Kingsway; Vancouver Quadra; Vancouver South
Next Election: Nov. 2011 (3 year terms)

Council
Gregor Robertson, Mayor
604-873-7621, Fax: 604-873-7685
info@vancouver.ca
Suzanne Anton, Councillor
604-873-7248, Fax: 604-873-7750
suzanne.anton@vancouver.ca
David Cadman, Councillor
604-873-7244, Fax: 604-873-7750
david.cadman@vancouver.ca
George Chow, Councillor
604-873-7245, Fax: 604-873-7750
george.chow@vancouver.ca
Heather Deal, Councillor
604-873-7242, Fax: 604-873-7750
heather.deal@vancouver.ca
Kerry Jang, Councillor
604-873-7621, Fax: 604-873-7685
kerry.jang@vancouver.ca

Raymond Louie, Councillor
604-873-7243, Fax: 604-873-7750
raymond.louie@vancouver.ca
Geoff Meggs, Councillor
604-873-7011, Fax: 604-873-7419
geoff.meggs@vancouver.ca
Andrea Reimer, Councillor
604-873-7011, Fax: 604-873-7419
andrea.reimer@vancouver.ca
Tim Stevenson, Councillor
604-873-7247, Fax: 604-873-7750
tim.stevenson@vancouver.ca
Ellen Woodsworth, Councillor
604-873-7245, Fax: 604-873-7750
ellen.woodsworth@vancouver.ca

Administration
Marg Coulson, City Clerk
604-873-7266, Fax: 604-873-7419
marg.coulson@vancouver.ca
Ken Bayne, General Manager, Business Planning & Services
ken.bayne@vancouver.ca
Penny Ballem, City Manager
604-873-7625, Fax: 604-873-7641
penny.ballem@vancouver.ca
Jim Chu, Chief Constable, Vancouver Police Department
604-717-3321, Fax: 604-873-7419
chief@vpd.ca
Garrick Bradshaw, Director, Facilities Design & Management
garrick.bradshaw@vancouver.ca
Sue Harvey, Managing Director, Cultural Services
604-871-6001
sue.harvey@vancouver.ca
Frances J. Connell, Director, Legal Services
604-873-7506, Fax: 604-873-7445
frances.connell@vancouver.ca
Trish Doge, Director, Risk & Emergency Management
604-873-7011, Fax: 604-873-7419
trish.doge@vancouver.ca
Peter Kuran, Acting General Manager, Board of Parks & Recreation
peter.kuran@vancouver.ca
Brent Toderian, Director, Planning Services
604-873-7011, Fax: 604-873-7419
brent.toderian@vancouver.ca
Shari Wallace, Director, Information Technology
shari.wallace@vancouver.ca
Chris Warren, Director, Development Services
604-873-7011, Fax: 604-873-7419
christine.warren@vancouver.ca
David McLellan, General Manager, Community Services
604-276-4083, Fax: 604-276-4222
david.mclellan@vancouver.ca
John McKearney, General Manager & Fire Chief, Vancouver Fire & Rescue Services
604-665-6051, Fax: 604-654-0623
john.mckearney@vancouver.ca
Patrice Impey, Chief Financial Officer & General Manager, Human R
604-873-7011, Fax: 604-873-7419
patrice.impey@vancouver.ca
Tom Timm, P.Eng., General Manager, Engineering Services
604-873-7300, Fax: 604-871-6119
tom.timm@vancouver.ca
Brian Davies, P.Eng., Assistant City Engineer, Solid Waste/Sanitation/Landfill Operations
604-873-7348
brian.davies@vancouver.ca
Sean Pander, Acting Manager, Sustainability Group
604-871-6619
Brian Crowe, P.Eng., Assistant City Engineer, Water & Sewers Utilities
604-873-7313
brian.crowe@vancouver.ca
Neal Carley, P.Eng., Assistant City Engineer, Streets Division
604-873-7360
neal.carley@vancouver.ca
Rowan Birch, P.Eng., Assistant City Engineer, Departmental Services Division
604-873-7280
rowan.birch@vancouver.ca
Chris Underwood, Manager, Solid Waste Management
604-873-7992

Vernon
3400 - 30 St.
Vernon, BC V1T 5E6
250-545-1361 Fax: 250-545-7876
admin@vernon.ca
www.vernon.ca
Municipal Type: City
Incorporated: Dec. 30, 1892; *Area:* 94.2 sq km
County or District: North Okanagan; *Population in 2006:* 35,944
Provincial Electoral District(s): Okanagan-Vernon
Federal Electoral District(s): Okanagan-Shuswap; Vancouver Island North
Next Election: Nov. 2011 (3 year terms)

Council
Wayne Lippert, Mayor

Administration
Patti Bridal, Manager, Corporate Services
James Rice, Manager, Public Works
jrice@vernon.ca
Tony Kopp, Manager, Utilities
250-545-1361
Kevin Bertles, Manager, Finance
Marg Bailey, General Manager, Corporate Services
Kim Flick, Manager, Planning, Development & Engineering Services

Victoria
1 Centennial Sq.
Victoria, BC V8W 1P6
250-385-5711 Fax: 250-361-0348
publicsrv@victoria.ca
www.victoria.ca
Municipal Type: City
Incorporated: Aug. 2, 1862; *Area:* 19.68 sq km
County or District: Capital Regional District; *Population in 2006:* 78,057
Provincial Electoral District(s): Victoria-Beacon Hill; Victoria-Hillside; Oak Bay-Gordon Head. In Greater Victoria: Esquimalt-Metchosin; Saanich South; Saanich North & the Islands; and Malahat-Juan de Fuca
Federal Electoral District(s): Victoria
Next Election: Nov. 2011 (3 year terms)

Council
Dean Fortin, B.A., LL.B., M.Ed., Mayor
250-361-0200
Sonya Chandler, R.N., Councillor
schandler@victoria.ca
Chris Coleman, B.A., M.B.A., LL.B., Councillor
ccoleman@victoria.ca
Lynn Hunter, Councillor
lhunter@victoria.ca
Phillipe Lucas, B.A., Councillor
plucas@victoria.ca
John Luton, B.A., Councillor
jluton@victoria.ca
Pamela Madoff, Councillor
pmadoff@victoria.ca
Charlayne Thornton-Joe, B.A., Councillor
cthornton-joe@victoria.ca
Geoff Young, B.A., Ph.D., Councillor
gyoung@victoria.ca

Administration
Robert Woodland, Director, Legislative & Regulatory Services
250-361-0203
Gail Stephens, City Manager
250-361-0202
Doug Angrove, Fire Chief
250-920-3353
Jamie Graham, Chief Constable
250-995-7217
John Basey, City Solicitor
250-361-0588, Fax: 250-361-0348
Deborah Day, Director, Planning & Development
250-361-0511
Trina Scott, Director, Human Resources
250-361-0229
Peter Sparanese, General Manager, Operations
250-361-0292
Jocelyn Jenkyns, General Manager, Victoria Conference Centre
250-361-1000
Ed Robertson, Assistant Director, Public Works
250-361-0457
Katie Josephson, Director, Communications
250-361-0210
Kate Friars, Director, Parks, Recreation & Community Development
250-361-0355
Scott Clark, Manager, Information Systems
250-361-0265
Glen Oberg, Manager, Supply Management Services
250-361-0271
Kim Fowler, Director, Sustainability
250-361-0290
Don Schaffer, Manager, Legislative Services
250-361-0549
Donald Reichert, Supervisor, Solid Waste & Recycling
250-361-0417, Fax: 250-361-0409

White Rock
15322 Buena Vista Ave.
White Rock, BC V4B 1Y6
604-541-2100 Fax: 604-541-9348
whiterockcouncil@city.whiterock.bc.ca
www.city.whiterock.bc.ca
Municipal Type: City
Incorporated: April 15, 1957; *Area:* 5.16 sq km
County or District: Greater Vancouver; *Population in 2006:* 18,755
Provincial Electoral District(s): Surrey-White Rock
Federal Electoral District(s): South Surrey-White Rock-Cloverdale
Next Election: Nov. 2011 (3 year terms)

Council
Catherine Ferguson, Mayor
cferguson@city.whiterock.bc.ca

Administration
Tracey Arthur, City Clerk
604-541-2212
tarthur@city.whiterock.bc.ca
Sandra Kurylo, Director
Financial Services
Peggy Clark, CAO
Peggy Clark, City Manager
pclark@city.whiterock.bc.ca
Phil Lemire, Fire Chief
604-541-2122
plemire@city.whiterock.bc.ca
David Pollock, Director, Municipal Operations
604-541-2181
dpollock@city.whiterock.bc.ca
Greg Scott, P.Eng., City Engineer
gscott@city.whiterock.bc.ca
Dale T. Kitsul, Manager, Parks
604-541-2181
dkitsul@city.whiterock.bc.ca
Paul Stanton, Director, Development Services
pstanton@city.whiterock.bc.ca

Williams Lake
450 Mart St.
Williams Lake, BC V2G 1N3
250-392-2311 Fax: 250-392-4408
corporateservices@williamslake.ca
www.williamslake.ca
Municipal Type: City
Incorporated: March 15, 1929; *Area:* 33.11 sq km
County or District: Cariboo; *Population in 2006:* 10,744
Provincial Electoral District(s): Cariboo North; Cariboo South
Federal Electoral District(s): Cariboo-Prince George
Next Election: Nov. 2011 (3 year terms)

Council
Kerry Cook, Mayor
mayor@williamslake.ca

Administration
Sue Moxey, Director, Corporate Services
250-392-1774
smoxey@williamslake.ca
Darcy Lazzarin, General Manager, Corporate Services
dlazzarin@williamslake.ca
Alberto De Feo, CAO
250-392-1775
adefeo@williamslake.ca
Randy Isfeld, Director, Protective Services
250-392-1778
risfeld@williamslake.ca
Geoff Goodall, Director, Development Services
250-392-1766
ggoodall@williamslake.ca
Brian Carruthers, General Manager, Community Services
250-392-1763
bcarruthers@williamslake.ca
Kevin Goldfuss, Director, Municipal Services
250-392-1783
kgoldfuss@williamslake.ca
Joe Engelberts, Manager, Water/Sewer Division

Other Municipalities in British Columbia

100 Mile House
P.O. Box 340
385 South Birch Ave.
100 Mile House, BC V0K 2E0
250-395-2434 Fax: 250-395-3625
district@dist100milehouse.bc.ca
www.100milehouse.com
Municipal Type: District
Incorporated: July 27, 1965; *Area:* 51.34 sq km
County or District: Cariboo; *Population in 2006:* 1,885
Provincial Electoral District(s): Cariboo South
Federal Electoral District(s): Kamloops-Thomson-Cariboo
Next Election: Nov. 2011 (3 year terms)
Mitch Campsall, Mayor
250-395-2434, Fax: 250-395-3625
mcampsall@dist100milehouse.bc.ca
Roy Scott, Director/CAO, Corporate Administration
250-395-2434, Fax: 250-395-3625
rscott@dist100milehouse.bc.ca

Alert Bay
P.O. Box 2800
Alert Bay, BC V0N 1A0
250-974-5213 Fax: 250-974-5470
info@alertbay.ca
www.alertbay.ca
Municipal Type: Village
Incorporated: Jan. 14, 1946; *Area:* 1.78 sq km
County or District: Mount Waddington; *Population in 2006:* 556
Provincial Electoral District(s): North Island
Federal Electoral District(s): Vancouver Island North
Next Election: Nov. 2011 (3 year terms)
Michael Berry, Mayor
250-974-5213, Fax: 250-974-5470
mberry@alertbay.ca
Madeline McDonald, CAO
250-974-5213, Fax: 250-974-5470
mmcdonald@alertbay.ca

Anmore
2697 Sunnyside Rd.
Anmore, BC V3H 3C8
604-469-9877 Fax: 604-469-0537
village.hall@anmore.com
www.anmore.com
Municipal Type: Village
Incorporated: Dec. 7, 1987; *Area:* 27.42 sq km

County or District: Greater Vancouver; *Population in 2006:* 1,785
Provincial Electoral District(s): Port Moody-Westwood
Federal Electoral District(s): Port Moody-Westwood-Port Coquitlam
Next Election: Nov. 2011 (3 year terms)
Hal Weinberg, Mayor
604-469-9877, Fax: 604-469-0537
hal_weinberg@sfu.ca
Howard Carley, Administrator
604-469-9877, Fax: 604-469-0537
howard.carley@anmore.com

Armstrong
P.O. Box 40
Armstrong, BC V0E 1B0
250-546-3023 Fax: 250-546-3710
info@cityofarmstrong.bc.ca
www.cityofarmstrong.bc.ca
Municipal Type: Town
Incorporated: March 31, 1913; *Area:* 5.24 sq km
County or District: North Okanagan; *Population in 2006:* 4,241
Provincial Electoral District(s): Shuswap
Federal Electoral District(s): Okanagan-Shuswap
Next Election: Nov. 2011 (3 year terms)
Chris Pieper, Mayor
mayor@cityofarmstrong.bc.ca
Patti Ferguson, CAO
pferguson@cityofarmstrong.bc.ca

Ashcroft
P.O. Box 129
Ashcroft, BC V0K 1A0
250-453-9161 Fax: 250-453-9664
admin@village.ashcroft.bc.ca
www.village.ashcroft.bc.ca
Municipal Type: Village
Incorporated: June 27, 1952; *Area:* 51.45 sq km
County or District: Thompson-Nicola; *Population in 2006:* 1,664
Provincial Electoral District(s): Cariboo South
Federal Electoral District(s): Chilliwack-Fraser Canyon
Next Election: Nov. 2011 (3 year terms)
Andy Anderson, Mayor
250-453-9161, Fax: 250-453-9664
Michelle Allen, CAO
250-453-9161, Fax: 250-453-9664
admin@village.ashcroft.bc.ca

Belcarra
4084 Bedwell Bay Rd.
Belcarra, BC V3H 4P8
604-937-4100 Fax: 604-939-5034
belcarra@belcarra.ca
www.belcarra.ca
Municipal Type: Village
Incorporated: Aug. 22, 1979; *Area:* 5.46 sq km
County or District: Greater Vancouver; *Population in 2006:* 676
Provincial Electoral District(s): Port Moody-Westwood
Federal Electoral District(s): Port Moody-Westwood-Port Coquitlam
Next Election: Nov. 2011 (3 year terms)
Ralph E. Drew, Mayor
604-937-4100, Fax: 604-939-5034
rdrew@belcarra.ca
Lynda Floyd, Administrator
604-937-4101, Fax: 604-939-5034
lfloyd@belcarra.ca

Bowen Island
981 Artisan Lane
Bowen Island, BC V0N 1G0
604-947-4255 Fax: 604-947-0193
bim@bimbc.ca
www.bimbc.ca
Municipal Type: Island Municipality
Incorporated: Dec. 4, 1999; *Area:* 49.94 sq km
County or District: Greater Vancouver; *Population in 2006:* 3,362
Provincial Electoral District(s): West Vancouver-Garibaldi
Federal Electoral District(s): West Vancouver-Sunshine Coast-Sea to Sky Country
Next Election: Nov. 2011 (3 year terms)
Bob Turner, Mayor
604-947-4255, Fax: 604-947-0193
Hendrik Slegtenhorst, CAO
caod@bimbc.ca

Burns Lake
P.O. Box 570
Burns Lake, BC V0J 1E0
250-692-7587 Fax: 250-692-3059
village@burnslake.org
www.burnslake.org
Municipal Type: Village
Incorporated: Dec. 6, 1923; *Area:* 7.17 sq km
County or District: Bulkley-Nechako; *Population in 2006:* 2,107
Provincial Electoral District(s): Bulkley Valley-Stikine
Federal Electoral District(s): Skeena-Buckley Valley
Next Election: Nov. 2011 (3 year terms)
Bernice Magee, Mayor
250-692-7587, Fax: 250-692-3059
Tim Palmer, CAO
250-692-7587, Fax: 250-692-3059
tpalmer@burnslake.ca

Cache Creek
P.O. Box 7
Cache Creek, BC V0K 1H0
250-457-6237 Fax: 250-457-9192
admin@cachecreek.info
www.cachecreekvillage.com
Municipal Type: Village
Incorporated: Nov. 28, 1967; *Area:* 10.57 sq km
County or District: Thompson-Nicola; *Population in 2006:* 1,037
Provincial Electoral District(s): Cariboo South
Federal Electoral District(s): Chilliwack-Fraser Canyon
Next Election: Nov. 2011 (3 year terms)
P.A. John Ranta, Mayor
250-457-6237, Fax: 250-457-9192
Tom Kadla, CAO
250-457-6237, Fax: 250-457-9192

Canal Flats
P.O. Box 159
Canal Flats, BC V0B 1B0
250-349-5462 Fax: 250-349-5460
village@canalflats.ca
www.canalflats.com
Municipal Type: Village
Incorporated: June 29, 2004; *Area:* 10.84 sq km
County or District: East Kootenay; *Population in 2006:* 700
Provincial Electoral District(s): Columbia River-Revelstoke
Federal Electoral District(s): Kootenay-Columbia
Next Election: Nov. 2011 (3 year terms)
Bruce Woodbury, Mayor
250-349-5462, Fax: 250-349-5460
Ruth Copeland, Chief Administrative Officer
250-349-5462, Fax: 250-349-5460

Castlegar
460 Columbia Ave.
Castlegar, BC V1N 1G7
250-365-7227 Fax: 250-365-4810
castlegar@castlegar.ca
www.castlegar.ca
Municipal Type: Town
Incorporated: Jan. 1, 1974; *Area:* 19.8 sq km
County or District: Central Kootenay; *Population in 2006:* 7,259
Provincial Electoral District(s): West Kootenay-Boundary
Federal Electoral District(s): British Columbia Southern Interior
Next Election: Nov. 2011 (3 year terms)
Lawrence Chernoff, Mayor
mayor@castlegar.ca
John Malcolm, CAO
jmalcolm@castlegar.ca

Central Saanich
1903 Mt. Newton Cross Rd.
Saanichton, BC V8M 2A9
250-652-4444 Fax: 250-652-0135
municipalhall@csaanich.ca
www.centralsaanich.ca
Municipal Type: District
Incorporated: Dec. 12, 1950; *Area:* 41.42 sq km
County or District: Capital; *Population in 2006:* 15,745
Provincial Electoral District(s): Saanich North & the Islands
Federal Electoral District(s): Saanich-Gulf Islands
Next Election: Nov. 2011 (3 year terms)
Jack Mar, Mayor
jack.mar@csaanich.ca
Sara C. Ribeiro, Corp. Administrator
sara.ribeiro@csaanich.ca
Nirmal Bhattacharya, P.Eng., Municipal Engineer, Public Works & Operationss
250-652-4444
nirmal@saanich.ca
Roy Thomassen, Chief Building Inspector
Ron French, Fire Chief
250-544-4227
ron.french@csaanich.ca
Hope V. Burns, Director, Planning & Building Services
hope.burns@csaanich.ca
Gary C. Nason, Administrator
gary.nason@csaanich.ca

Chase
P.O. Box 440
826 Okanagan Ave.
Chase, BC V0E 1M0
250-679-3238 Fax: 250-679-3070
chase@chasebc.ca
www.chasebc.ca
Municipal Type: Village
Incorporated: April 22, 1969; *Area:* 3.75 sq km
County or District: Thompson-Nicola; *Population in 2006:* 2,409
Provincial Electoral District(s): Kamloops-North Thompson
Federal Electoral District(s): Okanagan-Shuswap
Next Election: Nov. 2011 (3 year terms)
Harry Danyluk, Mayor
Martin Dalsin, CAO
mdalsin@chasebc.ca

Chetwynd
P.O. Box 357
Chetwynd, BC V0C 1J0
250-401-4100 Fax: 250-401-4101
d-chet@gochetwynd.com
www.gochetwynd.com
Municipal Type: District
Incorporated: Sept. 25, 1962; *Area:* 64.32 sq km
County or District: Peace River; *Population in 2006:* 2,633
Provincial Electoral District(s): Peace River South
Federal Electoral District(s): Prince George-Peace River
Next Election: Nov. 2011 (3 year terms)
Jannene Disher, Director, Corporate Administration
jdisher@gochetwynd.com
Evan Saugstad, Mayor

Clinton
P.O. Box 309
Clinton, BC V0K 1K0
250-459-2261 Fax: 250-459-2227
admin@village.clinton.bc.ca
www.village.clinton.bc.ca
Municipal Type: Village
Incorporated: July 16, 1963; *Area:* 4.36 sq km
County or District: Thompson-Nicola; *Population in 2006:* 578
Provincial Electoral District(s): Cariboo South
Federal Electoral District(s): Kamloops-Thompson-Cariboo
Next Election: Nov. 2011 (3 year terms)
Roland Stanke, Mayor
Valerie Bissat, Administrator
vbissat@village.clinton.bc.ca

Coldstream
9901 Kalamalka Rd.
Coldstream, BC V1B 1L6
250-545-5304 Fax: 250-545-4733
info@districtofcoldstream.ca
www.districtofcoldstream.ca
Municipal Type: District
Incorporated: Dec. 21, 1906; *Area:* 67.25 sq km
County or District: North Okanagan; *Population in 2006:* 9,471
Provincial Electoral District(s): Okanagan-Vernon
Federal Electoral District(s): Okanagan-Shuswap
Next Election: Nov. 2011 (3 year terms)
Jim Garlick, Mayor
mayor@district.coldstream.bc.ca
Michael Stamhuis, CAO

Creston
P.O. Box 1339
Creston, BC V0B 1G0
250-428-2214 Fax: 250-428-9164
info@creston.ca
www.creston.ca
Municipal Type: Town
Incorporated: May 14, 1924; *Area:* 8.48 sq km
County or District: Central Kootenay; *Population in 2006:* 4,826
Provincial Electoral District(s): Nelson-Creston
Federal Electoral District(s): Kootenay-Columbia
Next Election: Nov. 2011 (3 year terms)
Ron Toyota, Mayor
ron.toyota@creston.ca
James Thackray, Town Manager

Cumberland
P.O. Box 340
Cumberland, BC V0R 1S0
250-336-2291 Fax: 250-336-2321
www.cumberlandbc.net
Municipal Type: Village
Incorporated: Jan. 1, 1898; *Area:* 29.13 sq km
County or District: Comox-Strathcona; *Population in 2006:* 2,762
Provincial Electoral District(s): Comox Valley
Federal Electoral District(s): Vancouver Island North
Next Election: Nov. 2011 (3 year terms)
Fred Bates, Mayor
fbates@cumberlandbc.net
Anja Nurvo, CAO
anurvo@cumberlandbc.net

Delta
4500 Clarence Taylor Cres.
Delta, BC V4K 3E2
604-946-4141 Fax: 604-946-3390
clerks@corp.delta.bc.ca
www.corp.delta.bc.ca
Municipal Type: District
Incorporated: Nov. 10, 1879; *Area:* 183.7 sq km
County or District: Greater Vancouver; *Population in 2006:* 96,723
Provincial Electoral District(s): Delta North; Delta South
Federal Electoral District(s): Delta-Richmond East; Newton-North Delta
Next Election: Nov. 2011 (3 year terms)
Lois E. Jackson, Mayor
604-946-3210, Fax: 604-946-6055
mayor@corp.delta.bc.ca
Robert Campbell, Councillor
604-948-0623
rpc@telus.net
Scott Hamilton, Councillor
604-599-9261
shamilton@corp.delta.bc.ca
George Hawksworth, Councillor
604-946-4740
ghawksworth@corp.delta.bc.ca
Heather King, Councillor
604-946-4141
Bruce McDonald, Councillor
604-946-4141
Anne Peterson, Councillor
604-946-4141
Karl Preuss, Director, Finance
604-946-3230, Fax: 604-946-3962
kpreuss@corp.delta.bc.ca

Ken Kuntz, Director, Parks, Recreation & Culture
604-952-3537, Fax: 604-946-4693
kkuntz@corp.delta.bc.ca
Sean McGill, Director, Human Resources & Corporate Planning
604-946-3218, Fax: 604-946-3706
smcgill@corp.delta.bc.ca
Thomas Leathem, Director, Community Planning & Development
604-946-3380
tleathem@corp.delta.bc.ca
Dan Copeland, Fire Chief
604-952-3119
dcopeland@corp.delta.bc.ca
Jim Cessford, Chief Constable
604-946-3729, Fax: 604-946-3729
deltapolice@police.delta.bc.ca
George Harvie, CAO
604-946-3212, Fax: 604-946-3864
cao@corp.delta.bc.ca
Greg Vanstone, Municipal Solicitor
604-946-3213, Fax: 604-952-3801
gvanstone@corp.delta.bc.ca
Hugh Fraser, Deputy Director, Engineering
Ian Radnidge, Director, Engineering
604-946-3279, Fax: 604-946-2659
iradnidge@corp.delta.bc.ca
Verna Kucy, Manager, Environmental Services
604-946-3281, Fax: 604-946-3240
vkucy@corp.delta.bc.ca
Don Claybo, Manager, Purchasing
604-952-3640, Fax: 604-946-5796
dclybo@corp.delta.bc.ca
Wally Semenoff, Manager, Development
604-946-3384, Fax: 604-946-4148
wsemenoff@corp.delta.bc.ca
Marcy Sangret, Planning Manager, Environment & Agriculture
604-946-3219, Fax: 604-946-4148
msangret@corp.delta.bc.ca
Claudia Jesson, Acting Municipal Clerk
604-946-4141, Fax: 604-946-3390
cjesson@corp.delta.bc.ca

Duncan
P.O. Box 820
Duncan, BC V9L 3Y2
250-746-6126 Fax: 250-746-6129
duncan@duncan.ca
www.duncan.ca
Municipal Type: Town
Incorporated: March 4, 1912; *Area:* 2.05 sq km
County or District: Cowichan Valley; *Population in 2006:* 4,986
Provincial Electoral District(s): Cowichan-Ladysmith
Federal Electoral District(s): Nanaimo-Cowichan
Next Election: Nov. 2011 (3 year terms)
Phil Kent, Mayor
mayor@duncan.ca
Tom Ireland, CAO
tireland@duncan.ca
Peter de Verteuil, Director, Finance
peter@duncan.ca

Elkford
P.O. Box 340
Elkford, BC V0B 1H0
250-865-4000 Fax: 250-865-4001
info@elkford.ca
www.elkford.ca
Municipal Type: District
Incorporated: July 16, 1971; *Area:* 101.59 sq km
County or District: East Kootenay; *Population in 2006:* 2,463
Provincial Electoral District(s): East Kootenay
Federal Electoral District(s): Kootenay-Columbia
Next Election: Nov. 2011 (3 year terms)
Dean McKerracher, Mayor
mayor@elkford.ca
Corien L. Speaker, CAO
cspeaker@elkford.ca

Enderby
P.O. Box 400
Enderby, BC V0E 1V0
250-838-7230 Fax: 250-838-6007
enderbycity@sunwave.net
www.enderby.com
Municipal Type: Village
Incorporated: March 1, 1905; *Area:* 4.23 sq km
County or District: North Okanagan; *Population in 2006:* 2,828
Provincial Electoral District(s): Shuswap
Federal Electoral District(s): Okanagan-Shuswap
Next Election: Nov. 2011 (3 year terms)
Dee Wejr, Mayor
enderbycity@sunwave.net
Barry Gagnon, Administrator
bgagnon@sunwave.net

Esquimalt
1229 Esquimalt Rd.
Victoria, BC V9A 3P1
250-414-7100 Fax: 250-414-7111
info@esquimalt.ca
www.esquimalt.ca
Municipal Type: Township
Incorporated: Sept. 1, 1912; *Area:* 7.04 sq km
County or District: Capital; *Population in 2006:* 16,840
Provincial Electoral District(s): Esquimalt-Metchosin
Federal Electoral District(s): Esquimalt-Juan de Fuca
Next Election: Nov. 2011 (3 year terms)
Barbara Desjardins, Mayor
barb.desjardins@esquimalt.ca
Carolynne Evans, Municipal Clerk
Andy Katschor, Acting Director, Parks & Recreation
akatschor@esquimalt.ca
Barbara Snyder, Director, Development Services
barbara.snyder@esquimalt.ca
Paul Nelson, Fire Chief
250-414-7126, Fax: 250-414-7115
Trevor Parkes, Senior Planner, Development Services
Gilbert Cote, Director, Engineering & Public Works
gcote@esquimalt.ca
Vacant, Superintendent, Public Works
Andy Katschor, Manager, Parks
Paul Nelson, Coordinator, Emergency Program
250-414-7125
Laurie Hurst, Acting CAO
lhurst@esquimalt.ca

Fernie
P.O. Box 190
Fernie, BC V0B 1M0
250-423-6817 Fax: 250-423-3034
cityhall@fernie.ca
www.fernie.ca
Municipal Type: Town
Incorporated: July 28, 1904; *Area:* 16.05 sq km
County or District: East Kootenay; *Population in 2006:* 4,217
Provincial Electoral District(s): East Kootenay
Federal Electoral District(s): Kootenay-Columbia
Next Election: Nov. 2011 (3 year terms)
Cindy Corrigan, Mayor
cindy.corrigan@fernie.ca
Allan Chabot, CAO
250-423-2225
allan.chabot@fernie.ca

Fort Nelson
P.O. Box 399
Fort Nelson, BC V0C 1R0
250-774-2541 Fax: 250-774-6794
admin@northernrockies.org
www.northernrockies.org
Municipal Type: Town
Incorporated: Oct. 31, 1987; *Area:* 13.26 sq km
County or District: Northern Rockies; *Population in 2006:* 4,514
Provincial Electoral District(s): Peace River North
Federal Electoral District(s): Prince George-Peace River
Next Election: Nov. 2011 (3 year terms)
Bill Streeper, Mayor
mayor@northernrockies.org
Randy McLean, CAO
rmclean@northernrockies.org

Fort St. James
P.O. Box 640
477 Stuart Dr. West
Fort St James, BC V0J 1P0
250-996-8233 Fax: 250-996-2248
district@fortstjames.ca
www.fortstjames.ca
Municipal Type: District
Incorporated: Dec. 19, 1952; *Area:* 22.1 sq km
County or District: Bulkley-Nechako; *Population in 2006:* 1,355
Provincial Electoral District(s): Prince George-Omineca
Federal Electoral District(s): Skeena-Buckley Valley
Next Election: Nov. 2011 (3 year terms)
Sandra Harwood, Mayor
Nigel Black, CAO
cao@fortstjames.ca

Fraser Lake
P.O. Box 430
Fraser Lake, BC V0J 1S0
250-699-6257 Fax: 250-699-6469
village@fraserlake.ca
www.fraserlake.ca
Municipal Type: Village
Incorporated: Sept. 27, 1966; *Area:* 3.9 sq km
County or District: Bulkley-Nechako; *Population in 2006:* 1,113
Provincial Electoral District(s): Prince George-Omineca
Federal Electoral District(s): Skeena-Bulkley Valley
Next Election: Nov. 2011 (3 year terms)
Dwayne Lindstrom, Mayor
Donna Ward, Clerk-Treas.

Fruitvale
P.O. Box 370
Fruitvale, BC V0G 1L0
250-367-7551 Fax: 250-367-9267
karen@village.fruitvale.bc.ca
www.village.fruitvale.bc.ca
Municipal Type: Village
Incorporated: Nov. 4, 1952; *Area:* 36.86 sq km
County or District: Kootenay Boundary; *Population in 2006:* 1,952
Provincial Electoral District(s): West Kootenay-Boundary
Federal Electoral District(s): British Columbia Southern Interior
Next Election: Nov. 2011 (3 year terms)
Libby Nelson, Mayor
libbynelson@netidea.com
Lila Cresswell, Administrator
lila@village.fruitvale.bc.ca

Gibsons
P.O. Box 340
Gibsons, BC V0N 1V0
604-886-2274 Fax: 604-886-9735
info@gibsons.ca
www.gibsons.ca
Municipal Type: Town
Incorporated: March 4, 1929; *Area:* 4.33 sq km
County or District: Sunshine Coast; *Population in 2006:* 4,182
Provincial Electoral District(s): Powell River-Sunshine Coast
Federal Electoral District(s): West Vancouver-Sunshine Coast-Sea to Sky Country
Next Election: Nov. 2011 (3 year terms)
Barry Janyk, Mayor
bjanyk@gibsons.ca
Paul Gipps, CAO
pgipps@gibsons.ca

Gold River
P.O. Box 610
Gold River, BC V0P 1G0
250-283-2202 Fax: 250-283-7500
villageofgoldriver@cablerocket.com
www.goldriver.ca
Municipal Type: Village
Incorporated: Aug. 26, 1965; *Area:* 10.51 sq km
County or District: Comox-Strathcona; *Population in 2006:* 1,362
Provincial Electoral District(s): North Island
Federal Electoral District(s): Vancouver Island North
Next Election: Nov. 2011 (3 year terms)
Craig Anderson, Mayor
250-283-2202
villageofgoldriver@cablerocket.com
Larry Plourde, CAO
grlplourde@cablerocket.com

Golden
P.O. Box 350
Golden, BC V0A 1H0
250-344-2271 Fax: 250-344-6577
enquiries@town.golden.bc.ca
www.town.golden.bc.ca
Municipal Type: Town
Incorporated: June 26, 1957; *Area:* 11.02 sq km
County or District: Columbia-Shuswap; *Population in 2006:* 3,811
Provincial Electoral District(s): Columbia River-Revelstoke
Federal Electoral District(s): Kootenay-Columbia
Next Election: Nov. 2011 (3 year terms)
Magnus Magnusson, Mayor
mmagnusson@town.golden.bc.ca
Jamie Fitzgerald, Councillor
Chris Hambruch, Councillor
Jita Jaswal, Councillor
Magnus Magnusson, Councillor
Caleb Moss, Councillor
Mike Pecora, Councillor
Phil Taylor, CAO
cao@town.golden.bc.ca
Murray Martindale, CFO
treasurer@town.golden.bc.ca
Vacant, Manager, Operations
ops@town.golden.bc.ca
Cleo Corbett, Manager/Planner, Development Services
Shawn Tomash, Fire Chief
Jon Wilsgard, Manager, Corporate Administration
clerk@town.golden.bc.ca

Grand Forks
P.O. Box 220
Grand Forks, BC V0H 1H0
250-442-8266 Fax: 250-442-8000
info@city.grandforks.bc.ca
www.city.grandforks.bc.ca
Municipal Type: Town
Incorporated: April 15, 1897; *Area:* 10.44 sq km
County or District: Kootenay Boundary; *Population in 2006:* 4,036
Provincial Electoral District(s): West Kootenay-Boundary
Federal Electoral District(s): British Columbia Southern Interior
Next Election: Nov. 2011 (3 year terms)
Brian Taylor, Mayor
Lynne Burch, City Clerk
lburch@grandforks.ca
Cecile Arnott, CFO
carnott@grandforks.ca

Granisle
P.O. Box 128
Granisle, BC V0J 1W0
250-697-2248 Fax: 250-697-2306
garchambault@villageofgranisle.ca
www.villageofgranisle.ca
Municipal Type: Village
Incorporated: June 29, 1971; *Area:* 40.21 sq km
County or District: Bulkley-Nechako; *Population in 2006:* 364
Provincial Electoral District(s): Bulkley Valley-Stikine
Federal Electoral District(s): Skeena-Buckley Valley
Next Election: Nov. 2011 (3 year terms)
Frederick J. Clarke, Mayor
Gilles Archambault, CAO

Greenwood
P.O. Box 129
202 Government Ave.
Greenwood, BC V0H 1J0

250-445-6644 Fax: 250-445-6441
info@greenwoodcity.com
www.greenwoodcity.com
Municipal Type: Village
Incorporated: July 12, 1897; *Area:* 2.52 sq km
County or District: Kootenay Boundary; *Population in 2006:* 625
Provincial Electoral District(s): West Kootenay-Boundary
Federal Electoral District(s): British Columbia Southern Interior
Next Election: Nov. 2011 (3 year terms)
Colleen Lang, Mayor
Gerald A. Henke, Administrator
admin.greenwoodcity@shaw.ca

Harrison Hot Springs

P.O. Box 160
Harrison Hot Springs, BC V0M 1K0
604-796-2171 Fax: 604-796-2192
info@harrisonhotsprings.ca
www.harrisonhotsprings.ca
Municipal Type: Village
Incorporated: May 27, 1949; *Area:* 5.47 sq km
County or District: Fraser Valley; *Population in 2006:* 1,573
Provincial Electoral District(s): Chilliwack-Kent
Federal Electoral District(s): Chilliwack-Fraser Canyon
Next Election: Nov. 2011 (3 year terms)
Ken Becotte, Mayor
Larry Burk, CAO
lburk@harrisonhotsprings.ca

Hazelton

P.O. Box 40
Hazelton, BC V0J 1Y0
250-842-5991 Fax: 250-842-5152
info@village.hazelton.bc.ca
www.village.hazelton.bc.ca
Municipal Type: Village
Incorporated: Feb. 15, 1956; *Area:* 2.85 sq km
County or District: Kitimat-Stikine; *Population in 2006:* 293
Provincial Electoral District(s): Bulkley Valley-Stikine
Federal Electoral District(s): Skeena-Bulkley Valley
Next Election: Nov. 2011 (3 year terms)
Alice Maitland, Mayor
amaitland@village.hazelton.bc.ca
Kelly Mattson, Administrator
administrator@village.hazelton.bc.ca

Highlands

1980 Millstream Rd.
Victoria, BC V9B 6H1
250-474-1773 Fax: 250-474-3677
jcameron@highlands.ca
www.highlands.bc.ca
Municipal Type: District
Incorporated: Dec. 7, 1993; *Area:* 37.87 sq km
County or District: Capital; *Population in 2006:* 1,903
Provincial Electoral District(s): Malahat-Juan de Fuca
Federal Electoral District(s): Esquimalt-Juan de Fuca
Next Election: Nov. 2011 (3 year terms)
Jane Mendum, Mayor
jmendum@telus.net
Christopher D. Coates, Administrator
ccoates@highlands.ca

Hope

P.O. Box 609
Hope, BC V0X 1L0
604-869-5671 Fax: 604-869-2275
info@hope.ca
www.hope.ca
Municipal Type: District Municipality
Incorporated: April 6, 1929; *Area:* 41.42 sq km
County or District: Fraser Valley; *Population in 2006:* 6,185
Provincial Electoral District(s): Yale-Lillooet
Federal Electoral District(s): Chilliwack-Fraser Canyon
Next Election: Nov. 2011 (3 year terms)
Laurence (Laurie) French, Mayor
Karla Lanktree, Acting CAO
klanktree@hope.ca

Houston

P.O. Box 370
3367 - 12th St.
Houston, BC V0J 1Z0
250-845-2238 Fax: 250-845-3429
doh@houston.ca
www.houston.ca
Municipal Type: District
Incorporated: March 4, 1957; *Area:* 72.83 sq km
County or District: Bulkley-Nechako; *Population in 2006:* 3,163
Provincial Electoral District(s): Bulkley Valley-Stikine
Federal Electoral District(s): Skeena-Buckley Valley
Next Election: Nov. 2011 (3 year terms)
Bill Holmberg, Mayor
Gerry van der Wolf, CAO
cao@houston.ca

Hudson's Hope

P.O. Box 330
9904 Dudley Dr.
Hudson's Hope, BC V0C 1V0
250-783-9901 Fax: 250-783-5741
district@hudsonshope.ca
www.hudsonshope.ca
Municipal Type: District
Incorporated: Nov. 16, 1965; *Area:* 869.43 sq km
County or District: Peace River; *Population in 2006:* 1,012
Provincial Electoral District(s): Peace River North
Federal Electoral District(s): Prince George-Peace River
Next Election: Nov. 2011 (3 year terms)
Karen Anderson, Mayor
Carolyn Bonnick, Administrator

Invermere

P.O. Box 339
Invermere, BC V0A 1K0
250-342-9281 Fax: 250-342-2934
info@invermere.net
www.invermere.net
Municipal Type: District
Incorporated: May 22, 1951; *Area:* 10.18 sq km
County or District: East Kootenay; *Population in 2006:* 3,002
Provincial Electoral District(s): Columbia River-Revelstoke
Federal Electoral District(s): Kootenay-Columbia
Next Election: Nov. 2011 (3 year terms)
Gerry Taft, Mayor
mayor@invermere.net
Christopher Prosser, CAO
cao@invermere.net

Kaslo

P.O. Box 576
413 Fourth St.
Kaslo, BC V0G 1M0
250-353-2311 Fax: 250-353-7767
kaslomayor@netidea.com
www.kaslo.ca
Municipal Type: Village
Incorporated: Aug. 14, 1893; *Area:* 2.8 sq km
County or District: Central Kootenay; *Population in 2006:* 1,072
Provincial Electoral District(s): Nelson-Creston
Federal Electoral District(s): British Columbia Southern Interior
Next Election: Nov. 2011 (3 year terms)
Greg Lay, Mayor
kaslomayor@netidea.com
Rae Sawyer, CAO
kasloclerk@netidea.com

Kent

P.O. Box 70
7170 Cheam Ave.
Agassiz, BC V0M 1A0
604-796-2235 Fax: 604-796-9854
clee@district.kent.bc.ca
www.district.kent.bc.ca
Municipal Type: District
Incorporated: Jan. 1, 1895; *Area:* 166.51 sq km
County or District: Fraser Valley; *Population in 2006:* 4,738
Provincial Electoral District(s): Chilliwack-Kent
Federal Electoral District(s): Chilliwack-Fraser Canyon
Next Election: Nov. 2011 (3 year terms)
Lorne Fisher, Mayor
lfisher@district.kent.bc.ca
Wallace Mah, CAO
wmah@district.kent.bc.ca

Keremeos

P.O. Box 160
702 - 4th St.
Keremeos, BC V0X 1N0
250-499-2711 Fax: 250-499-5477
town@keremeos.ca
www.keremeos.ca
Municipal Type: Village
Incorporated: Oct. 30, 1956; *Area:* 2.11 sq km
County or District: Okanagan-Similkameen; *Population in 2006:* 1,289
Provincial Electoral District(s): Yale-Lillooet
Federal Electoral District(s): British Columbia Southern Interior
Next Election: Nov. 2011 (3 year terms)
Walter F. Despot, Mayor
Joni Heinrich, CAO
cao@keremeos.ca

Kimberley

340 Spokane St.
Kimberley, BC V1A 2E8
250-427-5311 Fax: 250-427-5252
info@city.kimberley.bc.ca
www.city.kimberley.bc.ca
Municipal Type: Town
Incorporated: March 29, 1944; *Area:* 58.31 sq km
County or District: East Kootenay; *Population in 2006:* 6,139
Provincial Electoral District(s): Columbia River-Revelstoke
Federal Electoral District(s): Kootenay-Columbia
Next Election: Nov. 2011 (3 year terms)
James E. Ogilvie, Mayor
mayor@city.kimberley.bc.ca
Michael Dodd, CAO
mdodd@city.kimberley.bc.ca
Holly Ronnquist, CFO
hronnquist@city.kimberley.bc.ca

Kitimat

270 City Centre
Kitimat, BC V8C 2H7
250-632-8900 Fax: 250-632-4995
districtofkitimat@kitimat.ca
www.city.kitimat.bc.ca
Municipal Type: District
Incorporated: March 31, 1953; *Area:* 242.63 sq km
County or District: Kitimat-Stikine; *Population in 2006:* 8,987
Provincial Electoral District(s): Skeena
Federal Electoral District(s): Skeena-Bulkley Valley
Next Election: Nov. 2011 (3 year terms)
Joanne Monaghan, Mayor
mayor@city.kitimat.bc.ca
Walter McLellan, Municipal Clerk
wmclellan@city.kitimat.bc.ca
Zoelita (Zo) Mulder, Treasurer
zmulder@kitimat.ca
John Klie, Fire Chief
jklie@city.kitimat.bc.ca
Steve Lawson, Manager, Information Systems & Procurement
slawson@city.kitimat.bc.ca
Tim Gleig, Director, Engineering Services
tgleig@city.kitimat.bc.ca
Diane Hewlett, Manager, Economic Promotion & Investor Services
dhewlett@kitimat.ca
Gwendolyn Sewell, Director, Planning and Development
gsewell@city.kitimat.bc.ca

Ladysmith

Town Hall
P.O. Box 220 Main
410 Esplanade
Ladysmith, BC V9G 1A2
250-245-6400 Fax: 250-245-6411
info@ladysmith.ca
www.ladysmith.ca
Municipal Type: Town
Incorporated: June 3, 1904; *Area:* 12.18 sq km
County or District: Cowichan Valley; *Population in 2006:* 7,538
Provincial Electoral District(s): Cowichan-Ladysmith
Federal Electoral District(s): Nanaimo-Cowichan
Next Election: Nov. 2011 (3 year terms)
Robert Hutchins, Mayor
rhutchins@ladysmith.ca
Ruth E. Malli, CAO
rmalli@ladysmith.ca

Lake Country

10150 Bottom Wood Lake Rd.
Lake Country, BC V4V 2M1
250-766-5650 Fax: 250-766-0116
admin@lakecountry.bc.ca
www.lakecountry.bc.ca
Municipal Type: District
Incorporated: May 2, 1995; *Area:* 122.16 sq km
County or District: Central Okanagan; *Population in 2006:* 9,606
Provincial Electoral District(s): Kelowna-Lake Country
Federal Electoral District(s): Kelowna-Lake Country
Next Election: Nov. 2011 (3 year terms)
James Baker, Mayor
mayorandcouncil@lakecountry.bc.ca
Hazel Christy, Director, Corporate Services
hchristy@lakecountry.bc.ca

Lake Cowichan

P.O. Box 860
39 South Shore Rd.
Lake Cowichan, BC V0R 2G0
250-749-6681 Fax: 250-749-3900
jfernandez@town.lakecowichan.bc.ca
www.town.lakecowichan.bc.ca
Municipal Type: Town
Incorporated: Aug. 19, 1944; *Area:* 8.25 sq km
County or District: Cowichan Valley; *Population in 2006:* 2,948
Provincial Electoral District(s): Cowichan-Ladysmith
Federal Electoral District(s): Nanaimo-Cowichan
Next Election: Nov. 2011 (3 year terms)
Ross Forrest, Mayor
rforrest@town.lakecowichan.bc.ca
Joseph A. Fernandez, CAO

Langley

20338 - 65 Ave.
Langley, BC V2Y 3J1
604-534-3211 Fax: 604-533-6052
info@tol.bc.ca
www.tol.bc.ca
Municipal Type: Township
Incorporated: April 26, 1873; *Area:* 306.93 sq km
County or District: Greater Vancouver; *Population in 2006:* 93,726
Provincial Electoral District(s): Fort Langely-Aldergrove
Federal Electoral District(s): Langley
Next Election: Nov. 2011 (3 year terms)
Rick Green, Mayor
Jordan Bateman, Councillor
Bev Dornan, Councillor
Steve Ferguson, Councillor
Charlie Fox, Councillor
Mel Kositsky, Councillor
Bob Long, Councillor
Kim Richter, Councillor
Grant Ward, Councillor
Mark Bakken, Administrator
604-533-6002
Hilary Tsikayi, Director, Finance
604-533-6156, Fax: 604-533-6130
htsikayi@tol.bc.ca
Ramin Sefi, Director, Community Development
604-533-6059, Fax: 604-533-6110
khoulden@tol.bc.ca

Christine Corfe, Director, Corporate Administration
604-533-6015, Fax: 604-533-6010
ccorfe@tol.bc.ca
Doug Wade, Fire Chief
604-532-7509, Fax: 604-532-7530
dwade@tol.bc.ca
Paul Crawford, Manager, Long Range Planning
604-533-6056
pcrawford@tol.bc.ca
Dellarae Sawchuk, Manager, Purchasing
604-533-7327, Fax: 604-533-6130
dsawchuk@tol.bc.ca
Shannon Harvey-Renner, Manager, Human Resources
604-533-6121, Fax: 604-533-6129

Lantzville
P.O. Box 100
7192 Lantzville Rd.
Lantzville, BC V0R 2H0
250-390-4006 Fax: 250-390-5188
district@lantzville.ca
www.lantzville.ca
Municipal Type: District
Incorporated: June 25, 2003; *Area:* 27.87 sq km
County or District: Nanaimo; *Population in 2006:* 3,661
Provincial Electoral District(s): Nanaimo-Parksville
Federal Electoral District(s): Nanaimo-Alberni
Next Election: Nov. 2011 (3 year terms)
Colin Haime, Mayor
Twyla Graff, CAO
twyla@lantzville.ca

Lillooet
P.O. Box 610
Lillooet, BC V0K 1V0
250-256-4289 Fax: 250-256-4288
cityhall@lillooetbc.com
www.lillooetbc.com
Municipal Type: District
Incorporated: Dec. 31, 1946; *Area:* 27.83 sq km
County or District: Squamish-Lillooet; *Population in 2006:* 2,324
Provincial Electoral District(s): Yale-Lillooet
Federal Electoral District(s): Chilliwack-Fraser Canyon
Next Election: Nov. 2011 (3 year terms)
Dennis Bontron, Mayor
Grant Loyer, CAO
gloyer@lillooetbc.com

Lions Bay
P.O. Box 141
Lions Bay, BC V0N 2E0
604-921-9333 Fax: 604-921-6643
reception@lionsbay.ca
www.lionsbay.ca
Municipal Type: Village
Incorporated: Dec. 17, 1970; *Area:* 2.55 sq km
County or District: Greater Vancouver; *Population in 2006:* 1,328
Provincial Electoral District(s): West Vancouver-Garibaldi
Federal Electoral District(s): West Vancouver-Sunshine Coast-Sea to Sky Country
Next Election: Nov. 2011 (3 year terms)
Brenda Broughton, Mayor
Rory Mandryk, Village Manager
admin@lionsbay.ca

Logan Lake
P.O. Box 190
Logan Lake, BC V0K 1W0
250-523-6225 Fax: 250-523-6678
districtofloganlake@loganlake.ca
www.loganlake.ca
Municipal Type: District
Incorporated: Nov. 10, 1970; *Area:* 325.4 sq km
County or District: Thompson-Nicola; *Population in 2006:* 2,162
Provincial Electoral District(s): Yale-Lillooet
Federal Electoral District(s): Okanagan-Coquihalla
Next Election: Nov. 2011 (3 year terms)
Marlon Dosch, Mayor
mdosch@loganlake.ca
David Allen, CAO
dallen@loganlake.ca

Lumby
P.O. Box 430
Lumby, BC V0E 2G0
250-547-2171 Fax: 250-547-6894
info@lumby.ca
www.lumby.ca
Municipal Type: Village
Incorporated: Dec. 20, 1955; *Area:* 5.27 sq km
County or District: North Okanagan; *Population in 2006:* 1,634
Provincial Electoral District(s): Okanagan-Vernon
Federal Electoral District(s): Okanagan-Shuswap
Next Election: Nov. 2011 (3 year terms)
Lori Mindnich, Mayor
mayor@lumby.ca
Frank Kosa, Village Administrator
fkosa@lumby.ca

Lytton
P.O. Box 100
380 Main St.
Lytton, BC V0K 1Z0
250-455-2355 Fax: 250-455-2142
hotspot@lytton.ca
www.lytton.ca
Municipal Type: Village
Incorporated: May 3, 1945; *Area:* 6.71 sq km
County or District: Thompson-Nicola; *Population in 2006:* 235
Provincial Electoral District(s): Yale-Lillooet
Federal Electoral District(s): Chilliwack-Fraser Canyon
Next Election: Nov. 2011 (3 year terms)
Jessoa Lightfoot, Mayor
lyttonlight@telus.net
Ian Hay, CAO

Mackenzie
P.O. Box 340
1 Mackenzie Blvd.
Mackenzie, BC V0J 2C0
250-997-3221 Fax: 250-997-5186
info@district.mackenzie.bc.ca
www.district.mackenzie.bc.ca
Municipal Type: District
Incorporated: May 19, 1966; *Area:* 159.09 sq km
County or District: Fraser-Fort George; *Population in 2006:* 4,539
Provincial Electoral District(s): Prince George North
Federal Electoral District(s): Prince George-Peace River
Next Election: Nov. 2011 (3 year terms)
Stephanie Killam, Mayor
stephanie@district.mackenzie.bc.ca
Warren Waycheshen, CAO
warren@district.mackenzie.bc.ca

Maple Ridge
11995 Haney Pl.
Maple Ridge, BC V2X 6A9
604-463-5221 Fax: 604-467-7329
enquiries@mapleridge.ca
www.mapleridge.ca
Municipal Type: District
Incorporated: Sept. 12, 1874; *Area:* 265.79 sq km
County or District: Fraser Valley; *Population in 2006:* 68,949
Provincial Electoral District(s): Maple Ridge-Pitt Meadows; Maple Ridge-Mission
Federal Electoral District(s): Pitt Meadows-Maple Ridge-Mission
Next Election: Nov. 2011 (3 year terms)
Ernie Daykin, Mayor
edaykin@mapleridge.ca
Cheryl Ashlie, Councillor
Judy Dueck, Councillor
Al Hogarth, Councillor
Linda King, Councillor
Mike Morden, Councillor
Craig Speirs, Councillor
James Rule, CAO
604-463-5221
jrule@mapleridge.ca
Mike Murray, General Manager, Community Development, Parks & Recreation Services
mmurray@mapleridge.ca
Frank Quinn, General Manager, Public Works & Development Services
fquinn@mapleridge.ca
Brock McDonald, Director, Licences, Permits & Bylaws
604-467-7370
bmcdonald@mapleridge.ca
Gary Manson, Manager, Communications
Paul Gill, General Manager, Corporate & Financial Services
pgill@mapleridge.ca
Jake Sorba, Director, Finance
604-467-7317
Jane Pickering, Director, Planning
604-467-7471
jpickering@mapleridge.ca
David Boag, Director, Parks & Facilities
604-467-7344
dboag@mapleridge.ca
Russ Carmichael, Director, Engineering Operations
604-467-7363
rcarmichael@mapleridge.ca
Andrew Wood, Municipal Engineer
604-467-7496, Fax: 604-467-7425
Jim Sheehan, Environmental Technician
604-467-7499
jsheehan@mapleridge.org
Rod Stott, Environmental Planner
604-467-7390
rstott@mapleridge.org
Chuck Goddard, Manager, Development & Environmental Services
604-467-7487
cgoddard@mapleridge.org
Terry Fryer, Manager, Corporate & Development Engineering
604-467-7450
Peter Grootendorst, Director, Fire Operations
604-463-5221
pgrootendorst@mapleridge.ca
John Bastaja, Chief Information Officer
604-467-7479
jbastaja@mapleridge.ca
Sue Wheeler, Director, Community Services
604-467-7308
swheeler@mapleridge.ca
Dave Walsh, Superintendent, Police Services
604-463-6251
Ceri Marlo, P.Eng., Manager, Legislative Services
604-467-7482, Fax: 604-467-7329
cmarlo@mapleridge.ca

Masset
P.O. Box 68
Masset, BC V0T 1M0
250-626-3995 Fax: 250-626-3968
vom@mhtv.ca
www.massetbc.com
Municipal Type: Village
Incorporated: May 11, 1961; *Area:* 19.45 sq km
County or District: Skeena-Queen Charlotte; *Population in 2006:* 940
Provincial Electoral District(s): North Coast
Federal Electoral District(s): Skeena-Bulkley Valley
Next Election: Nov. 2011 (3 year terms)
Barry Pages, Mayor
Trevor Jarvis, CAO

McBride
P.O. Box 519
McBride, BC V0J 2E0
250-569-2229 Fax: 250-569-3276
mcbride@mcbride.ca
www.mcbride.ca
Municipal Type: Village
Incorporated: April 7, 1932; *Area:* 4.43 sq km
County or District: Fraser-Fort George; *Population in 2006:* 660
Provincial Electoral District(s): Prince George-Mount Robson
Federal Electoral District(s): Prince George-Peace River
Next Election: Nov. 2011 (3 year terms)
Michael Frazier, Mayor
mfrazier@rdffg.bc.ca
Eliana Clements, CAO

Merritt
P.O. Box 189
2185 Voght St.
Merritt, BC V1K 1B8
250-378-4224 Fax: 250-378-2600
info@merritt.ca
www.merritt.ca
Municipal Type: Town
Incorporated: April 1, 1911; *Area:* 24.94 sq km
County or District: Thompson-Nicola; *Population in 2006:* 6,998
Provincial Electoral District(s): Yale-Lillooet
Federal Electoral District(s): Okanagan-Coquihalla
Next Election: Nov. 2011 (3 year terms)
Susan Roline, Mayor
mayor@merritt.ca
Jennifer Bridarolli, CAO
jbridarolli@merritt.ca
Marlie Worrin, Manager, Financial Services
mworrin@merritt.ca

Metchosin
4450 Happy Valley Rd.
Victoria, BC V9C 3Z3
250-474-3167 Fax: 250-474-6298
info@metchosin.ca
www.metchosin.ca
Municipal Type: District
Incorporated: Dec. 3, 1984; *Area:* 71.32 sq km
County or District: Capital; *Population in 2006:* 4,795
Provincial Electoral District(s): Esquimalt-Metchosin
Federal Electoral District(s): Esquimalt-Juan de Fuca
Next Election: Nov. 2011 (3 year terms)
John Ranns, Mayor
jranns@metchosin.ca
Dave Drummond, CAO
ddrummond@metchosin.ca

Midway
P.O. Box 160
661 Eighth Ave.
Midway, BC V0H 1M0
250-449-2222 Fax: 250-449-2258
midwaybc@shaw.ca
www.midwaybc.ca
Municipal Type: Village
Incorporated: May 25, 1967; *Area:* 12.16 sq km
County or District: Kootenay Boundary; *Population in 2006:* 621
Provincial Electoral District(s): West Kootenay-Boundary
Federal Electoral District(s): British Columbia Southern Interior
Next Election: Nov. 2011 (3 year terms)
Randy Kappes, Mayor
Jim Madder, Administrator

Mission
P.O. Box 20
8645 Stave Lake St.
Mission, BC V2V 4L9
604-820-3700 Fax: 604-826-1363
info@mission.ca
www.mission.ca
Municipal Type: District
Incorporated: June 2, 1892; *Area:* 225.78 sq km
County or District: Fraser Valley; *Population in 2006:* 34,505
Provincial Electoral District(s): Maple Ridge-Mission
Federal Electoral District(s): Pitt Meadows-Maple Ridge-Mission
Next Election: Nov. 2011 (3 year terms)
James Atebe, Mayor
Ian Fitzpatrick, Coordinator, Emergency Program
604-820-5390
Robert Ross, Director, Community Development
604-820-3751
RRoss@mission.ca

Beverly Endersby, Manager, Inspection Services
604-820-3732
bendersby@mission.ca
Brian Storrier, Director, Parks & Recreation
604-820-5355
Brian_Storrier@mission.ca
Michael Giesbrecht, Manager, Purchasing
604-820-3756
mgiesbrecht@mission.ca
Mike Hofer, Environmental Technician
604-820-3736
Mike_Hofer@mission.ca
Ken Bjorgaard, Director, Finance
Glenn Robertson, CAO
604-820-3704
grobertson@mission.ca
Ian Fitzpatrick, Fire Chief
604-820-5390
ifitzpatrick@mission.ca
Kim Allan, Director, Forest Management
604-820-3764
Kim_Allan@mission.ca
Greg Giles, Superintendent, Utilities
604-820-3765
Greg_Giles@mission.ca
Sharon Fletcher, Director, Planning
604-820-3752
sfletcher@mission.ca
Dennis Clark, Director, Corporate Administration
dclark@mission.ca
Rick Bomhof, Director, Engineering & Public Works
604-820-3736
rbomhof@mission.ca

Montrose
P.O. Box 510
Montrose, BC V0G 1P0
250-367-7234 Fax: 250-367-7288
montvill@telus.net
www.village.montrose.bc.ca
Municipal Type: Village
Incorporated: June 22, 1956; *Area:* 1.53 sq km
County or District: Kootenay Boundary; *Population in 2006:* 1,012
Provincial Electoral District(s): West Kootenay-Boundary
Federal Electoral District(s): British Columbia Southern Interior
Next Election: Nov. 2011 (3 year terms)
Griff Welsh, Mayor
Vacant, CAO

Nakusp
P.O. Box 280
91 - 1st St. NW
Nakusp, BC V0G 1R0
250-265-3689 Fax: 250-265-3788
info@nakusp.com
www.nakusp.com
Municipal Type: Village
Incorporated: Nov. 24, 1964; *Area:* 8 sq km
County or District: Central Kootenay; *Population in 2006:* 1,524
Provincial Electoral District(s): Nelson-Creston
Federal Electoral District(s): Kootenay-Columbia
Next Election: Nov. 2011 (3 year terms)
Karen Hamling, Mayor
khamling@nakusp.com
Robert Lafleur, CAO & Corporate Officer
blafleur@nakusp.com

Nelson
#101, 310 Ward St.
Nelson, BC V1L 5S4
250-352-5511 Fax: 250-352-2131
janet@nelson.ca
www.nelson.ca
Municipal Type: Town
Incorporated: March 18, 1897; *Area:* 11.72 sq km
County or District: Central Kootenay; *Population in 2006:* 9,258
Provincial Electoral District(s): Nelson-Creston
Federal Electoral District(s): British Columbia Southern Interior
Next Election: Nov. 2011 (3 year terms)
John Dooley, Mayor
mayor@nelson.ca
Janet Postelthwaite, Manager, Legislative & Administrative Services

New Denver
P.O. Box 40
115 Slocan Ave.
New Denver, BC V0G 1S0
250-358-2316 Fax: 250-358-7251
office@newdenver.ca
www.newdenver.ca
Municipal Type: Village
Incorporated: Jan. 12, 1929; *Area:* 1.1 sq km
County or District: Central Kootenay; *Population in 2006:* 512
Provincial Electoral District(s): Nelson-Creston
Federal Electoral District(s): British Columbia Southern Interior
Next Election: Nov. 2011 (3 year terms)
Gary Wright, Mayor
Carol Gordon, CAO

New Hazelton
P.O. Box 340
3026 Bowser St.
New Hazelton, BC V0J 2J0
250-842-6571 Fax: 250-842-6077
info@newhazelton.ca
www.newhazelton.ca
Municipal Type: District
Incorporated: Dec. 15, 1980; *Area:* 25.64 sq km
County or District: Kitimat-Stikine; *Population in 2006:* 627
Provincial Electoral District(s): Bulkley Valley-Stikine
Federal Electoral District(s): Skeena-Bulkley Valley
Next Election: Nov. 2011 (3 year terms)
Pieter Weeber, Mayor
250-842-6571
pweeber@newhazelton.ca
Brian Fassnidge, Administrator
bfassnidge@newhazelton.ca

North Cowichan
P.O. Box 278
7030 Trans Canada Hwy.
Duncan, BC V9L 3X4
250-746-3100 Fax: 250-746-3133
info@northcowichan.bc.ca
www.northcowichan.bc.ca
Municipal Type: District
Incorporated: June 18, 1873; *Area:* 193.66 sq km
County or District: Cowichan Valley; *Population in 2006:* 27,557
Provincial Electoral District(s): Cowichan-Ladysmith
Federal Electoral District(s): Nanaimo-Cowichan
Next Election: Nov. 2011 (3 year terms)
Tom Walker, Mayor
walker@northcowichan.bc.ca
Mark O. Ruttan, Director, Administration
ruttan@northcowichan.bc.ca
Mark Frame, Director, Finance
frame@northcowichan.bc.ca
Chris Hall, Director, Planning
hall@northcowichan.bc.ca
John Mackay, Director, Engineering
250-746-3103
mackay@northcowichan.bc.ca
Ernie Mansueti, Director, Parks & Recreation
mansueti@northcowichan.bc.ca
Darrell Frank, Forester
250-746-3104
frank@northcowichan.bc.ca
F.S. Rockwell, Medical Health Officer

North Saanich
1620 Mills Rd.
North Saanich, BC V8L 5S9
250-656-0781 Fax: 250-656-3155
admin@northsaanich.ca
www.northsaanich.ca
Municipal Type: District
Incorporated: Aug. 19, 1965; *Area:* 37.14 sq km
County or District: Capital; *Population in 2006:* 10,823
Provincial Electoral District(s): Saanich North & the Islands
Federal Electoral District(s): Saanich-Gulf Islands
Next Election: Nov. 2011 (3 year terms)
Alice Finall, Mayor
mayor@northsaanich.ca
Tim Tanton, Engineer
Curt Kingsley, Manager, Corporate Services
ckingsley@northsaanich.ca
Ralph Gillis, Director, Financial Services
rgillis@northsaanich.ca

North Vancouver
355 West Queens Rd.
North Vancouver, BC V7N 4N5
604-990-2311 Fax: 604-984-9637
infoweb@dnv.org
www.dnv.org
Municipal Type: District Municipality
Incorporated: Aug. 10, 1891; *Area:* 160.67 sq km
County or District: Greater Vancouver; *Population in 2006:* 82,562
Provincial Electoral District(s): N. Vancouver-Lonsdale; N. Vancouver-Seymour; W. Vancouver-Capilano; W. Vancouver-Garibaldi
Federal Electoral District(s): North Vancouver; West Vancouver-Sunshine Coast-Sea to Sky Country
Next Election: Nov. 2011 (3 year terms)
Richard Walton, Mayor
604-990-2208
council@dnv.org
Roger Bassam, Councillor
Robin Hicks, Councillor
Mike Little, Councillor
Doug Mackay-Dunn, Councillor
Lisa Muri, Councillor
Alan Nixon, Councillor
Agnes S. Hilsen, Municipal Clerk
604-990-2207
agnes_hilsen@dnv.org
Nicole Deveaux, CFO
604-990-2234
David Stuart, CAO
604-990-2209
dstuart@dnv.org
Doug Trussler, Chief, Fire & Rescue Services
604-990-3653
Jozsef Dioszeghy, Director, Environment, Parks & Engineering
604-990-3828
Margaret Eckenfelder, Director, Sustainability, Planning & Building
604-990-2398
Gavin Joyce, Director, Corporate Services
604-990-2336
Ken Bennett, Manager, Environment & Sustainability
604-990-2445
Richard Boulton, Manager, Parks & Environmental Services
604-990-3804
Brett Dwyer, Manager, Development Services
604-990-2247
Robert Huffman, P.Eng., Manager, Utilities
604-990-3861
Len Jensen, Manager, Engineering Operations
604-990-3845
Rick Pratt, Manager, Information Technology Services
604-990-2312
Cindy Rogers, Manager, Human Resources
604-990-2217
rogersc@dnv.org
Donna Howes, Section Manager, Transportation Planning
604-990-2450
Paula Huber, Section Manager, Planning Development
604-990-2328
Allen Lynch, Section Manager, Waste Reduction
604-984-9730
Graham Knell, Coordinator, Trails & Habitat
604-990-3806
Mark Brown, District Arborist

Oak Bay
2167 Oak Bay Ave.
Victoria, BC V8R 1G2
250-598-3311 Fax: 250-598-9108
lhilton@oakbaybc.org
www.oakbaybc.org
Municipal Type: District
Incorporated: July 2, 1906; *Area:* 10.38 sq km
County or District: Capital; *Population in 2006:* 17,908
Provincial Electoral District(s): Oak Bay-Gordon Head
Federal Electoral District(s): Victoria
Next Election: Nov. 2011 (3 year terms)
Christopher M. Causton, Mayor
mayor@oakbay.ca
Dave Marshall, Director, Engineering Services
Patricia A. Walker, Treasurer
pawalker@oakbay.ca
William E. Cochrane, CAO
bcochrane@oakbay.ca
Roy Thomassen, Director, Building & Planning
rthomassen@oakbay.ca
Agnes Szilos, Director, Parks & Recreation
250-595-7946
Phil Barnett, Superintendent, Public Works
250-598-4501
Gerry Adam, Fire Chief
250-592-9121
Lorne Middleton, Manager, Parks Services
250-592-7275
lmiddleton@oakbay.ca

Oliver
P.O. Box 638
35016 - 97th St.
Oliver, BC V0H 1T0
250-485-6200 Fax: 250-498-4466
admin@oliver.ca
www.oliver.ca
Municipal Type: Town
Incorporated: Dec. 31, 1945; *Area:* 4.95 sq km
County or District: Okanagan-Similkameen; *Population in 2006:* 4,370
Provincial Electoral District(s): Penticton-Okanagan Valley
Federal Electoral District(s): British Columbia Southern Interior
Next Election: Nov. 2011 (3 year terms)
Pat Hampson, Mayor
250-485-6205, Fax: 250-498-4466
phampson@oliver.ca
Tom Szalay, Municipal Manager
tszalay@oliver.ca

Osoyoos
P.O. Box 3010
8707 Main St.
Osoyoos, BC V0H 1V0
250-495-6515 Fax: 250-495-2400
tosoyoos@osoyoos.ca
www.osoyoos.ca
Municipal Type: Town
Incorporated: Jan. 14, 1946; *Area:* 8.76 sq km
County or District: Okanagan-Similkameen; *Population in 2006:* 4,752
Provincial Electoral District(s): Penticton-Okanagan Valley
Federal Electoral District(s): British Columbia Southern Interior
Next Election: Nov. 2011 (3 year terms)
Stu Wells, Mayor
Barry Romanko, CAO
bromanko@osoyoos.ca

Peachland
5806 Beach Ave.
Peachland, BC V0H 1X7
250-767-2647 Fax: 250-767-3433
ppalmer@peachland.ca
www.peachland.ca
Municipal Type: District
Incorporated: Jan. 1, 1909; *Area:* 15.98 sq km
County or District: Central Okanagan; *Population in 2006:* 4,883

Provincial Electoral District(s): Okanagan-Westside
Federal Electoral District(s): Okanagan-Coquihalla
Next Election: Nov. 2011 (3 year terms)
Keith Fielding, Mayor
250-767-6412
mayor@peachland.ca
Elsie Lemke, Administrator
elemke@peachland.ca

Pemberton
P.O. Box 100
7400 Prospect St.
Pemberton, BC V0N 2L0
604-894-6135 Fax: 604-894-6136
admin@pemberton.ca
www.pemberton.ca
Municipal Type: Village
Incorporated: July 20, 1956; *Area:* 4.45 sq km
County or District: Squamish-Lillooet; *Population in 2006:* 2,192
Provincial Electoral District(s): West Vancouver-Garibaldi
Federal Electoral District(s): Chilliwack-Fraser Canyon
Next Election: Nov. 2011 (3 year terms)
Jordan Sturdy, Mayor
jsturdy@pemberton.ca
Lori Pilon, CAO
lpilon@pemberton.ca
Nikki Gilmore, Manager, Finance

Port Alice
P.O. Box 130
1061 Marine Dr.
Port Alice, BC V0N 2N0
250-284-3391 Fax: 250-284-3416
info@portalice.ca
www.portalice.ca
Municipal Type: Village
Incorporated: June 16, 1965; *Area:* 7.65 sq km
County or District: Mount Waddington; *Population in 2006:* 821
Provincial Electoral District(s): North Island
Federal Electoral District(s): Vancouver Island North
Next Election: Nov. 2011 (3 year terms)
Gail Neely, Mayor
Gail Lind, CAO

Port Clements
P.O. Box 198
Port Clements, BC V0T 1R0
250-557-4295 Fax: 250-557-4568
office@portclements.com
www.portclements.com
Municipal Type: Village
Incorporated: Dec. 31, 1975; *Area:* 13.59 sq km
County or District: Skeena-Queen Charlotte; *Population in 2006:* 440
Provincial Electoral District(s): North Coast
Federal Electoral District(s): Skeena-Bulkley Valley
Next Election: Nov. 2011 (3 year terms)
Cory Delves, Mayor
cdelves@portclements.com
Heather Nelson-Smith, CAO
heather@portclements.com

Port Edward
P.O. Box 1100
770 Pacific Ave.
Port Edward, BC V0V 1G0
250-628-3667 Fax: 250-628-9225
info@portedward.ca
www.portedward.ca
Municipal Type: District
Incorporated: June 29, 1966; *Area:* 168.12 sq km
County or District: Skeena-Queen Charlotte; *Population in 2006:* 577
Provincial Electoral District(s): North Coast
Federal Electoral District(s): Skeena-Bulkley Valley
Next Election: Nov. 2011 (3 year terms)
Dave MacDonald, Mayor
dmacdonald@portedward.ca
Ron Bedard, CAO
rbedard@portedward.ca

Port Hardy
P.O. Box 68
Port Hardy, BC V0N 2P0
250-949-6665 Fax: 250-949-7433
general@porthardy.ca
www.porthardy.ca
Municipal Type: District
Incorporated: May 5, 1966; *Area:* 40.81 sq km
County or District: Mount Waddington; *Population in 2006:* 3,822
Provincial Electoral District(s): North Island
Federal Electoral District(s): Vancouver Island North
Next Election: Nov. 2011 (3 year terms)
Bev Parnham, Mayor
mayor@porthardy.ca
Deb Clipperton, Director, Financial Services
dclipperton@porthardy.ca
Gloria LeGal, Director, Corporate Services
gloria@porthardy.ca
Rick Davidge, CAO
rickd@porthardy.ca

Port McNeill
P.O. Box 728
Port McNeill, BC V0N 2R0
250-956-3111 Fax: 250-956-4300
reception.portmcneill@telus.net
www.town.portmcneill.bc.ca
Municipal Type: Town
Incorporated: Feb. 18, 1966; *Area:* 7.74 sq km
County or District: Mount Waddington; *Population in 2006:* 2,623
Provincial Electoral District(s): North Island
Federal Electoral District(s): Vancouver Island North
Next Election: Nov. 2011 (3 year terms)
Gerry Furney, Mayor
mayor.portmcneill@telus.net
Albert Sweet, Administrator & Treasurer
pmfinance@telus.net

Pouce Coupé
P.O. Box 190
Pouce Coupe, BC V0C 2C0
250-786-5794 Fax: 250-786-5257
admin@poucecoupe.ca
www.poucecoupe.ca
Municipal Type: Village
Incorporated: Jan. 5, 1932; *Area:* 2.06 sq km
County or District: Peace River; *Population in 2006:* 739
Provincial Electoral District(s): Peace River South
Federal Electoral District(s): Prince George-Peace River
Next Election: Nov. 2011 (3 year terms)
Lyman Clark, Mayor
mayor@poucecoupe.ca
Peter Thomas, CAO
cao@poucecoupe.ca

Princeton
P.O. Box 670
169 Bridge St.
Princeton, BC V0X 1W0
250-295-3135 Fax: 250-295-3477
admin@princeton.ca
www.princeton.ca
Municipal Type: Town
Incorporated: Sept. 11, 1951; *Area:* 10.25 sq km
County or District: Okanagan-Similkameen; *Population in 2006:* 2,677
Provincial Electoral District(s): Yale-Lillooet
Federal Electoral District(s): British Columbia Southern Interior
Next Election: Nov. 2011 (3 year terms)
Randy McLean, Mayor
Patrick Robins, CAO
probins@nethop.net

Qualicum Beach
P.O. Box 130
#201, 660 Primrose St.
Qualicum Beach, BC V9K 1S7
250-752-6921 Fax: 250-752-1243
qbtown@qualicumbeach.com
www.qualicumbeach.com
Municipal Type: Town
Incorporated: May 5, 1942; *Area:* 18 sq km
County or District: Nanaimo; *Population in 2006:* 8,502
Provincial Electoral District(s): Alberni-Qualicum
Federal Electoral District(s): Nanaimo-Alberni
Next Election: Nov. 2011 (3 year terms)
Teunis Westbroek, Mayor
mayor@qualicumbeach.com
Mark D. Brown, CAO
markb@qualicumbeach.com

Queen Charlotte
P.O. Box 478
903A Hwy. 33
Queen Charlotte, BC V0T 1S0
250-559-4765 Fax: 250-559-4742
office@queencharlotte.ca
www.queencharlotte.ca
Municipal Type: Village
Incorporated: Dec. 7, 2005; *Area:* 37.28 sq km
County or District: Skeena-Queen Charlotte; *Population in 2006:* 948
Provincial Electoral District(s): North Coast
Federal Electoral District(s): Skeena-Bulkley Valley
Next Election: Nov. 2011 (3 year terms)
Carol Kulesha, Mayor
250-559-4634
kulesha@qcislands.net
Eunice Ludlow, CAO
administrator@queencharlotte.ca

Quesnel
410 Kinchant St.
Quesnel, BC V2J 7J5
250-992-2111 Fax: 250-992-2206
cityhall@city.quesnel.bc.ca
www.city.quesnel.bc.ca
Municipal Type: Town
Incorporated: March 21, 1928; *Area:* 35.34 sq km
County or District: Cariboo; *Population in 2006:* 9,326
Provincial Electoral District(s): Cariboo North
Federal Electoral District(s): Cariboo-Prince George
Next Election: Nov. 2011 (3 year terms)
Mary Sjostrom, Mayor
mayorsjostrom@city.quesnel.bc.ca
Byron Johnson, CAO
bjohnson@city.quesnel.bc.ca
Kari Bolton, Director, Finance
kbolton@city.quesnel.bc.ca
Jack Marsh, Director, Public Works & Engineering
jmarsh@city.quesnel.bc.ca
Ric Raynor, Director, Emergency Services
rraynor@city.quesnel.bc.ca
Richard Bergey, Manager, Development Services
rbergey@city.quesnel.bc.ca
Tanya Turner, Planner
tturner@city.quesnel.bc.ca
Chris Coben, Superintendent, Utilities
ccoben@city.quesnel.bc.ca
Alec Darragh, Supervisor, Parks & Solid Waste
adarragh@city.quesnel.bc.ca
Coralee Oakes, Councillor & Member, Environmental Advisory Committee
Jeff Norburn, Director, Community Services
jnorburn@city.quesnel.bc.ca
Ken Coombs, Deputy Superintendent, Works
kcoombs@city.quesnel.bc.ca
Harlene Hunt, Manager, Quesnel Airport & Quesnel Transit
hhunt@city.quesnel.bc.ca

Radium Hot Springs
P.O. Box 340
4836A Radium Blvd.
Radium Hot Springs, BC V0A 1M0
250-347-6455 Fax: 250-347-9068
village@radiumhotsprings.com
www.radiumhotsprings.com
Municipal Type: Village
Incorporated: Dec. 10, 1990; *Area:* 6.31 sq km
County or District: East Kootenay; *Population in 2006:* 735
Provincial Electoral District(s): Columbia River-Revelstoke
Federal Electoral District(s): Kootenay Columbia
Next Election: Nov. 2011 (3 year terms)
Dee Conklin, Mayor
Mark Read, CAO
mark.read@radiumhotsprings.ca

Revelstoke
P.O. Box 170
216 Mackenzie Ave.
Revelstoke, BC V0E 2S0
250-837-2911 Fax: 250-837-4930
info@cityofrevelstoke.com
www.cityofrevelstoke.com
Municipal Type: Town
Incorporated: March 1, 1899; *Area:* 31.9 sq km
County or District: Columbia-Shuswap; *Population in 2006:* 7,230
Provincial Electoral District(s): Columbia River-Revelstoke
Federal Electoral District(s): Kootenay-Columbia
Next Election: Nov. 2011 (3 year terms)
David Raven, Mayor
draven@cityofrevelstoke.com
L. Ross McPhee, CAO
rmcphee@cityofrevelstoke.com
Graham Inglis, Director, Finance
ginglis@cityofrevelstoke.com

Rossland
P.O. Box 1179
Rossland, BC V0G 1Y0
250-362-7396 Fax: 250-362-5451
cityhall@rossland.ca
www.rossland.ca
Municipal Type: Town
Incorporated: March 18, 1897; *Area:* 57.97 sq km
County or District: Kootenay Boundary; *Population in 2006:* 3,278
Provincial Electoral District(s): West Kootenay-Boundary
Federal Electoral District(s): British Columbia Southern Interior
Next Election: Nov. 2011 (3 year terms)
Greg Granstrom, Mayor
Debra Timm, Interim CAO
dtimm@rossland.ca
Debra Timm, Manager, Finance
dtimm@rossland.ca

Saanich
770 Vernon Ave.
Victoria, BC V8X 2W7
250-475-1775 Fax: 250-475-5440
clerksec@saanich.ca
www.saanich.ca
Municipal Type: District Municipality
Incorporated: Dec. 12, 1950; *Area:* 103.44 sq km
County or District: Capital; *Population in 2006:* 108,265
Provincial Electoral District(s): Oak Bay-Gordon Head; Saanich N. & the Islands; Saanich S.
Federal Electoral District(s): Esquimalt-Juan de Fuca; Saanich-Gulf Islands; Victoria
Next Election: Nov. 2011 (3 year terms)
Frank Leonard, Mayor
250-475-5510
mayor@saanich.ca
Susan Brice, Councillor
Judy Brownoff, Councillor
Vic Derman, Councillor
Paul Gerrard, Councillor
Wayne Hunter, Councillor
Dean Murdock, Councillor
Vicki Sanders, Councillor
Leif Wergeland, Councillor
Carrie M. MacPhee, Manager, Legislative Services, Fax: 250-475-5440
macpheec@saanich.ca

Ken Kreiger, Director, Parks & Recreation
250-475-5422, Fax: 250-475-5411
kreigerk@saanich.ca
Russ Fuoco, Director, Planning
250-475-5472, Fax: 250-475-5430
fuocor@saanich.ca
Marie Van Dyk, Director, Purchasing, Fax: 250-475-5460
vandykm@saanich.ca
Tim Wood, Administrator
250-475-5555, Fax: 250-475-5440
woodt@saanich.ca
Colin Doyle, Director, Engineering
250-475-5447, Fax: 250-475-5450
colin.doyle@saanich.ca
Bonnie Cole, Manager, Human Resources, Fax: 250-475-5550
bonnie.cole@saanich.ca
Mike Chadwick, Chief Constable
250-475-4321, Fax: 250-475-6138
community@saanichpolice.ca
Chris Nation, Municipal Solicitor, Fax: 250-475-5444
chris.nation@saanich.ca
Dave Ward, Fire Chief
250-475-5423, Fax: 250-475-5588
dave.ward@saanich.ca
Dwayne Halldorson, Manager, Underground Services
250-475-5574, Fax: 250-475-5450
dwayne.halldorson@saanich.ca
Adriane Pollard, Manager, Environmental Services, Fax: 250-475-5430
Dave McAra, Manager, Solid Waste Services
250-475-5432, Fax: 250-475-5590
mcarad@saanich.ca
Mike Ippen, Manager, Public Works
250-475-1775, Fax: 250-475-5487
mike.ippen@saanich.ca
Al Keiser, Manager, Waterworks
250-475-1775, Fax: 250-475-5438
keisera@saanich.ca
Quenton Lehmann, Manager, Recreation
250-475-5441, Fax: 250-475-5411
quenton.lehmann@saanich.ca
Nathalie Dechaine, Officer, Environmental Education
250-475-5475
dechainn@saanich.ca
Anne Topp, Manager, Community Planning
250-475-1775, Fax: 250-457-5430
anne.topp@saanich.ca
Paul Murray, Director, Finance
250-475-5521, Fax: 250-475-5429
paul.murray@saanich.ca
Kristine Kelly, Manager, Forestry, Horticulture & Natural Areas
250-475-5539
kellyk@saanich.ca
Angela Evans, Officer, Environmental Planning
250-475-1775
evansa@saanich.ca
Donavon (Von) Bishop, Manager, Development & Municipal Facilities
Mike Lai, Manager, Transportation
250-475-5492, Fax: 250-475-5450

Salmo

P.O. Box 1000
Salmo, BC V0G 1Z0
250-357-9433 Fax: 250-357-9633
salvil@telus.net
www.salmovillage.ca/services.php
Municipal Type: Village
Incorporated: Oct. 30, 1946; *Area:* 2.38 sq km
County or District: Central Kootenay; *Population in 2006:* 1,007
Provincial Electoral District(s): Nelson-Creston
Federal Electoral District(s): British Columbia Southern Interior
Next Election: Nov. 2011 (3 year terms)
Ann Henderson, Mayor
Scott Sommerville, CAO

Sayward

P.O. Box 29
Sayward, BC V0P 1R0
250-282-5512 Fax: 250-282-5511
office@village.sayward.bc.ca
www.village.sayward.bc.ca
Municipal Type: Village
Incorporated: June 27, 1968; *Area:* 4.72 sq km
County or District: Comox-Strathcona; *Population in 2006:* 341
Provincial Electoral District(s): North Island
Federal Electoral District(s): Vancouver Island North
Next Election: Nov. 2011 (3 year terms)
John MacDonald, Mayor
Cameron Cairncross, CAO
ccairncross@saywardvalley.net

Sechelt

P.O. Box 129
5797 Cowrie St., 2nd Fl.
Sechelt, BC V0N 3A0
604-885-1986 Fax: 604-885-7591
info@sechelt.ca
www.sechelt.ca
Municipal Type: District Municipality
Incorporated: Feb. 15, 1956; *Area:* 39.71 sq km
County or District: Sunshine Coast; *Population in 2006:* 8,454
Provincial Electoral District(s): Powell River-Sunshine Coast
Federal Electoral District(s): West Vancouver-Sunshine Coast-Sea to Sky Country
Next Election: Nov. 2011 (3 year terms)
Darren Inkster, Mayor
dinkster@sechelt.ca
Warren Allan, Councillor
Alice Janisch, Councillor
Ann Kershaw, Councillor
Alice Lutes, Councillor
Fred Taylor, Councillor
Keith Thirkell, Councillor
Rob Brenner, Administrator
rbremner@district.sechelt.bc.ca

Sicamous

P.O. Box 219
1214 Riverside Ave.
Sicamous, BC V0E 2V0
250-836-2477 Fax: 250-836-4314
cityhall@sicamous.ca
www.sicamous.ca
Municipal Type: District
Incorporated: Dec. 4, 1989; *Area:* 14.68 sq km
County or District: Columbia-Shuswap; *Population in 2006:* 2,676
Provincial Electoral District(s): Shuswap
Federal Electoral District(s): Okanagan-Shuswap
Next Election: Nov. 2011 (3 year terms)
Malcolm MacLeod, Mayor
mayor@sicamous.ca
Alan Harris, CAO
aharris@sicamous.ca

Silverton

P.O. Box 14
421 Lake Ave.
Silverton, BC V0G 2B0
250-358-2472 Fax: 250-358-2321
village@silverton.ca
www.silverton.ca
Municipal Type: Village
Incorporated: May 6, 1930; *Area:* 0.44 sq km
County or District: Central Kootenay; *Population in 2006:* 185
Provincial Electoral District(s): Nelson-Creston
Federal Electoral District(s): British Columbia Southern Interior
Next Election: Nov. 2011 (3 year terms)
John Everett, Mayor
Junko Ida, Administrator

Slocan

P.O. Box 50
Slocan, BC V0G 2C0
250-355-2277 Fax: 250-355-2666 Toll Free Phone: 1-866-355-2023
info@slocancity.com
www.slocancity.com
Municipal Type: Village
Incorporated: June 1, 1901; *Area:* 0.75 sq km
County or District: Central Kootenay; *Population in 2006:* 314
Provincial Electoral District(s): Nelson-Creston
Federal Electoral District(s): British Columbia Southern Interior
Next Election: Nov. 2011 (3 year terms)
Madeline Perriere, Mayor
Shana Paivarinta, CAO
cao@villageofslocan.ca

Smithers

P.O. Box 879
1027 Aldous St.
Smithers, BC V0J 2N0
250-847-1600 Fax: 250-847-1601
general@smithers.ca
www.smithers.ca
Municipal Type: Town
Incorporated: Oct. 6, 1921; *Area:* 15.69 sq km
County or District: Bulkley-Nechako; *Population in 2006:* 5,217
Provincial Electoral District(s): Bulkley Valley-Stikine
Federal Electoral District(s): Skeena-Bulkley Valley
Next Election: Nov. 2011 (3 year terms)
Cress Farrow, Mayor
mayor@smithers.ca
Deborah Sargent, CAO
dsargent@smithers.ca

Sooke

2205 Otter Point Rd.
Sooke, BC V0S 1N0
250-642-1634 Fax: 250-642-0541
info@sooke.ca
www.sooke.ca
Municipal Type: District
Incorporated: Dec. 7, 1999; *Area:* 50.01 sq km
County or District: Capital; *Population in 2006:* 9,704
Provincial Electoral District(s): Malahat-Juan de Fuca
Federal Electoral District(s): Esquimalt-Juan de Fuca
Next Election: Nov. 2011 (3 year terms)
Janet Evans, Mayor
jevans@sooke.ca
Bonnie Sprinkling, Corporate Officer
bsprinkling@sooke.ca

Spallumcheen

4144 Spallumcheen Way
Spallumcheen, BC V0E 1B6
250-546-3013 Fax: 250-546-8878
mail@spallumcheentwp.bc.ca
www.spallumcheentwp.bc.ca
Municipal Type: Township
Area: 254.9 sq km
County or District: North Okanagan; *Population in 2006:* 4,960
Provincial Electoral District(s): Shuswap
Federal Electoral District(s): Okanagan-Shuswap
Next Election: Nov. 2011 (3 year terms)
Will Hansma, Mayor
mayor@spallumcheentwp.bc.ca
Lynda Shykora, Administrator
admin@spallumcheentwp.bc.ca

Sparwood

P.O. Box 520
136 Spruce Ave.
Sparwood, BC V0B 2G0
250-425-6271 Fax: 250-425-7277
sparwood@sparwood.bc.ca
www.sparwood.bc.ca
Municipal Type: District
Incorporated: Oct. 6, 1964; *Area:* 177.71 sq km
County or District: East Kootenay; *Population in 2006:* 3,618
Provincial Electoral District(s): East Kootenay
Federal Electoral District(s): Kootenay-Columbia
Next Election: Nov. 2011 (3 year terms)
David Wilks, Mayor
mayor@sparwood.bc.ca
Terry Melcer, Director, Corporate Services
tmelcer@sparwood.bc.ca

Squamish

P.O. Box 310
37955 Second Ave.
Squamish, BC V0N 3G0
604-892-5217 Fax: 604-892-1083
admdept@squamish.ca
www.squamish.ca
Municipal Type: District
Incorporated: May 18, 1948; *Area:* 106.11 sq km
County or District: Squamish-Lillooet; *Population in 2006:* 14,949
Provincial Electoral District(s): West Vancouver-Garibaldi
Federal Electoral District(s): West Vancouver-Sunshine Coast-Sea to Sky Country
Next Election: Nov. 2011 (3 year terms)
Greg Gardner, Mayor
ggardner@squamish.ca
Ray Saurette, Fire Chief
rsaurette@squamish.ca
Cameron Chalmers, Director, Planning
604-815-5010
cchalmers@squamish.ca
Rick Boulier, Manager, Technical Services
604-815-5015
rboulier@squamish.ca
Francesca Langford, Coordinator, Environment
604-815-5021
environment@squamish.ca
Kim Anema, CAO
604-815-5004
Ralph M. Hughes, Director, Finance
rhughes@squamish.ca
Mick Gottardi, Director, Community Development
604-815-5011
mgottardi@squamish.ca
Cliff Doherty, Director, Protective Services
cdoherty@squamish.ca
Rod Pleasance, Project Engineer
604-815-5016
rpleasance@squamish.ca
Gordon Prescott, Manager, Operations
gprescott@squamish.ca
Maurice Wutzke, Assistant Manager, Operations - Roads, Drainage & Parks
mwutzke@squamish.ca
Fred Hendy, Assistant Manager, Operations - Fleet & Buildings
fhendy@squamish.ca
Dennis Bell, Foreman, Waterworks
dbell@squamish.ca
Roy Mihalick, Chief Operator, Wastewater Treatment Plant
rmihalick@squamish.ca
Jim Lang, Coordinator, Emergency Program
jlang@squamish.ca

Stewart

P.O. Box 460
705 Brightwell St.
Stewart, BC V0T 1W0
250-636-2251 Fax: 250-636-2417
info@districtofstewart.com
www.districtofstewart.com
Municipal Type: District
Incorporated: May 16, 1930; *Area:* 571.5 sq km
County or District: Kitimat-Stikine; *Population in 2006:* 496
Provincial Electoral District(s): North Coast
Federal Electoral District(s): Skeena-Bulkley Valley
Next Election: Nov. 2011 (3 year terms)
Angela Brand Danuser, Mayor
mayor@districtofstewart.com
Maureen Tarrant, Accounting Clerk

Summerland

P.O. Box 159
11321 Henry Ave.
Summerland, BC V0H 1Z0
250-494-6451 Fax: 250-494-1415
info@summerland.ca
summerland@summerland.ca
Municipal Type: District
Incorporated: Dec. 21, 1906; *Area:* 73.88 sq km

County or District: Okanagan-Similkameen; *Population in 2006:* 10,828
Provincial Electoral District(s): Okanagan-Westside
Federal Electoral District(s): Okanagan-Coquihalla
Next Election: Nov. 2011 (3 year terms)
Janice Perrino, Mayor
mayor@summerland.ca
Ken Ostraat, Director, Finance
kostraat@summerland.ca
Gordon Morley, District Planner & Approving Officer
gmorley@summerland.ca
Dale McDonald, Director, Parks & Recreation
dmacdonald@summerland.ca
Lloyd Miskiman, Fire Chief
lmiskiman@summerland.ca
Dave Hill, Superintendent, Public Works
works@summerland.ca
Don De Gagne, CAO
ddegagne@summerland.ca
Don Darling, Director, Engineering & Public Works
ddarling@summerland.ca
Joe Fitzpatrick, Officer, Water Conservation
jfitzpatrick@summerland.ca
Greg Mealing, Superintendent, Water Operations
gmealing@summerland.ca

Tahsis
P.O. Box 519
Tahsis, BC V0P 1X0
250-934-6344 Fax: 250-934-6622
admin@villageoftahsis.com
www.villageoftahsis.com
Municipal Type: Village
Incorporated: June 17, 1970; *Area:* 5.73 sq km
County or District: Comox-Strathcona; *Population in 2006:* 366
Provincial Electoral District(s): North Island
Federal Electoral District(s): Vancouver Island North
Next Election: Nov. 2011 (3 year terms)
Corrine Dahling, Mayor
mayor@villageoftahsis.com
Harmony Nielsen, Corporate Officer, Corporate Administration

Taylor
P.O. Box 300
10007 - 100A St.
Taylor, BC V0C 2K0
250-789-3392 Fax: 250-789-3543
tjohnston@districtoftaylor.com
www.districtoftaylor.com
Municipal Type: District
Incorporated: Aug. 23, 1958; *Area:* 16.61 sq km
County or District: Peace River; *Population in 2006:* 1,384
Provincial Electoral District(s): Peace River South
Federal Electoral District(s): Prince George-Peace River
Next Election: Nov. 2011 (3 year terms)
Fred S. Jarvis, Mayor
Terry Johnston, Administrator

Telkwa
P.O. Box 220
1704 Riverside St.
Telkwa, BC V0J 2X0
250-846-5212 Fax: 250-846-9572
info@telkwa.com
www.telkwa.com
Municipal Type: Village
Incorporated: July 18, 1952; *Area:* 6.56 sq km
County or District: Bulkley-Nechako; *Population in 2006:* 1,295
Provincial Electoral District(s): Bulkley Valley-Stikine
Federal Electoral District(s): Skeena-Bulkley Valley
Next Election: Nov. 2011 (3 year terms)
Carman Graf, Mayor
mayor@telkwa.com
Tom Dall, CAO
administrator@telkwa.com

Tofino
P.O. Box 9
121 Third St.
Tofino, BC V0R 2Z0
250-725-3229 Fax: 250-725-3775
office@tofino.ca
www.tofino.ca
Municipal Type: District
Incorporated: Feb. 5, 1932; *Area:* 10.54 sq km
County or District: Alberni-Clayoquot; *Population in 2006:* 1,655
Provincial Electoral District(s): Alberni-Qualicum
Federal Electoral District(s): Nanaimo-Alberni
Next Election: Nov. 2011 (3 year terms)
John Fraser, Mayor
fraser@tofino.ca
Bob Long, CAO
cao@tofino.ca

Trail
1394 Pine Ave.
Trail, BC V1R 4E6
250-364-1262 Fax: 250-364-0830
info@trail.ca
www.trail.ca
Municipal Type: Town
Incorporated: June 14, 1901; *Area:* 34.78 sq km
County or District: Kootenay Boundary; *Population in 2006:* 7,237
Provincial Electoral District(s): West Kootenay-Boundary
Federal Electoral District(s): British Columbia Southern Interior
Next Election: Nov. 2011 (3 year terms)
Dieter Bogs, Mayor
dbogs@trail.ca
Michelle Ferraro, Corporate Administrator
mferraro@trail.ca

Tumbler Ridge
P.O. Box 100
305 Founders St.
Tumbler Ridge, BC V0C 2W0
250-242-4242 Fax: 250-242-3993
tradmin@dtr.ca
www.tumblerridge.ca
Municipal Type: District
Incorporated: April 9, 1981; *Area:* 1,574.45 sq km
County or District: Peace River; *Population in 2006:* 2,454
Provincial Electoral District(s): Peace River South
Federal Electoral District(s): Prince George-Peace River
Next Election: Nov. 2011 (3 year terms)
Larry White, Mayor
lwhite@dtr.ca
Kim Isaak, CAO

Ucluelet
P.O. Box 999
200 Main St.
Ucluelet, BC V0R 3A0
250-726-7744 Fax: 250-726-7335
info@ucluelet.ca
www.ucluelet.ca
Municipal Type: District
Incorporated: Feb. 26, 1952; *Area:* 6.55 sq km
County or District: Alberni-Clayoquot; *Population in 2006:* 1,487
Provincial Electoral District(s): Alberni-Qualicum
Federal Electoral District(s): Nanaimo-Alberni
Next Election: Nov. 2011 (3 year terms)
Eric Russcher, Mayor
Andrew Yeates, CAO
ayeates@ucluelet.ca

Valemount
P.O. Box 168
99 Gorse St.
Valemount, BC V0E 2Z0
250-566-4435 Fax: 250-566-4249
village@valemount.ca
www.valemount.ca
Municipal Type: Village
Incorporated: Dec. 13, 1962; *Area:* 4.96 sq km
County or District: Fraser-Fort George; *Population in 2006:* 1,018
Provincial Electoral District(s): Prince George-Mount Robson
Federal Electoral District(s): Kamloops-Thompson-Cariboo
Next Election: Nov. 2011 (3 year terms)
Bob Smith, Mayor
mayor@valemount.ca
Douglas B. Fleming, CAO
cao@valemount.ca

Vanderhoof
P.O. Box 900
160 Connaught St.
Vanderhoof, BC V0J 3A0
250-567-4711 Fax: 250-567-9169
info@district.vanderhoof.ca
www.vanderhoof.ca
Municipal Type: District
Incorporated: Jan. 22, 1926; *Area:* 54.85 sq km
County or District: Bulkley-Nechako; *Population in 2006:* 4,064
Provincial Electoral District(s): Prince George-Omineca
Federal Electoral District(s): Cariboo-Prince George
Next Election: Nov. 2011 (3 year terms)
Gerry Thiessen, Mayor
mayor@district.vanderhoof.ca
Marjorie Makow, Corporate Administrator
clerk@district.vanderhoof.ca

View Royal
45 View Royal Ave.
Victoria, BC V9B 1A6
250-479-6800 Fax: 250-727-9551
info@town.viewroyal.bc.ca
www.town.viewroyal.bc.ca
Municipal Type: Town
Incorporated: Dec. 5, 1988; *Area:* 14.48 sq km
County or District: Capital; *Population in 2006:* 8,768
Provincial Electoral District(s): Esquimalt-Metchosin
Federal Electoral District(s): Esquimalt-Juan de Fuca
Next Election: Nov. 2011 (3 year terms)
Graham Hill, Mayor
mayor@town.viewroyal.bc.ca
Mark Brennan, CAO
mbrennan@town.viewroyal.bc.ca

Warfield
555 Schofield Hwy.
Trail, BC V1R 2G7
250-368-8202 Fax: 250-368-9354
warfield@shawlink.ca
www.warfield.ca
Municipal Type: Village
Incorporated: Dec. 8, 1952; *Area:* 1.9 sq km
County or District: Kootenay Boundary; *Population in 2006:* 1,729
Provincial Electoral District(s): West Kootenay-Boundary
Federal Electoral District(s): British Columbia Southern Interior
Next Election: Nov. 2011 (3 year terms)
James Nelson, Mayor
Vince Morelli, CAO/Clerk/Treasurer

Wells
P.O. Box 219
Wells, BC V0K 2R0
250-994-3330 Fax: 250-994-3331
townhall@district.wells.bc.ca
www.district.wells.bc.ca
Municipal Type: District
Incorporated: June 29, 1998; *Area:* 159.15 sq km
County or District: Cariboo; *Population in 2006:* 236
Provincial Electoral District(s): Cariboo North
Federal Electoral District(s): Cariboo-Prince George
Next Election: Nov. 2011 (3 year terms)
Jay Vermette, Mayor
Gary Champagne, CAO
administrator@district.wells.bc.ca

West Vancouver
750 - 17 St.
West Vancouver, BC V7V 3T3
604-925-7000 Fax: 604-926-7006
info@westvancouver.ca
www.westvancouver.ca
Municipal Type: District
Incorporated: March 15, 1912; *Area:* 87.13 sq km
County or District: Greater Vancouver; *Population in 2006:* 42,131
Provincial Electoral District(s): N. Vancouver-Lonsdale; W. Vancouver-Capilano; W. Vancouver-Garibaldi
Federal Electoral District(s): West Vancouver-Sunshine Coast-Sea to Sky Country
Next Election: Nov. 2011 (3 year terms)
Pamela Goldsmith-Jones, Mayor
pgoldsmith-jones@westvancouver.ca
Anne Mooi, Director, Parks & Community Services
604-925-7206
Bob Sokol, Director, Planning, Lands & Permits
604-925-7058
Gareth Rowlands, Acting Manager, Transit
604-985-3500
Grant McRadu, CAO
604-925-7002
gmcradu@westvancouver.ca
Richard Laing, Director, Finance
Brent Dozzi, Manager, Roads & Transportation
604-925-7157
Jim Cook, Fire Chief
604-925-7370
Allen Lynch, Manager, North Shore Recycling Program
604-984-9730, Fax: 604-984-3563
Ray Fung, Director, Engineering & Transportation

Whistler
4325 Blackcomb Way
Whistler, BC V0N 1B4
604-932-5535 Fax: 604-935-8109
info@whistler.ca
www.whistler.ca
Municipal Type: Resort Municipality
Incorporated: Sept. 6, 1975; *Area:* 161.71 sq km
County or District: Squamish-Lillooet; *Population in 2006:* 9,248
Provincial Electoral District(s): West Vancouver-Garibaldi
Federal Electoral District(s): West Vancouver-Sunshine Coast-Sea to Sky Country
Next Election: Nov. 2011 (3 year terms)
Ken Melamed, Mayor
mayorsoffice@whistler.ca, kmelamed@whistler.ca
Bill Barrett, CAO
604-935-8181

Zeballos
P.O. Box 127
Zeballos, BC V0P 2A0
250-761-4229 Fax: 250-761-4331
zeballos@recn.ca
www.zeballos.com
Municipal Type: Village
Incorporated: June 27, 1952; *Area:* 130 sq km
County or District: Comox-Strathcona; *Population in 2006:* 189
Provincial Electoral District(s): North Island
Federal Electoral District(s): Vancouver Island North
Next Election: Nov. 2011 (3 year terms)
Edward (Ted) Lewis, Mayor
Holli Bellavie, CAO/Clerk/Treasurer

Indian Government District in British Columbia

Sechelt
P.O. Box 740
5555 Sunshine Coast Hwy.
Sechelt, BC V0N 3A0
604-885-2273 Fax: 604-885-3490
squinn@secheltnation.net
www.secheltnation.ca
Municipal Type: Metis Settlement
Incorporated: March 17, 1988; *Area:* 10.95 sq km
Population in 2006: 844
Next Election: Nov. 2011 (3 year terms)
Anthony Adcock, Chair
Barbara J. Joe, CAO

MANITOBA

All municipalities in Manitoba (except Winnipeg, which is governed by the City of Winnipeg Act) come under authority of the Manitoba Municipal Act.

In Manitoba there are no counties or regional governments; there are only urban & rural municipalities. Incorporation of a new municipality requires a population of at least 1,000 residents & a population density of at least 400 residents per square kilometre for an urban municipality & a population density of less than 400 residents per square kilometre for a rural municipality. Urban municipalities may be called cities, towns, villages & urban municipalities. The population requirement for a city is at least 7,500 residents.

All municipal elections are held every four years; thus, October 2010, October 2014 etc.

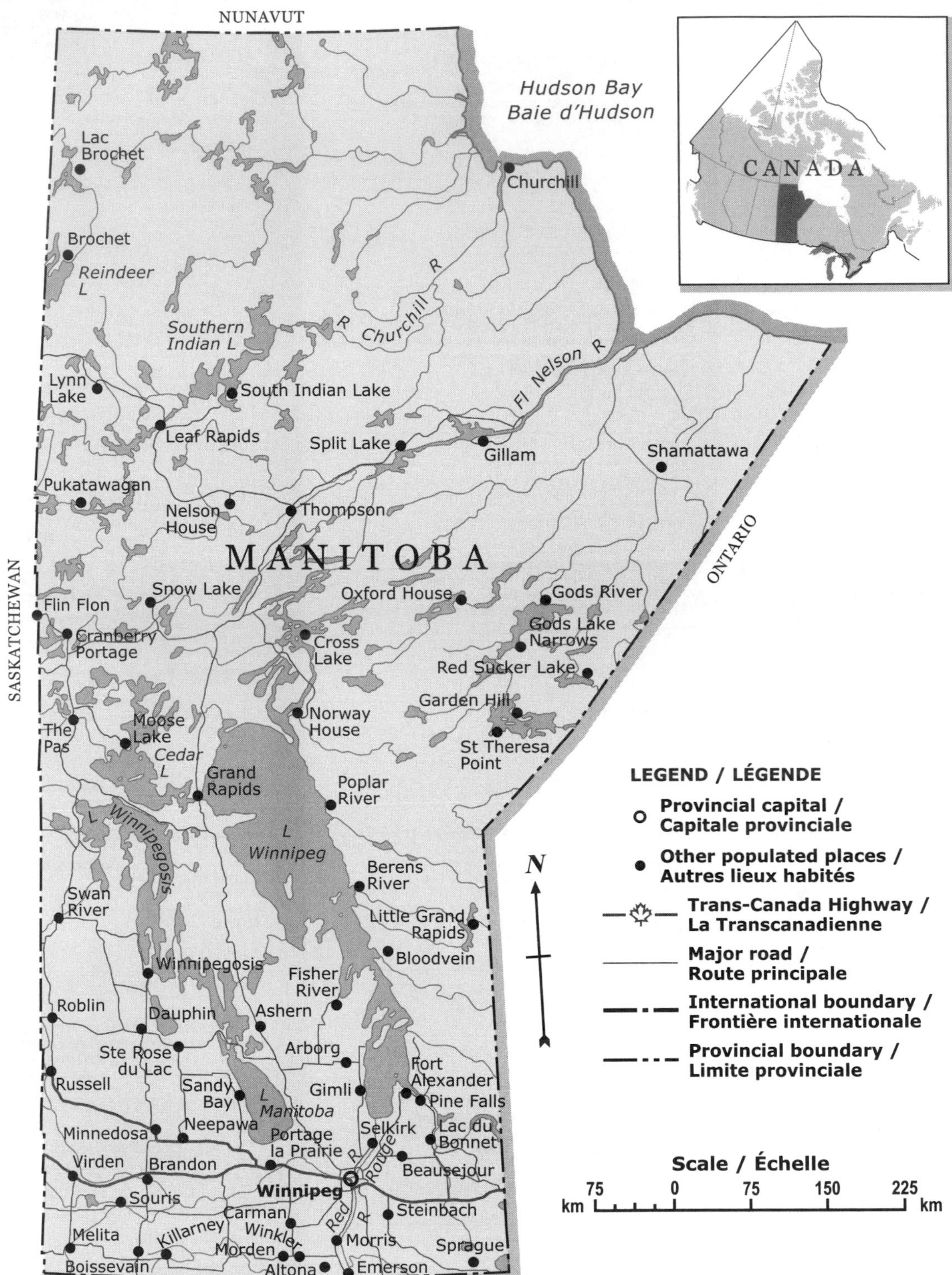

Manitoba

Major Municipalities in Manitoba

Brandon
410 - 9th St.
Brandon, MB R7A 6A2
204-729-2186 Fax: 204-729-8244
cityclerk@brandon.ca
www.brandon.ca
Municipal Type: City
Incorporated: May 3, 1882; *Area:* 76.89 sq km
Population in 2006: 41,511
Provincial Electoral District(s): Brandon East; Brandon West
Federal Electoral District(s): Brandon-Souris
Next Election: Oct. 2010 (4 year terms)

Council
Shari Decter Hirst, Mayor
mayor@brandon.ca
Jeff Fawcett, Councillor, Ward(s): 1. Assiniboine
Corey Roberts, Councillor, Ward(s): 2. Rosser
Murray Blight, Councillor, Ward(s): 3. Victoria
Jeff Harwood, Councillor, Ward(s): 4. University
James McCrae, Councillor, Ward(s): 5. Meadows
Garth Rice, Councillor, Ward(s): 6. South Centre
Shawn Berry, Councillor, Ward(s): 7. Linden Lanes
Stephen Montague, Councillor, Ward(s): 8. Richmond
Len Isleifson, Councillor, Ward(s): 9. Riverview
Jan Chaboyer, Councillor, Ward(s): 10. Green Acres

Administration
Conrad R. Arvisais, City Clerk
204-729-2207, Fax: 204-729-0975
c.arvisais@brandon.ca
Grant McMillan, General Manager & City Treasurer, Corporate Services
204-729-2209
g.mcmillan@brandon.ca
Brian MacRae, City Manager
204-729-2204, Fax: 204-729-0975
b.macrae@brandon.ca
Brian Kayes, Director, Emergency Coordination
best@brandon.ca
Rick Bailey, Director, Public Works
r.bailey@brandon.ca
Jeff Roziere, Director, Sanitation
204-573-6480
j.roziere@brandon.ca
Cathy Snelgrove, General Manager, Operations
204-729-2145, Fax: 204-729-2191
c.snelgrove@brandon.ca
Ted Snure, General Manager & City Engineer, Development Services
204-729-2214, Fax: 204-725-3235
t.snure@brandon.ca
Ian Christiansen, Manager, Engineering Services & Water Resources
i.christiansen@brandon.ca
Sandy Trudel, Officer, Economic Development
s.trudel@brandon.ca
Vivianne Lockerby, CPP, Supervisor, Purchasing
v.lockerby@brandon.ca
Brent Dane, Fire Chief
204-729-2404, Fax: 204-729-2153
b.dane@brandon.ca

Portage La Prairie
97 Saskatchewan Ave. East
Portage la Prairie, MB R1N 0L8
204-239-8337 Fax: 204-239-1532
tkirchener@city-plap.com
www.city-plap.com
Municipal Type: City
Incorporated: Jan. 3, 1907; *Area:* 24.67 sq km
Population in 2006: 12,728
Provincial Electoral District(s): Portage la Prairie
Federal Electoral District(s): Portage-Lisgar
Next Election: Oct. 2010 (4 year terms)

Council
Earl Porter, Mayor

Administration
Dale Lyle, City Manager
Kelly Braden, Director, Operations
204-239-8350, Fax: 204-857-7257
kbraden@city-plap.com
Dean Yaremchuk, Director, Economic & Community Development
dyaremchuk@city-plap.com
Dennis Nodrick, Chief, Fire
204-239-8340, Fax: 204-239-5154
dcnpes@escape.ca
Doug Campbell, Manager, Water Treatment
204-239-8373
dcampbell@city-plap.com
Dave Green, Manager, Parks
204-239-8325
dgreen@city-plap.com
Ian Milne, Manager, Engineering
204-239-8349
imilne@city-plap.com
Brian Taylor, Manager, Public Works
204-239-8352
btaylor@city-plap.com
Wayne Wall, Manager, Water Pollution Control Facility
204-239-8359
wwall@city-plap.com

Selkirk
200 Eaton Ave.
Selkirk, MB R1A 0W6
204-785-4900 Fax: 204-482-5448
info@cityofselkirk.com
www.cityofselkirk.com
Municipal Type: City
Incorporated: June 5, 1882; *Area:* 24.87 sq km
Population in 2006: 9,515
Provincial Electoral District(s): Selkirk
Federal Electoral District(s): Selkirk-Interlake
Next Election: Oct. 2010 (4 year terms)

Council
Larry Johannson, Mayor

Administration
Chris Luellman, CAO

Steinbach
225 Reimer Ave.
Steinbach, MB R5G 2J1
204-326-9877 Fax: 204-346-6235
info@steinbach.ca
www.steinbach.ca
Municipal Type: City
Incorporated: Jan. 3, 1946; *Area:* 25.57 sq km
Population in 2006: 11,066
Provincial Electoral District(s): Steinbach
Federal Electoral District(s): Provencher
Next Election: Oct. 2010 (4 year terms)

Council
Chris Goertzen, Mayor

Administration
Jack Kehler, CAO

Thompson
226 Mystery Lake Rd.
Thompson, MB R8N 1S6
204-677-7910 Fax: 204-677-7936
ltaylor@city.thompson.mb.ca
www.thompson.ca
Municipal Type: City
Incorporated: Jan. 5, 1970; *Area:* 17.18 sq km
Population in 2006: 13,446
Provincial Electoral District(s): Thompson
Federal Electoral District(s): Churchill
Next Election: Oct. 2010 (4 year terms)

Council
Tim Johnston, Mayor
johnston@city.thompson.mb.ca

Administration
Lynn Taylor, City Manager
Dennis Fenske, Director, Personnel & Community Development
dfenske@city.thompson.mb.ca
Ken Thevenot, Fire Chief
204-677-7915
fchief@city.thompson.mb.ca
Ken Allard, Superintendent, Public Works
204-677-7900
kallard@city.thompson.mb.ca
Ray Janzen, Engineering Technician, Water & Sewer
204-677-7905
rjanzen@city.thompson.mb.ca
Nathan Steuart, Engineering Technician, Roads & Buildings
nsteuart@city.thompson.mb.ca
Wayne Koversky, Agent, Purchasing
204-677-7973
koversky@city.thompson.mb.ca

Winkler
185 Main St.
Winkler, MB R6W 1B4
204-325-9524 Fax: 204-325-5915
admin@cityofwinkler.ca
www.cityofwinkler.ca
Municipal Type: City
Incorporated: Jan. 6, 1954; *Area:* 17.01 sq km
Population in 2006: 9,106
Provincial Electoral District(s): Pembina
Federal Electoral District(s): Portage-Lisgar
Next Election: Oct. 2010 (4 year terms)

Council
Martin Harder, Mayor
mayor@cityofwinkler.ca

Administration
Vince Anderson, CAO

Winnipeg
City Hall
510 Main St.
Winnipeg, MB R3B 1B9
204-986-6432 Fax: 204-947-3452 Phone or Fax: 311 for information on city services
www.winnipeg.ca
Municipal Type: City
Incorporated: Nov. 8, 1873; *Area:* 464.01 sq km
Population in 2006: 633,451
Provincial Electoral District(s): Assibonia; Burrows; Charleswood; Concordia; Elmwood; Ft. Garry-Riverview; Ft. Rouge; Ft. Whyte; Inkster; Kildonan; Kirkfield Park; Logan; Minto; Point Douglas; Radisson; Riel; River East; River Heights; Rossmere; Seine River; Southdale; St. Boniface; St. James; St. Johns; St. Norbert; St. Vital; The Maples; Transcona; Tuxedo; Tyndall Park; Wollseley
Federal Electoral District(s): Charleswood-St. James-Assiniboia; Elmwood-Transcona; Kildonan-St. Paul; Saint Boniface; Winnipeg Centre; Winnipeg North; Winnipeg South; Winnipeg South Centre
Next Election: Oct. 2010 (4 year terms)

Council
Sam Katz, Mayor
204-986-2171, Fax: 204-949-0566
feedback@winnipeg.ca
Paula Havixbeck, Councillor, Ward(s): Charleswood-Tuxedo
Harvey Smith, Councillor, Ward(s): Daniel McIntyre
204-986-5951, Fax: 204-986-7000
Thomas Steen, Councillor, Ward(s): Elmwood-East Kildonan
Jenny Gerbasi, Councillor, Ward(s): Fort Rouge-East Fort Garry
204-986-5878, Fax: 204-986-5636
Ross Eadie, Councillor, Ward(s): Mynarski
Jeff Browaty, Councillor, Ward(s): North Kildonan
204-986-5196, Fax: 204-986-3725
Devi Sharma, Councillor, Ward(s): Old Kildonan
Mike Pagtakhan, Councillor, Ward(s): Point Douglas
204-986-8401, Fax: 204-986-3531
John Orlikow, Councillor, Ward(s): River Heights-Fort Garry
204-986-5236, Fax: 204-986-3725
Daniel Vandal, Councillor, Ward(s): St. Boniface
204-986-5206, Fax: 204-986-3725
Grant Nordman, Councillor, Ward(s): St. Charles
204-986-5920, Fax: 204-986-7359
Scott Fielding, Councillor, Ward(s): St. James-Brooklands
204-986-5848, Fax: 204-986-4320
Justin Swandel, Councillor, Ward(s): St. Norbert
204-986-6824, Fax: 204-986-3725
Gord Steeves, Councillor, Ward(s): St. Vital
204-986-5088, Fax: 204-986-3725
Russ Wyatt, Councillor, Ward(s): Transcona
204-986-8087, Fax: 204-986-4530

Administration
Richard Kachur, City Clerk
204-986-2428, Fax: 204-947-3452
Jo-Anne Ferrier, City Treasurer
Michael P. Ruta, Deputy CAO/CFO
Glen Laubenstein, CAO
Jim Brennan, Chief, Winnipeg Fire Paramedic Service
Keith McCaskill, Chief of Police, Winnipeg Police Service
Linda Black, Director, Corporate Support Services
Nelson Karpa, Director, Assessment & Taxation
Bill Larkin, Director, Public Works
Barry MacBride, Director, Water & Waste
Deepak Joshi, Director, Planning, Property & Development
Dave Wardrop, Director, Winnipeg Transit
Clive Wightman, Director, Community Services
Kelly Kjartanson, Manager, Environmental Standards
Dave Domke, Manager, Parks & Open Space
Brad Sacher, Manager, Transportation

Other Municipalities in Manitoba

Altona
P.O. Box 1630
111 Centre Ave. East
Altona, MB R0G 0B0
204-324-6468 Fax: 204-324-1550
info@townofaltona.com
www.townofaltona.com
Municipal Type: Town
Incorporated: Jan. 1, 1956; *Area:* 9.39 sq km
Population in 2006: 3,709
Provincial Electoral District(s): Emerson
Federal Electoral District(s): Portage-Lisgar
Next Election: Oct. 2010 (4 year terms)
Russ Phillips, CAO
Melvin H. Klassen, Mayor

Arborg
P.O. Box 159
337 River Rd.
Arborg, MB R0C 0A0
204-376-2647 Fax: 204-376-5379
townofarborg@mts.net
www.townofarborg.com
Municipal Type: Town
Incorporated: 1964; *Area:* 2.26 sq km
Population in 2006: 1,021
Provincial Electoral District(s): Interlake
Federal Electoral District(s): Selkirk-Interlake
Next Election: Oct. 2010 (4 year terms)
Lorraine Bardarson, CAO
Randy Sigurdson, Mayor

Beausejour
P.O. Box 1028
639 Park Ave.
Beausejour, MB R0E 0C0
204-268-7550 Fax: 204-268-3107
townoffice@townofbeausejour.com
www.townofbeausejour.com
Municipal Type: Town
Incorporated: Jan. 2, 1912; *Area:* 5.35 sq km
Population in 2006: 2,823
Provincial Electoral District(s): Lac du Bonnet
Federal Electoral District(s): Selkirk-Interlake
Next Election: Oct. 2010 (4 year terms)
James Fenske, CAO
Don Mazur, Mayor

Benito
P.O. Box 369
126 Main St.
Benito, MB R0L 0C0
204-539-2634 Fax: 204-539-2221
benitov@mts.net
community.svcn.mb.ca/benito
Municipal Type: Village
Incorporated: Jan. 4, 1941; *Area:* 0.92 sq km
Population in 2006: 370
Provincial Electoral District(s): Swan River
Federal Electoral District(s): Dauphin-Swan River-Marquette
Next Election: Oct. 2010 (4 year terms)
Karon Harness, CAO
William C. Schneider, Mayor

Binscarth
P.O. Box 54
116 Russell St.
Binscarth, MB R0J 0G0
204-532-2223 Fax: 204-532-2153
vilbins@mts.net
www.binscarth.mb.com
Municipal Type: Village
Incorporated: Jan. 2, 1917; *Area:* 1.52 sq km
Population in 2006: 395
Provincial Electoral District(s): Russell
Federal Electoral District(s): Dauphin-Swan River-Marquette
Next Election: Oct. 2010 (4 year terms)
Sandra Birch, CAO
Peggy Bradshaw, Mayor

Birtle
P.O. Box 610
684 Main St.
Birtle, MB R0M 0C0
204-842-3234 Fax: 204-842-3496
birtle1@mts.net
www.town.birtle.mb.ca
Municipal Type: Town
Incorporated: Jan. 3, 1884; *Area:* 14.25 sq km
Population in 2006: 662
Provincial Electoral District(s): Russell
Federal Electoral District(s): Dauphin-Swan River-Marquette
Next Election: Oct. 2010 (4 year terms)
Joan E. Taylor, CAO
Ron Bell, Mayor

Boissevain
P.O. Box 490
420 South Railway
Boissevain, MB R0K 0E0
204-534-2433 Fax: 204-534-3710
boissevain@mts.net
www.boissevain.ca
Municipal Type: Town
Incorporated: 1906; *Area:* 2.77 sq km
Population in 2006: 1,497
Provincial Electoral District(s): Arthur-Virden
Federal Electoral District(s): Brandon-Souris
Next Election: Oct. 2010 (4 year terms)
Lloyd Leganchuk, CAO
M. Edward Anderson, Mayor

Bowsman
P.O. Box 244
105 - 2nd St.
Bowsman, MB R0L 0H0
204-238-4351 Fax: 204-238-4292
bowsman@mts.net
Municipal Type: Village
Incorporated: Jan. 7, 1949; *Area:* 2.63 sq km
Population in 2006: 315
Provincial Electoral District(s): Swan River
Federal Electoral District(s): Dauphin-Swan River-Marquette
Next Election: Oct. 2010 (4 year terms)
Patti Simpson, CAO
Theresa Rehaluk, Mayor

Carberry
P.O. Box 130
316 - 4th Ave.
Carberry, MB R0K 0H0
204-834-6600 Fax: 204-834-6604
town@townofcarberry.ca
www.townofcarberry.ca
Municipal Type: Town
Incorporated: Jan. 1, 1905; *Area:* 4.79 sq km
Population in 2006: 1,502
Provincial Electoral District(s): Turtle Mountain
Federal Electoral District(s): Brandon-Souris
Next Election: Oct. 2010 (4 year terms)
Brent McMillan, CAO
Wayne Blair, Mayor

Carman
P.O. Box 160
12 - 2nd Ave. SW
Carman, MB R0G 0J0
204-745-2443 Fax: 204-745-2903
townofcarman@mts.net
www.townofcarman.com
Municipal Type: Town
Incorporated: Jan. 1, 1905; *Area:* 4.12 sq km
Population in 2006: 2,880
Provincial Electoral District(s): Carman
Federal Electoral District(s): Portage-Lisgar
Next Election: Oct. 2010 (4 year terms)
Cheryl Young, CAO
Robert J. Mitchell, Mayor

Cartwright
P.O. Box 9
485 Curwen St.
Cartwright, MB R0K 0L0
204-529-2263 Fax: 204-529-2288
colleen@cartwrightmb.ca
www.cartwrightmb.ca
Municipal Type: Village
Incorporated: Jan. 5, 1948; *Area:* 1.86 sq km
Population in 2006: 282
Provincial Electoral District(s): Turtle Mountain
Federal Electoral District(s): Brandon-Souris
Next Election: Oct. 2010 (4 year terms)
Colleen Mullin, CAO
Bruce Leadbeater, Mayor

Churchill
P.O. Box 459
180 LaVerendrye Ave.
Churchill, MB R0B 0E0
204-675-8871 Fax: 204-675-2934
town@churchillmb.net
www.townofchurchill.ca
Municipal Type: Town
Incorporated: Jan. 4, 1997; *Area:* 53.96 sq km
Population in 2006: 923
Provincial Electoral District(s): Rupertsland
Federal Electoral District(s): Churchill
Next Election: Oct. 2010 (4 year terms)
Rod McKenzie, CAO
Michael Spence, Mayor

Crystal City
P.O. Box 310
26 South Railway Ave. East
Crystal City, MB R0K 0N0
204-873-2591 Fax: 204-873-2459
crystalcity@inetlink.ca
Municipal Type: Village
Incorporated: Dec. 4, 1947; *Area:* 2.84 sq km
Population in 2006: 400
Provincial Electoral District(s): Turtle Mountain
Federal Electoral District(s): Portage-Lisgar
Next Election: Oct. 2010 (4 year terms)
Scott Warrener, CAO
William H. McKitrick, Mayor

Dauphin
100 Main St. South
Dauphin, MB R7N 1K3
204-622-3200 Fax: 204-622-3290
cao@dauphin.ca
www.dauphin.ca
Municipal Type: Town
Incorporated: Jan. 7, 1898; *Area:* 12.65 sq km
Population in 2006: 7,906
Provincial Electoral District(s): Dauphin-Roblin
Federal Electoral District(s): Dauphin-Swan River-Marquette
Next Election: Oct. 2010 (4 year terms)
Brad D. Collett, CAO
Alex Paul, Mayor

Deloraine
P.O. Box 510
102 Broadway St. South
Deloraine, MB R0M 0M0
204-747-2655 Fax: 204-747-2927
deloraine@deloraine.org
www.deloraine.org
Municipal Type: Town
Incorporated: Jan. 6, 1904; *Area:* 2.25 sq km
Population in 2006: 977
Provincial Electoral District(s): Arthur-Virden
Federal Electoral District(s): Brandon-Souris
Next Election: Oct. 2010 (4 year terms)
Rick Branston, CAO
Brian Franklin, Mayor

Dunnottar
P.O. Box 321
44 Whytewold Rd.
Matlock, MB R0C 2B0
204-389-4962 Fax: 204-389-4966 Toll Free Phone: 1-800-665-1639
info@dunnottar.ca
www.dunnottar.ca
Municipal Type: Village
Area: 2.79 sq km
Population in 2006: 692
Provincial Electoral District(s): Interlake
Federal Electoral District(s): Selkirk-Interlake
Next Election: Oct. 2010 (4 year terms)
Janice Thevenot, CAO
Richard Gamble, Mayor

Elkhorn
P.O. Box 280
10 Grange St.
Elkhorn, MB R0M 0N0
204-845-2161 Fax: 204-845-2312
info@elkhorn.mb.ca
www.elkhorn.mb.ca
Municipal Type: Village
Incorporated: Jan. 2, 1906; *Area:* 2.73 sq km
Population in 2006: 461
Provincial Electoral District(s): Arthur-Virden
Federal Electoral District(s): Brandon-Souris
Next Election: Oct. 2010 (4 year terms)
Garth Mitchell, CAO
Roland Gagnon, Mayor

Emerson
P.O. Box 340
104 Church St.
Emerson, MB R0A 0L0
204-373-2002 Fax: 204-373-2486
emerson@mts.com
www.townofemerson.com
Municipal Type: Town
Incorporated: Nov. 3, 1879; *Area:* 22.28 sq km
Population in 2006: 689
Provincial Electoral District(s): Emerson
Federal Electoral District(s): Provencher
Next Election: Oct. 2010 (4 year terms)
Jeannette Sabourin, CAO
Wayne Arseny, Mayor

Erickson
P.O. Box 40
45 Main St.
Erickson, MB R0J 0P0
204-636-2431 Fax: 204-636-2516
erikclan@mts.net
www.townerickson.ca
Municipal Type: Town
Incorporated: Jan. 5, 1953; *Area:* 1.3 sq km
Population in 2006: 456
Provincial Electoral District(s): Russell
Federal Electoral District(s): Dauphin-Swan River-Marquette
Next Election: Oct. 2010 (4 year terms)
Kat Bridgeman, CAO
David Dauphinais, Mayor

Ethelbert
P.O. Box 185
5 - 2nd St.
Ethelbert, MB R0L 0T0
204-742-3301 Fax: 204-742-3228
vofethel@mts.net
Municipal Type: Village
Incorporated: Jan. 1, 1950; *Area:* 2.47 sq km
Population in 2006: 312
Provincial Electoral District(s): Swan River
Federal Electoral District(s): Dauphin-Swan River-Marquette
Next Election: Oct. 2010 (4 year terms)
Eleanor Kuzyk, CAO
Mitch Michaluk, Mayor

Flin Flon
20 - 1st Ave.
Flin Flon, MB R8A 0T7
204-684-7511 Fax: 204-681-7530
mkolt@city.flinflon.mb.ca
www.cityofflinflon.com
Municipal Type: Town
Incorporated: Jan. 1, 1933; *Area:* 13.88 sq km
Population in 2006: 5,836
Provincial Electoral District(s): Flin Flon
Federal Electoral District(s): Churchill
Next Election: Oct. 2010 (4 year terms)
Note: Flin Flon straddles a provincial boundary. The population shown represents Manitoba (5,594) & Saskatchewan (242) figures.
Marc Kolt, CAO
Tom Therien, Mayor

Gilbert Plains
P.O. Box 39
114 Main St. North
Gilbert Plains, MB R0L 0X0
204-548-2761 Fax: 204-548-2473
townofgp@mts.net
www.gilbertplains.com
Municipal Type: Town
Incorporated: July 1, 1906; *Area:* 2.66 sq km
Population in 2006: 760
Provincial Electoral District(s): Dauphin-Roblin
Federal Electoral District(s): Dauphin-Swan River-Marquette
Next Election: Oct. 2010 (4 year terms)

Lori Parker, CAO
Lyle Smith, Mayor

Gillam
P.O. Box 100
323 Railway Ave.
Gillam, MB R0B 0L0
204-652-2121 Fax: 204-652-2338
towncao@gillamnet.com
www.townofgillam.com
Municipal Type: Town
Area: 1,996.35 sq km
Population in 2006: 1,209
Provincial Electoral District(s): Rupertsland
Federal Electoral District(s): Churchill
Next Election: Oct. 2010 (4 year terms)
Jackie Clayton, CAO
Albert McTavish, Mayor
aamctavish@hydro.mb.ca

Gladstone
P.O. Box 25
48 Dennis St. West
Gladstone, MB R0J 0T0
204-385-2332 Fax: 204-385-2391
gladstone@mts.net
www.town.gladstone.mb.ca
Municipal Type: Town
Incorporated: Jan. 1, 1882; *Area:* 2.43 sq km
Population in 2006: 802
Provincial Electoral District(s): Ste. Rose
Federal Electoral District(s): Dauphin-Swan River-Marquette
Next Election: Oct. 2010 (4 year terms)
Louise E. Blair, CAO
Eileen Clarke, Mayor

Glenboro
P.O. Box 190
109 Broadway St.
Glenboro, MB R0K 0X0
204-827-2083 Fax: 204-827-2553
caormsc@mts.net
www.glenboromb.ca
Municipal Type: Village
Incorporated: Jan. 1, 1950; *Area:* 2.68 sq km
Population in 2006: 633
Provincial Electoral District(s): Turtle Mountain
Federal Electoral District(s): Brandon-Souris
Next Election: Oct. 2010 (4 year terms)
Eric C. Plaetinck, CAO
William R. Shackel, Mayor

Grand Rapids
P.O. Box 301
200 Grand Rapids Dr.
Grand Rapids, MB R0C 1E0
204-639-2260 Fax: 204-639-2475
towngra@xplornet.ca
Municipal Type: Town
Incorporated: Jan. 2, 1962; *Area:* 85.95 sq km
Population in 2006: 336
Provincial Electoral District(s): Swan River
Federal Electoral District(s): Churchill
Next Election: Oct. 2010 (4 year terms)
Valerie Fourre, CAO
Jim Allen, Mayor

Grandview
P.O. Box 219
531 Main St.
Grandview, MB R0L 0Y0
204-546-5250 Fax: 204-546-5269
townofgv@mts.net
www.grandviewmanitoba.net
Municipal Type: Town
Incorporated: Jan. 1, 1905; *Area:* 2.87 sq km
Population in 2006: 839
Provincial Electoral District(s): Dauphin-Roblin
Federal Electoral District(s): Dauphin-Swan River-Marquette
Next Election: Oct. 2010 (4 year terms)
Sharon Dalgleish, CAO
Ernest Gurica, Mayor

Gretna
P.O. Box 280
612 - 7th St.
Gretna, MB R0G 0V0
204-327-5578 Fax: 204-327-5458
info@gretna.ca
www.gretna.ca
Municipal Type: Town
Incorporated: Jan. 6, 1886; *Area:* 2.79 sq km
Population in 2006: 574
Provincial Electoral District(s): Emerson
Federal Electoral District(s): Portage-Lisgar
Next Election: Oct. 2010 (4 year terms)
Janine Wiebe, CAO
Dennis Loewen, Mayor

Hamiota
P.O. Box 100
44 Maple Ave. East
Hamiota, MB R0M 0T0
204-764-3050 Fax: 204-764-3055
info@hamiota.com
www.hamiota.com
Municipal Type: Town
Incorporated: 1907; *Area:* 3.38 sq km
Population in 2006: 823
Provincial Electoral District(s): Russell
Federal Electoral District(s): Dauphin-Swan River-Marquette
Next Election: Oct. 2010 (4 year terms)
Tom Mollard, CAO
Larry Oakden, Mayor

Hartney
P.O. Box 339
315 East Railway St.
Hartney, MB R0M 0X0
204-858-2429 Fax: 204-858-2681
hartney@mts.net
Municipal Type: Town
Incorporated: Jan. 1, 1905; *Area:* 2.45 sq km
Population in 2006: 400
Provincial Electoral District(s): Arthur-Virden
Federal Electoral District(s): Brandon-Souris
Next Election: Oct. 2010 (4 year terms)
Brad Coe, CAO
Bruce Evans, Mayor

Lac du Bonnet
P.O. Box 339
84 - 2nd St.
Lac du Bonnet, MB R0E 1A0
204-345-8693 Fax: 204-345-8694
townldb@mts.net
www.lacdubonnet.com
Municipal Type: Town
Incorporated: Jan. 4, 1947; *Area:* 2.25 sq km
Population in 2006: 1,009
Provincial Electoral District(s): Lac du Bonnet
Federal Electoral District(s): Provencher
Next Election: Oct. 2010 (4 year terms)
Colleen L. Johnson, CAO
Paul Chapman, Mayor

Leaf Rapids
Town Centre Complex
P.O. Box 340
Leaf Rapids, MB R0B 1W0
204-473-2436 Fax: 204-473-2566
administrator@townofleafrapids.ca
www.townofleafrapids.ca
Municipal Type: Town
Incorporated: Jan. 5, 1976; *Area:* 1,272.87 sq km
Population in 2006: 539
Provincial Electoral District(s): Flin Flon
Federal Electoral District(s): Churchill
Next Election: Oct. 2010 (4 year terms)
Bond Ryan, CAO
Ed Charrier, Mayor

Lynn Lake
P.O. Box 100
503 Sherritt Ave.
Lynn Lake, MB R0B 0W0
204-356-2418 Fax: 204-356-8297
info@lynnlake.ca
www.lynnlake.ca
Municipal Type: Town
Area: 910.23 sq km
Population in 2006: 714
Provincial Electoral District(s): Flin Flon
Federal Electoral District(s): Churchill
Next Election: Oct. 2010 (4 year terms)
Helen I. Gibson, CAO
Audie W. Dulewich, Mayor

MacGregor
P.O. Box 190
27 Hampton St. East
MacGregor, MB R0H 0R0
204-685-2211 Fax: 204-685-2616
office@villageofmacgregor.com
www.villageofmacgregor.com
Municipal Type: Village
Incorporated: Jan. 4, 1947; *Area:* 2.13 sq km
Population in 2006: 921
Provincial Electoral District(s): Turtle Mountain
Federal Electoral District(s): Portage-Lisgar
Next Election: Oct. 2010 (4 year terms)
Y. Ivan Bruneau, CAO
Doris Moore, Mayor

Manitou
P.O. Box 280
261 Main St.
Manitou, MB R0G 1G0
204-242-2515 Fax: 204-242-3281
manitou@goinet.ca
www.townofmanitou.ca
Municipal Type: Town
Incorporated: 1897; *Area:* 2.94 sq km
Population in 2006: 718
Provincial Electoral District(s): Pembina
Federal Electoral District(s): Portage-Lisgar
Next Election: Oct. 2010 (4 year terms)
Angie Klassen, CAO
Jake Goertzen, Mayor

McCreary
P.O. Box 267
436 - 2nd Ave.
McCreary, MB R0J 1B0
204-835-2341 Fax: 204-835-2658
villageofmccreary@hotmail.com
Municipal Type: Village
Incorporated: Jan. 4, 1964; *Area:* 1.7 sq km
Population in 2006: 487
Provincial Electoral District(s): Ste. Rose
Federal Electoral District(s): Dauphin-Swan River-Marquette
Next Election: Oct. 2010 (4 year terms)
Wendy L. Turko, Municipal Administrator
Carrie Walker, Mayor

Melita
P.O. Box 364
79 Main St.
Melita, MB R0M 1L0
204-522-3413 Fax: 204-522-3587
tofmel@mts.net
www.melitamb.ca
Municipal Type: Town
Incorporated: Jan. 2, 1906; *Area:* 2.96 sq km
Population in 2006: 1,051
Provincial Electoral District(s): Arthur-Virden
Federal Electoral District(s): Brandon-Souris
Next Election: Oct. 2010 (4 year terms)
Linda Cripps, CAO
R. F. (Bob) Walker, Mayor

Minitonas
P.O. Box 9
311 Main St.
Minitonas, MB R0L 1G0
204-525-4461 Fax: 204-525-4857
rmmin@mts.net
Municipal Type: Town
Incorporated: Jan. 5, 1948; *Area:* 2.01 sq km
Population in 2006: 497
Provincial Electoral District(s): Swan River
Federal Electoral District(s): Dauphin-Swan River-Marquette
Next Election: Oct. 2010 (4 year terms)
Carolyn Gordon, CAO
Henry Barkowski, Mayor

Minnedosa
P.O. Box 426
103 Main St. South
Minnedosa, MB R0J 1E0
204-867-2727 Fax: 204-867-2686
minnedosa@mts.net
Municipal Type: Town
Incorporated: Jan. 5, 1948; *Area:* 15.26 sq km
Population In 2006: 2,474
Provincial Electoral District(s): Minnedosa
Federal Electoral District(s): Dauphin-Swan River-Marquette
Next Election: Oct. 2010 (4 year terms)
Ken Jenkins, CAO
Duane LaCoste, Mayor

Morden
#100, 195 Stephen St.
Morden, MB R6M 1V3
204-822-4434 Fax: 204-822-6494
tmorden@mordenmb.com
www.mordenmb.com
Municipal Type: Town
Incorporated: Jan. 1, 1882; *Area:* 16.39 sq km
Population in 2006: 6,571
Provincial Electoral District(s): Pembina
Federal Electoral District(s): Portage-Lisgar
Next Election: Oct. 2010 (4 year terms)
Ernie Epp, CAO
Doug Wilson, Mayor

Morris
P.O. Box 28
233 Main St. North
Morris, MB R0G 1K0
204-746-2531 Fax: 204-746-6009
tomorris@mts.net
www.town.morris.mb.ca
Municipal Type: Town
Incorporated: Jan. 2, 1883; *Area:* 6.1 sq km
Population in 2006: 1,643
Provincial Electoral District(s): Morris
Federal Electoral District(s): Provencher
Next Election: Oct. 2010 (4 year terms)
Midge Anderson, CAO
Dale Hoffman, Mayor

Neepawa
P.O. Box 339
275 Hamilton St.
Neepawa, MB R0J 1H0
204-476-7600 Fax: 204-476-7624
neepawa@westman.wave.ca
www.neepawa.ca
Municipal Type: Town
Incorporated: Jan. 2, 1883; *Area:* 17.57 sq km
Population in 2006: 3,298
Provincial Electoral District(s): Ste. Rose

Federal Electoral District(s): Dauphin-Swan River-Marquette
Next Election: Oct. 2010 (4 year terms)
Sheila Mowat, CAO
Robert Durston, Mayor

Niverville
P.O. Box 267
86 Main St.
Niverville, MB R0A 1E0
204-388-4600 Fax: 204-388-6110
gjbuys@niverville.com
www.niverville.com
Municipal Type: Town
Incorporated: Jan. 4, 1969; *Area:* 8.79 sq km
Population in 2006: 2,464
Provincial Electoral District(s): Steinbach
Federal Electoral District(s): Provencher
Next Election: Oct. 2010 (4 year terms)
G. Jim Buys, CAO
Greg Fehr, Mayor

Notre Dame de Lourdes
P.O. Box 89
55 Rogers St.
Notre Dame de Lourdes, MB R0G 1M0
204-248-2348 Fax: 204-248-2677
villagend@mts.net
www.notre-dame-de-lourdes.ca
Municipal Type: Village
Incorporated: Jan. 3, 1963; *Area:* 2.58 sq km
Population in 2006: 589
Provincial Electoral District(s): Carman
Federal Electoral District(s): Portage-Lisgar
Next Election: Oct. 2010 (4 year terms)
Jolyne Bibault, CAO
Denis Bibault, Mayor

Oak Lake
P.O. Box 100
293 - 2nd Ave. West
Oak Lake, MB R0M 1P0
204-855-2423 Fax: 204-855-2836
cao_sifton@mts.net
www.oaklakeandarea.com
Municipal Type: Town
Incorporated: Jan. 3, 1907; *Area:* 2.73 sq km
Population in 2006: 363
Provincial Electoral District(s): Arthur-Virden
Federal Electoral District(s): Brandon-Souris
Next Election: Oct. 2010 (4 year terms)
Mary Smith, CAO
Jeff Sigurdson, Mayor

Pilot Mound
P.O. Box 39
219 Broadway Ave.
Pilot Mound, MB R0G 1P0
204-825-2587 Fax: 204-825-2362
vlgpm@mts.net
www.pilotmound.com
Municipal Type: Town
Incorporated: May 4, 1904; *Area:* 2.7 sq km
Population in 2006: 630
Provincial Electoral District(s): Turtle Mountain
Federal Electoral District(s): Portage-Lisgar
Next Election: Oct. 2010 (4 year terms)
Tannis Stevenson, CAO
R. Brent Checkley, Mayor

Plum Coulee
P.O. Box 36
253 Main Ave.
Plum Coulee, MB R0G 1R0
204-829-3419 Fax: 204-829-3436
pcoulee@mts.net
Municipal Type: Town
Incorporated: Jan. 6, 1901; *Area:* 2.48 sq km
Population in 2006: 770
Provincial Electoral District(s): Emerson
Federal Electoral District(s): Portage-Lisgar
Next Election: Oct. 2010 (4 year terms)
Dale Toews, CAO
Archie Heinrichs, Mayor

Powerview - Pine Falls
P.O. Box 220
277B Main St.
Powerview, MB R0E 1P0
204-367-8483 Fax: 204-367-4747
powerview.pinefalls@mts.net
Municipal Type: Town
Incorporated: Jan. 2, 1951; *Area:* 5.05 sq km
Population in 2006: 1,294
Provincial Electoral District(s): Lac du Bonnet
Federal Electoral District(s): Provencher
Next Election: Oct. 2010 (4 year terms)
Valerie P. Irving, CAO
Theodore Pichor, Mayor

Rapid City
P.O. Box 130
410 - 3rd Ave.
Rapid City, MB R0K 1W0
204-826-2679 Fax: 204-826-2652
rapcity@mts.net
www.rapidcitymb.ca
Municipal Type: Town
Incorporated: Jan. 2, 1883; *Area:* 5.38 sq km
Population in 2006: 416
Provincial Electoral District(s): Minnedosa
Federal Electoral District(s): Dauphin-Swan River-Marquette
Next Election: Oct. 2010 (4 year terms)
Donna Anderson, CAO
Terry Christie, Mayor

Rivers
P.O. Box 520
670 - 2nd Ave.
Rivers, MB R0K 1X0
204-328-5250 Fax: 204-328-5374
rivers@mts.net
www.townofrivers.mb.ca
Municipal Type: Town
Incorporated: Jan. 4, 1913; *Area:* 7.97 sq km
Population in 2006: 1,193
Provincial Electoral District(s): Minnedosa
Federal Electoral District(s): Brandon-Souris
Next Election: Oct. 2010 (4 year terms)
Dennis Higginson, CAO
Al Morken, Mayor

Riverton
P.O. Box 250
56 Laura Ave.
Riverton, MB R0C 2R0
204-378-2281 Fax: 204-378-5616
vilofriv@mts.net
Municipal Type: Village
Incorporated: Jan. 2, 1951; *Area:* 1.11 sq km
Population in 2006: 537
Provincial Electoral District(s): Interlake
Federal Electoral District(s): Selkirk-Interlake
Next Election: Oct. 2010 (4 year terms)
Nadine Eyjolfson, CAO
Colin Bjarnason, Mayor

Roblin
P.O. Box 730
125 - 1st Ave. NW
Roblin, MB R0L 1P0
204-937-8333 Fax: 204-937-4382
troblin@mts.net
Municipal Type: Town
Incorporated: Jan. 4, 1913; *Area:* 3.79 sq km
Population in 2006: 1,672
Provincial Electoral District(s): Dauphin-Roblin
Federal Electoral District(s): Dauphin-Swan River-Marquette; Brandon-Souris
Next Election: Oct. 2010 (4 year terms)
Marna J. Bulbuck, CAO
Doug Hazlitt, Mayor

Rossburn
P.O. Box 70
43 Main St. North
Rossburn, MB R0J 1V0
204-859-2762 Fax: 204-859-2959
town.rsb@mts.net
www.town.rossburn.mb.ca
Municipal Type: Town
Incorporated: Jan. 4, 1913; *Area:* 3.43 sq km
Population in 2006: 546
Provincial Electoral District(s): Russell
Federal Electoral District(s): Dauphin-Swan River-Marquette
Next Election: Oct. 2010 (4 year terms)
Leonard Mackedenski, CAO
Shirley Kalyniuk, Mayor

Russell
P.O. Box 10
178 Main St. North
Russell, MB R0J 1W0
204-773-2253 Fax: 204-773-3370
town@russellmb.com
www.russellmb.com
Municipal Type: Town
Incorporated: Jan. 4, 1913; *Area:* 3.15 sq km
Population in 2006: 1,428
Provincial Electoral District(s): Russell
Federal Electoral District(s): Dauphin-Swan River-Marquette
Next Election: Oct. 2010 (4 year terms)
Chris Radford, Mayor
Wally R. Melnyk, Chief Administrative Officer

Ste. Anne
181 Central Ave.
Ste. Anne, MB R5H 1G3
204-422-5293 Fax: 204-422-5459
nicole_champagne@steannemb.ca
www.steannemb.ca
Municipal Type: Town
Incorporated: Jan. 3, 1963; *Area:* 4.19 sq km
Population in 2006: 1,534
Provincial Electoral District(s): La Verendrye
Federal Electoral District(s): Provencher
Next Election: Oct. 2010 (4 year terms)
Nicole Champagne, CAO
Bernard Vermette, Mayor

St. Claude
P.O. Box 249
12 - 1st St.
St Claude, MB R0G 1Z0
204-379-2382 Fax: 204-379-2072
stclaude@mts.net
www.stclaude.ca
Municipal Type: Village
Incorporated: Jan. 3, 1963; *Area:* 1.8 sq km
Population in 2006: 588
Provincial Electoral District(s): Carman
Federal Electoral District(s): Portage-Lisgar
Next Election: Oct. 2010 (4 year terms)
Simone Dupasquier, CAO
Steve Kiefer, Mayor
204-379-2172

St. Lazare
P.O. Box 100
100 Chartier Ave. West
St Lazare, MB R0M 1Y0
204-683-2241 Fax: 204-683-2317
laz_ell@mts.net
Municipal Type: Village
Incorporated: Jan. 1, 1950; *Area:* 2.91 sq km
Population in 2006: 265
Provincial Electoral District(s): Russell
Federal Electoral District(s): Dauphin-Swan River-Marquette
Next Election: Oct. 2010 (4 year terms)
Richard W. Fouillard, CAO
Martin Dupont, Mayor

St. Pierre-Jolys
P.O. Box 218
466 Sabourin St.
St. Pierre-Jolys, MB R0A 1V0
204-433-7832 Fax: 204-433-7053
villstp@ratrivercomm.ca
www.granite.mb.ca/erdc/st.pierre-jolys
Municipal Type: Village
Incorporated: Jan. 4, 1947; *Area:* 2.6 sq km
Population in 2006: 839
Provincial Electoral District(s): Morris
Federal Electoral District(s): Provencher
Next Election: Oct. 2010 (4 year terms)
Rachelle Tessier, CAO
Réal Curé, Mayor

Ste. Rose du Lac
P.O. Box 445
722 Central Ave.
Ste. Rose du Lac, MB R0L 1S0
204-447-2229 Fax: 204-447-2875
sterose@mts.net
www.town.sterosedulac.mb.ca
Municipal Type: Town
Incorporated: Jan. 5, 1920; *Area:* 2.53 sq km
Population in 2006: 995
Provincial Electoral District(s): Ste. Rose
Federal Electoral District(s): Dauphin-Swan River-Marquette
Next Election: Oct. 2010 (4 year terms)
Marlene M. Bouchard, CAO
Rene L. Maillard, Mayor

Shoal Lake
P.O. Box 342
438 Station Rd.
Shoal Lake, MB R0J 1Z0
204-759-2270 Fax: 204-759-2690
tnshlake@mts.net
www.shoallake.ca
Municipal Type: Town
Incorporated: Jan. 6, 1909; *Area:* 2.58 sq km
Population in 2006: 680
Provincial Electoral District(s): Russell
Federal Electoral District(s): Dauphin-Swan River-Marquette
Next Election: Oct. 2010 (4 year terms)
Shirley Wowryk, CAO
Mike J. Blahy, Mayor

Snow Lake
P.O. Box 40
113 Elm St.
Snow Lake, MB R0B 1M0
204-358-2551 Fax: 204-358-2112
snowlake@mts.net
www.snowlake.com
Municipal Type: Town
Incorporated: 1947; *Area:* 1,211.89 sq km
Population in 2006: 837
Provincial Electoral District(s): Flin Flon
Federal Electoral District(s): Churchill
Next Election: Oct. 2010 (4 year terms)
Arnie Assoignon, CAO
Garry Zamzow, Mayor

Somerset
P.O. Box 187
307 - 3rd St.
Somerset, MB R0G 2L0
204-744-2171 Fax: 204-744-2618
somerset@mts.net
Municipal Type: Village
Incorporated: Jan. 2, 1962; *Area:* 2.45 sq km
Population in 2006: 432

Provincial Electoral District(s): Carman
Federal Electoral District(s): Portage-Lisgar
Next Election: Oct. 2010 (4 year terms)
Linda Talbot, CAO
Gerald Rondeau, Mayor

Souris
P.O. Box 518
100 - 2nd St. South
Souris, MB R0K 2C0
204-483-5200 Fax: 204-483-5203
tnsouris@mts.net
www.sourismanitoba.com
Municipal Type: Town
Incorporated: Jan. 6, 1904; *Area:* 3.64 sq km
Population in 2006: 1,772
Provincial Electoral District(s): Minnedosa
Federal Electoral District(s): Brandon-Souris
Next Election: Oct. 2010 (4 year terms)
William Hildebrand, CAO
Darryl Jackson, Mayor

Stonewall
P.O. Box 250
293 Main St.
Stonewall, MB R0C 2Z0
204-467-7979 Fax: 204-467-7999
info@stonewall.ca
www.stonewall.ca
Municipal Type: Town
Incorporated: Jan. 4, 1908; *Area:* 6.02 sq km
Population in 2006: 4,376
Provincial Electoral District(s): Lakeside
Federal Electoral District(s): Selkirk-Interlake
Next Election: Oct. 2010 (4 year terms)
Robert Potter, CAO
204-467-7960
cao@stonewall.ca
Ross Thompson, Mayor
rossthompson@mts.net

Swan River
P.O. Box 879
135 - 5th Ave. North
Swan River, MB R0L 1Z0
204-734-4586 Fax: 204-734-5166
townsr@town.swanriver.mb.ca
www.town.swanriver.mb.ca
Municipal Type: Town
Incorporated: Jan. 4, 1908; *Area:* 6.78 sq km
Population in 2006: 3,859
Provincial Electoral District(s): Swan River
Federal Electoral District(s): Dauphin-Swan River-Marquette
Next Election: Oct. 2010 (4 year terms)
Lawrence Hart, CAO
hart@town.swanriver.mb.ca
Glen McKenzie, Mayor

Teulon
P.O. Box 69
44 - 4 Ave. SE
Teulon, MB R0C 3B0
204-886-2314 Fax: 204-886-3918
teulon@mts.net
www.teulon.ca
Municipal Type: Town
Incorporated: Jan. 4, 1919; *Area:* 3.2 sq km
Population in 2006: 1,124
Provincial Electoral District(s): Lakeside
Federal Electoral District(s): Selkirk-Interlake
Next Election: Oct. 2010 (4 year terms)
Grant MacAulay, CAO
Bert Campbell, Mayor

The Pas
P.O. Box 870
81 Edwards Ave.
The Pas, MB R9A 1K8
204-627-1100 Fax: 204-623-5506
valm@townofthepas.ca
www.thepasarea.com
Municipal Type: Town
Incorporated: Jan. 2, 1912; *Area:* 47.83 sq km
Population in 2006: 5,589
Provincial Electoral District(s): The Pas
Federal Electoral District(s): Churchill
Next Election: Oct. 2010 (4 year terms)
Val Miron, CAO
Herb Jaques, Mayor

Treherne
P.O. Box 30
180 Broadway Ave.
Treherne, MB R0G 2V0
204-723-2044 Fax: 204-723-2719
info@treherne.ca
www.treherne.ca
Municipal Type: Town
Incorporated: Jan. 5, 1948; *Area:* 1.96 sq km
Population in 2006: 646
Provincial Electoral District(s): Carman
Federal Electoral District(s): Portage-Lisgar
Next Election: Oct. 2010 (4 year terms)
Jackie Jenkinson, CAO
James Knockaert, Mayor

Virden
P.O. Box 310
236 Wellington St. West
Virden, MB R0M 2C0
204-748-2440 Fax: 204-748-2501
virden_sec@mts.net
virden.cimnet.ca
Municipal Type: Town
Incorporated: Jan. 6, 1904; *Area:* 8.56 sq km
Population in 2006: 3,010
Provincial Electoral District(s): Arthur-Virden
Federal Electoral District(s): Brandon-Souris
Next Election: Oct. 2010 (4 year terms)
Rhonda Stewart, CAO
Bruce Dunning, Mayor

Waskada
P.O. Box 40
103 - 2nd St.
Waskada, MB R0M 2E0
204-673-2401 Fax: 204-673-2663
waskadan@mts.net
www.waskada.ca
Municipal Type: Village
Incorporated: Jan. 7, 1949; *Area:* 0.77 sq km
Population in 2006: 199
Provincial Electoral District(s): Arthur-Virden
Federal Electoral District(s): Brandon-Souris
Next Election: Oct. 2010 (4 year terms)
Ron Bertholet, Municipal Administrator
Gary Williams, Mayor

Wawanesa
P.O. Box 278
106 - 4th St.
Wawanesa, MB R0K 2G0
204-824-2244 Fax: 204-824-2244
vwawa@mts.net
www.wawanesa.ca
Municipal Type: Village
Incorporated: Jan. 6, 1909; *Area:* 2.26 sq km
Population in 2006: 535
Provincial Electoral District(s): Minnedosa
Federal Electoral District(s): Brandon-Souris
Next Election: Oct. 2010 (4 year terms)
Leonard Plett, CAO
Bruce Gullett, Mayor

Winnipeg Beach
P.O. Box 160
29 Robinson Ave.
Winnipeg Beach, MB R0C 3G0
204-389-2698 Fax: 204-389-2019
info@winnipegbeach.ca
www.winnipegbeach.ca
Municipal Type: Town
Incorporated: Jan. 5, 1914; *Area:* 3.88 sq km
Population in 2006: 1,017
Provincial Electoral District(s): Gimli
Federal Electoral District(s): Selkirk-Interlake
Next Election: Oct. 2010 (4 year terms)
Marion Grogan, CAO
cao@winnipegbeach.ca
Don Pepe, Mayor

Winnipegosis
P.O. Box 370
130 - 2nd St.
Winnipegosis, MB R0L 2G0
204-656-4791 Fax: 204-656-4751
vofwinnipegosis@mts.net
www.winnipegosis.ca
Municipal Type: Village
Incorporated: Jan. 6, 1915; *Area:* 2.5 sq km
Population in 2006: 628
Provincial Electoral District(s): Swan River
Federal Electoral District(s): Dauphin-Swan River-Marquette
Next Election: Oct. 2010 (4 year terms)
Terry Tomlinson, Village Administrator
Gloria Kostelnyk, Mayor

Rural Municipality

Albert
P.O. Box 70
14 Morris St.
Tilston, MB R0M 2B0
204-686-2271 Fax: 204-686-2335
rmalbert@mts.net
Municipal Type: Rural Municipality
Incorporated: Jan. 3, 1946; *Area:* 769.55 sq km
Population in 2006: 339
Provincial Electoral District(s): Arthur-Virden
Federal Electoral District(s): Brandon-Souris
Next Election: Oct. 2010 (4 year terms)
Carol Philip, CAO
Tom Campbell, Reeve

Alexander
P.O. Box 100
104058 Provincial Trunk Hwy. 11
St Georges, MB R0E 1V0
204-367-6170 Fax: 204-367-2257
margieb@wrac.ca
Municipal Type: Rural Municipality
Incorporated: Jan. 2, 1945; *Area:* 1,568.66 sq km
Population in 2006: 2,978
Provincial Electoral District(s): Lac du Bonnet; Selkirk
Federal Electoral District(s): Provencher; Brandon-Souris; Selkirk-Interlake
Next Election: Oct. 2010 (4 year terms)
Margaret Bonekamp, CAO
George Harbottle, Reeve

Alonsa
P.O. Box 127
20 Railway Ave.
Alonsa, MB R0H 0A0
204-767-2054 Fax: 204-767-2044
rmalonsa@inetlink.ca
Municipal Type: Rural Municipality
Area: 2,977.50 sq km
Population in 2006: 1,446
Provincial Electoral District(s): Ste. Rose
Federal Electoral District(s): Dauphin-Swan River-Marquette
Next Election: Oct. 2010 (4 year terms)
Pamela Sul, CAO
Stan Asham, Reeve

Archie
P.O. Box 67
202 Qu'Appelle St.
McAuley, MB R0M 1H0
204-722-2053 Fax: 204-722-2027
rmarchie@mb.sympatico.ca
Municipal Type: Rural Municipality
Incorporated: Jan. 2, 1883; *Area:* 577.68 sq km
Population in 2006: 330
Provincial Electoral District(s): Russell
Federal Electoral District(s): Dauphin-Swan River-Marquette
Next Election: Oct. 2010 (4 year terms)
Dawna Jamieson, CAO
Brian Bajus, Reeve

Argyle
P.O. Box 40
132 - 2nd St. North
Baldur, MB R0K 0B0
204-535-2176 Fax: 204-535-2176
gord@inetbiz.ca
Municipal Type: Rural Municipality
Incorporated: Jan. 1, 1882; *Area:* 770.44 sq km
Population in 2006: 1,073
Provincial Electoral District(s): Turtle Mountain
Federal Electoral District(s): Brandon-Souris; Selkirk-Interlake
Next Election: Oct. 2010 (4 year terms)
Gordon Dearsley, CAO
Bob Conibear, Reeve

Armstrong
P.O. Box 69
Inwood, MB R0C 1P0
204-278-3377 Fax: 204-278-3437
armstrong-RM@lakeshorewireless.ca
Municipal Type: Rural Municipality
Incorporated: Dec. 5, 1944; *Area:* 1,864.96 sq km
Population in 2006: 1,919
Provincial Electoral District(s): Interlake
Federal Electoral District(s): Selkirk-Interlake
Next Election: Oct. 2010 (4 year terms)
Don Rybachuk, CAO
Les Marchak, Reeve

Arthur
P.O. Box 429
138 Main St.
Melita, MB R0M 1L0
204-522-3263 Fax: 204-522-8706
rmarthur@mts.net
Municipal Type: Rural Municipality
Area: 765.77 sq km
Population in 2006: 440
Provincial Electoral District(s): Arthur-Virden
Federal Electoral District(s): Brandon-Souris
Next Election: Oct. 2010 (4 year terms)
Sandra Anderson, CAO
Jim Trewin, Reeve

Bifrost
P.O. Box 70
329 River Rd.
Arborg, MB R0C 0A0
204-376-2391 Fax: 204-376-2742
bifrost@mts.net
Municipal Type: Rural Municipality
Incorporated: Jan. 4, 1908; *Area:* 1,642.58 sq km
Population in 2006: 2,972
Provincial Electoral District(s): Interlake
Federal Electoral District(s): Selkirk-Interlake
Next Election: Oct. 2010 (4 year terms)
L. Grant Thorsteinson, CAO
Harold Foster, Reeve

Birtle
P.O. Box 70
678 Main St.
Birtle, MB R0M 0C0
204-842-3403 Fax: 204-842-3622
rmbirtle@mts.net

Municipal Type: Rural Municipality
Incorporated: Jan. 3, 1884; *Area:* 849.13 sq km
Population in 2006: 666
Provincial Electoral District(s): Russell
Federal Electoral District(s): Dauphin-Swan River-Marquette
Next Election: Oct. 2010 (4 year terms)
Debbie Jensen, CAO
Roger Wilson, Reeve

Blanshard
P.O. Box 179
10 Cochrane St.
Oak River, MB R0K 1T0
204-566-2146 Fax: 204-566-2126
blanshardcdc@inetlink.ca
www.rmofblanshard.ca
Municipal Type: Rural Municipality
Incorporated: Jan. 3, 1884; *Area:* 578.98 sq km
Population in 2006: 586
Provincial Electoral District(s): Russell
Federal Electoral District(s): Dauphin-Swan River-Marquette
Next Election: Oct. 2010 (4 year terms)
Diane Kuculym, CAO
Richard Heapy, Reeve

Brenda
P.O. Box 40
103 - 2nd St.
Waskada, MB R0M 2E0
204-673-2401 Fax: 204-673-2663
waskadan@mts.net
Municipal Type: Rural Municipality
Area: 766 sq km
Population in 2006: 549
Provincial Electoral District(s): Arthur-Virden
Federal Electoral District(s): Brandon-Souris
Next Election: Oct. 2010 (4 year terms)
Ron Bertholet, CAO
Dunc Stewart, Reeve

Brokenhead
P.O. Box 490
Beausejour, MB R0E 0C0
204-268-6700 Fax: 204-268-1504
rmbroken@granite.mb.ca
www.granite.mb.ca/erdc/brokenhead/main.html
Municipal Type: Rural Municipality
Incorporated: Jan. 2, 1900; *Area:* 750.54 sq km
Population in 2006: 3,940
Provincial Electoral District(s): Lac du Bonnet
Federal Electoral District(s): Selkirk-Interlake
Next Election: Oct. 2010 (4 year terms)
Christine Hutlet, CAO
Glen Dudek, Reeve

Cameron
P.O. Box 399
315 East Railway St.
Hartney, MB R0M 0X0
204-858-2590 Fax: 204-858-2681
hartney@mts.net
Municipal Type: Rural Municipality
Incorporated: Jan. 6, 1897; *Area:* 759.15 sq km
Population in 2006: 433
Provincial Electoral District(s): Arthur-Virden
Federal Electoral District(s): Brandon-Souris
Next Election: Oct. 2010 (4 year terms)
Brad Coe, CAO
Wayne Drummond, Reeve

Cartier
P.O. Box 117
28 Provincial Rd. 248 South
Elie, MB R0H 0H0
204-353-2214 Fax: 204-353-2335
info@rm-cartier.mb.ca
www.rm-cartier.mb.ca
Municipal Type: Rural Municipality
Incorporated: Jan. 5, 1914; *Area:* 553.42 sq km
Population in 2006: 3,162
Provincial Electoral District(s): Morris
Federal Electoral District(s): Portage-Lisgar
Next Election: Oct. 2010 (4 year terms)
Lynn Kauppila, CAO
Roland Rasmussen, Reeve

Clanwilliam
P.O. Box 40
44 Main St.
Erickson, MB R0J 0P0
204-636-2431 Fax: 204-636-2516
erikclan@mts.net
Municipal Type: Rural Municipality
Incorporated: Jan. 3, 1884; *Area:* 354.01 sq km
Population in 2006: 494
Provincial Electoral District(s): Russell
Federal Electoral District(s): Dauphin-Swan River-Marquette
Next Election: Oct. 2010 (4 year terms)
Kat Bridgeman, CAO
Victor Baraniuk, Reeve

Coldwell
P.O. Box 90
35 Main St.
Lundar, MB R0C 1Y0
204-762-5421 Fax: 204-762-5177
coldwell@mts.net
Municipal Type: Rural Municipality
Incorporated: Jan. 4, 1913; *Area:* 901.84 sq km
Population in 2006: 1,339
Provincial Electoral District(s): Lakeside
Federal Electoral District(s): Selkirk-Interlake
Next Election: Oct. 2010 (4 year terms)
K. Janet Isfeld, CAO
Brian Sigfusson, Reeve

Cornwallis
PO Box 10, Site 500, RR#5
Brandon, MB R7A 5Y5
204-725-8686 Fax: 204-725-3659
info@gov.cornwallis.mb.ca
www.gov.cornwallis.mb.ca
Municipal Type: Rural Municipality
Incorporated: Jan. 3, 1884; *Area:* 500.82 sq km
Population in 2006: 4,058
Provincial Electoral District(s): Minnedosa
Federal Electoral District(s): Brandon-Souris
Next Election: Oct. 2010 (4 year terms)
R.L. (Bob) Wallis, CAO
Kurt Wasserberg, Reeve

Daly
P.O. Box 538
645 - 2nd Ave.
Rivers, MB R0K 1X0
204-328-7410 Fax: 204-328-4431
rmdaly@mts.net
www.townofrivers.mb.ca
Municipal Type: Rural Municipality
Area: 562.44 sq km
Population in 2006: 868
Provincial Electoral District(s): Minnedosa
Federal Electoral District(s): Brandon-Souris
Next Election: Oct. 2010 (4 year terms)
Lorne Green, CAO
Evan Smith, Reeve

Dauphin
P.O. Box 574
Hwy. 20A East
Dauphin, MB R7N 2V4
204-638-4531 Fax: 204-638-7598
rmofdphn@mts.net
Municipal Type: Rural Municipality
Area: 1,516.1 sq km
Population in 2006: 2,328
Provincial Electoral District(s): Dauphin-Roblin
Federal Electoral District(s): Dauphin-Swan River-Marquette
Next Election: Oct. 2010 (4 year terms)
Marlene Durston, CAO
Dennis Forbes, Reeve

De Salaberry
P.O. Box 40
466 Sabourin St.
St Pierre Jolys, MB R0A 1V0
204-433-7406 Fax: 204-433-7063
info@rmdesalaberry.mb.ca
www.rmdesalaberry.mb.ca
Municipal Type: Rural Municipality
Incorporated: Jan. 2, 1883; *Area:* 670.29 sq km
Population in 2006: 3,349
Provincial Electoral District(s): Morris
Federal Electoral District(s): Provencher
Next Election: Oct. 2010 (4 year terms)
Luc Lahaie, CAO
Ron Musick, Reeve

Dufferin
P.O. Box 100
12 - 2nd Ave. SW
Carman, MB R0G 0J0
204-745-2301 Fax: 204-745-6348
rmduff@mts.net
Municipal Type: Rural Municipality
Incorporated: Feb. 7, 1880; *Area:* 915.72 sq km
Population in 2006: 2,199
Provincial Electoral District(s): Carman
Federal Electoral District(s): Portage-Lisgar
Next Election: Oct. 2010 (4 year terms)
Ruth Stege, CAO
Shawn McCutcheon

East St. Paul
3021 Bird's Hill Rd.
East St Paul, MB R2E 1A7
204-668-8112 Fax: 204-668-1987
administration@eaststpaul.com
www.eaststpaul.com
Municipal Type: Rural Municipality
Incorporated: May 2, 1916; *Area:* 42.1 sq km
Population in 2006: 8,733
Provincial Electoral District(s): Springfield
Federal Electoral District(s): Kildonan-St. Paul
Next Election: Oct. 2010 (4 year terms)
Lawrence Morris, Reeve
Jerome Mauws, CAO

Edward
P.O. Box 100
58 Railway Ave.
Pierson, MB R0M 1S0
204-634-2231 Fax: 204-634-2479
rmofedw@inethome.ca
Municipal Type: Rural Municipality
Incorporated: Jan. 1, 1905; *Area:* 769.14 sq km
Population in 2006: 621
Provincial Electoral District(s): Arthur-Virden
Federal Electoral District(s): Brandon-Souris
Next Election: Oct. 2010 (4 year terms)
Audrey Bird, CAO
Ralph J. Wang, Reeve

Ellice
P.O. Box 100
100 Chartier Ave. West
St Lazare, MB R0M 1Y0
204-683-2241 Fax: 204-683-2317
laz_ell@mts.net
Municipal Type: Rural Municipality
Incorporated: Jan. 2, 1883; *Area:* 572.74 sq km
Population in 2006: 423
Provincial Electoral District(s): Russell
Federal Electoral District(s): Dauphin-Swan River-Marquette
Next Election: Oct. 2010 (4 year terms)
Richard W. Fouillard, CAO
Guy Huberdeau, Reeve

Elton
Forest, MB R0K 0W0
204-728-7834 Fax: 204-725-1865
elton@inetlink.ca
Municipal Type: Rural Municipality
Incorporated: Jan. 2, 1883; *Area:* 571.85 sq km
Population in 2006: 1,285
Provincial Electoral District(s): Minnedosa
Federal Electoral District(s): Brandon-Souris
Next Election: Oct. 2010 (4 year terms)
Kathleen E.I. Steele, CAO
Jon B. Burton, Reeve

Eriksdale
P.O. Box 10
Eriksdale, MB R0C 0W0
204-739-2666 Fax: 204-739-2073
rm@eriksdale.com
www.eriksdale.com
Municipal Type: Rural Municipality
Incorporated: Jan. 6, 1904; *Area:* 784.76 sq km
Population in 2006: 911
Provincial Electoral District(s): Interlake
Federal Electoral District(s): Selkirk-Interlake
Next Election: Oct. 2010 (4 year terms)
Diane Friesen, CAO
Brian McKinnon, Reeve

Ethelbert
P.O. Box 115
5 Railway Ave. North
Ethelbert, MB R0L 0T0
204-742-3212 Fax: 204-742-3642
rmethelbert@inetlink.ca
Municipal Type: Rural Municipality
Incorporated: Jan. 1, 1905; *Area:* 1,134.5 sq km
Population in 2006: 383
Provincial Electoral District(s): Swan River
Federal Electoral District(s): Dauphin-Swan River-Marquette
Next Election: Oct. 2010 (4 year terms)
Janice C. Lagoski, CAO
Art Potoroka, Reeve

Fisher
P.O. Box 280
30 Tache St.
Fisher Branch, MB R0C 0Z0
204-372-6393 Fax: 204-372-8470
rmoffisher@mts.net
Municipal Type: Rural Municipality
Incorporated: Jan. 2, 1945; *Area:* 1,481.35 sq km
Population in 2006: 1,944
Provincial Electoral District(s): Interlake
Federal Electoral District(s): Selkirk-Interlake
Next Election: Oct. 2010 (4 year terms)
Linda Podaima, CAO
Denis Dandeneau, Reeve

Franklin
P.O. Box 66
115 Waddell Ave. East.
Dominion City, MB R0A 0H0
204-427-2557 Fax: 204-427-2224
rmfrank@mts.net
Municipal Type: Rural Municipality
Area: 953.34 sq km
Population in 2006: 1,768
Provincial Electoral District(s): Emerson
Federal Electoral District(s): Dauphin-Swan River-Marquette; Provencher
Next Election: Oct. 2010 (4 year terms)
Tracey French, CAO
Archie Hunter, Reeve

Gilbert Plains
P.O. Box 220
115 Main St. North
Gilbert Plains, MB R0L 0X0
204-548-2326 Fax: 204-548-2564
rmofgilbertplains@mts.net
www.gilbertplains.com
Municipal Type: Rural Municipality
Incorporated: Jan. 3, 1901; *Area:* 1,048.14 sq km
Population in 2006: 834
Provincial Electoral District(s): Dauphin-Roblin
Federal Electoral District(s): Dauphin-Swan River-Marquette
Next Election: Oct. 2010 (4 year terms)
Susan Boyachek, CAO
Larry Malowski, Reeve

Gimli
P.O. Box 1246
62 - 2nd St.
Gimli, MB R0C 1B0
204-642-6650 Fax: 204-642-6660
gimli@rmgimli.com
www.rmgimli.com
Municipal Type: Rural Municipality
Incorporated: Jan. 7, 1887; *Area:* 319.25 sq km
Population in 2006: 5,797
Provincial Electoral District(s): Gimli
Federal Electoral District(s): Selkirk-Interlake
Next Election: Oct. 2010 (4 year terms)
Note: Effective January 1, 2003, the Town & Rural Municipality of Gimli amalgamated, continuing as the Rural Municipality of Gimli.
Joann King, CAO
Tammy Axelsson, Reeve

Glenella
P.O. Box 10
50 Main St. North
Glenella, MB R0J 0V0
204-352-4281 Fax: 204-352-4281
rmofglen@mts.net
Municipal Type: Rural Municipality
Incorporated: Jan. 5, 1920; *Area:* 497.14 sq km
Population in 2006: 517
Provincial Electoral District(s): Ste. Rose
Federal Electoral District(s): Dauphin-Swan River-Marquette
Next Election: Oct. 2010 (4 year terms)
Wendy Wutzke, CAO
Tony Kushner, Reeve

Glenwood
P.O. Box 487
100 - 2nd St. South
Souris, MB R0K 2C0
204-483-2822 Fax: 204-483-2062
rmglenwood@mts.net
Municipal Type: Rural Municipality
Incorporated: 1883; *Area:* 577.58 sq km
Population in 2006: 640
Provincial Electoral District(s): Minnedosa
Federal Electoral District(s): Brandon-Souris
Next Election: Oct. 2010 (4 year terms)
Denis Bauldic, CAO
M.E. (Sandy) Sanderson, Reeve

Grahamdale
P.O. Box 160
23 Government Rd.
Moosehorn, MB R0C 2E0
204-768-2858 Fax: 204-768-3374
rm606@tcmsnet.com
www.grahamdale.ca
Municipal Type: Rural Municipality
Incorporated: Jan. 2, 1945; *Area:* 2,384.62 sq km
Population in 2006: 1,416
Provincial Electoral District(s): Interlake
Federal Electoral District(s): Selkirk-Interlake
Next Election: Oct. 2010 (4 year terms)
Beverley L. Yaworski, CAO
Brian Kiesman, Reeve

Grandview
P.O. Box 340
531 Main St.
Grandview, MB R0L 0Y0
204-546-5080 Fax: 204-546-5089
rmgra@inetlink.ca
www.rmofgrandview.ca
Municipal Type: Rural Municipality
Incorporated: Jan. 3, 1901; *Area:* 1,152.5 sq km
Population in 2006: 736
Provincial Electoral District(s): Dauphin-Roblin
Federal Electoral District(s): Dauphin-Swan River-Marquette
Next Election: Oct. 2010 (4 year terms)
Joan Scott, CAO
Clifford Kutzan, Reeve

Grey
P.O. Box 99
34 Main St. North
Elm Creek, MB R0G 0N0
204-436-2014 Fax: 204-436-2543
rmofgrey@mts.net
Municipal Type: Rural Municipality
Incorporated: Jan. 2, 1906; *Area:* 958.49 sq km
Population in 2006: 2,004
Provincial Electoral District(s): Carman
Federal Electoral District(s): Portage-Lisgar
Next Election: Oct. 2010 (4 year terms)
Ronald D. Hayward, CAO
Ted Tkachyk, Reeve

Hamiota
P.O. Box 100
44 Maple Ave. East
Hamiota, MB R0M 0T0
204-764-3050 Fax: 204-764-3055
info@hamiota.com
www.hamiota.com
Municipal Type: Rural Municipality
Area: 572.38 sq km
Population in 2006: 437
Provincial Electoral District(s): Russell
Federal Electoral District(s): Dauphin-Swan River-Marquette
Next Election: Oct. 2010 (4 year terms)
Tom Mollard, CAO
Randy Lints, Reeve

Hanover
P.O. Box 1720
28 Westland Dr.
Steinbach, MB R5G 1N4
204-326-4488 Fax: 204-326-4830
general@rmhanover.mb.ca
Municipal Type: Rural Municipality
Incorporated: Jan. 7, 1881; *Area:* 740.31 sq km
Population in 2006: 11,871
Provincial Electoral District(s): Steinbach
Federal Electoral District(s): Provencher
Next Election: Oct. 2010 (4 year terms)
Douglas E. Cavers, CAO
Stan Toews, Reeve

Harrison
P.O. Box 220
108 Main St.
Newdale, MB R0J 1J0
204-849-2107 Fax: 204-849-2190
rmharris@inetbiz.ca
Municipal Type: Rural Municipality
Incorporated: Jan. 2, 1883; *Area:* 476.73 sq km
Population in 2006: 812
Provincial Electoral District(s): Russell
Federal Electoral District(s): Dauphin-Swan River-Marquette
Next Election: Oct. 2010 (4 year terms)
Donna Memryk, CAO
Anthony Kowalchuk, Reeve

Headingley
#1, 126 Bridge Rd.
Headingley, MB R4H 1G9
204-837-5766 Fax: 204-831-7207
rmofheadingley@rmofheadingley.ca
www.rmofheadingley.ca
Municipal Type: Rural Municipality
Incorporated: Jan. 4, 1992; *Area:* 106.96 sq km
Population in 2006: 2,726
Provincial Electoral District(s): Morris
Federal Electoral District(s): Charleswood-St. James-Assiniboia
Next Election: Oct. 2010 (4 year terms)
Chris Fulsher, CAO
Wilfred R. Taillieu, Reeve

Hillsburg
P.O. Box 1180
130 - 2nd Ave. NW
Roblin, MB R0L 1P0
204-937-2155 Fax: 204-937-3317
rmhills@mts.net
Municipal Type: Rural Municipality
Incorporated: Jan. 2, 1912; *Area:* 656.76 sq km
Population in 2006: 484
Provincial Electoral District(s): Dauphin-Roblin
Federal Electoral District(s): Dauphin-Swan River-Marquette
Next Election: Oct. 2010 (4 year terms)
Robin Perchaluk, CAO
Robert Misko, Reeve

Kelsey
P.O. Box 578
264 Fischer Ave.
The Pas, MB R9A 1K6
204-623-7474 Fax: 204-623-4546
rmkelsey@mts.net
Municipal Type: Rural Municipality
Incorporated: Jan. 7, 1944; *Area:* 867.64 sq km
Population in 2006: 2,453
Provincial Electoral District(s): Flin Flon; The Pas
Federal Electoral District(s): Churchill
Next Election: Oct. 2010 (4 year terms)
Shirley Timm-Rudolph, CAO
Rod Berezowecki, Reeve

Killarney - Turtle Mountain
P.O. Box 10
415 Broadway Ave.
Killarney, MB R0K 1G0
204-523-7247 Fax: 204-523-4637
tmkly1@mts.net
Municipal Type: Rural Municipality
Incorporated: Jan. 1, 1882; *Area:* 925.13 sq km
Population in 2006: 3,299
Provincial Electoral District(s): Turtle Mountain
Federal Electoral District(s): Brandon-Souris
Next Election: Oct. 2010 (4 year terms)
Note: The municipalities of Killarney & Turtle Mountain amalgamated to form one entity effective Jan. 1, 2007.
Jim Dowsett, CAO
Brian Moore, Mayor

La Broquerie
P.O. Box 130
94 Principale St.
La Broquerie, MB R0A 0W0
204-424-5251 Fax: 204-424-5193
rmlabroq@labroquerie.com
www.labroquerie.com
Municipal Type: Rural Municipality
Incorporated: Jan. 2, 1883; *Area:* 578.2 sq km
Population in 2006: 3,659
Provincial Electoral District(s): Emerson
Federal Electoral District(s): Provencher
Next Election: Oct. 2010 (4 year terms)
Rose-Marie Blanchette, CAO
Marielle Wiebe, Reeve

Lac du Bonnet
P.O. Box 100
4187 Provincial Trunk Hwy. 317
Lac du Bonnet, MB R0E 1A0
204-345-2619 Fax: 204-345-6716
rmldb@mts.net
www.lacdubonnet.com
Municipal Type: Rural Municipality
Incorporated: Jan. 2, 1917; *Area:* 1,100.17 sq km
Population in 2006: 2,812
Provincial Electoral District(s): Lac du Bonnet
Federal Electoral District(s): Provencher
Next Election: Oct. 2010 (4 year terms)
Marlene Watson, CAO
Don Halbert, Reeve

Lakeview
P.O. Box 100
101 Main St.
Langruth, MB R0H 0N0
204-445-2243 Fax: 204-445-2162
rmlakeview@mts.net
Municipal Type: Rural Municipality
Incorporated: Jan. 5, 1920; *Area:* 567.87 sq km
Population in 2006: 342
Provincial Electoral District(s): Ste. Rose
Federal Electoral District(s): Dauphin-Swan River-Marquette
Next Election: Oct. 2010 (4 year terms)
Ron Brown, CAO
Philip Thordarson, Reeve

Langford
P.O. Box 280
275 Hamilton St.
Neepawa, MB R0J 1H0
204-476-7600 Fax: 204-476-7624
langford@westman.wave.ca
Municipal Type: Rural Municipality
Area: 561.95 sq km
Population in 2006: 787
Provincial Electoral District(s): Ste. Rose
Federal Electoral District(s): Dauphin-Swan River-Marquette
Next Election: Oct. 2010 (4 year terms)
Sheila Mowat, CAO
Kathy Jasienczyk, Reeve

Lansdowne
P.O. Box 141
302 Lansdowne Ave.
Arden, MB R0J 0B0
204-368-2202 Fax: 204-368-2278
rmlansdowne@inetlink.ca
Municipal Type: Rural Municipality
Incorporated: Jan. 3, 1884; *Area:* 766.29 sq km
Population in 2006: 750
Provincial Electoral District(s): Ste. Rose
Federal Electoral District(s): Dauphin-Swan River-Marquette
Next Election: Oct. 2010 (4 year terms)
Carol Henderson, CAO
Richard Funk, Reeve

Lawrence
P.O. Box 220
714 Main St.
Rorketon, MB R0L 1R0
204-732-2333 Fax: 204-732-2557
rmlaw@mts.net
Municipal Type: Rural Municipality
Incorporated: Jan. 5, 1914; *Area:* 761.64 sq km
Population in 2006: 501
Provincial Electoral District(s): Dauphin-Roblin
Federal Electoral District(s): Dauphin-Swan River-Marquette
Next Election: Oct. 2010 (4 year terms)
Elizabeth Tymchuk, CAO
Fred Taylor, Reeve

Lorne
P.O. Box 10
307 - 3rd St.
Somerset, MB R0G 2L0

204-744-2133 Fax: 204-744-2349
rmlorne@inetlink.ca
Municipal Type: Rural Municipality
Incorporated: Jan. 5, 1880; *Area:* 906.82 sq km
Population in 2006: 2,003
Provincial Electoral District(s): Carman
Federal Electoral District(s): Portage-Lisgar
Next Election: Oct. 2010 (4 year terms)
Val Turner, CAO
Robert Davy, Reeve

Louise
P.O. Box 310
26 South Railway Ave. East
Crystal City, MB R0K 0N0
204-873-2591 Fax: 204-873-2459
rmlouise@inetlink.ca
Municipal Type: Rural Municipality
Incorporated: Jan. 5, 1880; *Area:* 932.67 sq km
Population in 2006: 819
Provincial Electoral District(s): Turtle Mountain
Federal Electoral District(s): Portage-Lisgar
Next Election: Oct. 2010 (4 year terms)
Scott Warrener, CAO
Kenneth S. Buchanan, Reeve

Macdonald
P.O. Box 100
161 Mandan Dr.
Sanford, MB R0G 2J0
204-736-2255 Fax: 204-736-4335
info@rmofmacdonald.com
www.rmofmacdonald.com
Municipal Type: Rural Municipality
Incorporated: Jan. 7, 1881; *Area:* 1,156.62 sq km
Population in 2006: 5,653
Provincial Electoral District(s): Morris
Federal Electoral District(s): Portage-Lisgar
Next Election: Oct. 2010 (4 year terms)
W. Tom Raine, CAO
Rodney Burns, Reeve

McCreary
P.O. Box 338
432 - 1st Ave.
McCreary, MB R0J 1B0
204-835-2309 Fax: 204-835-2649
rmmccreary@inetlink.ca
Municipal Type: Rural Municipality
Incorporated: Jan. 6, 1909; *Area:* 522.69 sq km
Population in 2006: 476
Provincial Electoral District(s): Ste. Rose
Federal Electoral District(s): Dauphin-Swan River-Marquette
Next Election: Oct. 2010 (4 year terms)
Margaret I. Roncin, CAO
Larry McLauchlan, Reeve

Miniota
P.O. Box 70
111 Sarah Ave.
Miniota, MB R0M 1M0
204-567-3683 Fax: 204-567-3807
miniota@mts.net
Municipal Type: Rural Municipality
Incorporated: 1900; *Area:* 832.75 sq km
Population in 2006: 904
Provincial Electoral District(s): Russell
Federal Electoral District(s): Dauphin-Swan River-Marquette
Next Election: Oct. 2010 (4 year terms)
Tina Collier, CAO
William Clark, Reeve

Minitonas
P.O. Box 9
311 Main St.
Minitonas, MB R0L 1G0
204-525-4461 Fax: 204-525-4857
rmmin@mts.net
Municipal Type: Rural Municipality
Incorporated: Jan. 3, 1901; *Area:* 1,197.67 sq km
Population in 2006: 1,105
Provincial Electoral District(s): Swan River
Federal Electoral District(s): Dauphin-Swan River-Marquette
Next Election: Oct. 2010 (4 year terms)
Carolyn Gordon, CAO
Michael McIntosh, Reeve

Minto
P.O. Box 247
49 Main St. South
Minnedosa, MB R0J 1E0
204-867-3865 Fax: 204-867-1937
rmminto@mts.net
Municipal Type: Rural Municipality
Incorporated: Jan. 5, 1903; *Area:* 363.65 sq km
Population in 2006: 667
Provincial Electoral District(s): Minnedosa
Federal Electoral District(s): Brandon-Souris; Dauphin-Swan River-Marquette
Next Election: Oct. 2010 (4 year terms)
Aaren Robertson, CAO
Keith Syslak, Reeve

Montcalm
P.O. Box 300
46 - 1st St. East
Letellier, MB R0G 1C0
204-737-2271 Fax: 204-737-2326
montcalm@mts.net
Municipal Type: Rural Municipality
Incorporated: Jan. 1, 1882; *Area:* 469.41 sq km
Population in 2006: 1,317
Provincial Electoral District(s): Emerson
Federal Electoral District(s): Provencher
Next Election: Oct. 2010 (4 year terms)
Mitch Duval, CAO
Roger Vermette, Reeve

Morris
P.O. Box 518
207 Main St. North
Morris, MB R0G 1K0
204-746-2642 Fax: 204-746-8801
rmmorris@mts.net
Municipal Type: Rural Municipality
Incorporated: Jan. 5, 1880; *Area:* 1,041.15 sq km
Population in 2006: 2,662
Provincial Electoral District(s): Morris
Federal Electoral District(s): Provencher
Next Election: Oct. 2010 (4 year terms)
Ernest G. Buhler, CAO
Herm Martens, Reeve

Morton
P.O. Box 490
420 South Railway
Boissevain, MB R0K 0E0
204-534-2433 Fax: 204-534-3710
boissevain@mts.net
Municipal Type: Rural Municipality
Area: 1,089.88 sq km
Population in 2006: 718
Provincial Electoral District(s): Arthur-Virden
Federal Electoral District(s): Brandon-Souris
Next Election: Oct. 2010 (4 year terms)
Lloyd Leganchuk, CAO
Robert J.D. McCallum, Reeve

Mossey River
P.O. Box 80
Fork River, MB R0L 0V0
204-657-2331 Fax: 204-657-2202
rmmossey@inetlink.ca
Municipal Type: Rural Municipality
Incorporated: Jan. 2, 1906; *Area:* 1,123.06 sq km
Population in 2006: 614
Provincial Electoral District(s): Swan River
Federal Electoral District(s): Dauphin-Swan River-Mossey River
Next Election: Oct. 2010 (4 year terms)
Amelia Stefishen, CAO
Ron Kostyshyn, Reeve

Mountain
P.O. Box 155
200 Drury Ave.
Birch River, MB R0L 0E0
204-236-4222 Fax: 204-236-4773
rmmountn@mts.net
Municipal Type: Rural Municipality
Area: 2607.69 sq km
Population in 2006: 1,336
Provincial Electoral District(s): Swan River
Federal Electoral District(s): Dauphin-Swan River-Marquette
Next Election: Oct. 2010 (4 year terms)
Bev Ready, CAO
Marvin Kovachik, Reeve

Mystery Lake
P.O. Box 189
Thompson, MB R8N 1N1
204-677-4075 Fax: 204-778-7642
lgdmystlake@mts.net
Municipal Type: Local Goverment District
Incorporated: Jan. 1, 1956; *Area:* 3,464.06 sq km
Population in 2006: 147
Next Election: Oct. 2010 (4 year terms)
John E. Burden, Resident Administrator
Corinne Stewart, CAO

North Cypress
P.O. Box 130
316 - 4th Ave.
Carberry, MB R0K 0H0
204-834-6600 Fax: 204-834-6604
north.cypress@rmofnorthcypress.ca
www.rmofnorthcypress.ca
Municipal Type: Rural Municipality
Incorporated: Jan. 1, 1882; *Area:* 1,199.92 sq km
Population in 2006: 1,902
Provincial Electoral District(s): Turtle Mountain
Federal Electoral District(s): Brandon-Souris
Next Election: Oct. 2010 (4 year terms)
Brent McMillan, CAO
Brad Wells, Reeve

North Norfolk
P.O. Box 190
27 Hampton St. East
MacGregor, MB R0H 0R0
204-685-2211 Fax: 204-685-2616
ivan@villageofmacgregor.com
www.rm.north-norfolk.mb.ca
Municipal Type: Rural Municipality
Incorporated: Jan. 1, 1882; *Area:* 1,158.76 sq km
Population in 2006: 2,742
Provincial Electoral District(s): Turtle Mountain
Federal Electoral District(s): Portage-Lisgar
Next Election: Oct. 2010 (4 year terms)
Y. Ivan Bruneau, CAO
Neil Cristoffersen, Reeve

Oakland
P.O. Box 28
Nesbitt, MB R0K 1P0
204-824-2374 Fax: 204-824-2374
rm_of_oakland@hotmail.com
Municipal Type: Rural Municipality
Incorporated: Jan. 2, 1883; *Area:* 575.21 sq km
Population in 2006: 1,033
Provincial Electoral District(s): Minnedosa
Federal Electoral District(s): Brandon-Souris; Portage Lisgar
Next Election: Oct. 2010 (4 year terms)
Marlene Biles, CAO
David B. Inkster, Reeve

Ochre River
P.O. Box 40
206 MacKenzie Ave.
Ochre River, MB R0L 1K0
204-733-2423 Fax: 204-733-2259
rmochre@inetlink.ca
www.mts.net/~rmochre
Municipal Type: Rural Municipality
Incorporated: Jan. 3, 1901; *Area:* 535.59 sq km
Population in 2006: 929
Provincial Electoral District(s): Dauphin-Roblin
Federal Electoral District(s): Dauphin-Swan River-Marquette
Next Election: Oct. 2010 (4 year terms)
Laura Murray, CAO
Raymond Janssen, Reeve

Odanah
P.O. Box 1197
49 Main St. South
Minnedosa, MB R0J 1E0
204-867-3282 Fax: 204-867-1937
rmminto@mts.net
Municipal Type: Rural Municipality
Incorporated: Jan. 2, 1883; *Area:* 380.25 sq km
Population in 2006: 540
Provincial Electoral District(s): Minnedosa
Federal Electoral District(s): Dauphin-Swan River-Marquette
Next Election: Oct. 2010 (4 year terms)
Aaren Robertson, CAO
James A. Andersen, Reeve

Park
P.O. Box 190
43 Gateway St.
Onanole, MB R0J 1N0
204-848-7614 Fax: 204-848-2082
admin@rmpark.org
www.rmpark.org
Municipal Type: Rural Municipality
Incorporated: Jan. 6, 1954; *Area:* 793.38 sq km
Population in 2006: 1,291
Provincial Electoral District(s): Dauphin-Roblin; Russell
Federal Electoral District(s): Dauphin-Swan River-Marquette
Next Election: Oct. 2010 (4 year terms)
Sylvester Yakielashek, CAO
R. Boyd Robertson, Reeve

Pembina
P.O. Box 189
315 Main St.
Manitou, MB R0G 1G0
204-242-2838 Fax: 204-242-2798
admin@rmofpembina.com
www.rmofpembina.com
Municipal Type: Rural Municipality
Incorporated: Jan. 4, 1890; *Area:* 1,114.76 sq km
Population in 2006: 1,712
Provincial Electoral District(s): Pembina
Federal Electoral District(s): Portage-Lisgar
Next Election: Oct. 2010 (4 year terms)
Judy D. Young, CAO
Kim Taylor, Reeve

Pinawa
P.O. Box 100
36 Burrows Rd.
Pinawa, MB R0E 1L0
204-753-5100 Fax: 204-753-2770
info@pinawa.com
www.pinawa.com
Municipal Type: Local Goverment District
Incorporated: Jan. 3, 1963; *Area:* 128.47 sq km
Population in 2006: 1,450
Next Election: Oct. 2010 (4 year terms)
Gary Hanna, Resident Administrator

Blair Skinner, Mayor

Piney
P.O. Box 48
Vassar, MB R0A 2J0
204-437-2284 Fax: 204-437-2556
rmpiney@hotmail.com
www.rmofpiney.mb.ca
Municipal Type: Rural Municipality
Area: 2,433.77 sq km
Population in 2006: 1,755
Provincial Electoral District(s): Emerson
Federal Electoral District(s): Provencher
Next Election: Oct. 2010 (4 year terms)
Reynald Preteau, CAO
Marvin Hovorka, Reeve

Pipestone
P.O. Box 99
401 - 3rd Ave.
Reston, MB R0M 1X0
204-877-3327 Fax: 204-877-3999
admin@rmofpipestone.com
www.rmofpipestone.com
Municipal Type: Rural Municipality
Incorporated: Jan. 6, 1897; *Area:* 1,147.35 sq km
Population in 2006: 1,419
Provincial Electoral District(s): Arthur-Virden
Federal Electoral District(s): Brandon-Souris
Next Election: Oct. 2010 (4 year terms)
June Greggor, CAO
W. Ross Tycoles, Reeve

Portage la Prairie
35 Tupper St. South
Portage la Prairie, MB R1N 1W7
204-857-3821 Fax: 204-239-0069
rmptge@mts.net
www.rm.portage-la-prairie.mb.ca
Municipal Type: Rural Municipality
Incorporated: Jan. 4, 1879; *Area:* 1,964.32 sq km
Population in 2006: 6,793
Provincial Electoral District(s): Portage la Prairie; Carman
Federal Electoral District(s): Portage-Lisgar; Selkirk-Interlake
Next Election: Oct. 2010 (4 year terms)
Daryl Hrehirchuk, CAO
J. T. (Toby) Trimble, Reeve

Reynolds
P.O. Box 46
Hadashville, MB R0E 0X0
204-426-5305 Fax: 204-426-5552
rmreynol@mts.net
www.rmofreynolds.com
Municipal Type: Rural Municipality
Incorporated: Jan. 2, 1945; *Area:* 3,573.31 sq km
Population in 2006: 1,410
Provincial Electoral District(s): La Verendrye; Lac du Bonnet
Federal Electoral District(s): Provencher
Next Election: Oct. 2010 (4 year terms)
Holly Krysko, CAO
Donna Shandroski, Reeve

Rhineland
P.O. Box 270
72 - 2nd St. NE
Altona, MB R0G 0B0
204-324-5357 Fax: 204-324-1516
rhineland@mts.net
Municipal Type: Rural Municipality
Incorporated: Jan. 3, 1884; *Area:* 953.42 sq km
Population in 2006: 4,125
Provincial Electoral District(s): Emerson
Federal Electoral District(s): Portage-Lisgar
Next Election: Oct. 2010 (4 year terms)
Mike Rempel, CAO
John H. Falk, Reeve

Ritchot
352 Main St.
St Adolphe, MB R5A 1B9
204-883-2293 Fax: 204-883-2674
municipaloffice@ritchot.com
www.ritchot.com
Municipal Type: Rural Municipality
Incorporated: Jan. 4, 1890; *Area:* 333.53 sq km
Population in 2006: 5,051
Provincial Electoral District(s): La Verendrye; Morris
Federal Electoral District(s): Provencher; Winnipeg South
Next Election: Oct. 2010 (4 year terms)
Yves Sabourin, CAO
Valerie Rutherford, Deputy Mayor & Councillor
204-781-4458

Riverside
P.O. Box 126
110 Rea St.
Dunrea, MB R0K 0S0
204-776-2113 Fax: 204-776-2228
riverside@mts.net
www.rmriverside.ca
Municipal Type: Rural Municipality
Area: 577.34 sq km
Population in 2006: 809
Provincial Electoral District(s): Turtle Mountain
Federal Electoral District(s): Brandon-Souris; Provencher; Kildonan-St. Paul
Next Election: Oct. 2010 (4 year terms)
Meghan Cuvelier Klassen, CAO
Roger Renaud, Reeve

Roblin
P.O. Box 9
485 Curwen St.
Cartwright, MB R0K 0L0
204-529-2363 Fax: 204-529-2288
colleen@cartwrightmb.ca
www.cartwrightmb.ca
Municipal Type: Rural Municipality
Incorporated: Jan. 4, 1902; *Area:* 716.15 sq km
Population in 2006: 964
Provincial Electoral District(s): Turtle Mountain
Federal Electoral District(s): Brandon-Souris; Dauphin-Swan River-Marquette
Next Election: Oct. 2010 (4 year terms)
Colleen Mullin, CAO
David Lees, Reeve

Rockwood
P.O. Box 902
285 Main St.
Stonewall, MB R0C 2Z0
204-467-2272 Fax: 204-467-5329
rmrockwd@mts.net
www.rockwood.ca
Municipal Type: Rural Municipality
Incorporated: Jan. 7, 1881; *Area:* 1,199.76 sq km
Population in 2006: 7,692
Provincial Electoral District(s): Lakeside
Federal Electoral District(s): Selkirk-Interlake
Next Election: Oct. 2010 (4 year terms)
Jack Douglas, CAO
Garnet Thievin, Reeve
204-467-2652

Roland
P.O. Box 119
45 - 3rd St.
Roland, MB R0G 1T0
204-343-2061 Fax: 204-343-2001
rmroland@pmcnet.ca
Municipal Type: Rural Municipality
Incorporated: Jan. 4, 1908; *Area:* 485.06 sq km
Population in 2006: 1,002
Provincial Electoral District(s): Carman
Federal Electoral District(s): Portage-Lisgar
Next Election: Oct. 2010 (4 year terms)
Dianne Toews, CAO
W.M. (Bill) Whitehead, Reeve

Rosedale
P.O. Box 100
282 Hamilton St.
Neepawa, MB R0J 1H0
204-476-5414 Fax: 204-476-5431
rosedale@mts.net
Municipal Type: Rural Municipality
Incorporated: Jan. 3, 1884; *Area:* 865.58 sq km
Population in 2006: 1,658
Provincial Electoral District(s): Ste. Rose
Federal Electoral District(s): Dauphin-Swan River-Marquette
Next Election: Oct. 2010 (4 year terms)
Karen McDonald, CAO
Edward Levandoski, Reeve

Rossburn
P.O. Box 100
39 Main St. North
Rossburn, MB R0J 1V0
204-859-2779 Fax: 204-859-2959
rsbrm@mts.net
Municipal Type: Rural Municipality
Incorporated: Jan. 3, 1884; *Area:* 679.29 sq km
Population in 2006: 514
Provincial Electoral District(s): Russell
Federal Electoral District(s): Dauphin-Swan River-Marquette
Next Election: Oct. 2010 (4 year terms)
Ernie Antonow, CAO
Brian Brown, Reeve

Rosser
P.O. Box 131
Provincial Rd. 221
Rosser, MB R0H 1E0
204-467-5711 Fax: 204-467-5958
info@rmofrosser.com
www.rmofrosser.com
Municipal Type: Rural Municipality
Incorporated: Jan. 1, 1893; *Area:* 441.43 sq km
Population in 2006: 1,364
Provincial Electoral District(s): Lakeside
Federal Electoral District(s): Selkirk-Interlake
Next Election: Oct. 2010 (4 year terms)
Alice Bourgouin, Reeve
reeve@rmofrosser.com
Estelle Thornson, CAO

Russell
P.O. Box 220
362 Main St. North
Russell, MB R0J 1W0
204-773-2294 Fax: 204-773-3841
rmrussel@mts.net
Municipal Type: Rural Municipality
Incorporated: Jan. 1, 1882; *Area:* 567.83 sq km
Population in 2006: 661
Provincial Electoral District(s): Russell
Federal Electoral District(s): Dauphin-Swan River-Marquette
Next Election: Oct. 2010 (4 year terms)
Louise Ewankiw, CAO
Robert W. Muir, Reeve

St. Andrews
P.O. Box 130
500 Railway Ave.
Clandeboye, MB R0C 0P0
204-738-2264 Fax: 204-738-2500 Toll Free Phone: 1-866-738-2264
info@rmofstandrews.com
www.rmofstandrews.com
Municipal Type: Rural Municipality
Incorporated: Jan. 5, 1880; *Area:* 752.7 sq km
Population in 2006: 11,359
Provincial Electoral District(s): Gimli
Federal Electoral District(s): Selkirk-Interlake
Next Election: Oct. 2010 (4 year terms)
Danny Jo Sigmundson, CAO
cao@rmofstandrews.com
Don Forfar, Reeve
don@rmofstandrews.com
Ralph Bach, Chair, Public Works
Lawrie Hunt, Chair, Environment
Brad Pawluk, Superintendent, Public Works
Jack Robertson, District Fire Chief (St. Andrews South)
204-757-4748
Ray Kelsch, District Fire Chief (St. Andrews Central)
204-738-2607
Ron Lucyshen, District Fire Chief (St. Andrews North)
204-389-2004

Ste. Anne
141 Central Ave.
Ste. Anne, MB R5H 1C3
204-422-5929 Fax: 204-422-9723
rmstea@mts.net
Municipal Type: Rural Municipality
Incorporated: Feb. 3, 1881; *Area:* 477.65 sq km
Population in 2006: 4,509
Provincial Electoral District(s): La Verendrye
Federal Electoral District(s): Provencher
Next Election: Oct. 2010 (4 year terms)
Alice Y. De Baets, CAO
Art Bergmann, Reeve

St. Clements
PO Box 2, Group 35, RR#1
East Selkirk, MB R0E 0M0
204-482-3300 Fax: 204-482-3098
info@rmofstclements.com
www.rmofstclements.com
Municipal Type: Rural Municipality
Incorporated: July 7, 1883; *Area:* 728.67 sq km
Population in 2006: 9,706
Provincial Electoral District(s): Selkirk
Federal Electoral District(s): Selkirk-Interlake
Next Election: Oct. 2010 (4 year terms)
Jerome Mauws, CAO
Steve Strang, Reeve

St. François Xavier
1060 Hwy. 26
St François Xavier, MB R4L 1A5
204-864-2092 Fax: 204-864-2390
info@rm-stfrancois.mb.ca
www.rm-stfrancois.mb.ca
Municipal Type: Rural Municipality
Incorporated: Jan. 5, 1880; *Area:* 204.55 sq km
Population in 2006: 1,087
Provincial Electoral District(s): Morris
Federal Electoral District(s): Portage-Lisgar
Next Election: Oct. 2010 (4 year terms)
Colleen Atamanchuk, CAO
Roger Poitras, Reeve

St. Laurent
P.O. Box 220
436 St. Laurent Veterans Memorial Rd.
St Laurent, MB R0C 2S0
204-646-2259 Fax: 204-646-2705
rmstlaur@mts.net
www.stlaurentmb.ca
Municipal Type: Rural Municipality
Incorporated: Jan. 1, 1882; *Area:* 462.51 sq km
Population in 2006: 1,454
Provincial Electoral District(s): Lakeside
Federal Electoral District(s): Selkirk-Interlake
Next Election: Oct. 2010 (4 year terms)
Danielle Kerbrat, CAO
Denis Carrière, Reeve

Ste. Rose
P.O. Box 30
630 Central Ave.
Ste. Rose du Lac, MB R0L 1S0
204-447-2633 Fax: 204-447-2278
rmstrose@mts.net
www.mts.net/~rmstrose
Municipal Type: Rural Municipality
Incorporated: Nov. 7, 1902; *Area:* 626.03 sq km
Population in 2006: 791
Provincial Electoral District(s): Ste. Rose
Federal Electoral District(s): Dauphin-Swan River-Marquette
Next Election: Oct. 2010 (4 year terms)
Michelle Denys, CAO
Maurice Maguet, Reeve

Saskatchewan
P.O. Box 9
435 - 3rd Ave.
Rapid City, MB R0K 1W0
204-826-2515 Fax: 204-826-2274
rmsk@mts.net
Municipal Type: Rural Municipality
Incorporated: Jan. 2, 1883; *Area:* 563.73 sq km
Population in 2006: 593
Provincial Electoral District(s): Minnedosa
Federal Electoral District(s): Dauphin-Swan River-Marquette
Next Election: Oct. 2010 (4 year terms)
Lois Sharpe, CAO
Robert L. Sharpe, Reeve

Shell River
P.O. Box 998
213 - 2nd Ave. NW
Roblin, MB R0L 1P0
204-937-4430 Fax: 204-937-8496
shellrvr@mts.net
www.rm.shellriver.mb.ca
Municipal Type: Rural Municipality
Incorporated: Jan. 3, 1884; *Area:* 735.12 sq km
Population in 2006: 931
Provincial Electoral District(s): Dauphin-Roblin
Federal Electoral District(s): Dauphin-Swan River-Marquette
Next Election: Oct. 2010 (4 year terms)
Twyla Ludwig, CAO
Albert Nabe, Reeve

Shellmouth - Boulton
P.O. Box 110
118 Main St.
Inglis, MB R0J 0X0
204-564-2589 Fax: 204-564-2643
rmosb@mts.net
Municipal Type: Rural Municipality
Incorporated: Jan. 6, 1999; *Area:* 1,095.07 sq km
Population in 2006: 906
Provincial Electoral District(s): Russell
Federal Electoral District(s): Dauphin-Swan River-Marquette
Next Election: Oct. 2010 (4 year terms)
Raymond G. Bomback, CAO
Alvin Zimmer, Reeve

Shoal Lake
P.O. Box 278
306 Elm St.
Shoal Lake, MB R0J 1Z0
204-759-2565 Fax: 204-759-2740
shoalake@goinet.ca
Municipal Type: Rural Municipality
Area: 2.58 sq km
Population in 2006: 555
Provincial Electoral District(s): Russell
Federal Electoral District(s): Dauphin-Swan River-Marquette
Next Election: Oct. 2010 (4 year terms)
Nadine Gapka, CAO
Donald Yanick, Reeve

Sifton
P.O. Box 100
293 - 2nd Ave. West
Oak Lake, MB R0M 1P0
204-855-2423 Fax: 204-855-2836
cao_sifton@mts.net
Municipal Type: Rural Municipality
Incorporated: Jan. 3, 1884; *Area:* 768.11 sq km
Population in 2006: 796
Provincial Electoral District(s): Arthur-Virden
Federal Electoral District(s): Brandon-Souris; Dauphin-Swan River-Marquette
Next Election: Oct. 2010 (4 year terms)
Mary Smith, CAO
George Harrison, Reeve

Siglunes
P.O. Box 370
38 Main St.
Ashern, MB R0C 0E0
204-768-2641 Fax: 204-768-2301
siglunes@mts.net
Municipal Type: Rural Municipality
Incorporated: Jan. 2, 1917; *Area:* 837.42 sq km
Population in 2006: 1,480
Provincial Electoral District(s): Interlake
Federal Electoral District(s): Selkirk-Interlake
Next Election: Oct. 2010 (4 year terms)
Lori Postlethwaite, CAO
Lorne Park, Reeve

Silver Creek
P.O. Box 130
307 Main St.
Angusville, MB R0J 0A0
204-773-2449 Fax: 204-773-3101
silcreek@mts.net
Municipal Type: Rural Municipality
Incorporated: Jan. 3, 1884; *Area:* 525.46 sq km
Population in 2006: 483
Provincial Electoral District(s): Russell
Federal Electoral District(s): Dauphin-Swan River-Marquette
Next Election: Oct. 2010 (4 year terms)
Dianne Katchin, CAO
Fred Dunn, Reeve

South Cypress
P.O. Box 219
618 Railway Ave.
Glenboro, MB R0K 0X0
204-827-2252 Fax: 204-827-2123
caormsc@mts.net
Municipal Type: Rural Municipality
Incorporated: Jan. 7, 1881; *Area:* 1,095.08 sq km
Population in 2006: 834
Provincial Electoral District(s): Turtle Mountain
Federal Electoral District(s): Brandon-Souris
Next Election: Oct. 2010 (4 year terms)
Eric C. Plaetinck, CAO
Earl E. Malyon, Reeve

South Norfolk
P.O. Box 30
180 Broadway St.
Treherne, MB R0G 2V0
204-723-2044 Fax: 204-723-2719
treherne@mts.net
www.rmofsouthnorfolk.com
Municipal Type: Rural Municipality
Area: 726.76 sq km
Population in 2006: 1,170
Provincial Electoral District(s): Carman
Federal Electoral District(s): Portage-Lisgar
Next Election: Oct. 2010 (4 year terms)
Jackie Jenkinson, CAO
Tom Kelly, Reeve

Springfield
P.O. Box 219
628 Main St.
Oakbank, MB R0E 1J0
204-444-3321 Fax: 204-444-2137
ltetrault@rmofspringfield.ca
www.rmofspringfield.ca
Municipal Type: Rural Municipality
Incorporated: Jan. 4, 1873; *Area:* 1,100.81 sq km
Population in 2006: 12,990
Provincial Electoral District(s): Springfield
Federal Electoral District(s): Provencher; Selkirk-Interlake
Next Election: Oct. 2010 (4 year terms)
Laurent Tetrault, CAO
Peter Skrupski, Reeve
204-444-2970
pskrupski@mts.net
Shawn Tosh, Manager, Operations
204-444-2241
Tony Keoycga, Manager, Recreation
204-444-4119
David Donaghy, CAO

Stanley
#100, 379 Stephen St.
Morden, MB R6M 1V1
204-822-6251 Fax: 204-822-3596
rmstan@mts.net
www.rmofstanley.ca
Municipal Type: Rural Municipality
Incorporated: Nov. 7, 1890; *Area:* 835.59 sq km
Population in 2006: 6,367
Provincial Electoral District(s): Pembina
Federal Electoral District(s): Portage-Lisgar
Next Election: Oct. 2010 (4 year terms)
Rick Klippenstein, CAO
Art Patkau, Reeve
204-822-3877
petbeef@mts.net

Strathclair
P.O. Box 160
127 Minnedosa St.
Strathclair, MB R0J 2C0
204-365-2196 Fax: 204-365-2056
strathrm@inetbiz.ca
Municipal Type: Rural Municipality
Incorporated: Jan. 3, 1884; *Area:* 539.96 sq km
Population in 2006: 840
Provincial Electoral District(s): Russell
Federal Electoral District(s): Dauphin-Swan River-Marquette
Next Election: Oct. 2010 (4 year terms)
Shelley Glenn, CAO
Dianne Mistal, Reeve

Strathcona
P.O. Box 100
3rd St.
Belmont, MB R0K 0C0
204-537-2241 Fax: 204-537-2364
strathcona@inethome.ca
Municipal Type: Rural Municipality
Incorporated: Jan. 2, 1906; *Area:* 485.56 sq km
Population in 2006: 727
Provincial Electoral District(s): Turtle Mountain
Federal Electoral District(s): Brandon-Souris
Next Election: Oct. 2010 (4 year terms)
Barrie A. McGill, CAO
Dennis Schram, Reeve

Stuartburn
P.O. Box 59
108 Main St. North
Vita, MB R0A 2K0
204-425-3218 Fax: 204-425-3513
612rm@mts.net
Municipal Type: Rural Municipality
Incorporated: Jan. 4, 1997; *Area:* 1,161.65 sq km
Population in 2006: 1,629
Provincial Electoral District(s): Emerson
Federal Electoral District(s): Provencher
Next Election: Oct. 2010 (4 year terms)
Judy E. Reimer, CAO
Jim Swidersky, Reeve

Swan River
P.O. Box 610
216 Main St. West
Swan River, MB R0L 1Z0
204-734-3344 Fax: 204-734-3701
ruralm@mts.net
www.rmofswanriver.com
Municipal Type: Rural Municipality
Incorporated: Jan. 3, 1901; *Area:* 1,719.58 sq km
Population in 2006: 2,784
Provincial Electoral District(s): Swan River
Federal Electoral District(s): Dauphin-Swan River-Marquette
Next Election: Oct. 2010 (4 year terms)
Betty Nemetchek, CAO
Earl K. Fullerton, Reeve

Taché
P.O. Box 100
1294 Dawson Rd.
Lorette, MB R0A 0Y0
204-878-3321 Fax: 204-878-9977
info@rmtache.ca
Municipal Type: Rural Municipality
Incorporated: Jan. 5, 1880; *Area:* 581.52 sq km
Population in 2006: 9,083
Provincial Electoral District(s): La Verendrye
Federal Electoral District(s): Provencher
Next Election: Oct. 2010 (4 year terms)
Daniel Poersch, CAO
William Danylchuk, Reeve

Thompson
P.O. Box 190
531 Norton Ave.
Miami, MB R0G 1H0
204-435-2114 Fax: 204-435-2067
rmthompson@cici.mb.ca
Municipal Type: Rural Municipality
Incorporated: Jan. 6, 1909; *Area:* 528.57 sq km
Population in 2006: 1,259
Provincial Electoral District(s): Carman
Federal Electoral District(s): Portage-Lisgar
Next Election: Oct. 2010 (4 year terms)
Diane Chatwin, CAO
Brian Schwartz, Reeve

Victoria
P.O. Box 40
130 Broadway St.
Holland, MB R0G 0X0
204-526-2423 Fax: 204-526-2028
office@rmofvictoria.com
www.rmofvictoria.com
Municipal Type: Rural Municipality
Incorporated: Jan. 4, 1902; *Area:* 697.63 sq km
Population in 2006: 1,149
Provincial Electoral District(s): Carman
Federal Electoral District(s): Portage-Lisgar
Next Election: Oct. 2010 (4 year terms)
Corinne Henderson, CAO
Allan Steinke, Reeve

Victoria Beach
#303, 960 Portage Ave.
Winnipeg, MB R3G 0R4
204-774-4263 Fax: 204-774-9834
vicbeach@mts.net
Municipal Type: Rural Municipality
Incorporated: Jan. 4, 1902; *Area:* 20.28 sq km
Population in 2006: 388
Provincial Electoral District(s): Selkirk
Federal Electoral District(s): Selkirk-Interlake
Next Election: Oct. 2010 (4 year terms)
Raymond Moreau, CAO
William McDonald, Reeve

Wallace
P.O. Box 2200
305 Nelson St. West
Virden, MB R0M 2C0
204-748-1239 Fax: 204-748-3450
caodon@hotmail.com
Municipal Type: Rural Municipality
Incorporated: Jan. 6, 1909; *Area:* 1,148.75 sq km
Population in 2006: 1,501
Provincial Electoral District(s): Arthur-Virden
Federal Electoral District(s): Brandon-Souris
Next Election: Oct. 2010 (4 year terms)
Don Stephenson, CAO
Vince Heaman, Reeve

West St. Paul
3550 Main St.
West St Paul, MB R4A 5A3
204-338-0306 Fax: 204-334-9362
info@weststpaul.com
www.weststpaul.com
Municipal Type: Rural Municipality
Incorporated: Jan. 7, 1916; *Area:* 87.66 sq km
Population in 2006: 4,357
Provincial Electoral District(s): Gimli
Federal Electoral District(s): Kildonan-St. Paul
Next Election: Oct. 2010 (4 year terms)
Dorothy Thordarson, Clerk
dthordarson@weststpaul.com
Clifford Dearman, Reeve
WSPReeve@mts.net

Westbourne
P.O. Box 150
Hwy. 16 West
Gladstone, MB R0J 0T0
204-385-2388 Fax: 204-385-2780
info@rmwestbourne.mb.ca
Municipal Type: Rural Municipality
Incorporated: Jan. 2, 1877; *Area:* 1,261.79 sq km
Population in 2006: 1,906
Provincial Electoral District(s): Ste. Rose
Federal Electoral District(s): Dauphin-Swan River-Marquette
Next Election: Oct. 2010 (4 year terms)
Patricia McCaskill, Municipal Administrator
David Single, Reeve

Whitehead
P.O. Box 107
517 - 2nd Ave.
Alexander, MB R0K 0A0
204-752-2261 Fax: 204-752-2129
rmwhitehead@mts.net
www.marcd.mb.ca
Municipal Type: Rural Municipality
Incorporated: Jan. 2, 1883; *Area:* 562.82 sq km
Population in 2006: 1,402
Provincial Electoral District(s): Minnedosa
Federal Electoral District(s): Brandon-Souris
Next Election: Oct. 2010 (4 year terms)
John B. MacLellan, CAO
Wayne D. Dobbie, Reeve

Whitemouth
P.O. Box 248
47 Railway Ave.
Whitemouth, MB R0E 2G0
204-348-2221 Fax: 204-348-2576
rmwhite@mts.net
Municipal Type: Rural Municipality
Incorporated: Jan. 1, 1905; *Area:* 703.02 sq km
Population in 2006: 1,480
Provincial Electoral District(s): Lac du Bonnet
Federal Electoral District(s): Provencher
Next Election: Oct. 2010 (4 year terms)
Scott G. Spicer, CAO
Glenn Malkoske, Reeve

Whitewater
P.O. Box 53
201 South Railway St.
Minto, MB R0K 1M0
204-776-2172 Fax: 204-776-2252
whitewat@mts.net
Municipal Type: Rural Municipality
Incorporated: Jan. 6, 1897; *Area:* 584.25 sq km
Population in 2006: 648
Provincial Electoral District(s): Minnedosa
Federal Electoral District(s): Brandon-Souris
Next Election: Oct. 2010 (4 year terms)
Murray R. Jackson, CAO
Blair Woods, Reeve

Winchester
P.O. Box 387
129 Broadway St. North
Deloraine, MB R0M 0M0
204-747-2572 Fax: 204-747-2883
rmwin@mts.net
Municipal Type: Rural Municipality
Area: 725.58 sq km
Population in 2006: 594
Provincial Electoral District(s): Arthur-Virden
Federal Electoral District(s): Brandon-Souris
Next Election: Oct. 2010 (4 year terms)
Pamela Hainsworth, CAO
Michael Dillabough, Reeve

Woodlands
P.O. Box 10
57 Railway Ave.
Woodlands, MB R0C 3H0
204-383-5679 Fax: 204-383-5169
rmwdlds1@mts.net
www.rmwoodlands.info
Municipal Type: Rural Municipality
Incorporated: Jan. 5, 1880; *Area:* 1,160.45 sq km
Population in 2006: 3,562
Provincial Electoral District(s): Lakeside
Federal Electoral District(s): Selkirk-Interlake
Next Election: Oct. 2010 (4 year terms)
Beverley Wells, CAO
Donald Walsh, Reeve
204-375-6536

Woodworth
P.O. Box 148
220 Cornwall St.
Kenton, MB R0M 0Z0
204-838-2317 Fax: 204-838-2000
rmwdwo@inetlink.ca
Municipal Type: Rural Municipality
Incorporated: Jan. 2, 1883; *Area:* 817.84 sq km
Population in 2006: 890
Provincial Electoral District(s): Arthur-Virden
Federal Electoral District(s): Brandon-Souris
Next Election: Oct. 2010 (4 year terms)
Howard J. Norek, CAO
Denis Carter, Reeve

NEW BRUNSWICK

The provincial government of New Brunswick provides all services of a municipal nature for the rural area of the province while municipalities provide these services to their residents. For the rural area, an advisory committee may be elected at public meetings biennially to assist and advise the Minister. Municipal councils are elected to look after the affairs of the municipalities.

Acts of the legislature governing municipalities are the Municipalities Act, the Municipal Assistance Act, the Community Planning Act, the Assessment Act, the Municipal Capital Borrowing Act, the Municipal Elections Act, and the Control of Municipalities Act.

Population requirements for incorporation of municipalities are 10,000 for cities and 1,500 for towns. There are no specified requirements for villages.

Municipal elections are held every four years on the second Monday in May; thus, May 2008, May 2012 etc.

New Brunswick

Major Municipalities in New Brunswick

Bathurst
150 St. George St.
Bathurst, NB E2A 1B5
506-548-0400 Fax: 506-548-0581
city@bathurst.ca
www.bathurst.ca
Municipal Type: City
Area: 91.55 sq km
County or District: Gloucester; *Population in 2006:* 12,714
Provincial Electoral District(s): Bathurst
Federal Electoral District(s): Acadie-Bathurst
Next Election: May 2012 (4 year terms)

Council
Stephen J. Brunet, Mayor
506-548-2171
Bob Anderson, Councillor
506-548-3536
bobelva@nb.sympatico.ca
Hugh L. Comeau, Councillor
506-548-2255
2868@nb.sympatico.ca
Scott A. Ferguson, Councillor
506-547-8993
scott.ferguson@nbed.nb.ca
Anne-Marie Gammon, Councillor
506-545-6821
amgammon@nbnet.nb.ca
Daniel (Danny) Roy, Councillor
506-546-1588
Graham Wiseman, Councillor
506-548-3600
gwiseman3600@rogers.com
Hugh J. Young, Councillor
506-548-1815
HughJYoung@GMAIL.com

Administration
Lola Doucet, City Clerk
506-548-0417
André Doucet, City Manager
506-548-0733
Gerald Pettigrew, Manager, Operations, Parks, Recreation & Tourism Department
506-548-0410
kcregionalcenter@bathurst.ca
Vincent Wood, General Foreman, Utilities
506-548-0444
Vincent.Wood@bathurst.ca
Marc Losier, Director, Design & Construction
city.operationalservices@bathurst.ca
Paul Godin, General Engineer
Robert Langlais, Fire Chief
506-548-0439
city.fire@bathurst.ca
Danny White, Manager, Operation Planning
Barry Veniot, Supervisor, Purchasing
506-548-0700
Barry.Veniot@bathurst.ca
Lucien Cormier, Building Inspector
Lucien.Cormier@bathurst.ca
Donald McLaughlin, Technician, Planning
Dave Moran, General Foreman, Above Ground Operational Services

Dieppe
333, av Acadie
Dieppe, NB E1A 1G9
506-877-7900 Fax: 506-877-7910
info@dieppe.ca, communications@dieppe.ca
www.dieppe.ca
Municipal Type: City
Incorporated: Jan. 1, 1952; *Area:* 51.17 sq km
County or District: Westmorland; *Population in 2006:* 18,565
Provincial Electoral District(s): Dieppe Centre-Lewisville
Federal Electoral District(s): Moncton-Riverview-Dieppe; Beauséjour
Next Election: May 2012 (4 year terms)
Jody Dallaire, Councillor at Large
506-387-8738
jody.dallaire@dieppe.ca

Council
Jean G. LeBlanc, Mayor
jean.leblanc@dieppe.ca
Yvon Comeau, Councillor at Large
506-388-3245
yvon.comeau@dieppe.ca
Jean J. Gaudet, Councillor at Large
506-854-8409
jean.gaudet@dieppe.ca
Dave A. Maltais, Councillor, Ward(s): 1
506-855-4299
dave.maltais@dieppe.ca
Paul J.L. LeBlanc, Councillor, Ward(s): 2
506-853-3974
paul.leblanc@dieppe.ca
Paul N. Belliveau, Councillor, Ward(s): 3
506-855-2637
paul.belliveau@dieppe.ca
Hélène Boudreau, Councillor, Ward(s): 4
506-866-2739
helene.boudreau@dieppe.ca
Roger J. LeBlanc, Councillor, Ward(s): 5
506-850-1604
roger.leblanc@dieppe.ca

Administration
Marc Melanson, Chief Administrative Officer
Jacques LeBlanc, Director, Public Works
Marc Melanson, Director, Community Services
communityservices@dieppe.ca
Desimil Chalmessin, Superintendent, Public Works
David Knowles, Superintendent, Public Works

Edmundston
7, ch Canada
Edmundston, NB E3V 1T7
506-739-4636 Fax: 506-737-6902
communication@edmundston.ca
www.ville.edmundston.nb.ca
Municipal Type: City
Area: 106.92 sq km
County or District: Madawaska; *Population in 2006:* 16,643
Provincial Electoral District(s): Edmundston-Saint-Basile
Federal Electoral District(s): Madawaska-Restigouche
Next Election: May 2012 (4 year terms)

Council
Jacques P. Martin, Mayor
André Lang, Councillor, Ward(s): 1
Aldéo D. Nadeau, Councillor, Ward(s): 1
Ben Beaulieu, Councillor, Ward(s): 2
Denis M. Pelletier, Councillor, Ward(s): 2
Martin (Tin) Albert, Councillor, Ward(s): 3
Gérald G. Morneault, Councillor, Ward(s): 3
Michel Dubé, Councillor, Ward(s): 4
Jean Guy Marquis, Councillor, Ward(s): 4

Administration
Marc Michaud, Acting Chief Administrative Officer
Paul Dionne, Director, Public Works and Environment
506-739-2103

Fredericton
City Hall
P.O. Box 130
397 Queen St.
Fredericton, NB E3B 4Y7
506-460-2020 Fax: 506-460-2042
www.fredericton.ca
Municipal Type: City
Incorporated: 1848; *Area:* 130.68 sq km
County or District: York; *Population in 2006:* 50,535
Provincial Electoral District(s): Fredericton-Lincoln; Fredericton-Silverwood; Fredericton-Fort Nashwaak; Fredericton-Nashwaaksis
Federal Electoral District(s): Fredericton
Next Election: May 2012 (4 year terms)

Council
Brad S. Woodside, Mayor
506-460-2085, Fax: 506-460-2134
Daniel R. Keenan, Councillor, Ward(s): 1
Bruce N. Grandy, Deputy Mayor & Councillor, Ward(s): 2
Michael G. O'Brien, Councillor, Ward(s): 3
Eric Megarity, Councillor, Ward(s): 4
Steven Hicks, Councillor, Ward(s): 5
Marilyn K. Kerton, Councillor, Ward(s): 6
Scott McConaghy, Councillor, Ward(s): 7
Tony J. Whalen, Councillor, Ward(s): 8
Stephen A. Chase, Councillor, Ward(s): 9
Stephen T. Kelly, Councillor, Ward(s): 10
Jordan S. Graham, Councillor, Ward(s): 11
David A.J. Kelly, Councillor, Ward(s): 12

Administration
Pamela G. Hargrove, City Clerk
pam.hargrove@fredericton.ca
Marven Grant, City Treasurer & Director, Financial Services
marven.grant@fredericton.ca
Bruce A. Noble, City Solicitor
bruce.noble@fredericton.ca
Paul R. Stapleton, City Administrator
cityadmin@fredericton.ca
Barry MacKnight, Police Chief & Director, Emergency Measures Organization
506-460-2300
policechief@fredericton.ca
Philip E. Toole, Fire Chief & Deputy Director, Emergency Measures Organization
506-460-2500
fire@fredericton.ca
Jane Blakely, Director, Corporate Services
jane.blakely@fredericton.ca
W. Frank Flanagan, Director, Development Services
planning@fredericton.ca
Murray Jamer, P.Eng., Director, Engineering & Public Works
publicworks@fredericton.ca
Wayne Tallon, Director, Community Services
wayne.tallon@fredericton.ca
Ken Forrest, Manager, Policy & Planning
506-460-2110, Fax: 506-460-2894
Sandy MacNeill, Manager, Transit
506-460-2200
transit@fredericton.ca
Andy Holyoke, Superintendent, Water & Sewer
publicworks@fredericton.ca
Brian Cochrane, Superintendent, Parks & Trees Division
506-460-2230
recreation@fredericton.ca

Miramichi
141 Henry St.
Miramichi, NB E1V 2N5
506-623-2200 Fax: 506-623-2201
jim.lamkey@miramichi.org
www.miramichi.org
Municipal Type: City
Incorporated: Jan. 1, 1995; *Area:* 179.84 sq km
County or District: Northumberland; *Population in 2006:* 18,129
Provincial Electoral District(s): Miramichi-Bay du Vin; Miramichi-Centre; Miramichi Bay-Neguac; Southwest Miramichi
Federal Electoral District(s): Miramichi
Next Election: May 2012 (4 year terms)

Council
Gerry Cormier, Mayor
Rupert Bernard, Councillor
Derek Burchill, Councillor
Joan M. Cripps, Councillor
Jason J. Harris, Councillor
Brian J. King, Councillor
Nancy Lordon, Councillor
Michael J. (Tanker) Malley, Councillor
Michael J. McCoombs, Councillor
Bill Treadwell, Councillor
Robert B. Trevors, Councillor

Administration
James F. Lamkey, Clerk
Doug Chase, City Manager
doug.chase@miramichi.org
Kevin Kerr, P.Eng., Director, Engineering & Public Works
506-623-2020, Fax: 506-623-2025
kevin.kerr@miramichi.org
David Keating, Fire Chief
506-623-2225, Fax: 506-623-2226
david.keating@miramichi.org

Moncton / Ville de Moncton
655 Main St.
Moncton, NB E1C 1E8
506-853-3333 Fax: 506-389-5904
info@moncton.ca
www.moncton.ca
Municipal Type: City
Incorporated: 1890; *Area:* 141.17 sq km
County or District: Westmorland; *Population in 2006:* 64,128
Provincial Electoral District(s): Moncton East; Moncton North; Moncton West; Moncton Crescent
Federal Electoral District(s): Moncton-Riverview-Dieppe; Beauséjour
Next Election: May 2012 (4 year terms)

Council
George H. LeBlanc, Mayor
506-856-4343, Fax: 506-853-3553
info.mayor@moncton.ca
Kathryn M. Barnes, Councillor at Large
Pierre A. Boudreau, Councillor at Large
Steven Boyce, Councillor, Ward(s): 1
Paulette Thériault, Councillor, Ward(s): 1
Merrill A. Henderson, Councillor, Ward(s): 2
Nancy L. Hoar, Councillor, Ward(s): 2
Daniel Bourgeois, Councillor, Ward(s): 3
Brian A.Q. Hicks, Councillor, Ward(s): 3
René (Pepsi) Landry, Councillor, Ward(s): 4
Paul A. Pellerin, Councillor, Ward(s): 4

Administration
Barbara A. Quigley, City Clerk & Director, Legislative Support
info.clerk@moncton.ca
John Martin, City Treasurer & CFO
506-853-3566
john.martin@moncton.ca
Jacques Dubé, City Manager
506-853-3498
info.manager@moncton.ca
Stephen Trueman, City Solicitor
stephen.trueman@moncton.ca
Eric Arsenault, Fire Chief
506-857-8800, Fax: 506-856-4353
info.fire@moncton.ca
B. Butler, Constable, Codiac Regional RCMP
Bill Budd, Director, District Planning
C. Despres, Director, Corporate Planning & Policy Development
506-859-2608
info.support@moncton.ca
D. Morehouse, Director, Engineering Operations
info.engineering@moncton.ca
A. Richard, Director, Design & Construction
S. Sparks, Director, Building Inspection
info.inspection@moncton.ca
Paul Thomson, Director, Corporate Communications
info.communications@moncton.ca
Ian Fowler, General Manager, Recreation, Parks, Tourism & Culture
ian.fowler@moncton.ca

J. MacDonald, General Manager, Engineering & Public Works
info.publicworks@moncton.ca
T. Carter, Manager, Purchasing
506-853-3535
info.purchasing@moncton.ca
Catherine Dallaire, Assistant City Manager, Corporate Services
catherine.dallaire@moncton.ca
Donald MacLellan, Assistant City Manager
don.maclellan@moncton.ca
Rod Higgins, Assistant General Manager, Recreation, Parks, Tourism & Culture
rod.higgins@moncton.ca

Quispamsis

P.O. Box 21085
12 Landing Ct.
Quispamsis, NB E2E 4Z4
506-849-5778 Fax: 506-849-5799
quispamsis@quispamsis.ca
www.quispamsis.ca
Municipal Type: City
Area: 57.06 sq km
County or District: Kings; *Population in 2006:* 15,239
Provincial Electoral District(s): Quispamsis
Federal Electoral District(s): Fundy Royal; Saint John
Next Election: May 2012 (4 year terms)
Gary Losier, Director, Engineering & Works
506-849-5749
glosier@quispamsis.ca
Chris Vriezen, Supervisor, Utility
506-849-5734
cvriezen@quispamsis.ca
Phil Shedd, Superintendent, Works
506-849-5742
pshedd@quispamsis.ca
Beth Thompson, Councillor
506-849-2852
Margie McGrath, Secretary, Planning Advisory Committee
506-849-5745
mmcgrath@quispamsis.ca
Larry Greer, Fire Chief, Rothesay Regional Fire Dept.
506-848-6604, Fax: 506-848-6608
rrfd@nb.aibn.com

Council
Murray Driscoll, Mayor
506-849-5992
mayor@quispamsis.ca

Administration
Catherine Snow, Clerk
506-849-5738

Riverview

30 Honour House Ct.
Riverview, NB E1B 3Y9
506-387-2020 Fax: 506-387-2033
www.town.riverview.nb.ca
Municipal Type: City
Area: 33.88 sq km
County or District: Albert; *Population in 2006:* 17,832
Provincial Electoral District(s): Riverview
Federal Electoral District(s): Moncton-Riverview-Dieppe; Fundy Royal
Next Election: May 2012 (4 year terms)

Council
Clarence O. Sweetland, Mayor
506-386-1703
csweetland@town.riverview.nb.ca
Claude Curwin, Councillor, Ward(s): 1
506-860-6873
ccurwin@town.riverview.nb.ca
Ian Macdonald, Councillor, Ward(s): 2
506-386-8756
imacdonald@town.riverview.nb.ca
Bob Hyslop, Councillor, Ward(s): 3
506-866-2273
rhyslop@town.riverview.nb.ca
Wayne Bennett, Councillor, Ward(s): 4
506-386-3295
Don Lenehan, Councillor at Large
506-386-4483
lenehandon@yahoo.ca
Sherry Wilson, Councillor at Large
506-386-1133
swilson@town.riverview.nb.ca
Ann Seamans, Councillor at Large
506-386-4558
aseamans@town.riverview.nb.ca

Administration
David Muir, Chief Administrative Officer
506-387-2021
Denyse Richard, Deputy Town Clerk
506-387-2043
Robert Higson, Director, Finance
506-387-2023
Jim Steeves, Superintendent, Works
506-387-2027
Bob Clive, Director, Parks, Recreation & Community Relations
506-387-2031
Doug Hamer, Chief, Fire & Ambulance
506-387-2201
rivefire@nbnet.nb.ca

Kenneth L. Sharpe, Director, Works & Engineering
506-387-2035

Rothesay

70 Hampton Rd.
Rothesay, NB E2E 5L5
506-848-6600 Fax: 506-848-6677
info@rothesay.ca
www.rothesay.ca
Municipal Type: City
Incorporated: Jan. 1, 1998; *Area:* 34.73 sq km
County or District: Kings; *Population in 2006:* 11,637
Provincial Electoral District(s): Rothesay
Federal Electoral District(s): Saint John; Fundy Royal
Next Election: May 2012 (4 year terms)

Council
William J. Bishop, Mayor
BillBishop@rothesay.ca
Scott Cochrane, Councillor
jassco@rogers.com
Pat Gallagher Jette, Councillor
patgall@nbnet.nb.ca
Terry Kilfoil, Councillor
kilfoilt@nbnet.nb.ca
Norma Mullett, Councillor
normamullett@hotmail.com
Don Shea, Councillor
sheadoj@nbnet.nb.ca
Tom Young, Councillor
tomyoung@rogers.com

Administration
Mary Jane Banks, Clerk
MaryJaneBanks@rothesay.ca
Scott Hatcher, P.Eng., Director, Operations
506-848-6668
scotthatcher@rothesay.ca
Larry Greer, Fire Chief
506-848-6604
Gay Drescher, Director, Development Services
gaydrescher@rothesay.ca
Jeff Humphrey, Technologist, Engineering

Saint John

City Hall
P.O. Box 1971
15 Market Sq.
Saint John, NB E2L 4L1
506-649-6000
inquiries@saintjohn.ca
www.saintjohn.ca
Municipal Type: City
Incorporated: May 18, 1785; *Area:* 315.49 sq km
County or District: Saint John; *Population in 2006:* 68,043
Provincial Electoral District(s): Saint John East; Saint John Harbour; Saint John Portland; Saint John Lancaster; Saint John-Fundy
Federal Electoral District(s): Saint John
Next Election: May 2012 (4 year terms)

Council
Ivan Court, Mayor
ivan.court@saintjohn.ca
Stephen Chase, Deputy Mayor & Councillor
stephen.chase@saintjohn.ca
Christopher Titus, Councillor at Large
christopher.titus@saintjohn.ca
Bill Farren, Councillor, Ward(s): 1
bill.farren@saintjohn.ca
Peter McGuire, Councillor, Ward(s): 1
peter.mcguire@saintjohn.ca
Patricia (Patty) Higgins, Councillor, Ward(s): 2
patty.higgins@saintjohn.ca
H. Gary Sullivan, Councillor, Ward(s): 2
gary.sullivan@saintjohn.ca
Carl Killen, Councillor, Ward(s): 3
carl.killen@saintjohn.ca
Donnie Snook, Councillor, Ward(s): 3
donnie.snook@saintjohn.ca
Bruce Court, Councillor, Ward(s): 4
bruce.court@saintjohn.ca
Joe Mott, Councillor, Ward(s): 4
joe.mott@saintjohn.ca

Administration
J. Patrick Woods, City Manager
506-658-2913, Fax: 506-658-2802
citymanager@saintjohn.ca
Greg Yeomans, Treasurer & Commissioner, Finance & Corporate Services
506-658-2951, Fax: 506-649-7901
finance@saintjohn.ca
James R. Baird, Commissioner, Planning & Development
506-658-2835, Fax: 506-658-2837
planning@saintjohn.ca
William Edwards, Commissioner, Buildings & Inspection Services
506-658-2911, Fax: 506-632-6199
buildinginspection@saintjohn.ca
Paul Groody, P.Eng., Commissioner, Municipal Operations
506-658-4455, Fax: 506-658-4740
municipaloperations@saintjohn.ca
Margaret Totten, Manager, Tourism Saint John
506-658-2990, Fax: 506-632-6118
visitsj@saintjohn.ca

John Nugent, City Solicitor
506-658-2860, Fax: 506-649-7939
legal@saintjohn.ca
Allen Bodechon, Police Chief
506-648-3200, Fax: 506-648-3304
police@saintjohn.ca
Rob Simonds, Fire Chief
506-658-2910, Fax: 506-658-2916
fire@saintjohn.ca
Shayne Galbraith, Director, Works
506-658-2852
works@saintjohn.ca
Peter J. Hanlon, P.Eng., Manager, Water & Sewerage Services
506-658-2811, Fax: 506-658-4740
waterandsewerage@cityofsaintjohn.com
David Logan, Purchasing Agent, Material & Fleet Management
506-658-2930, Fax: 506-658-4742
mat-man@saintjohn.ca

Other Municipalities in New Brunswick

Alma

8 School St.
Alma, NB E4H 1L2
506-887-6123 Fax: 506-887-6124
almavill@nb.aibn.com
Municipal Type: Village
Area: 47.64 sq km
County or District: Albert; *Population in 2006:* 301
Provincial Electoral District(s): Albert
Federal Electoral District(s): Fundy Royal
Next Election: May 2012 (4 year terms)
Louise Butland, Clerk-Treasurer
Hilyard G. Rossiter, Mayor

Aroostook

383 Main St.
Aroostook, NB E7H 2Z4
506-273-6443 Fax: 506-273-3025
varoostk@nb.aibn.com
Municipal Type: Village
Area: 2.24 sq km
County or District: Victoria; *Population in 2006:* 346
Provincial Electoral District(s): Victoria-Tobique
Federal Electoral District(s): Tobique-Mactaquac
Next Election: May 2012 (4 year terms)
Marven Demmings, Mayor

Atholville

247, rue Notre-Dame
Atholville, NB E3N 4T1
506-789-2944 Fax: 506-789-2925
lyssa@nb.aibn.com
www.atholville.net
Municipal Type: Village
Incorporated: 1966; *Area:* 10.25 sq km
County or District: Restigouche; *Population in 2006:* 1,317
Provincial Electoral District(s): Campbellton-Restigouche Centre
Federal Electoral District(s): Madawaska-Restigouche
Next Election: May 2012 (4 year terms)
Lyssa Leclerc, Clerk-Administrator
J. Raymond Lagacé, Mayor

Baker Brook

3677, rue Principale, #A
Baker Brook, NB E7A 1V3
506-258-3030 Fax: 506-258-3017
villagebakerbrook@nb.aibn.com
Municipal Type: Village
Area: 12.4 sq km
County or District: Madawaska; *Population in 2006:* 525
Provincial Electoral District(s): Madawaska-les-Lacs
Federal Electoral District(s): Madawaska-Restigouche
Next Election: May 2012 (4 year terms)
Gertrude Albert, Gref.
Gilles Charette, Maire

Balmoral

CP 2531
1447, av des Pionniers
Balmoral, NB E8E 2W7
506-826-6060 Fax: 506-826-6037
vilbal@nbnet.nb.ca
www.balmoralnb.com
Municipal Type: Village
Incorporated: 1972; *Area:* 43.51 sq km
County or District: Restigouche; *Population in 2006:* 1,706
Provincial Electoral District(s): Dalhousie-Restigouche-East
Federal Electoral District(s): Madawaska-Restigouche
Next Election: May 2012 (4 year terms)
Gilles LePage, Greffier-Administrateur
Hébert Donald Arsenault, Maire

Bas-Caraquet

8185, rue St-Paul
Bas-Caraquet, NB E1W 6C4
506-726-2776 Fax: 506-726-2770
vilbasca@nbnet.nb.ca
www.bascaraquet.com
Municipal Type: Village
Area: 31 sq km
County or District: Gloucester; *Population in 2006:* 1,471
Provincial Electoral District(s): Caraquet

Federal Electoral District(s): Acadie-Bathurst
Next Election: May 2012 (4 year terms)
Richard Frigault, Gérant
Agnes Doiron, Mairesse

Bath

161 School St.
Bath, NB E7J 1C3
506-278-5293 Fax: 506-278-5932
bath@nbnet.nb.ca
Municipal Type: Village
Area: 2.03 sq km
County or District: Carleton; *Population in 2006:* 512
Provincial Electoral District(s): Carleton
Federal Electoral District(s): Tobique-Mactaquac
Next Election: May 2012 (4 year terms)
Christa Walton, Clerk
Troy F.J. Stone, Mayor

Belledune

P.O. Box 1006
2330 Main St.
Belledune, NB E8G 2X9
506-522-3700 Fax: 506-522-3704
bell001@nbnet.nb.ca
www.belledune.com
Municipal Type: Village
Incorporated: Jan. 1, 1968; *Area:* 189.03 sq km
County or District: Gloucester; *Population in 2006:* 1,711
Provincial Electoral District(s): Nigadoo-Chaleur
Federal Electoral District(s): Miramichi
Next Election: May 2012 (4 year terms)
Brenda Cormier, Clerk-Treas.
Nick Duivenvoorden, Mayor

Beresford

#2, 855, rue Principale
Beresford, NB E8K 1T3
506-542-2727 Fax: 506-542-2702
beresfor@nbnet.nb.ca
www.acadie-bathurst.com
Municipal Type: Town
Area: 19.2 sq km
County or District: Gloucester; *Population in 2006:* 4,264
Provincial Electoral District(s): Nigadoo-Chaleur
Federal Electoral District(s): Acadie-Bathurst
Next Election: May 2012 (4 year terms)
Norval Godin, Administrateur
Raoul Charest, Mayor

Bertrand

#1, 651, boul des Acadiens
Bertrand, NB E1W 1G5
506-726-2442 Fax: 506-726-2449
bertrand@nb.aibn.com
Municipal Type: Village
Area: 46.45 sq km
County or District: Gloucester; *Population in 2006:* 1,179
Provincial Electoral District(s): Caraquet
Federal Electoral District(s): Acadie-Bathurst
Next Election: May 2012 (4 year terms)
Mélanie Arseneau, CAO
Yvon Godin, Maire

Blacks Harbour

65 Wallace Cove Rd.
Blacks Harbour, NB E5H 1G9
506-456-4870 Fax: 506-456-4872
blkhvill@nbnet.nb.ca
www.villageofblacksharbour.com
Municipal Type: Village
Area: 8.9 sq km
County or District: Charlotte; *Population in 2006:* 952
Provincial Electoral District(s): Charlotte
Federal Electoral District(s): New Brunswick Southwest
Next Election: May 2012 (4 year terms)
Deanna Hunter, Manager
Terry James, Mayor

Blackville

136 Main St.
Blackville, NB E9B 1P1
506-843-6337 Fax: 506-843-6043
blackvl@nb.sympatico.ca
www.villageofblackville.com
Municipal Type: Village
Area: 21.73 sq km
County or District: Northumberland; *Population in 2006:* 931
Provincial Electoral District(s): Southwest Miramichi
Federal Electoral District(s): Miramichi
Next Election: May 2012 (4 year terms)
Kurt Marks, Clerk-Administrator
Glen A. Hollowood, Mayor

Bouctouche

211, boul Irving
Bouctouche, NB E4S 3K6
506-743-7260 Fax: 506-743-7261
ville@bouctouche.ca
www.bouctouche.org
Municipal Type: Town
Area: 18.34 sq km
County or District: Kent; *Population in 2006:* 2,383
Provincial Electoral District(s): Kent
Federal Electoral District(s): Beauséjour
Next Election: May 2012 (4 year terms)
Marc Landry, Gérant-Greffier
Aldéo Saulnier, Maire

Cambridge-Narrows

Municipal Bldg.
6 Municipal Lane
Cambridge-Narrows, NB E4C 4P4
506-488-3155 Fax: 506-488-1018
office@nbnet.nb.ca
www.cambridge-narrows.ca
Municipal Type: Village
Area: 106.94 sq km
County or District: Queens; *Population in 2006:* 717
Provincial Electoral District(s): Grand Lake-Gagetown
Federal Electoral District(s): New Brunswick Southwest
Next Election: May 2012 (4 year terms)
Alexis Trebble, Clerk
Peter W. Knight, Mayor

Campbellton

Campbellton City Centre
P.O. Box 100
76 Water St.
Campbellton, NB E3N 3G1
506-789-2700 Fax: 506-759-7403
manon.cloutier@campbellton.org
www.campbellton.org
Municipal Type: Town
Incorporated: 1889; *Area:* 18.66 sq km
County or District: Restigouche; *Population in 2006:* 7,384
Provincial Electoral District(s): Campbellton-Restigouche Centre
Federal Electoral District(s): Madawaska-Restigouche
Next Election: May 2012 (4 year terms)

Council
Bruce N. MacIntosh, Mayor
mayor@campbellton.org
Stephanie Marie Anglehart, Councillor
Diane M. Cyr, Councillor
Gilbert E. Cyr, Councillor
Greg Davis, Councillor
Sterling (Fuzzy) Loga, Councillor
Denis Turcotte, Councillor

Administration
Monique Cormier, Clerk
monique.cormier@campbellton.org

Canterbury

199 Main St.
Canterbury, NB E6H 1M6
506-279-2048 Fax: 506-279-9019
Municipal Type: Village
Area: 5.34 sq km
County or District: York; *Population in 2006:* 360
Provincial Electoral District(s): Woodstock
Federal Electoral District(s): Tobique-Mactaquac
Next Election: May 2012 (4 year terms)
Cara Hatton, Clerk
Léo Joseph Cloutier, Mayor

Cap-Pelé

33, ch St-André
Cap-Pelé, NB E4N 1Z4
506-577-2030 Fax: 506-577-2035
cappele@nb.aibn.com
www.cap-pele.com
Municipal Type: Village
Incorporated: 1969; *Area:* 23.78 sq km
County or District: Westmorland; *Population in 2006:* 2,279
Provincial Electoral District(s): Shediac-Cap-Pelé
Federal Electoral District(s): Beauséjour
Next Election: May 2012 (4 year terms)
Stéphane Dallaire, Administrateur/Greffier
stephane.dallaire@cappele.com
Debbie Dodier, Mairesse

Caraquet

CP 5695
10, rue du Colisée
Caraquet, NB E1W 1B7
506-726-2727 Fax: 506-726-2660
caraquet@nbnet.nb.ca
www.ville.caraquet.nb.ca
Municipal Type: Town
Incorporated: Nov. 15, 1961; *Area:* 68.26 sq km
County or District: Gloucester; *Population in 2006:* 4,156
Provincial Electoral District(s): Caraquet
Federal Electoral District(s): Acadie-Bathurst
Next Election: May 2012 (4 year terms)
Lucien Sonier, Directeur général
luciensonier@nb.aibn.com
Antonio (Antoine) Landry, Maire
antoinel@nb.aibn.com

Centreville

836 Central St.
Centreville, NB E7K 2E7
506-276-3671 Fax: 506-276-9891
clerk@nbnet.nb.ca
www.villageofcentreville.ca
Municipal Type: Village
Area: 2.69 sq km
County or District: Carleton; *Population in 2006:* 523
Provincial Electoral District(s): Carleton
Federal Electoral District(s): Tobique-Mactaquac; New Brunswick Southwest
Next Election: May 2012 (4 year terms)
Teresa Burtt, Administrator
Gary R. Thomas, Mayor

Charlo

614, rue Chaleur
Charlo, NB E8E 2G6
506-684-7850 Fax: 506-684-7855
vcharlo@nbnet.nb.ca
www.villagecharlo.com
Municipal Type: Village
Incorporated: 1966; *Area:* 30.75 sq km
County or District: Restigouche; *Population in 2006:* 1,376
Provincial Electoral District(s): Dalhousie-Restigouche East
Federal Electoral District(s): Madawaska-Restigouche
Next Election: May 2012 (4 year terms)
Adolphe Goulette, Administrateur
André J.C. Carrier, Maire

Chipman

#1, 10 Civic Ct.
Chipman, NB E4A 2H9
506-339-6601 Fax: 506-339-6197
villchip@nbnet.nb.ca
www.chipmannb.com
Municipal Type: Village
Area: 19.58 sq km
County or District: Queens; *Population in 2006:* 1,291
Provincial Electoral District(s): Grand Lake-Gagetown
Federal Electoral District(s): Fredericton
Next Election: May 2012 (4 year terms)
Brenda Barton, Clerk
Edward L. Farris, Mayor

Clair

809E, rue Principale
Clair, NB E7A 2H7
506-992-6030 Fax: 506-992-6041
vgeclair@nbnet.nb.ca
Municipal Type: Village
Area: 10.46 sq km
County or District: Madawaska; *Population in 2006:* 848
Provincial Electoral District(s): Madawaska-les-Lacs
Federal Electoral District(s): Madawaska-Restigouche
Next Election: May 2012 (4 year terms)
Nicole Michaud, Greffière-Trés.
Ludger Lang, Maire

Commission de gestion des déchets solides de la péninsule Acadienne (COGEDES)

#4, 149, boul St-Pierre ouest
Caraquet, NB E1W 1B6
506-726-2911 Fax: 506-726-2912
cogedes@nbnet.nb.ca
www.cogedes.com
Municipal Type: Waste Commission
Jean-Marie Gionet, Chair
Gary LeBlanc, General Manager

Commission de gestion enviro ressources du Nord-Ouest (COGERNO)

248, ch Clément Roy
Rivière-Verte, NB E7C 2W7
506-263-3470 Fax: 506-263-3476
jean@nbnet.nb.ca
www.cogerno.com
Municipal Type: Water Commission
Jean A. Bourque, General Manager
Pierre Michaud, Chair

Dalhousie

#1, 111 Hall St.
Dalhousie, NB E8C 1X2
506-684-7600 Fax: 506-684-7613
reception@dalhousienb.com
www.dalhousienb.com
Municipal Type: Town
Incorporated: 1905; *Area:* 14.51 sq km
County or District: Restigouche; *Population in 2006:* 3,676
Provincial Electoral District(s): Dalhousie-Restigouche East
Federal Electoral District(s): Madawaska-Restigouche
Next Election: May 2012 (4 year terms)
Michael J. Allain, Administrator
Clem Tremblay, Mayor

Doaktown

#2, 328 Main St.
Doaktown, NB E9C 1E3
506-365-7970 Fax: 506-365-7111
doaktown@nbnet.nb.ca
www.doaktown.com
Municipal Type: Village
Area: 28.74 sq km
County or District: Northumberland; *Population in 2006:* 888
Provincial Electoral District(s): Southwest Miramichi
Federal Electoral District(s): Miramichi
Next Election: May 2012 (4 year terms)
Marilyn E. Price, Clerk-Administrator
Charles Eric Stewart, Mayor

Dorchester
4984 Main St.
Dorchester, NB E4K 2Z1
506-379-3030 Fax: 506-379-3033
vilofdor@nb.sympatico.ca
www.dorchester.ca
Municipal Type: Village
Area: 5.74 sq km
County or District: Westmorland; *Population in 2006:* 1,119
Provincial Electoral District(s): Tantramar
Federal Electoral District(s): Beauséjour
Next Election: May 2012 (4 year terms)
Simonne Malenfant-Edgett, Clerk-Treas.
Melvin J. Goodland, Mayor

Drummond
1412, ch Tobique
Drummond, NB E3Y 1H7
506-475-4000 Fax: 506-475-4010
vildrum@nb.sympatico.ca
www.sn2000.nb.ca/comp/drummond
Municipal Type: Village
Area: 8.91 sq km
County or District: Victoria; *Population in 2006:* 839
Provincial Electoral District(s): Grand Falls-Drummond-Saint-André
Federal Electoral District(s): Tobique-Mactaquac
Next Election: May 2012 (4 year terms)
Annie Gagné, Administratrice
Cyril Rioux, Maire

Eel River Crossing
CP 159
20, rue Savoie
Eel River Crossing, NB E8E 1T8
506-826-6080 Fax: 506-826-6088
voerc@nbnet.nb.ca
Municipal Type: Village
Area: 17.43 sq km
Population in 2006: 1,168
Provincial Electoral District(s): Dalhousie-Restigouche East
Federal Electoral District(s): Madawaska-Restigouche
Next Election: May 2012 (4 year terms)
Kim Bujold, Administrateure
Denis D. Savoie, Maire

Florenceville-Bristol
4724 Juniper Rd.
Bristol, NB E7L 2W9
506-392-6013 Fax: 506-392-5211
vbristol@nb.sympatico.ca
www.villageofbristol.ca
Municipal Type: Village
Incorporated: 2008;
County or District: Carleton;
Provincial Electoral District(s): Carleton
Federal Electoral District(s): Tobique-Mactaquac
Next Election: May 2012 (4 year terms)
Note: The villages of Florenceville & Bristol amalgamated to create the municipality of Florenceville-Bristol.
Nancy Shaw, CAO-Clerk
Darrell R. Giggie, Mayor

Fredericton Junction
102 Wilsey Rd.
Fredericton Junction, NB E5L 1W7
506-368-2628 Fax: 506-368-1900
fredjct@nbnet.nb.ca
www.frederictonjunction.com
Municipal Type: Village
Area: 23.86 sq km
County or District: Sunbury; *Population in 2006:* 715
Provincial Electoral District(s): New Maryland-Sunbury West
Federal Electoral District(s): New Brunswick Southwest
Next Election: May 2012 (4 year terms)
Jocelyn Nason, Clerk
Gary W. Mersereau, Mayor

Fredericton Region Solid Waste Commission
P.O. Box 21 A
Fredericton, NB E3B 4Y2
506-453-9930 Fax: 506-453-9933
swc99@nbnet.nb.ca
www.frswc.ca
Municipal Type: Water Commission
Gordon Wilson, General Manager
506-444-0960
gordon@frswc.ca
Pierre Theriault, Operations Manager
506-453-9932
John Bigger, Chair

Fundy Region Solid Waste Commission
P.O. Box 3032
Grand-Bay Westfield, NB E5K 4V3
506-738-1212 Fax: 506-738-1207
hotline@fundyrecycles.com
www.fundyrecycles.com
Municipal Type: Water Commission
Jack Keir, General Manager
Rob Dean, Site Operations Supervisor, Crane Mountain Landfill
Ron Nelson, Environmental Coordinator
Chris Harned, Supervisor, Waste Diversion
Catherine Doucette, Officer, Public Education
Brenda MacCallum, Public Education Officer

Gagetown
68 Babbit St.
Gagetown, NB E5M 1C8
506-488-3567 Fax: 506-488-3543
gagetnvl@nbnet.nb.ca
www.villageofgagetown.ca
Municipal Type: Village
Incorporated: 1966; *Area:* 49.48 sq km
County or District: Queens; *Population in 2006:* 719
Provincial Electoral District(s): Grand Lake-Gagetown
Federal Electoral District(s): New Brunswick Southwest
Next Election: May 2012 (4 year terms)
Jane Trenholm, Clerk-Administrator
Randy A. Smith, Mayor

Grand Bay-Westfield
P.O. Box 3001
609 River Valley Dr.
Grand Bay-Westfield, NB E5K 4V3
506-738-6420 Fax: 506-738-6424
sgautreau@town.grandbay-westfield.nb.ca
www.town.grandbay-westfield.nb.ca
Municipal Type: Town
Incorporated: 1998; *Area:* 59.73 sq km
County or District: Kings; *Population in 2006:* 4,981
Provincial Electoral District(s): Fundy-River Valley
Federal Electoral District(s): New Brunswick Southwest
Next Election: May 2012 (4 year terms)
Sandra M. Gautreau, Town Manager & Clerk
M. Grace Losier, Mayor
losier@town.grandbay-westfield.nb.ca

Grand Falls / Grand-Sault
#200, 131, rue Pleasant
Grand-Sault, NB E3Z 1G6
506-475-7777 Fax: 506-475-7779
tgf@nbnet.nb.ca
www.grandfalls.com
Municipal Type: Town
Area: 18.06 sq km
County or District: Victoria; *Population in 2006:* 5,650
Provincial Electoral District(s): Grand Falls-Drummond-Saint-André
Federal Electoral District(s): Tobique-Mactaquac
Next Election: May 2012 (4 year terms)
Peter Michaud, CAO-Clerk
petergf@nb.aibn.com
Marcel Yvon Deschenes, Mayor

Grand Manan
23 Ingalls Head Rd.
Grand Manan, NB E5G 3G3
506-662-7059 Fax: 506-662-7060
grandmanan@villageofgrandmanan.com
www.villageofgrandmanan.com
Municipal Type: Village
Incorporated: May 8, 1995; *Area:* 150.78 sq km
County or District: Charlotte; *Population in 2006:* 2,460
Provincial Electoral District(s): Charlotte-The Isles
Federal Electoral District(s): New Brunswick Southwest
Next Election: May 2012 (4 year terms)
Linda Sullivan Brown, Clerk-Asst. Treas.
Dennis Clifton Greene, Mayor
dennisgreene@villageofgrandmanan.com

Grande-Anse
393, rue Acadie
Grande-Anse, NB E8N 1E2
506-732-3242 Fax: 506-732-3217
grande-anse@i-web.net
www.i-web.net/grande-anse
Municipal Type: Village
Incorporated: 1968; *Area:* 24.42 sq km
County or District: Gloucester; *Population in 2006:* 758
Provincial Electoral District(s): Caraquet
Federal Electoral District(s): Acadie-Bathurst
Next Election: May 2012 (4 year terms)
Rhéal Paulin, Administrateur
Roméo Thériault, Maire

Hampton
P.O. Box 1066
27 Centennial Rd.
Hampton, NB E5N 8H1
506-832-6065 Fax: 506-832-6098
brenda.collings@nb.aibn.com
www.townofhampton.ca
Municipal Type: Town
Area: 21 sq km
County or District: Kings; *Population in 2006:* 4,004
Provincial Electoral District(s): Hampton-Kings
Federal Electoral District(s): Fundy Royal
Next Election: May 2012 (4 year terms)
Megan O'Brien Harrison, Clerk & Development Officer
megan.obrienharrison@nb.aibn.com
Kenneth A. Chorley, Mayor
hampton@nbnet.nb.ca
Brenda Collings, CAO

Hartland
#1, 31 Orser St.
Hartland, NB E7P 1R4
506-375-4357 Fax: 506-375-8265
hartland@nbnet.nb.ca
www.town.hartland.nb.ca
Municipal Type: Town
Area: 9.63 sq km
County or District: Carleton; *Population in 2006:* 947
Provincial Electoral District(s): Carleton
Federal Electoral District(s): Tobique-Mactaquac
Next Election: May 2012 (4 year terms)
Judy Dee, Clerk
Wayne D. Britton, Mayor

Harvey Station
58 Hanselpacker Rd.
Harvey Station, NB E6K 1A3
506-366-6240 Fax: 506-366-6242
harveyst@nbnet.nb.ca
www.village.harvey-station.nb.ca
Municipal Type: Village
Incorporated: Nov. 9, 1966; *Area:* 2.46 sq km
County or District: York; *Population in 2006:* 352
Provincial Electoral District(s): York
Federal Electoral District(s): New Brunswick Southwest
Next Election: May 2012 (4 year terms)
Hubert Matheson, Clerk
Winston D. Gamblin, Mayor

Hillsborough
#1, 2849 Main St.
Hillsborough, NB E4H 2X7
506-734-3733 Fax: 506-734-3711
hillsborough@rogers.com
www.hillsboroughnb.ca
Municipal Type: Village
Incorporated: 1966; *Area:* 12.98 sq km
County or District: Albert; *Population in 2006:* 1,292
Provincial Electoral District(s): Albert
Federal Electoral District(s): Fundy Royal
Next Election: May 2012 (4 year terms)
Danny A. Jonah, Administrator-Clerk
Donna M. Bennett, Mayor

Kedgwick
114, rue Notre-Dame
Kedgwick, NB E8B 1H8
506-284-2160 Fax: 506-284-2859
villkedg@nbnet.nb.ca
Municipal Type: Village
Area: 4.28 sq km
County or District: Restigouche; *Population in 2006:* 1,146
Provincial Electoral District(s): Restigouche-La-Vallée
Federal Electoral District(s): Madawaska-Restigouche
Next Election: May 2012 (4 year terms)
Suzanne J. Cyr, Greffière
Jean Paul Savoie, Maire

Kent County Solid Waste Commission
2249 Rte. 134
Lakeville-Westmorland, NB E1H 1P3
506-384-9195 Fax: 506-384-6029 Toll Free Phone: 1-877-588-1125
Municipal Type: Water Commission
Roland Fougère, Chair
Florence Babineau, General Manager
fbabineau@rogers.com

Kings County Region Solid Waste Commission
P.O. Box 4861
Sussex, NB E4E 5L9
506-433-6502 Fax: 506-432-6435
kcrswc@nbnet.nb.ca
Municipal Type: Waste Commission
Garth Long, Chair
506-433-1341
gplong@nbnet.nb.ca

Lac-Baker
69, rue De La Pointe
Lac Baker, NB E7A 1J1
506-992-6060 Fax: 506-992-6061
lacbacac@nbnet.nb.ca
Municipal Type: Village
Area: 4.02 sq km
County or District: Madawaska; *Population in 2006:* 169
Provincial Electoral District(s): Madawaska-les-Lacs
Federal Electoral District(s): Madawaska-Restigouche
Next Election: May 2012 (4 year terms)
Doris Blanchard, Supervisor
Jean-Marc Nadeau, Mayor

Lamèque
28, rue de l'Hôpital
Lamèque, NB E8T 1C3
506-344-3222 Fax: 506-344-3266
info@lameque.ca
www.lameque.ca
Municipal Type: Town
Area: 12.45 sq km
County or District: Gloucester; *Population in 2006:* 1,422
Provincial Electoral District(s): Lamèque-Shippagan-Miscou
Federal Electoral District(s): Acadie-Bathurst
Next Election: May 2012 (4 year terms)
Henri-Paul Guignard, Administrateur
hplameque@nb.aibn.com
Rénald Haché, Maire

Le Goulet
1295, rue Principale
Le Goulet, NB E8S 2E9

506-336-3272 Fax: 506-336-3281
villagelegoulet@nb.aibn.com
www.legoulet.peninsuleacadienne.ca
Municipal Type: Village
Incorporated: May 12, 1986; *Area:* 5.46 sq km
County or District: Gloucester; *Population in 2006:* 908
Provincial Electoral District(s): Lamèque-Shippagan-Miscou
Federal Electoral District(s): Acadie-Bathurst
Next Election: May 2012 (4 year terms)
Line Roussel, Sec.-trés. adjointe
Ulysse Haché, Maire

Maisonnette
1512, rue Châtillon
Maisonnette, NB E8N 1S4
506-726-2717 Fax: 506-726-2718
maisonet@nbnet.nb.ca
www.maisonnette.ca
Municipal Type: Village
Incorporated: May 12, 1986; *Area:* 12.88 sq km
County or District: Gloucester; *Population in 2006:* 599
Provincial Electoral District(s): Caraquet
Federal Electoral District(s): Acadie-Bathurst
Next Election: May 2012 (4 year terms)
Lynne-Andrée Galarneau, Greffière
Lucio Cordisco, Maire

McAdam
146 Saunders Rd.
McAdam, NB E6J 1L2
506-784-2293 Fax: 506-784-1402
villageofmcadam@nb.aibn.com
www.mcadamnb.com
Municipal Type: Village
Area: 14.47 sq km
County or District: York; *Population in 2006:* 1,404
Provincial Electoral District(s): York
Federal Electoral District(s): New Brunswick Southwest
Next Election: May 2012 (4 year terms)
Ann Donahue, Clerk
Frank M. Carroll, Mayor
C.L. Nason, Manager

Meductic
10720 Rte. 2
Meductic, NB E6H 1J5
506-272-2098 Fax: 506-272-1883
villageofmeductic@nb.aibn.com
Municipal Type: Village
Area: 5.57 sq km
County or District: York; *Population in 2006:* 155
Provincial Electoral District(s): Woodstock
Federal Electoral District(s): Tobique-Mactaquac
Next Election: May 2012 (4 year terms)
Pamela Grant, Clerk-Treas.
Pamela E. Gavel, Mayor

Memramcook
540, rue Centrale
Memramcook, NB E4K 3S6
506-758-4078 Fax: 506-758-4079
village@memramcook.com
www.memramcook.com/English/index.html
Municipal Type: Village
Incorporated: 1995; *Area:* 185.71 sq km
County or District: Westmorland; *Population in 2006:* 4,638
Provincial Electoral District(s): Memramcook-Lakeville-Dieppe
Federal Electoral District(s): Beauséjour
Next Election: May 2012 (4 year terms)
Monique Bourque, Greffière
monique@memramcook.com
Donald Oscar LeBlanc, Maire

Millville
39 Howland Ridge Rd.
Millville, NB E6E 1Y3
506-463-2719 Fax: 506-463-8262
villageofmillville@nb.aibn.com
Municipal Type: Village
Area: 12.16 sq km
County or District: York; *Population in 2006:* 303
Provincial Electoral District(s): York North
Federal Electoral District(s): Tobique-Mactaquac
Next Election: May 2012 (4 year terms)
Karen Cooney, Clerk-Treas.
Beverly Herbert Forbes, Mayor

Minto
420 Pleasant Dr.
Minto, NB E4B 2T3
506-327-3383 Fax: 506-327-3041
minto@nb.aibn.com
www.village.minto.nb.ca
Municipal Type: Village
Area: 31.53 sq km
County or District: Sunbury-Queens; *Population in 2006:* 2,681
Provincial Electoral District(s): Grand Lake-Gagetown
Federal Electoral District(s): Fredericton
Next Election: May 2012 (4 year terms)
Trila McKenelley, Clerk-Administrator
Eric G. Barnett, Mayor

Nackawic
115 Otis Dr.
Nackawic, NB E6G 2P1
506-575-2241 Fax: 506-575-2035
townhall@nackawic.com
www.nackawic.com
Municipal Type: Town
Area: 8.4 sq km
County or District: York; *Population in 2006:* 977
Provincial Electoral District(s): York North
Federal Electoral District(s): Tobique-Mactaquac
Next Election: May 2012 (4 year terms)
Nancy Cronkhite, CAO
nancy.cronkhite@nackawic.com
Rowena E. Simpson, Mayor

Néguac
#1, 1175, rue Principale
Néguac, NB E9G 1T1
506-776-3950 Fax: 506-776-3975
village@nbnet.nb.ca
www.neguac.com
Municipal Type: Village
Incorporated: Aug. 23, 1967; *Area:* 26.69 sq km
County or District: Northumberland; *Population in 2006:* 1,623
Provincial Electoral District(s): Miramichi Bay-Neguac
Federal Electoral District(s): Miramichi
Next Election: May 2012 (4 year terms)
Denis Bujold, Administrateur
village.denis@nb.aibn.com
Roger Ward, Maire

Nepisiguit-Chaleur Solid Waste Commission
1300, rte 360
Allardville, NB E8L 1H5
506-725-2402 Fax: 506-725-2410
redpine@nb.sympatico.ca
Municipal Type: Waste Commission
Raymond Bryar, General Manager
Graham Wiseman, Chair

New Maryland
584 New Maryland Hwy.
New Maryland, NB E3C 1K1
506-451-8508 Fax: 506-450-1605
office@vonm.ca
www.vonm.ca
Municipal Type: Village
Incorporated: 1991; *Area:* 21.23 sq km
County or District: York; *Population in 2006:* 4,248
Provincial Electoral District(s): New Maryland-Sunbury West
Federal Electoral District(s): Fredericton; New Brunswick Southwest
Next Election: May 2012 (4 year terms)
Cynthia Geldart, CAO-Clerk
cynthia.geldart@vonm.ca
Frank C. Dunn, Mayor
mayor@vonm.ca

Nigadoo
#1, 385, rue Principale
Nigadoo, NB E8K 3R6
506-542-2626 Fax: 506-542-2678
nigadoov@nbnet.nb.ca
Municipal Type: Village
Incorporated: 1967; *Area:* 7.69 sq km
County or District: Gloucester; *Population in 2006:* 927
Provincial Electoral District(s): Nigadoo-Chaleur
Federal Electoral District(s): Acadie-Bathurst
Next Election: May 2012 (4 year terms)
Aline Morrison, Secrétaire
Gilberte Boudreau, Mairesse

Northumberland Solid Waste Commission
505 Old King George Hwy.
Miramichi, NB E1V 1J8
506-778-6646 Fax: 506-778-6642
info@nswc-cdsn.ca
www.nswc-cdsn.ca
Municipal Type: Waste Commission
Marie LeBlanc, Manager, Administration
Scotty Bernard, Chair
April Conroy, Coordinator, Waste Reduction

Norton
P.O. Box 335
Norton, NB E5T 1J7
506-839-3011 Fax: 506-839-3015
vnorton@nbnet.nb.ca
Municipal Type: Village
Area: 75.35 sq km
County or District: Kings; *Population in 2006:* 1,314
Provincial Electoral District(s): Hampton-Kings; Kings East
Federal Electoral District(s): Fundy Royal; New Brunswick Southwest
Next Election: May 2012 (4 year terms)
Anita Pollock, Clerk-Treas.
Wendy L. Alcorn, Mayor

Oromocto
4 Doyle Dr.
Oromocto, NB E2V 2V3
506-357-4400 Fax: 506-357-2266
gengov@oromocto.ca
www.oromocto.ca
Municipal Type: Town
Area: 22.37 sq km
County or District: Sunbury; *Population in 2006:* 8,402
Provincial Electoral District(s): Oromocto
Federal Electoral District(s): Fredericton
Next Election: May 2012 (4 year terms)
Fay Lillian Tidd, CAO-Clerk
Fay L. Tidd, Mayor

Paquetville
1094, rue du Parc
Paquetville, NB E8R 1J4
506-764-2500 Fax: 506-764-2504
loulou.blanchard@nb.ainb.com
www.paquetville.com
Municipal Type: Village
Incorporated: 1966; *Area:* 9.4 sq km
County or District: Gloucester; *Population in 2006:* 642
Provincial Electoral District(s): Centre-Péninsule-Saint-Sauveur
Federal Electoral District(s): Acadie-Bathurst
Next Election: May 2012 (4 year terms)
Marie-Louise (Loulou) Blanchard, Greffière & Secrétaire
André Gozzo, Maire
elitec@nbnet.nb.ca

Perth-Andover
1131 West Riverside Dr.
Perth-Andover, NB E7H 5G5
506-273-4959 Fax: 506-273-4947
info@perth-andover.com
www.perth-andover.com
Municipal Type: Village
Incorporated: 1966; *Area:* 8.89 sq km
County or District: Victoria; *Population in 2006:* 1,797
Provincial Electoral District(s): Victoria-Tobique
Federal Electoral District(s): Tobique-Mactaquac
Next Election: May 2012 (4 year terms)
Daniel Dionne, Chief Administrative Officer
dan.dionne@perth-andover.com
Rickey Allen Beaulieu, Mayor

Petit-Rocher
582, rue Principale
Petit-Rocher, NB E8J 1S5
506-542-2686 Fax: 506-542-2708
petit-rocher@nb.aibn.com
www.acadie-bathurst.com
Municipal Type: Village
Area: 4.49 sq km
County or District: Gloucester; *Population in 2006:* 1,949
Provincial Electoral District(s): Nigadoo-Chaleur
Federal Electoral District(s): Acadie-Bathurst
Next Election: May 2012 (4 year terms)
Guy Clavette, Gérant
Pierre Godin, Maire

Petitcodiac
P.O. Box 2507
63 Main St.
Petitcodiac, NB E4Z 6H4
506-756-3140 Fax: 506-756-3142
vop@nbnet.nb.ca
www.petitcodiac.ca
Municipal Type: Village
Area: 17.22 sq km
County or District: Westmorland; *Population in 2006:* 1,368
Provincial Electoral District(s): Petitcodiac
Federal Electoral District(s): Fundy Royal
Next Election: May 2012 (4 year terms)
Janice Conley, Clerk
Peter J. Saunders, Mayor

Plaster Rock
81 Ridgewell St.
Plaster Rock, NB E7G 2N6
506-356-6070 Fax: 506-356-6081
vilprock@nb.sympatico.ca
www.plasterrock.com
Municipal Type: Village
Area: 3.09 sq km
County or District: Victoria; *Population in 2006:* 1,150
Provincial Electoral District(s): Victoria-Tobique
Federal Electoral District(s): Tobique-Mactaquac
Next Election: May 2012 (4 year terms)
Barbara Wishart-Fawcett, Clerk
wishartbl@hotmail.com
Judy A. St. Peter, Mayor

Pointe-Verte
375, rue Principale
Pointe-Verte, NB E8J 2S8
506-542-2606 Fax: 506-542-2638
pverte@nbnet.nb.ca
www.acadie-bathurst.com
Municipal Type: Village
Area: 13.79 sq km
County or District: Gloucester; *Population in 2006:* 971
Provincial Electoral District(s): Nigadoo-Chaleur
Federal Electoral District(s): Acadie-Bathurst
Next Election: May 2012 (4 year terms)
Marie-Eve Cyr, Directrice generale
Paul Desjardins, Maire

Port Elgin
41 East Main St.
Port Elgin, NB E4M 2X8
506-538-2120 Fax: 506-538-2126
prtelgin@nbnet.nb.ca
www.villageofportelgin.com

Municipal Type: Village
Incorporated: 1922; *Area:* 2.61 sq km
County or District: Westmorland; *Population in 2006:* 451
Provincial Electoral District(s): Tantramar
Federal Electoral District(s): Beauséjour
Next Election: May 2012 (4 year terms)
Sonia M. Wells, Clerk-Treas.
Lynda Lukey, Mayor

Restigouche Solid Waste Corporation
P.O. Box 93
162B Water St.
Campbellton, NB E3N 3G1
506-789-2111 Fax: 506-789-2111
Municipal Type: Waste Commission
Ian Comeau, General Manager
comeai@nbnet.nb.ca
Jean Perron, Chair

Rexton
#1, 79 Main St.
Rexton, NB E4W 1Z9
506-523-6921 Fax: 506-523-7383
villageofrexton@nb.aibn.com
www.villageofrexton.com
Municipal Type: Village
Incorporated: Nov. 9, 1966; *Area:* 6.14 sq km
County or District: Kent; *Population in 2006:* 862
Provincial Electoral District(s): Kent
Federal Electoral District(s): Beauséjour
Next Election: May 2012 (4 year terms)
Barry Glencross, Clerk-Administrator
David L. Hanson, Mayor

Richibucto
9236, rue Main
Richibucto, NB E4W 4C6
506-523-7870 Fax: 506-523-7850
vtrcto@nbnet.nb.ca
www.richibucto.org
Municipal Type: Town
Incorporated: 1967; *Area:* 11.83 sq km
County or District: Kent; *Population in 2006:* 1,290
Provincial Electoral District(s): Rogersville-Kouchibouguac
Federal Electoral District(s): Beauséjour
Next Election: May 2012 (4 year terms)
Gilles Belleau, Gérant
Meldric J. Mazerolle, Mayor

Riverside-Albert
5823 King St.
Riverside-Albert, NB E4H 4B4
506-882-3022 Fax: 506-882-3016
villra@nbnet.nb.ca
www.bay-of-fundy.com/riverside-albert
Municipal Type: Village
Area: 3.41 sq km
County or District: Albert; *Population in 2006:* 320
Provincial Electoral District(s): Albert
Federal Electoral District(s): Fundy Royal
Next Election: May 2012 (4 year terms)
Deborah Murray, Clerk
Malcolm E. Fife, Mayor

Rivière-Verte
78, rue Principale
Rivière-Verte, NB E7C 2T8
506-263-1060 Fax: 506-263-1065
evelyne@nbnet.nb.ca
Municipal Type: Village
Area: 7 sq km
County or District: Madawaska; *Population in 2006:* 798
Provincial Electoral District(s): Restigouche-La-Vallée
Federal Electoral District(s): Madawaska-Restigouche
Next Election: May 2012 (4 year terms)
Evelyn Therrien, Greffière
Michel Leblond, Maire

Rogersville
#2, 28, rue de l'École
Rogersville, NB E4Y 1V7
506-775-2080 Fax: 506-775-2090
rogervil@nbnet.nb.ca
www.rogersville.info
Municipal Type: Village
Incorporated: Nov. 9, 1966; *Area:* 7.23 sq km
County or District: Kent; *Population in 2006:* 1,165
Provincial Electoral District(s): Rogersville-Kouchibouguac
Federal Electoral District(s): Miramichi
Next Election: May 2012 (4 year terms)
Hélène LeBlanc, Greffière & Administratrice
Bertrand LeBlanc, Maire

Sackville
P.O. Box 6191
110 East Main St.
Sackville, NB E4L 1G6
506-364-4930 Fax: 506-364-4975
b.carroll@sackville.com
www.sackville.com
Municipal Type: Town
Incorporated: Jan. 1903; *Area:* 74.32 sq km
County or District: Westmorland; *Population in 2006:* 5,411
Provincial Electoral District(s): Tantramar
Federal Electoral District(s): Beauséjour
Next Election: May 2012 (4 year terms)
Rhonda Tower, Clerk
r.tower@sackville.com
Pat A. Estabrooks, Mayor

Saint Léonard
108, rue du Pont
Saint Léonard, NB E7E 1Y1
506-423-3111 Fax: 506-423-3115
sleonard@nbnet.nb.ca
www.saint-leonard.ca
Municipal Type: Town
Incorporated: 1920; *Area:* 5.2 sq km
County or District: Madawaska; *Population in 2006:* 1,352
Provincial Electoral District(s): Restigouche-La-Vallée
Federal Electoral District(s): Madawaska-Restigouche
Next Election: May 2012 (4 year terms)
Charles Boucher, Directeur général
Carmel St-Amand, Maire

Saint-André
438, rue Lévesque
Saint-André, NB E3Y 3C7
506-473-7580 Fax: 506-473-7585
vilstand@nbnet.nb.ca
www.sn2000.nb.ca/comp/saint-andre
Municipal Type: Village
Area: 3.72 sq km
County or District: Madawaska; *Population in 2006:* 404
Provincial Electoral District(s): Grand Falls-Drummond-Saint-André
Federal Electoral District(s): Tobique-Mactaquac
Next Election: May 2012 (4 year terms)
Gisèle Ouellette, Sec.-Tres.
Lionel Poitras, Maire

Saint-Antoine
4599, rue Principale
Saint-Antoine, NB E4V 1P8
506-525-4020 Fax: 506-525-4027
village@village.stantoine.nb.ca
www.village.stantoine.nb.ca
Municipal Type: Village
Area: 6.43 sq km
County or District: Kent; *Population in 2006:* 1,546
Provincial Electoral District(s): Kent South
Federal Electoral District(s): Beauséjour
Next Election: May 2012 (4 year terms)
Bernadine Maillet-LeBlanc, Directrice générale
berniem@village.stantoine.nb.ca
Roseline M. Maillet, Mairesse

Saint-François-de-Madawaska
2033, rue Commerciale
Saint-François-de-Madawaska, NB E7A 1B3
506-992-6050 Fax: 506-992-6049
munstf@nb.aibn.com
Municipal Type: Village
Area: 6.34 sq km
County or District: Madawaska; *Population in 2006:* 585
Provincial Electoral District(s): Madawaska-les-Lacs
Federal Electoral District(s): Madawaska-Restigouche
Next Election: May 2012 (4 year terms)
Colette Lévesque, Greffière
Raoul Cyr, Maire

Saint-Hilaire
2190, rue Centrale
Saint-Hilaire, NB E3V 4W1
506-258-3307 Fax: 506-258-1802
Municipal Type: Village
Area: 5.67 sq km
County or District: Madawaska; *Population in 2006:* 231
Provincial Electoral District(s): Madawaska-les-Lacs
Federal Electoral District(s): Madawaska-Restigouche
Next Election: May 2012 (4 year terms)
Raymond Sirois, Maire

Saint-Isidore
3906, boul des Fondateurs
Saint-Isidore, NB E8M 1C2
506-358-6005 Fax: 506-358-6010
villasti@nbnet.nb.ca
www.saintisidore.ca
Municipal Type: Village
Incorporated: June 1, 1991; *Area:* 22.58 sq km
Population in 2006: 796
Provincial Electoral District(s): Centre-Péninsule-Saint-Sauveur
Federal Electoral District(s): Acadie-Bathurst
Next Election: May 2012 (4 year terms)
Dave Cowan, Directeur général
davecowan@t2way.com
Cécile Renaud, Mairesse

Saint-Léolin
117, rue des Prés
Saint-Léolin, NB E8N 2P9
506-732-3266 Fax: 506-732-3267
stleolin@nb.aira.com
Municipal Type: Village
Area: 19.78 sq km
County or District: Gloucester; *Population in 2006:* 733
Provincial Electoral District(s): Caraquet
Federal Electoral District(s): Acadie-Bathurst
Next Election: May 2012 (4 year terms)
Gérard Battah, Administrateur
Joseph Lanteigne, Maire

Saint-Louis-de-Kent
83, rue Beauséjour, #A
Saint-Louis-de-Kent, NB E4X 1A6
506-876-3420 Fax: 506-876-3477
vstlouis@nbnet.nb.ca
Municipal Type: Village
Area: 2 sq km
County or District: Kent; *Population in 2006:* 960
Provincial Electoral District(s): Rogersville-Kouchibouguac
Federal Electoral District(s): Beauséjour
Next Election: May 2012 (4 year terms)
Léo-Paul Frigault, Administrateur
Louis J. Arsenault, Maire

Saint-Quentin
10, rue Deschênes
Saint-Quentin, NB E8A 1M1
506-235-2425 Fax: 506-235-1952
ville@saintquentin.nb.ca
www.saintquentin.nb.ca
Municipal Type: Town
Incorporated: 1947; *Area:* 4.3 sq km
County or District: Restigouche; *Population in 2006:* 2,250
Provincial Electoral District(s): Restigouche-La-Vallée
Federal Electoral District(s): Madawaska-Restigouche
Next Election: May 2012 (4 year terms)
Note: Proclaimed as a town in 1992.
Suzanne Coulombe, Greffière
Robert Beaulieu, Maire

St. Andrews
212 Water St.
St Andrews, NB E5B 1B4
506-529-5120 Fax: 506-529-5183
thenderson@townofstandrews.ca
www.townofstandrews.ca
Municipal Type: Town
Area: 8.35 sq km
County or District: Charlotte; *Population in 2006:* 1,798
Provincial Electoral District(s): Charlotte-Campobello
Federal Electoral District(s): New Brunswick Southwest
Next Election: May 2012 (4 year terms)
W. Timothy Henderson, CAO & Development Officer
John D. Craig, Mayor

Sainte-Anne-de-Madawaska
75, rue Principale
Sainte-Anne-de-Madawaska, NB E7E 1A8
506-445-2449 Fax: 506-445-2405
Municipal Type: Village
Area: 9.21 sq km
County or District: Madawaska; *Population in 2006:* 1,073
Provincial Electoral District(s): Restigouche-La-Vallée
Federal Electoral District(s): Madawaska-Restigouche
Next Election: May 2012 (4 year terms)
Lise Deschênes, Clerk-Très.
Rodolphe R. Martin, Maire

Sainte-Marie-Saint-Raphaël
1541, boul de la Mer
Sainte-Marie-Saint-Raphaël, NB E8T 1P5
506-344-3210 Fax: 506-344-3213
smsr@nbnet.nb.ca
www.ste-marie-st-raphael.ca
Municipal Type: Village
Incorporated: May 12, 1986; *Area:* 15.61 sq km
County or District: Gloucester; *Population in 2006:* 993
Provincial Electoral District(s): Lamèque-Shippagan-Miscou
Federal Electoral District(s): Acadie-Bathurst
Next Election: May 2012 (4 year terms)
Denis Ducharme, Directeur général
Henri Pierre Duguay, Maire

St. George
1 School St.
St George, NB E5C 3N2
506-755-4321 Fax: 506-755-4329
stgeonb@nbnet.nb.ca
www.town.stgeorge.nb.ca
Municipal Type: Town
Incorporated: Oct. 17, 1904; *Area:* 16.13 sq km
County or District: Charlotte; *Population in 2006:* 1,309
Provincial Electoral District(s): Charlotte-The Isles
Federal Electoral District(s): New Brunswick Southwest
Next Election: May 2012 (4 year terms)
Ross A. Norman, Manager
Sharon E. Tucker, Mayor

St. Martins
#2, 73 Main St.
St Martins, NB E5R 1B4
506-833-2010 Fax: 506-833-2008
vilstmar@nbnet.nb.ca
www.stmartinscanada.com
Municipal Type: Village
Incorporated: Nov. 9, 1967; *Area:* 2.29 sq km
County or District: Saint John; *Population in 2006:* 386
Provincial Electoral District(s): Saint John-Fundy
Federal Electoral District(s): Fundy-Royal
Next Election: May 2012 (4 year terms)
Sandra Roy, Clerk
James Huttges, Mayor

St. Stephen
34 Milltown Blvd.
St Stephen, NB E3L 1G3
506-466-7700 Fax: 506-466-7701
jflewelling@town.ststephen.nb.ca
www.town.ststephen.nb.ca
Municipal Type: Town

County or District: Charlotte; *Population in 2006:* 4,780
Provincial Electoral District(s): Charlotte-Campobello
Federal Electoral District(s): New Brunswick Southwest
Next Election: May 2012 (4 year terms)
Joan Flewelling, Clerk
G.L. (Jed) Purcell, Mayor

Salisbury
56, rue Douglas
Salisbury, NB E4J 3E3
506-372-3230 Fax: 506-372-3225
vilsalisbury@nb.aibn.com
www.salisburynb.ca
Municipal Type: Village
Incorporated: 1966; *Area:* 13.68 sq km
County or District: Westmorland; *Population in 2006:* 2,036
Provincial Electoral District(s): Petitcodiac
Federal Electoral District(s): Fundy Royal
Next Election: May 2012 (4 year terms)
Pamela Cochrane, Clerk-Administrator
Terry A. Keating, Mayor

Shediac
#300, 290, rue Main
Shediac, NB E4P 2E3
506-532-7000 Fax: 506-532-6156
info@shediac.org
www.shediac.org
Municipal Type: Town
Area: 11.97 sq km
County or District: Westmorland; *Population in 2006:* 5,497
Provincial Electoral District(s): Shediac-Cap-Pelé
Federal Electoral District(s): Beauséjour
Next Election: May 2012 (4 year terms)
Jeannette Bourque, Greffière
Raymond Cormier, Mayor

Shippagan
200, av Hôtel de Ville
Shippagan, NB E8S 1M1
506-336-3900 Fax: 506 336-3901
shipadm@nbnet.nb.ca
www.ville.shippagan.com
Municipal Type: Town
Incorporated: 1947; *Area:* 9.94 sq km
County or District: Gloucester; *Population in 2006:* 2,754
Provincial Electoral District(s): Lamèque-Shippagan-Miscou
Federal Electoral District(s): Acadie-Bathurst
Next Election: May 2012 (4 year terms)
Note: Proclaimed as a town in 1958.
Nathalie Robichaud, Clerk
nathalie.robichaud@shippagan.com
Jonathan Roch Noël, Maire

South West Solid Waste Commission
P.O. Box 243
St Stephen, NB E3L 2X2
506-466-7830 Fax: 506-466-7833
crww@nbnet.nb.ca
www.swswc.com
Municipal Type: Waste Commission
Ken Landmaid, Chair, Managed Forest Committee
Glenn Greenlaw, Chair, Technical Committee
Peter Fenety, Chair, Environmental Monitoring Committee

Stanley
20 Main St.
Stanley, NB E6B 1A2
506-367-3245 Fax: 506-367-0006
vstanley@nbnet.nb.ca
Municipal Type: Village
Area: 17.34 sq km
County or District: York; *Population in 2006:* 433
Provincial Electoral District(s): York North
Federal Electoral District(s): Tobique-Mactaquac
Next Election: May 2012 (4 year terms)
Lorna Pinnock, Clerk-Administrator
Richard A. Storey, Mayor

Sussex
524 Main St.
Sussex, NB E4E 3E4
506-432-4540 Fax: 506-432-4566
townofsussex@sussex.ca
www.sussex.ca
Municipal Type: Town
Incorporated: 1904; *Area:* 9.03 sq km
County or District: Kings; *Population in 2006:* 4,241
Provincial Electoral District(s): Kings East
Federal Electoral District(s): Fundy Royal
Next Election: May 2012 (4 year terms)
Paul Maguire, Clerk-Treas.
paul.maguire@sussex.ca
Ralph A. Carr, Mayor

Sussex Corner
1067 Main St.
Sussex Corner, NB E4E 3A1
506-433-5184 Fax: 506-433-3785
sussex.corner@nb.aibn.com
www.sussexcorner.com
Municipal Type: Village
Incorporated: 1966; *Area:* 9.43 sq km
County or District: Kings; *Population in 2006:* 1,413
Provincial Electoral District(s): Kings East
Federal Electoral District(s): Fundy Royal
Next Election: May 2012 (4 year terms)
Don Smith, Clerk-Treas.
Eric C. Cunningham, Mayor

Tide Head
6 Mountain St.
Tide Head, NB E3N 4J9
506-789-6550 Fax: 506-789-6553
viltide@nb.sympatico.ca
Municipal Type: Village
Area: 19.57 sq km
County or District: Restigouche; *Population in 2006:* 1,075
Provincial Electoral District(s): Campbellton-Restigouche Centre
Federal Electoral District(s): Madawaska-Restigouche
Next Election: May 2012 (4 year terms)
Christine Babcock, Clerk-Administrator
Randy Hunter, Mayor

Tracadie-Sheila
CP 3600 Main
3620, rue Principale
Tracadie-Sheila, NB E1X 1G5
506-394-4020 Fax: 506-394-4025
info@tracadie-sheila.ca
www.tracadie-sheila.ca
Municipal Type: Town
Incorporated: Jan. 1, 1992; *Area:* 24.64 sq km
County or District: Gloucester; *Population in 2006:* 4,474
Provincial Electoral District(s): Tracadie-Sheila
Federal Electoral District(s): Acadie-Bathurst
Next Election: May 2012 (4 year terms)
Denis Poirier, Executive Director
Aldéoda Losier, Maire

Tracy
4435 Heritage Dr.
Tracy, NB E5L 1C1
506-368-2878 Fax: 506-368-1014
Municipal Type: Village
Area: 29.36 sq km
County or District: Sunbury; *Population in 2006:* 619
Provincial Electoral District(s): New Maryland-Sunbury West
Federal Electoral District(s): New Brunswick-Southwest
Next Election: May 2012 (4 year terms)
Susan Phillips, Clerk
Dale W. Mowry, Mayor

Valley Solid Waste Commission
P.O. Box 880
Hartland, NB E7P 3K4
506-375-3040 Fax: 506-375-3043 Toll Free Phone: 1-866-312-8800
vswc@nb.sympatico.ca
www.valleysolidwaste.com
Municipal Type: Water Commission
Denise Brown, Office Administrator

Westmorland-Albert Solid Waste Corporation
P.O. Box 1397
Moncton, NB E1C 8T6
506-877-1050 Fax: 506-877-1060
www.westmorlandalbert.com
Municipal Type: Waste Commission
Bill Slater, General Manager
Norman H. Crossman, Chair
Christa Methot, Coordinator, Community Relations
Yvon Gautreau, Vice-Chair
Greg Martin, Corporate Secretary
Trina Davidson, Supervisor, Site Operations

Woodstock
824 Main St.
Woodstock, NB E7M 2E8
506-325-4600 Fax: 506-325-4308
townhall@town.woodstock.nb.ca
www.town.woodstock.nb.ca
Municipal Type: Town
Incorporated: 1856; *Area:* 13.41 sq km
County or District: Carleton; *Population in 2006:* 5,113
Provincial Electoral District(s): Woodstock
Federal Electoral District(s): Tobique-Mactaquac
Next Election: May 2012 (4 year terms)
Ken Harding, CAO
ken.harding@town.woodstock.nb.ca
Arthur L. Slipp, Mayor

NEWFOUNDLAND & LABRADOR

The provincial government of Newfoundland and Labrador exercises control over the activities of all municipalities in accordance with the Executive Council Act and the Municipal Affairs Act. Under the provisions of the Municipalities Act, the Department exercises a certain degree of financial and administrative control over all municipalities with the exception of the Cities of St. John's, Corner Brook and Mount Pearl. The towns incorporated under the Municipalities Act do not require ministerial approval of their annual budgets, but the Department employs Municipal Analysts to oversee municipal activities. The province assumes responsibility for public health, welfare and law enforcement which are elsewhere generally considered to be municipal functions.

The cities and towns incorporated in Newfoundland are authorized to levy taxes and to provide a wide range of municipal services and to make appropriate bylaws or regulations for the implementation and administration of these services.

City and town councils in Newfoundland are elected on the last Tuesday in September every four years (2005, 2009, etc.).

Newfoundland & Labrador

Counties & Municipal Districts in Newfoundland & Labrador

Fogo Island Region
P.O. Box 159
Joe Batts Arm, NL A0G 2X0
709-266-1212 Fax: 709-266-1213
sosmond@nf.aibn.com
Municipal Type: Regional Municipality
Incorporated: March 1, 1996; *Area:* 173.48 sq km
Population in 2006: 488
Provincial Electoral District(s): Twillingate & Fogo
Federal Electoral District(s): Bonavista-Gander-Grand Falls-Windsor
Next Election: Sept. 2009 (4 year terms)
Shirley Osmond, Clerk
Gerald McKenna, Chair

Major Municipalities in Newfoundland & Labrador

Conception Bay South
106 Conception Bay Hwy.
Conception Bay South, NL A1W 3A5
709-834-6500 Fax: 709-834-8337
jmiller@conceptionbaysouth.ca
www.conceptionbaysouth.ca
Municipal Type: City
Incorporated: Sept. 1, 1971; *Area:* 59.27 sq km
Population in 2006: 21,966
Provincial Electoral District(s): Conception Bay South; Topsail
Federal Electoral District(s): St. John's East; Avalon
Next Election: Sept. 2009 (4 year terms)

Council
Woodrow French, Mayor
WFrench@conceptionbaysouth.ca

Administration
Keith Arns, CAO
karns@conceptionbaysouth.ca
Elaine Mitchell, Director, Planning
Ron Franey, Director, Public Works
Dave Tibbo, Director, Recreation & Leisure Services

Corner Brook
City Hall
P.O. Box 1080
Corner Brook, NL A2H 6E1
709-637-1500 Fax: 709-637-1625
cityhall@cornerbrook.com
www.cornerbrook.com
Municipal Type: City
Incorporated: April 27, 1955; *Area:* 148.27 sq km
Population in 2006: 20,083
Provincial Electoral District(s): Humber East; Humber West
Federal Electoral District(s): Humber-St. Barbe-Baie Verte
Next Election: Sept. 2009 (4 year terms)
Note: City Hall is located on Mount Bernard Ave. at Main St.

Council
Neville Greeley, Mayor
709-637-1537, Fax: 709-637-1543
ngreeley@cornerbrook.com
Leo Bruce, Councillor
lbruce@cornerbrook.com
Priscilla Boutcher, Councillor
pboutcher@cornerbrook.com
Donna Francis, Councillor
dfrancis@cornerbrook.com
Charlie Renouf, Councillor
crenouf@cornerbrook.com
Linda Chaisson, Councillor
lchaisson@cornerbrook.com

Administration
Marina Redmond, City Clerk
709-637-1534
mredmond@cornerbrook.com
Michael Dolter, CAO
709-637-1532
mdolter@cornerbrook.com
Neville Wheaton, Fire Chief
709-637-1615
nmwheaton@cornerbrook.com
Paul Barnable, Director, Community Services
709-637-1548, Fax: 709-637-1514
pbarnable@cornerbrook.com
Gerry Cole, Supervisor, Recreational Services
709-637-1232
gcole@cornerbrook.com
Trina Burden, Business Resource Manager
709-637-1558
tburden@cornerbrook.com
Steve May, Director, Operational Services
709-637-1541, Fax: 709-637-1502
smay@cornerbrook.com
Todd Pickett, Land Management Officer
709-637-1544
tpickett@cornerbrook.com
Colleen Humphries, Supervisor, Planning
709-637-1553
chumphries@cornerbrook.com
James Warford, P.Eng., Coordinator, Engineering Services
709-637-1626
jwarford@cornerbrook.com
Keith Costello, Superintendent, Water & Sewer
709-637-1595
kcostello@cornerbrook.com
Barry Ellsworth, Manager, Public Works
709-637-1509
bellsworth@cornerbrook.com
Percy Joyce, Officer, Land Management
709-637-1544
pjoyce@cornerbrook.com
Deon Rumbolt, Supervisor, Development & Inspection
709-637-1552
drumbolt@cornerbrook.com
Rhea Hutchings, Sustainable Development Officer, Operational Services
709-637-1574
rhutchings@cornerbrook.com
Craig Kennedy, Superintendent, Public Works
709-637-1607
ckennedy@cornerbrook.com

Grand Falls-Windsor
P.O. Box 439
Grand Falls-Windsor, NL A2A 2J8
709-489-0412 Fax: 709-489-0465
jrowsell@grandfallswindsor.com
www.grandfallswindsor.com
Municipal Type: City
Incorporated: Jan. 1, 1991; *Area:* 54.48 sq km
Population in 2006: 13,558
Provincial Electoral District(s): Grand Falls-Buchans; Windsor-Springdale
Federal Electoral District(s): Bonavista-Gander-Grand Falls-Windsor
Next Election: Sept. 2009 (4 year terms)

Council
Rex Barnes, Mayor
mayor@grandfallswindsor.com

Administration
Michael Pinsent, Town Manager
709-487-0407, Fax: 709-292-0018
mpinsent@grandfallswindsor.com
Jeff Saunders, Director, Engineering Works
709-489-0427, Fax: 709-489-0465
jsaunders@grandfallswindsor.com
Vince J. McKenzie, Fire Chief
709-489-0431, Fax: 709-489-0885
firechief@grandfallswindsor.com
Dave Nichols, Director, Parks & Recreation
709-489-0450, Fax: 709-489-0454
dnichols@grandfallswindsor.com
Robert Thompson, Supervisor, Engineering & Works
709-489-0421, Fax: 709-489-0467
rthompson@grandfallswindsor.com
Mark Kelly, Clerk, Purchasing
709-489-0422, Fax: 709-489-0465
purchasing@grandfallswindsor.com

Mount Pearl
3 Centennial St.
Mount Pearl, NL A1N 1G4
709-748-1000 Fax: 709-748-1150
info@mtpearl.nf.ca
info@mountpearl.ca
Municipal Type: City
Incorporated: Jan. 11, 1955; *Area:* 15.75 sq km
Population in 2006: 24,671
Provincial Electoral District(s): Mount Pearl; Waterford Valley
Federal Electoral District(s): St. John's South-Mount Pearl
Next Election: Sept. 2009 (4 year terms)

Council
Randy Simms, Mayor
rsimms@mountpearl.ca
Paul Lane, Deputy Mayor & Councillor
plane@mountpearl.ca
Ed Grant, Councillor
egrant@mountpearl.ca
Jim Locke, Councillor
jlocke@mountpearl.ca
Lucy Stoyles, Councillor
lstoyles@mountpearl.ca
Paula Tessier, Councillor
ptessier@mountpearl.ca
John Walsh, Councillor
jwalsh@mountpearl.ca

Administration
Gerard Lewis, CAO
709-748-1025
glewis@mountpearl.ca
Michelle Peach, C.A., City Treasurer
mpeach@mountpearl.ca
Stephen Jewcyzk, Director, Planning & Development
709-748-1029
sjewczyk@mountpearl.ca
James Oxford, Director, Infrastructure & Public Works
709-748-1028
joxford@mountpearl.ca
Raymond Osmond, Director, Community Services
709-748-1027
rosmond@mountpearl.ca
Bronda Aylward, Director, Economic Development
709-748-1096
baylward@mountpearl.ca

Paradise
28 McNamara Dr.
Paradise, NL A1L 0A6
709-782-1400 Fax: 709-782-3601
info@townofparadise.ca
www.townofparadise.ca
Municipal Type: City
Incorporated: Feb. 1, 1992; *Area:* 29.24 sq km
Population in 2006: 12,584
Provincial Electoral District(s): Conception Bay East & Bell Island; Topsail
Federal Electoral District(s): St. John's East; Bonavista-Gander-Grand Falls-Windsor; Labrador
Next Election: Sept. 2009 (4 year terms)

Council
Ralph Wiseman, Mayor
rwiseman@townofparadise.ca
Dan Bobbett, Councillor
dbobbett@townofparadise.ca
Allan English, Councillor
aenglish@townofparadise.ca
Ed Howlett, Councillor
ehowlett@townofparadise.ca
Fred Thornhill, Councillor
fthornhill@townofparadise.ca
Sterling Willis, Councillor
swillis@townofparadise.ca

Administration
Joyce Moss, Clerk
jmoss@townofparadise.ca

St. John's
City Hall
P.O. Box 908
10 New Gower St.
St. John's, NL A1C 5M2
709-754-2489 Fax: 709-576-7688 311 for city services
council@stjohns.ca
www.stjohns.ca
Municipal Type: City
Incorporated: Aug. 7, 1921; *Area:* 446.04 sq km
Population in 2006: 100,646
Provincial Electoral District(s): Kilbride; Signal Hill-Quidi Vidi; St. J. Centre; St. J. East; St. J. North; St. J. South; St. J. West; Virginia Waters; Mount Pearl North; Cape St. Francis
Federal Electoral District(s): St. John's East; St. John's South-Mount Pearl
Next Election: Sept. 2009 (4 year terms)

Council
Dennis O'Keefe, Mayor
709-576-8477, Fax: 709-576-8250
dokeefe@stjohns.ca
Shannie Duff, Deputy Mayor & Councillor
709-576 8583, Fax: 709-576-8474
sduff@stjohns.ca
Gerry Colbert, Councillor at Large
709-576-7689, Fax: 709-576-8474
gcolbert@stjohns.ca
Sheilagh O'Leary, Councillor at Large
709-576-8567, Fax: 709-576-8474
soleary@stjohns.ca
Tom Hann, Councillor at Large
709-576-8219, Fax: 709-576-8474
thann@stjohns.ca
Sandy Hickman, Councillor at Large
709-576-8045, Fax: 709-576-8474
shickman@stjohns.ca
Danny Breen, Councillor, Ward(s): 1
709-576-2332, Fax: 709-576-8474
dbreen@stjohns.ca
Frank Galgay, Councillor, Ward(s): 2
709-576-8577, Fax: 709-576-8474
fgalgay@stjohns.ca
Bruce Tilley, Councillor, Ward(s): 3
709-576-8643, Fax: 709-576-8474
btilley@stjohns.ca
Debbie Hanlon, Councillor, Ward(s): 4
709-576-2383, Fax: 709-576-8474
dhanlon@stjohns.ca
Wally Collins, Councillor, Ward(s): 5
709-576-8584, Fax: 709-576-8474
wcollins@stjohns.ca

Administration
Neil Martin, City Clerk, Director & Associate Commissioner, Corporate Services
709-576-8446, Fax: 709-576-8474
Robert Bishop, C.A., Treasurer & Director, Finance
709-576-8696, Fax: 709-576-8564
Ronald Penney, City Solicitor & City Manager
709-576-8557, Fax: 709-576-8561
legal@stjohns.ca
Walt Mills, Director, Engineering
709-576-8658, Fax: 709-576-8625

David Blackmore, Director, Building & Property Management
709-576-8701, Fax: 709-576-8160
Kevin Breen, Director, Human Resources
709-576-8213, Fax: 709-576-8575
Jill Brewer, Director, Recreation
709-576-8405, Fax: 709-576-8469
Cliff Johnston, Director, Planning
709-576-8383, Fax: 709-576-8625
Elizabeth Lawrence, Director, Economic Development, Tourism & Culture
709-576-8203, Fax: 709-576-8246
Paul Mackey, Director, Public Works & Parks
709-576-8303, Fax: 709-576-8026
Jim Clarke, Manager, Streets & Parks
709-576-8541, Fax: 709-576-8026
P.J. (Jim) Ford, Manager, Regulatory Services
709-576-8294, Fax: 709-576-8160
Gareth Griffiths, C.E.T., Manager, Real Estate Services
709-576-8440, Fax: 709-576-8561
Kevin Gushue, Manager, Tourism Development
709-567-8545, Fax: 709-576-8246
Geraldine King, Manager, Environmental Initiatives
709-576-8613, Fax: 709-576-8625
Joe Sampson, Manager, Development
Bob Wilson, Manager, Energy Efficiency
709-576-8238, Fax: 709-576-8160
Robin King, Transportation Engineer
709-576-8232, Fax: 709-576-8625

Other Municipalities in Newfoundland & Labrador

Admiral's Beach
P.O. Box 196
Admiral's Beach, NL A0B 3A0
709-521-2671 Fax: 709-521-2671
Municipal Type: Town
Incorporated: Jan. 16, 1968; *Area:* 24.42 sq km
Population in 2006: 185
Provincial Electoral District(s): Placentia & St. Mary's
Federal Electoral District(s): Avalon
Next Election: Sept. 2009 (4 year terms)
Mary Dobbin, Clerk
Theresa Bungay, Mayor

Anchor Point
P.O. Box 117
Anchor Point, NL A0K 1A0
709-456-2011 Fax: 709-456-2364
anchorpoint@nf.aibn.com
Municipal Type: Town
Incorporated: Sept. 10, 1974; *Area:* 2.41 sq km
Population in 2006: 309
Provincial Electoral District(s): St. Barbe
Federal Electoral District(s): Humber-St. Barbe-Baie Verte
Next Election: Sept. 2009 (4 year terms)
Sharon Gaulton, Clerk
Gerry Gros, Mayor

Appleton
PO Box 31, Site 4
Appleton, NL A0G 2K0
709-679-2289 Fax: 709-679-5552
townofappleton@personainternet.com
Municipal Type: Town
Incorporated: Feb. 27, 1962; *Area:* 6.39 sq km
Population in 2006: 582
Provincial Electoral District(s): Gander
Federal Electoral District(s): Bonavista-Gander-Grand Falls-Windsor
Next Election: Sept. 2009 (4 year terms)
Mavis Simms, Clerk
Derm Flynn, Mayor

Aquaforte
General Delivery
Aquaforte, NL A0A 1A0
709-363-2253 Fax: 709-363-2154
Municipal Type: Town
Incorporated: April 25, 1972; *Area:* 6.82 sq km
Population in 2006: 103
Provincial Electoral District(s): Ferryland
Federal Electoral District(s): Avalon
Next Election: Sept. 2009 (4 year terms)
Darlene George, Clerk
Donald Graham, Mayor

Arnold's Cove
P.O. Box 70
Arnolds Cove, NL A0B 1A0
709-463-2323 Fax: 709-463-2326
townofarnoldscove@nf.aibn.com
www.townofarnoldscove.com
Municipal Type: Town
Incorporated: June 3, 1967; *Area:* 4.93 sq km
Population in 2006: 1,003
Provincial Electoral District(s): Bellevue
Federal Electoral District(s): Avalon
Next Election: Sept. 2009 (4 year terms)
Wayne Slade, Clerk
Thomas Osbourne, Mayor

Avondale
P.O. Box 59
Avondale, NL A0A 1B0
709-229-4201 Fax: 709-229-4446
Municipal Type: Town
Incorporated: Nov. 26, 1974; *Area:* 29.93 sq km
Population in 2006: 667
Provincial Electoral District(s): Harbour Main-Whitbourne
Federal Electoral District(s): Avalon
Next Election: Sept. 2009 (4 year terms)
Lillian Healey, Clerk
Richard Chaulker, Mayor

Badger
P.O. Box 130
Badger, NL A0H 1A0
709-539-2406 Fax: 709-539-5262
Municipal Type: Town
Incorporated: Sept. 24, 1963; *Area:* 1.96 sq km
Population in 2006: 813
Provincial Electoral District(s): Grand Falls-Buchans
Federal Electoral District(s): Bonavista-Gander-Grand Falls-Windsor
Next Election: Sept. 2009 (4 year terms)
Pansy Hurley, Clerk
William Foley, Mayor

Baie Verte
P.O. Box 218
Baie Verte, NL A0K 1B0
709-532-8222 Fax: 709-532-4134
info@townofbaieverte.ca
www.townofbaieverte.ca
Municipal Type: Town
Incorporated: April 29, 1958; *Area:* 371.07 sq km
Population in 2006: 1,275
Provincial Electoral District(s): Baie Verte
Federal Electoral District(s): Humber-St. Barbe-Baie Verte
Next Election: Sept. 2009 (4 year terms)
Whit Kean, Clerk
Gerald Acreman, Mayor

Baine Harbour
General Delivery
Baine Harbour, NL A0E 1A0
709-443-2430
Municipal Type: Town
Incorporated: Dec. 1, 1970; *Area:* 4.82 sq km
Population in 2006: 134
Provincial Electoral District(s): Burin-Placentia West
Federal Electoral District(s): Random-Burin-St. George's
Next Election: Sept. 2009 (4 year terms)
Dinah Smith, Clerk
Leo Gaulton, Mayor

Bauline
2 Brook Path
Bauline, NL A1K 1E9
709-335-2483 Fax: 709-335-2053
bauline@nl.rogers.com
Municipal Type: Town
Incorporated: July 1, 1988; *Area:* 15.95 sq km
Population in 2006: 379
Provincial Electoral District(s): Cape St. Francis
Federal Electoral District(s): St. John's East
Next Election: Sept. 2009 (4 year terms)
Valeria McEvoy, Clerk
Rita King, Mayor

Bay Bulls
P.O. Box 70
Bay Bulls, NL A0A 1C0
709-334-3454 Fax: 709-334-3477
townofbaybulls@nf.aibn.com
www.baybulls.com
Municipal Type: Town
Incorporated: Jan. 1, 1986; *Area:* 30.74 sq km
Population in 2006: 1,078
Provincial Electoral District(s): Ferryland
Federal Electoral District(s): Avalon
Next Election: Sept. 2009 (4 year terms)
Janet O'Brien, Clerk
Don Drew, Mayor

Bay de Verde
P.O. Box 10
Bay de Verde, NL A0A 1E0
709-587-2260 Fax: 709-587-2049
baydeverde@nf.aibn.com
www.baydeverde.com
Municipal Type: Town
Incorporated: Aug. 22, 1950; *Area:* 13.28 sq km
Population in 2006: 470
Provincial Electoral District(s): Trinity-Bay de Verde
Federal Electoral District(s): Avalon
Next Election: Sept. 2009 (4 year terms)
Molly Walsh, Clerk
Gerald Murphy, Mayor

Bay L'Argent
P.O. Box 29
Bay L'Argent, NL A0E 1B0
709-461-2606 Fax: 709-461-2608
townofbaylargent@nf.aibn.com
Municipal Type: Town
Incorporated: July 13, 1971; *Area:* 3.56 sq km
Population in 2006: 287
Provincial Electoral District(s): Bellevue
Federal Electoral District(s): Random-Burin-St. George's
Next Election: Sept. 2009 (4 year terms)
Viola Pardy, Clerk
Roy Thornhill, Mayor

Bay Roberts
P.O. Box 114
Bay Roberts, NL A0A 1G0
709-786-2126 Fax: 709-786-2128
info@bayroberts.com
www.bayroberts.com
Municipal Type: Town
Incorporated: Feb. 17, 1951; *Area:* 23.92 sq km
Population in 2006: 5,414
Provincial Electoral District(s): Port de Grave
Federal Electoral District(s): Avalon
Next Election: Sept. 2009 (4 year terms)
Shirley Hawe, Clerk
Glenn Littlejohn, Mayor
glennlittlejohn@bayroberts.com

Baytona
P.O. Box 29
Baytona, NL A0G 2J0
709-659-6101 Fax: 709-659-6101
Municipal Type: Town
Incorporated: Aug. 1, 1975; *Area:* 15.38 sq km
Population in 2006: 276
Provincial Electoral District(s): Lewisporte
Federal Electoral District(s): Bonavista-Gander-Grand Falls-Windsor
Next Election: Sept. 2009 (4 year terms)
Patsy Lewis, Clerk
Jerden Bennett, Mayor

Beachside
112 Bayview Rd.
Beachside, NL A0J 1T0
709-267-5251 Fax: 709-267-5251
Municipal Type: Town
Incorporated: July 7, 1961; *Area:* 2.61 sq km
Population in 2006: 183
Provincial Electoral District(s): Baie Verte
Federal Electoral District(s): Humber-St. Barbe-Baie Verte
Next Election: Sept. 2009 (4 year terms)
Robert Stone, Clerk
Ada Locke, Mayor

Bellburns
General Delivery
Bellburns, NL A0K 1H0
709-898-2468 Fax: 709-898-2468
Municipal Type: Town
Incorporated: May 13, 1969; *Area:* 7.39 sq km
Population in 2006: 83
Provincial Electoral District(s): St. Barbe
Federal Electoral District(s): Humber-St. Barbe-Baie Verte
Next Election: Sept. 2009 (4 year terms)
D. House, Clerk
Norma House, Mayor

Belleoram
P.O. Box 29
Belleoram, NL A0H 1B0
709-881-6161 Fax: 709-881-6161
belloeam1946@yahoo.ca
Municipal Type: Town
Incorporated: March 19, 1946; *Area:* 2.1 sq km
Population in 2006: 421
Provincial Electoral District(s): Fortune Bay-Cape La Hune
Federal Electoral District(s): Random-Burin-St. George's
Next Election: Sept. 2009 (4 year terms)
Evelyn Savoury, Clerk
Steward May, Mayor

Bide Arm
P.O. Box 420
Bide Arm, NL A0K 1J0
709-457-2811 Fax: 709-457-2253
phyllis.randell@nf.aibn.com
Municipal Type: Town
Incorporated: June 2, 1970; *Area:* 29.85 sq km
Population in 2006: 192
Provincial Electoral District(s): The Straits & White Bay North
Federal Electoral District(s): Humber-St. Barbe-Baie Verte
Next Election: Sept. 2009 (4 year terms)
Phyllis Randell, Clerk
Wade Reid, Mayor

Birchy Bay
P.O. Box 40
Birchy Bay, NL A0G 1E0
709-659-3221 Fax: 709-659-2121
thetownofbirchybay@nf.sympatico.ca
Municipal Type: Town
Incorporated: Aug. 27, 1974; *Area:* 49.52 sq km
Population in 2006: 618
Provincial Electoral District(s): Lewisporte
Federal Electoral District(s): Bonavista-Gander-Grand Falls-Windsor
Next Election: Sept. 2009 (4 year terms)
Cynthia Baker, Clerk
Seymour Quinlan, Mayor

Bird Cove
67 Michael's Dr.
Bird Cove, NL A0K 1L0

709-247-2256 Fax: 709-247-2256
towncouncil.birdcove@nf.aibn.com
Municipal Type: Town
Incorporated: April 15, 1977; *Area:* 9.39 sq km
Population in 2006: 137
Provincial Electoral District(s): St. Barbe
Federal Electoral District(s): Humber-St. Barbe-Baie Verte
Next Election: Sept. 2009 (4 year terms)
Wanda Pittman, Clerk
Augustine Anscombe, Mayor

Bishop's Cove
P.O. Box 36
Bishop's Cove, NL A0A 3X0
709-589-2852
Municipal Type: Town
Incorporated: June 24, 1969; *Area:* 1.89 sq km
Population in 2006: 329
Provincial Electoral District(s): Port de Grave
Federal Electoral District(s): Avalon
Next Election: Sept. 2009 (4 year terms)
Irene Menchions, Clerk
Lori Ann Smith, Mayor

Bishop's Falls
P.O. Box 310
Bishops Falls, NL A0H 1C0
709-258-6581 Fax: 709-258-6346
info@bishopsfalls.com
Municipal Type: Town
Incorporated: Nov. 1, 1961; *Area:* 28.12 sq km
Population in 2006: 3,399
Provincial Electoral District(s): Exploits
Federal Electoral District(s): Bonavista-Gander-Grand Falls-Windsor
Next Election: Sept. 2009 (4 year terms)
Toni Elliott, Clerk
Jody Fancey, Mayor

Bonavista
P.O. Box 279
Bonavista, NL A0C 1B0
709-468-7747 Fax: 709-468-2495
town.bonavista@nf.sympatico.ca
Municipal Type: Town
Incorporated: Nov. 24, 1964; *Area:* 31.5 sq km
Population in 2006: 3,764
Provincial Electoral District(s): Bonavista South
Federal Electoral District(s): Bonavista-Gander-Grand Falls-Windsor
Next Election: Sept. 2009 (4 year terms)
David Hiscock, Clerk
Elizabeth Fitzgerald, Mayor

Botwood
P.O. Box 490
Botwood, NL A0H 1E0
709-257-2839 Fax: 709-257-3330
botwoodtowncouncil@@nf.aibn.com
www.town.botwood.nl.ca
Municipal Type: Town
Incorporated: June 21, 1960; *Area:* 15.05 sq km
Population in 2006: 3,052
Provincial Electoral District(s): Exploits
Federal Electoral District(s): Bonavista-Gander-Grand Falls-Windsor
Next Election: Sept. 2009 (4 year terms)
Edward Evans, Clerk
Jerry Dean, Mayor

Branch
P.O. Box 129
Branch, NL A0B 1E0
709-338-2920 Fax: 709-338-2921
townofbranch@nf.aibn.com
Municipal Type: Town
Incorporated: May 17, 1966; *Area:* 16.15 sq km
Population in 2006: 309
Provincial Electoral District(s): Placentia & St. Mary's
Federal Electoral District(s): Avalon
Next Election: Sept. 2009 (4 year terms)
Augustine Power, Clerk
Priscilla Corcoran Mooney, Mayor

Brent's Cove
General Delivery
Brents Cove, NL A0K 1R0
709-661-5301 Fax: 709-661-5303
Municipal Type: Town
Incorporated: April 12, 1966; *Area:* 1.02 sq km
Population in 2006: 204
Provincial Electoral District(s): Baie Verte
Federal Electoral District(s): Humber-St. Barbe-Baie Verte
Next Election: Sept. 2009 (4 year terms)
Ellen Butler, Clerk
Christopher Sullivan, Mayor

Brighton
304 Main St.
Brighton, NL A0J 1B0
709-263-7391 Fax: 709-263-7391
Municipal Type: Town
Incorporated: Jan. 1, 1986; *Area:* 2.23 sq km
Population in 2006: 203
Provincial Electoral District(s): Windsor-Springdale
Federal Electoral District(s): Humber-St. Barbe-Baie Verte
Next Election: Sept. 2009 (4 year terms)
Gloria Fudge, Clerk
Lindy Fudge, Mayor

Brigus
P.O. Box 220
Brigus, NL A0A 1K0
709-528-4588 Fax: 709-528-4588
info@brigus.net
www.brigus.net
Municipal Type: Town
Incorporated: July 21, 1964; *Area:* 11.57 sq km
Population in 2006: 794
Provincial Electoral District(s): Harbour Main-Whitbourne
Federal Electoral District(s): Avalon
Next Election: Sept. 2009 (4 year terms)
Wayne Rose, Town Clerk & Manager
Byron Rodway, Mayor
709-528-3201
byronrodway@personainternet.com

Bryant's Cove
PO Box 5, Site 3
Bryant's Cove, NL A0A 3P0
709-596-2291 Fax: 709-596-0015
Municipal Type: Town
Incorporated: July 29, 1977; *Area:* 4.87 sq km
Population in 2006: 417
Provincial Electoral District(s): Port de Grave
Federal Electoral District(s): Avalon
Next Election: Sept. 2009 (4 year terms)
Michelle Antle, Clerk
Denise Bloom, Mayor

Buchans
P.O. Box 190
Buchans, NL A0H 1G0
709-672-3972 Fax: 709-672-3702
townofbuchans@nf.aibn.com
Municipal Type: Town
Incorporated: April 24, 1963; *Area:* 4.88 sq km
Population in 2006: 761
Provincial Electoral District(s): Grand Falls-Buchans
Federal Electoral District(s): Bonavista-Gander-Grand Falls-Windsor
Next Election: Sept. 2009 (4 year terms)
David Whalen, Clerk
Derm Corbett, Mayor

Burgeo
P.O. Box 220
Burgeo, NL A0N 2H0
709-886-2250 Fax: 709-886-2166
townofburgeo@bbsict.ca
Municipal Type: Town
Incorporated: June 17, 1950; *Area:* 31.34 sq km
Population in 2006: 1,607
Provincial Electoral District(s): Burgeo & La Poile
Federal Electoral District(s): Random-Burin-St. George's
Next Election: Sept. 2009 (4 year terms)
Blaine Marke, Clerk
George Reid, Mayor

Burin
P.O. Box 370
Burin, NL A0E 1E0
709-891-1760 Fax: 709-891-2069
townofburin@persona.ca
www.burincanada.com
Municipal Type: Town
Incorporated: July 18, 1950; *Area:* 34.05 sq km
Population in 2006: 2,483
Provincial Electoral District(s): Burin-Placentia West; Grand Bank
Federal Electoral District(s): Random-Burin-St. George's
Next Election: Sept. 2009 (4 year terms)
Beth Hanrahan, Clerk
bhanrahan@persona.ca
Kevin Lundrigan, Mayor

Burlington
General Delivery
Burlington, NL A0K 1S0
709-252-2607 Fax: 709-252-2161
mbartlett@townofburlington.ca
www.townofburlington.ca
Municipal Type: Town
Incorporated: Oct. 20, 1953; *Area:* 4.1 sq km
Population in 2006: 376
Provincial Electoral District(s): Baie Verte
Federal Electoral District(s): Humber-St. Barbe-Baie Verte
Next Election: Sept. 2009 (4 year terms)
Mary Lou Bartlett, Clerk
George Kelly, Mayor
gkelly@townofburlington.ca

Burnt Islands
P.O. Box 39
Burnt Islands, NL A0M 1B0
709-698-3512 Fax: 709-698-3512
Municipal Type: Town
Incorporated: Oct. 31, 1975; *Area:* 9.52 sq km
Population in 2006: 703
Provincial Electoral District(s): Burgeo & La Poile
Federal Electoral District(s): Random-Burin-St. George's
Next Election: Sept. 2009 (4 year terms)
Rosetta Glover, Clerk
Kevin Hardy, Mayor

Campbellton
P.O. Box 70
Campbellton, NL A0G 1L0
709-261-2300 Fax: 709-261-2300
Municipal Type: Town
Incorporated: Oct. 21, 1972; *Area:* 35.71 sq km
Population in 2006: 494
Provincial Electoral District(s): Lewisporte
Federal Electoral District(s): Bonavista-Gander-Grand Falls-Windsor
Next Election: Sept. 2009 (4 year terms)
Gail Osmond, Clerk
Maisie Clarke, Mayor

Cape Broyle
P.O. Box 69
Cape Broyle, NL A0A 1P0
709-432-2288 Fax: 709-432-2794
townofcapebroyle@nf.aibn.com
Municipal Type: Town
Incorporated: Jan. 1, 1990; *Area:* 10.05 sq km
Population in 2006: 545
Provincial Electoral District(s): Ferryland
Federal Electoral District(s): Avalon
Next Election: Sept. 2009 (4 year terms)
Wendy Duggan, Clerk
Frank Hayden, Mayor

Cape St. George
P.O. Box 680
RR#3
Cape St George, NL A0N 1T0
709-644-2290 Fax: 709-644-2291
townofcapestgeorge@nf.aibn.com
Municipal Type: Town
Incorporated: June 24, 1969; *Area:* 33.46 sq km
Population in 2006: 893
Provincial Electoral District(s): Port au Port
Federal Electoral District(s): Random-Burin-St. George's
Next Election: Sept. 2009 (4 year terms)
Ian Renouf, Clerk
Peter Fenwick, Mayor

Carbonear
P.O. Box 999
Carbonear, NL A1Y 1C5
709-596-3831 Fax: 709-596-5021
info@carbonear.ca
www.carbonear.ca
Municipal Type: Town
Incorporated: July 13, 1948; *Area:* 11.81 sq km
Population in 2006: 4,723
Provincial Electoral District(s): Carbonear-Harbour Grace
Federal Electoral District(s): Avalon
Next Election: Sept. 2009 (4 year terms)
Cathy Somers, Clerk
csomers@@nf.aibn.com
Sam Slade, Mayor

Carmanville
P.O. Box 239
Carmanville, NL A0G 1N0
709-534-2814 Fax: 709-534-2425
townofcarmanville@nf.aibn.com
Municipal Type: Town
Incorporated: March 29, 1955; *Area:* 43.08 sq km
Population in 2006: 753
Provincial Electoral District(s): Bonavista North
Federal Electoral District(s): Bonavista-Gander-Grand Falls-Windsor
Next Election: Sept. 2009 (4 year terms)
Dianne Goodyear, Clerk
Ted Goodyear, Mayor

Cartwright
P.O. Box 129
Cartwright, NL A0K 1V0
709-938-7259 Fax: 709-938-7454
shopkins@nf.aibn.com
Municipal Type: Town
Incorporated: Oct. 10, 1956; *Area:* 3.27 sq km
Population in 2006: 552
Provincial Electoral District(s): Cartwright-L'Anse au Clair
Federal Electoral District(s): Labrador
Next Election: Sept. 2009 (4 year terms)
Shirley Hopkins, Clerk
Rosetta Holwell, Mayor

Centreville-Wareham-Trinity
P.O. Box 130
Centreville, NL A0G 4P0
709-678-2840 Fax: 709-678-2536
Municipal Type: Town
Incorporated: Jan. 1, 1992; *Area:* 37.25 sq km
Population in 2006: 1,122
Provincial Electoral District(s): Bonavista North
Federal Electoral District(s): Bonavista-Gander-Grand Falls-Windsor
Next Election: Sept. 2009 (4 year terms)
Gertrude Brown, Clerk
Malcolm Rogers, Mayor

Chance Cove
P.O. Box 133
Chance Cove, NL A0B 1K0
709-460-4151 Fax: 709-460-4151
Municipal Type: Town
Incorporated: Feb. 8, 1972; *Area:* 18.2 sq km

Population in 2006: 310
Provincial Electoral District(s): Bellevue
Federal Electoral District(s): Avalon
Next Election: Sept. 2009 (4 year terms)
Glenys Rowe, Clerk
Edgar Crann, Mayor

Change Islands
P.O. Box 67
Change Islands, NL A0G 1R0
709-621-4181 Fax: 709-621-3202
changeislandstc@nf.aibn.com
www.changeislands.ca
Municipal Type: Town
Incorporated: Oct. 16, 1951; *Area:* 5.31 sq km
Population in 2006: 300
Provincial Electoral District(s): Twillingate & Fogo
Federal Electoral District(s): Bonavista-Gander-Grand Falls-Windsor
Next Election: Sept. 2009 (4 year terms)
Sherry Diamond, Clerk
Bernice Diamond, Acting Mayor
709-621-3401

Channel-Port aux Basques
P.O. Box 70
Port aux Basques, NL A0M 1C0
709-695-2214 Fax: 709-695-9852
townofchannelpab@nf.aibn.com
www.portauxbasques.ca
Municipal Type: Town
Incorporated: Nov. 6, 1945; *Area:* 38.77 sq km
Population in 2006: 4,319
Provincial Electoral District(s): Burgeo & La Poile
Federal Electoral District(s): Random-Burin-St. George's
Next Election: Sept. 2009 (4 year terms)
Donna Bragg, Clerk
dbraggtown@nf.aibn.com
Brian Button, Mayor
bbutton@nf.sympatico.ca

Chapel Arm
68 Main Rd.
Chapel Arm, NL A0B 1L0
709-592-2720 Fax: 709-592-2800
Municipal Type: Town
Incorporated: Nov. 24, 1970; *Area:* 28.17 sq km
Population in 2006: 451
Provincial Electoral District(s): Bellevue
Federal Electoral District(s): Avalon
Next Election: Sept. 2009 (4 year terms)
Phyllis Pretty, Clerk
Helen Pretty, Mayor

Charlottetown
P.O. Box 151
Charlottetown, NL A0K 5Y0
709-949-0299 Fax: 709-949-0377
ctown@nf.sympatico.ca
Municipal Type: Town
Incorporated: March 4, 1988; *Area:* 30.53 sq km
Population in 2006: 366
Provincial Electoral District(s): Cartwright-L'Anse au Clair
Federal Electoral District(s): Bonavista-Gander-Grand Falls-Windsor; Labrador
Next Election: Sept. 2009 (4 year terms)
Zillah Kippenhuck, Clerk
Philip C. Snow, Mayor

Clarenville
99 Pleasant St.
Clarenville, NL A5A 1V9
709-466-7937 Fax: 709-466-2276
info@clarenville.net
www.clarenville.net
Municipal Type: Town
Incorporated: June 12, 1951; *Area:* 140.79 sq km
Population in 2006: 5,274
Provincial Electoral District(s): Trinity North
Federal Electoral District(s): Random-Burin-St.George's
Next Election: Sept. 2009 (4 year terms)
Marie Blackmore, Clerk
Fred Best, Mayor

Clarke's Beach
P.O. Box 159
Clarkes Beach, NL A0A 1W0
709-786-3993 Fax: 709-786-3994
joanwilcox@nf.aibn.com
Municipal Type: Town
Incorporated: Aug. 24, 1965; *Area:* 12.71 sq km
Population in 2006: 1,289
Provincial Electoral District(s): Harbour Main-Whitbourne
Federal Electoral District(s): Avalon
Next Election: Sept. 2009 (4 year terms)
Joan Wilcox, Clerk
Betty Moore, Mayor

Coachman's Cove
General Delivery
Coachmans Cove, NL A0K 1X0
709-253-5161
Municipal Type: Town
Incorporated: Nov. 24, 1970; *Area:* 18.15 sq km
Population in 2006: 93
Provincial Electoral District(s): Baie Verte
Federal Electoral District(s): Humber-St. Barbe-Baie Verte
Next Election: Sept. 2009 (4 year terms)
Susan Fitzgerald, Clerk
Theresa Kennedy, Mayor

Colinet
P.O. Box 8
Colinet, NL A0B 1M0
709-521-2300 Fax: 709-521-2482
Municipal Type: Town
Incorporated: Sept. 24, 1974; *Area:* 6.23 sq km
Population in 2006: 165
Provincial Electoral District(s): Placentia & St. Mary's
Federal Electoral District(s): Avalon
Next Election: Sept. 2009 (4 year terms)
Marie Bonia, Clerk
Herb Spurrell, Mayor

Colliers
P.O. Box 84
Colliers, NL A0A 1Y0
709-229-4333 Fax: 709-229-4033
townofcolliers@nl.aibn.com
Municipal Type: Town
Incorporated: Oct. 31, 1972; *Area:* 26.16 sq km
Population in 2006: 722
Provincial Electoral District(s): Harbour Main-Whitbourne
Federal Electoral District(s): Avalon
Next Election: Sept. 2009 (4 year terms)
Waneta Whelan, Clerk
Patrick L. Phillips, Mayor

Come By Chance
P.O. Box 89
Come By Chance, NL A0B 1N0
709-542-3240 Fax: 709-542-3121
bmulrooney@xplornet.com
Municipal Type: Town
Incorporated: July 22, 1969; *Area:* 41.16 sq km
Population in 2006: 260
Provincial Electoral District(s): Bellevue
Federal Electoral District(s): Avalon
Next Election: Sept. 2009 (4 year terms)
Wendy Coffin, Clerk
Joan Cleary, Mayor

Comfort Cove-Newstead
P.O. Box 10
Comfort Cove, NL A0G 3K0
709-244-4125 Fax: 709-244-4122
ccntown@thezone.net
Municipal Type: Town
Incorporated: Oct. 24, 1967; *Area:* 29.83 sq km
Population in 2006: 451
Provincial Electoral District(s): Lewisporte
Federal Electoral District(s): Bonavista-Gander-Grand Falls-Windsor
Next Election: Sept. 2009 (4 year terms)
Bobbi Ackerman, Clerk
Junior Eveleigh, Mayor

Conception Harbour
P.O. Box 128
Conception Harbour, NL A0A 1Z0
709-229-4781 Fax: 709-229-0432
charbour@nfld.com
Municipal Type: Town
Incorporated: Oct. 31, 1972; *Area:* 21.62 sq km
Population in 2006: 743
Provincial Electoral District(s): Harbour Main-Whitbourne
Federal Electoral District(s): Avalon
Next Election: Sept. 2009 (4 year terms)
Lillian Connors, Clerk
John Curran, Mayor

Conche
P.O. Box 59
Conche, NL A0K 1Y0
709-622-4531 Fax: 709-622-4491
townofconche@nf.aibn.com
Municipal Type: Town
Incorporated: Sept. 13, 1960; *Area:* 9.09 sq km
Population in 2006: 225
Provincial Electoral District(s): The Straits & White Bay North
Federal Electoral District(s): Humber-St. Barbe-Baie Verte
Next Election: Sept. 2009 (4 year terms)
Alice Flynn, Clerk
Gerald Bromley, Mayor

Cook's Harbour
P.O. Box 69
Cooks Harbour, NL A0K 1Z0
709-249-3111 Fax: 709-249-4105
Municipal Type: Town
Incorporated: Oct. 10, 1956; *Area:* 1.95 sq km
Population in 2006: 190
Provincial Electoral District(s): The Straits & White Bay North
Federal Electoral District(s): Humber-St. Barbe-Baie Verte
Next Election: Sept. 2009 (4 year terms)
Regina Short, Clerk
Barry Decker, Mayor

Cormack
280 Veterans Dr.
Cormack, NL A8A 2R4
709-635-7025 Fax: 709-635-7363
townofcormack@nf.aibn.com
Municipal Type: Town
Incorporated: April 14, 1964; *Area:* 135.23 sq km
Population in 2006: 657
Provincial Electoral District(s): Humber Valley
Federal Electoral District(s): Humber-St.Barbe-Baie Verte
Next Election: Sept. 2009 (4 year terms)
Cynthia Fry, Clerk
Warwick Hewitt, Mayor

Cottlesville
P.O. Box 10
Cottlesville, NL A0G 1S0
709-629-3505 Fax: 709-629-7411
vecassell@yahoo.ca
www.cottlesville.com
Municipal Type: Town
Incorporated: Oct. 24, 1972; *Area:* 11.17 sq km
Population in 2006: 279
Provincial Electoral District(s): Twillingate & Fogo
Federal Electoral District(s): Bonavista-Gander-Grand Falls-Windsor
Next Election: Sept. 2009 (4 year terms)
Shelly Abbott, Clerk
Larry Peddle, Mayor

Cow Head
P.O. Box 40
Cow Head, NL A0K 2A0
709-243-2446 Fax: 709-243-2590
info@cowhead.ca
www.cowhead.ca
Municipal Type: Town
Incorporated: Feb. 1, 1964; *Area:* 17.84 sq km
Population in 2006: 493
Provincial Electoral District(s): St. Barbe
Federal Electoral District(s): Humber-St. Barbe-Baie Verte
Next Election: Sept. 2009 (4 year terms)
Melinda King, Clerk
Garland Hutchings, Mayor

Cox's Cove
P.O. Box 100
Coxs Cove, NL A0L 1C0
709-688-2900 Fax: 709-688-2900
Municipal Type: Town
Incorporated: Nov. 11, 1969; *Area:* 7.21 sq km
Population in 2006: 646
Provincial Electoral District(s): Bay of Islands
Federal Electoral District(s): Humber-St. Barbe-Baie Verte
Next Election: Sept. 2009 (4 year terms)
Keon Noseworthy, Mayor
Michelle Restell, Clerk

Crow Head
P.O. Box 250
Crow Head, NL A0G 4M0
709-884-5651 Fax: 709-884-2344
Municipal Type: Town
Incorporated: Sept. 13, 1960; *Area:* 2.98 sq km
Population in 2006: 205
Provincial Electoral District(s): Twillingate & Fogo
Federal Electoral District(s): Bonavista-Gander-Grand Falls-Windsor
Next Election: Sept. 2009 (4 year terms)
Meta J. Hamlyn, Clerk
John Hamlyn, Mayor

Cupids
P.O. Box 99
Cupids, NL A0A 2B0
709-528-4428 Fax: 709-528-4430
Municipal Type: Town
Incorporated: April 13, 1965; *Area:* 11.02 sq km
Population in 2006: 790
Provincial Electoral District(s): Harbour Main-Whitbourne
Federal Electoral District(s): Avalon
Next Election: Sept. 2009 (4 year terms)
Ivy King, Clerk
Geraldine Curran, Mayor

Daniel's Harbour
P.O. Box 68
Daniels Harbour, NL A0K 2C0
709-898-2300 Fax: 709-898-2311
townofdanielsharbour@nf.aibn.com
Municipal Type: Town
Incorporated: March 9, 1965; *Area:* 8.19 sq km
Population in 2006: 288
Provincial Electoral District(s): St. Barbe
Federal Electoral District(s): Humber-St. Barbe-Baie Verte
Next Election: Sept. 2009 (4 year terms)
Melda Hann, Clerk
Stephen Carey, Mayor

Deer Lake
6 Crescent St.
Deer Lake, NL A8A 1E9
709-635-2451 Fax: 709-635-5857
deerlake@nf.aibn.com
www.town.deerlake.nf.ca
Municipal Type: Town
Incorporated: May 27, 1950; *Area:* 73.23 sq km
Population in 2006: 4,827
Provincial Electoral District(s): Humber Valley

Federal Electoral District(s): Humber-St. Barbe-Baie Verte
Next Election: Sept. 2009 (4 year terms)
Maxine Hayden, Clerk
Darryl Kelly, Mayor

Dover
P.O. Box 10
Dover, NL A0G 1X0
709-537-2139 Fax: 709-537-2190
dover@nf.aibn.com
Municipal Type: Town
Incorporated: July 13, 1971; *Area:* 11.55 sq km
Population in 2006: 688
Provincial Electoral District(s): Terra Nova
Federal Electoral District(s): Bonavista-Gander-Grand Falls-Windsor
Next Election: Sept. 2009 (4 year terms)
Wendy Elms, Clerk
Tony R. Keats, Mayor

Duntara
General Delivery
Duntara, NL A0C 1M0
709-447-3190
Municipal Type: Town
Incorporated: Nov. 14, 1961; *Area:* 17.78 sq km
Population in 2006: 72
Provincial Electoral District(s): Bonavista South
Federal Electoral District(s): Bonavista-Gander-Grand Falls-Windsor
Next Election: Sept. 2009 (4 year terms)
Dorothy Power, Clerk
Hilda Duggan, Mayor

Eastport
P.O. Box 119
Eastport, NL A0G 1Z0
709-677-2161 Fax: 709-677-2144
cynthia@eastport.ca
www.eastport.ca
Municipal Type: Town
Incorporated: Oct. 20, 1959; *Area:* 18.64 sq km
Population in 2006: 499
Provincial Electoral District(s): Terra Nova
Federal Electoral District(s): Bonavista-Gander-Grand Falls-Windsor
Next Election: Sept. 2009 (4 year terms)
Cynthia Bull, Clerk
Glenn Babstock, Mayor

Elliston
P.O. Box 115
Elliston, NL A0C 1N0
709-468-2649 Fax: 709-468-2867
town-elliston@yahoo.ca
www.rootcellars.com
Municipal Type: Town
Incorporated: June 15, 1965; *Area:* 10.05 sq km
Population in 2006: 306
Provincial Electoral District(s): Bonavista South
Federal Electoral District(s): Bonavista-Gander-Grand Falls-Windsor
Next Election: Sept. 2009 (4 year terms)
Wendy Baker, Clerk
Gary Baker, Mayor

Embree
P.O. Box 81
Embree, NL A0G 2A0
709-535-8712 Fax: 709-535-8716
Municipal Type: Town
Incorporated: Sept. 28, 1971; *Area:* 18.16 sq km
Population in 2006: 703
Provincial Electoral District(s): Lewisporte
Federal Electoral District(s): Bonavista-Gander-Grand Falls-Windsor
Next Election: Sept. 2009 (4 year terms)
Maxine Lane, Clerk
Wallace Fifield, Mayor

Englee
P.O. Box 160
Englee, NL A0K 2J0
709-866-2711 Fax: 709-866-2357
dorisenglee@nf.aibn.com
Municipal Type: Town
Incorporated: Dec. 23, 1948; *Area:* 28.76 sq km
Population in 2006: 618
Provincial Electoral District(s): The Straits & White Bay North
Federal Electoral District(s): Humber-St. Barbe-Baie Verte
Next Election: Sept. 2009 (4 year terms)
Doris Randell, Clerk
Edgar W. Fillier, Mayor

English Harbour East
P.O. Box 21
English Harbour East, NL A0E 1M0
709-245-4346 Fax: 709-245-4556
Municipal Type: Town
Incorporated: Feb. 5, 1974; *Area:* 3.2 sq km
Population in 2006: 169
Provincial Electoral District(s): Bellevue
Federal Electoral District(s): Random-Burin-St. George's
Next Election: Sept. 2009 (4 year terms)
Maxine Hackett, Clerk
Mary Hackett, Mayor

Fermeuse
General Delivery
Fermeuse, NL A0A 2G0
709-363-2400 Fax: 709-363-2308
Municipal Type: Town
Incorporated: Nov. 28, 1967; *Area:* 38.73 sq km
Population in 2006: 284
Provincial Electoral District(s): Ferryland
Federal Electoral District(s): Avalon
Next Election: Sept. 2009 (4 year terms)
Mary Kenny, Clerk
Patricia Coady, Mayor

Ferryland
P.O. Box 75
Ferryland, NL A0A 2H0
709-432-2127 Fax: 709-432-2209
town.ferryland@nf.aibn.com
Municipal Type: Town
Incorporated: Oct. 19, 1971; *Area:* 13.62 sq km
Population in 2006: 529
Provincial Electoral District(s): Ferryland
Federal Electoral District(s): Avalon
Next Election: Sept. 2009 (4 year terms)
Doris Kavanagh, Clerk
Leo Moriarty, Mayor

Flatrock
663 Wind Gap Rd.
Flatrock, NL A1K 1C7
709-437-6312 Fax: 709-437-6311
info@townofflatrock.com
www.townofflatrock.com
Municipal Type: Town
Incorporated: Oct. 31, 1975; *Area:* 18.12 sq km
Population in 2006: 1,214
Provincial Electoral District(s): Cape St. Francis
Federal Electoral District(s): St. John's East
Next Election: Sept. 2009 (4 year terms)
Rita Farrell, Clerk
Kevin Parsons, Mayor

Fleur de Lys
General Delivery
Fleur de Lys, NL A0K 2M0
709-253-3131 Fax: 709-253-2146
fleurdelys@nf.aibn.com
Municipal Type: Town
Incorporated: April 18, 1967; *Area:* 39.77 sq km
Population in 2006: 320
Provincial Electoral District(s): Baie Verte
Federal Electoral District(s): Humber-St. Barbe-Baie Verte
Next Election: Sept. 2009 (4 year terms)
Esther Lewis, Clerk
Millie Walsh, Mayor

Flower's Cove
P.O. Box 149
Flowers Cove, NL A0K 2N0
709-456-2124 Fax: 709-456-2086
townofflowerscove@nf.aibn.net
Municipal Type: Town
Incorporated: Dec. 12, 1961; *Area:* 7.64 sq km
Population in 2006: 270
Provincial Electoral District(s): The Straits & White Bay North
Federal Electoral District(s): Humber-St. Barbe-Baie Verte
Next Election: Sept. 2009 (4 year terms)
Bruce Way, Clerk
Keith Billard, Mayor

Fogo
P.O. Box 57
Fogo, NL A0G 2B0
709-266-2237 Fax: 709-266-2972
info@town-fogo.ca
www.town-fogo.ca
Municipal Type: Town
Incorporated: July 13, 1948; *Area:* 5.92
Population in 2006: 748
Provincial Electoral District(s): Twillingate & Fogo
Federal Electoral District(s): Bonavista-Gander-Grand Falls-Windsor
Next Election: Sept. 2009 (4 year terms)
Bruce Pomeroy, Clerk
Andrew Shea, Mayor
mayor@town-fogo.ca

Forteau
P.O. Box 99
Forteau, NL A0K 2P0
709-931-2241 Fax: 709-931-2037
Municipal Type: Town
Incorporated: Dec. 7, 1971; *Area:* 7.44 sq km
Population in 2006: 448
Provincial Electoral District(s): Cartwright-L'Anse au Clair
Federal Electoral District(s): Labrador
Next Election: Sept. 2009 (4 year terms)
Gail Flynn, Clerk
Reginald Hancock, Mayor

Fortune
P.O. Box 159
Fortune, NL A0E 1P0
709-832-2810 Fax: 709-832-2210
fortune@nf.sympatico.ca
Municipal Type: Town
Incorporated: Sept. 3, 1946; *Area:* 54.85 sq km
Population in 2006: 1,458
Provincial Electoral District(s): Grand Bank
Federal Electoral District(s): Random-Burin-St. George's
Next Election: Sept. 2009 (4 year terms)
Hedley Hillier, Clerk
Alec Noseworthy, Mayor

Fox Cove-Mortier
PO Box 17, Site 25, RR#1
Fox Cove-Mortier, NL A0E 1E0
709-891-1500 Fax: 709-891-1999
Municipal Type: Town
Incorporated: June 2, 1970; *Area:* 25.6 sq km
Population in 2006: 351
Provincial Electoral District(s): Burin-Placentia West
Federal Electoral District(s): Random-Burin-St. George's
Next Election: Sept. 2009 (4 year terms)
Gladys Kavanagh, Clerk
Wanda Antle, Mayor

Fox Harbour
P.O. Box 64
Fox Harbour PB, NL A0B 1V0
709-227-2271 Fax: 709-227-2271
Municipal Type: Town
Incorporated: Oct. 13, 1964; *Area:* 19.78 sq km
Population in 2006: 314
Provincial Electoral District(s): Placentia & St. Mary's
Federal Electoral District(s): Avalon
Next Election: Sept. 2009 (4 year terms)
Patricia Quilty, Clerk
John Maher, Mayor

Frenchman's Cove
P.O. Box 20
Frenchman's Cove, NL A0E 1R0
709-826-2190 Fax: 709-826-2190
Municipal Type: Town
Incorporated: May 28, 1974; *Area:* 68.55 sq km
Population in 2006: 166
Provincial Electoral District(s): Grand Bank; Bay of Islands
Federal Electoral District(s): Humber-St. Barbe-Baie Verte; Random-Burin-St. George's
Next Election: Sept. 2009 (4 year terms)
Nancy Grandy-Drake, Clerk
Charles Alexander, Mayor

Gallants
General Delivery
Gallants, NL A0L 1G0
709-646-2840 Fax: 709-646-2840
Municipal Type: Town
Incorporated: Aug. 16, 1966; *Area:* 6.34 sq km
Population in 2006: 54
Provincial Electoral District(s): Humber West
Federal Electoral District(s): Random-Burin-St. George's
Next Election: Sept. 2009 (4 year terms)
Marion Collier, Clerk
James Collier, Mayor

Gambo
P.O. Box 250
Gambo, NL A0G 1T0
709-674-4476 Fax: 709-674-5399
info@townofgambo.nf.net
www.townofgambo.com
Municipal Type: Town
Incorporated: July 10, 1962; *Area:* 92.07 sq km
Population in 2006: 2,072
Provincial Electoral District(s): Terra Nova
Federal Electoral District(s): Bonavista-Gander-Grand Falls-Windsor
Next Election: Sept. 2009 (4 year terms)
Jean Blackwood, Acting Town Clerk & Manager
Lloyd Noseworthy, Mayor

Gander
P.O. Box 280
Gander, NL A1V 1W6
709-651-2930 Fax: 709-256-5809
info@gandercanada.com
www.gandercanada.com
Municipal Type: Town
Incorporated: Dec. 28, 1954; *Area:* 104.25 sq km
Population in 2006: 9,951
Provincial Electoral District(s): Gander
Federal Electoral District(s): Bonavista-Gander-Grand Falls-Windsor
Next Election: Sept. 2009 (4 year terms)
Garry Brown, Town Clerk & Director, Finance
Claude Elliott, Mayor
Dermot Chafe, Director, Development
709-651-5912
dchafe@gandercanada.com
Dave Brett, Fire Chief
709-651-5928
Cluny Matchim, Director, Municipal Works & Services
709-651-5914
cmatchim@gandercanada.com
Kevin Waterman, Director, Parks, Recreation & Tourism
709-651-5928
kwatorman@gandercanada.com

Garnish
P.O. Box 70
Garnish, NL A0E 1T0
709-826-2330 Fax: 709-826-2173
townofgarnish@nf.aibn.com

Municipal Type: Town
Incorporated: Aug. 25, 1971; *Area:* 39.11 sq km
Population in 2006: 578
Provincial Electoral District(s): Grand Bank
Federal Electoral District(s): Random-Burin-St. George's
Next Election: Sept. 2009 (4 year terms)
Leslie Price, Clerk
Reuben Noseworthy, Mayor

Gaskiers-Point La Haye
P.O. Box 434
St Marys, NL A0B 3B0
709-525-2430 Fax: 709-525-2431
clydekielly@hotmail.com
Municipal Type: Town
Incorporated: Aug. 25, 1970; *Area:* 23.81 sq km
Population in 2006: 302
Provincial Electoral District(s): Placentia & St. Mary's
Federal Electoral District(s): Avalon
Next Election: Sept. 2009 (4 year terms)
Clyde Kielly, Clerk
Pearl Kielly, Mayor

Gaultois
P.O. Box 101
Gaultois, NL A0H 1N0
709-841-6546 Fax: 709-841-3521
Municipal Type: Town
Incorporated: Jan. 1, 1962; *Area:* 4.33 sq km
Population in 2006: 265
Provincial Electoral District(s): Fortune Bay-Cape La Hune
Federal Electoral District(s): Random-Burin-St. George's
Next Election: Sept. 2009 (4 year terms)
Sylvin Rose, Clerk
Murray Engram, Mayor

Gillams
P.O. Box 3968
RR#2
Corner Brook, NL A2H 6B9
709-783-2800 Fax: 709-783-2671
Municipal Type: Town
Incorporated: Aug. 17, 1971; *Area:* 6.7 sq km
Population in 2006: 402
Provincial Electoral District(s): Bay of Islands
Federal Electoral District(s): Humber-St. Barbe-Baie Verte
Next Election: Sept. 2009 (4 year terms)
Shelly Fillier, Clerk
Eddie Blanchard, Mayor

Glenburnie-Birchy Head-Shoal Brook
General Delivery
Birchy Head, NL A0K 1K0
709-453-7220 Fax: 709-453-7220
Municipal Type: Town
Incorporated: Sept. 1, 1978; *Area:* 6.57 sq km
Population in 2006: 275
Provincial Electoral District(s): Humber Valley
Federal Electoral District(s): Humber-St. Barbe-Baie Verte
Next Election: Sept. 2009 (4 year terms)
Ina Goosney, Clerk
Clarice Bursey, Mayor

Glenwood
P.O. Box 130
Glenwood, NL A0G 2K0
709-679-2159 Fax: 709-679-5470
Municipal Type: Town
Incorporated: June 12, 1962; *Area:* 6.92 sq km
Population in 2006: 762
Provincial Electoral District(s): Gander
Federal Electoral District(s): Bonavista-Gander-Grand Falls-Windsor
Next Election: Sept. 2009 (4 year terms)
Susan Gillingham, Clerk
Bradley Stuckless, Mayor

Glovertown
P.O. Box 224
Glovertown, NL A0G 2L0
709-533-2351 Fax: 709-533-2225
jperry@personainternet.com
www.glovertown.net
Municipal Type: Town
Incorporated: Dec. 28, 1954; *Area:* 70.33 sq km
Population in 2006: 2,062
Provincial Electoral District(s): Terra Nova
Federal Electoral District(s): Bonavista-Gander-Grand Falls-Windsor
Next Election: Sept. 2009 (4 year terms)
Joanne Perry, Clerk
David Saunders, Mayor

Goose Cove East
P.O. Box 208
Goose Cove, NL A0K 4S0
709-454-8393 Fax: 709-454-8393
Municipal Type: Town
Incorporated: Oct. 19, 1971; *Area:* 2.69 sq km
Population in 2006: 234
Provincial Electoral District(s): The Straits & White Bay North
Federal Electoral District(s): Humber-St. Barbe-Baie Verte
Next Election: Sept. 2009 (4 year terms)
Patricia Reardon, Clerk
Stephen Alyward, Mayor

Grand Bank
P.O. Box 640
56 Main St.
Grand Bank, NL A0E 1W0
709-832-1600 Fax: 709-832-1636
townofgrandbank@townofgrandbank.net
www.townofgrandbank.com
Municipal Type: Town
Incorporated: Dec. 28, 1943; *Area:* 16.97 sq km
Population in 2006: 2,580
Provincial Electoral District(s): Grand Bank
Federal Electoral District(s): Random-Burin-St. George's
Next Election: Sept. 2009 (4 year terms)
Cathy Follett, Town Clerk & Treas.
Rex C. Matthews, Mayor

Grand Le Pierre
P.O. Box 35
Grand Le Pierre, NL A0E 1Y0
709-662-2702 Fax: 709-662-2076
Municipal Type: Town
Incorporated: June 17, 1969; *Area:* 153.59 sq km
Population in 2006: 264
Provincial Electoral District(s): Bellevue
Federal Electoral District(s): Random-Burin-St. George's
Next Election: Sept. 2009 (4 year terms)
Martha Bolt, Clerk
Hazel Bolt, Mayor

Greenspond
P.O. Box 100
Greenspond, NL A0G 2N0
709-269-3111 Fax: 709-269-3191
dbragg@nf.aibn.com
Municipal Type: Town
Incorporated: Aug. 15, 1951; *Area:* 2.85 sq km
Population in 2006: 365
Provincial Electoral District(s): Bonavista North
Federal Electoral District(s): Bonavista-Gander-Grand Falls-Windsor
Next Election: Sept. 2009 (4 year terms)
Derrick Bragg, Clerk
Boyd E. Burton, Mayor

Hampden
P.O. Box 9
Hampden, NL A0K 2Y0
709-455-4212 Fax: 709-455-2117
townofhampden@nf.aibn.com
Municipal Type: Town
Incorporated: Dec. 8, 1959; *Area:* 32.97 sq km
Population in 2006: 489
Provincial Electoral District(s): Humber Valley
Federal Electoral District(s): Humber-St. Barbe-Baie Verte
Next Election: Sept. 2009 (4 year terms)
Ruth Jenkins, Clerk
Ross Pynn, Mayor

Hant's Harbour
P.O. Box 40
Hants Harbour, NL A0B 1Y0
709-586-2741 Fax: 709-586-2680
Municipal Type: Town
Incorporated: Oct. 13, 1970; *Area:* 32.31 sq km
Population in 2006: 401
Provincial Electoral District(s): Trinity-Bay de Verde
Federal Electoral District(s): Avalon
Next Election: Sept. 2009 (4 year terms)
Doris J. Short, Clerk
Terry H. Ash, Mayor

Happy Adventure
PO Box 1, Site 2
Happy Adventure, NL A0G 1Z0
709-677-2593 Fax: 709-677-2594
Municipal Type: Town
Incorporated: May 10, 1960; *Area:* 9.62 sq km
Population in 2006: 227
Provincial Electoral District(s): Terra Nova
Federal Electoral District(s): Bonavista-Gander-Grand Falls-Windsor
Next Election: Sept. 2009 (4 year terms)
Kim Babstock, Clerk
James Warren, Mayor

Happy Valley-Goose Bay
P.O. Box 40 B
Happy Valley-Goose Bay, NL A0P 1E0
709-896-3321 Fax: 709-896-9454
manager@happyvalley-goosebay.com
www.happyvalley-goosebay.com
Municipal Type: Town
Incorporated: March 15, 1955; *Area:* 305.85 sq km
Population in 2006: 7,572
Provincial Electoral District(s): Lake Melville
Federal Electoral District(s): Labrador
Next Election: Sept. 2009 (4 year terms)
Valerie Sheppard, Clerk
townclerk@happyvalley-goosebay.com
Leo Abbass, Mayor
labbass@cdli.ca

Harbour Breton
P.O. Box 130
Harbour Breton, NL A0H 1P0
709-885-2354 Fax: 709-885-2095
bernice@harbourbreton.com
www.harbourbreton.com
Municipal Type: Town
Incorporated: Dec. 16, 1952; *Area:* 13.74 sq km
Population in 2006: 1,877
Provincial Electoral District(s): Fortune Bay-Cape La Hune
Federal Electoral District(s): Random-Burin-St. George's
Next Election: Sept. 2009 (4 year terms)
Bernice Herritt, Clerk
Donald Stewart, Mayor

Harbour Grace
P.O. Box 310
Harbour Grace, NL A0A 2M0
709-596-3631 Fax: 709-596-1991
thg@nf.sympatico.ca
www.hrgrace.ca
Municipal Type: Town
Incorporated: July 10, 1945; *Area:* 33.71 sq km
Population in 2006: 3,074
Provincial Electoral District(s): Carbonear-Harbour Grace
Federal Electoral District(s): Avalon
Next Election: Sept. 2009 (4 year terms)
Lester Forward, Clerk
Don Coombs, Mayor

Harbour Main-Chapel Cove-Lakeview
P.O. Box 40
Harbour Main, NL A0A 2P0
709-229-6822 Fax: 709-229-6234
hmcouncil@persona.ca
Municipal Type: Town
Incorporated: June 1, 1965; *Area:* 21.05 sq km
Population in 2006: 1,090
Provincial Electoral District(s): Harbour Main-Whitbourne
Federal Electoral District(s): Avalon
Next Election: Sept. 2009 (4 year terms)
Gloria Brazil, Clerk
Paul Woodford, Mayor

Hare Bay
P.O. Box 130
Hare Bay BB, NL A0G 2P0
709-537-2187 Fax: 709-537-2987
Municipal Type: Town
Incorporated: Oct. 20, 1964; *Area:* 34.06 sq km
Population in 2006: 1,020
Provincial Electoral District(s): Terra Nova
Federal Electoral District(s): Bonavista-Gander-Grand Falls-Windsor
Next Election: Sept. 2009 (4 year terms)
George R. Collins, Clerk
James Payne, Mayor

Hawke's Bay
P.O. Box 33
Hawkes Bay, NL A0K 3B0
709-248-5216 Fax: 709-248-5201
hbcouncil@nf.aibn.com
Municipal Type: Town
Incorporated: Aug. 21, 1956; *Area:* 46.55 sq km
Population in 2006: 391
Provincial Electoral District(s): St. Barbe
Federal Electoral District(s): Humber-St. Barbe-Baie Verte
Next Election: Sept. 2009 (4 year terms)
Rosemary Offrey, Clerk
Lloyd Bennett, Mayor

Heart's Content
P.O. Box 31
Hearts Content, NL A0B 1Z0
709-583-2491 Fax: 709-583-2226
townofheartscontent@persona.ca
Municipal Type: Town
Incorporated: Aug. 25, 1967; *Area:* 62.81 sq km
Population in 2006: 418
Provincial Electoral District(s): Trinity-Bay de Verde
Federal Electoral District(s): Avalon
Next Election: Sept. 2009 (4 year terms)
Alice Cumby, Clerk
Donald Blundon, Mayor

Heart's Delight-Islington
P.O. Box 129
Hearts Delight, NL A0B 2A0
709-588-2708 Fax: 709-588-2235
Municipal Type: Town
Incorporated: Oct. 24, 1972; *Area:* 27.27 sq km
Population in 2006: 663
Provincial Electoral District(s): Trinity-Bay de Verde
Federal Electoral District(s): Avalon
Next Election: Sept. 2009 (4 year terms)
Emily Harnum, Clerk
John Sooley, Mayor

Heart's Desire
P.O. Box 10
Hearts Desire, NL A0B 2B0
709-588-2280 Fax: 709-588-2343
townofheartsdesire@persona.ca
Municipal Type: Town
Incorporated: Sept. 28, 1971; *Area:* 17.27 sq km
Population in 2006: 226
Provincial Electoral District(s): Trinity-Bay de Verde

Federal Electoral District(s): Avalon
Next Election: Sept. 2009 (4 year terms)
Eleanor Andrews, Clerk
Patrick Coombs, Mayor

Hermitage
P.O. Box 160
Hermitage, NL A0H 1S0
709-883-2343 Fax: 709-883-2150
info@hermitage-sandyville.ca
www.hermitage-sandyville.ca
Municipal Type: Town
Incorporated: Oct. 22, 1960; *Area:* 28.91 sq km
Population in 2006: 499
Provincial Electoral District(s): Fortune Bay-Cape La Hune
Federal Electoral District(s): Random-Burin-St. George's
Next Election: Sept. 2009 (4 year terms)
Josephine (Josie) Rideout Simms, Town Manager
Douglas Rose, Mayor

Holyrood
P.O. Box 100
Holyrood, NL A0A 2R0
709-229-7252 Fax: 709-229-7269
dkieley@townofholyrood.com
www.townofholyrood.com
Municipal Type: Town
Incorporated: March 23, 1969; *Area:* 125.57 sq km
Population in 2006: 2,005
Provincial Electoral District(s): Conception Bay South
Federal Electoral District(s): Avalon
Next Election: Sept. 2009 (4 year terms)
Scott Devereaux, CAO-Clerk
sdevereaux@townofholyrood.com
Curtis Buckle, Mayor

Hopedale
P.O. Box 189
Hopedale, NL A0P 1G0
709-933-3864 Fax: 709-933-3800
towncouncilhopedale@nf.aibn.com
Municipal Type: Town
Incorporated: Sept. 30, 1969; *Area:* 3.36 sq km
Population in 2006: 530
Provincial Electoral District(s): Torngat Mountains
Federal Electoral District(s): Labrador
Next Election: Sept. 2009 (4 year terms)
Tom Onalik, Clerk
Mary Sillet, Mayor

Howley
P.O. Box 40
Howley, NL A0K 3E0
709-635-5555 Fax: 709-635-5850
Municipal Type: Town
Incorporated: Feb. 4, 1958; *Area:* 19.91 sq km
Population in 2006: 241
Provincial Electoral District(s): Humber Valley
Federal Electoral District(s): Humber-St. Barbe-Baie Verte
Next Election: Sept. 2009 (4 year terms)
Blanche Gilley, Clerk
Calvin Samms, Mayor

Hughes Brook
P.O. Box 2527
RR#2
Corner Brook, NL A2H 6B9
709-783-2921 Fax: 709-783-2921
Municipal Type: Town
Incorporated: July 25, 1975; *Area:* 1.6 sq km
Population in 2006: 197
Provincial Electoral District(s): Bay of Islands
Federal Electoral District(s): Humber-St. Barbe-Baie Verte
Next Election: Sept. 2009 (4 year terms)
Melinda Murrin, Clerk
Vaughan Hefford, Mayor

Humber Arm South
P.O. Box 10
Benoits Cove, NL A0L 1A0
709-789-2981 Fax: 709-789-2918
humberarmsouth@nf.aibn.com
Municipal Type: Town
Incorporated: June 15, 1971; *Area:* 65.05 sq km
Population in 2006: 1,854
Provincial Electoral District(s): Bay of Islands
Federal Electoral District(s): Humber-St. Barbe-Baie Verte
Next Election: Sept. 2009 (4 year terms)
Marion Evoy, Clerk
Ronald Deluney, Mayor

Indian Bay
General Delivery
Indian Bay, NL A0G 2V0
709-678-2727 Fax: 709-678-2727
Municipal Type: Town
Incorporated: Oct. 19, 1971; *Area:* 86.24 sq km
Population in 2006: 196
Provincial Electoral District(s): Bonavista North
Federal Electoral District(s): Bonavista-Gander-Grand Falls-Windsor
Next Election: Sept. 2009 (4 year terms)
Thomas Easton, Clerk
Renee Easton, Mayor

Irishtown-Summerside
P.O. Box 2795
RR#2
Corner Brook, NL A2H 6B9
709-783-2146 Fax: 709-783-3220
Municipal Type: Town
Incorporated: Jan. 1, 1991; *Area:* 11.89 sq km
Population in 2006: 1,290
Provincial Electoral District(s): Bay of Islands
Federal Electoral District(s): Humber-St. Barbe-Baie Verte
Next Election: Sept. 2009 (4 year terms)
Rita Blanchard, Clerk
Tony Blanchard, Mayor

Isle aux Morts
P.O. Box 110
Isle-aux-Morts, NL A0M 1J0
709-698-3441 Fax: 709-698-3449
townhalliam@nf.aibn.com
Municipal Type: Town
Incorporated: Nov. 5, 1956; *Area:* 7.66 sq km
Population in 2006: 718
Provincial Electoral District(s): Burgeo & La Poile
Federal Electoral District(s): Random-Burin-St. George's
Next Election: Sept. 2009 (4 year terms)
Lydia Francis, Clerk
Raymond LeFrense, Mayor

Jackson's Arm
P.O. Box 10
Jacksons Arm, NL A0K 3H0
709-459-3122 Fax: 709-459-3173
info@townofjacksonsarm.com
Municipal Type: Town
Incorporated: June 19, 1982; *Area:* 7.02 sq km
Population in 2006: 374
Provincial Electoral District(s): Humber Valley
Federal Electoral District(s): Humber-St. Barbe-Baie Verte
Next Election: Sept. 2009 (4 year terms)
Rhonda Nicholas, Clerk
Claude Jones, Mayor

Joe Batt's Arm-Barr'd Islands-Shoal Bay
P.O. Box 28
Joe Batts Arm, NL A0G 2X0
709-658-3490 Fax: 709-658-3408
www.joebattsarm.ca
Municipal Type: Town
Incorporated: Oct. 24, 1972; *Area:* 26.02 sq km
Population in 2006: 778
Provincial Electoral District(s): Twillingate & Fogo
Federal Electoral District(s): Bonavista-Gander-Grand Falls-Windsor
Next Election: Sept. 2009 (4 year terms)
Anna Donahue, Clerk
Freeman Compton, Mayor

Keels
General Delivery
Keels, NL A0C 1R0
709-447-6127 Fax: 709-447-3155
Municipal Type: Town
Incorporated: June 14, 1966; *Area:* 6.54 sq km
Population in 2006: 73
Provincial Electoral District(s): Bonavista South
Federal Electoral District(s): Bonavista-Gander-Grand Falls-Windsor
Next Election: Sept. 2009 (4 year terms)
Glenys Byrne, Clerk
Annie Fitzgerald, Mayor

King's Cove
General Delivery
Kings Cove, NL A0C 1S0
709-477-4361 Fax: 709-477-4361
Municipal Type: Town
Incorporated: June 14,1966; *Area:* 21.48 sq km
Population in 2006: 121
Provincial Electoral District(s): Bonavista South
Federal Electoral District(s): Bonavista-Gander-Grand Falls-Windsor; Humber-St. Barbe-Baie Verte; Labrador
Next Election: Sept. 2009 (4 year terms)
Gerald Barron, Clerk
Tom Maddox, Mayor

King's Point
P.O. Box 10
Kings Point, NL A0J 1H0
709-268-3838 Fax: 709-358-3856
Municipal Type: Town
Incorporated: Oct. 1, 1957; *Area:* 46.31 sq km
Population in 2006: 670
Provincial Electoral District(s): Baie Verte
Federal Electoral District(s): Humber-St. Barbe-Baie Verte
Next Election: Sept. 2009 (4 year terms)
Dale Wright, Clerk
Baxter Newman, Mayor

Kippens
2 Juniper Ave.
Kippens, NL A2N 3H8
709-643-5281 Fax: 709-643-9773
townofkippens@nfld.net
www.kippens.ca
Municipal Type: Town
Incorporated: Dec. 31, 1968; *Area:* 14.32 sq km
Population in 2006: 1,739
Provincial Electoral District(s): Port au Port
Federal Electoral District(s): Random-Burin-St. George's
Next Election: Sept. 2009 (4 year terms)
Norma Childs, Clerk & Manager
Wayne Ruth, Mayor

L'Anse au Clair
P.O. Box 83
L'Anse au Clair, NL A0K 3K0
709-931-2481 Fax: 709-931-2488
townoflanseauclair@hotmail.com
Municipal Type: Town
Incorporated: June 2, 1970; *Area:* 61.92 sq km
Population in 2006: 226
Provincial Electoral District(s): Cartwright-L'Anse au Clair
Federal Electoral District(s): Labrador
Next Election: Sept. 2009 (4 year terms)
Loretta Griffin, Clerk
Nath Moores, Mayor

L'Anse au Loup
P.O. Box 101
L'Anse au Loup, NL A0K 3L0
709-927-5573 Fax: 709-927-5263
lanseauloup@nf.aibn.com
www.lanseauloup.ca
Municipal Type: Town
Incorporated: April 11, 1975; *Area:* 3.48 sq km
Population in 2006: 593
Provincial Electoral District(s): Cartwright-L'Anse au Clair
Federal Electoral District(s): Labrador; Random-Burin-St. George's
Next Election: Sept. 2009 (4 year terms)
Lawrence Normore, Town Clerk, Manager & Officer, Community Economic Development
Randy Earle, Mayor

La Scie
P.O. Box 130
La Scie, NL A0K 3M0
709-675-2266 Fax: 709-675-2168
townoflascie@nf.aibn.com
Municipal Type: Town
Incorporated: May 25, 1955; *Area:* 29.14 sq km
Population in 2006: 955
Provincial Electoral District(s): Baie Verte
Federal Electoral District(s): Humber-St. Barbe-Baie Verte
Next Election: Sept. 2009 (4 year terms)
Goldie White, Clerk
Clyde Saunders, Mayor

Labrador City
P.O. Box 280
Labrador City, NL A2V 2K5
709-944-2621 Fax: 709-944-6353
marilyn.dicks@labcity.nf.ca
www.labradorwest.com
Municipal Type: Town
Incorporated: June 27, 1961; *Area:* 38.83 sq km
Population in 2006: 7,240
Provincial Electoral District(s): Labrador West
Federal Electoral District(s): Labrador
Next Election: Sept. 2009 (4 year terms)
Diane Gear, Town Clerk
Graham Letto, Mayor

Lamaline
P.O. Box 40
Lamaline, NL A0E 2C0
709-857-2341 Fax: 709-857-2210
Municipal Type: Town
Incorporated: April 24, 1963; *Area:* 81.69 sq km
Population in 2006: 315
Provincial Electoral District(s): Grand Bank
Federal Electoral District(s): Random-Burin-St. George's
Next Election: Sept. 2009 (4 year terms)
Barbara King, Clerk
Maureen Fleming, Mayor

Lark Harbour
P.O. Box 40
Lark Harbour, NL A0L 1H0
709-681-2270 Fax: 709-681-2900
Municipal Type: Town
Incorporated: Jan. 22, 1974; *Area:* 12.92 sq km
Population in 2006: 565
Provincial Electoral District(s): Bay of Islands
Federal Electoral District(s): Humber-St. Barbe-Baie Verte
Next Election: Sept. 2009 (4 year terms)
Debra Park, Clerk
Paul Keetch, Mayor
Louise Darrigan, Co-Clerk

Lawn
P.O. Box 29
Lawn, NL A0E 2E0
709-873-2439 Fax: 709-873-3006
townoflawn@nf.aibn.com
Municipal Type: Town
Incorporated: Sept. 30, 1952; *Area:* 3.61 sq km
Population in 2006: 705
Provincial Electoral District(s): Grand Bank
Federal Electoral District(s): Random-Burin-St. George's
Next Election: Sept. 2009 (4 year terms)
Ruth M. Bennett, Clerk
Edgar Edwards, Mayor

Leading Tickles
P.O. Box 39
Leading Tickles West, NL A0H 1T0
709-483-2180 Fax: 709-483-2185
leadingtickles@nf.aibn.com
www.leadingtickles.ca
Municipal Type: Town
Incorporated: July 11, 1961; *Area:* 26.73 sq km
Population in 2006: 407
Provincial Electoral District(s): Exploits
Federal Electoral District(s): Bonavista-Gander-Grand Falls-Windsor
Next Election: Sept. 2009 (4 year terms)
Joanne Preston, Clerk
Harry Hallet, Mayor

Lewin's Cove
P.O. Box 40
Lewins Cove, NL A0E 2G0
709-894-4777 Fax: 709-894-4952
Municipal Type: Town
Incorporated: May 1, 1973; *Area:* 6.52 sq km
Population in 2006: 566
Provincial Electoral District(s): Grand Bank
Federal Electoral District(s): Random-Burin-St. George's
Next Election: Sept. 2009 (4 year terms)
Thomas Oldford, Clerk
John Moore, Mayor

Lewisporte
P.O. Box 219
Lewisporte, NL A0G 3A0
709-535-2737 Fax: 709-535-2695
info@lewisportecanada.com
www.lewisportecanada.com
Municipal Type: Town
Incorporated: July 2, 1946; *Area:* 36.91 sq km
Population in 2006: 3,308
Provincial Electoral District(s): Lewisporte
Federal Electoral District(s): Bonavista-Gander-Grand Falls-Windsor
Next Election: Sept. 2009 (4 year terms)
Elaine Bursey, Clerk
elaine@lewisportecanada.com
William Hooper, Mayor

Little Bay
P.O. Box 40
Little Bay, NL A0J 1J0
709-267-3200 Fax: 709-267-3200
Municipal Type: Town
Incorporated: April 19, 1966; *Area:* 1.45 sq km
Population in 2006: 116
Provincial Electoral District(s): Baie Verte
Federal Electoral District(s): Humber-St. Barbe-Baie Verte; Random-Burin-St. George's
Next Election: Sept. 2009 (4 year terms)
Jamie Winsor, Clerk
Bronson Webber, Mayor

Little Bay East
P.O. Box 15
Little Bay East, NL A0E 2J0
709-461-2724 Fax: 709-461-2724
Municipal Type: Town
Incorporated: April 27, 1979; *Area:* 1.48 sq km
Population in 2006: 140
Provincial Electoral District(s): Bellevue
Federal Electoral District(s): Random-Burin-St. George's
Next Election: Sept. 2009 (4 year terms)
Gail Clarke, Clerk

Little Bay Islands
P.O. Box 64
Little Bay Islands, NL A0J 1K0
709-626-3511 Fax: 709-626-3512
littlebayislandtowncouncil@nf.aibn.com
Municipal Type: Town
Incorporated: Oct. 25, 1955; *Area:* 7.16 sq km
Population in 2006: 152
Provincial Electoral District(s): Baie Verte
Federal Electoral District(s): Humber-St. Barbe-Baie Verte
Next Election: Sept. 2009 (4 year terms)
Kelly Roberts, Clerk
Perry Locke, Mayor

Little Burnt Bay
P.O. Box 40
Little Burnt Bay, NL A0G 3B0
709-535-6415 Fax: 709-535-6490
Municipal Type: Town
Incorporated: Sept. 19, 1975; *Area:* 8.5 sq km
Population in 2006: 325
Provincial Electoral District(s): Lewisporte
Federal Electoral District(s): Bonavista-Gander-Grand Falls-Windsor
Next Election: Sept. 2009 (4 year terms)
Maisie Wells, Clerk
Laverne Suppa, Mayor

Little Catalina
P.O. Box 59
Little Catalina, NL A0C 1W0
709-469-2795 Fax: 709-469-2795
thetownoflittlecatalina@hotmail.com
www.littlecatalina.com
Municipal Type: Town
Incorporated: May 18, 1965; *Area:* 11.15 sq km
Population in 2006: 458
Provincial Electoral District(s): Bonavista South
Federal Electoral District(s): Bonavista-Gander-Grand Falls-Windsor
Next Election: Sept. 2009 (4 year terms)
Marilyn Reid, Clerk
Annie G. Johnson, Mayor

Logy Bay-Middle Cove-Outer Cove
744 Logy Bay Rd.
Logy Bay, NL A1K 3B5
709-726-7930 Fax: 709-726-2178
office@townlb-mc-oc.nf.net
Municipal Type: Town
Incorporated: Sept. 1, 1986; *Area:* 16.98 sq km
Population in 2006: 1,978
Provincial Electoral District(s): Cape St. Francis
Federal Electoral District(s): St. John's East
Next Election: Sept. 2009 (4 year terms)
Richard Roache, Clerk
Robert Roche, Mayor

Long Harbour-Mount Arlington Heights
P.O. Box 40
Long Harbour, NL A0B 2J0
709-228-2920 Fax: 709-228-2900
longharbourtowncouncil@nf.aibn.com
Municipal Type: Town
Incorporated: Oct. 22, 1968; *Area:* 18.41 sq km
Population in 2006: 211
Provincial Electoral District(s): Bellevue
Federal Electoral District(s): Avalon
Next Election: Sept. 2009 (4 year terms)
Marie Pretty, Clerk
Gary Keating, Mayor

Lord's Cove
General Delivery
Lord's Cove, NL A0E 2C0
709-857-2316 Fax: 709-857-2031
Municipal Type: Town
Incorporated: May 17, 1966; *Area:* 30.91 sq km
Population in 2006: 207
Provincial Electoral District(s): Grand Bank
Federal Electoral District(s): Random-Burin-St. George's
Next Election: Sept. 2009 (4 year terms)
Susan Fitzpatrick, Clerk
John R. Hennebury, Mayor

Lourdes
P.O. Box 29
Lourdes, NL A0N 1R0
709-642-5812 Fax: 709-642-5812
townoflourdes@nf.aibn.com
Municipal Type: Town
Incorporated: July 17, 1969; *Area:* 8.1 sq km
Population in 2006: 550
Provincial Electoral District(s): Port au Port
Federal Electoral District(s): Random-Burin-St. George's
Next Election: Sept. 2009 (4 year terms)
Shelly Benoit, Clerk
Deborah Snook, Mayor

Lumsden
P.O. Box 100
Lumsden, NL A0G 3E0
709-530-2309 Fax: 709-530-2144
www.lumsdennl.ca
Municipal Type: Town
Incorporated: April 16, 1968; *Area:* 20.43 sq km
Population in 2006: 533
Provincial Electoral District(s): Bonavista North
Federal Electoral District(s): Bonavista-Gander-Grand Falls-Windsor
Next Election: Sept. 2009 (4 year terms)
Jeanie Stokes, Clerk
Jeanette Gibbons, Mayor

Lushes Bight-Beaumont-Beaumont North
P.O. Box 40
Beaumont, NL A0J 1A0
709-264-3271 Fax: 709-264-3191
townoflushesbightbeaumont@nf.aibn.com
Municipal Type: Town
Incorporated: Oct. 15, 1968; *Area:* 34.38 sq km
Population in 2006: 275
Provincial Electoral District(s): Windsor-Springdale
Federal Electoral District(s): Humber-St. Barbe-Baie Verte
Next Election: Sept. 2009 (4 year terms)
Joan Pittman, Clerk
Clyde Croucher, Mayor

Main Brook
P.O. Box 130
Main Brook, NL A0K 3N0
709-865-6561 Fax: 709-865-3279
Municipal Type: Town
Incorporated: June 1, 1948; *Area:* 28.51 sq km
Population in 2006: 293
Provincial Electoral District(s): The Straits & White Bay North
Federal Electoral District(s): Humber-St. Barbe-Baie Verte
Next Election: Sept. 2009 (4 year terms)
Ella R. Pilgrim, Clerk
David Gibbons, Mayor

Makkovik
P.O. Box 132
Makkovik, NL A0P 1J0
709-923-2221 Fax: 709-923-2126
townclerkmakkovik@nf.aibn.com
Municipal Type: Town
Incorporated: April 7, 1970; *Area:* 1.97 sq km
Population in 2006: 362
Provincial Electoral District(s): Torngat Mountains
Federal Electoral District(s): Labrador
Next Election: Sept. 2009 (4 year terms)
Terry Rice, Clerk
Herbert R. Jacque, Mayor

Mary's Harbour
P.O. Box 134
Mary's Harbour, NL A0K 3P0
709-921-6281 Fax: 709-921-6255
maryshbr@nf.aibn.com
Municipal Type: Town
Incorporated: April 11, 1975; *Area:* 38.16 sq km
Population in 2006: 417
Provincial Electoral District(s): Cartwright-L'Anse au Clair
Federal Electoral District(s): Labrador
Next Election: Sept. 2009 (4 year terms)
Glenys Rumbolt, Clerk
Ford Rumbolt, Mayor

Marystown
P.O. Box 1118
Marystown, NL A0E 2M0
709-279-1661 Fax: 709-279-2862
info@townofmarystown.ca
www.townofmarystown.ca
Municipal Type: Town
Incorporated: Dec. 18, 1951; *Area:* 61.97 sq km
Population in 2006: 5,436
Provincial Electoral District(s): Burin-Placentia West
Federal Electoral District(s): Random-Burin-St. George's
Next Election: Sept. 2009 (4 year terms)
Dennis P. Kelly, Clerk & Manager
dkelly@townofmarystown.ca
Sam Synard, Mayor
ssynard@townofmarystown.ca

Massey Drive
85 Massey Dr.
Massey Drive, NL A2H 7A2
709-634-2742 Fax: 709-634-2899
townmasseydr@nf.aibn.com
Municipal Type: Town
Incorporated: Sept. 28, 1971; *Area:* 2.48 sq km
Population in 2006: 1,170
Provincial Electoral District(s): Humber East
Federal Electoral District(s): Humber-St. Barbe-Baie Verte
Next Election: Sept. 2009 (4 year terms)
Catherine Munly, Clerk
Holly Walsh, Mayor

McIvers
P.O. Box 4375
RR#2
Corner Brook, NL A2H 6B9
709-688-2603 Fax: 709-688-2680
Municipal Type: Town
Incorporated: June 15, 1971; *Area:* 12.06 sq km
Population in 2006: 571
Provincial Electoral District(s): Bay of Islands
Federal Electoral District(s): Humber-St. Barbe-Baie Verte
Next Election: Sept. 2009 (4 year terms)
Bernice E. Parsons, Clerk
Warren Blanchard, Mayor

Meadows
P.O. Box 3529
RR#2
Corner Brook, NL A2H 6B9
709-783-2339 Fax: 709-783-2501
townofmeadows@nf.aibn.com
Municipal Type: Town
Incorporated: Jan. 13, 1970; *Area:* 3.79 sq km
Population in 2006: 637
Provincial Electoral District(s): Bay of Islands
Federal Electoral District(s): Humber-St. Barbe-Baie Verte
Next Election: Sept. 2009 (4 year terms)
Joy Taylor, Clerk
Kenneth Marche, Mayor

Middle Arm
P.O. Box 51
Middle Arm, NL A0K 3R0
709-252-2521 Fax: 709-252-2521
toma.66@hotmail.com
Municipal Type: Town
Incorporated: Nov. 29, 1966; *Area:* 25.19 sq km
Population in 2006: 517
Provincial Electoral District(s): Baie Verte
Federal Electoral District(s): Avalon; Humber-St. Barbe-Baie Verte
Next Election: Sept. 2009 (4 year terms)
Loretta Budgell, Clerk
Bennett Hull, Mayor

Miles Cove
General Delivery
Miles Cove, NL A0J 1L0

709-652-3685 Fax: 709-652-3685
Municipal Type: Town
Incorporated: Sept. 22, 1970; *Area:* 4.03 sq km
Population in 2006: 140
Provincial Electoral District(s): Windsor-Springdale
Federal Electoral District(s): Humber-St. Barbe-Baie Verte
Next Election: Sept. 2009 (4 year terms)
Gloria Reid, Clerk
Melvin Morey, Mayor

Millertown
P.O. Box 56
Millertown, NL A0H 1V0
709-852-6216 Fax: 709-852-5431
Municipal Type: Town
Incorporated: Dec. 15, 1959; *Area:* 3.24 sq km
Population in 2006: 100
Provincial Electoral District(s): Grand Falls-Buchans
Federal Electoral District(s): Bonavista-Gander-Grand Falls-Windsor
Next Election: Sept. 2009 (4 year terms)
Eileen M. Scott, Clerk
George Piercey, Mayor

Milltown-Head of Bay D'Espoir
P.O. Box 70
Milltown, NL A0H 1W0
709-882-2232 Fax: 709-882-2636
townofmhb@personainternet.com
Municipal Type: Town
Incorporated: Dec. 16, 1952; *Area:* 25.02 sq km
Population in 2006: 865
Provincial Electoral District(s): Fortune Bay-Cape La Hune
Federal Electoral District(s): Random-Burin-St. George's
Next Election: Sept. 2009 (4 year terms)
Kimberly Kendell, Clerk
Gordon Kearley, Mayor

Ming's Bight
P.O. Box 69
Mings Bight, NL A0K 3S0
709-254-6516 Fax: 709-254-6516
townmingsbight@nf.aibn.com
Municipal Type: Town
Incorporated: June 6, 1970; *Area:* 3.78 sq km
Population in 2006: 347
Provincial Electoral District(s): Baie Verte
Federal Electoral District(s): Humber-St. Barbe-Baie Verte
Next Election: Sept. 2009 (4 year terms)
Glenda Regular, Clerk
Gilbert Regular, Mayor

Morrisville
P.O. Box 19
Morrisville, NL A0H 1W0
709-882-2322
Municipal Type: Town
Incorporated: June 1, 1971; *Area:* 14.26 sq km
Population in 2006: 128
Provincial Electoral District(s): Fortune Bay-Cape La Hune
Federal Electoral District(s): Random-Burin-St. George's
Next Election: Sept. 2009 (4 year terms)
Karl Kendell, Clerk
Helen Kendell, Mayor

Mount Carmel-Mitchell's Brook-St. Catherines
General Delivery
Mount Carmel, NL A0B 2M0
709-521-2040 Fax: 709-521-2258
Municipal Type: Town
Incorporated: Oct. 6, 1970; *Area:* 61.55 sq km
Population in 2006: 438
Provincial Electoral District(s): Placentia & St. Mary's
Federal Electoral District(s): Avalon
Next Election: Sept. 2009 (4 year terms)
Geraldine Nolan, Clerk
Kim Mercer, Mayor

Mount Moriah
P.O. Box 31
Mount Moriah, NL A0L 1J0
709-785-5232 Fax: 709-785-5332
mtmoriahtownoffice@nf.aibn.com
Municipal Type: Town
Incorporated: Oct. 12, 1971; *Area:* 15.71 sq km
Population in 2006: 752
Provincial Electoral District(s): Bay of Islands
Federal Electoral District(s): Humber-St. Barbe-Baie Verte
Next Election: Sept. 2009 (4 year terms)
Carol Hussey, Clerk
James Gillam, Mayor

Musgrave Harbour
P.O. Box 159
Musgrave Harbour, NL A0G 3J0
709-655-2119 Fax: 709-655-2064
musgravetowncouncil@nf.aibn.com
www.musgraveharbour.com
Municipal Type: Town
Incorporated: Jan. 1, 1954; *Area:* 69.94 sq km
Population in 2006: 1,085
Provincial Electoral District(s): Bonavista North
Federal Electoral District(s): Bonavista-Gander-Grand Falls-Windsor
Next Election: Sept. 2009 (4 year terms)
Sophie Abbott, Clerk
Raymond Stokes, Mayor

Musgravetown
P.O. Box 129
Musgravetown, NL A0C 1Z0
709-467-2726 Fax: 709-467-2109
Municipal Type: Town
Incorporated: March 1, 1974; *Area:* 13.63 sq km
Population in 2006: 583
Provincial Electoral District(s): Terra Nova
Federal Electoral District(s): Bonavista-Gander-Grand Falls-Windsor
Next Election: Sept. 2009 (4 year terms)
Linda Fitzgerald, Clerk
Melvin Humby, Mayor

Nain
P.O. Box 59
Nain, NL A0P 1L0
709-922-2842 Fax: 709-922-2295
nainicg@nf.aibn.com
Municipal Type: Town
Incorporated: Nov. 24, 1970; *Area:* 94.58 sq km
Population in 2006: 1,034
Provincial Electoral District(s): Torngat Mountains
Federal Electoral District(s): Labrador
Next Election: Sept. 2009 (4 year terms)
Karen Dicker, Clerk
Sarah Erickson, Mayor

New Perlican
P.O. Box 130
New Perlican, NL A0B 2S0
709-583-2500 Fax: 709-583-2554
Municipal Type: Town
Incorporated: Sept. 28, 1971; *Area:* 24.47 sq km
Population in 2006: 188
Provincial Electoral District(s): Trinity-Bay de Verde
Federal Electoral District(s): Avalon
Next Election: Sept. 2009 (4 year terms)
Pauline Harris, Clerk
William Power Jr., Mayor

New Wes-Valley
P.O. Box 64
Badgers Quay, NL A0G 1B0
709-536-2010 Fax: 709-536-3481
new-wes-valley@sympatico.ca
www.townofnewwesvalley.com
Municipal Type: Town
Incorporated: Jan. 1, 1992; *Area:* 133.59 sq km
Population in 2006: 2,485
Provincial Electoral District(s): Bonavista North
Federal Electoral District(s): Bonavista-Gander-Grand Falls-Windsor
Next Election: Sept. 2009 (4 year terms)
Harry Winter, Clerk & Manager
Grant Burry, Mayor

Nipper's Harbour
P.O. Box 10
Nippers Harbour, NL A0K 3T0
709-255-3151 Fax: 709-255-3151
Municipal Type: Town
Incorporated: Nov. 10, 1964; *Area:* 1.93 sq km
Population in 2006: 151
Provincial Electoral District(s): Baie Verte
Federal Electoral District(s): Humber-St. Barbe-Baie Verte
Next Election: Sept. 2009 (4 year terms)
Beth Prole, Clerk
Hedley Randell, Mayor

Norman's Cove-Long Cove
P.O. Box 70
Normans Cove, NL A0B 2T0
709-592-2490 Fax: 709-592-2106
townofnormanscove@nf.aibn.com
Municipal Type: Town
Incorporated: June 2, 1970; *Area:* 19.98 sq km
Population in 2006: 773
Provincial Electoral District(s): Bellevue
Federal Electoral District(s): Avalon
Next Election: Sept. 2009 (4 year terms)
Dianne Hudson, Clerk
Calvin Peach, Mayor

Norris Arm
P.O. Box 70
Norris Arm, NL A0G 3M0
709-653-2519 Fax: 709-653-2163
norrisarm@nf.aibn.com
www.norrisarm.com
Municipal Type: Town
Incorporated: April 20, 1971; *Area:* 41.49 sq km
Population in 2006: 911
Provincial Electoral District(s): Lewisporte
Federal Electoral District(s): Bonavista-Gander-Grand Falls-Windsor
Next Election: Sept. 2009 (4 year terms)
Beverly Peyton, Clerk
Fred Budgell, Mayor

Norris Point
P.O. Box 119
Norris Point, NL A0K 3V0
709-458-2896 Fax: 709-458-2883
info@norrispoint.ca
www.norrispoint.ca
Municipal Type: Town
Incorporated: Oct. 25, 1960; *Area:* 4.91 sq km
Population in 2006: 699
Provincial Electoral District(s): St. Barbe
Federal Electoral District(s): Humber-St. Barbe-Baie Verte
Next Election: Sept. 2009 (4 year terms)
Regina Organ, Clerk
Joseph Reid, Mayor
mayor@norrispoint.ca

North River
P.O. Box 104
North River, NL A0A 3C0
709-786-6216 Fax: 709-786-6216
Municipal Type: Town
Incorporated: Aug. 11, 1964; *Area:* 4.32 sq km
Population in 2006: 557
Provincial Electoral District(s): Harbour Main-Whitbourne
Federal Electoral District(s): Avalon; Labrador
Next Election: Sept. 2009 (4 year terms)
Sheila Hall, Clerk
Anthony Morrissey, Mayor

North West River
P.O. Box 100
North West River, NL A0P 1M0
709-497-8533 Fax: 709-497-8228
manager@townofnwr.ca
www.townofnwr.ca
Municipal Type: Town
Incorporated: March 11, 1958; *Area:* 3.2 sq km
Population in 2006: 492
Provincial Electoral District(s): Lake Melville
Federal Electoral District(s): Labrador
Next Election: Sept. 2009 (4 year terms)
Ken Nelson, Clerk
Arthur Williams, Mayor

Northern Arm
P.O. Box 2006
Northern Arm, NL A0H 1E0
709-257-3482 Fax: 709-257-3482
ella@townofnorthernarm.ca
www.townofnorthernarm.ca
Municipal Type: Town
Incorporated: July 18, 1972; *Area:* 25.64 sq km
Population in 2006: 385
Provincial Electoral District(s): Exploits
Federal Electoral District(s): Bonavista-Gander-Grand Falls-Windsor
Next Election: Sept. 2009 (4 year terms)
Ella Humphries, Clerk
Deanna Gail Hancock, Mayor

Old Perlican
P.O. Box 39
Old Perlican, NL A0A 3G0
709-587-2266 Fax: 709-587-2261
townofoldperlican@persona.ca
Municipal Type: Town
Incorporated: March 30, 1971; *Area:* 14.47 sq km
Population in 2006: 676
Provincial Electoral District(s): Trinity-Bay de Verde
Federal Electoral District(s): Avalon
Next Election: Sept. 2009 (4 year terms)
Judi Barter, Clerk
Donald E. Burt, Mayor

Pacquet
General Delivery
Pacquet, NL A0K 3X0
709-251-5496 Fax: 709-251-5497
Municipal Type: Town
Incorporated: June 12, 1962; *Area:* 14.48 sq km
Population in 2006: 210
Provincial Electoral District(s): Baie Verte
Federal Electoral District(s): Humber-St. Barbe-Baie Verte
Next Election: Sept. 2009 (4 year terms)
Janet Sacrey, Clerk
Verna Geenham, Mayor

Parkers Cove
General Delivery
Parker's Cove, NL A0E 1H0
709-443-2216 Fax: 709-443-2216
Municipal Type: Town
Incorporated: Jan. 25, 1966; *Area:* 4.85 sq km
Population in 2006: 308
Provincial Electoral District(s): Burin-Placentia West
Federal Electoral District(s): Random-Burin-St. George's
Next Election: Sept. 2009 (4 year terms)
Jennifer Murphy, Clerk
Cyril Synard, Mayor

Parson's Pond
P.O. Box 39
Parsons Pond, NL A0K 3Z0
709-243-2564 Fax: 709-243-2254
towncouncilpp@nf.aibn.com
Municipal Type: Town
Incorporated: March 29, 1966; *Area:* 12.63 sq km
Population in 2006: 387
Provincial Electoral District(s): St. Barbe
Federal Electoral District(s): Humber-St. Barbe-Baie Verte
Next Election: Sept. 2009 (4 year terms)
Joan Parsons, Clerk
Brenda Biggin, Mayor

Pasadena
18 Tenth Ave.
Pasadena, NL A0L 1K0
709-686-2075 Fax: 709-686-2507
pasadena@nf.aibn.com
www.town.pasadena.nf.ca
Municipal Type: Town
Incorporated: Oct. 25, 1955; *Area:* 49.16 sq km
Population in 2006: 3,180
Provincial Electoral District(s): Humber East
Federal Electoral District(s): Humber-St. Barbe-Baie Verte
Next Election: Sept. 2009 (4 year terms)
Jim Merrigan, Clerk & Manager
jimmerrigan@nf.aibn.com
Bob Mercer, Mayor
bmercer@nf.aibn.com

Peterview
P.O. Box 10
Peterview, NL A0H 1Y0
709-257-2926 Fax: 709-257-2926
townofpeterview@nf.aibn.com
Municipal Type: Town
Incorporated: June 12, 1962; *Area:* 6.72 sq km
Population in 2006: 807
Provincial Electoral District(s): Exploits
Federal Electoral District(s): Bonavista-Gander-Grand Falls-Windsor
Next Election: Sept. 2009 (4 year terms)
Venus Samson, Clerk
James Samson, Mayor

Petty Harbour-Maddox Cove
P.O. Box 70
Petty Harbour, NL A0A 3H0
709-368-3959 Fax: 709-368-3994
ncostello@phmc.nf.net
www.pettyharbourmaddoxcove.ca
Municipal Type: Town
Incorporated: March 25, 1969; *Area:* 4.51 sq km
Population in 2006: 915
Provincial Electoral District(s): Ferryland
Federal Electoral District(s): St. John's South-Mount Pearl
Next Election: Sept. 2009 (4 year terms)
Noreen Costello, Clerk
Nat Hutchings, Mayor

Pilley's Island
P.O. Box 70
Pilleys Island, NL A0J 1M0
709-652-3555 Fax: 709-652-3852
townofpilleysisland@nf.aibn.com
Municipal Type: Town
Incorporated: April 11, 1975; *Area:* 34.67 sq km
Population in 2006: 317
Provincial Electoral District(s): Windsor-Springdale
Federal Electoral District(s): Humber-St. Barbe-Baie Verte
Next Election: Sept. 2009 (4 year terms)
Betty Traverse, Clerk
Michael Whalen, Mayor

Pinware
P.O. Box 37
Pinware, NL A0K 5S0
709-927-5422 Fax: 709-927-5422
Municipal Type: Town
Incorporated: May 18, 1978; *Area:* 4.37 sq km
Population in 2006: 114
Provincial Electoral District(s): Cartwright-L'Anse au Clair
Federal Electoral District(s): Labrador
Next Election: Sept. 2009 (4 year terms)
Mary Ellen Butt, Clerk
Neil Pike, Mayor

Placentia
P.O. Box 99
Placentia, NL A0B 2Y0
709-227-2151 Fax: 709-227-2323
townofplacentia@placentia.ca
www.placentia.ca
Municipal Type: Town
Incorporated: Nov. 6, 1945; *Area:* 58.05 sq km
Population in 2006: 3,898
Provincial Electoral District(s): Placentia & St. Mary's
Federal Electoral District(s): Avalon
Next Election: Sept. 2009 (4 year terms)
Frank Smith, Clerk
fsmith@placentia.ca
William P. Hogan, Mayor
wph@placentia.ca

Point au Gaul
P.O. Box 11
Point au Gaul, NL A0E 2C0
709-857-2514
Municipal Type: Town
Incorporated: Jan. 4, 1966; *Area:* 3.84 sq km
Population in 2006: 85
Provincial Electoral District(s): Grand Bank
Federal Electoral District(s): Random-Burin-St. George's
Next Election: Sept. 2009 (4 year terms)
Peter M. Lockyer, Clerk
Hubert Hillier, Mayor

Point Lance
P.O. Box 23
Point Lance, NL A0B 1E0
709-337-2355
mpower001@nf.sympatico.ca
Municipal Type: Town
Incorporated: Dec. 7, 1971; *Area:* 29.14 sq km
Population in 2006: 119
Provincial Electoral District(s): Placentia & St. Mary's
Federal Electoral District(s): Avalon
Next Election: Sept. 2009 (4 year terms)
Bernadette Careen, Clerk
Melvin Careen, Mayor

Point Leamington
P.O. Box 39
Point Leamington, NL A0H 1Z0
709-484-3421 Fax: 709-484-3556
Municipal Type: Town
Incorporated: Aug. 25, 1970; *Area:* 28.81 sq km
Population in 2006: 649
Provincial Electoral District(s): Exploits
Federal Electoral District(s): Bonavista-Gander-Grand Falls-Windsor
Next Election: Sept. 2009 (4 year terms)
Patricia Earle, Clerk
Robert Elliott, Mayor

Point May
P.O. Box 19
Point May, NL A0E 2C0
709-857-2640 Fax: 709-857-2640
Municipal Type: Town
Incorporated: Dec. 4, 1962; *Area:* 64.89 sq km
Population in 2006: 260
Provincial Electoral District(s): Grand Bank
Federal Electoral District(s): Random-Burin-St. George's
Next Election: Sept. 2009 (4 year terms)
Janice Haley, Clerk
Carmelita Hillier, Mayor

Point of Bay
P.O. Box 9
Point of Bay, NL A0H 2A0
709-257-3171 Fax: 709-257-3171
Municipal Type: Town
Incorporated: April 18, 1967; *Area:* 21.94 sq km
Population in 2006: 163
Provincial Electoral District(s): Exploits
Federal Electoral District(s): Bonavista-Gander-Grand Falls-Windsor
Next Election: Sept. 2009 (4 year terms)
Sybil Boone, Clerk
Clarence Sparkes, Mayor

Pool's Cove
P.O. Box 10
Pools Cove, NL A0H 2B0
709-665-3371 Fax: 709-665-3372
Municipal Type: Town
Incorporated: Nov. 25, 1969; *Area:* 2.64 sq km
Population in 2006: 189
Provincial Electoral District(s): Fortune Bay-Cape La Hune
Federal Electoral District(s): Random-Burin-St. George's
Next Election: Sept. 2009 (4 year terms)
Sharon May, Clerk
Janet Fiander, Mayor

Port Anson
General Delivery
Port Anson, NL A0J 1N0
709-652-3683 Fax: 709-652-3680
Municipal Type: Town
Incorporated: Dec. 12, 1961; *Area:* 7.69 sq km
Population in 2006: 155
Provincial Electoral District(s): Windsor-Springdale
Federal Electoral District(s): Humber-St. Barbe-Baie Verte
Next Election: Sept. 2009 (4 year terms)
Grace Burton, Clerk
Shawn Burton, Mayor

Port au Choix
P.O. Box 89
Port au Choix, NL A0K 4C0
709-861-3409 Fax: 709-861-3061
Municipal Type: Town
Incorporated: July 26, 1966; *Area:* 35.61 sq km
Population in 2006: 893
Provincial Electoral District(s): St. Barbe
Federal Electoral District(s): Humber-St. Barbe-Baie Verte
Next Election: Sept. 2009 (4 year terms)
Judy Billard Payne, Clerk
John White, Mayor

Port au Port East
P.O. Box 160
Port au Port East, NL A0N 1T0
709-648-2731 Fax: 709-648-9481
townofp.a.p.e@cablerocket.com
Municipal Type: Town
Incorporated: Dec. 16, 1952; *Area:* 24.76 sq km
Population in 2006: 608
Provincial Electoral District(s): Port au Port
Federal Electoral District(s): Random-Burin-St. George's
Next Election: Sept. 2009 (4 year terms)
Joanne Ryan, Clerk
Neil Duffy, Mayor

Port au Port West-Aguathuna-Felix Cove
P.O. Box 89
Aguathuna, NL A0N 1T0
709-648-2891 Fax: 709-648-9292
papwest@nf.aibn.com
Municipal Type: Town
Incorporated: Oct. 6, 1970; *Area:* 16.72 sq km
Population in 2006: 386
Provincial Electoral District(s): Port au Port
Federal Electoral District(s): Random-Burin-St. George's
Next Election: Sept. 2009 (4 year terms)
Vanessa Glasgow, Clerk
Phyllis Doucette, Mayor

Port Blandford
P.O. Box 70
Port Blandford, NL A0C 2G0
709-543-2170 Fax: 709-543-2153
vgreening@nf.aibn.com
www.portblandford.com
Municipal Type: Town
Incorporated: Sept. 28, 1971; *Area:* 50.56 sq km
Population in 2006: 521
Provincial Electoral District(s): Terra Nova
Federal Electoral District(s): Bonavista-Gander-Grand Falls-Windsor
Next Election: Sept. 2009 (4 year terms)
Vida Greening, Town Clerk & Manager
Reginald Penney, Mayor

Port Hope Simpson
P.O. Box 130
Port Hope Simpson, NL A0K 4E0
709-960-0236 Fax: 709-960-0387
porthopesimpson@nf.aibn.com
Municipal Type: Town
Incorporated: May 1, 1973; *Area:* 32.52 sq km
Population in 2006: 529
Provincial Electoral District(s): Cartwright-L'Anse au Clair
Federal Electoral District(s): Labrador
Next Election: Sept. 2009 (4 year terms)
Betty Sampson, Clerk
Margaret Burden, Mayor

Port Kirwan
PO Box 40, Site 2
Port Kirwan, NL A0A 2G0
709-363-2141 Fax: 709-363-2114
Municipal Type: Town
Incorporated: June 15, 1965; *Area:* 9.19 sq km
Population in 2006: 85
Provincial Electoral District(s): Ferryland
Federal Electoral District(s): Avalon
Next Election: Sept. 2009 (4 year terms)
Dana Boland, Clerk
Eugene Brothers, Mayor

Port Rexton
P.O. Box 55
Port Rexton, NL A0C 2H0
709-464-2006 Fax: 709-464-2006
portrexton.council@nf.aibn.com
Municipal Type: Town
Incorporated: April 22, 1969; *Area:* 11.78 sq km
Population in 2006: 351
Provincial Electoral District(s): Trinity North
Federal Electoral District(s): Bonavista-Gander-Grand Falls-Windsor
Next Election: Sept. 2009 (4 year terms)
Lois Long, Clerk
Alvin Piercey, Mayor

Port Saunders
P.O. Box 39
Port Saunders, NL A0K 4H0
709-861-3105 Fax: 709-861-2137
townofportsaunders@nf.aibn.com
Municipal Type: Town
Incorporated: Aug. 21, 1956; *Area:* 38.81 sq km
Population in 2006: 747
Provincial Electoral District(s): St. Barbe
Federal Electoral District(s): Humber-St. Barbe-Baie Verte
Next Election: Sept. 2009 (4 year terms)
Judy Quinlan, Clerk
Tony Ryan, Mayor
Co-Clerk , Helen
Hamlyn

Portugal Cove South
PO Box 8, Site 11
Trepassey, NL A0A 4B0
709-438-2092 Fax: 709-438-2092
jperry@nf.sympatico.ca
Municipal Type: Town
Incorporated: Aug. 6, 1963; *Area:* 1.14 sq km
Population in 2006: 222
Provincial Electoral District(s): Ferryland
Federal Electoral District(s): Avalon
Next Election: Sept. 2009 (4 year terms)
Ida Perry, Clerk
Clarence Molloy, Mayor

Portugal Cove-St Philip's
1119 Thorburn Rd.
Portugal Cove-St Philips, NL A1M 1T6

709-895-8000 Fax: 709-895-3780
pcsp@pcsp.ca
www.pcsp.ca
Municipal Type: Town
Incorporated: Feb. 1, 1992; *Area:* 57.35 sq km
Population in 2006: 6,575
Provincial Electoral District(s): Conception Bay East & Bell Island
Federal Electoral District(s): St. John's East
Next Election: Sept. 2009 (4 year terms)
Loretta Tucker, Town Clerk & Treas.
loretta.tucker@pcsp.ca
Norman Collins, Mayor
norm.collins@pcsp.ca

Postville
P.O. Box 74
Postville, NL A0P 1N0
709-479-9830 Fax: 709-479-9888
towncouncilpostville@hotmail.com
Municipal Type: Town
Incorporated: Aug. 1, 1975; *Area:* 1.96 sq km
Population in 2006: 219
Provincial Electoral District(s): Torngat Mountains
Federal Electoral District(s): Labrador
Next Election: Sept. 2009 (4 year terms)
Shirley Goudie, Clerk
Kieth Decker, Mayor

Pouch Cove
P.O. Box 59
Pouch Cove, NL A0A 3L0
709-335-2848 Fax: 709-335-2840
pouchcove@nf.aibn.com
www.pouchcove.ca
Municipal Type: Town
Incorporated: Dec. 22, 1970; *Area:* 58.34 sq km
Population in 2006: 1,756
Provincial Electoral District(s): Cape St. Francis
Federal Electoral District(s): St. John's East
Next Election: Sept. 2009 (4 year terms)
Barbara Tilley, Clerk
Sarah Patten, Mayor
709-335-2464

Raleigh
P.O. Box 119
Raleigh, NL A0K 4J0
709-452-4461 Fax: 709-452-2135
townofraleigh@nf.aibn.com
Municipal Type: Town
Incorporated: Oct. 2, 1973; *Area:* 11.12 sq km
Population in 2006: 248
Provincial Electoral District(s): The Straits & White Bay North
Federal Electoral District(s): Humber-St. Barbe-Baie Verte
Next Election: Sept. 2009 (4 year terms)
Valerie Taylor, Clerk
Cyril Taylor, Mayor

Ramea
P.O. Box 69
Ramea, NL A0N 2J0
709-625-2280 Fax: 709-625-2010
rameatowncouncil@nf.aibn.com
Municipal Type: Town
Incorporated: March 20, 1951; *Area:* 1.89 sq km
Population in 2006: 618
Provincial Electoral District(s): Fortune Bay-Cape La Hune
Federal Electoral District(s): Random-Burin-St. George's
Next Election: Sept. 2009 (4 year terms)
Minnie Organ, Clerk
Lloyd Rossiter, Mayor

Red Bay
P.O. Box 108
Red Bay, NL A0K 4K0
709-920-2197 Fax: 709-920-2103
redbaytowncouncil@nf.aibn.com
Municipal Type: Town
Incorporated: May 22, 1973; *Area:* 1.58 sq km
Population in 2006: 227
Provincial Electoral District(s): Cartwright-L'Anse au Clair
Federal Electoral District(s): Labrador
Next Election: Sept. 2009 (4 year terms)
Elizabeth Yetman, Clerk
Wade Earle, Mayor

Red Harbour
General Delivery
Red Harbour PB, NL A0E 2R0
709-443-2599 Fax: 709-443-2599
townofredhr@yahoo.ca
Municipal Type: Town
Incorporated: Nov. 9, 1969; *Area:* 11.35 sq km
Population in 2006: 210
Provincial Electoral District(s): Burin-Placentia West
Federal Electoral District(s): Random-Burin-St. George's
Next Election: Sept. 2009 (4 year terms)
Kevin Paddle, Clerk
Fred Keaway, Mayor

Reidville
2 Community Sq.
Reidville, NL A8A 2V7
709-635-5232 Fax: 709-635-4498
townofreidville@nf.aibn.com
www.reidville-nl.ca
Municipal Type: Town
Incorporated: Oct. 3, 1975; *Area:* 58.41 sq km
Population in 2006: 511
Provincial Electoral District(s): Humber Valley
Federal Electoral District(s): Humber-St. Barbe-Baie Verte
Next Election: Sept. 2009 (4 year terms)
Kimberly Reid, Clerk
Louie McDonald, Mayor

Rencontre East
P.O. Box 56
Rencontre East, NL A0H 2C0
709-848-4116 Fax: 709-848-4194
Municipal Type: Town
Incorporated: Feb. 8, 1972; *Area:* 2.62 sq km
Population in 2006: 165
Provincial Electoral District(s): Fortune Bay-Cape La Hune
Federal Electoral District(s): Random-Burin-St. George's
Next Election: Sept. 2009 (4 year terms)
Barbara Caines, Clerk
Tom Caines, Mayor

Renews-Cappahayden
P.O. Box 40
Renews, NL A0A 3N0
709-363-2500 Fax: 709-363-2143
Municipal Type: Town
Incorporated: Sept. 19, 1967; *Area:* 127.84 sq km
Population in 2006: 421
Provincial Electoral District(s): Ferryland
Federal Electoral District(s): Avalon
Next Election: Sept. 2009 (4 year terms)

Council
Roland Chidley, Mayor

Administration
Lena Bavis, Clerk

Rigolet
P.O. Box 69
Rigolet, NL A0P 1P0
709-947-3382 Fax: 709-947-3360
townmanager@thebigland.ca
www.thebigland.ca
Municipal Type: Town
Incorporated: Jan. 7, 1977; *Area:* 3.61 sq km
Population in 2006: 269
Provincial Electoral District(s): Torngat Mountains
Federal Electoral District(s): Labrador
Next Election: Sept. 2009 (4 year terms)
Sarah Blake, Town Clerk
townclerk@thebigland.ca
Daniel E. Michelin, Mayor

River of Ponds
P.O. Box 10
River of Ponds, NL A0K 4M0
709-225-3161 Fax: 709-225-3162
hollypatey@nf.sympatico.ca
Municipal Type: Town
Incorporated: May 26, 1970; *Area:* 4.69 sq km
Population in 2006: 251
Provincial Electoral District(s): St. Barbe
Federal Electoral District(s): Humber-St. Barbe-Baie Verte
Next Election: Sept. 2009 (4 year terms)
Holly Patey, Clerk
Eric Patey, Mayor

Riverhead
P.O. Box 266
RR#1
St Marys, NL A0B 3B0
709-525-2600 Fax: 709-525-2106
Municipal Type: Town
Incorporated: Dec. 20, 1966; *Area:* 105.6 sq km
Population in 2006: 220
Provincial Electoral District(s): Placentia & St. Mary's
Federal Electoral District(s): Avalon
Next Election: Sept. 2009 (4 year terms)
Anne Lee, Clerk
Gloria White, Mayor

Robert's Arm
P.O. Box 10
Roberts Arm, NL A0J 1R0
709-652-3331 Fax: 709-652-3079
town.robertsarm@nf.aibn.com
Municipal Type: Town
Incorporated: Sept. 7, 1954; *Area:* 35.79 sq km
Population in 2006: 841
Provincial Electoral District(s): Windsor-Springdale
Federal Electoral District(s): Humber-St. Barbe-Baie Verte
Next Election: Sept. 2009 (4 year terms)
Ada Rowsell, Clerk
Daphne Parsons, Mayor

Rocky Harbour
P.O. Box 24
Rocky Harbour, NL A0K 4N0
709-458-2376 Fax: 709-458-2293
info@rockyharbour.ca
www.rockyharbour.ca
Municipal Type: Town
Incorporated: April 5, 1966; *Area:* 12.08 sq km
Population in 2006: 978
Provincial Electoral District(s): St. Barbe
Federal Electoral District(s): Humber-St. Barbe-Baie Verte
Next Election: Sept. 2009 (4 year terms)
Myra Brown, Clerk
Keith Shears, Mayor

Roddickton
P.O. Box 10
Roddickton, NL A0K 4P0
709-457-2413 Fax: 709-457-2663
roddickton@nf.aibn.com
Municipal Type: Town
Incorporated: April 7, 1953; *Area:* 17.86 sq km
Population in 2006: 911
Provincial Electoral District(s): The Straits & White Bay North
Federal Electoral District(s): Humber-St. Barbe-Baie Verte
Next Election: Sept. 2009 (4 year terms)
Arthur A. Locke, Clerk
Raymond Norman, Mayor

Rose Blanche-Harbour Le Cou
P.O. Box 159
Rose Blanche, NL A0M 1P0
709-956-2540 Fax: 709-956-2541
Municipal Type: Town
Incorporated: Aug. 25, 1971; *Area:* 4.44 sq km
Population in 2006: 547
Provincial Electoral District(s): Burgeo & La Poile
Federal Electoral District(s): Random-Burin-St. George's
Next Election: Sept. 2009 (4 year terms)
Tammy Farrell, Clerk
Kerry Walters, Mayor

Rushoon
General Delivery
Rushoon, NL A0E 2S0
709-443-2572 Fax: 709-443-2572
townofrushoon@nf.aibn.com
Municipal Type: Town
Incorporated: Jan. 18, 1966; *Area:* 6.15 sq km
Population in 2006: 319
Provincial Electoral District(s): Burin-Placentia West
Federal Electoral District(s): Random-Burin-St. George's
Next Election: Sept. 2009 (4 year terms)
Jacqueline Gaulton, Clerk
Jill Mulrooney, Mayor
Margaret Whiffen, Mayor

St. Alban's
P.O. Box 10
St Albans, NL A0H 2E0
709-538-3132 Fax: 709-538-3683
inquiries@stalbans.ca
www.stalbans.ca
Municipal Type: Town
Incorporated: Sept. 1, 1953; *Area:* 20.85 sq km
Population in 2006: 1,278
Provincial Electoral District(s): Fortune Bay-Cape La Hune
Federal Electoral District(s): Random-Burin-St. George's
Next Election: Sept. 2009 (4 year terms)
Genevieve Tremblett, Clerk & Manager
Deborah Collier, Mayor

St. Anthony
P.O. Box 430
St Anthony, NL A0K 4S0
709-454-3454 Fax: 709-454-4154
bnbudgell@nf.aibn.com
www.town.stanthony.nf.ca
Municipal Type: Town
Incorporated: July 18, 1945; *Area:* 37.02 sq km
Population in 2006: 2,476
Provincial Electoral District(s): The Straits & White Bay North
Federal Electoral District(s): Humber-St. Barbe-Baie Verte
Next Election: Sept. 2009 (4 year terms)
Wallace Green, Clerk
Boyd Noel, Mayor

St. Bernard's-Jacques Fontaine
P.O. Box 70
St Bernards, NL A0E 2T0
709-461-2257 Fax: 709-461-2179
Municipal Type: Town
Incorporated: Nov. 21, 1967; *Area:* 16.44 sq km
Population in 2006: 525
Provincial Electoral District(s): Bellevue
Federal Electoral District(s): Random-Burin-St. George's
Next Election: Sept. 2009 (4 year terms)
Marie McCarthy, Clerk
Alice Parrott, Mayor

St. Brendan's
P.O. Box 54
St Brendans, NL A0G 3V0
709-669-4271 Fax: 709-669-4271
Municipal Type: Town
Incorporated: Sept. 1, 1953; *Area:* 10.14 sq km
Population in 2006: 203
Provincial Electoral District(s): Terra Nova

Federal Electoral District(s): Bonavista-Gander-Grand Falls-Windsor
Next Election: Sept. 2009 (4 year terms)
Rita White, Clerk
Kevin O'Reilly, Mayor

St. Bride's
General Delivery
St Brides, NL A0B 2Z0
709-337-2160 Fax: 709-337-2160
Municipal Type: Town
Incorporated: May 2, 1972; *Area:* 5.84 sq km
Population in 2006: 386
Provincial Electoral District(s): Placentia & St. Mary's
Federal Electoral District(s): Avalon
Next Election: Sept. 2009 (4 year terms)
Joan Morrissey, Clerk
Eugene Manning, Mayor

St. George's
P.O. Box 250
St Georges, NL A0N 1Z0
709-647-3283 Fax: 709-647-3180
townofstgeorges@nf.aibn.com
www.townofstgeorges.com
Municipal Type: Town
Incorporated: May 18, 1965; *Area:* 25.83 sq km
Population in 2006: 1,246
Provincial Electoral District(s): St. George's-Stephenville East
Federal Electoral District(s): Random-Burin-St. George's
Next Election: Sept. 2009 (4 year terms)
Debbie Woolridge, Clerk
Fintan Alexander, Mayor

St. Jacques-Coomb's Cove
P.O. Box 102
English Harbour West, NL A0H 1M0
709-888-6141 Fax: 709-888-6102
Municipal Type: Town
Incorporated: Nov. 15, 1971; *Area:* 83.76 sq km
Population in 2006: 669
Provincial Electoral District(s): Fortune Bay-Cape La Hune
Federal Electoral District(s): Random-Burin-St. George's
Next Election: Sept. 2009 (4 year terms)
Frances Courtney, Clerk
Max Taylor, Mayor

St. Joseph's
P.O. Box 9
St Josephs, NL A0B 3A0
709-521-2440 Fax: 709-521-2440
Municipal Type: Town
Incorporated: Aug. 18, 1970; *Area:* 32.31 sq km
Population in 2006: 144
Provincial Electoral District(s): Placentia & St. Mary's
Federal Electoral District(s): Avalon
Next Election: Sept. 2009 (4 year terms)
Maureen Healey, Clerk
Anthony Healey, Mayor

St. Lawrence
P.O. Box 128
St Lawrence, NL A0E 2V0
709-873-2222 Fax: 709-873-3352
townofstlawrence@nf.aibn.com
www.discoverstlawrence.com
Municipal Type: Town
Incorporated: Nov. 15, 1949; *Area:* 35.5 sq km
Population in 2006: 1,349
Provincial Electoral District(s): Grand Bank
Federal Electoral District(s): Random-Burin-St. George's
Next Election: Sept. 2009 (4 year terms)
Gregory Quirke, Clerk
Wayde Rowsell, Mayor

St. Lewis
P.O. Box 106
St. Lewis, NL A0K 4W0
709-939-2282 Fax: 709-939-2210
Municipal Type: Town
Incorporated: July 17, 1981; *Area:* 9.25 sq km
Population in 2006: 252
Provincial Electoral District(s): Cartwright-L'Anse au Clair
Federal Electoral District(s): Labrador
Next Election: Sept. 2009 (4 year terms)
Lorraine Poole, Clerk
Annie Rumbolt, Mayor

St. Lunaire-Griquet
P.O. Box 9
St Lunaire-Griquet, NL A0K 2X0
709-623-2323 Fax: 709-623-2170
stlunaire.griquet@nf.aibn.com
Municipal Type: Town
Incorporated: June 10, 1958; *Area:* 16.68 sq km
Population in 2006: 666
Provincial Electoral District(s): The Straits & White Bay North
Federal Electoral District(s): Humber-St. Barbe-Baie Verte
Next Election: Sept. 2009 (4 year terms)
Linda Hillier, Clerk
Todd Hedderson, Mayor

St. Mary's
P.O. Box 348
St Marys, NL A0B 3B0
709-525-2586 Fax: 709-525-2587
theresap@nf.aibn.com
Municipal Type: Town
Incorporated: Dec. 13, 1966; *Area:* 37.05 sq km
Population in 2006: 482
Provincial Electoral District(s): Placentia & St. Mary's
Federal Electoral District(s): Avalon
Next Election: Sept. 2009 (4 year terms)
Theresa Power, Clerk
Joseph Dillon, Mayor

St. Paul's
P.O. Box 9
St Pauls, NL A0K 4Y0
709-243-2279 Fax: 709-243-2299
Municipal Type: Town
Incorporated: July 30, 1968; *Area:* 5.35 sq km
Population in 2006: 309
Provincial Electoral District(s): St. Barbe
Federal Electoral District(s): Humber-St. Barbe-Baie Verte
Next Election: Sept. 2009 (4 year terms)
Monica Pittman, Clerk
Gary Bennett, Mayor

St. Shott's
General Delivery
St Shotts, NL A0A 3R0
709-438-2694 Fax: 709-438-2617
Municipal Type: Town
Incorporated: May 21, 1963; *Area:* 1.14 sq km
Population in 2006: 109
Provincial Electoral District(s): Placentia & St. Mary's
Federal Electoral District(s): Avalon
Next Election: Sept. 2009 (4 year terms)
Elizabeth Hewitt, Clerk
Patrick Hewitt, Mayor

St. Vincent's-St. Stephen's-Peter's River
P.O. Box 39
St Vincents, NL A0B 3C0
709-525-2540 Fax: 709-525-2110
svstpr@nf.aibn.com
Municipal Type: Town
Incorporated: Aug. 1, 1971; *Area:* 87.5 sq km
Population in 2006: 363
Provincial Electoral District(s): Placentia & St. Mary's
Federal Electoral District(s): Avalon
Next Election: Sept. 2009 (4 year terms)
Marilyn Gibbons, Clerk
Gus Stamp, Mayor

Salmon Cove
P.O. Box 240
Salmon Cove, NL A0A 3S0
709-596-2101 Fax: 709-596-1170
townof.salmoncove@nf.sympatico.ca
Municipal Type: Town
Incorporated: Aug. 27, 1974; *Area:* 4.21 sq km
Population in 2006: 707
Provincial Electoral District(s): Carbonear-Harbour Grace
Federal Electoral District(s): Avalon
Next Election: Sept. 2009 (4 year terms)
Bonnie Butt, Clerk
Gary Butt, Mayor

Salvage
General Delivery
Salvage, NL A0G 3X0
709-677-3535 Fax: 709-677-3535
Municipal Type: Town
Incorporated: Oct. 24, 1972; *Area:* 15.86 sq km
Population in 2006: 174
Provincial Electoral District(s): Terra Nova
Federal Electoral District(s): Bonavista-Gander-Grand Falls-Windsor
Next Election: Sept. 2009 (4 year terms)
Beverly Hunter, Clerk
Dave Brown, Mayor

Sandringham
43 Main St.
Sandringham, NL A0G 3Y0
709-677-2317 Fax: 709-677-2317
townofsandringham@yahoo.ca
Municipal Type: Town
Incorporated: April 30, 1968; *Area:* 9.6 sq km
Population in 2006: 255
Provincial Electoral District(s): Terra Nova
Federal Electoral District(s): Bonavista-Gander-Grand Falls-Windsor
Next Election: Sept. 2009 (4 year terms)
Audrey Penney, Clerk
Rayburn Fifield, Mayor

Sandy Cove
PO Box 37, Site 8
Eastport, NL A0G 1Z0
709-677-2731 Fax: 709-677-2731
sandycove@nf.sympatico.ca
www3.nf.sympatico.ca/sandycove
Municipal Type: Town
Incorporated: Sept. 18, 1956; *Area:* 9.01 sq km
Population in 2006: 133
Provincial Electoral District(s): Terra Nova; The Straits & White Bay North
Federal Electoral District(s): Bonavista-Gander-Grand Falls-Windsor; Humber-St. Barbe-Baie Verte
Next Election: Sept. 2009 (4 year terms)
Anne Benger, Clerk
Lisa Napier, Mayor

Seal Cove Fortune Bay
P.O. Box 156
Seal Cove Fortune Bay, NL A0H 2G0
709-851-4431 Fax: 709-851-4431
Municipal Type: Town
Incorporated: Jan. 25, 1972; *Area:* 2.42 sq km
Population in 2006: 315
Provincial Electoral District(s): Fortune Bay-Cape La Hune
Federal Electoral District(s): Random-Burin-St. George's
Next Election: Sept. 2009 (4 year terms)
Emily Loveless, Clerk
Ken Loveless, Mayor

Seal Cove White Bay
P.O. Box 119
Seal Cove White Bay, NL A0K 5E0
709-531-2550 Fax: 709-531-2551
sealcovewb@nf.aibn.com
Municipal Type: Town
Incorporated: Dec. 16, 1958; *Area:* 10.79 sq km
Population in 2006: 331
Provincial Electoral District(s): Baie Verte
Federal Electoral District(s): Humber-St. Barbe-Baie Verte
Next Election: Sept. 2009 (4 year terms)
Vanessa Osbourne, Clerk
Winston May, Mayor

Seldom-Little Seldom
P.O. Box 100
Seldom-Little Seldom, NL A0G 3Z0
709-627-3246 Fax: 709-627-3489
bbennett@nf.aibn.com
Municipal Type: Town
Incorporated: Feb. 8, 1972; *Area:* 14.6 sq km
Population in 2006: 444
Provincial Electoral District(s): Twillingate & Fogo
Federal Electoral District(s): Bonavista-Gander-Grand Falls-Windsor
Next Election: Sept. 2009 (4 year terms)
Blanche Bennett, Clerk
Gary Dawe, Mayor

Small Point-Adam's Cove-Blackhead-Broad Cove
P.O. Box 160
Broad Cove, NL A1Y 1C6
709-598-2610 Fax: 709-598-2618
towncouncil@nf.aibn.com
Municipal Type: Town
Incorporated: Oct. 24, 1972; *Area:* 22.22 sq km
Population in 2006: 438
Provincial Electoral District(s): Tinity-Bay de Verde
Federal Electoral District(s): Avalon
Next Election: Sept. 2009 (4 year terms)
Anne Wheadon, Clerk
Les Grover, Mayor

South Brook
P.O. Box 63
South Brook, NL A0J 1S0
709-657-2206 Fax: 709-657-2202
townofs.brk@nf.aibn.com
Municipal Type: Town
Incorporated: July 6, 1965; *Area:* 9.07 sq km
Population in 2006: 531
Provincial Electoral District(s): Windsor-Springdale
Federal Electoral District(s): Humber-St. Barbe-Baie Verte
Next Election: Sept. 2009 (4 year terms)
Blosson McKay, Clerk
Rockey Morey, Mayor

South River
P.O. Box 40
South River, NL A0A 3W0
709-786-6761 Fax: 709-786-6761
townofsouthriver@persona.com
Municipal Type: Town
Incorporated: June 7, 1966; *Area:* 6.06 sq km
Population in 2006: 649
Provincial Electoral District(s): Harbour Main-Whitbourne
Federal Electoral District(s): Avalon
Next Election: Sept. 2009 (4 year terms)
Arthur Petten, Mayor
Steven Rowe, Town Clerk & Manager

Southern Harbour
P.O. Box 10
Southern Harbour PB, NL A0B 3H0
709-463-2329 Fax: 709-463-2208
twnsouthernharbour@nf.aibn.com
Municipal Type: Town
Incorporated: Aug. 20, 1968; *Area:* 5.41 sq km
Population in 2006: 474
Provincial Electoral District(s): Bellevue
Federal Electoral District(s): Avalon
Next Election: Sept. 2009 (4 year terms)
Bernadette Power, Clerk
John Penney, Mayor

Spaniard's Bay
P.O. Box 190
Spaniards Bay, NL A0A 3X0

709-786-3568 Fax: 709-786-7273
spaniardsbay@nf.aibn.com
www.townofspaniardsbay.ca
Municipal Type: Town
Incorporated: June 8, 1965; *Area:* 65.73 sq km
Population in 2006: 2,540
Provincial Electoral District(s): Port de Grave
Federal Electoral District(s): Avalon
Next Election: Sept. 2009 (4 year terms)
Tony Ryan, Clerk & Manager
John W. Drover, Mayor

Springdale
P.O. Box 57
Springdale, NL A0J 1T0
709-673-3439 Fax: 709-673-4969
townoffice.springdale@nf.aibn.com
www.townofspringdale.ca
Municipal Type: Town
Incorporated: Oct. 23, 1961; *Area:* 17.6 sq km
Population in 2006: 2,764
Provincial Electoral District(s): Windsor-Springdale
Federal Electoral District(s): Humber-St. Barbe-Baie Verte
Next Election: Sept. 2009 (4 year terms)
Daphne Earle, Clerk & Manager
Kevin Pollard, Mayor

Steady Brook
P.O. Box 117
Steady Brook, NL A2H 2N2
709-634-7601 Fax: 709-634-7547
townoffice@steadybrook.com
www.steadybrook.com
Municipal Type: Town
Incorporated: April 7, 1953; *Area:* 1.22 sq km
Population in 2006: 435
Provincial Electoral District(s): Humber East
Federal Electoral District(s): Humber-St. Barbe-Baie Verte
Next Election: Sept. 2009 (4 year terms)
Rob Gosse, Clerk & Manager
townclerk@steadybrook.com
Tom Humphrey, Mayor

Stephenville
P.O. Box 420
Stephenville, NL A2N 2Z5
709-643-8360 Fax: 709-643-2770
manager@town.stephenville.nf.ca
www.town.stephenville.nf.ca
Municipal Type: Town
Incorporated: Oct. 1, 1952; *Area:* 35.69 sq km
Population in 2006: 6,588
Provincial Electoral District(s): St. George's-Stephenville East; Port au Port
Federal Electoral District(s): Random-Burin-St. George's
Next Election: Sept. 2009 (4 year terms)
Barry Coates, Clerk
ea@town.stephenville.nf.ca
Tom O'Brien, Mayor
mayor@town.stephenville.nf.ca

Stephenville Crossing
P.O. Box 68
Stephenville Crossing, NL A0N 2C0
709-646-2600 Fax: 709-646-2065
sxing@cablerocket.com
Municipal Type: Town
Incorporated: Oct. 20, 1958; *Area:* 31.2 sq km
Population in 2006: 1,960
Provincial Electoral District(s): St. George's-Stephenville East
Federal Electoral District(s): Random-Burin-St. George's
Next Election: Sept. 2009 (4 year terms)
Yvonne Young, Clerk
Brian Joy, Mayor

Summerford
P.O. Box 59
Summerford, NL A0G 4E0
709-629-3419 Fax: 709-629-7532
townofsummerford@nf.aibn.com
www.townofsummerford.com
Municipal Type: Town
Incorporated: Sept. 28, 1971; *Area:* 16.06 sq km
Population in 2006: 976
Provincial Electoral District(s): Twillingate & Fogo
Federal Electoral District(s): Bonavista-Gander-Grand Falls-Windsor
Next Election: Sept. 2009 (4 year terms)
Vicky Anstey, Clerk
Clayton LeDrew, Mayor

Sunnyside Trinity Bay
P.O. Box 09
Sunnyside, NL A0B 3J0
709-472-4506 Fax: 709-472-4182
town.sunnyside@nf.aibn.com
Municipal Type: Town
Incorporated: March 10, 1970; *Area:* 37.95 sq km
Population in 2006: 470
Provincial Electoral District(s): Bellevue
Federal Electoral District(s): Bonavista-Gander-Grand Falls-Windsor
Next Election: Sept. 2009 (4 year terms)
G. Philip Smith, Clerk
Gerard Lynch, Mayor

Terra Nova
PO Box 1, Site 3, RR#1
Terra Nova, NL A0C 1L0
709-265-6331 Fax: 709-265-6331
Municipal Type: Town
Incorporated: Sept. 13, 1960; *Area:* 2.46 sq km
Population in 2006: 68
Provincial Electoral District(s): Terra Nova
Federal Electoral District(s): Bonavista-Gander-Grand Falls-Windsor
Next Election: Sept. 2009 (4 year terms)
Linda Pelley, Clerk
Oliver Short, Mayor

Terrenceville
P.O. Box 100
Terrenceville, NL A0E 2X0
709-662-2204 Fax: 709-662-2071
terrancevilletownoffice@nf.aibn.com
Municipal Type: Town
Incorporated: Aug. 15, 1972; *Area:* 14.5 sq km
Population in 2006: 536
Provincial Electoral District(s): Bellevue
Federal Electoral District(s): Random-Burin-St. George's
Next Election: Sept. 2009 (4 year terms)
Joan Rideout, Clerk
Rebecca Hickey, Mayor

Tilt Cove
P.O. Box 22
Tilt Cove, NL A0K 3M0
709-675-2641
Municipal Type: Town
Incorporated: March 4, 1969; *Area:* 3.1 sq km
Population in 2006: 5
Provincial Electoral District(s): Baie Verte
Federal Electoral District(s): Humber-St. Barbe-Baie Verte
Next Election: Sept. 2009 (4 year terms)
Margaret Collins, Clerk
Donald Collins, Mayor

Tilting
P.O. Box 40
Tilting, NL A0G 4H0
709-658-7236 Fax: 709-658-7239
towncouncil@townoftilting.com
www.townoftilting.com
Municipal Type: Town
Incorporated: Oct. 10, 1975; *Area:* 17.63 sq km
Population in 2006: 248
Provincial Electoral District(s): Twillingate & Fogo
Federal Electoral District(s): Bonavista-Gander-Grand Falls-Windsor
Next Election: Sept. 2009 (4 year terms)
Amanda McGrath, Clerk
Gerard E. Foley, Mayor

Torbay
P.O. Box 1160
Torbay, NL A1K 1K4
709-437-6532 Fax: 709-437-1309
lotoole@town.torbay.nf.ca
www.town.torbay.nf.ca
Municipal Type: Town
Incorporated: Oct. 24, 1972; *Area:* 34.88 sq km
Population in 2006: 6,281
Provincial Electoral District(s): Cape St. Francis
Federal Electoral District(s): St. John's East
Next Election: Sept. 2009 (4 year terms)
Dawn Chaplin, CAO-Clerk
dchaplin@town.torbay.nf.ca
Robert Codner, Mayor

Traytown
1 Poplar Lane
Traytown, NL A0G 4K0
709-533-2156 Fax: 709-533-2156
traytown@thezone.net
Municipal Type: Town
Incorporated: June 15, 1971; *Area:* 13.31 sq km
Population in 2006: 302
Provincial Electoral District(s): Terra Nova
Federal Electoral District(s): Bonavista-Gander-Grand Falls-Windsor
Next Election: Sept. 2009 (4 year terms)
Leo Tulk, Mayor

Trepassey
P.O. Box 129
Trepassey, NL A0A 4B0
709-438-2641 Fax: 709-438-2749
terry@townoftrepassey.com
Municipal Type: Town
Incorporated: Aug. 1, 1967; *Area:* 55.81 sq km
Population in 2006: 763
Provincial Electoral District(s): Ferryland
Federal Electoral District(s): Avalon
Next Election: Sept. 2009 (4 year terms)
Jill McNeil, Clerk
Mary Coombs, Mayor

Trinity
P.O. Box 42
Trinity, NL A0C 2S0
709-464-3836 Fax: 709-464-3836
counciltrinity@netscape.net
Municipal Type: Town
Incorporated: May 13, 1969; *Area:* 12.92 sq km
Population in 2006: 191
Provincial Electoral District(s): Trinity North; Bonavista North
Federal Electoral District(s): Bonavista-Gander-Grand Falls-Windsor
Next Election: Sept. 2009 (4 year terms)
Linda Dalton, Clerk
Jim Miller, Mayor

Trinity Bay North
P.O. Box 91
Port Union, NL A0C 2J0
709-469-2571 Fax: 709-469-3444
town@trinitybaynorth.com
www.trinitybaynorth.com
Municipal Type: Town
Incorporated: Jan. 1, 2005; *Area:* 14.28 sq km
Population in 2006: 1,539
Provincial Electoral District(s): Bonavista South
Federal Electoral District(s): Bonavista-Gander-Grand Falls-Windsor
Next Election: Sept. 2009 (4 year terms)
Note: Effective January 1, 2005, the towns of Catalina, Port Union & Melrose amalgamated to form the new town of Trinity Bay North.
Austin Duffett, Mayor
Valerie Rogers, Clerk
tbn@personainternaet.com

Triton
P.O. Box 10
Triton, NL A0J 1V0
709-263-2264 Fax: 709-263-2381
townoftriton@nf.aibn.com
www.townoftriton.ca
Municipal Type: Town
Incorporated: March 11, 1958; *Area:* 7.55 sq km
Population in 2006: 1,029
Provincial Electoral District(s): Windsor-Springdale
Federal Electoral District(s): Humber-St. Barbe-Baie Verte
Next Election: Sept. 2009 (4 year terms)
Sandy Windsor, Clerk
Roy Williams, Mayor

Trout River
P.O. Box 89
Trout River, NL A0K 5P0
709-451-5376 Fax: 709-451-2127
townoftroutriver@nf.aibn.com
Municipal Type: Town
Incorporated: April 12, 1966; *Area:* 5.91 sq km
Population in 2006: 604
Provincial Electoral District(s): Humber Valley
Federal Electoral District(s): Humber-St. Barbe-Baie Verte
Next Election: Sept. 2009 (4 year terms)
Shelly Emily Butler, Clerk
Mildred Crocker, Mayor

Twillingate
P.O. Box 220
Twillingate, NL A0G 4M0
709-884-2438 Fax: 709-884-5278
Municipal Type: Town
Incorporated: Jan. 1, 1992; *Area:* 25.74 sq km
Population in 2006: 2,448
Provincial Electoral District(s): Twillingate & Fogo
Federal Electoral District(s): Bonavista-Gander-Grand Falls-Windsor
Next Election: Sept. 2009 (4 year terms)
David Burton, Clerk
Calla Guy, Mayor

Upper Island Cove
P.O. Box 149
Upper Island Cove, NL A0A 4E0
709-589-2503 Fax: 709-589-2522
townofuic@nf.aibn.com
Municipal Type: Town
Incorporated: Oct. 19, 1965; *Area:* 7.85 sq km
Population in 2006: 1,667
Provincial Electoral District(s): Port de Grave
Federal Electoral District(s): Avalon
Next Election: Sept. 2009 (4 year terms)
Baxter Drover, Clerk
George Adams, Mayor

Victoria
P.O. Box 130
Victoria, NL A0A 4G0
709-596-3783 Fax: 709-596-5020
townofvictoria@nf.sympatico.ca
Municipal Type: Town
Incorporated: July 1, 1971; *Area:* 17.64 sq km
Population in 2006: 1,769
Provincial Electoral District(s): Carbonear-Harbour Grace
Federal Electoral District(s): Avalon
Next Election: Sept. 2009 (4 year terms)
Sharon Snooks, Clerk
Arthur Burke, Mayor

Wabana
P.O. Box 1229
Wabana, NL A0A 4H0
709-488-2990 Fax: 709-488-3181
council@bellisland.net
www.bellisland.net
Municipal Type: Town
Incorporated: Aug. 28, 1950; *Area:* 14.5 sq km
Population in 2006: 2,418
Provincial Electoral District(s): Conception Bay East & Bell Island

Federal Electoral District(s): St. John's East
Next Election: Sept. 2009 (4 year terms)
Diane Butler, Clerk
dianebutler@aol.com
Gary Gosine, Mayor

Wabush
P.O. Box 190
Wabush, NL A0R 1B0
709-282-5696 Fax: 709-282-5142
fharnett@wabush.ca
www.labradorwest.com
Municipal Type: Town
Incorporated: April 11, 1967; *Area:* 46.25 sq km
Population in 2006: 1,739
Provincial Electoral District(s): Labrador West
Federal Electoral District(s): Labrador
Next Election: Sept. 2009 (4 year terms)
Martina Gale, Clerk & Treas.
townclerk@wabush.ca
James Farrell, Mayor

West St. Modeste
P.O. Box 78
West St Modeste, NL A0K 5S0
709-927-5583 Fax: 709-927-5898
townwsm@nf.sympatico.ca
Municipal Type: Town
Incorporated: Aug. 1, 1975; *Area:* 7.78 sq km
Population in 2006: 140
Provincial Electoral District(s): Cartwright-L'Anse au Clair
Federal Electoral District(s): Labrador
Next Election: Sept. 2009 (4 year terms)
Sandra O'Dell, Clerk
Agnes Pike, Mayor

Westport
P.O. Box 29
Westport, NL A0K 5R0
709-224-5501 Fax: 709-224-5501
Municipal Type: Town
Incorporated: July 18, 1967; *Area:* 5.13 sq km
Population in 2006: 246
Provincial Electoral District(s): Baie Verte
Federal Electoral District(s): Humber-St. Barbe-Baie Verte
Next Election: Sept. 2009 (4 year terms)
Peggy Randell, Clerk
Maxwell Warren, Mayor

Whitbourne
P.O. Box 119
Whitbourne, NL A0B 3K0
709-759-2780 Fax: 709-759-2016
whitbournetowncouncil@nf.aibn.com
Municipal Type: Town
Incorporated: April 16, 1968; *Area:* 21.41 sq km
Population in 2006: 855
Provincial Electoral District(s): Harbour Main-Whitbourne
Federal Electoral District(s): Avalon
Next Election: Sept. 2009 (4 year terms)
Juanita Gosse, Clerk
Lloyd Gosse, Mayor

Whiteway
Main St.
Whiteway, NL A0B 3L0
709-588-2948 Fax: 709-588-2985
townofwhiteway@nf.aibn.com
Municipal Type: Town
Incorporated: Oct. 3, 1975; *Area:* 22.64 sq km
Population in 2006: 220
Provincial Electoral District(s): Trinity-Bay de Verde
Federal Electoral District(s): Avalon
Next Election: Sept. 2009 (4 year terms)
Melinda Legge, Clerk
Kurt George, Mayor

Winterland
P.O. Box 10
Winterland, NL A0E 2Y0
709-279-3701 Fax: 709-583-3701
Municipal Type: Town
Incorporated: Nov. 24, 1970; *Area:* 54.34 sq km
Population in 2006: 337
Provincial Electoral District(s): Grand Bank
Federal Electoral District(s): Random-Burin-St. George's
Next Election: Sept. 2009 (4 year terms)
Marlyese Simms, Clerk
Ches Kenway, Mayor

Winterton
P.O. Box 59
Winterton, NL A0B 3M0
709-583-2010 Fax: 709-583-2099
wintertontowncouncil@nf.aibn.com
Municipal Type: Town
Incorporated: April 15, 1964; *Area:* 10.52 sq km
Population in 2006: 518
Provincial Electoral District(s): Trinity-Bay de Verde
Federal Electoral District(s): Avalon
Next Election: Sept. 2009 (4 year terms)
Joan Hiscock, Clerk
Jim Harnum, Mayor

Witless Bay
P.O. Box 130
Witless Bay, NL A0A 4K0
709-334-3407 Fax: 709-334-2377
townofwitlessbay@nf.aibn.com
Municipal Type: Town
Incorporated: Jan. 1, 1986; *Area:* 17.49 sq km
Population in 2006: 1,070
Provincial Electoral District(s): Ferryland
Federal Electoral District(s): Avalon
Next Election: Sept. 2009 (4 year terms)
Geraldine Caul, Clerk
Barbara Casey, Mayor

Woodstock
19 Park St.
Woodstock, NL A0K 5X0
709-251-3176 Fax: 709-251-3176
Municipal Type: Town
Incorporated: Sept. 29, 1970; *Area:* 10.09 sq km
Population in 2006: 199
Provincial Electoral District(s): Baie Verte
Federal Electoral District(s): Humber-St. Barbe-Baie Verte
Next Election: Sept. 2009 (4 year terms)
Charlene Randell, Clerk
Kirk Simms, Mayor

Woody Point
P.O. Box 100
Woody Point, NL A0K 1P0
709-453-2273 Fax: 709-453-2270
woodypoint@nf.aibn.com
www.townofwoodypoint.ca
Municipal Type: Town
Incorporated: March 27, 1956; *Area:* 2.91 sq km
Population in 2006: 355
Provincial Electoral District(s): Humber Valley
Federal Electoral District(s): Humber-St. Barbe-Baie Verte
Next Election: Sept. 2009 (4 year terms)
Heather Coates, Clerk
Everett Osmond, Mayor

York Harbour
136 Main St.
York Harbour, NL A0L 1L0
709-681-2280 Fax: 709-681-2799
Municipal Type: Town
Incorporated: June 27, 1972; *Area:* 3.9 sq km
Population in 2006: 346
Provincial Electoral District(s): Bay of Islands
Federal Electoral District(s): Humber-St. Barbe-Baie Verte
Next Election: Sept. 2009 (4 year terms)
Maria MacDonald, Clerk
Murray Sheppard, Mayor

NORTHWEST TERRITORIES

LEGISLATION: Cities, Towns and Villages Act; Hamlets Act; Charter Communities Act; Effective August 4, 2005 establishment of Tlicho Community Governments as a result of implementation of the Tlicho Self-Government and Land Claim; Settlements Act; Property Assessment and Taxation Act; Local Authorities Elections Act; Fire Protection Act; Civil Emergencies Act; Commissioner's Lands Act; Planning Act; Religious Societies Lands Act; Senior Citizens & Disabled Persons Property Tax Relief Act.

Incorporation as a city, town or village is determined by the value of all assessable land. Incorporation values: Village, $10 million; Town, $50 million; City, $200 million. All tax-based. Hamlets and Charter Communities may request tax-based status.

Local Authorities Elections: three years for cities, towns and villages; two years/staggered terms for hamlets and settlements; two to three years for charter communities. The Minister may extend or shorten terms on applications. Except for settlement councils, heads of councils are elected by separate ballot. First nations conduct their own electoral process.

Heads of Councils: Mayor, K'wati, Ehk'Wahtide, Chief, Chairperson.

First Nations provide municipal services as the main governing authority in several communities.

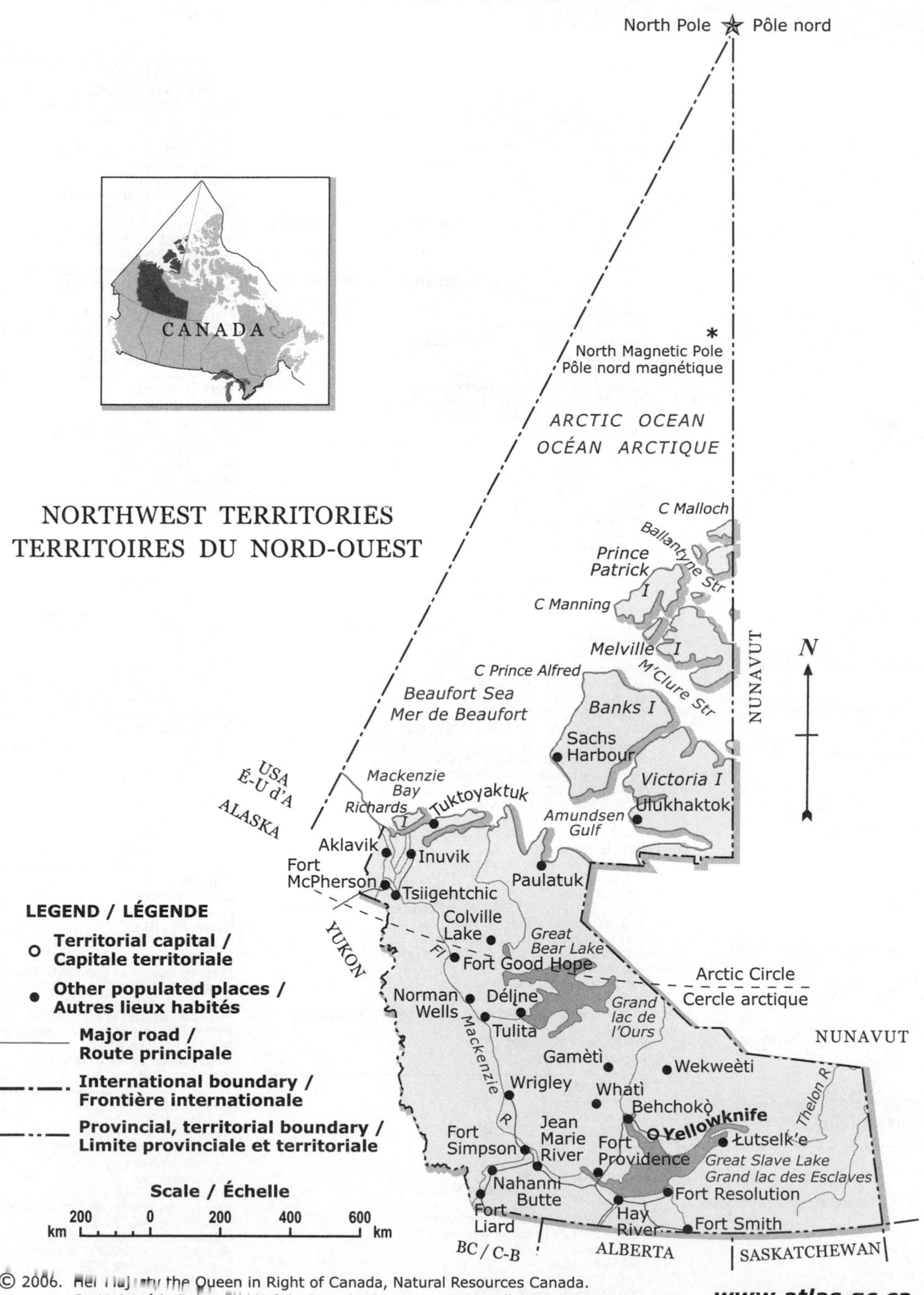

Northwest Territories

Major Municipalities in Northwest Territories

Yellowknife
P.O. Box 580
4807 - 52 St.
Yellowknife, NT X1A 2N4
867-920-5600 Fax: 867-920-5649
cityclerk@yellowknife.ca
www.yellowknife.ca
Municipal Type: City
Incorporated: Jan. 1, 1970; *Area:* 105.22 sq km
Population in 2006: 18,700
Provincial Electoral District(s): Yellowknife South; Yellowknife Centre; Frame Lake; Great Slave; Weledeh; Kam Lake, Range Lake
Federal Electoral District(s): Western Arctic
Next Election: Oct. 19, 2009

Council
Gordon Van Tighem, Mayor
gvantighem@yellowknife.ca
Lydia Bardak, City Councillor
lbardak@yellowknife.ca
Bob Brooks, City Councillor
bbrooks@yellowknife.ca
Paul Falvo, City Councillor
pfalvo@yellowknife.ca
Mark Heyck, City Councillor
mheyck@yellowknife.ca
Amanda Mallon, City Councillor
amallon@yellowknife.ca
Shelagh Montgomery, City Councillor
smontgomery@yellowknife.ca
Cory Vanthuyne, City Councillor
cvanthuyne@yellowknife.ca
David Wind, City Councillor
dwind@yellowknife.ca

Administration
Debbie Gillard, City Clerk
867-920-5646
debbie.gillard@yellowknife.ca
Max Hall, City Administrator
867-920-5624
mhall@yellowknife.ca
Darcy Hernblad, Fire Chief
867-766-5501
dhernblad@yellowknife.ca
Carl Bird, Director, Corporate Services
867-920-5666
cbird@yellowknife.ca
Jeffrey Humble, Director, Planning & Lands
867-920-5633
jhumble@yellowknife.ca
Dennis Kefalas, Director, Public Works
867-920-5639
dkefalas@yellowknife.ca
Dennis Marchiori, Director, Public Safety
867-920-5661
dmarchiori@yellowknife.ca
Peter Neugebauer, Director, Economic Development
867-920-5660
pneugebauer@yellowknife.ca
Grant White, Director, Community Services
867-920-5636
gwhite@yellowknife.ca
Kerry Penney, Manager, Legal Services
kpenney@yellowknife.ca
Nalini Naidoo, Manager, Planning & Lands
867-920-5675
nnaidoo@yellowknife.ca
Marie Couturier, Manager, Human Resources
mcouturier@yellowknife.ca
Clem Hand, Manager, Procurement Services
867-920-5617
chand@yellowknife.ca
Bruce Underhay, Manager, Solid Waste Management Facility
867-669-3404
bunderhay@yellowknife.ca
Sharolynn Woodward, Manager, Information Technology
867-920-5651
swoodward@yellowknife.ca
Dennis Althouse, Superintendent, Operations & Maintenance
867-766-5512
dalthouse@yellowknife.ca

Other Municipalities in Northwest Territories

Aklavik
P.O. Box 88
Aklavik, NT X0E 0A0
867-978-2351 Fax: 867-978-2434 Additional Phone: 867-978-2361
saoaklavik@permafrost.com
Municipal Type: Hamlet
Incorporated: Jan. 1, 1974; *Area:* 8.16 sq km
Population in 2006: 594
Provincial Electoral District(s): Mackenzie Delta
Federal Electoral District(s): Western Arctic
Next Election: Dec. 8, 2008
Knute Hansen, Mayor
Evelyn Storr, Sr. Admin. Officer

Behchoko
P.O. Box 68
Behchoko, NT X0E 0Y0
867-392-6500 Fax: 867-392-6139 Additional Phone: 867-392-6561
hamlet@arcticdata.ca
Municipal Type: Tlicho Community Government
Area: 75.08 sq km
Population in 2006: 1,894
Provincial Electoral District(s): Monfwi
Federal Electoral District(s): Western Arctic
Next Election: June 2009
Terry Testart, Sr. Admin. Officer
Leon Lafferty, Chief

Colville Lake
Behdzi Ahda First Nation
P.O. Box 53
Colville Lake, NT X0E 0L0
867-709-2200 Fax: 867-709-2202
Joseph_Kochon@airware.ca
Municipal Type: Settlement Corporation
Incorporated: Nov. 30, 1995; *Area:* 128.3 sq km
Population in 2006: 126
Provincial Electoral District(s): Sahtu
Federal Electoral District(s): Western Arctic
Next Election: Dec. 8, 2008
Joseph Kochon, Band Manager
Richard Kochon, Chief

Déline
General Delivery
Deline, NT X0E 0G0
867-589-4800 Fax: 867-589-4106 Additional Phone: 867-589-3604
erma_baton@gov.deline.ca
www.deline.ca
Municipal Type: Charter Community
Incorporated: April 1, 1993; *Area:* 79.33 sq km
Population in 2006: 525
Provincial Electoral District(s): Sahtu
Federal Electoral District(s): Western Arctic
Note: Déline sets its election date through its community charter.
Ronald Mackeinzo, Sr. Admin. Officer
Raymond Tutcho, Mayor

Detah
Yellowknife Dene First Nation
P.O. Box 2514
Yellowknife, NT X1A 2P8
867-873-4307 Fax: 867-873-5969
Municipal Type: First Nations/Governing Authority
Area: 1.34 sq km
Population in 2006: 247
Provincial Electoral District(s): Weledeh
Federal Electoral District(s): Western Arctic
Freddy Alfred Sangris, Chief

Enterprise
526 Robin Rd.
Enterprise, NT X0E 0R1
867-984-3491 Fax: 867-984-3400
sao_enterprise@airware.ca
Municipal Type: Settlement Corporation
Incorporated: July 1, 1988; *Area:* 286.9 sq km
Population in 2006: 97
Provincial Electoral District(s): Deh Cho
Federal Electoral District(s): Western Arctic
Next Election: Dec. 8, 2008
Scotty Edgerton, Sr. Admin Officer
Dave Richards, Mayor

Fort Good Hope
K'asho Got'ine Charter Community
P.O. Box 80
Fort Good Hope, NT X0E 0H0
867-598-2231 Fax: 867-598-2024 Additional Phone: 867-598-2232
fredrabisca@hotmail.com
Municipal Type: Charter Community
Incorporated: April 1, 1995; *Area:* 52.82 sq km
Population in 2006: 557
Provincial Electoral District(s): Sahtu
Federal Electoral District(s): Western Arctic
Note: Fort Good Hope sets its election date through its community charter.
Fred Rabesca, Sr. Admin. Officer
Lucy Jackson, Chief

Fort Liard
General Delivery
Fort Liard, NT X0G 0A0
867-770-4104 Fax: 867-770-4004
sao@fortliard.com
www.fortliard.com
Municipal Type: Hamlet
Incorporated: April 1, 1987; *Area:* 67.96 sq km
Population in 2006: 583
Provincial Electoral District(s): Nahendeh
Federal Electoral District(s): Western Arctic
Next Election: Dec. 8, 2008
Mike Drake, Mayor
myr@fortliard.com
John McKee, Sr. Admin. Officer

Fort McPherson
P.O. Box 57
Fort McPherson, NT X0E 0J0
867-952-2428 Fax: 867-952-2725
tjenkins@hamlet.fortmcpherson.nt.ca
Municipal Type: Hamlet
Incorporated: Nov. 1, 1986; *Area:* 53.06 sq km
Population in 2006: 776
Provincial Electoral District(s): Mackenzie Delta
Federal Electoral District(s): Western Arctic
Next Election: Dec. 8, 2008
Rebecca Blake, Mayor
Troy Jenkins, Sr. Admin. Officer

Fort Providence
P.O. Box 290
Fort Providence, NT X0E 0L0
867-699-3441 Fax: 867-699-3360
Albertl@ssimicro.com
Municipal Type: Hamlet
Incorporated: Jan. 1, 1987; *Area:* 256.33 sq km
Population in 2006: 727
Provincial Electoral District(s): Deh Cho
Federal Electoral District(s): Western Arctic
Next Election: Dec. 8, 2008
Tina Gargan, Mayor
Albert Lafferty, Sr. Admin. Officer

Fort Resolution
c/o Deninoo Community Council
General Delivery
Fort Resolution, NT X0E 0M0
867-394-4556 Fax: 867-394-5415
dcc_finance@airware.ca
Municipal Type: Settlement Corporation
Incorporated: April 1, 1988; *Area:* 455.06 sq km
Population in 2006: 484
Provincial Electoral District(s): Tu Nedhe
Federal Electoral District(s): Western Arctic
Tausia Lal, Sr. Admin. Officer
Elizabeth Ann Mckay, Mayor

Fort Simpson
P.O. Box 438
Fort Simpson, NT X0E 0N0
867-695-2253 Fax: 867-695-2005
sao@fortsimpson.com
www.fortsimpson.com
Municipal Type: Village
Incorporated: Jan. 1, 1973; *Area:* 78.32 sq km
Population in 2006: 1,216
Provincial Electoral District(s): Nahendeh
Federal Electoral District(s): Western Arctic
Next Election: Oct. 19, 2009
L. Beaulieu, Clerk
Duncan Canvin, Mayor
mayor@fortsimpson.com

Fort Smith
P.O. Box 147
174 McDougal Rd.
Fort Smith, NT X0E 0P0
867-872-8400 Fax: 867-872-8401
townoffortsmith@northwestel.net
www.town.fort-smith.nt.ca
Municipal Type: Town
Incorporated: Oct. 1, 1966; *Area:* 92.79 sq km
Population in 2006: 2,364
Provincial Electoral District(s): Thebacha
Federal Electoral District(s): Western Arctic
Next Election: Oct. 19, 2009
Roy Scott, Sr. Admin. Officer
roy.scott@northwestel.net
Peter Martselos, Mayor

Gamèti
Gameti First Nation
P.O. Box 1
Gameti, NT X0E 1R0
867-997-3441 Fax: 867-997-3411
sao@gameti.org
Municipal Type: Tlicho Community Government
Incorporated: Aug. 4, 2005; *Area:* 9.18 sq km
Population in 2006: 283
Provincial Electoral District(s): Monfwi
Federal Electoral District(s): Western Arctic
Next Election: June 2009
Annette Hastie, Sr. Admin. Officer
Henry Gon, Chief

Hay River
73 Woodland Dr.
Hay River, NT X0E 1G1
867-874-6522 Fax: 867-874-3237
townhall@hayriver.com
www.hayriver.com
Municipal Type: Town
Incorporated: June 16, 1963; *Area:* 132.58 sq km
Population in 2006: 3,648
Provincial Electoral District(s): Hay River North; Hay River South
Federal Electoral District(s): Western Arctic
Next Election: Oct. 19, 2009
Terry Molenkemp, Sr. Admin Officer
molenkamp@hayriver.com
John Pollard, Mayor

Hay River Reserve - K'atlodeeche First Nation
Katlodeechee First Nation
P.O. Box 3060
Hay River, NT X0E 1G0
867-874-6701 Fax: 867-874-3229
hrdb@ssimicro.com
Municipal Type: Reserve
Area: 134.21 sq km
Population in 2006: 309
Provincial Electoral District(s): Deh Cho
Federal Electoral District(s): Western Arctic
Keith Marshall, Band Manager
Alec Sunrise, Chief

Inuvik
P.O. Box 1160
2 Firth St.
Inuvik, NT X0E 0T0
867-777-8600 Fax: 867-777-8601
info@town.inuvik.nt.ca
www.inuvik.ca
Municipal Type: Town
Incorporated: Jan. 1, 1979; *Area:* 49.76 sq km
Population in 2006: 3,484
Provincial Electoral District(s): Inuvik Twin Lakes; Inuvik Boot Lake
Federal Electoral District(s): Western Arctic
Next Election: Oct. 19, 2009
Ken Crocker, Acting Sr. Admin. Officer & Director, Finance
KCrocker@town.inuvik.nt.ca
Derek Lindsay, Mayor
dlindsay@town.inuvik.nt.ca

Jean Marie River
TthedzedK'edili First Nation
General Delivery
Fort Simpson, NT X0E 0N0
867-809-2000 Fax: 867-809-2002
bandmanager@jmrfirstnation.com
www.jmrfirstnation.com
Municipal Type: First Nations/Governing Authority
Area: 37.26 sq km
Population in 2006: 81
Provincial Electoral District(s): Nahendeh
Federal Electoral District(s): Western Arctic
Tammy Neal, Band Manager
Stanley Sanguez, Chief

Kakisa
Ka'a'gee Tu First Nation
P.O. Box 4428
Hay River, NT X0E 1G4
867-825-2000 Fax: 867-825-2002
kakisa@ssimicro.com
Municipal Type: First Nations/Governing Authority
Area: 94.82 sq km
Population in 2006: 52
Provincial Electoral District(s): Deh Cho
Federal Electoral District(s): Western Arctic
Ruby Landry, Council Manager
Lloyd Chicot, Chief

Lutsel K'e
Lutsel K'e Dene Band
P.O. Box 28
Lutselk'e, NT X0E 1A0
867-370-7000 Fax: 867-370-3010
cyberia@mts.net
Municipal Type: First Nations/Governing Authority
Area: 43.01 sq km
Population in 2006: 318
Provincial Electoral District(s): Tu Nedhe
Federal Electoral District(s): Western Arctic
Janice Anderson, Sr. Admin. Officer & Band Manager
Adeline Jonasson, Chief

Nahanni Butte
Nahanni Butte First Nation
General Delivery
Fort Simpson, NT X0E 0N0
867-602-2900 Fax: 867-602-2910
j_ivey19@hotmail.com
Municipal Type: First Nations/Governing Authority
Area: 78.96 sq km
Population in 2006: 115
Provincial Electoral District(s): Nahendeh
Federal Electoral District(s): Western Arctic
Bernice Swanson, Band Manager
Eric Betsaka, Chief

Norman Wells
P.O. Box 5
Norman Wells, NT X0E 0V0
867-587-3700 Fax: 867-587-3701
info@normanwells.com
www.normanwells.com
Municipal Type: Town
Incorporated: April 12, 1992; *Area:* 93.28 sq km
Population in 2006: 761
Provincial Electoral District(s): Sahtu
Federal Electoral District(s): Western Arctic
Next Election: Oct. 19, 2009
Ian Fremantle, Town Manager
townmgr@normanwells.com
Peter Wilfred Guther, Mayor

Paulatuk
P.O. Box 98
Paulatuk, NT X0E 1N0
867-580-3531 Fax: 867-580-3703
hopaulatuk@hotmail.com
Municipal Type: Hamlet
Incorporated: April 1, 1987; *Area:* 66.76 sq km
Population in 2006: 294
Provincial Electoral District(s): Nunakput
Federal Electoral District(s): Western Arctic
Next Election: Dec. 8, 2008
Ray Ruben, Mayor
Debbie Gordon-Ruben, Sr. Admin. Officer

Sachs Harbour
General Delivery
Sachs Harbour, NT X0E 0Z0
867-690-4351 Fax: 867-690-4802
rkaslak@lycos.com
Municipal Type: Hamlet
Incorporated: April 1, 1986; *Area:* 290.94 sq km
Population in 2006: 122
Provincial Electoral District(s): Nunakput
Federal Electoral District(s): Western Arctic
Next Election: Dec. 8, 2008
Robert Eldridge, Mayor
Raymond Kaslak, Sr. Admin. Officer

Trout Lake
Sambaa K'e Dene Band
P.O. Box 10
Trout Lake, NT X0E 1Z0
867-206-2800 Fax: 867-206-2828
rjumbo@direcway.com
Municipal Type: First Nations/Governing Authority
Area: 119.42 sq km
Population in 2006: 86
Provincial Electoral District(s): Nahendeh
Federal Electoral District(s): Western Arctic
Rebecca Jumbo, Sr. Admin. Officer
Dolphus Jumbo, Chief

Tsiigehtchic
General Delivery
Tsiigehtchic, NT X0E 0B0
867-953-3201 Fax: 867-953-3302
dannylennie@msn.com
Municipal Type: Charter Community
Incorporated: June 21, 1993; *Area:* 48.98 sq km
Population in 2006: 175
Provincial Electoral District(s): Mackenzie Delta
Federal Electoral District(s): Western Arctic
Note: Tsiigehtchic sets its election date through its community charter.
Danny Lennie, Sr. Admin. Officer
Peter Ross, Chief

Tuktoyaktuk
P.O. Box 120
Tuktoyaktuk, NT X0E 1C0
867-977-2286 Fax: 867-977-2110
jnt@hamletoftuk.nt.ca
Municipal Type: Hamlet
Incorporated: April 1, 1970; *Area:* 11.07 sq km
Population in 2006: 870
Provincial Electoral District(s): Nunakput
Federal Electoral District(s): Western Arctic
Next Election: Dec. 8, 2008
Jackie Jacobson, Mayor
Debbie Raddi, Sr. Admin. Officer

Tulita
General Delivery
Tulita, NT X0E 0K0
867-588-4471 Fax: 867-588-4908
shorassi@allstream.net
Municipal Type: Hamlet
Incorporated: April 1, 1984; *Area:* 51.74 sq km
Population in 2006: 505
Provincial Electoral District(s): Sahtu
Federal Electoral District(s): Western Arctic
Next Election: Dec. 8, 2008
Gordon Yakeleya, Mayor
Peter Bahya, Sr. Admin. Officer

Ulukhaktok
P.O. Box 157
Ulukhaktok, NT X0E 0S0
867-396-8000 Fax: 867-396-8001
holmansao@yahoo.ca
Municipal Type: Hamlet
Incorporated: April 1, 1984; *Area:* 124.43 sq km
Population in 2006: 398
Provincial Electoral District(s): Nunakput
Federal Electoral District(s): Western Arctic
Next Election: Dec. 8, 2008
Note: Formerly known as Holman.
Peter Malgokak, Mayor
Ralph Butterworth, Sr. Admin. Officer

Wekweeti
Community Government of Wekweeti
P.O. Box 69
Wekweeti, NT X1A 1W0
867-713-2010 Fax: 867-713-2707
bandmanger@arcticdata.ca
Municipal Type: Tlicho Community Government
Incorporated: Aug. 4, 2005; *Area:* 14.66 sq km
Population in 2006: 137
Provincial Electoral District(s): Monfwi
Federal Electoral District(s): Western Arctic
Next Election: June 2009
Randy Bergen, Sr. Admin. Officer
Charlie Football, Chief

Whati
Community Government of Whati
P.O. Box 92
Whati, NT X0E 1P0
867-573-3401 Fax: 867-573-3222
whaticc@internorth.com
Municipal Type: Tlicho Community Government
Incorporated: Aug. 4, 2005; *Area:* 15.18 sq km
Population in 2006: 460
Provincial Electoral District(s): Monfwi
Federal Electoral District(s): Western Arctic
Next Election: June 2009
Charlie J. Nitsiza, Chief
Dan Moore, Sr. Admin. Officer

Wrigley
Pehdzeh Ki First Nation
General Delivery
Wrigley, NT X0E 1E0
867-581-3321 Fax: 867-581-3329 Additional Phone: 867-581-3581
Municipal Type: First Nations/Governing Authority
Area: 55.83 sq km
Population in 2006: 122
Provincial Electoral District(s): Nahendeh
Federal Electoral District(s): Western Arctic
Mike Canadian, Sr. Admin. Officer
Tim Lennie, Chief

NOVA SCOTIA

Nova Scotia is geographically divided into 18 counties. Twelve of these constitute separate municipalities (three are regional municipalities). The remaining six are each divided into two districts and each of these constitutes a separate municipality. Thus there are 21 rural municipalities. Within each of these areas are 31 autonomous incorporated towns and other local organizations with limited jurisdiction, including school boards, boards of school trustees, village commissions, local service commissions, rural fire districts and other special purpose forms.

Incorporation of a town is governed by the Municipal Government Act, Sections 383 to 393 (dissolution is governed by Sections 394 to 402).

The organization of municipalities and villages is governed by the Municipal Government Act. Additional regulation is provided by the Municipal Finance Corporation Act.

All general and special municipal elections, including elections for school board members, are governed by the Municipal Elections Act, 1979. The term of office for mayors, councillors, aldermen, and elective school board members is four years. Elections take place on the third Saturday in October in every fourth year, thus: October 2008, October 2012.

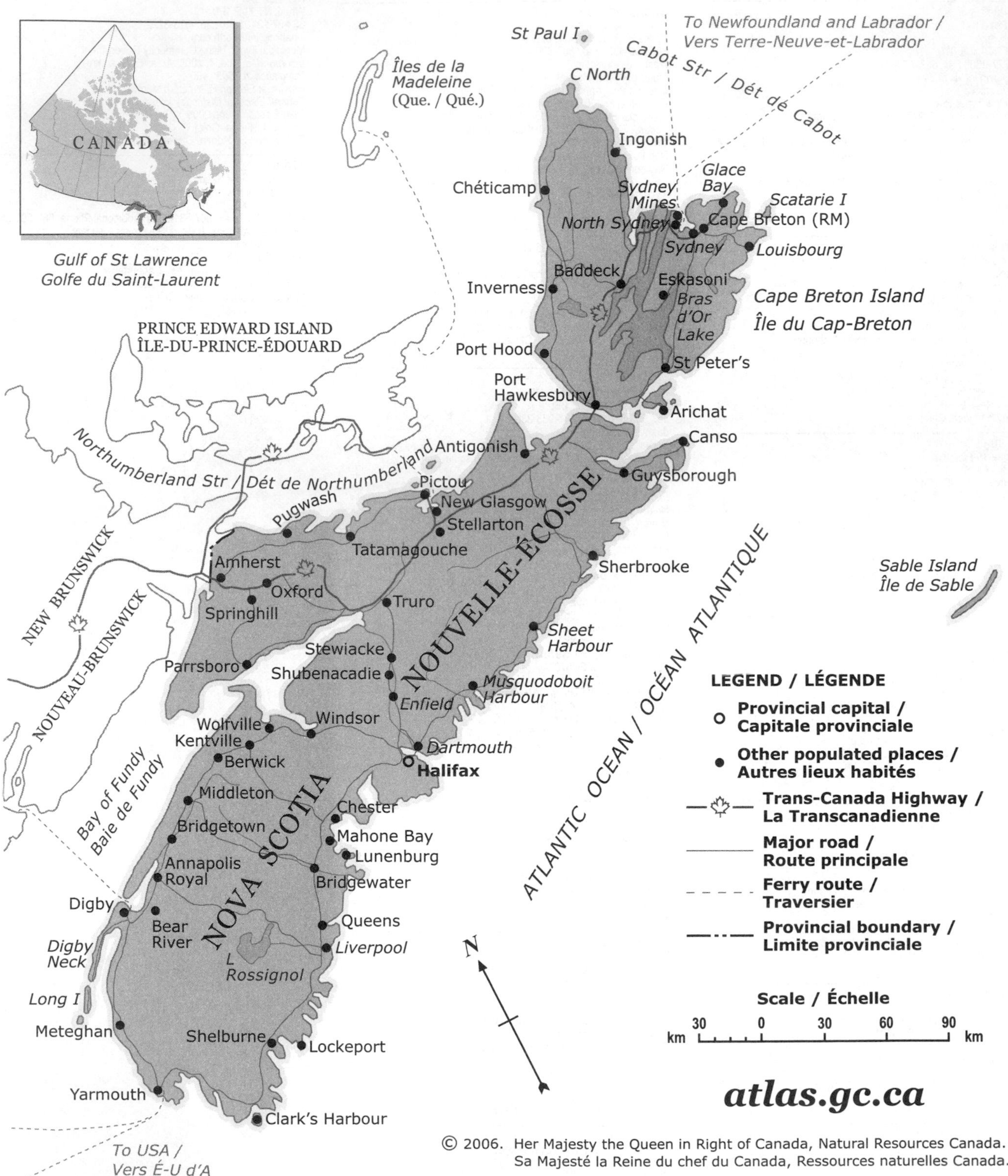

Nova Scotia

Counties & Municipal Districts in Nova Scotia

Cape Breton
Civic Centre
320 Esplanade
Sydney, NS B1P 7B9
902-563-5005 Fax: 902-564-0481
cbrm@cbrm.ns.ca
www.cbrm.ns.ca
Municipal Type: Regional Municipality
Incorporated: Aug. 1, 1995; *Area:* 2,433.33 sq km
County or District: Cape Breton; *Population in 2006:* 102,250
Provincial Electoral District(s): Cape Breton Centre; Cape Breton East; Cape Breton North; Cape Breton Nova; Cape Breton South; Cape Breton-The Lakes
Federal Electoral District(s): Cape Breton-Canso; Sydney-Victoria
Next Election: Oct. 2008 (4 year terms)
Gordon MacLeod, Councillor, Ward(s): District 14
gmacleod@cbrm.ns.ca

Council
John W. Morgan, Mayor
jwmorgan@cbrm.ns.ca
Brian Lahey, Councillor, Ward(s): District 1
blahey@cbrm.ns.ca
Kevin Saccary, Councillor, Ward(s): District 2
ksaccary@cbrm.ns.ca
Lee McNeil, Councillor, Ward(s): District 3
lmcneil@cbrm.ns.ca
George MacDonald, Councillor, Ward(s): District 4
gmmacdonald@cbrm.ns.ca
Darren Bruckschwaiger, Councillor, Ward(s): District 5
drbruckschwaiger@cbrm.ns.ca
Kim Desveaux, Councillor, Ward(s): District 6
kadesveaux@cbrm.ns.ca
Jim MacLeod, Councillor, Ward(s): District 7
jmacleod@cbrm.ns.ca
Ray Paruch, Councillor, Ward(s): District 8
frparuch@cbrm.ns.ca
Tom Wilson, Councillor, Ward(s): District 9
twilson@cbrm.ns.ca
Derek Mombourquette, Councillor, Ward(s): District 10
dcmombourquette@cbrm.ns.ca
Dave LeBlanc, Councillor, Ward(s): District 11
dfleblanc@cbrm.ns.ca
Claire Detheridge, Councillor, Ward(s): District 12
mcdetheridge@cbrm.ns.ca
Mae Rowe, Councillor, Ward(s): District 13
mjrowe@cbrm.ns.ca
Clarence Prince, Councillor, Ward(s): District 15
cprince@cbrm.ns.ca
Wesley Stubbert, Councillor, Ward(s): District 16
wstubbert@cbrm.ns.ca

Administration
Bernie White, Municipal Clerk
902-563-5010
bjwhite@cbrm.ns.ca
Marie Walsh, Director, Finance
902-563-5014
Jerry Ryan, CAO
Robin B. Campbell, Regional Solicitor
902-563-5045
rbcampbell@cbrm.ns.ca
Edgar MacLeod, Police Chief
902-563-5095
eamacleod@cbrmps.cape-breton.ns.ca
Angus Fleming, Director, Human Resources
902-563-5058
acfleming@cbrm.ns.ca
Doug Foster, Director, Planning
902-563-5070
Kevin MacDonald, Director, Engineering & Public Works
902-563-5051
Bernie MacKinnon, Director, Fire Services
902-563-5132
Bob McNeil, Director, Technology & Communications
902-563-5066
rjmcneil@cbrm.ns.ca
Fred Brooks, Sr. Manager, Recreation
902-563-5510
ftbrooks@cbrm.ns.ca
Malcolm Gillis, Manager, Planning & Development
Mike MacKeigan, Manager, Utilities
Roger Munroe, Manager, Solid Waste
902-563-5182

Halifax Regional Municipality
P.O. Box 1749
1841 Argyle St.
Halifax, NS B3J 3A5
902-490-4000 Fax: 902-490-4208 Toll Free Phone: 1-800-835-6428
www.halifax.ca
Municipal Type: Regional Municipality
Incorporated: April 1, 1996; *Area:* 5,490.18 sq km
Population in 2006: 372,679
Provincial Electoral District(s): Bedford-Birch Cove; Cole Harbour; Cole Harbour-Eastern Passage; Dartmouth E.; Dartmouth N.; Dartmouth S.-Portland Valley; Eastern Shore; Hlfx Atlantic; Hlfx Chebucto; Hlfx Citadel-Sable Island; Hlfx-Clayton Park; Hlfx Fairview; Hlfx Needham; Hammonds Plains-Upper Sackville; Preston; Sackville-Cobequid; Timberlea-Prospect; Waverly-Fall River-Beaver Bank
Federal Electoral District(s): Central Nova; Cumberland-Colchester-Musquodoboit Valley; Dartmouth-Cole Harbour; Halifax; Halifax West; Sackville-Eastern Shore; South Shore-St. Margaret's
Next Election: Oct. 2008 (4 year terms)

Council
Peter J. Kelly, M.B.A., Mayor
902-490-4010
kellyp@halifax.ca
Steve Streatch, Councillor, Ward(s): District 1
streats@halifax.ca
Barry Dalrymple, Councillor, Ward(s): District 2
barry.dalrymple@halifax.ca
David Hendsbee, Councillor, Ward(s): District 3
david.hendsbee@halifax.ca
Lorelei Nicoll, Councillor, Ward(s): District 4
lorelei.nicoll@halifax.ca
Gloria McCluskey, Councillor, Ward(s): District 5
mcclusg@halifax.ca
Darren Fisher, Councillor, Ward(s): District 6
darren.fisher@halifax.ca
Bill Karsten, Councillor, Ward(s): District 7
karsteb@halifax.ca
Jackie Barkhouse, Councillor, Ward(s): District 8
barkhoj@halifax.ca
Jim Smith, Councillor, Ward(s): District 9
smithj@halifax.ca
Mary Wile, Councillor, Ward(s): District 10
wilema@halifax.ca
Jerry Blumenthal, Councillor, Ward(s): District 11
blumenj@halifax.ca
Dawn Marie Sloane, Councillor, Ward(s): District 12
sloaned@halifax.ca
Sue Uteck, Councillor, Ward(s): District 13
utecks@halifax.ca
Jennifer Watts, Councillor, Ward(s): District 14
jennifer.watts@halifax.ca
Russell Walker, Councillor, Ward(s): District 15
walkerr@halifax.ca
Debbie Hum, Councillor, Ward(s): District 16
humd@halifax.ca
Linda Mosher, Councillor, Ward(s): District 17
mosherl@halifax.ca
Stephen Adams, Councillor, Ward(s): District 18
adamss@halifax.ca
Brad Johns, Councillor, Ward(s): District 19
brad.johns@halifax.ca
Robert (Bob) P. Harvey, Councillor, Ward(s): District 20
harveyb@halifax.ca
Tim Outhit, Councillor, Ward(s): District 21
outhitt@halifax.ca
Reg Rankin, Councillor, Ward(s): District 22
rankinr@halifax.ca
Peter Lund, Councillor, Ward(s): District 23
peter.lund@halifax.ca

Administration
Cathy Mellett, Acting Municipal Clerk
902-490-4210
clerks@halifax.ca
Cathie O'Toole, C.G.A., Director, Finance
Dan English, M.P.A., CAO
902-490-6430
Wayne Anstey, Q.C., B.Sc., LL.B., Deputy CAO, Operations
902-490-4426
Mike Labrecque, Deputy CAO, Corporate Services & Strategy
902-490-1520
Frank Beazley, Chief, Halifax Regional Police
902-490-6500
Bill Mosher, Chief Director, Fire & Emergency Services
Phillip Townsend, Director, Infrastructure & Asset Management
Brad Anguish, Director, Business Planning & Information Management and Harbour Solutions Project
Mary Ellen Donovan, B.Sc., LL.B., Director, Legal Services
902-490-4226
Paul Dunphy, B.A., Director, Community Development
Ken Reashor, Acting Director, Transportation & Public Works
Catherine Mullally, Director, Human Resources
Carl D. Yates, M.A.Sc., P.Eng., General Manager, Halifax Water
902-490-4827, Fax: 902-490-4808
general.manager@hrwc.ca
Jim Bauld, Manager, Solid Waste Resources
902-490-6606
Alan Brady, Manager, Wastewater Treatment
302-835-9566
Jim Donovan, Project Manager, Economic Strategy
902-490-1742
Shaune MacKinlay, Manager, Public Affairs
Cathie Osborne, P.Eng., Manager, Business Systems & Control
902-490-4093
John P. Sheppard, P.Eng., Manager, Environmental Engineering Services
902-490-6958, Fax: 902-490-4858
sheppaj@halifax.ca
Brian Taylor, Manager, Transit Services
902-490-6388
John Sibbald, Coordinator, Pollution Prevention
902-490-5527
sibbalj@halifax.ca
Peter Lund, Chair, Solid Waste Resource Advisory Committee

Queens
P.O. Box 1264
249 White Point Rd.
Liverpool, NS B0T 1K0
902-354-3453 Fax: 902-354-7473
nfo@regionofqueens.com
www.regionofqueens.com
Municipal Type: Regional Municipality
Incorporated: April 1, 1996; *Area:* 2,386.58 sq km
County or District: Queens; *Population in 2006:* 11,177
Provincial Electoral District(s): Queens
Federal Electoral District(s): South Shore-St. Margaret's
Next Election: Oct. 2008 (4 year terms)

Council
John G. Leefe, Mayor
jleefe@regionofqueens.com
Darlene Norman, Councillor, Ward(s): District 1
ross.surf@ns.sympatico.ca
Sheldon Brannen, Councillor, Ward(s): District 2
sbrannen@himmelman.ca
Owen Hamlin, Councillor, Ward(s): District 3
mrh@ns.sympatico.ca
Bruce Inglis, Councillor, Ward(s): District 4
bruceinglis@live.ca
Mervin Hartlen, Councillor, Ward(s): District 5
mhartlen@ns.sympatico.ca
Randi Dickie, Councillor, Ward(s): District 6
randidickie@eastlink.ca
John Croft, Councillor, Ward(s): District 7
jfcroft@ns.sympatico.ca
R. Douglas Adams, Councillor, Ward(s): District 8
doug.adams@ns.sympatico.ca
Peter Waterman, Councillor, Ward(s): District 9
pmwaterman@eastlink.ca

Administration
Kathleen Rafuse, Director, Finance
krafuse@regionofqueens.com

Major Municipalities in Nova Scotia

Truro
P.O. Box 427
695 Prince St.
Truro, NS B2N 5C5
902-895-4484 Fax: 902-893-0501
town@truro.ca
www.truro.ca
Municipal Type: City
Incorporated: May 6, 1875; *Area:* 37.63 sq km
County or District: Colchester; *Population in 2006:* 11,765
Provincial Electoral District(s): Truro-Bible Hill
Federal Electoral District(s): Cumberland-Colchester-Musquodoboit Valley
Next Election: Oct. 2008 (4 year terms)
W.R. (Bill) Mills, Mayor
Diane Bennett Cook, Councillor, Ward(s): 1
Raymond Tynes, Councillor, Ward(s): 1
Charles Cox, Councillor, Ward(s): 2
Brian Kinsman, Councillor, Ward(s): 2
Sharron Byers, Councillor, Ward(s): 3
Greg MacArthur, Councillor, Ward(s): 3
Jim Langille, CAO
jlangille@truro.ca
Andrew McKinnon, Director, Public Works & Traffic Authority
amackinnon@truro.ca
Audrey Buchanan, Senior Engineer
Doug MacKenzie, Director, Parks & Recreation Committee
dmackenzie@truro.ca
Tom Bremner, Chief, Fire
Juanita Bigelow, Administrator, Planning
jbigelow@truro.ca
Genevieve DeCoste, Superintendent, Water Treatment Plant
wpt@truro.ca

Other Municipalities in Nova Scotia

Amherst
P.O. Box 516
5 Ratchford St.
Amherst, NS B4H 4A1
902-667-3352 Fax: 902-667-3356
rpurdy@town.amherst.ns.ca
www.town.amherst.ns.ca
Municipal Type: Town
Incorporated: Dec. 18, 1889; *Area:* 12.02 sq km
County or District: Cumberland; *Population in 2006:* 9,505
Provincial Electoral District(s): Cumberland North
Federal Electoral District(s): Cumberland-Colchester-Musquodoboit Valley
Next Election: Oct. 2008 (4 year terms)
Gregory D. Herrett, CA, CAO
gherrett@town.amherst.ns.ca
Jerry A. Hallee, Mayor
jhallee@town.amherst.ns.ca

Annapolis Royal
P.O. Box 310
285 St. George St.
Annapolis Royal, NS B0S 1A0
902-532-2043 Fax: 902-532-7443
admin@annapolisroyal.com
www.annapolisroyal.com
Municipal Type: Town
Incorporated: Nov. 29, 1892; *Area:* 2.04 sq km
County or District: Annapolis; *Population in 2006:* 444
Provincial Electoral District(s): Annapolis
Federal Electoral District(s): West Nova
Next Election: Oct. 2008 (4 year terms)
John Kinsella, Mayor
Amery Boyer, CAO
cao@annapolisroyal.com

Antigonish
274 Main St.
Antigonish, NS B2G 2C4
902-863-2351 Fax: 902-863-9201
bmacneil@townofantigonish.ca
www.townofantigonish.ca
Municipal Type: Town
Incorporated: Jan. 9, 1889; *Area:* 5.15 sq km
County or District: Antigonish; *Population in 2006:* 4,236
Provincial Electoral District(s): Antigonish
Federal Electoral District(s): Central Nova
Next Election: Oct. 2008 (4 year terms)
Kathleen Chisholm, Mayor
Brian MacNeil, Clerk-Treas.

Aylesford
P.O. Box 91
Aylesford, NS B0P 1C0
902-847-0827 Fax: 902-847-0827
village.ayl@ns.sympatico.ca
Municipal Type: Village

County or District: Kings;
Provincial Electoral District(s): Kings West
Federal Electoral District(s): West Nova
Next Election: Oct. 2008 (4 year terms)
Trudie Spinney, Clerk-Treas.
Peter Sayers, Chair

Baddeck
P.O. Box 63
Baddeck, NS B0E 1B0
902-295-3666 Fax: 902-295-1729
erin.bradley@countyvictoria.ns.ca
www.baddeck.com
Municipal Type: Village

County or District: Victoria; *Population in 2006:* 982
Provincial Electoral District(s): Victoria-The Lakes
Federal Electoral District(s): Sydney-Victoria
Next Election: Oct. 2008 (4 year terms)
Erin Bradley, Clerk-Treas.
Eddie Keeling, Chair

Berwick
P.O. Box 130
236 Commercial St.
Berwick, NS B0P 1E0
902-538-8068 Fax: 902-538-3724
general@town.berwick.ns.ca
www.town.berwick.ns.ca
Municipal Type: Town
Incorporated: May 25, 1923; *Area:* 6.8 sq km
County or District: Kings; *Population in 2006:* 2,454
Provincial Electoral District(s): Kings West
Federal Electoral District(s): West Nova
Next Election: Oct. 2008 (4 year terms)
Bob Ashley, CAO
John P. Prall, Mayor

Bible Hill
67 Pictou Rd.
Bible Hill, NS B2N 2R9
902-893-8083 Fax: 902-897-0430
office@biblehill.ca
www.village.biblehill.ns.ca
Municipal Type: Village

County or District: Colchester; *Population in 2006:* 5,500
Provincial Electoral District(s): Truro-Bible Hill
Federal Electoral District(s): Cumberland-Colchester-Musquodoboit Valley
Next Election: Oct. 2008 (4 year terms)
Robert Christianson, Clerk-Treas.
chris@biblehill.ca
Richard Hilliard, Chair

Bridgetown
P.O. Box 609
271 Granville St.
Bridgetown, NS B0S 1C0
902-665-4637 Fax: 902-665-5011
bridgetown@ns.sympatico.ca
www.town.bridgetown.ns.ca
Municipal Type: Town
Incorporated: Sept. 15, 1897; *Area:* 3.54 sq km
County or District: Annapolis; *Population in 2006:* 972
Provincial Electoral District(s): Annapolis
Federal Electoral District(s): West Nova
Next Election: Oct. 2008 (4 year terms)
John F. Langmead, CAO
Art P. Marshall, Mayor

Bridgewater
60 Pleasant St.
Bridgewater, NS B4V 3X9
902-543-4651 Fax: 902-543-6876
admin@town.bridgewater.ns.ca
www.town.bridgewater.ns.ca
Municipal Type: Town
Incorporated: Feb. 13, 1899; *Area:* 13.6 sq km
County or District: Lunenburg; *Population in 2006:* 7,944
Provincial Electoral District(s): Lunenburg West
Federal Electoral District(s): South Shore-St. Margaret's
Next Election: Oct. 2008 (4 year terms)
Ken Smith, Town Manager
Carroll Publicover, Mayor

Canning
P.O. Box 9
2229 North Ave.
Canning, NS B0P 1H0
902-582-3768 Fax: 902-582-3068
village.canning@ns.sympatico.ca
Municipal Type: Village

County or District: Kings;
Provincial Electoral District(s): Kings North
Federal Electoral District(s): Kings-Hants
Next Election: Oct. 2008 (4 year terms)
Gloria Porter, Clerk-Treas.
Robert Churchill, Chair

Canso
P.O. Box 189
11 Telegraph St.
Canso, NS B0H 1H0
902-366-2525 Fax: 902-366-3093
michelle@townofcanso.com
www.townofcanso.com
Municipal Type: Town
Incorporated: May 14, 1901; *Area:* 5.42 sq km
County or District: Guysborough; *Population in 2006:* 911
Provincial Electoral District(s): Guysborough-Sheet Harbour
Federal Electoral District(s): Cape Breton-Canso
Next Election: Oct. 2008 (4 year terms)
Raymond White, Mayor
Michelle Hart, Town Clerk-Treas.

Chester
P.O. Box 620
Chester, NS B0J 1J0
902-275-4482 Fax: 902-275-2021
Municipal Type: Village

County or District: Lunenburg;
Provincial Electoral District(s): Chester-St.Margaret's
Federal Electoral District(s): South Shore-St. Margaret's
Next Election: Oct. 2008 (4 year terms)
Iris Tolliver, Clerk-Treas.
Tony Howlett, Chair

Clark's Harbour
P.O. Box 260
2648 Main St.
Clarks Harbour, NS B0W 1P0
902-745-2390 Fax: 902-745-1772
briancrowell@eastlink.ca
Municipal Type: Town
Incorporated: March 4, 1919; *Area:* 2.9 sq km
County or District: Shelburne; *Population in 2006:* 860
Provincial Electoral District(s): Shelburne
Federal Electoral District(s): South Shore-St. Margaret's
Next Election: Oct. 2008 (4 year terms)
Brian Crowell, Clerk-Treas.
Leigh B. Stoddart, Mayor

Cornwallis Square
P.O. Box 129
1415 Country Home Rd., Cambridge
Waterville, NS B0P 1V0
902-538-0325 Fax: 902-538-1683
Municipal Type: Village

County or District: Kings;
Provincial Electoral District(s): Kings North
Federal Electoral District(s): Kings-Hants
Next Election: Oct. 2008 (4 year terms)
George Foote, Chair
Bill Farrell, Clerk-Treas.

Digby
P.O. Box 579
147 First Ave.
Digby, NS B0V 1A0
902-245-4769 Fax: 902-245-2121
clerk.digby@tartannet.ns.ca
www.townofdigby.ns.ca
Municipal Type: Town
Incorporated: Feb. 28, 1890; *Area:* 3.14 sq km
County or District: Digby; *Population in 2006:* 2,092
Provincial Electoral District(s): Digby-Annapolis
Federal Electoral District(s): West Nova
Next Election: Oct. 2008 (4 year terms)
Tom Ossinger, Clerk-Treas.
Frank Mackintosh, Mayor

Freeport
P.O. Box 31
Freeport, NS B0V 1B0
902-839-2144
Municipal Type: Village

County or District: Digby;
Provincial Electoral District(s): Digby-Annapolis
Federal Electoral District(s): West Nova
Next Election: Oct. 2008 (4 year terms)
Vacant, Clerk-Treas.
Peter Morehouse, Chair

Greenwood
P.O. Box 1068
904 Central Ave.
Greenwood, NS B0P 1N0
902-765-8788 Fax: 902-765-4369
greenwoodns@eastlink.ca
www.greenwoodnovascotia.com
Municipal Type: Village

County or District: Kings; *Population in 2006:* 4,500
Provincial Electoral District(s): Kings West
Federal Electoral District(s): West Nova; Central Nova; South Shore-St. Margaret's
Next Election: Oct. 2008 (4 year terms)
Marian Elsworth, Clerk-Treas.
Al Belliveau, Chair

Hantsport
P.O. Box 399
20 Main St.
Hantsport, NS B0P 1P0
902-684-3211 Fax: 902-684-3227
Jeff@hantsportnovascotia.com
www.hantsportnovascotia.com
Municipal Type: Town
Incorporated: April 1, 1895; *Area:* 2.13 sq km
County or District: Hants; *Population in 2006:* 1,191
Provincial Electoral District(s): Hants West
Federal Electoral District(s): Kings-Hants
Next Election: Oct. 2008 (4 year terms)
Jeffrey Lawrence, CAO
H. Wayne Folker, Mayor

Havre Boucher
1318 Cape Jack Rd.
Havre Boucher, NS B0P 1P0
902-234-3088
rcarpenter@ns.sympatico.ca
www.havreboucher.com
Municipal Type: Village

County or District: Antigonish;
Provincial Electoral District(s): Antigonish
Federal Electoral District(s): Central Nova
Next Election: Oct. 2008 (4 year terms)
Raymond Carpenter, Clerk-Treas.
Sylvester Landry, Chair

Hebbville
47 Catidian Pl., RR#4
Bridgewater, NS B4V 2W3
902-543-5786 Fax: 902-543-7006
vcornish@eastlink.ca
Municipal Type: Village

County or District: Lunenburg;
Provincial Electoral District(s): Lunenburg West
Federal Electoral District(s): South Shore-St. Margaret's
Next Election: Oct. 2008 (4 year terms)
Vernon Cornish, Clerk-Treas.
Glen Whitehouse, Chair

Kentville
354 Main St.
Kentville, NS B4N 1K6
902-679-2500 Fax: 902-679-2375
info@town.kentville.ns.ca
www.town.kentville.ns.ca
Municipal Type: Town
Incorporated: May 1, 1886; *Area:* 17.35 sq km
County or District: Kings; *Population in 2006:* 5,815
Provincial Electoral District(s): Kings North
Federal Electoral District(s): Kings-Hants
Next Election: Oct. 2008 (4 year terms)
William Boyd, CAO & Clerk-Treas.
cao@town.kentville.ns.ca
Dave Corkum, Mayor
mayor@town.kentville.ns.ca

Kings County
P.O. Box 100
87 Cornwallis St.
Kentville, NS B4N 3W3
902-690-6133 Fax: 902-678-9279
inquiry@county.kings.ns.ca
www.county.kings.ns.ca

Municipal Type: Municipality
Incorporated: April 17, 1879; *Area:* 2,122.18 sq km
County or District: Kings; *Population in 2006:* 60,035
Provincial Electoral District(s): Kings North; Kings South; Kings West
Federal Electoral District(s): Kings-Hants; West Nova
Next Election: Oct. 2008 (4 year terms)

Council
Fred Whalen, Warden
902-690-6132
warden.whalen@county.kings.ns.ca
Jim Taylor, Councillor, Ward(s): District 1
councillor.taylor@county.kings.ns.ca
Janet Newton, Councillor, Ward(s): District 2
councillor.newton@county.kings.ns.ca
Dick Killam, Councillor, Ward(s): District 3
councillor.killam@county.kings.ns.ca
Fred Whalon, Councillor, Ward(s): District 4
Wayne Atwater, Councillor, Ward(s): District 5
councillor.atwater@county.kings.ns.ca
Diana Brothers, Councillor, Ward(s): District 6
councillor.brothers@county.kings.ns.ca
Dale Lloyd, Councillor, Ward(s): District 8
councillor.lloyd@county.kings.ns.ca
Basil Hall, Councillor, Ward(s): District 9
councillor.hall@county.kings.ns.ca
Chris Parker, Councillor, Ward(s): District 10
councillor.parker@county.kings.ns.ca
Eric Smith, Councillor, Ward(s): District 11
councillor.smith@county.kings.ns.ca
Mike Ennis, Councillor, Ward(s): District 12
902-542-5217
councillor.ennis@county.kings.ns.ca

Administration
Ann L. Longley, Municipal Clerk
alongley@county.kings.ns.ca
Brian Smith, CAO
902-690-6131, Fax: 902-678-9279
bsmith@county.kings.ns.ca
Bill Butler, Director, Community Development
902-690-6137
bbutler@county.kings.ns.ca
Richard Lloyd, Director, Engineering & Public Works
902-690-6111, Fax: 902-679-0911
rlloyd@county.kings.ns.ca
Bill McKennan, CMA, Director, Corporate Services
902-690-6130
bmckennan@county.kings.ns.ca
Kathleen Leslie, Manager, Information Technology
902-690-6155, Fax: 902-690-6165
kleslie@county.kings.ns.ca
Gary Smith, Manager, Protective & Emergency Services
902-690-6117
gsmith@county.kings.ns.ca
Bob Suffron, Coordinator, Parks & Open Spaces
902-690-6153
bsuffron@county.kings.ns.ca
Chrystal Fuller, Manager, Planning
902-690-6173
cfuller@county.kings.ns.ca
Scott Quinn, Project Engineer
902-690-6194, Fax: 902-679-0911
Zane Long, Manager, Properties
Brian Hazlett, Supervisor, Water & Wastewater
902-690-6198
bhazlett@county.kings.ns.ca

Kingston
P.O. Box 254
671 Main St.
Kingston, NS B0P 1R0
902-765-2800 Fax: 902-765-0807
kingsvil@ns.aliantzinc.ca
www.kingstonnovascotia.ca
Municipal Type: Village
Incorporated: 1957;
County or District: Kings; *Population in 2006:* 4,000
Provincial Electoral District(s): Kings West
Federal Electoral District(s): West Nova
Next Election: Oct. 2008 (4 year terms)
Kelly Rice, Clerk-Treas.
Murray Kinsman, Chair
902-765-3205

Lawrencetown
P.O. Box 38
83 Lawrencetown Lane
Lawrencetown, NS B0S 1M0
902-584-3559 Fax: 902-584-3878
villagelawrencetown@ns.sympatico.ca
Municipal Type: Village

County or District: Annapolis; *Population in 2006:* 750
Provincial Electoral District(s): Annapolis
Federal Electoral District(s): West Nova; Sackville-Eastern Shore
Next Election: Oct. 2008 (4 year terms)
Dene Marshall, Clerk-Treas.
Lynette Gilks, Chair

Lockeport
P.O. Box 189
26 North St.
Lockeport, NS B0T 1L0
902-656-2216 Fax: 902-656-2935
townoflockeport@ns.sympatico.ca
www.lockeport.ns.ca
Municipal Type: Town
Incorporated: Feb. 26, 1907; *Area:* 2.32 sq km
County or District: Shelburne; *Population in 2006:* 646
Provincial Electoral District(s): Shelburne
Federal Electoral District(s): South Shore-St. Margaret's
Next Election: Oct. 2008 (4 year terms)
Joyce Y. Young, Clerk-Treas.
Darian Huskilson, Mayor
902-875-7747

Lunenburg
P.O. Box 129
119 Cumberland St.
Lunenburg, NS B0J 2C0
902-634-4410 Fax: 902-634-4416
explorelunenburg@ns.sympatico.ca
www.town.lunenburg.ns.ca
Municipal Type: Town
Incorporated: Oct. 29, 1888; *Area:* 4.01 sq km
County or District: Lunenburg; *Population in 2006:* 2,317
Provincial Electoral District(s): Lunenburg
Federal Electoral District(s): South Shore-St. Margaret's
Next Election: Oct. 2008 (4 year terms)
Beatrice Renton, Town Manager & Clerk
D. Laurence Mawhinney, Mayor

Mahone Bay
P.O. Box 530
493 Main St.
Mahone Bay, NS B0J 2E0
902-624-8327 Fax: 902-624-8069
clerk@townofmahonebay.ca
Municipal Type: Town
Incorporated: March 31, 1919; *Area:* 3.13 sq km
County or District: Lunenburg; *Population in 2006:* 904
Provincial Electoral District(s): Lunenburg
Federal Electoral District(s): South Shore-St. Margaret's
Next Election: Oct. 2008 (4 year terms)
Jim Wentzell, CAO
C. Joseph Feeney, Mayor

Middleton
P.O. Box 340
131 Commercial St.
Middleton, NS B0S 1P0
902-825-4841 Fax: 902-825-6460
cao@town.middleton.ns.ca
www.discovermiddleton.ca
Municipal Type: Town
Incorporated: May 31, 1909; *Area:* 5.44 sq km
County or District: Annapolis; *Population in 2006:* 1,829
Provincial Electoral District(s): Annapolis
Federal Electoral District(s): West Nova; Central Nova; Cumberland—Colchester—Musquodoboit Valley
Next Election: Oct. 2008 (4 year terms)
Jemma Lambert, CAO
Calvin Eddy, Mayor
callyn@ns.sympatico.ca

Mulgrave
P.O. Box 129
457 MacLeod St.
Mulgrave, NS B0E 2G0
902-747-2243 Fax: 902-747-2585
scott.conrod@townofmulgrave.ca
www.townofmulgrave.ca
Municipal Type: Town
Incorporated: Dec. 1, 1923; *Area:* 17.81 sq km
County or District: Guysborough; *Population in 2006:* 879
Provincial Electoral District(s): Guysborough-Sheet Harbour
Federal Electoral District(s): Cape Breton-Canso
Next Election: Oct. 2008 (4 year terms)
Leonard MacDonald, Mayor
Scott Conrod, CAO

New Glasgow
111 Provost St.
New Glasgow, NS B2H 2P5
902-755-7788 Fax: 902-755-6242
dsmith@newglasgow.ca
www.newglasgow.ca
Municipal Type: Town
Incorporated: May 6, 1875; *Area:* 9.93 sq km
County or District: Pictou; *Population in 2006:* 9,455
Provincial Electoral District(s): Pictou Centre
Federal Electoral District(s): Central Nova
Next Election: Oct. 2008 (4 year terms)
David Smith, CAO
Ann MacLean, Mayor

New Minas
9209 Commercial St.
New Minas, NS B4N 3G1
902-681-0292 Fax: 902-681-0779
village.newminas@ns.sympatico.ca
www.newminas.com
Municipal Type: Village

County or District: Kings; *Population in 2006:* 4,200
Provincial Electoral District(s): Kings South
Federal Electoral District(s): Kings-Hants
Next Election: Oct. 2008 (4 year terms)
Terry Silver, Clerk-Treas.
newminas@ns.sympatico.ca
Dave Chaulk, Chair

Oxford
P.O. Box 338
5201 Main St.
Oxford, NS B0M 1P0
902-447-2170 Fax: 902-447-2485
dwhite@town.oxford.ns.ca
www.town.oxford.ns.ca
Municipal Type: Town
Incorporated: April 19, 1904; *Area:* 10.76 sq km
County or District: Cumberland; *Population in 2006:* 1,178
Provincial Electoral District(s): Cumberland South
Federal Electoral District(s): Cumberland-Colchester-Musquodoboit Valley
Next Election: Oct. 2008 (4 year terms)
Darrell White, Clerk-Treas.
Lloyd Jenkins, Mayor
lloyd.jenkins@ttownofoxford.ns.ca

Parrsboro
P.O. Box 400
4030 Eastern Ave.
Parrsboro, NS B0M 1S0
902-254-2036 Fax: 902-254-2313
town@town.parrsboro.ns.ca
www.town.parrsboro.ns.ca
Municipal Type: Town
Incorporated: July 15, 1889; *Area:* 14.88 sq km
County or District: Cumberland; *Population in 2006:* 1,401
Provincial Electoral District(s): Cumberland South
Federal Electoral District(s): Cumberland-Colchester-Musquodoboit Valley
Next Election: Oct. 2008 (4 year terms)
Ashley Brown, CAO
Douglas Robinson, Mayor

Pictou
P.O. Box 640
40 Water St.
Pictou, NS B0K 1H0
902-485-4372 Fax: 902-485-8110
pictou@munet.ns.ca
www.townofpictou.com
Municipal Type: Town
Incorporated: May 4, 1874; *Area:* 7.94 sq km
County or District: Pictou; *Population in 2006:* 3,813
Provincial Electoral District(s): Pictou West
Federal Electoral District(s): Central Nova
Next Election: Oct. 2008 (4 year terms)
Linda Ramsay, Interim CAO
lramsay@townofpictou.com
Joseph F. Hawes, Mayor

Port Hawkesbury
#1, 606 Reeves St.
Port Hawkesbury, NS B9A 2R7
902-625-0116 Fax: 902-625-0040
cjmacdonald@ns.sympatico.ca
www.porthawkesbury.straitareaonline.com
Municipal Type: Town
Incorporated: Jan. 22, 1889; *Area:* 8.11 sq km
County or District: Inverness; *Population in 2006:* 3,517
Provincial Electoral District(s): Inverness
Federal Electoral District(s): Cape Breton-Canso
Next Election: Oct. 2008 (4 year terms)
Colin J. MacDonald, CAO
W.J. (Billy Joe) MacLean, Mayor
billyjoe.maclean@townofporthawkesbury.ca

Port Williams
P.O. Box 153
1045 Main St.
Port Williams, NS B0P 1T0
902-542-4411 Fax: 902-542-4566
villageoffice@av.eastlink.ca
www.portwilliams.com
Municipal Type: Village

County or District: Kings;
Provincial Electoral District(s): Kings North
Federal Electoral District(s): Kings-Hants
Next Election: Oct. 2008 (4 year terms)
Diane Hancock, Clerk
Lewis Benedict, Chair

Pugwash
P.O. Box 220
124 Water St.
Pugwash, NS B0K 1L0
902-243-2946 Fax: 902-243-2126
villagecommission@pugwashvillage.com
www.pugwashvillage.com
Municipal Type: Village

County or District: Cumberland; *Population in 2006:* 900
Provincial Electoral District(s): Cumberland North
Federal Electoral District(s): Cumberland-Colchester-Musquodoboit Valley
Next Election: Oct. 2008 (4 year terms)
Randy Thompson, Clerk-Treas.
randythompson@pugwashvillage.com
Alan MacEachern, Chair

River Hebert
2724 Taylor Rd.
River Hebert, NS B0L 1G0
902-251-2250
Municipal Type: Village

County or District: Cumberland;
Provincial Electoral District(s): Cumberland South
Federal Electoral District(s): Cumberland-Colchester-Musquodoboit Valley
Next Election: Oct. 2008 (4 year terms)
Judy Jollymore, Clerk-Treas.
Dale Porter, Chair

St. Peter's
P.O. Box 452
60 Deny St.
St Peters, NS B0E 3B0
902-535-2155 Fax: 902-535-2330
stpeters.village@stpeterscable.com
Municipal Type: Village

County or District: Richmond; *Population in 2006:* 1200
Provincial Electoral District(s): Richmond
Federal Electoral District(s): Cape Breton-Canso
Next Election: Oct. 2008 (4 year terms)
Rena Burke, Clerk-Treas.
Esther McDonnell, Chair

Shelburne
P.O. Box 670
168 Water St.
Shelburne, NS B0T 1W0
902-875-2991 Fax: 902-875-3932
shelburnetown@ns.aliantzinc.ca
www.auracom.com/tnshelb
Municipal Type: Town
Incorporated: April 4, 1907; *Area:* 9 sq km
County or District: Shelburne; *Population in 2006:* 1,879
Provincial Electoral District(s): Shelburne
Federal Electoral District(s): South Shore-St. Margaret's
Next Election: Oct. 2008 (4 year terms)
Ed Crewson, Mayor
519-925-2600
John Telfer, Chief Administrative Officer & Town Clerk
jtelfer@townofshelburne.on.ca

Springhill
P.O. Box 1000
29 Main St.
Springhill, NS B0M 1X0
902-597-3751 Fax: 902-597-3637
dtabor@townofspringhill.ns.ca
www.town.springhill.ns.ca
Municipal Type: Town
Incorporated: March 30, 1889; *Area:* 11.15 sq km
County or District: Cumberland; *Population in 2006:* 3,941
Provincial Electoral District(s): Cumberland South
Federal Electoral District(s): Cumberland-Colchester-Musquodoboit Valley
Next Election: Oct. 2008 (4 year terms)
Donald F. Tabor, CAO
Guy Brown, Mayor

Stellarton
P.O. Box 2200
250 Foord St.
Stellarton, NS B0K 1S0
902-752-2114 Fax: 902-755-4105
townoffice@town.stellarton.ns.ca
www.stellarton.ca
Municipal Type: Town
Incorporated: Oct. 22, 1889; *Area:* 8.99 sq km
County or District: Pictou; *Population in 2006:* 4,717
Provincial Electoral District(s): Pictou Centre
Federal Electoral District(s): Central Nova
Next Election: Oct. 2008 (4 year terms)
Joyce Eaton, Clerk-Treas.
Joe Gennoe, Mayor

Stewiacke
P.O. Box 8
295 George St.
Stewiacke, NS B0N 2J0
902-639-2231 Fax: 902-639-2221
sdorey@stewiacke.net
www.stewiacke.net
Municipal Type: Town
Incorporated: Aug. 30, 1906; *Area:* 17.67 sq km
County or District: Colchester; *Population in 2006:* 1,421
Provincial Electoral District(s): Colchester-Musqodoboit Valley
Federal Electoral District(s): Cumberland-Colchester-Musquodoboit Valley
Next Election: Oct. 2008 (4 year terms)
Sheldon Dorey, CAO
Dereck Rhoddy, Mayor
drhoddy@stewiacke.net

Tatamagouche
P.O. Box 119
423 Main St.
Tatamagouche, NS B0K 1V0
902-657-3696
marilyn.ebsary@ns.sympatico.ca
www.tata.ns.ca
Municipal Type: Village

County or District: Colchester;
Provincial Electoral District(s): Colchester North
Federal Electoral District(s): Cumberland-Colchester-Musquodoboit Valley
Next Election: Oct. 2008 (4 year terms)
Marilyn Ebsary, Clerk-Treas.
Dale Semple, Chair

Tiverton
P.O. Box 16
RR#1
Tiverton, NS B0V 1G0
902-839-2369
Municipal Type: Village

County or District: Digby;
Provincial Electoral District(s): Digby-Annapolis
Federal Electoral District(s): West Nova
Next Election: Oct. 2008 (4 year terms)
Mary Cossaboom, Clerk-Treas.
Woodrow Outhouse, Chair

Trenton
P.O. Box 328
120 Main St.
Trenton, NS B0K 1X0
902-752-5311 Fax: 902-752-0090
trenton@town.trenton.ns.ca
www.town.trenton.ns.ca
Municipal Type: Town
Incorporated: March 18, 1911; *Area:* 6 sq km
County or District: Pictou; *Population in 2006:* 2,741
Provincial Electoral District(s): Pictou Centre
Federal Electoral District(s): Central Nova
Next Election: Oct. 2008 (4 year terms)
Debbie Kampen, Clerk-Treas.
Shannon MacInnis, Mayor

Westport
The Spouter Inn
P.O. Box 1192
263 Water St.
Westport, NS B0V 1H0
902-839-2219 Fax: 902-839-2219
Municipal Type: Village

County or District: Digby;
Provincial Electoral District(s): Digby-Annapolis
Federal Electoral District(s): West Nova
Next Election: Oct. 2008 (4 year terms)
Caroline Norwood, Clerk-Treas.
Glenda Welch, Chair

Westville
P.O. Box 923
2042 Queen St.
Westville, NS B0K 2A0
902-396-1500 Fax: 902-396-3986
www.westville.ca
Municipal Type: Town
Incorporated: Aug. 20, 1894; *Area:* 14.39 sq km
County or District: Pictou; *Population in 2006:* 3,805
Provincial Electoral District(s): Pictou East
Federal Electoral District(s): Central Nova
Next Election: Oct. 2008 (4 year terms)
Rick Ramsay, CAO
Sandy Cyr, Mayor

Weymouth
P.O. Box 121
5108 Hwy. 1
Weymouth, NS B0W 3T0
902-837-4976 Fax: 902- -
village@weymouthnovascotia.com
www.weymouthnovascotia.com
Municipal Type: Village

County or District: Digby;
Provincial Electoral District(s): Digby-Annapolis
Federal Electoral District(s): West Nova
Next Election: Oct. 2008 (4 year terms)
Murray Betts, Clerk-Treas.
Suzanne MacLean, Chair

Windsor
P.O. Box 158
100 King St.
Windsor, NS B0N 2T0
902-798-2275 Fax: 902-798-5679
info@town.windsor.ns.ca
www.town.windsor.ns.ca
Municipal Type: Town
Incorporated: April 4, 1878; *Area:* 9.06 sq km
County or District: Hants; *Population in 2006:* 3,709
Provincial Electoral District(s): Hants West
Federal Electoral District(s): Kings-Hants
Next Election: Oct. 2008 (4 year terms)
Louis Coutinho, CAO
lcoutinho@town.windsor.ns.ca
Anna Allen, Mayor

Wolfville
359 Main St.
Wolfville, NS B4P 1A1
902-542-5767 Fax: 902-542-4789
rbrideau@town.wolfville.ns.ca
www.town.wolfville.ns.ca
Municipal Type: Town
Incorporated: March 4, 1893; *Area:* 6.45 sq km
County or District: Kings; *Population in 2006:* 3,772
Provincial Electoral District(s): Kings South
Federal Electoral District(s): Kings-Hants
Next Election: Oct. 2008 (4 year terms)
J. Roy Brideau, CAO
Robert A. (Bob) Stead, Mayor

Yarmouth
400 Main St.
Yarmouth, NS B5A 1G2
902-742-8565 Fax: 902-742-6244
info@yarmouth-town.com
www.yarmouth-town.com
Municipal Type: Town
Incorporated: Aug. 6, 1890; *Area:* 10.56 sq km
County or District: Yarmouth; *Population in 2006:* 7,162
Provincial Electoral District(s): Yarmouth
Federal Electoral District(s): West Nova
Next Election: Oct. 2008 (4 year terms)
Jeffrey Gushue, CAO
Charles Crosby, Mayor

Rural Municipality

Annapolis County
P.O. Box 100
752 George St.
Annapolis Royal, NS B0S 1A0
902-532-2331 Fax: 902-532-2096
info@annapoliscounty.ns.ca
www.annapoliscounty.ns.ca
Municipal Type: Rural Municipality
Incorporated: April 17, 1879; *Area:* 3,184.97 sq km
County or District: Annapolis; *Population in 2006:* 21,438
Provincial Electoral District(s): Annapolis; Digby-Annapolis
Federal Electoral District(s): West Nova
Next Election: Oct. 2008 (4 year terms)
Peter A. Newton, Warden
warden@annapoliscounty.ns.ca
Tom Vitiello, Chair, Emergency Measures Advisory Committee
Reginald C. Ritchie, Chair, Municipal Services (Priorities & Planning) Committee
Brenda Orchard, Chief Administrative Officer
admin@annapoliscounty.ns.ca
Jacquie Farrow-Lawrence, Clerk
Gerald Hackenschmidt, Director, Finance
902-532-3135
ghackenschmidt@annapoliscounty.ns.ca
David McCoubrey, Coordinator, Regional Emergency Measures
remo@annapoliscounty.ns.ca
Laurie Emms, Director, Municipal Services
902-584-2188
lmemms@annapolisvalley.ns.ca
Nelson Porteous, Coordinator, Public Works
902-532-3141
pwork@annapoliscounty.ns.ca

Antigonish County
285 Beech Hill Rd.
Antigonish, NS B2G 0B4
902-863-1117 Fax: 902-863-5751
clerk@antigonishcounty.ns.ca
www.antigonishcounty.ns.ca
Municipal Type: Rural Municipality
Incorporated: April 17, 1879; *Area:* 1,457.82 sq km
County or District: Antigonish; *Population in 2006:* 18,836
Provincial Electoral District(s): Antigonish
Federal Electoral District(s): Central Nova
Next Election: Oct. 2008 (4 year terms)
Alan J. Bond, Clerk-Treas.
Herbert J. DeLorey, Warden
Michael O'Leary, Director, Public Works
publicworks@antigonishcounty.ns.ca
Kemp MacDonald, Municipal Planner
planning@antigonishcounty.ns.ca
Daryl Myers, Supervisor, Beech Hill Sanitary Landfill Site
902-863-4744
landfill@antigonishcounty.ns.ca

Argyle District
P.O. Box 10
27 Courthouse St.
Tusket, NS B0W 3M0
902-648-2311 Fax: 902-648-0367
admin@munargyle.com
www.munargyle.com
Municipal Type: Rural Municipality
Incorporated: April 17, 1879; *Area:* 1,527.1 sq km
County or District: Yarmouth; *Population in 2006:* 8,656
Provincial Electoral District(s): Argyle
Federal Electoral District(s): West Nova
Next Election: Oct. 2008 (4 year terms)
Aldric D'Entremont, Warden
Alain Muise, CAO
admuise@munargyle.com

Barrington District
P.O. Box 100
2447 Hwy. 3
Barrington, NS B0W 1E0
902-637-2015 Fax: 902-637-2075
munbar@eastlink.ca
www.barringtonmunicipality.com
Municipal Type: Rural Municipality
Incorporated: April 17, 1879; *Area:* 631.94 sq km
County or District: Shelburne; *Population in 2006:* 7,331
Provincial Electoral District(s): Shelburne
Federal Electoral District(s): South Shore-St. Margaret's
Next Election: Oct. 2008 (4 year terms)
Brian Holland, Clerk
mobclerk@eastlink.ca
Louise Halliday, Warden
mobwarden@eastlink.ca

Chester District
P.O. Box 369
151 King St.
Chester, NS B0J 1J0
902-275-3554 Fax: 902-275-4771
administration@district.chester.ns.ca
www.district.chester.ns.ca
Municipal Type: Rural Municipality
Incorporated: April 17, 1879; *Area:* 1,120.75 sq km
County or District: Lunenburg; *Population in 2006:* 10,741
Provincial Electoral District(s): Chester-St. Margaret's
Federal Electoral District(s): South Shore-St. Margaret's
Next Election: Oct. 2008 (4 year terms)
Allen Webber, Warden
awebber@district.chester.ns.ca
Pamela Myra, Clerk
Darrell Hiltz, CAO
darrell.hiltz@district.chester.ns.ca
Bruce Forest, Director, Public Works
902-275-1312
Earl Woodworth, Building Inspector
ewoodworth@district.chester.ns.ca
Geoff MacDonald, Planning Director
geoff.macdonald@district.chester.ns.ca
Karen Newton, Development Officer
colleen.clare@district.chester.ns.ca
Jennifer Veinotte, Recycling Coordinator
Chad Haughn, Director, Recreation & Parks

Clare District
P.O. Box 458
1185 Hwy. 1
Little Brook, NS B0W 1Z0
902-769-2031 Fax: 902-769-3773
council@municipality.clare.ns.ca
www.clarenovascotia.com
Municipal Type: Rural Municipality
Incorporated: April 17, 1879; *Area:* 852.82 sq km
County or District: Digby; *Population in 2006:* 8,813
Provincial Electoral District(s): Clare
Federal Electoral District(s): West Nova
Next Election: Oct. 2008 (4 year terms)
Connie Saulnier, CAO
Jean Melanson, Warden

Colchester County
P.O. Box 697
1 Church St.
Truro, NS B2N 5E7
902-897-3160 Fax: 902-895-9983
cao@colchester.ca
www.colchester.ca
Municipal Type: Rural Municipality
Incorporated: April 17, 1879; *Area:* 3,627.69 sq km
County or District: Colchester; *Population in 2006:* 50,023
Provincial Electoral District(s): Colchester-Musqudoboit Valley; Colchester North; Truro-Bible Hill
Federal Electoral District(s): Cumberland-Colchester-Musquodoboit Valley
Next Election: Oct. 2008 (4 year terms)
Bob Taylor, Mayor
mayor@colchester.ca
Christine Blair, Councillor, Ward(s): District 1
councillordistrict1@colchester.ca
Bill Masters, Councillor, Ward(s): District 2
councillordistrict2@colchester.ca
Gerry Buott, Councillor, Ward(s): District 3
councillordistrict3@colchester.ca
Mike Cooper, Councillor, Ward(s): District 4
councillordistrict4@colchester.ca
Glen Edwards, Councillor, Ward(s): District 5
councillordistrict5@colchester.ca
Karen MacKenzie, Councillor, Ward(s): District 6
kdmackenzie@tru.eastlink.ca
Le Fresne Jimmie, Councillor, Ward(s): District 7
councillordistrict7@colchester.ca
Ron Cavanaugh, Councillor, Ward(s): District 8
councillordistrict8@colchester.ca
Bob White, Councillor, Ward(s): District 9
councillordistrict9@colchester.ca
Tom Taggart, Councillor, Ward(s): District 10
councillordistrict10@colchester.ca
Earl D. McKenna, Councillor, Ward(s): District 11
councillordistrict11@colchester.ca
Dan McDougall, CAO
dmcdougall@colchester.ca
Bruce Purchase, Director, Corporate Services
bpurchase@colchester.ca
Crawford Macpherson, Director, Community Development
cmacpherson@colchester.ca
Donna Campbell, Manager, Finance
dcampbell@colchester.ca

Cumberland County
E.D. Fullerton Municipal Bldg.
P.O. Box 428
1395 Blair Lake Rd., RR#6
Amherst, NS B4H 3Y4
902-667-2313 Fax: 902-667-1352 Toll Free Phone: 1-888-756-6262
info@cumberlandcounty.ns.ca
www.cumberlandcounty.ns.ca
Municipal Type: Rural Municipality
Incorporated: April 17, 1879; *Area:* 4,271.14 sq km
County or District: Cumberland; *Population in 2006:* 32,046
Provincial Electoral District(s): Cumberland North; Cumberland South
Federal Electoral District(s): Cumberland-Colchester-Musquodoboit Valley
Next Election: Oct. 2008 (4 year terms)
Keith Hunter, Warden
Rennie Bugley, CAO
Connie Speight, Executive Secretary
Robert Streatch, Director, Public Works
902-667-3029
Jim Hannon, Coordinator, Emergency Measures
902-667-2313
jhannon@cumberlandcounty.ns.ca

Digby District
P.O. Box 429
Digby, NS B0V 1A0
902-245-4777 Fax: 902-245-5748
lfraser@municipality.digby.ns.ca
www.municipalities.com/digby
Municipal Type: Rural Municipality
Incorporated: April 17, 1879; *Area:* 1,655.93 sq km
County or District: Digby; *Population in 2006:* 7,986
Provincial Electoral District(s): Digby-Annapolis; Clare
Federal Electoral District(s): West Nova
Next Election: Oct. 2008 (4 year terms)
Linda Fraser, CAO
James Thurber, Warden

Guysborough District
Municipal Bldg.
P.O. Box 79
33 Pleasant St.
Guysborough, NS B0H 1N0
902-533-3705 Fax: 902-533-2749
dpmcdougall@municipality.guysborough.ns.ca
www.municipality.guysborough.ns.ca
Municipal Type: Rural Municipality
Incorporated: April 17, 1879; *Area:* 2,111.42 sq km
County or District: Guysborough; *Population in 2006:* 4,681
Provincial Electoral District(s): Guysborough-Sheet Harbour
Federal Electoral District(s): Cape Breton-Canso
Next Election: Oct. 2008 (4 year terms)
Dan McDougall, CAO
Lloyd P. Hines, Warden

Hants East District
P.O. Box 190
2361 Hwy. 2, Milford
Shubenacadie, NS B0N 2H0
902-758-2299 Fax: 902-758-3497
info@easthants.ca
www.easthants.ca
Municipal Type: Rural Municipality
Incorporated: April 17, 1879; *Area:* 1,787.64 sq km
County or District: Hants; *Population in 2006:* 21,387
Provincial Electoral District(s): Hants East
Federal Electoral District(s): Kings-Hants
Next Election: Oct. 2008 (4 year terms)
John Patterson, Warden
Ian Glasgow, CAO
iglasgow@easthants.ca
Edward Gillis, P.Eng., Director, Engineering Services
Roger Freeman, P.Eng., Engineer, Transportation
Andrea Trask, Coordinator & Educator, Waste Reduction
Heidi Achenbach, Manager, Solid Waste
902-758-2299
Jim Ashley, Manager, Public Works
Edward McQuillan, Operator, Water Distribution
John Woodford, Director, Planning & Development
902-758-2715
jwoodford@easthants.ca
Mike Brown, Foreman, Georgefield Municipal Landfill Site
902-261-2178
Krista Dewey, Director, Corporate & Residential Services
Terry Matheson, Officer, Environmental Compliance

Hants West District
Windsor-West Hants Industrial Park
P.O. Box 3000
76 Morrison Dr.
Windsor, NS B0N 2T0
902-798-8391 Fax: 902-798-8553
west.hants@westhants.ca
www.westhants.ca
Municipal Type: Rural Municipality
Incorporated: April 17, 1879; *Area:* 1,238.12 sq km
County or District: Hants; *Population in 2006:* 13,881
Provincial Electoral District(s): Hants West
Federal Electoral District(s): Kings-Hants
Next Election: Oct. 2008 (4 year terms)
Richard B. Dauphinee, Warden
admin@westhants.ca
Dwight Bennett, CAO
cao@westhants.ca
Rick Sherrard, Director, Public Works
public.works@westhants.ca
Paul DeMont, Operator, Water Treatment
drc@westhants.ca
Lynn Davis, Director, Planning
902-798-6900
ldavis@windsorwesthantsplanning.ns.ca
Doug MacInnes, Development Officer
dmacinnis@windsorwesthants.planning.ns.ca
Christine McClare, Coordinator, Waste Reduction
waste@westhants.ca

Inverness County
Municipal Bldg.
P.O. Box 179
375 Main St.
Port Hood, NS B0E 2W0
902-787-2274 Fax: 902-787-3110
joe.oconnor@invernesscounty.ca
www.invernesscounty.ca
Municipal Type: Rural Municipality
Incorporated: April 17, 1879; *Area:* 3,830.4 sq km
County or District: Inverness; *Population in 2006:* 19,036
Provincial Electoral District(s): Guysborough-Sheet Harbour; Inverness; Victoria-The Lakes
Federal Electoral District(s): Cape Breton-Canso; Sydney-Victoria
Next Election: Oct. 2008 (4 year terms)
Duart MacAulay, Warden
duartmaca@ns.sympatico.ca
Joe O'Connor, CAO
Joe O'Connor, Director, Public Works
902-787-3502, Fax: 902-787-2339
invworks@ns.sympatico.ca
William Gillis, Officer, Bylaw Enforcement

Lunenburg District
P.O. Box 200
210 Aberdeen Rd.
Bridgewater, NS B4V 4G8
902-543-8181 Fax: 902-543-7123
finance@municipality.lunenburg.ca
www.modl.ca
Municipal Type: Rural Municipality
Incorporated: April 17, 1879; *Area:* 1,759.14 sq km
County or District: Lunenburg; *Population in 2006:* 25,164
Provincial Electoral District(s): Chester-St. Margaret's Lunenburg; Lunenburg West
Federal Electoral District(s): South Shore-St. Margaret's
Next Election: Oct. 2008 (4 year terms)
Don Downe, Warden
Tammy Wilson, CAO
twilson@modl.ca
Pierre A. Breau, P.Eng., Municipal Engineer & Director, Engineering & Public Works
902-541-1331
pierrebreau@modl.ca
Ed Curran, Director, Planning & Development Services
902-541-1336
ecurran@modl.ca
Jim Annand, Manager, Solid Waste Operations
902-541-1325
jannand@modl.ca
Kevin Wentzell, Supervisor, Compost Plant
902-543-2991
Sally Steele, Coordinator, Recycling
902-543-2913
Bob Palmer, Emergency Measures
902-543-8650
emo@modl.ca
April Whynot-Lohnes, Officer, Development
awlohnes@modl.ca
Laura Barkhouse, Coordinator, Trails

Pictou County
P.O. Box 910
46 Municipal Dr.
Pictou, NS B0K 1H0
902-485-4311 Fax: 902-485-6475
cmacintosh@county.pictou.ns.ca
www.county.pictou.ns.ca
Municipal Type: Rural Municipality
Incorporated: April 17, 1879; *Area:* 2,845.26 sq km
County or District: Pictou; *Population in 2006:* 46,513
Provincial Electoral District(s): Pictou Centre; Pictou East; Pictou West
Federal Electoral District(s): Central Nova
Next Election: Oct. 2008 (4 year terms)
Ronald Baillie, Warden
Brian Cullen, CAO
Carol MacKenzie, Manager, Waste Reduction Program
902-396-1495
cmackenzie@pcwastemgmt.com
Lonnie Ferguson, General Manager, Mount William Landfill Site
902-396-5062, Fax: 902-396-4782
lferguson@pcwastemgmt.com

Richmond County
P.O. Box 120
2357 Hwy. 206
Arichat, NS B0E 1A0
902-226-2400 Fax: 902-226-1510
ldigout@richmondcounty.ca
www.richmondcounty.ca
Municipal Type: Rural Municipality
Incorporated: April 17, 1879; *Area:* 1,244.24 sq km
County or District: Richmond; *Population in 2006:* 9,740
Provincial Electoral District(s): Richmond
Federal Electoral District(s): Cape Breton-Canso
Next Election: Oct. 2008 (4 year terms)
Louis Digout, CAO
John Boudreau, Warden
Darrin McLean, Director, Public Works/Municipal Engineer
902-226-3988
dmclean@richmondcounty.ca
Jason MacMillan, Technologist, Engineering
902-226-3989
jmacmillan@richmondcounty.ca

St. Mary's District
P.O. Box 296
16 Main St.
Sherbrooke, NS B0J 3C0
902-522-2049 Fax: 902-522-2309
council@saint-marys.ca
www.saint-marys.ca
Municipal Type: Rural Municipality
Incorporated: April 17, 1879; *Area:* 1,909.59 sq km
County or District: Guysborough; *Population in 2006:* 2,587
Provincial Electoral District(s): Guysborough-Sheet Harbour
Federal Electoral District(s): Central Nova; Cape Breton-Canso
Next Election: Oct. 2008 (4 year terms)
David Gillis, Clerk-Treas.
Milton Jordan, Warden

Shelburne District
P.O. Box 280
136 Hammond Rd.
Shelburne, NS B0T 1W0
902-875-3544 Fax: 902-875-1278
munshel@ns.sympatico.ca
Municipal Type: Rural Municipality
Incorporated: April 17, 1879; *Area:* 1,818.49 sq km
County or District: Shelburne; *Population in 2006:* 4,828
Provincial Electoral District(s): Shelburne
Federal Electoral District(s): South Shore-St. Margaret's
Next Election: Oct. 2008 (4 year terms)
Penny Smith, Clerk-Treas.
Paulette Scott, Warden

Victoria County
P.O. Box 370
495 Chebucto St.
Baddeck, NS B0E 1B0
902-295-3659 Fax: 902-295-3331
sandy.hudson@countyvictoria.ns.ca
www.countyvictoria.ns.ca
Municipal Type: Rural Municipality
Incorporated: April 17, 1879; *Area:* 2,870.85 sq km
County or District: Victoria; *Population in 2006:* 7,594
Provincial Electoral District(s): Victoria-The Lakes
Federal Electoral District(s): Sydney-Victoria
Next Election: Oct. 2008 (4 year terms)
Wayne Budge, Warden
Alexander (Sandy) W. Hudson, Chief Administrative Officer

Yarmouth District
P.O. Box 21
932, Hwy 1
Hebron, NS B0W 1X0
902-742-7159 Fax: 902-742-3164
admin@district.yarmouth.ns.ca
www.district.yarmouth.ns.ca
Municipal Type: Rural Municipality
Incorporated: April 17, 1879; *Area:* 585.27 sq km
County or District: Yarmouth; *Population in 2006:* 10,304
Provincial Electoral District(s): Yarmouth
Federal Electoral District(s): West Nova
Next Election: Oct. 2008 (4 year terms)
Leland Anthony, Warden
warden@district.yarmouth.ns.ca
Ken Moses, CAO
cao@district.yarmouth.ns.ca
Greg Shay, Director, Finance
greg@district.yarmouth.ns.ca

NUNAVUT

The Department of Community & Government Services has legislative responsibility for 27 Territorial Acts & Regulations. These Acts include: Area Development; Business Licenses; Cities, Town & Villages; Civil Emergency Measures; Commissioner's Land; Community Employees Benefits Program Transfer; Conflict of Interest; Consumer Protection; Curfew; Dog; Film Classification; Fire Prevention; Hamlet; Homeowners Property; Local Authorities Election; Lotteries; Pawnbrokers & Second-hand Dealers; Planning; Property Assessments & Taxation; Real Estate Agents Licensing; Religious Societies; Residential Tenancies; Technical Standards & Safety; Senior Citizens & Disabled Persons Property Tax Relief Act; Settlement; Western Canada Lottery.

Incorporation as a city, town or village is determined by the value of all assessable land. Incorporation values: Village, $10 million; Town, $50 million; City, $200 million, all tax-based. Hamlets may request tax-based status. There is one City & 24 Hamlets in Nunavut.

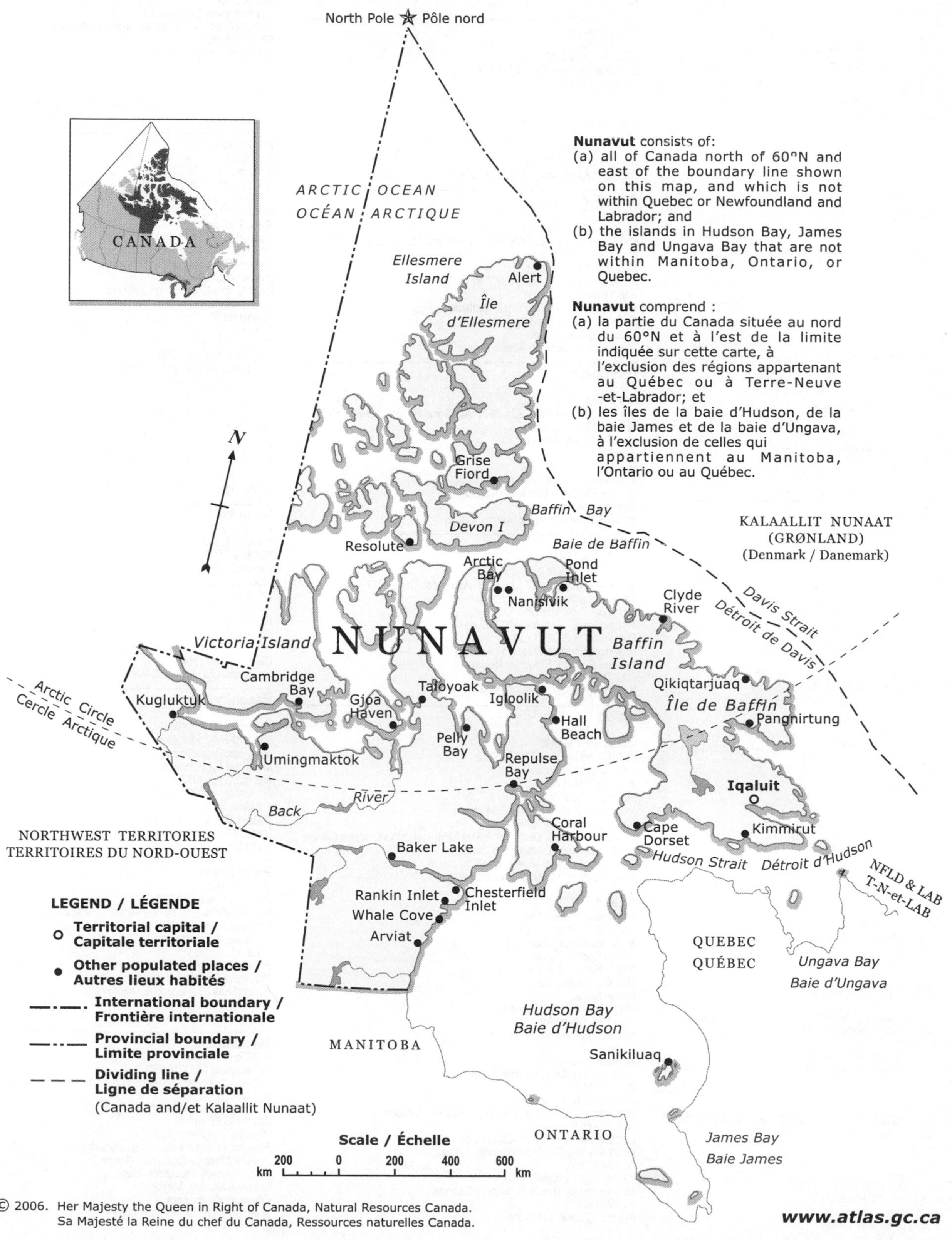

Nunavut

Other Municipalities in Nunavut

Arctic Bay
P.O. Box 150
Arctic Bay, NU X0A 0A0
867-439-9917 Fax: 867-439-8767 Additional Phone: 867-439-9918
sao_ab@qiniq.com
Municipal Type: Hamlet
Area: 247.5 sq km
Population in 2006: 690
Provincial Electoral District(s): Quttiktuq
Federal Electoral District(s): Nunavut
Darlene Willie, Mayor
mayor_ab@qiniq.com
Joelie Qamanirq, Sr. Admin. Officer

Arviat
P.O. Box 150
Arviat, NU X0C 0E0
867-857-2841 Fax: 867-857-2519
arviatsao@qiniq.com
Municipal Type: Hamlet
Incorporated: 1977; *Area:* 132 sq km
Population in 2006: 2,060
Provincial Electoral District(s): Arviat
Federal Electoral District(s): Nunavut
Note: Formerly known as Eskimo Point.
Johnny Mamgark, Mayor
Sheila Napayok, Acting Sr. Admin. Officer

Baker Lake
P.O. Box 149
Baker Lake, NU X0C 0A0
867-793-2874 Fax: 867-793-2509
blsao@netkaster.ca
www.bakerlake.org
Municipal Type: Hamlet
Incorporated: 1977; *Area:* 182.22 sq km
Population in 2006: 1,728
Provincial Electoral District(s): Baker Lake
Federal Electoral District(s): Nunavut
David Aksawnee, Mayor
blmayor@netkaster.ca
Dennis Zettler, Sr. Admin. Officer

Cambridge Bay
P.O. Box 16
Cambridge Bay, NU X0B 0C0
867-983-4650 Fax: 867-983-2193
danderson@cambridgebay.ca
www.cambridgebay.ca
Municipal Type: Hamlet
Incorporated: 1984; *Area:* 202.2 sq km
Population in 2006: 1,477
Provincial Electoral District(s): Cambridge Bay
Federal Electoral District(s): Nunavut
Michelle Gillis, Mayor
mayorycb@qiniq.com
Derek Anderson, Acting Sr. Admin. Officer

Cape Dorset
P.O. Box 30
Cape Dorset, NU X0A 0C0
867-897-8943 Fax: 867-897-8030 Additional Phone: 867-897-8981
muncdsao@capedorset.ca
www.capedorset.ca
Municipal Type: Hamlet
Incorporated: 1982; *Area:* 9.74 sq km
Population in 2006: 1,236
Provincial Electoral District(s): South Baffin
Federal Electoral District(s): Nunavut
Fred Schell, Mayor
Art Stewart, Sr. Admin. Officer

Chesterfield Inlet
P.O. Box 10
Chesterfield Inlet, NU X0C 0B0
867-898-9926 Fax: 867-898-9108
sao_hamlet@qiniq.com
www.chesterfieldinlet.net
Municipal Type: Hamlet
Incorporated: 1980; *Area:* 141.08 sq km
Population in 2006: 332
Provincial Electoral District(s): Nanulik
Federal Electoral District(s): Nunavut
Tony Amauyak, Mayor
Mike Rudkin, Sr. Admin. Officer

Clyde River
P.O. Box 89
Clyde River, NU X0A 0E0
867-924-6220 Fax: 867-924-6293 Additional Phone: 867-924-6301
saoclyde2004@yahoo.ca
Municipal Type: Hamlet
Area: 106.48 sq km
Population in 2006: 820
Provincial Electoral District(s): Uqqummiut
Federal Electoral District(s): Nunavut
Peter Paneak, Mayor
Terry Kalluk, Acting Sr. Admin. Officer

Coral Harbour
P.O. Box 30
Coral Harbour, NU X0C 0C0
867-925-8867 Fax: 867-925-8233
munch@qiniq.com
Municipal Type: Hamlet
Area: 137.83 sq km
Population in 2006: 769
Provincial Electoral District(s): Nanulik
Federal Electoral District(s): Nunavut
Armand Angootealuk, Mayor
Ronald Ladd, Sr. Admin. Officer

Gjoa Haven
P.O. Box 200
Gjoa Haven, NU X0B 1J0
867-360-7141 Fax: 867-360-6309
saogjoa@qiniq.com
Municipal Type: Hamlet
Incorporated: 1981; *Area:* 28.47 sq km
Population in 2006: 1,064
Provincial Electoral District(s): Nattilik
Federal Electoral District(s): Nunavut
Uriash Puqiqnak, Mayor
Raymond Kamookak, Sr. Admin. Officer

Grise Fiord
P.O. Box 77
Grise Fiord, NU X0A 0J0
867-980-9959 Fax: 867-980-9052 Additional Phone: 867-980-9060
gfsao@nv.sympatico.ca
Municipal Type: Hamlet
Incorporated: 1987; *Area:* 332.7 sq km
Population in 2006: 141
Provincial Electoral District(s): Quttiktuq
Federal Electoral District(s): Nunavut
Jarloo Kiguktak, Mayor
Marty Kuluguaqtuq, Sr. Admin. Officer

Hall Beach
P.O. Box 3
Hall Beach, NU X0A 0K0
867-928-8829 Fax: 867-928-8871 Additional Phone: 867-928-8945
hbhamlet@sympatico.ca
Municipal Type: Hamlet
Area: 16.52 sq km
Population in 2006: 654
Provincial Electoral District(s): Amittuq
Federal Electoral District(s): Nunavut
Sam Anguratsiaq, Mayor
Jayko Simonie, Acting Sr. Admin. Officer

Igloolik
P.O. Box 30
Igloolik, NU X0A 0L0
867-934-8940 Fax: 867-934-8757 Additional Phone: 867-934-8830
igloolik@magma.ca
Municipal Type: Hamlet
Incorporated: 1976; *Area:* 102.87 sq km
Population in 2006: 1,538
Provincial Electoral District(s): Amittuq
Federal Electoral District(s): Nunavut
Paul Quassa, Mayor
Brian Fleming, Sr. Admin. Officer

Iqaluit
P.O. Box 460
Iqaluit, NU X0A 0H0
867-979-5600 Fax: 867-979-5922
info@city.iqaluit.nu.ca
www.city.iqaluit.nu.ca
Municipal Type: Town
Incorporated: 2001; *Area:* 52.34 sq km
Population in 2006: 6,184
Provincial Electoral District(s): Iqaluit East; Iqaluit West; Iqaluit Centre
Federal Electoral District(s): Nunavut
Next Election: 2009 (3 year terms)
Note: Formerly known as Frobisher Bay.

Council
Elisapee Sheutiapik, Mayor
mayor@city.iqaluit.nu.ca
Mary Akpalialuk, Councillor
Jimmy Kilabuk, Councillor
Natsiq Kango, Councillor
Mat Knicklebein, Councillor
Simon Nattaq, Councillor
Mary Ekho Wilman, Councillor
David Ell, Councillor
Romeyn Stevenson, Councillor

Administration
John Hussey, Chief Administration Officer
867-979-5666
j.hussey@city.iqaluit.nu.ca
John Mabberi-Mudonyi, Director, Corporate Services
867-979-5675
j.mabberi-mudonyi@city.iqaluit.nu.ca
Doug Vincent, Chief Enforcement Officer
867-979-6363
d.vincent@city.iqaluit.nu.ca
Michèle Bertol, Director, Planning & Lands
867-979-6363
m.bertol@city.iqaluit.nu.ca
Amy Elgersma, Director, Recreation
867-979-5616
a.elgersma@city.iqaluit.nu.ca
Vacant, Director, Engineering & Public Works
Meagan Leach, Director, Engineering & Sustainability
867-979-6363
m.leach@city.iqaluit.nu.ca
Sean Tiessen, Coordinator, Materials
s.tiessen@city.iqaluit.nu.ca
Vacant, Superintendent, Operations
Geneva Chislett, Controller
867-979-5610
g.chislett@city.iqaluit.nu.ca
Walter Oliver, Fire Chief, Emergency Services
867-976-5657
w.oliver@city.iqaluit.nu.ca
Joamie Eegeesiak, Officer, Community Economic Development
867-979-6363
j.eegeesiak@city.iqaluit.nu.ca
Rob Hogan, Foreman, Utilidor Water Treatment Plant
867-975-8509

Kimmirut
P.O. Box 120
Kimmirut, NU X0A 0N0
867-939-2247 Fax: 867-939-2045 Additional Phone: 867-939-2002
cedkimm@qiniq.com
Municipal Type: Hamlet
Area: 2.27 sq km
Population in 2006: 411
Provincial Electoral District(s): South Baffin
Federal Electoral District(s): Nunavut
Joe Arlooktoo, Mayor
Cecil Marshall, Sr. Admin. Officer

Kugaaruk
P.O. Box 205
General Delivery
Kugaaruk, NU X0B 1K0
867-769-6281 Fax: 867-769-6069
asao_kug@qiniq.com
Municipal Type: Hamlet
Incorporated: 1972; *Area:* 4.97 sq km
Population in 2006: 688
Provincial Electoral District(s): Akulliq
Federal Electoral District(s): Nunavut
Note: Formerly known as Pelly Bay.
Canute Krejunark, Mayor
Guido Tigvareark, Sr. Admin. Officer

Kugluktuk
P.O. Box 271
Kugluktuk, NU X0B 0E0
867-982-6500 Fax: 867-982-3060 Additional Phone: 867-982-6505
saokug@qiniq.com
Municipal Type: Hamlet
Incorporated: 1981; *Area:* 549.61 sq km
Population in 2006: 1,302
Provincial Electoral District(s): Kugluktuk
Federal Electoral District(s): Nunavut
Note: Formerly known as Coppermine.
Derrick Power, Mayor
Linda Allen, Sr. Admin. Officer

Pangnirtung
P.O. Box 253
Pangnirtung, NU X0A 0R0
867-473-8953 Fax: 867-473-8832
pang_sao@qiniq.com
Municipal Type: Hamlet
Incorporated: 1972; *Area:* 7.54 sq km
Population in 2006: 1,325
Provincial Electoral District(s): Pangnirtung
Federal Electoral District(s): Nunavut
Manasa Evic, Mayor
Ron Mongeau, Sr. Admin. Officer

Pond Inlet
P.O. Box 180
Pond Inlet, NU X0A 0S0
867-899-8934 Fax: 867-899-8940 Additional Phone: 867-899-8935
hamletpond_sao@qiniq.com
Municipal Type: Hamlet
Area: 173.36 sq km
Population in 2006: 1,315
Provincial Electoral District(s): Tunnuniq
Federal Electoral District(s): Nunavut
David Q. Qamaniq, Mayor
Grant Scott, Sr. Admin. Officer

Qikiqtarjuaq
P.O. Box 4
Qikiqtarjuaq, NU X0A 0B0
867-927-8832 Fax: 867-927-8120 Additional Phone: 867-927-8178
munQik@qiniq.com
Municipal Type: Hamlet
Area: 130.65 sq km
Population in 2006: 473
Provincial Electoral District(s): Uqqummiut
Federal Electoral District(s): Nunavut
Note: Formerly Broughton Island.
Loasie Audlakiak, Mayor
Qikmayor@qiniq.com
Mike Richards, Sr. Admin. Officer

Rankin Inlet
P.O. Box 310
Rankin Inlet, NU X0C 0G0
867-645-2895 Fax: 867-645-2146
sao@rankininlet.ca
Municipal Type: Hamlet
Incorporated: 1975; *Area:* 20.24 sq km
Population in 2006: 2,358
Provincial Electoral District(s): Rankin Inlet North; Rankin Inlet South/Whale Cove
Federal Electoral District(s): Nunavut
Lorne Kusugak, Mayor
Paul Waye, Sr. Admin. Officer

Repulse Bay
P.O. Box 10
Repulse Bay, NU X0C 0H0
867-462-9952 Fax: 867-462-4411
saorepulse@qiniq.com
Municipal Type: Hamlet
Incorporated: 1978; *Area:* 423.74 sq km
Population in 2006: 748
Provincial Electoral District(s): Akulliq
Federal Electoral District(s): Nunavut
Johnny Tagornak, Mayor
Bob Aymont, Sr. Admin. Officer

Resolute Bay
P.O. Box 60
Resolute Bay, NU X0A 0V0
867-252-3616 Fax: 867-252-3749 Additional Phone: 867-252-3689
hamletsao@qiniq.com
Municipal Type: Hamlet
Incorporated: 1987; *Area:* 116.89 sq km
Population in 2006: 229
Provincial Electoral District(s): Quttiktuq
Federal Electoral District(s): Nunavut
Susan Salluviniq, Mayor
Josh Hunter, Sr. Admin. Officer

Sanikiluaq
General Delivery
Sanikiluaq, NU X0A 0W0
867-266-7900 Fax: 867-266-8903 Additional Phone: 867-266-7901
sanisao@qiniq.com
Municipal Type: Hamlet
Incorporated: 1976; *Area:* 114.98 sq km
Population in 2006: 744
Provincial Electoral District(s): Hudson Bay
Federal Electoral District(s): Nunavut
Eli Kavik, Mayor
Thomas Kutluk, Sr. Admin. Officer

Taloyoak
P.O. Box 8
Taloyoak, NU X0B 1B0
867-561-6341 Fax: 867-561-5057
hamoftal@qiniq.com
www.polarnet.ca/~taloyoak
Municipal Type: Hamlet
Incorporated: 1981; *Area:* 37.65 sq km
Population in 2006: 809
Provincial Electoral District(s): Nattilik
Federal Electoral District(s): Nunavut
Note: Formerly known as Spence Bay.
Jimmy Oleekatalik, Mayor
Stephen King, Sr. Admin. Officer

Whale Cove
P.O. Box 120
Whale Cove, NU X0C 0J0
867-896-9961 Fax: 867-896-9109
saowc@qiniq.com
Municipal Type: Hamlet
Incorporated: 1976; *Area:* 283.65 sq km
Population in 2006: 353
Provincial Electoral District(s): Rankin Inlet South/Whale Cove
Federal Electoral District(s): Nunavut
Percy Kabloona, Mayor
Clayton Croucher, Sr. Admin. Officer

ONTARIO

There are two types of municipal government structure in Ontario: two-tier municipalities, which consist of upper-tier municipalities known as either regions or counties plus their constituent lower-tier municipalities; & single-tier municipalities.

One-half of Ontario's population lives in the single-tier cities of Toronto, Ottawa & Hamilton & in areas with a regional system of government. The regional system was created for the more densely populated areas of this provinces. Regions have more servicing repsonsibilities than a county, & while there are variations, services usually provided by regions include arterial roads, transit, policing, sewer & water systems, waste disposal, region-wide land use planning & development, health & social services. Lower-tier municipalities within regions are generally responsible for local roads, fire protection, tax collection, garbage collection, recreation & local land use planning. All municipalities in a region participate in the regional system.

Counties exist only in southern Ontario. Lower-tier municipalities (known as cities, towns, villages, townships) within counties provide the majority of municipal services to their residents. The services provided by county governments are usually limited to arterial roads, health & social services & county land use planning. Local municipalities raise taxes for their own purposes, as well as for upper-tier & school board purposes.

Generally, membership of the upper-tier council comprises representatives from the lower tiers, although heads of council can be directly elected.

Single-tier municipalities exist across Ontario, & include separated municipalities that are located within a county but are not part of the county for municipal purposes (e.g. City of Windsor, Town of Smiths Falls, Township of Pelee). Single-tier municipalities also include all northern municipalities (e.g. City of Thunder Bay, Town of Blind River, Township of Cockburn Island). Single-tier municipalities also include those former counties or regional municipalities that have amalgamated into single-tier municipalities (e.g. Municipality of Chatham-Kent, County of Prince Edward, County of Brant, City of Kawartha Lakes, City of Toronto, City of Hamilton, City of Ottawa, City of Greater Sudbury, Haldimand County, Norfolk County). Single-tier municipalities have responsibilibities for their residents.

The more populated areas are incorporated into municipalitites; only 40,000 people (not including aboriginal peoples on reserves) live in areas not incorporated as municipalities. Services in the northern regions have been structured to optimize efficiencies in service delivery. District Social Service Administration Boards deliver core services in social assistance, child care & social housing, & may also provide optional health servies, land ambulances & public health. Some services in a limited number of unincorporated areas are provided by local service boards & local roads which are funded by the province.

Under the Municipal Elections Act, local government elections are held on the second Monday in November, for a three-year term (2006, 2009, etc.). The preliminary list of electors is compiled by the Municipal Property Assessment Corporation from assessment & other data. The Municipal Elections Act provides for alternative methods of voting, including touch screen, vote by mail, vote by telephone, & internet voting.

Ontario

Counties & Municipal Districts in Ontario

Brant
P.O. Box 160
26 Park Ave.
Burford, ON N0E 1A0
519-449-2451 Fax: 519-449-2454 Toll Free Phone: 1-888-250-2297
brant@county.brant.on.ca
www.brant.ca
Municipal Type: County
Incorporated: Jan. 1, 1999; *Area:* 843.1 sq km
Population in 2006: 34,415
Provincial Electoral District(s): Brant
Federal Electoral District(s): Brant
Next Election: Nov. 2010 (4 year terms)
Ron Eddy, Mayor
Steve Schmitt, Councillor, Ward(s): 1
John Wheat, Councillor, Ward(s): 1
Roy Haggart, Councillor, Ward(s): 2
Shirley Simons, Councillor, Ward(s): 2
Cliff Atfield, Councillor, Ward(s): 3
Murray Powell, Councillor, Ward(s): 3
Robert Chambers, Councillor, Ward(s): 4
Kevin Hodge, Councillor, Ward(s): 4
Brian Coleman, Councillor, Ward(s): 5
Joan Gatward, Councillor, Ward(s): 5
Jayne Carman, Clerk & Coordinator, Council Committee, Administration
Don Glassford, Chief Administrative Officer, Administration
Heather Mifflin, Treasurer, Administration
Fran Bell, Director, Corporate Services, Administration
Cynthia Compeau, Director, Public Works, Administration
David Johnston, Director, Development Services, Administration
Paul Boissonneault, Fire Chief, Administration
Kathy Ballantyne, Manager, Parks & Facilities, Administration
Alex Davidson, Manager, Water Division, Administration
Lee Robinson, Manager, Infrastructure Services, Administration
Ed Sharp, Manager, Environmental Services, Administration
Mike Tout, Manager, Roads Operations, Administration

Bruce
P.O. Box 70
30 Park St.
Walkerton, ON N0G 2V0
519-881-1291 Fax: 519-881-1619
www.brucecounty.on.ca
Municipal Type: County
Area: 4,079.17 sq km
Population in 2006: 65,349
Next Election: Nov. 2010 (4 year terms)

Council
Mike Smith, Warden & Councillor
Charlie Bagnato, Councillor
Bill Goetz, Councillor
Milt McIver, Councillor
Gwen Gilbert, Councillor
Larry Kraemer, Councillor
Mitch Twolan, Councillor
Ron Oswald, Councillor

Administration
J. Wayne Jamieson, Chief Administrative Officer, Administration
wjamieson@brucecounty.on.ca
Bettyanne Cobean, C.M.O., Clerk-Treasurer, Administration
bcobean@brucecounty.on.ca
Doug Harris, Director, Human Resources, Administration
Chris LaForest, Director, Planning, Administration
Terry Sanderson, Director, Social Services & Social Housing, Administration
Doug Smith, Director, Emergency Services, Administration
Brian Knox, County Engineer, Administration

Dufferin
51 Zina St.
Orangeville, ON L9W 1E5
519-941-2816 Fax: 519-941-4565 Toll Free Phone: 1-877-941-6991
info@dufferincounty.on.ca; treasury@dufferincounty.on.ca
www.dufferincounty.on.ca
Municipal Type: County
Incorporated: Jan. 24, 1881; *Area:* 1,485.58 sq km
Population in 2006: 54,436
Next Election: Nov. 2010 (4 year terms)

Council
Allen Taylor, Warden & Councillor, Ward(s): East Garafraxa
warden@dufferincounty.on.ca
Don MacIver, Councillor, Ward(s): Amaranth
Walter Kolodziechuk, Councillor, Ward(s): Amaranth
John Oosterhof, Councillor, Ward(s): East Luther Grand Valley
Debbie Fawcett, Councillor, Ward(s): Melancthon
Bill Hill, Councillor, Ward(s): Melancthon
Lorie Haddock, Councillor, Ward(s): Mono
Ken McGhee, Councillor, Ward(s): Mono
Sue Snider, Councillor, Ward(s): Mulmur
Gordon D. Montgomery, Councillor, Ward(s): Mulmur
Rob Adams, Councillor, Ward(s): Orangeville
Warren Maycock, Councillor, Ward(s): Orangeville
Ken Bennington, Councillor, Ward(s): Shelburne
Ed Crewson, Councillor, Ward(s): Shelburne

Administration
Pam Hillock, Clerk, Administration
clerk@dufferincounty.on.ca
Linda J. Dean, Chief Administrative Officer, Administration
cao@dufferincounty.on.ca
Alan Selby, Treasurer, Administration
treasurer@dufferincounty.on.ca
Trevor Lewis, Director, Public Works, Administration
directorofpublicworks@dufferincounty.on.ca
Michael A. Giles, Chief Building Official, Administration
cbo@dufferincounty.on.ca
Mark Bialkowski, Manager, Human Resources, Administration
hr@dufferincounty.on.ca
Melissa Kovacs-Reid, Coordinator, Waste Management, Administration
wastemgmt@dufferincounty.on.ca
Shara Bagnell, Officer, Health & Safety, Administration
health&safety@dufferincounty.on.ca

Durham
P.O. Box 623
605 Rossland Rd. East
Whitby, ON L1N 6A3
905-668-7711 Fax: 905-668-9963 Toll Free Phone: 1-800-372-1102
info@durham.ca; cishelp@durham.ca (Corporate Information)
www.durham.ca
Municipal Type: Regional Municipality
Incorporated: Jan. 1, 1974; *Area:* 2,523.15 sq km
Population in 2006: 561,258
Next Election: Nov. 2010 (4 year terms)

Council
Roger Anderson, Regional Chair & Chief Executive Officer, Councillor, Fax: 905-668-1567
chair@durham.ca
Scott Crawford, Councillor, Ward(s): Ajax
Steve Parish, Councillor, Ward(s): Ajax
Colleen Jordan, Councillor, Ward(s): Ajax
Debbie Bath, Councillor, Ward(s): Brock
John Grant, Councillor, Ward(s): Brock
Mary Novak, Councillor, Ward(s): Clarington 1 & 2
Willie Woo, Councillor, Ward(s): Clarington 3 & 4
John R. Aker, Councillor, Ward(s): Oshawa
Bob Chapman, Councillor, Ward(s): Oshawa
Nancy Diamond, Councillor, Ward(s): Oshawa
Amy England, Councillor, Ward(s): Oshawa
Tito-Dante Marimpietri, Councillor, Ward(s): Oshawa
John Neal, Councillor, Ward(s): Oshawa
Nester Pidwerbecki, Councillor, Ward(s): Oshawa
Jennifer O'Connell, Councillor, Ward(s): Pickering 1
Bill McLean, Councillor, Ward(s): Pickering 2
Peter Rodrigues, Councillor, Ward(s): Pickering 3
Bobbie Drew, Councillor, Ward(s): Scugog
Jack Ballinger, Councillor, Ward(s): Uxbridge
Lorne Earle Coe, Councillor, Ward(s): Whitby
Joe Drumm, Councillor, Ward(s): Whitby
Don Mitchell, Councillor, Ward(s): Whitby

Administration
Patricia M. Madill, Regional Clerk, Administration, Fax: 905-668-9963
clerks@durham.ca
Garry H. Cubitt, M.S.W., Chief Administrative Officer, Administration
cao@durham.ca
R. Jim Clapp, Commissioner, Finance Department, Administration, Fax: 905-666-6256
Cliff Curtis, Commissioner, Works Department, Administration, Fax: 905-668-2051
works@durham.ca
Hugh A. Drouin, Commissioner, Social Services Department, Administration, Fax: 905-666-6219
socserv@durham.ca
Alex L. Georgieff, Commissioner, Planning Department, Administration, Fax: 905-666-6208
planning@durham.ca
Garth S. Johns, Commissioner, Human Resources, Administration, Fax: 905-666-3327
Robert J. Kyle, Commissioner, Health Department & Medical Officer, Administration, Fax: 905-666-3327
health@durham.ca
Pat W. Olive, Commissioner, Economic Development & Tourism, Administration
800-413-0017, Fax: 905-666-6228
business@durham.ca; tourism@durham.ca
Ivan Ciuciura, Director, Durham Emergency Management Office, Administration
905-430-2792, Fax: 905-430-8635
demo@durham.ca
Sherri Munns-Audet, Director, Corporate Communications, Administration, Fax: 905-668-1468
corporatecommunications@durham.ca
Ted Galinis, General Manager, Durham Region Transit, Administration, Fax: 905-666-6193
transit@durham.ca

Elgin
450 Sunset Dr.
St Thomas, ON N5R 5V1
519-631-1460 Fax: 519-633-7661
www.elgin-county.on.ca
Municipal Type: County
Incorporated: 1852; *Area:* 1,880.84 sq km
Population in 2006: 85,351
Next Election: Nov. 2010 (4 year terms)
Note: Restructuring of the county occurred in 1998.

Council
Graham Warwick, Warden & Councillor
warden@elgin-county.on.ca
Lynn Acre, Councillor
Bob Habkirk, Councillor
Sylvia Hofhuis, Councillor
Tom Marks, Councillor
James McIntyre, Councillor
Dave Mennill, Councillor
Bonnie Vowel, Councillor
John R. Wilson, Councillor

Administration
Mark G. McDonald, Chief Administrative Officer, Administration
mmcdonald@elgin-county.on.ca
Jim Bundschuh, Director, Financial Services, Administration
Brian Masschaele, Director, Community & Cultural Services, Administration
Harley Underhill, Director, Human Resources, Administration
Clayton Watters, Director, Engineering Services, Administration

Essex
360 Fairview Ave. West
Essex, ON N8M 1Y6
519-776-6441 Fax: 519-776-4455 Fax, Planning Department: 519-776-1253
www.countyofessex.on.ca
Municipal Type: County
Incorporated: 1999; *Area:* 1,851.34 sq km
Population in 2006: 393,402
Next Election: Nov. 2010 (4 year terms)

Council
Nelson Santos, Warden & Councillor
519-733-9936
nsantos@kingsville.ca
John Adams, Deputy Warden, Councillor
519-326-7010
jadams@leamington.ca
Wayne Hurst, Councillor
519-736-7646
whurst@amherstburg.ca
Robert Bailey, Councillor
519-978-0974
rbailey@amherstburg.ca
Ron McDermott, Councillor
519-776-8150
rmcdermott@essex.ca
Richard Meloche, Councillor
519-776-5726
rmeloche@essex.ca
Katherine Gunning, Councillor, Fax: 519-839-6222
kayway@kelcom.net
Tom Bain, Councillor
519-728-2394
tbain@lakeshore.ca
Robert Sylvester, Councillor
519-727-3849
rsylvester@lakeshore.ca
Gary Baxter, Councillor
mayor@town.lasalle.on.ca
Bill Varga, Councillor
bvarga@town.lasalle.on.ca
Robert Schmidt, Councillor
519-326-7443
rschmidt@leamington.ca
Gary McNamara, Councillor
519-735-6654
gmcnamara@tecumseh.ca
Tom Burton, Councillor
519-979-2339
tburton@tecumseh.ca

Administration
Mary S. Brennan, Clerk & Director, Council Services, Administration
mbrennan@countyofessex.on.ca
Brian Gregg, Chief Administrative Officer, Administration
Robert Maisonville, Director, Corporate Services & Treasurer, Administration
Greg Schlosser, Director, Human Resources, Administration
Bill King, Manager, Planning Services, Administration
Tom Bateman, County Engineer, Administration
Phillip Berthiaume, Planner, Emergency Measures, Administration

Frontenac
2069 Battersea Rd., RR#1
Glenburnie, ON K0H 1S0
613-548-9400 Fax: 613-546-8460
info@frontenaccounty.ca; communications@frontenaccounty.ca
www.frontenaccounty.ca
Municipal Type: County
Incorporated: Jan. 1, 1998; *Area:* 3,672.49 sq km
Population in 2006: 143,865
Next Election: Nov. 2010 (4 year terms)

Council
Janet Gutowski, Warden & Councillor
cfmayor@frontenaccounty.ca
Gary Davison, Councillor
Ron Maguire, Councillor
Jim Vanden Hoek, Councillor

Administration
Liz Savill, Chief Administrative Officer & Clerk, Administration

Marian Van Bruinessen, Treasurer, Administration
Paul Charbonneau, Director, Emergency & Transportation Services & Ch, Administration
Anne Marie Young, Manager, Economic Development, Administration

Grey

County Administration Bldg.
595 Ninth Ave. East
Owen Sound, ON N4K 3E3
519-376-2205 Fax: 519-376-7970 Toll Free Phone: 1-800-567-4739
clerks@greycounty.ca; socialservices@greycounty.ca
www.greycounty.ca
Municipal Type: County
Incorporated: Jan. 1, 1852; *Area:* 4,508.12 sq km
Population in 2006: 92,411
Next Election: Nov. 2010 (4 year terms)

Council
Arlene Wright, Warden & Councillor
warden@grey.ca
Howard Greig, Mayor, Councillor, Ward(s): Chatsworth
howard.greig@grey.ca
Bob Pringle, Deputy Mayor & Councillor, Ward(s): Chatsworth
bob.pringle@grey.ca
Alan Barfoot, Mayor, Councillor, Ward(s): Georgian Bluffs
alan.barfoot@grey.ca
Dwight Burley, Deputy Mayor & Councillor, Ward(s): Georgian Bluffs
dwight.burley@grey.ca
Brian Mullin, Mayor, Councillor, Ward(s): Grey Highlands
brian.mullin@grey.ca
David Fawcett, Deputy Mayor & Councillor, Ward(s): Grey Highlands
david.fawcett@grey.ca
Kathi Maskell, Mayor, Councillor, Ward(s): Hanover
kathi.maskell@grey.ca
Gerald Rogers, Deputy Mayor & Councillor, Ward(s): Hanover
gerald.rogers@grey.ca
Francis Richardson, Mayor, Councillor, Ward(s): Meaford
francis.richardson@grey.ca
Michael Traynor, Deputy Mayor & Councillor, Ward(s): Meaford
michael.traynor@grey.ca
Ruth Lovell-Stanners, Mayor, Councillor, Ward(s): Owen Sound
ruth.lovell@grey.ca
Arlene Wright, City/County Councillor, Councillor, Ward(s): Owen Sound
arlene.wright@grey.ca
Don Lewis, Mayor, Councillor, Ward(s): Southgate
don.lewis@grey.ca
Brian Milne, Deputy Mayor & Councillor, Ward(s): Southgate
brian.milne@grey.ca
Ellen Anderson, Mayor, Councillor, Ward(s): The Blue Mountains
ellen.anderson@grey.ca
Duncan McKinlay, Deputy Mayor & Councillor, Ward(s): The Blue Mountains
duncan.mckinlay@grey.ca
Kevin Eccles, Mayor, Councillor, Ward(s): West Grey
kevin.eccles@grey.ca
Dan Sullivan, Deputy Mayor & Councillor, Ward(s): West Grey
dan.sullivan@grey.ca

Administration
Sharon Vokes, C.M.O., County Clerk & Director, Council Services, Administration
svokes@greycounty.ca
Lance Thurston, Chief Administrative Officer, Administration
lance.thurston@grey.ca
Kevin Weppler, Director, Finance, Administration
kevin.weppler@grey.ca
Barb Fedy, BA, Director, Social Services, Administration
barb.fedy@grey.ca; socialservices@grey.ca
Geoff Hogan, BSc, Director, Information Technology, Administration
geoff.hogan@grey.ca
Randy Scherzer, BES, MCIP, RPP, Director, Planning & Development, Administration
randy.scherzer@grey.ca; planning@grey.ca
Grant McLevy, Director, Human Resources, Administration
grant.mclevy@grey.ca; employment@grey.ca
Gary Shaw, Director, Transportation & Public Safety, Administration
gary.shaw@grey.ca; transportation@grey.ca

Haldimand

Cayuga Administration Bldg.
P.O. Box 400
45 Munsee St. North
Cayuga, ON N0A 1E0
905-318-5932 Fax: 905-772-3542 E-mail, Ops.: operations@haldimandcounty.on.ca
info@haldimandcounty.on.ca; clerk@haldimandcounty.on.ca
www.haldimandcounty.on.ca
Municipal Type: County
Incorporated: Jan. 1, 2001; *Area:* 1,251.58 sq km
Population in 2006: 45,212
Provincial Electoral District(s): Haldimand-Norfolk
Federal Electoral District(s): Haldimand-Norfolk
Next Election: Nov. 2010 (4 year terms)
Marie Trainer, Mayor
mayor@haldimandcounty.on.ca
Leroy Bartlett, Councillor, Ward(s): 1
lbartlett@haldimandcounty.on.ca
Buck Sloat, Councillor, Ward(s): 2
bsloat@haldimandcounty.on.ca
Craig Grice, Councillor, Ward(s): 3
cgrice@haldimandcounty.on.ca
Tony Dalimonte, Deputy Mayor & Councillor, Ward(s): 4
tdalimonte@haldimandcounty.on.ca
Don Ricker, Councillor, Ward(s): 5
dricker@haldimandcounty.on.ca
Lorne Boyko, Councillor, Ward(s): 6
lpboyko@haldimandcounty.on.ca
Janis Lankester, Clerk, Administration
jlankester@haldimandcounty.on.ca
D. Boyle, Chief Administrative Officer, Administration
K. General, General Manager, Corporate Services, Administration
R. Lane, General Manager, Community Services, Administration
C. Manley, General Manager, Planning & Economic Development, Administration
G. Rae, General Manager, Public Works, Administration

Haliburton

P.O. Box 399
11 Newcastle St.
Minden, ON K0M 2K0
705-286-1333 Fax: 705-286-4829 Toll Free: 1-866-886-8815
aballe@county.haliburton.on.ca
www.haliburtoncounty.ca
Municipal Type: County
Incorporated: Jan. 1, 2001; *Area:* 4,025.27 sq km
Population in 2006: 16,147
Next Election: Nov. 2010 (4 year terms)

Council
Dave Burton, Warden & Councillor
705-448-9355
dburton@highlandseast.ca
Eleanor Harrison, Councillor, Ward(s): Algonquin Highlands
705-489-2128
eharrison@algonquinhighlands.ca
Tom Gardner, Councillor, Ward(s): Algonquin Highlands
705-489-3703
tomgardner01@hotmail.com
Murray Fearrey, Councillor, Ward(s): Dysart et al
705-457-2557
mfearrey@dysartetal.ca
Bill Davis, Councillor, Ward(s): Dysart et al
705-457-1196
bdavis@county.haliburton.on.ca
James Mackie, Councillor, Ward(s): Highlands East
613-339-1714
james.mackie@sympatico.ca
James McMahon, Councillor, Ward(s): Minden Hills
705-286-2801
jmcmahon@mindenhills.ca
Cheryl Murdoch, Councillor, Ward(s): Minden Hills
705-286-1701

Administration
Tamara Wilbee, County Clerk & Coordinator, Human Resources, Administration
twilbee@county.haliburton.on.ca
Jim Wilson, Chief Administrative Officer, Administration
jwilson@county.haliburton.on.ca
Laura Janke, Treasurer, Administration
ljanke@county.haliburton.on.ca
Pat Kennedy, Director, Emergency Services, Administration
pkennedy@county.haliburton.on.ca
Doug Ray, Director, Public Works, Administration
dray@county.haliburton.on.ca
Robert Smith, Director, Economic Development & Tourism Marketing, Administration
rsmith@county.haliburton.on.ca
Jane Tousaw, Director, Planning, Administration
jtousaw@county.haliburton.on.ca
Roy Haig, Manager, Engineering, Administration
rhaig@county.haliburton.on.ca
Jim Young, Manager, Operations, Administration
jyoung@county.haliburton.on.ca

Halton

1151 Bronte Rd.
Oakville, ON L6M 3L1
905-825-6000 Fax: 905-825-9010 Toll Free Phone: 1-866-442-5866; TTY: 905-827-9833
accesshalton@halton.ca
www.halton.ca
Municipal Type: Regional Municipality
Incorporated: Jan. 1, 1974; *Area:* 967.17 sq km
Population in 2006: 439,256
Next Election: Nov. 2010 (4 year terms)

Council
Gary Carr, Regional Chair, Councillor
905-825-6115, Fax: 905-825-8273
gary.carr@halton.ca
Rick Goldring, Councillor, Ward(s): Burlington Mayor
Rick Craven, Councillor, Ward(s): Burlington 1
Marianne Meed Ward, Councillor, Ward(s): Burlington 2
John Taylor, Councillor, Ward(s): Burlington 3
Jack Dennison, Councillor, Ward(s): Burlington 4
Paul Sharman, Councillor, Ward(s): Burlington 5
Blair Lancaster, Councillor, Ward(s): Burlington 6
Rick Bonnette, Councillor, Ward(s): Halton Hills Mayor
Clark Somerville, Councillor, Ward(s): Halton Hills 1 & 2
Jane Fogal, Councillor, Ward(s): Halton Hills 3 & 4
Gordon Krantz, Councillor, Ward(s): Milton Mayor
Tony Lambert, Councillor, Ward(s): Milton 1, 6, 7, 8
Colin Best, Councillor, Ward(s): Milton 2, 3, 4, 5
Rob Burton, Councillor, Ward(s): Oakville Mayor
Alan Johnston, Councillor, Ward(s): Oakville 1
Cathy Duddeck, Councillor, Ward(s): Oakville 2
F. Keith Bird, Councillor, Ward(s): Oakville 3
Allan Elgar, Councillor, Ward(s): Oakville 4
Jeff Knoll, Councillor, Ward(s): Oakville 5
Tom Adams, Councillor, Ward(s): Oakville 6

Administration
Susan Lathan, Regional Clerk & Director, Council Services, Administration
regionalclerk@halton.ca
Pat Moyle, Chief Administrative Officer, Administration
J.E. MacCaskill, Regional Treasurer & Commissioner, Corporate Servi, Administration
Mark Meneray, Commissioner, Legislative & Planning Services & Co, Administration
Robert Nosal, Commissioner & Medical Officer of Health, Administration
Adelina Urbanski, Commissioner, Social & Community Services, Administration
M. Zamojc, Commissioner, Public Works, Administration

Hastings

County Administration Bldg.
P.O. Box 4400
235 Pinnacle St.
Belleville, ON K8N 3A9
613-966-1319 Fax: 613-966-2574 Toll Free Phone: 1-800-510-3306
www.hastingscounty.com
Municipal Type: County
Incorporated: 1850; *Area:* 5,977.64 sq km
Population in 2006: 130,474
Next Election: Nov. 2010 (4 year terms)

Council
Ron Emond, Warden & Councillor, Ward(s): Hastings Highlands
emondr@hastingscounty.com
Lloyd Churchill, Councillor, Ward(s): Bancroft
Dave Panabaker, Councillor, Ward(s): Carlow/Mayo
Tom Deline, Councillor, Ward(s): Centre Hastings
Norm Clark, Councillor, Ward(s): Deseronto
Carl Tinney, Councillor, Ward(s): Faraday
Dave Golem, Councillor, Ward(s): Limerick
Bob Sager, Councillor, Ward(s): Madoc
Terry Clemens, Councillor, Ward(s): Marmora & Lake
Peter Kooistra, Councillor, Ward(s): Stirling-Rawdon
Wanda Donaldson, Councillor, Ward(s): Tudor & Cashel
Jo-Anne Albert, Councillor, Ward(s): Tweed
Margaret Walsh, Councillor, Ward(s): Tyendinaga
Dan McCaw, Councillor, Ward(s): Wollaston

Administration
James Pine, Chief Administrative Officer & Clerk, Administration
pinej@hastingscounty.com
Sue Horwood, Treasurer, Director, Finance, Asset Management & S, Administration
Shaune Lightfoot, Director, Human Resources, Administration
Brian McComb, Director, Planning, Administration

Huron

1 Court House Sq.
Goderich, ON N7A 1M2
519-524-8394 Fax: 519-524-2044 Toll Free Phone: 1-888-524-8394 (in 519 area)
huronadmin@huroncounty.ca
www.huroncounty.ca
Municipal Type: County
Area: 3,396.68 sq km
Population in 2006: 59,325
Next Election: Nov. 2010 (4 year terms)

Council
Ken Oke, Warden & Councillor, Ward(s): South Huron
Ben Van Diepenbeek, Councillor, Ward(s): Ashfield-Colborne-Wawanosh
Neil Rintoul, Councillor, Ward(s): Ashfield-Colborne-Wawanosh
Bill Dowson, Councillor, Ward(s): Bluewater
Jim Fergusson, Councillor, Ward(s): Bluewater
Dave Johnston, Councillor, Ward(s): Bluewater
Bert Dykstra, Councillor, Ward(s): Central Huron
John Bezaire, Councillor, Ward(s): Central Huron
Tim Collyer, Councillor, Ward(s): Central Huron
Deb Shewfelt, Councillor, Ward(s): Goderich
John Grace, Councillor, Ward(s): Goderich
Max Demaray, Councillor, Ward(s): Howick
Joe Seili, Councillor, Ward(s): Huron East
Bernie MacLellan, Councillor, Ward(s): Huron East
Bill Siemon, Councillor, Ward(s): Huron East
Dorothy Kelly, Councillor, Ward(s): Morris-Turnberry
Neil Vincent, Councillor, Ward(s): North Huron
Murray Scott, Councillor, Ward(s): North Huron
George Robertson, Councillor, Ward(s): South Huron
Jim Dietrich, Councillor, Ward(s): South Huron

Administration
Barbara Wilson, Clerk, Administration
Dave Laurie, Director, Public Works, Administration
Scott Tousaw, Director, Planning & Development, Administration
Nancy Cameron, Medical Officer of Health, Administration

Lambton

P.O. Box 3000
789 Broadway St.
Wyoming, ON N0N 1T0
519-845-0801 Fax: 519-845-3160 Toll Free Phone: 1-866-324-6912
administration@county-lambton.on.ca
www.lambtononline.com

Municipal Type: County
Incorporated: 1853; *Area:* 3,001.7 sq km
Population in 2006: 128,204
Next Election: Nov. 2010 (4 year terms)

Council
Jim Burns, Warden & Councillor
jim.burns@county-lambton.on.ca
Anne Marie Gillis, Deputy Warden, Councillor
annemariegillis@sarnia.ca
Don McGugan, Councillor, Ward(s): Brooke-Alvinston
jdmcgugan@hotmail.com
William (Bill) Bilton, Councillor, Ward(s): Dawn-Euphemia
mayor@dawneuphemia.on.ca
Gord Minielly, Councillor, Ward(s): Lambton Shores
minielly1@execulink.com
Carolyn Jamieson, Councillor, Ward(s): Lambton Shores
cjscookies@execulink.com
Gord Perry, Councillor, Ward(s): Oil Springs
gord.perry@county-lambton.on.ca
John McCharles, Councillor, Ward(s): Petrolia
johnnyremax@bellnet.ca
Lonny Napper, Councillor, Ward(s): Plympton-Wyoming
lnapper@xcelco.on.ca
Dick Kirkland, Councillor, Ward(s): Point Edward
dkirkland@villageofpointedward.com
Mike Bradley, Councillor, Ward(s): Sarnia
mayor@city.sarnia.on.ca
David Boushy, Councillor, Ward(s): Sarnia
d.boushy@cogeco.ca
Jim Foubister, Councillor, Ward(s): Sarnia
jfoubister1@cogeco.ca
Bev MacDougall, Councillor, Ward(s): Sarnia
bevmacdougall@ebtech.net
Steve Arnold, Councillor, Ward(s): St. Clair
sarnold1@rogers.blackberry.net
Peter Gilliland, Councillor, Ward(s): St. Clair
pgillila@rivernet.net
Todd Case, Councillor, Ward(s): Warwick
cases@execulink.com

Administration
Ronald G. Van Horne, Chief Administrative Officer, Administration
Kenneth C.R. Dick, MSW, General Manager, Social & Health Services, Administration
Jim Kutyba, P.Eng., General Manager, Infrastructure & Development Serv, Administration
Cindy Thayer, General Manager, Community Services, Administration
Stephane Thiffeault, General Manager, Corporate Services, Administration
Andrew Taylor, MSW, Manager, Environmental Health & Prevention Service, Administration

Lanark
County Administration Bldg.
P.O. Box 37
99 Christie Lake Rd.
Perth, ON K7H 3E2
613-267-4200 Fax: 613-267-2964 Toll Free Phone: 1-888-952-6275
info@county.lanark.on.ca
www.county.lanark.on.ca
Municipal Type: County
Incorporated: Jan. 1st 1998; *Area:* 2,979.14 sq km
Population in 2006: 63,785
Next Election: Nov. 2010 (4 year terms)
John MacTavish, Councillor, Ward(s): Montague
johnmactavish@bellnet.ca

Council
Paul Dulmage, Warden & Councillor, Ward(s): Carleton Place
Richard Kidd, Councillor, Ward(s): Beckwith Township
rkidd@ripnet.com
Sharon Mousseau, Councillor, Ward(s): Beckwith Township
smousseau@ripnet.com
Ed Sonnenburg, Councillor, Ward(s): Carleton Place
e.sonnenburg@rogers.com
Aubrey Churchill, Councillor, Ward(s): Drummond / North Elmsley
achurchill@storm.ca
Gord McConnell, Councillor, Ward(s): Drummond / North Elmsley
gmcconnell@ripnet.com
Bob Fletcher, Councillor, Ward(s): Lanark Highlands
bob.fletcher@xplornet.com
Bruce Horlin, Councillor, Ward(s): Lanark Highlands
b.horlin@sympatico.ca
Al Lunney, Councillor, Ward(s): Mississippi Mills
al.lunney@sympatico.ca
Brenda Hurrle, Councillor, Ward(s): Mississippi Mills
unitedway@trytel.com
Bill Dobson, Councillor, Ward(s): Montague
bdobson@ripnet.com
John Fenik, Councillor, Ward(s): Perth
jfenik@cogeco.ca
John Gemmell, Councillor, Ward(s): Perth
jgemmell.lc@cogeco.ca
Keith Kerr, Councillor, Ward(s): Tay Valley Township
kmkk@ripnet.com
Susan Freeman, Councillor, Ward(s): Tay Valley Township
sfreeman@rideau.net

Administration
Cathie Ritchie, Clerk, Administration
clerk@county.lanark.on.ca
Peter Wagland, Chief Administrative Officer, Administration
cao@county.lanark.on.ca
Kurt Greaves, Treasurer & Director, Finance, Administration
Steve Allan, Director, Public Works, Administration
Lisa Crosbie-Larmon, Director, Human Resources, Administration
Nancy Green, Director, Social Services, Administration
Sam Law, Director, Information Technology, Administration

Lennox & Addington
P.O. Box 1000
97 Thomas St. East
Napanee, ON K7R 3S9
613-354-4883 Fax: 613-354-3112
www.lennox-addington.on.ca
Municipal Type: County
Area: 2,776.48 sq km
Population in 2006: 40,542
Next Election: Nov. 2010 (4 year terms)

Council
Gord Schermerhorn, Warden & Councillor
613-354-4883
Gary Hodson, Councillor
613-354-3664
Henry Hogg, Councillor
613-336-0227
Bill Lowry, Councillor
613-583-2412
Clayton McEwen, Councillor
613-354-4883
Todd Steele, Councillor
613-379-5664
Debbie Thompson, Councillor
613-378-1553
Helen Yanch, Councillor
613-336-8774

Administration
Larry Keech, Chief Administrative Officer & Clerk, Administration
lkeech@lennox-addington.on.ca
Stephen Fox, Director, Financial & Physical Services, Administration
sfox@lennox-addington.on.ca
Bill Bishop, Director, Human Resources, Administration
bbishop@lennox-addington.on.ca
Brian Elo-Sheperd, Director, Social Services, Administration
elo-shepherdb@pelass.org
Mary Anne Evans, Director, Information Services, Administration
mevans@lennox-addington.on.ca
Tom Bedford, Manager, Ambulance Services & Emergency Programs, Administration
tbedford@lennox-addington.on.ca
Linda Andoney, Coordinator, Environmental Services, Administration
landoney@lennox-addington.on.ca

Middlesex
399 Ridout St. North
London, ON N6A 2P1
519-434-7321 Fax: 519-434-0638
www.county.middlesex.on.ca
Municipal Type: County
Area: 3,317.15 sq km
Population in 2006: 422,333
Next Election: Nov. 2010 (4 year terms)

Council
Jim Maudsley, Warden & Councillor, Ward(s): Thames Centre
warden@county.middlesex.on.ca
David Bolton, Councillor, Ward(s): Adelaide Metcalfe
Paul Hodgins, Councillor, Ward(s): Lucan Biddulph
Al Edmondson, Councillor, Ward(s): Middlesex Centre
Albert Bannister, Councillor, Ward(s): Middlesex Centre
Wesley Hodgson, Councillor, Ward(s): North Middlesex
Ian Brebner, Councillor, Ward(s): North Middlesex
Doug Reycraft, Councillor, Ward(s): Southwest Middlesex
Vance Blackmore, Councillor, Ward(s): Southwest Middlesex
Mel Veale, Councillor, Ward(s): Strathroy Caradoc
Joanne Vanderheyden, Councillor, Ward(s): Strathroy Caradoc
Delia Reiche, Councillor, Ward(s): Thames Centre

Administration
Kathy Bunting, Clerk, Administration
kbunting@county.middlesex.on.ca
Bill Rayburn, Chief Administrative Officer, Administration
brayburn@county.middlesex.on.ca
Jim Gates, Treasurer, Administration
jgates@county.middlesex.on.ca
Sally Bennett, Director, Social Services, Administration
Steve Evans, Director, Planning & Economic Development & Deputy, Administration
Denis Merrall, Director, Emergency Services, Administration
Chris Traini, County Engineer, Administration
Doug Spettigue, Human Resource Officer, Administration
John Trott, Woodlands Conservation Officer & Weed Inspector, Administration

Muskoka
70 Pine St.
Bracebridge, ON P1L 1N3
705-645-2231 Fax: 705-645-5319 Toll Free Phone: 1-800-461-4210 (In 705 area code)
info@muskoka.on.ca
www.muskoka.on.ca
Municipal Type: Regional Municipality
Incorporated: Jan. 1, 1971; *Area:* 3,890.24 sq km
Population in 2006: 57,563
Next Election: Nov. 2010 (4 year terms)
Janet Peake, Councillor, Ward(s): Lake of Bays

Council
Gord Adams, District Chair, Councillor
gadams@muskoka.on.ca
Susan Pryke, Acting Chair, Councillor
Steven Clement, Councillor, Ward(s): Bracebridge
Don Coates, Councillor, Ward(s): Bracebridge
Graydon Smith, Councillor, Ward(s): Bracebridge
Scott Young, Councillor, Ward(s): Bracebridge
Larry Braid, Councillor, Ward(s): Georgian Bay
Greg Sutcliffe, Councillor, Ward(s): Georgian Bay
Jim Walden, Councillor, Ward(s): Georgian Bay
Mark Clairmont, Councillor, Ward(s): Gravenhurst
Bob Colhoun, Councillor, Ward(s): Gravenhurst
John Klinck, Councillor, Ward(s): Gravenhurst
Terry Pilger, Councillor, Ward(s): Gravenhurst
Fran Coleman, Councillor, Ward(s): Huntsville
Claude Doughty, Councillor, Ward(s): Huntsville
Brian Thompson, Councillor, Ward(s): Huntsville
George Young, Councillor, Ward(s): Huntsville
Ben Boivin, Councillor, Ward(s): Lake of Bays
Margaret Casey, Councillor, Ward(s): Lake of Bays
Mary Crady, Councillor, Ward(s): Muskoka Lakes
Stewart Martin, Councillor, Ward(s): Muskoka Lakes
Susan Pryke, Councillor, Ward(s): Muskoka Lakes
Nancy Thompson, Councillor, Ward(s): Muskoka Lakes

Administration
Christine Lees, District Clerk, Administration
clees@muskoka.on.ca
Jim Green, Chief Administrative Officer, Administration
jgreen@muskoka.on.ca
Stephen Cairns, Commissioner, Finance & Corporate Services, Administration
scairns@muskoka.on.ca
Tony White, Commissioner, Engineering & Public Works, Administration
705-645-6764
publicworks@muskoka.on.ca
Rick Williams, Commissioner, Community Services, Administration
705-645-2412
rwilliams@muskoka.on.ca; mcsinfo@muskoka.on.ca
Geoff Bache, Director, Environmental Services, Administration
Terri Burton, Director, Emergency Services, Administration
tburton@muskoka.on.ca
Herman Clemens, Director, Water & Sewer Operations, Administration
Anna Landry, Director, Human Resources, Administration, Fax: 705-645-4065
alandry@muskoka.on.ca
Noel Waters, Director, Roads & Waste Management, Administration

Niagara
P.O. Box 1042
2201 St. David's Rd.
Thorold, ON L2V 4T7
905-685-1571 Fax: 905-687-4977 Toll Free Phone: 1-800-263-7215; TTY: 905-984-3613
www.niagararegion.ca
Municipal Type: Regional Municipality
Incorporated: Jan. 1, 1970; *Area:* 1,854.17 sq km
Population in 2006: 427,421
Next Election: Nov. 2010 (4 year terms)

Council
Peter Partington, Regional Chair & Councillor
chairman@niagararegion.ca
Douglas Martin, Councillor, Ward(s): Fort Erie
mayor@town.forterie.ca
Shirley Cordiner, Councillor, Ward(s): Fort Erie
shirley.cordiner@niagararegion.ca
Bob Bentley, Councillor, Ward(s): Grimsby
bob.bentley@niagararegion.ca
Debbie M. Zimmerman, Councillor, Ward(s): Grimsby
debbie.zimmerman@niagararegion.ca
Bill Hodgson, Councillor, Ward(s): Lincoln
bhodgson@lincoln.ca
Mark Bylsma, Councillor, Ward(s): Lincoln
mark.bylsma@niagararegion.ca
R.T. (Ted) Salci, Councillor, Ward(s): Niagara Falls
tsalci@niagarafalls.ca
Barbara Greenwood, Councillor, Ward(s): Niagara Falls
barbara.greenwood@niagararegion.ca
Norm Puttick, Councillor, Ward(s): Niagara Falls
norm.puttick@niagararegion.ca; nputtick@cogeco.net
Willian (Bill) Smeaton, Councillor, Ward(s): Niagara Falls
william.smeaton@niagararegion.ca
Gary Burroughs, Councillor, Ward(s): Niagara on the Lake
gburroughs@notl.org
Dave Lepp, Councillor, Ward(s): Niagara on the Lake
dave.lepp@niagararegion.ca
Dave Augustyn, Councillor, Ward(s): Pelham
mayordave@pelham.ca
Brian Baty, Councillor, Ward(s): Pelham
brian.baty@niagararegion.ca; batyregion@cogeco.net
Vance Badawey, Councillor, Ward(s): Port Colborne
mayor@portcolborne.ca
Bob Saracino, Councillor, Ward(s): Port Colborne
bob.saracino@niagararegion.ca
Brian McMullan, Councillor, Ward(s): St Catharines
bmcmullan@stcatharines.ca
Judy Casselman, Councillor, Ward(s): St Catharines
judy.casselman@niagararegion.ca
Brian Heit, Councillor, Ward(s): St Catharines
brian.heit@niagararegion.ca

Ronna Katzman, Councillor, Ward(s): St Catharines
ronna.katzman@niagararegion.ca
Tim Rigby, Councillor, Ward(s): St Catharines
tim.rigby@niagararegion.ca
D. Bruce Timms, Councillor, Ward(s): St Catharines
bruce.timms@niagararegion.ca
Henry D'Angela, Councillor, Ward(s): Thorold
mayor@thorold.com
Robert Gabriel, Councillor, Ward(s): Thorold
robert.gabriel@niagararegion.ca
Barbara Henderson, Councillor, Ward(s): Wainfleet
bhenderson@township.wainfleet.on.ca
Damian Goulbourne, Councillor, Ward(s): Welland
mayor@welland.ca
Cindy Forster, Councillor, Ward(s): Welland
cindy.forster@niagararegion.ca
George Marshall, Councillor, Ward(s): Welland
george.marshall@niagararegion.ca
Katie Trombetta, Councillor, Ward(s): West Lincoln
jthrower@westlincoln.com

Administration
Kevin Bain, Regional Clerk, Administration
Michael Trojan, Chief Administrative Officer, Administration
Gord Lockyer, Treasurer & Director, Financial Management & Repor, Administration
John Bergsma, Commissioner, Corporate Services, Administration
Brian Hutchings, Commissioner, Social Services, Administration
Patrick Robson, Commissioner, Integrated Community Planning, Administration
patrick.robson@niagararegion.ca
Robin C. Williams, Commissioner, Public Health & Medical Officer of H, Administration
robin.williams@niagararegion.ca
Betty Matthews-Malone, Director, Water & Wastewater Services, Administration
Andrew Pollock, Director, Waste Management Services, Administration
Denise Papaiz, Senior Manager, Corporate Communications, Administration
denise.papaiz@niagararegion.ca

Norfolk
Main Administration Bldg.
P.O. Box 545
50 Colborne St. South
Simcoe, ON N3Y 4N5
519-426-5870 Fax: 519-426-8573 Delhi Customer Service Ctr., Phone: 519-582-2100
www.norfolkcounty.on.ca
Municipal Type: County
Incorporated: Jan. 1, 2001; *Area:* 1,606.91 sq km
Population in 2006: 62,563
Provincial Electoral District(s): Haldimand-Norfolk
Federal Electoral District(s): Haldimand-Norfolk
Next Election: Nov. 2010 (4 year terms)
Dennis Travale, Mayor
dennis.travale@norfolkcounty.ca
John Hunt, Councillor, Ward(s): 1
john.hunt@norfolkcounty.ca
Roger Geysens, Councillor, Ward(s): 2
roger.geysens@norfolkcounty.ca
Michael J. Columbus, Councillor, Ward(s): 3
michael.columbus@norfolkcounty.ca
Jim Oliver, Councillor, Ward(s): 4
jim.oliver@norfolkcounty.ca
Charlie Luke, Councillor, Ward(s): 5
charlie.luke@norfolkcounty.ca
Heidy Van Dyk, Councillor, Ward(s): 5
heidy.vandyk@norfolkcounty.ca
John Wells, Councillor, Ward(s): 6
john.wells@norfolkcounty.ca
Harold Sonnenberg, Councillor, Ward(s): 7
harold.sonnenberg@norfolkcounty.ca
Bev Wood, Clerk & Manager, Council Services, Administration
bev.wood@norfolkcounty.ca
William F. Allcock, County Manager, Administration
allcock@norfolkcounty.ca
John Ford, Treasurer & Manager, Financial Services, Administration
john.ford@norfolkcounty.ca
Christopher D. Baird, CET, CMMIII, Ec.D., General Manager, Planning & Economic Development, Administration
Eric R. D'Hondt, P.Eng., General Manager, Public Works & Environmental Serv, Administration, Fax: 519-582-4571
eric.dhondt@norfolkcounty.ca
Frank Gelinas, General Manager, Corporate Services, Administration
frank.gelinas@norfolkcounty.ca
Kevin Lichach, General Manager, Community Services, Administration
Patti Moore, General Manager, Health & Social Services, Administration
E. Bernard Dawtre, Manager, Environmental Services, Administration
bernard.dawtrey@norfolkcounty.ca
John Hamilton, Manager, Engineering, Administration
john.hamilton@norfolkcounty.ca
Frank Sams, Manager, Parks & Facilities, Administration
Terry Dicks, Fire Chief, Administration
519-426-4115, Fax: 519-426-4140

Northumberland
555 Courthouse Rd.
Cobourg, ON K9A 5J6
905-372-3329 Fax: 905-372-1696 Toll Free Phone: 1-800-354-7050
www.northumberland.ca
Municipal Type: County
Area: 1,902.97 sq km
Population in 2006: 80,963
Next Election: Nov. 2010 (4 year terms)

Council
Linda Thompson, Warden & Councillor, Ward(s): Port Hope
mayor@porthope.ca
William Finley, Councillor, Ward(s): Alnwick / Haldimand
finleyw@northumberlandcounty.ca
Christine Herrington, Councillor, Ward(s): Brighton
herringtonc@northumberlandcounty.ca
Peter Delanty, Councillor, Ward(s): Cobourg
delantyp@northumberlandcounty.ca
Marc Coombs, Councillor, Ward(s): Cramahe
coombsm@northumberlandcounty.ca
Mark Lovshin, Councillor, Ward(s): Hamilton
lovshinm@northumberlandcounty.ca
Hector Macmillan, Councillor, Ward(s): Trent Hills
macmillanh@northumberlandcounty.ca

Administration
Diane Cane, CMO, County Clerk, Administration
Bill Pyatt, Chief Administrative Officer, Administration
Jennifer Moore, Treasurer & Director, Finance, Administration
James Rogers, By-Law Officer, Forest Conservation, Administration
705-799-2470, Fax: 705-879-7297
Ken Stubbings, Coordinator, Emergency Management, Administration

Peel
10 Peel Centre Dr.
Brampton, ON L6T 4B9
905-791-7800 Fax: 905-791-7871 Toll Free Phone: 1-888-919-7800
info@peelregion.ca
www.peelregion.ca
Municipal Type: Regional Municipality
Incorporated: Oct. 15, 1973; *Area:* 1,242.40 sq km
Population in 2006: 1,159,405
Next Election: Nov. 2010 (4 year terms)

Council
Emil Kolb, Regional Chair & Councillor, Fax: 905-791-2567
chair@peelregion.ca
Susan Fennell, Mayor & Councillor, Ward(s): Brampton
susan.fennell@brampton.ca
Elaine Moore, Councillor, Ward(s): Brampton 1 & 5
elaine.moore@brampton.ca
Paul Palleschi, Councillor, Ward(s): Brampton 2 & 6
paul.palleschi@brampton.ca
John Sanderson, Councillor, Ward(s): Brampton 3 & 4
john.sanderson@brampton.ca
Gael Miles, Councillor, Ward(s): Brampton 7 & 8
gael.miles@brampton.ca
John Sprovieri, Councillor, Ward(s): Brampton 9 & 10
john.sprovieri@brampton.ca
Marolyn Morrison, Mayor, Ward(s): Caledon
marolyn.morrison@caledon.ca
Richard Paterak, Councillor, Ward(s): Caledon 1
richard.paterak@caledon.ca
Allan Thompson, Councillor, Ward(s): Caledon 2
allan.thompson@caledon.ca
Richard Whitehead, Councillor, Ward(s): Caledon 3 & 4
r.whitehead@sympatico.ca
Patti Foley, Councillor, Ward(s): Caledon 5
patti.foley@caledon.ca
Hazel McCallion, Mayor & Councillor, Ward(s): Mississauga
mayor@mississauga.ca
Jim Tovey, Councillor, Ward(s): Mississauga 1
jim.tovey@mississauga.ca
Patricia Mullin, Councillor, Ward(s): Mississauga 2
pat.mullin@mississauga.ca
Chris Fonseca, Councillor, Ward(s): Mississauga 3
chris.fonseca@mississauga.ca
Frank Dale, Councillor, Ward(s): Mississauga 4
frank.dale@mississauga.ca
Eve Adams, Councillor, Ward(s): Mississauga 5
eve.adams@mississauga.ca
Ron Starr, Councillor, Ward(s): Mississauga 6
ron.starr@mississauga.ca
Nando Iannicca, Councillor, Ward(s): Mississauga 7
nando.iannicca@mississauga.ca
Katie Mahoney, Councillor, Ward(s): Mississauga 8
katie.mahoney@mississauga.ca
Pat Saito, Councillor, Ward(s): Mississauga 9
pat.saito@mississauga.ca
Sue McFadden, Councillor, Ward(s): Mississauga 10
sue.mcfadden@mississauga.ca
George Carlson, Councillor, Ward(s): Mississauga 11
george.carlson@mississauga.ca

Administration
David Szwarc, Chief Administrative Officer, Administration
N. Trim, Chief Financial Officer & Commissioner, Corporate, Administration
R.K. Gillespie, Commissioner, Employee & Business Services, Administration
Dan Labrecque, Commissioner, Environment, Transportation, & Plann, Administration
Janette Smith, Commissioner, Health Services, Administration
Keith Ward, Commissioner, Human Services, Administration
D. Mowat, Medical Officer of Health, Administration
P. O'Connor, Regional Solicitor & Director, Legal & Risk Manage, Administration
Damian Albanese, Director, Transportation, Administration
Norman Lee, Director, Waste Management, Administration
norman.lee@peelregion.ca

Perth
Courthouse
1 Huron St.
Stratford, ON N5A 5S4
519-271-0531 Fax: 519-271-6265
info@perthcounty.ca
www.perthcounty.ca
Municipal Type: County
Incorporated: Jan. 1850; *Area:* 2,218.41 sq km
Population in 2006: 74,344
Next Election: Nov. 2010 (4 year terms)
Note: Restructuring occurred in Jan. 1998.

Council
Julie Behrns, Warden & Councillor, Ward(s): North Perth
warden@perthcounty.ca
Ed Hollinger, Councillor, Ward(s): North Perth
ehollinger@northperth.ca
Terry Seiler, Councillor, Ward(s): North Perth
tdseiler@wightman.ca
Ian Forrest, Councillor, Ward(s): Perth East
iforrest@pertheast.on.ca
Bob McMillan, Councillor, Ward(s): Perth East
mcmillan@cyg.net
Robert J. McTavish, Councillor, Ward(s): Perth East
rjmct@rogers.com
Ron McKay, Councillor, Ward(s): Perth South
rlmckay@rogers.com
Robert Wilhelm, Councillor, Ward(s): Perth South
ulchtran@quadro.net
John Van Bakel, Councillor, Ward(s): West Perth
mvb@omniglobe.ca
Gerry Kehl, Councillor, Ward(s): West Perth
gerry@riverroots.ca

Administration
Bill Arthur, Chief Administrative Officer & Clerk, Administration
cao@perthcounty.ca
Renato Pullia, Treasurer & Director, Corporate Services, Administration
treasurer@perthcounty.ca
Matt Ash, Director, Public Works, Administration
mash@perthcounty.ca
Dave Hanly, Director, Planning & Development, Administration
dhanly@perthcounty.ca
Linda Rockwood, Director, Emergency Medical Services, Administration
lrockwood@perthcounty.ca
Cliff Eggleton, Manager, Operations, Administration
ceggleton@perthcounty.ca
Ann McKnight Duralia, Manager, Human Resources, Administration
amcknight@perthcounty.ca

Peterborough
County Court House
470 Water St.
Peterborough, ON K9H 3M3
705-743-0380 Fax: 705-876-1730 Toll Free Phone: 1-800-710-9586
gking@county.peterborough.on.ca
www.county.peterborough.on.ca
Municipal Type: County
Area: 3,805.71 sq km
Population in 2006: 133,080
Next Election: Nov. 2010 (4 year terms)

Council
Ronald Gerow, Warden & Councillor, Ward(s): Havelock-Belmont-Methuen
ron.gerow@sympatico.ca
Douglas Pearcy, Councillor, Ward(s): Asphodel-Norwood
dpearcy@accel.net
Terry Low, Councillor, Ward(s): Asphodel-Norwood
terry.low@sympatico.ca
Neal Cathcart, Councillor, Ward(s): Cavan Monaghan
ncathcart@cavanmonaghan.net
Brian Fallis, Councillor, Ward(s): Cavan Monaghan
bfallis@nexicom.net
Brian Bartlett, Councillor, Ward(s): Cavan Monaghan
bbartlett@cavanmonaghan.net
James Jones, Councillor, Ward(s): Douro-Dummer
dumnews@nexicom.net
Karl Moher, Councillor, Ward(s): Douro-Dummer
kmoher@nexicom.net
Thomas Flynn, Councillor, Ward(s): Galway-Cavendish & Harvey
Madeline Pearson, Councillor, Ward(s): Galway-Cavendish & Harvey
madelinepearson@sympatico.ca
Andy Sharpe, Councillor, Ward(s): Havelock-Belmont-Methuen
2andysharpe@gmail.com
Jim Whelan, Councillor, Ward(s): North Kawartha
reeve@northkawartha.on.ca; mjdmwh@sympatico.ca
Barry Rand, Councillor, Ward(s): North Kawartha
sallyandbarry@aol.com.ca
David Nelson, Councillor, Ward(s): Otonabee- South Monaghan
Paul Heath, Councillor, Ward(s): Otonabee- South Monaghan
paul.heath@sympatico.ca
Ron Millen, Councillor, Ward(s): Smith-Ennismore-Lakefield
rmillen@nexicom.net
Mary Smith, Councillor, Ward(s): Smith-Ennismore-Lakefield
mjsmith@peterboro.net

Administration

Sally Saunders, Clerk, Administration
ssaunders@county.peterborough.on.ca
Gary King, Chief Administrative Officer & Deputy Clerk, Administration
gking@county.peterborough.on.ca
John Butler, Treasurer, Administration
jbutler@county.peterborough.on.ca
Chris Bradley, Director, Public Works, Administration
cbradley@county.peterborough.on.ca
Mary Percy, Director, Human Resources, Administration
mpercy@county.peterborough.on.ca
Bryan Weir, Director, Planning, Administration
bweir@county.peterborough.on.ca
Sheridan Graham, General Manager, Strategic Services & Corporate Pr, Administration
sgraham@county.peterborough.on.ca
Sherry Arcaro, Manager, Environmental Services, Administration
sarcaro@county.peterborough.on.ca
Bill Linnen, Manager, Operations, Administration
blinnen@county.peterborough.on.ca
Bob English, Chief, Emergency Medical Services (EMS), Administration
benglish@county.peterborough.on.ca
Mark Cross, Specialist, Waste Diversion Operations, Administration
mcross@county.peterborough.on.ca

Prince Edward

332 Main St.
Picton, ON K0K 2T0
613-476-2148 Fax: 613-476-8356
info@pecounty.on.ca; council@pecounty.on.ca
www.pecounty.on.ca
Municipal Type: County
Incorporated: Jan. 1, 1998; *Area:* 1,050.14 sq km
Population in 2006: 25,496
Provincial Electoral District(s): Prince Edward-Hastings
Federal Electoral District(s): Prince Edward-Hastings
Next Election: Nov. 2010 (4 year terms)
Leo P. Finnegan, Mayor
lfinnegan@pecounty.on.ca
Bev Campbell, Councillor, Ward(s): 1 - Picton
bcampbell@pecounty.on.ca
Laverne Bailey, Councillor, Ward(s): 1 - Picton
lbailey@pecounty.on.ca
Barry Turpin, Councillor, Ward(s): 2 - Bloomfield
bturpin@pecounty.on.ca
Peter Mertens, Councillor, Ward(s): 3 - Wellington
pmertens@pecounty.on.ca
Sandy Latchford, Councillor, Ward(s): 4 - Ameliasburgh
slatchford@pecounty.on.ca
Dianne O'Brien, Councillor, Ward(s): 4 - Ameliasburgh
dobrien@pecounty.on.ca
Lori Slik, Councillor, Ward(s): 4 - Ameliasburgh
lslik@pecounty.on.ca
Brian Marisett, Councillor, Ward(s): 5 - Athol
bmarisett@pecounty.on.ca
Richard Parks, Councillor, Ward(s): 6 - Hallowell
rparks@pecounty.on.ca
Keith MacDonald, Councillor, Ward(s): 6 - Hallowell
kmacdonald@pecounty.on.ca
Peggy Burris, Councillor, Ward(s): 7 - Hillier
pburris@pecounty.on.ca
Ray Best, Councillor, Ward(s): 8 - North Marysburgh
rbest@pecounty.on.ca
Monica Alyea, Councillor, Ward(s): 9 - South Marysburgh
malyea@pecounty.on.ca
Kevin Gale, Councillor, Ward(s): 10 - Sophiasburgh
kgale@pecounty.on.ca
John Thompson, Councillor, Ward(s): 10 - Sophiasburgh
jthompson@pecounty.on.ca
Victoria Leskie, Clerk, Administration
vleskie@pecounty.on.ca
Richard Shannon, Chief Administrative Officer, Administration
rshannon@pecounty.on.ca
James Hepburn, Treasurer, Administration
jhepburn@pecounty.on.ca
Barry Braun, Commissioner, Recreation, Parks, & Culture Departm, Administration
bbraun@pecounty.on.ca
Gerry Murphy, Commissioner, Planning Services Department, Administration
gmurphy@pecounty.on.ca
Susan Turnbull, Commissioner, Corporate Services & Finance, Administration
sturnbull@pecounty.on.ca
Joe Angelo, P.Eng., Manager, Public Works Department Projects, Administration
jangelo@pecounty.on.ca
Grant Currie, Manager, Human Resources, Administration
gcurrie@pecounty.on.ca
Scott Manlow, Fire Chief, Administration
smanlow@pecounty.on.ca

Renfrew

9 International Dr.
Pembroke, ON K8A 6W5
613-735-7288 Fax: 613-735-2081 Toll Free Phone: 1-800-273-0183
info@countyofrenfrew.on.ca
www.countyofrenfrew.on.ca
Municipal Type: County
Incorporated: June 8, 1861; *Area:* 7,403.46 sq km
Population in 2006: 97,545
Next Election: Nov. 2010 (4 year terms)

Council

Don Rathwell, Warden & Councillor, Ward(s): Whitewater
613-646-2282
Raye-Anne Briscoe, Councillor, Ward(s): Admaston / Bromley
613-432-2885
Walter Stack, Councillor, Ward(s): Arnprior
613-623-4231
Zig Mintha, Councillor, Ward(s): Bonnechere Valley
613-628-3101
Norm Lentz, Councillor, Ward(s): Brudenell, Lyndoch, & Raglan
613-758-2061
Ann Aikens, Councillor, Ward(s): Deep River
613-584-2000
Peter Emon, Councillor, Ward(s): Greater Madawaska
613-752-2222
Tammy Stewart, Councillor, Ward(s): Head, Clara & Maria
613-586-2526
Robert A. Johnston, Councillor, Ward(s): Horton
613-432-6271
Janice Visneskie, Councillor, Ward(s): Killaloe, Hagarty & Richards
613-757-2300
Vance Gutzman, Councillor, Ward(s): Laurentian Hills
613-584-3114
Jack Wilson, Councillor, Ward(s): Laurentian Valley
613-584-3114
John Hildebrandt, Councillor, Ward(s): Madawaska Valley
613-756-2747
Mary Campbell, Councillor, Ward(s): McNab / Braeside
613-623-5756
Harold Weckworth, Councillor, Ward(s): North Algona Wilberforce
613-628-2080
Bob Sweet, Councillor, Ward(s): Petawawa
613-687-5536
Audrey R. Green, Councillor, Ward(s): Renfrew
613-432-4848

Administration

Norm Lemke, Chief Administrative Officer & Clerk, Administration
James D. Kutschke, CA, Treasurer & Deputy Clerk, Administration
Bruce Beakley, Director, Human Resources, Administration
Dave Darch, Director, Public Works & Engineering, Administration
613-732-4353
Michael Nolan, Director, Emergency Services, Administration
Jeff Muzzi, Manager, Forestry Services, Administration
613-735-3204
jmuzzi@countyofrenfrew.on.ca

Simcoe

County of Simcoe Administration Centre
1110 Hwy. 26
Midhurst, ON L0L 1X0
705-726-9300 Fax: 705-726-3991 Toll Free Phone: 1-866-893-9300, 1-800-263-3199
info@simcoe.ca
www.simcoe.ca
Municipal Type: County
Incorporated: Jan. 1, 1850; *Area:* 4,840.56 sq km
Population in 2006: 422,204
Next Election: Nov. 2010 (4 year terms)

Council

Tony Guergis, Warden & Councillor
tony.guergis@simcoe.ca; Warden@simcoe.ca
Tom Walsh, Councillor, Ward(s): Adjala-Tosorontio
Doug Little, Councillor, Ward(s): Adjala-Tosorontio
Doug White, Councillor, Ward(s): Bradford West Gwillimbury
Dennis Roughley, Councillor, Ward(s): Bradford West Gwillimbury
Ken Ferguson, Councillor, Ward(s): Clearview
Alicia Savage, Councillor, Ward(s): Clearview
Chris Carrier, Councillor, Ward(s): Collingwood
Sandra Cooper, Councillor, Ward(s): Collingwood
David Guergis, Councillor, Ward(s): Essa
Terry Dowdall, Councillor, Ward(s): Essa
Brian Jackson, Councillor, Ward(s): Innisfil
Gord Wauchope, Councillor, Ward(s): Innisfil
James Downer, Councillor, Ward(s): Midland
Ruth Hackney, Councillor, Ward(s): Midland
Mike MacEachern, Councillor, Ward(s): New Tecumseth
Rick Milne, Councillor, Ward(s): New Tecumseth
Harry Huges, Councillor, Ward(s): Oro-Medonte
Ralph Hough, Councillor, Ward(s): Oro-Medonte
Anita Dubeau, Councillor, Ward(s): Penetanguishene
Doug Leroux, Councillor, Ward(s): Penetanguishene
Bill Duffy, Councillor, Ward(s): Ramara
Basil Clarke, Councillor, Ward(s): Ramara
Phil Sled, Councillor, Ward(s): Severn
Judith Cox, Councillor, Ward(s): Severn
Tony Guergis, Councillor, Ward(s): Springwater
Tony Hope, Councillor, Ward(s): Springwater
Scott Warnock, Councillor, Ward(s): Tay
Michael Ladouceur, Councillor, Ward(s): Tay
Peggy Breckenridge, Councillor, Ward(s): Tiny
George Lawrence, Councillor, Ward(s): Tiny
Cal Patterson, Councillor, Ward(s): Wasaga Beach
David Foster, Councillor, Ward(s): Wasaga Beach

Administration

Glen R. Knox, County Clerk, Administration
Glen.Knox@simcoe.ca
Mark Aitken, Chief Administrative Officer, Administration
CAO@simcoe.ca
Craig Elliott, General Manager, Finance & Administration, Administration
Craig.Elliott@simcoe.ca
Rick Newlove, General Manager, Corporate Services, Administration
Rick.Newlove@simcoe.ca
Jane Sinclair, General Manager, Health & Cultural Services, Administration
Jane.Sinclair@simcoe.ca
Terry Talon, General Manager, Social Services, Administration
Terry.Talon@simcoe.ca
Dawn Hipwell, Director, Purchasing, Fleet, & Property, Administration
Dawn.Hipwell@simcoe.ca
Jim Hunter, Director, Transportation Construction, Administration
Jim.Hunter@simcoe.ca
Bryan MacKell, Director, Planning & Development, Administration
Bryan.MacKell@simcoe.ca
Rob McCullough, Director, Environmental Services, Administration
Rob.McCullough@simcoe.ca
Michael Moffatt, Director, Human Resources, Administration
Michael.Moffatt@simcoe.ca

Waterloo

Regional Administration Bldg.
P.O. Box 9051 C
150 Frederick St.
Kitchener, ON N2G 4J3
519-575-4400 Fax: 519-575-4481 Phone, Regional Councillors: 519-575-4501
regionalinquiries@region.waterloo.on.ca
www.region.waterloo.on.ca
Municipal Type: Regional Municipality
Incorporated: Jan. 1, 1973; *Area:* 1,368.64 sq km
Population in 2006: 478,121
Next Election: Nov. 2010 (4 year terms)

Council

Ken Seiling, Regional Chair & Councillor
519-575-4585, Fax: 519-575-4440
sken@region.waterloo.on.ca
Jane Brewer, Councillor, Ward(s): Cambridge
bjane@region.waterloo.on.ca
Doug Craig, Councillor, Ward(s): Cambridge
cdoug@region.waterloo.on.ca
Claudette Millar, Councillor, Ward(s): Cambridge
mclaudette@region.waterloo.on.ca
Tom Galloway, Councillor, Ward(s): Kitchener
gtom@region.waterloo.on.ca
Jean Haalboom, Councillor, Ward(s): Kitchener
hjean@region.waterloo.on.ca
Jake Smola, Councillor, Ward(s): Kitchener
sjake@region.waterloo.on.ca
Jim Wideman, Councillor, Ward(s): Kitchener
wjim@region.waterloo.on.ca
Carl Zehr, Councillor, Ward(s): Kitchener
zcarl@region.waterloo.on.ca
Kim Denouden, Councillor, Ward(s): North Dumfries
dekim@region.waterloo.on.ca
Brenda Halloran, Councillor, Ward(s): Waterloo
hbrenda@region.waterloo.on.ca
Jane Mitchell, Councillor, Ward(s): Waterloo
mjane@region.waterloo.on.ca
Sean Strickland, Councillor, Ward(s): Waterloo
ssean@region.waterloo.on.ca
Ross Kelterborn, Councillor, Ward(s): Wellesley
kross@region.waterloo.on.ca
Wayne Roth, Councillor, Ward(s): Wilmot
rwayne@region.waterloo.on.ca
William Strauss, Councillor, Ward(s): Woolwich
sbill@region.waterloo.on.ca

Administration

Kris Fletcher, Regional Clerk & Director, Council & Administrativ, Administration
fkris@region.waterloo.on.ca
Mike Murray, Chief Administrative Officer
mmike@region.waterloo.on.ca
Larry Ryan, Chief Financial Officer, Administration
rlarry@region.waterloo.on.ca
Rob Horne, Commissioner, Planning, Housing & Community Servic, Administration
hrob@region.waterloo.on.ca
Thomas Schmidt, Commissioner, Transportation & Environmental Servi, Administration
sthomas@region.waterloo.on.ca
Michael Schuster, Commissioner, Social Services, Administration
scmike@region.waterloo.on.ca
Penny Smiley, Commissioner, Human Resources, Administration
spenny@region.waterloo.on.ca
Gary Sosnoski, Commissioner, Corporate Resources, Administration
sogary@region.waterloo.on.ca
James Archibald, Director, Waste Management, Administration
ajames@region.waterloo.on.ca
Debra Arnold, Director, Legal Services & Regional Solicitor, Administration
adebra@region.waterloo.on.ca
Lucille Bish, Director, Community Services, Administration
blucille@region.waterloo.on.ca
Kevin Eby, Director, Community Planning, Administration
ekevin@region.waterloo.on.ca
Eric Gillespie, Director, Transit Services, Administration
geric@region.waterloo.on.ca
Nancy Kodousek, Director, Water Services, Administration
konancy@region.waterloo.on.ca
Ken Noonan, Director, Facilities Management & Fleet Services, Administration
nken@region.waterloo.on.ca
Graham Vincent, Director, Transportation Planning, Administration
vgraham@region.waterloo.on.ca
Liana Nolan, Medical Officer of Health, Administration

Wellington

74 Woolwich St.
Guelph, ON N1H 3T9
519-837-2600 Fax: 519-837-1909 Toll Free Phone: 1-800-663-0750
finance@county.wellington.on.ca (Treasury)
www.wellington.ca
Municipal Type: County
Incorporated: Jan. 1, 1852; *Area:* 2,656.66 sq km
Population in 2006: 200,425
Next Election: Nov. 2010 (4 year terms)
Note: The council of the County of Wellington is comprised of the mayors of its seven municipalities, plus nine elected county ward councillors.

Council
Joanne Ross-Zuj, Warden & Councillor, Ward(s): Centre Wellington
519-846-0213, Fax: 519-846-8593
warden@wellington.ca; joanner@wellington.ca
Rod Finnie, Warden & Councillor, Ward(s): Erin
519-833-2380
rodf@wellington.ca
Chris White, Councillor, Ward(s): Guelph / Eramosa
519-856-0450
chrisw@wellington.ca
John Green, Councillor, Ward(s): Mapleton
519-638-2126
johngr@wellington.ca
David Anderson, Councillor, Ward(s): Minto
519-343-3883
davida@wellington.ca
Brad Whitcombe, Councillor, Ward(s): Puslinch
519-623-7970
bradw@wellington.ca
Mike Broomhead, Councillor, Ward(s): Wellington North
519-323-1981
mikeb@wellington.ca
Mark MacKenzie, Councillor, Ward(s): 1
519-338-2641
markm@wellington.ca
Carl Hall, Councillor, Ward(s): 2
519-846-5235
carlh@wellington.ca
Walter Trachsel, Councillor, Ward(s): 3
519-323-2794
waltert@wellington.ca
Lynda White, Councillor, Ward(s): 4
519-848-2806
lyndaw@wellington.ca
Jean Innes, Councillor, Ward(s): 5
519-846-8460
jeani@wellington.ca
Robert Wilson, Councillor, Ward(s): 6
519-843-3329
robertw@wellington.ca
Gordon Tosh, Councillor, Ward(s): 8
519-856-9056
gordt@wellington.ca
Lou Maieron, Councillor, Ward(s): 9
519-833-2559
loum@wellington.ca

Administration
Donna Van Wyck, Clerk, Administration
donnav@wellington.ca
Scott Wilson, Chief Administrative Officer, Administration
scottw@wellington.ca
Craig Dyer, Treasurer, Administration
craigd@county.wellington.on.ca
Andrea Lawson, Administrator, Human Resources, Administration, Fax: 519-837-8882
andreal@county.wellington.on.ca
Heather Burke, Director, Housing, Administration
heatherb@wellington.ca; wghsinfo@wellington.ca
Gary Cousins, Director, Planning, Administration, Fax: 519-823-1694
garyc@wellington.ca
Luisa Della Croce, Director, Child Care Services, Administration
luisad@wellington.ca
Bonnie Blackmore, Manager, Community Services, Administration
bonnieb@wellington.ca
Linda Dickson, Coordinator, Community Emergency Management, Administration
519-846-8058, Fax: 519-846-8482
lindad@wellington.ca
Rob Johnson, Coordinator, Forestry, Administration
robj@wellington.ca
Barb McKay, Councillor, Ward(s): 7
519-822-2984
barbm@wellington.ca

York

17250 Yonge St.
Newmarket, ON L3Y 6Z1
905-895-1231 Fax: 905-895-1238 Toll Free Phone: 1-877-464-9675
info@york.ca; twgeneral@york.ca (Transportation & Works)
www.york.ca
Municipal Type: Regional Municipality
Incorporated: Jan. 1, 1971; *Area:* 1,761.84 sq km
Population in 2006: 892,712
Next Election: Nov. 2010 (4 year terms)

Council
Bill Fisch, Regional Chair & Councillor
regional.chair@york.ca
Geoff Dawe, Councillor, Ward(s): Aurora Mayor
Virginia Hackson, Councillor, Ward(s): East Gwillimbury Mayor
Robert Grossi, Councillor, Ward(s): Georgina Mayor
Danny Wheeler, Councillor, Ward(s): Georgina
Steve Pellegrini, Councillor, Ward(s): King Mayor
Frank Scarpitti, Councillor, Ward(s): Markham Mayor
Jack Heath, Councillor, Ward(s): Markham
Jim Jones, Councillor, Ward(s): Markham
Gordon Landon, Councillor, Ward(s): Markham
Joe Li, Councillor, Ward(s): Markham
A.J. (Tony) Van Bynen, Councillor, Ward(s): Newmarket Mayor
John Taylor, Councillor, Ward(s): Newmarket
David Barrow, Councillor, Ward(s): Richmond Hill Mayor
Brenda Hogg, Councillor, Ward(s): Richmond Hill
Vito Spatafora, Councillor, Ward(s): Richmond Hill
Maurizio Bevilacqua, Councillor, Ward(s): Vaughan Mayor
Michael Di Biase, Councillor, Ward(s): Vaughan
Deb Schulte, Councillor, Ward(s): Vaughan
Gino Rosati, Councillor, Ward(s): Vaughan
Wayne Emmerson, Councillor, Ward(s): Whitchurch-Stouffville Mayor

Administration
Denis Kelly, Regional Clerk, Administration
regionalclerk@york.ca
Bruce Macgregor, Chief Administrative Officer, Administration
Lloyd Russell, Regional Treasurer & Commissioner, Finance, Administration
Jim Davidson, Commissioner, Corporate Services, Administration
Kathleen Llewellyn-Thomas, Commissioner, Transportation Services, Administration
Erin Mahoney, Commissioner, Environmental Services, Administration
Joann Simmons, Commissioner, Community & Health Services, Administration
Bryan Tuckey, Commissioner, Planning & Development Services, Administration
Patrick Casey, Director, Corporate Communications, Administration
patrick.casey@york.ca
Karen Close, Director, Human Resource Services, Administration
Karim Kurji, Medical Officer of Health & Director, Public Healt, Administration

Major Municipalities in Ontario

Ajax

65 Harwood Ave. South
Ajax, ON L1S 2H9
905-683-4550 Fax: 905-683-1061 Corporate Communications: 905-619-2529, ext. 3362
info@townofajax.com
www.townofajax.com
Municipal Type: City
Incorporated: 1955; *Area:* 67.09 sq km
County or District: Durham Regional Municipality; *Population in 2006:* 90,167
Provincial Electoral District(s): Ajax-Pickering
Federal Electoral District(s): Ajax-Pickering
Next Election: Nov. 2010 (4 year terms)

Council
Steve Parish, Mayor, Fax: 905-683-9450
Shaun Collier, Regional Councillor, Ward(s): 1 & 2
shaun.collier@townofajax.com
Colleen Jordan, Regional Councillor, Ward(s): 3 & 4
colleen.jordan@townofajax.com
Marilyn Crawford, Councillor, Ward(s): 1
Renrick Ashby, Councillor, Ward(s): 2
renrick.ashby@townofajax.com
Joanne Dies, Councillor, Ward(s): 3
joanne.dies@townofajax.com
Pat Brown, Councillor, Ward(s): 4
pat.brown@townofajax.com

Administration
Brian J. Skinner, Chief Administrative Officer, Administration
Rob Ford, Director, Finance & Treasurer, Administration
Finance@townofajax.com
John Fleck, Director, Human Resource Services, Administration
Dave Meredith, Director, Operations & Environmental Services, Administration
operations@townofajax.com

Amherstburg

271 Sandwich St. South
Amherstburg, ON N9V 2A5
519-736-0012 Fax: 519-736-5403 TTY: 519-736-9860
inquiry@amherstburg.ca
www.amherstburg.ca
Municipal Type: City
Incorporated: 1851; *Area:* 185.65 sq km
County or District: Essex; *Population in 2006:* 21,748
Provincial Electoral District(s): Essex
Federal Electoral District(s): Essex
Next Election: Nov. 2010 (4 year terms)
Note: Incorporated as a town in 1878.

Council
Wayne Hurst, Mayor
519-736-7646
whurst@amherstburg.ca
Carolyn Davies, Councillor
John Sutton, Councillor
jsutton@amherstburg.ca
Bart DiPasquale, Councillor
Diane Pouget, Councillor
Robert (Bob) Pillon, Councillor
rpillon@amherstburg.ca
Ron Sutherland, Councillor

Administration
Pam Malott, Chief Administrative Officer, Administration
pmalott@amherstburg.ca
Lou Zarlenga, P.Eng, Manager, Public Services, Administration
Antonietta Giofu, P.Eng, Engineer, Environmental Services, Administration
Dwayne Grondin, Superintendent, Sewer & Watermain, Administration
Tony DeThomasis, Superintendent, Roads & Parks, Administration

Aurora

P.O. Box 1000
1 Municipal Dr.
Aurora, ON L4G 6J1
905-727-1375 Fax: 905-726-4738 Alternative Phone: 905-727-3123; TTY: 905-726-4766
info@e-aurora.ca
www.e-aurora.ca
Municipal Type: City
Area: 49.62 sq km
County or District: York Regional Municipality; *Population in 2006:* 47,629
Provincial Electoral District(s): Newmarket-Aurora
Federal Electoral District(s): Newmarket-Aurora
Next Election: Nov. 2010 (4 year terms)

Council
Geoff Dawe, Mayor
John Abel, Councillor
Chris Ballard, Councillor
Evelyn Buck, Councillor
ebuck@e-aurora.ca.ca
Wendy Gaertner, Councillor
wgaertner@e-aurora.ca
John Gallo, Councillor
jgallo@e-aurora.ca
Sandra Humphries, Councillor
Paul Pirri, Councillor
Michael Thompson, Councillor

Administration
Lucille King, Town Clerk, Administration
905-727-3123
Ilmar Simanovskis, Director, Public Works, Administration
Peter Horvath, Manager, Operations Services, Administration

Barrie

P.O. Box 400
70 Collier St.
Barrie, ON L4M 4T5
705-726-4242 Fax: 705-739-4243 TTY: 705-792-7910; Council Info: 705-739-4204
cityinfo@barrie.ca
www.barrie.ca; www.facebook.com/cityofbarrie
Municipal Type: City
Incorporated: 1853; *Area:* 76.99 sq km
County or District: Simcoe; *Population in 2006:* 128,430
Provincial Electoral District(s): Barrie
Federal Electoral District(s): Barrie
Next Election: Nov. 2010 (4 year terms)

Council
Jeff Lehman, Mayor
705-792-7900
officeofthemayor@barrie.ca
Bonnie J. Ainsworth, Councillor, Ward(s): 1
Lynn M. Strachan, Councillor, Ward(s): 2
lstrachan@barrie.ca
Doug Shipley, Councillor, Ward(s): 3
Barry J. Ward, Councillor, Ward(s): 4
bward@barrie.ca
Peter Silveira, Councillor, Ward(s): 5
Michael Prowse, Councillor, Ward(s): 6
mprowse@barrie.ca
John Brassard, Councillor, Ward(s): 7
jbrassard@barrie.ca
Alison Eadie, Councillor, Ward(s): 8
Brian H. Jackson, Councillor, Ward(s): 9
Alexander Nuttall, Councillor, Ward(s): 10
anuttall@barrie.ca

Administration
Dawn McAlpine, City Clerk, Administration
705-739-4204
Jon Babulic, Chief Administrative Officer, Administration
Ed Archer, CMA, General Manager, Corporate Services, Administration
Richard Forward, M.Sc., P.Eng., General Manager, Infrastructure, Development & Cul, Administration
J.W. (Jim) Sales, General Manager, Community Operations, Administration
G. Allison, Director, Building Services & Chief Building Offic, Administration
Sandy Coulter, B.Sc., Acting Director, Operations - Water, Wastewater &, Administration
Dave Friary, Acting Director, Operations - Roads, Parks & Fleet, Administration
Hany Kirolos, Director, Strategy & Economic Development, Administration
Wendell McArthur, Director, Engineering, Administration
Debbie McKinnon, Director, Finance, Administration

Barbara Roth, Director, Leisure, Transit & Facilities, Administration
J. Taylor, Director, Planning Services Department, Administration
John Lynn, Fire Chief, Administration
Bruce L. Griffin, Community Emergency Planner, Administration

Belleville

City Hall
169 Front St.
Belleville, ON K8N 2Y8
613-968-6481 Fax: 613-967-3206
www.city.belleville.on.ca
Municipal Type: City
Area: 246.76 sq km
County or District: Hastings; *Population in 2006:* 48,821
Provincial Electoral District(s): Prince Edward-Hastings
Federal Electoral District(s): Prince Edward-Hastings
Next Election: Nov. 2010 (4 year terms)

Council
Neil R. Ellis, Mayor
613-967-3267, Fax: 613-967-3209
mayor.ellis@city.belleville.on.ca
Egerton Boyce, Councillor, Ward(s): 1
councillor.boyce@city.belleville.on.ca
Pat Culhane, Councillor, Ward(s): 1
councillor.culhane@city.belleville.on.ca
Jodie Jenkins, Councillor, Ward(s): 1
councillor.jenkins@city.belleville.on.ca
Tom Lafferty, Councillor, Ward(s): 1
councillor.lafferty@city.belleville.on.ca
Jack Miller, Councillor, Ward(s): 1
councillor.miller@city.belleville.on.ca
Garnet Thompson, Councillor, Ward(s): 1
councillor.thompson@city.belleville.on.ca
Taso Christopher, Councillor, Ward(s): 2
councillor.christopher@city.belleville.on.ca
Jackie Denyes, Councillor, Ward(s): 2
councillor.denyes@city.belleville.on.ca

Administration
Julie C. Oram, City Clerk & Director, Corporate Services, Administration
613-967-3271
joram@city.belleville.on.ca
Stephen G. Hyndman, Ec.D.(F), MCIP RPP, Chief Administrative Officer, Administration
shyndman@city.belleville.on.ca
Brian Cousins, Director, Finance & Treasurer, Administration
bcousins@city.belleville.on.ca
Mark Fluhrer, Director, Recreation Culture & Community Services, Administration
mfluhrer@city.belleville.on.ca
Rick Kester, Director, Engineering & Development Services, Administration
rkester@city.belleville.on.ca
John Martin, Director, Human Resources, Administration
jmartin@city.belleville.on.ca
Brad Wilson, Environmental & Operational Services, Administration
bwilson@city.belleville.on.ca
Ted Marecak, Chief Building Official, Administration
tmarecak@city.belleville.on.ca
Rhéaume Chaput, Fire Chief, Administration
rchaput@city.belleville.on.ca
Elizabeth Garrison, Manager, Transit Operations, Administration
phodgson@city.belleville.on.ca
Art MacKay, Manager, Policy Planning, Administration
amackay@city.belleville.on.ca
Pat McNulty, Manager, Transportation, Administration
pmcnulty@city.belleville.on.ca
Richard Reinert, Manager, Environmental Services, Administration
rreinert@city.belleville.on.ca

Bracebridge

1000 Taylor Ct.
Bracebridge, ON P1L 1R6
705-645-5264 Fax: 705-645-1262 Fax, Public Works: 705-645-4209
www.town.bracebridge.on.ca
Municipal Type: City
Area: 617.42 sq km
County or District: Muskoka Dist. Mun.; *Population in 2006:* 15,652
Provincial Electoral District(s): Parry Sound-Muskoka
Federal Electoral District(s): Parry Sound-Muskoka
Next Election: Nov. 2010 (4 year terms)

Council
Graydon Smith, Mayor
Steve Clement, District Councillor
Liam Craig, Councillor
Lori-Lynn Giaschi-Pacini, District Councillor
lpacini@sympatico.ca
Rick Maloney, Councillor
Barb McMurray, Councillor
Mark Quemby, Councillor
Gerry Tryon, Councillor
gtryon@vianet.ca
Scott Young, District Councillor
dsy4@vianet.ca

Administration
Lori McDonald, Clerk, Administration
mcdonald@town.bracebridge.on.ca
John R. Sisson, Chief Administrative Officer, Administration
Carol Wakefield, Treasurer, Administration
Kim Horrigan, Director, Development Services, Administration
Cheryl Kelley, Director, Economic Development, Administration
Ron Walton, Director, Public Works & Municipal Engineer, Administration
Murray Medley, Fire Chief, Administration

Bradford West Gwillimbury

Administration Centre
P.O. Box 160
3541 Line 11
Bradford, ON L3Z 2A8
905-775-5366 Fax: 905-775-0153
www.town.bradfordwestgwillimbury.on.ca
Municipal Type: City
Incorporated: 1857; *Area:* 201.03 sq km
County or District: Simcoe; *Population in 2006:* 24,039
Provincial Electoral District(s): York-Simcoe
Federal Electoral District(s): York-Simcoe
Next Election: Nov. 2010 (4 year terms)
Note: Incorporated as a town in 1960.

Council
Doug White, Mayor
dwhite@townofbwg.com
Rob Keffer, Deputy Mayor & Councillor
Raj Sandhu, Councillor, Ward(s): 1
Del Crake, Councillor, Ward(s): 2
Gary R. Lamb, Councillor, Ward(s): 3
Carl Hordyk, Councillor, Ward(s): 4
Ron Simpson, Councillor, Ward(s): 5
James Leduc, Councillor, Ward(s): 6
Peter Dykie, Jr., Councillor, Ward(s): 7

Administration
Patricia Nash, Municipal Clerk, Administration
pnash@townofbwg.com
Jay Currier, Chief Administrative Officer & Town Manager, Administration
Ian Goodfellow, Director, Finance & Treasurer, Administration
Debbie Korolnek, Director, Engineering Services, Administration
Geoff McKnight, Director, Planning & Development, Administration
Paul Feehely, Superintendent, Public Works, Administration
Edward O'Donnell, Supervisor, Water, Administration
Brad Sullivan, Supervisor, Waste Water, Administration
Lorne Arscott, Fire Chief, Administration

Brampton

2 Wellington St. West
Brampton, ON L6Y 4R2
905-874-2000 Fax: 905-874-2119 E-mail, Economic Development: edo@brampton.ca
cityhall@brampton.ca; tourism@brampton.ca (Tourism)
www.brampton.ca
Municipal Type: City
Incorporated: Jan. 1, 1974; *Area:* 266.71 sq km
County or District: Peel Reg. Mun.; *Population in 2006:* 433,806
Provincial Electoral District(s): Bramalea-Gore-Malton; Brampton Springdale; Brampton West; Brampton South-Mississauga
Federal Electoral District(s): Bramalea-Gore-Malton; Brampton Springdale; Brampton West; Mississauga-Brampton South
Next Election: Nov. 2010 (4 year terms)

Council
Susan Fennell, Mayor
mayor@brampton.ca
Grant Gibson, City Councillor, Ward(s): 1 & 5
John Hutton, City Councillor, Ward(s): 2 & 6
Bob Callahan, City Councillor, Ward(s): 3 & 4
Sandra Hames, City Councillor, Ward(s): 7 & 8
Vicky Dhillon, City Councillor, Ward(s): 9 & 10
Elaine Moore, Regional Councillor, Ward(s): 1 & 5
Paul Palleschi, Regional Councillor, Ward(s): 2 & 6
John Sanderson, Regional Councillor, Ward(s): 3 & 4
Gael Miles, Regional Councillor, Ward(s): 7 & 8
John Sprovieri, Regional Councillor, Ward(s): 9 & 10

Administration
Peter Fay, City Clerk, Administration
905-874-2100, Fax: 905-874-2119
cityclerksoffice@brampton.ca
Deborah Dubenofsky, City Manager, Administration
Mo Lewis, Commissioner, Finance, Administration
John Corbett, Commissioner, Planning, Design & Development, Administration
Dennis Cutajar, Commissioner, Economic Development & Communication, Administration
Jamie Lowery, Commissioner, Community Services, Administration
Tom Mulligan, Commissioner, Works & Transportation, Administration
Julian Patteson, Commissioner, Buildings & Property Management, Administration
Kathy Zammit, Commissioner, Corporate Services, Administration

Brantford

City Hall
P.O. Box 818
100 Wellington Sq.
Brantford, ON N3T 2M3
519-759-4150 Fax: 519-759-7840
new_webmaster@brantford.ca
www.brantford.ca
Municipal Type: City
Incorporated: May 31, 1877; *Area:* 72.47 sq km
County or District: Brant; *Population in 2006:* 90,192
Provincial Electoral District(s): Brant
Federal Electoral District(s): Brant
Next Election: Nov. 2010 (4 year terms)

Council
Chris Friel, Mayor
519-756-2242, Fax: 519-751-7109
Larry M. Kings, Councillor, Ward(s): 1
Jan C. Vander Stelt, Councillor, Ward(s): 1
Vince Bucci, Councillor, Ward(s): 2
John K. Utley, Councillor, Ward(s): 2
Debi Dignan-Rumble, Councillor, Ward(s): 3
Dan McCreary, Councillor, Ward(s): 3
Richard Carpenter, Councillor, Ward(s): 4
Dave Wrobel, Councillor, Ward(s): 4
Marguerite Ceschi-Smith, Councillor, Ward(s): 5
David E. Neumann, Councillor, Ward(s): 5

Administration
Darryl Lee, City Clerk, Administration
John Brown, City Manager, Administration
Sandra Lawson, General Manager, Engineering & Operational Service, Administration
Ted Salisbury, General Manager, Community Development Services, Administration
Dan Temprile, General Manager, Public Health, Safety, & Social S, Administration

Brighton, Municipality of

P.O. Box 189
35 Alice St.
Brighton, ON K0K 1H0
613-475-0670 Fax: 613-475-3453 Phone, Public Works & Planning: 613-475-1162
general@brighton.ca
www.brighton.ca
Municipal Type: City
Area: 222.52 sq km
County or District: Northumberland; *Population in 2006:* 10,253
Provincial Electoral District(s): Northumberland-Quinte West
Federal Electoral District(s): Northumberland-Quinte West
Next Election: Nov. 2010 (4 year terms)

Council
Mark Walas, Mayor
mayor@brighton.ca
Craig Kerr, Councillor
John Martinello, Councillor
Thomas Rittwage, Councillor
Emily Rowley, Councillor
Mary Tadman, Councillor
Mike Vandertoorn, Councillor

Administration
Gayle J. Frost, Chief Administrative Officer
gfrost@brighton.ca

Brockville

Victoria Bldg.
P.O. Box 5000
1 King St. West
Brockville, ON K6V 7A5
613-342-8772 Fax: 613-342-8780
info@brockville.com; tourism@brockvillechamber.com
www.brockville.com
Municipal Type: City
Area: 20.74 sq km
County or District: Leeds & Grenville; *Population in 2006:* 21,957
Provincial Electoral District(s): Leeds-Grenville
Federal Electoral District(s): Leeds-Grenville
Next Election: Nov. 2010 (4 year terms)

Council
David L. Henderson, Mayor
Jason Baker, Councillor
David E. Beatty, Councillor
Leigh Z. Bursey, Councillor
Jeffery Earle, Councillor
Jane Fullerton, Councillor
Larry F. Journal, Councillor
Mike Kalivas, Councillor
David D. Lesueur, Councillor
Mary Jane McFall, Councillor

Administration
Sandra M. Seale, City Clerk, Administration
smseale@brockville.com
Bob Casselman, City Manager, Administration
bcasselman@brockville.com
Donna Cyr, Director, Finance, Administration
dcyr@brockville.com
Jim Baker, Director, Human Resources, Administration
jbaker@brockville.com
Valerie Harvey, Director, Parks & Recreation, Administration
vharvey@brockville.com
David C. Paul, Director, Economic Development, Administration
dpaul@brockville.com
Maureen Pascoe Merkley, Director, Planning, Administration
mpmerkley@brockville.com
Harry Jones, Fire Chief, Administration
hjones@brockville.com

Burlington

City Hall
P.O. Box 5013
426 Brant St.
Burlington, ON L7R 3Z6

905-335-7777 Fax: 905-335-7881 Toll Free Phone: 1-877-213-3609
cob@burlington.ca
www.burlington.ca
Municipal Type: City
Incorporated: 1914; *Area:* 185.74 sq km
County or District: Halton Regional Municipality; *Population in 2006:* 164,415
Provincial Electoral District(s):
Ancaster-Dundas-Flamborough-Westdale; Burlington; Halton
Federal Electoral District(s): Burlington; Halton; Ancaster-Dundas-Flamborough-Westdale
Next Election: Nov. 2010 (4 year terms)
Note: Incorporated as a city in 1974.

Council
Rick Goldring, Mayor
905-335-7607, Fax: 905-335-7708
Rick Craven, Councillor, Ward(s): 1
cravenr@burlington.ca
Peter Thoem, Councillor, Ward(s): 2
thoemp@burlington.ca
John Taylor, Councillor, Ward(s): 3
taylorj@burlington.ca
Jack Dennison, Councillor, Ward(s): 4
dennisonj@burlington.ca
Paul Sharman, Councillor, Ward(s): 5
Blair Lancaster, Councillor, Ward(s): 6

Administration
Kim Phillips, City Clerk, Administration
905-335-7698, Fax: 905-335-7881
cityclerks@burlington.ca; phillipsk@burlington.ca
Roman Martiuk, City Manager, Administration
martiukr@burlington.ca
Steve Zorbas, City Treasurer, Administration
zorbass@burlington.ca
Leo DeLoyde, General Manager, Development & Infrastructure, Administration
Scott Stewart, General Manager, Community Services, Administration
Tom Eichenbaum, Director, Engineering, Administration
eichenbaumt@burlington.ca
Bruce Krushelnicki, Director, Planning & Building, Administration
krushelnickib@burlington.ca
Lynn Robichaud, Senior Coorindator, Environmental Services, Administration
robichaudl@burlington.ca

Caledon
Town Hall
6311 Old Church Rd.
Caledon, ON L7C 1J6
905-584-2272 Fax: 905-584-4325 Toll Free Phone: 1-888-225-3366
info@caledon.ca
www.caledon.ca
Municipal Type: City
Incorporated: Jan. 1, 1974; *Area:* 687.17 sq km
County or District: Peel Regional Municipality; *Population in 2006:* 57,050
Provincial Electoral District(s): Dufferin-Caledon
Federal Electoral District(s): Dufferin-Caledon
Next Election: Nov. 2010 (4 year terms)

Council
Marolyn Morrison, Mayor
marolyn.morrison@caledon.ca
Richard Paterak, Regional Councillor, Ward(s): 1
Allan Thompson, Regional Councillor, Ward(s): 2
Richard Whitehead, Regional Councillor, Ward(s): 3 & 4
Patti Foley, Regional Councillor, Ward(s): 5
Doug Beffort, Area Councillor, Ward(s): 1
Gord McClure, Area Councillor, Ward(s): 2
Nick deBoer, Area Councillor, Ward(s): 3 & 4
Rob Mezzapelli, Area Councillor, Ward(s): 5

Administration
Karen Landry, Town Clerk & Director, Administration, Administration
D. Barnes, Chief Administrative Officer, Administration
R. Kaufman, Treasurer, Deputy CAO, & Director, Corporate Servi, Administration
L. Koehle, Director, Public Works & Engineering, Administration
M. Hall, Director, Planning & Development, Administration
G. Middlebrook, Chief Building Official, Administration
J. Schembri, Officer, Environmental Progress, Administration

Cambridge
P.O. Box 669
73 Water St. North
Cambridge, ON N1R 5W8
519-623-1340 Fax: 519-740-3011 E-mail, Corporate Services: corpserv@cambridge.ca
questions@cambridge.ca; csd@cambridge.ca (Community Svs.)
www.cambridge.ca
Municipal Type: City
Incorporated: Jan. 1973; *Area:* 112.86 sq km
County or District: Waterloo Regional Municipality; *Population in 2006:* 120,371
Provincial Electoral District(s): Cambridge
Federal Electoral District(s): Cambridge
Next Election: Nov. 2010 (4 year terms)

Council
Doug Craig, Mayor
519-740-4517
mayor@cambridge.ca; craigd@cambridge.ca
Donna Reid, City Councillor, Ward(s): 1
Rick Cowsill, City Councillor, Ward(s): 2
cowsillr@cambridge.ca
Karl Kiefer, City Councillor, Ward(s): 3
kieferk@cambridge.ca
Ben Tucci, City Councillor, Ward(s): 4
tuccib@cambridge.ca
Pam Wolf, City Councillor, Ward(s): 5
wolfp@cambridge.ca
Gary Price, City Councillor, Ward(s): 6
priceg@cambridge.ca
Frank Monteiro, City Councillor, Ward(s): 7
Nicholas Ermeta, City Councillor, Ward(s): 8
Jane Brewer, Regional Councillor
Claudette Millar, Regional Councillor

Administration
Alex Mitchell, City Clerk, Administration
519-740-4680
clerks@city.cambridge.ca
Jim King, Chief Administrative Officer, Administration
519-740-4683
cao@cambridge.ca
Terry Allen, Commisssioner, Fire Services, Administration
Janet Babcock, Commisssioner, Planning Services, Administration
Steven Fairweather, Commisssioner, Corporate Services, Administration
Ed Kovacs, Commisssioner, Transportation & Public Works, Administration
Reg Weber, Commisssioner, Community Services, Administration

Clarence-Rockland
1560 Laurier St.
Rockland, ON K4K 1P7
613-446-6022 Fax: 613-446-1497
www.clarence-rockland.com
Municipal Type: City
Incorporated: Jan. 1, 1998; *Area:* 296.53 sq km
County or District: Prescott & Russell; *Population in 2006:* 20,790
Provincial Electoral District(s): Glengarry-Prescott-Russell
Federal Electoral District(s): Glengarry-Prescott-Russell
Next Election: Nov. 2010 (4 year terms)
Note: Amalgamation of the Town of Rockland and the Township of Clarence.

Council
Marcel Guibord, Mayor
613-446-4856
Michel Thivierge, Councillor, Ward(s): 1
André Henrie, Councillor, Ward(s): 2
Francine Mault, Councillor, Ward(s): 3
Raymond Serrurier, Councillor, Ward(s): 4
Kyle Cyr, Councillor, Ward(s): 5
Guy Desjardins, Councillor, Ward(s): 6
Jean-Pierre Chartrand, Councillor, Ward(s): 7
Garry M. Edwards, Councillor, Ward(s): 8

Administration
Daniel Gatien, Chief Administrative Officer & Clerk, Administration
dgatien@clarence-rockland.com
Chantal McLean-Leroux, Treasurer, Administration
cmcleanleroux@clarence-rockland.com
Thérèse Lefaivre, Director, Community Services, Administration
tlefaivre@clarence-rockland.com
Michael Michaud, Director, Planning, Administration
mmichaud@clarence-rockland.com
Yves Rivard, Director, By-law Enforcement, Administration
yrivard@clarence-rockland.com
Yves Rousselle, Director, Physical Services, Administration
yrousselle@clarence-rockland.com
Pierre Sabourin, Fire Chief, Administration
psabourin@clarence-rockland.com
Denis Longpré, Manager, Environment, Administration
dlongpre@clarence-rockland.com

Cobourg
55 King St. West
Cobourg, ON K9A 2M2
905-372-4301 Fax: 905-372-7421 Toll Free Phone: 1-888-262-6874
webmaster@cobourg.ca
www.cobourg.ca
Municipal Type: City
Area: 22.37 sq km
County or District: Northumberland; *Population in 2006:* 18,210
Provincial Electoral District(s): Northumberland-Quinte West
Federal Electoral District(s): Northumberland-Quinte West
Next Election: Nov. 2010 (4 year terms)

Council
Gil Brocanier, Mayor, Fax: 905-372-2910
gbrocanier@cobourg.ca
Stan Frost, Deputy Mayor & Councillor
stan.frost@sympatico.ca
John Henderson, Councillor
Miriam Mutton, Councillor
miriam.mutton@cogeco.ca
Forrest Rowden, Councillor
Larry E. Sherwin, Councillor
Donna Todd, Councillor

Administration
D.S. Robinson, Chief Administrative Officer, Administration
srobinson@cobourg.ca
Ian Davey, Director, Corporate Services, Administration
idavey@cobourg.ca
Glenn J. McGlashon, Director, Planning & Development Services, Administration
gmcglashon@cobourg.ca
Steven Peacock, Director, Public Works, Administration
speacock@cobourg.ca

Collingwood
P.O. Box 157
97 Hurontario St.
Collingwood, ON L9Y 3Z5
705-445-1030 Fax: 705-445-2448 Toll Free Phone, Economic Dev.: 1-888-265-9663
ddraper@collingwood.ca (Reception)
www.collingwood.ca
Municipal Type: City
Incorporated: 1858; *Area:* 33.46 sq km
County or District: Simcoe; *Population in 2006:* 17,290
Provincial Electoral District(s): Simcoe-Grey
Federal Electoral District(s): Simcoe-Grey
Next Election: Nov. 2010 (4 year terms)

Council
Sandra Cooper, Mayor
705-446-4704
scooper@collingwood.ca
Rick Lloyd, Deputy Mayor & Councillor
Ian Chadwick, Councillor
ichadwick@collingwood.ca
Sandy Cunningham, Councillor
Mike Edwards, Councillor
medwards@collingwood.ca
Joe Gardhouse, Councillor
Keith Hull, Councillor
Kevin Lloyd, Councillor
Dale West, Councillor

Administration
Sara J. Almas, Clerk, Administration
salmas@collingwood.ca
Gord Norris, Chief Administrative Officer, Administration
gnorris@collingwood.ca
Marjory Leonard, Treasurer, Administration
mleonard@collingwood.ca
Ed Houghton, Executive Director, Public Works, Administration
ehoughton@collingwood.ca
Peter Dunbar, Director, Leisure Services, Administration
pdunbar@collingwood.ca
Larry Irwin, Director, Information Technology, Administration
lirwin@collingwood.ca
Bill Plewes, Director, Building Services, Administration
bplewes@collingwood.ca
Gord Russell, Director, Planning Services, Administration
grussell@collingwood.ca
Trent Elyea, Fire Chief, Administration
telyea@collingwood.ca
Donald Green, Manager, Environmental Services, Administration
dgreen@collingwood.ca
Wendy Martin, Manager, Green Space, Administration
wmartin@collingwood.ca

Cornwall
P.O. Box 877
360 Pitt St.
Cornwall, ON K6H 5T9
613-932-6252 Fax: 613-932-8145 E-mail, Municipal Works: engineering@cornwall.ca
cityhall@cornwall.ca; ecodev@cornwall.ca (Economic Dev.)
www.cornwall.ca
Municipal Type: City
Incorporated: 1834; *Area:* 61.52 sq km
County or District: Stormont, Dundas & Glengarry; *Population in 2006:* 45,965
Provincial Electoral District(s): Stormont-Dundas-South Glengarry
Federal Electoral District(s): Stormont-Dundas-South Glengarry
Next Election: Nov. 2010 (4 year terms)
Note: Incorporated as a city in 1945.

Council
Bob Kilger, Mayor
mayor@cornwall.ca
Denis Carr, Councillor
Bernadette Clement, Councillor
Maurice Dupelle, Councillor
Syd Gardiner, Councillor
Glen Grant, Councillor
Elaine MacDonald, Councillor
David Murphy, Councillor
Leslie O'Shaugnessy, Councillor
André Rivette, Councillor
Denis Thibault, Councillor

Administration
Denise Labelle-Gelinas, City Clerk, Administration
dgelinas@cornwall.ca
Paul Fitzpatrick, Chief Administrative Officer, Administration
Maureen Adams, General Manager, Financial Services, Administration
Stephen Alexander, General Manager, Planning, Parks & Recreation Serv, Administration
Norm Levac, General Manager, Infrastructure & Municipal Works, Administration
Tom Gemmell, Division Manager, Municipal Works, Administration
Morris McCormick, Division Manager, Environment, Administration
Len Tapp, Division Manager, Transit, Administration
Mark Boileau, Manager, Economic Development, Administration

Myles Cassidy, Manager, Emergency Services & Chief, Fire, Administration
Patrick Carrière, Supervisor, Waste Water Treatment Facility, Administration
Neil Dixon, Supervisor, Waste Management, Administration
Owen O'Keefe, Supervisor, Water Purification Plant, Administration

East Gwillimbury

19000 Leslie St.
Sharon, ON L0G 1V0
905-478-4282 Fax: 905-478-2808 Alternate Fax: 905-478-8545
town@eastgwillimbury.ca; engineering@eastgwillimbury.ca
www.eastgwillimbury.ca
Municipal Type: City
Incorporated: 1850; *Area:* 245.06 sq km
County or District: York Regional Municipality; *Population in 2006:* 21,069
Provincial Electoral District(s): York-Simcoe
Federal Electoral District(s): York-Simcoe
Next Election: Nov. 2010 (4 year terms)

Council
Virginia Hackson, Mayor
John Eaton, Councillor
Marlene Johnston, Councillor
mjohnston@eastgwillimbury.ca
Cathy Morton, Councillor
cmorton@eastgwillimbury.ca
Tara Roy-Diclemente, Councillor

Administration
Anna Knowles, Acting Clerk, Administration
aknowles@eastgwillimbury.ca
Thomas R. Webster, Chief Administrative Officer, Administration
twebster@eastgwillimbury.ca
Mark Valcic, General Manager, Corporate & Financial Services &, Administration
mvalcic@eastgwillimbury.ca
Wayne Hunt, General Manager, Community Programs & Infrastructu, Administration
whunt@eastgwillimbury.ca
Don Sinclair, General Manager, Development & Legal Services, Administration
Ken Beckett, Fire Chief, Administration
Don Allan, Manager, Engineering Branch, Administration
dallan@eastgwillimbury.ca
Carolyn Kellington, Manager, Community Planning & Development Branch, Administration
ckellington@eastgwillimbury.ca
Steve Krystal, Manager, Capital Programs & Traffic Engineering Br, Administration
skrystal@eastgwillimbury.ca
Gary Shropshire, Manager, Community Parks & Programs Branch, Administration
gshropshire@eastgwillimbury.ca
Tim Gibson, Director, Building Approvals & Inspections, Administration
tgibson@eastgwillimbury.ca
Christopher Kalimootoo, Director, Engineering & Environmental Services, Administration
ckalimootoo@eastgwillimbury.ca
Robin Skinner, Environmental Planner, Administration
rskinner@eastgwillimbury.ca

Elliot Lake

45 Hillside Dr. North
Elliot Lake, ON P5A 1X5
705-848-2287 Fax: 705-461-7244
www.cityofelliotlake.com
Municipal Type: City
Area: 698.12 sq km
County or District: Algoma District; *Population in 2006:* 11,549
Provincial Electoral District(s): Algoma-Manitoulin
Federal Electoral District(s): Algoma-Manitoulin-Kapuskasing
Next Election: Nov. 2010 (4 year terms)

Council
Rick Hamilton, Mayor
Al Collett, Councillor
Tom Farquhar, Councillor
Sandy Finamore, Councillor
Norman Mann, Councillor
Chris Patrie, Councillor
Ken Rastin, Councillor

Administration
Lesley Sprague, City Clerk, Administration
Fred Bauthus, Chief Administrative Officer, Administration
Dawn Halcrow, Director, Finance, Administration
R. deBortoli, Director, Operations, Administration
D. Gagnon, Director, Economic Development, Administration
Paul Officer, Fire Chief, Administration

Erin

5684 Wellington Rd., RR#2
Hillsburgh, ON N0B 1Z0
519-855-4407 Fax: 519-855-4821 Toll Free Phone: 1-877-818-2888
council@erin.ca; cao@erin.ca (Town Manager)
www.erin.ca
Municipal Type: City
Incorporated: 1997; *Area:* 296.98 sq km
County or District: Wellington; *Population in 2006:* 11,148
Provincial Electoral District(s): Wellington-Halton Hills
Federal Electoral District(s): Wellington-Halton Hills
Next Election: Nov. 2010 (4 year terms)

Council
Lou Maieron, Mayor, Fax: 519-833-0208
John Brennan, Councillor, Fax: 519-833-0891
hejo@ca.inter.net
Deb Callaghan, Councillor
Barb Tocher, Councillor
barb.tocher@sympatico.ca
Josie Wintersinger, Councillor, Fax: 519-855-6927
jwintersinger@yahoo.ca

Administration
Kathryn Ironmonger, Clerk, Administration
Lisa Hass, Town Manager, Administration
Sharon Marshall, Director, Finance, Administration
Rhonda Buck, Administrator, Building & Planning, Administration
Louise Warn, Administrator, Water Compliance, Administration
Steve Goode, Fire Chief, Administration
Andrew Hartholt, Chief Building Official, Administration
Larry Van Wyck, Superintendent, Roads, Administration

Essex

33 Talbot St. South
Essex, ON N8M 1A8
519-776-7336 Fax: 519-776-8811
www.essex.ca
Municipal Type: City
Incorporated: 1883; *Area:* 277.95 sq km
County or District: Essex; *Population in 2006:* 20,032
Provincial Electoral District(s): Essex
Federal Electoral District(s): Essex
Next Election: Nov. 2010 (4 year terms)
Note: Incorporated as a town in 1890. Restructuring occurred in 1999.

Council
Ron McDermott, Mayor
519-776-8150
rmcdermott@essex.ca
Morley Bowman, Councillor, Ward(s): 1
Randy Voakes, Councillor, Ward(s): 1
Richard Meloche, Councillor, Ward(s): 2
Bill Baker, Councillor, Ward(s): 3
John Scott, Councillor, Ward(s): 3
Sherry Bondy, Councillor, Ward(s): 4

Administration
Cheryl Bondy, Clerk & Deputy-Treasurer, Administration
cbondy@essex.ca
Wayne Miller, Chief Administrative Officer, Administration
Donna Hunter, Director, Finance & Administration & Treasurer, Administration
Richard Beausoleil, Director, Public Works, Administration
Harry Hakim, Director, Parks & Recreation, Administration
Chris Nepszy, Director, Infastructure & Development, Administration
Ed Pillon, Fire Chief, Administration
519-776-6476, Fax: 519-776-7171
Heather Jablonski, Town Planner, Administration
Dan Boudreau, Superintendent, Drainage, Administration
Andy Graf, Superintendent, Water, Administration

Fort Erie

1 Municipal Centre Dr.
Fort Erie, ON L2A 2S6
905-871-1600 Fax: 905-871-4022 Fax, Corporate Services: 905-871-9984
townhall@town.forterie.on.ca
www.forterie.on.ca
Municipal Type: City
Incorporated: 1857; *Area:* 166.35 sq km
County or District: Niagara Regional Municipality; *Population in 2006:* 29,925
Provincial Electoral District(s): Niagara Falls
Federal Electoral District(s): Niagara Falls
Next Election: Nov. 2010 (4 year terms)

Council
Douglas G. Martin, Mayor
douglas.martin@town.forterie.ca
Stephen Passero, Councillor, Ward(s): 1
Richard Shular, Councillor, Ward(s): 2
rshular@town.forterie.ca
Bob Steckley, Councillor, Ward(s): 3
bsteckley@town.forterie.ca
John Hill, Councillor, Ward(s): 4
Don Lubberts, Councillor, Ward(s): 5
Paul Collard, Councillor, Ward(s): 6
John Teal, Regional Councillor

Administration
Carolyn J. Kett, Town Clerk, Administration
ckett@town.forterie.ca
H. Schlange, Chief Administrative Officer, Administration
H. Chamberlain, Director, Financial Services, Administration
R. Mostacci, Director, Community & Development Services, Administration
H. Salter, Director, Legal & Legislative Services & Town Soli, Administration
R. Tripp, Director, Infrastructure Services, Administration
Larry Coplen, Fire Chief & Coordinator, Community Emergency Mana, Administration
S. Hansen, Manager, Parks & Open Space Development, Administration

Georgina

Georgina Civic Centre
26557 Civic Centre Rd., RR#2
Keswick, ON L4P 3G1
905-476-4301 Fax: 905-476-8100 Alternative Phones: 905-722-6516; 705-437-2210
info@georgina.ca; events@georgina.ca
www.georgina.ca
Municipal Type: City
Area: 287.72 sq km
County or District: York Reg. Mun.; *Population in 2006:* 42,346
Provincial Electoral District(s): York-Simcoe
Federal Electoral District(s): York-Simcoe
Next Election: Nov. 2010 (4 year terms)
Note: Amalgamation of the Village of Keswick, the Township of Georgina & Village of Sutton.

Council
Robert Grossi, Mayor, Fax: 905-476-1475
rgrossi@georgina.ca
Danny Wheeler, Deputy Mayor & Regional Councillor
dwheeler@georgina.ca
Naomi Davison, Councillor, Ward(s): 1
Dan Fellini, Councillor, Ward(s): 2
Dave Szollosy, Councillor, Ward(s): 3
dszollosy@georgina.ca
Ken Hackenbrook, Councillor, Ward(s): 4
khackenbrook@georgina.ca
Brad Smockum, Councillor, Ward(s): 5
bsmockum@georgina.ca

Administration
Roland Chénier, A.M.C.T., Town Clerk, Administration
rchenier@georgina.ca
Susan Plamondon, Chief Administrative Officer, Administration
splamondon@georgina.ca
Rebecca Mathewson, C.G.A., Director, Administrative Services, Administration
rmathewson@georgina.ca
Harold Lenters, M.Sc.Pl., MCIP, RPP, Director, Planning & Building, Administration
hlenters@georgina.ca
Robert Magloughlen, P.Eng., Director, Engineering & Public Works, Administration
rmagloughlen@georgina.ca
Bill O'Neill, C.M.M. III, Director, Emergency Services & Fire Chief, Administration
boneill@georgina.ca
Faye Richardson, Director, Leisure Services, Administration
frichardson@georgina.ca
Claire Marsden, C.H.R.P., C.M.M. I, Manager, Human Resources, Administration
cmarsden@georgina.ca

Gravenhurst

190 Harvie St.
Gravenhurst, ON P1P 1S9
705-687-3412 Fax: 705-687-7016
reception@gravenhurst.ca
www.gravenhurst.ca
Municipal Type: City
Area: 517.99 sq km
County or District: Muskoka District Municipality; *Population in 2006:* 11,046
Provincial Electoral District(s): Parry Sound-Muskoka
Federal Electoral District(s): Parry Sound-Muskoka
Next Election: Nov. 2010 (4 year terms)

Council
Paisley Donaldson, Mayor
705-689-8334
Sandy Cairns, District Councillor
Bob Colhoun, District Councillor
colhoun@muskoka.com
Rosemary King, District Councillor
Heidi Lorenz, Councillor, Ward(s): 1
Lola Bratty, Councillor, Ward(s): 2
Joe Donoghue, Councillor, Ward(s): 3
Randy Jorgensen, Councillor, Ward(s): 4
Jeff Watson, Councillor, Ward(s): 5

Administration
Candace Thwaites, Clerk, Administration
Kenneth Watson, Treasurer, Administration
D. Broderick, Manager, Recreation, Community Services, & Centenn, Administration
N. Popovich, Manager, Development Services, Administration
B. Rundle, Manager, Arts & Culture, Administration
D. Saunders, Manager, Public Works & Operations, Administration
L. Sherk, Officer, Community Economic Development, Administration

Greater Napanee

P.O. Box 97
124 John St.
Napanee, ON K7R 3L4
613-354-3351 Fax: 613-354-6545 E-mail, Programs: recreation@greaternapanee.com
info@greaternapanee.com; roads@greaternapanee.com
www.greaternapanee.com
Municipal Type: City
Area: 459.71 sq km
County or District: Lennox-Addington; *Population in 2006:* 15,400
Provincial Electoral District(s): Lanark-Frontenac-Lennox & Addington
Federal Electoral District(s): Lanark-Frontenac-Lennox & Addington
Next Election: Nov. 2010 (4 year terms)

Council
Gord Schermerhorn, Mayor
613-354-0429
Roger Cole, Deputy Mayor & Councillor
613-354-3664
Shane Grant, Councillor, Ward(s): 2
613-354-5529
Marg Isbester, Councillor, Ward(s): 3
Shaune Lucas, Councillor, Ward(s): 5

Administration
Rebecca Murphy, Clerk & Director, Corporate & Legal Services, Administration
rmurphy@greaternapanee.com
Raymond Callery, Chief Administrative Officer, Administration
rcallery@greaternapanee.com
Mark Day, Director, Finance & Treasurer, Administration
mday@greaternapanee.com
Vern Amey, Director, Public Works, Administration
vamey@greaternapanee.com
George Hanmore, Director, Fire & Emergency Services, Administration
ghanmore@greaternapanee.com
Kevin Hill, Director, Parks, Recreation & Culture, Administration
khill@greaternapanee.com
Charles McDonald, Director, Development Services, Administration
cmcdonald@greaternapanee.com
Ron Vankoughnet, Supervisor, Roads & Landfill, Administration

Greater Sudbury / Grand Sudbury
Tom Davies Square
P.O. Box 5000 A
200 Brady St.
Sudbury, ON P3A 5P3
705-671-2489 Fax: 705-671-8118 Phone, Local Calls: 3-1-1
www.greatersudbury.ca
Municipal Type: City
Incorporated: Jan. 1, 2001; *Area:* 3,200.56 sq km
Population in 2006: 157,857
Provincial Electoral District(s): Nickel Belt; Sudbury
Federal Electoral District(s): Nickel Belt; Sudbury
Next Election: Nov. 2010 (4 year terms)

Council
Marianne Matichuk, Mayor
705-674-4455, Fax: 705-673-3096
mayor@greatersudbury.ca
Joe Cimino, Councillor, Ward(s): 1
joe.cimino@greatersudbury.ca
Jacques Barbeau, Councillor, Ward(s): 2
jacques.barbeau@greatersudbury.ca
Claude Berthiaume, Councillor, Ward(s): 3
claude.berthiaume@greatersudbury.ca
Evelyn Dutrisac, Councillor, Ward(s): 4
claude.berthiaume@greatersudbury.ca
Ron Dupuis, Councillor, Ward(s): 5
ron.dupuis@greatersudbury.ca
André Rivest, Councillor, Ward(s): 6
andre.rivest@greatersudbury.ca
Dave Kilgour, Councillor, Ward(s): 7
Fabio Belli, Councillor, Ward(s): 8
Doug Craig, Councillor, Ward(s): 9
doug.craig@greatersudbury.ca
Frances Caldarelli, Councillor, Ward(s): 10
frances.caldarelli@greatersudbury.ca
Terry Kett, Councillor, Ward(s): 11
Joscelyne Landry-Altmann, Councillor, Ward(s): 12
joscelyne.landry-altmann@greatersudbury.ca

Administration
Angie Hache, City Clerk, Administration
705-674-4455, Fax: 705-671-8118
angie.hache@greatersudbury.ca
Doug Nadorozny, Chief Administrative Officer, Administration
doug.nadorozny@greatersudbury.ca
Lorella M. Hayes, B.Comm., CA, Chief Financial Officer & Treasurer, Administration
lorella.hayes@greatersudbury.ca
Greg Clausen, P. Eng, General Manager, Infrastructure Services, Administration
greg.clausen@greatersudbury.ca
Bill Lautenbach, General Manager, Growth & Development, Administration
bill.lautenbach@greatersudbury.ca
Catherine Matheson, General Manager, Community Development, Administration
catherine.matheson@greatersudbury.ca
Bruno Mangiardi, Chief Information Officer, Administration
bruno.mangiardi@greatersudbury.ca
Tim P. Beadman, Chief, Emergency Services, Administration
tim.beadman@greatersudbury.ca
Marc Leduc, Fire Chief, Administration
marc.leduc@greatersudbury.ca
Nick Benkovich, Director, Water & Wastewater, Administration
nick.benkovich@greatersudbury.ca
Robert Falcioni, Director, Roads & Transportation, Administration
robert.falcioni@greatersudbury.ca
Guido Mazza, Director, Building Services, Administration
guido.mazza@greatersudbury.caa
Roger Sauvé, Director, Greater Sudbury Transit, Administration
roger.sauve@greatersudbury.ca
Kevin Shaw, Director, Engineering Services, Administration
kevin.shaw@greatersudbury.ca

Grimsby
P.O. Box 159
160 Livingston Ave.
Grimsby, ON L3M 4G3
905-945-9634 Fax: 905-945-5010 E-mail:
pw-general@town.grimsby.on.ca
administration-office-general@town.grimsby.on.ca
www.town.grimsby.on.ca
Municipal Type: City
Area: 68.94 sq km
County or District: Niagara Reg. Mun.; *Population in 2006:* 23,937
Provincial Electoral District(s): Niagara West-Glanbrook
Federal Electoral District(s): Niagara West-Glanbrook
Next Election: Nov. 2010 (4 year terms)

Council
Robert N. Bentley, Mayor
905-945-2710
bbentley@grimsby.ca
Steve Berry, Aldermen, Ward(s): 1
905-945-2578
sberry@grimsby.ca
Dave Wilson, Aldermen, Ward(s): 1
905-309-0905
dwilson@grimsby.ca
Dave Kadwell, Aldermen, Ward(s): 2
905-945-8259
dkadwell@grimsby.ca
Michelle Seaborn, Aldermen, Ward(s): 2
David Finch, Aldermen, Ward(s): 3
905-945-4545
Nick Andreychuk, Aldermen, Ward(s): 3
Nick DiFlavio, Aldermen, Ward(s): 4
905-309-4133
ndiflavio@grimsby.ca
Carolyn Mullins, Aldermen, Ward(s): 4

Administration
Kathryn J. Vout, Town Clerk, Administration
905-945-9634
Gary D. Shay, Town Manager, Administration
S. Gruninger, CGA, Town Treasurer & Director, Finance, Administration
B. Atkinson, CGA, Director, Recreation, Facilities, & Culture, Administration
R. LeRoux, P.Eng., Director, Public Works, Administration
J. Schonewille, Director, Building & Enforcement, Administration
K. Vogl, Director, Planning, Administration
C.H. Halliday, Fire Chief, Administration
Brandon Wartman, Manager, EHS Compliance, Administration
905-309-2016

Guelph
City Hall
1 Carden St.
Guelph, ON N1H 3A1
519-822-1260 Fax: 519-763-1269 TTY: 519-826-9771
info@guelph.ca; communications@guelph.ca
www.guelph.ca
Municipal Type: City
Incorporated: 1879; *Area:* 86.72 sq km
County or District: Wellington; *Population in 2006:* 114,943
Provincial Electoral District(s): Guelph; Wellington-Halton Hills
Federal Electoral District(s): Guelph; Wellington-Halton Hills
Next Election: Nov. 2010 (4 year terms)

Council
Karen Farbridge, Mayor
519-837-5643, Fax: 519-822-8277
mayor@guelph.ca
Jim J. Furfaro, Councillor, Ward(s): 1
Bob Bell, Councillor, Ward(s): 1
Ian Findlay, Councillor, Ward(s): 2
Andy Van Hellemond, Councillor, Ward(s): 2
Maggie Laidlaw, Councillor, Ward(s): 3
June Hofland, Councillor, Ward(s): 3
Gloria Kovach, Councillor, Ward(s): 4
Cam G. Guthrie, Councillor, Ward(s): 4
Leanne Piper, Councillor, Ward(s): 5
Lise Burcher, Councillor, Ward(s): 5
Karl Wettstein, Councillor, Ward(s): 6
Dinnis Todd, Councillor, Ward(s): 6

Administration
L.A. Giles, City Clerk & Director, Information Services, Administration
clerks@guelph.ca
Hans Loewig, Chief Administrative Officer, Administration
519-837-5602, Fax: 519-822-8277
administration@guelph.ca
M. Neubauer, Director, Finance, Administration
finance@guelph.ca
M. Amorosi, Director, Human Resources, Administration
hr@guelph.ca
S. Armstrong, Director, Emergency Services, Administration
J. Laird, Director, Environmental Services, Administration
D. McCaughan, Director, Operations, Administration
operations@guelph.ca
A. Pappert, Director, Community Services, Administration
L.E. Payne, Director, Corporate Services & City Solicitor, Administration
J. Riddell, Director, Community Design & Development Services, Administration

Halton Hills
1 Halton Hills Dr.
Georgetown, ON L7G 5G2
905-873-2601 Fax: 905-873-2347 Toll Free Phone: 1-877-712-2205
www.haltonhills.ca
Municipal Type: City
Area: 276.26 sq km
County or District: Halton Reg. Mun.; *Population in 2006:* 55,289
Provincial Electoral District(s): Wellington-Halton Hills
Federal Electoral District(s): Wellington-Halton Hills
Next Election: Nov. 2010 (4 year terms)

Council
Rick Bonnette, Mayor
Clark A. Somerville, Regional Councillor, Ward(s): 1 & 2
Jane Fogal, Regional Councillor, Ward(s): 3 & 4
Jon Hurst, Councillor, Ward(s): 1
Mike O'Leary, Councillor, Ward(s): 1
Joan Robson, Councillor, Ward(s): 2
Bryan Lewis, Councillor, Ward(s): 2
Moya Johnson, Councillor, Ward(s): 3
David Kentner, Councillor, Ward(s): 3
Bob Inglis, Councillor, Ward(s): 4
Ann Lawlor, Councillor, Ward(s): 4

Administration
Debbie Edmonds, Town Clerk, Administration
D. Perlin, Chief Administrative Officer, Administration
Ed DeSousa, Treasurer & Director, Corporate Services, Administration
Terry Alyman, Director, Recreation & Parks, Administration
Bruce D. MacLean, Director, Planning, Development, & Sustainability, Administration
Chris Mills, Director, Infrastructure Services & Town Engineer, Administration
D. Szybalski, Coordinator, Sustainability, Administration

Hamilton
Hamilton City Centre
P.O. Box 2040 LCD1
#220, 77 James St. North
Hamilton, ON L8R 2K3
905-546-2489 Fax: 905-546-2095 E-mail, Dev.:
economicdevelopment@hamilton.ca
askCITY@hamilton.ca; communications@hamilton.ca
www.hamilton.ca
Municipal Type: City
Incorporated: 1846; *Area:* 1,117.21 sq km
Population in 2006: 504,559
Provincial Electoral District(s):
Ancaster-Dundas-Flamborough-Westdale; Hamilton Centre; Hamilton East-Stoney Creek; Hamilton Mountain; Niagara West-Glanbrook
Federal Electoral District(s): Hamilton Centre; Hamilton East-Stoney Creek; Hamilton Mountain; Niagara West-Glanbrook; Ancaster-Dundas-Flamborough-Westdale
Next Election: Nov. 2010 (4 year terms)
Note: Incorporated as a city on Jan. 1, 2001.

Council
Bob Bratina, Mayor
Brian McHattie, Councillor, Ward(s): 1
bmchattie@hamilton.ca
Jason Farr, Councillor, Ward(s): 2
Bernie Morelli, Councillor, Ward(s): 3
bmorelli@hamilton.ca
Sam Merulla, Councillor, Ward(s): 4
smerulla@hamilton.ca
Chad Collins, Councillor, Ward(s): 5
ccollins@hamilton.ca
Tom Jackson, Councillor, Ward(s): 6
tjackson@hamilton.ca
Scott Duvall, Councillor, Ward(s): 7
sduvall@hamilton.ca
Terry Whitehead, Councillor, Ward(s): 8
twhitehead@hamilton.ca
Brad Clark, Councillor, Ward(s): 9
bclark@ghamilton.ca
Maria Pearson, Councillor, Ward(s): 10
mpearson@hamilton.ca
Brenda Johnson, Councillor, Ward(s): 11
Lloyd Ferguson, Councillor, Ward(s): 12
lferguson@hamilton.ca
Russ Powers, Councillor, Ward(s): 13
rpowers@hamilton.ca
Robert Pasuta, Councillor, Ward(s): 14
rpasuta@hamilton.ca
Judi Partridge, Councillor, Ward(s): 15

Administration
Rose Caterini, City Clerk, Administration
clerk@hamilton.ca
Chris Murray, City Manager, Administration
905-540-5420
Roberto Rossini, General Manager, Finance & Corporate Services, Administration
Jim Kay, General Manager, Hamilton Emergency Services, Administration
Tim McCabe, General Manager, Planning & Economic Development, Administration
Joe-Anne Priel, General Manager, Community Services, Administration
Scott Stewart, C.E.T., General Manager, Public Works, Administration

Hawkesbury

600 Higginson St.
Hawkesbury, ON K6A 1H1
613-632-0106 Fax: 613-632-2463
www.hawkesbury.ca
Municipal Type: City
Area: 9.46 sq km
County or District: Prescott & Russell; *Population in 2006:* 10,869
Provincial Electoral District(s): Glengarry-Prescott-Russell
Federal Electoral District(s): Glengarry-Prescott-Russell
Next Election: Nov. 2010 (4 year terms)

Council
Rene Berthiaume, Mayor
Michel A. Beaulne, Councillor
mbeaulne@hawkesbury.ca
André Chamaillard, Councillor
Alain Fraser, Councillor
Johanne Portelance, Councillor
Michel Thibodeau, Councillor
Marc Tourangeau, Councillor

Administration
Christine Groulx, Clerk, Administration
Normand Beaulieu, Chief Administrative Officer & Treasurer, Administration
Liette Valade, Director, Recreation & Culture, Administration
Gérald Campbell, Superintendent, Public Works, Administration
Richard Guertin, Superintendent, Water Treatment Plant, Administration
Jean-Claude Miner, Chief Building Official, Administration
Ghislain Pigeon, Fire Chief, Administration
Danielle Fredette-Thériault, Officer, Human Resources, Administration
Manon Belle-Isle, Planner, Administration

Huntsville

37 Main St. East
Huntsville, ON P1H 1A1
705-789-1751 Fax: 705-789-6689
administration@huntsville.ca
www.huntsville.ca
Municipal Type: City
Area: 703.23 sq km
County or District: Muskoka Dist. Mun.; *Population in 2006:* 18,280
Provincial Electoral District(s): Parry Sound-Muskoka
Federal Electoral District(s): Parry Sound-Muskoka
Next Election: Nov. 2010 (4 year terms)

Council
Claude Doughty, Mayor
council@huntsville.ca
Fran Coleman, District & Town Councillor
Brian Thompson, District & Town Councillor
Scott Aitchison, District & Town Councillor
Tim Withey, Councillor, Ward(s): Brunel
John Davis, Councillor, Ward(s): Chaffey
Karin Terziano, Councillor, Ward(s): Huntsville
Det Schumacher, Councillor, Ward(s): Stisted/Stephenson/Port Sydney
Chris Zanetti, Councillor, Ward(s): Stisted/Stephenson/Port Sydney

Administration
Kathleen Gilchrist, Municipal Clerk, Administration
corporateservices@huntsville.ca
Kelly Pender, Chief Administrative Officer, Administration
Dianne Leeder, Treasurer, Administration
Brian Crozier, Director, Community Services, Administration
Mike Gooch, Director, Development Services, Administration
developmentservices@huntsville.ca
Steve Hernen, Director, Protective Services, Administration
fire.chief@huntsville.ca
Steve Keeley, Director, Public Works, Administration
publicworks@huntsville.ca
Colleen MacDonald, Manager, Parks, Cemeteries & Environment, Administration
Lisa Smith, Manager, Human Resources, Administration

Ingersoll

130 Oxford St.
Ingersoll, ON N5C 2V5
519-485-0120 Fax: 519-485-3543
clerks@ingersoll.ca
www.ingersoll.ca
Municipal Type: City
Area: 12.9 sq km
County or District: Oxford; *Population in 2006:* 11,760
Provincial Electoral District(s): Oxford
Federal Electoral District(s): Oxford
Next Election: Nov. 2010 (4 year terms)

Council
Ted J. Comiskey, Mayor
mayor@ingersoll.ca
Fred Freeman, Deputy Mayor & Councillor
ffreeman@ingersoll.ca
John F. Fortner, Councillor
Gord Lesser, Councillor
glesser@ingersoll.ca
Dave McLeod, Councillor
dmcleod@ingersoll.ca
Cathy Mott, Councillor
Kristy Van Kooten-Bossence, Councillor
kvankootenbossence@ingersoll.ca

Administration
Elaine Clark, Clerk, Administration
clerks@ingersoll.ca
James Timlin, Chief Administrative Officer, Administration
jtimlin@ingersoll.ca
Gary Seitz, Treasurer & Director, Finance, Administration
Gene McLaren, Director, Engineering Services, Administration
John Phillips, Director, Public Works, Administration
Bonnie Ward, Director, Recreation, Administration
Darell Parker, Fire Chief, Administration

Innisfil

2101 Innisfil Beach Rd.
Innisfil, ON L9S 1A1
705-436-3710 Fax: 705-436-7120
www.innisfil.ca
Municipal Type: City
Incorporated: 1850; *Area:* 284.18 sq km
County or District: Simcoe; *Population in 2006:* 31,175
Provincial Electoral District(s): York Simcoe
Federal Electoral District(s): York-Simcoe; Barrie
Next Election: Nov. 2010 (4 year terms)

Council
Barb Baguley, Mayor
bbaguley@innisfil.ca
Dan Davidson, Deputy Mayor & Councillor
ddavidson@innisfil.ca
Doug Lougheed, Councillor, Ward(s): 1
dlougheed@innisfil.ca
Richard Simpson, Councillor, Ward(s): 2
rsimpson@innisfil.ca
Ken Simpson, Councillor, Ward(s): 3
ksimpson@innisfil.ca
Rod Boynton, Councillor, Ward(s): 4
rboynton@innisfil.ca
Bill Loughead, Councillor, Ward(s): 5
bloughead@innisfil.ca
Maria Baier, Councillor, Ward(s): 6
mbaierinnisfil.ca
Lynn Dollin, Councillor, Ward(s): 7
ldollin@innisfil.ca

Administration
John D. Leach, Clerk, Administration
Lawrence Allsion, Chief Administrative Officer, Administration
Ian Goodfellow, Treasurer, Administration
Kerry Columbus, Director, Community Services, Administration
Susan Downs, Director, Corporate Services & Chief Librarian, Administration
Robert McAuley, Director, Planning & Development, Administration
Michelle Collette, Manager, Human Resources, Administration
Ross Cotton, Manager, Planning, Administration
R. Wayne Young, Manager, Operational Services, Administration
Scott Griffith, Fire Chief, Administration

Kawartha Lakes

P.O. Box 9000
26 Francis St.
Lindsay, ON K9V 5R8
705-324-9411 Fax: 705-324-1750 Toll Free Phone: 1-888-822-2225
info@city.kawarthalakes.on.ca
www.city.kawarthalakes.on.ca
Municipal Type: City
Incorporated: Jan. 1, 2001; *Area:* 3,059.47 sq km
Population in 2006: 74,561
Provincial Electoral District(s): Haliburton-Kawartha Lakes-Brock
Federal Electoral District(s): Haliburton-Kawartha Lakes-Brock
Next Election: Nov. 2010 (4 year terms)
Note: Formerly the County of Victoria.

Council
Ric McGee, Mayor
rmcgee@city.kawarthalakes.on.ca
John Macklem, Councillor, Ward(s): 1
jmacklem@city.kawarthalakes.on.ca
Emmett Yeo, Councillor, Ward(s): 2
eyeo@city.kawarthalakes.on.ca
David Hodgson, Councillor, Ward(s): 3
dhodgson@city.kawarthalakes.on.ca
Glenn Campbell, Councillor, Ward(s): 4
gcampbell@city.kawarthalakes.on.ca
Stephen Strangway, Councillor, Ward(s): 5
sstrangway@city.kawarthalakes.on.ca
Doug Elmslie, Councillor, Ward(s): 6
delmslie@city.kawarthalakes.on.ca
Brian Junkin, Councillor, Ward(s): 7
bjunkin@city.kawarthalakes.on.ca
Donna Villemaire, Councillor, Ward(s): 8
dvillemaire@city.kawarthalakes.on.ca
Andy Luff, Councillor, Ward(s): 9
aluff@city.kawarthalakes.on.ca
Pat Dunn, Councillor, Ward(s): 10
pdunn@city.kawarthalakes.on.ca
Patrick O'Reilly, Councillor, Ward(s): 11
poreilly@city.kawarthalakes.on.ca
Gord James, Councillor, Ward(s): 12
gjames@city.kawarthalakes.on.ca
Pat Warren, Councillor, Ward(s): 13
pwarren@city.kawarthalakes.on.ca
Ron Ashmore, Councillor, Ward(s): 14
rashmore@city.kawarthalakes.on.ca
Gerald McGregor, Councillor, Ward(s): 15
gmcgregor@city.kawarthalakes.on.ca
Heather Stauble, Councillor, Ward(s): 16
hstauble@city.kawarthalakes.on.ca

Administration
Judy Currins, Administration
Jane Reynolds, Chief Administrative Officer, Administration
jreynolds@city.kawarthalakes.on.ca
Rudy Huisman, Director, Financial Services, Administration
rhuisman@city.kawarthalakes.on.ca
Ken Becking, Director, Public Works, Administration
kbecking@city.kawarthalakes.on.ca
Richard Danziger, Director, Development Services, Administration
rdanziger@city.kawarthalakes.on.ca
Bob Knight, Director, Health & Social Services, Administration
bknight@city.kawarthalakes.on.ca
Janice Platt, Director, Human Resources, Administration
jplatt@city.kawarthalakes.on.ca
Kevin Williams, Director, Community Services, Administration
dguilbault@city.kawarthalakes.on.ca
David Guilbault, Fire Chief, Administration
dguilbault@city.kawarthalakes.on.ca

Kenora

1 Main St. South
Kenora, ON P9N 3X2
807-467-2000 Fax: 807-467-2009
service@kenora.ca
www.kenora.ca
Municipal Type: City
Area: 210.91 sq km
County or District: Kenora District; *Population in 2006:* 15,177
Provincial Electoral District(s): Kenora-Rainy River
Federal Electoral District(s): Kenora
Next Election: Nov. 2010 (4 year terms)

Council
David S. Canfield, Mayor
Charito V. Drinkwalter, Councillor
Ron Lunny, Councillor
Rod McKay, Councillor
Rory McMillan, Councillor
807-468-4383
rmcmillan@kenora.ca
Louis Roussin, Councillor
Sharon L. Smith, Councillor

Administration
Joanne L. McMillin, Clerk, Administration
jmcmillin@kenora.ca
Bill Preisentanz, Chief Administrative Officer, Administration
billp@kenora.ca
Karen Brown, Manager, Finance & Administration, Administration
kbrown@kenora.ca
Warren Brinkman, Manager, Emergency Services, Administration
wbrinkman@kenora.ca
Sharen McDowall, Manager, Human Resources, Administration
smcdowall@kenora.ca
Colleen Neil, Manager, Recreation, Administration
cneil@kenora.ca
Rick Perchuk, Manager, Operations, Administration
rperchuk@kenora.ca
Mike Mostow, Supervisor, Fleet & Solid Waste, Administration
mmostow@kenora.ca
Warren Ortlieb, Supervisor, Sewer & Water, Administration
wortlieb@kenora.ca
Kevin Robertston, Chief Building Official, Administration
krobertson@kenora.ca
Jeff Port, City Planner, Administration
jport@kenora.ca
Marco Vogrig, Municipal Engineer, Administration
mvogrig@kenora.ca

Kingston

City Hall
216 Ontario St.
Kingston, ON K7L 2Z3
613-546-4291 Fax: 613-546-5232 TTY: 613-546-4889
contactus@cityofkingston.ca
www.cityofkingston.ca
Municipal Type: City
Incorporated: Jan. 1, 1998; *Area:* 450.39 sq km
County or District: Frontenac; *Population in 2006:* 117,207
Provincial Electoral District(s): Kingston & the Islands
Federal Electoral District(s): Kingston & the Islands
Next Election: Nov. 2010 (4 year terms)

Council
Mark Gerretsen, Mayor
Rick Downes, Councillor, Ward(s): Cataraqui District
Lisa Osanic, Councillor, Ward(s): Collins-Bayridge District
Jeff Scott, Councillor, Ward(s): Countryside District
Rob Hutchinson, Councillor, Ward(s): King's Town District
Sandy Berg, Councillor, Ward(s): Kingscourt-Strathcona District
Dorothy Hector, Councillor, Ward(s): Lakeside District
Kevin George, Councillor, Ward(s): Loyalist-Cataraqui District
Brian Reitzel, Councillor, Ward(s): Pittsburgh District
Liz Schell, Councillor, Ward(s): Portsmouth District
Bill Glover, Councillor, Ward(s): Sydenham District
Bryan Paterson, Councillor, Ward(s): Trillium District
Jim Neill, Councillor, Ward(s): Williamsville District

Administration
Carolyn Downs, City Clerk, Administration
Gerard Hunt, Chief Administrative Officer, Administration
Desiree Kennedy, Director, Financial Services, Administration

Cynthia Beach, Commissioner, Sustainability & Growth, Administration
Denis Leger, Commissioner, Corporate Services, Administration
James de Hoop, Director, Community & Family Services, Administration
Lanie Hurdle, Director, Recreation & Leisure Services, Administration
Paul MacLatchy, Director, Strategy, Environment, & Communications, Administration
Malcolm Morris, Director, Transportation, Administration
Mark Van Buren, Director, Engineering, Administration
George Wallace, Director, Planning & Development, Administration
Damon Wells, Director, Public Works, Administration
Terry Willing, Director, Building & Licensing, Administration
Harold Tulk, Fire Chief, Administration
John Cross, Manager, Emergency Services, Administration
John Giles, Manager, Solid Waste, Administration

Kingsville

2021 Division Rd. North
Kingsville, ON N9Y 2Y9
519-733-2305 Fax: 519-733-8108
www.kingsville.ca
Municipal Type: City
Incorporated: 1874; *Area:* 246.84 sq km
County or District: Essex; *Population in 2006:* 20,908
Provincial Electoral District(s): Essex
Federal Electoral District(s): Essex
Next Election: Nov. 2010 (4 year terms)
Note: Incorporated as a town in 1901. Restructuring occurred in 1999.

Council
Nelson Santos, Mayor
nsantos@kingsville.ca
Tamara Stomp, Deputy Mayor & Councillor
Ron Colasanti, Councillor
Gord Queen, Councillor
pgordonqueen@msn.com
Bob Peterson, Councillor
rpeterson9@cogeco.ca
Sandi McIntyre, Councillor
Gail Stiffler, Councillor

Administration
Linda Burling, Clerk, Administration
lburling@kingsville.ca
Dan DiGiovanni, Chief Administrative Officer, Administration
ddigiovanni@kingsville.ca
Sandra Ingratta, Director, Financial Services, Administration
singratta@kingsville.ca
Andrew Plancke, C.E.T., Director, Municipal Services, Administration
aplancke@kingsville.ca
Michael Arthur, Chief Building Official, Administration
marthur@kingsville.ca
Bob Kissner, Fire Chief, Administration
bkissner@kingsville.ca
Ron Steinwender, Manager, Public Works, Administration
rsteinwender@kingsville.ca
Dan Wood, Manager, Parks & Recreation, Administration
dwood@kingsville.ca

Kitchener

City Hall
P.O. Box 1118
200 King St. West
Kitchener, ON N2G 4G7
519-741-2286 Fax: 519-741-2705 TTY: 1-866-969-9994
info@kitchener.ca
www.kitchener.ca
Municipal Type: City
Incorporated: June 9, 1912; *Area:* 136.89 sq km
County or District: Waterloo Regional Municipality; *Population in 2006:* 204,668
Provincial Electoral District(s): Kitchener Centre; Kitchener-Waterloo; Waterloo-Wellington
Federal Electoral District(s): Kitchener Centre; Kitchener-Waterloo; Kitchener-Conestoga
Next Election: Nov. 2010 (4 year terms)

Council
Carl Zehr, Mayor
carl.zehr@kitchener.ca
Scott Davey, Councillor, Ward(s): 1
Berry Vrbanovic, Councillor, Ward(s): 2
John Gazzola, Councillor, Ward(s): 3
Yvonne Fernandes, Councillor, Ward(s): 4
Kelly Galloway, Councillor, Ward(s): 5
Paul Singh, Councillor, Ward(s): 6
Bil Ioannidis, Councillor, Ward(s): 7
Zyg Janecki, Councillor, Ward(s): 8
Frank Etherington, Councillor, Ward(s): 9
Daniel Glenn-Graham, Councillor, Ward(s): 10

Administration
Carla Ladd, Chief Administrative Officer, Administration
519-741-2350, Fax: 519-741-2705
carla.ladd@kitchener.ca
Dan Chapman, City Treasurer & General Manager, Financial Servic, Administration
519-741-2357
Pauline Houston, General Manager, Community Services, Administration
519-741-2646
Troy Speck, General Manager, Corporate Services, Administration
519-741-2279
Jeff Willmer, General Manager, Development & Technical Services, Administration
Grant Murphy, Director, Engineering Services, Administration
519-741-2410
Alain Pinard, Director, Planning, Administration
519-741-2426
Mike Seiling, Director, Building, Administration
519-741-2669
Tim Beckett, Fire Chief, Administration
519-741-2495

Lakeshore

419 Notre Dame Rd.
Belle River, ON N0R 1A0
519-728-2700 Fax: 519-728-9530
mmasse@lakeshore.ca
www.lakeshore.ca
Municipal Type: City
Incorporated: 1999; *Area:* 530.32 sq km
County or District: Essex; *Population in 2006:* 33,245
Provincial Electoral District(s): Essex
Federal Electoral District(s): Essex
Next Election: Nov. 2010 (4 year terms)
Note: Amalgamation of the former Town of Belle River & the former Townships of Maidstone, Rochester, Tilbury North & Tilbury West.

Council
Tom Bain, Mayor
tbain@lakeshore.ca
Al Fazio, Deputy Mayor & Councillor
afazio@lakeshore.ca
Len Janisse, Councillor, Ward(s): 1
ljanisse@lakeshore.ca
Dave Monk, Councillor, Ward(s): 2
dmonk@lakeshore.ca
Charles W. McLean, Councillor, Ward(s): 3
cmclean@lakeshore.ca
Steven Bezaire, Councillor, Ward(s): 4
sbezaire@lakeshore.ca
Dan Diemer, Councillor, Ward(s): 5
ddiemer@lakeshore.ca
Linda McKinlay, Councillor, Ward(s): 6
lmckinlay@lakeshore.ca

Administration
Mary Masse, Clerk, Administration
Ruth Coursey, Chief Administrative Officer, Administration
Sylvia Rammelaere, Director, Finance & Performance Service, Administration
Kirk Foran, Director, Corporate Services, Administration
kforan@lakeshore.ca
Lee Holling, Director, Community & Development Services, Administration
Dan Piescic, Director, Engineering & Infrastructure Services, Administration
Chuck Chevalier, Manager, Public Works, Administration
Kim Darroch, Manager, Development Services, Administration
Tony DiCiocco, Manager, Engineering Services, Administration
Tony Francisco, Manager, Environmental Services, Administration
Don Williamson, Fire Chief, Administration
Maureen Lesperance, Coordinator, Planning, Administration

LaSalle

5950 Malden Rd.
Lasalle, ON N9H 1S4
519-969-7770 Fax: 519-969-4469
webmaster@town.lasalle.on.ca
www.town.lasalle.on.ca
Municipal Type: City
Incorporated: 1924; *Area:* 65.25 sq km
County or District: Essex; *Population in 2006:* 27,652
Provincial Electoral District(s): Essex
Federal Electoral District(s): Essex
Next Election: Nov. 2010 (4 year terms)
Note: Dissolved into Township of Sandwich West in 1959. Status & name change to Town of LaSalle in 1991.

Council
Ken Antaya, Mayor
mayor@town.lasalle.on.ca
Mark Carrick, Deputy Mayor & Councillor
Marc Bondy, Councillor
mbondy@town.lasalle.on.ca
Terry Burns, Councillor
tburns@town.lasalle.on.ca
Sue Desjarlais, Councillor
sdesjarl@town.lasalle.on.ca
Crystal B. Meloche, Councillor
cmeloche@town.lasalle.on.ca
Ray Renaud, Councillor
rrenaud@town.lasalle.on.ca

Administration
Brenda Andreatta, Clerk, Administration
bandreat@town.lasalle.on.ca
Kevin Miller, Chief Administrative Officer, Administration
kmiller@town.lasalle.on.ca
Joe Milicia, Treasurer, Administration
jmilicia@town.lasalle.on.ca
Larry Silani, Director, Planning & Development Services, Administration
lsilani@town.lasalle.on.ca
Robert Hayes, P. Eng, Town Engineer, Administration
rhayes@town.lasalle.on.ca

Lincoln

4800 South Service Rd.
Beamsville, ON L0R 1B1
905-563-8205 Fax: 905-563-6566
info@lincoln.ca
www.lincoln.ca
Municipal Type: City
Incorporated: Jan. 1, 1970; *Area:* 162.86 sq km
County or District: Niagara Reg. Mun.; *Population in 2006:* 21,722
Provincial Electoral District(s): Niagara West-Glanbrook
Federal Electoral District(s): Niagara West-Glanbrook
Next Election: Nov. 2010 (4 year terms)
Note: Amalgamation of the Town of Beamsville, the Township of Clinton, & part of the Township of Louth.

Council
Bill Hodgson, Mayor
bhodgson@lincoln.ca
Dianne Rintjema, Councillor, Ward(s): 1
drintjema@lincoln.ca
Robert Foster, Councillor, Ward(s): 1
rfoster@lincoln.ca
John A. Kralt, Councillor, Ward(s): 2
jkralt@lincoln.ca
John D. Pachereva, Councillor, Ward(s): 2
jdpachereva@lincoln.ca
Robert Condotta, Councillor, Ward(s): 3
rcondotta@lincoln.ca
Dave A. Thomson, Councillor, Ward(s): 3
Geoffrey Barlow, Councillor, Ward(s): 4
gbarlow@lincoln.ca
Wayne MacMillan, Councillor, Ward(s): 4
wmacmillan@lincoln.ca

Administration
William J. Kolasa, Clerk & Director, Corporate Services, Administration
wkolasa@lincoln.ca
Anne Louise Heron, Chief Administrative Officer, Administration
aheron@lincoln.ca
Robert Spadoni, Director, Finance, Administration
bspadoni@lincoln.ca
Kathleen Dale, Director, Planning & Development, Administration
kdale@lincoln.ca
Doug Kerr, Director, Public Works, Administration
dkerr@lincoln.ca
Judy Pease, Director, Community Services, Administration
jpease@lincoln.ca
Scott Blake, Fire Chief, Administration
sblake@lincoln.ca
Andrew Greenaway, Chief Building Official, Administration
agreenaway@lincoln.ca
Greg Lancaster, Manager, Facilities & Parks, Administration
glancaster@lincoln.ca

London

City Hall
P.O. Box 5035
300 Dufferin Ave.
London, ON N6A 4L9
519-661-4500 Fax: 519-661-4892
webmaster@london.ca
www.london.ca
Municipal Type: City
Incorporated: 1855; *Area:* 420.57 sq km
County or District: Middlesex; *Population in 2006:* 352,395
Provincial Electoral District(s): London-Fanshawe; Elgin-Middlesex-London; London North Centre; London West
Federal Electoral District(s): London-Fanshawe; Elgin-Middlesex-London; London North Centre; London West
Next Election: Nov. 2010 (4 year terms)

Council
Joe Fontana, Mayor, Administration
Bud Polhill, Councillor, Ward(s): 1
Bill Armstrong, Councillor, Ward(s): 2
Joe Swan, Councillor, Ward(s): 3
Stephen Orser, Councillor, Ward(s): 4
Joni Baechler, Councillor, Ward(s): 5
Nancy Ann Branscombe, Councillor, Ward(s): 6
Matt Brown, Councillor, Ward(s): 7
Paul Hubert, Councillor, Ward(s): 8
Dale Henderson, Councillor, Ward(s): 9
Paul Van Meerbergen, Councillor, Ward(s): 10
Denise Brown, Councillor, Ward(s): 11
Harold Usher, Councillor, Ward(s): 12
Judy Bryant, Councillor, Ward(s): 13
Sandy White, Councillor, Ward(s): 14
Kevin Bain, City Clerk, Administration
Jeff Fielding, Chief Administrative Officer, Administration
Mike St. Amant, City Treasurer, Administration
Victor Cote, General Manager, Finance & Corporate Services, Administration
Ross Fair, General Manager, Community Services, Administration
Patrick McNally, P.Eng., General Manager, Environmental Engineering Service, Administration
Rob Panzer, General Manager, Planning & Development, Administration
William Coxhead, Director, Parks & Recreation, Administration
Karl Drysdale, Director, Technology Services, Administration
David Leckie, Director, Roads & Transportation, Administration
Veronica McAlea Major, Director, Human Resources, Administration
Ronald Standish, Director, Wastewater & Treatment, Administration
Jay Stanford, Director, Environmental Programs & Solid Waste, Administration

Markham

Markham Civic Centre
101 Town Centre Blvd.
Markham, ON L3R 9W3
905-477-7000 Fax: 905-479-7771 Language Phone Line: 905-477-5530 (150 languages)
customerservice@markham.ca; webmaster@markham.ca
www.markham.ca
Municipal Type: City
Incorporated: Jan. 1, 1971; *Area:* 212.58 sq km
County or District: York Reg. Mun.; *Population in 2006:* 261,573
Provincial Electoral District(s): Markham-Unionville; Oak Ridges-Markham; Thornhill
Federal Electoral District(s): Markham-Unionville; Oak Ridges-Markham; Thornhill
Next Election: Nov. 2010 (4 year terms)

Council
Frank Scarpitti, Mayor
905-475-4702
Jack Heath, Deputy Mayor & Regional Councillor
905-475-4872
Jim Jones, Regional Councillor
905-479-7757
Gordon Landon, Regional Councillor
905-415-7534
Joe Li, Regional Councillor
Valerie Burke, Councillor, Ward(s): 1
905-479-7747
Howard Shore, Councillor, Ward(s): 2
Don Hamilton, Councillor, Ward(s): 3
Carolina Moretti, Councillor, Ward(s): 4
905-479-7751
Colin Campbell, Councillor, Ward(s): 5
Alan Ho, Councillor, Ward(s): 6
Logan Kanapathi, Councillor, Ward(s): 7
905-479-7748
Alex Chiu, Councillor, Ward(s): 8

Administration
Kimberly Kitteringham, Town Clerk, Administration
905-475-4729
kkitteringham@markham.ca
John Livey, Chief Administrative Officer, Administration
905-479-7755
jlivey@markham.ca
Barbara Cribbett, Treasurer
905-475-4735
bcribbett@markham.ca
Jim Baird, Commissioner, Development Services, Administration
905-475-4875
Brenda Librecz, Commissioner, Community & Fire Services, Administration
905-479-7761
Andy Taylor, Commissioner, Corporate Services, Administration
905-475-4705
Nasir Kenea, Chief Information Officer, Administration
905-475-4733
Bill Snowball, Fire Chief, Fire & Emergency Services, Administration
905-305-5982
Alan Brown, Director, Engineering, Administration
905-415-7507
Sharon Laing, Director, Human Resources, Administration
905-475-4725
Peter Loukes, Director, Operations, Administration
905-475-4894
Valerie Shuttleworth, Director, Planning & Urban Design, Administration, Fax: 905-479-7768
John C. Wright, Director, Building Standards, Administration
905-475-4712
Jerry Klaus, General Manager, Waterworks, Administration
jklaus@markham.ca
Claudia Marsales, Manager, Waste Management, Administration
cmarsales@markham.ca

Midland

575 Dominion Ave.
Midland, ON L4R 1R2
705-526-4275 Fax: 705-526-9971 TTY: 705-526-4276, ext. 2824
info@midland.ca
www.midland.ca
Municipal Type: City
Area: 29.09 sq km
County or District: Simcoe; *Population in 2006:* 16,300
Provincial Electoral District(s): Simcoe North
Federal Electoral District(s): Simcoe North
Next Election: Nov. 2010 (4 year terms)

Council
Gordon A. McKay, Mayor
Stephan M. Kramp, Deputy Mayor & Councillor
Jim Attwood, Councillor, Ward(s): 1
Patricia A. File, Councillor, Ward(s): 1
Zena Pendlebury, Councillor, Ward(s): 1
Jack H. Charlebois, Councillor, Ward(s): 2
Bob Jeffery, Councillor, Ward(s): 2
Mike Ross, Councillor, Ward(s): 2
Glen M. Canning, Councillor, Ward(s): 3

Administration
Andrea Fay, Clerk, Administration
clerks@midland.ca
Ted Walker, Chief Administrative Officer, Administration
Sue Gignac, Treasurer
treasury@midland.ca
Wes Crown, Director, Planning & Development, Administration
wcrown@midland.ca; townplan@midland.ca
Doug Baker, General Manager, Public Works, & Town Engineer, Administration
engineering@midland.ca
Suzanne Beatty, Manager, Human Resources, Administration
hr@midland.ca
Kevin Foster, Fire Chief, Administration
fire@midland.ca

Milton

150 Mary St.
Milton, ON L9T 6Z5
905-878-7252 Fax: 905-878-6995
info@milton.ca
www.milton.ca
Municipal Type: City
Incorporated: 1857; *Area:* 366.61 sq km
County or District: Halton Regional Municipality; *Population in 2006:* 53,939
Provincial Electoral District(s): Halton
Federal Electoral District(s): Halton
Next Election: Nov. 2010 (4 year terms)

Council
Gordon A. Krantz, Mayor
Tony Lambert, Local & Regional Councillor, Ward(s): South
Colin Best, Local & Regional Councillor, Ward(s): North
Sharon Barkley, Councillor, Ward(s): 1
Andrew Salmons, Councillor, Ward(s): 1
Greg Nelson, Councillor, Ward(s): 2
Mike Broughton, Councillor, Ward(s): 2
Cindy Lunau, Councillor, Ward(s): 3
Jan Mowbray, Councillor, Ward(s): 3
jan@janmowbray.ca
Rick Malboeuf, Councillor, Ward(s): 4
Paul Scherer, Councillor, Ward(s): 4
Arnold Huffman, Councillor, Ward(s): 5
Michael Bugala, Councillor, Ward(s): 5
Mike Cluett, Councillor, Ward(s): 6
Maqsood A. Soomro, Councillor, Ward(s): 6
Rick Di Lorenzo, Councillor, Ward(s): 7
Paul Virdo, Councillor, Ward(s): 7
Zeeshan Hamid, Councillor, Ward(s): 8
Jefferey C. Belo, Councillor, Ward(s): 8

Administration
Troy McHarg, Clerk, Administration
townclerk@milton.ca
W.F. Mann, P.Eng., Director, Planning & Development, Administration
James G. McQueen, Director, Corporate Services, Administration
Jennifer Reynolds, Director, Community Services, Administration
Brian Elsworth, P.Eng., Fire Chief, Administration

Mississauga

Civic Centre
300 City Centre Dr.
Mississauga, ON L5B 3C1
905-896-5000 Fax: 905-615-4081 TTY: 905-896-5151
public.info@mississauga.ca
www.mississauga.ca
Municipal Type: City
Incorporated: Jan. 1, 1974; *Area:* 288.53 sq km
County or District: Peel Reg. Mun.; *Population in 2006:* 668,549
Provincial Electoral District(s): Bramalea-Gore-Malton; Mississauga-Brampton South; Mississauga-Erindale; Mississauga East-Cooksville; Mississauga South; Mississauga-Streetsville
Federal Electoral District(s): Bramalea-Gore-Malton; Mississauga-Brampton South; Mississauga-Erindale; Mississauga East-Cooksville; Mississauga South; Mississauga-Streetsville
Next Election: Nov. 2010 (4 year terms)

Council
Hazel McCallion, Mayor
Jim Tovey, Councillor, Ward(s): 1
Patricia Mullin, Councillor, Ward(s): 2
Chris Fonseca, Councillor, Ward(s): 3
Frank Dale, Councillor, Ward(s): 4
Eve Adams, Councillor, Ward(s): 5
Ron Starr, Councillor, Ward(s): 6
Nando Iannicca, Councillor, Ward(s): 7
Katie Mahoney, Councillor, Ward(s): 8
Pat Saito, Councillor, Ward(s): 9
Sue McFadden, Councillor, Ward(s): 10
George Carlson, Councillor, Ward(s): 11

Administration
Crystal Greer, City Clerk, Administration
Janice Baker, City Manager & Chief Administrative Officer, Administration
city.manager@mississauga.ca
Brenda Breault, Commissioner, Corporate Services, & Treasurer, Administration
Paul Mitcham, Commissioner, Community Services, Administration
Martin Powell, Commissioner, Transportation & Works, Administration
Ed Sajecki, Commissioner, Planning & Building, Administration
Garry W. Morden, Fire Chief, Administration

Mississippi Mills

P.O. Box 400
3131 Old Perth Rd., RR#2
Almonte, ON K0A 1A0
613-256-2064 Fax: 613-256-4887 Toll Free Phone: 1-888-779-8666
town@mississippimills.ca
www.mississippimills.ca
Municipal Type: City
Incorporated: Jan. 1, 1998; *Area:* 509.05 sq km
County or District: Lanark; *Population in 2006:* 11,734
Provincial Electoral District(s): Carleton-Mississippi Mills
Federal Electoral District(s): Carleton-Mississippi Mills
Next Election: Nov. 2010 (4 year terms)
Note: Merger of the Town of Almonte with the townships of Ramsay & Pakenham.

Council
John Levi, Mayor
Garry Dalgity, Councillor, Ward(s): Almonte
garry.dalgity@sympatico.ca
Rick Minnille, Councillor, Ward(s): Almonte
garry.dalgity@sympatico.ca
Bernard Cameron, Councillor, Ward(s): Almonte
Alex Gillis, Councillor, Ward(s): Almonte
Duncan A. Abbott, Councillor, Ward(s): Pakenham
Denzil Ferguson, Councillor, Ward(s): Pakenham
John H. Edwards, Councillor, Ward(s): Ramsay
Shaun J. McLaughlin, Councillor, Ward(s): Ramsay
Paul J. Watters, Councillor, Ward(s): Ramsay
Val Wilkinson, Councillor, Ward(s): Ramsay

Administration
Cynthia Halcrow, Town Clerk, Administration
chalcrow@mississippimills.ca
Diane Smithson, Chief Administrative Officer, Administration
dsmithson@mississippimills.ca
Rhonda Whitmarsh, Treasurer, Administration
rwhitmarsh@mississippimills.ca
Tim Kocialek, Director, Roads & Public Work, Administration
tkocialek@mississippimills.ca
Rod Cameron, Manager, Operations, Administration
rcameron@mississippimills.ca
Art Brown, Fire Chief, Administration
abrown@mississippimills.ca
Paul Lemay, Chief Building Official, Administration
plemay@mississippimills.ca

New Tecumseth

Town Administration Centre
P.O. Box 910
10 Wellington St. East
Alliston, ON L9R 1A1
705-435-6219 Fax: 705-435-2873 Alternative Phone: 905-729-0057
www.town.newtecumseth.on.ca
Municipal Type: City
Incorporated: Jan. 1991; *Area:* 274.18 sq km
County or District: Simcoe; *Population in 2006:* 27,701
Provincial Electoral District(s): Simcoe-Grey
Federal Electoral District(s): Simcoe-Grey
Next Election: Nov. 2010 (4 year terms)

Council
Mike MacEachern, Mayor
mayor@town.newtecumseth.on.ca
Rick Milne, Deputy Mayor & Councillor
deputymayor@town.newtecumseth.on.ca
Bob Marrs, Councillor, Ward(s): 1
ward.1@town.newtecumseth.on.ca
Jamie Smith, Councillor, Ward(s): 2
ward.2@town.newtecumseth.on.ca
J.J. Paul Whiteside, Councillor, Ward(s): 3
ward.3@town.newtecumseth.on.ca
Fran Sainsbury, Councillor, Ward(s): 4
ward.4@town.newtecumseth.on.ca
Donna Jebb, Councillor, Ward(s): 5
ward.5@town.newtecumseth.on.ca
Richard Norcross, Councillor, Ward(s): 6
ward.6@town.newtecumseth.on.ca
Bruce Haire, Councillor, Ward(s): 7
ward.7@town.newtecumseth.on.ca
Jim Stone, Councillor, Ward(s): 8
ward.8@town.newtecumseth.on.ca

Administration
Gayla McDonald, Clerk & Manager, Administration, Administration
Terri Caron, Chief Administrative Officer, Administration
Mark Sirr, Treasurer & Manager, Finance, Administration
Eric Chandler, Manager, Planning, Administration
Joyce Epstein, Manager, Parks, Recreation & Culture, Administration
Chad Horan, Manager, Public Works, Administration
Hilary McCormack, Manager, Human Resources, Administration
John Miller, Manager, Building Standards & Chief Building Offic, Administration
Rick Vatri, Manager, Engineering, Administration
Dan Heydon, Fire Chief, Administration

Newmarket

P.O. Box 328
395 Mulock Dr.
Newmarket, ON L3Y 4X7
905-895-5193 Fax: 905-953-5100
customerservice@newmarket.ca
www.newmarket.ca
Municipal Type: City
Incorporated: 1857; *Area:* 38.08 sq km
County or District: York Regional Municipality; *Population in 2006:* 74,295
Provincial Electoral District(s): Newmarket-Aurora
Federal Electoral District(s): Newmarket-Aurora

Next Election: Nov. 2010 (4 year terms)
Note: Incorporated as a town in 1880.

Council
Tony Van Bynen, Mayor
905-898-2876, Fax: 905-953-5102
mayor@newmarket.ca
John Taylor, Regional Councillor
jtaylor@newmarket.ca
Tom Vegh, Councillor, Ward(s): 1
tomvegh@gmail.com
Dave Kerwin, Councillor, Ward(s): 2
dkerwin@newmarket.ca
Jane Twinney, Councillor, Ward(s): 3
Tom Hempen, Councillor, Ward(s): 4
Joe Sponga, Councillor, Ward(s): 5
jsponga@newmarket.ca
Maddie Di Muccio, Councillor, Ward(s): 6
Chris Emanuel, Councillor, Ward(s): 7
cemanuel@newmarket.ca

Administration
Anita Moore, Town Clerk, Administration
clerks@newmarket.ca
Robert N. Shelton, Chief Administrative Officer, Administration
Mike Mayes, Treasurer, Administration
finance@newmarket.ca
Robert Dixon, Commissioner, Corporate & Financial Services, Administration
Robert Prentice, Commissioner, Community Services, Administration
Brian Jones, Director, Public Works Services, Administration
Jim Koutroubis, Director, Engineering Services, Administration
engineering@newmarket.ca
Ian McDougall, Director, Recreation & Culture Services, Administration
John Molyneaux, Director, Emergency Services, & Fire Chief, Administration
Rick Nethery, BES, MCIP, RPP, Director, Planning, Administration
905-953-5321, Fax: 905-953-5140
planning@newmarket.ca
Ron Tremblay, Director, Building & Bylaws, Administration
buildings@newmarket.ca
Wanda Bennett, Manager, Corporate Communications, Administration
communications@newmarket.ca
Lynn Georgeff, Manager, Human Resources, Administration

Niagara Falls
City Hall
P.O. Box 1023
4310 Queen St.
Niagara Falls, ON L2E 6X5
905-356-7521 Fax: 905-356-9083
www.niagarafalls.ca
Municipal Type: City
Incorporated: Jan. 1, 1904; *Area:* 209.58 sq km
County or District: Niagara Reg. Mun.; *Population in 2006:* 82,184
Provincial Electoral District(s): Niagara Falls
Federal Electoral District(s): Niagara Falls
Next Election: Nov. 2010 (4 year terms)

Council
Jim Diodati, Mayor
jdiodati@niagarafalls.ca
Wayne Thomson, City Councillor
wthomson@niagarafalls.ca
Victor Pietrangelo, City Councillor
vpietrangelo@niagarafalls.ca
Carolynn Ioannoni, City Councillor
ioannoni@niagarafalls.ca
Vince A. Kerrio, City Councillor
kerrio@overlookingthefalls.com s
Wayne Gates, City Councillor
Joyce Morocco, City Councillor
Janice Wing, City Councillor
jwing@niagarafalls.ca
Bart Maves, City & Regional Councillor
Barbara Greenwood, Regional Councillor
Selina Volpatti, Regional Councillor

Administration
Dean Iorfida, City Clerk & Director, Council Services, Administration
diorfida@niagarafalls.ca
Ken Todd, Chief Administrative Officer, Administration
ktodd@niagarafalls.ca
Ken Burden, Executive Director, Corporate Services, Administration
finance@niagarafalls.ca
Edward Dujlovic, Executive Director, Community Services, Administration
Serge Felicetti, Director, Business Development, Administration
sfelicetti@niagarafalls.ca
Alex Herlovitch, Director, Planning & Development, Administration
planning@niagarafalls.ca
Geoffrey Holman, Director, Municipal Works, Administration
Denyse Morrissey, Director, Parks, Recreation, & Culture, Administration
Lee Smith, Fire Chief, Administration

Niagara-on-the-Lake
P.O. Box 100
1593 Four Mile Creek Rd.
Virgil, ON L0S 1T0
905-468-3266 Fax: 905-468-2959
hdowd@notl.org
www.notl.org
Municipal Type: City
Area: 132.83 sq km
County or District: Niagara Reg. Mun.; *Population in 2006:* 14,587
Provincial Electoral District(s): Niagara Falls
Federal Electoral District(s): Niagara Falls
Next Election: Nov. 2010 (4 year terms)

Council
David Eke, Mayor
Gary Burroughs, Regional Councillor
Dennis Dick, Councillor
Terry Flynn, Councillor
Andrea Kaiser, Councillor
Jamie R. King, Councillor
Martin Mazza, Councillor
Gary Zalepa, Jr., Councillor
Maria Bau-Coote, Councillor
Jim Collard, Councillor

Administration
Holly Dowd, Town Clerk, Administration
hdowd@notl.org
Don Smith, Chief Administrative Officer, Administration
donsmith@notl.org
Scott Tipping, CMA, Director, Corporate Services, Administration
stipping@notl.org
S. Bedford, Director, Planning & Development, Administration
Clive Buist, Director, Parks & Recreation, Administration
cbuist@notl.org
E. Kuczera, Director, Public Works, Administration
ekuczera@notl.org
Ken Eden, Fire Chief, Administration
keden@notl.org
Larry Higgins, Supervisor, Water & Sewer, Administration
lhiggins@notl.org
J. Darren MacKenzie, Superintendent, Irrigation & Drainage, Administration
dmackenzie@notl.org

North Bay
City Hall
P.O. Box 360
200 McIntyre St. East
North Bay, ON P1B 8H8
705-474-0400 Fax: 705-495-4353 Toll Free Phone: 1-800-465-1882
info@cityofnorthbay.ca
www.city.north-bay.on.ca
Municipal Type: City
Incorporated: 1925; *Area:* 314.91 sq km
County or District: Nipissing District; *Population in 2006:* 53,966
Provincial Electoral District(s): Nipissing
Federal Electoral District(s): Nipissing-Timiskaming
Next Election: Nov. 2010 (4 year terms)

Council
Al McDonald, Mayor
Mayor@cityofnorthbay.ca
Peter Chirico, Councillor
Peter.Chirico@cityofnorthbay.ca
Mike Anthony, Councillor
Mike.Anthony@cityofnorthbay.ca
Mac Bain, Councillor
Mac.Bain@cityofnorthbay.ca
Sean Lawlor, Councillor
Sean.Lawlor@cityofnorthbay.ca
George Maroosis, Councillor
George.Maroosis@cityofnorthbay.ca
Judy Koziol, Councillor
Judy.Koziol@cityofnorthbay.ca
Chris Mayne, Councillor
Chris.Mayne@cityofnorthbay.ca
Dave Mendicino, Councillor
Dave.Mendicino@cityofnorthbay.ca
Daryl Vaillancourt, Councillor
Daryl.Vaillancourt@cityofnorthbay.ca
Tanya Vrebosch Merry, Councillor
Tanya.Vrebosch-Merry@cityofnorthbay.ca

Administration
Cathy Conrad, City Clerk, Administration
cathy.conrad@cityofnorthbay.ca
Dave Linkie, Chief Administration Officer, Administration
Brian Rogers, Chief Financial Officer, Administration
brian.rogers@cityofnorthbay.ca
Michael Burke, Managing Director, Corporate Services, Administration
Jerry Knox, Managing Director, Community Services, Administration
Alan Korell, Managing Director, Engineering, Environmental & Wo, Administration
David Euler, Director, Sewer & Water, Administration
Jamie Houston, Director, Parks, Recreation, & Leisure Services, Administration
Bob McGrath, Director, Human Resources, Administration
Peter Bullock, Manager, Environmental Services, Administration
Dorothea Carvell, Manager, Transit, Administration
Joe Germano, Manager, Road & Traffic, Administration
Ian Kilgour, Manager, Planning Services, Administration
Shawn Killins, Chief Building Official, Administration
Grant Love, Fire Chief, Administration

North Perth
330 Wallace Ave. North
Listowel, ON N4W 1L3
519-291-2950 Fax: 519-291-1804 Toll Free Phone: 1-888-714-1993
town@northperth.ca
www.northperth.ca
Municipal Type: City
Incorporated: 1998; *Area:* 493.18 sq km
County or District: Perth; *Population in 2006:* 12,254
Provincial Electoral District(s): Perth-Wellington
Federal Electoral District(s): Perth-Wellington
Next Election: Nov. 2010 (4 year terms)
Note: Amalgamation of Elma Township, Town of Listowel & Wallace Township.

Council
Julie Behrns, Mayor

Council
Vince Judge, Deputy Mayor & Councillor
Doug Kellum, Councillor, Ward(s): Listowel
Warren Howard, Councillor, Ward(s): Listowel
Matt Richardson, Councillor, Ward(s): Listowel
Kenneth Buchanan, Councillor, Ward(s): Elma
David Ludington, Councillor, Ward(s): Elma
Matt Duncan, Councillor, Ward(s): Elma
Meredith Schneider, Councillor, Ward(s): Wallace
Paul Horn, Councillor, Ward(s): Wallace

Administration
Patricia Berfelz, Clerk, Administration
519-292-2062
PBerfelz@northperth.ca
Frances Hale, Treasurer & Director, Finance, Administration
519-292-2045, Fax: 519-291-5611
FHale@northperth.ca
Steve Hardie, Director, Parks & Recreation, Administration
519-292-2055
SHardie@northperth.ca
Gary Pipe, Director, Public Works & Superintendent, Drainage, Administration
519-292-2066, Fax: 519-291-9643
GPipe@northperth.ca
Ed Podniewicz, Chief Building Official & Administrator, Zoning, Administration
519-292-2058
Ed@northperth.ca
Ed Smith, Fire Chief, Administration
519-292-2053
ESmith@northperth.ca

Oakville
P.O. Box 310
1225 Trafalgar Rd.
Oakville, ON L6J 5A6
905-845-6601 Fax: 905-815-2025 TTY: 905-338-4200
publicinquiry@oakville.ca; communications@oakville.ca
www.oakville.ca
Municipal Type: City
Incorporated: May 27, 1857; *Area:* 138.56 sq km
County or District: Halton Regional Municipality; *Population in 2006:* 165,613
Provincial Electoral District(s): Halton; Oakville
Federal Electoral District(s): Halton; Oakville
Next Election: Nov. 2010 (4 year terms)

Council
Rob Burton, Mayor, Fax: 905-815-2001
mayor@oakville.ca
Alan Johnston, Town & Regional Councillor, Ward(s): 1
Ralph Robinson, Town Councillor, Ward(s): 1
Cathy Duddeck, Town & Regional Councillor, Ward(s): 2
Pam Damoff, Town Councillor, Ward(s): 2
F. Keith Bird, Town & Regional Councillor, Ward(s): 3
Dave Gittings, Town Councillor, Ward(s): 3
Allan Elgar, Town & Regional Councillor, Ward(s): 4
Roger Lapworth, Town Councillor, Ward(s): 4
Jeff Knoll, Town & Regional Councillor, Ward(s): 5
Marc Grant, Town Councillor, Ward(s): 5
Tom Adams, Town & Regional Councillor, Ward(s): 6
Max Khan, Town Councillor, Ward(s): 6

Administration
Cathie Best, Town Clerk, Administration
clerks@oakville.ca; cbest@oakville.ca
Ray Green, Chief Administrative Officer, Administration
rgreen@oakville.ca
Patricia Elliott-Spencer, M.B.A., CMA, Treasurer & Director, Finance, Administration
pelliott-spencer@oakville.ca; finance@oakville.ca
David Bloomer, Commissioner, Infrastructure & Transportation Serv, Administration
dbloomer@oakville.ca
Jane Clohecy, Commissioner, Planning & Development Services, Administration
jclohecy@oakville.ca; planning@oakville.ca
Gord Lalonde, Commissioner, Corporate Services, Administration
glalonde@oakville.ca
Domenic Lunardo, Commissioner, Community Services, Administration
dlunardo@oakville.ca
Elizabeth Bourns, Director, Human Resources, Administration
ebourns@oakville.ca; humanresources@oakville.ca
Barry Cole, Director, Transit Services, Administration
bcole@oakville.ca; transit@oakville.ca
Daniel Cozzi, P.Eng., Director, Roads & Works Operations, Administration
dcozzi@oakville.ca

Darnell Lambert, C.E.T., Director, Engineering & Construction, Administration
dlambert@oakville.ca
Chris Mark, Director, Parks & Open Space, Administration
cmark@oakville.ca; parks@oakville.ca
Cindy Toth, Director, Environmental Policy, Administration
ctoth@oakville.ca; environment@oakville.ca
Sheldon Switzer, Director, Building Services & Chief Building Offic, Administration
sswitzer@oakville.ca; building@oakville.ca
John McNeil, Manager, Forestry & Cemetery Services, Administration
jmcneil@oakville.ca; forestry@oakville.ca
Richard Boyes, Fire Chief, Administration
rboyes@oakville.ca; fire@oakville.ca

Orangeville

87 Broadway St.
Orangeville, ON L9W 1K1
519-941-0440 Fax: 519-941-9033 Toll Free Phone: 1-866-941-0440; TTY: 519-943-0782
info@orangeville.ca
www.orangeville.ca
Municipal Type: City
Incorporated: Dec. 22, 1863; *Area:* 15.57 sq km
County or District: Dufferin; *Population in 2006:* 26,925
Provincial Electoral District(s): Dufferin-Caledon
Federal Electoral District(s): Dufferin-Caledon
Next Election: Nov. 2010 (4 year terms)
Note: Incorporated as a town on Dec. 15, 1873.

Council
Rob Adams, Mayor
radams@orangeville.ca
Warren Maycock, Deputy Mayor & Councillor
Sylvia Bradley, Councillor
Gail Campbell, Councillor
Mary Rose, Councillor
Jeremy Williams, Councillor
Scott Wilson, Councillor

Administration
Cheryl Johns, Clerk, Administration
cjohns@orangeville.ca
Rick Schwarzer, Chief Administrative Officer, Administration
rschwarzer@orangeville.ca
Karen Craggs, Deputy Treasurer, Administration
kcraggs@orangeville.ca
Vern Douglas, Director, Building & By-law Enforcement, Administration
vdouglas@orangeville.ca
Sonya Pritchard, Director, Parks & Recreation, Administration
spritchard@orangeville.ca
James Stiver, Director, Planning, Administration
jstiver@orangeville.ca
Jack Tupling, Director, Public Works, Administration
jtupling@orangeville.ca
Ed Gill, Managing Director, Operations & Transportation, Administration
egill@orangeville.ca
Doug Jones, Managing Director, Environmental & Development Ser, Administration
djones@orangeville.ca
Jennifer Gohn, Manager, Human Resources, Administration
jgohn@orangeville.ca
Andy Macintosh, Fire Chief, Administration
amacintosh@orangeville.ca

Orillia

Administration Office
#300, 50 Andrew St. South
Orillia, ON L3V 7T5
705-325-1311 Fax: 705-325-5178
corporate@city.orillia.on.ca
www.city.orillia.on.ca
Municipal Type: City
Incorporated: 1867; *Area:* 28.61 sq km
County or District: Simcoe; *Population in 2006:* 30,259
Provincial Electoral District(s): Simcoe North
Federal Electoral District(s): Simcoe North
Next Election: Nov. 2010 (4 year terms)
Note: Incorporated as a town in 1875 & as a city in 1969.

Council
Angelo Orsi, Mayor
mayor@city.orillia.on.ca
Patrick F. Kehoe, Councillor, Ward(s): 1
Donald W. Jenkins, Councillor, Ward(s): 1
Linda Murray, Councillor, Ward(s): 2
Pete Bowen, Councillor, Ward(s): 2
Michael Fogarty, Councillor, Ward(s): 3
Paul Spears, Councillor, Ward(s): 3
Tony Madden, Councillor, Ward(s): 4
Andrew Hill, Councillor, Ward(s): 4

Administration
Gayle Jackson, City Clerk, Administration
clerks@city.orillia.on.ca
Ian C.R. Brown, City Manager, Administration
clerks@city.orillia.on.ca
Bob Ripley, City Treasurer, Administration
treas@city.orillia.on.ca
Lori Bolton, Director, Human Resources, Administration
Peter Dance, Director, Public Works, Administration
publicworks@city.orillia.on.ca
Ray Merkley, Director, Parks & Recreation, Administration
parks@city.orillia.on.ca
Craig Metcalf, Director, Culture & Heritage, Administration
parks@city.orillia.on.ca
Ian Sugden, Director, Planning & Development, Administration
planning@city.orillia.on.ca
Ralph Dominell, Fire Chief, Administration
ord@city.orillia.on.ca
Kelly Smith, Chief Building Official, Administration
Jack Green, Manager, Transportation, Administration
Andrew Schell, Manager, Environmental Services, Administration
Percival Thomas, Manager, Water & Wastewater Systems, Administration

Oshawa

City Hall
50 Centre St. South
Oshawa, ON L1H 3Z7
905-436-3311 Fax: 905-436-5642 Toll Free Phone: 1-800-667-4292; TTY: 905-436 5627
service@oshawa.ca
www.oshawa.ca
Municipal Type: City
Incorporated: March 8, 1924; *Area:* 145.67 sq km
County or District: Durham Reg. Mun.; *Population in 2006:* 141,590
Provincial Electoral District(s): Whitby-Oshawa; Oshawa
Federal Electoral District(s): Whitby-Oshawa; Oshawa
Next Election: Nov. 2010 (4 year terms)

Council
John Henry, Mayor
John Aker, Regional Councillor
Bob Chapman, Regional Councillor
Nancy Diamond, Regional Councillor
Amy England, Regional Councillor
Tito-Dante Marimpietri, Regional Councillor
John Neal, Regional Councillor
Nester Pidwerbecki, Regional Councillor
Roger Bouma, City Councillor
Mike Nicholson, City Councillor
Bruce Wood, City Councillor

Administration
Sandra Kranc, City Clerk, Administration, Fax: 905-436-5697
Bob Duignan, City Manager, Administration
905-436-5622, Fax: 905-436-5623
oshawae@oshawa.ca
Chris Brown, Director, Finance Services, Administration, Fax: 905-436-5664
finance@oshawa.ca
Stan Bertoia, Commissioner, Community Services Department, Administration
sbertoia@oshawa.ca
Tom Hodgins, Commissioner, Development Services Department, Administration
planning@oshawa.ca
Rick Stockman, Commissioner, Corporate Services Department, Administration
rstockman@oshawa.ca
Ron Foster, Auditor General, Administration
rfoster@oshawa.ca
Tracy Adams, Director, Corporate Communications & Marketing, Administration
marketing@oshawa.ca
Jamie Bronsema, Director, Strategic & Business Services, Administration
jbronsema@oshawa.ca
Dan Carnegie, Director, Human Resource Services, Administration
humanresources@oshawa.ca
Gary Carroll, Director, Engineering Services, Administration
engineering@oshawa.ca
Mary Creighton, Director, Recreation & Culture Services, Administration
recreation@oshawa.ca
Craig Kelly, Director, Works & Transportation Services, Administration
ckelly@oshawa.ca
Mike Molinari, Director, Parks & Environmental Services, Administration
Paul Ralph, Director, Planning Services, Administration
planning@oshawa.ca
Mike Leonard, Chief Building Official, Administration
buildings@oshawa.ca
Steve Meringer, Fire Chief, Administration
fire@oshawa.ca

Ottawa

City Hall
110 Laurier Ave. West
Ottawa, ON K1P 1J1
613-580-2400 Fax: 613-560-1380 Toll Free Phone: 1-866-261-9799; or 311
info@ottawa.ca
www.ottawa.ca
Municipal Type: City
Incorporated: Jan. 1, 1855; *Area:* 2,778.13 sq km
Population in 2006: 812,129
Provincial Electoral District(s): Glengarry-Prescott-Russell; Nepean-Carleton; Ottawa Centre; Ottawa South; Ottawa-Vanier; Ottawa West-Nepean; Ottawa-Orléans; Carleton-Mississippi Mills
Federal Electoral District(s): Glengarry-Prescott-Russell; Nepean-Carleton; Ottawa Centre; Ottawa South; Ottawa-Vanier; Ottawa West-Nepean; Ottawa-Orléans; Carleton-Mississippi Mills
Next Election: Nov. 2010 (4 year terms)

Council
Jim Watson, Mayor
Bob Monette, Councillor, Ward(s): 1 - Orléans
613-580-2471
Bob.Monette@ottawa.ca
Rainer Bloess, Councillor, Ward(s): 2 - Innes
613-580-2472
Rainer.Bloess@ottawa.ca
Jan Harder, Councillor, Ward(s): 3 - Barrhaven
613-580-2473
Jan.Harder@ottawa.ca
Marianne Wilkinson, Councillor, Ward(s): 4 - Kanata North
613-580-2474
Marianne.Wilkinson@ottawa.ca
Eli El-Chantiry, Councillor, Ward(s): 5 - West Carleton-March
613-580-2475
Eli.El-Chantiry@ottawa.ca
Shad Qadri, Councillor, Ward(s): 6 - Stittsville-Kanata West
613-580-2476
Shad.Qadri@ottawa.ca
Mark Taylor, Councillor, Ward(s): 7 - Bay
Rick Chiarelli, Councillor, Ward(s): 8 - College
613-580-2478
Rick.Chiarelli@ottawa.ca
Keith Egli, Councillor, Ward(s): 9 - Knoxdale-Merivale
Diane Deans, Councillor, Ward(s): 10 - Gloucester-Southgate
613-580-2480
Diane.Deans@ottawa.ca
Tim Tierney, Councillor, Ward(s): 11 - Beacon Hill-Cyrville
Mathieu Fleury, Councillor, Ward(s): 12 - Rideau-Vanier
Peter Clark, Councillor, Ward(s): 13 - Rideau-Rockcliffe
Diane Holmes, Councillor, Ward(s): 14 - Somerset
613-580-2484
Diane.Holmes@ottawa.ca
Katherine Hobbs, Councillor, Ward(s): 15 - Kitchissippi
Maria McRae, Councillor, Ward(s): 16 - River
613-580-2486
Maria.Mcrae@ottawa.ca
David Chernushenko, Councillor, Ward(s): 17 - Capital
Peter Hume, Councillor, Ward(s): 18 - Alta Vista
613-580-2488
Peter.Hume@ottawa.ca
Stephen Blais, Councillor, Ward(s): 19 - Cumberland
Doug Thompson, Councillor, Ward(s): 20 - Osgoode
613-580-2490
Doug.Thompson@ottawa.ca
Scott Moffatt, Councillor, Ward(s): 21 - Rideau-Goulbourn
Steve Desroches, Councillor, Ward(s): 22 - Gloucester-South
613-580-2751
Steve.Desroches@ottawa.ca
Allan Hubley, Councillor, Ward(s): 23 - Kanata South

Administration
M. Rick O'Connor, City Clerk & Solicitor, Administration
Kent Kirkpatrick, City Manager, Administration
Marian Simulik, City Treasurer, Administration
Steve Kanellakos, Deputy City Manager, Administration
Nancy Schepers, Deputy City Manager, Administration
Chris Day, Chief, Corporate Communications, Administration
Catherine Frederick, Director, Human Resources, Administration
Donna L. Gray, Director, Organizational Development & Performance, Administration
Guy Michaud, Director, Information Technology & Chief Informati, Administration
Johanne Levesque, Director, Community Sustainability, Administration
Wayne Newell, Director, Infrastructure Services, Administration
Aaron Burry, General Manager, Community & Social Services, Administration
Dan Chenier, General Manager, Parks, Recreation & Cultural Serv, Administration
Susan Jones, General Manager, Emergency & Protective Services, Administration
John Manconi, General Manager, Public Works, Administration
Alain Mercier, General Manager, Transit Services, Administration
John Moser, General Manager, Planning & Growth Management, Administration
Dixon A. Weir, General Manager, Environmental Services, Administration
Isra Levy, Medical Officer of Health, Administration
Michel Chevalier, Manager, Wastewater & Drainage Operations, Administration
Felice Petti, Manager, Strategic & Environmental Services, Administration
Tammy Rose, Manager, Drinking Water Services, Administration

Owen Sound

City Hall
808 - 2nd Ave. East
Owen Sound, ON N4K 2H4
519-376-1440 Fax: 519-371-0511
cityadmin@e-owensound.com; communityservices@e-owensound.com
www.owensound.ca
Municipal Type: City
Incorporated: Jan. 1, 2001; *Area:* 24.22 sq km
County or District: Grey; *Population in 2006:* 21,753
Provincial Electoral District(s): Bruce-Grey-Owen Sound
Federal Electoral District(s): Bruce-Grey-Owen Sound
Next Election: Nov. 2010 (4 year terms)

Council
Deborah Haswell, Mayor

David Adair, Councillor
dadair@e-owensound.com
Ian C. Boddy, Councillor
Jan Chamberlain, Councillor
Peter Lemon, Councillor
plemon@e-owensound.com
Jim McManaman, Councillor
jmcmanaman@e-owensound.com
Colleen Purdon, Councillor
Bill Twaddle, Councillor
Arlene Wright, City & County Councillor
awright@e-owensound.com

Administration
Marion Koepke, C.M.O., City Clerk, Administration
mkoepke@owensound.ca
Jim Harrold, City Manager, Administration
Wayne Ritchie, CGA, Director, Financial Services, Administration
writchie@e-owensound.com
Pam Coulter, Director, Community Services, Administration
pcoulter@e-owensound.com
Glen Henry, C.M.O., Director, Corporate Services, Administration
ghenry@owensound.ca
John D. Johnston, C.E.T., Director, Operations, Administration
jdjohnson@e-owensound.com
Steve Furness, Manager, Economic Development & Tourism, Administration
business@e-owensound.com
Chris Webb, P.Eng., Manager, Engineering Services, Administration
Ed Nowak, Fire Chief, Administration
enowak@e-owensound.com

Pelham
P.O. Box 400
20 Pelham Town Sq.
Fonthill, ON L0S 1E0
905-892-2607 Fax: 905-892-5055
www.pelham.ca
Municipal Type: City
Incorporated: 1970; *Area:* 126.42 sq km
County or District: Niagara Reg. Mun.; *Population in 2006:* 16,155
Provincial Electoral District(s): Niagara West-Glanbrook
Federal Electoral District(s): Niagara West-Glanbrook
Next Election: Nov. 2010 (4 year terms)

Council
Dave Augustyn, Mayor
mayordave@pelham.ca
Larry Clark, Councillor, Ward(s): 1
Debbie Urbanowicz, Councillor, Ward(s): 1
Gary Accursi, Councillor, Ward(s): 2
Catherine King, Councillor, Ward(s): 2
John Durley, Councillor, Ward(s): 3
jjdurley@sympatico.ca
Peter Papp, Councillor, Ward(s): 3
peter.papp@sympatico.ca

Administration
Cheryl Miclette, Clerk, Administration
clerks@pelham.ca
Martin Yamich, Chief Administrative Officer, Administration
myamich@pelham.ca
Cari Pupo, Director, Financial Services, Administration
cpupo@pelham.ca
Craig Larmour, Director, Planning Services, Administration
clarmour@pelham.ca
Kelly Walsh, P.Eng., Director, Community & Infrastructure Services, Administration
kwalsh@pelham.ca
Keegan Gennings, Chief Building Official, Administration
kgennings@pelham.ca
Scott McLeod, Fire Chief, Administration
fire@pelham.ca
Alan Mannell, Manager, Engineering, Administration
amannell@pelham.ca

Pembroke
1 Pembroke St. East
Pembroke, ON K8A 3J5
613-735-6821 Fax: 613-735-3660
pembroke@pembroke.ca
www.pembroke.ca
Municipal Type: City
Incorporated: 1877; *Area:* 14.35 sq km
County or District: Renfrew; *Population in 2006:* 13,930
Provincial Electoral District(s): Renfrew-Nipissing-Pembroke
Federal Electoral District(s): Renfrew-Nipissing-Pembroke
Next Election: Nov. 2010 (4 year terms)
Note: Incorporated as a city in 1971.

Council
Ed Jacyno, Mayor
Dan Callaghan, Councillor
Ronald Gervais, Councillor
Bob Hackett, Councillor
Patricia Lafreniere, Councillor
Terry O'Neill, Councillor
Les Scott, Councillor
Gary Severin, Councillor
Colonel Towriss, Councillor

Administration
Terry Lapierre, Chief Administrative Officer, Administration
L. Eckford, Treasurer & Deputy Clerk, Administration
S. Ellis, Manager, Economic Development, Recreation, & Touri, Administration
T. Lapierre, Manager, Human Resources, Administration
Colleen Sauriol, Manager, Planning, Building, & Parking Authority, Administration
D. Sitland, Manager, Operations, Administration
D. Herback, Fire Chief, Administration
B. Hughes, Chief Building Official, Administration
R. Conroy, Supervisor, Parks & Facilities, Administration
B. Lewis, Supervisor, Roads & Fleet, Administration
C. Mick, Supervisor, Water & Sewer, Administration

Petawawa
1111 Victoria St.
Petawawa, ON K8H 2E6
613-687-5536 Fax: 613-687-5973
tspurrell@petawawa.ca (Executive Assistant)
www.petawawa.ca
Municipal Type: City
Incorporated: July 1, 1997; *Area:* 164.68 sq km
County or District: Renfrew; *Population in 2006:* 14,651
Provincial Electoral District(s): Renfrew-Nipissing-Pembroke
Federal Electoral District(s): Renfrew-Nipissing-Pembroke
Next Election: Nov. 2010 (4 year terms)
Note: Amalgamation of Petawawa Village & Petawawa Township.

Council
Robert Sweet, Mayor
mayor@petawawa.ca
Tom Mohns, Deputy Mayor & Councillor
James Carmody, Councillor
Frank Cirella, Councillor
Treena Lemay, Councillor
tlemay@petawawa.ca
Murray Rutz, Councillor
Theresa Sabourin, Councillor
tsabourin@petawawa.ca

Administration
Mitchell Stillman, Chief Administrative Officer & Clerk, Administration
mstillman@petawawa.ca
Daniel Scissons, Treasurer & Deputy Clerk, Administration
dscissons@petawawa.ca
Richard Bechamp, Chief Building Official, Administration
rbechamp@petawawa.ca
Steve Knott, Fire Chief, Administration
sknott@petawawa.ca
Tom Renaud, Supervisor, Public Works, Administration
works@petawawa.ca
Lynn Beatty, Coordinator, Economic Development, Administration
lbeatty@petawawa.ca
Karen Cronier, kcronier@petawawa.ca, Technician, Planning, Administration
kcronier@petawawa.ca

Peterborough
500 George St. North
Peterborough, ON K9H 3R9
705-742-7777 Fax: 705-742-4138 E-mail, Human Resources: hr@peterborough.ca
cityptbo@peterborough.ca; clerk@peterborough.ca
www.peterborough.ca
Municipal Type: City
Incorporated: 1850; *Area:* 58.40 sq km
County or District: Peterborough; *Population in 2006:* 74,898
Provincial Electoral District(s): Peterborough
Federal Electoral District(s): Peterborough
Next Election: Nov. 2010 (4 year terms)

Council
Daryl Bennett, Mayor
mayor@peterborough.ca
Dan McWilliams, Councillor, Ward(s): 1 - Otonabee
Lesley Parnell, Councillor, Ward(s): 1 - Otonabee
Henry Clarke, Councillor, Ward(s): 2 - Monaghan
hclarke@peterborough.ca
Jack Doris, Councillor, Ward(s): 2 - Monaghan
Bill J. Juby, Councillor, Ward(s): 3 - Town
Dean Pappas, Councillor, Ward(s): 3 - Town
dpappas@peterborough.ca
Keith G. Riel, Councillor, Ward(s): 4 - Ashburnham
Len Vass, Councillor, Ward(s): 4 - Ashburnham
lvass@peterborough.ca
Andrew Beamer, Councillor, Ward(s): 5 - Northcrest
Bob Hall, Councillor, Ward(s): 5 - Northcrest
bhall@peterborough.ca

Administration
Nancy Wright-Laking, City Clerk, Administration
nwright-laking@peterborough.ca
Linda Reed, Chief Administrative Officer, Administration
cao@peterborough.ca
Brian Horton, Senior Director, Corporate Services, Administration
bhorton@peterborough.ca
Ken Doherty, Director, Community Services, Administration
kdoherty@peterborough.ca
Malcolm Hunt, Director, Planning & Development Services, Administration
mhunt@peterborough.ca
Wayne Jackson, Director, Utility Services, Administration
wjackson@peterborough.ca
Trent Gervais, Fire Chief, Administration

Pickering
1 The Esplanade
Pickering, ON L1V 6K7
905-420-2222 Fax: 905-420-0515 Toll Free Phone: 1-866-683-2760; TTY: 905-420-1739
info@cityofpickering.com; customercare@cityofpickering.com
www.cityofpickering.com
Municipal Type: City
Incorporated: 1849; *Area:* 231.59 sq km
County or District: Durham Reg. Mun.; *Population in 2006:* 87,838
Provincial Electoral District(s): Ajax-Pickering; Pickering-Scarborough East
Federal Electoral District(s): Ajax-Pickering; Pickering-Scarborough East
Next Election: Nov. 2010 (4 year terms)
Note: Incorporated as a town in 1974 & as a city in 2000.

Council
Dave Ryan, Mayor
905-420-4600, Fax: 905-420-6064
mayor@cityofpickering.com
Jennifer O'Connell, Regional Councillor, Ward(s): 1
Kevin Ashe, City Councillor, Ward(s): 1
Bill McLean, Regional Councillor, Ward(s): 2
bmclean@cityofpickering.com
Doug Dickerson, City Councillor, Ward(s): 2
ddickerson@cityofpickering.com
Peter Rodrigues, Regional Councillor, Ward(s): 3
David Pickles, City Councillor, Ward(s): 3
dpickles@cityofpickering.com

Administration
Debi Wilcox, City Clerk, Administration
dwilcox@cityofpickering.com
Thomas J. Quinn, Chief Administrative Officer, Administration
905-420-4648, Fax: 905-420-6064
cao@cityofpickering.com
Gilles A. Paterson, Treasurer & Director, Corporate Services, Administration
905-420-4634, Fax: 905-420-5313
gpaterson@cityofpickering.com
Everett Buntsma, Director, Operations & Emergency Services, Administration
905-420-4624, Fax: 905-420-4650
ebuntsma@cityofpickering.com
Neil Carroll, Director, Planning & Development, Administration
905-420-4617, Fax: 905-420-7648
ncarroll@cityofpickering.com
Thomas E. Melymuk, Director, Office of Sustainability, Administration
905-420-4625, Fax: 905-420-4610
tmelymuk@cityofpickering.com
Richard W. Holborn, Division Head, Municipal Property & Engineering Di, Administration
90-542-0463, Fax: 905-420-4650
rholborn@cityofpickering.com
Jennifer Parent, Division Head, Human Resources, Administration
905-420-4627, Fax: 905-420-4638
hr@cityofpickering.com
Stephen Reynolds, Division Head, Culture & Recreation, Administration
905-420-4620, Fax: 905-420-2596
sreynolds@cityofpickering.com
William T. Douglas, Fire Chief, Administration
905-839-9968, Fax: 905-839-6327
fire@cityofpickering.com
Tim Moore, Chief Building Official, Administration
905-420-4617, Fax: 905-420-7648
tmoore@cityofpickering.com
Andrew C. Allison, City Solicitor, Administration
905-420-4626, Fax: 905-420-3534
aallison@cityofpickering.com

Port Colborne
66 Charlotte St.
Port Colborne, ON L3K 3C8
905-835-2900 Fax: 905-834-5746
www.portcolborne.ca
Municipal Type: City
Incorporated: 1870; *Area:* 121.97 sq km
County or District: Niagara Reg. Mun.; *Population in 2006:* 18,599
Provincial Electoral District(s): Welland
Federal Electoral District(s): Welland
Next Election: Nov. 2010 (4 year terms)
Note: Incorporated as a town in 1918 & as a city in 1966.

Council
Vance Badawey, Mayor, Fax: 905-835-2969
mayor@portcolborne.ca
David Barrick, Regional Councillor
David B. Elliott, Councillor, Ward(s): 1
Bill Steele, Councillor, Ward(s): 1
905-834-4483
billsteele@portcolborne.ca
Yvon A. Doucet, Councillor, Ward(s): 2
Angie Desmarais, Councillor, Ward(s): 2
Frank M. Danch, Councillor, Ward(s): 3
Bea Kenny, Councillor, Ward(s): 3
905-834-7685
beakenny@portcolborne.ca
Ron Bodner, Councillor, Ward(s): 4
Barbara Butters, Councillor, Ward(s): 4
905-834-4005
barbarabutters@portcolborne.ca

Administration

Janet Beckett, Clerk, Administration
janetbeckett@portcolborne.ca
Robert J. Heil, Chief Administrative Officer, Administration
cao@portcolborne.ca
Dan Aquilina, Director, Planning & Development, Administration
danaquilina@portcolborne.ca
Ron Hanson, Director, Engineering & Operations, Administration
hanson@portcolborne.cane.ca
Peter Sense, Director, Community & Corporate Services, Administration
petersenese@portcolborne.ca
Stephen Thompson, General Manager, Economic Development & Tourism, Administration
stephenthompson@portcolborne.ca
Thomas Cartwright, Fire Chief, Administration
firechief@portcolborne.ca
Ernie Cronier, Chief Building Official, Administration
erniecronier@portcolborne.ca
Tammy Morden, Coordinator, Human Resources, Administration
tammymorden@portcolborne.ca
Darlene Suddard, Coordinator, Water & Waste Water Compliance, Administration
darlenesuddard@portcolborne.ca
Martha Toscher, Coordinator, Health & Safety, Administration
marthatoscher@portcolborne.ca

Quinte West

P.O. Box 490
7 Creswell Dr.
Trenton, ON K8V 5R6
613-392-2841 Fax: 613-392-0714 Toll Free Phone: 1-866-485-2841
www.city.quintewest.on.ca
Municipal Type: City
Incorporated: Jan. 1, 1998; *Area:* 493.85 sq km
County or District: Hastings; *Population in 2006:* 42,697
Provincial Electoral District(s): Northumberland-Quinte West
Federal Electoral District(s): Northumberland-Quinte West
Next Election: Nov. 2010 (4 year terms)
Note: Amalgamation of the former municipalities of Trenton, Sidney, Murray & Frankford.

Council
John R. Williams, Mayor
866-987-2694, Fax: 613-392-5608
mayor@city.quintewest.on.ca
Sally Freeman, Councillor, Ward(s): 1 - Trenton
613-965-6769
Fred Kuypers, Councillor, Ward(s): 1 - Trenton
613-392-8588
Leslie Roseblade, Councillor, Ward(s): 1 - Trenton
Bob Wannamaker, Councillor, Ward(s): 1 - Trenton
613-392-8548
Doug Whitney, Councillor, Ward(s): 1 - Trenton
613-392-4779
Terry R.F. Cassidy, Councillor, Ward(s): 2 - Sidney
613-395-2031
Ron Hamilton, Councillor, Ward(s): 2 - Sidney
613-392-5369
Don Kuntze, Councillor, Ward(s): 2 - Sidney
613-962-6122
Paul Kyte, Councillor, Ward(s): 2 - Sidney
613-967-2134
Jim Alyea, Councillor, Ward(s): 3 - Murray
613-475-1519
Jim Harrison, Councillor, Ward(s): 3 - Murray
613-392-9437
Keith Reid, Councillor, Ward(s): 4 - Frankford
613-398-7991

Administration
Gary Dyke, CAO, City Clerk, & Manager, Corporate & Economic D, Administration
David Clazie, Treasurer & Director, Finance, Administration
Chris Angelo, Director, Public Works, Administration
613-392-7151
Charlie Murphy, Director, Planning & Development Services, Administration
613-392-7151
Tim Colasante, Manager, Engineering Services, Administration
Matt Tracey, Manager, Water & Wastewater, Administration
Cheryl Vandervoort, Manager, Human Resources, Administration
Ron Wardhaugh, Chief Building Official, Administration
John Whelan, Fire Chief, Administration
613-392-6567

Richmond Hill

225 East Beaver Creek Rd.
Richmond Hill, ON L4B 3P4
905-771-8800 Fax: 905-771-2502
info@richmondhill.ca
www.richmondhill.ca
Municipal Type: City
Incorporated: 1873; *Area:* 100.89 sq km
County or District: York Reg. Mun.; *Population in 2006:* 162,704
Provincial Electoral District(s): Richmond Hill; Oak Ridges-Markham
Federal Electoral District(s): Richmond Hill; Oak Ridges-Markham
Next Election: Nov. 2010 (4 year terms)

Council
Dave Barrow, Mayor, Fax: 905-771-2500
officemayor@richmondhill.ca
Brenda Hogg, Regional & Local Councillor
bhogg@richmondhill.ca
Vito Spatafora, Regional & Local Councillor
vspatafora@richmondhill.ca
Greg Beros, Councillor, Ward(s): 1
gberos@richmondhill.ca
Carmine Perrelli, Councillor, Ward(s): 2
Catro Liu, Councillor, Ward(s): 3
Lynn Foster, Councillor, Ward(s): 4
lfoster@richmondhill.ca
Nick Papa, Councillor, Ward(s): 5
npapa@richmondhill.ca
Godwin Chan, Councillor, Ward(s): 6
gchan@richmondhill.ca

Administration
D. McLarty, Town Clerk, Administration
clerks@richmondhill.ca
Joan Anderton, Chief Administrative Officer, Administration
905-771-2505, Fax: 905-771-2406
janderton@richmondhill.ca; cao@richmondhill.ca
David Dexter, Treasurer & Director, Financial Services, Administration
revenue@richmondhill.ca; budget@richmondhill.ca
A. Bassios, Commissioner, Planning, Administration
planning@richmondhill.ca
Italo Brutto, Commissioner, Engineering & Public Works, Administration
905-771-8830
epw@richmondhill.ca
D. Miller, Commissioner, Corporate & Financial Services, Administration
905-771-8830
epw@richmondhill.ca
J. DeVries, Director, Building Services, & Chief Building Offi, Administration
D. Joslin, Director, Recreation & Culture, Administration
K. Kwan, Director, Development, Administration

St. Catharines

City Hall
P.O. Box 3012
50 Church St.
St Catharines, ON L2R 7C2
905-688-5600 Fax: 905-682-3631
clerks@stcatharines.ca; hr@stcatharines.ca (Human Resources)
www.stcatharines.ca
Municipal Type: City
Incorporated: 1876; *Area:* 96.11 sq km
County or District: Niagara Reg. Mun.; *Population in 2006:* 131,989
Provincial Electoral District(s): St. Catharines; Welland
Federal Electoral District(s): St. Catharines; Welland
Next Election: Nov. 2010 (4 year terms)

Council
Brian McMullan, Mayor
905-688-5600
bmcmullan@stcatharines.ca
Jeff Burch, Councillor, Ward(s): 1. Merritton
905-988-3695
Jennifer Stevens, Councillor, Ward(s): 1. Merritton
905-641-5744
Matthew J. Harris, Councillor, Ward(s): 2. St. Andrew's
Joseph Kushner, Councillor, Ward(s): 2. St. Andrew's
905-685-1817
Peter Secord, Councillor, Ward(s): 3. St. Georges
905-937-0044
Greg Washuta, Councillor, Ward(s): 3. St. Georges
905-938-5123
Mark Elliott, Councillor, Ward(s): 4. St. Patricks
Mathew D. Siscoe, Councillor, Ward(s): 4. St. Patricks
Dawn Dodge, Councillor, Ward(s): 5. Grantham
905-934-9138
Bill Phillips, Councillor, Ward(s): 5. Grantham
905-937-7752
Len Stack, Councillor, Ward(s): 6. Port Dalhousie
Bruce Williamson, Councillor, Ward(s): 6. Port Dalhousie
905-934-2787

Administration
Kenneth R. Todd, City Clerk & Director, Corporate Services, Administration
ktodd@stcatharines.ca
Colin Briggs, Chief Administrative Officer, Administration
cbriggs@stcatharines.ca
Shelley Chemnitz, Director, Financial Management Services, Administration
fms@stcatharines.ca
Paul Chapman, Director, Planning Services, Administration
ps@stcatharines.ca
Richard Lane, Director, Recreation & Community Services, Administration
rcs@stcatharines.ca
Mark Mehlenbacher, Director, Fire & Emergency Management Services, Administration
Paul Mustard, Director, Transportation & Environmental Services, Administration
tes@stcatharines.ca
David Oakes, Director, Economic Development & Tourism Services, Administration
edts@stcatharines.ca
Annette Poulin, City Solicitor, Administration
Diane Garrington, Coordinator, Communications, Administration
dgarrington@stcatharines.ca

St. Thomas

City Hall
P.O. Box 520
545 Talbot St.
St Thomas, ON N5P 3V7
519-631-1680 Fax: 519-633-9019
info@city.st-thomas.on.ca
www.city.st-thomas.on.ca
Municipal Type: City
Incorporated: March 4, 1881; *Area:* 35.48 sq km
County or District: Elgin; *Population in 2006:* 36,110
Provincial Electoral District(s): Elgin-Middlesex-London
Federal Electoral District(s): Elgin-Middlesex-London
Next Election: Nov. 2010 (4 year terms)

Council
Heather Jackson-Chapman, Mayor
mayor@city.st-thomas.on.ca
Lori Baldwin-Sands, Alderman, Council
loribaldwinsands@live.com
Gord Campbell, Alderman, Council
jcampbell384@rogers.com
Mark Cosens, Alderman, Council
mark@markyourx.com
Tom Johnston, Alderman, Council
tomjohnston@execulink.com
Jeff Kohler, Alderman, Council
jkohler67@live.com
David Warden, Alderman, Council
warden_dave@hotmail.com
Sam Yusuf, Alderman, Council
sam@samyusuf.ca

Administration
Wendell Graves, City Clerk, Administration
wgraves@city.st-thomas.on.ca
Bill Day, City Treasurer, Administration
bday@city.st-thomas.on.ca
Graham Dart, Director, Human Resources, Administration
gdart@city.st-thomas.on.ca
John Dewancker, Director, Environmental Services, & City Engineer, Administration
jdewancker@city.st-thomas.on.ca
Patrick Keenan, Director, Planning, Administration
pkeenan@city.st-thomas.on.ca
Brian Clement, Manager, Engineering, Administration
bclement@city.st-thomas.on.ca
Edward Soldo, Manager, Operations & Compliance, Administration
esoldo@city.st-thomas.on.ca
Ross Tucker, Manager, Parks & Recreation, Administration
rtucker@city.st-thomas.on.ca
Bob Barber, Fire Chief, Administration
rbarber@city.st-thomas.on.ca
Jeff Jilek, Chief Building Official, Administration
jjilek@city.st-thomas.on.ca
Chuck Fiddy, Supervisor, Water & Wastewater, Administration
cfiddy@city.st-thomas.on.ca
Dave White, Supervisor, Roads & Transportation, Administration
dwhite@city.st-thomas.on.ca

Sarnia

City Hall
P.O. Box 3018
255 North Christina St.
Sarnia, ON N7T 7N2
519-332-0330 Fax: 519-332-3995 TTY: 519-332-2664
clerks@sarnia.ca; bylaws@sarnia.ca; legal@sarnia.ca
www.sarnia.ca
Municipal Type: City
Incorporated: May 7, 1914; *Area:* 164.63 sq km
County or District: Lambton; *Population in 2006:* 71,419
Provincial Electoral District(s): Sarnia-Lambton
Federal Electoral District(s): Sarnia-Lambton
Next Election: Nov. 2010 (4 year terms)

Council
Mike Bradley, Mayor
mayor@sarnia.ca
Dave Boushy, City / County Councillor
d.boushy@cogeco.ca
Jim Foubister, City / County Councillor
jimfoubister@sarnia.ca
Anne Marie Gillis, City / County Councillor
annemariegillis@sarnia.ca
Bev MacDougall, City / County Councillor
bevmacdougall@ebtech.net
Andy Bruziewicz, City Councillor
andybruziewicz@hotmail.com
Terry Burrell, City Councillor
terry@terryburrell.ca
Mike Kelch, City Councillor
mjkelch@mac.com
Jon McEachran, City Councillor
jonmceachran@hotmail.com

Administration
Brian Knott, Clerk & Solicitor, Administration
bknott@sarnia.ca
Lloyd Fennell, City Manager, Administration
lfennell@sarnia.ca
Brian McKay, Director, Finance, Administration
finance@.sarnia.ca
Kim Bresee, Director, Planning & Building, Administration
planning@sarnia.ca; buildept@sarnia.ca
Ian Smith, Director, Community Services, Administration
comserv@city.sarnia.on.ca
Jim Stevens, Director, Transit, Administration
transit@sarnia.ca

Peter Hungerford, Manager, Economic Development & Corporate Planning, Administration
pbh.edcp@sarnia.ca
Kathy Meade, Manager, Human Resources, Administration
hr@sarnia.ca
David Fielding, City Engineer, Administration
engineer@sarnia.ca
Doug Robertson, Superintendent, Public Works Department, Administration
Pat Cayen, Fire Chief, Fire Rescue Services, Administration
firerescue@sarnia.ca

Saugeen Shores

P.O. Box 820
600 Tomlinson Dr.
Port Elgin, ON N0H 2C0
519-832-2008 Fax: 519-832-2140
www.saugeenshores.ca
Municipal Type: City
Area: 170.58 sq km
County or District: Bruce; *Population in 2006:* 11,720
Provincial Electoral District(s): Huron-Bruce
Federal Electoral District(s): Huron-Bruce
Next Election: Nov. 2010 (4 year terms)

Council
Mike Smith, Mayor
mayor@town.saugeenshores.on.ca
Luke Charbonneau, Deputy Mayor & Councillor
lcharbonneau@bmts.com
Doug Gowanlock, Vice Deputy Mayor, Councillor
beaglerun@bmts.com
Marcel Legault, Councillor, Ward(s): Port Elgin
mlegaul@bmts.comcom
Fred Schildroth, Councillor, Ward(s): Port Elgin
schildrf@bmts.com
Gary R. Brown, Councillor, Ward(s): Saugeen
cargar@bmts.com
Taun Frosst, Councillor, Ward(s): Saugeen
sunset.taun@gmail.com
Diane Huber, Councillor, Ward(s): Southampton
dianehuber@bmts.com
Thead Seaman, Councillor, Ward(s): Southampton
t.j.seaman@bmts.com

Administration
Linda White, Clerk, Administration
whitel@town.saugeenshores.on.ca
Lawrence Allison, Chief Administrative Officer, Administration
allisonl@town.saugeenshores.on.ca
Lori Sweiger, Treasurer, Administration
sweigerl@town.saugeenshores.on.ca
Dave Burnside, Director, Engineering Services, Administration
burnsided@town.saugeenshores.on.ca
Bill Jones, Director, Public Works, Administration
jonesb@town.saugeenshores.on.ca
Mike Myatt, Director, Community Services, Administration
myattm@town.saugeenshores.on.ca
Lynn Worsley, Officer, Human Resources, Administration
worsleyl@town.saugeenshores.on.ca
Jim Bell, Chief Building Official, Administration
bellj@town.saugeenshores.on.ca
Phil Eagleson, Fire Chief, Administration
shores.fire@bmts.com
Cassie Coulson, Coordinator, Water & Sewer, Administration
coulsonc@town.saugeenshores.on.ca

Sault Ste. Marie

Civic Centre
P.O. Box 580
99 Foster Dr.
Sault Ste Marie, ON P6A 5N1
705-759-2500 Fax: 705-759-2310
webmaster@cityssm.on.
www.cityssm.on.ca
Municipal Type: City
Incorporated: 1912; *Area:* 221.71 sq km
County or District: Algoma District; *Population in 2006:* 74,948
Provincial Electoral District(s): Sault Ste. Marie
Federal Electoral District(s): Sault Ste. Marie
Next Election: Nov. 2010 (4 year terms)

Council
Debbie Amaroso, Mayor
705-759-7550
damaroso@shaw.ca
Steve Butland, Councillor, Ward(s): 1
s.butland@cityssm.on.ca
Paul Christian, Councillor, Ward(s): 1
paul.christian1@shaw.ca
Terry Sheehan, Councillor, Ward(s): 2
t.sheehan@cityssm.on.ca
Susan Myers, Councillor, Ward(s): 2
s.myers@cityssm.on.ca
Pat Mick, Councillor, Ward(s): 3
p.mick@cityssm.on.ca
Brian Watkins, Councillor, Ward(s): 3
brian@aoe.ca
Lou Turco, Councillor, Ward(s): 4
l.turco@cityssm.on.ca
Rick Niro, Councillor, Ward(s): 4
rick.niro@gmail.com
Frank Fata, Councillor, Ward(s): 5
f.fata@cityssm.on.ca
Marchy Bruni, Councillor, Ward(s): 5
Marchy_Bruni@hotmail.com
Frank Manzo, Councillor, Ward(s): 6
Joe Krmpotich, Councillor, Ward(s): 6
joekrmpotich@hotmail.com

Administration
Donna P. Irving, City Clerk, Administration
705-759-5388
cityclerk@cityssm.on.ca
Joseph M. (Joe) Fratesi, B.A., LL.B., Chief Administrative Officer, Administration
705-759-5347
j.fratesi@cityssm.on.ca
William Freiburger, Treasurer & Commissioner, Finance, Administration
705-759-5349
b.freiburger@cityssm.on.ca
Nicholas J. Apostle, Commissioner, Community Services, Administration
n.apostle@cityssm.on.ca
Jerry Dolcetti, Commissioner, Engineering & Planning, Administration
j.dolcetti@cityssm.on.ca
John R. Luszka, Commissioner, Human Resources, Administration
j.luszka@cityssm.on.ca
Patrick McAuley, P.Eng., Commissioner, Public Works & Transportation, Administration
p.mcauley@cityssm.on.ca
Kim Streich-Poser, Commissioner, Social Services, Administration
k.streich-poser@cityssm.on.ca
Lorie Bottos, City Solicitor, Administration
l.bottos@cityssm.on.ca
Marcel Provenzano, Fire Chief, Administration
m.provenzano@cityssm.on.ca

Stratford

City Hall
P.O. Box 818
1 Wellington St.
Stratford, ON N5A 6W1
519-271-0250 Fax: 519-273-5041 TTY: 519-271-5241
general@city.stratford.on.ca
www.city.stratford.on.ca
Municipal Type: City
Incorporated: 1854; *Area:* 25.28 sq km
County or District: Perth; *Population in 2006:* 30,461
Provincial Electoral District(s): Perth-Wellington
Federal Electoral District(s): Perth-Wellington
Next Election: Nov. 2010 (4 year terms)
Note: Incorporated as a city in 1886.

Council
Daniel Mathieson, Mayor
519-271-2783
dmathieson@city.stratford.on.ca
Brad Beatty, Councillor
George Brown, Councillor
gbrown@city.stratford.on.ca
Tom Clifford, Councillor
tclifford@city.stratford.on.ca
Keith Culliton, Councillor
kculliton@city.stratford.on.ca
Bonnie Henderson, Councillor
bhenderson@city.stratford.on.ca
Frank Mark, Councillor
fmark@city.stratford.on.ca
Kerry McManus, Councillor
Paul Nickel, Councillor
pnickel@city.stratford.on.ca
Martin Ritsma, Councillor
Karen Smythe, Councillor
ksmythe@city.stratford.on.ca

Administration
Joan Thomson, Clerk, Administration
clerks@city.stratford.on.ca
Ronald R. Shaw, Chief Administrative Officer, Administration
cao@city.stratford.on.ca
Larry Appel, Director, Economic Development, Administration
George Bowa, Director, Engineering & Public Works, Administration
Philip Buxton, Director, Corporate Services, Administration
Barbara Dembek, Director, Building & Planning, Administration
David St. Louis, Director, Community Services, Administration
Bill Tigert, Director, Social Services, Administration
Rick Young, Fire Chief, Administration
Jeff Bannon, City Planner, Administration
Randy Mattice, Economic Development Officer, Administration

Tecumseh

917 Lesperance Rd.
Tecumseh, ON N8N 1W9
519-735-2184 Fax: 519-735-6712
www.tecumseh.ca
Municipal Type: City
Incorporated: 1921; *Area:* 94.71 sq km
County or District: Essex; *Population in 2006:* 24,224
Provincial Electoral District(s): Windsor-Tecumseh
Federal Electoral District(s): Windsor-Tecumseh
Next Election: Nov. 2010 (4 year terms)
Note: Restructuring occurred in 1999.

Council
Gary McNamara, Mayor
519-735-6654
Cheryl M. Hardcastle, Deputy Mayor & Councillor
519-817-4864
Marcel (Pat) Blais, Councillor, Ward(s): 1
519-735-2686
Rita Ossington, Councillor, Ward(s): 1
519-735-8251
Guy Dorion, Councillor, Ward(s): 2
519-735-8580
Joe Bachetti, Councillor, Ward(s): 3
519-979-3339
Tania C. Jobin, Councillor, Ward(s): 4
519-735-9286

Administration
Laura Moy, Clerk & Director, Staff Services, Administration
Luc Gagnon, Treasurer & Director, Financial Services, Administration
George De Groot, Director, Public Works & Environmental Services, Administration
Shaun Fuerth, Director, Information Technology, Administration
Brian Hillman, Director, Planning & Building Services, Administration
Ken McMullen, Director, Fire Services, Administration
Denis Berthiume, Manager, Area Water Services, Administration
Casey Colthurst, Manager, Area Parks & Horticulture, Administration
Rob Filipov, Manager, Engineering Services, Administration
Kerri Rice, Manager, Area Recreation, Administration

Temiskaming Shores

Temiskaming Shores Administration Office
P.O. Box 2050
325 Farr Ave.
Haileybury, ON P0J 1K0
705-672-3363 Fax: 705-672-3200
coslund@temiskamingshores.ca
www.temiskamingshores.ca
Municipal Type: City
Incorporated: Jan. 1, 2004; *Area:* 177 sq km
County or District: Timiskaming District; *Population in 2006:* 10,732
Provincial Electoral District(s): Timiskaming-Cochrane
Federal Electoral District(s): Nipissing-Timiskaming
Next Election: Nov. 2010 (4 year terms)
Note: Amalgamation of the Town of Haileybury, the Town of New Liskeard & the Township of Dymond.

Council
Carman Kidd, Mayor
Bob Hobbs, Councillor
bhobbs@temiskamingshores.ca
Doug Jelly, Councillor
Mike McArthur, Councillor
mmcarthur@temiskamingshores.ca
Jamie Morrow, Councillor
Brian Thornton, Councillor
Danny Whalen, Councillor

Administration
Christopher W. Oslund, Clerk, Administration
coslund@temiskamingshores.ca
Brian J. Carré, Chief Administrative Officer, Administration
bcarre@temiskamingshores.ca
Chris Loughran, Director, Finance, Administration
cloughran@temiskamingshores.ca
Hani S. Asfur, Ph.D., P.Eng., Director, Public Works & City Engineer, Administration
hasfur@temiskamingshores.ca
Tammie Caldwell, Director, Leisure Services, Administration
tcaldwell@temiskamingshores.ca
Rick Barron, Manager, Parks & Facilities, Administration
rbarron@temiskamingshores.ca
John G. Brown, Manager, Planning & Development, Administration
jbrown@temiskamingshores.ca
Dan Harvey, Manager, Public Works Operations, Administration
dharvey@temiskamingshores.ca
David Treen, Manager, Environmental & Engineering Services, Administration
dtreen@temiskamingshores.ca
Tim Uttley, Fire Chief, Administration
tuttley@temiskamingshores.ca

Thorold

Thorold City Hall
P.O. Box 1044
3540 Schmon Pkwy.
Thorold, ON L2V 4A7
905-227-6613 Fax: 905-227-5590 E-mail, Deputy City Clerk: depclerk@thorold.com
secr@thorold.com (Administrative Assistant)
www.thorold.com
Municipal Type: City
Incorporated: 1798; *Area:* 83 sq km
County or District: Niagara Reg. Mun.; *Population in 2006:* 18,224
Provincial Electoral District(s): Welland
Federal Electoral District(s): Welland
Next Election: Nov. 2010 (4 year terms)
Note: Incorporated as a village in 1850, as a town in 1875, as a new town (amalgamating the Township of Thorold & the Town of Thorold) in 1970, & as a city in 1975.

Council
Ted Luciani, Mayor
mayor@thorold.com
Henry D'Angela, Regional Councillor
Arlene Arch, Councillor
Becky Day, Councillor
Jennifer Ferry, Councillor
Mike Murphy, Councillor

Norbert Preiner, Councillor
Tim Whalen, Councillor
twhalen1@cogeco.ca
Shawn Wilson, Councillor
shawn.wilson@thorold.com

Administration
Susan M. Daniels, AMCT, City Clerk, Administration
clerk@thorold.com
John Nicol, Chief Administrative Officer, Administration
adm@thorold.com
Maria J. Mauro, Director, Finance, Administration
finance@thorold.com
Adele Arbour, Director, Planning & Building Services, Administration
aarbour@thorold.com
Phillip Lambert, Director, Operations, Administration
905-227-3535, Fax: 905-227-3666
pubworks@thorold.com
Jeff Menard, A.Sc.T., B.Tech, Chief Building Official, Administration
jmenard@thorold.com
Dave Akrigg, Supervisor, Parks Operations, Administration
905-227-6544, Fax: 905-227-1149

Thunder Bay
City Hall
P.O. Box 800
500 Donald St. East
Thunder Bay, ON P7C 5K4
807-625-2230 Fax: 807-623-5468 TTY: 807-625-2230
cityinfo@thunderbay.ca
www.thunderbay.ca
Municipal Type: City
Incorporated: Jan 1, 1970; *Area:* 328.48 sq km
County or District: Thunder Bay District; *Population in 2006:* 109,140
Provincial Electoral District(s): Thunder Bay-Superior North; Thunder Bay-Atikokan
Federal Electoral District(s): Thunder Bay-Rainy River; Thunder Bay-Superior North
Next Election: Nov. 2010 (4 year terms)

Council
Keith Hobbs, Mayor
Iain Angus, Councillor at Large
Ken Boshcoff, Councillor at Large
Larry Hebert, Councillor at Large
Rebecca Johnson, Councillor at Large
Aldo. V. Ruberto, Councillor at Large
Andrew Foulds, Ward Councillor, Ward(s): Current River
Trevor Giertuga, Ward Councillor, Ward(s): McIntyre
Paul Pugh, Ward Councillor, Ward(s): McKellar
Linda Rydholm, Ward Councillor, Ward(s): Neebing
Mark Bentz, Ward Councillor, Ward(s): Northwood
Brian McKinnon, Ward Councillor, Ward(s): Red River
Joe Virdiramo, Ward Councillor, Ward(s): Westfort

Administration
John S. Hannam, City Clerk, Administration
807-623-2238, Fax: 807-623-5468
jhannam@thunderbay.ca
Tim Commisso, City Manager, Administration
807-625-2224, Fax: 807-623-1164
tcommisso@thunderbay.ca
Carol Busch, C.G.A., Treasurer & General Manager, Finance, Administration
807-625-2242
cbusch@thunderbay.ca
Greg Alexander, General Manager, Community Services, Administration
807-625-2315, Fax: 807-623-3292
galexander@thunderbay.ca
Rosalie Evans, General Manager, Corporate Services & City Solicit, Administration
807-625-2405, Fax: 807-623-2256
revans@thunderbay.ca
Alan Fydirchuk, General Manager, Facililties & Fleet, Administration
807-684-2774, Fax: 807-345-1909
afydirchuk@thunderbay.ca
Darrell Matson, General Manager, Transportation & Works, Administration
dmatson@thunderbay.ca
Mark Smith, General Manager, Development Services, Administration
807-625-2544, Fax: 807-625-2206
msmith@thunderbay.ca
Norm Gale, Chief, Emergency Medical Services, Administration
807-625-3259, Fax: 807-625-2698
ngale@thunderbay.ca
John Hay, Fire Chief, Administration
jhay@thunderbay.ca
Brad Loroff, Manager, Transit, Administration
807-684-2187
bloroff@thunderbay.ca
Alan Hjorth, Manager, Human Resources, Administration
807-625-2585, Fax: 807-625-3585
ahjorth@thunderbay.ca
Karen Lewis, Manager, Corporate Communications & Strategic Init, Administration
807-625-3859, Fax: 807-625-0181
klewis@thunderbay.ca
Kerri Marshall, Manager, Environment, Administration
807-625-2836, Fax: 807-625-3588
kmarshall@thunderbay.ca
Pat Mauro, Manager, Engineering, Administration
807-625-3022, Fax: 807-625-3588
pmauro@thunderbay.ca

Tillsonburg
200 Broadway St., 2nd Fl.
Tillsonburg, ON N4G 5A7
519-842-6428 Fax: 519-842-9431
dmorris@town.tillsonburg.on.ca
www.tillsonburg.ca
Municipal Type: City
Incorporated: 1872; *Area:* 22.34 sq km
County or District: Oxford; *Population in 2006:* 14,822
Provincial Electoral District(s): Oxford
Federal Electoral District(s): Oxford
Next Election: Nov. 2010 (4 year terms)

Council
John Lessif, Mayor
Mark Renaud, Deputy Mayor & Councillor
Dave Beres, Councillor
Mel Getty, Councillor
Marty Klein, Councillor
Chris (Chrissy) Rosehart, Councillor
Brian Stephenson, Councillor

Administration
David C. Morris, CAO
Steve Lund, P.Eng., Director, Operations
slund@town.tillsonburg.on.ca
Cynthia Hildebrand, Director, Community Services
childebrand@town.tillsonburg.on.ca
Bryan Drinkwater, Manager, Operations Utility
bdrinkwater@town.tillsonburg.on.ca
Peter Fung, Manager, Engineering
pfung@town.tillsonburg.on.ca
Kelly Batt, Manager, Parks & Facilities
kbatt@town.tillsonburg.on.ca
Bob Parsons, Fire Chief
519-842-2905
bparsons@town.tillsonburg.on.ca

Timmins
220 Algonquin Blvd. East
Timmins, ON P4N 1B3
705-264-1331 Fax: 705-360-2674
www.timmins.ca
Municipal Type: City
Incorporated: 1973; *Area:* 2,961.58 sq km
County or District: Cochrane District; *Population in 2006:* 42,997
Provincial Electoral District(s): Timmins-James Bay
Federal Electoral District(s): Timmins-James Bay
Next Election: Nov. 2010 (4 year terms)

Council
Thomas B. Laughren, Mayor
mayor@timmins.ca
Gary Scripnick, Councillor, Ward(s): 1
John P. Curley, Councillor, Ward(s): 2
Noella C. Rinaldo, Councillor, Ward(s): 3
Pat Bamford, Councillor, Ward(s): 4
Steven L. Black, Councillor, Ward(s): 5
Michael J.J. Doody, Councillor, Ward(s): 5
Todd Lever, Councillor, Ward(s): 5
Andrew Marks, Councillor, Ward(s): 5

Administration
R. Jack Watson, Clerk, Administration
Joe Torlone, Chief Administrative Officer, Administration
Bernie Christian, City Treasurer, Administration
Luc Duval, Director, Public Works & Engineering, Administration
Rock Foy, Director, Human Resources, Administration
Mark B Jensen, BA, MPL, MCIP, RPP, Director, Community & Development Services, Administration
David Laneville, Director, Information Technology, Administration
Mike Pintar, Fire Chief, Administration

Toronto
City Hall
100 Queen St. West
Toronto, ON M5H 2N2
Fax: 416-338-0685 In Toronto: 311; 416-392-2489; TTY: 416-338-0889
accesstoronto@toronto.ca
www.toronto.ca
Municipal Type: City
Incorporated: March 6, 1834; *Area:* 630.18 sq km
Population in 2006: 2,503,281
Provincial Electoral District(s): Beaches-East York; To.-Danforth; Davenport; Don V. East; Don V. West; Eglinton-Lawrence; Etob. Centre; Etob.-Lakeshore; Etob. North; Parkdale-High Park; St. Paul's; Scarb.-Agincourt; Scarb. Centre; Scarb. Southwest; Scarb.-Guildwood; Scarb.-Rouge River; To. Centre; Trinity-Spadina; Willowdale; York Centre; York South-Weston; York West
Federal Electoral District(s): Beaches-East York; Davenport; Don V. East; Don V. West; Eglinton-Lawrence; Etob. Centre; Etob.-Lakeshore; Etob. North; Parkdale-High Park; St. Paul's; Scarb.-Agincourt; Scarb. Centre; Scarb. Southwest; Scarb.-Guildwood; Scarb.-Rouge River; To. Centre; To.-Danforth; Trinity-Spadina; Willowdale; York Centre; York South-Weston, York West
Next Election: Nov. 2010 (4 year terms)
Note: Incorporated as a city on Jan. 1, 1998, & comprising the 6 former municipalities of: Etobicoke; North York; York; East York; Scarborough; & Old Toronto

Council
Rob Ford, Mayor
Vincent Crisanti, Councillor, Ward(s): 1 - Etobicoke North
Doug Ford, Councillor, Ward(s): 2 - Etobicoke North
Doug Holyday, Councillor, Ward(s): 3 - Etobicoke Centre
councillor_holyday@toronto.ca
Gloria Lindsay Luby, Councillor, Ward(s): 4 - Etobicoke Centre
councillor_lindsay_luby@toronto.ca
Peter Milczyn, Councillor, Ward(s): 5 - Etobicoke-Lakeshore
councillor_milczyn@toronto.ca
Mark Grimes, Councillor, Ward(s): 6 - Etobicoke-Lakeshore
councillor_grimes@toronto.ca
Giorgio Mammoliti, Councillor, Ward(s): 7 - York West
councillor_mammoliti@toronto.ca
Anthony Perruzza, Councillor, Ward(s): 8 - York West
councillor_perruzza@toronto.ca
Maria Augimeri, Councillor, Ward(s): 9 - York Centre
councillor_augimeri@toronto.ca
James Pasternak, Councillor, Ward(s): 10 - York Centre
Frances Nunziata, Councillor, Ward(s): 11 - York South-Weston
councillor_nunziata@toronto.ca
Frank Di Giorgio, Councillor, Ward(s): 12 - York South-Weston
councillor_digiorgio@toronto.ca
Sarah Doucette, Councillor, Ward(s): 13 - Parkdale-High Park
Gord Perks, Councillor, Ward(s): 14 - Parkdale-High Park
councillor_perks@toronto.ca
Josh Colle, Councillor, Ward(s): 15 - Eglinton-Lawrence
Karen Stintz, Councillor, Ward(s): 16 - Eglinton Lawrence
councillor_stintz@toronto.ca
Cesar Palacio, Councillor, Ward(s): 17 - Davenport
councillor_palacio@toronto.ca
Ana Bailao, Councillor, Ward(s): 18 - Davenport
Mike Layton, Councillor, Ward(s): 19 - Trinity-Spadina
Adam Vaughan, Councillor, Ward(s): 20 - Trinity-Spadina
councillor_vaughan@toronto.ca
Joe Mihevc, Councillor, Ward(s): 21 - St. Paul's
councillor_mihevc@toronto.ca
Josh Matlow, Councillor, Ward(s): 22 - St. Paul's
John Filion, Councillor, Ward(s): 23 - Willowdale
councillor_filion@toronto.ca
David Shiner, Councillor, Ward(s): 24 - Willowdale
councillor_shiner@toronto.ca
Jaye Robinson, Councillor, Ward(s): 25 - Don Valley West
John Parker, Councillor, Ward(s): 26 - Don Valley West
councillor_parker@toronto.ca
Kristyn Wong-Tam, Councillor, Ward(s): 27 - Toronto Centre-Rosedale
Pam McConnell, Councillor, Ward(s): 28 - Toronto Centre-Rosedale
councillor_mcconnell@toronto.ca
Mary Fragedakis, Councillor, Ward(s): 29 - Toronto-Danforth
Paula Fletcher, Councillor, Ward(s): 30 - Toronto-Danforth
councillor_fletcher@toronto.ca
Janet Davis, Councillor, Ward(s): 31 - Beaches-East York
councillor_davis@toronto.ca
Mary-Margaret McMahon, Councillor, Ward(s): 32 - Beaches-East York
Shelley Carroll, Councillor, Ward(s): 33 - Don Valley East
councillor_carroll@toronto.ca
Denzil Minnan-Wong, Councillor, Ward(s): 34 - Don Valley East
councillor_minnan-wong@toronto.ca
Michelle Berardinetti, Councillor, Ward(s): 35 - Scarborough Southwest
Gary Crawford, Councillor, Ward(s): 36 - Scarborough Southwest
Michael Thompson, Councillor, Ward(s): 37 - Scarborough Centre
councillor_thompson@toronto.ca
Glenn De Baeremaeker, Councillor, Ward(s): 38 - Scarborough Centre
councillor_debaeremaeker@toronto.ca
Mike Del Grande, Councillor, Ward(s): 39 - Scarborough-Agincourt
councillor_delgrande@toronto.ca
Norm Kelly, Councillor, Ward(s): 40 - Scarborough-Agincourt
councillor_kelly@toronto.ca
Chin Lee, Councillor, Ward(s): 41 - Scarborough-Rouge River
councillor_lee@toronto.ca
Raymond Cho, Councillor, Ward(s): 42 - Scarborough-Rouge River
councillor_cho@toronto.ca
Paul Ainslie, Councillor, Ward(s): 43 - Scarborough East
councillor_ainslie@toronto.ca
Ron Moeser, Councillor, Ward(s): 44 - Scarborough East
councillor_moeser@toronto.ca

Administration
Ulli S. Watkiss, City Clerk, Administration
416-392-8010, Fax: 416-392-2980
Joseph Pennachetti, City Manager, Administration
416-392-3551, Fax: 416-392-1827
Cam Weldon, Chief Financial Officer & Deputy City Manager, Administration
416-392-8773, Fax: 416-397-5236
Richard Butts, Deputy City Manager, Administration
416-338-7200, Fax: 416-392-4540
Sue Corke, Deputy City Manager, Administration
416-338-7205, Fax: 416-395-0388
Bruce L. Anderson, Executive Director, Human Resources, Administration
416-397-4112, Fax: 416-392-1524
Ann Borooah, Executive Director, Toronto Building, & Chief Buil, Administration
416-397-4446, Fax: 416-397-4383
Jim Hart, Executive Director, Municipal Licensing & Standard, Administration
416-392-8445, Fax: 416-397-5463
Gary Wright, Executive Director, City Planning, & Chief Planner, Administration
416-392-8772, Fax: 416-392-8115
Phil Brown, General Manager, Shelter, Support, & Housing Admin, Administration
416-392-7885, Fax: 416-392-0548

Lou Di Gironimo, General Manager, Toronto Water, Administration
416-392-8200, Fax: 416-302-4540
Bruce K. Farr, General Manager, Emergency Medical Services, & EMS, Administration
416-397-9240, Fax: 416-392-2115
Heather MacVicar, General Manager, Employment & Social Services, Administration
416-392-8952, Fax: 416-392-4214
Brenda Patterson, General Manager, Parks, Forestry, & Recreation, Administration
416-392-8182, Fax: 416-392-8565
parks@toronto.ca
Geoff Rathbone, General Manager, Solid Waste Management Services, Administration
416-392-4715, Fax: 416-392-4754
William (Bill) Stewart, General Manager, Fire Services & Fire Chief, Administration
416-338-9051, Fax: 416-338-9060
Gary Welsh, General Manager, Transportation Services, Administration
416-392-8431, Fax: 416-392-4455
Anna Kinastowski, City Solicitor, Administration
416-392-0080, Fax: 416-397-5624
David McKeown, Medical Officer of Health, Administration
416-338-7820, Fax: 416-392-0713

Vaughan

2141 Major Mackenzie Dr.
Vaughan, ON L6A 1T1
905-832-2281 Fax: 905-832-8535 Phone (Automated): 905-832-8585
clerks@vaughan.ca; resume@vaughan.ca (Human Resources)
www.vaughan.ca
Municipal Type: City
Incorporated: Jan. 1, 1971; *Area:* 273.58 sq km
County or District: York Regional Municipality; *Population in 2006:* 238,866
Provincial Electoral District(s): Vaughan; Thornhill
Federal Electoral District(s): Vaughan; Thornhill
Next Election: Nov. 2010 (4 year terms)

Council
Maurizio Bevilacqua, Mayor
mayor@vaughan.ca
Michael Di Biase, Regional Councillor
Gino Rosati, Regional Councillor
gino.rosati@vaughan.ca
Deb Schulte, Regional Councillor
Marilyn Iafrate, Councillor, Ward(s): 1
Tony Carella, Councillor, Ward(s): 2
tony.carella@vaughan.ca
Rosanna Defrancesca, Councillor, Ward(s): 3
Sandra Yeung Racco, Councillor, Ward(s): 4
sandra.racco@vaughan.ca
Alan Shefman, Councillor, Ward(s): 5
alan.shefman@vaughan.ca

Administration
Jeffrey A. Abrams, City Clerk, Administration
jeffrey.abrams@vaughan.ca
Michael DeAngelis, City Manager, Administration
michael.deangelis@vaughan.ca
Clayton D. Harris, Deputy City Manager & Commissioner, Finance & Corp, Administration
clayton.harris@vaughan.ca
Janet Atwood-Petkovski, Commissioner, Legal & Administrative Services, Administration
janice.atwood-petkovski@vaughan.ca
Marlon Kallideen, Commissioner, Community Services, Administration
marlon.kallideen@vaughan.ca
Bill Robinson, Commissioner, Engineering & Public Works, Administration
bill.robinson@city.vaughan.on.ca
John Zipay, Commissioner, Planning, Administration
commissionerofplanning@vaughan.ca
Marjie Fraser, Director, Parks & Forestry Operations, Administration
Jack Graziosi, Director, Engineering Services, Administration
jack.graziosi@vaughan.ca
Leo Grellette, Director, Building Standards, Administration
leo.grellette@vaughan.ca
Andrew D. Pearce, Director, Development & Transportation Engineering, Administration
andrew.pearce@vaughan.ca
Mary Reali, Director, Recreation & Culture, Administration
Madeline Zito, Director, Corporate Communications, Administration
madeline.zito@vaughan.ca
Gregory R. Senay, Fire Chief, Administration
firerescue@vaughan.ca

Wasaga Beach

30 Lewis St.
Wasaga Beach, ON L9Z 1A1
705-429-3844 Fax: 705-429-6732
cao@wasagabeach.com
www.wasagabeach.com
Municipal Type: City
Incorporated: 1947; *Area:* 58.43 sq km
County or District: Simcoe; *Population in 2006:* 15,029
Provincial Electoral District(s): Simcoe-Grey
Federal Electoral District(s): Simcoe-Grey
Next Election: Nov. 2010 (4 year terms)
Note: Incorporated as a village in 1951 & as a town in 1974.

Council
Cal Patterson, Mayor
mayor@wasagabeach.com
David Foster, Deputy Mayor & Councillor
Ron Anderson, Councillor
Morley Bercovitch, Councillor
Nina Bifolchi, Councillor
Connie Gray, Councillor
Stan Wells, Councillor

Administration
Audrey Johnstone, Clerk
clerk@wasagabeach.com
James A. McIntosh, Director, Public Works
705-429-2540, Fax: 705-429-8226
publicworks@wasagabeach.com
Gerry Reinders, Manager, Parks & Facilities
705-429-0412, Fax: 705-429-0413
parksandfac@wasagabeach.com
R. Kelso, Manager, Planning & Development
planning@wasagabeach.com
B. Smith, Economic Development Officer
705-429-3847
Donald Warden, Fire Chief
705-429-5281
fire@wasagabeach.com

Waterloo

City Hall
100 Regina St. South
Waterloo, ON N2J 4A8
519-886-1550 Fax: 519-747-8760 TTY Toll Free: 1-866-786-3942
elected@waterloo.ca (Elected Officials' Office)
www.city.waterloo.on.ca
Municipal Type: City
Incorporated: January 15, 1857; *Area:* 64.1 sq km
County or District: Waterloo Regional Municipality; *Population in 2006:* 97,475
Provincial Electoral District(s): Kitchener-Waterloo
Federal Electoral District(s): Kitchener-Waterloo
Next Election: Nov. 2010 (4 year terms)
Note: Incorporated as a town in 1876 & as a city on Jan 1, 1948.

Council
Brenda Halloran, Mayor
brenda.halloran@waterloo.ca
Scott Witmer, Councillor, Ward(s): 1
scott.witmer@waterloo.ca
Karen Scian, Councillor, Ward(s): 2
karen.scian@waterloo.ca
Angela Veith, Councillor, Ward(s): 3
angela.vieth@waterloo.ca
Diane Freeman, Councillor, Ward(s): 4
diane.freeman@waterloo.ca
Mark Whaley, Councillor, Ward(s): 5
mark.whaley@waterloo.ca
Jeff Henry, Councillor, Ward(s): 6
Melissa Durrell, Councillor, Ward(s): 7

Administration
Susan Greatrix, City Clerk, Administration
519-747-8705, Fax: 519-747-8510
Simon Farbrother, Chief Administrative Officer, Administration
519-747-8702, Fax: 519-747-8500
Bob Mavin, Chief Financial Officer, Administration
519-747-8722, Fax: 519-747-8541
David Calder, General Manager, Corporate Services, Administration
519-747-8542, Fax: 519-747-8553
Cameron Rapp, General Manager, Development Services, Administration
519-747-8763, Fax: 519-747-8523
David Smith, General Manager, Recreation & Leisure Services, Administration
519-747-8739, Fax: 519-747-8754
Mark Dykstra, Director, Environment & Parks Services, Administration
519-747-8611, Fax: 519-886-5788
Bill Garibaldi, Director, Water Services, Administration
519-747-8605, Fax: 519-886-5788
Phil Hewitson, Director, Transportation, Administration
519-747-8630, Fax: 519-886-5788
Patti McKague, Director, Corporate Communications, Administration
519-747-8748, Fax: 519-747-8646
Murray Kieswetter, Manager, Parks Operations, Administration
519-747-8607, Fax: 519-886-5788
Mary Thorpe, Manager, Human Resources, Administration
John DeHooge, Fire Chief, Administration

Welland

60 East Main St.
Welland, ON L3B 3X4
905-735-1700 Fax: 905-732-1919 E-mail, Bylaw Enforcement: bylaw_enforc@welland.ca
christine.mintoff@welland.ca (Communications Assistant)
www.welland.ca
Municipal Type: City
Incorporated: July 24, 1858; *Area:* 81.09 sq km
County or District: Niagara Regional Municipality; *Population in 2006:* 50,331
Provincial Electoral District(s): Welland
Federal Electoral District(s): Welland
Next Election: Nov. 2010 (4 year terms)
Note: Incorporated as a town on Jan. 1, 1878 & as a city on July 1, 1917.

Council
Barry Sharpe, Mayor
mayor@welland.ca
Mark Carl, Councillor, Ward(s): 1
Mary Ann Grimaldi, Councillor, Ward(s): 1
Frank Campion, Councillor, Ward(s): 2
David McLeod, Councillor, Ward(s): 2
Dan Fortier, Councillor, Ward(s): 3
Paul Grenier, Councillor, Ward(s): 3
Pat Chiocchio, Councillor, Ward(s): 4
Tony Dimarco, Councillor, Ward(s): 4
Rocky G. Létourneau, Councillor, Ward(s): 5
Michael Petrachenko, Councillor, Ward(s): 5
Jim Larouche, Councillor, Ward(s): 6
Bob Wright, Councillor, Ward(s): 6

Administration
Barbara Gallaccio, City Clerk, Administration
clerk@welland.ca
Craig A. Stirtzinger, City Manager, Administration
craig.stirtzinger@welland.ca
Bruno Silvestri, Treasurer & General Manager, Financial & Corporate, Administration
bruno.silvestri@welland.ca
Bill Fenwick, General Manager, Parks, Facilities, & Leisure Serv, Administration
bill.fenwick@welland.ca
Sal Iannello, General Manager, Engineering, Public Works, & Tran, Administration
sal.iannello@welland.ca
Rosanne Mantesso, General Manager, Human Resources, Administration
rosanne.mantesso@welland.ca
Donald Thorpe, General Manager, Planning & Development Services, Administration
don.thorpe@welland.ca
Dan Degazio, Manager, Economic Development, Administration
Mike Mantessp, Chief Building Official, Administration
mike.mantesso@welland.ca
Denys Prevost, Fire Chief, Administration
denys.prevost@welland.ca

Whitby

575 Rossland Rd. East
Whitby, ON L1N 2M8
905-668-5803 Fax: 905-686-7005 TTY: 905-430-1942
info@whitby.ca
www.whitby.ca
Municipal Type: City
Incorporated: 1855; *Area:* 146.52 sq km
County or District: Durham Reg. Mun.; *Population in 2006:* 111,184
Provincial Electoral District(s): Whitby-Oshawa
Federal Electoral District(s): Whitby-Oshawa
Next Election: Nov. 2010 (4 year terms)

Council
Pat Perkins, Mayor
council@whitby.ca
Tracy Hanson, Councillor, Ward(s): 1 - North
Elizabeth Roy, Councillor, Ward(s): 2 - West
Michael G. Emm, Councillor, Ward(s): 3 - Centre
Ken Montague, Councillor, Ward(s): 4 - East
Lorne Earl Coe, Regional Councillor
Joe Drumm, Regional Councillor
Don Mitchell, Regional Councillor

Administration
Paul Jones, Town Clerk
clerks@whitby.ca
K.R. Nix, Acting CAO, Treasurer & Director, Corporate Services
Robert B. Short, Director, Planning
planning@whitby.ca
Peter LeBel, Director, Community & Marketing Services
ecdev@whitby.ca
Suzanne Beale, Acting Director, Public Works
engineering@whitby.ca
Jennifer Morrison, Manager, Economic Development
905-655-4571
ecdev@whitby.ca
C. Collier, Manager, Human Resources
hr@whitby.ca
Steve Edwards, Manager, Parks, Marina, Long Range Planning, Special Events & Tourism
K.W. MacKarl, Fire Chief
905-668-3312
fire@whitby.ca

Whitchurch-Stouffville

37 Sandiford Dr., 4th Fl.
Stouffville, ON L4A 7X5
905-640-1900 Fax: 905-640-7957
michele.kennedy@townofws.com
www.townofws.com
Municipal Type: City
Incorporated: 1877; *Area:* 206.74 sq km
County or District: York Reg. Mun.; *Population in 2006:* 24,390
Provincial Electoral District(s): Oak Ridges-Markham
Federal Electoral District(s): Oak Ridges-Markham
Next Election: Nov. 2010 (4 year terms)
Note: Incorporated as a town in 1971, with the amalgamation of Whitchurch Township & the Village of Stouffville.

Council
Wayne Emmerson, Mayor
Ken Ferdinands, Councillor, Ward(s): 1
Phil Bannon, Councillor, Ward(s): 2

Clyde Smith, Councillor, Ward(s): 3
Susanne Hilton, Councillor, Ward(s): 4
Richard Bartley, Councillor, Ward(s): 5
Rob Hargrave, Councillor, Ward(s): 6

Administration
Michele Kennedy, Clerk

Administration
Nick Kristoffy, Treasurer & Administrator
Tom Parry, Chief Building Official & Director, Development Services
tom.parry@townofws.com
Paul Whitehouse, Director, Public Works
paul.whitehouse@townofws.com
Rob Raycroft, Manager, Facilities & Parks
rob.raycroft@townofws.com
Denis Chartrand, Manager, Operations
denis.chartrand@townofws.com
Andrew McNeely, Manager, Planning Services
andrew.mcneely@townofws.com
Chris Powers, Fire Chief

Windsor

City Hall
P.O. Box 1607
350 City Hall Sq. West
Windsor, ON N9A 6S1
Fax: 519-255-6868 Phone: 311; Toll Free Phone: 1-877-746-4311
311@city.windsor.on.ca; hrdiv@city.windsor.on.ca (HR Dept.)
www.citywindsor.ca
Municipal Type: City
Incorporated: 1854; *Area:* 146.91 sq km
County or District: Essex; *Population in 2006:* 216,473
Provincial Electoral District(s): Windsor-Tecumseh; Windsor-West
Federal Electoral District(s): Windsor-Tecumseh; Windsor-West
Next Election: Nov. 2010 (4 year terms)
Note: Incorporated as a town in 1858 & as a city in 1892.

Council
Eddie Francis, Mayor
mayoro@city.windsor.on.ca
Drew Dilkens, Councillor, Ward(s): 1
ddilkens@city.windsor.on.ca
Ronald Jones, Councillor, Ward(s): 2
rjones@city.windsor.on.ca
Fulvio Valentinis, Councillor, Ward(s): 3
fvalentinis@city.windsor.on.ca
Alan Halberstadt, Councillor, Ward(s): 4
Ed Sleiman, Councillor, Ward(s): 5
Jo-Anne Gignac, Councillor, Ward(s): 6
Percy Hatfield, Councillor, Ward(s): 7
Bill (Biagio) Marra, Councillor, Ward(s): 8
Hilary Payne, Councillor, Ward(s): 9
Al Maghneih, Councillor, Ward(s): 10

Administration
Valerie Critchley, City Clerk, Administration
519-255-6868
clerks@city.windsor.on.ca
Helga Reidel, Chief Administrative Officer, Administration
519-255-6349
caodept@city.windsor.on.ca
Michael Duben, General Manager, Community & Protective Services, Administration
Dev Tyagi, General Manager, Public Works, Administration
pubwork@city.windsor.on.ca
Ronna Warsh, General Manager, Social & Health Services, Administration
socserv@city.windsor.on.ca
Thom Hunt, MCIP, RPP, City Planner, Administration
thunt@city.windsor.on.ca
Mario Sonego, P. Eng., City Engineer, Administration
engineeringdept@city.windsor.on.ca
David T. Fields, Fire Chief, Windsor Fire & Rescue Service, Administration
519-253-6573, Fax: 519-255-6832
Josette Eugeni, Manager, Transportation Planning, Administration
Bill Lacasse, Manager, Lou Romano Water Reclamation Plant, Administration
519-253-7217
Jack MacRae, Manager, Little River Pollution Control Plant, Administration
519-948-1751
Jim Yanchula, MCIP, RPP, Manager, Urban Design & Community Development, Administration
jyanchula@city.windsor.on.ca

Woodstock

City Hall
P.O. Box 1539
500 Dundas St.
Woodstock, ON N4S 7W5
519-539-1291 Fax: 519-539-7705 E-mail, Works Department: 519-539-2382, ext. 3104
aash@city.woodstock.on.ca (Assistant to Mayor & CAO)
www.city.woodstock.on.ca
Municipal Type: City
Incorporated: Jan. 1, 1851; *Area:* 43.79 sq km
County or District: Oxford; *Population in 2006:* 35,480
Provincial Electoral District(s): Oxford
Federal Electoral District(s): Oxford
Next Election: Nov. 2010 (4 year terms)
Note: Incorporated as a city on July 1, 1901.

Council
Pat Sobeski, Mayor
mayor@city.woodstock.on.ca
Deb A. Tait, City / County Councillor
519-421-7449
dtait@city.woodstock.on.ca
Sandra J. Talbot, City / County Councillor
519-788-0639
stalbot@city.woodstock.on.ca
Bill M. Bes, City Councillor
Ron Fraser, City Councillor
Jim Northcott, City Councillor
519-539-3698
jnorthcott@city.woodstock.on.ca
Paul D. Plant, City Councillor

Administration
Louise Gartshore, City Clerk, Administration
lgartshore@city.woodstock.on.ca
Paul Bryan-Pulham, Chief Administrative Officer, Administration
pbryan-pulham@city.woodstock.on.ca
Patrice Hilderley, Treasurer, Administration
philderley@city.woodstock.on.ca
Len Magyar, Commissioner, Development, Administration
lmagyar@city.woodstock.on.ca
Bob McFarland, Director, Community Services, Administration
bmcfarland@city.woodstock.on.ca
David Creery, City Engineer, Administration
dcreery@city.woodstock.on.ca
Harold deHaan, Engineer, Development, Administration
hdehaan@city.woodstock.on.ca
Sil Nadalin, Engineer, Design & Construction, Administration
snadalin@city.woodstock.on.ca
Scott Tegler, Fire Chief, Administration
stegler@city.woodstock.on.ca
Terry Harrington, Manager, Water Department, Administration
tharrington@city.woodstock.on.ca
Tony Pihowich, Manager, Human Resources, Administration
tpihowich@city.woodstock.on.ca
Rick D'Entremont, Superintendent, Works, Administration
rdentremont@city.woodstock.on.ca
Dan Major, Supervisor, Parks, Administration
dmajor@city.woodstock.on.ca

Other Municipalities in Ontario

Addington Highlands

P.O. Box 89
Flinton, ON K0H 1P0
613-336-2286 Fax: 613-336-2847
www.addingtonhighlands.ca
Municipal Type: Township
Area: 1,288.47 sq km
County or District: Lennox & Addington; *Population in 2006:* 2,512
Provincial Electoral District(s): Lanark-Frontenac-Lennox & Addington
Federal Electoral District(s): Lanark-Frontenac-Lennox & Addington
Next Election: Nov. 2010 (4 year terms)
Henry Hogg, Reeve
henryh@sympatico.ca
Jack Pauhl, Clerk
jpauhl@mazinaw.on.ca

Adelaide Metcalfe

2340 Egremont Dr., RR#5
Strathroy, ON N7G 3H6
519-247-3687 Fax: 519-247-3411
info@adelaidemetcalfe.on.ca
www.adelaidemetcalfe.on.ca
Municipal Type: Township
Incorporated: Jan. 1, 2001; *Area:* 331.26 sq km
County or District: Middlesex; *Population in 2006:* 3,117
Provincial Electoral District(s): Lambton-Kent-Middlesex
Federal Electoral District(s): Lambton-Kent-Middlesex
Next Election: Nov. 2010 (4 year terms)
Note: Amalgamation of the former Township of Adelaide & the Township of Metcalfe.
David Bolton, Reeve
Fran Urbshott, Clerk, Administrator, & Treasurer
fran@adelaidemetcalfe.on.ca

Adjala-Tosorontio

7855 Sideroad 30, RR#1
Alliston, ON L9R 1V1
705-434-5055 Fax: 705-434-5051
www.townshipadjtos.on.ca
Municipal Type: Township
Incorporated: Jan. 1, 1994; *Area:* 372.33 sq km
County or District: Simcoe; *Population in 2006:* 10,695
Provincial Electoral District(s): Simcoe-Grey
Federal Electoral District(s): Simcoe-Grey
Next Election: Nov. 2010 (4 year terms)
Note: Amalgamation of the former Township of Adjala & the former Township of Tosorontio.
Tom Walsh, Mayor
905-729-2132
Doug Little, Deputy Mayor & Councillor
705-435-9020
Jack Jordan, Deputy Mayor & Councillor, Ward(s): 1
519-941-6687
jack.jordan@sympatico.ca
Ray Wallace, Councillor, Ward(s): 2
905-936-3116
Mary Brett, Councillor, Ward(s): 3
519-941-5828
marysmallbrett@sympatico.ca
Joy Webster, Councillor, Ward(s): 4
705-434-0355
joywebster@sympatico.ca
Tom Cook, Councillor, Ward(s): 5
705-424-2065
tcook@drlogick.com
Barbara Kane, Clerk, Administration
bkane@townshipadjtos.on.ca
Dorthy Bulman, Treasurer & Deputy Clerk, Administration
dbulman@townshipadjtos.on.ca
Gerry Caterer, Director, Planning, Administration
gcaterer@townshipadjtos.on.ca
Eric Wargel, Director, Public Works & Deputy CAO, Administration
ewargel@townshipadjtos.on.ca

Admaston/Bromley

477 Stone Rd., RR#2
Renfrew, ON K7V 3Z5
613-432-2885 Fax: 613-432-4052
www.admastonbromley.com
Municipal Type: Township
Incorporated: Jan. 1, 2000; *Area:* 520.5 sq km
County or District: Renfrew; *Population in 2006:* 2,716
Provincial Electoral District(s): Renfrew-Nipissing-Pembroke
Federal Electoral District(s): Renfrew-Nipissing-Pembroke
Next Election: Nov. 2010 (4 year terms)
Note: Amalgamation of Admaston Township & Bromley Township.
Raye-Anne Briscoe, Mayor
613-432-5728
Beverly Briscoe, Clerk-Treasurer
bbriscoe@admastonbromley.com

Alberton

#B2, RR#1
Fort Frances, ON P9A 3M2
807-274-6053 Fax: 807-274-8449
alberton@jam21.net
www.alberton.ca
Municipal Type: Township
Area: 115.3 sq km
County or District: Rainy River District; *Population in 2006:* 958
Provincial Electoral District(s): Kenora-Rainy River
Federal Electoral District(s): Thunder Bay-Rainy River; Ancaster-Dundas-Flamborough-Westdale
Next Election: Nov. 2010 (4 year terms)
Michael Hammond, Reeve
Dawn Hayes, CAO & Clerk-Treasurer

Alfred & Plantagenet

P.O. Box 350
205 Old Hwy. 17
Plantagenet, ON K0B 1L0
613-673-4797 Fax: 613-673-4812
www.alfred-plantagenet.com
Municipal Type: Township
Incorporated: Jan. 1, 1997; *Area:* 391.68 sq km
County or District: Prescott & Russell; *Population in 2006:* 8,654
Provincial Electoral District(s): Glengarry-Prescott-Russell
Federal Electoral District(s): Glengarry-Prescott-Russell
Next Election: Nov. 2010 (4 year terms)
Note: Amalgamation of the Township of Alfred, the Village of Alfred, the Township of North Plantagenet & the Village of Plantagenet.
Jean-Yves Lalonde, Mayor
Marc Daigneault, Chief Administrative Officer & Clerk

Algoma

c/o Algoma District Svs. Administration Bd.
1 Collver Rd., RR#1
Thessalon, ON P0R 1L0
705-842-3370 Fax: 705-842-3747
www.adsab.on.ca
Municipal Type: District
Area: 48,734.66 sq km
Population in 2006: 117,461
Provincial Electoral District(s): Algoma-Manitoulin
Federal Electoral District(s): Algoma-Manitoulin-Kapuskasing
Keith Bell, Chief Administrative Officer
kbell@adsab.on.ca

Algonquin Highlands

1123 North Shore Rd., RR#2
Minden, ON K0M 2K0
705-489-2379 Fax: 705-489-3491 Phone, Dorset Satellite Office: 705-766-2211
info@algonquinhighlands.ca
www.algonquinhighlands.ca
Municipal Type: Township
Area: 1,002.12 sq km
County or District: Haliburton; *Population in 2006:* 1,976
Provincial Electoral District(s): Haliburton-Kawartha Lakes-Brock
Federal Electoral District(s): Haliburton-Kawartha Lakes-Brock
Next Election: Nov. 2010 (4 year terms)
Carol Moffat, Reeve
Angela Bird, Clerk & Administrator, Planning

Alnwick-Haldimand

P.O. Box 70
10836 County Rd. No. 2
Grafton, ON K0K 2G0
905-349-2822 Fax: 905-349-3259 Phone, Roseneath Satellite Office: 905-352-3949

alnhald@eagle.ca
www.alnwickhaldimand.ca
Municipal Type: Township
Area: 398.08 sq km
County or District: Northumberland; *Population in 2006:* 6,435
Provincial Electoral District(s): Northumberland-Quinte West
Federal Electoral District(s): Northumberland-Quinte West
Next Election: Nov. 2010 (4 year terms)
Dalton McDonald, Mayor
905-349-2747
Terrence Korotki, B.A., A.M.C.T., Administrator-Clerk & Coordinator, Planning

Amaranth
374028 - 6th Line, RR#7
Orangeville, ON L9W 2Z3
519-941-1007 Fax: 519-941-1802
township@amaranth-eastgary.ca
www.amaranth-eastgary.ca
Municipal Type: Township
Incorporated: Jan. 2, 1854; *Area:* 264.35 sq km
County or District: Dufferin; *Population in 2006:* 3,845
Provincial Electoral District(s): Dufferin-Caledon
Federal Electoral District(s): Dufferin-Caledon
Next Election: Nov. 2010 (4 year terms)
Don MacIver, Mayor
519-925-3457
don.maciver@sympatico.ca
Susan M. Stone, AMCT, Chief Administrative Officer & Clerk-Treasurer
suestone@amaranth-eastgary.ca

Armour
Municipal Office
P.O. Box 533
56 Ontario St.
Burks Falls, ON P0A 1C0
705-382-3332 Fax: 705-382-2068 Alternative Phone: 705-382-2954
info@armourtownship.ca
www.armourtownship.ca
Municipal Type: Township
Area: 164.1 sq km
County or District: Parry Sound District; *Population in 2006:* 1,249
Provincial Electoral District(s): Parry Sound-Muskoka
Federal Electoral District(s): Parry Sound-Muskoka
Next Election: Nov. 2010 (4 year terms)
Bob MacPhail, Reeve
705-636-7678
aberdeen@surenet.net
Wendy Whitwell, Clerk-Administrator
clerk@armourtownship.ca

Armstrong
P.O. Box 546
35 Tenth St.
Earlton, ON P0J 1E0
705-563-2375 Fax: 705-563-2093
Municipal Type: Township
Area: 90.33 sq km
County or District: Timiskaming District; *Population in 2006:* 1,155
Provincial Electoral District(s): Timiskaming-Cochrane
Federal Electoral District(s): Timmins-James Bay
Next Election: Nov. 2010 (4 year terms)
Jules Gravel, Reeve
Reynald Rivard, Clerk-Treasurer
reynaldrivard@nt.net

Arnprior
P.O. Box 130
105 Elgin St. West
Arnprior, ON K7S 3H4
613-623-4231 Fax: 613-623-8091
arnprior@arnprior.ca
www.arnprior.ca
Municipal Type: Town
Area: 13.04 sq km
County or District: Renfrew; *Population in 2006:* 7,158
Provincial Electoral District(s): Renfrew-Nipissing-Pembroke
Federal Electoral District(s): Renfrew-Nipissing-Pembroke
Next Election: Nov. 2010 (4 year terms)
Terry Gibeau, Mayor
tgibeau@arnprior.ca
Monique Ouellet, Town Clerk
mouellet@arnprior.ca

Arran-Elderslie
P.O. Box 70
1925 Bruce Rd. 10
Chesley, ON N0G 1L0
519-363-3039 Fax: 519-363-2203
areld@bmts.com
www.arran-elderslie.com
Municipal Type: Municipality
Area: 460.13 sq km
County or District: Bruce; *Population in 2006:* 6,747
Provincial Electoral District(s): Bruce-Grey-Owen Sound
Federal Electoral District(s): Bruce-Grey-Owen Sound
Next Election: Nov. 2010 (4 year terms)
Paul Eagleson, Mayor
519-363-3559
A.P. Crawford, Clerk & Chief Administrative Officer

Ashfield-Colborne-Wawanosh
82133 Council Line, RR#5
Goderich, ON N7A 3Y2
519-524-4669 Fax: 519-524-1951
www.acwtownship.ca
Municipal Type: Township
Area: 587.07 sq km
County or District: Huron; *Population in 2006:* 5,409
Provincial Electoral District(s): Huron-Bruce
Federal Electoral District(s): Huron-Bruce
Next Election: Nov. 2010 (4 year terms)
Ben Van Diepenbeek, Reeve
Mark Becker, Administrator & Clerk-Treasurer
clerk@acwtownship.ca

Asphodel-Norwood
P.O. Box 29
2357 County Rd. 45
Norwood, ON K0L 2V0
705-639-5343 Fax: 705-639-1880
pquinlan@asphodelnorwood.com
www.asphodelnorwood.com
Municipal Type: Township
Incorporated: 1998; *Area:* 160.85 sq km
County or District: Peterborough; *Population in 2006:* 4,247
Provincial Electoral District(s): Peterborough
Federal Electoral District(s): Peterborough
Next Election: Nov. 2010 (4 year terms)
Note: Amalgamation of the Village of Norwood & the Township of Asphodel.
Doug Pearcy, Reeve
705-639-5510, Fax: 705-639-5388
dpearcy@accel.net
Valerie Przybilla, Chief Administrative Officer & Clerk
valeriep@asphodelnorwood.com

Assiginack
P.O. Box 238
25B Spragge St.
Manitowaning, ON P0P 1N0
705-859-3196 Fax: 705-859-3010 Toll Free Phone: 1-800-540-0179
assiginackinfo@amtelecom.net
www.assiginack.ca
Municipal Type: Township
Area: 227.44 sq km
County or District: Manitoulin District; *Population in 2006:* 914
Provincial Electoral District(s): Algoma-Manitoulin
Federal Electoral District(s): Algoma-Manitoulin-Kapuskasing
Next Election: Nov. 2010 (4 year terms)
Bud Rohn, Reeve
Alton Hobbs, Clerk-Treasurer
clerktreasurer@amtelecom.net

Athens
P.O. Box 189
1 Main St. West
Athens, ON K0E 1B0
613-924-2044 Fax: 613-924-2091
athens@ripnet.com
www.athenstownship.ca
Municipal Type: Township
Incorporated: 2001; *Area:* 126.46 sq km
County or District: Leeds & Grenville; *Population in 2006:* 3,086
Provincial Electoral District(s): Leeds-Grenville
Federal Electoral District(s): Leeds-Grenville
Next Election: Nov. 2010 (4 year terms)
Herb Scott, Mayor
Darlene Noonan, Chief Administrative Officer & Clerk Treasurer

Atikokan
P.O. Box 1330
120 Marks St.
Atikokan, ON P0T 1C0
807-597-2738 Fax: 807-597-6186
www.atikokan.ca
Municipal Type: Township
Area: 316.75 sq km
County or District: Rainy River District; *Population in 2006:* 3,293
Provincial Electoral District(s): Thunder Bay-Atikokan
Federal Electoral District(s): Thunder Bay-Rainy River
Next Election: Nov. 2010 (4 year terms)
Dennis Brown, Mayor
dennis.brown@atikokan.ca
Angela Sharbot, Clerk
angela.sharbot@atikokan.ca

Augusta
3560 County Rd. 26, RR#2
Prescott, ON K0E 1T0
613-925-4231 Fax: 613-925-3499
reception@augusta.ca
www.augusta.ca
Municipal Type: Township
Area: 314.06 sq km
County or District: Leeds & Grenville; *Population in 2006:* 7,510
Provincial Electoral District(s): Leeds-Grenville
Federal Electoral District(s): Leeds-Grenville
Next Election: Nov. 2010 (4 year terms)
Mel Campbell, Reeve
613-342-6962
reeve@augusta.ca
Linda Robinson, Clerk & Administrator, Planning

Aylmer
46 Talbot St. West
Aylmer, ON N5H 1J7
519-773-3164 Fax: 519-765-1446
www.aylmer.ca
Municipal Type: Town
Area: 6.22 sq km
County or District: Elgin; *Population in 2006:* 7,069
Provincial Electoral District(s): Elgin-Middlesex-London
Federal Electoral District(s): Elgin-Middlesex-London
Next Election: Nov. 2010 (4 year terms)
Jack Couckuyt, Mayor
mayor@town.aylmer.on.ca
Nancie Irving, Clerk & Officer, Lottery Licensing
nirving@town.aylmer.on.ca

Baldwin
P.O. Box 7095
11 Spooner St.
McKerrow, ON P0P 1M0
705-869-0225 Fax: 705-869-5049
www.townshipofbaldwin.ca
Municipal Type: Township
Area: 81.82 sq km
County or District: Sudbury District; *Population in 2006:* 554
Provincial Electoral District(s): Algoma-Manitoulin
Federal Electoral District(s): Algoma-Manitoulin-Kapuskasing
Next Election: Nov. 2010 (4 year terms)
Archie Boivin, Reeve
Joan Seidel, Clerk & Treasurer
joanseidel@townshipofbaldwin.c

Bancroft
P.O. Box 790
24 Flint Ave.
Bancroft, ON K0L 1C0
613-332-3331 Fax: 613-332-0384
bancroft@town.bancroft.on.ca
www.town.bancroft.on.ca
Municipal Type: Town
Incorporated: 1904; *Area:* 227.84 sq km
County or District: Hastings; *Population in 2006:* 3,838
Provincial Electoral District(s): Prince Edward-Hastings
Federal Electoral District(s): Prince Edward-Hastings
Next Election: Nov. 2010 (4 year terms)
Bernice Jenkins, Mayor
613-332-3782
Barry Wannamaker, Chief Administrative Officer & Clerk
bwannamaker@town.bancroft.on.ca

Bayham
P.O. Box 160
9344 Plank Rd.
Straffordville, ON N0J 1Y0
519-866-5521 Fax: 519-866-3884
bayham@bayham.on.ca
www.bayham.on.ca
Municipal Type: Municipality
Area: 244.99 sq km
County or District: Elgin; *Population in 2006:* 6,727
Provincial Electoral District(s): Elgin-Middlesex-London
Federal Electoral District(s): Elgin-Middlesex-London
Next Election: Nov. 2010 (4 year terms)
Paul Ens, Mayor
Lynn Acre, Mayor
519-866-3645
lynnacre@amtelecom.net

Beckwith
1702 - 9th Line, RR#2
Carleton Place, ON K7C 3P2
613-257-1539 Fax: 613-257-8996 Toll Free Phone: 1-800-535-4532 (in 613 area code)
www.twp.beckwith.on.ca
Municipal Type: Township
Area: 240.12 sq km
County or District: Lanark; *Population in 2006:* 6,387
Provincial Electoral District(s): Lanark-Frontenac-Lennox & Addington
Federal Electoral District(s): Lanark-Frontenac-Lennox & Addington
Next Election: Nov. 2010 (4 year terms)
Richard Kidd, Reeve
613-257-5409
rkidd@ripnet.com
Cynthia A.L. Moyle, Chief Administrative Officer
cmoyle@twp.beckwith.on.ca

Billings
Municipal Office
P.O. Box 34
15 Old Mill Rd.
Kagawong, ON P0P 1J0
705-282-2611 Fax: 705-282-3199
billingsadmin@xplornet.com
www.billingstwp.ca
Municipal Type: Township
Incorporated: 1884; *Area:* 209.15 sq km
County or District: Manitoulin District; *Population in 2006:* 539
Provincial Electoral District(s): Algoma-Manitoulin
Federal Electoral District(s): Algoma-Manitoulin-Kapuskasing
Next Election: Nov. 2010 (4 year terms)
Austin Hunt, Reeve
705-282-2684
Katherine McDonald, Clerk-Treasurer

Black River-Matheson
P.O. Box 601
429 Park Lane
Matheson, ON P0K 1N0

705-273-2313 Fax: 705-273-2140
reception@blackriver-matheson.com
www.blackriver-matheson.com
Municipal Type: Township
Area: 1,161.67 sq km
County or District: Cochrane District; *Population in 2006:* 2,619
Provincial Electoral District(s): Timiskaming-Cochrane
Federal Electoral District(s): Timmins-James Bay
Next Election: Nov. 2010 (4 year terms)
Mike Milinkovich, Mayor
mayor@blackriver-matheson.com
Heather Smith, Deputy Clerk & Treasurer
treasurer@blackriver-matheson.com

Blandford-Blenheim
P.O. Box 100
47 Wilmot St. South
Drumbo, ON N0J 1G0
519-463-5347 Fax: 519-463-5881
generalmail@twp.bla-ble.on.ca
www.twp.bla-ble.on.ca
Municipal Type: Township
Area: 382.34 sq km
County or District: Oxford; *Population in 2006:* 7,149
Provincial Electoral District(s): Oxford
Federal Electoral District(s): Oxford
Next Election: Nov. 2010 (4 year terms)
Marion Wearn, Mayor
Keith Reibling, Clerk-Administrator
kreibling@twp.bla-ble.on.ca

Blind River
P.O. Box 640
11 Hudson St.
Blind River, ON P0R 1B0
705-356-2251 Fax: 705-356-7343
www.blindriver.ca
Municipal Type: Town
Incorporated: 1906; *Area:* 520.59 sq km
County or District: Algoma District; *Population in 2006:* 3,780
Provincial Electoral District(s): Algoma-Manitoulin
Federal Electoral District(s): Algoma-Manitoulin-Kapuskasing
Next Election: Nov. 2010 (4 year terms)
Sue Jensen, Mayor
Ken Corbiere, Clerk

Bluewater, Municipality of
P.O. Box 250
14 Mill Ave.
Zurich, ON N0M 2T0
519-236-4351 Fax: 519-236-4329 Toll Free: 1-877-236-4351
bluewater@town.bluewater.on.ca
www.town.bluewater.on.ca
Municipal Type: Town
Area: 416.99 sq km
County or District: Huron; *Population in 2006:* 7,120
Provincial Electoral District(s): Huron-Bruce
Federal Electoral District(s): Huron-Bruce
Next Election: Nov. 2010 (4 year terms)
Bill Dowson, Mayor
Lori Wolfe, Chief Administrative Officer & Clerk

Bonfield
365 Hwy. 531
Bonfield, ON P0H 1E0
705-776-2641 Fax: 705-776-1154
monique@ebonfield.org
www.ebonfield.org
Municipal Type: Township
Incorporated: 1975; *Area:* 205.75 sq km
County or District: Nipissing District; *Population in 2006:* 2,009
Provincial Electoral District(s): Nipissing
Federal Electoral District(s): Nipissing-Timiskaming
Next Election: Nov. 2010 (4 year terms)
Randall McLaren, Mayor
Lise B. McMillan, Administrator, Clerk, & Treasurer

Bonnechere Valley
P.O. Box 100
49 Bonnechere St. East
Eganville, ON K0J 1T0
613-628-3101 Fax: 613-628-1336
admin@eganville.com
www.bonnecherevalleytwp.com
Municipal Type: Township
Incorporated: Jan. 1, 2001; *Area:* 589.87 sq km
County or District: Renfrew; *Population in 2006:* 3,665
Provincial Electoral District(s): Renfrew-Nipissing-Pembroke
Federal Electoral District(s): Renfrew-Nipissing-Pembroke
Next Election: Nov. 2010 (4 year terms)
Note: Amalgamation of Eganville Village, Grattan Township, Sebastopol Township & Algona South Township.
Jennifer Murphy, Mayor
613-628-3295
Bryan Martin, Chief Administrative Officer

Brethour
P.O. Box 537
51476 Brethour Rd.
Belle Vallee, ON P0J 1A0
705-647-1712 Fax: 705-647-6851
brethourtwp@ntl.sympatico.ca
Municipal Type: Township
Area: 82.05 sq km
County or District: Timiskaming District; *Population in 2006:* 117
Provincial Electoral District(s): Timiskaming-Cochrane
Federal Electoral District(s): Timmins-James Bay
Next Election: Nov. 2010 (4 year terms)
Maurice Chabot, Reeve

Brock
P.O. Box 10
1 Cameron St. East
Cannington, ON L0E 1E0
705-432-2355 Fax: 705-432-3487 Toll Free Phone: 1-866-223-7668
brock@townshipofbrock.ca
www.townshipofbrock.ca
Municipal Type: Township
Incorporated: 1973; *Area:* 423.31 sq km
County or District: Durham Reg. Mun.; *Population in 2006:* 11,979
Provincial Electoral District(s): Haliburton-Kawartha Lakes-Brock
Federal Electoral District(s): Haliburton-Kawartha Lakes-Brock
Next Election: Nov. 2010 (4 year terms)
Larry O'Connor, Mayor
loconnor@townshipofbrock.ca
John Grant, Regional Councillor
Mike Manchester, Councillor, Ward(s): 1
Randy Skinner, Councillor, Ward(s): 2
Anthony Woodruff, Councillor, Ward(s): 3
David Marquis, Councillor, Ward(s): 4
W.E. Ted Ted Smith, Councillor, Ward(s): 5
Thomas G. Gettinby, MA, MCIP, RPP, CMO, Municipal Clerk, Administration
tgettinby@townshipofbrock.ca
Kathryn McCann, BAS, AMCT, Chief Administrative Officer, Administration
kmccann@townshipofbrock.ca
Michael Legge, Treasurer, Administration
mlegge@townshipofbrock.ca
Judith S. Avery, Director, Public Works, Administration
javery@townshipofbrock.ca
Joseph J. Bonura, Chief Building Offical, Administration
jbonura@townshipofbrock.ca
Rick Harrison, Chief, Fire, Administration
rharrison@townshipofbrock.ca

Brockton
P.O. Box 68
100 Scott St.
Walkerton, ON N0G 2V0
519-881-2223 Fax: 519-881-2991 Toll Free Phone: 1-877-885-8084
info@brockton.ca
www.brockton.ca
Municipal Type: Municipality
Incorporated: Jan. 1, 1999; *Area:* 565.07 sq km
County or District: Bruce; *Population in 2006:* 9,641
Provincial Electoral District(s): Huron-Bruce
Federal Electoral District(s): Huron-Bruce
Next Election: Nov. 2010 (4 year terms)
Note: Amalgamation of the Town of Walkerton, Township of Brant, & the Township of Greenock.
David Inglis, Mayor
Richard W. Radford, Chief Administrative Officer & Clerk
rradford@brockton.ca

Brooke-Alvinston
P.O. Box 28
3236 River St.
Alvinston, ON N0N 1A0
519-898-2173 Fax: 519-898-5653 Toll Free Phone, Enforcement Unit: 1-866-344-9119
cswan@amtelecom.net (Administrative Assistant)
www.brookealvinston.com
Municipal Type: Township
Area: 311.3 sq km
County or District: Lambton; *Population in 2006:* 2,661
Provincial Electoral District(s): Lambton-Kent-Middlesex
Federal Electoral District(s): Lambton-Kent-Middlesex
Next Election: Nov. 2010 (4 year terms)
Don McGugan, Mayor
519-847-5606, Fax: 519-847-5607
jdmcgugan@hotmail.com
Cathy Case, Clerk
cathycase@amtelecom.net

Bruce Mines
P.O. Box 220
9180 Hwy. 17 East
Bruce Mines, ON P0R 1C0
705-785-3493 Fax: 705-785-3170
brucemines@bellnet.ca
www.brucemines.ca
Municipal Type: Town
Incorporated: 1903; *Area:* 6.13 sq km
County or District: Algoma District; *Population in 2006:* 584
Provincial Electoral District(s): Algoma-Manitoulin
Federal Electoral District(s): Sault Ste Marie
Next Election: Nov. 2010 (4 year terms)
Gordon Post, Mayor
Donna Brunke, Town Clerk
dbrunke@bellnet.ca

Brudenell, Lyndoch & Raglan
P.O. Box 40
42 Burnt Bridge Rd.
Palmer Rapids, ON K0J 2E0
613-758-2061 Fax: 613-758-2235
blrtownship@xplornet.com
www.countyofrenfrew.on.ca/municipalprofiles.htm
Municipal Type: Township
Incorporated: Jan. 1, 1999; *Area:* 702.77 sq km
County or District: Renfrew; *Population in 2006:* 1,497
Provincial Electoral District(s): Renfrew-Nipissing-Pembroke
Federal Electoral District(s): Renfrew-Nipissing-Pembroke
Next Election: Nov. 2010 (4 year terms)
Norman Lentz, Reeve
Michelle Mantifel, Clerk-Treasurer

Burk's Falls
P.O. Box 160
172 Ontario St.
Burks Falls, ON P0A 1C0
705-382-3138 Fax: 705-382-2273
villofbf@bellnet.ca
www.burksfalls.net
Municipal Type: Village
Incorporated: 1890; *Area:* 3.12 sq km
County or District: Parry Sound District; *Population in 2006:* 893
Provincial Electoral District(s): Parry Sound-Muskoka
Federal Electoral District(s): Parry Sound-Muskoka
Next Election: Nov. 2010 (4 year terms)
Cathy Still, Reeve
Jarvis W. Osborne, Clerk-Treasurer

Burpee & Mills
RR#1
Evansville, ON P0P 1E0
705-282-0624 Fax: 705-282-0624
burpeemills@xplornet.com
www.burpeemills.com
Municipal Type: Township
Area: 218.48 sq km
County or District: Manitoulin District; *Population in 2006:* 329
Provincial Electoral District(s): Algoma-Manitoulin
Federal Electoral District(s): Algoma-Manitoulin-Kapuskasing
Next Election: Nov. 2010 (4 year terms)
Ken Noland, Reeve
Bonnie J. Bailey, Clerk-Treasurer

Callander, Municipality of
P.O. Box 100
280 Main St. North
Callander, ON P0H 1H0
705-752-1410 Fax: 705-752-3116
info@callander.ca
www.callander.ca
Municipal Type: Township
Area: 100.96 sq km
County or District: Parry Sound District; *Population in 2006:* 3,249
Provincial Electoral District(s): Nipissing
Federal Electoral District(s): Nipissing-Timiskaming
Next Election: Nov. 2010 (4 year terms)
Note: Formerly North Himsworth Township.
Hector Lavigne, Mayor
705-845-5010
Jeffrey Celentano, Chief Administration Officer & Clerk

Calvin
1355 Peddlers Dr., RR#2
Mattawa, ON P0H 1V0
705-744-2700 Fax: 705-744-0309
info@calvintownship.info
www.calvintownship.info
Municipal Type: Township
Area: 139.17 sq km
County or District: Nipissing District; *Population in 2006:* 608
Provincial Electoral District(s): Nipissing
Federal Electoral District(s): Nipissing-Timiskaming
Next Election: Nov. 2010 (4 year terms)
Wayne Brown, Mayor
Lynda Kovacs, Clerk-Treasurer

Carleton Place
175 Bridge St.
Carleton Place, ON K7C 2V8
613-257-6200 Fax: 613-257-8170 E-mail, Public Works: dyoung@carletonplace.ca
info@carletonplace.ca; bylaw@carletonplace.ca (Bylaws)
www.carletonplace.ca
Municipal Type: Town
Area: 8.83 sq km
County or District: Lanark; *Population in 2006:* 9,453
Provincial Electoral District(s): Lanark-Frontenac-Lennox & Addington
Federal Electoral District(s): Lanark-Frontenac-Lennox & Addington
Next Election: Nov. 2010 (4 year terms)
Wendy LeBlanc, Mayor
613-257-6206
Duncan H. Rogers, Clerk
613-257-6211
drogers@carletonplace.ca

Carling
2 West Carling Bay Rd., RR#1
Nobel, ON P0G 1G0
705-342-5856 Fax: 705-342-9527 E-mail, Treasury: treasurer@carlingtownship.ca
reception@carlingtownship.ca; admin@carlingtownship.ca
www.carlingtownship.ca
Municipal Type: Township
Area: 243.94 sq km
County or District: Parry Sound District; *Population in 2006:* 1,123
Provincial Electoral District(s): Parry Sound-Muskoka
Federal Electoral District(s): Parry Sound-Muskoka
Next Election: Nov. 2010 (4 year terms)

Gord Harrison, Mayor
705-342-5230
Stephen Kaegi, Chief Administrative Officer & Clerk
cao@carlingtownship.ca

Carlow/Mayo

General Delivery, 3987 Boulter Rd.
Boulter, ON K0L 1G0
613-332-1760 Fax: 613-332-2175
carlowmayo@hughes.net
www.carlowmayo.ca
Municipal Type: Township
Incorporated: Jan. 1, 2001; *Area:* 388.36 sq km
County or District: Hastings; *Population in 2006:* 950
Provincial Electoral District(s): Prince Edward-Hastings
Federal Electoral District(s): Prince Edward-Hastings
Next Election: Nov. 2010 (4 year terms)
Note: Amalgamation of the former townships of Carlow & Mayo.
Bonnie Adams, Reeve
Arlene Cox, Clerk-Administrator

Casey

P.O. Box 460
Belle Vallee, ON P0J 1A0
705-647-7257 Fax: 705-647-6373
harlytwp@parolink.net; lise_chhk@parolink.net
www.casey.ca
Municipal Type: Township
Incorporated: 1909; *Area:* 80.75 sq km
County or District: Timiskaming District; *Population in 2006:* 385
Provincial Electoral District(s): Timiskaming-Cochrane
Federal Electoral District(s): Timmins-James Bay
Next Election: Nov. 2010 (4 year terms)
Guy Labonté, Reeve
Michel Lachapelle, Clerk-Treasurer

Casselman

P.O. Box 710
751 St. Jean St.
Casselman, ON K0A 1M0
613-764-3139 Fax: 613-764-5709
info@casselman.ca
www.casselman.ca
Municipal Type: Village
Area: 5.15 sq km
County or District: Prescott & Russell; *Population in 2006:* 3,294
Provincial Electoral District(s): Glengarry-Prescott-Russell
Federal Electoral District(s): Glengarry-Prescott-Russell
Next Election: Nov. 2010 (4 year terms)
Conrad Lamadeleine, Mayor
Gilles R. Lortie, Clerk
glortie@casselman.ca

Cavan Monaghan

988 County Rd. 10, RR#3
Millbrook, ON L0A 1G0
705-932-2929 Fax: 705-932-3458 Toll Free Phone: 1-877-906-5556
info@cavanmonaghan.net; services@cavanmonaghan.net
www.cavanmonaghan.net
Municipal Type: Township
Area: 306.13 sq km
County or District: Peterborough; *Population in 2006:* 8,828
Provincial Electoral District(s): Haliburton-Kawartha Lakes-Brock
Federal Electoral District(s): Haliburton-Kawartha Lakes-Brock
Next Election: Nov. 2010 (4 year terms)
Note: Formerly The Corporation of the Township of Cavan-Millbrook-North Monaghan.
Neal Cathcart, Reeve
705-742-7014
ncathcart@cavanmonaghan.net
Gail Empey, Clerk
705-932-9326
gempey@cavanmonaghan.net

Central Elgin

450 Sunset Dr.
St Thomas, ON N5R 5V1
519-631-4860 Fax: 519-631-4036
dwilson@centralelgin.org
www.centralelgin.org
Municipal Type: Municipality
Area: 280.22 sq km
County or District: Elgin; *Population in 2006:* 12,723
Provincial Electoral District(s): Elgin-Middlesex-London
Federal Electoral District(s): Elgin-Middlesex-London
Next Election: Nov. 2010 (4 year terms)
Sylvia Hofhuis, Mayor
519-782-3541
shofhuis@centralelgin.org
T. Marks, Deputy Mayor & Councillor
S. Carr, Councillor
S. Marr, Councillor
S. Martyn, Councillor
R. Matthews, Councillor
G. Reu, Councillor
Donald N. Leitch, Chief Administrative Officer & Clerk, Administration
dleitch@centralelgin.org
Sharon Larmour, Treasurer & Director, Financial Services, Administration
Donald Crocker, Director, Fire & Rescue Services, Administration
Lloyd Perrin, Director, Physical Services, Administration

Central Frontenac

P.O. Box 89
Sharbot Lake, ON K0H 2P0
613-279-2935 Fax: 613-279-2422
www.centralfrontenac.com
Municipal Type: Township
Incorporated: Jan. 1, 1998; *Area:* 970.07 sq km
County or District: Frontenac; *Population in 2006:* 4,665
Provincial Electoral District(s): Lanark-Frontenac-Lennox & Addington
Federal Electoral District(s): Lanark-Frontenac-Lennox & Addington
Next Election: Nov. 2010 (4 year terms)
Janet Gutowski, Mayor
613-374-1355
j.gutowski@sympatico.ca
John DuChene, Chief Administrative Officer & Clerk
clerk@centralfrontenac.com

Central Huron, Municipality of

P.O. Box 400
23 Albert St.
Clinton, ON N0M 1L0
519-482-3997 Fax: 519-482-9183
cao@centralhuron.com
www.centralhuron.com
Municipal Type: Township
Incorporated: Jan. 1, 2001; *Area:* 447.6 sq km
County or District: Huron; *Population in 2006:* 7,641
Provincial Electoral District(s): Huron-Bruce
Federal Electoral District(s): Huron-Bruce
Next Election: Nov. 2010 (4 year terms)
Note: Amalgamation of the Town of Clinton, the Township of Hullett, & the Township of Goderich.
Jim Ginn, Reeve
519-482-7811, Fax: 519-482-7487
Brenda MacIsaac, Clerk
clerk@centralhuron.com

Central Manitoulin

P.O. Box 187
6020 Hwy. 542
Mindemoya, ON P0P 1S0
705-377-5726 Fax: 705-377-5585 E-mail, Economic Dev.: centralecdev@amtelecom.net
centralm@amtelecom.net; centralinspections@amtelecom.net
www.centralmanitoulin.ca
Municipal Type: Township
Area: 431.53 sq km
County or District: Manitoulin District; *Population in 2006:* 1,944
Provincial Electoral District(s): Algoma-Manitoulin
Federal Electoral District(s): Algoma-Manitoulin-Kapuskasing
Next Election: Nov. 2010 (4 year terms)
Gerry Strong, Reeve
Ruth Frawley, Chief Administrative Officer & Clerk

Centre Hastings

11379 Hwy. 62, RR#5
Madoc, ON K0K 2K0
613-473-4030 Fax: 613-473-5444
www.centrehastings.com
Municipal Type: Municipality
Area: 222.09 sq km
County or District: Hastings; *Population in 2006:* 4,386
Provincial Electoral District(s): Prince Edward-Hastings
Federal Electoral District(s): Prince Edward-Hastings
Next Election: Nov. 2010 (4 year terms)
Owen Ketcheson, Reeve
613-473-4236
Doug Parks, Clerk
dparks@centrehastings.com

Centre Wellington

P.O. Box 10
1 MacDonald Sq.
Elora, ON N0B 1S0
519-846-9691 Fax: 519-846-2190
www.centrewellington.ca
Municipal Type: Township
Area: 407.33 sq km
County or District: Wellington; *Population in 2006:* 26,049
Provincial Electoral District(s): Wellington-Halton Hills
Federal Electoral District(s): Wellington-Halton Hills
Next Election: Nov. 2010 (4 year terms)
Joanne Ross-Zuj, Mayor
519-846-0213, Fax: 519-846-2825
mayor@centrewellington.ca
Shawn Watters, Councillor, Ward(s): 1
ward1@centrewellington.ca
Kirk McElwain, Councillor, Ward(s): 2
ward2@centrewellington.ca
Robert Foster, Councillor, Ward(s): 3
ward3@centrewellington.ca
Fred Morris, Councillor, Ward(s): 4
ward4@centrewellington.ca
Walt Visser, Councillor, Ward(s): 5
ward5@centrewellington.ca
Ron Hallman, Councillor, Ward(s): 6
ward6@centrewellington.ca
Marion Morris, Clerk, Administration
mmorris@centrewellington.ca
Michael K. Wood, Chief Administrative Officer, Administration
Wes Snarr, Chief Financial Officer & Treasurer, Administration
wsnarr@centrewellington.ca
Andrew Goldie, Director, Parks & Recreation, Administration
agoldie@centrewellington.ca
Brett Salmon, Director, Planning, Administration
bsalmon@centrewellington.ca
Brad Patton, Fire Chief, Administration
bpatton@centrewellington.ca
Ken Elder, Contact, Public Works, Administration
519-846-9801
kelder@centrewellington.ca

Chamberlain

RR#3
Englehart, ON P0J 1H0
705-544-8088 Fax: 705-544-1118
www.englehartpubliclibrary.ca/eplnew/Chamberlain/Frame.htm
Municipal Type: Township
Incorporated: 1908; *Area:* 110.13 sq km
County or District: Timiskaming District; *Population in 2006:* 322
Provincial Electoral District(s): Timiskaming-Cochrane
Federal Electoral District(s): Timmins-James Bay
Next Election: Nov. 2010 (4 year terms)
William Dickinson, Reeve
Barbara Cook, Township Clerk-Treasurer

Champlain

948 Pleasant Corners Rd. East
Vankleek Hill, ON K0B 1R0
613-678-3003 Fax: 613-678-3363
info@champlain.com
www.champlain.ca
Municipal Type: Township
Incorporated: Jan. 1, 1998; *Area:* 207.15 sq km
County or District: Prescott & Russell; *Population in 2006:* 8,683
Provincial Electoral District(s): Glengarry-Prescott-Russell
Federal Electoral District(s): Glengarry-Prescott-Russell
Next Election: Nov. 2010 (4 year terms)
Note: Amalgamation of the Village of L'Orignal, the Township of West Hawkesbury, the Township of Longueuil & the Village of Vankleek Hill.
Gary J. Barton, Mayor
613-678-3101
gary.barton@champlain.ca
Jean Thériault, Chief Administrative Officer & Clerk-Treasurer
jean.theriault@champlain.ca

Chapleau

Civic Centre
P.O. Box 129
20 Pine St.
Chapleau, ON P0M 1K0
705-864-1330 Fax: 705-864-1824
www.chapleau.ca
Municipal Type: Township
Area: 14.27 sq km
County or District: Sudbury District; *Population in 2006:* 2,354
Provincial Electoral District(s): Algoma-Manitoulin
Federal Electoral District(s): Algoma-Manitoulin-Kapuskasing
Next Election: Nov. 2010 (4 year terms)
Andre Byham, Mayor
mayorejf@township.chapleau.on.ca
Allan D. Pellow, Chief Administrative Officer
apellow@township.chapleau.on.ca

Chapple

P.O. Box 4
Barwick, ON P0W 1A0
807-487-2354 Fax: 807-487-2406
info@chapple.on.ca
www.chapple.on.ca
Municipal Type: Township
Area: 529.02 sq km
County or District: Rainy River District; *Population in 2006:* 856
Provincial Electoral District(s): Kenora-Rainy River
Federal Electoral District(s): Thunder Bay-Rainy River
Next Election: Nov. 2010 (4 year terms)
Peter Van Heyst, Reeve
Peggy Johnson, Chief Administrative Officer & Clerk-Treasurer

Charlton & Dack

RR#2
Englehart, ON P0J 1H0
705-544-7525 Fax: 705-544-2369
dack@ntl.sympatico.ca
www.charltonanddack.com
Municipal Type: Municipality
Incorporated: Jan. 1, 2003; *Area:* 92.33 sq km
County or District: Timiskaming District; *Population in 2006:* 613
Provincial Electoral District(s): Timiskaming-Cochrane
Federal Electoral District(s): Timmins-James Bay
Next Election: Nov. 2010 (4 year terms)
Note: Amalgamation of the Town of Charlton & the Township of Dack.
Reta Allen, Reeve
Louise Williams, Clerk-Treasurer

Chatham-Kent

Civic Centre
P.O. Box 640
315 King St. West
Chatham, ON N7M 5K8
519-360-1998 Fax: 519-436-3237 Toll Free Phone: 1-800-714-7497
CKinfo@chatham-kent.ca
www.chatham-kent.ca
Municipal Type: Municipality
Incorporated: Jan. 1, 1998; *Area:* 2,458.06 sq km
Population in 2006: 108,177
Provincial Electoral District(s): Chatham-Kent-Essex; Lambton-Kent-Middlesex
Federal Electoral District(s): Chatham-Kent-Essex; Lambton-Kent-Middlesex
Next Election: Nov. 2010 (4 year terms)
Note: Formerly the County of Kent.

Randy Hope, Mayor & Chief Executive Officer
519-436-3219, Fax: 519-436-3236
CKmayor@chatham-kent.ca
Bryon Fluker, Councillor, Ward(s): 1 - West Kent
Brian W. King, Councillor, Ward(s): 1 - West Kent
Karen Herman, Councillor, Ward(s): 2 - South Kent
Art Sterling, Councillor, Ward(s): 2 - South Kent
Frank Vercouteren, Councillor, Ward(s): 2 - South Kent
Jim Brown, Councillor, Ward(s): 3 - East Kent
Steve Pinsonneault, Councillor, Ward(s): 3 - East Kent
Joe Faas, Councillor, Ward(s): 4 - North Kent
Bill Weaver, Councillor, Ward(s): 4 - North Kent
Sheldon Parsons, Councillor, Ward(s): 5 - Wallaceburg
Tom McGregor, Councillor, Ward(s): 5 - Wallaceburg
Anne Gilbert, Councillor, Ward(s): 6 - Chatham
Larry Mansfield Robbins, Councillor, Ward(s): 6 - Chatham
Marjorie Crew, Councillor, Ward(s): 6 - Chatham
Don Clarke, Councillor, Ward(s): 6 - Chatham
Douglas Sulman, Councillor, Ward(s): 6 - Chatham
Steve Pickard, Councillor, Ward(s): 6 - Chatham
Elinor Mifflin, Clerk, Administration
Rob Browning, Chief Administrative Officer, Administration
Stuart Wood, CMA, Director, Financial Services & Treasurer, Administration
Lucy Brown, General Manager, Health & Family Services, Administration
lucyb@chatham-kent.ca
Leo Denys, General Manager, Infrastruture & Engineering Syste, Administration
Don Shropshire, General Manager. Community Development & Planning, Administration

Chatsworth
#316837, RR#1
Chatsworth, ON N0H 1G0
519-794-3232 Fax: 519-794-4499
office@chatsworth.ca
www.chatsworth.ca
Municipal Type: Township
Incorporated: Jan. 1, 2001; *Area:* 595.35 sq km
County or District: Grey; *Population in 2006:* 6,392
Provincial Electoral District(s): Bruce-Grey-Owen Sound
Federal Electoral District(s): Bruce-Grey-Owen Sound
Next Election: Nov. 2010 (4 year terms)
Note: Amalgamation of the Townships of Holland & Sullivan & the Village of Chatsworth.
Bob Pringle, Mayor
519-934-2330
Will Moore, Chief Administrative Officer & Clerk
519-794-3232
wmoore@chatsworth.ca

Chisholm
2847 Chiswick Line, RR#4
Powassan, ON P0H 1Z0
705-724-3526 Fax: 705-724-5099 Phone, Public Works: 705-724-5530
twpchisholm@ontera.net
www.chisholm.ca
Municipal Type: Township
Incorporated: 1912; *Area:* 205.26 sq km
County or District: Nipissing District; *Population in 2006:* 1,318
Provincial Electoral District(s): Nipissing
Federal Electoral District(s): Nipissing-Timiskaming
Next Election: Nov. 2010 (4 year terms)
Leo Jobin, Mayor
Linda M. Ringler, Clerk-Treasurer

Clarington
40 Temperance St.
Bowmanville, ON L1C 3A6
905-623-3379 Fax: 905-623-6506 Toll Free Phone: 1-800-563-1195
info@clarington.net; communications@clarington.net
www.clarington.net
Municipal Type: Municipality
Area: 611.1 sq km
County or District: Durham Reg. Mun.; *Population in 2006:* 77,820
Provincial Electoral District(s): Durham
Federal Electoral District(s): Durham
Next Election: Nov. 2010 (4 year terms)
Jim Abernethy, Mayor
mayor@clarington.net
Mary Novak, Regional Councillor, Ward(s): 1 & 2
mnovak@clarington.net
Charlie Trim, Regional Councillor, Ward(s): 3 & 4
ctrim@clarington.net
Adrian Foster, Local Councillor, Ward(s): 1
afoster@clarington.net
Ron Hooper, Local Councillor, Ward(s): 2
rhooper@clarington.net
Willie Woo, Local Councillor, Ward(s): 3
wwoo@clarington.net
Gord Robinson, Local Councillor, Ward(s): 4
grobinson@clarington.net
Patti L. Barrie, Municipal Clerk, Administration
pbarrie@clarington.net; clerks@clarington.net
Franklin Wu, Chief Administrative Officer, Administration
cao@clarington.net
Nancy Taylor, Treasurer & Director, Finance, Administration
ntaylor@clarington.net; finance@clarington.net
Tony Cannella, Director, Engineering Services, Administration
tcannella@clarington.net
Joseph Caruana, Director, Community Services, Administration
jcaruana@clarington.net
David Crome, Director, Planning Services, Administration
dcrome@clarington.net; planning@clarington.net
Fred Horvath, Director, Operations, Administration
fhorvath@clarington.net; operations@clarington.net
Marie Marano, Director, Corporate Services, Administration
mmarano@clarington.net
Gord Weir, Director, Emergency & Fire Services, Administration
gweir@clarington.net

Clearview
P.O. Box 200
217 Gideon St.
Stayner, ON L0M 1S0
705-428-6230 Fax: 705-428-0288
brenda.falls@clearview.ca (Administration)
www.clearviewtwp.on.ca
Municipal Type: Township
Area: 557.32 sq km
County or District: Simcoe; *Population in 2006:* 14,088
Provincial Electoral District(s): Simcoe-Grey
Federal Electoral District(s): Simcoe-Grey
Next Election: Nov. 2010 (4 year terms)
Ken Ferguson, Mayor
705-446-2323
kferguson@clearviewtwp.on.ca
Alicia Savage, Deputy Mayor & Councillor
asavage@clearviewtwp.on.ca
Doug Measures, Councillor, Ward(s): 1
dmeasures@clearviewtwp.on.ca
Orville Brown, Councillor, Ward(s): 2
obrown@clearviewtwp.on.ca
Mark Royal, Councillor, Ward(s): 3
mroyal@clearviewtwp.on.ca
Thom Paterson, Councillor, Ward(s): 4
tpaterson@clearviewtwp.on.ca
Robert Walker, Councillor, Ward(s): 5
rwalker@clearviewtwp.on.ca
Roger McGillvray, Councillor, Ward(s): 6
Rmcgillvray@clearviewtwp.on.ca
Shawn Davidson, Councillor, Ward(s): 7
sdavidson@clearviewtwp.on.ca
Bob Campbell, Clerk, Administration
bcampbell@clearview.ca
Susan McKenzie, Chief Administrative Officer, Administration
smckenzie@clearview.ca
Mitch Carruthers, Treasurer, Administration
mcarruthers@clearview.ca
Richard Spraggs, Director, Public Works, Administration
rspraggs@clearview.ca
Michael Wynia, Director, Planning & Development, Administration
mwynia@clearview.ca
Dave Carruthers, Fire Chief, Administration
dcarruthers@clearview.ca

Cobalt
P.O. Box 70
18 Silver St.
Cobalt, ON P0J 1C0
705-679-8877 Fax: 705-679-5050
cobalt@ntl.sympatico.ca
www.cobalt.ca
Municipal Type: Town
Area: 2.11 sq km
County or District: Timiskaming District; *Population in 2006:* 1,229
Provincial Electoral District(s): Timiskaming-Cochrane
Federal Electoral District(s): Nipissing-Timiskaming
Next Election: Nov. 2010 (4 year terms)
Andre Belanger, Mayor
Steph Palmateer, Chief Administrative Officer & Clerk-Treasurer

Cochrane
P.O. Box 490
171 Fourth Ave.
Cochrane, ON P0L 1C0
705-272-4361 Fax: 705-272-6068
townhall@town.cochrane.on.ca
www.town.cochrane.on.ca
Municipal Type: Town
Incorporated: 1910; *Area:* 538.76 sq km
County or District: Cochrane District; *Population in 2006:* 5,487
Provincial Electoral District(s): Timiskaming-Cochrane
Federal Electoral District(s): Timmins-James Bay
Next Election: Nov. 2010 (4 year terms)
Peter Politis, Mayor
Jean-Pierre Ouellette, Chief Administrative Officer & Clerk

Cochrane
Cochrane, ON

Municipal Type: District
Area: 141,247.30 sq km
Population in 2006: 82,503
David Landers, CAO, Cochrane District Social Services Administrat
705-268-7722, Fax: 705-268-8290
CAO@cdssab.on.ca

Cockburn Island
General Delivery
Walford, ON P0P 2E0
705-844-2289 Fax: 705-844-1101
Municipal Type: Township
Area: 167.6 sq km
County or District: Manitoulin District; *Population in 2006:* 10
Provincial Electoral District(s): Algoma-Manitoulin
Federal Electoral District(s): Algoma-Manitoulin-Kapuskasing
Next Election: Nov. 2010 (4 year terms)
David Haight, Reeve
Austin Clipperton, Clerk-Treasurer

Coleman
937907 Marsh Bay Rd.
Coleman, ON P0J 1C0
705-679-8833 Fax: 705-679-8300
toc@ontera.net
www.colemantownship.ca
Municipal Type: Township
Incorporated: 1906; *Area:* 177.6 sq km
County or District: Timiskaming District; *Population in 2006:* 431
Provincial Electoral District(s): Timiskaming-Cochrane
Federal Electoral District(s): Nipissing-Timiskaming
Next Election: Nov. 2010 (4 year terms)
Colleen Belanger, Mayor
Claire Bigelow, Clerk-Treasurer

Conmee
19 Holland Rd. West, RR#1
Kakabeka Falls, ON P0T 1W0
807-475-5229 Fax: 807-475-4793
conmee@tbaytel.net
www.conmee.com
Municipal Type: Township
Area: 167.53 sq km
County or District: Thunder Bay District; *Population in 2006:* 740
Provincial Electoral District(s): Thunder Bay-Atikokan
Federal Electoral District(s): Thunder Bay-Rainy River
Next Election: Nov. 2010 (4 year terms)
Kevin Holland, Reeve
Patricia Maxwell, Clerk-Treasurer

Cramahe
P.O. Box 357
1 Toronto St.
Colborne, ON K0K 1S0
905-355-2821 Fax: 905-355-3430 Toll Free Phone: 1-877-272-4263
www.visitcramahe.ca
Municipal Type: Township
Area: 201.56 sq km
County or District: Northumberland; *Population in 2006:* 5,950
Provincial Electoral District(s): Northumberland-Quinte West
Federal Electoral District(s): Northumberland-Quinte West
Next Election: Nov. 2010 (4 year terms)
Marc Coombs, Mayor
marc.coombs@airnet.ca
Christie Alexander, Chief Administrative Officer & Clerk

Dawn-Euphemia
4591 Lambton Line, RR#4
Dresden, ON N0P 1M0
519-692-5148 Fax: 519-692-5511
admin@dawneuphemia.on.ca
Municipal Type: Township
Area: 445.05 sq km
County or District: Lambton; *Population in 2006:* 2,190
Provincial Electoral District(s): Lambton-Kent-Middlesex
Federal Electoral District(s): Lambton-Kent-Middlesex
Next Election: Nov. 2010 (4 year terms)
William E. Bilton, Mayor
Michael Schnare, Administrator-Clerk

Dawson
P.O. Box 427
211 Fourth St.
Rainy River, ON P0W 1L0
807-852-3529 Fax: 807-852-3529
Municipal Type: Township
Area: 338.35 sq km
County or District: Rainy River District; *Population in 2006:* 620
Provincial Electoral District(s): Kenora-Rainy River
Federal Electoral District(s): Thunder Bay-Rainy River
Next Election: Nov. 2010 (4 year terms)
Eltjo Wiersema, Reeve
Patrick W. Giles, Clerk-Treasurer
gilesp@tbaytel.net

Deep River
P.O. Box 400
100 Deep River Rd.
Deep River, ON K0J 1P0
613-584-2000 Fax: 613-584-3237
clachance@deepriver.ca (Administrative Assistant)
www.deepriver.ca
Municipal Type: Town
Area: 50.84 sq km
County or District: Renfrew; *Population in 2006:* 4,216
Provincial Electoral District(s): Renfrew-Nipissing-Pembroke
Federal Electoral District(s): Renfrew-Nipissing-Pembroke
Next Election: Nov. 2010 (4 year terms)
Dave Thompson, Mayor
Gene Kiviaho, Chief Administrative Officer & Clerk
gkiviaho@deepriver.ca

Deseronto
P.O. Box 310
331 Main St.
Deseronto, ON K0K 1X0
613-396-2440 Fax: 613-396-3141 E-mail, Economic Dev.: dvalentyne@deseronto.ca
deseronto@on.aibn.com; aconger@deseronto.ca (Parks & Rec.)
www.deseronto.ca

Municipal Type: Town
Incorporated: 1889; *Area:* 2.52 sq km
County or District: Hastings; *Population in 2006:* 1,824
Provincial Electoral District(s): Prince Edward-Hastings
Federal Electoral District(s): Prince Edward-Hastings
Next Election: Nov. 2010 (4 year terms)
Norm Clark, Mayor
Bryan Brooks, Clerk-Treasurer
bbrooks@deseronto.ca

Dorion
170 Dorion Loop Rd., RR#1
Dorion, ON P0T 1K0
807-857-2289 Fax: 807-857-2203
office@doriontownship.ca
www.doriontownship.ca
Municipal Type: Township
Area: 212.07 sq km
County or District: Thunder Bay District; *Population in 2006:* 379
Provincial Electoral District(s): Thunder Bay-Superior North
Federal Electoral District(s): Thunder Bay-Superior North
Next Election: Nov. 2010 (4 year terms)
Ed Chambers, Reeve
807-627-0357
Helena Tamminen, Clerk-Treasurer
helena@doriontownship.ca

Douro-Dummer
P.O. Box 92
894 South St.
Warsaw, ON K0L 3A0
705-652-8392 Fax: 705-652-5044 Toll Free Phone: 1-800-899-8785
info@dourodummer.on.ca
www.dourodummer.on.ca
Municipal Type: Township
Area: 458.36 sq km
County or District: Peterborough; *Population in 2006:* 6,954
Provincial Electoral District(s): Peterborough
Federal Electoral District(s): Peterborough
Next Election: Nov. 2010 (4 year terms)
J. Murray Jones, Reeve
705-652-6325, Fax: 705-652-6325
jjones@dourodummer.on.ca
Linda Moher, Clerk & Coordinator, Planning
lindamo@dourodummer.on.ca

Drummond-North Elmsley
310 Port Elmsley Rd., RR#5
Perth, ON K7H 3L7
613-267-6500 Fax: 613-267-2083
admin@drummondnorthelmsley.com
www.drummondnorthelmsley.com
Municipal Type: Township
Incorporated: 1998; *Area:* 364.78 sq km
County or District: Lanark; *Population in 2006:* 7,118
Provincial Electoral District(s): Lanark-Frontenac-Lennox & Addington
Federal Electoral District(s): Lanark-Frontenac-Lennox & Addington
Next Election: Nov. 2010 (4 year terms)
Note: Amalgamation of the Townships of Drummond and North Elmsley.
Aubrey Churchill, Reeve
613-264-8404
Paul Snider, Clerk-Treasurer
psnider@drummondnorthelmsley.com

Dryden
30 Van Horne Ave.
Dryden, ON P8N 2A7
807-223-2225 Fax: 807-223-3999 Alternative Phone: 807-223-1126
generalinquiries@dryden.ca
www.dryden.ca
Municipal Type: Town
Area: 65.2 sq km
County or District: Kenora; *Population in 2006:* 8,195
Provincial Electoral District(s): Kenora-Rainy River
Federal Electoral District(s): Kenora
Next Election: Nov. 2010 (4 year terms)
Anne Krassilowsky, Mayor
807-223-6119
mayor@dryden.ca
Colleen Brosseau, City Clerk
807-223-1127
cbrosseau@dryden.ca

Dubreuilville
P.O. Box 367
23 Pine St.
Dubreuilville, ON P0S 1B0
705-884-2340 Fax: 705-884-2626
township@dubreuilville.ca
www.dubreuilville.ca
Municipal Type: Township
Incorporated: 1978; *Area:* 89.57 sq km
County or District: Algoma District; *Population in 2006:* 773
Provincial Electoral District(s): Algoma-Manitoulin
Federal Electoral District(s): Algoma-Manitoulin-Kapuskasing
Next Election: Nov. 2010 (4 year terms)
Louise Perrier, Mayor
Monique Ouellet, Chief Administrative Officer & Clerk
mouellet@dubreuilville.ca

Dutton-Dunwich
P.O. Box 329
199 Currie Rd.
Dutton, ON N0L 1J0
519-762-2204 Fax: 519-762-2278
htuffin@duttondunwich.on.ca
www.duttondunwich.on.ca
Municipal Type: Municipality
Area: 294.63 sq km
County or District: Elgin; *Population in 2006:* 3,821
Provincial Electoral District(s): Elgin-Middlesex-London
Federal Electoral District(s): Elgin-Middlesex-London
Next Election: Nov. 2010 (4 year terms)
Cameron McWilliam, Mayor
Ken Loveland, Administrator & Clerk-Treasurer

Dysart et al
P.O. Box 389
135 Maple Ave.
Haliburton, ON K0M 1S0
705-457-1740 Fax: 705-457-1964
www.dysartetal.ca
Municipal Type: Township
Incorporated: Jan. 7, 1867; *Area:* 1,474.07 sq km
County or District: Haliburton; *Population in 2006:* 5,526
Provincial Electoral District(s): Haliburton-Kawartha Lakes-Brock
Federal Electoral District(s): Haliburton-Kawartha Lakes-Brock
Next Election: Nov. 2010 (4 year terms)
Murray Fearrey, Reeve
Tammy McKelvey, Chief Administrative Officer & Clerk

Ear Falls
P.O. Box 309
1 Shelski Lane
Ear Falls, ON P0V 1T0
807-222-3624 Fax: 807-222-2384 E-mail, Public Services & Ops: pdyck@ear-falls.com
eftownship@ear-falls.com
www.ear-falls.com
Municipal Type: Township
Area: 330.99 sq km
County or District: Kenora District; *Population in 2006:* 1,153
Provincial Electoral District(s): Kenora-Rainy River
Federal Electoral District(s): Kenora
Next Election: Nov. 2010 (4 year terms)
Kevin Kahoot, Mayor
807-222-2408
Kimberly Ballance, Clerk-Treasurer & Administrator
807-222-3624
kballance@ear-falls.com

East Ferris
P.O. Box 85
390 Hwy. 94
Corbeil, ON P0H 1K0
705-752-2740 Fax: 705-752-2452
www.eastferris.ca
Municipal Type: Township
Area: 149.76 sq km
County or District: Nipissing District; *Population in 2006:* 4,200
Provincial Electoral District(s): Nipissing
Federal Electoral District(s): Nipissing-Timiskaming
Next Election: Nov. 2010 (4 year terms)
William Vrebosch, Mayor
John B. Fior, Clerk

East Garafraxa
374028 6th Line, RR#3
Orton, ON L0N 1N0
519-928-5298 Fax: 519-941-1802 Alternative Phone: 519-941-1007
township@amaranth-eastgary.ca
www.amaranth-eastgary.ca
Municipal Type: Township
Incorporated: Jan. 1, 1869; *Area:* 165.72 sq km
County or District: Dufferin; *Population in 2006:* 2,389
Provincial Electoral District(s): Dufferin-Caledon
Federal Electoral District(s): Dufferin-Caledon
Next Election: Nov. 2010 (4 year terms)
Allen Taylor, Mayor
519-941-4047
Susan M. Stone, AMCT, Chief Administrative Officer & Clerk-Treasurer
suestone@amaranth-eastgary.ca

East Hawkesbury
P.O. Box 340
St Eugene, ON K0B 1P0
613-674-2170 Fax: 613-674-2989 Toll Free Phone: 1.888.500.5749
webmaster@easthawkesbury.ca
www.easthawkesbury.ca
Municipal Type: Township
Incorporated: Jan. 1, 1850; *Area:* 235.09 sq km
County or District: Prescott & Russell; *Population in 2006:* 3,368
Provincial Electoral District(s): Glengarry-Prescott-Russell
Federal Electoral District(s): Glengarry-Prescott-Russell
Next Election: Nov. 2010 (4 year terms)
Robert Kirby, Mayor
613-632-4841, Fax: 613-632-4841
Linda Rozon, Chief Administrative Officer & Clerk-Treasurer
lrozon@easthawkesbury.ca

East Luther Grand Valley
P.O. Box 249
5 Main St. North
Grand Valley, ON L0N 1G0
519-928-5652 Fax: 519-928-2275
mail@eastluthergrandvalley.ca
www.eastluthergrandvalley.ca
Municipal Type: Township
Incorporated: Dec. 27, 1880; *Area:* 158.2 sq km
County or District: Dufferin; *Population in 2006:* 2,844
Provincial Electoral District(s): Dufferin-Caledon
Federal Electoral District(s): Dufferin-Caledon
Next Election: Nov. 2010 (4 year terms)
Note: Amalgamation of the Township of East Luther & the Village of Grand Valley on Jan. 1, 1995.
John K. Oosterhof, Mayor
519-928-3117
joosterhof@eastluthergrandvalley.ca
Jane M. Wilson, Chief Administrative Officer & Clerk-Treasurer
jwilson@eastluthergrandvalley.ca

East Zorra-Tavistock
P.O. Box 100
90 Loveys St.
Hickson, ON N0J 1L0
519-462-2697 Fax: 519-462-2961
ezt@twp.ezt.on.ca
www.twp.ezt.on.ca
Municipal Type: Township
Area: 247.42 sq km
County or District: Oxford; *Population in 2006:* 7,350
Provincial Electoral District(s): Oxford
Federal Electoral District(s): Oxford
Next Election: Nov. 2010 (4 year terms)
Don McKay, Mayor
519-532-2500
dmckay@twp.ezt.on.ca
Jeff Carswell, Chief Administrative Officer
jcarswell@twp.ezt.on.ca

Edwardsburgh/Cardinal
P.O. Box 129
18 Centre St.
Spencerville, ON K0E 1X0
613-658-3055 Fax: 613-658-3445 Toll Free Phone: 1-866-848-9099
mail@twpec.ca; rtrivett@twpec.ca (Administration & Treasury)
www.twpec.ca
Municipal Type: Township
Area: 311.83 sq km
County or District: Leeds & Grenville; *Population in 2006:* 6,689
Provincial Electoral District(s): Leeds-Grenville
Federal Electoral District(s): Leeds-Grenville
Next Election: Nov. 2010 (4 year terms)
Bill Sloane, Mayor
613-657-3102
mayor@twpec.ca
Debra McKinstry, Clerk & Administrator, Planning
dmckinstry@twpec.ca

Elizabethtown-Kitley
6544 New Dublin Rd., RR#2
Addison, ON K0E 1A0
613-345-7480 Fax: 613-345-7235 Toll Free Phone: 1-800-492-3175
mail@elizabethtown-kitley.on.ca
www.elizabethtown-kitley.on.ca
Municipal Type: Township
Area: 554.24 sq km
County or District: Leeds & Grenville; *Population in 2006:* 10,201
Provincial Electoral District(s): Leeds-Grenville
Federal Electoral District(s): Leeds-Grenville
Next Election: Nov. 2010 (4 year terms)
Jim Pickard, Mayor
613-342-5721
jimpickard@ripnet.com
John Johnston, Councillor
613-342-8952
Jim Miller, Councillor
613-924-9542
Eleanor Renaud, Councillor
613-275-2091
Earl F. Brayton, Councillor
613-345-2650
Susan Prettejohn, Councillor
613-498-2842
Herb Scott, Councillor
613-924-2133
Yvonne L. Robert, Administrator-Clerk, Administration
Melanie Kirkby, Director, Finance & Treasurer, Administration
Barbara Kalivas, Director, Planning & Development, Administration
Dale Kulp, Director, Public Works, Administration
Jim Donovan, Fire Chief, Administration
Ray Scissons, Chief Building Official, Administration

Emo
P.O. Box 520
39 Roy St.
Emo, ON P0W 1E0
807-482-2378 Fax: 807-482-2741
township@emo.ca
www.emo.ca
Municipal Type: Township
Incorporated: 1899; *Area:* 203.54 sq km
County or District: Rainy River District; *Population in 2006:* 1,305
Provincial Electoral District(s): Kenora-Rainy River
Federal Electoral District(s): Thunder Bay-Rainy River
Next Election: Nov. 2010 (4 year terms)
Vince Sheppard, Reeve
Brenda J. Cooke, Chief Administrative Officer & Clerk-Treasurer

Englehart
P.O. Box 399
61 Fifth Ave.
Englehart, ON P0J 1H0

705-544-2244 Fax: 705-544-8737
englehrt@ntl.sympatico.ca
www.englehart.ca
Municipal Type: Town
Incorporated: 1908; *Area:* 3.04 sq km
County or District: Timiskaming District; *Population in 2006:* 1,494
Provincial Electoral District(s): Timiskaming-Cochrane
Federal Electoral District(s): Timmins-James Bay
Next Election: Nov. 2010 (4 year terms)
Nina Wallace, Mayor
Jana VanOosten, Clerk

Enniskillen
4465 Rokeby Line, RR#1
Petrolia, ON N0N 1R0
519-882-2490 Fax: 519-882-3335
Municipal Type: Township
Area: 338.18 sq km
County or District: Lambton; *Population in 2006:* 3,122
Provincial Electoral District(s): Sarnia-Lambton
Federal Electoral District(s): Sarnia-Lambton
Next Election: Nov. 2010 (4 year terms)
Jim Burns, Mayor
Duncan McTavish, Administrator-Clerk

Espanola
#2, 100 Tudhope St.
Espanola, ON P5E 1S6
705-869-1540 Fax: 705-869-0083 E-mail, Public Works:
jyusko@town.espanola.on.ca
town@town.espanola.on.ca
www.town.espanola.on.ca
Municipal Type: Town
Incorporated: March 1, 1958; *Area:* 82.37 sq km
County or District: Sudbury District; *Population in 2006:* 5,314
Provincial Electoral District(s): Algoma-Manitoulin
Federal Electoral District(s): Algoma-Manitoulin-Kapuskasing
Next Election: Nov. 2010 (4 year terms)
Mike Lehoux, Mayor
Joel Mackenzie, Clerk-Treasurer & Administrator
jmackenzie@town.espanola.on.ca

Essa
5786 County Rd. 21
Utopia, ON L0M 1T0
705-424-9770 Fax: 705-424-2367 TTY: 705-424-5302; Canine Control: 1-888-624-6455
info@essatownship.on.ca
www.essatownship.on.ca
Municipal Type: Township
Incorporated: 1850; *Area:* 279.57 sq km
County or District: Simcoe; *Population in 2006:* 16,901
Provincial Electoral District(s): Simcoe-Grey
Federal Electoral District(s): Simcoe-Grey
Next Election: Nov. 2010 (4 year terms)
David Guergis, Mayor
705-424-0698
Terry Dowdall, Deputy Mayor & Councillor
705-423-1154
Sandie Macdonald, Councillor
705-424-6844
Rick Newlove, Councillor
705-458-1337
Ron Henderson, Councillor
705-424-9752
Mike Galloway, CMO, Clerk, Administration
mgalloway@essatownship.on.ca
Greg Murphy, CMO, Chief Administrative Officer & Manager, Public Wor, Administration
gmurphy@essatownship.on.ca
Julie Barrett, Treasurer & Deputy-Clerk, Administration
jbarrett@essatownship.on.ca
Colleen Healey, Manager, Planning & Development, Administration
chealey@essatownship.on.ca
Paul Macdonald, Fire Chief, Administration
fire@essatownship.on.ca
Heather Rutherford, Chief Building Official, Administration
hrutherford@essatownship.on.ca

Evanturel
P.O. Box 209
245453 Hwy. 659
Englehart, ON P0J 1H0
705-544-8200 Fax: 705-544-8206 E-mail, Building:
cbo@ntl.sympatico.ca
evantureladmin@parolink.net
www.evanturel.com
Municipal Type: Township
Incorporated: Jan. 1, 1904; *Area:* 88.99 sq km
County or District: Timiskaming District; *Population in 2006:* 473
Provincial Electoral District(s): Timiskaming-Cochrane
Federal Electoral District(s): Timmins-James Bay
Next Election: Nov. 2010 (4 year terms)
Jack Briggs, Reeve
Amy Vickery-Menard, Clerk-Treasurer
evanturelclerk@parolink.net

Faraday
P.O. Box 929
29860 Hwy. 28 South
Bancroft, ON K0L 1C0
613-332-3638 Fax: 613-332-3006
faraday@bellnet.ca
www.faraday.ca
Municipal Type: Township
Area: 215.23 sq km
County or District: Hastings; *Population in 2006:* 1,578
Provincial Electoral District(s): Prince Edward-Hastings
Federal Electoral District(s): Prince Edward-Hastings
Next Election: Nov. 2010 (4 year terms)
Carl A. Tinney, Reeve
613-332-2050
Brenda Vader, Clerk-Treasurer & Tax Collector

Fauquier-Strickland
P.O. Box 40
25 Grzela Rd.
Fauquier, ON P0L 1G0
705-339-2521 Fax: 705-339-2421
cdefauquier@vianet.ca
fauquierstrickland.com/en/index.asp
Municipal Type: Township
Area: 1,013.54 sq km
County or District: Cochrane District; *Population in 2006:* 568
Provincial Electoral District(s): Timmins-James Bay
Federal Electoral District(s): Algoma-Manitoulin-Kapuskasing
Next Election: Nov. 2010 (4 year terms)
Madeleine Tremblay, Reeve
Robert Courchesne, Administrator & Clerk-Treasurer

Fort Frances
320 Portage Ave.
Fort Frances, ON P9A 3P9
807-274-5323 Fax: 807-274-8479
town@fort-frances.com
www.fort-frances.com
Municipal Type: Town
Incorporated: 1903; *Area:* 26.85 sq km
County or District: Rainy River District; *Population in 2006:* 8,103
Provincial Electoral District(s): Kenora-Rainy River
Federal Electoral District(s): Thunder Bay-Rainy River
Next Election: Nov. 2010 (4 year terms)
Roy Avis, Mayor
ravis@fort-frances.com
Mark McCaig, Administrator
mmccaig@fort-frances.com

French River, Municipality of / Municipalité de la Rivière des Français
P.O. Box 156
17 Dollard St.
Noëlville, ON P0M 2N0
705-898-2294 Fax: 705-898-2181
mpellerin@frenchriver.ca
www.frenchriver.ca
Municipal Type: Town
Incorporated: Jan. 1, 1999; *Area:* 734.26 sq km
County or District: Sudbury District; *Population in 2006:* 2,659
Provincial Electoral District(s): Timiskaming-Cochrane; Nickle Belt
Federal Electoral District(s): Nickel Belt
Next Election: Nov. 2010 (4 year terms)
Claude Bouffard, Mayor
Michel V. Monette, CMA, Chief Administrative Officer & Clerk
mmonette@frenchriver.ca

Front of Yonge
P.O. Box 130
1514 County Rd. 2
Mallorytown, ON K0E 1R0
613-923-2251 Fax: 613-923-2421 Phone, Public Works: 613-923-5074
admin@frontofyonge.com
www.frontofyonge.com
Municipal Type: Township
Area: 127.85 sq km
County or District: Leeds & Grenville; *Population in 2006:* 2,803
Provincial Electoral District(s): Leeds-Grenville
Federal Electoral District(s): Leeds-Grenville
Next Election: Nov. 2010 (4 year terms)
Roger Haley, Reeve
Elaine A. Covey, Clerk
ecovey@frontofyonge.com

Frontenac Islands
P.O. Box 130
Rd. 96
Wolfe Island, ON K0H 2Y0
613-385-2216 Fax: 613-385-1032
www.municipality.frontenacislands.on.ca
Municipal Type: Township
Incorporated: Jan. 1, 1998; *Area:* 174.99 sq km
County or District: Frontenac; *Population in 2006:* 1,862
Provincial Electoral District(s): Kingston & the Islands
Federal Electoral District(s): Kingston & the Islands
Next Election: Nov. 2010 (4 year terms)
Note: Amalgamation of Howe Island & Wolfe Island.
Dennis Doyle, Mayor
613-385-1934
Terry J. O'Shea, AMCT, Chief Administrative Officer & Clerk
tjoshea@kos.net

Galway-Cavendish-Harvey
P.O. Box 820
701 County Rd. 36, RR#3
Bobcaygeon, ON K0M 1A0
705-738-3800 Fax: 705-738-3801 Toll Free Phone: 1-800-374-4009
lholtz@galwaycavendishharvey.ca
www.galwaycavendishharvey.ca
Municipal Type: Township
Area: 848.26 sq km
County or District: Peterborough; *Population in 2006:* 5,284
Provincial Electoral District(s): Haliburton-Kawartha Lakes-Brock
Federal Electoral District(s): Haliburton-Kawartha Lakes-Brock
Next Election: Nov. 2010 (4 year terms)
Janet Clarkson, Reeve
705-657-8569
Natalie Garnett, Clerk
ngarnett@galwaycavendishharvey.ca

Gananoque
Town Hall
P.O. Box 100
30 King St. East
Gananoque, ON K7G 2T6
613-382-2149 Fax: 613-382-8587
information@townofgananoque.ca
www.townofgananoque.com
Municipal Type: Separated for Municipal Purposes Only
Area: 7.01 sq km
County or District: Leeds & Grenville; *Population in 2006:* 5,285
Provincial Electoral District(s): Leeds-Grenville
Federal Electoral District(s): Leeds-Grenville
Next Election: Nov. 2010 (4 year terms)
Erika Demchuk, Mayor
mayor@townofgananoque.ca
Mike Larocque, CHRP, CMO, Chief Administrative Officer
mlarocque@townofgananoque.ca

Gauthier
P.O. Box 65
92 McPherson St.
Dobie, ON P0K 1B0
705-568-8951 Fax: 705-568-8951
Municipal Type: Township
Area: 88.36 sq km
County or District: Timiskaming District; *Population in 2006:* 133
Provincial Electoral District(s): Timiskaming-Cochrane
Federal Electoral District(s): Timmins-James Bay
Next Election: Nov. 2010 (4 year terms)
Marilyn Keith, Reeve
Dianne Quinn, Clerk-Treasurer
quinner@ntl.sympatico.ca

Georgian Bay
99 Lone Pine Rd.
Port Severn, ON L0K 1S0
705-538-2337 Fax: 705-538-1850 Toll Free Phone: 1-800-567-0187
clerks@township.georgianbay.on.ca
www.township.georgianbay.on.ca
Municipal Type: Township
Area: 535.48 sq km
County or District: Muskoka District Municipality; *Population in 2006:* 2,340
Provincial Electoral District(s): Parry Sound-Muskoka
Federal Electoral District(s): Parry Sound-Muskoka
Next Election: Nov. 2010 (4 year terms)
Larry Braid, Mayor
Susan Boonstra, Clerk
sboonstra@township.georgianbay.on.ca

Georgian Bluffs
177964 Grey Rd. 18, RR#3
Owen Sound, ON N4K 5N5
519-376-2729 Fax: 519-372-1620
office@georgianbluffs.on.ca
www.georgianbluffs.on.ca
Municipal Type: Township
Incorporated: Jan. 1, 2001; *Area:* 603.58 sq km
County or District: Grey; *Population in 2006:* 10,506
Provincial Electoral District(s): Bruce-Grey-Owen Sound
Federal Electoral District(s): Bruce-Grey-Owen Sound
Next Election: Nov. 2010 (4 year terms)
Note: Amalgamation of the Townships of Derby, Keppel & Sarawak.
Alan Barfoot, Mayor
Dwight Burley, Deputy Mayor & Councillor
Carol Barfoot, Councillor
Judy Gay, Councillor
Robert Lennox, Councillor
Ryan Thompson, Councillor
Tom Wiley, Councillor
Bruce Hoffman, Clerk, Administration
Bill White, Chief Administrative Officer, Administration
Holly Morrison, Treasurer, Administration
Rick Winters, Manager, Operations, Administration
Bill Klingenberg, Chief Building Official, Administration
Bev Nicolson, Planner, Administration
Martin Timmerman, Superintendent, Roads, Administration

Gillies
1092 Hwy. 595, RR#1
South Gillies, ON P0T 1W0
807-475-3185 Fax: 807-473-0767 E-mail, Building:
cmaki@xplornet.com
gillies@tbaytel.net
www.gilliestownship.ca
Municipal Type: Township
Area: 92.67 sq km
County or District: Thunder Bay District; *Population in 2006:* 544
Provincial Electoral District(s): Thunder Bay-Atikokan
Federal Electoral District(s): Thunder Bay-Rainy River
Next Election: Nov. 2010 (4 year terms)
Rick Kieri, Reeve
Karen Caren, Clerk-Treasurer
gillies@tbaytel.net

Goderich
Municipal Office, Town Hall
57 West St.
Goderich, ON N7A 2K5
519-524-8344 Fax: 519-524-7209 Phone, Public Works:
519-524-7222
townhall@goderich.ca
www.goderich.ca
Municipal Type: Town
Area: 7.91 sq km
County or District: Huron; *Population in 2006:* 7,563
Provincial Electoral District(s): Huron-Bruce
Federal Electoral District(s): Huron-Bruce
Next Election: Nov. 2010 (4 year terms)
Delbert (Deb) Shewfelt, Mayor
519-524-9581
Larry J. McCabe, Clerk-Administrator
lmccabe@goderich.ca

Gordon / Barrie Island
P.O. Box 680
29 Noble Side Rd.
Gore Bay, ON P0P 1H0
705-282-2702 Fax: 705-282-2722
gordon_admin@xplornet.com
gordontownship.manitoulin-link.com
Municipal Type: Municipality
Incorporated: Jan. 1, 2009;
County or District: Manitoulin District; *Population in 2006:* 459
Provincial Electoral District(s): Algoma-Manitoulin
Federal Electoral District(s): Algoma-Manitoulin-Kapuskasing
Next Election: Nov. 2010 (4 year terms)
Note: Amalgamation of the former Township of Gordon & Allan West & the Township of Barrie Island.
Carrie Lewis, Clerk-Treasurer

Gore Bay
P.O. Box 590
15 Water St.
Gore Bay, ON P0P 1H0
705-282-2420 Fax: 705-282-3076 E-mail, Treasury:
gbtreasurer@gorebaycable.com
tgorebay@gorebaycable.com
www.gorebay.ca
Municipal Type: Town
Incorporated: 1890; *Area:* 5.27 sq km
County or District: Manitoulin District; *Population in 2006:* 924
Provincial Electoral District(s): Algoma-Manitoulin
Federal Electoral District(s): Algoma-Manitoulin-Kapuskasing
Next Election: Nov. 2010 (4 year terms)
Ron Lane, Mayor
Annette Clarke, Clerk

Greater Madawaska
P.O. Box 180
1101 Francis St.
Calabogie, ON K0J 1H0
613-752-2222 Fax: 613-752-2617
greatermadawaska@on.aibn.com
www.townshipofgreatermadawaska.com
Municipal Type: Township
Incorporated: Jan. 1, 2001; *Area:* 1,011.67 sq km
County or District: Renfrew; *Population in 2006:* 2,751
Provincial Electoral District(s): Renfrew-Nipissing-Pembroke
Federal Electoral District(s): Renfrew-Nipissing-Pembroke
Next Election: Nov. 2010 (4 year terms)
Note: Amalgamation of Bagot, Blythfield & Brougham Township & Griffith & Matawatchan Township.
Peter Emon, Reeve
613-752-2922
peteremon@somuchmore.ca
Angela Yolkowskie, Chief Administrative Officer
ayolkowskie@bellnet.ca

Greenstone, Municipality of
P.O. Box 70
301 East St.
Geraldton, ON P0T 1M0
807-854-1100 Fax: 807-854-1947
megacity@astrocom-on.com
www.greenstone.ca
Municipal Type: Town
Area: 2,780.99 sq km
County or District: Thunder Bay; *Population in 2006:* 4,906
Provincial Electoral District(s): Thunder Bay-Superior North
Federal Electoral District(s): Thunder Bay-Superior North
Next Election: Nov. 2010 (4 year terms)
Renald Beaulieu, Mayor
Deborah B. Stevens, Clerk
stevens@astrocom-on.com

Grey Highlands, Municipality of
P.O. Box 409
#1, 206 Toronto St. South
Markdale, ON N0C 1H0
519-986-2811 Fax: 519-986-3643 Toll Free Phone: 1-888-342-4059
info@greyhighlands.ca
www.greyhighlands.ca
Municipal Type: Township
Incorporated: Jan. 1, 2001; *Area:* 880.6 sq km
County or District: Grey; *Population in 2006:* 9,480
Provincial Electoral District(s): Bruce-Grey-Owen Sound
Federal Electoral District(s): Bruce-Grey-Owen Sound
Next Election: Nov. 2010 (4 year terms)
Note: Amalgamation of Flesherton, Artemesia, Euphrasia, Markdale & Osprey.
Wayne Fitzgerald, Mayor
519-922-2078
Debbie Robertson, Clerk
519-986-1216
robertsond@greyhighlands.ca

Guelph-Eramosa
P.O. Box 700
8348 Wellington Rd. 124
Rockwood, ON N0B 2K0
519-856-9951 Fax: 519-856-2240 Toll Free Phone: 1-800-267-1465
general@get.on.ca
www.get.on.ca
Municipal Type: Township
Incorporated: Jan. 1, 1999; *Area:* 291.73 sq km
County or District: Wellington; *Population in 2006:* 12,066
Provincial Electoral District(s): Wellington-Halton Hills
Federal Electoral District(s): Wellington-Halton Hills
Next Election: Nov. 2010 (4 year terms)
Note: Amalgamation of the Townships of Guelph, Eramosa, Pilkington & Nichol.
Chris White, Mayor
whitecj@sympatico.ca
Meaghen Reid, Clerk
mreid@get.on.ca
Shawn Armstrong, Fire Chief
519-824-6590
Brad Roelfson, Manager, Property & Leisure Services
broelofson@get.on.ca
Ken Gagnon, Manager, Public Works
kgagnon@get.on.ca
Mark Thorpe, Officer, Bylaw Enforcement
mthorpe@get.on.ca
Mike Newark, Chief Building Official
mnewark@get.on.ca

Hamilton
P.O. Box 1060
8285 Majestic Hills Dr.
Cobourg, ON K9A 4W5
905-342-2810 Fax: 905-342-2818
info@hamiltontownship.ca
www.hamiltontownship.ca
Municipal Type: Township
Area: 256.11 sq km
County or District: Northumberland; *Population in 2006:* 10,972
Provincial Electoral District(s): Northumberland-Quinte West
Federal Electoral District(s): Northumberland-Quinte West
Next Election: Nov. 2010 (4 year terms)
Mark Lovshin, Deputy Mayor & Councillor
mlovshin@cogeco.ca
Isobel Hie, Mayor
oldhomestead1@gmail.com
Gary Woods, Councillor
woodsgj@gmail.com
Twila Marston, Councillor
tmarston@opseu.org
Pat McCourt, Councillor
mccourt@eagle.ca
Betty McIntosh, Chief Administrative Officer, Clerk, & Treasurer, Administration
bmcintosh@hamiltontownship.ca
Doug Murray, Director, Public Works, Administration
dmurray@hamiltontownship.ca
Ken Clapperton, Fire Chief, Baltimore, Administration
baltimorefire@hamiltontownship.ca
Reg Jackson, Fire Chief, Bewdley, Administration
bewdleyfire@hamiltontownship.ca
Pete Staples, Fire Chief, Harwood, Administration
harwoodfire@hamiltontownship.ca
Scott Jibb, Chief Building Official, Administration
sjibb@hamiltontownship.ca
Sandra Stothart, Coordinator, Planning, Administration
sstothart@hamiltontownship.ca
Doug Thompson, Manager, Water Operations, Administration
dthompson@hamiltontownship.ca

Hanover
341 - 10th St.
Hanover, ON N4N 1P5
519-364-2780 Fax: 519-364-6456
civic@hanover.ca
www.hanover.ca
Municipal Type: Town
Incorporated: Jan. 1, 2001; *Area:* 9.81 sq km
County or District: Grey; *Population in 2006:* 7,147
Provincial Electoral District(s): Bruce-Grey-Owen Sound
Federal Electoral District(s): Bruce-Grey-Owen Sound
Next Election: Nov. 2010 (4 year terms)
Kathi Maskell, Mayor
kmaskell@hanover.ca
Mike Dunlop, Chief Administrative Officer & Clerk
mdunlop@hanover.ca

Harley
903303 Hanbury Rd., RR#2
New Liskeard, ON P0J 1P0
705-647-5439 Fax: 705-647-6373
harleytwp@parolink.net
www.harley.ca
Municipal Type: Township
Incorporated: 1904; *Area:* 91.73 sq km
County or District: Timiskaming District; *Population in 2006:* 551
Provincial Electoral District(s): Timiskaming-Cochrane
Federal Electoral District(s): Timmins-James Bay
Next Election: Nov. 2010 (4 year terms)
Gerald Roy, Reeve
Michel Lachapelle, Clerk-Treasurer

Harris
Site 4-96, RR#3
New Liskeard, ON P0J 1P0
705-647-5094 Fax: 705-647-0041
harris@ntl.sympatico.ca
Municipal Type: Township
Area: 50.17 sq km
County or District: Timiskaming District; *Population in 2006:* 512
Provincial Electoral District(s): Timiskaming-Cochrane
Federal Electoral District(s): Nipissing-Timiskaming
Next Election: Nov. 2010 (4 year terms)
Martin Auger, Reeve
Kelly Sue Marshall, Clerk-Treasurer

Hastings Highlands
P.O. Box 130
33011 Hwy. 62 North
Maynooth, ON K0L 2S0
613-338-2811 Fax: 613-338-3292 Toll Free Phone: 1-877-338-2818
office@hastingshighlands.ca
www.hastingshighlands.ca
Municipal Type: Municipality
Area: 967.34 sq km
County or District: Hastings; *Population in 2006:* 4,033
Provincial Electoral District(s): Prince Edward-Hastings
Federal Electoral District(s): Prince Edward-Hastings
Next Election: Nov. 2010 (4 year terms)
Ronald J. Emond, Mayor
Craig Davidson, Chief Administrative Officer & Clerk-Treasurer
cdavidson@hastingshighlands.ca

Havelock-Belmont-Methuen
P.O. Box 10
1 Ottawa St. East
Havelock, ON K0L 1Z0
705-778-2308 Fax: 705-778-5248 Toll Free Phone: 1-877-767-2795
havbelmet@hbmtwp.ca
www.havelockbelmontmethuen.on.ca
Municipal Type: Township
Area: 526.02 sq km
County or District: Peterborough; *Population in 2006:* 4,637
Provincial Electoral District(s): Peterborough
Federal Electoral District(s): Peterborough
Next Election: Nov. 2010 (4 year terms)
Ronald Gerow, Reeve
705-778-2092
rgerow@hbmtwp.ca
Glenn Girven, Clerk
ggirven@hbmtwp.ca

Head, Clara & Maria
15 Township Hall Rd.
Stonecliffe, ON K0J 2K0
613-586-2526 Fax: 613-586-2596 Phone, Building Inspection:
613-586-1950
twpshcm@xplornet.com
www.townshipsofheadclaramaria.ca
Municipal Type: Township
Area: 727.96 sq km
County or District: Renfrew; *Population in 2006:* 228
Provincial Electoral District(s): Renfrew-Nipissing-Pembroke
Federal Electoral District(s): Renfrew-Nipissing-Pembroke
Next Election: Nov. 2010 (4 year terms)
Tammy Lea Stewart, Reeve
613-586-2750
Melinda Reith, Municipal Clerk

Hearst
Town Hall
P.O. Box 5000
925 Alexandra St.
Hearst, ON P0L 1N0
705-362-4341 Fax: 705-362-5902
townofhearst@hearst.ca
www.hearst.ca
Municipal Type: Town
Incorporated: 1922; *Area:* 98.67 sq km
County or District: Cochrane District; *Population in 2006:* 5,620
Provincial Electoral District(s): Timmins-James Bay
Federal Electoral District(s): Algoma-Manitoulin-Kapuskasing
Next Election: Nov. 2010 (4 year terms)
Roger Sigouin, Mayor
Claude J. Laflamme, Chief Administrative Officer & Clerk
705-372-2817

Highlands East, Municipality of
P.O. Box 295
County Rd. 648
Wilberforce, ON K0L 3C0
705-448-2981 Fax: 705-448-2532
highlands@highlandseast.ca
www.highlandseast.ca
Municipal Type: Township
Incorporated: Jan. 1, 2001; *Area:* 701.32 sq km
County or District: Haliburton; *Population in 2006:* 3,089
Provincial Electoral District(s): Haliburton-Kawartha Lakes-Brock
Federal Electoral District(s): Haliburton-Kawartha Lakes-Brock
Next Election: Nov. 2010 (4 year terms)

Note: Amalgamation of the Townships of Bicroft, Cardiff, Glamorgan & Monmouth.
Dave Burton, Reeve
705-448-9355
dburton@highlandseast.ca
Irene Cook, CMO, Clerk, Fax: 705-448-3211
icook@highlandseast.ca

Hilliard
P.O. Box 8
RR#3
Thornloe, ON P0J 1S0
705-563-2593 Fax: 705-563-8303
twphill@parolink.net
Municipal Type: Township
Area: 91.17 sq km
County or District: Timiskaming District; *Population in 2006:* 222
Provincial Electoral District(s): Timiskaming-Cochrane
Federal Electoral District(s): Timmins-James Bay
Next Election: Nov. 2010 (4 year terms)
Morgan Carson, Reeve
Janet Gore, Clerk-Treasurer

Hilton
P.O. Box 205
2983 Base Line
Hilton Beach, ON P0R 1G0
705-246-2472 Fax: 705-246-0132 Phone, Roads: 705-246-1781
admin@hiltontownship.ca; hiltontownship@xplornet.com
www.hiltontownship.ca
Municipal Type: Township
Incorporated: 1883; *Area:* 115.78 sq km
County or District: Algoma District; *Population in 2006:* 243
Provincial Electoral District(s): Algoma-Manitoulin
Federal Electoral District(s): Sault Ste Marie
Next Election: Nov. 2010 (4 year terms)
Rodney Wood, Reeve
Valerie Obarymskyj, Clerk-Treasurer
clerk@hiltontownship.ca

Hilton Beach
P.O. Box 25
Hilton Beach, ON P0R 1G0
705-246-2242 Fax: 705-246-2913
info@hiltonbeach.com
www.hiltonbeach.com
Municipal Type: Village
Area: 2.46 sq km
County or District: Algoma District; *Population in 2006:* 172
Provincial Electoral District(s): Algoma-Manitoulin
Federal Electoral District(s): Sault Ste Marie
Next Election: Nov. 2010 (4 year terms)
Wilfred Stevens, Mayor
Gloria Fischer, Clerk

Hornepayne
P.O. Box 370
68 Front St.
Hornepayne, ON P0M 1Z0
807-868-2020 Fax: 807-868-2787
www.hornepayne.com/township
Municipal Type: Township
Area: 204.52 sq km
County or District: Algoma District; *Population in 2006:* 1,209
Provincial Electoral District(s): Algoma-Manitoulin
Federal Electoral District(s): Algoma-Manitoulin-Kapuskasing
Next Election: Nov. 2010 (4 year terms)
Morley Forster, Mayor
Susan Smith, Township Clerk
smith.hpayne@xplornet.com

Horton
2253 Johnston Rd., RR#5
Renfrew, ON K7V 3Z8
613-432-6271 Fax: 613-432-7298
mjmhorton@storm.ca
www.hortontownship.ca
Municipal Type: Township
Area: 158.38 sq km
County or District: Renfrew; *Population in 2006:* 2,803
Provincial Electoral District(s): Renfrew-Nipissing-Pembroke
Federal Electoral District(s): Renfrew-Nipissing-Pembroke
Next Election: Nov. 2010 (4 year terms)
Robert A. Johnston, Reeve
Mackie J. McLaren, Chief Administrative Officer / Clerk

Howick
P.O. Box 89
44816 Hariston Rd.
Gorrie, ON N0G 1X0
519-335-3208 Fax: 519-335-6208
office@town.howick.on.ca
www.town.howick.on.ca
Municipal Type: Township
Area: 287.17 sq km
County or District: Huron; *Population in 2006:* 3,882
Provincial Electoral District(s): Huron-Bruce
Federal Electoral District(s): Huron-Bruce
Next Election: Nov. 2010 (4 year terms)
Amy Versteeg, Reeve
Ronna Lee Johnson, Clerk

Hudson
903303 Hanbury Rd., RR#2
New Liskeard, ON P0J 1P0
705-647-5439 Fax: 705-647-6373
harleytwp@parolink.net
www.hudson.ca
Municipal Type: Township
Area: 90.46 sq km
County or District: Timiskaming District; *Population in 2006:* 305
Provincial Electoral District(s): Timiskaming-Cochrane
Federal Electoral District(s): Nipissing-Timiskaming
Next Election: Nov. 2010 (4 year terms)
Larry Craig, Reeve
Michel Lachapelle, Clerk-Treasurer

Huron East, Municipality of
P.O. Box 610
72 Main St. South
Seaforth, ON N0K 1W0
519-527-0160 Fax: 519-527-2561 Toll Free Phone: 1-888-868-7513
jrmclachlan@huroneast.com
www.huroneast.com
Municipal Type: Town
Incorporated: Jan. 1, 2001; *Area:* 669.16 sq km
County or District: Huron; *Population in 2006:* 9,310
Provincial Electoral District(s): Huron-Bruce
Federal Electoral District(s): Huron-Bruce
Next Election: Nov. 2010 (4 year terms)
Note: Amalgamation of the Town of Seaforth, the Village of Brussels, & the Townships of Grey, McKillop and Tuckersmith.
Bernie MacLellan, Mayor
519-887-6289, Fax: 519-887-9500
mayor@huroneast.com
John R. McLachlan, Administrator-Clerk

Huron Shores
P.O. Box 460
7 Bridge St.
Iron Bridge, ON P0R 1H0
705-843-2033 Fax: 705-843-2035
email@huronshores.ca
www.huronshores.ca
Municipal Type: Municipality
Area: 455.33 sq km
County or District: Algoma District; *Population in 2006:* 1,696
Provincial Electoral District(s): Algoma-Manitoulin
Federal Electoral District(s): Algoma-Manitoulin-Kapuskasing
Next Election: Nov. 2010 (4 year terms)
Lionel Reeves, Mayor
Deborah Tonelli, Administrator-Clerk

Huron-Kinloss
P.O. Box 130
21 Queen St.
Ripley, ON N0G 2R0
519-395-3735 Fax: 519-395-4107
hurontwp@hurontel.on.ca
www.huronkinloss.com
Municipal Type: Township
Incorporated: 1999; *Area:* 440.59 sq km
County or District: Bruce; *Population in 2006:* 6,515
Provincial Electoral District(s): Huron-Bruce
Federal Electoral District(s): Huron-Bruce
Next Election: Nov. 2010 (4 year terms)
Note: Amalgamation of the Village of Lucknow & the Townships of Ripley-Huron & Kinloss.
Mitch Twolan, Mayor
519-395-0620
Sonya Watson, Clerk

Ignace
P.O. Box 248
34 Hwy. 17 West
Ignace, ON P0T 1T0
807-934-2202 Fax: 807-934-2864
administration@tbaytel.net
www.town.ignace.on.ca
Municipal Type: Township
Incorporated: 1908; *Area:* 72.66 sq km
County or District: Kenora District; *Population in 2006:* 1,431
Provincial Electoral District(s): Kenora-Rainy River
Federal Electoral District(s): Kenora
Next Election: Nov. 2010 (4 year terms)
Lee Kennard, Mayor
Wayne Hanchard, Administrator & Treasurer
admintreasurer@tbaytel.net

Iroquois Falls
P.O. Box 230
253 Main St.
Iroquois Falls, ON P0K 1G0
705-232-5700 Fax: 705-232-4241
www.iroquoisfalls.com
Municipal Type: Town
Area: 599.43 sq km
County or District: Cochrane District; *Population in 2006:* 4,729
Provincial Electoral District(s): Timiskaming-Cochrane
Federal Electoral District(s): Timmins-James Bay
Next Election: Nov. 2010 (4 year terms)
Gilles Forget, Mayor
mayor@iroquoisfalls.com
Michel S. Morrissette, Administrator-Clerk
morrissm@iroquoisfalls.com

James
P.O. Box 10
Third St.
Elk Lake, ON P0J 1G0
705-678-2237 Fax: 705-678-2495
elklake@ntl.sympatico.ca
www.elklake.ca
Municipal Type: Township
Incorporated: 1909; *Area:* 86.19 sq km
County or District: Timiskaming District; *Population in 2006:* 414
Provincial Electoral District(s): Timiskaming-Cochrane
Federal Electoral District(s): Timmins-James Bay
Next Election: Nov. 2010 (4 year terms)
Terry Fiset, Reeve
Myrna J. Hayes, Clerk-Treasurer

Jocelyn
RR#1
Richards Landing, ON P0R 1J0
705-246-2025 Fax: 705-246-3282
jocelynt@soonet.ca
Municipal Type: Township
Area: 131.37 sq km
County or District: Algoma District; *Population in 2006:* 277
Provincial Electoral District(s): Algoma-Manitoulin
Federal Electoral District(s): Sault Ste Marie
Next Election: Nov. 2010 (4 year terms)
Mark Henderson, Reeve
Janet Boucher, Clerk

Johnson
P.O. Box 160
1 Johnson Dr.
Desbarats, ON P0R 1E0
705-782-6601 Fax: 705-782-6780
johnsontwp@bellnet.ca
www.johnsontwp.ca
Municipal Type: Township
Area: 119.67 sq km
County or District: Algoma District; *Population in 2006:* 701
Provincial Electoral District(s): Algoma-Manitoulin
Federal Electoral District(s): Sault Ste Marie
Next Election: Nov. 2010 (4 year terms)
Ted Hicks, Mayor
Ruth Kelso, Clerk & Chief Administrative Officer

Joly
P.O. Box 519
871 Forest Lake Rd.
Sundridge, ON P0A 1Z0
705-384-5428 Fax: 705-384-0845
twpjoly@on.aibn.com
Municipal Type: Township
Area: 193.82 sq km
County or District: Parry Sound District; *Population in 2006:* 280
Provincial Electoral District(s): Parry Sound-Muskoka
Federal Electoral District(s): Parry Sound-Muskoka
Next Election: Nov. 2010 (4 year terms)
Mario Campese, Reeve
Gerry Whittington, Chief Administrative Officer & Clerk

Kapuskasing
Civic Centre
88 Riverside Dr.
Kapuskasing, ON P5N 1B3
705-335-2341 Fax: 705-337-1741
townkap@ntl.sympatico.ca
www.kapuskasing.ca
Municipal Type: Town
Incorporated: 1921; *Area:* 83.98 sq km
County or District: Cochrane District; *Population in 2006:* 8,509
Provincial Electoral District(s): Timmins-James Bay
Federal Electoral District(s): Algoma-Manitoulin-Kapuskasing
Next Election: Nov. 2010 (4 year terms)
Alan Spacek, Mayor
Barbara Major, Clerk & Officer, Economic Development

Kearney
P.O. Box 38
8 Main St.
Kearney, ON P0A 1M0
705-636-7752 Fax: 705-636-0527
kearney1@vianet.ca
www.townofkearney.com
Municipal Type: Town
Incorporated: 1908; *Area:* 529.5 sq km
County or District: Parry Sound District; *Population in 2006:* 798
Provincial Electoral District(s): Parry Sound-Muskoka
Federal Electoral District(s): Parry Sound-Muskoka
Next Election: Nov. 2010 (4 year terms)
Paul Tomlinson, Mayor
Yvonne Aubichon, Clerk Administrator
clerkadministrator@townofkearney.com

Kenora
Kenora District Services Board Admin Office
#1, 211 Princess St.
Dryden, ON P8N 3L5

Municipal Type: District
Area: 407,192.66 sq km
Population in 2006: 64,419
Rory McMillan, Chair, Kenora District Services Board of Directors
807-468-4383
rmcmillan@kenora.ca
Sten S. Lif, Chief Administrative Officer, Kenora District Serv
807-223-2100, Fax: 807-223-6500
kdsb@kdsb.on.ca; slif@kdsb.on.ca

Kerns
903303 Hanbury Rd., RR#2
New Liskeard, ON P0J 1P0
705-647-5439 Fax: 705-647-6373
harleytwp@parolink.net
www.kerns.ca
Municipal Type: Township
Incorporated: 1904; *Area:* 90.44 sq km
County or District: Timiskaming District; *Population in 2006:* 325
Provincial Electoral District(s): Timiskaming-Cochrane
Federal Electoral District(s): Timmins-James Bay
Next Election: Nov. 2010 (4 year terms)
Terry Phillips, Reeve
Michel Lachapelle, Clerk-Treasurer

Killaloe, Hagarty & Richards
P.O. Box 39
1 John St.
Killaloe, ON K0J 2A0
613-757-2300 Fax: 613-757-3634
khr@on.aibn.com
www.killaloe-hagarty-richards.ca
Municipal Type: Township
Incorporated: July 1, 2000; *Area:* 395.91 sq km
County or District: Renfrew; *Population in 2006:* 2,550
Provincial Electoral District(s): Renfrew-Nipissing-Pembroke
Federal Electoral District(s): Renfrew-Nipissing-Pembroke
Next Election: Nov. 2010 (4 year terms)
Note: Amalgamation of the Township of Hagarty & Richards & the former Village of Killaloe.
Janice Visneskie, Mayor
613-757-2470
Lorna Hudder, Chief Administrative Officer & Clerk-Treasurer

Killarney, Municipality of
32 Commissioner St.
Killarney, ON P0M 2A0
705-287-2424 Fax: 705-287-2660 Toll Free Phone: 1-888-597-2721
townkill@vianet.on.ca
www.municipality.killarney.on.ca
Municipal Type: Town
Incorporated: Jan. 1, 1999; *Area:* 1,513.58 sq km
County or District: Sudbury District; *Population in 2006:* 454
Provincial Electoral District(s): Algoma-Manitoulin
Federal Electoral District(s): Nickel Belt
Next Election: Nov. 2010 (4 year terms)
Morgan Pitfield, Mayor
Candy Beavais, Clerk-Treasurer

Kincardine
1475 Conc. 5, RR#5
Kincardine, ON N2Z 2X6
519-396-3468 Fax: 519-396-8288
ssmith@kincardine.net
www.kincardine.net
Municipal Type: Municipality
Area: 537.65 sq km
County or District: Bruce; *Population in 2006:* 11,173
Provincial Electoral District(s): Huron-Bruce
Federal Electoral District(s): Huron-Bruce
Next Election: Nov. 2010 (4 year terms)
Larry Kraemer, Mayor
519-395-3130
mayor@kincardine.net
Laura Haight, Deputy Mayor & Councillor
519-396-5204
Kenneth Craig, Councillor at Large
519-396-8767
Ron Hewitt, Councillor at Large
519-395-2774
Marsha Leggett, Councillor at Large
519-368-7644
Guy Anderson, Councillor, Ward(s): 1
519-396-3529
Mike Leggett, Councillor, Ward(s): 1
519-396-4529
Gordon Campbell, Councillor, Ward(s): 2
519-396-8075
Randy Roppel, Councillor, Ward(s): 3
519-368-7792
Donna MacDougall, Clerk, Administration
clerk@kincardine.net
John deRosenroll, Chief Administrative Officer, Administration
519-396-3018
Brenda French, Treasurer, Administration
519-396-3468
Michele Barr, Manager, Building & Planning, Administration
buildings@kincardine.net
Jim O'Rourke, Manager, Public Works, Administration
pwcasual@kincardine.net
Jamie MacKinnon, Fire Chief, Administration
kinfire@bmts.com
Steve Murray, Coordinator, Economic Development, & Manager, Tour, Administration
smurray@kincardine.net
Roberta Trelford, Coordinator, Community Emergency Management, & Hea, Administration
kinfirecemc@bmts.com
Donna Hardman, Compliance Officer, Water & Waste Water Administra, Administration
519-396-4660, Fax: 519-396-4673
waterservice@bmts.com

King
2075 King Rd.
King City, ON L7B 1A1
905-833-5321 Fax: 905-833-2300
online@king.ca
www.king.ca
Municipal Type: Township
Incorporated: 1850; *Area:* 333.04 sq km
County or District: York Reg. Mun.; *Population in 2006:* 19,487
Provincial Electoral District(s): Oak Ridges-Markham; York-Simcoe
Federal Electoral District(s): Oak Ridges-Markham; York-Simcoe
Next Election: Nov. 2010 (4 year terms)
Cleve Mortelliti, Mayor
mayor@king.ca
Cleve Mortelliti, Councillor, Ward(s): 1
cleve@kingcentric.ca
Jeff Laidlaw, Councillor, Ward(s): 2
kingribbit@gmail.com
Linda Pabst, Councillor, Ward(s): 3
csomerville@king.ca
Bill Cober, Councillor, Ward(s): 4
billcober@aol.com
Jane Underhill, Councillor, Ward(s): 5
janeunderhill@sympatico.ca
Jack Rupke, Councillor, Ward(s): 6
csomerville@king.ca
Chris Somerville, Clerk, Administration
csomerville@king.ca
Scott Somerville, Chief Administrative Officer, Administration
Donald Young, Director, Finance, Administration
Robert Flindall, Director, Engineering & Public Works, Administration
Catherine Purcell, Director, Parks, Recreation, & Culture, Administration
Marilyn Loan, Manager, Human Resources, Administration
Gaspare Ritacca, Manager, Planning & Development, Administration
Bryan Burbidge, Fire Chief, Administration
Jamie Smyth, Economic Development Officer, Administration

Kirkland Lake
P.O. Box 1757
3 Kirkland St. West
Kirkland Lake, ON P2N 3P4
705-567-9361 Fax: 705-567-3535
www.tkl.ca
Municipal Type: Town
Incorporated: 1972; *Area:* 262.24 sq km
County or District: Timiskaming District; *Population in 2006:* 8,248
Provincial Electoral District(s): Timiskaming-Cochrane
Federal Electoral District(s): Timmins-James Bay
Next Election: Nov. 2010 (4 year terms)
Note: Formerly known as the Township of Teck.
William Enouy, Mayor
bill.enouy@tkl.ca
Jo Ann Ducharme, Clerk, Department of Corporate Services

La Vallée
P.O. Box 99
56 Church Rd.
Devlin, ON P0W 1C0
807-486-3452 Fax: 807-486-3863
lavalley@nwonet.net
www.lavallee.ca
Municipal Type: Township
Area: 237.26 sq km
County or District: Rainy River District; *Population in 2006:* 1,067
Provincial Electoral District(s): Kenora-Rainy River
Federal Electoral District(s): Thunder Bay-Rainy River
Next Election: Nov. 2010 (4 year terms)
Ross Donaldson, Reeve
Sylvia Smeeth, Municipal Clerk

Laird
3 Pumpkin Point Rd., RR#4
Echo Bay, ON P0S 1C0
705-248-2395 Fax: 705-248-1138
lairdtwp@soonet.ca
www.lairdtownship.ca
Municipal Type: Township
Incorporated: 1891; *Area:* 101.77 sq km
County or District: Algoma District; *Population in 2006:* 1,078
Provincial Electoral District(s): Algoma-Manitoulin
Federal Electoral District(s): Sault Ste Marie
Next Election: Nov. 2010 (4 year terms)
Richard (Dick) Beitz, Mayor
Phyllis L. MacKay, Clerk-Treasurer, Tax Collector, & License Issuing

Lake of Bays
1012 Dwight Beach Rd., RR#1
Dwight, ON P0A 1H0
705-635-2272 Fax: 705-635-2132 Toll Free Phone: 1-877-566-0005
reception@lakeofbays.on.ca
www.lakeofbays.on.ca
Municipal Type: Township
Incorporated: 1971; *Area:* 671.46 sq km
County or District: Muskoka Dist. Mun.; *Population in 2006:* 3,570
Provincial Electoral District(s): Parry Sound-Muskoka
Federal Electoral District(s): Parry Sound-Muskoka
Next Election: Nov. 2010 (4 year terms)
Note: Amalgamation of the former Townships of Franklin, Ridout, McLean & Sinclair/Finlayson.
Bob Young, Mayor
705-767-2171
Michelle Percival, Clerk
clerk@lakeofbays.on.ca

Lake of the Woods
P.O. Box 427
211 Fourth St.
Rainy River, ON P0W 1L0
807-852-3529 Fax: 807-852-3529
www.lakeofthewoods.ca
Municipal Type: Township
Incorporated: Jan. 1, 1998; *Area:* 751.17 sq km
County or District: Rainy River District; *Population in 2006:* 323
Provincial Electoral District(s): Kenora-Rainy River
Federal Electoral District(s): Thunder Bay-Rainy River
Next Election: Nov. 2010 (4 year terms)
Note: Amalgamation of the Township of Morson & McCrosson-Tovell.
Valerie Pizey, Mayor
Patrick W. Giles, Clerk-Treasurer
gilesp@tbaytel.net

Lambton Shores
P.O. Box 610
7883 Amtelecom Pkwy.
Forest, ON N0N 1J0
519-786-2335 Fax: 519-786-2135
administration@lambtonshores.ca
www.lambtonshores.ca
Municipal Type: Municipality
Incorporated: 2001; *Area:* 331.08 sq km
County or District: Lambton; *Population in 2006:* 11,150
Provincial Electoral District(s): Lambton-Kent-Middlesex
Federal Electoral District(s): Lambton-Kent-Middlesex
Next Election: Nov. 2010 (4 year terms)
Note: Amalgamation of the Towns of Bosanquet & Forest, & the Villages of Thedford, Arkona & Grand Bend.
Gord Minielly, Mayor
519-786-4629
gminielly@lambtonshores.ca
Carolyn Jamieson, Deputy Mayor & Councillor
519-296-5810
cjamieson@lambtonshores.ca
John Dehondt, Councillor, Ward(s): 1
jdehondt@lambtonshores.ca
Bill Weber, Councillor, Ward(s): 2
bweber@lambtonshores.ca
Mark Simpson, Councillor, Ward(s): 3
msimpson@lambtonshores.ca
Ruth Illman, Councillor, Ward(s): 4
rillman@lambtonshores.ca
Gerry Rupke, Councillor, Ward(s): 5
grupke@lambtonshores.ca
Ken Evans, Councillor, Ward(s): 6
kevans@lambtonshores.ca
Carol McKenzie, Clerk, Administration
cpmckenzie@lambtonshores.ca
John Byrne, Chief Administrative Officer, Administration
jbyrne@lambtonshores.ca
Janet Ferguson, Treasurer, Administration
jferguson@lambtonshores.ca
Peggy Van Mierlo-West, Director, Community Services, Administration
pvmwest@lambtonshores.ca
Venkat Ramani, Manager, Infrastructure, Administration
vramani@lambtonshores.ca
Allan Little, Superintendent, Drainage, & Construction Inspector, Administration
alittle@lambtonshores.ca

Lanark Highlands
P.O. Box 340
75 George St.
Lanark, ON K0G 1K0
613-259-2398 Fax: 613-259-2291
mailbag@lanarkhighlands.ca
www.lanarkhighlands.ca
Municipal Type: Township
Incorporated: July 1, 1997; *Area:* 1,033.3 sq km
County or District: Lanark; *Population in 2006:* 5,180
Provincial Electoral District(s): Lanark-Frontenac-Lennox & Addington
Federal Electoral District(s): Lanark-Frontenac-Lennox & Addington
Next Election: Nov. 2010 (4 year terms)
Note: Amalgamation of North West Lanark Township & Darling Township.
Peter McLaren, Mayor
Amanda Mabo, Clerk & Deputy Chief Administrative Officer

Larder Lake
P.O. Box 40
13 Godfrey St.
Larder Lake, ON P0K 1L0
705-643-2158 Fax: 705-643-2311
llake@ntl.sympatico.ca
www.larderlake.net
Municipal Type: Township
Area: 228.73 sq km
County or District: Timiskaming District; *Population in 2006:* 735
Provincial Electoral District(s): Timiskaming-Cochrane
Federal Electoral District(s): Timmins-James Bay
Next Election: Nov. 2010 (4 year terms)
Patricia Bodick, Reeve
Anne Kmyta, Clerk-Treasurer & Chief Administration Office Mana
anne.kmyta@ntl.sympatico.ca

Latchford
P.O. Box 10
10 Main St.
Latchford, ON P0J 1N0

705-676-2416 Fax: 705-676-2121
bgibson@latchford.ca
www.latchford.ca
Municipal Type: Town
Incorporated: 1907; *Area:* 153.27 sq km
County or District: Timiskaming District; *Population in 2006:* 446
Provincial Electoral District(s): Timiskaming-Cochrane
Federal Electoral District(s): Nipissing-Timiskaming
Next Election: Nov. 2010 (4 year terms)
George Lefebvre, Mayor
Betty Gibson, Clerk-Treasurer
bgibson@latchford.ca

Laurentian Hills
34465 Hwy. 17, RR#1
Deep River, ON K0J 1P0
613-584-3114 Fax: 613-584-3285
info@town.laurentianhills.on.ca
www.town.laurentianhills.on.ca
Municipal Type: Town
Incorporated: Jan. 1, 2000; *Area:* 640.37 sq km
County or District: Renfrew; *Population in 2006:* 2,789
Provincial Electoral District(s): Renfrew-Nipissing-Pembroke
Federal Electoral District(s): Renfrew-Nipissing-Pembroke
Next Election: Nov. 2010 (4 year terms)
Note: Amalgamation of the United Townships of Rolph, Buchanan, Wylie & McKay & the Village of Chalk River.
Richard Rabishaw, Mayor
Wayne T. Kirby, Chief Administrative Officer & Clerk
cao@town.laurentianhills.on.ca

Laurentian Valley
460 Witt Rd., RR#4
Pembroke, ON K8A 6W5
613-735-6291 Fax: 613-735-5820
laurentian@laurvall.on.ca
www.laurentianvalleytwsp.on.ca
Municipal Type: Township
Incorporated: Jan. 1, 2000; *Area:* 552.44 sq km
County or District: Renfrew; *Population in 2006:* 9,265
Provincial Electoral District(s): Renfrew-Nipissing-Pembroke
Federal Electoral District(s): Renfrew-Nipissing-Pembroke
Next Election: Nov. 2010 (4 year terms)
Note: Amalgamation of the former Townships of Stafford-Pembroke & Alice & Fraser.
Jack Wilson, Mayor
John Baird, Chief Administrative Officer & Clerk

Leamington
38 Erie St. North
Leamington, ON N8H 2Z3
519-326-5761 Fax: 519-326 2481
info@leamington.ca
www.leamington.ca
Municipal Type: Municipality
Incorporated: 1874; *Area:* 261.92 sq km
County or District: Essex; *Population in 2006:* 28,833
Provincial Electoral District(s): Chatham-Kent-Essex
Federal Electoral District(s): Chatham-Kent-Essex
Next Election: Nov. 2010 (4 year terms)
Note: Incorporated as a town in 1890. Restructuring occurred in 1999.
John M. Adams, Mayor
councilmembers@leamington.ca
Rob Schmidt, Deputy Mayor & Councillor
Rick Atkin, Councillor
Bill Derbyshire, Councillor
Herb Enns, Councillor
Hilda MacDonald, Councillor
John Paterson, Councillor
Brian R. Sweet, B.A., LL.B, Municipal Clerk, Corporate Counsel & Director, Cor, Administration
clerk@leamington.ca
William J. Marck, B.A., LL.B, Chief Administrative Officer, Administration
bmarck@leamington.ca
Cheryl L. Horrobin, B.Comm, CA, AMCT, Director, Finance & Business Services, Administration
Douglas Morrish, Director, Development Services, Administration
John Tofflemire, Director, Community Services, Administration
Robert R. Bradt, Manager, Fire Services & Fire Chief, Administration
Bechara Daher, Manager, Building Services, Administration
Arthur Glab, Manager, Engineering, Administration
Cameron McKay, Manager, Public Works, Administration
Tracey Pillon-Abbs, Manager, Planning Services, Administration
Gary Foisy, Superintendent, Water Services, Administration
Kit Woods, Superintendent, Pollution Control Centre, Administration
Pauline Russell, MEd., IPMA-CP, Officer, Human Resources, Administration

Leeds & Grenville
#100, 25 Central Ave. West
Brockville, ON K6V 4N6
613-342-3840 Fax: 613-342-2101 Toll Free Phone: 1-800-770-2170
www.uclg.ca
Municipal Type: United County
Area: 3,350.18 sq km
Population in 2006: 99,206
Next Election: Nov. 2010 (4 year terms)

Council
Vacant, Warden & Councillor
Herb Scott, Councillor, Ward(s): Athens Township
Mel Campbell, Councillor, Ward(s): Augusta Township
William Sloan, Councillor, Ward(s): Edwardsburgh/Cardinal Township
Jim Pickard, Councillor, Ward(s): Elizabethtown-Kitley Township
Roger Haley, Councillor, Ward(s): Front of Yonge Township
Bruce Bryan, Councillor, Ward(s): Leeds & the Thousand Islands
J. Douglas Struthers, Councillor, Ward(s): Merrickville-Wolford
David Gordon, Councillor, Ward(s): North Grenville Municipality
Ronald E. Holman, Councillor, Ward(s): Rideau Lakes Township
William (Bill) L. Thake, Councillor, Ward(s): Westport

Administration
Lesley Todd, Clerk, Administration
Steven Silver, Chief Administrative Officer, Administration
Nigel White, Treasurer & Director, Corporate Services, Administration
Leslie Shepherd, Director, Works, Planning Services, & Asset Manage, Administration
Dorothy Theobald, Director, Human Services, Administration
James Alexander (Sandy) Hay, County Planner, Administration
Bob Cheetham, Manager, Economic Development, Administration
Dan Chevrier, Manager, Emergency Medical Services (EMS) Division, Administration
Kristen Hobbs, Manager, Human Resources, Administration
Geoff McVey, Manager, Forest, Administration

Leeds & The Thousand Islands
P.O. Box 129
1 Jessie St.
Lansdowne, ON K0E 1L0
613-659-2415 Fax: 613-659-3619 Toll Free Phone: 1-866-220-2327
www.townshipleeds.on.ca
Municipal Type: Township
Incorporated: Jan. 1, 2001; *Area:* 607.18 sq km
County or District: Leeds & Grenville; *Population in 2006:* 9,435
Provincial Electoral District(s): Leeds-Grenville
Federal Electoral District(s): Leeds-Grenville
Next Election: Nov. 2010 (4 year terms)
Note: Amalgamation of Front of Leeds & Lansdowne, Rear of Leeds & Lansdowne & Front of Escott.
Bruce Bryan, Mayor
Vanessa Latimer, AMCT, Clerk
vanessa@townshipleeds.on.ca

Limerick
89 Limerick Lake Rd., RR#2
Gilmour, ON K0L 1W0
613-474-2863 Fax: 613-474-0478
assistant@township.limerick.on.ca
www.township.limerick.on.ca
Municipal Type: Township
Incorporated: 1887; *Area:* 200.59 sq km
County or District: Hastings; *Population in 2006:* 364
Provincial Electoral District(s): Prince Edward-Hastings
Federal Electoral District(s): Prince Edward-Hastings
Next Election: Nov. 2010 (4 year terms)
David Golem, Reeve
613-474-0803
Jennifer Trumble, Clerk-Treasurer
613-474-286, Fax: 613-474-0478
clerk@township.limerick.on.ca

Loyalist
P.O. Box 70
263 Main St.
Odessa, ON K0H 2H0
613-386-7351 Fax: 613-386-3833
www.loyalisttownship.ca
Municipal Type: Township
Incorporated: 1998; *Area:* 340.02 sq km
County or District: Lennox & Addington; *Population in 2006:* 15,062
Provincial Electoral District(s): Lanark-Frontenac-Lennox & Addington
Federal Electoral District(s): Lanark-Frontenac-Lennox & Addington
Next Election: Nov. 2010 (4 year terms)
Note: Amalgamation of the Townships of Ernestown, Amherst Island & the Village of Bath.
Bill Lowry, Reeve
Bill Lowry, Deputy Reeve
Duncan Ashley, Councillor, Ward(s): 1 Amherst Island
Joe Hudacin, Councillor, Ward(s): 2 Bath
Carl Bresee, Councillor, Ward(s): 3 Ernestown
John Ibey, Councillor, Ward(s): 3 Ernestown
Ric Bresee, Councillor, Ward(s): 3 Ernestown
Brenda Hamilton, Township Clerk, Administration
Diane Pearce, Chief Administrative Officer, Administration
Alida Moffatt, Director, Finance, Administration
Cindy Lawson, Director, Recreation, Administration
David Thompson, Director, Engineering Services, Administration
Murray Beckel, Chief Building Official & Planner, Administration
Wayne Calver, Fire Chief, Administration
Bruce Hughson, Manager, Transportaton & Solid Waste, Administration
Lorie McFarland, Manager, Utilities, Administration
Brenda Martineau, Coordinator, Employee Relations, Administration

Lucan Biddulph
P.O. Box 190
33351 Richmond St., RR#3
Lucan, ON N0M 2J0
519-227-4491 Fax: 519-227-4998
info@lucanbiddulph.on.ca
www.lucanbiddulph.on.ca
Municipal Type: Township
Incorporated: Jan. 1, 1999; *Area:* 169.15 sq km
County or District: Middlesex; *Population in 2006:* 4,187
Provincial Electoral District(s): Lambton-Kent-Middlesex
Federal Electoral District(s): Lambton-Kent-Middlesex
Next Election: Nov. 2010 (4 year terms)
Note: Amalgamation of the Village of Lucan and the Township of Biddulph.
Paul Hodgins, Mayor
Lisa deBoer, Clerk
ldeboer@lucanbiddulph.on.ca

MacDonald, Meredith & Aberdeen Additional
P.O. Box 10
208 Church St.
Echo Bay, ON P0S 1C0
705-248-2441 Fax: 705-248-3091
twpmacd@onlink.net
hosting.soonet.ca/twpmacd/index.html
Municipal Type: Township
Incorporated: 1899; *Area:* 161.73 sq km
County or District: Algoma District; *Population in 2006:* 1,550
Provincial Electoral District(s): Algoma-Manitoulin
Federal Electoral District(s): Sault Ste Marie
Next Election: Nov. 2010 (4 year terms)
Lynn Watson, Mayor
Lynne Duguay, Clerk

Machar
P.O. Box 70
73 Municipal Rd. North
South River, ON P0A 1X0
705-386-7741 Fax: 705-386-0765
bpaulmachar@vianet.ca
www.machartownship.net
Municipal Type: Township
Area: 184.38 sq km
County or District: Parry Sound District; *Population in 2006:* 866
Provincial Electoral District(s): Parry Sound-Muskoka
Federal Electoral District(s): Parry Sound-Muskoka
Next Election: Nov. 2010 (4 year terms)
Douglas Maeck, Mayor
Brenda Paul, AMCT, Clerk-Treasurer

Machin
P.O. Box 249
75 Spruce St.
Vermilion Bay, ON P0V 2V0
807-227-2633 Fax: 807-227-5443
administrator@visitmachin.com
www.visitmachin.com
Municipal Type: Township
Area: 288.85 sq km
County or District: Kenora District; *Population in 2006:* 978
Provincial Electoral District(s): Kenora-Rainy River
Federal Electoral District(s): Kenora
Next Election: Nov. 2010 (4 year terms)
Gord Dingman, Mayor
Tammy Rob, Clerk-Treasurer
clerktreasurer@visitmachin.com

Madawaska Valley
P.O. Box 1000
85 Bay St.
Barrys Bay, ON K0J 1B0
613-756-2747 Fax: 613-756-0553 Toll Free Phone: 1-866-222-8699
info@madawaskavalley.on.ca
www.madawaskavalley.on.ca
Municipal Type: Township
Incorporated: Jan. 1, 2001; *Area:* 670.11 sq km
County or District: Renfrew; *Population in 2006:* 4,381
Provincial Electoral District(s): Renfrew-Nipissing-Pembroke
Federal Electoral District(s): Renfrew-Nipissing-Pembroke
Next Election: Nov. 2010 (4 year terms)
Note: Amalgamation of Barry's Bay Village, Radcliffe Township & Sherwood, Jones & Burns Township.
David M. Shulist, Reeve
613-756-0912
Pat Pilgrim, C.M.O., Chief Administrative Officer & Clerk
ppilgrim@madawaskavalley.on.ca

Madoc
P.O. Box 503
15651 Hwy. 62, RR#2
Madoc, ON K0K 2K0
613-473-2677 Fax: 613-473-5580
www.madoc.ca
Municipal Type: Township
Incorporated: 1850; *Area:* 269.98 sq km
County or District: Hastings; *Population in 2006:* 2,069
Provincial Electoral District(s): Prince Edward-Hastings
Federal Electoral District(s): Prince Edward-Hastings
Next Election: Nov. 2010 (4 year terms)
Robert Sager, Reeve
twpmad@sympatico.ca
W.G. (Bill) Lebow, B.A., AMCT, Clerk Administrator
clerk@madoc.ca

Magnetawan, Municipality of
P.O. Box 70
4304 Hwy. 520
Magnetawan, ON P0A 1P0
705-387-3947 Fax: 705-387-4875 E-mail, CAO: cao@magnetawan.com
info@magnetawan.com; admin@magnetawan.com
www.magnetawan.com
Municipal Type: Township
Incorporated: July 4, 1997; *Area:* 523.07 sq km
County or District: Parry Sound District; *Population in 2006:* 1,610
Provincial Electoral District(s): Parry Sound-Muskoka
Federal Electoral District(s): Parry Sound-Muskoka
Next Election: Nov. 2010 (4 year terms)
Sam Dunnett, Mayor

Mark Urbanski, Chief Administrative Officer & Clerk

Malahide
87 John St. South
Aylmer, ON N5H 2C3
519-773-5344 Fax: 519-773-5334
malahide@malahide.ca
www.malahide.ca
Municipal Type: Township
Incorporated: Jan. 1, 1998; *Area:* 395.07 sq km
County or District: Elgin; *Population in 2006:* 8,828
Provincial Electoral District(s): Elgin-Middlesex-London
Federal Electoral District(s): Elgin-Middlesex-London
Next Election: Nov. 2010 (4 year terms)
Note: Amalgamation of the Township of Malahide, Village of Springfield & Township of South Dorchester.
Dave Mennill, Mayor
519-269-3364
Michelle M. Casavecchia, Chief Administrative Officer & Clerk

Manitoulin
Gore Bay, ON

Municipal Type: District
Area: 4,759.74 sq km
Population in 2006: 13,090
Provincial Electoral District(s): Algoma-Manitoulin
Federal Electoral District(s): Algoma-Manitoulin-Kapuskasing
Note: The District incorporates the towns of Gore Bay, & Northeastern Manitoulin & the Islands; communities in the townships of Assiginack, Barrie Isl., Billing, Burpe & Mills, Central Manitoulin, Cockburn Isl., Gordon, & Tehkummah; & 1st Nations reserves

Manitouwadge
1 Mississauga Rd.
Manitouwadge, ON P0T 2C0
807-826-3227 Fax: 807-826-4592
www.manitouwadge.ca
Municipal Type: Township
Area: 351.97 sq km
County or District: Thunder Bay District; *Population in 2006:* 2,300
Provincial Electoral District(s): Algoma-Manitoulin
Federal Electoral District(s): Algoma-Manitoulin-Kapuskasing
Next Election: Nov. 2010 (4 year terms)
John MacEachern, Mayor
mayor@twp.manitouwadge.on.ca
Cecile Kerster, Municipal Manager Clerk
ckerster@manitouwadge.ca

Mapleton
P.O. Box 160
7275 Sideroad 3
Drayton, ON N0G 1P0
519-638-3313 Fax: 519-638-5113 Toll Free Phone: 1-800-385-7248
www.mapleton.ca
Municipal Type: Township
Incorporated: Jan. 1, 1999; *Area:* 534.71 sq km
County or District: Wellington; *Population in 2006:* 9,851
Provincial Electoral District(s): Perth-Wellington
Federal Electoral District(s): Perth-Wellington
Next Election: Nov. 2010 (4 year terms)
Note: Amalgamation of the Townships of Maryborough & Peel & the Village of Drayton.
Bruce Whale, Mayor
Patty Sinnamon, Chief Administrative Officer & Clerk
psinnamon@town.mapleton.on.ca

Marathon
P.O. Box TM
4 Hemlo Dr.
Marathon, ON P0T 2E0
807-229-1340 Fax: 807-229-1999
info@marathon.ca; clerk@marathon.ca
www.marathon.ca
Municipal Type: Town
Area: 170.48 sq km
County or District: Thunder Bay District; *Population in 2006:* 3,863
Provincial Electoral District(s): Thunder Bay-Superior North
Federal Electoral District(s): Thunder Bay-Superior North
Next Election: Nov. 2010 (4 year terms)
Rick Dumas, Mayor
Brian Tocheri, Chief Administrative Officer & Clerk
cao@marathon.ca

Markstay-Warren, Municipality of
P.O. Box 79
21 Main St. South
Markstay, ON P0M 2G0
705-853-4536 Fax: 705-853-4964 Toll Free Phone: 1-866-710-1065
info@markstay-warren.ca
www.markstay-warren.ca
Municipal Type: Town
Incorporated: Jan. 1, 1999; *Area:* 510.12 sq km
County or District: Sudbury District; *Population in 2006:* 2,475
Provincial Electoral District(s): Timiskaming-Cochrane
Federal Electoral District(s): Nickel Belt
Next Election: Nov. 2010 (4 year terms)
Note: Amalgamation of the Towns of Warren, Markstay & the Townships of Awrey, Street, Hawley, Loughrin & Henry.
Sonja Flynn, Mayor
Lorraine Demore, Chief Administrative Officer & Clerk
ldemore@markstay-warren.ca

Marmora & Lake, Municipality of
P.O. Box 459
12 Bursthall St.
Marmora, ON K0K 2M0
613-472-2629 Fax: 613-472-5330 Toll Free Phone: 1-866-518-2282
marmorajd@bellnet.ca
www.marmora.info
Municipal Type: Township
Area: 533.75 sq km
County or District: Hastings; *Population in 2006:* 3,912
Provincial Electoral District(s): Prince Edward-Hastings
Federal Electoral District(s): Prince Edward-Hastings
Next Election: Nov. 2010 (4 year terms)
Terry Clemens, Reeve
Judy Durbatch, Municipal Clerk

Matachewan
P.O. Box 177
Matachewan, ON P0K 1M0
705-565-2274 Fax: 705-565-2564
township@ntl.sympatico.ca
www.matachewan.com
Municipal Type: Township
Area: 543.63 sq km
County or District: Timiskaming District; *Population in 2006:* 375
Provincial Electoral District(s): Timiskaming-Cochrane
Federal Electoral District(s): Timmins-James Bay
Next Election: Nov. 2010 (4 year terms)
Beverley Hine, Reeve
Andrew Van Oosten, Chief Administrative Officer, Clerk, & Treasurer

Mattawa
P.O. Box 390
160 Water St.
Mattawa, ON P0H 1V0
705-744-5611 Fax: 705-744-0104
info@mattawa.info
www.mattawa.info
Municipal Type: Town
Area: 3.66 sq km
County or District: Nipissing District; *Population in 2006:* 2,003
Provincial Electoral District(s): Nipissing
Federal Electoral District(s): Nipissing-Timiskaming
Next Election: Nov. 2010 (4 year terms)
Dean Backer, Mayor
Wayne P. Belter, Administrator, Clerk, & Treasurer

Mattawan
P.O. Box 610
Mattawa, ON P0H 1V0
705-744-5680 Fax: 705-744-4141
info@mattawan.info
www.mattawan.info
Municipal Type: Township
Area: 199.52 sq km
County or District: Nipissing District; *Population in 2006:* 147
Provincial Electoral District(s): Nipissing
Federal Electoral District(s): Nipissing-Timiskaming
Next Election: Nov. 2010 (4 year terms)
Peter Murphy, Mayor
Barb Castellani, Clerk-Treasurer

Mattice-Val Côté
P.O. Box 129
500 Hwy. 11
Mattice, ON P0L 1T0
705-364-6511 Fax: 705-364-6431
mattice@ntl.sympatico.ca
www.nt.net/mattice
Municipal Type: Township
Area: 414.64 sq km
County or District: Cochrane District; *Population in 2006:* 772
Provincial Electoral District(s): Timmins-James Bay
Federal Electoral District(s): Algoma-Manitoulin-Kapuskasing
Next Election: Nov. 2010 (4 year terms)
Jean Louis Brunet, Reeve
Gilbert Brisson, Administrator-Clerk

McDougall
5 Barager Blvd., RR#3
Parry Sound, ON P2A 2W9
705-342-5252 Fax: 705-342-5573
www.municipalityofmcdougall.com
Municipal Type: Township
Incorporated: May 1, 1872; *Area:* 262.69 sq km
County or District: Parry Sound District; *Population in 2006:* 2,704
Provincial Electoral District(s): Parry Sound-Muskoka
Federal Electoral District(s): Parry Sound-Muskoka
Next Election: Nov. 2010 (4 year terms)
Dale Robinson, Mayor
Garfield Eaton, Chief Administrative Officer & Clerk

McGarry
P.O. Box 99
27 Webster St.
Virginiatown, ON P0K 1X0
705-634-2145 Fax: 705-634-2700
admin@mcgarry.ca
www.mcgarry.ca
Municipal Type: Township
Area: 86.05 sq km
County or District: Timiskaming District; *Population in 2006:* 674
Provincial Electoral District(s): Timiskaming-Cochrane
Federal Electoral District(s): Timmins-James Bay
Next Election: Nov. 2010 (4 year terms)
Clermont Lapointe, Reeve
Gary Cunnington, Clerk-Treasurer

McKellar
P.O. Box 69
701 Hwy. 124
McKellar, ON P0G 1C0
705-389-2842 Fax: 705-389-1244
www.township.mckellar.on.ca
Municipal Type: Township
Incorporated: 1873; *Area:* 177.48 sq km
County or District: Parry Sound District; *Population in 2006:* 1,080
Provincial Electoral District(s): Parry Sound-Muskoka
Federal Electoral District(s): Parry Sound-Muskoka
Next Election: Nov. 2010 (4 year terms)
Peter Hopkins, Reeve
Shawn Boggs, AMCT, Clerk Administrator

McMurrich-Monteith
P.O. Box 70
31 William St.
Sprucedale, ON P0A 1Y0
705-685-7901 Fax: 705-685-7393
mcmurric@surenet.net
www.mcmurrichmonteith.com
Municipal Type: Township
Area: 273.33 sq km
County or District: Parry Sound District; *Population in 2006:* 791
Provincial Electoral District(s): Parry Sound-Muskoka
Federal Electoral District(s): Parry Sound-Muskoka
Next Election: Nov. 2010 (4 year terms)
Glynn Robinson, Reeve
705-685-7779
Cheryl Marshall, Clerk

McNab-Braeside
2508 Russett Dr., RR#2
Arnprior, ON K7S 3G8
613-623-5756 Fax: 613-623-9138 Toll Free Phone: 1-800-957-4621
info@mcnabbraeside.com
www.mcnabbraeside.com
Municipal Type: Township
Incorporated: Jan. 1, 1998; *Area:* 253.87 sq km
County or District: Renfrew; *Population in 2006:* 7,222
Provincial Electoral District(s): Renfrew-Nipissing-Pembroke
Federal Electoral District(s): Renfrew-Nipissing-Pembroke
Next Election: Nov. 2010 (4 year terms)
Note: Amalgamation of Braeside Village & McNab Township.
Mary M. Campbell, Mayor
mcampbell@mcnabbraeside.com
Noreen C. Mellema, CMO, Chief Administrative Officer & Clerk
nmellema@mcnabbraeside.com

Meaford
21 Trowbridge St. West
Meaford, ON N4L 1A1
519-538-1060 Fax: 519-538-5240
info@meaford.ca
www.meaford.ca
Municipal Type: Municipality
Incorporated: Jan. 1, 2001; *Area:* 588.47 sq km
County or District: Grey; *Population in 2006:* 10,948
Provincial Electoral District(s): Bruce-Grey-Owen Sound
Federal Electoral District(s): Bruce-Grey-Owen Sound
Next Election: Nov. 2010 (4 year terms)
Note: Formerly the Town of Georgian Highlands. Amalgamation of Sydenham, St. Vincent & Meaford.
Francis Richardson, Mayor
519-538-5998
frichardson@meaford.ca
Michael Traynor, Deputy Mayor & Councillor
519-376-8791
mtraynor@meaford.ca
Harley Greenfield, Councillor
519-538-2570
hgreenfield@meaford.ca
Cynthia Lemon, Councillor
519-376-1013
clemon@meaford.ca
Jim McPherson, Councillor
519-538-0859
jmcpherson@meaford.ca
Gerald Shortt, Councillor
519-538-2648
gshortt@meaford.ca
Lynda Stephens, Councillor
519-538-1189
lstephens@meaford.ca
Peggy Rouse, Clerk, Administration
prouse@meaford.ca
Frank Miele, Chief Administrative Officer, Administration
Robert Armstrong, Director, Planning & Building, Administration
Karen Davies, Director, Human Resources, Administration
Stephen Vokes, Director, Operations, Administration
Rick Carefoot, Chief Building Official, Administration
Chris Collyer, Chief Operator, Environmental Services, Administration
Steve Nickels, Fire Chief, Administration

Melancthon
157101 Hwy. 10, RR#6
Shelburne, ON L0N 1S9
519-925-5525 Fax: 519-925-1110
info@melancthontownship.ca
www.melancthontownship.ca

Municipal Type: Township
Incorporated: Jan. 1, 1853; *Area:* 310.88 sq km
County or District: Dufferin; *Population in 2006:* 2,895
Provincial Electoral District(s): Dufferin-Caledon
Federal Electoral District(s): Dufferin-Caledon
Next Election: Nov. 2010 (4 year terms)
Bill Hill, Mayor
519-925-6293
Denise B. Holmes, Chief Administrative Officer & Clerk-Treasurer
dholmes@melancthontownship.ca

Merrickville-Wolford

P.O. Box 340
317 Brock St. West
Merrickville, ON K0G 1N0
613-269-4791 Fax: 613-269-3095 E-mail, Admin.:
admin@merrickville-wolford.ca
reception@merrickville-wolford.ca
www.merrickville-wolford.ca
Municipal Type: Village
Area: 213.77 sq km
County or District: Leeds-Grenville; *Population in 2006:* 2,867
Provincial Electoral District(s): Leeds-Grenville
Federal Electoral District(s): Leeds-Grenville
Next Election: Nov. 2010 (4 year terms)
J. Douglas Struthers, Mayor
mayor@merrickville-wolford.ca
Jill Eagle, Chief Administrative Officer & Clerk
cao@merrickville-wolford.ca

Middlesex Centre

10227 Ilderton Rd., RR#2
Ilderton, ON N0M 2A0
519-666-0190 Fax: 519-666-0271 Toll Free Phone: 1-800-220-8968
cormans@middlesexcentre.on.ca
www.middlesexcentre.on.ca
Municipal Type: Township
Incorporated: Jan. 1, 1998; *Area:* 588.05 sq km
County or District: Middlesex; *Population in 2006:* 15,589
Provincial Electoral District(s): Lambton-Kent-Middlesex
Federal Electoral District(s): Lambton-Kent-Middlesex
Next Election: Nov. 2010 (4 year terms)
Note: Amalgamation of the former Townships of Delaware, Lobo, & London.

Council

Al Edmondson, Mayor
wa.edmondson@sympatico.ca
Clare Bloomfield, Deputy Mayor
Stephen Harvey, Councillor, Ward(s): 1
John Brennan, Councillor, Ward(s): 2
519-666-0549
Sharon McMillan, Councillor, Ward(s): 3
Aina DeViet, Councillor, Ward(s): 4
Frank Berze, Councillor, Ward(s): 5
fberze@rogers.com

Administration

Cathy Saunders, Chief Administrative Officer & Clerk, Administration
saunders@middlesexcentre.on.ca
Greg Watterton, Treasurer & Deputy Clerk, Administration
wattertg@middlesexcentre.on.ca
Maureen A. Looby, Director, Public Works & Engineering, Administration
loobym@middlesexcentre.on.ca
Arnie Marsman, Director, Planning & Development Svs., & Chief Bui, Administration
marsmana@middlesexcentre.on.ca
John Elston, Fire Chief & Supervisor, Emergency Services, Administration
elstonj@middlesexcentre.on.ca
Jim Reeve, Superintendent, Drainage, Administration
reevej@middlesexcentre.on.ca
Mauro Castrilli, Coordinator, Transportation, Administration
castrilli@middlesexcentre.on.ca
Brian Hansen, Environmental Technologist, Administration
hansen@middlesexcentre.on.ca

Minden Hills

P.O. Box 359
7 Milne St.
Minden, ON K0M 2K0
705-286-1260 Fax: 705-286-4917 Treasury/Bldg./By-law/Planning, Fax: 705-286-6005
admin@mindenhills.ca
www.mindenhills.ca
Municipal Type: Township
Area: 847.76 sq km
County or District: Haliburton; *Population in 2006:* 5,556
Provincial Electoral District(s): Haliburton-Kawartha Lakes-Brock
Federal Electoral District(s): Haliburton-Kawartha Lakes-Brock
Next Election: Nov. 2010 (4 year terms)
Barb Reid, Reeve
Cheryl McCarroll, Clerk
cmccarroll@mindenhills.ca

Minto

5941 Hwy. 89
Harriston, ON N0G 1Z0
519-338-2511 Fax: 519-338-2005 E-mail, Treasury:
gordon@town.minto.on.ca
theresa@town.minto.on.ca (Deputy Clerk)
www.town.minto.on.ca
Municipal Type: Town
Area: 300.37 sq km
County or District: Wellington; *Population in 2006:* 8,504
Provincial Electoral District(s): Perth-Wellington
Federal Electoral District(s): Perth-Wellington
Next Election: Nov. 2010 (4 year terms)
George Bridge, Mayor
519-343-3883
Jane Steller, Clerk

Mono

347209 MonoCenter Rd., RR#1
Orangeville, ON L9W 2Y8
519-941-3599 Fax: 519-941-9490
info@townofmono.com
www.townofmono.com
Municipal Type: Town
Incorporated: June 1, 1999; *Area:* 277.67 sq km
County or District: Dufferin; *Population in 2006:* 7,071
Provincial Electoral District(s): Dufferin-Caledon
Federal Electoral District(s): Dufferin-Caledon
Next Election: Nov. 2010 (4 year terms)
Laura Ryan, Mayor
mayor@townofmono.com
Keith J. McNenly, Chief Administrative Officer & Clerk
keith@townofmono.com

Montague

P.O. Box 755
6547 Roger Stevens Dr.
Smiths Falls, ON K7A 4W6
613-283-7478 Fax: 613-283-3112
info@township.montague.on.ca
www.township.montague.on.ca
Municipal Type: Township
Area: 277.03 sq km
County or District: Lanark; *Population in 2006:* 3,595
Provincial Electoral District(s): Lanark-Frontenac-Lennox & Addington
Federal Electoral District(s): Lanark-Frontenac-Lennox & Addington
Next Election: Nov. 2010 (4 year terms)
Bill Dobson, Reeve
Murray Hackett, Chief Administrative Officer & Clerk
mhackett@township.montague.on.ca

Moonbeam

P.O. Box 330
53 St. Aubin Ave.
Moonbeam, ON P0L 1V0
705-367-2244 Fax: 705-367-2610
moonbeam@moonbeam.ca
www.moonbeam.ca
Municipal Type: Township
Area: 235.17 sq km
County or District: Cochrane District; *Population in 2006:* 1,298
Provincial Electoral District(s): Timmins-James Bay
Federal Electoral District(s): Algoma-Manitoulin-Kapuskasing
Next Election: Nov. 2010 (4 year terms)
Gilles Audet, Reeve
Carole Gendron, Clerk-Treasurer
cgendron@moonbeam.ca

Moosonee

P.O. Box 727
5 First St.
Moosonee, ON P0L 1Y0
705-336-2993 Fax: 705-336-2426
info@moosonee.ca
www.moosonee.ca
Municipal Type: Town
Area: 555.35 sq km
County or District: Cochrane District; *Population in 2006:* 2,006
Provincial Electoral District(s): Timmins-James Bay
Federal Electoral District(s): Timmins-James Bay
Next Election: Nov. 2010 (4 year terms)
Victor Mitchell, Mayor
Shelley L. Petten, Clerk-Treasurer
spetten@moosonee.ca

Morley

P.O. Box 40
Stratton, ON P0W 1N0
807-483-5455 Fax: 807-483-5882
morley@nwonet.net
www.townshipofmorley.ca
Municipal Type: Township
Incorporated: 1903; *Area:* 375.61 sq km
County or District: Rainy River District; *Population in 2006:* 492
Provincial Electoral District(s): Kenora-Rainy River
Federal Electoral District(s): Thunder Bay-Rainy River
Next Election: Nov. 2010 (4 year terms)
Vacant, Reeve
Anna H.M. Boily, CMO, Clerk-Treasurer

Morris-Turnberry

41342 Morris Rd., RR#4
Brussels, ON N0G 1H0
519-887-6137 Fax: 519-887-6424
morris@scsinternet.com
www.morris-turnberry.on.ca
Municipal Type: Township
Incorporated: Jan. 1, 2001; *Area:* 376.45 sq km
County or District: Huron; *Population in 2006:* 3,403
Provincial Electoral District(s): Huron-Bruce
Federal Electoral District(s): Huron-Bruce
Next Election: Nov. 2010 (4 year terms)
Note: Amalgamation of the Township of Morris & the Township of Turnberry.

Paul Gowing, Mayor
Nancy Michie, Administrator & Clerk-Treasurer

Mulmur

758070 2nd Line East, RR#2
Lisle, ON L0M 1M0
705-466-3341 Fax: 705-466-2922 Toll Free Phone: 1-866-472-0417 (In 519 area code)
info@mulmurtownship.ca
www.mulmurtownship.ca
Municipal Type: Township
Incorporated: 1851; *Area:* 286.73 sq km
County or District: Dufferin; *Population in 2006:* 3,318
Provincial Electoral District(s): Dufferin-Caledon
Federal Electoral District(s): Dufferin-Caledon
Next Election: Nov. 2010 (4 year terms)
Paul Mills, Mayor
Terry M. Horner, AMCT, Chief Administrative Officer & Clerk
thorner@mulmurtownship.ca

Muskoka Lakes

P.O. Box 129
1 Bailey St.
Port Carling, ON P0B 1J0
705-765-3156 Fax: 705-765-6755
www.muskokalakes.ca
Municipal Type: Township
Incorporated: Jan. 1971; *Area:* 781.55 sq km
County or District: Muskoka Dist. Mun.; *Population in 2006:* 6,467
Provincial Electoral District(s): Parry Sound-Muskoka
Federal Electoral District(s): Parry Sound-Muskoka
Next Election: Nov. 2010 (4 year terms)
Alice Murphy, Mayor
Cheryl Mortimer, AMCT, Clerk
cmortimer@muskokalakes.ca

Nairn & Hyman

64 McIntyre St.
Nairn Centre, ON P0M 2L0
705-869-4232 Fax: 705-869-5248
information@nairncentre.ca
www.nairncentre.ca
Municipal Type: Township
Incorporated: 1896; *Area:* 159.03 sq km
County or District: Sudbury District; *Population in 2006:* 493
Provincial Electoral District(s): Algoma-Manitoulin
Federal Electoral District(s): Algoma-Manitoulin-Kapuskasing
Next Election: Nov. 2010 (4 year terms)
Laurier P. Falldien, Mayor
Robert Deschene, Chief Administrative Officer & Clerk

Neebing, Municipality of

4766 Hwy. 61
Thunder Bay, ON P7L 0B5
807-474-5331 Fax: 807-474-5332 Information Phone Line: 807-474-5338
neebing@neebing.org
www.neebing.org
Municipal Type: Town
Area: 875.51 sq km
County or District: Thunder Bay District; *Population in 2006:* 2,184
Provincial Electoral District(s): Thunder Bay-Atikokan
Federal Electoral District(s): Thunder Bay-Rainy River
Next Election: Nov. 2010 (4 year terms)
Ziggy Polkowski, Mayor
807-964-2083
Delma Stajkowski, AMCT, Clerk
delma@neebing.org

Newbury

P.O. Box 130
22910 Hagerty Rd.
Newbury, ON N0L 1Z0
519-693-4941 Fax: 519-693-4340
vnewbury@on.aibn.com
www.newbury.ca
Municipal Type: Village
Incorporated: 1873; *Area:* 1.85 sq km
County or District: Middlesex; *Population in 2006:* 439
Provincial Electoral District(s): Lambton-Kent-Middlesex
Federal Electoral District(s): Lambton-Kent-Middlesex
Next Election: Nov. 2010 (4 year terms)
Diane Brewer, Reeve
Betty D. Gordon, Clerk-Treasurer

Nipigon

P.O. Box 160
25 Second St.
Nipigon, ON P0T 2J0
807-887-3135 Fax: 807-887-3564 E-mail, Recreation Inquiries:
nipigonrec@shaw.ca
info@nipigon.net; touristinfo@nipigon.net (Tourism Info.)
www.nipigon.net
Municipal Type: Township
Area: 109.14 sq km
County or District: Thunder Bay District; *Population in 2006:* 1,752
Provincial Electoral District(s): Thunder Bay-Superior North
Federal Electoral District(s): Thunder Bay-Superior North
Next Election: Nov. 2010 (4 year terms)
Richard Harvey, Mayor
richardharvey@nipigon.net
Lindsay Mannila, Chief Administrative Officer

Nipissing
General Delivery
Nipissing, ON P0H 1W0
705-724-2144 Fax: 705-724-5385
nipissingtwp@xplornet.com
www.nipissingtownship.com
Municipal Type: Township
Area: 387.4 sq km
County or District: Parry Sound District; *Population in 2006:* 1,642
Provincial Electoral District(s): Nipissing; Timiskaming-Cochrane
Federal Electoral District(s): Nipissing-Timiskaming
Next Election: Nov. 2010 (4 year terms)
Pat Haufe, Mayor
705-752-3139
Charles H. Barton, Chief Administrative Officer & Clerk

Nipissing
District Social Services Administration Bd.
P.O. Box 750
200 McIntyre St. East
North Bay, ON P1B 8J8

Municipal Type: District
Area: 17,065.07 sq km
Population in 2006: 84,688
George Jupp, Chair, District of Nipissing Social Services Admin
877-829-5121, Fax: 705-474-0136
William A. White, CAO, District of Nipissing Social Services Adminis
705-474-2151, Fax: 705-474-7155

North Algona Wilberforce
1091 Shaw Woods Rd., RR#1
Eganville, ON K0J 1T0
613-628-2080 Fax: 613-628-3341
naw@nalgonawil.com
www.nalgonawil.com
Municipal Type: Township
Incorporated: Jan. 1, 1999; *Area:* 378.53 sq km
County or District: Renfrew; *Population in 2006:* 2,840
Provincial Electoral District(s): Renfrew-Nipissing-Pembroke
Federal Electoral District(s): Renfrew-Nipissing-Pembroke
Next Election: Nov. 2010 (4 year terms)
Note: Amalgamation of North Algona Township & Wilberforce Township.
Harold Weckworth, Mayor
Marilyn M. Schruder, Clerk-Treasurer

North Dumfries
1171 Greenfield Rd., RR#4
Cambridge, ON N1R 5S5
519-621-0340 Fax: 519-623-7641
mail@township.northdumfries.on.ca
www.township.northdumfries.on.ca
Municipal Type: Township
Area: 187.22 sq km
County or District: Waterloo Regional Municipality; *Population in 2006:* 9,063
Provincial Electoral District(s): Cambridge
Federal Electoral District(s): Cambridge
Next Election: Nov. 2010 (4 year terms)
Robert Deutschmann, Mayor
Roger Mordue, Chief Administrative Officer & Clerk

North Dundas
P.O. Box 489
636 St. Lawrence St.
Winchester, ON K0C 2K0
613-774-2105 Fax: 613-774-5699
info@northdundas.com
www.northdundas.com
Municipal Type: Township
Incorporated: Jan. 1, 1998; *Area:* 503.18 sq km
County or District: Stormont, Dundas & Glengarry; *Population in 2006:* 11,095
Provincial Electoral District(s): Stormont-Dundas-South Glengarry
Federal Electoral District(s): Stormont-Dundas-South Glengarry
Next Election: Nov. 2010 (4 year terms)
Note: Amalgamation of the former Townships of Winchester & Mountain & the villages of Chesterville & Winchester.

Council
Eric Duncan, Mayor
Gerry Boyce, Deputy Mayor
Allan Armstrong, Councillor
alarmstrong@sympatico.ca
Tony Fraser, Councillor
John Thompson, Councillor
jthompsonelect@hotmail.com

Administration
Jo-Anne McCaslin, Clerk, Administration
jmccaslin@northdundas.com
Howard F. Smith, Chief Administrative Officer, Administration
hsmith@northdundas.com
John J. Gareau, CA, AMCT, Treasurer, Administration
jgareau@northdundas.com
Arden Carruthers, Director, Public Works, & Fire Chief, Morewood, Administration
acarruthers@northdundas.com
Mark Guy, Director, Recreation & Culture, Administration
mguy@northdundas.com
Calvin Pol, BES, MCIP, RPP, Director, Planning, Building, & Enforcement, Administration
cpol@northdundas.com
Angela Rutley, Manager, Water & Sewer Department, Administration
Doug Froats, Coordinator, Waste Management, Administration
dfroats@northdundas.com
Dan Kelly, Fire Chief, Winchester, Administration
Mike McMahon, Fire Chief, Chesterville, Administration
Scott Patterson, Fire Chief, Mountain, Administration

North Frontenac
P.O. Box 97
6648 Rd. 506
Plevna, ON K0H 2M0
613-479-2231 Fax: 613-479-2352 Toll Free Phone: 1-800-234-3953
info@northfrontenac.ca
www.northfrontenac.ca
Municipal Type: Township
Incorporated: Jan. 1, 1998; *Area:* 1,135.75 sq km
County or District: Frontenac; *Population in 2006:* 1,904
Provincial Electoral District(s): Hastings-Frontenac-Lennox & Addington
Federal Electoral District(s): Lanark-Frontenac-Lennox & Addington
Next Election: Nov. 2010 (4 year terms)
Bud Clayton, Mayor
613-479-0010
dundiggin@sympatico.ca
Brenda Defosse, Clerk & Coordinator, Planning

North Glengarry
P.O. Box 700
90 Main St. South
Alexandria, ON K0C 1A0
613-525-1110 Fax: 613-525-1649
www.northglengarry.ca
Municipal Type: Township
Area: 642.4 sq km
County or District: Stormont, Dundas & Glengarry; *Population in 2006:* 10,635
Provincial Electoral District(s): Glengarry-Prescott-Russell
Federal Electoral District(s): Glengarry-Prescott-Russell
Next Election: Nov. 2010 (4 year terms)

Council
Grant E. Crack, Mayor
Chris McDonell, Deputy Mayor & Councillor
Gary Shepherd, Councillor at Large
Jamie MacDonald, Councillor, Ward(s): Alexandria
Jim Picken, Councillor, Ward(s): Kenyon
Eric MacSweyn, Councillor, Ward(s): Lochiel
Carma Williams, Councillor, Ward(s): Maxville

Administration
Terry Hart, Clerk Administrator, Administration
Johanna (Annie) Levac, Treasurer, Administration
André Bachand, Manager, Public Works, Administration
Gerry Murphy, Manager, Planning & By-law Enforcement, & Chief Bu, Administration
Frank Flipsen, Fire Chief, Administration
Manson Barton, Superintendent, Drainage, Administration

North Grenville
P.O. Box 130
285 County Rd. 44
Kemptville, ON K0G 1J0
613-258-9569 Fax: 613-258-9620
www.northgrenville.ca
Municipal Type: MN
Incorporated: July 14, 2003; *Area:* 350.14 sq km
County or District: Leeds-Grenville; *Population in 2006:* 14,198
Provincial Electoral District(s): Leeds-Grenville
Federal Electoral District(s): Leeds-Grenville
Next Election: Nov. 2010 (4 year terms)

Council
David Gordon, Mayor
Terry Butler, Councillor
tbutler@can.rogers.com
Ken Finnerty
kfinnerty@northgrenville.on.ca
Tim Sutton, Councillor
tsutton@northgrenville.on.ca
Barb Tobin, Councillor
btobin@northgrenville.on.ca

Administration
Cahl Pominville, Clerk, Administration
cpominville@northgrenville.on.ca
Andy Brown, Chief Administrative Officer, Administration
abrown@northgrenville.on.ca
Sheila Kehoe, Treasurer, Administration
skehoe@northgrenville.on.ca
Karen Dunlop, Director, Public Works, Administration
Darren Patmore, Director, Parks, Recreation & Culture, Administration
Forbes Symon, Director, Planning & Development, Administration
Tim Bond, Fire Chief, Administration
Philip Gerrard, Chief Building Official, Administration
Jim Beeler, Chief Superintendent, Environmental Services, Administration
Gary Boal, Superintendent, Waste Site, Administration
Doug Scott, Superintendent, Roads, Administration
Jeff McEwen, Coordinator, Engineering, Administration
Gary Simser, Technician, Regulatory Water / Wastewater Complian, Administration

North Huron
P.O. Box 90
274 Josephine St.
Wingham, ON N0G 2W0
519-357-3550 Fax: 519-357-1110
www.northhuron.ca
Municipal Type: Township
Incorporated: Jan. 1, 2001; *Area:* 178.98 sq km
County or District: Huron; *Population in 2006:* 5,015
Provincial Electoral District(s): Huron-Bruce
Federal Electoral District(s): Huron-Bruce
Next Election: Nov. 2010 (4 year terms)
Note: Amalgamation of the Village of Blyth, the Township of East Wawanosh & the Town of Wingham.
Neil Vincent, Reeve
Gary Long, Chief Administrative Officer & Clerk

North Kawartha
P.O. Box 550
280 Burleigh St.
Apsley, ON K0L 1A0
705-656-4445 Fax: 705-656-4446 Toll Free Phone: 1-800-755-6931
d.page@northkawartha.on.ca (Reception)
www.northkawartha.on.ca
Municipal Type: Township
Area: 765.02 sq km
County or District: Peterborough; *Population in 2006:* 2,342
Provincial Electoral District(s): Haliburton-Kawartha Lakes-Brock
Federal Electoral District(s): Haliburton-Kawartha Lakes-Brock
Next Election: Nov. 2010 (4 year terms)
Jim Whelan, Reeve
reeve@northkawartha.on.ca
Connie Parent, Clerk

North Middlesex, Municipality of
Administrative Centre
P.O. Box 9
229 Parkhill Main St.
Parkhill, ON N0M 2K0
519-294-6244 Fax: 519-294-0573 Toll Free Phone: 1-888-793-9637
clerk@northmiddlesex.on.ca
www.northmiddlesex.on.ca
Municipal Type: Township
Incorporated: Jan. 1, 2001; *Area:* 597.86 sq km
County or District: Middlesex; *Population in 2006:* 6,740
Provincial Electoral District(s): Lambton-Kent-Middlesex
Federal Electoral District(s): Lambton-Kent-Middlesex
Next Election: Nov. 2010 (4 year terms)
Note: Amalgamation of the Townships of East Williams, West Williams & McGillivray, the Town of Parkhill & the Village of Ailsa Craig.
Don F. Shipway, Mayor
Linda Creaghe, Chief Administrative Officer

North Stormont
P.O. Box 99
15 Union St.
Berwick, ON K0C 1G0
613-984-2821 Fax: 613-984-2908 Toll Free Phone: 1-877-984-2821
admin@northstormont.ca
www.northstormont.ca
Municipal Type: Township
Area: 515.55 sq km
County or District: Stormont, Dundas & Glengarry; *Population in 2006:* 6,769
Provincial Electoral District(s): Stormont-Dundas-South Glengarry
Federal Electoral District(s): Stormont-Dundas-South Glengarry
Next Election: Nov. 2010 (4 year terms)
Dennis Fife, Mayor
fifeag@plantpioneer.com
Karen McPherson, Clerk
kmcpherson@northstormont.ca

Northeastern Manitoulin & the Islands
P.O. Box 2000
9050 Hwy. 6
Little Current, ON P0P 1K0
705-368-3500 Fax: 705-368-2245
info@townofnemi.on.ca
www.townofnemi.on.ca
Municipal Type: Town
Area: 495.04 sq km
County or District: Manitoulin District; *Population in 2006:* 2,711
Provincial Electoral District(s): Algoma-Manitoulin
Federal Electoral District(s): Algoma-Manitoulin-Kapuskasing
Next Election: Nov. 2010 (4 year terms)
Joe Chapman, Mayor
Janet Moore, Clerk
jmoore@townofnemi.on.ca

Northern Bruce Peninsula
56 Lindsay Rd. 5, RR#2
Lions Head, ON N0H 1W0
519-793-3552 Fax: 519-793-3823
northernbrucepen@amtelecom.net
www.northbrucepeninsula.ca
Municipal Type: Municipality
Incorporated: Jan. 1999; *Area:* 781.51 sq km
County or District: Bruce; *Population in 2006:* 3,850
Provincial Electoral District(s): Bruce-Grey-Owen Sound
Federal Electoral District(s): Bruce-Grey-Owen Sound
Next Election: Nov. 2010 (4 year terms)
Note: Amalgamation of of the former Townships of St. Edmunds, Lindsay, Eastnor & the Village of Lion's Head.
Milton McIver, Mayor
Mary Lynn Standen, Municipal Clerk
marylynn.nbp@amtelecom.net

Norwich
P.O. Box 100
210 Main St. East
Otterville, ON N0J 1R0
519-863-2709 Fax: 519-879-6385 Alternative Phone: 519-879-6568
www.twp.norwich.on.ca
Municipal Type: Township
Area: 431.28 sq km
County or District: Oxford; *Population in 2006:* 10,481
Provincial Electoral District(s): Oxford
Federal Electoral District(s): Oxford
Next Election: Nov. 2010 (4 year terms)

Council
Donald Doan, Mayor
ddoan@twp.norwich.on.ca
Pat Lee, Councillor, Ward(s): 1
plee@twp.norwich.on.ca
Lynne DePlancke, Councillor, Ward(s): 2
ldeplancke@twp.norwich.on.ca
Russell Jull, Councillor, Ward(s): 3
rjull@twp.norwich.on.ca
Susan Hampson, Councillor, Ward(s): 4

Administration
Michael Graves, Chief Administrativve Officer & Clerk, Administration
519-879-6568
mgraves@twp.norwich.on.ca
H. Roy Bauslaugh, Treasurer, Administration
rbauslaugh@twp.norwich.on.ca
Brian Reid, Chief Building Official, Property Standards, Administration
breid@twp.norwich.on.ca
Wray Ramsay, Superintendent, Drainage, Administration
519-879-6568
Ron Smith, Superintendent, Public Works, Administration
ronsmith@twp.norwich.on.ca
Ted Hunt, Officer, Economic Development, Administration
thunt@twp.norwich.on.ca

O'Connor
RR#1
Kakabeka Falls, ON P0T 1W0
807-476-1451 Fax: 807-473-0891
twpoconn@tbaytel.net
www.oconnortownship.ca
Municipal Type: Township
Incorporated: January 1, 1907; *Area:* 108.58 sq km
County or District: Thunder Bay District; *Population in 2006:* 720
Provincial Electoral District(s): Thunder Bay-Atikokan
Federal Electoral District(s): Thunder Bay-Rainy River
Next Election: Nov. 2010 (4 year terms)
Ron Nelson, Mayor
807-475-9213
Lorna Buob, Clerk-Treasurer
lorna@oconnortownship.ca

Oil Springs
P.O. Box 22
4591 Oil Springs Line
Oil Springs, ON N0N 1P0
519-834-2939 Fax: 519-834-2333
oilsprings@ciaccess.com
www.oilsprings.ca
Municipal Type: Village
Incorporated: 1865; *Area:* 8.18 sq km
County or District: Lambton; *Population in 2006:* 717
Provincial Electoral District(s): Sarnia-Lambton
Federal Electoral District(s): Sarnia-Lambton
Next Election: Nov. 2010 (4 year terms)
Ian Veen, Mayor
Christine Poland, Clerk-Treasurer

Oliver Paipoonge, Municipality of
P.O. Box 10
4569 Oliver Rd.
Murillo, ON P0T 2G0
807-935-2613 Fax: 807-935-2161
sharron.martyn@oliverpaipoonage.on.ca
www.oliverpaipoonge.on.ca
Municipal Type: Township
Incorporated: Jan. 1, 1998; *Area:* 350.27 sq km
County or District: Thunder Bay District; *Population in 2006:* 5,757
Provincial Electoral District(s): Thunder Bay-Atikokan
Federal Electoral District(s): Thunder Bay-Rainy River
Next Election: Nov. 2010 (4 year terms)
Note: Amalgamation of the Township of Oliver & the Township of Paipoonge.
Lucy Kloosterhuis, Mayor
807-473-5658
mayor.lucy@xplornet.com
Jamie Cressman, Chief Administrative Officer & Clerk
jamie.cressman@oliverpaipoonge.on.ca

Opasatika
P.O. Box 100
50 Government Rd.
Opasatika, ON P0L 1Z0
705-369-4531 Fax: 705-369-2002
twpopas@persona.ca
www.geocities.com/opasatika_ontario
Municipal Type: Township
Area: 329.98 sq km
County or District: Cochrane District; *Population in 2006:* 280
Provincial Electoral District(s): Timmins-James Bay
Federal Electoral District(s): Algoma-Manitoulin-Kapuskasing
Next Election: Nov. 2010 (4 year terms)
Françoise Lambert, Mayor
Denis Dorval, Clerk-Treasurer

Oro-Medonte
P.O. Box 100
148 Line 7 South
Oro, ON L0L 2X0
705-487-2171 Fax: 705-487-0133
www.oro-medonte.ca
Municipal Type: Township
Area: 586.65 sq km
County or District: Simcoe; *Population in 2006:* 20,031
Provincial Electoral District(s): Simcoe North
Federal Electoral District(s): Simcoe North
Next Election: Nov. 2010 (4 year terms)

Council
Harry Hughes, Mayor
Ralph Hough, Deputy Mayor & Councillor
705-835-2770
Mel Coutanche, Councillor, Ward(s): 1
705-835-5728
Kelly Meyer, Councillor, Ward(s): 2
Marty Lancaster, Councillor, Ward(s): 3
John Crawford, Councillor, Ward(s): 4
705-487-3373
Dwight Evans, Councillor, Ward(s): 5
705-325-1653

Administration
Doug Irwin, Clerk & Director, Corporate Services, Administration
Robin Dunn, Chief Administrative Officer, Administration
Paul Gravelle, Treasurer, Deputy CAO, & Director, Finance, Administration
Jerry Ball, Director, Transportation & Environmental Services, Administration
Shawn Binns, Director, Recreation & Community Services, Administration
Andria Leigh, Director, Development Services, Administration
Richard Playfair, Director, Fire & Emergency Services, Administration
Kim Allen, Chief Building Official, Administration
Glenn White, Senior Planner, Administration
Tamara Obee, Officer, Human Resources, Administration

Otonabee-South Monaghan
P.O. Box 70
20 Third St.
Keene, ON K0L 2G0
705-295-6852 Fax: 705-295-6405 Toll Free Phone: 1-800-999-4861 (In 705 area code)
info@otonabeesouthmonaghan.ca
www.otonabeesouthmonaghan.ca
Municipal Type: Township
Area: 349.22 sq km
County or District: Peterborough; *Population in 2006:* 6,934
Provincial Electoral District(s): Peterborough
Federal Electoral District(s): Peterborough
Next Election: Nov. 2010 (4 year terms)
David Nelson, Reeve
705-295-4628
Heather Scott, Clerk
hscott@otonabeesouthmonaghan.ca

Oxford
P.O. Box 1614
21 Givins St.
Woodstock, ON N4S 7Y3
519-539-9800 Fax: 519-421-4712
www.oxfordcounty.ca
Municipal Type: Restructured County
Area: 2,039.46 sq km
Population in 2006: 102,756
Next Election: Nov. 2010 (4 year terms)

Council
Vacant, Warden & Councillor
Marion Wearn, Councillor, Ward(s): Blandford-Blenheim
Don E. McKay, Councillor, Ward(s): East Zorra-Tavistock
519-462-2697
Ted J. Comiskey, Councillor, Ward(s): Ingersoll
519-462-2697
Donald Doan, Councillor, Ward(s): Norwich
519-863-2709
David Mayberry, Councillor, Ward(s): South-West Oxford
John Lessif, Councillor, Ward(s): Tillsonburg
Pat Sobeski, Councillor, Ward(s): Woodstock
Deb A. Tait, Councillor, Ward(s): Woodstock
Sandra J. Talbot, Councillor, Ward(s): Woodstock
519-539-6685
Margaret E. Lupton, Councillor, Ward(s): Zorra
519-485-2490

Administration
Michael Bragg, Chief Administrative Officer & Clerk, Administration
Lynn Buchner, Director, Corporate Services, Administration
Mary Metcalfe, Director, Public Health & Emergency Services, Administration
Robert Walton, Director, Public Works, Administration
Margaret Misek-Evans, Corporate Manager, Community & Strategic Planning, Administration
Janice Kubiak, Corporate Manager, Human Resources, Administration
Margaret Misek-Evans, Corporate Manager, Community & Strategic Planning, Administration

Papineau-Cameron
P.O. Box 630
4861 Hwy. 17
Mattawa, ON P0H 1V0
705-744-5610 Fax: 705-744-0434
info@papineau-cameron.info
www.papineau-cameron.info
Municipal Type: Township
Area: 561.37 sq km
County or District: Nipissing District; *Population in 2006:* 1,058
Provincial Electoral District(s): Nipissing
Federal Electoral District(s): Nipissing-Timiskaming
Next Election: Nov. 2010 (4 year terms)
Robert Corriveau, Mayor
705-744-2597
Sandra J. Morin, Clerk-Treasurer

Parry Sound
52 Seguin St.
Parry Sound, ON P2A 1B4
705-746-2101 Fax: 705-746-7461
middaugh@townofparrysound.com (Economic Dev. & Leisure Svs.)
www.townofparrysound.com
Municipal Type: Town
Area: 13.33 sq km
County or District: Parry Sound District; *Population in 2006:* 5,818
Provincial Electoral District(s): Parry Sound-Muskoka
Federal Electoral District(s): Parry Sound-Muskoka
Next Election: Nov. 2010 (4 year terms)
Jamie McGarvey, Mayor
Rob Mens, Chief Administrative Officer
rmens@townofparrysound.com

Parry Sound
District Social Services Administration Bd.
76 Church St., 2nd Fl.
Parry Sound, ON P2A 1Z1
705-746-7777 Fax: 705-746-7783
Municipal Type: District
Area: 9,222.04 sq km
Population in 2006: 40,918
Rick Rick Zanussi, Chair, ezanussi@zeuter.com
Janet Patterson, Chief Administrative Officer, District Social Serv
705-746-7777, Fax: 705-746-7783

Pelee
1045 West Shore Rd.
Pelee Island, ON N0R 1M0
519-724-2931 Fax: 519-724-2470
info@pelee.ca
www.pelee.org
Municipal Type: Township
Incorporated: 1869; *Area:* 41.79 sq km
County or District: Essex; *Population in 2006:* 287
Provincial Electoral District(s): Essex
Federal Electoral District(s): Essex
Next Election: Nov. 2010 (4 year terms)
Ricard Masse, Mayor
Ann Mitchell, Clerk-Treasurer

Penetanguishene
P.O. Box 5009
10 Robert St. West
Penetanguishene, ON L9M 2G2
705-549-7453 Fax: 705-549-3743
ctobey@penetanguishene.ca
www.penetanguishene.ca
Municipal Type: Town
Incorporated: Feb. 22, 1882; *Area:* 25.38 sq km
County or District: Simcoe; *Population in 2006:* 9,354
Provincial Electoral District(s): Simcoe North
Federal Electoral District(s): Simcoe North
Next Election: Nov. 2010 (4 year terms)
Gerry Marshall, Mayor
Holly Bryce, Town Clerk
hbryce@penetanguishene.ca

Perry
P.O. Box 70
Old Government Rd.
Emsdale, ON P0A 1J0
705-636-5941 Fax: 705-636-5759 Email Public Works: publicworks@townshipofperry.ca
info@townshipofperry.ca; council@townshipofperry.ca
www.townshipofperry.ca
Municipal Type: Township
Area: 186.63 sq km
County or District: Parry Sound District; *Population in 2006:* 2,010
Provincial Electoral District(s): Parry Sound-Muskoka
Federal Electoral District(s): Parry Sound-Muskoka
Next Election: Nov. 2010 (4 year terms)
John Dunn, Mayor
705-636-7833
mayor@townshipofperry.ca
Brenda J. Fraser, Clerk-Administrator

Perth
Town Hall
80 Gore St. East
Perth, ON K7H 1H9
613-267-3311 Fax: 613-267-5635
www.town.perth.on.ca
Municipal Type: Town
Area: 10.36 sq km
County or District: Lanark; *Population in 2006:* 5,907
Provincial Electoral District(s): Lanark-Frontenac-Lennox & Addington

Federal Electoral District(s): Lanark-Frontenac-Lennox & Addington
Next Election: Nov. 2010 (4 year terms)
John Fenik, Mayor
613-267-3311
jfenik@town.perth.on.ca
Lauren Walton, Clerk

Perth East

P.O. Box 455
25 Mill St. East
Milverton, ON N0K 1M0
519-595-2800 Fax: 519-595-2801
township@pertheast.on.ca
www.pertheast.on.ca
Municipal Type: Township
Area: 715.07 sq km
County or District: Perth; *Population in 2006:* 12,041
Provincial Electoral District(s): Perth-Wellinton
Federal Electoral District(s): Perth-Wellington
Next Election: Nov. 2010 (4 year terms)
Note: Amalgamation of North Easthope Township, South Easthope Township, Ellice Township, Village of Milverton & Mornington Township.

Council
Ian Forrest, Mayor
iforrest@pertheast.on.ca
Bob McMillan, Deputy Mayor & Councillor
Rhonda Ehgoetz, Councillor, Ward(s): Ellice
Jeremy Matheson, Councillor, Ward(s): Milverton
Don Brunk, Councillor, Ward(s): Mornington
Hugh McDermid, Councillor, Ward(s): North Easthope
Andrew MacAlpine, Councillor, Ward(s): South Easthope

Administration
Kerri Ann O'Rourke, Clerk, Administration
Glenn Schwendinger, Chief Administrative Officer, Administration
Rhonda Fischer, Treasurer, Administration
Wes Kuepfer, Manager, Public Works, Administration
Donna Chaffe, Coordinator, Human Resources, Administration
Bill Wilson, Coordinator, Operations, Administration
Darrell Reis, Fire Chief, Administration
Grant Schwartzentruber, Chief Building Official, Administration

Perth South

3204 Rd. 122
St Pauls, ON N0K 1V0
519-271-0619 Fax: 519-271-0647
township.perthsouth@cyg.net
www.perthsouth.ca
Municipal Type: Township
Area: 393.01 sq km
County or District: Perth; *Population in 2006:* 4,132
Provincial Electoral District(s): Perth-Wellington
Federal Electoral District(s): Perth-Wellington
Next Election: Nov. 2010 (4 year terms)
Note: Amalgamation of Blanshard Township & Downie Township.
Robert Wilhelm, Mayor
Tim Ivanyshyn, Chief Administrative Officer & Clerk, Fax: 519-271-0647
tivanyshyn@perthsouth.ca

Petrolia

P.O. Box 1270
411 Greenfield St.
Petrolia, ON N0N 1R0
519-882-2350 Fax: 519-882-3373
petrolia@town.petrolia.on.ca
www.town.petrolia.on.ca
Municipal Type: Town
Area: 12.68 sq km
County or District: Lambton; *Population in 2006:* 5,222
Provincial Electoral District(s): Lambton-Kent-Middlesex
Federal Electoral District(s): Sarnia-Lambton
Next Election: Nov. 2010 (4 year terms)
John McCharles, Mayor
519-882-2455
johnnyremax@bellnet.ca
Dianne Caryn, Chief Administrative Officer
dcaryn@town.petrolia.on.ca

Pickle Lake

P.O. Box 340
2 Anne St.
Pickle Lake, ON P0V 3A0
807-928-2034 Fax: 807-928-2708 Toll Free Phone: 1-800-565-9189
reception@picklelake.org
www.picklelake.ca
Municipal Type: Township
Incorporated: Dec. 1980; *Area:* 255.08 sq km
County or District: Kenora District; *Population in 2006:* 479
Provincial Electoral District(s): Kenora-Rainy River
Federal Electoral District(s): Kenora
Next Election: Nov. 2010 (4 year terms)
Roy Hoffman, Mayor
Paul Panciw, Clerk-Treasurer
clerktreasurer@picklelake.org

Plummer Additional

38 Railway Cres., RR#2
Bruce Mines, ON P0R 1C0
705-785-3479 Fax: 705-785-3135
Municipal Type: Township
Area: 221.31 sq km
County or District: Algoma District; *Population in 2006:* 625
Provincial Electoral District(s): Algoma-Manitoulin
Federal Electoral District(s): Sault Ste Marie
Next Election: Nov. 2010 (4 year terms)
Beth West, Mayor
Vicky Goertzen-Cooke, Clerk-Treasurer

Plympton-Wyoming

P.O. Box 250
546 Niagara St.
Wyoming, ON N0N 1T0
519-845-3939 Fax: 519-845-0597 Toll Free Phone: 1-877-313-3939
feedback@plympton-wyoming.com
www.plympton-wyoming.com
Municipal Type: Town
Incorporated: Jan. 1, 2001; *Area:* 318.76 sq km
County or District: Lambton; *Population in 2006:* 7,506
Provincial Electoral District(s): Sarnia-Lambton
Federal Electoral District(s): Sarnia-Lambton
Next Election: Nov. 2010 (4 year terms)
Note: Amalgamation of the Village of Wyoming & the Township of Plympton.
Lonny Napper, Mayor
lnapper@xcelco.on.ca
Caroline DeSchutter, A.M.C.T., Administrator-Clerk
cdeschutter@plympton-wyoming.ca

Point Edward

135 Kendall St.
Point Edward, ON N7V 4G6
519-337-3021 Fax: 519-337-5963
info@villageofpointedward.com
www.villageofpointedward.com
Municipal Type: Village
Incorporated: 1878; *Area:* 3.27 sq km
County or District: Lambton; *Population in 2006:* 2,019
Provincial Electoral District(s): Sarnia-Lambton
Federal Electoral District(s): Sarnia-Lambton
Next Election: Nov. 2010 (4 year terms)
Dick Kirkland, Mayor
Peggy Cramp, Chief Administrative Officer & Clerk-Treasurer
pcramp@villageofpointedward.com

Port Hope

56 Queen St.
Port Hope, ON L1A 3Z9
905-885-4544 Fax: 905-885-7698
admin@porthope.ca
www.porthope.ca
Municipal Type: Municipality
Incorporated: March 6, 1834; *Area:* 278.97 sq km
County or District: Northumberland; *Population in 2006:* 16,390
Provincial Electoral District(s): Northumberland-Quinte West
Federal Electoral District(s): Northumberland-Quinte West
Next Election: Nov. 2010 (4 year terms)

Council
Linda M. Thompson, Mayor
mayor@porthope.ca
Rick Austin, Councillor, Ward(s): 1
David Turck, Councillor, Ward(s): 1
dturck@porthope.ca
Jeff G. Lees, Councillor, Ward(s): 1
Greg W. Burns, Councillor, Ward(s): 2
Jeffrey S. Gilmer, Councillor, Ward(s): 2

Administration
Sue Dawe, Clerk & Director, Corporate Services, Administration
sdawe@porthope.ca
R. Carl Cannon, Chief Administrative Officer, Administration
Barbara Spry, Treasurer, Administration
bspry@porthope.ca
Peter Angelo, Director, Public Works, Administration
905-885-2431
publicworks@porthope.ca; pangelo@porthope.ca
Rob Collins, Director, Fire & Emergency Services, Administration
905-885-5323
rcollins@porthope.ca
Eugene Todd, Director, Parks, Recreation, & Culture, Administration
905-753-2230
etodd@porthope.ca
Ron Warne, Director, Planning & Development Services, Administration
905-885-2415
planning@porthope.ca
Ken Andrus, Chief Building Official, Administration
905-885-2415
cbo@porthope.ca
Gina Jackson, Manager, Human Resources, Administration
905-885-4544
gjackson@porthope.ca

Powassan, Municipality of

P.O. Box 250
466 Main St.
Powassan, ON P0H 1Z0
705-724-2813 Fax: 705-724-5533
info@powassan.net
www.powassan.net
Municipal Type: Town
Incorporated: Nov. 30, 1904; *Area:* 222.75 sq km
County or District: Parry Sound District; *Population in 2006:* 3,309
Provincial Electoral District(s): Nipissing
Federal Electoral District(s): Nipissing-Timiskaming
Next Election: Nov. 2010 (4 year terms)
Peter McIsaac, Mayor
Roger Labelle, Chief Administrative Officer & Clerk
rlabelle@powassan.net

Prescott

P.O. Box 160
360 Dibble St. West
Prescott, ON K0E 1T0
613-925-2812 Fax: 613-925-4381
info@prescott.ca
www.prescott.ca
Municipal Type: Separated for Municipal Purposes Only
Area: 4.95 sq km
County or District: Leeds & Grenville; *Population in 2006:* 4,180
Provincial Electoral District(s): Leeds-Grenville
Federal Electoral District(s): Leeds-Grenville
Next Election: Nov. 2010 (4 year terms)
Brett Todd, Mayor
Robert Haller, Chief Administrative Officer & Clerk
rhaller@prescott.ca

Prescott & Russell

P.O. Box 304
59 Court St.
L'Orignal, ON K0B 1K0
613-675-4661 Fax: 613-675-2519 Toll Free Phone: 1-800-667-6307
support@prescott-russell.on.ca
www.prescott-russell.on.ca
Municipal Type: United County
Incorporated: 1820; *Area:* 2,001.18 sq km
Population in 2006: 80,184
Next Election: Nov. 2010 (4 year terms)

Council
Vacant, Warden & Councillor

Council
Stéphane P. Parisien, Chief Administrative Officer & Clerk, Administration
spparisien@prescott-russell.on.ca
Jean-Yves Lalonde, Councillor, Ward(s): Alfred & Plantagenet
Louise Lepage-Gareau, Treasurer, Administration
llgareau@prescott-russell.on.ca
Claude Levac, Councillor, Ward(s): Casselman
Michel Chrétien, Director, Emergency Services, Administration
Gary J. Barton, Councillor, Ward(s): Champlain
Marc Clermont, Director, Public Works, Administration
Marcel Guibord, Councillor, Ward(s): Clarence-Rockland
Louis Prevost, Director, Planning & Forestry, Administration
Robert Kirby, Councillor, Ward(s): East Hawkesbury
Elizabeth Gauthier, Manager, Human Resources, Administration
Rene Berthiaume, Councillor, Ward(s): Hawkesbury
François St. Amour, Councillor, Ward(s): The Nation
Jean-Paul Saint-Pierre, Councillor, Ward(s): Russell

Prince

3042 2nd Line West, RR#6
Sault Ste Marie, ON P6A 6K4
705-779-2992 Fax: 705-779-2725
www.princetwp.ca
Municipal Type: Township
Area: 84.28 sq km
County or District: Algoma District; *Population in 2006:* 971
Provincial Electoral District(s): Algoma Manitoulin
Federal Electoral District(s): Sault Ste Marie
Next Election: Nov. 2010 (4 year terms)
Ken Lamming, Reeve
Brianna Coughlin, Chief Administrative Officer & Administrator

Puslinch

7404 Wellington Rd. 34, RR#3
Guelph, ON N1H 6H9
519-763-1226 Fax: 519-763-5846
admin@twp.puslinch.on.ca
www.twp.puslinch.on.ca
Municipal Type: Township
Incorporated: Jan. 1, 1850; *Area:* 214.44 sq km
County or District: Wellington; *Population in 2006:* 6,689
Provincial Electoral District(s): Wellington-Halton Hills
Federal Electoral District(s): Wellington-Halton Hills; Guelph
Next Election: Nov. 2010 (4 year terms)
Dennis Lever, Mayor
519-621-9239
Brenda Law, Chief Administrative Officer & Clerk-Treasurer

Rainy River

P.O. Box 488
200 Atwood Ave.
Rainy River, ON P0W 1L0
807-852-3244 Fax: 807-852-3553
rainyriver@tbaytel.net
www.rainyriver.ca
Municipal Type: Town
Incorporated: 1904; *Area:* 2.99 sq km
County or District: Rainy River District; *Population in 2006:* 909
Provincial Electoral District(s): Kenora-Rainy River
Federal Electoral District(s): Thunder Bay-Rainy River
Next Election: Nov. 2010 (4 year terms)
Deb Ewald, Mayor
Veldron Vogan, Chief Administrative Officer

Rainy River

District Social Services Administration Bd.
450 Scott St.
Fort Frances, ON P9A 1H2
807-274-5349 Toll Free Phone: 1-800-265-5349

Municipal Type: District
Area: 15,472.94 sq km
Population in 2006: 21,564
Michael Lewis, Chair, Rainy River District Social Services Admini
Donna Dittaro, CAO, Rainy River District Social Services Administ
donnad@rrdssab.on.ca

Ramara
P.O. Box 130
2297 Hwy. 12
Brechin, ON L0K 1B0
705-484-5374 Fax: 705-484-0441
ramara@township.ramara.on.ca
www.township.ramara.on.ca
Municipal Type: Township
Area: 417.25 sq km
County or District: Simcoe; *Population in 2006:* 9,427
Provincial Electoral District(s): Simcoe North
Federal Electoral District(s): Simcoe North
Next Election: Nov. 2010 (4 year terms)
Bill Duffy, Mayor
Janice McKinnon, Clerk
jconnor@township.ramara.on.ca

Red Lake
P.O. Box 1000
Balmertown, ON P0V 1C0
807-735-2096 Fax: 807-735-2286
municipality@red-lake.com
www.red-lake.com
Municipal Type: Municipality
Incorporated: July 1, 1998; *Area:* 610.38 sq km
County or District: Kenora District; *Population in 2006:* 4,526
Provincial Electoral District(s): Kenora-Rainy River
Federal Electoral District(s): Kenora
Next Election: Nov. 2010 (4 year terms)
Note: Amalgamation of the former Unorganized Territory of Madsen, the Township of Red Lake, & the Township of Golden.
Phil T. Vinet, Mayor
Brian Anderson, Chief Administrative Officer

Red Rock
P.O. Box 447
42 Salls St.
Red Rock, ON P0T 2P0
807-886-2245 Fax: 807-886-2793 Phone, Public Works: 807-886-2524
info@redrocktownship.com
www.redrocktownship.com
Municipal Type: Township
Area: 62.93 sq km
County or District: Thunder Bay District; *Population in 2006:* 1,063
Provincial Electoral District(s): Thunder Bay-Superior North
Federal Electoral District(s): Thunder Bay-Superior North
Next Election: Nov. 2010 (4 year terms)
Gary Nelson, Mayor
807-886-2503
Kal Pristanski, CAO, Clerk-Treasurer, Tax Collector, & Commissione
cao@shawbiz.ca

Renfrew
127 Raglan St. South
Renfrew, ON K7V 1P8
613-432-4848 Fax: 613-432-7245
info@town.renfrew.on.ca
www.renfrewontario.com
Municipal Type: Town
Area: 12.77 sq km
County or District: Renfrew; *Population in 2006:* 7,846
Provincial Electoral District(s): Renfrew-Nipissing-Pembroke
Federal Electoral District(s): Renfrew-Nipissing-Pembroke
Next Election: Nov. 2010 (4 year terms)
Bill Ringrose, Mayor
Kim R. Bulmer, Town Clerk
kbulmer@town.renfrew.on.ca
Audrey Green, Reeve

Rideau Lakes
P.O. Box 500
1439 County Rd. 8
Delta, ON K0E 1G0
613-928-2251 Fax: 613-928-3097 Toll Free Phone: 1-800-928-2250
info@twprideaulakes.on.ca
www.twprideaulakes.on.ca
Municipal Type: Township
Incorporated: Jan. 1, 1998; *Area:* 710.25 sq km
County or District: Leeds-Grenville; *Population in 2006:* 10,350
Provincial Electoral District(s): Leeds-Grenville
Federal Electoral District(s): Leeds-Grenville
Next Election: Nov. 2010 (4 year terms)
Note: Amalgamation of the former Townships of North Crosby, South Crosby, Bastard & South Burgess, South Elmsley & the Village of Newboro.

Council
Ronald Holman, Mayor
613-283-0724, Fax: 613-283-5517
mayor@twprideaulakes.on.ca; rholman@ripnet.com
Anders Carson, Councillor, Ward(s): Bastard & South Burgess
carson@rideau.net
Rob Dunfield, Councillor, Ward(s): Bastard & South Burgess
dunfield.robert@gmail.com
Cathy Monck, Councillor, Ward(s): Newboro
Ronald Pollard, Councillor, Ward(s): North Crosby
pollard.ron@sympatico.ca
Bob Lavoie, Councillor, Ward(s): North Crosby
Linda Carr, Councillor, Ward(s): South Crosby
councillor@rideaucondo.com
Robert Taylor, Councillor, Ward(s): South Crosby
Jeff Banks, Councillor, Ward(s): South Elmsley
Paul A.L. Smith, Councillor, Ward(s): South Elmsley
smith.paul@sympatico.ca

Administration
Dianna Bresee, Clerk & Officer, Administration
dianna@twprideaulakes.on.ca
Robert Maddocks, Chief Administrative Officer, Administration
cao@twprideaulakes.on.ca
Joseph Whyte, Treasurer, Administration
joe@twprideaulakes.on.ca
Susan Dunfield, Manager, Community & Leisure Services, Administration
susan@twprideaulakes.on.ca
Sheldon Laidman, Manager, Development Services, Administration
slaidman@twprideaulakes.on.ca
Michael Touw, Manager, Public Works, Administration
mtouw@twprideaulakes.on.ca
Jay DeBernardi, Fire Chief, Administration
fire.j@twprideaulakes.on.ca

Russell
717 Notre Dame St.
Embrun, ON K0A 1W1
613-443-3066 Fax: 613-443-1042
ginettebertrand@russell.ca (Ginette Bertrand)
www.russell.ca
Municipal Type: Township
Area: 198.96 sq km
County or District: Prescott & Russell; *Population in 2006:* 13,883
Provincial Electoral District(s): Glengarry-Prescott-Russell
Federal Electoral District(s): Glengarry-Prescott-Russell
Next Election: Nov. 2010 (4 year terms)
Ken Hill, Mayor
kenhill@russell.ca
Lorraine Dicaire, Councillor
lorrainedicaire@russell.ca
Jamie Laurin, Councillor
jlaurin@russell.ca
Donald St. Pierre, Councillor
dstpierre@russell.ca
Jean-Paul St. Pierre, Councillor
jpstpierre@russell.ca
Ginette Bertrand, Municipal Clerk, Administration
ginettebertrand@russell.ca
Jean Leduc, Chief Administrative Officer, Administration
jeanleduc@russell.ca
Christiane B. Brault, Director, Finance, Administration
christianebrault@russell.ca
Millie Bourdeau, Director, Public Safety & Enforcement, Administration
milliebourdeau@russell.ca
Lawrence Gangur, Director, Environmental Services, Administration
lawrencegangur@russell.ca
Jacques Lortie, Director, Public Works, Parks, & Recreation, Administration
jacqueslortie@russell.ca
Dominique Tremblay, Director, Planning, Administration
dominiquetremblay@russell.ca
Bruce Armstrong, Fire Chief, Russell, Administration
brucearmstrong@russell.ca
Jean-Luc Bourgie, Fire Chief, Embrun, Administration
bourgie@rogers.com
Julia Tuff, Chief Building Official, Administration
juliatuff@russell.ca

Ryerson
28 Midlothian Rd., RR#1
Burks Falls, ON P0A 1C0
705-382-3232 Fax: 705-382-3286
admin@ryersontownship.ca
www.ryersontownship.ca
Municipal Type: Township
Area: 186.79 sq km
County or District: Parry Sound District; *Population in 2006:* 686
Provincial Electoral District(s): Parry Sound-Muskoka
Federal Electoral District(s): Parry Sound-Muskoka
Next Election: Nov. 2010 (4 year terms)
Glenn Miller, Reeve
705-382-2898
Judy Kosowan, Clerk-Treasurer

Sables-Spanish Rivers
PO Box 5, Site 1, 11 Birch Lake Rd. RR#3
Massey, ON P0P 1P0
705-865-2646 Fax: 705-865-2736
inquiries@sables-spanish.ca
www.sables-spanish.ca
Municipal Type: Township
Incorporated: July 1998; *Area:* 806.27 sq km
County or District: Sudbury District; *Population in 2006:* 3,237
Provincial Electoral District(s): Algoma-Manitoulin
Federal Electoral District(s): Algoma-Manitoulin-Kapuskasing
Next Election: Nov. 2010 (4 year terms)
Leslie Gamble, Mayor
705-865-2655
Kim Sloss, Clerk-Administrator, Fax: 705-865-2736
kasloss@sables-spanish.ca

St. Clair
Civic Centre
1155 Emily St.
Mooretown, ON N0N 1M0
519-867-2021 Fax: 519-867-5509 Toll Free Phone: 1-800-809-0301 (Sombra & Lambton)
webmaster@twp.stclair.on.ca
www.twp.stclair.on.ca
Municipal Type: Township
Area: 619.3 sq km
County or District: Lambton; *Population in 2006:* 14,649
Provincial Electoral District(s): Sarnia-Lambton
Federal Electoral District(s): Sarnia-Lambton
Next Election: Nov. 2010 (4 year terms)

Council
Steve Arnold, Mayor
519-867-3333
Peter Gilliland, Deputy Mayor & Councillor
519-862-3534
Jeff Agar, Councillor, Ward(s): 1
519-862-5062
Patricia Carswell-Alexander, Councillor, Ward(s): 1
519-864-4006
Jim DeGurse, Councillor, Ward(s): 1
Steve Miller, Councillor, Ward(s): 2
519-677-5676
Darrell Randell, Councillor, Ward(s): 2
519-627-3764

Administration
John DeMars, Clerk & Director, Administration, Administration
J. Rodey, Chief Administrative Officer, Administration
C. Quenneville, Treasurer & Director, Finance, Administration
L. Burnham, Director, Public Works, Operations, & Engineering, Administration
R. Dewhirst, Director, Fire Services, Administration
G. Hackett, Director, Community Services, Administration

St. Joseph
P.O. Box 187
1669 Arthur St.
Richards Landing, ON P0R 1J0
705-246-2625 Fax: 705-246-3142
stjosephtwp@bellnet.ca
www.stjosephtownship.com
Municipal Type: Township
Area: 129.18 sq km
County or District: Algoma District; *Population in 2006:* 1,129
Provincial Electoral District(s): Algoma-Manitoulin
Federal Electoral District(s): Sault Ste Marie
Next Election: Nov. 2010 (4 year terms)
Jody Wildman, Mayor
Michael Jagger, Chief Administrative Officer & Clerk-Treasurer

St. Marys
P.O. Box 998
175 Queen St. East
St Marys, ON N4X 1B6
519-284-2340 Fax: 519-284-2881
townhall@townofstmarys.com
www.townofstmarys.com
Municipal Type: Separated for Municipal Purposes Only
Area: 12.48 sq km
County or District: Perth; *Population in 2006:* 6,617
Provincial Electoral District(s): Perth-Wellington
Federal Electoral District(s): Perth-Wellington
Next Election: Nov. 2010 (4 year terms)
Steve Grose, Mayor
Robert Brindley, Chief Administrative Officer
rbrindley@town.stmarys.on.ca

Schreiber
P.O. Box 40
608 Winnipeg St.
Schreiber, ON P0T 2S0
807-824-2711 Fax: 807-824-3231
executiveassistant@schreiber.ca
www.schreiber.ca
Municipal Type: Township
Area: 36.79 sq km
County or District: Thunder Bay District; *Population in 2006:* 901
Provincial Electoral District(s): Thunder Bay-Superior North
Federal Electoral District(s): Thunder Bay-Superior North
Next Election: Nov. 2010 (4 year terms)
Don McArthur, Mayor
mayor@schreiber.ca
Jonathan Hall, Clerk
clerk@schreiber.ca

Scugog
P.O. Box 780
181 Perry St.
Port Perry, ON L9L 1A7
905-985-7346 Fax: 905-985-1931
mail@township.scugog.on.ca
www.scugog.ca
Municipal Type: Township
Area: 474.63 sq km
County or District: Durham Regional Municipality; *Population in 2006:* 21,439
Provincial Electoral District(s): Durham
Federal Electoral District(s): Durham
Next Election: Nov. 2010 (4 year terms)

Council
Chuck Mercier, Mayor
Bobbie Drew, Regional Councillor
Larry Corrigan, Councillor, Ward(s): 1
John Hancock, Councillor, Ward(s): 2

Jim Howard, Councillor, Ward(s): 3
Wilma Wotten, Councillor, Ward(s): 4
Howard Danson, Councillor, Ward(s): 5

Administration
Kim Coates, Administration
Bev Hendry, Chief Administrative Officer, Administration
Kathryn McCann, Commissioner, Corporate Services, Administration
Gene Chartier, Commissioner, Planning & Public Works, Administration
John Sellars, Director, Parks, Recreation, & Culture, Administration
Richard Miller, Fire Chief, Administration

Seguin
5 Humphrey Dr., RR#2
Parry Sound, ON P2A 2W8
705-732-4300 Fax: 705-732-6347 Toll Free Phone: 1-877-473-4846
info@seguin.ca
www.seguin.ca
Municipal Type: Township
Incorporated: May 8, 1997; *Area:* 586.17 sq km
County or District: Parry Sound District; *Population in 2006:* 4,276
Provincial Electoral District(s): Parry Sound-Muskoka
Federal Electoral District(s): Parry Sound-Muskoka
Next Election: Nov. 2010 (4 year terms)
David Conn, Mayor
davidc@vianet.ca
Craig Jeffery, Clerk & Officer, Lottery Licensing

Severn
P.O. Box 159
1024 Hurlwood Lane
Orillia, ON L3V 6J3
705-325-2315 Fax: 705-327-5818
severn@encode.com
www.townshipofsevern.com
Municipal Type: Township
Incorporated: Jan. 1, 1994; *Area:* 534.78 sq km
County or District: Simcoe; *Population in 2006:* 12,030
Provincial Electoral District(s): Simcoe North
Federal Electoral District(s): Simcoe North
Next Election: Nov. 2010 (4 year terms)

Council
Mike H. Burkett, Mayor
Judith Cox, Deputy Mayor & Councillor
Mark Taylor, Councillor, Ward(s): 1
Jane Dunlop, Councillor, Ward(s): 2
Ian Crichton, Councillor, Ward(s): 3
Ron Stevens, Councillor, Ward(s): 4
Rob Ferguson, Councillor, Ward(s): 5

Administration
Henry Sander, Clerk-Treasurer & Director, Corporate Services, Administration
Eric Peterson, Chief Administrative Officer, Administration
Clayton Cameron, Director, Public Works, Administration
Eric Dowell, Director, Fire & Emergency Services, Administration
David Parks, Director, Planning & Development, Administration

Shelburne
P.O. Box 69
203 Main St. East
Shelburne, ON L0N 1S0
519-925-2600 Fax: 519-925-6134
shelburne@townofshelburne.on.ca
www.townofshelburne.on.ca
Municipal Type: Town
Incorporated: Mar. 22, 1879; *Area:* 6.44 sq km
County or District: Dufferin; *Population in 2006:* 5,149
Provincial Electoral District(s): Dufferin-Caledon
Federal Electoral District(s): Dufferin-Caledon
Next Election: Nov. 2010 (4 year terms)
Note: Incorporated as a town on Dec. 31, 1976.
Ed Crewson, Mayor
John Telfer, AMCT, Acting CAO, Town Clerk, & Economic Development Off
jtelfer@townofshelburne.on.ca

Shuniah
420 Leslie Ave.
Thunder Bay, ON P7A 1X8
807-683-4545 Fax: 807-683-6982 E-mail, Public Works: cbaumann@shuniah.org
shuniah@shuniah.org; ecollingwood@shuniah.org (CAO Office)
www.shuniah.org
Municipal Type: Township
Incorporated: 1873; *Area:* 569.18 sq km
County or District: Thunder Bay District; *Population in 2006:* 2,913
Provincial Electoral District(s): Thunder Bay-Superior North
Federal Electoral District(s): Thunder Bay-Superior North
Next Election: Nov. 2010 (4 year terms)
Maria Harding, Reeve
807-983-2276
mharding@tbaytel.net
Wendy Hamlin, Clerk
whamlin@shuniah.org

Sioux Lookout, Municipality of
P.O. Box 158
25 Fifth Ave.
Sioux Lookout, ON P8T 1A4
807-737-2700 Fax: 807-737-3436
admin@siouxlookout.ca
www.siouxlookout.ca
Municipal Type: Town
Incorporated: 1912; *Area:* 378.61 sq km
County or District: Kenora District; *Population in 2006:* 5,183
Provincial Electoral District(s): Kenora-Rainy River
Federal Electoral District(s): Kenora
Next Election: Nov. 2010 (4 year terms)
Dennis Leney, Mayor
Mary L. MacKenzie, Municipal Clerk

Sioux Narrows-Nestor Falls
P.O. Box 417
Sioux Narrows, ON P0X 1N0
807-226-5241 Fax: 807-226-5712
info@siouxnarrows-nestorfalls.ca
www.siouxnarrows-nestorfalls.ca
Municipal Type: Township
Area: 1,221.56 sq km
County or District: Kenora District; *Population in 2006:* 672
Provincial Electoral District(s): Kenora-Rainy River
Federal Electoral District(s): Kenora
Next Election: Nov. 2010 (4 year terms)
William (Bill) Thompson, Mayor
Wanda Kabel, Chief Administrative Officer

Smith-Ennismore-Lakefield
P.O. Box 270
1310 Centre Line, RR#4
Bridgenorth, ON K0L 1H0
705-292-9507 Fax: 705-292-8964 Toll Free Phone: 1-877-213-7419 (In 705 area code)
www.smithennismorelakefield.on.ca
Municipal Type: Township
Area: 318.77 sq km
County or District: Peterborough; *Population in 2006:* 17,413
Provincial Electoral District(s): Peterborough
Federal Electoral District(s): Peterborough
Next Election: Nov. 2010 (4 year terms)

Council
Mary Smith, Reeve
Andy Mitchell, Deputy Reeve
Donna Ballantyne, Councillor, Ward(s): Ennismore
dib1452@bell.net
Anita Locke, Councillor, Ward(s): Lakefield
anitalocke@anitalocke.ca; jasana@nexicom.net
Sherry Senis, Councillor, Ward(s): Lakefield
wssenis@sympatico.ca

Administration
Angela Chittick, Clerk, Administration
705-292-9507, Fax: 705-292-8964
Janice Lavalley, Chief Administrative Officer, Administration
R. Lane Vance, Treasurer & Manager, Financial Services, Administration
Ed Barber, Manager, Recreation, Administration
705-292-8774
Stephen Crough, Manager, Public Works, Administration
705-292-8621
Robert Lamarre, Manager, Building & Planning, Administration
Gord Jopling, Fire Chief, Administration
705-292-7282
Karen McGee, Coordinator, Human Resources, Administration

Smiths Falls
P.O. Box 695
77 Beckwith St. North
Smiths Falls, ON K7A 4T6
613-283-4124 Fax: 613-283-4764
info@smithsfalls.ca
www.smithsfalls.ca
Municipal Type: Separated for Municipal Purposes Only
Incorporated: 1854; *Area:* 8.2 sq km
County or District: Lanark; *Population in 2006:* 8,777
Provincial Electoral District(s): Lanark-Frontenac-Lennox & Addington
Federal Electoral District(s): Lanark-Frontenac-Lennox & Addington
Next Election: Nov. 2010 (4 year terms)
Note: Incorporated as a town on Jan. 1, 1883. In Dec. 1902, the Town of Smiths Falls became the Separated Town of Smiths Falls.
Dennis Staples, Mayor
mayor@smithsfalls.ca
Kerry Costello, Clerk
kcostello@smithsfalls.ca

Smooth Rock Falls
P.O. Box 249
142 First St.
Smooth Rock Falls, ON P0L 2B0
705-338-2717 Fax: 705-338-2584
francine.lévesque@townsrf.ca
www.townofsmoothrockfalls.ca
Municipal Type: Town
Incorporated: 1929; *Area:* 199.79 sq km
County or District: Cochrane District; *Population in 2006:* 1,473
Provincial Electoral District(s): Timmins-James Bay
Federal Electoral District(s): Algoma-Manitoulin-Kapuskasing
Next Election: Nov. 2010 (4 year terms)
Michel Arseneault, Mayor
Michelle Larose, Chief Administrative Officer
michelle.larose@townsrf.ca

South Algonquin
P.O. Box 217
Hay Creek Rd.
Whitney, ON K0J 2M0
613-637-2650 Fax: 613-637-5368 Toll Free Phone: 1-888-307-3187
southalgonquin@xplornet.com
www.township.southalgonquin.on.ca
Municipal Type: Township
Area: 871.31 sq km
County or District: Nipissing District; *Population in 2006:* 1,253
Provincial Electoral District(s): Renfrew-Nipissing-Pembroke
Federal Electoral District(s): Renfrew-Nipissing-Pembroke
Next Election: Nov. 2010 (4 year terms)
Jane Dumas, Mayor
Harold Luckasavitch, Clerk-Treasurer

South Bruce
P.O. Box 540
21 Gordon St. East
Teeswater, ON N0G 2S0
519-392-6623 Fax: 519-392-6266 Toll Free Phone, Westario Office; 1-866-978-2746
clerk@town.southbruce.on.ca
www.town.southbruce.on.ca
Municipal Type: Municipality
Incorporated: 1999; *Area:* 487.17 sq km
County or District: Bruce; *Population in 2006:* 5,939
Provincial Electoral District(s): Huron-Bruce
Federal Electoral District(s): Huron-Bruce
Next Election: Nov. 2010 (4 year terms)
Note: Amalgamation of the Village of Mildmay, the Township of Carrick, the Village of Teeswater, & the Township of Culross.
William Goetz, Mayor
Robert Small, Chief Administrative Officer & Clerk

South Bruce Peninsula
P.O. Box 310
315 George St.
Wiarton, ON N0H 2T0
519-534-1400 Fax: 519-534-4862 Toll Free Phone: 1-877-534-1400
admin@southbrucepeninsula.com
www.southbrucepeninsula.com
Municipal Type: Town
Area: 531.9 sq km
County or District: Bruce; *Population in 2006:* 8,415
Provincial Electoral District(s): Bruce-Grey-Owen Sound
Federal Electoral District(s): Bruce-Grey-Owen Sound
Next Election: Nov. 2010 (4 year terms)
John Close, Mayor
519-534-3067
Angela Cathrae, Clerk
cao@southbrucepeninsula.com

South Dundas
P.O. Box 160
4296 County Rd. 31
Williamsburg, ON K0C 2H0
613-535-2673 Fax: 613-535-2099 Toll Free Phone: 1-800-265-0619
mail@southdundas.com
www.southdundas.com
Municipal Type: Township
Area: 519.98 sq km
County or District: Stormont, Dundas & Glengarry; *Population in 2006:* 10,535
Provincial Electoral District(s): Stormont-Dundas-South Glengarry
Federal Electoral District(s): Stormont-Dundas-South Glengarry
Next Election: Nov. 2010 (4 year terms)

Council
Steven J. Byvelds, Mayor
Jim Locke, Deputy Mayor & Councillor
Evonne Delegarde, Councillor
613-652-1388
evonne_delegarde@hotmail.com
Archie L. Mellan, Councillor
Jim Graham, Councillor
613-543-3588
del_jones@sympatico.ca

Administration
Brenda M. Brunt, Clerk, Administration
bbrunt@southdundas.com
Stephen McDonald, Chief Administrative Officer, Administration
smcdonald@southdundas.com
Shannon Geraghty, Treasurer, Administration
sgeraghty@southdundas.com
Hugh Garlough, Manager, Public Works, Administration
hgarlough@southdundas.com
Don J.W. Lewis, Manager, Planning & Enforcement, Administration
dlewis@southdundas.com
Linda Wilson, Officer, Economic Development, Administration
lwilson@southdundas.com
Bill Shearing, Coordinator, Emergency Management, Administration
bill.shearing@sympatico.ca

South Frontenac
P.O. Box 100
4432 George St.
Sydenham, ON K0H 2T0
613-376-3027 Fax: 613-376-6657 Toll Free Phone: 1-800-559-5862
admin@township.southfrontenac.on.ca
www.township.southfrontenac.on.ca
Municipal Type: Township
Incorporated: Jan. 1, 1998; *Area:* 941.28 sq km
County or District: Frontenac; *Population in 2006:* 18,227
Provincial Electoral District(s): Lanark-Frontenac-Lennox & Addington
Federal Electoral District(s): Lanark-Frontenac-Lennox & Addington
Next Election: Nov. 2010 (4 year terms)

Council
Gary C Davison, Mayor
davison4544@yahoo.ca
Del Stowe, Councillor, Ward(s): Bedford
delstowe@yahoo.com
Mark Tinlin, Councillor, Ward(s): Bedford
Allan G. McPhail, Councillor, Ward(s): Loughborough
mcphail@queensu.ca
Ron W. Vandewal, Councillor, Ward(s): Loughborough
lakevalley@kos.net
John R. McDougall, Councillor, Ward(s): Portland
Bill W.L. Robinson, Councillor, Ward(s): Portland
sfronten@kingston.net
Cam L. Naish, Councillor, Ward(s): Storrington
Larry W. York, Councillor, Ward(s): Storrington
blue@reztel.net

Administration
Wayne Orr, Clerk & Administrator, Administration
worr@township.southfrontenac.on.ca
Deb Bracken, Treasurer, Administration
dbracken@township.southfrontenac.on.ca
Mark Segsworth, Manager, Public Works, Administration
msegsworth@township.southfrontenac.on.ca
Lindsay Mills, Coordinator, Planning, Administration
lmills@township.southfrontenac.on.ca
Rick Chesebrough, Fire Chief, Administration
rchesebrough@township.southfrontenac.on.ca
Alan Revill, Chief Building Inspector, Administration
rchesebrough@township.southfrontenac.on.ca

South Glengarry
P.O. Box 220
6 Oak St.
Lancaster, ON K0C 1N0
613-347-1166 Fax: 613-347-3411
info@southglengarry.com
www.southglengarry.com
Municipal Type: Township
Incorporated: Jan. 1, 1998; *Area:* 604.91 sq km
County or District: Stormont, Dundas & Glengarry; *Population in 2006:* 12,880
Provincial Electoral District(s): Stormont-Dundas-South Glengarry
Federal Electoral District(s): Stormont-Dundas-South Glengarry
Next Election: Nov. 2010 (4 year terms)

Council
Jim McDonell, Mayor
jim.mcdonell@bell.ca
Ian McLeod, Deputy Mayor & Councillor
Trevor Bougie, Councillor
Joyce Gravelle, Councillor
gravelle@cnwl.igs.net
Bill McKenzie, Councillor
613-347-3254, Fax: 613-347-3119

Administration
Marilyn Lebrun, Clerk, Administration
marilyn@southglengarry.com
Derik Brandt, Chief Administrative Officer, Administration
derik@southglengarry.com
Michel Samson, Treasurer & Deputy Clerk, Administration
mike@southglengarry.com
Joanne Haley, General Manager, Community Services, Administration
jhaley@southglengarry.com
J. Ewen MacDonald, General Manager, Infrastructure Services, Administration
ewen@southglengarry.com
Dwane Crawford, Manager, Development, Administration
dwane@southglengarry.com
Shawn Killoran, Manager, Water & Wastewater Operations, Administration
shawnkilloran@on.aibn.com

South Huron
P.O. Box 759
322 Main St. South
Exeter, ON N0M 1S6
519-235-0310 Fax: 519-235-3304 Toll Free: 1-877-204-0747
info@southhuron.ca
www.town.southhuron.on.ca
Municipal Type: Municipality
Incorporated: 2001; *Area:* 425.35 sq km
County or District: Huron; *Population in 2006:* 9,982
Provincial Electoral District(s): Huron-Bruce
Federal Electoral District(s): Huron-Bruce
Next Election: Nov. 2010 (4 year terms)
George Robertson, Mayor
Michael Di Lullo, Clerk & Manager, Corporate Services
m.dilullo@southhuron.ca

South River
P.O. Box 310
63 Marie St.
South River, ON P0A 1X0
705-386-2573 Fax: 705-386-0702 Phone, Public Works: 705-386-0245
info@southriverontario.com
www.southriverontario.com
Municipal Type: Village
Incorporated: 1907; *Area:* 4.04 sq km
County or District: Parry Sound District; *Population in 2006:* 1,069
Provincial Electoral District(s): Parry Sound-Muskoka
Federal Electoral District(s): Parry Sound-Muskoka
Next Election: Nov. 2010 (4 year terms)
Jim Coleman, Mayor
Susan Arnold, Administrator & Clerk

South Stormont
P.O. Box 340
4949 Country Rd. 14
Ingleside, ON K0C 1M0
613-537-2362 Fax: 613-537-8113 Toll Free Phone: 1-800-265-3915
info@southstormont.ca; bylawofficer@southstormont.ca
www.southstormont.ca
Municipal Type: Township
Area: 447.46 sq km
County or District: Stormont, Dundas & Glengarry; *Population in 2006:* 12,520
Provincial Electoral District(s): Stormont-Dundas-South Glengarry
Federal Electoral District(s): Stormont-Dundas-South Glengarry
Next Election: Nov. 2010 (4 year terms)

Council
Bryan McGillis, Mayor
mayor@southstormont.ca
Tammy Hart, Deputy Mayor & Councillor
Barry Brownlee, Councillor
613-537-9753
Richard Waldroff, Councillor
Cindy Woods, Councillor
cindy_woods@xplornet.com

Administration
Betty de Haan, Chief Administrative Officer & Clerk, Administration
betty@southstormont.ca
Johanna Barkley, Treasurer, Administration
johanna@southstormont.ca
Dan Pilon, Manager, Public Works, Administration
dan@southstormont.ca
Hilton Cryderman, Chief Building Official & Administrator, Planning, Administration
hilton@southstormont.ca
Roger Desjardins, Fire Chief, Administration
roger@southstormont.ca
Harry Hutchinson, Deputy Chief Building Official & Superintendent, D, Administration
buildinginspector@southstormont.ca

South-West Oxford
312915 Dereham Line, RR#1
Mount Elgin, ON N0J 1N0
519-485-0477 Fax: 519-485-2932 Phone, Works Department: 519-877-2953
dbarnes@swox.org (Office); dharnett@swox.org (Deputy Clerk)
www.swox.org
Municipal Type: Township
Area: 370.63 sq km
County or District: Oxford; *Population in 2006:* 7,589
Provincial Electoral District(s): Oxford
Federal Electoral District(s): Oxford
Next Election: Nov. 2010 (4 year terms)
David Mayberry, Mayor
Mary Ellen Greb, Chief Administrative Officer
megreb@swox.org

Southgate
RR#1
Dundalk, ON N0C 1B0
519-923-2110 Fax: 519-923-9262 Toll Free Phone: 1-888-560-6607
info@town.southgate.on.ca
www.town.southgate.on.ca
Municipal Type: Township
Incorporated: Jan. 1, 2001; *Area:* 643.95 sq km
County or District: Grey; *Population in 2006:* 7,167
Provincial Electoral District(s): Bruce-Grey-Owen Sound
Federal Electoral District(s): Bruce-Grey-Owen Sound
Next Election: Nov. 2010 (4 year terms)
Note: Amalgamation of the Village of Dundalk, the Township of Proton & the Township of Egremont.
Brian A. Milne, Mayor
519-334-3794
Carol Watson, Clerk
cwatson@town.southgate.on.ca

Southwest Middlesex, Municipality of
P.O. Box 218
153 McKellar St.
Glencoe, ON N0L 1M0
519-287-2015 Fax: 519-287-2359
info@southwestmiddlesex.ca
www.southwestmiddlesex.ca
Municipal Type: Township
Incorporated: Jan. 1, 2001; *Area:* 427.92 sq km
County or District: Middlesex; *Population in 2006:* 5,890
Provincial Electoral District(s): Lambton-Kent-Middlesex
Federal Electoral District(s): Lambton-Kent-Middlesex
Next Election: Nov. 2010 (4 year terms)
Note: Amalgamation of the Villages of Glencoe & Wardsville & the Townships of Ekfrid and Mosa.
Doug Reycraft, Mayor
dreycraft@southwestmiddlesex.ca
Janneke Newitt, Administrator & Clerk
jnewitt@southwestmiddlesex.ca

Southwold
General Delivery
35663 Fingal Line
Fingal, ON N0L 1K0
519-769-2010 Fax: 519-769-2837
southwold@twp.southwold.on.ca
twp.southwold.on.ca/council.shtml
Municipal Type: Township
Area: 301.71 sq km
County or District: Elgin; *Population in 2006:* 4,724
Provincial Electoral District(s): Elgin-Middlesex-London
Federal Electoral District(s): Elgin-Middlesex-London
Next Election: Nov. 2010 (4 year terms)
James McIntyre, Mayor
519-764-9764
Donna Ethier, Chief Administrative Officer-Clerk
cao@twp.southwold.on.ca

Spanish
P.O. Box 70
8 Trunk Rd.
Spanish, ON P0P 2A0
705-844-2300 Fax: 705-844-2622
info@town.spanish.on.ca
www.town.spanish.on.ca
Municipal Type: Town
Area: 106.02 sq km
County or District: Algoma District; *Population in 2006:* 728
Provincial Electoral District(s): Algoma-Manitoulin
Federal Electoral District(s): Algoma-Manitoulin-Kapuskasing
Next Election: Nov. 2010 (4 year terms)
Note: Formerly the Township of Shedden. Effective Oct. 1, 2004, the name was changed to the Town of Spanish.
Gary Bishop, Mayor
Brent St. Denis, Clerk-Treasurer & Administrator
brent.st.denis@ontera.net

Springwater
Simcoe County Administrative Centre
2231 Nursery Rd.
Minesing, ON L0L 1Y2
705-728-4784 Fax: 705-728-6957
info@springwater.ca; council@springwater.ca
www.springwater.ca
Municipal Type: Township
Incorporated: Jan. 1, 1994; *Area:* 536.3 sq km
County or District: Simcoe; *Population in 2006:* 17,456
Provincial Electoral District(s): Simcoe-Grey
Federal Electoral District(s): Simcoe-Grey
Next Election: Nov. 2010 (4 year terms)

Council
Linda Collins, Mayor
Dan McLean, Deputy Mayor & Councillor
Dan Clement, Councillor, Ward(s): 1
Perry Ritchie, Councillor, Ward(s): 2
Rick Webser, Councillor, Ward(s): 3
Sandy McConkey, Councillor, Ward(s): 4
Jack Hanna, Councillor, Ward(s): 5

Administration
John Daly, Clerk & Director, Corporate Services, Administration
Winanne Grant, Chief Administrative Officer, Administration
Laurie Kennard, Treasurer & Director, Finance, Administration
finance@springwater.ca
Ron Belcourt, Director, Recreation Services, Administration
recreation@springwater.ca
Brad Sokach, Director, Public Works, Administration
publicworks@springwater.ca
Nancy Tuckett, Director, Planning & Development, Administration
planning@springwater.ca
Tony Van Dam, Director, Fire & Emergency Services, Administration
fire@springwater.ca
Nick Ippolito, Chief Building Official, Administration
building@springwater.ca
Barb Fralick, Manager, Human Resources, Administration

St.-Charles, Municipality of
P.O. Box 70
2 King St. East
St Charles, ON P0M 2W0
705-867-2032 Fax: 705-867-5789 Toll Free Phone: 1-877-867-2032
cao@stcharlesontario.ca; tourism@stcharlesontario.ca
www.stcharlesontario.ca
Municipal Type: Town
Area: 318.47 sq km
County or District: Sudbury District; *Population in 2006:* 1,159
Provincial Electoral District(s): Timiskaming-Cochrane
Federal Electoral District(s): Nickel Belt
Next Election: Nov. 2010 (4 year terms)
Paul Schoppman, Mayor
Diane G. Charlebois-Howard, Chief Administrative Officer,
cao@stcharlesontario.ca

Stirling-Rawdon
P.O. Box 40
234 North St.
Stirling, ON K0K 3E0
613-395-3380 Fax: 613-395-0864
info@stirling-rawdon.com
www.stirling-rawdon.com
Municipal Type: Township
Area: 280.63 sq km
County or District: Hastings; *Population in 2006:* 4,906
Provincial Electoral District(s): Prince Edward-Hastings
Federal Electoral District(s): Prince Edward-Hastings
Next Election: Nov. 2010 (4 year terms)
Rodney Cooney, Mayor
Kevin Heath, Administrator-Clerk
cao@stirling-rawdon.com

Stone Mills
4504 County Rd. 4
Centreville, ON K0K 1N0
613-378-2475 Fax: 613-378-0033
caoclerk@stonemills.com
www.stonemills.com
Municipal Type: Township
Incorporated: Jan. 1, 1998; *Area:* 688.28 sq km
County or District: Lennox-Addington; *Population in 2006:* 7,568
Provincial Electoral District(s): Lanark-Frontenac-Lennox & Addington
Federal Electoral District(s): Lanark-Frontenac-Lennox & Addington
Next Election: Nov. 2010 (4 year terms)
Note: Amalgamation of the former Township of Camden East, Township of Sheffield & Village of Newburgh.
Douglas Bearance, Reeve
bearance@frontenac.net
Darlene Plumley, Chief Administrative Officer & Municipal Clerk
caoclerk@stonemills.com

Stormont, Dundas & Glengarry
26 Pitt St.
Cornwall, ON K6J 3P2
613-932-1515 Fax: 613-936-2913 Toll Free Phone: 1-800-267-7158
info@sdgcounties.ca
www.sdgcounties.ca
Municipal Type: United County
Area: 3,306.86 sq km
Population in 2006: 110,399
Next Election: Nov. 2010 (4 year terms)

Council
Eric Duncan, Mayor, Ward(s): North Dundas
Grant Crack, Mayor, Ward(s): North Glengarry
grantcrack@northglengarry.ca
Denis Fife, Mayor, Ward(s): North Stormont
fifeag@plantpioneer.com
Steven Byvelds, Mayor, Ward(s): South Dundas
Jim McDonell, Mayor, Ward(s): South Glengarry
jim.mcdonell@bell.ca
Bryan McGillis, Mayor, Ward(s): South Stormont
bryansouthstormont@hotmail.com

Administration
Helen Thomson, Clerk, Administration
hthomson@sdgcounties.ca
Michael S. Waddell, Chief Administrative Officer, Administration
mwaddell@sdgcounties.ca
Donald J. McDonald, County Engineer, Administration
Michael Otis, County Planner, Administration

Strathroy-Caradoc
52 Frank St.
Strathroy, ON N7G 2R4
519-245-1070 Fax: 519-245-6353
general@strathroy-caradoc.ca
www.strathroy-caradoc.ca
Municipal Type: Township
Incorporated: 2001; *Area:* 274.19 sq km
County or District: Middlesex; *Population in 2006:* 19,977
Provincial Electoral District(s): Lambton-Kent-Middlesex
Federal Electoral District(s): Lambton-Kent-Middlesex
Next Election: Nov. 2010 (4 year terms)
Note: Amalgamation of the Town of Strathroy & the Township of Caradoc.

Council
Joanne Vanderheyden, Mayor
Brad Richards, Deputy Mayor & Councillor
Marie Baker, Councillor, Ward(s): 1 - Strathroy
mbaker@strathroy-caradoc.caadoc.ca
John G. Brennan, Councillor, Ward(s): 1 - Strathroy
jbrennan@strathroy-caradoc.ca
Steve Pelkman, Councillor, Ward(s): 1 - Strathroy
spelkman@strathroy-caradoc.ca
Dave Cameron, Councillor, Ward(s): 1 - Strathroy
Steve Dausett, Councillor, Ward(s): 2 - Caradoc
sdausett@strathroy-caradoc.ca
Larry Cowan, Councillor, Ward(s): 2 - Caradoc
Neil Flegel, Councillor, Ward(s): 2 - Caradoc

Administration
Angela Toth, Clerk & Director, Corporate Services, Administration
atoth@strathroy-caradoc.ca
Jim Fairlie, Chief Administrative Officer, Administration
jfairlie@strathroy-caradoc.ca
Jane McPherson, Treasurer & Director, Financial Services, Administration
jmcpherson@strathroy-caradoc.ca
Bill Gibson, Director, Fire Services, & Fire Chief, Administration
bgibson@strathroy-caradoc.ca
Tim Hanna, Director, Recreation & Leisure Services, Administration
thanna@strathroy-caradoc.ca
Mark Harris, Director, Environmental Services, Administration
mharris@strathroy-caradoc.ca
Brad Dausett, Manager, Roads, Administration
bdausett@strathroy-caradoc.ca
Paul Hicks, Coordinator, Planning, Administration
dwalsh@strathroy-caradoc.ca
Andrew Meyer, Coordinator, Community Development, Administration
Leslie Pommer, Coordinator, Customer Services & Concession, Administration

Strong
P.O. Box 1120
1713 Hwy. 11 South
Sundridge, ON P0A 1Z0
705-384-5819 Fax: 705-384-5892
www.strongtownship.com
Municipal Type: Township
Area: 158.73 sq km
County or District: Parry Sound District; *Population in 2006:* 1,327
Provincial Electoral District(s): Parry Sound-Muskoka
Federal Electoral District(s): Parry Sound-Muskoka
Next Election: Nov. 2010 (4 year terms)
Christine Ellis, Mayor
Linda Maurer, Clerk & Treausurer

Sudbury District
c/o Manitoulin-Sudbury District Services Bd
210 Mead Blvd.
Espanola, ON P5E 1R9
www.msdsb.net
Municipal Type: District
Area: 38,504.53 sq km
Population in 2006: 21,392
Provincial Electoral District(s): Algoma-Manitoulin; Nickel Belt
Federal Electoral District(s): Nickel Belt; Algoma-Manitoulin-Kapuskasing
Note: Includes incorporated municipalities surrounding Greater Sudbury, unincorporated settlements, & First Nations reserves Chapleau 74A & 75, Duck Lake, Mattagami, Mountbatten, Whitefish Lake, & Whitefish River
J. Raymond (Ray) Chénier, Board Chair, Manitoulin-Sudbury District Services
705-862-7850
rchenier@msdsb.net
Fern Dominelli, Chief Administrative Officer, Manitoulin-Sudbury D
cao@msdsb.net

Sundridge
P.O. Box 129
110 Main St.
Sundridge, ON P0A 1Z0
705-384-5316 Fax: 705-384-7874
villageoffice@sundridge.ca
www.sundridge.ca
Municipal Type: Village
Incorporated: 1889; *Area:* 2.23 sq km
County or District: Parry Sound District; *Population in 2006:* 942
Provincial Electoral District(s): Parry Sound-Muskoka
Federal Electoral District(s): Parry Sound-Muskoka
Next Election: Nov. 2010 (4 year terms)
Elgin Schneider, Mayor
Lillian S. Fowler, Clerk-Treasurer & Tax Collector

Tarbutt & Tarbutt Additional
27 Barr Rd. South, RR#1
Desbarats, ON P0R 1E0
705-782-6776 Fax: 705-782-4274
tarbuttfire@hotmail.com
www.tarbutttownship.com
Municipal Type: Township
Incorporated: 1889; *Area:* 52.82 sq km
County or District: Algoma District; *Population in 2006:* 388
Provincial Electoral District(s): Algoma-Manitoulin
Federal Electoral District(s): Sault Ste Marie
Next Election: Nov. 2010 (4 year terms)
Ken Richie, Mayor
705-782-4386
Glenn Martin, Clerk-Treasurer

Tay
P.O. Box 100
450 Park St.
Victoria Harbour, ON L0K 2A0
705-534-7248 Fax: 705-534-4493
taytownship@tay.ca
www.tay.ca
Municipal Type: Township
Area: 138.93 sq km
County or District: Simcoe; *Population in 2006:* 9,748
Provincial Electoral District(s): Simcoe North
Federal Electoral District(s): Simcoe North
Next Election: Nov. 2010 (4 year terms)
Scott Warnock, Mayor
swarnock@tay.ca
Alison Thomas, Clerk
athomas@tay.ca
Wes Crown, Director, Planning
Herbert Proudley, Director, Public Works

Tay Valley
217 Harper Rd. RR#4
Perth, ON K7H 3C6
613-267-5353 Fax: 613-264-8516 Toll Free Phone: 1-800-810-0161
clerk@tayvalleytwp.ca; treasurer@tayvalleytwp.ca
www.tayvalleytwp.ca
Municipal Type: Township
Area: 527.46 sq km
County or District: Lanark; *Population in 2006:* 5,634
Provincial Electoral District(s): Lanark-Frontenac-Lennox & Addington
Federal Electoral District(s): Lanark-Frontenac-Lennox & Addington
Next Election: Nov. 2010 (4 year terms)
Note: Formerly the Township of Bathurst Burgess Sherbrooke.
Keith Kerr, Reeve
613-267-4025
kmkk@ripnet.com
Robert Tremblay, Clerk

Tehkummah
Municipal Bldg.
456 Hwy 542A
Tehkummah, ON P0P 2C0
705-859-3293 Fax: 705-859-2605
www.manitoulin-island.com/tehkummah/
Municipal Type: Township
Incorporated: 1881; *Area:* 132.48 sq km
County or District: Manitoulin District; *Population in 2006:* 382
Provincial Electoral District(s): Algoma-Manitoulin
Federal Electoral District(s): Algoma-Manitoulin-Kapuskasing
Next Election: Nov. 2010 (4 year terms)
Gary Brown, Reeve
gbrown@msdsb.net

Temagami
Welcome Centre
P.O. Box 220
Lakeshore Dr.
Temagami, ON P0H 2H0
705-569-3421 Fax: 705-569-2834 E-mail, Public Works: publicworks@temagami.ca
frontdesk@temagami.ca; visit@temagami.ca; EcDev@temagami.ca
www.temagami.ca
Municipal Type: Municipality
Incorporated: Jan. 1, 1998; *Area:* 1,906.42 sq km
County or District: Nipissing District; *Population in 2006:* 934
Provincial Electoral District(s): Timiskaming-Cochrane
Federal Electoral District(s): Nipissing-Timiskaming
Next Election: Nov. 2010 (4 year terms)
John Hodgson, Mayor
Patrick Cormier, Chief Administrative Officer
CAO@temagami.ca

Terrace Bay
Terrace Bay Community Centre
P.O. Box 40
1 Selkirk Ave.
Terrace Bay, ON P0T 2W0
807-825-3315 Fax: 807-825-9576 Toll Free Phone: 1-800-968-8616
info@terracebay.ca; m.hartling@terracebay.ca (Treasury)
www.terracebay.ca
Municipal Type: Township
Incorporated: Sept. 1, 1947; *Area:* 151.04 sq km
County or District: Thunder Bay District; *Population in 2006:* 1,625
Provincial Electoral District(s): Thunder Bay-Superior North
Federal Electoral District(s): Thunder Bay-Superior North
Next Election: Nov. 2010 (4 year terms)
Note: Incorporated as a municipality on July 1, 1959.
Michael King, Mayor
Carmelo Notarbartolo, Chief Administrative Officer
cao@terracebay.ca

Thames Centre
4305 Hamilton Rd.
Dorchester, ON N0L 1G3
519-268-7334 Fax: 519-268-3928 Toll Free Phone: 1-866-425-7306
inquiries@thamescentre.on.ca
www.thamescentre.on.ca
Municipal Type: Municipality
Incorporated: Jan. 1, 2001; *Area:* 433.8 sq km
County or District: Middlesex; *Population in 2006:* 13,085
Provincial Electoral District(s): Elgin-Middlesex-London
Federal Electoral District(s): Elgin-Middlesex-London
Next Election: Nov. 2010 (4 year terms)
Note: Amalgamation of the former Township of West Nissouri & the Township of North Dorchester.
Jim Maudsley, Mayor
jmaudsley@thamescentre.on.ca
Margaret Lewis, Clerk
Stewart M. Findlater, Director, Community Services & Development
sfindlater@thamescentre.on.ca
Steve McAuley, Director, Operations
smcauley@thamescentre.on.ca
Paul Hunter, Fire Chief
Dave Murray, Chief Building Official
Jarrod Craven, Area Superintendent, Water & Wastewater
Jarrod Craven, Superintendent, Environmental Services
Dennis Shand, Superintendent, Drainage
dshand@thamescentre.on.ca

The Archipelago
9 James St.
Parry Sound, ON P2A 1T4
705-746-4243 Fax: 705-746-7301
hgage@thearchipelago.on.ca
www.thearchipelago.on.ca
Municipal Type: Township
Area: 602.3 sq km
County or District: Parry Sound District; *Population in 2006:* 576
Provincial Electoral District(s): Parry Sound-Muskoka
Federal Electoral District(s): Parry Sound-Muskoka
Next Election: Nov. 2010 (4 year terms)
Peter Ketchum, Reeve
peter.ketchum@sympatico.ca
Stephen Kaegi, Chief Administrative Officer-Clerk
skaegi@thearchipelago.on.ca

The Blue Mountains
P.O. Box 310
26 Bridge St. East
Thornbury, ON N0H 2P0
519-599-3131 Fax: 519-599-7723 Toll Free Phone: 1-888-258-6867
info@town.thebluemountains.on.ca
www.thebluemountains.ca

Municipal Type: Town
Incorporated: Jan. 1, 2001; *Area:* 286.78 sq km
County or District: Grey; *Population in 2006:* 6,825
Provincial Electoral District(s): Simcoe-Grey
Federal Electoral District(s): Simcoe-Grey
Next Election: Nov. 2010 (4 year terms)
Note: Amalgamation of Collingwood & Thornbury.
Ellen Anderson, Mayor
mayor@thebluemountains.ca
Corrina Giles, Town Clerk
cgiles@thebluemountains.ca

The Nation
958 Rte. 500 West
Casselman, ON K0A 1M0
613-764-5444 Fax: 613-764-3310
mmccuaig@nationmun.ca
www.nationmun.ca
Municipal Type: Municipality
Incorporated: Jan. 1, 1998; *Area:* 657.16 sq km
County or District: Prescott & Russell; *Population in 2006:* 10,643
Provincial Electoral District(s): Glengarry-Prescott-Russell
Federal Electoral District(s): Glengarry-Prescott-Russell
Next Election: Nov. 2010 (4 year terms)
Note: Amalgamation of the Townships of Cambridge, South Plantagenet, Caledonia & the Village of St. Isidore.
François St. Amour, Mayor
Mary J. McCuaig, Clerk
mmccuaig@nationmun.ca
Guylain Laflèche, Municipal Planner
glafleche@nationmun.ca
Marc Legault, Superintendent, Roads
marclegault@nationmun.ca
Charles Bray, Chief Building Official
cbray@nationmun.ca

The North Shore
P.O. Box 108
1385 Hwy. 17 West
Algoma Mills, ON P0R 1A0
705-849-2213 Fax: 705-849-2428
twpns@ontera.net
www.townshipofthenorthshore.ca
Municipal Type: Township
Incorporated: March 1, 1973; *Area:* 230.79 sq km
County or District: Algoma District; *Population in 2006:* 549
Provincial Electoral District(s): Algoma-Manitoulin
Federal Electoral District(s): Algoma-Manitoulin-Kapuskasing
Next Election: Nov. 2010 (4 year terms)
Note: Incorporated as a township on Dec. 1, 1978.
Randi Condie, Mayor
Nancy Milne, Clerk

Thessalon
P.O. Box 220
169 Main St.
Thessalon, ON P0R 1L0
705-842-2217 Fax: 705-842-2572
townthess@bellnet.ca
www.townthessalon.ca
Municipal Type: Town
Area: 4.37 sq km
County or District: Algoma District; *Population in 2006:* 1,312
Provincial Electoral District(s): Algoma-Manitoulin
Federal Electoral District(s): Algoma-Manitoulin-Kapuskasing
Next Election: Nov. 2010 (4 year terms)
Brent Rankin, Mayor
Robert P. MacLean, Clerk-Treasurer

Thornloe
P.O. Box 30
Main St.
Thornloe, ON P0J 1S0
705-563-2593 Fax: 705-563-8303
twphill@parolink.net
Municipal Type: Village
Area: 6.49 sq km
County or District: Timiskaming District; *Population in 2006:* 105
Provincial Electoral District(s): Timiskaming-Cochrane
Federal Electoral District(s): Timmins-James Bay
Next Election: Nov. 2010 (4 year terms)
Ron Vottero, Reeve
Janet Gore, Clerk-Treasurer & Officer, Lottery Licensing

Thunder Bay
Thunder Bay, ON

Municipal Type: District
Area: 103,706.27 sq km
Population in 2006: 149,063

Timiskaming
Haileybury, ON

Municipal Type: District
Area: 13,279.88 sq km
Population in 2006: 33,283

Tiny
130 Balm Beach Rd. West, RR#1
Perkinsfield, ON L0L 2J0
705-526-4204 Fax: 705-526-2372 Toll Free Phone: 1-866-939-8469
tinytwsp@tiny.ca
www.tiny.ca
Municipal Type: Township
Area: 343.19 sq km
County or District: Simcoe; *Population in 2006:* 10,784
Provincial Electoral District(s): Simcoe North
Federal Electoral District(s): Simcoe North
Next Election: Nov. 2010 (4 year terms)
Ray Millar, Mayor
A. Ruth Coursey, Chief Administrative Officer-Clerk
rcoursey@tiny.ca

Trent Hills
P.O. Box 1030
66 Front St. South
Campbellford, ON K0L 1L0
705-653-1900 Fax: 705-653-5904
info@trenthills.ca
www.trenthills.ca
Municipal Type: Municipality
Area: 510.83 sq km
County or District: Northumberland; *Population in 2006:* 12,247
Provincial Electoral District(s): Northumberland-Quinte West
Federal Electoral District(s): Northumberland-Quinte West
Next Election: Nov. 2010 (4 year terms)
Hector MacMillan, Mayor
hecmacmillan@accel.net
Jim Peters, Director, Planning
jim.peters@trenthills.ca
Scott White, Manager, Water Operations
Shari Lang, Coordinator, Public Works
shari.lang@trendhills.ca
Joe Kelly, Manager, Wastewater
705-653-1480
Jim McIlmoyle, Manager, Roads
Shirley Preston, Deputy Clerk, Protective Services
shirley.preston@trenthills.ca
Tim Blake, Fire Chief, Campbellford/Seymour
705-653-1234
Bill Kelly, Fire Chief, Hastings & Warkworth
Margaret Montgomery, Clerk
marg.montgomery@trenthills.ca
Brenda Otto, Officer, Community Development
brenda.otto@trenthills.ca
David Rogers, Chief Building Official
dave.rogers@trenthills.ca

Tudor & Cashel
P.O. Box 436
371 Weslemkoon Lake Rd., RR#2
Gilmour, ON K0L 1W0
613-474-2583 Fax: 613-474-0664
clerk@tudorandcashel.com
www.tudorandcashel.com
Municipal Type: Township
Incorporated: 1869; *Area:* 433.49 sq km
County or District: Hastings; *Population in 2006:* 682
Provincial Electoral District(s): Prince Edward-Hastings
Federal Electoral District(s): Prince Edward-Hastings
Next Election: Nov. 2010 (4 year terms)
Wanda Donaldson, Reeve
Bernice Crocker, Clerk-Treasurer
clerk@tudorandcashel.com

Tweed
P.O. Box 729
255 Metcalf St.
Tweed, ON K0K 3J0
613-478-2535 Fax: 613-478-6457
info@twp.tweed.on.ca
www.twp.tweed.on.ca
Municipal Type: Municipality
Incorporated: 1998; *Area:* 896.98 sq km
County or District: Hastings; *Population in 2006:* 5,614
Provincial Electoral District(s): Prince Edward-Hastings
Federal Electoral District(s): Prince Edward-Hastings
Next Election: Nov. 2010 (4 year terms)
Jo-Anne Albert, Reeve
reeve@twp.tweed.on.ca
Patricia Bergeron, Clerk-Treasurer
plb@twp.tweed.on.ca

Tyendinaga
859 Melrose Rd., RR#1
Shannonville, ON K0K 3A0
613-396-1944 Fax: 613-396-2080
twp.tyend@sympatico.ca
www.tyendinagatownship.com
Municipal Type: Township
Area: 311.94 sq km
County or District: Hastings; *Population in 2006:* 4,070
Provincial Electoral District(s): Prince Edward-Hastings
Federal Electoral District(s): Prince Edward-Hastings
Next Election: Nov. 2010 (4 year terms)
Rick Phillips, Reeve
Steve Mercer, Clerk-Treasurer
clerk@tyendinagatownship.com

Uxbridge
P.O. Box 190
51 Toronto St. South
Uxbridge, ON L9P 1T1
905-852-9181 Fax: 905-852-9674
info@town.uxbridge.on.ca
www.town.uxbridge.on.ca
Municipal Type: Township
Incorporated: 1872; *Area:* 420.65 sq km
County or District: Durham Reg. Mun.; *Population in 2006:* 19,169
Provincial Electoral District(s): Durham
Federal Electoral District(s): Durham
Next Election: Nov. 2010 (4 year terms)
Note: Incorporated as a town in 1885, & town became part of Uxbridge Township in 1973.
Gerri Lynn O'Connor, Mayor
Debbie Leroux, Clerk & Officer, Lottery Licensing
dleroux@town.uxbridge.on.ca
Ron Mitchell, Treasurer
Alex Gant, Chief Administrator
agane@town.uxbridge.on.ca
Ben Kester, Director, Public Works
bkester@town.uxbridge.on.ca
Ingrid Svelnis, Director, Parks, Recreation & Culture
isvelnis@town.uxbridge.on.ca
Simon Almond, Fire Chief
905-852-3393

Val Rita-Harty
P.O. Box 100
2, av de l'Église
Val Rita, ON P0L 2G0
705-335-6146 Fax: 705-337-6292
valharty@hotmail.com
Municipal Type: Township
Area: 382.64 sq km
County or District: Cochrane District; *Population in 2006:* 939
Provincial Electoral District(s): Timmins-James Bay
Federal Electoral District(s): Algoma-Manitoulin-Kapuskasing
Next Election: Nov. 2010 (4 year terms)
Laurier Bourgeois, Mayor
Christiane Potvin, Administrator-Clerk-Treasurer

Wainfleet
P.O. Box 40
19M43 Hwy. 3
Wainfleet, ON L0S 1V0
905-899-3463 Fax: 905-899-2340
sluey@township.wainfleet.on.ca
www.township.wainfleet.on.ca
Municipal Type: Township
Area: 217.29 sq km
County or District: Niagara Reg. Mun.; *Population in 2006:* 6,601
Provincial Electoral District(s): Welland
Federal Electoral District(s): Welland
Next Election: Nov. 2010 (4 year terms)
April Jeffs, Mayor
Tanya Lamb, Township Clerk
tlamb@wainfleet.ca

Warwick
6332 Nauvoo Rd., RR#8
Watford, ON N0M 2S0
519-849-3926 Fax: 519-849-6136
info@warwicktownship.ca
www.warwicktownship.ca
Municipal Type: Township
Incorporated: 1998; *Area:* 290.2 sq km
County or District: Lambton; *Population in 2006:* 3,945
Provincial Electoral District(s): Lambton-Kent-Middlesex
Federal Electoral District(s): Lambton-Kent-Middlesex
Next Election: Nov. 2010 (4 year terms)
Todd Case, Mayor
Don R. Bruder, Administrator-Treasurer

Wawa
P.O. Box 500
40 Broadway Ave.
Wawa, ON P0S 1K0
705-856-2244 Fax: 705-856-2120 Toll Free Phone: 1-800-367-9292
info@wawa.cc
www.wawa.cc
Municipal Type: Township
Area: 417.78 sq km
County or District: Algoma District; *Population in 2006:* 3,204
Provincial Electoral District(s): Algoma-Manitoulin
Federal Electoral District(s): Algoma-Manitoulin-Kapuskasing
Next Election: Nov. 2010 (4 year terms)
Howard Whent, Mayor
Chris Wray, AMCT, Chief Administrative Officer & Clerk-Treasurer

Wellesley
4639 Lobsinger Line, RR#1
St Clements, ON N0B 2M0
519-699-4611 Fax: 519-699-4540
gkosch@township.wellesley.on.ca
www.township.wellesley.on.ca
Municipal Type: Township
Area: 277.84 sq km
County or District: Waterloo Regional Municipality; *Population in 2006:* 9,789
Provincial Electoral District(s): Kitchener-Conestoga
Federal Electoral District(s): Kitchener-Conestoga
Next Election: Nov. 2010 (4 year terms)
Ross Kelterborn, Mayor
kross@region.waterloo.on.ca
Susan Duke, CAO-Clerk & Director, Planning
sduke@township.wellesley.on.ca

Wellington North
P.O. Box 125
7490 Sideroad 7 West
Kenilworth, ON N0G 2E0

519-848-3620 Fax: 519-848-3228 Toll Free Phone: 1-866-848-3620
township@wellington-north.com
www.wellington-north.com
Municipal Type: Township
Incorporated: Jan. 1, 1999; *Area:* 524.38 sq km
County or District: Wellington; *Population in 2006:* 11,175
Provincial Electoral District(s): Perth-Wellington
Federal Electoral District(s): Perth-Wellington
Next Election: Nov. 2010 (4 year terms)
Note: Amalgamation of the Township of Arthur, Arthur Village, the Township of West Luther & the Town of Mount Forest.
Raymond T. Tout, Mayor
Lorraine (Lori) Heinbuch, Clerk
lheinbuch@wellington-north.com
Harold Knox, Chief Building Official
hknox@wellington-north.com
Gary Williamson, Superintendent, Works
garywil@wellington-north.com
Barry Trood, Foreman, Water & Sewer
519-848-5327
btrood@wellington-north.com
Melissa Irvine, Process/Compliance Analyst, Water & Sewer
Ronald MacEachern, Acting Fire Chief, Mount Forest
519-323-1441
Brent Barnes, Fire Chief, Arthur
519-848-3500

West Elgin

P.O. Box 490
22412 Hoskins Line
Rodney, ON N0L 2C0
519-785-0560 Fax: 519-785-0644
wtelgin@execulink.com
www.elginconnects.ca
Municipal Type: Municipality
Area: 322.52 sq km
County or District: Elgin; *Population in 2006:* 5,349
Provincial Electoral District(s): Elgin-Middlesex-London
Federal Electoral District(s): Elgin-Middlesex-London
Next Election: Nov. 2010 (4 year terms)
Bernie Wiehle, Mayor
Donald Leitch, Chief Administrative Officer & Clerk

West Grey

402813 Grey Rd., RR#2
Durham, ON N0G 1R0
519-369-2200 Fax: 519-369-5962 Toll Free Phone: 1-800-538-9647
info@westgrey.com
www.westgrey.com
Municipal Type: Municipality
Incorporated: Jan 1, 2001; *Area:* 875.37 sq km
County or District: Grey; *Population in 2006:* 12,193
Provincial Electoral District(s): Bruce-Grey-Owen Sound
Federal Electoral District(s): Bruce-Grey-Owen Sound
Next Election: Nov. 2010 (4 year terms)
Note: Amalgamation of Bentinck, Glenelg, Normanby, Neustadt & Durham.
Kevin Eccles, Mayor
Christine Robinson, Chief Administrative Officer & Clerk
robinsonc@westgrey.com
Ken Gould, Manager, Public Works
kgould@westgrey.com
Ray Holliday, Chief Building Official
rholliday@westgrey.com
Phillip Schwartz, Fire Chief & Coordinator, Health & Safety
durhamstation@bmts.com

West Lincoln

P.O. Box 400
318 Canborough St.
Smithville, ON L0R 2A0
905-957-3346 Fax: 905-957-3219 Toll Free Phone: 1-800-350-3876
jscime@westlincoln.com
www.westlincoln.com
Municipal Type: Township
Incorporated: Jan. 1, 1970; *Area:* 387.72 sq km
County or District: Niagara Reg. Mun.; *Population in 2006:* 13,167
Provincial Electoral District(s): Niagara West-Glanbrook
Federal Electoral District(s): Niagara West-Glanbrook
Next Election: Nov. 2010 (4 year terms)
Note: Amalgamation of the former Townships of South Grimsby, Caistor, & Gainsborough.
Douglas Joyner, Mayor
Carolyn Langley, Clerk
carolynlangley@westlincoln.ca
Stephanie Nagel, Treasurer & Director, Finance
snagel@westlincoln.ca
Derrick Thomas, Chief Administrative Officer
dthomson@westlincoln.ca
Sue-Ellen Merritt, Chair, Planning, Building & Environmental Committee
Anthony Boncori, Chief Building Official
aboncori@westlincoln.com
John Ganann, Fire Chief
905-957-3361
Kathy Desjardins, Director, Planning
kathyd@westlincoln.com
Kathy Sipos, Manager, Public Works
ksipos@westlincoln.com
Gary Ricker, Supervisor, Water & Sewer
John Branco, Operator, Water & Sewer

West Nipissing

#101, 225 Holditch St.
Sturgeon Falls, ON P2B 1T1
705-753-2250 Fax: 705-753-3950
jbarbeau@municipality.westnipissing.on.ca
www.westnipissingouest.ca
Municipal Type: Municipality
Area: 1,989.57 sq km
County or District: Nipissing District; *Population in 2006:* 13,410
Provincial Electoral District(s): Timiskaming-Cochrane
Federal Electoral District(s): Nickel Belt
Next Election: Nov. 2010 (4 year terms)
Joanne Savage, Mayor
jsavage@municipality.westnipissing.on.ca
Melanie Ducharme, Municipal Clerk & Planner
705-753-2250
mducharme@westnipissing.ca
Roger Lachance, Director, Planning
rlachance@municipality.westnipissing.on.ca
Rachel Prudhomme, Director, Public Works
rprudhomme@municipality.westnipissing.on.ca
Richard Savage, Fire Chief
rsavage@wnfs.ca
Denis Lafreniere, Manager, Solid Waste
Peter Ming, Manager, Water/Wastewater Operations
Lynne Duhaime, Coordinator, Community Services
lduhaime@municipality.westnipissing.on.ca
Rheal Levac, Superintendent, Roads

West Perth, Municipality of

P.O. Box 609
169 St. David St.
Mitchell, ON N0K 1N0
519-348-8429 Fax: 519-348-8935
info@westperth.com
www.westperth.com
Municipal Type: Township
Area: 579.4 sq km
County or District: Perth; *Population in 2006:* 8,839
Provincial Electoral District(s): Perth-Wellington
Federal Electoral District(s): Perth-Wellington
Next Election: Nov. 2010 (4 year terms)
Note: Amalgamation of Fullarton Township, Hibbert Township, Logan Township & the Town of Mitchell.
Walter McKenzie, Mayor
Susan Cronin, Municipal Clerk

Westport

P.O. Box 68
30 Bedford St.
Westport, ON K0G 1X0
613-273-2191 Fax: 613-273-3460
westport@rideau.net
www.village.westport.on.ca
Municipal Type: Village
Incorporated: 1904; *Area:* 1.71 sq km
County or District: Leeds & Grenville; *Population in 2006:* 645
Provincial Electoral District(s): Leeds-Grenville
Federal Electoral District(s): Leeds-Grenville
Next Election: Nov. 2010 (4 year terms)
William (Bill) L. Thake, Mayor
Scott Bryce, Clerk - Treasurer

White River

P.O. Box 307
102 Durham St.
White River, ON P0M 3G0
807-822-2450 Fax: 807-822-2719
winniempl@onlink.net
www.nwconx.net/~wrib/
Municipal Type: Township
Area: 96.94 sq km
County or District: Algoma District; *Population in 2006:* 841
Provincial Electoral District(s): Algoma-Manitoulin
Federal Electoral District(s): Algoma-Manitoulin-Kapuskasing
Next Election: Nov. 2010 (4 year terms)
Angelo Bazzoni, Mayor
Marilyn Parent Lethbridge, Chief Administrative Officer - Clerk & Director, Human Resources

Whitestone, Municipality of

General Delivery
21 Church St.
Dunchurch, ON P0A 1G0
705-389-2466 Fax: 705-389-1855
info@whitestone.ca
www.whitestone.ca
Municipal Type: Township
Incorporated: 2000; *Area:* 946.56 sq km
County or District: Parry Sound District; *Population in 2006:* 1,030
Provincial Electoral District(s): Parry Sound-Muskoka
Federal Electoral District(s): Parry Sound-Muskoka
Next Election: Nov. 2010 (4 year terms)
Chris Armstrong, Mayor
mayor.armstrong@whitestone.ca
Liliane Nolan, Chief Administrative Officer - Clerk
705-389-2466
clerk.administrator@whitestone.ca

Whitewater Region

P.O. Box 40
44 Main St.
Cobden, ON K0J 1K0
613-646-2282 Fax: 613-646-2283
info@whitewaterregion.ca
www.whitewaterregion.ca
Municipal Type: Township
Incorporated: Jan. 1, 2001; *Area:* 537.96 sq km
County or District: Renfrew; *Population in 2006:* 6,631
Provincial Electoral District(s): Renfrew-Nipissing-Pembroke
Federal Electoral District(s): Renfrew-Nipissing-Pembroke
Next Election: Nov. 2010 (4 year terms)
Note: Amalgamation of Beachburg Village, Cobden Village, Westmeath Township & Ross Township.
Jim Labow, Mayor
Donald Rathwell, Reeve
Dean Sauriol, Chief Administrative Officer - Clerk
dsauriol@whitewaterregion.ca

Wilmot

60 Snyder's Rd. West
Baden, ON N3A 1A1
519-634-8444 Fax: 519-634-5522 Toll Free Phone: 1-800-469-5576
info@wilmot.ca
www.wilmot.ca
Municipal Type: Township
Area: 263.73 sq km
County or District: Waterloo Regional Municipality; *Population in 2006:* 17,097
Provincial Electoral District(s): Kitchener-Conestoga
Federal Electoral District(s): Kitchener-Conestoga
Next Election: Nov. 2010 (4 year terms)
Les Armstrong, Mayor
Barbara McLeod, Clerk
barb.mcleod@wilmot.ca
John A. Hacking, Treasurer
Grant Whittington, Chief Administrative Officer
grant.whittington@wilmot.ca
John Ritz, Fire Chief
john.ritz@wilmot.ca
Doug Robertson, Chief Building Official
Gary Charbonneau, Director, Public Works
gary.charbonneau@wilmot.ca
Harold O'Krafka, Director, Development Services
harold.okrafka@wilmot.ca
Geoff Dubrick, Manager, Parks/Facilities
geoff.dubrick@wilmot.ca
Andrew Martin, Planner & Officer, Economic Development
andrew.martin@wilmot.ca
Derek Wallace, Officer, By-law Enforcement
Ken Dietrich, Foreman, Roads
Sean Montgomery, Foreman, Utilities
sean.montgomery@wilmot.ca

Wollaston

P.O. Box 99
Coe Hill, ON K0L 1P0
613-337-5731 Fax: 613-337-5789
wollaston@bellnet.ca
www.township.wollaston.on.ca
Municipal Type: Township
Incorporated: 1880; *Area:* 215.22 sq km
County or District: Hastings; *Population in 2006:* 730
Provincial Electoral District(s): Prince Edward-Hastings
Federal Electoral District(s): Prince Edward-Hastings
Next Election: Nov. 2010 (4 year terms)
Dan McCaw, Reeve
Marilyn Brickles, Chief Administrative Officer - Clerk - Treasurer &, Lottery Licensing

Woolwich

P.O. Box 158
69 Arthur St. South
Elmira, ON N3B 2Z6
519-669-1647 Fax: 519-669-1820
woolwich.mail@woolwich.ca
www.woolwich.ca
Municipal Type: Township
Incorporated: Jan. 1, 1973; *Area:* 326 sq km
County or District: Waterloo Regional Municipality; *Population in 2006:* 19,658
Provincial Electoral District(s): Kitchener-Conestoga
Federal Electoral District(s): Kitchener-Conestoga
Next Election: Nov. 2010 (4 year terms)
Todd Cowan, Mayor
Christine Broughton, Clerk & Director, Council & Information Services
Dan Chapman, Treasurer
Rod Kruger, Manager, Engineering Operations
rkruger@township.woolwich.on.ca
Earl Wideman, Fire Chief
519-664-2237
Peter Vanderbeek, Chief Building Official
pvanderbeek@township.woolwich.on.ca

Zorra

Municipal Office
P.O. Box 306
274620 - 27th Line
Ingersoll, ON N5C 3K5
519-485-2490 Fax: 519-485-2520 Toll Free Phone: 1-888-699-3868
zorra@zorra.on.ca
www.zorra.on.ca
Municipal Type: Township
Area: 528.78 sq km
County or District: Oxford; *Population in 2006:* 8,125
Provincial Electoral District(s): Oxford
Federal Electoral District(s): Oxford
Next Election: Nov. 2010 (4 year terms)
Margaret Lupton, Mayor
mlupton@zorra.on.ca
Donald W. MacLeod, Chief Administrative Officer
dmacleod@zorra.on.ca

PRINCE EDWARD ISLAND

Enabling legislation in P.E.I. includes the Charlottetown Area Municipalities Act, the City of Summerside Act, & the Municipalities Act. The first provides governance for three municipalities, the second provides governance for one municipality, & the third provides the framework for 71 municipalities. There are no population considerations for incorporation of a municipality, but a petition must be made by at least 25 residents of an area indicating their desire to incorporate; stating the boundaries of the area, whether it is to be a town or a community, and the services which are to be provided.

Municipal Elections are held every three years in November.

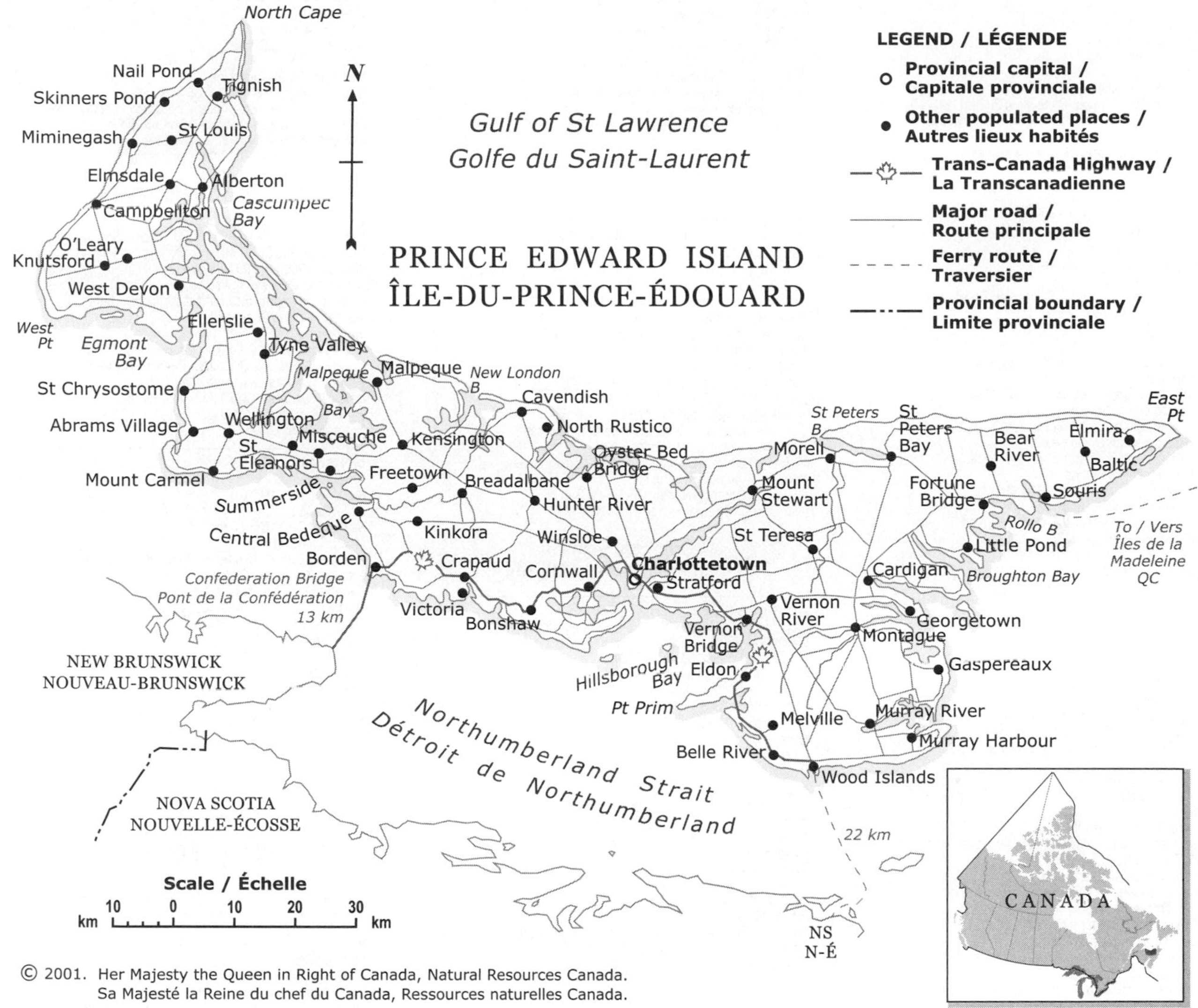

Prince Edward Island

Major Municipalities in Prince Edward Island

Charlottetown
P.O. Box 98
199 Queen St.
Charlottetown, PE C1A 4B7
902-566-5548 Fax: 902-566-4701
city@city.charlottetown.pe.ca
www.city.charlottetown.pe.ca
Municipal Type: City
Incorporated: 1855; *Area:* 44.33 sq km
County or District: Hillsborough; *Population in 2006:* 32,174
Provincial Electoral District(s): Charlottetown-Sherwood; Charlottetown-Parkdale; Charlottetown-Victoria Park; Charlottetown-Brighton; Charlottetown-Lewis Point
Federal Electoral District(s): Charlottetown
Next Election: Nov. 2010 (four year terms)

Council
Clifford J. Lee, Mayor
mayor@city.charlottetown.pe.ca
Kim Devine, B.A., Councillor, Ward(s): 1
kdevine@city.charlottetown.pe.ca
Daniel (Danny) J. Redmond, B.A., Councillor, Ward(s): 2
dredmond@city.charlottetown.pe.ca
Rob Lantz, B.Sc., Councillor, Ward(s): 3
rlantz@city.charlottetown.pe.ca
Mitchell G. Tweel, B.A., Councillor, Ward(s): 4
mitchell.tweel@pei.sympatico.ca
Sterling MacFadyen, Deputy Mayor & Councillor, Ward(s): 5
smacfadyen@city.charlottetown.pe.ca
David MacDonald, Councillor, Ward(s): 6
dmacdonald@city.charlottetown.pe.ca
Cecil F. Villard, Councillor, Ward(s): 7
cvillard@city.charlottetown.pe.ca
Peter F. McCloskey, Councillor, Ward(s): 8
pmccloskey@city.charlottetown.pe.ca
Melissa Hilton, B.A., Councillor, Ward(s): 9
mhilton@city.charlottetown.pe.ca
Terence H. Bernard, Councillor, Ward(s): 10
tbernard@city.charlottetown.pe.ca

Administration
Roy Main, Chief Administrative Officer
rmain@city.charlottetown.pe.ca
Joseph Coady, Director, Public Services
jcoady@city.charlottetown.pe.ca
Donna Waddell, Director, Corporate Services
dwaddell@city.charlottetown.pe.ca
Phil Handrahan, Director, Fiscal & Development Services
phandrahan@city.charlottetown.pe.ca
Craig Walker, Manager, Water & Sewer Utility
902-629-4014
cwalker@city.charlottetown.pe.ca
Bill Clair, Works Superintendent, Water & Sewer Utility
902-629-4015
bclair@city.charlottetown.pe.ca
Herman Van Omme, Superintendent, Waste Water Treatment Plant
902-628-6647, Fax: 902-628-6684
hvanomme@city.charlottetown.pe.ca
Ron Atkinson, Economic Development Officer, Economic Development, Tourism & Events
ratkinson@city.charlottetown.pe.ca
Dan Hughes, Manager, Human Resources
Don Poole, Manager of Planning, Planning & Development
dpoole@city.charlottetown.pe.ca
Vada Fernandez, Purchasing Officer, Finance
vfernandez@city.charlottetown.pe.ca
Mel Cheverie, Chief Building Inspector, Planning & Development
mcheverie@city.charlottetown.pe.ca
Jim Molyneux, Field Works Coordinator, Public Works
jmolyneux@city.charlottetown.pe.ca
Blair Kinch, Sr. Superintendent, Public Works
bkinch@city.charlottetown.pe.ca
Lance Jones, Streets Maintenance Supervisor, Public Works
ljones@city.charlottetown.pe.ca
Nancy McMinn, Parks Superintendent, Parks & Recreation
nmcminn@city.charlottetown.pe.ca
Scott Ryan, M.B.A., CMA, FCMA, Manager, Finance
sryan@city.charlottetown.pe.ca
Randy MacDonald, Fire Chief, Fire Services
rmacdonald@city.charlottetown.pe.ca
Paul Johnston, Manager, Public Works
902-894-5208
pjohnston@city.charlottetown.pe.ca
Sue Hendricken, Manager, Parks & Recreation
902-368-1025
shendricken@city.charlottetown.pe.ca
Paul Smith, Chief of Police
psmith@city.charlottetown.pe.ca

Summerside
275 Fitzroy St.
Summerside, PE C1N 1H9
902-432-1288 Fax: 902-436-9296
cityhall@city.summerside.pe.ca
www.city.summerside.pe.ca
Municipal Type: City
Incorporated: 1995; *Area:* 28.36 sq km
County or District: Egmont; *Population in 2006:* 14,500
Provincial Electoral District(s): Wilmot-Summerside; St. Eleanors-Summerside
Federal Electoral District(s): Egmont
Next Election: Nov. 2010 (four year terms)

Council
Basil L. Stewart, Mayor
mayor@city.summerside.pe.ca
Bruce MacDougall, Deputy Mayor & Councillor
bmacdougall@city.summerside.pe.ca
Cory Thomas, Councillor
cthomas@city.summerside.pe.ca
Brent Gallant, Councillor
bgallant@city.summerside.pe.ca
Ron Dowling, Councillor
rdowling@city.summerside.pe.ca
Garth Lyle, Councillor
glyle@city.summerside.pe.ca
Norma McColeman, Councillor
nmccoleman@city.summerside.pe.ca
Barry Chappell, Councillor
bchappell@city.summerside.pe.ca
Vance Bridges, Councillor
vbridges@pei.sympatico.ca

Administration
Terry Murphy, CAO
tmurphy@city.summerside.pe.ca
Malcolm Millar, Director, Financial Services
mmillar@city.summerside.pe.ca
David Morgan, Director, Community Services
dmorgan@city.summerside.pe.ca
James Peters, Director, Fire Services
jpeters@city.summerside.pe.ca
J. David Poirier, Director, Police Services
dpoirier@city.summerside.pe.ca
Gordon MacFarlane, Director, Human Resources
gmacfarlane@city.summerside.pe.ca
Michael Thususka, Director, Economic Development
miket@city.summerside.pe.ca
Aaron MacDonald, Director, Technical Services
aaronmac@city.summerside.pe.ca

Other Municipalities in Prince Edward Island

Abrams Village
P.O. Box 104
Wellington, PE C0B 2E0
902-854-2501 Fax: 902-854-2501
Municipal Type: Community
Incorporated: 1974; *Area:* 1.37 sq km
Population in 2006: 266
Provincial Electoral District(s): Evangeline-Miscouche
Federal Electoral District(s): Egmont
Next Election: Nov. 2010 (four year terms)
Desmond Arsenault, CAO
Roger Gallant, Chair

Afton
RR#2
Cornwall, PE C0A 1H0
902-675-3515
Municipal Type: Community
Incorporated: 1974;
Population in 2006: 826
Provincial Electoral District(s): Tracadie-Fort Augustus
Federal Electoral District(s): Malpeque
Next Election: Nov. 2010 (four year terms)
Joseph Clow, Administrator
Gina Rankin, Chair

Alberton
P.O. Box 153
10 Railway St.
Alberton, PE C0B 1B0
902-853-2720 Fax: 902-853-2314
info@townofalberton.ca
www.townofalberton.ca
Municipal Type: Town
Incorporated: May 1913; *Area:* 4.50 sq km
County or District: Egmont; *Population in 2006:* 1,081
Provincial Electoral District(s): Alberton-Miminegash
Federal Electoral District(s): Egmont
Next Election: Nov. 2010 (four year terms)
Susan Wallace-Flynn, CAO
Perry Morrell, Mayor

Alexandra
P.O. Box 2683
Charlottetown, PE C1A 8C3
902-569-4760
Municipal Type: Community
Incorporated: 1972;
County or District: Cardigan; *Population in 2006:* 280
Provincial Electoral District(s): Belfast-Pownal Bay
Federal Electoral District(s): Cardigan
Next Election: Nov. 2010 (four year terms)
Sheila Whiteway-McNeill, CAO
Dianne Wood, Chair

Annandale-Little Pond-Howe Bay
RR#4
Souris, PE C0A 2B0
902-583-2494
Municipal Type: Community
Incorporated: 1975;
County or District: Cardigan; *Population in 2006:* 370
Provincial Electoral District(s): Georgetown-Baldwin's Road
Federal Electoral District(s): Cardigan
Next Election: Nov. 2010 (four year terms)
Jim Mills, CAO
Arthur MacDonald, Chair

Bedeque
P.O. Box 4007
Bedeque, PE C0B 1C0
902-887-2244
Municipal Type: Community
Incorporated: 1978; *Area:* 0.68 sq km
County or District: Malpeque; *Population in 2006:* 139
Provincial Electoral District(s): Borden-Kinkora
Federal Electoral District(s): Malpeque
Next Election: Nov. 2010 (four year terms)
Clara Lockhart, Administrator
Edward Feehan, Chair

Belfast
RR#3
Belle River, PE C0A 1B0
902-659-2989 Fax: 902-659-2813
belfast.cap@pei.sympatico.ca
www3.pei.sympatico.ca/belfast.cap/public_html/
Municipal Type: Community
Incorporated: 1972;
County or District: Cardigan; *Population in 2006:* 1,839
Provincial Electoral District(s): Belfast-Pownal Bay
Federal Electoral District(s): Cardigan
Next Election: Nov. 2010 (four year terms)
Janice MacDonald, CAO
Norman Gillis, Chair

Bonshaw
RR#1
Bonshaw, PE C0A 1C0
902-675-4315
Municipal Type: Community
Incorporated: 1977;
County or District: Malpeque; *Population in 2006:* 250
Provincial Electoral District(s): Crapaud-Hazel Grove
Federal Electoral District(s): Malpeque
Next Election: Nov. 2010 (four year terms)
Elizabeth Glen, Administrator
John Jamieson, Chair

Borden-Carleton
P.O. Box 89
167 Industrial Dr.
Borden, PE C0B 1X0
902-437-2225 Fax: 902-437-2610
bcadmin@summerside.ca
Municipal Type: Community
Incorporated: July 1, 1995; *Area:* 13.16 sq km
County or District: Malpeque; *Population in 2006:* 786
Provincial Electoral District(s): Borden-Kinkora
Federal Electoral District(s): Malpeque
Next Election: Nov. 2010 (four year terms)
Charles McNally, CAO
John Bernard, Chair

Brackley
1 Cudmore Lane
Brackley, PE C1E 1Z3
902-368-8283
Municipal Type: Community
Incorporated: 1983; *Area:* 8.92 sq km
County or District: Malpeque; *Population in 2006:* 336
Provincial Electoral District(s): Stanhope-East Royalty
Federal Electoral District(s): Malpeque
Next Election: Nov. 2010 (four year terms)
Leo MacLeod, Administrator
Leonard MacCormack, Chair

Breadalbane
Breadalbane, PE C0A 1E0
902-626-7195
breadalbane@pei.sympatico.ca
Municipal Type: Community
Incorporated: 1991; *Area:* 12.57 sq km
Population in 2006: 172
Provincial Electoral District(s): Crapaud-Hazel Grove
Federal Electoral District(s): Malpeque
Next Election: Nov. 2010 (four year terms)
Kim MacLeod, CAO
Dawna MacLeod, Chair

Brudenell
P.O. Box 1183
Montague, PE C0A 1R0
902-838-8389
Municipal Type: Community
Incorporated: 1973;
County or District: Cardigan; *Population in 2006:* 358
Provincial Electoral District(s): Montague-Kilmuir
Federal Electoral District(s): Cardigan
Next Election: Nov. 2010 (four year terms)
Sandy Fraser, CAO
Gary Fraser, Chair

Cardigan
P.O. Box 40
Cardigan, PE C0A 1G0
902-583-2212 Fax: 902-583-2198
Municipal Type: Community
Incorporated: 1954; *Area:* 5.28 sq km
County or District: Cardigan; *Population in 2006:* 374
Provincial Electoral District(s): Georgetown-Baldwin's Road
Federal Electoral District(s): Cardigan
Next Election: Nov. 2010 (four year terms)
Mary Ann Donhoe, CAO
Ed MacAulay, Chair

Central Bedeque
P.O. Box 3964
Central Bedeque, PE C0B 1G0
902-887-2622
doug.macmurdo@pei.sympatico.ca
Municipal Type: Community
Incorporated: 1966; *Area:* 1.89 sq km
County or District: Malpeque; *Population in 2006:* 149
Provincial Electoral District(s): Borden-Kinkora
Federal Electoral District(s): Malpeque
Next Election: Nov. 2010 (four year terms)
Douglas MacMurdo, CAO
Earl Smith, Chair

Central Kings
RR#2
St. Peters Bay, PE C0A 2A0
902-583-2179 Fax: 902-583-2358
Municipal Type: Community
Incorporated: 1975;
Population in 2006: 565
Provincial Electoral District(s): Morell-Fortune Bay
Federal Electoral District(s): Cardigan
Next Election: Nov. 2010 (four year terms)
John Roach, Administrator
Colin Macleod, Chair
902-583-2358

Clyde River
P.O. Box 644
Cornwall, PE C0A 1H0
902-628-1550
Municipal Type: Community
Incorporated: 1974; *Area:* 16.05 sq km
County or District: Malpeque; *Population in 2006:* 618
Provincial Electoral District(s): Crapaud-Hazel Grove
Federal Electoral District(s): Malpeque
Next Election: Nov. 2010 (four year terms)
Janice McAlduff, Administrator
Peter McCrady, Chair

Cornwall
P.O. Box 430
29 Cornwall Rd.
Cornwall, PE C0A 1H0
902-566-2354 Fax: 902-566-5228
town.cornwall@pei.aibn.com
www.town.cornwall.pe.ca
Municipal Type: Town
Incorporated: 1995; *Area:* 28.2 sq km
County or District: Malpeque; *Population in 2006:* 4,677
Provincial Electoral District(s): North River-Rice Point
Federal Electoral District(s): Malpeque
Next Election: Nov. 2010 (four year terms)
Kevin McCarville, CAO
kmccarville@pei.aibn.com
Patrick MacFadyen, Mayor
pmacfadyen@pei.aibn.com

Crapaud
P.O. Box 30
Crapaud, PE C0A 1J0
902-658-2983
Municipal Type: Community
Incorporated: 1950; *Area:* 2.16 sq km
County or District: Malpeque; *Population in 2006:* 353
Provincial Electoral District(s): Crapaud-Hazel Grove
Federal Electoral District(s): Malpeque
Next Election: Nov. 2010 (four year terms)
Kathy Nicholson, CAO
Glenn Stewart, Chair

Darlington
760 Darlington Rd., RR#4
North Wiltshire, PE C0A 1Y0
902-964-2438
Municipal Type: Community
Incorporated: 1983;
County or District: Malpeque; *Population in 2006:* 78
Provincial Electoral District(s): Crapaud-Hazel Grove
Federal Electoral District(s): Malpeque
Next Election: Nov. 2010 (four year terms)
Bonnie MacDonald, Administrator
Warren MacDonald, Chair

Eastern Kings
RR#1
Elmira, PE C0A 1K0
902-357-2534 Fax: 902-357-2386
Municipal Type: Community
Incorporated: 1974;
County or District: Cardigan; *Population in 2006:* 950
Provincial Electoral District(s): Souris-Elmira
Federal Electoral District(s): Cardigan
Next Election: Nov. 2010 (four year terms)
Kay Sweeney, CAO
Paul Cheverie, Chair

Ellerslie-Bideford
P.O. Box 13
Ellerslie, PE C0B 1J0
902-831-2240
Municipal Type: Community
Incorporated: 1977;
County or District: Egmont; *Population in 2006:* 470
Provincial Electoral District(s): Cascumpec-Grand River
Federal Electoral District(s): Egmont
Next Election: Nov. 2010 (four year terms)
Susan Burleigh, CAO
Nan Ferrier, Chair

Georgetown
Llewellyn
P.O. Box 89
Kent St.
Georgetown, PE C0A 1L0
902-652-2924 Fax: 902-652-2701
georgetown@pei.sympatico.ca
www.georgetown.ca
Municipal Type: Town
Incorporated: 1912; *Area:* 1.65 sq km
County or District: Cardigan; *Population in 2006:* 634
Provincial Electoral District(s): Georgetown-Baldwin's Road
Federal Electoral District(s): Cardigan
Next Election: Nov. 2010 (four year terms)
Patsy Gotell, CAO
Peter Llewellyn, Mayor

Grand Tracadie
General Delivery
York, PE C0A 1P0
902-672-3429
Municipal Type: Community
Incorporated: 1984;
County or District: Cardigan; *Population in 2006:* 543
Provincial Electoral District(s): Tracadie-Fort Augustus
Federal Electoral District(s): Cardigan
Next Election: Nov. 2010 (four year terms)
Patsy MacKinnon, Administrator
Kim Meunier, Chair

Greenmount-Montrose
RR#2
Alberton, PE C0B 1B0
902-853-2455 Fax: 902-853-2583
Municipal Type: Community
Incorporated: 1977;
County or District: Egmont; *Population in 2006:* 319
Provincial Electoral District(s): Tignish-DeBlois
Federal Electoral District(s): Egmont
Next Election: Nov. 2010 (four year terms)
June Pridham, Administrator
Grant Wilkie, Chair

Hampshire
RR#2
North Wiltshire, PE C0A 1Y0
902-368-1144
Municipal Type: Community
Incorporated: 1974;
County or District: Malpeque; *Population in 2006:* 327
Provincial Electoral District(s): North River-Rice Point; Crapaud-Hazel Grove
Federal Electoral District(s): Malpeque
Next Election: Nov. 2010 (four year terms)
Gail Stewart, Administrator
Florence Nicholson, Chair

Hazelbrook
RR#1
Charlottetown, PE C1A 7J6
902-628-3846
Municipal Type: Community
Incorporated: 1974;
County or District: Cardigan; *Population in 2006:* 216
Provincial Electoral District(s): Belfast-Pownal Bay; Tracadie-Fort Augustus
Federal Electoral District(s): Cardigan
Next Election: Nov. 2010 (four year terms)
Kelly Mullaly, Administrator
Brian Gallant, Chair

Hunter River
P.O. Box 154
Hunter River, PE C0A 1N0
902-964-2417
Municipal Type: Community
Incorporated: 1974; *Area:* 6.08 sq km
County or District: Malpeque; *Population in 2006:* 319
Provincial Electoral District(s): Crapaud-Hazel Grove; Park Corner-Oyster Bed
Federal Electoral District(s): Malpeque
Next Election: Nov. 2010 (four year terms)
Wanita MacIntyre, CAO
Paul Ellis, Chair

Kensington
P.O. Box 418
Kensington, PE C0B 1M0
902-836-3781 Fax: 902-836-3741
townmanager@townofkensington.com
www.townofkensington.com
Municipal Type: Town
Incorporated: 1914; *Area:* 2.26 sq km
County or District: Malpeque; *Population in 2006:* 1,485
Provincial Electoral District(s): Kensington-Malpeque
Federal Electoral District(s): Malpeque
Next Election: Nov. 2010 (four year terms)
Don Smeltzer, Town Manager
townmanager@townofkensington.com
Ivan Gallant, Mayor
mayor@townofkensington.com

Kingston
RR#3
Cornwall, PE C0A 1H0
902-675-3231 Fax. 902-628-4024
Municipal Type: Community
Incorporated: 1974;
County or District: Malpeque; *Population in 2006:* 685
Provincial Electoral District(s): North River-Rice Point; Crapaud-Hazel Grove
Federal Electoral District(s): Malpeque
Next Election: Nov. 2010 (four year terms)
Marjorie MacDonald, Administrator
Kimberlee Trainor, Chair

Kinkora
P.O. Box 38
Kinkora, PE C0B 1N0
902-887-2868 Fax: 902-887-3514
commofkinkora@pei.aibn.com
Municipal Type: Community
Incorporated: 1955; *Area:* 3.82 sq km
County or District: Malpeque; *Population in 2006:* 326
Provincial Electoral District(s): Borden-Kinkora
Federal Electoral District(s): Malpeque
Next Election: Nov. 2010 (four year terms)
Rodney Gaudet, CAO
Roger Savoie, Chair

Lady Slipper
RR#2
Tyne Valley, PE C0B 2C0
902-831-3496
Municipal Type: Community
Incorporated: 1983;
County or District: Egmont; *Population in 2006:* 1076
Provincial Electoral District(s): Casumpec-Grand River
Federal Electoral District(s): Egmont
Next Election: Nov. 2010 (four year terms)
Douglas MacLeod, CAO
Deborah Cook, Chair

Linkletter
211 Glenn Dr.
Linkletter, PE C1N 5N2
902-888-5465 Fax: 902-436-1520
Municipal Type: Community
Incorporated: 1972; *Area:* 9.05 sq km
County or District: Egmont; *Population in 2006:* 321
Provincial Electoral District(s): St. Eleanors-Summerside
Federal Electoral District(s): Egmont
Next Election: Nov. 2010 (four year terms)
Gary Linkletter, Administrator
David Linkletter, Chair

Lorne Valley
RR#3
Cardigan, PE C0A 1G0
902-583-2759
Municipal Type: Community
Incorporated: 1978;
County or District: Cardigan; *Population in 2006:* 91
Provincial Electoral District(s): Georgetown-Baldwin's Road
Federal Electoral District(s): Cardigan
Next Election: Nov. 2010 (four year terms)
Susan Shaw, Administrator
Karen MacLeod, Chair

Lot 11 & Area
RR#2
Ellerslie, PE C0B 1J0
902-831-2787
Municipal Type: Community
Incorporated: 1982;
County or District: Egmont; *Population in 2006:* 780
Provincial Electoral District(s): Cascumpec-Grand River
Federal Electoral District(s): Egmont
Next Election: Nov. 2010 (four year terms)
Mary Williams, Administrator
Alfred Bridges, Chair

Lower Montague
P.O. Box 821
Montague, PE C0A 1R0
902-838-3359 Fax: 902-838-3617
bethnicholson@sympatico.ca
Municipal Type: Community
Incorporated: 1974;
County or District: Cardigan; *Population in 2006:* 950

Provincial Electoral District(s): Montague-Kilmuir
Federal Electoral District(s): Cardigan
Next Election: Nov. 2010 (four year terms)
Elizabeth Nicholson, Administrator
Heather Jamieson, Chair

Malpeque Bay
P.O. Box 405
Kensington, PE C0B 1M0
902-836-5029
Municipal Type: Community
Incorporated: 1973;
County or District: Malpeque; *Population in 2006:* 1,238
Provincial Electoral District(s): Kensington-Malpeque
Federal Electoral District(s): Malpeque
Next Election: Nov. 2010 (four year terms)
Joanne McCarvill, Administrator
David Smith, Chair

Meadowbank
P.O. Box 316
RR#2
Cornwall, PE C0A 1H0
902-894-2891
Municipal Type: Community
Incorporated: 1974; *Area:* 9.25 sq km
County or District: Malpeque; *Population in 2006:* 364
Provincial Electoral District(s): North River-Rice Point
Federal Electoral District(s): Malpeque
Next Election: Nov. 2010 (four year terms)
Eugene Murphy, Administrator
Helen MacPhail, Chair

Miltonvale Park
Lower Level, Winsloe Lions Hall
P.O. Box 38
Winsloe, PE C1E 1Z2
902-368-3090 Fax: 902-368-1152
admin@miltonvalepark.com
www.miltonvalepark.com
Municipal Type: Community
Incorporated: 1974; *Area:* 35.32 sq km
County or District: Malpeque; *Population in 2006:* 1,163
Provincial Electoral District(s): Winsloe-West Royalty
Federal Electoral District(s): Malpeque
Next Election: Nov. 2010 (four year terms)
Shari MacDonald, Administrator
Donald Aitken, Chair
chair@miltonvalepark.com

Miminegash
General Delivery
Miminegash, PE C0B 1S0
902-882-4298
ydeagle@islandtelecom.com
Municipal Type: Community
Incorporated: 1968; *Area:* 1.85 sq km
County or District: Egmont; *Population in 2006:* 176
Provincial Electoral District(s): Alberton-Miminegash
Federal Electoral District(s): Egmont
Next Election: Nov. 2010 (four year terms)
Yvonne Deagle, Administrator
Charlie Murphy, Chair

Miscouche
P.O. Box 70
Main Dr. East
Miscouche, PE C0B 1T0
902-436-4962 Fax: 902-436-4962
Municipal Type: Community
Incorporated: 1957; *Area:* 2.81 sq km
County or District: Egmont; *Population in 2006:* 769
Provincial Electoral District(s): Evangeline-Miscouche
Federal Electoral District(s): Egmont
Next Election: Nov. 2010 (four year terms)
Judy Gallant, CAO
Peter Gallant, Chair

Montague
P.O. Box 546
273 Queens Rd.
Montague, PE C0A 1R0
902-838-2528 Fax: 902-838-3392
info@montaguepei.ca
www.townofmontaguepei.com
Municipal Type: Town
Incorporated: 1917; *Area:* 3.04 sq km
County or District: Cardigan; *Population in 2006:* 1,802
Provincial Electoral District(s): Montague-Kilmuir
Federal Electoral District(s): Cardigan
Next Election: Nov. 2010 (four year terms)
Andrew Daggett, CAO
adaggett@montaguepei.ca
Patricia Patricia, Mayor

Morell
P.O. Box 173
25 Sunset Ct.
Morell, PE C0A 1S0
902-961-2900 Fax: 902-739-2900
morellcommunity@eastlink.ca
Municipal Type: Community
Incorporated: 1953; *Area:* 1.40 sq km
County or District: Cardigan; *Population in 2006:* 306
Provincial Electoral District(s): Morell-Fortune Bay
Federal Electoral District(s): Cardigan
Next Election: Nov. 2010 (four year terms)
Paula Sinnott, CAO
Bill Rooney, Chair

Mount Stewart
P.O. Box 143
Mount Stewart, PE C0A 1T0
902-676-2881 Fax: 902-676-2881
mtstewartoffice@eastlink.ca
Municipal Type: Community
Incorporated: 1953; *Area:* 1.22 sq km
County or District: Cardigan; *Population in 2006:* 261
Provincial Electoral District(s): Tracadie-Fort Augustus
Federal Electoral District(s): Cardigan
Next Election: Nov. 2010 (four year terms)
Edith Vissey, CAO
Connie Doucette, Chair

Murray Harbour
Murray Harbour Fire Hall, 2nd Fl.
P.O. Box 72
Main St.
Murray Harbour, PE C0A 1V0
902-962-3835 Fax: 902-962-3835
villoffice@eastlink.ca
www.murrayharbourpei.com
Municipal Type: Community
Incorporated: 1953; *Area:* 4.01 sq km
County or District: Cardigan; *Population in 2006:* 358
Provincial Electoral District(s): Murray River-Gaspereaux
Federal Electoral District(s): Cardigan
Next Election: Nov. 2010 (four year terms)
K. Jill Harris, Town Administrator
admin@murrayharbourpei.com
Faye Fraser, Chair

Murray River
P.O. Box 266
Murray River, PE C0A 1W0
902-962-2820 Fax: 902-962-3671
community@murrayrivercomm.pei.ca
Municipal Type: Community
Incorporated: 1955; *Area:* 1.43 sq km
County or District: Cardigan; *Population in 2006:* 430
Provincial Electoral District(s): Murray River-Gaspereaux
Federal Electoral District(s): Cardigan
Next Election: Nov. 2010 (four year terms)
Diane MacDonald, CAO
David Maclean, Chair

New Haven-Riverdale
RR#3
Bonshaw, PE C0A 1C0
902-675-3670 Fax: 902-368-1239
Municipal Type: Community
Incorporated: 1974;
County or District: Malpeque; *Population in 2006:* 500
Provincial Electoral District(s): Crapaud-Hazel Grove
Federal Electoral District(s): Malpeque
Next Election: Nov. 2010 (four year terms)
Dianne Dowling, CAO
Sharon Slauenwhite, Chair

North Rustico
P.O. Box 38
North Rustico, PE C0A 1X0
902-963-3211 Fax: 902-963-3321
northrustico@pei.aibn.com
Municipal Type: Community
Incorporated: 1954; *Area:* 2.45 sq km
County or District: Malpeque; *Population in 2006:* 599
Provincial Electoral District(s): Park Corner-Oyster Bed
Federal Electoral District(s): Malpeque
Next Election: Nov. 2010 (four year terms)
Margot Harris, CAO
David Blacquiere, Chair

North Shore
2490 Rte. 25
York, PE C0A 1P0
902-672-2363 Fax: 902-368-1620
WandapMyers@hotmail.com
www.stanhopecovehead.pe.ca
Municipal Type: Community
Incorporated: 1974;
County or District: Malpeque; *Population in 2006:* 737
Provincial Electoral District(s): Stanhope-East Royalty
Federal Electoral District(s): Malpeque
Next Election: Nov. 2010 (four year terms)
Wanda Myers, Administrator
Jim Lee, Chair
jlee@pei.symatico.ca

North Wiltshire
North Wiltshire, PE C0A 1Y0
902-621-1908
Municipal Type: Community
Incorporated: 1974;
County or District: Egmont; *Population in 2006:* 208
Provincial Electoral District(s): Crapaud-Hazel Grove
Federal Electoral District(s): Malpeque
Next Election: Nov. 2010 (four year terms)
Donald Parker, Administrator
Trevor Campbell, Chair

Northport
P.O. Box 466
Alberton, PE C0B 1B0
902-853-2551
Municipal Type: Community
Incorporated: 1974;
County or District: Egmont; *Population in 2006:* 210
Provincial Electoral District(s): Alberton-Miminegash
Federal Electoral District(s): Egmont
Next Election: Nov. 2010 (four year terms)
Paula Foley, Administrator
David Gaudet, Chair

O'Leary
P.O. Box 130
18 Community St.
O'Leary, PE C0B 1V0
902-859-3311 Fax: 902-859-3311
oleary@pei.sympatico.ca
www.community.oleary.pe.ca
Municipal Type: Community
Incorporated: 1951; *Area:* 1.57 sq km
County or District: Egmont; *Population in 2006:* 861
Provincial Electoral District(s): West Point-Bloomfield
Federal Electoral District(s): Egmont
Next Election: Nov. 2010 (four year terms)
Beverley Shaw, Administrator
Nancy Wallace, Chair
902-859-3633

Pleasant Grove
RR#1
York, PE C0A 1P0
902-672-3472
Municipal Type: Community
Incorporated: 1980;
County or District: Malpeque; *Population in 2006:* 194
Provincial Electoral District(s): Stanhope-East Royalty
Federal Electoral District(s): Malpeque
Next Election: Nov. 2010 (four year terms)
David Cairns, Administrator
Joe Doran, Chair

Resort Municipality
RR#2
Hunter River, PE C0A 1N0
902-963-2698 Fax: 902-963-2932
resort@pei.aibn.com
Municipal Type: Community
Incorporated: 1990; *Area:* 37.74 sq km
Population in 2006: 272
Provincial Electoral District(s): Park Corner-Oyster Bed
Federal Electoral District(s): Malpeque
Next Election: Nov. 2010 (four year terms)
Brenda MacDonald, CAO
Donald McKearney, Chair

Richmond
P.O. Box 7
Richmond, PE C0B 1Y0
902-854-2298 Fax: 902-854-3621
p-cbrown.rich.pe@pe.sympatico.ca
Municipal Type: Community
Incorporated: 1979;
County or District: Egmont; *Population in 2006:* 248
Provincial Electoral District(s): Cascumpec-Grand River; Evangeline-Miscouche
Federal Electoral District(s): Egmont
Next Election: Nov. 2010 (four year terms)
Carol Brown, CAO
Leonard Gallant, Chair

St. Felix
P.O. Box 22
Tignish, PE C0B 2B0
902-882-4015
Municipal Type: Community
Incorporated: 1977;
County or District: Egmont; *Population in 2006:* 359
Provincial Electoral District(s): Tignish-DeBlois
Federal Electoral District(s): Egmont
Next Election: Nov. 2010 (four year terms)
Joanne Gaudette, Administrator
Claude Gaudette, Chair

St. Louis
P.O. Box 40
St Louis, PE C0B 1Z0
902-882-2093
Municipal Type: Community
Incorporated: 1964; *Area:* 0.62 sq km
County or District: Egmont; *Population in 2006:* 80
Provincial Electoral District(s): Alberton-Miminegash; Tignish-DeBlois
Federal Electoral District(s): Egmont
Next Election: Nov. 2010 (four year terms)
Dorothy Gallant, CAO
Everett Wedge, Chair

St. Nicholas
3699 St. Nicholas
Miscouche, PE C0B 1T0
902-854-2731
Municipal Type: Community
Incorporated: 1991;
Population in 2006: 177

Provincial Electoral District(s): Evangeline-Miscouche
Federal Electoral District(s): Egmont
Next Election: Nov. 2010 (four year terms)
Corina Mundy, CAO
Shawn Jones, Chair

St. Peter's Bay
P.O. Box 51
St-Peters Bay, PE C0A 2A0
902-961-2268 Fax: 902-961-3148
stpeters@eastlink.ca
Municipal Type: Community
Incorporated: 1953; *Area:* 4.24 sq km
County or District: Cardigan; *Population in 2006:* 248
Provincial Electoral District(s): Morell-Fortune Bay
Federal Electoral District(s): Cardigan
Next Election: Nov. 2010 (four year terms)
Mary Burge, CAO
Ron MacInnis, Chair

Sherbrooke
P.O. Box 1344
Summerside, PE C1N 4K2
902-436-7005 Fax: 902-436-7005
Municipal Type: Community
Incorporated: 1972; *Area:* 8.83 sq km
Population in 2006: 168
Provincial Electoral District(s): Wilmot-Summerside
Federal Electoral District(s): Egmont
Next Election: Nov. 2010 (four year terms)
Peggy L. Kilbride, CAO
Errol Pauptit, Chair

Souris
P.O. Box 628
75 Main St.
Souris, PE C0A 2B0
902-687-2157 Fax: 902-687-4426
town@sourispei.com
www.sourispei.com
Municipal Type: Town
Incorporated: 1910; *Area:* 3.42 sq km
County or District: Cardigan; *Population in 2006:* 1,232
Provincial Electoral District(s): Souris-Elmira
Federal Electoral District(s): Cardigan
Next Election: Nov. 2010 (four year terms)
Dianne La Chapelle, Administrator
Joanne Reid, Mayor
sourismayor@joannereid.ca

Souris West
P.O. Box 680
Souris, PE C0A 2B0
902-687-2251
Municipal Type: Community
Incorporated: 1972;
County or District: Cardigan; *Population in 2006:* 327
Provincial Electoral District(s): Souris-Elmira
Federal Electoral District(s): Cardigan
Next Election: Nov. 2010 (four year terms)
Margaret MacDonald, Administrator
Paul A. Gallant, Chair

Stratford
234 Shakespeare Dr.
Stratford, PE C1B 2V8
902-569-1995 Fax: 902-569-5000
info@town.stratford.pe.ca
www.town.stratford.pe.ca
Municipal Type: Town
Incorporated: April 1, 1995; *Area:* 22.48 sq km
Population in 2006: 7,083
Provincial Electoral District(s): Glen Stewart-Bellevue Cove
Federal Electoral District(s): Cardigan
Next Election: Nov. 2010 (four year terms)

Council
Kevin Jenkins, Mayor
wkjenkin@gov.pe.ca

Administration
Robert Hughes, CAO
rhughes@town.stratford.pe.ca

Tignish
P.O. Box 57
209 Phillip St.
Tignish, PE C0B 2B0
902-882-2600 Fax: 902-882-2414
karen@village.tignish.pe.ca
www.tignish.com
Municipal Type: Community
Incorporated: 1952; *Area:* 5.86 sq km
County or District: Egmont; *Population in 2006:* 758
Provincial Electoral District(s): Tignish-DeBlois
Federal Electoral District(s): Egmont
Next Election: Nov. 2010 (four year terms)
Karen Gaudet-Gavin, CAO
Elmer Arsenault, Chair

Tignish Shore
Kildare Cape
Tignish, PE C0B 2B0
902-882-3811
Municipal Type: Community
Incorporated: 1975;
Population in 2006: 72
Provincial Electoral District(s): Tignish-DeBlois
Federal Electoral District(s): Egmont
Next Election: Nov. 2010 (four year terms)
Donna Pitre, Administrator
Alvin Pitre, Chair

Tyne Valley
P.O. Box 39
Tyne Valley, PE C0B 2C0
902-831-2938
Municipal Type: Community
Incorporated: 1966; *Area:* 1.74 sq km
County or District: Egmont; *Population in 2006:* 226
Provincial Electoral District(s): Cascumpec-Grand River
Federal Electoral District(s): Egmont
Next Election: Nov. 2010 (four year terms)
Marie Barlow, CAO
Matt McGuire, Chair

Union Road
P.O. Box 5908
2257 Horne Cross Rd., RR#3
Union Road, PE C1A 7J7
902-892-0197
richther@pei.sympatico.ca
Municipal Type: Community
Incorporated: 1977; *Area:* 9.95 sq km
County or District: Malpeque; *Population in 2006:* 245
Provincial Electoral District(s): Georgetown-Baldwin's Road
Federal Electoral District(s): Malpeque
Next Election: Nov. 2010 (four year terms)
Theresa Arsenault, Administrator
Fern Yeo, Chair

Valleyfield
RR#3
Montague, PE C0A 1R0
902-831-4238
Municipal Type: Community
Incorporated: 1974;
County or District: Cardigan; *Population in 2006:* 648
Provincial Electoral District(s): Georgetown-Baldwin's Road; Montague-Kilmuir; Belfast-Pownal Bay
Federal Electoral District(s): Cardigan
Next Election: Nov. 2010 (four year terms)
Donald Nicholson, Administrator
Graham Jones, Chair

Victoria
P.O. Box 7
Victoria, PE C0A 2G0
902-658-2541 Fax: 902-658-2541
len.keefe@pei.sympatico.ca
Municipal Type: Community
Incorporated: 1951; *Area:* 1.40 sq km
County or District: Malpeque; *Population in 2006:* 77
Provincial Electoral District(s): Crapaud-Hazel Grove
Federal Electoral District(s): Malpeque
Next Election: Nov. 2010 (four year terms)
Leonard Keefe, CAO
Ben Smith, Chair

Warren Grove
P.O. Box 963
Cornwall, PE C0A 1H0
902-675-2788
rodr@isn.net
Municipal Type: Community
Incorporated: 1985; *Area:* 10.32 sq km
County or District: Malpeque; *Population in 2006:* 341
Provincial Electoral District(s): North River-Rice Point
Federal Electoral District(s): Malpeque
Next Election: Nov. 2010 (four year terms)
Rod Raper, Administrator
Harvey Cairns, Chair

Wellington
P.O. Box 26
Wellington, PE C0B 2E0
902-854-2920
Municipal Type: Community
Incorporated: 1959; *Area:* 1.80 sq km
County or District: Egmont; *Population in 2006:* 401
Provincial Electoral District(s): Cascumpec-Grand River; Evangeline-Miscouche
Federal Electoral District(s): Egmont
Next Election: Nov. 2010 (four year terms)
Claudette Gallant, CAO
Gilles Painchaud, Chair

West River
P.O. Box 1008
Cornwall, PE C0A 1H0
902-675-3675 Fax: 902-368-0327
Municipal Type: Community
Incorporated: 1974;
County or District: Malpeque; *Population in 2006:* 296
Provincial Electoral District(s): North River-Rice Point
Federal Electoral District(s): Malpeque
Next Election: Nov. 2010 (four year terms)
Bill Grant, Administrator
Eric MacArthur, Chair

Winsloe South
RR#9
Winsloe, PE C1E 1Z3
902-368-1444
Municipal Type: Community
Incorporated: 1986; *Area:* 9.63 sq km
County or District: Malpeque; *Population in 2006:* 198
Provincial Electoral District(s): Winsloe-West Royalty
Federal Electoral District(s): Malpeque
Next Election: Nov. 2010 (four year terms)
Joanne Turner, CAO
Dave Cosh, Chair

York
P.O. Box 8910
York, PE C0A 1P0
902-629-1313
Municipal Type: Community
Incorporated: 1986;
Population in 2006: 296
Provincial Electoral District(s): Stanhope-East Royalty
Federal Electoral District(s): Malpeque
Next Election: Nov. 2010 (four year terms)
Sharon MacKinnon, CAO
Brenda MacDonald, Chair

QUÉBEC

(Source: Ministère des Affaires municipals et des Régions)

Québec legislation recognizes two levels of municipal organization: the local & the regional.

Major municipal reform has reduced the number of local municipalities from nearly 1,400 in 1998 to 1,087 on April 1, 2005. Of this number, 201 towns fall under the jurisdiction of the Cities & Towns Act (RSQ, chap. C-19). Nine of them have over 100,000 inhabitants & account for 53% of the Québec population. The 886 other local municipalities, which go by a variety of designations (township, united township, parish, municipality, village) are governed by the Municipal Code of Québec (RSQ, chap. C-27.1). Québec also has 96 unorganized territories, 39 Indian reserves, 14 Northern villages, eight Cree villages & one Naskapi village.

The regional level of municipal territorial organization includes the Montréal & Québec City metropolitan communities, the 86 regional county municipalities (RCMs), & the Kativik Regional Government. The metropolitan communities & RCMs are made up of local municipalities. RCMs may also include unorganized territories. As for the area under the administration of the Kativik Regional Government, it includes the Northern villages, the Naskapi village & one unorganized territory.

The regional organizations were created to ensure that issues that go beyond local boundaries were handled at the regional or metropolitan level. Although their structures, operation & powers vary, they are based on identical principles. The Montréal & Québec City metropolitan communities are responsible at their level for land use planning, economic development, international economic promotion, artistic & cultural development, regional orientations in public transit, waste management planning, establishing a tax base sharing program, as well as for determining & financing regional facilities, infrastructures, activities, services. RCMs also meet regional needs, including land use planning, & the pooling of services. In addition, they exercise certain powers in the areas of economic development, public security, & the environment. The Kativik Regional Government is in charge of local administration, police, transport, communications & labour force training & use, & may also set minimum standards by ordinance for things like house & building construction.

Eight local municipalities belong neither to a metropolitan community nor to one of the regional county municipalities. They do, however, wield some of the same powers as RCMs. This also holds true for six other cities, which although situated within one of the two metropolitan communities, nonetheless exercise certain of the powers of an RCM.

Ten cities are divided into boroughs. The boroughs have consultative & decision-making powers, are responsible for delivering certain neighbourhood services, & are represented by an elected borough council.

Québec

Major Municipalities in Québec

Alma
140, rue St-Joseph sud
Alma, QC G8B 3R1
418-669-5000 Fax: 418-669-5019
info@ville.alma.qc.ca
www.ville.alma.qc.ca
Municipal Type: City
Incorporated: 21 février 2001; *Area:* 202,10 km2
County or District: Lac-St-Jean-Est; *Population in 2006:* 29,998
Provincial Electoral District(s): Lac-Saint-Jean
Federal Electoral District(s): Jonquière-Alma
Next Election: 1er novembre 2013

Conseil
Gérald Scullion, Maire, 418-669-5005
Lucien Boily, Conseiller, District: 1
Jocelyn Fradette, Conseiller, District: 2
Claude Garneau, Conseiller, District: 3
Frédéric Tremblay, Conseiller, District: 4
Jean-Rock Pedneault, Conseiller, District: 5
Sylvie Beaumont, Conseiller, District: 6
Pascal Pilote, Conseiller, District: 7
Marc Asselin, Conseiller, District: 8

Administration
Jean Paradis, Greffier
Jean-Yves Lessard, Directeur, Travaux publics
Yves Thériault, Trésorier
Guy Simard, Directeur général
Bernard Dallaire, Directeur, Prévention des incendies, 418-669-5059
Marcel Guérin, Directeur, Loisirs/culture, 418-669-5111

Amos
182, 1e Rue est
Amos, QC J9T 2G1
819-732-3254 Fax: 819-727-9792
infos@ville.amos.qc.ca
www.ville.amos.qc.ca
Municipal Type: City
Incorporated: 17 janvier 1987; *Area:* 430,84 km2
County or District: Abitibi; *Population in 2009:* 12,729
Provincial Electoral District(s): Abitibi-Ouest
Federal Electoral District(s): Abitibi-Témiscamingue
Next Election: 1er novembre 2013

Conseil
Ulrick Chérubin, Maire
Marcel Labonté, Conseiller, Siège: 1
Léandre Paré, Conseiller, Siège: 2
André Goyette, Conseiller, Siège: 3
Denis Chandonnet, Conseiller, Siège: 4
Yvon Leduc, Conseiller, Siège: 5
Héliodore Arseneault, Conseiller, Siège: 6

Administration
Alain Plante, Greffier
Gérald Lavoie, Trésorier
Lucie Veillette, Responsable, Communications

Baie-Comeau
19, av Marquette
Baie-Comeau, QC G4Z 1K5
418-296-4931 Fax: 418-296-3759
vbc@ville.baie-comeau.qc.ca
www.ville.baie-comeau.qc.ca
Municipal Type: City
Incorporated: 23 juin 1982; *Area:* 371,69 km2
County or District: Manicouagan; *Population in 2006:* 22,554
Provincial Electoral District(s): René-Lévesque
Federal Electoral District(s): Manicouagan
Next Election: 1er novembre 2013

Conseil
Ivo Di Piazza, Maire, 418-296-8101
Alain Larouche, Conseiller, 418-589-2107, District: Saint-Sacrement
Raymond Coulombe, Conseiller, 418-589-8930, District: Mgr Bélanger
Christine Brisson, Conseiller, 418-295-2883, District: Trudel
Carole Deschênes, Conseiller, 418-589-8734, District: N.-A.-Labrie
Jean Thériault, Conseiller, 418-296-8637, District: La Chasse
Steve Ahern, Conseiller, 418-296-2245, District: Saint-Nom-de-Marie
Reina Savoie Jourdain, Conseiller, 418-296-5231, District: Sainte-Amélie
Yvon Boudreau, Conseiller, 418-296-2672, District: Saint-Georges

Administration
François Corriveau, Greffier, 418-296-8109, Fax: 418-296-8194
Danielle Bernatchez, Directrice, Finances, 418-296-8128, Fax: 418-296-3759
Paul Joncas, Directeur général, 418-296-8104, Fax: 418-296-8121
Jacques Comeau, Directeur, Service des communications, 418-296-8142, Fax: 418-296-3759
François Leblond, Directeur, Loisirs/sports/arts/culture/vie communautaire, 418-296-8358, Fax: 418-296-8399

Beaconsfield
303, boul Beaconsfield
Beaconsfield, QC H9W 4A7
514-428-4400 Fax: 514-428-4424
bob.benedetti@beaconsfield.ca
www.beaconsfield.ca
Municipal Type: City
Incorporated: 1er janvier 2006; *Area:* 10,64 km2
Population in 2006: 19,194
Provincial Electoral District(s): Jacques-Cartier
Federal Electoral District(s): Communauté-Urbaine-de-Montréal
Next Election: 1er janvier 2009

Conseil
Bob Benedetti, Maire
James Hasegawa, Conseiller, District: 1
Karen Messier, Conseillère, District: 2
Wade Staddon, Conseiller, District: 3
Kate Coulter, Conseillère, District: 4
Roy Baird, Conseiller, District: 5
David Pollock, Conseiller, District: 6

Administration
Helen Finn, Greffière

Beauharnois
#100, 660, rue Ellice
Beauharnois, QC J6N 1Y1
450-429-3546 Fax: 450-429-6663
manon.fortier@ville.beauharnois.qc.ca
www.ville.beauharnois.qc.ca
Municipal Type: City
Incorporated: 1er janvier 2002; *Area:* 73,05 km2
County or District: Beauharnois-Salaberry; *Population in 2006:* 11,918
Provincial Electoral District(s): Beauharnois
Federal Electoral District(s): Beauharnois-Salaberry
Next Election: 1er novembre 2013

Conseil
Daniel Charlesbois, Maire
Mario Tanguay, Conseiller, District: 1
Daniel Gervais, Conseiller, District: 2
Sylvie Guérin, Conseillère, District: 3
Henriette Fichault, Conseillère, District: 4
André Vinet, Conseiller, District: 5
Bruno Tremblay, Conseiller, District: 6

Administration
Manon Fortier, Directrice générale (par intérim) & Greffière
Guylaine Côte, Directrice, Services administratifs et financiers
Yves Magnan, Directeur, Travaux publics
Richard Plouffe, Directeur, Urbanisme
Jean-Maurice Marleau, Directeur, Service des incendies

Bécancour
1295, av Nicolas-Perrot
Bécancour, QC G9H 1A1
819-294-6500 Fax: 819-294-6535
becancour@ville.becancour.qc.ca
www.becancour.net
Municipal Type: City
Incorporated: 17 octobre 1965; *Area:* 434,28 km2
County or District: Bécancour; *Population in 2009:* 11,171
Provincial Electoral District(s): Nicolet-Yamaska
Federal Electoral District(s): Bas-Richelieu-Nicolet-Bécancour
Next Election: 1er novembre 2013

Conseil
Maurice Richard, Maire
Fernand Croteau, Conseiller, Secteur: Bécancour
Gaétane Désilets, Conseillère, Secteur: Saint-Grégoire
Alain Lévesque, Conseiller, Secteur: Sainte-Angèle
Guy Richard, Conseiller, Secteur: Sainte-Gertrude
Louise Labbée, Conseillère, Secteur: Gentilly
Mario Gagné, Conseiller, Secteur: Précieux-Sang

Administration
France Leclerc, Greffière
Daniel Brunelle, Directeur, Finances
Gaston Bélanger, Directeur général

Beloeil
777, rue Laurier
Beloeil, QC J3G 4S9
450-467-2835 Fax: 450-464-5445
info@ville.beloeil.qc.ca
www.ville.beloeil.qc.ca
Municipal Type: City
Incorporated: 9 décembre 1903; *Area:* 24 km2
County or District: La Vallée-du-Richelieu; *Population in 2006:* 18,927
Provincial Electoral District(s): Borduas
Federal Electoral District(s): Chambly-Borduas
Next Election: 1er novembre 2013

Conseil
Réal Jeannotte, Maire, 450-467-4679
Réginald Gagnon, Conseiller, 514-569-4500, District: 1
Jean-Guy Savard, Conseiller, 450-467-2545, District: 2
Gilles Gaucher, Conseiller, 450-446-5576, District: 3
Denis Corriveau, Conseiller, 450-464-2435, District: 4
Pierre Verret, Conseiller, 450-467-0630, District: 5
Bernard Cardinal, Conseiller, 450-467-7127, District: 6
Diane Lavoie, Conseillère, 450-464-3095, District: 7
Jean-Yves Labadie, Conseiller, 450-446-0347, District: 8

Administration
Sylvie Piérard, Greffière
Nathalie Guérin, Directrice, Finances
Martine Vallières, Directrice générale

Blainville
1000, ch du Plan-Bouchard
Blainville, QC J7C 3S9
450-434-5200 Fax: 450-434-8295
accueil@ville.blainville.qc.ca
www.ville.blainville.qc.ca
Municipal Type: City
Incorporated: 1er juillet 1855; *Area:* 54,62 km2
County or District: Thérèse-De Blainville; Communauté métropolitaine de Montréal; *Population in 2009:* 48,821
Provincial Electoral District(s): Blainville
Federal Electoral District(s): Terrebonne-Blainville
Next Election: 1er novembre 2013

Conseil
François Cantin, Maire, 450-434-5203
Michèle Murray, Conseillère, District: 1 Fontainebleau
Alain Portelance, Conseiller, District: 2 Côte-Saint-Louis
Serge Paquette, Conseiller, District: 3 Saint-Rédempteur
Guy Frigon, Conseiller, District: 4 Plan-Bouchard
Normand Dupont, Conseiller, District: 5 Notre-Dame-de-l'Assomption
Jeannette Lavoie, Conseillère, District: 6 Chante-Bois
Louis Lamarre, Conseiller, District: 7 Hirondelles
Richard Perreault, Conseiller, District: 8 Alençon
François Garand, Conseiller, District: 9 Renaissance
Marie-Claude Collin, Conseillère, District: 10 Blainvillier

Administration
Claude Bertrand, Greffier, 450-434-5215
Paul Allard, Directeur général, 450-434-5209
Claude Perrotte, Directeur, Finances, 450-434-5237

Boisbriand
940, boul de la Grande-Allée
Boisbriand, QC J7G 2J7
450-435-1954 Fax: 450-435-6398
www.ville.boisbriand.qc.ca
Municipal Type: City
Incorporated: 1er janvier 1946; *Area:* 26,43 km2
County or District: Thérèse-De Blainville; Communauté métropolitaine de Montréal; *Population in 2009:* 26,674
Provincial Electoral District(s): Groulx
Federal Electoral District(s): Rivière-des-Mille-Iles
Next Election: 1er novembre 2013

Conseil
Sylvie St-Jean, Mairesse
Lyne Levert, Conseillère, District: 1 Sanche
Gilles Sauriol, Conseiller, District: 2 Du Gué
Robert Frégeau, Conseiller, District: 3 Filion
Patrick Thifault, Conseiller, District: 4 Dubois
Louise Gauthier, Conseillère, District: 5 Brosseau
Louise Lemay, Conseillère, District: 6 Labelle
Mario Lavallée, Conseiller, District: 7 Desjardins
Marlene Cordato, Conseillère, District: 8 Dion

Administration
Lucie Mongeau, Greffière
Michel Lacasse, Directeur général
André Drainville, Directeur, Finances & Trésorerie

Boucherville
500, rue de la Rivière-aux-Pins
Boucherville, QC J4B 2Z7
450-449-8100 Fax: 450-655-0086
information@ville.boucherville.qc.ca
www.ville.boucherville.qc.ca
Municipal Type: City
Incorporated: 1er janvier 2006; *Area:* 69,33 km2
County or District: Communauté métropolitaine de Montréal; *Population in 2009:* 39,704
Provincial Electoral District(s): Marguerite-D'Youville
Federal Electoral District(s): Longueuil-Pierre-Boucher; Verchères-Les Patriotes
Next Election: 1er novembre 2013

Conseil
Francine Gadbois, Mairesse
Jean-Louis Richer, Conseiller, District: 1 Pierre-Viger
Monique Reeves, Conseillère, District: 2 Père-Le Jeune
Carl Chevalier, Conseiller, District: 3 Sainte Famille
Roger Saucier, Conseiller, District: 4 Découvreurs
Francine Guidi, Conseillère, District: 5 la Seigneurie
Richard Lalancette, Conseiller, District: 6 Saint-Louis
Armand Lefebvre, Conseiller, District: 7 Mortagne
Reynald Gagné, Conseillers, District: 8 Normandie

Administration
Claude Caron, Greffier

Brossard
2001, boul Rome
Brossard, QC J4W 3K5
450-923-6300 Fax: 450-923-7009
information@ville.brossard.qc.ca
www.ville.brossard.qc.ca
Municipal Type: City
Incorporated: 1er janvier 2006; *Area:* 44,77 km2
County or District: Communauté métropolitaine de Montréal; *Population in 2009:* 73,041
Provincial Electoral District(s): La Pinière

Federal Electoral District(s): Brossard-La Prairie
Next Election: 1er novembre 2013

Conseil
Jean-Marc Pelletier, Maire, 450-923-6300
Pierre O'Donoughue, Conseiller, District: 1
Gilbert Lizotte, Conseiller, District: 2
Monique Gagné, Conseillère, District: 3
Marc Benoit, Conseiller, District: 4
Serge Séguin, Conseiller, District: 5
Claudio Benedetti, Conseiller, District: 6
Zaki Thomas, Conseiller, District: 7
Antoine Assaf, Conseiller, District: 8
Pascal Forget, Conseiller, District: 9
Daniel Lucier, Conseiller, District: 10

Administration
Diane Lebrun, Greffière

Candiac
100, boul Montcalm nord
Candiac, QC J5R 3L8
450-444-6000 Fax: 450-444-6009
info@ville.candiac.qc.ca
www.ville.candiac.qc.ca
Municipal Type: City
Incorporated: 31 janvier 1957; *Area:* 16,40 km2
County or District: Roussillon; Communauté métropolitaine de Montréal; *Population in 2009:* 16,825
Provincial Electoral District(s): La Prairie
Federal Electoral District(s): Brossard-La Prairie
Next Election: 1er novembre 2013

Conseil
André J. Côté, Maire
Vincent Chatel, Conseiller, District: Saint-Laurent
Ronald Cormier, Conseiller, District: Taschereau
Normand Dyotte, Conseiller, District: Jean-Leman
Charles-André Fortier, Conseiller, District: Montcalm
Thérèse Gatien, Conseillère, District: La Promenade

Administration
Carole Lemaire, Greffière
Serge Drouin, Directeur général
Patrick Quirion, Trésorier

Chambly
56, rue Martel
Chambly, QC J3L 1V3
450-658-8788 Fax: 450-447-4525
information@ville.chambly.qc.ca
www.ville.chambly.qc.ca
Municipal Type: City
Incorporated: 26 octobre 1848; *Area:* 25,01 km2
County or District: La Vallée-du-Richelieu; *Population in 2006:* 22,608
Provincial Electoral District(s): Chambly
Federal Electoral District(s): Chambly-Borduas
Next Election: 1er novembre 2013

Conseil
Denis Lavoie, Maire
Ken Moquin, Conseiller, 450-658-8124, District: Antoine-Louis-Fréchette
Cécile Ouellet, Conseillère, 450-658-2045, District: Bassin
Jean Beauregard, Conseiller, 450-658-2213, District: Canton
Normand Houle, Conseiller, 450-658-0362, District: Charles-Michel-de Salaberry
Steeves Demers, Conseiller, 514-250-9960, District: Grandes Terres
Richard Tetreault, Conseiller, 450-658-4282, District: La Petite Rivière
Daniel Monast, Conseiller, 514-978-5405, District: Louis-Franquet
Jean Roy, Conseiller, 450-447-6152, District: Ruisseau

Administration
Louise Bouvier, Greffière
André Cholette, Directeur général
Annie Nepton, Directrice, Services des finances

Châteauguay
5, boul d'Youville
Châteauguay, QC J6J 2P8
450-698-3000 Fax: 450-698-3019
info@ville.chateauguay.qc.ca
www.ville.chateauguay.qc.ca
Municipal Type: City
Incorporated: 3 novembre 1975; *Area:* 35,37 km2
County or District: Roussillon; Communauté métropolitaine de Montréal; *Population in 2006:* 42,786
Provincial Electoral District(s): Châteauguay
Federal Electoral District(s): Châteauguay-St-Constant
Next Election: 1er novembre 2013

Conseil
Sergio Pavone, Maire
Anthony Boffice, Conseiller, 450-699-4613, District: 1 La Noue
Stephen Brisebois, Conseiller, 514-914-4945, District: 2 Filgate
Daniel Kabasele, Conseiller, 450-699-4883, District: 3 Robutel
Serge Dion, Conseiller, 450-691-6088, District: 4 Bumbray
Marcel Deschamps, Conseiller, 450-699-1120, District: 5 Salaberry
Mike Gendron, Conseiller, 514-829-1986, District: 6 Lang
André St-Pierre, Conseiller, 450-692-4979, District: 7 Le Moyne
Richard Motard, Conseiller, 450-699-6141, District: 8 D'Youville

Administration
Paul G. Brunet, Greffier & Directeur général

Coaticook
150, rue Child
Coaticook, QC J1A 2B3
819-849-2721 Fax: 819-849-9669
hoteldeville@ville.coaticook.qc.ca
www.ville.coaticook.qc.ca
Municipal Type: City
Incorporated: 30 décembre 1998; *Area:* 218,89 km2
County or District: Coaticook; *Population in 2006:* 9,204
Provincial Electoral District(s): St-François
Federal Electoral District(s): Compton-Stanstead
Next Election: 1er novembre 2013

Conseil
Bertrand Lamoureux, Maire
Charles Poulin, Conseiller, Siège: 1
Madeleine Drolet, Conseillère, Siège: 2
Sylvain Véronneau, Conseiller, Siège: 3
Raynald Drolet, Conseiller, Siège: 4
Lionel Giroux, Conseiller, Siège: 5
Gaétan Labelle, Conseiller, Siège: 6

Administration
Roger Garceau, Trés.

Côte-Saint-Luc
5801, boul Cavendish
Côte-Saint-Luc, QC H4W 3C3
514-485-6800 Fax: 514-485-6963
www.cotesaintluc.org
Municipal Type: City
Incorporated: 1er janvier 2006; *Area:* 7,35 km2
County or District: Communauté métropolitaine de Montréal; *Population in 2009:* 31,458
Provincial Electoral District(s): D'Arcy-McGee
Federal Electoral District(s): Mount Royal
Next Election: 1er novembre 2013

Conseil
Anthony Housefather, Maire, 514-485-6945
Sam Goldbloom, Conseiller, District: 1
Mike Cohen, Conseiller, District: 2
Dida Berku, Conseiller, District: 3
Steven Erdelyi, Conseiller, District: 4
Allan J. Levine, Conseiller, District: 5
Glenn J. Nashen, Conseiller, District: 6
Mitchell Brownstein, Conseiller, District: 7
Ruth Kovac, Conseillère, District: 8

Administration
Jonathan Shecter, Greffier
Ken Lerner, Directeur général
Angelo Marino, Trésorier

Cowansville
220, place Municipale
Cowansville, QC J2K 1T4
450-263-0141 Fax: 450-263-9357
hoteldeville@ville.cowansville.qc.ca
www.cowansville.org
Municipal Type: City
Incorporated: 1er janvier 1876; *Area:* 48,79 km2
County or District: Brome-Missisquoi; *Population in 2009:* 12,297
Provincial Electoral District(s): Brome-Missisquoi
Federal Electoral District(s): Brome-Missisquoi
Next Election: 1er novembre 2013

Conseil
Arthur Fauteux, Maire
Michel Charbonneau, Conseiller, District: Bruck
Yvon Pepin, Conseiller, District: Davignon
Jacqueline Caron, Conseillère, District: Fordyce
Denis Bourcier, Conseiller, District: Ruiter
Wayne Yates, Conseiller, District: Sweetsburg
Réal Plourde, Conseiller, District: Vilas

Administration
Joanne Skelling, Greffière
Pierre Bell, Trésorier

Deux-Montagnes
803, ch d'Oka
Deux-Montagnes, QC J7R 1L8
450-473-2796 Fax: 450-473-2417
www.ville.deux-montagnes.qc.ca
Municipal Type: City
Incorporated: 18 août 1921; *Area:* 5,82 km2
County or District: Deux-Montagnes; *Population in 2006:* 17,402
Provincial Electoral District(s): Deux-Montagnes
Federal Electoral District(s): Rivière-des-Mille-Iles
Next Election: 1er novembre 2013

Conseil
Marc Lauzon, Maire, 450-473-8898
Martin Bigras, Conseiller, District: Coteau
Nathalie Chayer, Conseillère, District: Gare
Denis Joannette, Conseiller, District: Olympia
Mario Saint-Charles, Conseiller, District: Lac
Gilles Saint-Marseille, Conseiller, District: Golf
Sylvain Sauvageau, Conseiller, District: Grand-Moulin

Administration
Nicolas Bouchard, Directeur général
Alexandre Verdy, Greffier
Marie-Josée Boissonneault, Directrice, Finances & Trésorerie

Dolbeau-Mistassini
1100, boul Wallberg
Dolbeau-Mistassini, QC G8L 1G7
418-276-0160 Fax: 418-276-8312
hotelville@ville.dolbeau-mistassini.qc.ca
www.ville.dolbeau-mistassini.qc.ca
Municipal Type: City
Incorporated: 17 décembre 1997; *Area:* 296,57 km2
County or District: Maria-Chapdelaine; *Population in 2009:* 14,474
Provincial Electoral District(s): Roberval
Federal Electoral District(s): Roberval-Lac-St-Jean
Next Election: 1er novembre 2013

Conseil
Georges Simard, Maire
Richard Hébert, Conseiller, Siège: 1
Marcel Gauthier, Conseiller, Siège: 2
Daniel Savard, Conseiller, Siège: 3
Daniel Lambert, Conseiller, Siège: 4
Claire Néron, Conseillère, Siège: 5
Patrice Bouchard, Conseiller, Siège: 6

Administration
André Côté, Greffier
Frédéric Lemieux, Directeur général
Suzy Gagnon, Trésorière

Dollard-Des-Ormeaux
12001, boul De Salaberry
Dollard-des-Ormeaux, QC H9B 2A7
514-684-1010 Fax: 514-684-6894
ville@ddo.qc.ca
www.ville.ddo.qc.ca
Municipal Type: City
Incorporated: 1er janvier 2006; *Area:* 15,20 km2
County or District: Communauté métropolitaine de Montréal; *Population in 2009:* 49,430
Provincial Electoral District(s): Robert-Baldwin
Federal Electoral District(s): Pierrefonds-Dollard
Next Election: 1er novembre 2013

Conseil
Edward Janiszewski, Maire
Zoé Bayouk, Conseiller, District: 1
Errol Johnson, Conseiller, District: 2
Howard Zingboim, Conseiller, District: 3
Herbert Brownstein, Conseiller, District: 4
Morris Vesely, Conseiller, District: 5
Peter Prassas, Conseiller, District: 6
Alex Bottausci, Conseiller, District: 7
Colette Gauthier, Conseillère, District: 8

Administration
Chantale Bilodeau, Greffière, 514-684-9244
Jack Benzaquen, Directeur général, 514-684-0879
Caroline Thall, Trésorière, 514-684-9391

Dorval
60, av Martin
Dorval, QC H9S 3R4
514-633-4040 Fax: 514-633-4138
dorval@ville.dorval.qc.ca
www.ville.dorval.qc.ca
Municipal Type: City
Incorporated: 1er janvier 2006; *Area:* 20,64 km2
County or District: Communauté métropolitaine de Montréal; *Population in 2009:* 18,238
Provincial Electoral District(s): Marquette
Federal Electoral District(s): Notre-Dame-de-Grâce-Lachine
Next Election: 1er novembre 2013

Conseil
Edgar Rouleau, Maire
Claude Valiquet, Conseiller, District: 1
Michel Hébert, Conseiller, District: 2
Daniel da Chao, Conseiller, District: 3
Robert Bourbeau, Conseiller, District: 4
Heather Allard, Conseillère, District: 5
Margo Heron, Conseillère, District: 6

Administration
Colette Gauthier, Greffière
Pierre Larivée, Directeur général
André Girard, Trésorier

Drummondville
CP 398
415, rue Lindsay
Drummondville, QC J2B 6W3
819-478-6550
communications@ville.drummondville.qc.ca
www.ville.drummondville.qc.ca
Municipal Type: City
Incorporated: 7 juillet 2004; *Area:* 249,80 km2
County or District: Drummond; *Population in 2006:* 67,392
Provincial Electoral District(s): Drummond
Federal Electoral District(s): Drummond
Next Election: 1er novembre 2013
Note: Effective July 7, 2004, the municipalities of St-Charles-de-Drummond & St-Joachim-de-Courval & the cities of St-Nicéphore & Drummondville regrouped to form the new city of Drummondville

Conseil
Francine Ruest Jutras, Mairesse
Mario Jacques, Conseiller, District: 1
Roberto Léveillée, Conseiller, District: 2
Jocelyn Gagné, Conseiller, District: 3
Jean Shooner, Conseiller, District: 4
Gilles Fontaine, Conseiller, District: 5
Christian Tourigny, Conseiller, District: 6
Alain Martel, Conseiller, District: 7
Yves Grondin, Conseiller, District: 8
Pierre-Yvan Aubé, Conseiller, District: 9
Denise Picotin, Conseillère, District: 10
Denis Chamberland, Conseiller, District: 11
Pierre Levasseur, Conseiller, District: 12

Administration
Thérèse Cajolet, Greffière, 819-478-6554, Fax: 819-478-3363
Claude Proulx, Directeur général, 819-478-6557, Fax: 819-478-3363
Gilles Bélisle, CGA, Trésorier, 819-478-6559, Fax: 819-478-3164

Gaspé
25, rue de l'Hôtel-de-Ville
Gaspé, QC G4X 2A5
418-368-2104 Fax: 418-368-8532
direction.generale@ville.gaspe.qc.ca
www.ville.gaspe.qc.ca
Municipal Type: City
Incorporated: 1er janvier 1971; *Area:* 1446,95 km2
County or District: La Côte-de-Gaspé; *Population in 2009:* 14,958
Provincial Electoral District(s): Gaspé
Federal Electoral District(s): Gaspésie-Iles-de-la-Madeleine
Next Election: 1er novembre 2013

Conseil
François Roussy, Maire
Luc Savage, Conseiller, Quartier: 1
Charles Aspirault, Conseiller, Quartier: 2
Nicole Perry Fortin, Conseillère, Quartier: 3
Denis Sinnett, Conseiller, Quartier: 4
Aline Perry, Conseillère, Quartier: 5
Brad McDonald, Conseiller, Quartier: 6

Administration
Sébastien Fournier, Greffier
Gaétan Lelièvre, Directeur général
Dave St-Croix, Trésorier

Gatineau
CP 1970 Hull
25, rue Laurier
Gatineau, QC J8X 3Y9
819-595-2002
info@gatineau.ca
www.gatineau.ca
Municipal Type: City
Incorporated: 1er janvier 2002; *Area:* 344,16 km2
Population in 2006: 242,124
Provincial Electoral District(s): Gatineau; Chapleau; Hull; Papineau; Pontiac
Federal Electoral District(s): Gatineau
Next Election: 1er novembre 2013

Conseil
Marc Bureau, Maire, 819-595-7100
Frank Thérien, Conseiller, District: Aylmer
Denis Tassé, Conseiller, District: Riverains
Alain Riel, Conseiller, District: Deschênes
Joseph De Sylva, Conseiller, District: Versant
Alain Pilon, Conseiller, District: Val-Tétreau
Luc Angers, Conseiller, District: Promenades
Richard Côté, Conseiller, District: Bellevue
Claude Millette, Conseillère, District: Orée-du-Parc
Yvon Boucher, Conseiller, District: Rivière-Blanche
Patrice Martin, Conseiller, District: Wright-Parc-de-la-Montagne
Aurèle Desjardins, Conseiller, District: Lac-Beauchamp
André Laframboise, Conseiller, District: Lucerne
Pierre Philion, Conseiller, District: Saint-Raymond-Vanier
Denise Laferrière, Conseillère, District: Hull
Simon Racine, Conseiller, District: Limbour
Luc Montreuil, Conseiller, District: Masson-Angers
Jocelyne Houle, Conseillère, District: Buckingham

Administration
Suzanne Ouellet, Greffière
Robert F. Weemaes, Directeur général
Roland Morin, Responsable, Travaux publics et environnement
Marc Pageau, Directeur, Service des ressources humaines
André Langelier, Coordonnateur, Mesures d'urgence
André Bonneau, Directeur, Service d'incendie
Claude Doucet, Directeur, Urbanisme
André Barbeau, Trésorier, Finances & trésorerie
Nicole Dumoulin, Directrice, Communications
Mario Harel, Directeur et Chef, Police

Granby
87, rue Principale
Granby, QC J2G 2T8
450-776-8282 Fax: 450-776-8278
communication@ville.granby.qc.ca
www.ville.granby.qc.ca
Municipal Type: City
Incorporated: 1er janvier 2007; *Area:* 156,68 km2
County or District: La Haute-Yamaska; *Population in 2006:* 47,637
Provincial Electoral District(s): Shefford
Federal Electoral District(s): Shefford
Next Election: 1er novembre 2013

Conseil
Richard Goulet, Maire, 450-776-8228, Fax: 450-776-8383
Louise Brodeur Comeau, Conseillère, District: 1
Claudette Hudon, Conseillère, District: 2
Pierre Breton, Conseiller, District: 3
Réal Bernard, Conseiller, District: 4
Denis Choinière, Conseiller, District: 5
Serges Ruel, Conseiller, District: 6
Jacques Gévry, Conseiller, District: 7
Guy Gaudor, Conseiller, District: 8
Yves Bélanger, Conseiller, District: 9
Michel Mailhot, Conseiller, District: 10

Administration
Catherine Bouchard, Greffière, 450-776-8275, Fax: 450-776-8278
Michel Pinault, Directeur général, 450-776-8232, Fax: 450-776-8279
Jean-Pierre Renaud, Trésorier, 450-776-8287, Fax: 450-776-8384
André Jean, Directeur, Travaux publics, 450-776-0300, Fax: 450-776-8370
Pierre Lacombe, Directeur, Service d'incendie, 450-776-8344, Fax: 450-776-8390
Patrice Faucher, Directeur, Loisir/arts/culture/vie communautaire, 450-776-8824

Joliette
614, boul Manseau
Joliette, QC J6E 3E4
450-753-8000 Fax: 450-753-8199
greffier@ville.joliette.qc.ca
www.ville.joliette.qc.ca
Municipal Type: City
Incorporated: 12 novembre 1966; *Area:* 22,36 km2
County or District: Joliette; *Population in 2006:* 19,044
Provincial Electoral District(s): Joliette
Federal Electoral District(s): Joliette
Next Election: 1er novembre 2013

Conseil
René Laurin, Maire
Alain Beaudry, Conseiller, Quartier: 1
Claude Savignac, Conseiller, Quartier: 2
Alain Lozeau, Conseiller, Quartier: 3
Diane Nicoletti, Conseillère, Quartier: 4
Richard Dugas, Conseiller, Quartier: 5
Yves Liard, Conseiller, Quartier: 6
Richard Leduc, Conseiller, Quartier: 7

Administration
Pierrick Sylvestre, Greffier
Robert Pépin, Directeur/Chef, Brigade des pompiers, 450-759-5222
Renald Gravel, Coordonnateur, Mesures d'urgence
Gilles Montambault, Inspecteur municipal de voirie

L'Assomption
399, rue Dorval
L'Assomption, QC J5W 1A1
450-589-5671 Fax: 450-589-4512
information@ville.lassomption.qc.ca
www.ville.lassomption.qc.ca
Municipal Type: City
Incorporated: 1er juillet 2000; *Area:* 100,09 km2
County or District: L'Assomption; *Population in 2006:* 16,738
Provincial Electoral District(s): L'Assomption
Federal Electoral District(s): Repentigny
Next Election: 1er novembre 2013

Conseil
Pierre Gour, Maire
René Langlais, Conseiller, District: 1
Micheline Martel-Richard, Conseillère, District: 2
Laurette Jobin-Morin, Conseillère, District: 3
Gilbert Gagnon, Conseiller, District: 4
Michel Rocray, Conseiller, District: 5
Louise T.-Francoeur, Conseillère, District: 6
Nathalie Lauzon, Conseillère, District: 7
Fernand Gendron, Conseiller, District: 8

Administration
Chantal Bédard, Greffière

L'Ile-Perrot
110, boul Perrot
L'Ile-Perrot, QC J7V 3G1
514-453-1751 Fax: 514-453-2432
ville@ile-perrot.qc.ca
www.ile-perrot.qc.ca
Municipal Type: City
Incorporated: 1er juillet 1855; *Area:* 4,86 km2
County or District: Vaudreuil-Soulanges; *Population in 2006:* 9,927
Provincial Electoral District(s): Vaudreuil
Federal Electoral District(s): Vaudreuil-Soulanges
Next Election: 1er novembre 2013

Conseil
Marc Roy, Maire
André Legault, Conseiller, District: 1
Poste vacant, District: 2
Marcel Rainville, Conseiller, District: 3
Michelle L. LeCavalier, Conseillère, District: 4
René Pinsonneault, Conseiller, District: 5
Daniel Leblanc, Conseiller, District: 6

Administration
Lucie Coallier, Greffière
André Morin, Directeur général, 514-453-1751

La Prairie
#400, 170, boul Taschereau
La Prairie, QC J5R 5H6
450-444-6600 Fax: 450-444-6636
info@ville.laprairie.qc.ca
www.ville.laprairie.qc.ca
Municipal Type: City
Incorporated: 30 mars 1846; *Area:* 43,53 km2
County or District: Roussillon; *Population in 2006:* 21,763
Provincial Electoral District(s): La Prairie
Federal Electoral District(s): Brossard-La Prairie
Next Election: 1er novembre 2013

Conseil
Lucie F. Roussel, Mairesse, 450-444-6618
Donat Serres, Conseiller, District: 1 la Milice
Christian Caron, Conseiller, District: 2 Christ-Roi
Laurent Blais, Conseiller, District: 3 Vieux La Prairie
Jacques Bourbonnais, Conseiller, District: 4 La Citière
Yvon Brière, Conseiller, District: 5 La Clairière
Pierre Vocino, Conseiller, District: 6 La Magdeleine
Yves Senécal, Conseiller, District: 7 la Bataille
Suzanne Perron, Conseillère, District: 8 la Briqueterie

Administration
Manon Thériault, Greffière, 450-444-6625
Jean Bergeron, Directeur général, 450-444-6619
Nathalie Guérin, Trésorière, 450-444-6603

La Tuque
375, rue St-Joseph
La Tuque, QC G9X 1L5
819-676-5091 Fax: 819-523-5419
infoservice@ville.latuque.qc.ca
www.ville.latuque.qc.ca
Municipal Type: City
Incorporated: 26 mars 2003; *Area:* 28 421,48 km2
Population in 2009: 11,759
Provincial Electoral District(s): Laviolette
Federal Electoral District(s): St-Maurice-Champlain
Next Election: 1er novembre 2013
Note: Dès le 26 mars 2003, la nouvelle ville de La Tuque regroupe La Tuque, les municipalités de La Croche, La Bostonnais, & Lac-Édouard, le village de Parent, & 8 autres territoires.

Conseil
Réjean Gaudreault, Maire
Michel Lachance, Conseiller, District: 1 Parent
Elzéar Lepage, Conseiller, District: 2 La Croche
Luc Martel, Conseiller, District: 3 Jacques-Buteux/Terrasse St-Maurice
Roger Pearson, Conseiller, District: 4 Polyvalente
Clément Lebel, Conseiller, District: 5 Bel-Air/Centre-ville/Lac St-Louis
Julien Boisvert, Conseiller, District: 6 Aéroport
Line Pilote, Conseillère, District: 7 Couronne rurale

Administration
Yves Tousignant, Directeur général
Jean-Sébastien Poirier, Greffier
Pierre Bouchard, Trésorier

Lachute
380, rue Principale
Lachute, QC J8H 1Y2
450-562-3781 Fax: 450-562-1431
lachute@ville.lachute.qc.ca
www.ville.lachute.qc.ca
Municipal Type: City
Incorporated: 30 avril 1966; *Area:* 111,20 km2
County or District: Argenteuil; *Population in 2009:* 11,889
Provincial Electoral District(s): Argenteuil
Federal Electoral District(s): Argenteuil-Papineau-Mirabel
Next Election: 1er novembre 2013

Conseil
Daniel Mayer, Maire
André Gauthier, Conseiller, District: 1
Carl Péloquin, Conseiller, District: 2
Denis Richer, Conseiller, District: 3
Stéphane Braney, Conseiller, District: 4
Guy Desforges, Conseiller, District: 5
Paul Cleary, Conseiller, District: 6

Administration
Louise Beaulieu, Greffière
Pierre Gionet, Directeur général
Nathalie Piret, Trésorière par intérim

Laval
Hôtel de Ville
CP 422 St-Martin
1, Place du Souvenir
Laval, QC H7V 3Z4
450-978-2900 Fax: 450-978-6569
info@ville.laval.qc.ca
www.ville.laval.qc.ca
Municipal Type: City
Incorporated: 6 août 1965; *Area:* 245,40 km2
County or District: Communauté métropolitaine de Montréal;
Population in 2009: 377,332
Provincial Electoral District(s): Chomedey; Fabre; Laval-des-Rapides;

Mille-Iles; Vimont
Federal Electoral District(s): Laval; Marc-Aurèle-Fortin; Alfred-Pellan; Laval-Les Iles
Next Election: 1er novembre 2013

Conseil
Gilles Vaillancourt, Maire
Jacques St-Jean, Conseiller, District: 1: Saint-François
Sylvie Clermont, Conseillère, District: 2 Saint-Vincent-de-Paul
Madeleine Sollazzo, Conseillère, District: 3 Val-des-Arbres
Michèle Des Trois Maisons, Conseillère, District: 4 Duvernay-Pont-Viau
Francine Légaré, Conseillère, District: 5 Marigot
Jean-Jacques Lapierre, Conseiller, District: 6 Concorde-Bois-de-Boulogne
Benoit Fradet, Conseiller, District: 7: Renaud
Norman Girard, Conseiller, District: 8: Vimont
Yvon Martineau, Conseiller, District: 9: Saint-Bruno
Lucie Hill Laroque, Conseillère, District: 10: Auteuil
Ginette Grisé, Conseillère, District: 11: Laval-des-Rapides
Jocelyne Guertin, Conseillère, District: 12: Souvenir-Labelle
Ginette Legault-Bernier, Conseillère, District: 13: Abord-à-Plouffe
Basile Angelopoulos,, Conseiller, District: 14: Chomedey
Alexandre Duplessis, Conseiller, District: 15: Saint-Martin
Pierre Cléroux, Conseiller, District: 16: Sainte-Dorothée
Jean-Jacques Beldié, Conseiller, District: 17: Laval-les-îles
Robert Plante, Conseiller, District: 18: Orée-des-bois
Yvon Bromley, Conseiller, District: 19: Marc-Aurèle-Fortin
André Boileau, Conseiller, District: 20: Fabreville
Denis Robillard, Conseiller, District: 21: Sainte-Rose

Administration
Richard Fleury, Directeur général
Robert Cadieux, Contentieux, 450-978-5866
Ernest Lépine, Évaluation, 450-978-8777
Suzanne Deshaies, Trésorière, Finances, 450-978-5700
Guy Collard, Greffier, 450-978-3950
Martin Fiset, Ressources humaines, 450-978-6560
Paul Lemay, Directeur, Vie communautaire, culture & communications, 450-662-4343
Jean-Pierre Gariépy, Directeur, Protection des citoyens, 450-662-4242
Pierre Pelletier, Directeur, Travaux publics, 450-662-4600
Gérard Poirier, Ingénierie, 450-978-6888
Sylvain Dubois, Directeur, Urbanisme, 450-978-6888
Denis Bertrand, Régime de rentes, 450-978-5876
Paul Martell, Systèmes & technologies
Martine Lachambre, Vérificatrice générale, 450-978-8715
Guy Courchesne, Environnement, 450-978-6888

Lavaltrie
1370, rue Notre-Dame
Lavaltrie, QC J5T 1M5
450-586-2921 Fax: 450-586-3939
mairie@ville.lavaltrie.qc.ca
www.ville.lavaltrie.qc.ca
Municipal Type: City
Incorporated: 16 mai 2001; *Area:* 68,61 km2
County or District: D'Autray; *Population in 2009:* 12,514
Provincial Electoral District(s): Berthier
Federal Electoral District(s): Berthier-Maskinongé
Next Election: 1er novembre 2013

Conseil
Norman Blackburn, Maire
Michèle Dawe, Conseillère, District: Terrasses
Robert Pellerin, Conseiller, District: Rivière
Jocelyne Vaillancourt, Conseillère, District: Chemin du Roy
Jean-Yves Pelletier, Conseiller, District: Érablière
Georges Bonin, Conseiller, District: Boisé
Francine Ranger, Conseillère, District: Golf
Denis Moreau, Conseiller, District: Chasse-galerie
Rénald Bédard, Conseiller, District: Saint-Antoine

Administration
Madeleine Barbeau, Greffière
Réjean Nantais, Trésorier
Yvon Mousseau, Directeur général

Lévis
2175, ch du Fleuve
Saint-Romuald, QC G6W 7W9
418-839-2002 Fax: 418-839-5548
levis@ville.levis.qc.ca
www.ville.levis.qc.ca
Municipal Type: City
Incorporated: 1er janvier 2002; *Area:* 443,65 km2
Population in 2006: 130,006
Provincial Electoral District(s): Chutes-de-la-Chaudière; Lévis
Federal Electoral District(s): Lévis-Bellechasse; Lotbinière-Chutes-de-la-Chaudière
Next Election: 1er novembre 2013

Conseil
Danielle Roy Marinelli, Mairesse
Philippe Laberge, Conseiller, District: 1 Chutes-de-la-Chaudière-Ouest
Dominique Maranda, Conseillère, District: 2 Chutes-de-la-Chaudière-Ouest
Anne Ladouceur, Conseillère, District: 3 Chutes-de-la-Chaudière-Ouest
Isabelle Demers, Conseillère, District: 4 Chutes-de-la-Chaudière-Ouest
Alain Lemaire, Conseiller, District: 5 Chutes-de-la-Chaudière-Est
Nicole Larouche, Conseillère, District: 6 Chutes-de-la-Chaudière-Est
Guy Dumoulin, Conseiller, District: 7 Chutes-de-la-Chaudière-Est
Jean-Pierre Bazinet, Conseiller, District: 8 Chutes-de-la-Chaudière-Est
Jean-Luc Daigle, Conseiller, District: 9 Chutes-de-la-Chaudière-Est
Simon Théberge, Conseiller, District: 10 Desjardins
Jean Girard, Conseiller, District: 11 Desjardins
André Hamel, Conseiller, District: 12 Desjardins
Robert Maranda, Conseiller, District: 13 Desjardins
Jean-Claude Bouchard, Conseiller, District: 14 Desjardins
Ann Jeffrey, Conseillère, District: 15 Desjardins

Administration
Danielle Bilodeau, Directrice, Affaires juridiques & du greffe, 418-839-2002
Sabin Tremblay, Directeur général adjoint, 418-839-2002
Marcel Rodrigue, Directeur, Finances & Services administratifs, 418-839-2002
Jean Dubé, Directeur général, 418-839-2002
Jean-François Roy, Directeur, Service de police, 418-839-2002
Christian Brière, Directeur, Communications, 418-839-2002
Claude Guérin, Directeur, Ressources humaines, 418-839-2002
René Tremblay, Directeur, Vie communautaire, 418-839-2002
Alain Francoeur, Directeur, Environnement & infrastructures, 418-839-2002
Dominique Fortin, Directeur, Sécurité incendie, 418-839-2002
Michel Bélanger, Vérificateur général, 418-839-2002
Robert Cooke, Directeur, Urbanisme & Arrondissements, 418-839-2002
Philippe Meurant, Directeur, Développement, 418-839-2002

Longueuil
4250, ch de la Savane
Saint-Hubert, QC J3Y 9G4
450-463-7000 Fax: 450-463-7403
information@ville.longueuil.qc.ca
www.longueuil.ca
Municipal Type: City
Incorporated: 1er janvier 2002; *Area:* 111,50 km2
County or District: Communauté métropolitaine de Montréal;
Population in 2006: 230,949
Provincial Electoral District(s): Marie-Victorin; Taillon; Laporte; Vachon
Federal Electoral District(s): Saint-Lambert; Brossard-LaPrairie; Longueuil-Pierre-Boucher; Saint-Bruno-Saint Hubert
Next Election: 1er novembre 2013

Conseil
Claude Gladu, Maire
Michel Desjardins, Conseiller, District: 1 Vieux-Longueuil
Simon Crochetière, Conseiller, District: 2 Vieux-Longueuil
Claudette Tessier, Conseillère, District: 3 Vieux-Longueuil
Jacques Goyette, Conseiller, District: 4 Vieux-Longueuil
Robert Charland, Conseiller, District: 5 Vieux-Longueuil
Alain St-Pierre, Conseiller, District: 6 Vieux-Longueuil
Marie-Lise Sauvé, Conseillère, District: 7 Vieux-Longueuil
Manon D. Hénault, Conseillère, District: 8 Vieux-Longueuil
Nicole Lafontaine, Conseillère, District: 9 Vieux-Longueuil
Nicole Béliveau, Conseillère, District: 10 Vieux-Longueuil
Johane Fontaine-Deshaies, Conseillère, District: 11 Vieux-Longueuil
Normand Caisse, Conseiller, District: 12 Vieux-Longueuil
Gilbert Côté, Conseiller, District: 13 Vieux-Longueuil
Robert Gladu, Conseiller, District: 14 Vieux-Longueuil
Gilles Grégoire, Conseiller, District: 15 Vieux-Longueuil
Mireille Carrière, Conseillère, District: 16 Greenfield Park
Robert Myles, Conseiller, District: 17 Greenfield Park
Bernard Constantini, Conseiller, District: 18 Greenfield Park
Jacques Lemire, Conseiller, District: 19 St-Hubert
Roger Roy, Conseiller, District: 20 St-Hubert
Jacques E. Poitras, Conseiller, District: 21 St-Hubert
Lise Bélisle Dutil, Conseillère, District: 22 St-Hubert
Stéphane Desjardins, Conseiller, District: 23 St-Hubert
Suzanne Charbonneau, Conseillère, District: 24 St-Hubert
Lorraine Guay-Boivin, Conseillère, District: 25 St-Hubert
Michel Latendresse, Conseiller, District: 26 St-Hubert

Administration
Guy Benedetti, Directeur général
Diane Boileau, Directrice, Ressources humaines
Daniel Carrier, Directeur, Services juridiques
Pierre D. Poisson, Vérificateur général
Alain Bissonnette, Directeur, Finances/Trésorier
Pierre Archambault, Directeur, Ressources informationnelles & matérielles
Gilles Côté, Directeur général adjoint, Développement
François Laramée, Directeur, Communications & relations avec le citoyen
Marc St-Laurent, Directeur, Service de police
Jean-Pierre Lacombe, Directeur, Service de sécurité incendie
Michel Binet, Directeur, Travaux publics
Hélène Ladouceur, Directrice, Urbanisme
Michel Vallée, Directeur, Évaluation
André Lachapelle, Directeur général adjoint, Services administratifs

Lorraine
33, boul De Gaulle
Lorraine, QC J6Z 3W9
450-621-8550 Fax: 450-621-4763
direction.generale@ville.lorraine.qc.ca
www.ville.lorraine.qc.ca
Municipal Type: City
Incorporated: 4 février 1960; *Area:* 5,96 km2
County or District: Thérèse-De Blainville; *Population in 2006:* 9,613
Provincial Electoral District(s): Blainville
Federal Electoral District(s): Marc-Aurèle-Fortin
Next Election: 1er novembre 2013

Conseil
Boniface Dalle-Vedove, Maire
Ramez Ayoub, Conseiller, District: 1
Lyne Rémillard, Conseillère, District: 2
André W. Bédard, Conseiller, District: 3
Sylvain Perron, Conseiller, District: 4
Lynn Dionne, Conseillère, District: 5
Marie José Magnin, Conseillère, District: 6

Administration
Sylvie Trahan, Greffière
Denis Leclerc, Directeur général
Guy Pelletier, Chef, Division des travaux publics

Magog
7, rue Principale est
Magog, QC J1X 1Y4
819-843-6501 Fax: 819-843-1091
info@ville.magog.qc.ca
www.ville.magog.qc.ca
Municipal Type: City
Incorporated: 9 octobre 2002; *Area:* 145,68 km2
County or District: Memphrémagog; *Population in 2006:* 23,880
Provincial Electoral District(s): Orford
Federal Electoral District(s): Brome-Missisquoi
Next Election: 1er novembre 2013
Note: Depuis le 9 oct., le canton de Magog, le village d'Omerville & la ville de Magog sont regroupés pour former la nouvelle ville de Magog.

Conseil
Marc Poulin, Maire, 819-843-2880
Michel Bombardier, Conseiller, District: 1 La Rivière
Stéphane Simard, Conseiller, 819-843-6389, District: 2 Omerville
Denise Poulin-Marcotte, Conseillère, 819-843-1146, District: 3 Des Sommets
Alain Vanden Eynden, Conseiller, 819-843-1706, District: 4 Du Marais
Vicki May Hamm, Conseillère, 819-347-7409, District: 5 Canton Ouest
Jacques Laurendeau, Conseiller, 819-843-3244, District: 6 Des Pionniers
Gilbert Kurt Boucher, Conseiller, 819-868-2006, District: 7 Centre
Gilles Robinson, Conseiller, 819-843-2364, District: 8 Monseigneur Vel
Serge Gosselin, Conseiller, 819-843-8203, District: 9 Des Marinas
Jocelyne Mongrain, Conseillère, 819-847-1577, District: 10 Des Deux-lacs

Administration
Martine Savard, Greffière
Anne Couturier, Trésorière
Gilles Bertrand, Directeur général, 819-843-2880

Mascouche
3034, ch Ste-Marie
Mascouche, QC J7K 1P1
450-474-4133 Fax: 450-474-6401
greffe@ville.mascouche.qc.ca
www.ville.mascouche.qc.ca
Municipal Type: City
Incorporated: 1er juillet 1855; *Area:* 107,95 km2
County or District: Les Moulins; Communauté métropolitaine de Montréal; *Population in 2009:* 35,755
Provincial Electoral District(s): Masson
Federal Electoral District(s): Montcalm
Next Election: 1er novembre 2013

Conseil
Richard Marcotte, Maire
Normand Pagé, Conseiller, 450-966-6326, District: 1 Louis-Hébert
Lise Gagnon, Conseillère, 450-474-4501, District: 2 Laurier
Siège vacant, Conseiller, District: 3 Le Gardeur
Donald Mailly, Conseiller, 450-966-1413, District: 4 La Vérendrye
Pierre Villeneuve, Conseiller, 450-474-3626, District: 5 Du Coteau
Denise Cloutier, Conseillère, 450-968-0325, District: 6 Des Hauts-Bois
Louise Fourtané Bordonado, Conseillère, 450-474-0847, District: 7 Du Rucher
Denise Paquette, Conseillère, 450-966-6044, District: 8 Du Manoir

Administration
Yvan Laberge, Greffier

Matane
230, av St-Jérôme
Matane, QC G4W 3A2
418-562-2333 Fax: 418-562-4869
mairie@ville.matane.qc.ca
www.ville.matane.qc.ca
Municipal Type: City
Incorporated: 26 septembre 2001; *Area:* 214,63 km2
County or District: Matane; *Population in 2006:* 14,742
Provincial Electoral District(s): Matane
Federal Electoral District(s): Haute-Gaspésie-La Mitis-Matane-Matapédia
Next Election: 1er novembre 2013

Conseil
Linda Cormier, Mairesse
Jérôme Landry Conseiller, District: 1
Poste vacant, District: 2
France Caron, Conseillère, District: 3
Mario Côté Conseiller, District: 4

Michel Savard Conseiller, District: 5
Mario Hamilton Conseiller, District: 6
Victor Truchon Conseiller, District: 7
Guy A. Gauthier Conseiller, District: 8

Administration
Dominique Tancrède, Greffière
Marie Pelletier, Directrice, Services financiers
Michel Barriault, Directeur général

Mercier
869, boul St-Jean-Baptiste, 2e étage
Mercier, QC J6R 2L3
450-691-6090 Fax: 450-691-6529
info@ville.mercier.qc.ca
www.ville.mercier.qc.ca
Municipal Type: City
Incorporated: 1er juillet 1855; *Area:* 45,89 km2
County or District: Roussillon; Communauté métropolitaine de Montréal; *Population in 2009:* 10,379
Provincial Electoral District(s): Châteauguay
Federal Electoral District(s): Châteauguay-St-Constant
Next Election: 1er novembre 2013

Conseil
Jacques Lambert, Maire
Anik Sauvé, Conseillère, District: 1
Martial Crête, Conseiller, District: 2
Gilles Desponts, Conseiller, District: 3
Daniel Pilon, Conseiller, District: 4
Gilles Beaudin, Conseiller, District: 5
Pierre Hébert, Conseiller, District: 6

Administration
Daniel Prince, Greffier & Directeur général

Mirabel
14111, rue Saint-Jean
Mirabel, QC J7J 1Y3
450-475-8653 Fax: 450-475-7195
communications@ville.mirabel.qc.ca
www.ville.mirabel.qc.ca
Municipal Type: City
Incorporated: 1er janvier 1971; *Area:* 477,86 km2
County or District: Mirabel; *Population in 2006:* 34,626
Provincial Electoral District(s): Mirabel
Federal Electoral District(s): Argenteuil-Papineau-Mirabel
Next Election: 1er novembre 2013

Conseil
Hubert Meilleur, Maire
Michel Lauzon, Conseiller, District: 1
Gérald Forget, Conseiller, District: 2
Jean Bouchard, Conseiller, District: 3
Luc St-Jean, Conseiller, District: 4
Daniel Gauthier, Conseiller, District: 5
Pierre-Paul Meloche, Conseiller, District: 6
François Bélanger, Conseiller, District: 7
Guy Laurin, Conseiller, District: 8

Administration
Suzanne Mireault, Greffière, 450-475-2002
Germain Paquette, Trésorier, 450-475-2003
Bernard Poulin, Directeur, Communications, 450-475-2001
Jean Gaudreault, Directeur, Loisirs/Culture/Vie communautaire, 450-475-8656
Louis Prud'homme, Directeur général, 450-475-2000, Fax: 450-475-2013

Mont-Laurier
485, rue Mercier
Mont-Laurier, QC J9L 3N8
819-623-1221 Fax: 819-623-4840
mlaurier@lino.com
www.villemontlaurier.qc.ca
Municipal Type: City
Incorporated: 8 janvier 2003; *Area:* 590,64 km2
County or District: Antoine-Labelle; *Population in 2009:* 13,394
Provincial Electoral District(s): Labelle
Federal Electoral District(s): Laurentides-Labelle
Next Election: 1er novembre 2013
Note: Dès le 8 janvier 2003, la ville de Mont-Laurier regroupe les municipalités de Des Ruisseaux & Saint-Aimé-du-Lac-des-Iles.

Conseil
Michel Adrien, Maire
Louis-Pierre Blais, Conseiller
Jocelyne Cloutier, Conseillère
Gilles Huberdeau, Conseiller
Gilles Lacelle, Conseiller
Benoit Pagé, Conseiller

Administration
Blandine Boulianne, Greffière
Jean-Yves Forget, Directeur général
Johanne Nantel, Trésorière

Mont-St-Hilaire
100, rue du Centre-Civique
Mont-Saint-Hilaire, QC J3H 3M8
450-467-2854 Fax: 450-467-6460
greffe@villemsh.ca
www.ville.mont-saint-hilaire.qc.ca
Municipal Type: City
Incorporated: 12 mars 1966; *Area:* 38,96 km2
County or District: La Vallée-du-Richelieu; Communauté métropolitaine de Montréal; *Population in 2009:* 16,177
Provincial Electoral District(s): Borduas
Federal Electoral District(s): Chambly-Borduas
Next Election: 1er novembre 2013

Conseil
Michel Gilbert, Maire
Denise Loiselle, Conseillère, District: 1 - du Déboulis
Rémi H. Lair, Conseiller, District: 2 - des Patriotes
André Ricard, Conseiller, District: 3 - du Piémont
Ginette Poirier, Conseillère, District: 4 - de Rouville
Lise Gauvin, Conseillère, District: 5 - de la Montagne
Fernand Brillant, Conseiller, District: 6 - de la Pommeraie

Administration
Estelle Simard, Greffière
Patrick Savard, Directeur général
Carmel Constant, Trésorier
Pierre Bergeron, Directeur, Communications/Loisirs/Culture

Montmagny
134, rue St-Jean-Baptiste est
Montmagny, QC G5V 1K6
418-248-3361 Fax: 418-248-4870
info@ville.montmagny.qc.ca
www.ville.montmagny.qc.ca
Municipal Type: City
Incorporated: 2 avril 1966; *Area:* 125,76 km2
County or District: Montmagny; *Population in 2006:* 11,353
Provincial Electoral District(s): Montmagny-L'Islet
Federal Electoral District(s): Montmagny-L'Islet-Kamouraska-Rivière-du-Loup
Next Election: 1er novembre 2013

Conseil
Jean-Guy Desrosiers, Maire
Jean-Paul Boivin, Conseiller, District: 1
Gaston Caron, Conseiller, District: 2
Michel Coulombe, Conseiller, District: 3
Michel Mercier, Conseiller, District: 4
Michel Paquet, Conseiller, District: 5
Jean-François Lachance, Conseiller, District: 6

Administration
Félix Michaud, Greffier
Bernard Létourneau, Directeur général
André Lévesque, CA, Directeur, Service des finances/Approvisionnement, 418-248-3361, Fax: 418-248-8468
Yves Chayer, Directeur, Service incendie, 418-248-5813, Fax: 418-248-2266

Montréal
Hôtel de Ville
275, rue Notre-Dame est
Montréal, QC H2Y 1C6
514-872-3142 Fax: 514-872-5655
www.ville.montreal.qc.ca
Municipal Type: City
Incorporated: 1er janvier 2002; *Area:* 363,52 km2
County or District: Communauté métropolitaine de Montréal; *Population in 2009:* 1,640,565
Provincial Electoral District(s): Acadie;Anjou;Bourassa-Sauvé;Bourget;Crémazie;D'Arcy McGee;Gouin;Hochelaga-Maisonneuve;Jeanne-Mance-Viger;LaFontaine;Laurier-Dorion;Marguerite-Bourgeoys;Mercier;Marquette;Mont-Royal;Nelligan;Notre-Dame-de-Grâce;Outremont;Pointe-aux-Trembles;Robert-Baldwin;Rosemont;St-Henri-Ste-Anne;St-Laurent;Ste-Marie-St-Jacques;Westmount-St-Louis;Verdun;Viau
Federal Electoral District(s): Ahuntsic; Bourassa; Hochelaga; Honoré-Mercier; Jeanne-Le Ber; Lac-Saint-Louis; LaSalle-Émard; Laurier-Ste-Marie; Mount Royal; Notre-Dame-de-Grâce-Lachine; Outremont; Papineau; Rosemont-La Petite-Patrie; Westmount-Ville-Marie; St-Laurent-Cartierville; St-Léonard-St-Michel; La Pointe-de-l'Ile; Pierrefonds-Dollard
Next Election: 1er novembre 2013

Conseil
Gérald Tremblay, Maire, 514-872-3101
André Bélisle, Conseiller de ville, Pointe-aux-Trembles, District: Rivière-des-Prairies-Pointe-aux-Trembles
Richard Bergeron, Conseiller de ville, De Lorimier, District: Le Plateau-Mont-Royal
Yvette Bissonnet, Conseillère de ville, Saint-Léonard, District: Saint-Léonard
Patricia Bittar, M.Sc., Conseillère de ville, Norman-McLaren, District: Saint-Laurent
Jean-Yves Cartier, Conseiller de ville, Saint-Paul-Émard, District: Le Sud-Ouest
Jane Cowell-Poitras, Conseillère de ville, District: Lachine
Laval Demers, CA, Conseiller de ville, Côte-de-Liesse, District: Saint-Laurent
Richard Deschamps, Conseiller de ville, Sault-St-Louis, District: LaSalle
Christian G. Dubois, Conseiller de ville, Est, District: Pierrefonds-Roxboro
Alvaro Farinacci, Conseiller de ville, Cecil-P.-Newman, District: LaSalle
Sammy Forcillo, Conseiller de ville, Ste-Marie-St-Jacques, District: Ville-Marie
Jean-Marc Gibeau, Conseiller de ville, Ovide-Clermont, District: Montréal-Nord
Line Hamel, Conseillère de ville, St-Henri-Petite-Bourgogne, District: Le Sud-Ouest
Andrée Hénault, Conseillère de ville, District: Anjou
James V. Infantino, Conseiller de ville, Marie-Clarac, District: Montréal-Nord
Michel Labrecque, Conseiller de ville, Mile-End, District: Le Plateau-Mont-Royal
Joe Magri, Conseiller de ville, Rivière-des-Prairies, District: Rivière-des-Prairies-Pointe-aux-Trembles
Ginette Marotte, Conseillère de ville, Champlain-L'Île-des-Soeurs, District: Verdun
Nicolas Montmorency, Conseiller de ville, Pointe-aux-Prairies, District: Rivière-des-Prairies-Pointe-aux-Trembles
Dominic Perri, B.Sc., M.A., Conseiller de ville, St-Léonard-Ouest, District: Saint-Léonard
Michel Prescott, Conseiller de ville, Jeanne-Mance, District: Le Plateau-Mont-Royal
Catherine Sévigny, Conseillère de ville, Peter-McGill, District: Ville-Marie
Alain Tassé, Conseiller de ville, Desmarchais-Crawford, District: Verdun
Bertrand A. Ward, Conseiller de ville, District: Pierrefonds-Roxboro
Warren Allmand, Conseiller, Loyola, District: Côte-des-Neiges-N.-D.-de-Grâce
Hasmig Belleli, Conseillère, Ahuntsic, District: Ahuntsic-Cartierville
Carle Bernier-Genest, Conseiller, Marie-Victorin, District: Rosemont-La Petite-Patrie
Laurent Blanchard, Conseiller, Hochelaga, District: Mercier-Hochelaga-Maisonneuve
Jocelyn Ann Campbell, Conseillère, Saint-Sulpice, District: Ahuntsic-Cartierville
Mary Deros, Conseillère, Parc-Extension, District: Villeray St-Michel-Parc-Extension
Richer Dompierre, Conseiller, Louis-Riel, District: Mercier-Hochelaga-Maisonneuve
Carole Du Sault, Conseillère, Étienne-Desmarteau, District: Rosemont-La Petite-Patrie
Noushig Eloyan, Conseillère, Bordeaux-Cartierville, District: Ahuntsic-Cartierville
Diane Gibb, Conseillère, Pierre-Foretier, District: L'île-Bizard-Ste-Geneviève
Gilles Grondin, Conseiller, Vieux-Rosemont, District: Rosemont-La Petite-Patrie
Sylvain Lachance, Conseiller, Villeray, District: Villeray St-Michel-Parc-Extens
Christopher Little, Conseiller, Denis-Benjamin-Viger, District: L'île-Bizard-Ste-Geneviève
Soraya Martinez, Conseillère, Saint-Michel, District: Villeray St-Michel-Parc-Extens
Louis Moffatt, Conseiller, Claude-Ryan, District: Outremont
Ana Nunes, Conseillère, Jeanne-Sauvé, District: Outremont
Claude B. Piquette, Conseiller, Joseph-Beaubien, District: Outremont
Marie Potvin, Conseillère, Robert-Bourassa, District: Outremont
Gaëtan Primeau, Conseiller, Tétreaultville, District: Mercier-Hochelaga-Maisonneuve
François Purcell, Conseiller, Saint-Édouard, District: Rosemont-La Petite-Patrie
François Robert, Conseiller, Jacques-Bizard, District: L'île-Bizard-Ste-Geneviève
Marvin Rotrand, Conseiller, Snowdon, District: Côte-des-Neiges-N.-D.-de-Grâce
Francine Senécal, Conseillère, Côte-des-Neiges, District: Côte-des-Neiges-N.-D.-de-Grâce
Claire St-Arnaud, Conseillère, Maisonneuve-Longue-Pointe, District: Mercier-Hochelaga-Maisonneuve
Jean-François St-Onge, Conseiller, Sault-au-Récollet, District: Ahuntsic-Cartierville
Marcel Tremblay, Conseiller, Notre-Dame-de-Grâce, District: Côte-des-Neiges-N.-D.-de-Grâce
Frank Venneri, Conseiller, François-Perrault, District: Villeray St-Michel-Parc-Extens
Philippe Voisard, Conseiller, Ste-Geneviève, District: L'île-Bizard-Ste-Geneviève
Saulie Zajdel, Conseiller, Darlington, District: Côte-des-Neiges-N.-D.-de-Grâce
Mario Battista, Conseiller d'arrondissement, St-Léonard-Ouest, District: Saint-Léonard
Gilles Beaudry, Conseiller d'arrondissement, Anjou Ouest, District: Anjou
Paul Beaupré, Conseiller d'arrondissement, Champlain-L'île-des-S, District: Verdun
Michèle D. Biron, Conseillère d'arrondissement, Norman-McLaren, District: Saint-Laurent
Ross Blackhurst, Conseiller d'arrondissement, Sault-St-Louis, District: LaSalle
Bernard Blanchet, Conseiller d'arrondissement, J.-Émery-Provost, District: Lachine
Ronald Bossy, Conseiller d'arrondissement, St-Paul-Émard, District: Le Sud-Ouest
Karim Boulos, Conseiller d'arrondissement, Peter-McGill, District: Ville-Marie
Maria Calderone, Conseillère d'arrondissement, Rivière-des-Prairies, District: Rivière.-des-Prairies-Pointe-aux-Trembles
Vincenzo Cesari, Conseiller d'arrondissement, Cecil-P.-Newman, District: LaSalle
Catherine Clément-Talbot, Conseillère d'arrondissement, District: Pierrefonds-Roxboro
Jean-François Cloutier, Conseiller d'arrondissement, Fort-Rolland, District: Lachine
Maurice Cohen, Conseiller d'arrondissement, Côte-de-Liesse, District: Saint-Laurent
Suzanne Décarie, Conseillère d'arrondissement, Pointe-aux-Trembles, District: Rivière-des-Prairies-Pointe-aux-Trembles
Joseph Di Pietro, Conseiller d'arrondissement, Pointe-aux-Prairies, District: Rivière-des-Prairies-Pointe-aux-Trembles
Isabel Dos Santos, Conseillère d'arrondissement, Jeanne-Mance, District: Le Plateau-Mont-Royal

Josée Duplessis, Conseillère d'arrondissement, De Lorimier, District: Le Plateau-Mont-Royal
Eleni Fakotakis, Conseillère d'arrondissement, Mile-End, District: Le Plateau-Mont-Royal
Normand Fortin, Conseiller d'arrondissement, Ovide-Clermont, District: Montréal-Nord
Pierre E. Fréchette, Conseiller d'arrondissement., St-Henri-Pte-Bourgogne, District: Le Sud-Ouest
Josée Lavigueur-Thériault, Conseillère d'arrondissement, Desmarchais-Crawford, District: Verdun
Pierre Mainville, Conseiller d'arrondissement, Ste-Marie-St-Jacques, District: Ville-Marie
Laura Palestini, Conseillère d'arrondissement, Sault-St-Louis, District: LaSalle
André Savard, Conseiller d'arrondissement, Desmarchais-Crawford, District: Verdun
Clementina Teti-Tomassi, Conseillère d'arrondissement, Marie-Clarac, District: Montréal-Nord
Rémy Tondreau, Conseiller d'arrondissement, Anjou Est, District: Anjou
Marc Touchette, Conseiller d'arrondissement, Champlain-L'île-des-S, District: Verdun
Roger Trottier, Conseiller d'arrondissement, District: Pierrefonds-Roxboro
Michael Vadacchino, Conseiller d'arrondissement, Cecil-P.-Newman, District: LaSalle
Elizabeth Verge, Conseillère d'arrondissement, Canal, District: Lachine
Robert L. Zambito, Conseiller d'arrondissement, St-Léonard-Est, District: Saint-Léonard
Michelle Zammit, Conseillère d'arrondissement, Anjou Centre, Conseillers et District: Anjou
Michael Applebaum, Maire d'arrondissement, District: Côte-des-Neiges-N.-D.-de-Grâce
Manon Barbe, Mairesse d'arrondissement/Conseillère de la ville, District: LaSalle
Marie-Andrée Beaudoin, Mairesse d'arrondissement, District: Ahuntsic-Cartierville
Richard Bélanger, Maire d'arrondissement/Conseiller de la ville, District: L'île-Bizard-Ste-Geneviève
Michel Bissonnet, Maire d'arrondissement, District: Saint-Léonard
Marie Cinq-Mars, Mairesse d'arrondissement/Conseillère de la ville, District: Outremont
Claude Dauphin, Maire d'arrondissement, District: Lachine
Alan DeSousa, FCA, Maire d'arrondissement, District: Saint-Laurent
Helen Fotopulos, Mairesse d'arrondissement, District: Le Plateau-Mont-Royal
Benoît Labonté, Maire d'arrondissement, District: Ville-Marie
André Lavallée, Maire d'arrondissement, District: Rosemont-La Petite-Patrie
Cosmo Maciocia, Maire d'arrondissement, District: Rivière-des-Prairies-Pointe-aux-Trembles
Luis Miranda, Maire d'arrondissement/Conseiller de la ville, District: Anjou
Jacqueline Montpetit, Mairesse d'arrondissement, District: Le Sud-Ouest
Marcel Parent, Maire d'arrondissement/Conseiller de la ville, District: Montréal-Nord
Anie Samson, Mairesse d'arrondissement, District: Villeray St-Michel-Parc-Extension
Lyn Thériault, Mairesse d'arrondissement, District: Mercier-Hochelaga-Maisonneuve
Claude Trudel, Maire d'arrondissement/Conseiller de ville, District: Verdun
Monique Worth, Mairesse d'arrondissement/Conseillère de la ville, District: Pierrefonds-Roxboro

Administration
Yves Saindon, Greffier, 514-872-3007
Claude Léger, Directeur général, 514-872-0589
Jacques Bergeron, Vérificateur général
Colombe Cliche, Directrice, Communications/Relations avec les citoyens
Pierre Reid, Directeur, Service du Capital humain
Robert Lamontagne, CA, MBA, Directeur, Finances & Trésorerie
Jacques Bergeron, CA, MBA, M.Sc., Vérificateur général
Denis Savard, CA, MBA, Directeur, Vérification financière & informatique
Robert Duquette, Chef de division, Vérification d'optimisation des ressources
Serge Vaillancourt, Chef de division, Vérification informatique
Denis Tremblay, Chef de division, Vérification -Autres organismes municipaux
Serge Tremblay, Directeur
Colombe Cliche, Directrice
Pierre Reid, Directeur
Claude Léger, Directeur général
Yvan Delorme, Directeur

Pincourt

919, ch Duhamel
Pincourt, QC J7V 4G8
514-453-8981 Fax: 514-453-8401
m.perrier@villepincourt.qc.ca
www.villepincourt.qc.ca
Municipal Type: City
Incorporated: 1er janvier 1950; *Area:* 8,36 km2
County or District: Vaudreuil-Soulanges; Communauté métropolitaine de Montréal; *Population in 2009:* 11,777
Provincial Electoral District(s): Vaudreuil
Federal Electoral District(s): Vaudreuil-Soulanges
Next Election: 1er novembre 2013

Conseil
Michel Kandyba, Maire
Stéphane Boyer, Conseiller, District: 1
Claude Comeau, Conseiller, District: 2
Marie-Andrée Laliberté, Conseillère, District: 3
Michel Pratte, Conseiller, District: 4
Jim Miron, Conseiller, District: 5
André D 'Aragon, Conseiller, District: 6

Administration
Michel Perrier, Directeur général
Nicole Drouin, Greffière

Prévost

2870, boul du Curé-Labelle
Prévost, QC J0R 1T0
450-224-8888 Fax: 450-224-8323
greffe@ville.prevost.qc.ca
www.ville.prevost.qc.ca
Municipal Type: City
Incorporated: 20 janvier 1973; *Area:* 34,32 km2
County or District: La Rivière-du-Nord; *Population in 2009:* 10,464
Provincial Electoral District(s): Prévost
Federal Electoral District(s): Rivière-du-Nord
Next Election: 1er novembre 2013

Conseil
Claude Charbonneau, Maire
Gaétan Bordeleau, Conseiller, District: 1
Jean-Pierre Joubert, Conseiller, District: 2
Germain Richer, Conseiller, District: 3
Sylvain Paradis, Conseiller, District: 4
Marcel Poirier, Conseiller, District: 5
Stéphane Parent, Conseiller, District: 6

Administration
Laurent Laberge, Greffier
Réal Martin, Directeur général

Québec

Hôtel de Ville
CP 700 Haute-Ville
2, rue des Jardins
Québec, QC G1R 4S9
418-691-6010 Fax: 418-641-6357
renseignements@ville.quebec.qc.ca
www.ville.quebec.qc.ca
Municipal Type: City
Incorporated: 1er janvier 2002; *Area:* 451,79 km2
Population in 2006: 491,142
Provincial Electoral District(s): Charlesbourg-Haute-Saint-Charles; Chauveau; Jean-Lesage; Jean-Talon; La Peltrie; Louis-Hébert; Montmorency; Taschereau; Vanier
Federal Electoral District(s): Québec; Louis-St-Laurent
Next Election: 1er novembre 2013

Conseil
Régis Labeaume, Maire, 418-641-6434
Arrondissement de Beauport
Carol Bégin Giroux, Conseillère, District: Chute-Montmorency
Lisette Lepage, Conseillère, District: Saint-Michel
André Letendre, Conseiller, District: Vieux-Bourg
Marc Simoneau, Conseiller, District: Vieux-Moulin
Marie-France Trudel, Conseillère, District: Laurentides
Arrondissement de Charlesbourg
Michel Fecteau, Conseiller, District: Sentiers
Jean-Marie Laliberté, Conseiller, District: Monts
Gilles Marcotte, Conseiller, District: Jean-Talon
Ralph Mercier, Conseiller, District: Charlesbourg-Centre
Denise Trudel, Conseillère, District: Saint-Rodrigue
Arrondissement de La Cité
Yvon Bussières, Conseiller, District: Saint-Sacrement
Anne Guérette, Conseillère, District: Montcalm
Jacques Joli-Coeur, Conseiller, District: Samuel-de-Champlain
Louise Lapointe, Conseillère, District: Saint-Sauveur
Pierre Maheux, Conseiller, District: Faubourgs
Arrondissement de La Haute-Saint-Charles
Pierre Blouin, Conseiller, District: Châtels
Raymond Dion, Conseiller, District: Loretteville
Jacques Teasdale, Conseiller, District: Lac-St-Charles
Steeve Verret, Conseiller, District: Saint-Émile
Arrondissement de Limoilou
Anne Beaulieu, Conseillère, District: Vieux-Limoilou
Anne Létourneau, Conseillère, District: Colisée
Alain Loubier, Conseiller, District: Maizerets
Ginette Picard Lavoie, Conseillère, District: Lairet
Arrondissement de Sainte-Foy-Sillery
Francine Bouchard, Conseillère, District: Pointe-de-Sainte-Foy
André Demers, Conseiller, District: Saint-Louis
Gérard Landry, Conseiller, District: Plateau
Paul Shoiry, Conseiller, District: Sillery
Jérôme Vaillancourt, Conseiller, District: Cité-universitaire
Arrondissement des Rivières
Richard Côté, Conseiller, District: Vanier
Patrick Paquet, Conseiller, District: Neufchâtel
François Picard, Conseiller, District: Lebourgneuf
Gérald Poirier, Conseiller, District: Saules
Poste vacant, Conseiller, District: Duberger
Arrondissement Laurentien
Jean-Marie Matte, Conseiller, District: Val-Bélair
Guy Perrault, Conseiller, District: Chauveau
Denise Tremblay Blanchette, Conseillère, District: Cap-Rouge
Conrad Verret, Conseiller, District: Champigny

Administration
Sylvain Ouellet, Greffier, 418-641-6212
Alain Marcoux, Directeur général
Annie Gaudreault, Directrice, Division du greffe de la cour municipale
Chantale Giguère, Directrice, Service des ressources humaines
Denis Deslauriers, Directeur, Service des technologies de l'information/télécommunication, 418-641-6239
Rhonda Rioux, Directrice, Service de la culture, 418-641-6181
Fernand Martin, Directeur, Service de l'aménagement du territoire, 418-641-6160
Marcel Roy, Directeur, Service des travaux publics, 418-641-6240
Pierre Huot, Directeur, Service de l'évaluation, 418-641-6193
Guy Bélanger, Directeur, Service des loisirs, des sports & vie communautaire
Jean-Yves Tellier, Directeur, Service du développement économique
Daniel Lessard, Directeur, Service de l'ingénierie
Richard Poitras, Directeur, Service de protection contre l'incendie, 418-641-6231
Serge Bélisle, Directeur, Service de la police, 418-641-6292
Pierre Gignac, Directeur, Service des communications, 418-641-6210
Daniel Maranda, Directeur, Service des approvisionnements, 418-641-6164
Gabriel Savard, Directeur, Office du tourisme et des congrès, 418-522-3511
François Gagnon, Vérificateur général
Serge Giasson, Directeur, Affaires juridiques
Gilles Noël, Directeur général adjoint, Services de soutien
Suzanne Canac Marquis, Directrice générale adjointe, Développement culturel, touristique, sportif & social
Guy Renaud, Directeur général adjoint, Développement durable
Chantale Giguère, Directrice générale adjointe, Sécurité publique
Alain Thériault, Directeur général adjoint, Coordination des arrondissements
Yves Courchesne, Directeur, Services des finances, 418-641-6203
Michel Beauchemin, Directeur

Repentigny

435, boul Iberville
Repentigny, QC J6A 2B6
450-470-3000 Fax: 450-470-3082
communication@ville.repentigny.qc.ca
www.ville.repentigny.qc.ca
Municipal Type: City
Incorporated: 1er juin 2002; *Area:* 68,42 km2
County or District: L'Assomption; Communauté métropolitaine de Montréal; *Population in 2009:* 78,812
Provincial Electoral District(s): L'Assomption; Masson
Federal Electoral District(s): Montcalm; Repentigny; Terrebonne-Blainville
Next Election: 1er novembre 2013

Conseil
Chantal Deschamps, Mairesse, 450-470-3103
André Cyr, Conseiller, 450-585-3410, District: 1
Georges Robinson, Conseiller, 450-654-9746, District: 2
Denyse Peltier, Conseillère, 450-581-5733, District: 3
Cécile Hénault, Conseillère, 450-654-3046, District: 4
Patrice Peltier-Rivest, Conseiller, 450-657-1255, District: 5
Daniel Labrecque, Conseiller, 450-841-2437, District: 6
Raymond Hénault, Conseiller, 450-581-0319, District: 7
Mario Morais, Conseiller, 450-654-4018, District: 8
Jean Langlois, Conseiller, 450-585-4285, District: 9
Jeannot Lemay, Conseiller, 450-585-6594, District: 10
Francine Payer, Conseillère, 450-582-7711, District: 11
Sylvie Langlois-Brouillette, Conseillère, 514-295-8376, District: 12

Administration
Louis-André Garceau, Greffier, 450-470-3130
Daniel L'Écuyer, Directeur général, 450-470-3110
Diane Pelchat, Trésorière, 450-470-3200
Michel Mailhot, Directeur, Ressources humaines, 450-470-3700
Serge Daoust, Directeur, Police (Administration), 450-470-3600
David Legault, Directeur, Permis, inspections & urbanisme, 450-470-3840
Denis Larose, Directeur, Service d'incendie, 450-470-3620
Sylvie Bouchard, Directrice, Travaux publics, 450-470-3800
Marlène Girard, Directrice, Communications, 450-470-3140
José Girard, Directeur, Transport collectif, 450-470-3860
Sylviane DiFolco, Directrice, Loisirs, culture & vie communautaire, 450-470-3400
Ghislain Bélanger, Directeur, Développement économique & services techniques, 450-470-3150

Rimouski

CP 710
205, av de la Cathédrale
Rimouski, QC G5L 7C7
418-724-3108 Fax: 418-724-3183
communications@ville.rimouski.qc.ca
www.ville.rimouski.qc.ca
Municipal Type: City
Incorporated: 1er janvier 2002; *Area:* 254,16 km2
County or District: Rimouski-Neigette; *Population in 2006:* 42,240
Provincial Electoral District(s): Rimouski
Federal Electoral District(s): Rimouski-Neigette-Témiscouata-Les Basques
Next Election: 1er novembre 2013

Conseil
Éric Forest, Maire, 418-724-3126
Marc St-Laurent, Conseiller, District: 1 Sacré-Coeur
Rodrigue Joncas, Conseiller, District: 2 Nazareth
Claude Mongrain, Conseiller, District: 3 Saint-Germain
Richard Caissy, Conseiller, District: 4 Rimouski-Est
Raymond-Marie Murray, Conseiller, District: 5 Pointe-au-Père
Donald Bélanger, Conseiller, District: 6 Sainte-Odile
Gisèle Saint-Pierre-Beaulieu, Conseillère, District: 7 Saint-Robert
Pierre Tourville, Conseiller, District: 8 Terrasse Arthur-Buies

Karol Francis, Conseillère, District: 9 Saint-Pie-X
Francis Proulx, Conseiller, District: 10 Sainte-Blanche/Mont-Lebel

Administration
Marc Doucet, Greffier, 418-724-3125, Fax: 418-724-9795
Jean Matte, Directeur général, 418-724-3171, Fax: 418-724-3183
Jean-Charles Fournier, Directeur, Service des finances, 418-724-3111, Fax: 418-724-3180

Rivière-du-Loup
CP 37
65, rue de l'Hôtel-de-Ville
Rivière-du-Loup, QC G5R 3Y7
418-867-6700 Fax: 418-862-2817
sylvie.roussel@ville.riviere-du-loup.qc.ca
www.ville.riviere-du-loup.qc.ca
Municipal Type: City
Incorporated: 30 décembre 1998; *Area:* 83,39 km2
County or District: Rivière-du-Loup; *Population in 2006:* 18,586
Provincial Electoral District(s): Rivière-du-Loup
Federal Electoral District(s):
Montmagny-L'Islet-Kamouraska-Rivière-du-Loup
Next Election: 1er novembre 2013

Conseil
Michel Morin, Maire, 418-867-6625
Claude Pelletier, Conseiller, District: la Rivière
Hervé Bouchard, Conseiller, District: Fraserville
Sylvie Vignet, Conseillère, District: la Plaine
Jacques Thériault, Conseiller, District: la Pointe
Gaëtan St-Pierre, Conseiller, District: l'Estuaire
Denis Tardif, Conseiller, District: Saint-Patrice

Administration
Georges Deschênes, Greffier, 418-867-6715
Marie Lapointe, Directrice, Service finances & Trésorerie, 418-867-6711
Jacques Poulin, Directeur général, 418-867-6707
Benoît Ouellet, Directeur, Loisirs, culture & vie communautaire, 418-862-0906

Roberval
851, boul St-Joseph
Roberval, QC G8H 2L6
418-275-0202 Fax: 418-275-5031
vroberval@ville.roberval.qc.ca
www.ville.roberval.qc.ca
Municipal Type: City
Incorporated: 23 décembre 1976; *Area:* 168,27 km2
County or District: Le Domaine-du-Roy; *Population in 2009:* 10,512
Provincial Electoral District(s): Roberval
Federal Electoral District(s): Roberval-Lac-St-Jean
Next Election: 1er novembre 2013

Conseil
Michel Larouche, Maire
Jocelyn Bouchard, Conseiller, District: 1
Gilles Veilleux, Conseiller, District: 2
Gilles Otis, Conseiller, District: 3
Michèle Claveau, Conseillère, District: 4
Rémy Leclerc, Conseiller, District: 5
Serge Hudon, Conseiller, District: 6

Administration
Jean-Guy Tardif, Greffier
Jeannot Gagnon, Directeur général
Nancy Boutin, Trésorière

Rosemère
100, rue Charbonneau
Rosemère, QC J7A 3W1
450-621-3500 Fax: 450-621-7601
info@ville.rosemere.qc.ca
www.ville.rosemere.qc.ca
Municipal Type: City
Incorporated: 1er janvier 1947; *Area:* 10,35 km2
County or District: Thérèse-De Blainville; Communauté métropolitaine de Montréal; *Population in 2009:* 14,284
Provincial Electoral District(s): Groulx
Federal Electoral District(s): Marc-Aurèle-Fortin
Next Election: 1er novembre 2013

Conseil
Hélène Daneault, Mairesse
Wendy Gurd, Conseillère, District: 1
Pierre Roussel, Conseiller, District: 2
Madeleine Leduc, Conseillère, District: 3
Louise Desjardins, Conseillère, District: 4
Eric Westram, Conseiller, District: 5
Claude Roy, Conseiller, District: 6

Administration
Patrick St-Amour, Greffier
Michel Gagné, Directeur général

Rouyn-Noranda
CP 220
100, rue Taschereau est
Rouyn-Noranda, QC J9X 5C3
819-797-7110 Fax: 819-797-7108
www.ville.rouyn-noranda.qc.ca
Municipal Type: City
Incorporated: 1er janvier 2002; *Area:* 6435,64 km2
Population in 2006: 39,924
Provincial Electoral District(s): Abitibi-Est; Rouyn-Noranda-Témiscamingue
Federal Electoral District(s): Abitibi-Témiscamingue
Next Election: 1er novembre 2013

Conseil
Mario Provencher, Maire
Léo Boisvert, Conseiller, District: Noranda-Nord/Lac-Dufault
Sylvie Turgeon, Conseillère, District: Rouyn-Noranda Ouest
André Philippon, Conseiller, District: Dallaire
Mario Provencher, Conseiller, District: Centre-ville
Bernard Duchesneau, Conseiller, District: Université
Marcel Loyer, Conseiller, District: Granada
Danielle Simard, Conseillère, District: Arntfield/Montbeillard/Rollet
Marcel Maheux, Conseiller, District: Bellecombe/Beaudry/Cloutier
Pierre Rodrigue, Conseiller, District: Alembert/Cléricy/Mt-Brun/Destr
Ronald Gaudet, Conseiller, District: McWatters
René Ducharme, Conseiller, District: Cadillac & T.N.O.
Siège vacant, Conseiller, District: Vieux-Noranda
Siège vacant, Conseiller, District: Des Pionniers
Siège vacant, Conseiller, District: Évain

Administration
Daniel Samson, Greffier
Poste vacant, Directeur, Finances
Denis Charron, Directeur général

Saguenay
CP 129
201, rue Racine est
Chicoutimi, QC G7H 5B8
418-698-3000 Fax: 418-541-4524
info@ville.saguenay.qc.ca
www.ville.saguenay.qc.ca
Municipal Type: City
Incorporated: 18 février 2002; *Area:* 1,166 km2
Population in 2006: 143,692
Provincial Electoral District(s): Dubuc; Chicoutimi; Jonquière
Federal Electoral District(s): Chicoutimi-Le Fjord
Next Election: 1er novembre 2013

Conseil
Jean Tremblay, Maire, 418-698-3330, Fax: 418-541-4510
Paul-Roger Cantin, Conseiller, District: 1 Jonquière
Réjean Laforest, Conseiller, District: 2 Jonquière
Sylvie Gaudreault, Conseillère, District: 3 Jonquière
Georges Bouchard, Conseiller, District: 4 Jonquière
Bernard Noël, Conseiller, District: 5 Jonquière
Raoul Simard, Conseiller, District: 6 Jonquière
Claude Tremblay, Conseiller, District: 7 Jonquière
Fabien Hovington, Conseiller, District: 8 Jonquière
Jean-Yves Provencher, Conseiller, District: 9 Chicoutimi
Carl Savard, Conseiller, District: 10 Chicoutimi
Marina Larouche, Conseillère, District: 11 Chicoutimi
Marcel Jean, Conseiller, District: 12 Chicoutimi
Jacques Cleary, Conseiller, District: 13 Chicoutimi
Denis Dahl, Conseiller, District: 14 Chicoutimi
Jacques Fortin, Conseiller, District: 15 Chicoutimi
Luc Blackburn, Conseiller, District: 16 Chicoutimi
Poste vacant, Conseiller, District: 17 La Baie
Marc-André Gagnon, Conseiller, District: 18 La Baie
Jean-Eudes Simard, Conseiller, District: 19 La Baie

Administration
Pierre Brassard, Greffier
Jean-François Boivin, Directeur général, 418-698-3320, Fax: 418-541-4524
Serges Chamberland, Directeur général adjoint, Opérations
Francine Maltais, Directrice, Services des arts, culture, communautaire & bibliothèque
Daniel Larouche, Directeur, Arrondissement de Jonquière
André Martin, Directeur, Arrondissement de Chicoutimi
Gaëtan Bergeron, Directeur, Arrondissement de La Baie
Christine Tremblay, Directrice, Trésorerie et Évaluation
Jeannot Allard, Directeur, Service des communications
Sylvie Jean, Directrice, Service des approvisionnements
Pierre A. Tremblay, Directeur, Service des ressources informationnelles
Robert Pépin, Directeur, Service des affaires juridiques & du greffe
Denis Coulombe, Directeur, Aménagement du territoire & urbanisme
Claude Bouchard, Directeur, Hydro-Jonquière
Jean Morneau, Directeur, Service des immeubles et équipements motorisés
Pierre Racine, Directeur, Service des sports & du plein air
Carol Girard, Directeur, Sécurité incendie
Mario Giroux, Directeur, Sécurité publique

Saint-Basile-le-Grand
204, rue Principale
Saint-Basile-le-Grand, QC J3N 1M1
450-461-8000 Fax: 450-461-8029
communciations@ville.saint-basile-le-grand.qc.ca
www.ville.saint-basile-le-grand.qc.ca
Municipal Type: City
Incorporated: 15 juin 1871; *Area:* 34,82 km2
County or District: La Vallée-du-Richelieu; Communauté métropolitaine de Montréal; *Population in 2009:* 16,088
Provincial Electoral District(s): Chambly
Federal Electoral District(s): Chambly-Borduas
Next Election: 1er novembre 2013

Conseil
Michel Carrières, Maire
Marie-Hélène Boisvert, Conseillère
Josée Laforest, Conseillère
Marie-Ginette Lafrance, Conseillère
Annie Lessard, Conseillère
Guy Raymond, Conseiller
Glenn Whitelaw, Conseiller

Administration
Luce Doucet, Greffière
Normand Lalande, Trésorier
Marc-André Lehoux, Directeur, Culture/Loisirs

Saint-Constant
147, rue St-Pierre
Saint-Constant, QC J5A 2G2
450-638-2010 Fax: 450-638-5919
communications@ville.saint-constant.qc.ca
www.ville.saint-constant.qc.ca
Municipal Type: City
Incorporated: 1er juillet 1855; *Area:* 56,58 km2
County or District: Roussillon; *Population in 2006:* 23,957
Provincial Electoral District(s): La Prairie
Federal Electoral District(s): Châteauguay-St-Constant
Next Election: 1er novembre 2013

Conseil
Gilles Pepin, Maire
Denise Poirier Rivard, Conseillère, District: 1
Raymond Létourneau, Conseiller, District: 2
Yvan Riendeau, Conseiller, District: 3
France Hébert, Conseillère, District: 4
André Sauvé, Conseiller, District: 5
Mignonne Pouliot, Conseillère, District: 6
Jean-François Ouellet, Conseiller, District: 7
Mario Arsenault, Conseiller, District: 8

Administration
Sophie Laflammme, Greffière
Susan McKercher, Directrice générale
Jean Gariépy, Directeur et chef, Brigade des pompiers
Bernard Armand, Coordonnateur, Mesures d'urgence

Saint-Eustache
145, rue St-Louis
Saint-Eustache, QC J7R 1X9
450-974-5000
www.ville.saint-eustache.qc.ca
Municipal Type: City
Incorporated: 15 janvier 1972; *Area:* 70,61 km2
County or District: Deux-Montagnes; Communauté métropolitaine de Montréal; *Population in 2009:* 42,762
Provincial Electoral District(s): Deux-Montagnes
Federal Electoral District(s): Rivière-des-Mille-Iles
Next Election: 1er novembre 2013

Conseil
Claude Carignan, Maire, 450-974-5014, Fax: 450-974-5203
Sylvain Mallette, Conseiller, District: 1 Vieux-Saint-Eustache
André Biard, Conseiller, 450-473-2214, District: 2 Carrefour
Patrice Paquette, Conseiller, 450-974-1120, District: 3 Rivière-Nord
Daniel Goyer, Conseiller, 450-974-9104, District: 4 Des Érables
Pierre Charron, Conseiller, 450-473-8054, District: 5 Clair Matin
Germain Lalonde, Conseiller, 450-472-5890, District: la Seigneurie
Pauline Harrison, Conseillère, 450-473-8141, District: Des Moissons
Raymond Tessier, Conseiller, 450-472-3951, District: Des ×les
Nicole Carignan Lefebvre, Conseillère, 450-623-5730, District: Plateau-des-Chênes
Sylvie Cloutier, Conseillère, 450-974-9379, District: Des Jardins

Administration
Marc Tourangeau, Greffier
Christian Bellemare, Directeur général, 450-974-5280, Fax: 450-974-5229
Ginette Lacoix, Directrice, Finances, 450-974-5070, Fax: 450-974-5077
Stéphanie Bouchard, Directrice, Communications, 450-974-5220, Fax: 450-974-5223
Yves Guillemette, Directeur général adjoint
Bastien Morin, Directeur, Services municipaux, 450-974-5284, Fax: 450-974-5229

Saint-Félicien
CP 7000
1209, boul Sacré-Coeur
Saint-Félicien, QC G8K 2R5
418-679-0251 Fax: 418-679-1449
dir.general@ville.stfelicien.qc.ca
www.ville.stfelicien.qc.ca
Municipal Type: City
Incorporated: 12 juin 1996; *Area:* 359,69 km2
County or District: Le Domaine-du-Roy; *Population in 2006:* 10,477
Provincial Electoral District(s): Roberval
Federal Electoral District(s): Roberval-Lac-St-Jean
Next Election: 1er novembre 2013

Conseil
Gilles Potvin, Maire
Bertrand Boutin, Conseiller, Siège #1
Bernard Boivin, Conseiller, Siège #2
Dany Larochelle, Conseiller, Siège #3
Luc Gibbons, Conseiller, Siège #4
Sonia Boudreault, Conseillère Siège #5
Michel Gagnon, Conseiller, Siège #6

Administration
Louise Ménard, Greffière
Luc Bergeron, Directeur général, 418-679-2100, Fax: 418-679-1449
Dany Coudé, Trésorier

Olivier de Launière, Directeur, Sécurité incendie, 418-679-0313, Fax: 418-679-8217
Paul-René Doucet, Directeur, Aménagement & entretien du territoire

Saint-Georges

11700, boul Lacroix
Saint-Georges, QC G5Y 1L3
418-228-5555 Fax: 418-228-3855
direction.generale@ville.saint-georges.qc.ca
www.ville.saint-georges.qc.ca
Municipal Type: City
Incorporated: 26 septembre 2001; *Area:* 199,51 km2
County or District: Beauce-Sartigan; *Population in 2006:* 29,616
Provincial Electoral District(s): Beauce-Sud
Federal Electoral District(s): Beauce
Next Election: 1er novembre 2013

Conseil
Roger Carette, Maire
Serge Paquet, Conseiller, District: 1
Daniel Lessard, Conseiller, District: 2
Jean Perron, Conseiller, District: 3
Irma Quirion, Conseillère, District: 4
Régis Drouin, Conseiller, District: 5
Marie-Ôve Dutil, Conseillère, District: 6
Karen Hilchey, Conseillère, District: 7
Marcel Bérubé, Conseiller, District: 8

Administration
Jean McCollough, Greffier
Clément Poulin, Directeur, Finances & Trésorerie

Saint-Hyacinthe

CP 10
700, av de l'Hôtel-de-Ville
Saint-Hyacinthe, QC J2S 5B2
450-778-8300 Fax: 450-778-5817
communications@ville.st-hyacinthe.qc.ca
www.ville.st-hyacinthe.qc.ca
Municipal Type: City
Incorporated: 27 décembre 2001; *Area:* 189,11 km2
County or District: Les Maskoutains; *Population in 2006:* 51,616
Provincial Electoral District(s): St-Hyacinthe
Federal Electoral District(s): St-Hyacinthe-Bagot
Next Election: 1er novembre 2013

Conseil
Claude Bernier, Maire, 450-778-8302, Fax: 450-778-5800
Johanne Delage, Conseillère, District: 1. Yamaska
Rosaire Martin, Conseiller, District: 2. Saint-Joseph
Bernard Barré, Conseiller, District: 3. La Providence
Sylvie Adam, Conseillère, District: 4. Cascades
Réal St-Pierre, Conseiller, District: 5. Notre-Dame
Nicole Dion-Audette, Conseillère, District: 6. Hertel
Siège vacant, Conseiller, District: 7. Douville
Ray-Marc Dumoulin, Conseiller, District: 8. Bois-Joli
Huguette Corbeil, Conseillère, District: 9. Deux-Clochers
Jean-Claude Patenaude, Conseiller, District: 10. Vanier
Léon Plante, Conseiller, District: 11. Sainte-Rosalie
Guylain Coulombe, Conseiller, District: 12. Saint-Thomas-d'Aquin
Réjean Veilleux, Conseiller, District: 13. Ceinture-Verte

Administration
Hélène Beauchesne, Notaire; OMA, Greffière, 450-778-8317
Louis Bilodeau, Directeur général
Chantal Frigon, Directrice, Communications, 450-778-8304
Patrice Furlan, Directeur, Service d'urbanisme, 450-778-8320, Fax: 450-778-5820
Daniel Dubois, Directeur, Sécurité incendie
Jean Bélisle, OMA, Directeur, Service des finances, 450-778-8387

Saint-Jean-sur-Richelieu

CP 1025
188, rue Jacques-Cartier nord
Saint-Jean-sur-Richelieu, QC J3B 7B2
450-357-2100 Fax: 450-357-2285
info@ville.saint-jean-sur-richelieu.qc.ca
www.ville.saint-jean-sur-richelieu.qc.ca
Municipal Type: City
Incorporated: 24 janvier 2001; *Area:* 225,61 km2
County or District: Le Haut-Richelieu; *Population in 2006:* 87,492
Provincial Electoral District(s): St-Jean; Iberville
Federal Electoral District(s): St-Jean
Next Election: 1er novembre 2013

Conseil
Gilles Dolbec, Maire, 450-357-2095, Fax: 450-357-2079
Philippe Lasnier, Conseiller, 450-347-1299, District: 1
Michel Gauthier, Conseiller, 450-515-9846, District: 2
Gaétan Gagnon, Conseiller, 450-347-3209, District: 3
Jean Fontaine, Conseiller, 450-346-3063, District: 4
Stéphane Legrand, Conseiller, 450-545-9515, District: 5
Germain Poissant, Conseiller, 450-347-8703, District: 6
Christiane Marcoux, Conseillère, 450-347-5277, District: 7
Marco Savard, Conseiller, 450-349-0473, District: 8
Yvan Berthelot, Conseiller, 450-349-0685, District: 9
Jean Lamoureux, Conseiller, 450-348-5014, District: 10
Michelle Power, Conseillère, 514-449-9614, District: 11
Robert Cantin, Conseiller, 450-349-6661, District: 12

Administration
François Lapointe, Greffier, 450-357-2077, Fax: 450-357-2362
Daniel Desroches, Directeur général, 450-357-2383, Fax: 450-357-2385
Michelle Hébert, Directrice générale adjointe

Serge Boulerice, Directeur, Service de police, 450-359-2529
Harold Ellefsen, Directeur, Service des finances

Saint-Jérôme

#301, 10, rue St-Joseph
Saint-Jérôme, QC J7Z 7G7
450-436-1511 Fax: 450-436-6626
info@vsj.ca
www.vsj.ca
Municipal Type: City
Incorporated: 1er janvier 2002; *Area:* 89,37 km2
County or District: La Rivière-du-Nord; *Population in 2006:* 63,729
Provincial Electoral District(s): Prévost
Federal Electoral District(s): Rivière-du-Nord
Next Election: 1er novembre 2013

Conseil
Marc Gascon, Maire
Louise Bouchard, Conseillère, 450-432-9625, District: 1 Rolland
Marcel Lachance, Conseiller, 450-432-4399, District: 2 Brière
Guy Lalande, Conseiller, 450-438-2021, District: 3 Laviolette
Bernard Bougie, Conseiller, 450-431-7227, District: 4 Labelle
Yves Legris, Conseiller, 450-438-1076, District: 5 Parent
Robert Carrière, Conseiller, 450-432-5629, District: 6 Desjardins
Benoît Delage, Conseiller, 450-436-6134, District: 7 Bouvrette
Stéphane Piché, Conseiller, 450-432-2791, District: 8 Lamontagne
Martin Pigeon, Conseiller, 450-436-1787, District: 9 Crispin
François Boyer, Conseiller, 450-224-1148, District: 10 Richer
Sylvain Gagné, Conseiller, 450-436-5357, District: 11 Forget
Manon Labrèche, Conseillère, 450-432-2733, District: 12 Schulz
Robert Rioux, Conseiller, 450-438-2057, District: 13 Dumont
Michèle Céclier, Conseillère, 450-438-1073, District: 14 Paquette

Administration
Marcel Bélanger, Greffier
Éric Lachapelle, Directeur général
René Lachance, Directeur, Finances
Richard Bégin, Directeur, Travaux publics
Pierre Bourgeois, Directeur, Service de police
Guy Meilleur, Directeur, Service de la sécurité incendie
Michel Larose, Directeur, Ressources humaines
Raymond Zizian, Directeur, Culture/Loisirs/Vie communautaire
Louis Parent, Directeur, Communications
Pierre Ratté, Directeur, Service de l'urbanisme

Saint-Lazare

1960, ch Ste-Angélique
Saint-Lazare, QC J7T 3A3
450-424-8000 Fax: 450-455-4712
info@ville.saint-lazare.qc.ca
www.ville.saint-lazare.qc.ca
Municipal Type: City
Incorporated: 29 décembre 1875; *Area:* 67,59 km2
County or District: Vaudreuil-Soulanges; *Population in 2006:* 17,016
Provincial Electoral District(s): Soulanges
Federal Electoral District(s): Vaudreuil-Soulanges
Next Election: 1er novembre 2013

Conseil
Paul Carzoli, Maire
Paul Laflamme, Conseiller, District: 1
Gaétan Aubé, Conseiller, District: 2
Brigitte Asselin, Conseillère District: 3
Michel St-Louis, Conseiller, District: 4
Gaétan Ménard, Conseiller, District: 5
Chico Levy, Conseiller, District: 6

Administration
Nathaly Rayneault, Greffière
Lucie Gendron, Directrice générale

Saint-Lin-Laurentides

900, 12e av
Saint-Lin-Laurentides, QC J5M 2W2
450-439-3130 Fax: 450-439-1525
s.martel@saint-lin-laurentides.com
saint-lin-laurentides.com
Municipal Type: City
Incorporated: 1er mars 2000; *Area:* 117,52 km2
County or District: Montcalm; *Population in 2006:* 14,159
Provincial Electoral District(s): Rousseau
Federal Electoral District(s): Montcalm
Next Election: 1er novembre 2013

Conseil
André Auger, Maire
Luc Cyr, Conseiller, District: 1
Raymond Martin, Conseiller, District: 2
André Malouin, Conseiller, District: 3
Patrick Massé, Conseiller, District: 4
Jean-Luc Arène, Conseiller, District: 5
Pierre Lortie, Conseiller, District: 6

Administration
Richard Dufort, Greffier & Directeur général
Sylvain Martel, Trésorier, Finance et trésoire
Jean-Pierre Desjardins, Directeur, Service des incendies

Sainte-Adèle

1381, boul de Sainte-Adèle
Sainte-Adèle, QC J8B 1A3
450-229-2921 Fax: 450-229-4179
dirgenerale@ville.sainte-adele.qc.ca
www.ville.sainte-adele.qc.ca
Municipal Type: City
Incorporated: 27 août 1997; *Area:* 122,19 km2
County or District: Les Pays-d'en-Haut; *Population in 2009:* 10,981
Provincial Electoral District(s): Bertrand
Federal Electoral District(s): Laurentides-Labelle
Next Election: 1er novembre 2013

Conseil
Claude Descôteaux, Maire
Victor Mainville, Conseiller, District: 1
Jean-Pierre Pariseau, Conseiller, District: 2
Gabriel D. Latour, Conseiller, District: 3
Gary Quenneville, Conseiller, District: 4
André Lamarche, Conseiller, District: 5
Nicole Durand, Conseillère, District: 6

Administration
Michel Rousseau, Greffier
Richard Blouin, Directeur général

Sainte-Anne-des-Plaines

139, boul Ste-Anne
Sainte-Anne-des-Plaines, QC J0N 1H0
450-478-0211 Fax: 450-478-5660
villesteannedesplaines@videotron.ca
www.ville.ste-anne-des-plaines.qc.ca
Municipal Type: City
Incorporated: 1er juillet 1855; *Area:* 92,22 km2
County or District: Thérèse-De Blainville; Communauté métropolitaine de Montréal; *Population in 2006:* 13,412
Provincial Electoral District(s): Blainville
Federal Electoral District(s): Terrebonne-Blainville
Next Election: 1er novembre 2013

Conseil
Catherine Collin, Mairesse
Isabelle Charbonneau, Conseillère, District: Siège 1
Mario Ronald Gauthier, Conseiller, District: Siège 2
Lyne Laramée, Conseillère, District: Siège 3
Daniel Latrémouille, Conseiller, District: Siège 4
Denys Gagnon, Conseiller, District: Siège 5
Michel Forget, Conseiller, District: Siège 6

Administration
Serge Lepage, Greffier & Directeur général
Christiane Joyal, Trésorière

Sainte-Catherine

5465, boul Marie-Victorin
Sainte-Catherine, QC J5C 1M1
450-632-0590 Fax: 450-632-3298
directiongenerale@ville.sainte-catherine.qc.ca
www.ville.sainte-catherine.qc.ca
Municipal Type: City
Incorporated: 30 octobre 1937; *Area:* 9,06 km2
County or District: Roussillon; Communauté métropolitaine de Montréal; *Population in 2009:* 16,306
Provincial Electoral District(s): Châteauguay
Federal Electoral District(s): Châteauguay-St-Constant
Next Election: 1er novembre 2013

Conseil
Jocelyne Bates, Mairesse
Daniel Lamanque, Conseiller, District: 1
Martin Gélinas, Conseiller, District: 2
Jocelyne Brossard, Conseillère, District: 3
Louise Cormier, Conseillère, District: 4
Michel Béland, Conseiller, District: 5
Daniel Gagnon, Conseiller, District: 6

Administration
Carole Cousineau, Greffière
Danielle Chevrette, Directrice générale
Serge Courchesne, Trésorier

Sainte-Julie

1580, ch du Fer-à-Cheval
Sainte-Julie, QC J3E 2M1
450-922-7111 Fax: 450-922-7108
communications@ville.sainte-julie.qc.ca
www.ville.sainte-julie.qc.ca
Municipal Type: City
Incorporated: 1er juillet 1855; *Area:* 47,78 km2
County or District: Lajemmerais; Communauté métropolitaine de Montréal; *Population in 2009:* 29,561
Provincial Electoral District(s): Marguerite-D'Youville
Federal Electoral District(s): Verchères-Les Patriotes
Next Election: 1er novembre 2013

Conseil
Suzanne Roy, Mairesse, mairie@ville.sainte-julie.qc.ca, 450-922-7053
Isabelle Poulet, Conseillère, District: 1 Belle-Rivière/Ringuet
André Lemay, Conseiller, District: 2 Moulin
Donald Savaria, Conseiller, District: 3 Vallée
Nicole Marchand, Conseillère, District: 4 Rucher
Mario Lemay, Conseiller, District: 5 Vieux-Village
Normand Varin, Conseiller, District: 6 Grand-Coteau
Henri Corbin, Conseiller, District: 7 Arc-en-Ciel
Lucie Bisson, Conseillère, District: 8 Montagne

Administration
Jean-François Gauthier, MBA, OMA, Greffier, 450-922-7050
Jean-Pierre Duplin, Trésorier, 450-922-7062
Claude Laperrière, Directeur général, 450-922-7102

Daniel Chagnon, Directeur, Service des loisirs, 450-922-7122

Sainte-Marie
270, av Marguerite-Bourgeoys
Sainte-Marie, QC G6E 3Z3
418-387-2301 Fax: 418-387-2454
administration@ville.sainte-marie.qc.ca
www.ville.sainte-marie.qc.ca
Municipal Type: City
Incorporated: 15 avril 1978; *Area:* 106,65 km2
County or District: La Nouvelle-Beauce; *Population in 2009:* 11,857
Provincial Electoral District(s): Beauce-Nord
Federal Electoral District(s): Beauce
Next Election: 1er novembre 2013

Conseil
Harold Guay, Maire
Christian Laroche, Conseiller, District: Siège 1
Mélanie Boissonneault, Conseillère, District: Siège 2
Rosaire Simoneau, Conseiller, District: Siège 3
Patrice Cossette, Conseiller, District: Siège 4
Paulin Nappert, Conseiller, District: Siège 5
Yves Chassé, Conseiller, District: Siège 6

Administration
Hélène Gagné, Greffière
Louis Normand, Directeur général
Jacques Boutin, Trésorier

Sainte-Marthe-sur-le-Lac
3000, ch d'Oka
Sainte-Marthe-sur-le-Lac, QC J0N 1P0
450-472-7310 Fax: 450-472-0109
info@ville.sainte-marthe-sur-le-lac.qc.ca
www.saintemarthesurlelac.qc.ca
Municipal Type: City
Incorporated: 1er janvier 1960; *Area:* 9,01 km2
County or District: Deux-Montagnes; Communauté métropolitaine de Montréal; *Population in 2009:* 12,089
Provincial Electoral District(s): Mirabel
Federal Electoral District(s): Rivière-des-Mille-Iles
Next Election: 1er novembre 2013

Conseil
Sonia Paulus, Mairesse
Francois Robillard, Conseiller, District: 1
Sylvain Goudreault, Conseiller, District: 2
Olivier Hamel, Conseiller, District: 3
Yves Legault, Conseiller, District: 4
Richard Paquette, Conseiller, District: 5
Daniel B. Bisson, Conseiller, District: 6

Administration
Sylvie Brunet, Greffière
Valérie Vivier, Trésorière
Marisol Charland, Directrice générale

Sainte-Thérèse
CP 100
6, rue de l'Église
Sainte-Thérèse, QC J7E 4H7
450-434-1440 Fax: 450-434-1499
info@sainte-therese.ca
www.ville.sainte-therese.qc.ca
Municipal Type: City
Incorporated: 1er juin 1849; *Area:* 8,62 km2
County or District: Thérèse-De Blainville; Communauté métropolitaine de Montréal; *Population in 2009:* 25,642
Provincial Electoral District(s): Groulx
Federal Electoral District(s): Marc-Aurèle-Fortin
Next Election: 1er novembre 2013

Conseil
Sylvie Surprenant, Mairesse
Denise Perreault-Théberge, Conseillère, District: 1 De Sève
Patrick Morin, Conseiller, District: 2 Verschelden
Marie-Andrée Petelle, Conseillère, District: 3 Morris
Marie-Noëlle Closson Duquette, Conseillère, District: 4 Chapleau
Luc Vézina, Conseiller, District: 5 Lonergan
Anne Lauzon, Conseillère, District: 6 Ducharme
Louis Lauzon, Conseiller, District: 7 Blanchard
Vincent Arseneau, Conseiller, District: 8 Marie-Thérèse

Administration
Jean-Luc Berthiaume, M.Sc., OMA, Greffier
Chantal Gauvreau, Directrice générale
Jean Pierre Gendron, Directeur, Finances

Salaberry-de-Valleyfield
61, rue Ste-Cécile
Salaberry-de-Valleyfield, QC J6T 1L8
450-370-4300
communications@ville.valleyfield.qc.ca
www.ville.valleyfield.qc.ca
Municipal Type: City
Incorporated: 24 avril 2002; *Area:* 100,96 km2
County or District: Beauharnois-Salaberry; *Population in 2006:* 39,672
Provincial Electoral District(s): Beauharnois
Federal Electoral District(s): Beauharnois-Salaberry
Next Election: 1er novembre 2013

Conseil
Denis Lapointe, Maire, 450-370-4819, Fax: 450-370-4343
Denis Laître, Conseiller, 450-373-0954, District: 1 Grande-Île
Jean-Marc Rochon, Conseiller, 450-377-2774, District: 2 Nitro
Siège vacant, Conseiller, District: 3 Georges-Leduc
Robert Savard, Conseiller, 450-371-1173, District: 4 Champlain
Jean-Jacques Leduc, Conseiller, 450-371-5099, District: 5 La Baie
Jacques Smith, Conseiller, 450-371-4975, District: 6 Robert-Cauchon
Pierre-Paul Messier, Conseiller, 450-373-5459, District: 7 Jules-Léger
Normand Amesse, Conseiller, 450-371-6895, District: 8 Saint-Timothée

Administration
Alain Gagnon, Greffier, 450-370-4304, Fax: 450-370-4388
Jacques Lemieux, CA, OMA, Trésorier, 450-370-4320, Fax: 450-370-4316
René Monette, Directeur, Service récréatif & communautaire, 450-370-4390, Fax: 450-370-4888

Sept-Iles
546, av De Quen
Sept-Iles, QC G4R 2R4
418-962-2525 Fax: 418-964-3213
info@ville.sept-iles.qc.ca
www.ville.sept-iles.qc.ca
Municipal Type: City
Incorporated: 12 février 2003; *Area:* 1 969,42 km2
County or District: Sept-Rivières; *Population in 2006:* 25,514
Provincial Electoral District(s): Duplessis
Federal Electoral District(s): Manicouagan
Next Election: 1er novembre 2013
Note: En 1970, Clarke City est fusionnée à Sept-Iles; le 12 fév., 2003, Moisie & Gallix sont fusionnées à Sept-Iles.

Conseil
Ghislain Lévesque, Maire
Gervais Gagné, Conseiller, District: 1 Clarke
Poste vacant, Conseiller, District: 2 Ferland
Jean Masse, Conseiller, District: 3 L'Anse
Denis Miousse, Conseiller, District: 4 Vieux-Poste
Gaby Gauthier, Conseiller, District: 5 Vigneault
Lorraine Dubuc-Johnson, Conseillère, District: 6 Mgr-Blanche
Martial Lévesque, Conseiller, District: 7 Sainte-Famille
Serge Lévesque, Conseiller, District: 8 La Rive
Guylaine Lejeune, Conseillère, District: 9 Gallix
Claude Lessard, Conseiller, District: 10 Moisie

Administration
Valérie Haince, Greffière, 418-964-3205
Claude Bureau, Directeur général, 418-964-3201
Serge Gagné, Directeur, Finances, 418-964-3215
Stéphanie Prévost, Directrice générale

Shawinigan
CP 400
550, av de l'Hôtel-de-Ville
Shawinigan, QC G9N 6V3
819-536-7200 Fax: 819-536-7255
information@shawinigan.qc.ca
www.shawinigan.qc.ca
Municipal Type: City
Incorporated: 1er janvier 2002; *Area:* 781,81 km2
Population in 2006: 51,904
Provincial Electoral District(s): St-Maurice; Laviolette
Federal Electoral District(s): Berthier-Maskinongé
Next Election: 1er novembre 2013
Note: 8 nouveaux districts seront en vigueur lors des élections municipal de nov/09.

Conseil
Lise Landry, Mairesse
Sylvain Trudel, Conseiller, District: 1
France Beaulieu, Conseillère, District: 2
Yves Bordeleau, Conseiller, District: 3
Josette Allard-Gignac, Conseillère, District: 4
Alain Beauparlant, Conseiller, District: 5
Robert Dupont, Conseiller, District: 6
Steve Martin, Conseiller, District: 7
Gilles Marchand, Conseiller, District: 8
Denis Lampron, Conseiller, District: 9
Alain Lord, Conseiller, District: 10

Administration
Yves Vincent, Greffier
François St-Onge, Directeur, Communications
Pierre Godin, Directeur, Travaux publics
Gaétan Béchard, Directeur général
Réal Beauchamp, Directeur général adjoint
Robert Y. Desjardins, Directeur, Loisirs, culture & vie communautaire
Sylvie Lavoie, Directrice, Finances
François Garceau, Directeur, Ressources humaines
Claude Larocque, Directeur, Services techniques

Sherbrooke
CP 610
191, rue du Palais
Sherbrooke, QC J1H 5H9
819-821-5969 Fax: 819-822-6131
mairie@ville.sherbrooke.qc.ca
www.ville.sherbrooke.qc.ca
Municipal Type: City
Incorporated: 1er janvier 2001; *Area:* 366,00 km2
Population in 2006: 147,427
Provincial Electoral District(s): St-François; Sherbrooke; Orford; Johnson
Federal Electoral District(s): Sherbrooke
Next Election: 1er novembre 2013

Conseil
Jean Perrault, Maire, 819-821-5969, Fax: 819-822-6131
Thomas A. Allen, Conseiller, District: Lennoxville/Fairview
Nicole Bergeron, Conseillère, District: Brompton
Pierre Boisvert, Conseiller, District: Mont-Bellevue/Croix-Lumineuse
Louida Brochu, Conseillère, District: Fleurimont/Lavigerie
Diane Délisle, Conseillère, District: Rock Forest-St-Élie-Deauville
Marc Denault, Conseiller, District: Jacques-Cartier/Montcalm
Benoît Dionne, Conseiller, District: Brompton/Beauvoir
Serge Forest, Conseiller, District: Rock Forest-St-Élie-Deauville
Mariette Fugère, Conseillère, District: Fleurimont/Pin-Solitaire
Francis Gagnon, Conseiller, District: Fleurimont/Desranleau
Chantal L'Espérance, Conseillère, District: Jacques-Cartier/Domaine-Howard
Roger Labrecque, Conseiller, District: Fleurimont/Quatre-Saisons
Dany Lachance, Conseiller, District: Jacques-Cartier/Carrefour
Julien Lachance, Conseiller, District: Rock Forest-St-Élie-Deauville
Michel Lamontagne, Conseiller, District: Brompton/Moulins
Douglas MacAulay, Conseiller, District: Lennoxville
Serge Paquin, Conseiller, District: Mont-Bellevue/Centre-Sud
Robert Y. Pouliot, Conseiller, District: Mont-Bellevue/Ascot
Jean-François Rouleau, Conseiller, District: Mont-Bellevue/Université
Bernard Sévigny, Conseiller, District: Rock Forest-St-Élie-Deauville
William Smith, Conseiller, District: Lennoxville/Uplands
Bernard F. Tanguay, Conseiller, District: Fleurimont/Marie-Rivier
Jacques Testulat, Conseiller, District: Jacques-Cartier/Beckett

Administration
Isabelle Sauvé, Greffière, Services des affaires juridiques et corporatives, 819-821-5500, Fax: 819-822-6064
Sylvie Lapointe, Directrice générale, 819-821-5618, Fax: 819-823-5121
François Poulette, Trésorier et Directeur, Service des finances, 819-821-5490, Fax: 819-822-6091
Marc Latendresse, Directeur, Services des loisirs, sports, culture et vie communautaire
Colette Ouellet, Directrice, Service des communications, 819-821-5572, Fax: 819-823-5153
Roger Vachon, Directeur, Service d'Hydro-Sherbrooke, 819-821-5726, Fax: 819-822-6085
Jacques Leduc, Directeur, Ressources humaines, 819-821-5677, Fax: 819-822-6086
Michel Richer, Directeur, Service de protection des incendies, 819-821-5514, Fax: 819-821-5516
Claude Marcoux, Directeur, Service de la planification et du développement urbain, 819-821-5901, Fax: 819-822-6070
Michel Caron, Directeur, Service des bâtiments et des équipements, 819-821-5630, Fax: 819-821-5426
Louis Daigle, Directeur, Service des technologies de l'information, 819-821-5623, Fax: 819-821-5470
Gaétan Labbé, Directeur, Service de police, 819-821-5555

Sorel-Tracy
CP 368
71, rue Charlotte
Sorel-Tracy, QC J3P 7K1
450-780-5600 Fax: 450-780-5625
info@ville.sorel-tracy.qc.ca
www.ville.sorel.qc.ca
Municipal Type: City
Incorporated: 15 mars 2000; *Area:* 56,58 km2
County or District: Pierre-De Saurel; *Population in 2009:* 34,308
Provincial Electoral District(s): Richelieu
Federal Electoral District(s): Bas-Richelieu-Nicolet-Bécancour
Next Election: 1er novembre 2013

Conseil
Marcel Robert, Maire
Michel Berthiaume, Conseiller, 450-742-0267, District: 1 Bourgchemin
Denis Gagné, Conseiller, 450-742-6481, District: 2 Richelieu
Yvon Bibeau, Conseiller, 450-746-8987, District: 3 Saint-Laurent
Corina Bastiani, Conseillère, 450-743-8484, District: 4 Vieux-Sorel
Marcel Lavallée, Conseiller, 450-742-3101, District: 5 Du Faubourg
André Bélanger, Conseiller, 450-742-9587, District: 6 Des Gouverneurs
Michèle Lacombe-Gauthier, Conseillère, 450-746-7710, District: 7 Des Patriotes
Yves Bérard, Conseiller, 450-746-8671, District: 8 Pierre-De Saurel

Administration
René Chevalier, Greffier
Diane Robillard, Directrice, Finances & Trésorerie
Alain Rouleau, Directeur, Sécurité incendie
Mario Lazure, Directeur général

Terrebonne
775, rue St-Jean-Baptiste
Terrebonne, QC J6W 1B5
450-961-2001
information@ville.terrebonne.qc.ca
www.ville.terrebonne.qc.ca
Municipal Type: City
Incorporated: 27 juin 2001; *Area:* 155,44 km2
County or District: Les Moulins; Communauté métropolitaine de Montréal; *Population in 2009:* 98,459
Provincial Electoral District(s): Terrebonne; Masson
Federal Electoral District(s): Terrebonne-Blainville
Next Election: 1er novembre 2013

Conseil
Jean-Marc Robitaille, Maire
Claude Lacasse, Conseiller, District: 1
Daniel L'Espérance, Conseiller, District: 2
Marie-Claude Lamarche, Conseillère, District: 3

Réal Leclerc, Conseiller, District: 4
Denis Poitras, Conseiller, District: 5
Michel Morin, Conseiller, District: 6
Paul Asselin, Conseiller, District: 7
Marie-Josée Beaupré, Conseillère, District: 8
Marc Campagna, Conseiller, District: 9
Frédéric Asselin, Conseiller, District: 10
Clermont Lévesque, Conseiller, District: 11
Jean-Luc Labrecque, Conseiller, District: 12
Sylvain Tousignant, Conseiller, District: 13
Michel Lefebvre, Conseiller, District: 14
Micheline Mathieu, Conseillère, District: 15
Jean-Guy Sénécal, Conseiller, District: 16

Administration
Denis Bouffard, Greffier
Raymond Champagne, Directeur, Finances, 450-492-2433
Denis Lévesque, Directeur général
Guy Dubois, Chef de police
Réal Lanoue, Directeur, Service de l'incendie
Michel Sarrazin, Directeur, Entretien du territoire

Thetford Mines
CP 489
144, rue Notre-Dame ouest
Thetford Mines, QC G6G 5T3
418-335-2981 Fax: 418-335-7089
infos@ville.thetfordmines.qc.ca
www.ville.thetfordmines.qc.ca
Municipal Type: City
Incorporated: 17 octobre 2001; *Area:* 224,37 km2
County or District: Les Appalaches; *Population in 2009:* 16,124
Provincial Electoral District(s): Frontenac
Federal Electoral District(s): Mégantic-L'Érable
Next Election: 1er novembre 2013

Conseil
Luc Berthold, Maire
Clément Boudreau, Conseiller, 418-423-2257, District: 1 Black Lake
Renaud Legendre, Conseiller, 418-423-2349, District: 2 Black Lake-Mitchell/Lacs
Ghyslain Cliche, Conseiller, 418-335-9267, District: 3 Thetford Mines
Luc Champagne, Conseiller, 418-338-2812, District: 4 Thetford Mines
Carmen Jalbert-Jacques, Conseillère, 418-338-1901, District: 5 Thetford Mines
Louis-Philippe Champagne, Conseiller, 418-335-7119, District: 6 Thetford Mines
Marco Tanguay, Conseiller, 418-338-8819, District: 7 Thetford Mines
Marc Vachon, Conseiller, 418-334-0340, District: 8 Thetford Mines
Paul-André Marchand, Conseiller, 418-335-9871, District: 9 Thetford-Sud
Gaétan Vachon, Conseiller, 418-335-9543, District: 10 Robertsonville/Pontbriand

Administration
Réjean Martin, Greffier
René Soucy, Directeur général
Sylvain Tremblay, Directeur, Service des ressources financières
François Gagnon, Directeur, Sécurité publique

Trois-Rivières
CP 368
1325, place de l'Hôtel-de-Ville
Trois-Rivières, QC G9A 5H3
819-374-2002 Fax: 819-372-4674
info@v3r.net
www.v3r.net
Municipal Type: City
Incorporated: 1er janvier 2002; *Area:* 288,50 km2
Population in 2006: 129,100
Provincial Electoral District(s): Trois-Rivières; Maskinongé; Champlain
Federal Electoral District(s): Trois-Rivières
Next Election: 1er novembre 2013

Conseil
Yves Lévesque, Maire
Denis Beaulieu, Conseiller, District: Sanctuaire
Ginette Bellemare, Conseillère, District: Rigaud
Michel Bronsard, Conseiller, District: St-Louis-de-France
Micheline Courteau, Conseillère, District: Ste-Marthe-du-Cap
Guy Daigle, Conseiller, District: Laviolette
Pierre A. Dupont, Conseiller, District: Ste-Marguerite
René Goyette, Conseiller, District: la Madeleine
Claude Lacroix, Conseiller, District: Chavigny
Fernand Lajoie, Conseiller, District: Estacades
Yves Landry, Conseiller, District: Terrasses
Monique Leclerc, Conseillère, District: Châteaudun
Joan Lefebvre, Conseillère, District: Plateaux
André Noël, Conseiller, District: Carmel
Sylvie Tardif, Conseillère, District: Marie de l'Incarnation
Michel Veillette, Conseiller, District: Pointe-du-lac
Françoise H. Viens, Conseillère, District: Vieilles-Forges

Administration
Michel Byette, Directeur général, 819-372-4608, Fax: 819-372-4631
Daniel Thibault, Directeur général adjoint, 819-372-4649, Fax: 819-372-0125
Gilles Poulin, Directeur, Service du greffe/Services juridiques, 819-372-4604, Fax: 819-372-4636
Alain Brouillette, Directeur, Finances et administration, 819-372-4642, Fax: 819-374-1243
Éric Chevalier, Directeur, Ressources humaines, 819-372-4603, Fax: 819-374-9005
Francis Gobeil, Directeur, Sécurité publique, 819-370-6700, Fax: 819-374-3506
Michel Lemieux, Directeur, Loisirs & services communautaires, 819-372-4621, Fax: 819-374-7133
Michel Jutras, Responsable, Arts et culture
Pierre Desjardins, Directeur, Aménagement, gestion & développement durable du territoire, 819-372-4626, Fax: 819-375-5865
Jacques St-Laurent, Directeur, Développement, 819-372-4642, Fax: 819-374-1243
François Roy, Directeur, Communications, 819-372-4602, Fax: 819-374-0210
Ghislain Lachance, Directeur, Travaux publics
Vincent Fortier, Directeur, Services techniques, 819-372-4627, Fax: 819-374-6646

Val-d'Or
CP 400
855, 2e av
Val-d'Or, QC J9P 4P4
819-824-9613 Fax: 819-825-6650
info@ville.valdor.qc.ca
www.ville.valdor.qc.ca
Municipal Type: City
Incorporated: 1er janvier 2002; *Area:* 3 958,13 km2
County or District: Vallée-de-l'Or; *Population in 2006:* 31,123
Provincial Electoral District(s): Abitibi-Est
Federal Electoral District(s): Abitibi-Baie-James-Nunavik-Eeyou
Next Election: 1er novembre 2013

Conseil
Fernand Trahan, Maire
Suzanne Couture Bordeleau, Conseillère, District: 1 Lac Blouin-Centre-ville
Yvon Frenette, Conseiller, District: 2 Paquinville-Fatima
Yolette Lévy, Conseillère, District: 3 Belvédère
Céline Brindamour, Conseillère, District: 4 Sullivan
Gilles Bérubé, Conseiller, District: 5 Val-Senneville-Vassan
Francis Murphy, Conseiller, District: 6 Bourlamaque-Louvicourt
André Gilbert, Conseiller, District: 7 Lemoine-Baie-Carrière
Claudia Chaput, Conseillère, District: 8 Dubuisson

Administration
Sophie Gareau, Greffière
Réal Houle, Trésorier
Alain Cloutier, Directeur, Ressources humaines/Communications
Danny Burbridge, Directeur, Infrastructures urbaines
Robert Migué, Directeur, Service culturel

Varennes
CP 5000
175, rue Ste-Anne
Varennes, QC J3X 1T5
450-652-9888 Fax: 450-652-2655
general@ville.varennes.qc.ca
www.ville.varennes.qc.ca
Municipal Type: City
Incorporated: 26 août 1972; *Area:* 93,96 km2
County or District: Lajemmerais; *Population in 2006:* 20,950
Provincial Electoral District(s): Verchères
Federal Electoral District(s): Verchères-Les Patriotes
Next Election: 1er novembre 2013

Conseil
Michel Tremblay, Maire
Gilles Lacroix, Conseiller, District: 1 La Guillaudière
Martin Damphousse, Conseiller, District: 2 La Sitière
Francis Rinfret, Conseiller, District: 3 Langloiserie
Denis Le Blanc, Conseiller, District: 4 Notre-Dame
Yves Tremblay, Conseiller, District: 5 Petite Prairie
Gilles Lebrun, Conseiller, District: 6 Les Seigneuries
Michel Lyons, Conseiller, District: 7 Saint-Charles
Brigitte Collin, Conseillère, District: 8 De Martigny

Administration
Marc Giard, Greffier
Claude Provost, ing., Responsable, Travaux publics
Denis Marchand, Responsable, Environnement

Vaudreuil-Dorion
#200, 2555, rue Dutrisac
Vaudreuil-Dorion, QC J7V 7E6
450-455-3371 Fax: 450-424-8540
courriel@ville.vaudreuil-dorion.qc.ca
www.ville.vaudreuil-dorion.qc.ca
Municipal Type: City
Incorporated: 16 mars 1994; *Area:* 73,18 km2
County or District: Vaudreuil-Soulanges; Communauté métropolitaine de Montréal; *Population in 2009:* 27,330
Provincial Electoral District(s): Vaudreuil
Federal Electoral District(s): Vaudreuil-Soulanges
Next Election: 1er novembre 2013

Conseil
Guy Pilon, Maire
Claude Beaudoin, Conseiller, District: 1
François Séguin, Conseiller, District: 2
Robert A. Laurence, Conseiller, District: 3
Denis Vincent, Conseiller, District: 4
Rénald Gabriele, Conseiller, District: 5
Gabriel Parent, Conseiller, District: 6
Guylène Duplessis, Conseillère, District: 7
Paul Dumoulin, Conseiller, District: 8

Administration
Jean St-Antoine, Greffier
Mona Dumouchel, Trésorière, 450-424-8532
Manon Bernard, Directrice générale

Victoriaville
CP 370
1, rue Notre-Dame ouest
Victoriaville, QC G6P 6T2
819-204-1571 Fax: 819-758-9292
info@ville.victoriaville.qc.ca
www.ville.victoriaville.qc.ca
Municipal Type: City
Incorporated: 23 juin 1993; *Area:* 81,96 km2
County or District: Arthabaska; *Population in 2006:* 40,486
Provincial Electoral District(s): Arthabaska
Federal Electoral District(s): Richmond-Arthabaska
Next Election: 1er novembre 2013

Conseil
Roger Richard, Maire, 819-758-1571
Bertrand Lambert, Conseiller, 819-752-5388, District: 1 Parc de l'Amitié
Jacques Gagnon, Conseiller, 819-758-8511, District: 2 Parc-de-l'île
Jacques Nadeau, Conseiller, 819-758-8530, District: 3 Charles-Édouard-Mailhot
Alexandre Côté, Conseiller, 819-357-3272, District: 4 Sainte-Famille
France Auger, Conseillère, 819-758-7330, District: 5 Parc-Terre-des-Jeunes
Siège vacant, Conseiller, District: 6 Parc-Victoria
Michel Allard, Conseiller, 819-752-6362, District: 7 Sainte-Victoire
Denis Morin, Conseiller, 819-357-7821, District: 8 Arthabaska-Nord
Donald Dumont, Conseiller, 819-758-9169, District: 9 Arthabaska-Ouest
Christian Lettre, Conseiller, 819-357-8573, District: 10 Arthabaska-Est

Administration
Jean Poirier, Greffier
Martin Lessard, Directeur général
Jean Mercier, Directeur, Service des ressources humaines, 819-758-1571
André Charest, Directeur, Services des travaux publics, 819-758-0651
Yves Fréchette, Directeur, Services administratifs

Other Municipalities in Québec

Abercorn
10, ch des Églises ouest
Abercorn, QC J0E 1B0
450-538-2664 Fax: 450-538-6295
mun.abercorn@bellnet.ca
Municipal Type: Village
Incorporated: 25 juin 1929; *Area:* 27,84 km2
County or District: Brome-Missisquoi; *Population in 2006:* 366
Provincial Electoral District(s): Brome-Missisquoi
Federal Electoral District(s): Brome-Missisquoi
Next Election: 1er novembre 2013
Danielle Corriveau, Sec.-Trés.

Abitibi
CP 214
571, 1re Rue est
Amos, QC J9T 2H3
819-732-5356 Fax: 819-732-9607
mrc@mrcabitibi.qc.ca
www.mrcabitibi.qc.ca
Municipal Type: Regional County Municipality

Population in 2009: 24,060
Note: 17 municipalités & 2 autres territoires.
Michel Roy, Directeur général

Abitibi-Ouest
#105, 6, 8e Av est
La Sarre, QC J9Z 1N6
819-339-5671 Fax: 819-339-5400
mrcao@mrcao.qc.ca
mrc.ao.ca
Municipal Type: Regional County Municipality

Population in 2009: 20,929
Note: 21 municipalités & 2 autres territoires.
Nicole Breton, Directrice générale

Acton
CP 99
1037, rue Beaugrand
Acton Vale, QC J0H 1A0
450-546-3256 Fax: 450-546-0525
info@mrcacton.qc.ca
www.mrcacton.qc.ca
Municipal Type: Regional County Municipality

Population in 2006: 15,289
Yvan Talbot, Sec.-Trés. & Directeur général

Acton-Vale
1025, rue Boulay
Acton Vale, QC J0H 1A0
450-546-2703 Fax: 450-546-4865
actonvale@ville.actonvale.qc.ca
www.ville.actonvale.qc.ca

Municipal Type: City
Incorporated: 26 janvier 2000; *Area:* 90,88 km2
County or District: Acton; *Population in 2006:* 7,797
Provincial Electoral District(s): Johnson
Federal Electoral District(s): St-Hyacinthe-Bagot
Next Election: 1er novembre 2013
Rita Parent, Greffière
Juliette Dupuis, Mairesse

Adstock
35, rue Principale ouest
Adstock, QC G0N 1S0
418-422-2135 Fax: 418-422-2134
info@municipaliteadstock.qc.ca
www.municipaliteadstock.qc.ca
Municipal Type: Municipality
Incorporated: 24e octobre 2001; *Area:* 289,220 km2
County or District: Les Appalaches; *Population in 2009:* 2,471
Provincial Electoral District(s): Frontenac
Federal Electoral District(s): Mégantic-L'Érable
Next Election: 1er novembre 2013
Bernardin Hamann, Directeur général

Aguanish
CP 47
106, rte Jacques-Cartier
Aguanish, QC G0G 1A0
418-533-2323 Fax: 418-533-2012
manug@globetrotter.net
Municipal Type: Municipality
Incorporated: 1er janvier 1957; *Area:* 594,40 km2
County or District: Minganie; *Population in 2006:* 303
Provincial Electoral District(s): Duplessis
Federal Electoral District(s): Manicouagan
Next Election: 1er novembre 2013
Aurore Lapierre, Sec.-Trés.

Akulivik
CP 50
Akulivik, QC J0M 1V0
819-496-2073 Fax: 819-496-2200
Municipal Type: Northern Village
Incorporated: 29 décembre 1979; *Area:* 79,37 km2
County or District: Nord-du-Québec; *Population in 2006:* 507
Provincial Electoral District(s): Ungava
Federal Electoral District(s): Abitibi-Baie-James-Nunavik-Eeyou
Next Election: 7 novembre 2007
Lydia Nappatuk, Sec.-Trés.

Albanel
160, rue Principale
Albanel, QC G8M 3J5
418-279-5250 Fax: 418-279-3147
albanel@msn.com
Municipal Type: Municipality
Incorporated: 11 avril 1990; *Area:* 195,69 km2
County or District: Maria-Chapdelaine; *Population in 2006:* 2,326
Provincial Electoral District(s): Roberval
Federal Electoral District(s): Roberval-Lac-Saint-Jean
Next Election: 1er novembre 2013
Gilles Lambert, Sec.-Trés.

Albertville
CP 9
1058, rue Principale
Albertville, QC G0J 1A0
418-756-3554 Fax: 418-756-3554
munipalite.albertville@globetrotter.net
Municipal Type: Municipality

County or District: La Matapédia; *Population in 2006:* 319
Provincial Electoral District(s): Matapédia
Federal Electoral District(s): Haute-Gaspésie-La Mitis-Matane-Matapédia
Next Election: 1er novembre 2013
Émile Pitre, Sec.-Trés. & Directrice-générale

Alleyn-et-Cawood
10, ch Jondée
Danford Lake, QC J0X 1P0
819-467-2941 Fax: 819-467-3133
administration@municipalite.alleyn-et-cawood.qc.ca
www.danfordlakevillage.qc.ca
Municipal Type: United Township (Cantons)
Incorporated: 1er janvier 1877; *Area:* 346,64 km2
County or District: Pontiac; *Population in 2006:* 248
Provincial Electoral District(s): Pontiac
Federal Electoral District(s): Pontiac
Next Election: 1er novembre 2013
Kim Cartier-Villeneuve, Sec.-Trés.

Amherst
CP 30
124, rue St-Louis
Saint-Rémi-d'Amherst, QC J0T 2L0
819-687-3355 Fax: 819-687-8430
bernard@cil.qc.ca
Municipal Type: Township
Incorporated: 9 mars 1887; *Area:* 260,82 km2
County or District: Les Laurentides; *Population in 2006:* 1,421
Provincial Electoral District(s): Labelle
Federal Electoral District(s): Laurentides-Labelle
Next Election: 1er novembre 2013
Bernard Davidson, Sec.-Trés.

Amqui
20, promenade de l'Hôtel-de-Ville
Amqui, QC G5J 1A1
418-629-4242 Fax: 418-629-4090
administration@ville.amqui.qc.ca
www.matapedia.net/amqui
Municipal Type: City
Incorporated: 16 janvier 1991; *Area:* 127,90 km2
County or District: La Matapédia; *Population in 2006:* 6,261
Provincial Electoral District(s): Matapédia
Federal Electoral District(s): Haute-Gaspésie-La Mitis-Matane-Matapédia
Next Election: 1er novembre 2013
Mario Lavoie, Greffier
Gaëtan Ruest, Maire

Ange-Gardien
249, rue St-Joseph
L'Ange-Gardien, QC J0E 1E0
450-293-7575 Fax: 450-293-6635
municipalite.ange-gardien@videotron.ca
Municipal Type: Municipality

County or District: Rouville; *Population in 2006:* 1,987
Provincial Electoral District(s): Iberville
Federal Electoral District(s): Shefford
Next Election: 1er novembre 2013
André Parent, Sec.-Trés.

Angliers
CP 9
14, rue de la Baie-Miller
Angliers, QC J0Z 1A0
819-949-4351 Fax: 819-949-4321
dir.gen_angliers@mrctemiscamingue.qc.ca
Municipal Type: Village
Incorporated: 24 mai 1945; *Area:* 378,20 km2
County or District: Témiscamingue; *Population in 2006:* 308
Provincial Electoral District(s): Rouyn-Noranda-Témiscamingue
Federal Electoral District(s): Abitibi-Témiscamingue
Next Election: 1er novembre 2013
Micheline Champoux, Sec.-Trés.

Antoine-Labelle
425, rue du Pont
Mont-Laurier, QC J9L 2R6
819-623-3485 Fax: 819-623-5052
administration@mrc-antoine-labelle.qc.ca
www.mrc-antoine-labelle.qc.ca
Municipal Type: Regional County Municipality

Population in 2009: 35,507
Note: 17 municipalités & 11 autres territoires.
Jacline Williams, Directrice générale

Argenteuil
430, rue Grace
Lachute, QC J8H 1M6
450-562-2474 Fax: 450-562-1911
mrc@argenteuil.qc.ca
www.argenteuil.qc.ca
Municipal Type: Regional County Municipality

Population in 2009: 30,267
Note: 9 municipalités.
Renée-Claude L'Allier, Greffière

Armagh
CP 87
5, rue de la Salle
Armagh, QC G0R 1A0
418-466-2916 Fax: 418-466-2409
munarma@globetrotter.net
Municipal Type: Municipality
Incorporated: 29 décembre 1993; *Area:* 168,15 km2
County or District: Bellechasse; *Population in 2006:* 1,613
Provincial Electoral District(s): Bellechasse
Federal Electoral District(s): Lévis-Bellechasse
Next Election: 1er novembre 2013
Sylvie Vachon, Sec.-Trés.

Arthabaska
40, rte de la Grande-Ligne
Victoriaville, QC G6T 0E6
819-752-2444 Fax: 819-752-3623
info@mrc-arthabaska.qc.ca
www.mrc-arthabaska.qc.ca
Municipal Type: Regional County Municipality

Population in 2009: 67,405
Note: 24 municipalités.
Frédérick Michaud, Directeur général

Arundel
2, rue du Village
Arundel, QC J0T 1A0
819-687-3991 Fax: 819-687-8760
bgoulet@qc.aibn.com
Municipal Type: Township
Incorporated: 1er janvier 1878; *Area:* 64,43 km2
County or District: Les Laurentides; *Population in 2006:* 601
Provincial Electoral District(s): Argenteuil
Federal Electoral District(s): Laurentides-Labelle
Next Election: 1er novembre 2013
Bernice Goulet, Sec.-Trés.

Asbestos
185, rue du Roi
Asbestos, QC J1T 1S4
819-879-7171 Fax: 819-879-2343
adm.mun@ville.asbestos.qc.ca
www.ville.asbestos.qc.ca
Municipal Type: City
Incorporated: 8 décembre 1999; *Area:* 29,55 km2
County or District: Asbestos; *Population in 2006:* 6,819
Provincial Electoral District(s): Richmond
Federal Electoral District(s): Richmond-Arthabaska
Next Election: 1er novembre 2013
Marie-Christine Fraser, Greffière
Jean-Philippe Bachand, Maire

Ascot-Corner
5655, rte 112
Ascot-Corner, QC J0B 1A0
819-560-8560 Fax: 819-560-8561
ascot.corner@hsfqc.ca
www.ascot-corner.qc.ca
Municipal Type: Municipality
Incorporated: 28 mars 1901; *Area:* 83,38 km2
County or District: Le Haut-St-François; *Population in 2009:* 2,620
Provincial Electoral District(s): Mégantic-Compton
Federal Electoral District(s): Compton-Stanstead
Next Election: 1er novembre 2013
Daniel St-Onge, Directeur général

Aston-Jonction
235, rue Vigneault
Aston-Jonction, QC G0Z 1A0
819-226-3459 Fax: 819-226-3459
mun.astonjonction@tlb.sympatico.ca
www.municipalite.aston-jonction.qc.ca
Municipal Type: Municipality
Incorporated: 26 mars 1997; *Area:* 26,43 km2
County or District: Nicolet-Yamaska; *Population in 2006:* 377
Provincial Electoral District(s): Nicolet-Yamaska
Federal Electoral District(s): Bas-Richelieu-Nicolet-Bécancour
Next Election: 1er novembre 2013
Jacqueline Leblanc, Sec.-Trés.

Auclair
773A, rue du Clocher
Auclair, QC G0L 1A0
418-899-2834 Fax: 418-899-6958
rstpierre@auclair.ca
www.auclair.ca
Municipal Type: Municipality
Incorporated: 1er janvier 1954; *Area:* 106,66 km2
County or District: Témiscouata; *Population in 2006:* 510
Provincial Electoral District(s): Kamouraska-Témiscouata
Federal Electoral District(s): Rimouski-Neigette-Témiscouata-Les-Basques
Next Election: 1er novembre 2013
Ryna St-Pierre, Directrice générale

Audet
CP 27
251, rue Principale
Audet, QC G0Y 1A0
819-583-1596 Fax: 819-583-5938
munaudet@axion.ca
Municipal Type: Municipality
Incorporated: 26 novembre 1903; *Area:* 132,86 km2
County or District: Le Granit; *Population in 2006:* 662
Provincial Electoral District(s): Mégantic-Compton
Federal Electoral District(s): Mégantic-L'Érable
Next Election: 1er novembre 2013
France Larochelle, Sec.-Trés.

Aumond
679, rte Principale
Aumond, QC J0W 1W0
819-449-4006 Fax: 819-449-7448
mun.aumond@lino.com
Municipal Type: Township
Incorporated: 12 décembre 1877; *Area:* 215,12 km2
County or District: La Vallée-de-la-Gatineau; *Population in 2006:* 775
Provincial Electoral District(s): Gatineau
Federal Electoral District(s): Pontiac
Next Election: 1er novembre 2013
Sonia Cronier, Directrice générale

Aupaluk
CP 4
Aupaluk, QC J0M 1X0
819-491-7070 Fax: 819-491-7035
Municipal Type: Northern Village
Incorporated: 2 février 1980; *Area:* 32,93 km2
County or District: Nord-du-Québec; *Population in 2006:* 174
Provincial Electoral District(s): Ungava
Federal Electoral District(s): Abitibi-Baie-James-Nunavik-Eeyou
Next Election: 7 novembre 2007
Sarah Annahatak, Sec.-Trés.

Austin
21, ch Millington
Austin, QC J0B 1B0
819-843-2388 Fax: 819-843-8211
austin@axion.ca
Municipal Type: Municipality
Incorporated: 5 novembre 1938; *Area:* 72,62 km2
County or District: Memphrémagog; *Population in 2006:* 1,404

Provincial Electoral District(s): Brome-Missisquoi
Federal Electoral District(s): Brome-Missisquoi
Next Election: 1er novembre 2013
Anne-Marie Ménard, Sec.-Trés.

Authier
605, av Principale
Authier, QC J0Z 1C0
819-782-3093 Fax: 819-782-3203
www.authier.ao.ca
Municipal Type: Municipality
Incorporated: 20 septembre 1918; *Area:* 139,72 km2
County or District: Abitibi-Ouest; *Population in 2006:* 247
Provincial Electoral District(s): Abitibi Ouest
Federal Electoral District(s): Abitibi-Témiscamingue
Next Election: 1er novembre 2013
Louise Lambert, Sec.-Trés.

Authier-Nord
452, rue Principale
Authier-Nord, QC J0Z 1E0
819-782-3914 Fax: 819-782-3914
m.authier-nord@tlb.sympatico.ca
www.authier-nord.ao.ca
Municipal Type: Municipality
Incorporated: 1er janvier 1983; *Area:* 289,79 km2
County or District: Abitibi-Ouest; *Population in 2006:* 317
Provincial Electoral District(s): Abitibi-Ouest
Federal Electoral District(s): Abitibi-Témiscamingue
Next Election: 1er novembre 2013
Diane Collard, Sec.-Trés.

Avignon
CP 128
470, rue Francoeur
Nouvelle, QC G0C 2E0
418-794-2221 Fax: 418-794-2076
info@mrcavignon.com
www.mrcavignon.com
Municipal Type: Regional County Municipality
Incorporated: 18 mars 1981;
Population in 2009: 13,219
Note: 11 municipalités & 2 autres territoires.
Gaétan Bernatchez, Directeur général

Ayer's Cliff
958, rue Main
Ayer's Cliff, QC J0B 1C0
819-838-5006 Fax: 819-838-4411
ayerclif@abacom.com
Municipal Type: Village
Incorporated: 24 février 1909; *Area:* 11,15 km2
County or District: Memphrémagog; *Population in 2006:* 1,096
Provincial Electoral District(s): Orford
Federal Electoral District(s): Compton-Stanstead
Next Election: 1er novembre 2013
Ghislaine Poulin-Doherty, Sec.-Trés.

Baie-D'Urfé
20410, ch Lakeshore
Baie-D'Urfé, QC H9X 1P7
514-457-5324 Fax: 514-457-5671
info@baie-durfe.qc.ca
Municipal Type: City
Incorporated: 1er janvier 2006; *Area:* 6,70 km2
County or District: Communauté métropolitaine de Montréal;
Population in 2009: 3,946
Provincial Electoral District(s): Jacques-Cartier
Federal Electoral District(s): Lac-Saint-Louis
Next Election: 1er novembre 2013
Richard White, Directeur général
Maria Tutino, Mairesse
Nathalie Hadida, Greffière

Baie-des-Sables
CP 39
20, rue du Couvent
Baie-des-Sables, QC G0J 1C0
418-772-6218 Fax: 418-772-6455
municipalitebds@globetrotter.net
Municipal Type: Municipality
Incorporated: 1er janvier 1859; *Area:* 64,54 km2
County or District: Matane; *Population in 2006:* 614
Provincial Electoral District(s): Matane
Federal Electoral District(s): Haute-Gaspésie-La Mitis-Matane-Matapédia
Next Election: 1er novembre 2013
Adam Coulombe, Sec.-Trés.

Baie-du-Febvre
CP 10
298, rte Marie-Victorin
Baie-du-Febvre, QC J0G 1A0
450-783-6422 Fax: 450-783-6423
municipalite@baie-du-febvre.net
www.baie-du-febvre.net
Municipal Type: Municipality
Incorporated: 26 mars 1983; *Area:* 96,04 km2
County or District: Nicolet-Yamaska; *Population in 2006:* 1,063
Provincial Electoral District(s): Nicolet-Yamaska
Federal Electoral District(s): Bas-Richelieu-Nicolet-Bécancour
Next Election: 1er novembre 2013
Maryse Baril, Sec.-Trés.

Baie-James
CP 500
110, boul de Matagami
Matagami, QC J0Y 2A0
819-739-2030 Fax: 819-739-2713
municipalite@baie-james.net
www.municipalite.baie-james.qc.ca
Municipal Type: Municipality
Incorporated: 14 juillet 1971; *Area:* 333 255,55 km2
Population in 2009: 2,010
Provincial Electoral District(s): Ungava
Federal Electoral District(s): Abitibi-Baie-James-Nunavik-Eeyou
Next Election: 1er novembre 2013
Stéphane Simard, Greffier

Baie-Johan-Beetz
20, rue Johan-Beetz
Baie-Johan-Beetz, QC G0G 1B0
418-539-0125 Fax: 418-539-0205
munbjb@globetrotter.net
Municipal Type: Municipality
Incorporated: 1er janvier 1966; *Area:* 425,31 km2
County or District: Minganie; *Population in 2006:* 95
Provincial Electoral District(s): Duplessis
Federal Electoral District(s): Manicouagan
Next Election: 1er novembre 2013
Sylvain Roy, Sec.-Trés.

Baie-Saint-Paul
15, rue Forget
Baie-Saint-Paul, QC G3Z 3G1
418-435-2205 Fax: 418-435-2688
ville@baiesaintpaul.com
www.baiesaintpaul.com
Municipal Type: City
Incorporated: 3 janvier 1996; *Area:* 546,73 km2
County or District: Charlevoix; *Population in 2009:* 7,317
Provincial Electoral District(s): Charlevoix
Federal Electoral District(s): Montmorency-Charlevoix-Haute-Côte-Nord
Next Election: 1er novembre 2013
Émilien Bouchard, Greffier
Jean Fortin, Maire
Martin Bouchard, Directeur général

Baie-Ste-Catherine
CP 10
308, rue Leclerc
Baie-Sainte-Catherine, QC G0T 1A0
418-237-4241 Fax: 418-237-4223
baie.ste-catherine@qc.aira.com
Municipal Type: Municipality
Incorporated: 4 novembre 1903; *Area:* 232,16 km2
County or District: Charlevoix-Est; *Population in 2006:* 227
Provincial Electoral District(s): Charlevoix
Federal Electoral District(s): Montmorency-Charlevoix-Haute-Côte-Nord
Next Election: 1er novembre 2013
Brigitte Boulianne, Sec.-Trés.

Baie-Trinité
CP 100
28, rte 138
Baie-Trinité, QC G0H 1A0
418-939-2231 Fax: 418-939-2616
municipalite.baie.trinite@globetrotter.net
Municipal Type: Village
Incorporated: 1er janvier 1955; *Area:* 425,32 km2
County or District: Manicouagan; *Population in 2006:* 526
Provincial Electoral District(s): René-Lévesque
Federal Electoral District(s): Manicouagan
Next Election: 1er novembre 2013
Manon Comeau, Sec.-Trés.

Barkmere
CP 11
182, ch de Barkmere
Barkmere, QC J0T 1A0
819-687-3373 Fax: 819-687-3383
info.barkmere@sympatico.ca
Municipal Type: City
Incorporated: 24 mars 1926; *Area:* 18,07 km2
County or District: Les Laurentides; *Population in 2006:* 87
Provincial Electoral District(s): Argenteuil
Federal Electoral District(s): Laurentides-Labelle
Next Election: 1er novembre 2013
Robert Mearns, Sec.-Trés.
Charles Huot, Maire

Barnston-Ouest
Way's Mills
741, ch Hunter
Ayer's Cliff, QC J0B 1C0
819-838-4334 Fax: 819-838-1717
mun45@abacom.com
Municipal Type: Municipality
Incorporated: 1er janvier 1946; *Area:* 97,90 km2
County or District: Coaticook; *Population in 2006:* 583
Provincial Electoral District(s): Orford
Federal Electoral District(s): Compton-Stanstead
Next Election: 1er novembre 2013
Manon Bergeron, Sec.-Trés.

Barraute
CP 299
481, 8e Av
Barraute, QC J0Y 1A0
819-734-6574 Fax: 819-734-5186
mun.barraute@cableamos.com
Municipal Type: Municipality
Incorporated: 5 janvier 1994; *Area:* 495,51 km2
County or District: Abitibi; *Population in 2009:* 2,069
Provincial Electoral District(s): Abitibi-Est
Federal Electoral District(s): Abitibi-Témiscamingue
Next Election: 1er novembre 2013
Richard Nantel, Directeur général

Batiscan
395, rue Principale
Batiscan, QC G0X 1A0
418-362-2421 Fax: 418-362-3174
municipalite@batiscan.ca
www.batiscan.ca
Municipal Type: Municipality
Incorporated: 1er juillet 1855; *Area:* 44,02 km2
County or District: Les Chenaux; *Population in 2006:* 949
Provincial Electoral District(s): Champlain
Federal Electoral District(s): St-Maurice-Champlain
Next Election: 1er novembre 2013
Caroline Cyr, Sec.-Trés.

Béarn
CP 369
28, 2e rue nord
Béarn, QC J0Z 1G0
819-726-4121 Fax: 819-726-2121
dg.bearn@mrctemiscamingue.qc.ca
www.temiscamingue.net/bearn
Municipal Type: Municipality
Incorporated: 3 octobre 1912; *Area:* 566,48 km2
County or District: Témiscamingue; *Population in 2006:* 883
Provincial Electoral District(s): Rouyn-Noranda-Témiscamingue
Federal Electoral District(s): Abitibi-Témiscamingue
Next Election: 1er novembre 2013
Lynda Gaudet, Sec.-Trés.

Beauce-Sartigan
2727, 6e Av
Saint-Georges, QC G5Y 3Y1
418-228-8418 Fax: 418-228-3709
mrcbsart@globetrotter.net
Municipal Type: Regional County Municipality

Population in 2009: 50,229
Note: 16 municipalités.
Éric Paquet, Directeur général

Beauceville
540, boul Renault
Beauceville, QC G5X 1N1
418-774-9137 Fax: 418-774-9141
beauceville@ville.beauceville.qc.ca
www.ville.beauceville.qc.ca
Municipal Type: City
Incorporated: 25 février 1998; *Area:* 167,76 km2
County or District: Robert-Cliche; *Population in 2006:* 6,226
Provincial Electoral District(s): Beauce-Nord
Federal Electoral District(s): Beauce
Next Election: 1er novembre 2013
Roger Longchamps, Greffier
Jean-Guy Bolduc, Maire

Beauharnois-Salaberry
#200, 660, rue Ellice
Beauharnois, QC J6N 1Y1
450-225-0870 Fax: 450-225-0872
info@mrc-beauharnois-salaberry.com
www.mrc-beauharnois-salaberry.com
Municipal Type: Regional County Municipality

Population in 2009: 61,531
Note: 7 municipalités.
Linda Phaneuf, Directrice générale

Beaulac-Garthby
96, rte 112
Beaulac-Garthby, QC G0Y 1B0
418-458-2375 Fax: 418-458-1127
municipalitedebeaulac@bellnet.ca
www.beaulac-garthby.com
Municipal Type: Municipality
Incorporated: 15 mars 2000; *Area:* 76,810 km2
County or District: Les Appalaches; *Population in 2009:* 873
Provincial Electoral District(s): Richmond
Federal Electoral District(s): Mégantic-L'Érable
Next Election: 1er novembre 2013
Cynthia Gagné, Directrice générale

Beaumont
48, ch du Domaine
Beaumont, QC G0R 1C0
418-833-3369 Fax: 418-833-4788
info.generale@municipalite.beaumont.qc.ca
www.municipalitedebeaumont.com
Municipal Type: Municipality
Incorporated: 1er juillet 1855; *Area:* 45,29 km2
County or District: Bellechasse; *Population in 2009:* 2,153
Provincial Electoral District(s): Bellechasse

Federal Electoral District(s): Lévis-Bellechasse
Next Election: 1er novembre 2013
Patrice Bissonnette, Directeur général

Beaupré
216, rue Prévost
Beaupré, QC G0A 1E0
418-827-4541 Fax: 418-827-3818
mairie@ville.beaupre.qc.ca
www.ville.beaupre.qc.ca
Municipal Type: City
Incorporated: 23 avril 1928; *Area:* 22,53 km2
County or District: La Côte-de-Beaupré; *Population in 2006:* 3,006
Provincial Electoral District(s): Charlevoix
Federal Electoral District(s):
Montmorency-Charlevoix-Haute-Côte-Nord
Next Election: 1er novembre 2013
Johanne Gagnon, Greffière
Henri Cloutier, Maire

Bécancour
#1, 3689, boul Bécancour
Bécancour, QC G9H 3W7
819-298-2070 Fax: 819-298-2041
info@mrcbecancour.qc.ca
Municipal Type: Regional County Municipality
Incorporated: 1 janvier 1982;
Population in 2009: 18,816
Note: 12 municipalités.
Laval Dubois, Directeur général

Bedford
1, rue Principale
Bedford, QC J0J 1A0
450-248-2440 Fax: 450-248-3220
bertrand@ville.bedford.qc.ca
Municipal Type: City
Incorporated: 21 novembre 1866; *Area:* 4,57 km2
County or District: Brome-Missisquoi; *Population in 2006:* 2,612
Provincial Electoral District(s): Brome-Missisquoi
Federal Electoral District(s): Brome-Missisquoi
Next Election: 1er novembre 2013
Bertrand Déry, Sec.-Trés.
Claude Dubois, Maire

Bedford
237, rte 202 est
Canton de Bedford, QC J0J 1A0
450-248-7576 Fax: 450-248-0135
canton.bedford@qc.aira.com
Municipal Type: Township
Incorporated: 4 mars 1919; *Area:* 31,06 km2
County or District: Brome-Missisquoi; *Population in 2006:* 736
Provincial Electoral District(s): Brome-Missisquoi
Federal Electoral District(s): Brome-Missisquoi
Next Election: 1er novembre 2013
Louise Desautels, Sec.-Trés. & Directrice générale

Bégin
126, rue Brassard
Bégin, QC G0V 1B0
418-672-4270 Fax: 418-672-6161
munbegin@hotmail.com
begin.chez.tiscali.fr/index.html
Municipal Type: Municipality
Incorporated: 8 février 1922; *Area:* 191,81 km2
County or District: Le Fjord-du-Saguenay; *Population in 2006:* 862
Provincial Electoral District(s): Dubuc
Federal Electoral District(s): Jonquière-Alma
Next Election: 1er novembre 2013
Claude Marceau, Sec.-Trés.

Belcourt
CP 22
219, rue Communautaire
Belcourt, QC J0Y 2M0
819-737-8894 Fax: 819-737-8894
g.m.a@munbelcourt.ca
Municipal Type: Municipality
Incorporated: 24 octobre 1918; *Area:* 411,23 km2
County or District: La Vallée-de-l'Or; *Population in 2006:* 256
Provincial Electoral District(s): Abitibi-Est
Federal Electoral District(s): Abitibi-Baie-James-Nunavik-Eeyou
Next Election: 1er novembre 2013
Nathalie Lizotte, Sec.-Trés.

Bellechasse
100, rue Monseigneur-Bilodeau
Saint-Lazare-de-Bellechasse, QC G0R 3J0
418-883-3347 Fax: 418-883-2555
clement@mrcbellechasse.qc.ca
www.mrcbellechasse.qc.ca
Municipal Type: Regional County Municipality
Incorporated: 1 janvier 1982;
Population in 2009: 33,792
Note: 20 municipalités.
Clément Fillion, Directeur général

Belleterre
CP 130
265, 1re av
Belleterre, QC J0Z 1L0
819-722-2122 Fax: 819-722-2527
villebelleterre@hotmail.com
vbelleterre.tripod.com/Belleterre/page0003.html
Municipal Type: City
Incorporated: 13 mai 1942; *Area:* 606,33 km2
County or District: Témiscamingue; *Population in 2006:* 350
Provincial Electoral District(s): Rouyn-Noranda-Témiscamingue
Federal Electoral District(s): Abitibi-Témiscamingue
Next Election: 1er novembre 2013
Liliane Rochon, Sec.-Trés.
Jean-Pierre Charron, Maire

Berry
274, rte 399
Berry, QC J0Y 2G0
819-732-1815 Fax: 819-732-3289
munberry85@hotmail.com
Municipal Type: Municipality
Incorporated: 1er janvier 1982; *Area:* 583,36 km2
County or District: Abitibi; *Population in 2006:* 560
Provincial Electoral District(s): Abitibi-Ouest
Federal Electoral District(s): Abitibi-Témiscamingue
Next Election: 1er novembre 2013
Caroline Tessier, Sec.-Trés.

Berthier-sur-Mer
5, rue du Couvent
Berthier-sur-Mer, QC G0R 1E0
418-259-7343 Fax: 418-259-2038
berthier-sur-mer@montmagny.com
www.berthiersurmer.ca
Municipal Type: Municipality
Incorporated: 1er juillet 1855; *Area:* 26,05 km2
County or District: Montmagny; *Population in 2006:* 1,239
Provincial Electoral District(s): Montmagny-L'Islet
Federal Electoral District(s):
Montmagny-L'Islet-Kamouraska-Rivière-du-Loup
Next Election: 1er novembre 2013
Suzanne Blais, Sec.-Trés.

Berthierville
CP 269
588, rue De Montcalm
Berthierville, QC J0K 1A0
450-836-7035 Fax: 450-836-1446
info@ville.berthierville.qc.ca
www.ville.berthierville.qc.ca
Municipal Type: City
Incorporated: 14 avril 1852; *Area:* 7,20 km2
County or District: D'Autray; *Population in 2006:* 4,007
Provincial Electoral District(s): Berthier
Federal Electoral District(s): Berthier-Maskinongé
Next Election: 1er novembre 2013
Jean Tremblay, Greffier
Yvon Poirier, Maire

Béthanie
1321, ch de Béthanie
Roxton Falls, QC J0H 1E0
450-548-2826 Fax: 450-548-5693
bethanie@cooptel.qc.ca
Municipal Type: Municipality
Incorporated: 2 mars 1920; *Area:* 47,29 km2
County or District: Acton; *Population in 2006:* 331
Provincial Electoral District(s): Johnson
Federal Electoral District(s): St-Hyacinthe-Bagot
Next Election: 1er novembre 2013
Heidi Bédard, Directrice générale & Sec.-Trés.

Biencourt
CP 70
2, rue St-Marc
Biencourt, QC G0K 1T0
418-499-2423 Fax: 418-499-2708
municipalitebiencourt@bellnet.ca
Municipal Type: Municipality
Incorporated: 1er janvier 1947; *Area:* 187,80 km2
County or District: Témiscouata; *Population in 2006:* 596
Provincial Electoral District(s): Rimouski
Federal Electoral District(s): Rimouski-Neigette-Témiscouata-Les Basques
Next Election: 1er novembre 2013
Lucette Viel, Sec.-Trés.

Blanc-Sablon
CP 400
1149, boul Dr.-Camille-Marcoux
Lourdes-de-Blanc-Sablon, QC G0G 1W0
418-461-2707 Fax: 418-461-2529
mbsablon@globetrotter.net
Municipal Type: Municipality
Incorporated: 1er janvier 1990; *Area:* 254,49
Population in 2009: 1,269
Provincial Electoral District(s): Duplessis
Federal Electoral District(s): Manicouagan
Next Election: 1er novembre 2013
Réjean L. Dumas, Directeur général

Blue Sea
CP 99
7, rue Principale
Blue Sea, QC J0X 1C0
819-463-2261 Fax: 819-463-4345
blue-sea@ireseau.com
Municipal Type: Municipality
Incorporated: 31 janvier 1921; *Area:* 76,89 km2
County or District: La Vallée-de-la-Gatineau; *Population in 2006:* 608
Provincial Electoral District(s): Gatineau
Federal Electoral District(s): Pontiac
Next Election: 1er novembre 2013
Manon Guilbault, Sec.-Trés.

Boileau
702, ch de Boileau
Boileau, QC J0V 1N0
819-687-3436 Fax: 819-687-3745
mun.boileau@sympatico.ca
www.petite-nation.qc.ca/boileau
Municipal Type: Municipality
Incorporated: 8 mars 1882; *Area:* 136,22 km2
County or District: Papineau; *Population in 2006:* 499
Provincial Electoral District(s): Papineau
Federal Electoral District(s): Argenteuil-Papineau-Mirabel
Next Election: 1er novembre 2013
Ghyslaine Lauzon, Sec.-Trés.

Bois-des-Filion
60, 36e av sud
Bois-des-Filion, QC J6Z 2G6
450-621-1460 Fax: 450-621-8483
ville@ville.bois.filion.qc.ca
www.ville.bois-des-filion.qc.ca
Municipal Type: City
Incorporated: 1er janvier 1949; *Area:* 4,34 km2
County or District: Thérèse-De Blainville; *Population in 2006:* 8,383
Provincial Electoral District(s): Blainville
Federal Electoral District(s): Marc-Aurèle-Fortin
Next Election: 1er novembre 2013
Martine Baribeau, Greffière
Paul Larocque, Maire

Bois-Franc
466, rte 105
Bois-Franc, QC J9E 3A9
819-449-2252 Fax: 819-449-4407
mun.bois-franc@ireseau.com
Municipal Type: Municipality
Incorporated: 17 novembre 1920; *Area:* 73,24 km2
County or District: La Vallée-de-la-Gatineau; *Population in 2006:* 449
Provincial Electoral District(s): Gatineau
Federal Electoral District(s): Pontiac
Next Election: 1er novembre 2013
Louise Pelletier, Sec.-Trés.

Boischatel
45, rue Bédard
Boischatel, QC G0A 1H0
418-822-4500 Fax: 418-822-4512
Info@municipalitedeboischatel.ca
www.municipalitedeboischatel.ca
Municipal Type: Municipality
Incorporated: 3 avril 1920; *Area:* 19,64
County or District: La Côte de Beaupré; Communauté métropolitaine de Québec; *Population in 2009:* 5,664
Provincial Electoral District(s): Montmorency
Federal Electoral District(s):
Montmorency-Charlevoix-Haute-Côte-Nord
Next Election: 1er novembre 2013
Carl Michaud, Directeur général

Bolton-Est
858, rte Missisquoi
Bolton-Est, QC J0E 1G0
450-292-3444 Fax: 450-292-4224
info@boltonest.ca
www.boltonest.ca
Municipal Type: Municipality
Incorporated: 28 décembre 1876; *Area:* 80,78
County or District: Memphrémagog; *Population in 2006:* 704
Provincial Electoral District(s): Brome-Missisquoi
Federal Electoral District(s): Brome-Missisquoi
Next Election: 1er novembre 2013
Lucy Edward, Directrice générale & Sec.-Trés.

Bolton-Ouest
9, ch Town Hall
Bolton-Ouest, QC J0E 2T0
450-242-2704 Fax: 450-242-2705
bolton-ouest@qc.aira.com
www.municipalitedeboltonouest.com
Municipal Type: Municipality
Incorporated: 28 décembre 1876; *Area:* 103,59
County or District: Brome-Missisquoi; *Population in 2006:* 723
Provincial Electoral District(s): Brome-Missisquoi
Federal Electoral District(s): Brome-Missisquoi
Next Election: 1er novembre 2013
Carrol Kralik, Sec.-Trés.

Bonaventure
127, av de Louisbourg
Bonaventure, QC G0C 1E0
418-534-2313 Fax: 418-534-4336
bonavent@globetrotter.qc.ca
www.bononaventuregaspesie.com
Municipal Type: City
Incorporated: 1er janvier 1884; *Area:* 109,20 km2
County or District: Bonaventure; *Population in 2006:* 2,673
Provincial Electoral District(s): Bonaventure
Federal Electoral District(s): Gaspésie-Iles-de-la-Madeleine
Next Election: 1er novembre 2013
Rollande Roy, Greffière
Serge Arsenault, Maire

Bonaventure
CP 310
51, rue Notre-Dame
New Carlisle, QC G0C 1Z0
418-752-6601 Fax: 418-752-6657
mrcbonav@globetrotter.net
www.mrcbonaventure.com
Municipal Type: Regional County Municipality
Incorporated: 8 avril 1981;
Population in 2009: 17,987
Note: 13 municipalités & 1 autre territoire.
Anne-Marie Flowers, Directrice générale

Bonne-Espérance
CP 40
Rivière-Saint-Paul, QC G0G 2P0
418-379-2911 Fax: 418-379-2959
munbon@globetrotter.net
Municipal Type: Municipality
Incorporated: 1er janvier 1990; *Area:* 721,28 km2
Population in 2006: 834
Provincial Electoral District(s): Duplessis
Federal Electoral District(s): Manicouagan
Next Election: 1er novembre 2013
René Fequet, Sec.-Trés.

Bonsecours
691, rte 220
Bonsecours, QC J0E 1H0
450-532-3139 Fax: 450-532-3953
mbonsecours@cooptel.qc.ca
www.bonsecours.ca
Municipal Type: Municipality
Incorporated: 20 mars 1905; *Area:* 59,92 km2
County or District: Le Val-St-François; *Population in 2006:* 547
Provincial Electoral District(s): Brome-Missisquoi
Federal Electoral District(s): Shefford
Next Election: 1er novembre 2013
Lyne Gaudreau, Sec.-Trés.

Bouchette
CP 59
36, rue Principale
Bouchette, QC J0X 1E0
819-465-2555 Fax: 819-465-2318
mun.bouchette@ireseau.com
Municipal Type: Municipality
Incorporated: 22 mars 1980; *Area:* 131,97 km2
County or District: La Vallée-de-la-Gatineau; *Population in 2006:* 718
Provincial Electoral District(s): Gatineau
Federal Electoral District(s): Pontiac
Next Election: 1er novembre 2013
Claudia Lacroix, Sec.-Trés.

Bowman
214, rte 307
Bowman, QC J0X 3C0
819-454-2421 Fax: 819-454-2133
munbowman@infonet.ca
Municipal Type: Municipality
Incorporated: 27 juin 1913; *Area:* 166,99 km2
County or District: Papineau; *Population in 2006:* 676
Provincial Electoral District(s): Papineau
Federal Electoral District(s): Argenteuil-Papineau-Mirabel
Next Election: 1er novembre 2013
Lucie Morisette, Directrice générale

Brébeuf
217, rte 323
Brébeuf, QC J0T 1B0
819-425-9833 Fax: 819-425-6611
secretariat@brebeuf.ca
Municipal Type: Parish (Paroisse)
Incorporated: 4 juin 1910; *Area:* 36,71 km2
County or District: Les Laurentides; *Population in 2006:* 939
Provincial Electoral District(s): Labelle
Federal Electoral District(s): Laurentides-Labelle
Next Election: 1er novembre 2013
Lynda Foisy, Sec.-Trés.

Brigham
118, av des Cèdres
Brigham, QC J2K 4K4
450-263-5942 Fax: 450-263-8380
direction@municipalitedebrigham.com
www.municipalitedebrigham.com
Municipal Type: Municipality
Incorporated: 1er juillet 1855; *Area:* 84,80 km2
County or District: Brome-Missisquoi; *Population in 2006:* 2,408
Provincial Electoral District(s): Brome-Missisquoi
Federal Electoral District(s): Brome-Missisquoi
Next Election: 1er novembre 2013
Stéphan F. Dulude, Sec.-Trés.

Bristol
32, ch d'Aylmer
Bristol, QC J0X 1G0
819-647-5555 Fax: 819-647-2424
info@bristolmunicipality.com
www.bristolmunicipality.com
Municipal Type: Municipality
Incorporated: 1er juillet 1855; *Area:* 224,08 km2
County or District: Pontiac; *Population in 2006:* 1,210
Provincial Electoral District(s): Pontiac
Federal Electoral District(s): Pontiac
Next Election: 1er novembre 2013
Keith R. Emmerson, Sec.-Trés.

Brome
330, ch Stage Coach
Brome, QC J0E 1K0
450-243-0489 Fax: 450-243-1091
bromevillage@qc.aibn.com
Municipal Type: Village
Incorporated: 20 juin 1923; *Area:* 11,75 km2
County or District: Brome-Missisquoi; *Population in 2006:* 286
Provincial Electoral District(s): Brome-Missisquoi
Federal Electoral District(s): Brome-Missisquoi
Next Election: 1er novembre 2013
Carmen Forgues, Sec.-Trés.

Brome-Missisquoi
749, rue Principale
Cowansville, QC J2K 1J8
450-266-4900 Fax: 450-266-6141
administration@mrcbm.qc.ca
www.brome-missisquoi.ca
Municipal Type: Regional County Municipality

Population in 2009: 47,127
Note: 20 municipalités.
Robert Desmarais, Directeur général

Bromont
88, boul de Bromont
Bromont, QC J2L 1A1
450-534-2021 Fax: 450-534-1025
ville@bromont.com
www.bromont.com
Municipal Type: City
Incorporated: 27 janvier 1973; *Area:* 108,36 km2
County or District: La Haute-Yamaska; *Population in 2009:* 6,400
Provincial Electoral District(s): Brome-Missisquoi
Federal Electoral District(s): Brome-Missisquoi
Next Election: 1er novembre 2013
Catherine Nadeau, Greffière
Pauline Quinlan, Mairesse
Jacques DesOrmeaux, Directeur général
Richard Joyal, Trésorier

Brownsburg-Chatham
300, rue de l'Hôtel de Ville
Brownsburg-Chatham, QC J8G 3B4
450-533-6687 Fax: 450-533-5795
secretariat@brownsburgchatham.ca
Municipal Type: City
Incorporated: 6 octobre 1999; *Area:* 249,31 km2
County or District: Argenteuil; *Population in 2006:* 6,664
Provincial Electoral District(s): Argenteuil
Federal Electoral District(s): Argenteuil-Papineau-Mirabel
Next Election: 1er novembre 2013
Jean Vachon, Sec.-Trés.
Lise Bourgault, Maire

Bryson
CP 190
770, rue Centrale
Bryson, QC J0X 1H0
819-648-5940 Fax: 819-648-5297
munbryson@personainternet.com
Municipal Type: Municipality
Incorporated: 1er janvier 1873; *Area:* 3,10 km2
County or District: Pontiac; *Population in 2006:* 618
Provincial Electoral District(s): Pontiac
Federal Electoral District(s): Pontiac
Next Election: 1er novembre 2013
Tracey Hérault, Sec.-Trés.

Bury
563, rue Main
Bury, QC J0B 1J0
819-872-3692 Fax: 819-872-3675
bury@qc.aira.com
Municipal Type: Municipality
Incorporated: 1er juillet 1855; *Area:* 232,52 km2
County or District: Le Haut-St-François; *Population in 2006:* 1,249
Provincial Electoral District(s): Mégantic-Compton
Federal Electoral District(s): Compton-Stanstead
Next Election: 1er novembre 2013
Marilyn Matheson, Sec.-Trés.

Cabano
79, rue Commerciale
Cabano, QC G0L 1E0
418-854-2116 Fax: 418-854-0118
ville.cabano@qc.aira.com
www.ville.cabano.qc.ca
Municipal Type: City
Incorporated: 19 juillet 1969; *Area:* 121,78 km2
County or District: Témiscouata; *Population in 2006:* 3,199
Provincial Electoral District(s): Kamouraska-Témiscouata
Federal Electoral District(s): Rimouski-Neigette-Témiscouata-Les Basques
Next Election: 1er novembre 2013
Gilles Desrosiers, Sec.-Trés. & Directeur général
Jacques Asselin, Mairesse

Cacouna
415, rue St-Georges
Cacouna, QC G0L 1G0
418-867-1781 Fax: 418-867-5677
mun.cacouna@bellnet.ca
Municipal Type: Municipality
Incorporated: 22 mars 2006; *Area:* 62,49 km2
County or District: Rivière-du-Loup; *Population in 2006:* 1,847
Provincial Electoral District(s): Rivière-du-Loup
Federal Electoral District(s):
Montmagny-L'Islet-Kamouraska-Rivière-du-Loup
Next Election: 1er novembre 2013
Thérèse Dubé, Directrice générale

Calixa-Lavallée
771, ch de la Beauce
Calixa-Lavallée, QC J0L 1A0
450-583-6470 Fax: 450-583-5508
directeur@calixa-lavallee.org
Municipal Type: Parish (Paroisse)
Incorporated: 24 juillet 1878; *Area:* 32,42 km2
County or District: Lajemmerais; *Population in 2006:* 533
Provincial Electoral District(s): Verchères
Federal Electoral District(s): Verchères-Les Patriotes
Next Election: 1er novembre 2013
Serge Woods, Sec.-Trés.

Campbell's Bay
CP 157
59, rue Leslie
Campbell's Bay, QC J0X 1K0
819-648-5811 Fax: 819-648-2045
administration@municipalite.campbell'sbay.qc.ca
Municipal Type: Municipality
Incorporated: 23 février 1904; *Area:* 3,08 km2
County or District: Pontiac; *Population in 2006:* 745
Provincial Electoral District(s): Pontiac
Federal Electoral District(s): Pontiac
Next Election: 1er novembre 2013
Colleen Larivière, Sec.-Trés.

Caniapiscau
CP 1420
100, place Daviault
Fermont, QC G0G 1J0
418-287-5339 Fax: 418-287-3420
mrc@caniapiscau.net
www.caniapiscau.net/mrc/
Municipal Type: Regional County Municipality
Incorporated: 1 janvier 1982;
Population in 2009: 2,892
Note: 2 municipalités & 4 autres territoires.
Jimmy Morneau, Directeur général

Cantley
8, ch River
Cantley, QC J8V 2Z9
819-827-3434 Fax: 819-827-4328
municipalite@cantley.ca
www.cantley.ca
Municipal Type: Municipality
Incorporated: 1er janvier 1989; *Area:* 134 km2
County or District: Les Collines-de-l'Outaouais; *Population in 2009:* 8,436
Provincial Electoral District(s): Gatineau
Federal Electoral District(s): Pontiac
Next Election: 1er novembre 2013
Vincent Tanguay, Directeur général

Cap-Chat
CP 279
53, rue Notre-Dame
Cap-Chat, QC G0J 1E0
418-786-5537 Fax: 418-786-5540
ville.capchat@globetrotter.net
Municipal Type: City
Incorporated: 15 mars 2000; *Area:* 183,13 km2
County or District: La Haute-Gaspésie; *Population in 2006:* 2,777
Provincial Electoral District(s): Matane
Federal Electoral District(s): Haute-Gaspésie-La Mitis-Matane-Matapédia
Next Election: 1er novembre 2013
Jacques Fournier, Greffier
Judes Landry, Maire

Cap-Santé
194, rte 138
Cap-Santé, QC G0A 1L0
418-285-1207 Fax: 418-285-0009
villecapsante@globetrotter.net
www.capsante.qc.ca
Municipal Type: City
Incorporated: 1er juillet 1855; *Area:* 54,38 km2
County or District: Portneuf; *Population in 2006:* 2,666
Provincial Electoral District(s): Portneuf
Federal Electoral District(s): Portneuf-Jacques-Cartier
Next Election: 1er novembre 2013
Jacques Blais, Sec.-Trés.
Jeanne Noreau, Mairesse

Cap-St-Ignace
850, rte du Souvenir
Cap-Saint-Ignace, QC G0R 1H0

418-246-5631 Fax: 418-246-5663
dg@capsaintignace.ca
www.capsaintignace.ca
Municipal Type: Municipality
Incorporated: 1er juillet 1855; *Area:* 227,76 km2
County or District: Montmagny; *Population in 2006:* 3,204
Provincial Electoral District(s): Montmagny-L'Islet
Federal Electoral District(s):
Montmagny-L'Islet-Kamouraska-Rivière-du-Loup
Next Election: 1er novembre 2013
Chantal Caron, Sec.-Trés. & Directrice générale

Caplan
CP 360
17, boul Perron est
Caplan, QC G0C 1H0
418-388-2075 Fax: 418-388-2429
caplan@globetrotter.net
municipalitecaplan.tripod.com
Municipal Type: Municipality
Incorporated: 1er janvier 1875; *Area:* 85,05 km2
County or District: Bonaventure; *Population in 2006:* 1,884
Provincial Electoral District(s): Bonaventure
Federal Electoral District(s): Gaspésie-Iles-de-la-Madeleine
Next Election: 1er novembre 2013
Lise Castilloux, Directrice générale

Carignan
2555, ch Bellevue
Carignan, QC J3L 6G8
450-658-1066 Fax: 450-658-6079
info@villedecarignan.org
www.villedecarignan.org
Municipal Type: City
Incorporated: 1er juillet 1855; *Area:* 62,39 km2
County or District: La Vallée-du-Richelieu; *Population in 2006:* 7,426
Provincial Electoral District(s): Chambly
Federal Electoral District(s): Chambly-Borduas
Next Election: 1er novembre 2013
Rémi Raymond, Greffier
Jean-Guy Legendre, Maire

Carleton-sur-Mer
629, boul Perron
Carleton, QC G0C 1J0
418-364-7073 Fax: 418-364-7314
direction@carletonsurmer.com
www.carletonsurmer.com
Municipal Type: City
Incorporated: 4 octobre 2000; *Area:* 214,78 km2
County or District: Avignon; *Population in 2006:* 4,077
Provincial Electoral District(s): Bonaventure
Federal Electoral District(s): Gaspésie-Iles-de-la-Madeleine
Next Election: 1er novembre 2013
Gilles Desjardins, Sec.-Trés. & Directeur général
Yvan Côté, Maire

Cascapédia-St-Jules
55, rte Gallagher
Cascapédia-Saint-Jules, QC G0C 1T0
418-392-4042 Fax: 418-392-6004
cascapediastjules.loisirs@globetrotter.net
Municipal Type: Municipality
Incorporated: 2 juin 1999; *Area:* 168 km2
County or District: Bonaventure; *Population in 2006:* 714
Provincial Electoral District(s): Bonaventure
Federal Electoral District(s): Gaspésie-Iles-de-la-Madeleine
Next Election: 1er novembre 2013
Susan Legouffe, Directrice générale

Causapscal
1, rue St-Jacques nord
Causapscal, QC G0J 1J0
418-756-3444 Fax: 418-756-3344
muncausa@globetrotter.net
www.causapscal.net
Municipal Type: City
Incorporated: 31 décembre 1997; *Area:* 163,88 km2
County or District: La Matapédia; *Population in 2006:* 2,458
Provincial Electoral District(s): Matapédia
Federal Electoral District(s): Haute-Gaspésie-La Mitis-Matane-Matapédia
Next Election: 1er novembre 2013
Jean-Noël Barriault, Sec.-Trés.
Denis Bastien, Maire

Cayamant
6, ch Lachapelle
Lac-Cayamant, QC J0X 1Y0
819-463-3587 Fax: 819-463-4020
mun.caymant@ireseau.com
Municipal Type: Municipality
Incorporated: 10 octobre 1906; *Area:* 411,13 km2
County or District: La Vallée-de-la-Gatineau; *Population in 2006:* 811
Provincial Electoral District(s): Gatineau
Federal Electoral District(s): Pontiac
Next Election: 1er novembre 2013
Suzanne Vallières, Sec.-Trés. & Directrice générale

Chambord
1526, rue Principale
Chambord, QC G0W 1G0
418-342-6274 Fax: 418-342-8438
tresorier@munchambord.ca
www.munchambord.ca
Municipal Type: Municipality
Incorporated: 8 décembre 1973; *Area:* 157,03 km2
County or District: Le Domaine-du-Roy; *Population in 2006:* 1,690
Provincial Electoral District(s): Roberval
Federal Electoral District(s): Roberval-Lac-Saint-Jean
Next Election: 1er novembre 2013
Bruno Laroche, Maire

Champlain
CP 250
819, rue Notre-Dame
Champlain, QC G0X 1C0
819-295-3979 Fax: 819-295-3032
municipalite.champlain@infoteck.qc.ca
Municipal Type: Municipality
Incorporated: 11 décembre 1982; *Area:* 58,59 km2
County or District: Les Chenaux; *Population in 2006:* 1,566
Provincial Electoral District(s): Champlain
Federal Electoral District(s): St-Maurice-Champlain
Next Election: 1er novembre 2013
Jean Houde, Sec.-Trés.

Champneuf
12, 6e av nord
Champneuf, QC J0Y 1E0
819-754-2053 Fax: 819-754-5749
munichampneuf@tlb.sympatico.ca
Municipal Type: Municipality
Incorporated: 1er janvier 1964; *Area:* 241,38 km2
County or District: Abitibi; *Population in 2006:* 130
Provincial Electoral District(s): Abitibi-Ouest
Federal Electoral District(s): Abitibi-Témiscamingue
Next Election: 1er novembre 2013
Diane Fleurent, Sec.-Trés.

Chandler
CP 459
35, rue Commerciale ouest
Chandler, QC G0C 1K0
418-689-2221 Fax: 418-689-3073
hdvchan@globetrotter.net
www.villedechandler.com
Municipal Type: City
Incorporated: 27 juin 2001; *Area:* 424,90 km2
County or District: Le Rocher-Percé; *Population in 2009:* 7,893
Provincial Electoral District(s): Gaspé
Federal Electoral District(s): Gaspésie-Iles-de-la-Madeleine
Next Election: 1er novembre 2013
Roch Giroux, Greffier & Directeur général
Claude Cyr, Maire

Chapais
CP 380
145, boul Springer
Chapais, QC G0W 1H0
418-745-2511 Fax: 418-745-3871
villedechapais@lino.com
Municipal Type: City
Incorporated: 16 novembre 1955; *Area:* 62,78 km2
Population in 2006: 1,630
Provincial Electoral District(s): Ungava
Federal Electoral District(s): Abitibi-Baie-James-Nunavik-Eeyou
Next Election: 1er novembre 2013
Daniel Dufour, Greffier
Jacques Bérubé, Maire

Charette
390, rue St-Édouard
Charette, QC G0X 1E0
819-221-2095 Fax: 819-221-3493
municipalitedecharette@hotmail.com
Municipal Type: Municipality
Incorporated: 9 février 1918; *Area:* 42,55 km2
County or District: Maskinongé; *Population in 2006:* 924
Provincial Electoral District(s): Maskinongé
Federal Electoral District(s): Berthier-Maskinongé
Next Election: 1er novembre 2013
Danielle D. Villemure, Sec.-Trés.

Charlemagne
84, rue du Sacré-Coeur
Charlemagne, QC J5Z 1W8
450-581-2541 Fax: 450-581-0597
info@ville.charlemagne.qc.ca
www.ville.charlemagne.qc.ca
Municipal Type: City
Incorporated: 13 novembre 1906; *Area:* 1,95 km2
County or District: L'Assomption; *Population in 2006:* 5,594
Provincial Electoral District(s): Masson
Federal Electoral District(s): Repentigny
Next Election: 1er novembre 2013
Bernard Boudreau, Greffier & Directeur général
Normand Grenier, Maire

Charlevoix
#201, 4, place de l'Église
Baie-Saint-Paul, QC G3Z 1T2
418-435-2639 Fax: 418-435-2666
mrc@charlevoix.net
www.mrc-charlevoix.com
Municipal Type: Regional County Municipality
Incorporated: 1 janvier 1982;
Population in 2009: 13,228
Note: 6 municipalités & 1 autre territoire.
Karine Horvath, Directrice générale

Charlevoix-Est
172, boul Notre-Dame
Clermont, QC G4A 1G1
418-439-3947 Fax: 418-439-2502
direction@mrccharlevoixest.ca
www.mrccharlevoixest.ca
Municipal Type: Regional County Municipality
Incorporated: 1 janvier 1982;
Population in 2009: 16,347
Note: 7 municipalités & 2 autres territoires.
Pierre Girard, Directeur général

Chartierville
27, rue St-Jean-Baptiste
Chartierville, QC J0B 1K0
819-656-2323 Fax: 819-656-1067
munichartier@bellnet.ca
Municipal Type: Municipality
Incorporated: 1er janvier 1879; *Area:* 139,13 km2
County or District: Le Haut-St-François; *Population in 2006:* 378
Provincial Electoral District(s): Mégantic-Compton
Federal Electoral District(s): Compton-Stanstead
Next Election: 1er novembre 2013
Maryse Prud'homme, Sec.-Trés.

Château-Richer
8006, av Royale
Château-Richer, QC G0A 1N0
418-824-4294 Fax: 418-824-3277
chateau.richer@videotron.ca
Municipal Type: City
Incorporated: 1er juillet 1855; *Area:* 228,99 km2
County or District: La Côte-de-Beaupré; *Population in 2006:* 3,563
Provincial Electoral District(s): Montmorency
Federal Electoral District(s):
Montmorency-Charlevoix-Haute-Côte-Nord
Next Election: 1er novembre 2013
Lucie Gagnon, Greffière
Frédéric Dancause, Maire

Chazel
335, rue Principale
Chazel, QC J0Z 1N0
819-333-4758 Fax: 819-333-4758
municipalitedechazel@hotmail.com
chazel.ao.ca
Municipal Type: Municipality
Incorporated: 19 février 1938; *Area:* 134,57 km2
County or District: Abitibi-Ouest; *Population in 2006:* 321
Provincial Electoral District(s): Abitibi-Ouest
Federal Electoral District(s): Abitibi-Témiscamingue
Next Election: 1er novembre 2013
Manon Therrien, Sec.-Trés.

Chelsea
100, ch d'Old Chelsea
Chelsea, QC J9B 1C1
819-827-1124 Fax: 819-827-2672
info@chelsea.ca
www.chelsea.ca
Municipal Type: Municipality
Incorporated: 1er janvier 1875; *Area:* 111,2 km2
County or District: Les Collines-de-l'Outaouais; *Population in 2009:* 6,816
Provincial Electoral District(s): Gatineau
Federal Electoral District(s): Pontiac
Next Election: 1er novembre 2013
Paul St-Louis, Directeur général

Chénéville
63, rue de l'Hôtel-de-Ville
Chénéville, QC J0V 1E0
819-428-3583 Fax: 819-428-4838
adm.cheneville@mrcpapineau.com
www.ville.cheneville.qc.ca
Municipal Type: Municipality
Incorporated: 21 août 1996; *Area:* 65,22 km2
County or District: Papineau; *Population in 2006:* 784
Provincial Electoral District(s): Papineau
Federal Electoral District(s): Argenteuil-Papineau-Mirabel
Next Election: 1er novembre 2013
Jacques Maillé, Sec.-Trés. & Directeur général

Chertsey
333, av de l'Amitié
Chertsey, QC J0K 3K0
450-882-2920 Fax: 450-882-3333
general@municipalite.chertsey.qc.ca
www.municipalite.chertsey.qc.ca
Municipal Type: Municipality
Incorporated: 13 novembre 1991; *Area:* 313,22 km2
County or District: Matawinie; *Population in 2009:* 4,961
Provincial Electoral District(s): Bertrand
Federal Electoral District(s): Joliette
Next Election: 1er novembre 2013
Pierre Mercier, Directeur général

Chester-Est
3456, rue Principale
Sainte-Hélène-de-Chester, QC G0P 1H0
819-382-2650 Fax: 819-382-9933
chestest@ivic.qc.ca
Municipal Type: Township
Incorporated: 1er janvier 1859; *Area:* 82,87 km2
County or District: Arthabaska; *Population in 2006:* 357

Provincial Electoral District(s): Arthabaska
Federal Electoral District(s): Richmond-Arthabaska
Next Election: 1er novembre 2013
Diane Beauchesne, Sec.-Trés.

Chesterville
261, rue de l'Accueil
Chesterville, QC G0P 1J0
819-382-2059 Fax: 819-382-2073
munches@videotron.ca
Municipal Type: Municipality
Incorporated: 18 décembre 1982; *Area:* 114,89 km2
County or District: Arthabaska; *Population in 2006:* 894
Provincial Electoral District(s): Arthabaska
Federal Electoral District(s): Richmond-Arthabaska
Next Election: 1er novembre 2013
Lyse Côté, Directrice générale & Trés.

Chibougamau
650, 3e rue
Chibougamau, QC G8P 1P1
418-748-2688 Fax: 418-748-6562
www.ville.chibougamau.qc.ca
Municipal Type: City
Incorporated: 8 novembre 1952; *Area:* 1,041,97 km2
Population in 2009: 7,696
Provincial Electoral District(s): Ungava
Federal Electoral District(s): Abitibi-Baie-James-Nunavik-Eeyou
Next Election: 1er novembre 2013
Mario Asselin, Greffier
Donald Bubar, Maire
Luc Mongeau, Directeur général
Pascale Vézina, Trésorière

Chichester
CP 158
75, rue Notre-Dame
Chapeau, QC J0X 1M0
819-689-2266 Fax: 819-689-5619
administration@municipalite.lisle-aux-allumettes.qc.ca
Municipal Type: Township
Incorporated: 1er janvier 1857; *Area:* 225,71 km2
County or District: Pontiac; *Population in 2006:* 388
Provincial Electoral District(s): Pontiac
Federal Electoral District(s): Pontiac
Next Election: 1er novembre 2013
Richard Vaillancourt, Sec.-Trés.

Chisasibi
CP 150
Chisasibi, QC J0M 1E0
819-855-2878 Fax: 819-855-2875
Municipal Type: Villages Cris

Provincial Electoral District(s): Ungava
Federal Electoral District(s): Abitibi-Baie-James-Nunavik-Eeyou
Abraham Rupert, Maire

Chute-aux-Outardes
2, rue de l'École
Chute-aux-Outardes, QC G0H 1C0
418-567-2144 Fax: 418-567-4478
municipalitecao@internetsaco.com
Municipal Type: Village
Incorporated: 7 mars 1951; *Area:* 8,31 km2
County or District: Manicouagan; *Population in 2006:* 1,853
Provincial Electoral District(s): René-Lévesque
Federal Electoral District(s): Manicouagan
Next Election: 1er novembre 2013
Rick Tanguay, Sec.-Trés. & Directeur général

Chute-Saint-Philippe
592, ch du Progrès
Chute-Saint-Philippe, QC J0W 1A0
819-585-3397 Fax: 819-585-4949
chute.st-philippe@tlb.sympatico.ca
Municipal Type: Municipality
Incorporated: 26 octobre 1940; *Area:* 282,28 km2
County or District: Antoine-Labelle; *Population in 2006:* 890
Provincial Electoral District(s): Labelle
Federal Electoral District(s): Laurentides-Labelle
Next Election: 1er novembre 2013
Ginette Ippersiel, Sec.-Trés. & Directrice générale

Clarendon
CP 777
427C, rte 148
Shawville, QC J0X 2Y0
819-647-3862 Fax: 819-647-3822
Municipal Type: Municipality
Incorporated: 1er juillet 1855; *Area:* 327,27 km2
County or District: Pontiac; *Population in 2006:* 1,248
Provincial Electoral District(s): Pontiac
Federal Electoral District(s): Pontiac
Next Election: 1er novembre 2013
Ruth Potter Strutt, Sec.-Trés.

Clermont
722, 4e rang
Saint-Vital-de-Clermont, QC J0Z 3M0
819-333-6129 Fax: 819-333-3811
clermont@mrcao.qc.ca
www.clermont.ao.ca
Municipal Type: Township
Incorporated: 4 mars 1936; *Area:* 155,89 km2
County or District: Abitibi-Ouest; *Population in 2006:* 534
Provincial Electoral District(s): Abitibi-Ouest
Federal Electoral District(s): Abitibi-Témiscamingue
Next Election: 1er novembre 2013
Yvette Portelance, Sec.-Trés.

Clermont
2, rue Maisonneuve
Clermont, QC G4A 1G6
418-439-3931 Fax: 418-439-4889
villedeclermont@qc.aira.com
Municipal Type: City
Incorporated: 16 février 1935; *Area:* 52,99 km2
County or District: Charlevoix-Est; *Population in 2006:* 3,041
Provincial Electoral District(s): Charlevoix
Federal Electoral District(s):
Montmorency-Charlevoix-Haute-Côte-Nord
Next Election: 1er novembre 2013
Guy-Raymond Savard, Sec.-Trés.
Jean-Pierre Gagnon, Maire

Clerval
579, 2e rang
Clerval, QC J0Z 1R0
819-783-2640 Fax: 819-783-2640
clerval@mrcao.qc.ca
www.clerval.ao.ca
Municipal Type: Municipality
Incorporated: 12 septembre 1927; *Area:* 101,60 km2
County or District: Abitibi-Ouest; *Population in 2006:* 358
Provincial Electoral District(s): Abitibi-Ouest
Federal Electoral District(s): Abitibi-Témiscamingue
Next Election: 1er novembre 2013
Lise Roy, Sec.-Trés.

Cleveland
292, ch de la Rivière
Cleveland, QC J0B 2H0
819-826-3546 Fax: 819-826-2827
cleveland.dir.gen@b2b2c.ca
Municipal Type: Township
Incorporated: 1er juillet 1855; *Area:* 120,82 km2
County or District: Le Val-St-François; *Population in 2006:* 1,590
Provincial Electoral District(s): Richmond
Federal Electoral District(s): Richmond-Arthabaska
Next Election: 1er novembre 2013
Claudette Lapointe, Sec.-Trés.

Cloridorme
CP 100
472, rte 132
Cloridorme, QC G0E 1G0
418-395-2808 Fax: 418-395-2228
munclori@globetrotter.net
Municipal Type: Township
Incorporated: 1er janvier 1885; *Area:* 162,10 km2
County or District: La Côte-de-Gaspé; *Population in 2006:* 764
Provincial Electoral District(s): Gaspé
Federal Electoral District(s): Gaspésie-Iles-de-la-Madeleine
Next Election: 1er novembre 2013
Marie Dufresne, Sec.-Trés.

Coaticook
294, rue St-Jacques nord
Coaticook, QC J1A 2R3
819-849-9166 Fax: 819-849-4320
secretariat@mrcdecoaticook.qc.ca
www.mrcdecoaticook.qc.ca
Municipal Type: Regional County Municipality
Incorporated: 1 janvier 1982;
Population in 2009: 18,680
Note: 12 municipalités.
Nancy Bilodeau, Greffière

Colombier
CP 69
568, rue Principale
Colombier, QC G0H 1P0
418-565-3343 Fax: 418-565-3289
info@municipalite.colombier.qc.ca
www.municipalite.colombier.qc.ca
Municipal Type: Municipality
Incorporated: 1er janvier 1946; *Area:* 313,20 km2
County or District: La Haute-Côte-Nord; *Population in 2006:* 817
Provincial Electoral District(s): René-Lévesque
Federal Electoral District(s):
Montmorency-Charlevoix-Haute-Côte-Nord
Next Election: 1er novembre 2013
Rémi Tremblay, Sec.-Trés. & Directeur général

Compton
3, ch de Hatley
Compton, QC J0B 1L0
819-835-5584 Fax: 819-835-5750
muncompton@bellnet.ca
Municipal Type: Municipality
Incorporated: 8 décembre 1999; *Area:* 205,72 km2
County or District: Coaticook; *Population in 2006:* 2,818
Provincial Electoral District(s): St-François
Federal Electoral District(s): Compton-Stanstead
Next Election: 1er novembre 2013
Serge Caron, Sec.-Trés. & Directeur général

Contrecoeur
5000, rte Marie-Victorin
Contrecoeur, QC J0L 1C0
450-587-5901 Fax: 450-587-5855
beaulieuy@ville.contrecoeur.qc.ca
www.ville.contrecoeur.qc.ca
Municipal Type: City
Incorporated: 1er janvier 1976; *Area:* 61,56 km2
County or District: Lajemmerais; *Population in 2006:* 5,678
Provincial Electoral District(s): Verchères
Federal Electoral District(s): Verchères-Les Patriotes
Next Election: 1er novembre 2013
Yves Beaulieu, Sec.-Trés.
Suzanne Dansereau, Mairesse

Cookshire-Eaton
220, rue Principale est
Cookshire, QC J0B 1M0
819-875-3165 Fax: 819-875-5311
ville@cookshire-eaton.qc.ca
www.cookshire-eaton.qc.ca
Municipal Type: City
Incorporated: 24 juillet 2002; *Area:* 297,60 km2
County or District: Le Haut-St-François; *Population in 2006:* 5,004
Provincial Electoral District(s): Mégantic-Compton
Federal Electoral District(s): Compton-Stanstead
Next Election: 1er novembre 2013
André Croisetière, Sec.-Trés. & Directeur général
Normand Potvin, Maire

Côte-Nord-du-Golfe-du-St-Laurent
Chevery, QC G0G 1G0
418-787-2244 Fax: 418-787-2241
mcngsl@globetrotter.net
Municipal Type: Municipality
Incorporated: 22 juin 1963; *Area:* 2783,59 km2
Population in 2006: 1,028
Provincial Electoral District(s): Duplessis
Federal Electoral District(s): Manicouagan
Next Election: 1er novembre 2013
Richmond Monger, Administrateur

Coteau-du-Lac
20, ch Rivière Delisle
Coteau-du-Lac, QC J0P 1B0
450-763-5822 Fax: 450-763-0938
info@coteau-du-lac.com
www.coteau-du-lac.com
Municipal Type: Municipality
Incorporated: 6 février 1982; *Area:* 46,57 km2
County or District: Vaudreuil-Soulanges; *Population in 2009:* 6,595
Provincial Electoral District(s): Soulanges
Federal Electoral District(s): Vaudreuil-Soulanges
Next Election: 1er novembre 2013
Johanne Lamothe, Trésorière

Courcelles
CP 160
116, av du Domaine
Courcelles, QC G0M 1C0
418-483-5540 Fax: 418-483-3540
municipal@telcourcelles.net
www.muncourcelles.qc.ca
Municipal Type: Parish (Paroisse)
Incorporated: 6 avril 1904; *Area:* 92,25 km2
County or District: Le Granit; *Population in 2006:* 928
Provincial Electoral District(s): Beauce-Sud
Federal Electoral District(s): Mégantic-L'Érable
Next Election: 1er novembre 2013
Renée Mathieu, Sec.-Trés. & Directrice générale

Crabtree
CP 660
111, 4e Av
Crabtree, QC J0K 1B0
450-754-3434 Fax: 450-754-2172
info@municipalitecrabtree.qc.ca
www.municipalitecrabtree.qc.ca
Municipal Type: Municipality
Incorporated: 23 octobre 1996; *Area:* 24,71 km2
County or District: Joliette; *Population in 2009:* 3,532
Provincial Electoral District(s): Joliette
Federal Electoral District(s): Joliette
Next Election: 1er novembre 2013
Pierre Rondeau, Directeur général

D'Autray
CP 1500
550, rue De Montcalm
Berthierville, QC J0K 1A0
450-836-7007 Fax: 450-836-1576
mrcautray@mrcautray.com
mrcautray.com
Municipal Type: Regional County Municipality

Population in 2009: 41,052
Note: 15 municipalités.
Danielle Joyal, Directrice générale

Danville
CP 310
150, rue Water
Danville, QC J0A 1A0

819-839-2771 Fax: 819-839-2918
info@villededanville.com
www.villededanville.com
Municipal Type: City
Incorporated: 17 mars 1999; *Area:* 149,51 km2
County or District: Asbestos; *Population in 2006:* 4,041
Provincial Electoral District(s): Richmond
Federal Electoral District(s): Richmond-Arthabaska
Next Election: 1er novembre 2013
Michel Lecours, Sec.-Trés. & Directeur général
Jacques Hémond, Maire

Daveluyville
CP 187
337, rue Principale
Daveluyville, QC G0Z 1C0
819-367-3395 Fax: 819-367-3550
villededaveluyville@lino.com
Municipal Type: City
Incorporated: 13 novembre 1901; *Area:* 2,25 km2
County or District: Arthabaska; *Population in 2006:* 1,005
Provincial Electoral District(s): Nicolet-Yamaska
Federal Electoral District(s): Richmond-Arthabaska
Next Election: 1er novembre 2013
Huguette Lafrenière, Sec.-Trés.
Normand Beaudoin, Maire

Dégelis
369, av Principale
Dégelis, QC G5T 2G3
418-853-2332 Fax: 418-853-3464
info@ville.degelis.qc.ca
www.ville.degelis.qc.ca
Municipal Type: City
Incorporated: 13 décembre 1969; *Area:* 562,84 km2
County or District: Témiscouata; *Population in 2006:* 3,209
Provincial Electoral District(s): Kamouraska-Témiscouata
Federal Electoral District(s): Rimouski-Neigette-Témiscouata-Les Basques
Next Election: 1er novembre 2013
Claire Bérubé, Greffière
Émelien Nadeau, Maire

Déléage
175, rte 107, RR#1
Maniwaki, QC J9E 3A8
819-449-1979 Fax: 819-449-7441
municipalitedeleage@bellnet.ca
Municipal Type: Municipality
Incorporated: 1er janvier 1881; *Area:* 249,44 km2
County or District: La Vallée-de-la-Gatineau; *Population in 2006:* 1,964
Provincial Electoral District(s): Gatineau
Federal Electoral District(s): Pontiac
Next Election: 1er novembre 2013
Jacinthe St-Amour-Labelle, Sec.-Trés. & Directrice générale

Delson
50, rue Ste-Thérèse
Delson, QC J5B 2B2
450-632-1050 Fax: 450-632-1571
info@ville.delson.qc.ca
www.ville.delson.qc.ca
Municipal Type: City
Incorporated: 4 janvier 1918; *Area:* 7,76 km2
County or District: Roussillon; *Population in 2006:* 7,322
Provincial Electoral District(s): La Prairie
Federal Electoral District(s): Châteauguay-St-Constant
Next Election: 1er novembre 2013
Nicole Lafontaine, Greffière
Georges Gagné, Maire

Denholm
419, ch du Poisson-Blanc
Denholm, QC J8N 9C8
819-457-2992 Fax: 819-457-9862
mairie.denholm@qc.aira.com
Municipal Type: Municipality
Incorporated: 27 février 1924; *Area:* 191,65 km2
County or District: La Vallée-de-la-Gatineau; *Population in 2006:* 604
Provincial Electoral District(s): Gatineau
Federal Electoral District(s): Pontiac
Next Election: 1er novembre 2013
Marc Langevin, Sec.-Trés.

Desbiens
CP 9
925, rue Hébert
Desbiens, QC G0W 1N0
418-346-5571 Fax: 418-346-5422
administration@ville.desbiens.qc.ca
www.ville.desbiens.qc.ca
Municipal Type: City
Incorporated: 16 août 1926; *Area:* 10,35 km2
County or District: Lac-St-Jean-Est; *Population in 2006:* 1,074
Provincial Electoral District(s): Lac-St-Jean
Federal Electoral District(s): Roberval-Lac-St-Jean
Next Election: 1er novembre 2013
Fernand Lapointe, Sec.-Trés.
Johanne Vézina, Mairesse

Deschaillons-sur-St-Laurent
1596, rte Marie-Victorin
Deschaillons-sur-Saint-Laurent, QC G0S 1G0
819-292-2085 Fax: 819-292-3194
mun.deschaillons@qc.aira.com
Municipal Type: Municipality
Incorporated: 23 mai 1990; *Area:* 37,70 km2
County or District: Bécancour; *Population in 2006:* 1,009
Provincial Electoral District(s): Lotbinière
Federal Electoral District(s): Bas-Richelieu-Nicolet-Bécancour
Next Election: 1er novembre 2013
Sylvie Dubois, Sec.-Trés.

Deschambault-Grondines
CP 220
120, rue St-Joseph
Deschambault, QC G0A 1S0
418-286-4511 Fax: 418-286-6511
deschambault@csportneuf.qc.ca
www.municipalite.deschambault.qc.ca
Municipal Type: Municipality
Incorporated: 27 février 2002; *Area:* 123,60 km2
County or District: Portneuf; *Population in 2006:* 2,032
Provincial Electoral District(s): Portneuf
Federal Electoral District(s): Portneuf-Jacques-Cartier
Next Election: 1er novembre 2013
Claire St-Arnaud, Sec.-Trés.

Deux-Montagnes
#301, 1, place de la Gare
Saint-Eustache, QC J7R 0B4
450-491-1818 Fax: 450-491-3040
info@mrc2m.qc.ca
www.clddm.com/mrc.php
Municipal Type: Regional County Municipality

Population in 2009: 90,638
Note: 7 municipalités.
Nicole Loiselle, Directrice générale

Disraéli
CP 2050
550, av Jacques-Cartier
Disraéli, QC G0N 1E0
418-449-2771 Fax: 418-449-4299
hoteldeville@villededisraeli.com
www.villededisraeli.com
Municipal Type: Town
Incorporated: 19e novembre 1904; *Area:* 6,470 km2
County or District: Les Appalaches; *Population in 2009:* 2,699
Provincial Electoral District(s): Frontenac
Federal Electoral District(s): Mégantic-L'Érable
Next Election: 1er novembre 2013
Francyne Gagné, Directrice générale

Disraéli
8306, rte 112
Disraéli, QC G0N 1E0
418-449-5329 Fax: 418-449-5459
paroissedisraeli@tlb.sympatico.ca
www.paroissedisraeli.com
Municipal Type: Parish (Paroisse)
Incorporated: 1ère janvier 1883; *Area:* 93,880 km2
County or District: Les Appalaches; *Population in 2009:* 1,020
Provincial Electoral District(s): Frontenac
Federal Electoral District(s): Mégantic-L'Érable
Next Election: 1er novembre 2013
Magda Matteau, Directrice générale

Dixville
251, rue Parker
Dixville, QC J0B 1P0
819-849-3037 Fax: 819-849-9520
bureaumunicipal@dixville.ca
www.dixville.ca
Municipal Type: Municipality
Incorporated: 27 septembre 1995; *Area:* 76,17 km2
County or District: Coaticook; *Population in 2006:* 685
Provincial Electoral District(s): Mégantic-Compton
Federal Electoral District(s): Compton-Stanstead
Next Election: 1er novembre 2013
Mary Brus, Sec.-Trés.

Donnacona
138, av Pleau
Donnacona, QC G3M 1A1
418-285-0110 Fax: 418-285-0020
naudb@villededonnaconna.com
www.villededonnacona.com
Municipal Type: City
Incorporated: 21 janvier 1967; *Area:* 20,12 km2
County or District: Portneuf; *Population in 2006:* 5,564
Provincial Electoral District(s): Portneuf
Federal Electoral District(s): Portneuf-Jacques-Cartier
Next Election: 1er novembre 2013
Sonya Dion, Greffière
André Marcoux, Maire

Dosquet
179, rte St-Joseph
Dosquet, QC G0S 1H0
418-728-3653 Fax: 418-728-3338
dosquet@globetrotter.net
Municipal Type: Municipality
Incorporated: 9 février 1918; *Area:* 67,26 km2
County or District: Lotbinière; *Population in 2006:* 907
Provincial Electoral District(s): Lotbinière
Federal Electoral District(s): Lotbinière-Chutes-de-la-Chaudière
Next Election: 1er novembre 2013
Louisette Chartrand, Sec.-Trés.

Drummond
436, rue Lindsay
Drummondville, QC J2B 1G6
819-477-2230 Fax: 819-477-8442
courriel@mrcdrummond.qc.ca
www.mrcdrummond.qc.ca
Municipal Type: Regional County Municipality

Population in 2009: 94,559
Note: 18 municipalités.
Michel Gagnon, Directeur général

Dudswell
CP 180
76, rue Main
Bishopton, QC J0B 1G0
819-884-5926 Fax: 819-884-5777
dudswell@bellnet.ca
Municipal Type: Municipality
Incorporated: 11 octobre 1995; *Area:* 214,76 km2
County or District: Le Haut-St-François; *Population in 2006:* 1,712
Provincial Electoral District(s): Mégantic-Compton
Federal Electoral District(s): Compton-Stanstead
Next Election: 1er novembre 2013
Hélène Leroux, Sec.-Trés.

Duhamel
CP 117
1890, rue Principale
Duhamel, QC J0V 1G0
819-428-7100 Fax: 819-428-1941
dinelc@municipalité.duhamel.qc.ca
www.municipalite.duhamel.qc.ca
Municipal Type: Municipality
Incorporated: 15 août 1936; *Area:* 449,45 km2
County or District: Papineau; *Population in 2006:* 483
Provincial Electoral District(s): Papineau
Federal Electoral District(s): Argenteuil-Papineau-Mirabel
Next Election: 1er novembre 2013
Claire Dinel, Sec.-Trés. & Directrice générale

Duhamel-Ouest
361, rte 101 sud
Duhamel-Ouest, QC J9V 1A2
819-629-2522 Fax: 819-629-2422
caldo@cablevision.qc.ca
Municipal Type: Municipality
Incorporated: 20 février 1911; *Area:* 127,61 km2
County or District: Témiscamingue; *Population in 2006:* 870
Provincial Electoral District(s): Rouyn-Noranda-Témiscamingue
Federal Electoral District(s): Abitibi-Témiscamingue
Next Election: 1er novembre 2013
Lise Gosselin, Sec.-Trés.

Dundee
3296, montée Smallman
Dundee, QC J0S 1L0
450-264-4674 Fax: 450-264-8044
mun.dundee@rocler.qc.ca
Municipal Type: Township
Incorporated: 1er juillet 1855; *Area:* 94,20 km2
County or District: Le Haut-St-Laurent; *Population in 2006:* 436
Provincial Electoral District(s): Huntingdon
Federal Electoral District(s): Beauharnois-Salaberry
Next Election: 1er novembre 2013
Marco Pilon, Sec.-Trés. & Directeur général

Dunham
CP 70
3777, rue Principale
Dunham, QC J0E 1M0
450-295-2418 Fax: 450-295-2182
info@ville.dunham.qc.ca
www.ville.dunham.qc.ca
Municipal Type: City
Incorporated: 25 septembre 1971; *Area:* 200,99 km2
County or District: Brome-Missisquoi; *Population in 2006:* 3,396
Provincial Electoral District(s): Brome-Missisquoi
Federal Electoral District(s): Brome-Missisquoi
Next Election: 1er novembre 2013
Pierre Loiselle, Greffier
Marcel Poirier, Maire

Duparquet
86, rue Principale
Duparquet, QC J0Z 1W0
819-948-2266 Fax: 819-948-2466
duparquet@mrcao.qc.ca
www.duparquet.ao.ca
Municipal Type: City
Incorporated: 13 avril 1933; *Area:* 157,40 km2
County or District: Abitibi-Ouest; *Population in 2006:* 639
Provincial Electoral District(s): Abitibi-Ouest
Federal Electoral District(s): Abitibi-Témiscamingue
Next Election: 1er novembre 2013
Éric Bergeron, Sec.-Trés.
Gilbert Rivard, Maire

Dupuy
CP 59
2 av du Chemin-de-Fer
Dupuy, QC J0Z 1X0
819-783-2595 Fax: 819-783-2595
dupuy@mrcao.qc.ca
www.dupuy.ao.ca
Municipal Type: Municipality
Incorporated: 20 septembre 1918; *Area:* 123,48 km2
County or District: Abitibi-Ouest; *Population in 2006:* 955
Provincial Electoral District(s): Abitibi-Ouest
Federal Electoral District(s): Abitibi-Témiscamingue
Next Election: 1er novembre 2013
Pascale Lavigne, Directrice générale

Durham-Sud
CP 70
70, rue de l'Hôtel-de-Ville
Durham-Sud, QC J0H 2C0
819-858-2044 Fax: 819-858-2044
mun@durham-sud.com
www.durham-sud.com
Municipal Type: Municipality
Incorporated: 1er novembre 1975; *Area:* 92,02 km2
County or District: Drummond; *Population in 2006:* 1,018
Provincial Electoral District(s): Johnson
Federal Electoral District(s): Drummond
Next Election: 1er novembre 2013
Christiane Bastien, Sec.-Trés.

East-Angus
49, rue Angus nord
East Angus, QC J0B 1R0
819-832-2868 Fax: 819-832-2938
eastangus@biz.videotron.ca
www.ville.east-angus.qc.ca
Municipal Type: City
Incorporated: 14 mars 1912; *Area:* 8,10 km2
County or District: Le Haut-St-François; *Population in 2006:* 3,357
Provincial Electoral District(s): Mégantic-Compton
Federal Electoral District(s): Compton-Stanstead
Next Election: 1er novembre 2013
Yves Desrochers, Greffier
Martin Mailhot, Maire

East Broughton
600, 10e av sud
East Broughton, QC G0N 1H0
418-427-2608 Fax: 418-427-3414
municipaliteeastbroughton@bellnet.ca
Municipal Type: Municipality
Incorporated: 5 janvier 1994; *Area:* 9,310 km2
County or District: Les Appalaches; *Population in 2009:* 2,365
Provincial Electoral District(s): Frontenac
Federal Electoral District(s): Mégantic-L'Érable
Next Election: 1er novembre 2013
Natalie Tanguay, Directrice générale

East Farnham
228, rue Principale
East Farnham, QC J2K 4T5
450-263-4252 Fax: 450-263-6131
eastfarnham@videotron.ca
www.eastfarnham.com
Municipal Type: Village
Incorporated: 27 août 1914; *Area:* 5,29 km2
County or District: Brome-Missisquoi; *Population in 2006:* 484
Provincial Electoral District(s): Brome-Missisquoi
Federal Electoral District(s): Brome-Missisquoi
Next Election: 1er novembre 2013
Madelyn Marcoux, Sec.-Trés.

East Hereford
15, rue de l'Église
East Hereford, QC J0B 1S0
819-844-2463 Fax: 819-844-2463
dlrioux@municipalite.easthereford.qc.ca
www.municipalite.easthereford.qc.ca
Municipal Type: Municipality
Incorporated: 1er juillet 1855; *Area:* 71,56 km2
County or District: Coaticook; *Population in 2006:* 401
Provincial Electoral District(s): Mégantic-Compton
Federal Electoral District(s): Compton-Stanstead
Next Election: 1er novembre 2013
Diane Lauzon-Rioux, Sec.-Trés.

Eastmain
147, Shabow Meskino
Eastmain, QC J0M 1W0
819-977-0211 Fax: 819-977-0281
Municipal Type: Villages Cris

Provincial Electoral District(s): Ungava
Federal Electoral District(s): Abitibi-Baie-James-Nunavik-Eeyou
Edwardh Gilpin, Jr., Maire

Eastman
160, ch George-Bonnallie
Eastman, QC J0E 1P0
450-297-3440 Fax: 450-297-3448
municipaliteeastman@bellnet.ca
Municipal Type: Municipality
Incorporated: 30 mai 2001; *Area:* 68,87 km2
County or District: Memphrémagog; *Population in 2006:* 1,585
Provincial Electoral District(s): Brome-Missisquoi
Federal Electoral District(s): Brome-Missisquoi
Next Election: 1er novembre 2013
Yvan Provencher, Directeur général

Egan-Sud
95, rte 105
Egan-Sud, QC J9E 3A9
819-449-1702 Fax: 819-449-7423
mun.egansud@ireseau.com
Municipal Type: Municipality
Incorporated: 17 novembre 1920; *Area:* 50,67 km2
County or District: La Vallée-de-la-Gatineau; *Population in 2006:* 508
Provincial Electoral District(s): Gatineau
Federal Electoral District(s): Pontiac
Next Election: 1er novembre 2013
Mariette Rochon, Sec.-Trés.

Elgin
933, 2e Concession
Elgin, QC J0S 1A0
450-264-2320 Fax: 450-264-6846
munelgin@rocler.qc.ca
Municipal Type: Township
Incorporated: 1er juillet 1855; *Area:* 69,38 km2
County or District: Le Haut-St-Laurent; *Population in 2006:* 458
Provincial Electoral District(s): Huntingdon
Federal Electoral District(s): Beauharnois-Salaberry
Next Election: 1er novembre 2013
Josée Taillefer, Sec.-Trés.

Entrelacs
2351, ch d'Entrelacs
Entrelacs, QC J0T 2E0
450-228-2529 Fax: 450-228-4866
info@entrelacs.com
www.entrelacs.com
Municipal Type: Municipality
Incorporated: 1er janvier 1860; *Area:* 51,78 km2
County or District: Matawinie; *Population in 2006:* 952
Provincial Electoral District(s): Bertrand
Federal Electoral District(s): Joliette
Next Election: 1er novembre 2013
Claude Comtois, Sec.-Trés. & Directeur général

Escuminac
13, rue de l'Église
Pointe-à-la-Garde, QC G0C 2M0
418-788-5644 Fax: 418-788-2613
munescuminac@globetrotter.net
Municipal Type: Municipality
Incorporated: 10 octobre 1907; *Area:* 109,55 km2
County or District: Avignon; *Population in 2006:* 645
Provincial Electoral District(s): Bonaventure
Federal Electoral District(s): Gaspésie-Iles-de-la-Madeleine
Next Election: 1er novembre 2013
Barbara Borris, Sec.-Trés.

Esprit-Saint
121, rue Principale
Esprit-Saint, QC G0K 1A0
418-779-2716 Fax: 418-779-2716
muni.esprit@globetrotter.net
Municipal Type: Municipality
Incorporated: 13 mai 1972; *Area:* 169,28 km2
County or District: Rimouski-Neigette; *Population in 2006:* 397
Provincial Electoral District(s): Rimouski
Federal Electoral District(s): Rimouski-Neigette-Témicouata-Les Basques
Next Election: 1er novembre 2013
Diane Ouellet, Sec.-Trés.

Estérel
CP 142
115, ch Dupuis
Estérel, QC J0T 1L0
450-228-3232 Fax: 450-228-3737
info@villedesterel.com
Municipal Type: City
Incorporated: 1er janvier 2006; *Area:* 12,06 km2
County or District: Les Pays-d'en-Haut; *Population in 2006:* 256
Provincial Electoral District(s): Bertrand
Federal Electoral District(s): Laurentides-Labelle
Next Election: 1er novembre 2013
André Nadeau, Maire
Luc Lafontaire, Sec.-Trés.

Farnham
477, rue de l'Hôtel-de-Ville
Farnham, QC J2N 2H3
450-293-3178 Fax: 450-293-2989
administration@ville.farnham.qc.ca
www.ville.farnham.qc.ca
Municipal Type: City
Incorporated: 8 mars 2000; *Area:* 92,53 km2
County or District: Brome-Missisquoi; *Population in 2006:* 7,809
Provincial Electoral District(s): Brome-Missisquoi
Federal Electoral District(s): Brome-Missisquoi
Next Election: 1er novembre 2013
Marielle Benoit, Greffière
Josef Hüsler, Maire

Fassett
19, rue Gendron
Fassett, QC J0V 1H0
819-423-6943 Fax: 819-423-5388
munfassett@videotron.ca
Municipal Type: Municipality
Incorporated: 1er juillet 1855; *Area:* 13,98 km2
County or District: Papineau; *Population in 2006:* 468
Provincial Electoral District(s): Papineau
Federal Electoral District(s): Argenteuil-Papineau-Mirabel
Next Election: 1er novembre 2013
Mireille Séguin, Sec.-Trés. & Directrice générale

Ferland-et-Boileau
CP 70
461, rte 381
Ferland-et-Boilleau, QC G0V 1H0
418-676-2282 Fax: 418-676-2681
munfb@royaume.com
www.royaume.com/~ferland
Municipal Type: Municipality
Incorporated: 1er janvier 1978; *Area:* 418,85 km2
County or District: Le Fjord-du-Saguenay; *Population in 2006:* 626
Provincial Electoral District(s): Dubuc
Federal Electoral District(s): Chicoutimi-Le Fjord
Next Election: 1er novembre 2013
Sylvie Gagnon, Sec.-Trés.

Ferme-Neuve
70, 12e rue
Ferme-Neuve, QC J0W 1C0
819-587-3400 Fax: 819-587-4733
bureau@municipalite.ferme-neuve.qc.ca
www.municipalite.ferme-neuve.qc.ca
Municipal Type: Municipality
Incorporated: 24 décembre 1997; *Area:* 1031,55 km2
County or District: Antoine-Labelle; *Population in 2006:* 3,006
Provincial Electoral District(s): Labelle
Federal Electoral District(s): Laurentides-Labelle
Next Election: 1er novembre 2013
Thérèse Boivin, Sec.-Trés. & Directrice générale

Fermont
CP 520
100, place Daviault
Fermont, QC G0G 1J0
418-287-5411 Fax: 418-287-5413
administration@villedefermont.qc.ca
Municipal Type: City
Incorporated: 15 octobre 1974; *Area:* 497,45 km2
County or District: Caniapiscau; *Population in 2006:* 2,633
Provincial Electoral District(s): Duplessis
Federal Electoral District(s): Manicouagan
Next Election: 1er novembre 2013
Carolle Bourque, Greffière
Lise Pelletier, Mairesse

Forestville
1, 2e av
Forestville, QC G0T 1E0
418-587-2285 Fax: 418-587-6212
forestville@forestville.ca
www.forestville.ca
Municipal Type: City
Incorporated: 5 janvier 1980; *Area:* 241,73 km2
County or District: La Haute Côte-Nord; *Population in 2006:* 3,543
Provincial Electoral District(s): René-Lévesque
Federal Electoral District(s): Montmorency-Charlevoix-Haute-Côte-Nord
Next Election: 1er novembre 2013
Jacques Beaulieu, Sec.-Trés. & Directeur général
Gaston Tremblay, Maire

Fort-Coulonge
CP 640
134, rue Principale
Fort-Coulonge, QC J0X 1V0
819-683-2259 Fax: 819-683-3627
m.fortin@bellnet.ca
www.fortcoulonge.qc.ca
Municipal Type: Village
Incorporated: 15 décembre 1888; *Area:* 3,44 km2
County or District: Pontiac; *Population in 2006:* 1,369
Provincial Electoral District(s): Pontiac
Federal Electoral District(s): Pontiac
Next Election: 1er novembre 2013
Ken Rose, Sec.-Trés.

Fortierville
198, rue de la Fabrique
Fortierville, QC G0S 1J0
819-287-5922 Fax: 819-287-0322
municipalite@fortierville.com
www.fortierville.com
Municipal Type: Municipality
Incorporated: 3 juin 1998; *Area:* 45,53 km2
County or District: Bécancour; *Population in 2006:* 702
Provincial Electoral District(s): Lotbinière
Federal Electoral District(s): Bas-Richelieu-Nicolet-Bécancour
Next Election: 1er novembre 2013
Annie Jacques, Sec.-Trés. & Directrice générale

Fossambault-sur-le-Lac
145, rue Gingras
Fossambault-sur-le-Lac, QC G0A 3M0
418-875-3133 Fax: 418-875-3544
fossam@coopcscf.com
www.fossambault-sur-le-lac.com

Municipal Type: City
Incorporated: 10 mars 1949; *Area:* 10,96 km2
County or District: La Jacques-Cartier; *Population in 2006:* 1,532
Provincial Electoral District(s): Portneuf
Federal Electoral District(s): Portneuf-Jacques-Cartier
Next Election: 1er novembre 2013
Johanne Bédard, Sec.-Trés.
Guy Maranda, Maire

Frampton
107, rue Ste-Anne
Frampton, QC G0R 1M0
418-479-5363 Fax: 418-479-5364
munframpton@globetrotter.net
Municipal Type: Municipality
Incorporated: 1er juillet 1855; *Area:* 150,76 km2
County or District: La Nouvelle-Beauce; *Population in 2006:* 1,314
Provincial Electoral District(s): Beauce-Nord
Federal Electoral District(s): Beauce
Next Election: 1er novembre 2013
Josée Audet, Sec.-Trés.

Franklin
1670, rte 202
Franklin, QC J0S 1E0
450-827-2538 Fax: 450-827-2640
franklin@qc.aira.com
Municipal Type: Municipality
Incorporated: 31 mars 1973; *Area:* 112,19 km2
County or District: Le Haut-St-Laurent; *Population in 2006:* 1,651
Provincial Electoral District(s): Huntingdon
Federal Electoral District(s): Beauharnois-Salaberry
Next Election: 1er novembre 2013
Francine Rivest, Directrice générale

Franquelin
CP 10
27, rue des Érables
Franquelin, QC G0H 1E0
418-296-1406 Fax: 418-296-6946
munic.franq@globetrotter.net
Municipal Type: Municipality
Incorporated: 1er janvier 1978; *Area:* 529,84 km2
County or District: Manicouagan; *Population in 2006:* 346
Provincial Electoral District(s): René-Lévesque
Federal Electoral District(s): Manicouagan
Next Election: 1er novembre 2013
Diane Cyr, Sec.-Trés. & Directrice générale

Frelighsburg
2, place de l'Hôtel-de-Ville
Frelighsburg, QC J0J 1C0
450-298-5133 Fax: 450-298-5557
municipalitefrelighsburg@qc.aira.com
Municipal Type: Municipality
Incorporated: 28 septembre 1985; *Area:* 123,27 km2
County or District: Brome-Missisquoi; *Population in 2006:* 1,030
Provincial Electoral District(s): Brome-Missisquoi
Federal Electoral District(s): Brome-Missisquoi
Next Election: 1er novembre 2013
Anne Pouleur, Sec.-Trés.

Frontenac
2430, rue St-Jean
Frontenac, QC G6B 2S1
819-583-3295 Fax: 819-583-0855
adm@municipalitefrontenac.qc.ca
www.municipalitefrontenac.qc.ca
Municipal Type: Municipality
Incorporated: 1er janvier 1882; *Area:* 225,71 km2
County or District: Le Granit; *Population in 2006:* 1,622
Provincial Electoral District(s): Mégantic-Compton
Federal Electoral District(s): Mégantic-L'Érable
Next Election: 1er novembre 2013
Bruno Turmel, Directeur général

Fugèreville
CP 831
43, rue Principale
Fugèreville, QC J0Z 2A0
819-748-3241 Fax: 819-748-2422
dg.fugereville@mrctemiscamingue.qc.ca
Municipal Type: Municipality
Incorporated: 5 février 1904; *Area:* 163,79 km2
County or District: Témiscamingue; *Population in 2006:* 301
Provincial Electoral District(s): Rouyn-Noranda-Témiscamingue
Federal Electoral District(s): Abitibi-Témiscamingue
Next Election: 1er novembre 2013
Marguerite Lachance, Sec.-Trés.

Gallichan
CP 38
207, ch de la Rivière ouest
Gallichan, QC J0Z 2B0
819-787-6092 Fax: 819-787-6015
gallichan@mrca.qc.ca
www.gallichan.ao.ca
Municipal Type: Municipality
Incorporated: 1er janvier 1958; *Area:* 73,32 km2
County or District: Abitibi-Ouest; *Population in 2006:* 458
Provincial Electoral District(s): Abitibi-Ouest
Federal Electoral District(s): Abitibi-Témiscamigue
Next Election: 1er novembre 2013
Johanne Shink, Sec.-Trés.

Girardville
180, rue Principale
Girardville, QC G0W 1R0
418-258-3293 Fax: 418-258-3473
admin@ville.girardville.qc.ca
ville.girardville.qc.ca
Municipal Type: Municipality
Incorporated: 11 novembre 1921; *Area:* 125,80 km2
County or District: Maria-Chapdelaine; *Population in 2006:* 1,186
Provincial Electoral District(s): Roberval
Federal Electoral District(s): Roberval-Lac-St-Jean
Next Election: 1er novembre 2013
Denis Desmeules, Sec.-Trés.

Godbout
CP 248
144, rue Pascal-Comeau
Godbout, QC G0H 1G0
418-568-7581 Fax: 418-568-7401
Municipal Type: Village
Incorporated: 1er janvier 1955; *Area:* 204,34 km2
County or District: Manicouagan; *Population in 2006:* 361
Provincial Electoral District(s): René-Lévesque
Federal Electoral District(s): Manicouagan
Next Election: 1er novembre 2013
Carolle Vallée, Sec.-Trés.

Godmanchester
2282, ch Ridge
Godmanchester, QC J0S 1H0
450-264-4116 Fax: 450-264-9749
godmanchester@intermobilex.com
Municipal Type: Township
Incorporated: 1er juillet 1855; *Area:* 138,77 km2
County or District: Le Haut-St-Laurent; *Population in 2006:* 1,457
Provincial Electoral District(s): Huntingdon
Federal Electoral District(s): Beauharnois-Salaberry
Next Election: 1er novembre 2013
Élaine Duhème, Sec.-Trés.

Gore
9, ch Cambria
Lakefield, QC J0V 1K0
450-562-2025 Fax: 450-562-5424
dchales@cantondegore.qc.ca
www.cantondegore.qc.ca
Municipal Type: Township
Incorporated: 1er juillet 1855; *Area:* 93,86 km2
County or District: Argenteuil; *Population in 2006:* 1,540
Provincial Electoral District(s): Argenteuil
Federal Electoral District(s): Argenteuil-Papineau-Mirabel
Next Election: 1er novembre 2013
Ron Kelley, Directeur général

Gracefield
CP 329
3, rue de la Polyvalente
Gracefield, QC J0X 1W0
819-463-3458 Fax: 819-463-4236
villedegracefield@bellnet.ca
Municipal Type: City
Incorporated: 13 mars 2002; *Area:* 386,95 km2
County or District: La Vallée-de-la-Gatineau; *Population in 2006:* 2,439
Provincial Electoral District(s): Gatineau
Federal Electoral District(s): Pontiac
Next Election: 1er novembre 2013
Note: Formerly known as Wright-Gracefield-Northfield.
Jean-Marie Gauthier, Greffier
Réal Rochon, Maire

Grand-Calumet
CP 130
8, rue Brizard
Ile-du-Grand-Calumet, QC J0X 1J0
819-648-5965 Fax: 819-648-2659
calumet@renc.igs.net
Municipal Type: Municipality
Incorporated: 1er juillet 1855; *Area:* 130,61 km2
County or District: Pontiac; *Population in 2006:* 785
Provincial Electoral District(s): Pontiac
Federal Electoral District(s): Pontiac
Next Election: 1er novembre 2013
Jacques Mantha, Sec.-Trés.

Grand-Métis
70, ch Kempt
Grand-Métis, QC G0J 1Z0
418-775-6485 Fax: 418-775-3591
grand-metis@globetrotter.net
Municipal Type: Municipality
Incorporated: 13 septembre 1855; *Area:* 25,85 km2
County or District: La Mitis; *Population in 2006:* 268
Provincial Electoral District(s): Matapédia
Federal Electoral District(s): Haute-Gaspésie-La Mitis-Matane-Matapédia
Next Election: 1er novembre 2013
Pierret Roy, Directrice générale

Grand-Remous
1508, rte Transcanadienne
Grand-Remous, QC J0W 1E0
819-438-2877 Fax: 819-438-2364
info@grandremous.ca
Municipal Type: Municipality
Incorporated: 29 avril 1937; *Area:* 386,55 km2
County or District: La Vallée-de-la-Gatineau; *Population in 2006:* 1,249
Provincial Electoral District(s): Gatineau
Federal Electoral District(s): Pontiac
Next Election: 1er novembre 2013
Betty McCarthy, Sec.-Trés.

Grand-St-Esprit
5410, rte Principale
Grand-Saint-Esprit, QC J0G 1B0
819-289-2410 Fax: 819-289-2029
municipalite@grandsaintesprit.qc.ca
www.grandsaintesprit.qc.ca
Municipal Type: Municipality
Incorporated: 14 mai 1938; *Area:* 28,41 km2
County or District: Nicolet-Yamaska; *Population in 2006:* 466
Provincial Electoral District(s): Nicolet-Yamaska
Federal Electoral District(s): Bas-Richelieu-Nicolet-Bécancour
Next Election: 1er novembre 2013
Nicole Larochelle, Sec.-Trés.

Grande-Rivière
CP 188
108, rue de l'Hôtel de Ville
Grande-Rivière, QC G0C 1V0
418-385-2282 Fax: 418-385-2290
villegr@globetrotter.net
Municipal Type: City
Incorporated: 21 septembre 1974; *Area:* 87,15 km2
County or District: Le Rocher Percé; *Population in 2006:* 3,409
Provincial Electoral District(s): Gaspé
Federal Electoral District(s): Gaspésie-Iles-de-la-Madeleine
Next Election: 1er novembre 2013
Romuald Boutin, Maire
Éliane Hotton-Beaulieu, Greffière

Grande-Vallée
CP 98
3, rue St-François-Xavier est
Grande-Vallée, QC G0E 1K0
418-393-2161 Fax: 418-393-2274
gvdiane@globetrotter.net
www.grande-vallee.ca
Municipal Type: Municipality
Incorporated: 15 septembre 1927; *Area:* 154,67 km2
County or District: La Côte-de-Gaspé; *Population in 2006:* 1,230
Provincial Electoral District(s): Gaspé
Federal Electoral District(s): Gaspésie-Iles-de-la-Madeleine
Next Election: 1er novembre 2013
Diane C.-Chicoine, Sec.-Trés. adjointe & Directrice générale adjointe

Grandes-Piles
630, 4e av
Grandes-Piles, QC G0X 1H0
819-538-9708 Fax: 819-538-6947
claire.angers@grandespiles.qc.ca
www.grandespiles.qc.ca
Municipal Type: Village
Incorporated: 10 août 1885; *Area:* 115,38 km2
County or District: Mékinac; *Population in 2006:* 350
Provincial Electoral District(s): Laviolette
Federal Electoral District(s): St-Maurice-Champlain
Next Election: 1er novembre 2013
Claire Angers, Directrice générale

Grenville
21, rue Tri-Jean
Grenville, QC J0V 1J0
819-242-2146 Fax: 819-242-5891
info@grenville.ca
www.grenville.ca
Municipal Type: Village
Incorporated: 1er janvier 1876; *Area:* 3,05 km2
County or District: Argenteuil; *Population in 2006:* 1,398
Provincial Electoral District(s): Argenteuil
Federal Electoral District(s): Argenteuil-Papineau-Mirabel
Next Election: 1er novembre 2013
Alain Léveillé, Directeur général

Grenville-sur-la-Rouge
40, rue Maple
Grenville, QC J0V 1J0
819-242-8762 Fax: 819-242-9341
info@grenvillesurlarouge.ca
www.grenvillesurlarouge.ca
Municipal Type: Municipality
Incorporated: 24 avril 2002; *Area:* 321,81 km2
County or District: Argenteuil; *Population in 2006:* 2,721
Provincial Electoral District(s): Argenteuil
Federal Electoral District(s): Argenteuil-Papineau-Mirabel
Next Election: 1er novembre 2013
Roger Brunette, Sec.-Trés. & Directeur général

Gros-Mécatina
CP 9
La Tabatière, QC G0G 1T0
418-773-2263 Fax: 418-773-2696
mun.grosmecatina@globetrotter.net
Municipal Type: Municipality
Incorporated: 1er janvier 1994; *Area:* 961,46 km2
Population in 2006: 566
Provincial Electoral District(s): Duplessis

Federal Electoral District(s): Manicouagan
Next Election: 1er novembre 2013
Randy Jones, Maire

Grosses-Roches
CP 69
122, rue de la Mer
Grosses-Roches, QC G0J 1K0
418-733-4273 Fax: 418-733-4273
mungrossesroches@globetrotter.net
Municipal Type: Municipality
Incorporated: 19 août 1939; *Area:* 63,99 km2
County or District: Matane; *Population in 2006:* 416
Provincial Electoral District(s): Matane
Federal Electoral District(s): Haute-Gaspésie-La Mitis-Matane-Matapédia
Next Election: 1er novembre 2013
Linda Imbeault, Sec.-Trés.

Guérin
CP 1040
#101, 516, rue St-Gabriel ouest
Guérin, QC J0Z 2E0
819-784-7011 Fax: 819-784-7012
mun.guerin@tlb.sympatico.ca
Municipal Type: Township
Incorporated: 8 novembre 1911; *Area:* 203,10 km2
County or District: Témiscamingue; *Population in 2006:* 295
Provincial Electoral District(s): Rouyn-Noranda-Témiscamingue
Federal Electoral District(s): Abitibi-Témiscamingue
Next Election: 1er novembre 2013
Doris Gauthier, Sec.-Trés.

Ham-Nord
CP 1271
474, rue Principale
Ham-Nord, QC G0P 1A0
819-344-2424 Fax: 819-344-2805
hamnord@nplus.ca
Municipal Type: Township
Incorporated: 1er janvier 1864; *Area:* 101,60 km2
County or District: Arthabaska; *Population in 2006:* 890
Provincial Electoral District(s): Richmond
Federal Electoral District(s): Richmond-Arthabaska
Next Election: 1er novembre 2013
Aline Lemieux, Sec.-Trés.

Hampden
CP 1055
863, rte 257 nord
Hampden, QC J0B 1Y0
819-657-4942 Fax: 819-657-2974
info@municipalitehampden.ca
Municipal Type: Township
Incorporated: 1er janvier 1874; *Area:* 110,10 km2
County or District: Le Haut-St-François; *Population in 2006:* 209
Provincial Electoral District(s): Mégantic-Compton
Federal Electoral District(s): Compton-Stanstead
Next Election: 1er novembre 2013
Diane Carrier, Directrice générale

Harrington
2811, rte 327
Harrington, QC J8G 2T1
819-687-2122 Fax: 819-687-8610
l.lafontaine@harrington.ca
www.harrington.ca
Municipal Type: Township
Incorporated: 1er juillet 1855; *Area:* 243,87 km2
County or District: Argenteuil; *Population in 2006:* 777
Provincial Electoral District(s): Argenteuil
Federal Electoral District(s): Argenteuil-Papineau-Mirabel
Next Election: 1er novembre 2013
Luc Lafontaine, Sec.-Trés.

Hatley
135, rue Main
North Hatley, QC J0B 2C0
819-842-2977 Fax: 819-842-2639
cantondehatley@municipalite.org
www.cantondehatley.ca
Municipal Type: Township
Incorporated: 1er juillet 1855; *Area:* 71,51 km2
County or District: Memphrémagog; *Population in 2009:* 1,809
Provincial Electoral District(s): Orford
Federal Electoral District(s): Compton-Stanstead
Next Election: 1er novembre 2013
Liane Breton, Directrice générale

Hatley
2100, rte 143
Hatley, QC J0B 4B0
819-838-5877 Fax: 819-838-4646
hatley@xplornet.com
Municipal Type: Municipality
Incorporated: 27 juillet 1995; *Area:* 60,67 km2
County or District: Memphrémagog; *Population in 2009:* 804
Provincial Electoral District(s): Orford
Federal Electoral District(s): Compton-Stanstead
Next Election: 1er novembre 2013
Roland Gascon, Directeur général

Havelock
481, rte 203
Havelock, QC J0S 2C0
450-826-4741 Fax: 450-826-4800
mun.havelock@bellnet.ca
Municipal Type: Township
Incorporated: 1er avril 1863; *Area:* 87,98 km2
County or District: Le Haut-St-Laurent; *Population in 2006:* 761
Provincial Electoral District(s): Huntingdon
Federal Electoral District(s): Beauharnois-Salaberry
Next Election: 1er novembre 2013
Linda Logan, Sec.-Trés.

Havre-Saint-Pierre
#01, 1235, rue de la Digue
Hâvre-Saint-Pierre, QC G0G 1P0
418-538-2717 Fax: 418-538-3439
info@havresaintpierre.com
www.havresaintpierre.com
Municipal Type: Municipality
Incorporated: 1er janvier 1873; *Area:* 3779,89 km2
County or District: Minganie; *Population in 2006:* 3,150
Provincial Electoral District(s): Duplessis
Federal Electoral District(s): Manicouagan
Next Election: 1er novembre 2013
Roger Vigneault, Sec.-Trés.

Hébertville
351, rue Turgeon
Hébertville, QC G8N 1S8
418-344-1302 Fax: 418-344-4618
guy@ville.hebertville.qc.ca
www.ville.hebertville.qc.ca
Municipal Type: Municipality
Incorporated: 16 décembre 1972; *Area:* 263,88 km2
County or District: Lac-St-Jean-Est; *Population in 2006:* 2,421
Provincial Electoral District(s): Lac-St-Jean
Federal Electoral District(s): Roberval-Lac-St-Jean
Next Election: 1er novembre 2013
Guy Larouche, Sec.-Trés.

Hébertville-Station
6, rue Tremblay
Hébertville-Station, QC G0W 1T0
418-343-3961 Fax: 418-343-2349
serge@hebertvillestation.com
Municipal Type: Village
Incorporated: 18 février 1903; *Area:* 33,28 km2
County or District: Lac-St-Jean-Est; *Population in 2006:* 1,230
Provincial Electoral District(s): Lac-St-Jean
Federal Electoral District(s): Roberval-Lac-St-Jean
Next Election: 1er novembre 2013
Serge Martel, Directeur général

Hemmingford
#3, 505, rue Frontière
Hemmingford, QC J0L 1H0
450-247-2050 Fax: 450-247-3283
greffe_canton_hemmingford@bellnet.ca
Municipal Type: Township
Incorporated: 1er juillet 1855; *Area:* 155,78 km2
County or District: Les Jardins-de-Napierville; *Population in 2006:* 1,763
Provincial Electoral District(s): Huntingdon
Federal Electoral District(s): Beauharnois-Salaberry
Next Election: 1er novembre 2013
Margaret Hess, Directrice générale

Hemmingford
#5, 505, rue Frontière
Hemmingford, QC J0L 1H0
450-247-3310 Fax: 450-247-2389
villagehford@b2b2c.ca
Municipal Type: Village
Incorporated: 1er janvier 1878; *Area:* 0,85 km2
County or District: Les Jardins-de-Napierville; *Population in 2006:* 757
Provincial Electoral District(s): Huntingdon
Federal Electoral District(s): Beauharnois-Salaberry
Next Election: 1er novembre 2013
Diane Lawrence, Sec.-Trés.

Henryville
165, rue de l'Église
Henryville, QC J0J 1E0
450-299-2655 Fax: 450-299-2355
cveilleux.munhenryville@netc.net
www.municipalite-henryville.com
Municipal Type: Municipality
Incorporated: 15 décembre 1999; *Area:* 64,87 km2
County or District: Le Haut-Richelieu; *Population in 2006:* 1,529
Provincial Electoral District(s): Iberville
Federal Electoral District(s): Brome-Missisquoi
Next Election: 1er novembre 2013
Diane Lemieux, Sec.-Trés.

Hérouxville
1060, rue St-Pierre
Hérouxville, QC G0X 1J0
418-365-7135 Fax: 418-365-7041
herouxville@regionmekinac.com
Municipal Type: Parish (Paroisse)
Incorporated: 13 avril 1904; *Area:* 54,51 km2
County or District: Mékinac; *Population in 2006:* 1,235
Provincial Electoral District(s): Laviolette
Federal Electoral District(s): St-Maurice-Champlain
Next Election: 1er novembre 2013
Denise Cossette, Sec.-Trés.

Hinchinbrooke
1056, ch Brook
Hinchinbrooke, QC J0S 1A0
450-264-5353 Fax: 450-264-3787
munhinch@rocler.qc.ca
Municipal Type: Township
Incorporated: 1er juillet 1855; *Area:* 148,95 km2
County or District: Le Haut-St-Laurent; *Population in 2006:* 2,369
Provincial Electoral District(s): Huntingdon
Federal Electoral District(s): Beauharnois-Salaberry
Next Election: 1er novembre 2013
Kevin Neal, Sec.-Trés.

Honfleur
320, rue St-Jean
Honfleur, QC G0R 1N0
418-885-9195 Fax: 418-885-9195
livro@globetrotter.qc.ca
Municipal Type: Municipality
Incorporated: 5 mars 1915; *Area:* 50,99 km2
County or District: Bellechasse; *Population in 2006:* 794
Provincial Electoral District(s): Bellechasse
Federal Electoral District(s): Lévis-Bellechasse
Next Election: 1er novembre 2013
Jocelyne G. Paré, Sec.-Trés. & Directrice générale

Hope
330, rte 132
Hope, QC G0C 2K0
418-752-3212 Fax: 418-752-6986
mun.hope@globetrotter.net
Municipal Type: Township
Incorporated: 1er juillet 1855; *Area:* 71,45 km2
County or District: Bonaventure; *Population in 2006:* 878
Provincial Electoral District(s): Bonaventure
Federal Electoral District(s): Gaspésie-Iles-de-la-Madeleine
Next Election: 1er novembre 2013
Nancy Castilloux, Directrice générale

Hope Town
CP 146
209, rte 132 ouest
Hope Town, QC G0C 3C0
418-752-2137 Fax: 418-752-2137
Municipal Type: Municipality
Incorporated: 21 novembre 1936; *Area:* 49,80 km2
County or District: Bonaventure; *Population in 2006:* 347
Provincial Electoral District(s): Bonaventure
Federal Electoral District(s): Gaspésie-Iles-de-la-Madeleine
Next Election: 1er novembre 2013
Gisèle Delarosbil, Sec.-Trés.

Howick
51, rue Colville
Howick, QC J0S 1G0
450-825-2032 Fax: 450-825-0026
municipalite@villagehowick.com
Municipal Type: Village
Incorporated: 29 octobre 1915; *Area:* 0,89 km2
County or District: Le Haut-St-Laurent; *Population in 2006:* 606
Provincial Electoral District(s): Huntingdon
Federal Electoral District(s): Beauharnois-Salaberry
Next Election: 1er novembre 2013
Yves Galbrand, Sec.-Trés. & Directeur général

Huberdeau
101, rue du Pont
Huberdeau, QC J0T 1G0
819-687-8321 Fax: 819-687-8808
info@municipalite.huberdeau.qc.ca
Municipal Type: Municipality
Incorporated: 8 juin 1926; *Area:* 57,18 km2
County or District: Les Laurentides; *Population in 2006:* 924
Provincial Electoral District(s): Labelle
Federal Electoral District(s): Laurentides-Labelle
Next Election: 1er novembre 2013
Guylaine Maurice, Sec.-Trés.

Hudson
CP 550
481, rue Principale
Hudson, QC J0P 1H0
450-458-5348 Fax: 450-458-4922
vdh@videotron.ca
www.ville.hudson.qc.ca
Municipal Type: City
Incorporated: 7 juin 1969; *Area:* 21,62 km2
County or District: Vaudreuil-Soulanges; *Population in 2006:* 5,088
Provincial Electoral District(s): Vaudreuil
Federal Electoral District(s): Vaudreuil-Soulanges
Next Election: 1er novembre 2013
Louise L.-Villandré, Sec.-Trés.
Élizabeth Corker, Mairesse

Huntingdon
23, rue King
Huntingdon, QC J0S 1H0
450-264-5389 Fax: 450-264-6826
directiongenerale@villehuntingdon.com
Municipal Type: City
Incorporated: 9 octobre 1848; *Area:* 2,58 km2
County or District: Le Haut-St-Laurent; *Population in 2006:* 2,587
Provincial Electoral District(s): Huntingdon
Federal Electoral District(s): Beauharnois-Salaberry
Next Election: 1er novembre 2013

Diane Giguère, Greffière
Stéphane Gendron, Maire

Inukjuak
CP 234
Inukjuak, QC J0M 1M0
819-254-8822 Fax: 819-254-8779
cnaktialuk@nvinukjuak.ca
www.nvinukjuak.ca
Municipal Type: Northern Village
Incorporated: 7 juin 1980; *Area:* 64,45 km2
County or District: Nord-du-Québec; *Population in 2006:* 1,597
Provincial Electoral District(s): Ungava
Federal Electoral District(s): Abitibi-Baie-James-Nunavil-Eeyou
Next Election: 7 novembre 2007
Caroline Naktialuk, Sec.-Trés.

Inverness
CP 129
1799, rte Dublin
Inverness, QC G0S 1K0
418-453-2512 Fax: 418-453-2554
muni.inverness@bellnet.ca
www.municipaliteinverness.ca
Municipal Type: Municipality
Incorporated: 9 septembre 1998; *Area:* 176,35 km2
County or District: L'Érable; *Population in 2006:* 838
Provincial Electoral District(s): Lotbinière
Federal Electoral District(s): Mégantic-L'Érable
Next Election: 1er novembre 2013
Sonia Tardif, Sec.-Trés. & Directrice générale

Irlande
157, ch Gosford
Irlande, QC G6H 2N7
418-428-9216 Fax: 418-428-4262
mundirlande@bellnet.ca
Municipal Type: Municipality
Incorporated: 1er juillet 1855; *Area:* 110,200 km2
County or District: Les Appalaches; *Population in 2009:* 988
Provincial Electoral District(s): Frontenac
Federal Electoral District(s): Mégantic-L'Érable
Next Election: 1er novembre 2013
Christiane Laroche, Directrice générale

Ivujivik
CP 20
Ivujivik, QC J0M 1H0
819-922-9940 Fax: 819-922-3045
aulla@nvivujivik.ca
www.nvivujivik.ca
Municipal Type: Northern Village
Incorporated: 27 juin 1981; *Area:* 36,59 km2
County or District: Kativik; *Population in 2006:* 349
Provincial Electoral District(s): Ungava
Federal Electoral District(s): Abitibi-Baie-James-Nunavik-Eeyou
Next Election: 7 novembre 2007
Aulla Qaunnaaluk, Sec.-Trés.

Joliette
632, rue De Lanaudière
Joliette, QC J6E 3M7
450-759-2237 Fax: 450-759-2597
info@mrcjoliette.qc.ca
www.mrcjoliette.qc.ca
Municipal Type: Regional County Municipality

Population in 2009: 59,329
Note: 10 municipalités.
Line Laporte, Directrice générale

Kamouraska
67, av Morel
Kamouraska, QC G0L 1M0
418-492-6523 Fax: 418-492-6523
munkam@videotron.ca
www.kamouraska.ca
Municipal Type: Municipality
Incorporated: 25 avril 1987; *Area:* 40,81 km2
County or District: Kamouraska; *Population in 2006:* 705
Provincial Electoral District(s): Kamouraska-Témiscouata
Federal Electoral District(s):
Montmagny-L'Islet-Kamouraska-Rivière-du-Loup
Next Election: 1er novembre 2013
Mychelle Lévesque, Sec.-Trés.

Kamouraska
CP 1120
425, av Patry
Saint-Pascal, QC G0L 3Y0
418-492-1660 Fax: 418-492-2220
info@mrckamouraska.com
www.mrckamouraska.com
Municipal Type: Regional County Municipality
Incorporated: 1 janvier 1982;
Population in 2009: 22,055
Note: 17 municipalités & 2 autres territoires.
Guy Lavoie, Directeur général

Kangiqsualujjuaq
CP 120
Kangiqsualujjuaq, QC J0M 1N0
819-337-5271 Fax: 819-337-5200
www.nvkangiqsualujjuaq.ca
Municipal Type: Northern Village
Incorporated: 2 février 1980; *Area:* 36,23 km2
County or District: Nord-du-Québec; *Population in 2006:* 735
Provincial Electoral District(s): Ungava
Federal Electoral District(s): Abitibi-Baie-James-Nunavik-Eeyou
Next Election: 7 novembre 2007
Tommy Annanack, Sec.-Trés.

Kangiqsujuaq
CP 60
Kangiqsujuaq, QC J0M 1K0
819-338-3342 Fax: 819-338-3237
mayor@nvkangiqsujuaq.ca
Municipal Type: Northern Village
Incorporated: 20 septembre 1980; *Area:* 12,47 km2
County or District: Nord-du-Québec; *Population in 2006:* 605
Provincial Electoral District(s): Ungava
Federal Electoral District(s): Abitibi-Baie-James-Nunavik-Eeyou
Next Election: 7 novembre 2007
Pasa Kiatainaq, Sec.-Trés.

Kangirsuk
CP 90
Kangirsuk, QC J0M 1A0
819-935-4388 Fax: 819-935-4287
Municipal Type: Northern Village
Incorporated: 17 janvier 1981; *Area:* 58,73 km2
County or District: Nord-du-Québec; *Population in 2006:* 466
Provincial Electoral District(s): Ungava
Federal Electoral District(s): Abitibi-Baie-James-Nunavik-Eeyou
Next Election: 7 novembre 2007
Alec Kudluk, Sec.-Trés.

Kawawachikamach
CP 5111
Kawawachikamach, QC G0G 2Z0
418-585-2686 Fax: 418-585-3130
kawawa@naskapi.ca
www.naskapi.ca
Municipal Type: Villages Naskapi
Area: 284.7 sq. km
County or District: Kativik;
Provincial Electoral District(s): Duplessis
Federal Electoral District(s): Manicouagan
Jimmy James Einish, Maire

Kazabazua
CP 10
30, ch Begley
Kazabazua, QC J0X 1X0
819-467-2852 Fax: 819-467-3872
munkaz@qc.aibn.com
Municipal Type: Municipality
Incorporated: 1er janvier 1862; *Area:* 175,49 km2
County or District: La Vallée-de-la-Gatineau; *Population in 2006:* 839
Provincial Electoral District(s): Gatineau
Federal Electoral District(s): Pontiac
Next Election: 1er novembre 2013
Josée Parsons, Sec.-Trés. & Directeur général

Kiamika
3, ch Valiquette
Kiamika, QC J0W 1G0
819-585-3225 Fax: 819-585-3992
mun.kiamika@tlb.sympatico.ca
Municipal Type: Municipality
Incorporated: 3 janvier 1898; *Area:* 348,25 km2
County or District: Antoine-Labelle; *Population in 2006:* 779
Provincial Electoral District(s): Labelle
Federal Electoral District(s): Laurentides-Labelle
Next Election: 1er novembre 2013
Josée Lacasse, Directrice générale

Kingsbury
370, rue du Moulin
Kingsbury, QC J0B 1X0
819-826-2527 Fax: 819-826-2520
kingsbury@qc.aira.com
Municipal Type: Village
Incorporated: 7 juillet 1896; *Area:* 6,26 km2
County or District: Le Val-St-François; *Population in 2006:* 99
Provincial Electoral District(s): Richmond
Federal Electoral District(s): Richmond-Arthabaska
Next Election: 1er novembre 2013
Yves Barthe, Sec.-Trés.

Kingsey Falls
CP 270
15, rue Caron
Kingsey Falls, QC J0A 1B0
819-363-3810 Fax: 819-363-3819
villedekingsey@cablovision.com
Municipal Type: City
Incorporated: 31 décembre 1997; *Area:* 70,14 km2
County or District: Arthabaska; *Population in 2006:* 2,086
Provincial Electoral District(s): Richmond
Federal Electoral District(s): Richmond-Arthabaska
Next Election: 1er novembre 2013
Gino Dubé, Greffier & Directeur général
Micheline Pinard-Lampron, Mairesse

Kinnear's Mills
120, rue des Églises
Kinnear's Mills, QC G0N 1K0
418-424-3377 Fax: 418-424-3015
munikin@gabskycom.com
www.kinnearsmills.com
Municipal Type: Municipality
Incorporated: 1er juillet 1855; *Area:* 93,180 km2
County or District: Les Appalaches; *Population in 2009:* 359
Provincial Electoral District(s): Frontenac
Federal Electoral District(s): Mégantic-L'Érable
Next Election: 1er novembre 2013
Nancy Richard, Directrice générale

Kipawa
15, rue Principale
Kipawa, QC J0Z 2H0
819-627-3500 Fax: 819-627-1067
kipawa@mrctemiscamingue.qc.ca
Municipal Type: Municipality
Incorporated: 1er janvier 1985; *Area:* 47,20 km2
County or District: Témiscamingue; *Population in 2006:* 565
Provincial Electoral District(s): Rouyn-Noranda-Témiscamingue
Federal Electoral District(s): Abitibi-Témiscamingue
Next Election: 1er novembre 2013
Monique Savard, Directrice générale

Kuujjuaq
CP 210
528, rue Airport
Kuujjuaq, QC J0M 1C0
819-964-2943 Fax: 819-964-2980
webmail@nvkuujjuaq.qc.ca
www.nvkuujjuaq.ca
Municipal Type: Northern Village
Incorporated: 29 décembre 1979; *Area:* 390,33 km2
County or District: Kativik; *Population in 2006:* 2,132
Provincial Electoral District(s): Ungava
Federal Electoral District(s): Abitibi-Baie-James-Nunavik-Eeyou
Next Election: 7 novembre 2007
Ian D. Robertson, Sec.-Trés.

Kuujjuarapik
CP 360
403, av Katimavik
Kuujjuarapik, QC J0M 1G0
819-929-3360 Fax: 819-929-3453
proussel@nkuujjaraapik.ca
Municipal Type: Northern Village
Incorporated: 7 juin 1980; *Area:* 7,46 km2
County or District: Kativik; *Population in 2006:* 568
Provincial Electoral District(s): Ungava
Federal Electoral District(s): Abitibi-Baie-James-Nunavik-Eeyou
Next Election: 7 novembre 2007
Pierre Roussel, Sec.-Trés.

L'Ange-Gardien
870, ch Donaldson
L'Ange-Gardien, QC J8L 2W7
819-986-7470 Fax: 819-986-8349
adm@ville.lange-gardien.qc.ca
www.ville.lange-gardien.qc.ca
Municipal Type: Municipality
Incorporated: 17 mai 1979; *Area:* 224,17 km2
County or District: Les Collines-de-l'Outaouais; *Population in 2006:* 4,348
Provincial Electoral District(s): Papineau
Federal Electoral District(s): Pontiac
Next Election: 1er novembre 2013
Alain Descarreaux, Sec.-Trés.

L'Ange-Gardien
6405, av Royale
L'Ange-Gardien, QC G0A 2K0
418-822-1555 Fax: 418-822-2526
mun-langegardien@bellnet.ca
www.langegardien.qc.ca
Municipal Type: Parish (Paroisse)
Incorporated: 1er juillet 1855; *Area:* 50,67 km2
County or District: La Côte-de-Beaupré; *Population in 2006:* 3,008
Provincial Electoral District(s): Montmorency
Federal Electoral District(s):
Montmorency-Charlevoix-Haute-Côte-Nord
Next Election: 1er novembre 2013
Lise Drouin, Sec.-Trés. & Directrice générale

L'Anse-St-Jean
3, rue du Couvent
L'Anse-Saint-Jean, QC G0V 1J0
418-272-2633 Fax: 418-272-3148
lansesaintjean@royaume.com
www.lanse-saint-jean.ca
Municipal Type: Municipality
Incorporated: 1er janvier 1859; *Area:* 527,06 km2
County or District: Le Fjord-du-Saguenay; *Population in 2006:* 1,088
Provincial Electoral District(s): Dubuc
Federal Electoral District(s): Chicoutimi-Le Fjord
Next Election: 1er novembre 2013
Lolita Boudreault, Sec.-Trés.

L'Ascension
CP 30
59, rue de l'Hôtel-de-Ville
L'Ascension, QC J0T 1W0
819-275-3027 Fax: 819-275-3489
ascensiondg@xplornet.com
Municipal Type: Municipality
Incorporated: 23 septembre 1905; *Area:* 342,83 km2

County or District: Antoine-Labelle; *Population in 2006:* 861
Provincial Electoral District(s): Labelle
Federal Electoral District(s): Laurentides-Labelle
Next Election: 1er novembre 2013
Hélène Beauchamp, Directrice générale

L'Ascension-de-Notre-Seigneur
CP 100
1000, 1re rue est
L'Ascension-de-Notre-Seigneur, QC G0W 1Y0
418-347-3482 Fax: 418-347-4253
normand.desgagne@ville.ascension.qc.ca
www.ville.ascension.qc.ca
Municipal Type: Parish (Paroisse)
Incorporated: 25 février 1919; *Area:* 131,83 km2
County or District: Lac-St-Jean-Est; *Population in 2006:* 1,976
Provincial Electoral District(s): Lac-St-Jean
Federal Electoral District(s): Roberval-Lac-St-Jean
Next Election: 1er novembre 2013
Normand Desgagné, Sec.-Trés.

L'Ascension-de-Patapédia
CP 9
82, rue Principale
L'Ascension-de-Patapédia, QC G0J 1R0
418-299-2024 Fax: 418-299-2027
munic@globetrotter.qc.ca
Municipal Type: Municipality
Incorporated: 1er janvier 1968; *Area:* 95,38 km2
County or District: Avignon; *Population in 2006:* 214
Provincial Electoral District(s): Bonaventure
Federal Electoral District(s): Gaspésie-Iles-de-la-Madeleine
Next Election: 1er novembre 2013
Marie-Jeanne Gallant, Sec.-Trés.

L'Assomption
300A, rue Dorval
L'Assomption, QC J5W 3A1
450-589-2288 Fax: 450-589-9430
mrcinfo@mrclassomption.qc.ca
www.mrclassomption.qc.ca
Municipal Type: Regional County Municipality

Population in 2009: 113,413
Note: 6 municipalités.
Michel C. Gagnon, Directeur général

L'Avenir
545, rue Principale
L'Avenir, QC J0C 1B0
819-394-2422 Fax: 819-394-2222
municipaliteavenir@9bit.com
Municipal Type: Municipality
Incorporated: 23 décembre 1976; *Area:* 96,47 km2
County or District: Drummond; *Population in 2006:* 1,262
Provincial Electoral District(s): Johnson
Federal Electoral District(s): Drummond
Next Election: 1er novembre 2013
Andrée Béland, Sec.-Trés.

L'Épiphanie
331, rang du Bas-de-l'Achigan
L'Épiphanie, QC J5X 1E1
450-588-5547 Fax: 450-588-6050
mun@paroisse-lepiphanie.com
www.epiphanie.net
Municipal Type: Parish (Paroisse)
Incorporated: 1er juillet 1855; *Area:* 55,32 km2
County or District: L'Assomption; *Population in 2006:* 3,129
Provincial Electoral District(s): Rousseau
Federal Electoral District(s): Repentigny
Next Election: 1er novembre 2013
Nicole Renaud, Sec.-Trés.

L'Épiphanie
66, rue Notre-Dame
L'Épiphanie, QC J5X 1A1
450-588-5515 Fax: 450-588-6171
courrier@ville.lepiphanie.qc.ca
www.ville.lepiphanie.qc.ca
Municipal Type: City
Incorporated: 30 juin 1967; *Area:* 2,46 km2
County or District: L'Assomption; *Population in 2006:* 4,606
Provincial Electoral District(s): Rousseau
Federal Electoral District(s): Repentigny
Next Election: 1er novembre 2013
Luc Amireault, Greffier & Directeur général
Benoît Verstraete, Maire

L'Érable
#300, 1783, av St-Édouard
Plessisville, QC G6L 3S7
819-362-2333 Fax: 819-362-9150
info@mrc-erable.qc.ca
www.mrc-erable.qc.ca
Municipal Type: Regional County Municipality
Incorporated: 1 janvier 1982;
Population in 2009: 23,209
Note: 11 municipalités.
Rick Lavergne, Directeur général

L'Ile-Cadieux
50, ch de l'Ile
Ile-Cadieux, QC J7V 8P3
450-424-4273 Fax: 450-424-6327
secretaire.ilecadieux@videotron.ca
www.ilecadieux.ca
Municipal Type: City
Incorporated: 21 mars 1922; *Area:* 0,62 km2
County or District: Vaudreuil-Soulanges; *Population in 2006:* 128
Provincial Electoral District(s): Vaudreuil
Federal Electoral District(s): Vaudreuil-Soulanges
Next Election: 1er novembre 2013
Sylvie La Barre, Sec.-Trés.
Marc-André Léger, Maire

L'Ile-d'Anticosti
CP 119
25B, ch des Forestiers
Port-Menier, QC G0G 2Y0
418-535-0311 Fax: 418-535-0381
munanticosti@xplornet.com
Municipal Type: Municipality
Incorporated: 1er janvier 1984; *Area:* 7923,16 km2
County or District: Minganie; *Population in 2006:* 281
Provincial Electoral District(s): Duplessis
Federal Electoral District(s): Manicouagan
Next Election: 1er novembre 2013
Gilles Ruest, Sec.-Trés.

L'Isle-aux-Allumettes
CP 100
75, rue Notre-Dame
L'Isle-aux-Allumettes, QC J0X 1M0
819-689-2266 Fax: 819-689-5619
administration@municipalite.lisle-aux-allumettes.qc.ca
Municipal Type: Municipality
Incorporated: 30 décembre 1998; *Area:* 190,19 km2
County or District: Pontiac; *Population in 2006:* 1,443
Provincial Electoral District(s): Pontiac
Federal Electoral District(s): Pontiac
Next Election: 1er novembre 2013
Richard Vaillancourt, Sec.-Trés.

L'Isle-aux-Coudres
1026, ch des Coudriers
L'Isle-aux-Coudres, QC G0A 3J0
418-438-2583 Fax: 418-438-2750
municipaliteiac@charlevoix.qc.ca
Municipal Type: Municipality
Incorporated: 23 août 2000; *Area:* 29,54 km2
County or District: Charlevoix; *Population in 2006:* 1,296
Provincial Electoral District(s): Charlevoix
Federal Electoral District(s):
Montmorency-Charevoix-Haute-Côte-Nord
Next Election: 1er novembre 2013
Marie Dufour, Sec.-Trés.

L'Isle-Verte
CP 159
141, rue St-Jean-Baptiste
L'Isle-Verte, QC G0L 1K0
418-898-2812 Fax: 418-898-2788
munisle.verte@qc.aira.com
www.municipalite-isle-verte.qc.ca
Municipal Type: Municipality
Incorporated: 9 février 2000; *Area:* 112,33 km2
County or District: Rivière-du-Loup; *Population in 2006:* 1,464
Provincial Electoral District(s): Rivière-du-Loup
Federal Electoral District(s):
Montmagny-L'Islet-Kamouraska-Rivière-du-Loup
Next Election: 1er novembre 2013
Guy Bérubé, Sec.-Trés. & Directeur général

L'Islet
284, boul Nilus-Leclerc
L'Islet, QC G0R 2C0
418-247-3060 Fax: 418-247-5085
muni-islet@globetrotter.net
www.lislet.com
Municipal Type: Municipality
Incorporated: 1er janvier 2000; *Area:* 176,800 km2
County or District: L'Islet; *Population in 2009:* 3,904
Provincial Electoral District(s): Montmagny-L'Islet
Federal Electoral District(s):
Montmagny-L'Islet-Kamouraska-Rivière-du-Loup
Next Election: 1er novembre 2013
Colette Lord, Sec.-trés.

L'Islet
364, rue Verreault
Saint-Jean-Port-Joli, QC G0R 3G0
418-598-3076 Fax: 418-598-6880
administration@mrclislet.com
www.mrclislet.com
Municipal Type: Regional County Municipality
Incorporated: 1er janvier 1982; *Area:* 2 091,92 km2
Population in 2009: 19,010
Note: 14 municipalités.
Michel Pelletier, Directeur général

L'Ile-d'Orléans
3896, ch Royal
Sainte-Famille, QC G0A 3P0
418-829-1011 Fax: 418-829-2513
www.mrcio.qc.ca
Municipal Type: Regional County Municipality
Incorporated: 1 janvier 1982;
Population in 2009: 6,893
Note: 6 municipalités.
Chantale Cormier, Directrice générale

La Conception
1371, rue du Centenaire
La Conception, QC J0T 1M0
819-686-3016 Fax: 819-686-5808
jdlarocque@municipalite.laconception.qc.ca
Municipal Type: Municipality
Incorporated: 1er janvier 1882; *Area:* 142,61 km2
County or District: Les Laurentides; *Population in 2006:* 1,283
Provincial Electoral District(s): Labelle
Federal Electoral District(s): Laurentides-Labelle
Next Election: 1er novembre 2013
Jean-Denis Larocque, Directeur général

La Corne
324, rte 111
La Corne, QC J0Y 1R0
819-799-3571 Fax: 819-799-3572
mun.lacorne@cableamos.com
Municipal Type: Municipality
Incorporated: 2 août 1975; *Area:* 331,54 km2
County or District: Abitibi; *Population in 2006:* 682
Provincial Electoral District(s): Abitibi-Ouest
Federal Electoral District(s): Abitibi-Témiscamingue
Next Election: 1er novembre 2013
Kathleen Guévin, Sec.-Trés.

La Côte-de-Beaupré
3, rue de la Seigneurie
Château-Richer, QC G0A 1N0
418-824-3444 Fax: 418-824-3917
info@mrccotedebeaupre.qc.ca
Municipal Type: Regional County Municipality
Incorporated: 1 janvier 1982;
Population in 2009: 23,675
Note: 9 municipalités & 2 autres territoires.
Chantal Hamel, Greffière

La Côte-de-Gaspé
CP 57
187, boul Renard ouest
Rivière-au-Renard, QC G4X 5B1
418-269-7718 Fax: 418-269-5419
mrc@mrccotegaspe.net
Municipal Type: Regional County Municipality
Incorporated: 1 janvier 1982;
Population in 2009: 18,060
Note: 5 municipalités & 2 autres territoires.
Pierre R. Charron, Directeur général

La Doré
5000, rue des Peupliers
La Doré, QC G8J 1E8
418-256-3545 Fax: 418-256-3496
info@municipalite.ladore.qc.ca
www.municipalite.ladore.qc.ca
Municipal Type: Parish (Paroisse)
Incorporated: 16 mars 1906; *Area:* 280,83 km2
County or District: Le Domaine-du-Roy; *Population in 2006:* 1,454
Provincial Electoral District(s): Roberval
Federal Electoral District(s): Roberval-Lac-St-Jean
Next Election: 1er novembre 2013
Jacques Asselin, Maire

La Durantaye
539, rue du Piedmont
La Durantaye, QC G0R 1W0
418-884-3465 Fax: 418-884-3048
par.ladurantaye@globetrotter.net
Municipal Type: Parish (Paroisse)
Incorporated: 4 août 1910; *Area:* 33,78 km2
County or District: Bellechasse; *Population in 2006:* 703
Provincial Electoral District(s): Bellechasse
Federal Electoral District(s): Lévis-Bellechasse
Next Election: 1er novembre 2013
Marie-Josée Blais, Sec.-Trés.

La Guadeloupe
483, 9e rue est
La Guadeloupe, QC G0M 1G0
418-459-3342 Fax: 418-459-3507
lagua@tlb.sympatico.ca
Municipal Type: Village
Incorporated: 6 août 1929; *Area:* 31,67 km2
County or District: Beauce-Sartigan; *Population in 2006:* 1,758
Provincial Electoral District(s): Beauce-Sud
Federal Electoral District(s): Beauce
Next Election: 1er novembre 2013
Marc-André Doyle, Sec.-Trés.

La Haute-Côte-Nord
#101, 26, rue de la Rivière
Les Escoumins, QC G0T 1K0
418-233-2102 Fax: 418-233-3010
info@mrchcn.qc.ca
www.mrchcn.qc.ca
Municipal Type: Regional County Municipality
Incorporated: 1 janvier 1982;
Population in 2009: 12,053
Note: 8 municipalités & 1 autre territoire.
Alain Tremblay, Directeur général

La Haute-Gaspésie
464, boul Ste-Anne ouest
Sainte-Anne-des-Monts, QC G4V 1T5
418-763-7791 Fax: 418-763-7737
mrc.haute-gaspesie@globetrotter.net
www.hautegaspesie.com
Municipal Type: Regional County Municipality
Incorporated: 18 mars 1981;
Population in 2009: 12,233
Note: 8 municipalités & 2 autres territoires.

La Haute-Yamaska
#100, 142, rue Dufferin
Granby, QC J2G 4X1
450-378-9975 Fax: 450-378-2465
mrc@haute-yamaska.ca
www.haute-yamaska.ca
Municipal Type: Regional County Municipality

Population in 2009: 87,405
Note: 9 municipalités.
Johanne Gaouette, Directrice générale

La Jacques-Cartier
60, rue St-Patrick
Shannon, QC G0A 4N0
418-844-2160 Fax: 418-844-2664
fbreton@mrc.lajacquescartier.qc.ca
www.mrc.lajacquescartier.qc.ca
Municipal Type: Regional County Municipality
Incorporated: 1 avril 1981;
Population in 2009: 31,258
Note: 9 municipalités & 1 autre territoire.
Francine Breton, Directrice générale

La Malbaie
280, rue John-Nairne
La Malbaie, QC G5A 1L9
418-665-3747 Fax: 418-665-4935
dg@ville.lamalbaie.qc.ca
www.ville.lamalbaie.qc.ca
Municipal Type: City
Incorporated: 1er décembre 1999; *Area:* 470,57 km2
County or District: Charlevoix-Est; *Population in 2006:* 8,959
Provincial Electoral District(s): Charlevoix
Federal Electoral District(s):
Montmorency-Charlevoix-Haute-Côte-Nord
Next Election: 1er novembre 2013
Daniel Lavoie, Directeur général
Jean-Luc Simard, Maire

La Martre
9, av du Phare
La Martre, QC G0E 2H0
418-288-5605 Fax: 418-288-5144
lamartre@globetrotter.net
Municipal Type: Municipality
Incorporated: 18 décembre 1923; *Area:* 185,69 km2
County or District: La Haute-Gaspésie; *Population in 2006:* 253
Provincial Electoral District(s): Matane
Federal Electoral District(s): Haute-Gaspésie-La Mitis-Matane-Matapédia
Next Election: 1er novembre 2013
Claire St-Laurent, Sec.-Trés.

La Matapédia
#501, 123, rue Desbiens
Amqui, QC G5J 3P9
418-629-2053 Fax: 418-629-3195
administration@mrcmatapedia.qc.ca
www.lamatapedia.com/mrc
Municipal Type: Regional County Municipality
Incorporated: 1 janvier 1982;
Population in 2009: 19,316
Note: 18 municipalités & 7 autres territoires.
Mario Lavoie, Directeur général

La Minerve
6, rue Mailloux
La Minerve, QC J0T 1S0
819-274-2364 Fax: 819-274-2031
bureau@municipalite.laminerve.qc.ca
www.municipalite.laminerve.qc.ca
Municipal Type: Municipality
Incorporated: 30 décembre 1892; *Area:* 297,78 km2
County or District: Les Laurentides; *Population in 2006:* 1,295
Provincial Electoral District(s): Labelle
Federal Electoral District(s): Laurentides-Labelle
Next Election: 1er novembre 2013
Gilbert Forget, Sec.-Trés. & Directeur général

La Mitis
300, av du Sanatorium
Mont-Joli, QC G5H 1V7
418-775-8445 Fax: 418-775-9303
mrcmitis@mitis.qc.ca
www.lamitis.ca
Municipal Type: Regional County Municipality
Incorporated: 1 janvier 1982;
Population in 2009: 19,425
Note: 16 municipalités & 2 autres territoires.
Marcel Moreau, Directeur général

La Morandière
204, rte 397
La Morandière, QC J0Y 1S0
819-734-6143 Fax: 819-734-6143
lamorandiere@tlb.sympatico.ca
Municipal Type: Municipality
Incorporated: 1er janvier 1983; *Area:* 430 km2
County or District: Abitibi; *Population in 2006:* 262
Provincial Electoral District(s): Abitibi-Ouest
Federal Electoral District(s): Abitibi-Témiscamingue
Next Election: 1er novembre 2013
Sandra Hardy, Sec.-Trés.

La Motte
CP 644
349, ch St-Luc
La Motte, QC J0Y 1T0
819-732-2878 Fax: 819-727-4248
municipalite.lamotte@cableamos.com
Municipal Type: Municipality
Incorporated: 30 mai 1921; *Area:* 224,03 km2
County or District: Abitibi; *Population in 2006:* 395
Provincial Electoral District(s): Abitibi-Ouest
Federal Electoral District(s): Abitibi-Témiscamingue
Next Election: 1er novembre 2013
Rachelle Cossette, Sec.-Trés. & Directrice générale

La Nouvelle-Beauce
#B, 700, rue Notre-Dame nord
Sainte-Marie, QC G6E 2K9
418-387-3444 Fax: 418-387-7060
mrc@nouvellebeauce.com
www.nouvellebeauce.com
Municipal Type: Regional County Municipality
Incorporated: 1 janvier 1982;
Population in 2009: 32,042
Note: 11 municipalités.
Mario Caron, Directeur général

La Patrie
18, rue Chartier
La Patrie, QC J0B 1Y0
819-888-2691 Fax: 819-888-2697
munilapatrie@qc.aira.com
Municipal Type: Municipality
Incorporated: 24 décembre 1997; *Area:* 206,95 km2
County or District: Le Haut-St-François; *Population in 2006:* 805
Provincial Electoral District(s): Mégantic-Compton
Federal Electoral District(s): Compton-Stanstead
Next Election: 1er novembre 2013
Brigitte April, Sec.-Trés. & Directrice générale

La Pêche
1, rue Principale ouest
La Pêche, QC J0X 2W0
819-456-2161 Fax: 819-456-4534
reception@villelapeche.qc.ca
www.villelapeche.qc.ca
Municipal Type: Municipality
Incorporated: 1er janvier 1975; *Area:* 597,14 km2
County or District: Les Collines-de-l'Outaouais; *Population in 2009:* 7,609
Provincial Electoral District(s): Gatineau
Federal Electoral District(s): Pontiac
Next Election: 1er novembre 2013
Charles Ricard, Directeur général

La Pocatière
412, 9e rue
La Pocatière, QC G0R 1Z0
418-856-3394 Fax: 418-856-5465
michael.schmouth@lapocatiere.ca
www.lapocatiere.ca
Municipal Type: City
Incorporated: 1er janvier 1960; *Area:* 22,71 km2
County or District: Kamouraska; *Population in 2006:* 4,575
Provincial Electoral District(s): Kamouraska-Témiscouata
Federal Electoral District(s):
Montmagny-L'Islet-Kamouraska-Rivière-du-Loup
Next Election: 1er novembre 2013
Danielle Caron, Greffière
Bernard Généreux, Maire

La Présentation
772, rue Principale
La Présentation, QC J0H 1B0
450-796-2317 Fax: 450-796-1707
lapresentation@mrcmaskoutains.qc.ca
Municipal Type: Parish (Paroisse)
Incorporated: 1er juillet 1855; *Area:* 104,71 km2
County or District: Les Maskoutains; *Population in 2006:* 2,115
Provincial Electoral District(s): Verchères
Federal Electoral District(s): St-Hyacinthe-Bagot
Next Election: 1er novembre 2013
Lise Lapalme, Sec.-Trés.

La Rédemption
CP 39
68, rue Soucy
La Rédemption, QC G0J 1P0
418-776-5311 Fax: 418-776-5711
redemption@mitis.qc.ca
Municipal Type: Parish (Paroisse)
Incorporated: 1er janvier 1956; *Area:* 116,29 km2
County or District: La Mitis; *Population in 2006:* 515
Provincial Electoral District(s): Matapédia
Federal Electoral District(s): Haute-Gaspésie-La Mitis-Matane-Matapédia
Next Election: 1er novembre 2013
Annie Dubé, Directrice générale

La Reine
CP 40
1, 3e av ouest
La Reine, QC J0Z 2L0
819-947-5271 Fax: 819-947-5271
lareine@lareine.ao.ca
www.lareine.ao.ca
Municipal Type: Municipality
Incorporated: 19 septembre 1981; *Area:* 100,01 km2
County or District: Abitibi-Ouest; *Population in 2006:* 362
Provincial Electoral District(s): Abitibi-Ouest
Federal Electoral District(s): Abitibi-Témiscamingue
Next Election: 1er novembre 2013
Diane Sévigny-East, Sec.-Trés.

La Rivière-du-Nord
#200, 161, rue de la Gare
Saint-Jérôme, QC J7Z 2B9
450-436-9321 Fax: 450-436-1977
info@mrcrivieredunord.qc.ca
www.mrcrivieredunord.qc.ca
Municipal Type: Regional County Municipality

Population in 2009: 105,087
Note: 5 municipalités.
Pierre Godin, Directeur général

La Sarre
6, 4e av est
La Sarre, QC J9Z 1J9
819-333-2282 Fax: 819-333-3090
info@ville.lasarre.qc.ca
www.ville.lasarre.qc.ca
Municipal Type: City
Incorporated: 19 avril 1980; *Area:* 148,21 km2
County or District: Abitibi-Ouest; *Population in 2006:* 7,336
Provincial Electoral District(s): Abitibi-Ouest
Federal Electoral District(s): Abitibi-Témiscamingue
Next Election: 1er novembre 2013
Normand Houde, Maire
François Casaubon, Greffier & Directeur général

La Trinité-des-Monts
CP 9
12, rue Principale ouest
La Trinité-des-Monts, QC G0K 1B0
418-779-2421 Fax: 418-779-2454
muntrinite@globetrotter.net
Municipal Type: Parish (Paroisse)
Incorporated: 1er janvier 1965; *Area:* 233,09 km2
County or District: Rimouski-Neigette; *Population in 2006:* 278
Provincial Electoral District(s): Rimouski
Federal Electoral District(s): Rimouski-Neigette-Témiscouata-Les Basques
Next Election: 1er novembre 2013
Thérèse Dumont, Sec.-Trés.

La Vallée-de-l'Or
42, place Hammond
Val-d'Or, QC J9P 3A9
819-825-7733 Fax: 819-825-4137
info@mrcvo.qc.ca
www.mrcvo.qc.ca
Municipal Type: Regional County Municipality

Population in 2009: 41,497
Note: 6 municipalités & 5 autres territoires.
Louis Bourget, Directeur général

La Vallée-de-la-Gatineau
CP 307
7, rue de la Polyvalente
Gracefield, QC J0X 1W0
819-463-3241 Fax: 819-463-3632
info@mrcvg.qc.ca
www.mrcvg.qc.ca
Municipal Type: Regional County Municipality
Incorporated: 1 janvieer 1983;
Population in 2009: 19,264
Note: 17 municipalités & 5 autres territoires.
André Beauchemin, Directeur général

La Vallée-du-Richelieu
#100, 255, boul Laurier
McMasterville, QC J3G 0B7
450-464-0339 Fax: 450-464-3827
mrcvr@vallee-du-richelieu.ca
www.vallee-du-richelieu.ca
Municipal Type: Regional County Municipality

Population in 2009: 109,996
Note: 13 municipalités.
Bernard Roy, Directeur général

La Visitation-de-l'Ile-Dupas
113, rue de l'Église
La Visitation-de-l'Ile-Dupas, QC J0K 2P0
450-836-6019 Fax: 450-836-6019
admin@ile-dupas.ca

Municipal Type: Municipality
Incorporated: 1er juillet 1855; *Area:* 24,86 km2
County or District: D'Autray; *Population in 2006:* 612
Provincial Electoral District(s): Berthier
Federal Electoral District(s): Joliette
Next Election: 1er novembre 2013
Isabelle Perreault, Sec.-Trés. & Directrice générale

La Visitation-de-Yamaska
21, rue Principale
La Visitation, QC J0G 1C0
450-564-2818 Fax: 450-564-9923
municipalite@lavisitationdeyamaska.net
www.lavisitationdeyamaska.net
Municipal Type: Municipality
Incorporated: 2 février 1899; *Area:* 41,86 km2
County or District: Nicolet-Yamaska; *Population in 2006:* 348
Provincial Electoral District(s): Nicolet-Yamaska
Federal Electoral District(s): Bas-Richelieu-Nicolet-Bécancour
Next Election: 1er novembre 2013
Suzanne Bibeau, Sec.-Trés.

Labelle
1, rue du Pont
Labelle, QC J0T 1H0
819-681-3371 Fax: 819-686-3820
info@municipalite.labelle.qc.ca
www.municipalite.labelle.qc.ca
Municipal Type: Municipality
Incorporated: 27 janvier 1973; *Area:* 217,11 km2
County or District: Les Laurentides; *Population in 2006:* 2,258
Provincial Electoral District(s): Labelle
Federal Electoral District(s): Laurentides-Labelle
Next Election: 1er novembre 2013
Christiane Cholette, Sec.-Trés. & Directrice générale

Labrecque
3425, rue Ambroise
Labrecque, QC G0W 2S0
418-481-2022 Fax: 418-481-1210
municipalite@ville.labrecque.qc.ca
www.ville.labrecque.qc.ca
Municipal Type: Municipality
Incorporated: 6 octobre 1925; *Area:* 147,37 km2
County or District: Lac-St-Jean-Est; *Population in 2006:* 1,295
Provincial Electoral District(s): Lac-St-Jean
Federal Electoral District(s): Roberval-Lac-St-Jean
Next Election: 1er novembre 2013
Suzanne Couture, Sec.-Trés. & Directrice générale

Lac-au-Saumon
CP 98
36, rue Bouillon
Lac-au-Saumon, QC G0J 1M0
418-778-3378 Fax: 418-778-3706
lacausaumon@globetrotter.net
www.lacausaumon.com
Municipal Type: Municipality
Incorporated: 17 décembre 1997; *Area:* 79,74 km2
County or District: La Matapédia; *Population in 2006:* 1,495
Provincial Electoral District(s): Matapédia
Federal Electoral District(s): Haute-Gaspésie-La Mitis-Matane-Matapédia
Next Election: 1er novembre 2013
Nadia Saint-Pierre, Directrice générale

Lac-aux-Sables
820, rue St-Alphonse
Lac-aux-Sables, QC G0X 1M0
418-336-2331 Fax: 418-336-2500
lac-aux-sables@regionmekinac.com
www.lac-aux-sables.qc.ca
Municipal Type: Parish (Paroisse)
Incorporated: 24 avril 1899; *Area:* 285,45 km2
County or District: Mékinac; *Population in 2006:* 1,312
Provincial Electoral District(s): Portneuf
Federal Electoral District(s): St-Maurice-Champlain
Next Election: 1er novembre 2013
Madeleine Hébert, Secrétaire

Lac-Beauport
65, ch du Tour-du-Lac
Lac-Beauport, QC G3B 0A1
418-849-7141 Fax: 418-849-0361
adm@lacbeauport.net
www.lac-beauport.ca
Municipal Type: Municipality
Incorporated: 1er juillet 1855; *Area:* 62,72 km2
County or District: La Jacques-Cartier; Communauté métropolitaine de Québec; *Population in 2009:* 6,378
Provincial Electoral District(s): Chauveau
Federal Electoral District(s): Portneuf-Jacques-Cartier
Next Election: 1er novembre 2013
Hélène Renaud, Directrice générale

Lac-Bouchette
249, rue Principale
Lac-Bouchette, QC G0W 1V0
418-348-6306 Fax: 418-348-9477
munilac@lac-bouchette.com
Municipal Type: Municipality
Incorporated: 25 septembre 1971; *Area:* 919,99 km2
County or District: Le Domaine-du-Roy; *Population in 2006:* 1,311
Provincial Electoral District(s): Roberval
Federal Electoral District(s): Roberval-Lac-St-Jean
Next Election: 1er novembre 2013
Jean-Pierre Tremblay, Sec.-Trés.

Lac-Brome
122, ch Lakeside
Lac-Brome, QC J0E 1V0
450-243-6111 Fax: 450-243-5300
reception@ville.lac-brome.qc.ca
ville.lac-brome.qc.ca
Municipal Type: City
Incorporated: 2 janvier 1971; *Area:* 209,37 km2
County or District: Brome-Missisquoi; *Population in 2006:* 5,629
Provincial Electoral District(s): Brome-Missisquoi
Federal Electoral District(s): Brome-Missisquoi
Next Election: 1er novembre 2013
Alain Roy, Greffier
Richard Wisdom, Maire

Lac-Delage
24, rue du Pied-des-Pentes
Lac-Delage, QC G0A 4P0
418-848-2417 Fax: 418-848-1948
villelacdelage@ccapcable.com
Municipal Type: City
Incorporated: 11 février 1959; *Area:* 1,46 km2
County or District: La Jacques-Cartier; *Population in 2006:* 530
Provincial Electoral District(s): Chauveau
Federal Electoral District(s): Portneuf-Jacques-Cartier
Next Election: 1er novembre 2013
Guylaine Thibault, Sec.-Trés.
Marc Boiteau, Maire

Lac-des-Aigles
CP 70
75, rue Principale
Lac-des-Aigles, QC G0K 1V0
418-779-2300 Fax: 418-779-3024
munlda@globetrotter.net
Municipal Type: Municipality
Incorporated: 1er janvier 1948; *Area:* 85,10 km2
County or District: Témiscouata; *Population in 2006:* 609
Provincial Electoral District(s): Rimouski
Federal Electoral District(s): Rimouski-Neigette-Témiscouata-Les Basques
Next Election: 1er novembre 2013
Francine Beaulieu, Directrice générale

Lac-des-Écorces
330, rte 117 est
Lac-des-Écorces, QC J0W 1H0
819-585-4600 Fax: 819-585-4610
lacdesecorces@lino.com
Municipal Type: Municipality
Incorporated: 10 octobre 2002; *Area:* 143,59 km2
County or District: Antoine-Labelle; *Population in 2006:* 2,884
Provincial Electoral District(s): Labelle
Federal Electoral District(s): Laurentides-Labelle
Next Election: 1er novembre 2013
Note: Effective October 10, 2002, the Municipality of Beaux-Rivages, the Village of Lac-des-Écorces & the Village of Val-Barrette amalgamated to create the new Municipality of Beaux-Rivages-Lac-des-Écorces-Val-Barrette. Effective June 21, 2003, name change
Pierre Flamand, Maire

Lac-des-Plages
2053, ch Tour-du-Lac
Lac-des-Plages, QC J0T 1K0
819-426-2391 Fax: 819-426-2085
admin@lacdesplages.com
www.lacdesplages.com/ldp
Municipal Type: Municipality
Incorporated: 1er janvier 1950; *Area:* 121,78 km2
County or District: Papineau; *Population in 2006:* 403
Provincial Electoral District(s): Papineau
Federal Electoral District(s): Argenteuil-Papineau-Mirabel
Next Election: 1er novembre 2013
Denis Dagenais, Directeur général

Lac-des-Seize-Iles
47, rue de l'Église
Lac-des-Seize-Iles, QC J0T 2M0
450-226-3117 Fax: 450-226-1461
munlac16iles@qc.aira.com
Municipal Type: Municipality
Incorporated: 19 février 1914; *Area:* 8,49 km2
County or District: Les Pays-d'en-Haut; *Population in 2006:* 160
Provincial Electoral District(s): Argenteuil
Federal Electoral District(s): Argenteuil-Papineau-Mirabel
Next Election: 1er novembre 2013
Luce Bergeron, Sec.-Trés. & Directrice générale

Lac-Drolet
CP 148
685, rue Principale
Lac-Drolet, QC G0Y 1C0
819-549-2332 Fax: 819-549-2626
munlacdrolet@axion.ca
www.lacdrolet.ca
Municipal Type: Municipality
Incorporated: 1er janvier 1885; *Area:* 124,94 km2
County or District: Le Granit; *Population in 2006:* 1,148
Provincial Electoral District(s): Mégantic-Compton
Federal Electoral District(s): Mégantic-L'Érable
Next Election: 1er novembre 2013
Maryse Champagne, Directrice générale

Lac-du-Cerf
19, ch de l'Église
Lac-du-Cerf, QC J0W 1S0
819-597-2424 Fax: 819-597-4036
municipalite.lacducerf@tlb.sympatico.ca
Municipal Type: Municipality
Incorporated: 1er janvier 1955; *Area:* 78,45 km2
County or District: Antoine-Labelle; *Population in 2006:* 424
Provincial Electoral District(s): Labelle
Federal Electoral District(s): Laurentides-Labelle
Next Election: 1er novembre 2013
Jacinthe Valiquette, Sec.-Trés.

Lac-Etchemin
208, 2e Av
Lac-Etchemin, QC G0R 1S0
418-625-4521 Fax: 418-625-3175
munetchemin@sogetel.net
www.municipalite.lac-etchemin.qc.ca
Municipal Type: Municipality
Incorporated: 10 octobre 2001; *Area:* 160,57 km2
County or District: Les Etchemins; *Population in 2009:* 4,088
Provincial Electoral District(s): Bellechasse
Federal Electoral District(s): Lévis-Bellechasse
Next Election: 1er novembre 2013
Laurent Rheault, Directeur général/Greffier

Lac-Frontière
22, rue de l'Église
Lac-Frontière, QC G0R 1T0
418-245-3553 Fax: 418-245-3553
municipalitelac-frontiere@globetrotter.net
Municipal Type: Municipality
Incorporated: 7 février 1916; *Area:* 51,33 km2
County or District: Montmagny; *Population in 2006:* 197
Provincial Electoral District(s): Montmagny-L'Islet
Federal Electoral District(s): Montmagny-L'Islet-Kamouraska-Rivière-du-Loup
Next Election: 1er novembre 2013
Dany Robert, Sec.-Trés.

Lac-Mégantic
#200, 5527, rue Frontenac
Lac-Mégantic, QC G6B 1H6
819-583-2441 Fax: 819-583-5920
greffier@ville.lac-megantic.qc.ca
www.ville.lac-megantic.qc.ca
Municipal Type: City
Incorporated: 14 mars 1907; *Area:* 20,33 km2
County or District: Le Granit; *Population in 2006:* 5,967
Provincial Electoral District(s): Mégantic-Compton
Federal Electoral District(s): Mégantic-L'Érable
Next Election: 1er novembre 2013
Jean-François Grandmont, Greffier
Colette Roy Laroche, Mairesse

Lac-Poulin
CP 1019
Saint-Benoît-Labre, QC G0M 1P0
418-228-7585 Fax: 418-222-6931
munlacpoulin@globetrotter.net
Municipal Type: Village
Incorporated: 5 mars 1959; *Area:* 1,08 km2
County or District: Beauce-Sartigan; *Population in 2006:* 135
Provincial Electoral District(s): Beauce-Sud
Federal Electoral District(s): Beauce
Next Election: 1er novembre 2013
Jeanne Faucher, Sec.-Trés.

Lac-Saguay
257A, rte 117
Lac-Saguay, QC J0W 1L0
819-278-3972 Fax: 819-278-0260
lac.saguay@lincsat.com
www.lacsaguay.qc.ca
Municipal Type: Village
Incorporated: 1er juillet 1951; *Area:* 176,26 km2
County or District: Antoine-Labelle; *Population in 2006:* 492
Provincial Electoral District(s): Labelle
Federal Electoral District(s): Laurentides-Labelle
Next Election: 1er novembre 2013
Richard Gagnon, Sec.-Trés.

Lac-Saint-Jean-Est
625, rue Bergeron ouest
Alma, QC G8B 1V3
418-668-3023 Fax: 418-668-5112
sabin.larouche@mrclac.qc.ca
www.mrclacsaintjeanest.qc.ca
Municipal Type: Regional County Municipality

Population in 2009: 51,606
Note: 14 municipalités & 4 autres territoires.
Sabin Larouche, Directeur général

Lac-St-Joseph
1048, ch Thomas-Maher, RR#1
Lac-St-Joseph, QC G0A 3M0
418-875-3355 Fax: 418-875-0444
villedulacstjospeh@bellnet.ca

Municipal Type: City
Incorporated: 10 juin 1936; *Area:* 32,81 km2
County or District: La Jacques-Cartier; *Population in 2006:* 266
Provincial Electoral District(s): Portneuf
Federal Electoral District(s): Portneuf-Jacques-Cartier
Next Election: 1er novembre 2013
Vivian Viviers, Sec.-Trés. & Directrice générale
O'Donnell Bédard, Maire

Lac-Ste-Marie
CP 97
106, ch de Lac-Ste-Marie
Lac-Sainte-Marie, QC J0X 1Z0
819-467-5437 Fax: 819-467-3691
municipalitestemarie@qc.aira.com
www.geocities.com/municipalitelacstemarie
Municipal Type: Municipality
Incorporated: 1er janvier 1872; *Area:* 211,13 km2
County or District: La Vallée-de-la-Gatineau; *Population in 2006:* 647
Provincial Electoral District(s): Gatineau
Federal Electoral District(s): Pontiac
Next Election: 1er novembre 2013
Yvon Blanchard, Sec.-Trés.

Lac-Sergent
1149, ch Tour-du-Lac nord
Lac-Sergent, QC G0A 2J0
418-875-4854 Fax: 418-875-3805
lac-sergent@bellnet.ca
Municipal Type: City
Incorporated: 25 février 1921; *Area:* 3,52 km2
County or District: Portneuf; *Population in 2006:* 423
Provincial Electoral District(s): Portneuf
Federal Electoral District(s): Portneuf-Jacques-Cartier
Next Election: 1er novembre 2013
Josée Brouillette, Sec.-Trés.
Denis Racine, Maire

Lac-Simon
CP 3550
849, ch du Tour-du-Lac
Chénéville, QC J0V 1E0
819-428-3906 Fax: 819-428-3455
mun.lacsimon@mrcpapineau.com
www.lacsimon.com/lacsim
Municipal Type: Municipality
Incorporated: 1er janvier 1881; *Area:* 96,83 km2
County or District: Papineau; *Population in 2006:* 869
Provincial Electoral District(s): Papineau
Federal Electoral District(s): Argenteuil-Papineau-Mirabel
Next Election: 1er novembre 2013
Gisèle Prévost, Sec.-Trés. & Directrice générale

Lac-St-Paul
388, rue Principale
Lac-Saint-Paul, QC J0W 1K0
819-587-4283 Fax: 819-587-4892
mun.lacstpaul@ireseau.com
Municipal Type: Municipality
Incorporated: 11 septembre 1922; *Area:* 173,06 km2
County or District: Antoine-Labelle; *Population in 2006:* 521
Provincial Electoral District(s): Labelle
Federal Electoral District(s): Laurentides-Labelle
Next Election: 1er novembre 2013
Suzanne Raymond, Directrice générale

Lac-Supérieur
1281, ch du lac-Supérieur
Lac-Supérieur, QC J0T 1J0
819-681-3370 Fax: 819-688-3010
directiongenerale@muni.lacsuperieur.qc.ca
Municipal Type: Municipality
Incorporated: 1er janvier 1881; *Area:* 380,36 km2
County or District: Les Laurentides; *Population in 2006:* 1,745
Provincial Electoral District(s): Labelle
Federal Electoral District(s): Laurentides-Labelle
Next Election: 1er novembre 2013
Diane Taillon, Sec.-Trés. & Directrice générale

Lacolle
1, rue de l'Église sud
Lacolle, QC J0J 1J0
450-246-3201 Fax: 450-246-4412
admin@lacolle.com
www.lacolle.com
Municipal Type: Municipality
Incorporated: 13 septembre 2001; *Area:* 49,17 km2
County or District: Le Haut-Richelieu; *Population in 2006:* 2,512
Provincial Electoral District(s): Huntingdon
Federal Electoral District(s): St-Jean
Next Election: 1er novembre 2013
Georgette Chèvrefils, Sec.-Trés. & Directrice générale

Laforce
CP 25
703, ch du Village
Laforce, QC J0Z 2J0
819-722-2461 Fax: 819-722-2462
dir.genlaforce@mrctemiscamingue.qc.ca
Municipal Type: Municipality
Incorporated: 1er janvier 1979; *Area:* 612,65 km2
County or District: Témiscamingue; *Population in 2006:* 174
Provincial Electoral District(s): Rouyn-Noranda-Témiscamingue
Federal Electoral District(s): Abitibi-Témiscamingue
Next Election: 1er novembre 2013
Nathalie Breton, Sec.-Trés.

Lajemmerais
609, rte Marie-Victorin
Verchères, QC J0L 2R0
450-583-3301 Fax: 450-583-3592
info@mrclajemmerais.qc.ca
www.mrclajemmerais.qc.ca
Municipal Type: Regional County Municipality

Population in 2009: 71,385
Note: 6 municipalités.
Sylvain Berthiaume, Directeur général

Lamarche
100, rue Principale
Lamarche, QC G0W 1X0
418-481-2861 Fax: 418-481-1412
mun.lamarche@ville.lamarche.qc.ca
www.ville.lamarche.qc.ca
Municipal Type: Municipality
Incorporated: 1er janvier 1967; *Area:* 94,79 km2
County or District: Lac-St-Jean-Est; *Population in 2006:* 562
Provincial Electoral District(s): Lac-St-Jean
Federal Electoral District(s): Roberval-Lac-St-Jean
Next Election: 1er novembre 2013
Fabienne Girard, Sec.-Trés.

Lambton
CP 206
230, rue du Collège
Lambton, QC G0M 1H0
418-486-7438 Fax: 418-486-7440
munilambton@tellambton.net
www.munilambton.qc.ca
Municipal Type: Municipality
Incorporated: 23 décembre 1976; *Area:* 106,86 km2
County or District: Le Granit; *Population in 2006:* 1,623
Provincial Electoral District(s): Mégantic-Compton
Federal Electoral District(s): Mégantic-L'Érable
Next Election: 1er novembre 2013
Jocelyne Boulanger, Sec.-Trés.

Landrienne
158, av Principale est
Landrienne, QC J0Y 1V0
819-732-4357 Fax: 819-732-3866
jperron@landrienne.com
Municipal Type: Township
Incorporated: 15 juillet 1918; *Area:* 276,22 km2
County or District: Abitibi; *Population in 2006:* 986
Provincial Electoral District(s): Abitibi-Ouest
Federal Electoral District(s): Abitibi-Témiscamingue
Next Election: 1er novembre 2013
Jacques Perron, Sec.-Trés.

Lanoraie
57, rue Laroche
Lanoraie, QC J0K 1E0
450-887-1100 Fax: 450-887-2077
info@lanoraie.ca
www.municipalite.lanoraie.qc.ca
Municipal Type: Municipality
Incorporated: 6 décembre 2000; *Area:* 102,04 km2
County or District: D'Autray; *Population in 2009:* 4,237
Provincial Electoral District(s): Berthier
Federal Electoral District(s): Berthier-Maskinongé
Next Election: 1er novembre 2013
Michel Dufort, Directeur général

Lantier
CP 39
118, croissant des Trois-Lacs
Lantier, QC J0T 1V0
819-326-2674 Fax: 819-326-5204
direction@municipalite.lantier.qc.ca
www.municipalite.lantier.qc.ca
Municipal Type: Municipality
Incorporated: 1er janvier 1948; *Area:* 43,57 km2
County or District: Les Laurentides; *Population in 2006:* 825
Provincial Electoral District(s): Bertrand
Federal Electoral District(s): Laurentides-Labelle
Next Election: 1er novembre 2013
Benoit Charbonneau, Sec.-Trés.

Larouche
709, rue Gauthier
Larouche, QC G0W 1Z0
418-695-2201 Fax: 418-695-4989
administration@villedelarouche.qc.ca
www.villedelarouche.qc.ca
Municipal Type: Municipality
Incorporated: 21 mars 1922; *Area:* 88 km2
County or District: Le Fjord-du-Saguenay; *Population in 2006:* 1,200
Provincial Electoral District(s): Lac-St-Jean
Federal Electoral District(s): Jonquière-Alma
Next Election: 1er novembre 2013
Paul-Henri Munger, Sec.-Trés. & Directeur général

Latulipe-et-Gaboury
CP 9
1, rue Principale est
Latulipe-et-Gaboury, QC J0Z 2N0
819-747-4281 Fax: 819-747-2194
dir.gen_latulipe@mrctemiscamingue.qc.ca
www.temiscamingue.net/decouvrir/municipalite/latulipe.html
Municipal Type: United Township (Cantons)
Incorporated: 18 novembre 1924; *Area:* 298,38 km2
County or District: Témiscamingue; *Population in 2006:* 333
Provincial Electoral District(s): Rouyn-Noranda-Témiscamingue
Federal Electoral District(s): Abitibi-Témiscamingue
Next Election: 1er novembre 2013
Julie Gilbert, Sec.-Trés.

Launay
843, rue des Pionniers
Launay, QC J0Y 1W0
819-796-2545 Fax: 819-796-2545
Municipal Type: Township
Incorporated: 18 mai 1921; *Area:* 252,44 km2
County or District: Abitibi; *Population in 2006:* 226
Provincial Electoral District(s): Abitibi-Ouest
Federal Electoral District(s): Abitibi-Témiscamingue
Next Election: 1er novembre 2013
Claudette Laroche, Sec.-Trés.

Laurier-Station
121, rue St-André
Laurier-Station, QC G0S 1N0
418-728-3852 Fax: 418-728-4801
mun.laurier@globetrotter.net
www.ville.laurier-station.qc.ca
Municipal Type: Village
Incorporated: 1er janvier 1951; *Area:* 12,43 km2
County or District: Lotbinière; *Population in 2006:* 2,403
Provincial Electoral District(s): Lotbinière
Federal Electoral District(s): Lotbinière-Chutes-de-la-Chaudière
Next Election: 1er novembre 2013
Valérie Boucher, Sec.-Trés.

Laurierville
CP 159
140, rue Grenier
Laurierville, QC G0S 1P0
819-365-4646 Fax: 819-365-4200
munlauri@ivic.qc.ca
Municipal Type: Municipality
Incorporated: 26 novembre 1997; *Area:* 110,62 km2
County or District: L'Érable; *Population in 2006:* 1,404
Provincial Electoral District(s): Lotbinière
Federal Electoral District(s): Mégantic-L'Érable
Next Election: 1er novembre 2013
Réjean Gingras, Sec.-Trés. & Directeur général

Laval
CP 422 Saint-Martin
1, Place du Souvenir
Laval, QC H7V 3Z4
450-978-3951 Fax: 450-978-3966
info@ville.laval.qc.ca
www.ville.laval.qc.ca
Municipal Type: Regional County Municipality

Population in 2009: 377,332
Guy Collard, Sec.-Trés.

Laverlochère
CP 159
11, rue St-Isidore ouest
Laverlochère, QC J0Z 2P0
819-765-5111 Fax: 819-765-2564
dg.lave@mrctemiscamingue.qc.ca
www.temiscamingue.net/laverlochere
Municipal Type: Municipality
Incorporated: 3 octobre 1912; *Area:* 107,01 km2
County or District: Témiscamingue; *Population in 2006:* 732
Provincial Electoral District(s): Rouyn-Noranda-Témiscamingue
Federal Electoral District(s): Abitibi-Témiscamingue
Next Election: 1er novembre 2013
Monique Rivest, Sec.-Trés.

Lawrenceville
2100, rue Dandenault
Lawrenceville, QC J0E 1W0
450-535-6398 Fax: 450-535-6537
munlaw@cooptel.qc.ca
Municipal Type: Village
Incorporated: 27 avril 1905; *Area:* 17,40 km2
County or District: Le Val-St-François; *Population in 2006:* 642
Provincial Electoral District(s): Brome-Missisquoi
Federal Electoral District(s): Shefford
Next Election: 1er novembre 2013
Sylvie Lachance, Sec.-Trés. & Directrice générale

Le Bic
79, rue St-Jean-Baptiste
Le Bic, QC G0L 1B0
418-736-5833 Fax: 418-736-4034
dirgen.munlebic@globetrotter.net
www.municipalitedubic.com
Municipal Type: Municipality
Incorporated: 29 janvier 1972; *Area:* 81,17 km2
County or District: Rimouski-Neigette; *Population in 2006:* 2,946
Provincial Electoral District(s): Rimouski
Federal Electoral District(s): Rimouski-Neigette-Témiscouata-Les Basques
Next Election: 1er novembre 2013
Raymond Côté, Sec.-Trés. & Directeur général

Le Domaine-du-Roy
901, boul St-Joseph
Roberval, QC G8H 2L8
418-275-5044 Fax: 418-275-4049
administration@mrcdomaineduroy.ca
www.domaineduroy.ca
Municipal Type: Regional County Municipality
Incorporated: 1 janvier 1983;
Population in 2009: 30,346
Note: 9 municipalités & 1 autre territoire.
Denis Taillon, Directeur général

Le Fjord-du-Saguenay
3110, boul Martel
St. Honoré-de-Chicoutimi, QC G0V 1L0
418-673-1705 Fax: 418-673-7205
reception@mrc-fjord.qc.ca
www.mrc-fjord.qc.ca
Municipal Type: Regional County Municipality

Population in 2009: 20,312
Note: 13 municipalités & 3 autres territoires.
Christine Dufour, Directrice générale

Le Granit
5090, rue Frontenac
Lac-Mégantic, QC G6B 1H3
819-583-0181 Fax: 819-583-5327
administration@mrcgranit.qc.ca
www.mrcgranit.qc.ca
Municipal Type: Regional County Municipality
Incorporated: 26 mai 1982;
Population in 2009: 22,527
Note: 20 municipalités.
Serge Bilodeau, Directeur général

Le Haut-Richelieu
380, 4e av
Saint-Jean-sur-Richelieu, QC J2X 1W9
450-346-3636 Fax: 450-346-8464
info@mrchr.qc.ca
www.mrchr.qc.ca
Municipal Type: Regional County Municipality
Incorporated: 1 janvier 1982;
Population in 2009: 111,093
Note: 14 municipalités.
Joane Saulnier, Directrice générale

Le Haut-St-François
85, rue du Parc
Cookshire, QC J0B 1M0
819-560-8400 Fax: 819-560-8479
direction.mrc@hsfqc.ca
www.mrchsf.com
Municipal Type: Regional County Municipality
Incorporated: 1 janvier 1982;
Population in 2009: 22,181
Note: 14 municipalités.
Dominic Provost, Directeur général

Le Haut-St-Laurent
#400, 10, rue King
Huntingdon, QC J0S 1H0
450-264-5411 Fax: 450-264-6885
mrchsl@mrchsl.com
www.mrchsl.com
Municipal Type: Regional County Municipality
Incorporated: 1 janvier 1982;
Population in 2009: 21,829
Note: 13 municipalités.
François Landreville, Directeur général

Le Rocher-Percé
CP 128
129, boul René-Lévesque ouest
Chandler, QC G0C 1K0
418-689-4313 Fax: 418-689-5807
mrc@rocherperce.qc.ca
www.rocherperce.qc.ca
Municipal Type: Regional County Municipality
Incorporated: 1 avril 1981;
Population in 2009: 18,375
Note: 5 municipalités & 1 autre territoire.
Mario Grenier, Directeur général

Le Val-St-François
810, montée du Parc
Richmond, QC J0B 2H0
819-826-6505 Fax: 819-826-3484
mrc@val-saint-francois.qc.ca
www.val-saint-francois.qc.ca
Municipal Type: Regional County Municipality
Incorporated: 26 mai 1982;
Population in 2009: 29,335
Note: 18 municipalités.
Manon Fortin, Directrice générale

Lebel-sur-Quévillon
CP 430
500, place Quévillon
Lebel-sur-Quévillon, QC J0Y 1X0
819-755-4826 Fax: 819-755-8124
ville@lebel-sur-quevillon.com
www.lebel-sur-quevillon.com
Municipal Type: City
Incorporated: 6 août 1965; *Area:* 44,74 km2
Population in 2006: 2,729
Provincial Electoral District(s): Ungava
Federal Electoral District(s): Abitibi-Baie-James-Nunavik-Eeyou
Next Election: 1er novembre 2013
Réal Lavigne, Greffier & Directeur général
Gérald Lemoyne, Maire

Leclercville
8053, rte Marie-Victorin
Leclercville, QC G0S 2K0
819-292-2331 Fax: 819-292-2639
mun.leclercville@videotron.ca
Municipal Type: Municipality
Incorporated: 26 janvier 2000; *Area:* 135,40 km2
County or District: Lotbinière; *Population in 2006:* 524
Provincial Electoral District(s): Lotbinière
Federal Electoral District(s): Lotbinière-Chutes-de-la-Chaudière
Next Election: 1er novembre 2013
Francine B. Demers, Sec.-Trés. & Directrice générale

Lefebvre
186, 10e rang
Lefebvre, QC J0H 2C0
819-394-2782 Fax: 819-394-2186
lefebvre@mrcdrummond.qc.ca
Municipal Type: Municipality
Incorporated: 10 octobre 1922; *Area:* 65,75 km2
County or District: Drummond; *Population in 2006:* 806
Provincial Electoral District(s): Johnson
Federal Electoral District(s): Drummond
Next Election: 1er novembre 2013
Julie Yergeau, Sec.-Trés.

Lejeune
CP 40
69, rue de la Grande-Coulée
Lejeune, QC G0L 1S0
418-855-2428 Fax: 418-855-2428
munlejeune@qcaira.com
Municipal Type: Municipality
Incorporated: 1er janvier 1964; *Area:* 269,40 km2
County or District: Témiscouata; *Population in 2006:* 357
Provincial Electoral District(s): Kamouraska-Témiscouata
Federal Electoral District(s): Rimouski-Neigette-Témiscouata-Les Basques
Next Election: 1er novembre 2013
Lucie Gilbert, Mairesse

Lemieux
530, rue de l'Église
Lemieux, QC G0X 1S0
819-283-2506 Fax: 819-283-2506
info@municipalitelemieux.ca
Municipal Type: Municipality
Incorporated: 14 août 1922; *Area:* 74,79 km2
County or District: Bécancour; *Population in 2006:* 323
Provincial Electoral District(s): Lotbinière
Federal Electoral District(s): Bas-Richelieu-Nicolet-Bécancour
Next Election: 1er novembre 2013
France Hénault, Sec.-Trés.

Léry
1, rue de l'Hôtel-de-Ville
Léry, QC J6N 1E8
450-692-6861 Fax: 450-692-6881
villedelery@videotron.ca
Municipal Type: City
Incorporated: 1er juin 1914; *Area:* 10,98 km2
County or District: Roussillon; *Population in 2006:* 2,385
Provincial Electoral District(s): Châteauguay
Federal Electoral District(s): Châteauguay-St-Constant
Next Election: 1er novembre 2013
Rose-Hélène Langlais, Sec.-Trés. & Directrice générale
Yvon Mailhot, Maire

Les Appalaches
3830, boul Frontenac ouest
Thetford Mines, QC G6H 2L8
418-423-2757 Fax: 418-423-5122
info@mrcdesappalaches.ca
www.mrcdesappalaches.ca
Municipal Type: Regional County Municipality

Population in 2009: 43,602
Note: 19 municipalités.
Alain Gravel, Directeur général

Les Basques
#400, 2, rue Jean-Rioux
Trois-Pistoles, QC G0L 4K0
418-851-3206 Fax: 418-851-3171
mrc@mrcdesbasques.com
www.mrcdesbasques.com
Municipal Type: Regional County Municipality
Incorporated: 1 avril 1981;
Population in 2009: 9,464
Note: 11 municipalités & 1 autre territoire.
François Gosselin, Directeur général

Les Bergeronnes
CP 158
424, rue de la Mer
Les Bergeronnes, QC G0T 1G0
418-232-6244 Fax: 418-232-6602
info@bergeronnes.com
www.bergeronnes.net
Municipal Type: Municipality
Incorporated: 29 décembre 1999; *Area:* 291,89 km2
County or District: La Haute Côte-Nord; *Population in 2006:* 655
Provincial Electoral District(s): René-Lévesque
Federal Electoral District(s):
Montmorency-Charlevoix-Haute-Côte-Nord
Next Election: 1er novembre 2013
Carole Perron, Sec.-Trés. & Directrice générale

Les Cèdres
1060, ch du Fleuve
Les Cèdres, QC J7T 1A1
450-452-4651 Fax: 450-452-4605
dgenerale@ville.lescedres.qc.ca
www.ville.lescedres.qc.ca
Municipal Type: Municipality
Incorporated: 9 mars 1985; *Area:* 78,31 km2
County or District: Vaudreuil-Soulanges; *Population in 2006:* 5,732
Provincial Electoral District(s): Soulanges
Federal Electoral District(s): Vaudreuil-Soulanges
Next Election: 1er novembre 2013
Stéphane Plante, Sec.-Trés. & Directeur général

Les Chenaux
630, rue Principale
Saint-Luc-de-Vincennes, QC G0X 3K0
819-840-0704 Fax: 819-295-5117
info@mrcdeschenaux.ca
www.mrcdeschenaux.ca
Municipal Type: Regional County Municipality
Incorporated: 1 janvier 2002;
Population in 2009: 17,199
Note: 10 municipalités.
Pierre St-Onge, Directeur général

Les Collines-de-l'Outaouais
216, ch Old Chelsea
Chelsea, QC J9B 1J4
819-827-0516 Fax: 819-827-9272
gpoulin@mrcdescollines.com
www.mrcdescollines.com
Municipal Type: Regional County Municipality

Population in 2009: 43,358
Note: 7 municipalités.
Ghislain Poulin, Directeur général

Les Coteaux
65, rte 338
Les Coteaux, QC J7X 1A2
450-267-3531 Fax: 450-267-3532
municipalitedescoteaux@videotron.ca
Municipal Type: Municipality
Incorporated: 18 mai 1994; *Area:* 12,11 km2
County or District: Vaudreuil-Soulanges; *Population in 2006:* 3,764
Provincial Electoral District(s): Soulanges
Federal Electoral District(s): Vaudreuil-Soulanges
Next Election: 1er novembre 2013
Réal Boisvert, Maire

Les Éboulements
CP 130
248, rue du Village
Les Éboulements, QC G0A 2M0
418-635-2755 Fax: 418-635-2520
munieboul@bellnet.ca
www.leseboulements.com
Municipal Type: Municipality
Incorporated: 19 septembre 2001; *Area:* 153,99 km2
County or District: Charlevoix; *Population in 2006:* 1,264
Provincial Electoral District(s): Charlevoix
Federal Electoral District(s):
Montmorency-Charlevoix-Haute-Côte-Nord
Next Election: 1er novembre 2013
Linda Gauthier, Sec.-Trés. & Directrice générale

Les Escoumins
2, rue Sirois
Les Escoumins, QC G0T 1K0
418-233-2766 Fax: 418-233-3273
administration.muni@escoumins.ca
www.ihcn.qc.ca/escoumins
Municipal Type: Municipality
Incorporated: 5 mai 1863; *Area:* 267,33 km2
County or District: La Haute-Côte-Nord; *Population in 2006:* 2,073
Provincial Electoral District(s): René-Lévesque
Federal Electoral District(s):
Montmorency-Charlevoix-Haute-Côte-Nord
Next Election: 1er novembre 2013
Chantale Otis, Sec.-Trés. & Directrice générale

Les Etchemins
1137, rte 277
Lac-Etchemin, QC G0R 1S0
418-625-9000 Fax: 418-625-9005
mrcetchemins@sogetel.net
www.mrcetchemins.qc.ca
Municipal Type: Regional County Municipality
Incorporated: 1 janvier 1982;
Population in 2009: 17,613
Note: 13 muncipalités.
Fernand Heppell, Directeur général

Les Hauteurs
50, rue de l'Église
Les Hauteurs, QC G0K 1C0
418-798-8266 Fax: 418-798-4707
9015@globetrotter.net
Municipal Type: Municipality
Incorporated: 7 novembre 1918; *Area:* 105,41 km2
County or District: La Mitis; *Population in 2006:* 576
Provincial Electoral District(s): Matapédia
Federal Electoral District(s): Haute-Gaspésie-La Mitis-Matane-Matapédia
Next Election: 1er novembre 2013
Diane Bernier, Sec.-Trés. & Directrice générale

Les Iles-de-la-Madeleine
460, ch Principal
Cap-aux-Meules, QC G4T 1A1
418-986-3100 Fax: 418-986-6962
jlebreux@muniles.ca
www.muniles.ca
Municipal Type: Municipality
Incorporated: 1er janvier 2002; *Area:* 166,39 km2
Population in 2009: 12,628
Provincial Electoral District(s): Iles-de-la-Madeleine
Federal Electoral District(s): Gaspésie-Iles-de-la-Madeleine
Next Election: 1er novembre 2013
Joël Arseneau, Maire

Les Jardins-de-Napierville
1767, rue Principale
Saint-Michel, QC J0L 2J0
450-454-0559 Fax: 450-454-0560
info@mrcjardinsdenapierville.ca
Municipal Type: Regional County Municipality

Population in 2009: 24,745
Provincial Electoral District(s): Huntington
Federal Electoral District(s): Beauharnois-Salaberry
Note: 11 municipalités.
Nicole Inkel, Directrice générale

Les Laurentides
1255, ch des Lacs
Saint-Faustin-Lac-Carré, QC J0T 1J2
819-425-5555 Fax: 819-688-6590
adm@mrclaurentides.qc.ca
www.mrclaurentides.qc.ca
Municipal Type: Regional County Municipality

Population in 2009: 43,467
Note: 20 municipalités.
Michel Bélanger, Directeur général

Les Maskoutains
805, av du Palais
Saint-Hyacinthe, QC J2S 5C6
450-774-3141 Fax: 450-774-7161
admin@mrcmaskoutains.qc.ca
www.mrcmaskoutains.qc.ca
Municipal Type: Regional County Municipality

Population in 2009: 81,937
Note: 17 municipalités.
Francine Morin, Préfète

Les Méchins
108, rte des Fonds
Les Méchins, QC G0J 1T0
418-729-3952 Fax: 418-729-3585
mechins@globetrotter.net
www.lesmechins.com
Municipal Type: Municipality
Incorporated: 27 novembre 1982; *Area:* 452 km2
County or District: Matane; *Population in 2006:* 1,148
Provincial Electoral District(s): Matane
Federal Electoral District(s): Haute-Gaspésie-La Mitis-Matane-Matapédia
Next Election: 1er novembre 2013
Lyne Fortin, Directrice générale

Les Moulins
148, rue St-André
Terrebonne, QC J6W 3C3
450-471-9576 Fax: 450-471-8193
info@mrclesmoulins.ca
www.mrclesmoulins.ca
Municipal Type: Regional County Municipality

Population in 2009: 134,214
Note: 2 municipalités.
Daniel Pilon, Directeur général

Les Pays-d'en-Haut
1014, rue Valiquette
Sainte-Adèle, QC J8B 2M3
450-229-6637 Fax: 450-229-5203
info@mrcpdh.org
www.mrcpdh.com
Municipal Type: Regional County Municipality
Incorporated: 1 janvier 1983;
Population in 2009: 37,456
Note: 10 municipalités.
Yvan Genest, Directeur général

Les Sources
309, rue Chassé
Asbestos, QC J1T 2B4
819-879-6661 Fax: 819-879-5188
mrcdessources@mrcdessources.com
www.mrcdessources.com
Municipal Type: Regional County Municipality

Population in 2009: 14,569
Note: 7 municipalités.
Yvan Provencher, Directeur général

Lingwick
72, rte 108
Lingwick, QC J0B 2Z0
819-877-3311 Fax: 819-877-3315
cantondelingwick@globetrotter.net
Municipal Type: Township
Incorporated: 1er juillet 1855; *Area:* 242,83 km2
County or District: Le Haut-St-François; *Population in 2006:* 611
Provincial Electoral District(s): Mégantic-Compton
Federal Electoral District(s): Compton-Stanstead
Next Election: 1er novembre 2013
Monique Polard, Sec.-Trés. & Directrice générale

Litchfield
CP 340
1362, rte 148
Campbell's Bay, QC J0X 1K0
819-648-5511 Fax: 819-648-5575
litchfield@renc.igs.net
Municipal Type: Municipality
Incorporated: 1er juillet 1855; *Area:* 178,96 km2
County or District: Pontiac; *Population in 2006:* 483
Provincial Electoral District(s): Pontiac
Federal Electoral District(s): Pontiac
Next Election: 1er novembre 2013
Jacqueline Brisebois, Sec.-Trés.

Lochaber
164, rte 148 est
Lochaber, QC J0X 3B0
819-985-3291 Fax: 819-985-3291
munlochaber@qc.aira.com
Municipal Type: Township
Incorporated: 1er juillet 1855; *Area:* 62,17 km2
County or District: Papineau; *Population in 2006:* 497
Provincial Electoral District(s): Papineau
Federal Electoral District(s): Argenteuil-Papineau-Mirabel
Next Election: 1er novembre 2013
Marthe Thibaudeau, Sec.-Trés.

Lochaber-Partie-Ouest
#11, 161, rue Galipeau
Thurso, QC J0X 3B0
819-985-1553 Fax: 819-985-0790
municipalitedelochaberouest@videotron.ca
Municipal Type: Township
Incorporated: 20 avril 1891; *Area:* 61,22 km2
County or District: Papineau; *Population in 2006:* 514
Provincial Electoral District(s): Papineau
Federal Electoral District(s): Argenteuil-Papineau-Mirabel
Next Election: 1er novembre 2013
Alain Hotte, Sec.-Trés.

Longue-Pointe-de-Mingan
CP 68
878, ch du Roi
Longue-Pointe-de-Mingan, QC G0G 1V0
418-949-2053 Fax: 418-949-2166
dgst@globetrotter.net
Municipal Type: Municipality
Incorporated: 1er janvier 1966; *Area:* 417,60 km2
County or District: Minganie; *Population in 2006:* 430
Provincial Electoral District(s): Duplessis
Federal Electoral District(s): Manicouagan
Next Election: 1er novembre 2013
Célyne B.-Loiselle, Sec.-Trés.

Longue-Rive
3, rue de l'Église
Longue-Rive, QC G0T 1Z0
418-231-2344 Fax: 418-231-2577
munlonguerive@bellnet.ca
Municipal Type: Municipality
Incorporated: 28 mai 1997; *Area:* 295,35 km2
County or District: La Haute-Côte-Nord; *Population in 2006:* 1,259
Provincial Electoral District(s): René-Lévesque
Federal Electoral District(s): Montmorency-Charlevoix-Haute-Côte-Nord
Next Election: 1er novembre 2013
Mario Tremblay, Maire

Lorrainville
CP 218
2, rue St-Jean-Baptiste est
Lorrainville, QC J0Z 2R0
819-625-2167 Fax: 819-625-2380
lorrainville@mrctemiscamingue.qc.ca
www.lorrainville.ca
Municipal Type: Municipality
Incorporated: 16 février 1994; *Area:* 85,12 km2
County or District: Témiscamingue; *Population in 2006:* 1,325
Provincial Electoral District(s): Rouyn-Noranda-Témiscamingue
Federal Electoral District(s): Abitibi-Témiscamingue
Next Election: 1er novembre 2013
Marc Giroux, Sec.-Trés. & Directeur général

Lotbinière
10, rue Commerciale
Lotbinière, QC G0S 1S0
418-796-2103 Fax: 418-796-2198
secretariat@municipalite.lotbiniere.qc.ca
www.municipalite.lotbiniere.qc.ca
Municipal Type: Municipality
Incorporated: 1er janvier 1979; *Area:* 78,47 km2
County or District: Lotbinière; *Population in 2006:* 931
Provincial Electoral District(s): Lotbinière
Federal Electoral District(s): Lotbinière-Chutes-de-la-Chaudière
Next Election: 1er novembre 2013
Bernard Lepage, Directeur général

Lotbinière
6375, rue Garneau
Sainte-Croix, QC G0S 2H0
418-926-3407 Fax: 418-926-3409
info@mrclotbiniere.org
www.mrclotbiniere.org
Municipal Type: Regional County Municipality
Incorporated: 1 janvier 1982;
Population in 2009: 27,819
Note: 18 municipalités.
Daniel Patry, Directeur général

Louiseville
105, av St-Laurent
Louiseville, QC J5V 1J6
819-228-9437 Fax: 819-228-2263
directiongenerale@ville.louiseville.qc.ca
Municipal Type: City
Incorporated: 31 décembre 1988; *Area:* 62,56 km2
County or District: Maskinongé; *Population in 2006:* 7,433
Provincial Electoral District(s): Maskinongé
Federal Electoral District(s): Berthier-Maskinongé
Next Election: 1er novembre 2013
Martine St-Yves, Greffière & Directrice générale
Guy Richard, Mairesse

Low
4A, ch d'Amour
Low, QC J0X 2C0
819-422-3528 Fax: 819-422-3796
info@lowquebec.ca
www.lowquebec.ca
Municipal Type: Township
Incorporated: 1er janvier 1858; *Area:* 259,95 km2
County or District: La Vallée-de-la-Gatineau; *Population in 2006:* 956
Provincial Electoral District(s): Gatineau
Federal Electoral District(s): Pontiac
Next Election: 1er novembre 2013
Liette Hickey, Sec.-Trés.

Lyster
CP 250
2375, rue Bécancour
Lyster, QC G0S 1V0
819-389-5787 Fax: 819-389-5981
municipalite.lyster@ivic.qc.ca
www.municipalite.lyster.qc.ca
Municipal Type: Municipality
Incorporated: 18 septembre 1976; *Area:* 162,35 km2
County or District: L'Érable; *Population in 2006:* 1,644
Provincial Electoral District(s): Lotbinière
Federal Electoral District(s): Mégantic-L'Érable
Next Election: 1er novembre 2013
Guy Leroux, Directeur général

Macamic
1, 7e av ouest
Macamic, QC J0Z 2S0
819-782-4604 Fax: 819-782-4283
villemacamic@cablevision.qc.ca
Municipal Type: City
Incorporated: 6 mars 2002; *Area:* 191,95 km2
County or District: Abitibi-Ouest; *Population in 2006:* 2,726
Provincial Electoral District(s): Abitibi-Ouest
Federal Electoral District(s): Abitibi-Témiscamingue
Next Election: 1er novembre 2013
Denis Bédard, Sec.-Trés. & Directeur général
Daniel Rancourt, Maire

Maddington
CP 339
572, rte Principale
Daveluyville, QC G0Z 1C0
819-367-2818 Fax: 819-367-2143
Municipal Type: Township
Incorporated: 11 janvier 1902; *Area:* 23,38 km2
County or District: Arthabaska; *Population in 2006:* 412
Provincial Electoral District(s): Nicolet-Yamaska
Federal Electoral District(s): Richmond-Arthabaska
Next Election: 1er novembre 2013
Robert Desaulniers, Sec.-Trés.

Malartic
CP 3090
901, rue Royale
Malartic, QC J0Y 1Z0

819-757-3611 Fax: 819-757-2403
rcadieux@ville.malartic.qc.ca
www.ville.malartic.qc.ca
Municipal Type: City
Incorporated: 28 avril 1939; *Area:* 159,31 km2
County or District: La Vallée-de-l'Or; *Population in 2006:* 3,640
Provincial Electoral District(s): Abitibi-Est
Federal Electoral District(s): Abitibi-Baie-James-Nunavik-Eeyou
Next Election: 1er novembre 2013
Robert Cadieux, Greffier
Fernand Carpentier, Maire

Mandeville
162, boul Desjardins
Saint-Charles-de-Mandeville, QC J0K 1L0
450-835-2055 Fax: 450-835-7795
mandeville@intermonde.net
municipalite.mandeville.qc.ca
Municipal Type: Municipality
Incorporated: 20 avril 1904; *Area:* 330,85 km2
County or District: D'Autray; *Population in 2006:* 2,221
Provincial Electoral District(s): Berthier
Federal Electoral District(s): Joliette
Next Election: 1er novembre 2013
Danielle Lambert, Sec.-Trés.

Manicouagan
768, rue Bossé
Baie-Comeau, QC G5C 1L6
418-589-9594 Fax: 418-589-6383
info@mrcmanicouagan.qc.ca
www.mrcmanicouagan.qc.ca
Municipal Type: Regional County Municipality
Incorporated: 1 avril 1981;
Population in 2009: 33,689
Note: 8 municipalités & 1 autre territoire.
Patricia Huet, Directrice générale

Maniwaki
186, rue Principale sud
Maniwaki, QC J9E 1Z9
819-449-2800 Fax: 819-449-7078
maniwaki@ville.maniwaki.qc.ca
www.ville.maniwaki.qc.ca
Municipal Type: City
Incorporated: 15 mars 1904; *Area:* 5,60 km2
County or District: La Vallée-de-la-Gatineau; *Population in 2006:* 4,102
Provincial Electoral District(s): Gatineau
Federal Electoral District(s): Pontiac
Next Election: 1er novembre 2013
Andrée Loyer, Greffière
Robert Coulombe, Maire

Manseau
CP 200
200, rue Roux
Manseau, QC G0X 1V0
819-356-2450 Fax: 819-356-2721
directiongenerale@manseau.ca
www.manseau.ca
Municipal Type: Municipality
Incorporated: 31 décembre 1997; *Area:* 102,5 km2
County or District: Bécancour; *Population in 2006:* 934
Provincial Electoral District(s): Lotbinière
Federal Electoral District(s): Bas-Richelieu-Nicolet-Bécancour
Next Election: 1er novembre 2013
Gérard Cossette, Sec.-Trés. & Directeur général

Mansfield-et-Pontefract
300, rue Principale
Mansfield, QC J0X 1V0
819-683-2944 Fax: 819-683-3590
mansfield@personainternet.com
Municipal Type: Municipality
Incorporated: 1er janvier 1868; *Area:* 420,79 km2
County or District: Pontiac; *Population in 2006:* 2,064
Provincial Electoral District(s): Pontiac
Federal Electoral District(s): Pontiac
Next Election: 1er novembre 2013
Donald Marion, Sec.-Trés.

Maria
545, boul Perron
Maria, QC G0C 1Y0
418-759-3883 Fax: 418-759-3059
munmaria@globetrotter.net
www.mariaquebec.com
Municipal Type: Municipality
Incorporated: 1er juillet 1855; *Area:* 96,34 km2
County or District: Avignon; *Population in 2006:* 2,401
Provincial Electoral District(s): Bonaventure
Federal Electoral District(s): Gaspésie-Iles-de-la-Madeleine
Next Election: 1er novembre 2013
Gilbert Leblanc, Sec.-Trés. & Directeur général

Maria-Chapdelaine
173, boul St-Michel
Dolbeau-Mistassini, QC G8L 4N9
418-276-2131 Fax: 418-276-7043
portail@mrcmaria.qc.ca
www.mrcdemaria-chapdelaine.ca
Municipal Type: Regional County Municipality
Population in 2009: 25,737
Note: 12 municipalités & 2 autres territoires.
Christian Bouchard, Directeur général

Maricourt
1195, 3e rang nord
Maricourt, QC J0E 1Y0
450-532-2243 Fax: 450-532-2246
munmari@cooptel.qc.ca
Municipal Type: Municipality
Incorporated: 1er janvier 1864; *Area:* 62,03 km2
County or District: Le Val-St-François; *Population in 2006:* 432
Provincial Electoral District(s): Johnson
Federal Electoral District(s): Shefford
Next Election: 1er novembre 2013
Yves Barthe, Sec.-Trés.

Marieville
682, rue Saint-Charles
Marieville, QC J3M 1P9
450-460-4444 Fax: 450-460-2770
administration@ville.marieville.qc.ca
www.ville.marieville.qc.ca
Municipal Type: City
Incorporated: 14 juin 2000; *Area:* 64,25 km2
County or District: Rouville; *Population in 2006:* 7,904
Provincial Electoral District(s): Iberville
Federal Electoral District(s): Chambly-Borduas
Next Election: 1er novembre 2013
Nancy Forget, Greffière
Michel Marchand, Maire

Marsoui
CP 130
8, rte Principale est
Marsoui, QC G0E 1S0
418-288-5552 Fax: 418-288-5104
municipalite.marsoui@globetrotter.net
www.marsoui.com
Municipal Type: Village
Incorporated: 1er janvier 1950; *Area:* 182,95 km2
County or District: La Haute-Gaspésie; *Population in 2006:* 341
Provincial Electoral District(s): Matane
Federal Electoral District(s): Haute-Gaspésie-La Mitis-Matane-Matapédia
Next Election: 1er novembre 2013
Nancy Leclerc, Sec.-Trés.

Marston
CP 15
175, rte 263 sud
Marston, QC G0Y 1G0
819-583-0435 Fax: 819-583-6604
marston@axion.ca
Municipal Type: Township
Incorporated: 1er janvier 1874; *Area:* 71,77 km2
County or District: Le Granit; *Population in 2006:* 683
Provincial Electoral District(s): Mégantic-Compton
Federal Electoral District(s): Mégantic-L'Érable
Next Election: 1er novembre 2013
Jeanne-Mance Roy, Sec.-Trés.

Martinville
233, rue Principale est
Martinville, QC J0B 2A0
819-835-5390 Fax: 819-835-0171
martinville@qc.aira.com
Municipal Type: Municipality
Incorporated: 21 décembre 1895; *Area:* 48,64 km2
County or District: Coaticook; *Population in 2006:* 467
Provincial Electoral District(s): Mégantic-Compton
Federal Electoral District(s): Compton-Stanstead
Next Election: 1er novembre 2013
Diane Mercier, Sec.-Trés. & Directrice générale

Maskinongé
154, boul Ouest, rte 138
Maskinongé, QC J0K 1N0
819-227-2243 Fax: 819-227-2097
mun.maskinonge@infoteck.qc.ca
www.mun-maskinonge.ca
Municipal Type: Municipality
Incorporated: 25 avril 2001; *Area:* 75,98 km2
County or District: Maskinongé; *Population in 2009:* 2,256
Provincial Electoral District(s): Maskinongé
Federal Electoral District(s): Berthier-Maskinongé
Next Election: 1er novembre 2013
France Gervais, Directrice générale

Maskinongé
651, boul St-Laurent est
Louiseville, QC J5V 1J1
819-228-9461 Fax: 819-228-2193
mrcinfo@mrc-maskinonge.qc.ca
www.mrc-maskinonge.qc.ca
Municipal Type: Regional County Municipality
Incorporated: 1 janvier 1982;
Population in 2009: 36,048
Note: 17 municipalités.
Janyse L. Pichette, Directrice générale

Massueville
CP 90
881, rue Royale
Massueville, QC J0G 1K0
450-788-2957 Fax: 450-788-2050
massueville@bas-richelieu.net
www.village-massueville.com
Municipal Type: Village
Incorporated: 25 mars 1903; *Area:* 1,29 km2
County or District: Pierre-De Saurel; *Population in 2009:* 504
Provincial Electoral District(s): Richelieu
Federal Electoral District(s): Bas-Richelieu-Nicolet-Bécancour
Next Election: 1er novembre 2013
France Saint-Pierre, Directrice générale

Matane
145, rue Soucy
Matane, QC G4W 2E1
418-562-6734 Fax: 418-562-7265
mrcmatane@mrcdematane.qc.ca
Municipal Type: Regional County Municipality
Incorporated: 1 janvier 1982;
Population in 2009: 22,378
Note: 11 municipalités & 1 autre territoire.
Line Ross, Directrice générale

Matagami
CP 160
195, boul Matagami
Matagami, QC J0Y 2A0
819-739-2541 Fax: 819-739-4278
matagami@matagami.com
www.matagami.com
Municipal Type: City
Incorporated: 1er avril 1963; *Area:* 64,75 km2
Population in 2006: 1,555
Provincial Electoral District(s): Ungava
Federal Electoral District(s): Abitibi-Baie-James-Nunavik-Eeyou
Next Election: 1er novembre 2013
Pierre Deslauriers, Greffier & Directeur général
Robert Labelle, Maire

Matapédia
CP 207
1, rue de l'Hôtel-de-Ville
Matapédia, QC G0J 1V0
418-865-2917 Fax: 418-865-2828
munmata@globetrotter.net
Municipal Type: Parish (Paroisse)
Incorporated: 4 novembre 1905; *Area:* 70,75 km2
County or District: Avignon; *Population in 2006:* 696
Provincial Electoral District(s): Bonaventure
Federal Electoral District(s): Gaspésie-Iles-de-la-Madeleine
Next Election: 1er novembre 2013
Carole Bélanger, Sec.-Trés.

Matawinie
3184, 1re Av
Rawdon, QC J0K 1S0
450-834-5441 Fax: 450-834-6560
administration@mrcmatawinie.qc.ca
www.matawinie.org
Municipal Type: Regional County Municipality

Population in 2009: 48,309
Note: 15 municipalités & 12 autres territoires.
Lyne Arbour, Directrice générale

Mayo
CP 3000 Buckingham
140, rue Joseph
Gatineau, QC J8L 2X5
819-986-3199 Fax: 819-986-2586
Municipal Type: Municipality
Incorporated: 1er août 1864; *Area:* 72,67 km2
County or District: Papineau; *Population in 2006:* 549
Provincial Electoral District(s): Papineau
Federal Electoral District(s): Argenteuil-Papineau-Mirabel
Next Election: 1er novembre 2013
Michel Vézina, Sec.-Trés.

McMasterville
255, boul Constable
McMasterville, QC J3G 6N9
450-467-3580 Fax: 450-467-2493
hoteldeville@municipalitemcmasterville.qc.ca
www.mcmasterville.ca
Municipal Type: Municipality
Incorporated: 31 juillet 1917; *Area:* 3 km2
County or District: La Vallée-du-Richelieu; Communauté métropolitaine de Montréal; *Population in 2009:* 5,496
Provincial Electoral District(s): Borduas
Federal Electoral District(s): Chambly-Borduas
Next Election: 1er novembre 2013
Lyne Savaria, Directrice générale

Mékinac
560, rue Notre-Dame
Saint-Tite, QC G0X 3H0
418-365-5151 Fax: 418-365-7377
mrcmekinac@mrcmekinac.com
www.regionmekinac.com
Municipal Type: Regional County Municipality
Incorporated: 1 janvier 1982;
Population in 2009: 12,666
Note: 10 municipalités & 4 autres territoires.
Claude Beaulieu, Directeur général

Melbourne
CP 4
1257, rte 243
Melbourne, QC J0B 2B0
819-826-3555 Fax: 819-826-3981
melcan@qc.aibn.com
www.melbournecanton.ca
Municipal Type: Township
Incorporated: 1er juillet 1855; *Area:* 170,29 km2
County or District: Le Val-St-François; *Population in 2006:* 1,095
Provincial Electoral District(s): Richmond
Federal Electoral District(s): Richmond-Arthabaska
Next Election: 1er novembre 2013
John Barley, Sec.-Trés.

Memphrémagog
#200, 455, rue MacDonald
Magog, QC J1X 1M2
819-843-9292 Fax: 819-843-7295
info@mrcmemphremagog.com
www.mrcmemphremagog.com
Municipal Type: Regional County Municipality

Population in 2009: 46,041
Note: 17 municipalités.
Guy Jauron, Directeur général

Messines
CP 69
3, ch de la Ferme
Messines, QC J0X 2J0
819-465-2323 Fax: 819-465-2943
info@messines.ca
www.messines.ca
Municipal Type: Municipality
Incorporated: 19 août 1921; *Area:* 108,46 km2
County or District: La Vallée-de-la-Gatineau; *Population in 2006:* 1,610
Provincial Electoral District(s): Gatineau
Federal Electoral District(s): Pontiac
Next Election: 1er novembre 2013
Jim Smith, Directeur général

Métabetchouan-Lac-à-la-Croix
87, rue St-André
Métabetchouan-Lac-à-la-Croix, QC G8G 1A1
418-349-2060 Fax: 418-349-2395
bouchard.mario@ville.metabetchouan.qc.ca
www.ville.metabetchouan.qc.ca
Municipal Type: City
Incorporated: 6 janvier 1999; *Area:* 185,86 km2
County or District: Lac-St-Jean-Est; *Population in 2006:* 4,084
Provincial Electoral District(s): Lac-St-Jean
Federal Electoral District(s): Roberval-Lac-St-Jean
Next Election: 1er novembre 2013
Mario Bouchard, Greffier
Lawrence Potvin, Maire

Métis-sur-Mer
30, du Couvent
Métis-sur-Mer, QC G0J 1S0
418-936-3255 Fax: 418-936-3117
municipalitemetis@globetrotter.net
Municipal Type: City
Incorporated: 4 juillet 2002; *Area:* 48,01 km2
County or District: La Mitis; *Population in 2006:* 604
Provincial Electoral District(s): Matapédia
Federal Electoral District(s): Haute-Gaspésie-La Mitis-Matane-Matapédia
Next Election: 1er novembre 2013
Raymond Tremblay, Maire
Pierre Séguin, Greffier & Directeur général

Milan
CP 54
403, rang Ste-Marie
Milan, QC G0Y 1E0
819-657-4527 Fax: 819-657-2987
munmilan@axion.ca
Municipal Type: Municipality
Incorporated: 1er juin 1948; *Area:* 130,06 km2
County or District: Le Granit; *Population in 2006:* 299
Provincial Electoral District(s): Mégantic-Compton
Federal Electoral District(s): Mégantic-L'Érable
Next Election: 1er novembre 2013
Noëlla Bergeron, Sec.-Trés.

Mille-Isles
1262, ch de Mille-Isles
Mille-Isles, QC J0R 1A0
450-438-2958 Fax: 450-438-6157
cstpierre@mille-isles.ca
Municipal Type: Municipality
Incorporated: 1er juillet 1855; *Area:* 59,98 km2
County or District: Argenteuil; *Population in 2006:* 1,480
Provincial Electoral District(s): Argenteuil
Federal Electoral District(s): Argenteuil-Papineau-Mirabel
Next Election: 1er novembre 2013
Chantal St-Pierre, Sec.-Trés. & Directrice générale

Minganie
1303, rue de la Digue
Hâvre-Saint-Pierre, QC G0G 1P0
418-538-2732 Fax: 418-538-3711
info@mrc.minganie.org
www.mrc.minganie.org
Municipal Type: Regional County Municipality
Incorporated: 1 janvier 1982;
Population in 2009: 5,167
Note: 8 municipalités & 2 autres territoires.
Nathalie de Grandpré, Directice générale

Mirabel
14111, rue Saint-Jean
Mirabel, QC J7J 1Y3
450-475-8653 Fax: 450-475-7195
www.ville.mirabel.qc.ca/mrc-mirabel.asp
Municipal Type: Regional County Municipality
Incorporated: 1 janvier 1985; *Area:* 477,86 km2
Population in 2009: 36,436
Note: 1 municipalité.
Louis Prud'homme, Directeur général

Mistissini
Isaac Shecapio Sr. Administration Bldg.
187, rue Main
Mistissini, QC G0W 1C0
418-923-3253 Fax: 418-923-3115
legislative@nation.mistissini.qc.ca
Municipal Type: Villages Cris

Provincial Electoral District(s): Ungava
Federal Electoral District(s): Abitibi-Baie-James-Nunavik-Eeyou
Nellie Petawabano, Sec.-Trés

Moffet
CP 89
14D, rue Principale
Moffet, QC J0Z 2W0
819-747-6116 Fax: 819-747-6116
munmoffet@tlb.sympatico.ca
Municipal Type: Municipality
Incorporated: 1er janvier 1953; *Area:* 431,46 km2
County or District: Témiscamingue; *Population in 2006:* 208
Provincial Electoral District(s): Rouyn-Noranda-Témiscamingue
Federal Electoral District(s): Abitibi-Témiscamingue
Next Election: 1er novembre 2013
Linda Roy, Sec.-Trés.

Mont-Carmel
22, rue de la Fabrique
Mont-Carmel, QC G0L 1W0
418-498-2050 Fax: 418-489-2522
municmt-carmel@videotron.ca
Municipal Type: Municipality
Incorporated: 1er juillet 1855; *Area:* 435,29 km2
County or District: Kamouraska; *Population in 2006:* 1,198
Provincial Electoral District(s): Kamouraska-Témiscouata
Federal Electoral District(s): Montmagny-L'Islet-Kamouraska-Rivière-du-Loup
Next Election: 1er novembre 2013
Robert Bérubé, Directeur général

Mont-Joli
40, av de l'Hôtel-de-Ville
Mont-Joli, QC G5H 1W8
418-775-7285 Fax: 418-775-6320
mont-joli@ville.mont-joli.qc.ca
www.ville.mont-joli.qc.ca
Municipal Type: City
Incorporated: 13 juin 2001; *Area:* 22,64 km2
County or District: La Mitis; *Population in 2006:* 6,568
Provincial Electoral District(s): Matapédia
Federal Electoral District(s): Huate-Gaspésie-La Mitis-Matane-Matapédia
Next Election: 1er novembre 2013
Joël Harrisson, Directeur général
Jean Bélanger, Maire

Mont-St-Grégoire
225, rue St-Joseph
Mont-Saint-Grégoire, QC J0J 1K0
450-347-5376 Fax: 450-347-9200
direction@mmsg.ca
www.mont-saint-gregoire.ca
Municipal Type: Municipality
Incorporated: 21 décembre 1994; *Area:* 79,92 km2
County or District: Le Haut-Richelieu; *Population in 2006:* 2,922
Provincial Electoral District(s): Iberville
Federal Electoral District(s): St-Jean
Next Election: 1er novembre 2013
Christianne Pouliot, Sec.-Trés. & Directeur générale

Mont-St-Michel
94, rue de l'Église
Mont-Saint-Michel, QC J0W 1P0
819-587-3093 Fax: 819-587-3781
mun.mont-st-michel@tlb.sympatico.ca
Municipal Type: Municipality
Incorporated: 11 septembre 1928; *Area:* 137,65 km2
County or District: Antoine-Labelle; *Population in 2006:* 625
Provincial Electoral District(s): Labelle
Federal Electoral District(s): Laurentides-Labelle
Next Election: 1er novembre 2013
Lucie Gagnon, Sec.-Trés.

Mont-St-Pierre
CP 9
102, rue Cloutier
Mont-Saint-Pierre, QC G0E 1V0
418-797-2898 Fax: 418-797-2307
mont-st-pierre@globetrotter.net
Municipal Type: Village
Incorporated: 1er janvier 1947; *Area:* 60,45 km2
County or District: La Haute-Gaspésie; *Population in 2006:* 230
Provincial Electoral District(s): Matane
Federal Electoral District(s): Haute-Gaspésie-La Mitis-Matane-Matapédia
Next Election: 1er novembre 2013
Marianne Ouellet, Sec.-Trés.

Mont-Tremblant
1145, rue de St-Jovite
Mont-Tremblant, QC J8E 1V1
819-425-8614 Fax: 819-425-2528
info@villedemont-tremblant.qc.ca
www.villedemont-tremblant.qc.ca
Municipal Type: City
Incorporated: 22 novembre 2000; *Area:* 235,97 km2
County or District: Les Laurentides; *Population in 2009:* 9,059
Provincial Electoral District(s): Labelle
Federal Electoral District(s): Laurentides-Labelle
Next Election: 1er novembre 2013
Isabelle Grenier, Greffière
Pierre Pilon, Maire
Lise Julien, Directrice générale

Montcalm
10, rue de l'Hôtel-de-Ville
Montcalm, QC J0T 2V0
819-687-2836 Fax: 819-687-2374
direction@municipalite.montcalm.qc.ca
www.municipalite.montcalm.qc.ca
Municipal Type: Municipality
Incorporated: 6 mars 1907; *Area:* 119,65 km2
County or District: Les Laurentides; *Population in 2006:* 652
Provincial Electoral District(s): Argenteuil
Federal Electoral District(s): Laurentides-Labelle
Next Election: 1er novembre 2013
Lucie Côté, Directrice générale

Montcalm
1540, rue Albert
Sainte-Julienne, QC J0K 2T0
450-831-2182 Fax: 450-831-2647
info@mrcmontcalm.com
www.mrcmontcalm.com
Municipal Type: Regional County Municipality

Population in 2009: 44,201
Note: 11 municipalités.
Gaétan Hudon, Directeur général

Montcerf-Lytton
18, rue Principale nord
Montcerf-Lytton, QC J0W 1N0
819-449-4578 Fax: 819-449-7310
mun.montcerf@ireseau.com
www.montcerf-lytton.com
Municipal Type: Municipality
Incorporated: 19 septembre 2001; *Area:* 358,34 km2
County or District: La Vallée-de-la-Gatineau; *Population in 2006:* 739
Provincial Electoral District(s): Gatineau
Federal Electoral District(s): Pontiac
Next Election: 1er novembre 2013
Liliane Crytes, Sec.-Trés.

Montebello
550, rue Notre-Dame
Montebello, QC J0V 1L0
819-423-5123 Fax: 819-423-5703
mun.montebello@videotron.ca
www.ville.montebello.qc.ca
Municipal Type: Municipality
Incorporated: 29 août 1878; *Area:* 7,95 km2
County or District: Papineau; *Population in 2006:* 987
Provincial Electoral District(s): Papineau
Federal Electoral District(s): Argenteuil-Papineau-Mirabel
Next Election: 1er novembre 2013
Charles-Guy Beauchamp, Sec.-Trés.

Montmagny
159, rue Saint-Louis
Montmagny, QC G5V 1N5
418-248-5985 Fax: 418-248-4624
mrc@montmagny.com
www.montmagny.com
Municipal Type: Regional County Municipality
Incorporated: 1 janvier 1982;
Population in 2009: 23,155
Note: 14 municipalités.
Nancy Labrecque, Directrice générale

Montpellier
4, rue du Bosquet
Montpellier, QC J0V 1M0
819-428-3663 Fax: 819-428-1221
dg.montpellier@mrcpapineau.com
www.montpellier.ca
Municipal Type: Municipality
Incorporated: 11 octobre 1920; *Area:* 249,16 km2

County or District: Papineau; *Population in 2006:* 966
Provincial Electoral District(s): Papineau
Federal Electoral District(s): Argenteuil-Papineau-Mirabel
Next Election: 1er novembre 2013
Henriette Dupuis, Sec.-Trés.

Morin-Heights
567, ch du Village
Morin-Heights, QC J0R 1H0
450-226-3232 Fax: 450-226-8786
municipalite@morinheights.com
www.morinheights.com
Municipal Type: Municipality
Incorporated: 1er juillet 1855; *Area:* 55,42 km2
County or District: Les Pays-d'en-Haut; *Population in 2006:* 3,503
Provincial Electoral District(s): Argenteuil
Federal Electoral District(s): Argenteuil-Papineau-Mirabel
Next Election: 1er novembre 2013
Yves Desmarais, Sec.-Trés. & Directeur général

Mulgrave-et-Derry
CP 3000 Buckingham
140, rue Joseph
Gatineau, QC J8L 2X5
819-986-9519 Fax: 819-986-2586
Municipal Type: Municipality
Incorporated: 1er janvier 1870; *Area:* 297,74 km2
County or District: Papineau; *Population in 2006:* 389
Provincial Electoral District(s): Papineau
Federal Electoral District(s): Argenteuil-Papineau-Mirabel
Next Election: 1er novembre 2013
Michel-A. Vézina, Sec.-Trés.

Murdochville
CP 1120
635, 5e rue
Murdochville, QC G0E 1W0
418-784-2536 Fax: 418-784-2607
dgmurd@globetrotter.net
www.murdochville.com
Municipal Type: City
Incorporated: 15 juillet 1953; *Area:* 64,68 km2
County or District: La Côte-de-Gaspé; *Population in 2006:* 812
Provincial Electoral District(s): Gaspé
Federal Electoral District(s): Gaspésie-Iles-de-la-Madeleine
Next Election: 1er novembre 2013
Jean-Marie Chrétien, Sec.-Trés. & Directrice générale
Délisca Roussy, Mairesse

Namur
996, rue du Centenaire
Namur, QC J0V 1N0
819-426-2457 Fax: 819-426-3074
dirgeneral.namur@mrcpapineau.com
Municipal Type: Municipality
Incorporated: 1er janvier 1964; *Area:* 57,07 km2
County or District: Papineau; *Population in 2006:* 487
Provincial Electoral District(s): Papineau
Federal Electoral District(s): Argenteuil-Papineau-Mirabel
Next Election: 1er novembre 2013
Danielle Longtin, Directrice générale adjointe

Nantes
CP 60
1244, rue Principale
Nantes, QC G0Y 1G0
819-547-3655 Fax: 819-547-3755
munantes@axion.ca
Municipal Type: Municipality
Incorporated: 1er janvier 1874; *Area:* 120,47 km2
County or District: Le Granit; *Population in 2006:* 1,436
Provincial Electoral District(s): Mégantic-Compton
Federal Electoral District(s): Mégantic-L'Érable
Next Election: 1er novembre 2013
Lucie Lortitch, Sec.-Trés. & Directrice générale

Napierville
CP 1120
260, rue de l'Église
Napierville, QC J0J 1L0
450-245-7210 Fax: 450-245-7691
mun.napierville@qc.aira.com
www.napierville.ca
Municipal Type: Village
Incorporated: 1er janvier 1873; *Area:* 4,53 km2
County or District: Les Jardins-de-Napierville; *Population in 2006:* 3,352
Provincial Electoral District(s): Huntingdon
Federal Electoral District(s): Beauharnois-Salaberry
Next Election: 1er novembre 2013
Ginette Leblanc-Pruneau, Sec.-Trés. & Directrice générale

Natashquan
CP 99
29, ch d'en-Haut
Natashquan, QC G0G 2E0
418-726-3362 Fax: 418-726-3698
muninatashquan@globetrotter.net
Municipal Type: Township
Incorporated: 16 septembre 1907; *Area:* 193,20 km2
County or District: Minganie; *Population in 2006:* 264
Provincial Electoral District(s): Duplessis
Federal Electoral District(s): Manicouagan
Next Election: 1er novembre 2013
Léonard Landry, Sec.-Trés.

Nédélec
CP 70
33, rue Principale
Nédélec, QC J0Z 2Z0
819-784-3311 Fax: 819-784-2126
nedelec@mrctemiscamingue.qc.ca
Municipal Type: Township
Incorporated: 1er février 1909; *Area:* 369,90 km2
County or District: Témiscamingue; *Population in 2006:* 416
Provincial Electoral District(s): Rouyn-Noranda-Témiscamingue
Federal Electoral District(s): Abitibi-Témiscamingue
Next Election: 1er novembre 2013
Mireille St-Amour, Sec.-Trés. & Directrice générale

Némiscau
1, rue Lakeshore
Némiscau, QC J0Y 3B0
819-673-2512 Fax: 819-673-2542
nation@nemaska.ca
www.nemaska.ca
Municipal Type: Villages Cris

Provincial Electoral District(s): Ungava
Federal Electoral District(s): Abitibi-Baie-James-Nunavik-Eeyou
Josie Jimiken, Maire

Neuville
230, rue du Père-Rhéaume
Neuville, QC G0A 2R0
418-876-2280 Fax: 418-876-3349
mun@ville.neuville.qc.ca
www.ville.neuville.qc.ca
Municipal Type: City
Incorporated: 2 janvier 1997; *Area:* 72,04 km2
County or District: Portneuf; *Population in 2006:* 3,638
Provincial Electoral District(s): Portneuf
Federal Electoral District(s): Portneuf-Jacques-Cartier
Next Election: 1er novembre 2013
Normand Bolduc, Maire
Nicole Béland, Greffière

New Carlisle
CP 40
138, boul Gérard-D.-Levesque
New Carlisle, QC G0C 1Z0
418-752-3141 Fax: 418-752-3140
newcarlisle@globetrotter.net
Municipal Type: Municipality
Incorporated: 1er février 1877; *Area:* 66,12 km2
County or District: Bonaventure; *Population in 2006:* 1,370
Provincial Electoral District(s): Bonaventure
Federal Electoral District(s): Gaspésie-Iles-de-la-Madeleine
Next Election: 1er novembre 2013
Donald Kerr, Directeur général

New Richmond
99, place Suzanne-Guité
New Richmond, QC G0C 2B0
418-392-7000 Fax: 418-392-5331
dpaquet@villenewrichmond.com
www.villenewrichmond.com
Municipal Type: City
Incorporated: 1er juillet 1855; *Area:* 168,63 km2
County or District: Bonaventure; *Population in 2006:* 3,748
Provincial Electoral District(s): Bonaventure
Federal Electoral District(s): Gaspésie-Iles-de-la-Madeleine
Next Election: 1er novembre 2013
Line Cormier, Greffière
Nicole Appleby, Mairesse

Nicolet
180, rue Monseigneur-Panet
Nicolet, QC J3T 1S6
819-293-6901 Fax: 819-293-6767
maire@ville.nicolet.qc.ca
www.ville.nicolet.qc.ca
Municipal Type: City
Incorporated: 27 décembre 2000; *Area:* 94,50 km2
County or District: Nicolet-Yamaska; *Population in 2006:* 7,827
Provincial Electoral District(s): Nicolet-Yamaska
Federal Electoral District(s): Bas-Richelieu-Nicolet-Bécancour
Next Election: 1er novembre 2013
Pierre Genest, Directeur général
Alain Drouin, Maire

Nicolet-Yamaska
#257, 1, rue de Mgr-Courchesne
Nicolet, QC J3T 2C1
819-293-2997 Fax: 819-293-5367
mrcny@mrcnicolet-yamaska.qc.ca
www.mrcnicolet-yamaska.qc.ca
Municipal Type: Regional County Municipality
Incorporated: 1 janvier 1982;
Population in 2009: 22,557
Note: 16 municipalités.
Donald Martel, Directeur général

Nominingue
2110, ch du Tour-du-Lac
Nominingue, QC J0W 1R0
819-278-3384 Fax: 819-278-4967
mun.nominingue@expresso.qc.ca
www.expresso.qc.ca/nominingue
Municipal Type: Municipality
Incorporated: 30 octobre 1971; *Area:* 308,34 km2
County or District: Antoine-Labelle; *Population in 2006:* 2,317
Provincial Electoral District(s): Labelle
Federal Electoral District(s): Laurentides-Labelle
Next Election: 1er novembre 2013
Robert Charette, Sec.-Trés.

Norbertville
250, rte de la Rivière
Norbertville, QC G0P 1B0
819-369-9294 Fax: 819-369-8296
stnorber@ivic.qc.ca
Municipal Type: Village
Incorporated: 27 juillet 1940; *Area:* 2,84 km2
County or District: Arthabaska; *Population in 2006:* 266
Provincial Electoral District(s): Arthabaska
Federal Electoral District(s): Richmond-Arthabaska
Next Election: 1er novembre 2013
René Savoie, Sec.-Trés. & Directeur général

Normandin
1048, rue St-Cyrille
Normandin, QC G8M 4R9
418-274-2004 Fax: 418-274-7171
admin@ville.normandin.qc.ca
www.ville.normandin.qc.ca
Municipal Type: City
Incorporated: 10 mars 1979; *Area:* 211,96 km2
County or District: Maria-Chapdelaine; *Population in 2006:* 3,220
Provincial Electoral District(s): Roberval
Federal Electoral District(s): Roberval-Lac-St-Jean
Next Election: 1er novembre 2013
Guy Mailloux, Greffier & Directeur général
Lucien Guillemette, Maire

Normétal
CP 308
59, 1re rue
Normétal, QC J0Z 3A0
819-788-2550 Fax: 819-788-2730
normetal@normetal.ao.ca
www.normetal.ao.ca
Municipal Type: Municipality
Incorporated: 1er janvier 1945; *Area:* 55,89 km2
County or District: Abitibi-Ouest; *Population in 2006:* 886
Provincial Electoral District(s): Abitibi-Ouest
Federal Electoral District(s): Abitibi-Témiscamingue
Next Election: 1er novembre 2013
Gaétan Petit, Sec.-Trés.

North Hatley
3125, ch Capelton
North Hatley, QC J0B 2C0
819-842-2754 Fax: 819-842-4501
villagenorthhatley@qc.aira.com
www.northhatley.org
Municipal Type: Village
Incorporated: 25 octobre 1897; *Area:* 3,23 km2
County or District: Memphrémagog; *Population in 2006:* 722
Provincial Electoral District(s): Orford
Federal Electoral District(s): Compton-Stanstead
Next Election: 1er novembre 2013
Léonard Castagner, Sec.-Trés. & Directeur général

Notre-Dame-Auxiliatrice-de-Buckland
CP 40
4340, rue Principale
Buckland, QC G0R 1G0
418-789-3119 Fax: 418-789-3535
buckland@globetrotter.net
Municipal Type: Parish (Paroisse)
Incorporated: 1er janvier 1885; *Area:* 96,32 km2
County or District: Bellechasse; *Population in 2006:* 815
Provincial Electoral District(s): Bellechasse
Federal Electoral District(s): Lévis-Bellechasse
Next Election: 1er novembre 2013
Jocelyne Nadeau, Sec.-Trés.

Notre-Dame-de-Bonsecours
220A, rue Bonsecours
Montebello, QC J0V 1L0
819-423-5575 Fax: 819-423-5571
mun.ndbonsecours@mrcpapineau.com
Municipal Type: Municipality
Incorporated: 7 mars 1918; *Area:* 265,75 km2
County or District: Papineau; *Population in 2006:* 275
Provincial Electoral District(s): Papineau
Federal Electoral District(s): Argenteuil-Papineau-Mirabel
Next Election: 1er novembre 2013
Suzie Latourelle, Sec.-Trés.

Notre-Dame-de-Ham
25, rue de l'Église
Notre-Dame-de-Ham, QC G0P 1C0
819-344-5806 Fax: 819-344-5807
munndham@ivic.qc.ca
Municipal Type: Municipality
Incorporated: 7 octobre 1898; *Area:* 32,34 km2
County or District: Arthabaska; *Population in 2006:* 424
Provincial Electoral District(s): Richmond
Federal Electoral District(s): Richmond-Arthabaska
Next Election: 1er novembre 2013
Christiane Leblanc, Sec.-Trés.

Notre-Dame-de-l'Ile-Perrot
21, rue de l'Église
Notre-Dame-de-l'Ile-Perrot, QC J7V 8P4
514-453-4128 Fax: 514-453-8961
info@ndip.org
www.ndip.org
Municipal Type: Municipality
Incorporated: 14 avril 1984; *Area:* 28,14 km2
County or District: Vaudreuil-Soulanges; Communauté métropolitaine de Montréal; *Population in 2009:* 10,264
Provincial Electoral District(s): Vaudreuil
Federal Electoral District(s): Vaudreuil-Soulanges
Next Election: 1er novembre 2013
Jacques Robichaud, Greffier

Notre-Dame-de-la-Merci
1900, montée de la Réserve
Notre-Dame-de-la-Merci, QC J0T 2A0
819-424-2113 Fax: 819-424-7347
municipalitendm@netaxis.ca
www.municipalitenotredamedelamerci.com
Municipal Type: Municipality
Incorporated: 1er janvier 1950; *Area:* 251,22 km2
County or District: Matawinie; *Population in 2006:* 1,056
Provincial Electoral District(s): Bertrand
Federal Electoral District(s): Joliette
Next Election: 1er novembre 2013
Chantal Soucy, Sec.-Trés. & Directrice générale

Notre-Dame-de-la-Paix
267, rue Notre-Dame
Notre-Dame-de-la-Paix, QC J0V 1P0
819-522-6610 Fax: 819-522-6710
mun.ndlapaix@mrcpapineau.com
Municipal Type: Municipality
Incorporated: 3 octobre 1902; *Area:* 105,90 km2
County or District: Papineau; *Population in 2006:* 719
Provincial Electoral District(s): Papineau
Federal Electoral District(s): Argenteuil-Papineau-Mirabel
Next Election: 1er novembre 2013
Monique Côté, Sec.-Trés. & Directrice générale

Notre-Dame-de-la-Salette
CP 59
45, rue des Saules
Notre-Dame-de-la-Salette, QC J0X 2L0
819-766-2533 Fax: 819-766-2983
nds@infonet.ca
Municipal Type: Municipality
Incorporated: 17 mai 1979; *Area:* 117,54 km2
County or District: Les Collines-de-l'Outaouais; *Population in 2006:* 774
Provincial Electoral District(s): Papineau
Federal Electoral District(s): Pontiac
Next Election: 1er novembre 2013
Sylvie Gratton, Sec.-Trés.

Notre-Dame-de-Lorette
22, rue Principale
Notre-Dame-de-Lorette, QC G0W 1B0
418-276-1934 Fax: 418-276-1934
Municipal Type: Municipality
Incorporated: 1er janvier 1966; *Area:* 225,32 km2
County or District: Maria-Chapdelaine; *Population in 2006:* 175
Provincial Electoral District(s): Roberval
Federal Electoral District(s): Roberval-Lac-St-Jean
Next Election: 1er novembre 2013
Michèle Tremblay, Sec.-Trés.

Notre-Dame-de-Lourdes
830, rue Principale
Lourdes, QC G0S 1T0
819-385-4315 Fax: 819-385-4315
lourdes1@ivic.qc.ca
Municipal Type: Parish (Paroisse)
Incorporated: 7 octobre 1897; *Area:* 83,39 km2
County or District: L'Érable; *Population in 2006:* 716
Provincial Electoral District(s): Lotbinière
Federal Electoral District(s): Mégantic-L'Érable
Next Election: 1er novembre 2013
Hélène Lessard, Sec.-Trés.

Notre-Dame-de-Lourdes
4050, rue Principale
Notre Dame de Lourdes, QC J0K 1K0
450-759-2277 Fax: 450-759-2055
munindl@intermonde.net
Municipal Type: Municipality
Incorporated: 28 octobre 1925; *Area:* 35,48 km2
County or District: Joliette; *Population in 2006:* 2,201
Provincial Electoral District(s): Joliette
Federal Electoral District(s): Joliette
Next Election: 1er novembre 2013
Micheline Miron, Sec.-Trés.

Notre-Dame-de-Montauban
CP 69
555, av des Loisirs
Notre-Dame-de-Montauban, QC G0X 1W0
418-336-2640 Fax: 418-336-2353
nd-montauban@regionmekinac.com
www.municipalite.notre-dame-de-montauban.qc.ca
Municipal Type: Municipality
Incorporated: 3 janvier 1976; *Area:* 163,53 km2
County or District: Mékinac; *Population in 2006:* 846
Provincial Electoral District(s): Portneuf
Federal Electoral District(s): St-Maurice-Champlain
Next Election: 1er novembre 2013
Manon Frenette, Sec.-Trés. & Directrice générale

Notre-Dame-de-Pontmain
1027, rue Principale
Notre-Dame-de-Pontmain, QC J0W 1S0
819-597-2382 Fax: 819-597-2231
mun.pontmain@ireseau.com
Municipal Type: Municipality
Incorporated: 26 janvier 1894; *Area:* 267,92 km2
County or District: Antoine-Labelle; *Population in 2006:* 712
Provincial Electoral District(s): Labelle
Federal Electoral District(s): Laurentides-Labelle
Next Election: 1er novembre 2013
Suzanne Robinson, Sec.-Trés.

Notre-Dame-de-Stanbridge
CP 209
900, rue Principale
Notre-Dame-de-Stanbridge, QC J0J 1M0
450-296-4710 Fax: 450-296-5001
notre-dame@netc.net
www.notredamedestanbridge.qc.ca
Municipal Type: Parish (Paroisse)
Incorporated: 21 mars 1889; *Area:* 44,67 km2
County or District: Brome-Missisquoi; *Population in 2006:* 728
Provincial Electoral District(s): Brome-Missisquoi
Federal Electoral District(s): Brome-Missisquoi
Next Election: 1er novembre 2013
Béatrice Travers, Sec.-Trés. & Directrice générale

Notre-Dame-des-Anges
260, boul Langelier
Québec, QC G1K 5N1
418-529-0931 Fax: 418-524-7162
mamj@mediom.com
Municipal Type: Parish (Paroisse)
Incorporated: 1er juillet 1855; *Area:* 0,06 km2
Population in 2006: 437
Provincial Electoral District(s): Taschereau
Federal Electoral District(s): Québec
Next Election: 1er novembre 2013
Colette Huot, Sec.-Trés.

Notre-Dame-des-Bois
35, rte de l'Église
Notre-Dame-des-Bois, QC J0B 2E0
819-888-2724 Fax: 819-888-2904
mun.notredamedesbois@axion.ca
Municipal Type: Municipality
Incorporated: 1er janvier 1877; *Area:* 190,90 km2
County or District: Le Granit; *Population in 2006:* 964
Provincial Electoral District(s): Mégantic-Compton
Federal Electoral District(s): Mégantic-L'Érable
Next Election: 1er novembre 2013
Guylaine Blais, Sec.-Trés.

Notre-Dame-des-Monts
15, rue Principale
Notre-Dame-des-Monts, QC G0T 1L0
418-439-3452 Fax: 418-439-0883
municipalitenddm@coopnddm.com
www.notredamedesmonts.com
Municipal Type: Municipality
Incorporated: 11 avril 1935; *Area:* 56,15 km2
County or District: Charlevoix-Est; *Population in 2006:* 764
Provincial Electoral District(s): Charlevoix
Federal Electoral District(s):
Montmorency-Charlevoix-Haute-Côte-Nord
Next Election: 1er novembre 2013
Émilie Tremblay, Sec.-Trés.

Notre-Dame-des-Neiges
4, 2e rang Centre
Trois-Pistoles, QC G0L 4K0
418-851-3009 Fax: 418-851-3169
Municipal Type: Municipality
Incorporated: 1er juillet 1855; *Area:* 92,87 km2
County or District: Les Basques; *Population in 2006:* 1,209
Provincial Electoral District(s): Rivière-du-Loup
Federal Electoral District(s): Rimouski-Neigette-Témiscouata-Les Basques
Next Election: 1er novembre 2013
Danielle Ouellet, Sec.-Trés.

Notre-Dame-des-Pins
CP 100
2790, 1re av
Notre-Dame-des-Pins, QC G0M 1K0
418-774-9718 Fax: 418-774-9718
notredamedespins@globetrotter.net
Municipal Type: Parish (Paroisse)
Incorporated: 29 juin 1926; *Area:* 24,60 km2
County or District: Beauce-Sartigan; *Population in 2006:* 1,065
Provincial Electoral District(s): Beauce-Sud
Federal Electoral District(s): Beauce
Next Election: 1er novembre 2013
François Fontaine, Sec.-Trés.

Notre-Dame-des-Prairies
225, boul Antonio-Barrette
Notre-Dame-des-Prairies, QC J6E 1E7
450-759-7741 Fax: 450-759-6255
prairies@notre-dame-des-prairies.org
www.notre-dame-des-prairies.org
Municipal Type: City
Incorporated: 1er janvier 1957; *Area:* 17,74 km2
County or District: Joliette; *Population in 2006:* 8,230
Provincial Electoral District(s): Joliette
Federal Electoral District(s): Joliette
Next Election: 1er novembre 2013
Sylvie Malo, Greffière
Alain Larue, Maire

Notre-Dame-des-Sept-Douleurs
École Fraser
69B, ch de l'Ile
Ile Verte, QC G0L 1K0
418-898-3451 Fax: 418-898-3492
ndsd-ileverte@bellnet.ca
www.ileverte.qc.ca
Municipal Type: Parish (Paroisse)
Incorporated: 1er janvier 1874; *Area:* 11,18 km2
County or District: Rivière-du-Loup; *Population in 2006:* 62
Provincial Electoral District(s): Rivière-du-Loup
Federal Electoral District(s):
Montmagny-L'Islet-Kamouraska-Rivière-du-Loup
Next Election: 1er novembre 2013
Denis Cusson, Sec.-Trés. & Directeur général

Notre-Dame-du-Bon-Conseil
1428, rte 122
Notre-Dame-du-Bon-Conseil, QC J0C 1A0
819-336-5374 Fax: 819-336-2389
vaubin@cgocable.ca
Municipal Type: Parish (Paroisse)
Incorporated: 15 février 1898; *Area:* 86,42 km2
County or District: Drummond; *Population in 2006:* 912
Provincial Electoral District(s): Richmond
Federal Electoral District(s): Drummond
Next Election: 1er novembre 2013
Valérie Aubin, Sec.-Trés.

Notre-Dame-du-Bon-Conseil
CP 128
541, rue Notre-Dame
Notre-Dame-du-Bon-Conseil, QC J0C 1A0
819-336-2744 Fax: 819-336-2030
nb.bonconseil@cgocable.ca
www.ndbc.qc.ca
Municipal Type: Village
Incorporated: 1er janvier 1957; *Area:* 4,22 km2
County or District: Drummond; *Population in 2006:* 1,426
Provincial Electoral District(s): Richmond
Federal Electoral District(s): Drummond
Next Election: 1er novembre 2013
Isabelle Dumont, Directrice générale

Notre-Dame-du-Lac
5, rue de l'Hôtel-de-Ville
Notre-Dame-du-Lac, QC G0L 1X0
418-899-6743 Fax: 418-899-2041
ville.nddl@globetrotter.net
Municipal Type: City
Incorporated: 14 décembre 1968; *Area:* 106,13 km2
County or District: Témiscouata; *Population in 2006:* 2,060
Provincial Electoral District(s): Kamouraska-Témiscouata
Federal Electoral District(s): Rimouski-Nigette-Témiscouata-Les Basques
Next Election: 1er novembre 2013
Colomba Lebel, Sec.-Trés.
Gilles Garon, Maire

Notre-Dame-du-Laus
CP 10
66, rue Principale
Notre-Dame-du-Laus, QC J0X 2M0
819-767-2247 Fax: 819-767-3102
mun.notre-dame-du-laus@tlb.sympatico.ca
www.municipalite.notre-dame-du-laus.qc.ca
Municipal Type: Municipality
Incorporated: 1er janvier 1876; *Area:* 866,02 km2
County or District: Antoine-Labelle; *Population in 2006:* 1,564
Provincial Electoral District(s): Labelle
Federal Electoral District(s): Laurentides-Labelle
Next Election: 1er novembre 2013
Yves Larocque, Sec.-Trés.

Notre-Dame-du-Mont-Carmel
3860, rue de l' Hôtel de Ville
Notre-Dame-du-Mont-Carmel, QC G0X 3J0
819-375-9856 Fax: 819-373-4045
municipalite@mont-carmel.org
www.mont-carmel.org
Municipal Type: Parish (Paroisse)
Incorporated: 30 décembre 1858; *Area:* 126,61 km2
County or District: Les Chenaux; *Population in 2006:* 5,299
Provincial Electoral District(s): St-Maurice
Federal Electoral District(s): St-Maurice-Champlain
Next Election: 1er novembre 2013
Jean Lachance, Directeur général

Notre-Dame-du-Nord
CP 160
71, rue Principale
Notre-Dame-du-Nord, QC J0Z 3B0

819-723-2294 Fax: 819-723-2483
municipalitenddunord@mrctemiscamingue.qc.ca
www.municipalite.notre-dame-du-nord.qc.ca
Municipal Type: Municipality
Incorporated: 23 septembre 1919; *Area:* 103,60 km2
County or District: Témiscamingue; *Population in 2006:* 1,116
Provincial Electoral District(s): Rouyn-Noranda-Témiscamingue
Federal Electoral District(s): Abitibi-Témiscamingue
Next Election: 1er novembre 2013
Réjean Pelletier, Sec.-Trés. & Directeur général

Notre-Dame-du-Portage
560, rte de la Montagne
Notre-Dame-du-Portage, QC G0L 1Y0
418-862-9163 Fax: 418-862-5240
municipalite.portage@videotron.ca
www.municipalite.notre-dame-du-portage.qc.ca
Municipal Type: Municipality
Incorporated: 19 juillet 1856; *Area:* 39,55 km2
County or District: Rivière-du-Loup; *Population in 2006:* 1,262
Provincial Electoral District(s): Rivière-du-Loup
Federal Electoral District(s):
Montmagny-L'Islet-Kamouraska-Rivière-du-Loup
Next Election: 1er novembre 2013
Éric Bérubé, Sec.-Trés.

Notre-Dame-du-Rosaire
144, rue Principale
Notre-Dame-du-Rosaire, QC G0R 2H0
418-469-2802 Fax: 418-469-2802
munndr@globetrotter.net
Municipal Type: Municipality
Incorporated: 18 décembre 1894; *Area:* 158,53 km2
County or District: Montmagny; *Population in 2006:* 394
Provincial Electoral District(s): Montmagny-L'Islet
Federal Electoral District(s):
Montmagny-L'Islet-Kamouraska-Rivière-du-Loup
Next Election: 1er novembre 2013
Danye Anctil, Directrice générale

Notre-Dame-du-Sacré-Coeur-d'Issoudun
268, rue Principale
Issoudun, QC G0S 1L0
418-728-2006 Fax: 418-728-2303
munissoudun@globetrotter.net
Municipal Type: Parish (Paroisse)
Incorporated: 4 janvier 1909; *Area:* 60,81 km2
County or District: Lotbinière; *Population in 2006:* 794
Provincial Electoral District(s): Lotbinière
Federal Electoral District(s): Lotbinière-Chutes-de-la-Chaudière
Next Election: 1er novembre 2013
Suzanne Therrien-Croteau, Directrice générale

Nouvelle
CP 68
470, rue Francoeur
Nouvelle, QC G0C 2E0
418-794-2253 Fax: 418-794-2254
munouv@globetrotter.net
www.nouvellegaspesie.com
Municipal Type: Municipality
Incorporated: 10 octobre 1907; *Area:* 230,63 km2
County or District: Avignon; *Population in 2006:* 1,815
Provincial Electoral District(s): Bonaventure
Federal Electoral District(s): Gaspésie-Iles-de-la-Madeleine
Next Election: 1er novembre 2013
Daniel Bujold, Sec.-Trés.

Noyan
1312, ch de la Petite-France
Noyan, QC J0J 1B0
450-294-2689 Fax: 450-294-2175
info@ville.noyan.qc.ca
www.ville.noyan.qc.ca
Municipal Type: Municipality
Incorporated: 1er juillet 1855; *Area:* 43,79 km2
County or District: Le Haut-Richelieu; *Population in 2006:* 1,354
Provincial Electoral District(s): Iberville
Federal Electoral District(s): Brome-Missisquoi
Next Election: 1er novembre 2013
Marie-France Saucier, Sec.-Trés.

Ogden
70, ch Ogden
Ogden, QC J0B 3E3
819-876-7117 Fax: 819-876-2121
Municipal Type: Municipality
Incorporated: 23 janvier 1932; *Area:* 75,49 km2
County or District: Memphrémagog; *Population in 2006:* 762
Provincial Electoral District(s): Orford
Federal Electoral District(s): Compton-Stanstead
Next Election: 1er novembre 2013
Renée Donaldson, Sec.-Trés.

Oka
183, rue des Anges
Oka, QC J0N 1E0
450-479-8333 Fax: 450-479-1886
info@municipalite.oka.qc.ca
municipalite.oka.qc.ca/fr/index.php
Municipal Type: Municipality
Incorporated: 8 septembre 1999; *Area:* 67,21 km2
County or District: Deux-Montagnes; *Population in 2006:* 3,300
Provincial Electoral District(s): Mirabel
Federal Electoral District(s): Argenteuil-Papineau-Mirabel
Next Election: 1er novembre 2013
Marie Daoust, Directrice générale

Orford
2530, ch du Parc
Orford, QC J1X 8R8
819-843-3111 Fax: 819-843-2707
beaupre@canton.orford.qc.ca
www.canton.orford.qc.ca
Municipal Type: Township
Incorporated: 1er juillet 1855; *Area:* 135,25 km2
County or District: Memphrémagog; *Population in 2006:* 2,979
Provincial Electoral District(s): Orford
Federal Electoral District(s): Brome-Missisquoi
Next Election: 1er novembre 2013
Brigitte Boisvert, Greffière

Ormstown
81, rue Lambton
Ormstown, QC J0S 1K0
450-829-2625 Fax: 450-829-4162
ormstown@rocler.qc.ca
Municipal Type: Municipality
Incorporated: 26 janvier 2000; *Area:* 142,39 km2
County or District: Le Haut-St-Laurent; *Population in 2006:* 3,651
Provincial Electoral District(s): Huntingdon
Federal Electoral District(s): Beauharnois-Salaberry
Next Election: 1er novembre 2013
John McCaig, Maire

Otter Lake
CP 70
15, av Palmer
Otter Lake, QC J0X 2P0
819-453-7049 Fax: 819-453-7311
munleslie@renc.igs.net
Municipal Type: Municipality
Incorporated: 1er janvier 1877; *Area:* 496,21 km2
County or District: Pontiac; *Population in 2006:* 972
Provincial Electoral District(s): Pontiac
Federal Electoral District(s): Pontiac
Next Election: 1er novembre 2013
Anita Lafleur, Sec.-Trés.

Otterburn Park
472, rue Prince-Edward
Otterburn Park, QC J3H 1W4
450-536-0303 Fax: 450-467-8260
info@ville.otterburnpark.qc.ca
www.ville.otterburnpark.qc.ca
Municipal Type: City
Incorporated: 1er juillet 1855; *Area:* 5,20 km2
County or District: La Vallée-du-Richelieu; *Population in 2006:* 8,464
Provincial Electoral District(s): Borduas
Federal Electoral District(s): Chambly-Borduas
Next Election: 1er novembre 2013
Clément Vautour, Greffier
Guy Dubé, Maire

Oujé-Bougoumou Village
Headquarters Office, Oujé-Bougoumou Cree Na
203, Opemiska Meskino
Oujé-Bougoumou, QC G0W 3C0
418-745-3911 Fax: 418-745-3544
tourism@ouje.ca
www.ouje.ca
Municipal Type: Villages Cris

Provincial Electoral District(s): Ungava
Federal Electoral District(s): Roberval-Lac-St-Jean
Sam Bosum, Chief

Packington
35A, rue Principale
Packington, QC G0L 1Z0
418-853-2269 Fax: 418-853-6427
packing@municipalite.packington.qc.ca
www.municipalite.packington.qc.ca
Municipal Type: Parish (Paroisse)
Incorporated: 6 octobre 1925; *Area:* 117,89 km2
County or District: Témiscouata; *Population in 2006:* 657
Provincial Electoral District(s): Kamouraska-Témiscouata
Federal Electoral District(s): Rimouski-Neigette-Témiscouata-Les Basques
Next Election: 1er novembre 2013
Denis Moreau, Sec.-Trés.

Padoue
CP 15
215, rue Beaulieu
Padoue, QC G0J 1X0
418-775-8188 Fax: 418-775-8177
Municipal Type: Municipality
Incorporated: 31 janvier 1911; *Area:* 67,57 km2
County or District: La Mitis; *Population in 2006:* 283
Provincial Electoral District(s): Matapédia
Federal Electoral District(s): Haute-Gaspésie-La Mitis-Matane-Matapédia
Next Election: 1er novembre 2013
Line Fillion, Sec.-Trés.

Palmarolle
CP 309
499, rte 393
Palmarolle, QC J0Z 3C0
819-787-2303 Fax: 819-787-2412
palmarolle@palmarolle.ao.ca
www.palmarolle.ao.ca
Municipal Type: Municipality
Incorporated: 14 avril 1930; *Area:* 118,36 km2
County or District: Abitibi-Ouest; *Population in 2006:* 1,453
Provincial Electoral District(s): Abitibi-Ouest
Federal Electoral District(s): Abitibi-Témiscamingue
Next Election: 1er novembre 2013
Claude Marquis, Sec.-Trés.

Papineau
266, rue Viger
Papineauville, QC J0V 1R0
819-427-6243 Fax: 819-427-8318
info@mrcpapineau.com
www.mrcpapineau.com
Municipal Type: Regional County Municipality
Incorporated: 1 janvier 1983;
Population in 2009: 21,895
Note: 24 municipalités.
Ghislain Ménard, Directeur général

Papineauville
#100, 188, rue Jeanne-D'Arc
Papineauville, QC J0V 1R0
819-427-5511 Fax: 819-427-5590
papineauville@mrcpapineau.com
www.mun-papineauville.qc.ca
Municipal Type: Municipality
Incorporated: 29 novembre 2000; *Area:* 48,52 km2
County or District: Papineau; *Population in 2006:* 2,167
Provincial Electoral District(s): Papineau
Federal Electoral District(s): Argenteuil-Papineau-Mirabel
Next Election: 1er novembre 2013
Jocelyn Robinson, Directeur général

Parisville
CP 69
975, rue Principale ouest
Parisville, QC G0S 1X0
819-292-2222 Fax: 819-292-1514
info@municipalite.parisville.qc.ca
www.municipalite.parisville.qc.ca
Municipal Type: Parish (Paroisse)
Incorporated: 18 mars 1901; *Area:* 36,85 km2
County or District: Bécancour; *Population in 2006:* 487
Provincial Electoral District(s): Lotbinière
Federal Electoral District(s): Bas-Richelieu-Nicolet-Bécancour
Next Election: 1er novembre 2013
Ginette C.-Bisaillon, Sec.-Trés. & Directrice générale

Paspébiac
CP 130
178, 9e rue
Paspébiac, QC G0C 2K0
418-752-2277 Fax: 418-752-6566
paspebia@globetrotter.net
www.paspebiac.com
Municipal Type: City
Incorporated: 20 août 1997; *Area:* 94,59 km2
County or District: Bonaventure; *Population in 2006:* 3,159
Provincial Electoral District(s): Bonaventure
Federal Electoral District(s): Gaspésie-Iles-de-la-Madeleine
Next Election: 1er novembre 2013
Annie Chapados, Sec.-Trés.
Gino Lebrasseur, Maire

Percé
CP 99
137, rte 132 ouest
Percé, QC G0C 2L0
418-782-2933 Fax: 418-782-5487
vilp@globetrotter.net
www.ville.perce.qc.ca
Municipal Type: City
Incorporated: 1er janvier 1971; *Area:* 427,94 km2
County or District: Le Rocher-Percé; *Population in 2006:* 3,419
Provincial Electoral District(s): Gaspé
Federal Electoral District(s): Gaspésie-Iles-de-la-Madeleine
Next Election: 1er novembre 2013
Gemma Vibert, Greffière
Georges Mamelonet, Maire

Péribonka
312, rue Édouard-Niquet
Péribonka, QC G0W 2G0
418-374-2967 Fax: 418-374-2355
mun.per@qc.aira.com
Municipal Type: Municipality
Incorporated: 19 septembre 1908; *Area:* 113,46 km2
County or District: Maria-Chapdelaine; *Population in 2006:* 541
Provincial Electoral District(s): Roberval
Federal Electoral District(s): Roberval-Lac-St-Jean
Next Election: 1er novembre 2013
Normand Fortin, Sec.-Trés.

Petit-Saguenay
CP 40
35, ch du Quai
Petit-Saguenay, QC G0V 1N0

418-272-2323 Fax: 418-272-2346
munps@royaume.com
www.petit-saguenay.com
Municipal Type: Municipality
Incorporated: 12 août 1919; *Area:* 328,72 km2
County or District: Le Fjord-du-Saguenay; *Population in 2006:* 780
Provincial Electoral District(s): Dubuc
Federal Electoral District(s): Chicoutimi-Le Fjord
Next Election: 1er novembre 2013
Alexis Lavoie, Sec.-Trés. & Directeur général

Petite-Rivière-St-François
CP 10
1067, rue Principale
Petite-Rivière-Saint-François, QC G0A 2L0
418-632-5831 Fax: 418-632-5886
munprsf@charlevoix.net
www.petiteriviere.com
Municipal Type: Municipality
Incorporated: 1er juillet 1855; *Area:* 135,66 km2
County or District: Charlevoix; *Population in 2006:* 703
Provincial Electoral District(s): Charlevoix
Federal Electoral District(s):
Montmorency-Charlevoix-Haute-Côte-Nord
Next Election: 1er novembre 2013
Francine Dufour, Sec.-Trés.

Petite-Vallée
CP 1067
45, rue Principale
Petite-Vallée, QC G0E 1Y0
418-393-2949 Fax: 418-393-2949
bibliopv@globetrotter.qc.ca
Municipal Type: Municipality
Incorporated: 1er janvier 1957; *Area:* 37,83 km2
County or District: La Côte-de-Gaspé; *Population in 2006:* 248
Provincial Electoral District(s): Gaspé
Federal Electoral District(s): Gaspésie-Iles-de-la-Madeleine
Next Election: 1er novembre 2013
Simon Côté, Sec.-Trés.

Piedmont
670, rue Principale
Piedmont, QC J0R 1K0
450-227-1888 Fax: 450-227-6716
info@municipalite.piedmont.qc.ca
www.municipalite.piedmont.qc.ca
Municipal Type: Municipality
Incorporated: 22 septembre 1923; *Area:* 23,66 km2
County or District: Les Pays-d'en-Haut; *Population in 2006:* 2,386
Provincial Electoral District(s): Bertrand
Federal Electoral District(s): Laurentides-Labelle
Next Election: 1er novembre 2013
Gilbert Aubin, Sec.-Trés.

Pierre-De Saurel
50, rue du Fort
Sorel-Tracy, QC J3P 7X7
450-743-2703 Fax: 450-743-7313
mrc@pierredesaurel.com
www.mrcpierredesaurel.com
Municipal Type: Regional County Municipality
Incorporated: 1 janvier 1982;
Population in 2009: 50,286
Note: 12 municipalités.
Denis Boisvert, Directeur général

Pierreville
CP 300
26, rue Ally
Pierreville, QC J0G 1J0
450-568-2139 Fax: 450-568-0689
info@municipalitepierreville.qc.ca
Municipal Type: Municipality
Incorporated: 13 juin 2001; *Area:* 79,54 km2
County or District: Nicolet-Yamaska; *Population in 2006:* 2,337
Provincial Electoral District(s): Nicolet-Yamaska
Federal Electoral District(s): Bas-Richelieu-Nicolet-Bécancour
Next Election: 1er novembre 2013
Micheline C. Laforce, Sec.-Trés. & Directrice générale

Piopolis
403, rue Principale
Piopolis, QC G0Y 1H0
819-583-3953 Fax: 819-583-1467
mun.piopolis@axion.ca
www.piopolis.ca
Municipal Type: Municipality
Incorporated: 1er janvier 1880; *Area:* 104,14 km2
County or District: Le Granit; *Population in 2006:* 376
Provincial Electoral District(s): Mégantic-Compton
Federal Electoral District(s): Mégantic-L'Érable
Next Election: 1er novembre 2013
Julie Cloutier, Sec.-Trés. & Directrice générale

Plaisance
274, rue Desjardins
Plaisance, QC J0V 1S0
819-427-5363 Fax: 819-427-5015
ville.plaisance@videotron.ca
www.ville.plaisance.qc.ca
Municipal Type: Municipality
Incorporated: 31 octobre 1900; *Area:* 42,61 km2
County or District: Papineau; *Population in 2006:* 1,024
Provincial Electoral District(s): Papineau
Federal Electoral District(s): Argenteuil-Papineau-Mirabel
Next Election: 1er novembre 2013
Benoit Hébert, Sec.-Trés. & Directeur général

Plessisville
CP 245
290, rte 165 sud
Plessisville, QC G6L 2Y7
819-362-2712 Fax: 819-362-9185
info@paroisseplessisville.com
Municipal Type: Parish (Paroisse)
Incorporated: 1er juillet 1855; *Area:* 136,29 km2
County or District: L'Érable; *Population in 2006:* 2,557
Provincial Electoral District(s): Arthabaska
Federal Electoral District(s): Mégantic-L'Érable
Next Election: 1er novembre 2013
Johanne Dubois, Sec.-Trés. & Directrice générale

Plessisville
1700, rue St-Calixte
Plessisville, QC G6L 1R3
819-362-3284 Fax: 819-362-6421
info@ville.plessisville.qc.ca
www.ville.plessisville.qc.ca
Municipal Type: City
Incorporated: 27 avril 1855; *Area:* 4,44 km2
County or District: L'Érable; *Population in 2006:* 6,677
Provincial Electoral District(s): Arthabaska
Federal Electoral District(s): Mégantic-L'Érable
Next Election: 1er novembre 2013
René Turcotte, Sec.-Trés.
Jacques Martineau, Maire

Pohénégamook
1309, rue Principale
Pohénégamook, QC G0L 1J0
418-859-2222 Fax: 418-859-3465
villedepohenegamook@bellnet.ca
www.pohenegamook.net
Municipal Type: City
Incorporated: 3 novembre 1973; *Area:* 351,97 km2
County or District: Témiscouata; *Population in 2006:* 2,940
Provincial Electoral District(s): Kamouraska-Témiscouata
Federal Electoral District(s): Rimouski-Neigette-Témiscouata-Les Basques
Next Election: 1er novembre 2013
Denise Pelletier, Greffière
Guy Leblanc, Maire

Pointe-à-la-Croix
CP 159
30, rue Chouinard
Pointe-à-la-Croix, QC G0C 1L0
418-788-2011 Fax: 418-788-2916
pointe-a-la-croix@globetrotter.net
www.pointe-a-la-croix.com
Municipal Type: Municipality
Incorporated: 7 mai 1983; *Area:* 394,03 km2
County or District: Avignon; *Population in 2006:* 1,587
Provincial Electoral District(s): Bonaventure
Federal Electoral District(s): Gaspésie-Iles-de-la-Madeleine
Next Election: 1er novembre 2013
Claude Audet, Sec.-Trés. & Directeur général

Pointe-aux-Outardes
471, ch Principal
Pointe-aux-Outardes, QC G0H 1H0
418-567-2203 Fax: 418-567-4409
munpao@satcomcolibri.com
Municipal Type: Village
Incorporated: 1er janvier 1964; *Area:* 71,56 km2
County or District: Manicouagan; *Population in 2006:* 1,443
Provincial Electoral District(s): René-Lévesque
Federal Electoral District(s): Manicouagan
Next Election: 1er novembre 2013
Dania Hovington, Sec.-Trés. & Directrice générale

Pointe-Calumet
300, av Basile-Routhier
Pointe-Calumet, QC J0N 1G2
450-473-5930 Fax: 450-473-6571
info@municipalite.pointe-calumet.qc.ca
www.municipalite.pointe-calumet.qc.ca
Municipal Type: Municipality
Incorporated: 12 février 1953; *Area:* 4,89 km2
County or District: Deux-Montagnes; Communauté métropolitaine de Montréal; *Population in 2009:* 6,847
Provincial Electoral District(s): Mirabel
Federal Electoral District(s): Argenteuil-Papineau-Mirabel
Next Election: 1er novembre 2013
Chantal Pilon, Directrice générale

Pointe-des-Cascades
105, ch du Fleuve
Pointe-des-Cascades, QC J0P 1M0
450-455-3414 Fax: 450-455-9671
pointe-des-cascades@videotron.ca
Municipal Type: Village
Incorporated: 1er mai 1961; *Area:* 2,66 km2
County or District: Vaudreuil-Soulanges; *Population in 2006:* 1,046
Provincial Electoral District(s): Soulanges
Federal Electoral District(s): Vaudreuil-Soulanges
Next Election: 1er novembre 2013
Christiane Cyr, Sec.-Trés.

Pointe-Fortune
694, rue du Tisseur
Pointe-Fortune, QC J0P 1N0
450-451-5178 Fax: 450-451-4649
mpf@qc.aira.com
www.pointefortune.ca
Municipal Type: Village
Incorporated: 28 août 1880; *Area:* 9,09 km2
County or District: Vaudreuil-Soulanges; *Population in 2006:* 507
Provincial Electoral District(s): Soulanges
Federal Electoral District(s): Vaudreuil-Soulanges
Next Election: 1er novembre 2013
Diane Héroux, Sec.-Trés. & Directrice générale

Pointe-Lebel
365, rue Granier
Pointe-Lebel, QC G0H 1N0
418-589-8073 Fax: 418-589-6154
municipalite.pointelebel@globetrotter.net
www.pointe-lebel.com
Municipal Type: Village
Incorporated: 1er janvier 1964; *Area:* 91,16 km2
County or District: Manicouagan; *Population in 2006:* 1,958
Provincial Electoral District(s): René-Lévesque
Federal Electoral District(s): Manicouagan
Next Election: 1er novembre 2013
Gervais Boucher, Directeur général

Pont-Rouge
212, rue Dupont
Pont-Rouge, QC G3H 1A1
418-873-4481 Fax: 418-873-3494
info@ville.pontrouge.qc.ca
www.ville.pontrouge.qc.ca
Municipal Type: City
Incorporated: 3 janvier 1996; *Area:* 121,02 km2
County or District: Portneuf; *Population in 2006:* 7,518
Provincial Electoral District(s): Portneuf
Federal Electoral District(s): Portneuf-Jacques-Cartier
Next Election: 1er novembre 2013
Claude Bégin, Maire
Jocelyne Laliberté, Greffière

Pontiac
2024, rte 148
Pontiac, QC J0X 2G0
819-455-2401 Fax: 819-455-9756
municipalite_pontiac@videotron.ca
Municipal Type: Municipality
Incorporated: 1er janvier 1975; *Area:* 446,87 km2
County or District: Les Collines-de-l'Outaouais; *Population in 2006:* 5,238
Provincial Electoral District(s): Pontiac
Federal Electoral District(s): Pontiac
Next Election: 1er novembre 2013
Sylvain Bertrand, Sec.-Trés.

Pontiac
CP 460
602, rte 301
Campbell's Bay, QC J0X 1K0
819-648-5689 Fax: 819-648-5810
mrc@mrcpontiac.qc.ca
www.mrcpontiac.qc.ca
Municipal Type: Regional County Municipality
Incorporated: 1 janvier 1983; *Area:* 13 848,26 km2
Population in 2009: 14,608
Note: 18 municipalités & 1 autre territoire.
Rémi Bertrand, Directeur général

Port-Cartier
40, av Parent
Port-Cartier, QC G5B 2G5
418-766-2343 Fax: 418-766-6236
dgport-cartier@globetrotter.net
Municipal Type: City
Incorporated: 19 février 2003; *Area:* 1073,70 km2
County or District: Sept-Rivières; *Population in 2006:* 6,758
Provincial Electoral District(s): Duplessis
Federal Electoral District(s): Manicouagan
Next Election: 1er novembre 2013
Note: Effective February 19, 2003, the City of Port-Cartier & the Municipality of Rivière-Pentecôte amalgamated to create the new City of Port-Cartier
Pierre St-Onge, Greffier
Laurence Méthot Losier, Maire

Port-Daniel-Gascons
CP 130
494, rte 132
Port-Daniel, QC G0C 2N0
418-396-5225 Fax: 418-396-5588
municipalitedeport-daniel@globetrotter.net
Municipal Type: Municipality
Incorporated: 17 janvier 2001; *Area:* 305,34 km2
County or District: Le Rocher Percé; *Population in 2006:* 2,586
Provincial Electoral District(s): Bonaventure
Federal Electoral District(s): Gaspésie-Iles-de-la-Madeleine
Next Election: 1er novembre 2013
Thérèse Roussy, Sec.-Trés. & Directrice générale

Portage-du-Fort
CP 130
24, rue Church
Portage-du-Fort, QC J0X 2T0

819-647-2767 Fax: 819-647-1910
Municipal Type: Village
Incorporated: 1er janvier 1863; *Area:* 4,24 km2
County or District: Pontiac; *Population in 2006:* 280
Provincial Electoral District(s): Pontiac
Federal Electoral District(s): Pontiac
Next Election: 1er novembre 2013
Tracey Hérault, Sec.-Trés.

Portneuf
185, rte 138
Cap-Santé, QC G0A 1L0
418-285-3744 Fax: 418-285-1703
portneuf@mrc-portneuf.qc.ca
www.portneuf.com
Municipal Type: Regional County Municipality

Population in 2009: 47,206
Note: 18 municipalités & 3 autres territoires.
Daniel Le Pape, Directeur général

Portneuf
297, 1re Av
Portneuf, QC G0A 2Y0
418-286-3844 Fax: 418-286-4304
info@villedeportneuf.com
www.villedeportneuf.com
Municipal Type: City
Incorporated: 4 juillet 2002; *Area:* 110,43 km2
County or District: Portneuf; *Population in 2006:* 3,086
Provincial Electoral District(s): Portneuf
Federal Electoral District(s): Portneuf-Jacques-Cartier
Next Election: 1er novembre 2013
France Marcotte, Greffière
Pierre de Savoye, Maire
Yves Landry, Directeur général

Portneuf-sur-Mer
CP 98
170, rue Principale
Portneuf-sur-Mer, QC G0T 1P0
418-238-2642 Fax: 418-238-5319
muniport@bellnet.ca
www.fjord-best.com/portneuf
Municipal Type: Municipality
Incorporated: 12 septembre 1902; *Area:* 241,23 km2
County or District: La Haute-Côte-Nord; *Population in 2006:* 835
Provincial Electoral District(s): René-Lévesque
Federal Electoral District(s):
Montmorency-Charlevoix-Haute-Côte-Nord
Next Election: 1er novembre 2013
Note: Formerly Municipality of Ste-Anne-de-Portneuf.
Gontran Tremblay, Sec.-Trés.

Potton
CP 330
2, rue de Vale Perkins
Mansonville, QC J0E 1X0
450-292-3313 Fax: 450-292-5555
potton@axion.ca
Municipal Type: Township
Incorporated: 1er juillet 1855; *Area:* 264,10 km2
County or District: Memphrémagog; *Population in 2006:* 1,790
Provincial Electoral District(s): Brome-Missisquoi
Federal Electoral District(s): Brome-Missisquoi
Next Election: 1er novembre 2013
Danielle Gilbert, Sec.-Trés. & Directrice générale

Poularies
CP 58
990, rue Principale
Poularies, QC J0Z 3E0
819-782-5159 Fax: 819-782-5063
poularies@mrcao.qc.ca
www.poularies.ao.ca
Municipal Type: Municipality
Incorporated: 7 mai 1924; *Area:* 164,95 km2
County or District: Abitibi-Ouest; *Population in 2006:* 693
Provincial Electoral District(s): Abitibi-Ouest
Federal Electoral District(s): Abitibi-Témiscamingue
Next Election: 1er novembre 2013
Hélène Richer, Directrice générale

Preissac
6, rue des Rapides
Preissac, QC J0Y 2E0
819-732-4938 Fax: 819-732-4909
munic.preissac@coopwifi.com
www.preissac.com
Municipal Type: Municipality
Incorporated: 1er janvier 1979; *Area:* 489,50 km2
County or District: Abitibi; *Population in 2006:* 726
Provincial Electoral District(s): Abitibi-Ouest
Federal Electoral District(s): Abitibi-Témiscamingue
Next Election: 1er novembre 2013
Pierre Goyette, Sec.-Trés.

Price
CP 340
18, rue Fournier
Price, QC G0J 1Z0
418-775-2144 Fax: 418-775-2459
price@globetrotter.qc.ca
www.municipaliteprice.cjb.net
Municipal Type: Village
Incorporated: 3 mars 1926; *Area:* 2,35 km2
County or District: La Mitis; *Population in 2006:* 1,777
Provincial Electoral District(s): Matapédia
Federal Electoral District(s):
Haute-Gaspésie-La-Mitis-Matane-Matapédia
Next Election: 1er novembre 2013
Louise Furlong, Sec.-Trés.

Princeville
50, rue St-Jacques ouest
Princeville, QC G6L 4Y5
819-364-3333 Fax: 819-364-5198
info@villedeprinceville.qc.ca
www.villedeprinceville.qc.ca
Municipal Type: City
Incorporated: 23 février 2000; *Area:* 198 km2
County or District: L'Érable; *Population in 2006:* 5,571
Provincial Electoral District(s): Arthabaska
Federal Electoral District(s): Mégantic-L'Érable
Next Election: 1er novembre 2013
Gilles Fortier, Maire
Mario Juaire, Greffier & Directeur général

Puvirnituq
CP 150
Puvirnituq, QC J0M 1P0
819-988-2825 Fax: 819-988-2751
www.nvpuvirnituq.ca
Municipal Type: Northern Village
Incorporated: 2 septembre 1989; *Area:* 111 km2
County or District: Kativik; *Population in 2006:* 1,457
Provincial Electoral District(s): Ungava
Federal Electoral District(s): Abitibi-Baie-James-Nunavik-Eeyou
Next Election: 7 novembre 2007
Sarah Beaulne, Sec.-Trés.

Quaqtaq
CP 107
Quaqtaq, QC J0M 1J0
819-492-9912 Fax: 819-492-9935
stukkiapik@nvquaqtaq.ca
www.nvquaqtaq.ca
Municipal Type: Northern Village
Incorporated: 1er novembre 1980; *Area:* 26,49 km2
County or District: Kativik; *Population in 2006:* 315
Provincial Electoral District(s): Ungava
Federal Electoral District(s): Abitibi-Baie-James-Nunavik-Eeyou
Next Election: 7 novembre 2007
Sammy Tukkiapik, Sec.-Trés.

Racine
348, rue de L'Église
Racine, QC J0E 1Y0
450-532-2876 Fax: 450-532-2865
munracin@cooptel.qc.ca
www.municipalite.racine.qc.ca
Municipal Type: Municipality
Incorporated: 15 février 1995; *Area:* 107,87 km2
County or District: Le Val-St-François; *Population in 2006:* 1,265
Provincial Electoral District(s): Johnson
Federal Electoral District(s): Jonquière-Alma
Next Election: 1er novembre 2013
André Courtemanche, Sec.-Trés.

Ragueneau
523, rte 138
Ragueneau, QC G0H 1S0
418-567-2345 Fax: 418-567-2344
ragueneau@satcomcolibri.com
www.municipalite.ragueneau.qc.ca
Municipal Type: Parish (Paroisse)
Incorporated: 7 mars 1951; *Area:* 215,92 km2
County or District: Manicouagan; *Population in 2006:* 1,520
Provincial Electoral District(s): René-Lévesque
Federal Electoral District(s): Manicouagan
Next Election: 1er novembre 2013
Colette Girard, Sec.-Trés.

Rapide-Danseur
535, rue du Village
Rapide-Danseur, QC J0Z 3G0
819-948-2152 Fax: 819-948-2265
rapide-danseur@rapide-danseur.ao.ca
www.rapide-danseur.ao.ca
Municipal Type: Municipality
Incorporated: 1er janvier 1981; *Area:* 185,18 km2
County or District: Abitibi-Ouest; *Population in 2006:* 273
Provincial Electoral District(s): Abitibi-Ouest
Federal Electoral District(s): Abitibi-Témiscamingue
Next Election: 1er novembre 2013
Yvette Fournier-Boutin, Sec.-Trés.

Rapides-des-Joachims
CP 92
48, rue de l'Église
Rapides-des-Joachims, QC J0X 3M0
613-586-2532 Fax: 613-586-2720
rapidjoa@magma.ca
Municipal Type: Municipality
Incorporated: 1er janvier 1955; *Area:* 248,92 km2
County or District: Pontiac; *Population in 2006:* 172
Provincial Electoral District(s): Pontiac
Federal Electoral District(s): Pontiac
Next Election: 1er novembre 2013
Noreen Loos, Sec.-Trés.

Rawdon
3647, rue Queen
Rawdon, QC J0K 1S0
450-834-2596 Fax: 450-834-3031
www.rawdon.ca
Municipal Type: Municipality
Incorporated: 28 mai 1998; *Area:* 179,73 km2
County or District: Matawinie; *Population in 2009:* 10,251
Provincial Electoral District(s): Rousseau
Federal Electoral District(s): Joliette
Next Election: 1er novembre 2013
Marie Andrée Tremblay, Greffière

Rémigny
1304, ch de l'Église
Rémigny, QC J0Z 3H0
819-761-2421 Fax: 819-761-2421
mun.remigny@mrctemiscamingue.qc.ca
Municipal Type: Municipality
Incorporated: 1er janvier 1978; *Area:* 985,03 km2
County or District: Témiscamingue; *Population in 2006:* 318
Provincial Electoral District(s): Rouyn-Noranda-Témiscamingue
Federal Electoral District(s): Abitibi-Témiscamingue
Next Election: 1er novembre 2013
Josée Dubeau, Sec.-Trés.

Richelieu
200, boul Richelieu
Richelieu, QC J3L 3R4
450-658-1157 Fax: 450-658-5096
n.poirier@villederichelieu.org
www.villederichelieu.org
Municipal Type: City
Incorporated: 15 mars 2000; *Area:* 29,75 km2
County or District: Rouville; *Population in 2006:* 5,208
Provincial Electoral District(s): Chambly
Federal Electoral District(s): Chambly-Borduas
Next Election: 1er novembre 2013
Nancy Poirier, Greffière
Jacques Ladouceur, Maire

Richmond
745, rue Gouin
Richmond, QC J0B 2H0
819-826-3789 Fax: 819-826-2813
admin@ville.richmond.qc.ca
www.ville.richmond.qc.ca
Municipal Type: City
Incorporated: 29 décembre 1999; *Area:* 7,76 km2
County or District: Le Val-St-François; *Population in 2006:* 3,336
Provincial Electoral District(s): Richmond
Federal Electoral District(s): Richmond-Arthabaska
Next Election: 1er novembre 2013
Colette Létourneau, Sec.
Marc-André Martel, Maire

Rigaud
391, ch de la Mairie
Rigaud, QC J0P 1P0
450-451-0869 Fax: 450-451-4227
rigaud@ville.rigaud.qc.ca
www.ville.rigaud.qc.ca
Municipal Type: Municipality
Incorporated: 29 novembre 1995; *Area:* 97,15 km2
County or District: Vaudreuil-Soulanges; *Population in 2009:* 7,057
Provincial Electoral District(s): Soulanges
Federal Electoral District(s): Vaudreuil-Soulanges
Next Election: 1er novembre 2013
Hélène Therrien, Greffière

Rimouski-Neigette
220, av de la Cathédrale
Rimouski, QC G5L 5J2
418-724-5154 Fax: 418-725-4567
administration@mrcrimouskineigette.qc.ca
Municipal Type: Regional County Municipality

Population in 2009: 53,878
Note: 10 municipalités & 1 autre territoire.
Louise Audet, Directrice générale

Ripon
#101, 31, rue Coursol
Ripon, QC J0V 1V0
819-983-2000 Fax: 819-983-1327
ripon@tlb.sympatico.ca
www.ville.ripon.qc.ca
Municipal Type: Municipality
Incorporated: 3 mai 2000; *Area:* 140,57 km2
County or District: Papineau; *Population in 2006:* 1,497
Provincial Electoral District(s): Papineau
Federal Electoral District(s): Argenteuil-Papineau-Mirabel
Next Election: 1er novembre 2013
Lorraine Sabourin, Sec.-Trés.

Ristigouche-Partie-Sud-Est
35, ch Kempt, RR#2
Matapédia, QC G0J 1V0
418-788-5769 Fax: 418-788-2598
ristigouchesudest@globetrotter.net
www.ristigouchesudest.ca
Municipal Type: Township
Incorporated: 30 juin 1906; *Area:* 48,95 km2

County or District: Avignon; *Population in 2006:* 173
Provincial Electoral District(s): Bonaventure
Federal Electoral District(s): Gaspésie-Iles-de-la-Madeleine
Next Election: 1er novembre 2013
Suzanne Bourdages, Sec.-Trés.

Rivière-à-Claude
520, rue Principale est
Rivière-à-Claude, QC G0E 1Z0
418-797-2422 Fax: 418-797-2455
munirac@globetrotter.net
Municipal Type: Municipality
Incorporated: 18 décembre 1923; *Area:* 155,39 km2
County or District: La Haute-Gaspésie; *Population in 2006:* 171
Provincial Electoral District(s): Matane
Federal Electoral District(s): Haute-Gaspésie-La Mitis-Matane-Matapédia
Next Election: 1er novembre 2013
Claudine Auclair, Sec.-Trés.

Rivière-à-Pierre
CP 69
830, rue Principale
Rivière-à-Pierre, QC G0A 3A0
418-323-2112 Fax: 418-323-2111
rivapier@globetrotter.net
Municipal Type: Municipality
Incorporated: 11 octobre 1897; *Area:* 521,31 km2
County or District: Portneuf; *Population in 2006:* 694
Provincial Electoral District(s): Portneuf
Federal Electoral District(s): Portneuf-Jacques-Cartier
Next Election: 1er novembre 2013
Sylvie Trahan, Sec.-Trés.

Rivière-au-Tonnerre
CP 129
473, rue Jacques Cartier
Rivière-au-Tonnerre, QC G0G 2L0
418-465-2255 Fax: 418-465-2956
municipaliterivauton@globetrotter.net
Municipal Type: Municipality
Incorporated: 14 décembre 1925; *Area:* 1331,17 km2
County or District: Minganie; *Population in 2006:* 390
Provincial Electoral District(s): Duplessis
Federal Electoral District(s): Manicouagan
Next Election: 1er novembre 2013
Carmelle Anglehart, Sec.-Trés.

Rivière-Beaudette
663, ch de la Frontière
Rivière-Beaudette, QC J0P 1R0
450-269-2931 Fax: 450-269-2815
munrivbeaudette@qc.aira.com
Municipal Type: Municipality
Incorporated: 17 janvier 1990; *Area:* 19,62 km2
County or District: Vaudreuil-Soulanges; *Population in 2006:* 1,720
Provincial Electoral District(s): Soulanges
Federal Electoral District(s): Vaudreuil-Soulanges
Next Election: 1er novembre 2013
Céline Chayer, Directrice générale

Rivière-Bleue
32, rue des Pins est
Rivière-Bleue, QC G0L 2B0
418-893-5559 Fax: 418-893-5530
info@riviere-bleue.ca
Municipal Type: Municipality
Incorporated: 14 juin 1975; *Area:* 179,93 km2
County or District: Témiscouata; *Population in 2006:* 1,407
Provincial Electoral District(s): Kamouraska-Témiscouata
Federal Electoral District(s): Rimouski-Neigette-Témiscouata-Les Basques
Next Election: 1er novembre 2013
Claude-A. Dubé, Sec.-Trés. & Directeur général

Rivière-du-Loup
310, rue St-Pierre
Rivière-du-Loup, QC G5R 3V3
418-867-2485 Fax: 418-867-3100
administration@mrc-riviere-du-loup.qc.ca
www.riviereduloup.ca
Municipal Type: Regional County Municipality
Incorporated: 1 janvier 1982; *Area:* 1 267,45 km2
Population in 2009: 33,947
Note: 13 municipalités.
Raymond Duval, Directeur général

Rivière-Éternité
418, rte Principale
Rivière-Éternité, QC G0V 1P0
418-272-2860 Fax: 418-272-3454
munriv.denis@royaume.com
mun.riveternite@royaume.com
Municipal Type: Municipality
Incorporated: 20 juillet 1974; *Area:* 496,88 km2
County or District: Le Fjord-du-Saguenay; *Population in 2006:* 557
Provincial Electoral District(s): Dubuc
Federal Electoral District(s): Chicoutimi-Le Fjord
Next Election: 1er novembre 2013
Denis Houde, Sec.-Trés. & Directeur général

Rivière-Héva
CP 60
740, rte St-Paul nord
Rivière-Héva, QC J0Y 2H0
819-735-3521 Fax: 819-735-4251
nathalie@mun.r-h.com
Municipal Type: Municipality
Incorporated: 1er janvier 1982; *Area:* 193 km2
County or District: La Vallée-de-l'Or; *Population in 2006:* 1,056
Provincial Electoral District(s): Abitibi-Est
Federal Electoral District(s): Abitibi-Baie-James-Nunavik-Eeyou
Next Election: 1er novembre 2013
Nathalie Savard, Sec.-Trés. & Directrice générale

Rivière-Ouelle
CP 99
106, rue de l'Église
Rivière-Ouelle, QC G0L 2C0
418-856-3829 Fax: 418-856-1790
munrivierouelle@videotron.ca
Municipal Type: Municipality
Incorporated: 1er juillet 1855; *Area:* 54,72 km2
County or District: Kamouraska; *Population in 2006:* 1,165
Provincial Electoral District(s): Kamouraska-Témiscouata
Federal Electoral District(s): Montmagny-L'Islet-Kamouraska-Rivière-du-Loup
Next Election: 1er novembre 2013
André Lacombe, Sec.-Trés.

Rivière-Rouge
25, rue L'Annonciation sud
Rivière-Rouge, QC J0T 1T0
819-275-2929 Fax: 819-275-3676
greffe@riviere-rouge.ca
www.riviere-rouge.ca
Municipal Type: City
Incorporated: 18 décembre 2002; *Area:* 463,18 km2
County or District: Antoine-Labelle; *Population in 2006:* 4,152
Provincial Electoral District(s): Labelle
Federal Electoral District(s): Laurentides-Labelle
Next Election: 1er novembre 2013
Note: Effective December 18, 2002, the Municipality of La Macaza, the Village of L'Annonciation, the Municipality of Marchand & the Village of Ste-Véronique amalgamated to create the new City of Rivière-Rouge.
Claire Coulombe, Greffière
Déborah Bélanger, Mairesse

Rivière-St-Jean
116, rue du Quai
Rivière-Saint-Jean, QC G0G 2N0
418-949-2464 Fax: 418-949-2489
munrsj@xplornet.com
Municipal Type: Municipality
Incorporated: 1er janvier 1966; *Area:* 652,54 km2
County or District: Minganie; *Population in 2006:* 260
Provincial Electoral District(s): Duplessis
Federal Electoral District(s): Manicouagan
Next Election: 1er novembre 2013
Louise Rodgers, Sec.-Trés.

Robert-Cliche
111A, 107e Rue
Beauceville, QC G5X 2P9
418-774-9828 Fax: 418-774-4057
www.beaucerc.com
Municipal Type: Regional County Municipality
Incorporated: 1 janvier 1982; *Area:* 829,03 km2
Population in 2009: 19,001
Note: 10 municipalités.
Gilbert Caron, Directeur général

Rochebaucourt
20, rue du Chanoine-Girard
Rochebaucourt, QC J0Y 2J0
819-754-2083 Fax: 819-754-2083
muniroche@tlb.sympatico.ca
Municipal Type: Municipality
Incorporated: 1er janvier 1983; *Area:* 185 km2
County or District: Abitibi; *Population in 2006:* 177
Provincial Electoral District(s): Abitibi-Ouest
Federal Electoral District(s): Abitibi-Témiscamingue
Next Election: 1er novembre 2013
Diane Fleurent, Sec.-Trés.

Roquemaure
15, rue Raymond est
Roquemaure, QC J0Z 3K0
819-787-6311 Fax: 819-787-6383
roquemaure@mrcao.qc.ca
www.roquemaure.ao.ca
Municipal Type: Municipality
Incorporated: 1er janvier 1952; *Area:* 121,67 km2
County or District: Abitibi-Ouest; *Population in 2006:* 402
Provincial Electoral District(s): Abitibi-Ouest
Federal Electoral District(s): Abitibi-Témiscamingue
Next Election: 1er novembre 2013
Annick Lavoie, Sec.-Trés. & Directrice générale

Rougemont
61, ch de Marieville
Rougemont, QC J0L 1M0
450-469-3790 Fax: 450-469-0309
municipalite.rougemont@videotron.ca
www.rougemont.ca
Municipal Type: Municipality
Incorporated: 26 janvier 2000; *Area:* 44,48 km2
County or District: Rouville; *Population in 2006:* 2,622
Provincial Electoral District(s): Iberville
Federal Electoral District(s): Shefford
Next Election: 1er novembre 2013
Vacant, Sec.-Trés. & Directrice générale

Roussillon
#200, 260, rue Saint-Pierre
Saint-Constant, QC J5A 2A5
450-638-1221 Fax: 450-638-4499
admin@mrcroussillon.qc.ca
www.mrcroussillon.qc.ca
Municipal Type: Regional County Municipality

Population in 2009: 153,382
Note: 11 municipalités.
Pierre Largy, Directeur général

Rouville
#100, 500 rue Desjardins
Marieville, QC J3M 1E1
450-460-2127 Fax: 450-460-7169
mrcrouville@on.aira.com
www.mrcrouville.qc.ca
Municipal Type: Regional County Municipality
Incorporated: 1 janvier 1982; *Area:* 484,99 km2
Population in 2009: 31,926
Note: 8 municipalités.

Roxton
216, rang Ste-Geneviève
Roxton Falls, QC J0H 1E0
450-548-2500 Fax: 450-548-2412
canrox@cooptel.qc.ca
Municipal Type: Township
Incorporated: 1er juillet 1855; *Area:* 149,07 km2
County or District: Acton; *Population in 2006:* 1,016
Provincial Electoral District(s): Johnson
Federal Electoral District(s): St-Hyacinthe-Bagot
Next Election: 1er novembre 2013
Caroline Choquette, Directrice générale

Roxton Falls
26, rue du Marché
Roxton Falls, QC J0H 1E0
450-548-5790 Fax: 450-548-5881
roxton@cooptel.qc.ca
www.cooptel.qc.ca/~roxton
Municipal Type: Village
Incorporated: 1er janvier 1863; *Area:* 5,25 km2
County or District: Acton; *Population in 2006:* 1,305
Provincial Electoral District(s): Johnson
Federal Electoral District(s): St-Hyacinthe-Bagot
Next Election: 1er novembre 2013
Julie Gagné, Sec.-Trés.

Roxton Pond
901, rue St-Jean
Roxton Pond, QC J0E 1Z0
450-372-6875 Fax: 450-372-1205
munroxtonpond@qc.aira.com
Municipal Type: Municipality
Incorporated: 17 décembre 1997; *Area:* 102,11 km2
County or District: La Haute-Yamaska; *Population in 2006:* 3,599
Provincial Electoral District(s): Johnson
Federal Electoral District(s): Shefford
Next Election: 1er novembre 2013
Francois Giasson, Sec.-Trés. & Directeur général

Sacré-Coeur
CP 159
88, rue Principale nord
Sacré-Coeur, QC G0T 1Y0
418-236-4621 Fax: 418-236-9144
s-c@municipalite.sacre-coeur.qc.ca
www.municipalite.sacre-coeur.qc.ca
Municipal Type: Municipality
Incorporated: 30 juin 1976; *Area:* 341,74 km2
County or District: La Haute-Côte-Nord; *Population in 2006:* 2,024
Provincial Electoral District(s): René-Lévesque
Federal Electoral District(s): Montmorency-Charlevoix-Haute-Côte-Nord
Next Election: 1er novembre 2013
Sarto Simard, Directeur général

Sacré-Coeur-de-Jésus
4118, rte 112
East Broughton, QC G0N 1G0
418-427-3447 Fax: 418-427-4774
sacrecoeurjesus@bellnet.ca
www.sacrecoeurdejesus.qc.ca
Municipal Type: Parish (Paroisse)
Incorporated: 11 décembre 1889; *Area:* 103,850 km2
County or District: Les Appalaches; *Population in 2009:* 553
Provincial Electoral District(s): Frontenac
Federal Electoral District(s): Mégantic-L'Érable
Next Election: 1er novembre 2013
Marie-France Létourneau, Directrice générale

Saint-Adalbert
55, rue Principale
Saint-Adalbert, QC G0R 2M0
418-356-5271 Fax: 418-356-5317
mstadalb@globetrotter.net
Municipal Type: Municipality
Incorporated: 26 août 1911; *Area:* 213,95 km2
County or District: L'Islet; *Population in 2006:* 596

Provincial Electoral District(s): Montmagny-L'Islet
Federal Electoral District(s):
Montmagny-L'Islet-Kamouraska-Rivière-du-Loup
Next Election: 1er novembre 2013
Magguy Mathault, Sec.-Trés.

Saint-Adelme
CP 39
138, rue Principale
Saint-Adelme, QC G0J 2B0
418-733-4044 Fax: 418-733-4111
munstadelme@globetrotter.net
www.saint-adelme.com
Municipal Type: Parish (Paroisse)
Incorporated: 9 septembre 1933; *Area:* 100,20 km2
County or District: Matane; *Population in 2006:* 497
Provincial Electoral District(s): Matane
Federal Electoral District(s): Haute-Gaspésie-La Mitis-Matane-Matapédia
Next Election: 1er novembre 2013
Annick Hudon, Directrice générale

Saint-Adelphe
150, rue Baillargeon
Saint-Adelphe-de-Champlain, QC G0X 2G0
418-322-5721 Fax: 418-322-5434
st-adelphe@regionmekinac.com
Municipal Type: Parish (Paroisse)
Incorporated: 19 octobre 1891; *Area:* 135,35 km2
County or District: Mékinac; *Population in 2006:* 1,013
Provincial Electoral District(s): Laviolette
Federal Electoral District(s): St-Maurice-Champlain
Next Election: 1er novembre 2013
Daniel Bacon, Directeur général

Saint-Adolphe-d'Howard
1881, ch du Village
Saint-Adolphe-d'Howard, QC J0T 2B0
819-327-2044 Fax: 819-327-2282
info@stadolphedhoward.qc.ca
www.stadolphedhoward.qc.ca
Municipal Type: Municipality
Incorporated: 1er janvier 1883; *Area:* 144,41 km2
County or District: Les Pays-d'en-Haut; *Population in 2006:* 3,563
Provincial Electoral District(s): Argenteuil
Federal Electoral District(s): Argenteuil-Papineau-Mirabel
Next Election: 1er novembre 2013
Michel Binette, Sec.-Trés. & Directeur général

Saint-Adrien
1589, rue Principale
Saint-Adrien, QC J0A 1C0
819-828-2872 Fax: 819-828-0442
munstadrien@cgocable.ca
Municipal Type: Municipality
Incorporated: 1er janvier 1879; *Area:* 97,59 km2
County or District: Les Sources; *Population in 2006:* 488
Provincial Electoral District(s): Richmond
Federal Electoral District(s): Richmond-Arthabaska
Next Election: 1er novembre 2013
Maryse Ducharme, Sec.-Trés.

Saint-Adrien-d'Irlande
152, rue Municipale
Saint-Adrien-d'Irlande, QC G0N 1M0
418-335-2585 Fax: 418-335-2585
muadrien@globetrotter.net
Municipal Type: Municipality
Incorporated: 1er janvier 1873; *Area:* 52,780 km2
County or District: Les Appalaches; *Population in 2009:* 419
Provincial Electoral District(s): Frontenac
Federal Electoral District(s): Mégantic-L'Érable
Next Election: 1er novembre 2013
Ghislaine Leblanc, Directrice générale

Saint-Agapit
1186, rue Principale
Saint-Agapit, QC G0S 1Z0
418-888-4620 Fax: 418-888-4791
stagapit@globetrotter.net
Municipal Type: Municipality
Incorporated: 14 avril 1979; *Area:* 65,91 km2
County or District: Lotbinière; *Population in 2006:* 2,965
Provincial Electoral District(s): Lotbinière
Federal Electoral District(s): Lotbinière-Chutes-de-la-Chaudière
Next Election: 1er novembre 2013
Michèle Bouchard, Sec.-Trés.

Saint-Aimé
CP 240
285, rue Bonsecours
Massueville, QC J0G 1K0
450-788-2737 Fax: 450-788-3337
staime@bas-richelieu.net
Municipal Type: Municipality
Incorporated: 1er juillet 1855; *Area:* 61,33 km2
County or District: Pierre-De Saurel; *Population in 2006:* 523
Provincial Electoral District(s): Richelieu
Federal Electoral District(s): Bas-Richelieu-Nicolet-Bécancour
Next Election: 1er novembre 2013
Francine B. Lambert, Sec.-Trés.

Saint-Aimé-des-Lacs
119, rue Principale
Saint-Aimé-des-Lacs, QC G0T 1S0
418-439-2229 Fax: 418-439-1475
mun.sadl@qc.aira.com
Municipal Type: Municipality
Incorporated: 1er janvier 1950; *Area:* 101,57 km2
County or District: Charlevoix-Est; *Population in 2006:* 1,076
Provincial Electoral District(s): Charlevoix
Federal Electoral District(s):
Montmorency-Charlevoix-Haute-Côte-Nord
Next Election: 1er novembre 2013
Suzanne Gaudreault, Sec.-Trés.

Saint-Alban
204, rue Principale
Saint-Alban, QC G0A 3B0
418-268-8026 Fax: 418-268-5073
st-alban@globetrotter.net
www.st-alban.qc.ca
Municipal Type: Municipality
Incorporated: 31 décembre 1991; *Area:* 150,55 km2
County or District: Portneuf; *Population in 2006:* 1,138
Provincial Electoral District(s): Portneuf
Federal Electoral District(s): Portneuf-Jacques-Cartier
Next Election: 1er novembre 2013
Andrée Gosselin, Sec.-Trés.

Saint-Albert
CP 100
25, rue des Loisirs
Saint-Albert, QC J0A 1E0
819-353-3300 Fax: 819-353-3313
stalbert@telwarwick.net
Municipal Type: Municipality
Incorporated: 1er janvier 1864; *Area:* 70,36 km2
County or District: Arthabaska; *Population in 2006:* 1,501
Provincial Electoral District(s): Richmond
Federal Electoral District(s): Richmond-Arthabaska
Next Election: 1er novembre 2013
Suzanne Crête, Sec.-Trés.

Saint-Alexandre
453, rue St-Denis
Saint-Alexandre, QC J0J 1S0
450-346-6641 Fax: 450-346-0538
villedestalexandre@qc.aira.com
www.ville.saint-alexandre.qc.ca
Municipal Type: Municipality
Incorporated: 17 septembre 1988; *Area:* 76,55 km2
County or District: Le Haut-Richelieu; *Population in 2006:* 2,340
Provincial Electoral District(s): Iberville
Federal Electoral District(s): St-Jean
Next Election: 1er novembre 2013
Maryse Boucher, Sec.-Trés.

Saint-Alexandre-de-Kamouraska
CP 10
629, rte 289
Saint-Alexandre-de-Kamouraska, QC G0L 2G0
418-495-2440 Fax: 418-495-2659
stalex.kamouraska@bellnet.ca
www.stalex.kamouraska.qc.ca
Municipal Type: Municipality
Incorporated: 1er juillet 1855; *Area:* 115,95 km2
County or District: Kamouraska; *Population in 2006:* 1,880
Provincial Electoral District(s): Kamouraska-Témiscouata
Federal Electoral District(s):
Montmagny-L'Islet-Kamouraska-Rivière-du-Loup
Next Election: 1er novembre 2013
Lyne Dumont, Sec.-Trés. & Directrice générale

Saint-Alexandre-des-Lacs
17, rue de l'Église
Saint-Alexandre-des-Lacs, QC G0J 2C0
418-778-3532 Fax: 418-778-1315
alexlacs@globetrotter.net
Municipal Type: Parish (Paroisse)
Incorporated: 1er janvier 1965; *Area:* 92,98 km2
County or District: La Matapédia; *Population in 2006:* 275
Provincial Electoral District(s): Matapédia
Federal Electoral District(s): Haute-Gaspésie-La Mitis-Matane-Matapédia
Next Election: 1er novembre 2013
Caroline Savoie, Sec.-Trés.

Saint-Alexis
232, rue Principale
Saint-Alexis, QC J0K 1T0
450-839-7277 Fax: 450-839-6241
info@st-alexis.com
Municipal Type: Parish (Paroisse)
Incorporated: 1er juillet 1855; *Area:* 36,59 km2
County or District: Montcalm; *Population in 2006:* 722
Provincial Electoral District(s): Rousseau
Federal Electoral District(s): Montcalm
Next Election: 1er novembre 2013
Robert Perreault, Maire

Saint-Alexis
232, rue Principale
Saint-Alexis, QC J0K 1T0
450-839-7277 Fax: 450-839-6241
info@st-alexis.com
Municipal Type: Village
Incorporated: 16 novembre 1920; *Area:* 6,60 km2
County or District: Montcalm; *Population in 2006:* 556
Provincial Electoral District(s): Rousseau
Federal Electoral District(s): Montcalm
Next Election: 1er novembre 2013
Rémy Lanoue, Directeur général

Saint-Alexis-de-Matapédia
CP 99
190, rue Principale
Saint-Alexis-de-Matapédia, QC G0J 2E0
418-299-2030 Fax: 418-299-3011
plateau1@globetrotter.qc.ca
Municipal Type: Municipality
Incorporated: 1er juillet 1855; *Area:* 83,37 km2
County or District: Avignon; *Population in 2006:* 625
Provincial Electoral District(s): Bonaventure
Federal Electoral District(s): Gaspésie-Iles-de-la-Madeleine
Next Election: 1er novembre 2013
Lise Pitre, Sec.-Trés.

Saint-Alexis-des-Monts
101, rue de l'Hôtel-de-Ville
Saint-Alexis-des-Monts, QC J0K 1V0
819-265-2046 Fax: 819-265-2481
info@saint-alexis-des-monts.ca
www.saint-alexis-des-monts.ca
Municipal Type: Parish (Paroisse)
Incorporated: 21 avril 1984; *Area:* 1153,85 km2
County or District: Maskinongé; *Population in 2006:* 3,118
Provincial Electoral District(s): Maskinongé
Federal Electoral District(s): Berthier-Maskinongé
Next Election: 1er novembre 2013
Gilles Frappier, Sec.-Trés.

Saint-Alfred
194, rang Ste-Marie
Saint-Alfred, QC G0M 1L0
418-774-2068 Fax: 418-774-2068
municipalitestalfred@sogetel.net
Municipal Type: Municipality
Incorporated: 1er janvier 1950; *Area:* 42,42 km2
County or District: Robert-Cliche; *Population in 2006:* 458
Provincial Electoral District(s): Beauce-Nord
Federal Electoral District(s): Beauce
Next Election: 1er novembre 2013
Diane Jacques, Sec.-Trés.

Saint-Alphonse
127, rue Principale est
Saint-Alphonse, QC G0C 2V0
418-388-5214 Fax: 418-388-2435
st-alphonsemuni@globetrotter.net
www.st-alphonsegaspesie.com
Municipal Type: Municipality
Incorporated: 9 mai 1902; *Area:* 113,13 km2
County or District: Bonaventure; *Population in 2006:* 731
Provincial Electoral District(s): Bonaventure
Federal Electoral District(s): Gaspésie-Iles-de-la-Madeleine
Next Election: 1er novembre 2013
Reina Goulet, Sec.-Trés.

Saint-Alphonse
360, rue Principale
Saint-Alphonse-de-Granby, QC J0E 2A0
450-375-4570 Fax: 450-375-4717
infos@st-alphonse.qc.ca
Municipal Type: Parish (Paroisse)
Incorporated: 30 décembre 1890; *Area:* 50,52 km2
County or District: La Haute-Yamaska; *Population in 2006:* 2,918
Provincial Electoral District(s): Brome-Missisquoi
Federal Electoral District(s): Shefford
Next Election: 1er novembre 2013
Réal Pitt, Directeur général

Saint-Alphonse-Rodriguez
101, rue de la Plage
Saint-Alphonse-Rodriguez, QC J0K 1W0
450-883-2264 Fax: 450-883-0833
fdauphin@munsar.ca
www.munsar.ca
Municipal Type: Municipality
Incorporated: 1er juillet 1855; *Area:* 101,37 km2
County or District: Matawinie; *Population in 2006:* 3,152
Provincial Electoral District(s): Berthier
Federal Electoral District(s): Joliette
Next Election: 1er novembre 2013
Jacques Y. Lachapelle, Sec.-Trés. & Directeur général

Saint-Amable
616, rue de l'Église
Saint-Amable, QC J0L 1N0
450-649-3555 Fax: 450-922-0728
ville@st-amable.qc.ca
www.st-amable.qc.ca
Municipal Type: Municipality
Incorporated: 13 juin 1921; *Area:* 38,04 km2
County or District: Lajemmerais; Communauté métropolitaine de Montréal; *Population in 2009:* 8,980
Provincial Electoral District(s): Verchères
Federal Electoral District(s): Verchères-Les-Patriotes
Next Election: 1er novembre 2013
Nicolas-Marie Moukhaiber, Directeur général

Saint-Ambroise
330, rue Gagnon
Saint-Ambroise, QC G7P 2P9

418-672-4765 Fax: 418-672-6126
info@st-ambroise.qc.ca
www.st-ambroise.qc.ca
Municipal Type: Municipality
Incorporated: 25 septembre 1971; *Area:* 148,61 km2
County or District: Le Fjord-du-Saguenay; *Population in 2006:* 3,484
Provincial Electoral District(s): Dubuc
Federal Electoral District(s): Jonquière-Alma
Next Election: 1er novembre 2013
Michel Perreault, Sec.-Trés. & Directeur général

Saint-Ambroise-de-Kildare
CP 57
850, rue Principale
Kildare, QC J0K 1C0
450-755-4782 Fax: 450-755-4784
ambroise@qc.aira.com
www.saintambroisedekildare.qc.ca
Municipal Type: Parish (Paroisse)
Incorporated: 1er juillet 1855; *Area:* 66,89 km2
County or District: Joliette; *Population in 2006:* 3,491
Provincial Electoral District(s): Joliette
Federal Electoral District(s): Joliette
Next Election: 1er novembre 2013
Yvon Ducharme, Sec.-Trés. & Directeur général

Saint-Anaclet-de-Lessard
318, rue Principale ouest
Saint-Anaclet, QC G0K 1H0
418-723-2816 Fax: 418-723-0436
munstana@globetrotter.net
www.saintanacletdelessard.qc.ca
Municipal Type: Parish (Paroisse)
Incorporated: 9 mai 1859; *Area:* 126,26 km2
County or District: Rimouski-Neigette; *Population in 2006:* 2,644
Provincial Electoral District(s): Rimouski
Federal Electoral District(s): Rimouski-Neigette-Témiscouata-Les Basques
Next Election: 1er novembre 2013
Alain Lapierre, Directeur général

Saint-André
122A, rue Principale
Saint-André-de-Kamouraska, QC G0L 2H0
418-493-2085 Fax: 418-493-2373
munand@bellnet.ca
Municipal Type: Municipality
Incorporated: 14 février 1987; *Area:* 68,94 km2
County or District: Kamouraska; *Population in 2006:* 618
Provincial Electoral District(s): Kamouraska-Témiscouata
Federal Electoral District(s):
Montmagny-L'Islet-Kamouraska-Rivière-du-Loup
Next Election: 1er novembre 2013
Claudine Lévesque, Directrice générale

Saint-André-Avellin
119, rue Principale
Saint-André-Avellin, QC J0V 1W0
819-983-2318 Fax: 819-983-2344
info@ville.st-andre-avellin.qc.ca
www.ville.st-andre-avellin.qc.ca
Municipal Type: Municipality
Incorporated: 17 décembre 1997; *Area:* 131,05 km2
County or District: Papineau; *Population in 2006:* 3,435
Provincial Electoral District(s): Papineau
Federal Electoral District(s): Argenteuil-Papineau-Mirabel
Next Election: 1er novembre 2013
Claire Tremblay, Sec.-Trés. & Directrice générale

Saint-André-d'Argenteuil
10, rue de la Mairie
Saint-André-d'Argenteuil, QC J0V 1X0
450-537-3527 Fax: 450-537-3070
munst-andre@qc.aira.com
Municipal Type: Municipality
Incorporated: 29 décembre 1999; *Area:* 98,45 km2
County or District: Argenteuil; *Population in 2006:* 3,097
Provincial Electoral District(s): Argenteuil
Federal Electoral District(s): Argenteuil-Papineau-Mirabel
Next Election: 1er novembre 2013
Linne Roquebrune, Sec.-Trés.

Saint-André-de-Restigouche
CP 4
163, rue Principale
Saint-André-de-Restigouche, QC G0J 2G0
418-865-2234 Fax: 418-865-1393
m.st.and.restigouche@globetrotter.net
Municipal Type: Municipality
Incorporated: 1er juillet 1855; *Area:* 146,07 km2
County or District: Avignon; *Population in 2006:* 192
Provincial Electoral District(s): Bonaventure
Federal Electoral District(s): Gaspésie-Iles-de-la-Madeleine
Next Election: 1er novembre 2013
Blandine Parent, Sec.-Trés.

Saint-André-du-Lac-St-Jean
11, rue du Collège
Saint-André-du-Lac-Saint-Jean, QC G0W 2K0
418-349-8167 Fax: 418-349-1019
municipalitedestandre@bellnet.ca
Municipal Type: Village
Incorporated: 29 novembre 1969; *Area:* 157,75 km2
County or District: Le Domaine-du-Roy; *Population in 2006:* 484
Provincial Electoral District(s): Lac-St-Jean
Federal Electoral District(s): Roberval-Lac-St-Jean
Next Election: 1er novembre 2013
Maude Tremblay, Sec.-Trés.

Saint-Anicet
335, av Jules-Léger
Saint-Anicet, QC J0S 1M0
450-264-2555 Fax: 450-264-2395
stanicet@citenet.net
www.municipalite-saint-anicet.com
Municipal Type: Parish (Paroisse)
Incorporated: 1er juillet 1855; *Area:* 136,25 km2
County or District: Le Haut-St-Laurent; *Population in 2006:* 2,717
Provincial Electoral District(s): Huntingdon
Federal Electoral District(s): Beauharnois-Salaberry
Next Election: 1er novembre 2013
Lyne Viau, Sec.-Trés. & Directrice générale

Saint-Anselme
134, rue Principale
Saint-Anselme, QC G0R 2N0
418-885-4977 Fax: 418-885-9834
municipalite@st-anselme.ca
www.st-anselme.ca
Municipal Type: Municipality
Incorporated: 7 janvier 1998; *Area:* 74,45 km2
County or District: Bellechasse; *Population in 2006:* 3,220
Provincial Electoral District(s): Bellechasse
Federal Electoral District(s): Lévis-Bellechasse
Next Election: 1er novembre 2013
Louis Felteau, Directeur général

Saint-Antoine de l'Isle-aux-Grues
107, ch de la Volière
L'Isle-aux-Grues, QC G0R 1P0
418-248-8060 Fax: 418-248-7955
municipaliteiag@globetrotter.net
www.isle-aux-grues.com
Municipal Type: Parish (Paroisse)
Incorporated: 1er janvier 1860; *Area:* 26,40 km2
County or District: Montmagny; *Population in 2006:* 163
Provincial Electoral District(s): Montmagny-L'Islet
Federal Electoral District(s):
Montmagny-L'Islet-Kamouraska-Rivière-du-Loup
Next Election: 1er novembre 2013
Hélène Painchaud, Sec.-Trés.

Saint-Antoine-de-Tilly
CP 10
3870, ch de Tilly
Saint-Antoine-de-Tilly, QC G0S 2C0
418-886-2441 Fax: 418-886-2075
saint-antoine@globetrotter.net
www.saintantoinedetilly.com
Municipal Type: Municipality
Incorporated: 1er juillet 1855; *Area:* 60,29 km2
County or District: Lotbinière; *Population in 2006:* 1,449
Provincial Electoral District(s): Lotbinière
Federal Electoral District(s): Lotbinière-Chutes-de-la-Chaudière
Next Election: 1er novembre 2013
Diane Laroche, Directrice générale

Saint-Antoine-sur-Richelieu
1060, rue des Ormes
Saint-Antoine-sur-Richelieu, QC J0L 1R0
450-787-3497 Fax: 450-787-2852
municipalite@saint-antoine-sur-richelieu.ca
www.saint-antoine-sur-richelieu.ca
Municipal Type: Municipality
Incorporated: 6 novembre 1982; *Area:* 65,26 km2
County or District: La Vallée-du-Richelieu; *Population in 2006:* 1,594
Provincial Electoral District(s): Verchères
Federal Electoral District(s): Verchères-Les Patriotes
Next Election: 1er novembre 2013
Gertrude Therrien, Sec.-Trés.

Saint-Antonin
CP 340
261, rue Principale
Saint-Antonin, QC G0L 2J0
418-862-1056 Fax: 418-862-3268
municipalitedestantonin@videotron.ca
Municipal Type: Parish (Paroisse)
Incorporated: 30 août 1856; *Area:* 182,66 km2
County or District: Rivière-du-Loup; *Population in 2006:* 3,780
Provincial Electoral District(s): Rivière-du-Loup
Federal Electoral District(s):
Montmagny-L'Islet-Kamouraska-Rivière-du-Loup
Next Election: 1er novembre 2013
Gina Dionne, Sec.-Trés.

Saint-Apollinaire
94, rue Principale
Saint-Apollinaire, QC G0S 2E0
418-881-3996 Fax: 418-881-4152
martine.couture@st-apollinaire.com
www.st-apollinaire.com
Municipal Type: Municipality
Incorporated: 6 avril 1974; *Area:* 96,63 km2
County or District: Lotbinière; *Population in 2006:* 4,425
Provincial Electoral District(s): Lotbinière
Federal Electoral District(s): Lotbinière-Chutes-de-la-Chaudière
Next Election: 1er novembre 2013
Ginette Moreau, Mairesse

Saint-Armand
444, ch Bradley
Saint-Armand, QC J0J 1T0
450-248-2344 Fax: 450-248-3820
starmand@bellnet.ca
Municipal Type: Municipality
Incorporated: 3 février 1999; *Area:* 84,26 km2
County or District: Brome-Missisquoi; *Population in 2006:* 1,166
Provincial Electoral District(s): Brome-Missisquoi
Federal Electoral District(s): Brome-Missisquoi
Next Election: 1er novembre 2013
Jacqueline Chisholm, Sec.-Trés.

Saint-Arsène
#101, 49, rue de l'Église
Saint-Arsène, QC G0L 2K0
418-867-2205 Fax: 418-867-2025
munstarsene@qc.aira.com
Municipal Type: Parish (Paroisse)
Incorporated: 1er juillet 1855, *Area:* 71,01 km2
County or District: Rivière-du-Loup; *Population in 2006:* 1,151
Provincial Electoral District(s): Rivière-du-Loup
Federal Electoral District(s):
Montmagny-L'Islet-Kamouraska-Rivière-du-Loup
Next Election: 1er novembre 2013
François Michaud, Sec.-Trés.

Saint-Athanase
CP 40
6081, ch de l'Église
Saint-Athanase, QC G0L 2L0
418-859-2575 Fax: 418-859-3415
st-athanase@qc.aira.com
www.saint-athanase.com
Municipal Type: Municipality
Incorporated: 1er janvier 1955; *Area:* 289,08 km2
County or District: Témiscouata; *Population in 2006:* 321
Provincial Electoral District(s): Kamouraska-Témiscouata
Federal Electoral District(s): Rimouski-Neigette-Témiscouata-Les Basques
Next Election: 1er novembre 2013
Nicole Gosselin, Sec.

Saint-Aubert
14, rue des Loisirs
Saint-Aubert, QC G0R 2R0
418-598-3368 Fax: 418-598-3369
munstaub@videotron.qc.ca
Municipal Type: Municipality
Incorporated: 1er juillet 1857; *Area:* 97,15 km2
County or District: L'Islet; *Population in 2006:* 1,468
Provincial Electoral District(s): Montmagny-L'Islet
Federal Electoral District(s):
Montmagny-L'Islet-Kamouraska-Rivière-du-Loup
Next Election: 1er novembre 2013
Serge Roussel, Sec.-Trés.

Saint-Augustin
CP 279
Saint-Augustin, QC G0G 2R0
418-947-2404 Fax: 418-947-2533
jgalliboismsa@globetrotter.net
Municipal Type: Municipality
Incorporated: 1er janvier 1993; *Area:* 1435,82 km2
Population in 2006: 599
Provincial Electoral District(s): Duplessis
Federal Electoral District(s): Roberval-Lac-St-Jean
Next Election: 1er novembre 2013
Jackie Gallibois, Sec.-Trés.

Saint-Augustin
686, rue Principale
Saint-Augustin, QC G0W 1K0
418-374-2147 Fax: 418-374-2984
mun.sta@derytele.com
Municipal Type: Parish (Paroisse)
Incorporated: 14 mai 1925; *Area:* 103,96 km2
County or District: Maria-Chapdelaine; *Population in 2006:* 393
Provincial Electoral District(s): Roberval
Federal Electoral District(s): Roberval-Lac-St-Jean
Next Election: 1er novembre 2013
Maud Larouche, Sec.-Trés. & Directrice générale

Saint-Augustin-de-Woburn
590, rue St-Augustin
Woburn, QC G0Y 1R0
819-544-4211 Fax: 819-544-9236
mun.woburn@axion.ca
Municipal Type: Parish (Paroisse)
Incorporated: 13 janvier 1900; *Area:* 280,80 km2
County or District: Le Granit; *Population in 2006:* 701
Provincial Electoral District(s): Mégantic-Compton
Federal Electoral District(s): Mégantic-L'Érable
Next Election: 1er novembre 2013
Gaétane Allard-Lavoie, Sec.-Trés.

Saint-Barnabé
CP 250
70, rue Duguay
Saint-Barnabé, QC G0X 2K0
819-264-2085 Fax: 819-264-2079
municipalitest-barnabe@telmilot.net
Municipal Type: Parish (Paroisse)
Incorporated: 1er juillet 1855; *Area:* 58,81 km2
County or District: Maskinongé; *Population in 2006:* 1,207

Provincial Electoral District(s): Maskinongé
Federal Electoral District(s): Berthier-Maskinongé
Next Election: 1er novembre 2013
Denis Gélinas, Sec.-Trés.

Saint-Barnabé-Sud
251, rang de Michaudville
Saint-Barnabé-Sud, QC J0H 1G0
450-792-3030 Fax: 450-792-3759
munstbarnabesud@mrcmaskoutains.qc.ca
Municipal Type: Municipality
Incorporated: 1er juillet 1855; *Area:* 57,08 km2
County or District: Les Maskoutains; *Population in 2006:* 864
Provincial Electoral District(s): St-Hyacinthe
Federal Electoral District(s): St-Hyacinthe-Bagot
Next Election: 1er novembre 2013
Nicole Bélanger, Sec.-Trés. & Directrice générale

Saint-Barthélemy
1980, rue Bonin
Saint-Barthélémy, QC J0K 1X0
450-885-3511 Fax: 450-885-2165
municipalite@stbarthelemy.ca
Municipal Type: Parish (Paroisse)
Incorporated: 1er juillet 1855; *Area:* 98,80 km2
County or District: D'Autray; *Population in 2006:* 2,037
Provincial Electoral District(s): Berthier
Federal Electoral District(s): Berthier-Maskinongé
Next Election: 1er novembre 2013
Jean Charland, Sec.-Trés.

Saint-Basile
20, rue St-Georges
Saint-Basile, QC G0A 3G0
418-329-2204 Fax: 418-329-2788
greffe@saintbasile.qc.ca
www.saintbasile.qc.ca
Municipal Type: City
Incorporated: 1er mars 2000; *Area:* 97,69 km2
County or District: Portneuf; *Population in 2006:* 2,560
Provincial Electoral District(s): Portneuf
Federal Electoral District(s): Portneuf-Jacques-Cartier
Next Election: 1er novembre 2013
Roger Proulx, Sec.-Trés.
Jean Poirier, Maire

Saint-Benjamin
CP 100
440, av du Collège
Saint-Benjamin, QC G0M 1N0
418-594-8156 Fax: 418-594-6068
mun.st-ben@globetrotter.net
Municipal Type: Municipality
Incorporated: 9 janvier 1897; *Area:* 110,53 km2
County or District: Les Etchemins; *Population in 2006:* 865
Provincial Electoral District(s): Beauce-Sud
Federal Electoral District(s): Beauce
Next Election: 1er novembre 2013
France Veilleux, Sec.-Trés.

Saint-Benoît-du-Lac
Abbaye-Saint-Benoît
Saint-Benoît-du-Lac, QC J0B 2M0
819-843-4080 Fax: 819-868-1861
abbaye@st-benoit-du-lac.com
www.st-benoit-du-lac.com
Municipal Type: Municipality
Incorporated: 16 mars 1939; *Area:* 2,27 km2
County or District: Memphrémagog; *Population in 2006:* 48
Provincial Electoral District(s): Brome-Missisquoi
Federal Electoral District(s): Brome-Missisquoi
Next Election: 1er novembre 2013
André Blanchet, Directeur général

Saint-Benoît-Labre
216, rte 271
Saint-Benoît-Labre, QC G0M 1P0
418-228-9250 Fax: 418-228-0518
munstben@globetrotter.net
Municipal Type: Municipality
Incorporated: 4 janvier 1894; *Area:* 83,92 km2
County or District: Beauce-Sartigan; *Population in 2006:* 1,613
Provincial Electoral District(s): Beauce-Sud
Federal Electoral District(s): Beauce
Next Election: 1er novembre 2013
Gaétane Vallée, Sec.-Trés.

Saint-Bernard
CP 70
1512, rue St-Georges
Saint-Bernard, QC G0S 2G0
418-475-6060 Fax: 418-475-6069
mun.stbernard@globetrotter.net
Municipal Type: Municipality
Incorporated: 9 mai 1987; *Area:* 87,56 km2
County or District: La Nouvelle-Beauce; *Population in 2006:* 1,920
Provincial Electoral District(s): Beauce-Nord
Federal Electoral District(s): Beauce
Next Election: 1er novembre 2013
Marie-Ôve Parent, Sec.-Trés.

Saint-Bernard-de-Lacolle
116, rang St-Claude
Saint-Bernard-de-Lacolle, QC J0J 1V0
450-246-3348 Fax: 450-246-4380
mun.st-bernard-de-lacolle@bellnet.ca
Municipal Type: Parish (Paroisse)
Incorporated: 1er juillet 1855; *Area:* 112,63 km2
County or District: Les Jardins-de-Napierville; *Population in 2006:* 1,537
Provincial Electoral District(s): Huntingdon
Federal Electoral District(s): Beauharnois-Salaberry
Next Election: 1er novembre 2013
Daniel Striletsky, Sec.-Trés.

Saint-Bernard-de-Michaudville
410, rue Principale
Saint-Bernard-de-Michaudville, QC J0H 1C0
450-792-3190 Fax: 450-792-3591
munstbernard@mrcmaskoutains.qc.ca
Municipal Type: Municipality
Incorporated: 31 août 1908; *Area:* 64,80 km2
County or District: Les Maskoutains; *Population in 2006:* 486
Provincial Electoral District(s): Richelieu
Federal Electoral District(s): St-Hyacinthe-Bagot
Next Election: 1er novembre 2013
Nathalie Audette, Sec.

Saint-Blaise-sur-Richelieu
795, rue des Loisirs
Saint-Blaise-sur-Richelieu, QC J0J 1W0
450-291-5944 Fax: 450-291-3832
info.st-blaise@videotron.ca
Municipal Type: Municipality
Incorporated: 20 juin 1892; *Area:* 68,42 km2
County or District: Le Haut-Richelieu; *Population in 2006:* 2,050
Provincial Electoral District(s): St-Jean
Federal Electoral District(s): St-Jean
Next Election: 1er novembre 2013
Francine Milot, Sec.-Trés.

Saint-Bonaventure
720, rue Plante
Saint-Bonaventure, QC J0C 1C0
819-396-2335 Fax: 819-396-2335
st-bonaventure@mrcdrummond.qc.ca
Municipal Type: Municipality
Incorporated: 1er janvier 1867; *Area:* 78,83 km2
County or District: Drummond; *Population in 2006:* 983
Provincial Electoral District(s): Nicolet-Yamaska
Federal Electoral District(s): Drummond
Next Election: 1er novembre 2013
Claire Côté, Sec.-Trés. & Directrice générale

Saint-Boniface
140, rue Guimont
Saint-Boniface, QC G0X 2L0
819-535-3811 Fax: 819-535-1242
loji@cgocable.ca
Municipal Type: Municipality
Incorporated: 1er janvier 1962; *Area:* 112,12 km2
County or District: Maskinongé; *Population in 2006:* 4,180
Provincial Electoral District(s): St-Maurice
Federal Electoral District(s): Berthier-Maskinongé
Next Election: 1er novembre 2013
Jacques Caron, Sec.-Trés.

Saint-Bruno
563, av St-Alphonse
Saint-Bruno, QC G0W 2L0
418-343-2303 Fax: 418-343-2662
info@ville.saint-bruno.qc.ca
www.ville.saint-bruno.qc.ca
Municipal Type: Municipality
Incorporated: 12 juillet 1975; *Area:* 77,88 km2
County or District: Lac-St-Jean-Est; *Population in 2006:* 2,353
Provincial Electoral District(s): Lac-St-Jean
Federal Electoral District(s): Roberval-Lac-St-Jean
Next Election: 1er novembre 2013
Gilles Boudreault, Sec.-Trés.

Saint-Bruno-de-Guigues
CP 130
21, rue Principale nord
Saint-Bruno-de-Guigues, QC J0Z 2G0
819-728-2186 Fax: 819-728-2404
dg.guigues@mrctemiscamingue.qc.ca
www.temiscamingue.net/guigues
Municipal Type: Municipality
Incorporated: 3 octobre 1912; *Area:* 188,99 km2
County or District: Témiscamingue; *Population in 2006:* 1,076
Provincial Electoral District(s): Rouyn-Noranda-Témiscamingue
Federal Electoral District(s): Abitibi-Témiscamingue
Next Election: 1er novembre 2013
Serge Côté, Sec.-Trés.

Saint-Bruno-de-Kamouraska
CP 10
4, rue du Couvent
Saint-Bruno-de-Kamouraska, QC G0L 2M0
418-492-2612 Fax: 418-492-2612
mun.stbrunokam@globetrotter.net
Municipal Type: Municipality
Incorporated: 1er janvier 1887; *Area:* 186,79 km2
County or District: Kamouraska; *Population in 2006:* 534
Provincial Electoral District(s): Kamouraska-Témiscouata
Federal Electoral District(s): Montmagny-L'Islet-Kamouraska-Rivière-du-Loup
Next Election: 1er novembre 2013
Gilles Bois, Maire

Saint-Calixte
6230, rue de l'Hôtel-de-Ville
Saint-Calixte, QC J0K 1Z0
450-222-2782 Fax: 450-222-2789
stresorier@mscalixte.qc.ca
www.municipalite.sanit-calixte.qc.ca
Municipal Type: Municipality
Incorporated: 1er juillet 1855; *Area:* 147,68 km2
County or District: Montcalm; *Population in 2006:* 5,687
Provincial Electoral District(s): Rousseau
Federal Electoral District(s): Montcalm
Next Election: 1er novembre 2013
Vacant, Sec.-Trés. & Directeur général

Saint-Camille
87, rue Desrivières
Saint-Camille, QC J0A 1G0
819-828-3222 Fax: 819-828-3723
munstcamille@cgocable.ca
Municipal Type: Township
Incorporated: 1er janvier 1860; *Area:* 81,27 km2
County or District: Asbestos; *Population in 2006:* 448
Provincial Electoral District(s): Richmond
Federal Electoral District(s): Richmond-Arthabaska
Next Election: 1er novembre 2013
Caroline Poirier, Directrice générale

Saint-Camille-de-Lellis
CP 70
217, rue Principale
Saint-Camille-de-Lellis, QC G0R 2S0
418-595-2233 Fax: 418-595-2238
mustcam@sogetel.net
Municipal Type: Parish (Paroisse)
Incorporated: 11 janvier 1904; *Area:* 252,08 km2
County or District: Les Etchemins; *Population in 2006:* 904
Provincial Electoral District(s): Bellechasse
Federal Electoral District(s): Lévis-Bellechasse
Next Election: 1er novembre 2013
Nicole Mathieu, Sec.-Trés. & Directrice générale

Saint-Casimir
CP 220
220, boul de la Montagne
Saint-Casimir, QC G0A 3L0
418-339-2543 Fax: 418-339-3105
st-casimir@infoteck.qc.ca
Municipal Type: Municipality
Incorporated: 21 juin 2000; *Area:* 65,93 km2
County or District: Portneuf; *Population in 2006:* 1,528
Provincial Electoral District(s): Portneuf
Federal Electoral District(s): Portneuf-Jacques Cartier
Next Election: 1er novembre 2013
Carole Germain, Sec.-Trés.

Saint-Célestin
990, rang du Pays-Brûlé
Saint-Célestin, QC J0C 1G0
819-229-3745 Fax: 819-229-1386
info@saint-celestin.net
www.saint-celestin.net
Municipal Type: Municipality
Incorporated: 1er juillet 1864; *Area:* 78,72 km2
County or District: Nicolet-Yamaska; *Population in 2006:* 624
Provincial Electoral District(s): Nicolet-Yamaska
Federal Electoral District(s): Bas-Richelieu-Nicolet-Bécancour
Next Election: 1er novembre 2013
Gisèle Plourde, Sec.-Trés. & Directrice générale

Saint-Célestin
510, rue Marquis
Saint-Célestin, QC J0C 1G0
819-229-3642 Fax: 819-229-1149
info@village-st-celestin.net
Municipal Type: Village
Incorporated: 25 novembre 1896; *Area:* 1,61 km22
County or District: Nicolet-Yamaska; *Population in 2006:* 762
Provincial Electoral District(s): Nicolet-Yamaska
Federal Electoral District(s): Bas-Richelieu-Nicolet-Bécancour
Next Election: 1er novembre 2013
Pascale Lamoureux, Directrice générale

Saint-Césaire
1111, av St-Paul
Saint-Césaire, QC J0L 1T0
450-469-3108 Fax: 450-469-5275
ville-st-cesaire@bellnet.ca
www.ville.saint-cesaire.qc.ca
Municipal Type: City
Incorporated: 26 janvier 2000; *Area:* 84,14 km2
County or District: Rouville; *Population in 2006:* 5,151
Provincial Electoral District(s): Iberville
Federal Electoral District(s): Shefford
Next Election: 1er novembre 2013
Louise Benoit, Greffière
Yvon Boucher, Maire

Saint-Charles-Borromée
525, rue de la Visitation
Saint-Charles-Borromée, QC J6E 4P2
450-759-4415 Fax: 450-759-3393
info@st-charles-borromee.org
www.st-charles-borromee.org

Municipal Type: Municipality
Incorporated: 1er juillet 1855; *Area:* 18,60 km2
County or District: Joliette; *Population in 2009:* 12,345
Provincial Electoral District(s): Joliette
Federal Electoral District(s): Joliette
Next Election: 1er novembre 2013
François Thériault, Directeur général

Saint-Charles-de-Bellechasse
2815, av Royale
Saint-Charles-de-Bellechasse, QC G0R 2T0
418-887-6600 Fax: 418-887-6779
munstcha@globetrotter.net
www.saint-charles.ca
Municipal Type: Municipality
Incorporated: 22 décembre 1993; *Area:* 94,73 km2
County or District: Bellechasse; *Population in 2006:* 2,159
Provincial Electoral District(s): Bellechasse
Federal Electoral District(s): Lévis-Bellechasse
Next Election: 1er novembre 2013
Denis Labbé, Sec.-Trés. & Directeur général

Saint-Charles-de-Bourget
357, 2e rang
Saint-Charles-de-Bourget, QC G0V 1G0
418-672-2624 Fax: 418-672-4403
bourget@saglac.qc.ca
saglac.qc.ca/~bourget/
Municipal Type: Municipality
Incorporated: 29 septembre 1885; *Area:* 62,31 km2
County or District: Le Fjord-du-Saguenay; *Population in 2006:* 659
Provincial Electoral District(s): Dubuc
Federal Electoral District(s): Jonquière-Alma
Next Election: 1er novembre 2013
Marlène Néron, Sec.-Trés.

Saint-Charles-Garnier
CP 39
38, rue Principale
Saint-Charles-Garnier, QC G0K 1K0
418-798-4305 Fax: 418-798-4499
stcharles@globetrotter.net
Municipal Type: Parish (Paroisse)
Incorporated: 1er janvier 1966; *Area:* 83,73 km2
County or District: La Mitis; *Population in 2006:* 298
Provincial Electoral District(s): Matapédia
Federal Electoral District(s): Haute-Gaspésie-La Mitis-Matane-Matapédia
Next Election: 1er novembre 2013
Josette Bouillon, Sec.-Trés.

Saint-Charles-sur-Richelieu
#101, 405, ch des Patriotes
Saint-Charles-sur-Richelieu, QC J0H 2G0
450-584-3484 Fax: 450-584-2965
direction@saint-charles-sur-richelieu.ca
www.saint-charles-sur-richelieu.ca
Municipal Type: Municipality
Incorporated: 22 mars 1995; *Area:* 63,59 km2
County or District: La Vallée-du-Richelieu; *Population in 2006:* 1,742
Provincial Electoral District(s): Verchères
Federal Electoral District(s): Verchères-Les-Patriotes
Next Election: 1er novembre 2013
Denis R. Dufour, Sec.-Trés. & Directeur général.

Saint-Christophe-d'Arthabaska
418, av Pie-X
Saint-Christophe-d'Arthabaska, QC G6P 6S1
819-357-9031 Fax: 819-357-9087
christo@lino.com
Municipal Type: Parish (Paroisse)
Incorporated: 1er juillet 1855; *Area:* 74,87 km2
County or District: Arthabaska; *Population in 2006:* 2,709
Provincial Electoral District(s): Arthabaska
Federal Electoral District(s): Richmond-Arthabaska
Next Election: 1er novembre 2013
Francine Moreau, Sec.-Trés.

Saint-Chrysostome
624, rue Notre-Dame, 2e étage
Saint-Chrysostome, QC J0S 1R0
450-826-3911 Fax: 450-826-0568
dg@mun-sc.ca
Municipal Type: Municipality
Incorporated: 29 septembre 1999; *Area:* 99,54 km2
County or District: Le Haut-St-Laurent; *Population in 2006:* 2,584
Provincial Electoral District(s): Huntingdon
Federal Electoral District(s): Beauharnois-Salaberry
Next Election: 1er novembre 2013
Céline Ouimet, Directrice générale

Saint-Claude
295, rte de l'Église
Saint-Claude, QC J0B 2N0
819-845-7795 Fax: 819-845-2479
st-claude@qc.aira.com
Municipal Type: Municipality
Incorporated: 15 novembre 1912; *Area:* 120,38 km2
County or District: Le Val-St-François; *Population in 2006:* 1,104
Provincial Electoral District(s): Richmond
Federal Electoral District(s): Richmond-Arthabaska
Next Election: 1er novembre 2013
France Lavertu, Sec.-Trés.

Saint-Clément
CP 40
25A, rue St-Pierre
Saint-Clément, QC G0L 2N0
418-963-2258 Fax: 418-963-2619
st_clement@videotron.ca
www.info-basques.com/st-clement
Municipal Type: Parish (Paroisse)
Incorporated: 1er janvier 1885; *Area:* 80,44 km2
County or District: Les Basques; *Population in 2006:* 521
Provincial Electoral District(s): Rivière-du-Loup
Federal Electoral District(s): Rimouski-Neigette-Témiscouata-Les Basques
Next Election: 1er novembre 2013
Line Caron, Directrice générale

Saint-Cléophas
350, rue Principale
Saint-Cléophas, QC G0J 3N0
418-536-3023 Fax: 418-536-3023
liseturbide@globetrotter.net
Municipal Type: Parish (Paroisse)
Incorporated: 19 mai 1921; *Area:* 97,46 km2
County or District: La Matapédia; *Population in 2006:* 367
Provincial Electoral District(s): Matapédia
Federal Electoral District(s): Haute-Gaspésie-La Mitis-Matane-Matapédia
Next Election: 1er novembre 2013
Lise Turbide, Sec.-Trés.

Saint-Cléophas-de-Brandon
750, rue Principale
Saint-Cléophas-de-Brandon, QC J0K 2A0
450-889-5683 Fax: 450-889-8007
st-cleo@megacom.net
www.st-cleophas.qc.ca
Municipal Type: Municipality
Incorporated: 7 octobre 1897; *Area:* 14,76 km2
County or District: D'Autray; *Population in 2006:* 284
Provincial Electoral District(s): Berthier
Federal Electoral District(s): Berthier-Maskinongé
Next Election: 1er novembre 2013
Lorraine Cloutier-Gamelin, Sec.-Trés.

Saint-Clet
4, rue du Moulin
Saint-Clet, QC J0P 1S0
450-456-3363 Fax: 450-456-3879
st-clet@videotron.ca
Municipal Type: Municipality
Incorporated: 31 août 1974; *Area:* 38,61 km2
County or District: Vaudreuil-Soulanges; *Population in 2006:* 1,725
Provincial Electoral District(s): Soulanges
Federal Electoral District(s): Vaudreuil-Soulanges
Next Election: 1er novembre 2013
Nathalie Pharand, Sec.-Trés.

Saint-Colomban
330, montée de l'Église
Saint-Colomban, QC J5K 1A1
450-436-1453 Fax: 450-436-5955
info@st-colomban.qc.ca
www.st-colomban.qc.ca
Municipal Type: Municipality
Incorporated: 1er juillet 1855; *Area:* 94,24 km2
County or District: La Rivière-du-Nord; *Population in 2006:* 10,973
Provincial Electoral District(s): Argenteuil
Federal Electoral District(s): Rivière-du-Nord
Next Election: 1er novembre 2013
Claude Panneton, Directeur général

Saint-Côme
1673, 55e rue
Saint-Côme, QC J0K 2B0
450-883-2726 Fax: 450-883-6431
stcome@pandore.qc.ca
www.stcomelanaudiere.ca
Municipal Type: Parish (Paroisse)
Incorporated: 1er janvier 1873; *Area:* 167,26 km2
County or District: Matawinie; *Population in 2006:* 2,161
Provincial Electoral District(s): Berthier
Federal Electoral District(s): Joliette
Next Election: 1er novembre 2013
Alice Riopel, Sec.-Trés. & Directrice générale

Saint-Côme-Linière
1375, 18e rue
Saint-Côme-Linière, QC G0M 1J0
418-685-3825 Fax: 418-685-2566
st-come@globetrotter.net
Municipal Type: Municipality
Incorporated: 13 avril 1994; *Area:* 151,24 km2
County or District: Beauce-Sartigan; *Population in 2006:* 3,260
Provincial Electoral District(s): Beauce-Sud
Federal Electoral District(s): Beauce
Next Election: 1er novembre 2013
Yvan Bélanger, Sec.-Trés.

Saint-Cuthbert
CP 100
1891, rue Principale
Saint-Cuthbert, QC J0K 2C0
450-836-4852 Fax: 450-836-4833
mairie@municipalite.saint-cuthbert.qc.ca
www.megacom.net/~biordi/municipalite.html
Municipal Type: Municipality
Incorporated: 7 janvier 1998; *Area:* 133,71 km2
County or District: D'Autray; *Population in 2006:* 1,938
Provincial Electoral District(s): Berthier
Federal Electoral District(s): Berthier-Maskinongé
Next Election: 1er novembre 2013
Richard Lauzon, Sec.-Trés.

Saint-Cyprien
CP 9
101B, rue Collin
Saint-Cyprien, QC G0L 2P0
418-963-2730 Fax: 418-963-3490
municipalitestcyprien@bellnet.ca
www.municipalite.saint-cyprien.qc.ca
Municipal Type: Municipality
Incorporated: 1er janvier 1883; *Area:* 136,14 km2
County or District: Rivière-du-Loup; *Population in 2006:* 1,262
Provincial Electoral District(s): Rivière-du-Loup
Federal Electoral District(s): Montmagny-L'Islet-Kamouraska-Rivière-du-Loup
Next Election: 1er novembre 2013
Sanny Beaulieu, Greffière

Saint-Cyprien
CP 100
399, rue Principale
Saint-Cyprien-des-Etchemins, QC G0R 1B0
418-383-5274 Fax: 418-383-5269
corpmun@sogetel.net
www.st-cyprien.qc.ca
Municipal Type: Parish (Paroisse)
Incorporated: 22 février 1918; *Area:* 92,82 km2
County or District: Les Etchemins; *Population in 2006:* 630
Provincial Electoral District(s): Bellechasse
Federal Electoral District(s): Lévis-Bellechasse
Next Election: 1er novembre 2013
Pauline Fortier, Sec.-Trés.

Saint-Cyprien-de-Napierville
121, rang Cyr
Saint-Cyprien-de-Napierville, QC J0J 1L0
450-245-3658 Fax: 450-245-7824
paroissest-cyprien@qc.aira.com
Municipal Type: Parish (Paroisse)
Incorporated: 1er juillet 1855; *Area:* 97,62 km2
County or District: Les Jardins-de-Napierville; *Population in 2006:* 1,570
Provincial Electoral District(s): Huntingdon
Federal Electoral District(s): Beauharnois-Salaberry
Next Election: 1er novembre 2013
Nancy Trottier, Sec.-Trés.

Saint-Cyrille-de-Lessard
282, rue Principale
Saint-Cyrille-de-Lessard, QC G0R 2W0
418-247-5186 Fax: 418-247-7086
Municipal Type: Parish (Paroisse)
Incorporated: 1er juillet 1855; *Area:* 228,95 km2
County or District: L'Islet; *Population in 2006:* 778
Provincial Electoral District(s): Montmagny-L'Islet
Federal Electoral District(s): Montmagny-L'Islet-Kamouraska-Rivière-du-Loup
Next Election: 1er novembre 2013
Josée Godbout, Sec.-Trés.

Saint-Cyrille-de-Wendover
4055, rue Principale
Saint-Cyrille-de-Wendover, QC J1Z 1C8
819-397-4226 Fax: 819-397-5505
municipalite@stcyrille.qc.ca
www.stcyrille.qc.ca
Municipal Type: Municipality
Incorporated: 6 septembre 1905; *Area:* 112,24 km2
County or District: Drummond; *Population in 2006:* 4,079
Provincial Electoral District(s): Richmond
Federal Electoral District(s): Drummond
Next Election: 1er novembre 2013
Mario Picotin, Directeur général

Saint-Damase
223, rue Principale
Saint-Damase, QC J0H 1J0
450-797-3341 Fax: 450-797-3543
svfrechette@st-damase.qc.ca
www.st-damase.qc.ca
Municipal Type: Municipality
Incorporated: 5 octobre 2001; *Area:* 79,06 km2
County or District: Les Maskoutains; *Population in 2006:* 2,486
Provincial Electoral District(s): St-Hyacinthe
Federal Electoral District(s): St-Hyacinthe-Bagot
Next Election: 1er novembre 2013
Note: Effective October 10, 2001, the Village & Parish of St-Damase amalgamated to create the Municipality of St-Damase.
Sylvie V. Fréchette, Sec.-Trés. & Directrice générale

Saint-Damase-de-L'Islet
CP 10
26, rue du Village est
Saint-Damase-de-L'Islet, QC G0R 2X0
418-598-9370 Fax: 418-598-9370
stdamase3@hotmail.com
Municipal Type: Municipality
Incorporated: 9 novembre 1898; *Area:* 259,72 km2
County or District: L'Islet; *Population in 2006:* 593

Provincial Electoral District(s): Montmagny-L'Islet
Federal Electoral District(s):
Montmagny-L'Islet-Kamouraska-Rivière-du-Loup
Next Election: 1er novembre 2013
Dany Marois, Sec.-Trés.

Saint-Damien
6850, ch Montauban
Saint-Damien, QC J0K 2E0
450-835-3419 Fax: 450-835-5538
stdamien@pandore.qc.ca
www.st-damien.com
Municipal Type: Parish (Paroisse)
Incorporated: 6 septembre 1870; *Area:* 260,38 km2
County or District: Matawinie; *Population in 2006:* 2,178
Provincial Electoral District(s): Berthier
Federal Electoral District(s): Joliette
Next Election: 1er novembre 2013
Josée Tellier, Sec.-Trés. & Directrice générale

Saint-Damien-de-Buckland
75, rte St-Gérard
Saint-Damien-de-Buckland, QC G0R 2Y0
418-789-2526 Fax: 418-789-2125
j.thibault@globetrotter.net
Municipal Type: Parish (Paroisse)
Incorporated: 20 décembre 1890; *Area:* 85,17 km2
County or District: Bellechasse; *Population in 2006:* 1,946
Provincial Electoral District(s): Bellechasse
Federal Electoral District(s): Lévis-Bellechasse
Next Election: 1er novembre 2013
Jacques Thibault, Sec.-Trés.

Saint-David
11, rue de la Rivière-David
Saint-David, QC J0G 1L0
450-789-2288 Fax: 450-789-3023
stdavid@bas-richelieu.net
www.stdavid.qc.ca
Municipal Type: Municipality
Incorporated: 1er juillet 1855; *Area:* 91,08 km2
County or District: Pierre-De Saurel; *Population in 2009:* 812
Provincial Electoral District(s): Nicolet-Yamaska
Federal Electoral District(s): Bas-Richelieu-Nicolet-Bécancour
Next Election: 1er novembre 2013
Sylvie Letendre, Directrice générale

Saint-David-de-Falardeau
CP 130
140, boul St-David
Saint-David-de-Falardeau, QC G0V 1C0
418-673-4647 Fax: 418-673-3266
villefalardeau@videotron.ca
pages.infinit.net/falardau/
Municipal Type: Municipality
Incorporated: 1er janvier 1948; *Area:* 379,23 km2
County or District: Le Fjord-du-Saguenay; *Population in 2006:* 2,555
Provincial Electoral District(s): Dubuc
Federal Electoral District(s): Jonquière-Alma
Next Election: 1er novembre 2013
Daniel Hudon, Directeur général

Saint-Denis
CP 69
2, rte de la Grève
Saint-Denis, QC G0L 2R0
418-498-2968 Fax: 418-498-2948
municipalitestdenis1@microbranche.com
Municipal Type: Parish (Paroisse)
Incorporated: 1er juillet 1855; *Area:* 33,84 km2
County or District: Kamouraska; *Population in 2006:* 523
Provincial Electoral District(s): Kamouraska-Témiscouata
Federal Electoral District(s):
Montmagny-L'Islet-Kamouraska-Rivière-du-Loup
Next Election: 1er novembre 2013
Mélanie Lévesque, Sec.-Trés.

Saint-Denis-de-Brompton
CP 120
2050, rue Ernest-Camiré
Saint-Denis-de-Brompton, QC J0B 2P0
819-846-2744 Fax: 819-846-0915
mstdenis@videotron.ca
Municipal Type: Parish (Paroisse)
Incorporated: 6 mars 1935; *Area:* 70,25 km2
County or District: Le Val-St-François; *Population in 2006:* 3,090
Provincial Electoral District(s): Johnson
Federal Electoral District(s): Brome-Missisquoi; Richmond-Arthabaska
Next Election: 1er novembre 2013
Marc Laflamme, Sec.-Trés.

Saint-Denis-sur-Richelieu
599, ch des Patriotes
Saint-Denis-sur-Richelieu, QC J0H 1K0
450-787-2244 Fax: 450-787-2635
municipalitedestdenis@bellnet.ca
Municipal Type: Municipality
Incorporated: 24 décembre 1997; *Area:* 82,20 km2
County or District: La Vallée-du-Richelieu; *Population in 2006:* 2,243
Provincial Electoral District(s): Verchères
Federal Electoral District(s): Verchères-Les Patriotes
Next Election: 1er novembre 2013
Pierre Pétrin, Sec.-Trés.

Saint-Didace
380, rue Principale
Saint-Didace, QC J0K 2G0
450-835-4184 Fax: 450-835-0602
stdidace@megacom.net
Municipal Type: Parish (Paroisse)
Incorporated: 27 août 1863; *Area:* 99,66 km2
County or District: D'Autray; *Population in 2006:* 668
Provincial Electoral District(s): Berthier
Federal Electoral District(s): Berthier-Maskinongé
Next Election: 1er novembre 2013
André Allard, Sec.-Trés.

Saint-Dominique
467, rue Deslandes
Saint-Dominique, QC J0H 1L0
450-774-9939 Fax: 450-774-1595
admin@municipalite.saint-dominique.qc.ca
Municipal Type: Municipality
Incorporated: 1er juillet 1855; *Area:* 70,16 km2
County or District: Les Maskoutains; *Population in 2006:* 2,132
Provincial Electoral District(s): St-Hyacinthe
Federal Electoral District(s): St-Hyacinthe-Bagot
Next Election: 1er novembre 2013
Christine Massé, Sec.-Trés. & Directrice générale

Saint-Dominique-du-Rosaire
235, rue Principale
Saint-Dominique-du-Rosaire, QC J0Y 2K0
819-727-9544 Fax: 819-727-4344
mun.stdomrosaire@cableamos.com
Municipal Type: Municipality
Incorporated: 1er janvier 1978; *Area:* 512,24 km2
County or District: Abitibi; *Population in 2006:* 447
Provincial Electoral District(s): Abitibi-Ouest
Federal Electoral District(s): Abitibi-Témiscamingue
Next Election: 1er novembre 2013
Lucille Ferron, Sec.-Trés.

Saint-Donat
CP 70
194, av du Mont-Comi
Saint-Donat-de-Rimouski, QC G0K 1L0
418-739-4634 Fax: 418-739-5003
municipalite@saintdonat.ca
www.saintdonat.ca
Municipal Type: Parish (Paroisse)
Incorporated: 10 mars 1869; *Area:* 93,23 km2
County or District: La Mitis; *Population in 2006:* 892
Provincial Electoral District(s): Matapédia
Federal Electoral District(s): Haute-Gaspésie-La Mitis-Matane-Matapédia
Next Election: 1er novembre 2013
Gil Bérubé, Sec.-Trés.

Saint-Donat
490, rue Principale
Saint-Donat, QC J0T 2C0
819-424-2383 Fax: 819-424-5020
dg@saint-donat.ca
www.saint-donat.ca
Municipal Type: Municipality
Incorporated: 19 février 1904; *Area:* 361,42 km2
County or District: Matawinie; *Population in 2006:* 4,297
Provincial Electoral District(s): Bertrand
Federal Electoral District(s): Joliette
Next Election: 1er novembre 2013
Michel Hamel, Sec.-Trés. & Directeur général

Saint-Edmond-de-Grantham
1393, rue Notre-Dame-de-Lourdes
Saint-Edmond-de-Grantham, QC J0C 1K0
819-395-2562 Fax: 819-395-2666
muned@tellabaie.net
Municipal Type: Parish (Paroisse)
Incorporated: 9 février 1918; *Area:* 48,79 km2
County or District: Drummond; *Population in 2006:* 621
Provincial Electoral District(s): Drummond
Federal Electoral District(s): Drummond
Next Election: 1er novembre 2013
Hélène Ruel, Sec.-Trés. & Directrice générale

Saint-Edmond-les-Plaines
561, ch Principale
Saint-Edmond-les-Plaines, QC G0W 2M0
418-274-3069 Fax: 418-274-5629
stedmond@destination.ca
Municipal Type: Municipality
Incorporated: 3 septembre 1938; *Area:* 87,15 km2
County or District: Maria-Chapdelaine; *Population in 2006:* 432
Provincial Electoral District(s): Roberval
Federal Electoral District(s): Roberval-Lac-St-Jean
Next Election: 1er novembre 2013
Danielle Bernard, Sec.-Trés.

Saint-Édouard
CP 120
405C, montée Lussier
Saint-Édouard, QC J0L 1Y0
450-454-6333 Fax: 450-454-4921
Municipal Type: Parish (Paroisse)
Incorporated: 1er juillet 1855; *Area:* 52,91 km2
County or District: Les Jardins-de-Napierville; *Population in 2006:* 1,212
Provincial Electoral District(s): Huntingdon
Federal Electoral District(s): Beauharnois-Salaberry
Next Election: 1er novembre 2013
Lucie Riendeau, Sec.-Trés.

Saint-Édouard-de-Fabre
CP 70
620, rue de l'Église
Saint-Édouard-de-Fabre, QC J0Z 1Z0
819-634-4441 Fax: 819-634-2646
municipalitefabre@mrctemiscamingue.qc.ca
Municipal Type: Parish (Paroisse)
Incorporated: 3 octobre 1912; *Area:* 216,18 km2
County or District: Témiscamingue; *Population in 2006:* 701
Provincial Electoral District(s): Rouyn-Noranda-Témiscamingue
Federal Electoral District(s): Abitibi-Témiscamingue
Next Election: 1er novembre 2013
Aline Desjardins, Sec.-Trés.

Saint-Edouard-de-Lotbinière
105, rte Soucy
Saint-Edouard-de-Lotbinière, QC G0S 1Y0
418-796-2971 Fax: 418-796-2228
st-edouar@municipalite.st-edouard.qc.ca
www.municipalite.st-edouard.qc.ca
Municipal Type: Parish (Paroisse)
Incorporated: 1er décembre 1862; *Area:* 98,57 km2
County or District: Lotbinière; *Population in 2006:* 1,261
Provincial Electoral District(s): Lotbinière
Federal Electoral District(s): Lotbinière-Chutes-de-la-Chaudière
Next Election: 1er novembre 2013
Anna Blondin, Directrice générale

Saint-Édouard-de-Maskinongé
3851, rue Notre-Dame
Saint-Édouard-de-Maskinongé, QC J0K 2H0
819-268-2833 Fax: 819-268-2883
municipalitestedouard@telmilot.net
Municipal Type: Municipality
Incorporated: 1er janvier 1950; *Area:* 55,06 km2
County or District: Maskinongé; *Population in 2006:* 800
Provincial Electoral District(s): Maskinongé
Federal Electoral District(s): Berthier-Maskinongé
Next Election: 1er novembre 2013
Nadia Béland, Directrice générale

Saint-Élie-de-Caxton
52, ch des Loisirs
Saint-Élie, QC G0X 2N0
819-221-2839 Fax: 819-221-4039
saintelie@telmilot.net
www.saint-elie-de-caxton.com
Municipal Type: Municipality
Incorporated: 12 avril 1865; *Area:* 118,75 km2
County or District: Maskinongé; *Population in 2006:* 1,676
Provincial Electoral District(s): Maskinongé
Federal Electoral District(s): Berthier-Maskinongé
Next Election: 1er novembre 2013
Micheline Allard, Sec.-Trés.

Saint-Éloi
CP 9
183, rue Principale
Saint-Éloi, QC G0L 2V0
418-898-2734 Fax: 418-898-2305
st-eloi@qc.aira.com
www.info-basques.com/ste-eloi
Municipal Type: Parish (Paroisse)
Incorporated: 1er juillet 1855; *Area:* 67,69 km2
County or District: Les Basques; *Population in 2006:* 338
Provincial Electoral District(s): Rivière-du-Loup
Federal Electoral District(s): Rimouski-Neigette-Témiscouata-Les Basques
Next Election: 1er novembre 2013
Annie Roussel, Sec.-Trés.

Saint-Elphege
245, rang St-Antoine
Saint-Elphege, QC J0G 1J0
450-568-0288 Fax: 450-568-0288
Municipal Type: Parish (Paroisse)
Incorporated: 12 mars 1886; *Area:* 40,32 km2
County or District: Nicolet-Yamaska; *Population in 2006:* 271
Provincial Electoral District(s): Nicolet-Yamaska
Federal Electoral District(s): Bas-Richelieu-Nicolet-Bécancour
Next Election: 1er novembre 2013
France Dionne, Sec.-Trés.

Saint-Elzéar
CP 40
148, ch Principal
Saint-Elzéar-de-Bonaventure, QC G0C 2W0
418-534-2611 Fax: 866-499-8558
muni@saint-elzear.com
www.saint-elzear.com
Municipal Type: Municipality
Incorporated: 1er janvier 1965; *Area:* 198,75 km2
County or District: Bonaventure; *Population in 2006:* 508
Provincial Electoral District(s): Bonaventure
Federal Electoral District(s): Gaspésie-Iles-de-la-Madeleine
Next Election: 1er novembre 2013
Marjolaine St-Pierre, Sec.-Trés.

Saint-Elzéar
672, av Principale
Saint-Elzéar, QC G0S 2J0

418-387-2534 Fax: 418-387-4378
munst-elzear@nouvellebeauce.com
Municipal Type: Municipality
Incorporated: 30 novembre 1994; *Area:* 85,12 km2
County or District: La Nouvelle-Beauce; *Population in 2006:* 1,864
Provincial Electoral District(s): Beauce-Nord
Federal Electoral District(s): Beauce
Next Election: 1er novembre 2013
Solange Marcoux, Sec.-Trés.

Saint-Elzér-de-Témiscouata
209, rue de l'Église
Saint-Elzér-de-Témiscouata, QC G0L 2W0
418-854-7690 Fax: 418-854-3279
muni.stelzear@qc.aibn.com
Municipal Type: Municipality
Incorporated: 19 novembre 1938; *Area:* 151,54 km2
County or District: Témiscouata; *Population in 2006:* 334
Provincial Electoral District(s): Kamouraska-Témiscouata
Federal Electoral District(s): Rimouski-Neigette-Témiscouata-Les Basques
Next Election: 1er novembre 2013
Denise Dubé, Sec.-Trés.

Saint-Émile-de-Suffolk
299, rte des Cantons
Saint-Émile-de-Suffolk, QC J0V 1Y0
819-426-2987 Fax: 819-426-3447
admstemile@sympatico.ca
Municipal Type: Municipality
Incorporated: 1er janvier 1881; *Area:* 54,07 km2
County or District: Papineau; *Population in 2006:* 537
Provincial Electoral District(s): Papineau
Federal Electoral District(s): Argenteuil-Papineau-Mirabel
Next Election: 1er novembre 2013
Gisèle Éthier, Sec.-Trés.

Saint-Éphrem-de-Beauce
#3, 2, rue de la Clinique
Saint-Éphrem-de-Beauce, QC G0M 1R0
418-484-5716 Fax: 418-484-2305
munise@telstep.net
Municipal Type: Municipality
Incorporated: 24 décembre 1997; *Area:* 115,35 km2
County or District: Beauce-Sartigan; *Population in 2006:* 2,627
Provincial Electoral District(s): Beauce-Sud
Federal Electoral District(s): Beauce
Next Election: 1er novembre 2013
Charlotte Poulin, Sec.-Trés.

Saint-Épiphane
280, rue Bernier
Saint-Épiphane, QC G0L 2X0
418-862-0052 Fax: 418-862-7753
directionmunepi@mail4fun.ca
Municipal Type: Municipality
Incorporated: 1er juillet 1855; *Area:* 82,36 km2
County or District: Rivière-du-Loup; *Population in 2006:* 874
Provincial Electoral District(s): Rivière-du-Loup
Federal Electoral District(s):
Montmagny-L'Islet-Kamouraska-Rivière-du-Loup
Next Election: 1er novembre 2013
Francine Labelle, Sec.-Trés. & Directrice générale

Saint-Esprit
21, rue Principale
Saint-Esprit, QC J0K 2L0
450-839-3629 Fax: 450-839-6070
precourt@megacom.net
www.municipalite-saint-esprit.com
Municipal Type: Municipality
Incorporated: 1er juillet 1855; *Area:* 54,36 km2
County or District: Montcalm; *Population in 2006:* 1,868
Provincial Electoral District(s): Rousseau
Federal Electoral District(s): Montcalm
Next Election: 1er novembre 2013
Diane Précourt, Sec.-Trés. & Directrice générale

Saint-Étienne-de-Beauharnois
489, ch St-Louis
Saint-Étienne-de-Beauharnois, QC J0S 1S0
450-225-1000 Fax: 450-225-1011
stetienne@videotron.ca
Municipal Type: Municipality
Incorporated: 1er janvier 1867; *Area:* 41,62 km2
County or District: Beauharnois-Salaberry; *Population in 2006:* 774
Provincial Electoral District(s): Beauharnois
Federal Electoral District(s): Beauharnois-Salaberry
Next Election: 1er novembre 2013
Ginette Prud'Homme, Directrice générale

Saint-Étienne-de-Bolton
9, rang de la Montagne
Saint-Étienne-de-Bolton, QC J0E 2E0
450-297-3353 Fax: 450-297-0412
secretaire@cooptel.qc.ca
Municipal Type: Municipality
Incorporated: 27 mai 1939; *Area:* 47,99 km2
County or District: Memphrémagog; *Population in 2006:* 496
Provincial Electoral District(s): Brome-Missisquoi
Federal Electoral District(s): Brome-Missisquoi
Next Election: 1er novembre 2013
Pauline Desautels, Sec.-Trés.

Saint-Étienne-des-Grès
1230, rue Principale
Saint-Étienne-des-Grès, QC G0X 2P0
819-535-3113 Fax: 819-535-1246
saint-etienne-des-gres@mun-stedg.qc.ca
Municipal Type: Parish (Paroisse)
Incorporated: 14 avril 1859; *Area:* 103,52 km2
County or District: Maskinongé; *Population in 2006:* 3,881
Provincial Electoral District(s): Maskinongé
Federal Electoral District(s): Berthier-Maskinongé
Next Election: 1er novembre 2013
Fabienne Bouchard, Sec.-Trés.

Saint-Eugène
CP 120
1065, rang de l'Église
Saint-Eugène, QC J0C 1J0
819-396-3000 Fax: 819-396-3576
st-eugene@mrcdrummond.qc.ca
Municipal Type: Municipality
Incorporated: 31 octobre 1879; *Area:* 76,37 km2
County or District: Drummond; *Population in 2006:* 1,133
Provincial Electoral District(s): Drummond
Federal Electoral District(s): Drummond
Next Election: 1er novembre 2013
Maryse Desbiens, Sec.-Trés. & Directrice générale

Saint-Eugène-d'Argentenay
CP 70
439, rue Principale
Saint-Eugène-d'Argentenay, QC G0W 1B0
418-276-1787 Fax: 418-276-9356
argentenay@qc.aira.com
Municipal Type: Municipality
Incorporated: 14 novembre 2009; *Area:* 83,37 km2
County or District: Maria-Chapdelaine; *Population in 2006:* 572
Provincial Electoral District(s): Roberval
Federal Electoral District(s): Roberval-Lac-St-Jean
Next Election: 1er novembre 2013
Karine Ouellet, Sec.-Trés.

Saint-Eugène-de-Guigues
CP 1070
4, rue Notre-Dame ouest
Saint-Eugène-de-Guigues, QC J0Z 3L0
819-785-2301 Fax: 819-785-2301
munst-eugene@mrctemiscamingue.qc.ca
Municipal Type: Municipality
Incorporated: 20 novembre 1912; *Area:* 113,02 km2
County or District: Témiscamingue; *Population in 2006:* 474
Provincial Electoral District(s): Rouyn-Noranda-Témiscamingue
Federal Electoral District(s): Abitibi-Témiscamingue
Next Election: 1er novembre 2013
Hugo Bellemare, Sec.-Trés.

Saint-Eugène-de-Ladrière
155, rue Principale
Saint-Eugène-de-Ladrière, QC G0L 1P0
418-869-2582 Fax: 418-869-2582
ladriere@globetrotter.net
www.ladriere.qc.ca
Municipal Type: Parish (Paroisse)
Incorporated: 1er janvier 1962; *Area:* 355,09 km2
County or District: Rimouski-Neigette; *Population in 2006:* 441
Provincial Electoral District(s): Rimouski
Federal Electoral District(s): Rimouski-Neigette-Témiscouata-Les Basques
Next Election: 1er novembre 2013
Colette D'Astous, Directrice générale

Saint-Euphémie-sur-Rivière-du-Sud
220, rue Principal est
Ste-Euphémie-sur-Rivière-du-Su, QC G0R 2Z0
418-469-3427 Fax: 418-469-3427
municipalitesteeuphemie@globetrotter.net
Municipal Type: Municipality
Incorporated: 20 juillet 1907; *Area:* 93,21 km2
County or District: Montmagny; *Population in 2006:* 358
Provincial Electoral District(s): Montmagny-L'Islet
Federal Electoral District(s):
Montmagny-L'Islet-Kamouraska-Rivière-du-Loup
Next Election: 1er novembre 2013
Lynda Pruneau, Sec.-Trés. & Directrice générale

Saint-Eusèbe
222, rue Principale
Saint-Eusèbe, QC G0L 2Y0
418-899-2762 Fax: 418-899-0194
municipalite.st_eusebe@qc.aira.com
Municipal Type: Parish (Paroisse)
Incorporated: 5 janvier 1911; *Area:* 120,12 km2
County or District: Témiscouata; *Population in 2006:* 620
Provincial Electoral District(s): Kamouraska-Témiscouata
Federal Electoral District(s): Rimouski-Neigette-Témiscouata-Les Basques
Next Election: 1er novembre 2013
Chantal Bouchard, Sec.-Trés.

Saint-Évariste-de-Forsyth
CP 39
495, rue Principale
Saint-Évariste-de-Forsyth, QC G0M 1S0
418-459-6488 Fax: 418-459-6268
Municipal Type: Municipality
Incorporated: 1er mars 1870; *Area:* 111,36 km2
County or District: Beauce-Sartigan; *Population in 2006:* 647
Provincial Electoral District(s): Beauce-Sud
Federal Electoral District(s): Beauce
Next Election: 1er novembre 2013
Claude Poulin, Sec.-Trés.

Saint-Fabien
CP 9
10, 7e av
Saint-Fabien, QC G0L 2Z0
418-869-2950 Fax: 418-869-3265
informations@saintfabien.net
www.saintfabien.net
Municipal Type: Parish (Paroisse)
Incorporated: 1er juillet 1855; *Area:* 128,07 km2
County or District: Rimouski-Neigette; *Population in 2006:* 1,952
Provincial Electoral District(s): Rimouski
Federal Electoral District(s): Rimouski-Neigette-Témiscouata-Les Basques
Next Election: 1er novembre 2013
Murielle Cloutier, Sec.-Trés. & Directrice générale

Saint-Fabien-de-Panet
195, rue Bilodeau
Saint-Fabien-de-Panet, QC G0R 2J0
418-249-4471 Fax: 418-249-4470
munpanet@globetrotter.net
www.montmagny.com/fabien/index.html
Municipal Type: Parish (Paroisse)
Incorporated: 26 mars 1907; *Area:* 185,31 km2
County or District: Montmagny; *Population in 2006:* 1,057
Provincial Electoral District(s): Montmagny-L'Islet
Federal Electoral District(s):
Montmagny-L'Islet-Kamouraska-Rivière-du-Loup
Next Election: 1er novembre 2013
Julie Lapointe, Sec.-Trés.

Saint-Faustin-Lac-Carré
100, Place de la Mairie
Saint-Faustin-Lac-Carré, QC J0T 1J2
819-688-2161 Fax: 819-688-6791
dirgen@munipalite.stfaustin.qc.ca
www.municipalite.stfaustin.qc.ca
Municipal Type: Municipality
Incorporated: 3 janvier 1996; *Area:* 119,86 km2
County or District: Les Laurentides; *Population in 2006:* 2,985
Provincial Electoral District(s): Labelle
Federal Electoral District(s): Laurentides-Labelle
Next Election: 1er novembre 2013
Richard Daveluy, Sec.-Trés. & Directeur général

Saint-Félix-d'Otis
455, rue Principale
Saint-Félix-d'Otis, QC G0V 1M0
418-544-5543 Fax: 418-544-9122
municipalite@st-felix-dotis.qc.ca
www.st-felix-dotis.qc.ca
Municipal Type: Municipality
Incorporated: 3 octobre 1923; *Area:* 235,94 km2
County or District: Le Fjord-du-Saguenay; *Population in 2006:* 1,007
Provincial Electoral District(s): Dubuc
Federal Electoral District(s): Chicoutimi-Le Fjord
Next Election: 1er novembre 2013
Éric Dallaire, Sec.-Trés. & Directeur général

Saint-Felix-de-Dalquier
CP 219
41, rue de L'Aqueduc
Saint-Felix-de-Dalquier, QC J0Y 1G0
819-727-1732 Fax: 819-727-9685
mun.stfelixdedalquier@cableamos.com
Municipal Type: Municipality
Incorporated: 29 octobre 1932; *Area:* 112,12 km2
County or District: Abitibi; *Population in 2006:* 936
Provincial Electoral District(s): Abitibi-Ouest
Federal Electoral District(s): Abitibi-Témiscamingue
Next Election: 1er novembre 2013
Richard Michaud, Sec.-Trés. & Directeur général

Saint-Félix-de-Kingsey
CP 30
1205, rue de l'Église
Saint-Félix-de-Kingsey, QC J0B 2T0
819-848-2321 Fax: 819-848-2202
munsaintfelixdekingsey@qc.aira.com
Municipal Type: Municipality
Incorporated: 1er juillet 1855; *Area:* 125,38
County or District: Drummond; *Population in 2006:* 1,430
Provincial Electoral District(s): Richmond
Federal Electoral District(s): Drummond
Next Election: 1er novembre 2013
Paul-Ernest Deslandes, Maire

Saint-Félix-de-Valois
600, ch de Joliette
Saint-Félix-de-Valois, QC J0K 2M0
450-889-5589 Fax: 450-889-5259
municipalite@st-felix-de-valois.com
Municipal Type: Municipality
Incorporated: 24 décembre 1997; *Area:* 85,79 km2
County or District: Matawinie; *Population in 2006:* 5,755
Provincial Electoral District(s): Berthier
Federal Electoral District(s): Joliette
Next Election: 1er novembre 2013
René Charbonneau, Sec.-Trés. & Directeur général

Saint-Ferdinand
821, rue Principale
Saint-Ferdinand, QC G0N 1N0
418-428-3480 Fax: 418-428-9724
st-ferdi@ivic.qc.ca
www.municipalite.saint-ferdinand.qc.ca
Municipal Type: Municipality
Incorporated: 29 novembre 2000; *Area:* 137,07 km2
County or District: L'Érable; *Population in 2006:* 2,195
Provincial Electoral District(s): Lotbinière
Federal Electoral District(s): Mégantic-L'Érable
Next Election: 1er novembre 2013
Sylvie Tardif, Directrice générale

Saint-Ferréol-les-Neiges
33, rue de l'Église
Saint-Ferréol-les-Neiges, QC G0A 3R0
418-826-2253 Fax: 418-826-0489
info@saintferreollesneiges.qc.ca
www.saintferreollesneiges.qc.ca
Municipal Type: Municipality
Incorporated: 1er juillet 1855; *Area:* 82,28 km2
County or District: La Côte-de-Beaupré; *Population in 2006:* 2,546
Provincial Electoral District(s): Charlevoix
Federal Electoral District(s):
Montmorency-Charlevoix-Haute-Côte-Nord
Next Election: 1er novembre 2013
François Drouin, Sec.-Trés. & Directeur général

Saint-Flavien
177, rue Prinipale
Saint-Flavien, QC G0S 2M0
418-728-4190 Fax: 418-728-3775
st-flavien@globetrotter.net
www.st-flavien.com
Municipal Type: Municipality
Incorporated: 29 décembre 1999; *Area:* 67,56 km2
County or District: Lotbinière; *Population in 2006:* 1,585
Provincial Electoral District(s): Lotbinière
Federal Electoral District(s): Lotbinière-Chutes-de-la-Chaudière
Next Election: 1er novembre 2013
Mario Roy, Directeur général & Sec.-Trés.

Saint-Fortunat
156, rue Principale
Saint-Fortunat, QC G0P 1G0
819-344-5399 Fax: 819-344-5399
munfort@ivic.qc.ca
www.st-fortunat.com
Municipal Type: Municipality
Incorporated: 1er janvier 1873; *Area:* 75,520 km2
County or District: Les Appalaches; *Population in 2009:* 324
Provincial Electoral District(s): Richmond
Federal Electoral District(s): Mégantic-L'Érable
Next Election: 1er novembre 2013
Brigitte Pelletier, Directrice générale

Saint-François-d'Assise
457, ch Central
Saint-François-d'Assise, QC G0J 2N0
418-299-2066 Fax: 418-299-3037
munstfrs@globetrotter.net
Municipal Type: Municipality
Incorporated: 3 septembre 1926; *Area:* 171,97 km2
County or District: Avignon; *Population in 2006:* 743
Provincial Electoral District(s): Bonaventure
Federal Electoral District(s): Gaspésie-Iles-de-la-Madeleine
Next Election: 1er novembre 2013
Pauline Gallant, Sec.-Trés.

Saint-François-de-l'Ile-d'Orléans
337, ch Royal
Saint-François, QC G0A 3S0
418-829-3100 Fax: 418-829-1004
stfrancois@oricom.ca
Municipal Type: Municipality
Incorporated: 1er juillet 1855; *Area:* 30,76 km2
County or District: L'Ile-d'Orléans; *Population in 2006:* 573
Provincial Electoral District(s): Montmorency
Federal Electoral District(s):
Montmorency-Charlevoix-Haute-Côte-Nord
Next Election: 1er novembre 2013
Marco Langlois, Sec.-Trés. & Directeur général

Saint-François-de-la-Rivière-du-Sud
CP 68
534, ch St-François ouest
St-François-de-la-Riv.-du-Sud, QC G0R 3A0
418-259-7228 Fax: 418-259-2056
munist-frs@globetrotter.net
Municipal Type: Municipality
Incorporated: 1er juillet 1855; *Area:* 95,49 km2
County or District: Montmagny; *Population in 2006:* 1,574
Provincial Electoral District(s): Montmagny-L'Islet
Federal Electoral District(s):
Montmagny-L'Islet-Kamouraska-Rivière-du-Loup
Next Election: 1er novembre 2013
Yves Laflamme, Sec.-Trés.

Saint-François-de-Sales
541, rue Principale
Saint-François-de-Sales, QC G0W 1M0
418-348-6736 Fax: 418-348-9439
munstfrs@destination.ca
Municipal Type: Municipality
Incorporated: 14 mai 1888; *Area:* 200,56 km2
County or District: Le Domaine-du-Roy; *Population in 2006:* 731
Provincial Electoral District(s): Roberval
Federal Electoral District(s): Roberval-Lac-St-Jean
Next Election: 1er novembre 2013
Renaud Blanchette, Sec.-Trés.

Saint-François-du-Lac
CP 60
400, rue Notre-Dame
Saint-François-du-Lac, QC J0G 1M0
450-568-2124 Fax: 450-568-7465
municipalite@saint-francois-du-lac.ca
Municipal Type: Municipality
Incorporated: 31 décembre 1997; *Area:* 63,11 km2
County or District: Nicolet-Yamaska; *Population in 2006:* 2,002
Provincial Electoral District(s): Nicolet-Yamaska
Federal Electoral District(s): Bas-Richelieu-Nicolet-Bécancour
Next Election: 1er novembre 2013
Peggy Péloquin, Sec.-Trés.

Saint-François-Xavier-de-Brompton
CP 10
94, rue Principale
St-François-Xavier-de-Brompton, QC J0B 2V0
819-845-3954 Fax: 819-845-7711
xavier@axion.ca
Municipal Type: Parish (Paroisse)
Incorporated: 28 décembre 1887; *Area:* 96,11 km2
County or District: Le Val-St-François; *Population in 2006:* 2,018
Provincial Electoral District(s): Johnson
Federal Electoral District(s): Richmond-Arthabaska
Next Election: 1er novembre 2013
Sylvie Champagne, Sec.-Trés.

Saint-François-Xavier-de-Viger
123, rue Principale
Saint-François-Xavier-de-Viger, QC G0L 3C0
418-497-2302 Fax: 418-497-2302
stfxcaci@globetrotter.net
pages.globetrotter.net/munstfrancoisxv
Municipal Type: Municipality
Incorporated: 1er janvier 1950; *Area:* 110,19 km2
County or District: Rivière-du-Loup; *Population in 2006:* 277
Provincial Electoral District(s): Rivière-du-Loup
Federal Electoral District(s):
Montmagny-L'Islet-Kamourask-Rivière-du-Loup
Next Election: 1er novembre 2013
Yvette Beaulieu, Sec.-Trés. & Directrice générale

Saint-Frédéric
850, rue de l'Hôtel-de-Ville
Saint-Frédéric, QC G0N 1P0
418-426-3357 Fax: 418-426-1259
jacqueline.lehoux@bellnet.ca
Municipal Type: Parish (Paroisse)
Incorporated: 1er juillet 1855; *Area:* 71,58 km2
County or District: Robert-Cliche; *Population in 2006:* 1,049
Provincial Electoral District(s): Beauce-Nord
Federal Electoral District(s): Beauce
Next Election: 1er novembre 2013
Jacqueline Lehoux, Sec.-Trés.

Saint-Fulgence
253, rue du Saguenay
Saint-Fulgence, QC G0V 1S0
418-674-2588 Fax: 418-674-9213
admin@ville.st-fulgence.qc.ca
www.ville.st-fulgence.qc.ca
Municipal Type: Municipality
Incorporated: 1er mai 1973; *Area:* 354,68 km2
County or District: Le Fjord-du-Saguenay; *Population in 2006:* 2,024
Provincial Electoral District(s): Dubuc
Federal Electoral District(s): Chicoutimi-Le Fjord
Next Election: 1er novembre 2013
Fabienne Larouche, Sec.-Trés.

Saint-Gabriel
45, rue Beausoleil
Saint-Gabriel, QC J0K 2N0
450-835-2212 Fax: 450-835-9852
villesaintgabriel@intermonde.net
Municipal Type: City
Incorporated: 17 décembre 1892; *Area:* 2,9 km2
County or District: D'Autray; *Population in 2006:* 2,828
Provincial Electoral District(s): Berthier
Federal Electoral District(s): Berthier-Maskinongé
Next Election: 1er novembre 2013
Jean-Maurice Gadoury, Greffier & Directeur général
Gaétan Gravel, Maire

Saint-Gabriel-de-Brandon
5111, ch du Lac
Saint-Gabriel-de-Brandon, QC J0K 2N0
450-835-3494 Fax: 450-835-3495
info@munstgab.com
Municipal Type: Parish (Paroisse)
Incorporated: 30 juin 1864; *Area:* 95,87 km2
County or District: D'Autray; *Population in 2006:* 2,800
Provincial Electoral District(s): Berthier
Federal Electoral District(s): Berthier-Maskinongé
Next Election: 1er novembre 2013
Jeanne Pelland, Sec.-Trés.

Saint-Gabriel-de-Rimouski
248, rue Principale
Saint-Gabriel-de-Rimouski, QC G0K 1M0
418-798-4938 Fax: 418-798-4108
mun.st-gabriel@globetrotter.net
Municipal Type: Municipality
Incorporated: 7 janvier 1989; *Area:* 132,10 km2
County or District: La Mitis; *Population in 2006:* 1,228
Provincial Electoral District(s): Matapédia
Federal Electoral District(s): Haute-Gaspésie-La Mitis-Matane-Matapédia
Next Election: 1er novembre 2013
Martin Norman, Directeur générale

Saint-Gabriel-de-Valcartier
1743, boul Valcartier
Saint-Gabriel-de-Valcartier, QC G0A 4S0
418-844-1218 Fax: 418-844-3030
admin@munsgdv.ca
www.saint-gabriel-de-valcartier.ca
Municipal Type: Municipality
Incorporated: 5 octobre 1985; *Area:* 441,17 km2
County or District: La Jacques-Cartier; *Population in 2006:* 2,827
Provincial Electoral District(s): Chauveau
Federal Electoral District(s): Portneuf-Jacques-Cartier
Next Election: 1er novembre 2013
Joan Sheehan, Sec.-Trés. & Directrice générale

Saint-Gabriel-Lalemant
CP 9
20, rue Principale
Saint-Gabriel-Lalemant, QC G0L 3E0
418-852-2801 Fax: 418-852-3390
munstgab@globetrotter.net
Municipal Type: Municipality
Incorporated: 27 mai 1939; *Area:* 80,49 km2
County or District: Kamouraska; *Population in 2006:* 788
Provincial Electoral District(s): Kamouraska-Témiscouata
Federal Electoral District(s):
Montmagny-L'Islet-Kamouraska-Rivière-du-Loup
Next Election: 1er novembre 2013
Gina Lévesque, Sec.-Trés.

Saint-Gédéon
208, rue De Quen
Saint-Gédéon, QC G0W 2P0
418-345-8001 Fax: 418-345-2306
mairie@ville.st-gedeon.qc.ca
www.ville.st-gedeon.qc.ca
Municipal Type: Municipality
Incorporated: 6 décembre 1975; *Area:* 64,17 km2
County or District: Lac-St-Jean-Est; *Population in 2006:* 1,931
Provincial Electoral District(s): Lac-St-Jean
Federal Electoral District(s): Roberval-Lac-St-Jean
Next Election: 1er novembre 2013
Dany Dallaire, Directeur général & Sec.-Trés.

Saint-Gédéon-de-Beauce
102 - 1re av sud
Saint-Gédéon-de-Beauce, QC G0M 1T0
418-582-3341 Fax: 418-582-6016
stgedeon@globetrotter.net
Municipal Type: Municipality
Incorporated: 12 février 1003; *Area:* 193,45 km2
County or District: Beauce-Sartigan; *Population in 2006:* 2,351
Provincial Electoral District(s): Beauce-Sud
Federal Electoral District(s): Beauce
Next Election: 1er novembre 2013
Note: Effective October 12, 2003, the Municipality of St-Gédéon-de-Beauce & the Parish of St-Gédéon amalgamated to create the new Municipality of St-Gédéon-de-Beauce.
Pierre-Alain Pelchat, Sec.-Trés. & Directeur général

Saint-Georges-de-Clarenceville
1350, ch Middle
Saint-Georges-de-Clarenceville, QC J0J 1B0
450-294-2464 Fax: 450-294-2016
st-georges@qc.aira.com
Municipal Type: Municipality
Incorporated: 27 décembre 1989; *Area:* 63,76 km2
County or District: Le Haut-Richelieu; *Population in 2006:* 1,106
Provincial Electoral District(s): Iberville
Federal Electoral District(s): Brome-Missisquoi
Next Election: 1er novembre 2013
Thérèse Lacombe, Sec.-Trés.

Saint-Georges-de-Windsor
485, rue Principale
Saint-Georges-de-Windsor, QC J0A 1J0
819-828-2716 Fax: 819-828-0213
mungeorges@cgocable.ca
Municipal Type: Municipality
Incorporated: 30 novembre 2009; *Area:* 126,57 km2
County or District: Les Sources; *Population in 2006:* 911
Provincial Electoral District(s): Richmond
Federal Electoral District(s): Richmond-Arthabaska
Next Election: 1er novembre 2013
Armande Perreault, Sec.-Trés. & Directrice générale

Saint-Gérard-Majella
435, rang St-Antoine
Saint-Gérard-Majella, QC J0G 1X0
450-789-5777 Fax: 450-789-1188
info@munistgerardmajella.com

Municipal Type: Parish (Paroisse)
Incorporated: 18 février 1907; *Area:* 37,81 km2
County or District: Pierre-De Saurel; *Population in 2009:* 230
Provincial Electoral District(s): Nicolet-Yamaska
Federal Electoral District(s): Bas-Richelieu-Nicolet-Bécancour
Next Election: 1er novembre 2013
François Léveillée, Directeur général

Saint-Germain
146, rang des Côtes
Saint-Germain, QC G0L 3G0
418-492-9771 Fax: 418-492-9772
Municipal Type: Parish (Paroisse)
Incorporated: 29 juin 1893; *Area:* 26,70 km2
County or District: Kamouraska; *Population in 2006:* 301
Provincial Electoral District(s): Kamouraska-Témiscouata
Federal Electoral District(s):
Montmagny-L'Islet-Kamouraska-Rivière-du-Loup
Next Election: 1er novembre 2013
Hélène B.-Bernier, Sec.-Trés.

Saint-Germain-de-Grantham
233, ch Yamaska
Saint-Germain-de-Grantham, QC J0C 1K0
819-395-5496 Fax: 819-395-5200
municipalitestgermain@cgocable.ca
Municipal Type: Municipality
Incorporated: 22 février 1995; *Area:* 86,29 km2
County or District: Drummond; *Population in 2006:* 3,993
Provincial Electoral District(s): Drummond
Federal Electoral District(s): Drummond
Next Election: 1er novembre 2013
Jocelyn Légaré, Sec.-Trés.

Saint-Gervais
CP 9
150, rue Principale
Saint-Gervais, QC G0R 3C0
418-887-6116 Fax: 418-887-6312
mungerv@globetrotter.net
www.saint-gervais.ca
Municipal Type: Municipality
Incorporated: 1er juillet 1855; *Area:* 87,23 km2
County or District: Bellechasse; *Population in 2006:* 1,926
Provincial Electoral District(s): Bellechasse
Federal Electoral District(s): Lévis-Bellechasse
Next Election: 1er novembre 2013
Jérôme Fortier, Sec.-Trés.

Saint-Gilbert
110, rue Principale
Saint-Gilbert, QC G0A 3T0
418-268-8194 Fax: 418-268-6466
saint-gilbert@globetrotter.net
www.municipalite.saint-gilbert.qc.ca
Municipal Type: Parish (Paroisse)
Incorporated: 27 avril 1893; *Area:* 36,95 km2
County or District: Portneuf; *Population in 2006:* 292
Provincial Electoral District(s): Portneuf
Federal Electoral District(s): Portneuf-Jacques-Cartier
Next Election: 1er novembre 2013
Réjeanne Plamondon, Sec.-Trés. & Directrice générale

Saint-Gilles
161, rue O'Hurley
Saint-Gilles, QC G0S 2P0
418-888-3198 Fax: 418-888-5145
st-gilles@globetrotter.net
Municipal Type: Parish (Paroisse)
Incorporated: 1er juillet 1855; *Area:* 174,74 km2
County or District: Lotbinière; *Population in 2006:* 1,813
Provincial Electoral District(s): Lotbinière
Federal Electoral District(s): Lotbinière-Chutes-de-la-Chaudière
Next Election: 1er novembre 2013
Aline Martin, Sec.-Trés.

Saint-Godefroi
CP 157
109C, rte 132
Saint-Godefroi, QC G0C 3C0
418-752-6316 Fax: 418-752-6396
st.godefroi@globetrotter.net
Municipal Type: Township
Incorporated: 16 décembre 1913; *Area:* 60,32 km2
County or District: Bonaventure; *Population in 2006:* 370
Provincial Electoral District(s): Bonaventure
Federal Electoral District(s): Gaspésie-Iles-de-la-Madeleine
Next Election: 1er novembre 2013
Jocelyne Joseph, Sec.-Trés.

Saint-Guillaume
106, rue St-Jean-Baptiste
Saint-Guillaume, QC J0C 1L0
819-396-2403 Fax: 819-396-0184
adm@municipalite.st-guillaume.qc.ca
Municipal Type: Municipality
Incorporated: 8 novembre 1995; *Area:* 86,83 km2
County or District: Drummond; *Population in 2006:* 1,578
Provincial Electoral District(s): Nicolet-Yamaska
Federal Electoral District(s): Drummond
Next Election: 1er novembre 2013
Nathalie Lussier, Sec.-Trés.

Saint-Guy
52, rue Principal
Saint-Guy, QC G0K 1W0
418-963-2601 Fax: 418-963-2601
municipalitest-guy@qc.aira.com
Municipal Type: Municipality
Incorporated: 1er janvier 1958; *Area:* 140,09 km2
County or District: Les Basques; *Population in 2006:* 89
Provincial Electoral District(s): Rivière-du-Loup
Federal Electoral District(s): Rimouski-Neigette-Témiscouata-Les Basques
Next Election: 1er novembre 2013
Marie-Eve Chouinard, Sec.-Trés.

Saint-Henri
219, rue Commerciale
Saint-Henri, QC G0R 3E0
418-882-2401 Fax: 418-882-0302
munhenri@globetrotter.net
www.municipalite.saint-henri.qc.ca
Municipal Type: Municipality
Incorporated: 9 octobre 1976; *Area:* 121,78 km2
County or District: Bellechasse; *Population in 2006:* 4,094
Provincial Electoral District(s): Bellechasse
Federal Electoral District(s): Lévis-Bellechasse
Next Election: 1er novembre 2013
Jacques Risler, Sec.-Trés.

Saint-Henri-de-Taillon
401, rue de l'Hôtel-de-Ville
Saint-Henri-de-Taillon, QC G0W 2X0
418-347-3243 Fax: 418-347-1138
municipalite@ville.st-henri-de-taillon.qc.ca
Municipal Type: Municipality
Incorporated: 12 août 1903; *Area:* 62,95 km2
County or District: Lac-St-Jean-Est; *Population in 2006:* 739
Provincial Electoral District(s): Lac-St-Jean
Federal Electoral District(s): Roberval-Lac-St-Jean
Next Election: 1er novembre 2013
Rachel Bourget, Sec.-Trés.

Saint-Herménégilde
776, rue Principale
Saint-Herménégilde, QC J0B 2W0
819-849-4443 Fax: 819-849-6924
municipalite@st-hermenegilde.qc.ca
Municipal Type: Municipality
Incorporated: 12 octobre 1985; *Area:* 169,90 km2
County or District: Coaticook; *Population in 2006:* 718
Provincial Electoral District(s): Mégantic-Compton
Federal Electoral District(s): Compton-Stanstead
Next Election: 1er novembre 2013
Nathalie Isabelle, Sec.-Trés.

Saint-Hilaire-de-Dorset
847, rue Principale
Saint-Hilaire-de-Dorset, QC G0M 1G0
418-459-6872 Fax: 418-459-6882
munstahilaire@telcourcelles.net
Municipal Type: Parish (Paroisse)
Incorporated: 12 avril 1916; *Area:* 252,52 km2
County or District: Beauce-Sartigan; *Population in 2006:* 104
Provincial Electoral District(s): Beauce-Sud
Federal Electoral District(s): Beauce
Next Election: 1er novembre 2013
Johanne Jacques, Sec.-Trés.

Saint-Hilarion
306, ch Cartier Nord
Saint-Hilarion, QC G0A 3V0
418-457-3463 Fax: 418-457-3805
munsthil@cabletel.net
Municipal Type: Parish (Paroisse)
Incorporated: 1er juillet 1855; *Area:* 97,77 km2
County or District: Charlevoix; *Population in 2006:* 1,191
Provincial Electoral District(s): Charlevoix
Federal Electoral District(s):
Montmorency-Charlevoix-Haute-Côte-du-Loup
Next Election: 1er novembre 2013
Madeleine Tremblay, Sec.-Trés.

Saint-Hippolyte
2253, ch des Hauteurs
Saint-Hippolyte, QC J8A 1A1
450-563-2505 Fax: 450-563-2362
munsthippolyte@questzones.com
Municipal Type: Parish (Paroisse)
Incorporated: 1er juillet 1855; *Area:* 121,19 km2
County or District: La Rivière-du-Nord; *Population in 2006:* 7,219
Provincial Electoral District(s): Bertrand
Federal Electoral District(s): Rivière-du-Nord
Next Election: 1er novembre 2013
Christiane Côté, Sec.-Trés. & Directrice générale

Saint-Honoré
3611, boul Martel
Saint-Honoré, QC G0V 1L0
418-673-3405 Fax: 418-673-3871
admin@ville.sthonore.qc.ca
www.ville.sthonore.qc.ca
Municipal Type: Municipality
Incorporated: 16 décembre 1972; *Area:* 189,82 km2
County or District: Le Fjord-du-Saguenay; *Population in 2006:* 4,727
Provincial Electoral District(s): Dubuc
Federal Electoral District(s): Chicoutimi-Le Fjord
Next Election: 1er novembre 2013
Stéphane Leclerc, Sec.-Trés. & Directeur général

Saint-Honoré-de-Shenley
CP 128
499, rue Principale
Saint-Honoré-de-Shenley, QC G0M 1V0
418-485-6738 Fax: 418-485-6171
st.honore@tlb.sympatico.ca
Municipal Type: Municipality
Incorporated: 19 avril 2000; *Area:* 136,46 km2
County or District: Beauce-Sartigan; *Population in 2006:* 1,664
Provincial Electoral District(s): Beauce-Sud
Federal Electoral District(s): Beauce
Next Election: 1er novembre 2013
Edith Quirion, Sec.-Trés.

Saint-Honoré-de-Témiscouata
99, rue Principale
Saint-Honoré-de-Témiscouata, QC G0L 3K0
418-497-2588 Fax: 418-497-1656
mun.st-honore@qc.aira.com
membres.lycos.fr/munsthonore/
Municipal Type: Municipality
Incorporated: 1er janvier 1881; *Area:* 251,58 km2
County or District: Témiscouata; *Population in 2006:* 807
Provincial Electoral District(s): Kamouraska-Témiscouata
Federal Electoral District(s): Rimouski-Neigette-Témiscouata-Les Basques
Next Election: 1er novembre 2013
Lucie April, Directrice générale

Saint-Hubert-Rivière-du-Loup
CP 218
10, rue Saint-Rosaire
Saint-Hubert-Rivière-du-Loup, QC G0L 3L0
418-497-3394 Fax: 418-497-1187
mun.st-hubert@bellnet.ca
www.municipalite.saint-hubert-de-riviere-du-loup.qc.ca
Municipal Type: Municipality
Incorporated: 4 janvier 1894; *Area:* 183,99 km2
County or District: Rivière-du-Loup; *Population in 2006:* 1,422
Provincial Electoral District(s): Rivière-du-Loup
Federal Electoral District(s):
Montmagney-L'Islet-Kamouraska-Rivière-du-Loup
Next Election: 1er novembre 2013
Sylvie Samson, Sec.-Trés. & Directrice générale

Saint-Hugues
508, rue Notre-Dame
Saint-Hugues, QC J0H 1N0
450-794-2030 Fax: 450-794-2474
munst-huguesdirection@mrcmaskoutains.qc.ca
Municipal Type: Municipality
Incorporated: 6 novembre 1982; *Area:* 89,39 km2
County or District: Les Maskoutains; *Population in 2006:* 1,310
Provincial Electoral District(s): St-Hyacinthe
Federal Electoral District(s): St-Hyacinthe-Bagot
Next Election: 1er novembre 2013
Yolande Simoneau, Sec.-Trés. & Directrice générale

Saint-Ignace-de-Loyola
25, rue Laforest
Saint-Ignace-de-Loyola, QC J0K 2P0
450-836-3376 Fax: 450-836-1400
st.ignace.loyola@intermonde.net
Municipal Type: Parish (Paroisse)
Incorporated: 11 février 1897; *Area:* 30,76 km2
County or District: D'Autray; *Population in 2006:* 1,925
Provincial Electoral District(s): Berthier
Federal Electoral District(s): Berthier-Maskinongé
Next Election: 1er novembre 2013
Fabrice St-Martin, Sec.-Trés.

Saint-Ignace-de-Stanbridge
678, rang de l'Église nord
Saint-Ignace-de-Stanbridge, QC J0J 1Y0
450-296-4467 Fax: 450-296-4461
stignace@citenet.net
Municipal Type: Parish (Paroisse)
Incorporated: 21 mars 1889; *Area:* 69,33 km2
County or District: Brome-Missisquoi; *Population in 2006:* 631
Provincial Electoral District(s): Brome-Missisquoi
Federal Electoral District(s): Brome-Missisquoi
Next Election: 1er novembre 2013
Monique Aubry-Santerre, Sec.-Trés. & Directrice générale

Saint-Irénée
CP 68
122, rue Principale
Saint-Irénée, QC G0T 1V0
418-452-3231 Fax: 418-452-8221
munstirenee@bellnet.ca
Municipal Type: Parish (Paroisse)
Incorporated: 1er juillet 1855; *Area:* 60,29 km2
County or District: Charlevoix-Est; *Population in 2006:* 727
Provincial Electoral District(s): Charlevoix
Federal Electoral District(s):
Montmorency-Charlevoix-Haute-Côte-Nord
Next Election: 1er novembre 2013
Marie-Claude Lavoie, Sec.-Trés. & Directrice générale

Saint-Isidore
671, rue St-Régis
Saint-Isidore, QC J0L 2A0
450-454-3919 Fax: 450-454-7485
mun.stisidore@videotron.ca
Municipal Type: Parish (Paroisse)
Incorporated: 1er juillet 1855; *Area:* 52,00 km2
County or District: Roussillon; *Population in 2006:* 2,489
Provincial Electoral District(s): Châteauguay
Federal Electoral District(s): Châteauguay-St Constant
Next Election: 1er novembre 2013
Daniel Vinet, Sec.-Trés. & Directeur général

Saint-Isidore
128, route Coulombe
Saint-Isidore, QC G0S 2S0
418-882-5670 Fax: 418-882-5902
isidore@clic.net
Municipal Type: Municipality
Incorporated: 22 septembre 1993; *Area:* 101,18 km2
County or District: La Nouvelle-Beauce; *Population in 2006:* 2,503
Provincial Electoral District(s): Beauce-Nord
Federal Electoral District(s): Beauce
Next Election: 1er novembre 2013
Louise Trachy, Sec.-Trés. & Directrice générale

Saint-Isidore-de-Clifton
66, ch Auckland
Saint-Isidore-de-Clifton, QC J0B 2X0
819-658-3637 Fax: 819-658-9070
mun32@globetrotter.net
www.st-isidore-clifton.qc.ca
Municipal Type: Municipality
Incorporated: 24 décembre 1997; *Area:* 178,43 km2
County or District: Le Haut-St-François; *Population in 2006:* 781
Provincial Electoral District(s): Mégantic-Compton
Federal Electoral District(s): Compton-Stanstead
Next Election: 1er novembre 2013
Gaétan Perron, Sec.-Trés.

Saint-Jacques
16, rue Maréchal
Saint-Jacques, QC J0K 2R0
450-839-3671 Fax: 450-839-2387
info@st-jacques.org
www.st-jacques.org
Municipal Type: Municipality
Incorporated: 20 mai 1998; *Area:* 64,69 km2
County or District: Montcalm; *Population in 2006:* 3,706
Provincial Electoral District(s): Joliette
Federal Electoral District(s): Montcalm
Next Election: 1er novembre 2013
Josée Philibert, Sec.-Trés.

Saint-Jacques-de-Leeds
355, rue Principale
Saint-Jacques-de-Leeds, QC G0N 1J0
418-424-3321 Fax: 418-424-0126
mun.leeds@bellnet.ca
www.stjacquesdeleeds.com
Municipal Type: Municipality
Incorporated: 23 septembre 1929; *Area:* 81,830 km2
County or District: Les Appalaches; *Population in 2009:* 795
Provincial Electoral District(s): Frontenac
Federal Electoral District(s): Mégantic-L'Érable
Next Election: 1er novembre 2013
Nathalie Laflamme, Directrice générale

Saint-Jacques-le-Majeur-de-Wolfstown
877, rte 263
Saint-Jacques-le-Majeur, QC G0N 1E0
418-449-1531 Fax: 418-449-1876
mun.st-jacques-le-majeur@globetrotter.net
Municipal Type: Parish (Paroisse)
Incorporated: 30 septembre 1909; *Area:* 59,330 km2
County or District: Les Appalaches; *Population in 2009:* 182
Provincial Electoral District(s): Frontenac
Federal Electoral District(s): Mégantic-L'Érable
Next Election: 1er novembre 2013
Linda Bolduc, Directrice générale

Saint-Jacques-le-Mineur
91, rue Principale
Saint-Jacques-le-Mineur, QC J0J 1Z0
450-347-5446 Fax: 450-347-5754
saintjacqueslemineur@qc.aira.com
Municipal Type: Parish (Paroisse)
Incorporated: 1er juillet 1855; *Area:* 65,19 km2
County or District: Les Jardins-de-Napierville; *Population in 2006:* 1,628
Provincial Electoral District(s): Huntingdon
Federal Electoral District(s): Beauharnois-Salaberry
Next Election: 1er novembre 2013
Jean-Pierre Cayer, Sec.-Trés. & Directeur général

Saint-Janvier-de-Joly
729, rue des Loisirs
Saint-Janvier-de-Joly, QC G0S 1M0
418-728-2984 Fax: 418-728-2997
joly33065@globetrotter.net
Municipal Type: Municipality
Incorporated: 1er janvier 1944; *Area:* 109,86 km2
County or District: Lotbinière; *Population in 2006:* 890
Provincial Electoral District(s): Lotbinière
Federal Electoral District(s): Lotbinière-Chutes-de-la-Chaudière
Next Election: 1er novembre 2013
Céline Biron, Sec.-Trés. & Directrice générale

Saint-Jean-Baptiste
3041, rue Principale
Saint-Jean-Baptiste, QC J0L 2B0
450-467-3456 Fax: 450-467-8813
info@msjb.qc.ca
www.msjb.qc.ca
Municipal Type: Municipality
Incorporated: 1er juillet 1855; *Area:* 75,98 km2
County or District: La Vallée-du-Richelieu; *Population in 2006:* 3,035
Provincial Electoral District(s): 2006uas
Federal Electoral District(s): Chambly-Borduas
Next Election: 1er novembre 2013
Denis Meunier, Directeur général

Saint-Jean-de-Brébeuf
844, rue de l'Église
Saint-Jean-de-Brébeuf, QC G6G 0A1
418-453-7774 Fax: 418-453-2339
stjeandebrebeuf@bellnet.ca
Municipal Type: Municipality
Incorporated: 1er janvier 1946; *Area:* 79,680 km2
County or District: Les Appalaches; *Population in 2009:* 378
Provincial Electoral District(s): Frontenac
Federal Electoral District(s): Mégantic-L'Érable
Next Election: 1er novembre 2013
Caroline Gagné, Directrice générale

Saint-Jean-de-Cherbourg
10, 8e rang
Saint-Jean-de-Cherbourg, QC G0J 2R0
418-733-8177 Fax: 418-733-8177
muni.st-jean@globetrotter.net
Municipal Type: Parish (Paroisse)
Incorporated: 1er mai 1954; *Area:* 113,23 km2
County or District: Matane; *Population in 2006:* 218
Provincial Electoral District(s): Matane
Federal Electoral District(s): Haute-Gaspésie-La Mitis-Matane-Matapédia
Next Election: 1er novembre 2013
Jacinthe Imbeault, Sec.-Trés. & Directrice générale

Saint-Jean-de-Dieu
32, rue Principale sud
Saint-Jean-de-Dieu, QC G0L 3M0
418-963-3529 Fax: 418-963-2903
stjeandd@intermobilex.com
Municipal Type: Municipality
Incorporated: 1er janvier 1865; *Area:* 151,32 km2
County or District: Les Basques; *Population in 2006:* 1,671
Provincial Electoral District(s): Rivière-du-Loup
Federal Electoral District(s): Rimouski-Neigette-Témisouata-Les Basques
Next Election: 1er novembre 2013
Normand Morency, Directeur général & Sec.-Trés.

Saint-Jean-de-l'Ile-d'Orléans
2336, ch Royal
Saint-Jean-de-l'Ile-d'Orléans, QC G0A 3W0
418-829-2206 Fax: 418-829-0997
munsaintjeanileorleans@qc.aira.com
Municipal Type: Municipality
Incorporated: 1er juillet 1855; *Area:* 43,64 km2
County or District: L'Ile-d'Orléans; *Population in 2006:* 968
Provincial Electoral District(s): Montmorency
Federal Electoral District(s): Montmorency-Charlevoix-Haute-Côte-Nord
Next Election: 1er novembre 2013
Lucie Lambert, Sec.-Trés. & Directrice générale

Saint-Jean-de-la-Lande
810, rue Principale
Saint-Jean-de-la-Lande, QC G0L 3N0
418-853-3703 Fax: 418-853-3475
munst.j.dlandre@qc.aira.com
Municipal Type: Municipality
Incorporated: 1er janvier 1965; *Area:* 108,80 km2
County or District: Témiscouata; *Population in 2006:* 293
Provincial Electoral District(s): Kamouraska-Témiscouata
Federal Electoral District(s): Rimouski-Neigette-Témiscouata-Les Basques
Next Election: 1er novembre 2013
Danielle Rousseau, Sec.-Trés. & Directrice générale

Saint-Jean-de-Matha
170, rue Ste-Louise
Saint-Jean-de-Matha, QC J0K 2S0
450-886-3867 Fax: 450-886-3398
matha@qc.aira.com
www.municipalitestjeandematha.com
Municipal Type: Municipality
Incorporated: 1er juillet 1855; *Area:* 117,01 km2
County or District: Matawinie; *Population in 2006:* 4,152
Provincial Electoral District(s): Berthier
Federal Electoral District(s): Joliette
Next Election: 1er novembre 2013
Nicole D. Archambault, Sec.-Trés. & Directrice générale

Saint-Jean-Port-Joli
7, place de l'Église
Saint-Jean-Port-Joli, QC G0R 3G0
418-598-3084 Fax: 418-598-3085
munisjpj@globetrotter.net
www.saintjeanportjoli.com
Municipal Type: Municipality
Incorporated: 1er juillet 1855; *Area:* 68,55 km2
County or District: L'Islet; *Population in 2006:* 3,363
Provincial Electoral District(s): Montmagny-L'Islet
Federal Electoral District(s): Montmagny-L'Islet-Kamouraska-Rivière-du-Loup
Next Election: 1er novembre 2013
Denis Gaudreault, Sec.-Trés. & Directeur général

Saint-Joachim
172, rue de l'Église
Saint-Joachim, QC G0A 3X0
418-827-3755 Fax: 418-827-8574
munst-j@qc.aira.com
Municipal Type: Parish (Paroisse)
Incorporated: 1er juillet 1855; *Area:* 40,68 km2
County or District: La Côte-de-Beaupré; *Population in 2006:* 1,362
Provincial Electoral District(s): Charlevoix
Federal Electoral District(s): Montmorency-Charlevoix-Haute-Côte-Nord
Next Election: 1er novembre 2013
Suzanne Cyr, Sec.-Trés. & Directrice générale

Saint-Joachim-de-Shefford
567, 1er rang ouest
Saint-Joachim-de-Shefford, QC J0E 2G0
450-539-3201 Fax: 450-539-3145
mairie@st-joachim.ca
www.st-joachim.ca
Municipal Type: Parish (Paroisse)
Incorporated: 10 juin 1884; *Area:* 126,98 km2
County or District: La Haute-Yamaska; *Population in 2006:* 1,089
Provincial Electoral District(s): Johnson
Federal Electoral District(s): Shefford
Next Election: 1er novembre 2013
France Lagrandneur, Sec.-Trés. & Directrice générale

Saint-Joseph-de-Beauce
843, av du Palais
Saint-Joseph-de-Beauce, QC G0S 2V0
418-397-4358 Fax: 418-397-5715
vsjoseph@globetrotter.qc.ca
www.ville.stjosephdebeauce.qc.ca
Municipal Type: City
Incorporated: 27 janvier 1999; *Area:* 108,54 km2
County or District: Robert-Cliche; *Population in 2006:* 4,454
Provincial Electoral District(s): Beauce-Nord
Federal Electoral District(s): Beauce
Next Election: 1er novembre 2013
Michel Cliche, Maire
Jean-Louis Lessard, Greffier

Saint-Joseph-de-Coleraine
88, av St-Patrick
Saint-Joseph-de-Coleraine, QC G0N 1B0
418-423-4000 Fax: 418-423-4150
coleraine@bellnet.ca
www.coleraine.qc.ca
Municipal Type: Municipality
Incorporated: 11 novembre 1891; *Area:* 125,11 km2
County or District: Les Appalaches; *Population in 2009:* 2,030
Provincial Electoral District(s): Frontenac
Federal Electoral District(s): Mégantic-L'Érable
Next Election: 1er novembre 2013
Martin Cadorette, Directeur général

Saint-Joseph-de-Ham-Sud
9, ch Gosford sud
Saint-Joseph-de-Ham-Sud, QC J0B 3J0
819-877-3258 Fax: 819-877-5121
ham-sud@qc.aira.com, ham-sud@cgocable.ca
Municipal Type: Parish (Paroisse)
Incorporated: 1er janvier 1879; *Area:* 150,45 km2
County or District: Les Sources; *Population in 2006:* 219
Provincial Electoral District(s): Richmond
Federal Electoral District(s): Richmond-Arthabaska
Next Election: 1er novembre 2013
France L. Maurice, Sec.-Trés. & Directrice générale

Saint-Joseph-de-Kamouraska
300, rue Principale ouest
Saint-Joseph-de-Kamouraska, QC G0L 3P0
418-493-2214 Fax: 418-493-1126
stjosephkam@bellnet.ca
Municipal Type: Parish (Paroisse)
Incorporated: 14 janvier 1924; *Area:* 84,61 km2
County or District: Kamouraska; *Population in 2006:* 402
Provincial Electoral District(s): Kamouraska-Témiscouata
Federal Electoral District(s): Montmagny-L'Islet-Kamouraska-Rivière-du-Loup
Next Election: 1er novembre 2013
Ginette Castonguay, Directrice générale & Sec.-Trés.

Saint-Joseph-de-Lepage
70, rue de la Rivière
Mont-Joli, QC G5H 3N8
418-775-4171 Fax: 418-775-3004
Municipal Type: Parish (Paroisse)
Incorporated: 29 septembre 1873; *Area:* 30,27 km2
County or District: La Mitis; *Population in 2006:* 545
Provincial Electoral District(s): Matapédia
Federal Electoral District(s): Haute-Gaspésie-La

Mitis-Matane-Matapédia
Next Election: 1er novembre 2013
Renée Roy, Sec.-Trés.

Saint-Joseph-de-Sorel
700, rue Montcalm
Saint-Joseph-de-Sorel, QC J3R 1C9
450-742-3744 Fax: 450-742-1315
ville@vsjs.ca
www.vsjs.ca
Municipal Type: City
Incorporated: 1er mai 1907; *Area:* 1,4 km2
County or District: Pierre-De Saurel; *Population in 2009:* 1,669
Provincial Electoral District(s): Richelieu
Federal Electoral District(s): Bas-Richelieu-Nicolet-Bécancour
Next Election: 1er novembre 2013
Martin Valois, Directeur général
Olivar Gravel, Maire

Saint-Joseph-des-Érables
370A, rang des Érables
Saint-Joseph-des-Érables, QC G0S 2V0
418-397-4772 Fax: 418-397-1555
stjosephdeserables@globetrotter.net
Municipal Type: Municipality
Incorporated: 26 novembre 2009; *Area:* 50,01 km2
County or District: Robert-Cliche; *Population in 2006:* 417
Provincial Electoral District(s): Beauce-Nord
Federal Electoral District(s): Beauce
Next Election: 1er novembre 2013
Huguette Rodrique, Sec.-Trés. & Directrice générale

Saint-Joseph-du-Lac
1110, ch Principal
Saint-Joseph-du-Lac, QC J0N 1M0
450-623-1072 Fax: 450-623-2889
info@sjdl.qc.ca
www.sjdl.qc.ca
Municipal Type: Municipality
Incorporated: 1er juillet 1855; *Area:* 40,81 km2
County or District: Deux-Montagne; *Population in 2006:* 4,958
Provincial Electoral District(s): Mirabel
Federal Electoral District(s): Argenteuil-Papineau-Mirabel
Next Election: 1er novembre 2013
Guylaine Comtois, Sec.-Trés. & Directrice générale

Saint-Jude
940, rue du Centre
Saint-Jude, QC J0H 1P0
450-792-3855 Fax: 450-792-3828
munstjude@mrcmaskoutains.qc.ca
Municipal Type: Municipality
Incorporated: 1er juillet 1855; *Area:* 77,36 km2
County or District: Les Maskoutains; *Population in 2006:* 1,130
Provincial Electoral District(s): Richelieu
Federal Electoral District(s): St-Hyacinthe-Bagot
Next Election: 1er novembre 2013
Sylvie Beauregard, Sec.-Trés. & Directrice générale

Saint-Jules
390, rte Principale
Saint-Jules, QC G0N 1R0
418-397-5444 Fax: 418-397-5007
mun.st-jules@globetrotter.net
Municipal Type: Parish (Paroisse)
Incorporated: 28 mai 1919; *Area:* 57,08 km2
County or District: Robert-Cliche; *Population in 2006:* 534
Provincial Electoral District(s): Beauce-Nord
Federal Electoral District(s): Beauce
Next Election: 1er novembre 2013
Claire Roy, Sec.-Trés. & Directrice générale

Saint-Julien
787, ch St-Julien
Saint-Julien, QC G0N 1B0
418-423-4295 Fax: 418-423-2384
st-julien@globetrotter.net
Municipal Type: Municipality
Incorporated: 1er juillet 1855; *Area:* 82,300 km2
County or District: Les Appalaches; *Population in 2009:* 409
Provincial Electoral District(s): Frontenac
Federal Electoral District(s): Mégantic-L'Érable
Next Election: 1er novembre 2013
Réjean Gouin, Directeur général

Saint-Juste-du-Lac
CP 38
28, ch Principal
Saint-Juste-du-Lac, QC G0L 3R0
418-899-2855 Fax: 418-899-2938
munijuste@bellnet.ca
Municipal Type: Municipality
Incorporated: 23 mai 1923; *Area:* 170,11 km2
County or District: Témiscouata; *Population in 2006:* 653
Provincial Electoral District(s): Kamouraska-Témiscouata
Federal Electoral District(s):
Montmagny-L'Islet-Kamouraska-Rivière-du-Loup
Next Election: 1er novembre 2013
Nicole Dubé-Chouinard, Sec.-Trés. & Directrice générale

Saint-Just-de-Bretenières
CP 668
250, rue Principale
Saint-Just-de-Bretenières, QC G0R 3H0
418-244-3637 Fax: 418-244-3637
st-just-de-bretenieres@globetrotter.net
www.saintjustdebretenieres.com
Municipal Type: Municipality
Incorporated: 27 mai 1918; *Area:* 132,35 km2
County or District: Montmagny; *Population in 2006:* 794
Provincial Electoral District(s): Montmagny-L'Islet
Federal Electoral District(s): Lévis-Bellechasse
Next Election: 1er novembre 2013
Isabelle Simard, Sec.-Trés. & Directrice générale

Saint-Justin
1281, rue Gérin
Saint-Justin, QC J0K 2V0
819-227-2838 Fax: 819-227-4876
saint-justin@infoteck.qc.ca
Municipal Type: Parish (Paroisse)
Incorporated: 1er juillet 1855; *Area:* 82,46 km2
County or District: Maskinongé; *Population in 2006:* 1,051
Provincial Electoral District(s): Maskinongé
Federal Electoral District(s): Berthier-Maskinongé
Next Election: 1er novembre 2013
Raymonde Bastien, Directrice générale & Sec.-Trés.

Saint-Lambert
CP 86
509, rte 5e-au-8e Rang
Des Méloizes, QC J0Z 1V0
819-788-2491 Fax: 819-788-2491
st-lambert@mrcao.qc.ca
www.st-lambert.ao.ca
Municipal Type: Parish (Paroisse)
Incorporated: 14 mai 1938; *Area:* 101,76 km2
County or District: Abitibi-Ouest; *Population in 2006:* 222
Provincial Electoral District(s): Abitibi-Ouest
Federal Electoral District(s): Abitibi-Témiscamingue
Next Election: 1er novembre 2013
Nicole Garant, Sec.-Trés. & Directrice générale

Saint-Lambert-de-Lauzon
1200, rue du Pont
Saint-Lambert-de-Lauzon, QC G0S 2W0
418-889-9715 Fax: 418-889-0660
info@municipalite.saint-lambert-de-lauzon.qc.ca
www.municipalite.saint-lambert-de-lauzon.qc.ca
Municipal Type: Parish (Paroisse)
Incorporated: 1er juillet 1855; *Area:* 107,32 km2
County or District: La Nouvelle-Beauce; *Population in 2006:* 5,401
Provincial Electoral District(s): Beauce-Nord
Federal Electoral District(s): Lotbinière-Chutes-de-la-Chaudière
Next Election: 1er novembre 2013
Magdalen Blanchet, Sec.-Trés. & Directrice générale

Saint-Laurent-de-l'Ile-d'Orléans
1430, ch Royal
St-Laurent-de-l'Ile-d'Orléans, QC G0A 3Z0
418-828-2322 Fax: 418-828-2170
stlaurentorleans@videotron.ca
Municipal Type: Municipality
Incorporated: 1er juillet 1855; *Area:* 35,32 km2
County or District: L'Ile-d'Orléans; *Population in 2006:* 1,601
Provincial Electoral District(s): Montmorency
Federal Electoral District(s):
Montmorency-Charlevoix-Haute-Côte-Nord
Next Election: 1er novembre 2013
Claudette Pouliot, Sec.-Trés. & Directrice générale

Saint-Lazare-de-Bellechasse
116, rue de la Fabrique
Saint-Lazare-de-Bellechasse, QC G0R 3J0
418-883-3841 Fax: 418-883-2551
munstlaz@globetrotter.net
Municipal Type: Municipality
Incorporated: 1er juillet 1855; *Area:* 85,53 km2
County or District: Bellechasse; *Population in 2006:* 1,155
Provincial Electoral District(s): Bellechasse
Federal Electoral District(s): Lévis-Bellechasse
Next Election: 1er novembre 2013
Richard Côté, Sec.-Trés. & Directeur général

Saint-Léandre
2005, rue de l'Église
Saint-Léandre, QC G0J 2V0
418-737-4973 Fax: 418-737-4972
mun.stleandre@globetrotter.net
Municipal Type: Parish (Paroisse)
Incorporated: 20 mars 1912; *Area:* 102,62 km2
County or District: Matane; *Population in 2006:* 401
Provincial Electoral District(s): Matane
Federal Electoral District(s): Haute-Gaspésie-La
Mitis-Matane-Matapédia
Next Election: 1er novembre 2013
Guylaine Ouellet, Directrice générale

Saint-Léon-de-Standon
CP 130
100A, rue St-Pierre
Saint-Léon-de-Standon, QC G0R 4L0
418-642-5034 Fax: 418-642-2570
mun.st-leon@globetrotter.net
www.stleondestandon.qc.ca
Municipal Type: Parish (Paroisse)
Incorporated: 1er janvier 1874; *Area:* 136,90 km2
County or District: Bellechasse; *Population in 2006:* 1,237
Provincial Electoral District(s): Bellechasse
Federal Electoral District(s): Lévis-Bellechasse
Next Election: 1er novembre 2013
Gérald Patry, Sec.-Trés. & Directeur général

Saint-Léon-le-Grand
CP 188
277, rue Plourde
Saint-Léon-le-Grand, QC G0J 2W0
418-743-2914 Fax: 418-743-2914
munistlg@globetrotter.net
Municipal Type: Parish (Paroisse)
Incorporated: 12 août 1903; *Area:* 127,73 km2
County or District: La Matapédia; *Population in 2006:* 1,073
Provincial Electoral District(s): Matapédia
Federal Electoral District(s): Haute-Gaspésie-La
Mitis-Matane-Matapédia
Next Election: 1er novembre 2013
Suzanne Poirier, Sec.-Trés. & Directrice générale

Saint-Léon-le-Grand
49, rue de la Fabrique
Saint-Léon-le-Grand, QC J0K 2W0
819-228-3236 Fax: 819-228-8088
glessard@st-leon.com
Municipal Type: Parish (Paroisse)
Incorporated: 1er juillet 1855; *Area:* 72,57 km2
County or District: Maskinongé; *Population in 2006:* 965
Provincial Electoral District(s): Maskinongé
Federal Electoral District(s): Berthier-Maskinongé
Next Election: 1er novembre 2013
Gabrielle Lessard, Sec.-Trés. & Directrice générale

Saint-Léonard-d'Aston
370, rue Principale
Saint-Léonard-d'Aston, QC J0C 1M0
819-399-2596 Fax: 819-399-2333
municipalite@saint-leonard-daston.net
www.saint-leonard-daston.net
Municipal Type: Municipality
Incorporated: 13 avril 1994; *Area:* 81,83 km2
County or District: Nicolet-Yamaska; *Population in 2006:* 2,146
Provincial Electoral District(s): Nicolet-Yamaska
Federal Electoral District(s): Bas-Richelieu-Nicolet-Bécancour
Next Election: 1er novembre 2013
Danielle Leduc, Sec.-Trés.

Saint-Léonard-de-Portneuf
260, rue Pettigrew
Saint-Léonard-de-Portneuf, QC G0A 4A0
418-337-6741 Fax: 418-337-6742
saintleonard@csportneuf.qc.ca
www.municipalite.st-leonard.qc.ca
Municipal Type: Municipality
Incorporated: 22 juillet 1899; *Area:* 138,71 km2
County or District: Portneuf; *Population in 2006:* 1,046
Provincial Electoral District(s): Portneuf
Federal Electoral District(s): Portneuf-Jacques-Cartier
Next Election: 1er novembre 2013
Eddy Alain, Directeur-général

Saint-Liboire
CP 120
21, place Mauriac
Saint-Liboire, QC J0H 1R0
450-793-2811 Fax: 450-793-4428
admin@municipalite.st-liboire.qc.ca
www.municipalite.st-liboire.qc.ca
Municipal Type: Municipality
Incorporated: 17 août 1994; *Area:* 72,90 km2
County or District: Les Maskoutains; *Population in 2006:* 2,895
Provincial Electoral District(s): St-Hyacinthe
Federal Electoral District(s): St-Hyacinthe-Bagot
Next Election: 1er novembre 2013
Lucie Chevrier, Sec.-Trés. & Directrice générale

Saint-Liguori
750, rue Principale
Saint-Liguori, QC J0K 2X0
450-753-3570 Fax: 450-753-4638
liguori@megacom.net
Municipal Type: Parish (Paroisse)
Incorporated: 1er juillet 1855; *Area:* 50,91 km2
County or District: Montcalm; *Population in 2006:* 1,887
Provincial Electoral District(s): Joliette
Federal Electoral District(s): Montcalm
Next Election: 1er novembre 2013
Edith Gagné, Sec.-Trés. & Directrice générale

Saint-Louis
765B, rue St-Joseph
Saint-Louis, QC J0G 1K0
450-788-2631 Fax: 450-788-2231
mstlouis@mrcmaskoutains.qc.ca
Municipal Type: Parish (Paroisse)
Incorporated: 29 août 1881; *Area:* 45,92 km2
County or District: Les Maskoutains; *Population in 2006:* 726
Provincial Electoral District(s): Richelieu
Federal Electoral District(s): St-Hyacinthe-Bagot
Next Election: 1er novembre 2013
Jaqueline Lavallée, Sec.-Trés. adjointe & Directrice générale

Saint-Louis-de-Blandford
CP 140
80, rue Principale
Saint-Louis-de-Blandford, QC G0Z 1B0

819-364-7007 Fax: 819-364-2781
munstlb@gabskycom.com
Municipal Type: Parish (Paroisse)
Incorporated: 1er juillet 1855; *Area:* 106,70 km2
County or District: Arthabaska; *Population in 2006:* 985
Provincial Electoral District(s): Lotbinière
Federal Electoral District(s): Richmond-Arthabaska
Next Election: 1er novembre 2013
Annie Poirier, Sec.-Trés. & Directrice générale

Saint-Louis-de-Gonzague
108, rue de l'Église
Ravignan, QC G0R 2L0
418-267-5931 Fax: 418-267-5930
munstlouis@sogetel.net
Municipal Type: Municipality
Incorporated: 17 mars 1923; *Area:* 116,36 km2
County or District: Les Etchemins; *Population in 2006:* 442
Provincial Electoral District(s): Bellechasse
Federal Electoral District(s): Lévis-Bellechasse; Beauharnois-Salaberry
Next Election: 1er novembre 2013
Odette Poulin, Sec.-Trés. & Directrice générale

Saint-Louis-de-Gonzague
CP 382
140, rue Principale
Saint-Louis-de-Gonzague, QC J0S 1T0
450-371-0523 Fax: 450-371-6229
munstlouisdegonzague@intermobilex.com
Municipal Type: Parish (Paroisse)
Incorporated: 1er juillet 1855; *Area:* 78,52 km2
County or District: Beauharnois-Salaberry; *Population in 2006:* 1,404
Provincial Electoral District(s): Beauharnois
Federal Electoral District(s): Beauharnois-Salaberry
Next Election: 1er novembre 2013
Micheline J.-Carrière, Sec.-Trés. & Directrice générale

Saint-Louis-de-Gonzague-du-Cap-Tourmente
CP 460 Haute-Ville
1, rue des Remparts
Québec, QC G1R 4R7
418-692-3981 Fax: 418-692-4345
jroberge@globetrotter.net
Municipal Type: Parish (Paroisse)
Incorporated: 1er janvier 1917;
County or District: La Côte-de-Beaupré; *Population in 2006:* 2
Provincial Electoral District(s): Charlevoix
Federal Electoral District(s): Charlevoix-Montmorency-Haute-Côte-Nord
Next Election: 1er novembre 2013
Jacques Roberge, Administrateur

Saint-Louis-du-Ha!-Ha!
95, rue St-Charles
Saint-Louis-du-Ha!-Ha!, QC G0L 3S0
418-854-2260 Fax: 418-854-0717
municipalite@saintlouisduhaha.com
www.saintlouisduhaha.com
Municipal Type: Parish (Paroisse)
Incorporated: 14 juillet 1874; *Area:* 114,45 km2
County or District: Témiscouata; *Population in 2006:* 1,348
Provincial Electoral District(s): Kamouraska-Témiscouata
Federal Electoral District(s): Rimouski-Neigette-Témiscouata-Les Basques
Next Election: 1er novembre 2013
Gratien Ouellet, Sec.-Trés. & Directeur général

Saint-Luc-de-Bellechasse
230A, rue Principale
Saint-Luc-de-Bellechasse, QC G0R 1L0
418-636-2176 Fax: 418-636-2176
munstluc@sogetel.net
www.st-luc-bellechasse.qc.ca
Municipal Type: Municipality
Incorporated: 12 août 1921; *Area:* 160,03 km2
County or District: Les Etchemins; *Population in 2006:* 490
Provincial Electoral District(s): Bellechasse
Federal Electoral District(s): Lévis-Bellechasse
Next Election: 1er novembre 2013
Lorette S.-Jolin, Sec.-Trés. & Directrice générale

Saint-Luc-de-Vincennes
CP 450
660, rue Principale
Saint-Luc-de-Vincennes, QC G0X 3K0
819-295-3782 Fax: 819-295-3782
municipalite@stlucdevincennes.com
www.stlucdevincennes.com
Municipal Type: Municipality
Incorporated: 19 janvier 1865; *Area:* 52,73 km2
County or District: Les Chenaux; *Population in 2006:* 553
Provincial Electoral District(s): Champlain
Federal Electoral District(s): St-Maurice-Champlain
Next Election: 1er novembre 2013
Rita Massicotte, Directrice générale & Sec.-Trés.

Saint-Lucien
5350, 7e rang
Saint-Lucien, QC J0C 1N0
819-397-4679 Fax: 819-397-2732
lynda.lalancette@municipalite.saint-lucien.qc.ca
Municipal Type: Parish (Paroisse)
Incorporated: 11 novembre 1907; *Area:* 113,61 km2
County or District: Drummond; *Population in 2006:* 1,508
Provincial Electoral District(s): Richmond
Federal Electoral District(s): Drummond
Next Election: 1er novembre 2013
Lynda Lalancette, Sec.-Trés. & Directrice générale

Saint-Ludger
212, rue La Salle
Saint-Ludger, QC G0M 1W0
819-548-5408 Fax: 819-548-5743
munstludger@sogetel.net
www.st-ludger.qc.ca
Municipal Type: Municipality
Incorporated: 25 février 1998; *Area:* 124,46 km2
County or District: Le Granit; *Population in 2006:* 1,197
Provincial Electoral District(s): Beauce-Sud
Federal Electoral District(s): Beauce
Next Election: 1er novembre 2013
Julie Létourneau, Sec.-Trés. & Directrice générale

Saint-Ludger-de-Milot
739, rue Gaudreault
Saint-Ludger-de-Milot, QC G0W 2B0
418-373-2266 Fax: 418-373-2554
stludgerdemilot_mun@hotmail.com
www.ville.st-ludger-de-milot.qc.ca
Municipal Type: Municipality
Incorporated: 1er janvier 1948; *Area:* 106,81 km2
County or District: Lac-St-Jean-Est; *Population in 2006:* 727
Provincial Electoral District(s): Lac-St-Jean
Federal Electoral District(s): Roberval-Lac-St-Jean
Next Election: 1er novembre 2013
Rita Ouellet, Sec.-Trés. & Directrice générale

Saint-Magloire
130, rue Principale
Saint-Magloire, QC G0R 3M0
418-257-4421 Fax: 418-257-4422
stmagloire@sogetel.net
www.saint-magloire.com
Municipal Type: Municipality
Incorporated: 1er janvier 1875; *Area:* 208,64 km2
County or District: Les Etchemins; *Population in 2006:* 745
Provincial Electoral District(s): Bellechasse
Federal Electoral District(s): Lévis-Bellechasse
Next Election: 1er novembre 2013
Francine Chabot, Sec.-Trés. & Directrice générale

Saint-Majorique-de-Grantham
1966, boul St-Joseph ouest
Saint-Majorique-de-Grantham, QC J2B 8A8
819-478-7058 Fax: 819-478-8479
municipalite.st-majorique@dr.cgocable.ca
Municipal Type: Parish (Paroisse)
Incorporated: 13 juillet 1901; *Area:* 57,26 km2
County or District: Drummond; *Population in 2006:* 1,136
Provincial Electoral District(s): Drummond
Federal Electoral District(s): Drummond
Next Election: 1er novembre 2013
Francine Gagnon, Directrice générale & Sec.-Trés.

Saint-Malachie
610, 7e rue
Saint-Malachie, QC G0R 3N0
418-642-2102 Fax: 418-642-2231
munimala@globetrotter.net
Municipal Type: Parish (Paroisse)
Incorporated: 1er juin 1874; *Area:* 100,59 km2
County or District: Bellechasse; *Population in 2006:* 1,413
Provincial Electoral District(s): Bellechasse
Federal Electoral District(s): Lévis-Bellechasse
Next Election: 1er novembre 2013
Hélène Bissonnette, Sec.-Trés. & Directrice générale

Saint-Malo
228, rte 253 sud
Saint-Malo, QC J0B 2Y0
819-658-2174 Fax: 819-658-1169
saint-malo@axion.ca
Municipal Type: Municipality
Incorporated: 1er janvier 1870; *Area:* 129,30 km2
County or District: Coaticook; *Population in 2006:* 516
Provincial Electoral District(s): Mégantic-Compton
Federal Electoral District(s): Compton-Stanstead
Next Election: 1er novembre 2013
Edith Rouleau, Sec.-Trés. & Directrice générale

Saint-Marc-de-Figuery
CP 12
10, av Michaud
Saint-Marc-de-Figuery, QC J0Y 1J0
819-732-8501 Fax: 819-732-4324
mun.stmard@cableamos.com
Municipal Type: Parish (Paroisse)
Incorporated: 10 novembre 1926; *Area:* 91,10 km2
County or District: Abitibi; *Population in 2006:* 692
Provincial Electoral District(s): Abitibi-Ouest
Federal Electoral District(s): Abitibi-Témiscamingue
Next Election: 1er novembre 2013
Aline Guénette, Sec.-Trés. & Directrice générale

Saint-Marc-des-Carrières
965, av Bona-Dussault
Saint-Marc-des-Carrières, QC G0A 4B0
418-268-3862 Fax: 418-268-8776
stmarc01@globetrotter.qc.ca
www.st-marc-des-carrieres.qc.ca
Municipal Type: City
Incorporated: 24 octobre 1918; *Area:* 16,73 km2
County or District: Portneuf; *Population in 2006:* 2,774
Provincial Electoral District(s): Portneuf
Federal Electoral District(s): Portneuf-Jacques-Cartier
Next Election: 1er novembre 2013
Maryon Leclerc, Sec.-Trés. & Directeur général
Michel Matte, Maire

Saint-Marc-du-Lac-Long
12, rue de l'Église
Saint-Marc-du-Lac-Long, QC G0L 1T0
418-893-2643 Fax: 418-893-7228
munstmarc@videotron.ca
Municipal Type: Parish (Paroisse)
Incorporated: 11 juin 1938; *Area:* 147,16 km2
County or District: Témiscouata; *Population in 2006:* 479
Provincial Electoral District(s): Kamouraska-Témiscouata
Federal Electoral District(s): Rimouski-Neigette-Témiscouata-Les Basques
Next Election: 1er novembre 2013
Karine Plourde, Directrice générale & Sec.-Trés.

Saint-Marc-sur-Richelieu
102, rue de la Fabrique
Saint-Marc-sur-Richelieu, QC J0L 2E0
450-584-2258 Fax: 450-584-2795
sburelle@ville.saint-marc-sur-richelieu.qc.ca
www.ville.saint.marc-sur-richelieu.qc.ca
Municipal Type: Municipality
Incorporated: 1er juillet 1855; *Area:* 59,51 km2
County or District: Le Vallée-du-Richelieu; *Population in 2006:* 1,876
Provincial Electoral District(s): Verchères
Federal Electoral District(s): Verchères-Les Patriotes
Next Election: 1er novembre 2013
Sylvie Burelle, Sec.-Trés. & Directrice générale

Saint-Marcel
CP 10
48, ch Taché est
Saint-Marcel, QC G0R 3R0
418-356-2691 Fax: 418-356-2820
mun.sm@globetrotter.net
Municipal Type: Municipality
Incorporated: 30 juillet 1904; *Area:* 178,86 km2
County or District: L'Islet; *Population in 2006:* 527
Provincial Electoral District(s): Montmagny-L'Islet
Federal Electoral District(s): Montmagny-L'Islet-Kamouraska-Rivière-du-Loup
Next Election: 1er novembre 2013
Normande Bélanger, Sec.-Trés. & Directrice générale

Saint-Marcel-de-Richelieu
500, rue de l'École
Saint-Marcel-de-Richelieu, QC J0H 1T0
450-794-2832 Fax: 450-794-1140
munst-marcel@mrcmaskoutains.qc.ca
Municipal Type: Municipality
Incorporated: 1er juillet 1855; *Area:* 50,21 km2
County or District: Les Maskoutains; *Population in 2006:* 580
Provincial Electoral District(s): Nicolet-Yamaska
Federal Electoral District(s): St-Hyacinthe-Bagot
Next Election: 1er novembre 2013
Christiane Janelle, Sec.-Trés. & Directrice générale

Saint-Marcellin
336, rte 234
Saint-Marcellin, QC G0K 1R0
418-798-4382 Fax: 418-798-4383
munstmar@globetrotter.net
Municipal Type: Parish (Paroisse)
Incorporated: 19 novembre 1924; *Area:* 117,01 km2
County or District: Rimouski-Neigette; *Population in 2006:* 357
Provincial Electoral District(s): Rimouski
Federal Electoral District(s): Rimouski-Neigette-Témiscouata-Les Basques
Next Election: 1er novembre 2013
Brigitte Rouleau, Sec.-Trés. & Directrice générale

Saint-Martin
131, 1e av est
Saint-Martin, QC G0M 1B0
418-382-5035 Fax: 418-382-5561
municipalite@st-martin.qc.ca
www.st-martin.qc.ca
Municipal Type: Parish (Paroisse)
Incorporated: 12 octobre 1911; *Area:* 119,34 km2
County or District: Beauce-Sartigan; *Population in 2006:* 2,543
Provincial Electoral District(s): Beauce-Sud
Federal Electoral District(s): Beauce
Next Election: 1er novembre 2013
Brigitte Quirion, Sec.-Trés. & Directrice générale

Saint-Mathias-sur-Richelieu
300, ch des Patriotes
Saint-Mathias-sur-Richelieu, QC J3L 6Z5
450-658-2841 Fax: 450-447-1416
information@st-mathias.org
Municipal Type: Municipality
Incorporated: 1er juillet 1855; *Area:* 48,22 km2
County or District: Rouville; *Population in 2006:* 4,506
Provincial Electoral District(s): Chambly

Federal Electoral District(s): Chambly-Borduas
Next Election: 1er novembre 2013
Catherine Chartrand, Sec.-Trés. & Directrice général

Saint-Mathieu
299, ch St-Édouard
Saint-Mathieu, QC J0L 2H0
450-632-9528 Fax: 450-632-9544
stmathieu@cstsm.net
www.st-mathieu.qc.ca
Municipal Type: Municipality
Incorporated: 1er août 1917; *Area:* 32,27 km2
County or District: Roussillon; *Population in 2006:* 1,894
Provincial Electoral District(s): La Prairie
Federal Electoral District(s): Châteauguay-St-Constant
Next Election: 1er novembre 2013
Cynthia Bossé, Sec.-Trés. & Directrice générale

Saint-Mathieu-d'Harricana
CP 63
203, ch Lanoix
Saint-Mathieu-d'Harricana, QC J0Y 1M0
819-727-9557 Fax: 819-727-9557
mun.st-mathieu@cableamos.com
Municipal Type: Municipality
Incorporated: 1er janvier 1943; *Area:* 104,09 km2
County or District: Abitibi; *Population in 2006:* 716
Provincial Electoral District(s): Abitibi-Ouest
Federal Electoral District(s): Abitibi-Témiscamingue
Next Election: 1er novembre 2013
Nancy Fortier, Sec.-Trés. & Directrice générale

Saint-Mathieu-de-Beloeil
5000, rue des Loisirs
Saint-Mathieu-de-Beloeil, QC J3G 2C9
450-467-7490 Fax: 450-467-2999
reception@munstmathbel.ca
Municipal Type: Municipality
Incorporated: 1er juillet 1855; *Area:* 39,26 km2
County or District: La Vallée-du-Richelieu; *Population in 2006:* 2,288
Provincial Electoral District(s): Borduas
Federal Electoral District(s): Chambly-Borduas
Next Election: 1er novembre 2013
Doris Parent, Directrice générale & Sec.-Trés.

Saint-Mathieu-de-Rioux
41, rue de l'Église
Saint-Mathieu-de-Rioux, QC G0L 3T0
418-738-2953 Fax: 418-738-2454
st-mathieuderioux@globetrotter.net
www.saint-mathieu.com
Municipal Type: Parish (Paroisse)
Incorporated: 18 août 1865; *Area:* 102,35 km2
County or District: Les Basques; *Population in 2006:* 672
Provincial Electoral District(s): Rivière-du-Loup
Federal Electoral District(s): Rimouski-Neigette-Témiscouata-Les Basques
Next Election: 1er novembre 2013
Michelle Lafontaine, Directrice générale & Sec.-Trés.

Saint-Mathieu-du-Parc
561, ch Déziel
Saint-Mathieu-du-Parc, QC G0X 1N0
819-532-2205 Fax: 819-532-2415
stmathieu@qc.aira.com
www.stmathieuduparc.org
Municipal Type: Municipality
Incorporated: 30 juin 1886; *Area:* 196,45 km2
County or District: Maskinongé; *Population in 2006:* 1,376
Provincial Electoral District(s): St-Maurice
Federal Electoral District(s): Berthier-Maskinongé
Next Election: 1er novembre 2013
Sylvie Courchesne, Sec.-Trés.

Saint-Maurice
CP 9
2510, rang St-Jean
Saint-Maurice, QC G0X 2X0
819-374-4525 Fax: 819-374-9132
municipalite@st-maurice.ca
Municipal Type: Parish (Paroisse)
Incorporated: 1er juillet 1855; *Area:* 90,33 km2
County or District: Les Chenaux; *Population in 2006:* 2,338
Provincial Electoral District(s): Champlain
Federal Electoral District(s): St-Maurice-Champlain
Next Election: 1er novembre 2013
Andrée Neault, Sec.-Trés. & Directrice générale

Saint-Maxime-du-Mont-Louis
CP 130
1, 1re av ouest
Saint-Maxime-du-Mont-Louis, QC G0E 1T0
418-797-2310 Fax: 418-797-2928
munst-maxime@globetrotter.net
www.municipalitest-maxime.qc.ca
Municipal Type: Municipality
Incorporated: 10 juin 1884; *Area:* 220,38 km2
County or District: La Haute-Gaspésie; *Population in 2006:* 1,194
Provincial Electoral District(s): Matane
Federal Electoral District(s): Haute-Gaspésie-La Mitis-Matane-Matapédia
Next Election: 1er novembre 2013
Hilaire Lemieux, Sec.-Trés. & Directeur général

Saint-Médard
1B, rue Principale est
Saint-Médard, QC G0L 3V0
418-963-6276 Fax: 418-963-6468
munstmedard@globetrotter.net
Municipal Type: Municipality
Incorporated: 1er janvier 1949; *Area:* 67,59 km2
County or District: Les Basques; *Population in 2006:* 252
Provincial Electoral District(s): Rivière-du-Loup
Federal Electoral District(s): Rimouski-Neigette-Témiscouata-Les Basques
Next Election: 1er novembre 2013
Andrée O. Beaulieu, Sec.-Trés. & Directrice générale

Saint-Michel
1700, rue Principale
Saint-Michel, QC J0L 2J0
450-454-4502 Fax: 450-454-7508
stmichel@cstsm.net
Municipal Type: Parish (Paroisse)
Incorporated: 1er juillet 1855; *Area:* 57,36 km2
County or District: Les Jardins-de-Napierville; *Population in 2006:* 2,637
Provincial Electoral District(s): Huntingdon
Federal Electoral District(s): St-Léonard-St-Michel
Next Election: 1er novembre 2013
Micheline Lemay, Sec.-Trés. & Directrice générale

Saint-Michel-de-Bellechasse
129, rte 132 est
Saint-Michel-de-Bellechasse, QC G0R 3S0
418-884-2865 Fax: 418-884-2866
munstmic@globetrotter.net
www.saintmicheldebellechasse.com
Municipal Type: Municipality
Incorporated: 1er juillet 1855; *Area:* 53,43 km2
County or District: Bellechasse; *Population in 2006:* 1,669
Provincial Electoral District(s): Bellechasse
Federal Electoral District(s): Lévis-Bellechasse
Next Election: 1er novembre 2013
Ronald Gonthier, Sec.-Trés. & Directeur général

Saint-Michel-des-Saints
441, rue Brassard
Saint-Michel-des-Saints, QC J0K 3B0
450-833-6941 Fax: 450-833-6081
stmichel@satelcom.qc.ca
www.saintmicheldesaints.com
Municipal Type: Municipality
Incorporated: 3 mars 1979; *Area:* 563,72 km2
County or District: Matawinie; *Population in 2006:* 2,713
Provincial Electoral District(s): Berthier
Federal Electoral District(s): Joliette
Next Election: 1er novembre 2013
Alain Bellerose, Sec.-Trés. & Directeur général

Saint-Michel-du-Squatec
CP 280
150, rue St-Joseph
Saint-Michel-du-Squatec, QC G0L 4H0
418-855-2185 Fax: 418-855-2935
accueil.squatec@bellnet.ca
www.squatec.qc.ca
Municipal Type: Parish (Paroisse)
Incorporated: 16 avril 1928; *Area:* 363,10 km2
County or District: Témiscouata; *Population in 2006:* 1,263
Provincial Electoral District(s): Kamouraska-Témiscouata
Federal Electoral District(s): Rimouski-Neigette-Témiscouata-Les Basques
Next Election: 1er novembre 2013
Danielle Albert, Directrice générale & Sec.-Trés. & Greffière

Saint-Modeste
312, rue Principale
Saint-Modeste, QC G0L 3W0
418-867-2352 Fax: 418-867-5359
munst-modeste@bellnet.ca
http://www.municipalite.saint-modeste.qc.ca/
Municipal Type: Parish (Paroisse)
Incorporated: 1er juillet 1855; *Area:* 107,91 km2
County or District: Rivière-du-Loup; *Population in 2006:* 942
Provincial Electoral District(s): Rivière-du-Loup
Federal Electoral District(s): Montmagny-L'Islet-Kamouraska-Rivière-du-Loup
Next Election: 1er novembre 2013
Claudie Malouin, Sec.-Trés. & Directrice générale

Saint-Moïse
CP 8
120-B, rue Principale
Saint-Moïse, QC G0J 2Z0
418-776-2833 Fax: 418-776-2833
Municipal Type: Parish (Paroisse)
Incorporated: 1er janvier 1878; *Area:* 106,83 km2
County or District: La Matapédia; *Population in 2006:* 625
Provincial Electoral District(s): Matapédia
Federal Electoral District(s): Haute-Gaspésie-La Mitis-Matane-Matapédia
Next Election: 1er novembre 2013
Monique Bouchard, Sec.-Trés. & Directrice générale

Saint-Narcisse
353, rue Notre-Dame
Saint-Narcisse, QC G0X 2Y0
418-328-8645 Fax: 418-328-4348
municipalite@saint-narcisse.com
Municipal Type: Parish (Paroisse)
Incorporated: 1er juillet 1855; *Area:* 103,49 km2
County or District: Les Chenaux; *Population in 2006:* 1,806
Provincial Electoral District(s): Champlain
Federal Electoral District(s): St-Maurice-Champlain
Next Election: 1er novembre 2013
René Pinard, Sec.-Trés. & Directeur général

Saint-Narcisse-de-Beaurivage
#1, 508, rue de l'École
Saint-Narcisse-de-Beaurivage, QC G0S 1W0
418-475-6842 Fax: 418-475-6880
saintnarcisse@globetrotter.net
Municipal Type: Parish (Paroisse)
Incorporated: 1er mai 1874; *Area:* 60,83 km2
County or District: Lotbinière; *Population in 2006:* 975
Provincial Electoral District(s): Lotbinière
Federal Electoral District(s): Lotbinière-Chutes-de la Chaudière
Next Election: 1er novembre 2013
Solange Boulanger, Sec.-Trés. & Directrice générale

Saint-Narcisse-de-Rimouski
7, rue du Pavillon
Saint-Narcisse-de-Rimouski, QC G0K 1S0
418-735-2638 Fax: 418-735-6021
informations@saintnarcisse.net
www.saintnarcisse.net
Municipal Type: Parish (Paroisse)
Incorporated: 13 février 1922; *Area:* 166,83 km2
County or District: Rimouski-Neigette; *Population in 2006:* 1,088
Provincial Electoral District(s): Rimouski
Federal Electoral District(s): Rimouski-Neigette-Témiscouata-Les Basques
Next Election: 1er novembre 2013
Gilles Lepage, Sec.-Trés. & Directeur général

Saint-Nazaire
199, rue Principale
Saint-Nazaire, QC G0W 2V0
418-662-4154 Fax: 418-662-5467
ktremblay@ville.saint-nazaire.qc.ca
www.ville.saint-nazaire.qc.ca
Municipal Type: Municipality
Incorporated: 23 septembre 1905; *Area:* 147,78 km2
County or District: Lac-St-Jean-Est; *Population in 2006:* 1,866
Provincial Electoral District(s): Lac-St-Jean
Federal Electoral District(s): Roberval-Lac-St-Jean
Next Election: 1er novembre 2013
Kathy Tremblay, Sec.-Trés. & Directrice générale

Saint-Nazaire-d'Acton
750, rue des Loisirs
Saint-Nazaire-d'Acton, QC J0H 1V0
819-392-2347 Fax: 819-392-2039
municipalite@mun-nazaire.qc.ca
Municipal Type: Parish (Paroisse)
Incorporated: 8 janvier 1894; *Area:* 57,49 km2
County or District: Acton; *Population in 2006:* 832
Provincial Electoral District(s): Johnson
Federal Electoral District(s): St-Hyacinthe-Bagot
Next Election: 1er novembre 2013
Guylaine Bourgoin, Sec.-Trés. & Directrice générale

Saint-Nazaire-de-Dorchester
61A, rue Principale
Saint-Nazaire, QC G0R 3T0
418-642-1305 Fax: 418-642-2945
mun_st_nazaire@globetrotter.net
Municipal Type: Parish (Paroisse)
Incorporated: 9 mars 1906; *Area:* 51,43 km2
County or District: Bellechasse; *Population in 2006:* 385
Provincial Electoral District(s): Bellechasse
Federal Electoral District(s): Lévis-Bellechasse
Next Election: 1er novembre 2013
Francine Brochu, Sec.-Trés. & Directrice générale

Saint-Nérée
1990, rte Principale
Saint-Nérée, QC G0R 3V0
418-243-2735 Fax: 418-243-2136
muneree@globetrotter.net
Municipal Type: Parish (Paroisse)
Incorporated: 29 mars 1887; *Area:* 75,73 km2
County or District: Bellechasse; *Population in 2006:* 789
Provincial Electoral District(s): Bellechasse
Federal Electoral District(s): Lévis-Bellechasse
Next Election: 1er novembre 2013
Jean-Louis Chabot, Sec.-Trés. & Directeur général

Saint-Noël
CP 99
51, rue de l'Église
Saint-Noël, QC G0J 3A0
418-776-2936 Fax: 418-776-5521
muni.stnoel@globetrotter.net
Municipal Type: Village
Incorporated: 2 octobre 1906; *Area:* 45,68 km2
County or District: La Matapédia; *Population in 2006:* 459
Provincial Electoral District(s): Matapédia
Federal Electoral District(s): Haute-Gaspésie-La Mitis-Matane-Matapédia
Next Election: 1er novembre 2013
Manon Caron, Sec.-Trés. & Directrice générale

Saint-Norbert
2150, rue Principale
Saint-Norbert, QC J0K 3C0
450-836-4700 Fax: 450-836-4004
municipalite@saint-norbert.com
www.saint-norbert.com
Municipal Type: Parish (Paroisse)
Incorporated: 1er juillet 1855; *Area:* 77,31 km2
County or District: D'Autray; *Population in 2006:* 1,067
Provincial Electoral District(s): Berthier
Federal Electoral District(s): Berthier-Maskinongé
Next Election: 1er novembre 2013
Martine Laberge, Sec.-Trés. & Directrice générale

Saint-Norbert-d'Arthabaska
250, rte de la Rivière
Norbertville, QC G0P 1B0
819-369-9318 Fax: 819-369-8686
stnorber@ivic.qc.ca
Municipal Type: Municipality
Incorporated: 30 novembre 1994; *Area:* 113,66 km2
County or District: Arthabaska; *Population in 2006:* 857
Provincial Electoral District(s): Arthabaska
Federal Electoral District(s): Richmond-Arthabaska
Next Election: 1er novembre 2013
René Savoie, Sec.-Trés. & Directeur général

Saint-Octave-de-Métis
201A, rue de l'Église
Saint-Octave-de-Métis, QC G0J 3B0
418-775-2996 Fax: 418-775-0099
stoctave@mitis.qc.ca
Municipal Type: Parish (Paroisse)
Incorporated: 25 avril 1908; *Area:* 74,63 km2
County or District: La Mitis; *Population in 2006:* 488
Provincial Electoral District(s): Matapédia
Federal Electoral District(s): Haute-Gaspésie-La Mitis-Matane-Matapédia
Next Election: 1er novembre 2013
Mylene-Julie Lavoie, Sec.-Trés.

Saint-Odilon-de-Cranbourne
CP 100
111, rue de l'Hôtel-de-Ville
Saint-Odilon, QC G0S 3A0
418-464-4801 Fax: 418-464-4800
mun.stodilon@sogetel.net
www.saint-odilon.qc.ca
Municipal Type: Parish (Paroisse)
Incorporated: 1er juillet 1855; *Area:* 128,77 km2
County or District: Robert-Cliche; *Population in 2006:* 1,440
Provincial Electoral District(s): Beauce-Nord
Federal Electoral District(s): Beauce
Next Election: 1er novembre 2013
Suzie Turcotte, Sec.-Trés. & Directrice générale

Saint-Omer
243, rang des Pelletier
Saint-Omer, QC G0R 4R0
418-356-5634 Fax: 418-356-5634
municipalitest-omer@globetrotter.net
Municipal Type: Municipality
Incorporated: 1er janvier 1954; *Area:* 125,35 km2
County or District: L'Islet; *Population in 2006:* 343
Provincial Electoral District(s): Montmagny-L'Islet
Federal Electoral District(s): Montmagny-L'Islet-Kamouraska-Rivière-du-Loup
Next Election: 1er novembre 2013
Lise Bastien, Sec.-Trés. & Directrice générale

Saint-Onésime-d'Ixworth
12, rue de l'Église
Saint-Onésime-d'Ixworth, QC G0R 3W0
418-856-3018 Fax: 418-856-6626
mun.stonesime@videotron.ca
Municipal Type: Parish (Paroisse)
Incorporated: 13 mai 1895; *Area:* 103,59 km2
County or District: Kamouraska; *Population in 2006:* 577
Provincial Electoral District(s): Kamouraska-Témiscouata
Federal Electoral District(s): Montmagny-L'Islet-Kamouraska-Rivière-du-Loup
Next Election: 1er novembre 2013
Isabelle Saint-Laurent, Sec.-Trés. & Directrice générale

Saint-Ours
CP 129
2540, rue de l'Immaculée-Conception
Saint-Ours, QC J0G 1P0
450-785-2203 Fax: 450-785-2254
villestours@bas-richelieu.net
Municipal Type: City
Incorporated: 17 avril 1991; *Area:* 58,50 km2
County or District: Pierre-De Saurel; *Population in 2009:* 1,704
Provincial Electoral District(s): Richelieu
Federal Electoral District(s): Bas-Richelieu-Nicolet-Bécancour
Next Election: 1er novembre 2013
Diane Graveline-Bélanger, Directrice générale
Daniel Arpin, Maire

Saint-Pacôme
CP 370
27, rue St-Louis
Saint-Pacôme, QC G0L 3X0
418-852-2356 Fax: 418-852-2977
stpacome@bellnet.ca
www.st-pacome.ca
Municipal Type: Municipality
Incorporated: 5 janvier 1980; *Area:* 29,31 km2
County or District: Kamouraska; *Population in 2006:* 1,685
Provincial Electoral District(s): Kamouraska-Témiscouata
Federal Electoral District(s): Montmagny-L'Islet-Kamouraska-Rivière-du-Loup
Next Election: 1er novembre 2013
Hélène Lévesque, Sec.-Trés. & Directrice générale

Saint-Pamphile
3, rte Elgin sud
Saint-Pamphile, QC G0R 3X0
418-356-5501 Fax: 418-356-5502
pamphile@globetrotter.qc.ca
Municipal Type: City
Incorporated: 21 janvier 1888; *Area:* 136,80 km2
County or District: L'Islet; *Population in 2006:* 2,704
Provincial Electoral District(s): Montmagny-L'Islet
Federal Electoral District(s): Montmagny-L'Islet-Kamouraska-Rivière-du-Loup
Next Election: 1er novembre 2013
Richard Pelletier, Directeur général & Sec.-Trés.
Réal Laverdiére, Maire

Saint-Pascal
CP 250
405, rue Taché
Saint-Pascal, QC G0L 3Y0
418-492-2312 Fax: 418-492-9862
hoteldeville@villestpascal.com
www.villesaintpascal.qc.ca
Municipal Type: City
Incorporated: 1er mars 2000; *Area:* 57,75 km2
County or District: Kamouraska; *Population in 2006:* 3,504
Provincial Electoral District(s): Kamouraska-Témiscouata
Federal Electoral District(s): Montmagny-L'Islet-Kamouraska-Rivière-du-Loup
Next Election: 1er novembre 2013
Louise Saint-Pierre, Greffière
Cécile Joseph, Mairesse

Saint-Patrice-de-Beaurivage
530, rue Principale
Saint-Patrice-de-Beaurivage, QC G0S 1B0
418-596-2362 Fax: 418-596-2430
st.patrice@globetrotter.net
www.ville.saint-patrice-de-beaurivage.qc.ca
Municipal Type: Municipality
Incorporated: 29 septembre 1984; *Area:* 86,18 km2
County or District: Lotbinière; *Population in 2006:* 1,037
Provincial Electoral District(s): Lotbinière
Federal Electoral District(s): Lotbinière-Chutes-de-la-Chaudière
Next Election: 1er novembre 2013
Josée Martineau, Sec.-Trés. & Directrice générale

Saint-Patrice-de-Sherrington
300, rue St-Patrice
Saint-Patrice-de-Sherrington, QC J0L 2N0
450-454-4959 Fax: 450-454-5677
municipalitesherrington@intermobilex.com
Municipal Type: Parish (Paroisse)
Incorporated: 1er juillet 1855; *Area:* 91,47 km2
County or District: Les Jardins-de-Napierville; *Population in 2006:* 1,911
Provincial Electoral District(s): Huntingdon
Federal Electoral District(s): Beauharnois-Salaberry
Next Election: 1er novembre 2013
Francine Fleurent, Sec.-Trés. & Directrice générale

Saint-Paul
18, boul Brassard
Saint-Paul, QC J0K 3E0
450-759-4040 Fax: 450-759-6396
mairie@municipalitestpaul.qc.ca
www.municipalitestpaul.qc.ca
Municipal Type: Municipality
Incorporated: 1er juillet 1855; *Area:* 48,17 km2
County or District: Joliette; *Population in 2006:* 3,987
Provincial Electoral District(s): Joliette
Federal Electoral District(s): Joliette
Next Election: 1er novmbre 2009
Richard-B. Morasse, Sec.-Trés. & Directeur général

Saint-Paul-d'Abbotsford
926, rue Principale est
Saint-Paul-d'Abbotsford, QC J0E 1A0
450-379-5408 Fax: 450-379-9905
dg.rainville@videotron.ca, stpauldabbotsford@videotron.ca
Municipal Type: Parish (Parcisse)
Incorporated: 1er juillet 1855; *Area:* 79,59 km2
County or District: Rouville; *Population in 2006:* 2,824
Provincial Electoral District(s): Iberville
Federal Electoral District(s): Shefford
Next Election: 1er novembre 2013
Daniel Rainville, Sec.-Trés. & Directeur général

Saint-Paul-de-l'Ile-aux-Noix
959, rue Principale
Saint-Paul-de-l'Ile-aux-Noix, QC J0J 1G0
450-291-3166 Fax: 450-291-5930
mairie_stpaul@netc.net
www.ile-aux-noix.qc.ca
Municipal Type: Parish (Paroisse)
Incorporated: 18 novembre 1898; *Area:* 29,47 km2
County or District: Le Haut-Richelieu; *Population in 2006:* 1,996
Provincial Electoral District(s): Huntingdon
Federal Electoral District(s): St-Jean
Next Election: 1er novembre 2013
Marie-Lili Lenoir, Directrice générale & Sec.-Trés.

Saint-Paul-de-la-Croix
CP 70
1A, rue du Parc
Saint-Paul-de-la-Croix, QC G0L 3Z0
418-898-2031 Fax: 418-898-2322
munstpaul@intermobilex.com
st-paul-de-la-croix.qc.ca
Municipal Type: Parish (Paroisse)
Incorporated: 1er janvier 1873; *Area:* 84,25 km2
County or District: Rivière-du-Loup; *Population in 2006:* 370
Provincial Electoral District(s): Rivière-du-Loup
Federal Electoral District(s): Montmagny-L'Islet-Kamouraska-Rivière-du-Loup
Next Election: 1er novembre 2013
Hélène Malenfant, Sec.-Trés. & Directrice générale

Saint-Paul-de-Montminy
CP 160
309, 4e av
Saint-Paul-de-Montminy, QC G0R 3Y0
418-469-3120 Fax: 418-469-3358
municipalitest-paul@globetrotter.net
www.stpauldemontminy.com
Municipal Type: Municipality
Incorporated: 1er janvier 1862; *Area:* 162,80 km2
County or District: Montmagny; *Population in 2006:* 840
Provincial Electoral District(s): Montmagny-L'Islet
Federal Electoral District(s): Montmagny-L'Islet-Kamouraska-Rivière-du-Loup
Next Election: 1er novembre 2013
Nathalie Boutin, Directrice générale & Sec.-Trés.

Saint-Paulin
CP 120
3051, rue Bergeron
Saint-Paulin, QC J0K 3G0
819-268-2026 Fax: 819-268-2890
munistpaulindg@telmilot.net
www.st-paulin.qc.ca
Municipal Type: Municipality
Incorporated: 27 février 1988; *Area:* 96,40 km2
County or District: Maskinongé; *Population in 2006:* 1,622
Provincial Electoral District(s): Maskinongé
Federal Electoral District(s): Berthier-Maskinongé
Next Election: 1er novembre 2013
Ghislain Lemay, Sec.-Trés. & Directeur général

Saint-Philémon
1531, rue Principale
Saint-Philémon, QC G0R 4A0
418-469-2890 Fax: 418-469-2726
munphile@globetrotter.net
www.saint-philemon.com
Municipal Type: Parish (Paroisse)
Incorporated: 1er janvier 1867; *Area:* 146,51 km2
County or District: Bellechasse; *Population in 2006:* 790
Provincial Electoral District(s): Bellechasse
Federal Electoral District(s): Lévis-Bellechasse
Next Election: 1er novembre 2013
Diane Labrecque, Sec.-Trés. & Directrice générale

Saint-Philibert
CP 9
329, rue Principale
Saint-Philibert, QC G0M 1X0
418-228-8759 Fax: 418-228-0432
ouellet.mj@st-philibert.qc.ca
www.st-philibert.qc.ca
Municipal Type: Municipality
Incorporated: 25 février 1921; *Area:* 57,26 km2
County or District: Beauce-Sartigan; *Population in 2006:* 387
Provincial Electoral District(s): Beauce-Sud
Federal Electoral District(s): Beauce
Next Election: 1er novembre 2013
Marie-Jeanne Ouellet, Sec.-Trés. & Directrice générale

Saint-Philippe
2225, rte Édouard-VII
Saint-Philippe, QC J0L 2K0
450-659-7701 Fax: 450-659-7702
mairiestphilippe@bellnet.ca
Municipal Type: Municipality
Incorporated: 1er juillet 1855; *Area:* 61,66 km2
County or District: Roussillon; *Population in 2006:* 5,121
Provincial Electoral District(s): La Prairie
Federal Electoral District(s): Brossard-La Prairie
Next Election: 1er novembre 2013
Claudine Cormier, Greffière

Saint-Philippe-de-Néri
CP 130
12, côte de l'Église
Saint-Philippe-de-Néri, QC G0L 4A0
418-498-2744 Fax: 418-498-2193
munic.s.phil.neri@qc.aira.com
Municipal Type: Parish (Paroisse)
Incorporated: 29 décembre 1875; *Area:* 33,08 km2

County or District: Kamouraska; *Population in 2006:* 889
Provincial Electoral District(s): Kamouraska-Témiscouata
Federal Electoral District(s):
Montmagny-L'Islet-Kamouraska-Rivière-du-Loup
Next Election: 1er novembre 2013
Pierre Leclerc, Sec.-Trés. & Directeur général

Saint-Pie
77, rue St-Pierre
Saint-Pie, QC J0H 1W0
450-772-2488 Fax: 450-772-2233
st-pie@villest-pie.ca
www.villest-pie.ca
Municipal Type: City
Incorporated: 28 février 2003; *Area:* 106,47 km2
County or District: Les Maskoutains; *Population in 2006:* 5,109
Provincial Electoral District(s): Iberville
Federal Electoral District(s): St-Hyacinthe-Bagot
Next Election: 1er novembre 2013
Note: Effective February 28, 2003, the Parish & the Village of St-Pie amalgamated to create the new City of St-Pie.
Denise Breton, Greffière
Robert Bergeron, Maire

Saint-Pie-de-Guire
445B, rue Principale
Saint-Pie-de-Guire, QC J0G 1R0
450-784-2278 Fax: 450-784-0133
mun.stpie-guire@nplus.ca
Municipal Type: Parish (Paroisse)
Incorporated: 14 juin 1866; *Area:* 52,34 km2
County or District: Drummond; *Population in 2006:* 453
Provincial Electoral District(s): Nicolet-Yamaska
Federal Electoral District(s): Drummond
Next Election: 1er novembre 2013
Claire Roy, Sec.-Trés. & Directrice générale

Saint-Pierre
485, ch du Village-de-St-Pierre nord
Joliette, QC J6E 3Z1
450-756-2592 Fax: 450-756-2735
villagestpierre@qc.aira.com
Municipal Type: Village
Incorporated: 24 avril 1922; *Area:* 10,60 km2
County or District: Joliette; *Population in 2006:* 304
Provincial Electoral District(s): Joliette
Federal Electoral District(s): Joliette
Next Election: 1er novembre 2013
Édith Gagné, Sec.-Trés. & Directrice générale

Saint-Pierre-Baptiste
532B, rte de l'Église
Saint-Pierre-Baptiste, QC G0P 1K0
418-453-2286 Fax: 418-453-2286
mun32050@ivic.qc.ca
www.saintpierrebaptiste.qc.ca
Municipal Type: Parish (Paroisse)
Incorporated: 1er janvier 1874; *Area:* 80,72 km2
County or District: L'Érable; *Population in 2006:* 422
Provincial Electoral District(s): Lotbinière
Federal Electoral District(s): Mégantic-L'Érable
Next Election: 1er novembre 2013
Suzanne Savage, Sec.-Trés. & Directrice générale

Saint-Pierre-de-Broughton
CP 68
29, rue de la Fabrique
Saint-Pierre-de-Broughton, QC G0N 1T0
418-424-3572 Fax: 418-424-0389
muni.stpierre@ville.st-pierre-de-broughton.qc.ca
www.ville.st-pierre-de-broughton.qc.ca
Municipal Type: Municipality
Incorporated: 12 octobre 1974; *Area:* 147,460 km2
County or District: Les Appalaches; *Population in 2009:* 838
Provincial Electoral District(s): Frontenac
Federal Electoral District(s): Mégantic-L'Érable
Next Election: 1er novembre 2013
Sylvie Mercier, Directrice générale

Saint-Pierre-de-la-Rivière-du-Sud
645 - 2e av
St-Pierre-de-la-Rivière-du-Sud, QC G0R 4B0
418-248-8277 Fax: 418-248-7068
st-pierre.rivsud@globetrotter.net
Municipal Type: Parish (Paroisse)
Incorporated: 1er juillet 1855; *Area:* 92,28 km2
County or District: Montmagny; *Population in 2006:* 1,014
Provincial Electoral District(s): Montmagny-L'Islet
Federal Electoral District(s):
Montmagny-L'Islet-Kamouraska-Rivière-du-Loup
Next Election: 1er novembre 2013
Georges Baillargeon, Sec.-Trés. & Directeur général

Saint-Pierre-de-Lamy
115, rte de l'Église
Saint-Pierre-de-Lamy, QC G0L 4B0
418-497-2447 Fax: 418-497-2447
munpierre@bellnet.ca
Municipal Type: Municipality
Incorporated: 4 juin 1977; *Area:* 115,46 km2
County or District: Témiscouata; *Population in 2006:* 123
Provincial Electoral District(s): Kamouraska-Témiscouata
Federal Electoral District(s): Rimouski-Neigette-Témiscouata-Les Basques
Next Election: 1er novembre 2013
Mireille Plourde, Directrice générale & Sec.-Trés.

Saint-Pierre-de-Véronne-à-Pike-River
CP 93
548, rte 202
St-Pierre-de-Véronne, QC J0J 1P0
450-248-2120 Fax: 450-248-4772
stpierredeveronne@qc.aira.com
www.pikeriver.com
Municipal Type: Municipality
Incorporated: 3 avril 1912; *Area:* 43,58 km2
County or District: Brome-Missisquoi; *Population in 2006:* 542
Provincial Electoral District(s): Brome-Missisquoi
Federal Electoral District(s): Brome-Missisquoi
Next Election: 1er novembre 2013
Lyne Boivin, Sec.-Trés. & Directrice générale

Saint-Pierre-Ile-d'Orléans
515, rte des Prêtres
Saint-Pierre-Ile-d'Orléans, QC G0A 4E0
418-828-2855 Fax: 418-828-0724
munst-pierreiledorleans@qc.aira.com
Municipal Type: Municipality
Incorporated: 1er juillet 1855; *Area:* 31,13 km2
County or District: L'Ile-d'Orléans; *Population in 2006:* 1,816
Provincial Electoral District(s): Montmorency
Federal Electoral District(s):
Montmorency-Charlevoix-Haute-Côte-Nord
Next Election: 1er novembre 2013
Marie-Paule Corriveau, Sec.-Trés. & Directrice générale

Saint-Pierre-les-Becquets
110, rue des Loisirs
Saint-Pierre-les-Becquets, QC G0X 2Z0
819-263-2622 Fax: 819-263-0798
municipalite@st-pierre-les-becquets.qc.ca
Municipal Type: Municipality
Incorporated: 22 février 1986; *Area:* 43,00 km2
County or District: Bécancour; *Population in 2006:* 1,183
Provincial Electoral District(s): Lotbinière
Federal Electoral District(s): Bas-Richelieu-Nicolet-Bécancour
Next Election: 1er novembre 2013
Michèle Laquerre, Sec.-Trés. & Directrice générale

Saint-Placide
281, montée St-Vincent
Saint-Placide, QC J0V 2B0
450-258-2305 Fax: 450-258-3059
infosp@municipalite.st-placide.qc.ca
www.municipalite.saint-placide.qc.ca
Municipal Type: Municipality
Incorporated: 3 août 1994; *Area:* 41,95 km2
County or District: Deux-Montagnes; *Population in 2006:* 1,642
Provincial Electoral District(s): Mirabel
Federal Electoral District(s): Argenteuil-Papineau-Mirabel
Next Election: 1er novembre 2013
Marisol Charland, Directrice générale & Directrice générale

Saint-Polycarpe
CP 380
1263, ch Élie-Auclair
Saint-Polycarpe, QC J0P 1X0
450-265-3777 Fax: 450-265-3010
mdery@munstpolycarpe.qc.ca
Municipal Type: Municipality
Incorporated: 31 décembre 1988; *Area:* 70,80 km2
County or District: Vaudreuil-Soulanges; *Population in 2006:* 1,708
Provincial Electoral District(s): Soulanges
Federal Electoral District(s): Vaudreuil-Soulanges
Next Election: 1er novembre 2013
Micheline Déry, Sec.-Trés. & Directrice générale

Saint-Prime
599, rue Principale
Saint-Prime, QC G8J 1T2
418-251-2116 Fax: 418-251-2823
rgirard@saint-prime.ca
www.saint-prime.ca
Municipal Type: Municipality
Incorporated: 29 juin 1968; *Area:* 147,43 km2
County or District: Le Domaine-du-Roy; *Population in 2006:* 2,661
Provincial Electoral District(s): Roberval
Federal Electoral District(s): Roberval-Lac-St-Jean
Next Election: 1er novembre 2013
Régis Girard, Sec.-Trés. & Directeur général

Saint-Prosper
2025, 29e rue
Saint-Prosper, QC G0M 1Y0
418-594-8135 Fax: 418-594-8865
stpros@globetrotter.qc.ca
www.saint-prosper.com
Municipal Type: Municipality
Incorporated: 26 septembre 1887; *Area:* 136, 95 km2
County or District: Les Etchemins; *Population in 2006:* 3,612
Provincial Electoral District(s): Beauce-Sud
Federal Electoral District(s): Beauce
Next Election: 1er novembre 2013
Johanne Nadeau, Sec.-Trés. & Directrice générale

Saint-Prosper
CP 68
375, rue St-Joseph
Saint-Prosper, QC G0X 3A0
418-328-8449 Fax: 418-328-4267
municipalite@st-prosper.ca
Municipal Type: Parish (Paroisse)
Incorporated: 1er juillet 1855; *Area:* 92,03 km2
County or District: Les Chenaux; *Population in 2006:* 541
Provincial Electoral District(s): Champlain
Federal Electoral District(s): St-Maurice-Champlain
Next Election: 1er novembre 2013
Micheline Duchesne, Directrice générale

Saint-Raphaël
CP 1091
19, av Chanoine-Audet
Saint-Raphaël, QC G0R 4C0
418-243-2853 Fax: 418-243-2605
muraph@globetrotter.net
www.municipalite.saint-raphael.qc.ca
Municipal Type: Municipality
Incorporated: 8 décembre 1993; *Area:* 120,06 km2
County or District: Bellechasse; *Population in 2006:* 2,301
Provincial Electoral District(s): Bellechasse
Federal Electoral District(s): Lévis-Bellechasse
Next Election: 1er novembre 2013
Paul Beaudoin, Sec.-Trés. & Directeur général

Saint-Raymond
375, rue St-Joseph
Saint-Raymond, QC G3L 1A1
418-337-2202 Fax: 418-337-2203
christiane.noreau@ville.st-raymond.qc.ca
www.ville.st-raymond.qc.ca
Municipal Type: City
Incorporated: 29 mars 1995; *Area:* 684,65 km2
County or District: Portneuf; *Population in 2006:* 9,273
Provincial Electoral District(s): Portneuf
Federal Electoral District(s): Portneuf-Jacques-Cartier
Next Election: 1er novembre 2013
Rolland Dion, Maire
Réjeanne Julien, Greffière

Saint-Rémi
105, rue Perras
Saint-Rémi, QC J0L 2L0
450-454-3993 Fax: 450-454-7978
administration@ville.saint-remi.qc.ca
www.ville.saint-remi.qc.ca
Municipal Type: City
Incorporated: 20 septembre 1975; *Area:* 79,66 km2
County or District: Les Jardins-de-Napierville; *Population in 2006:* 6,136
Provincial Electoral District(s): Huntingdon
Federal Electoral District(s): Beauharnois-Salaberry
Next Election: 1er novembre 2013
Diane Soucy, Greffier
Michel Lavoie, Maire

Saint-Rémi-de-Tingwick
141A, rue Principale
Saint-Rémi-de-Tingwick, QC J0A 1K0
819-359-2731 Fax: 819-359-3532
mstremi@nplus.ca
Municipal Type: Parish (Paroisse)
Incorporated: 1er janvier 1882; *Area:* 72,18 km2
County or District: Arthabaska; *Population in 2006:* 468
Provincial Electoral District(s): Richmond
Federal Electoral District(s): Richmond-Arthabaska
Next Election: 1er novembre 2013
Renée Vaudreuil, Sec.-Trés. & Directrice générale

Saint-René
778, rte Principale
Saint-René, QC G0M 1Z0
418-382-5226 Fax: 418-382-3655
muni.st.rene@globetrotter.net
Municipal Type: Parish (Paroisse)
Incorporated: 1er janvier 1945; *Area:* 61,53 km3
County or District: Beauce-Sartigan; *Population in 2006:* 612
Provincial Electoral District(s): Beauce-Sud
Federal Electoral District(s): Beauce
Next Election: 1er novembre 2013
Michel Gilbert, Directeur général & Sec.-Trés.

Saint-René-de-Matane
CP 58
178, av St-René
Saint-René-de-Matane, QC G0J 3E0
418-224-3306 Fax: 418-224-3259
mustrene@globetrotter.net
Municipal Type: Municipality
Incorporated: 18 décembre 1982; *Area:* 255,58 km2
County or District: Matane; *Population in 2006:* 1,070
Provincial Electoral District(s): Matane
Federal Electoral District(s): Haute-Gaspésie-La Mitis-Matane-Matapédia
Next Election: 1er novembre 2013
Yvette Boulay, Sec.-Trés. & Directrice générale

Saint-Robert
CP 150
650, ch de St-Robert
Saint-Robert, QC J0G 1S0
450-782-2844 Fax: 450-782-2733
strobert@bas-richelieu.net
Municipal Type: Municipality
Incorporated: 17 octobre 1857; *Area:* 64,93 km2

County or District: Pierre-De Saurel; *Population in 2009:* 1,757
Provincial Electoral District(s): Richelieu
Federal Electoral District(s): Bas-Richelieu-Nicolet-Bécanour
Next Election: 1er novembre 2013
Nathalie Lussier, Directrice générale

Saint-Robert-Bellarmin
10, rue Nadeau
Saint-Robert-Bellarmin, QC G0M 2E0
418-582-3420 Fax: 418-582-3420
mun-st-robert@globetrotter.net
Municipal Type: Municipality
Incorporated: 1er janvier 1949; *Area:* 234,82 km2
County or District: Le Granit; *Population in 2006:* 645
Provincial Electoral District(s): Beauce-Sud
Federal Electoral District(s): Beauce
Next Election: 1er novembre 2013
Suzanne Lescomb, Directrice générale & Sec.-Trés.

Saint-Roch-de-l'Achigan
CP 480
30, rue du Dr.-Wilfrid-Locat nord
Saint-Roch-de-l'Achigan, QC J0K 3H0
450-588-2211 Fax: 450-588-4478
info@strochlachigan.com
www.strochlachigan.com
Municipal Type: Parish (Paroisse)
Incorporated: 1er juillet 1855; *Area:* 78,83 km2
County or District: Montcalm; *Population in 2006:* 4,449
Provincial Electoral District(s): Rousseau
Federal Electoral District(s): Montcalm
Next Election: 1er novembre 2013
Philippe Riopelle, Sec.-Trés. & Directeur général

Saint-Roch-de-Mékinac
1210, rte Ducharme
Saint-Roch-de-Mékinac, QC G0X 2E0
819-646-5635 Fax: 819-646-5635
mekin363@globetrotter.net
Municipal Type: Parish (Paroisse)
Incorporated: 2 novembre 2009; *Area:* 155,39 km2
County or District: Mékinac; *Population in 2006:* 324
Provincial Electoral District(s): Laviolette
Federal Electoral District(s): St-Maurice-Champlain
Next Election: 1er novembre 2013
Robert Jourdain, Sec.-Trés. & Directeur général

Saint-Roch-de-Richelieu
1111, rue du Parc
Saint-Roch-de-Richelieu, QC J0L 2M0
450-785-2755 Fax: 450-785-3098
stroch@bas-richelieu.net
Municipal Type: Municipality
Incorporated: 4 juin 1859; *Area:* 34,86 km2
County or District: Pierre-De Saurel; *Population in 2009:* 1,915
Provincial Electoral District(s): Verchères
Federal Electoral District(s): Bas-Richelieu-Nicolet-Bécancour
Next Election: 1er novembre 2013
Claude Gratton, Directeur général

Saint-Roch-des-Aulnaies
379, rte de l'Église
Saint-Roch-des-Aulnaies, QC G0R 4E0
418-354-2892 Fax: 418-354-2059
munirock@globetrotter.net
Municipal Type: Parish (Paroisse)
Incorporated: 1er juillet 1855; *Area:* 48,28 km2
County or District: L'Islet; *Population in 2006:* 939
Provincial Electoral District(s): Kamouraska-Témiscouata
Federal Electoral District(s):
Montmorency-Charlevoix-Haute-Côte-Nord
Next Election: 1er novembre 2013
Cécile Morin, Sec.-Trés. & Directrice générale

Saint-Roch-Ouest
806, rang de la Rivière sud, RR#2
Saint-Roch-Ouest, QC J0K 3H0
450-588-6060 Fax: 450-588-0975
stroch_ouest@hotmail.com
Municipal Type: Municipality
Incorporated: 4 juin 1921; *Area:* 20,90 km2
County or District: Montcalm; *Population in 2006:* 285
Provincial Electoral District(s): Rousseau
Federal Electoral District(s): Montcalm
Next Election: 1er novembre 2013
Jacinthe Mercier, Sec.-Trés. & Directrice générale

Saint-Romain
355, rue Principale
Saint-Romain, QC G0Y 1L0
418-486-7374 Fax: 418-486-7875
municipalite-st-romain@tellambton.net
Municipal Type: Municipality
Incorporated: 1er janvier 1858; *Area:* 112,92 km2
County or District: Le Granit; *Population in 2006:* 628
Provincial Electoral District(s): Mégantic-Compton
Federal Electoral District(s): Mégantic-L'Érable
Next Election: 1er novembre 2013
Nicole P. Roy, Sec.-Trés. & Directrice générale

Saint-Rosaire
208, 6e rang
Saint-Rosaire, QC G0Z 1K0
819-752-6178 Fax: 819-752-3959
munstros@nplus.ca
Municipal Type: Parish (Paroisse)
Incorporated: 23 mai 1896; *Area:* 109,84 km2
County or District: Arthabaska; *Population in 2007:* 776
Provincial Electoral District(s): Arthabaska
Federal Electoral District(s): Richmond-Arthabaska
Next Election: 1er novembre 2013
Céline Raymond, Sec.-Trés. & Directrice générale

Saint-Samuel
141, rue de l'Église
Saint-Samuel, QC G0Z 1G0
819-353-1242 Fax: 819-353-1499
stsamuel@telwarwick.net
Municipal Type: Parish (Paroisse)
Incorporated: 9 mars 1878; *Area:* 42,89 km2
County or District: Arthabaska; *Population in 2006:* 673
Provincial Electoral District(s): Richmond
Federal Electoral District(s): Richmond-Arthabaska
Next Election: 1er novembre 2013
Suzie Constant, Sec.-Trés. & Directrice générale

Saint-Sauveur
1, place de la Mairie
Saint-Sauveur, QC J0R 1R2
450-227-4633 Fax: 450-227-3834
directiongenerale@ville.saint-sauveur.qc.ca
www.ville.saint-sauveur.qc.ca
Municipal Type: City
Incorporated: 11 septembre 2002; *Area:* 47,99 km2
County or District: Les Pays-d'en-Haut; *Population in 2006:* 9,191
Provincial Electoral District(s): Bertrand
Federal Electoral District(s): Laurentides-Labelle
Next Election: 1er novembre 2013
Note: Effective September 9, 2002, the Parish of St-Sauveur & the Village of St-Sauveur-des-Monts amalgamated to create the City of St-Sauveur.
Normand Patrice, Greffier
Michel Lagacé, Maire

Saint-Sébastien
582, rue Principale
Saint-Sébastien, QC G0Y 1M0
819-652-2727 Fax: 819-652-2584
st-sebastien@bellnet.ca
www.st-sebastien.com
Municipal Type: Municipality
Incorporated: 15 mars 1975; *Area:* 91,19 km2
County or District: Le Granit; *Population in 2006:* 752
Provincial Electoral District(s): Mégantic-Compton
Federal Electoral District(s): Mégantic-L'Érable
Next Election: 1er novembre 2013
Martine Rouleau, Sec.-Trés. & Directrice générale

Saint-Sébastien
CP 126
176, rue Dussault
Saint-Sébastien, QC J0J 2C0
450-244-5237 Fax: 450-244-6264
muniseba@netc.net
Municipal Type: Parish (Paroisse)
Incorporated: 17 février 1865; *Area:* 62,56 km2
County or District: Le Haut-Richelieu; *Population in 2006:* 682
Provincial Electoral District(s): Iberville
Federal Electoral District(s): Brome-Missisquoi
Next Election: 1er novembre 2013
Micheline Benoit, Sec.-Trés. & Directrice générale

Saint-Sévère
47, rue Principale
Saint-Sévère, QC G0X 3B0
819-264-5656 Fax: 819-264-5656
paroissestsevere@hotmail.com
Municipal Type: Parish (Paroisse)
Incorporated: 1er juillet 1855; *Area:* 31,83 km2
County or District: Maskinongé; *Population in 2006:* 329
Provincial Electoral District(s): Maskinongé
Federal Electoral District(s): Berthier-Maskinongé
Next Election: 1er novembre 2013
Anne-Marie Sauvageau, Sec.-Trés. & Directrice générale

Saint-Séverin
900, rue des Lacs
Saint-Séverin, QC G0N 1V0
418-426-2423 Fax: 418-426-1274
munseverin@globetrotter.net
Municipal Type: Parish (Paroisse)
Incorporated: 24 décembre 1875; *Area:* 56,22 km2
County or District: Robert-Cliche; *Population in 2006:* 279
Provincial Electoral District(s): Beauce-Nord
Federal Electoral District(s): Beauce
Next Election: 1er novembre 2013
Marie Giguère, Sec.-Trés. & Directrice générale

Saint-Séverin
CP 120
1986, place du Centre
Saint-Séverin, QC G0X 2B0
418-365-5844 Fax: 418-365-7544
st-severin@regionmekinac.com
Municipal Type: Parish (Paroisse)
Incorporated: 11 avril 1890; *Area:* 61,97 km2
County or District: Mékinac; *Population in 2006:* 859
Provincial Electoral District(s): Laviolette
Federal Electoral District(s): St-Maurice-Champlain
Next Election: 1er novembre 2013
Ginette Hamelin, Sec.-Trés. & Directrice générale

Saint-Siméon
CP 98
502, rue St-Laurent
Saint-Siméon, QC G0T 1X0
418-638-2691 Fax: 418-638-5145
munstsimeon@bellnet.ca
Municipal Type: Municipality
Incorporated: 25 avril 2001; *Area:* 289,73 km2
County or District: Charlevoix-Est; *Population in 2006:* 1,360
Provincial Electoral District(s): Charlevoix
Federal Electoral District(s):
Montmorency-Charlevoix-Haute-Côte-Nord
Next Election: 1er novembre 2013
Sylvie Foster, Sec.-Trés. & Directrice générale

Saint-Siméon
CP 39
111, av de l'Église
Saint-Siméon, QC G0C 3A0
418-534-2155 Fax: 418-534-3830
munsseon@globetrotter.net
Municipal Type: Parish (Paroisse)
Incorporated: 29 octobre 1914; *Area:* 56,12 km2
County or District: Bonaventure; *Population in 2006:* 1,174
Provincial Electoral District(s): Bonaventure
Federal Electoral District(s): Gaspésie-Iles-de-la-Madeleine
Next Election: 1er novembre 2013
Jean-Guy Poirier, Maire

Saint-Simon
CP 40
30, rue de l'Église
Saint-Simon, QC G0L 4C0
418-738-2896 Fax: 418-738-2934
munstsimon@globetrotter.net
Municipal Type: Parish (Paroisse)
Incorporated: 1er juillet 1855; *Area:* 75,62 km2
County or District: Les Basques; *Population in 2006:* 437
Provincial Electoral District(s): Rivière-du-Loup
Federal Electoral District(s): Rimouski-Neigette-Témiscouata-Les Basques
Next Election: 1er novembre 2013
Yolande Théberge, Sec.-Trés. & Directrice générale

Saint-Simon
49, rue du Couvent
Saint-Simon-de-Bagot, QC J0H 1Y0
450-798-2276 Fax: 450-798-2498
st-simon@mrcmaskoutains.qc.ca
Municipal Type: Parish (Paroisse)
Incorporated: 1er juillet 1855; *Area:* 68,66 km2
County or District: Les Maskoutains; *Population in 2006:* 1,228
Provincial Electoral District(s): St-Hyacinthe
Federal Electoral District(s): St-Hyacinthe-Bagot
Next Election: 1er novembre 2013
Suzanne Francoeur, Sec.-Trés. & Directrice générale

Saint-Simon-les-Mines
3338, rue Principale
Saint-Simon-les-Mines, QC G0M 1K0
418-774-3317 Fax: 418-774-3317
municipalitestsimonlesmines@sogetel.net
Municipal Type: Municipality
Incorporated: 1er juin 1950; *Area:* 44,80 km2
County or District: Beauce-Sartigan; *Population in 2006:* 473
Provincial Electoral District(s): Beauce-Sud
Federal Electoral District(s): Beauce
Next Election: 1er novembre 2013
Francine Poulin, Sec.-Trés. & Directrice générale

Saint-Sixte
5, rue Emery
Saint-Sixte, QC J0X 3B0
819-983-3155 Fax: 819-983-3409
mun.st-sixte@tlb.sympatico.ca
Municipal Type: Municipality
Incorporated: 7 février 1893; *Area:* 83,44 km2
County or District: Papineau; *Population in 2006:* 466
Provincial Electoral District(s): Papineau
Federal Electoral District(s): Argenteuil-Papineau-Mirabel
Next Election: 1er novembre 2013
Alain Hotte, Sec.-Trés. & Directeur général

Saint-Stanislas
33, rue du Pont
Saint-Stanislas, QC G0X 3E0
418-328-3245 Fax: 418-328-4121
municipalite@saint-stanislas.ca
www.saint-stanislas.ca
Municipal Type: Municipality
Incorporated: 17 avril 1976; *Area:* 86,37 km2
County or District: Les Chenaux; *Population in 2006:* 1,033
Provincial Electoral District(s): Champlain
Federal Electoral District(s): St-Maurice-Champlain
Next Election: 1er novembre 2013
Raymonde Bordeleau, Directrice générale & Sec.-Trés.

Saint-Stanislas
953, rue Principale
Saint-Stanislas, QC G8L 7B4
418-276-4476 Fax: 418-276-9947
municipalite.st-stanislas@caramail.com
sadcmaria.qc.ca/pac/stanislas/municipalite/index.html

Municipal Type: Municipality
Incorporated: 24 octobre 1931; *Area:* 159,45 km2
County or District: Maria-Chapdelaine; *Population in 2006:* 345
Provincial Electoral District(s): Roberval
Federal Electoral District(s): Roberval-Lac-St-Jean
Next Election: 1er novembre 2013
Caroline Gagnon, Sec.-Trés. & Directrice générale

Saint-Stanislas-de-Kostka
CP 120
221, rue Centrale
Saint-Stanislas-de-Kostka, QC J0S 1W0
450-373-8944 Fax: 450-373-8949
st-stan@intermobilex.com
Municipal Type: Parish (Paroisse)
Incorporated: 1er juillet 1855; *Area:* 62,16 km2
County or District: Beauharnois-Salaberry; *Population in 2006:* 1,668
Provincial Electoral District(s): Beauharnois
Federal Electoral District(s): Beauharnois-Salaberry
Next Election: 1er novembre 2013
Louise Maheu Denis, Sec.-Trés. & Directrice générale

Saint-Sulpice
1089, rue Notre-Dame
Saint-Sulpice, QC J5W 1G1
450-589-4450 Fax: 450-589-9647
mun.paroissestsulpice@videotron.ca
Municipal Type: Parish (Paroisse)
Incorporated: 1er juillet 1855; *Area:* 37 km2
County or District: L'Assomption; *Population in 2006:* 3,332
Provincial Electoral District(s): L'Assomption
Federal Electoral District(s): Repentigny
Next Election: 1er novembre 2013
Marie-Josée Masson, Sec.-Trés. & Directrice générale

Saint-Sylvère
837, 8e rang
Saint-Sylvère, QC G0Z 1H0
819-285-2075 Fax: 819-285-2075
mun.st.sylvere@infoteck.qc.ca
Municipal Type: Municipality
Incorporated: 18 septembre 1976; *Area:* 85,02 km2
County or District: Bécancour; *Population in 2006:* 686
Provincial Electoral District(s): Nicolet-Yamaska
Federal Electoral District(s): Bas-Richelieu-Nicolet-Bécancour
Next Election: 1er novembre 2013
Ginette Richard, Directrice générale & Sec.-Trés.

Saint-Sylvestre
CP 70
423B, rue Principale
Saint-Sylvestre, QC G0S 3C0
418-596-2384 Fax: 418-596-2375
munisylvestre@altanet.ca
www.ville.saint-sylvestre.qc.ca
Municipal Type: Municipality
Incorporated: 4 décembre 1996; *Area:* 143,34 km2
County or District: Lotbinière; *Population in 2006:* 973
Provincial Electoral District(s): Lotbinière
Federal Electoral District(s): Lotbinière-Chutes-de-la-Chaudière
Next Election: 1er novembre 2013
Céline Bilodeau, Sec.-Trés. & Directrice générale

Saint-Télesphore
1425, rte 340
Saint-Télesphore, QC J0P 1Y0
450-269-2999 Fax: 450-269-2257
st-telesphore@rocler.qc.ca
Municipal Type: Parish (Paroisse)
Incorporated: 10 avril 1877; *Area:* 59,62 km2
County or District: Vaudreuil-Soulanges; *Population in 2006:* 769
Provincial Electoral District(s): Soulanges
Federal Electoral District(s): Vaudreuil-Soulanges
Next Election: 1er novembre 2013
Danielle Bourgon, Sec.-Trés. & Directrice générale

Saint-Tharcisius
CP 10
55, rue Principale
Saint-Tharcisius, QC G0J 3G0
418-629-4727 Fax: 418-629-4727
munsttharcisius@hotmail.com
Municipal Type: Parish (Paroisse)
Incorporated: 4 décembre 2009; *Area:* 79,61 km2
County or District: La Matapédia; *Population in 2006:* 480
Provincial Electoral District(s): Matapédia
Federal Electoral District(s): Haute-Gaspésie-La Mitis-Matane-Matapédia
Next Election: 1er novembre 2013
Nancy Gagné, Sec.-Trés. & Directrice générale

Saint-Théodore-d-Acton
1661, rue Principale
Saint-Théodore-d-Acton, QC J0H 1Z0
450-546-2634 Fax: 450-546-2526
mun.st-theo@mrcacton.qc.ca
www.st-theodore.com
Municipal Type: Parish (Paroisse)
Incorporated: 1er janvier 1864; *Area:* 83,60 km2
County or District: Acton; *Population in 2006:* 1,494
Provincial Electoral District(s): Johnson
Federal Electoral District(s): St-Hyacinthe-Bagot
Next Election: 1er novembre 2013
France Desjardins, Sec.-Trés. & Directrice générale

Saint-Théophile
CP 10
644, rue du Collège
Saint-Théophile, QC G0M 2A0
418-597-3998 Fax: 418-597-3015
muntheo@globetrotter.net
Municipal Type: Municipality
Incorporated: 28 juin 1975; *Area:* 429,58 km2
County or District: Beauce-Sartigan; *Population in 2006:* 776
Provincial Electoral District(s): Beauce-Sud
Federal Electoral District(s): Beauce
Next Election: 1er novembre 2013
Paula Lacoursière, Sec.-Trés. & Directrice générale

Saint-Thomas
770, rue Principale
Saint-Thomas, QC J0K 3L0
450-759-3405 Fax: 450-759-0059
munisth@videotron.ca
www.saintthomas.qc.ca
Municipal Type: Municipality
Incorporated: 1er juillet 1855; *Area:* 97,26 km2
County or District: Joliette; *Population in 2006:* 2,861
Provincial Electoral District(s): Joliette
Federal Electoral District(s): Joliette
Next Election: 1er novembre 2013
Roger Drainville, Directeur général

Saint-Thomas-Didyme
9, av du Moulin
Saint-Thomas-Didyme, QC G0W 1P0
418-274-3638 Fax: 418-274-4176
jmparadis@stthomasdidyme.qc.ca
www.stthomasdidyme.qc.ca
Municipal Type: Municipality
Incorporated: 11 mai 1923; *Area:* 325,36 km2
County or District: Maria-Chapdelaine; *Population in 2006:* 708
Provincial Electoral District(s): Roberval
Federal Electoral District(s): Roberval-Lac-St-Jean
Next Election: 1er novembre 2013
Jean-Marc Paradis, Sec.-Trés. & Directeur général

Saint-Thuribe
CP 69
385, rue Principale
Saint-Thuribe, QC G0A 4H0
418-339-2171 Fax: 418-339-3435
municipalitestthuribe@globetrotter.net
Municipal Type: Parish (Paroisse)
Incorporated: 14 février 1898; *Area:* 50,81 km2
County or District: Portneuf; *Population in 2006:* 303
Provincial Electoral District(s): Portneuf
Federal Electoral District(s): Portneuf-Jacques-Cartier
Next Election: 1er novembre 2013
Sylvie Groleau, Sec.-Trés. & Directrice générale

Saint-Tite
540, rue Notre-Dame
Saint-Tite, QC G0X 3H0
418-365-5143 Fax: 418-365-4020
hoteldeville@villest-tite.com
Municipal Type: City
Incorporated: 23 décembre 1998; *Area:* 91,01 km2
County or District: Mékinac; *Population in 2006:* 3,826
Provincial Electoral District(s): Laviolette
Federal Electoral District(s): St-Maurice-Champlain
Next Election: 1er novembre 2013
Pierre Massicotte, Directeur général & Sec.-Trés.
Raynald Périgny, Maire

Saint-Tite-des-Caps
1, rue Leclerc
Saint-Tite-des-Caps, QC G0A 4J0
418-823-2239 Fax: 418-823-2527
sainttitedescaps@videotron.ca
www.sainttitedescaps.com
Municipal Type: Municipality
Incorporated: 24 décembre 1872; *Area:* 130,01 km2
County or District: La Côte-de-Beaupré; *Population in 2006:* 1,440
Provincial Electoral District(s): Charlevoix
Federal Electoral District(s): Montmorency-Charlevoix-Haute-Côte-Nord
Next Election: 1er novembre 2013
Mathieu Genest, Sec.-Trés. & Directeur général

Saint-Ubalde
427B, boul Chabot
Saint-Ubalde, QC G0A 4L0
418-277-2124 Fax: 418-277-2055
stubalde@globetrotter.net
www.st-ubalde.qc.ca
Municipal Type: Municipality
Incorporated: 3 mars 1973; *Area:* 141,28 km2
County or District: Portneuf; *Population in 2006:* 1,458
Provincial Electoral District(s): Portneuf
Federal Electoral District(s): Portneuf-Jacques-Cartier
Next Election: 1er novembre 2013
Serge Deraspe, Sec.-Trés. & Directeur général

Saint-Ulric
128, av Ulric-Tessier
Saint-Ulric, QC G0J 3H0
418-737-4341 Fax: 418-737-9242
munpulr@globetrotter.net
www.st-ulric.ca

Municipal Type: Municipality
Incorporated: 12 janvier 2000; *Area:* 118,68 km2
County or District: Matane; *Population in 2006:* 1,696
Provincial Electoral District(s): Matane
Federal Electoral District(s): Haute-Gaspésie-La Mitis-Matane-Matapédia
Next Election: 1er novembre 2013
Louise Coll, Sec.-Trés. & Directrice générale

Saint-Urbain
CP 100
917, rue St-Édouard
Saint-Urbain, QC G0A 4K0
418-639-2467 Fax: 418-639-1063
munsturb@charlevoix.net
Municipal Type: Parish (Paroisse)
Incorporated: 1er juillet 1855; *Area:* 327,68 km2
County or District: Charlevoix; *Population in 2006:* 1,448
Provincial Electoral District(s): Charlevoix
Federal Electoral District(s): Montmorency-Charlevoix-Haute-Côte-Nord
Next Election: 1er novembre 2013
Josée Desmeules, Sec.-Trés. & Directrice générale

Saint-Urbain-Premier
204, rue Principale
Saint-Urbain-Premier, QC J0S 1Y0
450-427-3987 Fax: 450-427-2056
sainturbainpremier@qc.aira.com
Municipal Type: Municipality
Incorporated: 1er juillet 1855; *Area:* 52,24
County or District: Beauharnois-Salaberry; *Population in 2006:* 1,129
Provincial Electoral District(s): Huntingdon
Federal Electoral District(s): Beauharnois-Salaberry
Next Election: 1er novembre 2013
Nicole Sainte-Marie, Sec.-Trés. & Directrice générale

Saint-Valentin
790, ch de la Quatrième-Ligne
Saint-Valentin, QC J0J 2E0
450-291-5422 Fax: 450-291-5327
administration@municipalite.saint-valentin.qc.ca
Municipal Type: Parish (Paroisse)
Incorporated: 1er juillet 1855; *Area:* 40,09 km2
County or District: Le Haut-Richelieu; *Population in 2006:* 478
Provincial Electoral District(s): Huntingdon
Federal Electoral District(s): St-Jean
Next Election: 1er novembre 2013
Serge Gibeau, Sec.-Trés. & Directeur général

Saint-Valère
2, rue du Parc
Saint-Valère, QC G0P 1M0
819-353-3450 Fax: 819-353-3459
stvalere@msvalere.qc.ca
www.msvalere.qc.ca
Municipal Type: Municipality
Incorporated: 1er janvier 1862; *Area:* 108,13 km2
County or District: Arthabaska; *Population in 2006:* 1,299
Provincial Electoral District(s): Arthabaska
Federal Electoral District(s): Richmond-Arthabaska
Next Election: 1er novembre 2013
Jocelyn Jutras, Sec.-Trés. & Directeur général

Saint-Valérien
CP 9
181, rte Centrale
Saint-Valérien-de-Rimouski, QC G0L 4E0
418-736-5047 Fax: 418-736-5922
valerien@globetrotter.net
Municipal Type: Parish (Paroisse)
Incorporated: 19 juin 1885; *Area:* 149,69 km2
County or District: Rimouski-Neigette; *Population in 2006:* 835
Provincial Electoral District(s): Rimouski
Federal Electoral District(s): Rimouski-Neigette-Témiscouata-Les Basques
Next Election: 1er novembre 2013
Marie-Paule Cimon, Directrice générale & Sec.-Trés.

Saint-Valérien-de-Milton
960, ch de Milton
Saint-Valérien-de-Milton, QC J0H 2B0
450-549-2463 Fax: 450-549-2993
administration.st-valerien@mrcmaskoutains.qc.ca
Municipal Type: Township
Incorporated: 1er janvier 1864; *Area:* 106,44 km2
County or District: Les Maskoutains; *Population in 2006:* 1,718
Provincial Electoral District(s): Johnson
Federal Electoral District(s): St-Hyacinthe-Bagot
Next Election: 1er novembre 2013
Élise Guertin, Sec.-Trés. & Directrice générale

Saint-Vallier
375, montée de la Station
Saint-Vallier, QC G0R 4J0
418-884-2559 Fax: 418-884-2454
svallier@globetrotter.net
www.stvallierbellechasse.qc.ca
Municipal Type: Municipality
Incorporated: 10 mars 1993; *Area:* 42,24 km2
County or District: Bellechasse; *Population in 2006:* 1,044
Provincial Electoral District(s): Bellechasse
Federal Electoral District(s): Lévis-Bellechasse
Next Election: 1er novembre 2013
Caroline Gendron, Sec.-Trés. & Directrice générale

Saint-Venant-de-Paquette
5, ch du Village
Saint-Venant-de-Paquette, QC J0B 1S0
819-658-3660 Fax: 819-658-0985
stvenant@axion.ca
www.regioncoaticook.qc.ca/stvenant
Municipal Type: Municipality
Incorporated: 11 juin 1917; *Area:* 58,17 km2
County or District: Coaticook; *Population in 2006:* 81
Provincial Electoral District(s): Mégantic-Compton
Federal Electoral District(s): Compton-Stanstead
Next Election: 1er novembre 2013
Robert Plante, Directeur général

Saint-Vianney
CP 39
170, av Centrale
Saint-Vianney, QC G0J 3J0
418-629-4082 Fax: 418-629-4821
munvia@globetrotter.net
Municipal Type: Municipality
Incorporated: 27 août 1926; *Area:* 145,24 km2
County or District: La Matapédia; *Population in 2006:* 489
Provincial Electoral District(s): Matapédia
Federal Electoral District(s): Haute-Gaspésie-La Mitis-Matane-Matapédia
Next Election: 1er novembre 2013
Roselle Caron, Sec.-Trés. & Directrice générale

Saint-Victor
CP 40
287, rue Marchand
Saint-Victor, QC G0M 2B0
418-588-6854 Fax: 418-588-6855
saint-vic@telvic.net
Municipal Type: Municipality
Incorporated: 31 décembre 1996; *Area:* 120,94 km2
County or District: Robert-Cliche; *Population in 2006:* 2,553
Provincial Electoral District(s): Beauce-Nord
Federal Electoral District(s): Beauce
Next Election: 1er novembre 2013
Marc Bélanger, Sec.-Trés. & Directeur général

Saint-Wenceslas
1065, rue Richard
Saint-Wenceslas, QC G0Z 1J0
819-224-7784 Fax: 819-224-4036
mun.stwen@sogetel.net
Municipal Type: Municipality
Incorporated: 11 octobre 1995; *Area:* 78,42 km2
County or District: Nicolet-Yamaska; *Population in 2006:* 1,101
Provincial Electoral District(s): Nicolet-Yamaska
Federal Electoral District(s): Bas-Richelieu-Nicolet-Bécancour
Next Election: 1er novembre 2013
Carole Hélie, Directrice générale & Sec.-Trés.

Saint-Zacharie
735, 15e rue
Saint-Zacharie, QC G0M 2C0
418-593-3185 Fax: 418-593-3085
munzac@sogetel.net
Municipal Type: Municipality
Incorporated: 18 avril 1990; *Area:* 189,70 km2
County or District: Les Etchemins; *Population in 2006:* 1,918
Provincial Electoral District(s): Beauce-Sud
Federal Electoral District(s): Beauce
Next Election: 1er novembre 2013
Brigitte Larivière, Dirctrice générale & Sec.-Trés.

Saint-Zénon
6101, rue Principale
Saint-Zénon, QC J0K 3N0
450-884-5987 Fax: 450-884-5285
municipalite@st-zenon.net
www.st-zenon.net
Municipal Type: Municipality
Incorporated: 7 octobre 1895; *Area:* 488,69 km2
County or District: Matawinie; *Population in 2006:* 1,379
Provincial Electoral District(s): Berthier
Federal Electoral District(s): Joliette
Next Election: 1er novembre 2013
Alain St-Vincent-Rioux, Sec.-Trés. & Directeur général

Saint-Zénon-du-Lac-Humqui
CP 39
156, rte 195
Lac-Humqui, QC G0J 1N0
418-743-2177 Fax: 418-743-2177
cachum@globetrotter.net
Municipal Type: Parish (Paroisse)
Incorporated: 28 avril 1920; *Area:* 112,97 km2
County or District: La Matapédia; *Population in 2006:* 426
Provincial Electoral District(s): Matapédia
Federal Electoral District(s): Haute-Gaspésie-La Mitis-Matane-Matapédia
Next Election: 1er novembre 2013
Maryline Pronovost, Sec.-Trés. & Directrice générale

Saint-Zéphirin-de-Courval
CP 40
1471, rue St-Pierre
Saint-Zéphirin-de-Courval, QC J0G 1V0
450-564-2188 Fax: 450-564-2339
municipalite@saint-zephirin.ca
www.saint-zephirin.ca
Municipal Type: Parish (Paroisse)
Incorporated: 1er juillet 1855; *Area:* 71,01 km2
County or District: Nicolet-Yamaska; *Population in 2006:* 825
Provincial Electoral District(s): Nicolet-Yamaska
Federal Electoral District(s): Bas-Richelieu-Nicolet-Bécancour
Next Election: 1er novembre 2013
Hélène Chassé, Directrice générale & Sec.-Trés.

Saint-Zotique
1250, rue Principale
Saint-Zotique, QC J0P 1Z0
450-267-9335 Fax: 450-267-0907
dg@st-zotique.com
www.st-zotique.com
Municipal Type: Village
Incorporated: 27 mai 1967; *Area:* 24,24 km2
County or District: Vaudreuil-Soulanges; *Population in 2006:* 5,251
Provincial Electoral District(s): Soulanges
Federal Electoral District(s): Vaudreuil-Soulanges
Next Election: 1er novembre 2013
Pierre Chevrier, Sec.-Trés. & Directeur général

Sainte-Agathe-de-Lotbinière
CP 159
254, rue St-Pierre
Sainte-Agathe-de-Lotbinière, QC G0S 2A0
418-599-2605 Fax: 418-599-2905
admin@ste-agathelotb.org
Municipal Type: Municipality
Incorporated: 3 février 1999; *Area:* 169,50 km2
County or District: Lotbinière; *Population in 2006:* 1,202
Provincial Electoral District(s): Lotbinière
Federal Electoral District(s): Lotbinière-Chutes-de-la-Chaudière
Next Election: 1er novembre 2013
André Castonguay, Directeur général

Sainte-Agathe-des-Monts
50, rue St-Joseph
Sainte-Agathe-des-Monts, QC J8C 1M9
819-326-4595 Fax: 819-326-5784
info@ville.sainte-agathe-des-monts.qc.ca
www.ville.sainte-agathe-des-monts.qc.ca
Municipal Type: City
Incorporated: 27 février 2002; *Area:* 129,03 km2
County or District: Les Laurentides; *Population in 2006:* 9,679
Provincial Electoral District(s): Bertrand
Federal Electoral District(s): Laurentides-Labelle
Next Election: 1er novembre 2013
Benoît Fugère, Greffier
Laurent Paquette, Maire

Sainte-Angèle-de-Mérici
CP 129
23, rue de la Fabrique
Sainte-Angèle-de-Mérici, QC G0J 2H0
418-775-7733 Fax: 418-775-5722
municipalitesteangele@globetrotter.net
Municipal Type: Municipality
Incorporated: 26 avril 1989; *Area:* 108,41 km2
County or District: La Mitis; *Population in 2006:* 1,068
Provincial Electoral District(s): Matapédia
Federal Electoral District(s): Haute-Gaspésie-La Mitis-Matane-Matapédia
Next Election: 1er novembre 2013
Marielle Dionne, Sec.-Trés. & Directrice générale

Sainte-Angèle-de-Monnoir
7, ch du Vide
Sainte-Angèle-de-Monnoir, QC J0L 1P0
450-460-7838 Fax: 450-460-3853
steangeledemonnoir@videotron.ca
Municipal Type: Parish (Paroisse)
Incorporated: 15 mars 1865; *Area:* 45,49 km2
County or District: Rouville; *Population in 2006:* 1,163
Provincial Electoral District(s): Iberville
Federal Electoral District(s): Shefford
Next Election: 1er novembre 2013
Jacqueline Houle, Directrice générale

Sainte-Angèle-de-Prémont
2451, rue Camirand
Sainte-Angèle-de-Prémont, QC J0K 1R0
819-268-5526 Fax: 819-268-5536
ste-angele@infoteck.qc.ca
Municipal Type: Municipality
Incorporated: 28 août 1917; *Area:* 38,51 km2
County or District: Maskinongé; *Population in 2006:* 663
Provincial Electoral District(s): Maskinongé
Federal Electoral District(s): Berthier-Maskinongé
Next Election: 1er novembre 2013
Josée Deschesnes, Sec.-Trés.

Sainte-Anne-de-Beaupré
9336, av Royale
Sainte-Anne-de-Beaupré, QC G0A 3C0
418-827-3191 Fax: 418-827-8275
steannedebeaupre@bellnet.ca
Municipal Type: City
Incorporated: 27 janvier 1973; *Area:* 64,38 km2
County or District: La Côte-de-Beaupré; *Population in 2006:* 2,803
Provincial Electoral District(s): Charlevoix
Federal Electoral District(s): Montmorency-Charlevoix-Haute-Côte-Nord
Next Election: 1er novembre 2013
Frédéric Drolet-Gervais, Sec.-Trés & Directeur général
Jean-Luc Fortin, Maire

Sainte-Anne-de-la-Pérade
200, rue Principale
Sainte-Anne-de-la-Pérade, QC G0X 2J0
418-325-2841 Fax: 418-325-3070
municipalite@sainteannedelaperade.net
www.sainteannedelaperade.net
Municipal Type: Municipality
Incorporated: 10 mai 1989; *Area:* 107,94 km2
County or District: Les Chenaux; *Population in 2006:* 1,991
Provincial Electoral District(s): Champlain
Federal Electoral District(s): St-Maurice-Champlain
Next Election: 1er novembre 2013
René Roy, Sec.-Trés.

Sainte-Anne-de-la-Pocatière
395, ch des Sables est
Sainte-Anne-de-la-Pocatière, QC G0R 1Z0
418-856-3192 Fax: 418-856-9936
ste-anne-de-la-pocatiere@bellnet.ca
Municipal Type: Parish (Paroisse)
Incorporated: 1er juillet 1855; *Area:* 53,68 km2
County or District: Kamouraska; *Population in 2006:* 1,843
Provincial Electoral District(s): Kamouraska-Témiscouata
Federal Electoral District(s): Montmagny-L'Islet-Kamouraska-Rivière-du-Loup
Next Election: 1er novembre 2013
Sylvie Dionne, Sec.-Trés.

Sainte-Anne-de-la-Rochelle
145, rue l'Église
Sainte-Anne-de-la-Rochelle, QC J0E 2B0
450-539-1654 Fax: 450-539-2317
mun.steannedelarochelle@qc.aira.com
Municipal Type: Municipality
Incorporated: 1er juillet 1855; *Area:* 60,96 km2
County or District: Le Val-St-François; *Population in 2006:* 642
Provincial Electoral District(s): Brome-Missisquoi
Federal Electoral District(s): Shefford
Next Election: 1er novembre 2013
Magella René, Sec.-Trés.

Sainte-Anne-de-Sabrevois
CP 60
1218, rte 133
Sabrevois, QC J0J 2G0
450-347-0066 Fax: 450-347-4040
info.sabrevois@videotron.ca
Municipal Type: Parish (Paroisse)
Incorporated: 1er mars 1888; *Area:* 45,24 km2
County or District: Le Haut-Richelieu; *Population in 2006:* 1,889
Provincial Electoral District(s): Iberville
Federal Electoral District(s): St-Jean
Next Election: 1er novembre 2013
Fredy Serreyn, Sec.-Trés.

Sainte-Anne-de-Sorel
1685, ch du Chenal-du-Moine
Sainte-Anne-de-Sorel, QC J3P 5N3
450-742-1616 Fax: 450-742-1118
info@sainteannedesorel.ca
www.sainteannedesorel.ca
Municipal Type: Municipality
Incorporated: 14 mai 1877; *Area:* 36,51 km2
County or District: Pierre-De Saurel; *Population in 2009:* 2,803
Provincial Electoral District(s): Richelieu
Federal Electoral District(s): Bas-Richelieu-Nicolet-Bécancour
Next Election: 1er novembre 2013
Maxime Dauplaise, Directeur général

Sainte-Anne-des-Lacs
773, ch de Ste-Anne-des-Lacs
Sainte-Anne-des-Lacs, QC J0R 1B0
450-224-2675 Fax: 450-224-8672
info@sadl.qc.ca
Municipal Type: Parish (Paroisse)
Incorporated: 28 mars 1946; *Area:* 23,45 km2
County or District: Les Pays-d'en-Haut; *Population in 2006:* 3,029
Provincial Electoral District(s): Bertrand
Federal Electoral District(s): Laurentides-Labelle
Next Election: 1er novembre 2013
Jean-François René, Sec.-Trés. & Directeur général

Sainte-Anne-des-Monts
6, 1re av ouest
Sainte-Anne-des-Monts, QC G4V 1A1
418-763-5511 Fax: 418-763-3473
sadmonts@globetrotter.net
www.villesainte-anne-des-monts.qc.ca
Municipal Type: City
Incorporated: 2 février 2000; *Area:* 263,62 km2
County or District: La Haute-Gaspésie; *Population in 2006:* 6,772
Provincial Electoral District(s): Matane
Federal Electoral District(s): Haute-Gaspésie-La Mitis-Matane-Matapédia
Next Election: 1er novembre 2013
Micheline Pelletier, Mairesse
Sylvie Lepage, Greffière

Sainte-Anne-du-Lac
1, rue St-François-Xavier
Sainte-Anne-du-Lac, QC J0W 1V0

819-586-2110 Fax: 819-586-2203
sainte.anne.du.lac.municipalite@tlb.sympatico.ca
www.municipalite.sainte-anne-du-lac.qc.ca
Municipal Type: Municipality
Incorporated: 30 décembre 1976; *Area:* 345,28 km2
County or District: Antoine-Labelle; *Population in 2006:* 613
Provincial Electoral District(s): Labelle
Federal Electoral District(s): Laurentides-Labelle
Next Election: 1er novembre 2013
Denise Bélec, Sec.-Trés. & Directrice générale

Sainte-Anne-du-Sault
539, rte Principale
Sainte-Anne-du-Sault, QC G0Z 1C0
819-367-2210 Fax: 819-367-4011
munstann@tlb.sympatico.ca
Municipal Type: Municipality
Incorporated: 21 mars 1889; *Area:* 56,09 km2
County or District: Arthabaska; *Population in 2006:* 1,315
Provincial Electoral District(s): Nicolet-Yamaska
Federal Electoral District(s): Richmond-Arthabaska
Next Election: 1er novembre 2013
Lyne Bertrand, Sec.-Trés.

Sainte-Apolline-de-Patton
105, rte de l'Église
Sainte-Apolline-de-Patton, QC G0R 2P0
418-469-3031 Fax: 418-469-3051
munapoli@globetrotter.net
Municipal Type: Parish (Paroisse)
Incorporated: 14 décembre 1909; *Area:* 255,70 km2
County or District: Montmagny; *Population in 2006:* 678
Provincial Electoral District(s): Montmagny-L'Islet
Federal Electoral District(s):
Montamagny-L'Islet-Kamouraska-Rivière-du-Loup
Next Election: 1er novembre 2013
Doris Godbout, Sec.-Trés.

Sainte-Aurélie
151A, ch des Bois Francs
Sainte-Aurélie, QC G0M 1M0
418-593-3021 Fax: 418-593-3961
munsteau@sogetel.net
Municipal Type: Municipality
Incorporated: 3 avril 1909; *Area:* 78,52 km2
County or District: Les Etchemins; *Population in 2006:* 965
Provincial Electoral District(s): Beauce-Sud
Federal Electoral District(s): Beauce
Next Election: 1er novembre 2013
Sophie Fortin, Sec.-Trés. & Directrice générale

Sainte-Barbe
470, ch de l'Église
Sainte-Barbe, QC J0S 1P0
450-371-2504 Fax: 450-371-2575
info@ste-barbe.com
Municipal Type: Parish (Paroisse)
Incorporated: 12 juin 1882; *Area:* 39,78 km2
County or District: Le Haut-St-Laurent; *Population in 2006:* 1,453
Provincial Electoral District(s): Huntingdon
Federal Electoral District(s): Beauharnois-Salaberry
Next Election: 1er novembre 2013
Chantal Girouard, Sec.-Trés.

Sainte-Béatrix
861, rue de l'Église
Sainte-Béatrix, QC J0K 1Y0
450-883-2245 Fax: 450-883-1772
mun.stebeatrix@qc.aira.com
Municipal Type: Municipality
Incorporated: 11 mai 1864; *Area:* 83,52 km2
County or District: Matawinie; *Population in 2006:* 1,788
Provincial Electoral District(s): Berthier
Federal Electoral District(s): Joliette
Next Election: 1er novembre 2013
Michel St-Laurent, Sec.-Trés. & Directeur général

Sainte-Brigide-d'Iberville
480, rue de l'Hôtel-de-Ville
Sainte-Brigide-d'Iberville, QC J0J 1X0
450-293-7511 Fax: 450-293-1077
ste_brigide@bellnet.ca
www.sainte-brigide.qc.ca
Municipal Type: Municipality
Incorporated: 1er juillet 1855; *Area:* 68,89 km2
County or District: Le Haut-Richelieu; *Population in 2006:* 1,223
Provincial Electoral District(s): Iberville
Federal Electoral District(s): St-Jean
Next Election: 1er novembre 2013
Murielle Papineau, Directrice générale

Sainte-Brigitte-de-Laval
414, av Ste-Brigitte
Sainte-Brigitte-de-Laval, QC G0A 3K0
418-825-2515 Fax: 418-825-3114
gbussieres@sbdl.net
www.sbdl.net
Municipal Type: Municipality
Incorporated: 11 février 1875; *Area:* 111,49 km2
County or District: La Jacques-Cartier; *Population in 2006:* 3,790
Provincial Electoral District(s): Montmorency
Federal Electoral District(s): Portneuf-Jacques Cartier
Next Election: 1er novembre 2007
Pierre Vallée, Maire

Sainte-Brigitte-des-Saults
CP 1051
400, rue Principale
Sainte-Brigitte-des-Saults, QC J0C 1E0
819-336-4460 Fax: 819-336-4410
muni.ste-brigitte@mrcdrummond.qc.ca
Municipal Type: Parish (Paroisse)
Incorporated: 9 mars 1878; *Area:* 69,23
County or District: Drummond; *Population in 2006:* 739
Provincial Electoral District(s): Nicolet-Yamaska
Federal Electoral District(s): Drummond
Next Election: 1er novembre 2013
Nicole Comtois, Directrice générale

Sainte-Catherine-de-Hatley
CP 30
35, ch de North Hatley
Sainte-Catherine-de-Hatley, QC J0B 1W0
819-843-1935 Fax: 819-843-8527
munstecatherinehatley@qc.aira.com
Municipal Type: Municipality
Incorporated: 28 mars 1901; *Area:* 81,43 km2
County or District: Memphrémagog; *Population in 2006:* 2,318
Provincial Electoral District(s): Orford
Federal Electoral District(s): Compton-Stanstead
Next Election: 1er novembre 2013
Colette St-Martin, Sec.-Trés.

Sainte-Catherine-de-la-Jacques-Cartier
CP 250
1, rue Rouleau
Ste-Catherine-de-la-J-Cartier, QC G0A 3M0
418-875-2758 Fax: 418-875-2170
sainte-catherine-de-la-jacques-cartier@coopcscf.com
Municipal Type: City
Incorporated: 1er juillet 1855; *Area:* 120,61 km2
County or District: La Jacques-Cartier; *Population in 2006:* 5,021
Provincial Electoral District(s): Portneuf
Federal Electoral District(s): Portneuf-Jacques-Cartier
Next Election: 1er novembre 2013
Marcel Grenier, Sec.-Trés. & Directeur général
Jacques Marcotte, Maire

Sainte-Cécile-de-Lévrard
235, rue Principale
Sainte-Cécile-de-Lévrard, QC G0X 2M0
819-263-2104 Fax: 819-263-1043
munstececilelvrd@bellnet.ca
Municipal Type: Parish (Paroisse)
Incorporated: 11 septembre 1908; *Area:* 33,35 km2
County or District: Bécancour; *Population in 2006:* 417
Provincial Electoral District(s): Lotbinière
Federal Electoral District(s): Bas-Richelieu-Nicolet-Bécancour
Next Election: 1er novembre 2013
Réjean Poisson, Sec.-Trés.

Sainte-Cécile-de-Milton
CP 195
136, rue Principale
Sainte-Cécile-de-Milton, QC J0E 2C0
450-378-1942 Fax: 450-378-4621
mun@stececiledemilton.qc.ca
Municipal Type: Township
Incorporated: 1er janvier 1864; *Area:* 74,04 km2
County or District: La Haute-Yamaska; *Population in 2006:* 2,024
Provincial Electoral District(s): Johnson
Federal Electoral District(s): Shefford
Next Election: 1er novembre 2013
Monique Fortin, Sec.-Trés. & Directrice générale

Sainte-Cécile-de-Whitton
4557, rue Principale
Sainte-Cécile-de-Whitton, QC G0Y 1J0
819-583-0770 Fax: 819-583-4149
muncecilewhitton@axion.ca
www.mrcgranit.qc.ca/stececile.html
Municipal Type: Municipality
Incorporated: 19 septembre 1889; *Area:* 146,59 km2
County or District: Le Granit; *Population in 2006:* 899
Provincial Electoral District(s): Mégantic-Compton
Federal Electoral District(s): Mégantic-L'Érable
Next Election: 1er novembre 2013
Linda Deschiever, Sec.-Trés. & Directrice générale

Sainte-Christine
629, rue des Loisirs
Sainte-Christine, QC J0H 1H0
819-858-2828 Fax: 819-858-9911
france.tetreault@mrcacton.qc.ca
Municipal Type: Parish (Paroisse)
Incorporated: 8 janvier 1894; *Area:* 89,40 km2
County or District: Acton; *Population in 2006:* 560
Provincial Electoral District(s): Johnson
Federal Electoral District(s): St-Hyacinthe-Bagot
Next Election: 1er novembre 2013
France Tétreault, Sec.-Trés.

Sainte-Christine-d'Auvergne
80, rue Principale
Sainte-Christine-d'Auvergne, QC G0A 1A0
418-329-3304 Fax: 418-329-3356
ste-christine@globetrotter.net
Municipal Type: Municipality
Incorporated: 10 avril 1896; *Area:* 145,58 km2
County or District: Portneuf; *Population in 2006:* 462
Provincial Electoral District(s): Portneuf
Federal Electoral District(s): Portneuf-Jacques Cartier
Next Election: 1er novembre 2013
Nathalie Matte, Sec.-Trés. & Directrice générale

Sainte-Claire
135, rue Principale
Sainte-Claire, QC G0R 2V0
418-883-3314 Fax: 418-883-3845
msclaire@globetrotter.qc.ca
www.municipalite.sainte-claire.qc.ca
Municipal Type: Municipality
Incorporated: 1er octobre 1977; *Area:* 88,63 km2
County or District: Bellechasse; *Population in 2006:* 3,097
Provincial Electoral District(s): Bellechasse
Federal Electoral District(s): Lévis-Bellechasse
Next Election: 1er novembre 2013
Serge Gagnon, Sec.-Trés. & Directeur général

Sainte-Clotilde-de-Beauce
307B, rue du Couvent
Sainte-Clotilde-de-Beauce, QC G0N 1C0
418-427-2637 Fax: 418-427-4303
steclotilde@hotmail.com
www.ste-clotilde.com
Municipal Type: Municipality
Incorporated: 19 novembre 1938; *Area:* 58,680 km2
County or District: Les Appalaches; *Population in 2009:* 569
Provincial Electoral District(s): Beauce-Sud
Federal Electoral District(s): Mégantic-L'Érable
Next Election: 1er novembre 2013
Sandy Grenier, Directrice générale

Sainte-Clotilde-de-Châteauguay
2452, ch de l'Église
Sainte-Clotilde-de-Châteauguay, QC J0L 1W0
450-826-3129 Fax: 450-826-3217
mun.steclotilde@rocler.qc.ca
Municipal Type: Parish (Paroisse)
Incorporated: 2 avril 1885; *Area:* 78,96 km2
County or District: Les Jardins-de-Napierville; *Population in 2006:* 1,608
Provincial Electoral District(s): Huntingdon
Federal Electoral District(s): Beauharnois-Salaberry
Next Election: 1er novembre 2013
Nicole Marcil, Sec.-Trés.

Sainte-Clotilde-de-Horton
CP 29
17, rte 122
Sainte-Clotilde-de-Horton, QC J0A 1H0
819-336-5344 Fax: 819-336-5440
info@steclotildedehorton.ca
www.steclotildedehorton.ca
Municipal Type: Municipality
Incorporated: 26 mars 1997; *Area:* 118,44 km2
County or District: Arthabaska; *Population in 2006:* 1,560
Provincial Electoral District(s): Richmond
Federal Electoral District(s): Richmond-Arthabaska
Next Election: 1er novembre 2013
Marlène Langlois, Directrice générale

Sainte-Croix
6310, rue Principale
Sainte-Croix, QC G0S 2H0
418-926-3494 Fax: 418-926-2570
stecroix@globetrotter.net
www.ville.sainte-croix.qc.ca
Municipal Type: Municipality
Incorporated: 5 octobre 2001; *Area:* 69,64 km2
County or District: Lotbinière; *Population in 2006:* 2,390
Provincial Electoral District(s): Lotbinière
Federal Electoral District(s): Lotbinière-Chutes-de-la-Chaudière
Next Election: 1er novembre 2013
Bertrand Fréchette, Directeur général

Sainte-Edwidge-de-Clifton
203, rue Principale Nord
Sainte-Edwidge-de-Clifton, QC J0B 2R0
819-849-7740 Fax: 819-849-4212
steedwidge@axion.ca
Municipal Type: Township
Incorporated: 21 décembre 1895; *Area:* 99,35 km2
County or District: Coaticook; *Population in 2006:* 440
Provincial Electoral District(s): Mégantic-Compton
Federal Electoral District(s): Compton-Stanstead
Next Election: 1er novembre 2013
Réjean Fauteux, Sec.-Trés.

Sainte-Élisabeth
2270, rue Principale
Sainte-Élisabeth, QC J0K 2J0
450-759-2875 Fax: 450-756-4312
steelisabeth@qc.aira.com
www.ste-elisabeth.qc.ca
Municipal Type: Parish (Paroisse)
Incorporated: 1er juillet 1855; *Area:* 81,66 km2
County or District: D'Autray; *Population in 2006:* 1,440
Provincial Electoral District(s): Berthier
Federal Electoral District(s): Joliette
Next Election: 1er novembre 2013
Pauline Ladouceur, Sec.-Trés. & Directrice générale

Sainte-Elizabeth-de-Warwick
230, rue Principale
Sainte-Elizabeth-de-Warwick, QC J0A 1M0
819-358-5162 Fax: 819-358-9192
munstelizw@telwarwick.net
Municipal Type: Parish (Paroisse)
Incorporated: 18 mai 1887; *Area:* 50,51 km2
County or District: Arthabaska; *Population in 2006:* 368
Provincial Electoral District(s): Richmond
Federal Electoral District(s): Richmond-Arthabaska
Next Election: 1er novembre 2013
Josée Leblond, Directrice générale

Sainte-Émélie-de-l'Énergie
241, rue Coutu
Sainte-Émélie-de-l'Énergie, QC J0K 2K0
450-886-3823 Fax: 450-886-9175
stemelie@intermonde.net
Municipal Type: Municipality
Incorporated: 10 juin 1884; *Area:* 170,68 km2
County or District: Matawinie; *Population in 2006:* 1,681
Provincial Electoral District(s): Berthier
Federal Electoral District(s): Joliette
Next Election: 1er novembre 2013
Brigitte Belleville, Sec.-Trés. & Directrice générale

Sainte-Eulalie
757, rue des Bouleaux
Sainte-Eulalie, QC G0Z 1E0
819-225-4345 Fax: 819-225-4078
municipalite@sainte-eulalie.net
www.sainte-eulalie.net
Municipal Type: Municipality
Incorporated: 1er juillet 1864; *Area:* 90,79 km2
County or District: Nicolet-Yamaska; *Population in 2006:* 894
Provincial Electoral District(s): Nicolet-Yamaska
Federal Electoral District(s): Bas-Richelieu-Nicolet-Bécancour
Next Election: 1er novembre 2013
Lucie Blanchette, Sec.

Sainte-Famille
3894, ch Royal
Sainte-Famille, QC G0A 3P0
418-829-3572 Fax: 418-829-2513
stefamille@hotmail.com
Municipal Type: Parish (Paroisse)
Incorporated: 1er juillet 1855; *Area:* 46,43 km2
County or District: L'Ile-d'Orléans; *Population in 2006:* 844
Provincial Electoral District(s): Montmorency
Federal Electoral District(s):
Montmorency-Charlevoix-Haute-Côte-Nord
Next Election: 1er novembre 2013
Sylvie Beaulieu, Sec.-Trés.

Sainte-Félicité
5, rte de l'Église nord
Sainte-Félicité, QC G0R 4P0
418-359-2321 Fax: 418-359-2321
mun.ste-felicite@globetrotter.net
Municipal Type: Municipality
Incorporated: 1er janvier 1950; *Area:* 95,82 km2
County or District: L'Islet; *Population in 2006:* 422
Provincial Electoral District(s): Montmagny-L'Islet
Federal Electoral District(s):
Montmagny-l'Islet-Kamouraska-Rivière-du-Loup
Next Election: 1er novembre 2013
Julie Bélanger, Sec.-Trés.

Sainte-Félicité
CP 9
192, rue St-Joseph
Sainte-Félicité, QC G0J 2K0
418-733-4628 Fax: 418-733-8377
mustefelicite@globetrotter.net
Municipal Type: Municipality
Incorporated: 10 janvier 1996; *Area:* 89,76 km2
County or District: Matane; *Population in 2006:* 1,201
Provincial Electoral District(s): Matane
Federal Electoral District(s): Haute-Gaspésie-La Mitis-Matane-Matapédia
Next Election: 1er novembre 2013
Yves Chassé, Sec.-Trés.

Sainte-Flavie
775, rte Jacques-Cartier
Sainte-Flavie, QC G0J 2L0
418-775-7050 Fax: 418-775-5672
munflavie@globetrotter.net
www.municipalite.sainte-flavie.qc.ca
Municipal Type: Parish (Paroisse)
Incorporated: 1er juillet 1855; *Area:* 37,62 km2
County or District: La Mitis; *Population in 2006:* 943
Provincial Electoral District(s): Matapédia
Federal Electoral District(s): Haute-Gaspésie-La Mitis-Matane-Matapédia
Next Election: 1er novembre 2013
Suzanne Landreville, Sec.-Trés.

Sainte-Florence
CP 9
29, rue des Loisirs
Sainte-Florence, QC G0J 2M0
418-756-3491 Fax: 418-756-5079
munisflo@globetrotter.net
Municipal Type: Municipality
Incorporated: 12 avril 1911; *Area:* 103,00 km2
County or District: La Matapédia; *Population in 2006:* 458
Provincial Electoral District(s): Matapédia
Federal Electoral District(s): Haute-Gaspésie-La Mitis-Matane-Matapédia
Next Election: 1er novembre 2013
Huguette Gagné, Sec.-Trés.

Sainte-Françoise
563, 11e rang est
Sainte-Françoise-de-Lotbinière, QC G0S 2N0
819-287-5755 Fax: 819-287-5838
municipalite@ste-francoise.com
Municipal Type: Municipality
Incorporated: 1er janvier 1947; *Area:* 89,12 km2
County or District: Bécancour; *Population in 2006:* 471
Provincial Electoral District(s): Lotbinière
Federal Electoral District(s): Bas-Richelieu-Nicolet-Bécancour
Next Election: 1er novembre 2013
Isabelle Dubois, Sec.-Trés.

Sainte-Françoise
156, rue Jérémie-Beaulieu
Sainte-Françoise, QC G0L 3B0
418-851-1502 Fax: 418-851-0926
stefrancoise@intermobilex.com
Municipal Type: Parish (Paroisse)
Incorporated: 6 décembre 1873; *Area:* 88,54 km2
County or District: Les Basques; *Population in 2006:* 431
Provincial Electoral District(s): Rivière-du-Loup
Federal Electoral District(s): Rimouski-Neigette-Témiscouata-Les Basques
Next Election: 1er novembre 2013
Véronique Pelletier, Sec.-Trés. & Directrice générale

Sainte-Geneviève-de-Batiscan
30, rue St-Charles
Sainte-Geneviève-de-Batiscan, QC G0X 2R0
418-362-2078 Fax: 418-362-2111
municipalite@stegenevieve.ca
www.stegenevieve.ca
Municipal Type: Parish (Paroisse)
Incorporated: 1er juillet 1855; *Area:* 97,09 km2
County or District: Les Chenaux; *Population in 2006:* 1,036
Provincial Electoral District(s): Champlain
Federal Electoral District(s): St-Maurice-Champlain
Next Election: 1er novembre 2013
Line Blais, Sec.-Trés.

Sainte-Geneviève-de-Berthier
400, rang de la Rivière-Bayonne sud
Sainte-Geneviève-de-Berthier, QC J0K 1A0
450-836-4333 Fax: 450-836-7260
munisgb@autray.net
Municipal Type: Parish (Paroisse)
Incorporated: 1er juillet 1855; *Area:* 74,67
County or District: D'Autray; *Population in 2006:* 2,307
Provincial Electoral District(s): Berthier
Federal Electoral District(s): Berthier-Maskinongé
Next Election: 1er novembre 2013
Réjean Marsolais, Sec.-Trés. & Directeur général

Sainte-Germaine-Boulé
CP 5 Boulé
199, rue Roy
Sainte-Germaine-Boulé, QC J0Z 1M0
819-787-6221 Fax: 819-787-2560
stegermaine@ste-germaine.ao.ca
www.ste-germaine.ao.ca
Municipal Type: Municipality
Incorporated: 1er janvier 1954; *Area:* 108,46 km2
County or District: Abitibi-Ouest; *Population in 2006:* 942
Provincial Electoral District(s): Abitibi-Ouest
Federal Electoral District(s): Abitibi-Témiscamingue
Next Election: 1er novembre 2013
Gisèle Bisson-Lapointe, Sec.-Trés. & Directrice générale

Sainte-Gertrude-Manneville
391, rte 395
Sainte-Gertrude-Manneville, QC J0Y 2L0
819-727-2244 Fax: 819-727-3293
stegertman@hotmail.com
Municipal Type: Municipality
Incorporated: 1er janvier 1980; *Area:* 329,84 km2
County or District: Abitibi; *Population in 2006:* 811
Provincial Electoral District(s): Abitibi-Ouest
Federal Electoral District(s): Abitibi-Témiscamingue
Next Election: 1er novembre 2013
Gertrude Bilodeau, Sec.-Trés.

Sainte-Hedwidge
1090, rue Principale
Sainte-Hedwidge, QC G0W 2R0
418-275-3020 Fax: 418-275-4163
mustehed@destination.ca
Municipal Type: Municipality
Incorporated: 10 mars 1909; *Area:* 469,07 km2
County or District: Le Domaine-du-Roy; *Population in 2006:* 820
Provincial Electoral District(s): Roberval
Federal Electoral District(s): Roberval-Lac-St-Jean
Next Election: 1er novembre 2013
Sylvain Privé, Sec.-Trés.

Sainte-Hélène
CP 216
531, rue de l'Église sud
Sainte-Hélène, QC G0L 3J0
418-492-6830 Fax: 418-492-1854
munhel@bellnet.ca
Municipal Type: Parish (Paroisse)
Incorporated: 1er juillet 1855; *Area:* 60,34 km2
County or District: Kamouraska; *Population in 2006:* 897
Provincial Electoral District(s): Kamouraska-Témiscouata
Federal Electoral District(s):
Montmagny-L'Islet-Kamourask-Rivière-du-Loup
Next Election: 1er novembre 2013
Nathalie Blais, Sec.-Trés.

Sainte-Hélène-de-Bagot
379, 7e av
Sainte-Hélène-de-Bagot, QC J0H 1M0
450-791-2455 Fax: 450-791-2550
line.lupien@mrcmaskoutains.qc.ca
Municipal Type: Municipality
Incorporated: 9 juillet 1977; *Area:* 73,53 km2
County or District: Les Maskoutains; *Population in 2006:* 1,446
Provincial Electoral District(s): Johnson
Federal Electoral District(s): St-Hyacinthe-Bagot
Next Election: 1er novembre 2013
Line Lupien, Sec.-Trés.

Sainte-Hélène-de-Mancebourg
451, rang 2e-et-3e
Mancebourg, QC J0Z 2T0
819-333-5766 Fax: 819-333-9514
mancebourg@mrcao.qc.ca
www.ste-helene.ao.ca
Municipal Type: Parish (Paroisse)
Incorporated: 10 mai 1941; *Area:* 68,29 km2
County or District: Abitibi-Ouest; *Population in 2006:* 375
Provincial Electoral District(s): Abitibi-Ouest
Federal Electoral District(s): Abitibi-Témiscamingue
Next Election: 1er novembre 2013
Sylvie Boutin-Bergeron, Sec.-Trés.

Sainte-Hénédine
CP 6
111, rue Principale
Sainte-Hénédine, QC G0S 2R0
418-935-7125 Fax: 418-935-3113
munisthe@globetrotter.net
Municipal Type: Parish (Paroisse)
Incorporated: 1er juillet 1855; *Area:* 53,06
County or District: La Nouvelle-Beauce; *Population in 2006:* 1,073
Provincial Electoral District(s): Beauce-Nord
Federal Electoral District(s): Beauce
Next Election: 1er novembre 2013
Yvon Marcoux, Sec.-Trés.

Sainte-Irène
362, rue de la Fabrique
Sainte-Irène, QC G0J 2P0
418-629-5705 Fax: 418-629-3220
steirene@globetrotter.net
Municipal Type: Parish (Paroisse)
Incorporated: 1er janvier 1953; *Area:* 134,03
County or District: La Matapédia; *Population in 2006:* 350
Provincial Electoral District(s): Matapédia
Federal Electoral District(s): Haute-Gaspésie-La Mitis-Matane-Matapédia
Next Election: 1er novembre 2013
Lucie Desjardins, Sec.-Trés.

Sainte-Jeanne-d'Arc
CP 40
205, rue Principale
Sainte-Jeanne-d'Arc, QC G0J 2T0
418-776-5660 Fax: 418-776-5660
stejeanne@mitis.qc.ca
Municipal Type: Parish (Paroisse)
Incorporated: 30 janvier 1922; *Area:* 110,82 km2
County or District: La Mitis; *Population in 2006:* 322
Provincial Electoral District(s): Matapédia
Federal Electoral District(s): Haute-Gaspésie-La Mitis-Matane-Matapédia
Next Election: 1er novembre 2013
Louise Boivin, Sec.-Trés. & Directrice générale

Sainte-Jeanne-d'Arc
378, rue François-Bilodeau
Sainte-Jeanne-d'Arc, QC G0W 1E0
418-276-3166 Fax: 418-276-7648
jeannerm@destination.ca
Municipal Type: Village
Incorporated: 24 janvier 1970; *Area:* 270,88 km2
County or District: Maria-Chapdelaine; *Population in 2006:* 1,139
Provincial Electoral District(s): Roberval
Federal Electoral District(s): Roberval-Lac-St-Jean
Next Election: 1er novembre 2013
Régis Martin, Sec.-Trés.

Sainte-Julienne
1400, rte 125
Sainte-Julienne, QC J0K 2T0
450-831-2688 Fax: 450-831-4433
municipalite@sainte-julienne.com
www.sainte-julienne.com

Municipal Type: Municipality
Incorporated: 1er juillet 1855; *Area:* 102,10 km2
County or District: Montcalm; *Population in 2009:* 8,303
Provincial Electoral District(s): Rousseau
Federal Electoral District(s): Montcalm
Next Election: 1er novembre 2013
Claude Arcoragi, Directeur général

Sainte-Justine
167, rte 204
Sainte-Justine, QC G0R 1Y0
418-383-5397 Fax: 418-383-5398
sjustine@sogetel.net
www.stejustine.net
Municipal Type: Municipality
Incorporated: 1er janvier 1870; *Area:* 124,55 km2
County or District: Les Etchemins; *Population in 2006:* 1,825
Provincial Electoral District(s): Bellechasse
Federal Electoral District(s): Lévis-Bellechasse
Next Election: 1er novembre 2013
Gilles Vézina, Sec.-Trés.

Sainte-Justine-de-Newton
CP 270
2627, rue Principale
Sainte-Justine-de-Newton, QC J0P 1T0
450-764-3573 Fax: 450-764-3180
ste-justine@rocler.qc.ca
Municipal Type: Parish (Paroisse)
Incorporated: 1er juillet 1855; *Area:* 84,14 km2
County or District: Vaudreuil-Soulanges; *Population in 2006:* 929
Provincial Electoral District(s): Soulanges
Federal Electoral District(s): Vaudreuil-Soulanges
Next Election: 1er novembre 2007
Denis Perrier, Directeur général

Sainte-Louise
CP 2130
80, rte de la Station
Sainte-Louise, QC G0R 3K0
418-354-2509 Fax: 418-354-7730
ste-louise@globetrotter.net
www.saintelouise.qc.ca
Municipal Type: Parish (Paroisse)
Incorporated: 11 décembre 1860; *Area:* 73,03 km2
County or District: L'Islet; *Population in 2006:* 704
Provincial Electoral District(s): Kamouraska-Témiscouata
Federal Electoral District(s):
Montmagny-L'Islet-Kamouraska-Rivière-du-Loup
Next Election: 1er novembre 2013
Ghislain Lizotte, Sec.-Trés.

Sainte-Luce
1, rue Langlois
Sainte-Luce, QC G0K 1P0
418-739-4317 Fax: 418-739-4823
mun.ste-luce@cgocable.ca
www.municipalite.sainte-luce.qc.ca
Municipal Type: Municipality
Incorporated: 29 octobre 2001; *Area:* 74,88 km2
County or District: La Mitis; *Population in 2006:* 2,934
Provincial Electoral District(s): Matapédia
Federal Electoral District(s): Haute-Gaspédie-La
Mitis-Matane-Matapédia
Next Election: 1er novembre 2013
Alain Landry, Sec.-Trés.

Sainte-Lucie-de-Beauregard
21, rte des Chutes
Sainte-Lucie-de-Beauregard, QC G0R 3L0
418-223-3122 Fax: 418-223-3121
ste-lucie@globetrotter.net
www.sainteluciedebeauregard.com
Municipal Type: Municipality
Incorporated: 18 novembre 1924; *Area:* 80,18 km2
County or District: Montmagny; *Population in 2006:* 336
Provincial Electoral District(s): Montagny-L'Islet
Federal Electoral District(s):
Montmagny-L'Islet-Kamouraska-Rivière-du-Loup
Next Election: 1er novembre 2013
Yvon Leclerc, Sec.-Trés. & Directeur général

Sainte-Lucie-des-Laurentides
2121, ch des Hauteurs
Sainte-Lucie-des-Laurentides, QC J0T 2J0
819-326-3198 Fax: 819-326-0592
dg@municipalite.sainte-lucie-des-laurentides.qc.ca
Municipal Type: Municipality
Incorporated: 1er janvier 1874; *Area:* 115,15 km2
County or District: Les Laurentides; *Population in 2006:* 1,138
Provincial Electoral District(s): Bertrand
Federal Electoral District(s): Laurentides-Labelle
Next Election: 1er novembre 2013
Ghislain Schoeb, Maire

Sainte-Madeleine
850, rue St-Simon
Sainte-Madeleine, QC J0H 1S0
450-795-3822 Fax: 450-795-3736
administration@villestemadeleine.qc.ca
Municipal Type: Village
Incorporated: 30 décembre 1919; *Area:* 5,39 km2
County or District: Les Maskoutains; *Population in 2006:* 2,175
Provincial Electoral District(s): Verchères
Federal Electoral District(s): St-Hyacinthe-Bagot
Next Election: 1er novembre 2013
Carole Dulude, Sec.-Trés. & Directrice générale

Sainte-Madeleine-de-la-Rivière-Madeleine
104, rte Principale
Madeleine-Centre, QC G0E 1P0
418-393-2428 Fax: 418-393-2869
munste-madeleine@globetrotter.net
Municipal Type: Municipality
Incorporated: 27 février 1915; *Area:* 269,35 km2
County or District: La Haute-Gaspésie; *Population in 2006:* 373
Provincial Electoral District(s): Matane
Federal Electoral District(s): Haute-Gaspésie-La
Mitis-Matane-Matapédia
Next Election: 1er novembre 2013
Suzanne Roy, Directrice générale

Sainte-Marcelline-de-Kildare
500, rue Principale
Sainte-Marcelline-de-Kildare, QC J0K 2Y0
450-883-2241 Fax: 450-883-2242
info@ste-marcelline.com
www.ste-marcelline.com
Municipal Type: Municipality
Incorporated: 1er janvier 1956; *Area:* 33,66 km2
County or District: Matawinie; *Population in 2006:* 1,423
Provincial Electoral District(s): Joliette
Federal Electoral District(s): Joliette
Next Election: 1er novembre 2013
Catherine Haulard, Sec.-Trés. & Directrice générale

Sainte-Marguerite
15, rte de La Vérendrye
Sainte-Marguerite-Marie, QC G0J 2Y0
418-756-3364 Fax: 418-756-3364
sainte.marguerite@globetrotter.net
Municipal Type: Municipality
Incorporated: 1er janvier 1957; *Area:* 83,94 km2
County or District: La Matapédia; *Population in 2006:* 222
Provincial Electoral District(s): Matapédia
Federal Electoral District(s): Haute-Gaspésie-La
Mitis-Matane-Matapédia
Next Election: 1er novembre 2013
Odette Corbin, Sec.-Trés.

Sainte-Marguerite
235, rue St-Jacques
Sainte-Marguerite, QC G0S 2X0
418-935-7103 Fax: 418-935-3709
ste.marguerite@globetrotter.net
Municipal Type: Parish (Paroisse)
Incorporated: 1er juillet 1855; *Area:* 82,56 km2
County or District: La Nouvelle-Beauce; *Population in 2006:* 1,060
Provincial Electoral District(s): Beauce-Nord
Federal Electoral District(s): Beauce
Next Election: 1er novembre 2013
Nicole Chabot, Sec.-Trés.

Sainte-Marguerite-du-Lac-Masson
414, rue de Baron-Louis-Empain
Ste-Marguerite-du-Lac-Masson, QC J0T 1L0
450-228-2543 Fax: 450-228-4008
adm@lacmasson.com
www.ste-marguerite.qc.ca
Municipal Type: City
Incorporated: 17 octobre 2001; *Area:* 98,65 km2
County or District: Les Pays-d'en-Haut; *Population in 2006:* 2,498
Provincial Electoral District(s): Bertrand
Federal Electoral District(s): Laurentides-Labelle
Next Election: 1er novembre 2013
Denis Lemay, Directeur général, Sec.-Trés. & Greffier
André Charbonneau, Maire

Sainte-Marie-de-Blandford
492, rte des Bosquets
Sainte-Marie-de-Blandford, QC G0X 2W0
819-283-2127 Fax: 819-283-2169
munsmb@tlb.sympatico.ca
Municipal Type: Municipality
Incorporated: 23 décembre 1976; *Area:* 68,29 km2
County or District: Bécancour; *Population in 2006:* 517
Provincial Electoral District(s): Lotbinière
Federal Electoral District(s): Bas-Richelieu-Nicolet-Bécancour
Next Election: 1er novembre 2013
Josée Charest, Sec.-Trés.

Sainte-Marie-Madeleine
3541, boul Laurier
Sainte-Marie-Madeleine, QC J0H 1S0
450-795-6272 Fax: 450-795-3180
stemariemadeleine@mrcmaskoutains.qc.ca
Municipal Type: Parish (Paroisse)
Incorporated: 13 août 1879; *Area:* 49,53 km2
County or District: Les Maskoutains; *Population in 2006:* 2,678
Provincial Electoral District(s): Verchères
Federal Electoral District(s): St-Hyacinthe-Bagot
Next Election: 1er novembre 2013
Sylvie Viens, Sec.-Trés. & Directrice générale

Sainte-Marie-Salomé
690, ch St-Jean
Sainte-Marie-Salomé, QC J0K 2Z0
450-839-6212 Fax: 450-839-6106
smsalome@pandore.qc.ca
Municipal Type: Parish (Paroisse)
Incorporated: 27 décembre 1888; *Area:* 34,44 km2
County or District: Montcalm; *Population in 2006:* 1,256
Provincial Electoral District(s): Joliette
Federal Electoral District(s): Montcalm
Next Election: 1er novembre 2013
Denise Desmarais, Sec.-Trés. & Directrice générale

Sainte-Marthe
776, rue des Loisirs
Sainte-Marthe, QC J0P 1W0
450-459-4284 Fax: 450-459-4627
municipalite-stemarthe@sympatico.ca
www.sainte-marthe.ca
Municipal Type: Municipality
Incorporated: 27 décembre 1980; *Area:* 80,23 km2
County or District: Vaudreuil-Soulanges; *Population in 2006:* 1,080
Provincial Electoral District(s): Soulanges
Federal Electoral District(s): Vaudreuil-Soulanges
Next Election: 1er novembre 2013
Bernard Chalebois, Directeur générale

Sainte-Martine
3, rue des Copains
Sainte-Martine, QC J0S 1V0
450-427-3050 Fax: 450-427-7331
info@municipalite.sainte-martine.qc.ca
www.municipalite.sainte-martine.qc.ca
Municipal Type: Municipality
Incorporated: 8 septembre 1999; *Area:* 59,79 km2
County or District: Beauharnois-Salaberry; *Population in 2006:* 4,237
Provincial Electoral District(s): Huntingdon
Federal Electoral District(s): Beauharnois-Salaberry
Next Election: 1er novembre 2013
Luc Laberge, Sec.-Trés. & Directeur général

Sainte-Mélanie
10, rue Louis-Charles-Panet
Sainte-Mélanie, QC J0K 3A0
450-889-5871 Fax: 450-889-4527
info@sainte-melanie.ca
www.sainte-melanie.ca
Municipal Type: Municipality
Incorporated: 1er juillet 1855; *Area:* 77,05 km2
County or District: Joliette; *Population in 2006:* 2,765
Provincial Electoral District(s): Berthier
Federal Electoral District(s): Joliette
Next Election: 1er novembre 2013
Fredette Gilles, Sec.-Trés. & Directrice générale

Sainte-Monique
101, rue Honfleur
Sainte-Monique-de-Honfleur, QC G0W 2T0
418-347-3592 Fax: 418-347-3335
ste-monique@qc.aira.com
Municipal Type: Municipality
Incorporated: 30 octobre 1930; *Area:* 155,15 km2
County or District: Lac-St-Jean-Est; *Population in 2006:* 914
Provincial Electoral District(s): Lac-St-Jean
Federal Electoral District(s): Roberval-Lac-St-Jean
Next Election: 1er novembre 2013
Jean-Claude Duchesne, Sec.-Trés.

Sainte-Monique
247, rue Principale
Sainte-Monique, QC J0G 1N0
819-289-2051 Fax: 819-289-2344
municipalite@municipalitesaintemonique.com
Municipal Type: Municipality
Incorporated: 3 janvier 1996; *Area:* 58,79 km2
County or District: Nicolet-Yamaska; *Population in 2006:* 536
Provincial Electoral District(s): Nicolet-Yamaska
Federal Electoral District(s): Bas-Richelieu-Nicolet-Bécancour
Next Election: 1er novembre 2013
Line Camiré, Sec.-Trés.

Sainte-Paule
191, rue de l'Église
Sainte-Paule, QC G0J 3C0
418-737-4296 Fax: 418-737-9460
munstpau@globetrotter.net
www.municipalite.sainte-paule.qc.ca
Municipal Type: Municipality
Incorporated: 1er janvier 1968; *Area:* 86,64 km2
County or District: Matane; *Population in 2006:* 229
Provincial Electoral District(s): Matane
Federal Electoral District(s): Haute-Gaspésie-La
Mitis-Matane-Matapédia
Next Election: 1er novembre 2013
Gilles Desjardins, Sec.-Trés.

Sainte-Perpétue
#201, 366, rue Principale sud
Sainte-Perpétue, QC G0R 3Z0
418-359-2966 Fax: 418-359-2707
munistep@globetrotter.net
www.sainteperpetue.com
Municipal Type: Municipality
Incorporated: 21 janvier 1888; *Area:* 284,51 km2
County or District: L'Islet; *Population in 2006:* 1,895
Provincial Electoral District(s): Montmagny-L'Islet
Federal Electoral District(s):
Montmagny-L'Islet-Kamouraska-Rivière-du-Loup;
Bas-Richelieu-Nicolet-Bécancour
Next Election: 1er novembre 2013

Marie-Claude Chouinard, Directrice générale

Sainte-Perpétue
CP 98
2480, rang St-Joseph
Sainte-Perpétue, QC J0C 1R0
819-336-6740 Fax: 819-336-6770
municipalite@ste-perpetue.qc.ca
Municipal Type: Parish (Paroisse)
Incorporated: 9 mars 1878; *Area:* 71,14 km2
County or District: Nicolet-Yamaska; *Population in 2006:* 959
Provincial Electoral District(s): Nicolet-Yamaska
Federal Electoral District(s): Bas-Richelieu-Nicolet-Bécancour
Next Election: 1er novembre 2013
Silvie Leclerc, Sec.-Trés.

Sainte-Pétronille
3, ch de l'Église
Sainte-Pétronille, QC G0A 4C0
418-828-2270 Fax: 418-828-1364
ste-petronille@qc.aira.com
Municipal Type: Village
Incorporated: 1er janvier 1874; *Area:* 4,50
County or District: L'Ile-d'Orléans; *Population in 2006:* 1,060
Provincial Electoral District(s): Montmorency
Federal Electoral District(s):
Montmorency-Charlevoix-Haute-Côte-Nord
Next Election: 1er novembre 2013
Gaston Lebel, Sec.-Trés.

Sainte-Praxède
4795, rte 263
Sainte-Praxède, QC G0N 1E0
418-449-2250 Fax: 418-449-2251
mun.stepraxede@globetrotter.net
Municipal Type: Municipality
Incorporated: 1er janvier 1944; *Area:* 135,680 km2
County or District: Les Appalaches; *Population in 2009:* 341
Provincial Electoral District(s): Frontenac
Federal Electoral District(s): Mégantic-L'Érable
Next Election: 1er novembre 2013
Josée Vachon, Directrice générale

Sainte-Rita
CP 39
5, rue de l'Église ouest
Sainte-Rita, QC G0L 4G0
418-963-2967 Fax: 418-963-6539
mun.ste-rita@globetrotter.net
Municipal Type: Municipality
Incorporated: 1er janvier 1948; *Area:* 142,88 km2
County or District: Les Basques; *Population in 2006:* 355
Provincial Electoral District(s): Rivière-du-Loup
Federal Electoral District(s): Rimouski-Neigette-Témiscouata-Les Basques
Next Election: 1er novembre 2013
Brigitte Pelletier, Sec.-Trés.

Sainte-Rose-de-Watford
CP 39
695, rue Carrier
Sainte-Rose-de-Watford, QC G0R 4G0
418-267-5811 Fax: 418-267-5812
municipaliteste-rose@sogetel.net
Municipal Type: Municipality
Incorporated: 17 novembre 1897; *Area:* 112,74 km2
County or District: Les Etchemins; *Population in 2006:* 750
Provincial Electoral District(s): Bellechasse
Federal Electoral District(s): Lévis-Bellechasse
Next Election: 1er novembre 2013
Lyse Audet, Sec.-Trés.

Sainte-Rose-du-Nord
126, rue de la Descente-des-Femmes
Sainte-Rose-du-Nord, QC G0V 1T0
418-675-2250 Fax: 418-675-1149
admin@ste-rosedunord.qc.ca
www.ste-rosedunord.qc.ca
Municipal Type: Parish (Paroisse)
Incorporated: 1er janvier 1942; *Area:* 119,03 km2
County or District: Le Fjord-du-Saguenay; *Population in 2006:* 441
Provincial Electoral District(s): Dubuc
Federal Electoral District(s): Chicoutimi-Le Fjord
Next Election: 1er novembre 2013
Maryse Girard, Sec.-Trés. & Directrice générale

Sainte-Sabine
4, rue St-Charles
Sainte-Sabine, QC G0R 4H0
418-383-5488 Fax: 418-383-5484
munisabine@sogetel.net
pages.globetrotter.net/ste-sabine
Municipal Type: Parish (Paroisse)
Incorporated: 26 août 1908; *Area:* 67,28 km2
County or District: Les Etchemins; *Population in 2006:* 408
Provincial Electoral District(s): Bellechasse
Federal Electoral District(s): Lévis-Bellechasse
Next Election: 1er novembre 2013
Réjeanne Ruel, Sec.-Trés.

Sainte-Sabine
185, rue Principale
Sainte-Sabine, QC J0J 2B0
450-293-7686 Fax: 450-293-7604
ste-sabine@endirect.qc.ca
Municipal Type: Parish (Paroisse)
Incorporated: 19 mars 1921; *Area:* 55,42 km2
County or District: Brome-Missisquoi; *Population in 2006:* 1,053
Provincial Electoral District(s): Brome-Missisquoi
Federal Electoral District(s): Brome-Missisquoi
Next Election: 1er novembre 2013
Johanne Duval, Sec.-Trés.

Sainte-Séraphine
2660, rue du Centre-Communautaire
Sainte-Séraphine, QC J0A 1E0
819-336-3200 Fax: 819-336-3800
munisera@9bit.qc.ca
Municipal Type: Parish (Paroisse)
Incorporated: 7 mars 1931; *Area:* 75,73 km2
County or District: Arthabaska; *Population in 2006:* 401
Provincial Electoral District(s): Richmond
Federal Electoral District(s): Richmond-Arthabaska
Next Election: 1er novembre 2013
Lynda Desrochers, Sec.-Trés.

Sainte-Sophie
2212, rue de l'Hôtel-de-Ville
Sainte-Sophie, QC J5J 1A1
450-438-7784 Fax: 450-438-1080
courrier@municipalite.sainte-sophie.qc.ca
www.municipalite.sainte-sophie.qc.ca
Municipal Type: Municipality
Incorporated: 3 mai 2000; *Area:* 108,98 km2
County or District: La Rivière-du-Nord; *Population in 2009:* 10,962
Provincial Electoral District(s): Rousseau
Federal Electoral District(s): Rivière-du-Nord
Next Election: 1er novembre 2013
André Charron, Directeur général

Sainte-Sophie-d'Halifax
10, rue de l'Église
Sainte-Sophie-d'Halifax, QC G0P 1L0
819-362-2225 Fax: 819-362-2225
Municipal Type: Municipality
Incorporated: 17 décembre 1997; *Area:* 91,11 km2
County or District: L'Érable; *Population in 2006:* 638
Provincial Electoral District(s): Lotbinière
Federal Electoral District(s): Mégantic-L'Érable
Next Election: 1er novembre 2013
Doris Turgeon, Sec.-Trés.

Sainte-Sophie-de-Lévrard
174A, rang St-Antoine
Sainte-Sophie-de-Lévrard, QC G0X 3C0
819-288-5804 Fax: 819-288-5804
municipalite@ste-sophie-de-levrard.com
Municipal Type: Parish (Paroisse)
Incorporated: 23 avril 1875; *Area:* 82,38 km2
County or District: Bécancour; *Population in 2006:* 775
Provincial Electoral District(s): Lotbinière
Federal Electoral District(s): Bas-Richelieu-Nicolet-Bécancour
Next Election: 1er novembre 2013
Micheline St-Onge, Sec.-Trés.

Sainte-Thècle
301, rue St-Jacques
Sainte-Thècle, QC G0X 3G0
418-289-2070 Fax: 418-289-3014
ste-thecle@regionmekinac.com
www.ste-thecle.qc.ca
Municipal Type: Municipality
Incorporated: 7 juin 1989; *Area:* 216,64 km2
County or District: Mékinac; *Population in 2006:* 2,486
Provincial Electoral District(s): Laviolette
Federal Electoral District(s): St-Maurice-Champlain
Next Election: 1er novembre 2013
Louise T.-Rompré, Sec.-Trés.

Sainte-Thérèse-de-Gaspé
CP 160
374, rte 132
Sainte-Thérèse-de-Gaspé, QC G0C 3B0
418-385-3313 Fax: 418-385-3799
muniste@globetrotter.net
Municipal Type: Municipality
Incorporated: 6 septembre 1930; *Area:* 34,36 km2
County or District: Le Rocher-Percé; *Population in 2006:* 1,109
Provincial Electoral District(s): Gaspé
Federal Electoral District(s): Gaspésie-Iles-de-la-Madeleine
Next Election: 1er novembre 2013
Luc Lambert, Sec.-Trés. & Directeur général

Sainte-Thérèse-de-la-Gatineau
CP 155
27, ch Principal
Sainte-Thérèse-de-la-Gatineau, QC J0X 2X0
819-449-4134 Fax: 819-449-2194
mun.ste.therese@ireseau.com
Municipal Type: Municipality
Incorporated: 1er janvier 1946; *Area:* 67,85 km2
County or District: La Vallée-de-la-Gatineau; *Population in 2006:* 335
Provincial Electoral District(s): Gatineau
Federal Electoral District(s): Pontiac
Next Election: 1er novembre 2013
Mélanie Lyrette, Sec.-Trés.

Sainte-Ursule
CP 60
215, rue Lessard
Sainte-Ursule, QC J0K 3M0
819-228-4345 Fax: 819-228-8326
ste-ursule@infoteck.qc.ca
www.ste-ursule.ca
Municipal Type: Parish (Paroisse)
Incorporated: 1er juillet 1855; *Area:* 65,37 km2
County or District: Maskinongé; *Population in 2006:* 1,419
Provincial Electoral District(s): Maskinongé
Federal Electoral District(s): Berthier-Maskinongé
Next Election: 1er novembre 2013
Diane Faucher, Directrice générale

Sainte-Victoire-de-Sorel
517, ch Ste-Victoire
Sainte-Victoire-de-Sorel, QC J0G 1T0
450-782-3111 Fax: 450-782-2687
stevictoire@bas-richelieu.net
Municipal Type: Parish (Paroisse)
Incorporated: 1er juillet 1855; *Area:* 74,90 km2
County or District: Pierre-De Saurel; *Population in 2009:* 2,454
Provincial Electoral District(s): Richelieu
Federal Electoral District(s): Bas-Richelieu-Nicolet-Bécancour
Next Election: 1er novembre 2013
Michel Saint-Martin, Directeur général

Saints-Anges
CP 157
317, rue des Érables
Saints-Anges, QC G0S 3E0
418-253-5230 Fax: 418-253-5613
munsts-anges@nouvellebeauce.com
Municipal Type: Parish (Paroisse)
Incorporated: 29 décembre 1880; *Area:* 68,61 km2
County or District: La Nouvelle-Beauce; *Population in 2006:* 1,032
Provincial Electoral District(s): Beauce-Nord
Federal Electoral District(s): Beauce
Next Election: 1er novembre 2013
Marie-Paule Marquis, Directrice générale & Sec.-Trés.

Saints-Martyrs-Canadiens
13, ch du Village
Saints-Martyrs-Canadiens, QC G0Y 1B0
819-344-5171 Fax: 819-344-5171
bmsmc@ivic.qc.ca
Municipal Type: Parish (Paroisse)
Incorporated: 1er janvier 1943; *Area:* 109,37 km2
County or District: Arthabaska; *Population in 2006:* 253
Provincial Electoral District(s): Richmond
Federal Electoral District(s): Richmond-Arthabaska
Next Election: 1er novembre 2013
Thérèse Lemay, Sec.-Trés. & Directrice générale

Salluit
CP 240
18, Aqqutituqaq Rd.
Salluit, QC J0M 1S0
819-255-8953 Fax: 819-255-8802
nvstreasurer@nvsalluit.ca
www.nvsalluit.ca
Municipal Type: Northern Village
Incorporated: 29 décembre 1979; *Area:* 14,33 km2
County or District: Kativik; *Population in 2006:* 1,241
Provincial Electoral District(s): Ungava
Federal Electoral District(s): Abitibi-Baie-James-Nunavik-Eeyou
Next Election: 7 novembre 2007
Susie P. Alaku, Sec.-Trés.

Sayabec
3, rue Keable
Sayabec, QC G0J 3K0
418-536-5440 Fax: 418-536-5572
municipalitesayabec@globetrotter.net
Municipal Type: Municipality
Incorporated: 24 décembre 1982; *Area:* 130,29 km2
County or District: La Matapédia; *Population in 2006:* 1,953
Provincial Electoral District(s): Matapédia
Federal Electoral District(s): Haute-Gaspésie-La Mitis-Matane-Matapédia
Next Election: 1er novembre 2013
Francis Ouellet, Sec.-Trés. & Directeur général

Schefferville
CP 1600
505, rue Fleming
Schefferville, QC G0G 2T0
418-585-2471 Fax: 418-585-2256
municipalite.schefferville@infonik.net
Municipal Type: City
Incorporated: 1er août 1955; *Area:* 39,02 km2
County or District: Caniapiscau; *Population in 2006:* 202
Provincial Electoral District(s): Duplessis
Federal Electoral District(s): Manicouagan
Next Election: 1er novembre 2013
Marcella Beaudoin, Administratrice
Marcella Beaudoin, Maire

Scotstown
101, ch Victoria ouest
Scotstown, QC J0B 3B0
819-657-4965 Fax: 819-657-1196
scotstown@qc.aira.com

Municipal Type: City
Incorporated: 24 juin 1892; *Area:* 12,40 km2
County or District: Le Haut-St-François; *Population in 2006:* 588
Provincial Electoral District(s): Mégantic-Compton
Federal Electoral District(s): Compton-Stanstead
Next Election: 1er novembre 2013
Claudette Cloutier, Sec.-Trés. & Directrice générale
Solange Bouffard, Mairesse

Scott
1070, rte Kennedy
Scott, QC G0S 3G0
418-387-2037 Fax: 418-387-1837
nthibodeau@municipalitescott.com
Municipal Type: Municipality
Incorporated: 29 mars 1995; *Area:* 32,91 km2
County or District: La Nouvelle-Beauce; *Population in 2006:* 1,796
Provincial Electoral District(s): Beauce-Nord
Federal Electoral District(s): Beauce
Next Election: 1er novembre 2013
Nicole Thibodeau, Sec.-Trés. & Directrice générale

Senneterre
CP 789
551, 10e av
Senneterre, QC J0Y 2M0
819-737-2296 Fax: 819-737-4215
info@ville.senneterre.qc.ca
www.ville.senneterre.qc.ca
Municipal Type: City
Incorporated: 13 juin 1919; *Area:* 16 524,89 km2
County or District: Vallée-de-l'Or; *Population in 2006:* 2,993
Provincial Electoral District(s): Abitibi-Est
Federal Electoral District(s): Abitibi-Baie-James-Nunavik-Eeyou
Next Election: 1er novembre 2013
Hélène Veillette, Greffière
Jean-Maurice Matte, Maire

Senneterre
CP 700
100, rue le Portage
Senneterre, QC J0Y 2M0
819-737-2842 Fax: 819-737-4668
info@paroissesenneterre.qc.ca
Municipal Type: Parish (Paroisse)
Incorporated: 23 mars 1923; *Area:* 432,98 km2
County or District: Vallée-de-l'Or; *Population in 2006:* 1,186
Provincial Electoral District(s): Abitibi-Est
Federal Electoral District(s): Abitibi-Baie-James-Nunavik-Eeyou
Next Election: 1er novembre 2013
Céline Taillefer, Mairesse

Sept-Rivières
#400, 106, rue Napoléon
Sept-Iles, QC G4R 3L7
418-962-1900 Fax: 418-962-3365
mrcsept@globetrotter.net
Municipal Type: Regional County Municipality
Incorporated: 18 mars 1981; *Area:* 32 153,95 km2
Population in 2009: 32,823
Note: 2 municipalités & 2 autres territoires.

Shannon
50, rue St-Patrick
Shannon, QC G0A 4N0
418-844-3778 Fax: 418-844-2111
municipalite@shannon.ca
www.shannon.ca
Municipal Type: Municipality
Incorporated: 1er janvier 1947; *Area:* 61,79 km2
County or District: La Jacques-Cartier; *Population in 2006:* 3,825
Provincial Electoral District(s): Chauveau
Federal Electoral District(s): Portneuf-Jacques-Cartier
Next Election: 1er novembre 2013
Dale Feeney, Directrice générale

Shawville
CP 339
350, rue Main
Shawville, QC J0X 2Y0
819-647-2979 Fax: 819-647-6895
ddowe@town.shawville.qc.ca
www.town.shawville.qc.ca
Municipal Type: Municipality
Incorporated: 1er janvier 1874; *Area:* 5,25 km2
County or District: Pontiac; *Population in 2006:* 1,587
Provincial Electoral District(s): Pontiac
Federal Electoral District(s): Pontiac
Next Election: 1er novembre 2013
Denise Dowe, Sec.-Trés. & Directrice générale

Sheenboro
59, ch de Sheen
Sheenboro, QC J0X 2Z0
819-683-2944 Fax: 819-683-3590
Municipal Type: Municipality
Incorporated: 1er janvier 1860; *Area:* 571,01 km2
County or District: Pontiac; *Population in 2006:* 167
Provincial Electoral District(s): Pontiac
Federal Electoral District(s): Pontiac
Next Election: 1er novembre 2013
Donald Marion, Sec.-Trés. & Directeur général

Shefford
245, ch Picard
Shefford, QC J2M 1J2
450-539-2258 Fax: 450-539-4951
info@cantonshefford.qc.ca
www.cantonshefford.qc.ca
Municipal Type: Township
Incorporated: 1er juillet 1855; *Area:* 116,62 km2
County or District: La Haute-Yamaska; *Population in 2006:* 5,941
Provincial Electoral District(s): Shefford
Federal Electoral District(s): Shefford
Next Election: 1er novembre 2013
Sylvie Gougeon, Sec.-Trés. & Directrice générale

Shigawake
334, rte 132
Shigawake, QC G0C 3E0
418-752-2474 Fax: 418-752-7474
Municipal Type: Municipality
Incorporated: 15 décembre 1924; *Area:* 77,36 km2
County or District: Bonaventure; *Population in 2006:* 357
Provincial Electoral District(s): Bonaventure
Federal Electoral District(s): Gaspésie-Iles-de-la-Madeleine
Next Election: 1er novembre 2013
Elton Hayes, Sec.-Trés. & Directeur général

Stanbridge East
12, rue Maple
Stanbridge East, QC J0J 2H0
450-248-3188 Fax: 450-248-7744
stanbridge@axion.ca
Municipal Type: Municipality
Incorporated: 1er juillet 1855; *Area:* 49,05 km2
County or District: Brome-Missisquoi; *Population in 2006:* 833
Provincial Electoral District(s): Brome-Missisquoi
Federal Electoral District(s): Brome-Missisquoi
Next Election: 1er novembre 2013
Vera Gendreau, Sec.-Trés. & Directrice générale

Stanbridge Station
229, ch Principal
Stanbridge Station, QC J0J 2J0
450-248-2125 Fax: 450-248-1132
sergetherrien@bellnet.ca
Municipal Type: Municipality
Incorporated: 21 mars 1889; *Area:* 18,11 km2
County or District: Brome-Missisquoi; *Population in 2006:* 309
Provincial Electoral District(s): Brome-Missisquoi
Federal Electoral District(s): Brome-Missisquoi
Next Election: 1er novembre 2013
Serge Therrien, Sec.-Trés. & Directeur général

Stanstead
425, rue Dufferin
Stanstead, QC J0B 3E2
819-876-7181 Fax: 819-876-5560
villestanstead@bellnet.ca
www.stanstead.ca
Municipal Type: City
Incorporated: 15 février 1995; *Area:* 21,93 km2
County or District: Memphrémagog; *Population in 2006:* 2,957
Provincial Electoral District(s): Orford
Federal Electoral District(s): Compton-Stanstead
Next Election: 1er novembre 2013
Me Guillaume Labbé, Greffière
Raymond Yates, Maire

Stanstead
778, ch Sheldon
Fitch Bay, QC J1X 3W4
819-876-2948 Fax: 819-876-7007
cantonstanstead@axion.ca
Municipal Type: Township
Incorporated: 1er juillet 1855; *Area:* 113,93 km2
County or District: Memphrémagog; *Population in 2006:* 1,065
Provincial Electoral District(s): Orford
Federal Electoral District(s): Compton-Stanstead
Next Election: 1er novembre 2013
Suzanne Ménard, Sec.-Trés. & Directrice générale

Stanstead-Est
7015, route 143
Stanstead-Est, QC J0B 3E0
819-876-7292 Fax: 819-876-7170
stansteadest@bellnet.ca
Municipal Type: Municipality
Incorporated: 16 juillet 1932; *Area:* 111,70 kme
County or District: Coaticook; *Population in 2006:* 628
Provincial Electoral District(s): Orford
Federal Electoral District(s): Compton-Stanstead
Next Election: 1er novembre 2013
Suzanne Boislard Côté, Sec.-Trés. & Directrice générale

Stoke
403, rue Principale
Stoke, QC J0B 3G0
819-878-3790 Fax: 819-878-3804
mun.stoke@videotron.ca
pages.infinit.net/munstoke/
Municipal Type: Municipality
Incorporated: 1er janvier 1864; *Area:* 239,89 km2
County or District: Le Val-St-François; *Population in 2006:* 2,708
Provincial Electoral District(s): Johnson
Federal Electoral District(s): Compton-Stanstead
Next Election: 1er novembre 2013
Adèle Madore, Sec.-Trés. & Directrice générale

Stoneham-et-Tewkesbury
325, ch du Hibou
Stoneham-et-Tewkesbury, QC G0A 4P0
418-848-2381 Fax: 418-848-1748
mairie@villestoneham.com
www.villestoneham.com
Municipal Type: United Township (Cantons)
Incorporated: 1er juillet 1855; *Area:* 684,75 km2
County or District: La Jacques-Cartier; *Population in 2006:* 5,866
Provincial Electoral District(s): Chauveau
Federal Electoral District(s): Portneuf-Jacques-Cartier
Next Election: 1er novembre 2013
Michel Chatigny, Sec.-Trés.

Stornoway
CP 98
507, rte 108 ouest
Stornoway, QC G0Y 1N0
819-652-2800 Fax: 819-652-2105
munstornoway@xplornet.com
Municipal Type: Municipality
Incorporated: 1er janvier 1858; *Area:* 178,32 km2
County or District: Le Granit; *Population in 2006:* 584
Provincial Electoral District(s): Mégantic-Compton
Federal Electoral District(s): Mégantic-L'Érable
Next Election: 1er novembe 2009
Sylvie Gauthier, Directrice générale & Sec.-Trés.

Stratford
165, av Centrale nord
Stratford, QC G0Y 1P0
418-443-2307 Fax: 418-443-2603
mun.stratford@qc.aira.com
Municipal Type: Township
Incorporated: 1er janvier 1874; *Area:* 125,61 km2
County or District: Le Granit; *Population in 2006:* 1,086
Provincial Electoral District(s): Mégantic-Compton
Federal Electoral District(s): Mégantic-L'Érable
Next Election: 1er novembre 2013
Hélène Lessard, Directrice générale

Stukely-Sud
101, place de la Mairie
Stukely-Sud, QC J0E 2J0
450-297-3407 Fax: 450-297-3759
info@stukely-sud.com
Municipal Type: Village
Incorporated: 19 septembre 1934; *Area:* 66,31 km2
County or District: Memphrémagog; *Population in 2006:* 941
Provincial Electoral District(s): Brome-Missisquoi
Federal Electoral District(s): Brome-Missisquoi
Next Election: 1er novembre 2013
Carol Enright-Knips, Directrice générale & Sec.-Trés.

Sutton
11, rue Principale sud
Sutton, QC J0E 2K0
450-538-2290 Fax: 450-538-0930
p.menard@sutton.caa
Municipal Type: City
Incorporated: 4 juillet 2002; *Area:* 243,51 km2
County or District: Brome-Missisquoi; *Population in 2006:* 3,805
Provincial Electoral District(s): Brome-Missisquoi
Federal Electoral District(s): Brome-Missisquoi
Next Election: 1er novembre 2013
Suzanne Lessard-Gilbert, Sec.-Trés. & Directrice générale
Kenneth Hill, Maire

Tadoussac
162, rue des Jésuites
Tadoussac, QC G0T 2A0
418-235-4446 Fax: 418-235-4433
ville@tadoussac.com
www.tadoussac.com
Municipal Type: Village
Incorporated: 10 octobre 1899; *Area:* 74,59 km2
County or District: La Haute-Côte-Nord; *Population in 2006:* 850
Provincial Electoral District(s): René-Lévesque
Federal Electoral District(s):
Montmorency-Charlevoix-Haute-Côte-Nord
Next Election: 1er novembre 2013
Louis-Philippe Guay, Sec.-Trés. & Directeur général

Taschereau
CP 150
52, rue Morin
Taschereau, QC J0Z 3N0
819-796-2219 Fax: 819-796-2220
taschereau@mrcao.qc.ca
www.taschereau.ao.ca
Municipal Type: Municipality
Incorporated: 27 décembre 2001; *Area:* 265,62 km2
County or District: Abitibi-Ouest; *Population in 2006:* 996
Provincial Electoral District(s): Abitibi-Ouest
Federal Electoral District(s): Abitibi-Témiscamingue
Next Election: 1er novembre 2013
Yves Aubut, Sec.-Trés. & Directeur général

Tasiujaq
CP 54
Tasiujaq, QC J0M 1T0
819-633-9924 Fax: 819-633-5026
www.nvtasiujaq.ca

Municipal Type: Northern Village
Incorporated: 2 février 1980; *Area:* 68,08 km2
County or District: Kativik; *Population in 2006:* 248
Provincial Electoral District(s): Ungava
Federal Electoral District(s): Abitibi-Baie-James-Nunavik-Eeyou
Next Election: 7 novembre 2007
Mary Berthe, Sec.-Trés.

Témiscaming
CP 730
20, rue Humphrey
Témiscaming, QC J0Z 3R0
819-627-3273 Fax: 819-627-3019
ville.temiscaming@temiscaming.net
www.temiscaming.net
Municipal Type: City
Incorporated: 26 mars 1988; *Area:* 861,77 km2
County or District: Témiscamingue; *Population in 2009:* 2,652
Provincial Electoral District(s): Rouyn-Noranda-Témiscamingue
Federal Electoral District(s): Abitibi-Témiscamingue
Next Election: 1er novembre 2013
Maurice Paquin, Directeur général
Philippe Barette, Maire

Témiscamingue
#209, 21, rue Notre-Dame-de-Lourdes
Ville-Marie, QC J9V 1X8
819-629-2829 Fax: 819-629-3472
mrc@mrctemiscamingue.qc.ca
www.temiscamingue.net
Municipal Type: Regional County Municipality
Incorporated: 15 avril 1981; *Area:* 19 243,88 km2
Population in 2009: 16,218
Note: 20 municipalités & 2 autres territoires.
Denis Clermont, Directeur général

Témiscouata
5, rue de l'Hôtel de Ville, 2e étage
Notre-Dame-du-Lac, QC G0L 1X0
418-899-6725 Fax: 418-899-2000
admin@mrctemis.ca
www.mrctemiscouata.qc.ca
Municipal Type: Regional County Municipality
Incorporated: 1 janvier 1982; *Area:* 3 920,90 km2
Population in 2009: 21,791
Note: 20 municipalités.
Jean-Pierre Laplante, Directeur général

Terrasse-Vaudreuil
74, 7e av
Terrasse-Vaudreuil, QC J7V 3M9
514-453-8120 Fax: 514-453-1180
terrassevaudreuil@qc.aira.com
www.terrassevaudreuil.ca
Municipal Type: Municipality
Incorporated: 1er janvier 1952; *Area:* 1,08 km2
County or District: Vaudreuil-Soulanges; *Population in 2006:* 1,985
Provincial Electoral District(s): Vaudreuil
Federal Electoral District(s): Vaudreuil-Soulanges
Next Election: 1er novembre 2013
Georges Robitaille, Sec.-Trés. & Directeur général

Thérèse-De Blainville
479, boul Adolphe-Chapleau
Bois-des-Filion, QC J6Z 1J9
450-621-5546 Fax: 450-621-2628
reception@mrc-tdb.org
www.mrctheresedeblainville.qc.ca
Municipal Type: Regional County Municipality

Population in 2009: 147,403
Note: 7 municipalités.
Perrine Lapierre, Directrice générale

Thorne
775, rte 366
Ladysmith, QC J0X 2A0
819-647-3206 Fax: 819-647-2086
munthorn@netrover.com
Municipal Type: Municipality
Incorporated: 1er janvier 1860; *Area:* 177,33 km2
County or District: Pontiac; *Population in 2006:* 427
Provincial Electoral District(s): Pontiac
Federal Electoral District(s): Pontiac
Next Election: 1er novembre 2013
Karen Kelly, Sec.-Trés. & Directrice générale

Thurso
161, rue Galipeau
Thurso, QC J0X 3B0
819-985-2701 Fax: 819-985-0134
ville.thurso@mrcpapineau.com
www.ville.thurso.qc.ca
Municipal Type: City
Incorporated: 16 janvier 1886; *Area:* 6,77 km2
County or District: Papineau; *Population in 2006:* 2,299
Provincial Electoral District(s): Papineau
Federal Electoral District(s): Argenteuil-Papineau-Mirabel
Next Election: 1er novembre 2013
Mario Boyer, Directeur général & Greffier
Maurice Boivin, Maire

Tingwick
CP 150
12, rue de l'Hôtel-de-Ville
Tingwick, QC J0A 1L0
819-359-2454 Fax: 819-359-2233
c.ramsay@tingwick.ca
www.tingwick.ca
Municipal Type: Municipality
Incorporated: 12 décembre 1981; *Area:* 168,93 km2
County or District: Arthabaska; *Population in 2006:* 1,458
Provincial Electoral District(s): Richmond
Federal Electoral District(s): Richmond-Arthabaska
Next Election: 1er novembre 2013
Chantale Ramsay, Sec.-Trés. & Directrice générale

Tourville
946, rue Principale
Tourville, QC G0R 4M0
418-359-2106 Fax: 418-359-3671
municipal.tourville@globetrotter.net
Municipal Type: Municipality
Incorporated: 14 novembre 1918; *Area:* 161,51 km2
County or District: L'Islet; *Population in 2006:* 730
Provincial Electoral District(s): Montmagny-L'Islet
Federal Electoral District(s):
Montmagny-L'Islet-Kamouraska-Rivière-du-Loup
Next Election: 1er novembre 2013
Normand Blier, Directeur général & Sec.-Trés.

Trécesson
CP 9
314, rue Sauvé
Villemontel, QC J0Y 2S0
819-732-8524 Fax: 819-732-8322
mun.trecesson@cableamos.com
www.mrcabitibi.qc.ca
Municipal Type: Township
Incorporated: 15 juillet 1918; *Area:* 198,38 km2
County or District: Abitibi; *Population in 2006:* 1,195
Provincial Electoral District(s): Abitibi-Ouest
Federal Electoral District(s): Abitibi-Témiscamingue
Next Election: 1er novembre 2013
Colette Hamelin, Sec.-Trés. & Directrice générale

Très-St-Rédempteur
769, rte Principale
Très-St-Rédempteur, QC J0P 1P0
450-451-5203 Fax: 450-451-8894
mun.tsr@qc.aira.com
www.tressaintredempteur.ca
Municipal Type: Parish (Paroisse)
Incorporated: 30 décembre 1880; *Area:* 25,40 km2
County or District: Vaudreuil-Soulanges; *Population in 2006:* 733
Provincial Electoral District(s): Soulanges
Federal Electoral District(s): Vaudreuil-Soulanges
Next Election: 1er novembre 2013
Lise Couët, Sec.-Trés. & Directrice générale

Très-St-Sacrement
CP 160
1180, rte 203
Howick, QC J0S 1G0
450-825-0192 Fax: 450-825-0193
mun-trst@videotron.ca
Municipal Type: Parish (Paroisse)
Incorporated: 2 avril 1885; *Area:* 97,30 km2
County or District: Le Haut-Saint-Laurent; *Population in 2006:* 1,213
Provincial Electoral District(s): Huntingdon
Federal Electoral District(s): Beauharnois-Salaberry
Next Election: 1er novembre 2013
Suzanne Côté, Sec.-Trés. & Directrice générale

Tring-Jonction
100, av Commerciale
Tring-Jonction, QC G0N 1X0
418-426-2497 Fax: 418-426-2498
tring@bellnet.ca
Municipal Type: Village
Incorporated: 21 novembre 1918; *Area:* 25,71 km2
County or District: Robert-Cliche; *Population in 2006:* 1,380
Provincial Electoral District(s): Beauce-Nord
Federal Electoral District(s): Beauce
Next Election: 1er novembre 2013
Marcel Poulin, Sec.-Trés. & Directeur général

Trois-Pistoles
5, rue Notre-Dame est
Trois-Pistoles, QC G0L 4K0
418-851-1995 Fax: 418-851-3567
administration@ville-trois-pistoles.ca
www.ville-trois-pistoles.ca
Municipal Type: City
Incorporated: 9 mars 1916; *Area:* 7,74 km2
County or District: Les Basques; *Population in 2006:* 3,500
Provincial Electoral District(s): Rivière-du-Loup
Federal Electoral District(s): Rimouski-Neigette-Témiscouata-Les Basques
Next Election: 1er novembre 2013
Marc Lemay, Greffier
Jean-Pierre Rioux, Maire

Trois-Rives
258, ch St-Joseph
Trois-Rives, QC G0X 2E0
819-646-5686 Fax: 819-646-5686
trois-rives@regionmekinac.com
www.trois-rives.com
Municipal Type: Municipality
Incorporated: 2 septembre 1972; *Area:* 675,09 km2
County or District: Mékinac; *Population in 2006:* 411
Provincial Electoral District(s): Laviolette
Federal Electoral District(s): St-Maurice-Champlain
Next Election: 1er novembre 2013
Lucien Mongrain, Maire

Ulverton
151, rte 143
Ulverton, QC J0B 2B0
819-826-5049 Fax: 819-826-5181
municipalite.ulverton@bellnet.ca
Municipal Type: Municipality
Incorporated: 1er juillet 1855; *Area:* 51,28 km2
County or District: Le Val-St-François; *Population in 2006:* 363
Provincial Electoral District(s): Johnson
Federal Electoral District(s): Richmond-Arthabaska
Next Election: 1er novembre 2013
France Côté, Sec.-Trés. & Directrice générale

Umiujaq
CP 108
Umiujaq, QC J0M 1Y0
819-331-7000 Fax: 819-331-7057
sec.treasurer@nvumiujaq.ca
www.nvumiujaq.ca
Municipal Type: Northern Village
Incorporated: 20 décembre 1986; *Area:* 25,50 km2
County or District: Kativik; *Population in 2006:* 390
Provincial Electoral District(s): Ungava
Federal Electoral District(s): Abitibi-Baie-James-Nunavik-Eeyou
Next Election: 7 novembre 2007
Sam Nuktie, Sec.-Trés.

Upton
863, rue Lanoie
Upton, QC J0H 2E0
450-549-5611 Fax: 450-549-5045
mun.upton@mrcacton.qc.ca
Municipal Type: Municipality
Incorporated: 25 février 1998; *Area:* 51,02 km2
County or District: Acton; *Population in 2006:* 1,954
Provincial Electoral District(s): Johnson
Federal Electoral District(s): St-Hyacinthe-Bagot
Next Election: 1er novembre 2013
Robert Leclerc, Sec.-Trés. & Directeur général

Val-Alain
CP 10
1245, 2e rang
Val-Alain, QC G0S 3H0
819-744-3222 Fax: 819-744-1330
municipalitevalalain@globetrotter.net
Municipal Type: Municipality
Incorporated: 1er janvier 1950; *Area:* 103,80 km2
County or District: Lotbinière; *Population in 2006:* 901
Provincial Electoral District(s): Lotbinière
Federal Electoral District(s): Lotbinière-Chutes-de-la-Chaudière
Next Election: 1er novembre 2013
France Bisson, Directrice générale & Sec.-Trés.

Val-Brillant
CP 220
11, rue St-Pierre ouest
Val-Brillant, QC G0J 3L0
418-742-3212 Fax: 418-742-3624
valbrillant@globetrotter.net
www.valbrillant.ca
Municipal Type: Municipality
Incorporated: 20 décembre 1986; *Area:* 80,00 km2
County or District: La Matapédia; *Population in 2006:* 1,003
Provincial Electoral District(s): Matapédia
Federal Electoral District(s): Haute-Gaspésie-La Mitis-Matane-Matapédia
Next Election: 1er novembre 2013
Lise Tremblay, Sec.-Trés. & Directrice générale

Val-David
2579, rue de l'Église
Val-David, QC J0T 2N0
819-322-2900 Fax: 819-322-6327
info@valdavid.com
www.valdavid.com
Municipal Type: Village
Incorporated: 10 mai 1921; *Area:* 43,17 km2
County or District: Les Laurentides; *Population in 2006:* 4,216
Provincial Electoral District(s): Bertrand
Federal Electoral District(s): Laurentides-Labelle
Next Election: 1er novembre 2013
André Desjardins, Sec.-Trés. & Directeur général

Val-des-Bois
CP 69
595, rte 309
Val-des-Bois, QC J0X 3C0
819-454-2280 Fax: 819-454-2211
mun.valdesbois@mrcpapineau.com
Municipal Type: Municipality
Incorporated: 1er janvier 1885; *Area:* 224,34 km2
County or District: Papineau;
Provincial Electoral District(s): Papineau

Federal Electoral District(s): Argenteuil-Papineau-Mirabel
Next Election: 1er novembre 2013
Line Sarrazin, Directrice générale & Sec.-Trés.

Val-des-Lacs
349, ch de Val-des-Lacs
Val-des-Lacs, QC J0T 2P0
819-326-5624 Fax: 819-326-7065
info@municipalite.val-des-lacs.qc.ca
municipalite.val-des-lacs.qc.ca
Municipal Type: Municipality
Incorporated: 6 février 1932; *Area:* 121,82 km2
County or District: Les Laurentides; *Population in 2006:* 778
Provincial Electoral District(s): Bertrand
Federal Electoral District(s): Laurentides-Labelle
Next Election: 1er novembre 2013
Sylvain Michaudville, Sec.-Trés. & Directeur général

Val-des-Monts
1, rte du Carrefour
Val-des-Monts, QC J8N 4E9
819-457-9400 Fax: 819-457-4141
administration@val-des-monts.net
www.val-des-monts.net
Municipal Type: Municipality
Incorporated: 1er janvier 1975; *Area:* 457,31 km2
County or District: Les Collines-de-l'Outaouais; *Population in 2006:* 9,539
Provincial Electoral District(s): Papineau
Federal Electoral District(s): Pontiac
Next Election: 1er novembre 2013
Patricia Fillet, Sec.-Trés. & Directrice générale

Val-Joli
500, rte 249
Val-Joli, QC J1S 2L5
819-845-7663 Fax: 819-845-4399
val-jolidg@axion.ca
Municipal Type: Municipality
Incorporated: 1er juillet 1855; *Area:* 90,61 km2
County or District: Le Val-Saint-François; *Population in 2006:* 1,479
Provincial Electoral District(s): Johnson
Federal Electoral District(s): Richmond-Arthabaska
Next Election: 1er novembre 2013
Lucie Camiré, Sec.-Trés. & Directrice générale

Val-Morin
6120, rue Morin
Val-Morin, QC J0T 2R0
819-322-5670 Fax: 819-322-3923
municipalite@val-morin.ca
www.val-morin.ca
Municipal Type: Municipality
Incorporated: 27 juin 1922; *Area:* 39,00 km2
County or District: Les Laurentides; *Population in 2006:* 2,756
Provincial Electoral District(s): Bertrand
Federal Electoral District(s): Laurentides-Labelle
Next Election: 1er novembre 2013
Pierre Delage, Directeur général & Sec.-Trés.

Val-Racine
CP 1
2991, ch St-Léon
Val-Racine, QC G0Y 1E0
819-657-4790 Fax: 819-657-4790
vracine@bellnet.ca
www.municipalite.val-racine.qc.ca
Municipal Type: Parish (Paroisse)
Incorporated: 26 avril 1907; *Area:* 116,80 km2
County or District: Le Granit; *Population in 2006:* 142
Provincial Electoral District(s): Mégantic-Compton
Federal Electoral District(s): Mégantic-L'Érable
Next Election: 1er novembre 2013
Chantal Grégoire, Directrice générale & Sec.-Trés.

Val-St-Gilles
801, rue Principale
Val-Saint-Gilles, QC J0Z 3T0
819-333-2158 Fax: 819-333-3116
valstgilles@mrcao.qc.ca
www.valst-gilles.ao.ca
Municipal Type: Municipality
Incorporated: 1er avril 1939; *Area:* 110,54 km2
County or District: Abitibi-Ouest; *Population in 2006:* 171
Provincial Electoral District(s): Abitibi-Ouest
Federal Electoral District(s): Abitibi-Témiscamingue
Next Election: 1er novembre 2013
Hélène Richer, Directrice générale & Sec.-Trés.

Valcourt
1155, rue St-Joseph
Valcourt, QC J0E 2L0
450-532-3313 Fax: 450-532-3424
ville.valcourt@valcourt.ca
www.ville.valcourt.qc.ca
Municipal Type: City
Incorporated: 19 octobre 1929; *Area:* 5,17 km2
County or District: Le Val-St-François; *Population in 2006:* 2,349
Provincial Electoral District(s): Johnson
Federal Electoral District(s): Shefford
Next Election: 1er novembre 2013
Manon Beauchemin, Greffière
Laurian Gagné, Maire

Valcourt
9040B, rue de la Montagne
Valcourt, QC J0E 2L0
450-532-2688 Fax: 450-532-5570
canton@cooptel.qc.ca
Municipal Type: Township
Incorporated: 1er juillet 1855; *Area:* 79,64 km2
County or District: Le Val-St-François; *Population in 2006:* 1,025
Provincial Electoral District(s): Johnson
Federal Electoral District(s): Shefford
Next Election: 1er novembre 2013
Sylvie Courtemanche, Directrice générale & Sec.-Trés.

Vallée-Jonction
218, rue Labbé
Vallée-Jonction, QC G0S 3J0
418-253-5515 Fax: 418-253-6731
munivj@globetrotter.net
Municipal Type: Municipality
Incorporated: 22 mars 1989; *Area:* 24,41 km2
County or District: La Nouvelle-Beauce; *Population in 2006:* 1,868
Provincial Electoral District(s): Beauce-Nord
Federal Electoral District(s): Beauce
Next Election: 1er novembre 2013
Gervais Boily, Sec.-Trés. & Directeur général

Vaudreuil-Soulanges
420, av Saint-Charles
Vaudreuil-Dorion, QC J7V 2N1
450-455-5753 Fax: 450-455-0145
info@mrcvs.ca
www.mrcvs.ca
Municipal Type: Regional County Municipality

Population in 2009: 125,404
Note: 23 municipalités.
Guy-Lin Beaudoin, Directeur général

Vaudreuil-sur-le-Lac
44, rue de l'Église
Vaudreuil-sur-le-Lac, QC J7V 8P3
450-455-1133 Fax: 450-455-8614
vsll@videotron.ca
www.vsll.ca
Municipal Type: Village
Incorporated: 29 mai 1920; *Area:* 1,73 km2
County or District: Vaudreuil-Soulanges; *Population in 2006:* 1,290
Provincial Electoral District(s): Vaudreuil
Federal Electoral District(s): Vaudreuil-Soulanges
Next Election: 1er novembre 2013
Claudia Chebin, Directrice générale & Sec.-Trés.

Venise-en-Québec
CP 270
237, 16e av ouest
Venise-en-Québec, QC J0J 2K0
450-244-5838 Fax: 450-244-5550
begind@venise-en-quebec.ca
www.municipalite.venise-en-quebec.qc.ca
Municipal Type: Municipality
Incorporated: 1er janvier 1950; *Area:* 13,57 km2
County or District: Le Haut-Richelieu; *Population in 2006:* 1,319
Provincial Electoral District(s): Iberville
Federal Electoral District(s): Brome-Missisquoi
Next Election: 1er novembre 2013
Diane Bégin, Sec.-Trés. & Directrice générale

Verchères
581, rte Marie-Victorin
Verchères, QC J0L 2R0
450-583-3307 Fax: 450-583-3637
mairie@ville.vercheres.qc.ca
www.ville.vercheres.qc.ca
Municipal Type: Municipality
Incorporated: 18 septembre 1971; *Area:* 72,77 km2
County or District: Lajemmerais; *Population in 2006:* 5,243
Provincial Electoral District(s): Verchères
Federal Electoral District(s): Verchères-Les Patriotes
Next Election: 1er novembre 2013
Luc Forcier, Sec.-Trés. & Directeur général

Ville-Marie
Édifice Gérard-Caron
21, rue St-Gabriel sud
Ville-Marie, QC J9V 1A1
819-629-2881 Fax: 819-629-3215
vvm.dgst@mrctemiscamingue.qc.ca
www.ville-marie.ca
Municipal Type: City
Incorporated: 13 octobre 1897; *Area:* 11,94 km2
County or District: Témiscamingue; *Population in 2006:* 2,696
Provincial Electoral District(s): Rouyn-Noranda-Témiscamingue
Federal Electoral District(s): Abitibi-Témiscamingue
Next Election: 1er novembre 2013
Jean-Yves Gauthier, Sec.-Trés. & Directeur général
Sylvain Trudel, Maire

Villeroy
378, rue Principale
Villeroy, QC G0S 3K0
819-385-4605 Fax: 819-385-4754
munville@ivic.qc.ca
www.municipalite-villeroy.ca
Municipal Type: Municipality
Incorporated: 22 septembre 1924; *Area:* 100,41 km2
County or District: L'Érable; *Population in 2006:* 496
Provincial Electoral District(s): Lotbinière
Federal Electoral District(s): Mégantic-L'Érable
Next Election: 1er novembre 2013
Angèle Germain, Directrice générale & Sec.-Trés.

Waltham
CP 29
69, rue de l'Hôtel-de-Ville
Waltham, QC J0X 3H0
819-683-3027 Fax: 819-683-1815
Municipal Type: Municipality
Incorporated: 1er janvier 1859; *Area:* 451,43 km2
County or District: Pontiac; *Population in 2006:* 360
Provincial Electoral District(s): Pontiac
Federal Electoral District(s): Pontiac
Next Election: 1er novembre 2013
Fernand Roy, Directeur général & Sec.-Trés.

Warden
172, rue Principale
Warden, QC J0E 2M0
450-539-1349 Fax: 450-539-0096
villagedewarden@qc.aira.com
Municipal Type: Village
Incorporated: 31 mars 1916; *Area:* 5,28 km2
County or District: La Haute-Yamaska; *Population in 2006:* 346
Provincial Electoral District(s): Shefford
Federal Electoral District(s): Shefford
Next Election: 1er novembre 2013
Jacqueline Giroux, Sec.-Trés. & Directrice générale

Warwick
8, rue de l'Hôtel-de-Ville
Warwick, QC J0A 1M0
819-358-4300 Fax: 819-358-4319
ville@ville.warwick.qc.ca
Municipal Type: City
Incorporated: 15 mars 2000; *Area:* 114,01 km2
County or District: Arthabaska; *Population in 2006:* 4,804
Provincial Electoral District(s): Richmond
Federal Electoral District(s): Richmond-Arthabaska
Next Election: 1er novembre 2013
Lise Lemieux, Sec.-Trés. & Directrice générale
Claude Desrochers, Maire

Waskaganish
CP 60
19, rue Nottaway
Waskaganish, QC J0M 1R0
819-895-8650 Fax: 819-895-8901
Municipal Type: Villages Cris

Provincial Electoral District(s): Ungava
Federal Electoral District(s): Abitibi-Baie-James-Nunavik-Eeyou
Robert Weistche, Maire

Waswanipi
Édifice Diom-Blacksmith
CP 8
Waswanipi, QC J0Y 3C0
819-753-2587 Fax: 819-753-2555
council@waswanipi.com
www.waswanipi.com
Municipal Type: Villages Cris

Provincial Electoral District(s): Ungava
Federal Electoral District(s): Abitibi-Baie-James-Nunavik-Eeyou
Robert Kitchen, Maire

Waterloo
CP 50
417, rue de la Cour
Waterloo, QC J0E 2N0
450-539-2282 Fax: 450-539-3257
administration@ville.waterloo.qc.ca, d.belanger@ville.waterl
www.ville.waterloo.qc.ca
Municipal Type: City
Incorporated: 1er janvier 1867; *Area:* 11,52 km2
County or District: La Haute-Yamaska; *Population in 2006:* 4,054
Provincial Electoral District(s): Shefford
Federal Electoral District(s): Shefford
Next Election: 1er novembre 2013
Denyse Bélanger, Greffière
Pascal Russell, Maire

Waterville
170, rue Principale sud
Waterville, QC J0B 3H0
819-837-2456 Fax: 819-837-0786
kesmith@sympatico.ca
Municipal Type: City
Incorporated: 1er janvier 1876; *Area:* 44,53 km2
County or District: Coaticook; *Population in 2006:* 1,926
Provincial Electoral District(s): St-François
Federal Electoral District(s): Compton-Stanstead
Next Election: 1er novembre 2013
Kimball Smith, Sec.-Trés. & Directeur général
Gérald Boudreau, Maire

Weedon
525, 2e av
Weedon, QC J0B 3J0

819-877-2727 Fax: 819-877-2255
weedon@bellnet.ca
www.weedon.info
Municipal Type: Municipality
Incorporated: 9 février 2000; *Area:* 215,02 km2
County or District: Le Haut-St-François; *Population in 2006:* 2,739
Provincial Electoral District(s): Mégantic-Compton
Federal Electoral District(s): Compton-Stanstead
Next Election: 1er novembre 2013
Émile Royer, Sec.-Trés. & Directeur général

Wemindji

CP 60
16, rue Beaver
Wemindji, QC J0M 1L0
819-978-0264 Fax: 819-978-0258
tgull@wemindji-nation.qc.ca
www.wemindji-nation.qc.ca
Municipal Type: Villages Cris
Incorporated: 28 juin 1978; *Area:* 186,22 km2
Population in 2006: 1,215
Provincial Electoral District(s): Ungava
Federal Electoral District(s): Abitibi-Baie-James-Nunavik-Eeyou
Next Election: 1er septembre 2009
Reggie Mark, Maire

Wentworth

114, ch Louisa
Wentworth, QC J8H 0C7
450-562-0701 Fax: 450-562-0703
info@wentworth.ca
Municipal Type: Township
Incorporated: 1er juillet 1855; *Area:* 88,99 km2
County or District: Argenteuil; *Population in 2006:* 483
Provincial Electoral District(s): Argenteuil
Federal Electoral District(s): Argenteuil-Papineau-Mirabel
Next Election: 1er novembre 2013
Paula Knudsen, Directrice générale

Wentworth-Nord

3488, rte Principale
Wentworth-Nord, QC J0T 1Y0
450-226-2416 Fax: 450-226-2109
info@went-nord.qc.ca
www.went-nord.qc.ca
Municipal Type: Municipality
Incorporated: 1er janvier 1958; *Area:* 155,71 km2
County or District: Les Pays-d'en-Haut; *Population in 2006:* 1,353
Provincial Electoral District(s): Argenteuil
Federal Electoral District(s): Argenteuil-Papineau-Mirabel
Next Election: 1er novembre 2013
René Tousignant, Sec.-Trés. & Directeur général

Westbury

168, rte 112
Westbury, QC J0B 1R0
819-832-3966 Fax: 819-832-3962
westbury@abacom.com
Municipal Type: Township
Incorporated: 16 août 1858; *Area:* 65,78 km2
County or District: Le Haut-St-François; *Population in 2006:* 932
Provincial Electoral District(s): Mégantic-Compton
Federal Electoral District(s): Compton-Stanstead
Next Election: 1er novembre 2013
Ghislaine Giard, Directrice générale & Sec.-Trés.

Whapmagoostui

CP 390
Whapmagoostui, QC J0M 1G0
819-929-3384 Fax: 819-929-3203
Municipal Type: Villages Cris

Provincial Electoral District(s): Ungava
Federal Electoral District(s): Abitibi-Baie-James-Nunavik-Eeyou
David Masty, Maire

Wickham

893, rue Moreau
Wickham, QC J0C 1S0
819-398-6878 Fax: 819-398-7166
wickham@bellnet.ca
www.wickham.ca
Municipal Type: Municipality
Incorporated: 23 décembre 1972; *Area:* 97,72 km2
County or District: Drummond; *Population in 2006:* 2,503
Provincial Electoral District(s): Johnson
Federal Electoral District(s): Drummond
Next Election: 1er novembre 2013
Réal Dulmaine, Sec.-Trés. & Directeur général

Windsor

CP 90
22, rue St-Georges
Windsor, QC J1S 2L7
819-845-7888 Fax: 819-845-7606
info@villedewindsor.qc.ca
www.villedewindsor.qc.ca
Municipal Type: City
Incorporated: 29 décembre 1999; *Area:* 13,78 km2
County or District: Le Val-St-François; *Population in 2006:* 5,239
Provincial Electoral District(s): Johnson
Federal Electoral District(s): Richmond-Arthabaska
Next Election: 1er novembre 2013
Judith Desmeules, Directrice générale & Greffière
Malcolm Wheeler, Maire

Wotton

CP 60
396, rue Monseigneur-L'Heureux
Wotton, QC J0A 1N0
819-828-2112 Fax: 819-828-3594
municipalite.wotton@cgocable.ca
Municipal Type: Municipality
Incorporated: 10 mars 1993; *Area:* 142,41 km2
County or District: Asbestos; *Population in 2006:* 1,540
Provincial Electoral District(s): Richmond
Federal Electoral District(s): Richmond-Arthabaska
Next Election: 1er novembre 2013
Carole Vaillancourt, Sec.-Trés. & Directrice générale

Yamachiche

366, rue Ste-Anne
Yamachiche, QC G0X 3L0
819-296-3795 Fax: 819-296-3542
hoteldeville@municipalite.yamachiche.qc.ca
www.municipalite.yamachiche.qc.ca
Municipal Type: Municipality
Incorporated: 26 décembre 1987; *Area:* 106,30 km2
County or District: Maskinongé; *Population in 2006:* 2,760
Provincial Electoral District(s): Maskinongé
Federal Electoral District(s): Berthier-Maskinongé
Next Election: 1er novembre 2013
Paul Desaulniers, Sec.-Trés. & Directeur général

Yamaska

CP 120
100, rue Guilbault
Yamaska, QC J0G 1X0
450-789-2489 Fax: 450-789-2970
yamaska@bas-richelieu.net
Municipal Type: Municipality
Incorporated: 19 décembre 2001; *Area:* 74,44 km2
County or District: Pierre-De Saurel; *Population in 2009:* 1,615
Provincial Electoral District(s): Richelieu; Nicolet-Yamaska
Federal Electoral District(s): Bas-Richelieu-Nicolet-Bécancour
Next Election: 1er novembre 2013
Brigitte Vachon, Directrice générale

SASKATCHEWAN

Acts governing the municipal system in Saskatchewan are The Urban Municipality Act, 1984; The Rural Municipality Act, 1989; and The Northern Municipalities Act. In the province there are the following types of incorporated municipalities: Rural Municipalities, Villages, Resort Villages, Towns, and Cities, as well as Northern Towns, Northern Villages, Northern Hamlets, Northern Settlements, Resort Hamlets and Organized Hamlets. The incorporation of these municipalities is voluntary. Thus a Village that qualifies to be named a Town, can remain a Village if the population so wishes.

Rural Municipalities: are divided into divisions. A Reeve is elected at large every two years. Councillors are also elected every two years but in "staggered" sequence. Rural municipal nominations are received until the third Monday in October and elections are held on the third Wednesday after the nomination period.

Villages: are defined as communities with not less than 100 permanent residents and not less than 50 dwellings and/or business premises. The Village is represented by a Mayor and at least two Councillors.

Towns: are defined as communities with not less that 500 permanent residents. They are represented by a Mayor and at least two Councillors.

Cities: are defined as communities with not less than 5,000 residents. They are represented by a Mayor and Councillors (the number varies).

Elections for all members of council in urban municipalities occur every three years. Nominations are held in cities, towns, and villages on the second Wednesday in October and elections on the fourth Wednesday in October. In resort villages, nomination day will be the last Saturday in June and the election will be held on the fourth Saturday in July.

Northern Hamlets: have a population of 50 or more and must contain 25 or more separate dwelling units or business premises. They are governed by a Mayor and two Aldermen, although they may pass a bylaw to increase the number of Aldermen to four.

Northern Villages: contain a minimum population of 100 and at least 50 dwelling units or business premises. Their council consists of a Mayor and four Councillors; although they may pass bylaws to either decrease the number of Councillors to two, or increase the number of Councillors by any even number.

Northern Towns: will have a minimum population of 500 and are governed by a Mayor and six Councillors. The council may pass a bylaw increasing or decreasing the size of council by any even number, provided the number of Councillors does not fall below two.

Election for all members of council in northern municipalities occur every three years. Council will determine the date of the election, which shall be held the second last Wednesday in September, the last Wednesday in September, or the first Wednesday in October. Nomination day is five weeks prior to the date on which the election is to be held.

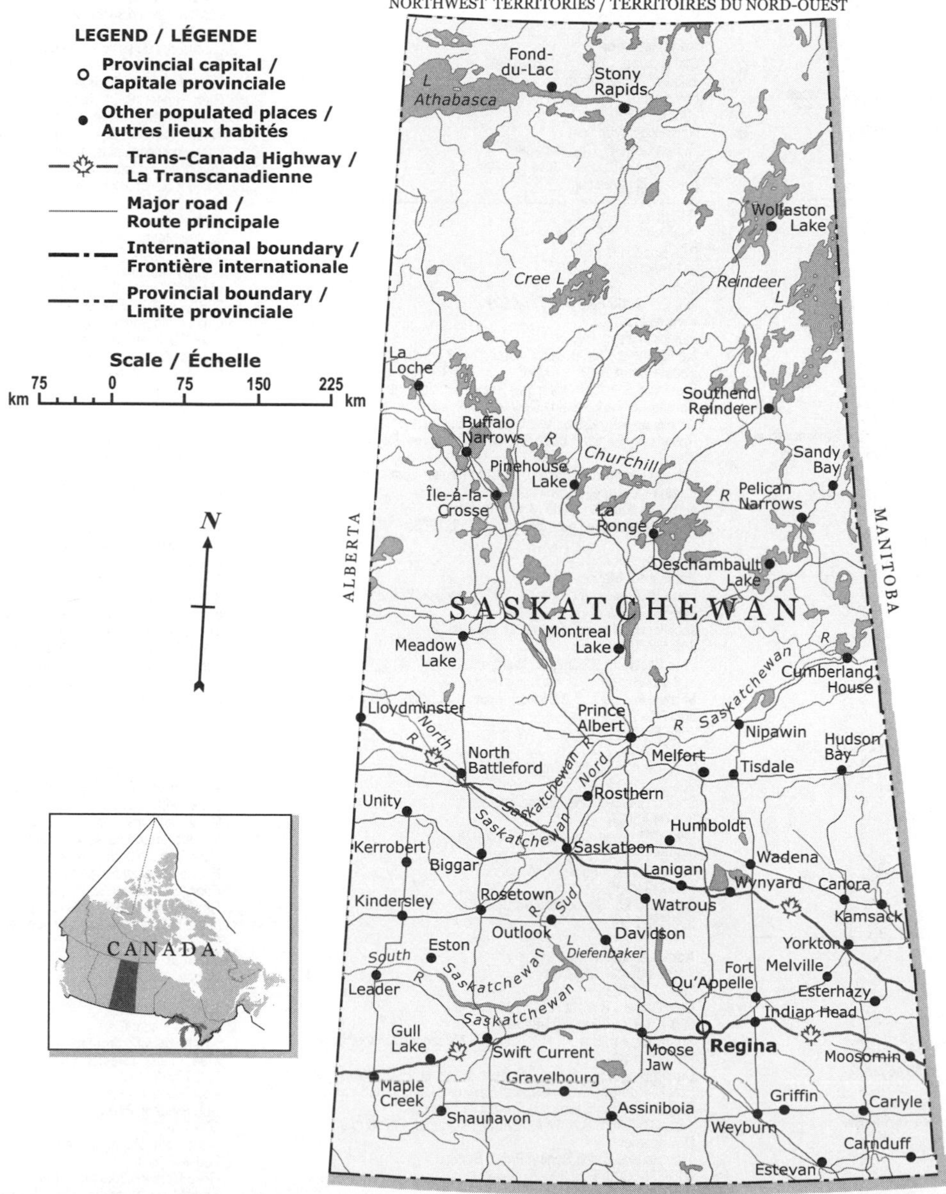

UNITED STATES OF AMERICA
ÉTATS-UNIS D'AMÉRIQUE

Saskatchewan

Major Municipalities in Saskatchewan

Estevan
1102 - 4 St.
Estevan, SK S4A 0W7
306-634-1800 Fax: 306-634-9790
citymanager@estevan.ca
www.estevan.ca
Municipal Type: City
Incorporated: Nov. 2, 1899; *Area:* 17.56 sq km
Population in 2006: 10,084
Provincial Electoral District(s): Estevan
Federal Electoral District(s): Souris-Moose Mountain
Next Election: Oct. 2009 (3 year terms)
Note: Incorporated as city on March 1, 1957.

Council
Gary St. Onge, Mayor

Administration
Lyndon Stachoski, Clerk
administration@estevan.ca
Greg Wock, Manager, Engineering Services
306-634-1823
engman@estevan.ca
Rick Perry, Fire Chief
306-634-1850
rperry@estevan.ca
Jim Puffalt, City Manager
306-634-1803
Les Naka, Manager, Public Works Services
306-634-1818
Kevin Sutter, Manager, Water/Wastewater Treatment Services
wt.manager@estevan.ca
Rob Denys, Manager, Land Development Services
306-634-1821
Dan Chestney, Foreman, Roads & Drainage
306-634-1829

Lloydminster
City Hall
4420 - 50 Ave.
Lloydminster, SK T9V 0W2
306-875-6184 Fax: 306-871-8346
tomlysyk@telusplanet.net
www.lloydminster.ca
Municipal Type: City
Incorporated: Nov. 25, 1903; *Area:* 17.34 sq km
Population in 2006: 24,028
Provincial Electoral District(s): Lloydminster
Federal Electoral District(s): Battlefords-Lloydminster
Next Election: Oct. 2009 (3 year terms)
Note: Population figure represents both the Alberta & Saskatchewan populations. Incorporated as a city on Jan. 1, 1958.

Council
Ken Baker, Mayor

Administration
Tom Lysyk, City Clerk

Moose Jaw
228 Main St. North
Moose Jaw, SK S6H 3J8
306-694-4400 Fax: 306-694-4400
webmaster@moosejaw.ca
www.moosejaw.ca
Municipal Type: City
Incorporated: Jan. 19, 1884; *Area:* 46.82 sq km
Population in 2006: 32,132
Provincial Electoral District(s): Moose Jaw North; Moose Jaw Wakamow
Federal Electoral District(s): Palliser
Next Election: Oct. 2009 (3 year terms)
Note: Incorporated as a city on Nov. 20, 1903.

Council
Dale McBain, Mayor

Administration
Myron Gulka-Tiechko, Clerk

North Battleford
P.O. Box 460
North Battleford, SK S9A 2Y6
306-445-1700 Fax: 306-445-0411
jtoye@cityofnb.ca
www.cityofnb.ca
Municipal Type: City
Incorporated: March 21, 1906; *Area:* 33.55 sq km
Population in 2006: 13,190
Provincial Electoral District(s): The Battlefords
Federal Electoral District(s): Battlefords-Lloydminster
Next Election: Oct. 2009 (3 year terms)
Note: Proclaimed as a city on May 1, 1913.

Council
Julian Sadlowski, Mayor
jsadlowski@cityofnb.ca

Administration
Elaine Kostiuk, Clerk
ejkostiuk@cityofnb.ca
Tim LaFreniere, City Planner
tlafreniere@citynb.ca
Stewart Schafer, Director, Public Works & Engineering
sschafer@cityofnb.ca
Alan Parkin, Director, Parks & Recreation
306-445-1740
aparkin@cityofnb.ca
Pat MacIsaac, Chief, Fire
nbfire@citynb.ca

Prince Albert
City Hall
1084 Central Ave.
Prince Albert, SK S6V 7P3
306-953-4305 Fax: 306-953-4313
cskauge@citypa.com
www.citypa.ca
Municipal Type: City
Incorporated: Oct. 8, 1885; *Area:* 65.68 sq km
Population in 2006: 34,138
Provincial Electoral District(s): Prince Albert Carlton; Prince Albert Northcote
Federal Electoral District(s): Prince Albert
Next Election: Oct. 2009 (3 year terms)
Note: Incorporated as a city on Oct. 8, 1904.

Council
Jim Scarrow, Mayor
mayor@citypa.com

Administration
Cliff Skauge, Clerk
cskauge@citypa.com
Les Karpluk, Fire Chief
306-953-4200
lkarpluk@citypa.com
Robert Cotterill, City Manager
306-953-4300
rcotterill@citypa.com

Regina
City Hall
P.O. Box 1790
2476 Victoria Ave.
Regina, SK S4P 3C8
306-777-7000 Fax: 306-777-6809
www.regina.ca
Municipal Type: City
Incorporated: Dec. 1, 1883; *Area:* 118.87 sq km
Population in 2006: 179,246
Provincial Electoral District(s): Regina Elphinstone-Centre; Regina Coronation Park; Regina Dewdney; Regina Douglas Park; Regina Lakeview; Regina Northeast; Regina Qu'Appelle Valley; Regina Rosemont; Regina South; Regina Walsh Acres; Regina Wascana Plains
Federal Electoral District(s): Palliser; Regina-Lumsden-Lake Centre; Regina-Qu'Appelle; Wascana
Next Election: Oct. 2009 (3 year terms)
Note: Incorporated as a city on June 19, 1903.

Council
Pat Fiacco, Mayor
Louis Browne, B.A.(Hons.), LL.B., Councillor, Ward(s): 1
306-531-5151
Jocelyn Hutchinson, Councillor, Ward(s): 2
306-584-1739
Fred Clipsham, Councillor, Ward(s): 3
306-757-8212
Michael Fougere, B.A.(Hons.), M.Sc., Councillor, Ward(s): 4
306-789-5586
John Findura, Councillor, Ward(s): 5
306-536-4250
Wade Murray, Councillor, Ward(s): 6
306-596-1035
Sharron Bryce, R.N., Councillor, Ward(s): 7
306-949-5025
Mike O'Donnell, Councillor, Ward(s): 8
306-545-7300
Terry Hincks, Councillor, Ward(s): 9
306-949-9690
Chris Szarka, Councillor, Ward(s): 10
306-551-2766

Administration
Joni Swidnicki, City Clerk
306-777-7262
Glen Davies, B.A., M.A., City Manager
306-777-7314, Fax: 306-949-7210
Bonny Bryant, B.A., M.P.A., General Manager, Community & Protective Services
Dorian Wandzura, P.Eng., General Manager, Public Works Division
Brent Sjoberg, C.M.A., General Manager, Corporate Services
Rick McCullough, Director, Protective Services
Jason Carlston, B.A., M.A., General Manager, Planning & Development
Troy Hagen, Chief, Regina Police Service
306-777-6500, Fax: 306-757-5461
rps@police.regina.sk.ca
Jim Nicol, Chief of Staff, City Manager's Office

Saskatoon
City Hall
222 - 3rd Ave. North
Saskatoon, SK S7K 0J5
306-975-3200 Fax: 306-975-2784
city.clerks@saskatoon.ca
www.saskatoon.ca
Municipal Type: City
Incorporated: Nov. 16, 1901; *Area:* 170.83 sq km
Population in 2006: 202,340
Provincial Electoral District(s): Saskatoon Centre; Saskatoon Eastview; Saskatoon Fairview; Saskatoon Greystone; Saskatoon Massey Place; Saskatoon Meewasin; Saskatoon Northwest; Saskatoon Nutana; Saskatoon Riversdale; Saskatoon Silver Springs; Saskatoon Southeast; Saskatoon Sutherland
Federal Electoral District(s): Blackstrap; Saskatoon-Humboldt; Saskatoon-Rosetown-Biggar; Saskatoon-Wanuskewin
Next Election: Oct. 2009 (3 year terms)
Note: Incorporated as a city on May 26, 1906.

Council
Donald J. Atchison, Mayor
306-975-3202, Fax: 306-975-3144
Darren Hill, Councillor, Ward(s): 1
darren.hill@saskatoon.ca
Pat Lorje, B.A., M.A., Councillor, Ward(s): 2
pat.lorje@saskatoon.ca
Maurice (Moe) Neault, Councillor, Ward(s): 3
maurice.neault@saskatoon.ca
Myles Heidt, Councillor, Ward(s): 4
myles.heidt@saskatoon.ca
Gordon Wyant, B.A., LL.B., Councillor, Ward(s): 5
gordon.wyant@saskatoon.ca
Charlie Clark, B.Ed., M.E.S., Councillor, Ward(s): 6
charlie.clark@saskatcoon.ca
Bob Pringle, B.S.W., M.S.W., Councillor, Ward(s): 7
bob.pringle@saskatoon.ca
Glen Penner, B.Ed., M.Ed., Councillor, Ward(s): 8
glen.penner@saskatoon.ca
Tiffany Paulsen, B.A., LL.B., Councillor, Ward(s): 9
tiffany.paulsen@saskatoon.ca
Bev Dubois, Councillor, Ward(s): 10
bev.dubois@saskatoon.ca

Administration
Janice Mann, City Clerk
306-975-3240, Fax: 306-975-2784
Shelley Sutherland, Treasurer
Marlys Bilanski, General Manager, Corporate Services
306-975-3206, Fax: 306-975-7975
Gaston Gourdeau, General Manager, Infrastructure Services
Paul Gauthier, General Manager, Community Services
Murray Totland, City Manager
Lorne Sully, Manager, City Planning
Brian Bentley, General Manager, Fire & Protective Services
306-975-2575, Fax: 306-975-2689
fire.protective.services@city.saskatoon.sk.ca
Cal Sexsmith, Manager, Municipal Engineering
Wayne Briant, Manager, Parks
Gaston Gourdeau, Manager, Public Works
Pawel Kerc, Contact, Environmental Compliance
306-975-2486
Tim Sedgewick, Contact, Wastewater Treatment
Mark Keller, Contact, Water Treatment & Meters
Randy Grauer, Manager, Development Services
Clive Weighill, Police Chief
306-975-8300
police.service@city.saskatoon.sk.ca
Theresa Dust, City Solicitor
306-975-3270, Fax: 306-975-7828
Jeff Jorgenson, General Manager, Utility Services

Swift Current
P.O. Box 340
177 - 1st Ave. NE
Swift Current, SK S9H 3W1
306-778-2777 Fax: 306-773-2194
admin@swiftcurrent.ca; m.johnson@swiftcurrent.ca
www.swiftcurrent.ca
Municipal Type: City
Incorporated: Feb. 4, 1904; *Area:* 24.04 sq km
Population in 2006: 14,946
Provincial Electoral District(s): Swift Current
Federal Electoral District(s): Cypress Hills-Grasslands
Next Election: Oct. 2009 (3 year terms)
Note: Incorporated as a city on Jan. 15, 1914.

Council
Sandy Larson, Mayor

Administration
Dianne Hahn, Clerk
d.hahn@swiftcurrent.ca
Mac Forster, Director, Engineering
306-778-2740
eng@swiftcurrent.ca
Bob Rindahl, Fire Chief
306-778-2760
Andy Toth, Manager, Parks
306-778-2787
Greg Parsons, Manager, Public Works
Stuart Kyle, Superintendent, Streets & Transportation
306-778-2748
Tim Cox, Superintendent, Water & Wastewater Division
306-778-2748

Rudy Holland, Superintendent, Water Treatment
306-778-2755
Trevor Feicht, Manager, Engineering Services
Dean Robson, Director, Recreation & Parks

Weyburn
P.O. Box 370
157 - 3rd St. NE
Weyburn, SK S4H 2K6
306-848-3200 Fax: 306-842-2001
rsmith@weyburn.ca
www.weyburn.ca
Municipal Type: City
Incorporated: Oct. 22, 1900; *Area:* 15.78 sq km
Population in 2006: 9,433
Provincial Electoral District(s): Weyburn-Big Muddy
Federal Electoral District(s): Souris-Moose Mountain
Next Election: Oct. 2009 (3 year terms)
Note: Incorporated as a city on Sept. 1, 1913.

Council
Debra Button, Mayor
mayor@weyburn.ca

Administration
Donette Rasmussen, Clerk
drasmussen@weyburn.ca

Yorkton
P.O. Box 400
Yorkton, SK S3N 2W3
306-786-1700 Fax: 306-786-6880
bschenher@yorkton.ca
www.yorkton.ca
Municipal Type: City
Incorporated: July 11, 1894; *Area:* 24.57 sq km
Population in 2006: 15,038
Provincial Electoral District(s): Yorkton
Federal Electoral District(s): Yorkton-Melville
Next Election: Oct. 2009 (3 year terms)
Note: Incorporated as a city on Feb. 1, 1928.

Council
Chris Whyatt, Mayor

Administration
Bonnie Schenher, City Clerk
Lonnie Kaal, Director, Finance
306-786-1721, Fax: 306-786-6880
lkaal@yorkton.ca
Roger Hunter, Director, Planning & Engineering
306-786-1730
Dean Clark, Fire Chief, Fire Protective Services
306-786-1795, Fax: 306-786-6588
dclark@yorkton.ca
Faisal Anwar, Officer, Economic Development
306-786-1747
econdev@yorkton.ca
Trent Mandzuk, Manager, Public Works
306-786-1760
tmanzuk@yorkton.ca
Michael Buchholzer, Manager, Water Works
306-786-1771, Fax: 306-782-4990
mbuchholzer@yorkton.ca
Maureen Berard, Manager, Building Services
306-786-1710, Fax: 306-786-6880
mberard@yorkton.ca
David Putz, CGA, City Manager
306-786-1703, Fax: 306-786-6880
dputz@yorkton.ca
Darcy McLeod, Director, Leisure Services
306-786-1750, Fax: 306-786-6880
dmcleod@yorkton.ca

Other Municipalities in Saskatchewan

Abbey
P.O. Box 210
Abbey, SK S0N 0A0
306-689-2412 Fax: 306-689-2901
rm229@sasktel.net
Municipal Type: Village
Incorporated: Sept. 2, 1913; *Area:* 0.77 sq km
Population in 2006: 130
Provincial Electoral District(s): Cypress Hills
Federal Electoral District(s): Cypress Hills-Grasslands
Next Election: Oct. 2009 (3 year terms)
Jan Stern, Administrator
Bruce Walker, Mayor

Aberdeen
P.O. Box 130
207 Main St.
Aberdeen, SK S0K 0A0
306-253-4311 Fax: 306-253-4201
townaberdeen@sasktel.net
Municipal Type: Town
Incorporated: March 13, 1907; *Area:* 1.95 sq km
Population in 2006: 527
Provincial Electoral District(s): Humboldt
Federal Electoral District(s): Saskatoon-Humboldt
Next Election: Oct. 2009 (3 year terms)
Note: Proclaimed as town on Nov. 1, 1988.
Glen Ogilvy, Mayor
Susan Thompson, Administrator

Abernethy
P.O. Box 189
Abernethy, SK S0A 0A0
306-333-2271 Fax: 306-333-2271
Municipal Type: Village
Incorporated: July 26, 1904; *Area:* 1.03 sq km
Population in 2006: 197
Provincial Electoral District(s): Last Mountain-Touchwood
Federal Electoral District(s): Regina-Qu'Appelle
Next Election: Oct. 2009 (3 year terms)
Leona Ward, Clerk
Brian Wilkes, Mayor

Air Ronge
P.O. Box 100
328 Husky Ave.
Air Ronge, SK S0J 3G0
306-425-2107 Fax: 306-425-3108
vill.airronge@sasktel.net
www.villageofairronge.com
Municipal Type: Northern Village
Incorporated: Oct. 1, 1983; *Area:* 6.00 sq km
Population in 2006: 1,032
Provincial Electoral District(s): Cumberland
Federal Electoral District(s): Desnethé-Missinippi-Churchill River
Next Election: 2009 (3 year terms)
Gordon Stomp, Mayor
Louise Baht, Administrator

Alameda
P.O. Box 36
Alameda, SK S0C 0A0
306-489-2077 Fax: 306-489-4602
townofalameda@sasktel.net
www.townofalameda.ca
Municipal Type: Town
Incorporated: Dec. 29, 1898; *Area:* 2.55 sq km
Population in 2006: 308
Provincial Electoral District(s): Cannington
Federal Electoral District(s): Souris-Moose Mountain
Next Election: Oct. 2009 (3 year terms)
Note: Proclaimed as town on April 15, 1907.
Allan Faber, Mayor
Lynne Hewitt, Administrator

Albertville
General Delivery
Albertville, SK S0J 0A0
306-929-2110 Fax: 306-929-4744
albertville@inet2000.com
Municipal Type: Village
Incorporated: Jan. 1, 1986; *Area:* 1.11 sq km
Population in 2006: 110
Provincial Electoral District(s): Saskatchewan Rivers
Federal Electoral District(s): Prince Albert
Next Election: Oct. 2009 (3 year terms)
Jacki Leason, Clerk
Louis Hradecki, Mayor

Alida
P.O. Box 6
Alida, SK S0C 0B0
306-443-2228 Fax: 306-443-2568
villageofalida@sasktel.net
Municipal Type: Village
Incorporated: Feb. 19, 1926; *Area:* 0.35 sq km
Population in 2006: 106
Provincial Electoral District(s): Cannington
Federal Electoral District(s): Souris-Moose Mountain
Next Election: Oct. 2009 (3 year terms)
Sheri-Lee Patton, Clerk

Allan
P.O. Box 159
224 Main St.
Allan, SK S0K 0C0
306-257-3272 Fax: 306-257-3337
townofallan@sasktel.net
www.allan.ca
Municipal Type: Town
Incorporated: June 9, 1910; *Area:* 1.78 sq km
Population in 2006: 631
Provincial Electoral District(s): Humboldt
Federal Electoral District(s): Blackstrap
Next Election: Oct. 2009 (3 year terms)
Note: Proclaimed as town on Dec. 1, 1965.
Christine Dyck, Administrator
Larry Sommerfeld, Mayor

Alsask
P.O. Box 219
Alsask, SK S0L 0A0
306-968-2394 Fax: 306-968-2300
alsask.village@sasktel.net
Municipal Type: Village
Incorporated: Nov. 22, 1910; *Area:* 1.66 sq km
Population in 2006: 129
Provincial Electoral District(s): Kindersley
Federal Electoral District(s): Battlefords-Lloydminster
Next Election: Oct. 2009 (3 year terms)
Ernie Pushkarenko, Administrator
Ed Sonmor, Mayor

Alvena
P.O. Box 8
Alvena, SK S0K 0E0
306-943-2101 Fax: 306-943-2155
rm369@sasktel.net
Municipal Type: Village
Incorporated: July 1, 1936; *Area:* 0.43 sq km
Population in 2006: 55
Provincial Electoral District(s): Batoche
Federal Electoral District(s): Saskatoon-Humboldt
Next Election: Oct. 2009 (3 year terms)
Lucille Cousin, Clerk
Val Matheson, Mayor

Aneroid
P.O. Box 226
Aneroid, SK S0N 0C0
306-588-2300 Fax: 306-588-2300
mgervais@xplornet.com
Municipal Type: Village
Incorporated: Aug. 7, 1913; *Area:* 1.05 sq km
Population in 2006: 45
Provincial Electoral District(s): Wood River
Federal Electoral District(s): Cypress Hills-Grasslands
Next Election: Oct. 2009 (3 year terms)
Marcel Gervais, Clerk
Elton Meikle, Mayor

Annaheim
P.O. Box 70
Annaheim, SK S0K 0G0
306-598-2122 Fax: 306-598-4526
rm369@sasktel.net
www.ctreda.ca/webpage/towns/annaheim/annaheimhome.htm
Municipal Type: Village
Incorporated: April 1, 1977; *Area:* 0.78 sq km
Population in 2006: 218
Provincial Electoral District(s): Melfort
Federal Electoral District(s): Saskatoon-Humboldt
Next Election: Oct. 2009 (3 year terms)
Brenda Nagy, Administrator
Julius LePoudre, Mayor

Antler
P.O. Box 83
Antler, SK S0C 0E0
306-452-3533 Fax: 306-452-6114
Municipal Type: Village
Incorporated: March 15, 1905; *Area:* 0.72 sq km
Population in 2006: 40
Provincial Electoral District(s): Cannington
Federal Electoral District(s): Souris-Moose Mountain
Next Election: Oct. 2009 (3 year terms)
Bonnie Rutten, Clerk
James Duncan, Mayor

Arborfield
P.O. Box 280
201 Main St.
Arborfield, SK S0E 0A0
306-769-8533 Fax: 306-769-8301
arborfieldrm456@sasktel.net
www.arborfieldsk.ca
Municipal Type: Town
Incorporated: June 16, 1933; *Area:* 0.88 sq km
Population in 2006: 329
Provincial Electoral District(s): Carrot River Valley
Federal Electoral District(s): Prince Albert
Next Election: Oct. 2009 (3 year terms)
Note: Proclaimed as town on June 1, 1950.
Randal Rusk, Mayor
Allan Frisky, Administrator

Archerwill
P.O. Box 130
Archerwill, SK S0E 0B0
306-323-2161 Fax: 306-323-2101
www.newsaskcfdc.ca/archerwill.htm
Municipal Type: Village
Incorporated: Jan. 1, 1947; *Area:* 0.83 sq km
Population in 2006: 185
Provincial Electoral District(s): Kelvington-Wadena
Federal Electoral District(s): Yorkton-Melville
Next Election: Oct. 2009 (3 year terms)
Paulette Althouse, Administrator
Robert Wilson, Mayor

Arcola
P.O. Box 359
127 Main St.
Arcola, SK S0C 0G0
306-455-2212 Fax: 306-455-2445
arcadmin@sasktel.net
www.creda.sk.ca/arcola
Municipal Type: Town
Incorporated: April 11, 1901; *Area:* 2.59 sq km
Population in 2006: 504
Provincial Electoral District(s): Cannington
Federal Electoral District(s): Souris-Moose Mountain
Next Election: Oct. 2009 (3 year terms)
Note: Proclaimed as town on Nov. 20, 1903.
Harry Laurent, Mayor
Glenda Johnson, Administrator

Arran
P.O. Box 40
Arran, SK S0A 0B0
306-595-4521 Fax: 306-595-4531
rm331@sasktel.net
Municipal Type: Village
Incorporated: Sept. 21, 1916; *Area:* 0.69 sq km
Population in 2006: 40
Provincial Electoral District(s): Canora-Pelly
Federal Electoral District(s): Yorkton-Melville
Next Election: Oct. 2009 (3 year terms)
Yvonne Bilsky, Administrator
Rick Nahnybida, Mayor

Asquith
P.O. Box 160
Asquith, SK S0K 0J0
306-329-4341 Fax: 306-329-4969
town.asquith@sasktel.net
Municipal Type: Town
Incorporated: Dec. 10, 1907; *Area:* 1.23 sq km
Population in 2006: 576
Provincial Electoral District(s): Biggar
Federal Electoral District(s): Saskatoon-Rosetown-Biggar
Next Election: Oct. 2009 (3 year terms)
Note: Proclaimed as a town on Aug. 15, 1908.
Charles Chappell, Mayor
Holly Cross, Administrator

Assiniboia
P.O. Box 670
131 - 3rd Ave. West
Assiniboia, SK S0H 0B0
306-642-3382 Fax: 306-642-5622
townofassiniboia@sasktel.net
www.assiniboia.net
Municipal Type: Town
Incorporated: Dec. 19, 1912; *Area:* 3.78 sq km
Population in 2006: 2,305
Provincial Electoral District(s): Wood River
Federal Electoral District(s): Cypress Hills-Grasslands
Next Election: Oct. 2009 (3 year terms)
Note: Proclaimed as a town on Oct. 1, 1913.
Paul Topola, Mayor
Kim Eklund, Administrator

Atwater
P.O. Box 45
Atwater, SK S0A 0C0
306-745-3443
Municipal Type: Village
Incorporated: Aug. 12, 1910; *Area:* 1.79 sq km
Population in 2006: 25
Provincial Electoral District(s): Melville-Saltcoats
Federal Electoral District(s): Yorkton-Melville
Next Election: Oct. 2009 (3 year terms)
Sharon Gelowitz, Clerk
James Ferguson, Mayor

Avonlea
P.O. Box 209
Avonlea, SK S0H 0C0
306-868-2221 Fax: 306-868-2221
avonlea@sasktel.net
www.avonlea.biz
Municipal Type: Village
Incorporated: Feb. 10, 1912; *Area:* 0.96 sq km
Population in 2006: 381
Provincial Electoral District(s): Indian Head-Milestone
Federal Electoral District(s): Palliser
Next Election: Oct. 2009 (3 year terms)
Tim Forer, Administrator
Alex Getzlaf, Mayor

Aylesbury
P.O. Box 151
Aylesbury, SK S0G 0B0
306-734-5125
susy632@sasktel.net
www.craik.ca/aylesbury.html
Municipal Type: Village
Incorporated: March 31, 1910; *Area:* 1.28 sq km
Population in 2006: 45
Provincial Electoral District(s): Thunder Creek
Federal Electoral District(s): Regina-Lumsden-Lake Centre
Next Election: Oct. 2009 (3 year terms)
Doris Adrienne Florness, Administrator
Nigel McAlpine, Mayor

Aylsham
P.O. Box 64
Aylsham, SK S0E 0C0
306-862-9415
Municipal Type: Village
Incorporated: Aug. 4, 1947; *Area:* 0.48 sq km
Population in 2006: 92
Provincial Electoral District(s): Carrot River Valley
Federal Electoral District(s): Prince Albert
Next Election: Oct. 2009 (3 year terms)
Dorothy E. Blue, Clerk
Elizabeth F. Archer, Mayor

Balcarres
P.O. Box 130
Balcarres, SK S0G 0C0
306-334-2566 Fax: 306-334-2907
balcarrestown@sasktel.net
Municipal Type: Town
Incorporated: Nov. 21, 1904; *Area:* 1.57 sq km
Population in 2006: 598
Provincial Electoral District(s): Last Mountain-Touchwood
Federal Electoral District(s): Regina-Qu'Appelle
Next Election: Oct. 2009 (3 year terms)
Note: Proclaimed as a town on Jan. 1, 1951.
Dwight Dixon, Mayor
Bev Gelech, Administrator

Balgonie
P.O. Box 310
129 South Railway St. East
Balgonie, SK S0G 0E0
306-771-2284 Fax: 306-771-2899
townofbalgonie@sasktel.net
www.townofbalgonie.ca
Municipal Type: Town
Incorporated: April 20, 1903; *Area:* 3.15 sq km
Population in 2006: 1,384
Provincial Electoral District(s): Indian Head-Milestone
Federal Electoral District(s): Regina-Qu'Appelle
Next Election: Oct. 2009 (3 year terms)
Note: Proclaimed as a town on Jan. 1, 1951.
Tim Sterzer, Mayor
Val Hubbard, Administrator

Bangor
P.O. Box 35
Bangor, SK S0A 0E0
306-728-4084
Municipal Type: Village
Incorporated: June 8, 1911; *Area:* 1.65 sq km
Population in 2006: 50
Provincial Electoral District(s): Melville-Saltcoats
Federal Electoral District(s): Yorkton-Melville
Next Election: Oct. 2009 (3 year terms)
Joan C. Bomberak, Clerk
Jerome Bomberak, Mayor

Battleford
P.O. Box 40
Battleford, SK S0M 0E0
306-937-6200 Fax: 306-937-2450
admin@battleford.ca
www.battleford.ca
Municipal Type: Town
Incorporated: Jan. 6, 1899; *Area:* 23.33 sq km
Population in 2006: 3,685
Provincial Electoral District(s): The Battlefords
Federal Electoral District(s): Battlefords-Lloydminster
Next Election: Oct. 2009 (3 year terms)
Note: Proclaimed as a town on June 15, 1904.
Chris Odishaw, Mayor
Sheryl Ballendine, Administrator

Beatty
P.O. Box 51
Beatty, SK S0J 0C0
306-752-3980
www.newsaskcfdc.ca/beatty.htm
Municipal Type: Village
Incorporated: March 31, 1921; *Area:* 0.82 sq km
Population in 2006: 61
Provincial Electoral District(s): Melfort
Federal Electoral District(s): Prince Albert
Next Election: Oct. 2009 (3 year terms)
Pam Armstrong, Clerk
Harvey Rainville, Mayor

Beauval
P.O. Box 19
Lavoie St.
Beauval, SK S0M 0G0
306-288-2110 Fax: 306-288-2348
admin.beauval@sasktel.net
Municipal Type: Northern Village
Incorporated: Oct. 1, 1983; *Area:* 6.71 sq km
Population in 2006: 806
Provincial Electoral District(s): Athabasca
Federal Electoral District(s): Desnethé-Missinippi-Churchill River
Next Election: Oct. 2009 (3 year terms)
Alex Maurice, Mayor
Angus McKay, Clerk

Beechy
P.O. Box 153
Beechy, SK S0L 0C0
306-859-2205 Fax: 306-859-2290
info@beechysask.ca
www.beechysask.ca
Municipal Type: Village
Incorporated: May 11, 1925; *Area:* 1.06 sq km
Population in 2006: 243
Provincial Electoral District(s): Rosetown-Elrose
Federal Electoral District(s): Cypress Hills-Grasslands
Next Election: Oct. 2009 (3 year terms)
Mel Hanke, Clerk
beechy@yourlink.ca
Francis Fleuter, Mayor

Belle Plaine
P.O. Box 63
Belle Plaine, SK S0G 0G0
306-693-0378
Municipal Type: Village
Incorporated: Aug. 12, 1910; *Area:* 1.34 sq km
Population in 2006: 64
Provincial Electoral District(s): Thunder Creek
Federal Electoral District(s): Palliser
Next Election: Oct. 2009 (3 year terms)
Debra Day, Clerk
Donald Firomski, Mayor

Bengough
P.O. Box 188
181 Main St.
Bengough, SK S0C 0K0
306-268-2927 Fax: 306-268-2988
town.bengough@sasktel.net
www.bengough.com
Municipal Type: Town
Incorporated: March 15, 1912; *Area:* 1.07 sq km
Population in 2006: 337
Provincial Electoral District(s): Weyburn-Big Muddy
Federal Electoral District(s): Souris-Moose Mountain
Next Election: Oct. 2009 (3 year terms)
Note: Proclaimed as a town on April 1, 1958.
Madonna Unterreiner, Mayor
Penny Nergard, Administrator

Bethune
P.O. Box 209
519 Main St.
Bethune, SK S0G 0H0
306-638-3188 Fax: 306-638-3188
villageofbethune@sasktel.net
www.villageofbethune.com
Municipal Type: Village
Incorporated: Aug. 2, 1912; *Area:* 1.04 sq km
Population in 2006: 369
Provincial Electoral District(s): Thunder Creek
Federal Electoral District(s): Regina-Lumsden-Lake Centre
Next Election: Oct. 2009 (3 year terms)
Patti Vance, Administrator
Doug Patience, Mayor

Bienfait
P.O. Box 220
Bienfait, SK S0C 0M0
306-388-2969 Fax: 306-388-2449
bienfait@sasktel.net
Municipal Type: Town
Incorporated: April 16, 1912; *Area:* 3.09 sq km
Population in 2006: 748
Provincial Electoral District(s): Estevan
Federal Electoral District(s): Souris-Moose Mountain
Next Election: Oct. 2009 (3 year terms)
Note: Proclaimed as a town on March 1, 1957.
Garry Hammett, Mayor
Laurel Gilroy, Administrator

Big River
P.O. Box 220
606 - 1st St. North
Big River, SK S0J 0E0
306-469-2112 Fax: 306-469-4856
bigriver@sasktel.net
www.bigriver.ca
Municipal Type: Town
Incorporated: Aug. 18, 1923; *Area:* 2.11 sq km
Population in 2006: 728
Provincial Electoral District(s): Saskatchewan Rivers
Federal Electoral District(s): Desnethé-Missinippi-Churchill River
Next Election: Oct. 2009 (3 year terms)
Note: Proclaimed as a town on Oct. 1, 1966.
Sandra Gilbert, Mayor
Gail L. Gear, Administrator

Biggar
P.O. Box 489
202 - 3rd Ave. West
Biggar, SK S0K 0M0
306-948-3317 Fax: 306-948-5134
townoffice@townofbiggar.com
www.townofbiggar.com
Municipal Type: Town
Incorporated: May 18, 1909; *Area:* 15.75
Population in 2006: 2,033
Provincial Electoral District(s): Biggar
Federal Electoral District(s): Saskatoon-Rosetown-Biggar
Next Election: Oct. 2009 (3 year terms)
Note: Proclaimed as a town on Nov. 1, 1911.
Raymond Sadler, Mayor
R.G. (Bob) Tyler, Administrator

Birch Hills
P.O. Box 206
Birch Hills, SK S0J 0G0
306-749-2232 Fax: 306-749-2545
birchills.town@sasktel.net
www.birchhills.ca
Municipal Type: Town
Incorporated: July 19, 1907; *Area:* 1.82 sq km
Population in 2006: 935
Provincial Electoral District(s): Batoche

Federal Electoral District(s): Prince Albert
Next Election: Oct. 2009 (3 year terms)
Note: Proclaimed as a town on Aug. 1, 1960.
Shirley Ulvild, Mayor
Darlene Cochrane, Administrator

Bjorkdale
P.O. Box 27
Bjorkdale, SK S0E 0E0
306-886-2167 Fax: 306-886-2167
www.newsaskcfdc.ca/bjorkdale.htm
Municipal Type: Village
Incorporated: April 1, 1968; *Area:* 1.39 sq km
Population in 2006: 201
Provincial Electoral District(s): Kelvington-Wadena
Federal Electoral District(s): Yorkton-Melville
Next Election: Oct. 2009 (3 year terms)
Joanne Kehrig, Administrator
Brad Wearing, Mayor

Bladworth
P.O. Box 90
Bladworth, SK S0G 0J0
306-567-4364
Municipal Type: Village
Incorporated: July 27, 1906; *Area:* 0.84 sq km
Population in 2006: 70
Provincial Electoral District(s): Arm River-Watrous
Federal Electoral District(s): Blackstrap
Next Election: Oct. 2009 (3 year terms)
Marion Bessey, Clerk
Ron Bessey, Mayor

Blaine Lake
P.O. Box 10
Blaine Lake, SK S0J 0J0
306-497-2531 Fax: 306-497-2511
blainelake@sasktel.net
Municipal Type: Town
Incorporated: March 15, 1912; *Area:* 1.75 sq km
Population in 2006: 472
Provincial Electoral District(s): Rosthern-Shellbrook
Federal Electoral District(s): Saskatoon-Wanuskewin
Next Election: Oct. 2009 (3 year terms)
Note: Proclaimed as a town on March 1, 1954.
Ernie Crowder, Mayor
Anna Brad, Administrator

Borden
P.O. Box 210
Borden, SK S0K 0N0
306-997-2134 Fax: 306-997-2134
borden@sasktel.net
www.bordensask.com
Municipal Type: Village
Incorporated: July 19, 1907; *Area:* 0.76 sq km
Population in 2006: 223
Provincial Electoral District(s): Biggar
Federal Electoral District(s): Saskatoon-Wanuskewin
Next Election: Oct. 2009 (3 year terms)
Sandra Long, Administrator
John Rawlych, Mayor

Bracken
P.O. Box 41
Bracken, SK S0N 0G0
306-293-2700 Fax: 306-293-2221
Municipal Type: Village
Incorporated: Jan. 4, 1926; *Area:* 0.60 sq km
Population in 2006: 25
Provincial Electoral District(s): Wood River
Federal Electoral District(s): Cypress Hills-Grasslands
Next Election: Oct. 2009 (3 year terms)
Ron Johnson, Administrator
Steve Dueck, Mayor

Bradwell
P.O. Box 100
Bradwell, SK S0K 0P0
306-257-4141 Fax: 306-257-3303
rm343@sasktel.net
Municipal Type: Village
Incorporated: July 13, 1910; *Area:* 0.42 sq km
Population in 2006: 182
Provincial Electoral District(s): Humboldt
Federal Electoral District(s): Blackstrap
Next Election: Oct. 2009 (3 year terms)
Robert Thurmeier, Administrator
Ken Hartz, Mayor

Bredenbury
P.O. Box 87
Bredenbury, SK S0A 0H0
306-898-2055 Fax: 306-898-2103
bredenbury@sasktel.net
Municipal Type: Town
Incorporated: May 3, 1911; *Area:* 4.80 sq km
Population in 2006: 329
Provincial Electoral District(s): Melville-Saltcoats
Federal Electoral District(s): Yorkton-Melville
Next Election: Oct. 2009 (3 year terms)
Note: Proclaimed as a town on May 1, 1913.
Glenn Langford, Mayor
Kim Varga, Administrator

Briercrest
P.O. Box 25
Briercrest, SK S0H 0K0
306-799-2066 Fax: 306-799-2067
villageofbriercrest@sasktel.net
Municipal Type: Village
Incorporated: April 17, 1912; *Area:* 0.62 sq km
Population in 2006: 117
Provincial Electoral District(s): Indian Head-Milestone
Federal Electoral District(s): Palliser
Next Election: Oct. 2009 (3 year terms)
Sandra Warnock, Administrator
Russ Adams, Mayor

Broadview
P.O. Box 430
Broadview, SK S0G 0K0
306-696-2533 Fax: 306-696-3573
town.of.broadview@sasktel.net
www.broadview.ca
Municipal Type: Town
Incorporated: Dec. 29, 1898; *Area:* 2.45 sq km
Population in 2006: 611
Provincial Electoral District(s): Moosomin
Federal Electoral District(s): Souris-Moose Mountain
Next Election: Oct. 2009 (3 year terms)
Note: Proclaimed as a town on May 15, 1907.
Sidney Criddle, Mayor
Mervin J. Schmidt, Administrator

Brock
P.O. Box 70
Brock, SK S0L 0H0
306-379-2116 Fax: 306-463-4577
kathy.l@kindersley.ca
Municipal Type: Village
Incorporated: July 7, 1910; *Area:* 0.74 sq km
Population in 2006: 115
Provincial Electoral District(s): Rosetown-Elrose
Federal Electoral District(s): Battlefords-Lloydminster
Next Election: Oct. 2009 (3 year terms)
Kathy Leidl, Clerk
Jim Gartner, Mayor

Broderick
P.O. Box 29
Broderick, SK S0H 0L0
306-867-8036 Fax: 306-867-9620
egnadeau@sasktel.net
Municipal Type: Village
Incorporated: Sept. 13, 1909; *Area:* 0.91 sq km
Population in 2006: 77
Provincial Electoral District(s): Rosetown-Elrose
Federal Electoral District(s): Blackstrap
Next Election: Oct. 2009 (3 year terms)
Kim Olson, Clerk

Brownlee
P.O. Box 89
Brownlee, SK S0H 0M0
306-759-2302
Municipal Type: Village
Incorporated: Dec. 29, 1908; *Area:* 2.42 sq km
Population in 2006: 50
Provincial Electoral District(s): Thunder Creek
Federal Electoral District(s): Regina-Lumsden-Lake Centre
Next Election: Oct. 2009 (3 year terms)
Jackie Leggott, Clerk
Lyle Swanson, Mayor

Bruno
P.O. Box 370
Bruno, SK S0K 0S0
306-369-2514 Fax: 306-369-2878
bruno@sasktel.net
Municipal Type: Town
Incorporated: March 9, 1909; *Area:* 0.95 sq km
Population in 2006: 495
Provincial Electoral District(s): Humboldt
Federal Electoral District(s): Saskatoon-Humboldt
Next Election: Oct. 2009 (3 year terms)
Note: Proclaimed as a town on Jan. 1, 1962.
Audrey Ludwig, Mayor
Kim Sopotyk, Administrator

Buchanan
P.O. Box 479
Buchanan, SK S0A 0J0
306-592-2144 Fax: 306-592-4471
buchananvillage@sasktel.net
www.goodspiritreda.com/profiles/buchanan.html
Municipal Type: Village
Incorporated: June 11, 1907; *Area:* 1.29 sq km
Population in 2006: 225
Provincial Electoral District(s): Canora-Pelly
Federal Electoral District(s): Yorkton-Melville
Next Election: Oct. 2009 (3 year terms)
Eleanor May Hadubiak, Administrator
Adam Kosar, Mayor

Buena Vista
1050 Grand Ave.
Buena Vista, SK S2V 1A2
306-729-4385 Fax: 306-729-4518
buenavista@sasktel.net
www.lumsden.ca/buenavista
Municipal Type: Village
Incorporated: Nov. 18, 1983; *Area:* 3.61 sq km
Population in 2006: 490
Provincial Electoral District(s): Thunder Creek
Federal Electoral District(s): Regina-Lumsden-Lake Centre
Next Election: Oct. 2009 (3 year terms)
Larry Hall, Mayor
Anne Fink, Administrator

Buffalo Narrows
P.O. Box 98
Waite St.
Buffalo Narrows, SK S0M 0J0
306-235-4225 Fax: 306-235-4699
www.sasked.gov.sk.ca/schools/twin_lakes/bn.html
Municipal Type: Northern Village
Incorporated: Oct. 1, 1983; *Area:* 34.10 sq km
Population in 2006: 1,081
Provincial Electoral District(s): Athabasca
Federal Electoral District(s): Churchill River/Rivière Churchill
Next Election: 2009 (3 year terms)
Bobby Woods, Mayor
Therese Chartier, Administrator

Bulyea
P.O. Box 37
Bulyea, SK S0G 0L0
306-725-4936
info@bulyea.com
www.bulyea.com
Municipal Type: Village
Incorporated: March 9, 1909; *Area:* 1.28 sq km
Population in 2006: 104
Provincial Electoral District(s): Last Mountain-Touchwood
Federal Electoral District(s): Regina-Lumsden-Lake Centre
Next Election: Oct. 2009 (3 year terms)
Janice Ritter, Clerk
Darren Cameron, Mayor

Burstall
P.O. Box 250
Burstall, SK S0N 0H0
306-679-2000 Fax: 306-679-2275
burstall@sasktel.net
www.burstall.ca
Municipal Type: Town
Incorporated: May 31, 1921; *Area:* 1.11 sq km
Population in 2006: 315
Provincial Electoral District(s): Cypress Hills
Federal Electoral District(s): Cypress Hills-Grasslands
Next Election: Oct. 2009 (3 year terms)
Note: Proclaimed as a town on Nov. 1, 1976.
Ken Hook, Mayor
Lucein Stuebing, Administrator

Cabri
P.O. Box 200
Cabri, SK S0N 0J0
306-587-2500 Fax: 306-587-2392
townofcabri@sasktel.net
www.cabri.sasktelwebsite.net
Municipal Type: Town
Incorporated: May 13, 1912; *Area:* 1.33 sq km
Population in 2006: 439
Provincial Electoral District(s): Cypress Hills
Federal Electoral District(s): Cypress Hills-Grasslands
Next Election: Oct. 2009 (3 year terms)
Note: Proclaimed as a town on April 16, 1917.
Robert Oldhaver, Mayor
Kristi Jamieson, Administrator

Cadillac
P.O. Box 189
Cadillac, SK S0N 0K0
306-785-2100 Fax: 306-785-2101
v.cadillac@sasktel.net
Municipal Type: Village
Incorporated: July 2, 1914; *Area:* 1.05 sq km
Population in 2006: 80
Provincial Electoral District(s): Wood River
Federal Electoral District(s): Cypress Hills-Grasslands
Next Election: Oct. 2009 (3 year terms)
Betty Moller, Clerk
Holly Franklin, Mayor

Calder
P.O. Box 47
Calder, SK S0A 0K0
306-742-2158 Fax: 306-742-2158
Municipal Type: Village
Incorporated: Jan. 18, 1911; *Area:* 0.75 sq km
Population in 2006: 80
Provincial Electoral District(s): Melville-Saltcoats
Federal Electoral District(s): Yorkton-Melville
Next Election: Oct. 2009 (3 year terms)
Kendra Busch, Administrator
Walter Balabuk, Mayor

Canora
P.O. Box 717
418 Main St.
Canora, SK S0A 0L0

306-563-5773 Fax: 306-563-4336
admin.canora@sasktel.net
www.canora.com
Municipal Type: Town
Incorporated: April 8, 1905; *Area:* 7.31 sq km
Population in 2006: 2,013
Provincial Electoral District(s): Canora-Pelly
Federal Electoral District(s): Yorkton-Melville
Next Election: Oct. 2009 (3 year terms)
Note: Proclaimed as a town on Nov. 1, 1910.
Terry Dennis, Mayor
306-563-6485
Michael Mykytyshyn, Administrator

Canwood
P.O. Box 172
Canwood, SK S0J 0K0
306-468-2016 Fax: 306-468-2666
canwood.town@sasktel.net
Municipal Type: Village
Incorporated: July 18, 1916; *Area:* 2.56 sq km
Population in 2006: 337
Provincial Electoral District(s): Rosthern-Shellbrook
Federal Electoral District(s): Desnethé-Missinippi-Churchill River
Next Election: Oct. 2009 (3 year terms)
Lorna Benson, Administrator
Arthur Young, Mayor

Carievale
P.O. Box 88
128 Broadway St.
Carievale, SK S0C 0P0
306-928-2033 Fax: 306-928-2021
village.carievale@sasktel.net
Municipal Type: Village
Incorporated: March 14, 1903; *Area:* 0.88 sq km
Population in 2006: 241
Provincial Electoral District(s): Cannington
Federal Electoral District(s): Souris-Moose Mountain
Next Election: Oct. 2009 (3 year terms)
Donalene McMillen, Administrator
Eric Hoefer, Mayor

Carlyle
P.O. Box 10
Carlyle, SK S0C 0R0
306-453-2363 Fax: 306-453-6380
towncarlyle@sasktel.net
www.townofcarlyle.com
Municipal Type: Town
Incorporated: March 13, 1902; *Area:* 3.03 sq km
Population in 2006: 1,257
Provincial Electoral District(s): Cannington
Federal Electoral District(s): Souris-Moose Mountain
Next Election: Oct. 2009 (3 year terms)
Note: Proclaimed as a town on Jan. 1, 1906.
Don Shirley, Mayor
Huguette Lutz, Administrator

Carmichael
P.O. Box 420
Gull Lake, SK S0N 1A0
306-672-3501 Fax: 306-672-3879
rm109@sasktel.net
Municipal Type: Village
Incorporated: May 25, 1917; *Area:* 0.67 sq km
Population in 2006: 10
Provincial Electoral District(s): Cypress Hills
Federal Electoral District(s): Cypress Hills-Grasslands
Next Election: Oct. 2009 (3 year terms)
Collette Jones, Clerk
Miles C. Wells, Mayor

Carnduff
P.O. Box 100
Carnduff, SK S0C 0S0
306-482-3300 Fax: 306-482-3422
town.carnduff@sasktel.net
www.carnduff.ca
Municipal Type: Town
Incorporated: March 29, 1899; *Area:* 2.05 sq km
Population in 2006: 1,012
Provincial Electoral District(s): Cannington
Federal Electoral District(s): Souris-Moose Mountain
Next Election: Oct. 2009 (3 year terms)
Note: Proclaimed as a town on Aug. 12, 1905.
John McFarlane, Mayor
Rodney Audette, Administrator

Caronport
P.O. Box 550
Caronport, SK S0H 0S0
306-756-2225 Fax: 306-756-5007
vcoffice@sasktel.net
Municipal Type: Village
Incorporated: Jan. 1, 1988; *Area:* 1.90 sq km
Population in 2006: 919
Provincial Electoral District(s): Thunder Creek
Federal Electoral District(s): Palliser
Next Election: Oct. 2009 (3 year terms)
Paul Blankestijn, Mayor
Brenda Thiessen, Administrator

Carrot River
P.O. Box 147
5 Main St.
Carrot River, SK S0E 0L0
306-768-2515 Fax: 306-768-2930
t.carrotriver@sasktel.net
www.town.carrotriver.sk.ca
Municipal Type: Town
Incorporated: Nov. 6, 1941; *Area:* 1.46 sq km
Population in 2006: 941
Provincial Electoral District(s): Carrot River Valley
Federal Electoral District(s): Prince Albert
Next Election: Oct. 2009 (3 year terms)
Note: Proclaimed as a town on April 1, 1948.
Jim Doherty, Mayor
Duril Touet, Administrator

Central Butte
P.O. Box 10
Central Butte, SK S0H 0T0
306-796-2288 Fax: 306-796-4627
townofcentralbutte@sasktel.net
www.centralb.sasktelwebsite.net
Municipal Type: Town
Incorporated: April 9, 1915; *Area:* 2.24 sq km
Population in 2006: 372
Provincial Electoral District(s): Thunder Creek
Federal Electoral District(s): Cypress Hills-Grasslands
Next Election: Oct. 2009 (3 year terms)
Note: Proclaimed as a town on July 1, 1967.
Alvin Klassen, Mayor
Joyce Aitken, Administrator

Ceylon
P.O. Box 188
Ceylon, SK S0C 0T0
306-454-2202 Fax: 306-454-2627
rmgap39@sasktel.net
Municipal Type: Village
Incorporated: Sept. 26, 1911; *Area:* 0.75 sq km
Population in 2006: 90
Provincial Electoral District(s): Weyburn-Big Muddy
Federal Electoral District(s): Souris-Moose Mountain
Next Election: Oct. 2009 (3 year terms)
Yvonne Johnston, Administrator
Larry Harkes, Mayor

Chamberlain
P.O. Box 8
Chamberlain, SK S0G 0R0
306-638-4680 Fax: 306-638-3108
chamberlain_sk@yahoo.com
Municipal Type: Village
Incorporated: Jan. 31, 1911; *Area:* 0.70 sq km
Population in 2006: 108
Provincial Electoral District(s): Thunder Creek
Federal Electoral District(s): Regina-Lumsden-Lake Centre
Next Election: Oct. 2009 (3 year terms)
Rhonda Lang, Clerk
Kevin Uhrich, Mayor

Chaplin
P.O. Box 210
Chaplin, SK S0H 0V0
306-395-2221 Fax: 306-395-2555
village.chaplin@sasktel.net
Municipal Type: Village
Incorporated: Oct. 8, 1912; *Area:* 1.26 sq km
Population in 2006: 235
Provincial Electoral District(s): Thunder Creek
Federal Electoral District(s): Cypress Hills-Grasslands
Next Election: Oct. 2009 (3 year terms)
Julie Gerbrandt, Administrator
Michael Forsberg, Mayor

Choiceland
P.O. Box 279
100 Railway Ave. East
Choiceland, SK S0J 0M0
306-428-2070 Fax: 306-428-2071
choiceland.town@sasktel.net
www.choicelandsk.com
Municipal Type: Town
Incorporated: Sept. 8, 1944; *Area:* 1.12 sq km
Population in 2006: 346
Provincial Electoral District(s): Saskatchewan Rivers
Federal Electoral District(s): Desnethé-Missinippi-Churchill River
Next Election: Oct. 2009 (3 year terms)
Note: Proclaimed as a town on Jan. 1, 1979.
Elaine L. McLean, Administrator
Wayne Debler, Mayor

Christopher Lake
P.O. Box 163
Christopher Lake, SK S0J 0N0
306-982-4242 Fax: 306-982-4242
vilchr@sasktel.net
Municipal Type: Village
Incorporated: March 1, 1985; *Area:* 3.47 sq km
Population in 2006: 215
Provincial Electoral District(s): Saskatchewan Rivers
Federal Electoral District(s): Desnethé-Missinippi-Churchill River
Next Election: Oct. 2009 (3 year terms)
Audrey Veer, Administrator
Denis Daughton, Mayor

Churchbridge
P.O. Box 256
116 Vincent Ave.
Churchbridge, SK S0A 0M0
306-896-2240 Fax: 306-896-2910
churchbridge@sasktel.net
www.churchbridge.com
Municipal Type: Town
Incorporated: Sept. 17, 1903; *Area:* 2.76 sq km
Population in 2006: 704
Provincial Electoral District(s): Melville-Saltcoats
Federal Electoral District(s): Yorkton-Melville
Next Election: Oct. 2009 (3 year terms)
Note: Proclaimed as a town on March 1, 1964.
Walter Karau, Mayor
Gail Welygan, Administrator

Clavet
P.O. Box 68
Clavet, SK S0K 0Y0
306-933-2425 Fax: 306-933-1995
clavetvillage@sasktel.net
Municipal Type: Village
Incorporated: Dec. 21, 1908; *Area:* 0.61 sq km
Population in 2006: 345
Provincial Electoral District(s): Humboldt
Federal Electoral District(s): Blackstrap
Next Election: Oct. 2009 (3 year terms)
Monica Buddecke, Clerk
Blair Bentley, Mayor

Climax
P.O. Box 30
Climax, SK S0N 0N0
306-293-2124 Fax: 306-293-2702
Municipal Type: Village
Incorporated: Dec. 11, 1923; *Area:* 1.00 sq km
Population in 2006: 182
Provincial Electoral District(s): Cypress Hills
Federal Electoral District(s): Cypress Hills-Grasslands
Next Election: Oct. 2009 (3 year terms)
Shawna-Lee Bertram, Administrator
Nancy Kirk, Mayor

Coderre
P.O. Box 9
Coderre, SK S0H 0X0
306-394-2070
Municipal Type: Village
Incorporated: Aug. 26, 1925; *Area:* 0.85 sq km
Population in 2006: 40
Provincial Electoral District(s): Wood River
Federal Electoral District(s): Cypress Hills-Grasslands
Next Election: Oct. 2009 (3 year terms)
Faye Johnstone, Clerk
David Duckworth, Mayor

Codette
P.O. Box 100
Codette, SK S0E 0P0
306-862-9551 Fax: 306-862-2432
rm487@sasktel.net
Municipal Type: Village
Incorporated: March 9, 1929; *Area:* 0.37 sq km
Population in 2006: 221
Provincial Electoral District(s): Carrot River Valley
Federal Electoral District(s): Prince Albert
Next Election: Oct. 2009 (3 year terms)
Eunice Rudy, Clerk
Natalie Hipkins, Mayor

Cole Bay
P.O. Box 80
Canoe Rd.
Cole Bay, SK S0M 0M0
306-829-4232 Fax: 306-829-4312
Municipal Type: Northern Village
Incorporated: Jan. 1, 1990; *Area:* 4.95 sq km
Population in 2006: 156
Provincial Electoral District(s): Athabasca
Federal Electoral District(s): Desnethé-Missinippi-Churchill River
Next Election: 2009 (3 year terms)
Delphine Bouvier, Clerk
Harold Aubichon, Mayor

Coleville
P.O. Box 249
Coleville, SK S0L 0K0
306-965-2281 Fax: 306-965-2466
Municipal Type: Village
Incorporated: July 1, 1953; *Area:* 1.27 sq km
Population in 2006: 248
Provincial Electoral District(s): Kindersley
Federal Electoral District(s): Battlefords-Lloydminster
Next Election: Oct. 2009 (3 year terms)
Gloria Johnson, Administrator
Mike Smith, Mayor

Colonsay
P.O. Box 190
513 Railway Ave.
Colonsay, SK S0K 0Z0
306-255-2313 Fax: 306-255-2291
town.colonsay@sasktel.net
www.townofcolonsay.com

Municipal Type: Town
Incorporated: Oct. 6, 1910; *Area:* 2.46 sq km
Population in 2006: 425
Provincial Electoral District(s): Humboldt
Federal Electoral District(s): Blackstrap
Next Election: Oct. 2009 (3 year terms)
Note: Proclaimed as a town on Jan. 1, 1977.
James Gray, Mayor
Deborah Prosper, Administrator

Conquest
P.O. Box 250
Conquest, SK S0L 0L0
306-856-2114 Fax: 306-856-2114
conquest@sasktel.net
Municipal Type: Village
Incorporated: Oct. 24, 1911; *Area:* 1 sq km
Population in 2006: 167
Provincial Electoral District(s): Rosetown-Elrose
Federal Electoral District(s): Cypress Hills-Grasslands
Next Election: Oct. 2009 (3 year terms)
L. Jean Jones, Administrator
Doug Lemon, Mayor

Consul
P.O. Box 185
Consul, SK S0N 0P0
306-299-2030 Fax: 306-299-2031
consul@sasktel.net
Municipal Type: Village
Incorporated: June 12, 1917; *Area:* 0.65 sq km
Population in 2006: 93
Provincial Electoral District(s): Cypress Hills
Federal Electoral District(s): Cypress Hills-Grasslands
Next Election: Oct. 2009 (3 year terms)
Carrie Funk, Administrator
Linda Brown, Mayor

Coronach
P.O. Box 90
Coronach, SK S0H 0Z0
306-267-2150 Fax: 306-267-2296
townoffice@coronach.ca
www.coronach.ca
Municipal Type: Town
Incorporated: Feb. 3, 1928; *Area:* 2.33 sq km
Population in 2006: 770
Provincial Electoral District(s): Weyburn-Big Muddy
Federal Electoral District(s): Souris-Moose Mountain
Next Election: Oct. 2009 (3 year terms)
Note: Proclaimed as a town on Jan. 1, 1977.
Alexander (Skip) McBain, Mayor
Murray H. Setrum, Administrator

Craik
P.O. Box 60
Craik, SK S0G 0V0
306-734-2250 Fax: 306-734-2688
town.craik@sasktel.net
www.craik.ca
Municipal Type: Town
Incorporated: Oct. 22, 1903; *Area:* 5.41 sq km
Population in 2006: 408
Provincial Electoral District(s): Thunder Creek
Federal Electoral District(s): Regina-Lumsden-Lake Centre
Next Election: Oct. 2009 (3 year terms)
Note: Proclaimed as a town on Aug. 1, 1907.
Rodney Haugerud, Mayor
Tallie Ehman, Administrator

Craven
P.O. Box 30
Craven, SK S0G 0W0
306-731-3452 Fax: 306-731-3162
Municipal Type: Village
Incorporated: April 11, 1905; *Area:* 1.16 sq km
Population in 2006: 274
Provincial Electoral District(s): Last Mountain-Touchwood
Federal Electoral District(s): Regina-Lumsden-Lake Centre
Next Election: Oct. 2009 (3 year terms)
Audrey Webb, Clerk
Adri Vandeven, Mayor

Creelman
P.O. Box 177
Creelman, SK S0G 0X0
306-433-2011 Fax: 306-433-2011
creelmanvillage@sasktel.net
www.creda.sk.ca/creelman
Municipal Type: Village
Incorporated: April 6, 1906; *Area:* 1.14 sq km
Population in 2006: 81
Provincial Electoral District(s): Cannington
Federal Electoral District(s): Souris-Moose Mountain
Next Election: Oct. 2009 (3 year terms)
Vernna Wiggins, Administrator
Don Anslow, Mayor

Creighton
P.O. Box 100
Creighton, SK S0P 0A0
306-688-8253 Fax: 306-688-4764
townofcreighton@sasktel.net
www.townofcreighton.ca
Municipal Type: Northern Town
Incorporated: Oct. 1, 1983; *Area:* 14.39 sq km
Population in 2006: 1,502
Provincial Electoral District(s): Cumberland
Federal Electoral District(s): Desnethé-Missinippi-Churchill River
Next Election: 2009 (3 year terms)
Bruce Fidler, Mayor
Paula Muench, Administrator

Cudworth
P.O. Box 69
223 Main St.
Cudworth, SK S0K 1B0
306-256-3492 Fax: 306-256-3515
town.cudworth@sasktel.net
www.townofcudworth.com
Municipal Type: Town
Incorporated: Oct. 23, 1911; *Area:* 2.21 sq km
Population in 2006: 730
Provincial Electoral District(s): Batoche
Federal Electoral District(s): Saskatoon-Humboldt
Next Election: Oct. 2009 (3 year terms)
Note: Proclaimed as a town on Oct. 1, 1961.
Harold Mueller, Mayor
Yvonne Gobolos, Clerk

Cumberland House
P.O. Box 190
Cumberland St.
Cumberland House, SK S0E 0S0
306-888-2066 Fax: 306-888-2103
northernvillageofchouse@sasktel.net
Municipal Type: Northern Village
Incorporated: Oct. 1, 1983; *Area:* 15.69 sq km
Population in 2006: 810
Provincial Electoral District(s): Cumberland
Federal Electoral District(s): Desnethé-Missinippi-Churchill River
Next Election: Oct. 2009 (3 year terms)
Andy McKay, Mayor
Rachel Fiddler, Clerk

Cupar
P.O. Box 397
Cupar, SK S0G 0Y0
306-723-4324 Fax: 306-723-4644
townofcupar@sasktel.net
www.townofcupar.com
Municipal Type: Town
Incorporated: March 21, 1906; *Area:* 0.80 sq km
Population in 2006: 566
Provincial Electoral District(s): Last Mountain-Touchwood
Federal Electoral District(s): Regina-Qu'Appelle
Next Election: Oct. 2009 (3 year terms)
Note: Proclaimed as a town on Jan. 1, 1961.
Val Orb, Mayor
Linda Nameth, Administrator

Cut Knife
P.O. Box 70
Cut Knife, SK S0M 0N0
306-398-2363 Fax: 306-398-2839
rm439@sasktel.net
Municipal Type: Town
Incorporated: May 17, 1912; *Area:* 1.99 sq km
Population in 2006: 532
Provincial Electoral District(s): Cut Knife-Turtleford
Federal Electoral District(s): Battlefords-Lloydminster
Next Election: Oct. 2009 (3 year terms)
Note: Proclaimed as a town on Aug. 1, 1968.
Germaine Vany, Mayor
Don McCallum, Administrator

Dafoe
P.O. Box 142
Dafoe, SK S0K 1C0
306-554-3250
Municipal Type: Village
Incorporated: May 28, 1920; *Area:* 0.80 sq km
Population in 2006: 10
Provincial Electoral District(s): Rosetown-Elrose
Federal Electoral District(s): Regina-Qu'Appelle
Next Election: Oct. 2009 (3 year terms)
Lana M. Bolt, Clerk
Ron Jordan, Mayor

Dalmeny
P.O. Box 400
301 Railway Ave.
Dalmeny, SK S0K 1E0
306-254-2133 Fax: 306-254-2142
dalmenytownoffice@sasktel.net
www.towndalmeny.ca
Municipal Type: Town
Incorporated: June 17, 1912; *Area:* 2.27 sq km
Population in 2006: 1,560
Provincial Electoral District(s): Weyburn-Big Muddy
Federal Electoral District(s): Saskatoon-Wanuskewin
Next Election: Oct. 2009 (3 year terms)
Note: Proclaimed as a town on April 1, 1983.
Allan Earle, Mayor
Shelley Funk, Administrator

Davidson
P.O. Box 340
Davidson, SK S0G 1A0
306-567-2040 Fax: 306-567-4730
townofdavidson@sasktel.net
www.townofdavidson.com
Municipal Type: Town
Incorporated: March 7, 1904; *Area:* 4.49 sq km
Population in 2006: 958
Provincial Electoral District(s): Arm River-Watrous
Federal Electoral District(s): Regina-Lumsden-Lake Centre
Next Election: Oct. 2009 (3 year terms)
Note: Proclaimed as a town on Nov. 15, 1906.
Mary Jane Morrison, Mayor
Gary Edom, Administrator

Debden
P.O. Box 400
Debden, SK S0J 0S0
306-724-2040 Fax: 306-724-2220
vdebden@sasktel.net
Municipal Type: Village
Incorporated: June 7, 1922; *Area:* 1.39 sq km
Population in 2006: 348
Provincial Electoral District(s): Saskatchewan Rivers
Federal Electoral District(s): Desnethé-Missinippi-Churchill River
Next Election: Oct. 2009 (3 year terms)
Carmen Jean, Administrator
Ron Reres, Mayor

Delisle
P.O. Box 40
201 - 1st St. West
Delisle, SK S0L 0P0
306-493-2242 Fax: 306-493-2263
delisle@sasktel.net
www.townofdelisle.com
Municipal Type: Town
Incorporated: Dec. 29, 1908; *Area:* 2.35 sq km
Population in 2006: 898
Provincial Electoral District(s): Biggar
Federal Electoral District(s): Saskatoon-Rosetown-Biggar
Next Election: Oct. 2009 (3 year terms)
Note: Proclaimed as a town on Nov. 1, 1913.
Rita Pfoh, Mayor
306-493-2652
Mark Dubkowski, Administrator

Denare Beach
P.O. Box 70
512 - 7th Ave.
Denare Beach, SK S0P 0B0
306-362-2054 Fax: 306-362-2257
denarebeach@aski.ca
Municipal Type: Northern Village
Incorporated: April 1, 1984; *Area:* 5.84 sq km
Population in 2006: 785
Provincial Electoral District(s): Cumberland
Federal Electoral District(s): Desnethé-Missinippi-Churchill River
Next Election: Oct. 2009 (3 year terms)
Carl Lentowicz, Mayor
Bev Wheeler, Administrator

Denholm
P.O. Box 71
Denholm, SK S0M 0R0
306-446-0478
Municipal Type: Village
Incorporated: June 25, 1912; *Area:* 0.33 sq km
Population in 2006: 61
Provincial Electoral District(s): Biggar
Federal Electoral District(s): Battlefords-Lloydminster
Next Election: Oct. 2009 (3 year terms)
Lila Yuhasz, Clerk
Terry Welch, Mayor

Denzil
P.O. Box 100
Denzil, SK S0L 0S0
306-358-2118 Fax: 306-358-4828
villageofdenzil@sasktel.net
Municipal Type: Village
Incorporated: May 3, 1911; *Area:* 0.55 sq km
Population in 2006: 142
Provincial Electoral District(s): Kindersley
Federal Electoral District(s): Battlefords-Lloydminster
Next Election: Oct. 2009 (3 year terms)
Kathy Reschny, Administrator
Murray Sieben, Mayor

Dilke
P.O. Box 100
Dilke, SK S0G 1C0
306-488-4866 Fax: 306-488-4866
Municipal Type: Village
Incorporated: Dec. 30, 1912; *Area:* 1.28 sq km
Population in 2006: 80
Provincial Electoral District(s): Thunder Creek
Federal Electoral District(s): Regina-Lumsden-Lake Centre
Next Election: Oct. 2009 (3 year terms)
Colleen R. Duesing, Clerk
Arnold Ball, Mayor

Dinsmore
P.O. Box 278
100 Main St.
Dinsmore, SK S0L 0T0

306-846-2220 Fax: 306-846-2999
dinsmore@sasktel.net
www.dinsmore.ca
Municipal Type: Village
Incorporated: Nov. 3, 1913; *Area:* 2.59 sq km
Population in 2006: 269
Provincial Electoral District(s): Rosetown-Elrose
Federal Electoral District(s): Cypress Hills-Grasslands
Next Election: Oct. 2009 (3 year terms)
Jim Main, Administrator
Janice Thomson, Mayor
j.thomson.cma@sasktel.net

Disley
P.O. Box 184
Bethune, SK S0G 0H0
306-638-3188
Municipal Type: Village
Incorporated: June 24, 1907; *Area:* 0.65 sq km
Population in 2006: 62
Provincial Electoral District(s): Thunder Creek
Federal Electoral District(s): Regina-Lumsden-Lake Centre
Next Election: Oct. 2009 (3 year terms)
Norman Noel, Mayor
Patti Vance, Clerk

Dodsland
P.O. Box 400
Dodsland, SK S0L 0V0
306-356-2106 Fax: 306-356-2085
rmwinslow319@xplornet.com
Municipal Type: Village
Incorporated: Aug. 23, 1913; *Area:* 2.93 sq km
Population in 2006: 207
Provincial Electoral District(s): Rosetown-Elrose
Federal Electoral District(s): Battlefords-Lloydminster
Next Election: Oct. 2009 (3 year terms)
Regan MacDonald, Administrator
Kevin McCarthy, Mayor

Dore Lake
P.O. Box 608
Dore Ave.
Big River, SK S0J 0E0
306-832-4528 Fax: 306-832-4525
northern.dore@sasktel.net
Municipal Type: Northern Hamlet
Incorporated: Jan. 11, 1985; *Area:* 8.03 sq km
Population in 2006: 30
Provincial Electoral District(s): Athabasca
Federal Electoral District(s): Desnethé-Missinippi-Churchill River
Next Election: 2009 (3 year terms)
Eugenie Lafleur, Administrator
Carl Feszyk, Mayor

Dorintosh
P.O. Box 40
301 1st St. East
Dorintosh, SK S0M 0T0
306-236-5166 Fax: 306-236-5166
vill.dor@sasktel.net
Municipal Type: Village
Incorporated: Jan. 1, 1989; *Area:* 0.88 sq km
Population in 2006: 127
Provincial Electoral District(s): Meadow Lake
Federal Electoral District(s): Desnethé-Missinippi-Churchill River
Next Election: Oct. 2009 (3 year terms)
Pam Dallyn, Assistant Administrator
John Osborne, Mayor

Drake
P.O. Box 18
Drake, SK S0K 1H0
306-363-2109 Fax: 306-363-2102
villageofdrake@sasktel.net
www.drake.ca
Municipal Type: Village
Incorporated: Sept. 19, 1910; *Area:* 0.72 sq km
Population in 2006: 232
Provincial Electoral District(s): Arm River-Watrous
Federal Electoral District(s): Blackstrap
Next Election: Oct. 2009 (3 year terms)
Stuart Jantz, Administrator
Peter Nicholson, Mayor

Drinkwater
P.O. Box 66
Drinkwater, SK S0H 1G0
306-693-5093 Fax: 306-693-5093
villageofdrinkwater@sasktel.net
Municipal Type: Village
Incorporated: June 7, 1904; *Area:* 2.64 sq km
Population in 2006: 65
Provincial Electoral District(s): Indian Head-Milestone
Federal Electoral District(s): Palliser
Next Election: Oct. 2009 (3 year terms)
Sandra Warnock, Clerk
Steve Gilroy, Mayor

Dubuc
P.O. Box 126
Bernier St.
Dubuc, SK S0A 0R0
306-877-2172
villageofdubuc@sasktel.net
www.spreda.sk.ca/community_Dubuc.htm
Municipal Type: Village
Incorporated: May 29, 1905; *Area:* 0.63 sq km
Population in 2006: 55
Provincial Electoral District(s): Melville-Saltcoats
Federal Electoral District(s): Yorkton-Melville
Next Election: Oct. 2009 (3 year terms)
Marilyn Parker, Clerk
Melba McAlpine, Mayor

Duck Lake
P.O. Box 430
Duck Lake, SK S0K 1J0
306-467-2277 Fax: 306-467-4434
town.ducklake@sasktel.net
www.ducklake.ca
Municipal Type: Town
Incorporated: Dec. 29, 1898; *Area:* 2.86 sq km
Population in 2006: 610
Provincial Electoral District(s): Batoche
Federal Electoral District(s): Saskatoon-Wanuskewin
Next Election: Oct. 2009 (3 year terms)
Note: Proclaimed as a town on Nov. 1, 1911.
Lloyd Debray, Mayor
Betty Fiolleau, Administrator

Duff
P.O. Box 57
Duff, SK S0A 0S0
306-728-3570
www.spreda.sk.ca/community_Duff.htm
Municipal Type: Village
Incorporated: May 28, 1920; *Area:* 0.22 sq km
Population in 2006: 30
Provincial Electoral District(s): Last Mountain-Touchwood
Federal Electoral District(s): Yorkton-Melville
Next Election: Oct. 2009 (3 year terms)
Tracey Schuman, Clerk
David Hollinger, Mayor

Dundurn
P.O. Box 185
300 Third Ave.
Dundurn, SK S0K 1K0
306-492-2202 Fax: 306-492-2360
town.dundurn@sasktel.net
www.townofdundurn.ca
Municipal Type: Town
Incorporated: July 7, 1905; *Area:* 0.88 sq km
Population in 2006: 647
Provincial Electoral District(s): Arm River-Watrous
Federal Electoral District(s): Blackstrap
Next Election: Oct. 2009 (3 year terms)
Note: Proclaimed as a town on Nov. 1, 1980.
Doug Narraway, Mayor
Janet Patry, Administrator

Duval
P.O. Box 70
Duval, SK S0G 1G0
306-725-3767 Fax: 306-725-4339
jeff.jones@sasktel.net
Municipal Type: Village
Incorporated: Dec. 21, 1910; *Area:* 0.75 sq km
Population in 2006: 94
Provincial Electoral District(s): Arm River-Watrous
Federal Electoral District(s): Regina-Lumsden-Lake Centre
Next Election: Oct. 2009 (3 year terms)
Jeff Jones, Clerk
Dale Campbell, Mayor

Dysart
P.O. Box 70
Dysart, SK S0G 1H0
306-432-2100 Fax: 306-432-2265
dysartsk@sasktel.net
www.dysartsk.com
Municipal Type: Village
Incorporated: April 6, 1909; *Area:* 1.19 sq km
Population in 2006: 198
Provincial Electoral District(s): Last Mountain-Touchwood
Federal Electoral District(s): Regina-Qu'Appelle
Next Election: Oct. 2009 (3 year terms)
Gerry Burym, Clerk
Gary Kayter, Mayor

Earl Grey
P.O. Box 100
Earl Grey, SK S0G 1J0
306-939-2062 Fax: 306-939-2036
earlgreyvillage@sasktel.net
earl.sasktelwebhosting.com
Municipal Type: Village
Incorporated: July 27, 1906; *Area:* 1.31 sq km
Population in 2006: 264
Provincial Electoral District(s): Last Mountain-Touchwood
Federal Electoral District(s): Regina-Lumsden-Lake Centre
Next Election: Oct. 2009 (3 year terms)
Murray Cook, Administrator
Allan H. Johnson, Mayor

Eastend
P.O. Box 520
Eastend, SK S0N 0T0
306-295-3322 Fax: 306-295-3571
eastend@sasktel.net
www.dinocountry.com
Municipal Type: Town
Incorporated: Feb. 26, 1914; *Area:* 2.71 sq km
Population in 2006: 471
Provincial Electoral District(s): Cypress Hills
Federal Electoral District(s): Cypress Hills-Grasslands
Next Election: Oct. 2009 (3 year terms)
Note: Proclaimed as a town on March 15, 1920.
Scott Morvik, Mayor
Deb Lewis, Administrator

Eatonia
P.O. Box 237
Eatonia, SK S0L 0Y0
306-967-2251 Fax: 306-967-2267
eatonia@yourlink.ca
www.townofeatonia.com
Municipal Type: Town
Incorporated: Jan. 28, 1920; *Area:* 1.68 sq km
Population in 2006: 449
Provincial Electoral District(s): Kindersley
Federal Electoral District(s): Cypress Hills-Grasslands
Next Election: Oct. 2009 (3 year terms)
Note: Proclaimed as a town on Jan. 1, 1954.
R.W. (Bob) Peters, Mayor
Cheryl Bailey, Administrator

Ebenezer
P.O. Box 97
Ebenezer, SK S0A 0T0
306-783-1217 Fax: 306-793-1218
village.ebenezer@sasktel.net
Municipal Type: Village
Incorporated: July 1, 1948; *Area:* 0.62 sq km
Population in 2006: 139
Provincial Electoral District(s): Canora-Pelly
Federal Electoral District(s): Yorkton-Melville
Next Election: Oct. 2009 (3 year terms)
Angela Filipchuk, Administrator
Ray Miller, Mayor

Edam
P.O. Box 203
Edam, SK S0M 0V0
306-397-2223 Fax: 306-397-2626
edamvill@sasktel.net
Municipal Type: Village
Incorporated: Oct. 12, 1911; *Area:* 1.13 sq km
Population in 2006: 399
Provincial Electoral District(s): Cut Knife-Turtleford
Federal Electoral District(s): Battlefords-Lloydminster
Next Election: Oct. 2009 (3 year terms)
Trudy McMurphy, Administrator
Larry McDaid, Mayor

Edenwold
P.O. Box 130
Edenwold, SK S0G 1K0
306-771-4121 Fax: 306-771-4121
Municipal Type: Village
Incorporated: Oct. 3, 1912; *Area:* 0.68 sq km
Population in 2006: 242
Provincial Electoral District(s): Indian Head-Milestone
Federal Electoral District(s): Regina-Qu'Appelle
Next Election: Oct. 2009 (3 year terms)
Christine Galbraith, Clerk
Kevin Lindenbach, Mayor

Elbow
P.O. Box 8
Elbow, SK S0H 1J0
306-854-2277 Fax: 306-854-2229
info@elbowsask.com
www.elbowsask.com
Municipal Type: Village
Incorporated: April 6, 1909; *Area:* 3.92 sq km
Population in 2006: 294
Provincial Electoral District(s): Thunder Creek
Federal Electoral District(s): Blackstrap
Next Election: Oct. 2009 (3 year terms)
Yvonne Jess, Administrator
David Cross, Mayor

Elfros
P.O. Box 40
Elfros, SK S0A 0V0
306-328-2123 Fax: 306-328-4490
rm307@sasktel.net
Municipal Type: Village
Incorporated: Dec. 1, 1909; *Area:* 2.52 sq km
Population in 2006: 110
Provincial Electoral District(s): Kelvington-Wadena
Federal Electoral District(s): Regina-Qu'Appelle
Next Election: Oct. 2009 (3 year terms)
Glenn Thompson, Administrator
Karilee Zemlak, Mayor

Elrose
P.O. Box 458
Elrose, SK S0L 0Z0

306-378-2202 Fax: 306-378-2966
townofelrose@sasktel.net
Municipal Type: Town
Incorporated: Oct. 24, 1913; *Area:* 2.76 sq km
Population in 2006: 453
Provincial Electoral District(s): Rosetown-Elrose
Federal Electoral District(s): Cypress Hills-Grasslands
Next Election: Oct. 2009 (3 year terms)
Note: Proclaimed as a town on Feb. 1, 1951.
June Hintze, Mayor
Chris Hopkins, Administrator

Elstow
P.O. Box 29
Elstow, SK S0K 1M0
306-257-3889 Fax: 306-257-3709
Municipal Type: Village
Incorporated: Dec. 17, 1908; *Area:* 0.58 sq km
Population in 2006: 91
Provincial Electoral District(s): Humboldt
Federal Electoral District(s): Blackstrap
Next Election: Oct. 2009 (3 year terms)
Elva Greschuk, Clerk
Jed Bruce, Mayor

Endeavour
P.O. Box 307
Endeavour, SK S0A 0W0
306-547-3484 Fax: 306-547-3484
endeavour@sasktel.net
Municipal Type: Village
Incorporated: April 29, 1953; *Area:* 0.99 sq km
Population in 2006: 118
Provincial Electoral District(s): Canora-Pelly
Federal Electoral District(s): Yorkton-Melville
Next Election: Oct. 2009 (3 year terms)
Kathleen Ambrose, Administrator
Roy Sheets, Mayor

Englefeld
P.O. Box 44
Englefeld, SK S0K 1N0
306-287-3151 Fax: 306-287-9902
vengle@sasktel.net
www.englefeld.ca
Municipal Type: Village
Incorporated: June 13, 1916; *Area:* 0.65 sq km
Population in 2006: 227
Provincial Electoral District(s): Melfort
Federal Electoral District(s): Saskatoon-Humboldt
Next Election: Oct. 2009 (3 year terms)
Roman Zimmerman, Clerk
Darrell Athmer, Mayor

Ernfold
P.O. Box 340
Morse, SK S0H 3C0
306-629-3300 Fax: 306-629-3212
rm165@sasktel.net
Municipal Type: Village
Incorporated: Dec. 4, 1912; *Area:* 1.19 sq km
Population in 2006: 35
Provincial Electoral District(s): Thunder Creek
Federal Electoral District(s): Cypress Hills-Grasslands
Next Election: Oct. 2009 (3 year terms)
Mark Wilson, Administrator
Christine Bauck, Mayor

Esterhazy
P.O. Box 490
Esterhazy, SK S0A 0X0
306-745-3942 Fax: 306-745-6797
town.esterhazy@sasktel.net
www.town.esterhazy.sk.ca
Municipal Type: Town
Incorporated: Dec. 3, 1903; *Area:* 4.75 sq km
Population in 2006: 2,336
Provincial Electoral District(s): Melville-Saltcoats
Federal Electoral District(s): Yorkton-Melville
Next Election: Oct. 2009 (3 year terms)
Note: Proclaimed as a town on March 1, 1957.
Herb Hozjan, Mayor
Lois Kubik, Administrator

Eston
P.O. Box 757
Eston, SK S0L 1A0
306-962-4444 Fax: 306-962-4224
townofeston@sasktel.net
www.eston.ca
Municipal Type: Town
Incorporated: March 28, 1916; *Area:* 2.72 sq km
Population in 2006: 971
Provincial Electoral District(s): Rosetown-Elrose
Federal Electoral District(s): Cypress Hills-Grasslands
Next Election: Oct. 2009 (3 year terms)
Note: Proclaimed as a town on Dec. 1, 1928.
Allan Heron, Mayor
Gary Johnson, Administrator

Eyebrow
P.O. Box 159
Eyebrow, SK S0H 1L0
306-759-2167 Fax: 306-759-2388
eyebrowvillage@sasktel.net
www.eyebrowvillage.ca
Municipal Type: Village
Incorporated: Jan. 8, 1909; *Area:* 2.70 sq km
Population in 2006: 135
Provincial Electoral District(s): Thunder Creek
Federal Electoral District(s): Regina-Lumsden-Lake Centre
Next Election: Oct. 2009 (3 year terms)
Joy Harms, Clerk
Don Linton, Mayor

Fairlight
P.O. Box 55
Fairlight, SK S0G 1M0
306-646-4439 Fax: 306-646-2272
village_of_fairlight@yahoo.ca
Municipal Type: Village
Incorporated: Oct. 5, 1909; *Area:* 2.71 sq km
Population in 2006: 40
Provincial Electoral District(s): Cannington
Federal Electoral District(s): Souris-Moose Mountain
Next Election: Oct. 2009 (3 year terms)
Nadia Metz, Administrator
Gerald Toupich, Mayor

Fenwood
P.O. Box 66
Fenwood, SK S0A 0Y0
306-728-4069
www.spreda.sk.ca/community_Fenwood.htm
Municipal Type: Village
Incorporated: June 30, 1909; *Area:* 1.74 sq km
Population in 2006: 35
Provincial Electoral District(s): Last Mountain-Touchwood
Federal Electoral District(s): Yorkton-Melville
Next Election: Oct. 2009 (3 year terms)
Doreen Dohms, Clerk
Byron Dohms, Mayor

Fillmore
P.O. Box 185
Fillmore, SK S0G 1N0
306-722-3330 Fax: 306-722-3340
v.fillmore@sasktel.net
www.creda.sk.ca/fillmore
Municipal Type: Village
Incorporated: June 10, 1905; *Area:* 1.33 sq km
Population in 2006: 193
Provincial Electoral District(s): Cannington
Federal Electoral District(s): Souris-Moose Mountain
Next Election: Oct. 2009 (3 year terms)
Donna E. Pringle, Administrator
Marvin J. Chambers, Mayor

Findlater
P.O. Box 10
Findlater, SK S0G 1P0
306-638-4630 Fax: 306-638-4630
Municipal Type: Village
Incorporated: Sept. 27, 1911; *Area:* 1.20 sq km
Population in 2006: 49
Provincial Electoral District(s): Thunder Creek
Federal Electoral District(s): Regina-Lumsden-Lake Centre
Next Election: Oct. 2009 (3 year terms)
Colleen Ball, Clerk
Harold Kutcher, Mayor

Flaxcombe
P.O. Box 136
Flaxcombe, SK S0L 1E0
306-463-2004
hopkg.sasktelwebsite.net
Municipal Type: Village
Incorporated: June 4, 1913; *Area:* 1.49 sq km
Population in 2006: 111
Provincial Electoral District(s): Kindersley
Federal Electoral District(s): Battlefords-Lloydminster
Next Election: Oct. 2009 (3 year terms)
Charlotte Helfrich, Clerk
Dolores Doolittle, Mayor

Fleming
P.O. Box 129
Fleming, SK S0G 1R0
306-435-4244
Municipal Type: Town
Incorporated: July 2, 1896; *Area:* 2.17 sq km
Population in 2006: 75
Provincial Electoral District(s): Moosomin
Federal Electoral District(s): Souris-Moose Mountain
Next Election: Oct. 2009 (3 year terms)
Note: Proclaimed as a town on June 15, 1907.
Lisa Chorney, Clerk
Philip Hamm, Mayor

Foam Lake
P.O. Box 57
Foam Lake, SK S0A 1A0
306-272-3359 Fax: 306-272-3738
foamlaketown@sasktel.net
www.foamlake.com
Municipal Type: Town
Incorporated: Oct. 12, 1908; *Area:* 6.06 sq km
Population in 2006: 1,123
Provincial Electoral District(s): Kelvington-Wadena
Federal Electoral District(s): Yorkton-Melville
Next Election: Oct. 2009 (3 year terms)
Note: Proclaimed as a town on March 1, 1924.
Bob Johnson, Mayor
Gloria Leader, Administrator

Forget
P.O. Box 522
Stoughton, SK S0G 4T0
306-457-2277 Fax: 306-457-3149
rmtec@sasktel.net
Municipal Type: Village
Incorporated: Nov. 21, 1904; *Area:* 1.39 sq km
Population in 2006: 40
Provincial Electoral District(s): Cannington
Federal Electoral District(s): Souris-Moose Mountain
Next Election: Oct. 2009 (3 year terms)
Zandra Slater, Administrator
Don Shakotko, Mayor

Fort Qu'Appelle
P.O. Box 309
Fort Qu'appelle, SK S0G 1S0
306-332-5266 Fax: 306-332-5087
forttownoffice@sasktel.net
www.fortquappelle.com
Municipal Type: Town
Incorporated: June 25, 1898; *Area:* 5.28 sq km
Population in 2006: 1,919
Provincial Electoral District(s): Indian Head-Milestone
Federal Electoral District(s): Regina-Qu'Appelle
Next Election: Oct. 2009 (3 year terms)
Note: Proclaimed as a town on Jan. 1, 1951.
Ron Osika, Mayor
Ed Sigmeth, Administrator

Fosston
P.O. Box 160
Fosston, SK S0E 0V0
306-322-4521 Fax: 306-322-4442
www.newsaskcfdc.ca/fosston.htm
Municipal Type: Village
Incorporated: Jan. 1, 1965; *Area:* 0.59 sq km
Population in 2006: 55
Provincial Electoral District(s): Kelvington-Wadena
Federal Electoral District(s): Yorkton-Melville
Next Election: Oct. 2009 (3 year terms)
Kathleen Ambrose, Administrator
Ron Einarson, Mayor

Fox Valley
P.O. Box 207
Fox Valley, SK S0N 0V0
306-666-3020 Fax: 306-666-3020
villoffoxvalley@sasktel.net
Municipal Type: Village
Incorporated: Aug. 30, 1928; *Area:* 0.60 sq km
Population in 2006: 295
Provincial Electoral District(s): Cypress Hills
Federal Electoral District(s): Cypress Hills-Grasslands
Next Election: Oct. 2009 (3 year terms)
Michelle Sehn, Administrator
Larry Hudec, Mayor

Francis
P.O. Box 128
Francis, SK S0G 1V0
306-245-3624 Fax: 306-245-3326
town.francis@sasktel.net
Municipal Type: Town
Incorporated: Oct. 24, 1904; *Area:* 0.59 sq km
Population in 2006: 148
Provincial Electoral District(s): Indian Head-Milestone
Federal Electoral District(s): Wascana
Next Election: Oct. 2009 (3 year terms)
Note: Proclaimed as a town on Sept. 24, 1906.
Joyce A. Carroll, Clerk
Cliff Knoll, Mayor

Frobisher
P.O. Box 235
Frobisher, SK S0C 0Y0
306-486-2140 Fax: 306-486-4504
Municipal Type: Village
Incorporated: July 4, 1904; *Area:* 1.35 sq km
Population in 2006: 145
Provincial Electoral District(s): Cannington
Federal Electoral District(s): Souris-Moose Mountain
Next Election: Oct. 2009 (3 year terms)
Bill Ringguth, Clerk
Lawrence Herzberg, Mayor

Frontier
P.O. Box 270
Frontier, SK S0N 0W0
306-296-2250 Fax: 306-296-4586
village.frontier@sasktel.net
Municipal Type: Village
Incorporated: July 10, 1930; *Area:* 0.93 sq km
Population in 2006: 283
Provincial Electoral District(s): Cypress Hills
Federal Electoral District(s): Cypress Hills-Grasslands
Next Election: Oct. 2009 (3 year terms)
Barb Webber, Administrator

Connie Korsberg, Mayor

Gainsborough
P.O. Box 120
Gainsborough, SK S0C 0Z0
306-685-2010 Fax: 306-685-2161
rm.1@sasktel.net
www.creda.sk.ca/gainsborough
Municipal Type: Village
Incorporated: May 25, 1894; *Area:* 0.87 sq km
Population in 2006: 250
Provincial Electoral District(s): Cannington
Federal Electoral District(s): Souris-Moose Mountain
Next Election: Oct. 2009 (3 year terms)
Valerie A. Olney, Administrator
Colin J. Bennett, Mayor

Gerald
P.O. Box 155
Gerald, SK S0A 1B0
306-745-6786 Fax: 306-745-6590
vofger@sasktel.net
Municipal Type: Village
Incorporated: March 25, 1953; *Area:* 0.80 sq km
Population in 2006: 124
Provincial Electoral District(s): Melville-Saltcoats
Federal Electoral District(s): Yorkton-Melville
Next Election: Oct. 2009 (3 year terms)
Lila R.A. Sippola, Administrator
Rudy Lonoway, Mayor

Gladmar
P.O. Box 54
Gladmar, SK S0C 1A0
306-969-4952
Municipal Type: Village
Incorporated: Feb. 15, 1968; *Area:* 0.55 sq km
Population in 2006: 53
Provincial Electoral District(s): Weyburn-Big Muddy
Federal Electoral District(s): Souris-Moose Mountain
Next Election: Oct. 2009 (3 year terms)
Randy Hoimyr, Clerk
Dale Ehrhardt, Mayor

Glaslyn
P.O. Box 279
Glaslyn, SK S0M 0Y0
306-342-2144 Fax: 306-342-2135
villageofglaslyn@sasktel.net
Municipal Type: Village
Incorporated: April 16, 1929; *Area:* 1.97 sq km
Population in 2006: 369
Provincial Electoral District(s): Cut Knife-Turtleford
Federal Electoral District(s): Battlefords-Lloydminster
Next Election: Oct. 2009 (3 year terms)
Jamey Kuhmayer, Clerk
Ken Morrison, Mayor

Glen Ewen
P.O. Box 99
Glen Ewen, SK S0C 1C0
306-925-2211 Fax: 306-925-2210
rm3@sasktel.net
Municipal Type: Village
Incorporated: March 24, 1904; *Area:* 2.77 sq km
Population in 2006: 120
Provincial Electoral District(s): Cannington
Federal Electoral District(s): Souris-Moose Mountain
Next Election: Oct. 2009 (3 year terms)
Myrna-Jean Babbings, Administrator
George Shain, Mayor

Glenavon
P.O. Box 327
Glenavon, SK S0G 1Y0
306-429-2011 Fax: 306-429-2260
Municipal Type: Village
Incorporated: April 13, 1910; *Area:* 1.32 sq km
Population in 2006: 183
Provincial Electoral District(s): Moosomin
Federal Electoral District(s): Souris-Moose Mountain
Next Election: Oct. 2009 (3 year terms)
James Hoff, Administrator
Herb Schmidt, Mayor

Glenside
P.O. Box 99
Glenside, SK S0H 1T0
306-867-8932
Municipal Type: Village
Incorporated: March 30, 1911; *Area:* 0.77 sq km
Population in 2006: 86
Provincial Electoral District(s): Rosetown-Elrose
Federal Electoral District(s): Blackstrap
Next Election: Oct. 2009 (3 year terms)
Sharon Tomecek, Clerk
Rod Simonson, Mayor

Golden Prairie
P.O. Box 9
Golden Prairie, SK S0N 0Y0
306-662-2883 Fax: 306-662-3954
rm141@sasktel.net
Municipal Type: Village
Incorporated: April 15, 1942; *Area:* 0.41 sq km
Population in 2006: 35
Provincial Electoral District(s): Cypress Hills
Federal Electoral District(s): Cypress Hills-Grasslands
Next Election: Oct. 2009 (3 year terms)
Quinton Jacksteit, Administrator
Delmar Beck, Mayor

Goodeve
P.O. Box 160
Goodeve, SK S0A 1C0
306-795-2272 Fax: 306-795-3330
www.spreda.sk.ca/community_Goodeve.htm
Municipal Type: Village
Incorporated: Aug. 18, 1910; *Area:* 2.62 sq km
Population in 2006: 50
Provincial Electoral District(s): Last Mountain-Touchwood
Federal Electoral District(s): Yorkton-Melville
Next Election: Oct. 2009 (3 year terms)
Diana Lee, Clerk
Craig Sawchuk, Mayor

Goodsoil
P.O. Box 176
Goodsoil, SK S0M 1A0
306-238-2094 Fax: 306-238-2098
villageofgoodsoil@sasktel.net
www.goodsoil.sasktelwebsite.net
Municipal Type: Village
Incorporated: Jan. 1, 1960; *Area:* 1.76 sq km
Population in 2006: 253
Provincial Electoral District(s): Meadow Lake
Federal Electoral District(s): Desnethé-Missinippi-Churchill River
Next Election: Oct. 2009 (3 year terms)
Rita Rogers, Administrator
Dean Kuypers, Mayor

Goodwater
P.O. Box 280
Weyburn, SK S4H 2K1
306-456-2566 Fax: 306-456-2440
rm37@sasktel.net
Municipal Type: Village
Incorporated: May 8, 1911; *Area:* 0.59 sq km
Population in 2006: 25
Provincial Electoral District(s): Estevan
Federal Electoral District(s): Souris-Moose Mountain
Next Election: Oct. 2009 (3 year terms)
Kevin Melle, Administrator
Greg Collins, Mayor

Govan
P.O. Box 160
Govan, SK S0G 1Z0
306-484-2011 Fax: 306-484-2113
govan@sasktel.net
www.govansk.com
Municipal Type: Town
Incorporated: Aug. 21, 1907; *Area:* 1.35 sq km
Population in 2006: 232
Provincial Electoral District(s): Arm River-Watrous
Federal Electoral District(s): Regina-Lumsden-Lake Centre
Next Election: Oct. 2009 (3 year terms)
Note: Proclaimed as a town on Nov. 1, 1911.
Kelly Holbrook, Administrator
Wesley Pearce, Mayor

Grand Coulee
PO Box 72, GBS 200, RR#2
Regina, SK S4P 2Z2
306-352-8694 Fax: 306-352-6659
grandcoulee.cap@sasktel.net
Municipal Type: Village
Incorporated: April 10, 1908; *Area:* 0.30 sq km
Population in 2006: 435
Provincial Electoral District(s): Regina Qu'Appelle Valley
Federal Electoral District(s): Regina-Lumsden-Lake Centre
Next Election: Oct. 2009 (3 year terms)
Irv Brunas, Mayor
Tobi Duck, Administrator

Gravelbourg
P.O. Box 359
Gravelbourg, SK S0H 1X0
306-648-3301 Fax: 306-648-3400
gravelbourg.adm@sasktel.net
www.gravelbourg.ca
Municipal Type: Town
Incorporated: Dec. 30, 1912; *Area:* 3.23 sq km
Population in 2006: 1,089
Provincial Electoral District(s): Wood River
Federal Electoral District(s): Cypress Hills-Grasslands
Next Election: Oct. 2009 (3 year terms)
Note: Proclaimed as a town on Nov. 1, 1916.
Fernand Bouvier, Mayor
Suzy Martin, Administrator

Grayson
P.O. Box 9
Railway Ave.
Grayson, SK S0A 1E0
306-794-2011 Fax: 306-794-2261
www.spreda.sk.ca/community_Grayson.htm
Municipal Type: Village
Incorporated: April 19, 1906; *Area:* 1.47 sq km
Population in 2006: 179
Provincial Electoral District(s): Melville-Saltcoats
Federal Electoral District(s): Yorkton-Melville
Next Election: Oct. 2009 (3 year terms)
Lawrence J. Kreiser, Administrator
Neil Ottenbreit, Mayor

Green Lake
P.O. Box 128
110 North St.
Green Lake, SK S0M 1B0
306-832-2131 Fax: 306-832-2124
green.lake@sasktel.net
www.nvgreenlake.ca
Municipal Type: Northern Village
Incorporated: Oct. 1, 1983; *Area:* 121.92 sq km
Population in 2006: 361
Provincial Electoral District(s): Athabasca
Federal Electoral District(s): Desnethé-Missinippi-Churchill River
Next Election: Oct. 2009 (3 year terms)
Tina Rasmussen, Administrator
Fred McCallum, Mayor

Grenfell
P.O. Box 1120
Grenfell, SK S0G 2B0
306-697-2815 Fax: 306-697-2484
townofgrenfell@sasktel.net
www.grenfell.ca
Municipal Type: Town
Incorporated: April 12, 1894; *Area:* 3.17 sq km
Population in 2006: 947
Provincial Electoral District(s): Moosomin
Federal Electoral District(s): Souris-Moose Mountain
Next Election: Oct. 2009 (3 year terms)
Note: Proclaimed as a town on Nov. 1, 1911.
Marc Saleski, Mayor
Leslie McGhie, Administrator

Gull Lake
P.O. Box 150
Gull Lake, SK S0N 1A0
306-672-3361 Fax: 306-672-3777
gulllaketown@sasktel.net
www.gulllakesk.ca
Municipal Type: Town
Incorporated: Jan. 12, 1909; *Area:* 2.5 sq km
Population in 2006: 965
Provincial Electoral District(s): Cypress Hills
Federal Electoral District(s): Cypress Hills-Grasslands
Next Election: Oct. 2009 (3 year terms)
Note: Proclaimed as a town on Nov. 1, 1911.
Bob Francis, Mayor
Dawnette Peterson, Administrator

Hafford
P.O. Box 220
Hafford, SK S0J 1A0
306-549-2331 Fax: 306-549-2331
hafto@sasktel.net
Municipal Type: Town
Incorporated: Dec. 16, 1913; *Area:* 0.80 sq km
Population in 2006: 360
Provincial Electoral District(s): Rosthern-Shellbrook
Federal Electoral District(s): Saskatoon-Wanuskewin
Next Election: Oct. 2009 (3 year terms)
Note: Proclaimed as a town on Jan. 1, 1981.
Charles W. Linnell, Administrator
Peter Kingsmill, Mayor

Hague
P.O. Box 180
Hague, SK S0K 1X0
306-225-2155 Fax: 306-225-4410
town.hague@sasktel.net
www.townofhague.com
Municipal Type: Town
Incorporated: Aug. 25, 1903; *Area:* 1.03 sq km
Population in 2006: 707
Provincial Electoral District(s): Martensville
Federal Electoral District(s): Saskatoon-Wanuskewin
Next Election: Oct. 2009 (3 year terms)
Note: Proclaimed as a town on Nov. 1, 1991.
Patricia Wagner, Mayor
pat@townofhague.com
Deanna Braun, Administrator

Halbrite
P.O. Box 10
Halbrite, SK S0C 1H0
306-458-2252 Fax: 306-458-2657
Municipal Type: Village
Incorporated: Feb. 26, 1904; *Area:* 1.20 sq km
Population in 2006: 98
Provincial Electoral District(s): Estevan
Federal Electoral District(s): Souris-Moose Mountain
Next Election: Oct. 2009 (3 year terms)
Joy M. Guider, Clerk
Dwayne Carlson, Mayor

Hanley
P.O. Box 270
Hanley, SK S0G 2E0
306-544-2223 Fax: 306-544-2261
townahanley@sasktel.net

Municipal Type: Town
Incorporated: April 27, 1905; *Area:* 2.65 sq km
Population in 2006: 464
Provincial Electoral District(s): Arm River-Watrous
Federal Electoral District(s): Blackstrap
Next Election: Oct. 2009 (3 year terms)
Note: Proclaimed as a town on Dec. 1, 1906.
Marvin Gerbrandt, Mayor
Darice Carlson, Clerk

Harris
P.O. Box 124
Harris, SK S0L 1K0
306-656-2122 Fax: 306-656-2151
villageofharris@sasktel.net
Municipal Type: Village
Incorporated: Aug. 10, 1909; *Area:* 0.72 sq km
Population in 2006: 187
Provincial Electoral District(s): Rosetown-Elrose
Federal Electoral District(s): Saskatoon-Rosetown-Biggar
Next Election: Oct. 2009 (3 year terms)
Rhonda Leonard, Clerk
Ron Genest, Mayor

Hawarden
P.O. Box 7
Hawarden, SK S0H 1Y0
306-855-2020
Municipal Type: Village
Incorporated: July 16, 1909; *Area:* 1.24 sq km
Population in 2006: 75
Provincial Electoral District(s): Arm River-Watrous
Federal Electoral District(s): Blackstrap
Next Election: Oct. 2009 (3 year terms)
Darice Carlson, Clerk
Dean Blenkinsop, Mayor

Hazenmore
P.O. Box 36
Hazenmore, SK S0N 1C0
306-264-3218 Fax: 306-264-3218
villageofkincaid@hotmail.com
Municipal Type: Village
Incorporated: Aug. 20, 1913; *Area:* 0.80 sq km
Population in 2006: 57
Provincial Electoral District(s): Wood River
Federal Electoral District(s): Cypress Hills-Grasslands
Next Election: Oct. 2009 (3 year terms)
Barbara Hunter, Administrator
Gary Loverin, Mayor

Hazlet
P.O. Box 150
Hazlet, SK S0N 1E0
306-678-2131 Fax: 306-678-2132
hazlet@sasktel.net
www.hazletsask.com
Municipal Type: Village
Incorporated: Jan. 1, 1963; *Area:* 0.55 sq km
Population in 2006: 85
Provincial Electoral District(s): Cypress Hills
Federal Electoral District(s): Cypress Hills-Grasslands
Next Election: Oct. 2009 (3 year terms)
Terry Erdelyan, Administrator
Robert Hansen, Mayor

Hepburn
P.O. Box 217
311 Main St.
Hepburn, SK S0K 1Z0
306-947-2170 Fax: 306-947-4202
hepburnvillage@sasktel.net
Municipal Type: Village
Incorporated: July 5, 1919; *Area:* 1.02 sq km
Population in 2006: 530
Provincial Electoral District(s): Martensville
Federal Electoral District(s): Saskatoon-Wanuskewin
Next Election: Oct. 2009 (3 year terms)
Barbara Adams-Eichendorf, Mayor
Del Cunningham, Administrator

Herbert
P.O. Box 370
218 Dennis St.
Herbert, SK S0H 2A0
306-784-2400 Fax: 306-784-2402
t.o.herbert@sasktel.net
www.townofherbertsk.ca
Municipal Type: Town
Incorporated: June 11, 1907; *Area:* 3.78 sq km
Population in 2006: 742
Provincial Electoral District(s): Thunder Creek
Federal Electoral District(s): Cypress Hills-Grasslands
Next Election: Oct. 2009 (3 year terms)
Note: Proclaimed as a town on Nov. 1, 1912.
Albert Kildaw, Mayor
Reagan Funk, Administrator

Heward
P.O. Box 10
Heward, SK S0G 2G0
306-457-2277 Fax: 306-457-3149
rmtec@sasktel.net
Municipal Type: Village
Incorporated: Nov. 21, 1904; *Area:* 0.99 sq km
Population in 2006: 20
Provincial Electoral District(s): Cannington
Federal Electoral District(s): Souris-Moose Mountain
Next Election: Oct. 2009 (3 year terms)
Zandra Slater, Clerk
John Griffin, Mayor

Hodgeville
P.O. Box 307
Hodgeville, SK S0H 2B0
306-677-2223 Fax: 306-677-2466
cooper.hodge@sasktel.net
Municipal Type: Village
Incorporated: June 22, 1921; *Area:* 1.35 sq km
Population in 2006: 142
Provincial Electoral District(s): Wood River
Federal Electoral District(s): Cypress Hills-Grasslands
Next Election: Oct. 2009 (3 year terms)
Sheila Cooper, Administrator
Leanne Sabasch, Mayor

Holdfast
P.O. Box 160
Roberts St.
Holdfast, SK S0G 2H0
306-488-2000 Fax: 306-488-4609
rm.sarnia@sasktel.net
www.holdfastsask.com
Municipal Type: Village
Incorporated: Oct. 5, 1911; *Area:* 1.29 sq km
Population in 2006: 173
Provincial Electoral District(s): Thunder Creek
Federal Electoral District(s): Regina-Lumsden-Lake Centre
Next Election: Oct. 2009 (3 year terms)
John H. J. Eberl, Administrator
William Gardiner, Mayor

Hubbard
P.O. Box 190
Ituna, SK S0A 1N0
306-795-2202 Fax: 306-795-2202
rmofituna@sasktel.net
Municipal Type: Village
Incorporated: June 11, 1910; *Area:* 1.25 sq km
Population in 2006: 43
Provincial Electoral District(s): Last Mountain-Touchwood
Federal Electoral District(s): Regina-Qu'Appelle
Next Election: Oct. 2009 (3 year terms)
Diane M. Olech, Administrator
Ron Rokosh, Mayor

Hudson Bay
P.O. Box 730
304 Main St.
Hudson Bay, SK S0E 0Y0
306-865-2261 Fax: 306-865-2800
hudson.bay@sasktel.net
www.townofhudsonbay.com
Municipal Type: Town
Incorporated: Sept. 25, 1907; *Area:* 17.35 sq km
Population in 2006: 1,646
Provincial Electoral District(s): Carrot River Valley
Federal Electoral District(s): Yorkton-Melville
Next Election: Oct. 2009 (3 year terms)
Note: Proclaimed as a town on Nov. 30, 1946.
Elvina Rumak, Mayor
Richard Dolezsar, Administrator

Humboldt
P.O. Box 640
715 Main St.
Humboldt, SK S0K 2A0
306-682-2525 Fax: 306-682-3144
cityofhumboldt@sasktel.net
www.cityofhumboldt.ca
Municipal Type: Town
Incorporated: June 30, 1905; *Area:* 11.72 sq km
Population in 2006: 4,998
Provincial Electoral District(s): Humboldt
Federal Electoral District(s): Saskatoon-Humboldt
Next Election: Oct. 2009 (3 year terms)
Note: Incorporated as a city on Nov. 7, 2000.
Malcolm Eaton, Mayor
Sandra Pauli, Clerk

Hyas
P.O. Box 40
Hyas, SK S0A 1K0
306-594-2817 Fax: 306-594-2817
hyas@sasktel.net
Municipal Type: Village
Incorporated: May 23, 1919; *Area:* 1.17 sq km
Population in 2006: 111
Provincial Electoral District(s): Canora-Pelly
Federal Electoral District(s): Yorkton-Melville
Next Election: Oct. 2009 (3 year terms)
Ingrid Wildman, Administrator
Lawrence Ostafichuk, Mayor

Ile à la Crosse
P.O. Box 280
Lajeunesse Ave.
Ile-a-la-Crosse, SK S0M 1C0
306-833-2122 Fax: 306-833-2132
village.of.ilealacrosse@sasktel.net
Municipal Type: Northern Village
Incorporated: Oct. 1, 1983; *Area:* 23.84 sq km
Population in 2006: 1,341
Provincial Electoral District(s): Athabasca
Federal Electoral District(s): Desnethé-Missinippi-Churchill River
Next Election: 2009 (3 year terms)
Dianne McCallum, Administrator
Duane Favel, Mayor

Imperial
P.O. Box 90
Imperial, SK S0G 2J0
306-963-2220 Fax: 306-963-2445
town.imperial@sasktel.net
www.imperial.ca
Municipal Type: Town
Incorporated: July 4, 1911; *Area:* 1.23 sq km
Population in 2006: 321
Provincial Electoral District(s): Arm River-Watrous
Federal Electoral District(s): Regina-Lumsden-Lake Centre
Next Election: Oct. 2009 (3 year terms)
Note: Proclaimed as a town on April 1, 1962.
Sheila Newlove, Administrator
Fred Grigg, Mayor

Indian Head
P.O. Box 460
Indian Head, SK S0G 2K0
306-695-3344 Fax: 306-695-2398
townofindianhead@sasktel.net
www.townofindianhead.com
Municipal Type: Town
Incorporated: April 19, 1902; *Area:* 3.17 sq km
Population in 2006: 1,634
Provincial Electoral District(s): Indian Head-Milestone
Federal Electoral District(s): Regina-Qu'Appelle
Next Election: Oct. 2009 (3 year terms)
Allan Hubbs, Mayor
Erinn Kaun, Administrator

Invermay
P.O. Box 234
Invermay, SK S0A 1M0
306-593-2242 Fax: 306-593-2242
Municipal Type: Village
Incorporated: Sept. 1, 1908; *Area:* 1.22 sq km
Population in 2006: 262
Provincial Electoral District(s): Kelvington-Wadena
Federal Electoral District(s): Yorkton-Melville
Next Election: Oct. 2009 (3 year terms)
Veronica L. Wolski, Clerk
Kim C. Rioch, Mayor

Ituna
P.O. Box 580
Ituna, SK S0A 1N0
306-795-2272 Fax: 306-795-3330
townofituna@sasktel.net
www.town.ituna.sk.ca
Municipal Type: Town
Incorporated: May 30, 1910; *Area:* 1.56 sq km
Population in 2006: 622
Provincial Electoral District(s): Last Mountain-Touchwood
Federal Electoral District(s): Regina-Qu'Appelle
Next Election: Oct. 2009 (3 year terms)
Note: Proclaimed as a town on Oct. 1, 1961.
Glenn Leontowich, Mayor
Diana Lee, Administrator

Jans Bay
Maurice Ave., General Delivery
Canoe Narrows, SK S0M 0K0
306-829-4320 Fax: 306-829-4424
jansbay@sasktel.net
Municipal Type: Northern Village
Incorporated: Oct. 1, 1983; *Area:* 5.94 sq km
Population in 2006: 181
Provincial Electoral District(s): Athabasca
Federal Electoral District(s): Desnethé-Missinippi-Churchill River
Next Election: Oct. 2009 (3 year terms)
Vicky Gardiner, Clerk
Patsy Laliberte, Mayor

Jansen
P.O. Box 116
Jansen, SK S0K 2B0
306-364-2013 Fax: 306-364-2088
jansen@jansen.ca
www.jansen.ca
Municipal Type: Village
Incorporated: Oct. 19, 1908; *Area:* 0.85 sq km
Population in 2006: 140
Provincial Electoral District(s): Arm River-Watrous
Federal Electoral District(s): Blackstrap
Next Election: Oct. 2009 (3 year terms)
Joni Mack, Clerk
David Renwick, Mayor

Kamsack
P.O. Box 729
161 Queen Elizabeth Blvd. West
Kamsack, SK S0A 1S0
306-542-2155 Fax: 306-542-2975
town.of.kamsack@sasktel.net
www.town.kamsack.sk.ca

Municipal Type: Town
Incorporated: March 14, 1905; *Area:* 5.85 sq km
Population in 2006: 1,713
Provincial Electoral District(s): Canora-Pelly
Federal Electoral District(s): Yorkton-Melville
Next Election: Oct. 2009 (3 year terms)
Note: Proclaimed as a town on Nov. 1, 1911.
Darryl Binkley, Mayor
Rona Seidle, Administrator

Keeler
P.O. Box 33
Keeler, SK S0H 2E0
306-759-2302
Municipal Type: Village
Incorporated: July 5, 1910; *Area:* 1.02 sq km
Population in 2006: 5
Provincial Electoral District(s): Thunder Creek
Federal Electoral District(s): Regina-Lumsden-Lake Centre
Next Election: Oct. 2009 (3 year terms)
Jackie Leggott, Clerk
Duncan Keeler, Mayor

Kelliher
P.O. Box 190
Kelliher, SK S0A 1V0
306-675-2226 Fax: 306-675-2240
villageofkelliher@sasktel.net
www.kelliher.ca
Municipal Type: Village
Incorporated: April 27, 1909; *Area:* 2.81 sq km
Population in 2006: 257
Provincial Electoral District(s): Last Mountain-Touchwood
Federal Electoral District(s): Regina-Qu'Appelle
Next Election: Oct. 2009 (3 year terms)
Pauline Hallwas, Clerk
Vic Maydonick, Mayor

Kelvington
P.O. Box 10
201 Main St.
Kelvington, SK S0A 1W0
306-327-4482 Fax: 306-327-4946
tkelv@sasktel.net
www.townofkelvington.com
Municipal Type: Town
Incorporated: Nov. 18, 1921; *Area:* 3.89 sq km
Population in 2006: 866
Provincial Electoral District(s): Kelvington-Wadena
Federal Electoral District(s): Yorkton-Melville
Next Election: Oct. 2009 (3 year terms)
Note: Proclaimed as a town on May 1, 1944.
Ed Tetelowski, Mayor
Loretta Nagy, Administrator

Kenaston
P.O. Box 129
Kenaston, SK S0G 2N0
306-252-2211 Fax: 306-252-2248
kenaston@sasktel.net
www.kenaston.ca
Municipal Type: Village
Incorporated: July 18, 1910; *Area:* 1.17 sq km
Population in 2006: 259
Provincial Electoral District(s): Arm River-Watrous
Federal Electoral District(s): Blackstrap
Next Election: Oct. 2009 (3 year terms)
Mark J. Zdunich, Administrator
Dan O'Handley, Mayor

Kendal
P.O. Box 97
115 Main St.
Kendal, SK S0G 2P0
306-424-2722 Fax: 306-424-2722
villageofkendal@sasktel.net
Municipal Type: Village
Incorporated: Feb. 17, 1919; *Area:* 0.65 sq km
Population in 2006: 59
Provincial Electoral District(s): Indian Head-Milestone
Federal Electoral District(s): Wascana
Next Election: Oct. 2009 (3 year terms)
Carrie Kotylak, Clerk
Shannon Gray, Mayor

Kennedy
P.O. Box 93
Kennedy, SK S0G 2R0
306-538-2194 Fax: 306-538-4522
village.kennedy@sasktel.net
www.angelfire.com/ca/kennedysk
Municipal Type: Village
Incorporated: Nov. 5, 1907; *Area:* 1.60 sq km
Population in 2006: 187
Provincial Electoral District(s): Moosomin
Federal Electoral District(s): Souris-Moose Mountain
Next Election: Oct. 2009 (3 year terms)
Helen Gurski, Administrator
Tye Cancade, Mayor

Kenosee Lake
P.O. Box 30
Kenosee Lake, SK S0C 2S0
306-577-2139 Fax: 306-577-2261
village.kenosee@sasktel.net
Municipal Type: Village
Incorporated: Oct. 1, 1987; *Area:* 0.35 sq km
Population in 2006: 194
Provincial Electoral District(s): Cannington
Federal Electoral District(s): Souris-Moose Mountain
Next Election: Oct. 2009 (3 year terms)
Helen Gurski, Administrator
Lyle Basken, Mayor

Kerrobert
P.O. Box 558
433 Manitoba Ave.
Kerrobert, SK S0L 1R0
306-834-2361 Fax: 306-834-2633
kerrobert@sasktel.net
www.kerrobertsk.com
Municipal Type: Town
Incorporated: Nov. 9, 1910; *Area:* 7.49 sq km
Population in 2006: 1,001
Provincial Electoral District(s): Kindersley
Federal Electoral District(s): Battlefords-Lloydminster
Next Election: Oct. 2009 (3 year terms)
Note: Proclaimed as a town on Nov. 1, 1911.
William Scott, Mayor
Michele Schmidt, Administrator

Killaly
P.O. Box 69
Railway Ave.
Killaly, SK S0A 1X0
306-748-2457
www.spreda.sk.ca/community_Killaly.htm
Municipal Type: Village
Incorporated: April 28, 1909; *Area:* 2.59 sq km
Population in 2006: 77
Provincial Electoral District(s): Melville-Saltcoats
Federal Electoral District(s): Yorkton-Melville
Next Election: Oct. 2009 (3 year terms)
Linda Hanowski, Clerk
Angie Rogalski, Mayor

Kincaid
P.O. Box 177
Kincaid, SK S0H 2J0
306-264-3910 Fax: 306-264-3903
villageofkincaid@hotmail.com
Municipal Type: Village
Incorporated: July 19, 1913; *Area:* 0.82 sq km
Population in 2006: 135
Provincial Electoral District(s): Wood River
Federal Electoral District(s): Cypress Hills-Grasslands
Next Election: Oct. 2009 (3 year terms)
Barbara Hunter, Administrator
Cynthia Gross, Mayor

Kindersley
P.O. Box 1269
106 - 5th Ave. East
Kindersley, SK S0L 1S0
306-463-2675 Fax: 306-463-4577
office@kindersley.ca
www.kindersley.ca
Municipal Type: Town
Incorporated: Jan. 10, 1910; *Area:* 12.55 sq km
Population in 2006: 4,412
Provincial Electoral District(s): Kindersley
Federal Electoral District(s): Battlefords-Lloydminster
Next Election: Oct. 2009 (3 year terms)
Note: Proclaimed as a town on Nov. 1, 1910.
John K. Boquist, Mayor
Sherry Magnuson, Town Administrator

Kinistino
P.O. Box 10
Kinistino, SK S0J 1H0
306-864-2461 Fax: 306-864-2880
townofkinistino@sasktel.net
www.townofkinistino.ca
Municipal Type: Town
Incorporated: July 30, 1905; *Area:* 0.89 sq km
Population in 2006: 643
Provincial Electoral District(s): Batoche
Federal Electoral District(s): Prince Albert
Next Election: Oct. 2009 (3 year terms)
Note: Proclaimed as a town on Feb. 7, 1952.
Leonard Margolis, Mayor
Shirley Jackson, Administrator

Kinley
P.O. Box 51
Kinley, SK S0K 2E0
306-237-4337 Fax: 306-237-4337
Municipal Type: Village
Incorporated: Jan. 7, 1909; *Area:* 1.18 sq km
Population in 2006: 35
Provincial Electoral District(s): Biggar
Federal Electoral District(s): Saskatoon-Rosetown-Biggar
Next Election: Oct. 2009 (3 year terms)
Pam McMahon, Administrator
John Evers, Mayor

Kipling
P.O. Box 299
301 - 6th Ave.
Kipling, SK S0G 2S0
306-736-2515 Fax: 306-736-8448
kiptown@sasktel.net
www.townofkipling.ca
Municipal Type: Town
Incorporated: Sept. 13, 1909; *Area:* 2.15 sq km
Population in 2006: 973
Provincial Electoral District(s): Moosomin
Federal Electoral District(s): Souris-Moose Mountain
Next Election: Oct. 2009 (3 year terms)
Note: Proclaimed as a town on Jan. 1, 1954.
Kevin Hassler, Mayor
Gail Dakue, Administrator

Kisbey
P.O. Box 249
Kisbey, SK S0C 1L0
306-462-2212 Fax: 306-462-2279
vill.kisbey@sasktel.net
www.creda.sk.ca/kisbey
Municipal Type: Village
Incorporated: May 8, 1907; *Area:* 2.77 sq km
Population in 2006: 185
Provincial Electoral District(s): Cannington
Federal Electoral District(s): Souris-Moose Mountain
Next Election: Oct. 2009 (3 year terms)
Judy Graham, Administrator
John Houston, Mayor

Krydor
P.O. Box 160
Hafford, SK S0J 1A0
306-549-2333 Fax: 306-549-2333
rm435@sasktel.net
Municipal Type: Village
Incorporated: Aug. 25, 1914; *Area:* 0.82 sq km
Population in 2006: 25
Provincial Electoral District(s): Rosthern-Shellbrook
Federal Electoral District(s): Saskatoon-Wanuskewin
Next Election: Oct. 2009 (3 year terms)
Lisa Tanchak Prescesky, Clerk
Arnold Bahniuk, Mayor

Kyle
P.O. Box 520
Kyle, SK S0L 1T0
306-375-2525 Fax: 306-375-2525
townofkyle@sasktel.net
www.kylesaskatchewan.ca
Municipal Type: Town
Incorporated: April 13, 1926; *Area:* 1.01 sq km
Population in 2006: 423
Provincial Electoral District(s): Rosetown-Elrose
Federal Electoral District(s): Cypress Hills-Grasslands
Next Election: Oct. 2009 (3 year terms)
Note: Proclaimed as a town on Jan. 1, 1959.
Audrey Blohm, Administrator
Ansgar Tynning, Mayor

La Loche
P.O. Box 310
La Loche, SK S0M 1G0
306-822-2032 Fax: 306-822-2078
nor.vill.laloche@sasktel.net
Municipal Type: Northern Village
Incorporated: Oct. 1, 1983; *Area:* 15.59 sq km
Population in 2006: 2,348
Provincial Electoral District(s): Athabasca
Federal Electoral District(s): Desnethé-Missinippi-Churchill River
Next Election: 2009 (3 year terms)
Georgina Jolibois, Mayor
Doug Gailey, Clerk

La Ronge
P.O. Box 5680
1212 Hildebrandt Dr.
La Ronge, SK S0J 1L0
306-425-2066 Fax: 306-425-3883
town.of.laronge@sasktel.net
www.townoflaronge.ca
Municipal Type: Northern Town
Incorporated: May 3, 1905; *Area:* 11.86 sq km
Population in 2006: 2,725
Provincial Electoral District(s): Cumberland
Federal Electoral District(s): Desnethé-Missinippi-Churchill River
Next Election: 2009 (3 year terms)
Note: Proclaimed as a northern town on Oct. 1, 1983.
Davidie Zarazun, Administrator
laronge.administrator@sasktel.net
Joe Hordyski, Mayor

Lafleche
P.O. Box 250
Lafleche, SK S0H 2K0
306-472-5292 Fax: 306-472-3706
town.of.lafleche@sasktel.net
www.town.lafleche.sk.ca
Municipal Type: Town
Incorporated: Sept. 3, 1913; *Area:* 1.51 sq km
Population in 2006: 370
Provincial Electoral District(s): Wood River
Federal Electoral District(s): Cypress Hills-Grasslands
Next Election: Oct. 2009 (3 year terms)
Note: Proclaimed as a town on June 1, 1953.
Lorraine McIvor, Administrator
Raymond Clermont, Mayor

Laird
P.O. Box 189
Laird, SK S0K 2H0
306-223-4343 Fax: 306-223-4349
lairdvillage@sasktel.net
Municipal Type: Village
Incorporated: May 4, 1911; *Area:* 1.29 sq km
Population in 2006: 207
Provincial Electoral District(s): Rosthern-Shellbrook
Federal Electoral District(s): Saskatoon-Wanuskewin
Next Election: Oct. 2009 (3 year terms)
Gloria Landell, Clerk
Gary Fischer, Mayor

Lake Alma
P.O. Box 163
Lake Alma, SK S0C 1M0
306-447-2002
Municipal Type: Village
Incorporated: Jan. 1, 1949; *Area:* 0.47 sq km
Population in 2006: 30
Provincial Electoral District(s): Estevan
Federal Electoral District(s): Souris-Moose Mountain
Next Election: Oct. 2009 (3 year terms)
Kyla Robinson, Clerk
Wilfred Jacobson, Mayor

Lake Lenore
P.O. Box 148
Lake Lenore, SK S0K 2J0
306-368-2344 Fax: 306-368-2226
lakelenorevil@sasktel.net
www.newsaskcfdc.ca/lakelenore.htm
Municipal Type: Village
Incorporated: April 28, 1921; *Area:* 0.97 sq km
Population in 2006: 306
Provincial Electoral District(s): Batoche
Federal Electoral District(s): Saskatoon-Humboldt
Next Election: Oct. 2009 (3 year terms)
Barb Politeski, Clerk
Kerry Haeusler, Mayor

Lampman
P.O. Box 70
Lampman, SK S0C 1N0
306-487-2462 Fax: 306-487-2285
browning.lampman@sasktel.net
www.lampman.sasktelwebsite.net
Municipal Type: Town
Incorporated: Aug. 16, 1910; *Area:* 2.23 sq km
Population in 2006: 634
Provincial Electoral District(s): Cannington
Federal Electoral District(s): Souris-Moose Mountain
Next Election: Oct. 2009 (3 year terms)
Note: Proclaimed as a town on June 1, 1963.
Gerry Perkowitsch, Mayor
Greg Wallin, Administrator

Lancer
P.O. Box 3
Lancer, SK S0N 1G0
306-689-2925 Fax: 306-689-2890
Municipal Type: Village
Incorporated: Sept. 11, 1913; *Area:* 1.33 sq km
Population in 2006: 65
Provincial Electoral District(s): Cypress Hills
Federal Electoral District(s): Cypress Hills-Grasslands
Next Election: Oct. 2009 (3 year terms)
Karen Hartman, Clerk
Ernest Wagner, Mayor

Landis
P.O. Box 153
Landis, SK S0K 2K0
306-658-2155 Fax: 306-658-2156
villageoflandis@sasktel.net
Municipal Type: Village
Incorporated: May 17, 1909; *Area:* 0.80 sq km
Population in 2006: 119
Provincial Electoral District(s): Biggar
Federal Electoral District(s): Battlefords-Lloydminster
Next Election: Oct. 2009 (3 year terms)
Sandra Beckett, Administrator
Bernard J. Ochs, Mayor

Lang
P.O. Box 97
223 Main St.
Lang, SK S0G 2W0
306-464-2024 Fax: 306-464-2024
lang@sasktel.net
www.langsk.com
Municipal Type: Village
Incorporated: July 27, 1906; *Area:* 0.64 sq km
Population in 2006: 172
Provincial Electoral District(s): Indian Head-Milestone
Federal Electoral District(s): Souris-Moose Mountain
Next Election: Oct. 2009 (3 year terms)
Joanne Broderick, Administrator
Al Broderick, Mayor

Langenburg
P.O. Box 400
Langenburg, SK S0A 2A0
306-743-2432 Fax: 306-743-2723
langenburgt@sasktel.net
www.town.langenburg.sk.ca
Municipal Type: Town
Incorporated: March 30, 1903; *Area:* 3.46 sq km
Population in 2006: 1,048
Provincial Electoral District(s): Melville-Saltcoats
Federal Electoral District(s): Yorkton-Melville
Next Election: Oct. 2009 (3 year terms)
Note: Proclaimed as a town on Sept. 15, 1959.
Dave Schappert, Mayor
Howard McCullough, Administrator

Langham
P.O. Box 289
230 Main St. East
Langham, SK S0K 2L0
306-283-4842 Fax: 306-283-4772
admin@langham.ca
www.langham.ca
Municipal Type: Town
Incorporated: June 8, 1906; *Area:* 3.98 sq km
Population in 2006: 1,120
Provincial Electoral District(s): Biggar
Federal Electoral District(s): Saskatoon-Rosetown-Biggar; Saskatoon-Wanuskewin
Next Election: Oct. 2009 (3 year terms)
Note: Proclaimed as a town on Aug. 1, 1907.
Glen Thiessen, Mayor
Randy J. Sherstobitoff, Administrator

Lanigan
P.O. Box 280
Lanigan, SK S0K 2M0
306-365-2809 Fax: 306-365-2960
town.lanigan@sasktel.net
www.town.lanigan.sk.ca
Municipal Type: Town
Incorporated: Aug. 21, 1907; *Area:* 8.34 sq km
Population in 2006: 1,233
Provincial Electoral District(s): Humboldt
Federal Electoral District(s): Blackstrap
Next Election: Oct. 2009 (3 year terms)
Note: Proclaimed as a town on April 15, 1908.
Bernie Bishop, Mayor
Jack R. Dvernichuk, Administrator

Lashburn
P.O. Box 328
Lashburn, SK S0M 1H0
306-285-3533 Fax: 306-285-3358
townoflashburn@sasktel.net
Municipal Type: Town
Incorporated: Dec. 8, 1906; *Area:* 3.11 sq km
Population in 2006: 914
Provincial Electoral District(s): Cut Knife-Turtleford
Federal Electoral District(s): Battlefords-Lloydminster
Next Election: Oct. 2009 (3 year terms)
Note: Proclaimed as a town on March 1, 1979.
Steven Turnbull, Mayor
Vicki Seabrook, Administrator

Leader
P.O. Box 39
151 - 1st St. West
Leader, SK S0N 1H0
306-628-3868 Fax: 306-628-4337
town.leader@sasktel.net
www.leader.ca
Municipal Type: Town
Incorporated: Sept. 13, 1913; *Area:* 1.70 sq km
Population in 2006: 881
Provincial Electoral District(s): Cypress Hills
Federal Electoral District(s): Cypress Hills-Grasslands
Next Election: Oct. 2009 (3 year terms)
Note: Proclaimed as a town on May 1, 1947.
Craig Tondevold, Mayor
Rochelle Francis, Administrator

Leask
P.O. Box 190
Leask, SK S0J 1M0
306-466-2229 Fax: 306-466-2000
rm464.leask@sasktel.net
www.leask.ca
Municipal Type: Village
Incorporated: Sept. 3, 1912; *Area:* 0.75 sq km
Population in 2006: 418
Provincial Electoral District(s): Rosthern-Shellbrook
Federal Electoral District(s): Saskatoon-Wanuskewin
Next Election: Oct. 2009 (3 year terms)
Robert Hryniuk, Mayor
Wanda Boon, Administrator

Lebret
P.O. Box 40
Lebret, SK S0G 2Y0
306-332-6545 Fax: 306-332-5338
Municipal Type: Village
Incorporated: Oct. 14, 1912; *Area:* 1.32 sq km
Population in 2006: 203
Provincial Electoral District(s): Last Mountain-Touchwood
Federal Electoral District(s): Regina-Qu'Appelle
Next Election: Oct. 2009 (3 year terms)
Mavis Webster, Administrator
Carl Olson, Mayor

Lemberg
P.O. Box 399
332 Main St.
Lemberg, SK S0A 2B0
306-335-2244 Fax: 306-335-2911
townoffice.lemberg@sasktel.net
www.spreda.sk.ca/community_Lemberg.htm
Municipal Type: Town
Incorporated: July 12, 1904; *Area:* 2.67 sq km
Population in 2006: 255
Provincial Electoral District(s): Last Mountain-Touchwood
Federal Electoral District(s): Yorkton-Melville
Next Election: Oct. 2009 (3 year terms)
Note: Proclaimed as a town on Sept. 1, 1907.
Joyce Hauck, Clerk
Herbert MacDonald, Mayor

Leoville
P.O. Box 280
Leoville, SK S0J 1N0
306-984-2140 Fax: 306-984-2337
leoville@sasktel.net
Municipal Type: Village
Incorporated: June 26, 1944; *Area:* 1.11 sq km
Population in 2006: 341
Provincial Electoral District(s): Meadow Lake
Federal Electoral District(s): Desnethé-Missinippi-Churchill River
Next Election: Oct. 2009 (3 year terms)
Mona Chalifour, Clerk
Ron Craswell, Mayor

Leross
P.O. Box 68
Leross, SK S0A 2C0
306-675-4429 Fax: 306-675-2097
Municipal Type: Village
Incorporated: Dec. 1, 1909; *Area:* 1.21 sq km
Population in 2006: 42
Provincial Electoral District(s): Last Mountain-Touchwood
Federal Electoral District(s): Regina-Qu'Appelle
Next Election: Oct. 2009 (3 year terms)
Elaine Klyne, Clerk
Francis Klyne, Mayor

Leroy
P.O. Box 40
Leroy, SK S0K 2P0
306-286-3288 Fax: 306-286-3400
leroy@bogend.ca
www.leroy.ca
Municipal Type: Town
Incorporated: Dec. 5, 1922; *Area:* 1.06 sq km
Population in 2006: 412
Provincial Electoral District(s): Melfort
Federal Electoral District(s): Saskatoon-Humboldt
Next Election: Oct. 2009 (3 year terms)
Note: Proclaimed as a town on March 1, 1963.
Morris Hartman, Mayor
Ann-Marie Block, Administrator

Lestock
P.O. Box 209
320 Touchwood Hills Ave.
Lestock, SK S0A 2G0
306-274-2277 Fax: 306-274-2277
Municipal Type: Village
Incorporated: April 17, 1912; *Area:* 0.87 sq km
Population in 2006: 138
Provincial Electoral District(s): Last Mountain-Touchwood
Federal Electoral District(s): Regina-Qu'Appelle
Next Election: Oct. 2009 (3 year terms)
Susan Ross, Administrator
Kelly Komodowski, Mayor

Liberty
P.O. Box 59
Liberty, SK S0G 3A0
306-963-2402 Fax: 306-963-2405
rm251@sasktel.net
Municipal Type: Village
Incorporated: Jan. 23, 1912; *Area:* 1.37 sq km
Population in 2006: 73
Provincial Electoral District(s): Arm River-Watrous
Federal Electoral District(s): Regina-Lumsden-Lake Centre
Next Election: Oct. 2009 (3 year terms)
Yvonne Carrick, Administrator
Donald Anderson, Mayor

Limerick
P.O. Box 129
Limerick, SK S0H 2P0
306-263-2020 Fax: 306-263-2013
rm73@sasktel.net
Municipal Type: Village
Incorporated: July 10, 1913; *Area:* 0.79 sq km
Population in 2006: 130
Provincial Electoral District(s): Wood River
Federal Electoral District(s): Cypress Hills-Grasslands
Next Election: Oct. 2009 (3 year terms)
Tammy Franks, Administrator
Robert Smith, Mayor

Lintlaw
P.O. Box 10
Lintlaw, SK S0A 2H0
306-325-2006 Fax: 306-325-2006
villageoflintlaw@sasktel.net
Municipal Type: Village
Incorporated: Dec. 14, 1921; *Area:* 1.23 sq km
Population in 2006: 145
Provincial Electoral District(s): Kelvington-Wadena
Federal Electoral District(s): Yorkton-Melville
Next Election: Oct. 2009 (3 year terms)
Kathleen Ambrose, Administrator
Leonard Johnson, Mayor

Lipton
P.O. Box 219
Lipton, SK S0G 3B0
306-336-2505 Fax: 306-336-2505
villip@sasktel.net
Municipal Type: Village
Incorporated: May 15, 1905; *Area:* 0.75 sq km
Population in 2006: 342
Provincial Electoral District(s): Last Mountain-Touchwood
Federal Electoral District(s): Regina-Qu'Appelle
Next Election: Oct. 2009 (3 year terms)
Marlene L. Bausmer, Clerk
Doug Blatter, Mayor

Loon Lake
P.O. Box 220
Loon Lake, SK S0M 1L0
306-837-2090 Fax: 306-837-4735
loonlake@sasktel.net
Municipal Type: Village
Incorporated: Jan. 1, 1950; *Area:* 0.66 sq km
Population in 2006: 306
Provincial Electoral District(s): Meadow Lake
Federal Electoral District(s): Churchill River/Rivière Churchill
Next Election: Oct. 2009 (3 year terms)
Meredith Chuiko, Clerk
Brian Hirschfeld, Mayor

Loreburn
P.O. Box 177
Loreburn, SK S0H 2S0
306-644-2097 Fax: 306-644-4847
villageofloreburn@yourlink.ca
Municipal Type: Village
Incorporated: May 20, 1909; *Area:* 0.62 sq km
Population in 2006: 113
Provincial Electoral District(s): Arm River-Watrous
Federal Electoral District(s): Blackstrap
Next Election: Oct. 2009 (3 year terms)
Muriel Stronski, Clerk
Bruce Hagen, Mayor

Love
P.O. Box 94
Love, SK S0J 1P0
306-276-2525
www.cybervillagemall.com/sk/love
Municipal Type: Village
Incorporated: June 2, 1945; *Area:* 0.46 sq km
Population in 2006: 55
Provincial Electoral District(s): Saskatchewan Rivers
Federal Electoral District(s): Desnethé-Missinippi-Churchill River
Next Election: Oct. 2009 (3 year terms)
Valerie Rodgers, Clerk
Duane Tempel, Mayor

Lucky Lake
P.O. Box 99
Lucky Lake, SK S0L 1Z0
306-858-2234 Fax: 306-858-2234
rm225.vll@sasktel.net
Municipal Type: Village
Incorporated: Nov. 23, 1920; *Area:* 0.66 sq km
Population in 2006: 295
Provincial Electoral District(s): Rosetown-Elrose
Federal Electoral District(s): Cypress Hills-Grasslands
Next Election: Oct. 2009 (3 year terms)
Edna A. Laturnus, Administrator
Tom Luchenski, Mayor

Lumsden
P.O. Box 160
300 James Street North
Lumsden, SK S0G 3C0
306-731-2404 Fax: 306-731-3572
town.lumsden@sasktel.net
www.lumsden.ca
Municipal Type: Town
Incorporated: Dec. 29, 1898; *Area:* 3.82 sq km
Population in 2006: 1,523
Provincial Electoral District(s): Thunder Creek
Federal Electoral District(s): Regina-Lumsden-Lake Centre
Note: Proclaimed as a town on March 15, 1905.
Verne Barber, Mayor
Wayne Zerff, Administrator

Luseland
P.O. Box 130
Luseland, SK S0L 2A0
306-372-4218 Fax: 306-347-4700
luseland@sasktel.net
www.townofluseland.com
Municipal Type: Town
Incorporated: Dec. 10, 1910; *Area:* 1.53 sq km
Population in 2006: 571
Provincial Electoral District(s): Kindersley
Federal Electoral District(s): Battlefords-Lloydminster
Next Election: Oct. 2009 (3 year terms)
Note: Proclaimed as a town on Jan. 1, 1954.
Len Schlosser, Mayor
E. Lynne Tolley, Administrator

Macklin
P.O. Box 69
Macklin, SK S0L 2C0
306-753-2256 Fax: 306-753-3234
town.macklin@sasktel.net
www.macklin.ca
Municipal Type: Town
Incorporated: Nov. 8, 1909; *Area:* 2.85 sq km
Population in 2006: 1,290
Provincial Electoral District(s): Kindersley
Federal Electoral District(s): Battlefords-Lloydminster
Next Election: Oct. 2009 (3 year terms)
Note: Proclaimed as a town on Nov. 1, 1912.
Patrick Doetzel, Mayor
Kim G. Gartner, Administrator

MacNutt
P.O. Box 10
MacNutt, SK S0A 2K0
306-742-4391 Fax: 306-742-4391
Municipal Type: Village
Incorporated: Feb. 22, 1913; *Area:* 0.81 sq km
Population in 2006: 80
Provincial Electoral District(s): Melville-Saltcoats
Federal Electoral District(s): Yorkton-Melville
Next Election: Oct. 2009 (3 year terms)
Kendra Busch, Clerk
Fred Peppler, Mayor

Macoun
P.O. Box 58
Macoun, SK S0C 1P0
306-634-9352 Fax: 306-634-9352
Municipal Type: Village
Incorporated: Oct. 16, 1903; *Area:* 1.68 sq km
Population in 2006: 168
Provincial Electoral District(s): Estevan
Federal Electoral District(s): Souris-Moose Mountain
Next Election: Oct. 2009 (3 year terms)
Lorna Vollmin, Clerk
Lisa Kuntz, Mayor

Macrorie
P.O. Box 37
Main St.
Macrorie, SK S0L 2E0
306-243-2010 Fax: 306-243-2010
villageofmacrorie@sasktel.net
www.macrorie.com
Municipal Type: Village
Incorporated: Feb. 8, 1912; *Area:* 0.77 sq km
Population in 2006: 78
Provincial Electoral District(s): Rosetown-Elrose
Federal Electoral District(s): Cypress Hills-Grasslands
Next Election: Oct. 2009 (3 year terms)
Kate Johnson, Administrator
Lorne Arthur, Mayor

Maidstone
P.O. Box 208
112 - 1st Ave. West
Maidstone, SK S0M 1M0
306-893-2373 Fax: 306-893-4378
townofmaidstone@sasktel.net
www.townofmaidstone.com
Municipal Type: Town
Incorporated: July 19, 1907; *Area:* 4.56 sq km
Population in 2006: 1,037
Provincial Electoral District(s): Cut Knife-Turtleford
Federal Electoral District(s): Battlefords-Lloydminster
Next Election: Oct. 2009 (3 year terms)
Note: Proclaimed as a town on March 1, 1955.
Valerie Kenyon, Mayor
Don Wildeman, Administrator

Major
P.O. Box 179
Major, SK S0L 2H0
306-834-5668
ssteele@yourlink.ca
Municipal Type: Village
Incorporated: Sept. 29, 1914; *Area:* 2.78 sq km
Population in 2006: 67
Provincial Electoral District(s): Kindersley
Federal Electoral District(s): Battlefords-Lloydminster
Next Election: Oct. 2009 (3 year terms)
Stacey Steele, Clerk
Veryl Richelhoff, Mayor

Makwa
P.O. Box 159
Makwa, SK S0M 1N0
306-236-3919 Fax: 306-236-3919
Municipal Type: Village
Incorporated: June 1, 1965; *Area:* 0.66 sq km
Population in 2006: 96
Provincial Electoral District(s): Meadow Lake
Federal Electoral District(s): Desnethé-Missinippi-Churchill River
Next Election: Oct. 2009 (3 year terms)
Patricia Tatlow, Clerk
Cecile Bertrand, Mayor

Mankota
P.O. Box 336
Mankota, SK S0H 2W0
306-478-2331 Fax: 306-478-2525
village.mankota@sasktel.net
Municipal Type: Village
Incorporated: Feb. 3, 1941; *Area:* 1.55 sq km
Population in 2006: 238
Provincial Electoral District(s): Wood River
Federal Electoral District(s): Cypress Hills-Grasslands
Next Election: Oct. 2009 (3 year terms)
Janet Viker, Administrator
Judy Smith, Mayor

Manor
P.O. Box 295
45 Main St.
Manor, SK S0C 1R0
306-448-2273 Fax: 306-448-2273
admin.manor@sasktel.net
Municipal Type: Village
Incorporated: April 15, 1902; *Area:* 2.79 sq km
Population in 2006: 312
Provincial Electoral District(s): Cannington
Federal Electoral District(s): Souris-Moose Mountain
Next Election: Oct. 2009 (3 year terms)
Joan Mills, Administrator
Anthony Hortness, Mayor

Maple Creek
P.O. Box 428
205 Jasper St.
Maple Creek, SK S0N 1N0
306-662-2244 Fax: 306-662-4131
townofmaplecreek@sasktel.net
www.maplecreek.ca
Municipal Type: Town
Incorporated: April 28, 1896; *Area:* 4.42 sq km
Population in 2006: 2,198
Provincial Electoral District(s): Cypress Hills
Federal Electoral District(s): Cypress Hills-Grasslands
Next Election: Oct. 2009 (3 year terms)
Note: Proclaimed as a town on April 30, 1903.
Anne Weisgerber, Mayor
Mark Caswell, Administrator

Marcelin
P.O. Box 39
100 - 1st Ave. North
Marcelin, SK S0J 1R0
306-226-2168 Fax: 306-226-2171
vmarcelin@sasktel.net
Municipal Type: Village
Incorporated: Sept. 25, 1911; *Area:* 1.32 sq km
Population in 2006: 169
Provincial Electoral District(s): Rosthern-Shellbrook
Federal Electoral District(s): Saskatoon-Wanuskewin
Next Election: Oct. 2009 (3 year terms)
Nicole Pool, Administrator
E.W. Dale Butler, Mayor

Marengo
P.O. Box 70
Marengo, SK S0L 2K0
306-968-2922 Fax: 306-968-2278
rm292.rm322@sasktel.net
Municipal Type: Village
Incorporated: Nov. 5, 1910; *Area:* 0.87 sq km
Population in 2006: 51
Provincial Electoral District(s): Kindersley
Federal Electoral District(s): Battlefords-Lloydminster
Next Election: Oct. 2009 (3 year terms)
Shelley Mohr, Administrator
Robert Lee, Mayor

Margo
P.O. Box 28
Margo, SK S0A 2M0
306-324-2134 Fax: 306-324-4563
Municipal Type: Village
Incorporated: April 24, 1911; *Area:* 0.80 sq km
Population in 2006: 90
Provincial Electoral District(s): Kelvington-Wadena
Federal Electoral District(s): Yorkton-Melville
Next Election: Oct. 2009 (3 year terms)
Faye H. Kucheran, Clerk
Neil Trach, Mayor

Markinch
P.O. Box 29
Markinch, SK S0G 3J0
306-726-4355
Municipal Type: Village
Incorporated: Feb. 16, 1911; *Area:* 0.68 sq km
Population in 2006: 59

Provincial Electoral District(s): Last Mountain-Touchwood
Federal Electoral District(s): Regina-Qu'Appelle
Next Election: Oct. 2009 (3 year terms)
Rita T. Orb, Clerk
Wendell Langford, Mayor

Marquis
P.O. Box 40
Marquis, SK S0H 2X0
306-788-2022 Fax: 306-788-2168
rm191@sasktel.net
Municipal Type: Village
Incorporated: March 21, 1910; *Area:* 0.63 sq km
Population in 2006: 71
Provincial Electoral District(s): Thunder Creek
Federal Electoral District(s): Regina-Lumsden-Lake Centre
Next Election: Oct. 2009 (3 year terms)
Ronald J. Gasper, Administrator
Nicolas J. Kettel, Mayor

Marsden
P.O. Box 69
Marsden, SK S0M 1P0
306-826-5215 Fax: 306-826-5512
rm442@sasktel.net
Municipal Type: Village
Incorporated: April 24, 1931; *Area:* 0.94 sq km
Population in 2006: 234
Provincial Electoral District(s): Cut Knife-Turtleford
Federal Electoral District(s): Battlefords-Lloydminster
Next Election: Oct. 2009 (3 year terms)
Joanne Loy, Administrator
Tracy Kurtz, Mayor

Marshall
P.O. Box 125
Marshall, SK S0M 1R0
306-387-6340 Fax: 306-387-6161
office@townofmarshall.com
www.townofmarshall.com
Municipal Type: Town
Incorporated: Jan. 21, 1914; *Area:* 1.01 sq km
Population in 2006: 608
Provincial Electoral District(s): Lloydminster
Federal Electoral District(s): Battlefords-Lloydminster
Next Election: Oct. 2009 (3 year terms)
Note: Proclaimed as a town on Oct. 26, 2006.
Noella Hill, Mayor
Lorne Kachur, Administrator

Martensville
P.O. Box 970
515 Centennial Dr. South
Martensville, SK S0K 2T0
306-931-2166 Fax: 306-933-2468
manager@martensville.ca
www.martensville.ca
Municipal Type: Town
Incorporated: Sept. 1, 1966; *Area:* 4.78 sq km
Population in 2006: 4,968
Provincial Electoral District(s): Martensville
Federal Electoral District(s): Saskatoon-Wanuskewin
Next Election: Oct. 2009 (3 year terms)
Note: Proclaimed as a town on Jan. 1, 1969.
Giles Saulnier, Mayor
saulnier@martensville.ca
Scott Blevins, Town Manager
manager@martensville.ca

Maryfield
P.O. Box 58
Maryfield, SK S0G 3K0
306-646-2143 Fax: 306-646-2193
vom.ward@sasktel.net
Municipal Type: Village
Incorporated: Aug. 21, 1907; *Area:* 2.69 sq km
Population in 2006: 347
Provincial Electoral District(s): Cannington
Federal Electoral District(s): Souris-Moose Mountain
Next Election: Oct. 2009 (3 year terms)
Ward Frazer, Administrator
David Hill, Mayor

Maymont
P.O. Box 160
Maymont, SK S0M 1T0
306-389-2112 Fax: 306-389-2162
rm406@sasktel.net
Municipal Type: Village
Incorporated: June 24, 1907; *Area:* 0.66 sq km
Population in 2006: 130
Provincial Electoral District(s): Biggar
Federal Electoral District(s): Saskatoon-Wanuskewin
Next Election: Oct. 2009 (3 year terms)
Laurie DuBois, Administrator
Denise Bernier, Mayor

McLean
P.O. Box 56
McLean, SK S0G 3E0
306-699-7279 Fax: 306-699-2347
lylagrad@sasktel.net
www.mcleansask.com
Municipal Type: Village
Incorporated: Jan. 24, 1913; *Area:* 1.33 sq km
Population in 2006: 275
Provincial Electoral District(s): Indian Head-Milestone
Federal Electoral District(s): Regina-Qu'Appelle
Next Election: Oct. 2009 (3 year terms)
Lyla Grad, Administrator
Cliff Ebenal, Mayor

McTaggart
P.O. Box 134
McTaggart, SK S0G 3G0
306-869-3245
Municipal Type: Village
Incorporated: Oct. 5, 1909; *Area:* 0.69 sq km
Population in 2006: 114
Provincial Electoral District(s): Weyburn-Big Muddy
Federal Electoral District(s): Souris-Moose Mountain
Next Election: Oct. 2009 (3 year terms)
Darlene Paquin, Administrator
John Dyck, Mayor

Meacham
P.O. Box 9
Meacham, SK S0K 2V0
306-376-2003
Municipal Type: Village
Incorporated: June 19, 1912; *Area:* 1.27 sq km
Population in 2006: 70
Provincial Electoral District(s): Humboldt
Federal Electoral District(s): Blackstrap
Next Election: Oct. 2009 (3 year terms)
Elizabeth Saretzky, Clerk
Perry Thiessen, Mayor

Meadow Lake
120 - 1st St. East
Meadow Lake, SK S9X 1P8
306-236-3622 Fax: 306-236-4299
meadowlake_townml@sasktel.net
www.meadowlake.ca
Municipal Type: Town
Incorporated: Aug. 24, 1931; *Area:* 7.95 sq km
Population in 2006: 4,771
Provincial Electoral District(s): Meadow Lake
Federal Electoral District(s): Desnethé-Missinippi-Churchill River
Next Election: Oct. 2009 (3 year terms)
Note: Proclaimed as a town on Feb. 1, 1936.
Darwin Obrigewitsch, Mayor
Rosalee Brown, Administrator

Meath Park
P.O. Box 255
Meath Park, SK S0J 1T0
306-929-2112 Fax: 306-929-2281
villpark@sasktel.net
Municipal Type: Village
Incorporated: May 23, 1938; *Area:* 0.77 sq km
Population in 2006: 179
Provincial Electoral District(s): Saskatchewan Rivers
Federal Electoral District(s): Prince Albert
Next Election: Oct. 2009 (3 year terms)
Elaine Esopenko, Administrator
Darryl Sachkowski, Mayor

Medstead
P.O. Box 148
Medstead, SK S0M 1W0
306-342-4609 Fax: 306-342-2067
rm497@sasktel.net
Municipal Type: Village
Incorporated: April 23, 1931; *Area:* 0.67 sq km
Population in 2006: 148
Provincial Electoral District(s): Rosthern-Shellbrook
Federal Electoral District(s): Battlefords-Lloydminster
Next Election: Oct. 2009 (3 year terms)
Christin Baynes, Administrator
Robert Bosnan, Mayor

Melfort
City Hall
P.O. Box 2230
202 Burrows Ave. West
Melfort, SK S0E 1A0
306-752-5911 Fax: 306-752-5556
city@cityofmelfort.ca
www.cityofmelfort.ca
Municipal Type: Town
Incorporated: Nov. 4, 1903; *Area:* 14.78 sq km
Population in 2006: 5,192
Provincial Electoral District(s): Melfort
Federal Electoral District(s): Prince Albert
Next Election: Oct. 2009 (3 year terms)
Note: Incorporated as a city on Sept. 2, 1980.
Kevin Phillips, Mayor
Heather Audette, Clerk
h.audette@cityofmelfort.ca

Melville
P.O. Box 1240
430 Main St.
Melville, SK S0A 2P0
306-728-6840 Fax: 306-728-5911
mhotsko@melville.ca
www.city.melville.sk.ca
Municipal Type: Town
Incorporated: Dec. 21, 1908; *Area:* 14.82 sq km
Population in 2006: 4,149
Provincial Electoral District(s): Melville-Saltcoats
Federal Electoral District(s): Yorkton-Melville
Next Election: Oct. 2009 (3 year terms)
Note: Incorporated as a city on Aug. 1, 1960.
Walter Streelasky, Mayor
Michael Hotsko, City Manager
mhotsko@melville.ca

Mendham
P.O. Box 69
Mendham, SK S0N 1P0
306-679-2000 Fax: 306-679-2275
Municipal Type: Village
Incorporated: April 1, 1930; *Area:* 0.5 sq km
Population in 2006: 35
Provincial Electoral District(s): Cypress Hills
Federal Electoral District(s): Cypress Hills-Grasslands
Next Election: Oct. 2009 (3 year terms)
Lucein Stuebing, Clerk
Kevin Angerman, Mayor

Meota
P.O. Box 80
Meota, SK S0M 1X0
306-892-2061 Fax: 306-892-2449
rm.468@sasktel.net
Municipal Type: Village
Incorporated: July 6, 1911; *Area:* 1.55 sq km
Population in 2006: 297
Provincial Electoral District(s): Cut Knife-Turtleford
Federal Electoral District(s): Battlefords-Lloydminster
Next Election: Oct. 2009 (3 year terms)
Maryann Germann, Administrator
Terry Tait, Mayor

Mervin
P.O. Box 35
Mervin, SK S0M 1Y0
306-845-2784 Fax: 306-845-3563
mervin.lib@sasktel.net
Municipal Type: Village
Incorporated: March 17, 1920; *Area:* 0.73 sq km
Population in 2006: 228
Provincial Electoral District(s): Cut Knife-Turtleford
Federal Electoral District(s): Battlefords-Lloydminster
Next Election: Oct. 2009 (3 year terms)
David Woof, Administrator
Kenneth Knowlton, Mayor

Michel Village
Sylvestre Place
P.O. Box 250
Dillon, SK S0M 0S0
306-282-4401 Fax: 306-282-2155
hamletofmichelvillage@sasktel.net
Municipal Type: Northern Hamlet
Incorporated: Nov. 1, 1983; *Area:* 3.73 sq km
Population in 2006: 79
Provincial Electoral District(s): Athabasca
Federal Electoral District(s): Desnethé-Missinippi-Churchill River
Next Election: 2009 (3 year terms)
Seraphine Montgrand, Clerk
Ernest Sylvestre, Mayor

Midale
P.O. Box 128
233 Main St.
Midale, SK S0C 1S0
306-458-2400 Fax: 306-458-2209
lindugan@sasktel.net
Municipal Type: Town
Incorporated: Aug. 10, 1907; *Area:* 1.53 sq km
Population in 2006: 462
Provincial Electoral District(s): Estevan
Federal Electoral District(s): Souris-Moose Mountain
Next Election: Oct. 2009 (3 year terms)
Note: Proclaimed as a town on March 1, 1962.
Allan Hauglum, Mayor
Linda M. Dugan, Administrator

Middle Lake
P.O. Box 119
Middle Lake, SK S0K 2X0
306-367-2149
www.ctreda.ca/webpage/towns/middlelake/middlelakehome.htm
Municipal Type: Village
Incorporated: Jan. 1, 1963; *Area:* 1.26 sq km
Population in 2006: 277
Provincial Electoral District(s): Batoche
Federal Electoral District(s): Saskatoon-Humboldt
Next Election: Oct. 2009 (3 year terms)
Donna Hauser, Clerk
Gordon Koeferle, Mayor

Milden
P.O. Box 70
202 Centre St.
Milden, SK S0L 2L0
306-935-2131 Fax: 306-935-2020
vmilden@sasktel.net
www.villageofmilden.com
Municipal Type: Village
Incorporated: July 20, 1911; *Area:* 1.18 sq km
Population in 2006: 172

Provincial Electoral District(s): Rosetown-Elrose
Federal Electoral District(s): Cypress Hills-Grasslands
Next Election: Oct. 2009 (3 year terms)
Penny Aadland, Clerk
Glen Adair, Mayor

Milestone
P.O. Box 74
105 Main St.
Milestone, SK S0G 3L0
306-436-2130 Fax: 306-436-2051
milcal@sasktel.net
www.milestonesk.ca
Municipal Type: Town
Incorporated: March 14, 1903; *Area:* 2.17 sq km
Population in 2006: 562
Provincial Electoral District(s): Indian Head-Milestone
Federal Electoral District(s): Souris-Moose Mountain
Next Election: Oct. 2009 (3 year terms)
Note: Proclaimed as a town on Aug. 15, 1906.
Richard Galbraith, Mayor
Stephen Schury, Administrator

Minton
P.O. Box 52
Minton, SK S0C 1T0
306-969-2144 Fax: 306-969-2127
rm.09@sasktel.net
Municipal Type: Village
Incorporated: Jan. 1, 1951; *Area:* 0.3 sq km
Population in 2006: 60
Provincial Electoral District(s): Weyburn-Big Muddy
Federal Electoral District(s): Souris-Moose Mountain
Next Election: Oct. 2009 (3 year terms)
Joyce Axten, Clerk
Orville Corbin, Mayor

Missinipe
P.O. Box 1617
38 Otter St.
La Ronge, SK S0J 1L0
306-635-4540 Fax: 306-635-4434
msnpoffice@sasktel.net
Municipal Type: Northern Hamlet
Incorporated: Feb. 1, 1984; *Area:* 1.87 sq km
Population in 2006: 5
Provincial Electoral District(s): Cumberland
Federal Electoral District(s): Desnethé-Missinippe-Churchill River
Next Election: 2009 (3 year terms)
Mel Piper, Clerk
Zack Adams, Mayor

Mistatim
P.O. Box 145
Mistatim, SK S0E 1B0
306-889-2008
www.newsaskcfdc.ca/mistatim.htm
Municipal Type: Village
Incorporated: July 1, 1952; *Area:* 0.47 sq km
Population in 2006: 89
Provincial Electoral District(s): Carrot River Valley
Federal Electoral District(s): Yorkton-Melville
Next Election: Oct. 2009 (3 year terms)
Krista Biro, Clerk
Gene Legare, Mayor

Montmartre
P.O. Box 146
136 Cemtral Ave.
Montmartre, SK S0G 3M0
306-424-2040 Fax: 306-424-2065
rm126@sasktel.net
www.montmartre-sk.com
Municipal Type: Village
Incorporated: Oct. 19, 1908; *Area:* 1.63 sq km
Population in 2006: 413
Provincial Electoral District(s): Moosomin
Federal Electoral District(s): Wascana
Next Election: Oct. 2009 (3 year terms)
Calvin D. Abrahamson, Mayor
Dale Brenner, Administrator

Moosomin
P.O. Box 730
701 Main St.
Moosomin, SK S0G 3N0
306-435-2988 Fax: 306-435-3343
twn.moosomin@sasktel.net
www.moosomin.com
Municipal Type: Town
Incorporated: March 20, 1889; *Area:* 5.97 sq km
Population in 2006: 2,257
Provincial Electoral District(s): Moosomin
Federal Electoral District(s): Souris-Moose Mountain
Next Election: Oct. 2009 (3 year terms)

Morse
P.O. Box 270
Morse, SK S0H 3C0
306-629-3300 Fax: 306-629-3235
morse@sasktel.net
Municipal Type: Town
Incorporated: March 11, 1910; *Area:* 1.45 sq km
Population in 2006: 236
Provincial Electoral District(s): Thunder Creek
Federal Electoral District(s): Cypress Hills-Grasslands
Next Election: Oct. 2009 (3 year terms)
Note: Proclaimed as a town on Nov. 1, 1912.
Gloria Weppler, Administrator
Louis Fafard, Mayor

Mortlach
P.O. Box 10
Mortlach, SK S0H 3E0
306-355-2233 Fax: 306-355-2351
mortlach@sasktel.net
www.mortlach.ca
Municipal Type: Village
Incorporated: April 19, 1906; *Area:* 2.76 sq km
Population in 2006: 254
Provincial Electoral District(s): Thunder Creek
Federal Electoral District(s): Cypress Hills-Grasslands
Next Election: Oct. 2009 (3 year terms)
Elaine Salikin, Administrator
Ron Locke, Mayor

Mossbank
P.O. Box 370
Mossbank, SK S0H 3G0
306-354-2294 Fax: 306-354-7725
townofmossbank@sasktel.net
Municipal Type: Town
Incorporated: Dec. 14, 1915; *Area:* 1.75 sq km
Population in 2006: 330
Provincial Electoral District(s): Wood River
Federal Electoral District(s): Palliser
Next Election: Oct. 2009 (3 year terms)
Note: Proclaimed as a town on May 15, 1959.
Lise Costley, Administrator
Carl Weiss, Mayor

Muenster
P.O. Box 98
Muenster, SK S0K 2Y0
306-682-2794 Fax: 306-682-4179
muenster@sasktel.net
www.ctreda.ca/webpage/towns/muenster/muensterhome.htm
Municipal Type: Village
Incorporated: Aug. 18, 1908; *Area:* 1.24 sq km
Population in 2006: 342
Provincial Electoral District(s): Humboldt
Federal Electoral District(s): Saskatoon-Humboldt
Next Election: Oct. 2009 (3 year terms)
Rose M. Haeusler, Administrator
Benno Korte, Mayor

Naicam
P.O. Box 238
Naicam, SK S0K 2Z0
306-874-2280 Fax: 306-874-5444
naicam@sasktel.net
www.townofnaicam.ca
Municipal Type: Town
Incorporated: April 28, 1921; *Area:* 1.69 sq km
Population in 2006: 690
Provincial Electoral District(s): Melfort
Federal Electoral District(s): Saskatoon-Humboldt
Next Election: Oct. 2009 (3 year terms)
Note: Proclaimed as a town on Sept. 1, 1954.
Rodger Hayward, Mayor
Lowell Prefontaine, Administrator

Neilburg
P.O. Box 280
39 Centre St.
Neilburg, SK S0M 2C0
306-823-4321 Fax: 306-823-4477
neilburg@sasktel.net
Municipal Type: Village
Incorporated: Jan. 1, 1947; *Area:* 1.16 sq km
Population in 2006: 394
Provincial Electoral District(s): Cut Knife-Turtleford
Federal Electoral District(s): Battlefords-Lloydminster
Next Election: Oct. 2009 (3 year terms)
Janet L. Black, Administrator
Ernest Ducherer, Mayor

Netherhill
P.O. Box 2706
Kindersley, SK S0L 1S0
306-463-3562
Municipal Type: Village
Incorporated: April 28, 1910; *Area:* 0.73 sq km
Population in 2006: 30
Provincial Electoral District(s): Rosetown-Elrose
Federal Electoral District(s): Battlefords-Lloydminster
Next Election: Oct. 2009 (3 year terms)
Vacant, Clerk
Winston Jones, Mayor

Neudorf
P.O. Box 187
Neudorf, SK S0A 2T0
306-748-2551
vneudorf@sasktel.net
www.village.neudorf.sk.ca
Municipal Type: Village
Incorporated: April 25, 1905; *Area:* 2.05 sq km
Population in 2006: 281
Provincial Electoral District(s): Last Mountain-Touchwood
Federal Electoral District(s): Yorkton-Melville
Next Election: Oct. 2009 (3 year terms)
Crystal Campbell, Administrator
Murray J. Hanowski, Mayor

Neville
P.O. Box 88
Neville, SK S0N 1T0
306-627-3255 Fax: 306-627-3546
village.neville@sasktel.net
Municipal Type: Village
Incorporated: July 5, 1912; *Area:* 1.10 sq km
Population in 2006: 65
Provincial Electoral District(s): Wood River
Federal Electoral District(s): Cypress Hills-Grasslands
Next Election: Oct. 2009 (3 year terms)
Linda Hornung, Clerk
Harvey Linnen, Mayor

Nipawin
P.O. Box 2134
210 Second Ave. East
Nipawin, SK S0E 1E0
306-862-9866 Fax: 306-862-3076 Toll Free Phone: 306-877-647-2946
townoffice@nipawin.com; info@nipawin.com
www.nipawin.com
Municipal Type: Town
Incorporated: May 7, 1925; *Area:* 8.03 sq km
Population in 2006: 4,061
Provincial Electoral District(s): Carrot River Valley
Federal Electoral District(s): Prince Albert
Next Election: Oct. 2009 (3 year terms)
Note: Proclaimed as a town on May 1, 1937.
Glen Day, Mayor
Steven Piermantier, Administrator
s.piermantier@nipawin.com

Nokomis
P.O. Box 189
101 - 3rd Ave. West
Nokomis, SK S0G 3R0
306-528-2010 Fax: 306-528-2024
townofnokomis@sasktel.net
www.geocities.com/nokomis_website
Municipal Type: Town
Incorporated: March 5, 1908; *Area:* 2.61 sq km
Population in 2006: 404
Provincial Electoral District(s): Arm River-Watrous
Federal Electoral District(s): Regina-Lumsden-Lake Centre
Next Election: Oct. 2009 (3 year terms)
Note: Proclaimed as a town on Aug. 15, 1908.
Willard Beeler, Mayor
Joanne Hamilton, Administrator

Norquay
P.O. Box 327
25 Main St.
Norquay, SK S0A 2V0
306-594-2101 Fax: 306-594-2347
norquay@sasktel.net
www.townofnorquay.ca
Municipal Type: Town
Incorporated: June 4, 1913; *Area:* 1.69 sq km
Population in 2006: 412
Provincial Electoral District(s): Canora-Pelly
Federal Electoral District(s): Yorkton-Melville
Next Election: Oct. 2009 (3 year terms)
Note: Proclaimed as a town on March 1, 1963.
Don Tower, Mayor
Rodney C. Johnson, Administrator

North Portal
P.O. Box 15
North Portal, SK S0C 1W0
306-927-5050 Fax: 306-927-5052
villagen@sasktel.net
Municipal Type: Village
Incorporated: Nov. 16, 1903; *Area:* 2.49 sq km
Population in 2006: 123
Provincial Electoral District(s): Estevan
Federal Electoral District(s): Souris-Moose Mountain
Next Election: Oct. 2009 (3 year terms)
Arnold Lindsay, Clerk
Murray Arnold, Mayor

Odessa
P.O. Box 91
Odessa, SK S0G 3S0
306-957-2020 Fax: 306-957-4502
villageofodessa@sasktel.net
Municipal Type: Village
Incorporated: March 14, 1911; *Area:* 1.18 sq km
Population in 2006: 201
Provincial Electoral District(s): Indian Head-Milestone
Federal Electoral District(s): Wascana
Next Election: Oct. 2009 (3 year terms)
Sheila Leurer, Clerk
Phillip Selinger, Mayor

Ogema
P.O. Box 159
Ogema, SK S0C 1Y0

306-459-2262 Fax: 306-459-2762
townofogema@sasktel.net
www.ogema.ca
Municipal Type: Town
Incorporated: Jan. 18, 1911; *Area:* 1.43 sq km
Population in 2006: 304
Provincial Electoral District(s): Weyburn-Big Muddy
Federal Electoral District(s): Souris-Moose Mountain
Next Election: Oct. 2009 (3 year terms)
Note: Proclaimed as a town on Jan. 7, 1913.
Peggy Tuchscherer, Administrator
Wayne Myren, Mayor

Osage
P.O. Box 96
Osage, SK S0G 3T0
306-722-3747
Municipal Type: Village
Incorporated: May 8, 1906; *Area:* 0.59 sq km
Population in 2006: 20
Provincial Electoral District(s): Indian Head-Milestone
Federal Electoral District(s): Souris-Moose Mountain
Next Election: Oct. 2009 (3 year terms)
Linda R. Kreutzer, Clerk
Garry Kreutzer, Mayor

Osler
P.O. Box 190
Osler, SK S0K 3A0
306-239-2155 Fax: 306-239-2194
townofosler@yourlink.ca
www.osler-sk.ca
Municipal Type: Town
Incorporated: April 9, 1904; *Area:* 0.98 sq km
Population in 2006: 926
Provincial Electoral District(s): Martensville
Federal Electoral District(s): Saskatoon-Wanuskewin
Next Election: Oct. 2009 (3 year terms)
Note: Proclaimed as a town on Nov. 1, 1985.
Ben Buhler, Mayor
Sandra MacArthur, Administrator

Outlook
P.O. Box 518
400 Saskatchewan Ave. West
Outlook, SK S0L 2N0
306-867-8663 Fax: 306-867-9898
town@town.outlook.sk.ca
www.town.outlook.sk.ca
Municipal Type: Town
Incorporated: Dec. 19, 1908; *Area:* 7.83 sq km
Population in 2006: 1,938
Provincial Electoral District(s): Rosetown-Elrose
Federal Electoral District(s): Blackstrap; Cypress Hills-Grasslands
Next Election: Oct. 2009 (3 year terms)
Note: Proclaimed as a town on Nov. 1, 1909.
Robert T. Stephenson, Mayor
Trent Michelman, Administrator
michelman@town.outlook.sk.ca

Oxbow
P.O. Box 149
517 Prospect Ave.
Oxbow, SK S0C 2B0
306-483-2300 Fax: 306-483-5277
townofoxb@sasktel.net
www.town-oxbow.ca
Municipal Type: Town
Incorporated: March 7, 1899; *Area:* 3.1 sq km
Population in 2006: 1,139
Provincial Electoral District(s): Cannington
Federal Electoral District(s): Souris-Moose Mountain
Next Election: Oct. 2009 (3 year terms)
Note: Proclaimed as a town on May 30, 1904.
Dale Ching, Mayor
Brad Vanbeselaere, Administrator

Paddockwood
P.O. Box 188
Paddockwood, SK S0J 1Z0
306-989-2033 Fax: 306-989-2033
vpaddockwood@inet2000.com
Municipal Type: Village
Incorporated: Jan. 1, 1949; *Area:* 0.65 sq km
Population in 2006: 125
Provincial Electoral District(s): Saskatchewan Rivers
Federal Electoral District(s): Prince Albert
Next Election: Oct. 2009 (3 year terms)
Diana Siurko, Clerk
Reg Hintz, Mayor

Pangman
P.O. Box 189
Pangman, SK S0C 2C0
306-442-2131 Fax: 306-442-2144
rm.69@sasktel.net
Municipal Type: Village
Incorporated: May 17, 1911; *Area:* 0.73 sq km
Population in 2006: 200
Provincial Electoral District(s): Weyburn-Big Muddy
Federal Electoral District(s): Souris-Moose Mountain
Next Election: Oct. 2009 (3 year terms)
Wayne W. Lozinsky, Administrator
Cory Henheffer, Mayor

Paradise Hill
P.O. Box 270
Paradise Hill, SK S0M 2G0
306-344-2206 Fax: 306-344-4941
paradisehill@sasktel.net
www.paradisehill.ca
Municipal Type: Village
Incorporated: Jan. 1, 1947; *Area:* 1.99 sq km
Population in 2006: 483
Provincial Electoral District(s): Lloydminster
Federal Electoral District(s): Battlefords-Lloydminster
Next Election: Oct. 2009 (3 year terms)
Alvin Form, Mayor
Marion Hougham, Clerk

Parkside
P.O. Box 48
Parkside, SK S0J 2A0
306-747-2235 Fax: 306-747-3395
Municipal Type: Village
Incorporated: Feb. 21, 1913; *Area:* 0.92 sq km
Population in 2006: 129
Provincial Electoral District(s): Rosthern-Shellbrook
Federal Electoral District(s): Saskatoon-Wanuskewin
Next Election: Oct. 2009 (3 year terms)
Gwen Olson, Clerk
David K. Moe, Mayor

Patuanak
P.O. Box 180
Shagwenaw Dr.
Patuanak, SK S0M 2H0
306-396-2020 Fax: 306-396-2092
nhofpatuanak@sasktel.net
Municipal Type: Northern Hamlet
Incorporated: Dec. 1, 1983; *Area:* 1.34 sq km
Population in 2006: 84
Provincial Electoral District(s): Athabasca
Federal Electoral District(s): Desnethé-Missinippi-Churchill River
Next Election: Oct. 2009 (3 year terms)
Marie Lariviere, Clerk
Ernie Laliberte, Mayor

Paynton
P.O. Box 10
Paynton, SK S0M 2J0
306-895-2023 Fax: 306-895-4800
rm470@sasktel.net
Municipal Type: Village
Incorporated: May 2, 1907; *Area:* 0.85 sq km
Population in 2006: 151
Provincial Electoral District(s): Cut Knife-Turtleford
Federal Electoral District(s): Battlefords-Lloydminster
Next Election: Oct. 2009 (3 year terms)
Nicole Walker, Administrator
Ken (Mack) McDonald, Mayor

Pelican Narrows
P.O. Box 10
Bear St.
Pelican Narrows, SK S0P 0E0
306-632-2225 Fax: 306-632-2006
Municipal Type: Northern Village
Incorporated: Jan. 1, 1989; *Area:* 3.70 sq km
Population in 2006: 599
Provincial Electoral District(s): Cumberland
Federal Electoral District(s): Desnethé-Missinippi-Churchill River
Next Election: Oct. 2009 (3 year terms)
Ovide Michel, Mayor
Doreen Linklater, Clerk

Pelly
P.O. Box 220
Pelly, SK S0A 2Z0
306-595-2124 Fax: 306-595-2050
town.pelly@sasktel.net
www.pelly.ca
Municipal Type: Village
Incorporated: May 4, 1911; *Area:* 0.96 sq km
Population in 2006: 287
Provincial Electoral District(s): Canora-Pelly
Federal Electoral District(s): Yorkton-Melville
Next Election: Oct. 2009 (3 year terms)
Victoria Makohoniuk, Administrator
Sharon Nelson, Mayor

Pennant
P.O. Box 57
Pennant, SK S0N 1X0
306-626-3255 Fax: 306-626-3661
pennant@t2.net
Municipal Type: Village
Incorporated: July 29, 1912; *Area:* 0.65 sq km
Population in 2006: 119
Provincial Electoral District(s): Swift Current
Federal Electoral District(s): Cypress Hills-Grasslands
Next Election: Oct. 2009 (3 year terms)
Debra Shaw, Administrator
Leslie Bayliss, Mayor

Pense
P.O. Box 125
Pense, SK S0G 3W0
306-345-2332 Fax: 306-345-2340
pensevillage@sasktel.net
www.pense.ca
Municipal Type: Village
Incorporated: March 7, 1904; *Area:* 1.32 sq km
Population in 2006: 507
Provincial Electoral District(s): Thunder Creek
Federal Electoral District(s): Palliser
Next Election: Oct. 2009 (3 year terms)
Linda Goetz, Mayor
Jennifer Lendvay, Administrator

Penzance
P.O. Box 68
Penzance, SK S0G 3X0
306-488-4669
Municipal Type: Village
Incorporated: July 13, 1912; *Area:* 0.62 sq km
Population in 2006: 30
Provincial Electoral District(s): Thunder Creek
Federal Electoral District(s): Regina-Lumsden-Lake Centre
Next Election: Oct. 2009 (3 year terms)
Ellen Frohlick, Clerk
John Thorson, Mayor

Perdue
P.O. Box 190
1103 - 9th St.
Perdue, SK S0K 3C0
306-237-4337 Fax: 306-237-4337
vill.per@sasktel.net
www.villageofperdue.com
Municipal Type: Village
Incorporated: July 15, 1909; *Area:* 1.10 sq km
Population in 2006: 364
Provincial Electoral District(s): Biggar
Federal Electoral District(s): Saskatoon-Rosetown-Biggar
Next Election: Oct. 2009 (3 year terms)
Pam McMahon, Administrator
Kelly Dwyer, Mayor

Pierceland
P.O. Box 39
177 Main St.
Pierceland, SK S0M 2K0
306-839-2015 Fax: 306-839-2057
plandvillage@sasktel.net
Municipal Type: Village
Incorporated: Jan. 1, 1973; *Area:* 2.69 sq km
Population in 2006: 498
Provincial Electoral District(s): Lloydminster
Federal Electoral District(s): Desnethé-Missinippi-Churchill River
Next Election: Oct. 2009 (3 year terms)
Jim Krushelnitzky, Mayor
Jane Eistetter, Clerk

Pilger
P.O. Box 24
Pilger, SK S0K 3G0
306-367-4631 Fax: 306-367-4621
www.ctreda.ca/webpage/towns/pilger/pilgerhome.htm
Municipal Type: Village
Incorporated: Jan. 1, 1969; *Area:* 0.52 sq km
Population in 2006: 74
Provincial Electoral District(s): Batoche
Federal Electoral District(s): Saskatoon-Humboldt
Next Election: Oct. 2009 (3 year terms)
Diane Forster, Clerk
Gloria Struck, Mayor

Pilot Butte
P.O. Box 253
Pilot Butte, SK S0G 3Z0
306-781-4547 Fax: 306-781-4477
pilotbutteadmin@sasktel.net
www.pilotbutte.ca
Municipal Type: Town
Incorporated: Nov. 8, 1913; *Area:* 4.69 sq km
Population in 2006: 1,867
Provincial Electoral District(s): Regina Wascana Plains
Federal Electoral District(s): Regina-Qu'Appelle
Next Election: Oct. 2009 (3 year terms)
Note: Proclaimed as a town on Nov. 1, 1980.
Ed Zsombor, Mayor
Laurie Rudolph, Administrator

Pinehouse
P.O. Box 298
Pinehouse Ave.
Pinehouse, SK S0J 2B0
306-884-2030 Fax: 306-884-2021
nvp@sasktel.net
Municipal Type: Northern Village
Incorporated: Oct. 1, 1983; *Area:* 6.84 sq km
Population in 2006: 1,076
Provincial Electoral District(s): Athabasca
Federal Electoral District(s): Desnethé-Missinippi-Churchill River
Next Election: 2009 (3 year terms)
Mike Natomagan, Mayor
Marie LaVallee, Administrator

Pleasantdale
P.O. Box 147
Pleasantdale, SK S0K 3H0

306-874-5743 Fax: 306-874-5743
www.newsaskcfdc.ca/pleasantdale.htm
Municipal Type: Village
Incorporated: Jan. 1, 1987; *Area:* 0.56 sq km
Population in 2006: 85
Provincial Electoral District(s): Melfort
Federal Electoral District(s): Saskatoon-Humboldt
Next Election: Oct. 2009 (3 year terms)
Dianne M. Dodd, Clerk
Kenneth Myhre, Mayor

Plenty
P.O. Box 177
Plenty, SK S0L 2R0
306-932-2045 Fax: 306-932-2044
vop@sasktel.net
Municipal Type: Village
Incorporated: March 25, 1911; *Area:* 0.65 sq km
Population in 2006: 126
Provincial Electoral District(s): Rosetown-Elrose
Federal Electoral District(s): Battlefords-Lloydminster
Next Election: Oct. 2009 (3 year terms)
Lorraine McDonald, Administrator
Corey Kingwell, Mayor

Plunkett
P.O. Box 149
Plunkett, SK S0K 3J0
306-944-4514 Fax: 306-944-4512
Municipal Type: Village
Incorporated: Dec. 28, 1921; *Area:* 0.64 sq km
Population in 2006: 75
Provincial Electoral District(s): Humboldt
Federal Electoral District(s): Blackstrap
Next Election: Oct. 2009 (3 year terms)
Helen Miller, Clerk
Richard Hayes, Mayor

Ponteix
P.O. Box 330
213 Centre St.
Ponteix, SK S0N 1Z0
306-625-3222 Fax: 306-625-3204
town.ponteix@sasktel.net
www.townofponteix.com
Municipal Type: Town
Incorporated: June 24, 1914; *Area:* 1.09 sq km
Population in 2006: 531
Provincial Electoral District(s): Wood River
Federal Electoral District(s): Cypress Hills-Grasslands
Next Election: Oct. 2009 (3 year terms)
Note: Proclaimed as a town on April 1, 1957.
Etiennette Binette, Mayor
Lynne Lemieux, Administrator
admin@townofponteix.com

Porcupine Plain
P.O. Box 310
151 McAllister Ave.
Porcupine Plain, SK S0E 1H0
306-278-2262 Fax: 306-278-3378
porcupineplain@sasktel.net
www.porcupineplain.com
Municipal Type: Town
Incorporated: April 9, 1942; *Area:* 2.27 sq km
Population in 2006: 783
Provincial Electoral District(s): Kelvington-Wadena
Federal Electoral District(s): Yorkton-Melville
Next Election: Oct. 2009 (3 year terms)
Note: Proclaimed as a town on Jan. 1, 1968.
Terry Zip, Mayor
Alicia Kwasney-Curle, Administrator

Preeceville
P.O. Box 560
239 Highway Ave. East
Preeceville, SK S0A 3B0
306-547-2810 Fax: 306-547-3116
preeceville@sasktel.net
www.townofpreeceville.ca
Municipal Type: Town
Incorporated: Feb. 6, 1912; *Area:* 2.79 sq km
Population in 2006: 1,050
Provincial Electoral District(s): Canora-Pelly
Federal Electoral District(s): Yorkton-Melville
Next Election: Oct. 2009 (3 year terms)
Note: Incorporated as a town on Nov. 30, 1946.
Garth Harris, Mayor
Lorelei Karcha, Administrator

Prelate
P.O. Box 40
Prelate, SK S0N 2B0
306-673-2340 Fax: 306-673-2340
Municipal Type: Village
Incorporated: Oct. 25, 1913; *Area:* 0.87 sq km
Population in 2006: 126
Provincial Electoral District(s): Cypress Hills
Federal Electoral District(s): Cypress Hills-Grasslands
Next Election: Oct. 2009 (3 year terms)
Darlene Wagner, Clerk
Jeannine Schmaltz, Mayor

Primate
P.O. Box 6
Primate, SK S0L 2S0
306-753-2897 Fax: 306-753-2971
tjcl@lincsat.com
Municipal Type: Village
Incorporated: April 5, 1922; *Area:* 0.94 sq km
Population in 2006: 50
Provincial Electoral District(s): Kindersley
Federal Electoral District(s): Battlefords-Lloydminster
Next Election: Oct. 2009 (3 year terms)
Dianne Latendresse, Clerk
Donald Sieben, Mayor

Prud'homme
P.O. Box 38
Prud'Homme, SK S0K 3K0
306-654-2001 Fax: 306-654-2001
prudhommevillage@sasktel.net
Municipal Type: Village
Incorporated: Nov. 15, 1922; *Area:* 0.84 sq km
Population in 2006: 167
Provincial Electoral District(s): Humboldt
Federal Electoral District(s): Saskatoon-Humboldt
Next Election: Oct. 2009 (3 year terms)
Holly Williams, Administrator
Preston Tkatch, Mayor

Punnichy
P.O. Box 250
Punnichy, SK S0A 3C0
306-835-2135 Fax: 306-835-2100
punnichy@aski.ca
Municipal Type: Village
Incorporated: Oct. 22, 1909; *Area:* 0.68 sq km
Population in 2006: 277
Provincial Electoral District(s): Last Mountain-Touchwood
Federal Electoral District(s): Regina-Qu'Appelle
Next Election: Oct. 2009 (3 year terms)
Aaron Millar, Administrator
Victor Senft, Mayor

Qu'Appelle
P.O. Box 60
Qu'Appelle, SK S0G 4A0
306-699-2279 Fax: 306-699-2306
townquappelle@sasktel.net
www.townofquappelle.ca
Municipal Type: Town
Incorporated: Feb. 20, 1904; *Area:* 4.22 sq km
Population in 2006: 624
Provincial Electoral District(s): Indian Head-Milestone
Federal Electoral District(s): Regina-Qu'Appelle
Next Election: Oct. 2009 (3 year terms)
Allan Arthur, Mayor
Carol Wickenheiser, Administrator

Quill Lake
P.O. Box 9
60 Main St.
Quill Lake, SK S0A 3E0
306-383-2592 Fax: 306-383-2255
quilllake@sasktel.net
www.quill-lakes.com/quilllake/village
Municipal Type: Village
Incorporated: Dec. 8, 1906; *Area:* 1.30 sq km
Population in 2006: 413
Provincial Electoral District(s): Melfort
Federal Electoral District(s): Saskatoon-Humboldt
Next Election: Oct. 2009 (3 year terms)
Robert Walker, Mayor
Judy L. Kanak, Administrator

Quinton
P.O. Box 128
Quinton, SK S0A 3G0
306-835-2515 Fax: 306-835-2515
quinton@sasktel.net
Municipal Type: Village
Incorporated: March 1, 1910; *Area:* 0.96 sq km
Population in 2006: 108
Provincial Electoral District(s): Arm River-Watrous
Federal Electoral District(s): Regina-Qu'Appelle
Next Election: Oct. 2009 (3 year terms)
Aaron Millar, Administrator
Ralph Brockman, Mayor

Rabbit Lake
P.O. Box 9
Rabbit Lake, SK S0M 2L0
306-824-2044 Fax: 306-824-2044
Municipal Type: Village
Incorporated: April 13, 1928; *Area:* 0.92 sq km
Population in 2006: 113
Provincial Electoral District(s): Rosthern-Shellbrook
Federal Electoral District(s): Battlefords-Lloydminster
Next Election: Oct. 2009 (3 year terms)
Cindy Miller, Administrator
Don Unger, Mayor

Radisson
P.O. Box 69
Radisson, SK S0K 3L0
306-827-2218 Fax: 306-827-2218
tradisson@sasktel.net
radisson.sasktelwebhosting.com
Municipal Type: Town
Incorporated: Feb. 3, 1906; *Area:* 2.07 sq km
Population in 2006: 421
Provincial Electoral District(s): Biggar
Federal Electoral District(s): Saskatoon-Wanuskewin
Next Election: Oct. 2009 (3 year terms)
Note: Proclaimed as a town on July 1, 1913.
Myrna Condon, Mayor
Darrin Beaudoin, Administrator

Radville
P.O. Box 339
Radville, SK S0C 2G0
306-869-2477 Fax: 306-869-3100
town.radville@sasktel.net
www.radville.ca
Municipal Type: Town
Incorporated: Jan. 3, 1911; *Area:* 1.86 sq km
Population in 2006: 755
Provincial Electoral District(s): Estevan
Federal Electoral District(s): Souris-Moose Mountain
Next Election: Oct. 2009 (3 year terms)
Note: Proclaimed as a town on May 1, 1913.
David Bellavance, Mayor
Shauna Bourassa, Administrator

Rama
P.O. Box 205
Rama, SK S0A 3H0
306-593-6065 Fax: 306-593-2273
Municipal Type: Village
Incorporated: Dec. 18, 1919; *Area:* 0.67 sq km
Population in 2006: 75
Provincial Electoral District(s): Kelvington-Wadena
Federal Electoral District(s): Yorkton-Melville
Next Election: Oct. 2009 (3 year terms)
Nicole Monchamp, Administrator
Darrell Dutchak, Mayor

Raymore
P.O. Box 10
Raymore, SK S0A 3J0
306-746-2100 Fax: 306-746-4314
raymoretown@aski.ca
Municipal Type: Town
Incorporated: Aug. 11, 1909; *Area:* 2.75 sq km
Population in 2006: 581
Provincial Electoral District(s): Arm River-Watrous
Federal Electoral District(s): Regina-Qu'Appelle
Next Election: Oct. 2009 (3 year terms)
Note: Proclaimed as a town on Aug. 1, 1963.
Keith Bentz, Mayor
Gail R. Braman, Administrator

Redvers
P.O. Box 249
Redvers, SK S0C 2H0
306-452-3533 Fax: 306-452-3701
town.of.redvers@sasktel.net
www.redvers.org
Municipal Type: Town
Incorporated: July 9, 1904; *Area:* 2.83 sq km
Population in 2006: 878
Provincial Electoral District(s): Cannington
Federal Electoral District(s): Souris-Moose Mountain
Next Election: Oct. 2009 (3 year terms)
Note: Proclaimed as a town on July 6, 1960.
Omer Carriere, Mayor
Janice Burnett, Administrator

Regina Beach
P.O. Box 10
218 Centre St.
Regina Beach, SK S0G 4C0
306-729-2202 Fax: 306-729-3411
townofreginabeach@sasktel.net
www.reginabeach.ca
Municipal Type: Town
Incorporated: Sept. 30, 1920; *Area:* 2.58 sq km
Population in 2006: 1,195
Provincial Electoral District(s): Thunder Creek
Federal Electoral District(s): Regina-Lumsden-Lake Centre
Next Election: Oct. 2009 (3 year terms)
Note: Proclaimed as a town on Nov. 1, 1980.
Duane Klippenstine, Mayor
306-729-3010
Pearl Peters, Administrator

Rhein
P.O. Box 40
Rhein, SK S0A 3K0
306-273-2155 Fax: 306-273-2155
Municipal Type: Village
Incorporated: March 10, 1913; *Area:* 1.09 sq km
Population in 2006: 161
Provincial Electoral District(s): Canora-Pelly
Federal Electoral District(s): Yorkton-Melville
Next Election: Oct. 2009 (3 year terms)
Kim Engel, Administrator
Craig Walsh, Mayor

Richard
P.O. Box 202
Hafford, SK S0J 1A0
306-549-2266 Fax: 306-549-2266
vrichard@sasktel.net
Municipal Type: Village
Incorporated: Oct. 11, 1916; *Area:* 0.73 sq km
Population in 2006: 25
Provincial Electoral District(s): Rosthern-Shellbrook
Federal Electoral District(s): Saskatoon-Wanuskewin
Next Election: Oct. 2009 (3 year terms)
Lisa Prescesky, Administrator
Merilyn Wawryk, Mayor

Richmound
P.O. Box 29
Richmound, SK S0N 2E0
306-669-4415 Fax: 306-669-2052
richmound.village@sasktel.net
Municipal Type: Village
Incorporated: May 5, 1947; *Area:* 0.47 sq km
Population in 2006: 159
Provincial Electoral District(s): Cypress Hills
Federal Electoral District(s): Cypress Hills-Grasslands
Next Election: Oct. 2009 (3 year terms)
Melinda Hammer, Administrator
Barry Manz, Mayor
Al Korol, Alderman
Glen Nickell, Alderman

Ridgedale
P.O. Box 27
Ridgedale, SK S0E 1L0
306-277-2002
www.newsaskcfdc.ca/ridgedale.htm
Municipal Type: Village
Incorporated: Dec. 15, 1921; *Area:* 0.72 sq km
Population in 2006: 66
Provincial Electoral District(s): Carrot River Valley
Federal Electoral District(s): Prince Albert
Next Election: Oct. 2009 (3 year terms)
Barbara Messenger, Clerk
Murray Leveque, Mayor

Riverhurst
P.O. Box 116
324 Teck St.
Riverhurst, SK S0H 3P0
306-353-2220 Fax: 306-353-2220
villageofriverhurst@sasktel.net
www.riverhurst.ca
Municipal Type: Village
Incorporated: June 22, 1916; *Area:* 0.91 sq km
Population in 2006: 121
Provincial Electoral District(s): Thunder Creek
Federal Electoral District(s): Cypress Hills-Grasslands
Next Election: Oct. 2009 (3 year terms)
Jo-Ann Turner, Administrator
Joe Dumonceau, Mayor
306-796-2006

Rocanville
P.O. Box 265
Rocanville, SK S0A 3L0
306-645-2022 Fax: 306-645-4492
rocanville.town@sasktel.net
www.rocanvilletown.ca
Municipal Type: Town
Incorporated: March 24, 1904; *Area:* 2.43 sq km
Population in 2006: 869
Provincial Electoral District(s): Moosomin
Federal Electoral District(s): Souris-Moose Mountain
Next Election: Oct. 2009 (3 year terms)
Note: Incorporated as a town on Aug. 1, 1967.
Daryl Fingas, Mayor
Monica M. Merkosky, Administrator

Roche Percée
P.O. Box 237
Bienfait, SK S0C 0M0
306-634-4661 Fax: 306-634-4693
Municipal Type: Village
Incorporated: Jan. 12, 1909; *Area:* 2.59 sq km
Population in 2006: 149
Provincial Electoral District(s): Estevan
Federal Electoral District(s): Souris-Moose Mountain
Next Election: Oct. 2009 (3 year terms)
Barry Katschke, Administrator
Reg Jahn, Mayor

Rockglen
P.O. Box 267
Rockglen, SK S0H 3R0
306-476-2144 Fax: 306-476-2339
rockglen1@sasktel.net
Municipal Type: Town
Incorporated: July 12, 1927; *Area:* 2.85 sq km
Population in 2006: 366
Provincial Electoral District(s): Wood River
Federal Electoral District(s): Cypress Hills-Grasslands
Next Election: Oct. 2009 (3 year terms)
Note: Proclaimed as a town on Sept. 1, 1957.
Diane Griffin, Administrator
Leonard Davey, Mayor

Rockhaven
P.O. Box 9
Rockhaven, SK S0M 2R0
306-398-2734 Fax: 306-398-2929
Municipal Type: Village
Incorporated: March 19, 1913; *Area:* 1.58 sq km
Population in 2006: 20
Provincial Electoral District(s): Cut Knife-Turtleford
Federal Electoral District(s): Battlefords-Lloydminster
Next Election: Oct. 2009 (3 year terms)
Karri Risling, Clerk
Tom Hollman, Mayor

Rose Valley
P.O. Box 460
Rose Valley, SK S0E 1M0
306-322-2232 Fax: 306-322-4461
rosevalley@sasktel.net
www.newsaskcfdc.ca/rosevalley.htm
Municipal Type: Town
Incorporated: Sept. 24, 1940; *Area:* 1.12 sq km
Population in 2006: 338
Provincial Electoral District(s): Kelvington-Wadena
Federal Electoral District(s): Yorkton-Melville
Next Election: Oct. 2009 (3 year terms)
Note: Proclaimed as a town on Jan. 1, 1962.
Marjorie A. Zarowny, Clerk
Daniel Veilleux, Mayor

Rosetown
P.O. Box 398
Rosetown, SK S0L 2V0
306-882-2214 Fax: 306-882-3166
townofrosetown@sasktel.net
www.rosetown.ca
Municipal Type: Town
Incorporated: Aug. 24, 1909; *Area:* 10.59 sq km
Population in 2006: 2,277
Provincial Electoral District(s): Rosetown-Elrose
Federal Electoral District(s): Saskatoon-Rosetown-Biggar
Next Election: Oct. 2009 (3 year terms)
Note: Proclaimed as a town on Nov. 1, 1911.
Brian Gerow, Mayor
Darcy Olson, Administrator

Rosthern
P.O. Box 416
Rosthern, SK S0K 3R0
306-232-4826 Fax: 306-232-5638
townofrosthern@sasktel.net
www.rosthern.com
Municipal Type: Town
Incorporated: Dec. 29, 1898; *Area:* 4.01 sq km
Population in 2006: 1,382
Provincial Electoral District(s): Rosthern-Shellbrook
Federal Electoral District(s): Saskatoon-Wanuskewin
Next Election: Oct. 2009 (3 year terms)
Note: Proclaimed as a town on Nov. 20, 1903.
Doug Knoll, Mayor
Nicole LaChance, Administrator

Rouleau
P.O. Box 250
Rouleau, SK S0G 4H0
306-776-2270 Fax: 306-776-2482
info@townofrouleau.com
www.townofrouleau.com
Municipal Type: Town
Incorporated: July 23, 1903; *Area:* 1.65 sq km
Population in 2006: 400
Provincial Electoral District(s): Indian Head-Milestone
Federal Electoral District(s): Palliser
Next Election: Oct. 2009 (3 year terms)
Note: Proclaimed as a town on March 1, 1907.
Allen Kuhlmann, Mayor
Guy Lagrandeur, Administrator

Ruddell
P.O. Box 7
Ruddell, SK S0M 2S0
306-445-4601 Fax: 306-445-4611
Municipal Type: Village
Incorporated: March 18, 1914; *Area:* 0.47 sq km
Population in 2006: 20
Provincial Electoral District(s): Biggar
Federal Electoral District(s): Saskatoon-Wanuskewin
Next Election: Oct. 2009 (3 year terms)
Betty Prescesky, Administrator
Byron Olsen, Mayor

Rush Lake
P.O. Box 126
Rush Lake, SK S0H 3S0
306-784-3504 Fax: 306-773-0331
a.steinley@sasktel.net
Municipal Type: Village
Incorporated: Oct. 16, 1911; *Area:* 0.74 sq km
Population in 2006: 50
Provincial Electoral District(s): Thunder Creek
Federal Electoral District(s): Cypress Hills-Grasslands
Next Election: Oct. 2009 (3 year terms)
Adeline Steinley, Clerk
Stacey Beisel, Mayor

Ruthilda
P.O. Box 90
Ruthilda, SK S0K 3S0
306-932-4408
Municipal Type: Village
Incorporated: Feb. 3, 1921; *Area:* 0.67 sq km
Population in 2006: 5
Provincial Electoral District(s): Biggar
Federal Electoral District(s): Battlefords-Lloydminster
Next Election: Oct. 2009 (3 year terms)
Anita Gilles, Clerk
Jerry Gilles, Mayor

St. Benedict
P.O. Box 99
St Benedict, SK S0K 3T0
306-289-2072 Fax: 306-289-2077
Municipal Type: Village
Incorporated: Jan. 1, 1964; *Area:* 0.54 sq km
Population in 2006: 78
Provincial Electoral District(s): Batoche
Federal Electoral District(s): Saskatoon-Humboldt
Next Election: Oct. 2009 (3 year terms)
Helen Martinka, Clerk
Edward Martin, Mayor

St. Brieux
P.O. Box 249
300 Main St.
St Brieux, SK S0K 3V0
306-275-2257 Fax: 306-275-4949
brieux@sasktel.net
Municipal Type: Town
Incorporated: Nov. 11, 1913; *Area:* 2.02 sq km
Population in 2006: 492
Provincial Electoral District(s): Batoche
Federal Electoral District(s): Saskatoon-Humboldt
Next Election: Oct. 2009 (3 year terms)
Note: Proclaimed as a town on Nov. 8, 2006.
Pauline Boyer, Mayor
Jennifer Thompson, Administrator

St. George's Hill
P.O. Box 160
Desjarlais St.
Dillon, SK S0M 0S0
306-282-4408 Fax: 306-282-2002
sgh123@sasktel.net
Municipal Type: Northern Hamlet
Incorporated: Dec. 1, 1983; *Area:* 1.46 sq km
Population in 2006: 19
Provincial Electoral District(s): Athabasca
Federal Electoral District(s): Desnethé-Missinippi-Churchill River
Next Election: 2009 (3 year terms)
Tom Bekkattla, Clerk
Donna Janvier, Mayor

St. Gregor
P.O. Box 19
St Gregor, SK S0K 3X0
306-366-2129 Fax: 306-366-2128
stgregorsk@sasktel.net
www.ctreda.ca/webpage/towns/stgregor/gregor.htm
Municipal Type: Village
Incorporated: March 26, 1920; *Area:* 0.91 sq km
Population in 2006: 102
Provincial Electoral District(s): Melfort
Federal Electoral District(s): Saskatoon-Humboldt
Next Election: Oct. 2009 (3 year terms)
Darlene Kuz, Administrator
Doug Hogemann, Mayor

St. Louis
P.O. Box 40
172 Riverside Dr.
St Louis, SK S0J 2C0
306-422-8471 Fax: 306-422-8450
villageofstlouis@sasktel.net
www.villageofstlouis.com
Municipal Type: Village
Incorporated: May 19, 1959; *Area:* 1.08 sq km
Population in 2006: 431
Provincial Electoral District(s): Batoche
Federal Electoral District(s): Saskatoon-Humboldt
Next Election: Oct. 2009 (3 year terms)
Les Rancourt, Acting Mayor
Robin Boyer, Clerk

St. Walburg
P.O. Box 368
St Walburg, SK S0M 2T0
306-248-3232 Fax: 306-248-3484
townofstwalburg@sasktel.net
www.stwalburg.com
Municipal Type: Town
Incorporated: Jan. 18, 1922; *Area:* 2.12 sq km
Population in 2006: 672
Provincial Electoral District(s): Meadow Lake
Federal Electoral District(s): Battlefords-Lloydminster
Next Election: Oct. 2009 (3 year terms)
Note: Proclaimed as a town on Feb. 1, 1953.
Gordon Lee Hall, Mayor
Susan Hamm, Administrator

Saltcoats
P.O. Box 120
Saltcoats, SK S0A 3R0
306-744-2212 Fax: 306-744-2239
saltcoats.town@sasktel.net
www.stown.sasktelwebsite.net
Municipal Type: Town
Incorporated: April 4, 1894; *Area:* 1.35 sq km
Population in 2006: 467
Provincial Electoral District(s): Melville-Saltcoats
Federal Electoral District(s): Yorkton-Melville
Next Election: Oct. 2009 (3 year terms)
Note: Proclaimed as a town on Nov. 1, 1910.
Woodrow Bjarnason, Mayor
Ernie Pushkarenko, Administrator

Sandy Bay
P.O. Box 130
Sandy Bay, SK S0P 0G0
306-754-2165 Fax: 306-754-2157
nvsb@sasktel.net
Municipal Type: Northern Village
Incorporated: Oct. 1, 1983; *Area:* 14.85 sq km
Population in 2006: 1,175
Provincial Electoral District(s): Cumberland
Federal Electoral District(s): Desnethé-Missinippi-Churchill River
Next Election: 2009 (3 year terms)
Ina Fietz-Ray, Mayor
Ramona Nateweyes, Administrator

Sceptre
P.O. Box 128
Sceptre, SK S0N 2H0
306-623-4244 Fax: 306-623-4244
sceptrevillage@xplornet.com
Municipal Type: Village
Incorporated: April 30, 1913; *Area:* 1.23 sq km
Population in 2006: 99
Provincial Electoral District(s): Cypress Hills
Federal Electoral District(s): Cypress Hills-Grasslands
Next Election: Oct. 2009 (3 year terms)
Sherry Egeland, Clerk
Charlene King, Mayor

Scott
P.O. Box 96
104 Main St.
Scott, SK S0K 4A0
306-247-2033 Fax: 306-247-2055
townofscott@xplornet.com
Municipal Type: Town
Incorporated: Nov. 17, 1908; *Area:* 4.39 sq km
Population in 2006: 91
Provincial Electoral District(s): Kindersley
Federal Electoral District(s): Battlefords-Lloydminster
Next Election: Oct. 2009 (3 year terms)
Note: Proclaimed as a town on Nov. 1, 1910.
Stacy Hawkins, Administrator
Eric Schell, Mayor

Sedley
P.O. Box 130
Sedley, SK S0G 4K0
306-885-2133 Fax: 306-885-2132
villageofsedley@sasktel.net
Municipal Type: Village
Incorporated: Aug. 3, 1907; *Area:* 1.31 sq km
Population in 2006: 319
Provincial Electoral District(s): Indian Head-Milestone
Federal Electoral District(s): Wascana
Next Election: Oct. 2009 (3 year terms)
Barbara Marcia, Clerk
David Mayer, Mayor

Semans
P.O. Box 113
Semans, SK S0A 3S0
306-524-2144 Fax: 306-524-2145
semans@aski.ca
Municipal Type: Village
Incorporated: Dec. 14, 1908; *Area:* 1.18 sq km
Population in 2006: 195
Provincial Electoral District(s): Arm River-Watrous
Federal Electoral District(s): Regina-Lumsden-Lake Centre
Next Election: Oct. 2009 (3 year terms)
Charmayne Szatkowski, Administrator
Ray Lamontagne, Mayor

Senlac
P.O. Box 93
Senlac, SK S0L 2Y0
306-228-4330
Municipal Type: Village
Incorporated: Oct. 11, 1916; *Area:* 0.60 sq km
Population in 2006: 45
Provincial Electoral District(s): Cut Knife-Turtleford
Federal Electoral District(s): Battlefords-Lloydminster
Next Election: Oct. 2009 (3 year terms)
Maureen Forbes, Clerk
Joe Murrell, Mayor

Shackleton
P.O. Box 7
Shackleton, SK S0N 2L0
306-587-2910
rwcator@sasktel.net
Municipal Type: Village
Incorporated: May 29, 1919; *Area:* 0.66 sq km
Population in 2006: 10
Provincial Electoral District(s): Cypress Hills
Federal Electoral District(s): Cypress Hills-Grasslands
Next Election: Oct. 2009 (3 year terms)
Marjorie A. Cator, Clerk
Ronald J. Heron, Mayor

Shamrock
P.O. Box 119
Shamrock, SK S0H 3W0
306-648-2736 Fax: 306-648-2798
Municipal Type: Village
Incorporated: April 30, 1924; *Area:* 0.79 sq km
Population in 2006: 20
Provincial Electoral District(s): Wood River
Federal Electoral District(s): Cypress Hills-Grasslands
Next Election: Oct. 2009 (3 year terms)
Sharon Arnold, Clerk
Rene Fortin, Mayor

Shaunavon
P.O. Box 820
401 - 3rd St. West
Shaunavon, SK S0N 2M0
306-297-2605 Fax: 306-297-2608
shaunavon@sasktel.net
www.shaunavon.com
Municipal Type: Town
Incorporated: Nov. 27, 1913; *Area:* 5.10 sq km
Population in 2006: 1,691
Provincial Electoral District(s): Cypress Hills
Federal Electoral District(s): Cypress Hills-Grasslands
Next Election: Oct. 2009 (3 year terms)
Note: Proclaimed as a town on Nov. 1, 1914.
Sharon J. Dickie, Mayor
Charmaine Bernath, Administrator
bernath.shaunavon@sasktel.net

Sheho
P.O. Box 130
Sheho, SK S0A 3T0
306-849-2044
Municipal Type: Village
Incorporated: June 30, 1905; *Area:* 1.95 sq km
Population in 2006: 121
Provincial Electoral District(s): Kelvington-Wadena
Federal Electoral District(s): Yorkton-Melville
Next Election: Oct. 2009 (3 year terms)
Ron Sebulsky, Clerk
Dennis Zoski, Mayor

Shell Lake
P.O. Box 280
Shell Lake, SK S0J 2G0
306-427-2272 Fax: 306-427-4800
village.sl@sasktel.net
www.rkc.ca/shell_lake/
Municipal Type: Village
Incorporated: Oct. 18, 1940; *Area:* 1.09 sq km
Population in 2006: 152
Provincial Electoral District(s): Rosthern-Shellbrook
Federal Electoral District(s): Desnethé-Missinippi-Churchill River
Next Election: Oct. 2009 (3 year terms)
Shirley Dauvin, Clerk
Paula Stalwick, Mayor

Shellbrook
P.O. Box 40
71 Main St.
Shellbrook, SK S0J 2E0
306-747-2177 Fax: 306-747-3111
shellbrook@sasktel.net
www.shellbrook.net
Municipal Type: Town
Incorporated: Nov. 18, 1909; *Area:* 2.13 sq km
Population in 2006: 1,215
Provincial Electoral District(s): Rosthern-Shellbrook
Federal Electoral District(s): Prince Albert
Next Election: Oct. 2009 (3 year terms)
Note: Proclaimed as a town on April 1, 1948.
John Young, Mayor
Tara Kerber, Administrator

Silton
P.O. Box 1
Silton, SK S0G 4L0
306-731-3222
Municipal Type: Village
Incorporated: July 2, 1914; *Area:* 1.07 sq km
Population in 2006: 91
Provincial Electoral District(s): Last Mountain-Touchwood
Federal Electoral District(s): Regina-Lumsden-Lake Centre
Next Election: Oct. 2009 (3 year terms)
Janice Ritter, Clerk
Warren Wild, Mayor

Simpson
P.O. Box 10
303 George St.
Simpson, SK S0G 4M0
306-836-2020 Fax: 306-836-4460
rm281@sasktel.net
Municipal Type: Village
Incorporated: July 11, 1911; *Area:* 1.41 sq km
Population in 2006: 118
Provincial Electoral District(s): Arm River-Watrous
Federal Electoral District(s): Regina-Lumsden-Lake Centre
Next Election: Oct. 2009 (3 year terms)
Darlene Mann, Administrator
Kurt Vanthuyne, Mayor

Sintaluta
P.O. Box 150
Sintaluta, SK S0G 4N0
306-727-2100 Fax: 306-727-2100
www.sintaluta.ca
Municipal Type: Town
Incorporated: Oct. 27, 1898; *Area:* 2.70 sq km
Population in 2006: 98
Provincial Electoral District(s): Indian Head-Milestone
Federal Electoral District(s): Regina-Qu'Appelle
Next Election: Oct. 2009 (3 year terms)
Note: Proclaimed as a town on June 1, 1907.
Sandra McLaren, Administrator
Keith Rathgerber, Mayor

Smeaton
P.O. Box 70
Smeaton, SK S0J 2J0
306-426-2044 Fax: 306-426-2291
www.newsaskcfdc.ca/smeaton.htm
Municipal Type: Village
Incorporated: March 7, 1944; *Area:* 1.38 sq km
Population in 2006: 183
Provincial Electoral District(s): Saskatchewan Rivers
Federal Electoral District(s): Desnethé-Missinippi-Churchill River
Next Election: Oct. 2009 (3 year terms)
Diana M. Jensen, Administrator
Joe Bernhard, Mayor

Smiley
P.O. Box 90
Smiley, SK S0L 2Z0
306-838-2020 Fax: 306-838-4343
rm321@sasktel.net
Municipal Type: Village
Incorporated: Nov. 26, 1913; *Area:* 0.64 sq km
Population in 2006: 50
Provincial Electoral District(s): Kindersley
Federal Electoral District(s): Battlefords-Lloydminster
Next Election: Oct. 2009 (3 year terms)
Lee Torrance, Administrator
Barry Lowe, Mayor

Southey
P.O. Box 248
Southey, SK S0G 4P0
306-726-2202 Fax: 306-726-2916
townofsouthey@sasktel.net
www.southey.ca
Municipal Type: Town
Incorporated: Nov. 9, 1907; *Area:* 1 sq km
Population in 2006: 711
Provincial Electoral District(s): Last Mountain-Touchwood
Federal Electoral District(s): Regina-Qu'Appelle
Next Election: Oct. 2009 (3 year terms)
Note: Proclaimed as a town on Nov. 1, 1980.
Martin Lingelbach, Mayor
Karen Herman, Administrator

Spalding
P.O. Box 280
Spalding, SK S0K 4C0
306-872-2276 Fax: 306-872-2275
spalding.village@sasktel.net
www.newsaskcfdc.ca/spalding.htm
Municipal Type: Village
Incorporated: March 11, 1924; *Area:* 1.18 sq km
Population in 2006: 237
Provincial Electoral District(s): Melfort
Federal Electoral District(s): Saskatoon-Humboldt
Next Election: Oct. 2009 (3 year terms)
Cathy Holt, Administrator
Olwen Hoffman, Mayor

Speers
P.O. Box 974
Speers, SK S0M 2V0
306-246-2114 Fax: 306-246-2173
rm436@littleloon.ca
Municipal Type: Village
Incorporated: Dec. 24, 1915; *Area:* 0.69 sq km
Population in 2006: 74
Provincial Electoral District(s): Rosthern-Shellbrook
Federal Electoral District(s): Saskatoon-Wanuskewin
Next Election: Oct. 2009 (3 year terms)
Dean Nicholson, Clerk
Thomas E. Nicholson, Mayor

Spiritwood
P.O. Box 460
Spiritwood, SK S0J 2M0
306-883-2161 Fax: 306-883-3212
tos@sasktel.net
www.townofspiritwood.ca

Municipal Type: Town
Incorporated: Oct. 1, 1935; *Area:* 2.95 sq km
Population in 2006: 911
Provincial Electoral District(s): Rosthern-Shellbrook
Federal Electoral District(s): Desnethé-Missinippi-Churchill River
Next Election: Oct. 2009 (3 year terms)
Note: Proclaimed as a town on Sept. 1, 1965.
Gary von Holwede, Mayor
Kathy Aumack, Administrator

Springside
P.O. Box 414
Springside, SK S0A 3V0
306-792-2022 Fax: 306-792-2210
springside.town@sasktel.net
Municipal Type: Town
Incorporated: Nov. 11, 1909; *Area:* 0.64 sq km
Population in 2006: 494
Provincial Electoral District(s): Canora-Pelly
Federal Electoral District(s): Yorkton-Melville
Next Election: Oct. 2009 (3 year terms)
Note: Proclaimed as a town on Nov. 1, 1985.
Tom Gall, Mayor
Joan M. Popoff, Administrator

Spy Hill
P.O. Box 69
Spy Hill, SK S0A 3W0
306-534-2255 Fax: 306-534-4520
spyhillvillage@sasktel.net
vila.sasktelwebsite.net
Municipal Type: Village
Incorporated: April 22, 1910; *Area:* 1.19 sq km
Population in 2006: 201
Provincial Electoral District(s): Melville-Saltcoats
Federal Electoral District(s): Yorkton-Melville
Next Election: Oct. 2009 (3 year terms)
Lila R.A. Sippola, Administrator
Allan Perrin, Mayor

Star City
P.O. Box 250
Star City, SK S0E 1P0
306-863-2282 Fax: 306-863-2277
town.starcity@sasktel.net
www.townofstarcity.com
Municipal Type: Town
Incorporated: April 6, 1906; *Area:* 0.7 sq km
Population in 2006: 428
Provincial Electoral District(s): Melfort
Federal Electoral District(s): Prince Albert
Next Election: Oct. 2009 (3 year terms)
Note: Proclaimed as a town on Nov. 1, 1921.
Lorne Campbell, Mayor
Rachel Kunz, Administrator

Stenen
P.O. Box 160
Stenen, SK S0A 3X0
306-548-4334 Fax: 306-548-4334
villageofstenen@sasktel.net
Municipal Type: Village
Incorporated: Aug. 14, 1912; *Area:* 0.58 sq km
Population in 2006: 91
Provincial Electoral District(s): Canora-Pelly
Federal Electoral District(s): Yorkton-Melville
Next Election: Oct. 2009 (3 year terms)
Melody M. Mills, Administrator
Garry Giesbrecht, Mayor

Stewart Valley
P.O. Box 10
Stewart Valley, SK S0N 2P0
306-778-3611 Fax: 306-778-3688
vlg.stvalley@sasktel.net
Municipal Type: Village
Incorporated: Jan. 1, 1958; *Area:* 0.86 sq km
Population in 2006: 100
Provincial Electoral District(s): Swift Current
Federal Electoral District(s): Cypress Hills-Grasslands
Next Election: Oct. 2009 (3 year terms)
Val Ferguson, Administrator
Mike Moen, Mayor

Stockholm
P.O. Box 265
Stockholm, SK S0A 3Y0
306-793-2151 Fax: 306-793-2151
stockholm@sasktel.net
www.villagestockholm.com
Municipal Type: Village
Incorporated: June 30, 1905; *Area:* 1.64 sq km
Population in 2006: 323
Provincial Electoral District(s): Melville-Saltcoats
Federal Electoral District(s): Yorkton-Melville
Next Election: Oct. 2009 (3 year terms)
Heather Szakacs, Administrator
Brandon Banga, Mayor

Stony Rapids
P.O. Box 120
Johnson St.
Stony Rapids, SK S0J 2R0
306-439-2173 Fax: 306-439-2098
stony.rapids@sasktel.net
Municipal Type: Northern Hamlet
Incorporated: April 1, 1992; *Area:* 3.96 sq km
Population in 2006: 255
Provincial Electoral District(s): Athabasca
Federal Electoral District(s): Desnethé-Missinippi-Churchill River
Next Election: 2009 (3 year terms)
Lillian Laprise, Clerk
Daniel Powder, Mayor

Storthoaks
P.O. Box 40
Storthoaks, SK S0C 2K0
306-449-2262 Fax: 306-449-2210
rm31@sasktel.net
Municipal Type: Village
Incorporated: June 5, 1940; *Area:* 0.49 sq km
Population in 2006: 82
Provincial Electoral District(s): Cannington
Federal Electoral District(s): Souris-Moose Mountain
Next Election: Oct. 2009 (3 year terms)
Erin McMillen, Administrator
Eileen Jenkins, Mayor

Stoughton
P.O. Box 397
Stoughton, SK S0G 4T0
306-457-2413 Fax: 306-457-3162
stoughtontown@sasktel.net
Municipal Type: Town
Incorporated: Feb. 26, 1904; *Area:* 2.13 sq km
Population in 2006: 653
Provincial Electoral District(s): Cannington
Federal Electoral District(s): Souris-Moose Mountain
Next Election: Oct. 2009 (3 year terms)
Note: Proclaimed as a town on June 1, 1960.
Heather Balon-Barmann, Mayor
Chris Miskolczi, Administrator

Strasbourg
P.O. Box 369
Strasbourg, SK S0G 4V0
306-725-3707 Fax: 306-725-3613
strasbourg@sasktel.net
www.townofstrasbourg.ca
Municipal Type: Town
Incorporated: April 19, 1906; *Area:* 5.70 sq km
Population in 2006: 732
Provincial Electoral District(s): Last Mountain-Touchwood
Federal Electoral District(s): Regina-Lumsden-Lake Centre
Next Election: Oct. 2009 (3 year terms)
Note: Proclaimed as a town on July 1, 1907.
Carol Schultz, Mayor
Barbara Griffin, Administrator

Strongfield
P.O. Box 87
Strongfield, SK S0H 3Z0
306-857-4801 Fax: 306-857-4801
strongfield@sasktel.net
Municipal Type: Village
Incorporated: May 3, 1912; *Area:* 0.8 sq km
Population in 2006: 47
Provincial Electoral District(s): Arm River-Watrous
Federal Electoral District(s): Blackstrap
Next Election: Oct. 2009 (3 year terms)
Darice Carlson, Clerk
George Bristow, Mayor

Sturgis
P.O. Box 520
209 - 1st Ave. SE
Sturgis, SK S0A 4A0
306-548-2108 Fax: 306-548-2948
townofsturgis@sasktel.net
www.townofsturgis.com
Municipal Type: Town
Incorporated: Sept. 3, 1912; *Area:* 3.39 sq km
Population in 2006: 575
Provincial Electoral District(s): Canora-Pelly
Federal Electoral District(s): Yorkton-Melville
Next Election: Oct. 2009 (3 year terms)
Note: Proclaimed as a town on March 1, 1951.
Don Olson, Mayor
Olivia (Bim) Bartch, Administrator

Success
P.O. Box 40
Success, SK S0N 2R0
306-773-1345 Fax: 306-773-1345
Municipal Type: Village
Incorporated: Oct. 25, 1912; *Area:* 1.38 sq km
Population in 2006: 40
Provincial Electoral District(s): Swift Current
Federal Electoral District(s): Cypress Hills-Grasslands
Next Election: Oct. 2009 (3 year terms)
Rhonda Cameron, Clerk
John Kroeker, Mayor

Tantallon
P.O. Box 70
Tantallon, SK S0A 4B0
306-643-2112 Fax: 306-643-2113
tantallon@sasktel.net
Municipal Type: Village
Incorporated: June 17, 1904; *Area:* 0.84 sq km
Population in 2006: 105
Provincial Electoral District(s): Melville-Saltcoats
Federal Electoral District(s): Yorkton-Melville
Next Election: Oct. 2009 (3 year terms)
Charlene Swanton, Administrator
Michael Swanton, Mayor

Tessier
P.O. Box 34
Tessier, SK S0L 3G0
306-656-4580
Municipal Type: Village
Incorporated: Aug. 24, 1909; *Area:* 1 sq km
Population in 2006: 20
Provincial Electoral District(s): Rosetown-Elrose
Federal Electoral District(s): Saskatoon-Rosetown-Biggar
Next Election: Oct. 2009 (3 year terms)
Rhonda Leonard, Clerk
L.B. Johnson, Mayor

Theodore
P.O. Box 417
102 Main St.
Theodore, SK S0A 4C0
306-647-2315 Fax: 306-647-2476
theodore.village@sasktel.net
theovill.sasktelwebsite.net
Municipal Type: Village
Incorporated: July 5, 1907; *Area:* 1.73 sq km
Population in 2006: 339
Provincial Electoral District(s): Kelvington-Wadena
Federal Electoral District(s): Yorkton-Melville
Next Election: Oct. 2009 (3 year terms)
Ron Sebulsky, Clerk
Fred Dowholis, Mayor

Timber Bay
General Delivery
Timber Bay, SK S0J 2T0
306-663-5885 Fax: 306-663-5052
Municipal Type: Northern Hamlet
Incorporated: Oct. 1, 1983; *Area:* 4.44 sq km
Population in 2006: 139
Provincial Electoral District(s): Cumberland
Federal Electoral District(s): Desnethé-Missinippi-Churchill River
Next Election: Oct. 2009 (3 year terms)
Sylvia LaVallee, Clerk
Peggy Hennie, Mayor

Tisdale
P.O. Box 1090
901 - 100 St.
Tisdale, SK S0E 1T0
306-873-2681 Fax: 306-873-5700
townoffice@townoftisdale.com
www.townoftisdale.com
Municipal Type: Town
Incorporated: May 15, 1905; *Area:* 4.62 sq km
Population in 2006: 2,981
Provincial Electoral District(s): Carrot River Valley
Federal Electoral District(s): Prince Albert
Next Election: Oct. 2009 (3 year terms)
Note: Proclaimed as a town on Nov. 1, 1920.
Roland (Rolly) Zimmer, Mayor
Brad Hvidston, Administrator

Togo
P.O. Box 100
Togo, SK S0A 4E0
306-597-2114 Fax: 306-597-2114
Municipal Type: Village
Incorporated: Sept. 4, 1906; *Area:* 1.5 sq km
Population in 2006: 100
Provincial Electoral District(s): Canora-Pelly
Federal Electoral District(s): Yorkton-Melville
Next Election: Oct. 2009 (3 year terms)
Rosemarie G. Hamell, Administrator
Amanda Burback, Mayor

Tompkins
P.O. Box 247
5 - 2nd St.
Tompkins, SK S0N 2S0
306-622-2020 Fax: 306-622-2025
villageoftompkins@sasktel.net
www.villageoftompkins.ca
Municipal Type: Village
Incorporated: June 2, 1910; *Area:* 2.65 sq km
Population in 2006: 173
Provincial Electoral District(s): Cypress Hills
Federal Electoral District(s): Cypress Hills-Grasslands
Next Election: Oct. 2009 (3 year terms)
Tammy Todd, Clerk
John Woodward, Mayor

Torquay
P.O. Box 6
Torquay, SK S0C 2L0
306-923-2172 Fax: 306-923-2172
Municipal Type: Village
Incorporated: Dec. 11, 1923; *Area:* 1.35 sq km
Population in 2006: 184
Provincial Electoral District(s): Estevan
Federal Electoral District(s): Souris-Moose Mountain
Next Election: Oct. 2009 (3 year terms)

Thera-Lee Deschner, Clerk
Ken Sutherland, Mayor

Tramping Lake
P.O. Box 157
Tramping Lake, SK S0K 4H0
306-755-2002 Fax: 306-755-2022
Municipal Type: Village
Incorporated: April 10, 1917; *Area:* 1.39 sq km
Population in 2006: 60
Provincial Electoral District(s): Kindersley
Federal Electoral District(s): Battlefords-Lloydminster
Next Election: Oct. 2009 (3 year terms)
Rose Simon, Clerk
Joe Fruhstuk, Mayor

Tribune
P.O. Box 61
Tribune, SK S0C 2M0
306-456-2213 Fax: 306-456-2213
Municipal Type: Village
Incorporated: Feb. 18, 1914; *Area:* 1.61 sq km
Population in 2006: 35
Provincial Electoral District(s): Estevan
Federal Electoral District(s): Souris-Moose Mountain
Next Election: Oct. 2009 (3 year terms)
Dallas Locken, Clerk
Glenn Walkeden, Mayor

Tugaske
P.O. Box 159
Tugaske, SK S0H 4B0
306-759-2211 Fax: 306-759-2249
info@tugaske.com
www.tugaske.com
Municipal Type: Village
Incorporated: May 7, 1909; *Area:* 0.76 sq km
Population in 2006: 105
Provincial Electoral District(s): Thunder Creek
Federal Electoral District(s): Regina-Lumsden-Lake Centre
Next Election: Oct. 2009 (3 year terms)
Daryl Dean, Administrator
Clayton Cave, Mayor

Turnor Lake
P.O. Box 130
Turnor Lake, SK S0M 3E0
306-894-2080 Fax: 306-894-2138
Municipal Type: Northern Hamlet
Incorporated: Oct. 1, 1984; *Area:* 4.62 sq km
Population in 2006: 115
Provincial Electoral District(s): Athabasca
Federal Electoral District(s): Desnethé-Missinippi-Churchill River
Next Election: Oct. 2009 (3 year terms)
Jean Montgrand, Commissioner
John L. Montgrand, Mayor

Turtleford
P.O. Box 38
Turtleford, SK S0M 2Y0
306-845-2156 Fax: 306-845-3320
townofturtleford@sasktel.net
Municipal Type: Town
Incorporated: Oct. 9, 1914; *Area:* 1.64 sq km
Population in 2006: 461
Provincial Electoral District(s): Cut Knife-Turtleford
Federal Electoral District(s): Battlefords-Lloydminster
Next Election: Oct. 2009 (3 year terms)
Note: Proclaimed as a town on July 1, 1983.
Roland Olson, Mayor
Deanna M. Kahl Lundberg, Administrator

Tuxford
P.O. Box 28
Tuxford, SK S0H 4C0
306-692-3390
Municipal Type: Village
Incorporated: July 19, 1907; *Area:* 0.62 sq km
Population in 2006: 88
Provincial Electoral District(s): Thunder Creek
Federal Electoral District(s): Regina-Lumsden-Lake Centre
Next Election: Oct. 2009 (3 year terms)
Reg E. McKee, Clerk
Allison Koch, Mayor

Unity
P.O. Box 1030
#2, 100 First Ave. West
Unity, SK S0K 4L0
306-228-2621 Fax: 306-228-4221
townofunity@sasktel.net
www.townofunity.com
Municipal Type: Town
Incorporated: May 18, 1909; *Area:* 9.77 sq km
Population in 2006: 2,147
Provincial Electoral District(s): Kindersley
Federal Electoral District(s): Battlefords-Lloydminster
Next Election: Oct. 2009 (3 year terms)
Note: Proclaimed as a town on Nov. 1, 1919.
Kathryn Johnson, Mayor
Aileen Garrett, Administrator

Val Marie
P.O. Box 178
Val Marie, SK S0N 2T0
306-298-2022 Fax: 306-298-2062
vovm@sasktel.net
www.vovm.sasktelwebsite.net
Municipal Type: Village
Incorporated: Sept. 13, 1926; *Area:* 0.42 sq km
Population in 2006: 137
Provincial Electoral District(s): Wood River
Federal Electoral District(s): Cypress Hills-Grasslands
Next Election: Oct. 2009 (3 year terms)
Cathy Facette, Administrator
Roland Facette, Mayor

Valparaiso
P.O. Box 473
Star City, SK S0E 1P0
306-863-2522 Fax: 306-863-2255
www.newsaskcfdc.ca/valparaiso.htm
Municipal Type: Village
Incorporated: July 18, 1924; *Area:* 0.69 sq km
Population in 2006: 20
Provincial Electoral District(s): Melfort
Federal Electoral District(s): Prince Albert
Next Election: Oct. 2009 (3 year terms)
Ann Campbell, Clerk
Margaret Emro, Mayor

Vanguard
P.O. Box 187
Vanguard, SK S0N 2V0
306-582-2295 Fax: 306-582-2296
vill.vanguard@sasktel.net
www.vanguardsask.com
Municipal Type: Village
Incorporated: July 8, 1912; *Area:* 1.86 sq km
Population in 2006: 152
Provincial Electoral District(s): Wood River
Federal Electoral District(s): Cypress Hills-Grasslands
Next Election: Oct. 2009 (3 year terms)
Marie Burton, Administrator
Dorothy Saunderson, Mayor

Vanscoy
P.O. Box 480
109 Main St.
Vanscoy, SK S0L 3J0
306-668-2008 Fax: 306-978-0237
vanscoy@sasktel.net
Municipal Type: Village
Incorporated: June 17, 1919; *Area:* 1.49 sq km
Population in 2006: 339
Provincial Electoral District(s): Biggar
Federal Electoral District(s): Saskatoon-Rosetown-Biggar
Next Election: Oct. 2009 (3 year terms)
Dawn Steeves, Administrator
Keith Lensen, Mayor

Vibank
P.O. Box 204
Vibank, SK S0G 4Y0
306-762-2130 Fax: 306-762-4722
village.of.vibank@sasktel.net
Municipal Type: Village
Incorporated: June 23, 1911; *Area:* 0.73 sq km
Population in 2006: 361
Provincial Electoral District(s): Indian Head-Milestone
Federal Electoral District(s): Wascana
Next Election: Oct. 2009 (3 year terms)
Jeanette Schaeffer, Administrator
Wesley Wolfe, Mayor

Viscount
P.O. Box 99
Viscount, SK S0K 4M0
306-944-2199 Fax: 306-944-2198
viscount.office@sasktel.net
Municipal Type: Village
Incorporated: Dec. 17, 1908; *Area:* 1.18 sq km
Population in 2006: 251
Provincial Electoral District(s): Humboldt
Federal Electoral District(s): Blackstrap
Next Election: Oct. 2009 (3 year terms)
Valerie Schlosser, Clerk
Moe Kirzinger, Mayor

Vonda
P.O. Box 308
204 Main St.
Vonda, SK S0K 4N0
306-258-2035 Fax: 306-258-4420
vonda.to@baudoux.ca
Municipal Type: Town
Incorporated: Aug. 29, 1905; *Area:* 2.86 sq km
Population in 2006: 322
Provincial Electoral District(s): Humboldt
Federal Electoral District(s): Saskatoon-Humboldt
Next Election: Oct. 2009 (3 year terms)
Note: Proclaimed as a town on May 6, 1907.
Linda Denis, Clerk
Laurent Loiselle, Mayor

Wadena
P.O. Box 730
Wadena, SK S0A 4J0
306-338-2145 Fax: 306-338-3804
wadadmin@sasktel.net
www.wadena.ca
Municipal Type: Town
Incorporated: Oct. 6, 1906; *Area:* 2.91 sq km
Population in 2006: 1,315
Provincial Electoral District(s): Kelvington-Wadena
Federal Electoral District(s): Yorkton-Melville
Next Election: Oct. 2009 (3 year terms)
Note: Proclaimed as a town on April 1, 1912.
Greg Chaykowski, Mayor
Barb Barteski, Administrator

Wakaw
P.O. Box 669
121 Main St.
Wakaw, SK S0K 4P0
306-233-4223 Fax: 306-233-5234
town.wakaw@sasktel.net
www.townofwakaw.com
Municipal Type: Town
Incorporated: Dec. 26, 1911; *Area:* 3.12 sq km
Population in 2006: 864
Provincial Electoral District(s): Batoche
Federal Electoral District(s): Saskatoon-Humboldt
Next Election: Oct. 2009 (3 year terms)
Note: Proclaimed as a town on Aug. 1, 1953.
Ed Kidd, Mayor
Rick Kindrachuk, Administrator

Waldeck
P.O. Box 97
Waldeck, SK S0H 4J0
306-773-6275 Fax: 306-773-6275
villageofwaldeck@sasktel.net
Municipal Type: Village
Incorporated: Dec. 23, 1913; *Area:* 2 sq km
Population in 2006: 294
Provincial Electoral District(s): Thunder Creek
Federal Electoral District(s): Cypress Hills-Grasslands
Next Election: Oct. 2009 (3 year terms)
Susan Chase, Clerk
Bill Martens, Mayor

Waldheim
P.O. Box 460
Waldheim, SK S0K 4R0
306-945-2161 Fax: 306-945-2360
town.waldheim@sasktel.net
www.waldheim.ca
Municipal Type: Town
Incorporated: June 10, 1912; *Area:* 1.97 sq km
Population in 2006: 868
Provincial Electoral District(s): Martensville
Federal Electoral District(s): Saskatoon-Wanuskewin
Next Election: Oct. 2009 (3 year terms)
Note: Proclaimed as a town on March 1, 1967.
Barbara Schultz, Mayor
D. Chris Adams, Administrator

Waldron
P.O. Box 87
Waldron, SK S0A 4K0
306-794-4521
www.spreda.sk.ca/community_Waldron.htm
Municipal Type: Village
Incorporated: July 17, 1909; *Area:* 1.45 sq km
Population in 2006: 20
Provincial Electoral District(s): Melville-Saltcoats
Federal Electoral District(s): Yorkton-Melville
Next Election: Oct. 2009 (3 year terms)
Monica Haas, Clerk
Raymond Kitch, Mayor

Wapella
P.O. Box 189
Wapella, SK S0G 4Z0
306-532-4343
webmaster@townofwapella.com
www.townofwapella.com
Municipal Type: Town
Incorporated: Dec. 29, 1898; *Area:* 2.56 sq km
Population in 2006: 311
Provincial Electoral District(s): Moosomin
Federal Electoral District(s): Souris-Moose Mountain
Next Election: Oct. 2009 (3 year terms)
Note: Proclaimed as a town on Nov. 20, 1903.
Nancy Campbell, Clerk
townofwapella@hotmail.com
Alison Prokopiw, Mayor

Warman
P.O. Box 340
107 Central St. West
Warman, SK S0K 4S0
306-933-2133 Fax: 306-933-1987
town.warman@sasktel.net
www.townofwarman.ca
Municipal Type: Town
Incorporated: Aug. 3, 1906; *Area:* 5.34 sq km
Population in 2006: 4,764
Provincial Electoral District(s): Martensville
Federal Electoral District(s): Saskatoon-Wanuskewin
Next Election: Oct. 2009 (3 year terms)
Note: Proclaimed as a town on July 1, 1966.

Sheryl Spence, Mayor
Judi Thurlow, Town Clerk
judi.townofwarman@sasktel.net

Waseca
Douglas Place
P.O. Box 88
Waseca, SK S0M 3A0
306-893-2211 Fax: 306-893-4193
Municipal Type: Village
Incorporated: March 15, 1911; *Area:* 0.68 sq km
Population in 2006: 144
Provincial Electoral District(s): Cut Knife-Turtleford
Federal Electoral District(s): Battlefords-Lloydminster
Next Election: Oct. 2009 (3 year terms)
Sandra Sutherland, Administrator
Curtis Sutherland, Mayor

Watrous
P.O. Box 730
Watrous, SK S0K 4T0
306-946-3369 Fax: 306-946-2974
townofwatrous@sasktel.net
www.watrousmanitou.com
Municipal Type: Town
Incorporated: Oct. 15, 1908; *Area:* 11.17 sq km
Population in 2006: 1,743
Provincial Electoral District(s): Arm River-Watrous
Federal Electoral District(s): Blackstrap
Next Election: Oct. 2009 (3 year terms)
Note: Proclaimed as a town on Dec. 30, 1909.
Ed Collins, Mayor
Orrin Redden, Administrator

Watson
P.O. Box 276
Watson, SK S0K 4V0
306-287-3224 Fax: 306-287-3442
town.watson@sasktel.net
Municipal Type: Town
Incorporated: Oct. 6, 1906; *Area:* 2.83 sq km
Population in 2006: 719
Provincial Electoral District(s): Melfort
Federal Electoral District(s): Saskatoon-Humboldt
Next Election: Oct. 2009 (3 year terms)
Note: Proclaimed as a town on Aug. 1, 1908.
Ted Reifferscheid, Mayor
Cathy Coloman, Administrator

Wawota
P.O. Box 58
308 Railway Ave.
Wawota, SK S0G 5A0
306-739-2216 Fax: 306-739-2216
wawota.town@sasktel.net
www.wawota.com
Municipal Type: Town
Incorporated: Dec. 10, 1907; *Area:* 1.24 sq km
Population in 2006: 522
Provincial Electoral District(s): Cannington
Federal Electoral District(s): Souris-Moose Mountain
Next Election: Oct. 2009 (3 year terms)
Note: Proclaimed as a town on Feb. 1, 1975.
Norman Oliver, Mayor
Diane Smith, Administrator

Webb
P.O. Box 100
Webb, SK S0N 2X0
306-674-2230 Fax: 306-674-2324
rm138@xplornet.com
Municipal Type: Village
Incorporated: June 18, 1910; *Area:* 1.41 sq km
Population in 2006: 44
Provincial Electoral District(s): Cypress Hills
Federal Electoral District(s): Cypress Hills-Grasslands
Next Election: Oct. 2009 (3 year terms)
Connie A. Sorenson, Administrator
John Martens, Mayor

Weekes
P.O. Box 159
Weekes, SK S0E 1V0
306-278-2800 Fax: 306-278-2395
www.newsaskcfdc.ca/weekes.htm
Municipal Type: Village
Incorporated: Jan. 13, 1947; *Area:* 0.59 sq km
Population in 2006: 55
Provincial Electoral District(s): Kelvington-Wadena
Federal Electoral District(s): Yorkton-Melville
Next Election: Oct. 2009 (3 year terms)
Betty Dagnon, Clerk
Kenneth Harris, Mayor

Weirdale
General Delivery
Albertville, SK S0J 0A0
306-929-4832
Municipal Type: Village
Incorporated: April 1, 1948; *Area:* 1.36 sq km
Population in 2006: 83
Provincial Electoral District(s): Saskatchewan Rivers
Federal Electoral District(s): Prince Albert
Next Election: Oct. 2009 (3 year terms)
Jacki Leason, Clerk
Garry Sumlic, Mayor

Weldon
P.O. Box 190
Weldon, SK S0J 3A0
306-887-2070 Fax: 306-752-3882
weldon@sasktel.net
www.newsaskcfdc.ca/weldon.htm
Municipal Type: Village
Incorporated: Jan. 24, 1914; *Area:* 1.1 sq km
Population in 2006: 205
Provincial Electoral District(s): Batoche
Federal Electoral District(s): Prince Albert
Next Election: Oct. 2009 (3 year terms)
Shelley L. Holmes, Administrator
Neil Ball, Mayor

Welwyn
P.O. Box 118
Welwyn, SK S0A 4L0
306-733-2077 Fax: 306-435-4313
rm121@sasktel.net
Municipal Type: Village
Incorporated: June 11, 1907; *Area:* 0.64 sq km
Population in 2006: 142
Provincial Electoral District(s): Moosomin
Federal Electoral District(s): Souris-Moose Mountain
Next Election: Oct. 2009 (3 year terms)
Elaine Olsen, Administrator
Joe Santer, Mayor

Weyakwin
P.O. Box 295
Weyakwin Rd.
Weyakwin, SK S0J 1W0
306-663-5820 Fax: 306-663-5112
Municipal Type: Northern Hamlet
Incorporated: Dec. 1, 1983; *Area:* 8.2 sq km
Population in 2006: 99
Provincial Electoral District(s): Cumberland
Federal Electoral District(s): Desnethé-Missinippi-Churchill River
Next Election: Oct. 2009 (3 year terms)
Diane Smith, Clerk
Stella Brown, Mayor

Weyburn No. 67
23 - 6 St. NE
Weyburn, SK S4H 1A7
306-842-2314 Fax: 306-842-1002
rm.67@sasktel.net
Municipal Type: Municipality
Incorporated: Dec. 13, 1909; *Area:* 811.70 sq km
Population in 2006: 888
Next Election: Oct 2010; staggered 2 yr term
Note: URL:
www.saskbiz.ca/communityprofiles/CommunityProfile.Asp?CommunityID=1024
Carmen Sterling, Reeve
Kim McIvor, Administrator

White City
P.O. Box 220 Main
14 Ramm Ave. East
White City, SK S4L 5B1
306-781-2355 Fax: 306-781-2194
whitecity@sasktel.net
www.townofwhitecity.com
Municipal Type: Town
Incorporated: March 1, 1967; *Area:* 4.64 sq km
Population in 2006: 1,113
Provincial Electoral District(s): Regina Wascana Plains
Federal Electoral District(s): Regina-Qu'Appelle
Next Election: Oct. 2009 (3 year terms)
Note: Proclaimed as a town on Nov. 1, 2000.
Bruce Evans, Mayor
els2000@accesscomm.ca
Barbara Marcia, Administrator

White Fox
P.O. Box 38
116 Main St.
White Fox, SK S0J 3B0
306-276-2106 Fax: 306-276-2131
villageofwhitefox@sasktel.net
www.wfox.sasktelwebsite.net
Municipal Type: Village
Incorporated: July 21, 1941; *Area:* 0.85 sq km
Population in 2006: 348
Provincial Electoral District(s): Saskatchewan Rivers
Federal Electoral District(s): Desnethé-Missinippi-Churchill River
Next Election: Oct. 2009 (3 year terms)
Kimberley Issacson, Administrator
Gary Vidnes, Mayor

Whitewood
P.O. Box 129
Whitewood, SK S0G 5C0
306-735-2210 Fax: 306-735-2262
general@townofwhitewood.ca
www.townofwhitewood.ca
Municipal Type: Town
Incorporated: Dec. 31, 1892; *Area:* 3.04 sq km
Population in 2006: 869
Provincial Electoral District(s): Moosomin
Federal Electoral District(s): Souris-Moose Mountain
Next Election: Oct. 2009 (3 year terms)
Malcolm Green, Mayor
Sharon Rodgers, Administrator

Wilcox
P.O. Box 130
Wilcox, SK S0G 5E0
306-732-2030 Fax: 306-732-4495
rm129@sasktel.net
www.wilcox.ca
Municipal Type: Village
Incorporated: April 20, 1907; *Area:* 1.48 sq km
Population in 2006: 222
Provincial Electoral District(s): Indian Head-Milestone
Federal Electoral District(s): Palliser
Next Election: Oct. 2009 (3 year terms)
Kevin Ritchie, Village Clerk
Ryan Matity, Mayor

Wilkie
P.O. Box 580
Wilkie, SK S0K 4W0
306-843-2692 Fax: 306-843-3151
contact@townofwilkie.com
www.townofwilkie.com
Municipal Type: Town
Incorporated: July 18, 1908; *Area:* 9.48 sq km
Population in 2006: 1,222
Provincial Electoral District(s): Biggar
Federal Electoral District(s): Battlefords-Lloydminster
Next Election: Oct. 2009 (3 year terms)
Note: Proclaimed as a town on Nov. 1, 1910.
Walter Lorenz, Mayor
Julie Brooks, Administrator
julieb@townofwilkie.com

Willow Bunch
P.O. Box 189
16 - 5th Edouard Beaupre St. East
Willow Bunch, SK S0H 4K0
306-473-2450 Fax: 306-473-2773
willowbunch.town@sasktel.net
www.willowbunch.ca
Municipal Type: Town
Incorporated: Nov. 15, 1929; *Area:* 0.84 sq km
Population in 2006: 297
Provincial Electoral District(s): Weyburn-Big Muddy
Federal Electoral District(s): Cypress Hills-Grasslands
Next Election: Oct. 2009 (3 year terms)
Note: Proclaimed as a town on Oct. 1, 1960.
Colette Walter, Clerk
Renaud Bissonnette, Mayor

Willowbrook
P.O. Box 98
Willowbrook, SK S0A 4P0

Municipal Type: Village
Incorporated: March 12, 1919; *Area:* 0.48 sq km
Population in 2006: 46
Provincial Electoral District(s): Yorkton
Federal Electoral District(s): Yorkton-Melville
Next Election: Oct. 2009 (3 year terms)
Shirley Biro, Clerk
William Kish, Mayor

Windthorst
P.O. Box 98
202 Angus St.
Windthorst, SK S0G 5G0
306-224-2033 Fax: 306-224-4610
village.windthorst@sasktel.net
www.windthorstvillage.ca
Municipal Type: Village
Incorporated: Aug. 21, 1907; *Area:* 1.43 sq km
Population in 2006: 194
Provincial Electoral District(s): Moosomin
Federal Electoral District(s): Souris-Moose Mountain
Next Election: Oct. 2009 (3 year terms)
Denise Swallow, Administrator
Tim Dew, Mayor

Wiseton
P.O. Box 160
Wiseton, SK S0L 3M0
306-357-2022 Fax: 306-357-2027
villageofwiseton@sasktel.net
Municipal Type: Village
Incorporated: Sept. 23, 1913; *Area:* 0.77 sq km
Population in 2006: 96
Provincial Electoral District(s): Rosetown-Elrose
Federal Electoral District(s): Cypress Hills-Grasslands
Next Election: Oct. 2009 (3 year terms)
Cheryl Joel, Administrator
James R. McDonald, Mayor

Wolseley
P.O. Box 310
Wolseley, SK S0G 5H0
306-698-2477 Fax: 306-698-2953
townofwolseley@sasktel.net
www.wolseley.ca
Municipal Type: Town
Incorporated: Oct. 20, 1898; *Area:* 5.93 sq km

Population in 2006: 782
Provincial Electoral District(s): Moosomin
Federal Electoral District(s): Regina-Qu'Appelle
Next Election: Oct. 2009 (3 year terms)
Denton Keating, Mayor
Teri Scaife, Administrator

Wood Mountain
P.O. Box 89
Wood Mountain, SK S0H 4L0
306-266-4810 Fax: 306-266-2020
wmtvillage@sasktel.net
www.woodmountain.ca
Municipal Type: Village
Incorporated: March 4, 1930; *Area:* 0.61 sq km
Population in 2006: 20
Provincial Electoral District(s): Wood River
Federal Electoral District(s): Cypress Hills-Grasslands
Next Election: Oct. 2009 (3 year terms)
Richard Aupperle, Clerk
Michael Klein, Mayor

Wynyard
P.O. Box 220
435 Bosworth St.
Wynyard, SK S0A 4T0
306-554-2123 Fax: 306-554-3224
town.office.wynyard@sasktel.net
www.town.wynyard.sk.ca
Municipal Type: Town
Incorporated: Oct. 9, 1908; *Area:* 5.29 sq km
Population in 2006: 1,744
Provincial Electoral District(s): Arm River-Watrous
Federal Electoral District(s): Regina-Qu'Appelle
Next Election: Oct. 2009 (3 year terms)
Note: Proclaimed as a town on Nov. 1, 1911.

Yarbo
P.O. Box 96
Yarbo, SK S0A 4V0
306-745-3532
Municipal Type: Village
Incorporated: July 1, 1964; *Area:* 0.83 sq km
Population in 2006: 72
Provincial Electoral District(s): Melville-Saltcoats
Federal Electoral District(s): Yorkton-Melville
Next Election: Oct. 2009 (3 year terms)
Joan Kerr, Clerk
Robert Prazma, Mayor

Yellow Creek
P.O. Box 219
Yellow Creek, SK S0K 4X0
306-279-2191
Municipal Type: Village
Incorporated: May 13, 1943; *Area:* 0.64 sq km
Population in 2006: 45
Provincial Electoral District(s): Batoche
Federal Electoral District(s): Saskatoon-Humboldt
Next Election: Oct. 2009 (3 year terms)
Betty Ann Fossen, Clerk
Ken Pacholko, Mayor

Yellow Grass
P.O. Box 270
102 Coteau Ave. West
Yellow Grass, SK S0G 5J0
306-465-2400 Fax: 306-465-2802
yellowgrass@signaldirect.ca
Municipal Type: Town
Incorporated: July 22, 1903; *Area:* 2.68 sq km
Population in 2006: 371
Provincial Electoral District(s): Weyburn-Big Muddy
Federal Electoral District(s): Souris-Moose Mountain
Next Election: Oct. 2009 (3 year terms)
Note: Proclaimed as a town on Feb. 15, 1906.
Trudy Richards, Administrator
William Wilke, Mayor

Young
P.O. Box 359
Young, SK S0K 4Y0
306-259-2242 Fax: 306-259-2247
villageofyoung2@sasktel.net
Municipal Type: Village
Incorporated: June 7, 1910; *Area:* 2.51 sq km
Population in 2006: 263
Provincial Electoral District(s): Arm River-Watrous
Federal Electoral District(s): Blackstrap
Next Election: Oct. 2009 (3 year terms)
Belinda Rowan, Administrator
Robert Speiser, Mayor

Zealandia
P.O. Box 52
Zealandia, SK S0L 3N0
306-882-3825 Fax: 306-882-4178
townofzealandia@yahoo.com
Municipal Type: Town
Incorporated: May 22, 1909; *Area:* 1.38 sq km
Population in 2006: 90
Provincial Electoral District(s): Rosetown-Elrose
Federal Electoral District(s): Saskatoon-Rosetown-Biggar
Next Election: Oct. 2009 (3 year terms)
Note: Proclaimed as a town on Nov. 1, 1911.
Lynn Farquharson, Clerk
Darren Haugen, Mayor

Zelma
Zelma GMB #14
Allan, SK S0K 0C0
306-257-3927 Fax: 306-257-4125
Municipal Type: Village
Incorporated: Aug. 10, 1910; *Area:* 0.72 sq km
Population in 2006: 30
Provincial Electoral District(s): Humboldt
Federal Electoral District(s): Blackstrap
Next Election: Oct. 2009 (3 year terms)
Maxine A. Fischer, Clerk
R. Glen Crockett, Mayor

Zenon Park
P.O. Box 278
Zenon Park, SK S0E 1W0
306-767-2233 Fax: 306-767-2226
vofzenon@sasktel.net
www.newsaskcfdc.ca/zenonpark.htm
Municipal Type: Village
Incorporated: July 28, 1941; *Area:* 0.56 sq km
Population in 2006: 192
Provincial Electoral District(s): Carrot River Valley
Federal Electoral District(s): Prince Albert
Next Election: Oct. 2009 (3 year terms)
Connie Chabot, Clerk
Amy Shipley, Mayor

Rural Municipality

Aberdeen No. 373
P.O. Box 40
Aberdeen, SK S0K 0A0
306-253-4312 Fax: 306-253-4445
rm373@sasktel.net
saskbiz.ca/communityprofiles/CommunityProfile.Asp?CommunityID=748
Municipal Type: Rural Municipality
Incorporated: Dec. 13, 1909; *Area:* 673.43 sq km
Population in 2006: 765
Next Election: Oct 2010; staggered 2 yr term
Real Hamoline, Reeve
Gary Dziadyk, Administrator

Abernethy No. 186
P.O. Box 249
Abernethy, SK S0A 0A0
306-333-2044 Fax: 306-333-2285
rm186@sasktel.net
www.townofbalcarres.ca/rm186/information.htm
Municipal Type: Rural Municipality
Incorporated: Dec. 11, 1911; *Area:* 779.42 sq km
Population in 2006: 375
Next Election: Oct 2010; staggered 2 yr term
Karissa Lingelbach, Administrator
George Noble, Reeve

Antelope Park No. 322
P.O. Box 70
Marengo, SK S0L 2K0
306-968-2922 Fax: 306-968-2278
rm292.rm322@sasktel.net
Municipal Type: Rural Municipality
Incorporated: Dec. 11, 1911; *Area:* 612.66 sq km
Population in 2006: 151
Next Election: Oct 2010; staggered 2 yr term
Shelley Mohr, Administrator
Roger Hawkins, Reeve

Antler No. 61
P.O. Box 70
Redvers, SK S0C 2H0
306-452-3263 Fax: 306-452-3518
rm61@sasktel.net
www.creda.sk.ca/antler
Municipal Type: Rural Municipality
Incorporated: Dec. 13, 1909; *Area:* 832.23 sq km
Population in 2006: 506
Next Election: Oct 2010; staggered 2 yr term
David Hutton, Reeve
Jane Laich, Administrator

Arborfield No. 456
P.O. Box 280
Arborfield, SK S0E 0A0
306-769-8533 Fax: 306-769-8301
arborfieldrm456@sasktel.net
Municipal Type: Rural Municipality
Incorporated: Jan. 1, 1913; *Area:* 1,416.01 sq km
Population in 2006: 429
Next Election: Oct 2010; staggered 2 yr term
Alec J. Black, Reeve
Allan Frisky, Administrator

Argyle No. 1
P.O. Box 120
Gainsborough, SK S0C 0Z0
306-685-2010 Fax: 306-685-2161
rm.1@sasktel.net
www.creda.sk.ca/argyle
Municipal Type: Rural Municipality
Incorporated: Dec. 19, 1912; *Area:* 579.99 sq km
Population in 2006: 267
Next Election: Oct 2010; staggered 2 yr term
Valerie A. Olney, Administrator
Robert Meredith, Reeve

Arlington No. 79
P.O. Box 1115
264 Centre St.
Shaunavon, SK S0N 2M0
306-297-2108 Fax: 306-297-2144
rm79@sasktel.net
saskbiz.ca/communityprofiles/CommunityProfile.Asp?CommunityID=754
Municipal Type: Rural Municipality
Incorporated: Jan. 1, 1913; *Area:* 846.79 sq km
Population in 2006: 413
Next Election: Oct 2010; staggered 2 yr term
Donald L. Lundberg, Reeve
Richard E. Goulet, Administrator

Arm River No. 252
P.O. Box 250
Davidson, SK S0G 1A0
306-567-3103 Fax: 306-567-3266
rm253@sasktel.net
Municipal Type: Rural Municipality
Incorporated: Dec. 13, 1909; *Area:* 725.26 sq km
Population in 2006: 240
Next Election: Oct 2010; staggered 2 yr term
Norman Sagen, Administrator
Lorne E. Willner, Reeve

Auvergne No. 76
P.O. Box 60
Ponteix, SK S0N 1Z0
306-625-3210 Fax: 306-625-3681
rm76@sasktel.net
Municipal Type: Rural Municipality
Incorporated: Jan. 1, 1913; *Area:* 853.40 sq km
Population in 2006: 329
Next Election: Oct 2010; staggered 2 yr term
Roxanne Empey, Administrator
Allan R. Oliver, Reeve

Baildon No. 131
P.O. Box 1902
Moose Jaw, SK S6H 7N6
306-693-2166 Fax: 306-693-2166
rm131@sasktel.net
saskbiz.ca/communityprofiles/CommunityProfile.Asp?CommunityID=757
Municipal Type: Rural Municipality
Incorporated: Dec. 9, 1912; *Area:* 846.21 sq km
Population in 2006: 548
Next Election: Oct 2010; staggered 2 yr term
Terry R. Anthony, Reeve
Glenda Smith, Administrator

Barrier Valley No. 397
P.O. Box 246
Archerwill, SK S0E 0B0
306-323-2101 Fax: 306-323-2106
rm397@sasktel.net
saskbiz.ca/communityprofiles/CommunityProfile.Asp?CommunityID=758
Municipal Type: Rural Municipality
Incorporated: Oct. 29, 1917; *Area:* 819.99 sq km
Population in 2006: 576
Next Election: Oct 2010; staggered 2 yr term
Quentin Ralph Hanson, Reeve
Fern Lucas, Administrator

Battle River No. 438
P.O. Box 159
Battleford, SK S0M 0E0
306-937-2235 Fax: 306-937-2235
rm438@sasktel.net
saskbiz.ca/communityprofiles/CommunityProfile.Asp?CommunityID=759
Municipal Type: Rural Municipality
Incorporated: Dec. 12, 1910; *Area:* 1,061.40 sq km
Population in 2006: 1,053
Next Election: Oct 2010; staggered 2 yr term
Joseph Beckman, Reeve
Betty Johnson, Administrator

Bayne No. 371
P.O. Box 130
Bruno, SK S0K 0S0
306-369-2511 Fax: 306-369-2528
rm371@sasktel.net
Municipal Type: Rural Municipality
Incorporated: Dec. 12, 1910; *Area:* 802.93 sq km
Population in 2006: 505
Next Election: Oct 2010; staggered 2 yr term
Melvin Strasser, Reeve
Lonnie Sowa, Administrator

Beaver River No. 622
P.O. Box 129
159 Main St.
Pierceland, SK S0M 2K0

306-839-2060 Fax: 306-839-2178
rm622@sasktel.net
Municipal Type: Rural Municipality
Incorporated: Jan. 1, 1978; *Area:* 2,370.25 sq km
Population in 2006: 1,108
Next Election: Oct 2010; staggered 2 yr term
Murray Rausch, Reeve
Rita Rogers, Administrator

Bengough No. 40
P.O. Box 429
Bengough, SK S0C 0K0
306-268-2055 Fax: 306-268-2054
rm40@sasktel.net
www.rm40.com
Municipal Type: Rural Municipality
Incorporated: Jan. 1, 1913; *Area:* 1,036.91 sq km
Population in 2006: 337
Next Election: Oct 2010; staggered 2 yr term
Lara Scott, Administrator
Steven King, Reeve
306-268-4230

Benson No. 35
P.O. Box 69
Benson, SK S0C 0L0
306-634-9410 Fax: 306-634-8804
rm35@sasktel.net
saskbiz.ca/communityprofiles/CommunityProfile.Asp?CommunityID=762
Municipal Type: Rural Municipality
Incorporated: Dec. 13, 1909; *Area:* 836.39 sq km
Population in 2006: 434
Next Election: Oct 2010; staggered 2 yr term
David Hoffort, Reeve
Laureen Keating, Administrator

Big Arm No. 251
P.O. Box 10
Stalwart, SK S0G 4R0
306-963-2402 Fax: 306-963-2405
rm251@sasktel.net
Municipal Type: Rural Municipality
Incorporated: Dec. 11, 1911; *Area:* 699.47 sq km
Population in 2006: 237
Next Election: Oct 2010; staggered 2 yr term
Yvonne Carrick, Administrator
Paul Remlinger, Reeve

Big Quill No. 308
P.O. Box 898
Wynyard, SK S0A 4T0
306-554-2533 Fax: 306-554-3935
rm308@sasktel.net
Municipal Type: Rural Municipality
Incorporated: Dec. 13, 1909; *Area:* 739.86 sq km
Population in 2006: 635
Next Election: Oct 2010; staggered 2 yr term
Bob Gudnason, Reeve
Gail Wolfe, Administrator

Big River No. 555
Big River Community Centre
P.O. Box 219
606 First St. North
Big River, SK S0J 0E0
306-469-2323 Fax: 306-469-2428
rm555@sasktel.net
www.bigriver.ca
Municipal Type: Rural Municipality
Incorporated: Oct. 1, 1977; *Area:* 2,488.22 sq km
Population in 2006: 851
Next Election: Oct 2010; staggered 2 yr term
Doug Panter, Reeve
Donna Tymiak, Administrator

Big Stick No. 141
P.O. Box 9
Golden Prairie, SK S0N 0Y0
306-662-2883 Fax: 306-662-3954
rm141@sasktel.net
Municipal Type: Rural Municipality
Incorporated: Dec. 11, 1911; *Area:* 821.40 sq km
Population in 2006: 182
Next Election: Oct 2010; staggered 2 yr term
Quinton Jacksteit, Administrator
Edward Feil, Reeve

Biggar No. 347
P.O. Box 280
Biggar, SK S0K 0M0
306-948-2422 Fax: 306-948-2250
rm347@sasktel.net
Municipal Type: Rural Municipality
Incorporated: Dec. 11, 1911; *Area:* 1,597.87 sq km
Population in 2006: 867
Next Election: Oct 2010; staggered 2 yr term
Louise Singer, Reeve
Wendy Davis, Administrator

Birch Hills No. 460
P.O. Box 369
Birch Hills, SK S0J 0G0
306-749-2233 Fax: 306-749-2220
rm460@sasktel.net
Municipal Type: Rural Municipality
Incorporated: Dec. 11, 1911; *Area:* 554.52 sq km
Population in 2006: 701
Next Election: Oct 2010; staggered 2 yr term
Earl Mickelson, Reeve
Sandra Barber, Administrator

Bjorkdale No. 426
P.O. Box 10
Crooked River, SK S0E 0R0
306-873-2470 Fax: 306-873-2365
rm.426.bjork@xplornet.com
saskbiz.ca/communityprofiles/CommunityProfile.Asp?CommunityID=769
Municipal Type: Rural Municipality
Incorporated: Jan. 1, 1913; *Area:* 1,458.79 sq km
Population in 2006: 997
Next Election: Oct 2010; staggered 2 yr term
Wayne Dmytriw, Reeve
Lisa Hamelin, Administrator

Blaine Lake No. 434
P.O. Box 38
Blaine Lake, SK S0J 0J0
306-497-2282 Fax: 306-497-2511
rm434@sasktel.net
saskbiz.ca/communityprofiles/CommunityProfile.Asp?CommunityID=770
Municipal Type: Rural Municipality
Incorporated: Dec. 9, 1912; *Area:* 799.89 sq km
Population in 2006: 302
Next Election: Oct 2010; staggered 2 yr term
James V. Burak, Administrator
John Reban, Reeve

Blucher No. 343
P.O. Box 100
Bradwell, SK S0K 0P0
306-257-3344 Fax: 306-257-3303
rm343@sasktel.net
www.rm343.com
Municipal Type: Rural Municipality
Incorporated: Dec. 13, 1909; *Area:* 789.28 sq km
Population in 2006: 1,593
Next Election: Oct 2010; staggered 2 yr term
Daniel Greschuk, Reeve
R. Doran Scott, Administrator

Bone Creek No. 108
P.O. Box 459
Shaunavon, SK S0N 2M0
306-297-2570 Fax: 306-297-6270
rmbc@sasktel.net
Municipal Type: Rural Municipality
Incorporated: Dec. 11, 1911; *Area:* 847.16 sq km
Population in 2006: 321
Next Election: Oct 2010; staggered 2 yr term
Rhonda Bellefeuille, Administrator
Ben Lewans, Reeve

Bratt's Lake No. 129
P.O. Box 130
Wilcox, SK S0G 5E0
306-732-2030 Fax: 306-732-4495
rm129@sasktel.net
Municipal Type: Rural Municipality
Incorporated: Jan. 1, 1913; *Area:* 844.94 sq km
Population in 2006: 362
Next Election: Oct 2010; staggered 2 yr term
Kevin S. Ritchie, Administrator
J. Barry Hamdorf, Reeve

Britannia No. 502
P.O. Box 661
4824 - 47th St.
Lloydminster, SK S9V 0Y7
306-825-2610 Fax: 306-825-8894
rm502@sasktel.net
www.rmbritannia.com
Municipal Type: Rural Municipality
Incorporated: Dec. 13, 1909; *Area:* 950.87 sq km
Population in 2006: 1,501
Next Election: Oct 2010; staggered 2 yr term
Arvid Eskelson, Reeve
Patti Volk, Clerk
patti.rm502@sasktel.net

Brock No. 64
P.O. Box 247
Kisbey, SK S0C 1L0
306-462-2010 Fax: 306-462-2016
rm64@sasktel.net
www.creda.sk.ca/brock
Municipal Type: Rural Municipality
Incorporated: Dec. 12, 1910; *Area:* 827.53 sq km
Population in 2006: 279
Next Election: Oct 2010; staggered 2 yr term
Michael Rattray, Administrator
Allan Brigden, Reeve

Brokenshell No. 68
23 - 6th St. NE
Weyburn, SK S4H 1A7
306-842-2314 Fax: 306-842-1002
rm.67@sasktel.net
saskbiz.ca/communityprofiles/CommunityProfile.Asp?CommunityID=776
Municipal Type: Rural Municipality
Incorporated: Dec. 13, 1909; *Area:* 850.01 sq km
Population in 2006: 324
Next Election: Oct 2010; staggered 2 yr term
Kim McIvor, Administrator
Don Watson, Reeve

Browning No. 34
P.O. Box 40
Lampman, SK S0C 1N0
306-487-2444 Fax: 306-487-2496
browning.lampman@sasktel.net
www.creda.sk.ca/browning
Municipal Type: Rural Municipality
Incorporated: Dec. 11, 1911; *Area:* 823.39 sq km
Population in 2006: 426
Next Election: Oct 2010; staggered 2 yr term
Randy Fleck, Reeve
Greg Wallin, Administrator

Buchanan No. 304
P.O. Box 10
Buchanan, SK S0A 0J0
306-592-2055 Fax: 306-592-4436
rm304@sasktel.net
Municipal Type: Rural Municipality
Incorporated: Jan. 1, 1913; *Area:* 738.80 sq km
Population in 2006: 435
Next Election: Oct 2010; staggered 2 yr term
Gerald Wolkowski, Reeve
Twila Hadubiak, Administrator

Buckland No. 491
99 River St. East
Prince Albert, SK S6V 0A1
306-763-2585 Fax: 306-763-6369
rm491@sasktel.net
Municipal Type: Rural Municipality
Incorporated: Dec. 11, 1911; *Area:* 791.55 sq km
Population in 2006: 3,429
Next Election: Oct 2010; staggered 2 yr term
Wes Stubbs, Reeve
Wendy Gowda, Administrator

Buffalo No. 409
P.O. Box 100
Wilkie, SK S0K 4W0
306-843-2342 Fax: 306-843-2455
rm409@sasktel.net
Municipal Type: Rural Municipality
Incorporated: Dec. 13, 1909; *Area:* 1,222.08 sq km
Population in 2006: 525
Next Election: Oct 2010; staggered 2 yr term
Arthur J. Mann, Reeve
Sherry Huber, Administrator

Calder No. 241
P.O. Box 10
Wroxton, SK S0A 4S0
306-742-4233 Fax: 306-742-4559
calderrm@sasktel.net
Municipal Type: Rural Municipality
Incorporated: Jan. 1, 1913; *Area:* 807.15 sq km
Population in 2006: 423
Next Election: Oct 2010; staggered 2 yr term
Dennis Elaschuk, Reeve
Linda Napady, Administrator

Caledonia No. 99
P.O. Box 328
Milestone, SK S0G 3L0
306-436-2050 Fax: 306-436-2051
milcal@sasktel.net
Municipal Type: Rural Municipality
Incorporated: Dec. 13, 1909; *Area:* 845.68 sq km
Population in 2006: 286
Next Election: Oct 2010; staggered 2 yr term
Ernest P. Audette, Administrator
Richard Linton, Reeve

Cambria No. 6
P.O. Box 210
Torquay, SK S0C 2L0
306-923-2000 Fax: 306-923-2099
rm.cambria@sasktel.net
saskbiz.ca/communityprofiles/CommunityProfile.Asp?CommunityID=783
Municipal Type: Rural Municipality
Incorporated: Dec. 13, 1909; *Area:* 814.14 sq km
Population in 2006: 268
Next Election: Oct 2010; staggered 2 yr term
Graham Bell, Administrator
James Phillips, Reeve

Cana No. 214
P.O. Box 550
Melville, SK S0A 2P0
306-728-5645 Fax: 306-728-3807
rmcana@sasktel.net
www.spreda.sk.ca/community_RM_of_Cana.htm
Municipal Type: Rural Municipality
Incorporated: Dec. 13, 1909; *Area:* 820.81 sq km

Population in 2006: 850
Next Election: Oct 2010; staggered 2 yr term
Robert Almasi, Reeve
Audrey Law, Administrator

Canaan No. 225
P.O. Box 99
Lucky Lake, SK S0L 1Z0
306-858-2234 Fax: 306-858-2234
rm225.vll@sasktel.net
Municipal Type: Rural Municipality
Incorporated: Jan. 1, 1913; *Area:* 549.09 sq km
Population in 2006: 165
Next Election: Oct 2010; staggered 2 yr term
Edna A. Laturnus, Administrator
William Sheppard, Reeve

Canwood No. 494
P.O. Box 10
Canwood, SK S0J 0K0
306-468-2014 Fax: 306-468-2666
rm494@sasktel.net
Municipal Type: Rural Municipality
Incorporated: Jan. 1, 1913; *Area:* 1,945.20 sq km
Population in 2006: 1,535
Next Election: Oct 2010; staggered 2 yr term
Richard Porter, Reeve
Hugh Otterson, Administrator

Carmichael No. 109
P.O. Box 420
Gull Lake, SK S0N 1A0
306-672-3501 Fax: 306-672-3879
rm109@sasktel.net
saskbiz.ca/communityprofiles/CommunityProfile.Asp?CommunityID=787
Municipal Type: Rural Municipality
Incorporated: Dec. 9, 1912; *Area:* 846.40 sq km
Population in 2006: 450
Next Election: Oct 2010; staggered 2 yr term
Howard Wedrick, Reeve
Collette Jones, Administrator

Caron No. 162
P.O. Box 85
Caron, SK S0H 0R0
306-756-2353 Fax: 306-756-2250
rm162@sasktel.net
saskbiz.ca/communityprofiles/CommunityProfile.Asp?CommunityID=788
Municipal Type: Rural Municipality
Incorporated: Dec. 9, 1912; *Area:* 569.87 sq km
Population in 2006: 500
Next Election: Oct 2010; staggered 2 yr term
Gregory McKeown, Reeve
Sandra Sparkes, Administrator

Chaplin No. 164
P.O. Box 60
Chaplin, SK S0H 0V0
306-395-2244 Fax: 306-395-2767
rm164@sasktel.net
saskbiz.ca/communityprofiles/CommunityProfile.Asp?CommunityID=789
Municipal Type: Rural Municipality
Incorporated: Jan. 1, 1913; *Area:* 802.74 sq km
Population in 2006: 138
Next Election: Oct 2010; staggered 2 yr term
Kathy Mealing, Administrator
Michael Michael, Reeve

Chester No. 125
P.O. Box 180
Glenavon, SK S0G 1Y0
306-429-2110 Fax: 306-429-2260
rmchester125@sasktel.net
Municipal Type: Rural Municipality
Incorporated: Dec. 13, 1909; *Area:* 837.08 sq km
Population in 2006: 386
Next Election: Oct 2010; staggered 2 yr term
James R. Hoff, Administrator
Stan Muchowski, Reeve

Chesterfield No. 261
P.O. Box 70
Eatonia, SK S0L 0Y0
306-967-2222 Fax: 306-967-2424
rm261@sasktel.net
saskbiz.ca/communityprofiles/CommunityProfile.Asp?CommunityID=790
Municipal Type: Rural Municipality
Incorporated: Dec. 9, 1912; *Area:* 1,942.72 sq km
Population in 2006: 475
Next Election: Oct 2010; staggered 2 yr term
Dennis Hyland, Reeve
Beverly Dahl, Administrator

Churchbridge No. 211
P.O. Box 211
Churchbridge, SK S0A 0M0
306-896-2522 Fax: 306-896-2743
rmchurchbridge@sasktel.net
Municipal Type: Rural Municipality
Incorporated: Jan. 1, 1913; *Area:* 958.98 sq km

Population in 2006: 679
Next Election: Oct 2010; staggered 2 yr term
Neil Mehrer, Reeve
Brenda A. Goulden, Administrator

Clayton No. 333
P.O. Box 220
Hyas, SK S0A 1K0
306-594-2832 Fax: 306-594-2832
rm_333@xplornet.com
Municipal Type: Rural Municipality
Incorporated: Jan. 1, 1913; *Area:* 1,401.69 sq km
Population in 2006: 753
Next Election: Oct 2010; staggered 2 yr term
Valerie Koroluk, Reeve
Douglas W. Ferder, Administrator

Clinworth No. 230
P.O. Box 120
Sceptre, SK S0N 2H0
306-623-4229 Fax: 306-623-4229
rm230@xplornet.com
Municipal Type: Rural Municipality
Incorporated: Dec. 9, 1912; *Area:* 1,432.75 sq km
Population in 2006: 228
Next Election: Oct 2010; staggered 2 yr term
Linda Boser, Administrator
Ken Dietz, Reeve

Coalfields No. 4
P.O. Box 190
Bienfait, SK S0C 0M0
306-388-2723 Fax: 306-388-2330
rm.04@sasktel.net
Municipal Type: Rural Municipality
Incorporated: Jan. 1, 1913; *Area:* 819.76 sq km
Population in 2006: 396
Next Election: Oct 2010; staggered 2 yr term
Barry Katschke, Administrator
Stanley Lainton, Reeve

Colonsay No. 342
P.O. Box 130
Colonsay, SK S0K 0Z0
306-255-2233 Fax: 306-255-2291
rm342@sasktel.net
www.townofcolonsay.com/RM.htm
Municipal Type: Rural Municipality
Incorporated: Dec. 13, 1909; *Area:* 549.99 sq km
Population in 2006: 275
Next Election: Oct 2010; staggered 2 yr term
Deborah Prosper, Administrator
Pius Steckler, Reeve

Connaught No. 457
P.O. Box 25
Tisdale, SK S0E 1T0
306-873-2657 Fax: 306-873-4442
rm457@sasktel.net
saskbiz.ca/communityprofiles/CommunityProfile.Asp?CommunityID=797
Municipal Type: Rural Municipality
Incorporated: Dec. 11, 1911; *Area:* 853.11 sq km
Population in 2006: 656
Next Election: Oct 2010; staggered 2 yr term
Francis Chabot, Reeve
Keith Hummel, Administrator

Corman Park No. 344
111 Pinehouse Dr.
Saskatoon, SK S7K 5W1
306-242-9303 Fax: 306-242-6965
rm344@rmcormanpark.ca
www.rmcormanpark.ca
Municipal Type: Rural Municipality
Incorporated: Jan. 1, 1970; *Area:* 1,978.14 sq km
Population in 2006: 8,349
Next Election: Oct 2010; staggered 2 yr term
Ed Hobday, Reeve
Tammy Knuttila, Administrator
tammy.knuttila@rmcormanpark.ca

Cote No. 271
P.O. Box 669
Kamsack, SK S0A 1S0
306-542-2121 Fax: 306-542-2428
rm271@sasktel.net
Municipal Type: Rural Municipality
Incorporated: Dec. 12, 1910; *Area:* 880.23 sq km
Population in 2006: 551
Next Election: Oct 2010; staggered 2 yr term
Herb Harper, Reeve
Barry Hvidston, Administrator

Coteau No. 255
P.O. Box 30
Birsay, SK S0L 0G0
306-573-2047 Fax: 306-573-2111
rm255@sasktel.net
Municipal Type: Rural Municipality
Incorporated: Dec. 12, 1910; *Area:* 899.27 sq km
Population in 2006: 468
Next Election: Oct 2010; staggered 2 yr term
Clayton Ylioja, Reeve
Linda Van Den Bosch, Administrator

Coulee No. 136
1680 Chaplin St. East
Swift Current, SK S9H 1K8
306-773-5420 Fax: 306-773-1859
rm136@sasktel.net
Municipal Type: Rural Municipality
Incorporated: Dec. 12, 1910; *Area:* 842.95 sq km
Population in 2006: 509
Next Election: Oct 2010; staggered 2 yr term
Greg Targerson, Reeve
Ken Hollinger, Administrator

Craik No. 222
P.O. Box 420
Craik, SK S0G 0V0
306-734-2242 Fax: 306-734-2257
rm222@sasktel.net
www.craik.ca
Municipal Type: Rural Municipality
Incorporated: Dec. 9, 1912; *Area:* 883.02 sq km
Population in 2006: 288
Next Election: Oct 2010; staggered 2 yr term
Leslee Winchester, Administrator
Hilton Spencer, Reeve

Cupar No. 218
P.O. Box 400
Cupar, SK S0G 0Y0
306-723-4726 Fax: 306-723-4726
rm218@sasktel.net
Municipal Type: Rural Municipality
Incorporated: Dec. 13, 1909; *Area:* 919.01 sq km
Population in 2006: 502
Next Election: Oct 2010; staggered 2 yr term
Raymond Orb, Reeve
Loretta Young, Administrator

Cut Knife No. 439
P.O. Box 70
Cut Knife, SK S0M 0N0
306-398-2353 Fax: 306-398-2839
rm439@sasktel.net
Municipal Type: Rural Municipality
Incorporated: Dec. 13, 1909; *Area:* 651.43 sq km
Population in 2006: 390
Next Election: Oct 2010; staggered 2 yr term
Donald McCallum, Administrator
Milton Bingham, Reeve

Cymri No. 36
P.O. Box 238
Midale, SK S0C 1S0
306-458-2244 Fax: 306-458-2699
rmcymri@sasktel.net
saskbiz.ca/communityprofiles/CommunityProfile.Asp?CommunityID=805
Municipal Type: Rural Municipality
Incorporated: Dec. 13, 1909; *Area:* 832.36 sq km
Population in 2006: 455
Next Election: Oct 2010; staggered 2 yr term
Joe Vilcu, Reeve
Pamela Scott, Administrator

Deer Forks No. 232
P.O. Box 250
Burstall, SK S0N 0H0
306-679-2000 Fax: 306-679-2275
rm232@sasktel.net
Municipal Type: Rural Municipality
Incorporated: Jan. 1, 1913; *Area:* 735.49 sq km
Population in 2006: 213
Next Election: Oct 2010; staggered 2 yr term
Tim C. Lozinsky, Administrator
Doug Smith, Reeve

Douglas No. 436
P.O. Box 964
Speers, SK S0M 2V0
306-246-2171 Fax: 306-246-2173
rm436@littleloon.ca
saskbiz.ca/communityprofiles/CommunityProfile.Asp?CommunityID=807
Municipal Type: Rural Municipality
Incorporated: Dec. 13, 1909; *Area:* 820.37 sq km
Population in 2006: 383
Next Election: Oct 2010; staggered 2 yr term
Ronald A. Tanchak, Administrator
Nick W. Partyka, Reeve

Duck Lake No. 463
P.O. Box 250
Duck Lake, SK S0K 1J0
306-467-2011 Fax: 306-476-4423
rm463@sasktel.net
Municipal Type: Rural Municipality
Incorporated: Jan. 1, 1913; *Area:* 1,046.57 sq km
Population in 2006: 776
Next Election: Oct 2010; staggered 2 yr term
Lois McCormick, Administrator
Raymond Gauthier, Reeve

Dufferin No. 190
P.O. Box 67
Bethune, SK S0G 0H0

306-638-3112 Fax: 306-638-3102
rm190@sasktel.net
Municipal Type: Rural Municipality
Incorporated: Dec. 9, 1912; *Area:* 961.44 sq km
Population in 2006: 540
Next Election: Oct 2010; staggered 2 yr term
Donald McDonald, Reeve
Rick Hicks, Administrator

Dundurn No. 314
P.O. Box 159
Dundurn, SK S0K 1K0
306-492-2132 Fax: 306-492-4758
rm314@sasktel.net
Municipal Type: Rural Municipality
Incorporated: Dec. 13, 1909; *Area:* 800.91 sq km
Population in 2006: 632
Next Election: Oct 2010; staggered 2 yr term
R. Fred Wilson, Reeve
Violet P. Barna, Administrator

Eagle Creek No. 376
P.O. Box 278
Asquith, SK S0K 0J0
306-237-4424 Fax: 306-237-4294
rm376@sasktel.net
Municipal Type: Rural Municipality
Incorporated: Dec. 13, 1909; *Area:* 833.08 sq km
Population in 2006: 552
Next Election: Oct 2010; staggered 2 yr term
Russel Pashovitz, Reeve
Lloyd Cross, Administrator

Edenwold No. 158
P.O. Box 10
Balgonie, SK S0G 0E0
306-771-2522 Fax: 306-771-2631
rm158@sasktel.net
Municipal Type: Rural Municipality
Incorporated: Dec. 9, 1912; *Area:* 882.67 sq km
Population in 2006: 3,611
Next Election: Oct 2010; staggered 2 yr term
Mitchell Huber, Huber
Gail Sloan, Administrator

Elcapo No. 154
P.O. Box 668
Broadview, SK S0G 0K0
306-696-2474 Fax: 306-696-3573
rm154@sasktel.net
Municipal Type: Rural Municipality
Incorporated: Dec. 12, 1910; *Area:* 846.54 sq km
Population in 2006: 489
Next Election: Oct 2010; staggered 2 yr term
Larry Parrott, Reeve
Mervin J. Schmidt, Administrator

Eldon No. 471
P.O. Box 130
212 Main St.
Maidstone, SK S0M 1M0
306-893-2391 Fax: 306-893-4644
rm471@sasktel.net
www.rmeldon.ca
Municipal Type: Rural Municipality
Incorporated: Dec. 13, 1909; *Area:* 1,007.59 sq km
Population in 2006: 750
Next Election: Oct 2010; staggered 2 yr term
Garry Taylor, Reeve
Ken E. Reiter, Administrator

Elfros No. 307
P.O. Box 40
Elfros, SK S0A 0V0
306-328-2011 Fax: 306-328-4490
rm307@sasktel.net
Municipal Type: Rural Municipality
Incorporated: Dec. 13, 1909; *Area:* 696.71 sq km
Population in 2006: 481
Next Election: Oct 2010; staggered 2 yr term
Henry Bzdel, Reeve
Glenn Thompson, Administrator

Elmsthorpe No. 100
P.O. Box 240
Avonlea, SK S0H 0C0
306-868-2221 Fax: 306-868-2221
rm.100@sasktel.net
Municipal Type: Rural Municipality
Incorporated: Dec. 12, 1910; *Area:* 843.12 sq km
Population in 2006: 258
Next Election: Oct 2010; staggered 2 yr term
Tim Forer, Administrator
Ken Miller, Reeve

Emerald No. 277
P.O. Box 160
Wishart, SK S0A 4R0
306-576-2002 Fax: 306-576-2132
rm277@sasktel.net
www.rm277emerald.ca
Municipal Type: Rural Municipality
Incorporated: Dec. 12, 1910; *Area:* 854.44 sq km
Population in 2006: 549
Next Election: Oct 2010; staggered 2 yr term
Gerald Faye, Reeve
Sharolyn Prisiak, Administrator

Enfield No. 194
P.O. Box 70
Central Butte, SK S0H 0T0
306-796-2025 Fax: 306-796-2025
rm194@sasktel.net
Municipal Type: Rural Municipality
Incorporated: Dec. 13, 1909; *Area:* 1,014.10 sq km
Population in 2006: 301
Next Election: Oct 2010; staggered 2 yr term
Joe Van Leuken, Administrator
Ron Kurz, Reeve

Enniskillen No. 3
P.O. Box 179
Oxbow, SK S0C 2B0
306-483-2277 Fax: 306-483-2598
rm3@sasktel.net
saskbiz.ca/communityprofiles/CommunityProfile.Asp?CommunityID=819
Municipal Type: Rural Municipality
Incorporated: Dec. 13, 1909; *Area:* 834.78 sq km
Population in 2006: 430
Next Election: Oct 2010; staggered 2 yr term
Brian Northeast, Reeve
Myrna-Jean Babbings, Administrator

Enterprise No. 142
P.O. Box 150
Richmound, SK S0N 2E0
306-669-2000 Fax: 306-669-2052
rm142@sasktel.net
Municipal Type: Rural Municipality
Incorporated: April 18, 1913; *Area:* 988.80 sq km
Population in 2006: 160
Next Election: Oct 2010; staggered 2 yr term
Brandi Trembath, Administrator
Wayne Freitag, Reeve

Estevan No. 5
721 Henry St.
Estevan, SK S4A 2B7
306-634-2222 Fax: 306-634-2223
rm5@sasktel.net
Municipal Type: Rural Municipality
Incorporated: Dec. 12, 1910; *Area:* 774.67 sq km
Population in 2006: 1,051
Next Election: Oct 2010; staggered 2 yr term
Marie Dukart, Reeve
Greg Hoffort, Administrator

Excel No. 71
P.O. Box 100
Viceroy, SK S0H 4H0
306-268-4555 Fax: 306-268-4547
rm71@sasktel.net
Municipal Type: Rural Municipality
Incorporated: Jan. 1, 1913; *Area:* 1,122.02 sq km
Population in 2006: 466
Next Election: Oct 2010; staggered 2 yr term
Glenn Roszell, Reeve
Mervin A. Guillemin, Administrator

Excelsior No. 166
P.O. Box 180
Rush Lake, SK S0H 3S0
306-784-3121 Fax: 306-784-3479
rm166@sasktel.net
Municipal Type: Rural Municipality
Incorporated: Dec. 13, 1909; *Area:* 1,198.35 sq km
Population in 2006: 825
Next Election: Oct 2010; staggered 2 yr term
Harold Martens, Reeve
Christina Patoine, Administrator

Eye Hill No. 382
P.O. Box 69
Macklin, SK S0L 2C0
306-753-2075 Fax: 306-753-2075
rm382@sasktel.net
saskbiz.ca/communityprofiles/CommunityProfile.Asp?CommunityID=823
Municipal Type: Rural Municipality
Incorporated: Dec. 12, 1910; *Area:* 797.96 sq km
Population in 2006: 650
Next Election: Oct 2010; staggered 2 yr term
Robert Brost, Reeve
Calvin Giggs, Administrator

Eyebrow No. 193
P.O. Box 99
Eyebrow, SK S0H 1L0
306-759-2101 Fax: 306-759-2026
rm193@sasktel.net
saskbiz.ca/communityprofiles/CommunityProfile.Asp?CommunityID=746
Municipal Type: Rural Municipality
Incorporated: Dec. 13, 1909; *Area:* 835.04 sq km
Population in 2006: 245
Next Election: Oct 2010; staggered 2 yr term
Herbert A. White, Administrator
Raymond L. Carrick, Reeve

Fertile Belt No. 183
P.O. Box 190
100 Ohlen St.
Stockholm, SK S0A 3Y0
306-793-2061 Fax: 306-793-2063
rm183@sasktel.net
www.yellowheadreda.com/rmfertilebelt.htm
Municipal Type: Rural Municipality
Incorporated: January 1, 1913; *Area:* 1,006.68 sq km
Population in 2006: 771
Next Election: Oct 2010; staggered 2 yr term
Arlynn Kurtz, Reeve
Lorie Jackson, Administrator

Fertile Valley No. 285
P.O. Box 70
Conquest, SK S0L 0L0
306-856-2037 Fax: 306-856-2211
fv285@sasktel.net
Municipal Type: Rural Municipality
Incorporated: Dec. 13, 1909; *Area:* 1,016.37 sq km
Population in 2006: 609
Next Election: Oct 2010; staggered 2 yr term
Alvin Barrington, Reeve
Yvonne Arntsen, Administrator

Fillmore No. 96
P.O. Box 130
Fillmore, SK S0G 1N0
306-722-3251 Fax: 306-722-3775
rm96@sasktel.net
Municipal Type: Rural Municipality
Incorporated: Dec. 13, 1909; *Area:* 828.33 sq km
Population in 2006: 256
Next Election: Oct 2010; staggered 2 yr term
Vernna Wiggins, Administrator
Robert Clay, Reeve

Fish Creek No. 402
P.O. Box 160
Wakaw, SK S0K 4P0
306-233-4412 Fax: 306-233-5234
rm402@sasktel.net
www.ctreda.ca/webpage/mempages/rmfish/rmfish.htm
Municipal Type: Rural Municipality
Incorporated: Jan. 1, 1913; *Area:* 597.90 sq km
Population in 2006: 307
Next Election: Oct 2010; staggered 2 yr term
Richard Kindrachuk, Administrator
Dennis Sawitsky, Reeve

Flett's Springs No. 429
P.O. Box 160
Melfort, SK S0E 1A0
306-752-3606 Fax: 306-752-3882
rm429@sasktel.net
Municipal Type: Rural Municipality
Incorporated: Dec. 13, 1909; *Area:* 844.61 sq km
Population in 2006: 736
Next Election: Oct 2010; staggered 2 yr term
Blaine Forsyth, Reeve
Shelley L. Holmes, Administrator

Foam Lake No. 276
P.O. Box 490
Foam Lake, SK S0A 1A0
306-272-3334 Fax: 306-272-4722
rm276@sasktel.net
Municipal Type: Rural Municipality
Incorporated: Dec. 12, 1910; *Area:* 1,345.91 sq km
Population in 2006: 598
Next Election: Oct 2010; staggered 2 yr term
Chris Gislason, Reeve
Ron Kostiuk, Administrator

Fox Valley No. 171
P.O. Box 190
Fox Valley, SK S0N 0V0
306-666-2055 Fax: 306-666-2074
rm.171@sasktel.net
Municipal Type: Rural Municipality
Incorporated: Oct. 29, 1913; *Area:* 1,253.79 sq km
Population in 2006: 368
Next Election: Oct 2010; staggered 2 yr term
Daniel Steven Buye, Administrator
Anthony Hoffart, Reeve

Francis No. 127
P.O. Box 36
Francis, SK S0G 1V0
306-245-3256 Fax: 306-245-3203
rm127@sasktel.net
Municipal Type: Rural Municipality
Incorporated: Dec. 13, 1909; *Area:* 1,106.80 sq km
Population in 2006: 672
Next Election: Oct 2010; staggered 2 yr term
George R. Leier, Reeve
Gwen C. Johnston, Administrator

Frenchman Butte No. 501
P.O. Box 180
Paradise Hill, SK S0M 2G0
306-344-2034 Fax: 306-344-4434
rm501@sasktel.net
www.rmfrenchmanbutte.ca

Municipal Type: Rural Municipality
Incorporated: Jan. 1, 1954; *Area:* 1,928.32 sq km
Population in 2006: 1,223
Next Election: Oct 2010; staggered 2 yr term
George Larre, Reeve
Isabelle Jasper, Administrator

Frontier No. 19
P.O. Box 30
Frontier, SK S0N 0W0
306-296-2030 Fax: 306-296-2175
rm19@sasktel.net
saskbiz.ca/communityprofiles/Select_a_Community.asp?Region_ID=5
Municipal Type: Rural Municipality
Incorporated: Jan. 1, 1913; *Area:* 1,675.02 sq km
Population in 2006: 323
Next Election: Oct 2010; staggered 2 yr term
Barb Webber, Administrator
Brian Onerheim, Reeve

Garden River No. 490
P.O. Box 70
Meath Park, SK S0J 1T0
306-929-2020 Fax: 306-929-2281
rm490@sasktel.net
Municipal Type: Rural Municipality
Incorporated: Jan. 1, 1913; *Area:* 662.90 sq km
Population in 2006: 633
Next Election: Oct 2010; staggered 2 yr term
Bernard Zurkowski, Reeve
Elaine Esopenko, Administrator

Garry No. 245
P.O. Box 10
Jedburgh, SK S0A 1R0
306-647-2450 Fax: 306-647-2450
rm245@yourlink.ca
Municipal Type: Rural Municipality
Incorporated: Jan. 1, 1913; *Area:* 853.59 sq km
Population in 2006: 426
Next Election: Oct 2010; staggered 2 yr term
Garry Dubiel, Reeve
Tanis Ferguson, Administrator

Glen Bain No. 105
P.O. Box 39
Glen Bain, SK S0N 0X0
306-264-3607 Fax: 306-264-3956
rm105@xplornet.com
Municipal Type: Rural Municipality
Incorporated: Dec. 11, 1911; *Area:* 843.40 sq km
Population in 2006: 232
Next Election: Oct 2010; staggered 2 yr term
Marilyn Scheller, Administrator
Ross Turnbull, Reeve

Glen McPherson No. 46
P.O. Box 277
Mankota, SK S0H 2W0
306-478-2323 Fax: 306-478-2606
rm45.46@sasktel.net
Municipal Type: Rural Municipality
Incorporated: Jan. 1, 1913; *Area:* 848.29 sq km
Population in 2006: 112
Next Election: Oct 2010; staggered 2 yr term
Michael E. Sherven, Administrator
Gordon Kruger, Reeve

Glenside No. 377
P.O. Box 1084
Biggar, SK S0K 0M0
306-948-3681 Fax: 306-948-3684
rm377@sasktel.net
saskbiz.ca/communityprofiles/CommunityProfile.Asp?CommunityID=838
Municipal Type: Rural Municipality
Incorporated: Dec. 13, 1909; *Area:* 905.74 sq km
Population in 2006: 367
Next Election: Oct 2010; staggered 2 yr term
Shantell Redlick, Administrator
Elmer Ermolenko, Reeve

Golden West No. 95
P.O. Box 70
Corning, SK S0G 0T0
306-224-4456 Fax: 306-224-2196
goldwest@sasktel.net
Municipal Type: Rural Municipality
Incorporated: Dec. 13, 1909; *Area:* 790.13 sq km
Population in 2006: 322
Next Election: Oct 2010; staggered 2 yr term
Edward A. Mish, Administrator
J. Garth Allan, Reeve

Good Lake No. 274
P.O. Box 896
401 Main St.
Canora, SK S0A 0L0
306-563-5244 Fax: 306-563-5005
rm274@sasktel.net
www.goodlakerm.com
Municipal Type: Rural Municipality
Incorporated: Jan. 1, 1913; *Area:* 800.06 sq km
Population in 2006: 748
Next Election: Oct 2010; staggered 2 yr term
David Popowich, Reeve
Grant Doupe, Administrator

Grandview No. 349
P.O. Box 39
Kelfield, SK S0K 2C0
306-932-4911 Fax: 306-932-4923
rm349@xplornet.com
Municipal Type: Rural Municipality
Incorporated: Dec. 11, 1911; *Area:* 712.05 sq km
Population in 2006: 355
Next Election: Oct 2010; staggered 2 yr term
Patti J. Turk, Administrator
Vacant, Reeve

Grant No. 372
P.O. Box 190
Vonda, SK S0K 4N0
306-258-2022 Fax: 306-258-2011
rm372@sasktel.net
Municipal Type: Rural Municipality
Incorporated: Dec. 13, 1909; *Area:* 666.16 sq km
Population in 2006: 406
Next Election: Oct 2010; staggered 2 yr term
Julien Denis, Reeve
Brenda Skakun, Administrator

Grass Lake No. 381
P.O. Box 40
Reward, SK S0K 3N0
306-228-2988 Fax: 306-228-4188
rm381@sasktel.net
Municipal Type: Rural Municipality
Incorporated: Dec. 13, 1909; *Area:* 801.29 sq km
Population in 2006: 433
Next Election: Oct 2010; staggered 2 yr term
Scott Vetter, Reeve
Brenda M. Kasas, Administrator

Grassy Creek No. 78
P.O. Box 400
Shaunavon, SK S0N 2M0
306-297-2520 Fax: 306-297-3162
rm77.78@sasktel.net
Municipal Type: Rural Municipality
Incorporated: Jan. 1, 1913; *Area:* 837.40 sq km
Population in 2006: 305
Next Election: Oct 2010; staggered 2 yr term
Grace Potter, Administrator
Philip A. Fritz, Reeve

Gravelbourg No. 104
P.O. Box 510
Gravelbourg, SK S0H 1X0
306-648-2412 Fax: 306-648-2603
rm104@sasktel.net
saskbiz.ca/communityprofiles/CommunityProfile.Asp?CommunityID=744
Municipal Type: Rural Municipality
Incorporated: Dec. 9, 1912; *Area:* 842.08 sq km
Population in 2006: 329
Next Election: Oct 2010; staggered 2 yr term
Edgerton Sam, Administrator
Elwood Biech, Reeve

Grayson No. 184
P.O. Box 69
Boswell St.
Grayson, SK S0A 1E0
306-794-2044 Fax: 306-794-4655
grayson184@sasktel.net
www.rmofgrayson.com
Municipal Type: Rural Municipality
Incorporated: Jan. 1, 1913; *Area:* 875.22 sq km
Population in 2006: 542
Next Election: Oct 2010; staggered 2 yr term
Wilfred Schultz, Reeve
Darlene Paquin, Administrator

Great Bend No. 405
P.O. Box 150
200 Shepard St.
Borden, SK S0K 0N0
306-997-2101 Fax: 306-997-2201
rm405@sasktel.net
saskbiz.ca/communityprofiles/CommunityProfile.Asp?CommunityID=846
Municipal Type: Rural Municipality
Incorporated: Dec. 12, 1910; *Area:* 830.57 sq km
Population in 2006: 458
Next Election: Oct 2010; staggered 2 yr term
Ron Saunders, Reeve
Ken Tanchak, Administrator

Griffin No. 66
P.O. Box 70
Griffin, SK S0C 1G0
306-842-6298 Fax: 306-842-6400
rm66@sasktel.net
Municipal Type: Rural Municipality
Incorporated: Dec. 13, 1909; *Area:* 816.59 sq km
Population in 2006: 334
Next Election: Oct 2010; staggered 2 yr term
Audrey L. Trombley, Administrator
Marvin Eddy, Reeve

Gull Lake No. 139
P.O. Box 180
Gull Lake, SK S0N 1A0
306-672-4430 Fax: 306-672-3879
rm139@sasktel.net
saskbiz.ca/communityprofiles/CommunityProfile.Asp?CommunityID=849
Municipal Type: Rural Municipality
Incorporated: Jan. 1, 1913; *Area:* 836.41 sq km
Population in 2006: 221
Next Election: Oct 2010; staggered 2 yr term
Ida-Mae Leek, Administrator
Doug Steele, Reeve

Happy Valley No. 10
P.O. Box 39
Big Beaver, SK S0H 0G0
306-267-4540 Fax: 306-267-4540
rm11@coronach.ca
Municipal Type: Rural Municipality
Incorporated: Jan. 1, 1913; *Area:* 812.74 sq km
Population in 2006: 174
Next Election: Oct 2010; staggered 2 yr term
Vernon R. Palmer, Administrator
Dean Holbrook, Reeve

Happyland No. 231
P.O. Box 339
Leader, SK S0N 1H0
306-628-3800 Fax: 306-628-4228
rm231@sasktel.net
Municipal Type: Rural Municipality
Incorporated: Jan. 1, 1913; *Area:* 1,259 sq km
Population in 2006: 297
Next Election: Oct 2010; staggered 2 yr term
Tim C. Lozinsky, Administrator
Timothy Geiger, Reeve

Harris No. 316
P.O. Box 146
Harris, SK S0L 1K0
306-656-2072 Fax: 306-656-2151
rm316@sasktel.net
Municipal Type: Rural Municipality
Incorporated: Dec. 12, 1910; *Area:* 805.42 sq km
Population in 2006: 195
Next Election: Oct 2010; staggered 2 yr term
Jim Angus, Administrator
Ted Gross, Reeve

Hart Butte No. 11
P.O. Box 210
Coronach, SK S0H 0Z0
306-267-2005 Fax: 306-267-2391
rm11@accesscomm.ca
www.coronach.ca/RM__11/rm__11.html
Municipal Type: Rural Municipality
Incorporated: Jan. 1, 1913; *Area:* 841.98 sq km
Population in 2006: 272
Next Election: Oct 2010; staggered 2 yr term
Vernon R. Palmer, Administrator
Donald Kirby, Reeve

Hazel Dell No. 335
P.O. Box 87
Okla, SK S0A 2X0
306-325-4315 Fax: 306-352-4314
rm335@sasktel.net
Municipal Type: Rural Municipality
Incorporated: Jan. 1, 1913; *Area:* 1,394.02 sq km
Population in 2006: 611
Next Election: Oct 2010; staggered 2 yr term
Richard Radawetz, Reeve
Miranda Serhan, Administrator

Hazelwood No. 94
P.O. Box 270
Kipling, SK S0G 2S0
306-736-8121 Fax: 306-736-2496
rm94@sasktel.net
Municipal Type: Rural Municipality
Incorporated: Jan. 1, 1913; *Area:* 780.68 sq km
Population in 2006: 272
Next Election: Oct 2010; staggered 2 yr term
Gary Vargo, Administrator
Allan LaRose, Reeve

Heart's Hill No. 352
P.O. Box 458
Luseland, SK S0L 2A0
306-372-4224 Fax: 306-372-4770
rm352@sasktel.net
Municipal Type: Rural Municipality
Incorporated: Nov. 15, 1910; *Area:* 838.20 sq km
Population in 2006: 285
Next Election: Oct 2010; staggered 2 yr term
Vern Gintaut, Administrator
Lawrence Loehndorf, Reeve

Hillsborough No. 132
403 Coteau St. West
Moose Jaw, SK S6H 5E1

306-693-1329 Fax: 306-693-2810
rm.132@sasktel.net
Municipal Type: Rural Municipality
Incorporated: Jan. 1, 1913; *Area:* 445.25 sq km
Population in 2006: 122
Next Election: Oct 2010; staggered 2 yr term
Charlene Loos, Administrator
Ernest Doyle, Reeve

Hillsdale No. 440
P.O. Box 280
Neilburg, SK S0M 2C0
306-823-4321 Fax: 306-823-4477
rm440@sasktel.net
saskbiz.ca/communityprofiles/CommunityProfile.Asp?CommunityID=857
Municipal Type: Rural Municipality
Incorporated: Jan. 1, 1913; *Area:* 1,028.75 sq km
Population in 2006: 530
Next Election: Oct 2010; staggered 2 yr term
Glenn Goodfellow, Reeve
Janet L. Black, Administrator

Hoodoo No. 401
P.O. Box 250
Cudworth, SK S0K 1B0
306-256-3281 Fax: 306-256-7147
rm401@yourlink.ca
Municipal Type: Rural Municipality
Incorporated: Jan. 1, 1913; *Area:* 810.61 sq km
Population in 2006: 804
Next Election: Oct 2010; staggered 2 yr term
Linus Hackl, Reeve
David Yorke, Administrator

Hudson Bay No. 394
P.O. Box 520
Hudson Bay, SK S0E 0Y0
306-865-2691 Fax: 306-865-2857
rm394@sasktel.net
saskbiz.ca/communityprofiles/CommunityProfile.Asp?CommunityID=859
Municipal Type: Rural Municipality
Incorporated: May 1, 1977; *Area:* 12,460.90 sq km
Population in 2006: 1,359
Next Election: Oct 2010; staggered 2 yr term
Neal Hardy, Reeve
Tracy Smith, Administrator

Humboldt No. 370
P.O. Box 420
Humboldt, SK S0K 2A0
306-682-2242 Fax: 306-682-3239
r.m.humboldt@sasktel.net
Municipal Type: Rural Municipality
Incorporated: Jan. 1, 1913; *Area:* 798.51 sq km
Population in 2006: 842
Next Election: Oct 2010; staggered 2 yr term
Jordan Bergermann, Reeve
Corinne Nimegeers, Administrator

Huron No. 223
P.O. Box 159
Tugaske, SK S0H 4B0
306-759-2211 Fax: 306-759-2249
rm223@sasktel.net
Municipal Type: Rural Municipality
Incorporated: Dec. 12, 1910; *Area:* 842.11 sq km
Population in 2006: 233
Next Election: Oct 2010; staggered 2 yr term
Daryl Dean, Administrator
Corey Doerksen, Reeve

Indian Head No. 156
P.O. Box 39
Indian Head, SK S0G 2K0
306-695-3464 Fax: 306-695-3462
rm156@sasktel.net
Municipal Type: Rural Municipality
Incorporated: Aug. 6, 1884; *Area:* 759.98 sq km
Population in 2006: 356
Next Election: Oct 2010; staggered 2 yr term
Lorelei Theaker, Administrator
Lorne Scott, Reeve

Insinger No. 275
P.O. Box 179
Insinger, SK S0A 1L0
306-647-2422 Fax: 306-647-2740
rm275@sasktel.net
Municipal Type: Rural Municipality
Incorporated: Jan. 1, 1913; *Area:* 849.38 sq km
Population in 2006: 373
Next Election: Oct 2010; staggered 2 yr term
Sonya Butuk, Administrator
Barry Koshman, Reeve

Invergordon No. 430
P.O. Box 40
Crystal Springs, SK S0K 1A0
306-749-2852 Fax: 306-749-2499
rm430@sasktel.net
Municipal Type: Rural Municipality
Incorporated: Dec. 11, 1911; *Area:* 853.55 sq km
Population in 2006: 570
Next Election: Oct 2010; staggered 2 yr term
Dennis Shulhan, Reeve
Sally Wojcichowsky, Administrator

Invermay No. 305
P.O. Box 130
Invermay, SK S0A 1M0
306-593-2152 Fax: 306-593-2152
rm.inv.305@sasktel.net
Municipal Type: Rural Municipality
Incorporated: Dec. 11, 1911; *Area:* 728.23 sq km
Population in 2006: 379
Next Election: Oct 2010; staggered 2 yr term
Sandra Leitch, Administrator
Jack Prychak, Reeve

Ituna Bon Accord No. 246
P.O. Box 190
Ituna, SK S0A 1N0
306-795-2202 Fax: 306-795-2202
rmofituna@sasktel.net
www.town.ituna.sk.ca
Municipal Type: Rural Municipality
Incorporated: Jan. 1, 1913; *Area:* 837.23 sq km
Population in 2006: 453
Next Election: Oct 2010; staggered 2 yr term
Orest Zrymiak, Reeve
Wilma Hrenyk, Administrator

Kellross No. 247
P.O. Box 10
Leross, SK S0A 2C0
306-675-4423 Fax: 306-675-2097
rm247@sasktel.net
saskbiz.ca/communityprofiles/CommunityProfile.Asp?CommunityID=867
Municipal Type: Rural Municipality
Incorporated: Dec. 13, 1909; *Area:* 834.09 sq km
Population in 2006: 390
Next Election: Oct 2010; staggered 2 yr term
Edith Goddard, Administrator
John Olinik, Reeve

Kelvington No. 366
P.O. Box 519
Kelvington, SK S0A 1W0
306-327-4222 Fax: 306-327-4222
rm366@sasktel.net
saskbiz.ca/communityprofiles/CommunityProfile.Asp?CommunityID=868
Municipal Type: Rural Municipality
Incorporated: Jan. 1, 1913; *Area:* 907.37 sq km
Population in 2006: 514
Next Election: Oct 2010; staggered 2 yr term
Stanley Elmy, Reeve
Tim G. Leurer, Administrator

Key West No. 70
P.O. Box 159
Ogema, SK S0C 1Y0
306-459-2262 Fax: 306-459-2762
rm.70@sasktel.net
Municipal Type: Rural Municipality
Incorporated: Dec. 12, 1910; *Area:* 825.26 sq km
Population in 2006: 309
Next Election: Oct 2010; staggered 2 yr term
Peggy Tuchscherer, Administrator
Darryl Wiles, Reeve

Keys No. 303
P.O. Box 899
Canora, SK S0A 0L0
306-563-5331 Fax: 306-563-6759
rm303@sasktel.net
Municipal Type: Rural Municipality
Incorporated: Jan. 1, 1913; *Area:* 661.61 sq km
Population in 2006: 397
Next Election: Oct 2010; staggered 2 yr term
Sharon Ciesielski, Administrator
James Hallick, Reeve

Kindersley No. 290
P.O. Box 1210
Kindersley, SK S0L 1S0
306-463-2524 Fax: 306-463-4197
rm290@sasktel.net
Municipal Type: Rural Municipality
Incorporated: Dec. 12, 1910; *Area:* 2,113.36 sq km
Population in 2006: 1,042
Next Election: Oct 2010; staggered 2 yr term
Glen Harrison, Reeve
Glenda M. Giles, Administrator

King George No. 256
P.O. Box 100
Dinsmore, SK S0L 0T0
306-846-2022 Fax: 306-846-2032
rm256@sasktel.net
Municipal Type: Rural Municipality
Incorporated: Dec. 11, 1911; *Area:* 831.97 sq km
Population in 2006: 234
Next Election: Oct 2010; staggered 2 yr term
Jamie McIntosh, Administrator
Fred Jaskela, Reeve

Kingsley No. 124
P.O. Box 239
Kipling, SK S0G 2S0
306-736-2272 Fax: 306-736-2798
rm124@sasktel.net
saskbiz.ca/communityprofiles/CommunityProfile.Asp?CommunityID=873
Municipal Type: Rural Municipality
Incorporated: Dec. 12, 1910; *Area:* 844.61 sq km
Population in 2006: 439
Next Election: Oct 2010; staggered 2 yr term
Lorne Rygh, Reeve
Holly Kemp, Administrator

Kinistino No. 459
P.O. Box 310
Kinistino, SK S0J 1H0
306-864-2474 Fax: 306-864-2880
rm459@sasktel.net
Municipal Type: Rural Municipality
Incorporated: Dec. 11, 1911; *Area:* 949.13 sq km
Population in 2006: 713
Next Election: Oct 2010; staggered 2 yr term
Raymond Hawrish, Reeve
Tina M. Douglas, Administrator

Lac Pelletier No. 107
P.O. Box 70
Neville, SK S0N 1T0
306-627-3226 Fax: 306-627-3641
rm107@sasktel.net
Municipal Type: Rural Municipality
Incorporated: Jan. 1, 1913; *Area:* 849.27 sq km
Population in 2006: 524
Next Election: Oct 2010; staggered 2 yr term
Cornie Martens, Reeve
Rose Lawrence, Administrator

Lacadena No. 228
P.O. Box 39
Lacadena, SK S0L 1V0
306-574-2008 Fax: 306-574-4753
rm228@xplornet.com
Municipal Type: Rural Municipality
Incorporated: Dec. 12, 1910; *Area:* 1,890.08 sq km
Population in 2006: 613
Next Election: Oct 2010; staggered 2 yr term
Bradley Sander, Reeve
Wilma Moen, Administrator

Laird No. 404
P.O. Box 160
Waldheim, SK S0K 4R0
306-945-2133 Fax: 306-945-4824
rmlaird@sasktel.net
Municipal Type: Rural Municipality
Incorporated: Dec. 12, 1910; *Area:* 729.98 sq km
Population in 2006: 1,136
Next Election: Oct 2010; staggered 2 yr term
Kenneth Petkau, Reeve
Sandra Galambos, Administrator

Lajord No. 128
P.O. Box 36
Lajord, SK S0G 2V0
306-781-2744 Fax: 306-781-1023
rm128@yourlink.ca
Municipal Type: Rural Municipality
Incorporated: Dec. 13, 1909; *Area:* 943.87 sq km
Population in 2006: 977
Next Election: Oct 2010; staggered 2 yr term
Erwin Beitel, Reeve
Rod J. Heise, Administrator

Lake Alma No. 8
P.O. Box 100
Lake Alma, SK S0C 1M0
306-447-2022 Fax: 306-447-4802
rmalma@sasktel.net
Municipal Type: Rural Municipality
Incorporated: May 5, 1913; *Area:* 822.47 sq km
Population in 2006: 240
Next Election: Oct 2010; staggered 2 yr term
Myrna Lohse, Administrator
Lyle Hoimyr, Reeve

Lake Johnston No. 102
P.O. Box 160
Mossbank, SK S0H 3G0
306-354-2414 Fax: 306-354-7725
rm102.103@sasktel.net
Municipal Type: Rural Municipality
Incorporated: Dec. 9, 1912; *Area:* 567.24 sq km
Population in 2006: 161
Next Election: Oct 2010; staggered 2 yr term
Sherry D. Green, Administrator
Harold Ray, Reeve

Lake Lenore No. 399
P.O. Box 280
St Brieux, SK S0K 3V0
306-275-2066 Fax: 306-275-4667
rmll@sasktel.net
Municipal Type: Rural Municipality
Incorporated: Jan. 1, 1913; *Area:* 724.06 sq km

Population in 2006: 513
Next Election: Oct 2010; staggered 2 yr term
Jerry Briens, Reeve
Gailene Gallais, Administrator

Lake of the Rivers No. 72
P.O. Box 610
Assiniboia, SK S0H 0B0
306-642-3533 Fax: 306-642-4382
rm72@sasktel.net
saskbiz.ca/communityprofiles/CommunityProfile.Asp?CommunityID=747
Municipal Type: Rural Municipality
Incorporated: Dec. 11, 1911; *Area:* 677.51 sq km
Population in 2006: 326
Next Election: Oct 2010; staggered 2 yr term
Mervin A. Guillemin, Administrator
Gerald Leduc, Reeve

Lakeland No. 521
P.O. Box 27
Christopher Lake, SK S0J 0N0
306-982-2010 Fax: 306-982-2589
rm.521@sasktel.net
www.rmlakeland521.ca
Municipal Type: Rural Municipality
Incorporated: Aug. 1, 1977; *Area:* 494.06 sq km
Population in 2006: 1,043
Next Election: Oct 2010; staggered 2 yr term
Al Christensen, Reeve
Andrew J. Springs, Administrator

Lakeside No. 338
P.O. Box 9
Quill Lake, SK S0A 3E0
306-383-2261 Fax: 306-383-2255
rm338@sasktel.net
Municipal Type: Rural Municipality
Incorporated: Dec. 12, 1910; *Area:* 636.80 sq km
Population in 2006: 444
Next Election: Oct 2010; staggered 2 yr term
Arnold Boyko, Reeve
Judy Kanak, Administrator

Lakeview No. 337
P.O. Box 220
Wadena, SK S0A 4J0
306-338-2341 Fax: 306-338-2595
rm337@sasktel.net
saskbiz.ca/communityprofiles/CommunityProfile.Asp?CommunityID=885
Municipal Type: Rural Municipality
Incorporated: Dec. 13, 1909; *Area:* 724.89 sq km
Population in 2006: 393
Next Election: Oct 2010; staggered 2 yr term
Betty Ann Bjarnason, Administrator
Mervin Kryzanowski, Reeve

Langenburg No. 181
P.O. Box 489
Langenburg, SK S0A 2A0
306-743-2341 Fax: 306-743-5282
rm181@sasktel.net
saskbiz.ca/communityprofiles/CommunityProfile.Asp?CommunityID=886
Municipal Type: Rural Municipality
Incorporated: Jan. 1, 1913; *Area:* 675.66 sq km
Population in 2006: 558
Next Election: Oct 2010; staggered 2 yr term
Ken Apland, Reeve
Darwyn MacKenzie, Administrator

Last Mountain Valley No. 250
P.O. Box 160
Govan, SK S0G 1Z0
306-484-2011 Fax: 306-484-2113
rm250@sasktel.net
Municipal Type: Rural Municipality
Incorporated: Dec. 13, 1909; *Area:* 871.17 sq km
Population in 2006: 362
Next Election: Oct 2010; staggered 2 yr term
Kelly Holbrook, Administrator
Allan Magel, Reeve

Laurier No. 38
P.O. Box 219
Radville, SK S0C 2G0
306-869-2255 Fax: 306-869-2524
rm.38@sasktel.net
Municipal Type: Rural Municipality
Incorporated: Dec. 13, 1909; *Area:* 840.86 sq km
Population in 2006: 350
Next Election: Oct 2010; staggered 2 yr term
Shannon Herman, Administrator
Gene Gilmore, Reeve

Lawtonia No. 135
P.O. Box 10
Hodgeville, SK S0H 2B0
306-677-2266 Fax: 306-677-2446
rm135@sasktel.net
saskbiz.ca/communityprofiles/CommunityProfile.Asp?CommunityID=889
Municipal Type: Rural Municipality
Incorporated: Dec. 12, 1910; *Area:* 845.28 sq km
Population in 2006: 356
Next Election: Oct 2010; staggered 2 yr term
Art Thompson, Administrator
Barry Leisle, Reeve

Leask No. 464
P.O. Box 190
Leask, SK S0J 1M0
306-466-2000 Fax: 306-466-2000
rmleask464@sasktel.net
saskbiz.ca/communityprofiles/CommunityProfile.Asp?CommunityID=890
Municipal Type: Rural Municipality
Incorporated: Dec. 9, 1912; *Area:* 1,257.36 sq km
Population in 2006: 846
Next Election: Oct 2010; staggered 2 yr term
Jim Joanette, Reeve
Wanda Boon, Administrator

Leroy No. 339
P.O. Box 100
Leroy, SK S0K 2P0
306-286-3261 Fax: 306-286-3400
rm339@sasktel.net
Municipal Type: Rural Municipality
Incorporated: Jan. 1, 1913; *Area:* 840.40 sq km
Population in 2006: 544
Next Election: Oct 2010; staggered 2 yr term
Jerry McGrath, Reeve
Joan Fedak, Administrator

Lipton No. 217
P.O. Box 40
Lipton, SK S0G 3B0
306-336-2244 Fax: 306-336-2244
rm.217@sasktel.net
Municipal Type: Rural Municipality
Incorporated: Dec. 11, 1911; *Area:* 813.69 sq km
Population in 2006: 427
Next Election: Oct 2010; staggered 2 yr term
Corey Senft, Reeve
Nikki Czemeres, Administrator

Livingston No. 331
P.O. Box 40
Arran, SK S0A 0B0
306-595-4521 Fax: 306-595-4531
rm331@sasktel.net
Municipal Type: Rural Municipality
Incorporated: Jan. 1, 1913; *Area:* 1,338.64 sq km
Population in 2006: 355
Next Election: Oct 2010; staggered 2 yr term
Yvonne Bilsky, Administrator
Paul Abrahamson, Reeve

Lomond No. 37
P.O. Box 280
Weyburn, SK S4H 2K1
306-456-2566 Fax: 306-456-2440
rm37@sasktel.net
saskbiz.ca/communityprofiles/CommunityProfile.Asp?CommunityID=894
Municipal Type: Rural Municipality
Incorporated: Dec. 11, 1911; *Area:* 833.95 sq km
Population in 2006: 301
Next Election: Oct 2010; staggered 2 yr term
Kevin Melle, Administrator
John McKenzie, Reeve

Lone Tree No. 18
P.O. Box 30
Climax, SK S0N 0N0
306-293-2124 Fax: 306-293-2702
Municipal Type: Rural Municipality
Incorporated: Dec. 8, 1913; *Area:* 838 sq km
Population in 2006: 150
Next Election: Oct 2010; staggered 2 yr term
Ronald J. Johnson, Administrator
Larry Jarman, Reeve

Longlaketon No. 219
P.O. Box 100
Earl Grey, SK S0G 1J0
306-939-2144 Fax: 306-939-2036
rm219@sasktel.net
Municipal Type: Rural Municipality
Incorporated: Dec. 12, 1910; *Area:* 1,024.61 sq km
Population in 2006: 899
Next Election: Oct 2010; staggered 2 yr term
Ken Gellner, Reeve
Murray Cook, Administrator

Loon Lake No. 561
P.O. Box 40
Loon Lake, SK S0M 1L0
306-837-2076 Fax: 306-837-2282
rm561@sasktel.net
Municipal Type: Rural Municipality
Incorporated: Jan. 1, 1978; *Area:* 2,802.51 sq km
Population in 2006: 815
Next Election: Oct 2010; staggered 2 yr term
Harvey Dimond, Reeve
Jackie Regnier, Administrator

Loreburn No. 254
P.O. Box 40
Loreburn, SK S0H 2S0
306-644-2022 Fax: 306-644-2064
rm254@sasktel.net
www.rmloreburn.ca
Municipal Type: Rural Municipality
Incorporated: Dec. 12, 1910; *Area:* 966.78 sq km
Population in 2006: 350
Next Election: Oct 2010; staggered 2 yr term
Nona Stronski, Administrator
Kevin Vollmer
mbarv@sasktel.net

Lost River No. 313
P.O. Box 159
Allan, SK S0K 0C0
306-257-3272 Fax: 306-257-3337
rm313@sasktel.net
saskbiz.ca/communityprofiles/CommunityProfile.Asp?CommunityID=899
Municipal Type: Rural Municipality
Incorporated: Dec. 11, 1911; *Area:* 549.90 sq km
Population in 2006: 188
Next Election: Oct 2010; staggered 2 yr term
Christine Dyck, Administrator

Lumsden No. 189
P.O. Box 160
300 James Street North
Lumsden, SK S0G 3C0
306-731-2404 Fax: 306-731-3572
rm189@sasktel.net
www.lumsden.ca
Municipal Type: Rural Municipality
Incorporated: Dec. 9, 1912; *Area:* 818.66 sq km
Population in 2006: 1,627
Next Election: Oct 2010; staggered 2 yr term
Jim Hipkin, Reeve
Wayne Zerff, Administrator

Manitou Lake No. 442
P.O. Box 69
Marsden, SK S0M 1P0
306-826-5215 Fax: 306-826-5512
rm442@sasktel.net
saskbiz.ca/communityprofiles/CommunityProfile.Asp?CommunityID=901
Municipal Type: Rural Municipality
Incorporated: Dec. 12, 1910; *Area:* 850.32 sq km
Population in 2006: 590
Next Election: Oct 2010; staggered 2 yr term
Grant Wightman, Reeve
Joanne Loy, Administrator

Mankota No. 45
P.O. Box 148
Mankota, SK S0H 2W0
306-478-2323 Fax: 306-478-2606
rm45.46@sasktel.net
Municipal Type: Rural Municipality
Incorporated: Jan. 1, 1913; *Area:* 1,696.22 sq km
Population in 2006: 382
Next Election: Oct 2010; staggered 2 yr term
Michael E. Sherven, Administrator
Doug Williamson, Reeve

Maple Bush No. 224
P.O. Box 160
Riverhurst, SK S0H 3P0
306-353-2292 Fax: 306-353-2292
rm224@sasktel.net
Municipal Type: Rural Municipality
Incorporated: Dec. 13, 1909; *Area:* 811.95 sq km
Population in 2006: 186
Next Election: Oct 2010; staggered 2 yr term
Garry L. Gross, Administrator
Dennis R. O'Brien, Reeve

Maple Creek No. 111
P.O. Box 188
Maple Creek, SK S0N 1N0
306-662-2300 Fax: 306-662-3566
rm111@sasktel.net
Municipal Type: Rural Municipality
Incorporated: Dec. 10, 1917; *Area:* 3,242.96 sq km
Population in 2006: 1,167
Next Election: Oct 2010; staggered 2 yr term
Greg Link, Reeve
Barbi-Rose Weisgerber, Administrator

Mariposa No. 350
P.O. Box 228
603 Atlantic Ave.
Kerrobert, SK S0L 1R0
306-834-5037 Fax: 306-834-5047
rm350@sasktel.net
Municipal Type: Rural Municipality
Incorporated: Dec. 12, 1910; *Area:* 636.73 sq km
Population in 2006: 225
Next Election: Oct 2010; staggered 2 yr term
Terry Bohn, Administrator
Stew Seversen, Reeve

Marquis No. 191
P.O. Box 40
Marquis, SK S0H 2X0
306-788-2022 Fax: 306-788-2168
rm191@sasktel.net
saskbiz.ca/communityprofiles/CommunityProfile.Asp?CommunityID=906
Municipal Type: Rural Municipality
Incorporated: Dec. 11, 1911; *Area:* 805.48 sq km
Population in 2006: 404
Next Election: Oct 2010; staggered 2 yr term
Kenneth Waldenberger, Reeve
Ronald J. Gasper, Administrator

Marriott No. 317
P.O. Box 366
Rosetown, SK S0L 2V0
306-882-4030 Fax: 306-882-4401
rm317@sasktel.net
Municipal Type: Rural Municipality
Incorporated: Dec. 12, 1910; *Area:* 843.29 sq km
Population in 2006: 410
Next Election: Oct 2010; staggered 2 yr term
Colin Ahrens, Reeve
Michelle McQueen, Administrator

Martin No. 122
P.O. Box 1109
Moosomin, SK S0G 3N0
306-532-3113 Fax: 306-435-4313
rm121@sasktel.net
saskbiz.ca/communityprofiles/CommunityProfile.Asp?CommunityID=908
Municipal Type: Rural Municipality
Incorporated: Jan. 1, 1913; *Area:* 556.50 sq km
Population in 2006: 339
Next Election: Oct 2010; staggered 2 yr term
Elaine M. Olsen, Administrator
Mark Bateman, Reeve

Maryfield No. 91
P.O. Box 70
Maryfield, SK S0G 3K0
306-646-2033 Fax: 306-646-2033
rm91@sasktel.net
Municipal Type: Rural Municipality
Incorporated: Dec. 9, 1912; *Area:* 759.63 sq km
Population in 2006: 341
Next Election: Oct 2010; staggered 2 yr term
Anna Macksymchuk, Administrator
Gary Sweeting, Reeve

Mayfield No. 406
P.O. Box 100
Maymont, SK S0M 1T0
306-389-2112 Fax: 306-389-2162
rm406@sasktel.net
Municipal Type: Rural Municipality
Incorporated: Dec. 13, 1909; *Area:* 782.50 sq km
Population in 2006: 394
Next Election: Oct 2010; staggered 2 yr term
Laurie DuBois, Administrator
Ernest Voegeli, Reeve

McCraney No. 282
P.O. Box 129
Kenaston, SK S0G 2N0
306-252-2240 Fax: 306-252-2248
rm282@sasktel.net
Municipal Type: Rural Municipality
Incorporated: Dec. 13, 1909; *Area:* 948.36 sq km
Population in 2006: 346
Next Election: Oct 2010; staggered 2 yr term
Mark Zdunich, Administrator
Reginald Zdunich, Reeve

McKillop No. 220
P.O. Box 369
Strasbourg, SK S0G 4V0
306-725-3230 Fax: 306-725-3613
rm220@sasktel.net
saskbiz.ca/communityprofiles/CommunityProfile.Asp?CommunityID=912
Municipal Type: Rural Municipality
Incorporated: Dec. 13, 1909; *Area:* 668.45 sq km
Population in 2006: 566
Next Election: Oct 2010; staggered 2 yr term
Nelson Swanston, Reeve
Barbara Griffin, Administrator

McLeod No. 185
P.O. Box 130
Neudorf, SK S0A 2T0
306-748-2233 Fax: 306-748-2647
www.village.neudorf.sk.ca/RM%20OF%20MCLEOD.htm
Municipal Type: Rural Municipality
Incorporated: Jan. 1, 1913; *Area:* 886.6 sq km
Population in 2006: 508
Next Election: Oct 2010; staggered 2 yr term
Wilfred G. Goebel, Reeve
Murray J. Hanowski, Administrator

Meadow Lake No. 588
P.O. Box 668
#1, 225 Centre St.
Meadow Lake, SK S9X 1L5
306-236-5651 Fax: 306-236-3115
rm.588@sasktel.net
saskbiz.ca/communityprofiles/CommunityProfile.Asp?CommunityID=914
Municipal Type: Rural Municipality
Incorporated: Feb. 1, 1976; *Area:* 6,303.31 sq km
Population in 2006: 2,627
Next Election: Oct 2010; staggered 2 yr term
Raymond Wilfing, Reeve
Gina Bernier, Administrator

Medstead No. 497
P.O. Box 148
Medstead, SK S0M 1W0
306-342-4609 Fax: 306-342-2067
rm497@sasktel.net
Municipal Type: Rural Municipality
Incorporated: Jan. 1, 1913; *Area:* 1,203.22 sq km
Population in 2006: 524
Next Election: Oct 2010; staggered 2 yr term
Archie Latimer, Reeve
Christin Baynes, Administrator

Meeting Lake No. 466
P.O. Box 26
Mayfair, SK S0M 1S0
306-246-4228 Fax: 306-246-4974
rm466@sasktel.net
Municipal Type: Rural Municipality
Incorporated: Jan. 1, 1913; *Area:* 1,066.74 sq km
Population in 2006: 429
Next Election: Oct 2010; staggered 2 yr term
Lyle Prescesky, Reeve
Janelle Lavallee, Administrator

Meota No. 468
P.O. Box 80
Meota, SK S0M 1X0
306-892-2061 Fax: 306-892-2449
rm.468@sasktel.net
saskbiz.ca/communityprofiles/CommunityProfile.Asp?CommunityID=917
Municipal Type: Rural Municipality
Incorporated: Dec. 13, 1909; *Area:* 651.09 sq km
Population in 2006: 984
Next Election: Oct 2010; staggered 2 yr term
Wilbert Fennig, Reeve
Maryann Germann, Administrator

Mervin No. 499
P.O. Box 130
Turtleford, SK S0M 2Y0
306-845-2045 Fax: 306-845-2950
rm499@sasktel.net
saskbiz.ca/communityprofiles/CommunityProfile.Asp?CommunityID=918
Municipal Type: Rural Municipality
Incorporated: Jan. 1, 1913; *Area:* 1,594.64 sq km
Population in 2006: 1,331
Next Election: Oct 2010; staggered 2 yr term
Harold Kivimaa, Reeve
L. Ryan Domotor, Administrator

Milden No. 286
P.O. Box 160
113 Centre St.
Milden, SK S0L 2L0
306-935-2181 Fax: 306-935-2046
rm286@sasktel.net
Municipal Type: Rural Municipality
Incorporated: Dec. 12, 1910; *Area:* 735.31 sq km
Population in 2006: 215
Next Election: Oct 2010; staggered 2 yr term
Melody Nieman, Administrator
Arnold Somerville, Reeve

Milton No. 292
P.O. Box 70
Marengo, SK S0L 2K0
306-968-2922 Fax: 306-968-2278
rm292.rm322@sasktel.net
Municipal Type: Rural Municipality
Incorporated: Dec. 11, 1911; *Area:* 655.76 sq km
Population in 2006: 181
Next Election: Oct 2010; staggered 2 yr term
Shelley Mohr, Administrator
Kenneth Weisbrod, Reeve

Miry Creek No. 229
P.O. Box 210
Abbey, SK S0N 0A0
306-689-2281 Fax: 306-689-2901
rm229@sasktel.net
saskbiz.ca/communityprofiles/CommunityProfile.Asp?CommunityID=921
Municipal Type: Rural Municipality
Incorporated: Jan. 1, 1913; *Area:* 1,220.38 sq km
Population in 2006: 458
Next Election: Oct 2010; staggered 2 yr term
Morgan Powell, Reeve
Jan Stern, Administrator

Monet No. 257
P.O. Box 370
Elrose, SK S0L 0Z0
306-378-2212 Fax: 306-378-2212
rm257@sasktel.net
Municipal Type: Rural Municipality
Incorporated: Dec. 13, 1909; *Area:* 1,591.75 sq km
Population in 2006: 479
Next Election: Oct 2010; staggered 2 yr term
George Myers, Reeve
Lori A. McDonald, Administrator

Montmartre No. 126
P.O. Box 120
136 Central Ave.
Montmartre, SK S0G 3M0
306-424-2040 Fax: 306-424-2065
rm126@sasktel.net
www.montmartre-sk.com
Municipal Type: Rural Municipality
Incorporated: Dec. 13, 1909; *Area:* 853.91 sq km
Population in 2006: 503
Next Election: Oct 2010; staggered 2 yr term
Rodney Baumgartner, Reeve
Dale Brenner, Administrator

Montrose No. 315
P.O. Box 755
Delisle, SK S0L 0P0
306-493-2694 Fax: 306-493-2694
rm315@sasktel.net
Municipal Type: Rural Municipality
Incorporated: Dec. 13, 1909; *Area:* 898.38 sq km
Population in 2006: 648
Next Election: Oct 2010; staggered 2 yr term
Gordon Ross, Reeve
Ray French, Administrator

Moose Creek No. 33
P.O. Box 10
Alameda, SK S0C 0A0
306-489-2044 Fax: 306-489-2112
rm33@sasktel.net
www.creda.sk.ca/moosecreek
Municipal Type: Rural Municipality
Incorporated: Dec. 12, 1910; *Area:* 842.03 sq km
Population in 2006: 365
Next Election: Oct 2010; staggered 2 yr term
Betty Ann Rattray, Administrator
Murray Rossow, Reeve

Moose Jaw No. 161
170 Fairford St. West
Moose Jaw, SK S6H 1V3
306-692-3446 Fax: 306-691-0015
rm161@sasktel.net
www.moosejawrm161.ca
Municipal Type: Rural Municipality
Incorporated: Dec. 11, 1911; *Area:* 797.60 sq km
Population in 2006: 1,228
Next Election: Oct 2010; staggered 2 yr term
Darol Owens, Reeve
John Eberl, Administrator

Moose Mountain No. 63
P.O. Box 445
Carlyle, SK S0C 0R0
306-453-6175 Fax: 306-453-2430
rm63@sasktel.net
Municipal Type: Rural Municipality
Incorporated: Dec. 11, 1911; *Area:* 740.91 sq km
Population in 2006: 482
Next Election: Oct 2010; staggered 2 yr term
Note: URL:
www.creda.sk.ca/moosemountain/moose_mountain_community_profile.htm
Lyle Brown, Reeve
Ron Matsalla, Administrator

Moose Range No. 486
P.O. Box 699
Carrot River, SK S0E 0L0
306-768-2212 Fax: 306-768-2211
rm486@sasktel.net
www.rmmooserange.sasktelwebsite.net
Municipal Type: Rural Municipality
Incorporated: Dec. 11, 1916; *Area:* 2,419.06 sq km
Population in 2006: 1,086
Next Election: Oct 2010; staggered 2 yr term
Herman Enns, Reeve
Richard C. Colborn, Administrator

Moosomin No. 121
P.O. Box 1109
Moosomin, SK S0G 3N0
306-435-3113 Fax: 306-435-4313
rm121@sasktel.net
saskbiz.ca/communityprofiles/CommunityProfile.Asp?CommunityID=929
Municipal Type: Rural Municipality
Incorporated: Jan. 1, 1913; *Area:* 566.39 sq km
Population in 2006: 518
Next Election: Oct 2010; staggered 2 yr term
Ken Mannle, Reeve
Kendra L. Lawrence, Administrator

Morris No. 312
P.O. Box 130
Young, SK S0K 4Y0
306-259-2211 Fax: 306-259-2225
rm312@sasktel.net
saskbiz.ca/communityprofiles/CommunityProfile.Asp?CommunityID=930
Municipal Type: Rural Municipality
Incorporated: Dec. 13, 1909; *Area:* 847.16 sq km
Population in 2006: 347
Next Election: Oct 2010; staggered 2 yr term
Rolande Davis, Administrator
Gordon Dengler, Reeve

Morse No. 165
P.O. Box 340
Morse, SK S0H 3C0
306-629-3282 Fax: 306-629-3212
rm165@sasktel.net
Municipal Type: Rural Municipality
Incorporated: Dec. 11, 1911; *Area:* 1,244.38 sq km
Population in 2006: 435
Next Election: Oct 2010; staggered 2 yr term
Glen Solberg, Reeve
Mark Wilson, Administrator

Mount Hope No. 279
P.O. Box 190
Semans, SK S0A 3S0
306-524-2055 Fax: 306-524-4526
rm279@sasktel.net
Municipal Type: Rural Municipality
Incorporated: Dec. 11, 1911; *Area:* 1,669.29 sq km
Population in 2006: 633
Next Election: Oct 2010; staggered 2 yr term
Ernie Oblander, Reeve
Jim Down, Administrator

Mount Pleasant No. 2
P.O. Box 278
820 Railway Ave.
Carnduff, SK S0C 0S0
306-482-3313 Fax: 306-482-5278
rm.2@sasktel.net
Municipal Type: Rural Municipality
Incorporated: Dec. 11, 1911; *Area:* 781.48 sq km
Population in 2006: 418
Next Election: Oct 2010; staggered 2 yr term
Slade Boyes, Reeve
Valerie A. Olney, Administrator

Mountain View No. 318
P.O. Box 130
Herschel, SK S0L 1L0
306-377-2144 Fax: 306-377-2023
rm318@sasktel.net
Municipal Type: Rural Municipality
Incorporated: Dec. 13, 1909; *Area:* 838.67 sq km
Population in 2006: 333
Next Election: Oct 2010; staggered 2 yr term
Karen F. Martin, Administrator
William A. Bradley, Reeve

Newcombe No. 260
P.O. Box 40
Glidden, SK S0L 1H0
306-463-3338 Fax: 306-463-4748
rm260@yourlink.ca
Municipal Type: Rural Municipality
Incorporated: Dec. 11, 1911; *Area:* 1,075.6 sq km
Population in 2006: 361
Next Election: Oct 2010; staggered 2 yr term
Michele A. Schmidt, Administrator
John Hebert, Reeve

Nipawin No. 487
P.O. Box 250
Codette, SK S0E 0P0
306-862-9551 Fax: 306-862-2432
rm487@sasktel.net
Municipal Type: Rural Municipality
Incorporated: Dec. 9, 1912; *Area:* 886.73 sq km
Population in 2006: 1,166
Next Election: Oct 2010; staggered 2 yr term
Lyle L. Larsen, Reeve
Eunice Rudy, Administrator

North Battleford No. 437
1101 - 101 St.
North Battleford, SK S9A 0Z5
306-445-3604 Fax: 306-445-3694
rm437@sasktel.net
saskbiz.ca/communityprofiles/CommunityProfile.Asp?CommunityID=937
Municipal Type: Rural Municipality
Incorporated: Dec. 12, 1910; *Area:* 797.20 sq km
Population in 2006: 737
Next Election: Oct 2010; staggered 2 yr term
Lorne Kemp, Reeve
Debbie Arsenault, Administrator

North Qu'Appelle No. 187
P.O. Box 99
Fort Qu'appelle, SK S0G 1S0
306-332-5202 Fax: 306-332-6028
rm187@sasktel.net
www.fortquappelle.com/rm187
Municipal Type: Rural Municipality
Incorporated: Dec. 12, 1910; *Area:* 494.98 sq km
Population in 2006: 852
Next Election: Oct 2010; staggered 2 yr term
Arthur N. Foster, Reeve
Beverly van der Breggen, Administrator

Norton No. 69
P.O. Box 189
Pangman, SK S0C 2C0
306-442-2131 Fax: 306-442-2144
rm.69@sasktel.net
Municipal Type: Rural Municipality
Incorporated: Dec. 13, 1909; *Area:* 844.8 sq km
Population in 2006: 248
Next Election: Oct 2010; staggered 2 yr term
Wayne Lozinsky, Administrator
Chuck Jacques, Reeve

Oakdale No. 320
P.O. Box 249
Coleville, SK S0L 0K0
306-965-2281 Fax: 306-965-2466
rm320@sasktel.net
Municipal Type: Rural Municipality
Incorporated: Dec. 13, 1909; *Area:* 806.52 sq km
Population in 2006: 290
Next Election: Oct 2010; staggered 2 yr term
Gloria Johnson, Administrator
Darwin Whitfield, Reeve

Old Post No. 43
P.O. Box 70
Wood Mountain, SK S0H 4L0
306-266-2002 Fax: 306-266-2020
rm43@sasktel.net
Municipal Type: Rural Municipality
Incorporated: Jan. 1, 1967; *Area:* 1,757 sq km
Population in 2006: 394
Next Election: Oct 2010; staggered 2 yr term
Vickie Greffard, Clerk
Warren Spagrud, Reeve

Orkney No. 244
26 - 5 Ave. North
Yorkton, SK S3N 0Y8
306-782-2333 Fax: 306-782-5177
orkney@sasktel.net
Municipal Type: Rural Municipality
Incorporated: Jan. 1, 1913; *Area:* 815.87 sq km
Population in 2006: 1,721
Next Election: Oct 2010; staggered 2 yr term
Barclay Westerhaug, Reeve
Donna Westerhaug, Administrator

Paddockwood No. 520
P.O. Box 187
Paddockwood, SK S0J 1Z0
306-989-2124 Fax: 306-989-4625
rm520@sasktel.net
Municipal Type: Rural Municipality
Incorporated: Jan. 1, 1978; *Area:* 2,456.51 sq km
Population in 2006: 976
Next Election: Oct 2010; staggered 2 yr term

Parkdale No. 498
P.O. Box 310
Glaslyn, SK S0M 0Y0
306-342-2015 Fax: 306-342-4442
rm498@sasktel.ca
saskbiz.ca/communityprofiles/CommunityProfile.Asp?CommunityID=944
Municipal Type: Rural Municipality
Incorporated: Jan. 1, 1913; *Area:* 1,388.91 sq km
Population in 2006: 711
Next Election: Oct 2010; staggered 2 yr term
Daniel W. Hicks, Reeve
Linda Sandwick, Administrator

Paynton No. 470
P.O. Box 10
Paynton, SK S0M 2J0
306-895-2020 Fax: 306-895-4800
rm470@sasktel.net
Municipal Type: Rural Municipality
Incorporated: Jan. 1, 1913; *Area:* 593.95 sq km
Population in 2006: 254
Next Election: Oct 2010; staggered 2 yr term
Nicole Walker, Administrator
Don Ferguson, Reeve

Pense No. 160
P.O. Box 190
324 Elder St.
Pense, SK S0G 3W0
306-345-2303 Fax: 306-345-2583
rm160@sasktel.net
www.pense160.ca
Municipal Type: Rural Municipality
Incorporated: Jan. 1, 1913; *Area:* 841.48 sq km
Population in 2006: 490
Next Election: Oct 2010; staggered 2 yr term
Tom Lemon, Reeve
Carolynn Meadows, Administrator

Perdue No. 346
P.O. Box 208
Perdue, SK S0K 3C0
306-237-4202 Fax: 306-237-4202
rm346@sasktel.net
Municipal Type: Rural Municipality
Incorporated: Dec. 13, 1909; *Area:* 826.14 sq km
Population in 2006: 432
Next Election: Oct 2010; staggered 2 yr term
Bill Peters, Reeve
Allan Kirzinger, Administrator

Piapot No. 110
P.O. Box 100
Piapot, SK S0N 1Y0
306-558-2011 Fax: 306-558-2125
rm110@sasktel.net
saskbiz.ca/communityprofiles/CommunityProfile.Asp?CommunityID=948
Municipal Type: Rural Municipality
Incorporated: Dec. 8, 1913; *Area:* 1,912.81 sq km
Population in 2006: 392
Next Election: Oct 2010; staggered 2 yr term
Barry W. Dixon, Administrator
John Wagner, Reeve

Pinto Creek No. 75
P.O. Box 239
Kincaid, SK S0H 2J0
306-264-3277 Fax: 306-264-3254
rm75@sasktel.net
Municipal Type: Rural Municipality
Incorporated: Jan. 1, 1913; *Area:* 845.01 sq km
Population in 2006: 204
Next Election: Oct 2010; staggered 2 yr term
Roxanne Empey, Administrator
R. Alan Snyder, Reeve

Pittville No. 169
P.O. Box 150
Hazlet, SK S0N 1E0
306-678-2131 Fax: 306-678-2132
rm169@sasktel.net
www.hazletsask.com/RM.htm
Municipal Type: Rural Municipality
Incorporated: Jan. 1, 1913; *Area:* 1,258.06 sq km
Population in 2006: 216
Next Election: Oct 2010; staggered 2 yr term
Terry Erdelyan, Administrator
Larry Sletten, Reeve

Pleasant Valley No. 288
P.O. Box 2080
Rosetown, SK S0L 2V0
306-882-4030 Fax: 306-882-4401
rm317@sasktel.net
Municipal Type: Rural Municipality
Incorporated: Dec. 11, 1911; *Area:* 830.53 sq km
Population in 2006: 346
Next Election: Oct 2010; staggered 2 yr term
Jim P. Reiter, Administrator
Jerry Spence, Reeve

Pleasantdale No. 398
P.O. Box 70
Naicam, SK S0K 2Z0
306-874-5732 Fax: 306-874-2225
rm398@sasktel.net
saskbiz.ca/communityprofiles/CommunityProfile.Asp?CommunityID=951
Municipal Type: Rural Municipality
Incorporated: Dec. 11, 1911; *Area:* 757.91 sq km
Population in 2006: 607
Next Election: Oct 2010; staggered 2 yr term
Forrest Pederson, Reeve
Lowell Prefontaine, Administrator

Ponass Lake No. 367
P.O. Box 98
Rose Valley, SK S0E 1M0
306-322-2162 Fax: 306-322-2168
rm367@sasktel.net
saskbiz.ca/communityprofiles/CommunityProfile.Asp?CommunityID=953
Municipal Type: Rural Municipality
Incorporated: Jan. 1, 1913; *Area:* 770.21 sq km
Population in 2006: 618
Next Election: Oct 2010; staggered 2 yr term
Allan Nelson, Reeve
Bonnie W. Lengyel, Administrator

Poplar Valley No. 12
P.O. Box 190
Rockglen, SK S0H 3R0
306-476-2062 Fax: 306-476-2175
rm12@sasktel.net
Municipal Type: Rural Municipality
Incorporated: Jan. 1, 1913; *Area:* 769.37 sq km
Population in 2006: 245
Next Election: Oct 2010; staggered 2 yr term
Carol Allingham, Administrator
Nairn Nielsen, Reeve

Porcupine No. 395
P.O. Box 190
Porcupine Plain, SK S0E 1H0
306-278-2368 Fax: 306-278-3473
rm395@sasktel.net
saskbiz.ca/communityprofiles/CommunityProfile.Asp?CommunityID=955
Municipal Type: Rural Municipality
Incorporated: Feb. 28, 1944; *Area:* 2,339.96 sq km
Population in 2006: 949
Next Election: Oct 2010; staggered 2 yr term
Wes Black, Reeve
Shandy Wegwitz, Administrator

Prairie Rose No. 309
P.O. Box 89
Main St.
Jansen, SK S0K 2B0
306-364-2013 Fax: 306-364-2088
rm309@sasktel.net
www.jansen.ca
Municipal Type: Rural Municipality
Incorporated: Dec. 12, 1910; *Area:* 839.08 sq km
Population in 2006: 292
Next Election: Oct 2010; staggered 2 yr term
Dennis C. McBurney, Administrator
Bruce Elke, Reeve
306-364-2077

Prairiedale No. 321
P.O. Box 90
Smiley, SK S0L 2Z0
306-838-2020 Fax: 306-838-4343
rm321@sasktel.net
saskbiz.ca/communityprofiles/CommunityProfile.Asp?CommunityID=956
Municipal Type: Rural Municipality
Incorporated: Dec. 13, 1909; *Area:* 546.74 sq km
Population in 2006: 271
Next Election: Oct 2010; staggered 2 yr term
Lee Torrance, Administrator
Tim Richelhoff, Reeve

Preeceville No. 334
P.O. Box 439
Preeceville, SK S0A 3B0
306-547-2029 Fax: 306-547-2081
rm334@sasktel.net
saskbiz.ca/communityprofiles/CommunityProfile.Asp?CommunityID=958
Municipal Type: Rural Municipality
Incorporated: Jan. 1, 1913; *Area:* 1,394.80 sq km
Population in 2006: 960
Next Election: Oct 2010; staggered 2 yr term
Earl Pottle, Reeve
Lynn Larsen, Administrator

Prince Albert No. 461
99 River St. East
Prince Albert, SK S6V 0A1
306-763-2469 Fax: 306-763-6369
rm461@sasktel.net
www.rmprincealbert.ca
Municipal Type: Rural Municipality
Incorporated: Dec. 9, 1912; *Area:* 1,019.01 sq km
Population in 2006: 2,918
Next Election: Oct 2010; staggered 2 yr term
Leonard Blocka, Reeve
Terry-Lynn Zahara, Administrator

Progress No. 351
P.O. Box 130
Luseland, SK S0L 2A0
306-372-4322 Fax: 306-372-4700
rm351@sasktel.net
Municipal Type: Rural Municipality
Incorporated: Dec. 12, 1910; *Area:* 803.09 sq km
Population in 2006: 289
Next Election: Oct 2010; staggered 2 yr term
Lynne Tolley, Administrator
Dennis Gintaut, Reeve

Reciprocity No. 32
P.O. Box 70
Alida, SK S0C 0B0
306-443-2212 Fax: 306-443-2287
rm.of.reciprocity@sasktel.net
www.creda.sk.ca/reciprocity
Municipal Type: Rural Municipality
Incorporated: Dec. 11, 1911; *Area:* 733.06 sq km
Population in 2006: 352
Next Election: Oct 2010; staggered 2 yr term
Kathy Anthony, Administrator
Alan Arthur, Reeve

Redberry No. 435
P.O. Box 160
Hafford, SK S0J 1A0
306-549-2333 Fax: 306-549-2435
rm435@sasktel.net
saskbiz.ca/communityprofiles/CommunityProfile.Asp?CommunityID=962
Municipal Type: Rural Municipality
Incorporated: Jan. 1, 1913; *Area:* 1,015.53 sq km
Population in 2006: 451
Next Election: Oct 2010; staggered 2 yr term
Victor Hupaelo, Reeve
Alan Tanchak, Administrator

Redburn No. 130
P.O. Box 250
Rouleau, SK S0G 4H0
306-776-2270 Fax: 306-776-2482
redrou@sasktel.net
Municipal Type: Rural Municipality
Incorporated: Jan. 1, 1913; *Area:* 847.91 sq km
Population in 2006: 245
Next Election: Oct 2010; staggered 2 yr term
Jacquelin Dobson, Administrator
Arnold Cornea, Reeve

Reford No. 379
P.O. Box 100
Wilkie, SK S0K 4W0
306-843-2342 Fax: 306-843-2455
rm409@sasktel.net
Municipal Type: Rural Municipality
Incorporated: Dec. 12, 1910; *Area:* 707.06 sq km
Population in 2006: 296
Next Election: Oct 2010; staggered 2 yr term
Sherry Huber, Administrator
Charles Robert Clay, Reeve

Reno No. 51
P.O. Box 90
Consul, SK S0N 0P0
306-299-2133 Fax: 306-299-4433
rm51@sasktel.net
Municipal Type: Rural Municipality
Incorporated: Dec. 11, 1911; *Area:* 3,460.66 sq km
Population in 2006: 462
Next Election: Oct 2010; staggered 2 yr term
Brian McMillan, Reeve
Kim Lacelle, Administrator

Riverside No. 168
P.O. Box 129
Pennant, SK S0N 1X0
306-626-3255 Fax: 306-626-3661
rmriverside168@xplornet.com
saskbiz.ca/communityprofiles/CommunityProfile.Asp?CommunityID=966
Municipal Type: Rural Municipality
Incorporated: Jan. 1, 1913; *Area:* 1,295.21 sq km
Population in 2006: 511
Next Election: Oct 2010; staggered 2 yr term
Richard Bye, Reeve
Brandi Trembath, Administrator

Rocanville No. 151
P.O. Box 298
Rocanville, SK S0A 3L0
306-645-2055 Fax: 306-645-2697
rm151@sasktel.net
Municipal Type: Rural Municipality
Incorporated: Dec. 9, 1912; *Area:* 758.64 sq km
Population in 2006: 554
Next Election: Oct 2010; staggered 2 yr term
Murray D. Reid, Reeve
Sylvia Anderson, Administrator

Rodgers No. 133
P.O. Box 70
Courval, SK S0H 1A0
306-394-4305 Fax: 306-394-4305
rm133@sasktel.net
saskbiz.ca/communityprofiles/CommunityProfile.Asp?CommunityID=968
Municipal Type: Rural Municipality
Incorporated: Dec. 9, 1912; *Area:* 719.80 sq km
Population in 2006: 115
Next Election: Oct 2010; staggered 2 yr term
Linda K. Coates, Administrator
Lawrence Johnstone, Reeve

Rosedale No. 283
P.O. Box 150
107 Lincoln St.
Hanley, SK S0G 2E0
306-544-2202 Fax: 306-544-2252
rm283@sasktel.net
Municipal Type: Rural Municipality
Incorporated: Dec. 13, 1909; *Area:* 921.50 sq km
Population in 2006: 455
Next Election: Oct 2010; staggered 2 yr term
Nick Patkau, Reeve
Paulette Wolkowski, Administrator

Rosemount No. 378
P.O. Box 184
Landis, SK S0K 2K0
306-658-2034 Fax: 306-658-2034
rm378@sasktel.net
Municipal Type: Rural Municipality
Incorporated: Dec. 12, 1910; *Area:* 571.35 sq km
Population in 2006: 230
Next Election: Oct 2010; staggered 2 yr term
Kara Kirilenko, Administrator
A. Ed Egert, Reeve

Rosthern No. 403
P.O. Box 126
2022 - 6th St.
Rosthern, SK S0K 3R0
306-232-4393 Fax: 306-232-5321
rm403@sasktel.net
www.rmofrosthern.ca
Municipal Type: Rural Municipality
Incorporated: Dec. 9, 1912; *Area:* 954.66 sq km
Population in 2006: 1,840
Next Election: Oct 2010; staggered 2 yr term
Bruce K. Fehr, Reeve
James F. Spriggs, Administrator

Round Hill No. 467
P.O. Box 9
Rabbit Lake, SK S0M 2L0
306-824-2044 Fax: 306-824-2044
rm467@sasktel.net
Municipal Type: Rural Municipality
Incorporated: Dec. 11, 1911; *Area:* 815.21 sq km
Population in 2006: 374
Next Election: Oct 2010; staggered 2 yr term
Cindy Miller, Administrator
Henry Siemens, Reeve

Round Valley No. 410
P.O. Box 538
Unity, SK S0K 4L0
306-228-2248 Fax: 306-228-3483
rm410@sasktel.net
saskbiz.ca/communityprofiles/CommunityProfile.Asp?CommunityID=973
Municipal Type: Rural Municipality
Incorporated: Dec. 13, 1909; *Area:* 810.57 sq km
Population in 2006: 355
Next Election: Oct 2010; staggered 2 yr term
Mervin Bosch, Administrator
Francis Boskill, Reeve

Rudy No. 284
P.O. Box 1010
400 Saskatchewan Ave. West
Outlook, SK S0L 2N0
306-867-9349 Fax: 306-867-9898
rmrudy@sasktel.net
www.rmrudy.ca
Municipal Type: Rural Municipality
Incorporated: Dec. 13, 1909; *Area:* 813.86 sq km
Population in 2006: 434
Next Election: Oct 2010; staggered 2 yr term
D. Wayne Vaxvick, Reeve
Trent Michelman, Administrator

St. Andrews No. 287
P.O. Box 488
Rosetown, SK S0L 2V0
306-882-2314 Fax: 306-882-3287
rm.287@sasktel.net
Municipal Type: Rural Municipality
Incorporated: Dec. 12, 1910; *Area:* 805.30 sq km
Population in 2006: 582
Next Election: Oct 2010; staggered 2 yr term
Garry Nisbet, Reeve
Joan Babecy, Administrator

St. Louis No. 431
P.O. Box 28
Hoey, SK S0J 1E0
306-422-6170 Fax: 306-422-8520
rm431@sasktel.net
Municipal Type: Rural Municipality
Incorporated: Jan. 1, 1913; *Area:* 790.18 sq km
Population in 2006: 1,006
Next Election: Oct 2010; staggered 2 yr term
Henry Gareau, Reeve
Louise Hodgson, Administrator

St. Peter No. 369
P.O. Box 70
Annaheim, SK S0K 0G0
306-598-2122 Fax: 306-598-4526
rm369@sasktel.net
Municipal Type: Rural Municipality
Incorporated: Dec. 11, 1911; *Area:* 823.22 sq km
Population in 2006: 901
Next Election: Oct 2010; staggered 2 yr term
Danny Breker, Reeve
Brenda Nagy, Administrator

St. Philips No. 301
P.O. Box 220
Pelly, SK S0A 2Z0
306-595-2050 Fax: 306-595-2050
town.pelly@sasktel.net
Municipal Type: Rural Municipality
Incorporated: Jan. 1, 1913; *Area:* 655.79 sq km
Population in 2006: 258
Next Election: Oct 2010; staggered 2 yr term
Victoria Makohoniuk, Administrator
Ron Sorrell, Reeve

Saltcoats No. 213
P.O. Box 150
Saltcoats, SK S0A 3R0

306-744-2202 Fax: 306-744-2455
rm.saltcoats@sasktel.net
Municipal Type: Rural Municipality
Incorporated: Dec. 9, 1912; *Area:* 830.58 sq km
Population in 2006: 746
Next Election: Oct 2010; staggered 2 yr term
Don Taylor, Reeve
Ronald R. Risling, Administrator

Sarnia No. 221
P.O. Box 160
Roberts St.
Holdfast, SK S0G 2H0
306-488-2033 Fax: 306-488-4609
rm.sarnia@sasktel.net
Municipal Type: Rural Municipality
Incorporated: Dec. 13, 1909; *Area:* 870.11 sq km
Population in 2006: 254
Next Election: Oct 2010; staggered 2 yr term
John H.J. Eberl, Administrator
Brian Gottselig, Reeve

Saskatchewan Landing No. 167
P.O. Box 40
Stewart Valley, SK S0N 2P0
306-778-2105 Fax: 306-778-2152
rm167@sasktel.net
Municipal Type: Rural Municipality
Incorporated: Jan. 1, 1913; *Area:* 797.52 sq km
Population in 2006: 480
Next Election: Oct 2010; staggered 2 yr term
Dan Barber, Reeve
Larry Wightman, Administrator

Sasman No. 336
P.O. Box 130
Kuroki, SK S0A 1Y0
306-338-2263 Fax: 306-338-2048
rm336@yourlink.ca
saskbiz.ca/communityprofiles/CommunityProfile.Asp?CommunityID=982
Municipal Type: Rural Municipality
Incorporated: Jan. 1, 1913; *Area:* 1,006.49 sq km
Population in 2006: 960
Next Election: Oct 2010; staggered 2 yr term
Borden Woloshyn, Reeve
Lynette Figeland, Administrator

Scott No. 98
P.O. Box 210
Yellow Grass, SK S0G 5J0
306-465-2512 Fax: 306-465-2802
rm98@signaldirect.ca
Municipal Type: Rural Municipality
Incorporated: Dec. 13, 1909; *Area:* 850.08 sq km
Population in 2006: 176
Next Election: Oct 2010; staggered 2 yr term
Paul P. Thiele, Administrator
Douglas Watson, Reeve

Senlac No. 411
P.O. Box 130
Senlac, SK S0L 2Y0
306-228-3339 Fax: 306-228-2264
rm411@sasktel.net
Municipal Type: Rural Municipality
Incorporated: Jan. 1, 1913; *Area:* 1,026.25 sq km
Population in 2006: 225
Next Election: Oct 2010; staggered 2 yr term
Lois Haug, Administrator
Della Purser, Reeve

Shamrock No. 134
P.O. Box 40
Shamrock, SK S0H 3W0
306-648-3594 Fax: 306-648-3687
rm134@sasktel.net
www.shamrockpark.ca/html/rm134.html
Municipal Type: Rural Municipality
Incorporated: Dec. 9, 1912; *Area:* 757.52 sq km
Population in 2006: 226
Next Election: Oct 2010; staggered 2 yr term
Jody Kennedy, Administrator
Dwayne James, Reeve

Shellbrook No. 493
P.O. Box 40
Shellbrook, SK S0J 2E0
306-747-2177 Fax: 306-747-3111
rm493@sasktel.net
www.shellbrook.net
Municipal Type: Rural Municipality
Incorporated: Jan. 1, 1913; *Area:* 1,237.29 sq km
Population in 2006: 1,636
Next Election: Oct 2010; staggered 2 yr term
Robert Strube, Reeve
Tara Kerber, Administrator

Sherwood No. 159
1840 Cornwall St.
Regina, SK S4P 2K2
306-525-5237 Fax: 306-352-1760
admin@rmsherwood.ca
www.rmofsherwood.ca
Municipal Type: Rural Municipality
Incorporated: Dec. 11, 1911; *Area:* 719.32 sq km
Population in 2006: 1,075
Next Election: Oct 2010; staggered 2 yr term
Douglas Harle, Reeve
Ron Hilton, Administrator

Silverwood No. 123
P.O. Box 700
Whitewood, SK S0G 5C0
306-735-2500 Fax: 306-735-2524
rm123@sasktel.net
Municipal Type: Rural Municipality
Incorporated: Oct. 31, 1911; *Area:* 844.61 sq km
Population in 2006: 449
Next Election: Oct 2010; staggered 2 yr term
William MacPherson, Reeve
Jennalee Beutler, Administrator

Sliding Hills No. 273
P.O. Box 70
Mikado, SK S0A 2R0
306-563-5285 Fax: 306-563-4447
slidinghills_rm273@sasktel.net
Municipal Type: Rural Municipality
Incorporated: Jan. 1, 1913; *Area:* 853.76 sq km
Population in 2006: 462
Next Election: Oct 2010; staggered 2 yr term
Harvey Malanowich, Reeve
Todd Steele, Administrator

Snipe Lake No. 259
P.O. Box 786
Eston, SK S0L 1A0
306-962-3214 Fax: 306-962-4330
rm259admin@sasktel.net
Municipal Type: Rural Municipality
Incorporated: Dec. 11, 1911; *Area:* 1,573.80 sq km
Population in 2006: 427
Next Election: Oct 2010; staggered 2 yr term
T. A. (Ted) Koester, Reeve
Debbie Shaw, Administrator

Souris Valley No. 7
P.O. Box 40
Oungre, SK S0C 1Z0
306-456-2676 Fax: 306-456-2480
rm07@eclipsewireless.ca
Municipal Type: Rural Municipality
Incorporated: Dec. 13, 1909; *Area:* 817.52 sq km
Population in 2006: 230
Next Election: Oct 2010; staggered 2 yr term
Jo Ann Larsen, Administrator
Dallas Pederson, Reeve

South Qu'Appelle No. 157
P.O. Box 66
Qu'Appelle, SK S0G 4A0
306-699-2257 Fax: 306-699-2856
rm157@sasktel.net
www.rm157.ca
Municipal Type: Rural Municipality
Incorporated: Aug. 6, 1884; *Area:* 889.73 sq km
Population in 2006: 1,066
Next Election: Oct 2010; staggered 2 yr term
Ken MacPherson, Reeve
Brian Shauf, Administrator

Spalding No. 368
P.O. Box 10
Spalding, SK S0K 4C0
306-872-2166 Fax: 306-872-2275
bob368@sasktel.net
saskbiz.ca/communityprofiles/CommunityProfile.Asp?CommunityID=993
Municipal Type: Rural Municipality
Incorporated: Dec. 11, 1911; *Area:* 811.47 sq km
Population in 2006: 425
Next Election: Oct 2010; staggered 2 yr term
Eugene Eggerman, Reeve
Cathy Holt, Administrator

Spiritwood No. 496
P.O. Box 340
Spiritwood, SK S0J 2M0
306-883-2034 Fax: 306-883-2557
rm496@sasktel.net
Municipal Type: Rural Municipality
Incorporated: Dec. 9, 1929; *Area:* 2,410.62 sq km
Population in 2006: 1,277
Next Election: Oct 2010; staggered 2 yr term
Grant Cadieu, Reeve
Gloria Teer, Administrator

Spy Hill No. 152
P.O. Box 129
Spy Hill, SK S0A 3W0
306-534-2022 Fax: 306-534-2230
rm152@sasktel.net
Municipal Type: Rural Municipality
Incorporated: Dec. 11, 1911; *Area:* 679.28 sq km
Population in 2006: 365
Next Election: Oct 2010; staggered 2 yr term
Carey Nicholauson, Administrator
Bernard Mikolas, Reeve

Stanley No. 215
P.O. Box 70
238 - 3rd Ave. West
Melville, SK S0A 2P0
306-728-2818 Fax: 306-728-2818
rm.ofstanley@sasktel.net
www.spreda.sk.ca/community_RM_of_Stanley.htm
Municipal Type: Rural Municipality
Incorporated: Jan. 1, 1913; *Area:* 855.40 sq km
Population in 2006: 509
Next Election: Oct 2010; staggered 2 yr term
Kenneth Petlock, Reeve
Marie Steiner, Administrator

Star City No. 428
P.O. Box 370
Star City, SK S0E 1P0
306-863-2522 Fax: 306-863-2255
r.m.starcity@sasktel.ca
saskbiz.ca/communityprofiles/CommunityProfile.Asp?CommunityID=997
Municipal Type: Rural Municipality
Incorporated: Jan. 1, 1913; *Area:* 824.85 sq km
Population in 2006: 936
Next Election: Oct 2010; staggered 2 yr term
Kenneth Naber, Reeve
Ann T. Campbell, Administrator

Stonehenge No. 73
P.O. Box 129
Limerick, SK S0H 2P0
306-263-2020 Fax: 306-263-2013
rm73@sasktel.net
Municipal Type: Rural Municipality
Incorporated: Dec. 11, 1911; *Area:* 985.74 sq km
Population in 2006: 442
Next Election: Oct 2010; staggered 2 yr term
Kelvin Ruzicka, Reeve
Tammy A. Franks, Administrator

Storthoaks No. 31
P.O. Box 40
Storthoaks, SK S0C 2K0
306-449-2262 Fax: 306-449-2210
rm31@sasktel.net
www.creda.sk.ca/storthoaks
Municipal Type: Rural Municipality
Incorporated: Dec. 11, 1911; *Area:* 582.57 sq km
Population in 2006: 312
Next Election: Oct 2010; staggered 2 yr term
Erin McMillen, Administrator
James E. Lorette, Reeve

Surprise Valley No. 9
P.O. Box 52
Minton, SK S0C 1T0
306-969-2144 Fax: 306-969-2127
rm.09@sasktel.net
Municipal Type: Rural Municipality
Incorporated: Jan. 1, 1913; *Area:* 813.38 sq km
Population in 2006: 199
Next Election: Oct 2010; staggered 2 yr term
Note: URL:
www.saskbiz.ca/communityprofiles/CommunityProfile.Asp?CommunityID=1000
Joyce Axten, Administrator
Herb Axten, Reeve

Sutton No. 103
P.O. Box 100
Mossbank, SK S0H 3G0
306-354-2414 Fax: 306-354-7725
rm102.103@sasktel.net
Municipal Type: Rural Municipality
Incorporated: Dec. 11, 1911; *Area:* 822.40 sq km
Population in 2006: 294
Next Election: Oct 2010; staggered 2 yr term
Sherry D. Green, Administrator
Richard Nagel, Reeve

Swift Current No. 137
2024 South Service Rd. West
Swift Current, SK S9H 5J5
306-773-7314 Fax: 306-773-9538
rmsc137@sasktel.net
Municipal Type: Rural Municipality
Incorporated: Dec. 12, 1910; *Area:* 1,107.7 sq km
Population in 2006: 1,587
Next Election: Oct 2010; staggered 2 yr term
James W. Parsons, Reeve
Dave E. Dmytruk, Administrator

Tecumseh No. 65
P.O. Box 300
Stoughton, SK S0G 4T0
306-457-2277 Fax: 306-457-3149
rmtec@sasktel.net
www.creda.sk.ca/tecumseh
Municipal Type: Rural Municipality
Incorporated: Dec. 13, 1909; *Area:* 826.11 sq km
Population in 2006: 270
Next Election: Oct 2010; staggered 2 yr term
Zandra Slater, Administrator
Hugh Goudy, Reeve

Terrell No. 101
P.O. Box 60
Spring Valley, SK S0H 3X0
306-475-2803 Fax: 306-475-2805
street101@sasktel.net
Municipal Type: Rural Municipality
Incorporated: Jan. 1, 1913; *Area:* 864.06 sq km
Population in 2006: 257
Next Election: Oct 2010; staggered 2 yr term
Lloyd Muma, Administrator
M. Owen Labuik, Reeve

The Gap No. 39
P.O. Box 188
Ceylon, SK S0C 0T0
306-454-2202 Fax: 306-454-2627
rmgap39@sasktel.net
Municipal Type: Rural Municipality
Incorporated: Dec. 12, 1903; *Area:* 830.92 sq km
Population in 2006: 245
Next Election: Oct 2010; staggered 2 yr term
Yvonne Johnston, Administrator
Keith Kaufmann, Reeve

Three Lakes No. 400
P.O. Box 100
Middle Lake, SK S0K 2X0
306-367-2172 Fax: 306-367-2011
rm400@sasktel.net
Municipal Type: Rural Municipality
Incorporated: Jan. 1, 1913; *Area:* 772.49 sq km
Population in 2006: 659
Next Election: Oct 2010; staggered 2 yr term
Allen Baumann, Reeve
Tim Schmidt, Administrator

Tisdale No. 427
P.O. Box 128
Tisdale, SK S0E 1T0
306-873-2334 Fax: 306-873-4442
rm427@sasktel.net
Municipal Type: Rural Municipality
Incorporated: Dec. 9, 1912; *Area:* 849.24 sq km
Population in 2006: 938
Next Election: Oct 2010; staggered 2 yr term
Robert C. Jackson, Reeve
Terry Hvidston, Administrator

Torch River No. 488
P.O. Box 40
White Fox, SK S0J 3B0
306-276-2066 Fax: 306-276-2099
rm488@sasktel.net
Municipal Type: Rural Municipality
Incorporated: Jan. 1, 1950; *Area:* 5,179 sq km
Population in 2006: 1,559
Next Election: Oct 2010; staggered 2 yr term
Note: URL:
www.saskbiz.ca/communityprofiles/CommunityProfile.Asp?CommunityID=1008
Dennis Scott, Reeve
Wendy Nycholat, Administrator

Touchwood No. 248
P.O. Box 160
Punnichy, SK S0A 3C0
306-835-2110 Fax: 306-835-2100
rm248@aski.ca
Municipal Type: Rural Municipality
Incorporated: Dec. 12, 1910; *Area:* 706.72 sq km
Population in 2006: 287
Next Election: Oct 2010; staggered 2 yr term
Lorelei Paulsen, Administrator
Larry Dosdall, Reeve

Tramping Lake No. 380
P.O. Box 129
104 Main St.
Scott, SK S0K 4A0
306-247-2033 Fax: 306-247-2055
rmtrampinglake@xplornet.com
Municipal Type: Rural Municipality
Incorporated: Dec. 12, 1910; *Area:* 615.56 sq km
Population in 2006: 403
Next Election: Oct 2010; staggered 2 yr term
Peter Volk, Reeve
Stacy Hawkins, Administrator

Tullymet No. 216
P.O. Box 190
Balcarres, SK S0G 0C0
306-334-2366 Fax: 306-334-2930
rm216@sasktel.net
Municipal Type: Rural Municipality
Incorporated: Jan. 1, 1913; *Area:* 562.99 sq km
Population in 2006: 245
Next Election: Oct 2010; staggered 2 yr term
Sheila Keisig, Administrator
Larry Jankoski, Reeve

Turtle River No. 469
P.O. Box 128
Edam, SK S0M 0V0
306-397-2311 Fax: 306-397-2346
rm469@sasktel.net
Municipal Type: Rural Municipality
Incorporated: Dec. 9, 1912; *Area:* 664.49 sq km
Population in 2006: 336
Next Election: Oct 2010; staggered 2 yr term
Joseph McMurphy, Administrator
Louis McCaffrey, Reeve

Usborne No. 310
P.O. Box 310
Lanigan, SK S0K 2M0
306-365-2924 Fax: 306-365-2129
rm310@sasktel.net
Municipal Type: Rural Municipality
Incorporated: Dec. 13, 1909; *Area:* 810.38 sq km
Population in 2006: 566
Next Election: Oct 2010; staggered 2 yr term
Don Bowman, Reeve
Keith Schulze, Administrator

Val Marie No. 17
P.O. Box 59
Val Marie, SK S0N 2T0
306-298-2009 Fax: 306-298-2224
rm17@sasktel.net
Municipal Type: Rural Municipality
Incorporated: Jan. 1, 1969; *Area:* 3,105.26 sq km
Population in 2006: 479
Next Election: Oct 2010; staggered 2 yr term
Mike Waldner, Reeve
Cathy Legault, Administrator

Vanscoy No. 345
P.O. Box 187
Vanscoy, SK S0L 3J0
306-668-2060 Fax: 306-668-1338
rm345@sasktel.net
Municipal Type: Rural Municipality
Incorporated: Dec. 13, 1909; *Area:* 866.68 sq km
Population in 2006: 2,629
Next Election: Oct 2010; staggered 2 yr term
Floyd Chapple, Reeve
Shawn Antosh, Administrator

Victory No. 226
P.O. Box 100
Beechy, SK S0L 0C0
306-859-2270 Fax: 306-859-2271
rm.226@yourlink.ca
Municipal Type: Rural Municipality
Incorporated: Dec. 8, 1919; *Area:* 1,375.44 sq km
Population in 2006: 428
Next Election: Oct 2010; staggered 2 yr term
Wes Jansen, Reeve
Diane Watt, Administrator

Viscount No. 341
P.O. Box 100
215 Bangor Ave.
Viscount, SK S0K 4M0
306-944-2044 Fax: 306-944-2016
patrm341@sasktel.net
Municipal Type: Rural Municipality
Incorporated: Dec. 13, 1909; *Area:* 831.23 sq km
Population in 2006: 386
Next Election: Oct 2010; staggered 2 yr term
Patrick T. Clavelle, Administrator
Russell Deneiko, Reeve

Wallace No. 243
26 - 5 Ave. North
Yorkton, SK S3N 0Y8
306-782-2455 Fax: 306-782-5177
wallace@sasktel.net
Municipal Type: Rural Municipality
Incorporated: Dec. 11, 1911; *Area:* 832.01 sq km
Population in 2006: 901
Next Election: Oct 2010; staggered 2 yr term
Garry Liebrecht, Reeve
Kim Waddell, Administrator

Walpole No. 92
P.O. Box 117
Wawota, SK S0G 5A0
306-739-2545 Fax: 306-739-2777
rm92@sasktel.net
Municipal Type: Rural Municipality
Incorporated: Dec. 12, 1910; *Area:* 844.66 sq km
Population in 2006: 348
Next Election: Oct 2010; staggered 2 yr term
Rhonda M. Hall, Administrator
Denis Lamontagne, Reeve

Waverley No. 44
P.O. Box 70
Glentworth, SK S0H 1V0
306-266-4920 Fax: 306-266-2077
rm44@yourlink.ca
Municipal Type: Rural Municipality
Incorporated: Feb. 1, 1913; *Area:* 1,429.30 sq km
Population in 2006: 422
Next Election: Oct 2010; staggered 2 yr term
Lloyd Anderson, Reeve
Deidre Downie, Administrator

Wawken No. 93
P.O. Box 90
Wawota, SK S0G 5A0
306-739-2332 Fax: 306-739-2222
rm93@sasktel.net
Municipal Type: Rural Municipality
Incorporated: Jan. 1, 1913; *Area:* 766.53 sq km
Population in 2006: 613
Next Election: Oct 2010; staggered 2 yr term
Lester Brickley, Reeve
Debbie Saville, Administrator

Webb No. 138
P.O. Box 100
Webb, SK S0N 2X0
306-674-2230 Fax: 306-674-2324
rm138@xplornet.com
Municipal Type: Rural Municipality
Incorporated: Dec. 13, 1909; *Area:* 1,098.78 sq km
Population in 2006: 556
Next Election: Oct 2010; staggered 2 yr term
Dennis Fiddler, Reeve
Connie A. Sorenson, Administrator

Wellington No. 97
P.O. Box 1390
Weyburn, SK S4H 3J9
306-842-5606 Fax: 306-842-5601
rm97@sasktel.net
Municipal Type: Rural Municipality
Incorporated: Dec. 13, 1909; *Area:* 838.68 sq km
Population in 2006: 357
Next Election: Oct 2010; staggered 2 yr term
Tammie Kwochka, Administrator
Bruce Wagner, Reeve

Wheatlands No. 163
P.O. Box 129
Mortlach, SK S0H 3E0
306-355-2233 Fax: 306-355-2351
rm163@sasktel.net
Municipal Type: Rural Municipality
Incorporated: Dec. 13, 1909; *Area:* 827.4 sq km
Population in 2006: 164
Next Election: Oct 2010; staggered 2 yr term
Elaine Salikin, Administrator
Gary Stirling, Reeve

Whiska Creek No. 106
P.O. Box 10
Vanguard, SK S0N 2V0
306-582-2133 Fax: 306-582-4950
rm106@sasktel.net
Municipal Type: Rural Municipality
Incorporated: Jan. 1, 1913; *Area:* 851.89 sq km
Population in 2006: 520
Next Election: Oct 2010; staggered 2 yr term
Keith Carleton, Reeve
Kathy Countryman, Administrator

White Valley No. 49
P.O. Box 520
Eastend, SK S0N 0T0
306-295-3553 Fax: 306-295-3571
rm49@sasktel.net
Municipal Type: Rural Municipality
Incorporated: Jan. 1, 1913; *Area:* 2,026.88 sq km
Population in 2006: 518
Next Election: Oct 2010; staggered 2 yr term
Note: URL:
www.saskbiz.ca/communityprofiles/CommunityProfile.Asp?CommunityID=1027
Richard Girard, Reeve
Deb Lewis, Administrator

Willner No. 253
P.O. Box 250
Davidson, SK S0G 1A0
306-567-3103 Fax: 306-567-3266
rm253@sasktel.net
Municipal Type: Rural Municipality
Incorporated: Jan. 1, 1913; *Area:* 834.97 sq km
Population in 2006: 254
Next Election: Oct 2010; staggered 2 yr term
Norman Sagen, Administrator
David Greene, Reeve

Willow Bunch No. 42
P.O. Box 220
Willow Bunch, SK S0H 4K0
306-473-2302 Fax: 306-473-2312
rm.42@sasktel.net
Municipal Type: Rural Municipality
Incorporated: Nov. 21, 1912; *Area:* 1,047.8 sq km
Population in 2006: 407
Next Election: Oct 2010; staggered 2 yr term
Kirby David, Reeve
Margaret L. Brown, Administrator

Willow Creek No. 458
P.O. Box 5
Brooksby, SK S0E 0H0
306-863-4143 Fax: 306-863-2366
rm458@sasktel.net

Municipal Type: Rural Municipality
Incorporated: Dec. 9, 1912; *Area:* 845.18 sq km
Population in 2006: 719
Next Election: Oct 2010; staggered 2 yr term
Note: URL:
www.saskbiz.ca/communityprofiles/CommunityProfile.Asp?CommunityID=1030
Mark Miazga, Reeve
Vicki Baptist, Administrator

Willowdale No. 153
P.O. Box 58
Whitewood, SK S0G 5C0
306-735-2344 Fax: 306-735-4495
rm153@sasktel.net
Municipal Type: Rural Municipality
Incorporated: Jan. 1, 1913; *Area:* 605.06 sq km
Population in 2006: 333
Next Election: Oct 2010; staggered 2 yr term
Delsey Roske, Administrator
Kenneth Aldous, Reeve

Wilton No. 472
P.O. Box 40
Marshall, SK S0M 1R0
306-387-6244 Fax: 306-387-6598
rm472@sasktel.net
www.rmwilton.ca
Municipal Type: Rural Municipality
Incorporated: Dec. 13, 1909; *Area:* 1,042.72 sq km
Population in 2006: 1,473
Next Election: Oct 2010; staggered 2 yr term
Glen Dow, Reeve
Darren Elder, Administrator

Winslow No. 319
P.O. Box 310
Dodsland, SK S0L 0V0
306-356-2106 Fax: 306-356-2085
rmwinslow319@xplornet.com
Municipal Type: Rural Municipality
Incorporated: Dec. 13, 1909; *Area:* 798.07 sq km
Population in 2006: 296
Next Election: Oct 2010; staggered 2 yr term
Regan MacDonald, Administrator
Ken MacDonald, Reeve

Wise Creek No. 77
P.O. Box 400
Shaunavon, SK S0N 2M0
306-297-2520 Fax: 306-297-3162
rm77.78@sasktel.net
Municipal Type: Rural Municipality
Incorporated: Jan. 1, 1913; *Area:* 843.85 sq km
Population in 2006: 222
Next Election: Oct 2010; staggered 2 yr term
Grace Potter, Administrator
Frank Dunham, Reeve

Wolseley No. 155
P.O. Box 370
Wolseley, SK S0G 5H0
306-698-2522 Fax: 306-698-2664
rm155@sasktel.net
Municipal Type: Rural Municipality
Incorporated: Dec. 13, 1909; *Area:* 774.26 sq km
Population in 2006: 438
Next Election: Oct 2010; staggered 2 yr term
Edward Dureault, Reeve
Rose Zimmer, Administrator

Wolverine No. 340
P.O. Box 28
Burr, SK S0K 0T0
306-682-3640 Fax: 306-682-3640
rm340@sasktel.net
Municipal Type: Rural Municipality
Incorporated: Dec. 13, 1909; *Area:* 834.78 sq km
Population in 2006: 480
Next Election: Oct 2010; staggered 2 yr term
Bryan Gibney, Reeve
Sandi Dunne, Administrator

Wood Creek No. 281
P.O. Box 10
303 George St.
Simpson, SK S0G 4M0
306-836-2020 Fax: 306-836-4460
rm281@sasktel.net
Municipal Type: Rural Municipality
Incorporated: Dec. 13, 1909; *Area:* 832.34 sq km
Population in 2006: 274
Next Election: Oct 2010; staggered 2 yr term
Darlene Mann, Administrator
Milton Sather, Reeve

Wood River No. 74
P.O. Box 250
35 - 2nd Ave. East
Lafleche, SK S0H 2K0
306-472-5235 Fax: 306-472-3706
rm74@sasktel.net
www.town.lafleche.sk.ca
Municipal Type: Rural Municipality
Incorporated: Dec. 9, 1912; *Area:* 838.45 sq km
Population in 2006: 387
Next Election: Oct 2010; staggered 2 yr term
Louis Genest, Administrator
Duane Filson, Reeve

Wreford No. 280
P.O. Box 99
Nokomis, SK S0G 3R0
306-528-2202 Fax: 306-528-4411
rm280@sasktel.net
Municipal Type: Rural Municipality
Incorporated: Dec. 12, 1910; *Area:* 798.55 sq km
Population in 2006: 175
Next Election: Oct 2010; staggered 2 yr term
Penny O'Carroll, Administrator
Clayton G. Hobman, Reeve

YUKON TERRITORY

LEGISLATION: Municipal Act, Municipal Finance & Community Grants Act, Assessment and Taxation Act.

Requirements for municipal incorporation in the Yukon are based on population: town 300-2,500, city over 2,500. Any community may become a Local Advisory Area, an advisory body to the minister, as a first step in local governance. A community may also incorporate as a Rural Government with limited powers, as a developmental step in becoming a full municipality. The Yukon Municipal Act does not include provisions for unorganized settlements or First Nation communities.

Municipal elections are held every three years and polling day is the third Thursday of October in each election year. Mayors and councillors are elected for a three-year period.

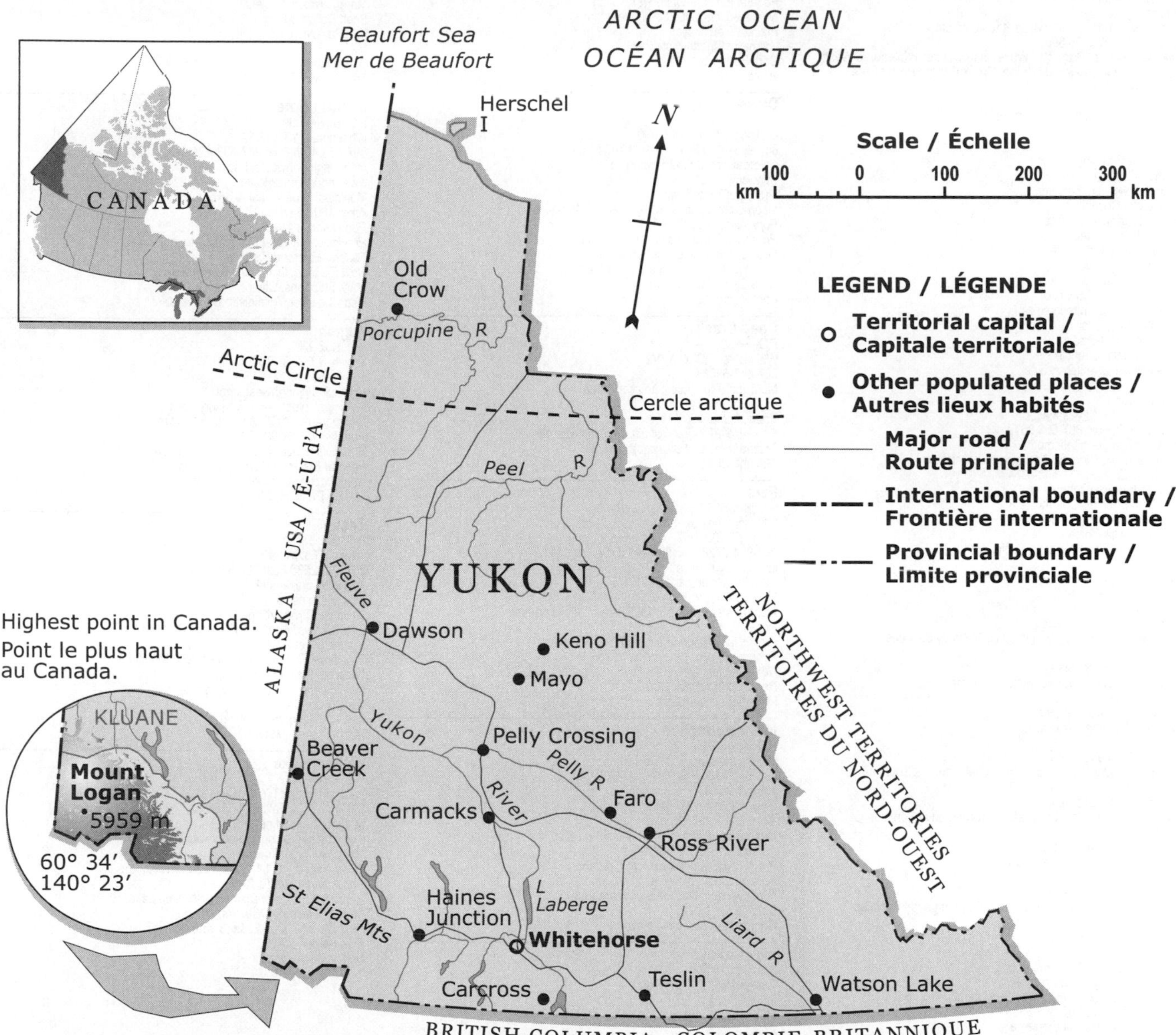

www.atlas.gc.ca

Yukon Territory

Major Municipalities in Yukon Territory

Whitehorse
2121 Second Ave.
Whitehorse, YT Y1A 1C2
867-667-6401 Fax: 867-668-8384
council.services@whitehorse.ca
www.city.whitehorse.yk.ca
Municipal Type: City
Incorporated: June 1, 1950; *Area:* 416.43 sq km
Population in 2009: 25,690
Provincial Electoral District(s): Whitehorse Centre; Whitehorse West; Copperbelt; McIntyre-Takhini; Porter Creek Centre; Porter Creek North; Porter Creek South; Riverdale North; Riverdale South
Federal Electoral District(s): Yukon
Next Election: Oct. 2012 (3 year terms)

Council
Bev Buckway, Mayor
867-668-8626
bev.buckway@whitehorse.ca
Dave Austin, Councillor
dave.austin@whitehorse.ca
Doug Graham, Councillor
doug.graham@whitehorse.ca
Betty Irwin, Councillor
betty.irwin@whitehorse.ca
Florence Roberts, Councillor
florence.roberts@whitehorse.ca
Ranj Pillai, Councillor
ranj.pillai@whitehorse.ca
Dave Stockdale, Councillor
dave.stockdale@whitehorse.ca

Administration
Dennis Shewfelt, City Manager
867-668-8650, Fax: 867-668-8639
dennis.shewfelt@whitehorse.ca
Robert Fendrick, Director, Administrative Services
867-668-8612, Fax: 867-668-8384
robert.fendrick@whitehorse.ca
Brian Crist, Director, Operations
867-668-8301, Fax: 867-668-8386
brian.crist@whitehorse.ca
James D. MacLeod, Manager, Public Works
867-668-8351
james.mcleod@Whitehorse.ca
Clive Sparks, Fire Chief
867-668-8383
clive.sparks@whitehorse.ca
George White, Manager, Maintenance & Safety Services
867-668-8345
george.white@whitehorse.ca
Mike Stevely, Manager, Information Systems
867-334-2100
mike.stevely@whitehorse.ca
Dave Muir, Manager, Transit
867-668-8391
dave.muir@whitehorse.ca
Sheila Dodd, Supervisor, Economic Development & Tourism
867-668-8660
sheila.dodd@whitehorse.ca
Sabine Schweiger, Co-Coordinator, Environmental Services
867-668-8312
environment@whitehorse.ca
John Taylor, Manager, Bylaw Services
867-668-8318
john.taylor@whitehorse.ca
Wayne Tuck, Manager, Engineering & Environmental Services
867-668-8306
wayne.tuck@whitehorse.ca
Linda Rapp, Manager, Parks & Recreation
867-668-8325, Fax: 867-668-8675
parks.recreation@whitehorse.ca
Mike Gau, Manager, Planning & Development Services
867-668-8333, Fax: 867-668-8395
planning.services@whitehorse.ca
Pippa McNeil, Co-Coordinator, Environmental Services
867-668-8312
environment@whitehorse.ca
Ray Osborne, Supervisor, Utility Stations
867-668-8669
ray.osborne@whitehorse.ca

Other Municipalities in Yukon Territory

Carcross
P.O. Box 130
Carcross, YT Y0B 1B0
867-821-4251 Fax: 867-668-4802
pat.hiebert@ctfn.ca
www.ctfn.ca
Municipal Type: Local Advisory Area
Incorporated: 2005; *Area:* 15.96 sq km
Population in 2006: 331
Provincial Electoral District(s): Southern Lakes
Federal Electoral District(s): Yukon
Next Election: Oct. 2009 (3 year terms)
Darla Jean Lindstrom, Acting Director

Carmacks
P.O. Box 113
Carmacks, YT Y0B 1C0
867-863-6271 Fax: 867-863-6606
carmacks@northwestel.net
www.carmacks.ca
Municipal Type: Village
Incorporated: Nov. 1, 1984; *Area:* 36.90 sq km
Population in 2006: 425
Provincial Electoral District(s): Mayo-Tatchun
Federal Electoral District(s): Yukon
Next Election: Oct. 2009 (3 year terms)
Elaine Wyatt, Mayor
vocmayor@northwestel.net
Cory Bellmore, CAO
voccao@northwestel.net

Dawson City
P.O. Box 308
Dawson City, YT Y0B 1G0
867-993-7400 Fax: 867-993-7434
cityofdawson@cityofdawson.ca
www.dawsoncity.ca
Municipal Type: Town
Incorporated: Jan. 9, 1902; *Area:* 32.45 sq km
Population in 2006: 1,327
Provincial Electoral District(s): Klondike
Federal Electoral District(s): Yukon
Next Election: Oct. 2009 (3 year terms)
John Steins, Mayor
Paul Moore, CAO

Deep Creek
P.O. Box 20264
Whitehorse, YT Y1A 7V2
867-667-6966
Municipal Type: Local Advisory Area

Population in 2006: 150
Provincial Electoral District(s): Lake LaBerge
Federal Electoral District(s): Yukon
Vacant, Chair

Faro
P.O. Box 580
200 Campbell St.
Faro, YT Y0B 1K0
867-994-2728 Fax: 867-994-3154
info@faroyukon.ca
www.faroyukon.ca
Municipal Type: Town
Incorporated: June 13, 1969; *Area:* 203.57 sq km
Population in 2006: 341
Provincial Electoral District(s): Pelly-Nisutlin
Federal Electoral District(s): Yukon
Next Election: Oct. 2009 (3 year terms)
Hermann Minderlein, CAO
Michelle Vainio, Mayor

Haines Junction
P.O. Box 5339
Haines Junction, YT Y0B 1L0
867-634-7100 Fax: 867-634-2008
vhj@yknet.ca
www.hainesjunctionyukon.com
Municipal Type: Village
Incorporated: Oct. 1, 1984; *Area:* 34.08 sq km
Population in 2006: 589
Provincial Electoral District(s): Kluane
Federal Electoral District(s): Yukon
Next Election: Oct. 2009 (3 year terms)
Colin Dean, CAO
George Nassiopoulos, Mayor

Ibex Valley
P.O. Box 20624
Whitehorse, YT Y1A 7A2
867-667-7844
Municipal Type: Local Advisory Area
Area: 209.06 sq km
Population in 2006: 376
Provincial Electoral District(s): Kluane-Lake LaBerge
Federal Electoral District(s): Yukon
Next Election: Oct. 2009 (3 year terms)
Bob Atkins, Chair

Marsh Lake
P.O. Box 1325
Marsh Lake, YT Y0B 1Y1
867-660-5116
marshlakelac@mail.com
www.marshlakeyukon.net
Municipal Type: Local Advisory Area

Population in 2006: 367
Provincial Electoral District(s): Southern Lakes
Federal Electoral District(s): Yukon
Next Election: Oct. 2009 (3 year terms)
Malcolm Taggart, Chair
mtaggart@northwestel.net
Helen Smith, Sec.-Treas.

Mayo
P.O. Box 160
Mayo, YT Y0B 1M0
867-996-2317 Fax: 867-996-2907
mayo@northwestel.net
www.yukonweb.com/community/mayo
Municipal Type: Village
Incorporated: June 1, 1984; *Area:* 0.87 sq km
Population in 2006: 248
Provincial Electoral District(s): Mayo/Tatchun
Federal Electoral District(s): Yukon
Next Election: Oct. 2009 (3 year terms)
Margrit Wozniak, CAO
Scott Bolton, Mayor
Kris Pavlovich, Councillor
Michael McGinnis, Councillor
Dick Ewing, Councillor
Trevor Ellis, Councillor

Mount Lorne
P.O. Box 10009
Whitehorse, YT Y1A 7A1
867-633-4211 Fax: 867-633-4211
mtlorne@northwestel.net
www.mountlorne.yk.net
Municipal Type: Local Advisory Area
Area: 160.15 sq km
Population in 2006: 370
Provincial Electoral District(s): Mount Lorne
Federal Electoral District(s): Yukon
Next Election: Oct. 2009 (3 year terms)
Mark Stephens, Chair
Lisa Chevalier, Administrative Assistant

Tagish
P.O. Box 92
Tagish, YT Y0B 1T0
867-399-3036
tagishclub@northwestel.net
Municipal Type: Local Advisory Area
Incorporated: 2005; *Area:* 43.38 sq km
Population in 2006: 222
Provincial Electoral District(s): Southern Lakes
Federal Electoral District(s): Yukon
Next Election: Oct. 2009 (3 year terms)
Claude Dastous, Chair

Teslin
P.O. Box 32
Teslin, YT Y0A 1B0
867-390-2530 Fax: 867-390-2104
vteslin@northwestel.net
www.teslin.ca
Municipal Type: Village
Incorporated: Aug. 1, 1984; *Area:* 2.22 sq km
Population in 2006: 141
Provincial Electoral District(s): Pelly-Nisutlin
Federal Electoral District(s): Yukon
Next Election: Oct. 2009 (3 year terms)
Wes Wirth, CAO
wes.wirth@northwestel.net
Robin Smarch, Mayor

Watson Lake
P.O. Box 590
Watson Lake, YT Y0A 1C0
867-536-8000 Fax: 867-536-7522
twl@northwestel.net
www.yukoninfo.com/watson/watsonlakeinfo.htm
Municipal Type: Town
Incorporated: April 1, 1984; *Area:* 5.16 sq km
Population in 2006: 846
Provincial Electoral District(s): Watson Lake
Federal Electoral District(s): Yukon
Next Election: Oct. 2009 (3 year terms)
Rick Harder, CAO
Nancy Moore, Mayor

SECTION 9
GOVERNMENT/JUDICIAL

Following the Federal listings, this section is arranged by Province. Within each Province, listings are by type of Court, then by City.

Federal

Supreme Court of Canada

301 Wellington St., Ottawa, ON K1A 0J1

613-995-4330, Fax: 613-996-3063, 888-551-1185, reception@scc-csc.gc.ca; media@scc-csc.gc.ca
www.scc-csc.gc.ca

Other Communications: Teletypewriter: 613-944-7895; Registry, E-mail: registry-greffe@scc-csc.gc.ca; Court Library, E-mail: library-bibliotheque@scc-csc.gc.ca; Tours, E-mail: tour-visite@scc-csc.gc.ca

In 1875, the Supreme Court of Canada was created by an Act of Parliament. The Court is a general court of appeal, which consists of nine judges. The Governor in Council appoints the judges, who remain in the position until the age of seventy-five. There is a Chief Justice of Canada, plus eight puisne judges. A Registrar is also appointed by the Governor in Council. The Registrar is responsible for all the administrative work in the Court, & answers directly to the Chief Justice. There are approximately 200 employees of the Supreme Court. The Supreme Court sits in Ottawa where, each year, three sessions are held. Approximately eighty appeals are heard by the Court every year. The hearings are open to the public. Cases for review come from the provincial & territorial appellate courts & the Federal Court of Appeal, in criminal, civil, constitutional, & administrative law matters. Decisions of the Supreme Court of Canada may be unanimous, or a majority may decide.

Chief Justice of Canada: The Rt. Hon. Madam Chief Justice Beverley McLachlin, 613-992-6940, Fax: 613-952-3092

Puisne Judges (The Honourable Mr. / Madam Justice) Ian Corneil Binnie, Louis LeBel, Marie Deschamps, Morris J. Fish, Rosalie Silberman Abella, Louise Charron, Marshall Rothstein, Thomas Albert Cromwell

Administration:

Registrar: Roger Bilodeau, 613-996-9277, Fax: 613-996-9138

Deputy Registrar: Louise Meagher, 613-996-7521, Fax: 613-941-5817

Director General: Corporate Services Sector, Lynn Potter, 613-996-0429, Fax: 613-947-2860

Director: Library Branch, Rosalie Fox, 613-996-9971, Fax: 613-991-0258

Director: Finance & Administrative Branch, Cathy Gaudet, 613-992-1765, Fax: 613-947-2860

Director: Information Management & Technology, Catherine Laforce, 613-947-0682, Fax: 613-991-0258

Director: Human Resources, Anne-Marie Larivière, 613-995-4224, Fax: 613-996-7266

Director: Security Services Branch, Louis Lahaie, 613-947-3700

Federal Court of Appeal
Cour d'appel fédérale

Courts Administration Service, Ottawa, ON K1A 0H9

613-996-6795, Fax: 613-952-7226, reception@cas-satj.gc.ca (enquiries concerning web site)
www.fca-caf.gc.ca

Other Communications: Text telephone for the hearing impaired: 613-995-4640; Media Enquiries, E-mail: media-fca@fca-caf.gc.ca

The Federal Court of Appeal was established by Parliament in accordance with provision of section 101 of the Constitution Act, 1867. The Court is a bilingual tribunal, which sits & hears cases anywhere in Canada. Both common law & civil law are administered by the Federal Court of Appeal. Decisions of the Federal Court of Appeal impact all Canadians. Responsibilities of the Court include enforcing rights & obligations between Canadians & the federal government, & interpreting & implementing Canada's international obligations.

Chief Justice of the Federal Court of Appeal: The Hon. Pierre Blais, 613-995-5106

Judges (The Hon. Mr. / Madam Justice): Gilles Létourneau(Supernumerary), Marc Noël, Marc Nadon, J. Edgar Sexton(Supernumerary), John Maxwell Evans, Karen Sharlow, J.D. Denis Pelletier, Eleanor R. Dawson, Carolyn Layden-Stevenson, Johanne Trudel, David W. Stratas, Robert M. Mainville

Administration:

Judicial Administrator: Suzelle Bazinet, 613-995-5117, Fax: 613-952-6439

Federal Court
Cour fédérale

Courts Administration Service, 90 Sparks St., Ottawa, ON K1A 0H9

613-992-4238, Fax: 613-952-3653, reception@cas-satj.gc.ca (Web Site Comments)
www.fct-cf.gc.ca

Other Communications: TDD: 613-995-4640; Media Enquiries, E-mail: media-fct@fct-cf.gc.ca

The Federal Court is a trial court. The jurisdiction of the Federal Court is conferred by the Federal Courts Act, as well as close to one hundred other applicable federal statutes. Its broad federal jurisdiction includes the following: Crown litigation, access to information, admiralty & maritime disputes, citizenship, communications, customs, immigration & refugee matters, intellectual property rights, labour relations, national security, parole & penitentiary proceedings, tax, transportation & aeronautics, war veterans, & limited criminal jurisdiction. The Court conducts hearings & renders decisions in disputes anywhere in Canada.

Chief Justice of the Federal Court: The Hon. Mr. Justice Allan Lufty, 613-996-5901, Yvon Pinard(Supernumerary), Sandra J. Simpson, Danièle Tremblay-Lamer(Supernumerary), Douglas R. Campbell, François Lemieux(Supernumerary), John A. O'Keefe, Elizabeth Heneghan, Dolores Hansen, Edmond P. Blanchard, Michael A. Kelen, Michel Beaudry, Luc Martineau, Simon Noël, Judith A. Snider, James Russell, Johanne Gauthier, James W. O'Reilly, Sean J. Harrington, Richard Mosley, Michel M.J. Shore, Michael L. Phelan, Anne L. Mactavish, Yves de Montigny, Roger T. Hughes, Robert L. Barnes, Leonard S. Mandamin, Russel W. Zinn, David G. Near, Richard Boivin, Paul S. Crampton, Marie-Josée Bédard, James K. Hugessen, Max M. Teitelbaum, Frederick E. Gibson, Maurice E. Lagacé, Orville Frenette, Louis S. Tannenbaum

Prothonotaries:

Richard Morneau, 514-496-7840

Roza Aronovitch, 613-947-3356

Roger Lafrenière, 604-666-7435

Mireille Tabib, 613-947-2453

Martha Milczynski, 416-954-9006

Kevin R. Aalto, 416-954-9009

Registrar of the Federal Court: Manon Pitre

Judicial Administrator: Giovanna Calamo, 613-995-1285

Court Martial Appeal Court of Canada
Cour d'Appel de la Cour Mart

Thomas D'Arcy McGee Building, 90 Sparks St., Ottawa, ON K1A 0H9

613-996-6795, Fax: 613-952-7226, reception@cas-satj.gc.ca (Web site enquiries)
www.cmac-cacm.ca

Other Communications: TDD: 613-947-0407

The Court Martial Appeal Court of Canada was established by the Parliament of Canada, pursuant to its authority under section 101 of the Constitution Act,1867. The Court administers the National Defence Act & the Criminal Code. The Court Martial Appeal Court of Canada hears appeals from military courts. Military courts, known as courts martial, try members of the Canadian Forces, as well as civilians accompanying military personnel abroad, for crimes & offences against the Code of Service Discipline. The Code of Service Discipline is found in Part III & Part VII of the National Defence Act. Military personnel are subjected to military law, except when the offence has little to do with their military role. Offences, such as murder & manslaughter, are tried in civilian courts. There is a right of appeal to the Supreme Court of Canada from the Court Martial Appeal Court of Canada on questions of law.

Chief Justice: The Hon. Mr. Justice Edmond P. Blanchard, 613-995-7886

Designated Judges (The Hon. Mr. / Madam Justice): Edward C. Malone, Yvon Pinard, Elizabeth McFadyen, Joanne B. Veit(Supernumerary Judge), Gilles Létourneau, Marc Noël, Sandra J. Simpson, Marc Nadon, Danièle Tremblay-Lamer, Karen M. Weiler, Eugene Glen Ewaschuk, Douglas R. Campbell, Allan Lutfy, J. Edgar Sexton, Pierre Blais, John Maxwell Evans, François Lemieux, Karen Sharlow, Carol Mahood Huddart, Ross Goodwin, Elizabeth A. Bennett, John A. O'Keefe, J.D. Denis Pelletier, Eleanor R. Dawson, Dolores M. Hansen, Elizabeth Heneghan, Michael A. Kelen, Michel Beaudry, Luc Martineau, Luc Martineau, Carloyn Layden-Stevenson, Simon Noël, Judith A. Snider, Johanne Gauthier, James O'Reilly, James Russell, J. David Watt, A. Donald K. MacKenzie, Joseph T. Robertson, Deborah J. McCawley, Sean J. Harrington, Richard G. Mosley, Michel M.J. Shore, Michael L. Phelan, Anne L. Mactavish, Yves de Montigny, Roger T. Hughes, Robert L. Barnes, Johanne Trudel, Leonard S. Mandamin, Russel W. Zinn, Alexandre Deschênes, J. Douglas Cunningham, Guy Cournoyer, Douglas N. Abra, Richard Boivin, David Near, Robert Mainvile, Jamie W.S. Saunders

Administration:

Administrator of the Court: Raymond P. Guenette, 613-996-4778

Assistant Administrator: Suzanne Labbé, 613-947-5506

Judicial Administratorr: Dorothée Paquin, 613-995-7886

Contact: Media, Chantelle Bowers, 613-995-5063, Fax: 613-941-9454
media-fca@fca-caf.gc.ca

Tax Court of Canada

200 Kent St., Ottawa, ON K1A 0H9

613-992-0901, Fax: 613-957-9034, 800-927-5499, web@tcc-cci.gc.ca (Comments regarding web site)
www.tcc-cci.gc.ca

Other Communications: TDD: 613-943-0946; After Hours, Phone: 613-850-5021

In 1983, the Tax Court of Canada was established, pursuant to the Tax Court of Canada Act. The Court operates independently of the Canada Revenue Agency & other departments of the Government of Canada. Many of the appeals to the Tax Court of Canada are related to income tax, the goods & services tax, & employment insurance. References are also heard from the Canada Revenue Agency to provide interpretations of the legislation within its jurisdiction.

Chief Justice: The Honourable Mr. Justice Gerald J. Rip, 613-992-1994

Judges in order of seniority (The Honourable Mr./Madam Justice): Theodore E. Margeson(Supernumerary Judge), Pierre Archambault, Cameron Hugh McArthur(Supernumerary Judge), Lucie Lamarre, Alain Tardif, Eric A. Bowie(Supernumerary Judge), Joe E. Hershfield, Diane Campbell, Campbell J. Miller, François M. Angers, Leslie M. Little, Brent Paris, Judith Woods, Georgette Anne Sheridan, Paul Bédard, Réal Favreau, Wyman W. Webb, Gaston Jorré, Patrick J. Boyle, Valerie Miller, Robert James Hogan, Steven K. D'Arcy, Frank J. Pizzitelli

Administration:

Registrar of the Court: Roula Eatrides, 613-944-7758
roula.eatrides@cas-satj.gc.ca

Judicial Administrator: Louise Rochon, 613-992-0942

Legal Information Officer: Danielle Lebeau, 613-947-3691

Courts Administration Service
Service administratif des tr

434 Queen St., Ottawa, ON K1A 0H9

613-996-4778, Fax: 613-941-6197, reception@cas-satj.gc.ca (Enquiries concerning the web site)
www.cas-satj.gc.ca

Other Communications: Internal Audit Division, Phone: 613-996-4778

In 2003, the Courts Administration Service was established by the Courts Administration Service Act, S.C. 2002, c. 8. The Courts Administration Service provides administrative services to the following courts of law: the Federal Court, the Federal Court of Appeal, the Tax Court of Canada, & the Court Martial Appeal Court of Canada. Examples of the duties of the Courts Administration Service are as follows: providing support services, such as library services, to judges, prothonotaries, & staff; maintaining courts records; providing facilities & security for judges, prothonotaries, & staff; & informing litigants on rules of practice & procedures.

Administration:

Chief Administrator: Raymond P. Guenette, 613-996-4778

Deputy Chief Administrator, Registry Services: Murielle Brazeau, 613-943-3458

Deputy Chief Administrator, Corporate Services: Francine Côté, 613-996-1611

Deputy Chief Administrator, Judicial Services: Suzanne Labbé, 613-992-4439

Registrar, Registry of the Tax Court of Canada: Roula Eatrides, 613-944-7758
roula.eatrides@tcc-cci.gc.ca

Registrar: Federal Court of Appeal & Court Martial Appeal Court, Alain Le Gal, 613-992-8867
alain.le_gal@cas-satj.gc.ca

Registrar, Registry of the Federal Court: Manon Pitre, 613-992-4238
manon.pitre@cas-satj.gc.ca

Executive Director, Project Management: Gerry R. Montpetit, 613-992-9104

Director General: Information Management & Information Technology, Eric Cloutier, 613-992-9393

Director General: Administrative, Facilities, & Security Services, Eric R. Delage, 613-944-6614, Fax: 613-943-7948

Director General, Human Resources: Nathalie Dunn, 613-995-4453

Director General, Finance & Contracting Services: Paul Waksberg, 613-992-1745, Fax: 613-941-4915

Director, Corporate Secretariat: Alan Ritchie, 613-943-4782

Director, Library Services: Jean Weerasinghe, 613-995-1382

Manager, Communications: Isabelle Rodier, 613-943-4355
isabelle.rodier@cas-satj.gc.ca Registry of the Courts Administration Service

Principal Office, Ottawa, ON K1A 0H9

Other Communications: Federal Court of Appeal: 613-996-6795; Federal Court: 613-992-4238; Court Martial Appeal Court of Canada: 613-996-6795; Tax Court of Canada: 613-992-0901; Duty Officers (after hours): 613-769-3079

Local Offices:

Calgary

Canadian Occidental Tower, 635 - Eighth Ave. SW, Calgary, AB T2P 3M3

403-292-5329, 800-665-3329,
Other Communications: TDD: 403-292-5992; Duty Officers (for matters of an urgent nature which arise after regular business hours), Phone: 403-292-5920
Director: Cheryl Braden, 403-292-5328
Senior Registry Officer: Nancy Gagné, 403-292-5417
Registry Officer: Marjorie M. MacDonald, 902-368-0179

Charlottetown
Sir Henry Louis Davies Law Courts, 42 Water St., P.O. Box 2000, Charlottetown, PE C1A 8B9
902-368-0179, Fax: 902-368-0266, 800-565-0541
Registry Officer: Gloria Panting, 902-368-0179
Director: Kathy Dobransky, 780-495-2216

Edmonton
Tower 1, Scotia Place, #530, 10060 Jasper Ave., P.O. Box 51, Edmonton, AB T5J 3R8
Fax: 780-495-4681, 800-665-3329,
Other Communications: TDD: 780-495-2428; Duty Officers (for matters of an urgent nature which arise after regular business hours), Phone: 780-495-4651
Director: Willa Doyle, 506-452-3016
Registry Officer: Michel Morneault, 506-452-3016

Fredericton
Westmorland Place, #100, 82 Westmorland St., Fredericton, NB E3B 3L3
Fax: 506-452-3584, 800-565-0541,
Other Communications: TDD: 506-452-3036; Duty Officers (for matters of an urgent nature which arise after regular business hours), Phone: 506-452-3016
Director: Elizabeth Caverly, 902-426-3282
Registry Officer: Michael Kowalchuk, 902-426-3282

Halifax
#1720, 1801 Hollis St., 17th Fl., Halifax, NS B3J 3N4
Fax: 902-426-5514, 800-565-0541,
Other Communications: TDD: 902-426-9776; Duty Officers (for matters of an urgent nature which arise after regular business hours), Phone: 902-229-3719

Montréal
Registry of the Federal Courts, 30, rue McGill, Montréal, QC H2Y 3Z7
800-927-5499,
Other Communications: Duty Officers (for matters of an urgent nature which arise after regular business hours), Phone: 514-346-7884
Director: Claire Drolet, 418-648-7778
Registry Officer: Donald Ringuette, 418-648-5127
Registry Officer: Isabelle Sanfacon, 418-648-8469

Québec
Palais de Justice, #500A, 300, boul Jean Lesage, Québec, QC G1K 8K6
Fax: 418-648-4051,
Other Communications: TDD: 418-648-4644; Duty Officers (for matters of an urgent nature which arise after regular business hours), Phone: 418-648-4920
Director: Gordon C. Dauncey, 306-787-5380
Registry Officer: Gregory Jenkins, 306-787-5403
Registry Officer: Margaret Pelletier, 306-787-5421

Regina
Court House, 2425 Victoria Ave., Regina, SK S4P 3V7
306-780-5268, Fax: 306-787-7217, 800-663-2096
Registry Officer: Edward Joas, 506-636-4990
Registry Officer: Kathy Tobin, 506-636-4990

Saint John
Provincial Building, #413, 110 Charlotte St., 4th Fl., Saint John, NB E2L 2J4
506-636-4990, Fax: 506-658-3070, 800-565-0541
Deputy District Administrator: Darlene Wells, 709-772-2811
Registry Officer: Daphne Lewis, 709-772-2884

St. John's
The Court House, Duckworth St., P.O. Box 937, St. John's, NL A1C 5M3
709-772-2884, Fax: 709-772-6351, 800-565-0541
Director: Dennis Berezowsky, 306-933-5139
Registry Officer: Diane Papuzynski, 306-933-6642

Saskatoon
The Court House, 520 Spadina Cres. East, Saskatoon, SK S7K 2H6
306-975-4509, Fax: 306-975-4818, 800-663-2096
Regional Director General: Ontario, Gerry Montpetit

Toronto
Registry of the Federal Courts, #200, 180 Queen St. West, Toronto, ON M5V 3L6
416-973-3356, 800-927-5499,
Other Communications: Duty Officers (for matters of an urgent nature which arise after regular business hours), Phone: 416-677-1054
Regional Director General: Western, Gail MacIver

Vancouver
The Pacific Centre, 701 West Georgia St., P.O. Box 10065, Vancouver, BC V7Y 1B6
604-666-3232,
Other Communications: Duty Officers (for matters of an urgent nature which arise after regular business hours), Phone: 604-512-4471
District Administrator: Shauna Curtin, 867-667-5441
Registry Officer: Sue Bergren, 867-667-5441

Whitehorse
Andrew A. Phillipsen Law Centre, 2134 Second Ave., P.O. Box 2703, Whitehorse, YT Y1A 2C6
867-667-5441, Fax: 867-393-6212, 800-665-3329
Director: Jennifer MacGillivray, 204-983-7610
Registry Officer: Robert M'vondo, 204-983-2509
Registry Officer: Renée Taillefer, 204-983-2509

Winnipeg
363 Broadway St., 4th Fl., Winnipeg, MB R3C 3N9
Fax: 204-983-7636,
Other Communications: TDD: 204-984-4440; Duty Officers (for matters of an urgent nature which arise after regular business hours), Phone: 204-983-2509
District Administrator: Robin Anne Mould, 867-873-2044
Registry Officer: Bernice Dillman, 867-873-2044

Yellowknife
Court House, 4905 - 49th St., P.O. Box 1320, Yellowknife, NT X1A 2L9
867-873-2044, Fax: 867-873-0291, 800-665-3329

Alberta

Alberta Court of Appeal
Law Courts, 1A Sir Winston Churchill Sq., Edmonton, AB T5J 0R2
780-422-2416, Fax: 780-422-4127,
www.albertacourts.ab.ca/ca
The Alberta Court of Appeal hears appeals from the following courts: the Provincial Court; the Court of Queen's Bench; & administrative tribunals. The Court of Appeal also provides opinions on questions referred from the Lieutenant Governor under the Judicature Act. Court of Appeal justices are appointed by the federal government. Sittings are held in Edmonton & Calgary.
Chief Justice of Alberta: The Honourable Catherine A. Fraser
Justices of the Court of Appeal (The Hon. Mr. / Madam Justice): Jean E. Côté, Ellen I. Picard, Ronald L. Berger, Peter T. Costigan, Keith G. Ritter, Jack Watson, Frans F. Slatter, Myra B. Bielby
Administration:
Registrar: Sue Stushnoff, 780-422-7710, Fax: 780-427-5507
sue.stushnoff@gov.ab.ca
Deputy Registrar: Danielle Umrysh, 780-422-7714, Fax: 780-422-4127
danielle.umrysh@gov.ab.ca
Office Manager: Julie Ulmer, 780-422-4223, Fax: 780-422-4127
julie.ulmer@gov.ab.ca

Courts:
Calgary: Court of Appeal
TransCanada Pipelines Tower, #2600, 450 - 1st St. SW, Calgary, AB T2P 5H1
403-297-2206, Fax: 403-297-5294,
www.albertacourts.ab.ca/ca
Justices of the Court of Appeal (The Hon. Mr. / Madam Justice): Carole M. Conrad, Elizabeth A. McFadyen, Constance D. Hunt, Marina S. Paperny, Constance D. O'Brien, Peter W.L. Martin
Justices of the Court of Appeal (The Hon. Mr. / Madam Justice): Patricia A. Rowbotham, J.D. Bruce McDonald
Administration:
Deputy Registrar: Ileen Moore, 403-297-3949, Fax: 403-297-5294
ileen.moore@gov.ab.ca
Administration:
Director, Operations: Bev Thomson, 403-297-6077, Fax: 403-297-7528
bev.thomson@gov.ab.ca

Alberta Provincial Court
Law Courts, 1A Sir Winston Churchill Sq., Edmonton, AB T5J 0R2
780-427-8713, Fax: 780-422-9736,
www.albertacourts.ab.ca
The Provincial Court of Alberta serves as the point of entry to the justice system in the following areas of law: civil matters (Small Claims Court), related to damages & debt & pretrial conferences; criminal law; family law, such as Parenting & Contact Orders; traffic offences, under federal statutes, provincial statutes, & municipal bylaws; & Criminal Code offences committed by youth from ages twelve to seventeen. Circuit point courts are situated throughout the province.
A.G. Vickery(Chief Judge), A.H. Lefever(Deputy Chief Judge), J.M. Fililce(Assistant Chief Judge (Family & Youth)), N.R. Hess(Assistant Chief Judge (Civil)), A.G Vickery(Chief Judge), N.R. Hess(Assistant Chief Judge (Civil)), V.T. Tousignant(Assistant Chief Judge (Family & Youth))
Administration:
Senior Manager: Basem Hage, 403-297-3681, Fax: 403-592-4896
basem.hage@gov.ab.ca

Calgary - Civil, Criminal, Family, Regional, Traffic, & Youth
Calgary Courts Centre, #402S, 601 - 5th St. SW, Calgary, AB T2P 5P7
403-297-3122, Fax: 403-297-2932,
www.albertacourts.ab.ca
N.R. Hess(Assistant Chief Judge), L.L. Burt, M.A. McCorquodale, B.K. O'Ferrall
Administrator: Marilyn Clisdell, 403-297-7217, Fax: 403-297-7374
marilyn.clisdell@gov.ab.ca

Calgary - Civil
Calgary Courts Centre, #606S, 601 - 5th St. SW, Calgary, AB T2P 5P7
403-297-7217, Fax: 403-297-7374,
www.albertacourts.ab.ca
A.G. Vickery(Chief Judge), R.J. Wilkins(Assistant Chief Judge (Calgary & Calgary Region))
Administration:
Manager: Barb McCullough, 403-297-3122, Fax: 403-297-3106
barb.mccullough@gov.ab.ca
Administration:
Administrator, Criminal Hearing Office & Document Control: Julia Hiebert, 403-297-3127, Fax: 403-297-6405
Administration:
Administrator: Criminal Justice Clerks, Jo-Ann Larson, 403-297-3128, Fax: 403-297-3179

Calgary - Criminal
Calgary Courts Centre, #402S, 601 5th St. SW, Calgary, AB T2P 5P7
403-297-3122, Fax: 403-297-3179,
www.albertacourts.ab.ca
V.T. Tousignant(Assistant Chief Judge), G.J. Burrell, E.R.R. Carruthers, L.T.L. Cook-Stanhope, K.J. Jordan, T. LaRochelle, S.E. Lipton

Calgary - Family
Calgary Courts Centre, #704N, 601 - 5th St. SW, Calgary, AB T2P 5P7
403-297-3471, Fax: 403-297-3461,
www.albertacourts.ab.ca
L.K. McLellan, R.J. O'Gorman, S. Prowse O'Ferrall, J.R. Shaw
Manager: Lisa Lindquist, 403-297-3926, Fax: 403-297-3461
lisa.lindquist@gov.ab.ca
Administrator: Nadia Gates, 403-297-3925, Fax: 403-297-4892
nadia.gates@gov.ab.ca
Judges: R.J. Wilkins(Assistant Chief Judge, Calgary & Calgary Regional)
Judges: P.B. Barley
Judges: E.J. Creighton
Judges: L.R. Grieve
Judges: P.M. McIlhargey
Judges: J. Shriar
Administration:
Manager, Victims Services: Carol Lemieux, 780-422-3566, Fax: 780-422-4213
carol.lemieux@gov.ab.ca

Calgary - Regional
Calgary Courts Centre, #607S, 601 - 5th St. SW, Calgary, AB T2P 5P7
403-297-3010, Fax: 403-297-3237,
www.albertacourts.ab.ca
Circuit point courts are located in the following places: Airdrie (#113, 104 - 1 Ave.), Banff (#350, 208 Wolf St.), Canmore (#101, 800 Railway Ave.), Cochrane (213 - 1 St., West), Didsbury (1611 - 15 Ave.), Okotoks (98 McRae St.), & Tsuu T'ina Nation (9911 Chula Blvd., Sarcee).
Traffic Commissioner: M.A. Brown, V.T. Tousignant(Assistant Chief Judge)
Traffic Commissioner: J.K. Conley, G.J. Burrell
Traffic Commissioner: D.C. Elliott, E.R.R. Carruthers
Traffic Commissioner: J.G. Szekeres, L.T.L. Cook-Stanhope
Administrator: Lynn Quinton, 403-297-4771, Fax: 403-591-4820
lynn.quinton@gov.ab.ca, K.J. Jordan, T. LaRochelle, S.E. Lipton, L.K. McLellan, R.J. O'Gorman, S. Prowse O'Ferrall, J.R. Shaw
Manager: Lisa Lindquist, 403-297-3926, Fax: 403-297-3461
lisa.lindquist@gov.ab.ca
Administrator: Nadia Gates, 403-297-3925, Fax: 403-297-4892
nadia.gates@gov.ab.ca

Calgary - Traffic
Calgary Courts Centre, #203S, 601 - 5th St. SW, Calgary, AB T2P 5P7
403-297-2283, Fax: 403-297-2220,
www.albertacourts.ab.ca

Calgary - Youth
Calgary Courts Centre, #201N, 601 - 5th St. SW, Calgary, AB T2P 5P7
403-297-3473, Fax: 403-297-4892,
www.albertacourts.ab.ca
Judges: H.D. Gaede
Judges: W.A. Andreassen
Judges: K.L. Rostad
Administration:
Manager: Debbie Tkachuk, 780-644-8411, Fax: 780-644-8424
debbie.tkachuk@gov.ab.ca

Camrose
Court House, 5210 - 49 Ave., Camrose, AB T4V 3Y2
780-679-1240, Fax: 780-679-1253,
www.albertacourts.ab.ca
A circuit point court is located in Killam (4903 - 50 St.).
Administration:
Manager: Janice McGuckin, 403-820-7300, Fax: 403-823-6073
janice.mcguckin@gov.ab.ca

Drumheller
Court House, 511 - 3 Ave. West, P.O. Box 759, Drumheller, AB T0J 0Y0
403-820-7300, Fax: 403-823-6073,
www.albertacourts.ab.ca
Circuit point courts are situated in the following places: Hanna (401 Centre St.), Siksika Nation (Junction of Highways 901 & 547), & Strathmore (226 - 2 Ave.).
A.G. Vickery(Chief Judge), A.H. Lefever(Deputy Chief Judge), J.M. Filice(Assistant Chief Judge (Family & Youth)), N.R. Hess(Assistant Chief Judge (Civil)), D.R. Pahl(Assistant Chief Judge (Edmonton Region))
Senior Manager: Brenda Haynes, 780-427-7869, Fax: 780-422-9736
brenda.haynes@gov.ab.ca

Edmonton - Civil, Criminal, Family & Youth, & Traffic
Law Courts, 1A Sir Winston Churchill Sq., Edmonton, AB T5J 0R2
780-427-8713, Fax. 780-422-9736,
www.albertacourts.ab.ca
N.R. Hess(Assistant Chief Judge), M.M. Donnelly, K. Haymour, K.D. Hope, J.L. Skitsko, L.D. Young
Administration:
Administrator: Clarice Cameron, 780-422-2508, Fax: 780-427-4348
clarice.cameron@gov.ab.ca

Edmonton - Civil
Law Courts, 1A Sir Winston Churchill Sq., Edmonton, AB T5J 0R2
780-422-2508, Fax: 780-427-4348,
www.albertacourts.ab.ca
A.G. Vickery(Chief Judge), A.H. Lefever(Deputy Chief Judge), J.K. Wheatley(Assistant Chief Judge), D.R. Pahl(Assistant Chief Judge (Edmonton Region))
Administration:
Manager: Kerri McPhee, 780-427-7869, Fax: 780-422-9736
kerri.mcphee@gov.ab.ca

Edmonton - Criminal
Law Courts, 1A Sir Winston Churchill Sq., Edmonton, AB T5J 0R2
780-427-7868, Fax: 780-422-9736,
www.albertacourts.ab.ca
J.M. Filice(Assistant Chief Judge), D.J. Buchanan, M.J. Burch, D. Dalton, J.G. Easton, J.D. Franklin, G.B.N. Ho, J.C. Koshman, P.E. Kvill, S.C. Miller, L.S. Witten
Manager: Barbara Petryk, 780-427-2743, Fax: 780-427-5797
barb.petryk@gov.ab.ca
Administrator: Donna Blauel, 780-427-8337, Fax: 780-427-5797
donna.blauel@gov.ab.ca

Edmonton - Family & Youth
Law Courts, 1A Sir Winston Churchill Sq., Edmonton, AB T5J 0R2
780-427-2743, Fax: 780-427-5797,
www.albertacourts.ab.ca
Traffic Commissioner: D.R. Ackroyd
Traffic Commissioner: W.S. Andrew
Traffic Commissioner: I. Yaverbaum
Linda Hawryluk, 780-427-5913, Fax: 780-427-5791
linda.hawryluk@gov.ab.ca

Edmonton - Traffic & Civil
Law Courts, 1A Sir Winston Churchill Sq., Edmonton, AB T5J 0R2
780-427-5913, Fax: 780-427-5791,
www.albertacourts.ab.ca

S.A. Cleary, J.R. Jacques
Manager: Michelle Campbell, 780-743-7136, Fax: 780-743-7395
michelle.l.campbell@gov.ab.ca

Fort McMurray
Court House, 9700 Franklin Ave., Fort McMurray, AB T9H 4W3
780-743-7195, Fax: 780-743-7395,
www.albertacourts.ab.ca
A circuit point court is located in Fort Chipewyan (Multi-Plex, Flett St.).
D.G. Rae
Manager: Bonnie Matvichuk, 780-998-1200, Fax: 780-998-7222
bonnie.matvichuk@gov.ab.ca

Fort Saskatchewan
Court House, 10504 - 100 Ave., Fort Saskatchewan, AB T8L 3S9
780-998-1200, Fax: 780-998-7222,
www.albertacourts.ab.ca
A circuit point court is located in Boyle (5006 - 3 St.).
M.B. Golden, B.R. Hougestol, J.A. Watson
Manager: Rogena Hunt, 780-538-5360, Fax: 780-538-5454
rogena.hunt@gov.ab.ca

Grande Prairie
Court House, 10260 - 99 St., Grande Prairie, AB T8V 6J4
780-538-5360, Fax: 780-538-5454,
www.albertacourts.ab.ca
Circuit point courts are located in the following places: Fox Creek (100 - 4 Ave.) & Valleyview (5102 - 50 Ave.).
Administrator: Shelly Rendle, 780-926-3715, Fax: 780-926-4068
shelly.rendle@gov.ab.ca

High Level
Court House, 10106 - 100 Ave., P.O. Box 1560, High Level, AB T0H 1Z0
780-926-3715, Fax: 780-926-4068,
www.albertacourts.ab.ca
Circuit point courts are located in the following places: Assumption (Court House, Chateh) & Fort Vermilion (4607 River Rd.).
T.R. Goodson
Manager: Mae Fjeld, 780-523-6600, Fax: 780-523-6643
mae.fjeld@gov.ab.ca

High Prairie
Court House, 4911 - 53 Ave., P.O. Box 1470, High Prairie, AB T0G 1E0
780-523-6600, Fax: 780-523-6643,
www.albertacourts.ab.ca
Circuit point courts are located in the following places: Red Earth Creek (122 Forestry Rd.), Slave Lake (101 - 3 St., SW), & Wabasca-Desmarais (867 Stony Point Rd.).
D.C. Norheim
Administrator: Karen Hanington, 780-865-8280, Fax: 780-865-8253
karen.hanington@gov.ab.ca

Hinton
Court House, 237 Jasper St. West, P.O. Box 6450, Hinton, AB T7V 1X7
780-865-8280, Fax: 780-865-8253,
www.albertacourts.ab.ca
Circuit point courts are located in the following places: Edson (111 - 54 St.), Grande Cache (Provincial Building, Hoppe Ave.), & Jasper (629 Patricia St.).
M.M. White
Manager: Marilea McMullen, 780-986-6911, Fax: 780-986-0345
marilea.mcmullen@gov.ab.ca

Leduc
Court House, 4612 - 50 St., Leduc, AB T9E 6L1
780-986-6911, Fax: 780-986-0345,
www.albertacourts.ab.ca
Circuit point courts are located in the following places: Breton (4911 - 50 Ave.) & Drayton Valley (5136 - 51 Ave.).
E.W. Peterson(Assistant Chief Judge, Southern Region), F.W. Coward, G.R. DeBow, T.G. Hironaka, L.B. Hogan, R.A. Jacobson, J.N. LeGrandeur, S.L. Oishi, D.G. Redman
Administrator: M, McCulloch, 403-381-5525, Fax: 403-381-5763
maria.mcculloch@gov.ab.ca

Lethbridge
Court House, 320 - 4th St. South, Lethbridge, AB T1J 1Z8
403-381-5223, Fax: 403-381-5763,
www.albertacourts.ab.ca
Circuit point courts are located in the following places: Cardston (576 Main St.), Fort Macleod (244 Chief Red Crow Blvd.), Pincher Creek (782 Main St.), & Taber (5126 - 49 Ave.).
Dietrich Brand, F.C. Fisher, D.J. Greaves, G.K. Krinke
Administrator: Miles Weatherall, 403-529-8647, Fax: 403-529-8606
miles.weatherall@gov.ab.ca

Medicine Hat
Law Courts, 460 - First St. SE, Medicine Hat, AB T1A 0A8
403-529-8644, Fax: 403-529-8606,
www.albertacourts.ab.ca
A circuit point court is located in Brooks (220 - 4 Ave., West).
E.J. Simpson(Assistant Chief Judge, Northern Region), J.R. McIntosh, G.W. Paul
Administrator: Pam Testawich, 780-624-6256, Fax: 780-624-6175
pam.testawich@gov.ab.ca

Peace River
Court House, 9905 - 97 Ave., P.O. Box 900-34, Peace River, AB T8S 1T4
780-624-6256, Fax: 780-624-6175,
www.albertacourts.ab.ca
Circuit point courts are located in the following places: Fairview (10209 - 109 St.) & Falher (028 Main St., SE).
W.A. Skinner(Assistant Chief Judge, Central Region), N.P. Lawrence, T.G. Schollie, G.E. Deck, J.D. Holmes, J.A. Hunter, J.B. Mitchell, D.J. Plosz, E.D. Riemer
Manager: Sandra Mitchell, 403-340-5250, Fax: 403-340-7985
sandra.mitchell@gov.ab.ca

Red Deer
Court House, 4909 - 48 Ave., Red Deer, AB T4N 3T5
403-340-5250, Fax: 403-340-7985,
www.albertacourts.ab.ca
Circuit point courts are located in the following places: Coronation (4909 Royal St.), Rimbey (5025 - 55 St.), Rocky Mountain House (4919 - 51 St.), & Stettler (4705 - 49 Ave.).
B.H. Fraser, N.A.F. Mackie
Manager: Joanne McNeilly, 780-458-7300, Fax: 780-460-2963
joanne.mcneilly@gov.ab.ca

St Albert
Court House, 3 St. Anne St., St Albert, AB T8N 2E8
780-458-7305, Fax: 780-460-2963,
www.albertacourts.ab.ca
Circuit point courts are located in the following places: Athabasca (4903 - 50 St.), Barrhead (6203 - 49 St.), Morinville (10008 - 107 St.), & Westlock (10003 - 100 St.).
D.E. Demetrick, K.D. Williams
Manager: Wanda Whelan, 780-645-6324, Fax: 780-645-6273
wanda.whelan@gov.ab.ca

St Paul
Court House, 4704 - 50 St., P.O. Box 1900, St Paul, AB T0A 3A0
780-645-6324, Fax: 780-645-6273,
www.albertacourts.ab.ca
Circuit point courts are located in the following places: Bonnyville (4902 - 50 Ave.), Cold Lake (5323 - 48 Ave.), & Lac La Biche (9503 Beaver Hill Rd.).
J. Maher, S.G. Peck
Administrator: Bonnie Matvichuk, 780-464-0114, Fax: 780-449-1490
bonnie.matvichuk@gov.ab.ca

Sherwood Park
Court House, 190 Chippewa Rd., Sherwood Park, AB T8A 4H5
780-464-0114, Fax: 780-449-1490,
www.albertacourts.ab.ca
P. Ayotte, H.W.A. Fuller, V.H. Myers, K.E. Tjosvold
Manager: Brenda Majeau, 780-968-6401, Fax: 780-963-6402
brenda.majeau@gov.ab.ca

Stony Plain
Court House, 4711 - 44 Ave., Stony Plain, AB T7Z 1N5
780-963-6205, Fax: 780-963-6402,
www.albertacourts.ab.ca
Circuit point courts are located in the following places: Evansburg (4921 - 50 St.), Glenevis (Administration Office, Alexis Reserve), Mayerthorpe (5013 - 50 St.), & Whitecourt (5020 - 52 Ave.).
R.L. Tibbitt, P.T. Johnston
Administrator: Ruth Westman, 780-853-8130, Fax: 780-853-8200
ruth.westman@gov.ab.ca

Vermilion
Provincial Building, 4701 - 52nd St., P.O. Box 30, Vermilion, AB T9X 1J9
780-853-8130, Fax: 780-853-8200,
www.albertacourts.ab.ca
Circuit point courts are located in the following places: Lloydminster (5124 - 50 St.), Vegreville (4809 - 50 St.), & Wainwright (738 - 2 Ave.).
B.D. Rosborough
Manager: Edwina Segboer, 780-361-1204, Fax: 780-361-1338
edwina.segboer@gov.ab.ca

Wetaskiwin
Law Courts, 4605 - 51 St., Wetaskiwin, AB T9A 1K7

780-361-1204, Fax: 780-361-1338,
www.albertacourts.ab.ca
A circuit point court is located in Ponoka (5110 - 49 Ave.).

Alberta Court of Queen's Bench
Calgary Courts Centre, #705N, 601 - 5th St. SW, Calgary, AB T2P 5P7
403-297-7538, Fax: 403-297-8617,
www.albertacourts.ab.ca
In Alberta, the Court of Queen's Bench is the Superior Trial Court. The Court hears trials in both civil & criminal matters, as well as appeals from decisions of the Provincial Court. The Chief Justice & other Justices are also judges of Surrogate Matters. Sittings of the Court of Queen's Bench are held in various areas throughout Alberta.
Chief Justice: The Honourable Neil C. Wittmann
Justices (The Honourable Mr. / Madam Justice): Allen B. Sulatycky, Arthur M. Lutz, Bonnie L. Rawlins, T.F. McMahon, Suzanne M. Bensler, Lloyd David Wilkins(Supernumerary Judge), C. Adele Kent, Peter J. McIntyre, Carolyn S. Phillips, Peter Macdonnell Clark, Sal Joseph LoVecchio, William P. Sullivan, Colleen Lynn Kenny, Gerard C. Hawco, C. Scott Brooker, Barbara E.C. Romaine, Rosemary E. Nation, Aexander G. Park, Bryan E. Mahoney, Elizabeth A. Hughes, Marshsa C. Erb, Karen M. Horner, Sheilah L. Martin, Alan D. Macleod, K.M. Eidsvik, E.C. Wilson, J. Strekaf, R.G. Stevens, P.R. Jeffrey, S.L. Hunt McDonald, J.T. McCarthy, R.J. Hall, G.H. Poelman
Administration: Kathleen McAusland(Senior Manager), Bonita Dueck(Director, Judicial Administration), Shoana Holt(Criminal Supervisor), Audrey Jeske(Exhibits Supervisor), Lise Spilloway(Administrator, Procedure Control), Christine Urquhart(Supervisor, Judicial Assistants)
Manager: Janice McGuckin, 403-820-7300, Fax: 403-823-6073
janice.mcguckin@gov.ab.ca

Drumheller: Court of Queen's Bench
Court House, 511 - 3 Ave. West, P.O. Box 759, Drumheller, AB T0J 0Y0
403-820-7300, Fax: 403-823-6073,
www.albertacourts.ab.ca
Justices (The Honourable Mr. / Madam Justice): Joanne B. Veit, Edward P. MacCallum(Supernumerary Judge), Ernest A. Marshall(Supernumerary Judge), Myra B. Bielby, Lawrie J. Smith, Donald Lee, Mary T. Moreau, Richard P. Marceau, R. Paul Belzil, Mel A. Binder, Sterling M. Sanderman, Doreen A. Sulyma, Brian R. Burrows, Gerald A. Verville, L. Darlene Acton, Terrance D. Clackson, Andrea B. Moen, S.J. Greckol

Edmonton: Court of Queen's Bench
Law Courts, 1A Sir Winston Churchill Sq., Edmonton, AB T5J 0R2
780-422-2492, Fax: 780-422-9742,
www.albertacourts.ab.ca
Eric F. Macklin, Vital O. Ouellette, Donna C. Read, Stephen D. Hillier, Juliana E. Topolniski, Adam W. Germain, June M. Ross, John J. Gill, Dennis R.G. Thomas, R.A. Graesser, D.L. Shelley, K.G. Nielsen, M.G. Crighton, D.J. Manderscheid, K.D. Yamauchi, Beverley A. Browne, J.H. Goss
Senior Manager: Maria Lavorato, 780-422-2492, Fax: 780-427-0629
maria.lavorato@gov.ab.ca
Manager: Diane Royan, 780-422-2492, Fax: 780-427-0629
diane.royan@gov.ab.ca
Manager: Susan Logan, 780-422-9475, Fax: 780-427-0629
susan.logan@gov.ab.ca
Administrator: Leanne Malcolm, 780-415-2672, Fax: 780-422-9742
leanne.malcolm@gov.ab.ca
Manager: M. Campbell

Fort McMurray: Court of Queen's Bench
Court House, 9700 Franklin Ave., Fort McMurray, AB T9H 4W3
780-743-7136, Fax: 780-743-7135,
www.albertacourts.ab.ca
Manager: Rogena Hunt, 780-538-5340, Fax: 780-538-5493
rogena.hunt@gov.ab.ca
Senior Judicial Clerk: Jaime Bressler, 780-538-5340, Fax: 780-538-5493
jaime.bressler@gov.ab.ca
Senior Judicial Clerk: Chervaughn Shirto, 780-538-5340, Fax: 780-538-5493
chervaughn.shirto@gov.ab.ca
Senior Judicial Clerk: Michelle Wilmott, 780-538-5340, Fax: 780-538-5493
michelle.wilmott@gov.ab.ca

Grande Prairie: Court of Queen's Bench
Court House, 10260 - 99 St., Grande Prairie, AB T8V 2H4
780-538-5340, Fax: 780-538-5493,
www.albertacourts.ab.ca
Manager: S. Rendle

High Level: Court of Queen's Bench
Court House, 10106 - 100 Ave., P.O. Box 1560, High Level, AB T0H 1Z0
780-926-3715, Fax: 780-926-4068,
www.albertacourts.ab.ca
Criminal sittings are held as required.
Manager: K. Hanington

Hinton: Court of Queen's Bench
Court House, 237 Jasper St. West, P.O. Box 6450, Hinton, AB T7V 1X7
780-865-8280, Fax: 780-865-8253,
www.albertacourts.ab.ca
W. Vaughan Hembroff
Justices (The Honourable Mr. / Madam Justice): J.H. Langston
Justices (The Honourable Mr. / Madam Justice): D.K. Miller
Administration: Gwen Chadsey(Manager)
Administration: Evina Frankish(Senior Judicial Clerk)

Lethbridge: Court of Queen's Bench
Court House, 320 - 4 St. South, Lethbridge, AB T1J 1Z8
403-381-5196, Fax: 403-381-5128,
www.albertacourts.ab.ca
Manager: Shauna Jobagyu, 403-529-8710, Fax: 403-529-8607
shauna.jobagy@gov.ab.ca

Medicine Hat: Court of Queen's Bench
Law Courts, 460 First St. SE, Medicine Hat, AB T1A 0A8
403-529-8710, Fax: 403-529-8607,
www.albertacourts.ab.ca
Manager: Pam Testawich, 780-624-6256, Fax: 780-624-7101
pam.testawich@gov.ab.ca

Peace River: Court of Queen's Bench
Court House, 9905 - 97 Ave., P.O. Box 900-34, Peace River, AB T8S 1T4
780-624-6256, Fax: 780-624-7101,
www.albertacourts.ab.ca
James L. Foster
Justices (The Honourable Mr. / Madam Justice): K.L. Sisson
Justices (The Honourable Mr. / Madam Justice): Monica R. Bast
Administration: Sandra Mitchell(Senior Manager)
Administration: W. Darda(Manager)

Red Deer: Court of Queen's Bench
Court House, 4909 - 48 Ave., Red Deer, AB T4N 3T5
403-340-5220, Fax: 403-340-7984,
www.albertacourts.ab.ca
Manager: Wanda Whelan, 780-645-6324, Fax: 780-645-6273
wanda.whelan@gov.ab.ca

St. Paul: Court of Queen's Bench
Court House, 4704 - 50 St., P.O. Box 1900, St Paul, AB T0A 3A0
780-645-6324, Fax: 780-645-6273,
www.albertacourts.ab.ca
Manager: Edwina Segboer, 780-361-1204, Fax: 780-361-1338
edwina.segboer@gov.ab.ca

Wetaskiwin: Court of Queen's Bench
Law Courts, 4605 - 51 St., Wetaskiwin, AB T9A 1K7
780-361-1258, Fax: 780-361-1319,
www.albertacourts.ab.ca

British Columbia

British Columbia Court of Appeal
The Law Courts, #400, 800 Hornby St., Vancouver, BC V6Z 2C5
604-660-2468, Fax: 604-660-1951,
www.courts.gov.bc.ca/Court_of_Appeal
The Court of Appeal is the highest court in the province. It hears appeals from the Supreme Court, & from the Provincial Court on some criminal matters. It also hears reviews and appeals from some administrative boards and tribunals.
Chief Justice: The Hon. Lance S.G. Finch
Justices of Appeal (The Hon. Mr./Madam Justice): E.A. Bennett, E.C. Chiasson, I.T. Donald, S.D. Frankel, N.J. Garson, H.M. Groberman, J.E. Hall, C.E. Hinkson, C.M. Huddart, P.A. Kirkpatrick, R.E. Levine, R.T.A. Low, P.D. Lowry, K.C. Mackenzie, K.E. Neilson, M.V. Newbury, J.E. Prowse, M. Rowles, C.A. Ryan, M. Saunders, D.M. Smith, K.J. Smith, D.F. Tysoe
Administration:
Registrar: Jennifer Jordan, 604-660-2729

British Columbia Supreme Court
The Law Courts, 800 Smithe St., Vancouver, BC V6Z 2E1
604-660-2800, Fax: 604-660-1723,
www.courts.gov.bc.ca/supreme_court
The Supreme Court is a trial court of original jurisdiction for all civil & criminal matters arising in B.C., save & except matters expressly excluded by statute. It hears most appeals from the Provincial Court.
Chief Justice: The Hon. Robert J. Bauman
Judges (The Hon. Mr./Madam Justice): E.J. Adair, M.J. Allan, W.G. Baker, S.K. Ballance, G.T.W. Bowden, M. Boyd, B. Brown, C.J. Bruce, G.D. Burnyeat, B. Butler, B.I. Cohen, F.W. Cole, A.F. Cullen, V.R. Curtis, D.J. Dardi, B.M. Davies, G. Dickson, J.R. Dillon, W. Ehrcke, L.A. Fenlon, B. Fisher, S.C. Fitzpatrick, L.B. Gerow, R.B.T. Goepel, J.C. Grauer, V. Gray, B.M. Greyell, S.A. Griffin, J.M. Gropper, J.R. Groves, D.D. Harris, H.J. Holmes, M.A. Humphries, S.F. Kelleher, D. Kloegman, P.D. Leask, L.A. Loo, M.A. Mainsonville, D.M. Masuhara, N. Morrison, E.M. Myers, P.J. Pearlman, E. Rice, S.R. Romilly, C.J. Ross, L.D. Russell, J.E.D. Savage, R.J. Sewell, J.S. Sigurdson, A.H. Silverman, H.A. Slade, W.B. Smart, C.L. Smith, N.H. Smith, A.M. Stewart, S.S. Stromberg-Stein, P.G. Voith, Paul W. Walker, C.A. Wedge, P.M. Willcock, R.S.K. Wong
District Manager: Michael Hammell
michael.hammell@gov.bc.ca

Campbell River
500 - 13 Ave., Campbell River, BC V9W 6P1
250-286-7510, Fax: 250-286-7512
Registry (County): Vancouver Island
W. Grist, B. Joyce
District Manager: Marian Moore, 604-795-8300, Fax: 604-795-8345

Chilliwack
Court House, 46085 Yale Rd., Chilliwack, BC V2P 2L8
604-795-8350, Fax: 604-795-8393
Registry (County): Westminster
District Manager: R. Krayenhoff
rolph.krayenhoff@gov.bc.ca

Courtenay
Court House, #100, 420 Cumberland Rd., Courtenay, BC V9N 2C4
250-334-1115, Fax: 250-334-1191
Registry (County): Vancouver Island
T. Melnick
Deputy District Registrar: Debbie Schroeter
debbie.schroeter@gov.bc.ca

Cranbrook
Court House, 102 - 11 Ave. South, Cranbrook, BC V1C 2P3
250-426-1234, Fax: 250-426-1352
Registry (County): Kootenay
District Manager: Joanne Power
joanne.power@gov.bc.ca

Duncan
Court House, 238 Government St., Duncan, BC V9L 1A5
250-746-1227, Fax: 250-746-1244
Registry (County): Vancouver Island
Court Administrator: Linda Brekelmans
linda.brekelmans@gov.bc.ca

Fort Nelson
4604 Sunset Dr., P.O. Box 1000, Fort Nelson, BC V0C 1R0
250-774-5999, Fax: 250-774-6904
Registry (County): Cariboo
Deputy Registrar: Gloria Carew
gloria.carew@gov.bc.ca

Fort St. John
Court House, 10600 - 100 St., Fort St John, BC V1J 4L6
250-787-3231, Fax: 250-787-3518
Registry (County): Cariboo
Court Administrator: Lori-Ann Roseberry
loriann.roseberry@gov.bc.ca

Golden
837 Park Dr., P.O. Box 1500, Golden, BC V0A 1H0
250-344-7581, Fax: 250-344-7715
Registry (County): Kootenay
R. Blair, S.D. Dley, H. Hyslop, I.C. Meiklem, R. Powers
Manager, Scheduling: David McCoy, 250-828-4021, Fax: 250-828-4080
sc.scheduling_ka@courts.gov.bc.ca

Kamloops
Court House, #223 - 455 Columbia St., Kamloops, BC V2C 6K4
250-828-4344, Fax: 250-828-4332
Registry (County): Yale
G. Barrow, A. Beames, T. Brooke, P. Rogers
Manager, Scheduling: Barb Turik
sc.scheduling_ok@courts.gov.bc.ca

Kelowna
Court House, 1355 Water St., Kelowna, BC V1Y 9R3
250-470-6900, Fax: 250-470-6939
Registry (County): Yale
D.A. Halfyard, B.D. MacKenzie, J. Power, S. Shabbits

Senior Manager: Tanya Hingley, 250-741-3812, Fax: 250-741-3809
tanya.hingley@gov.bc.ca

Nanaimo
Court House, 35 Front St., Nanaimo, BC V9R 5J1
250-741-3805, Fax: 250-741-3809
Registry (County): Vancouver Island
T. McEwan
District Manager: Wendy Schwab, 250-354-6165, Fax: 250-354-6539
wendy.schwab@gov.bc.ca

Nelson
Court House, 320 Ward St., Nelson, BC V1L 1S6
250-354-6165, Fax: 250-354-6133
Registry (County): Kootenay
E. Arnold-Bailey, L. Bernard, N. Brown, R. Crawford, J.S. Harvey, I.B. Josephson, K.M. Ker, R. McKinnon, A. Saunders, T. Schultes, J. Truscott, F. Verhoeven, J. Williams, L.P. Williamson
Administrator: Laura Mayes, 604-660-8557, Fax: 604-660-2047
laura.mayes@gov.bc.ca

New Westminster
Court House, Begbie Sq., 651 Carnarvon St., New Westminster, BC V3M 1C9
604-660-8551, Fax: 604-660-2072
Registry (County): Vancouver
District Manager: Sylvia Judge
sylvia.judge@gov.bc.ca

Penticton
Court House, #116, 100 Main St., Penticton, BC V2A 5A5
250-492-1231, Fax: 250-492-1378, 888-526-8555
Registry (County): Yale
District Manager: Lowell Boran
lowell.boran@gov.bc.ca

Port Alberni
2999 - 4 Ave., Port Alberni, BC V9Y 8A5
250-720-2424, Fax: 250-720-2426, 877-741-3820
Registry (County): Vancouver Island
District Manager: Bryna Ary
bryna.ary@gov.bc.ca

Powell River
#103, 6953 Alberni St., Powell River, BC V8A 2B8
604-485-3630, Fax: 604-485-3637, 877-741-3820
Registry (County): Vancouver Island
W. Parrett
Senior District Manager: Patty Walker, 250-614-2700, Fax: 250-614-2737
patricia.walker@gov.bc.ca

Prince George
Court House
J.O. Wilson Sq., 250 George St., Prince George, BC V2L 5S2
250-614-2700, Fax: 250-614-2737
Registry (County): Cariboo
R.D. Punnett
Manager, Scheduling: Crystal Foerster, 250-624-7474, Fax: 250-624-7538
sc.scheduling_pr@courts.gov.bc.ca

Prince Rupert
Court House, 100 Market Pl., Prince Rupert, BC V8J 1B8
250-624-7525, Fax: 250-624-7538
Registry (County): Prince Rupert
District Manager: Einar Gunnarson
einar.gunnarson@gov.bc.ca

Quesnel
Court House, #305, 350 Barlow Ave., Quesnel, BC V2J 2C1
250-992-4256, Fax: 250-992-4171
Registry (County): Cariboo
District Manager: Trudy Williams
trudy.williams@gov.bc.ca

Rossland
Court House, 2288 Columbia Ave., P.O. Box 639, Rossland, BC V0G 1Y0
250-362-7368, Fax: 250-362-9632
Registry (County): Kootenay
Manager, Scheduling: David McCoy
sc.scheduling_ka@courts.gov.bc.ca

Salmon Arm
Court House, #550, 2nd Ave. NE, Salmon Arm, BC V1E 4S4
250-832-1610, Fax: 250-832-1749
Registry (County): Yale
District Manager: J. Caird
janet.caird@gov.bc.ca

Smithers
3793 Alfred St., P.O. Box 5000, Smithers, BC V0J 2N0
250-847-7376, Fax: 250-847-7710
Registry (County): Prince Rupert
District Manager: Laura Pistell
laura.pistell@gov.bc.ca

Terrace
Court House, 3408 Kalum St., Terrace, BC V8G 2N6
250-638-2111, Fax: 250-638-2123
Registry (County): Prince Rupert
District Manager: Sheree Marshall, 250-549-5420
sheree.marshall@gov.bc.ca

Vernon
Court House, 3001 - 27th St., Vernon, BC V1T 4W5
250-549-5422, Fax: 205-549-5621
Registry (County): Yale
K. Bracken, J. Dorgan, R. Johnston, M.D. Macaulay, R.W. Metzger, D. Wilson, R. Wilson
Senior District Manager: Charlene Kornaga, 250-356-1461
charlene.kornaga@gov.bc.ca

Victoria
Court House, #2, 850 Burdett Ave., Victoria, BC V8W 1B4
250-356-1478, Fax: 250-356-6279
Registry (County): Vancouver Island
Deputy Registrar: Rhonda Hykawy, 250-398-4308, Fax: 250-398-4459

Williams Lake
Court House, 540 Borland St., Williams Lake, BC V2G 1R8
250-398-4301, Fax: 250-398-4459
Registry (County): Cariboo

British Columbia Provincial Court

Pacific Centre, #602, 700 West Georgia St., P.O. Box 10287, Vancouver, BC V7Y 1E8
604-660-2864, Fax: 604-660-1108,
www.provincialcourt.bc.ca

The Provincial Court is a statutory, trial court. It hears cases in criminal, family, youth, small claims & traffic matters.
Acting Chief Judge: The Hon. Jim Threlfall
Judges (The Hon.): T. Crabtree, T. Shupe, K. Walker
Ad Hoc Judicial Justices of the Peace: Cheryl Harvey, David Maihara, Linda Mayner, Candice Rogers, Jane Wakefield
Administration:
Executive Director: Judicial Administration, Jan Rossley
Administrator: Justice of the Peace Program, Kevin Purdy, R.B. Caryer, D. Gardner, B.G. Hoy, C.G. Maltby

Abbotsford
32203 South Fraser Way, Abbotsford, BC V2T 1W6
604-855-3200, Fax: 604-855-3232
R.R. Romano, J. Rounthwaite, K.D. Skilnick
Judicial Case Manager: Healther Holt, B. Saunderson
Judicial Case Manager: Christine M. Ballman

Campbell River
500 - 13 Ave., Campbell River, BC V9W 6P1
250-286-7650, Fax: 250-286-7512
T.J. Crabtree, R. MacKay, W.A. Young
Judicial Case Manager: Andrea Schulz

Chilliwack
46085 Yale Rd., Chilliwack, BC V2P 2L8
604-795-8350, Fax: 604-795-8345
P. Doherty
Judicial Case Manager: Christine M. Ballman

Courtenay
#100, 420 Cumberland Rd., Courtenay, BC V9N 2C4
250-334-1115, Fax: 250-334-1191
W.G. Sheard, R.J. Webb
Judicial Case Manager: Megan Jensen

Cranbrook
#147, 102 - 11 Ave. South, Cranbrook, BC V1C 2P3
250-426-1234, Fax: 250-426-1352
R.R. Blaskovits
Judicial Case manager: Faye Campbell

Dawson Creek
#205, 1201 - 103 Ave., Dawson Creek, BC V1G 4J2
250-784-2278, Fax: 250-784-2339
J. Wood
Judicial Case Manager: Shannon L. Cole

Duncan
238 Government St., Duncan, BC V9L 1A5
250-746-1219, Fax: 250-746-1244
R.S. Bowry, B.A. Daley
Judicial Case Manager: Faye Campbell

Fort St. John
10600 - 100 St., Fort St John, BC V1J 4L6
250-787-3231, Fax: 250-787-3518

Golden
837 Park Dr., P.O. Box 1500, Golden, BC V0A 1H0
250-344-7581, Fax: 250-344-7715
C.D. Cleaveley, D. Dley, S. Frame(Admin. Judge), S.R. Harrison, H. Rohrmoser, J.E. Hughes
Judicial Case Manager: Sheila D. Paul

Kamloops
#223, 455 Columbia St., Kamloops, BC V2C 6K4
250-828-4344, Fax: 250-828-4332
E.M. Burdett, J.P. Cartwright, B.J. Chapman, P.V. Hogan, W.W. Klinger, R.R. Smith, J.J. Threlfall(Acting Chief Judge), A. Wallace
Judicial Case Manager: Kathy Bullach

Kelowna
#1, 1355 Water St., Kelowna, BC V1Y 9R3
250-470-6900, Fax: 250-470-6939

Mackenzie
64 Centennial Dr., P.O. Box 2050, Mackenzie, BC V0J 2C0
250-997-3377, Fax: 250-997-5617

Masset
1666 Orr St., P.O. Box 230, Masset, BC V0T 1M0
250-626-5512, Fax: 250-626-5491

Nakusp
415 Broadway St., P.O. Box 328, Nakusp, BC V0G 1R0
250-265-4253, Fax: 250-265-4413
J.D. Cowling, T.A. Dohm(Admin. Judge), R.A. Gould, E.L. Iverson, J.I.D. Joe, B.R. Klaver, John Dodd
Judicial Case Manager: Veronica Mitchell

Nanaimo
Court House, 35 Front St., Nanaimo, BC V9R 5J1
250-741-3805, Fax: 250-741-3809
L.J. Mrozinski
Judicial Case Manager: Sandra Hadikin

Nelson
320 Ward St., Nelson, BC V1L 1S6
250-354-6165, Fax: 250-354-6539
T. Alexander, G.P. Angelomatis, D.M.B. Steinberg, C.M. Proctor
Judicial Case Manager: Lila MacDonald

New Westminster
Law Courts, Begbie Sq., New Westminster, BC V3M 1C9
604-660-8522, Fax: 604-660-8977
J. Auxier, C.C. Baird Ellan, J. Challenger, J. Gedye, D.E. Moss, W.J. Rodgers(Admin. Judge), Phillip Lim
Judicial Case Manager: Suzanne McLarty

North Vancouver
200 East 23 St., North Vancouver, BC V7L 4R4
604-981-0200, Fax: 604-981-0234
G.G. Sinclair
Judicial Case Manager: Mar Warwick

Penticton
100 Main St., Penticton, BC V2A 5A5
250-492-1231, Fax: 250-492-1378
J.E. Saunders

Port Alberni
2999 - 4 Ave., Port Alberni, BC V9Y 8A5
250-720-2424, Fax: 250-720-2426
M.R. Buller-Bennett, P.L.J. de Couto, S. Dossa, A. Dyer, D.D. Pothecary, D.A. St. Pierre, A.J. Spence, D. Stone
Judicial Case Manager: Marylynn deKeruzec

Port Coquitlam
2620 Mary Hill Rd., #A, Port Coquitlam, BC V3C 3B2
604-927-2100, Fax: 604-927-2222

Port Hardy
9300 Trustee Rd., P.O. Box 279, Port Hardy, BC V0N 2P0
604-949-6122, Fax: 604-949-9283

Powell River
#103, 6953 Alberni St., Powell River, BC V8A 2B8
604-485-3630, Fax: 604-485-3637
M.J. Brecknell, B.L. Dollis, M.A. Gray, D. O'Byrne(Admin. Judge), R.S. Tindale, R.E. Walker, D.H. Weatherly, C.D. Jolly
Judicial Case Manager: Debra Pillipow

Prince George
J.O. Wilson Square, 250 George St., Prince George, BC V2L 5S2
250-614-2700, Fax: 250-614-2717
A.K. Krantz, H.J. Seidemann III(Admin. Judge)
Judicial Case Manager: Crystal M. Foerster

Prince Rupert
#200, 100 Market Pl., Prince Rupert, BC V8J 1B8
250-624-7525, Fax: 250-627-7538
R.D. Morgan
Judicial Case Manager: Sherry Jasper

Quesnel
#115, 350 Barlow Ave., Quesnel, BC V2J 2C2
250-992-4256, Fax: 250-992-4171
R.D. Fratkin, J.E. McKinnon, P.R. Meyers, M. Rae, E.D. Schmidt, P.L. Dodwell

Judicial Case Manager: Candace Goodrich

Richmond
7577 Elmridge Way, Richmond, BC V6X 4J2
604-660-6900, Fax: 604-660-1797
D.L. Sperry

Rossland
Court House, 2288 Columbia Ave., P.O. Box 639, Rossland, BC V0G 1Y0
250-362-7368, Fax: 250-362-9632
E.F. de Walle

Salmon Arm
#550, 2nd Ave. NE, P.O. Box 100 Main, Salmon Arm, BC V1E 4S4
250-832-1610, Fax: 250-832-1749
A. Rounthwaite

Sechelt
5480 Shorncliffe Ave., Sechelt, BC V0N 3A0
604-740-8929, Fax: 604-740-8924
C. Birnie, J.R. Milne
Judicial Case Manager: Sharon Portsch

Smithers
3793 Alfred St., P.O. Box 5000, Smithers, BC V0J 2N0
250-847-7376, Fax: 250-847-7710
K.W. Ball, M.C. Borowicz, J.G. Cohen, P.M. Dohm, H. Field, G. Gill(Assoc. Chief Judge), E. Gordon, P. Gulbransen(Admin. Judge), R.P. Harris, M.B. Hicks, P.A. Hyde, J.F. Lenaghan, J.R. Lytwyn, W.G. MacDonald, S.K. MacGregor, R.D. Miller, R. Raven, A. Rounthwaite

Surrey
14340 - 57 Ave., Surrey, BC V3X 1B2
604-572-2200, Fax: 604-572-2280
W.F. Stewart, K. Walker, J.O. Wingham
Judicial Case Manager: Doreen J. Hodge
Judicial Case Manager: Judith Jenvey
Judicial Case Manager: Sandra Thorne
Judicial Case Manager: Bianca L. West
Judicial Case Manager: Lyne Leonardes

Terrace
3408 Kalum St., Terrace, BC V8G 2N6
250-638-2111, Fax: 250-638-2123

Valemount
38 Dogwood St., Valemount, BC V0E 2Z0
250-566-4652, Fax: 250-566-9732
B.K. Davis, H.K. Dhillon, A. Ehrcke, E.A. Ferbey, R.M. Gallagher, D.R. Pendleton, N.N. Phillips(Assoc. Chief Judge), V. Romilly, A.R. Tweedale, J.F. Werier, W.F.W. Yee, J. Arntsen

Vancouver
Robson Sq., 800 Hornby St., P.O. Box 21, Vancouver, BC V6Z 2C5
604-660-8989, Fax: 604-660-8950
M. Kobiljski, Z. Makhdoom
Judicial Case Manager: Barbara Brown
Judicial Case Manager: Clare Mayhew
Judicial Case Manager: Judith Norton, C.L. Bagnall, B.E. Bastin, G.T.W. Bowden, E. Burgess, R.P. Chen, J. Galati, M.F. Giardini, J.E. Godfrey, T.J. Gove, F.E. Howard, W.J. Kitchen, R.R. Low(Admin. Judge), M.O. MacLean, T.D. McGee, M. McMillan, J.F. Palmer, G.M. Rideout, D. Senniw, D.I. Smyth, C.E. Warren, J.E. Watchuk, H. Weitzel

Vancouver - Criminal Division
222 Main St., Vancouver, BC V6A 2S8
604-660-4200, Fax: 604-775-1134
Judicial Case Manager: Kelly Butler
Judicial Case Manager: Laura Caporale
Judicial Case Manager: Johnny Ceraldi
Judicial Case Manager: Teresa L. Hill
Judicial Case Manager: Catherine J. Johnstone
Judicial Case Manager: Jovanka Mihic
Judicial Case Manager: Lori Stokes, D.A. Betton(Admin. Judge), M.G. Takahashi
Judicial Case Manager: D.C. Krenz

Vernon
3001 - 27 St., Vernon, BC V1T 4W5
250-549-5422, Fax: 250-549-5621
E.C. Blake, A.F. Brooks, L.F.E. Chaperon, L.J.M. Harvey, R.A. Higinbotham, J.M. Hubbard, J.N. Kay, B.D. MacKenzie, B.M. Neal, E.J. Quantz(Admin. Judge), L.W. Smith, S.E. Wishart, G.E. Madrick

Victoria
#2, 850 Burdett Ave., Victoria, BC V8W 1B4
250-356-1478, Fax: 250-356-6279
Judicial Case Manager: A. Bruce
Judicial Case Manager: Deborah Henry
Judicial Case Manager: Yvonne Locke, A.J. Palmer
Judicial Case Manager: Shannon Cole

Victoria - Western Communities
1756 Island Hwy., Victoria, BC V9B 1H8
250-391-2888, Fax: 250-391-2877
E.L. Bayliff, R. Walters
Judicial Case Manager: Sherry Jasper

Williams Lake
540 Borland St., Williams Lake, BC V2G 1R8
250-398-4310, Fax: 250-398-4459

Manitoba

Manitoba Court of Appeal
Law Courts Bldg., #100E, 408 York Ave., Winnipeg, MB R3C 0P9
204-945-2647, Fax: 204-948-2072,
www.manitobacourts.mb.ca
The Court is the senior & final court in the province & has appellate jurisdiction in all civil & criminal cases adjudicated by the Court of Queen's Bench & indictable offences adjudicated by the Provincial Court. The Court hears, in limited circumstances & as mandated by statute, appeals from professional bodies & some government boards & tribunals.
Chief Justice: The Hon. Mr. Richard J. Scott
Justices of Appeal (The Hon. Mr./Madam Justice): Martin H. Freedman, Barbara M. Hamilton, Richard J.F. Chartier, Alan D. MacInnes, Michael A. Monnin, Freda M. Steel, Holly C. Beard

Manitoba Court of Queen's Bench
Law Courts Bldg., 408 York Ave., Winnipeg, MB R3C 0P9
204-945-0344, Fax: 204-948-2369,
www.manitobacourts.mb.ca
The highest trial court for the province, The Court of Queen's Bench is a court of original jurisdiction & hears all civil & criminal cases arising in Manitoba, except matters expressly excluded by statute. The Court is comprised of the General Division, and the Family Division; it also has appellate jurisdiction & hears appeals from decisions of the Provincial Court in less serious criminal & quasi-criminal matters, decisions of the Hearing Officers in small claims matters, & decisions made by Masters of the court.
Chief Justice: The Hon. Mr. Marc M. Monnin, Robert Carr(Supernumerary), A.R. Clearwater(Supernumerary), Léa A. Duval, Shawn D. Greenberg, Kenneth R. Hanssen(Supernumerary), Morris Kaufman, Brenda L. Keyser, Deborah J. McCawley, Rodney H. Mykle, Perry Schulman(Supernumerary), Karen I. Simonsen, C. Murray Sinclair, Lori T. Spivak, Colleen Suche, Laurie P. Allen, Frank Aquila, Douglas N. Abra, Robert A. Dewar, Robyn M. Diamond, Robert B. Doyle, A. Catherine Everett, Marilyn E. Goldberg, Sylvia Guertin-Riley(Supernumerary), William Johnston, Donald M. Little, Joan G. McKelvey, Joan A. MacPhail, Chris W. Martin, John A. Menzies, Gerald W. Mercier, Brian Midwinter, Jeffrey J. Oliphant(Supernumerary), Marianne Rivoalen, Richard A. Saull, Kris Stefanson(Supernumerary), Michael A. Thomson, Douglas D. Yard, Donald P. Bryk, William J. Burnett, Robert G. Cummings

Courts:
Brandon
Court of Queen's Bench, 1104 Princess Ave., P.O. Box 68, Brandon, MB R7A 0P9
204-726-6240, Fax: 204-726-6547
R. Mykle, J.A. Menzies
Master/Registrar in Bankruptcy: Errick G. Harrison, D. Bryk

Dauphin
Court of Queen's Bench, 114 River Ave. West, Dauphin, MB R7N 0J7
204-622-2087, Fax: 204-622-2099

Portage la Prairie
Court of Queen's Bench, 20 3rd St. SE, Portage la Prairie, MB R1N 1M9
204-239-3383, Fax: 204-239-3402

The Pas
Court of Queen's Bench, 300 - 3rd St. East, P.O. Box 1259, The Pas, MB R9A 1L2
204-627-8420, Fax: 204-623-6528

Thompson
Court of Queen's Bench, 59 Elizabeth Dr., P.O. Box 34, Thompson, MB R8N 1X4
204-677-6757, Fax: 204-677-6686

Manitoba Provincial Court
Law Courts Bldg., 408 York Ave., Main Fl., Winnipeg, MB R3C 0P9
204-945-3454, Fax: 204-945-7130
The Provincial Court has jurisdiction in youth & select family & criminal matters, including summary conviction offences.
Chief Judge: The Hon. Kenneth Champagne
Judges (His/Her Hon.): Herbert Lawrence Allen, Catherine Carlson, Sandra L. Chapman, Brian G. Colli, John Combs, Brian M. Corrin, Kathlyn Mary A. Curtis, Judith A. Elliott, Robin A. Finlayson, Marvin F. Garfinkel, Wanda M. Garreck, John P. Guy, Christine Harapiak, Mary Kate Harvie, Robert M. Heinrichs, Shauna Hewitt-Michta, Sidney B. Lerner, Theodore J. Lismer, Tracey M. Lord, Lee Ann M. Martin, Jean McBride, Malcolm W. McDonald, Kelly Moar, Timothy Preston, Heather R. Pullan, Doreen Redhead, Fred H. Sandhu, Dale C. Schille, Donald R. Slough, Marva J. Smith, Lynn A. Stannard, Brent D. Stewart, Krystyna D. Tarwid, Patti-Anne L. Umpherville, Raymond E. Wyant

Courts:
Brandon
Provincial Court, 1104 Princess Ave., Brandon, MB R7A 0P9
J. Combs, B.D. Giesbrecht, K. Tarwid
Sheriff: M. Drosdoski, 204-726-6552, R.W. Thompson

Dauphin
Provincial Court, 114 River Ave. West, Dauphin, MB R7N 0J7
C. Harapiak
Sheriff: D. Werbiski, 204-622-2088, R.G. Cummings
Sheriff: R. Sim, 204-239-3379

Portage la Prairie
Provincial Court, 25 Tupper St., Portage la Prairie, MB R1N 3K1
Roger Grégoire, B.D. Stewart
Sheriff: R.A. Gray, 204-627-8431

The Pas
300 - 3 St. East, The Pas, MB R9A 1L2
B.G. Colli, M. Thompson
Sheriff: Dale Manning, 204-677-6764

Thompson
Provincial Court, 59 Elizabeth Dr., Thompson, MB R8N 1X4

New Brunswick

New Brunswick Court of Appeal
Justice Bldg., #202, 427 Queen St., P.O. Box 6000, Fredericton, NB E3B 5H1
506-453-2452, Fax: 506-453-7921,
www.gnb.ca/cour
The Court of Appeal has appellate jurisdiction in civil & criminal matters.
Chief Justice: The Hon. Mr. J. Ernest Drapeau
Justices of Appeal (The Hon. Mr./Madam Justice): Alexandre Deschênes(Supernumerary), Joseph Z. Daigle, Margaret E.L. Larlee(Supernumerary), J.C. Marc Richard, Joseph T. Robertson, Wallace S. Turnbull(Supernumerary), B. Richard Bell, Kathleen A. Quigg, Bradley V. Green

New Brunswick Court of Queen's Bench
Justice Bldg., 427 Queen St., P.O. Box 6000, Fredericton, NB E3B 5H1
www.gnb.ca/cour
The Court of Queen's Bench is a court of original jurisdiction, having jurisdiction in all civil & criminal matters arising in New Brunswick, except those expressly excluded by statute. The Court is comprised of two divisions: Trial & Family.
Moncton: **Chief Justice:** The Hon. David D. Smith, 506-856-2300, Fax: 506-856-2751
Administration:
Registrar: Bankruptcy/Divorce & Matrimonial Causes, Michael J. Bray, 506-453-2452
Deputy Registrar: Bankruptcy, Elizabeth Nicholas, 506-453-2452

Courts:
Bathurst
Court House, 254 St. Patrick St., P.O. Box 5001, Bathurst, NB E2A 3Z9
506-547-2151, Fax: 506-547-2966
G.W. Boisvert, Réginald Léger, J.R. McIntyre
Regional Manager: R.G. Boudreau
Clerk (Trial Division) & Administrator (Family Division): Donald Arseneau
Sheriff/Coroner: Edgar Aubé, Raymond J. Guerette

Campbellton
Court House, 157 Water St., P.O. Box 5001, Campbellton, NB E3N 3H5
506-789-2368, Fax: 506-789-2062
Gladys J. Young
Clerk (Trial Division) & Administrator (Family Division): Johanne Martin
Sheriff/Coroner: Walter Thompson, Thomas E. Cyr, Lucie Lavigne

Edmundston
121 Church St., P.O. Box 5001, Edmundston, NB E3V 3L3
506-753-2025, Fax: 506-737-4419
Clerk, Administrator (Family Division) & Regional Manager: Jean-François Cyr
Clerk, Administrator (Family Division) & Regional Manager: Sylvie Dumont
Sheriff/Coroner: Paul Ringuette, Myrna Athey, Paulette Garnett, D.H. Russell

Fredericton
Court House, 427 Queen St., P.O. Box 6000, Fredericton, NB E3B 5H1
506-453-2015,
Other Communications: Fax: 506/453-7921 (Family); 506/444-4392 (Trial)
Regional Manager: Dominique Laundry
Sheriff/Coroner: Keith Ball
Clerk (Trial Division) & Administrator (Family Division): Jean-Marie Goguen
Clerk (Trial Division) & Administrator (Family Division): Joy Toole, Thomas Riordon, Stephen J. McNally
Administrator: Cynthia Goulette
Clerk: Matthew Cripps
Sheriff/Coroner:Vacant

Miramichi
Court House, 599 King George Hwy., Miramichi, NB E1V 1N6
506-627-4021, Fax: 506-627-4134
Colette M. d'Entremont, B.M. Robichaud, P.S. Creaghan, J. Alfred Landry

Moncton
770 Main St., P.O. Box 5001, Moncton, NB E1C 8R3
506-856-2305, Fax: 506-856-2951
Guy A. Richard, George S. Rideout, Roger Savoie, Jacques A. Sirois, C.J. David D. Smith
Regional Director, Court Services: David Léger
Clerk (Trial Division) & Administrator (Family Division): Anne Richard
Sheriff/Coroner: Rhéal LeBlanc, Anne D. Wooder, Robert L. Tuck, P.S. Glennie, William T. Grant, Robert J. Higgins, H.H. McLellan

Saint John
110 Charlotte St., P.O. Box 5001, Saint John, NB E2L 4Y9
506-658-2400, Fax: 506-658-3070
J.W. Turnbull
Regional Manager: Tom Bishop
Clerk (Trial Division) & Administrator (Family Division): Sharon LeBlanc
Clerk (Trial Division) & Administrator (Family Division): George S. Thériault
Sheriff/Coroner: Joan Collins, Judy L. Clendening
Deputy Clerk (Trial Division) & Deputy Administrator (Fam: Andrea Hull
Sheriff/Coroner: Tim Wiebe

Woodstock
Court House, 689 Main St., P.O. Box 5001, Woodstock, NB E7M 5C6
506-325-4414, Fax: 506-325-4447

New Brunswick Provincial Court
Justice Bldg., #105, 427 Queen St., P.O. Box 6000, Fredericton, NB E3B 5H1
506-453-2935,
www.gnb.ca/cour
The Provincial Court has jurisdiction in select criminal matters as well as youth matters.
Chief Judge: His Hon. R. Leslie Jackson

Courts:

Carleton County
689 Main St., P.O. Box 5001, Woodstock, NB E7M 5C6
506-325-4415, Fax: 506-325-3906
R. Leslie Jackson(Chief Judge), David C. Walker

Charlotte County
41 King St., P.O. Box 5001, St Stephen, NB E3L 2C1
506-466-7507, Fax: 506-466-7508
Frederic Arsenault(Supernumerary)

Gloucester County (Bathurst)
#223, 254 St. Patrick St., P.O. Box 5001, Bathurst, NB E2A 3Z9
506-547-2155, Fax: 506-547-7448
Donald J. LeBlanc

Gloucester County (Tracadie-Sheila)
Place Tracadie, 3514 Main St., 1st Fl., Tracadie, NB E1X 1C9
506-394-3700, Fax: 506-394-3696
Joseph C. Michaud(Supernumerary)

Kent County
#1, 9358 Main St., P.O. Box 5001, Richibucto, NB E4W 5R5
506-523-7611, Fax: 506-526-7155
Henrik G. Tonning

Kings County
#2, 648 Main St., Hampton, NB E5N 6C8
506-832-6015, Fax: 506-832-6079
George S. Pérusse(Surnuméraire)

Madawaska County
Carrefour Assomption, #235, 121 rue de l'Église, P.O. Box 5001, Edmundston, NB E3V 3L3
506-735-2026, Fax: 506-735-2396
Denis T. Lordon, John C. Friel

Northumberland County
673 King George Hwy., Miramichi, NB E1V 1N6
506-627-4018
Pierre F. Dubé, Steven M. Hutchinson

Restigouche County
#202, 157 Water St., P.O. Box 5001, Campbellton, NB E3N 3H5
506-789-2337, Fax: 506-789-2186
Alfred H. Brien, Anne M. Jeffries, William J. McCarroll, James G. McNamee(Supernumerary), W. Andrew LeMesurier

Saint John County
15 Market Square, 3rd Fl., P.O. Box 5001, Saint John, NB E2L 1E8
506-658-2568
Patricia L. Cumming

Sunbury-Queens Counties
P.O. Box 94, Oromocto, NB E2V 2G4
506-347-4020, Fax: 506-357-4032
The courthouse is located at 23 Route 102 Highway, River Road, in Burton, NB.
Jacques Desjardins(Supernumerary)

Victoria County
426 Broadway, P.O. Box 5001, Grand Falls, NB E3Z 1G1
506-473-7700, Fax: 506-473-7379
Pierre W. Arseneault(Assoc. Chief Judge), Jolène Richard, Anne Dugas-Horsman, Irwin E. Lampert, Michael McKee(Supernumerary), J. Camille Vautour

Westmorland County
Assumption Place, 770 Main St., P.O. Box 5001, Moncton, NB E1C 8R3
506-856-2301, Fax: 506-856-3226
Mary Jane Richards, Julian Dickson

York County
Justice Bldg., #105, 427 Queen St., P.O. Box 6000, Fredericton, NB E3B 5H1
506-453-2120

New Brunswick Probate Court
Justice Bldg., 423 Queen St., P.O. Box 6000, Fredericton, NB E3B 5H1
506-453-2015,
www.gnb.ca/cour
The Probate Court has jurisdiction in estate matters. Clerks of the Court of Queen's Bench are, ex officio, Clerks of Probate Court. Court locations throughout New Brunswick; contact: Clerk of Probate, Court Services Office (Queen's Bench).

Newfoundland & Labrador

Supreme Court of Newfoundland & Labrador: Court of Appeal
287 Duckworth St., P.O. Box 937, St. John's, NL A1C 5M3
709-729-0066, Fax: 709-729-7909
The Court of Appeal has appellate jurisdiction in criminal & civil matters from decisions of the lower courts & designated administrative boards & tribunals.
Chief Justice: The Hon. J.D. Green
Justices of Appeal (The Hon. Mr./Madam Justice): L. Barry, M.F. Harrington, L.R. Hoegg, K.J. Mercer, M. Rowe, C.K. Wells, G. Welsh, C.W. White

Supreme Court of Newfoundland & Labrador: Trial Division
Court House, 309 Duckworth St., P.O. Box 937, St. John's, NL A1C 5M3
709-729-1137, Fax: 709-729-6623,
www.court.nl.ca/supreme/trial
The Trial Division is a court of original jurisdiction having jurisdiction in all civil & criminal matters arising in Newfoundland, except those excluded by statute. With the exception of the judicial area of St. John's, the Trial Division's original jurisdiction extends to particular family matters. The Registrar,and staff in the Estates Division of the Supreme Court, carrys out public guardian, guardian ad litem and public trustree functions.
Chief Justice: The Hon. David B. Orsborn
Judges (The Hon.): J.S. Adams, G.D. Butler, W.G. Dymond, A.E. Faour, R.A. Fowler, D.E. Fry, R.M. Hall, R.J. Halley, L.R. Hoegg(Supernumerary), R.D. LeBlanc, D.L. Russell, C.R. Thompson

Supreme Court of Newfoundland & Labrador: Judicial Centres
Courthouse, 309 Duckworth St., P.O. Box 937, St. John's, NL A1C 5M3
709-729-1137, Fax: 709-729-6623
The Supreme Court also has jurisdiction in Bankruptcy.
Administration:
Registrar: Christopher P. Curran
Senior Deputy Registrar: Bankruptcy, Darlene Wells
darlenewells@gov.nl.ca
Director: Supreme Court Services, William F. Barron
Estate Administrator: W.H. John Baird, W.H.N. Goodridge, D. Peddle
Deputy Registrar: Sandra Oxford, 709-637-2224, Fax: 709-637-2569

Corner Brook
Courthouse, 82 Mt. Bernard Ave., P.O. Box 2006, Corner Brook, NL A2H 6J8
709-637-2485, Fax: 709-637-2569
R.P. Whalen
Asst. Deputy Registrar: Lynetta Payne, 709-256-1115, Fax: 709-256-1120

Gander
Law Court Bldg., 98 Airport Blvd., P.O. Box 2222, Gander, NL A1V 2N9
709-256-1115, Fax: 709-256-1120
G.A. Handrigan
Asst. Deputy Registrar: Wilson Crowley, 709-832-1720, Fax: 709-832-2755

Grand Bank
T. Alex Hickman Courthouse, P.O. Box 910, Grand Bank, NL A0E 1W0
709-832-1720, Fax: 709-832-2755
A. Schwartz(Supernumerary), K.J. Goulding
Asst. Deputy Registrar: Edward Lannon, 709-292-4260, Fax: 709-292-4224

Grand Falls - Windsor
The Law Courts, 55 Cromer Ave., Grand Falls, NL A2A 1W9
709-292-4260, Fax: 709-292-4224
R.P. Stack
Asst. Deputy Registrar: Paula Parsons, 709-896-7891, Fax: 709-896-9212

Happy Valley - Goose Bay
Courthouse, 214 Hamilton River Rd., P.O. Box 1139 B, Happy Valley-Goose Bay, NL A0P 1E0
709-896-7892, Fax: 709-896-9212

Supreme Court of Newfoundland & Labrador: United Family Court
21 King's Bridge Rd., St. John's, NL A1C 3K4
709-729-2258, Fax: 709-729-0784
Judicial matters regarding families are shared/divided between the Supreme & Provincial Courts along geographical boundaries. The United Family Court, a division of the Supreme Court, has exclusive jurisdiction for all family matters on the Avalon Peninsula (including Bell Is.). In the "expanded service area" of the United Family Court (from Holyrood to Port Blandford & Bonavista Peninsula), however, there is concurrent jurisdiction.
Judges (The Hon.): J.D. Cook, M. Dunn, S.B. O'Regan

Provincial Court of Newfoundland & Labrador
Atlantic Place, 215 Water St., P.O. Box 68, St. John's, NL A1C 6C9
709-729-1004, Fax: 709-729-2161,
inquiries@provincial.court.nl.ca
www.court.nl.ca/provincial
The Provincial Court has jurisdiction in select criminal & family (outside the judicial area of St. John's) matters as well as small claims & youth matters.
Chief Judge: The Hon. D. Mark Pike
Judges (The Hon.): G.O. Brown, C.J. Flynn, G. Harding, D. Orr, D. Power, L. Skanes, R. Smith, L. Spracklin, J. Woodrow
Administration:
Director: Court Services, Pamela Ryder-Lahey
plahey@provincial.court.nl, W.A. Trahey

Wabush
Whiteway Dr., P.O. Box 1060, Wabush, NL A0R 1B0
709-282-6617, Fax: 709-282-6905

Courts:

Clarenville
47 Marine Dr., Clarenville, NL A5A 1M5
709-466-2635, Fax: 709-466-3147
P.J. Kennedy, C. Allen-Westby

Corner Brook
84 Mt. Bernard Ave., P.O. Box 2006, Corner Brook, NL A2H 6J8
709-637-2323, Fax: 709-637-2656
W. Gorman, K. Howe, M. Madden, B. Short

Gander
98 Airport Rd., P.O. Box 2222, Gander, NL A1V 2N9
709-256-1100, Fax: 709-256-1097
H. Porter

Grand Bank
Grand Bank-Fortune Hwy., P.O. Box 339, Grand Bank, NL A0E 1W0
709-832-1450, Fax: 709-832-1758
T. Chalker, R.J. Whiffen

Grand Falls
Law Courts Bldg., Grand Falls, NL A2A 1W9
709-292-4212, Fax: 709-292-4388
W. English

Happy Valley-Goose Bay
P.O. Box 3014 B, Happy Valley-Goose Bay, NL A0P 1E0
709-896-7870, Fax: 709-896-8767
J. Joy, J. Brazil

Harbour Grace
Harvey St., P.O. Box 519, Harbour Grace, NL A0A 2M0
709-596-6141, Fax: 709-596-4304,
www.hrgrace.ca/court.html
J. Jenkins

Stephenville
35 Alabama Dr., Stephenville, NL A2N 3K9
709-643-2966, Fax: 709-643-4022

Northwest Territories

Northwest Territories Court of Appeal
Court House, P.O. Box 550, Yellowknife, NT X1A 2N4
867-873-7643, Fax: 867-873-0291
The Court of Appeal has appellate jurisdiction in criminal & civil matters from the Supreme Court & Territorial Court.
Chief Justice: The Hon. C.A. Fraser
Justices of Appeal (The Hon. Mr./Madam Justice): Ronald L. Berger, Beverley A. Browne, J.E. Côté, C.M. Conrad, Peter T. Costigan, Adelle Fruman, L.F. Gower, C. Hunt, E.D. Johnson, Robert G. Kilpatrick, P. Martin, J.W. McClung, E.A. McFadyen, C.D. O'Brien, W. O'Leary, M.S. Paperny, E. Picard, J.E. Richard, K.G. Ritter, A.H. Russell, Virginia A. Schuler, Ronald S. Veale, J.Z. Vertes, Neil C. Wittmann
Administration:
Registrar: Anne Mould

Northwest Territories Supreme Court
P.O. Box 550, Yellowknife, NT X1A 2N4
867-873-7643, Fax: 867-873-0291
The Supreme Court is a court of original jurisdiction & has jurisdiction in all civil & criminal matters arising in the Northwest Territories, except those expressly excluded by statute.
Senior Judge: The Hon. J.E. Richard
Judges (The Hon. Mr./Madam Justice): V.A. Schuler, J.Z. Vertes
Deputy Judges (The Hon. Mr./Madam Justice): Lucien Beaulieu, Jean-Guy Boilard, C. Scott Brooker, Paul Chrumka, Carole M. Conrad, Alan T. Cooke, Wallace M. Darichuk, R.P. Foisy, Tellex W. Gallant, J.K. Hugessen, Howard L. Irving, Cecilia I. Johnstone, Daniel P. Kennedy, Colleen L. Kenny, Douglas H. Lissaman, Arthur M. Lutz, E.P. MacCallum, Elizabeth McFadyen, Ernest A. Marshall, Mary Moreau, Mary E. Noonan, Terrance P. O'Connor, Vital Ouellette, R.F. Paul, Ellen I. Picard, M.L. Rothman, P. Lawrie J. Smith, William J. Vancise, Joanne B. Veit, A.H. Wachowich, Randall S.K. Wong
Ex-Officio Judges (The Hon. Mr./Madam Justice): B.A. Browne, E.D. Johnson, Leigh F. Gower, R.G. Kilpatrick, Ronald S. Veale
Administration:
Court Administrator: Anne Mould

Northwest Territorial Court
P.O. Box 550, Yellowknife, NT X1A 2N4
867-873-7643, Fax: 867-873-0291
The Territorial Court has jurisdiction in small claims, youth, family & select criminal matters.
Chief Judge: The Hon. B.A. Bruser
Judges (His/Her Hon.): R.D. Gorin, B.A. Schmaltz
Administration:
Court Administrator: Anne Mould

Northwest Territories: Justice of the Peace Court
P.O. Box 550, Yellowknife, NT X1A 2N4
867-920-8020, Fax: 867-873-0203
The Justices of the Peace have jurisdiction in summary conviction matters arising out of territorial statute, municipal by-law & select criminal matters.
Administration:
JP Program Administrator: The Hon. Judge Vacant
JP Coordinator: Ramona Sorenson

Nova Scotia

Nova Scotia Court of Appeal
The Law Courts Bldg., 1815 Upper Water St., Halifax, NS B3J 1S7
902-424-4900, Fax: 902-424-0524,
www.courts.ns.ca/Appeals/index_ca.htm
The Nova Scotia Court of Appeal is the province's highest court and has appellate jurisdiction in civil & criminal matters. It sits only in Halifax and hears appeals from both the Supreme and Provincial Courts.
Chief Justice: The Hon. Michael MacDonald
Justices of Appeal (The Hon. Justice): Duncan R. Beveridge, Peter M.S. Bryson, David P.S. Farrar, Joel E. Fichaud, M. Jill Hamilton, Linda L. Oland, Jamie W.S. Saunders
Administration:
Registrar: Court of Appeal, Annette M. Boucher, 902-424-6187 boucheam@gov.ns.ca

Nova Scotia Supreme Court
The Law Courts Bldg., 1815 Upper Water St., Halifax, NS B3J 1S7
902-424-4900, Fax: 902-424-0524,
www.courts.ns.ca/supreme/index_sc.htm
The Supreme Court is the highest trial court in the province with jurisdiction in all civil & criminal matters, except those expressly excluded by statute. It hears appeals on Provincial Court, Small Claims Court and Residential Tenancies Board matters.
Chief Justice: The Hon. Joseph P. Kennedy, 902-424-6939, Fax: 902-424-0536
Judges (The Hon. Mr./Madam Justice): A.P. Boudreau(Supernumerary), F.A. Cacchione(Supernumerary), K. Coady, C.R. Coughlan, P.J. Duncan(Supernumerary), S.M. Hood, A.J. LeBlanc, A.D. MacAdam(Supernumerary), G.G. McDougall, G. Moir, J.D. Murphy, A.W.D. Pickup, M.H. Robertson, P. Rosinski, Robert Wright
Judges, Family Division (The Hon. Mr./Madam Justice): D.C. Campbell, L.J. Dellapinna, D. Gass, E. Jollimore, M.C. Legere-Sers, M. Lynch, B.A. MacDonald, L.I. O'Neil, R.J. Williams
Administration:
Registrar in Bankruptcy: Richard W. Cregan, 902-424-6908

Courts:

Amherst
16 Church St., 3 Fl., Amherst, NS B4H 3A6
902-667-2256, Fax: 902-667-5498
J.E. Scanlon, C.E. Haliburton(Supernumerary)

Annapolis Royal
Justice Centre, 377 St. George St., Annapolis Royal, NS B0S 1A0
902-532-5462, Fax: 902-532-7225
D.L. MacLellan(Supernumerary), N.M. Scaravelli

Antigonish
Justice Centre, 11 James St., Antigonish, NS B2G 1R6
902-863-7394, Fax: 902-863-7479
M. Stewart

Bridgewater
Court House, 141 High St., Bridgewater, NS B4V 1W2
902-543-4679, Fax: 902-543-0678
C.E. Haliburton(Supernumerary), P.L. Muise

Digby
Justice Centre, 119 Queen St., Digby, NS B0V 1A0
902-245-7134, Fax: 902-245-6722
G.M. Warner

Kentville
Justice Centre, 87 Cornwallis St., Kentville, NS B4N 2E5
902-679-6070, Fax: 902-679-6178
D.L. MacLellan(Supernumerary), N.M. Scaravelli

Pictou/New Glasgow
Court House, 69 Water St., P.O. Box 1750, Pictou, NS B0K 1H0
902-485-6373, Fax: 902-485-6737

Port Hawkesbury
#201, 15 Kennedy St., Port Hawkesbury, NS B9A 2Y1
902-625-4218, Fax: 902-625-4084
C.A. Bourgeois, F.C. Edwards(Supernumerary), S.J. MacDonald, P.J. Murray, T.M. Forgeron, K. Haley, M.C. MacLellan, D.W. Wilson

Sydney
Justice Centre, #6, 136 Charlotte St., Sydney, NS B1P 1C3
902-563-3550, Fax: 902-563-2224
J.E. Scanlan

Truro
Justice Centre, 1 church St., Truro, NS B2N 3Z5
902-893-3953, Fax: 902-893-6114
P.L. Muise

Yarmouth
Justice Centre, 164 Main St., Yarmouth, NS B5A 1C2
902-742-0500, Fax: 902-742-0678

Nova Scotia Provincial Court
5250 Spring Garden Rd., Halifax, NS B3J 1E7
902-424-8718, Fax: 902-424-0551,
www.courts.ns.ca/provincial/index_pc.htm
The Provincial Court has jurisdiction over almost all indictable charges under provincial & federal statutes and regulations. When judges are not available, presiding Justices of the Peace deal with release or detention of those arrested.
Chief Judge: The Hon. Patrick H. Curran
Judges (The Hon.): B.J. Beach, J.S. Campbell, M.C. Chisholm, A.S. Derrick, W.B. Digby, T. Gabriel, G.H. Randall, M.B. Sherar, C.H.F. Williams

Courts:

Amherst
16 church St., 3rd Fl., Amherst, NS B4H 3A6
902-667-2256, Fax: 902-667-1108
C.A. Beaton

Annapolis Royal
Justice Centre, 377 St. George St., Annapolis Royal, NS B0S 1A0
902-245-4567
J.D. Embree

Antigonish
11 James St., Antigonish, NS B2G 1R6
902-863-3676, Fax: 902-863-7479
J.H. Burrill, A. Crawford

Bridgewater
Justice Centre, 141 High St., Bridgewater, NS B4V 1W2
902-543-4679, Fax: 902-543-0678
F.I. Buchan, R.B. Gibson, F.P. Hoskins, W. MacDonald

Dartmouth
#200, 277 Pleasant St., Dartmouth, NS B2Y 3S2
902-424-2390, Fax: 902-424-0677
A. Murphy, T.K. Tax, P.S. Williams, J. Batiot

Digby
119 Queen St., P.O. Box 1089, Digby, NS B0V 1A0
902-245-4567, Fax: 902-245-6722
C. MacDonald, M.L. Melvin, A.T. Tufts

Kentville
Justice Centre, 87 Cornwallis St., Kentville, NS B4N 2E5
902-679-6070, Fax: 902-679-6190

New Glasgow
Justice Centre, 115 MacLean St., New Glasgow, NS B2H 4M5
902-755-5106, Fax: 902-755-7181
L. Halfpenny-MacQuarrie

Port Hawkesbury
Justice Centre, #201, 15 Kennedy St., Port Hawkesbury, NS B9A 2Y1
902-625-2605, Fax: 902-625-4084
A.P. Ross, D.J. Ryan, J.M. Whalen, B.D. Williston

Sydney
Harbour Place, #6, 136 Charlotte St., Sydney, NS B1P 1C3
902-563-3510, Fax: 902-563-3421
J.G. MacDougall, R.J. MacKinnon

Truro
Justice Centre, 540 Prince St., Truro, NS B2N 1G1
902-893-5840, Fax: 902-893-6261
R.M.J. Prince

Yarmouth
Justice Centre, 164 Main St., Yarmouth, NS B5A 1C2
902-742-0500, Fax: 902-742-0678

Nova Scotia: Probate Court
Law Courts Bldg, 1815 Upper Water St., Halifax, NS B3J 1S7
902-424-7422, Fax: 902-424-0524
The Probate Court has jurisdiction in respect of estate matters.
Registrar: Anne Marie LeBlanc

Amherst
Justice Centre, 16 Church St., 3rd Fl., Amherst, NS B4H 3A6
902-667-2256, Fax: 902-667-1108
Registrar: Sandra Gennette

Annapolis Royal
Justice Centre, 377 St. George St., P.O. Box 129, Annapolis Royal, NS B0S 1A0
902-532-5462, Fax: 902-532-7225
Registrar: Lorna Chisholm

Antigonish
Justice Centre, 11 James St., Antigonish, NS B2G 1R6
902-863-7396, Fax: 902-863-7479
Registrar: Claire Feener

Bridgewater
Justice Centre, 141 High St., Bridgewater, NS B4V 1W2
902-543-0816, Fax: 902-543-0678
Registrar: Sandra Gennette

Digby
Court House, Queen St., P.O. Box 1089, Digby, NS B0V 1A0
902-245-7134, Fax: 902-245-6722
Registrar: Sharron Atton

Halifax
Law Courts Bldg., 1815 Upper Water St., Halifax, NS B3J 1S7
902-424-7422, Fax: 902-424-0524
Registrar: Susan Campbell-Baltzer

Kentville
Justice Centre, 87 Cornwallis St., Kentville, NS B4N 2E5
902-679-5540, Fax: 902-679-6178
Registrar: Laura Lannon

Pictou/New Glasgow
69 Water St., P.O. Box 1750, Pictou, NS B0K 1H0
902-485-4351, Fax: 902-485-6737
Registrar: Karen Gillies

Port Hawkesbury
Justice Centre, #201, 15 Kennedy St., Port Hawkesbury, NS B9A 2Y1
902-625-4269, Fax: 902-625-4084
Registrar: Shauna Wilson

Sydney
Justice Centre, #6, 136 Charlotte St., Sydney, NS B1P 1C3
902-563-3545, Fax: 902-563-5701
Registrar: Anne Marie LeBlanc

Truro
Justice Centre, 1 Church St., Truro, NS B2N 3Z5
902-893-5870, Fax: 902-893-6114
Registrar: Ruth Hulbert

Yarmouth
Justice Centre, 164 Main St., Yarmouth, NS B5A 1C2
902-742-5469, Fax: 902-742-0678

Nova Scotia: Family Court
1815 Upper Water St., Halifax, NS B3J 1S7
The Family Court has jurisdiction in family matters & also functions as a Youth Court for cases involving youths aged 12 to 15 years.
Chief Judge: His Hon. Patrick H. Curran
Administration:
Director: Court Services, Judith McPhee, 902-424-4632, Fax: 902-424-7596
mcpheeja@gov.ns.ca, C.A. Beaton, J.M. Dewolfe

Amherst
Justice Centre, 16 Church St., 3rd Fl., Amherst, NS B4H 3A6
902-667-2256, Fax: 902-667-1108
Senior Officer: Patrick Dornan, James C. Wilson

Antigonish
Justice Centre, 11 James St., Antigonish, NS B2G 1R6
902-863-7312, Fax: 902-863-7479
J.H. Burrill, W. Dyer

Bridgewater
Justice Centre, 141 High St., Bridgewater, NS B4V 1W2
902-543-4679, Fax: 902-543-0678
R. Levy, M.L. Melvin

Kentville
136 Exhibition St., Kentville, NS B4N 4E5
902-679-6075, Fax: 902-679-6081
D.R. Hubley, J.G. MacDonald, R.J. MacKinnon
Officer: Keith Mumford

Truro
542 Prince St., Truro, NS B2N 1G1
902-893-5840, Fax: 902-893-6261
J.D. Comeau
Officer: Bob LeBlanc

Yarmouth
Justice Centre, 164 Main St., Yarmouth, NS B5A 1C2
902-742-0550, Fax: 902-742-0678

Nova Scotia Justice Centres
NS

Amherst
16 Church St., 3rd Fl., Amherst, NS B4H 3A6
902-667-2256, Fax: 902-667-1108
Court Administrator: Lynn Sorensen
Court Administrator: Janice Gillis-MacLean

Antigonish
11 James St., Antigonish, NS B2G 1R6
902-863-3676, Fax: 902-863-7479
Court Administrator: Paul Fay

Bridgewater
141 High St., Bridgewater, NS B4V 1W2
902-543-4679, Fax: 902-543-0678
Court Administrator: Alan Hamilton

Digby/Annapolis
119 Queen St., P.O. Box 1089, Digby, NS B0V 1A0
902-245-4567, Fax: 902-245-6722
Prothonotary: Annette Boucher
Court Administrator: Court of Appeal/Supreme Court, Wayne Stewart
Court Administrator: Supreme Court, Family Div., John Campbell
Court Administrator: Provincial Court, Peter James

Halifax
1815 Upper Water St., Halifax, NS B3J 1S7
902-424-6900, Fax: 902-424-0524
Court Administrator: Laurie Wanamaker

Kentville
87 Cornwallis St., Kentville, NS B4N 2E5
902-679-6070, Fax: 902-679-6178
Court Administrator: Jim Hahnen

Pictou/New Glasgow
115 MacLean St., 1st Fl., New Glasgow, NS B2H 4M5
902-755-7364, Fax: 902-755-7783
Acting Court Administrator: Janice Gillis-MacLean

Port Hawkesbury
#201, 15 Kennedy St., Port Hawkesbury, NS B9A 2Y1
902-625-4793, Fax: 902-625-4084
Court Administrator: Pam Kachafanas

Sydney
Harbour Place, #6, 136 Charlotte St., Sydney, NS B1P 1C3
902-563-3510, Fax: 902-563-3421
Court Administrator: Lynn Sorensen

Truro
540 Prince St., Truro, NS B2N 1G1
902-893-5840, Fax: 902-893-6261
Court Administrator: Alan Hamilton

Yarmouth
Court House, 164 Main St., Yarmouth, NS B5A 1C2
902-742-0500, Fax: 902-742-0678

Nunavut

Nunavut Court of Appeal
#224, Arnakallak Bldg., P.O. Box 297, Iqaluit, NU X0A 0H0
867-975-6100, Fax: 867-975-6168,
www.nunavutcourtofjustice.ca
Chief Justice: The Hon. Catherine Anne Fraser
Justices of Appeal (The Hon. Mr./Madam Justice): Carole Conrad, Adelle Fruman, Constance D. Hunt, Peter Martin, Clifton O'Brien, Neil C. Wittmann, Ronald L. Berger, Peter T. Costigan, Jean E. Côté, Keith Ritter, Anne Helen Russell, Beverley Browne, Earl Johnson, Robert Kilpatrick, Ronald Veale, John Edward Richard, Virginia A. Schuler, John Z. Vertes

Nunavut Court of Justice
#224, Arnakallak Bldg., P.O. Box 297, Iqaluit, NU X0A 0H0
867-975-6120, Fax: 867-975-6169,
www.nunavutcourtofjustice.ca
Deputy Judges appointed as required.
Resident Judges (The Hon. Mr./Madam Justice): Beverley A. Browne(Sr. Judge), Earl D. Johnson, Robert G. Kilpatrick

Ontario

Court of Appeal for Ontario
Osgoode Hall, 130 Queen St. West, Toronto, ON M5H 2N5
416-327-5020, Fax: 416-327-5032,
www.ontariocourts.on.ca/coa/en/index.htm
The Court of Appeal is the final court of appeal for Ontario. Appeals from the Court of Appeal may be pursued in the Supreme Court of Canada.
Chief Justice: The Hon. Mr. Warren K. Winkler
Justices (The Hon. Mr./Madam Justice): Robert P. Armstrong, Robert A. Blair, Eleanore A. Cronk, David H. Doherty, Gloria J. Epstein, Kathryn N. Feldman, Eileen E. Gillese, Stephen T. Goudge, Russell G. Juriansz, Andromache Karakatsanis, Harry S. LaForme, Susan E. Lang, John I. Laskin, Jean L. MacFarland, James MacPherson, Michael J. Moldaver, Marc Rosenberg, Paul S. Rouleau, Robert J. Sharpe, Janet M. Simmons, David Watt, Karen M. Weiler
Administration:
Senior Legal Officer: John Kromkamp, 416-327-5276
Registrar & Manager: Court Operations, Huguette Thomson
Deputy Registrar & Supervisor of Court Operations: Sandra Theroulde
Deputy Registrar & Acting Supervisor of Judicial Support: Carole Ibsen

Ontario Superior Court of Justice
Osgoode Hall, 130 Queen St. West, Toronto, ON M5H 2N5
Fax: 416-327-6209,
www.ontariocourts.on.ca/scj/en/index.htm
In addition to its regular trial court functions, the Superior Court of Justice has two branches: the Divisional Court which generally hears appeals from a final order of a Judge of the Superior Court involving disputes of up to $25,000, & the Small Claims Court which generally hears cases involving claims up to $10,000. The Governor General appoints the Judges to all but the Ontario Court of Justice.
Chief Justice: The Hon. Heather F. Smith, 416-327-5000, J. dePencier Wright, J.S. Fregeau, J.F. McCartney, T.A. Platana Northwest Region
277 Camelot St., Thunder Bay, ON P7A 4B3
807-343-2710
D.C. Shaw, G.P. Smith, E.W. Stach, B. Warkentin, R.P. Boissonneault, F.R Caputo, R.R.D. Cornell, R.G. Del Frate Northeast Region
155 Elm St. West, Sudbury, ON P3C 1T9
705-564-7600
E.E. Gareau, R.D. Gordon, I.M. Gordon, P.C. Hennessy, N.M.J. Karam, E.J. Koke, C.A.M. Macdonald, I.S. McMillan, D.J. Nadeau, J.S. O'Neill, J.S. Poupore, R.A. Riopelle, P.U. Rivard, G.W. Tranmer, G.T. Valin, W.L. Whalen, J.A.S. Wilcox, C.D. Aitken, P.B. Annis, R.N. Beaudoin, D.M. Belch, J.A. Blishen, W.J.L. Brennan, R.G. Byers, M.Z. Charbonneau, R.C. Desmarais, J.A. Forget, M.S. James, P.B. Kane, R. Kealey East Region
161 Elgin St., Ottawa, ON K2P 2K1
613-239-1560
S.J. Kershman, J. Lafrance-Cardinal, P.F. Lalonde, R. Leroy, H.S. Levenson Polowin, M.T. Linhares de Sousa, V.J. MacKinnon, H.K. MacLeod-Beliveau, B.J. Manton, R.L. Maranger, C. McKinnon, H.R. McLean, J.A. McMunagle, J. McNamara, M. Métivier, J.A. Parfett, K.D. Pedlar, R. Pelletier, D. Power, M. Quigley, L.D. Ratushny, T.D. Ray, C. Robertson, G.T. Roccamo, A.J. Roy, D.J.A. Rutherford, R.F. Scott, A.D. Sheffield, R.J. Smith, A.C. Trousdale, R.C. Boswell, J.C. Corkery, G.P. DiTomaso, M.P. Eberhard, M.L. Edwards, J.E. Ferguson Central East Region
50 Eagle St. West, 4th Fl., Newmarket, ON L3Y 6B1
905-853-4801
M.K. Fuerst, C.A. Gilmore, B. Glass, F. Graham, D.S. Gunsolus, M.J. Hatton, S.E. Healey, P.H. Howden, A.P. Ingram, R.P. Kaufman, M.L. Lack, P. Lauwers, B.G. MacDougall, J.R. MacKinnon, P.Z. Magda, T.J. McEwen, H.A. McGee, J.R. McIsaac, E.B. Minden, G.M. Mulligan, A. Mullins, C.S. Nelson, H.K. O'Connell, L. Olah, E. Quinlan, S. Rogers, A.R. Rowsell, D. Salmers, M.A.C. Scott, J.B. Shaughnessy, A. Sosna, A.J. Stong, D.R. Timms, R.A. Wildman, T.M. Wood, D.F. Baltman, J.R. Bellegham, T.A. Bielby, J.H. Clarke, K.D. Coats, D.L. Corbett, P.A. Daley, F. Dawson, T.M. Dunn, S.B. Durno, J.M. Fragomeni, D.K. Gray Central West Region
#100, 7755 Hurontario St., Brampton, ON L6W 4T1
905-456-4700
C.N. Herold, S.C. Hill, C.W. Hourigan, E. Kruzick, K.A. Langdon, G.D. Lemon, A.D.K. MacKenzie, G.M. Miller, N.M. Mossip, C. Murray, T.P. O'Connor, D. Price, M.G. Quigley, L. Ricchetti, S.S. Seppi, L.L. Snowie, J.R. Sproat, R.G. Thomas, R.M. Thompson, M.H. Tulloch, K.M. van Rensburg, B.J. Wein, H.S. Arrell, C.E. Brown, K.A. Carpenter-Gunn, J.J. Cavarzan, David S. Crane Central South Region
45 Main St. East, Hamilton, ON L8N 2B7
905-645-5252
W.J. Festeryga, P.J. Flynn, D.J. Gordon, P.B. Hambly, C.R. Harris, J.R. Henderson, J.C. Kent, C. Lafrenière, T.R. Lofchik, W.L. MacPherson, T. Maddalena, B.H. Matheson, Randolph Mazza, M.J. McLaren, J.A. Milanetti, D. Parayeski, A. Pazaratz, J.W. Quinn, J.A. Ramsay, R.D. Reilly, J.W. Scott, D.M. Steinberg, D.J. Taliano, C.A. Tucker, J.R.H. Turnbull, L.M. Walters, A.C.R. Whitten, A.W. Bryant, G.A. Campbell, S.K. Campbell, A.E. Cusinato, John Desotti, J.M.W. Donohue, R.C. Gates, K.A. Gorman, B.T. Granger, J. Harper, R.J. Haines, T.A. Heeney, Peter B. Hockin, W.A. Jenkins,

J.C. Kennedy, L. Leitch, T.D. Little, M. Marshman, D.R. McDermid, J.F. McGarry, J.N. Morissette, M.J. Nolan, T.L.J. Patterson, R.M. Pomerance, J.G. Quinn, H.A. Rady Southwest Region
80 Dundas St. East, London, ON N6A 6A3
519-660-3000, Fax: 519-660-3087
S. Rogin, W. Tausendfreund, L.C. Templeton, B.G. Thomas, G.I. Thomson, H. Vogelsang, B.A. Allen, T.L. Archibald, D. Aston, N.L. Backhouse, D. Bellamy, E.P. Belobaba, M. Benotto, D.M. Brown, C.L. Campbell, S. Chapnik, R.A. Clark, M. Code, B.A. Conway, K.B. Corrick, B.L. Croll, P.A. Cumming, G. Czutrin, M.R. Dambrot, T. Ducharme, T. Dunnet, R.S. Echlin, E.G. Ewaschuk, L.K. Ferrier, M.D. Forestell, E.E. Frank, A.M. Gans, N.E. Garton, S.R. Goodman, A.D. Grace, S.E. Greer, P.A. Grossi, J.F. Hamilton, A.L. Harvison Young, T.P. Herman, S. Himel, C. Horkins, A. Hoy, P.G. Jarvis, J.R.R. Jennings Metropolitan Toronto
361 University Ave., Toronto, ON M5G 1T3
416-327-5990, Fax: 416-327-6056
J.E. Kelly, F.P. Kiteley, G.R. Klowak, J. Lax, T.R. Lederer, S.N. Lederman, W. Low, E.M. Macdonald, J.A.B. Macdonald, I.A. MacDonnell, F.N. Marrocco, P.T. Matlow, J.D. McCombs, J.B. McMahon, F.E. McWatt, R.E. Mesbur, A.M. Molloy, J.P. Moore, G.B. Morawetz, F.J.C. Newbould, I.V.B. Nordheimer, A.J. O'Marra, V. Paisley, G.I. Pardu, L.A. Pattillo, M.A. Penny, S.E. Pepall, P.M. Perell, C. Perkins, R.W.M. Pitt, A. Pollack, L.B. Roberts, H.E. Sachs, M.A. Sanderson, H.J.W. Siegel, G.F. Speigel, C.M. Speyer, N.J. Spies, N.J. Spence, E.M. Stewart, D.G. Stinson, G.R. Strathy, K. Swinton, J.A. Thornburn, W.B. Trafford, G.T. Trotter, J.C. Wilkins, D.A. Wilson, J. Wilson

Ontario Court of Justice
#2300, 1 Queen St. East, P.O. Box 91, Toronto, ON M5C 2W5
416-327-5660,
www.ontariocourts.on.ca/ocj/en/index.htm
The Ontario Court of Justice generally performs functions assigned to it by Acts such as the Criminal Code, the Provincial Offences Act, the Family Law Act, the Children's Law Reform Act & the Child & Family Services Act & is a youth court. The Lieutenant Governor in Council, on the recommendation of the Attorney General, appoints the justices.
Chief Justice: The Hon. Annemarie E. Bonkalo, D.P. Baig, P.T. Bishop Northwest Region
1805 East Arthur St., 1st Fl., Thunder Bay, ON P7E 5N7
807-625-1620
J. Elder, D. Di Giuseppe, D.G. Fraser, J.R. Hoshizaki, J. Little, A.T. McKay, J.L. Pelletier, F. Valente, E.K. Bignell, R.D.J. Boivin Northeast Region
#303, 159 Cedar St., Sudbury, ON P3E 6A5
705-564-7600
P.J. Boucher, A. Buttazzoni, R.E.W. Carr, L. Duchesneau-McLachlan, W.F. Fitzgerald, G.N. Glaude, N. Gregson, A.L. Guay, J.D. Keast, L. Klein, J. Kukurin, R.W. Lalande, M.P. Lambert, J. Lebel, M. McLeod, Y. Renaud, M. Rocheleau, G.P. Rodgers, L. Serré, R.P. Villeneuve, P.R. Adams, A. Alder, C.D. Anderson East Region
161 Elgin St., 6th Fl., Ottawa, ON K2P 2L1
613-239-1560
E. Deluzio, D.W. Dempsey, C.S. Dorval, R.N. Fournier, H.L. Fraser, G. Griffin, S.J. Hunter, C.A. Kehoe, R. Lajoie, B.W. Lennox, W. Malcolm, B.E. MacPhee, L. Maisonneuve, S.A.J. March, R.G. Masse, P.H. Megginson, J.D. Nadelle, D.M. Nicholas, H.E. Perkins-Walters, S.G. Radley-Walters, G. Renaud, R.G. Selkirk, J.D. Wake, J.D.G. Waugh, J.N. Wilson, J.P. Wright, S.C. Armstrong Central East Region
440 Kent St. West, Lindsay, ON K9V 6G8
705-324-1400
G.W. Beatty, R.W. Beninger, P.L. Bellefontaine, M. Block, R. Blouin, P.N. Bourque, L.E. Chester, H.I. Chisvin, J.C. Crawford, N.A. Dawson, J.A. De Filippis, P. De Freitas, M.T.E. Devlin, J.A. Douglas, J.D. Evans, L. Favret, W.A. Gorewich, R. Graydon, D.J. Halikowski, M. Harpur, C.R. Harris, A. Hourigan, J.F. Kenkel, G.D. Krelove, S.C. MacLean, R.P. Main, R. McCreary, R.A. Minard, J.R. Morgan, K. Mulligan, R.J. Richards, E. Rosenberg, D.M. Stone, Peter Tetley, G. Wakefield, P.C. West, T.C. Whetung, J.B. Wilson, P.J. Wright, P.H.M. Agro, J.E. Allen, I.W. André Central West Region
#762, 45 Main St. East, Hamilton, ON L8N 2B7
905-645-5252
H.K. Atwood, J.C. Baldock, L.M. Baldwin, J.C. Blacklock, L. Botham, S.D. Brown, F.M. Campling, S.R. Clark, T. Colvin, D.S. Cooper, S. Coroza, I. Cowan, T.A. Culver, P.R. Currie, B. Duncan, P.W. Dunn, G.B. Edward, F.L. Forsyth, G.S. Gage, D. Harris, R. Jennis, N.S. Kastner, J.J. Keaney, R. Kelly, J. Kerrigan Brownridge, M.F. Khoorshed, R.J. LeDressay, K.G. Lenz, J. Maresca, E. Martin, D.B. Maund, K.L. McLeod, J. Nadel, C.A. Nelson, M. Pawagi, B.E. Pugsley, E. Ready, R.H.K. Schwarzl, B.R. Shilton, M. Speyer, J.D. Takach, L.P. Thibideau, D.T. Vyse, A. Watson, P.H. Wilkie, B.E. Zabel, R. Zisman, M. Ziolak, D.J. Austin, S.S. Bondy, G.J. Brophy West Region
80 Dundas St. East, 15th Fl., #G, London, ON N6A 6A3
519-660-3013, Fax: 519-660-3087
G.A. Campbell, D.G. Carr, J. Caspers, L.C. Dean, G.F. DeMarco, N. Douglas, M. Epstein, B. Frazer, S.J. Fuerth, J.L. Getliffe, L. Glenn, P.A. Hardman, G.F. Hearn, G.M. Hornblower, M. Hoffman, R.G.E. Hunter, P.R.W. Isaacs, P.J.S. Kowalyshyn, D.K. Livingstone, J.T. Lynch, R.S. MacKenzie, A.E.E. McFadyen, E.J. McGrath, K.L. McKerlie, M.A. McSorley, J. Morneau, S.M. Nicklas, M. O'Dea, D.W. Phillips, G.A. Pockele, W.G. Rabley, M. Rawlins, M.L.D. Roberts, L.J. Rogers, R.W. Rogerson, E.M. Schnall, J.S. Skowronski, B. Tobin, C.R. Westman, M.F. Woolcott, K.N. Barnes, W.P. Bassel, P. Bentley, F. Bhabha, M. Bloomenfeld, H. Borenstein, J.W. Bovard Toronto
Old City Hall, 60 Queen St. West, Toronto, ON M5H 2M4
416-327-6064
C. Brewer, B.A. Brown, Harvey P. Brownstone, L.M. Budzinski, K.J. Caldwell, B. Cavion, A.P. Chapin, T.P. Cleary, S.F. Clements, M.L. Cohen, D.P. Cole, C. Curtis, A. Di Zio, S.G. Dobney, D. Fairgrieve, L.T. Feldman, F.M. Finnestad, R.J. Flaherty, S.E. Foster, P. French, M. Green, M.B. Greene, J.M. Grossman, D.G. Hackett, P.A.J. Harris, M.L. Hogan, W.B. Horkins, P. Hryn, P. Jones, H.L. Katarynych, R. Khawly, B. Knazan, N.L. Kozloff, A.T. Lacavera, G.S. Lapkin(Senior Judge), E.N. Libman, S.B. Linden, T.R. Lipson, S.E. Marin, S. Merenda, C. Mocha, J.C. Moore, E.B. Murray, S.S. Nakatsuru, P.E. Newton, F.C. O'Donnell, D.I. Oleskiw, M. Omatsu, E.F. Ormston, R.J. Otter, D.A.W. Paulseth, L.C. Pringle, S. Ray, P.H. Reinhardt, J.M. Ritchie, P. Robertson, R. Rutherford, R. Schneider, B.M. Scully, S.R. Shamai, S.B. Sherr, G. Sparrow, R.J. Spence, J. Sutherland, P.M. Taylor, A. Tuck-Jackson, C.H. Vaillancourt, G. Waldman, B. Weagant, F.M. Weinper, W.R. Wolski, M. Wong, K.. Wright, B.J. Young, M.A. Zuker

Court Services Division
McMurtry-Scott Bldg., #204, 720 Bay St., Toronto, ON M7A 2S9
416-326-4263, Fax: 416-326-2652,
www.attorneygeneral.jus.gov.on.ca/english/courts
Court Services Division manages the court offices in communities across Ontario: scheduling court cases, maintaining records & files, collecting fines & fees, enforcing civil orders, and providing information to the public. It also provides administration support to judicial offices in the Superior Court of Justice & the Ontario Court of Justice: providing clerks, court reporters, registrars and interpreters for court proceedings.
Director: Court Operations, Paul Langlois Regional Court: North East
#501, 159 Cedar St., Sudbury, ON P3E 6A5
705-564-7675, Fax: 705-564-7664
Areas served include: Kapuskasing, Kirkland Lake, Moosonee, North Bay, Parry Sound, Sault Ste. Marie, Sturgeon Falls, Sudbury, Timmins. Court services are regularly provided in French, Ojibway & Cree. Total court locations: 35.
Director: Court Operations, Robert Gordon Regional Court: North West
277 Camelot St., Thunder Bay, ON P7A 4B3
807-343-2747, Fax: 807-345-6383
Areas served include: Dryden, Fort Severn, Kenora, Nipigon, Rainy River, Thunder. There are significant Aboriginal populations in this region and court services are regularly provided in Ojibway and Oji-Cree. Many locations are fly-in. Total court locations: 42.
Director: Court Operations, Thomas Fagan Regional Court: East
#100, Preston St., Ottawa, ON K1S 1N4
613-239-1551, Fax: 613-239-1273
Areas served include: Bancroft, Belleville, Brockville, Cornwall, Kingston, Ottawa, Pembroke, Perth. Total court locations: 29.
Acting Director: Court Operations, Sarina Kashak Regional Court: Central East
#210, 1091 Gorham St., Newmarket, ON L3Y 8X7
905-836-5621, Fax: 905-836-5620
Areas served include: Barrie, Bracebridge, Huntsville, Lindsay, Kawartha Lakes, Muskoka, Newmarket, Orillia, Peterborough, Whitby, York Region. Total court locations: 24.
Acting Director: Court Operations, Lou Bartucci Regional Court: Toronto
#1601, 720 Bay St., Toronto, ON M5G 1Z6
416-326-4249, Fax: 416-326-2073
Areas served: Greater Toronto Area. Total court locations: 11.
Director: Court Operations, Joanne Spriet Regional Court: Central West
John Sopinka Courthouse, #518B, 45 Main St. East, Hamilton, ON L8N 2B7
905-645-5333, Fax: 905-645-5375
Areas served include: Brampton, Brantford, Burlington, Hamilton, Niagara Region, Oakville, Orangeville, St. Catharines, Welland. Total court locations: 15.
Director: Court Operations, Len Griffiths Regional Court: West
80 Dundas St., #D, London, ON N6A 6A4
519-660-3090, Fax: 519-660-3098
Areas served include: Cambridge, Chatham, Fergus, Guelph, Kitchener, London, Owen Sound, Sarnia, Waterloo, Windsor. Total court locations: 24.

Prince Edward Island

Prince Edward Island Supreme Court: Trial Division
Sir Louis Davies Law Courts Bldg., 42 Water St., P.O. Box 2000, Charlottetown, PE C1A 7N8
The Supreme Court is a Court of original jurisdiction & has jurisdiction in all civil (including family, estate & small claims) & criminal matters arising in Prince Edward Island.
Chief Justice: The Hon. Madam Jacqueline Matheson
Justices (The Hon. Mr./Madam Justice): Gordon Campbell, Wayne Cheverie, David Jenkins, Benjamin Taylor
Administration:
Registrar: Charles Thompson, 902-368-6669
Deputy Registrar: Estates Section, Gloria Panting
Deputy Registrar: General Section, Marjorie MacDonald
Deputy Registrar: Small Claims Section, Roxanne Smith
Deputy Registrar: Family Section, Sandra Mitchell
Deputy Registrar: Trial Division, Mary MacLeod
Court Services Manager: Tanya Tynski, 902-368-6005

Prince Edward Island Supreme Court: Court of Appeal
Sir Louis Henry Davies Law Courts, 42 Water St., P.O. Box 2000, Charlottetown, PE C1A 7N8
The Court of Appeal has appellate jurisdiction in criminal & civil matters.
Chief Justice: The Hon. Mr. Gerard E. Mitchell, John McQuaid, Linda Webber
Deputy Registrar: Appeal Division, Gloria Panting

Prince Edward Island Supreme Court
Sir Louis Henry Davies Law Courts, 42 Water St., P.O. Box 2000, Charlottetown, PE C1A 7N8
902-368-6000, Fax: 902-368-0266
Chief Justice: The Hon. Gerard E. Mitchell

Prince Edward Island Provincial Court
Kelly Bldg., 3 Harbourside Access Rd., Charlottetown, PE C1A 8R4
902-368-6000
The Provincial Court has jurisdiction in select criminal matters as well as youth matters.
Chief Judge: The Hon. John R. Douglas, 902-368-6011

Courts:
Queens & Kings Counties: Provincial Court
Law Courts Bldg., P.O. Box 2290, Charlottetown, PE C1A 8C1
Jeffrey Lantz

Prince County: Provincial Court
Law Courts Bldg., P.O. Box 2020, Summerside, PE C1N 4M1
Nancy K. Orr

Prince Edward Island: Judicial Officers
PE

Courts:
Kings County
Court House, Kent St., P.O. Box 89, Georgetown, PE C0A 1L0
902-652-2924, Fax: 902-652-2701,
georgetown@pei.sympatico.ca
www.georgetown.ca/courthouse.html
Deputy Registrar: Shirley Clory, 902-652-8990
Sheriff: Ron Dowling, 902-888-8191

Prince County
Court House, P.O. Box 2020, Summerside, PE C1N 4M1
Chief Sheriff: Frank Driscoll, 902-368-6055

Queens County
Law Courts, P.O. Box 2000, Charlottetown, PE C1A 7N8
Prothonotary: Charles P. Thompson
Court Services Manager: Tanya Tynski, 902-368-6005

Québec

Cour d'Appel du Québec
Québec Court of Appeal
Édifice Ernest-Cormier, 100, rue Notre-Dame Est, Montréal, QC H2Y 4B6
514-393-2022,
courdappelqc@justice.gouv.qc.ca
www.tribunaux.qc.ca/c-appel

Le plus haut tribunal du Québec; la cour est la gardienne de l'intégrité du droit civil de la province; en matière civile, la cour entend les appels des jugements finals de la Cour supérieure et de la Cour du Québec lorsque la valeur de l'objet du litige en appel est to 50 000$ ou plus; outrage, adoption, évaluation psychiatrique, garde en établissement, faillite, et divorce.
Juge en chef: L'hon. J.J. Michel Robert
Juges (Les honorables): Marc Beauregard(Juge surnuméraire), Marie-France Bich, Jean Bouchard, André Brossard(Juge surnuméraire), Jacques Chamberland, Lise Côté, Pierre J. Dalphond, François Doyon, Jacques Dufresne, Julie Dutil, Nicole Duval Hesler, André Forget(Juge surnuméraire), Guy Gagnon, Paul-Arthur Gendreau(Juge surnuméraire), Lorne Giroux, Allan Ross Hilton, Nicholas Kasirer, Jacques A. Léger, Benoît Morin(Juge surnuméraire), Yves-Marie Morissette, François Pelletier, Louis Rochette, André Rochon, France Thibault, Paul Vézina(Juge surnuméraire)

Montréal
Édifice Ernest-Cormier, #2.22, 100, rue Notre-Dame est, Montréal, QC H2Y 4B6
514-393-2022, Fax: 514-864-7270
Coordonnatrice juridique: Lysanne P. Legault
Coordonnatrice juridique: Claire Roberge

Québec
Palais de justice de Québec, #4.27, 300, boul Jean-Lesage, Québec, QC G1K 8K6
418-649-3401, Fax: 418-646-6961

Cour Supérieure du Québec
Québec Superior Court
300, boul Jean-Lesage, Québec, QC G1K 8K6
418-649-3400, Fax: 418-528-0932,
www.tribunaux.qc.ca/c-superieure

Affaires civiles et commerciales dont l'enjeu est de 70 000$ ou plus; litiges en matières administratives et familiale, faillite, procès devant jury en matière pénale, et appels en matière de poursuites sommaires
Juge en chef: L'hon. François Rolland

Abitibi—Rouyn-Noranda—Témiscamingue
QC
Robert Dufresne, Jocelyn Geoffroy, Laurent Guertin, Ivan St-Julien(Juge surnuméraire), Jacques Viens(Juge surnuméraire), Gratien Duchesne

Alma
QC
Jules Allard(Juge surnuméraire)

Arthabaska
QC
Paul Corriveau

Baie-Comeau—Mingan
QC
Jean-Roch Landry

Bonaventure
QC
Jacques Babin, Roger Banford(Juge surnuméraire), Martin Dallaire, Carl Lachance, Jean-Claude Larouche(Juge surnuméraire)

Chicoutimi
QC
Paul-Marcel Bellavance, Suzanne Mireault

Granby
Martin Bédard, Pierre Dallaire, Dominique Goulet, Pierre Isabelle, Louis-Philippe Landry(Juge surnuméraire), Jean-Pierre Plouffe(Juge surnuméraire), Suzanne Tessier

Hull—Pontiac—Labelle
QC
Michel Déziel, Jacques R. Fournier, Pierre Journet(Juges surnuméraire)

Laval
QC
Jean-Jude Chabot, Carole Julien, Gilles Mercure, Réjean F. Paul(Juge surnuméraire)

Longueuil
QC
Christiane Alary, Louisa Arcand, Claude Auclair, Roger E. Baker(Juge surnuméraire), Guylène Beaugé, Pierre Béliveau, Nicole Bénard(Juge surnuméraire), Marc-André Blanchard, Jean-Guy Boilard(Juge surnuméraire), Sylviane W. Borenstein(Juge surnuméraire), Sophie Bourque

Montréal
QC
James L. Brunton, Jean-François Buffoni, Pepita G. Capriolo, Michel A. Caron, Kirkland Casgrain, Robert Castiglio, Martin Castonguay, Claude Champagne, Paul G. Chaput(Juge surnuméraire), France Charbonneau, Jean-Pierre Chrétien, Carol Cohen, Chantal Corriveau, Guy Cournoyer, Suzanne Courteau, Marie-France Courville, Louis Crête(Juge surnuméraire), Louis-Paul Cullen, Claude Dallaire, Marc David, Wilbrod Claude Décarie, Jean-François de Grandpré, Michel Delorme, André Denis(Juge surnuméraire), Sylvie Devito, Marc De Wever, Kevin Downs(Juge surnuméraire), Gérard Dugré, Benoît Emery, Lucie Fournier, William Fraiberg, Pierre-C. Gagnon, Clément Gascon, Marie Gaudreau, Jacques Gauthier, Nicole M. Gibeau, Danielle Grenier(Juge surnuméraire), Jean Guibault(Juge surnuméraire), Carole Hallée, Gilles Hébert(Juge surnuméraire), Pierre Jasmin(Juge surnuméraire), Marie-Christine Laberge, Louis Lacoursière, Jean-Yves Lalonde, Julien Lanctôt, Hélène Langlois, Claude Larouche(Juge surnuméraire), Hélène Le Bel(Juge surnuméraire), Luc Lefebvre, Louise Lemelin, Johanne Mainville(Juge surnuméraire), Catherine Mandeville, Diane Marcelin(Juge surnuméraire), Geneviève Marcotte, J. Fraser Martin(Juge surnuméraire), Israel Mass(Juge surnuméraire), Chantal Masse, Lise Matteau, Paul Mayer, Danièle Mayrand, Michèle Monast, Richard Mongeau, Robert Mongeon, Richard Nadeau, Francine Nantel, Pierre Nollet, Daniel W. Payette, Mark G. Peacock, Micheline Perrault, Eva Petras, Claudette Picard, Sophie Picard, Ginette Piché(Juge surnuméraire), Yves Poirier, Hélène Poulin, André Prévost, Steve J. Reimnitz, Danielle Richer, Brian J. Riordan, Jeannine M. Rousseau(Juge surnuméraire), André Roy, Claudine Roy, Manon Savard, Jean-Pierre Sénécal, Joel Avery Silcoff, Marie St-Pierre, Pierre Tessier(Juge surnuméraire), Daniel H. Tingley(Juge surnuméraire), Anne-Marie Trahan, Clément Trudel(Juge surnuméraire), Danielle Turcotte, Martin Vauclair, Jocelyn Verrier, André Vincent, Richard Wagner, Dionysia Zerbisias(Juge surnuméraire), Jerry Zigman(Juge surnuméraire), Gilles Blanchet, Claude-Henri Gendreau

Rimouski
QC
Pierre Boily(Juge surnuméraire), Martin Bureau, Léo Daigle, Gaétan Dumas, Line Samoisette, Yves Tardif, François Tôth

Sherbrooke
QC
Raymond W. Pronovost

St-Maurice
QC
Alain Bolduc, Ivan Godin, Guy Lebrun(Juge surnuméraire), Robert Legris(Juge surnuméraire), Michel Richard, Marc St-Pierre

Trois-Rivières
850, rue Hart, Trois-Rivières, QC G9A 1T9
819-372-4153,
www.justice.gouv.qc.ca; www.tribunaux.qc.ca/c-superieure

Cour du Québec
Court of Québec
300, boul Jean-Lesage, Québec, QC G1K 8K6
418-649-3400, Fax: 418-528-0932,
www.tribunaux.qc.ca/c-quebec/

Composée d'au plus 270 juges dont la juge en chef, le juge en chef associé, 4 juges en chef adjoints, et 18 juges coordonnateurs et coordonnateurs adjoints; matières civile, criminelle et pénale; matière de jeunesse; matière administrative ou en appel dans les cas prévus par la loi; cour d'archives.
Juge en chef: L'honorable Élizabeth Corte, Maurice Abud(Juge coordonnateur), Paul Chevalier(Juge coordonnateur), Jean-Paul Decoste(Juge coordonnateur), Pierre Labbé(Juge coordonnateur), Micheline Laliberté(Juge coordonnatrice), Daniel Bédard(Juge coordonnateur), Lynne Landry(Juge coordonnatrice), Patrick Théroux(Juge coordonnateur), Ruth Veillet(Juge coordonnatrice), Suzanne Villeneuve(Juge coordonnatrice), Normand Amyot(Juge coordonnateur adjoint), Pierre E. Audet(Juge coordonnateur adjoint), Marc Bisson(Juge coordonnateur adjoint), Claude Parent(Juge coordonnateur adjoint), Charles-G. Grenier(Juge coordonnateur adjoint), Chantale Pelletier(Juge coordonnatrice adjointe), Jean Lebel(Juge coordonnateur adjoint), Denis Saulnier(Juge coordonnateur adjoint), Anne Bélanger(Directrice déléguée à l'administration)
Juges (Les honorables): Michel Auger, Andrée Bergeron, Lina Bond, Rémi Bouchard, Hélène Bouillon, Christian Boulet, Peter Bradley, André-J. Brochet, Gilles Charest, André Cloutier, Pierre Coderre, René de la Sablonnière, Jean-François Dionne, Colette Duford, Jean-Pierre Dumais, Paule Gaumond, Marie-Claude Gilbert, François Godbout, Line Gosselin, Charles G. Grenier(Juge coordonnateur adjoint), Anne Laberge, Judith Landry, Daniel Lavoie, Jean Lebel(Juge coordonnateur adjoint), Jean-Louis Lemay, Bernard Lemieux, Alain Morand, Chantale Pelletier(Juge coordonnatrice adjointe), André Plante, Lucie Rondeau, Pierre-L. Rousseau, Carol St Cyr, Claude Tremblay, Jacques Tremblay, Alain Turgeon, Suzanne Villeneuve(Juge coordonnatrice), Réna Émond(Juge de paix magistrat), Sylvie Marcotte(Juge de paix magistrat), Nicole Martin(Juge de paix magistrat)

Abitibi-Témiscamingue - Amos
Claude P. Bigué, Lucille Chabot, Jean-Pierre Gervais, Marc E. Grimard

Abitibi-Témiscamingue - Rouyn-Noranda
Richard Laflamme, Nancy McKenna, Marie-Claude Bélanger(Juge de paix magistrat), Daniel Bédard(Juge coordonnateur), Denyse Leduc

Abitibi-Témiscamingue - Val d'Or
Renée Lemoine, François Boisjoli, Michel Dionne

Est du Québec - Baie-Comeau
VACANTE

Est du Québec - Matane
Jean Bécu, Robert Lévesque, Luc Marchildon(Juge de paix magistrat)

Est du Québec - New-Carlisle
Embert Whittom

Est du Québec - Percé
Richard Côté, Jean-Paul Decoste(Juge coordonnateur), James Rondeau, Lucie Morissette(Juge de paix magistrat)

Est du Québec - Rimouski
Martin Gagnon, Luce Kennedy, Guy Ringuet, Julie Dionne(Juge de paix magistrat)

Est du Québec - Rivière-du-Loup
Nathalie Aubry, Gabriel de Pokomandy(Coordonnateur), Michel Parent, Louise Gallant(Juge de paix magistrat)

Est du Québec - Sept-Iles
Gilles Lafrenière, Marie-Josée Ménard

Estrie - Drummondville
Pierre Bachand, Serge Champoux, Johanne Denis, François Marchand, Monique Perron(Juge de paix magistrat)

Estrie - Granby
Michel Beauchemin, Conrad Chapdelaine, Danielle Côté, Alain Désy, Michel DuBois, Paul Dunnigan, Michel Durand, Hélène Fabi, Lise Gagnon, Patrick Théroux(Juge coordonnateur), Sylvie Desmeules(Juge de paix magistrat)

Estrie - Sherbrooke
Normand Bonin, François Landry, Richard Landry, Denis Le Reste, Maurice Parent, Jean Roy, Marc Vanasse, Danielle Michaud(Juge de paix magistrat)

Laval—Lanaudière—Laurentides - Joliette
Jean-Pierre Archambault, Lise Gaboury, Françoise Garneau-Fournier, Dominique Larochelle, Marie-Suzanne Lauzon, Julie Messier, Micheline Sasseville, Gaby Dumas(Juge de paix magistrat)

Laval—Lanaudière—Laurentides - Laval
Pierre E. Audet(Juge coordonnateur adjoint), François Beaudoin, Jean R. Beaulieu, Valmont Beaulieu, Omer Boudreau, Paul Chevalier(Juge coordonnateur), Antoine Cloutier, Monique Fradette, Jean-Claude Gagnon, Diane Girard, Normand Lafond, Marie Lapointe, Jean La Rue, Ginette Maillet, Georges Massol

Laval—Lanaudière—Laurentides - Saint-Jérôme
Claude Melançon, Carol Richer, Jean Sirois, Michèle Toupin, Nathalie DuPerron Roy(Juge de paix magistrat), Jean-Georges Laliberté(Juge de paix magistrat), Richard Poudrier

Mauricie—Bois-Francs - Shawinigan
Yvan Cousineau, Jacques Lacoursière, Guy Lambert, Nicole Mallette, Daniel Perreault, Jacques Rioux, Dominique Slater, Guylaine Tremblay, Alain Trudel, Jacques Trudel, Pierre Verrette(Juge de paix magistrat)

Mauricie—Bois-Francs - Trois-Rivières
Pierre Labbé(Juge coordonnateur), Gaétan Ratté(Juge de paix magistrat)

Mauricie—Bois-Francs - Victoriaville
Mireille Allaire, Pierre Bélisle, Marc Bisson(Juge coordonnateur adjoint), Virgile Buffoni, Mario Gervais, Jean Gravel, Anne-Marie Jacques, Micheline Laliberté(Juge coordonnatrice), Claude Laporte, Louise Leduc, Richard Marleau, Nancy Moreau, Denys Noël, Ellen Paré, Robert Proulx, Claude Provost, Jean-Pierre Saintonge, Chantal Sirois, Marie-Josée Hénault(Juge de paix magistrat)

Montérégie - Longueuil
Marc Renaud(Juge de paix magistrat), Guy Fortier, Yves Morier, Viviane Primeau, Robert Lanctôt(Juge de paix magistrat)

Montérégie - Saint-Hyacinthe
Michel Bédard, Éric Simard

Montérégie - Saint-Jean-sur-Richelieu
Linda Despots, Marie-Chantal Doucet, Gilbert Lanthier, Michel Mercier, Claude Montpetit, Odette Perron, Marie-Andrée Villeneuve, Patricia Compagnone(Juge de paix magistrat)

Montérégie - Salaberry-de-Valleyfield
VACANTE

Montérégie - Sorel-Tracy
Juges (Les honorables): Normand Amyot(Juge coordonnateur adjoint), Denis Asselin, Armando Aznar, Normand Bastien, Lucille Beauchemin, Michel Bellehumeur, Serge Boisvert, Louise Bourdeau, François Bousquet, Jean-Pierre Boyer, Jean-Paul Braun, Alain Breault, Carole Brosseau, Gilles Cadieux, David L. Cameron, Brigitte Charron, Louise Comeau, Suzanne Coupal, Sylvain Coutlée, Antonio De Michele, Taya Di Pietro, Daniel Dortélus, Sylvie Durand, Jean-B. Falardeau

Montréal
Gilles Garneau, Lucie Godin, Brigitte Gouin, Louis Grégoire, Yves Hamel, Suzanne Handman, Patrick Healy, Martin Hébert, Patrice Hurtubise, Michel Jasmin, Ann-Marie Jones, Jean-F. Keable, Pierre E. Labelle, Céline Lacerte-Lamontagne, Gilson Lachance, Sylvie Lachapelle, Claude Lamoureux, Gilles Lareau, Denis Lavergne, Daniel Lavery, Marie Michelle Lavigne, Claude Leblond, Guy Lecompte, Michèle Lefebvre, Louis A. Legault, Gérald Locas, Robert Marchi, Eliana Marengo, Salvatore Mascia, Rolande Matte, Claude Millette, Hélène V. Morin, Jacques A. Nadeau, Gilles L. Ouellet, Manon Ouimet, Jacques Paquet, Claude Parent(Juge coordonnateur adjoint (criminelle/pénale)), Michèle Pauzé(Présidente), Michel A. Pinsonnault(Président), Louise Provost(Présidente), Diane Quenneville, André Renaud, Isabelle Rheault, Henri Richard, Robert Sansfaçon, Denis Saulnier(Juge coordonnateur adjoint (jeunesse)), Mark Shamie, Christian M. Tremblay, Suzanne Vadboncoeur, Ruth Veillet(Juge coordonnatrice), Julie Veilleux, Louise Villemure, Lori Renée Weitzman, Juanita Westmoreland-Traoré, Dominique Wilhelmy, Gaétan Zonato, Gatien Fournier, Nicole Gibeault, Jean-François Gosselin, Lynne Landry(Juge coordonnatrice), Réal R. Lapointe, Serge Laurin, Rosemarie Millar, Michel Séguin, Louise Turpin, Christine Auger(Juge de paix magistrat), Georges Benoît(Juge de paix magistrat)

Outaouais - Gatineau
Jogues Lavoie

Québec—Chaudière-Appalaches - Montmagny
Hubert Couture, Yannick Couture(Juge de paix magistrat)

Québec—Chaudière-Appalaches - Saint-Joseph-de-Beauce
Maurice Abud(Juge coordonnateur)

Saguenay—Lac-Saint-Jean - Alma
Jean-Paul Aubin, Paul Casgrain, Richard P. Daoust, Pierre Lortie, Micheline Paradis, Johanne Roy, Pierre Simard, Doris Thibault, Réjean Bédard(Juge de paix magistrat)

Saguenay—Lac-Saint-Jean - Saguenay (Chicoutimi)
Rosaire Larouche, Michel Boissonneault(Juge de paix magistrat)

Saguenay—Lac-Saint-Jean - Roberval
Pierre G. Geoffroy

Cours municipales du Québec
Québec Municipal Courts

Ministère de la Justice du Québec, 1200, route de l'Église, 6e étage, Québec, QC G1K 8K6
418-643-5140, 866-536-5140,
informations@justice.gouv.gc.ca
www.justice.gouv.qc.ca

Les cours municipales ont une compétence limitée en matière civile, notamment dans le domaine des réclamations de taxes; en matière pénale en ce qui concerne les infractions aux règlements municipaux et les infractions aux lois québécoises; et pour entendre et juger les infractions visées par la partie XXVII du Code criminel.. infractions punissables sur déclaration de culpabilité par procédure sommaire.
Juge responsable: André Perreault, Paulin Cloutier(Juge-président)

Québec
285, rue de la Maréchausée, Québec, QC G1K 8W5
418-691-6340, Fax: 418-641-6512,
greffecourmunicipale@ville.quebec.qc.ca
www.ville.quebec.qc.ca
Louis-B. Grignon

Acton Vale
1025, rue Boulay, P.O. Box 640, Acton Vale, QC J0H 1A0
450-546-2704,
www.paquette.qc.ca
Jean-M. Morency

Alma
140, rue St-Joseph S., Alma, QC G8B 3R1
418-669-5020, Fax: 418-669-5019,
www.paquette.qc.ca

Asbestos
#201, 185, rue du Roi, Asbestos, QC J1T 1S4
819-879-6971, Fax: 819-879-4102,
www.paquette.qc.ca
Micheline Fournier

Baie-Comeau
1000, rue de Mingan, Baie-Comeau, QC G5C 3C3
418-589-1518, Fax: 418-589-1556,
www.paquette.qc.ca

Barkmère
RR#1, P.O. Box 11, Argenteuil, QC J0T 1A0
Alain Boisvert

Bedford
1, rue Principale, Bedford, QC J0J 1A0
450-248-7742, Fax: 450-248-3220,
www.paquette.qc.ca
Claude Fortin

Bellechasse MRC
100, Monseigneur Bilodeau, P.O. Box 130, St-Lazare-de-Bellechasse, QC G0R 3J0
418-883-3347,
www.paquette.qc.ca
Luc Alarie, Morton S. Minc(Juge-président), Nathalie Haccoun, Richard Starck

Beloeil
777, rue Laurier, Beloeil, QC J3G 4S9
450-467-2835, Fax: 450-464-5445,
cour-mun@ville.beloeil.qc.ca
www.paquette.qc.ca

Montréal
#101, 775, rue Gosford, Montréal, QC H2Y 3B9
514-872-2534, Fax: 514-872-8271,
cour-municipale@ville.montreal.qc.ca
www.ville.montreal.qc.ca; www.paquette.qc.ca
Guy Saulnier

Blainville
Hôtel de ville, 1000, ch du Plan-Bouchard, Blainville, QC J7C 3S9
450-434-5224, Fax: 450-434-8285,
www.ville.blainville.qc.ca, www.paquette.qc.ca
André Hotte

Boisbriand
940, boul de la Grande-Allée, Boisbriand, QC J7G 2J7
450-435-1954, Fax: 450-435-6398,
service.cour.municipale@ville.boisbriand.qc.ca
www.paquette.qc.ca
Jean-Pierre Dépelteau

Candiac
100, boul Montcalm N., Candiac, QC J5R 3L8
450-444-6060, Fax: 450-444-0789,
www.paquette.qc.ca
Gilles R. Pelletier

Chambly
1, Place de la Mairie, Chambly, QC J3L 4X1
450-658-8788, Fax: 450-658-4214,
www.paquette.qc.ca
Jean-Pierre Gignac

Charlesbourg
160, rue 76e est, Charlesbourg, QC G1H 7H5
418-641-6179, Fax: 418-641-6594
Raymond Lavoie

Charny
5333, rue de la Symphonie, Charny, QC G6X 3B6
Paul Lemieux

Châteauguay
#101, 265, boul d'Anjou, Châteauguay, QC J6J 5J9
450-698-3245, Fax: 450-698-3259,
courmun@ville.chateauguay.qc.ca
www.ville.chateauguay.qc.ca
La cour a le mandat de veiller à l'application des lois et des règlements municipaux, provinciaux et fédéraux pour Châteauguay, Mercier, Léry et Beauharnois.
Frédérique Lalancette

Chibougamau
650, 3e rue, Chibougamau, QC G8P 1P1
418-748-3132, Fax: 418-748-6562,
www.paquette.qc.ca
Pierre A. Cloutier

Coaticook
14, rue Adams, #14, Coaticook, QC J1A 1K3
819-849-2721, Fax: 819-849-4883,
www.paquette.qc.ca
Slobodan Delev

Colline-de-L'Outaouais
216, ch Haute-Chelsea, Chelsea, QC J9B 1J4
819-827-0516, Fax: 819-827-5712,
lst-pierre@mrcdescollines.co
www.paquette.qc.ca
M. Jacques Ouellet

Côte-de-Beaupré MRC
3, rue de la Seigneurie, Château-Richer, QC G0A 1N0
418-824-3444, Fax: 418-824-3917
Pierre Raiche

Cowansville
220, Place Municipale, Cowansville, QC J2K 1T4
450-263-5434, Fax: 450-263-4332,
www.paquette.qc.ca
Marguerite M. Brochu

D'Autray MRC
118, Notre-Dame, Le Gardeur, QC J5Z 3C3
Fax: 450-585-7035
Jacques Laurier

Delson
50, Ste-Thérèse, Delson, QC J0L 1G0
Jacques Lamontagne

Deux-Montagnes
#101, 400, boul Deux-Montagnes, Deux-Montagnes, QC J7R 5C2
450-473-8688, Fax: 450-473-0094,
www.paquette.qc.ca
Jacquelin Légaré

Dolbeau-Mistassini
1100, boul Walberg, Dolbeau-Mistassini, QC J7R 5C2
450-473-8688,
www.paquette.qc.ca
Claude Fournier

Donnacona
138, av Pleau, P.O. Box 609, Donnacona, QC G01 1T0
418-285-3163, Fax: 418-285-0020,
www.paquette.qc.ca
Manon Bourbonnais

Dorion
190, St-Charles, P.O. Box 70, Dorion, QC J7V 5V8
Georges É. Laurin, Jean-Pierre Dépelteau

Dorval
530, boul Bouchard, Dorval, QC H9S 1B2
514-633-4146,
www.paquette.qc.ca
Michel Houle

Drummondville
415, rue Lindsay, P.O. Box 398, Drummondville, QC J2B 6W3
819-478-6556, Fax: 819-478-0920,
courmunicipale@ville.drummondville.qc.ca
www.paquette.qc.ca
Pierre-A. Cloutier

Haut-St-François MRC
146, Angus Nord, East Angus, QC J0B 1R0
819-832-2868, Fax: 819-832-2868
Claude Hamann

Farnham
477, de l'Hôtel-de-Ville, Farnham, QC J2N 2H3
450-293-3178, Fax: 450-260-1376,
www.paquette.qc.ca
François Gravel, Yves Daoust

Gatineau
La Mairie- 280, boul. Maloney E., Gatineau, QC J8P 1C6
819-243-2345, Fax: 819-595-4289,
www.paquette.qc.ca
Pierre G. Geoffroy

Granby
125, Simonds S., Granby, QC J2J 1P7
450-776-8340, Fax: 450-776-8342,
www.paquette.qc.ca
Jean-Marc Champagne, Jocelyn Crête

Grand'Mère
333, av 5e, P.O. Box 350, Grand-Mère, QC G9T 5L1
819-538-1614,
www.paquette.qc.ca
Jean-Guy Clément, Denis Boudrias

Greenfield Park
156, boul Churchill, Greenfield Park, QC J4V 2M3
450-446-8108,
www.paquette.qc.ca
Lison Asseraf, Pierre Mondor

Hampstead
5569, ch. De la Reine-Marie, Hampstead, QC H3X 1W5

514-369-8200,
www.paquette.qc.ca
Vacant

Haut-Saint Laurent MRC
23, Laurier, 6e étage, Hull, QC J8X 4C8
819-595-7272,
www.paquette.qc.ca
Robert La Haye

Hudson
rue Principale, Hudson, QC J0P 1H0
Pierre-Armand Tremblay, Denis Boudrias

Iberville
855, 1ère, Iberville, QC J2X 3C7
450-357-2744,
www.paquette.qc.ca
Louis Laporte

Joliette
245, Papineau, Joliette, QC J6E 2K8
450-753-8123,
www.paquette.qc.ca
Other Communications: Email:
cour.municipale@ville.joliette.qc.ca
Jean-Jacques Turcotte, Alain Côté

Jonquière
2201, rue de Montfort, P.O. Box 278, Jonquière, QC G7X 4P6
418-546-2238,
www.paquette.qc.ca
Jacques Laverdure

Ile-Perrot
110, boul Perrot, Ile-Perrot, QC J7V 3G1
Alain Côté, Jean-Jacques Turcotte

La-Baie
422, rue Victoria, La Baie, QC G7B 3M4
418-697-5000,
www.paquette.qc.ca
Jacques Ouellet

La Pocatière
412, 9e rue, P.O. Box 668, La Pocatière, QC G0R 1Z0
418-856-3394, Fax: 418-856-5465,
www.paquette.qc.ca
Claude Céré

La Prairie
170, boul. Taschereau, #400, La Prairie, QC J5R 5H6
450-444-0540,
www.paquette.qc.ca
Gabriel Garneau

Lac Mégantic
#201, 5527, rue Frontenac, Lac-Mégantic, QC G6B 1H6
819-583-2815, Fax: 819-583-2841,
cour.municipale@ville.lac-megantic.qc.ca
www.ville.lac-megantic.qc.ca; www.paquette.qc.ca
Sophie Beauchemin, Manon Bourbonnais

Lachine
1800, boul St-Joseph, Lachine, QC H8S 2N4
514-634-3471,
www.paquette.qc.ca
Guy Saulnier

Lachute
380, rue Principale, Lachute, QC J8H 1Y2
450-562-3781, Fax: 450-562-1431,
www.paquette.qc.ca
Denis Laberge

Lasalle
55, av Dupras, Lasalle, QC H8R 4A8
514-367-6270,
www.paquette.qc.ca
Gilles Thouin

L'Assomption
399, rue Dorval, L'Assomption, QC J5W 1A1
450-589-5671, Fax: 450-589-4512,
courmunicipale@ville.lassomption.qc.ca
www.ville.lassomption.qc.ca; www.paquette.qc.ca
Claude Trudel

La Tuque
558, rue Commerciale, La Tuque, QC G9X 3A9
819-523-2052, Fax: 819-523-4536,
www.paquette.qc.ca
Bernard Caron, Jean H. Charbonneau, Yves Fournier

Laval
55, boul des Laurentides, Laval, QC H7G 2T1
450-662-4466, Fax: 450-662-8501,
www.paquette.qc.ca

Lévis
5333, rue de la Symphonie, Charny, QC G6X 3B6
418-832-4695,
www.ville.levis.qc.ca
Jacques Ouellet, Jacques Ouellet

L'Islet MRC
364, rue Verreault, Saint-Jean-Port-Joli, QC G0R 3G0
418-598-3076, Fax: 418-598-6880,
www.paquette.qc.ca
Richard Alary, Guy Houle, Bruno Themens

Longueuil
100, Place Charles-Lemoyne, Longueuil, QC J4K 2T4
450-463-7006, Fax: 450-646-8897,
www.longueuil.ca
Louis-M. Vachon, Claude Fournier, Jean-Pierre Gignac, Paulin Cloutier

Loretteville
305, rue Racine, Loretteville, QC G2B 1E7
418-842-1921,
www.paquette.qc.ca
Paulin Cloutier

Lotbinière MRC
#4, 372, rue St-Joseph, P.O. Box 40, Laurier-Station, QC G0S 1N0
418-728-2787, Fax: 418-728-2501,
www.paquette.qc.ca
Jocelyn Crête

Louiseville
105, av St-Laurent ouest, Louiseville, QC J5V 1J6
819-228-9437
Pierre Geoffroy

Magog
7, rue Principale E., Magog, QC J1X 1Y4
819-843-6501, Fax: 819-843-3599,
www.paquette.qc.ca
Louis-B. Grignon

Marieville
682, rue St-Charles, Marieville, QC J3M 1P9
450-460-4444,
www.paquette.qc.ca
Claude Lemire

Mascouche
3034, Ste-Marie, Mascouche, QC J7K 1P1
450-474-4133,
www.paquette.qc.ca
Michel Lalande

Matawinie MRC
3184, 1e av, P.O. Box 1239, Rawdon, QC J0K 1S0
450-834-5441,
cour@mrcmatawinie.qc.ca
www.paquette.qc.ca
Michel Paquin

Mirabel
14 026, boul du Curé-Labelle, Mirabel, QC J7J 1A1
450-435-6408,
www.paquette.qc.ca
Michel J. Lapointe, Jacquelin Légaré

Mistassini
173, St-Michel, P.O. Box 219, Mistissini, QC G0W 2C0
Pierre-G. Bouchard, Jacques Laurier

Mont-Royal
20, av Roosevelt, Mount-Royal, QC H3R 1Z4
514-734-2907
Marguerite M. Brochu

Montcalm
1530, rue Albert, P.O. Box 308, Sainte-Julienne, QC J0K 2T0
450-831-2182,
www.paquette.qc.ca
Louis-Marie Vachon

Montmagny
134, rue St-Jean-Baptiste est, Montmagny, QC G5V 1K6
418-248-3361,
www.paquette.qc.ca
Florent Bisson, Jean Hébert

Montréal-Est
11 370, rue Notre-Dame est, Montréal, QC H1B 2W6
514-645-7431,
www.paquette.qc.ca
Jacques Lamontagne, Robert Diamond

Montréal-Nord
11 211 av. Hébert, Montréal-Nord, QC H1H 3X5
514-328-4079,
www.paquette.qc.ca
Frank Schlesinger

Montréal-Ouest
50, av Westminster S., Montréal, QC H4X 1Y7
514-481-8125
Jacques Desaulniers

Nicolet
180, Mgr. Panet, Nicolet, QC J3T 1S6
819-293-6901, Fax: 819-293-6767,
www.paquette.qc.ca
Pierre-J. Raîche, Georges-E. Laurin

Outremont
1433. ave. Van Horne, Outremont, QC H2V 1K9
514-495-6250,
www.paquette.qc.ca
Philippe Clément, Pierre Mondor

Pierrefonds
13 665, boul Pierrefonds, Pierrefonds, QC H9H 2Z4
514-624-1124,
www.paquette.qc.ca
Robert La Haye

Pincourt
919, ch Duhamel, Pincourt, QC J7V 4G8
Jules Bellavance

Plessisville
1700, rue St-Calixte, Plessisville, QC G6L 1R3
819-362-3284,
www.paquette.qc.ca
Pierre Mondor, Philippe Clément

Pointe-Claire
401, boul. Saint-Jean, Pointe-Claire, QC H9R 3J2
514-630-1205,
www.paquette.qc.ca
Claude Caron

Princeville
50, St-Jacques ouest, Princeville, QC G6L 4Y5
819-364-5179, Fax: 819-364-5198,
www.paquette.qc.ca
Gilles Thouin

Repentigny
435, boul d'Iberville, Repentigny, QC J6A 2B6
450-654-2358,
www.paquette.qc.ca
Jean Blouin

Rimouski
205, av de la Cathédrale, P.O. Box 710, Rimouski, QC G5L 7C7
418-724-3181, Fax: 418-724-9795,
greffe@ville.rimouski.qc.ca
www.paquette.qc.ca
Jacquelin Légaré

Roberval
851, boul Saint-Joseph, Roberval, QC G8H 2L6
418-275-0202, Fax: 418-275-5031,
www.paquette.qc.ca
Robert Diamond

Rosemère
100, rue Charbonneau, Rosemère, QC J7A 3W1
450-621-3500, Fax: 450-472-3607,
www.paquette.qc.ca
Ronald J. Montcalm, Philippe Clément

Roxboro
13 Centre Commercial, Roxboro, QC H8Y 2N9
514-684-0555,
www.paquette.qc.ca

Saguenay
201, rue Racine est, P.O. Box 129, Chicoutimi, QC G7H 5B8
418-698-3161,
www.paquette.qc.ca
Jacques Laverdure

Ste-Adèle
1381, boul Sainte-Adele, Sainte-Adèle, QC J8B 1A3
450-229-2921, Fax: 450-229-4179,
www.paquette.qc.ca
J.H. Denis Gagnon

Ste-Agathe-des-Monts
50, rue St-Joseph, Sainte-Agathe-des-Monts, QC J8C 1M9
819-326-4595, Fax: 819-326-6331,
www.paquette.qc.ca
Pascal Pillarella, Jacques Ghanimé

Ste-Anne-de-Bellevue
109, Ste-Anne, P.O. Box 40, Sainte-Anne-de-Bellevue, QC H9X 1M2
514-457-5500,
www.paquette.qc.ca
Guy Houle, Marc Gravel

St-Bruno-de-Montarville
1585, boul Montarville, St-Bruno-de-Montarville, QC J3V 3T8
450-441-8303,
www.paquette.qc.ca
Michel Brun

St-Césaire
1111, St-Paul, Saint-Césaire, QC J0L 1T0
450-469-3108, Fax: 450-469-5275,
www.paquette.qc.ca
Jacques Laurier

St-Constant
147, rue St-Pierre, P.O. Box 130, Saint-Constant, QC J5A 2G2
450-638-2010, Fax: 450-632-0788,
www.paquette.qc.ca
Guy Saulnier

St-Eustache
168, Dorion, Saint-Eustache, QC J7R 2G2
450-472-4440
Frédérique Lalancette

St-Félicien
1058, boul. Sacré-Coeur, P.O. Box 7000, Saint-Félicien, QC G8K 2R5
418-679-0251, Fax: 418-679-1449,
www.paquette.qc.ca

Sainte-Foy
1130, rte de l'Église, Sainte-Foy, QC G1V 4X6
418-641-6179, Fax: 418-641-6539,
www.ville.quebec.qc.ca
Gabriel Garneau

St-Georges
11 700, boul. LaCroix, St-Georges, QC G5Y 1L3
418-228-5555, Fax: 418-226-2282,
www.paquette.qc.ca

Mont-Saint-Hilaire
Hôtel de Ville, 100, rue du Centre-Civique, Mont-Saint-Hilaire, QC J3H 3M8
450-467-2854,
courmunicipale@villemsh.ca
www.ville.mont-saint-hilaire.qc.ca
Jean Herbert, Claude Céré

St-Hubert
4800, Leckie, Saint-Hubert, QC J3Z 1H4
450-445-7862,
www.paquette.qc.ca
Gilles Charpentier

Saint-Hyacinthe
700, de l'Hôtel-de-Ville, Saint-Hyacinthe, QC J2S 5B2
450-778-8319, Fax: 450-778-8628,
cour-municipale@ville.st-hyacinthe.qc.ca
www.paquette.qc.ca
Claude Fortin, Jean-Pierre Gignac

St-Jean-Chrysostome
959, rue de l'Hotel de Ville, St-Jean-Chrysostome-de-Lév, QC G6Z 2N8
418-839-9417,
www.paquette.qc.ca
Pierre-Armand Tremblay

Saint-Jean-sur-Richelieu
188, Jacques-Cartier N., P.O. Box 1025, Saint-Jean-sur-Richelieu, QC J3B 7B2
450-357-2087, Fax: 450-357-2750,
cour.municipale@ville.saint-jean-sur-richelieu.qc.ca
www.paquette.qc.ca
Jacques Laverdure

St-Jérôme MRC
280, Labelle, Saint-Jérome, QC J7Z 5L1
450-436-1511, Fax: 450-436-4506
Marc Gravel, Guy Houle

St-Lambert
55, Argyle, Saint-Lambert, QC J4P 2H3
450-923-6555,
www.paquette.qc.ca
Pierre G. Bouchard, Lison Asseraf

Saint-Laurent
1405, de l'Église, Saint-Laurent, QC H4L 2H4
514-855-6060,
www.paquette.qc.ca
Robert LaHaye, Richard Chassé

St-Léonard-de-Port-Maurice
8400, boul Lacordaire, St-Léonard, QC H1R 3B1
514-328-8447,
www.paquette.qc.ca
Denis Boudrias, Pascal Pillarella

St-Luc
347, boul St-Luc, Saint-Luc, QC J2W 2A2
450-359-2444,
www.paquette.qc.ca
Paul Routhier

Ste-Marie
270, av Marguerite Bourgeos, P.O. Box 1750, Sainte-Marie, QC G6E 3C7
418-387-2301, Fax: 418-387-2454,
www.paquette.qc.ca
Jacques Ouellet, Louis-Marie Vachon

St-Rédempteur
85, rue 19e, St-Rédempteur, QC G6K 1C3
418-836-4400,
www.paquette.qc.ca; www.barreau.qc.ca
Commune St-Nicholas, St-Rédempteur, Bernières et St-Étienne de Lauzon.
Pierre G. Bouchard

St-Pierre
69, av 5e, Saint-Pierre, QC H8R 1P1
514-364-5153,
www.paquette.qc.ca
Jean-R. Côté

St-Raymond
375, rue St-Joseph, Saint-Raymond, QC G3L 1A1
418-337-2202, Fax: 418-337-2203,
www.paquette.qc.ca
Pascal Pillarella

St-Rémi
105, Perras, Saint-Rémi, QC J0L 2L0
450-454-3994, Fax: 450-454-6898,
www.paquette.qc.ca
Guy Saulnier

Ste-Thérèse
6, rue de l'Église, P.O. Box 100, Sainte-Thérèse, QC J7E 4H7
450-434-1440, Fax: 450-434-1499,
www.paquette.qc.ca
Claude Trudel

St-Tite
540, rue Notre-Dame, Saint-Tite, QC G0X 3H0
418-365-5143
Paul Lemieux

Salaberry-de-Valleyfield
61, Sainte-Cécile, Salaberry-de-Valleyfield, QC J6T 1L8
450-370-4305, Fax: 450-370-4868,
www.paquette.qc.ca
Pierre Mondor, Philippe Clément

Senneville
35, ch. Senneville, Senneville, QC H9X 1B8
514-457-6020,
www.paquette.qc.ca
Guy Pettigrew

Sept-Iles
546, av Dequen, Sept-Iles, QC G4R 2R4
418-964-3249, Fax: 418-964-3259,
www.paquette.qc.ca
Claude Trudel

Shawinigan MRC
550, de l'Hôtel de Ville, P.O. Box 400, Shawinigan, QC G9N 6V3
819-536-7216, Fax: 819-536-2797
Claude Trudel, Jocelyn Crête

Shawinigan
1550, rue 118e, P.O. Box 400, Shawinigan, QC G9P 3V3
819-536-7216,
www.paquette.qc.ca
Roland Lamoureux

Sherbrooke
191, rue Palais, P.O. Box 1614, Sherbrooke, QC J1H 5M4
819-821-5600, Fax: 819-821-5599,
www.paquette.qc.ca
René Paquet, Jean-Pierre Gignac

Sillery
1445, av Maguire, Sillery, QC G1T 2W9
418-684-2134,
www.paquette.qc.ca
Jacques Guertin

Sorel-Tracy
3025, boul de Tracy, Sorel-Tracy, QC J3R 1C2
450-742-7775, Fax: 450-742-2420,
www.agcmq.qc.ca
Michel Paquin

Terrebonne
Édifice Louis Lepage, 754, rue Saint-Pierre, Terrebonne, QC J6W 1E4
450-471-4192,
www.paquette.qc.ca
Gilles Ouellet

Thetford-Mines
144, rue Notre-Dame ouest, P.O. Box 489, Thetford Mines, QC G6G 5T3
418-335-2981, Fax: 418-335-7089,
www.paquette.qc.ca
Jocelyn Crête

Trois-Rivières
1401, Royale, 2 étage, P.O. Box 969, Trois-Rivières, QC G9A 5K2
819-372-4628, Fax: 819-379-7551,
www.paquette.qc.ca
Jocelyn Crête, Claude Trudel

Trois-Rivières-Ouest
500, Côte du Richelieu, Trois-Rivières, QC G9A 2Z1
819-375-7731,
www.paquette.qc.ca
Jean-Pierre Gignac, Claude Fortin

Val-Bélair
1105, av de l'Église N., Val-Bélair, QC G3K 1X5
418-842-7184,
www.paquette.qc.ca
Jacques Barbès

Val-d'Or
855, 2e Ave., P.O. Box 400, Val-d'Or, QC J9P 4P4
819-824-9613, Fax: 819-825-6650,
courmunicipale@ville.valdor.
www.paquette.qc.ca
Pierre G. Geoffroy

Val-St-François MRC
#101, 3, Greenlay S., Sainte-Grégoire-de-Greenlay, QC J1S 2J1
819-845-2016, Fax: 819-845-3209,
www.paquette.qc.ca
Manon Bourbonnais

Vaudreuil-Soulanges MRC
190, Saint-Charles, Vaudreuil-Dorion, QC J7V 2L3
450-455-9480, Fax: 450-373-7967,
www.paquette.qc.ca
Jacques Ghanimé, Pascal Pillarella

Verdun
#104, 4555, av Verdun, Verdun, QC H4G 1M4
514-765-7060,
www.paquette.qc.ca
Michel Houle

Victoriaville
1, Notre-Dame O., P.O. Box 370, Victoriaville, QC G6P 6T2
819-758-4338, Fax: 819-758-9292,
www.paquette.qc.ca
Michel Brun

Waterloo
417, rue de la Cour, #210, P.O. Box 430, Waterloo, QC J0E 2N0
450-539-2422, Fax: 450-539-3257,
www.paquette.qc.ca
Keith A. Ham, Ronald Montcalm

Westmount
21, rue Stanton, Westmount, QC H3Y 3B1
514-989-5260,
www.paquette.qc.ca

Québec: Les Palais de justice et Points de service de justice
Courts & Judicial Service Ce
QC

Alma
725, rue Harvey ouest, Alma, QC G8B 1P5
418-668-3334, Fax: 418-662-3697

Amos
891, rue 3e ouest, Amos, QC J9T 2T4
819-444-5063, Fax: 819-444-5204

Baie Comeau
71, av Mance, Baie-Comeau, QC G4Z 1N2
418-296-5534, Fax: 418-294-8717, 866-854-4075

Campbell's Bay
30, rue John, Campbell's Bay, QC J0X 1K0
819-648-5222, Fax: 819-648-5931

Chicoutimi
227, rue Racine est, 1er étage, Chicoutimi, QC G7H 7B4
418-696-9926, Fax: 418-698-3558

Cowansville

920, rue Principale, Cowansville, QC J2K 0E3
450-263-3520, Fax: 450-266-1415
Drummondville
1680, boul St-Joseph, Drummondville, QC J2C 2G3
819-478-2513, Fax: 819-475-8459
Granby
Édifice Roger-Paré, #1.32, 77, rue Principale, Granby, QC J2G 9B3
450-776-7110, Fax: 450-776-4080
Hâvre-Aubert
#102, 405, ch d'En-Haut, Hâvre-Aubert, QC G4T 9A7
418-937-2201, Fax: 418-937-9038
Hull
17, rue Laurier, Gatineau, QC J8X 4C1
819-776-8100, Fax: 819-772-3347
Joliette
200, rue Saint-Marc, Joliette, QC J6E 8C2
450-753-4807, Fax: 450-752-1733
Lac-Mégantic
#316, 5527, rue Frontenac, Lac-Mégantic, QC G6B 1H6
819-583-1268, Fax: 819-583-0703
La Malbaie
30, ch de la Vallée, La Malbaie, QC G5A 1A3
418-665-3991, Fax: 418-665-1125
La Tuque
290, rue Saint-Joseph, P.O. Box 6, La Tuque, QC G9X 3Z8
819-523-9533, Fax: 819-523-3603
Laval
2800, boul Saint-Martin ouest, Laval, QC H7T 2S9
450-686-5015, Fax: 450-686-5005
Longueuil
1111, boul Jacques-Cartier est, Longueuil, QC J4M 2J6
450-646-4010, Fax: 450-928-7982
Maniwaki
266, rue Notre-Dame, 1er étage, Maniwaki, QC J9E 2J8
819-449-3222, Fax: 819-449-6085
Mont-Laurier
645, rue de la Madone, Mont-Laurier, QC J9L 1T1
819-623-9666, Fax: 819-623-6859
Montmagny
25, rue du Palais de Justice, Montmagny, QC G5V 1P6
418-248-0909, Fax: 418-248-2437
Montréal
1, rue Notre-Dame est, Montréal, QC H2Y 1B6
514-393-2721, Fax: 514-873-4760
New Carlisle
87, rue Gérard-D.-Lévesque, New Carlisle, QC G0C 1Z0
418-752-3376, Fax: 418-752-6979
Percé
124, rte 132, P.O. Box 188, Percé, QC G0C 2L0
418-782-2055, Fax: 418-782-2906
Québec
300, boul Jean-Lesage, Québec, QC G1K 8K6
418-649-3400, Fax: 418-528-0932
Rimouski
183, av de la Cathédrale, Rimouski, QC G5L 5J1
418-727-3852, Fax: 418-727-3635
Rivière-du-Loup
33, rue de la Cour, Rivière-du-Loup, QC G5R 1J1
418-862-3579, Fax: 418-867-8794, 800-463-8009
Roberval
750, boul St-Joseph, Roberval, QC G8H 2L5
418-275-3666, Fax: 418-275-6169
Rouyn-Noranda
2, av du Palais, Rouyn-Noranda, QC J9X 2N9
819-763-3058, Fax: 819-763-3389
Saint-Hyacinthe
1550, rue Dessaulles, Saint-Hyacinthe, QC J2S 2S8
450-778-6559, Fax: 450-778-6557
Saint-Jean-sur-Richelieu
109, rue Saint-Charles, Saint-Jean-sur-Richelieu, QC J3B 2C2
450-347-1392, Fax: 450-346-8437
Saint-Jérôme
25, rue de Martigny ouest, Saint-Jérôme, QC J7Y 4Z1
514-431-4406, Fax: 514-569-3143
Saint-Joseph-de-Beauce
795, av du Palais, Saint-Joseph-de-Beauce, QC G0S 2V0
418-397-7187, Fax: 418-397-7968
Salaberry-de-Valleyfield
180, rue Salaberry ouest, Salaberry-de-Valleyfield, QC J6T 2J2
450-370-4006, Fax: 450-370-3022
Sept-Iles
425, boul Laure, Sept-Iles, QC G4R 1X6
418-962-3044, Fax: 418-964-8714, 866-405-7951
Shawinigan
212, 6e rue, Shawinigan, QC G9N 8B6
819-536-2571, Fax: 819-536-2992
Sherbrooke
375, rue King ouest, Sherbrooke, QC J1H 6B9
819-822-6910, Fax: 819-820-3134
Sorel-Tracy
46, rue Charlotte, Sorel-Tracy, QC J3P 6N5
450-742-2786, Fax: 450-746-7394
Thetford Mines
#1.23, 693, rue St-Alphonse ouest, Thetford Mines, QC G6G 3X3
418-338-2118, Fax: 418-335-7756
Trois-Rivières
850, rue Hart, Trois-Rivières, QC G9A 1T9

Other Communications: Fax civile: 819/371-6096; Fax criminel: 819/371-6111
Victoriaville
800, boul Bois-Francs sud, Victoriaville, QC G6P 5W5
819-357-2054, Fax: 819-357-5517
Ville-Marie
8, rue Saint-Gabriel nord, Ville-Marie, QC J9V 1Z9
819-629-6473, Fax: 819-622-6367

Points de service:
Amqui
29, boul Saint-Benoît ouest, Amqui, QC G5J 2E4
418-629-4488, Fax: 418-629-6450

Carleton
17, rue Lacroix, Carleton, QC G0C 1J0
418-364-3442, Fax: 418-364-7036

Dolbeau-Mistassini
1420, boul Walberg, 1er étage, Dolbeau-Mistassini, QC G8L 1H4
418-276-0683, Fax: 418-276-6110

Forestville
Édifice Renato, 24, rte 138 ouest, P.O. Box 400, Forestville, QC G0T 1E0
418-587-4471, Fax: 418-587-6639, 866-854-4075

Gaspé
11, rue de la Cathédrale, Gaspé, QC G4X 2V9
418-368-5756, Fax: 416-360-8030

Jonquière
Édifice Marguerite-Belley, 3950, boul Harvey, RC, Jonquière, QC G7X 8L6
418-695-7991, Fax: 418-698-3558

Lachute
#216, 505, rue Béthany, Lachute, QC J8H 4A6
450-562-3711, Fax: 450-569-7645

Magog
Hôtel de Ville, #127, 7, rue Principale est, Magog, QC J1X 1Y4
819-843-7323, Fax: 819-843-4533

Matane
382, av Saint-Jérôme, Matane, QC G4W 3B3
418-562-2497, Fax: 418-560-8746

Mont-Joli
40, rue de l'Hôtel-de-Ville, Mont-Joli, QC G5H 1W8
418-775-8811, Fax: 418-775-7517

Sainte-Agathe-des-Monts
85, rue Saint-Vincent, Sainte-Agathe-des-Monts, QC J8C 2A8
819-326-6462, Fax: 819-569-7645

Sainte-Anne-des-Monts
10-B, boul Sainte-Anne ouest, Sainte-Anne-des-Monts, QC G4V 1P3
418-763-2791, Fax: 418-763-3107

Saskatchewan

Saskatchewan: Court of Appeal
Court House, 2425 Victoria Ave., Regina, SK S4P 3V7
306-787-5382, Fax: 306-787-5817,
www.sasklawcourts.ca
The Court of Appeal has appellate jurisdiction with respect to any judgement, order or decree made by the Court of Queen's Bench & any matter granted to it by statute.
Chief Justice of Saskatchewan: The Hon. John Klebuc
Justices of Appeal (The Hon. Mr./Madam Justice): S.J. Cameron, W.J. Vancise, M.A. Gerwing, R.G. Richards, N.W. Sherstobitoff, G.A. Smith, J.G. Lane, G.R. Jackson
Administration:
Registrar: Maurice Herauf

Saskatchewan Court of Queen's Bench
2425 Victoria Ave., Regina, SK S4P 3V7
306-787-5377, Fax: 306-787-7217,
www.sasklawcourts.ca/default.asp?pg=queens_ben
The Court of Queen's Bench is a court of original jurisdiction having jurisdiction in civil & criminal matters arising in Saskatchewan, except those matters expressly excluded by statute.
Chief Justice: The Hon. R.D. Laing
Justices (The Hon. Mr./Madam Justice): D.P. Ball, R.L. Barclay(Supernumerary), C.L. Dawson, W.F. Gerein(Supernumerary), E.J. Gunn, D.C. Hunter, G.M. Kraus, L.A. Kyle, F.J. Kovach, E.C. Malone(Supernumerary), D.E.W. McIntyre, I.D. McLellan(Supernumerary), J.E. McMurtry, N.S. Sandomirsky, E.A. Scheibel(Supernumerary), D.L. Wilson, C.R. Wimmer(Supernumerary), T.C. Zarzeczny
Administration:
Registrar, the Court of Queen's Bench & Provincial Court: Sharon Pratchler
Local Registrar: Gordon Dauncey
Sheriff: J. Rhinelander

Battleford
Court House, 291 - 23 St. West, P.O. Box 340, Battleford, SK S0M 0E0
306-446-7670, Fax: 306-446-7737
D.K. Kreuger(Supernumerary)
Sheriff, Local Registrar: Linda Popp, G.A. Chicoine
Deputy Sheriff & Local Registrar: Peggy Boxrud

Estevan
Court House, 1016 - 4 St., Estevan, SK S4A 0W5
306-637-4530, Fax: 306-637-4536
Sheriff & Local Registrar: Patricia Buttner
Sheriff & Local Registrar: Eleanor Neigel
Deputy Sheriff & Deputy Local Registrar: Elaine Lange

Humboldt
Court House, 805 - 8 Ave., P.O. Box 490, Humboldt, SK S0K 2A0
306-682-6730, Fax: 306-682-3536
Deputy Sheriff & Deputy Local Registrar: D. Willenborg

Melfort
Court House, 409 Main St., P.O. Box 850, Melfort, SK S0E 1A0
306-752-6265, Fax: 306-752-6264
L.B. MacDonald

Moose Jaw
Court House, 64 Ominica St. West, Moose Jaw, SK S6H 1W9
306-694-3602, Fax: 306-694-3056
R.D. Maher, A.R. Rothery
Sheriff & Local Registrar: Maria Lynn Freeland

Prince Albert
Court House, Prince Albert, SK S6V 4W7
306-953-3200, Fax: 306-953-3210
G.N. Allbright, G.W. Baynton(Supernumerary), G.M. Currie, M.L. Dovell, P. Foley, N.G. Gabrielson, I. Goldenberg(Supernumerary)

Saskatoon
520 Spadina Cres. East, Saskatoon, SK S7K 2H6
306-933-5137, Fax: 306-975-4818
P. Hrabinsky(Supernumerary), J. Klebuc, J.D. Koch, R.C. Mills, G.A. Smith, D.H. Wright(Supernumerary)
Local Registrar: D. Berezowsky
Sheriff: G. Laing, J.A. Ryan-Froslie, R.S. Smith, Y.G.K. Wilkinson, M.R. Wright
Local Registrar: Dennis Berezowsky
Deputy Local Registrar: Kathy Brower

Saskatoon Family Law Division
224 - 4 Ave. South, 9th Fl., Saskatoon, SK S7K 5M5
306-933-5174, Fax: 306-933-5703
D.B. Konkin
Sheriff & Local Registrar: R. Peterson

Swift Current
Court House, 121 Lorne St. West, Swift Current, SK S9H 0J4
306-778-8400, Fax: 306-778-8581
Sheriff & Local Registrar: Patricia Buttner

Weyburn
Court House, 301 Prairie Ave., Weyburn, SK S4H 0L4
306-848-2359, Fax: 306-848-2540
Deputy Sheriff/Local Registrar & Court Clerk: Stan Urbanoski

Wynyard
Court House, 410 Ave. C East, P.O. Box 369, Wynyard, SK S0A 4T0
306-554-2561, Fax: 306-554-3405
J.L.G. Pritchard
Sheriff, Court Clerk & Local Registrar: S. Urbanoski

Yorkton
Court House, 29 Darlington St. East, Yorkton, SK S3N 0C2
306-786-1515, Fax: 306-786-1521

Saskatchewan Provincial Court
1815 Smith St., Regina, SK S4P 3V7

306-787-5500, Fax: 306-787-3933, www.sasklawcourts.ca/default.asp?pg=provincial

The Provincial Court has jurisdiction in both civil (including small claims & family) & select criminal (including young offender) matters.

Chief Judge: The Hon. G.T.G. Seniuk

Courts:

Estevan
Court House, 1016 - 4th St., Estevan, SK S4A 0W5
306-637-4528, Fax: 306-637-4536
J. Benison, Sid Robinson

La Ronge
1320 La Ronge Ave., P.O. Box 5000, La Ronge, SK S0J 1L0
306-425-4505, Fax: 306-425-4269
W.K. Tucker, K.J. Young

Lloydminster
4815 - 50 St., Lloydminster, SK S9V 0M8
306-825-6420, Fax: 306-825-6497
J. Nightingale, E. Kalenith

Meadow Lake
#3, 212 - 1 St. East, Meadow Lake, SK S9X 1T7
306-236-7575, Fax: 306-236-7598
L. Dyck, B. Morgan

Melfort
107 Crawford Ave. East, P.O. Box 6500, Melfort, SK S0E 1A0
306-752-6230, Fax: 306-752-6126
D. Kovatch, D. Orr

Moose Jaw
#211, 110 Ominica St. West, Moose Jaw, SK S6H 6V2
306-694-3612, Fax: 306-694-3043
D. Kaiser, V.H. Meekma, D. O'Hanlon

North Battleford
3 Railway Ave. East, North Battleford, SK S9A 2P9
306-446-7400, Fax: 306-446-7432
T.B. Bekolay, Stephen Carter, T.W. Ferris, H.W. Goliath, G.M. Morin, H.R.E. Weisgerber

Prince Albert
188 -11th St. West, P.O. Box 3003, Prince Albert, SK S6V 6G1
306-953-2640, Fax: 306-953-2819
K.E. Bellerose, D. Bogdasavich, A. Crugnole-Reid, D.E. Fenwick, L. Halliday, B.D. Henning, D. Morris, L.J. Smith

Regina
1815 Smith St., Regina, SK S4P 3V7
306-787-5250, Fax: 306-787-7037
L.C.A. Snell, C. Toth, R.G. Bell, B.P. Carey, B.L. Huculak, R.D. Jackson, M.D. Irwin, P. Kolenick, D.A. Lavoie, G.T. Seniuk, B. Singer

Saskatoon
220 - 19 St. East, Saskatoon, SK S7K 2H6
306-933-5250, Fax: 306-933-7043
M.E. Turpel-Lafond, S.P. Whelan, T.W. White, L.A. Matsulla

Swift Current
Court House, 121 Lorne St. West, Swift Current, SK S9H 0J4
306-778-8390, Fax: 306-778-8581
D. Ebert

Wynyard
Court House, 410 Ave. C East, P.O. Box 1449, Wynyard, SK S0A 4T0
306-554-2155, Fax: 306-554-3405
K.A. Andrychuck, R. Green, P.R. Koskie

Yorkton
Court House, 120 Smith St. East, Yorkton, SK S3N 3V3
306-786-1400, Fax: 306-786-1422

Yukon Territory

Yukon Territory: Court of Appeal
Court Registry, 2134 Second Ave. (Ground Fl.), Whitehorse, YT Y1A 5H6
867-667-3429, Fax: 867-393-6212, 800-661-0408, courtservices@gov.yk.ca
www.yukoncourts.ca/courts/appeal

The Court of Appeal has appellate jurisdiction in all civil & criminal matters from decisions by the Territorial Court & Supreme Court.

Justices of Appeal (The Hon. Mr./Madam Justice): Beverley A. Browne, Earl Johnson, Robert G. Kilpatrick, T. Braidwood, I.T. Donald, William A. Esson, L.S.G. Finch, J. Hall, H.A. Hollinrake, C. Huddart, J.D. Lambert, R.E. Levine, R.T.A. Low, P.D. Lowry, K. Mackenzie, M. Newbury, W.T. Oppal, J. Prowse, M.A. Rowles, C.A. Ryan, M.E. Saunders, K.J. Smith, M.F. Southin, A.D. Thackray, L.F. Gower, R.S. Veale, John Edward Richard, V.A. Schuler, John Z. Vertes

Administration:
Acting Registrar: Sharon Kerr

Yukon Territory: Supreme Court
Court Services J-3, 2134 Second Ave., P.O. Box 2703, Whitehorse, YT Y1A 2C6
867-667-3524, Fax: 867-667-3079, 800-661-0408, courtserivces@gov.yk.ca
www.justice.gov.yk.ca/prog/cs/supr/supremecrt.html

The Supreme Court is a superior court of record having original jurisdiction in all civil & criminal matters arising in the Yukon, unless excluded by statute.

Judges (The Hon. Mr./Madam Justice): Leigh F. Gower, Ronald S. Veale

Ex-Officio Judges (The Hon. Mr./Madam Justice): Beverley A. Browne, Earl Johnson, Robert G. Kilpatrick, John Edward Richard, Virginia A. Schuler, John Z. Vertes

Deputy Judges (The Hon. Mr./Madam Justice): C. Scott Brooker, Paul S. Chrumka, Carole M. Conrad, Mary M. Hetherington, Colleen L. Kenny, Arthur M. Lutz, Peter McIntyre, René P. Foisy, William J. Girgulis, Cecilia I. Johnstone, Edward P. MacCallum, Richard P. Marceau, Ernest A. Marshall, Mary Moreau, Allan H. Wachowich, R.J. Haines, James D. Taylor, Ross Goodwin, Edward D. Bayda, Lucien A. Beaulieu, Stephen Borins, Dennis O'Connor, John D. Watt, Marion Jean Allan, George Peter Fraser, D.J. Martinson, Kathryn E. Neilson, Wallace T. Oppal, Randall S.K. Wong, John C. Bouck, David Vickers, Wallace M. Darichuk, Guy J. Kroft

Administration:
Acting Registrar: Bankruptcy, Sue Christianson
Acting Sheriff: Linda Balcaen

Yukon Territory: Territorial Court
Court Services J-3, 2134 Second Ave., P.O. Box 2703, Whitehorse, YT Y1A 2C6
867-667-5441, Fax: 867-393-6212, 800-661-0408, courtservices@gov.yk.ca
www.justice.gov.yk.ca/prog/cs/terr/index.html

The Territorial Court has jurisdiction in family, youth & select criminal matters.

Chief Judge: The Hon. John E. Faulkner

Judges (The Hon. Mr./Madam Justice): Heino Lilles, K. Ruddy

Administration:
Senior Court Clerk: Sharon Kerr
Territorial Court Clerk: Tara Boland
Territorial Court Clerk: Dawson City, Susan Coulson
Territorial Court Clerk: Lucretia Flemming
Territorial Court Clerk: Watson Lake, Stella Hearty
Territorial Court Clerk: Dorothy Irwin
Territorial Court Clerk: Karin Keeley-Eriksson
Territorial Court Clerk: Sharon Kerr
Territorial Court Clerk: Arlene Ogden

SECTION 10
HOSPITALS & HEALTH CARE FACILITIES

Listings in this section are arranged by Province, and then by City. Each Provincial section includes the following six categories.

Government Department

Regional Health Authorities

Hospitals

Community Health Centres

Long Term/Retirement Care

Mental Health Facilities

Alberta

Government Departments in Charge

ALBERTA: Alberta Health & Wellness
Telus Plaza North Tower, PO Box 1360 Main, 10025 Jasper Ave., 22nd Fl., Edmonton, AB T5J 2N3
780-427-7164 Fax: 780-427-1171
health.ahinform.gov.ab.ca
www.health.gov.ab.ca
Ronald Liepert, Minister of Health

Regional Health Authorities

***Edmonton:* Alberta Health Services/AHS**
AHS Corporate Office, Manulife Place, #700, 10180 - 101 St., Edmonton, AB T5J 3S4
780-342-2000 Fax: 780-342-2060 www.albertahealthservices.ca
Year Founded: 2009
Note: Specialty: Provincial governance board, overseeing hospitals, other health facilities, & ground ambulance service in Alberta. Number of Employees: 90,000 (7,200 physicians). Note: Alberta Health Services brings together the following former Alberta health entities: Chinook Health, Palliser Health Region, Calgary Health Region, David Thompson Health Region, East Central Health, Capital Health, Aspen Regional Health, Peace Country Health, Northern Lights Health Region, Alberta Mental Health Board, Alberta Alcohol & Drug Abuse Commission, & the Alberta Cancer Board.
J.M. Turc, President; CEO

Hospitals

Hospitals - General

***Athabasca:* Athabasca Healthcare Centre**
3100 - 48 Ave., Athabasca, AB T9S 1M9
780-675-6000 Fax: 780-675-7050
www9.albertahealthservices.ca
Parent: Alberta Health Services
Number of Beds: 26 acute care beds; 1 palliative care bed; 23 continuing care beds
Note: Hospital Specialties: Emergency services; Diagnostic imaging; Laboratory services; Acute care; Obstetrics; Pediatrics; Continuing care; Rehabilitation; Recreation services; Palliative care
Mary Proskie, Manager, Healthcare Centre
Brian Oldale, Chief, Medical Staff

***Banff:* Banff Mineral Springs Hospital**
PO Box 1050, 305 Lynx St., Banff, AB T1L 1H7
403-762-2222 Fax: 403-762-4193
info@banffmineralspringshospital.ca
www.banffmineralspringshospital.ca
Division of: Covenant Health
Year Founded: 1930
Note: Hospital Specialties: Emergency services; Surgery; Acute care; Maternal & child care; Physiotherapy; Occupational therapy; Recreation therapy; Music therapy; Mental health services; P.A.R.T.Y. program, to Prevent Alcohol & Risk-Related Trauma in Youth; Continuing care; Outpatient clinics; Palliative care
Cindy Mulherin, Executive Director

***Barrhead:* Barrhead Healthcare Centre**
4815 - 51 Ave., Barrhead, AB T7N 1M1
780-674-2221 Fax: 780-674-3541 www.albertahealthservices.ca
Parent: Alberta Health Services
Number of Beds: 34 beds
Note: Hospital specialties: Emergency services; Diagnostic imaging; Laboratory Services; Obstetrics; Community cancer centre; Rehabilitation services; Social work; Diet counselling; Education programs; Outpatient clinics; Palliative care
Heather Thompson, Manager, Healthcare Centre
Elizabeth Thompson, Chief, Medical Staff

***Bassano:* Bassano Health Centre**
608 - 5 Ave., Bassano, AB T0J 0B0
403-641-6100 Fax: 403-641-2157 www.albertahealthservices.ca
Parent: Alberta Health Services
Year Founded: 1914
Number of Beds: 3 acute care beds; 7 continuting care beds; 1 palliative care bed
Note: Hospital specialties: Emergency services; Diagnostic imaging; Acute care; Physiotherapy; Occupational therapy; Physiotherapy; Mental health services; Nutrition services; Social work; Continuing care; Respite care; Palliative care

***Beaverlodge:* Beaverlodge Municipal Hospital**
PO Box 480, 422 - 10A St., Beaverlodge, AB T0H 0C0
780-354-2136 Fax: 780-354-8355 www.albertahealthservices.ca
Parent: Alberta Health Services
Number of Beds: 18 acute care beds
Note: Hospital Specialties: Emergency services; Radiology; Medical laboratory; Acute care; Obstetrics; Physiotherapy; Occupational therapy; Palliative care

***Black Diamond:* Oilfields General Hospital**
717 Government Rd., Black Diamond, AB T0L 0H0
403-933-2222 www.albertahealthservices.ca
Parent: Alberta Health Services
Note: Specialties: Acute care; Long-term care; Public health; Mental health services; Adult day support program; Physical therapy; Occupational therapy; Tuberculosis testing & immunization; Palliative care
Tom Sawyer, Maintenance

***Black Diamond:* Oilfields General Hospital**
PO Box 1, 717 Government Rd., Black Diamond, AB T0L 0H0
403-933-2222 Fax: 403-933-2031
Murray Kobe, Administrator

***Blairmore:* Crowsnest Pass Health Centre**
2001 - 107th St., Blairmore, AB T0K 0E0
403-562-5011 Fax: 403-562-8992 www.albertahealthservices.ca
Parent: Alberta Health Services
Note: Specialties: Emergency services (403-562-2831); Diagnostic imaging services; Laboratory services; Surgery; Obstetrics; Neonatal intensive care nursery; Pediatrics; Critical care services; Acute care; Rehabilitation services, including occupational therapy & therapeutic recreation; Southern Alberta Renal Program (403-564-4661); Continuing care; Palliative care

***Bonnyville:* Bonnyville Healthcare Centre**
5001 Lakeshore Dr., Bonnyville, AB T9N 2J7
780-826-3311 Fax: 780-826-6526 www.albertahealthservices.ca
Parent: Alberta Health Services
Year Founded: 1986
Number of Beds: 24 acute care beds; 30 continuing care beds; 9 day care beds
Note: Hospital Specialties: Emergency services; Regional laboratory services (780-826-3311 ext. 265); Diagnostic imaging; Pathology; Surgery; Acute care; Community Cancer Centre (780-826-3311, ext. 227); Cardiac stress testing(780-826-3311, ext. 255); Obstetrics; Rehabilitation; Medical accupunture; Occupational therapy (780-826-8266); Respiratory therapy (780-826-3311, ext. 304); Continuing care (780-826-3311, Ext 272); Palliative care (780-826-3311, ext. 286); Number of Employees: 281

***Bow Island:* Bow Island Health Centre**
938 Centre St., Bow Island, AB T0K 0G0
403-545-3200 Fax: 403-545-2281 www.albertahealthservices.ca
Parent: Alberta Health Services
Number of Beds: 10 acute care beds; 20 continuing care beds
Note: Hospital Specialties: Emergency services; Diagnostic imaging & laboratory services (403-545-3209); Acute care; Maternal child services; Physiotherapy (403-545-3207); Occupational therapy (403-529-8851); Continuing care; Respite Services (403-545-3208)

***Boyle:* Boyle Healthcare Centre**
PO Box 330, 5004 Lakeview Rd., Boyle, AB T0A 0M0
780-689-3731 Fax: 780-689-3951 www.albertahealthservices.ca
Parent: Alberta Health Services
Year Founded: 1966
Number of Beds: 19 acute care beds; 1 palliative care bed
Note: Hospital specialties: Emergency services; Diagnostic imaging; Laboratory services; Acute care services; Nutrition services (780-675-2231); Community health; Social work; Palliative care
Carol Ulliac, Manager, Healthcare Centre
Marthinius Doman, Chief, Medical Staff

***Brooks:* Brooks Health Centre**
440 - 3rd St. East, Brooks, AB T1R 1B3
403-501-3232 Fax: 403-362-6039
Parent: Alberta Health Services
Number of Beds: 40 acute care beds; 75 long term care beds
Note: Hospital Specialties: Emergency services; Ambulatory care; Acute care; Obstetrics; Pediatrics (403-501-3211); Physiotherapy; Occupational therapy; Recreational therapy; Living Healthy Program / Cardiac rehabilitation (403-793-6659); Diabetes education; Community health; Social work (403-501-3266); Continuing care (403-501-3227); Palliative care

***Calgary:* Alberta Children's Hospital**
West Campus, University of Calgary, 2888 Shaganappi Trail NW, Calgary, AB T3B 6A8
403-955-7211
943.Link@calgaryhealthregion.ca
www.calgaryhealthregion.ca/ACH
Old Name: Alberta Crippled Children's Hospital; Junior Red C
Parent: Alberta Health Services
Year Founded: 1922
Note: Hospital Specialties: Pediatrics (birth to age 18); Emergency services (403-955-7070); Sugery; Complex Pain Service (403-955-7430); Diagnostic imaging (403-955-7656); Burn treatment (403-955-7853); Eating disorder program - day treatment (403-943-1500); Therapeutic arts; Child health information (Family & Community Resource Centre)

***Calgary:* Foothills Medical Centre**
1403 - 29 St. NW, Calgary, AB T2N 2T9
403-944-1110 www.albertahealthservices.ca
Parent: Alberta Health Services
Note: Hospital Specialties: Emergency services (403-944-1405); Trauma services (403-944-4339); Diagnostic imaging; Acute care; Gynecology (403-944-1301); Newborn care (403-944-1352); Cardiology (403-944-1381); Gastrointestinal services (403-944-4711); Hematology (403-944-1157); Adult neuropsychology service (403-944-1340); Neurology (403-944-1312); Psychiatry (403-944-1321); Renal services (403-944-1137); Movement Disorders Program (403-944-4364); Occupational therapy (403-944-1432); Respiratory services (403-944-1319); Social work (403-944-1560); Addiction services (403-943-1500)

***Calgary:* Peter Lougheed Centre**
3500 - 26 Ave. NE, Calgary, AB T1Y 6J4
403-943-4555 Fax: 403-943-4878
Parent: Alberta Health Services
Number of Beds: 513 beds

***Calgary:* Rockyview General Hospital**
7007 - 14 St. SW, Calgary, AB T2V 1P9
403-943-3000 Fax: 403-943-3434
www.albertahealthservices.ca/facilities.asp?pid=facility&rid=3
Parent: Alberta Health Services
Number of Beds: 566 beds
Note: Services include: emergency, acute care, addiction network, CT imaging, cardiac intensive care/coronary care units, colorectal surgery, cystoscopy, diagnostic imaging, electroencephalography, endoscopy, geriatric assessment and rehabilitation, obstetrics/gynecology outpatient.
Stephen Duckett, President/CEO, AHS
Nancy Guebert, Vice-President
Teresa Davidson, Site Director

***Camrose:* St. Mary's Hospital**
4607 - 53 St., Camrose, AB T4V 1Y5
780-679-6100 Fax: 780-679-6196 www.stmaryscamrose.com
Parent: Alberta Health Services
Year Founded: 1924
Number of Beds: 76 beds
Note: An acute care facility with services including emergency, cardiology, diabetic education, diagnostic imaging (CT scans, fluoroscopy, radiology, mammography, ultrasound), community cancer clinic, women's health, pediatrics, palliative care, respiratory therapy, occupational therapy, mental health, urology. The facility operates under the governance of Covenant Health, a Catholic provider of healthcare.
R. Patrick Dumelie, President/CEO, Covenant Health
Rosa Rudelich, Vice-President/CFO, Covenant Health
Fran Ross, Vice-President, Communications, Covenant Health

***Canmore:* Canmore General Hospital**
1100 Hospital Pl., Canmore, AB T1W 1N2
403-678-5536 Fax: 403-678-9874 www.albertahealthservices.ca
Parent: Alberta Health Services
Note: Hospital Specialties: Emergency services; Diagnostic imaging (403-678-7216); Laboratory services; Surgical services; Obstetrics; Newborn care; Acute care; Cardiology; Audiology; Chemotherapy treatments; Wound centre; Occupational therapy; Physical therapy; Recreation therapy; Speech language pathology; Mental health; Aboriginal hospital Liaison; Diabetes prevention; Adult day support program (403-678-7200); Respite care; Long term care; Palliative care

***Castor:* Our Lady of the Rosary Hospital**
PO Box 329, 5402 - 47 St., Castor, AB T0C 0X0
403-882-3434 Fax: 403-882-2751
Parent: Alberta Health Services
Number of Beds: 5 acute care, 20 continuing care beds, 2 respite
Marilyn Weber, Executive Director
Barry Straub, Maintenance

***Claresholm:* Claresholm General Hospital**
221 - 43 Ave., Claresholm, AB T0L 0T0
403-682-3750 www.albertahealthservices.ca
Parent: Alberta Health Services
Note: Hospital Specialties: Emergency services (403-682-3700); Diagnostic imaging (403-682-3725); Cardiology electrocardiogram services; Acute care; Occupational therapy (403-625-8640); Physiotherapy (403-625-8617); Recreation

therapy (403-625-8613); Mental health services; Respite care; Palliative care

Cold Lake: Cold Lake Healthcare Centre
314 - 25 St., Cold Lake, AB T9M 1G6
780-639-3322 Fax: 780-639-2255 www.albertahealthservices.ca
Parent: Alberta Health Services
Number of Beds: 31 continuing care beds; 24 acute care beds; 2 palliative care beds
Note: Hospital Specialties: Emergency services; Diagnostic imaging services; Laboratory services; Surgical services; Acute care; Ambulatory care; Obstetrics; Pediatrics; Eating disorder services (780-998-5225); Rehabilitation services, including physiotherapy, occupational therapy, recreation therapy, & respiratory therapy; Continuing care (780-639-6515); Dementia care; Respite services; Palliative care
James Murray, Manager, Cold Lake Healthcare Centre
Siegfried Heydenrych, Chief, Medical Staff

Consort: Consort Hospital & Care Centre
5402 - 52 Ave., Consort, AB T0C 1B0
403-577-3555 Fax: 403-577-3950 www.albertahealthservices.ca
Parent: Alberta Health Services
Note: Hospital Specialties: Emergency services; Diagnostic imaging; Laboratory services; Acute care; Occupational therapy; Physiotherapy; Recreation therapy; Continuing care; Palliative care

Coronation: Coronation Hospital & Care Centre
5000 Municipal Rd., Coronation, AB T0C 1C0
403-577-3803 Fax: 403-578-3474 www.albertahealthservices.ca
Parent: Alberta Health Services
Note: Hospital Specialties: Emergency services (403-578-3200); Diagnostic imaging (403-578-3804); Laboratory services (403-578-3804, ext. 308); Acute care; Nutrition services (403-309-6199); Diabetes education (403-314-5780); Occupational therapy; Physical therapy; Recreation therapy; Speech language pathology (403-343-4822); Continuing care (403-343-4822); Supportive living; Seniors Mental Health Program; Palliative care (403-578-3680)

Daysland: Daysland Health Centre
5920 - 51st Ave., Daysland, AB T0B 1A0
780-374-3746 Fax: 780-374-2111 www.albertahealthservices.ca
Parent: Alberta Health Services
Number of Beds: 16 acute care beds; 10 rehabilitation beds
Note: Hospital Specialties: Emergency services; Laboratory services; Surgery; Acute care; Obstetrics; Rehabilitation services, including occupational therapy, physiotherapy, & respiratory therapy; Pediatric speech language services; Social work; Respite care; Palliative care
Mariann Wolbeck, Health Centre Coordinator
mariann.wolbeck@albertahealthservice

Devon: Devon General Hospital
101 Erie St. South, Devon, AB T9G 1A6
780-342-7000 www.albertahealthservices.ca
Parent: Alberta Health Services
Number of Beds: 9 acute care beds; 10 continuing care beds; 2 respite beds
Note: Hospital Specialties: Emergency services; Laboratory services; Radiology services (780-342-7075); Acute care; Rehabilitation services; Mental health therapy (780-963-6151); Public health (780-342-7069); Tuberculosis testing & immunization (780-342-7069); Diabetes education; Nutrition information; Social work (780-987-8200); Adult day program; Home care (780-342-7020); Continuing care

Devon: Devon Health Unit
101 Erie St. South, Devon, AB T9G 1A6
780-987-8224 Fax: 780-987-8232 www.capitalhealth.ca
Parent: Alberta Health Services

Didsbury: Didsbury District Health Services
1210 - 20th Ave., Didsbury, AB T0M 0W0
403-335-9393 Fax: 403-335-4816 www.albertahealthservices.ca
Parent: Alberta Health Services
Note: Hospital Specialties: Emergency services; Laboratory services (403-335-7224;); Diagnostic imaging; Acute care; Rehabilitation, including occupational therapy & physiotherapy; Speech language pathology (403-335-7623); Clinical nutrition services (403-335-9437); Public health services; Respite care; Long term care; Palliative care

Drayton Valley: Drayton Valley Hospital & Care Centre
4550 Madsen Ave., Drayton Valley, AB T7A 1N8
780-542-5321 Fax: 780-621-4966 www.albertahealthservices.ca
Parent: Alberta Health Services
Number of Beds: 34 acute care beds; 50 long term care beds
Note: Hospital Specialties: Emergency services; Diagnostic imaging (780-621-4945); Laboratory services (780-542-5321); Acute care; Obstetrics (780-542-5321); Northern Alberta Renal Program (780-542-2010); Occupational therapy, physiotherapy, & recreation therapy (780-542-4415); Asthma education (780-621-4866); Diabetes education(403-314-5780); Nutrition services (403-309-6199); Long-term care; Palliative care (780-621-4917)

Drumheller: Drumheller Health Centre
351 - 9 St. NW, Drumheller, AB T0J 0Y1
403-823-6500 Fax: 403-823-5076 www.albertahealthservices.ca
Parent: Alberta Health Services
Note: Hospital services: Emergency services; Diagnostic imaging; Acute care; Obstetrics; Cardiac Rehabilitation Program (403-820-7201); Chemotherapy treatments (403-820-7985); Occupational therapy, physical therapy, & recreation therapy; Mental health services (403-820-7863); Nutrition Services (403-309-6199); Public health (403-820-6004); Diabetes education (403-314-5780); Asthma education (403-820-7264); Continuing care (403-820-7245); Respite care (403-820-6020); Home care (403-820-6004); Palliative care (403-820-7241)

Edmonton: Grey Nuns Community Hospital
1100 Youville Dr. West, Edmonton, AB T6L 5X8
780-735-7000 www.capitalhealth.ca
Old Name: Grey Nuns Community Hospital & Health Centre
Parent: Alberta Health Services
Number of Beds: 267 beds

Edmonton: Misericordia Community Hospital
16940 - 87 Ave., Edmonton, AB T5R 4H5
780-735-2611 Fax: 780-930-5774 www.capitalhealth.ca
Old Name: Misericordia Community Hospital & Health Centre
Parent: Alberta Health Services
Number of Beds: 259 beds

Edmonton: Royal Alexandra Hospital
10240 Kingsway Ave., Edmonton, AB T5H 3V9
780-735-4111
www.albertahealthservices.ca/facilities.asp?pid=facility&rid=6598
Parent: Alberta Health Services
Number of Beds: 678 beds
Note: Emergency, acute care of the elderly, adolescent pregnancy clinic, otolaryngology, angiography, child & adolescent psychiatry, colonoscopy, diabetic foot clinic, diagnostic imaging, electroencephalography, gastroscopy, radiology, intensive care unit, liver clinic, mental health clinic, ophthalmology, prenatal nutrition counselling, plastics surgery, recto/colo Clinic, rehabilitation services, rheumatology, sexual assault response team, ultrasound, urology. Located in this hospital is the Lois Hole Hospital for Women.
Stephen Duckett, President/CEO, AHS
Joanna Pawlyshyn, Vice-President
Lois Stefaniuk, Site Director

Edmonton: University of Alberta Hospital & Stollery Children's Hospital
8440 - 112 St. NW, Edmonton, AB T6G 2B7
780-735-7000
www.albertahealthservices.ca/facilities.asp?pid=facility&rid=6600
Parent: Alberta Health Services
Number of Beds: 687 beds
Note: A clinical, research and teaching facility, its specialized services include cardiac sciences, neurosciences, surgery, medicine, renal, critical and trauma care, burn unit. Other areas of focus include amyotrophic lateral sclerosis, anaesthesiology, angiography, audiology, bronchoscopy, cardiology, cardiovascular intensive care unit, CT scans, continence, dental clinic, E. Garner King Critical Care Unit, ECG/Holter monitoring, ENT, ears nose & throat surgery, eating disorders, echocardiography, endoscopy, fluoroscopy, gastroenterology and hepatology, general surgery, geriatric assessment, hemodialysis, hepatitis, laboratory, MRI, medical microbiology, multiple sclerosis, neurosurgery, nuclear medicine, nutrition counselling, occupational therapy, orthopaedic surgery, palliative care, pediatric chronic pain, physical therapy, plastic surgery, psychiatry, pulmonary medicine, radiology, respiratory therapy, rheumatology, sexual assault response, social work, speech language pathology, spine assessment, spiritual care, stress, stroke, surgery, pediatric sleep disturbance, teleStroke, transplantation, tuberculosis, ultrasound, urology. Also located within the facility are the Mazankowski Alberta Heart Institute and the Stollery Children's Hospital, specializing in pediatric cardiac surgery and organ transplantation.
Stephen Duckett, President/CEO, AHS
David Megren, CMO/Executive Vice-President, AHS
Glenda Coleman-Miller, Site Vice-President
Amelda Foster, Site Director

Edson: Edson Healthcare Centre
4716 - 5th Ave., Edson, AB T7E 1S8
780-723-3331 Fax: 780-723-7787 www.albertahealthservices.ca
Parent: Alberta Health Services
Note: Hospital Specialties: Emergency services; Diagnostic imaging; Laboratory services (780-712-6840); Surgical services & recovery; Acute care; Ambulatory care; Obstetrics; Pediatrics; Rehabilitation services; Social work (780-712-6862, ext. 324); Respite care; Continuing care (780-723-2229); Palliative care

Elk Point: Elk Point Healthcare Centre
5310 - 50th Ave., Elk Point, AB T0A 1A0
780-724-3847 Fax: 780-724-3085 www.albertahealthservices.ca
Parent: Alberta Health Services
Number of Beds: 30 continuing care beds; 11 acute care beds; 1 palliative care bed
Note: Hospital Specialties: Diagnostic imaging; Laboratory services; Acute care; Ambulatory care; Obstetrics; Rehabilitation services, including physical therapy & recreation therapy; Community health services; Social work (780-645-3396); Continuing care; Respite care; Palliative care
Paulette Levasseur, Manager, Healthcare Centre
D. Ramful, Medical Director

Fairview: Fairview Health Centre
PO Box 2201, 10628 - 110 St., Fairview, AB T0H 1L0
780-835-4951 Fax: 780-835-5789
Parent: Alberta Health Services
Cal Kindon, Director, Health Services

Fairview: Fairview Health Complex
10628 - 110 St., Fairview, AB T0H 1L0
780-835-6100 www.albertahealthservices.ca
Parent: Alberta Health Services
Number of Beds: 25 beds
Note: Hospital Specialties: Emergency services; Intensive care unit; Acute care; Obstetrics; Pediatrics; Rehabilitation services, including occupational therapy, physiotherapy, & therapeutic recreation; Mental health services (780-835-6149); Cardiac education (780-835-6117); Prenatal education & counselling (780-835-4951); Healthy Families Program (780-835-6139); Diabetes Prevention & Wellness Program (780-835-6117); Environmental Public Health Program (780-835-4951); Social work (780-835-6112); Nutrition services; Continuing care (780-835-6180); Palliative care (780-835-4951)

Fairview: Fairview Mental Health Clinic
Bag 2201, Fairview, AB T0H 1L0
780-835-6149 Fax: 780-835-3879
Parent: Alberta Health Services

Fort McMurray: Northern Lights Regional Health Centre
7 Hospital St., Fort McMurray, AB T9H 1P2
780-791-6161 Fax: 780-791-6029
Parent: Alberta Health Services
Number of Beds: 94 beds
Patricia L. Eelton, CEO

Fort Saskatchewan: Fort Saskatchewan Health Centre
9430 - 95 St., Fort Saskatchewan, AB T8L 1R8
780-998-2256 www.albertahealthservices.ca
Parent: Alberta Health Services
Number of Beds: 32 beds
Note: Specialties: Emergency services; Surgical services; Acute care; Obstetrics; Respiratory therapy; COPD Rehabilitation Program (780 992-5801); Neurological physical therapy services (780-992-5824); Occupational therapy; Nutritional counselling (780-992-5812); Social work

Fort Vermilion: St. Theresa General Hospital
4506 - 46 Ave., Fort Vermilion, AB T0H 1N0
780-927-3761 Fax: 780-927-4271
www.albertahealthservices.ca/facilities.asp?pid=facility&rid=1000199
Parent: Alberta Health Services
Number of Beds: 10 long-term care, 21 acute care beds
Note: Services include emergency, blood collection, clinical nutrition, continuing care, diagnostic imaging, interpretive services, lab, maternity, mental health, occupational therapy, palliative care, pediatrics, physical therapy, school dental services, spiritual care.
Stephen Duckett, President/CEO, AHS
David Megren, Executive Vice-President/CMO, AHS
Kerry Williamson, Senior Media Relations Advisor, AHS
780-407-2602

Fox Creek: Fox Creek Health Care Centre
600 - 3rd St., Fox Creek, AB T0H 1P0
780-622-3545 www.albertahealthservices.ca
Parent: Alberta Health Services
Number of Beds: 4 acute care beds
Note: Specialties: Emergency services; Laboratory services; Acute care; Prenatal classes & Healthy Beginnings Program (780-622-3730); Pediatrics; Cardiac & diabetes education (780-524-7027); Home care & palliative care (780-622-3730)

Grande Cache: Grande Cache Community Health Complex
PO Box 629, 10200 Shand Ave., Grande Cache, AB T0E 0Y0
780-827-3701 Fax: 780-827-2859
tracy.peddy@pchr.ca
Parent: Alberta Health Services
Number of Beds: 12 acute care, 4 continuing care beds
Tracy Peddy, Director, Health Services

Grande Prairie: Queen Elizabeth II Hospital
10409 - 98 St., Grande Prairie, AB T8V 2E8
780-538-7100 Fax: 780-538-1500
Parent: Alberta Health Services
Number of Beds: 48 med, 10 NICU, 22 Obs/Gen, 14 Ped, 26 psy, 8 rehab, 40 sur
Diane Calvert, Chief Operating Officer

Grimshaw: Grimshaw/Berwyn & District Community Health Centre
PO Box 648, 5612 Wilcox Rd., Grimshaw, AB T0H 1W0
780-332-6500 Fax: 780-618-4522
Parent: Alberta Health Services
Number of Beds: 4 beds, 10 continuing care beds
Carmen Johnson, Chairperson

Hanna: Hanna Health Centre
PO Box 730, 904 Centre St. North, Hanna, AB T0J 1P0
403-854-3331 Fax: 403-854-3253
Parent: Alberta Health Services
Number of Beds: 18 acute care, 49 continuing care beds, 12 assisted living beds
Ken Hansenen, Site Leader

Hardisty: Hardisty Health Centre
PO Box 269, 4531 - 47 Ave., Hardisty, AB T0B 1V0
780-888-3742 Fax: 780-888-2427
evelyn.scott@eastcentralhealth.com
www.ech.ab.ca
Parent: Alberta Health Services
Number of Beds: 5 acute care, 15 continuing care beds
Evelyn Scott, Health Centre Coordinator

High Level: Ranchlands Village Mall
1829 Ranchlands Blvd. NW, High Level, AB T0H 1Z0
403-943-9700 Fax: 403-943-9735
Old Name: High Level General Hospital; Northwest Health Cent
Parent: Alberta Health Services
Number of Beds: 30 beds
Patricia Pelton, CEO

High Prairie: High Prairie Health Complex
4620 - 53 Ave, High Prairie, AB T0G 1E0
780-523-6440 Fax: 780-523-6642
Parent: Alberta Health Services
Number of Beds: 25 acute care, 35 long-term care, continuing care 35
Kate Butler, Director, Health Services

High River: High River General Hospital
560 - 9 Ave. SW, High River, AB T1V 1B3
403-652-2200 Fax: 403-652-0199 www.calgaryhealthregion.ca
Parent: Alberta Health Services
Number of Beds: 103 beds
Rosemary Burness, Community Health Services Leader
Gesina Allan, Purchasing Manager
Geraldine Polanchek, Director, Finance & Support Services

Hinton: Hinton Healthcare Centre
1280 Switzer Dr., Hinton, AB T7V 1V2
780-865-3333 Fax: 780-865-1099
lisa.mcconnell@aspenrha.com
aspenrha.com
Parent: Alberta Health Services
Number of Beds: 21 beds
Lisa McConnell, Health Centre Manager
Doug Johnson, Supervisor, Environmental Services

Innisfail: Innisfail Health Centre
5023 - 42 St., Innisfail, AB T4G 1A9
403-227-7800 Fax: 403-227-7801
Parent: Alberta Health Services
Number of Beds: 102 beds
Cindy Mulherin, Site Leader

Jasper: Seton Jasper Healthcare Centre
PO Box 310, 518 Robson St., Jasper, AB T0E 1E0
780-852-3344 Fax: 780-852-3413
www9.albertahealthservices.ca/Default.aspx?cid=156&lang=1
Parent: Alberta Health Services
Number of Beds: 11 beds; 10 for acute care and 1 for palliative care
Note: Emergency, acute care services, diagnostic imaging, eating disorder services, mental health services, occupational therapy, palliative care, physiotherapy, social work
Stephen Duckett, President; CEO, AHS
Lorna Chisholm, Site Manager
Mark Addison, Chief, Medical Staff

Killam: Killam Healthcare Centre
PO Box 40, 5203 - 49 Ave., Killam, AB T0B 2L0
780-385-3741 Fax: 780-385-3904 www.ech.ab.ca
Parent: Alberta Health Services
Number of Beds: 5 acute care, 45 continuing care beds, 4 other
Geri Clark, Chief Executive Director

Lac La Biche: William J. Cadzow Health Centre
PO Box 507, 9200 - 95 St., Lac La Biche, AB T0A 2C0
780-623-4404 Fax: 780-623-5904
Parent: Alberta Health Services
Number of Beds: 23 acute care, 41 long-term care beds

Lac La Biche: William J. Cadzow Lac La Biche Healthcare Centre
PO Box 507, 9110 - 93 St., Lac La Biche, AB T0A 2C0
780-623-4404 Fax: 780-623-5904
Old Name: Lac La Biche Health Care Centre
Parent: Alberta Health Services
Number of Beds: 65 beds
Gislind Moehrle, Healthcare Centre Manager

Lamont: Lamont Health Care Centre
5216 - 53 St., Lamont, AB T0B 2R0
780-895-2211 Fax: 780-895-7305 www.ech.ab.ca
Parent: Alberta Health Services
Number of Beds: 14 acute, 105 continuing care beds
Harold James, Executive Director

Leduc: Leduc Community Hospital
4210 - 48 St., Leduc, AB T9E 5Z3
780-986-7711 www.capitalhealth.ca
Old Name: Leduc Community Hospital & Health Centre
Parent: Alberta Health Services
Number of Beds: 54 beds

Lethbridge: Lethbridge Regional Hospital
960 - 19 St. South, Lethbridge, AB T1J 1W5
403-382-6111 Fax: 403-388-6011
Parent: Alberta Health Services
Number of Beds: 236 acute care, 41 mental health
Cheryl Dick, CEO

Magrath: Magrath Hospital
PO Box 550, 37E - 2 Ave. North, Magrath, AB T0K 1J0
403-758-3331 Fax: 403-758-3332
Parent: Alberta Health Services
Number of Beds: 3 acute care beds, 21 auxiliary beds
Pam Whitnack, CEO
Grace Navratil, Housekeeping Supervisor

Manning: Manning Community Health Centre
Bag 1260, 600 - 2 St. NE, Manning, AB T0H 2M0
780-836-3391 Fax: 780-836-7352
Parent: Alberta Health Services
Number of Beds: 11 acute care, 16 long-term care beds
Jo Kelemen, Director of Health Services

Mayerthorpe: Mayerthorpe Healthcare Centre
PO Box 30, 4417 - 45 St., Mayerthorpe, AB T0E 1N0
780-786-2261 Fax: 780-786-2023
Parent: Alberta Health Services
Number of Beds: 25 acute care, 30 long-term care beds
Karen Kyle, Facility Supervisor
Gwen Hunt, Purchasing Agent

McLennan: McLennan Sacred Heart Community Health Centre
Bag 2000, McLennan, AB T0H 2L0
780-324-3730 Fax: 780-324-4206
barbara.mader@pchr.ca
www.pchr.ca
Parent: Alberta Health Services
Number of Beds: 20 acute care, 45 long-term care beds
Note: community health centre; nursing home
Barbara Mader, Director, Health Services

Medicine Hat: Medicine Hat Regional Hospital
666 - 5 St. SW, Medicine Hat, AB T1A 4H6
403-529-8000 Fax: 403-529-8998 www.palliserhealth.ca
Parent: Alberta Health Services
Number of Beds: 177 beds
L. Iwasiw, Senior Vice-President
G. Lukasiewich, Director, Physical Plant/Maintenance

Milk River: Milk River Health Centre
PO Box 90, 517 Centre Ave. East, Milk River, AB T0K 1M0
403-647-3500
Old Name: Milk River Hospital
Parent: Alberta Health Services
Number of Beds: 21 auxiliary beds, 3 community support beds, 1 respite
Brad Moser, Head of Housekeeping

Mundare: Mary Immaculate Hospital
PO Box 349, Mundare, AB T0B 3H0
780-764-3730 Fax: 780-764-3039 www.ech.ab.ca
Parent: Alberta Health Services
Number of Beds: 30 continuing care
Note: auxiliary/clinic (out patient)
Rhonda McCarty, Executive Director

New Westminster: Royal Columbian Hospital
330 East Columbia St., New Westminster, AB V3L 3W7
604-520-4253 Fax: 604-520-4827
feedback@fraserhealth.ca
www.fraserhealth.ca/find_us/locations/our_locations?site_id=1789
Parent: Fraser Health Authority
Year Founded: 1862
Number of Beds: 352 acute care beds
Note: Emergency, acute care services, care for the elderly, angiography, antepartum care services, bone densitometry, cardiac services, diabetes education, bronchoscopy services, ultrasound, fluoroscopy, respiratory unit, radiography, surgery unit, hand clinic, haemodialysis, psychiatry, intensive care unit, intrapartum care, magnetic resonance imaging, mammography, oncology, neonatal intensive care, neurological services, orthopaedic surgery, paediatrics, pantomography, family counselling, physiotherapy, plastic surgery, respiratory therapy, social work services, ultrasound, vascular and thoracic surgery
Nigel Murray, President/CEO, FHA
Andrew Webb, Vice-President, FHA, Medicine
Brian Woods, CFO, FHA
Gillian Harwood, Executive Director, FHA
Miriam Stewart, Director, Health Services

Olds: Olds Hospital & Care Centre
3901 - 57 Ave., Olds, AB T4H 1T4
403-556-3381 Fax: 403-556-2199
Parent: Alberta Health Services
Number of Beds: 81 beds
Colleen Simon, Site Leader

Oyen: Big Country Hospital
312 - 3 Ave. East, Oyen, AB T0J 2J0
403-664-3651 Fax: 403-502-8649
Parent: Alberta Health Services
Number of Beds: 10 acute care, 30 continuing care beds
Lynne Baisley, Director, Health Services Northern Area
Wayne Trembley, Supervisor, Physical Plant

Peace River: Peace River Community Health Centre
Bag 400, 10101 - 68 St., Peace River, AB T8S 1T6
780-624-7500 Fax: 780-618-3472
hrabb@telusplanet.net
www.pchr.ca
Parent: Alberta Health Services
Number of Beds: 30 acute care, 40 long-term care beds
Note: long-term care facility, nursing home, outpatient services, treatment centre, community health centre, home care office
Sandra Herritt, Director, Health Services

Picture Butte: Piyami Place
301 Cowan Ave., Picture Butte, AB T0K 1V0
403-732-4811 Fax: 403-388-6011
Old Name: Picture Butte Hospital
Parent: Alberta Health Services
Number of Beds: 15 suites
Pam Whitnack, CEO

Pincher Creek: Pincher Creek Health Centre
1222 Bev McLachlin Dr., Pincher Creek, AB T0K 1W0
403-627-1234 Fax: 403-627-5275 www.chr.ab.ca
Old Name: Pincher Creek Hospital
Parent: Alberta Health Services
Number of Beds: 16 acute care beds, 3 auxiliary beds
Pam Whitnack, CEO
Brian Meaney, Acting Maintenance Supervisor

Ponoka: Ponoka Hospital & Healthcare Centre
5800 - 57 Ave., Ponoka, AB T4J 1P1
403-783-3341 Fax: 403-783-6907
Parent: Alberta Health Services
Number of Beds: 75 beds
Sue MacKenzie, Site Leader
Hardy Kohlman, Director, Physical Plant

Provost: Provost Health Centre
PO Box 270, 5002 - 54 Ave., Provost, AB T0B 3S0
780-753-2291 Fax: 780-608-8850 www.ech.ab.ca
Parent: Alberta Health Services

Number of Beds: 15 acute care, 37 continuing care beds, 10 alternative housing
Lana Clark, Health Services Coordinator

Raymond: Raymond Hospital
PO Box 599, 150 North 4th St. E, Raymond, AB T0K 2S0
403-752-4561 Fax: 403-627-5275
www.albertahealthservices.ca/facilities.asp?pid=facility&rid=3306
Parent: Alberta Health Services
Number of Beds: 12 acute care, 35 auxiliary beds
Note: Emergency, obstetrics, and palliative care, diagnostic imaging, rehabilitation
Stephen Duckett, President; CEO, AHS
David Megran, Executive Vice-President, CMO, AHS

Red Deer: Red Deer Regional Hospital Centre
3942 - 50A Ave., Red Deer, AB T4N 4E7
403-343-4422 Fax: 403-341-8632
www.albertahealthservices.ca/facilities.asp?pid=facility&rid=1000 342
Parent: Alberta Health Services
Number of Beds: 365 beds
Note: Emergency, dialysis clinic, cancer clinic and a pediatric and special care nursery
Stephen Duckett, President/ CEO, AHS
David Megran, Executive Vice-President, CMO, AHS

Redwater: Redwater Health Centre
4812 - 58 St., Redwater, AB T0A 2W0
780-942-3932 Fax: 780-942-2373
www.albertahealthservices.ca/facilities.asp?pid=facility&rid=8928
Parent: Alberta Health Services
Number of Beds: 13 beds
Note: 24-hour emergency services, palliative care, lab services, respiratory services, radiology, nutritional counselling, and a visiting optometrist office
David S. Diamond, Chief Operating Officer, AHS

Slave Lake: Slave Lake Healthcare Centre
309 - 6 St. NE, Slave Lake, AB T0G 2A2
780-805-3500 Fax: 780-805-3574
www.albertahealthservices.ca/facilities.asp?pid=facility&rid=1024 257
Parent: Alberta Health Services
Number of Beds: 43 beds (24 acute care beds including 2 labor and delivery beds, 1 palliative care bed, 2 special care beds, plus 20 continuing care beds)
Note: Emergency, acute care, continuing care, pharmacy, renal dialysis, rehabilitation, obstetrics, occupational therapy, pediatrics, respiratory therapy, social work, ultrasound and X-Ray
Stephen Duckett, President/CEO, AHS
Steve Marcotte, Healthcare Centre Manager
Paul Caffaro, Chief, Medical Staff

Smoky Lake: Smoky Lake - George McDougall Memorial Healthcare Centre
PO Box 340, 4212 - 55 Ave., Smoky Lake, AB T0A 3C0
780-656-3034 Fax: 780-656-5010 www.albertahealthservices.ca
Parent: Alberta Health Services
Number of Beds: 12 acute care beds, including 1 palliative care bed; 23 continuing care beds
Note: Hospital Specialties: Emergency services; Diagnostic imaging; Laboratory services; Ambulatory services; Acute care; Rehabilitation; Occupational therapy; Physical therapy services; Respiratory therapy; Therapeutic recreation; Community health services; Nutrition services; Social work; Continuing care; Palliative care
David Ponich, Manager, Healthcare Centre
Anton Raubenheimer, Chief, Medical Staff

Spirit River: Central Peace Health Complex
5010 - 45th Ave., Spirit River, AB T0H 3G0
780-864-3993 www.albertahealthservices.ca
Parent: Alberta Health Services
Number of Beds: 10 acute care beds; 16 continuing care beds
Note: Hospital Specialties: Emergency care; Laboratory services; Acute care; Newborn hearing screening program; Pediatrics; Rehabilitation; Physical therapy; Nutrition counselling (780-864-3063); Continuing care; Palliative care

St Albert: Sturgeon Community Hospital
201 Boudreau Rd., St Albert, AB T8N 6C4
780-418-8200 Fax: 780-460-6262
www.albertahealthservices.ca/facilities.asp?pid=facility&rid=1000 932
Old Name: Sturgeon Community Hospital & Health Centre
Parent: Alberta Health Services
Number of Beds: 167 beds
Note: A comprehensive health facility with services including emergency, cardiac rehabilitation, diagnostic imaging (CT scans, radiology, fluoroscopy), geriatric evaluation, intensive care unit, mental health emergency, nutrition counselling, obstetrical outpatient clinic, physical therapy/occupational therapy, prenatal program, sexual assault response team, spiritual care, surgery.
Stephen Duckett, President/CEO, AHS
Linda Cargill, Executive Director, Community & Rural Hospitals, AHS

St. Paul: St. Therese/St. Paul Healthcare Centre
4713 - 48 Ave., St. Paul, AB T0A 3A3
780-645-3331 Fax: 780-645-1702
www9.albertahealthservices.ca/Default.aspx?cid=162&lang=1
Parent: Alberta Health Services
Number of Beds: 80 beds (30 acute care beds, including 3 special care beds, 2 palliative care beds; there is also a 30-bed continuing care facility and a 20-bed psych
Note: Services include emergency, diagnostic imaging (ultrasound, x-ray), eating disorder services, obstetrics, pharmacy, rehabilitation, renal dialysis, and laboratory.

Stephen Duckett, President/CEO, AHS
Bev Belland, Site Manager
Albert Harmse, Chief of Medical Staff

Stettler: Stettler Hospital & Care Centre
5912 - 47 Ave., Stettler, AB T0C 2L0
403-742-7400 Fax: 403-742-1244
www.albertahealthservices.ca/services.asp?pid=facility&rid=100 0353
Parent: Alberta Health Services
Number of Beds: 150 beds (with 50 acute care, 40 long-term care, 2 respite beds)
Note: Services include emergency, continuing care, diabetes education, diagnostic imaging, enterostomal therapy, homecare, mental health, obstetrics, occupational therapy (for acute & continuing care), palliative care, pharmacy, physical therapy, respiratory therapy, sleep program, speech language pathology
Stephen Duckett, President/CEO, AHS
Donna Stelmachovich, Vice-President, Seniors Health, AHS
Diane Ecklund, Site Program Supervisor

Stony Plain: Westview Health Centre
4405 South Park Dr., Stony Plain, AB T7Z 0A1
780-968-3600 Fax: 780-963-7612 www.capitalhealth.ca
Parent: Alberta Health Services
Number of Beds: 68 beds
Joy Myskiw, Area Team Leader

Strathmore: Strathmore District Health Services
200 Brent Blvd., Strathmore, AB T1P 1J9
403-934-4204 Fax: 403-934-3948
www.albertahealthservices.ca/facilities.asp?pid=facility&rid=1000 943
Parent: Alberta Health Services
Number of Beds: 25 acute care, 23 long-term care beds
Note: An acute care hospital with services incuding cardiology, nutrition services, continuing care, diabetes education, diagnostic imaging, fluoroscopy, Holter monitoring, home care, laboratory, medical genetics, occupational therapy, palliative care, pharmacy, physical therapy, psychiatric assessment, respiratory services, respite care, speech language pathology
Stephen Duckett, President/CEO, AHS
Donna Stelmachovich, Vice-President, Seniors Health, AHS
Jim Silvius, Senior Medical Director, AHS

Sundre: Sundre Hospital & Care Centre
709 - 1 St. NE, Sundre, AB T0M 1X0
403-638-3033 Fax: 403-638-4971
www.albertahealthservices.ca/facilities.asp?pid=facility&rid=1000 359
Parent: Alberta Health Services
Number of Beds: 13 acute care, 15 continuing care beds
Note: A facility offering long-term and acute care with services including emergency, clinical nutrition, continuing care counseling, diabetes education, diagnostic imaging, enterostomal therapy, laboratory, obstetrics, occupational therapy, palliative care, pharmacy, physical therapy, speech language pathology.
Stephen Duckett, President/CEO, AHS
Linda Cargill, Executive Director, Community & Rural Hospitals, AHS
Bonny Jones, Site Coordinator

Swan Hills: Swan Hills Healthcare Centre
PO Box 266, 29 Freeman Dr., Swan Hills, AB T0G 2C0
780-333-7000 Fax: 780-333-7009
www9.albertahealthservices.ca/Default.aspx?cid=163&lang=1
Parent: Alberta Health Services
Year Founded: 1985
Number of Beds: 4 acute care beds
Note: A community centre with services including emergency, general medicine, laboratory, nutrition services pharmacy, radiology.
Stephen Duckett, President/CEO, AHS
Patricia Baker, Site Manager
J. Hankinson, Site Medical Director

Taber: Taber Health Centre
4326 - 50 Ave., Taber, AB T0K 2G0
403-223-7211 Fax: 403-388-6011
www.albertahealthservices.ca/facilities.asp?pid=facility&rid=3307
Old Name: Taber Hospital
Parent: Alberta Health Services
Number of Beds: 19 acute care, 15 auxiliary, 55 nursing home beds
Note: This acute and continuing care facility has services including emergency, diagnostic imaging, home care, laboratory, neonatal intensive care, occupational therapy, pediatrics, therapeutic recreation.
Stephen Duckett, CEO, AHS
Bruce Conway, Senior Media Relations Advisor, South, AHS
403-943-1212

Tofield: Tofield Health Centre
PO Box 1200, 5543 - 44 St., Tofield, AB T0B 4J0
780-662-3263 Fax: 780-662-3835
www.albertahealthservices.ca/facilities.asp?pid=facility&rid=1000 176
Parent: Alberta Health Services
Number of Beds: 16 acute care, 50 continuing care beds
Note: Services include emergency, acute care, communicable disease control, continuing care, home care, laboratory, occupational therapy, palliative care, physiotherapy, prenatal education, radiology, respiratory therapy, respite care, speech language services, surgery
Stephen Duckett, President/CEO, AHS
Dave Megren, Executive Vice-President/CMO, AHS
Roman Cooney, Senior Vice-President, Communications, AHS
Betty Kolewaski, Site Administrator

Two Hills: Two Hills Health Centre
PO Box 458, 4401 - 53 Ave., Two Hills, AB T0B 4K0
780-657-3344 Fax: 780-657-2508
www.albertahealthservices.ca/facilities.asp?pid=facility&rid=1001 613
Parent: Alberta Health Services
Year Founded: 1986
Number of Beds: 75 beds (6 acute care, 60 continuing care, 9 stroke rehabilitation beds)
Note: A multi-level care complex with services including emergency, acute care, communicable disease control, genetics, mental health clinics, nutrition, continuing care, diabetes education, home care, laboratory, occupational therapy, adult community rehab program, oral health, palliative care, pharmacy, prenatal education, radiology, respiratory therapy, respite care, social work, stroke & geriatric empowerment unit
Stephen Duckett, President/CEO, AHS
Cheryl Knight, Executive Director, Continuing Care, Integrated Services Rural, AHS
Kathy Miskew, Interm Site Coordinator

Valleyview: Valleyview Health Complex
4802 Highway St., Valleyview, AB T0H 3N0
780-524-3356 Fax: 780-524-4462
Parent: Alberta Health Services
Number of Beds: 15 acute care, 17 long-term care beds
Tracy Brown, Site Manager
Debbie Stewart, Chairman

Vegreville: St. Joseph's General Hospital
5241 - 43 St., Vegreville, AB T9C 1R5
780-632-2811 Fax: 780-603-4401
www.albertahealthservices.ca/facilities.asp?pid=facility&rid=1000 160
Parent: Alberta Health Services
Number of Beds: 35 beds; 6 station dialysis unit
Note: An acute care facility offering services in emergency, medicine, laboratory, diagnostic imaging (x-ray, ultrasound), dialysis, diabetic education, occupational therapy, respiratory therapy, surgery and day support
Stephen Duckett, President/CEO, AHS
David Megren, Executive Vice-President/CMO, AHS
Kerry Williamson, Senior Media Relations Advisor, North Region, AHS
780-407-2602

Vermilion: Vermilion Health Centre
5720 - 50 Ave., Vermilion, AB T9X 1K7
780-853-5305 Fax: 780-853-4786 www.ech.ab.ca
Parent: Alberta Health Services
Number of Beds: 25 acute care, 48 continuing care beds
Debora Okrainetz, Health Centre Coordinator

Viking: Viking Health Centre
PO Box 60, 5110 - 57 Ave., Viking, AB T0B 4N0
780-336-4786 Fax: 780-336-4983 www.ech.ab.ca
Parent: Alberta Health Services

Number of Beds: 16 acute care beds
Note: Community health care services; acute & continuing care facilities
Kathryn Miskew, Health Centre Coordinator

Vulcan: Vulcan Community Health Centre
610 Elizabeth St. South, Vulcan, AB T0L 2B0
403-485-3333 Fax: 403-485-2336
Number of Beds: 8 acute care, 15 long-term care beds
Patty Greene, Executive Leader

Wabasca: Wabasca/Desmarais Healthcare Centre
PO Box 450, Wabasca, AB T0G 2K0
780-891-3007 Fax: 780-891-3784
trisslin@aspenrha.ab.ca
www.aspenrha.ab.ca
Old Name: Wabasca/Desmarais General Hospital
Parent: Alberta Health Services
Number of Beds: 10 beds
Kirk Richardson

Wainwright: Wainwright Health Centre
530 - 6 Ave., Wainwright, AB T9W 1R6
780-842-3324 Fax: 780-842-4290 www.ech.ab.ca
Parent: Alberta Health Services
Number of Beds: 25 acute care, 69 continuing care beds
Cheryl Huxley, Health Centre Coordinator

Westlock: Westlock Healthcare Centre
#103, 10030 - 106 St., Westlock, AB T7P 2G4
780-349-3301 Fax: 780-349-6973
Parent: Alberta Health Services
Number of Beds: 45 beds
Joyce Nadeau, Site Supervisor
Richard Baker, Director of Plant Operations; Maintenance

Wetaskiwin: Wetaskiwin Hospital & Health Centre
6910 - 47 St., Wetaskiwin, AB T9A 3N3
780-361-7100 Fax: 780-361-4107 www.dthr.ab.ca
Old Name: Crossroads Hospital & Health Centre - Wetaskiwin
Parent: Alberta Health Services
Number of Beds: 76 acute care, 79 long-term care beds
Bruce Finkel, Site Leader

Whitecourt: Whitecourt Healthcare Centre
20 Sunset Blvd., Whitecourt, AB T7S 1M8
780-778-2285 Fax: 780-778-5161
Parent: Alberta Health Services
Number of Beds: 24 beds
Marj Stockwell, Facility Supervisor

Auxiliary Hospitals

Breton: Breton Health Centre
4919 - 49th Ave., Breton, AB T0C 0P0
780-696-4701 Fax: 780-696-4747 www.albertahealthservices.ca
Parent: Alberta Health Services
Year Founded: 1994
Number of Beds: 23 long term care beds
Note: Hospital Specialties: Laboratory services (780-696-3731); Occupational therapy; Physical therapy; Recreational therapy; Speech language pathology; Clinical nutrition services (403-309-6199); Continuing care (780-696-3731); Home care; Palliative care (780-696-4713)

Cardston: Cardston Health Centre
PO Box 1440, 144 - 2nd St. West, Cardston, AB T0K 0K0
403-653-5234 www.albertahealthservices.ca
Parent: Alberta Health Services
Note: Hospital Specialties: Emergency services (403-653-4399); Diagnostic imaging (403-653-4399); Surgery; Obstetrics: Acute care; Rehabilitation; Therapeutic Recreation (403-653-5253); Speech language pathology; Continuing care (403-653-5262); Palliative care
Cindy Baker, Manager, Cardston Acute Care
403-653-4411, CBaker@chr.ab.ca

Carmangay: Little Bow Continuing Care Centre
316 Armstrong St., Carmangay, AB T0L 0N0
403-643-3511 Fax: 403-643-4222
Number of Beds: 20 beds
Pete Sherstabetoff, Supervisor, Plant Maintenance

Claresholm: Willow Creek Continuing Care Centre
4221 - 8 St., Claresholm, AB T0L 0T0
403-625-3361 Fax: 403-625-3822
Parent: Alberta Health Services
Number of Beds: 100 beds
Pat Manderville, Health Services Leader
Pat Manderville, Community Care Leader

Lacombe: Lacombe Community Health Centre
5010 - 51 St., Lacombe, AB T4L 1W2
403-782-3218 Fax: 403-782-2866
Parent: Alberta Health Services
Kerry Bales, Community Care Home Care Manager

Lethbridge: St. Michael's Health Centre
1400 - 9 Ave. South, Lethbridge, AB T1J 4V5
403-382-6400 Fax: 403-382-6433
Parent: Alberta Health Services
Year Founded: 1929
Number of Beds: 202 beds (148 continuing care, 36 rehabilitation, 18 palliative)
Note: A long-term care (continuing care) facility focusing on assisted living, palliative care, post-acute rehabilitative program, Bridges program (care for the elderly in their own home). It operates under the governance of Covenant Health, a Catholic healthcare provider.
R. Patrick Dumelie, President/CEO, Covenant Health
Al Pierog, Vice-President, Seniors Health, Covenant Health
Fran Ross, Vice-President, Communications, Covenant Health

Trochu: St. Mary's Health Care Centre
PO Box 100, 451 de Chauney Ave., Trochu, AB T0M 2C0
403-442-3955 Fax: 403-341-8632
Parent: Alberta Health Services
Number of Beds: 28 beds
Kathryn Kane-Upton, CEO

Westlock: Westlock Long Term Care Centre
9732 - 100 Ave., Westlock, AB T7P 2G3
780-349-3306 Fax: 780-349-5647
Parent: Alberta Health Services
Number of Beds: 103 beds
Susan Gokiert, Coninuing Care Centre Manager
Brian Hyndman, Supervisor, Plant Maintenance

Community Health Centres

Community Health Care Centres

Airdrie: Airdrie Regional Health Centre
604 Main St. South, Airdrie, AB T4B 1C9
403-912-8400 Fax: 403-948-6284 www.calgaryhealthregion.ca
Parent: Alberta Health Services

Athabasca: Athabasca Community Health Services
3401 - 48 Ave., Athabasca, AB T9S 1M7
780-675-2231 Fax: 780-675-3111
Parent: Alberta Health Services
Rosalie Stobee, Supervisor

Banff: Banff Public Health & Community Care
PO Box 1266, 301 Lynx St., Banff, AB T1L 1B3
403-762-2990 Fax: 403-762-5570
Dr. Judith MacDonald, Designated Physician

Barrhead: Barrhead Community Health Services
6203 - 49 Ave., Barrhead, AB T7N 1A1
780-674-3408 Fax: 780-674-3941
Parent: Alberta Health Services
Lorraine Lindberg, CHS Supervisor

Bashaw: Bashaw
4909 - 50 St., Bashaw, AB T0B 0H0
780-372-3731 Fax: 780-372-4050 www.ech.ab.ca
Parent: Alberta Health Services
Lee Fredeen-Kohlert, Contact

Bashaw: Hospital Bashaw
PO Box 449, 4909 - 50 St., Bashaw, AB T0B 0H0
780-372-3731 Fax: 780-372-4050 www.ech.ab.ca
Parent: Alberta Health Services
Number of Beds: 25 beds, 4 program beds
Evelyn Kraft, Interim Health Centre Coordinator

Beaumont: Beaumont Public Health Authority
4918 - 50 Ave., Beaumont, AB T4X 1J9
780-929-4822 Fax: 780-929-4828 www.capitalhealth.ca
Parent: Alberta Health Services

Beaverlodge: Beaverlodge Public Health Centre
PO Box 120, 412 - 10A St., Beaverlodge, AB T0H 0C0
780-354-2647 Fax: 780-354-1550
Parent: Alberta Health Services
Janet Wallace, Director, Health Services

Black Diamond: Black Diamond Health Unit
PO Box 1, 717 Government Rd. S, Black Diamond, AB T0L 0H0
403-933-8505 Fax: 403-933-2031
Parent: Alberta Health Services

Blairmore: Community Health - Crowsnest Pass
12501 - 26 St., Blairmore, AB T0K 0E0
403-388-6009 Fax: 403-388-6011
Parent: Alberta Health Services
Pam Whitnack, CEO

Bonnyville: Bonnyville Community Health Services
4904 - 50 Ave., Bonnyville, AB T9N 2G4
780-826-3381 Fax: 780-826-6470
Parent: Alberta Health Services
Joan Panteluk, Community Health Services Supervisor

Bow Island: Bow Island Public Health/Home Care
PO Box 949, Bow Island, AB T0K 0G0
403-525-2296 Fax: 403-525-6357 www.palliserhealth.org
Parent: Alberta Health Services

Boyle: Boyle Community Health Services
5004 Lakeview Rd., Boyle, AB T0A 0M0
780-689-2677 Fax: 780-689-2835
Parent: Alberta Health Services
Note: home care office

Brooks: Brooks Home Care
#11 - 311 Ninth St. SE, Brooks, AB T1A 8E3
403-362-7766 Fax: 403-362-7778
Parent: Alberta Health Services

Calgary: Bowness Community Health Centre
6328 - 35 Ave. NW, Calgary, AB T3B 1S4
403-288-7744 Fax: 403-288-3223
Parent: Alberta Health Services

Calgary: East Community Health Centre
112 - 28 St. SE, Calgary, AB T2A 5J9
403-248-8868 Fax: 403-273-3219
Parent: Alberta Health Services

Calgary: 8th & 8th Health Centre
912 - 8 Ave. SW, Calgary, AB T2P 1H9
403-781-1200 Fax: 403-205-4979
Parent: Alberta Health Services

Calgary: Forest Lawn District Office
3810 - 17 Ave. SE, Calgary, AB T1X 1E1
403-944-7300 Fax: 403-248-0429
Parent: Alberta Health Services
Lisa Oake, Secretary

Calgary: Millican-Odgen Community Health Centre
2880 Glenmore Trail SE, Calgary, AB T2C 2E6
403-944-7225
Parent: Alberta Health Services
Lorraine Dunn, Manager

Calgary: North Hill Community Health Centre
1920 - 14 Ave. NW, Calgary, AB T2N 1M5
403-282-1612 Fax: 403-282-0039
Parent: Alberta Health Services

Calgary: Northwest Health Centre
#109, 1829 Ranchlands Blvd. NW, Calgary, AB T3G 2A7
403-943-9700 Fax: 403-943-9735
Parent: Alberta Health Services

Calgary: Shaganappi District Office
3415 - 8th Ave. SW, Calgary, AB T3C 0E8
403-944-7373 Fax: 403-246-0326
Parent: Alberta Health Services

Calgary: South Calgary Health District
31 Sunpark Plaza SE, Calgary, AB T2X 3W5
403-943-9501 Fax: 403-944-2224
Parent: Alberta Health Services

Calgary: Thornhill District Office
6617 Centre St. NW, Calgary, AB T2K 4Y5
403-274-4515 Fax: 403-944-2224
Parent: Alberta Health Services

Calgary: Village Square Community Health Centre
2623 - 56 St. NE, Calgary, AB T1Y 6E7
403-944-7000 Fax: 403-285-6304
Parent: Alberta Health Services

Calling Lake: Calling Lake Community Health Services
Highway 813, Calling Lake, AB T0G 0G0
780-331-3760 Fax: 780-331-2200
Parent: Alberta Health Services

Camrose: Camrose Public Health, Home Care, Rehab
4615 - 56 St., Camrose, AB T4V 4M5
780-679-2900 Fax: 780-679-2929 www.ech.ab.ca
Parent: Alberta Health Services
Monica O'Gorman

Canmore: **Canmore Public Health Office**
Provincial Building, #104, 800 Railway Ave., Canmore, AB T1W 1P1
403-678-5656 Fax: 403-678-5068
Note: public health programs

Cardston: **Cardston Community & Wellness Site**
Provincial Bldg., PO Box 1590, 576 Main St., Cardston, AB T0K 0K0
403-388-6099 Fax: 403-388-6011
Parent: Alberta Health Services
Note: community health centre & home care office
Pam Whitnack, CEO

Claresholm: **Claresholm Public Health & Community Care**
PO Box 1391, 5221 - 2nd St. West, Claresholm, AB T0L 0T0
403-625-4061 Fax: 403-625-4062
Parent: Alberta Health Services
Pat Manderville, Facility Coordinator

Coaldale: **Coaldale Community Health**
PO Box 1000, 2012 - 18 St., Coaldale, AB T1M 1M8
403-345-6507 Fax: 403-345-2043
Parent: Alberta Health Services
Number of Beds: 40 continuing care, 4 community care beds
Bob Parker, Environmental Services

Coaldale: **Community Health - Coaldale**
PO Box 1000, 2012 - 18 St., Coaldale, AB T1M 1M8
403-345-3000 Fax: 403-345-2043 866-345-8800
Parent: Alberta Health Services

Cochrane: **Cochrane Community Health Centre**
Provincial Bldg., 213 - 1 St. West, Cochrane, AB T4C 1A6
403-932-8700 Fax: 403-932-7219
Parent: Alberta Health Services
Note: home care public health programs

Cold Lake: **Cold Lake Community Health Services**
4720 - 55 St., Cold Lake, AB T9M 1V9
780-594-4404 Fax: 780-594-2404
Parent: Alberta Health Services
Anne Tucker, Supervisor

Cold Lake: **Elizabeth Settlement Community Health Services**
4720 - 55 St., Cold Lake, AB T9M 1V8
780-594-3383
Parent: Alberta Health Services
Anne Tucker, Supervisor

Consort: **Consort Community Health Centre**
5410 - 52 Ave., Consort, AB T0C 1B0
403-577-3770 Fax: 403-577-2235 www.albertahealthservices.ca
Parent: Alberta Health Services
Note: Specialties: Public health promotion & services, including nutrition services & postnatal follow-up; Education programs, including diabetes & car seat education; Immunization clinics; Alberta Aids to Daily Living Program; Home care; Respite care; Continuing care counselling & placement coordination

Coronation: **Coronation Community Health Centre**
PO Box 338, 4909 Royal St., Coronation, AB T0C 1C0
403-578-3803 Fax: 403-578-2702
Parent: Alberta Health Services
Carolee Tkach

Drayton Valley: **Drayton Valley Community Health Centre**
4110 - 50 Ave., Drayton Valley, AB T7A 0B3
780-542-4415 Fax: 780-621-4998 www.dthr.ab.ca
Parent: Alberta Health Services

Drumheller: **Drumheller Health Unit**
601 - 7 St. East, Drumheller, AB T0J 0Y5
403-823-3341 Fax: 403-823-6657
Parent: Big Country Health Unit

Eckville: **Eckville Community Health Centre**
PO Box 150, 5120 - 51 Ave., Eckville, AB T0M 0X0
403-746-2201 Fax: 403-341-8632
Parent: Alberta Health Services
Number of Beds: 20 beds
Kevin McEntee, Administrator
Ken Kissick, Maintenance

Edmonton: **Bonnie Doon Public Health Centre**
8314 - 88 Ave. NW, Edmonton, AB T6C 1L1
780-413-5670 Fax: 780-466-3110 www.capitalhealth.ca
Parent: Alberta Health Services

Edmonton: **Capital Health Home Care**
10216 - 124th St., Edmonton, AB T5N 4A3
780-408-5465 Fax: 780-488-3401 www.capitalhealth.ca
Parent: Alberta Health Services
Linda Killick, Director

Edmonton: **Castle Downs Public Health Centre**
214-10807 Castle Downs Rd. NW, Edmonton, AB T5X 3N7
780-413-5787 Fax: 780-413-9746 www.capitalhealth.ca
Parent: Alberta Health Services

Edmonton: **Eastwood Public Health Centre**
7919 - 118 Ave. NW, Edmonton, AB T5B 0R5
780-413-5645 Fax: 780-474-5760 www.capitalhealth.ca
Parent: Alberta Health Services

Edmonton: **Mill Woods Public Health Centre**
7525 - 38 Ave. NW, Edmonton, AB T6K 3X9
780-413-5685 Fax: 780-461-2504 www.capitalhealth.ca
Parent: Alberta Health Services
Marianne Stewart, Sr. Operating Officer

Edmonton: **North Central Public Health Centre**
25-9204 - 144th Ave. NW, Edmonton, AB T5E 6A3
780-413-5600 Fax: 780-457-5638 www.capitalhealth.ca
Parent: Alberta Health Services

Edmonton: **Northeast Community Health Centre**
14007 - 50 St., Edmonton, AB T5A 5E4
780-472-5000 Fax: 780-472-5188 866-408-5465
www.capitalhealth.ca
Parent: Alberta Health Services

Edmonton: **Twin Brooks Public Health Centre**
201-1110 - 113 St. NW, Edmonton, AB T6J 7J4
780-413-5630 Fax: 780-437-6270 www.capitalhealth.ca
Parent: Alberta Health Services

Edmonton: **West Jasper Place Public Health Centre**
9720 - 182 St. NW, Edmonton, AB T5T 3T9
780-413-5700 Fax: 780-484-9516 www.capitalhealth.ca
Parent: Alberta Health Services

Edmonton: **Woodcroft Public Health Centre**
13221 - 115 Ave. NW, Edmonton, AB T5M 4B7
780-413-5720 Fax: 780-451-5886 www.capitalhealth.ca
Parent: Alberta Health Services

Edson: **Edson Community Health Services**
5028 - 3 Ave., Edson, AB T7E 1X4
780-723-4421 Fax: 780-852-3413
Parent: Alberta Health Services
Margaret Fern, CHS Supervisor

Elk Point: **Elk Point Community Health Services**
5310 - 50 Ave., Elk Point, AB T0A 1A0
780-724-3532 Fax: 780-943-2575
Parent: Alberta Health Services
Joan Panteluk, Community Health Services Supervisor

Elnora: **Elnora Community Health Centre**
PO Box 659, 425 - 8 Ave., Elnora, AB T0M 0Y0
403-773-3636 Fax: 403-341-8632
Parent: Alberta Health Services

Evansburg: **Evansburg Health Centre**
5225 - 50 St., Evansburg, AB T0E 0T0
780-727-2288 Fax: 780-727-2809 www.capitalhealth.ca
Parent: Alberta Health Services

Fishing Lake: **Fishing Lake Community Health Services**
General Delivery, Fishing Lake, AB T0A 3G0
780-943-2202 Fax: 780-943-2575
community.dev@gishinglake.ca
Parent: Alberta Health Services
Joan Panteluk, Community Health Services Supervisor

Fort MacLeod: **Fort Macleod Community Health**
Fort Macleod Health Centre, PO Box 820, 744 - 26 St. South, Fort MacLeod, AB T0L 0Z0
403-553-5351 Fax: 403-553-4567 www.albertahealthservices.ca
Parent: Alberta Health Services
Note: Specialties: Community mental health services (403-553-5340); Home care services (403-553-5300); Prenatal education & immunization program (403-553-5351)

Fort MacLeod: **Fort Macleod Health Centre**
744 - 26 St. South, Fort MacLeod, AB T0L 0Z0
403-553-5311 www.albertahealthservices.ca
Parent: Alberta Health Services
Note: Specialties: Emergency services (403-553-4487); Diagnostic imaging services (403-553-4487); Laboratory services (403-553-4487); Occupational therapy; Services to persons with developmental disabilities; Southern Alberta Renal Program (403-553-3690)

Fort Saskatchewan: **Fort Saskatchewan Health Unit**
10420 - 98th Ave., Fort Saskatchewan, AB T8L 2N6
780-998-3366 www.albertahealthservices.ca
Parent: Alberta Health Services
Note: Specialties: Audiology service (780-992-5801); Mental health services (780-342-2388); Health for Two Program (780-342-2366); Immunization services (780-342-2366)

Fort Vermilion: **Fort Vermilion Mental Health Clinic**
PO Box 68, Fort Vermilion, AB T0H 1N0
780-927-3391 Fax: 780-927-4440

Fox Creek: **Aspen Health Services**
PO Box 430, Fox Creek, AB T0H 1P0
780-622-3730 Fax: 780-622-4169

Gibbons: **Gibbons Health Unit**
4720 50 Ave., Gibbons, AB T0A 1N0
780-923-3700 Fax: 780-923-2373 www.capitalhealth.ca
Parent: Alberta Health Services

Gift Lake: **Public Health Centre**
PO Box 60, Gift Lake, AB T0G 1B0
780-767-2101 Fax: 780-767-2095
Parent: Alberta Health Services
Kate Butler, Director, Health Services

Glendon: **Glendon Community Health Clinic**
PO Box 570, Glendon, AB T0A 1P0
780-635-3861 Fax: 780-635-4213
Parent: Alberta Health Services
Joan Panteluk, Home Care Services Manager

Grande Cache: **Public Health Centre/Mistahia Health Unit**
1001 Hoppe Ave., Grande Cache, AB T0E 0Y0
780-827-3504 Fax: 780-827-2728
Parent: Alberta Health Services
Tracy Peddy, Director, Health Services

Grande Prairie: **College & Community Health Centre**
10620 - 104 Ave., Grande Prairie, AB T8V 8J8
780-518-7500 Fax: 780-538-4400
Parent: Alberta Health Services
Peter Lindsay

Grande Prairie: **Public Health Centre**
10320 - 99 St., Grande Prairie, AB T8V 6J4
780-513-7500 Fax: 780-532-1550
Parent: Alberta Health Services

Grande Prairie: **Public Health Centre**
10121 - 97 Ave., Grande Prairie, AB T8V 0N5
780-532-4447 Fax: 780-864-4187
Parent: Alberta Health Services

Hanna: **Hanna Health Unit**
PO Box 730, 904 Centre St. North, Hanna, AB T0J 1P0
403-854-3331 Fax: 403-854-3233
Old Name: Hanna Health Unit
Parent: Alberta Health Services

High Level: **Health Care Centre**
PO Box 2000, 10207 - 103 St., High Level, AB T0H 1Z0
780-926-7000 Fax: 780-926-7001

High Level: **Paddle Prairie Health Centre**
PO Box 46, High Level, AB T0H 2W0
780-981-2188 Fax: 780-981-2190 www.capitalhealth.ca
Parent: Alberta Health Services

High Prairie: **Community Health Services**
PO Bag 1, High Prairie, AB T0G 1E0
780-523-6450 Fax: 780-523-6458

High River: **High River Public Health**
PO Box 5638, 310 Macleod Trail, High River, AB T1V 1M7
403-652-5450 Fax: 403-652-5455
Lori Anderson
403/652-0142

Hobbema: **Hobbema Community Health Clinic**
PO Box 189, Hobbema, AB T0C 1N0
780-585-2020 Fax: 780-585-3965
Parent: Carewest Health Authority
Helen Littlechild, Nurse in Charge

Hughenden: **Hughenden Public Health: Home Care**
PO Box 25, 33 Mackenzie Ave., Hughenden, AB T0B 2E0
780-753-6180 Fax: 780-753-2064 www.ech.ab.ca
Parent: Alberta Health Services
Lana Clark

Jasper: **Jasper Community Health Services**
529 Turret St., Jasper, AB T0E 1E0

780-852-4759 Fax: 780-852-3413
Parent: Alberta Health Services
Joan Connors, Supervisor

Kinuso: **Kinuso Public Health Centre**
PO Box 208, Kinuso, AB T0G 1K0
780-775-3501 Fax: 780-775-3944
Parent: Alberta Health Services
Kate Butler, Director, Health Services

Kitscoty: **Kitscoty Public Health**
PO Box 508, 4922 - 59 Ave., Kitscoty, AB T0B 2P0
780-846-2824 Fax: 780-846-2731 www.ech.ab.ca
Parent: Alberta Health Services
Note: community health & home care office
Randey Ferster

La Crete: **La Crete Health Centre**
PO Box 295, 10601 - 100th Ave., La Crete, AB T0H 1H0
780-928-3242 Fax: 780-928-3080
Parent: Alberta Health Services

Lac La Biche: **Buffalo Lake Settlement Health Unit**
c/o Lac La Biche Health Unit, PO Box 869, 9503 Beaverhill Rd., Lac La Biche, AB T0A 2C0
780-689-4471 Fax: 780-689-2615
Parent: Alberta Health Services
Tracy Smith, Supervisor

Lac La Biche: **Community Health Services**
PO Box 297, 9503 Beaver Hill Rd., Lac La Biche, AB T0A 2C0
780-623-4471 Fax: 780-623-4212
Parent: Alberta Health Services
Tracy Smith, Supervisor

Lac La Biche: **Kikino Settlement Community Health Services**
c/o Lac La Biche Health Unit, PO Box 869, 9503 Beaverhill Rd., Lac La Biche, AB T0A 2C0
780-623-7797 Fax: 780-623-4212
Parent: Alberta Health Services
Tracy Smith, Supervisor

Lacombe: **Lacombe Hospital & Care Centre**
5430 - 47 Ave., Lacombe, AB T4L 1G8
403-782-3336 Fax: 403-782-2818
Parent: Alberta Health Services
Number of Beds: 101 beds
M. Stotz, Site Leader
Rob Grodaes, Plant Maintenance Director

Lamont: **Lamont Public Health, Home Care**
Bag 10, 5216 - 53 St., Lamont, AB T0B 2R0
780-895-2211 Fax: 780-895-2200 www.ech.ab.ca
Parent: Alberta Health Services
Janet Kiist, Contact

Leduc: **Leduc Public Health Centre**
4219 - 50 St., Leduc, AB T9E 8C9
780-980-4644 Fax: 780-980-4666 www.capitalhealth.ca
Parent: Alberta Health Services

Lethbridge: **Community Health**
960 19 St. South, Lethbridge, AB T1J 0C6
403-388-6009 Fax: 403-388-6011
Parent: Alberta Health Services
Pam Whitnack, CEO

Lethbridge: **Lethbridge Community Health - Lethbridge Centre Tower**
400 - 4th Ave. South, Lethbridge, AB T1J 4E1
403-388-6009 Fax: 403-388-6011
Parent: Alberta Health Services
Pam Whitnack, CEO

Lethbridge: **Lethbridge Community Health Site/Health Unit**
806 - 2 Ave. South, Lethbridge, AB T1J 4L5
403-388-6666 Fax: 403-627-5275
Parent: Alberta Health Services
Pam Whitnack, CEO
Brian Dalshary, Coordinator, Environmental Services

Magrath: **Magrath Community & Wellness Site**
PO Box 126, 135 West Civic Ave., Magrath, AB T0K 1J0
403-388-6009 Fax: 403-388-6011
Parent: Alberta Health Services
Pam Whitnack, CEO

Manning: **Peace Country Health Unit**
PO Box 1260, 118 - 2 Ave., Manning, AB T0H 2M0
780-836-3391 Fax: 780-836-2860
Parent: Alberta Health Services

Mannville: **Mannville Home Care, Public Health/Rehab**
PO Box 1000, 5007 - 46 St., Mannville, AB T0B 2W0
780-763-3989 Fax: 780-736-3678 www.ech.ab.ca
Parent: Alberta Health Services
Gladys Burrows
780/632-3331

Mayerthorpe: **Mayerthorpe Community Health Services**
4417 - 45 St., Mayerthorpe, AB T0E 1N0
780-786-4198 Fax: 780-786-2023
Parent: Alberta Health Services
Doug Kemp, Supervisor

McLennan: **Peace Country Health Unit - McLennan**
c/o Sacred Heart Community Health Centre, 350 - 3 Ave., McLennan, AB T0H 2L0
780-324-3750 Fax: 780-324-4256
Parent: Alberta Health Services

Medicine Hat: **Medicine Hat Community Health Services**
2948 Dunmore Rd. SE, Medicine Hat, AB T1A 8E3
403-502-8200 Fax: 403-528-2250
Parent: Alberta Health Services

Milk River: **Milk River/Warner Community & Wellness Site**
PO Box 90, 517 Centre Ave., Milk River, AB T0K 1M0
403-647-3500 Fax: 403-627-5275
Parent: Alberta Health Services

Morinville: **Morinville Public Health Centre**
10008 - 107 St., Morinville, AB T8R 1L3
780-939-3388 Fax: 780-939-7126 www.capitalhealth.ca
Old Name: Morinville Health Services
Parent: Alberta Health Services

Myrnam: **Myrnam Home Care**
PO Box 220, 4802 - 49 Ave., Myrnam, AB T0B 3K0
780-366-3891 Fax: 780-366-3919 www.ech.ab.ca
Parent: Alberta Health Services
Judy Flessau, Contact
780/632-3331

Okotoks: **Okotoks Health & Wellness Centre**
11 Cimarron Common, Okotoks, AB T1S 2E9
403-995-2600
Parent: Alberta Health Services
Peer Mikelsen, Public Health Inspector

Olds: **Olds Community Health Centre**
#103, 5030 - 50th St., Olds, AB T4H 1S1
403-556-8441 Fax: 403-556-6842
Parent: Alberta Health Services
Denise McBain, Vice-President, Community Health Services

Onoway: **Onoway Community Health Servics**
PO Box 1047, 4919 Lac Ste Anne Trail, Onoway, AB T0E 1V0
780-967-4440 Fax: 780-967-2547
Parent: Alberta Health Services
Doug Kemp, Supervisor

Oyen: **Oyen Community Health Services**
c/o Big Country Hospital, PO Box 296, 315 - 3 St. East, Oyen, AB T0J 2J0
403-664-3651 Fax: 403-664-2934
Parent: Alberta Health Services

Peerless Lake: **Peerless Lake Community Health Services**
PO Box 90, Peerless Lake, AB T0G 2W0
780-869-3930 Fax: 780-869-2053
Parent: Alberta Health Services
Cindy Harmata, Supervisor

Picture Butte: **Community Health**
301 Cowan Ave., Picture Butte, AB T0K 1V0
403-732-4762 Fax: 403-627-5275
Parent: Alberta Health Services

Pincher Creek: **Community Health**
1222 Bev McLachlin Dr., Pincher Creek, AB T0K 1W0
403-388-6009 Fax: 403-388-6011
Parent: Alberta Health Services
Pam Whitnack, CEO

Ponoka: **Ponoka Community Health Centre**
5900 Hwy. 2A, Ponoka, AB T4J 1P6
403-783-4491 Fax: 403-341-8632
Parent: Alberta Health Services
Denise McBain, Vice-President, Community Health Services

Provost: **Provost Public Health, Home Care**
5419 - 44 St., Provost, AB T0B 3S0
780-753-6180 Fax: 780-753-2064 www.ech.ab.ca
Parent: Alberta Health Services
Lana Clark

Rainbow Lake: **Rainbow Lake Health Centre**
PO Box 177, Rainbow Lake, AB T0H 2Y0
780-956-3646 Fax: 780-926-3338 www.nlhr.ca
Parent: Alberta Health Services

Raymond: **Community Health**
PO Box 251, 200N - 2nd St. West, Raymond, AB T0K 2S0
403-752-3303 Fax: 403-752-4655
Parent: Alberta Health Services
Pam Whitnack, CEO

Red Deer: **Red Deer 49th Street Community Health Centre**
4755 - 49th St., Red Deer, AB T4N 1T6
403-314-5225 www.albertahealthservices.ca
Parent: Alberta Health Services
Note: Specialties: Public health; Diabetes education (403-314-5780); Audiology (403-314-5225); Pediatric rehabilitation (403-314 5240); Speech language pathology (403-314-5250); Hanen parent program (403-314-5250)

Red Deer: **Red Deer Community Health Centre**
2845 Bremner Ave., Red Deer, AB T4R 1S2
403-341-2100 Fax: 403-341-8632
Parent: Alberta Health Services
John Vogelzans, President/CEO

Red Earth Creek: **Red Earth Creek Community Health Services**
PO Box 109, Red Earth Creek, AB T0G 1X0
780-649-2242 Fax: 780-649-2029
Parent: Alberta Health Services
Cindy Harmata

Redwater: **Redwater Health Care Centre**
4812 - 58 St., Redwater, AB T0A 2W0
780-942-3801 Fax: 780-942-2024 www.capitalhealth.ca
Parent: Alberta Health Services

Rimbey: **Rimbey Community Health Centre**
4709 - 51 Ave., Rimbey, AB T0C 2J0
403-843-2288 Fax: 403-843-3050
Parent: Alberta Health Services
Denise McBain, Administrator

Rocky Mountain House: **Rocky Mountain House Community Health Centre**
5016 - 52 Ave., Rocky Mountain House, AB T0M 1T0
403-845-3030 Fax: 403-845-4975
Parent: Alberta Health Services
Number of Beds: 30 continuing care beds

Sedgewick: **Sedgewick Public Health, Home Care, Rehab**
PO Box 12, 4822 - 50 St., Sedgewick, AB T0B 4C0
780-384-3652 Fax: 780-608-8850 www.ech.ab.ca
Parent: Alberta Health Services
Marlene Adam

Sherwood Park: **Health First Strathcona Primary Care Centre**
140 - 80 Chippewa Rd., Sherwood Park, AB T0B 4C0
780-449-5380 Fax: 780-942-2373 www.capitalhealth.ca
Parent: Alberta Health Services

Sherwood Park: **Strathcona County Health Centre**
2 Brower Dr., Sherwood Park, AB T8H 1V4
780-467-5571 Fax: 780-449-1338
Parent: Alberta Health Services

Slave Lake: **Slave Lake Community Health Services**
309 - 6 St. NE, Slave Lake, AB T0G 2A4
780-849-3947 Fax: 780-805-3550
Parent: Alberta Health Services
Cindy Harmata, Community Health Services Supervisor

Smoky Lake: **Smoky Lake Community Health Services**
4212 - 55 Ave., Smoky Lake, AB T0A 3C0
780-656-3595 Fax: 780-943-2575
Parent: Alberta Health Services
Gloria Strachan, Supervisor

Spirit River: **Public Health Centre**
PO Box 187, Spirit River, AB T0H 3G0
780-864-3063 Fax: 780-864-4187
Old Name: Mistahia Health Unit - Spirit River
Parent: Alberta Health Services

Karen Osborne, Director, Health Services

***St Albert:* St. Albert Public Health Centre**
23 Sir Winston Churchill Ave., St Albert, AB T8N 2S7
780-459-6671 Fax: 780-460-7062 www.capitalhealth.ca
Parent: Alberta Health Services

***St Paul:* St Paul Community Health Services**
5610 - 50 Ave., St Paul, AB T0A 3A1
780-645-3396 Fax: 780-943-2575
Parent: Alberta Health Services
Leanne Betts, Community Health Services Supervisor

***Stettler:* Stettler Community Health Center**
5911 - 50 Ave. SS 2, Stettler, AB T0C 2L0
403-742-3326 Fax: 403-641-8632 www.dthr.ab.ca
Parent: Alberta Health Services
Jenn Currie, Director of Public Health

***Sundre:* Sundre Community Health Centre**
212 - 6 Ave. NE, Sundre, AB T0M 1X0
403-638-4063 Fax: 403-341-8632
Parent: Alberta Health Services
Note: health unit
Rudy Zimmer

***Swan Hills:* Swan Hills Community Health Services**
29 Freeman Dr., Swan Hills, AB T0G 2C0
780-333-7077 Fax: 780-891-3784
Parent: Alberta Health Services
Lorraine Lindberg, Supervisor

***Sylvan Lake:* Sylvan Lake Community Health Centre**
4602 - 49 Ave, Sylvan Lake, AB T4S 1M7
403-887-2241 www.albertahealthservices.ca
Parent: Alberta Health Services
Note: Specialties: Public health services; Health promotion; Car seat education program; Child & adolescent services; Speech language pathology; Mental health services; Continuing care counselling; Environmental public health program; Breast health program; Prenatal education program; Communicable disease control; Home care; Physiotherapy; Immunization clinics; Tobacco reduction program; Respite care
Lori Sparrow, Coordinator

***Taber:* Community Health**
5009 - 56th St., Taber, AB T1G 1M8
403-223-4403 Fax: 403-627-5275
Parent: Alberta Health Services
Pam Whitnack, CEO

***Thorhild:* Thorhild Community Health Services**
302 - 2 Ave., Thorhild, AB T0A 3J0
780-398-3879 Fax: 780-398-2671
Parent: Alberta Health Services
Gloria Strachan, Supervisor

***Thorsby:* Thorsby Public Health Centre**
4825 Hankin St., Thorsby, AB T0C 2P0
780-789-4800 Fax: 780-789-4811 www.capitalhealth.ca
Parent: Alberta Health Services

***Two Hills:* Two Hills Public Health, Home Care, Rehab**
c/o Two Hills Health Centre, PO Box 458, 4401 - 53 Ave., Two Hills, AB T0B 4K0
780-657-3361 Fax: 780-608-8850 www.ech.ab.ca
Parent: Alberta Health Services
Judy Flessau, Contact
780/632-3331

***Valleyview:* Valleyview Public Health Centre**
5112 - 50 Ave., Valleyview, AB T0H 3N0
780-524-3338 Fax: 780-524-3153
Old Name: Mistahia Health Unit, Valleyview; Valleyview Distr
Parent: Alberta Health Services
Tracy Brown, Director, Health Services

***Vauxhall:* Vauxhall Community Care**
408 - 1 Ave., Vauxhall, AB T0K 2K0
403-388-6009 Fax: 403-388-6011
Parent: Alberta Health Services
Note: home care office, public health office
Pam Whitnack, CEO

***Vegreville:* Vegreville Public Health, Home Care, Rehab**
5318 - 50 St., Vegreville, AB T9C 1R1
780-632-3331 Fax: 780-632-4334 www.ech.ab.ca
Parent: Alberta Health Services
Bonnie Litwin, Contact

***Vermilion:* Vermilion Public Health, Home Care, Rehab**
4701 - 52nd St., Vermilion, AB T9X 1J9
780-853-5270 Fax: 780-853-7362 www.ech.ab.ca
Parent: Alberta Health Services
Note: community health & home care office
Gladys Burrows

***Viking:* Viking Home Care/Public Health/Rehab Office**
5110 - 57 Ave., Viking, AB T0B 4N0
780-336-4782 Fax: 780-608-8850 www.ech.ab.ca
Parent: Alberta Health Services
Hilda Tucker

***Vilna:* Vilna Community Health Services**
5103 Dr. Frobb Ave., Vilna, AB T0A 3L0
780-636-3533 Fax: 780-943-2575
Old Name: Our Lady's Health Centre

***Vulcan:* Vulcan Health Unit**
Vulcan Community Health Centre, PO Box 214, Vulcan, AB T0L 2B0
403-485-2285 Fax: 403-485-2639
Parent: Alberta Health Services
Wendy Shearer, Health Services Access Coordinator

***Wabasca:* Wabasca/Desmarais Community Health Services**
PO Box 9, Wabasca, AB T0G 2K0
780-891-3931 Fax: 780-891-3011
Parent: Alberta Health Services
Brenda Jenkins, Supervisor

***Wainwright:* Wainwright Public Health, Home Care**
Public Health #22, 810 - 14 Ave., Wainwright, AB T9W 1R2
780-842-4077 Fax: 780-842-3151 www.ech.ab.ca
Parent: Alberta Health Services
Randey Ferster

***Westlock:* Westlock Community Health Services**
10024 - 107 St., Westlock, AB T7P 1H7
780-349-3316 Fax: 780-349-5725
Parent: Alberta Health Services
Rick Saint, Community Health Services Supervisor

***Wetaskiwin:* Wetaskiwin Community Health Centre**
5610 - 40 Ave., Wetaskiwin, AB T9A 3E4
780-361-4333 Fax: 780-361-8554
Parent: Alberta Health Services
Malcolm Maxwell, CEO
Lucy Beck, Coordinator, Environmental Services

***Whitecourt:* Whitecourt Community Health Services**
20 Sunset Blvd., Whitecourt, AB T7S 1M8
780-778-5555 Fax: 780-778-3852
Parent: Alberta Health Services

***Willingdon:* Willingdon Home Care**
5303 - 49 St., Willingdon, AB T0B 4R0
780-367-2928 Fax: 780-367-2379 www.ech.ab.ca
Old Name: Mary Immaculate Hospital
Parent: Alberta Health Services
Judy Flessau, Manager, Health Services

***Winfield:* Winfield Community Health Centre**
PO Box 114, Winfield, AB T0C 2X0
780-682-4757 Fax: 780-682-4750
Old Name: Crossroads Health Unit - Winfield
Parent: Alberta Health Services

Nursing Stations

***Chateh:* Assumption Nursing Station**
PO Box 90, Chateh, AB T0H 0S0
780-321-3971 Fax: 780-321-3820
Number of Beds: 1 bed
Joanne Smith, Nurse in Charge

***Fort Chipewyan:* Fort Chipewyan Nursing Station**
PO Box 350, Fort Chipewyan, AB T0P 1B0
780-697-3650 Fax: 780-697-3565
ftchipmedical@hotmail.com

***Rocky Mountain House:* Rocky Mountain House**
Big Horn Health Station, PO Box 1617, Rocky Mountain House, AB T4T 1A1
403-845-3660 Fax: 403-845-3011

***Trout Lake:* Trout Lake Health Station**
General Delivery, Trout Lake, AB T0G 2N0
780-869-3922 Fax: 780-869-2054 www.albertahealthservices.ca
Parent: Alberta Health Services
Note: Specialties: Public health services; Community care nursing; Health education; Environmental health services; Healthy Beginnings, a support program for families with new infants; Immunization; Nutrition services; Social work; Rehabilitation services

***Worsley:* Worsley Health Centre**
General Delivery, Worsley, AB T0H 3W0
780-685-3752 Fax: 780-685-2007
rmacdonald@mhr.ab.ca
Parent: Alberta Health Services
Rose Mary McDonald, Nurse

Special Treatment Centre

***Calgary:* Carewest Dr. Vernon Fanning Extended Care Centre**
722 - 16 Ave. NE, Calgary, AB T2E 6V7
403-230-6900 Fax: 403-230-6902 www.carewest.org
Parent: Alberta Health Services
Number of Beds: 294 beds
Mark Ewan, Director

***Calgary:* Tom Baker Cancer Centre/TBCC**
1331 - 29 St. NW, Calgary, AB T2N 4N2
403-521-3723 Fax: 403-521-3245 866-238-3735
support@albertabreast.com (Alberta Breast Cancer Program)
www.albertahealthservices.ca
Parent: Alberta Health Services
Note: Specialties: Medical oncology; Surgery (E-mail, Alberta Radiosurgery Centre: arcinfo@cancerboard.ab.ca); Radiation oncology; Radiology; Chemotherapy treatments; Psychosocial resources; Pathology; Genetics; Research
George Browman, Director

***Calgary:* Women's Health Centre**
1441 - 29 St. NW, Calgary, AB T2N 4JB
403-944-2200 Fax: 403-944-2190
www.crha-health.ab.ca/clin/women
Old Name: Grace Women's Health Centre
Parent: Alberta Health Services
Patricia DeWitt, Manager

***Camrose:* Rosehaven Care Center (The Bethany Group)**
4612 - 53 St., Camrose, AB T4V 1Y5
780-679-2000 Fax: 780-679-2001 www.thebethanygroup.ca
Parent: Alberta Health Services
Number of Beds: 100 beds
Note: Faith-based organization that operates a wide range of homes and services for older, disabled and vulnerable people in the Central Alberta area, serving over 1000 residents through over 600 staff members.
Marilyn Wood, Administrator

***Edmonton:* Cross Cancer Institute**
11560 University Ave. NW, Edmonton, AB T6G 1Z2
780-432-8771 Fax: 780-432-8411 www.cancerboard.ab.ca
Parent: Alberta Health Services
Number of Beds: 46 beds
Note: cancer treatment
Carol Cass

***Edmonton:* Glenrose Rehabilitation Hospital**
10230 - 111 Ave., Edmonton, AB T5G 0B7
780-735-7999 Fax: 780-735-7976
ihender@cha.ab.ca
www.cha.ab.ca/glenrose
Parent: Alberta Health Services
Number of Beds: 240 beds
Note: rehabilitation centre

***Edmonton:* McConnell Place North**
9113 - 144 Ave., Edmonton, AB T5E 6K2
780-496-2575 Fax: 780-472-6699
Year Founded: 1995
Number of Beds: 36 beds
Note: Specialty: Residential care for persons with Alzheimer disease; Reminiscence therapy
Nat Mitchell, Manager

***Edmonton:* Woman's Health Options**
12409 - 109A Ave., Edmonton, AB T5M 4A7
780-484-1124 Fax: 780-489-3379
info@whol.ca
www.womanshealthoptions.com
Old Name: Morgentaler Clinic of Edmonton
Note: abortion clinic
Kim Cholewa, Manager

***Grande Prairie:* Grande Prairie Cancer Centre**
10409 - 98 St., Grande Prairie, AB T8V 2E8
780-538-7588 Fax: 780-532-9120
Parent: Alberta Health Services
Note: cancer treatment; outpatient facility
Marie Moreau, Medical Director

***Lethbridge:* Children's Centre**
#A252, 200 - 5 Ave. South, 2nd Fl., Lethbridge, AB T1J 4C7
403-388-6009 Fax: 403-388-6011

Parent: Alberta Health Services
Note: children's assessment, rehabilitation & education centre
Pam Whitnack, CEO

Lethbridge: Lethbridge Cancer Centre
#2H209, 960 - 19th St. South, Lethbridge, AB T1J 1W5
403-329-0633 Fax: 403-320-0508
Parent: Alberta Health Services
Note: cancer treatment
David R. Holland, Medical Director

Medicine Hat: Medicine Hat Cancer Clinic
Medicine Hat Regional Hospital, 666 - 5th St. SW, Medicine Hat, AB T1A 4H6
403-529-8817
Parent: Alberta Health Services
Year Founded: 1989
Number of Beds: 4 treatment beds + 10 treatment chairs
Note: Specialties: Colposcopy screening; Diagnostic imaging; Chemotherapy; Pain management; Counselling; Palliative treatment
Josh Foley, Director

Peace River: Peace River Community Cancer Centre
PO Box Bag 400, 10101, 68 St., Peace River, AB T8S 1T6
780-624-7500 Fax: 780-624-7593
jillwood@cancerboard.ab.ca
Number of Beds: 3 treatment chairs
Note: cancer treatment

Red Deer: Central Alberta Cancer Centre
3942 - 50A Ave., Red Deer, AB T4N 4E7
403-343-4526 Fax: 403-346-1160
Parent: Alberta Health Services
Note: cancer treatment outpatient facility
Neil Graham, Director

Nursing Homes

Athabasca: Athabasca Extendicare
PO Box 119, 4517 - 53 St., Athabasca, AB T9S 1K4
780-675-2291 Fax: 780-675-3833
Parent: Alberta Health Services
Number of Beds: 50 beds
Note: Private; affiliated with Regional Health Authority
Joan Cody, Administrator

Barrhead: Barrhead Continuing Care Centre
5336 - 59 Ave., Barrhead, AB T7N 1L2
780-674-4506 Fax: 780-674-3003
Old Name: Keir Care Centre
Parent: Alberta Health Services
Number of Beds: 115 beds
Note: auxiliary
Susan Oleskiw, Site Supervisor

Blairmore: York Creek Lodge
1810 - 112 St., Blairmore, AB T0K 0J0
403-562-2102 Fax: 403-562-2106
Parent: Alberta Health Services
Number of Beds: 20 beds

Bonnyville: Extendicare - Bonnyville
4602 - 47 Ave., Bonnyville, AB T9N 2E8
780-826-3341 Fax: 780-826-4890 www.extendicare.com
Parent: Alberta Health Services
Number of Beds: 50 beds
Steve Krim, Administrator

Calgary: Beverly Centre - Glenmore
1729 - 90 Ave. SW, Calgary, AB T2V 4S1
403-253-8806 Fax: 403-212-3532
Parent: Alberta Health Services
Number of Beds: 200 beds

Calgary: Bow View Manor
4628 Montgomery Blvd. NW, Calgary, AB T3B 0K7
403-288-4446 Fax: 403-288-8522
Parent: Alberta Health Services
Number of Beds: 193 beds
Norma J. Jackson, Administrator

Calgary: Bow-Crest Health Centre
5927 Bowness Rd. NW, Calgary, AB T3B 0C7
403-288-2373 Fax: 403-288-2403
bowcrestcare@shaw.ca
Parent: Alberta Health Services
Number of Beds: 150 beds
Michael Harris, Administrator

Calgary: Carewest George Boyack
1203 Centre Ave. NE, Calgary, AB T2E 0A5
403-267-2750 Fax: 403-267-2757 www.carewest.org
Parent: Alberta Health Services
Number of Beds: 221 beds

Marg Marlin, Administrator

Calgary: Extendicare - Cedars Villa
3330 - 8 Ave. SW, Calgary, AB T3C 0E7
403-249-8915 Fax: 403-246-7561
Parent: Alberta Health Services
Number of Beds: 248 beds
Lori Young, Administrator

Calgary: Extendicare - Hillcrest
1512 - 8 Ave. NW, Calgary, AB T2N 1C1
403-289-0236 Fax: 403-289-2350
Parent: Alberta Health Services
Number of Beds: 112 beds
Pierre Poirier, Administrator

Calgary: Father Lacombe Nursing Home
332 - 146 Ave. SE, Calgary, AB T2X 2A3
403-256-4641 Fax: 403-254-6297
Parent: Alberta Health Services
Number of Beds: 110 beds
Note: adult day support program offered M-F, 15 clients/day
Bill Ruckdashel, Site Pastoral Care Coordinator

Calgary: Forest Grove Care Centre, Ltd.
4726 - 8 Ave. SE, Calgary, AB T2A 0A8
403-272-9831 Fax: 403-248-5788
fgcc@fgcc.ab.ca
www.fgcc.ab.ca
Parent: Alberta Health Services
Number of Beds: 246 beds
Jack A. King, Administrator

Calgary: Glamorgan Care Centre
105 Galbraith Dr. S, Calgary, AB T3E 4Z5
403-242-5911 Fax: 403-242-7613
glamorgan@shaw.ca
Parent: Alberta Health Services
Number of Beds: 52 beds
Joel Bond, Administrator

Calgary: Intercare/Brentwood Care Centre
2727 - 16 Ave. NW, Calgary, AB T2N 3Y6
403-289-2576 Fax: 403-282-7027
Parent: Alberta Health Services
Number of Beds: 120 beds
Michela Smith, Director, Care

Calgary: Intercare/Chinook Care Centre
1261 Glenmore Trail SW, Calgary, AB T2V 4Y8
403-252-0141 Fax: 403-253-0292
Parent: Alberta Health Services
Number of Beds: 149 beds
Lorraine Nygard, Director, Care

Calgary: Intercare/Southwood Care Centre
211 Heritage Dr. SE, Calgary, AB T2H 1M9
403-252-1194 Fax: 403-253-0393
Parent: Alberta Health Services
Number of Beds: 177 beds
Oriel Morrison, Regional Director

Calgary: Mayfair Nursing Home
211 Heritage Dr. SW, Calgary, AB T2H 1M9
403-252-1194 Fax: 403-253-0393
Parent: Alberta Health Services
Number of Beds: 142 beds
Joel Bond, Administrator

Calgary: Mount Royal Care Centre
1813 - 9 St. SW, Calgary, AB T2T 3C2
403-244-8994 Fax: 403-244-5939
Parent: Alberta Health Services
Number of Beds: 107 beds
Colin McMillan, Administrator

Camrose: Bethany Long Term Care Centre
4501 - 47 St., Camrose, AB T4V 1H9
780-679-1000 Fax: 780-679-1020 www.ech.ab.ca
Parent: Alberta Health Services
Number of Beds: 130 beds; 78 supportive housing
B. Olsen, Manager, Health Support Services

Cardston: Chinook Lodge
451 - 3rd St. West, Cardston, AB T0K 0K0
403-653-4324 Fax: 403-653-1506
Parent: Alberta Health Services
Number of Beds: 20 beds

Cardston: Grandview Nursing Home
PO Box 1440, 990 Main St., Cardston, AB T0K 0K0
403-653-4054 Fax: 403-627-5275
Parent: Alberta Health Services
Number of Beds: 40 nursing home beds
Pam Whitnack, CEO

Ron Schow, Director, Physical Plant

Coaldale: Sunny South Lodge
Green Acres Foundation Housing for Seniors, 1122 - 20 Ave., Coaldale, AB T1M 1L4
403-345-5955
Parent: Alberta Health Services
Number of Beds: 20 beds

Edmonton: Good Samaritan Millwoods Centre
Mill Woods Centre, 101 Youville Dr. East NW, Edmonton, AB T6L 7A4
780-413-3501 Fax: 780-963-9808
Number of Beds: 60 beds

Fort MacLeod: Extendicare - Fort Macleod
654 - 29 St., Fort MacLeod, AB T0L 0Z0
403-553-3955 Fax: 403-553-2812 www.extendicare.com
Parent: Alberta Health Services
Number of Beds: 50 beds
Greg Guyn, Administrator

Grande Prairie: Grande Prairie Care Centre
10039 - 98 St., Grande Prairie, AB T8V 2E7
780-532-3525 Fax: 780-532-6504
Parent: Alberta Health Services
Number of Beds: 60 beds
Dorothy Brown, Administrator; Director, Nursing

High Prairie: J.B. Wood Extended Care Unit
Bag 1, High Prairie, AB T0G 1E0
780-523-6470 Fax: 780-523-6642
Parent: Alberta Health Services
Number of Beds: 35 beds
Ron Benson, CEO

Lethbridge: Columbia House - Enhanced
785 Columbia Blvd. West, Lethbridge, AB T1K 4T8
Parent: Alberta Health Services
Number of Beds: 50 beds

Lethbridge: Edith Cavell Care Centre
1255 - 5 Ave. South, Lethbridge, AB T1J 0V6
403-328-6631 Fax: 403-627-5275
Parent: Alberta Health Services
Number of Beds: 120 beds
Marian Teierle, Administrator

Lethbridge: Extendicare - Lethbridge
1821 - 13 St. North, Lethbridge, AB T1H 2V4
403-328-6664 Fax: 403-328-9294
Parent: Alberta Health Services
Number of Beds: 120 beds
Joyce Adachi, Administrator

Lethbridge: Golden Acres Lodge
1615 - 13 St. North, Lethbridge, AB T1H 2V2
403-328-5111 Fax: 403-327-8909
Parent: Alberta Health Services
Number of Beds: 45 beds

Lethbridge: Good Sam's - Park Meadow
1511 - 15th Ave. North, Lethbridge, AB T1H 1W2
403-328-9404 Fax: 403-328-8208
Parent: Alberta Health Services
Number of Beds: 40 nursing home, 44 DAL, 1 community support beds

Lethbridge: Good Sam's - West Highlands
2867 Gary Dr. West, Lethbridge, AB T1J 5A3
403-380-6275 Fax: 403-380-6732
Parent: Alberta Health Services
Number of Beds: 10 nursing home, 60 DAL, 30 enhanced beds

Linden: Linden Nursing Home
PO Box 220, Linden, AB T0M 1J0
403-546-3966 Fax: 403-546-4061 http://www.dthr.ab.ca/
Parent: Alberta Health Services
Number of Beds: 37 beds
Roland Toews, Administrator
Leonard Toeurs, Director, Physical Plant

Mayerthorpe: Mayerthorpe Extendicare
4706 - 54 St., Mayerthorpe, AB T0E 1N0
780-786-2211 Fax: 780-786-4710
Parent: Alberta Health Services
Number of Beds: 50 beds
Note: private, affiliated with Regional Health Authority
Michael Belanger, Administrator

Picture Butte: Piyami Lodge
301 Rogers Ave., Picture Butte, AB T0K 1V0

403-732-4811
info@greenacres.ab.ca
www.greenacres.ab.ca
Parent: Green Acres Foundation
Number of Beds: 32 rooms
Note: Independent living & enhanced care options
Linda McFalls, Manager

Pincher Creek: Good Sam's - Vista Villa
1240 Ken Thornton Blvd., Pincher Creek, AB T0K 1W0
403-627-1900 Fax: 403-627-3939
Parent: Alberta Health Services
Number of Beds: 10 nursing home, 40 DAL, 5 community support beds

Ponoka: Northcott Care Centre
4209 - 48 Ave., Ponoka, AB T4J 1P4
403-783-4764 Fax: 403-341-8632
Parent: Alberta Health Services
Number of Beds: 72 beds
Arthur Ulveland, Managing Director

Red Deer: Red Deer Nursing Home
Bag 5030, 4736 - 30 St., Red Deer, AB T4N 5H8
403-343-4458 Fax: 403-341-4988
Parent: Alberta Health Services
Number of Beds: 117 beds
Chris Hume, Clinical Manager

Spruce Grove: Good Samaritan Spruce Grove Care Centre
5600 - 50 St., Spruce Grove, AB T7X 3Y8
780-962-3415 Fax: 780-962-3416 www.gss.org
Number of Beds: 30 beds
Alice Sears, Director, Operations

St Paul: Extendicare - St. Paul
4614 - 47 Ave., St Paul, AB T0A 3A0
780-645-3375 Fax: 780-645-4290
Parent: Alberta Health Services
Number of Beds: 75 beds
Steve Krim, Administrator

Stony Plain: Good Samaitan George Henning Place
4808 - 57 Ave., Stony Plain, AB T7Z 2J9
780-963-3403 Fax: 780-963-9808 www.gss.org
Number of Beds: 30 beds
Alice Sears, Director, Operations

Taber: Clearview Lodge - Enhanced
4730 - 50th Ave., Taber, AB T1G 1N6
780-963-3403 Fax: 780-963-9808
Parent: Alberta Health Services
Number of Beds: 20 beds

Viking: Extendicare - Vicking
PO Box 430, 5020 - 57 Ave., Viking, AB T0B 4N0
780-336-4790 Fax: 780-336-4004 www.ech.ab.ca
Parent: Alberta Health Services
Number of Beds: 60 beds
Brant Poirier, Administrator

Long Term/Retirement Care

Long Term Care Facility

Airdrie: Bethany Airdrie
1736 - 1st Ave. NW, Airdrie, AB T4B 2C4
403-948-6022 Fax: 403-912-0958
info@bethanycare.com
www.bethanycare.com
Parent: Alberta Health Services
Number of Beds: 124 beds
Heath Miller, Administrator

Bentley: Bentley Care Centre
4834 - 52 Ave., Bentley, AB T0C 0J0
403-748-4115 Fax: 403-748-2727 www.albertahealthservices.ca
Parent: Alberta Health Services
Note: Specialties: Continuing Care services; Physiotherapy; Occupational therapy; Recreational therapy; Palliative care

Blackie: Nanton Mountain View Estates
PO Box 50, Blackie, AB T0L 0J0
403-684-3805
Note: private support home

Bon Accord: Oak Hills Boys Ranch
PO Box 97, Bon Accord, AB T0A 0K0
403-921-2121 Fax: 403-921-2379 www.oakhillboysranch.ca
Number of Beds: 30 beds
Note: group home
Anton Smith, Executive Director

Calgary: Bethany Calgary
916 - 18A St. NW, Calgary, AB T2N 1C6
403-284-6000 Fax: 403-284-6085
info@bethanycare.com
www.bethanycare.com
Parent: Alberta Health Services
Number of Beds: 476 beds
Note: respite care
Ian West, Administrator

Calgary: Bethany Harvest Hills
19 Harvest Gold Manor NE, Calgary, AB T3K 4Y1
403-226-8200 Fax: 403-226-7265
info@bethanycare.com
www.bethanycare.com
Parent: Alberta Health Services
Number of Beds: 60 long-term care beds
Note: provides a familiar home environment for residents in middle to late stages of Alzheimer disease & related dementias
Shelagh Slater, Administrator

Calgary: Bow Park Court
200 - 200 Scenic Bow Pl. NW, Calgary, AB T3L 1S5
403-297-6539 Fax: 403-287-4651
Parent: Alberta Health Services
Number of Beds: 24 beds
D. Grant, Manager

Calgary: Carewest - Cross Bow
1011 Centre Ave. NE, Calgary, AB T2E 0A3
403-267-2950 Fax: 403-267-2995
Parent: Alberta Health Services
Number of Beds: 98 beds
Note: continuing care

Calgary: Carewest - Glenmore Park
6909 - 14 St. SW, Calgary, AB T2V 1P8
403-258-7650 Fax: 403-258-7676
Parent: Alberta Health Services
Number of Beds: 147 beds
Note: continuing care

Calgary: Carewest - Royal Park
4222 Sarcee Rd. SW, Calgary, AB T3E 7J8
403-240-7475 Fax: 403-240-7476
Parent: Alberta Health Services
Number of Beds: 50 beds

Calgary: Margaret House Residential Treatment Centre
404 - 94 Ave. SE, Calgary, AB T2J 0E8
403-253-2291 Fax: 403-253-6974
astc@autism.ca
www.autism.ca
Parent: Alberta Health Services
Number of Beds: 20 beds
Note: group home
Dave Mikkelsen, Executive Director

Calgary: Salvation Army Agape Hospice
1302 - 8 Ave. NW, Calgary, AB T2N 1B8
403-282-6588 Fax: 403-284-1778
ab.salvationarmy.ca/calgary/health.html
Parent: Alberta Health Services
Number of Beds: 18 beds
Note: hospice for terminally ill
David Luginbuhl, Executive Director

Camrose: Bethany Group
4612 - 53 St., Camrose, AB T4V 1Y6
780-679-2000 Fax: 780-679-2001 www.thebethanygrp.ca
Parent: Alberta Health Services
Number of Beds: 288 beds
Marilyn Wood, Director Health Services

Cochrane: Bethany Cochrane
302 Quigley Dr., Cochrane, AB T4C 1X9
403-932-6422 Fax: 403-932-4617
info@bethanycare.com
www.bethanycare.com
Parent: Alberta Health Services
Number of Beds: 78 long-term care, 50 residential care beds
Note: adult day support program; residential care
Barb Fredrich, Administrator

Edmonton: Allen Gray Continuing Care Centre
5005 - 28 Ave. NW, Edmonton, AB T6L 7G1
780-469-2371 Fax: 780-465-2073 www.capitalhealth.ca
Parent: Alberta Health Services

Edmonton: L'Arche Association of Edmonton
7708 - 83 St., Edmonton, AB T6C 2Y8
780-465-0618 Fax: 780-465-8091
edmoffice@larcheedmonton.org
www.larcheedmonton.org
Parent: Alberta Health Services
Number of Beds: 24 beds
Note: group home
Grant Kaminski, Executive Director

Edmonton: CapitalCare Dickinsfield
14225 - 94 St. NW, Edmonton, AB T5E 6C6
780-496-3300 Fax: 780-476-4585 www.albertahealthservices.ca; www.capitalcare.net
Parent: Alberta Health Services
Year Founded: 1979
Number of Beds: 275
Note: Specialties: Continuing care; Secure units for residents with dementia; Supportive & comfort units fo residents in middle to later stages of dementia; Care for young adults who are disabled; Young adult day support program
Betty Thompson, Administrator

Edmonton: CapitalCare Grandview
6215 - 124 St. NW, Edmonton, AB T6H 3V1
780-496-7100 Fax: 780-496-7150 www.albertahealthservices.ca; www.capitalcare.net
Parent: Alberta Health Services
Year Founded: 1973
Number of Beds: 149 beds
Note: Specialties: Continuing care for persons with dementia & who are chronically disabled; Secure unit for residents wtih dementia who are at risk of leaving the building; Supportive & comfort units for residents in middle to later stages of dementia; Orthopedic sub-acute program

Edmonton: CapitalCare Lynnwood
8740 - 165 St., Edmonton, AB T5R 2R8
780-496-2500 Fax: 780-484-8089 www.albertahealthservices.ca; www.capitalcare.net
Parent: Alberta Health Services
Year Founded: 1966
Number of Beds: 296 beds
Note: Specialties: Continuing care; Behavioural assessment & stabilization uit; Secure unit for residents with dementia; Supportive & comfore care units for rsidents in middle to later stages of dementia; Mental health services
Iris Neumann, Administrator
Ralph Anderson, Manager, Maintenance

Edmonton: CapitalCare Norwood
10410 - 111 Ave., Edmonton, AB T5G 3A2
780-496-3200 Fax: 780-474-9806 www.albertahealthservices.ca; www.capitalcare.net
Parent: Alberta Health Services
Year Founded: 1963
Number of Beds: 235 beds
Note: Specialties: Continuing care; Brian injury unit; Chronic ventilator unit; Medical sub-acute program; Transition program; Palliative care

Edmonton: Devonshire Care Centre
1808 - 142 St., Edmonton, AB T6R 3H2
780-665-8050 Fax: 780-665-8051 www.capitalhealth.ca
Parent: Alberta Health Services

Edmonton: Edmonton Chinatown Care Centre
9539 - 102A Ave. NW, Edmonton, AB T5H 0G2
780-429-0888 www.capitalhealth.ca
Parent: Alberta Health Services

Edmonton: Edmonton General Continuing Care Centre
11111 Jasper Ave., Edmonton, AB T5K 0L4
780-482-8111 www.caritas.ab.ca
Parent: Alberta Health Services

Edmonton: Eric Cormack Centre
9835 - 112 St., Edmonton, AB T5K 2E7
403-427-2764 Fax: 403-422-2815
paulette.killam@gov.ab.ca
Number of Beds: 80 beds
Note: institution
Paulette Killam, Executive Director

Edmonton: Extendicare - Holyrood
8008 - 95 Ave., Edmonton, AB T6C 2T1
780-469-1307 Fax: 780-469-5196 www.capitalhealth.ca
Parent: Alberta Health Services
Note: continuing care centre

Edmonton: Extendicare - Somerset
13210 - 114 St., Edmonton, AB T5E 5E2
780-454-8616 Fax: 780-447-5906 www.capitalhealth.ca
Parent: Alberta Health Services

***Edmonton:* Good Samaritan Dr. Gerald Zetter Centre**
9649 - 71 Ave., Edmonton, AB T6E 5J2
780-431-3621 Fax: 780-431-3699
qchoo@gss.org
www.gss.org
Parent: Alberta Health Services

***Edmonton:* Good Samaritan Mount Pleasant Care Centre**
10530 - 56 Ave. NW, Edmonton, AB T6H 0X7
780-431-3600 Fax: 780-431-3949
goodsaminfo@gss.org
www.gss.org
Parent: Alberta Health Services

***Edmonton:* Good Samaritan Southgate Care Centre**
4225 - 107 St. NW, Edmonton, AB T6J 2P1
780-431-3600 Fax: 780-431-3898
goodsaminfo@gss.org
www.gss.org
Parent: Alberta Health Services

***Edmonton:* Hardisty Nursing Home**
6420 - 101 Ave. NW, Edmonton, AB T6A 0H5
780-466-9267 Fax: 780-450-9457 www.capitalhealth.ca
Parent: Alberta Health Services

***Edmonton:* Kensington Village**
12603 - 135 Ave., Edmonton, AB T5L 5B1
780-447-3840 Fax: 780-482-6532 www.capitalhealth.ca
Parent: Alberta Health Services

***Edmonton:* Kipnes Centre for Veterans**
4470 McCrae Ave., Edmonton, AB T5E 6M8
780-442-5700 Fax: 780-442-5711 www.capitalhealth.ca
Parent: Alberta Health Services

***Edmonton:* McConnell Place West**
8720 - 165 St., Edmonton, AB T5R 5Y8
780-413-4770 Fax: 780-413-4773 www.capitalhealth.ca
Parent: Alberta Health Services
Number of Beds: 36 beds
Gwenne Tweddle, Manager

***Edmonton:* Miller Crossing Continuing Care Services**
145251 - 50 St., Edmonton, AB T5E 6M8
780-478-9212 Fax: 780-478-2894 www.capitalhealth.ca
Parent: Alberta Health Services

***Edmonton:* Millwoods Shepherd's Care Centre**
6620 - 28th Ave. NW, Edmonton, AB T6K 2R1
780-463-9810 Fax: 780-462-1643 www.capitalhealth.ca
Parent: Alberta Health Services

***Edmonton:* Rosecrest Home**
10205 - 134 Ave., Edmonton, AB T5E 1J2
403-427-0927 Fax: 403-427-4408 www.capitalhealth.ca
Parent: Alberta Health Services
Number of Beds: 22 beds
Note: institution
MaryAnn Sinclair, Executive Director

***Edmonton:* St. Joseph's Auxiliary Hospital**
10707 - 29 Ave. NW, Edmonton, AB T6J 6W1
780-430-9110 Fax: 780-430-9777 www.stjosephs.ab.ca
Parent: Alberta Health Services

***Edmonton:* St. Michael's Long Term Care Centre**
7404 - 139 Ave. NW, Edmonton, AB T5C 3H7
780-473-5621 Fax: 780-472-4506
smeccs@smhg.ca
www.smhg.ca
Parent: Alberta Health Services
Number of Beds: 153 beds
Stan C. Fisher, President; CEO

***Edmonton:* Salvation Army Sunset Lodge**
11034 - 124 St., Edmonton, AB T5X 6C4
780-454-5484 Fax: 780-455-7196 www.capitalhealth.ca
Parent: Alberta Health Services
Number of Beds: 108 beds
Note: intermediate care
Blake Mooney, Executive Director

***Edmonton:* South Terrace Continuing Care Centre**
5905 - 112 St. NW, Edmonton, AB T6H 3J4
780-434-1451 Fax: 780-436-4300 www.capitalhealth.ca
Parent: Alberta Health Services
Number of Beds: 134 beds
C.W. Dillane, President/CEO

***Edmonton:* South Terrace Continuing Care Centre**
5905 - 112 St. NW, Edmonton, AB T6H 3J4
780-434-1451 Fax: 780-436-4300
southterrace@reveraliving.com
www.reveraliving.com

***Edmonton:* Venta Nursing Home**
13525 - 102 St. NW, Edmonton, AB T5E 4K3
780-476-6633 Fax: 780-476-6943 www.capitalhealth.ca
Old Name: Venta Nursing Home
Parent: Alberta Health Services

***Edmonton:* Victoria: Salvation Army Sunset Lodge**
952 Arm Street, Edmonton, AB V9A 4G7
250-385-3422 Fax: 250-385-3183
Parent: Vancouver Island Health Authority
Number of Beds: 41 beds
Note: seniors' lodge with residential mental health program
Blake Mooney, Executive Director

***Evansburg:* Good Samaritan Pembina Village**
5225 - 50 St., Evansburg, AB T0E 0T0
780-727-4441 Fax: 780-727-2410 www.capitalhealth.ca
Parent: Alberta Health Services

***Fort Saskatchewan:* Rivercrest Care Centre**
10104 - 101 Ave., Fort Saskatchewan, AB T8L 2A5
780-998-2425 Fax: 780-992-9432 www.capitalhealth.ca
Old Name: Rivercrest Lodge Nursing Home
Parent: Alberta Health Services
Eleanor Low, Administrator

***Grande Prairie:* Mackenzie Place Continuing Care**
10409 - 98 St., Grande Prairie, AB T8V 2E8
780-538-7100 Fax: 780-538-1500 www.capitalhealth.ca
Parent: Alberta Health Services
Number of Beds: 128 beds
Shana Hammy-Bugarin, Director, Continuing Care

***Hythe:* Hythe Continuing Care Centre**
PO Box 100, Hythe, AB T0H 2C0
780-356-3818 Fax: 780-356-3633
Parent: Alberta Health Services
Number of Beds: 29 long-term care beds
Note: continuing care centre
Donna Turner, Director, Health Services

***Islay:* Islay Care Centre**
PO Box 55, Islay, AB T0B 2J0
780-744-3795 Fax: 780-608-8850 www.ech.ab.ca
Parent: Alberta Health Services
Number of Beds: 12 continuing care beds, 8 assisted living
Audrey Cusack, Health Centre Coordinator

***Leduc:* Extendicare - Leduc**
PO Box 280, 4309 - 50 St., Leduc, AB T9E 6K6
780-986-2245 Fax: 780-986-0669 www.capitalhealth.ca
Parent: Alberta Health Services

***Leduc:* Salem Manor Nursing Home**
4419 - 46 St., Leduc, AB T9E 6L2
780-986-8654 Fax: 780-986-4130 www.capitalhealth.ca
Parent: Alberta Health Services
Bernie Pankonin, Administrator

***Lethbridge:* Sifton Family & Youth Services**
528 Stafford Dr. North, Lethbridge, AB T1H 2B2
403-381-5411 Fax: 403-382-4565
Number of Beds: 12 beds
Note: group home
Ross Wakelen, Director

***Mannville:* Mannville Care Centre**
5007 - 46 St., Mannville, AB T0B 2W0
780-763-3621 Fax: 780-608-8850 www.ech.ab.ca
Parent: Alberta Health Services
Number of Beds: 23 beds
Debora Okrainetz, Nursing Manager

***Medicine Hat:* Dr. Dan McCharles Extended Care Centre**
666 - 5 St. SW, Medicine Hat, AB T1A 4H6
403-529-7000 Fax: 403-529-8950
Parent: Alberta Health Services
Number of Beds: 42 beds
Barb Cameron, Manager, Extended/Home Care

***Medicine Hat:* Riverview**
603 Prospect Dr. SW, Medicine Hat, AB T1A 4C2
403-527-5531 Fax: 403-527-5175
riverview@reveraliving.com
www.reveraliving.com
Goldie Boyd, Administrator
Audrey Powers, Care Coordinator

***Morinville:* Aspen House**
9706 - 100 Ave., Morinville, AB T8R 1T2
780-939-7482 Fax: 780-939-6144
Number of Beds: 40 beds; 4 respite beds
Note: assisted living
Grace Regnier, Site Manager

***Radway:* Radway Continuing Care Centre**
PO Box 70, 5002 - 52 St., Radway, AB T0A 2V0
780-736-3740 Fax: 780-736-2353
Parent: Alberta Health Services
Number of Beds: 20 permanent, 4 waiting beds
Gloria Strachan

***Red Deer:* Valley Park Manor**
5505 - 60 Ave., Red Deer, AB T4N 4W2
403-343-4722 Fax: 403-341-5938
Parent: Alberta Health Services
Number of Beds: 100 beds
Note: elderly, medically frail
Candace Spurell, Vice-President

***Red Deer:* West Park Lodge**
5715 - 41 St. Crescent, Red Deer, AB T4N 1B3
403-343-7471 Fax: 403-343-3424
westparklodge@telusplanet.net
www.westparklodge.com
Parent: Alberta Health Services
Number of Beds: 37 beds
Note: senior's lodge; assisted living
Evelyne Gaudet, Administrator

***Sherwood Park:* CapitalCare Strathcona**
12 Brower Dr., Sherwood Park, AB T8H 1V3
780-467-3366 Fax: 780-467-4095 www.albertahealthservices.ca; www.capitalcare.net
Parent: Alberta Health Services
Year Founded: 1994
Number of Beds: 75 beds
Note: Specialties: Continuing care; Secure dementia unit; Eden Alternative philosophy of care; Recreational programs; Occupational therapy; Respite program; Adult community day support program

***Sherwood Park:* Sherwood Park Care Center**
2020 Brentwood Blvd., Sherwood Park, AB T8A 0X1
780-467-2281 Fax: 780-449-1529
admin@advhealth.org
Parent: Alberta Health Services

***Smoky Lake:* Smoky Lake Continuing Care Centre**
47607 - 52 Ave., Smoky Lake, AB T0A 3C0
780-656-3818 Fax: 780-656-3010
Parent: Alberta Health Services
Number of Beds: 32 beds
David Ponich, Continuing Care Centre Supervisor

***St Albert:* Youville Home**
9 St Vital Ave., St Albert, AB T8N 1K1
780-460-6900 Fax: 780-459-4139
youville@telusplanet.net
www.capitalhealth.ca
Parent: Alberta Health Services

***Standoff:* Kainai Continuing Care Centre**
PO Box 380, Standoff, AB T0L 1Y0
403-737-3652 Fax: 403-737-3487
ceciliabthealth@telusplanet.net
Number of Beds: 50 beds
Note: Blood Tribe Dept. of Health
Cecilia Black Water, Director, Health Services

***Stony Plain:* Good Samaritan Care Centre**
5600 - 50 St., Stony Plain, AB T7Z 1P8
780-963-2261 Fax: 780-963-5156
goodsaminfo@gss.org
www.gss.org
Parent: Alberta Health Services
Bob Taillefer, Coordinator, Environmental Services

***Vegreville:* Heritage Home**
4570 Maple St., Vegreville, AB T9C 1X2
780-603-0853 Fax: 780-603-0867 www.ech.ab.ca
Parent: Alberta Health Services
Wanda White, Site Manager

***Vegreville:* Vegreville Care Centre**
5225 - 43 St., Vegreville, AB T9C 1S1
780-632-2871 Fax: 780-632-6680 www.ech.ab.ca
Parent: Alberta Health Services
Number of Beds: 87 beds
Peggy Standen, Coordinator, Health Care

***Youngstown:* Youngstown House**
PO Box 9, Youngstown, AB T0J 3P0
403-779-3920 Fax: 403-779-3946

Number of Beds: 50 beds
Note: group home
Dianne Bradley, Manager

Nursing Homes

Calgary: Carewest Sarcee
3504 - 29th St. SW, Calgary, AB T3E 2L3
403-686-8100 Fax: 403-686-8104 www.carewest.ca; www.albertahealthservices.ca
Parent: Alberta Health Services
Note: Specialties: Comprehensive community care for seniors; Short stay rehabilitation; Long term care; Alzheimer's & dementia services; Palliative care at Sarcee Hospice, which has 15 hospice rooms

Galahad: Galahad Care Centre
PO Box 88, 1 Main St., Galahad, AB T0B 1R0
780-583-3788 Fax: 780-583-2105
Parent: Alberta Health Services
Note: Specialties: Continuing care; Respite care; Palliative care

Retirement Residences

Calgary: Carewest Colonel Belcher Veterans' Care Centre & Seniors' Care Residence
1939 Veterans Way NW, Calgary, AB T3B 5Y8
403-944-7800 www.carewest.ca; www.albertahealthservices.ca
Parent: Alberta Health Services
Year Founded: 2003
Number of Beds: 175 residents in seniors' residence, most of whom are veterans
Note: Specialties: Continuing care services; Care centre offering areas for persons with Alzheimer's disease & other dementias; Day support program for seniors (403-944-7852)

Mental Health Facilities

Mental Health Hospital/Clinic/Facility

Airdrie: Airdrie Mental Health Clinic
112 - 1 Ave. NW, Airdrie, AB T4B 2B3
403-948-3878 Fax: 403-948-7926
maureen.gilberg@calgaryhealthregion.ca
Parent: Alberta Health Services

Athabasca: Athabasca Mental Health Clinic
3401 - 48 Ave., Athabasca, AB T9S 1M7
780-675-5404 Fax: 780-675-3994
Parent: Alberta Health Services

Banff: Banff Mental Health Clinic
301 Lynx St., Banff, AB T1L 1A1
403-762-4451 Fax: 403-762-5570
Note: outpatient clinic

Barrhead: Barrhead Mental Health Clinic
PO Box 4054, 6203 - 49 St., Barrhead, AB T7N 1A1
780-674-8243 Fax: 780-674-8352
Parent: Alberta Health Services
Lorraine Lindberg

Black Diamond: Black Diamond Mental Health Clinic
Oilfields General Hospital, PO Box 1, 717 Government Road, Black Diamond, AB T0L 0H0
403-933-3800 Fax: 403-933-4353 1-877-652-4700

Blairmore: Community Health
PO Box 67, 12501 - 20 Ave., Blairmore, AB T0K 0E0
403-562-7378 Fax: 403-562-7379
Parent: Alberta Health Services

Bonnyville: Bonnyville Mental Health Clinic
PO Box 6917, 5201 - 44 St., Bonnyville, AB T9N 2H4
780-826-2404 Fax: 780-826-6114
Parent: Alberta Health Services
Joan Panteluk

Bow Island: Bow Island Mental Health Clinic
802 - 6 St., Bow Island, AB T0K 0G0
403-545-5120 Fax: 403-545-6357
Parent: Alberta Health Services

Brooks: Brooks Community Mental Health Services
Bag 300, Brooks, AB T1R 1C5
403-793-6655 Fax: 403-795-6656
Parent: Alberta Health Services

Calgary: Central Calgary Mental Health Clinic
1000 - 8 Ave. SW, Calgary, AB T2P 3M7
403-297-7311 Fax: 403-297-5354
Parent: Alberta Health Services

Calgary: Northwest Calgary Mental Health Clinic
#280, 1620 - 29th St. NW, Calgary, AB T2N 4L7
403-297-7345 Fax: 403-297-4543
Parent: Alberta Health Services

Calgary: Wood's Homes (Alberta) Mental Health & Child Welfare Services
9400 - 48 Ave. NW, Calgary, AB T3B 2B2
403-247-6751 Fax: 403-268-0878
jane.matheson@woodshomes.ca
www.woodshomes.ca
Parent: Alberta Health Services
Number of Beds: 110 beds
Jane Matheson, CEO

Calgary: Wood's Homes Child & Adolescent Mental Health Services
805 - 37 St. NW, Calgary, AB T2N 4N8
403-270-4102 Fax: 403-286-0878
kathryn.osterberg@woodshomes.ca
www.woodshomes.ca
Parent: Alberta Health Services
Number of Beds: 150 beds
Note: day treatment, educational, outreach services; longterm care: permanent care (child welfare services) residential; treatment centre for adolescents & families; services for street youth, educational/day treatment services, caregiver services
Jane Matheson, CEO

Camrose: Mental Health Centre
4911 - 49 St., Camrose, AB T4V 1J9
780-679-1764 Fax: 780-608-8850 www.ech.ab.ca
Parent: Alberta Health Services
Brenda Nelson
780/679-1765

Canmore: Mental Health Clinic
Provincial Building, 3rd Floor, 302 - 800 Railway Ave., Canmore, AB T1W 1P1
403-678-4696 Fax: 403-678-1951 www.ech.ab.ca
Parent: Alberta Health Services

Cardston: Cardston Mental Health Clinic
Provincial Building, PO Box 1590, 576 Main St., Cardston, AB T0K 0K0
403-653-5115 Fax: 403-653-2926
Parent: Alberta Health Services

Chestermere: Chestermere Lake Mental Health Clinic
#250, 124 East Chestermere Dr., Chestermere, AB T1X 1M1
403-207-8770 Fax: 403-944-2224
Parent: Alberta Health Services

Claresholm: Claresholm Care Centre
PO Box 490, 139 - 43 Ave. West, Claresholm, AB T0L 0T0
403-625-8500 Fax: 403-625-4318
Parent: Alberta Health Services
Darrell Contes, Administrator

Claresholm: Claresholm Mental Health Clinic
PO Box 2198, 4901 - 2 St. West, Claresholm, AB T0L 0T0
403-625-4068 Fax: 403-625-4177

Cochrane: Cochrane Mental Health Clinic
PO Box 807, Cochrane, AB T4C 1A9
403-932-3455 Fax: 403-932-2971
Parent: Alberta Health Services

Cold Lake: Cold Lake Mental Health Clinic
#208, 314 - 25th St., Cold Lake, AB T9M 1G6
780-639-4922 Fax: 780-639-4990
Parent: Alberta Health Services
Anne Tucker

Consort: Consort Mental Health Clinic
5410 - 52 Ave., Consort, AB T0C 1B0
403-577-3770 Fax: 403-577-2235
Parent: Alberta Health Services

Didsbury: Didsbury Mental Health Clinic
1210 - 20 Ave., Didsbury, AB T0M 0W0
403-335-7285 Fax: 403-335-7227
Parent: Alberta Health Services

Drayton Valley: Drayton Valley Mental Health Clinic
PO Box 7276, 5136 - 51 Ave., Drayton Valley, AB T7A 1S5
780-542-3140 Fax: 780-542-4461 www.dthr.ab.ca
Parent: Alberta Health Services

Edmonton: Alberta Hospital Edmonton
PO Box 307, 17480 Fort Rd., Edmonton, AB T5J 2J7
780-472-5555 Fax: 780-472-5508 www.capitalhealth.ca
Parent: Alberta Health Services
Year Founded: 1923
Number of Beds: 410 beds
Note: Provides assessment, diagnosis, treatment, education & consultation. Conducts research. Programs include: Adult Psychiatry, Geriatric Psychiatry, & the Northern Alberta Forensic Psychiatry Program.

Edmonton: Edmonton Mental Health Clinic
9942 - 108th St., Edmonton, AB T5K 2J5
780-427-4444 Fax: 780-427-0424 www.capitalhealth.ca
Parent: Alberta Health Services

Edson: Edson Mental Health Centre
Provincial Bldg., #100, 111 - 54 St., Edson, AB T7E 1T2
780-723-8294 Fax: 780-723-8297
Parent: Alberta Health Services
Margaret Fern

Fort McMurray: Fort McMurray Mental Health Services
7 Hospital St., Fort McMurray, AB T9H 1P2
780-791-6194 Fax: 780-791-6219
Parent: Alberta Health Services

Gibbons: Gibbons Mental Health Clinic
5018 - 50 St., Gibbons, AB T0A 1N0
780-923-3700 Fax: 780-923-3939

Grande Cache: Grande Cache Mental Health Clinic
702 Pine Plaza, Grande Cache, AB T0E 0Y0
780-827-4998 Fax: 780-827-4787
Note: community clinic

Grande Prairie: Grande Prairie Mental Health Clinic
#600, 10014 - 99th St., Grande Prairie, AB T8V 3N4
780-538-5160 Fax: 780-538-6279

Hanna: Hanna Mental Health Clinic
904 Centre St. North, Hanna, AB T0J 1P0
403-854-5276 Fax: 403-854-5280
Parent: Alberta Health Services

Hardisty: Hardisty Mental Health Clinic
PO Box 269, 4531 - 47 St., Hardisty, AB T0B 1V0
780-888-8306 Fax: 780-888-2427
carol.roberts@ech.ab.ca
www.ech.ab.ca
Parent: Alberta Health Services
Brenda Nelson
780/679-1765

High Level: High Level Mental Health Clinic
PO Box 400, High Level, AB T0H 1Z0
780-926-3791 Fax: 780-926-2944 www.capitalhealth.ca
Parent: Alberta Health Services

High Prairie: High Prairie Mental Health Clinic
High Prairie Health Complex, PO Box 1, 4444 - 53 Ave., High Prairie, AB T0G 1E0
780-926-3791 Fax: 780-767-6491 www.capitalhealth.ca
Parent: Alberta Health Services

High River: High River Mental Health Clinic
PO Box 5309, 310 Macleod Trail, 2nd Floor, High River, AB T1V 1M5
403-652-8340 Fax: 403-652-1456

Hinton: Hinton Mental Health Clinic
1280A Switzer Dr., Hinton, AB T7V 1T5
780-865-8247 Fax: 780-865-8327
Old Name: Hinton Mental Health Centre
Parent: Alberta Health Services
Louise Maurik

Innisfail: Innisfail Mental Health Clinic
5023 - 42 St., Innisfail, AB T4G 1A9
403-227-4601 Fax: 403-227-5683
Parent: Alberta Health Services

Jasper: Jasper Mental Health Clinc
PO Box 310, 518 Robson St., Jasper, AB T0E 1E0
780-852-6616 Fax: 780-852-3413
Parent: Alberta Health Services
Joan Connors

Killam: Killam Mental Health Club
4811 - 49 Ave., Killam, AB T0B 2L0
780-385-7160 Fax: 780-608-8850 www.ech.ab.ca
Parent: Alberta Health Services
Brenda Nelson
780-679-1765

La Crete: La Crete Mental Health Club
Unit 2, 10001 - 100 Av., La Crete, AB T0H 2H0
780-928-4215 Fax: 780-928-4237 www.nlhr.ca
Parent: Alberta Health Services

Lac La Biche: **Lac La Biche Mental Health Clinic**
9503 Beaver Hill Rd., Lac La Biche, AB T0A 2C0
780-623-5230 Fax: 780-623-5232
Parent: Alberta Health Services
Tracy Smith

Leduc: **Leduc Mental Health Clinic**
4210 - 48 St., Leduc, AB T9E 5Z3
780-986-2660 Fax: 780-986-9292 www.capitalhealth.ca
Parent: Alberta Health Services

Lethbridge: **Lethbridge Mental Health Clinic**
200 - 5 Ave. South, Lethbridge, AB T1K 4L1
403-381-5260 Fax: 403-382-4518
mhc-leth@amhb.ab.ca
Diane Conley, Administrator

Mayerthorpe: **Mayerthorpe Mental Health Clinic**
PO Box 30, 4417 - 45 St., Mayerthorpe, AB T0E 1N0
780-786-2279 Fax: 780-786-2023
Parent: Alberta Health Services
Doug Kemp

Medicine Hat: **Medicine Hat Mental Health Clinic**
#4, 181 Carry Dr. SE, Medicine Hat, AB T1B 3T2
403-529-3500 Fax: 403-529-3562

Morinville: **Morinville Mental Health Clinic**
10008 - 107 St., Morinville, AB T8R 1L3
780-939-3388 Fax: 780-939-1216 www.capitalhealth.ca
Parent: Alberta Health Services

Olds: **Olds Mental Health Centre**
Olds Provincial Bldg., 5025 - 50th St., Olds, AB T4H 1R9
403-556-4204 www.albertahealthservices.ca
Parent: Alberta Health Services
Note: Specialties: Mental health services; Crisis response; Counselling; Telemental health psychiatric consultation service

Onoway: **Onoway Mental Health Clinic**
PO Box 1047, 5115 Lac Ste Anne Trail, Onoway, AB T0E 1V0
780-967-9117 Fax: 780-967-2547
Parent: Alberta Health Services
Doug Kemp

Oyen: **Oyen Mental Health Clinic**
312 - 3 Ave. E, Oyen, AB T0J 2J0
403-664-3651 Fax: 403-664-2934
Parent: Alberta Health Services

Peace River: **Peace River Mental Health Clinic**
10015 - 98 St., 3rd Floor, Peace River, AB T8S 1T4
780-624-6151 Fax: 780-624-6565
Parent: Alberta Health Services
Brenda Nelson

Pincher Creek: **Pincher Creek Mental Health Clinic**
PO Box 1052, 696 Kerrle Street, Pincher Creek, AB T0K 1W0
403-627-1121 Fax: 403-627-1145
mhc-pinchercreek@amhb.ab.ca

Ponoka: **Ponoka Mental Health Clinic**
#223, 5110 - 49th Ave., Ponoka, AB T4J 1R6
403-783-7903 Fax: 403-783-7926
dorothy.ranta@amhb.ab.ca
Parent: Alberta Health Services

Provost: **Provost Mental Health Centre**
5419 - 44 St., Provost, AB T0B 3S0
780-753-2575 Fax: 780-753-8096 www.ech.ab.ca
Parent: Alberta Health Services
Brenda Nelson
780/679-1765

Raymond: **Raymond Care Centre**
PO Box 260, Raymond, AB T0K 2S0
403-752-3316 Fax: 403-752-4147
Parent: Alberta Health Services
Number of Beds: 30 beds
Note: geriatric psychiatric facility (longterm & rehab)

Raymond: **Raymond Mental Health Clinic**
150N - 4 St. East, Raymond, AB T0K 2S0
403-752-7960 Fax: 403-627-5275
Parent: Alberta Health Services

Red Deer: **Red Deer Mental Health Centre**
4755 - 49 St., Red Deer, AB T4N 1T6
403-340-5466 Fax: 403-340-4874
Parent: Alberta Health Services
Di Uosburgh, Executive Director

Rimbey: **Rimbey Mental Health Centre**
PO Box 471, 5025 - 55 St., Rimbey, AB T0C 2J0
403-843-2406 Fax: 403-843-2337
Parent: Alberta Health Services

Sherwood Park: **Sherwood Park Mental Health Clinic**
2 Brower Dr., Sherwood Park, AB T8A 3Y1
780-449-5380 Fax: 780-464-3705
mhcsherwoodpark@cha.ab.ca
www.capitalhealth.ca
Division of: Capital Health Region
Anita Murphy, Manager

Slave Lake: **Slave Lake Mental Health Clinic**
309 - 6 St., Slave Lake, AB T0G 2A2
780-805-3502 Fax: 780-805-3550
Parent: Alberta Health Services
Cindy Harmata

Smoky Lake: **Smoky Lake Mental Health Clinic**
4212 - 55 Ave., Smoky Lake, AB T0A 3C0
780-656-3034 Fax: 780-656-5010
Parent: Alberta Health Services
Gloria Strachan

St Albert: **St. Albert Mental Health Clinic**
Sir Winston Churchill Ave., St Albert, AB T8N 3A4
780-459-2820 Fax: 780-460-7152 www.capitalhealth.ca
Parent: Alberta Health Services

St Paul: **St. Paul Mental Health Clinic**
4713 - 48 Ave., St Paul, AB T0A 3A4
780-645-1850 Fax: 780-645-2788
Parent: Alberta Health Services
Leanne Betts

Stettler: **Stettler Mental Health Clinic**
PO Box 600, 4835 - 50 Ave. SS, Stettler, AB T0C 2L0
403-742-7591 Fax: 403-742-7916
Parent: Alberta Health Services

Stony Plain: **Stony Plain Mental Health Clinic**
Westview Health Centre, 4405 South Park Dr., Stony Plain, AB T7Z 1A1
780-968-3600 Fax: 780-963-7186

Strathmore: **Strathmore Mental Health Clinic**
Hilton Plaza, PO Box 2002, 209 - 3 St., Strathmore, AB T1P 1K2
403-934-5174 Fax: 403-934-2685
Old Name: Strathmore Mental Health Centre

Swan Hills: **Swan Hills Mental Health Clinic**
PO Box 261, 29 Freeman Dr., Swan Hills, AB T0G 2C0
780-333-4241 Fax: 780-333-7009
Parent: Alberta Health Services
Lorraine Lindberg

Sylvan Lake: **Sylvan Lake Mental Health Centre**
4602 - 49 Ave., Sylvan Lake, AB T4S 1M7
403-887-2241 Fax: 403-887-2641
Parent: Alberta Health Services

Taber: **Taber Mental Health Clinic**
5011 - 49 Ave., Taber, AB T1G 1V9
403-223-7932 Fax: 403-223-7902

Three Hills: **Three Hills Mental Health Centre**
PO Box 1717, 160 - 3 Ave. South, Three Hills, AB T0M 2A0
403-443-8532 Fax: 403-443-8541
Parent: Alberta Health Services

Tofield: **Tofield Mental Health Clinic & Children's Resource Centre**
5024 - 51 Ave., Tofield, AB T0B 4J0
780-662-7061 Fax: 780-662-3854 www.albertahealthservices.ca
Parent: Alberta Health Services
Brenda Nelson

Valleyview: **Valleyview Mental Health Clinic**
PO Box 358, 4802 Highway St., Valleyview, AB T0H 3N0
780-524-7050
Parent: Alberta Health Services

Vegreville: **Vegreville Mental Health Clinic**
5318 - 50 Ave., Vegreville, AB T9C 1R1
780-632-2714 Fax: 780-632-4954
Parent: Alberta Health Services
Brenda Nelson
780/679-1765

Vegreville: **Vegreville Mental Health Clinic**
PO Box 90, 5318 - 50 St., Vegreville, AB T9C 1R1
780-632-2714 Fax: 780-632-4954 www.ech.ab.ca
Parent: Alberta Health Services
Note: 24-hour crisis line: 780-632-7070
Brenda Nelson

Vermilion: **Vermilion Mental Health Clinic**
Provincial Building, PO Box 14, 4701 - 52 St., Vermilion, AB T9X 1J9
780-853-8168 Fax: 780-853-8279 www.ech.ab.ca
Parent: Alberta Health Services
Brenda Nelson
780/679-1765

Wainwright: **Wainwright Mental Health Clinic**
PO Box 20, 810 - 14 Ave., Wainwright, AB T9W 1R2
780-842-7522 Fax: 780-842-7520 www.ech.ab.ca
Parent: Alberta Health Services
Brenda Nelson

Wetaskiwin: **Wetaskiwin Mental Health Clinic**
5201 - 50 Ave., Wetaskiwin, AB T9A 0S7
780-361-1245 Fax: 780-361-1387
mhc-wetaskiwin@amhb.ab.ca
Parent: Alberta Health Services

Special Care Home

Lloydminster: **Dr. Cooke Extended Care Centre**
3915 - 56 Ave., Lloydminster, AB T9V 0Z7
780-871-7900 Fax: 780-875-3505
Parent: Prairie North Health Region
Number of Beds: 105 beds
Joan Zimmer, Director, Continuing Care

British Columbia

Government Departments in Charge

BRITISH COLUMBIA: Ministry of Health Services
1515 Blanshard St., 6th Fl., Victoria, BC V8W 3C8
250-952-1297 Fax: 250-952-1052 www.gov.bc.ca/health
Division of: Performance Management & Improvement Division

Regional Health Authorities

Kelowna: **Interior Health Authority**
Corporate Office, 220-1815 Kirschner Rd., Kelowna, BC V1Y 4N7
250-862-4200 Fax: 250-862-4201
feedback@interiorhealth.ca; patient.concerns@interiorhealth.ca
www.interiorhealth.ca
Note: Facilities: 20 community health centres; 16 community hospitals; 4 service area hospitals; 2 tertiary referral hospitals. Area Served: Thompson Cariboo Shuswap Health Service Area; Okanagan Health Service Area; Kootenay Boundary Health Service Area; East Kootenay Health Service Area
Robert Halpenny, President; Chief Executive Officer
Cathy Renkas, Vice-President, Communications / Public Affairs
Allan Sinclair, Vice-President, Acute Services
Norman Embree, Board Chair
Keith
Hutchison, Chair, Health Authority Medical Advisory Committee
Donna Lommer, Chief Financial Officer
& Vice-President, Residential Services
Jeremy Etherington, Vice-President, Medicine / Quality
Joanne Konnert, Vice-President, Tertiary Services
Martin McMahon, Vice-President, Planning / Strategic Services
Andrew Neuner, Vice-President, Community Integration
Brenda Rebman, Vice-President, People / Clinical Services

Prince George: **Northern Health Authority**
299 Victoria St., Prince George, BC V2L 5B8
250-565-2649 Fax: 250-565-2640 866-565-2999
communications@northernhealth.ca
www.northernhealth.ca
Note: Formerly Northern Interior Health Board; services administered through 3 service delivery areas: Northwest, Northeast, Northern Interior
Malcolm Maxwell, CEO

Surrey: **Fraser Health Authority**
Corporate Office, #300, 10233 - 152A St., Surrey, BC V3R 7P8
604-587-4600 Fax: 604-587-4666 1-877-935-5669
feedback@fraserhealth.ca
www.fraserhealth.ca
Note: Number of Employees: 23,000 employees, 2,300 physicians, & approximately 5,000 volunteers. Population Served: 1,600,000+. Area Served: Burnaby to White Rock to Hope in British Columbia
Nigel Murray, President; Chief Executive Officer
Kathleen Butler, Director, Corporate Communications
David Plug, Director, Public Affairs
Gordon Barefoot, Board Chair
Brian Woods, Chief Financial Officer; Vice-President, Corporate Services Integration
Philip Barker, Vice-President, Information Management

Geoffrey Crampton, Vice-President, People & Organization Development
Peter Goldthorpe, Vice-President, Capital Projects, Real Estate, & Facilities, Lo
Barbara Korabek, Vice-President, Clinical Operations
Marc Pelletier, Vice-President, Clinical Operations & Clinical Support

Andrew Webb, Vice-President, Medicine

Vancouver: Provincial Health Services Authority/PHSA
700 - 1380 Burrard St., Vancouver, BC V6Z 2H3
604-675-7400 Fax: 604-708-2000 www.phsa.ca
Note: Manages BC Cancer Agency, BC Centre for Disease Control, BC Drug & Poison Information Centre, BC Mental Health Society (Riverview Hospital), BC Provincial Renal Agency, BC Transplant Society, BC Cardiac Program; Children's & Women's Health Centre of British Columbia, Forensic Psychiatric Services Commission
Lynda Cranston, President/CEO

Vancouver: Vancouver Coastal Health
Vancouver Coastal Health Corporate Office, 601 West Broadway, 11th Fl., Vancouver, BC V5Z 4C2
604-736-2033 Fax: 604-736-7601 1-866-884-0888; feedback@vch.ca; pcqo@vch.ca (Patient Care Quality Office)
www.vch.ca
Note: Number of Employees: 22,000 staff; 2,500 physicians; 5,000 volunteers. Population Served: 1,000,000+. Area Served: Vancouver; Richmond; the North Shore; Coast Garibaldi; Sea-to-Sky; Sunshine Coast; Powell River; Bella Bella; Bella Coola
Kip Woodward, Board Chair
Maureen Whyte, Vice-President, Strategic Community Initiatives
Gavin Wilson, Director, Public Affairs
604-708-5312, gavin.wilson@vch.ca
David N. Ostrow, President; Chief Executive Officer
Mary
Ackenhusen, Chief Operating Officer
Duncan Campbell, Chief Financial Officer; Vice-President, Systems Development; Performance
Patricia Daly, Chief Medical Health Officer; Vice-President, Public Health
Susan Wannamaker, Chief Nursing Officer; Executive Lead, Professional Practice
Clay
Adams, Vice-President, Communications & Public Affairs
Jeff Coleman, Vice-President, Regional Programs & Service Integration
Patrick O'Connor, Vice-President, Medicine, Quality, & Safety

Victoria: Vancouver Island Health Authority
1952 Bay St., Victoria, BC V8R 1J8
250-370-8000 Fax: 250-370-8750 877-370-8699
info@viha.ca
www.viha.ca
Number of Beds: 1307 acute care; 4593 residential, VIHA & contracted beds
Note: Formerly Capital Health Region
Howard Waldner, President; CEO

Hospitals

Hospitals - General

Alert Bay: Cormorant Island Health Centre
PO Box 223, 49 School Rd., Alert Bay, BC V0N 1A0
250-974-5585 Fax: 250-974-5422
info@viha.ca
www.viha.ca
Parent: Vancouver Island Health Authority
Number of Beds: 10 multi-purpose beds
Note: Hospital Specialties: Emergency services; Acute care; Medical imaging; General laboratory services (250-974-5585, ext. 3); Adult mental health & addiction services; Care to adults with developmental or physical disabilities; Public health services; Rural health services (250-755-6281)

Richard Stanwick, Chief Medical Health Officer, Vancouver Island Health Authority

Ashcroft: Ashcroft & District General Hospital
700 Ash-Cache Creek Hwy., Ashcroft, BC V0K 1A0
250-453-2211 Fax: 250-453-9685 www.interiorhealth.ca
Parent: Interior Health Authority
Year Founded: 1970
Number of Beds: Number of beds: 24

Bella Bella: R.W. Large Memorial Hospital
88 Waglisla St., Bella Bella, BC V0T 1Z0
250-957-2314 Fax: 250-957-2612
feedback@vch.ca
www.vch.ca/EN/find_locations/find_locations/?&site_id=2136
Parent: Vancouver Coastal Health Authority
Number of Beds: 16 beds
Note: Provincial hospital offering ltc/acute care, pharmacy, diagnostic imaging services, telehealth services
David N. Ostrow, President; CEO, VCH

Bella Coola: Bella Coola General Hospital/BCGH
PO Box 434, 1025 Elcho St., Bella Coola, BC V0T 1C0
250-799-5311 Fax: 250-799-5635
feedback@vch.ca
www.vch.ca
Number of Beds: 10 acute care beds; 5 extended care beds
Note: Hospital Specialties: Emergency services; Walk-in clinic; Laboratory services; Acute care; Long term care; Mental health services; Public health; Physiotherapy; Home support
Michel Bazille, Administrator, Health Services
250-799-5308
Lorinda Andersen, Director, Patient Care
250-799-5311, lorinda.andersen@vch.ca

Burnaby: Burnaby Hospital
3935 Kincaid St., Burnaby, BC V5G 2X6
604-412-6131 Fax: 604-412-6190 www.fraserhealth.ca
Parent: Fraser Health Authority
Number of Beds: 309 acute care beds
Note: Hospital Specialties: Emergency services; Diagnostic testing; General surgery; Perinatal services; Neonatal intensive care; Oncology; Mental health services; Critical care; Palliative care
Arden Krystal, Executive Director

Campbell River: Campbell River & District Regional Hospital
375 - 2nd Ave., Campbell River, BC V9W 3V1
250-850-2141 Fax: 250-286-9675 www.viha.ca
Also Known As: Campbell River General Hospital
Parent: Vancouver Island Health Authority
Note: Hospital Specialties: Emergency care; Surgical services: Intensive care; Cardiac care; Laboratory services; Acute care; Rehabilitation services (250-286-7045); Aboriginal health; Diabetes education (250-850-2607); Nutrition services (250-286-7013)
Richard Crow, Executive Vice-President; Chief Medical Officer, Vancouver Island Health Authority
Sandy Murphy, Nurse, Aboriginal Health
250-850-2602, sandy.murphy@viha.ca

Chetwynd: Chetwynd Hospital & Health Centre
PO Box 507, 5500 Hospital Rd., Chetwynd, BC V0C 1J0
250-788-2236 Fax: 250-788-7247
hello@northernhealth.ca
www2.northernhealth.ca
Parent: Northern Health Authority
Note: Hospital Specialty: Acute care
Betty McCracken Morris, Chief Operating Officer, Northeast Health Service Delivery Area, Northern He

Chilliwack: Chilliwack General Hospital
45600 Menholm Rd., Chilliwack, BC V2P 1P7
604-795-4141 Fax: 604-795-4110
feedback@fraserhealth.ca
www.fraserhealth.ca
Parent: Fraser Health Authority
Note: Hospital Specialties: Emergency services; Laboratory services; Ambulatory care; Rehabilitation services
Andrew Webb, Vice-President, Medicine, Fraser Health

Clearwater: Dr. Helmcken Memorial Hospital/DHM
640 Park Dr., RR#1, Clearwater, BC V0E 1N0
250-674-2244 Fax: 250-674-2477 www.interiorhealth.ca
Parent: Interior Health Authority
Number of Beds: 6 beds
Note: Hospital Specialties: Community hospital level 1 services; Emergency services; Acute care; Physiotherapy; Recreation therapy; Dietician services; Public health; Environmental health protection services; Home care nursing
Nicole Lacroix, Coordinator, Recreation Therapy
Nicole.Lacroix@interiorhealth.ca

Comox: St. Joseph's General Hospital
2137 Comox Ave., Comox, BC V9M 1P2
250-339-2242 Fax: 250-339-1432 www.sjghcomox.ca
Parent: Vancouver Island Health Authority
Year Founded: 1913
Number of Beds: 235 beds (110 in acute care and 125 in complex care)
Note: A comprehensive health facility with services in emergency, colposcopy, dermatology, diabetes, diagnostic imaging (mammography, radiology, ultrasound), extended care, general surgery, gastroenterology, internal medicine, maternity, obstetrics/gynaecology, oncology, ophthalmology, orthopaedics, paediatrics, palliative care, pathology, psychiatry and urology
Michael Pontus, President /CEO
250-339-1409
Stefan Schovanek, President, Medical Staff

Cranbrook: East Kootenay Regional Hospital/EKRH
13 - 24th Ave. North, Cranbrook, BC V1C 3H9
250-426-5281 Fax: 250-426-5285 866-288-8082
www.interiorhealth.ca
Parent: Interior Health Authority
Note: Hospital Specialties: Emergency services; Laboratory services; Diagnostic imaging; General surgery; Intensive care unit; Obstetrics; Pediatrics; Oncology (250-417-6228); Ophthalmology; Orthopedics; Urology; Otolaryncology; Rehabilitation services; Psychiatry
Jeremy Etherington, Vice-President, Medicine / Quality, Interior Health
Allan Sinclair, Vice-President, Acute Services, Interior Health
Kate Fox, Coordinator, Volunteers, East Kootenay Regional Hospital
250-417-2746, katefox@shaw.ca

Creston: Creston Valley Hospital/CVH
PO Box 3000, 312 - 15th Ave. North, Creston, BC V0B 1G0
250-428-2286 Fax: 250-428-4860 www.interiorhealth.ca
Parent: Interior Health Authority
Number of Beds: 16 beds
Note: Hospital Specialties: Emergency services; Trauma care; Diagnostic imaging; Laboratory services; Acute care; Ambulatory care; Obstetrics; Pediatrics; Rehabilitation services, including occupational therapy & physiotherapy; Mental health services; Diabetes education; Dietitian services; Outpatient renal dialysis unit; Chronic disease management; Adult day care; Number of Employees: 150
Cindy Kozak-Campbell, Interior Health Authority Health Services Administrator, Creston
Atma Persad, Chief of Staff
Deryn Collier, Coordinator, Recruitment

Dawson Creek: Dawson Creek & District Hospital
11100 - 13th St., Dawson Creek, BC V1G 3W8
250-782-8501 Fax: 250-783-7301
hello@northernhealth.ca
www2.northernhealth.ca
Parent: Northern Health Authority
Number of Beds: 62 acute care beds
Note: Hospital Specialties: Emergency services (250-784-7393); Diagnostic imaging; Laboratory services; General surgery; Intensive care unit; Acute care; Maternity services; Rehabilitation services, including physiotherapy, occupational, & respiratory therapy; Adult psychiatry inpatient unit (250-784-7369); Diabetes education

Cathy Ulrich, Chief Executive Officer, Northern Health
Betty McCracken Morris, Chief Operating Officer, Northern Health Northeast Health Service Delivery A

Delta: Delta Hospital
5800 Mountain View Blvd., Delta, BC V4K 3V6
604-946-1121 Fax: 604-538-3320
feedback@fraserhealth.ca
www.fraserhealth.ca
Parent: Fraser Health Authority
Note: Hospital Specialties: Emergency services; General surgery; Ambulatory care; Cardiac services; Occupational therapy; Physiotherapy; Respiratory therapy; Speech language pathology services; Diabetes education; Asthma education; Nutrition counselling; Social work; Palliative care
Arden Krystal, Vice-President, Clinical Operations, Fraser Health
Andrew Webb, Vice-President, Medicine, Fraser Health
Andrew.Webb@fraserhealth.ca

Duncan: Cowichan District Hospital/CDH
3045 Gibbins Rd., Duncan, BC V9L 1E5
250-737-2030 Fax: 250-715-1212 www.viha.ca
Parent: Vancouver Island Health Authority
Number of Beds: 95 beds
Note: Hospital Specialties: Emergency services; Laboratory services; Medical imaging: Intensive care unit; Acute care; Maternity; Rehabilitation services; Adult mental health & addiction services; Breast Health Hereditary Cancer Program; Hemodialysis; Occupational therapy & physiotherapy (250-709-3000); Nutrition services (250-370-8111); Respiratory ambulatory service; Palliative care
Richard Crow, Chief Medical Officer; Executive Vice-President, Vancouver Island Health Authority
Catherine Mackay, Chief Operating Officer; Executive Vice President, Vancouver Island Health Authority
Gerry Giles, Chair, Cowichan Valley Regional Hospital District
Jim Potts, Manager, CDH Pharmacy

Fernie: Elk Valley Hospital
PO Box 670, 1501 - 5th Ave., Fernie, BC V0B 1M0
250-423-4453 Fax: 250-423-3732 www.interiorhealth.ca
Parent: Interior Health Authority
Number of Beds: 20 beds
Note: Hospital Specialties: Emergency services; Diagnostic imaging; Laboratory services; Ambulatory care; Acute care; Obstetrics; Pediatrics; Occupational therapy; Physiotherapy; Mental health services; Dietitian services; Pain management education; Public health; Home support services. Number of Employees: 100

Fort Nelson: Fort Nelson Hospital
PO Box 60, 5315 Liard Street, Fort Nelson, BC V0C 1R0
250-774-8100 Fax: 250-774-8110
hello@northernhealth.ca
www2.northernhealth.ca
Parent: Northern Health Authority
Note: Hospital Specialties: Emergency care; Intensive care; Medical imaging; Addictions counselling services (250-565-2649); Adult day centre (250-565-7451); Diabetes education (250-774-6916)
Betty McCracken Morris, Chief Operating Officer, Northern Health, Northeast Health Service Delivery

Fort St James: Stuart Lake Hospital
PO Box 1060, 600 Stuart Dr. East, Fort St James, BC V0J 1P0
250-996-8201 Fax: 250-996-8777
hello@northernhealth.ca
www2.northernhealth.ca/Contact_Us/Northern_Interior/FraserLakeandVanderhoofcontacts.asp
Parent: Northern Health Authority
Number of Beds: 12 beds (6 acute care, 6 long-term care beds)
Note: Services include emergency, laboratory and x-ray facilities.
Cathy Ulrich, CEO, NHA
250-565-2649
Michael McMillan, COO, Northern Interior, NHA
Bruna Schnepf., Director, Patient Care
250-567-2211

Fort St John: Fort St. John Hospital & Health Centre
9636 - 100th Ave., Fort St John, BC V1J 1Y3
250-262-5200 Fax: 250-262-5294 www2.northernhealth.ca
Parent: Northern Health Authority
Number of Beds: 44 beds
Note: Hospital Specialties: Diagnostics; Surgery; Intensive care; Acute care; Maternity services; Rehabilitation; Hemo dialysis; Palliative care
Betty McCracken Morris, Chief Operating Officer, Northern Health, Northeast Health Service Delivery

Golden: Golden & District General Hospital
835 - 9th St. North RR 2, Golden, BC V0A 1H2
250-344-5271 Fax: 250-344-2511
Parent: Interior Health Authority
Number of Beds: 8 beds
Tish Smith

Grand Forks: Boundary Hospital
7649 - 22nd St., Grand Forks, BC V0H 1H2
250-443-2100 Fax: 250-442-8331 www.interiorhealth.ca
Parent: Interior Health Authority
Number of Beds: 12 acute care beds
Note: Hospital specialties: Emergency services; Laboratory services; Radiology; Acute care; Chemotherapy; Renal dialysis; Ambulatory care
Louise Fitzgerald, Social Worker
250-443-2162, Louise.Fitzgerald@interiorhealth.ca

Hazelton: Wrinch Memorial Hospital
#999, 2510 Highway 62, Hazelton, BC V0J 1Y0
250-842-5339 Fax: 250-842-5685
Parent: Northern Health Authority

Hope: Fraser Canyon Hospital
1275 - 7th Ave., Hope, BC V0X 1L4
604-869-5656 Fax: 604-860-7732
feedback@fraserhealth.ca
www.fraserhealth.ca
Parent: Fraser Health Authority
Note: Hospital Specialties: Emergency services; Diagnostic laboratory services (604-860-7702); Acute care; Social work; Nutrition counselling; Palliative care (604-860-7713)

Invermere: Invermere & District Hospital
850 - 10th Ave., Invermere, BC V0A 1K0
250-342-9201 Fax: 250-342-6303
Parent: Interior Health Authority
Number of Beds: 8 acute care, 35 residential beds
Colleen Wagner, Contact
250-342-9201

Kamloops: Royal Inland Hospital
311 Columbia St., Kamloops, BC V2C 2T1
250-374-5111 Fax: 250-314-2333 877-288-5688
patient.concerns@interiorhealth.ca
www.interiorhealth.ca/health-services.aspx?id=284
Parent: Interior Health Authority
Number of Beds: 226 beds
Note: Tertiary acute care hospital; angiography/interventional radiology, bone density, CT scan, mammography, MRI, nuclear medicine, ultrasound, X-Ray
Robert Halpenny, President/CEO, IHA
Donna Lommer, CFO, IHA, Medical Services

Kelowna: Kelowna General Hospital
2268 Pandosy St., Kelowna, BC V1Y 1T2
250-862-4000 Fax: 250-862-4201 www.interiorhealth.ca
Parent: Interior Health Authority
Number of Beds: 329 beds
Rick Riley, COO
Dave Macintosh, Director, Purchasing Services

Kitimat: Kitimat General Hospital & Health Centre
920 Lahakas Blvd. South, Kitimat, BC V8C 2S3
250-632-2121 Fax: 250-632-8726
Parent: Northern Health Authority
Number of Beds: 54 beds

Ladysmith: Ladysmith & District General Hospital
1111 - 4 Ave., Ladysmith, BC V0R 2E0
250-739-5777 Fax: 250-245-3238
Parent: Vancouver Island Health Authority
Number of Beds: 42 beds
Chuck Rowe, CEO

Langley: Langley Memorial Hospital
22051 Fraser Hwy., Langley, BC V3A 4H4
604-534-4121 Fax: 604-534-8283
Old Name: Langley Health Services
Parent: Fraser Health Authority
Number of Beds: 166 acute care beds, 230 residential care beds
Leanne Heppill, Executive Director
Harry Berglund, Director of Purchasing

Lillooet: Lillooet District Hospital & Community Health Programs
951 Murray St., Lillooet, BC V0K 1V0
250-256-4233 Fax: 250-256-1336
Parent: Interior Health Authority
Number of Beds: 6 beds
Jennifer Thur

MacKenzie: MacKenzie & District Hospital
45 Centennial Dr., MacKenzie, BC V0J 2C0
250-997-3263 Fax: 250-997-3940
Parent: Northern Health Authority
Number of Beds: 5 beds
Raelene Shea, Exec. Dir.

Maple Ridge: Ridge Meadows Hospital
PO Box 5000, 11666 Laity St., Maple Ridge, BC V2X 7G5
604-463-4111 Fax: 604-463-1888
feedback@fraserhealth.ca
www.fraserhealth.ca/find_us/locations/our_locations?site_id=1787
Old Name: Ridge Meadows Hospice Society
Parent: Fraser Health Authority
Number of Beds: 104 acute care, 150 residential care beds, 20-bed psychiatric care unit
Nigel Murray, President/CEO, FHA
Greg Kotylak, Head, Surgery
Valerie Spurrell, Director, Acute Care

McBride: McBride & District Hospital
1126, 5th Ave., McBride, BC V0J 2E0
250-569-2251 Fax: 250-569-3369
Parent: Northern Health Authority
Number of Beds: 16 beds
Vic Chicoine, Administrator

Merritt: Nicola Valley General Hospital
3451 Voght St., Merritt, BC V1K 1C6
250-378-3271 Fax: 250-378-3287
Parent: Interior Health Authority
Number of Beds: 8 beds
Doug Sage

Mission: Mission Memorial Hospital
7324 Hurd St., Mission, BC V2V 3H5
604-826-6261 Fax: 604-826-9513
Parent: Fraser Health Authority
Number of Beds: 20 acute care, 75 residential care beds
Vivian Giglio, Executive Director, Health Services

Nakusp: Arrow Lakes Hospital
97 East 1st Ave., Nakusp, BC V0G 1R0
250-265-3622 Fax: 250-265-4435 www.interiorhealth.ca
Parent: Interior Health Authority
Number of Beds: 6 acute inpatient beds; 14 residential beds (Minto House residential unit)
Note: Hospital Specialties: Emergency services; Acute care; Public health; Physiotherapy; Occupational therapy; Home care; Mental health services; Palliative care Number of Employees: 50

Nanaimo: Nanaimo Regional General Hospital
1200 Dufferin Cres., Nanaimo, BC V9S 2B7
250-754-2141 Fax: 250-755-7633
Parent: Vancouver Island Health Authority
Number of Beds: 329 beds
Allison Cutler, Executive Director, Medicine, Chronic Disease Management/Primary Health

Nelson: Kootenay Lake Hospital
3 View St., Nelson, BC V1L 2V1
250-352-3111 Fax: 250-354-2320 866-352-3111
www.interiorhealth.ca
Parent: Interior Health Authority
Number of Beds: 30 beds
Dorothy Wayling, Site Director

New Denver: Slocan Community Health Centre
401 Galena Ave., New Denver, BC V0G 1S0
250-358-7911 Fax: 250-358-7117
www.interiorhealth.ca/health-services.aspx?id=350&terms=slocan
Parent: Interior Health Authority
Number of Beds: 30 beds
Note: Primary, long-term care facilty with services including emergency, mental health services, occupational therapy, physiotherapy, podiatry, respiratory therapy, X-ray & ECG
Robert Halpenny, CEO, IHA
Ann Weir, Health Centre Manager
Fax: 250-358-7801, ann.weir@interiorhealth.ca

North Vancouver: Lions Gate Hospital
231 - 15 St. East, North Vancouver, BC V7L 2L7
604-988-3131 Fax: 604-984-5838 www.vch.ca
Parent: Vancouver Coastal Health Authority
Number of Beds: 268 beds
Ellen Pekeles, COO

Oliver: South Okanagan General Hospital
7139 - 362nd Ave., Oliver, BC V0H 1T0
250-498-5000 Fax: 250-498-5004
www.interiorhealth.ca/health-services.aspx?id=11846
Parent: Interior Health Authority
Number of Beds: 18 beds
Note: A level 1, community hospital with services including emergency, radiology, acute care, outpatient ambulatory care
Robert Halpenny, President/CEO, IHA
Allan Sinclair, Vice-President, Acute Services, IHA
Mary Doughtery, Patient Care Quality Officer, South Okanagan
250-862-4300, mary.dougherty@interiorhealth.ca

Penticton: Penticton Regional Hospital
550B Carmi Ave., Penticton, BC V2A 3G6
250-492-4000 Fax: 250-492-9068
Parent: Interior Health Authority
Number of Beds: 148 beds
Lorraine Ferguson

Port Alberni: West Coast General Hospital
3949 Port Alberni Hwy., Port Alberni, BC V9Y 7L1
250-723-2135 Fax: 250-723-8805
Parent: Vancouver Island Health Authority
Number of Beds: 43 acute care, 32 extended care beds
Jim Latham, Director, Physical Plant

Port Alice: Port Alice Hospital
1090 Marine Dr., Port Alice, BC V0N 2N0
250-284-3555 Fax: 250-284-6163
pahospital@capescott.net
Parent: Vancouver Island Health Authority
Number of Beds: 3 beds
Jean Wheeler, Manager

Port Hardy: Port Hardy Hospital
9120 Granville, Port Hardy, BC V0N 2P0
250-949-6161 Fax: 250-949-7000
phhospital@capescott.net
Parent: Vancouver Island Health Authority
Number of Beds: 17 beds
Ron Benson, CEO

Port McNeill: Port McNeill & District Hospital
2750 Kingcome Place, Port McNeill, BC V0N 2R0

250-956-4461 Fax: 250-956-4823
pmhosp@island.net
Parent: Vancouver Island Health Authority
Number of Beds: 10 beds

Port Moody: Eagle Ridge Hospital/ERH
475 Guildford Way, Port Moody, BC V3H 3W9
604-461-2022 Fax: 604-461-9972
feedback@fraserhealth.ca
www.fraserhealth.ca
Parent: Fraser Health Authority
Year Founded: 1984
Note: Hospital Specialties: Emergency services; General surgery unit; Acute care; Ambulatory care; Cardiac care; Medical oncology unit; Rehabilitation services, including physiotherapy & occupational therapy; Respiratory therapy; Diabetes education; Asthma education; Nutrition counselling; Palliative care
Arden Krystal, Vice-President, Clinical Operations
Andrew Webb, Vice-President, Medicine, Fraser Health

Powell River: Powell River General Hospital
5000 Joyce Ave., Powell River, BC V8A 5R3
604-485-3211 Fax: 604-485-3245
Parent: Vancouver Coastal Health Authority
Number of Beds: 33 beds
Jerry Causier, Manager, Acute Services

Prince George: Prince George Regional Hospital
1475 Edmonton St., Prince George, BC V2M 1S2
250-565-2000 Fax: 250-565-2343
Parent: Northern Health Authority
Number of Beds: 338 beds
Ginger Brown, Executive Director
Adrian Van Peenen, Director, Physical Plant

Prince Rupert: Prince Rupert Regional Hospital
1305 Summit Ave., Prince Rupert, BC V8J 2A6
250-624-2171 Fax: 250-624-2195
Parent: Northern Health Authority
Number of Beds: 71 beds

Princeton: Princeton General Hospital
98 Ridgewood Ave., Princeton, BC V0X 1W0
250-295-3233 Fax: 250-295-3344
mharkness@oshr.org
Parent: Interior Health Authority
Number of Beds: 6 acute care beds
Marilyn Harkness, Administrator
Alex Smith, Head, Plant Maintenance

Queen Charlotte: Queen Charlotte Islands General Hospital
PO Box 9, 3203 3rd Ave., Queen Charlotte, BC V0T 1S0
250-559-4300 Fax: 250-559-4312
chcexec@qcislands.net
Division of: Queen Charlotte City Site
Parent: Northern Health Authority
Number of Beds: 21 beds
George Cheyne, CEO

Quesnel: GR Baker Memorial Hospital
543 Front St., Quesnel, BC V2J 2K7
250-985-5600 Fax: 250-992-5652 www2.northernhealth.ca
Parent: Northern Health Authority
Year Founded: 1955
Number of Beds: 38 beds
Note: Hospital Specialties: Emergency services; Intensive care; Crisis stabilization; Acute care; Maternity services; Occupational therapy; Physiotherapy
Michael McMillan, Chief Operating Officer, Northern Health, Northern Interior Health Service D

Revelstoke: Queen Victoria Hospital & Health Centre
1200 Newlands Rd., Revelstoke, BC V0E 2S0
250-837-2131 Fax: 250-837-4788 www.interiorhealth.ca
Parent: Interior Health Authority
Number of Beds: 38 beds
Dorothy Schiller
Andrew Neuner
Ron Hawkins, Maintenance Supervisor

Richmond: Richmond Hospital
7000 Westminster Hwy., Richmond, BC V6X 1A2
604-278-9711 Fax: 604-244-5191
feedback@vch.ca
www.vch.ca/find_locations/find_locations/?&site_id=135
Old Name: The Richmond Hospital
Parent: Vancouver Coastal Health Authority
Number of Beds: 175 beds
Note: Emergency, ambulatory care, diagnostics, intensive care and coronary care, maternity, psychiatry and surgery
David N. Ostrow, President/CEO, VCH
Duncan Adams, Vice-President, Communications & Public Affairs, VCH

Saanichton: Saanich Peninsula Hospital
2166 Mount Newton Cross Rd., Saanichton, BC V8M 2B2
250-544-7676 Fax: 250-652-7521
www.viha.ca/finding_care/facilities/saanich_peninsula_hospital.htm
Parent: Vancouver Island Health Authority
Number of Beds: 48 acute beds, 144 extended care beds
Note: Emergency, breast surgical oncology, imaging - bone mineral densitometry, CT scan; 10-bed palliative care unit; acute & extended care
Howard Waldner, President; CEO, VIHA
William Boomer, Vice-President; CFO, VIHA
Catherine Mackay, Executive Vice-President; COO, VIHA

Salmon Arm: Shuswap Lake General Hospital
601 - 10th St. NE, Salmon Arm, BC V1E 4N6
250-833-3600 Fax: 250-833-3611 877-299-1599
lab.interiorhealth.ca/site_gi.aspx?id=32
Parent: Interior Health Authority
Number of Beds: 40 beds
Note: Emergency, acute care beds, diagnostic imaging, radiology, obstetrical care
Robert Halpenny, CEO, IHA
Warren Bell, President, Medical Staff

Salt Spring Island: The Lady Minto Gulf Islands Hospital
135 Crofton Rd., Salt Spring Island, BC V8K 1T1
250-538-4800 Fax: 250-538-4870
www.viha.ca/finding_care/facilities/lady_minto_gulf_islands_hospital.htm
Old Name: Lady Minto Hospital
Parent: Vancouver Island Health Authority
Number of Beds: 50 beds (19 acute care, 31 extended care beds)
Note: Services include emergency, laboratory, diagnostic imaging (fluoroscope, ultrasound, x-rays), breast oncology, surgery
Howard Waldner, President/CEO, VIHA
250-370-8692
Bill Boomer, Vice-President/CFO, VIHA
250-370-8602
Shannon Marshall, Communications Officer, VIHA
250-370-8270, shannon.marshall@viha.ca
Bill Relph, Site Manager

Sechelt: St. Mary's Hospital
5544 Sunshine Coast Highway, Sechelt, BC V0N 3A0
604-885-2224 Fax: 604-885-8628
feedback@vch.ca
www.vch.ca/EN/find_locations/find_locations/?&site_id=152
Parent: Vancouver Coastal Health Authority
Number of Beds: 31 beds
Note: Services include emergency, tomography, fluoroscopy, mammography, renal program (dialysis units), ultrasound, laboratory, radiology, youth clinic.
David N. Ostrow, President/CEO, VCHA
Duncan Campbell, CFO/Vice-President, Systems Devlopment, VCHA
Trudi Beutel, Public Affairs Officer, VCHA
604 -08-5282, trudi.beutel@vch.ca

Smithers: Bulkley Valley District Hospital
PO Box 370, 3950 - 8th Ave., Smithers, BC V0J 2N0
250-847-2611 Fax: 250-847-2446 www.northernhealth.ca
Parent: Northern Health Authority
Number of Beds: 25 beds
Note: Hospital Specialties: Emergency services; Medical imaging; Acute care; Maternity services; Long term care; Palliative care

Sparwood: Sparwood General Hospital & Health Care Centre
PO Box 9, 570 Pine Ave., Sparwood, BC V0B 2G0
250-425-6212 Fax: 250-425-2313
www.interiorhealth.ca/health-services.aspx?id=352
Parent: Interior Health Authority
Note: A primary health care centre with services including emergency, medical clinic, on-site lab & x-ray, dialysis, wellness centre focusing on diabetic, cardiac and respiratory education, as well as nutrition counselling and pain management counselling
Robert Halpenny, President/CEO, IHA
Jeremy Etherington, Vice-President, Medicine/Quality, IHA
Donna Lommer, CFO/Vice-President, Residential Services, IHA

Squamish: Squamish General Hospital
38140 Behrner Dr., Squamish, BC V0N 3G0
604-892-5211 Fax: 604-892-9417
feedback@vch.ca
www.vch.ca/EN/find_locations/find_locations/?&site_id=150
Parent: Vancouver Coastal Health Authority
Number of Beds: 21 beds
Note: Services include emergency, general medicine and surgery, obstetrics, palliative care, physiotherapy, pharmacy, diagnostic imaging, laboratory, ambulatory care, chemotherapy, fluoroscopy, diabetic day clinic, residential care
David N. Ostrow, President/CEO, VCHA
Duncan Campbell, CFO/Vice-President, Systems Development, VCHA
Tina Hua, Manager, Acute Services, VCHA

Stewart: Stewart Health Centre
PO Box 8, 904 Brightwell St., Stewart, BC V0T 1W0
250-636-2221 Fax: 250-636-2715
www2.northernhealth.ca/Contact_Us/Northwest/Stewartcontacts.asp
Parent: Northern Health Authority
Number of Beds: 3 beds
Note: Services include acute care, home support, physicians, counseling services, pharmacy, visiting specialists, mammography, ambulance services.
Cathy Ulrich, CEO, NHA
Shawn Terlson, CFO, NHA
Marina Ellinson, COO, Northwest, NHA
Ronald Chapman, Chief Medical Health Officer, NHA
Suzanne Johnston, Chief Nursing Officer, NHA

Summerland: Summerland Memorial Health Centre
PO Box 869, 12815 Atkinson Rd., Summerland, BC V0H 1Z0
250-404-8000 Fax: 250-404-8005
www.interiorhealth.ca/health-services.aspx?id=268
Also Known As: Summerland Health Centre
Old Name: Summerland General Hospital
Parent: Interior Health Authority
Year Founded: 1967
Number of Beds: 50 beds
Note: A community health and residential care facility with services including surgery (cataract, ear, nose & throat, and dental), occupational therapy, physical therapy, laboratory services, x-ray, home support, social work, diabetes education, long-term case management.
Robert Halpenny, President/CEO, IHA
Cathy Renkas, Vice-President, Communications/Public Affairs, IHA
Bob Heise, Community Health Services Administrator

Surrey: Matsqui-Sumas-Abbotsford General Hospital
10334, 152A Street, Surrey, BC V3R 7P8
604-587-4600 Fax: 604-587-4666
Parent: Fraser Health Authority
Number of Beds: 202 beds
Vivian Giglio, Executive Director
Ed Towndow, Supervisor, Building Services/Environmental Dept.
Jeri Lynch, Purchasing Agent

Surrey: Surrey Memorial Hospital
13750 - 96 Ave., Surrey, BC V3V 1Z2
604-581-2211 Fax: 604-588-3320
feedback@fraserhealth.ca
www.fraserhealth.ca/find_us/locations/our_locations?site_id=1792
Parent: Fraser Health Authority
Number of Beds: 450 acute care, 186 residential care beds
Note: A comprehensive health centre with services including emergency, adolescent psychiatry, angiography, antepartum care, asthma education, diagnostic imaging (CT scans, bone densitometry, fluoroscopy, mammography, MRI, radiology, ultrasound), cardiology, outpatient speech language pathology, dental surgery, drug and alcohol resource team, hospice palliative care, intensive care, neonatal intensive care, ophthalmology, otolaryngology, paediatric oncology, pharmacy, plastic surgery, postpartum care, psychiatry, respiratory therapy, STI/HIV clinic, sexual assault, sleep lab, social work, speech language pathology, spiritual care, urological surgery, vascular and thoracic surgery, youth wellness centre.
Nigel Murray, President/CEO, FHA
Andrew Webb, Vice-President, Medicine, FHA
Loretta Solomon, Site Executive Director
Loretta.Solomon@fraserhealth.ca
Urbain Ip, Site Medical Director

Terrace: Mills Memorial Hospital
4720 Haugland Ave., Terrace, BC V8G 2W7
250-635-2211 Fax: 250-635-7639
cholly.boland@northernhealth.ca
Parent: Northern Health Authority
Number of Beds: 52 beds
Cholly Boland, Health Services Administrator

Tofino: Tofino General Hospital
PO Box 190, 261 Neill St., Tofino, BC V0R 2Z0
250-725-3212 Fax: 250-725-3150
info@viha.ca
www.viha.ca/finding_care/facilities/tofino_general_hospital.htm
Parent: Vancouver Island Health Authority
Year Founded: 1954
Number of Beds: 10 beds
Note: Services include emergency, echocardiography, laboratory, mental health, physiotherapy, radiology
Howard Waldner, President/CEO, VIHA
250-370-8692
Brian Jackson, Director, Rural Health Services, VIHA
Kathryn Kilpatrick, Site Manager
Monica E. MacDonald, Site Administrative Assistant
250-725.3204, monica.macdonald@viha.ca

Trail: Kootenay Boundary Regional Hospital
1200 Hospital Bench, Trail, BC V1R 4M1
250-368-3311 Fax: 250-364-3422 866-368-2314
info@kbrh.ca
www.kbrh.ca
Old Name: Trail Regional Hospital
Parent: Interior Health Authority
Number of Beds: 75 beds
Lynn Johnstone

Vancouver: Children's & Women's Health Centre of British Columbia
4500 Oak St., Vancouver, BC V6H 3N1
604-875-2345 Fax: 604-875-5381 www.bcwomens.ca
Division of: BC Children's Hospital
Parent: Provincial Health Services Authority
Sharon Toohey, President

Vancouver: Children's & Women's Heatlh Centre of British Columbia
4480 Oak St., Vancouver, BC V6H 3V4
604-875-2345 Fax: 604-875-5381 www.bcchildrens.ca
Division of: BC Children's Hospital
Parent: Provincial Health Services Authority
Sharon Toohey, President

Vancouver: Providence Health Care
7801 Argyle St., Vancouver, BC V5P 3L6
604-321-2661 Fax: 604-321-6886
www.providencehealthcare.org
Division of: Holy Family Hospital
Parent: Vancouver Coastal Health Authority
Number of Beds: 218 beds
Note: Rehabilitation
Dianne Doyle, President; CEO

Vancouver: Providence Health Care
3080 Prince Edward St., Vancouver, BC V5T 3N4
604-874-1141 Fax: 604-877-8125
www.providencehealthcare.org
Division of: Mount Saint Joseph Hospital
Parent: Vancouver Coastal Health Authority
Number of Beds: 208 beds
Dianne Doyle, President; CEO

Vancouver: Providence Health Care
1081 Burrard St., Vancouver, BC V6Z 1Y6
604-682-2344 Fax: 604-684-6532
Division of: St. Paul's Hospital
Parent: Vancouver Coastal Health Authority
Number of Beds: 520 acute care beds
Dianne Doyle, President; CEO

Vancouver: UBC Hospital
2211 Westbrook Mall, Vancouver, BC V6T 2B5
604-822-7121 Fax: 604-822-7268
feedback@vch.ca
www.vch.ca/EN/find_locations/find_locations/?&site_id=164
Also Known As: UBC Health Sciences Centre Hospital
Parent: Vancouver Coastal Health Authority
Year Founded: 1968
Number of Beds: 191 beds
Note: Divided into 3 buildings, the Detwiller Pavilion is known for its psychiatric unit, the Purdy Pavilion offers operational stress injury clinic, MRI, movement disorder clinic, residential care, while the Koerner Pavilion offers acute neurology, Alzheimer clinic, angiography, bladder care, brain research, breast reconstruction, CT scans, fluoroscopy, Huntington disease clinic, laboratory, multiple sclerosis clinic, nuclear medicine, nutrition counselling, radiology, sleep disorders program, speech language pathology, spirometry, surgical clinic, ultrasound, urgent care centre.
David N. Ostrow, President/CEO, VCHA
Anne Sutherland Boal, COO, Vancouver Acute, VCHA
Susan Stromberg, Medical Director, Urgent Care Centre, UBC
Tiffany Akins, Regional Communications Leader, VCHA
604-319-7530

Vancouver: Vancouver General Hospital
855 West 12th Avenue, Vancouver, BC V5Z 1M9
604-875-4111 Fax: 604-875-4035 http://www.vanhosp.bc.ca/
Parent: Vancouver Coastal Health Authority
Number of Beds: 583 beds
Susan Wannamaker, Senior Operating Officer
C. Roach, Manager, Physical Plant
Maggie Sinclair, Waste Management, Physical Plant

Vanderhoof: St. John Hospital
3255 Hospital Rd., Vanderhoof, BC V0J 3A0
250-567-2211 Fax: 250-567-9713
hello@northernhealth.ca
www.northernhealth.ca
Parent: Northern Health Authority
Year Founded: 1941
Number of Beds: 24 acute care
Note: Services include emergency, labor & delivery, diagnostic imaging (X-ray, ultrasound), orthopedic surgery, general surgeries, physiotherapy, visiting specialists
Cathy Ulrich, CEO, NHA
Michael McMillan, COO, Northern Interior Region, NHA

Vernon: Vernon Jubilee Hospital
2101 - 32 St. South, Vernon, BC V1T 5L2
250-558-1200 Fax: 250-545-0369
Parent: Interior Health Authority
Number of Beds: 123 beds
Peter Dutoit
R. Lediet, Manager, Physical Plant

Victoria: Glengarry Extended Care Hospital
1780 Fairfield Rd., Victoria, BC V8S 1G7
250-595-4321 Fax: 250-370-5727
Parent: Vancouver Island Health Authority
Number of Beds: 212 beds
Carrie Peter, Coordinator, Volunteer Resources

Victoria: Mount Tolmie Extended Care Hospital
3690 Richmond Rd., Victoria, BC V8P 4R6
250-370-5626 Fax: 250-370-5755
Parent: Vancouver Island Health Authority
Number of Beds: 75 beds
Note: extended care hospital

Victoria: Priory Hospital
567 Goldstream Ave., Victoria, BC V9B 2W4
250-370-5626 Fax: 250-370-5779
Parent: Vancouver Island Health Authority
Number of Beds: 75 beds
Note: extended care hospital

Victoria: Queen Alexandra Centre for Children's Health
2400 Arbutus Rd., Victoria, BC V8N 1V7
250-519-5390 Fax: 250-721-6837
Parent: Vancouver Island Health Authority
Number of Beds: 20 beds
Note: acute & extended care

Victoria: Royal Jubilee Hospital
1952 Bay St., Victoria, BC V8R 1J8
250-370-8000 Fax: 250-370-8804
info@viha.ca
www.viha.ca/finding_care/facilities/royal_jubilee_hospital.htm
Parent: Vancouver Island Health Authority
Number of Beds: 425 beds
Note: Acute care, cystic fibrosis clinic, rehabilitation services, breast physiotherapy, breast surgical oncology. Located in Memorial Pavilion.
Howard Waldner, President/CEO, VIHA
Catherine Mackay, Executive Vice-President/COO, VIHA
Shannon Marshall, Media Contact, Communications, VIHA
250-370-8270

Victoria: Victoria General Hospital
1 Hospital Way, Victoria, BC V8Z 6R5
250-727-4212 Fax: 250-727-4106
Parent: Vancouver Island Health Authority
Number of Beds: 349 including 50 paeds
Note: acute care

White Rock: Peace Arch Hospital
15521 Russell Ave., White Rock, BC V4B 2R4
604-531-5512 Fax: 604-531-0726 www.peacearchhospital.com
Parent: Fraser Health Authority
Number of Beds: 475 acute care, 300 residential care beds
Jackie Smith, Executive Director

Williams Lake: Cariboo Memorial Hospital
517 North 6th Ave., Williams Lake, BC V2G 2G8
250-392-4411 Fax: 250-392-2157 www.interiorhealth.ca
Parent: Interior Health Authority
Note: Hospital Specialties: Emergency services: Diagnostic imaging; Laboratory services (250-392-8215); Ambulatory care; Acute care; Obstetrics
Deb Runge, Site Manager
Deborah.Runge@interiorhealth.ca

Federal

Abbotsford: Pacific Institution / Regional Treatment Centre
PO Box 3000, 33344 King Rd., Abbotsford, BC V2S 4P4
604-870-7700 Fax: 604-870-7746
www.csc-scc.gc.ca/text/facilit/institutprofiles/pacific-eng.shtml
Also Known As: Pacific Institution
Old Name: Regional Health Centre (Pacific)
Division of: Correctional Services Canada, Dept. of the Solicitor General
Year Founded: 1972
Number of Beds: 122 beds
Note: Psychiatric care unit, health centre, rehabilitation unit, regional reception/assessment centre and intensive program unit; a mens' facility
Zender Katz, Executive Director

Private

Abbotsford: Menno Hospital
32945 Marshall Rd., Abbotsford, BC V2S 1K1
604-859-7631 Fax: 604-859-6931 www.mennoplace.ca
Parent: Fraser Health Authority
Number of Beds: 150 beds
Robert V. Turnbull, Chief Operating Officer
Chris Dean, Director, Environmental Services

Burnaby: Willingdon Park Hospital
4435 Grange St., Burnaby, BC V5H 1P4
604-433-2455 Fax: 604-433-5804
Old Name: Willingdon Private Hospital
Parent: Fraser Health Authority
Number of Beds: 95 beds
Arnold Bennewith, Administrator
Joy Lee, Superintendent

Coquitlam: Como Lake Private Hospital & Nursing Home
657 Gatensbury St., Coquitlam, BC V3J 5G9
604-939-9277 Fax: 604-939-6518
Number of Beds: 95 beds
Note: Specialties: Complex health care & personal assistance in a residential setting; Adult day program

Coquitlam: Lakeshore Care Centre
657 Gatensbury St., Coquitlam, BC V3J 5G9
604-939-9277 Fax: 604-939-6518
Parent: Fraser Health Authority
Number of Beds: 95 beds
Lynn Aarvold, Administrator

Kelowna: Still Waters Private Hospital
1450 Sutherland Ave., Kelowna, BC V1Y 5Y5
250-860-2216 Fax: 250-860-3655
Number of Beds: 79 beds
Note: A long-term care home for seniors and the disabled. Rooms are rented and geared to income. Licensed care included. Other services include 24-hr. emergency response, laundry, housekeeping. There is a fulltime resident manager.
David Kornell, Executive Director

Langley: Simpson Manor
PO Box 40, 8838 Glover Rd., Langley, BC V1M 2R4
604-888-0711 Fax: 604-888-1218
inquiries@simpsonmanor.ca
www.simpsonmanor.ca
Old Name: Simpsons Private Hospital
Parent: Fraser Health Authority
Note: Long-term care for seniors, permanent and semi-premament residency; adult day program, 9-5 pm weekdays; a 2-storey facility with 42 resident rooms per floor, mostly single occupancy, and 18 double rooms
Debbie Eglsaer, Director, Resident Care
Director@SimpsonManor.ca
Ingo Riesen, Administrator
604-888-4699, Administrator@SimpsonManor.ca

Maple Ridge: Holyrood Manor
22710 Holyrood Ave., Maple Ridge, BC V2X 3E6
604-467-8831 Fax: 604-467-8262
holyrood@reveraliving.com
Parent: Fraser Health Authority
Number of Beds: 123 beds
Ann MacMillan, Administrator

North Vancouver: North Shore Private Hospital & Lynn Valley Care Centre
1070 Lynn Valley Rd., North Vancouver, BC V7J 1Z8
604-988-4181 Fax: 604-988-0814
gailwilson@nsph.ca
www.lynnvalleycare.com
Number of Beds: 142 beds
Mehdi Sherkat, Administrator

Vancouver: Amherst Private Hospital & Nursing Home
375 West 59th Ave., Vancouver, BC V5X 1X3
604-321-6777 Fax: 604-322-0123
Year Founded: 1964
Number of Beds: 74 beds
Note: Hospital Specialties: Complex care

Vancouver: Point Grey Private Hospital
2423 Cornwall Ave., Vancouver, BC V6K 1B9
604-733-7133 Fax: 604-733-8298
pghosp@telus.net
Number of Beds: 52 beds
Maureen McIntosh, Administrator

Victoria: Wayside House
550 Foul Bay Rd., Victoria, BC V8S 4H1
250-598-4521 Fax: 250-598-4547
inquiries@waysidehousevictoria.org
Division of: Christian Science Care Facility
Parent: Vancouver Island Health Authority
Number of Beds: 9 beds
Susan Waterman, Administrator

Auxiliary Hospitals

100 Mile House: 100 Mile District General Hospital
South Cariboo Health Centre, PO Box 399, 555 Cedar Ave. South, 100 Mile House, BC V0K 2E0
250-395-7600 Fax: 250-395-7578 www.interiorhealth.ca
Parent: Interior Health Authority
Note: Hospital Specialties: Maternity; Diagnostic imaging; Physiotherapy; MMental health; Public health; Diabetic education; Adult day service; Home support
Gayle Dunsmuir, Contact, Hospice
gayle.hospice@shawbiz.ca
Wendy Reilly, Contact, Residential Care
Wendy.Reilly@interiorhealth.ca

Vancouver: BC Children's Hospital
4480 Oak St., Vancouver, BC V6H 3N1
604-875-2000 888-300-3088
comm@cw.bc.ca
www.bcchildrens.ca
Old Name: Crippled Children's Hospital; Children's Hospital
Parent: Provincial Health Services Authority
Year Founded: 1928
Note: Hospital Specialties: Emergency services; Ambulatory care; Pediatric surgery; Specialized pediatric health services; Intensive & trauma care; Specialized programs for children with congenital or acquired heart disease; Onclogy; Kidney transplants; Bone marrow transplants; Cochlear implant service; Medical genetics program; Mental health services for children & youth; Assessment & diagnosis for children with complex developmental behavioural conditions; Healthy Buddies, a child-centred health promotion program; Centre for Healthy Weights; Safe Start, an injury prevention program; Research; Child health information (Family Resource Library)
Larry Gold, President

Vancouver: BC Women's Hospital & Health Centre
4500 Oak St., Vancouver, BC V6H 3N1
604-875-2424 1-888-300-3088
comm@cw.bc.ca (Communications)
www.bcwomens.ca
Parent: Provincial Health Services Authority
Note: Hospital Specialties: Health care for women, newborn, & families; Gynecological & reproductive health services; Sexual assault service; HIV care of women & children; Birth control & abortion support & counselling; Substance dependency; Psychology; Social work; Aboriginal Health Program; Osteoporois
Jan Christilaw, President

Victoria: Aberdeen Hospital
1450 Hillside Ave., Victoria, BC V8T 2B7
250-370-5626 Fax: 250-370-5612 www.viha.ca
Parent: Vancouver Island Health Authority
Note: Hospital Specialty: Extended care for the elderly & young adults with neurological challenges
Helene Driscoll, Coordinator, Therapy / Seniors Health

Community Health Centres

Community Health Care Centres

Alexis Creek: Alexis Creek Health Centre
2591 Morton St., Alexis Creek, BC V0L 1A0
250-394-4313 Fax: 250-964-5179
Parent: Interior Health Authority

Armstrong: Pleasant Valley Health Centre
3800 Patten Dr., Armstrong, BC V0E 1B2
250-546-4720 Fax: 250-546-9821
Parent: Interior Health Authority
Number of Beds: 40 beds
Peter DuToit

Barriere: Barriere & District Health Centre
PO Box 659, 537 Barriere Town Rd., Barriere, BC V0E 1M0
250-672-9731 Fax: 250-672-5144
Parent: Interior Health Authority
Linda Basran

Castlegar: Castlegar & District Community Health Centre
709 - 10th St., Castlegar, BC V1N 2H7
250-365-7711 Fax: 250-365-1236 www.interiorhealth.ca
Parent: Interior Health Authority
Note: Specialties: Ambulatory care; Family medicine; Laboratory services

Chase: Chase Health Centre
825 Thompson Ave., Chase, BC V0E 1M0
250-679-3312 Fax: 250-679-5329
Parent: Interior Health Authority
Bonnie Lee

Chemainus: Chemainus Health Authority
PO Box 499, 9909 Esplanade St., Chemainus, BC V0R 1K0
250-246-3291 Fax: 250-246-3844
Parent: Vancouver Island Health Authority
Number of Beds: 75 beds
Note: diagnostic & treatment centre, multilevel care facility
Joan Roberts, Director

Cumberland: Cumberland Health Care Centre
PO Box 400, 2696 Windermere Ave., Cumberland, BC V0R 1S0
250-336-8531 Fax: 250-336-2100
Parent: Vancouver Island Health Authority
Number of Beds: 75 beds
Don Brown, CEO

Elkford: Elkford Health Centre
PO Box 640, 212 Alpine Way, Elkford, BC V0B 1H0
250-865-2247 Fax: 250-865-2797
Parent: Interior Health Authority
Number of Beds: 4 beds
Wendy Timmerman, Site Manager

Fort Smith: Fort Smith Public Health Unit
PO Box 1080, Fort Smith, BC Z0E 0P0
867-872-6203 Fax: 867-872-6260
Parent: Fort Smith Health & Social Services Authority

Fraser Lake: Fraser Lake Community Health Centre
130 Chowsunket St., Fraser Lake, BC V0J 1S0
250-699-7742 Fax: 250-699-6987
Parent: Northern Health Authority
Kay Scott, CEO

Gold River: Gold River Health Clinic
601 Trumpeter Dr., Gold River, BC V0P 1G0
250-283-2626 Fax: 250-283-7561
Parent: Vancouver Island Health Authority
Enid O'Hara, Area Director of Rural Services, Campbell River/Nootka/Comac Valley

Hudson's Hope: Hudson's Hope Gething Diagnostic & Treatment Centre
PO Box 599, 10309 Kyllo St., Hudson's Hope, BC V0C 1V0
250-783-9991 Fax: 250-783-9125
Parent: Northern Health Authority
Number of Beds: 2 emergency beds
Andrew Neuner, CEO
Susan Mochoruk, Nurse Manager

Kaslo: Victorian Community Health Centre of Kaslo
673 A Ave., Kaslo, BC V0G 1M0
250-353-2291 Fax: 250-353-2738
Old Name: Victoria Hospital of Kaslo
Parent: Interior Health Authority
Number of Beds: 20 beds
Christie Heuston, Site Director

Logan Lake: Logan Lake Primary Health Care Organization
5 Beryl Ave., Logan Lake, BC V0K 1W0
250-523-9414 Fax: 250-523-6869
Old Name: Logan Lake Health Centre
Parent: Interior Health Authority
Number of Beds: 4 beds
Marsha Wilson, Care Coordinator

Lytton: St. Bartholomew's Health & Healing Centre
PO Box 1089, Lytton, BC V0K 1Z0
250-455-2221 Fax: 250-455-6621
Parent: Interior Health Authority
Jennifer Thur, Manager, Health Services

Pemberton: Pemberton Health Centre
PO Box 8, 1403 Portage Rd., Pemberton, BC V0N 2L0
604-894-6939 Fax: 604-894-6918
Old Name: Pemberton Diagnostic & Treatment Centre
Parent: Vancouver Coastal Health Authority
Number of Beds: 5 beds
Rebecca Lindley, President, Med Staff

Sparwood: Sparwood General Healthcare Centre
PO Box 9, 570 Pine Ave., Sparwood, BC V0B 2G0
250-425-6212 Fax: 250-425-2313
wendy.timmerman@interiorhealth.ca
Parent: Interior Health Authority
Number of Beds: 12 beds
Wendy Timmerman, Site Manager

Tahsis: Tahsis Health Centre
PO Box 399, 1085 Maquinna Dr., Tahsis, BC V0P 1X0
250-934-6322 Fax: 250-934-6404
Parent: Vancouver Island Health Authority
Enid O'Hara, Area Director of Rural Health Services, Campbell River/Nootka/Comoc Valley

Tatla Lake: West Chilcotin Health Centre
Tatla Lake Nursing Station, 16452 Chilcotin Highway 20, Tatla Lake, BC V0L 1V0
250-476-1114 Fax: 250-476-1266
Parent: Interior Health Authority

Tumbler Ridge: Tumbler Ridge Health Care Centre
PO Box 80, 220 Front St., Tumbler Ridge, BC V0C 2W0
250-242-5271 Fax: 250-242-3889
Parent: Northern Health Authority
Number of Beds: 2 holding beds
Note: diagnostic & treatment centre
Beth Kidd, COO

Valemount: Valemount Health Centre
PO Box 697, 1445 - 5 Ave., Valemount, BC V0E 2Z0
250-566-9138 Fax: 250-566-4319
health@valemount.com
www.nirhb.bc.ca
Parent: Northern Health Authority
Note: outpatient health centre
Marilyn Harknes, Administrator
Vic Chicoine, Executive Director

Nursing Stations

Alexis Creek: Red Cross Outpost Nursing Station
PO Box 39, 2591 Morton Rd., Alexis Creek, BC V0L 1A0
250-394-4313 Fax: 250-394-5179
Number of Beds: 1 beds
Note: Red Cross Outpost Nursing Stations correspondence should be sent to Manager of Outpost Hospital Program, Canadian Red Cross Society, 4750 Oak St., 3rd Fl., Vancouver BC V6H 2N9
Pat Kermeen, Manager

Anahim Lake: Anahim Lake Nursing Station
Hudson Rd., Anahim Lake, BC V0L 1C0
250-742-3305 Fax: 250-742-3336
anahim_lake_nursing_station@hc-sc.gc.ca
Parent: Interior Health Authority

Atlin: Atlin Health Centre
PO Box 330, 3rd St., Atlin, BC V0W 1A0
250-651-7677 Fax: 250-651-7687
atlinoph@atlin.net
Old Name: Red Cross Outpost Hospital
Number of Beds: 1 bed

Bamfield: Red Cross Outpost Nursing Station
353 Bamfield Rd., Bamfield, BC V0R 1B0
250-728-3312 Fax: 250-728-3054
Parent: Vancouver Island Health Authority
Number of Beds: 3 beds
Pat Kermeen, Manager, Outpost Hospital Program

Blue River: **Red Cross Outpost Hospital**
PO Box 18, 858 Main St., Blue River, BC V0E 1J0
250-673-8311 Fax: 250-673-2380
Pat Kermeen, Manager, Outpost Hospital Program

Edgewood: **Red Cross Outpost Nursing Station**
322 Monashee Ave., Edgewood, BC V0G 1J0
250-269-7313 Fax: 250-269-7520
Pat Kermeen, Manager, Outpost Hospital Program

Hartley Bay: **Hartley Bay Nursing Station**
General Delivery, Hartley Bay, BC V0V 1A0
250-841-2556 Fax: 250-841-2554
angelacliftonrhealth@yahoo.ca
Number of Beds: 1 bed
Angela Clifton, Health Director

Iskut: **Iskut Nursing Station**
PO Box 9, Iskut, BC V0J 1K0
250-234-3511 Fax: 250-234-3512 866-660-6607
feddie.louie@ivhs.ca
www.ivhs.ca
Parent: Northern Health Authority
Freddie Carlick, Health Director

Kincolith: **Kincolith Nursing Station**
General Delivery, Kincolith, BC V0V 1B0
250-326-4258

Kitkatla: **Kitkatla Nursing Station**
General Delivery, Kitkatla, BC V0V 1C0
250-848-2254 Fax: 250-848-2263
kitkatla_nursing_station@hc-sc.gc.ca

Klemtu: **Klemtu Nursing Station**
General Delivery, Klemtu, BC V0T 1L0
250-839-1221 Fax: 250-839-1184
alma_wert@hc-sc.gc.ca

Kyuquot: **Red Cross Outpost Nursing Station**
100 Okime Island, Kyuquot, BC V0P 1J0
250-332-5289 Fax: 250-332-5215
Pat Kermeen, Manager, Outpost Hospital Program

Takla Landing: **Takla Landing Nursing Station**
General Delivery, Takla Landing, BC V0J 2T0
250-564-9334 Fax: 250-564-9334

Telegraph Creek: **Telegraph Creek Nursing Station**
PO Box 112, Telegraph Creek, BC V0J 2W0
250-235-3211 Fax: 250-235-3213

Special Treatment Centre

Burnaby: **Burnaby Family Court Centre - Outpatient Clinic**
3405 Willingdon Ave., Burnaby, BC V5G 3H4
604-660-5870 Fax: 604-660-1109
Number of Beds: 9 beds
Fred Bannon, Director

Houston: **Houston Health Centre**
3150 - 14 St., Houston, BC V0J 1Z0
250-845-2294 Fax: 250-845-2005
Parent: Northern Health Authority
Number of Beds: 2 holding beds
Hanna White, Administrator

Kamloops: **Phoenix Centre**
922 - 3 Ave., Kamloops, BC V2C 6W5
250-374-4634 Fax: 250-374-4621
ksad@phoenixcentre.org
www.phoenixcentre.org
Number of Beds: 20 beds
Note: detox centre

Vancouver: **Arthritis Society**
895 - 10 Ave. West, Vancouver, BC V5Z 1L7
604-879-7511 Fax: 604-871-4500
Parent: Vancouver Coastal Health Authority
Melanie Crombie, Executive Director

Vancouver: **British Columbia Cancer Agency**
600 - 10 Ave. West, Vancouver, BC V5Z 4E6
604-877-6000 Fax: 604-872-4596 www.bccancer.bc.ca
Parent: Provincial Health Services Authority
Note: cancer treatment
Simon B. Sutcliffe, President
Mohan Bains, Supervisor, Biomedical Waste
Tom Bennett, Supervisor, Waste Management

Vancouver: **Elizabeth Bagshaw Women's Clinic**
200 - 1177 West Broadway, Vancouver, BC V6H 1G3
604-736-7878 Fax: 604-736-8081 877-736-7171
www.elizabethbagshawclinic.ca
Parent: Vancouver Coastal Health Authority
Note: abortion clinic
Cheryl Davies, Administrator

Vancouver: **Everywoman's Health Centre**
210 - 2525 Commercial Dr., Vancouver, BC V5A 4C1
604-322-6692 Fax: 604-322-6632
ehc@axion.net
www.everywomanshealthcentre.ca
Division of: Abortion Control Clinic
Parent: Vancouver Coastal Health Authority
Number of Beds: 6 recovery room, 2 procedure room beds
Note: abortion clinic
J. Foley, Executive Director

Vancouver: **G.F. Strong Centre**
4255 Laurel St., Vancouver, BC V5Z 2G9
604-734-1313 Fax: 604-737-6359 www.gfstrong.com
Parent: Vancouver Coastal Health Authority
Number of Beds: 92 beds
Note: rehabilitation treatment centre
Patti Flaherty, Senior Operation Officer

Vancouver: **Sunny Hill Health Centre for Children**
3644 Slocan St., Vancouver, BC V5M 3E8
604-453-8300 Fax: 604-453-8301
Parent: Provincial Health Services Authority
Number of Beds: 18 beds
Note: Provincial rehabilitation & assessment centre for children with disabilities

Victoria: **British Columbia Cancer Agency**
2410 Lee Ave., Victoria, BC V8R 6V5
250-519-5500 Fax: 250-519-2012 800-670-3322
www.bccancer.bc.ca
Parent: Vancouver Coastal Health Authority
Note: comprehensive cancer centre
B. Weinerman, Vice-President

Whistler: **Diagnostic & Treatment Centre**
4380 Lorimer Rd., Whistler, BC V0N 1B4
604-932-4911 Fax: 604-932-4992
Old Name: Whistler Diagnostic & Treatment Centre
Parent: Vancouver Coastal Health Authority
Number of Beds: 13 beds
Tina Hua, Manager, Acute Services

Nursing Homes

Abbotsford: **Menno Home**
32910 Brundige Ave., Abbotsford, BC V2S 1N2
604-853-2411 Fax: 604-859-0751
Parent: Fraser Health Authority
Number of Beds: 196 beds
Arthur J. Enns, Administrator

Abbotsford: **Sunrise Special Care Facility**
2411 Railway St., Abbotsford, BC V2S 2E3
604-853-3078
Number of Beds: 8 beds
Mona McMillan, Head Nursing

Burnaby: **St. Michael's Centre**
7451 Sussex Ave., Burnaby, BC V5J 5C2
604-434-1323 Fax: 604-434-6469
reception@stmichaels.bc.ca
www.saintmichaelscentre.org
Parent: Fraser Health Authority
Number of Beds: 128 extended care, 16 hospice beds
Helene Elias, Acting Executive Director
Severino Tolfo, Director, Environmental Services

Chilliwack: **Eden Care Centre**
9100 Charles St., Chilliwack, BC V2P 5K6
604-792-8166 Fax: 604-792-1111
edencare@telus.net
Old Name: Eden Rest Home
Parent: Fraser Health Authority
Number of Beds: 89 beds
Elaine Price, Administrator

Coquitlam: **Burquitlam Lions Care Centre**
560 Sydney Ave., Coquitlam, BC V3K 6A4
604-939-6485 Fax: 604-939-4728
ceo@burquitlamlionscare.com
www.burquitlamlionscare.com
Parent: Fraser Health Authority
Number of Beds: 76 beds
Renee Danylczuk, Administrator

Duncan: **Cowichan Lodge**
3045 Gibbins Rd., Duncan, BC V9L 1E5
250-748-3331 Fax: 250-748-3032 www.viha.ca
Parent: Vancouver Island Health Authority
Number of Beds: 85 beds
, Laurie, Chisholm

Gibsons: **Kiwanis Village Care Home**
841 Kiwanis Way, Gibsons, BC V0N 1V9
604-886-8132 Fax: 604-886-8483
kiwanis@uniserve.com
Number of Beds: 37 beds
Dennis Regnier, Site Manager

Kamloops: **Extendicare - Pine Grove Lodge**
313 McGowan Ave., Kamloops, BC V2B 2N8
250-376-5701 Fax: 250-376-5770
cnh-pinegrove@extendicare.com
www.motimahal.ca
Parent: Interior Health Authority
Number of Beds: 75 beds
Robert S. Moffitt, Administrator

Kamloops: **Kamloops Personal Care Home Ltd. - Garden Manor**
63 Nicola St. West, Kamloops, BC V2C 1J5
250-374-7612 Fax: 250-374-7605
Number of Beds: 24 beds
John H. Stewart, Administrator

Kamloops: **Overlander Extended Care Hospital**
953 Southill St., Kamloops, BC V2B 7Z9
250-554-2323 Fax: 250-554-5557
Parent: Interior Health Authority
Number of Beds: 189 beds

Kelowna: **Gordon House**
3091 Walnut Rd., Kelowna, BC V1W 3V2
250-763-5290 Fax: 250-763-5207
Number of Beds: 8 beds
Valerie Bosch, Administrator

Langley: **Murrayville Manor Ltd.**
21616 - 46 Ave., Langley, BC V3A 3J4
604-530-9033 Fax: 604-530-9023
Number of Beds: 39 beds
Wayne Mills, Administrator

Nanaimo: **Columbian Centre Society**
2356 Rosstown Rd., Nanaimo, BC V9T 3R7
250-758-8711 Fax: 250-751-1128
Number of Beds: 10 beds
Tom Grauman, Administrator

Nelson: **Mount St. Francis Hospital**
1300 Gordon Rd., Nelson, BC V1L 3M5
250-352-3531 Fax: 250-352-6942
Parent: Interior Health Authority
Number of Beds: 79 beds
Cydney Higgins

Parksville: **Trillium Lodge**
PO Box 940, 401 Moilliet St., Parksville, BC V9P 2G9
250-248-8353 Fax: 250-248-8388
Parent: Vancouver Island Health Authority
Number of Beds: 106 beds
Gillian Forsyth, Director, Care

Pouce Coupe: **Pouce Coupe Care Home**
PO Box 98, 5216 - 50 Ave., Pouce Coupe, BC V0C 2C0
250-786-6116 Fax: 250-786-0197
Parent: Northern Helath Authority
Number of Beds: 55 beds
Dave Price, Resident Care Manager

Salmon Arm: **Bastion Place**
700 - 11 St. NE, Salmon Arm, BC V1E2S5
250-833-3616 Fax: 250-833-3605
Number of Beds: 101 beds
Brenda Veerman

Sidney: **Rest Haven Lodge**
2281 Mills Rd., Sidney, BC V8L 2C3
250-656-0717 Fax: 250-656-4745
Number of Beds: 75 beds
Bernard Skoretz, Administrator

Surrey: **Argyll Lodge**
14590 - 106A Ave., Surrey, BC V3R 1T4
604-581-4174 Fax: 604-582-6348
Number of Beds: 25 beds
Baljit Kandola, Administrator

Surrey: **Cherington Place**
13453 - 111A Ave., Surrey, BC V3R 2C5
604-581-2885 Fax: 604-582-9028
cherington@telus.net
seniorshome.com
Parent: Fraser Health Authority

Number of Beds: 75 beds
Annamae Clarke, Administrator

Surrey: **K & C Care Ltd.**
1504 - 160 St., Surrey, BC V4A 4N9
604-531-7900 Fax: 604-531-2338
Number of Beds: 10 beds
Kwan-Ying Jen, President

Terrace: **Terraceview Lodge**
4103 North Sparks South, Terrace, BC V8G 5G9
250-638-0223 Fax: 250-635-9775
Parent: Northern Health Authority
Number of Beds: 75 beds
Doris Mitchell, Administrator

Vancouver: **Ananda**
1249 - 8 Ave. East, Vancouver, BC V5T 1V3
604-872-7134 Fax: 604-872-8420
Number of Beds: 20 beds
Darrell Burnham, Executive Director

Vancouver: **Britannia Lodge**
1090 Victoria Dr., Vancouver, BC V5L 4G2
604-255-3711 Fax: 604-255-3712
britannia.lodge@shaw.ca
Number of Beds: 45 beds
A. Filsoof, Administrator

Vancouver: **Louis Brier Home & Hospital**
1055 West 41st Ave., Vancouver, BC V6M 1W9
604-261-9376 Fax: 604-266-8712
Parent: Vancouver Coastal Health Authority
Number of Beds: 93 beds
Peter Kafka, CEO
Patrick Chan, Director, Administration

Vancouver: **St. Jude's Anglican Home**
810 - 27 Ave. East, Vancouver, BC V5Z 2G7
604-874-3200 Fax: 604-874-3459
info@stjudes.ca
www.stjudes.ca
Parent: Vancouver Coastal Health Authority
Number of Beds: 55 beds
Chris Norman, Administrator

Vernon: **Sunshine Lodge**
9604 Shamanski Dr., Vernon, BC V1B 2L7
250-542-9350
Number of Beds: 18 beds
C. Baziw, Administrator

Vernon: **Twin Cedars Rest Home**
3201 - 37 Ave., Vernon, BC V1T 2Y4
250-542-4983 Fax: 250-542-4924
Number of Beds: 29 beds
Charlene Fair, Administrator

Victoria: **Glenwarren Lodge**
1230 Balmoral Rd., Victoria, BC V8T 1B3
250-383-2323 Fax: 250-383-6359
glenwarren@cplodges.com
www.cplcanada.com
Number of Beds: 131 beds
Note: intermediate & extended care
Norman Carelius, Administrator

West Vancouver: **Capilano Care Centre**
525 Clyde Ave., West Vancouver, BC V7T 1C4
604-926-6856 Fax: 604-926-9169
Parent: Vancouver Coastal Health Authority
Number of Beds: 215 beds
Ann MacMillan, Administrator

West Vancouver: **West Vancouver Care Centre**
1675 - 27 St., West Vancouver, BC V7V 4K9
604-925-1247 Fax: 604-925-3507
Parent: Vancouver Coastal Health Authority
Number of Beds: 75 beds
Courtenay Woodworth, Administrator

White Rock: **Buena Vista Rest Home**
15109 Buena Vista Ave., White Rock, BC V4B 1Y2
604-536-6752
Number of Beds: 12 beds
Elaine Lasoto, Administrator

Long Term/Retirement Care

Long Term Care Facility

100 Mile House: **Mill Site Lodge**
76 Horse Lake Road, 100 Mile House, BC V0K 2E0
250-395-3366 Fax: 250-395-7692
Number of Beds: 26 beds
Allison Ruault, Director, Health Services

Abbotsford: **Bevan Lodge**
33386 Bevan Ave., Abbotsford, BC V2S 5G6
604-850-5416 Fax: 604-850-5418
Parent: Fraser Health Authority
Number of Beds: 15 beds
Hendrik Van Ryk, Administrator

Abbotsford: **M.S.A. Manor Society**
2510 Gladwin Rd., Abbotsford, BC V2T 3N9
604-853-5831 Fax: 604-853-1647
Parent: Fraser Health Authority
Number of Beds: 34 beds
Dennis Magnusson, Administrator

Abbotsford: **Maplewood House**
1919 Jackson St., Abbotsford, BC V2S 2Z8
604-853-5585 Fax: 604-853-4224
Parent: Fraser Health Authority
Number of Beds: 76 beds
Dennis Magnusson, Director

Abbotsford: **Sherwood Crescent Manor Ltd.**
32073 Sherwood Cres., Abbotsford, BC V2T 1C1
604-853-7854 Fax: 604-853-9910
sherwoodcrescentmanor@telus.net
Parent: Fraser Health Authority
Number of Beds: 41 permanent, 10 transitional care, 3 respite beds
Note: intermediate/residential care
Marilyn Smart, Director, Care

Abbotsford: **Tabor Home**
31944 Sunrise Cres., Abbotsford, BC V2T 1N5
604-859-8715 Fax: 604-859-6695
Parent: Fraser Health Authority
Number of Beds: 121 beds
Jack Pauls, Administrator

Abbotsford: **Valhaven Rest Home**
4212 Balmoral St., Abbotsford, BC V4X 1Y5
604-856-2812 Fax: 604-856-3243
Parent: Fraser Health Authority
Number of Beds: 22 beds
Barb Schmidt

Agassiz: **Glenwood Home**
PO Box 15, 1458 Glenwood Dr., RR#2, Agassiz, BC V0M 1A2
604-796-9202
Number of Beds: 19 beds
Anne Marie Leyen, Administrator

Agassiz: **Glenwood Home**
PO Box 15, Agassiz, BC V0M 1A0
604-796-9202 Fax: 604-796-9186
Parent: Fraser Health Authority
Number of Beds: 37 beds complete care; 32 units assisted living
Anne Marie Leyen, Administrator

Aldergrove: **Jackman Manor**
27447 - 28 Ave., Aldergrove, BC V4W 3L9
604-856-4161 Fax: 604-856-2562
Parent: Fraser Health Authority
Number of Beds: 87 beds
Sheila Bridger, Administrator

Aldergrove: **La Rosa de Matsqui**
28711 Huntington Rd., Aldergrove, BC V0X 1A0
604-856-1555 Fax: 604-856-3252
Number of Beds: 15 beds
Carlos Arthur, Manager

Armstrong: **Pioneer Square**
2865 Willowdale Dr., Armstrong, BC V0E 1B1
250-546-3396 Fax: 250-546-9033
Parent: Willowdale Guest Home
Number of Beds: 20 beds
Kevin Svoboda, Administrator

Burnaby: **L'Arche Greater Vancouver**
7401 Sussex Ave., Burnaby, BC V5J 3V6
604-435-9544 Fax: 604-434-1933
larchez@larchevancouver.org
www.larchevancouver.org
Number of Beds: 27 beds
Note: services for developmentally disabled adults
Landys Klyne, Executive Director

Burnaby: **Canada Way Care Centre & Lodge**
7195 Canada Way, Burnaby, BC V5E 3R7
604-525-9444 Fax: 604-526-4746
hmannis@agecare.ca
www.agecare.ca
Parent: Fraser Health Authority
Number of Beds: 80 beds
Note: intermediate care facility
Heidi Mannis, Administrator

Burnaby: **Carlton Gardens**
4125 Canada Way, Burnaby, BC V5G 1G9
604-438-8224 Fax: 604-438-6571
Parent: Fraser Health Authority
Number of Beds: 152 beds
Gwen Gordon, General Manager

Burnaby: **Dania Home Society**
4279 Norland Ave., Burnaby, BC V5G 3Z6
604-299-2414 Fax: 604-299-7775
margaretd@dania.bc.ca
Parent: Fraser Health Authority
Number of Beds: 67 beds
Margaret Douglas-Matthews, Administrator

Burnaby: **Fair Haven United Church Homes**
7557 Sussex Ave., Burnaby, BC V5J 3V6
604-435-0525 Fax: 604-435-7031
mharrison@fairhaven.bc.ca
Parent: Fraser Health Authority
Number of Beds: 100 beds
Maureen Harrison, Administrator

Burnaby: **Fellburn Care Centre**
6050 Hastings St. East, Burnaby, BC V5B 1R6
604-412-6510 Fax: 604-299-1015
Parent: Fraser Health Authority
Number of Beds: 110 beds
Note: extended care facility
Carol Wheeler, Administrator

Burnaby: **Finnish Manor**
3460 Kalyk Ave., Burnaby, BC V5G 3B2
604-434-2666 Fax: 604-439-7448
Parent: Fraser Health Authority
Number of Beds: 60 beds
Sinikka Seppanen, Administrator

Burnaby: **George Derby Centre**
7550 Cumberland St., Burnaby, BC V3N 3X5
604-521-2676 Fax: 604-521-0220 www.georgederbycentre.ca
Parent: Fraser Health Authority
Number of Beds: 300 beds
Janice Mitchell, Executive Director

Burnaby: **New Vista Care Home**
7550 Rosewood St., Burnaby, BC V5E 3Z3
604-521-7764 Fax: 604-527-6001
patk@newvista.bc.ca
www.newvista.bc.ca
Parent: Fraser Health Authority
Number of Beds: 236 beds
Pat Kasprow, CEO

Burnaby: **Normanna Rest Home**
7725 - 4 St., Burnaby, BC V3N 5B6
604-522-5812 Fax: 604-522-5803
Parent: Fraser Health Authority
Number of Beds: 100 beds
Note: multi level care
Margaret Douglas-Matthews, Administrator

Burns Lake: **Pines Care Home**
PO Box 479, 800 Center St., Burns Lake, BC V0J 1E0
250-692-7752 Fax: 250-692-7462
Parent: Northern Health Authority
Number of Beds: 30 beds
Note: multi-level care

Campbell River: **Yucalta Lodge**
555 - 2 Ave., Campbell River, BC V9W 3V1
250-286-1051 Fax: 250-850-0328
linda.harley@crncare.org
Parent: Vancouver Island Health Authority
Number of Beds: 100 beds
Note: multi-level care
Linda Harley, Manager, Residential services

Castlegar: **Castleview Care Centre**
2300 - 14 Ave., Castlegar, BC V1N 4A6
250-365-7277 Fax: 250-365-3291
Parent: Interior Health Authority
Number of Beds: 61 beds
Kimberly Hunter, Administrator

Castlegar: **Talarico Place**
709 - 10 St., Castlegar, BC V1N 1A1
250-365-7221 Fax: 250-304-1238
Parent: Interior Health Authority

Number of Beds: 60 beds
Meg Milner

Chilliwack: McIntosh Lodge
44586 McIntosh Dr., Chilliwack, BC V2P 7W8
604-795-2500 Fax: 604-795-5693
Parent: Fraser Health Authority
Number of Beds: 25 beds
Lynda Marlett, Administrator

Chilliwack: Valleyhaven Guest Home
45450 Menholm Rd., Chilliwack, BC V2P 1M2
604-792-0037 Fax: 604-792-6766
Parent: Fraser Health Authority
Number of Beds: 52 beds
Gillian McCunnie, Director of Care

Chilliwack: Waverly of Chilliwack
8445 Young Rd. South, Chilliwack, BC V2P 4P2
604-792-6340 Fax: 604-792-5611
Parent: Fraser Health Authority
Number of Beds: 15 beds
Debbie Davidson, Administrator

Coquitlam: Cartier House
1419 Cartier Ave., Coquitlam, BC V3K 2C6
604-939-4654 Fax: 604-939-6442
Parent: Fraser Health Authority
Number of Beds: 78 beds
Linda Clary, Administrator

Coquitlam: Foyer Maillard
1010 Alderson Ave., Coquitlam, BC V3K 1W1
604-937-5578 Fax: 604-937-7133
services@foyermaillard.com
Parent: Fraser Health Authority
Number of Beds: 45 beds
Doris Brisebois, Administrator

Courtenay: Glacier View Lodge
2450 Back Rd., Courtenay, BC V9N 9G8
250-338-1451 Fax: 250-338-1115
swolden@sjgh.hnet.bc.ca
Number of Beds: 100 beds
Michael Pontus, President/CEO

Courtenay: Laurel Lodge
280 - 2nd St., Courtenay, BC V9N 1B7
250-334-3083 Fax: 250-338-2253
Number of Beds: 27 beds
Note: seniors' support home
David Reghr, Administrator

Cranbrook: F.W. Green Memorial Home
1700 - 4th St. South, Cranbrook, BC V1C 6E1
250-426-3710 Fax: 250-426-3622
Number of Beds: 86 beds
Allan Sinclair

Cranbrook: Rocky Mountain Lodge
20 - 23rd Ave. South, Cranbrook, BC V1C 5V1
250-489-3361 Fax: 250-489-3545
Number of Beds: 63 beds
Allan Sinclair

Creston: Pioneer Villa
1909 Ash St., RR#5, Creston, BC V0B 1G5
250-428-7188 Fax: 250-428-5192
Parent: Interior Health Authority
Number of Beds: 31 beds
Cheryl Comin, Manager

Creston: Swan Valley Lodge
818 Vancouver St., Creston, BC V0B 1G0
250-428-2283 Fax: 250-428-9318
Parent: Interior Health Authority
Number of Beds: 105 beds
Note: residential care
Cindy Kozak-Campbell

Dawson Creek: Rotary Manor
1121 - 90 Ave., Dawson Creek, BC V1G 5A3
250-719-3480 Fax: 250-719-3781
rmanor@pris.ca
Parent: Northern Health Authority
Number of Beds: 44 beds
Elaine Washington, Residential Program Manager

Delta: Delta Lodge
4501 Arthur Dr., Delta, BC V4K 2X3
604-946-6221 Fax: 604-946-6542
Number of Beds: 21 beds
Jesus Supnet, Administrator

Delta: Delta View Habilitation Centre
9341 Burns Dr., Delta, BC V4K 3N3
604-596-8842 Fax: 604-596-8858
jdevji@deltaview.ca
www.deltaview.ca
Number of Beds: 80 beds
Note: cares for peoples with Alzheimer's disease; specializing in caring for people with difficult behaviour
Jane Devji, Manager

Delta: Heritage Home
5681 Ladner Trunk Rd., Delta, BC V4K 1X3
604-946-4013 Fax: 604-946-4034
heritagehome@dccnet.com
Parent: Fraser Health Authority
Number of Beds: 29 beds
Jasmine Barredo, Director of Care

Delta: Kinsmen Retirement Centre
5410 - 10 Ave., Delta, BC V4M 3X8
604-943-0155 Fax: 604-943-0947
kinsmen@istar.ca
Parent: Fraser Health Authority
Number of Beds: 101 beds
Gerald Arksey, Chairman

Delta: Northcrest Care Centre
6771 - 120th St., Delta, BC V4E 2A7
604-597-7878 Fax: 604-597-7805
general@northcrestcare.ca
Parent: Fraser Health Authority
Number of Beds: 106 beds
Sue Emmons, Executive Director

Delta: West Shore Laylum
4900 Central Ave., Delta, BC V4K 2G7
604-946-2822 Fax: 604-946-2217
Parent: Fraser Health Authority
Number of Beds: 55 beds
Kris Coonfer, Administrator

Duncan: Cairnsmore Place
250 Cairnsmore St., Duncan, BC V9L 4H2
250-709-3080 Fax: 250-746-0351
Parent: Vancouver Island Health Authority
Number of Beds: 100 beds

Enderby: Parkview Place
PO Box 129, Granville St., Enderby, BC V0E 1V0
250-546-6131 Fax: 250-546-9943
Parent: Interior Health Authority
Number of Beds: 31 beds
Peter DuToit

Fort Langley: Simpson Private Hospital
PO Box 40, 8838 Glover Rd., Fort Langley, BC V1M 2R4
604-888-0711 Fax: 604-888-1218
Parent: Fraser Health Authority
Number of Beds: 55 beds
Note: intermediate & extended care
Ingo Riesen, Controller

Fort St John: North Peace Care Centre
9907 - 110 Ave., Fort St John, BC V1J 2S9
250-785-8941 Fax: 250-785-2296 www.northernhealth.ca
Parent: Northern Health Authority
Number of Beds: 95 beds
Note: complex care special care unit
Larry Tokarchuk, COO
Bob Smalley, Director, Plant Services

Golden: Durand Manor
8th Ave. & 9th St., Golden, BC V0A 1H0
250-344-5271 Fax: 250-344-2511
Number of Beds: 27 beds
Note: group home for the elderly mainly who are no longer able to live in the community

Grand Forks: Boundary Lodge Assisted Living
7130 - 9th St., Grand Forks, BC V0H 1H4
250-443-0006 Fax: 250-443-0015
Number of Beds: 18 assisted living units

Grand Forks: Hardy View Lodge
2320 - 78 Ave., Grand Forks, BC V0H 1H0
250-443-2080 Fax: 250-442-3663
Parent: Interior Health Authority
Number of Beds: 35 beds
Trish Hallstrom, Director of Care

Invermere: Columbia House
850 - 10th St., Invermere, BC V0A 1K0
250-342-2329 Fax: 250-342-2319
Number of Beds: 20 beds
Rose Bard

Kamloops: Liberty Manor
470 Hilltop Ave., Kamloops, BC V2B 2S3
250-376-3788
Note: group home
Claire Ann Brodie, Executive Director, Continuing Care Services

Kamloops: Panderosa Lodge
425 Columbia St., Kamloops, BC V2C 2T4
250-374-5671 Fax: 250-374-8873
Number of Beds: 157 beds
Claire Ann Brodie, Director

Kelowna: Avonlea Care Centre Limited
1658 Blondeaux Cres., Kelowna, BC V1Y 4J7
250-762-4378 Fax: 250-762-0167
avonleahouse@avonleacare.com
www.avonleacare.com
Division of: Avonlea House
Parent: Interior Health Authority
Number of Beds: 14 beds
Note: specialized care home for severely brain-injured
Abbas Moledina, Managing Director/Administrator
Lunda Asselstine, Director of Care/Manager

Kelowna: David Lloyd Jones Home
934 Bernard Ave., Kelowna, BC V1Y 6P8
250-762-2706 Fax: 250-762-5961
Number of Beds: 64 beds
Rick Riley

Kelowna: May Bennett Home
965 West Highway 33, Kelowna, BC V1X 1Y8
250-763-6277 Fax: 250-763-6262
Parent: Interior Health Authority
Number of Beds: 24 beds
Nancy Kilpatrick, Director

Kelowna: Parkside Residence Ltd.
265 Gray Rd., Kelowna, BC V1X 1W8
250-765-8482 Fax: 250-765-8213
Parent: Interior Health Authority
Number of Beds: 23 beds
Alena Merhaut, Administrator

Kelowna: Sutherland Hills Rest Home
3081 Hall Rd., Kelowna, BC V1W 2R5
250-860-2330 Fax: 250-860-2399
shrhbob@silk.net
Parent: Interior Health Authority
Number of Beds: 100 beds
Wendy Calhoun, Facility Director

Kelowna: Three Links Manor
1449 Kelglen Cres., Kelowna, BC V1Y 8P4
250-763-2585 Fax: 250-763-6773
Parent: Interior Health Authority
Number of Beds: 81 beds
Rick Riley

Kelowna: Windsor Manor Care Centre
355 Terai Ct., Kelowna, BC V1X 5X6
250-979-6000 Fax: 250-979-6002
Parent: Interior Health Authority
Number of Beds: 149 beds
Bev Powell, Administrator

Kimberley: Kimberley Special Care Home
386 - 2nd Ave., Kimberley, BC V1A 2Z8
250-427-4807 Fax: 250-427-5377
Parent: Interior Health Authority
Number of Beds: 51 beds, 15 mental health
Allan Sinclair, Site Manager

Ladysmith: Four All Seasons Retirement Lodge
3464 Yellowpoint Rd., Ladysmith, BC V0R 1E6
250-245-4237 Fax: 250-245-7757
4allseasons@telus.net
Parent: Vancouver Island Health Authority
Number of Beds: 22 beds
Gerard B. Huard, Administrator

Langley: Highland Lodge
20619 Eastleigh Cres., Langley, BC V3A 4C3
604-534-7186 Fax: 604-534-7139
hlodge@idirect.ca
Parent: Fraser Health Authority
Number of Beds: 60 beds
Dave Stott, Director, Care

Langley: Langley Gardens
8888 - 202nd St., Langley, BC V1M 4A7
604-881-8122 Fax: 604-881-8199 www.cpac-care.com
Parent: Fraser Health Authority

Number of Beds: 73 beds
Lisa Kachur, General Manager

***Langley:* Langley Lodge**
5451 - 204th St., Langley, BC V3A 5M9
604-530-2305 Fax: 604-532-4205
wpauls@langleylodge.org
www.langleylodge.org
Parent: Fraser Health Authority
Number of Beds: 153 beds
Note: seniors
Werner Pauls, Administrator

***Lillooet:* Mountain View Lodge**
844 Main Street, Lillooet, BC V0K 1V0
250-455-2221 Fax: 250-455-6621
Parent: Interior Health Authority
Number of Beds: 22 beds
Jennifer Thur

***Maple Ridge:* Golden Ears Retirement Centre**
12155 Edge St., Maple Ridge, BC V2X 6G7
604-467-5511 Fax: 604-467-0510
Parent: Fraser Health Authority
Number of Beds: 52 beds
Doreen Fleming, Administrator

***Merritt:* Coquihalla/Gillis House**
3451 Voght St., Merritt, BC V1K 1C6
250-378-3271 Fax: 250-378-3252
Parent: Interior Health Authority
Number of Beds: 92 beds
Doug Sage, Administrator

***Mission:* Grand Street Lodge**
7755 Grand St., Mission, BC V2V 3T6
604-826-6646 Fax: 604-820-8550
Parent: Fraser Health Authority
Number of Beds: 23 beds
Annamae Clark, Administrator

***Mission:* Pleasant View Care Home**
7530 Hurd St., Mission, BC V2V 3H9
604-826-2154 Fax: 604-826-8672
j.ray@pvhs.ca
www.pvhs.ca
Parent: Fraser Health Authority
Number of Beds: 76 beds
Judith E. Ray, Administrator

***Nakusp:* Halcyon Community Home**
PO Box 910, 83 - 8th Ave., Nakusp, BC V0G 1R0
250-265-3692 Fax: 250-265-4141
Number of Beds: 14 beds
Note: Intermediate care
Deborah Austin

***Nanaimo:* Kiwanis Village Lodge**
1221 Kiwanis Crescent, Nanaimo, BC V9S 5Y1
250-753-6471 Fax: 250-740-2816
Parent: Vancouver Island Health Authority
Number of Beds: 102 beds
Virginia Ostrand, Administrator

***Nanaimo:* Malaspina Gardens Inc.**
388 Machleary St., Nanaimo, BC V9R 2G9
250-754-7711 Fax: 250-754-2175
Parent: Vancouver Island Health Authority
Number of Beds: 133 beds
Diane DeRepentigny, General Manager

***Nanaimo:* Travellers Lodge**
1298 Nelson St., Nanaimo, BC V9S 2K5
250-758-4676 Fax: 250-758-4698
ot@nantralodge.bc.ca
Parent: Vancouver Island Health Authority
Number of Beds: 93 beds
Sandra Rummy, Administrator/Director

***Nelson:* Nelson Jubilee Manor**
500 Beasley St., Nelson, BC V1L 6G9
250-352-7011 Fax: 250-352-7044
Parent: Interior Health Authority
Number of Beds: 39 beds
Kim Irving

***New Westminster:* Blue Spruce Cottage**
509 St. George St., New Westminster, BC V3L 1L1
604-521-4316 Fax: 604-521-6600
Parent: Fraser Health Authority
Number of Beds: 15 beds
Betty Dewitte, Manager

***New Westminster:* Buchanan Lodge**
409 Blair Ave., New Westminster, BC V3L 4A4
604-522-7033 Fax: 604-522-3689
Parent: Fraser Health Authority
Number of Beds: 112 beds
Penny Lang, Administrator

***New Westminster:* Kiwanis Intermediate Care Centre**
35 Clute St., New Westminster, BC V3L 1Z5
604-525-6471 Fax: 604-525-8522
sbrowne@kiwaniscarecentre.com
Parent: Fraser Health Authority
Number of Beds: 74 beds, 2 respite beds
Note: intermediate care
Shirley Brown, Administrator

***New Westminster:* Queen's Park Care Centre**
260 Sherbrooke St., New Westminster, BC V3L 5E8
604-520-0911 Fax: 604-517-8651
cspeers@sfhr.hnet.bc.ca
Parent: Fraser Health Authority
Number of Beds: 219 beds
Note: extended care facility
Carol Wheeler, Director

***New Westminster:* Royal City Manor**
77 Jamieson Ct., New Westminster, BC V3L 5P8
604-522-6699 Fax: 604-522-1022
royalcitymanor@reveraliving.com
www.reveraliving.com
Kevin Perry, Administrator

***New Westminster:* Salvation Army Buchanan Lodge**
409 Blair Ave., New Westminster, BC V3L 4A4
604-522-7033 Fax: 604-522-3689
Parent: Fraser Health Authority
Number of Beds: 112 beds
Penny Lang

***North Vancouver:* Cedarview Lodge**
1200 Cedar Village Close, North Vancouver, BC V7J 3P3
604-904-6400 Fax: 604-904-6411
Parent: Vancouver Coastal Health Authority
Number of Beds: 90 beds, 30 assisted living units
Note: intermediate care
Lynne Pentland, Manager

***North Vancouver:* Evergreen House**
231 - 15 St. East, North Vancouver, BC V7L 2L7
604-988-3131 Fax: 604-984-5838
Parent: Vancouver Coastal Health Authority
Number of Beds: 293 beds
Rizwan Damji, Director of Seniors

***North Vancouver:* H & H Total Care Services**
4530 Meadowbank Close, North Vancouver, BC V7K 2L2
604-987-7569 Fax: 604-597-8032
Parent: Vancouver Coastal Health Authority
Note: specializing in Huntington & brain injury care
Hank Van Ryk, Manager

***North Vancouver:* N.S. Kiwanis Care Centre**
2444 Burr Pl., North Vancouver, BC V7H 3A5
604-924-8300 Fax: 604-924-8325
Parent: Vancouver Coastal Health Authority
Number of Beds: 192 beds
Carol Mothersill, Admin.
Cathy Baxter, Clinical Manager

***North Vancouver:* United Lodge**
116 West 23rd St., North Vancouver, BC V7M 2A9
604-987-5010 Fax: 604-987-9378
Parent: Vancouver Coastal Health Authority
Number of Beds: 22 beds
Abraham Calaguian, Administrator

***Oliver:* Sunnybank Retirement Centre**
36657 - 79th St., Oliver, BC V0H 1T0
250-498-4951 Fax: 250-498-2287
Number of Beds: 51 beds
Janice Little, Care Coordinator

***Osoyoos:* Country Squire Retirement Villa**
9707 - 87th St., RR#2, Osoyoos, BC V0H 1V0
250-495-6568 Fax: 250-495-7466
Number of Beds: 31 beds
G. Munro, Administrator

***Osoyoos:* Sagebrush Lodge**
4816 - 89 St., Osoyoos, BC V0H 1V1
250-495-2666 Fax: 250-495-2605
Parent: Vancouver Island Health Authority
Number of Beds: 52 beds
Lorraine Ferguson

***Parksville:* Arrowsmith Lodge**
266 Moilliet St., Parksville, BC V9P 1M9
250-248-4331 Fax: 250-248-4813
Parent: Vancouver Island Health Authority
Number of Beds: 58 beds
Pam Swanson, Administrator

***Parksville:* Halliday House of BC**
188 McCarter St., Parksville, BC V9P 1A1
250-248-2835 Fax: 250-248-2403
Parent: Vancouver Island Health Authority
Number of Beds: 20 beds
Louise Hughes, Manager

***Penticton:* Haven Hill Retirement Centre**
415 Haven Hill Rd., Penticton, BC V2A 4E9
250-492-2600 Fax: 250-492-2498
bwyatt@shawcable.com
Parent: Interior Health Authority
Number of Beds: 83 beds
Brian Wyatt, Administrator

***Penticton:* Penticton & District Retirement Centre**
439 Winnipeg St., Penticton, BC V2A 6P5
250-770-7400 Fax: 250-492-1091
Parent: Interior Health Authority
Number of Beds: 101 beds
Betty Ashton, Care Unit Coordinator

***Port Alberni:* Echo Village**
4200 - 10th Ave., Port Alberni, BC V9Y 4X3
250-724-1090 Fax: 250-724-2115
Parent: Vancouver Island Health Authority
Number of Beds: 65 beds
Barbara A. Stevenson, Administrator

***Port Alberni:* Fir Park Village**
4411 Wallace St., Port Alberni, BC V9Y 7Y5
250-724-6541 Fax: 250-724-6543
bstevenson@acccs.ca
Parent: Vancouver Island Health Authority
Number of Beds: 62 beds
Barb Stevenson, Executive Director

***Port Alberni:* Tsawaayuus-Rainbow Gardens**
6151 Russell Pl., Port Alberni, BC V9Y 7W3
250-724-5655 Fax: 250-724-5666
Parent: Vancouver Island Health Authority
Number of Beds: 30 beds
Lillian Thomas, Administrator

***Port Coquitlam:* Hawthorne Care Centre**
2111 Hawthorne Ave., Port Coquitlam, BC V3C 1W3
604-941-4051 Fax: 604-941-5829
Parent: Fraser Health Authority
Number of Beds: 125 beds
Lenore Pickering, Administrator

***Port Coquitlam:* Melissa Park Lodge**
2175 Mary Hill Rd., Port Coquitlam, BC V3C 3A2
604-942-4325 Fax: 604-526-2984
Parent: Fraser Health Authority
Number of Beds: 20 beds
Ronald Wong, Manager

***Pouce Coupe:* Peace River Haven**
PO Box 188, 5213 - 50th Ave., Pouce Coupe, BC V0C 2C0
250-786-6100 Fax: 250-786-6107
Parent: Northern Health Authority
Number of Beds: 60 beds
Note: intermediate level
Elaine Washington, Resident Care Manager

***Prince George:* AiMHi - Prince George Association for Community Living**
500 Victoria St., 3rd Fl., Prince George, BC V2L 2J9
250-564-6408 Fax: 250-564-6801
aimhi@aimhi.ca
www.aimhi.ca
Number of Beds: 47 beds
Note: non-profit, supports individuals with developmental disabilities & children with special needs
Carol Burbee, Contact

***Prince George:* Simon Fraser Lodge**
2410 Laurier Cres., Prince George, BC V2M 2B3
250-563-3413 Fax: 250-563-7209
Number of Beds: 131 beds
Kathy Giene, Administrator

***Prince Rupert:* Acropolis Manor**
1325 Summit Ave., Prince Rupert, BC V8J 4C1
250-627-8497 Fax: 250-627-1490
Parent: Northern Health Authority
Number of Beds: 50 beds
Karen Inkpen, Clinical Coordinator

***Princeton:* Ridgewood Lodge**
98 Ridgewood Dr., Princeton, BC V0X 1W0
250-295-5551 Fax: 250-295-4081
Number of Beds: 37 beds
Marilyn Harkness, Administrator

***Qualicum Beach:* Arranglen Lodge**
2300 Fowler Rd., Qualicum Beach, BC V9K 2A5
250-752-9277 Fax: 250-752-5525
dderepentigny@cpac-care.com
Parent: vancouver Island Health Authority
Number of Beds: 85 beds
Diane Derepentigny, Administrator

***Qualicum Beach:* Eagle Park Health Care Facility**
777 Jones St., Qualicum Beach, BC V9K 2L1
250-752-7075 Fax: 250-752-8316
Parent: Vancouver Island Health Authority
Number of Beds: 10 beds
Jill Forsythe, Director, Residential Care

***Quesnel:* Dunrovin Park Lodge**
351 Murphy St., Quesnel, BC V2J 3S3
250-992-5263 Fax: 250-992-5277
Parent: Northern Health Authority
Number of Beds: 75 beds
Val Waymark, Program Manager, Home & Community Care

***Revelstoke:* Shuswap Lake General Hospital**
601 - 10th St. NE, Revelstoke, BC V1E 4N6
250-833-3600 Fax: 250-833-3611
Parent: Interior Health Authority
Number of Beds: 21 beds
Dorothy Schiller

***Richmond:* Courtyard Gardens**
7051 Moffatt Rd., Richmond, BC V6Y 3W2
604-273-1225 Fax: 604-273-9253
courtyardgardens_info@diversicare.ca
www.diversicare.ca
Parent: Vancouver Coastal Health Authority
Number of Beds: 31 intermediate care beds, 107 assisted living apts, 1 respi
Note: 107 suites of assisted living
Maggie Keatley, General Manager

***Richmond:* Fraserview Intermediate Care Lodge Co. Ltd.**
9580 Williams Rd., Richmond, BC V7A 1H2
604-274-3510 Fax: 604-275-0996
Parent: Vancouver Coastal Health Authority
Number of Beds: 105 beds
A.M. Baron, Administrator

***Richmond:* Pinegrove Place**
11331 Mellis Dr., Richmond, BC V6X 1L8
604-278-1296 Fax: 604-273-0050
Parent: Vancouver Coastal Health Authority
Number of Beds: 75 beds
Gordon Milner, Administrator

***Richmond:* Richmond Lions Manor**
11771 Fentiman Pl., Richmond, BC V7E 3M4
604-274-6311 Fax: 604-274-2543
Parent: Vancouver Coastal Health Authority
Number of Beds: 132 beds
S. Garrison, Medical Coordinator

***Richmond:* Rosewood Manor**
6260 Blundell Rd., Richmond, BC V7C 5C4
604-271-3590 Fax: 604-271-3551
Parent: Vancouver Coastal Health Authority
Number of Beds: 120 beds
Note: intermediate & complex care
Deborah Goegan, Administrator

***Salt Spring Island:* Greenwoods**
133 Blain Rd., Salt Spring Island, BC V8K 1Z9
250-537-5561 Fax: 250-537-1124
catherinb53@yahoo.ca
Parent: Vancouver Island Health Authority
Number of Beds: 50 beds
Andrew Brown, Administrator

***Sechelt:* Shorncliffe**
5847 Medusa St., Sechelt, BC V0N 3A0
604-885-5126 Fax: 604-885-5140
dennis.regnier@cgh.bc.ca
Number of Beds: 60 beds
Dennis Regnier, Coordinator

***Shawnigan Lake:* Acacia Ty Mawr Lodge**
2655 Shawnigan Lake Rd. East, Shawnigan Lake, BC V0R 2W0
250-743-2124 Fax: 250-743-2130
administration@acaciatymawr.com
Number of Beds: 35 beds
J. Neil Stuart, Administrator

***Sidney:* Sidney Intermediate Care Home Ltd.**
9888 - 5th St., Sidney, BC V8L 2X3
250-656-0121 Fax: 250-656-0189
Number of Beds: 52 beds
Susan Irvine, Administrator

***Smithers:* Buckley Lodge**
3668 - 11th Ave., Smithers, BC V0J 2N0
250-847-4443 Fax: 250-847-3895
Parent: Northern Health Authority
Number of Beds: 73 beds
Heather Hodson, Administrator

***South Surrey:* Peace Portal Lodge**
15441 - 16th Ave., South Surrey, BC V4A 8T8
604-535-2273 Fax: 604-535-3051
swilson@retirementconcepts.com
www.retirementconcepts.com
Parent: Fraser Health Authority
Number of Beds: 27 beds
Susan Wilson, Administrator

***Squamish:* Hilltop House**
38146 Behrner Dr., Squamish, BC V8B 0J3
604-892-9337 Fax: 604-892-6091
Parent: Vancouver Coastal Health Authority
Number of Beds: 10 beds for dementia care, 31 intermediate care, 20 extended
Note: long term care
Marian Biln

***Summerland:* Kelly Care Centre**
12801 Kelly Ave., Summerland, BC V0H 1Z0
250-494-7911 Fax: 250-494-4027
Number of Beds: 79 beds
Lorraine Ferguson

***Surrey:* Bear Creek Lodge**
13646 - 94A Ave., Surrey, BC V3V 1N1
604-581-4028 Fax: 604-581-8523
info@bearcreek-lodge.com
www.bearcreek-lodge.com
Parent: Fraser Health Authority
Number of Beds: 115 beds
Hendrik Van Ryk, COO

***Surrey:* Centennial Park Lodge**
11861 - 99 Ave., Surrey, BC V3V 2M3
604-584-6811 Fax: 604-581-4768
kahmon@telus.net
Parent: Fraser Health Authority
Number of Beds: 26 beds
Kevin Ahmon, Administrator

***Surrey:* Crescent Gardens**
1222 King George Hwy., Surrey, BC V4A 9W6
604-541-8861 Fax: 604-541-8871
bcosta@cpac-care.com
www.chartwellreit.ca
Parent: Fraser Health Authority
Number of Beds: 53 beds
Ann Varona, Director of Care

***Surrey:* Evergreen Cottages**
15660 - 84th Ave., Surrey, BC V3A 2N5
604-597-7906 Fax: 604-597-9025 www.evergreen-cottages.com
Parent: Fraser Health Authority
Number of Beds: 33 beds
Marion Butte, Administrator

***Surrey:* Fleetwood Place**
16011 - 83rd Ave., Surrey, BC V3S 8M2
604-590-6860 Fax: 604-590-6861
messages@fleetwoodplace.ca
Parent: Fraser Health Authority
Number of Beds: 75 beds
Kevin Ahmon, Administrator

***Surrey:* Guildford Seniors Village**
14584 - 104A Ave., Surrey, BC V3R 1R3
604-582-0808 Fax: 604-582-7011
Parent: Fraser Health Authority
Number of Beds: 60 beds
Leslie Karmazinuk, Administrator

***Surrey:* Hilton Villa Care Centre**
13525 Hilton Rd., Surrey, BC V3R 5J3
604-588-3424 Fax: 604-588-3433
Parent: Fraser Health Authority
Number of Beds: 124 beds
Al Jina, Administrator

***Surrey:* Kinsmen Place Lodge**
13333 Old Yale Rd., Surrey, BC V3T 5A2
604-588-0445 Fax: 604-588-7211 www.kinsmenplace.org
Parent: Fraser Health Authority
Number of Beds: 143 beds
Note: intermediate care
Karen Holt, Director, Resident Care

***Surrey:* Morgan Place**
3288 - 156A St., Surrey, BC V3S 9T1
604-535-7328 Fax: 604-535-7386 www.morganplace.ca
Parent: Fraser Health Authority
Number of Beds: 122 beds
Betty Ahmon, Administrator

***Surrey:* Newton Regency**
13855 - 68 Ave., Surrey, BC V3W 2G9
604-597-9333 Fax: 604-597-8032
reception@newtonregency.ca
www.newtonregency.ca
Parent: Fraser Health Authority
Number of Beds: 136 beds
Note: adults, resdential care
Rudy Young, Director of Care
Rudi Young, Manager of Facility

***Surrey:* Zion Park Manor**
5939 - 180th St., Surrey, BC V3S 4L2
604-576-2891 Fax: 604-576-8046
Parent: Fraser Health Authority
Number of Beds: 142 beds
Thomas Crump, Administrator

***Trail:* Columbia View Lodge**
2920 Laburnum Dr., Trail, BC V1R 4N2
250-364-1271 Fax: 250-364-0911
Parent: Interior Health Authority
Number of Beds: 77 beds
Note: complex care facility
Norma Mildenberger, Director, Residential Care

***Trail:* Kiro Manor**
1500 Columbia Ave., Trail, BC V1R 1J9
250-364-1214 Fax: 250-364-1261
Parent: Interior Health Authority
Number of Beds: 9 beds
Norman Mildenberger

***Trail:* Poplar Ridge Pavillion**
1200 Hospital Bench, Trail, BC V1R 4M1
250-368-3311 Fax: 250-364-3422
Parent: Interior Health Authority
Number of Beds: 50 beds
Frank Marino, Health Service Administrator

***Vancouver:* Adanac Park Lodge**
851 Boundary Rd., Vancouver, BC V5K 4T2
604-299-7567 Fax: 604-299-7424
Parent: Vancouver Coastal Health Authority
Number of Beds: 72 beds
Dan Levitt, Executive Director

***Vancouver:* Amica at Arbutus Manor**
2125 Eddington Dr., Vancouver, BC V6L 3A9
604-736-8936 Fax: 604-731-8933
Parent: Vancouver Coastal Health Authority
Number of Beds: 125 beds
Holly Goldsmith, Facilities Manager

***Vancouver:* Arbutus Care Centre**
4505 Valley Dr., Vancouver, BC V6L 2L1
604-261-4292 Fax: 604-261-7849
arbutus@reveraliving.com
www.reveraliving.com
Parent: Vancouver Coastal Health Authority
Number of Beds: 161 beds
Note: Specialty: Complex residential care; Nursing care; Foot care; Social work; Recreational therapy; Music therapy

***Vancouver:* Balfour House**
1490 Balfour St., Vancouver, BC V6H 1Y1
604-733-0222 Fax: 604-714-1386
Parent: Vancouver Coastal Health Authority
Number of Beds: 18 beds
D. Morton, Administrator

***Vancouver:* Blenheim Lodge**
3263 Blenheim St., Vancouver, BC V6L 2X7
604-732-8717 Fax: 604-732-7316
Parent: Vancouver Coastal Health Authority
Number of Beds: 109 beds

Derek Morton, Administrator

Vancouver: Braddan Private Hospital
2450 - 2nd Ave., Vancouver, BC V6K 1J6
604-731-2127 Fax: 604-731-0283
mcintosh@axion.net
Parent: Vancouver Coastal Health Authority
Number of Beds: 51 beds
Maureen McIntosh, Administrator

Vancouver: Broadway Pentecostal Lodge
1377 Lamey's Mill Rd., Vancouver, BC V6H 3S9
604-733-1441 Fax: 604-731-1484
Parent: Vancouver Coastal Health Authority
Number of Beds: 114 beds
Jeanette Thompson, Administrator

Vancouver: Chalmers Lodge Personal Care Home
1450 - 12th Ave. West, Vancouver, BC V6H 1M9
604-731-3178 Fax: 604-731-3140
info@chalmerslodge.ca
www.chalmerslodge.ca
Parent: Vancouver Coastal Health Authority
Number of Beds: 130 beds
Note: personal care home
K.P.S. Aujlay, CEO

Vancouver: City Centre Care Society - Central City Lodge
415 West Pender St., Vancouver, BC V6B 1V2
604-681-9111 Fax: 604-681-5546
Parent: Vancouver Coastal Health Authority
Number of Beds: 122 beds
Note: multilevel care; supportive housing - addictions recovery
Catherine Adair, Executive Director

Vancouver: City Centre Care Society - Cooper Place
306 Cordova St. East, Vancouver, BC V6A 1L5
604-684-2545 Fax: 604-684-2575
Parent: Vancouver Coastal Health Authority
Number of Beds: 72 beds
Antonia Reynolds, Manager, Assisted Living

Vancouver: Columbus Residence
704 West 69th Ave., Vancouver, BC V6P 2W3
604-321-4405 Fax: 604-321-4543
Parent: Vancouver Coastal Health Authority
Number of Beds: 76 beds
Peter Horsfield, Executive Director

Vancouver: Crofton Manor
2803 - 41 Ave. West, Vancouver, BC V6N 4B4
604-263-0921 Fax: 604-263-7719
cm.mkg@lra.ca
www.lrc.ca/crofton.asp
Parent: Vancouver Coastal Health Authority
Number of Beds: 194 suites
Carol Omstead, General Manager

Vancouver: Dogwood Lodge
500 West 57th Ave., Vancouver, BC V6P 6E8
604-324-6882 Fax: 604-324-7226
Parent: Vancouver Coastal Health Authority
Number of Beds: 113 beds
Susan Fong, Administrator

Vancouver: Fair Haven United Church Home
2720 East 48th St., Vancouver, BC V5S 1G7
604-433-2939 Fax: 604-433-4547
mharrison@fairhaven.bc.ca
Parent: Vancouver Coastal Health Authority
Number of Beds: 69 beds
Maureen Harrison, COO

Vancouver: False Creek Residence
1167 Forge Walk, Vancouver, BC V6H 3R1
604-731-0401 Fax: 604-731-9546
info@rils.ca
www.rils.ca
Parent: Vancouver Coastal Health Authority
Number of Beds: 24 beds
Kathleen Mason, Executive Director

Vancouver: George Pearson Centre
700 West 57th Ave., Vancouver, BC V6P 1S1
604-321-3231 Fax: 604-321-7833
Parent: Vancouver Coastal Health Authority
Number of Beds: 120 beds
Maureen White, COO

Vancouver: German-Canadian Care Home
2010 Harrison Dr., Vancouver, BC V5P 2P6
604-713-6500 Fax: 604-713-6548
Parent: Vancouver Coastal Health Authority
Number of Beds: 144 beds
Donna Dougan, CEO

Vancouver: Haro Park Centre
1233 Haro St., Vancouver, BC V6E 3Y5
604-687-5584 Fax: 604-687-0645
info@haropark.org
www.haropark.org
Parent: Vancouver Coastal Health Authority
Number of Beds: 190 suites
Shayne Ramsay, Chief Executive Officer

Vancouver: Icelandic Care Home
2020 Harrison Dr., Vancouver, BC V5P 2P6
604-321-3812 Fax: 604-321-3863
Parent: Vancouver Coastal Health Authority
Number of Beds: 64 beds
Marlene Wynes, Administrator

Vancouver: Kopernik Lodge
3150 Rosemont Dr., Vancouver, BC V5S 2C9
604-438-2474 Fax: 604-438-5344
admin@kopernik-lodge.bc.ca
www.kopernik-foundation.org
Division of: Kopernik Nicolaus Foundation
Parent: Vancouver Coastal Health Authority
Number of Beds: 87 beds
Note: intermediate care facility
Diana Ollmann, Administrator/CEO

Vancouver: L & T Rehabilitation Services Ltd.
3103 Kings Way, Vancouver, BC V5R 5J9
604-439-7545 Fax: 604-439-1326
Parent: Vancouver Coastal Health Authority
Number of Beds: 19 beds
Joan Grimsrud, Administrator

Vancouver: Lakeview Care Centre
3490 Porter St., Vancouver, BC V5N 4H2
604-874-2803 Fax: 604-874-7744
Number of Beds: 165 beds
Pat May, Administrator

Vancouver: Little Mountain Place
330 East 36th Ave., Vancouver, BC V5W 3Z4
604-325-2298 Fax: 604-325-3655 www.littlemountaincare.ca
Parent: Vancouver Coastal Health Authority
Number of Beds: 117 beds
Dan Levitt, Executive Director

Vancouver: Providence Health Care
255 - 62nd Ave. West, Vancouver, BC V5X 4V4
604-325-4116 Fax: 604-877-3081
www.providencehealthcare.org
Division of: St. Vincent's Hospital Langara
Parent: Vancouver Coastal Health Authority
Number of Beds: 221 beds
Note: long-term care facility
Carl Roy, President; CEO

Vancouver: Providence Health Care
4650 Oak St., Vancouver, BC V6H 4J4
604-877-3220 Fax: 604-877-3215
Division of: St. Vincent's Hospital
Parent: Vancouver Coastal Health Authority
Number of Beds: 150 beds
Note: extended care facility
Carl Roy, President; CEO

Vancouver: Providence Health Care
4950 Heather, Vancouver, BC V5Z 3L9
604-261-9371 Fax: 604-261-9047
www.providencehealthcare.org
Division of: Youville Residence
Parent: Vancouver Coastal Health Authority
Number of Beds: 84 beds
Note: intermediate care facility with Alzheimer ward
Carl Roy, President; CEO

Vancouver: Renfrew Care Centre
1880 Renfrew St., Vancouver, BC V5M 3H9
604-255-7723 Fax: 604-255-2045
Parent: Vancouver Coastal Health Authority
Number of Beds: 88 beds
Loraine Coffin, Administrator

Vancouver: Royal Arch Masonic Home
7850 Champlain Cres., Vancouver, BC V5S 4C7
604-437-7343 Fax: 604-437-7373
Parent: Vancouver Coastal Health Authority
Number of Beds: 151 beds
Gregory Runzer, Administrator

Vancouver: Royal Ascot Care Centre
2455 Broadway East, Vancouver, BC V5M 1Y7
604-254-5559 Fax: 604-254-5523
Parent: Vancouver Coastal Health Authority
Number of Beds: 82 beds
Cheryl Scarlett, Administrator

Vancouver: St. Bernard House
547 - 12th Ave. East, Vancouver, BC V5T 2H6
604-874-8657 Fax: 604-984-7933
Parent: Vancouver Coastal Health Authority
Number of Beds: 12 beds
David A. Russell, Administrator

Vancouver: Salvation Army Southview Terrace
3131 East 58th Ave., Vancouver, BC V5S 4V2
604-438-3367 Fax: 604-438-0262
Parent: Vancouver Coastal Health Authority
Note: personal care facility

Vancouver: South Granville Park Lodge
1645 West 14th Ave., Vancouver, BC V6J 2J4
604-732-8633 Fax: 604-732-9833
jack@smartt.com
www.sgplodge.com
Parent: Vancouver Coastal Health Authority
Number of Beds: 120 beds
Zdenka Votrubova, Director, Nursing

Vancouver: Three Links Care Centre
2934 East 22nd Ave., Vancouver, BC V5M 2Y4
604-434-7211 Fax: 604-438-7563
info@threelinks.com
www.threelinks.com
Parent: Vancouver Coastal Health Authority
Number of Beds: 90 beds
Note: complex care facility
Tom Novak, CEO

Vancouver: Villa Cathay Care Home
970 Union St., Vancouver, BC V6A 3V1
604-254-5621 Fax: 604-254-5230 www.villacathay.ca
Parent: Vancouver Coastal Health Authority
Number of Beds: 188 beds
Hudson Chong, COO

Vancouver: Windermere Care Centre
900 West 12th Ave., Vancouver, BC V5Z 1N3
604-736-8676 Fax: 604-736-8682
sugimoto@portal.ca
Parent: Vancouver Coastal Health Authority
Number of Beds: 196 beds
Note: complex care
Ross Sugimoto, Administrator

Vancouver: Yaletown House Society
1099 Cambie St., Vancouver, BC V6B 5A8
604-689-0022 Fax: 604-662-7954
Parent: Vancouver Coastal Health Authority
Number of Beds: 130 beds
Carol Crichton, Executive Director

Vanderhoof: Omineca Lodge
Bag 5000, 242 Louvain St., Vanderhoof, BC V0J 3A0
250-567-2216 Fax: 250-567-2677
Parent: Northern Health Authority
Number of Beds: 36 beds
Note: intermediate care
Ray Scott, Administrator, Health Services

Vernon: Bethany House
3904 - 27 St., Vernon, BC V1T 4X7
250-545-2060 Fax: 250-545-4060
Parent: Interior Health Authority
Number of Beds: 37 beds
Kevin Svoboda, Facilities Manager

Vernon: Birch Lodge
7446 Hwy. 6, Vernon, BC V1B 3H4
250-545-6849
Parent: Interior Health Authority
Number of Beds: 29 beds
T. Huber, Facilities Manager

Vernon: Gateby Intermediate Care Facility
3000 Gateby Pl., Vernon, BC V1T 8V8
250-545-4456 Fax: 250-545-4439
Parent: Interior Health Authority
Number of Beds: 75 beds
Peter DuToit

Vernon: Noric House Extended Care
1400 Mission Rd., Vernon, BC V1T 9C3

250-545-9167 Fax: 250-545-4980
mary.napier@interiorhealth.ca
Parent: Interior Health Authority
Number of Beds: 85 beds
Peter DuToit

Victoria: Beacon Hill Villa
635 Superior St., Victoria, BC V8V 1V1
250-383-5447 Fax: 250-361-4395
Number of Beds: 80 beds
May Sauder, Administrator

Victoria: Beckley Farm Lodge
530 Simcoe St., Victoria, BC V8V 1V1
250-381-4421 Fax: 250-381-0112
jrobertson@beckleyfarmlodge.com
Parent: Vancouver Island Health Authority
Number of Beds: 70 beds
Note: complex care & adult day centre
Jan Robertson, Administrator

Victoria: Central Care Home
844 Johnston St., Victoria, BC V8W 1N3
250-384-1313 Fax: 250-384-9760
torr@baptisthousing.org
Parent: Vancouver Island Health Authority
Number of Beds: 147 beds
Note: intermediate care
Tim Orr, Administrator

Victoria: Chinatown Care Centre
555 Herald St., Victoria, BC V8W 1S5
250-381-4322 Fax: 250-920-0318
Number of Beds: 31 beds
May Sauder, Executive Director

Victoria: Craigdarroch Care Home
1048 Craigdarroch Rd., Victoria, BC V8W 1N3
250-595-3813 Fax: 250-595-3836
Parent: Vancouver Island Health Authority
Number of Beds: 18 beds
J.O. Scott, Administrator

Victoria: Hart Home Seniors Residence
1961 Fairfield Rd., Victoria, BC V8S 1H5
250-598-3542 Fax: 250-598-2594
harthouse@shaw.ca
Parent: Vancouver Island Health Authority
Number of Beds: 20 beds
Note: intermediate care home
Melanie Sundquist, Manager

Victoria: James Bay Lodge
336 Simcoe St., Victoria, BC V8V 1L2
250-388-6457 Fax: 250-381-2969
Parent: Vancouver Island Health Authority
Number of Beds: 208 beds
Note: intermediate care
Stan Dubas, Administrator

Victoria: The Kensington
3965 Shelbourne St., Victoria, BC V8N 6J4
250-477-1232 Fax: 250-472-1271
kv.mkg@lrc.ca
www.lrc.ca
Number of Beds: 116 suites
Alaine Reimer, General Manager

Victoria: Kiwanis Pavilion
3034 Cedar Hill Rd., Victoria, BC V8T 3J3
250-598-2022 Fax: 250-598-0023 www.obkp.org
Old Name: Oak Bay Kiwanis Pavilion
Parent: Vancouver Island Health Authority
Number of Beds: 117 beds
Note: multi level care facility
William B. Cuthill, Administrator

Victoria: Lodge at Broadmead
4579 Chatterton Way, Victoria, BC V8X 4Y7
250-658-0311 Fax: 250-658-0948 www.tvcs.ca
Parent: Vancouver Island Health Authority
Number of Beds: 229 beds
Evelyn Stewart, Executive Director

Victoria: Luther Court
1525 Cedar Hill Cross Rd., Victoria, BC V8P 5M1
250-477-7241 Fax: 250-477-5740
jsolomon@luthercourtsociety.org
Parent: Vancouver Island Health Authority
Number of Beds: 66 beds
Joanne Solomonson, CEO

Victoria: Mount Edwards Court Care Home
1002 Vancouver St., Victoria, BC V8V 3V8
250-385-2241 Fax: 250-385-4842
torr@baptisthousing.org
Parent: Vancouver Island Health Authority
Number of Beds: 83 beds
Tim Orr, Administrator

Victoria: Mount St. Mary Hospital
861 Fairfield Rd., Victoria, BC V8V 5A9
250-480-3100 Fax: 250-480-3110 www.mtstmary.victoria.bc.ca
Parent: Vancouver Island Health Authority
Number of Beds: 200 beds
Note: extended care
Colleen Black, CEO
Doug Moffatt, Physical Plant

Victoria: Oak Bay Lodge
2251 Cadboro Bay Rd., Victoria, BC V8R 5H3
250-370-6600 Fax: 250-370-6601
Parent: Vancouver Island Health Authority
Number of Beds: 245 beds
Heather Cook
Heather.cook@gov.bc.ca

Victoria: Rose Manor
857 Rupert Terrace, Victoria, BC V8V 3E5
250-383-0414 Fax: 250-360-2039 www.rosemanor.ca
Parent: Vancouver Island Health Authority
Number of Beds: 128 beds
James Baird, Administrator

Victoria: Sandringham Hospital
1650 Fort St., Victoria, BC V8R 1H9
250-595-2313 Fax: 250-595-4137
Parent: Vancouver Island Health Authority
Number of Beds: 85 beds
Stan Dubas, Administrator

West Vancouver: Capilano Care Centre
525 Clyde Ave., West Vancouver, BC V7T 1C4
604-926-6856 Fax: 604-926-0245
Parent: Vancouver Island Health Authority
Number of Beds: 217 beds
Donna Moroz, Administrator

West Vancouver: Hollyburn House
2095 Marine Dr., West Vancouver, BC V7V 4V5
604-922-7616 Fax: 604-922-9163
Parent: Vancouver Coastal Health Authority
Number of Beds: 102 suites
June Messmer, General Manager

West Vancouver: Inglewood Care Centre
725 Inglewood Ave., West Vancouver, BC V7T 1X5
604-922-9394 Fax: 604-922-2709
Parent: Vancouver Coastal Health Authority
Number of Beds: 231 beds
Note: multi-level care
Nick Whittle, Administrator

Westbank: Brookhaven Extended Care Centre
1775 Shannon Lake Rd., Westbank, BC V4T 2N7
250-862-4040 Fax: 250-862-4048
dolorese.rudnicki@interiorhealth.ca
www.interiorhealth.ca
Parent: Interior Health Authority
Number of Beds: 168 beds
Dolorese Rudnicki, Primary Contact

Westbank: Pine Acres Home
1902 Pheasant Lane, Westbank, BC V4T 2H4
250-768-7676 Fax: 250-768-3234
Parent: Interior Health Authority
Number of Beds: 40 community beds, 23 private care beds
Note: complex care
JoAnn Derrickson, Administrator

Westbank: Westside Care Centre
3324 Old Okanagan Hwy., Westbank, BC V4T 1N3
250-768-0488 Fax: 250-768-4777
Parent: Interior Health Authority
Number of Beds: 98 beds
Elizabeth Harris, Managing Director

White Rock: Bel Air Rest Home
14824 North Bluff Rd., White Rock, BC V4B 3E2
604-536-1224 Fax: 604-536-1267
Parent: Fraser Health Authority
Number of Beds: 31 beds
Karen Armitage, Director

White Rock: Evergreen Baptist Home
1550 Oxford St., White Rock, BC V4B 3R5
604-536-3344 Fax: 604-541-3803 www.evergreen-home.com
Parent: Fraser Health Authority
Number of Beds: 157 beds
Linda Ingham, Administrator

White Rock: Ocean View Care Home
15628 Buena Vista Ave., White Rock, BC V4B 1Z4
604-531-2273 Fax: 604-531-8782
Parent: Fraser Health Authority
Number of Beds: 71 beds
Note: Specialty: Residential care for seniors; Secure unit for persons with dementia
Pat Mulcahy, Administrator

Williams Lake: Jubilee Care Home
196 - 2nd Ave. North, Williams Lake, BC V2G 1Z6
250-398-7736 Fax: 250-398-7736
Parent: Interior Health Authority
Number of Beds: 7 beds
Note: mental health group home
Doris Foote, Administrator

Winfield: Lake Country Lodge
10163 Konschuh Rd., Winfield, BC V4V 2M2
250-766-3007 Fax: 250-766-3178
admin@lakecountrylodge.ca
www.lakecountrylodge.ca
Number of Beds: 34 beds
Cathy Redden, Facilities Manager

Nursing Homes

Coquitlam: Belvedere Care Centre
739 Alderson Ave., Coquitlam, BC V3K 7B3
604-939-5991 Fax: 604-939-5910
belvederecare@telus.net
www.belvederecare.com
Also Known As: Belvedere Care Centre & Residences at Belvedere
Parent: Fraser Health Authority
Number of Beds: 148 complex care beds at care centre; 114 units for seniors at assisted living centre, including a secure unit for 11 residents
Note: Specialties: Complex care for seniors; Assisted living for residents with mild cognitive impairment; Wellness programs; Diabetes management; Therapy; Rehabilitation; Dementia care; Chronic care; Palliative care
Berton B. Evertt, Chair; Chief Executive Officer
Greg Graham, Controller
Gayle Vanags, Registered Dietitian
Annamae Clarke, Vice-President
Andrew Butler, Manager, Strategic Planning
Jennifer Cuvelier, Manager, Administration Services
Aileen Mellors-Luyt, Manager, Support Services
Karen Slutsken, Manager, Resident Relations
Fay Woodward, Manager, Resident Services
Azim Ladhani, Medical Coordinator
Linda Tod, Coordinator, Quality Improvement

Coquitlam: Dufferin Care Centre
1131 Dufferin St., Coquitlam, BC V3B 7X5
604-552-1166 Fax: 604-552-3116 www.retirementconcepts.com
Division of: Retirement Concepts
Number of Beds: 153 beds
Note: Specialties: Continuing care; Nursing care; Physiotherapy; Recreation therapy; Music therapy
Pat Kittler, General Manager
pkittler@retirementconcepts.com
Shannon Johnson, Director, Care
Elaine Drysdale, Coordinator, Administration
edrysdale@retirementconcepts.com
Doris Robinson, Coordinator, Marketing
604-375-9193, drobinson@retirementconcepts.com

Vancouver: George Pearson Centre/GPC
700 West 57th Ave., Vancouver, BC V6P 1S1
604-321-3231 Fax: 604-321-7833
feedback@vch.ca
www.vch.ca
Parent: Vancouver Coastal Health Authority
Year Founded: 1952
Number of Beds: 120 beds; 1 respite bed
Note: Specialties: Residential & complex medical care for adults with severe disabilities, such as cerebral palsy, multiple sclerosis, & spinal cord & traumatic brain injury; Special care units for ventilator dependent residents & persons with tracheostomies; Occupational therapy, physical therapy, pool therapy, music therapy, & respiratory therapy; Speech language pathology; Social work

Retirement Residences

Burnaby: CPAC (Carlton Gardens) Inc.
4125 Canada Way, Burnaby, BC V5G 1G9
604-438-8224 Fax: 604-438-6571
Note: Specialty: Care for the elderly

Coquitlam: **Parkwood Manor**
1142 Dufferin St., Coquitlam, BC V3B 6V4
604-941-7651 Fax: 604-941-4223
parkwoodmanor@lrc.ca
www.reveraliving.com
Number of Beds: 139 suites
Note: Independent living, convalescent & respite options
Wilma Mitchell, General Manager

Surrey: **Whitecliff**
15501 - 16th Ave., Surrey, BC V4A 9M5
604-538-7227 Fax: 604-538-4919
whiteclif@lrc.ca
www.reveraliving.com
Number of Beds: 133 suites; 18 beds
Note: Independent living, convalescent & respite options
Sherry Fossum, General Manager

Victoria: **Parkwood Court**
3000 Shelbourne St., Victoria, BC V8R 4M8
250-598-1575 Fax: 250-598-7372
parkwoodcourt@lrc.ca
www.reveraliving.com
Number of Beds: 83 suites
Note: Assisted living, respite & convalescent options
Jan Bard, General Manager

Victoria: **Parkwood Place**
3051 Shelbourne St., Victoria, BC V8R 6T2
250-598-1565 Fax: 250-598-8222
parkwoodplace@lrc.ca
www.reveraliving.com
Linda Bartel, Director, Marketing

Mental Health Facilities

Mental Health Hospital/Clinic/Facility

Burnaby: **Craigend Rest Home**
5480 Patterson Ave., Burnaby, BC V5H 2M5
604-433-8600
Number of Beds: 10 beds
Sayo Gardenia, Manager

Kamloops: **Forensic Psychiatric Services Commission (B.C.)**
#5, 1315 Summit Dr., Kamloops, BC V2C 5R9
250-377-2660 Fax: 250-371-3894
www.bcmhas.ca/ForensicService/ForensicRegionalServices.htm
Division of: Kamloops Clinic
Rose Dumont, Coordinator

Kamloops: **Kamloops Youth Forensic Psychiatric Services**
#8, 1315 Summit Dr., Kamloops, BC V2C 5R9
250-828-4940 Fax: 250-828-4946
Note: for young offenders directed by court/probation to assessment/treatment
Judie Hogg, Regional Office Manager
250/861-7601,

Kelowna: **White Heather Manor**
3728 Casorso Rd., Kelowna, BC V1W 4M8
250-763-6554 Fax: 250-763-6754
Number of Beds: 24 beds
Peter White, Manager

Maple Ridge: **Trejan Lodge Ltd.**
25402 Johnson Ave., Maple Ridge, BC V4R 1G3
604-467-3377 Fax: 604-467-0705
Note: Specialty: Long-term care
Mary Blume, Care Manager

Mission: **Waddell's Haven Guest Home**
12459 Dewdney Trunk Rd., Mission, BC V2V 5X4
604-826-7420
Number of Beds: 30 beds
Betty Baird, Manager

Nanaimo: **Forensic Psychiatric Services Commission (B.C.)**
#101, 190 Wallace St., Nanaimo, BC V9R 5B1
250-739-5000 Fax: 250-739-5001
www.bcmhas.ca/ForensicService/ForensicRegionalServices.htm
Old Name: Nanaimo Adult Forensic Psychiatric Community Servi
Division of: Nanaimo Clinic
Angus Monaghan, Regional Manager

Nanaimo: **Nanaimo Youth Forensic Psychiatric Services**
#101, 190 Wallace St., Nanaimo, BC V9R 5B1
250-741-5733 Fax: 250-741-5740
Note: youth forensic psychiatric outpatient clinic
André Picard, Coordinator

Port Coquitlam: **Forensic Psychiatric Services Commission (B.C.)**
70 Colony Farm Rd., Port Coquitlam, BC V3C 5X9
604-524-7700 Fax: 604-524-7905
www.bcmhas.ca/ForensicService/ForensicHospital/default.htm
Division of: Forensic Psychiatric Hospital
Number of Beds: 190 beds
Note: State-of-the-art facility which provides specialized clinical services & comprehensive rehabilitative & vocational programs.
Leslie Arnold, President, Mental Health

Port Coquitlam: **Riverview Hospital**
500 Lougheed Hwy., Port Coquitlam, BC V3C 4J2
604-524-7000 Fax: 604-524-7016 www.bcmhs.bc.ca
Number of Beds: 256 beds
Note: psychiatric teaching hospital
Leslie Arnold, President, Mental Health

Prince George: **Forensic Psychiatric Services Commission (B.C.)**
1594 - 7 Ave., 2nd Fl., Prince George, BC V2L 3P4
250-561-8060 Fax: 250-561-8075
www.bcmhas.ca/ForensicService/ForensicRegionalServices.htm
Division of: Prince George Clinic
Julia Thompson, Acting Regional Director

Richmond: **Westminster House**
11675 Bird Rd., Richmond, BC V6X 1N7
604-270-9510 Fax: 604-270-3539
Parent: Vancouver Coastal Health Authority
Number of Beds: 10 beds
André Chevrier, Director

Victoria: **Pacific Operational Trauma & Stress Support Centre/OTSSC**
PO Box 17000 Forces, Victoria, BC V9A 7N2
250-363-4411
Also Known As: Canadian Forces Health Services, Operational Be
Division of: Canadian Forces Health Services
Year Founded: 1999
Note: Specialties: Assistance to serving members of the Canadian Forces & their families, who are dealing with psychological, emotional, spiritual, & social problems stemming from military operations, especially deployments abroad; Psychiatry; Psychology; Social work; Community health nursing; Educational programs; Chaplain services

Victoria: **Victoria Youth Forensic Psychiatric Services**
1515 Quadra St., Victoria, BC V8V 3P3
250-387-1465 Fax: 250-387-3217
www.mcf.gov.bc.ca/yfps/index.htm
Gregg Badger, Regional Manager

Manitoba

Government Departments in Charge

MANITOBA: Manitoba Health
300 Carlton St., Winnipeg, MB R3B 3M9
204-786-7301 Fax: 204-775-3412
www.gov.mb.ca/health/index.html
Division of: Regional Affairs Division
Donna Forbes, Asst. Deputy Minister, Regional Affairs

Regional Health Authorities

Brandon: **Brandon Regional Health Authority**
150A - 7th St., Brandon, MB R7A 7M2
204-571-8400 Fax: 204-726-8505
turnbullp@brandonrha.mb.ca
www.brandonrha.mb.ca
Number of Beds: 186 acute care, 430 PCH, 99 EPH beds
Note: Services include: public health, home care, long term care, mental health services, comprehensive health services (cancer care, cardiac, birthing & neonatal, rehabilitation, surgery).
Carmel Olson, CEO

Churchill: **Churchill Regional Health Authority Inc./Churchil**
Corporate Office, PO Box 2500, 162 Laverendrye St., Churchill, MB R0B 0E0
204-675-8881 Fax: 204-675-2243 (
humanresources@churchillrha.mb.ca
www.churchillrha.com
Note: Area Served: Churchill; the communities of the Keewatin Region of the Territory of Nunavut
Verna Flett, Board Chair
David Merry, Supervisor, Material Management
204-675-8332, dmerry@churchillrha.mb.ca
Jukeepa Nowdlak, Supervisor, Health Information Systems
204-675-8309, jnowdlak@churchillrha.mb.ca
Derry Martens, Chief Executive Officer
204-675-8325, dmartens@churchillrha.mb.ca
Bobbi Sigurdson, Chief Financial Officer
204-675-8305, bsigurds@churchillrha.mb.ca
Patti MacEwan, Director, Clinical Services
204-675-8312, pmacewan@churchillrha.mb.ca
Michel Petit, Director, Community Services & Planning
204-675-8387, mpetit@churchillrha.mb.ca
Ron Sweeney, Director, Human Resources
204-675-8307, rsweeney@churchillrha.mb.ca
Amy Goulet, Manager, EMS
204-675-8356, agoulet@churchillrha.mb.ca
Debbie Leggett, Manager, Community Wellness
204-675-8383, dleggett@churchillrha.mb.ca
Ken Slobodesky, Manager, Support Services
204-675-8333, kslobodesky@churchillrha.mb.ca

Dauphin: **Parkland Regional Health Authority Inc.**
#112, 27 - 2nd Ave. SW, Dauphin, MB R7N 3E5
204-622-6222 Fax: 204-622-6232 800-259-7541
prha@prha.mb.ca
www.prha.mb.ca
Number of Beds: 214 acute care, 545 long-term care beds
Andre Remillard, CEO

Flin Flon: **Nor-Man Regional Health Authority Inc.**
PO Box 130, 84 Church St., Flin Flon, MB R8A 1M7
204-687-1300 Fax: 204-687-6405
nrha@normanrha.mb.ca
www.norman-rha.mb.ca
Number of Beds: 264 beds
Note: Serves a population of 26,000 across 72,000 square kilometers
Drew Lockhart, CEO

La Broquerie: **South Eastman Health/Santé Sud-Est Inc.**
PO Box 470, La Broquerie, MB R0A 0W0
204-424-5880 Fax: 204-424-5888 866-716-5633
corp@sehealth.mb.ca
www.sehealth.mb.ca
Monique Vielfaure MacKenz, CEO

Pinawa: **North Eastman Health Association Inc.**
PO Box 339, 24 Aberdeen Ave., Pinawa, MB R0E 1L0
204-753-2012 Fax: 204-753-2015 877-753-2012
neha@neha.mb.ca
www.neha.mb.ca
Note: Provides services to over 38,000 people
Jim Hayes, CEO

Souris: **Assiniboine Regional Health Authority Office régional de la santé Assiniboine**
Corporate Office, PO Box 579, 192 - 1st Ave. West, Souris, MB R0K 2C0
204-483-5000 Fax: 204-483-5005 1-888-682-2253
assiniboinerha@arha.ca
www.assiniboine-rha.ca
Note: Facilities: 20 acute care facilities; 28 long term care facilities; 7 housing units for elderly persons; 1 transitional care unit. Number of Employees: 3,000+, including 64 physicians. Population served: 69,371
Penny Gilson, Chief Executive Officer

Michelle Clark, Executive Director, Primary Care & Medical Services

Garlen Maxwell, Executive Director, Facility Services
Glenda Short, Executive Director, Allied Health Services
Lara Bossert, Chief Officer, Human Resources & Communications
Deb Clevett, Vice-President, Community Health Services
Pat Cockburn, Vice-President, Programs & Standards
Kerry Takvam, Vice-President, Corporate Services

Stonewall: **Interlake Regional Health Authority**
589 - 3rd Ave. South, Stonewall, MB R0C 2Z0
204-467-4742 Fax: 204-467-4750 1-888-488-2299
info@irha.mb.ca
www.irha.mb.ca
Note: Population Served: 77,500. Area Served: 26,000 square kilometers, covering the R.M. of Rosser to the 53rd parallel, & Lake Manitoba on the west to Lake Winnipeg on the east (14 rural municipalities, 9 First Nation communities, 5 towns, 2 villages, 1 city, plus unorganized territories)
Kevin Beresford, Chief Executive Officer
204-467-4742, kberesford@irha.mb.ca
Dela Irwin, Director, Human Resources
204-785-7436, dirwin@irha.mb.ca

Kim Olver, Director, Home Based Programs & Services to Seniors
204-785-5504, kolver@irha.mb.ca
Kevin
O'Donovan, Manager, Public Relations
204-467-4747, kodonovan@irha.mb.ca
Jim Rodger, Chair, Board of Directors
Tim Hilderman, Medical Officer of Health
204-467-4400, Tim.Hilderman@gov.mb.ca
Cary Chapnick, Vice-President, Medical Services
204-642-4524, cchapnick@irha.mb.ca
Lorne
Charbonneau, Vice-President, Health Services
204-467-4749, lcharbonneau@irha.mb.ca
Doreen
Fey, Vice-President, Planning
204-467-4748, dfey@irha.mb.ca
Sherry Lees, Vice-President, Corporate Services
204 785 7431, slees@irha.mb.ca
Angela Charison, Director, Finance
204-785-7432, acharison@irha.mb.ca
Gary Dandeneau, Director, Physical Facilities
204-372-7318, gdandeneau@irha.mb.ca

***Thompson:* Burntwood Regional Health Authority/BRHA**
867 Thompson Dr. South, Thompson, MB R8N 1Z4
204-677-5350 Fax: 204-778-1424 1-888-442-9264
brha@brha.mb.ca
www.brha.mb.ca
Note: Population Served: 45,798
Gloria King, Chief Executive Officer
204-677-5399, gking@brha.mb.ca
Marion Ellis, Chief Nursing Officer; Vice-President, Acute Care
204-677-5351, mellis@brha.mb.ca
Paul
Therrien, Chief Officer, Human Resources
204-778-1519, ptherrien@brha.mb.ca
Rajinder Thethy, Chief Officer, Finance & Operations
204-677-5346, rthethy@brha.mb.ca
Lisa Richards, Medical Officer of Health
204-778-1494, lrichards@brha.mb.ca
Hussam Azzam, Vice-President, Medical Services
204-677-5376, hazzam@brha.mb.ca
Rusty
Beardy, Vice-President, Aboriginal Services
204-778-1435, rbeardy@brha.mb.ca

***Winnipeg:* Winnipeg Regional Health Authority**
#1800, 155 Carlton St., Winnipeg, MB R3C 4Y1
204-926-7000 Fax: 204-926-7007
info@wrha.mb.ca
www.wrha.mb.ca
Brian Postl, President; CEO
Milton Sussman, Chief Operating Officer, Vice-President, Community Health Services

Hospitals

Hospitals - General

***Altona:* Altona Community Memorial Health Centre/Eastview Place**
PO Box 660, 240 - 5 Ave. NE, Altona, MB R0G 0B0
204-324-6411 Fax: 204-324-8482
Parent: Regional Health Authority - Central Manitoba Inc.
Number of Beds: 22 acute care, 65 long-term care beds
Edith Calder, Facility Contact
e.calder@ahc.rha-central.mb.ca

***Arborg:* Arborg & District Health Centre**
PO Box 10, Arborg, MB R0C 0A0
204-376-5247 Fax: 204-376-5669 www.irha.mb.ca
Parent: Interlake Regional Health Authority Inc.
Number of Beds: 16 beds + 40 long term care beds in an attached personal care home
Note: Specialties: Diagnostic services

***Ashern:* Lakeshore General Hospital**
PO Box 110, Ashern, MB R0C 0E0
204-768-2461 Fax: 204-768-2337
Parent: Interlake Regional Health Authority Inc.
Number of Beds: 15 beds
Jan O'Flanagan, District Director

***Beausejour:* Beausejour District Hospital**
PO Box 1178, Beausejour, MB R0E 0C0
204-268-1076 Fax: 204-268-1207 www.neha.mb.ca
Parent: North Eastman Health Association Inc.
Number of Beds: 30 acute care beds
Note: Hospital Specialties: Imaging; Physiotherapy; Occupational therapy; Number of Employees: 86
Glennda Gould, Manager, Care Team

***Boissevain:* Boissevain Health Centre**
PO Box 899, 305 Mill Rd., Boissevain, MB R0K 0E0
204-534-2451 Fax: 204-534-6487
dgraham@arha.ca (Area Manager)
www.assiniboine-rha.ca
Parent: Assiniboine Regional Health Authority
Number of Beds: 20 beds
Note: Specialties: Emergency services; Diagnostic services; Acute care; Mental health services; Public health services; Home care; Respite care

***Brandon:* Brandon Regional Health Centre**
150 McTavish Ave. East, Brandon, MB R7A 2B3
204-578-4219 Fax: 204-578-4969 www.brandonrha.mb.ca
Parent: Brandon Regional Health Authority
Number of Beds: 336 beds
Note: A regional referral acute care hospital & teaching facility. Services include in- & out-patient care, rehabilitation, diagnositics, & clinics.
Kathy McPhail, Vice-President, Acute Care & Diagnostic Services
K. Martinook, Director, Physical Plant

***Carman:* Carman Memorial Hospital**
PO Box 610, 350 - 4 St., SW, Carman, MB R0G 0J0
204-745-2021 Fax: 204-745-2756 www.rha-central.mb.ca
Parent: Regional Health Authority - Central Manitoba Inc.
Number of Beds: 25 beds
Note: Hospital Specialties: Surgerey; Acute care; Obstetrics Physiotherapy; Diabetes education; Dietitian service; Palliative care; Number of Employees: 190 at Carman Hospital & the nearby Boyne Lodge personal care home
Mary Heard
, Director, Health Services - Carman

m.heard@rha-central.mb.ca

***Crystal City:* Rock Lake Hospital/Rock Lake Health District**
PO Box 130, 135 Machray Ave., Crystal City, MB R0K 0N0
204-873-2132 Fax: 204-873-2185
pking@rlh.rha-central.mb.ca
Parent: Regional Health Authority - Central Manitoba Inc.
Number of Beds: 16 acute care beds
Pam King, Facility Contact

***Dauphin:* Dauphin Regional Health Centre/DRHC**
625 - 3rd St. SW, Dauphin, MB R7N 1R7
204-638-3010 1-800-259-7541 www.prha.mb.ca
Parent: Parkland Regional Health Authority Inc.
Note: Hospital Specialties: Emergency medical services; Computed Tomography (CT) services; Ultrasound service; Surgical services; Acute care; Obstetrics; Chemotherapy; Hemodialysis; 10 bed acute care psychiatric unit; Manitoba Telehealth site
Kevin McKnight, Chief Executive Officer, Parkland Regional Health Authority
Blaine Kraushaar, Coordinator, Community Relations
204-622-6237, Fax: 204-622-6232, bkraushaar@prha.mb.ca

***Deloraine:* Deloraine Health Centre**
PO Box 447, Deloraine, MB R0M 0M0
204-747-2745 Fax: 204-747-2160 www.assiniboine-rha.ca
Parent: Assiniboine Regional Health Authority
Note: Hospital Specialties: Emergency medical services; Diagnostic services (204-747-2431); Deloraine Community Cancer Program (204-747-1836); Acute care; Mental health services; Public health services; Home care
D. Graham, Area Manager
dgraham@arha.ca

***Eriksdale:* E.M. Crowe Memorial Hospital**
PO Box 130, 1st St. NE, Eriksdale, MB R0C 0W0
204-739-2611 Fax: 204-739-2065
Note: Hospital Specialties: Emergency services; X-ray services; Doppler ultrasound carotid artery scans
Jan O'Flanagan, Director, North West District, Interlake Regional Health Auth
Kevin O'Donovan, Manager, Public Relations, Interlake Regional Health Authori

***Eriksdale:* Elizabeth M. Crowe Memorial Hospital**
PO Box 130, Eriksdale, MB R0C 0W0
204-739-2611 Fax: 204-739-2065
Parent: Interlake Regional Health Authority Inc.
Jan O'Flanagan, District Director

***Flin Flon:* Flin Flon General Hospital Inc.**
PO Box 340, Flin Flon, MB R8A 1N2
204-687-7591 Fax: 204-687-8494 www.norman-rha.mb.ca
Parent: Nor-Man Regional Health Authority Inc.
Number of Beds: 44 acute care beds
Note: Hospital Specialty: Acute care
Lois Moberly, Executive Director, Clinical Services
204-687-9610

***Gillam:* Gillam Hospital Incorporated**
PO Box 2000, 15 Gillam Dr., Gillam, MB R0B 0L0
204-652-2600 Fax: 204-652-2536
Parent: Burntwood Regional Health Authority Inc.
Number of Beds: 10 beds, including 3 long term beds
Note: Hospital Specialties: Emergency services; Laboratory services; Acute care; Public health; Long term care

***Gimli:* Gimli Community Health Centre/GCHC**
Johnson Memorial Hospital, PO Box 250, 120 - 6th Ave., Gimli, MB R0C 1B0
204-642-5116 Fax: 204-642-5860
info@irha.mb.ca
www.irha.mb.ca
Parent: Interlake Regional Health Authority Inc.
Year Founded: 2004
Number of Beds: 14 acute beds; 4 special care beds; 2 palliative care beds
Note: Specialties: Diagnostic services (204-642-4519); Laboratory services; Acute care; Chemotherapy program (204-642-4520); Physiotherapy; Occupational therapy; Community health (204-642-6051); Adult day program; Palliative care
Cary Chapnick, Vice-President, Medical Services, Interlake Regional Health Authori
204-642-4524, cchapnick@irha.mb.ca
Lorne Charbonneau, Vice-President, Health Services, Interlake Regional Health Authorit
204-467-4749, lcharbonneau@irha.mb.ca

***Gladstone:* Seven Regions Health Centre**
PO Box 1000, 24 Mill St., Gladstone, MB R0J 0T0
204-385-2968 Fax: 204-385-3053
Parent: Regional Health Authority - Central Manitoba Inc.
Number of Beds: 14 acute care beds
Dorothy Doell, Facility Contact
d.doell@srhc.rha-central.mb.ca

***Grandview:* Grandview District Hospital**
PO Box 339, 644 Mill St., Grandview, MB R0L 0Y0
204-546-2425 Fax: 204-546-3269
Parent: Parkland Regional Health Authority Inc.
Number of Beds: 18 beds
John Kelly, COO

***Hodgson:* Percy E. Moore Hospital**
PO Box 190, Hodgson, MB R0C 1N0
204-372-8444 Fax: 204-372-6991
Parent: Interlake Regional Health Authority Inc.
Number of Beds: 16 beds
Note: Specialties: Dialysis services
Carol Hartog, Acting Administrator
Joe Malenchak, Head of Maintenance
L. McCorrister, Purchasing Agent

***Killarney:* Tri-Lake Health Centre**
PO Box 5000, Killarney, MB R0K 1G0
204-523-3210 Fax: 204-523-8948 www.assiniboine-rha.ca
Parent: Assiniboine Regional Health Authority
Number of Beds: 22 beds
Note: Specialties: Acute care; Diagnostic services; Mental health services; Public health services; Home care
Bev Towler, Area Manager

***Lynn Lake:* Lynn Lake District Hospital**
PO Box 2030, 640 Camp St., Lynn Lake, MB R0B 0W0
204-356-2474 Fax: 204-356-8023
dtitterson@brha.mb.ca
www.thompson.ca/dbs/brha
Parent: Burntwood Regional Health Authority Inc.
Number of Beds: 11 general beds + 6 long term care beds + 2 chronic beds
Note: Specialties: Public health services; Mental health services; Medical clinic; Long-term care. Number of employees: 22

***McCreary:* McCreary/Alonsa Health Centre**
PO Box 250, 613 Government Rd., McCreary, MB R0J 1B0
204-835-2482 Fax: 204-835-2713
Parent: Parkland Regional Health Authority Inc.
Number of Beds: 13 beds
Note: Specialties: Acute care; Diagnostic services
Charlie Sitwell, Administrator

***Melita:* Melita Health Centre**
PO Box 459, Melita, MB R0M 1L0
204-522-8197 Fax: 204-522-3161
Parent: Assiniboine Regional Health Authority
Number of Beds: 11 beds
Note: Specialties: Diagnostic services; Acute care; Outreach

services; Mental health services; Physiotherapy; Occupational therapy
Georgina Henuset, Area Manager

Morris: Morris General Hospital
PO Box 519, 215 Railroad Ave. East, Morris, MB R0G 1K0
204-746-2301 Fax: 204-746-2197 www.rha-central.mb.ca
Parent: Regional Health Authority - Central Manitoba Inc.
Number of Beds: 23 acute care beds
Brad Street, Facility Contact
b.street@mgh.rha-central.mb.ca

Norway House: Norway House Hospital
General Delivery, Norway House, MB R0B 1B0
204-359-6731 Fax: 204-359-6599 www.nhhsinc.ca
Year Founded: 1925
Leonard York, Administrator

Pinawa: Pinawa Hospital
PO Box 220, 30 Vanier Dr., Pinawa, MB R0E 1L0
204-753-2334
Parent: North Eastman Health Association Inc.
Year Founded: 1964
Number of Beds: 17 beds
Note: Specialties: Acute care; Community cancer care program; Physiotherapy; Occupational therapy; Palliative care
May Fast, Care Team Manager

Pine Falls: Pine Falls Health Complex
PO Box 2000, 37 Maple St., Pine Falls, MB R0E 1M0
204-367-4441 www.neha.mb.ca
Parent: North Eastman Health Association Inc.
Number of Beds: 23 inpatient beds + 20 personal care home beds
Note: Specialties: Health & social services; Primary medical care combined with traditional aboriginal approaches to health care; Hemodialysis; Physiotherapy; Occupational therapy; Mental health services; Palliative care
Brenda Neufeld, Director of Acute Care

Portage la Prairie: Portage District General Hospital
524 - 5 St. SE, Portage la Prairie, MB R1N 3A8
204 239-2211 Fax: 204-239-1941
Parent: Regional Health Authority - Central Manitoba Inc.
Number of Beds: 89 acute care beds
Note: 660 staff
Pat Nodrick, Director, Health Services
p.nodrick@pdgh.rha-central.mb.ca

Roblin: Roblin District Health Centre
PO Box 940, 15 Hospital St., Roblin, MB R0L 1P0
204-937-2142 Fax: 204-937-8892
rdhc@prha.mb.ca
www.prha.mb.ca
Parent: Parkland Regional Health Authority Inc.
Number of Beds: 25 bed hospital, 60 bed personal care home
Note: Emergency & diagnostic services, X-ray and EKG testing, ultrasound & mammography, podiatry, speech therapy, occupational therapy, physiotherapy
Cheryl Jerome, COO

Russell: Russell District Health Centre
Bag Service 2, Russell, MB R0J 1W0
204-773-2125 Fax: 204-773-2142
Parent: Assiniboine Regional Health Authority
Number of Beds: 32 acute care beds; 40 PCH
Barb Kostesky, Community Health Director

Selkirk: Selkirk & District General Hospital
PO Box 5000, 100 Easton Dr., Selkirk, MB R1A 2M2
204-482-5800 Fax: 204-785-9113 www.irha.mb.ca/programs.htm
Parent: Interlake Regional Health Authority Inc.
Year Founded: 1907
Number of Beds: 49 beds
Note: Emergency & outpatient services, acute care, surgery, obstetrics, physiotherapy, diagnostic imaging, chemotherapy, dialysis, palliative care, mental health services
Kevin Beresford, CEO, IRHA
204-467-4742, kberesford@irha.mb.ca
Dianne Mestdagh, Director, South East District, IRHA
204-785-7430, dmestdagh@irha.mb.ca
Edie Telenko, Executive Assistant, Selkirk
204-785-7424, etelenko@irha.mb.ca

Shoal Lake: Shoal Lake - Strathclair Health Centre
PO Box 490, Shoal Lake, MB R0J 1Z0
204-759-2336 Fax: 204-759-2230
assiniboinerha@arha.ca
www.assiniboine-rha.ca/index.php/health_sites/view?id=36
Number of Beds: 40 personal care home beds
Note: Emergency, acute care, diagnostic services, mental Health Services, home care services, regional palliative care program, regional occupational & physiotherapy services
Roseanne Yaremchuk, Area Manager
ryaremchuk@arha.ca

St Claude: St. Claude Health District
PO Box 400, 33 Roy St., St Claude, MB R0G 1Z0
204-379-2585 Fax: 204-379-2655
Parent: Regional Health Authority - Central Manitoba Inc.
Number of Beds: 10 beds; 18 long-term care beds
Mona Spencer, Facility Contact

Ste Anne: Hôpital Ste Anne Hospital
52 St Gerard St., Ste Anne, MB R5H 1C4
204-422-8837 Fax: 204-422-9929
clavack@schealth.mb.ca
Parent: South Eastman Health/Santé Sud-Est Inc.
Number of Beds: 21 beds
Carole Lavack, Facility Manager

Ste Rose du Lac: Ste Rose General Hospital
Hôpital général de Ste-Rose
PO Box 60, 480 - 3rd Ave. East, Ste Rose du Lac, MB R0L 1S0
204-447-2131
Note: Specialty: Diagnostic services
Glen Kozak, Executive Director

Steinbach: Bethesda Hospital / Bethesda Place Complex
316 Henry St., Steinbach, MB R5G 0P9
204-326-6411 www.sehealth.mb.ca
Parent: South Eastman Health/Santé Sud-Est Inc.
Number of Beds: 64 acute care beds; 20 rehabilitation beds
Note: Specialties: Emergency services; Diagnostic services; Laboratory services; Acute care; Cardiac care; Cancer care; Obstetrics; Physiotherapy; Occupational therapy; Speech-language pathology services; Social work; Personal care at Bethesda Place; Palliative care; Number of Employees: 471
Patti Fries, Manager, Facility
204-346-5168
Don Fast, Clinical Manager, Medicine, ER, & CancerCare
Debbie Harms, Clinical Manager, Surgery, Obstetrics, Rehabilitation, & Therapy
Ginette Morgan, Clinical Manager, Long Term Care (Bethesda Place)
Wally Driedger
, Manager, Physical Plant
Marie Lacey, Manager, Nutrition & Food Services
Pam Beaudoin, Coordinator, Recreation
Ruth Campbell, Coordinator, Human Resources

Swan Lake: Lorne Memorial Hospital
9 - 2nd St. North, Swan Lake, MB R0G 2S0
204-836-2132 Fax: 204-836-2044
Parent: Regional Health Authority - Central Manitoba Inc.
Number of Beds: 18 acute care beds
Note: Hospital Specialties: Imaging health unit; Advanced palliative care program. Number of Employees: 60
Kristal McKitrick-Bazin, Facility Contact
k.mckitrick-bazin@lmh.rha-central.mb

Swan River: Swan Valley Health Centre
PO Box 1450, 1011 Main St., Swan River, MB R0L 1Z0
204-734-3441 Fax: 204-734-9081
www.prha.mb.ca/Hospitals.aspx
Parent: Parkland Regional Health Authority Inc.
Year Founded: 2005
Number of Beds: 52 acute-care beds
Note: Services include acute care, ambulatory care, audiology, chemotherapy, diabetes education, diagnostics, dialysis, emergency service, mental health, physiotherapy, occupational therapy, speech language pathology, surgery.
Allan Bradley, CEO, PRHA
Blaine Kraushaar, Coordinator, Community Relations, PRHA
204-622-6237, Fax: 204-622-6232, bkraushaar@prha.mb.ca
Neoma Stiegler, Clinical Services Manager
204-734-6664, nstiegler@prha.mb.ca

Teulon: Teulon Hunter Memorial Hospital
PO Box 89, 3rd Ave. SE, Teulon, MB R0C 3B0
204-886-2433 Fax: 204-886-2653
info@irha.mb.ca
www.irha.mb.ca
Parent: Interlake Regional Health Authority Inc.
Number of Beds: 20 beds
Note: Services include emergency, ambulatory care, acute care, diagnostic imaging, laboratory, pharmacy, surgery, physiotherapy, dietary services, occupational therapy, opthamology.
Kevin Beresford, CEO, IRHA
204-467-4742, kberesford@irha.mb.ca
Shannon Montgomery, South West District Director, IRHA
smontgomery@irha.mb.ca
Kevin O'Donovan, Public Relations Manager, IRHA
204-467-4747, kodonovan@irha.mb.ca
Abdalla Rizk, Site Chief of Staff

The Pas: The Pas Health Complex Inc.
PO Box 240, 67 - 1st St. West, The Pas, MB R9A 1K4
204-623-6431 Fax: 204-623-9263
Old Name: St. Anthony's General Hospital
Parent: Nor-Man Regional Health Authority Inc.
Year Founded: 1969
Number of Beds: 118 beds
Note: Specialties: Acute care; Ambulatory clinic program; Dialysis; Physiotherapy; Occupational therapy; Social services; Chronic care; Long-term care
Drew Lockhart, CEO

Thompson: Thompson General Hospital
871 Thompson Dr. South, Thompson, MB R8N 0C8
204-677-2381 Fax: 204-778-1413
brha@brha.mb.ca
www.brha.mb.ca
Parent: Burntwood Regional Health Authority Inc.
Number of Beds: 74 beds
Note: A community facility with services including emergency, aboriginal interpretive services, cancer care, diagnostics, dialysis, obstetrics, palliative care, psychiatric acute care unit, rehabilitation, respiratory therapy, spiritual care, surgery
Gloria King, CEO, BRHA
204-677-5399, gking@brha.mb.ca
Hussam Azzam, Vice-President, Medical Services, BRHA
204-677-5376, hazzam@brha.mb.ca
Hisham Tassi, Site Head, Medical Services
204-677-5314, htassi@brha.mb.ca

Winkler: Boundary Trails Health Centre
PO Box 2000 Main, Winkler, MB R6W 1H8
204-331-8800 Fax: 204-331-8801 www.rha-central.mb.ca
Parent: Regional Health Authority - Central Manitoba Inc.
Number of Beds: 40 medical beds; 25 rehabilitation beds; 18 surgical services beds; 7 obstetrics / birthing beds; 4 intensive care unit beds
Note: Hospital specialties: Emergency services; Diagnostics, Laboratory services; Surgery; Intensive care; Acute care; Chemotherapy; Dialysis; Physiotherapy; Occupational therapy; Audiology; Mental health services; Public health; Home care Number of Employees: 450
Linda Buhr, Director, Health Services
l.buhr@rha-central.mb.ca
Kristy Radke
, Director, Support Services
k.radke@rha-central.mb.ca

Winnipeg: Concordia Hospital
1095 Concordia Ave., Winnipeg, MB R2K 3S8
204-667-1560 Fax: 204-667-1049 www.concordiahospital.mb.ca
Parent: Winnipeg Regional Health Authority
Note: Hospital Specialties: Emergency services; Diagnostic imaging; Laboratory services (204-661-7174); Surgery (a major centre for hip and knee replacements); Intensive care; A.M.I. (Acute Myocardial Infarct) Program; Occupational therapy (204-661-7216); Physiotherapy (204-661-7354); Respiratory therapy (204-661-7346); Oncology haematology service; Social work (204-661-7185); Cardiac Teaching Program (nurse home visit); Lifeline personal response & support services
Henry Tessman, President; Chief Operating Officer

Winnipeg: Health Sciences Centre
820 Sherbrook St., Winnipeg, MB R3A 1R9
204-774-6511 Fax: 204-787-3912 www.hsc.mb.ca
Parent: Winnipeg Regional Health Authority
Number of Beds: 850 beds
Note: teaching hospital
Adam Topp, COO
Dana Erickson, Vice-President; CAO
Perry Gray, Vice-President; Chief Medical Officer

Winnipeg: Riverview Health Centre
1 Morley Ave. East, Winnipeg, MB R3L 2P4
204-478-6203 Fax: 204-478-6212
enquiries@rhc.mb.ca
www.rhc.mb.ca
Parent: Winnipeg Regional Health Authority
Number of Beds: 388 beds
Note: Long-term care, catering to the needs of the elderly and rehabilitation patients
Norman R. Kasian, President/CEO
Sheldon Mindell, Development Officer
smindell@rhc.mb.ca

Winnipeg: St. Boniface General Hospital
L'Hôpital général Saint-Boniface
409 Taché Ave., Winnipeg, MB R2H 2A6

204-233-8563 Fax: 204-231-0640
sbghweb@sbgh.mb.ca
www.sbgh.mb.ca
Parent: Winnipeg Regional Health Authority
Year Founded: 1871
Number of Beds: 524 beds
Note: Catholic tertiary care facility & teaching hospital affiliated with the University of Manitoba & dedicated to the values of care of the Sisters of Charity of Montreal (Grey Nuns). Emergency services, family medicine, mental health, geriatrics & rehabilitation, surgery, women's health, paediatrics. Number of staff, including support & healthcare staff: 4,000+
Michel Tétreault, President/CEO

Winnipeg: The Salvation Army Grace General Hospital
300 Booth Dr., Winnipeg, MB R3J 3M7
204 837 0111
hrs@ggh.mb.ca (Human Resources); pr@ggh.mb.ca (Public relations)
www.gracehospital.ca
Parent: Winnipeg Regional Health Authority
Year Founded: 1904
Number of Beds: 270 beds
Note: Specialties: Emergency & critical care programs; Surgery program; Mental health services; Hospice care
John McFarlane, President; CEO
204/837-0143
Scott Wichenko, Director, Materials Management
Art Isaak, Director, Housekeeping

Winnipeg: Seven Oaks General Hospital
2300 McPhillips St., Winnipeg, MB R2V 3M3
204-632-7133 Fax: 204-697-2106 www.sogh.winnipeg.mb.ca
Parent: Winnipeg Regional Health Authority
Year Founded: 1981
Number of Beds: 275 beds
Note: Comprehensive health services, including emergency, surgery, rehabilitation/geriatric/mental health services, intensive care, dialysis, pulmonary rehabilitation program, hearing centre, dental services
Carrie Solmundson, President; COO
Ricardo Lobato de Faria, Chief Medical Officer
Monique Constant, Chief Administrative Officer

Winnipeg: Victoria General Hospital
2340 Pembina Hwy., Winnipeg, MB R3T 2E8
204-269-3570 Fax: 204-261-0223
info@vgh.mb.ca
www.vgh.mb.ca
Parent: Winnipeg Regional Health Authority
Number of Beds: 231 beds
Note: Comprehensive health care. Number of staff: 1,200
Ray J. Racette, President; CEO

Winnipegosis: Winnipegosis General Hospital
PO Box 280, 230 Bridge St., Winnipegosis, MB R0L 2G0
204-656-4881 Fax: 204-656-4402
Parent: Parkland Regional Health Authority Inc.
Number of Beds: 14 acute care, 20 long-term care beds
Glen Kozak, COO

Community Health Centres

Community Health Care Centres

Baldur: Baldur Health Centre/Baldur Health District
PO Box 128, Baldur, MB R0K 0B0
204-535-2373 Fax: 204-535-2116
Parent: Assiniboine Regional Health Authority
Number of Beds: 14 beds
Bev Towler

Benito: Benito Primary Health Centre
PO Box 490, 200 - 1st St. East, Benito, MB R0L 0C0
204-539-2815 Fax: 204-539-2482 www.prha.mb.ca
Parent: Parkland Regional Health Authority Inc.
Note: Specialties: Community health; Mental health services

Birtle: Birtle Health Centre
PO Box 10, Birtle, MB R0M 0C0
204-842-3317 Fax: 204-842-3375
Parent: Assiniboine Regional Health Authority
Number of Beds: 14 acute care, 20 long-term care beds
Roseanne Yaremchuk, Area Manager

Brandon: 7th Street Health Access Centre
20 - 7th St., Brandon, MB R7A 6M8
204-578-4800 Fax: 204-578-4950 www.brandonrha.mb.ca
Parent: Brandon Regional Health Authority
Note: Community Health Nurse; Adult Community Mental Health Worker; Community Social Worker; Addictions Services; Housing Resource Worker; Cultural Facilitators; Supports to Services in Group Living; Supports to Seniors living at Home; Mental Health Peer Support Educator; Community Volunteer Income Tax Program; YWCA Family Violence Outreach Program.
Vicky Legassie, Program Manager

Carberry: Carberry Plains District Health Centre
Bag Service #1, 1st Ave., Carberry, MB R0K 0H0
204-834-2144 Fax: 204-834-3333
Parent: Assiniboine Regional Health Authority
Number of Beds: 10 acute care, 36 PCH beds
Deb Obach, Director

Cartwright: Davidson Memorial Health Centre
PO Box 118, Cartwright, MB R0K 0L0
204-529-2483 Fax: 204-529-2562
Old Name: Cartwright & District Hospital
Parent: Assiniboine Regional Health Authority
Number of Beds: 10 beds
Bev Towler

Churchill: Churchill Health Centre
General Delivery, Churchill, MB R0B 0E0
204-675-8318 Fax: 204-675-2243 www.churchillrha.com
Parent: Churchill Regional Health Authority Inc.
Note: Specialties: Primary care; Public health services
Derry Martens, Chief Executive Officer, Churchill Regional Health Authority Inc.

Deloraine: Deloraine Health Centre
PO Box 447, 109 Kellett St., Deloraine, MB R0M 0M0
204-747-2745 Fax: 204-747-2160
John Rekai, Manager

Emerson: Emerson Hospital/Personal Care Home
PO Box 428, 26 Main St., Emerson, MB R0A 0L0
204-373-2109 Fax: 204-373-2748
Parent: Regional Health Authority - Central Manitoba Inc.
Number of Beds: 4 acute care, 20 long-term care beds
Paulette Goossen, Facility Contact

Erickson: Erickson District Health Centre
PO Box 25, Erickson, MB R0J 0P0
204-636-7777 Fax: 204-636-2471
Parent: Assiniboine Regional Health Authority
Number of Beds: 9 acute care, 16 PCH beds
Judith McDowell, Community Health Director

Glenboro: Glenboro Health District Hospital
PO Box 310, Glenboro, MB R0K 0X0
204-827-2438 Fax: 204-827-2199
Parent: Assiniboine Regional Health Authority
Number of Beds: 11 beds
Note: acute care, personal home care
Marilyn McGregor, Manager

Hamiota: Hamiota District Health Centre
177 Birch Ave., Hamiota, MB R0M 0T0
204-764-2412 Fax: 204-764-2049
Parent: Assiniboine Regional Health Authority
Number of Beds: 20 acute care, 30 PCH beds
Greg Paddock, Area Manager

Hamiota: Hamiota District Health Centre
177 Birch Ave., Hamiota, MB R0M 0T0
204-764-2412 Fax: 204-764-2049
mandrew@mrha.mb.ca
Parent: Assiniboine Regional Health Authority

Hartney: Hartney Medical Nursing Unit
PO Box 28, Hartney, MB R0M 0X0
204-858-2054 Fax: 204-858-2303
Number of Beds: 9 beds
Shirley Kloon, Manager

Lac du Bonnet: Lac du Bonnet District Health Centre
PO Box 1030, Lac du Bonnet, MB R0E 1A0
204-345-1219 Fax: 204-268-8609
Parent: North Eastman Health Association Inc.
Mary Power, Home Care Manager

Leaf Rapids: Leaf Rapids Health Centre
PO Box 370, Leaf Rapids, MB R0B 1W0
204-473-2441 Fax: 204-473-8273
lrhcadm@cancom.net
Parent: Burntwood Regional Health Authority Inc.
Number of Beds: 8 beds
Bernette Alexander, Manager, Leaf Rapids Health Program

MacGregor: MacGregor Health Centre
PO Box 250, 87 Grafton St. South, MacGregor, MB R0H 0R0
204-685-2850 Fax: 204-685-2529
Parent: Regional Health Authority - Central Manitoba Inc.
Number of Beds: 6 beds
Note: Specialties: Respite care; convalescent care; Palliative services; Number of Employees: 52
Sharon Stewart, Facility Contact

Manitou: Pembina-Manitou Health Centre
PO Box 129, 232 Carrie St., Manitou, MB R0G 1G0
204-242-2744 Fax: 204-242-3062
Parent: Regional Health Authority - Central Manitoba Inc.
Number of Beds: 8 acute care, 18 long-term care beds
Linda Pearce, Facility Contact

Minnedosa: Minnedosa Health Centre
PO Box 960, Minnedosa, MB R0J 1E0
204-867-2701 Fax: 204-867-2239
Parent: Assiniboine Regional Health Authority
Number of Beds: 27 acute care
Judith McDowell

Neepawa: Neepawa District Memorial Hospital
PO Box 1240, Neepawa, MB R0J 1H0
204-476-2394 Fax: 204-476-5007
Parent: Assiniboine Regional Health Authority
Number of Beds: 38 beds
K.D. Braden, Community Health Director

Notre Dame de Lourdes: Notre Dame Medical Nursing Inc.
PO Box 190, Notre Dame de Lourdes, MB R0G 1M0
204-248-2112 Fax: 204-248-2499
Parent: Regional Health Authority - Central Manitoba Inc.
Note: Specialty: Acute care
Cheryl Harrison, Facility Contact
c.harrison@fnd.rha-central.mb.ca

Rivers: Riverdale Health Centre/Riverdale Health Services District
PO Box 428, 512 Quebec St., Rivers, MB R0K 1X0
204-328-5321 Fax: 204-328-7130
Parent: Assiniboine Regional Health Authority
Number of Beds: 14 acute care, 20 PCH beds, 12 Elderly Persons Housing units
Greg Paddock, Community Health Director

Roblin: Roblin District Health Centre
PO Box 940, 15 Hospital St., Roblin, MB R0L 1P0
204-937-2142 Fax: 204-937-8892
rdhc@prha.mb.ca
www.prha.mb.ca
Parent: Parkland Regional Health Authority Inc.
Number of Beds: 25 bed hospital, 60 bed personal care home
Note: Emergency & diagnostic services, podiatry, speech therapy, physiotherapy, dietician. Number of employees: 125
Cheryl Jerome, COO

Roblin: Roblin District Health District
PO Box 940, Roblin, MB R0L 1P0
204-937-2142 Fax: 204-937-8892
Parent: Parkland Regional Health Authority Inc.
Note: The Roblin District Health Centre is comprised of a 25 bed hospitaland a 60 bed personal care home, with 125 staff and 3.5 full time physicians
Cheryl Jerome, COO

Rossburn: Rossburn District Health Centre
PO Box 40, Rossburn, MB R0J 1V0
204-859-2413 Fax: 204-859-2526
Parent: Assiniboine Regional Health Authority
Number of Beds: 10 acute care, 20 long-term care beds
Barb Kostesky, Area Manager

Shoal Lake: Shoal Lake-Strathclair Health Centre
PO Box 490, Shoal Lake, MB R0J 1Z0
204-759-2336 Fax: 204-759-2480
Parent: Assiniboine Regional Health Authority
Number of Beds: 12 acute care, 40 long-term care beds
Roseanne Yaremchuk, Community Health Director

Snow Lake: Snow Lake Health Centre
PO Box 453, Snow Lake, MB R0B 1M0
204-358-2597 Fax: 204-358-7310
Parent: Nor-Man Regional Health Authority Inc.
Number of Beds: 6 beds
Mae de Graff, Site Administrator

Souris: Souris Health District
PO Box 10, Souris, MB R0K 2C0
204-483-2121 Fax: 204-483-2310
Parent: Deloraine Health Centre
Number of Beds: 30 beds
Shirley Kloon, Manager

***St Pierre Jolys:* Centre Medico-Social De Salaberry District Health Centre**
PO Box 320, St Pierre Jolys, MB R0A 1V0
204-433-7611 Fax: 204-433-7455
Parent: South Eastman Health/Santé Sud-Est Inc.
Number of Beds: 14 beds
Note: acute care & emergency with personal care home
Elaine McPherson, Facility Manager

***Stonewall:* Stonewall & District Health Centre**
589 - 3rd Ave. South, Stonewall, MB R0C 2Z0
204-467-5514
Parent: Interlake Regional Health Authority Inc.
Number of Beds: 15 beds
Note: Specialties: Clinic services; Community health services; Emergency outpatient services
Keith Bytheway, District Services

***Thompson:* Burntwood Community Health Resource Centre**
50 Selkirk Avenue, Thompson, MB R8N 0M7
204-677-1777 Fax: 204-677-1755
smacdonald@brha.mb.ca
Parent: Burntwood Regional Health Authority Inc.
Shane MacDonald, Manager
204/677-1796, smacdonald@brha.mb.ca

***Treherne:* Tiger Hills Health District**
PO Box 130, Treherne, MB R0G 2V0
204-723-2133 Fax: 204-723-2869
Parent: Assiniboine Regional Health Authority
Number of Beds: 13 acute beds; 20 pch
Deb Obach, Area Manager

***Virden:* Virdin Health Centre**
PO Box 400, Virden, MB R0M 2C0
204-748-1230 Fax: 204-748-2053
mcarson@arha.ca
Parent: Assiniboine Regional Health Authority
Number of Beds: 25 acute; 100 long-term care
Meegan Carson, Manager

***Vita:* Vita & District Health Centre Inc.**
217 First Ave. West, Vita, MB R0A 2K0
204-425-7763 Fax: 204-425-3545
Parent: South Eastman Health/Santé Sud-Est Inc.
Number of Beds: 10 acute care, 44 long-term care beds
Note: with personal care home
Shawny Elyk Prevost, Facility Manager

***Wawanesa:* Wawanesa & District Memorial Health Centre**
PO Box 309, Wawanesa, MB R0K 2G0
204-824-2335 Fax: 204-824-2148
Parent: Assiniboine Regional Health Authority
Number of Beds: 6 acute beds; 20 pch
Deb Obach, Manager

***Whitemouth:* Whitemouth District Health Centre**
PO Box 160, Whitemouth, MB R0E 2G0
204-348-7191 Fax: 204-348-7911
Parent: North Eastman Health Association Inc.
Number of Beds: 24 beds, 1 palliative, 1 respite
Heather Frederick, Care Team Manager

***Winnipeg:* Aboriginal Health & Wellness Centre**
#214-215, 181 Higgins Ave., Winnipeg, MB R3B 3G1
204-925-3700 Fax: 204-925-3709 www.abcentre.org
Parent: Winnipeg Regional Health Authority
Darlene Hall, Executive Director

***Winnipeg:* Centre de santé Saint-Boniface**
#D-1048, 409, av Taché, Winnipeg, MB R2H 2A6
204-235-3910 Fax: 204-237-9057
access@centredesante.mb.ca
www.centredesante.mb.ca
Note: community health care office
Micheline St-Hilaire, Acting Executive Director

***Winnipeg:* Health Action Centre - Health Sciences Centre**
425 Elgin Ave., Winnipeg, MB R3A 1P2
204-940-1626 Fax: 204-942-7828
healthac@mb.sympatico.ca
Parent: Winnipeg Regional Health Authority
Note: community health care centre
Joan Dawkins, Community Area Director
Roy Becket, Manager of Administration
Kathryn Kisil, Medical Coordinator

***Winnipeg:* Hope Centre Health Care Inc.**
1644 Dublin Ave., Winnipeg, MB R3H 0X5
204-982-4673 Fax: 204-953-3510
admin@hopecentreinc.org
www.hopecentreinc.org
Parent: Winnipeg Regional Health Authority
Jeannette DeLong, Executive Director
jdelong@hopecentreinc.org

***Winnipeg:* Klinic Community Health Centre**
870 Portage Ave., Winnipeg, MB R3G 0P1
204-784-4090 Fax: 204-772-7998
klinic@klinic.mb.ca
www.klinic.mb.ca
Parent: Winnipeg Regional Health Authority
Note: community health centre & mental health facility
Lori Johnson, Executive Director

***Winnipeg:* MFL Occupational Health Centre, Inc.**
#102, 275 Broadway, Winnipeg, MB R3C 4M6
204-949-0811 Fax: 204-956-0848 888-843-1229 (i
mflohc@mflohc.mb.ca
www.mflohc.mb.ca
Parent: Winnipeg Regional Health Authority
Year Founded: 1983
Note: Specialties: Occupational health (health issues related to work experiences); Improvement of workplace health & safety conditions & elimination of hazards
Carol Loveridge, Executive Director

***Winnipeg:* Misericordia Health Centre**
99 Cornish Ave., Winnipeg, MB R3C 1A2
204-774-6581 Fax: 204-783-6052
info@miseri.winnipeg.mb.ca
www.misericordia.mb.ca
Parent: Winnipeg Regional Health Authority
Number of Beds: 250
Note: nursing home, outpatient services
Rosie Jacuzzi, President; CEO

***Winnipeg:* Mount Carmel Clinic**
886 Main St., Winnipeg, MB R2W 5L4
204-582-2311 Fax: 204-582-1341 www.mountcarmel.ca
Parent: Winnipeg Regional Health Authority
Brenda Slobozian, Executive Director

***Winnipeg:* Nine Circles Community Health Centre**
705 Broadway, Winnipeg, MB R3G 0X2
204-940-6000 Fax: 204-940-6027 888-305-8647
ninecircles@ninecircles.ca
www.ninecircles.ca
Parent: Winnipeg Regional Health Authority
Note: Non-profit centre specializing in STI/HIV prevention and care services
John C. Stinson, Executive Director

***Winnipeg:* Nor'west Cooperative Health & Social Service Centre Inc.**
#103, 61 Tyndall Ave., Winnipeg, MB R2X 2T4
204-633-5955 Fax: 204-633-4666
Parent: Winnipeg Regional Health Authority
Nancy Henrichs, Executive Director

***Winnipeg:* Women's Health Clinic Inc.**
419 Graham Ave., Unit A, Winnipeg, MB R3C 0M3
204-947-1517 Fax: 204-943-3844 www.womenshealthclinic.org
Parent: Winnipeg Regional Health Authority
Jennifer Howard, Executive Director
Carolyn Clarke, Nurse Practioner

***Winnipeg:* Youville Centre - Community Health Resource Centre**
33 Marion St., Winnipeg, MB R2H 0S8
204-233-0262 Fax: 204-233-1520 www.youville.ca
Sylvia Oosterveen, Executive Director

Nursing Stations

***Bloodvein:* Bloodvein Nursing Station**
General Delivery, Bloodvein, MB R0C 0J0
204-395-2161 Fax: 204-395-2087

***Brochet:* Brochet Nursing Station**
General Delivery, Brochet, MB R0B 0B0
204-323-2120 Fax: 204-323-2650

***Cross Lake:* Cross Lake Nursing Station**
General Delivery, Cross Lake, MB R0B 0J0
204-676-2011 Fax: 204-676-3179

***Easterville:* Easterville Nursing Station**
PO Box 122, Easterville, MB R0C 0V0
204-329-2212 Fax: 204-329-2337
Ethel McKay, Community Health Representative

***Fisher Branch:* Fisher Medical Facilities Inc.**
PO Box 370, Fisher Branch, MB R0C 0Z0
204-372-6228 Fax: 204-372-6207
Bev Fisher, Sec.-Treas.

***God's Narrows:* God's Lake Narrows Nursing Station**
General Delivery, God's Narrows, MB R0B 0M0
204-335-2557

***Gods River:* God's River Health Station**
General Delivery, Gods River, MB R0B 0N0
204-366-2355 Fax: 204-366-2474

***Grand Rapids:* Grand Rapids Nursing Station**
PO Box 53, Grand Rapids, MB R0C 1E0
204-639-2215 Fax: 204-639-2448

***Ilford:* Ilford Nursing Station**
General Delivery, Ilford, MB R0B 0S0
204-288-4348 Fax: 204-288-4360

***Island Lake:* Garden Hill Nursing Station**
General Delivery, Island Lake, MB R0B 0T0
204-456-2454 Fax: 204-456-2866

***Lac Brochet:* Lac Brochet Nursing Station**
General Delivery, Lac Brochet, MB R0B 2E0
204-337-2161 Fax: 204-337-2143

***Little Grand Rapids:* Little Grand Rapids Nursing Station**
General Delivery, Little Grand Rapids, MB R0B 0V0
204-397-2115 Fax: 204-397-2016
Note: Number of Employees: 1 community health worker

***Little Grand Rapids:* Pauingassi Nursing Station**
PO Box 32, Little Grand Rapids, MB R0B 2G0
204-397-2395 Fax: 204-397-2104

***Moose Lake:* Moose Lake Nursing Station**
General Delivery, Moose Lake, MB R0B 0Y0
204-678-2252 Fax: 204-678-2343

***Negginan:* Poplar River Nursing Station**
General Delivery, Negginan, MB R0B 0Z0
204-244-2102 Fax: 204-244-2001

***Oxford House:* Oxford House Nursing Station**
General Delivery, Oxford House, MB R0B 1C0
204-538-2347 Fax: 204-538-2445
Parent: Burntwood Regional Health Authority
Note: Specialties: Acute care; Public health programs. Number of Employees: 5 nurses + an administrative clerk + a maintenance person
Helen Weenusk, Secretary

***Pikwitonei:* Pikwitonei Health Centre**
General Delivery, Pikwitonei, MB R0B 1E0
204-288-4348 Fax: 204-458-2468 www.thompson.ca/dbs/brha
Parent: Burntwood Regional Health Authority Inc.
Marion Ellis, Director

***Pukatawagan:* Pukatawagan Nursing Station**
General Delivery, Pukatawagan, MB R0B 1G0
204-553-2271 Fax: 204-553-2402
Also Known As: Nikawiy Nursing Station
Note: Serving the Mathias Colomb Cree Nation

***Red Sucker Lake:* Red Sucker Lake Nursing Station**
General Delivery, Red Sucker Lake, MB R0B 1H0
204-469-5351 Fax: 204-469-5769
Note: Number of staff: 2 nurses, visiting physician, dentist, optometrist, pediatrician, & psychologist

***Shamattawa:* Shamattawa Nursing Station**
General Delivery, Shamattawa, MB R0B 1K0
204-565-2370 Fax: 204-565-2519

***South Indian Lake:* South Indian Lake Nursing Station**
General Delivery, South Indian Lake, MB R0B 1N0
204-374-2013 Fax: 204-374-2039

***Split Lake:* Split Lake Nursing Station**
General Delivery, Split Lake, MB R0B 1P0
204-342-2033 Fax: 204-342-2319

***St Theresa Point:* St Theresa Point Nursing Station**
General Delivery, St Theresa Point, MB R0B 1J0
204-462-2473 Fax: 204-462-2642
Richard Hopper, Clerk

***Thicket Portage:* Thicket Portage Health Centre**
PO Box 39, Thicket Portage, MB R0B 0L0
204-286-3254 Fax: 204-286-3216 www.thompson.ca/dbs/brha
Marion Ellis, Director

***Wabowden:* Wabowden Health Centre**
PO Box 160, General Delivery, Wabowden, MB R0B 1S0
204-689-2600 Fax: 204-689-2180
Marion Ellis, Director

***Wasagamack Bay:* Wasagamack Nursing Station**
General Delivery, Wasagamack Bay, MB R0B 1Z0
204-457-2024 Fax: 204-457-2348

***York Landing:* York Landing Nursing Station**
General Delivery, York Landing, MB R0B 2B0
204-341-2325 Fax: 204-341-2179

Special Treatment Centre

***Brandon:* Westman Crisis Centre**
Town Centre, B13 - 800 Rosser Avenue, Brandon, MB R7A 6N5
888-379-7699
Parent: Brandon Regional Health Authority
Number of Beds: 8 beds
Allison Done, Program Manager

***Reston:* Reston District Health Centre**
PO Box 250, Reston, MB R0M 1X0
204-877-3925 Fax: 204-877-3998
Parent: Assiniboine Regional Health Authority
Number of Beds: 13 beds
Meegan Carson

***Winnipeg:* CancerCare Manitoba**
675 McDermot Ave., Winnipeg, MB R3E 0V9
204-787-2241 Fax: 204-787-1184 www.cancercare.mb.ca
Note: cancer treatment, ambulatory care only
Dhali Dhaliwal, President; CEO
204/787-2241
Vivian Painter, Director of Nursing
204/787-4155

***Winnipeg:* Jane's Clinic**
883 Corydon Ave., Winnipeg, MB R3M 0W7
204-477-1887 Fax: 204-447-1888
Note: abortion clinic

***Winnipeg:* Manitoba Cardiac Institute (Reh-Fit Centre)**
1390 Taylor Ave., Winnipeg, MB R3M 3V8
204-488-8023 Fax: 204-488-4819
rehfit@reh-fit.com
www.reh-fit.com
Note: rehabilitation centre
Donald Fletcher, Executive Director
M. Grace, Director of Nursing
Al Coot, Maintenance Supervisor

***Winnipeg:* New Directions for Children, Youth, Adults & Families**
#400, 491 Portage Ave., Winnipeg, MB R3B 2E4
204-786-7051 Fax: 204-774-6468 www.newdirections.mb.ca
Old Name: Children's Home of Winnipeg
Note: 19 programs: residential, day & family support services
Elizabeth Adkins, Executive Director

Long Term/Retirement Care

Long Term Care Facility

***Arborg:* Riverdale Place Homes Inc.**
PO Box 968, Arborg, MB R0C 0A0
204-376-2940 Fax: 204-376-5051
riverdale@mts.net
Number of Beds: 19 beds
Note: Provides residential services to adults with intellectual disabilities.
K. Finnson, Executive Director

***Saint Malo:* Chalet Malouin Inc.**
14 Hilaire St., Saint Malo, MB R0A 1T0
204-347-5753 Fax: 204-347-5107
Number of Beds: 38 beds assisted living
Note: EPH & assisted living facility
Aline Sveinson, Administrator

***Swan River:* Association for Community Living - Swan River**
PO Box 1282, Swan River, MB R0L 1Z0
204-734-9114 Fax: 204-734-3704
Number of Beds: 17 beds
G. Mitchell, Services Coordinator

***Winnipeg:* L'Arche Winnipeg Inc.**
118 Regent Ave. East., Winnipeg, MB R2C 0C1
204-237-0300 Fax: 204-237-0316
office@larchewinnipeg.org
www.larchewinnipeg.org
Number of Beds: 28 beds
Note: group homes for persons with a developmental disability
Dennis Butcher, Executive Director

***Winnipeg:* Deer Lodge Centre**
2109 Portage Ave., Winnipeg, MB R3J 0L3
204-837-1301
info@deerlodge.mb.ca
(www.deerlodge.mb.ca
Parent: Winnipeg Regional Health Authority
Number of Beds: 487 beds, including 155 personal care beds for veterans
Note: Specialties: Rehabilitation services, including physiotherapy, occupational therapy, respiratory therapy, & therapeutic recreation services; Speech-language pathology; Services for ALS patients; Peritoneal dialysis; Operational Stress Injuries Clinic; Movement Disorders Clinic; Audiological services; Assistive technology products & services; Outreach programs in geriatric mental health; Social work; Day hospital & adult day care for cognitively impaired clients; Long term care; Geriatric research
Réal Cloutier, Chief Operating Officer; Winnipeg Regional Health, Long Term Care
204-831-2110, rcloutier@deerlodge.mb.ca
Ed
Courcelles, Chief Financial Officer,
ecourcelles@deerlodge.mb.ca
204-831-2116
Jo-Ann LaPointe-McKenzie, Chief Nursing Officer
204-831-2529, JlapointeMcKenzie@deerlodge.mb.ca
David Strang, Chief Medical Officer
204-831-2920, dstrang@deerlodge.mb.ca
Janet Clark, Director, Allied Health Services
204-831-2570, jeclark@deerlodge.mb.ca
Cheryl
LeBlue, Director, Human Resources
204-831-2103, cleblue@deerlodge.mb.ca
Sylvia
Ptashnik, Director, Resident Services
204-831-2108, sptashnik@deerlodge.mb.ca

***Winnipeg:* Parkview Place**
440 Edmonton St., Winnipeg, MB R3B 2M4
204-942-5291 Fax: 204-947-1969
parkviewplace@reveraliving.com
www.reveralving.com
Number of Beds: 277 beds
Donald M. Solar, Administrator
Noel Gray, Director of Nursing

***Winnipeg:* Poseidon Care Centre**
70 Poseidon Bay, Winnipeg, MB R3M 3E5
204-452-6204 Fax: 204-474-2173
poseidon@reveraliving.com
www.reveraliving.com
Number of Beds: 218 beds
Marg Fisher, Administrator

***Winnipeg:* St. Amant Inc.**
440 River Rd., Winnipeg, MB R2M 3Z9
204-256-4301 Fax: 204-257-4349
inquiries@stamant.mb.ca
www.stamant.mb.ca
Parent: Winnipeg Regional Health Authority
Number of Beds: 216 beds
Note: Developmental disability resource centre
Carl Stephens, President; CEO

***Winnipeg:* The Wellington**
3161 Grant Ave., Winnipeg, MB R3R 3R1
204-831-0788 Fax: 204-896-0576
thewellington@lrc.ca
www.reveraliving.com
Number of Beds: 117 suites
Note: Independent living
Warren Stephenson, Executive Director

Retirement Residences

***Winnipeg:* Metropolitan Kiwanis Courts**
2300 Ness Ave., Winnipeg, MB R3J 1A2
204-885-7700 Fax: 204-831-1022
shunter@kiwaniscourts.ca
Year Founded: 2000
Note: Specialties: Assisted living
Heather Ritchie, Exec. Dir.

Personal Care Homes

***Arborg:* Arborg Pioneer Health**
PO Box 10, Arborg, MB R0C 0A0
204-376-5226 Fax: 204-376-5669
Old Name: Pioneer Health Services Inc
Parent: Interlake Regional Health Authority
Number of Beds: 40 beds
Ruby Tretiak, District Director
C. Cherepak, Head Nurse

***Ashern:* Ashern Personal Care Home**
PO Box 110, Ashern, MB R0C 0E0
204-768-2461 Fax: 204-768-2337
Parent: Interlake Regional Health Authority
Number of Beds: 20 beds
Jan O'Flanagan, District Director

***Baldur:* Baldur Manor Inc.**
PO Box 128, Baldur, MB R0K 0B0
204-535-2456 Fax: 204-535-2116
Parent: Assiniboine Regional Health Authority
Number of Beds: 20 beds
Bev Towler

***Beausejour:* East-Gate Lodge**
PO Box 1690, 646 James Ave., Beausejour, MB R0E 0C0
204-268-1029 Fax: 204-268-3525
Parent: North Eastman Health Association Inc.
Number of Beds: 80 beds
Mary Ann Austman, Care Team Manager

***Benito:* Benito Health Centre Personal Care Home**
PO Box 490, Benito, MB R0L 0C0
204-539-2815 Fax: 204-539-2482
Parent: Parkland Regional Health Authority
Number of Beds: 20 beds

***Birtle:* Birtle Personal Care Home**
PO Box 10, Birtle, MB R0M 0C0
204-842-3323 Fax: 204-842-3375
Number of Beds: 20 beds
Gerry Berry, Director

***Boissevain:* Evergreen Place**
PO Box 899, Boissevain, MB R0K 0E0
204-534-2451 Fax: 204-534-6487
Parent: Assiniboine Regional Health Authority
Number of Beds: 20 beds
Marilyn McGregor, Area Manager

***Boissevain:* Westview Lodge**
200 Student Street, Boissevain, MB R0K 0E0
204-534-2455 Fax: 204-534-6633
Parent: Assiniboine Regional Health Authority
Number of Beds: 42 beds

***Brandon:* Dinsdale Personal Care Home**
510 - 6th St., Brandon, MB R7A 3N9
204-727-3636 Fax: 204-727-2103
Parent: Brandon Regional Health Authority
Number of Beds: 60 beds
Wilson Perrin, Administrator

***Brandon:* Fairview Home**
1351 - 13th St., Brandon, MB R7A 4S5
204-728-6696 Fax: 204-727-7616
Parent: Brandon Regional Health Authority
Number of Beds: 248 beds
Trudy Curtis, Coordinator, Resident Services

***Brandon:* Hillcrest Place**
930 - 26th St., Brandon, MB R7B 2B8
204-728-6690 Fax: 204-726-0089
Parent: Brandon Regional Health Authority
Number of Beds: 100 beds
Kathy Traill, Administrator

***Brandon:* Rideau Park Personal Care Home**
525 Victoria Ave. East, Brandon, MB R7A 6S9
204-727-1734 Fax: 204-726-6690 www.brandonrha.mb.ca
Parent: Brandon Regional Health Authority
Number of Beds: 98 beds
Cheryl Bourdeau d'Hui, Coordinator, Resident Services

***Carberry:* Carberry Personal Care Home**
Bag Service #1, Carberry, MB R0K 0H0
204-834-2144 Fax: 204-834-3333
Number of Beds: 36 beds

***Carman:* Boyne Lodge Personal Care Home**
120 - 4th Ave. SW, Carman, MB R0G 0J0
204-745-6715 Fax: 204-745-6152
Parent: Central Regional Health Authority
Number of Beds: 70 long-term care beds
Janet Wigley, Facility Contact
j.wigley@bvl.rha-central.mb.ca

***Dauphin:* Dauphin Personal Care Home Inc.**
625 Third St. SW, Dauphin, MB R7N 1R7
204-638-3010 Fax: 204-638-2199
Parent: Parkland Regional Health Authority
Number of Beds: 90 beds
Melodie Powell, Site Manager

***Dauphin:* St. Paul's Home**
703 Jackson St., Dauphin, MB R7N 2N2
204-638-3129 Fax: 204-638-9294
Parent: Parkland Regional Health Authority
Number of Beds: 70 beds
G. Karpinka, Administrator

***Deloraine:* Bren-Del-Win Lodge**
103 Kellet St. South, Deloraine, MB R0M 0M0
204-747-2119 Fax: 204-747-2160
Parent: Assiniboine Regional Health Authority
Number of Beds: 30 beds
Miriam Nichol, Community Health Manager

***Elkhorn:* Elkwood Manor Personal Care Home**
PO Box 70, Elkhorn, MB R0M 0N0
204-845-2575 Fax: 204-845-2371
Parent: Assiniboine Regional Health Authority
Number of Beds: 24 beds
Meegan Carson, Manager

***Emerson:* Emerson Personal Care Home**
PO Box 428, 26 Main St., Emerson, MB R0A 0L0
204-373-2109 Fax: 204-373-2748
Number of Beds: 20 beds
Paulette Goossen, Nurse Manager

***Erickson:* Erickson Personal Care Home**
60 Queen E Rd., Erickson, MB R0J 0P0
204-636-7777
Number of Beds: 16 beds

***Eriksdale:* Eriksdale Personal Care Home**
PO Box 130, 40 Railway Ave., Eriksdale, MB R0C 0W0
204-739-2611 Fax: 204-739-2065
Parent: Interlake Regional Health Authority Inc.
Number of Beds: 20 beds
Patty Johnson, District Director
Helen Melville, Director of Nursing

***Fisher Branch:* Fisher Personal Care Home**
PO Box 119, Fisher Branch, MB R0C 0Z0
204-372-8703 Fax: 204-372-8710
Parent: Interlake Regional Health Authority Inc.
Number of Beds: 30 beds
Ruby Tretiak, District Director

***Flin Flon:* Flin Flon Personal Care Corporation**
PO Box 340, Flin Flon, MB R8A 1N2
204-687-9630 Fax: 204-687-8494
Parent: Nor-Man Regional Health Authority Inc.
Number of Beds: 30 beds

***Flin Flon:* Northern Lights Manor**
PO Box 14, 274 Bracken St., Flin Flon, MB R8A 1P4
204-687-7325 Fax: 204-687-8494
Parent: Nor-Man Regional Health Authority Inc.
Number of Beds: 36 beds
Note: Personal care home
Shauna Cupples, Unit Manager

***Gilbert Plains:* Gilbert Plains Health Centre**
PO Box 368, Gilbert Plains, MB R0L 0X0
204-548-2161 Fax: 204-548-2516
gphc@mb.sympatico.ca
Parent: Parkland Regional Health Authority Inc.
Number of Beds: 30 beds
Joan Gryba, Site Manager

***Gimli:* Betel Home Foundation**
PO Box 10, Gimli, MB R0C 1B0
204-642-5004 Fax: 204-642-7243 www.betelhomefoundation.ca
Parent: Interlake Regional Health Authority Inc.
Number of Beds: 80 beds
Brenna Raemer, Executive Director

***Gladstone:* Third Crossing Manor**
PO Box 1000, 24 Mill St., Gladstone, MB R0J 0T0
204-385-2474 Fax: 204-385-2163 www.rha-central.mb.ca
Parent: Regional Health Authority - Central Manitoba Inc.
Year Founded: 1974
Number of Beds: 50 residential capacity
Shirley Guenther, Facility Contact
s.guenther@tcm.rha-central.mb.ca

***Glenboro:* Glenboro Personal Care Home Inc.**
PO Box 310, Glenboro, MB R0K 0X0
204-827-2268 Fax: 204-827-2199
Parent: Assiniboine Regional Health Authority
Number of Beds: 20 beds
Marilyn McGregor

***Grandview:* Grandview Personal Care Home Inc.**
PO Box 130, 308 Jackson St., Grandview, MB R0L 0Y0
204-546-2769 Fax: 204-546-2207
Parent: Parkland Regional Health Authority Inc.
Number of Beds: 39 beds
John Kelly, COO

***Grunthal:* Menno Home for the Aged**
235 Park St., Grunthal, MB R0A 0R0
204-434-6496 www.sehealth.mb.ca
Parent: South Eastman Health / Santé Sud-Est Inc.
Year Founded: 1960
Number of Beds: 40 beds
Ken Knaggs, Administrator

***Hamiota:* Hamiota Personal Care Home**
177 Birch Ave., Hamiota, MB R0M 0T0
204-764-2011 Fax: 204-764-2049
mandrew@mrha.mb.ca
Number of Beds: 30 beds
Marlene Andrew, Area Manager

***Killarney:* Bayside Personal Care Home Inc.**
PO Box 400, Killarney, MB R0K 1G0
204-523-4661 Fax: 204-523-8948
Parent: Assiniboine Regional Health Authority
Number of Beds: 60 beds
L. Blixhavn, Head Nurse

***Lac du Bonnet:* Lac du Bonnet Personal Care Home**
PO Box 1030, Lac du Bonnet, MB R0E 1A0
204-345-8675 Fax: 204-345-9245
Parent: North Eastman Health Association Inc.
Number of Beds: 30 beds
Merle Fischer, Care Team Manager

***Lundar:* Lundar Personal Care Home**
97 - 1st St. South, Lundar, MB R0C 1Y0
204-762-5663
Parent: Interlake Regional Health Authority Inc.
Number of Beds: 20 beds
Patty Johnson, District Director
Patty Johnson, Director of Nursing

***MacGregor:* MacGregor Personal Care Home**
PO Box 250, 87 Grafton St. South, MacGregor, MB R0H 0R0
204-685-2850 Fax: 204-685-2529
Parent: Regional Health Authority - Central Manitoba Inc.
Number of Beds: 20 beds
Garry Mattin, Executive Director

***McCreary:* McCreary/Alonsa Personal Care Home Inc.**
PO Box 250, McCreary, MB R0J 1B0
204-835-2482 Fax: 204-835-2713
Parent: Parkland Regional Health Authority Inc.
Number of Beds: 20 beds
Charlie Sitwell, Administrator

***Melita:* Melita & Area Personal Care Home**
147 Summit St., Melita, MB R0M 1L0
204-522-3403
Parent: Assiniboine Regional Health Authority
Number of Beds: 20 beds
Note: Specialties: Long-term care; Respite care
Georgina Henuset

***Morden:* Tabor Home Inc.**
230 - 9th St. South, Morden, MB R6M 1Y3
204-822-4848 Fax: 204-822-5289
info@taborhome.ca
www.taborhome.ca
Parent: Regional Health Authority - Central Manitoba Inc.
Year Founded: 1951
Number of Beds: 60 residential capacity
Note: Specialties: Nursing services for persons who require long-term care; Activity program; Social work; Alternative needs area, for residents who experience difficulties in the areas of thought, memory, & perception; Adult day program
Sherry Hildebrand, Facility Director
s.hildebrand@taborhome.ca

***Morris:* Red River Valley Lodge Inc.**
PO Box 507, 136 Ottawa St. West, Morris, MB R0G 1K0
204-746-2394 Fax: 204-746-2123
Parent: Regional Health Authority - Central Manitoba Inc.
Number of Beds: 40 long-term care beds
Clara Wiebe, Facility Contact
c.wiebe@rrvl.rha-central.mb.ca

***Neepawa:* East View Lodge**
PO Box 1240, Neepawa, MB R0J 1H0
204-476-2383 Fax: 204-476-3645
Parent: Assiniboine Regional Health Authority
Number of Beds: 124 beds
Judy Gabler, Area Manager

***Nelson House:* Nisichawaysihk Personal Care Home**
PO Box 460, Nelson House, MB R0B 1A0
204-484-2350 Fax: 204-484-2011
Number of Beds: 24 beds

***Norway House:* Pinaow Wachi Inc. Personal Care Home**
PO Box 98, Norway House, MB R0B 1B0
204-359-6606 Fax: 204-359-6949
Number of Beds: 26 beds
B. Rowden, Administrator

***Notre Dame de Lourdes:* Foyer Notre Dame Inc.**
PO Box 190, 40 Rodgers St., Notre Dame de Lourdes, MB R0G 1M0
204-248-2092 Fax: 204-248-2499
Parent: Regional Health Authority - Central Manitoba Inc.
Number of Beds: 60 long-term care beds
Marcie Dupasquier, Facility Contact
m.dupasquier@fnd.rha-central.mb.ca

***Oakbank:* Kin Place**
PO Box 28, Oakbank, MB R0E 1J0
204-444-6128 Fax: 204-444-7868
Parent: North Eastman Health Association Inc.
Number of Beds: 40 beds
Liz Hogue, Care Team Manager

***Pilot Mound:* Prairie View Lodge**
#26, 424 Broadway Ave. West, Pilot Mound, MB R0G 1P0
204-825-2717 Fax: 204-825-2267
Parent: Regional Health Authority - Central Manitoba Inc.
Number of Beds: 30 long-term care beds (24 EPH units)
Pam King, Health Services Leader
p.king@rlh.rha-central.mb.ca

***Pilot Mound:* Rock Lake Personal Care Home Inc.**
#27, 115 Brown St. South, Pilot Mound, MB R0G 1P0
204-825-2246 Fax: 204-825-2267
rlhd@mts.net
Parent: Regional Health Authority - Central Manitoba Inc.
Number of Beds: 24 long-term care beds
Pam King, Health Services Leader
p.king@rlh.rha-central.mb.ca

***Pine Falls:* Sunnywood Personal Care Home**
PO Box 2000, Spruce St., Pine Falls, MB R0E 1M0
204-367-8201 www.neha.mb.ca
Parent: North Eastman Health Association Inc.
Number of Beds: 20 beds
Note: Specialties: Nursing care; Recreation services; Occupational therapy; Physiotherapy; Podiatry; Mental health services; Respite care
Lorraine Dent-Prychun, Director of Long Term Care

***Portage la Prairie:* Douglas Campbell Lodge**
150 - 9 St. SE, Portage la Prairie, MB R1N 3T6
204-239-6006 Fax: 204-239-0055
Parent: Regional Health Authority - Central Manitoba Inc.
Number of Beds: 60 long-term care beds
Colleen Fletcher, Facility Contact
c.fletcher@dcl.rha-central.mb.ca

***Portage la Prairie:* Lions Prairie Manor**
24 - 9th St. SE, Portage la Prairie, MB R1N 3V4
204-857-7864 Fax: 204-857-8207
Parent: Regional Health Authority - Central Manitoba Inc.
Number of Beds: 150 beds
Cathy Asham, Facility Contact

***Reston:* Willowview Home**
PO Box 250, Reston, MB R0M 1X0
204-877-3921 Fax: 204-877-3998
Parent: Assiniboine Regional Health Authority
Number of Beds: 20 beds
Meegan Carson

***Roblin:* Crocus Court Personal Care Home**
PO Box 940, 15 Hospital St., Roblin, MB R0L 1P0
204-937-2142 Fax: 204-937-8892
Number of Beds: 60 beds
C. Jerome, Site Manager

***Rossburn:* Rossburn Personal Care Home Inc.**
PO Box 40, Rossburn, MB R0J 1V0
204-859-2413 Fax: 204-859-2526
Number of Beds: 20 beds

Russell: **Russell & District Personal Care Home Inc.**
PO Box 400, Russell, MB R0J 1W0
204-773-3117 Fax: 204-773-2232
Parent: Assiniboine Regional Health Authority
Number of Beds: 40 beds
Barb Kostesky, Area Manager

Sandy Lake: **Sandy Lake Medical Nursing Home Inc.**
PO Box 7, Sandy Lake, MB R0J 1X0
204-585-2107 Fax: 204-585-5352
gkowaluk@arha.ca
Parent: Assiniboine Regional Health Authority
Number of Beds: 36 beds
Barb Kostesky, Area Manager

Selkirk: **Betel Personal Care Home, Selkirk**
212 Manchester Ave., Selkirk, MB R1A 0B6
204-482-4171 Fax: 204-482-4651
www.betelhomefoundation.ca/selkirk.html
Parent: Interlake Regional Health Authority Inc.
Number of Beds: 92 beds
Brenna Raemer, Administrator
B. Armstrong, Plant Manager

Selkirk: **Red River Place**
133 Manchester Ave., Selkirk, MB R1A 0B5
204-482-3036 Fax: 204-482-9499
mgd_redriverplace@extendicare.com
www.ltcam.mb.ca
Parent: Interlake Regional Health Authority Inc.
Number of Beds: 104 beds
Note: Personal care facility, member of the Long Term Care Association of Manitoba
M.S. Fages, Executive Director
J. Chennell, Director of Nursing

Selkirk: **Tudor House Personal Care Home**
800 Manitoba Ave., Selkirk, MB R3C 2C9
204-482-6601 Fax: 204-482-4369
tudor@geriatricare.ca
www.geriatricare.ca/tudorhouse
Parent: Interlake Regional Health Authority Inc.
Year Founded: 1971
Number of Beds: 76 beds
Note: Specialties: Care for seniors, physically & mentally handicapped adults, & persons with dementia; Hospice-type care for the dying
Ashley Martyniw, CEO/Administrator

Souris: **Souris District Personal Care Home**
PO Box 10, Souris, MB R0L 2C0
204-483-2730 Fax: 204-483-2310
Parent: Assiniboine Regional Health Authority
Number of Beds: 43 beds
Marilyn McGregor

St Adolphe: **St. Adolphe Personal Care Home**
PO Box 40, St Adolphe, MB R5A 1A1
204-883-2181 Fax: 204-883-2394
stadolphepch@mts.net
Parent: South Eastman Health/Santé Sud-Est Inc.
Number of Beds: 42 beds
Robert Brosseau, Administrator

St Pierre Jolys: **Repos Jolys**
PO Box 320, St Pierre Jolys, MB R0A 1V0
204-433-7611 Fax: 204-433-7455
Parent: South Eastman Health/Santé Sud-Est Inc.
Year Founded: 1995
Number of Beds: 22 beds
Note: this personal care home is justaposed to Centre Medico-Spcial De Salaberry District Health Centre
Elaine McPherson, Facility Manager

Ste Anne: **Villa Youville Inc.**
208 Central Ave., Ste Anne, MB R0A 1R0
204-422-5624 Fax: 204-422-5842
Parent: South Eastman Health/Santé Sud-Est Inc.
Number of Beds: 66 beds
Claude Lachance, Executive Director
Noel Deslauriers, Coordinator, Environmental Services

Ste Rose du Lac: **Dr. Gendreau Memorial Personal Care Home Inc.**
PO Box 420, Ste Rose du Lac, MB R0L 1S0
204-447-2019 Fax: 204-447-2267
Parent: Parkland Regional Health Authority Inc.
Number of Beds: 65 beds
Glen Kozak, Administrator

Steinbach: **Rest Haven Care Services**
185 Woodhaven Ave., Steinbach, MB R5G 1K7
204-326-2206 Fax: 204-326-3521
Parent: South Eastman Health/Santé Sud-Est Inc.
Number of Beds: 60 long-term care beds
Note: Owned and operated by seven area Evangelical Mennonite Conference churches
Marlin J. Roth, CEO

Stonewall: **Rosewood Lodge**
436 - 1 Ave. North, Stonewall, MB R0C 2Z0
204-467-5257 Fax: 204-467-4763
knattrass@irha.mb.ca
www.irha.mb.ca
Parent: Interlake Regional Health Authority Inc.
Number of Beds: 50 beds
Note: Personal care home
Keith Bytheway, South West District Director

Swan River: **Swan River Valley Lodge (1991) Inc.**
1013 Main St., Swan River, MB R0L 1Z0
204-734-3441 Fax: 204-734-9081 www.svhf.mb.ca
Parent: Parkland Regional Health Authority Inc.
Number of Beds: 70 beds
Note: Number of staff: 7 Registered Nurses, 41 other staff
Mary Ellen Parsons, Clinical Services Manager
204-734-3441, mparsons@prha.mb.ca

Swan River: **Swan River Valley Personal Care Home Inc.**
334 - 8 Ave. South, Swan River, MB R0L 1Z0
204-734-4521 Fax: 204-734-9965 www.svhf.mb.ca
Parent: Parkland Regional Health Authority Inc.
Number of Beds: 60 beds
Note: Personal care home. Number of staff: 8 Registered Nurses, 31 Nurses' Aides, 5 other staff
Michelle Vandepoele, Nurse Manager
mvandepoele@prha.mb.ca

Teulon: **Goodwin Lodge**
PO Box 89, 3rd Ave. SE, Teulon, MB R0C 3B0
204-886-2433 Fax: 204-886-2653
Parent: Interlake Regional Health Authority Inc.
Number of Beds: 20 beds
Keith Bytheway, District Director

The Pas: **St. Paul's Personal Care Home**
PO Box 240, The Pas, MB R9A 1K4
204-623-9226
Old Name: St. Paul's Residence
Number of Beds: 60 beds
Shauna Cupples, Regional Manager

Thompson: **Cambridge Residence**
PO Box 81, 65 McGill, Thompson, MB R8N 1M9
204-778-7582
Number of Beds: 8 beds
Johanna Fudge, Manager

Treherne: **Tiger Hills Manor Inc.**
PO Box 130, Treherne, MB R0G 2V0
204-723-2023 www.assiniboine-rha.ca
Parent: Assiniboine Regional Health Authority
Number of Beds: 22 beds
Note: Specialties: Long-term care
Deb Obach

Virden: **Sherwood Nursing Home**
223 Hargrave St. East, Virden, MB R0M 2C0
204-748-1546 www.assiniboine-rha.ca
Parent: Assiniboine Regional Health Authority
Number of Beds: 50 beds
Note: Specialties: Long-term personal care; Respite care
Meegan Carson, Area Manager

Virden: **West Man Nursing Home Inc.**
PO Box 1630, 427 Frame St. E, Virden, MB R0M 2C0
204-748-1230 Fax: 204-748-3432
mcarson@arha.ca
Parent: Assiniboine Regional Health Authority
Number of Beds: 50 beds
Meegan Carson

Wawanesa: **Wawanesa Personal Care Home Inc.**
PO Box 309, Wawanesa, MB R0K 2G0
204-824-2335 Fax: 204-824-2148
Parent: Assiniboine Regional Health Authority
Number of Beds: 20 beds
Deb Obach, Area Manager

Whitemouth: **Whitemouth District Health Centre Personal Care Home**
PO Box 160, Whitemouth, MB R0E 2G0
204-348-7191 Fax: 204-348-7911
Parent: North Eastman Health Association Inc.
Number of Beds: 24 PCH beds
Heather Frederick, Care Team Manager

Winkler: **Salem Home Inc.**
165 - 15 St., Winkler, MB R6W 1T8
204-325-4316 Fax: 204-325-5442
salem@salemhome.net
www.salemhome.net
Parent: Regional Health Authority - Central Manitoba Inc.
Number of Beds: 145 long-term care beds
Note: Personal care home owned and operated by 14 Mennonite churches
Sherry Janzen, Facility Contact
s.janzen@salemhome.net

Winnipeg: **Beacon Hill Lodge**
190 Fort St., Winnipeg, MB R3C 1C9
204-942-7541 Fax: 204-944-0136
Parent: Winnipeg Regional Health Authority
Number of Beds: 175 beds
Shelley Gurvey, Administrator

Winnipeg: **Bethania Mennonite Personal Care Home Inc.**
1045 Concordia Ave., Winnipeg, MB R2K 3S7
204-667-0795 Fax: 204-667-7078
Parent: Winnipeg Regional Health Authority
Number of Beds: 148 beds
Anita Kampen, Executive Director

Winnipeg: **Calvary Place Personal Care Home**
1325 Erin St., Winnipeg, MB R3E 3R6
204-943-4424 Fax: 204-783-7524
Parent: Winnipeg Regional Health Authority
Number of Beds: 100 beds
Dale Berry

Winnipeg: **Charleswood Care Centre**
5501 Roblin Blvd., Winnipeg, MB R3R 0G8
204-888-3363 Fax: 204-896-4763
Parent: Winnipeg Regional Health Authority
Number of Beds: 155 beds

Winnipeg: **Concordia Place Personal Care Home**
1000 Molson St., Winnipeg, MB R2K 4L5
204-661-7372 Fax: 204-661-7297
Number of Beds: 140 beds
Les Janzen, COO

Winnipeg: **Convalescent Home of Winnipeg**
276 Hugo St. North, Winnipeg, MB R3M 2N6
204-453-4663 Fax: 204-453-7149 www.wrha.mb.ca
Parent: Winnipeg Regional Health Authority
Number of Beds: 84 residents
Note: Specialty: Long-term care
A.L. (Tony) Fraser, Executive Director
Rhonda Crane, Director of Nursing

Winnipeg: **Deaf Centre Manitoba**
#101, 285 Pembina Hwy., Winnipeg, MB R3L 2E1
204-284-0802 Fax: 204-284-9373
Number of Beds: 57 beds
Doug Momotiuk, Exec. Dir.

Winnipeg: **Donwood Manor Personal Care Home**
171 Donwood Dr., Winnipeg, MB R2G 0V9
204-668-4410 Fax: 204-663-5429
jheinrichs@donwoodmanor.org
www.donwoodmanor.org
Parent: Winnipeg Regional Health Authority
Number of Beds: 121 beds
James Heinrichs, Executive Director

Winnipeg: **Extendicare - Oakview Place**
2395 Ness Ave., Winnipeg, MB R3J 1A5
204-888-3005 Fax: 204-831-8101
cnh_oakviewplace@extendicare.com
www.extendicarecanada.com
Parent: Winnipeg Regional Health Authority
Number of Beds: 245 beds
Note: Specialties: Nursing & supportive care; Rehabilitation & rehabilitative services; Optometry services; Dental services; Social & therapeutic programs; Adult day program; Care for persons with Alzheimer's disease and related dementias; Palliative care
Terry Vanbocquestal, Administrator
Carol Rowley, Director of Care

Winnipeg: **Extendicare - Tuxedo Villa**
2060 Corydon Ave., Winnipeg, MB R3P 0N3
204-889-2650 Fax: 204-896-0258
cnh_tuxedovilla@extendicare.com
www.extendicarecanada.com
Parent: Winnipeg Regional Health Authority
Number of Beds: 213 beds
Note: Specialties: Professional nursing & supportive care; Rehabilitation services; Care for persons with Alzheimer's

disease & related dementias; Optometry services; Social & therapeutic programs
Ronald Parent, Administrator

Winnipeg: Fort Garry Care Centre Ltd.
1776 Pembina Hwy., Winnipeg, MB R3T 2G2
204-269-6939 Fax: 204-275-2192
Parent: Winnipeg Regional Health Authority
Number of Beds: 64 beds
Gerald Kalef, Executive Director
Germain Sicotte, Maintenance Manager

Winnipeg: Foyer Valade Inc.
450 River Rd., Winnipeg, MB R2M 5M4
204-254-3332 Fax: 204-254-0329
Parent: Winnipeg Regional Health Authority
Number of Beds: 115 beds
Francis LaBossière, Executive Director
C. Dupuis, Environmental Services

Winnipeg: Fred Douglas Society Inc.
1275 Burrows Ave., Winnipeg, MB R2X 0B8
204-586-8541 Fax: 204-589-0110 www.freddouglassociety.com
Old Name: Fred Douglas Lodge
Parent: Winnipeg Regional Health Authority
Number of Beds: 136 beds
Theresa Jachnycky, Chief Executive Officer
Marilyn Allan, Director of Resident Care

Winnipeg: Golden Door Geriatric Centre
1679 Pembina Hwy., Winnipeg, MB R3T 2G6
204-269-6308 Fax: 204-275-3185
Parent: Winnipeg Regional Health Authority
Number of Beds: 78 beds
Lorrie LeBlanc, Administrator
Mary P. Entwistle, Director, Nursing

Winnipeg: Golden Links Lodge
PO Box 248, 2280 St. Mary's Rd., Winnipeg, MB R2M 4A5
204-257-9947 Fax: 204-257-2405
Parent: Winnipeg Regional Health Authority
Number of Beds: 88 beds
Dorene Rosmus, Administrator

Winnipeg: Golden West Centennial Lodge
811 School Rd., Winnipeg, MB R2Y 0S8
204-888-3311 Fax: 204-831-0544
Parent: Winnipeg Regional Health Authority
Number of Beds: 116 beds
Don Maye, Executive Director

Winnipeg: Heritage Lodge Personal Care Home
3555 Portage Ave., Winnipeg, MB R3K 0X2
204-888-7940 Fax: 204-832-6544
heritagelodge@reveraliving.com
www.retirementresidencesreit.com/homes/82/
Old Name: Heritage Lodge Personal Care Home Inc
Number of Beds: 86 beds
Kim Hykawy, Administrator
Mary Baranski, Assistant Director of Nursing
Len Falco, Maintenance Supervisor

Winnipeg: Holy Family Nursing Home
165 Aberdeen Ave., Winnipeg, MB R2W 1T9
204-589-7381 Fax: 204-589-8605
Number of Beds: 276 beds
Jean Piche, Executive Director
Mike Ostryniuk, Plant Supt.

Winnipeg: Kildonan Personal Care Centre Inc.
1970 Henderson Hwy., Winnipeg, MB R2G 1P2
204-334-4633 Fax: 204-334-4632
kildonan@reveraliving.com
Number of Beds: 120 beds
Edward Bird, Administrator

Winnipeg: Lions Personal Care Centre
320 Sherbrook St., Winnipeg, MB R3B 2W6
204-784-1240 Fax: 204-784-2723
Parent: Winnipeg Regional Health Authority
Number of Beds: 116 rooms
Helmut Epp, CEO

Winnipeg: Luther Home
1081 Andrews St., Winnipeg, MB R2V 2G9
204-338-4641 Fax: 204-338-4643
info@lutherhome.mb.ca
www.lutherhome.com
Parent: Winnipeg Regional Health Authority
Year Founded: 1969
Number of Beds: 80 personal care home beds, including a respite bed
Note: Specialties: Physio, occupational, massage, & music therapy; Foot care;
Ray Koop, Director of Care

Winnipeg: Maples Personal Care Home
500 Mandalay Dr., Winnipeg, MB R2P 1V4
204-632-8570 Fax: 204-697-0249
Parent: Winnipeg Regional Health Authority
Number of Beds: 200 beds
Linda Norton, Administrator
Nancy Coey, Director, Nursing

Winnipeg: Meadowood Manor
577 St. Anne's Rd., Winnipeg, MB R2M 5B2
204-257-2394
info@meadowood.ca
www.meadowood.ca
Parent: Winnipeg Regional Health Authority
Number of Beds: 88 beds
Note: Specialties: Long-term care; Rehabilitation services; Foot care services; Social work; Recreation programs; Respite care; Palliative care
Charles Kunze, Administrator
E. Verplaetse, Director of Resident Services

Winnipeg: Middlechurch Home of Winnipeg Inc.
280 Balderstone Ave., Winnipeg, MB R4A 4A6
204-339-1947 Fax: 204-338-3498
www.middlechurchhome.mb.ca
Parent: Winnipeg Regional Health Authority
Year Founded: 1884
Number of Beds: 197 beds
Note: Specialties: Care of older people; Activity centre; Physiotherapy; Occupational therapy; Pet therapy; Adult day program; Respite care. Number of employees: 320
Heather Temple, Executive Director

Winnipeg: Park Manor Personal Care Home Inc.
301 Redonda St., Winnipeg, MB R2C 1L7
204-222-3251 Fax: 204-222-3237 www.parkmanor.ca
Parent: Winnipeg Regional Health Authority
Number of Beds: 44 private rooms + 20 semi-private rooms + 4 four-bed rooms
Note: Specialties: Therapeutic recreation; Education sessions for residents & families; Adult day program; Palliative care
Charles L. Toop, Executive Director
Robert Ivany, Director, Nursing
B. Gmiterek, Maintenance Director

Winnipeg: Pembina Place Mennonite Personal Care Home
285 Pembina Hwy., Winnipeg, MB R3L 2E1
204-284-0802 Fax: 204-474-0073
Parent: Winnipeg Regional Health Authority
Number of Beds: 57 beds

Winnipeg: River East Personal Care Home Ltd.
1375 Molson St., Winnipeg, MB R2K 4K8
204-668-7460 Fax: 204-668-7459
Parent: Winnipeg Regional Health Authority
Number of Beds: 120 beds
Virginia Zazula, Administrator

Winnipeg: St. Joseph's Residence Inc.
1149 Leila Ave., Winnipeg, MB R2P 1S6
204-697-8031 Fax: 204-697-8075
stjosephs@primus.ca
Parent: Winnipeg Regional Health Authority
Number of Beds: 100 beds
Note: Personal care home
Marianna Muzyka, Executive Director
Luba Sirdar, Director, Nursing Services
Ben Korving, Director, Direct Services

Winnipeg: St. Norbert Personal Care Home
50 St Pierre St., Winnipeg, MB R3V 1J6
204-269-4538 Fax: 204-269-6374
Parent: Winnipeg Regional Health Authority
Number of Beds: 91 beds
Robert Brousseau, Administrator
Shirley Beaulieu, Director, Nursing

Winnipeg: The Sharon Home Inc.
1 Falconridge Dr., Winnipeg, MB R3Y 1V9
204-586-9781 Fax: 204-589-9760
Also Known As: The Simkin Centre
Division of: The Saul and Claribel Simkin Centre
Parent: Winnipeg Regional Health Authority
Year Founded: 2002
Number of Beds: 200 beds
Note: Specialties: Care for elders of Jewish community; Therapeutic recreation; Walking track for residents recovering from hip surgery or a stroke; Tracking program for resident safety; Adult day program

Winnipeg: Vista Park Lodge
144 Novavista Dr., Winnipeg, MB R2N 1P8
204-257-6688 Fax: 204-257-0446
Parent: Winnipeg Regional Health Authority
Year Founded: 1981
Number of Beds: 100 beds
Betty Jane Jones, Administrator; Director, Nursing

Winnipeg: West Park Manor
3199 Grant Ave., Winnipeg, MB R3R 1X2
204-889-3330 Fax: 204-832-9555
krcimchewpm@mts.net
Parent: Winnipeg Regional Health Authority
Number of Beds: 150 beds
K.D. Reimche, Administrator
M. Gutierrez, A/Director of Nursing

Winnipegosis: Winnipegosis-Mossey River Personal Care Home
PO Box 280, 230 Bridge St., Winnipegosis, MB R0L 2G0
204-656-4481 Fax: 204-656-4402
Parent: Parkland Regional Health Authority Inc.
Number of Beds: 20 beds
Glen Kozak, COO

Mental Health Facilities

Mental Health Hospital/Clinic/Facility

Altona: Altona & District Association for the Mentally Handicapped Inc.
PO Box 330, 122 - 10th Ave. NW, Altona, MB R0G 0B0
204-324-5401
otc@mts.net
Number of Beds: 5 beds
Anne Klassen, General Manager

Brandon: Centre for Adult Psychiatry
AP1, 150 McTavish Ave. East, Brandon, MB R7A 2B3
204-726-2923 Fax: 204-728-9633
Parent: Brandon Regional Health Authority
Number of Beds: 25 beds
Lynda Stiles, Program Manager

Brandon: Centre for Geriatric Psychiatry
Assiniboine Centre, 150 McTavish Ave. East, Brandon, MB R7A 2B3
204-726-2900 Fax: 204-725-0911
Parent: Brandon Regional Health Authority
Number of Beds: 22
Wendy Dryburgh, Program Manager

Brandon: Child & Adolescent Treatment Centre
1240 - 10 St., Brandon, MB R7A 7L6
204-727-3445 Fax: 204-727-3451
Parent: Brandon Regional Health Authority
Number of Beds: 10 beds
Doug Crookshanks, Program Manager

Brandon: Community Mental Health Services
The Town Centre, #B13, 800 Rosser Ave., Brandon, MB R7A 6N5
204-571-8300 Fax: 204-726-8684
Albert Hajes, Coordinator

Portage la Prairie: Manitoba Developmental Centre
PO Box 1190, 3rd St. NE, Portage la Prairie, MB R1N 3C6
204-856-4200 Fax: 204-856-4258 800/473-4603
dbjore@gov.mb.ca
Number of Beds: 375 beds
Note: developmental centre for residents with intellectual disabilities
Donna Bjore, CEO

Selkirk: Selkirk Mental Health Centre
PO Box 9600, 825 Manitoba Ave., Selkirk, MB R1A 2B5
204-482-3810 Fax: 204-785-8936 800-881-3073
smhc@gov.mb.ca
www.gov.mb.ca/health/smhc/
Number of Beds: 269 beds
Note: Long term mental health inpatient care & rehabilitation
K. Nattrass, CEO

Winkler: Eden Health Care Services
PO Box 129, 204 Main St., Winkler, MB R6W 4A4
204-325-5355 Fax: 204-325-8742
edencare@valleycable.com
edenhealth.mb.ca
Parent: Regional Health Authority - Central Manitoba Inc.
Number of Beds: 40 beds
Eckhard Goerz, Facility Contact

Winkler: Eden Mental Health Centre
1500 Pembina Ave., Winkler, MB R6W 1T4

204-325-4325 Fax: 204-325-8429
edenment@edenhealth.mb.ca
edenhealth.mb.ca
Parent: Regional Health Authority - Central Manitoba Inc.
Number of Beds: 30 beds
Les Zacharias, Administrator
les.zacharias@edenhealth.mb.ca

***Winnipeg:* Manitoba Adolescent Treatment Centre Inc.**
120 Tecumseh St., Winnipeg, MB R3E 2A9
204-477-6391 Fax: 204-783-8948
info@matc.ca
www.matc.ca
Parent: Winnipeg Regional Health Authority
Number of Beds: 25 beds
Note: Mental health services for children, youth, and families
Keith Hildahl, CEO

New Brunswick

Government Departments in Charge

NEW BRUNSWICK: Dept. of Health
PO Box 5100, Fredericton, NB E3B 5G8
506-453-2536 Fax: 506-444-4697
HealthInfo@gnb.ca; InfoSante@gnb.ca
Old Name: Dept. of Health & Community Services
Division of: Communications
Carole Payne, Director, Communications

Regional Health Authorities

***Bathurst:* Vitalité Health Network**
Réseau de santé Vitalité
#600, 275 Main St., Bathurst, NB E2A 1A9
506-544-2133 Fax: 506-544-2145 1-888-472-2220
info@rrsa.ca
www.santevitalitehealth.ca
Old Name: Restigouche Health Authority/Régie de la santé du
Year Founded: 2008
Number of Beds: 1,124
Note: The Vitalité Health Network amalgamates Regional Health Authority 4, the Restigouche Health Authority, the Acadie-Bathurst Health Authority, and the Beauséjour Health Authority; 7,600 employees; 470 physicians; 1,200 volunteers. The network is comprised of 11 hospitals, 6 community health centres, and a centre for psychiatric care.
Andrée Robichaud, President/CEO
Aldéa Landry, President of the Board of Directors

***Miramichi:* Horizon Health Network**
Réseau de santé Horizon
155 Pleasant St., Miramichi, NB E1V 1Y3
506-623-5500 Fax: 506-623-5533 www.rhab-rrsb.ca
Old Name: Regional Health Authority B
Year Founded: 2008
Number of Beds: 1,675 beds
Note: Along with the Vitalité Health Network, the Horizon Health Network amalgamates the 8 former regional health authorities in New Brunswick. Horizon Health Network servies the Moncton, Saint John, Fredericton and Miramichi areas, as well as communities in Nova Scotia and Prince Edward Island; 924 physicians; 5,000 nurses; 25 nurse practitioners; 2,175 health care professionals; 4,800 support staff; 3,500 volunteers.
Donald J. Peters, President/CEO

Hospitals

Hospitals - General

***Bath:* Northern Carleton Hospital**
82 Hospital St., Bath, NB E7J 1B9
506-278-2400 Fax: 506-278-2449
Number of Beds: 17 beds
Denise Gray, Facilities Manager
Peter Byron, Manager, Housekeeping

***Bathurst:* Hôpital régional Chaleur**
1745, promenade Vallée Lourdes, Bathurst, NB E2A 4L7
506-544-3000 Fax: 506-544-2440
Old Name: Centre hospitalier régional
Parent: Regional Health Authority A
Number of Beds: 215 beds
Stéphane Legacy, Administrateur d'établissement

***Blacks Harbour:* Fundy Health Centre**
34 Hospital St., Blacks Harbour, NB E5H 1K2
506-456-4200 Fax: 506-456-4222
Parent: Horizon Health Network
Note: Specialties: Primary care; Rehabilitation services

***Campbellton:* Campbellton Regional Hospital**
Hôpital régional de Campbellton
PO Box 880, 189 Lily Lake Rd., Campbellton, NB E3N 3H3
506-789-5000 Fax: 506-789-5025
www.santerestigouchehealth.com; www.santevitalitehealth.ca
Parent: Regional Health Authority A
Year Founded: 1991
Number of Beds: 166 beds/lits
Note: The hospital is part of the Vitalité Health Network, one of 2 regional health authorities formed in 2008 to amalgamate the provincial health authority structure in New Brunswick; 900 employees; 17 family physicians; 200 nurses; 27 specialists; 35 health care professionals; emergency and ambulatory care; obstetrics and gynecology; pediatrics; psychiatry; geriatric medicine; rehabilitation; orthopedics; palliative care.
Ruth Lyons, Facility Director

***Edmundston:* Hôpital régional d'Edmundston**
Edmundston Regional Hospital
275, boul Hébert, Edmundston, NB E3V 4E4
506-739-2200 Fax: 506-739-2231
Parent: Regional Health Authority A
Number of Beds: 169 lits
Édouard Hendriks, Administrateur d'établissement

***Fredericton:* Dr. Everett Chalmers Regional Hospital**
PO Box 9000, 700 Priestman St., Fredericton, NB E3B 5N5
506-452-5400 Fax: 506-452-5670 www.rhab-rrsb.ca
Year Founded: 1976
Number of Beds: 314 beds
Note: Hospital Specialties: Emergency services; Diagnostic services; Surgery; Intensive care; Primary care; Obstetrics; Neonatology; Pediatrics; Reconstructive & restorative medicine; Cardiac care; Rheumatology; Oncology; Dermatology; Gastroenterology; Neurology; Dialysis; Psychiatry; Geriatric care. Number of Employees: 2,000+ nurses, health care professionals, & support staff; 58 family physicians; 88 specialists
Ward Murdock, Chief of Staff, Fredericton, Horizon Health Network
Peter Feero, Chief of Surgery, Fredericton, Horizon Health Network
David Addleman, Chief of Psychiatry, Fredericton, Horizon Health Network

***Grand Manan:* Grand Manan Hospital Ltd.**
196 Rte. 776, Grand Manan, NB E5G 1A3
506-662-4060 Fax: 506-662-4050
Parent: Regional Health Authority B
Number of Beds: 8 beds
Karen Thomas, Facility Manager

***Grand-Sault:* Hôpital général de Grand-Sault inc.**
Grand Falls General Hospital Inc.
CP 7061, 625, boul Evérard H. Daigle, Grand-Sault, NB E3Z 2R9
506-473-7555 Fax: 506-473-7530
Parent: Regional Health Authority A
Number of Beds: 20 lits
Solange Bossé, Directrice d'établissement

***Harvey Station:* Harvey Community Hospital Ltd.**
2019 Rte. 3, Harvey Station, NB E6K 3E9
506-366-6400 Fax: 506-366-6403
Parent: Regional Health Authority B
Shirley Moffatt, Nurse Manager

***Lamèque:* Hôpital de Lamèque/Centre de santé communautaire de Lamèque**
29, rue de l'Hôpital, Lamèque, NB E8T 1C5
506-344-2261 Fax: 506-344-3403
Parent: Regional Health Authority A
Number of Beds: 12 lits
Dina Chiasson, Directrice d'établissement

***Miramichi:* Miramichi Regional Hospital**
500 Water St., Miramichi, NB E1V 3G5
506-623-3000 Fax: 506-623-3465
Parent: Regional Health Authority B
Number of Beds: 161 beds
Gary Foley, Acting President/CEP

***Moncton:* Hôpital régional Dr.-Georges-L.-Dumont**
330, av Université, Moncton, NB E1C 2Z3
506-862-4000 Fax: 506-862-4256 www.beausejour-nb.ca
Parent: Regional Health Authority A
Number of Beds: 362 lits
Louis-Marie Simard, Président et Directeur général par intérim
Blondine Arseneau, Conseillère en environnement

***Moncton:* The Moncton Hospital**
L'Hôpital de Moncton
135 MacBeath Ave., Moncton, NB E1C 6Z8
506-857-5520 Fax: 506-857-5545
generalinquiries@serha.ca
www.serha.ca
Parent: Regional Health Authority B
Number of Beds: 381 beds
Note: Comprehensive health care, including trauma care, intensive care units for cardiac care, neonatal care, medical/surgical care; child & adolescent psychiatric unit; burn unit; ambulance service
Donald J. Peters, President/CEO

***Oromocto:* Oromocto Public Hospital**
103 Winnebago St., Oromocto, NB E2V 1C6
506-357-4700 Fax: 506-357-4735 www.rivervalleyhealth.nb.ca
Parent: Regional Health Authority B
Number of Beds: 45 beds
Note: Specialties: Day surgery; Breast cancer screening centre; Close observation unit; William R. Duffie Unit, a healthy aging & restorative program. Number of employees: 15 family physicians + 1 radiologist + visiting surgeons + nurses, & professional & support staff
Darlene Cogswell, Facility Coordinator
John Swanwick, Lab Manager

***Perth-Andover:* Hôtel-Dieu of Saint-Joseph**
10 Woodland Hill, Perth-Andover, NB E7H 5H5
506-273-7100 Fax: 506-273-7200
Old Name: Hôtel-Dieu Saint-Joseph de Perth-Andover
Parent: Regional Health Authority B
Number of Beds: 27 beds
Joy Van Tassel, Facility Manager

***Plaster Rock:* Tobique Valley Hospital Inc.**
120 Main St., Plaster Rock, NB E7G 2E5
506-356-6600 www.rivervalleyhealth.nb.ca
Parent: Regional Health Authority B
Year Founded: 1957
Note: Specialties: Nursing care service; Physiotherapy
Susan Kukurski, Facility Coordinator
Ron Lewis, Plant Manager

***Sackville:* Sackville Memorial Hospital**
L'Hôpital mémorial de Sackville
8 Main St., Sackville, NB E4L 4A3
506-364-4100 Fax: 506-536-1983
generalinquiries@serha.ca
www.serha.ca/sackville_hospital
Parent: Regional Health Authority B
Number of Beds: 21 beds
France Gauthier, Acting Manager

***Saint John:* Saint John Regional Hospital**
PO Box 2100, Tucker Park Rd., Saint John, NB E2L 4L2
506-648-6000 Fax: 506-648-6364
Parent: Regional Health Authority B
Number of Beds: 524 beds
Note: Teaching hospital affiliated with Dalhousie University, New Brunswick Community College, University of New Brunswick and Memorial University in St. John's Newfoundland
Dora Nicinski, President/CEO

***Saint John:* Saint John Regional Hospital - Ridgewood Veterans Wing**
PO Box 2100, 422 Bay St., Saint John, NB E2L 4L2
506-635-2420 Fax: 506-635-2425
www.ahsc.health.nb.ca/AboutUs/OurFacilities/facvets.shtml
Parent: Regional Health Authority B
Year Founded: 1976
Number of Beds: 80 beds
Note: A facility for veterans who require long-term care; maintains a close relationship with Veteran Affairs Canada and the Royal Canadian Legion.
Maxine Walsh, Regional Manager, Veterans Care, AHSC
506-635-2150, walma@reg2.health.nb.ca
Michael Park, Regional Manager, Long Term Mental Health Services, AHSC
parmi@reg2.health.nb.ca

***Saint John:* St. Joseph's Hospital**
130 Bayard Dr., Saint John, NB E2L 3L6
506-632-5555 Fax: 506-632-5551
Parent: Regional Health Authority B
Number of Beds: 62 beds
Daryl Steeves, Facility Manager

***Saint-Quentin:* Hôtel-Dieu de St-Quentin**
21, rue Canada, Saint-Quentin, NB E8A 2P6
506-235-2300 Fax: 506-235-7201
nicole-d.labrie@rrs4.ca
Parent: Regional Health Authority A
Number of Beds: 6 lits
Nicole Labrie, Directrice d'établissement
Monette Dupéré, Chef de service à l'entretien ménager

St Stephen: Charlotte County Hospital
4 Garden St., St Stephen, NB E3L 2L9
506-465-4444
Parent: Regional Health Authority B
Number of Beds: 44 beds
Note: Specialties: Ambulatory care; Diagnostic services; Rehabilitative services; Restorative health; Physiotherapy; Speech-language pathology; Respiratory therapy; Occupational therapy; Adult & youth addiction counselling; Diabetic education; Oncology outreach services; Sexual health clinic; Cardiac risk clinic; Healthy lung clinic; Palliative care
Yvonne Bartlette, Facility Manager

Ste-Anne-de-Kent: Hôpital Stella Maris de Kent
7714, rte 134, Ste-Anne-de-Kent, NB E4S 1H5
506-743-7800 Fax: 506-743-7813 www.beausejour-nb.ca
Number of Beds: 20 lits
Lise Guerrette-Daigle, Directeur d'établissement
Gloria Melanson, Chef, Entretien mén.

Sussex: Sussex Health Centre
75 Leonard Dr., Sussex, NB E4E 2P7
506-432-3100 www.ahsc.health.nb.ca
Parent: Regional Health Authority B
Number of Beds: 25 beds
Note: Specialties: Acute care; Family medicine; Dialysis; IV therapy day hospital; Rehabilitative services; Palliative care
Elspeth Stanley, Facility Adminstrator

Tracadie-Sheila: Hôpital de Tracadie-Sheila
400, rue des Hospitalières, Tracadie-Sheila, NB E1X 1G5
506-394-3000 Fax: 506-394-3034
Parent: Regional Health Authority A
Number of Beds: 59 lits
Odette Robichaud, Directrice d'établissement
A. Saulnier, Directeur, Installations matériels

Community Health Centres

Community Health Care Centres

Baie-Sainte-Anne: Baie-Ste-Anne Health Centre
Centre de santé Baie-Ste-Anne
13, rue de l'Église, Baie-Sainte-Anne, NB E9A 1A9
506-228-2004 Fax: 506-228-2008 www.rha7.ca
Parent: Regional Health Authority B
Note: Patients may access the services of a physician who works 3 days per week, & a full time nurse on site; monthly public health & diabetic clinics; weekly lab.
Monica Lloyd, Contact

Bathurst: NB Extra Mural Program
1750 Sunset Dr., Bathurst, NB E2Z 4L7
506-455-3030
Division of: Bathurst Unit
Parent: Regional Health Authority A
Norma McGraw, Manager

Belledune: Centre de santé de Jacquet River Health Centre
41 Mack St., Belledune, NB E8G 2R3
506-237-3222 Fax: 506-237-3224
Parent: Regional Health Authority A
Lynn DeGroot, Administratrice d'établissement

Blackville: Blackville Health Centre
2 Shaffer Lane, Blackville, NB E9B 1P4
506-843-2910 Fax: 506-843-2911
Parent: Regional Health Authority B
Ann Dickison, Contact

Boiestown: Upper Miramichi Health Services Centre - Boiestown
#2, 6154, rte 8, Boiestown, NB E6A 1M4
506-369-2700 Fax: 506-369-2702
Parent: Regional Health Authority B
Lori Amos, Nurse Manager

Campobello: NB Extra Mural Program
640, rte 774, Welshpool, Campobello, NB E5E 1A5
506-752-4110 Fax: 506-752-4106
Division of: St Stephen Unit - Campobello Office
Parent: Regional Health Authority B
Sue Ness, Manager

Caraquet: Centre de santé communautaire de l'Enfant-Jésus
1, boul St-Pierre, Caraquet, NB E1W 1B7
506-726-2100 Fax: 506-726-2188
Old Name: Hôpital de l'Enfant-Jésus-RHSJT
Parent: Regional Health Authority A
Dina Chiasson, Directrice d'établissement
Guy Gallien, Chef de service, Installations matériels

Caraquet: Programme extra mural du NB Acadian Peninsula Unit
442, blvd. Saint-Pierre ouest, Caraquet, NB E1W 1A3
506-726-2800 Fax: 506-726-2808
Division of: Unite de la Penisule Acadienne - Bureau de Caraquet
Parent: Regional Health Authority A
Norma McGraw, Manager

Chipman: Chipman Health Centre
9 Civic Ct., Chipman, NB E4A 2H8
506-339-7650 Fax: 506-339-7652
Parent: Regional Health Authority B
Roddy Barton, Nurse Manager

Dalhousie: Centre de santé communautaire St. Joseph
St. Joseph Community Health Centre
#1, 280, rue Victoria, Dalhousie, NB E8C 2R6
506-684-7000 Fax: 506-684-4751
www.santerestigouchehealth.com; www.santevitalitehealth.ca
Parent: Regional Health Authority A
Note: Le Réseau de santé Vitalité regroupe les huit anciennes régies régionales dans la province. Le Centre a pour mission d'améliorer l'accès aux soins de santé primaires, et l'état de santé des collectivités; promotion de la santé, prévention des maladies et blessures, et traitement des maladies chroniques; services diagnostiques; soins ambulatoires.
Lynn Kelly deGroot, Directrice d'établissement

Dalhousie: NB Extra Mural Program
#2, 280 Victoria St., Dalhousie, NB E8C 2R6
506-684-7060 Fax: 506-684-7334
Division of: Restigouche Unit
Parent: Regional Health Authority A
Claire Dennie, Manager

Deer Island: Deer Island Health Centre
999 Rte. 772, Deer Island, NB E5V 1P2
506-747-4150 Fax: 506-747-4151
Parent: Regional Health Authority B
Susan Ness, Facility Manager

Dieppe: Programme extra mural du NB
30, rue Englehart, Unité B, Dieppe, NB E1A 8H3
506-862-4400 Fax: 506-862-4415
Division of: Blanche Bourgeois Unit
Parent: Regional Health Authority A
Rino Lang, Manager

Doaktown: Central Miramichi Community Health Centre
PO Box 1039, 8 Miramichi St., Doaktown, NB E9C 1C8
506-365-6100 Fax: 506-365-6104
Old Name: Upper Miramichi Health Services Centre - Doaktown
Parent: Regional Health Authority B
Lorri Amos, Nurse Manager

Edmundston: Programme extra mural du NB
275, boul Hebert, 4e étage, Edmundston, NB E3V 4N4
506-739-2160 Fax: 506-739-2163
Division of: Unite d'Edmundston
Parent: Regional Health Authority A
Carlene Pelletier, Manager

Fredericton: NB Extra Mural Program
PO Box 9000, 700 Priestman St., Fredericton, NB E3B 5N5
506-452-5800 Fax: 506-452-5858
Division of: Fredericton Unit
Parent: Regional Health Authority B
Christine DeJong, Manager

Fredericton: NB Extra Mural Program
Health Services Complex, #4, 20 Kennedy Dr., Fredericton, NB E4E 2P1
506-432-3280 Fax: 506-432-3250
Division of: Sussex Unit
Parent: Regional Health Authority B
Sue Ness, Manager

Fredericton: NB Extra Mural Program
c/o Fredericton Unit, PO Box 9000, 700 Priestman St., Fredericton, NB E3B 5N5
506-369-2711 Fax: 506-369-2722
Division of: Fredericton Unit - Boiestown Office
Parent: Regional Health Authority B
Christine DeJong, Manager

Fredericton Junction: Fredericton Junction Health Centre
233 Sunbury Dr., Fredericton Junction, NB E3L 1S1
506-368-6501 Fax: 506-368-6502
Parent: Regional Health Authority B
Ruth Richardson, Nurse Manager

Grand Manan: NB Extra Mural Program
Grand Manan Hospital, 196 Rte. 776, Grand Manan, NB E5G 1A3
506-662-4055 Fax: 506-662-4054
Division of: Eastern Charlotte Unit - Grand Manan
Parent: Regional Health Authority B
Sue Ness, Manager

Grand-Sault: Programme extra mural du NB
CP 7812, 532, ch Madawaska, Grand-Sault, NB E3Z 3E8
506-473-7492 Fax: 506-473-7476
Division of: Unite de Grand-Sault
Parent: Regional Health Authority A
Carlene Pelletier, Manager

Kedgwick: Programme extra mural du NB
CP 1002, Kedgwick, NB E8B 1Z7
506-284-3444 Fax: 506-284-3446
Division of: Unite de Grand-Sault - Kedgwick Office
Carlene Pelletier, Manager

Lamèque: Programme extra mural du NB
29, rue l'hopital Lemeque, Lamèque, NB E8T 1C5
506-344-3000 Fax: 506-344-3001
Division of: Unte de la Peninsule Acadienne - Bureau de Lameque
Parent: Regional Health Authority A
Norma McGraw, Manager

McAdam: MacLean Memorial Hospital
PO Box 311, 15 Saunders Rd., McAdam, NB E6J 1K9
506-784-6300 Fax: 506-784-6306
Shirley Moffat, Nurse Manager

Minto: Queens North Community Health Centre
PO Box 1004, 1100 Pleasant Dr., Minto, NB E4B 3Y6
506-327-7800 Fax: 506-327-7850
Parent: Regional Health Authority B
Sandra Parker, Nurse Manager
Kivon Snihur, Supervisor, Housekeeping

Miramichi: NB Extra Mural Program
500 Water St., Miramichi, NB E1V 3G5
506-623-6350 Fax: 506-623-6370
Division of: Miramichi Unit
Parent: Regional Health Authority B
Joanne Sonier, Manager

Miramichi: NB Extra Mural Program
500 Water St., Miramichi, NB E1V 3G5
506-623-6312 Fax: 506-623-6370
Division of: Miramichi Unit - Blackville Office
Parent: Regional Health Authority B
Joanne Sonier, Manager

Miramichi: NB Extra Mural Program
500 Water St., Miramichi, NB E1V 3G5
506-623-6311 Fax: 506-623-6370
Division of: Miramichi Unit - Neguac Office
Parent: Regional Health Authority B
Joanne Sonier, Manager

Miscou: Centre de santé de Miscou Health Centre
10482, rte 113, Miscou, NB E8T 1Y8
506-344-3434
Parent: Regional Health Authority A

Moncton: NB Extra Mural Program
Programme extra-mural - unité Driscoll
#107, 1600 Main St., Moncton, NB E1E 1G5
506-867-6500 Fax: 506-867-6509
generalinquiries@serha.ca
www.serha.ca/extra_mural
Division of: Driscoll Unit
Parent: Regional Health Authority B
Note: Home healthcare program for eligible residents
Fonda Kazi, Vice President, Community Health

Nackawic: Nackawic Community Health Centre
Nackawic Shopping Centre, Upper Floor, #201, 135 Otis Dr., Nackawic, NB E6G 1H1
506-575-6600 Fax: 506-575-6603
Parent: Regional Health Authority B
Shirley Moffatt, Nurse Manager

Néguac: Neguac Health Centre
38 Otho St., Néguac, NB E9C 4H3
506-776-3876 Fax: 506-776-3877
Anna Stymiest, Contact

Oromocto: NB Extra Mural Program
275A Restigouche Rd., Oromocto, NB E2V 2H1
506-357-4900 Fax: 506-357-4904

Division of: Oromocto Unit
Parent: Regional Health Authority B
Christine DeJong, Manager

***Oromocto:* NB Extra Mural Program**
c/o NB Extra Mural Program, 275A Restigouche Rd., Oromocto, NB E2V 2H1
506-327-4900 Fax: 506-327-4904
Division of: Oromocto Unit - Minto Office
Parent: Regional Health Authority B
Christine DeJong, Manager

***Paquetville:* Centre de santé de Paquetville**
1096, du Parc, Paquetville, NB E8R 1J4
506-764-2424 Fax: 506-764-2425
Parent: Regional Health Authority A

***Perth-Andover:* NB Extra Mural Program**
#2, 500 East Riverside Dr., Perth-Andover, NB E7H 1Z1
506-273-7222 Fax: 506-273-7220
Division of: Woodstock Unit - Perth-Andover Sub Unit
Parent: Regional Health Authority B
Christine DeJong, Manager

***Petitcodiac:* Petitcodiac Health Centre**
Centre de santé de Petitcodiac
25 Railway Ave., Petitcodiac, NB E4Z 6H4
506-756-3400 Fax: 506-756-3406
generalinquiries@serha.ca
www.serha.ca/petitcodiac
Parent: Regional Health Authority B
Note: Number of staff: 3 physicians, 1 dentist. Foot care & diabetes clinics by appointment, drop-in services, visiting dietician
Heather Steeves, Nurse Manager

***Pointe-Verte:* Centre de santé de Chaleur Health Centre**
382, rue Principale, Pointe-Verte, NB E8J 2X6
506-542-2434 Fax: 506-783-8623
Old Name: Centre de santé Pointe Verte
Parent: Regional Health Authority A

***Quispamsis:* NB Extra Mural Program**
PO Box 21025, 175 Old Hampton Hwy., Quispamsis, NB E2E 4Z4
506-848-4600 Fax: 506-848-4620
Division of: Kennebecasis Valley Unit
Parent: Regional Health Authority B
Sue Ness, Manager

***Rexton:* Health Services Centre Rexton**
Le Centre de santé de Rexton
82 Main St., Rexton, NB E4W 5N4
506-523-7940 Fax: 506-523-7949
generalinquiries@serha.ca
www.serha.ca
Parent: Regional Health Authority B
Year Founded: 1974
Note: Drop-in services, clinics, immunization, nutrition & diabetes education
Lucille Cormier, Nurse Manager

***Riverside-Albert:* Albert County Health & Wellness Centre**
Le Centre de santé & de mieux-être du comté d'Albert
8 Forestdale Rd., Riverside-Albert, NB E4H 3Y7
506-882-3100 Fax: 506-882-3101
generalinquiries@serha.ca
www.serha.ca/albert_county
Parent: Regional Health Authority B
Year Founded: 1961
Note: Multidisciplinary, primary health care services
Marlene Hueston, Nurse Manager

***Rogersville:* Rogersville Health Centre**
9, rue des Ormes, Rogersville, NB E4Y 1S6
506-775-2030 Fax: 506-775-2025
Parent: Regional Health Authority B
Glorine Caissie, Contact

***Sackville:* NB Extra Mural Program**
Programme extra-mural - unité Tantramar
8 Main St., Sackville, NB E4L 4A3
506-364-4400 Fax: 506-364-4405
generalinquiries@serha.ca
www.serha.ca/extra_mural
Division of: Tantramar Unit
Parent: Regional Health Authority B
Year Founded: 1979
Note: Home healthcare program for eligible residents
Fonda Kazi, Vice President, Community Health

***Saint John:* Hospice Greater Saint John**
385 Dufferin Row, Saint John, NB E2M 2J9
506-632-5593 Fax: 506-632-5592
info@hospicesj.ca
www.hospicesj.ca
Old Name: Hospice Saint John & Sussex
Note: Number of employees: 4
Sandy Johnson, Executive Director

***Saint John:* NB Extra Mural Program**
West End Office Park, 1490 Manawagonish Rd., Saint John, NB E2M 3Y4
506-649-2626 Fax: 506-649-2540
Division of: Saint John Unit
Parent: Regional Health Authority B
Note: in-home support
Sue Ness, Manager

***Saint John:* St. Joseph's Community Health Centre**
116 Coburg St., Saint John, NB E2L 3K1
506-632-5537 www.ahsc.health.nb.ca/CHC
Parent: Regional Health Authority B
Dawn Marie Buck, Contact

***Saint John:* Senior Watch Inc.**
33 Hanover St., Saint John, NB E2L 3G1
506-634-8906 Fax: 506-633-2992
senior@seniorwatch.com
www.seniorwatch.com
Note: New Brunswick-based firm specializing in developing and managing new programs for Seniors
Jean E. Porter Mowatt, President/CEO

***Sainte-Anne-de-Madawaska:* Centre de santé Ste-Anne**
1, rue de la Clinique, Sainte-Anne-de-Madawaska, NB E7E 1B9
506-445-6200 Fax: 506-445-6201
Parent: Regional Health Authority A
Édouard Hendriks, Administrateur d'établissement (par intérim)

***Shediac:* Centre médical régional de Shédiac**
419, rue Main, Shediac, NB E4P 2B8
506-533-2700 Fax: 506-533-2710
Parent: Regional Health Authority A
Lise Guerrette-Daigle, Administrateur d'établissement

***Shediac:* Programme extra mural du NB**
423 Main St., Shediac, NB E4P 2B6
506-533-2800
Division of: Shediac Unit
Parent: Regional Health Authority A
Rino Lang, Manager

***St George:* NB Extra Mural Program**
#401, 124 Main St., St George, NB E5C 3S3
506-755-4660 Fax: 506-755-4665
Division of: Eastern Charlotte Unit
Parent: Regional Health Authority B
Sue Ness, Manager

***St Stephen:* NB Extra Mural Program**
#100, 73 Milltown Blvd., St Stephen, NB E3L 1G5
506-465-4520 Fax: 506-465-4523
Division of: St Stephen Unit
Parent: Regional Health Authority B
Sue Ness, Manager

***Stanley:* Stanley Health Services Centre**
PO Box 340, Stanley, NB E6B 2K5
506-367-7730 Fax: 506-367-7738
Parent: Regional Health Authority B
Charlene Merrill, Nurse Manager
Penny Higgs, Director, Nursing
Ronald Hay, Maintenance Supervisor

***Ste-Anne de Kent:* Programme extra mural du NB**
7717, route 134, Livraison Générale, Ste-Anne de Kent, NB E4S 1H5
506-743-2000
Division of: Kent Unit
Parent: Regional Health Authority A
Rino Lang, Manager

***Tracadie Sheila:* Progrmme extra mural du NB**
Centre hospitalier de Tracadie, PO Box 3180 Bureau-Chef, 3512-2, rue Principale, Tracadie Sheila, NB E1X 1G5
506-394-4100 Fax: 506-394-4117
Division of: Unite de la Peninsule Acadienne - Bureau de Tracadie
Parent: Regional Health Authority A
Norma McGraw, Manager

***Welshpool:* Campobello Health Centre**
640, rte 774, Welshpool, NB E5E 1A5
506-752-4100 Fax: 506-752-2654
Parent: Regional Health Authority B
Susan Ness, Facility Manager

***Woodstock:* NB Extra Mural Program**
Nurses' Residence, #310, 787 Main St., Woodstock, NB E7M 2E9
506-325-6838 Fax: 506-325-6862
Division of: Woodstock Unit
Parent: Regional Health Authority B
Christine DeJong, Manager

Special Treatment Centre

***Edmundston:* Services de toxicomanie**
62, rue Queen, Edmundston, NB E3V 1A1
506-735-2092 Fax: 506-835-2700 www.rrs4-rha4.nb.ca
Parent: Regional Health Authority A
Number of Beds: 10 lits
Note: Service de désintoxification interne
Carmen Bouchard
Carmen.Bouchard@chr4.health.nb.ca

***Fredericton:* Addiction Services**
c/o Victoria Health Centre, 65 Brunswick St., Fredericton, NB E3B 1G5
506-452-5558 Fax: 506-452-5533
Gordon Skead, Regional Director

***Fredericton:* The Morgentaler Clinic**
554 Brunswick St., Fredericton, NB E3B 1H5
506-451-9060 Fax: 506-451-9062
nbclinic@nb.aibn.com
www.morgentalernb.ca
Division of: Fredericton Site
Note: Specialties: Abortion care services; Abortion aftercare

***Fredericton:* Stan Cassidy Centre for Rehabilitation**
180 Woodbridge St., Fredericton, NB E3B 4R3
506-452-5225 Fax: 506-452-5190
Parent: Regional Health Authority B
Number of Beds: 20 beds
Ron Harris, Administrative Director
Calvin Gesner, Maintenance Director

***Moncton:* Addiction Services**
Services de traitement des dépendances
125 Mapleton Rd., Moncton, NB E1C 9G8
506-856-2333 Fax: 506-856-6057
generalinquiries@serha.ca
www.serha.ca/addiction_services
Number of Beds: 20 beds
Note: Detoxification unit, methadone maintenance treatment program, addiction prevention & education, counseling, assessments
Michelina Mancuso, Regional Manager

***Petit-Rocher:* Services Résidentiels Nepisiguit Inc.**
#312, 702, rue Principale, Petit-Rocher, NB E8J 1V1
506-542-2404 Fax: 506-542-2406
srninc@nb.aibn.com
www.gnb.ca
Number of Beds: 22 lits
Note: Service résidentiel à toutes les personnes ayant des handicaps de la région Nepisiguit
Luc DeRoche, Directeur général

***Saint John:* Workers' Rehabilitation Centre**
PO Box 160, 1 Portland St., Saint John, NB E2L 3X9
506-738-8411 Fax: 506-738-3470 www.whscc.nb.ca
Note: occupational rehabilitation
R. Brian Connell, Vice-President, Compensation & Rehabilitation

***Saint John West:* Ridgewood Addiction Services**
PO Box 3566 B, 416 Bay St., Saint John West, NB E2M 4Y1
506-674-4300 Fax: 506-658-3774 www.ahsc.health.nb.ca
Number of Beds: 90 beds
Note: Comprehensive addiction treatment programs, detoxification, outpatient & short term residential services, addiction prevention & education, community reintegration
Bonnie Lambert, Executive Director
lambo@reg2.health.nb.ca

Nursing Homes

***Albert:* Forest Dale Home Inc.**
5836 King St., Albert, NB E4H 4B9
506-882-3015 Fax: 506-882-3014
Number of Beds: 40 beds
Debbie Smith, Administrator
506/882-3018
Ethel Duffy, Director, Nursing

***Baker Brook:* Foyer Ste. Elizabeth Inc.**
25, rue des Ormes, Baker Brook, NB E7A 2J6
506-258-3020 Fax: 506-258-3010
Number of Beds: 50 lits
Paul Couturier, Directeur général

***Bath:* River View Manor Inc.**
96 Hospital St., Bath, NB E7J 1B9
506-278-6030 Fax: 506-278-5962 www.riverviewmanor.ca
Year Founded: 1981
Number of Beds: 40 beds
Note: Nursing home
Kay Simonds, Administrator
Randy Giberson, Supervisor, Plant Maintenance

***Bathurst:* Le Foyer Notre-Dame de Lourdes Inc.**
2055, Vallée-Lourdes, Bathurst, NB E2A 4P8
506-549-5085 Fax: 506-548-5052
dg.fndl@health.nb.ca
Number of Beds: 100 lits
Claire Savoie, Directeur général
506/549-5071

***Bathurst:* Robert L. Knowles Veterans Unit, Villa Chaleur**
795, rue Champlain, Bathurst, NB E2A 4M8
506-549-5582 Fax: 506-545-6424
Number of Beds: 13 beds
Lucie Fournier, Administrator

***Blacks Harbour:* Fundy Nursing Home**
34 Hospital St., Blacks Harbour, NB E5H 1C2
506-456-4218 Fax: 506-456-4259
Number of Beds: 26 beds
Debbie Harris, Administrator
506/456-4213

***Boiestown:* Central New Brunswick Nursing Home Inc.**
3458 Rte. 625, Boiestown, NB E6A 1C8
506-369-7262 Fax: 506-369-2331
Number of Beds: 30 beds
Manley Black, Administrator

***Bouctouche:* Manoir Saint-Jean Baptiste**
5, av Richard, Bouctouche, NB E4S 3T2
506-743-7344 Fax: 506-743-7343
Number of Beds: 50 lits
Robert Allain, Administrateur
506/743-7346
Edmond Babineau, Chef, Installations matériels

***Campbellton:* Campbellton Nursing Home Inc.**
PO Box 850, 101 Dover St., Campbellton, NB E3N 3K6
506-789-7350 Fax: 506-789-7360
Number of Beds: 100 beds
Ken Murray, Executive Director
506/789-7351
Randy Johnson, Supervisor, Plant Maintenance

***Caraquet:* Villa Beauséjour Inc.**
CP 5608, 253, boul St-Pierre ouest, Caraquet, NB E1W 1B7
506-726-2744 Fax: 506-726-2745
Number of Beds: 62 lits
Roger Landry, Directeur général
506/726-2741
Annette Chiasson, Director, Nursing
Dennis Power, Maintenance Supervisor

***Dalhousie:* Dalhousie Nursing Home Inc.**
#1, 296 Victoria St., Dalhousie, NB E8C 2R8
506-684-7800 Fax: 506-684-7832
Number of Beds: 105 beds
Diane Léger, Administrator
506/684-7805
Maurice Savoie, Director, Physical Plant

***Edmundston:* Villa des Jardins Inc.**
50, rue Queen, Edmundston, NB E3V 3N4
506-735-2112 Fax: 506-735-2462
Number of Beds: 30 lits
Carole Ouellette, Administrateur
506/735-2115

***Fredericton:* Pine Grove**
521 Woodstock Rd., Fredericton, NB E3B 2J2
506-444-3400 Fax: 506-444-3407
Pam Bowen, Administrator

***Fredericton:* York Manor Inc.**
100 Sunset Dr., Fredericton, NB E3A 1A3
506-444-3880 Fax: 506-444-3544
info@yorkmanor.nb.ca
www.yorkmanor.nb.ca
Number of Beds: 198 beds
Ken McGeorge, Administrator

***Fredericton Junction:* White Rapids Manor Inc.**
233 Sunbury Dr., Fredericton Junction, NB E5L 1S1
613-368-6508 Fax: 613-368-6512
Number of Beds: 36 beds
Kathy Jenkins, Administrator

***Gagetown:* Gagetown Nursing Home Ltd.**
2230 Rte 102, Gagetown, NB E5M 1A1
506-488-3544 Fax: 506-488-3551
khamilto@health.nb.ca
Number of Beds: 40 beds
Kathy Hamilton, Administrator
506/488-3586
S. Douthwright, Maintenance Supervisor

***Grand Falls:* Grand Falls Manor Inc.**
55, rue Gagnon, Grand Falls, NB E3Z 3E5
506-473-7726 Fax: 506-473-7849
manoirgs@health.nb.ca
Number of Beds: 69 lits
Maurice Richard, Administrateur
506/473-7726
Gaetan Theriult, Director, Physical Plant

***Grand Manan:* Grand Manan Nursing Home Inc.**
266, Rte. 776, Grand Manan, NB E5G 1A5
506-662-7111 Fax: 506-662-7117
urquharts@nb.aibn.com
Number of Beds: 30 beds
Sharon Urquhart, Administrator
Larry Clowater, Maintenance Supervisor

***Hampton:* Dr. V.A. Snow Centre Inc.**
54 Demille Ct., Hampton, NB E5N 5S7
506-832-6210 Fax: 506-832-7674
adminvasnow@nb.aibn.com
Number of Beds: 50 beds
Terry MacNeill, Administrator
506/832-6214
Bill Bettle, Maintenance Supervisor

***Hartland:* Central Carleton Nursing Home Inc.**
139 Rockland Rd., Hartland, NB E7P 1E9
506-375-3033 Fax: 506-375-3035
cullinsg@health.nb.ca
Number of Beds: 30 beds
Gwen Cullins-Jones, Administrator

***Inkerman:* Résidences Inkerman Inc.**
1171, ch Pallot, Inkerman, NB E8P 1C2
506-336-3909 Fax: 506-336-3912
Number of Beds: 30 lits
Michel Haché, Directeur général
Paul Doucet, Coordinateur, Services environnementaux

***Lamèque:* Les Résidences Lucien Saindon Inc.**
26, rue de l-Hôpital, Lamèque, NB E8T 1C3
506-344-3232 Fax: 506-344-3240
dir.gen.rlsaindon@health.nb.ca
Number of Beds: 54 lits
Gaëtan Haché, Directeur général
506/344-3245

***Memramcook:* Foyer St. Thomas de la Vallée de Memramcook Inc.**
100, rue Notre-Dame, Memramcook, NB E3K 3W3
506-758-2110 Fax: 506-758-9489
Number of Beds: 30 lits
Pierre Landry, Directeur général
Alexandre Gaudet, Directrice, Installations matériels

***Mill Cove:* Mill Cove Nursing Home Inc.**
5647 Rte 105, Mill Cove, NB E4C 3A5
506-488-3033 Fax: 506-488-3037
mcceo@millcovenh.com
www.millcovenh.com
Note: Specialties: Nursing care for persons with special needs; Podiatry; Psychology; Rehabilitation; Snoezelen rooms
G. Paul Mills, Administrator
506/488-3033

***Minto:* W.G. Bishop Nursing Home**
1100 Pleasant Dr., Minto, NB E4B 3Y6
506-327-7853 Fax: 506-327-7812
llbetts@health.nb.ca
www.wgbishopnursinghome.org
Number of Beds: 30 beds
Kathy Donaldson, Acting CEO
506/327-7809

***Miramichi:* Miramichi Senior Citizens Home Inc.**
1400 Water St., Miramichi, NB E1N 1A4
506-778-6810 Fax: 506-778-6860
msch@nb.aibn.com
www.miramichiseniorshome.com
Number of Beds: 81 beds
Margaret Manderson, Administrator
Macrena Jardine, Director, Plant Maintenance

***Miramichi:* Mount Saint Joseph Nursing Home**
PO Box 1002, 51 Lobban Ave., Miramichi, NB E1N 3W4
506-778-6550 Fax: 506-778-0193
Number of Beds: 133 beds
Robert B. Stewart, Executive Director
506/778-6555
Jan Flieger, Director, Support Services

***Moncton:* Kenneth E. Spencer Memorial Home Inc.**
35 Atlantic Baptist Ave., Moncton, NB E1E 4N3
506-858-7870 Fax: 506-858-9674
info@abschi.com
Number of Beds: 200 beds
Barbara Cook, Administrator
Byron Cole, Director of Support Services

***Moncton:* Villa du Repos Inc.**
474, promenade Elmwood, Moncton, NB E1A 2X3
506-857-3560 Fax: 506-859-1619
Number of Beds: 126 lits
Paul Williams, Directeur général
Louis Audet, Directeur, Installations matériels

***Paquetville:* Manoir Édith B. Pinet Inc.**
1189, rue des Fondateurs, Paquetville, NB E8R 1A9
506-764-2444 Fax: 506-764-2451
sec.mebp@health.nb.ca
Number of Beds: 30 lits
Léonard Légère, Administrateur
506/764-2445
Guy Thériault, Directeur, Installations phys.

***Perth-Andover:* Victoria Glen Manor Inc.**
30 Beech Glen Rd., Perth-Andover, NB E7H 1J9
506-273-4885 Fax: 506-273-4975
office@vgm.ca
www.vgm.ca
Number of Beds: 65 beds
Note: Long-term care home
Eric Haddad, Administrator
506/273-4824

***Port Elgin:* Westford Nursing Home**
57 West Main St., Port Elgin, NB E4M 1L7
506-538-2307 Fax: 506-538-7293
admwnh@nb.aibn.com
www.westfordnursinghome.com
Year Founded: 1986
Number of Beds: 30 beds
Note: Home for seniors and physically and mentally challenged adults
Judith White, Executive Director
Ian Hurley, Manager, Environmental Support Services

***Rexton:* Rexton Lions Nursing Home Inc.**
84 Main St., Rexton, NB E4W 2B3
506-523-7720 Fax: 506-523-7703
rex_general@nb.aibn.com
Number of Beds: 30 beds
Dianne Robichaud, Administrator
506/523-7778

***Riverview:* The Salvation Army Lakeview Manor**
50 Suffolk St., Riverview, NB E1B 4K6
506-387-2012 Fax: 506-387-7200
www.maritime.salvationarmy.ca
Number of Beds: 50 beds
Note: Specialties: Geriatric care; Care for persons with dementia
Shirley King, Executive Director

***Rivière-Verte:* Foyer de l'Age d'Or**
55, rue Principale, Rivière-Verte, NB E7C 2T7
506-263-8851

***Rogersville:* Foyer Assomption**
CP 296, 62, rue Assomption, Rogersville, NB E4Y 1S5
506-775-2040 Fax: 506-775-2053
Number of Beds: 50 lits
Anne Cormier, Directrice générale
506/775-2043
Ronald Poirier, Chef, Installations matériels

***Saint John:* Carleton-Kirk Lodge**
3 Carleton Kirk Pl., Saint John, NB E2M 5B8

506-635-7040 Fax: 506-635-7038
Number of Beds: 70 beds
Tim Stevens, Executive Director

Saint John: Church of St. John & St. Stephen Home Inc.
130 University Ave., Saint John, NB E2K 4K3
506-634-6001 Fax: 506-634-6126
Note: Specialty: Long-term care
Darlene Cannell, Administrator

Saint John: Kennebec Manor Inc.
475 Woodward Ave., Saint John, NB E2K 4N1
506-632-9628 Fax: 506-658-9376
kennebecman@health.nb.ca
Number of Beds: 70 beds
Judith Ann Lane, Administrator
506/658-0591,

Saint John: Loch Lomond Villa, Inc.
185 Loch Lomond Rd., Saint John, NB E2J 3S3
506-643-7175 Fax: 506-643-7198
bwilkins@lochlomondvilla.nb.ca (Executive Assistant)
www.lochlomondvilla.com
Year Founded: 1973
Number of Beds: 196 beds
Note: Specialties: Specialized units for Alzheimers & Psychogeriatric needs
Cindy Donovan, Administrator
506/643-7130
Valerie O'Leary, Director, Nursing
Paul Mills, Director, Operations

Saint John: Rocmaura Inc.
10 Park St., Saint John, NB E2K 4P1
506-643-7050 Fax: 506-643-7053
reception@rocmaura.com
www.rocmaura.com
Year Founded: 1972
Number of Beds: 150 beds
Note: Christian nursing home; affiliated with the Sisters of Charity of the Immaculate Conception (SCIC)
Susan Quinn, Administrator
506/643-7060
Harry Seele, Maintenance Supervisor

Saint John: Turnbull Nursing Home Inc.
231 Britain St., Saint John, NB E2L 0A4
506-643-7200 Fax: 506-648-9786
turnbulloffice@nb.aibn.com
Old Name: Turnbull Home
Number of Beds: 50 beds
Note: Specialty: Long-term care
Elizabeth Crouchman, Administrator
506/643-7211
Brian Worden, Director, Physical Plant

Saint-Antoine: Foyer Saint-Antoine
7, av de l'Église, Saint-Antoine, NB E4V 1L6
506-525-4040 Fax: 506-525-4090
dg_fsa@health.nb.ca
www3.nbnet.nb.ca/fsa
Number of Beds: 30 lits
Gilles C. Ouellette, Administrateur
Gérard-Eugene Richard, Chef, Installations matériels

Saint-Basile: Foyer Saint-Joseph de Saint-Basile Inc.
475, rue Principale, Saint-Basile, NB E7C 1J2
506-263-3462 Fax: 506-263-3467
Number of Beds: 126 lits
Louisette Landry-Bouchard, Directrice générale
506/263-3465
Roger Lévesque, Directeur, Installations matériels

Saint-Léonard: Foyer Notre-Dame de Saint-Léonard Inc.
604, rue Principale, Saint-Léonard, NB E7E 2H5
506-423-3151 Fax: 506-423-3152
Number of Beds: 45 lits
Denis J. Michaud, Administrateur
506/423-3150

Saint-Louis-de-Kent: Villa Maria Inc.
19, rue du College, Saint-Louis-de-Kent, NB E4X 1C2
506-876-3488 Fax: 506-876-3466
Number of Beds: 73 lits
Jean Paul Mazerolle, Administrateur
Sylvio Gigou, Directeur, Installations matériels

Saint-Quentin: Résidence Mgr. Melanson Inc.
11, rue Levesque, Saint-Quentin, NB E8A 1T1
506-235-6030 Fax: 506-235-6075
Number of Beds: 42 lits
Susie Roy, Directrice générale
Rejeanne Chouinere, Superviseur
Claude Paquet, Chef, Installations

Shediac: Villa Providence Shédiac Inc.
403, rue Main, Shediac, NB E4P 2B9
506-532-4484 Fax: 506-532-5909
roger.hebert@vp-vr.ca
Number of Beds: 190 lits
Roger T. Hébert, Directeur général
Regin LeBlanc, Chef, Entretien ménager

Shippagan: Les Résidences Mgr. Chiasson Inc.
128, rue Mgr Chiasson, Shippagan, NB E8S 1X7
506-336-3266 Fax: 506-336-3099
Number of Beds: 100 lits
Octave Haché, Directeur général

St Andrews: Passamaquoddy Lodge Inc.
230 Sophia St., St Andrews, NB E5B 2C2
506-529-5240 Fax: 506-529-5258
lezlie.leblanc@nb.aibn.com
www.passamaquoddylodge.ca
Number of Beds: 60 beds
Note: Nursing home
Catherine Smith, Administrator
506/529-5242
F. Meredith, Supervisor, Plant Maintenance

St Stephen: Lincourt Manor Inc.
PO Box 116, 1 Chipman St., St Stephen, NB E3L 2W9
506-466-7855 Fax: 506-466-7853
Note: Specialty: Long term care
Jane Lyons, Administrator
Ron Hall, Maintenance Supervisor

St Stephen: Maria F. Ganong Seniors Residence
28 Union St., St Stephen, NB E3L 1T1
506-466-1471
lonicerahall@nb.aibn.com
www.lonicerahall.com
Also Known As: Lonicera Hall
Old Name: Maria F. Ganong Old Folks Home
Number of Beds: 19 rooms
Pat Steves, Administrator

Stanley: Nashwaak Villa Inc.
PO Box 340, 32 Lime Kiln Rd., Stanley, NB E6B 2K5
506-367-7731 Fax: 506-367-7745
Number of Beds: 30 beds
Bonnie MacNeil, Administrator
506/367-7734

Sussex: Kiwanis Nursing Home Inc.
11 Bryant Dr., Sussex, NB E4E 2P3
506-432-3118 Fax: 506-432-3104
knhi@nb.aibn.com
Number of Beds: 70 beds
Arthur Hetherington, Administrator
Ralph Mayfield, Director, Plant Maintenance

Tabusintac: Tabusintac Nursing Home
10 Old Manse Rd., Tabusintac, NB E9H 1G4
506-779-4100 Fax: 506-779-8149
Betty Blake, Administrator

Tracadie-Sheila: Villa Saint-Joseph Inc.
3400, rue Albert, Tracadie-Sheila, NB E1X 1C8
506-394-4800 Fax: 506-394-4826
Number of Beds: 64 lits
Paul Arseneau, Directeur général
506/394-4820

Welshpool: Campobello Lodge
640 Rte. 774, #2, Welshpool, NB ESE 1A5
506-752-7101 Fax: 506-752-7105
Number of Beds: 30 beds
Sherry Johnston, Administrator
506/752-7030
Raye Brown, Maintenance Supervisor

Woodstock: Carleton Manor Inc.
106 Elizabeth St., Woodstock, NB E7M 1R1
506-325-4373 Fax: 506-325-4618
macneilp@health.nb.ca
Number of Beds: 89 beds
Kay Simonds, Administrator
506/325-4376

Long Term/Retirement Care

Long Term Care Facility

Acadieville: Villa Acadie Ltée
4057, rte. 480, Acadieville, NB E4Y 1Z3
506-775-6088
Number of Beds: 13 lits
Bernice Doiron, Proprietor

Baker Brook: Résidence Notre Dame
CP 38, 3741, rue Principale, Baker Brook, NB E7A 2A5
506-258-3322
Number of Beds: 18 lits
Roland Bouchard, Directeur général

Chatham: Howard Henderson House Inc.
225 Wellington St., Chatham, NB E1N 1N1
506-773-6522
Number of Beds: 9 beds
Cathy McDonald, Executive Director

Kedgwick: Maison Notre-Dame
38, rue St. Paul, Kedgwick, NB E8B 2A7
506-284-2318
Number of Beds: 23 lits
Solange Borris, Administratrice

Moncton: Alternative Residences Inc.
257 Lutz St., Moncton, NB E1C 5G4
506-854-7229 Fax: 506-853-6051
Number of Beds: 83 beds
Joanne LeBreton, Executive Director

Moncton: Birchmount Lodge
144 Birchmount Dr., Moncton, NB E1C 8E7
506-384-7573 Fax: 506-384-8143
Number of Beds: 29 beds
Donald Vossburgh, Administrator

Moncton: Moncton Community Residences
357 Collishaw St., Moncton, NB E1C 9R2
506-858-0550 Fax: 506-858-0271
mcri3@nb.aibn.com
Number of Beds: 30 beds
Jerry Kirkpatrick, General Manager

Moncton: Moncton Community Residences Inc.
357 Collishaw St., Moncton, NB E1C 9R2
506-858-0550 Fax: 506-858-0271
mcri3@nb.aibn.com
Old Name: Reade House
Number of Beds: 5 beds
Note: Provides residential services to people with developmental challenges, ranging from group homes to assistance with independent living
Jerry Kirkpatrick, Administrator

Moncton: Moncton Community Residences Inc.
357 Collishaw St., Moncton, NB E1C 9R2
506-858-0550 Fax: 506-858-0271
mcri3@nb.aibn.com
Old Name: West Lane House
Number of Beds: 8 beds
Note: Provides residential services to developmentally challenged adults
Jerry Kirkpatrick, Administrator

Moncton: Moncton Community Residences, Inc.
357 Collishaw St., Moncton, NB E1C 9R2
506-858-0550 Fax: 506-858-0271
mcri3@nb.aibn.com
Old Name: Norwood House
Number of Beds: 6 beds
Note: Provides residential services to people with developmental challenges
Jerry Kirkpatrick, Administrator

Paquetville: Foyer Simonne Butler
1137, rue des Fondateurs, Paquetville, NB E8R 1B3
506-764-2105
Number of Beds: 5
Simonne Butler, Administratrice

Pennfield: Collingwood Home
RR#2, Pennfield, NB E0G 2R0
506-456-3533
Number of Beds: 20 beds
Dan Drost, Administrator

Riverview: Grass Home
774 Coverdale Rd., Riverview, NB E1B 3L5
506-386-1740 Fax: 506-386-7040
Old Name: N-Joy Homes Ltd.
Number of Beds: 24 beds

John Grass, Proprietor/Administrator

***Robertville:* La Villa Sormany Inc.**
1730, ch. Ste Thérèse, Rte. 322, Robertville, NB E8K 2V8
506-542-2731 Fax: 506-542-2733
dg.vsormany@health.nb.ca
Number of Beds: 40 lits
Lucie Marteau, Directrice générale

***Sackville:* Drew Nursing Home**
165 Main St., Sackville, NB E4L 4S2
506-364-4900 Fax: 506-364-4921
office@drewnursinghome.ca
www.drewnursinghome.ca
Number of Beds: 130 beds
Note: senior apartments
Linda Leroux, Administrator
506/364-4822
Ray Letcher, Director, Environmental Services

***Saint John:* New Direction Inc.**
PO Box 549, Saint John, NB E2L 3Z8
506-643-6207 Fax: 506-643-6209
newdir@nb.aibn.com
Number of Beds: 43 beds
Note: Provides housing and support services to persons suffering from mental illness
Gayle Capson, Executive Director

***Saint John:* Westport Residential Facility**
427 Prince St., Saint John, NB E2M 1R2
506-674-2069 Fax: 506-832-0808
beverlyr@nb.sympatico.ca
Number of Beds: 18 beds
Beverly Rideout, Administrator

***Saint-Jacques:* Foyer Georgette St-Onge**
CP 484, 11, rue Babineau, Saint-Jacques, NB E0L 1K0
506-735-8511
Number of Beds: 6 lits
Georgette St-Onge, Propriétaire

***Sainte-Anne-de-Madawaska:* Foyer Mont St-Joseph**
8, rue St-Joseph, Sainte-Anne-de-Madawaska, NB E7E 1L1
506-445-2755
Number of Beds: 16 lits
Florida Lavoie, Directrice générale

***Tabusintac:* Foyer Prime Breau**
14 Covedell Rd., Tabusintac, NB E9H 1E6
506-779-4445
Number of Beds: 4 lits
Roséanna Breau, Propriétrice

***Woodstock:* Women's Institute Home**
129 Chapel St., Woodstock, NB E7M 1G7
506-328-2148
Number of Beds: 21 beds
Marion Briand, Supervisor

Mental Health Facilities

Mental Health Hospital/Clinic/Facility

***Campbellton:* Centre Hospitalier Restigouche Restigouche Hospital Centre**
CP 10, 63, ch Gallant, Campbellton, NB E3N 3G2
506-789-7000 Fax: 506-789-7065
www.santerestigouchehealth.com
Parent: Regional Health Authority A
Number of Beds: 150 lits
Bertrand Collin, Directeur d'établissement
Jean Bouloy, Vice-President, Administration Services

***Saint John:* Centracare Saint John Inc.**
PO Box 3220 B, 414 Bay St., Saint John, NB E2M 4H7
506-649-2550 Fax: 506-649-2570
Parent: Regional Health Authority B
Number of Beds: 50 beds
Joanne Lewis, Acting Regional Manager

***Shippagan:* Pavillon St-Jér"me Inc.**
150, 17e rue, Shippagan, NB E8S 1G4
506-336-8609 Fax: 506-336-8652
Number of Beds: 12 lits
Note: résidence pour adultes handicapés intellectuels
Louise Pichette, Directrice

Special Care Home

***Campbellton:* Duguay's Special Care Home**
20 Dover St., Campbellton, NB E3N 1P3
506-789-1208
Number of Beds: 9 beds
Susan Duguay, Administrator

***Harvey Station:* Swanhaven Adult Residential Facility**
1915, Rte. 3, Harvey Station, NB E6K 3K1
506-366-2950 Fax: 506-366-1010
Number of Beds: 25 units
Note: Specialty: Long-term care
Frances P. Ward, Owner

***Moncton:* Castle Manor**
271 Mountain Rd., Moncton, NB E1C 2L7
506-382-5713 Fax: 506-383-4330
Number of Beds: 48 beds
Myrtle Rogers, Administrator

***Moncton:* Ritchie V Manor II**
2031 Mountain Rd., Moncton, NB E1G 1B1
506-384-7658
Number of Beds: 20 beds
Debbie Teakles, Proprietor

***Moncton:* Smith Special Care Home Ltd.**
56 Dorchester St., Moncton, NB E1E 3A7
506-383-2826 Fax: 506-383-2826
Number of Beds: 10 beds
Eric Smith

***Ratter Corner:* Wilson's Special Care Home**
510 Drurys Cove Rd., Ratter Corner, NB E4E 3L4
506-433-5532
Number of Beds: 3 beds
Sharon Wilson, Proprietor

***Saint John:* Champlain House**
18 Hayes Ave., Saint John, NB E2M 5K3
506-672-4651
Number of Beds: 8 beds
Barbara McMullin, Administrator

***Saint John:* Forest Hills Special Care Home**
30 Mountain Rd., Saint John, NB E2J 2W8
506-633-0743
Number of Beds: 10 beds
Janet Hebert, Proprietor

***Saint John:* Seale Special Care Home**
295 Millidge Ave., Saint John, NB E2K 2M9
506-693-3719
Number of Beds: 5 beds
Verna Seale, Proprietor

***Titusville:* Yvonne's Special Care Home**
1773 Hwy. 860, Titusville, NB E0G 1Z0
506-832-7186
Number of Beds: 14 beds
Yvonne Clark, Proprietor

Newfoundland & Labrador

Government Departments in Charge

NEWFOUNDLAND & LABRADOR: Newfoundland & Labrador Department of Health & Community Services
1st Floor West Block, Confederation Bldg., PO Box 8700, St. John's, NL A1B 4J6
709-729-4984 Fax: 709-729-5824
healthinfo@gov.nl.ca
www.gov.nl.ca/health
Loretta Chard, Asst., Board Services

Regional Health Authorities

***Corner Brook:* Western Health**
PO Box 2005, 1 Brookfield Ave., Western Memorial Hosp, Corner Brook, NL A2H 6C7
709-637-5245 Fax: 709-637-5159
info@hcsw.nf.ca
www.westernhealth.nl.ca
Old Name: Western Regional Integrated Health Authority
Number of Beds: 226 acute care, 441 long-term care
Note: Provides health and community services to over 79,000 people
Susan Gillam, CEO

***Grand Falls-Windsor:* Central Health**
Regional Office, 21 Carmelite Rd., Grand Falls-Windsor, NL A2A 1Y4
709-292-1289 www.centralhealth.nl.ca
Number of Beds: 519 long term care beds; 269 acute care beds; 32 residential units; 28 bassinets
Note: Number of Employees: 3,179 (140 physicians). Population Served: 94,000
Karen McGrath, Chief Executive Officer
Michael Zuckerman, Vice-President, Medical Services
Stephanie Power, Director, Communications
Ann Roberts, Medical Officer of Health
Sherry Freake, Chief Operating Officer, Gander
Sean Tulk, Chief Operating Officer, Grand Falls-Windsor
Trudy Stuckless, Chief Nursing Officer; Vice-President, Professional Standards
Rosemarie Goodyear, Senior Vice-President, Quality, Planning, & Priorities
Heather Brown, Vice-President, Rural Health
Terry Ings, Vice-President, Human Resources
John Kattenbusch, Vice-President, Finance & Corporate Services

***Happy Valley-Goose Bay:* Labrador-Grenfell Health**
PO Box 7000 C, Labrador Health Centre, Happy Valley-Goose Bay, NL A0P 1C0
709-897-2349 Fax: 709-896-4032 www.hlc.nl.ca
Michael Jong, Vice-President, Medical Affairs
Boyd Rowe, CEO

***St. John's:* Eastern Health Integrated Health Authority**
Health Sciences Centre, Prince Philip Dr., St. John's, NL A1B 3V6
709-777-1399 1-877-444-1399
employment@easternhealth.ca;
client.relations@easternhealth.ca
www.easternhealth.ca
Also Known As: Eastern Health
Number of Beds: 1,696 long term care beds; 987 acute care beds; 9 observation beds
Note: Facilities: 80+ hospitals, health care centres, long-term care facilities, & community care sites. Number of Employees: 12,000+ health care & support services professionals. Population served: 293,790. Area Covered: Region of Newfoundland & Labrador east of Port Blandford, including Port Blandford, the Avalon, Burin, & Bonavista Peninsulas, & Bell Island (111 incorporated municipalities, 69 local service districts, & 66 unincorporated municipal units)
Vickie Kaminski, President; Chief Executive Officer
709-777-1301, ceo@easternhealth.ca
Oscar Howell, Vice-President, Medical Services & Diagnostics
Wayne Miller, Vice-President, Planning, Quality, & Research

Michael J. O'Keefe, Chair
Norma Baker, Chief Operating Officer, Adult Acute Care (St. John's)
Beverley Clarke, Chief Operating Officer, Community, Children & Women, & Mental Healt
Pat Coish-Snow, Chief Operating Officer, Peninsulas
Alice Kennedy, Chief Operating Officer, Long Term Care (St. John's), Community Living &
Fay Matthews, Chief Operating Officer, Rural Avalon Child Youth & Family Services
George Butt, Vice-President, Corporate Services
Stephen Dodge, Vice-President, People & Information Services

Hospitals

Hospitals - General

***Burin:* Burin Peninsula Health Care Centre**
PO Box 340, Burin, NL A0E 1E0
709-891-1040 Fax: 709-891-3375 www.easternhealth.ca
Parent: Eastern Regional Integrated Health Authority
Number of Beds: 42 beds
Note: Hospital Specialties: Diagnostic imaging; Laboratory services; General surgery; Acute care; Gynecology; Obstetrics; Pediatrics; Psychiatry; Speech pathology, Physiotherapy, Occupational therapy; Respiratory therapy; Palliative care
Kim Green, Manager, Acute Care
709-891-3490, Fax: 709-891-3375, kim.green@easternhealth.ca

***Clarenville:* Dr. G.B. Cross Memorial Hospital**
67 Manitoba Dr., Clarenville, NL A5A 1K3
709-466-3411 www.easternhealth.ca
Parent: Eastern Regional Integrated Health Authority
Note: Hospital Specialties: Surgery; Intensive care; Obstetrics; Respiratory therapy; Physiotherapy; Dietitian services; Palliative care
Oscar Howell, Vice-President, Medical Services & Diagnostics, Eastern Health

***Corner Brook:* Western Memorial Regional Hospital**
PO Box 2005, Corner Brook, NL A2H 6J7
709-637-5000 Fax: 709-637-5410
Parent: Western Health
Number of Beds: 192 acute care beds
M. Wasmeier

Fogo: **Fogo Island Health Centre**
PO Box 9, Fogo, NL A0G 2B0
709-266-2221 www.centralhealth.nl.ca
Parent: Central Regional Integrated Health Authority
Year Founded: 1953
Note: Hospital Specialties: Primary care; Public health
Karen McGrath, Chief Executive Officer, Central Regional Health Authority

Gander: **James Paton Memorial Hospital**
125 TransCanada Hwy., Gander, NL A1V 1P7
709-256-2500 Fax: 709-256-7800
Parent: Central Regional Integrated Health Authority
Number of Beds: 92 acute care beds
J. Horwood

Grand Falls-Windsor: **Central Newfoundland Regional Health Centre**
50 Union St., Grand Falls-Windsor, NL A2A 2E1
709-292-2500 Fax: 709-292-2249 www.centralhealth.nl.ca
Parent: Central Regional Integrated Health Authority
Note: Hospital Specialties: Emergency services; Radiology; Surgical care; Ambulatory care services; Maternal / newborn unit; Cardiology; Neurology; Otolaryngology; Rehabilitation services; Physiotherapy; Occupational therapy; Pharmacy services
Janelle Hillier
, Regional Director, Medical Services

709-292-2450, Fax: 709-292-2249, janelle.hillier@centralhealth.nl.ca

Happy Valley-Goose Bay: **Labrador Health Centre**
PO Box 7000 C, Happy Valley-Goose Bay, NL A0P 1C0
709-897-2000 Fax: 709-896-4032
Old Name: Melville Hospital
Parent: Labrador-Grenfell Regional Integrated Health Authority
Number of Beds: 25 beds
Note: Full diagnostic services; Rehabilitation
E. Harding
Ed Sharpe, Supervisor, Plant Maintenance

Labrador City: **Captain William Jackman Memorial Hospital/CWJ**
410 Booth Ave., Labrador City, NL A2V 2K1
709-944-2632 www.lghealth.ca
Parent: Labrador-Grenfell Regional Integrated Health Authority
Year Founded: 1965
Number of Beds: 14 acute care beds; 6 long term care beds
Note: Hospital Specialties: Emergency services; Diagnostic imaging; Intensive care; Acute care; Obstetrics; Physiotherapy; Occupational therapy; Speech therapy; Respiratory therapy; Health education; Respite care; Long term care; Palliative care

St. Anthony: **Charles S. Curtis Memorial Hospital**
178-200 West St., St. Anthony, NL A0K 4S0
709-454-3333 www.lghealth.ca
Also Known As: Curtis Hospital
Parent: Labrador-Grenfell Regional Integrated Health Authority
Number of Beds: 50 hospital beds; 48 long term care beds at the John M. Gray Centre, which is adjoined to Charles S. Curtis Memorial Hospital
Note: Hospital Specialties: General surgery; Radiology; Pathology; Obstetrics; Gynecology; Genetics research; Pediatrics; Ophthalmology; Chemotherapy services; Orthopedics; Urology; Psychiatry; Rehabilitation services, including occupational therapy & physiotherapy; Acute care; Diabetes education; Social work
Michael Jong, Vice-President, Medical Services, Labrador-Grenfell Health

St. John's: **Dr. Leonard A. Miller Centre**
100 Forest Rd., St. John's, NL A1A 1E5
709-777-6555
Also Known As: The Miller Centre
Old Name: Quidi Vidi Hospital
Year Founded: 1851
Note: Specialty: Continuing care; Rehabilitation; Residential care for veterans of Newfoundland & Labrador; Centre for Nursing Studies

St. John's: **The General Hospital/Health Sciences Centre**
300 Prince Phillip Dr., St. John's, NL A1B 3V6
709-777-6300 Fax: 709-777-6770
www.easternhealth.ca/OurServices.aspx?d=2&id=118&p=75
Parent: Eastern Regional Integrated Health Authority
Number of Beds: 344 acute care beds
Note: A tertiary acute care facility & teaching hospital affiliated with Memorial University Schools of Medicine, Nursing, & Pharmacy.
Vickie Kaminski, President/CEO, ERIHA
709-777-1301, ceo@easternhealth.ca
Deborah Collins, Manager, Media Relations, ERIHA
709-777-1339, deborah.collins@easternhealth.ca

St. John's: **Janeway Children's Health and Rehabilitation Centre**
300 Prince Philip Dr., St. John's, NL A1B 3V6
709-777-6300 Fax: 709-777-4446
carol.chafe@easternhealth.ca
www.easternhealth.ca
Parent: Eastern Regional Integrated Health Authority
Number of Beds: 83 beds
Note: teaching hospital
Carol Chafe, Program Director
Keith Collins, Environmental Services Manager
709/778-4222

St. John's: **St. Clare's Mercy Hospital**
154 LeMarchant Rd., St. John's, NL A1C 5B8
709-777-1317 Fax: 709-777-5470
hcc.jonlo@hccsj.nf.ca
Parent: Eastern Regional Integrated Health Authority
Year Founded: 1922
Number of Beds: 216 acute care beds
Note: tertiary hospital
Ernie Power, Director, Plant Maintenance
L. Jones, CEO

Stephenville: **Sir Thomas Roddick Hospital**
142 Minnesota Dr., Stephenville, NL A2N 1H0
709-643-5111 Fax: 709-643-2700
westernhealth.nl.ca/index.php/locations/hospitals/sir-thomas-roddick-hospital
Parent: Western Health
Year Founded: 2003
Number of Beds: 44 acute care beds
Note: A comprehensive care facility, with services including emergency, surgery, obstetrics, gynecaelogy, renal care
Karen Alexander, Site Manager
Alan McComiskey, Chief of Staff

Community Health Centres

Community Health Care Centres

Badgers Quay: **Brookfield/Bonnews Health Care Centre**
PO Box 209, Badgers Quay, NL A0G 1B0
709-536-2405 Fax: 709-536-3334 www.cehcib.nf.ca
Parent: Central Regional Integrated Health Authority
Year Founded: 1944
Number of Beds: 12 beds
Kevin Green, Facility Manager
Winston Perry, Director, Maintenance Services

Baie Verte: **Baie Verte Peninsula Health Centre**
Baie Verte, NL A0K 1B0
709-532-4281 Fax: 709-532-4939
Parent: Central Regional Integrated Health Authority
Number of Beds: 7 acute care, 18 long-term care beds, 1 respite bed
Joyce Barker, Facility Director

Bell Island: **Dr. Walter Templeman Community Health Centre**
PO Box 580, Wabana, Bell Island, NL A0A 4H0
709-488-2821 Fax: 709-488-2600
Parent: Eastern Regional Integrated Health Authority
Number of Beds: 20 Beds
T. O'Brien
Jerry Butler, Director, Plant Maintenance

Bonavista: **Bonavista Peninsula Health Centre**
PO Box 1, Bonavista, NL A0C 1B0
709-468-7881 Fax: 709-468-7223
Old Name: Bonavista Community Health Centre
Parent: Eastern Regional Integrated Health Authority
Pauline Pardy, Director, Patient/Resident Care

Burgeo: **Calder Health Care Centre**
PO Box 190, Burgeo, NL A0M 1A0
709-886-3350 Fax: 709-886-3382
Parent: Western Health
Number of Beds: 3 acute care, 18 continuing care beds
Laurie Porter, Director of Nursing/Site Coordinator

Churchill Falls: **Churchill Falls Community Health Centre**
General Delivery, Churchill Falls, NL A0R 1A0
709-925-3381 Fax: 709-925-3246
Parent: Labrador-Grenfell Regional Integrated Health Authority
Joan Paul Kent, Nurse in Charge

Flowers Cove: **Strait of Belle Isle Health Centre**
General Delivery, Flowers Cove, NL A0K 2N0
709-456-2401 www.lghealth.ca
Parent: Labrador-Grenfell Regional Integrated Health Authority
Number of Beds: 3 beds
Note: Specialties: Ambulatory care; Family medicine; Public health services; Pre-natal classes; Post-natal visiting; Preschool & baby assessments; Dental services; Rehabilitation services; Home care
Judy Applin Poole

Grand Bank: **Grand Bank Community Health Centre**
PO Box 310, Grand Bank, NL A0E 1W0
709-832-2500 Fax: 709-832-1164
Parent: Eastern Regional Integrated Health Authority
Joan Penney, Director, Patient/Resident Care
Cyril Parsons, Utility Supervisor

Harbour Breton: **Connaigre Peninsula Health Centre**
PO Box 70, Harbour Breton, NL A0H 1P0
709-885-2359 Fax: 709-885-2358 www.cwhc.nl.ca/cp.htm
Old Name: Harbour Breton Health Centre
Parent: Central Regional Integrated Health Authority
Number of Beds: 20 beds: 6 acute, 12 continuing, 1 palliative, 1 respite
Sharon Skinner, Facility Director

Norris Point: **Bonne Bay Health Centre**
Norris Point, NL A0K 3V0
709-458-2201 Fax: 709-458-2074
Parent: Western Health
Number of Beds: 8 acute care, 14 continuing care beds

Northwest River: **NorthWest River Clinic**
General Delivery, Northwest River, NL A0P 1M0
709-497-8351 Fax: 709-497-8521
Parent: Labrador-Grenfell Regional Integrated Health Authority

Old Perlican: **Dr. A.A. Wilkinson Memorial Health Centre**
PO Box 70, Old Perlican, NL A0A 3G0
709-587-2200 Fax: 709-587-2275
Parent: Eastern Regional Integrated Health Authority
Number of Beds: 4 beds
M. Oliver

Port Saunders: **Rufus Guinchard Health Care Centre**
PO Box 40, Port Saunders, NL A0K 4H0
709-861-3533 Fax: 709-861-3772
Parent: Western Health
Number of Beds: 1 palliative care, 6 acute care, 22 continuing care beds
Paulette Lavers, Director of Nursing/Site Coordinator

Port aux Basques: **Dr. Charles L. LeGrow Health Centre**
PO Box 250, Port aux Basques, NL A0M 1C0
709-695-2175 Fax: 709-695-3118
Parent: Western Health
Number of Beds: 14 acute care, 30 continuing care beds
S. Savoury, Director of Nursing/Site Coordinator

Springdale: **Green Bay Community Health Centre**
PO Box 280, Springdale, NL A0J 1T0
709-673-3911 Fax: 709-673-3186
Parent: Central Regional Integrated Health Authority
Number of Beds: 8 beds; 1 special care, 2 convalescent, 1 palliative
Rose Saunders, Facility Director

Twillingate: **Notre Dame Bay Memorial Health Centre**
General Delivery, Twillingate, NL A0G 4M0
709-884-2131 Fax: 709-884-2586
Parent: Central Regional Integrated Health Authority
Number of Beds: 31 long-term care beds + 18 acute care beds
Note: Specialties: Outpatient services; Social work; Physiotherapy; Recreation therapy; Dietetics; Diabetes education; Health promotion & protection; Respite care, for children with special needs
Katherine Walters, Director, Health Services
B. Hamlyn, Supervisor, Plant Maintenance

Whitbourne: **Dr. W. H. Newhook Community Health Centre**
General Delivery, Whitbourne, NL A0B 3K0
709-759-2300 Fax: 709-759-2387
Parent: Eastern Regional Integrated Health Authority
L. English

Nursing Stations

Black Tickle: **Black Tickle Nursing Station**
General Delivery, Black Tickle, NL A0K 1N0

709-471-8872 Fax: 709-471-8893
Parent: Labrador-Grenfell Regional Integrated Health Authority

Cartwright: Cartwright Nursing Station
General Delivery, Cartwright, NL A0K 1V0
709-938-7285 Fax: 709-938-7286
Parent: Labrador-Grenfell Regional Integrated Health Authority

Charlottetown: Charlottetown Nursing Station
Charlottetown, NL A0K 5Y0
709-949-0259 Fax: 709-949-0259
Old Name: Charlottetown Nursing Station
Parent: Labrador-Grenfell Regional Integrated Health Authority
Number of Beds: 3 beds

Forteau: Labrador South Health Centre
Forteau, NL A0K 2P0
709-931-2450 Fax: 709-931-2000
Parent: Labrador-Grenfell Regional Integrated Health Authority
Number of Beds: 15 long-term care beds; 5 in-patient beds
Cornelia Linstead

Hopedale: Hopedale Nursing Station
General Delivery, Hopedale, NL A0P 1G0
709-933-3857 Fax: 709-933-3744
Parent: Labrador-Grenfell Regional Integrated Health Authority
Number of Beds: 3 beds

Makkovik: Makkovik Nursing Station & Community Service
General Delivery, Makkovik, NL A0P 1J0
709-923-2229 Fax: 709-923-2428
Parent: Labrador-Grenfell Regional Integrated Health Authority
Note: Specialties: Pharmaceutical services; Social work. Number of Employees: 2 nurses + 1 part time physician

Mary's Harbour: Mary's Harbour Community Clinic
Mary's Harbour, NL A0K 3P0
709-921-6228 Fax: 709-921-6975
jbudgell@grhs.nf.ca
www.lghealth.ca
Parent: Labrador-Grenfell Regional Integrated Health Authority
Number of Beds: 1 holding bed + 1 crib
Note: Number of Employees: 3 nurses + 1 social worker + 1 personal care attendant + 1 maintenance person

Nain: Nain Nursing Station
General Delivery, Nain, NL A0P 1L0
709-922-2912 Fax: 709-922-2103
Parent: Labrador-Grenfell Regional Integrated Health Authority

Natuashish: Natuashish Nursing Station
General Delivery, Natuashish, NL A0P 1A0
709-478-8842 Fax: 709-478-8817
Old Name: Davis Inlet Nursing Station
Parent: Labrador-Grenfell Regional Integrated Health Authority

Port Hope Simpson: Port Hope Simpson Community Clinic
General Delivery, Port Hope Simpson, NL A0K 4E0
709-960-0271 Fax: 709-960-0392 www.lghealth.ca
Parent: Labrador-Grenfell Health
Year Founded: 1975
Note: Specialties: Emergency room, basic trauma, cardiac monitoring & resuscitation, dental suite. Number of staff: 9

Postville: Postville Community Clinic
General Delivery, Postville, NL A0P 1N0
709-479-9851 Fax: 709-479-9715 www.lghealth.ca
Parent: Labrador-Grenfell Health
Number of Beds: 1 bed, 1 crib
Note: Number of staff: 3

Rigolet: Rigolet Nursing Station
General Delivery, Rigolet, NL A0P 1P0
709-947-3386 Fax: 709-947-3401
Parent: Labrador-Grenfell Regional Integrated Health Authority
Note: Number of staff: 2 Registered Nurses; visiting physician, dentist & specialists

Roddickton: White Bay Central Health Centre
Roddickton, NL A0K 4P0
709-457-2215 Fax: 709-457-2076
Parent: Labrador-Grenfell Regional Integrated Health Authority
Number of Beds: 5 beds

St Lewis: St. Lewis Nursing Station
General Delivery, St Lewis, NL A0K 4W0
709-939-2230 Fax: 709-939-2342
Parent: Labrador-Grenfell Regional Integrated Health Authority

Special Treatment Centre

St. John's: Dr. H. Bliss Murphy Cancer Centre
Newfoundland Cancer Treatment & Research Foundatio, 300 Prince Philip Dr., St. John's, NL A1B 3V6
709-777-6480 Fax: 709-753-0927 www.nctrf.nf.ca
Bertha Paulse, CEO

St. John's: The Morgentaler Clinic
#408, 59 Hamlyn Rd. Plaza, St. John's, NL A1E 5X7
709-754-3572 Fax: 709-754-6626 800-755-2044
sjmc@nf.aibn.com
Division of: St. John's Site
Year Founded: 1990
Note: Specialties: Abortion services; Counselling

Nursing Homes

Botwood: Dr. Hugh Twomey Health Care Centre
PO Box 250, Botwood, NL A0H 1E0
709-257-2874 Fax: 709-257-4613
Parent: Central Regional Integrated Health Authority
Number of Beds: 77 long-term care, 2 respite, 1 palliative care beds
Brenda Kelly, Facility Director

Buchans: A.M. Guy Memorial Health Centre
PO Box 10, Buchans, NL A0H 1G0
709-672-3326 Fax: 709-672-3390
Parent: Central Regional Integrated Health Authority
Number of Beds: 22 beds: 18 long-term, 2 acute care, 1 holding, 1 palliative
Roslyn Lane, Facility Director

Carbonear: Harbour Lodge Nursing Home
86 Highroad South, Carbonear, NL A1Y 1A4
709-945-5400
www.easternhealth.ca/OurServices.aspx?d=2&id=142&p=76
Parent: Eastern Regional Integrated Health Authority
Number of Beds: 127 beds
Debbie Farrell, Facility Manager
Harry Meados, Director, Environmental Services

Carbonear: Inter Faith Citizens Home
41 Water St., Carbonear, NL A1Y 1B1
709-945-5300 Fax: 709-945-5323
Parent: Eastern Regional Integrated Health Authority
Number of Beds: 53 beds
Deborah Farrell, Facility Manager

Clarke's Beach: Pentecostal Senior Citizen's Home
PO Box 130, Clarke's Beach, NL A0A 1W0
709-786-2993 www.easternhealth.ca
Parent: Eastern Regional Integrated Health Authority
Number of Beds: 75 beds
Note: Specialties: Nursing care for persons who require Level I, II, & III type care; Social work; Physiotherapy; Occupational therapy; Podiatry; Hearing & vision care
Beverley Bellefleur, Facility Manager

Corner Brook: Inter Faith Home for Senior Citizens
Churchill St., Corner Brook, NL A2H 5L8
709-639-9247 Fax: 709-639-1126
Parent: Western Health
Number of Beds: 103 long-term care beds
P. Griffin, Director of Nursing/Site Coordinator

Corner Brook: J.I. O'Connell Centre
PO Box 2005, Corner Brook, NL A2H 6J7
709-637-5606 Fax: 709-634-3047
Parent: Western Health
Number of Beds: 104 beds
P. Griffin, Director of Nursing/Site Coordinator

Gander: Lakeside Homes
95 Airport Blvd., Gander, NL A1V 2L7
709-256-8850 Fax: 709-256-4259
www.cehcib.nf.ca/web/lakeside.htm
Parent: Central Regional Integrated Health Authority
Number of Beds: 102 beds; 1 respite
Marlyce Greene, Facility Manager
Sam Butt, Maintenance Supervisor

Gander Bay South: Riverview Retirement Home Ltd.
Gander Bay South, NL A0G 2H0
709-676-2773
Also Known As: Gander Bay Retirement Home
Number of Beds: 40 beds
Shaun Lane

Goulds: Hefferman Boarding Home
PO Box 56, Goulds, NL A1S 1G3
709-745-5398
Number of Beds: 15 beds
Theresa Hefferman, Administrator

Grand Bank: Blue Crest Inter Faith Home
PO Box 160, Grand Bank, NL A0E 1W0
709-832-1660 Fax: 709-832-2103
Parent: Eastern Regional Integrated Health Authority
Number of Beds: 70 long-term care beds
Joan Penney, Director, Patient/Resident Care
Cyril Parsons, Maintenance Manager

Grand Falls-Windsor: Carmelite House
50 Union St., Grand Falls-Windsor, NL A2A 2E4
709-292-2528 Fax: 709-489-5778
Parent: Central Regional Integrated Health Authority
Number of Beds: 60 longterm care beds
Cynthia Burt, Facility Director

Happy Valley-Goose Bay: Harry L. Paddon Memorial Home
PO Box 766 B, Happy Valley-Goose Bay, NL A0P 1E0
709-896-3615 Fax: 709-896-5241
searle@hlc.nf.ca
Parent: Labrador-Grenfell Regional Integrated Health Authority
Number of Beds: 48 beds
K. White
Ronald Lyall, Supervisor, Maintenance

Lewisporte: North Haven Manor Senior Citizens' Home
PO Box 880, 21 Centennial Dr., Lewisporte, NL A0G 3A0
709-535-6767 Fax: 709-535-8383
Parent: Central Regional Integrated Health Authority
Number of Beds: 62 long-term care, 1 palliative, 2 respite beds
Debbie Colbourne, Facility Director

Mount Pearl: Masonic Park Nursing Home
#4000, Bldg. 15, Masonic Park, Mount Carson Ave., Mount Pearl, NL A1N 3K6
709-368-6081 www.masonicpark.ca; www.easternhealth.ca
Old Name: Masonic Park Senior Citizen's Home
Parent: Eastern Regional Integrated Health Authority
Year Founded: 1982
Number of Beds: 40 long term beds + 200 self-contained cottage & apt. units
Note: Specialties: Long-term care for seniors
Rolanda Ryan, Resident Care Manager

Springdale: Valley Vista Senior Citizens' Home
PO Box 130, Springdale, NL A0J 1T0
709-673-3936 Fax: 709-673-2832
Parent: Central Regional Integrated Health Authority
Number of Beds: 75 long-term care beds, 3 respite
Rose Saunders, Facility Director

St Anthony: John M. Gray Centre
PO Box 69, St Anthony, NL A0K 4S0
709-454-0371 Fax: 709-454-4134
Old Name: St. Anthony Interfaith Home
Parent: Labrador-Grenfell Regional Integrated Health Authority
Year Founded: 1998
Number of Beds: 48 long-term care beds
Michael Jong, Vice President Medical Affairs
Boyd Rowe, Chief Executive Officer

St. John's: Agnes Pratt Home
239 Topsail Rd., St. John's, NL A1E 2B4
709-579-0185 Fax: 709-739-5457
www.easternhealth.ca/AboutEH.aspx?d=2&id=150&p=76
Parent: Eastern Regional Integrated Health Authority
Number of Beds: 128 long-term care beds
Linda Colllingwood, Administrator

St. John's: Glenbrook Lodge
105 Torbay Rd., St. John's, NL A1A 2G9
709-726-1575 Fax: 709-726-0610
smatchem@sjnhb.nf.ca
www.sjnhb.nf.ca/glenbrooklodge.asp
Parent: Eastern Regional Integrated Health Authority
Number of Beds: 114 beds
Charles Granter, Executive Director

St. John's: Hoyles-Escasoni Complex
10 Escasoni Pl., St. John's, NL A1A 3R6
709-753-7590 Fax: 709-753-9620
Parent: Eastern Regional Integrated Health Authority
Number of Beds: 377 beds
Annette Clarke, Manager, Resident Care

St. John's: Saint Luke's Home
24 Road Deluxe, St. John's, NL A1E 5Z3
709-579-0052 Fax: 709-579-7317
Parent: Eastern Regional Integrated Health Authority
Number of Beds: 126 beds
Note: Nursing homel also owns and operates 54 independent

living cottages and the 76-unit Bishop John Meaden Manor Complex
Barbara Ivany, Administrator

***St. John's:* St. Patrick's Mercy Home**
146 Elizabeth Ave., St. John's, NL A1B 1S5
709-726-2687 Fax: 709-726-0722
Parent: Eastern Regional Integrated Health Authority
Number of Beds: 214 beds
Note: Long-term care facility affiliated with the Roman Catholic Diocese of St. John's
Phyllis Corbett, Administrator

***Stephenville Crossing:* Bay St. George Long Term Care Centre**
PO Box 250, Stephenville Crossing, NL A0N 2C0
709-646-5800 Fax: 709-646-2375
Old Name: Bay St. George Senior Citizens Home
Parent: Western Health
Number of Beds: 114 beds
Anne Doyle, Nursing

Long Term/Retirement Care

Long Term Care Facility

***Bonavista:* Golden Heights Manor**
Postal Service #1, Bonavista, NL A0C 1B0
709-468-2043 Fax: 709-468-1549
Parent: Eastern Regional Integrated Health Authority
Number of Beds: 62 beds
Pauline Pardy

***Placentia:* Placentia Health Centre**
PO Box 480, Placentia, NL A0B 2Y0
709-227-2061 Fax: 709-227-5476 www.easternhealth.ca
Parent: Eastern Regional Integrated Health Authority
Number of Beds: 10 acute care, 75 long term care beds
Note: Acute care, long term care (Lions Manor Nursing Home), on an in-patient & out-patient basis
Diane Reid, Facility Manager
W. Whittle, Director, Environmental Services

***St Brides:* Bay View Manor**
General Delivery, St Brides, NL A0B 2Z0
709-337-2569
Number of Beds: 10 beds
Note: personal care home
Jerome Quinlan
Beverly Russell

***St Lawrence:* U.S. Memorial Community Health Centre**
PO Box 398, St Lawrence, NL A0E 2V0
709-873-2220 Fax: 709-873-2390 www.easternhealth.ca
Parent: Eastern Regional Integrated Health Authority
Number of Beds: 40 beds
Note: Long term & protective care units, ambulatory care clinic, nutritional services, pharmacy, visiting specialty clinics
Jocelyn Dunphy, Co-ordinator, Patient/Resident Care
Elizabeth Degruchy-Lace, Manager, Environmental Services

Personal Care Homes

***Arnolds Cove:* Hilltop Manor**
PO Box 280, Arnolds Cove, NL A0B 1A0
709-463-5000 Fax: 709-463-1005
hollismetcalge@hotmail.com
Number of Beds: 32 beds
Trey Metcalfe

***Baie Verte:* Baie Verte Manor Ltd.**
PO Box 561, 20 High St., Baie Verte, NL A0K 1B0
709-532-4615 Fax: 709-532-4643
Number of Beds: 30 beds
Donna Rideout, Owner/Administrator

***Baie Verte:* H. Pardy Manor**
PO Box 1, Baie Verte, NL A0K 1B0
709-532-4603 Fax: 709-329-3281
Number of Beds: 22 beds
Kim Sacrey, Manager

***Bay Bulls:* Glynn's Rest Home**
PO Box 6, Bay Bulls, NL A0A 1C0
709-334-2241
Old Name: White's Rest Home
Number of Beds: 13 beds
Kathy White, Contact

***Bay Bulls:* Walsh's Personal Care Home**
PO Box 42, Rte. 10, Bay Bulls, NL A0A 1C0
709-334-2619
Number of Beds: 10 beds
Delores Walsh, Proprietor

***Bell Island:* Island Manor**
PO Box 728, Bell Island, NL A0A 4H0
709-488-2966
Number of Beds: 10 beds
Jocelyn Russell

***Bishop's Cove:* Smith's Personal Care Home**
PO Box 86, RR#1, Bishop's Cove, NL A0A 3X0
709-589-2189
Number of Beds: 4 beds
Mildred Naomi Smith

***Bishops Falls:* Exploits Manor**
PO Box 850, Bishops Falls, NL A0H 1C0
709-258-6446
Number of Beds: 30 beds
Alex Faulkner

***Cape Anguille:* Hilliard's Personal Care Home**
PO Box 18, Cape Anguille, NL A0N 1H0
709-955-2339
Number of Beds: 14 beds
Minnie Hilliard, Owner/Administrator

***Carmanville:* Carmanville Manor**
PO Box 42, Carmanville, NL A0G 1N0
709-534-2244 Fax: 709-534-2337
carmanvillemanor@nf.sympatico.ca
Number of Beds: 21 beds
Jeanne Clarke

***Catalina:* Seaside Lodge**
PO Box 182, Catalina, NL A0C 1J0
709-469-3160 Fax: 709-469-3161
Number of Beds: 50 beds
Note: Personal care home
Shirley Barney

***Catalina:* Shirley's Haven**
PO Box 182, Catalina, NL A0C 1J0
709-469-3160 Fax: 709-469-3161
Number of Beds: 50 beds
Shirley Barney

***Clarenville:* Clarenville Rest Home**
PO Box 951, Clarenville, NL A0E 1J0
709-466-2447
Number of Beds: 30 beds
Michelle Holloway, Proprietor/Administrator

***Clarkes Beach:* Brigus Personal Care Home**
PO Box 515, Clarkes Beach, NL A0A 1W0
709-786-9693 Fax: 709-786-4757
Number of Beds: 9 beds
Denise Smith, Co-owner
Keith Smith, Co-owner

***Clarkes Beach:* Calling Wood Downs**
PO Box 160, Clarkes Beach, NL A0A 1W0
709-786-1850
Number of Beds: 87 beds
Jerome Russell

***Clarkes Beach:* Smith's Country Villa Inc.**
PO Box 515, Clarkes Beach, NL A0A 1W0
709-786-7861
Number of Beds: 17 beds
Denise Smith

***Conception Bay South:* Greenslade's Personal Care Home**
12 Wettlaufer Rd., Conception Bay South, NL A1X 7P6
709-834-3047 Fax: 709-834-3087
Old Name: Greenslade Special Care Home
Number of Beds: 14 beds
Wayne Greenslade
Marilyn Greenslade

***Conception Bay South:* Halliday's Personal Care Home**
91 Cherry Lane, Conception Bay South, NL A1W 3B5
709-834-2349
Number of Beds: 20 beds
Donna Meeker, Manager

***Corner Brook:* Brake's Personal Care Home**
292 Curling St., Corner Brook, NL A2H 3J7
709-785-5092
Number of Beds: 6 beds
Vera Brake
Vivian Brake

***Corner Brook:* Mountain View Estates**
161 Premier Dr., Corner Brook, NL A2H 7M6
709-637-7960 Fax: 709-634-0235 www.mountainviewestates.ca
Number of Beds: 84 beds
Note: Nursing home
Byron Brake

***Corner Brook:* Mountain View House**
PO Box 3850, RR#2, Corner Brook, NL A2H 6B9
709-783-2019
Number of Beds: 30 beds
Note: Nursing home
Byron Brake

***Corner Brook:* Xavier House Inc.**
19 Mount Bernard Ave., Corner Brook, NL A2H 6K7
709-634-2787
Number of Beds: 20 beds
Rosalie Carey, Administrator

***Cow Head:* Cowhead Personal Care Home**
PO Box 145, Cow Head, NL A0K 2A0
709-243-2016
Number of Beds: 9 beds
Violet Nicolle

***Deer Lake:* Deer Lake Manor**
#119, 123 Nicholsville Rd., Deer Lake, NL A8A 1W6
709-635-2868
Number of Beds: 31 Beds
Dwight Ball, Contact

***Dunville:* Gateway Residence**
PO Box 280, Dunville, NL A0B 1S0
709-227-3814 Fax: 709-227-2346
polar@roadrunner.nf.net
Number of Beds: 22 beds
Maxine Dawe, Administrator

***Embree:* Parson's Retirement Home**
PO Box 82, Embree, NL A0G 2A0
709-535-6094
Number of Beds: 16 beds
Robert Parsons

***Fermeuse:* Fahey's Personal Care Home**
General Delivery, Fermeuse, NL A0A 2G0
709-363-2250 Fax: 709-363-2231
Old Name: Fahey Boarding Home
Number of Beds: 22 beds
Gerald Fahey

***Flowers Cove:* Ivey Durley Place**
PO Box 157, Flowers Cove, NL A0K 2N0
709-456-9104
Old Name: Straits-St Barbe Chronic Care
Number of Beds: 20 beds
Judy Way, Contact
709-456-2022,
Dennis Coates, Contact
704/456-2022

***Fogo:* Riverhead Manor**
PO Box 375, Fogo, NL A0G 2B0
709-266-2336
Number of Beds: 17 beds
Luther Piercey

***Gander:* Nightingale Manor**
11 Hadfield St., Gander, NL A1V 2V6
709-256-3711
Number of Beds: 60 beds
Lawrence Guy

***Glovertown:* Baywatch Manor**
PO Box 120, Glovertown, NL A0G 2M0
709-533-2600
baywatchmanor@nf.aibn.com
www.baywatchmanor.ca
Number of Beds: 38 beds
Denise Button

***Glovertown:* Oram's Birchview Manor**
PO Box 10, Glovertown, NL A0G 2L0
709-266-2336
Number of Beds: 50 beds
Note: Specialty: Personal care
Paul Oram

***Goulds:* Kelly's Personal Care Home**
478 Main Road, Goulds, NL A1S 1G3
709-745-5343
Old Name: Kelly Boarding Home
Number of Beds: 19 beds

Linda Spurrell, Proprietor
709/745-5343

Goulds: Lawlor's Personal Care Home
PO Box 419, Goulds, NL A1S 1G5
709-745-1956

Number of Beds: 14 beds
Albert Lawlor

Goulds: Maloney's Personal Care Home
PO Box 568, Barton's Rd., Goulds, NL A1S 1G3
709-745-4986

Number of Beds: 10 beds
Note: Nursing Home
Mary Maloney, Contact

Grand Falls-Windsor: Golden Years Estate
348 Grenfell Heights, Grand Falls-Windsor, NL A2H 2R8
709-489-7263 Fax: 709-489-7306
zettalane@tgyestate.com
www.thegoldenyearsestate.com

Number of Beds: 67 beds
Zetta Lane, Owner

Grand Falls-Windsor: Islandside Manor
PO Box 814, Grand Falls-Windsor, NL A2A 2P7
709-483-2121

Number of Beds: 24 beds
Max Arnold

Grand Falls-Windsor: Twin Town Manor
15 King St., Grand Falls-Windsor, NL A1B 1J6
709-489-0988 Fax: 709-489-1880

Number of Beds: 96 beds
Guy Bailey, Contact

Happy Valley-Goose Bay: Pine Lodge Personal Care Home
PO Box 264 C, 3 Spruce Ave., Happy Valley-Goose Bay, NL A0P 1C0
709-896-5512 Fax: 709-896-5465

Note: Specialties: Personal care for seniors & person with an intellectual disability
Diane Oliver-Scales

Harbour Breton: Hillside Manor
PO Box 687, Harbour Breton, NL A0H 1P0
709-885-2693

Number of Beds: 16 beds
Luther Piercey

Hickmans Harbour: Blundons' Personal Care Home
PO Box 90, Hickmans Harbour, NL A0C 1P0
709-466-2189

Number of Beds: 20 beds
Effie Blundon, Proprietor

Holyrood: Kennedy's Riverside Boarding Home Ltd.
PO Box 114, Holyrood, NL A0A 2R0
709-229-6886

Old Name: Kennedy's Riverside Manor Limited
Number of Beds: 33 beds
Geneviève Kennedy

Holyrood: Tobin's Guest Home Inc.
PO Box 95, Holyrood, NL A0A 2R0
709-229-7464

Number of Beds: 30 beds
Betty Tobin
Walter Tobin

Holyrood: Woodford's Golden Care
PO Box 158, Holyrood, NL A0A 2R0
709-229-3343

Number of Beds: 10 beds
Josephine Woodford

Holyrood: Woodford's Golden Care Home
PO Box 158, Holyrood, NL A0A 2R0
709-229-3343

Number of Beds: 10 beds
Josephine Woodford, Contact

Kelligrews: Gully Pond Manor
39 Gully Pond Rd., Kelligrews, NL A1X 6Z2
709-834-8083

Number of Beds: 20 beds
Ruby Hennessey

Kilbride: Hennessey's Personal Care Home
222 Old Bay Bulls Rd., Kilbride, NL A1G 1E1
709-368-5558 Fax: 709-368-4910

Number of Beds: 16 beds
Catherine Hennessey, Proprietor

Lark Harbour: Guardian Angel Seniors Home
PO Box 91, Lark Harbour, NL A0L 1L0
709-681-2288

Number of Beds: 20 beds
Brian Park

Lewisporte: Pleasantville Manor
PO Box 207, Lewisporte, NL A0G 3A0
709-535-0941

Number of Beds: 60 beds
Ron Sheppard

Long Pond: Allison's Manor
PO Box 14099, 332 Ancorage Rd., Long Pond, NL A0A 2Y0
709-834-8541 Fax: 709-834-6336

Number of Beds: 42 beds
Sharon Stone, Administrator

Mary's Harbour: Harbourview Manor
PO Box 153, Mary's Harbour, NL A0K 3P0
709-921-6440

Number of Beds: 20 beds
Elaine Rumbolt

Mount Carmel: Silverdale Manor
PO Box 86, Mount Carmel, NL A0B 2M0
709-521-2377

Number of Beds: 25 beds
Angela DeCaria

Mount Pearl: Cradea Manor
1234 Topsail Rd., Mount Pearl, NL A1N 2C1
709-364-5265

Number of Beds: 20 beds
Madeline Sturge

Mount Pearl: Pearl House
163 Park Ave., Mount Pearl, NL A1N 1K6
709-368-3850

Number of Beds: 44 beds
Lawrence Guy

Musgrave Harbour: Hillcrest Manor
PO Box 100, Musgrave Harbour, NL A0G 3J0
709-655-2777

Number of Beds: 30 beds
Lawrence Guy

Musgravetown: Greenwood Rest Home Ltd.
PO Box 9, Bunyan's Cove Rd., Musgravetown, NL A0C 1Z0
709-467-5243 Fax: 709-467-5578

Number of Beds: 20 beds
Wilfred Greening

New Harbour: Honeysuckle Estates Inc.
PO Box 46, New Harbour, NL A0B 2P0
709-582-3604

Number of Beds: 14 beds
Joan Hillier

New Harbour: Jackson's Country Manor
New Harbour Barrens, New Harbour, NL A0B 2P0
709-588-2382

Number of Beds: 39 Beds
Wallace Jackson, Contact
709/582-2888

Norris Point: Crockers Retirement Home
PO Box 1, Norris Point, NL A0K 3V0
709-458-2429

Number of Beds: 20 beds
Gerald Crocker

Paradise: Shady Rest Lodge
PO Box 3034, Paradise, NL A1L 3W2
709-895-6786

Number of Beds: 21 beds
Cavell Murphy, Contact

Pollards Point: Main River Manor Ltd.
General Delivery, Pollards Point, NL A0K 4B0
709-482-2334

Old Name: Golden Crest Haven
Number of Beds: 20 beds
Dale Gillingham, Contact

Port aux Basques: Mountain Hope Manor
PO Box 957, Port aux Basques, NL A0M 1C0
709-695-3458 Fax: 709-695-3751

Number of Beds: 32 beds
Ida Lawrence

Porterville: Bayside Manor
PO Box 134, RR#1, Porterville, NL A0G 3A0
709-654-3171 Fax: 709-654-2176

Number of Beds: 50 beds
Ron Sheppard, Proprietor

Roddickton: Roddickton House
PO Box 40, Roddickton, NL A0K 4P0
709-457-2166 Fax: 709-457-2079

Old Name: Claudelle Manor
Number of Beds: 22 beds
Note: Nursing home
Chris Decker

Shearstown: Maple Lodge
PO Box 10, Shearstown, NL A0A 3V0
709-786-7051

Number of Beds: 16 beds
Note: Nursing home
William Tetford, Proprietor

St Albans: K.M. Homes Limited
8 Meadow Pl, St Albans, NL A0H 2E0
709-538-3162

Number of Beds: 30 beds
Shirley Ingram

St Anthony: Shirley's Haven #2
St Anthony, NL A0K 4S0
709-454-1070

Number of Beds: 60 beds
Shirley Barney

St Lawrence: Mount Margaret Manor
PO Box 278, St Lawrence, NL A0E 2V0
709-873-3199

Number of Beds: 31 beds
Mildred Marsden

St Marys: Lewis' Personal Care Home, Inc.
PO Box 219, St Marys, NL A0B 3B0
709-525-2244

Number of Beds: 20 beds
Carolann Lewis, Proprietor

St Marys: Neville's Special Care Home
General Delivery, St Marys, NL A0B 3B0
709-525-2098

Number of Beds: 21 beds
Paul Neville

St. John's: Katherine House
90 Lemarchant Rd., St. John's, NL A1E 1P1
709-754-3864

Number of Beds: 10 beds
Barry Oliver
709/754-3864
Linda Ebsary, Proprietor
709/754-3864

St. John's: Margaret's Manor
57 Bonaventure Ave., St. John's, NL A1C 3Z3
709-722-4040

Number of Beds: 40 beds
Note: Nursing home
William Clarke

St. John's: North Pond Home
34 Virginia Place, St. John's, NL A1A 3G6
709-437-1415 Fax: 709-726-8187

Number of Beds: 35 beds
Maxine Isaacs
Barry Isaacs

Stephenville: Silverwood Manor
42 Kippens Rd., Stephenville, NL A2N 1A7
709-643-6550

Number of Beds: 30 beds
Judy Gallant

Trepassey: Ocean View Rest Home
PO Box 5, Trepassey, NL A0A 4B0
709-438-2227

Number of Beds: 19 beds
Anne Pennell, Contact
Jerome Devereaux, Contact

Twillingate: Sunset Manor
PO Box 638, Twillingate, NL A0G 4M0
709-884-5301

Number of Beds: 23 beds
Note: Rest home
Margaret Woods

Wesleyville: Otterbury Manor
PO Box 42, 428 Main St., Wesleyville, NL A0G 4R0
709-536-3383

Number of Beds: 30 beds

Elsie Carter

***White Bay:* Hamlyn Manor Inc.**
PO Box 59, Seal Cove, White Bay, NL A0K 5E0
709-531-2085
Number of Beds: 17 beds
Calvin Hamlyn

***Witless Bay:* Alderwood Estates**
PO Box 10, Witless Bay, NL A0A 4K0
709-334-2183 Fax: 709-334-2058 www.alderwoodestates.ca
Old Name: Dunn's Personal Care Home
Number of Beds: 52 beds
Debbie Dunne

Mental Health Facilities

Mental Health Hospital/Clinic/Facility

***St. John's:* Waterford Hospital**
Waterford Bridge Rd., St. John's, NL A1E 4J8
709-777-3300 Fax: 709-777-3993 www.easternhealth.ca
Parent: Eastern Regional Integrated Health Authority
Number of Beds: 80 acute care, 104 continuing care beds
Note: Mental Health Program, acute & outpatient care; dialysis services, blood collection, x-ray clinics
Beverley Clarke, COO, Community & Children, Mental Health & Addic
Louise Jones, Interim President/CEO, Eastern Health

Northwest Territories

Government Departments in Charge

NORTHWEST TERRITORIES: Dept. of Health & Social Services
PO Box 1320, Centre Square Tower, Yellowknife, NT X1A 2L9
867-920-6173 Fax: 867-873-0266
sandra_pearce@gov.nt.ca
www.hlthss.gov.nt.ca
Norman M. Hatlevik, Director, Population Health & Board Development

Regional Health Authorities

***Fort Simpson:* Dehcho Health & Social Services Authority/DHSSA**
PO Box 246, Fort Simpson, NT X0E 0N0
867-695-3815 Fax: 867-695-2920
health_beat@gov.nt.ca
www.dhssa.ca
Old Name: Deh Cho Health & Social Services Board
Year Founded: 1997
Note: Population Served: 3,409. Area Served: Fort Liard; Fort Providence; Fort Simpson; Hay River Reserve; Jean Marie River; Kakisa; Nahanni Butte; Trout Lake; Wrigley, Dehcho Region, NWT.
Allan J. Landry, Chair
Kathy Tsetso, Chief Executive Officer
KATHY_TSETSO@gov.nt.ca
David Humphrey, Director, Finance & Administration
Fax: 867-695-2054
Minnie Letcher, Director, Community Programs
MINNIE_LETCHER@gov.nt.ca
Claude Gingras, Manager, Social Services
Cindy MacDonald, Manager, Health Services
CINDY_MACDONALD@gov.nt.ca
Tracy Humphrey, Coordinator, Risk Management & Planning
TRACY_HUMPHREY@gov.nt.ca
Rene Lamothe, Coordinator, Traditional Healing
RENE_LAMOTHE@gov.nt.ca

***Hay River:* Hay River Health & Social Services Authority/HRHSSA**
3 Gaetz Dr., Hay River, NT X0E 0R8
867-874-7115 Fax: 867-874-7118 www.hrhssa.org
Note: Facilities: Hay River Emergency Group Home; Hay River Public Health Unit; Hay River Social Services Office; H.H. Williams Memorial Hospital (29 acute / extended care beds); Hay River Medical Clinic; Woodland Manor (15 long term care beds); Hay River Reserve Health Station; Hay River Reserve Social Services; Enterprise Social Services. Population Served: 3,832. Area Served: Southern shore of Great Slave Lake, Northwest Territories, including the communities of Enterprise & Hay River
Sue Cullen, Chief Executive Officer
867-874-7110, SUE_CULLEN@gov.nt.ca
George Blandford, Director, Finance & Administration
867-874-7119, GEORGE_BLANDFORD@gov.nt.ca
Joletta Larocque, Director, Employment & Community Service
867-874-7117, JOLETTA_LAROCQUE@gov.nt.ca
Jennifer Croucher, Physician Administrator
867-874-7160, JENNIFER_CROUCHER@gov.nt.ca
Sheryl Courtoreille, Coordinator, Quality Improvment
867-874-7168, SHERYL_COURTOREILLE@gov.nt.ca

***Inuvik:* Beaufort-Delta Health & Social Services Authority**
Bag 2, Inuvik, NT X0E 0T0
867-777-8000 Fax: 867-777-8062 bdhssa.nt.ca
Old Name: Inuvik Regional Health & Social Services Authority
Note: Serves the communities of Aklavik, Fort McPherson, Inuvik, Paulatuk, Sachs Harbour, Tsiigehtchic, Tuktoyaktuk, & Ulukhaktok. Services provided through the Inuvik Regional Hospital & community clinics, & include continuing care, health promotion, counselling, social programs, nutrition, telehealth, rehabilitation & diabetes education.
Deborah Tynes, CEO
deborah_tynes@gov.nt.ca

***Norman Wells:* Sahtu Health & Social Services Authority**
PO Box 340, Norman Wells, NT X0E 0V0
867-587-3438 Fax: 867-587-3436 www.shssa.org
Note: provides numerous health and social services to 2,700 people on the Mackenzie Valley
Chad Fehr, CEO
chad_fehr@gov.nt.ca

***Yellowknife:* Stanton Territorial Health Authority**
PO Box 10, Yellowknife, NT X1A 2N1
867-669-4224 Fax: 867-669-4128 www.srhb.org
Old Name: Stanton Regional Health Board
Sylvia Haener, CEO
sylvia_haener@gov.nt.ca

***Yellowknife:* Yellowknife Health & Social Services Authority**
PO Box 608, Yellowknife, NT X1A 2N5
867-873-7276 Fax: 867-873-0289
greg_cummings@gov.nt.ca
Old Name: Yellowknife Health & Social Services Board
Note: community health & social services board
Greg Cummings, CEO

Hospitals

Hospitals - General

***Hay River:* H.H. Williams Memorial Hospital**
3 Gaetz Dr., Hay River, NT X0E 0R8
867-874-7100 Fax: 867-874-7118
Parent: Hay River Health & Social Service Authority
Number of Beds: 23 acute, 8 extended care beds
Note: long-term care facility
Paul Vieira, CEO

***Inuvik:* Inuvik Regional Hospital**
Bag 2, Inuvik, NT X0E 0T0
867-777-8000 Fax: 867-777-8054 bdhssa.nt.ca
Parent: Beaufort-Delta Health & Social Services Authority
Number of Beds: 51 beds
Note: Location: 285 Mackenzie Rd., Inuvik. Provides emergency services, surgery, obstetrics, acute care, long term care, pharmacy, diagnostic imaging & lab, physician clinics, visiting specialists, & referral.

Community Health Centres

Community Health Care Centres

***Aklavik:* Susie Husky Health & Social Services Centre**
PO Box 114, Aklavik, NT X0E 0A0
867-978-2516 Fax: 867-978-2160 www.bdhssa.nt.ca
Old Name: Susie Husky Health Centre
Parent: Beaufort-Delta Health & Social Services Authority
Note: Specialties: Clinics, such as chronic disease & well child, woman, & man clinics; School health program; Health promotion; Dental therapy; Home care; Immunization programs; Rehabilitative services; Child protection; Child & family services; Palliative care. Number of Employees: 1 nurse in charge + 3 community health nurses + 2 community social service workers; 1 dental therapist + 1 community health representative + 1 home support worker + 1 clerk + 1 caretaker

***Behchoko:* Behchoko Health Centre**
General Delivery, Behchoko, NT X0E 0Y0
867-392-6351 Fax: 867-392-6612
Old Name: Rae Health Centre
Parent: Dogrib Community Services Authority

***Deline:* Deline Health Centre**
PO Box 119, General Delivery, Deline, NT X0E 0G0
867-589-3111 Fax: 867-589-3406
Parent: Sahtu Health & Social Services Authority

***Fort Good Hope:* Fort Good Hope Health Centre**
PO Box 9, Fort Good Hope, NT X0E 0H0
867-598-2211 Fax: 867-598-2605
Parent: Sahtu Health & Social Services Authority

***Fort Liard:* Fort Liard Health Centre**
General Delivery, Fort Liard, NT X0G 0A0
867-770-4301 Fax: 867-770-3235
Parent: Deh Cho Health & Social Services Authority

***Fort McPherson:* William Firth Health Centre**
PO Box 56, Fort McPherson, NT X0E 0J0
867-952-2586 Fax: 867-952-2620
Parent: Beaufort-Delta Health & Social Services Authority

***Fort Providence:* Fort Providence Health Centre**
PO Box 260, Fort Providence, NT X0E 0L0
867-699-4311 Fax: 867-699-3811
Parent: Deh Cho Health & Social Services Authority

***Fort Simpson:* Fort Simpson Health Centre**
PO Box 246, Fort Simpson, NT X0E 0N0
867-695-7000 Fax: 867-695-7017
Parent: Deh Cho Health & Social Services Authority

***Fort Smith:* Fort Smith Health Centre**
c/o Fort Smith Health & Social Services, PO Box 1080, Fort Smith, NT X0E 0P0
867-872-6203 Fax: 867-872-6260
Parent: Fort Smith Health & Social Services Authority
Number of Beds: 25 beds

***Gameti:* Gameti Health Centre**
General Delivery, Gameti, NT X0E 1R0
867-997-3141 Fax: 867-997-3045
Old Name: Gameti/Rae Lakes Outpatient Centre
Parent: Dogrib Community Services Authority

***Hay River:* Hay River Public Health Unit**
3 Gaetz Dr., Hay River, NT X0E 0R8
867-874-7201 Fax: 867-874-7211
Parent: Hay River Health & Social Service Authority

***Inuvik:* Inuvik Public Health Unit**
PO Bag 2, Inuvik, NT X0E 0T0
867-777-7246 Fax: 867-777-3255
Parent: Beaufort-Delta Health & Social Services Authority

***Inuvik:* Inuvik Public Health Unit**
Bag 2, Inuvik, NT X0E 0T0
867-777-7246 Fax: 867-777-3255
Barb Lennie, Nurse-in-Charge

***Jean Marie River:* Jean Marie River Health Cabin**
General Delivery, Jean Marie River, NT X0E 0N0
867-809-2900 Fax: 867-809-2902

***Lutselk'e:* Lutselk'e Health Centre**
PO Box 56, Lutselk'e, NT X0E 1A0
867-370-3111 Fax: 867-370-3022
Parent: Yellowknife Health & Social Services Authority
Note: Specialties: Public health programs; Counselling & crisis intervention & referrals

***Nahanni Butte:* Nahanni Butte Medical Health Clinic**
General Delivery, Nahanni Butte, NT X0E 0N0
867-602-2203 Fax: 867-602-2021
Parent: Deh Cho Health & Social Services Authority

***Norman Wells:* Norman Wells Health Centre**
PO Box 8, Norman Wells, NT X0E 0V0
867-587-2250 Fax: 867-587-2934
Parent: Sahtu Health & Social Services Authority

***Paulatuk:* Paulatuk Health Centre**
PO Box 114, General Delivery, Paulatuk, NT X0E 1N0
867-580-3231 Fax: 867-580-3300
Parent: Beaufort-Delta Health & Social Services Authority
Number of Beds: 1 bed

***Sachs Harbour:* Sachs Harbour Health Centre**
PO Box 14, Sachs Harbour, NT X0E 0Z0
867-690-4181 Fax: 867-690-3802
Parent: Beaufort-Delta Health & Social Services Authority

***Tuktoyaktuk:* Rosie Ovayouk Health Centre**
Bag 1000, Tuktoyaktuk, NT X0E 1C0
867-977-2321 Fax: 867-977-2535
Parent: Beaufort-Delta Health & Social Services Authority

***Tulita:* Tulita Health Centre**
PO Box 145, Tulita, NT X0E 0K0
867-588-4251 Fax: 867-588-3000 www.shssa.org

Parent: Sahtu Health & Social Services Authority
Note: Specialties: Primary care; Health promotion & prevention. Number of Employees: 3 nurses + 2 prevention & health promotion workers + 1 community social service worker + 1 mental health & addictions worker + 1 home support worker + support staff

Ulukhaktok: Emegak Health Centre
PO Box 160, Ulukhaktok, NT X0E 0S0
867-396-3111 Fax: 867-396-3221
Parent: Beaufort-Delta Health & Social Services Authority

Ulukhaktok: Ulukhaktok Community Wellness Centre
c/o Emegak Health & Social Services Centre, PO Box 160, Ulukhaktok, NT X0E 0S0
867-396-4688 Fax: 867-396-2934
Parent: Beaufort-Delta Health & Social Services Authority
Note: Specialties: Assessments; Crisis intervention; Therapeutic counselling; Education & awareness. Number of Employees: 1 mental health & addictions counsellor + 1 community wellness worker

Wekweti: Wekweti Health Centre
General Delivery, Wekweti, NT X0E 1W0
867-713-2904 Fax: 867-713-2904

Wha Ti: Wha Ti Health Centre
General Delivery, Wha Ti, NT X0E 1P0
867-573-3261 Fax: 867-573-3701
Old Name: Wha Ti Outpatient Health Centre
Parent: Dogrib Community Services Authority

Wrigley: Wrigley Health Centre
PO Box 58, General Delivery, Wrigley, NT X0E 1E0
867-581-3441 Fax: 867-581-3200
Parent: Deh Cho Health & Social Services Authority

Yellowknife: Yellowknife Public Health Centre
PO Box 608, Yellowknife, NT X1A 2N5
867-920-6570 Fax: 867-873-0158
Parent: Yellowknife Health & Social Services Authority

Nursing Stations

Colville Lake: Colville Lake Health Station
PO Box 50, General Delivery, Colville Lake, NT X0E 0L0
867-709-2409 Fax: 867-709-2504

Fort Resolution: Fort Resolution Health Centre
General Delivery, Fort Resolution, NT X0E 0M0
867-394-4511 Fax: 867-394-3117

Trout Lake: Trout Lake Health Station
Trout Lake Health Cabin, PO Box 39, Trout Lake, NT X0E 1Z0
867-206-2838 Fax: 867-206-2024
Parent: Deh Cho Health & Social Services Authority
Versa Vendron

Tsiigehtchic: Tsiigehtchic Health & Social Services Centre
General Delivery, Tsiigehtchic, NT X0E 0B0
867-953-3361 Fax: 867-777-8049
Parent: Beaufort-Delta Health & Social Services Authority

Special Treatment Centre

Fort Liard: Fort Liard Mental Health & Addictions Program
General Delivery, Fort Liard, NT X0G 0A0
867-770-4770 Fax: 867-770-4813

Fort Simpson: Fort Simpson Mental Health & Addictions Program
PO Box 246, Fort Simpson, NT X0E 0N0
867-695-7085 Fax: 867-695-7071
Elsie Gresl, Coordinator

Hay River: Hay River Reserve Wellness Centre
PO Box 3092, Hay River, NT X0E 1G4
867-874-2838 Fax: 867-874-6305
Anne Firth-Jones, Community Wellness Worker

Inuvik: Inuvik Homeless Shelter
PO Box 2570, Inuvik, NT X0E 0T0
867-777-2726 Fax: 867-777-4597
Joanna Christie, Executive Director

Nursing Homes

Fort Smith: Northern Lights Special Care Home
PO Box 1319, Fort Smith, NT X0E 0P0
867-872-5403 Fax: 867-872-5404
Parent: Fort Smith Health & Social Services Authority
Number of Beds: 21 beds
Suzanne Sihikal, Administrator

Yellowknife: Aven Manor
#1, 5710 - 50th Ave., Yellowknife, NT X1A 1E9
867-920-2443 Fax: 867-873-9915
yaccs@theedge.ca
Parent: Yellowknife Health & Social Services Authority
Number of Beds: 29 beds
Greg Debogorski, Executive Director

Long Term/Retirement Care

Long Term Care Facility

Aklavik: Joe Greenland Centre
PO Box 162, Aklavik, NT X0E 0A0
867-978-2381 Fax: 867-978-2943
Parent: Beaufort-Delta Health & Social Services Authority
Number of Beds: 8 beds
Judy Semple, Facility Manager

Fort Simpson: Fort Simpson Long Term Care Home
PO Box 246, Fort Simpson, NT X0E 0N0
867-695-7080 Fax: 867-695-7083
Parent: Deh Cho Health & Social Services Authority

Fort Simpson: Stanley Isaiah Support of Living Home
PO Box 240, Fort Simpson, NT X0E 0N0
867-695-2365 Fax: 867-695-2364
Parent: Deh Cho Health & Social Services Authority
Note: independent living adult

Hay River: Judith Fabian Group Home
PO Box 3052, Hay River, NT X0E 0R0
867-874-3844 Fax: 867-847-3814
Parent: Deh Cho Health & Social Services Authority

Hay River: Woodland Manor
52 Woodland Dr., Hay River, NT X0E 0R8
867-874-7226 Fax: 867-874-7234
ruth_budgel@gov.nt.ca
Parent: Hay River Health & Social Service Authority
Number of Beds: 15 beds
Janet Leask, Coordinator, Residential Care

Inuvik: Billy Moore Home
PO Box 1078, Inuvik, NT X0E 0T0
867-777-2472 Fax: 867-777-2472
Parent: Beaufort-Delta Health & Social Services Authority

Inuvik: Charlotte Vehus Home
PO Box 1800, Inuvik, NT X0E 0T0
867-777-4780 Fax: 867-777-4687
Parent: Beaufort-Delta Health & Social Services Authority

Mental Health Facilities

Mental Health Hospital/Clinic/Facility

Yellowknife: Yellowknife Mental Health Clinic
PO Box 10, Yellowknife, NT X1A 2N5
867-873-7042 Fax: 867-873-0487
Corliss McCloskey, Manager, Psychiatric Services

Nova Scotia

Government Departments in Charge

NOVA SCOTIA: Nova Scotia Department of Health
Joseph Howe Bldg., PO Box 488, 1690 Hollis St., Halifax, NS B3J 2R8
902-424-5818 Fax: 902-424-0730 800-387-6665
dohweb@gov.ns.ca
www.gov.ns.ca/health
Nancy Maguire

Regional Health Authorities

Amherst: Cumberland Health Authority
PO Box CHA, 34 Prince Arthur St., Amherst, NS B4H 3B3
902-661-1090 Fax: 902-667-1125 www.cha.nshealth.ca
Year Founded: 2001
Note: Area Served: Cumberland County, NS
Bruce Saunders, Chair
H. Bruce Quigley, Chief Executive Officer, bruce.quigley@cha.nshealth.ca
Darla MacPherson, Vice-President, Community Health
Darla.MacPherson@cha.nshealth.ca
Rakesh Minocha, Vice-President, Operations
rakesh.minocha@cha.nshealth.ca
Cheryl Northcott, Vice-President, Patient Care Services
cheryl.northcott@cha.nshealth.ca
Ann Keddy, Director, Public Relations
902-661-1090, ann.keddy@cha.nshealth.ca

Antigonish: Guysborough Antigonish Strait Health Authority #7/GASHA
25 Bay St., Antigonish, NS B2G 2G5
902-867-4500 Fax: 902-863-1176 1-800-565-2511
Donalda.Macgillivary@gasha.nshealth.ca
www.gasha.nshealth.ca
Year Founded: 2001
Number of Beds: 89 beds at St. Martha's Regional Hospital; 31 beds at Strait Richmond Hospital; 10 beds at Guysborough Memorial Hospital; 6 beds at St. Mary's Memoria
Note: Facilities: St. Martha's Regional Hospital; Strait Richmond Hospital, Evanston, Richmond County; Guysborough Memorial Hospital; St. Mary's Memorial Hospital; Eastern Memorial Hospital, Canso. Number of Employees: 1,000+. Population Served: 44,515. Area Served: Town of Antigonish; Town of Canso; Town of Mulgrave; Town of Port Hawkesbury; Municipality of the County of Antigonish; Municipality of the District of Guysborough; Municipality of the County of Richmond; Municipality of the District of St. Mary's; Municipality of the County of Inverness, Nova Scotia
Kevin MacDonald, Chief Executive Officer
902-867-4500, Kevin.Macdonald@gasha.nshealth.ca
David Samson, Chair

Jeremy Hillyard, District Medical Chief of Staff
902-867-4500, Jeremy.Hillyard@gasha.nshealth.ca
Madonna MacDonald, Vice-President, Community Health
902-867-4500, Madonna.Macdonald@gasha.nshealth.ca
Heather MacKay, Director, Public Relations
902-867-4500, Fax: 902-867-1059, Heather.MacKay@gasha.nshealth.ca
David MacKenzie, Vice-President, Operations
902-867-4500, David.mackenzie@gasha.nshealth.ca
Liz Millett, Vice-President, Patient Care
902-867-4500, Liz.Millett@gasha.nshealth.ca
Helen Muir, Coordinator, Human Resources
902-867-4500, Fax: 902-863-6455, humanresources@gasha.nshealth.ca

Bridgewater: South Shore District Health Authority #1
90 Glen Allan Dr., Bridgewater, NS B4V 3S6
902-527-2266 Fax: 902-527-5269
thawkesworth@ssdha.nshealth.ca
www.ssdha.nshealth.ca
Note: South Shore Regional Hospital (Bridgewater), Fishermen's Memorial Hospital (Lunenburg), & Queens General Hospital (Liverpool). Community-based programs for addiction services, palliative care, public health, mental health
Kevin McNamara, CEO

Halifax: Capital Health District
#2142, 1796 Summer St., Halifax, NS B3H 3A7
EXJW@cdha.nshealth.ca
www.cdha.nshealth.ca
Note: Number of Employees: 11,000. Population Served: 400,000
Chris Power, President; Chief Executive Officer
902-473-2240
John McCarthy, Officer, Board Development
902-473-1143, Fax: 902-473-3368, John.McCarthy@cdha.nshealth.ca
Anne Bereziuk, Patient Representative
902-473-2133, anne.bereziuk@cdha.nshealth.ca
Gaynor Watson-Creed, Medical Officer of Health
902-481-5800
Catherine Gaulton, General Counsel; Vice-President, Performance Excellence
902-473-2626
Paula Bond, Vice-President, People Centred Care
902-473-7084
Lea Bryden, Citizen Engagement; Accountability
902-473-2194
Brendan Carr, Vice-President, Medicine

902-473-7066
Ray LeBlanc, Vice-President, Innovation & Learning

902-473-7310
Kathy MacNeil, Vice-President, People
902-473-7995
Amanda Whitewood, Vice-President, Sustainability
902-473-3317

Kentville: Annapolis Valley Health/AVH
15 Chipman Dr., Kentville, NS B4N 3V7

902-678-7381 1-800-886-9757 www.avdha.nshealth.ca
Note: Number of Medical Staff: 170 physicians; Population Served: 84,000
Janet Knox, President; Chief Executive Officer
902-538-3431, Fax: 902-538-7609, ceo@avdha.nshealth.ca
David
Logie, Board Chair

902-538-3431, Fax: 902-538-7609, lbobbitt@avdha.nshealth.ca (Linda Bo
Lynne Harrigan, Vice-President, Medicine
902-538-3424, Fax: 902-538-3432
Tamara Gilley, Director, Public Relations
902-538-3468, Fax: 902-678-9553, tgilley@avdha.nshealth.ca

New Glasgow: Pictou County District Health Authority #6
c/o Aberdeen Hospital, 835 East River Rd., New Glasgow, NS B2H 3S6
902-752-7600 www.pcha.nshealth.ca
Patrick Flinn, CEO

Sydney: Cape Breton District Health Authority
1482 George St, Sydney, NS B1P 1P3
902-567-8000 Fax: 902-563-2717 www.cbdha.nshealth.ca
Number of Beds: 466 acute care beds; 207 veteran & continuing care beds
Note: Number of Employees: 3,300 health care providers working with 270 hospital & community based physicians
John Malcom, Chief Executive Officer
902-567-7802
Yvon LeBlanc, Chair
M.A. Naqvi, Chief of Staff; Medical Director
902-567-7806
Evelyn Schaller, Chief Nursing Officer; Vice-President, Patient Services
902-567-7814
Jim Merkley, Vice-President, Diagnostic & Support Services
902-842-2842
Mary Lou O'Neil, Vice-President, Clinical Services
902-563-2711
Lindsay Peach, Vice-President, Population Health & Continuing Care
902-794-5449
Greg Boone, Director, Public Affairs
902-567-7791

Truro: Colchester East Hants Health Authority/CEHHA
207 Willow St., Truro, NS B2N 5A1
902-893-5554 Fax: 902-893-0040; 1-800-460-2110
humanresources-cehha@cehha.nshealth.ca
www.cehha.nshealth.ca
Year Founded: 2001
Note: Facilities: Colchester Regional Hospital, Truro, NS; Lillian Fraser Memorial Hospital, Tatamagouche, NS; East Hants Resource Centre, Elmsdale, NS. Population Served: 73,000. Area Served: Colchester County; Municipality of East Hants
John K. MacDonald, Chair
Peter MacKinnon, Chief Executive Officer
Martin Dzierzanowski, Head, Surgery
Krista Wood, Director, Public Relations
902-893-5554, krista.wood@cehha.nshealth.ca
Wendy Mosher, Manager, Volunteer Resources
902-893-5554, Wendy.Mosher@cehha.nshealth.ca

Yarmouth: Southwest Health
c/o Yarmouth Regional Hospital, 60 Vancouver St., Yarmouth, NS B4A 2P5
902-742-3541 Fax: 902-742-0369 www.swndha.nshealth.ca
Old Name: Western Regional Health Board
Number of Beds: 536 beds
Blaise MacNeil, CEO

Hospitals

Hospitals - General

Amherst: Cumberland Regional Health Care Centre/CRHCC
19428 Hwy. #2, RR#6, Amherst, NS B4H 1N6
902-667-3361 Fax: 902-667-6306 www.cha.nshealth.ca
Parent: Cumberland Health Authority #5
Year Founded: 2002
Note: Hospital Specialties: Level 2 emergency services; Diagnostic imaging; Laboratory services; Surgery; Intensive care unit; Maternal / child unit (902-667-5400, ext. 6144); Acute care; Ambulatory care; Physiotherapy; Occupational therapy; Respiratory therapy; Diabetes education; Social work (902-667-5400, ext. 6219); Palliative care (902-667-5400, ext. 6373)
David Gass, Chief of Staff, Cumberland Health Authority
david.gass@cha.nshealth.ca
Cheryl Northcott, Vice-President, Patient Care Services, Cumberland Health Authority
cheryl.northcott@cha.nshealth.ca
Ann Keddy, Director, Public Relations, Cumberland Health Authority
902-661-1090, ann.keddy@cha.nshealth.ca

Antigonish: St. Martha's Regional Hospital
25 Bay St., Antigonish, NS B2G 2G5
902-863-2830 Fax: 902-867-1059
www.erhb.ns.ca/Facilities/St_Marthas/default.htm
Parent: Guysborough Antigonish Strait Health Authority #7
Number of Beds: 80 beds
Note: regional hospital
Liz Millett, Vice President, Patient Care
David MacKenzie, Vice President, Operations

Baddeck: Victoria County Memorial Hospital
PO Box 220, 30 Old Margaree Rd., Baddeck, NS B0E 1B0
902-295-2112 Fax: 902-295-3432 www.cbdha.nshealth.ca
Parent: Cape Breton District Health Authority #8
Number of Beds: 12 beds
Diane Grant, Administrator

Bridgewater: South Shore Regional Hospital
90 Glen Allan Dr., Bridgewater, NS B4V 3S6
902-543-4603 Fax: 902-543-4719
www.ssdha.nshealth.ca/ssrh.htm
Old Name: Health Services Association of the South Shore
Parent: South Shore District Health Authority #1
Number of Beds: 80 beds
Note: A primary and secondary care hospital and designated district trauma centre, services include emergency & ambulatory care, diagnostic imaging (radiography/fluoroscopy, ultrasound, mammography, CT scanning, nuclear medicine), intensive care, surgery, EKG, gastroenterology, mental health services, obstetrics, opthalmology, pediatrics, cardiac care, respiratory therapy, rheumatology, rehabilitation, palliative, pharmacy, walk-in clinic
Alice Leverman, CEO, SSDHA
aleverman@ssdha.nshealth.ca
Peter Vaughan, Medical Director, SSDHA
Theresa Hawkesworth, Communications Officer, SSDHA
902-527-2266, thawkesworth@ssdha.nshealth.ca

Canso: Eastern Memorial Hospital
PO Box 10, 1746 Union St., Canso, NS B0H 1H0
902-366-2794 Fax: 902-366-2740 www.gasha.nshealth.ca
Parent: Guysborough Antigonish Strait Health Authority #7
Year Founded: 1948
Number of Beds: 6 beds
Note: Hospital Specialties: Emergency services; Diagnostic imaging; Physiotherapy; Psychology services; Social services; Nutritional counselling; Diabetes education; Outreach nursing; Palliative care
Rose Richardson, Manager, Eastern Memorial Hospital Facility
Rose.Richardson@gasha.nshealth.ca

Cheticamp: Sacred Heart Community Health Centre
PO Box 129, 15102 Cabot Trail, Cheticamp, NS B0E 1H0
902-224-1500 Fax: 902-224-2903 www.cbdha.nshealth.ca
Old Name: Sacred Heart Hospital
Parent: Cape Breton District Health Authority #8
Number of Beds: 10 beds
Note: Emergency & outpatient services, lab, physiotherapy, nutrition counseling, foot & eye clinics, diagnostic imaging, palliative care
John Malcom, CEO, CBDHA
Mary Lou O'Neil, Vice-President, Clinical Services, CBDHA
M. A. Naqvi, Medical Director; Chief of Staff, CBDHA

Cleveland: Strait Richmond Hospital
138 Hospital Rd., RR#1, Cleveland, NS B0E 1J0
902-625-3100 Fax: 902-625-3804 www.gasha.nshealth.ca
Parent: Guysborough Antigonish Strait Health Authority #7
Year Founded: 1980
Number of Beds: 20 beds
Note: Specialties: Inpatient unit for addiction services; Mental health services; Social work services; Physiotherapy; Occupational therapy; Physicians clinics, such as pediatrics & orthopedics; Ambulatory care clinics, such as a living with stroke program, a well men's clinic, & a well women's clinic
Andrea Boyd-White, Facility Manager
Andy Parland, Director, Maintenance & Chief Engineer

Dartmouth: Dartmouth General Hospital/DGH
325 Pleasant St., Dartmouth, NS B2Y 4G8
902-465-8300 www.cdha.nshealth.ca
Parent: Capital District Health Authority #9
Note: Hospital Specialties: Emergency services (902-465-8333); Diagnostic services; Laboratory services; Surgery; Critical care; Gynaecology; Urology; Orthopedics; Ophthalmology; Ear, nose, & throat; Renal dialysis; Nutrition counselling; Osteoporosis Multidisciplinary Education Program
Gaynor Watson-Creed, Medical Officer of Health
, Capital Health

902-481-5800
Laura
Brine, Patient Representative
902-460-4544, Fax: 902-465-2729, laura.brine@cdha.nshealth.ca
Natalie Morris, Contact, Dartmouth Osteoporosis Multidisciplinary Education
902-860-3719, morrisn@cdha.nshealth.ca
Marlene Regan, Contact, DGH Nutrition Counselling Department
902-465-8514

Digby: Digby General Hospital
75 Warwick St., Digby, NS B0V 1A0
902-245-2501 Fax: 902-245-5517 www.swndha.nshealth.ca
Parent: Southwest Health
Note: Hospital Specialties: Emergency services (902-245-1303); Diagnostic imaging (1-877-742-2571); Laboratory services (902-245-2502, ext. 3213); Primary care; Ambulatory care; Cardiac & respiratory services (902-245-2502, ext. 3264); Restorative care (902-245-2502, ext. 3337); Physiotherapy & occupational therapy (902-245-2502, ext. 3257); Recreation therapy (902-245-2502, ext. 3280); Mental health services (902-245-4709); Diabetes education (902-245-2502, ext. 3274); Nutrition counselling (902-245-2502, ext. 3341); Public health (902-245-2557); Hearing & Speech Centre (902-245-2502, ext. 3265); Palliative care (902-245-2502, ext. 3335)
Hubert d'Entremont, Manager, Digby General Hospital Site
902)-245-250, Fax: 902-245-2803, hubertdentremont@swndha.nshealth.ca

Guysborough: Guysborough Memorial Hospital
PO Box 170, Guysborough, NS B0H 1N0
902-533-3702 Fax: 902-533-4066
Parent: Guysborough Antigonish Strait Health Authority #7
Number of Beds: 10 beds
Elaine MacMaster, Facility Manager
emacmaster@gasha.nshealth.ca
Tom DeLorey, Supervisor, Plant Maintenance

Halifax: IWK Health Centre
PO Box 9700, 5980 University Ave., Halifax, NS B3K 6R8
902-470-8888
feedback@iwk.nshealth.ca
www.iwk.nshealth.ca
Number of Beds: 324 beds
Anne McGuire, President/CEO
Anne Cogdon, Director, Primary Health
902/420-6770

Halifax: Queen Elizabeth II Health Sciences Centre
1796 Summer St., Halifax, NS B3H 2A7
902-473-2700 Fax: 902-473-4183
capitalnews@cdha.nshealth.ca
www.cdha.nshealth.ca
Parent: Capital District Health Authority #9
Number of Beds: 983 beds
Note: The largest teaching hospital in Atlantic Canada, the QEII provides general & specialized medical care, including mental health programs, cancer care, long-term care, geriatric assessment & restorative care
Karen MacRury-Sweet, Health Services Director, Nursing, Cardiac, Thoracic & Emergency Care

Inverness: Inverness Consolidated Memorial Hospital
PO Box 610, 39 James St., Inverness, NS B0E 1N0
902-258-2100 Fax: 902-258-3025
Old Name: Inverness Consolidated Hospital
Parent: Cape Breton District Health Authority #8
Number of Beds: 48 beds
Note: Acute & continuing care
Claire MacQuarrie, Facilities Manager
Sandy Gillis, Head, Plant Services

Kentville: Valley Regional Hospital
150 Exhibition St., Kentville, NS B4N 5E3
902-678-7381 Fax: 902-679-1904
Parent: Annapolis Valley District Health Authority #3
Year Founded: 1992
Note: Medicine, surgery, obstetrics, pediatrics, intensive care, emergency services, psychiatry, addictions. Number of staff: 700 staff, 100 physicians
Janet Knox, President/CEO, Annapolis Valley Health

Liverpool: Queens General Hospital
PO Box 370, 175 School St., Liverpool, NS B0T 1K0
902-354-3436 Fax: 902-354-4614

Parent: South Shore District Health Authority #1
Number of Beds: 22 beds
Anne Kelley, Site Manager

Lunenburg: Fishermen's Memorial Hospital
PO Box 1180, 14 High St., Lunenburg, NS B0J 2C0
902-634-8801 www.ssdha.nshealth.ca
Parent: South Shore District Health Authority #1
Number of Beds: 23 beds for veterans' care; 10 addiction services beds; 12 restorative care beds; 12 alternate level of care beds; 6 acute care beds; 2 observation be
Note: Hospital Specialties: Laboratory services; Diagnostic imaging; Acute care; Ambulatory care; Addiction services; Rehabilitation services; Restorative care; Respiratory therapy; Asthma Care Centre; Palliative care
Peter Vaughan, Medical Director, South Shore Health
902-527-5271, Fax: 902-527-5269,
Phil Langford, Vice-President, Operations, South Shore Health
902-634-7308, Fax: 902-634-3668,
plangford@ssdha.nshealth.ca

Middle Musquodoboit: Musquodoboit Valley Memorial Hospital
492 Archibald Brook Rd., Middle Musquodoboit, NS B0N 1X0
902-384-2220 Fax: 902-384-3310
Parent: Capital District Health Authority #9
Number of Beds: 8 beds
Sheila Martin, Director, Health Services

Middleton: Soldiers Memorial Hospital
PO Box 730, Middleton, NS B0S 1P0
902-825-3411 Fax: 902-825-0599 www.avdha.nshealth.ca/smh
Parent: Annapolis Valley District Health Authority #3
Number of Beds: 62 beds (25 medical/surgical beds, 25 long term care beds, 12 beds for transitional patients)
Note: Services include emergency, acute care, addictions care, enterostomal therapy, surgery, diagnostic imaging, occupational & physiotherapy, nutrition services, diabetes education, speech language pathology services
Janet Knox, President/CEO, AVH
902-538-3431, ceo@avdha.nshealth.ca
Tamara Gilley, Public Relations Director, AVH
902-538-3468, Fax: 902-678-9553, tgilley@avdha.nshealth.ca
Joanne Wentzell, Site Manager

Musquodoboit Harbour: Twin Oaks Memorial Hospital
7702 - 7 Hwy., Musquodoboit Harbour, NS B0J 2L0
902-889-4110 Fax: 902-889-4144
www.cdha.nshealth.ca/default.aspx?page=SubPage¢erContent.Id.0=9233&category.Categories.1=22
Parent: Capital District Health Authority #9
Year Founded: 1976
Number of Beds: 14 beds
Note: Services include emergency, acute care, addiction services, diabetic and foot clinics, diagnostic imaging, hearing and speech clinic, Home Care Nova Scotia, laboratory, nutrition counseling, occupational therapy, outpatient services, palliative & respite care, physiotherapy, social services; Twin Oaks/Birches Continuting Care Centre. A helipad is located at the back of the hospital.
Chris Power, President/CEO, CDHA
Sheila Martin, Director, Health Services
902-889-2200, sheila.martin@cdha.nshealth.ca
Marilyn Cipak, Manager, Health Services
902-889-4106, Fax: 902-889-4140,
marilyn.cipak@cdha.nshealth.ca

Neils Harbour: Buchanan Memorial Community Health Centre
32610 Cabot Trail, Neils Harbour, NS B0C 1N0
902-336-2200 Fax: 902-336-2399 www.cbdha.nshealth.ca
Parent: Cape Breton District Health Authority #8
Note: Specialty: Acute care

North Sydney: Northside General Hospital
PO Box 399, 520 Purves St., North Sydney, NS B2A 3M4
506-794-8521 Fax: 506-794-3355
Parent: Cape Breton District Health Authority #8
Number of Beds: 21 beds
Note: Emergency & ambulatory care, diagnostic imaging, lab, day surgery, diabetic education, respiratory therapy, mental health clinic; Taigh Solas, a 21-bed continuing care facility, comprises the 3rd floor of the hospital
Sharon Sheppard, Director, Continuing Care

Pictou: Sutherland Harris Memorial Hospital
PO Box 1059, 222 Haliburton Rd., Pictou, NS B0K 1H0
902-485-4324 Fax: 902-485-8835
www.pcha.nshealth.ca/sutherlandharris/aboutus/default.htm
Parent: Pictou County District Health Authority #6
Year Founded: 1928
Number of Beds: 20 long-term beds for veterans, 12 restorative care beds
Note: A community facility with services incuding the Northumberland Veterans Unit, Restorative Care Unit, geriatric consultation, occupational therapy, palliative care, physiotherapy, social work, speech language therapy, special clinics (for dermatology, diabetes education, podiatry, vascularity, women's health).
Patrick Lee, CEO, PCHA
pat.lee@pcha.nshealth.ca
Nicole Boutilier, Interim Vice-President, Medical Affairs, PCHA
nicole.boutilier@pcha.nshealth.ca
Eileen MacIsaac, Public Relations Officer, PCHA
902-752-7600, eileen.macisaac@pcha.nshealth.ca

Sheet Harbour: Eastern Shore Memorial Hospital
22737 Hwy. #7, Sheet Harbour, NS B0J 3B0
902-885-2554 Fax: 902-885-3200 www.cdha.nshealth.ca
Parent: Capital District Health Authority #9
Year Founded: 1976
Number of Beds: 16 beds
Note: Hospital Specialties: Emergency services; Diagnostic imaging; Laboratory services; Ambulatory care; Acute care; Physiotherapy; Occupational therapy; Social services; Diabetes education (902-885-3606); Respite care; Palliative care
Harold Taylor, Manager, Health Services
902-885-3616, harold.taylor@cdha.nshealth.ca
Natasha Sharpe, Facility Secretary

902-885-3678, Fax: 902-885-3200, natasha.sharpe@cdha.nshealth.ca

Shelburne: Roseway Hospital
PO Box 610, 1606 Sandy Point Rd., Shelburne, NS B0T 1W0
902-875-3011 Fax: 902-875-1580
www.swndha.nshealth.ca/pages/roseway.htm
Parent: Southwest Nova District Health Authority #2
Number of Beds: 19 beds
Note: Emergency, diagnostic services, physiotherapy, nutrition counseling, mental health & addiction services, speech therapy, continuing care, VON, visiting specialists
Jodi Ybarra, Site Manager
jybarra@swndha.nshealth.ca

Sherbrooke: St. Mary's Memorial Hospital
PO Box 299, 91 Hospital Rd., Sherbrooke, NS B0J 3C0
902-522-2882 Fax: 902-522-2556
Parent: Guysborough Antigonish Strait Health Authority #7
Number of Beds: 6 beds
Teresa MacInnis, Facility Manager

Sydney: Cape Breton Regional Hospital
1482 George St., Sydney, NS B1P 1P3
902-567-8000 www.cbdha.nshealth.ca
Parent: Cape Breton District Health Authority #8
Year Founded: 1995
Note: Hospital Specialties: Emergency services; Diagnostic imaging; Laboratory services; Ambulatory care; Surgery; Intensive care; Acute care; Obstetrics; Oncology; Renal dialysis; Physical therapy; Occupational therapy; Speech therapy; Respiratory therapy; Diabetes education; Social work; Mental health; Mi'kmaq liaison; Geriatrics; Palliative care

Tatamagouche: Lillian Fraser Memorial Hospital
PO Box 40, 110 Blair Ave., Tatamagouche, NS B0K 1V0
902-657-2382 Fax: 902-657-3745 www.cehha.nshealth.ca/LillianFraser/index.cfm
Parent: Colchester East Hants Health Authority #4
Number of Beds: 10 beds
Bain Brown, Maintenance Supervisor

Truro: Colchester Regional Hospital
207 Willow St., Truro, NS B2N 5A1
902-893-4321 Fax: 902-893-5559 1-800-460-2110
humanresources-cehha@cehha.nshealth.ca (Human Resources, Colchester
www.cehha.nshealth.ca
Parent: Colchester East Hants Health Authority #4
Number of Beds: 126 beds
Note: Hospital Specialties: Emergency services; Diagnostic imaging; Laboratory services; Acute care; Maternal / child services; Coronary care; Hearing & speech centre; Ophthalmology
Occupational therapy; Physiotherapy; Wound management; Asthma care centre; Diabetes centre; Social work; Veterans' unit; Palliative care
Krista Wood, Director, Public Relations

902-893-5554, krista.wood@cehha.nshealth.ca

Windsor: Hants Community Hospital
89 Payzant Dr., Windsor, NS B0N 2T0
902-792-2000 Fax: 902-798-6002 www.cdha.nshealth.ca
Parent: Capital District Health Authority #9
Number of Beds: 34 acute care beds
Sherri Parker, Director, Health Services
sherri.parker@cdha.nshealth.ca

Yarmouth: Yarmouth Regional Hospital
60 Vancouver St., Yarmouth, NS B5A 2P5
902-742-3541 Fax: 902-742-0369
Parent: Southwest Nova District Health Authority #2
Number of Beds: 139 beds
Blaise MacNeil, President; CEO
John Sullivan, Director, Physical Plant
Chris Newell, Director, Environmental Services

Community Health Centres

Community Health Care Centres

Annapolis Royal: Annapolis Community Health Centre
PO Box 426, 821 St. George St., Annapolis Royal, NS B0S 1A0
902-532-2381 Fax: 902-532-2113
duggan.achc@avdha.nshealth.ca
www.avdha.nshealth.ca/achc/
Parent: Annapolis Valley District Health Authority #3

Berwick: Western Kings Memorial Health Centre
PO Box 490, 121 Orchard St., Berwick, NS B0P 1E0
902-538-3111 Fax: 902-538-9590 www.avdha.nshealth.ca
Parent: Annapolis Valley District Health Authority #3
Note: Outpatient department, lab, diagnostic imaging, physiotherapy, nutritional counseling, dialysis, mental health clinic, VON Adult Day Care
Cheryl Grosvold, Site Manager

Dartmouth: Regional Residential Services Society/RRSS
#LKD1, 202 Brownlow Ave., Dartmouth, NS B3B 1T5
902-465-4022 Fax: 902-465-3124
beverley.wicks@rrss.ns.ca
www.rrss.ns.ca
Number of Beds: 185 beds
Note: Developmental residences & group homes, supported apartments, short & long term respite services, personal support planning, counseling, assessment. Number of staff: 400+
Carol Ann Brennan, Executive Director
carolann.brennan@rrss.ns.ca

Lower Sackville: Cobequid Community Health Centre
70 Memory Lane, Lower Sackville, NS B4C 2J3
902-869-6100 Fax: 902-865-4816
Parent: Capital District Health Authority #9
Margaret Merlin, Health Facility Manager

Parrsboro: South Cumberland Community Care Centre
PO Box 489, 50 Jenks Ave., Parrsboro, NS B0M 1S0
902-254-2540 Fax: 902-254-2504
Parent: Cumberland Health Authority #5
Number of Beds: 14 beds
Connie Ellis, Site Manager

Pugwash: North Cumberland Memorial Hospital
PO Box 242, 260 Church St., Pugwash, NS B0K 1L0
902-243-2521 Fax: 902-243-2941
Parent: Cumberland Health Authority #5
Number of Beds: 4 beds
Beryl MacLean, Site Manager

Springhill: All Saints Springhill Hospital
PO Box 700, 10 Princess St., Springhill, NS B0M 1X0
902-597-3773 Fax: 902-597-3440
Old Name: All Saint's Hospital
Parent: Cumberland Health Authority #5
Number of Beds: 20 beds
Note: Beds are provided for restorative care, transitional care, & palliative care. There is also a 10-bed inpatient addictions treatment program.
Beryl MacLean, Site Manager

Sydney: Public Health Services
235 Townsend St., Sydney, NS B1P 5E7
902-563-2400 Fax: 902-563-0508
Parent: Guysborough Antigonish Strait Health Authority #7
Eileen Woodford

***Wolfville:* Eastern Kings Memorial Community Health Centre**
PO Box 1180, Wolfville, NS B0P 1X0
902-542-2266 Fax: 902-542-4619
www.go.ednet.ns.ca/~healthque/
Old Name: Eastern Kings Community Health Centre
Parent: Annapolis Valley District Health Authority #3
Marg Blakeney, Site Manager

Special Treatment Centre

***Halifax:* IWK Mental Health Program**
#1001, 6080 Young St., Halifax, NS B3K 5L2
902-464-4110 Fax: 902-464-3008 www.iwk.nshealth.ca
Old Name: Atlantic Child Guidance Center
Wayne Hollett, Interim Executive Director

***Halifax:* Nova Scotia Hearing & Speech Centres**
Provincial Centre, Park Lane Terraces, PO Box 120, #401, 5657 Spring Garden Rd., Halifax, NS B3J 3R4
902-492-8289 Fax: 902-423-0532
info@nshsc.ns.ca
www.nshsc.ns.ca
Note: Specialties: Speech-language pathology services; Audiology services Augmentative communication program; Cochlear implant program; Industrial & community audiology; Newborn hearing screening program
Anne Mason-Browne, Vice-President, Speech

***Waterville:* Kings Regional Rehabilitation Centre**
PO Box 128, 1349 County Home Rd., Waterville, NS B0P 1V0
902-538-3103 Fax: 902-538-7022
Number of Beds: 199 beds
Note: residential rehab
Betty E. Mattson, Administrator

***Yarmouth:* Addiction Services**
c/o Yarmouth Regional Hospital, 60 Vancouver St., Yarmouth, NS B5A 2P5
902-742-2406 Fax: 902-742-0684
addictions-yrh@swndha.nshealth.ca
Old Name: Western Drug Dependency Program
Division of: District Health Authorities 1, 2, & 3
Hubert Devine, Regional Program Manager

Nursing Homes

***Annapolis Royal:* Annapolis Royal Nursing Home**
9745, St. George St., RR#2, Annapolis Royal, NS B0S 1A0
902-532-2240 Fax: 902-532-7151
arnh@tartannet.ns.ca
annapolisroyalnursinghome.ca
Number of Beds: 51 beds + 2 respite
Linda R. Bailey, Administrator

***Annapolis Royal:* Northhills Nursing Home Ltd.**
PO Box 220, 5038 Granville Rd., Annapolis Royal, NS B0S 1A0
902-532-5555 Fax: 902-532-7449
nhnhltd@ns.sympatico.ca
Number of Beds: 50 beds
Note: adult residential centre
Leonard S. Tedds, Administrator

***Arichat:* St. Anne Community & Nursing Care Centre**
2313 Main St., PO Box Drawer 30, Arichat, NS B0E 1A0
902-226-2826 Fax: 902-226-1529
eric.burke@sacentre.nshealth.ca
Parent: Guysborough Antigonish Strait Health Authority #7
Number of Beds: 24 beds
Eric Burke, Administrator

***Beaverbank:* Scotia Nursing Homes Ltd.**
125 Knowles Cres., Beaverbank, NS B4G 1E7
902-865-6364 Fax: 902-865-3582
julie.frail@rosecrest.ca
www.scotianursinghomes.ca
Old Name: Scotia Nursing Homes Ltd.
Parent: Capital District Health Authority #9
Number of Beds: 49 beds + 1 respite
Patricia Bland, Administrator

***Berwick:* Grand View Manor**
110A Commercial St., Berwick, NS B0P 1E0
902-538-3118 Fax: 902-538-3998
admin@grandviewmanor.org
www.grandviewmanor.org
Number of Beds: 142 beds
Graham E. Hardy, Administrator

***Bridgetown:* Mountain Lea Lodge**
170 Church St., RR#1, Bridgetown, NS B0S 1C0
902-665-4489 Fax: 902-665-2900
larrymarsters@ns.sympatico.ca
Number of Beds: 106 beds + 1 respite
Larry Marsters, Administrator

***Bridgewater:* Hillside Pines**
77 Exhibition Dr., Bridgewater, NS B4V 3K6
902-543-1525 Fax: 902-543-8083
Number of Beds: 50 beds
Sheila MacKinnon, Administrator

***Caledonia:* North Queens Nursing Home**
9565 Highway #8, Caledonia, NS B0T 1B0
902-682-2553 Fax: 902-682-2602 www.nqnh.ca
Number of Beds: 42 beds + 2 respite
Note: adult residential centre
Norma Lenco, Administrator

***Canso:* Canso Seaside Manor**
PO Box 70, 1748 Union St., Canso, NS B0H 1H0
902-366-3030 Fax: 902-366-2154
dbennett@gosha.nshealth.ca
Number of Beds: 15 beds
Darren Bennett, Administrator

***Chester:* Shoreham Village**
3777 North St., RR#1, Chester, NS B0J 1J0
902-275-5631 Fax: 902-275-2586 www.shorehamvillage.com
Number of Beds: 83 beds
Brian M. Selig, Administrator
Joan Regimbal, Director, Environmental Services

***Dartmouth:* Oakwood Terrace**
10 Mount Hope Ave., Dartmouth, NS B2Y 4K1
902-469-3702 Fax: 902-469-3824 www.oakwoodterrace.ns.ca
Parent: Capital District Health Authority #9
Year Founded: 1982
Number of Beds: 111 beds
Note: Specialties: Physiotherapy; Adult Day Program; Medical services; Palliative care
Leonard Tedds, Administrator
Pat Nightingale, Nurse Manager
Gary Comeau, Coordinator, Recreation Therapy & Volunteer Services

***Dartmouth:* Woodside Manor**
351 Pleasant St., Dartmouth, NS B2Y 3S4
902-463-5845
Number of Beds: 29 beds
Cathy Prothro, Site Manager

***Digby:* Tideview Terrace**
PO Box 1120, 51 West St., Digby, NS B0V 1A0
902-245-4718 Fax: 902-245-6674
Parent: Southwest Nova District Health Authority #2
Number of Beds: 89 beds
Note: Specialties: Long-term care (level II); Dementia care; Adult day programs; Respite care; Palliative care
Lynda Casey, Administrator

***Eastern Passage:* Ocean View Manor**
PO Box 130, 1909 Caldwell Rd., Eastern Passage, NS B3G 1M4
902-465-6020 Fax: 902-465-4929
admin@ovm.ca
www.ovm.ca
Parent: Capital District Health Authority #9
Year Founded: 1967
Number of Beds: 176 residents
Note: Specialties: Physiotherapy; Occupational therapy; Recreation therapy; Social work; Respite care; Palliative care
Dion Mouland, Administrator

***Glace Bay:* Victoria Haven Nursing Home**
PO Box 219, 5 Third St., Glace Bay, NS B1A 5V2
902-849-4127 Fax: 902-849-8826 www.victoriahaven.ca
Number of Beds: 50 beds, 4 respite
Marie McPhee, Administrator

***Glenwood:* Nakile Home for Special Care**
35 Nakile Dr., RR#1, Glenwood, NS B0W 1W0
902-643-2707 Fax: 902-643-2862
bertha@nakile.ns.ca
www.nakilehome.ca
Old Name: Nakile Home for the Aged
Parent: Southwest Nova District Health Authority #2
Number of Beds: 35 beds + 1 respite
Bertha Brannen, Administrator

***Halifax:* Arborstone Enhanced Care**
126 Purcell's Cove Rd., Halifax, NS B3P 1B5
902-477-8051 Fax: 902-477-5726 www.shannex.com
Old Name: Arbourstone Enhanced Care
Parent: Capital District Health Authority #9
Number of Beds: 190 beds
Chris Labréche, Administrator
Sean Skinner, Director, Environmental Services

***Halifax:* Glades Lodge**
25 Alton Dr., Halifax, NS B3N 1M1
902-477-1777 Fax: 902-477-8174
glades.lodge@gemhealth.com
Parent: Capital District Health Authority #9
Number of Beds: 123 beds + 1 respite
Bonnie Kay-Griffin, Administrator

***Halifax:* Maplestone Enhanced Care**
245 Main Ave., Halifax, NS B3M 1B7
902-443-1971 Fax: 902-443-9037
Parent: Capital District Health Authority #9
Number of Beds: 87 beds
Note: Nursing home
Renee Donovan-Grey, Administrator
Debbie Thompson, Environmental Services

***Halifax:* Maplestone Enhanced Care**
245 Main Ave., Halifax, NS B3M 1B7
902-443-1971 Fax: 902-443-9037
Parent: Capital District Health Authority #9
Number of Beds: 87 beds
Renee Donovan-Gray, Administrator

***Halifax:* Melville Lodge Long Term Care Center**
50 Shoreham Lane, Halifax, NS B3P 2R3
902-479-1030 Fax: 902-477-1663 www.gemhealth.com
Year Founded: 1984
Number of Beds: 122 beds
Bernice Clake-Dibblee, Administrator

***Halifax:* Northwoodcare Inc.**
2615 Northwood Terrace, Halifax, NS B3K 3S5
902-454-8311 Fax: 902-455-6408
information@nwood.ns.ca
www.nwood.ns.ca
Parent: Capital District Health Authority #9
Number of Beds: 406 beds
Note: Adult residental centre
Lloyd O. Brown, Administrator

***Halifax:* Parkstone Enhanced Care**
156 Parkland Dr., Halifax, NS B3S 1N9
902-446-7275 Fax: 902-446-4044
dryan@shannex.com
Parent: Capital District Health Authority #9
Number of Beds: 185 beds, 5 respite beds
Note: Nursing home
Carol Ann Gallant, Administrator

***Halifax:* Saint Vincent's Nursing Home**
2080 Windsor St., Halifax, NS B3K 5B2
902-429-0550 Fax: 902-492-3703
info@svnh.ca
www.svnh.ca
Old Name: Saint Vincent Guest Home
Parent: Capital District Health Authority #9
Number of Beds: 149 beds
Note: Nursing home affiliated with the Roman Catholic Archdiocese of Halifax
Kristin Schmitz, Administrator

***Inverness:* Inverary Manor**
PO Box 460, 72 Maple St., Inverness, NS B0E 1N0
902-258-2842 Fax: 902-258-3865
inverary.manor@ns.sympatico.ca
Parent: Cape Breton District Health Authority #8
Number of Beds: 60 beds
Joan MacLellan, Administrator

***Kentville:* Evergreen Home for Special Care**
655 Park St., Kentville, NS B4N 3V7
902-678-7355 Fax: 902-678-5292
evergreen@evergreenhome.ns.ca
evergreenhome.ns.ca
Number of Beds: 97 beds plus 20 children's beds & 2 respite beds
Note: adult residential centre
Fred Houghton, Administrator

***Liverpool:* Queens Manor**
PO Box 1283, 20 Hollands Dr., Liverpool, NS B0T 1K0
902-354-3451 Fax: 902-354-5383 www.queensmanor.ca
Number of Beds: 60 beds + 1 respite
Norma Lenco, Administrator

***Lockeport:* Surf Lodge Nursing Home**
PO Box 160, 73 Howe St., Lockeport, NS B0T 1L0
902-656-2014 www.surflodge.ca
Parent: Southwest Nova District Health Authority #2

Note: Specialties: Long-term care; Massage therapy; Activity program; Physiotherapy
Margaret Coates, Administrator

***Lunenburg:* Harbour View Haven**
PO Box 1480, 25 Blockhouse Hill Rd., Lunenburg, NS B0J 2C0
902-634-8836 Fax: 902-634-8792 www.hvh.ca
Number of Beds: 129 beds + 1 respite
Barry Granter, Administrator

***Mahone Bay:* Mahone Nursing Home**
PO Box 320, 640 Main St., Mahone Bay, NS B0J 2E0
902-624-8341 Fax: 902-624-6338
www.mahonenursinghome.com
Year Founded: 1965
Note: Specialties: Long-term care Physiotherapy & occupational therapy; Palliative care
Anne Kennedy, Administrator

***Meteghan:* Villa Acadienne**
CP 248, 8403 Hwy. 1, Meteghan, NS B0W 2J0
902-645-2065 Fax: 902-645-3899 www.villaacadienne.com
Parent: Southwest Nova District Health Authority #2
Number of Beds: 84 beds + 2 respite
Lucille Maillet, Administrator

***Middle Musquodoboit:* Musquodoboit Valley Home for Special Care (Braeside)**
126 Higginsville Rd., Middle Musquodoboit, NS B0N 1X0
902-384-3007 Fax: 902-384-3310
Parent: Capital District Health Authority #9
Number of Beds: 28 beds + 1 respite
Diana Graham-Lentz, Site Manager

***Musquodoboit Harbour:* The Birches Nursing Home**
#7702, 7 Hwy. RR#2, Musquodoboit Harbour, NS B0J 2L0
902-889-3474
Parent: Capital District Health Authority #9
Number of Beds: 42 residents
Note: Specialties: Long-term care for older adults; Community outreach adult day programs
Sheila Martin, Manager, Health Care Facility

***New Germany:* Rosedale Home for Special Care**
Trunk 10, #4927, RR#2, New Germany, NS B0R 1E0
902-644-2008 Fax: 902-644-3260
Old Name: Rosedale Home
Year Founded: 1984
Number of Beds: 29 beds
Maureen Wade, Administrator

***New Glasgow:* Glen Haven Manor**
739 East River Rd., New Glasgow, NS B2H 5E9
902-752-2588 Fax: 902-752-0053
Parent: Pictou County District Health Authority #6
Number of Beds: 202 beds
Note: adult residential centre
James Ferguson, Administrator

***New Waterford:* Maple Hill Manor**
700 King St., New Waterford, NS B1H 3Z5
902-862-6495 Fax: 902-862-9294
maplehillmanor1@ns.sympatico.ca
www.maplehillmanor.ca
Parent: Cape Breton District Health Authority #8
Number of Beds: 50 beds
Note: Long term & secured care
Cathy MacPhee, Administrator

***North Sydney:* Northside Community Guest Home**
11 Queen St., North Sydney, NS B2A 1A2
902-794-4733 Fax: 902-794-9021
www.northsideguesthome.com
Parent: Cape Breton District Health Authority #8
Number of Beds: 105 beds
Joanne MacNeil, Administrator

***Pictou:* Maritime Odd Fellows Home**
PO Box 850, 143 Haliburton Rd., Pictou, NS B0K 1H0
902-485-5492 Fax: 902-485-6868
Parent: Pictou County District Health Authority #6
Number of Beds: 47 beds
Note: Specialty: Long-term care; Therapeutic recreation
Janet Johnston, Administrator

***Sheet Harbour:* Duncan MacMillan Nursing Home**
PO Box 68, 22639 7 Hwy., Sheet Harbour, NS B0J 3B0
902-885-2545 Fax: 902-885-3289
Old Name: Duncan MacMillan Home for the Aged
Parent: Capital District Health Authority #9
Number of Beds: 25 beds + 1 respite
Sheila Martin, Health Care Facility Manager

***Shelburne:* Roseway Manor Inc.**
PO Box 518, 1604 Lake Rd., Sandy Point, Shelburne, NS B0T 1W0
902-875-4707 Fax: 902-875-4105
admin@rosewaymanor.ca
Parent: Southwest Nova District Health Authority #2
Number of Beds: 65 beds + 1 respite
Jerry Fraser, Administrator

***Sherbrooke:* High-Crest Sherbrooke Home for Special Care**
PO Box 284, 53 Court St., Sherbrooke, NS B0J 3C0
902-522-2147 Fax: 902-522-2628
high-crestsherbrooke@high-crest.com
www.high-crest.com/highcresther.html
Parent: Guysborough Antigonish Strait Health Authority #7
Number of Beds: 39 beds
Marion Carroll, Administrator

***Stellarton:* Valley View Villa**
6125 Trafalgar Rd., RR#1, Stellarton, NS B0K 1S0
902-755-5780 Fax: 902-755-3104
jmacsonald@vvvilla.ca
www.valleyviewvilla.com
Parent: Pictou County District Health Authority #6
Year Founded: 1978
Number of Beds: 109 beds + 4 respite
Note: Home for special care
Norman Ferguson, Administrator

***Sydney:* Breton Bay Nursing Home**
70 St. Anthony Dr., Sydney, NS B1S 2R5
902-539-4560 Fax: 902-567-6234
Number of Beds: 264 beds
Ellen Stoddard, Administrator

***Sydney:* Cove Guest Home**
320 Alexander St., Sydney, NS B1S 2G1
902-539-5267 Fax: 902-539-7565 www.coveguesthome.com
Parent: Cape Breton District Health Authority #8
Year Founded: 1944
Archie MacKeigan, CEO

***Sydney:* Harbourstone Enhanced Care**
84 Kenwood Dr., Sydney, NS B1S 3V7
902-539-4560 Fax: 902-567-6234
www.shannex.com/enhanced_care/harbourstone.html
Parent: Cape Breton District Health Authority #8
Year Founded: 2002
Number of Beds: 268 beds + 4 respite
Ellen Stoddard, Administrator

***Sydney:* New Dawn Guest Home**
50 Military Rd., Sydney, NS B1N 3K6
902-539-2221 Fax: 902-564-8309
Number of Beds: 30 beds + 1 respite
Note: Residential care facility
Janet Gillis-Hussey, Administrator

***Sydney:* R.C. MacGillivray Guest Home Society**
25 Xavier Dr., Sydney, NS B1S 2R9
902-539-6110 Fax: 902-567-0437
Parent: Cape Breton District Health Authority #8
Number of Beds: 78 beds, 2 respite, 1 adult protection
John W. Coffey, Administrator

***Sydney Mines:* Miner's Memorial Manor**
15 Lorne St., Sydney Mines, NS B1V 3B9
902-736-1992 Fax: 902-736-0667
Parent: Cape Breton District Health Authority #8
Number of Beds: 35 beds + 2 respite
Harry Blinkhorn, Administrator

***Tatamagouche:* Willow Lodge**
PO Box 249, 100 Blair Ave., Tatamagouche, NS B0X 1V0
902-657-3101 Fax: 902-657-3859
douglas.cunningham@willowlodge.ca
Parent: Colchester East Hants Health Authority #4
Number of Beds: 51 beds
Douglas Cunningham, Administrator

***Truro:* Cedarstone Enhanced Care**
378 Young St., Truro, NS B2N 7H2
902-895-2891 Fax: 902-893-2361
powerk@shannex.acl.ca
Parent: Colchester East Hants Health Authority #4
Number of Beds: 122 beds + 2 respite
Kim Power, Administrator

***Truro:* The Mira Long Term Care Center**
426 Young St., Truro, NS B2N 7B1
902-895-8715 Fax: 902-897-1903
mira@gemhealth.com
www.gemhealth.com
Year Founded: 1999
Number of Beds: 90 beds
Note: Specialty: Long-term care for seniors; Medication administration; Peritoneal dialysis unit; Seniors' dental clinic; Palliative care
Lynn Smith, Administrator

***Windsor:* Dykeland Lodge/Hants County Residence for Senior Citizens**
124 Cottage St., Windsor, NS B0N 2T0
902-798-8346 Fax: 902-798-8312
dykelandlodge@ns.sympatico.ca
Old Name: Dykeland Lodge
Parent: Capital District Health Authority #9
Number of Beds: 110 beds
M. Emily Samson, Administrator

***Windsor:* Haliburton Place**
89 Payzant Dr., Windsor, NS B0N 2T0
902-792-2026 Fax: 902-798-6002
Parent: Capital District Health Authority #9
Number of Beds: 30 beds + 2 respite
Theresa Fillatre, Healthcare Facility Manager

***Windsor:* Windsor Elms United Church Senior Citizens' Home**
590 King St., Windsor, NS B0N 2T0
902-798-2251 Fax: 902-798-0914
Parent: Capital District Health Authority #9
Number of Beds: 107 beds + 1 respite
Sherry Keen, Administrator

***Windsor:* Windsor House**
PO Box 938, 16 Wentworth St., Windsor, NS B0N 2T0
902-798-2115
Number of Beds: 16 beds
Gordon Armsworthy, Proprietor

***Wolfville:* Wolfville Nursing Home**
601 Main St., Comp. C5, Site 11, RR#2, Wolfville, NS B0P 1X0
902-542-2429 Fax: 902-542-4048
wnh.home@ns.sympatico.ca
Number of Beds: 66 beds + 1 respite bed
Paul MacDonald, Administrator

***Yarmouth:* Harbourside Lodge**
60 Vancouver St., Yarmouth, NS B5A 2P5
902-742-3328 Fax: 902-742-1427
Number of Beds: 32 beds
Sandra M. Boudreau, Executive Director

***Yarmouth:* Villa Saint Joseph-du-Lac**
PO Box 810, Yarmouth, NS B5A 4A5
902-742-7128 Fax: 902-742-4230
rickatkinson@villasaintjoseph.com
www.villasaintjoseph.com
Parent: Southwest Nova District Health Authority #2
Number of Beds: 79 beds
Barry Granter, Administrator

***Yarmouth:* Villa St-Joseph-du-Lac**
CP 810, RR#1, Yarmouth, NS B5A 4A5
902-742-7128 Fax: 902-742-4230
rickatkinson@villasaintjoseph.com
www.villasaintjoseph.com
Parent: Southwest Nova District Health Authority #2
Number of Beds: 79 lits
Barry Granter, Administrator

Long Term/Retirement Care

Long Term Care Facility

***Advocate Harbor:* Bayview Memorial Health Centre**
Advocate Harbor, NS B0M 1A0
902-392-2859 Fax: 902-392-2625
Parent: Cumberland Health Authority #5
Number of Beds: 12 beds
Note: also community health services
Connie Ells, Site Manager

***Advocate Harbour:* Chignecto Manor Co-op Ltd.**
Residential Care Facility, Box 63, Advocate Harbour, NS B0M 1A0
902-392-2028 Fax: 902-392-2434
Number of Beds: 14 beds
Note: residential care facility
Shirley Morris, Administrator

***Antigonish:* L'Arche Antigonish**
4 West St., Antigonish, NS B2G 1R8
902-863-5000 Fax: 902-863-8224

Number of Beds: 13 beds
Note: residential care facility
Gus Leuschner, Executive Director

Antigonish: Highland Crest Home
44 Hillcrest St., Antigonish, NS B2G 1Z3
902-863-3855 Fax: 902-863-1833
highlandcres@high-crest.com
www.high-crest.com/highlandcresthome.html
Parent: Guysborough Antigonish Strait Health Authority #7
Number of Beds: 40 beds
Note: residential care facility
Mary Beaver, Administrator

Barrington: Bayside Home Adult Residential Centre
PO Box 238, Barrington, NS B0W 1E0
902-637-2098 Fax: 902-637-3151
Number of Beds: 20 beds
Note: adult residential centre
Joanne Rose, Administrator

Bridgetown: Annapolis County Adult Residential Centre
PO Box 548, Bridgetown, NS B0S 1C0
902-665-4566 Fax: 902-665-5265
Number of Beds: 34 beds
Note: adult residential centre
Patricia A. MacDougall, Administrator

Bridgetown: Grace Haven Enterprises Ltd.
RR#4, Bridgetown, NS B0S 1C0
902-665-4224 Fax: 902-825-1400
Number of Beds: 20 beds
Note: residential care facility
Donna Hatt, Administrator

Bridgetown: Saunders Rest Home
PO Box 114, 9 Freeman St., Bridgetown, NS B0S 1C0
902-665-4331 Fax: 902-665-4768
patricia_saunders@lycos.com
Number of Beds: 8 beds
Shaun Saunders, Administrator

Bridgewater: La Have Manor Corp. Adult Residential Centre
PO Box 270, Bridgewater, NS B4V 2W9
902-543-7851 Fax: 902-543-8332
Number of Beds: 97 beds
Note: adult residential centre
Thomas Wright, Executive Director

Bridgewater: LaHave Manor Corp. Group Home
58 Alexandra Ave., Bridgewater, NS B4V 1H1
902-543-7712 Fax: 902-543-1816
sclo@ns.sympatico.ca
Number of Beds: 9 beds
Note: group home for mentally challenged adults
Lorelei Mason, House Coordinator

Bridgewater: Pleasant Rest Home
45 Pleasant St., Bridgewater, NS B4V 1M9
902-543-2675 Fax: 902-543-3779
djbreid@eastlink.ca
Parent: Southwest Nova District Health Authority #2
Number of Beds: 22 beds
Note: residential care facility
Deborah Reid, Administrator

Chester: Bonny Lea Farm
PO Box 560, 5 Collicutt Rd., Chester, NS B0J 1J0
902-275-5622 Fax: 902-275-2567
sscsa@tallships.ca
www.ChesterBound.com/bonnylea
Number of Beds: 35 beds
Note: adult residential centre; small option units & apartments
Jim MacFarlane, Director

Dartmouth: Harbour Glen Manor Ltd.
229 Pleasant St., Dartmouth, NS B2Y 3R5
902-465-5770
Number of Beds: 18 beds
Note: residential care facility
Deborah Morgan-Downey, Administrator

Dartmouth: Hilltop Villa
200 Main St., Dartmouth, NS B2X 1S3
902-435-6186 Fax: 902-435-9354
hilltopvilla@hotmail.com
Parent: Capital District Health Authority #9
Number of Beds: 24 beds
Jin Young Jung, Administrator
Yoo Kyung Jung, Administrator

Glace Bay: Charlotte's Guest Home
25 Dominion St., Glace Bay, NS B1A 3P6
902-842-9797 Fax: 902-849-3774
charlottesguesthome@aliantzinc.com
Parent: Cape Breton District Health Authority #8
Number of Beds: 10 beds + 1 respite
Martha Matheson, Administrator

Glace Bay: Terrace Manor
208 South St., Glace Bay, NS B1A 1W1
902-849-2849 Fax: 902-842-0359
John MacAulay, Administrator

Greenfield: Hillsview Acres
PO Box 4, 14 Middlefield Rd., RR#1, Greenfield, NS B0T 1E0
902-685-2966 Fax: 902-685-2446
Number of Beds: 28 beds + 1 respite
Raymond Fiske, Administrator

Halifax: Basinview Drive Developmental Residence
3838 Basinview Dr., Halifax, NS B3K 5A2
902-455-7421
Number of Beds: 8 beds
Ruth McIver, Supervisor

Halifax: Haven Manor
6411 Cobourg Rd., Halifax, NS B3H 2A6
902-421-1167 Fax: 902-421-1168
Number of Beds: 17 beds
Hilda Stevens, Administrator

Halifax: Homes for Independent Living
2505 Oxford St., Halifax, NS B3L 2T5
902-422-9591 Fax: 902-425-3151
hil@hfx.eastlink.ca
www.nsnet.org/hil/
Year Founded: 1980
Number of Beds: 6 group home beds, with 1 respite bed
Note: Specialty: Programs & accommodation for young adults with physical disabilities; Community outreach programs
JoAnne Abraham, Supervisor

Halifax: Joseph Howe Drive Group Home
Tower 1, #215, 7001 Mumford Rd., Halifax, NS B3L 4N9
902-454-0630
Number of Beds: 9 beds
Note: group home
Cathy Krause, Executive Director

Halifax: Lynden Rest Home
1019 Lucknow St., Halifax, NS B3H 2T2
902-420-0697 Fax: 902-492-3936

Halifax: Melville Gardens Residential & Level 2 Nursing Care Facility
11 Ramsgate Lane, Halifax, NS B3P 2S9
902-477-3135 Fax: 902-477-2718 www.gemhealth.com
Year Founded: 1991
Paul Hussain, Administrator
Syed Hussain, GEM Management Group, Owner

Halifax: Point Pleasant Lodge
1121 South Park St., Halifax, NS B3H 2W6
902-421-1599 Fax: 902-429-9722
guestservices@pointpleasantlodge.com
www.pointpleasantlodge.com
Number of Beds: 104 guest rooms
Note: A specialty hotel, with guest rooms for people directly or indirectly associated with medical attention in the Halifax area
Robert S. Manuel, CEO

Halifax: Robert Allen Drive Development Residence
31 Robert Allen Dr., Halifax, NS B3M 3G9
902-443-6804
Number of Beds: 7 beds
Note: developmental residence
Angela Fraser, Supervisor

Halifax: Vernon St. Group Home
1648 Vernon St., Halifax, NS B3H 3N1
902-422-6742
Number of Beds: 7 beds
Note: group home

Howie Center: My Cape Breton Home for Seniors
PO Box 856, 171 Curry St., Howie Center, NS B1P 6J1
902-564-4461 Fax: 902-564-4247
Parent: Cape Breton District Health Authority #8
Number of Beds: 7 beds
Sherry MacNeil, Owner/Operator

Kentville: Wedgewood House
19 Leverett Ave., Kentville, NS B4N 2K5
902-678-1242 Fax: 902-679-2808
Number of Beds: 15 beds
Note: Residential care facility
Ingrid Althouse, Administrator

Lantz: Corridor Community Options Society
21 Convent Rd., Lantz, NS B2S 1T4
902-883-9404 Fax: 902-883-1251
ccosdirector@gmail.com
Old Name: Lantz Residential Programs
Number of Beds: 14 beds
Note: group home/small options home
Robin C. Strickland, Executive Director

Lower West Pubnico: Pont du Marais Home Ltd.
PO Box 236, Lower West Pubnico, NS B0W 2C0
902-762-3099 Fax: 902-762-2072
pdm@auracom.com
Parent: Southwest Nova District Health Authority #2
Number of Beds: 23 beds + 2 respite
Note: Residential care facility
Charlene LeBlanc, Administrator

Margaree Valley: Brookside Residential Care Facility
PO Box 83, Margaree Valley, NS B0E 2C0
902-248-2181 Fax: 902-248-2056
brook@ns.sympatico.ca
Number of Beds: 11 beds, 2 respite beds
Note: residential care facility
Lorraine Robertson, Administrator

Meteghan: Au Logis Meteghan Ltd.
PO Box 128, 8405 Hwy. 1, Meteghan, NS B0W 2J0
902-645-3594 Fax: 902-645-3594
Parent: Southwest Nova District Health Authority #2
Number of Beds: 20 beds, 2 respite
Note: residential care
Joanne Deveau, Administrator

Meteghan: Cottage Celeste
PO Box 314, 8064 Hwy. 31, Meteghan, NS B0W 2J0
902-645-2248
Parent: Southwest Nova District Health Authority #2
Number of Beds: 19 beds
Kathy MacDonald, Administrator

Middle Musquodoboit: Musquodoboit Valley Home for Special Care - Braeside
126 Higginsville Rd., Middle Musquodoboit, NS B0N 1X0
902-384-3007 Fax: 902-384-3310
Number of Beds: 28 beds
Diana Graham-Lentz, Site Manager

New Glasgow: High-Crest Home New Glasgow
253 Forbes St., New Glasgow, NS B2G 4P5
902-752-3461 Fax: 902-752-2672
high_crest@hotmail.com
www.high-crest.com
Old Name: Sunset Haven Home
Parent: Pictou County District Health Authority #6
Number of Beds: 36 beds
Note: Specialties: Medication monitoring; Recreational program
Rosalie Parsons, Administrator

New Glasgow: Highland Community Residential Services
483 East River Rd., New Glasgow, NS B2H 3R3
902-752-1755 Fax: 902-752-4256
Number of Beds: 68 beds
Note: residential care facility
Hilary Amit, Executive Director

Oxford: Four Seasons Manor
General Delivery, Oxford, NS B0M 1P0
902-447-2819
Number of Beds: 24 beds
Note: residential care facility
Herbert Hochhold, Administrator

Oxford: Shady Rest Ltd.
237 Water St., Oxford, NS B0M 1P0
902-447-2786
Note: residential care facility

Pugwash: Residential & Rehabilitation Services Inc.
PO Box 130, Pugwash, NS B0K 1L0
902-243-2571 Fax: 902-243-3222
Note: Specialties: Residential care & support services for persons who are mentally challenged & disabled; Day programs; Life & vocational skills programs; Social development programs; Advocacy services
Ronald Langille, CEO

Saulnierville: La Maison au Coucher du Soleil Ltd.
RR#1, Saulnierville, NS B0W 2Z0

902-769-2270 Fax: 902-769-3850
Number of Beds: 32 lits
Note: residential care facility
Nicole Amirault, Administrator

Shelburne: Mary's Abide-A-While Home Ltd.
PO Box 609, 188 Water St., Shelburne, NS B0T 1W0
902-875-4384 Fax: 902-875-4384
Parent: Southwest Nova District Health Authority #2
Number of Beds: 16 beds
Mary Davis, Administrator

South Berwick: New Visions Home for Seniors
PO Box 566, 4507 Hwy. 1, South Berwick, NS B0P 1E0
902-538-9579 Fax: 902-538-0390
newvision2@ns.sympatico.ca
www.newvision2.ca
Year Founded: 1993
Number of Beds: 25 beds + 1 respite
Helen B. Walsh, Administrator

Stellarton: Riverview Home Corp.
6105 Trafalgar Rd., RR#1, Stellarton, NS B0K 1S0
902-755-4884 Fax: 902-755-3207
riverview@eastlink.ca
Number of Beds: 106 beds + 3 community homes & supervised depts.
Note: Residential care facility for mentally and/or physically challenged adults, group homes, & developmental residence.
Number of staff: 150
Nancy Clarke, CEO

Stewiacke: Elmwood Manor Limited
PO Box 189, 98 Riverside Ave., Stewiacke, NS B0N 2J0
902-639-9003
Number of Beds: 14 beds
Note: residential care facility
Germaine M. Roberts, Administrator

Sydney: Cape Breton Community Housing Association
PO Box 1292, Sydney, NS B1P 6K3
902-539-0025 Fax: 902-562-5476
communityhousing@auracom.com
Number of Beds: 50 beds
Note: residential care facility
Jane Crawley, Executive Director

Sydney: Mayfair Guest Home
37 George St., Sydney, NS B1P 1H4
902-539-5611
Rosemary Ingraham-MacEache, Proprietor/Administrator

Sydney: Resi-Care (Cape Breton) Association
146 Vulcan Ave., Sydney, NS B1P 5W5
902-539-0935 Fax: 902-562-0717
Number of Beds: 60 beds
Note: group home
Michael Walsh, Executive Director

Sydney River: Braemore Home
PO Box 515, Sydney River, NS B1P 6H4
902-539-7640 Fax: 902-539-5340
admin@braemorehome.ns.ca
www.braemorehome.ns.ca
Number of Beds: 124 beds
Note: adult residential & rehabilitation
Debra MacPherson, Administrator

Tatamagouche: Maplewood Manor
PO Box 208, 150 Blair Ave., Tatamagouche, NS B0K 1V0
902-657-2876 Fax: 902-657-1022
maplewood.manor@ns.aliantzinc.ca
Parent: Colchester East Hants Health Authority #4
Number of Beds: 7 beds
Helen E. Williams, Administrator

Truro: Karlaine Place Ltd.
PO Box 691, 104 Pictou Rd., Truro, NS B2N 5E5
902-895-5111 Fax: 902-893-1513
Parent: Colchester East Hants Health Authority #4
Number of Beds: 8 beds
Note: residential care facility
Robert Barnhill, Administrator

Truro: Townsview Estates
PO Box 1825, 310 Abenaki Rd., Truro, NS B2N 5Z5
902-895-9559 Fax: 902-893-8094
sheila_peck@hotmail.com
Parent: Colchester East Hants Health Authority #4
Number of Beds: 85 beds
Note: Residential care facility
Sheila Peck, Administrator

Truro: Westside Villa
421 Prince St., Truro, NS B2N 1E6
902-893-8463 Fax: 902-893-8107
Parent: Colchester East Hants Health Authority #4
Number of Beds: 26 beds
E. Louise Boyle, Administrator

Windsor: Kendall Lane Housing Society
PO Box 556, Windsor, NS B0N 2T0
902-798-4375 Fax: 902-798-4378
vpghinc@gmail.com
www.vpgh.ca/klhs.html
Year Founded: 1993
Number of Beds: 6 beds
Note: small option home
Dorothy Blakely, Manager

Windsor: Kings Meadows Residence
RR#1, Windsor, NS B0N 2T0
902-798-4657
kingsmeadow@ns.sympatico.ca
Number of Beds: 10 beds
Barbara Campbell, Administrator

Windsor: Victoria Park Guest House
PO Box 556, 350 King St., Windsor, NS B0N 2T0
902-798-4375 Fax: 902-798-4378
vpghinc@@gmail.com
www.vpgh.ca
Parent: Capital District Health Authority #9
Year Founded: 1989
Number of Beds: 15 beds
Note: Adult residential care facility
Dorothy Blakely, Administrator
Tom Blakely, Administrator

Wolfville: Wolfville Elms Residential Care Facility
705 Main St., Wolfville, NS B4P 2N4
902-542-2420 Fax: 902-542-1048
wnh.home@ns.sympatico.ca
Number of Beds: 26 beds + 2 respite
Paul MacDonald, Administrator

Yarmouth: Glo Estates
36 Grove Rd., 143, Rte. 304, Yarmouth, NS B5A 4J7
902-742-7583 Fax: 902-742-2463
holson@ns.sympatico.ca
Parent: Southwest Nova District Health Authority #2
Number of Beds: 12 beds
Evelyn Spurr, Assistant
Hazel Olson, Administrator

Yarmouth: Sunset Terrace
8 James St., Yarmouth, NS B5A 2V1
902-742-3322
Janet Doucette, Administration

Nursing Homes

Antigonish: R.K. MacDonald Nursing Home
64 Pleasant St., Antigonish, NS B2G 1W7
902-863-2578 Fax: 902-863-4437
lcrocker@rkmacdonald.ca
www.gov.ns.ca/health/
Parent: Guysborough Antigonish Strait Health Authority #7
Number of Beds: 108 beds + 1 respite
Lorna Crocker, Administrator

Cheticamp: Foyer Père Fiset
CP 219, 15092 Cabot Trail, Cheticamp, NS B0E 1H0
902-224-2087 Fax: 902-224-1188 www.cbdha.nshealth.ca
Parent: Cape Breton District Health Authority #8
Number of Beds: 60 lits
Betty Ann Aucoin, Administrator

Glace Bay: Seaview Manor
275 South St., Glace Bay, NS B1A 1W6
902-849-7300 Fax: 902-849-7401
seaviews@ns.sympatico.ca
www.seaviewmanor.ca
Parent: Cape Breton District Health Authority #8
Number of Beds: 101 beds, 2 respite
Catherine Power, Administrator

Glace Bay: Taigh Na Mara
974 Main St., Glace Bay, NS B1A 4L8
902-842-3900 Fax: 902-842-3926
Parent: Cape Breton District Health Authority #8
Number of Beds: 67 beds
Note: Continuing care for residents & veterans
Sharon Sheppard, Administrator

Inverness: Aite Curam
PO Box 610, 39 James St., Inverness, NS B0E 1N0
902-258-1914 Fax: 902-258-3025
www.cbdha.nshealth.ca/HL_AiteCuram.htm
Parent: Cape Breton District Health Authority #8
Number of Beds: 11 beds
Note: Part of Inverness Consolidated Memorial Hospital
Clare MacQuarrie, Facility Manager

New Waterford: Waterford Heights
c/o New Waterford Consolidated Hospital, 716 King St., New Waterford, NS B1H 3Z5
902-862-6411 Fax: 902-862-8277
Parent: Cape Breton District Health Authority #8
Number of Beds: 24 beds
Sharon Sheppard, Administrator

Pictou: Shiretown Nursing Home
PO Box 250, 270 Haliburton Rd., Pictou, NS B0K 1H0
902-485-4341 Fax: 902-485-9203
bonniel@shiretown.ca
www.shiretown.ca
Parent: Pictou County District Health Authority #6
Number of Beds: 89 beds
Note: Nursing & residential care
Bonnie Linkletter, Administrator
Tammy MacKenzie, Director of Care

Port Hawkesbury: Port Hawkesbury Nursing Home
2 MacQuarrie Dr. Extension, Port Hawkesbury, NS B9A 3A2
902-625-1460 Fax: 902-625-3232
www.porthawkesburynursinghome.ca
Parent: Guysborough Antigonish Strait Health Authority #7
Number of Beds: 50 beds + 4 respite
Note: Adult residential centre
Leona Wilneff, Administrator

St Peters: Richmond Villa
PO Box 250, 9361 Pepperell St., St Peters, NS B0E 3B0
902-535-3030 Fax: 902-535-2256
richmondvilla@ns.sympatico.ca
www.richmondvilla.ca
Parent: Guysborough Antigonish Strait Health Authority #7
Number of Beds: 59 nursing home beds, 8 resident care beds
Note: Nursing & residential care centre
Margaret Morrison, Administrator
Heather MacQueen, Director of Care

Mental Health Facilities

Mental Health Hospital/Clinic/Facility

Dartmouth: East Coast Forensic Psychiatric Hospital
88 Gloria McClusky Ave., Dartmouth, NS B3B 2B8
902-460-7300 Fax: 902-460-7337
louise.bradley@cdha.nshealth.ca
Parent: Capital District Health Authority #9
Number of Beds: 92 beds
Louise Bradley, Director, Forensic Services

Dartmouth: Nova Scotia Hospital
PO Box 1004, 300 Pleasant St., Dartmouth, NS B2Y 3Z9
902-464-3111 Fax: 902-464-6032
shelley.peterson@cdha.nshealth.ca (Volunteer services)
www.cdha.nshealth.ca
Parent: Capital District Health Authority #9
Note: Specialties: Mental health programs
Linda Judge, Director, Capital District Mental Health Programs

Halifax: Metro Community Housing Association
Tower 1, #215, 7001 Mumford Rd., Halifax, NS B3L 4N9
902-453-6444 Fax: 902-453-1188
info@mcha.ns.ca
www.mcha.ns.ca
Number of Beds: 165 residential capacity
Note: Specialties: Support & residential services to persons who have experienced mental health difficulties
Cathy Crouse, Executive Director

Special Care Home

Glace Bay: Jones Manor
1 Minto St., Glace Bay, NS B1Z 5B2
902-849-1605
Parent: Cape Breton District Health Authority #8
Number of Beds: 7 beds
Calvin Jones, Administrator

Kingston: Tibbetts Home Wilmot
PO Box 519, 15074 Hwy. #1, Kingston, NS B0P 1R0
902-765-6614 Fax: 902-765-3807
tibbco2001@yahoo.com
Number of Beds: 25 beds
Wanda Tibbetts, Administrator

Nunavut

Government Departments in Charge

NUNAVUT: Dept. of Health & Social Services
PO Box 1000 1000, 1107 Sivummut Bldg., 3rd Fl., Iqaluit, NU X0A 0H0
867-975-5700 Fax: 867-975-5705
health@gov.nu.ca
www.gov.nu.ca/health

Regional Health Authorities

Behchok": **Tłîch" Community Services Agency**
PO Box 5, Behchok", NW X0E 0Y0
867-392-3000 Fax: 867-392-3001
tcsa@tlicho.net
www.tlicho.ca/tlichocommunityservices
Old Name: Dogrib Community Services Board; Dogrib Divisional
Year Founded: 2005
Note: Facilities: Rae Lakes Health Centre, Gamètì; Jimmy Erasmus Seniors Home, Rae; Mary Adele Bishop Health Centre, Rae; Tłîchô Healing Path Wellness Centre, Rae; Tłîchô Healing Path Wellness Centre, Whatì; Lac La Martre Health Centre, Whatì; Dechi Laoti Health Centre, Wekweètì; Area Covered: Behchokö; Gamètì; Wekweètì; Whatì, Tłîchô Region, NWT
Alfonz Nitsiza, Chair
Jim Martin, Chief Executive Officer
jmartin@tlicho.net
Kevin Armstrong, Manager, Finance
karmstrong@tlicho.net
Dave Harnum, Manager, Ambulance
867-392-6075, Fax: 867-392-6612, dharnum@tlicho.net
Ryan Hewlett, Manager, Health Services
Nora Wedzin, Manager, Continuing Care & Independent Living
nwedzin@tlicho.net
Nancy Gibson, Coordinator, Community Health
ngibson@tlicho.net

Fort Smith: **Fort Smith Health & Social Services Authority/Fort Smi**
PO Box 1080, Fort Smith, NW X0E 0P0
867-872-6200 Fax: 867-872-6275
www.hlthss.gov.nt.ca/english/our_system/authorities
Note: Facilities: Fort Smith Health & Social Services Centre; Northern Lights Special Care Home; Polar Crescent Group Home; Sutherland House; Tapwe House; Trailcross Treatment Centre; Fort Smith Wellness Centre. Population Served: 2,466. Area Covered: Southern Northwest Territories, including the Town of Fort Smith, Salt River First Nations, & Métis Nation Local 50
Robert Tordiff, Chief Executive Officer
867-872-6201, Fax: 867-872-6291,
ROBERT_TORDIFF@gov.nt.ca
Natalie Campbell, Director, Quality Assurance & Risk Management
867-872-6237, NATALIE_CAMPBELL@gov.nt.ca
Julie Lys, Director, Patient Services
867-872-6217, JULIE_LYS@gov.nt.ca
Phyllis Mawdsley, Director, Community Services
867-872-6300, PHYLLIS_MAWDSLEY@gov.nt.ca
Suzanne Sihikal, Director, Northern Lights Special Care Home
867-872-6296, SUZANNE_SIHIKAL@gov.nt.ca
Katerina Tsaknaki, Director, Finance
867-872-6235, KATERINA_TSAKNAKI@gov.nt.ca
Linda McDevitt, Officer, Human Resources
867-872-6507, LINDA_MCDEVITT@gov.nt.ca

Hospitals

Hospitals - General

Dryden: **Dryden Regional Health Centre/DRHC**
PO Box 3003, 58 Goodall St., Dryden, NU P8N 2Z6
807-223-8200 Fax: 807-223-2370 www.dh.dryden.on.ca
Number of Beds: 31 acute care beds; 10 chronic / rehabilitation care beds
Note: Hospital Specialties: Emergency services; Diagnostic imaging (807-223-8253); Acute care; Obstetrics; Critical care; Mental health & addiction services (807-223-6678); Occupational therapy (807-223-8214); Physiotherapy (807-223-8259); Sexual assault & domestic violence services (807-223-7427); Diabetes education (807-223-8208); Counselling; Chronic care
Karen Mazurski, Chief of Staff
Mark Dahmer, Chief, Emergency
Steven Viherjoki, Chief, Inpatient Services
Siobain Moore, Administrative Director, Workplace Culture & Organizational Health
807-223-8829, smoore@dh.dryden.on.ca

Iqaluit: **Baffin Regional Hospital**
PO Box 200, Iqaluit, NU X0A 0H0
867-979-7300 Fax: 867-979-7347
Number of Beds: 25 inpatient beds; 19 acute care adult beds; 6 pediatric beds; 8 newborn bassinets
Note: Hospital Specialties: Emergency & outpatient department; X-ray department; Laboratory; Acute care; Pediatrics

Iqaluit: **Qikiqtani General Hospital**
PO Box 1000 1040, Iqaluit, NU X0A 0H0
867-975-8600
Number of Beds: 35 beds
Note: Birthing rooms, surgery, diagnostic imaging & lab, state-of-the-art community health care
Katherine Walters, Director

Community Health Centres

Community Health Care Centres

Arctic Bay: **Arctic Bay Health Centre**
PO Box 60, Arctic Bay, NU X0A 0A0
867-439-8816 Fax: 867-439-8315
Gail Redpath, Nurse Manager

Arviat: **Arviat Health Centre**
General Delivery, Arviat, NU X0C 0E0
867-857-2816 Fax: 867-857-2980
Sandy Ranahan, Nurse Manager

Baker Lake: **Baker Lake Health Centre**
PO Box 120, Baker Lake, NU X0C 0A0
867-793-2816 Fax: 867-793-2812
Donna Brown, Nurse Manager

Cambridge Bay: **Cambridge Bay Health Centre**
PO Box 83, Cambridge Bay, NU X0E 0C0
867-983-2531 Fax: 867-983-2262
Number of Beds: 2 beds

Cape Dorset: **Cape Dorset Health Centre**
PO Box 40, Cape Dorset, NU X0A 0C0
867-897-8820 Fax: 867-897-8914

Chesterfield Inlet: **Chesterfield Inlet Health Centre**
PO Box 9, Chesterfield Inlet, NU X0C 0B0
867-898-9968 Fax: 867-898-9122

Clyde River: **Clyde River Health Centre**
PO Box 180, Clyde River, NU X0A 0E0
867-924-6377 Fax: 867-924-6244

Coral Harbour: **Coral Harbour Health Centre**
PO Box 120, Coral Harbour, NU X0C 0C0
867-925-9916 Fax: 867-925-8380

Gjoa Haven: **Gjoa Haven Haputtit Health Centre**
General Delivery, Gjoa Haven, NU X0E 1J0
867-360-7441 Fax: 867-360-6110

Grise Fjord: **Grise Fjord Health Centre**
PO Box 81, Grise Fjord, NU X0A 0J0
867-980-9923 Fax: 867-980-9067

Hall Beach: **Hall Beach Health Centre**
General Delivery, Hall Beach, NU X0A 0K0
867-928-8827 Fax: 867-928-8847

Igloolik: **Igloolik Health Centre**
PO Box 240, Igloolik, NU X0A 0L0
867-934-8837 Fax: 867-934-8901

Iqaluit: **Iqaluit Public Health Clinic**
PO Box 200, Iqaluit, NU X0A 0H0
867-979-5306 Fax: 867-979-4830

Kimmirut: **Kimmirut Health Centre**
PO Box 30, Kimmirut, NU X0A 0N0
867-939-2217 Fax: 867-939-2068

Kugaaruk: **St. Theresa Kugaaruk Health Centre**
General Delivery, Kugaaruk, NU X0E 1K0
867-769-6441 Fax: 867-769-6059

Kugluktuk: **Kugluktuk Health Centre**
General Delivery, Kugluktuk, NU X0E 0E0
867-982-4531 Fax: 867-982-3115

Pangnirtung: **Pangnirtung Health Centre**
PO Box 454, Pangnirtung, NU X0A 0R0
867-473-8977 Fax: 867-473-8519
Note: Specialty: General health care by registered nurses; Individual counseling & referral; Massage therapy; Workshops for stress relief

Pond Inlet: **Pond Inlet Health Centre**
PO Box 216, Pond Inlet, NU X0A 0S0
867-899-8840 Fax: 867-899-8997
Year Founded: 2004
Note: Comprehensive health care. Number of employees: 20
Di Schulze, Supervisor, Health & Community Programs

Qikiqtarjuaq: **Qikiqtarjuaq Health Centre**
PO Box 911, Qikiqtarjuaq, NU X0A 0B0
867-927-8916 Fax: 867-927-8217

Rankin Inlet: **Rankin Inlet Health Centre**
Bag 008, Rankin Inlet, NU X0C 0G0
867-645-2816 Fax: 867-645-2688
gbecker@auroranet.nt.ca

Repulse Bay: **Repulse Bay Health Centre**
General Delivery, Repulse Bay, NU X0C 0H0
867-462-9916 Fax: 867-462-4212
Number of Beds: 2 beds

Resolute: **Resolute Health Centre**
PO Box 180, Resolute, NU X0A 0V0
867-252-3844 Fax: 867-252-3601

Sanikiluaq: **Sanikiluaq Health Centre**
PO Box 145, Sanikiluaq, NU X0A 0W0
867-266-8965 Fax: 867-266-8802
http://webmail.gov.nu.ca
Note: Provides general health care, counseling & referral. Services in Inuktitut & English
Joanne Watson, Nurse in Charge

Taloyoak: **Taloyoak Judy Hill Memorial Health Centre**
General Delivery, Taloyoak, NU X0E 1B0
867-561-5111

Whale Cove: **Whale Cove Health Centre**
PO Box 3, Whale Cove, NU X0C 0J0
867-896-9916 Fax: 867-896-9115

Nursing Stations

Broughton Island: **Qikiqtarjuaq Health Centre**
PO Box 911, Broughton Island, NU X0A 0B0
867-927-8916 Fax: 867-927-8217
Christine Kellett, Nursing Supervisor

Long Term/Retirement Care

Long Term Care Facility

Arviat: **Andy Aulatjut Elders' Centre**
PO Box 147, Arviat, NU X0C 0E0
867-857-2667 Fax: 867-857-2668

Chesterfield Inlet: **St. Therese Home**
PO Box 1, Chesterfield Inlet, NU X0C 0B0
867-898-9917 Fax: 867-898-9080
Note: Homecare facility

Iqaluit: **Iqaluit Elders' Facility**
Pairijait Tigumivik Society, PO Box 640, Iqaluit, NU X0A 0H0
867-979-7408 Fax: 867-979-8864

Mental Health Facilities

Mental Health Hospital/Clinic/Facility

Iqaluit: **Akausisarvik Mental Health Facilty**
Baffin Hospital, PO Box 1000 1048, Iqaluit, NU X0A 0H0
867-979-7379
Number of Beds: 13 beds
Katherine Walters, Director, Hospital Services

Ontario

Government Departments in Charge

ONTARIO: Ministry of Health & Long-Term Care
Hepburn Block, Queen's Park, 80 Grosvenor St., 10th Fl., Toronto, ON M7A 1S2
416-327-4327 Fax: 416-314-8721 800-268-1153
www.health.gov.on.ca

Regional Health Authorities

Ajax: **Central East Local Health Integration Network/Central**
Harwood Plaza, #204A, 314 Harwood Ave. South, Ajax, ON L1S 2J1
905-427-5497 Fax: 905-427-9659 1-866-804-5446
centraleast@lhins.on.ca
www.centraleastlhin.on.ca
Note: Population Served: 1,400,000
Deborah Hammons, Chief Executive Officer

Foster Loucks, Chair
Paul Barker, Senior Director, Performance, Contracts, & Allocation
James Meloche, Senior Director, Planning, Integration & Community Engagement

Belleville: South East Local Health Integration Network
#2, 48 Dundas St. West, Belleville, ON K8P 1A3
613-967-0196 866-831-5446
Paul Huras, CEO
Georgina Thompson, Chair

Brampton: Central West Local Health Integration Network/Central RLISS du Centre-Ouest
#300, 8 Nelson St. West, Brampton, ON L6X 4J2
905-455-1281
centralwest@lhins.on.ca
www.centralwestlhin.on.ca
Note: Facilities: 23 long term care homes; 13 community support services; 8 mental health & addiction agencies; 2 hospitals (4 sites); 2 community health centres; 1 community care access centre. Population Served: 800,144
Mimi Lowi-Young, Chief Executive Officer
905-455-1281, Mimi.lowi-young@lhins.on.ca
Joe McReynolds, Chair
David Colgan, Senior Director, Planning, Integration, & Community Development
Pat Stoddart, Senior Director, Performance Contract & Allocation
Chuck Ferguson, Director, Communications & Community Engagement

905-455-1281, chuck.ferguson@lhins.on.ca

Chatham: Erie St. Clair Local Health Integration Network/Erie St. RLISS d'Érié St. Clair
180 Riverview Dr., Chatham, ON N7M 5Z8
519-351-5677 Fax: 519-351-9672 1-866-231-5446
eriestclairlhin@lhins.on.ca
www.eriestclairlhin.on.ca
Note: Population Served: 649,000+. Area Served: Regions of Chatham-Kent, Sarnia / Lambton, & Windsor / Essex
Gary Switzer, Chief Executive Officer
1-866-231-54, gary.switzer@lhins.on.ca

Mina Grossman-Ianni, Chair
mailto:mina.grossman-ianni@lhins.on.
Ralph Ganter, Senior Director, Planning & Integration
1-866-231-54, ralph.ganter@lhins.on.ca
Brad Keeler, Senior Director, Performance, Contracts, & Allocation

1-866-231-54, brad.keeler@lhins.on.ca
Shannon
Sasseville, Director, Communications & Community Engagement
1-866-231-54, shannon.sasseville@lhins.on.ca
Eli Malus, Lead, Critical Care
519-973-4411, eli.malus@hdgh.org
David Ng, Lead, Emergency Department
519-973-4411, dng14@cogeco.ca
Ruth Augi, Corporate Coordinator
1-866-231-54, ruth.augi@lhins.on.ca
Matthew Little, Corporate Controller; Manager, Business Support
1-866-231-54, matthew.little@lhins.on.ca

Grimsby: Hamilton Niagara Haldimand Brant Local Health Integration Network/HNHB LHI RLISS de Hamilton Niagara Haldimand Brant
264 Main St. East, Grimsby, ON L3M 1P8
905-945-4930 Fax: 905-945-1992 1-866-363-5446
hamiltonniagarahaldimandbrant@lhins.on.ca
www.hnhblhin.on.ca
Note: Facilities: 88 long term care homes; 10 hospitals (23 hospital sites); 8 community health centres (10 sites); 1 community care access centre. Programs: 81 community support services; 50 community mental health & addictions programs. Area Served: Brant, Burlington, Haldimand, Hamilton, Niagara, Norfolk
Pat Mandy, Chief Executive Officer
905-945-4930, pat.mandy@lhins.on.ca
Juanita Gledhill, Chair
Marion Emo, Senior Director, Planning, Integration, & Community Engagement
905-945-4930, marion.emo@lhins.on.ca
Alan Iskiw, Senior Director, Performance, Contract, & Allocation
905-945-4930, alan.iskiw@lhins.on.ca
Patricia Ciccarelli, Team Lead, Funding & Allocation
905.945.4930, patricia.ciccarelli@lhins.on.ca
Jennifer Everson, Physician Lead, Planning & Integration
905.945.4930, jennifer.everson@lhins.on.ca
Trish Nelson, Team Lead, Communications
905-945-4930, trish.nelson@lhins.on.ca
Rosalind Tarrant, Team Lead, Performance & Integration
905-945-4930, rosalind.tarrant@lhins.on.ca

Guelph: Waterloo Wellington Local Health Integration Network
#212, 55 Wyndham St. North, Guelph, ON N1H 7T8
519-822-6208 Fax: 519-822-5807 866-306-5446
waterloowellington@lhins.on.ca
www.waterloowellingtonlhin.on.ca
Note: Not-for-profit organization that works to plan, integrate, and fund local health services
Sandra Hanmer, CEO
Kathryn Durst, Chair

London: South West Local Health Integration Network
#700, 201 Queens Ave., London, ON N6A 1J1
519-672-0445 866-294-5446
Tony Woolgar, CEO
Norm Gamble, Chair

Markham: Central Local Health Integration Network/Central
#210, 140 Allstate Pkwy., Markham, ON L3R 5Y8
905-948-1872 Fax: 905-948-8011 1-866-392-5446
Central@lhins.on.ca
www.centrallhin.on.ca
Note: Population Served: 1,600,000
Kim Baker, Chief Executive Officer

Kenneth A. Morrison, Chair
Shaukat Moloo, Senior Director, Performance, Contracts, & Allocations
Victoria van Hemert, Senior Director, Planning, Integration, & *Community Engagement*
Naj Hassam, Director, Performance & Funding, Hospital Programs
Frances Murphy, Director, Clinical Services Development & Organization
Frances.Murphy@lhins.on.ca
Thomas O'Shaughnessy, Director, System Integration & Engagement
Kate Blackwell, Coordinator, Communications
kate.blackwell@lhins.on.ca
Peter Sit, Controller
peter.sit@lhins.on.ca

North Bay: North East Local Health Integration Network
555 Oak St. East, 3rd Fl., North Bay, ON P1B 8E3
705-840-2872 866-906-5446 www.nelhin.on.ca
Note: Provides services to over 560,000 people across 400,000 square kilometers
Dave Murray, CEO
Mathilde Gravelle, Chair

Oakville: Mississauga Halton Local Health Integration Network/MH LHIN
#500, 700 Dorval Dr., Oakville, ON L6K 3V3
905-337-7131 Fax: 905-337-8330 866-371-5446
mississaugahalton@lhins.on.ca
www.mississaugahaltonlhin.on.ca
Michael Fenn, CEO
John Magill, Chair

Orillia: North Simcoe Muskoka Local Health Integration Network
#127-130, 210 Memorial Ave., Orillia, ON L3V 7V1
705-326-7750 Fax: 705-326-1392 866-903-5446
northsimcoemuskoka@lhins.on.ca
www.nsmlhin.on.ca
Note: Plans and funds health services for over 400,000 people in the District of Muskoka, County of Simcoe, and Grey County
Jean Trimnell, CEO
Ruben Rosen, Chair

Ottawa: Champlain Local Health Integration Network/Champlai RLISS de Champlain
#204, 1900 City Park Dr., Ottawa, ON K1J 1A3
613-747-6784 Fax: 613-747-6519 1-866-902-5446
champlain@lhins.on.ca
www.champlainlhin.on.ca; www.rlisschamplain.on.ca
Year Founded: 2005
Note: Facilities: 100+ community support services, including mental health & addictions agencies; 61 long-term care homes; 21 hospitals; 7 community health centres plus satellites, 1 community care access centre. Population Served: 1,147,000. Area Served: Renfrew County; City of Ottawa; Prescott & Russell; Stormont; Dundas & Glengarry; North Grenville; four parts of North Lanark
Robert Cushman, Chief Executive Officer
613-747-6784
Michael LeMay, Board Chair
613-747-3201, Michael.LeMay@lhins.on.ca
Glenn Alexander, Chief Information Officer
613-747-3244, Glenn.Alexander@lhins.on.ca
Suzanne Dionne, Senior Director, Performance, Contract, & Allocation
Chantale LeClerc, Senior Director, Planning, Integration, & Community Engagement
Amir Afkham, Senior Manager, Projects
613-747-3235, Amir.Afkham@lhins.on.ca

Thunder Bay: North West Local Health Integration Network
#201, 975 Alloy Dr., Thunder Bay, ON P7B 5Z8
807-684-9425 Fax: 807-684-9533 866-907-5446
northwest@lhins.on.ca.
www.northwestlhin.on.ca
Note: Works with healthcare providers, communities and the public to set prioritiesand plan health services in Northwestern Ontario
Gwen DuBois-Wing, CEO
John Whitfield, Chair

Toronto: Toronto Central Local Health Integration Network/LHIN
#201, 425 Bloor St. East, Toronto, ON M4W 3R4
416-921-7453 Fax: 416-921-0117 866-383-5446
torontocentral@lhins.on.ca
www.torontocentrallhin.on.ca
Note: Specialties: Planning, integrating, & funding local health services
Barry Monaghan, CEO
Penny Thomsen, Chair

Hospitals - General

Chapleau: Chapleau Health Services/SSCHS Services de sante de Chapleau
6 Broomhead Rd., Chapleau, ON P0M 1K0
705-864-1520 Fax: 705-864-0449
chapleauhr@sschs.ca
Number of Beds: 14 acute care beds at Chapleau General Hospital; 19 long term care beds, 4 chronic care beds, & 2 respite beds at the Bignucolo Residence; 23 apartmen
Note: Specialties: Emergency services; Acute care; Occupational therapy; Rehabilitation services; Adult mental health services; Counselling; Services for the for the developmentally disabled; Diabetes education; Community services, such as Meals on Wheels, home support services, & Lifeline; Operation of a nursing station in Foleyet; Long term care; Chronic care; Respite care
Gail Bignucolo, Chief Executive Officer
705-864-3050
Robin Greer, Manager, Diabetes Education
rgreer@sschs.ca

Hospitals

Hospitals - General

Ajax: Rouge Valley Ajax & Pickering
580 Harwood Ave. South, Ajax, ON L1S 2J4
905-683-2320 Fax: 905-683-2618 www.rougevalley.ca
Parent: Rouge Valley Health System
Number of Beds: 130 beds
Note: Emergency, cancer care, cardiac care, continuing care & rehabilitation, diagnostic imaging, maternal, paediatrics, surgery
Rik Ganderton, President/CEO, RVHS
boardofdirectors@rougevalley.ca
David Brazeau, Director, RVHS, Public Affairs & Community Relations
647-294-8885, dbrazeau@rougevalley.ca

Alexandria: Glengarry Memorial Hospital
20260 County Road 43, Alexandria, ON K0C 1A0
613-525-2222 Fax: 613-525-4515 www.hgmh.on.ca
Number of Beds: 37 beds
Linda Morrow, CEO

Alliston: Stevenson Memorial Hospital/SMH
PO Box 4000, 200 Fletcher Cres., Alliston, ON L9R 1W7
705-435-6281 Fax: 705-434-5138
information@smhosp.on.ca
www.smhosp.on.ca
Number of Beds: 36 beds
Note: Specialties: Acute care; Day surgery; Diagnostic imaging; Ambulatory care clinics; Obstetrics / Gynaecology
Edward Takacs, President/CEO

***Almonte:* Almonte General Hospital/AGH**
75 Spring St., Almonte, ON K0A 1A0
613-256-2500 Fax: 613-256-8549
tmclelland@agh-fvm.com
www.almontegeneral.com
Note: Hospital Specialties: Emergency services; Diagnostic services; Acute care; Physiotherapy
Ray K. Timmons, Executive Director
613-256-2514, rtimmons@agh-fvm.com

Donna Leafloor
, Assistant Executive Director, Patient & Resident Services
dleafloor@agh-fvm.com

Randy Shaw, Assistant Executive Director, Support Services

rshaw@agh-fvm.com

Jamie Welsford
, Assistant Executive Director, Finance & Information Technology
jwelsford@agh-fvm.com

Rena L. Bowen, Director, Special Services

rbowen@agh-fvm.com
Michael Doyle, Director, Human Resources

mdoyle@agh-fvm.com

Beth Lepack
, Director, Medical Records

blepack@agh-fvm.com

Nina Mukerjee
, Director, Physiotherapy

nmukerjee@agh-fvm.com

Pam Murphy, Director, Long-Term Care
pmurphy@agh-fvm.com

***Arnprior:* Arnprior & District Memorial Hospital**
350 John St. North, Arnprior, ON K7S 2P6
613-623-3166 Fax: 613-623-4844
lab@arnpriorhospital.com
www.arnpriorhospital.com
Note: Hospital Specialties: Emergency services; Diagnostic imaging; Acute care; Ontario Breast Screening Program; Diabetes clinic; Physiotherapy; Speech therapy; Urotherapy; Palliative care
Eric Hanna, Chief Executive Officer
eric.hanna@arnpriorhospital.com
Leah Levesque, Director, Patient & Resident Services
Michelle Lewis, Director, Human Resources

michelle.lewis@arnpriorhospital.com
Tim Sonnenburg, Director, Finance & Support Services
tim.sonnenburg@arnpriorhospital.com
Wendy Knechtel, Manager, Public Relations & Fundraising
wknechtel@arnpriorhospital.com
Cindy O'Greysik, Manager, Health Records
cindy.ogreysik@arnpriorhospital.com
Karen Graham, Supervisor, Food Services
karen.graham@arnpriorhospital.com

***Atikokan:* Atikokan General Hospital**
120 Dorothy St., Atikokan, ON P0T 1C0
807-597-4215 Fax: 807-597-4305 (www.aghospital.on.ca
Number of Beds: 41 beds
Note: Hospital services: Emergency services; Diagnostic services; Acute care; Cardiac care; Rehabilitation services; Counselling & addictions program; Diabetic counselling; Complex continuing care; Long-term care; Number of Employees: 100
Robert G. Wilson, Chief Executive Officer
robert.wilson@aghospital.on.ca
Kim Cross, Assistant Executive Director, Finance
kim.cross@aghospital.on.ca
Wayne Smith, Assistant Executive Director, Patient Care Services
wayne.smith@aghospital.on.ca
Marie Cornell
, Manager, Lab
marie.cornell@aghospital.on.ca
Bridget Davidson, Manager, Health Records & Privacy
bridget.davidson@aghospital.on.ca
Donna Mallard, Nurse, Diabetic Health
donna.mallard@aghospital.on.ca

***Attawapiskat:* James Bay General Hospital**
General Delivery, Attawapiskat, ON P0L 1A0
705-997-2150 Fax: 705-997-2121
hr@jbgh.org
www.jbgh.org
Number of Beds: 16 beds
Cecile Rose, Wing Director

***Bancroft:* Quinte Health Care North Hastings**
PO Box 157, 1-H Manor Lane, Bancroft, ON K0L 1C0
613-332-2825 Fax: 613-332-3847
www.qhc.on.ca/Default.aspx?cid=275&lang=1
Old Name: North Hastings District Hospital
Division of: Quinte Health Care
Number of Beds: 6 beds
Note: Primary healthcare facility; acute care/emergency; dialysis unit
Pat Tresierra, Interim Site Administrator

***Barrie:* Royal Victoria Hospital**
201 Georgian Dr., Barrie, ON L4M 6M2
705-728-9802 Fax: 705-726-0822
webmaster@rvh.on.ca
www.rvh.on.ca
Number of Beds: 299 beds
Note: Comprehensive services, including emergency, cardiology, intensive care unit, renal services, chronic disease management, imaging (CT scans, MRIs, mammograms, BMDs, ultrasound, angiography); specializing in cancer care, surgical services, critical care, mental health rehabilitation services, as well as women and children's programs; 280 physicians, staff of 2,300.
Janice Skot, President; CEO
Laura Freeman, Senior Vice-President; CFO
Sandy McFarlane, Vice-President; Chief Nursing Executive, Patient Programs

***Barry's Bay:* St. Francis Memorial Hospital**
PO Box 129, 7 St. Francis Memorial Dr., Barry's Bay, ON K0J 1B0
613-756-3044 Fax: 613-756-0106 www.sfmhosp.com
Year Founded: 1960
Number of Beds: 27 beds (13 continuing care beds, 14 active care beds)
Note: A comprehensive care facility with services including emergency, complex continuing care, physiotherapy, dialysis, diagnostic imaging (ultrasound, mammography, bone densitometry), holter monitor, respirology, diabetic clinic, foot care clinic, general surgery, ear, nose & throat, mental health, orthotist. Private, semi-private and ward rooms are available.
Randy Penney, CEO
Jeremy Stevenson, COO
Joanne Pecarskie, Executive Assistant
pecarskiej@sfmhosp.com
Darlene Sernoskie, Director, Operations
Joan Kuiack, Director, Patient Care Services

***Belleville:* Quinte Health Care Belleville General**
265 Dundas St. East, Belleville, ON K8N 5A9
613-969-7400 Fax: 613-968-8234
www.qhc.on.ca/Default.aspx?cid=273&lang=1
Division of: Quinte Health Care
Year Founded: 1886
Number of Beds: 192 beds
Note: Emergency, cardiology, children's treatment centre, intensive care, obstetrics, oncology, outpatient clinics, orthopaedics, psychiatry/mental health services, rehabilitation, radiology, surgical services, District Stroke Centre
Mary Clare Egberts, President; CEO, Quinte Health Care
Mohamed Gaber, Chief of Staff

***Blind River:* Blind River District Health Centre/BRDHC**
Pavillion Santé du District de Blind River
525 Causley St., Blind River, ON P0R 1B0
705-356-2265 Fax: 705-356-1220
webinfo@brdhc.on.ca
www.brdhc.on.ca
Old Name: Robb Hospital; St. Joseph's General Hospital
Year Founded: 1928
Number of Beds: 16 acute care beds
Note: Hospital Specialties: Emergency services; Acute care; Diagnostic imaging; Medical laboratory services; Long term care; Health promotion; Physiotherapy; Diabetes education; Dietician services; Social work; Palliative care
Gaston Lavigne, Chief Executive Officer
705-356-2265, glavigne@brdhc.on.ca
Chris Barnes, Chief of Staff
705-356-1666, cstjules@brdhc.on.ca
Mary Ellen Luukkonen, Chief Nursing Officer; Director, Clinical Services
705-356-2265, mluukkonen@brdhc.on.ca
Jennifer Stanton Smith, Chief Financial Officer
705-356-2265, jsmith@brdhc.on.ca
Dan Lewis, Director, Environmental Services
705-356-2265, dlewis@brdhc.on.ca

***Bowmanville:* Lakeridge Health Corporation**
47 Liberty St. South, Bowmanville, ON L1C 2N4
905-623-3331 Fax: 905-623-0681 www.lakeridgehealth.on.ca
Division of: Bowmanville Site
Number of Beds: 686 beds
C. Kooy, COO

***Bracebridge:* Muskoka Algonquin Healthcare - South Muskoka Memorial Hospital Site**
75 Ann St., Bracebridge, ON P1L 2E4
705-645-4400 Fax: 705-645-4594
info@mahc.ca
www.mahc.ca/Content.cfm?C=6169&SC=1&SCM=0&MI=4181&L1M=4150
Also Known As: South Muskoka Memorial Hospital
Parent: Muskoka Algonquin Healthcare
Number of Beds: 75 beds
Note: Services include emergency, intensive care unit, surgery, endoscopy/gastroenterology, urology, ophthamology, oncology, obstetrics, antenatal, paediatrics, diabetes centre, social work, occupational therapy, speech/language therapy, pathology, complex continuing care, laboratory services, diagnostic imaging (radiography, tomography, ultrasound, bone densitometry, mammography), cardio-respiratory services, pharmacy

Barry Monaghan, CEO, MAHC
barry.monaghan@mahc.ca
David Mathies, Chief of Staff, MAHC
liz.parrott@mahc.ca
Bev McFarlane, Chief Nursing Officer, MAHC
bev.mcfarlane@mahc.ca

***Brampton:* William Osler Health Centre - Brampton Civic Hospital Campus**
2100 Bovaird Dr. East, Brampton, ON L6R 3J7
905-494-2120 www.williamoslerhc.on.ca
Year Founded: 2007
Number of Beds: 479
Note: Comprehensive health care. The William Osler Health Centre is comprised of the Brampton Civic Hospital, Etobicoke General, & the Peel Memorial Hospital (currently in re-development)
Ken White, Supervisor

***Brantford:* Brantford General Hospital Site**
200 Terrace Hill St., Brantford, ON N3R 1G9
519-752-7871 www.bchsys.org
Division of: Brant Community Healthcare System
Year Founded: 1885
Number of Beds: 300+ beds
Note: Hospital Specialties: Emergency medicine; Acute care; Critical care; Surgery; Ambulatory care; Obstetrics; Paediatrics; Brant Community Cancer Clinic; S.C. Johnson Dialysis Clinic; Mental health; Gynaecology; Number of Employees: 1,282 (175 physicians & 26 members of the Department of Dentistry)
James Hornell, President; Chief Executive Officer, Brant Community Healthcare System
519-751-5500
Robert Davidson, Manager, Human Resources
519-751-5544
Jill Randall, Manager, Critical Care
519-751-5544
Lina Rinaldi, Vice-President, Patient Services

519-751-5544
Charmaine Roye, Chief, Medical Staff

519-751-5544
David Cameron, Director, Medical Affairs

519-751-5544
Patricia Debrusk, Director, Surgical & Ambulatory Services
519-751-5544
Diane Draper, Director, Critical Care, Maternal / Child Care, Dialysis, Med
519-751-5544
Don Manning, Director, Diagnostic Services

519-751-5544
Heather Riddell, Director, Emergency Services & Urgent Care
519-751-5544
Terry Dalimonte, Manager, Dialysis, Diabetic Education, Paediatrics, & Ma
519-751-5544

Brockville: Brockville General Hospital/BGH
75 Charles St., Brockville, ON K6V 1S8
613-345-5649 Fax: 613-345-8336 www.bgh-on.ca
Year Founded: 1889
Number of Beds: 141 beds
Note: Hospital Specialties: Emergency services; Diagnostic services; Laboratory services; Acute care; Child development program; Rehabilitation services, including physiotherapy, occupational therapy, & speech therapy; Respiratory therapy; Stroke prevention clinic; Ontario breast screening clinic; Pain clinic; Complex continuing care; Palliative care
Hugh Bates, Chair
chair.of.the.board@bgh-on.ca
Ray Marshall, President; Chief Executive Officer
marra@bgh-on.ca
Robert Beveridge
, Chief, Medical Staff
bevro@bgh-on.ca
Heather Crawford, Chief Nursing Executive; Vice-President, Clinical Services
Maggie Wheeler, Officer, Communications
613-345-5649

Burk's Falls: Burk's Falls & District Health Centre
PO Box 520, 150 Huston St., Burk's Falls, ON P0A 1C0
705-382-2900 Fax: 705-382-2257 1-800-661-2900
info@mahc.ca
www.mahc.ca
Old Name: Almaguin Health Centre
Parent: Muskoka Algonquin Healthcare
Number of Beds: 7 sub-acute care beds
Note: Specialties: Physiotherapy; Nutritional counselling; Palliative care
Barry Monaghan, Chief Executive Officer, Muskoka Algonquin Healthcare
705-789-0022, barry.monaghan@mahc.ca

Burlington: Joseph Brant Memorial Hospital
1230 North Shore Blvd., Burlington, ON L7R 4C4
905-632-3730 Fax: 905-336-6480
corporatecommunications@jbmh.com
www.jbmh.com
Number of Beds: 285 beds
Don Scott, President/CEO

Cambridge: Cambridge Memorial Hospital
700 Coronation Blvd., Cambridge, ON N1R 3G2
519-621-2330 Fax: 519-740-4938
information@cmh.org; patientrelations@cmh.org (Patient relations)
www.cmh.org
Old Name: South Waterloo Memorial Hospital
Year Founded: 1953
Note: Hospital Specialties: Emergency services; Surgical services; Women's & Children's Services; Cardio Respiratory Unit; Oncology; Rehabilitation; Palliative care; Number of Employees: 1,200 (283 medical staff)
Patrick Gaskin, Chief Executive Officer
519-621-2330
Scott Hutchings, Program Manager, ICU & Medicine
519-621-2330
Ruth McKinley, Program Manager, Diagnostic Imaging
519-621-2330
Deb Snider, Program Manager, Women's & Children's Health
Michael Lawrie, Chief, Staff
519-621-2330
Katrina Power, Chief Finance Officer
519-621-2330
Susan Gregoroff, Chief Nursing Executive; Vice-President, Clinical Programs
519-621-2330
Ann Bartlett, Director, Patient Services
519-621-2330
Karen Anderson Keith, Program Manager, Mental Health
519-621-2330
Charles Bauman, Program Manager, Palliative Care, Rehabilitation & Oncology
519-621-2330, Fax: 519-740-4950
Alan Clay, Program Manager, Public Affairs & Communications
519-621-2330
Susan Harris-Howe, Program Manager, Emergency
519-621-2330,

Campbellford: Campbellford Memorial Hospital/CMH
146 Oliver Rd., Campbellford, ON K0L 1L0
705-653-1140 Fax: 705-653-4371 (ltinney@cmh.ca (The Office of the Board of Directors)
www.cmh.ca
Number of Beds: 34 beds
Note: Hospital Specialties: Emergency services; Radiology (705-653-1140, ext. 2125); Laboratory services; Ambulatory care (705-653-1140, ext. 2100); Acute care; Occupational therapy (705-653-1140, ext. 2111); Ontario Breast Screening Program (705-653-3104); Nutrition clinic (705-653-1140, ext. 2132)
Derek Nice, Chair
Kelly Isfan, President; Chief Executive Officer
Paul Williams, Chief, Staff
Norm Bartlett, Chief, Emergency Services
Glenn Gibson, President, Medical Staff

Carleton Place: Carleton Place & District Memorial Hospital
211 Lake Ave. East, Carleton Place, ON K7C 1J4
613-257-2200 Fax: 613-257-3026
info@carletonplacehosp.com
www.carletonplacehospital.ca
Note: Hospital Specialties: Diagnostic imaging (613-253-3804); Laboratory services (613-257-2200, ext. 152); Physiotherapy (613-253-3822); Speech & language (613-253-3823)
Dewar Burnett
, Chair
Martin White, Chief, Staff
Roger Drake, President, Medical Staff
Toni Surko, Secretary to the Board
613-253-3825, tsurko@carletonplacehosp.com

Chatham: Chatham-Kent Health Alliance
PO Box 2030, 80 Grand Ave. W., Chatham, ON N7M 5L9
519-352-6400 Fax: 519-436-2543 www.ckha.on.ca
Old Name: Public General Hospital Society of Chatham
Number of Beds: 300 beds
Colin Patey, President/CEO

Chatham: Chatham-Kent Health Alliance/CKHA
PO Box 2030, 80 Grand Ave. West, Chatham, ON N7M 5L9
519-352-6400
howarewedoing@ckha.on.ca
www.ckha.on.ca
Year Founded: 1998
Number of Beds: 300 beds
Note: Hospital Specialties: Emergency services; District Stroke Centre; Sexual Assault Treatment Centre; Diagnostic imaging; Ontario Breast Screening Program; Surgery; Orthopedics; Women & children's health care services; Asthma Care Centre; Rehabilitation services, including physiotherapy & occupational therapy; Mental health services, including an Early Psychosis Intervention Program for youth; Dialysis; Post coronary classes; Diabetes education; Nutritional counselling; Complex continuing care; Number of Employees: 1,300
Colin Patey, President; Chief Executive Officer, cpatey@ckha.on.ca

Anthony DiCaita, Chief Financial Officer
& Vice-President
adicaita@ckha.on.ca
Shona Elliott, Chief Human Resource Officer
& Vice-President
selliott@ckha.on.ca
Crystal Houze, Chief Nursing Executive; Chief Health Professions
chouze@ckha.on.ca
Gary Tithecott, Chief of Staff

chiefofstaff@ckha.on.ca
Kim Bossy, Director, Communications & Public Affairs

kbossy@ckha.on.ca

Chesley: Chesley Centre
PO Box 40, 39 Second St. SE, Chesley, ON N0G 1L0
519-363-2340 Fax: 519-363-2340
Number of Beds: 20 beds
M. Jackson, CEO

Chesley: South Bruce Grey Health Centre - Chesley Site
39 - 2nd St. SE, Chesley, ON N0G 1L0
519-363-2340 Fax: 519-363-9871 www.sbghc.on.ca
Parent: Chesley & District Memorial Hospital
Year Founded: 1944
Number of Beds: 15 beds
Note: A rural health centre with services including emergency, internal medicine, nutrition services, diagnostic imaging (ultrasound, ECG, radiography), lab, physiotherapy, spirometry, healthy heart program, prenatal and postnatal care
Paul L. Davies, President/CEO, SBGHC
pdavies@sbghc.on.ca
Rhonda Ridgeway, Site Manager/Director, Patient Care
rridgeway@sbghc.on.ca

Clinton: Clinton Public Hospital
98 Shipley St., Clinton, ON N0M 1L0
519-482-3440 Fax: 519-482-5960
administration@hpha.ca; humanresources@hpha.ca
www.hpha.ca
Parent: Huron Perth Healthcare Alliance
Number of Beds: 17 acute care beds
Note: Hospital Specialties: Emergency services; Ambulatory care; Acute care; Physiotherapy; Diabetes education
Maarten Bokhout, Chief, Clinton Public Hospital Site
Bonnie Royal, Administrator, Clinton Public Hospital Site
bonnie.royal@hpha.ca
Greg Stewart, Chair, Local Advisory Committee

Cobourg: Northumberland Hills Hospital
1000 DePalma Dr., Cobourg, ON K9A 5W6
905-372-6811 Fax: 905-372-4243
info@nhh.ca
www.nhh.ca
Old Name: Northumberland Health Care Corp.
Number of Beds: 80 acute care, 39 complex care, 18 rehabilitation beds
Note: community hospital
Joan Ross, CEO

Cochrane: The Lady Minto Hospital
PO Box 4000, 241 - 8 St., Cochrane, ON P0L 1C0
705-272-7200 Fax: 705-272-5486
www.micsgroup.com/Site_Published/Micsgroup/minto_about.asp x
Year Founded: 1915
Number of Beds: 66 beds (20 acute, 8 complex continuing care, 2 OBS, 2 paediatrics, 1 special care and 33 long-term care beds)
Note: An acute general facility with services including emergency, complex continuing care, out-patient, ambulatory care, obstetrics, paediatrics, surgery, and long-term care services. The Villa Minto chronic care wing houses a long-term care unit.
Dan O'Mara, CEO, MICs Group of Health Services
dan.omara@micsgroup.com
Rita Affleck, Chief of Staff
Lawrence McPherrin, President, Medical Staff

Cornwall: Cornwall Community Hospital - McConnell Avenue Site
Hôpital communautaire de Cornwall
840 McConnell Ave., Cornwall, ON K6H 5S5
613-938-4240 Fax: 613-930-4502
communications@cornwallhospital.ca
www.cornwallhospital.ca
Note: Hospital Specialties: Emergency services; Diagnostic imaging; Surgery; Cardio-respiratory therapy; Critical care; Maternal Child Program; Rehabilitation services, including occupational therapy, physiotherapy, social work, & speech-language pathology; Neurology; Orthopaedics; Ambulatory care; Geriatric services; Palliative care
Fernand Hamelin, Chair
Jeanette Despatie, Chief Executive Officer
Ashley Cook, Chief of Staff
Julie Lampron, Director, Diagnostic Imaging Department
julie.lampron@cornwallhospital.ca

Cornwall: Cornwall Community Hospital - Second Street Site
Hôpital communautaire de Cornwall
510 Second St. East, Cornwall, ON K6H 1Z6
613-932-3300 www.cornwallhospital.ca
Note: Hospital Specialties: Assault & Sexual Abuse Program (Phone: 613-932-3300, ext. 4202; Toll-Free Phone: 1-866-263-1560; TTY: 613-936-4643; E-mail: asap@cornwallhospital.ca); Psychiatric care (613-932-3300, ext. 4204); Outpatient Mental Health Program (613-932-3300, ext. 4278); Withdrawal management services (613-938-8506)
Fernand Hamelin, Chair
Jeanette Despatie, Chief Executive Officer

Deep River: Deep River & District Hospital/DRDH
117 Banting Dr., Deep River, ON K0J 1P0
613-584-3333 Fax: 613-584-4920 1-866-571-8168 www.drdh.org
Year Founded: 1974
Note: Hospital Specialties: Emergency department (613-584-1266 ext. 166); Laboratory services (613-584-1266, ext 120); Diagnostic imaging (613-584-1266, ext 160); Cardiac care services; Physiotherapy; Nutritional counselling; Long term care
Paul Fehrenbach, Chair
Sean Patterson, Manager, Support Services
Ralph Roloff, Certified Orthotist
613-582-7219
Ericia Van Drunen, Contact, Clinical Nutrition
613-584-1266
Larry Schruder, Chief Executive Officer
Stacey Mortson, Chief Financial Officer
Elizabeth Noulty, Chief of Staff
Lianne Wheeler, Chief Nursing Officer
Allison Felix, Director, Rehabilitation Services
Terry Corbett, Manager, Laboratory / DI
Garry Hartlin, Manager, IT

Cara McGuire, Manager, Medical Records, Reception, & Admitting

Dunnville: Haldimand War Memorial Hospital
206 John St., Dunnville, ON N1A 2P7
905-774-7431 Fax: 905-774-6776
kanger@hwmh.ca
www.hwmh.ca
Number of Beds: 34 beds
David Montgomery, CEO

Durham: South Bruce Grey Health Centre - Durham Site
PO Box 638, 320 College St., Durham, ON N0G 1R0
519-369-2340 Fax: 519-369-6180 www.sbghc.on.ca
Parent: Durham Memorial Hospital
Year Founded: 1946
Number of Beds: 19 beds
Note: A rural health centre with services incuding emergency, audiology, cardiorespiratory care, bone densitometry, dermatology, ear/nose/throat, hearing aid testing, urology, nutrition services, diagnostic imaging (ultrasound, ECG, radiography), lab, physiotherapy, healthy heart program, prenatal and postnatal care
Paul L. Davies, President/CEO, SBGHC
pdavies@sbghc.on.ca
Maureen Rydall, Site Manager/Director, Patient Care
mrydall@sbghc.on.ca

Elliot Lake: St. Joseph's General Hospital
70 Spine Rd., Elliot Lake, ON P5A 1X2
705-848-7181 Fax: 705-848-4414 www.sjgh.ca
Year Founded: 1958
Number of Beds: 57 beds, plus 12 day-surgery beds
Note: Services include emergency, bone density, cardiology, chemotherapy, chiropody, clinical nutrition, diabetes education, ears, nose, & throat, electrocardiogram, endoscopy, gastroenterology, gerontology, intensive care, mental health, nephrology, obstetrics, ophthamology, orthopedics, paediatrics, palliative care, pastoral care, physiotherapy, radiology, renal dialysis (as a satellite of Sudbury Regional Hospital), speech therapy, social work, surgery, urology, ultrasound. The hospital corporation also manages St. Joseph's Manor long term care facility, & the Oaks Substance Abuse Treatment Centre.
Michael Hukezalie, CEO
mhukezalie@sjgh.ca

Englehart: Englehart & District Hospital Inc.
PO Box 69, 61 Fifth St., Englehart, ON P0J 1H0
705-544-2301 Fax: 705-544-5222
dmitchell@edhospital.on.ca
www.edhospital.on.ca
Note: Hospital Specialties: Emergency services; Diagnostic imaging; Laboratory services; Physiotherapy; Occupational therapy; Respiratory therapy; Chronic care (14 chronic care beds)
Mary Lynn Kirkey, Chair
Lois Kozak, Chief Executive Officer
A. Vera, Chief of Staff

Espanola: Espanola General Hospital/EGH Hôpital Général d' Espanola
825 McKinnon Dr., Espanola, ON P5E 1R4
705-869-1420 Fax: 705-869-2608
info@esphosp.on.ca
www.esphosp.on.ca
Year Founded: 1949
Note: Hospital Specialties: Primary care; Therapeutic care; Preventive services; Diabetes education; Social work services; Assisted living; Long term care
Gisele Guenard, Chief Executive Officer
Catherine Gray, Director, Care

Exeter: South Huron Hospital Association
24 Huron St. West, Exeter, ON N0M 1S2
519-235-2700 Fax: 519-235-3405
shha.administration@shha.on.ca
www.shha.on.ca
Year Founded: 1953
Number of Beds: 19 beds (11 acute, 4 rehab, 4 chronic care)
Note: Serving the municipalities of South Huron and Bluewater, services include emergency care, acute, in-patient services, diagnostic imaging (x-ray, ultrasound, bone mineral density, ECG, Holter monitors, pulmonary testing), physiotherapy, speech/language therapy, complex continuing care, and a range of out-patient clinics.
Debra Hunt, CEO/Chief Nursing Executive

Fergus: Groves Memorial Community Hospital
235 Union St. East, Fergus, ON N1M 1W3
519-843-2010 Fax: 519-843-5331
info@gmch.fergus.net
www.gmch.ca
Number of Beds: 42 beds
Jerome Quenneville, President; CEO

Fort Albany: James Bay General Hospital
General Delivery, Fort Albany, ON P0L 1H0
705-278-3330 Fax: 705-278-1121
hr@jbgh.org
www.jbgh.org
Division of: Fort Albany Wing
Number of Beds: 17 beds
Andrew Poonae, Wing Dir.
Alexandra Sutherland, Administrator

Fort Erie: Niagara Health System - Douglas Memorial Hospital Site in Fort Erie/NHS
230 Bertie St., Fort Erie, ON L2A 1Z2
905-378-4647 Fax: 905-871-7765 (www.niagarahealth.on.ca
Division of: Niagara Health System / Système de santé de Niagara
Year Founded: 1931
Number of Beds: 46 beds
Note: Hospital Specialties: Urgent Care Centre; Acute care; Outpatient programs, including a methadone clinic & a satellite Ontario Breast Screening Program; Complex continuing care
Debbie Sevenpifer, President; Chief Executive Officer, Niagara Health System
Frank Demizio, Vice-President, Patient Services, *Douglas Memorial Hospital*
Christine Clark, Chief Communications Officer, Niagara Health System
Bala Kathiresan, Chief Operating Officer, Niagara Health System
Angela *Zangari, Chief Financial Officer, Niagara Health System*

Fort Frances: Riverside Health Care Facilities Inc.
110 Victoria Ave., Fort Frances, ON P9A 2B7
807-274-3266 Fax: 807-274-2898 www.riversidehealthcare.ca
Year Founded: 1989
Number of Beds: 55 beds (Fort Frances), 15 beds (Emo), 24 beds (Rainy River)
Note: Operates the La Verendrye General Hospital (Fort Frances- acute care, continuing care, obstetrics & surgery); the Emo Health Centre (Emo- acute care, urgent care, long tern care, diagnostic imaging, physiotherapy, dental clinic); & Rainy River Health Centre (Rainy River- acute care, long term care, diagnostic imaging, dental clinic)
Wayne Woods, President/CEO

Georgetown: Halton Healthcare Services Corp. - Georgetown Hospital
1 Princess Anne Dr., Georgetown, ON L7G 2B8
905-873-0111 Fax: 905-873-9653 www.haltonhealthcare.com
Old Name: Georgetown & District Memorial Hospital
Year Founded: 1961
Number of Beds: 33 acute care beds, 20 continuing care beds
Note: Number of staff: 346, 20 family physicians, 14 specialists
Cindy McDonell, COO

Geraldton: Geraldton District Hospital
500 Hogarth Ave., Geraldton, ON P0T 1M0
807-854-1862 Fax: 807-854-1568 www.tbrhsc.net
Year Founded: 1963
Number of Beds: 23 acute care beds; 26 long term care beds
Note: Hospital Specialties: Emergency services; Diagnostic imaging; Laboratory services; Acute care; Physiotherapy; Occupational therapy; Social work; Diabetes education; Long term care
Kurt Pristanski, Chief Executive Officer
kpristanski@geraldtondh.com
R. Laine, Chief of Staff

Goderich: Alexandra Marine & General Hospital/AMGH
120 Napier St., Goderich, ON N7A 1W5
519-524-8689 Fax: 519-524-5579
stephanie.page@amgh.on.ca
www.amgh.on.ca
Number of Beds: 54 acute, long-term, & psychiatric care beds
Note: Hospital Specialties: Emergency services; Ambulatory care; Psychiatry; Diagnostic imaging; Physiotherapy; Occupational therapy; Speech & language pathology; Diabetes education; Social work; Number of employees: 250
William R. Thibert, President; Chief Executive Officer
william.thibert@amgh.on.ca
Patrick Conlon, Chief of Staff
Mike Dawson, President, Medical Staff

Grimsby: West Lincoln Memorial Hospital
169 Main St. East, Grimsby, ON L3M 1P3
905-945-2253 Fax: 905-945-0504
comments@wlmh.on.ca
www.wlmh.on.ca
Number of Beds: 60 beds
Note: Number of staff: 385, 15 medical staff
David Bird, CEO

Guelph: Guelph General Hospital
115 Delhi St., Guelph, ON N1E 4J4
519-822-5350 Fax: 519-822-2170
info@gghorg.ca
www.gghorg.ca
Number of Beds: 165 beds; 11 critical care, 55 surgery, 22 obstetrics
Note: Total employees: 1200, 224 physicians
Richard Ernst, President; CEO

Guelph: St. Joseph's Health Centre
100 Westmount Rd., Guelph, ON N1H 5H8
519-824-6000 Fax: 519-763-0264
info@sjhcg.ca
www.sjhh.guelph.on.ca
Year Founded: 1861
Number of Beds: 235 beds (144 long-term care beds and 91 specialty beds)
Note: Residential long-term & respite care, complex continuing care, rehabilitation, community outreach, nutrition & food services, outpatient clinics, palliative care, recreation therapy, speech/language pathology services, social worker
Marianne Walker, President/CEO
president@sjhcg.ca

Hagersville: West Haldimand General Hospital
75 Parkview Rd., Hagersville, ON N0A 1H0
905-768-3311 Fax: 905-768-1820
webmaster@whgh.ca
www.whgh.ca
Year Founded: 1964
Number of Beds: 33 beds
Note: Acute & complex continuing care, surgery, diagnostic imaging, senior support services
Paul Mailloux, CEO

Haliburton: Haliburton Highlands Health Service/HHHS
PO Box 115, 7199 Gellert Rd., Haliburton, ON K0M 1S0
705-457-1392 Fax: 705-457-2398
info@hhhs.on.ca; physio@hhhs.on.ca (Physiotherapy)
www.hhhs.on.ca
Division of: Haliburton Site
Year Founded: 2000
Number of Beds: 13 acute care beds + 1 maternity bed
Note: Specialties: Acute care; Physiotherapy
Keith Sansford, Pres./CEO

Hamilton: Hamilton Health Sciences
PO Box 2000 A, Sanitorium Road, MPO, Hamilton, ON L8N 3Z5
905-521-2100 Fax: 905-521-7959
www.hamiltonhealthsciences.ca
Division of: Chedoke Hospital
Number of Beds: 129 beds
Murray T. Martin, President/CEO

Hamilton: Hamilton Health Sciences Corp.
237 Barton St. East, Hamilton, ON L8L 2X2
905-521-2100 Fax: 905-527-1941
Old Name: Hamilton Health Sciences Corp, Hamilton General Di
Division of: Hamilton General Hospital
Year Founded: 1848
Number of Beds: 304 beds
Note: Hospital Specialty: Cardiac & Vascular; Neurosciences & Trauma; Population Health Institute.

Hamilton: Hamilton Health Sciences Corp.
711 Concession St., Hamilton, ON L8V 1C3
905-527-4322 Fax: 905-575-2662
Division of: Juravinski Hospital
Year Founded: 1917
Number of Beds: 228
Note: Hospital Specialty: Oncology; Orthopedics; Rehabilitation; Palliative Care; Nuclear medecine; Infectious diseases; Diagnostic imaging; General surgery

Hamilton: St. Joseph's Healthcare
50 Charlton Ave. East, Hamilton, ON L8N 4A6
905-522-1155 Fax: 905-521-6066 www.stjosham.on.ca
Number of Beds: 600 acute care
Kevin Smith, President/CEO

Hamilton: St. Peter's Hospital
88 Maplewood Ave., Hamilton, ON L8M 1W9
905-777-3837 Fax: 905-549-7003
info@stpetes.ca
www.hhsc.ca/body.cfm?id=1575
Year Founded: 1890
Number of Beds: 250 beds

Note: A complex, continuing care hospital, with speciality programs in behavioural health, palliative care, rehabilitation, and community services. The facility operates under the umbrella of Hamilton Health Sciences.
Murray T. Martin, President/CEO, HHS
Murray Glendining, Executive Vice-President, Corporate Affairs, HHS
Donna Cripps, President, St. Peter's Hospital
Richard Seeley, Chief of Staff, St. Peter's Hospital

***Hanover:* Hanover & District Hospital**
90 - 7 Ave., Hanover, ON N4N 1N1
519-364-2340 Fax: 519-364-6602 www.hanoverhospital.on.ca
Number of Beds: 80 beds; 36 acute care, 2 obstetrics, 2 palliative
Katrina Wilson, President; CEO

***Hawkesbury:* Hôpital Général de Hawkesbury & District General Hospital**
1111 Ghislain St., Hawkesbury, ON K6A 3J7
613-632-1111 Fax: 613-636-6183 www.hawkesburyhospital.com
Year Founded: 1984
Number of Beds: 69 beds
Luc Séguin, Vice-President, Administration

***Hearst:* Hôpital N"tre-Dame Hospital**
1405 Edward St., Bag 8000, Hearst, ON P0L 1N0
705-362-4291 Fax: 705-372-2923 www.ndh.on.ca
Number of Beds: 44 lits
France Dallaire, CEO

***Hornepayne:* Hornepayne Community Hospital**
PO Box 190, 278 Front St., Hornepayne, ON P0M 1Z0
807-868-2442 Fax: 807-868-2697
www.hornepayne.com/Hospital/hospital.htm
Number of Beds: 20 beds; 12 Long-term care, 8 Acute care
Lisa Verrino, CEO
Lisa.Verrino@hornepaynehospital.ca

***Huntsville:* Huntsville District Memorial Hospital**
100 Frank Miller Dr., Huntsville, ON P1H 1H7
705-789-2311 Fax: 705-789-0557
info@mahc.ca
www.mahc.ca
Parent: Muskoka Algonquin Healthcare
Number of Beds: 76 beds, 6 special care beds
Barry Monaghan, CEO

***Ingersoll:* Alexandra Hospital**
29 Noxon St., Ingersoll, ON N5C 3V6
519-485-1700 Fax: 519-485-9606
feedback@ah.tvh.ca; Robin.Schultz@ah.tvh.ca
www.alexandrahospital.on.ca
Year Founded: 1909
Number of Beds: 35 acute care beds
Note: Hospital Specialties: Emergency services; Diagnostic & laboratory services; Outpatient rehabilitation; Number of Employees: 168
Tom McHugh, Chief Executive Officer
519-485-1732, tom.mchugh@ah.tvh.ca
Jill Matsuo, President, Medical Staff
Martha Bancroft, Contact, Human Resources
519-485-9603, Martha.Bancroft@ah.tvh.ca

***Iroquois Falls:* Anson General Hospital**
58 Anson Dr., Iroquois Falls, ON P0K 1E0
705-258-3911 Fax: 705-258-3221
Number of Beds: 21 active care beds; 15 chronic care beds; 4 palliative or long-term rehabilitation care beds
Note: Hospital Specialties: Emergency services; Chronic care; Diabetes education; Palliative care; Snoezelen room

***Kapuskasing:* Sensenbrenner Hospital**
101 Progress Cres., Kapuskasing, ON P5N 3H5
705-337-6111 Fax: 705-337-4021
info@sensenbrennerhospital.on.ca
www.senhosp.ca
Number of Beds: 30 active care
Allan Yarush, CEO

***Kemptville:* Kemptville District Hospital**
PO Box 2007, 2675 Concession Rd., Kemptville, ON K0G 1J0
613-258-6133 www.kdh.on.ca
Number of Beds: 23 acute care beds
Colin Goodfellow, Chief Executive Officer
613/258-6133, Fax: 613/258-7853

***Kenora:* Lake of the Woods District Hospital**
21 Sylvan St. West, Kenora, ON P9N 3W7
807-468-9861 Fax: 807-468-3939
admin@lwdh.on.ca
www.lwdh.on.ca
Number of Beds: 104 beds
Mark Balcaen, CEO

***Kincardine:* South Bruce Grey Health Centre - Kincardine Site**
43 Queen St., Kincardine, ON N2Z 1G6
519-396-3331 Fax: 519-396-3699 www.sbghc.on.ca
Division of: Kincardine & District General Hospital
Year Founded: 1908
Number of Beds: 36 beds
Note: A rural health centre with services including emergency, cardiorespiratory care, dental services, bone densitometry, gynecology, internal medicine, pediatrics, respirology, rheumatology, surgery, urology, nutrition services, diagnostic imaging (ultrasound, ECG, radiography), lab, physiotherapy, pharmacy, healthy heart program, prenatal and postnatal care
Paul L. Davies, President/CEO, SBGHC
pdavies@sbgh.on.ca
Kate Kincaid, Site Manager/Director, Patient Care
kkincaid@sbghc.on.ca

***Kingston:* Kingston General Hospital**
76 Stuart St., Kingston, ON K7L 2V7
613-548-3232 Fax: 613-548-6042
web@kgh.kari.net
www.kgh.kari.net
Year Founded: 1838
Number of Beds: 456 beds
Note: Teaching hospital; Research hospital; Total employees: 3,737; Medical Staff: 546
Janet Davidson, President/CEO
Paul Belliveau, President, Medical Staff

***Kingston:* The Religious Hospitaliers of Saint-Joseph of the Hotel Dieu of Kingston**
166 Brock St., Kingston, ON K7L 5G2
613-544-3310 Fax: 613-544-9897
holdenc@hdh.kari.net
www.hoteldieu.com
Year Founded: 1845
Note: An ambulatory care teaching facility with services including emergency, audiology, breast assessment, detoxification centre, diabetes education, ophthalmology, pastoral care, pediatrics, psychiatry, sexual assault/domestic violence program, day surgery, urgent care and mental health programs. It is affiliated with Queen's University and is partnered with Kingston's university hospitals.
David Pichora, CEO
Steve Miller, CFO
Sandi Cox, Chief, Patient Care
Elizabeth Bardon, Chief, Pubilc Relations & Community Engagement

***Kirkland Lake:* Kirkland & District Hospital**
145 Government Rd. East, Kirkland Lake, ON P2N 3P4
705-567-5251 Fax: 705-568-2115 www.kdhospital.com
Number of Beds: 62 beds
Hal Fjeldsted, CEO
hfjelsted@kdhospital.com
Mark Spiller, Chief of Staff
aallison@kdhospital.com
Louis Gravel, Manager, Information Systems
lgravel@kdhospital.com

***Kitchener:* Grand River Hospital Corp.**
PO Box 9056, 835 King St. West, Kitchener, ON N2G 1G3
519-749-4300 Fax: 519-749-4208
info@grhosp.on.ca
www.grandriverhospital.on.ca
Division of: Kitchener-Waterloo Health Centre
Number of Beds: 495 beds (including Freeport Health Centre site)
Note: Hospital Specialty: acute, complex continuing & cancer care
Malcolm Maxwell, President/CEO
malcolm.maxwell@grhosp.on.ca

***Kitchener:* Grand River Hospital Corp.**
PO Box 9056, 3570 King St. East, Kitchener, ON N2A 2W1
519-749-4300 Fax: 519-894-8349 www.grandriverhospital.on.ca
Division of: Freeport Health Centre
Number of Beds: 139 continuing care, 32 short-term rehab beds
Note: Complex continuing care, chronic care, rehabilitation & restoration
Malcolm Maxwell, President/CEO
malcolm.maxwell@grhosp.on.ca

***Kitchener:* St. Mary's General Hospital**
911 Queen's Blvd., Kitchener, ON N2M 1B2
519-744-3311 Fax: 519-749-6426
info@smgh.ca
www.smgh.ca
Number of Beds: 191 acute care beds
Note: Catholic hospital, home to the Regional Cardiac Care Centre
Bruce M. Antonello, President/CEO

***Leamington:* Leamington District Memorial Hospital**
194 Talbot St. West, Leamington, ON N8H 1N9
519-322-2501 Fax: 519-322-1677 www.leamingtonhospital.com
Number of Beds: 81 beds
Note: complex continuing care & rehab
J. Stenger, CEO

***Lindsay:* Ross Memorial Hospital**
10 Angeline St. North, Lindsay, ON K9V 4M8
705-324-6111 Fax: 705-328-2817 800-510-7365 www.rmh.org
Year Founded: 1902
Number of Beds: 175 beds: 36 continuing care; 16 rehabilitation; 10 palliative; 8 intensive care; 40 adult beds; 36 adult surgical beds
Note: Emergency, mental health services, complex continuing care, rehabilitation, palliative care, surgery, women's health, pediatrics, physiotherapy, diagnostic imaging, cardiac & diabetes care, outpatient pain clinic
Brian Payne, President/CEO
Varouj Eskedjian, Vice-President, Diagnostics & Support

***Lions Head:* Grey Bruce Health Services**
22 Moore St., Lions Head, ON N0H 1W0
519-793-3424 www.gbhs.on.ca/lionshead.php
Division of: Lion's Head Hospital
Number of Beds: 6 inpatient beds
Note: Specialties: Acute care; Preschool speech therapy; Diabetes education; Physiotherapy Palliative care. Number of employees: 25
Sue McCutcheon, Site Director

***Listowel:* Listowel Memorial Hospital**
255 Elizabeth St. East, Listowel, ON N4W 2P5
519-291-3120 Fax: 519-291-5440 www.lwha.ca
Parent: Listowel & Wingham Hospitals Alliance
Year Founded: 1919
Number of Beds: 51 beds
Note: Acute & complex continuing care. Number of staff: 10 physicians
Liz Phelan, CEO (Interim)
liz.phelan@lwha.ca

***Little Current:* Manitoulin Health Centre**
PO Box 640, 11-13 Meredith St. West, Little Current, ON P0P 1K0
705-368-2300 Fax: 705-368-3566 www.mhc.on.ca
Number of Beds: 16 beds
James D. Van Camp, CEO

***London:* London Health Sciences Centre**
339 Windermere Rd., London, ON N6A 5A5
519-685-8500
motslhsc@lhsc.on.ca (general transplant inquiries)
www.lhsc.on.ca
Division of: University Hospital Site
Note: Hospital Specialties: Emergency services; Medical-surgical intensive care; Cardiac surgery; Regional Stroke Centre for the Southwestern Ontario Region; London Health Sciences Centre cochlear implant program; Orthopaedics program; London Multiple Sclerosis Clinic; Multi-organ transplant program
Tony Dagnone, President/CEO

***London:* London Health Sciences Centre**
PO Box 5010, 800 Commissioners Rd. East, London, ON N6A 5W9
519-685-8500
leanne.siebenmorgen@lhsc.on.ca (Trauma program)
www.lhsc.on.ca
Division of: Victoria Hospital Site
Year Founded: 1995
Note: Hospital Specialties: Emergency services; Critical Care Trauma Center; Bleeding disorders program; Maternal newborn care; Prostate cancer centre; Trauma progam
Tony Dagnone, President/CEO

***London:* London Health Sciences Centre**
375 South St., London, ON N6A 4G5
519-685-8500 www.lhsc.on.ca
Division of: South Street Hospital Site
Note: Hospital Specialties: Adult mental health care program
Cliff Nordal, President; CEO

***London:* London Health Sciences Centre**
800 Commissioners Rd. East, London, ON N6A 5W9
519-685-8484 www.lhsc.on.ca
Old Name: Children's Hospital of Western Ontario
Division of: Children's Hospital Site

Note: Hospital Specialties: Specialized paediatric inpatient & outpatient services; Paediatric critical care unit; Child & adolescent mental health care program; Acute paediatric rehabilitation services; Gastroenterology, transplant, hepatology, & nutrition; Medical genetics; Respiratory therapy; Asthma clinic; Cystic fibrosis; Hematology & oncology

***London:* Parkwood Hospital**
801 Commissioners Rd. East, London, ON N6C 5J1
519-685-4000 Fax: 519-685-4052
Communications.Department@sjhc.london.on.ca
www.sjhc.london.on.ca
Parent: St. Joseph's Health Care, London
Number of Beds: 530 beds

***London:* St. Joseph's Health Care, London**
268 Grosvenor St., London, ON N6A 4V2
519-646-6000 Fax: 519-646-6006 www.sjhc.london.on.ca
Number of Beds: 1,660 beds
Note: Includes St. Joseph's Hospital; Mount Hope Centre for Long Term Care; Parkwood Hospital (chronic, longterm & veterans facility); Lawson Health Research Institute; Regional Mental Health Care, London & Regional Mental Health Care, St Thomas
Cliff Nordal, President/CEO

***London:* St. Joseph's Hospital**
PO Box 5777, 268 Grosvenor St., London, ON N6A 4V2
519-646-6000
Parent: St. Joseph's Health Care, London
Number of Beds: 177 beds

***Manitouwadge:* Manitouwadge General Hospital**
1 Health Care Lane, Manitouwadge, ON P0T 2C0
807-826-3251 Fax: 807-826-4216
infoserv@mh.on.ca
www.mh.on.ca
Number of Beds: 18 beds
Judith C. Harris, CEO

***Marathon:* Wilson Memorial General Hospital**
26 Peninsula Rd., PO Bag W, Marathon, ON P0T 2E0
807-229-1740 Fax: 807-229-1721
wilson@wmgh.net
www.wmgh.net
Year Founded: 1971
Number of Beds: 25 beds
Note: Number of staff: 7 physicians
Paul Paradis, CEO

***Markdale:* Grey Bruce Health Services**
PO Box 406, 55 Isla St., Markdale, ON N0C 1H0
519-986-3040 www.gbhs.on.ca/markdale.php
Also Known As: Centre Grey Hospital
Division of: Markdale Hospital
Number of Beds: 18 inpatient beds
Note: Specialties: Day surgery service; Acute care; Physiotherapy services; Diabetes education; Palliative care
Pat Campbell, President; CEO

***Markham:* Markham-Stouffville Hospital/MSH**
PO Box 1800, 381 Church St., Markham, ON L3P 7P3
905-472-7000
myhospital@msh.on.ca
www.msh.on.ca
Year Founded: 1990
Note: Specialties: Emergency medicine; Surgical care; Child, adolescent, & adult mental health services; Genetics counselling; Obstetrical assessment; The Childbirth Centre; Paediatrics; Occupational therapy & Physiotherapy; Geriatrics; Sleep disorders; Speech language pathology; Palliative care. Number of Employees: 275 physicians + 1,700 staff
Janet M. Beed, President/CEO

***Matheson:* Bingham Memorial Hospital**
PO Box 70, 507 - 8th Ave., Matheson, ON P0K 1N0
705-273-2424 Fax: 705-273-1617
Year Founded: 1955
Number of Beds: 11 acute care beds; 6 chronic care beds
Note: Hospital Specialties: Emergency services; Laboratory services; Radiology services; Acute care; Chemotherapy; Physiotherapy; Respiratory therapy; Dietician services; Diabetes education; Chronic care; Palliative care; Number of Employees: 72 (Bingham Memorial Hospital & adjoined Rosedale Centre)
Daniel O'Mara, Chief Executive Officer
705-273-2424, micsceo@puc.net
Sharon Hill, Coordinator, Human Resources
705-273-2424
Beverley Magee, Coordinator, Diabetes Program
Beverley.magee@micsgroup.com

***Mattawa:* Mattawa Hospital**
Hôpital de Mattawa
PO Box 70, 217 Turcotte Park Rd., Mattawa, ON P0H 1V0
705-744-5511 Fax: 705-744-6020
admin@mattawahospital.ca
www.mhsmattawa.on.ca
Year Founded: 1878
Number of Beds: 19 beds
Note: Specialties: Primary care; Acute care; Ambulatory programs; Diabetic resource centre; Adult & children's mental health services; Paediatric, urology, psychiatry, & women's clinic; Physiotherapy services; Palliative care
Edward Darby, CEO

***Meaford:* Grey Bruce Health Services**
229 Nelson St. West, Meaford, ON N4L 1A3
519-538-1311 www.gbhs.on.ca/meaford.php
Division of: Meaford Hospital
Number of Beds: 20 inpatient beds
Note: Specialties: Diagnostic support; Laboratory services; Inpatient primary care; Ambulatory care services; Diabetes education; Physiotherapy; Palliative care. Number of Employees: 116
Carol Gouett, Site Director

***Midland:* Huronia District Hospital**
PO Box 760, 1112 St. Andrews Dr., Midland, ON L4R 4P4
705-526-1300 Fax: 705-526-2007 www.nsha.on.ca
Number of Beds: 72 acute care beds, 8 ICU beds
Carol Lambie, Interim CEO

***Milton:* Halton Healthcare Services Corp. - Milton District Hospital**
30 Derry Rd. East, Milton, ON L9T 2X5
905-878-2383 Fax: 905-878-7047
Number of Beds: 43 acute care beds, 25 complex continuing care beds
Note: Number of staff: 385, 29 physicians, 30 specialists
Allan Halls, COO

***Mindemoya:* Manitoulin Health Centre**
PO Box 156, Mindemoya, ON P0P 1S0
705-377-5371 Fax: 705-377-5372
Division of: Mindemoya Medical Clinic
Number of Beds: 14 beds
Dan Charette, Pat. Care Coord.

***Minden:* Haliburton Highlands Health Service/HHHS**
PO Box PO Box 30, 6 McPherson St, Minden, ON K0M 2K0
705-286-2140 Fax: 705-286-6384
info@hhhs.on.ca; physio@hhhs.on.ca (Physiotherapy)
www.hhhs.on.ca
Division of: Minden Site
Note: Specialties: Physiotherapy; Diabetes education
Keith Sansford, Executive Director

***Mississauga:* The Credit Valley Hospital**
2200 Eglinton Ave. West, Mississauga, ON L5M 2N1
905-813-2200 Fax: 905-813-4444 1-877-292-4284
cvhpr@cvh.on.ca
www.cvh.on.ca
Year Founded: 1985
Number of Beds: 471 beds
Note: A comprehensive health care facility with services including emergency, Addictions and Concurrent Disorders Centre, ambulatory care, asthma education, cancer care, cardiopulmonary, complex continuing care, critical care, diabetes care centre, diagnostic imaging, eating disorders program, endoscopy, genetics, geriatric assessment, laboratory, maternal child services, mental health, music therapy, occupational therapy, paediatrics, physiotherapy, psychology, renal program, social work, spiritual care, surgery.
Michelle DiEmanuele, President/CEO
905-813-1100, mdiemanuele@cvh.on.ca
Matt Gysler, Chief, Medical Staff
mgysler@cvh.on.ca
Wendy Johnson, Chief, Communications & Public Affairs
905-813-2617, wjohnson@cvh.on.ca

***Mississauga:* Trillium Health Centre - Mississauga Site**
100 Queensway West, Mississauga, ON L5B 1B8
905-848-7100 Fax: 905-848-7140
publicrelations@thc.on.ca
www.trilliumhealthcentre.org
Old Name: Queensway General Hospital
Number of Beds: 748 beds (for acute, rehabilitation and chronic care)
Note: Inpatient services include emergency care centre, birthing centre, critical care, intensive care, neurosurgery, stroke & cardiac care, sexual assault & domestic violence services, women's & children's health (Colonel Harland Sanders Family Care Centre)
Janet M. Davidson, President /CEO
May Chang, CFO/Vice-President, Corporate Services
Gopal Bhatnagar, Chief of Staff
Larry Roberts, Media Relations Consultant
905-848-7580, lroberts@thc.on.ca

***Moose Factory:* Weeneebayko General Hospital**
PO Box 34, Moose Factory, ON P0L 1W0
705-658-4544 Fax: 705-658-4917
pat.chilton@wha.on.ca
www.wha.on.ca
Number of Beds: 58 beds
Pat Chilton, CEO

***Moosonee:* James Bay General Hospital**
PO Box 370, Moosonee, ON P0L 1Y0
705-336-2947 Fax: 705-336-2637
administrator@jbgh.org
www.jbgh.org
Year Founded: 1969
Number of Beds: 33 beds
Note: sites in Moosonee, Fort Albany, Attawapiska
Wes Drodge, Executive Director

***Mount Forest:* North Wellington Health Care**
630 Dublin St., Mount Forest, ON N0G 2L3
519-323-2210 Fax: 519-323-3741 www.nwhealthcare.ca
Division of: Louise Marshall Hospital Site
Number of Beds: 19 beds
Pierre Noel, CEO

***Napanee:* Lennox & Addington County General Hospital**
PO Box 300, 8 Richmond Park Dr., Napanee, ON K7R 2Z4
613-354-3301 Fax: 613-354-7157 web.lacgh.napanee.on.ca
Number of Beds: 33 beds; 25 active care; 8 chronic care
Note: Number of employees: 200
Wayne Coveyduck, Executive Director
Tom Touzel, Chief of Staff

***New Liskeard:* Temiskaming Hospital**
421 Shepherdson Rd., New Liskeard, ON P0J 1P0
705-647-8121 Fax: 705-647-5800
www.temiskaming-hospital.com
Year Founded: 1980
Number of Beds: 59 beds (40 acute, 11 chronic, 5 obstetric & 3 special care unit beds)
Note: This community facility offers services including emergency, cardiac rehabilitation, diagnostic imaging (CT scans), laboratory, nutrition services, occupational therapy, pastoral care, pharmacy, physiotherapy, respiratory therapy, speech language pathology and Telestroke Program. Visiting specialists conduct services in neurology, nephrology, obstetrics and gynecology, orthotics, rehab/physical medicine, psychiatry, ophthalmology and pediatrics.
Bruce Cunningham, CEO
Lenord Alfred, Director, Support Services
Sylvie Lavictoire, Director, Clinical Services
Raymond Rahn, President, Medical Staff
Céline Léger-Nolet, Hospital Stroke Leader
705-647-1088

***Newbury:* Four Counties Health Services Site/FCHS**
1824 Concession Dr., RR#3, Newbury, ON N0L 1Z0
519-693-7111 www.mhalliance.on.ca
Division of: Middlesex Hospital Alliance
Note: Specialties: Emergency care; Diagnostic services; Physiotherapy (519-693-7111, ext. 2441); Diabetes Education Centre (519-693-7111, ext. 2489); Adult Day Centre
Michael A. Mazza, Chief Executive Officer
, Middlesex Hospital Alliance
Jon Dreyer, Chief of Staff, Four Counties Health Services Site

***Newmarket:* Southlake Regional Health Centre**
596 Davis Dr., Newmarket, ON L3Y 2P9
905-895-4521 Fax: 905-830-5972
communications@southlakeregional.org
www.southlakeregional.org
Old Name: York County Hospital
Year Founded: 1922
Number of Beds: 375 beds
Note: Comprehensive health care services including emergency, cancer care, cardiac care centre, arthritis care, birthing unit, diabetes education, diagnostic imaging (bone densitometry, CT scan, MRI, mammography, nuclear medicine, ultrasound, x-ray), eating disorders, mental health programs, neonatal intensive care unit, obstetrics, pediatrics & perinatal care, palliative care, respiratory therapy, thoracic surgery
Daniel P. Carriere, President/CEO
Terry Kuula, CFO/Vice-President, Finance
Paul Clarry, Vice-President, Facilities & Paramedical Services
Nancy Merrow, Chief of Staff

***Niagara Falls:* Niagara Health System - Greater Niagara General Site in Niagara Falls/NHS**
5546 Portage Rd., Niagara Falls, ON L2E 6X2
905-378-4647 Fax: 905-358-8435 (www.niagarahealth.on.ca
Division of: Niagara Health System / Système de santé de Niagara
Year Founded: 1907
Number of Beds: 180+ beds
Note: Hospital Specialties: Emergency services; Intensive care; Ambulatory care; Acute care; Maternal / child care services; Women's Health Centre, including the Ontario Breast Screening Program; Mental health services; Geriatric assessment; Regional Stroke Program; Complex continuing care
Debbie Sevenpifer, President; Chief Executive Officer, Niagara Health System
Frank Demizio, Vice-President, Patient Services, Greater Niagara General Site
Su Bolibruck, Director, Clinical Programs (Chronic Kidney Disease, Cardiolo
905-378-4647
Heather Scott, Director, Clinical Programs (Mental Health)
905-378-4647,

***Niagara on the Lake:* Niagara Health System - Niagara-on-the-Lake Site/NHS**
176 Wellington St., Niagara on the Lake, ON L0S 1J0
905-378-4647 Fax: 905-468-7690 www.niagarahealth.on.ca
Division of: Niagara Health System / Système de santé de Niagara
Year Founded: 1921
Number of Beds: 22 beds
Note: Hospital Specialties: Acute care; Walk-in clinic; Complex continuing care
Debbie
Sevenpifer, President; Chief Executive Officer, Niagara Health System
Linda Boich, Vice-President, Patient Services, Niagara-on-the-Lake Hospital Site
Joanna Hope, Chief of Staff, Niagara Health System

***Nipigon:* Nipigon District Memorial Hospital**
PO Box 37, 125 Hogan Rd., Nipigon, ON P0T 2J0
807-887-3026 Fax: 807-887-2800
lenders@ndmh.ca
www.ndmh.ca
Number of Beds: 37 beds
Lori Marshall, Site Administrator

***North Bay:* North Bay General Hospital**
PO Box 2500, 750 Scollard St., North Bay, ON P1B 5A4
705-474-8600 Fax: 705-495-7956
mhurst@nbgh.on.ca
www.nbgh.on.ca
Number of Beds: 204 beds
Mark Hurst, Pres./CEO

***North Bay:* North Bay General Hospital**
PO Box 2500, 720 McLaren St., North Bay, ON P1B 3L9
705-474-8600 888-602-2222 www.nbgh.on.ca
Division of: McLaren Site
Denis Labelle, Executive Director

***Oakville:* Halton Healthcare Services Corp. - Oakville-Trafalgar Memorial Hospital**
327 Reynolds St., Oakville, ON L6J 3L7
905-845-2571 Fax: 905-338-4636
Number of Beds: 262 acute care beds, 39 rehab beds, 21 continuing care beds
Note: Full service acute care hospital. Number of staff: 2,056, 96 physicians, 101 specialists
Dale Clement, COO

***Orangeville:* Headwaters Orangeville**
100 Rolling Hills Dr., Orangeville, ON L9W 4X9
519-941-2410 Fax: 519-942-0483 www.headwatershealth.ca
Number of Beds: 108 beds
Cholly Boland, President; CEO

***Orillia:* Orillia Soldiers' Memorial Hospital/OSMH**
170 Colborne St. West, Orillia, ON L3V 2Z3
705-325-2201
administration@osmh.on.ca; tadyni@osmh.on.ca (Community relations)
www.osmh.on.ca
Number of Beds: 230 inpatient beds
Note: Specialties: Paediatric & neonatal services; Regional diagnostic imaging centre of excellence; Surgical services; Critical care; Dialysis; Oncology; Chronic disease management; Complex continuing care; Diabetes education; Sexual & domestic violence services; Mental health services; Outpatient clinics. Number of Employees: 300 physicians + 1,200 staff + 400+ volunteers
Glen H. Penwarden, Executive Director

***Oshawa:* Lakeridge Health Corporation**
1 Hospital Ct., Oshawa, ON L1G 2B9
905-576-8711 Fax: 905-721-4735 www.lakeridgehealth.on.ca
Division of: Oshawa Site
Number of Beds: 437 beds
J. Dusek, COO

***Ottawa:* Children's Hospital of Eastern Ontario/CHEO**
401 Smyth Rd., Ottawa, ON K1H 8L1
613-737-7600
kouri@cheo.on.ca (Patient Representative Office)
www.cheo.on.ca
Year Founded: 1974
Number of Beds: 112 pediatric, oncology, adolescent medicine, & surgery beds; 25 psychiatry beds; 20 neonatal intensive care unit beds; 10 intensive care unit beds
Note: Hospital Specialties: Pediatric health for children & youth aged 0 to 18 years; Emergency services; Surgery; Ontario Newborn Screening Program; Neonatal intensive care; Genetics; Oncology; Dialysis; Cardiology; Neurology; Provincial Centre of Excellence for Child & Youth Mental Health; Number of Employees: 1,500 administrative, service, & allied health staff; 630 nursing staff; 183 physicians
Michel Bilodeau, President; Chief Executive Officer

Carrol Pitters, Chief of Staff

Jerry Bisson, Chief Financial Officer; Senior Vice-President
Pat Elliott-Miller, Chief Nursing Executive; Vice-President, Patient Services
Tyson Roffey, Chief Information Officer
Ginette Champagne, Vice-President, Human Resources
Martin H. Osmond, Vice-President, Research
Susan Richardson, Vice-President, Professional Services
Ann
Fuller, Director, Public Relations

***Ottawa:* Hôpital Montfort**
713, ch Montréal, Ottawa, ON K1K 0T2
613-746-4621 Fax: 613-748-4947 800-276-0161
montfort@montfort.on.ca
www.hopitalmontfort.com
Number of Beds: 208 lits
Gérald Savoie, Président/Directeur général

***Ottawa:* The Ottawa Hospital L'Hôpital d'Ottawa**
1053 Carling Ave., Ottawa, ON K1Y 4E9
613-722-7000
webmaster@ottawahospital.on.ca
www.ottawahospital.on.ca
Division of: Civic Campus
Number of Beds: 1,066 beds across the system
Note: Comprehensive, patient-focussed care; University of Ottawa Heart Institute. Number of staff total TOH: 11,566 staff, 1,150 physicians
Jack Kitts, President/CEO
Jeffrey Turnbull, Chief of Staff

***Ottawa:* The Ottawa Hospital L'Hôpital d'Ottawa**
501 Smyth Rd., Ottawa, ON K1H 8L6
613-722-7000 Fax: 613-737-8470 www.ottawahospital.on.ca
Division of: General Campus
Number of Beds: 1,066 beds across the system
Note: Comprehensive, patient-focussed care, including the University of Ottawa Eye Institute. Number of staff total TOH: 11,566 staff, 1,150 physicians
Jack Kitts, President/CEO
Jeffrey Turnbull, Chief of Staff

***Ottawa:* The Ottawa Hospital L'Hôpital d'Ottawa**
1967 Riverside Dr., Ottawa, ON K1H 7W9
613-722-7000 Fax: 613-738-8526
Division of: Riverside Campus
Number of Beds: 1,066 beds across the system
Note: Comprehensive, patient-focussed care, including Eye Care Centre, & the Shirley E. Greenberg Women's Health Centre. Number of staff total TOH: 11,566 staff, 1,150 physicians
Jack Kitts, President/CEO
Jeffrey Turnbull, Chief of Staff

***Ottawa:* Queensway Carleton Hospital**
3045 Baseline Rd., Ottawa, ON K2H 8P4
613-721-2000 Fax: 613-721-4770
communications@qch.on.ca
www.qch.on.ca
Number of Beds: 264 beds
Note: Diagnostic imaging, emergency services, family medicine, geriatrics, lab, rehabilitation, obstetrics & gynaecology, paediatrics, psychiatry, surgery. Number of staff: 1,798, 234 physicians, 3 midwives.
Tom Schonberg, President/CEO
Andrew Falconer, Chief of Staff

***Owen Sound:* Grey Bruce Health Services**
1800 - 8 St. East, Owen Sound, ON N4K 6M9
519-376-2121
web@gbhs.on.ca
www.gbhs.on.ca
Pat Campbell, President; CEO

***Owen Sound:* Grey Bruce Health Services**
PO Box 1800, 1800 - 8th St. East, Owen Sound, ON N4K 6M9
519-376-2121
library@gbhs.on.ca
www.gbhs.on.ca/owensound.php
Division of: Owen Sound Hospital
Note: Specialties: Community addiction treatment services; Community mental health services; Community outreach; Critical care services; Grey Bruce District Stroke Centre; Grey Bruce Huron paramedic base hospital program; Ontario breast screening program; Preschool speech & language service; Sleep lab; Sexual assault & partner abuse care; Surgical services; Nuclear medicine; Psychogeriatric unit; Palliative care. Number of Employees: 60 specialists + 21 family physicians + 1,129 nurses, therapists, technologists, & support staff

***Palmerston:* North Wellington Health Care Corporation**
500 Whites Rd., Palmerston, ON N0G 2P0
519-343-2030 Fax: 519-343-3821 www.nwhealthcare.ca
Division of: Palmerston & District Hospital Site
Number of Beds: 19 beds
Pierre Noel, Administrator/CEO

***Paris:* Willett Hospital Site**
238 Grand River St. North, Paris, ON N3L 2N7
519-442-2251 www.bchsys.org
Also Known As: The Willett
Division of: Brant Community Healthcare System (BCHS)
Year Founded: 1922
Number of Beds: A total of 350 beds are part of The Brant Community Healthcare System, which consists of The Willett Hospital in Paris, Ontario & the Brantford Genera
Note: Hospital Specialties: Urgent care; Diagnostic imaging; Recreational therapy; Physiotherapy; Occupational therapy; Counselling services; Community health, including health & wellness education
James Hornell, President; Chief Executive Officer, Brant Community Healthcare System
519-751-5500
Andrew McRobert, Director, Health & Addiction Services & Pastoral Care
519-751-5544
Heather Riddell, Director, Emergency Services / Urgent Care

519-751-5544
Jill Berridge, Manager, Rehabilitation Services
519-751-5544
Karen Kuzmich, Manager, Wellness & Healthcare Integration

519-442-4000
Nancy Wheeler, Manager, Imaging
519-751-5547

***Pembroke:* Pembroke General Hospital**
705 MacKay St., Pembroke, ON K8A 1G8
613-732-2811 Fax: 613-732-9986
pr@pemgenhos.org
www.pemgenhos.org
Number of Beds: 165 beds
Lloyd Koch, President/CEO

***Penetanguishene:* Penetanguishene General Hospital**
25 Jeffery St., Penetanguishene, ON L9M 1K6
705-549-7431 Fax: 705-549-4031 www.nsha.on.ca
Number of Beds: 51 beds
Note: hospital, regional rehab. & complex continuing care, dialysis
Doris Shirriff, Executive Director
Robert Robitaille, Director, Environmental Services

***Perth:* Perth & Smiths Falls District Hospital**
33 Drummond St. West, Perth, ON K7H 2K1
613-267-1500 Fax: 613-264-0365
webinquiry@psfdh.on.ca
www.psfdh.on.ca
Also Known As: Great War Memorial Site
Division of: Perth Site

Note: Specialties: Acute care; Health promotion programs; Ambulatory care; Rehabilitation services; Chronic care; Palliative care

Peterborough: Peterborough Regional Health Centre/PRHC
1 Hospital Dr., Peterborough, ON K9J 7C6
705-743-2121 Fax: 705-876-5120
info@prhc.on.ca
www.prhc.on.ca
Number of Beds: 494 beds
Note: Specialties: Acute care; Emergency services; Diagnostic imaging; Surgical services; Regional renal program; Mental health services; Maternal child services. Number of Employees: 2,000 staff; 350 physicians with privileges; 600 volunteers
Wendy Fucile, Interim President/CEO

Petrolia: Charlotte Eleanor Englehart Hospital of Bluewater Health/CEEH of
450 Blanche St., Petrolia, ON N0N 1R0
519-882-4325 Fax: 519-882-3711 www.bluewaterhealth.ca
Old Name: Charlotte Eleanor Englehart Hospital
Division of: Bluewater Health
Year Founded: 1911
Number of Beds: 23 acute care beds; 18 continuing care beds
Note: Hospital Specialties: Emergency services; Acute care; Ambulatory care; Continuing care services
Sue Denomy, President; Chief Executive Officer, Bluewater Health
519-464-4400, Fax: 519-336-8780, sdenomy@bluewaterhealth.ca

Picton: Quinte Health Care Prince Edward County Memorial
403 Main St. East, Picton, ON K0K 2T0
613-476-1008 Fax: 613-476-8600
www.qhc.on.ca/Default.aspx?cid=276&lang=1
Division of: Quinte Health Care
Year Founded: 1959
Number of Beds: 24 beds
Note: Emergency services, obstetrics, physiotherapy, outpatient clinics, radiology, pharmacy
Mary Clare Egberts, President; CEO, Quinte Health Care

Port Colborne: Niagara Health System - Port Colborne Site/NHS
260 Sugarloaf St., Port Colborne, ON L3K 2N7
905-378-4647 Fax: 905-834-0404 (www.niagarahealth.on.ca
Division of: Niagara Health System / Système de santé de Niagara
Year Founded: 1951
Number of Beds: 46 beds inpatient beds for complex continuing care; 35 beds at the New Port Centre for addiction recovery
Note: Hospital Specialties: Urgent Care Centre; Ontario Breast Screening Program; Eating Disorders Clinic; Addiction recovery, including a methadone clinic; Complex continuing care
Debbie
Sevenpifer, President; Chief Executive Officer, Niagara Health System
Bala Kathiresan, Chief Operating Officer, Niagara Health System
Sue Matthews, Chief Nursing Executive; Vice-President, Patient Services, Port Colborne Site
Norma Medulun, Director, Clinical Program (Addiction Recovery)
905-378-4647

Port Perry: Lakeridge Health Corporation
451 Paxton St., Port Perry, ON L9L 1A8
905-985-7321 Fax: 905-985-5829 www.lakeridgehealth.on.ca
Division of: Port Perry Site
Number of Beds: 24 beds
Carol Anderson, Site Leader

Rainy River: Rainy River Health Centre
114 - 4th St., Rainy River, ON P0W 1L0
807-852-3232 Fax: 807-852-3565
riverside@rhcf.on.ca
www.riversidehealthcare.ca
Parent: Riverside Health Care Facilities Inc.
Number of Beds: 24 beds
Note: Emergency, diagnostic imaging, acute and long term care facility
Tammie McNally, Nurse Manager

Red Lake: Red Lake Margaret Cochenour Memorial Hospital
PO Box 5005, 51 Hwy. 105, Red Lake, ON P0V 2M0
807-727-2066 Fax: 807-727-2923
info@redlakehospital.ca
www.redlakehospital.ca
Also Known As: Red Lake Hospital
Year Founded: 1973
Number of Beds: 14 acute care beds, 4 long term care beds
Note: Emergency services, lab, radiology & ultrasound, rehabilitation, sugery, endoscopy, nutritional services, chemotherapy, telehealth.
Janice Mullin, Chief Executive Officer

Renfrew: Renfrew Victoria Hospital
499 Raglan St. North, Renfrew, ON K7V 1P6
613-432-4851 Fax: 613-432-8649 www.renfrewhosp.com
Year Founded: 1897
Number of Beds: 101 beds
Note: Birthing room & obstetrical care, pediatrics, chronic care, geriatric care, surgery, physiotherapy, palliative care, nephrology, urology, cardiac care, dialysis services, satellite oncology service, diagnostic imaging & ultrasound, dermatology, ophthalmology
Randy Penney, President/CEO
Julia Boudreau, Vice-President, Corporate Services

Richmond Hill: York Central Hospital
10 Trench St., Richmond Hill, ON L4C 4Z3
905-883-1212 Fax: 905-883-2455 www.yorkcentral.on.ca
Number of Beds: 427 beds, 116 long-term care beds
Note: Total staff: 1732 Employees
William M. Leacy, President/CEO

Sarnia: Bluewater Health
Norman Site, 89 Norman St., Sarnia, ON N7T 6S3
519-464-4400 Fax: 519-336-8780 www.bluewaterhealth.ca
Old Name: Charlotte Eleanor Englehart Hospital; Sarnia Gener
Year Founded: 2002
Number of Beds: 211 acute care beds; 88 complex continuing care beds
Note: Hospital Specialties: Emergency medicine; Laboratory services; Surgery; Acute care; Obstetrics; Pediatrics; Rehabilitation; Mental health services; Dialysis; Diabetes education; Nutrition services; Sexual & Domestic Assault Treatment Centre; Complex continuing care; Palliative care; Number of Employees: 2,070
Sue Denomy, President; Chief Executive Officer
519-464-4470, Fax: 519-336-8780, sdenomy@bluewaterhealth.ca
Stephen Anema, Chief Financial Officer
519-464-4400, Fax: 519-346-4600, sanema@bluewaterhealth.ca
Kim Bossy, Chief, Communications & Public
Affairs
519-464-4400, Fax: 519-346-4600, kbossy@bluewaterhealth.ca
Michael Lapaine, Chief Operating Officer; Vice-President, Operations

519-464-4400, Fax: 519-336-8780, mlapaine@bluewaterhealth.ca
Martin Lees, Chief, Professional Staff & Quality / Risk Management
519-464-4400, Fax: 519-464-4501, mlees@bluewaterhealth.ca
Barb O'Neil, Chief

, Nursing, Interprofessional Practice & Organizat
519-464-4400, Fax: 519-346-4600, boneil@bluewaterhealth.ca

Sault Ste Marie: Sault Area Hospital
969 Queen St. East, Sault Ste Marie, ON P6A 2C4
705-759-3434 Fax: 705-759-3640
publicaffairs@sah.on.ca
www.sah.on.ca
Number of Beds: 289 beds
Note: Acute care hospital with over 1900 employees, 400 volunteers, and 125 physicians on staff.
Ron Gagnon, Interim President; CEO

Seaforth: Huron-Perth Healthcare Alliance
PO Box 99, 24 Centennial Dr., Seaforth, ON N0K 1W0
519-527-1650 Fax: 519-527-8414 www.hpha.ca
Division of: Seaforth Community Hospital
Number of Beds: 34 beds
Andrew Williams, CEO
andrew.williams@hpha.ca

Seaforth: Seaforth Community Hospital
PO Box 99, 24 Centennial Dr., Seaforth, ON N0K 1W0
519-527-1650 Fax: 519-527-8414
administration@hpha.ca
www.hpha.ca/default.aspx?cid=48&lang=1
Parent: Huron Perth Healthcare Alliance
Year Founded: 1965
Number of Beds: 18 beds
Note: Emergency & ambulatory care, cardiorespiratory, diagnostic imaging, lab, physiotherapy, occupational therapy, chemotherapy, nutrition, diabetes education, dialysis, women's care & pediatrics, general surgery, intensive care & telemetry units, mental health services, dentistry. Heliport & Seaforth Medical Clinic
Andrew Williams, CEO, HPHA
519-272-8202, andrew.williams@hpha.ca
Ken Haworth, Vice-President; CFO, Operations, HPHA
519-272-8210, ken.haworth@hpha.ca
Bonnie Royal, Site Administrator; Program Director, Seaforth
519-527-3000, bonnie.royal@hpha.ca

Simcoe: Norfolk General Hospital
365 West St., Simcoe, ON N3Y 1T7
519-426-0130 Fax: 519-429-6998
wlewis@ngh.on.ca
www.ngh.on.ca
Number of Beds: 121 beds
J. William C. Lewis, Executive Director

Sioux Lookout: Sioux Lookout Meno Ya Win Health Centre - 5th Avenue Site
PO Box 909, 5th Ave. South, Sioux Lookout, ON P8T 1B4
807-737-3030 Fax: 807-737-3454 www.slmhc.on.ca
Year Founded: 2002
Number of Beds: 36 acute care beds, 5 chronic care beds, 20 extended care beds
Note: Emergency & ambulatory care, primary care services, specialized community-based programs, such as suicide prevention, addiction & mental health, long term care (William Bill George Extended Care facility), & integrated modern & traditional medicine. Services in English, Ojibway, Oji-Cree & Cree.
Douglas Semple, CEO (interim)
Doug Moynihan, Vice-President, Corporate Services
dmoynihan@slmhc.on.ca
Terry O'Driscoll, Chief of Staff
Renee Southwind, Manager, Communications and Community Development
807-737-5133, rsouthwind@slmhc.on.ca

Sioux Lookout: Sioux Lookout Meno Ya Win Health Centre - 7th Avenue Site
PO Box 909, 60 - 7th Ave., Sioux Lookout, ON P8T 1B4
807-737-3030 Fax: 807-737-5127 www.slmhc.on.ca
Number of Beds: 35 beds
Note: Cancer care, cardiac care, lab, diagnostic imaging, pharmacy, telemedicine, library & education centre
Douglas Semple, CEO (interim)
Doug Moynihan, Vice-President, Corporate Services
Terry O'Driscoll, Chief of Staff
Renee Southwind, Manager, Communications & Community Development
807-737-5133, rsouthwind@slmhc.on.ca

Smiths Falls: Perth & Smiths Falls District Hospital
60 Cornelia St. West, Smiths Falls, ON K7A 2H9
613-283-2330 Fax: 613-283-8990
webinquiry@psfdh.on.ca
www.psfdh.on.ca
Division of: Smiths Falls Site
Note: Specialties: Acute care; Ambulatory care; Dialysis unit; Cataract surgery; Diabetes counselling; Children's mental health services; Sexual assault & domestic violence program; Vascular protection clinic; Chronic care; Palliative care. Number of Employees: 560
Todd Stepanuik, President/CEO

Smooth Rock Falls: Hôpital de Smooth Rock Falls Hospital
PO Box 219, 107 Kelly Road, Smooth Rock Falls, ON P0L 2B0
705-338-2781 Fax: 705-338-4410
info@srfhosp.ca
www.srfhosp.ca
Number of Beds: 14 acute care beds, 23 long term care beds
Note: Primary care, including the North Cochrane Detoxification Centre. Number of staff: 85 staff, 1 FT & 3 PT physicians
Fabien L. Hébert, CEO

Southampton: Grey Bruce Health Services
340 High St., Southampton, ON N0H 2L0
519-797-3230 www.gbhs.on.ca/southampton.php
Division of: Southampton Hospital
Number of Beds: 16 inpatient beds
Note: Specialties: Day surgery services; Outpatient services, such as a women's health clinic; Home & community support services, such as the Day Away Program; Diabetes education; Physiotherapy; Palliative care. Number of employees: 105
Carolyn Zacharuk, Site Director

St Catharines: Niagara Health System - Ontario Street Site in St. Catharines
155 Ontario St., St Catharines, ON L2R 5K3
905-378-4647 Fax: 905-682-5533 (www.niagarahealth.on.ca
Old Name: Hotel Dieu Hospital
Division of: Niagara Health System / Système de santé de Niagara
Year Founded: 1948
Number of Beds: 43 beds for addiction management

Note: Hospital Specialties: Urgent Care Centre; Dialysis Program, including peritoneal dialysis, hemodialysis, & a pre-renal clinic; Addiction management services, including counselling, detoxification, & post-addiction services
Debbie Sevenpifer, President; Chief Executive Officer, Niagara Health System
Anne Atkinson, Vice-President, Patient Services, Ontario Street Site
Norma Medulun, Director, Clinical Program (Addiction Recovery)
905-378-4647

St Catharines: Niagara Health System - St. Catharines General Site/NHS
142 Queenston St., St Catharines, ON L2R 2Z7
905-378-4647 Fax: 905-684-1468 (www.niagarahealth.on.ca
Division of: Niagara Health System / Système de santé de Niagara
Year Founded: 1865
Number of Beds: 200+ beds
Note: Hospital Specialties: Emergency services; Surgery; Acute care; Ambulatory care; Maternal & child services; Oncology; Ontario Breast Screening Program; Sexual Assault / Domestic Violence Treatment Centre; Mental health services; Critical care; Palliative care
Debbie
Sevenpifer, President; Chief Executive Officer, Niagara Health System
Patty Welychka, Director, Clinical Program (Surgical Services)
905-378-4647
Anne
Atkinson, Vice-President, Patient Services, St. Catharines General Site
Terry McMahon, Vice-President, Human Resources, Niagara Health System
Joanna Hope, Chief of Staff, Niagara Health System
Bala Kathiresan, Chief Operating Officer, Niagara Health System
Donna Rothwell, Chief Nursing; Professional Practice Officer, Maternal; Child Care
Angela Zangari, Chief Financial Officer, Niagara Health System
Patricia
Morka, Director, Clinical Program (Emergency & Critical Care) 905-378-4647
Heather Scott, Director, Clinical Program (Mental Health)
905-378-4647

St Marys: St. Marys Memorial Hospital
PO Box 940, 267 Queen St. West, St Marys, ON N4X 1B6
519-284-1332 Fax: 519-284-8324
smmh.administration@hphp.org
www.hpha.ca
Parent: Huron Perth Healthcare Alliance
Year Founded: 1950
Number of Beds: 21 beds
Note: Primary care services include emergency, cardiac care, gynecology & pediatrics, rehabilitation, diagnostic imaging, orthopedic care
Andrew Williams, CEO, HPHA
519-272-8202, andrew.williams@hpha.ca.
Laurel Moore, Chief Of Staff, HPHA
519-272-8210, dr.laurel.moore@hpha.ca
Shirley Veenendaal, Site Administrator
shirley.veenendaal@hpha.ca

St Thomas: St. Thomas Elgin General Hospital
189 Elm St., St Thomas, ON N5R 5C4
519-631-2020 Fax: 519-631-1825
publicrelations@stegh.on.ca
www.stegh.on.ca
Year Founded: 1954
Number of Beds: 166 beds
Note: A comprehensive health care facility with services including emergency, rehabiltation, complex Care, social work, diagnostic imaging, laboratory, pharmacy, surgery, diabetes education, cardiac intensive care, maternal care unit
Paul Collins, President /CEO
pcollins@stegh.on.ca
Malcolm Hopkins, Vice-President, Corporate Services
mhopkins@stegh.on.ca
Nancy Whitmore, Vice-President, Medical Affairs & Chief of Staff
nwhitmor@stegh.on.ca
Brenda Lambert, Vice-President, Patient Services
blambert@stegh.on.ca

Stratford: Stratford General Hospital
46 General Hospital Dr., Stratford, ON N5A 2Y6
519-271-2120 Fax: 519-271-7137
administration@hpha.ca
www.hpha.ca/default.aspx?cid=49&lang=1
Parent: Huron Perth Healthcare Alliance
Year Founded: 1896
Number of Beds: 153 beds (110 acute care beds, 25 chronic care beds, 15 rehab beds, 3 neonatal intensive care beds)
Note: A comprehensive care facility with services including emergency & ambulatory care, diagnostic imaging (CT scans, x-ray, ultrasound, mammography), obstetrics, gynecology, pediatrics, psychiatry, ophthalmology, complex continuing care, palliative care, rehabilitation, maternity, satellite dialysis unit, speech language pathology, surgery.
Andrew Williams, CEO, HPHA
519-272-8202, andrew.williams@hpha.ca

Laurel Moore, Chief of Staff, HPHA
519-272-8210, dr.laurel.moore@hpha.ca

Strathroy: Strathroy Middlesex General Hospital
395 Carrie St., Strathroy, ON N7G 3J4
519-245-5295 Fax: 519-245-0366 www.mhalliance.on.ca
Parent: Middlesex Hospital Alliance
Year Founded: 1914
Number of Beds: 77 beds (of which 60 are acute care beds)
Note: A full-service, community hospital with comprehensive outpatient services, primary & secondary care. Services include emergency & trauma care, cataract surgery, diagnostic imaging (bone mineral density, CT scans, x-rays, mammography, ultrasound), intensive care/coronary care unit, obstetrics, urology, orthopedics, gynecology, otolaryngology, ophthalmology and some operative dental.
Michael A. Mazza, CEO, MHA
Marc Raymond, President, Medical Staff
Paul Ferner, Chief of Staff

Sturgeon Falls: The West Nipissing General Hospital L'Hôpital général de Nipissing Ouest
725 Coursol Rd., Sturgeon Falls, ON P2B 2Y6
705-753-3110 Fax: 705-753-0210
marthe.levac@wngh.ca
www.wngh.ca
Year Founded: 1977
Number of Beds: 56 beds
Note: Number of staff: 9 physicians, 1 nurse practitioner
Yves Campeau, Executive Director

Sudbury: Sudbury Regional Hospital - Laurentian Site
Hôpital régional de Sudbury - Emplacement Laurentien
41 Ramsey Lake Rd., Sudbury, ON P3E 5J1
705-523-7100 Fax: 705-523-7112 1-866-469-0822
communications@hrsrh.on.ca
www.hrsrh.on.ca
Number of Beds: 530 acute care beds
Note: Complex continuing care, assistive communication clinic, chiropody clinic, eating disorders clinic, HIV/AIDS clinic, intensive rehabilitation, physiotherapy, occupational therapy
Vickie Kaminski, President/CEO

Sudbury: Sudbury Regional Hospital - Memorial Site
Hôpital régional de Sudbury - Emplacement Mémorial
865 Regent St. South, Sudbury, ON P3E 3Y9
705-523-7100 1-866-469-0822
communications@hrsrh.on.ca
www.hrsrh.on.ca
Number of Beds: 189 beds
Vickie Kaminski, CEO
Chris McKibbon, Chief of Staff

Sudbury: Sudbury Regional Hospital - St. Joseph's Health Centre
Hôpital régional de Sudbury - Centre de santé de St-Joseph
700 Paris St., Sudbury, ON P3B 3B5
705-523-7100 Fax: 0
communications@hrsrh.on.ca
www.hrsrh.on.ca
Jo-Anne Palkovits, CEO

Terrace Bay: The McCausland Hospital
20B Cartier Rd., Terrace Bay, ON P0T 2W0
807-825-3273 Fax: 807-825-9623
admin@mccauslandhospital.com
www.mccauslandhospital.com
Year Founded: 1980
Number of Beds: 45 beds (23 community beds, 22 long-term beds)
Note: Services include emergency, cancer care, diabetes program, diagnostic imaging (ECG, Holter monitors, radiology, ultrasound), laboratory, obstetrics & gynecology, physiotherapy, seniors drop-in program, surgery.
Paul Paradis, CEO
ceo@mccauslandhospital.com
David Hurst, Chief of Staff

Thunder Bay: Hogarth-Westmount Hospital
300 Lillie St., Thunder Bay, ON P7C 4Y7
807-625-1110 Fax: 807-623-4520
Number of Beds: 228 beds
Barry Brown, Executive Director
Richard Roberts, Director, Physical Plant

Thunder Bay: St. Joseph's Care Group
PO Box 3251, 35 North Algoma St., Thunder Bay, ON P7B 5G7
807-343-2431 Fax: 807-345-4994 www.sjcg.net
Old Name: St. Joseph's Care Group
Number of Beds: 224 beds
Carl White, President
Jack Tallon, Director, Materials Management

Thunder Bay: Thunder Bay Regional Health Sciences Centre
980 Oliver Rd., Thunder Bay, ON P7B 6V4
807-684-6000
tbrhsc@tbh.net
www.tbrhsc.com
Year Founded: 2004
Number of Beds: 375 acute care beds (28 beds for anesthetic recovery, 40 beds for day surgery recovery)
Note: A comprehensive, multi-disciplinary, acute care facility with services incuding emergency, ambulatory care, asthma education, cardiology, critical care unit, dentistry, diagnostic imaging (breast MRI, CT scans, radiology), dietitians, forensics, Holter monitoring, Hospice Northwest, ICU, laboratory, maternity, oncology (brachytherapy), paediatrics, renal program, respiratory therapy, surgery, trauma rooms.
The TBRHSC amalgamates the former Port Arthur & McKellar sites of the Thunder Bay Regional Hospital.
Andrée Robichaud, President/CEO
Lori Marshall, Vice-President, Medicine, Cardiology, Mental Health and Maternal/Ch
Blair Schoales, Chief of Staff
Don Edwards, Director, Communications
807-684-6010,

Tillsonburg: Tillsonburg District Memorial Hospital
PO Box 3100, 167 Rolph St., Tillsonburg, ON N4G 3Y9
519-842-3611 Fax: 519-688-1031
mail@tillsonburghospital.on.ca
www.tillsonburghospital.on.ca
Number of Beds: 79 beds
Note: Services include emergency, ambulatory care, Community Care Access Centre, complex continuing care, diagnostic imaging (ultrasound, nuclear medicine, mammography, x-ray, fluoroscopy), diabetes education, dialysis, dietitian, geriatric rehab therapy program, intensive coronary care, interpreter services, mental health, palliative care, pastoral care, pharmacy, physiotherapy, surgery.
Tom McHugh, President/CEO
Gerry Rowland, President, Medical Staff
Frank Deutsch, Senior Executive Leader/CFO
Julie Ellery, Senior Executive Leader, Patient Services

Timmins: Timmins & District Hospital L'Hôpital de Timmins et du district
700 Ross Ave. East, Timmins, ON P4N 8P2
705-267-2131 Fax: 705-267-6311
evainio@tadh.com
www.tadh.com
Number of Beds: 159 beds
Note: Level C referral hospital, providing services in English & French; mental health services; medical, surgical, obstetrics & pediatrics, intensive care; complex continuing care & interim long term care
Esko Vainio, President/CEO

Toronto: The Hospital for Sick Children
555 University Ave., Toronto, ON M5G 1X8
416-813-1500
inquiry.patientrep@sickkids.ca; hr.recruiter@sickkids.ca
www.sickkids.ca
Also Known As: SickKids
Note: Specialties: Paediatric academic health sciences; Paediatric emergency medicine; Trauma; Developmental paediatrics; Fetal cardiac program, cardiac transplants, cardiovascular surgery, & cardiac critical care; Neonatology; Clinical & metabolic genetics; Cleft lip & palate; Neurology & neurosurgery; Cochlear implants; Haematology / Oncology; Communication disorders; Infectious diseases; Immunology & allergy; Gastroenterology, hepatology, & nutrition; Orthotics & medical devices; Rehabilitation; Child & youth counselling; Program for international patients (cindy.fiore@sickkids.ca)
Mary Jo Haddad, Pres./CEO
Scott Menzies, Director, Environmental & Central Services
Valerie O'Grady, Waste Management Coordinator

Toronto: Humber River Regional Hospital
200 Church St., Toronto, ON M9N 1N8
416-249-8111 Fax: 416-243-4547 www.hrrh.on.ca
Division of: Church St. Site

Reuben Devlin, President; CEO
Jack Barkin, Chief of Staff

Toronto: Humber River Regional Hospital
2175 Keele St., Toronto, ON M6M 3Z4
416-249-8111 www.hrrh.on.ca
Division of: Keele St. Site

Toronto: Humber River Regional Hospital
2111 Finch Ave. West, Toronto, ON M3N 1N1
416-744-2500 Fax: 416-747-3882
administration@hrrh.on.ca
www.hrrh.on.ca
Division of: Finch Ave. Site
Number of Beds: 610 beds
Reuben Devlin, President/CEO
Barbara Collins, COO; Vice-President, Planning; Support Services
Scott Jarrett, Vice-President, Patient Programs
Richard Kelly, Vice-President, Human Resources & Support Services
Peter Wegener, Vice-President, Finance & Information Systems

Toronto: Humber River Regional Hospital - Keele St. Site
2175 Keele St., Toronto, ON M6M 3Z4
416-651-6111 Fax: 416-658-2192 www.hrrh.on.ca

Toronto: Mount Sinai Hospital
#334, 600 University Ave., Toronto, ON M5G 1X5
416-596-4200 Fax: 416-586-8555
patientrelationsunit@mtsinai.on.ca
www.mountsinai.on.ca
Number of Beds: 472 beds
Note: Teaching and research Hospital; Home to five Centres of Excellence
Joseph Mapa, Pres./CEO

Toronto: North York General Hospital - Branson Site
555 Finch Ave. West, Toronto, ON M2R 1N5
416-633-9420 Fax: 416-635-2537 www.nygh.on.ca
Number of Beds: 205 beds
Note: Urgent & ambulatory care, Ontario Breast Screening Program site, pediatric speech & language services, diagnostic imaging, geriatric medicine & psychiatry, Gale & Graham Wright Prostrate Centre
Bonnie Adamson, President/CEO

Toronto: North York General Hospital - General Site
4001 Leslie St., Toronto, ON M2K 1E1
416-756-6000 Fax: 416-756-6384 www.nygh.on.ca
Number of Beds: 400 beds
Note: Community teaching hospital affiliated with the University of Toronto. Comprehensive health care services including full service emergency unit
Bonnie Adamson, President/CEO

Toronto: Rouge Valley Centenary
2867 Ellesmere Rd., Toronto, ON M1E 4B9
416-284-8131 Fax: 416-281-7323 www.rougevalley.ca
Parent: Rouge Valley Health System
Year Founded: 1967
Number of Beds: 285 beds
Note: Emergency, cardiac care, mental health, paediatrics.
Rik Ganderton, President/CEO, RVHS
boardofdirectors@rougevalley.ca
David Brazeau, Director, RVHS, Public Affairs & Community Relations
647-294-8885, dbrazeau@rougevalley.ca

Toronto: St. Joseph's Health Centre
30 The Queensway, Toronto, ON M6R 1B5
416-530-6000 Fax: 416-530-6346 www.stjoe.on.ca
Year Founded: 1921
Number of Beds: 376 beds
Note: Services include emergency & critical care, women/children/family health, seniors' care, surgery, oncology, diagnostic imaging, rehabilitation. This teaching hospital was founded by the Sisters of St. Joseph.
Carolyn Baker, President/CEO
Dale McGregor, Executive Vice-President/CFO
Tom Harmantas, Chief of Staff

Toronto: St. Michael's Hospital
1 Queen Wing, 30 Bond St., Toronto, ON M5B 1W8
416-360-4000 Fax: 416-360-7304 www.stmichaelshospital.com
Number of Beds: 527 inpatient
Note: Catholic hospital with a focus on teaching and research affiliated with the University of Toronto
Jeffrey Lozon, President; CEO
William Rosenitsch, Director, Material Management

Toronto: The Salvation Army Toronto Grace Health Centre
650 Church St., Toronto, ON M4Y 2G5
416-925-2251 Fax: 416-925-3211
info@torontograce.org
www.torontograce.org
Also Known As: Toronto Grace Hospital
Year Founded: 1905
Number of Beds: 119 beds
Note: A patient-centred, palliative and complex continuing care facility focusing on holistic and respite care for patients, families and friends through inpatient and community outreach programs.
Marilyn Rook, President/CEO
Monica Codjoe, Vice-President, Patient Services
David Van Der Hout, Medical Director
Alexis Dishaw, Director, Communications, Community Engagement and Strategic
Beth D'Angelo, Manager, Patient Care
edangelo@torontograce.org
John P. Murray, Spokesperson, Public Relations and Development
416-998-0117, John_Murray@can.salvationarmy.org

Toronto: The Scarborough Hospital - Birchmount Campus
3030 Birchmount Rd., Toronto, ON M1W 3W3
416-495-2400 Fax: 416-431-8204
info@tsh.to
www.tsh.to
Old Name: The Scarborough Hospital - Grace Campus
Number of Beds: 650 beds total
Note: A health facility with emphasis on emergency outpatient psychiatric concerns, notably its Regional Crisis Program, an emergency response team to acute psychiatric crises. Total staff: 3,700
John Wright, President/CEO
Steven Jackson, Chief of Medical Staff
Ester Lipnicki, Executive Director, Patient Services & Quality Care
Dave Bourne, Manager, Corporate Communications
dbourne@tsh.to
Sara Kirkup, Manager, Regional Crisis Program
416-495-2891, Fax: 416-495-2880, skirkup@tsh.to

Toronto: The Scarborough Hospital - General Campus
3050 Lawrence Ave. East, Toronto, ON M1P 2V5
416-438-2911 Fax: 416-431-8204 www.tsh.to
Number of Beds: 556 beds (medical 266, surgical 134, paediatric 14, ICU/CCU 32, obstetric 44, mental health 50, rehab 16 beds)
Note: A comprehensive community facility with services including emergency, cardio-respiratory & critical care, specialized geriatrics, family medicine & community services, maternal/newborn & child care, mental health, nephrology & dialysis, oncology, surgery, sexual assault care & domestic violence program, orthopedics & rehabilitation. Total staff: 3,700
John Wright, President/CEO
Ralph Anstey, Vice-President/CFO
Lindsey Crawford, Vice-President, Patient Services
Cara Fleming, Vice-President/CIO, Performance
Steven Jackson, Chief of Medical Staff
Dave Bourne, Manager, Corporate Communications
dbourne@tsh.to

Toronto: Sunnybrook Health Sciences Centre
2075 Bayview Ave., Toronto, ON M4N 3M5
416-480-6100
questions@sunnybrook.ca
www.sunnybrook.ca
Year Founded: 1948
Number of Beds: 1,212 beds
Note: A comprehensive health facility with a focus on cancer care (Odette Cancer Centre), cardiac care (Schulich Heart Centre), musculoskeletal care (Holland Musculoskeletal Program), brain science program (stroke, dementias, mood disorders), women's health, infertility, perinatal care, pediatrics, emergency services, trauma & critical care, veterans' care & residence, research & education. Number of staff: 10,000
Barry A. McLellan, President/CEO
Michael Julius, Vice-President, Research
Wendy Levinson, Physician-in-Chief
Gordon Rubenfeld, Chief, Trauma, Emergency and Critical Care

Toronto: Sunnybrook Health Sciences Centre - Perinatal & Gynaecology Unit
New Women's College Hospital, 76 Grenville St., Toronto, ON M5S 1B2
416-323-6400 Fax: 416-323-7314 www.sunnybrook.ca
Note: The facility focuses on perinatal care (labour, delivery, newborn care), gynaecological conditions, mature women's health, infertility, cancers with an aim to high quality, individualized care. On site are a pregnancy & birth unit, high risk unit, NICU, HPV Vaccine Clinic.
Barry A. McLellan, President/CEO

Toronto: Toronto East General Hospital
825 Coxwell Ave., Toronto, ON M4C 3E7
416-461-8272 Fax: 416-469-6106
ptrep@tegh.on.ca (Patients); community@tegh.on.ca (Community)
www.tegh.on.ca
Year Founded: 1929
Note: Specialties: Ambulatory & community services; Emergency; Diagnostic imaging; Laboratory medicine; Surgery; Maternal & newborn care; Diabetes education community network; Mental health services; Complex continuing care & rehabilitation; Progressive weaning centre
Robert Devitt, President; CEO
Joanne Holgate, Director, Environmental Services
416/469-6471

Toronto: Trillium Health Centre - West Toronto Site
150 Sherway Dr., Toronto, ON M9C 1A5
416-259-6671 Fax: 416-253-2500
publicrelations@thc.on.ca
www.trilliumhealthcentre.org
Note: An ambulatory care facility with services including urgent care centre (8:00 a.m.-10:00 p.m. only, daily), day surgery, diabetes management centre, cardiac wellness & rehabilitation, Kingsway Financial Spine Centre, The Betty Wallace Women's Health Centre (focusing on osteoporosis and breast disease). There is no emergency centre here; it is located at branch in Mississauga.
Janet M. Davidson, President /CEO
Ruby Brown, Executive Vice-President/COO
Gopal Bhatnagar, Chief of Staff
Larry Roberts, Media Relations Consultant
905-848-7580, lroberts@thc.on.ca

Toronto: University Health Network
190 Elizabeth St., Toronto, ON M5G 2C4
416-340-3388 Fax: 416-340-4896
uhn.info@uhn.on.ca
www.uhn.ca
Old Name: The Toronto Hospital
Number of Beds: 1,093 beds (total, all sites)
Note: Comprised of Princess Margaret Hospital, Toronto General Hospital, & Toronto Western Hospital, UHN is a comprehensive health care, research & teaching facility with fields of focus including cancer care, cardiac care, musculoskeletal health & arthritis, neuroscience, ophthalmology, surgical & critical care, transplantation. The network is affiliated with the University of Toronto, Faculty of Medicine.
Robert S. Bell, President /CEO
416-340-3300
Kevin Empey, Executive Vice President, Clinical Support & Corporate Services
Mary Ferguson Paré, Chief Nurse Executive/Vice-President, Professional Affairs
Gillian Howard, Vice-President, Public Affairs & Communications
416-340-4838, gillian.howard@uhn.on.ca

Toronto: University Health Network - Toronto General Hospital
200 Elizabeth St., Toronto, ON M5G 2C4
416-340-4800 Fax: 416-340-5054
uhn.info@uhn.on.ca
www.uhn.ca/applications/TGH/iNews/default.aspx
Year Founded: 1829
Number of Beds: 471 beds
Note: A comprehensive, health care and teaching facility, its specialties include cardiac care (Peter Munk Cardiac Centre), transplantation, kidney diseases & care, tropical disease, eating disorders, nephrology, psychiatry, HIV/AIDS care, telemedicine. It is home to the MaRS Discovery District, a not-for-profit research corporation with funding from both private and public sectors.
Robert Bell, President/CEO, UHN
416-340-3300
Charlie Chan, Vice-President, Medical Affairs, UHN
Marnie Escaf, Site Lead/Vice-President, UHN
Gillian Howard, Vice-President, Public Affairs & *Communications, UHN*
416-340-4838, gillian.howard@uhn.on.ca

Toronto: University Health Network - Toronto Western Hospital
399 Bathurst St., Toronto, ON M5T 2S8
416-603-5800
uhn.info@uhn.on.ca
www.uhn.ca/applications/TWH/iNews/default.aspx
Year Founded: 1905
Number of Beds: 256 beds
Note: The facility focuses on neural/sensory science research &

treatment, musculoskeletal health. Other fields of specialty include acupuncture for addictions, Asian Initiative in Mental Health program, asthma care, cardiac/pulmonary wellness centre, chronic pain, dermatology, diabetes education, epilepsy, geriatrics, memory, neuro-ophthalmology, neuro-otology, neurosurgery, occupational lung disease, outpatient physiotherapy, peritoneal dialysis, plastic surgery, Portuguese mental health & addictions, psychiatry, renal clinic, sleep, spinal cord, Tourette's syndrome, tuberculosis, urology.
Robert Bell, President/CEO, UHN
416-340-3300
Charlie Chan, Vice-President, Medical Affairs, UHN
Kathy Sabo, Site Lead/Vice-President
kathy.sabo@uhn.on.ca
Gillian Howard, Vice-President, Public Affairs & *Communications, UHN*
416-340-4838, gillian.howard@uhn.on.ca

Toronto: William Osler Health Centre - Etobicoke General Hospital Campus
101 Humber College Blvd., Toronto, ON M9V 1R8
416-747-2120 Fax: 0
Number of Beds: 250 beds
Note: Comprehensive health care services. The William Osler Health Centre is comprised of the Etobicoke General Hospital, Brampton Civic Hospital, & the Peel Memorial Hospital (in re-development)
Dawne Barbiei, Site Executive; Chief Nursing Officer

Trenton: Quinte Health Care Trenton Memorial
242 King St., Trenton, ON K8V 5S6
613-392-2540 Fax: 613-392-3749
www.qhc.on.ca/Default.aspx?cid=274&lang=1
Division of: Quinte Health Care
Year Founded: 1951
Number of Beds: 33 beds
Note: Emergency services, intensive care, outpatient clinics, lab, pharmacy, radiology, surgical service, psychiatry
Wendy Parker, Site Administrator
Ext. 5376,

Uxbridge: Markham-Stouffville Hospital
PO Box 5003, 4 Campbell Dr., Uxbridge, ON L9P 1S4
905-852-9771
myhospital@msh.on.ca
www.msh.on.ca
Old Name: Uxbridge Cottage Hospital
Division of: Uxbridge Site
Year Founded: 1959
Number of Beds: 20 beds
Note: Specialties: Diagnostic services; Rhabilitation services, such as physiotherapy & diabetes education
Lorne Zen, Actg. COO

Walkerton: South Bruce Grey Health Centre - Walkerton Site
PO Box 1300, 21 McGivern St. W., Walkerton, ON N0G 2V0
519-881-1220 Fax: 519-881-0452 www.sbghc.on.ca
Division of: Walkerton Hospital
Year Founded: 1900
Number of Beds: 38 beds
Note: A rural health centre with services including emergency, cardio-respiratory care, dental care, ear/nose/throat, family birthing centre, internal medicine, pediatrics, surgery, urology, nutrition services, diagnostic imaging, lab, physiotherapy, healthy heart program
Paul L. Davies, President/CEO, SBGHC
pdavies@sbghc.on.ca
Jill Machan, Site Manager/Director, Patient Care
jmachan@sbghc.on.ca

Wawa: Lady Dunn Health Centre
PO Box 179, 17 Government Rd., Wawa, ON P0S 1K0
705-856-2335 Fax: 705-856-7533 866-832-3321 www.ldhc.com
Number of Beds: 26 beds
Sally Garland, CEO
Gary Trudeau, Chair, Environmental Committee
Holly Morrison-Smith, Manager, Environmental Services

Welland: Niagara Health System
65 Third St., Welland, ON L3B 4W6
905-378-4647 Fax: 905-732-3268 www.niagarahealth.on.ca
Division of: Welland Hospital Site
Number of Beds: 119 acure care; 56 continuing care; 16 mental health
K. Scott, Director, Environmental Services

Whitby: Lakeridge Health Corporation
300 Gordon St., Whitby, ON L1N 5T2
905-668-6831 Fax: 905-665-2406 www.lakeridgehealth.on.ca
Division of: Whitby Site
Number of Beds: 74 beds
Carol Anderson, Site Lead

Wiarton: Grey Bruce Health Services
369 Mary St., Wiarton, ON N0H 2T0
519-534-1260 Fax: 519-534-4450 www.gbhs.on.ca/wiarton.php
Division of: Wiarton Hospital
Number of Beds: 18 inpatient beds
Note: Specialties: Acute care; Dental surgery; Diabetes education; Physiotherapy; Mental health & addictions programs; Palliative care. Number of employees: 107
Pat Campbell, Pres./CEO

Winchester: Winchester District Memorial Hospital
566 Louise St., Winchester, ON K0C 2K0
613-774-2422 Fax: 613-774-0453 www.wdmh.on.ca
Number of Beds: 70 beds
Note: Teaching hospital with emergency care, general surgery, cardiac & respiratory care, diabetes care, obstetrics & pediatrics, rehabilitation, palliative care, chemotherapy, diagnostic imaging
Trudy Reid, President/CEO
treid@wdmh.on.ca

Windsor: Hôtel Dieu Grace Hospital
1030 Ouellette Ave., Windsor, ON N9A 1E1
519-973-4444 Fax: 519-973-0803 www.hdgh.org
Number of Beds: 305 beds
John Coughlin, Pres./CEO
Patricia Somers, Vice President of Operations

Windsor: The Windsor Regional Hospital - Metropolitan Campus
1995 Lens Ave., Windsor, ON N8W 1L9
519-254-5577 Fax: 519-254-2317 www.wrh.on.ca
Year Founded: 1928
Number of Beds: 669 beds (total of all WRH sites)
Note: An acute care facility with services including emergency, ambulatory care, intensive care, Breast Health Centre, cardiac & critical care, diagnostic imaging (nuclear medicine/MRI), endoscopy, family birthing centre, Oncology Inpatient Program, paediatrics, regional cancer services, surgery
David Musyj, President/CEO
Gary Ing, Medical Chief of Staff
Karen McCullough, Vice-President/Chief Nursing Executive, Acute Care Services
Ron Foster, Vice-President, Public Affairs, Communication and Philanthropy
fosterr@wrh.on.ca

Windsor: The Windsor Regional Hospital - Western Campus
1453 Prince Rd., Windsor, ON N9C 3Z4
519-254-5577 Fax: 519-254-2317 www.wrh.on.ca
Year Founded: 1910
Number of Beds: 669 beds (total of all WRH sites)
Note: Services include inter-disciplinary rehabilitation, complex continuing care, long term care, specialized mental health services, audiology, speech language pathology, acquired brain injury treatment, geriatric assessment & consultation program, physiotherapy, occupational therapy and chiropody. The Malden Park Continuing Care Centre is also located at this campus.
David Musyj, President/CEO
Gary Ing, Medical Chief of Staff
Sharon Pillon, Vice-President, Complex Continuing Care/Rehabilitation
Ron Foster, Vice-President, Public Affairs, Communications and Philanthropy

fosterr@wrh.on.ca

Wingham: Wingham & District Hospital
270 Carling Terrace, Wingham, ON N0G 2W0
519-357-3210 Fax: 519-357-3522 www.lwha.ca
Parent: Listowel & Wingham Hospitals Alliance
Number of Beds: 50 beds
Note: Acute care facility, emergency services, surgery, obstetrics & pediatrics, rehabilitation, specialist clinics; affiliated with the London Regional Cancer Centre; air ambulance service; medical clinic. Number of staff: 6 physicians, resident surgeon, 2 anesthetists
Margret Comack, CEO
margret.comack@lwha.ca

Woodstock: Woodstock General Hospital
270 Riddell St., Woodstock, ON N4S 6N4
519-421-4211 Fax: 519-537-5142 www.wgh.on.ca
Number of Beds: 120 beds
Natasa Veljovic, President/CEO

Federal

Ottawa: Canadian Forces Health Care Centre Ottawa/CF H Svc
713 Montreal Rd., Ottawa, ON K1K 0T2
945-1140; 61 Fax: 613-991-1543 www.forces.gc.ca/health-sante
Note: Hospital Specialties: Primary health care services to the military community in the National Capital Region (613-945-1502); Laboratory services; Surgery; Cardio Pulmonary Unit; Operational Trauma & Stress Support Centre (613-945-1060); Mental health (613-945-1060); Addiction counselling (613-945-1060); Ophthalmology (613-945-1550); Physiotherapy (613-945-1585); Preventive medicine (613-945-1604); Public health
LCol Gisele Fontaine, Commanding Officer
LCol Michel P. Deilgat, NCR Surgeon
CPO2 Mario Richard, Clinic Sergeant-Major
Nathalie Tremblay, Officer, Patient Relations
Fax: 613-945-1836

Private

Penetanguishene: Hôpital Privé Beechwood Private Hospital
58 Church St., Penetanguishene, ON L9M 1B3
705-549-7473 Fax: 705-549-7194
bph@bellnet.ca
Number of Beds: 20 beds
L. Bellisle, CEO

Thornhill: Shouldice Hospital Ltd.
PO Box 370, 7750 Bayview Ave., Thornhill, ON L3T 4A3
905-889-1125 Fax: 905-889-4216 800-291-7750
postoffice@shouldice.com
www.shouldice.com
Year Founded: 1945
Number of Beds: 89 beds
Note: Specializes in hernia repair; walk-in clinic
Cassim Degani, Chief Surgeon

Toronto: Don Mills Surgical Unit Inc./DMSU
#208, 20 Wynford Dr., Toronto, ON M3C 1J4
416-441-2111 Fax: 416-441-2114 1-888-857-6069
info@dmsu.com
www.dmsu.com
Division of: Centric Health Group
Number of Beds: 20 in-patient beds
Note: Hospital Specialties: Opthamology; Orthopedic surgery; Plastic & reconstructive surgery; Number of Employees: 16 surgeons; 10 anesthesiologists
Robert G. Gordon, Superintendent

Toronto: St. Joseph's Infirmary
3377 Bayview Ave., Toronto, ON M2M 2S4
416-222-1101 Fax: 416-222-0186
Old Name: St. Joseph's Morrow Park Infirmary & Private Hospi
Number of Beds: 57 beds
Catherine McDonough, Administrator
Diane Hibrant, Nursing Administrator

Woodbridge: Cosmetic Surgery Hospital/CSH
The Manor, 4650 Hwy. 7, Woodbridge, ON L4L 1S7
905-851-7701 Fax: 905-856-4406
info@cosmeticsurgeryhospital.com
www.cosmeticsurgeryhospital.com
Year Founded: 1970
Note: Hospital Specialties: Plastic & cosmetic surgery; Clinical obesity
Lloyd N. Carlsen, Director
Paul Braude, Medical Director, Ageless

Woodstock: Woodstock Private Hospital
369 Huron St., Woodstock, ON N4S 7A5
519-537-8162 Fax: 519-537-7204
wph@gtn.net
Number of Beds: 16 beds
Note: Chronic care hospital
Irma C. Vander Zwaag, Administrator
Marg Atkinson, Head, Housekeeping

Auxiliary Hospitals

Toronto: Baycrest Hospital
3560 Bathurst St., Toronto, ON M6A 2E1
416-785-2500 Fax: 416-785-2378
webmaster@baycrest.org
www.baycrest.org
Division of: Baycrest Geriatric Health Care System
Year Founded: 1986
Number of Beds: 300 hospital beds
Note: Hospital Specialties: Acute geriatric care; Rehabilitation; Psychiatry; Behavioural neurology; Complex continuing care for the elderly; Palliative care
William Reichman, President; Chief Executive Officer
David Conn, Vice-President, Education
Laurie Harrison
, Chief Financial Officer

& Vice-President, Corporate Services
Paul Katz, Chief of Staff

& Vice-President, Medical Services

Joni Kent, Vice-President, Human *Resources & Organizational*

Effectiveness

Karima Velji, Chief Nursing Executive; Vice-President, Clinical; Residential Programs
Nancy Webb
, Vice-President, Public Affairs &

Stakeholders Relations

Welland: Niagara Health System - Welland Hospital Site/NHS
Third St., Welland, ON L3B 4W6
905-378-4647 Fax: 905-732-3268 (www.niagarahealth.on.ca
Division of: Niagara Health System / Système de santé de Niagara
Year Founded: 1908
Number of Beds: 160 beds
Note: Hospital Specialties: Emergency service; Intensive care; Acute care; Ambulatory care; Maternal & child care services; Ontario Breast Screening Program; Dialysis; Nephrology; Mental health services; Complex continuing care
Debbie
Sevenpifer, President; Chief Executive Officer, Niagara Health System
Christine Clark, Chief Communications Officer, Niagara Health System
Sue Matthews, Chief Nursing Executive; Vice-President, Patient Services, Welland Hospital Site
Su Bolibruck, Director, Clinical Programs (Chronic Kidney Disease, Cardiolo
905-378-4647
Patricia Morka, Director, Clinical Programs (Emergency & Critical Care)
905-378-4647
Debbie Smith, Director, Clinical Programs (Primary Care Services & Inpa
905-378-4647

Community Health Centres

Community Health Care Centres

Ajax: Barbara Black Centre for Youth Resources
#5, 360 Bayly St. West, Ajax, ON L1S 1P1
905-428-1212 Fax: 905-428-9151
Also Known As: The Youth Centre
Susan Bland, Executive Director

Barrie: Barrie Community Health Centre
56 Bayfield St., Barrie, ON L4M 3A5
705-734-9690 Fax: 705-734-0239
bchc@csolve.net
www.bchc.ca
Note: Community-focused health promotion, illness prevention, & primary care services. Services provided by physicians, registered nurses, social workers, physiotherapists, & dietitians. North Innisfil office located at: 902 Lockhart Rd., 705-431-9245.
Carla Palmer, Executive Director

Barrie: CCAC North Simcoe Muskoka
#100, 15 Sperling Dr., Barrie, ON L4M 6K9
705-721-8010 Fax: 705-792-6294 888-721-2222
www.ccac-ont.ca
Note: With offices in Barrie & Huntsville, provides health & personal support services for individuals living independently at home or making the transition to alternative care settings; information & referral, advocacy
Al Scarth, Board Chair

Belleville: CCAC South East - Belleville Branch Office
Bayview Mall, 470 Dundas St. East, Belleville, ON K8N 1G1
613-966-3530 Fax: 613-966-0996 1-800-668-0901
www.ccac-ont.ca
John Hill, Board Chair

Brampton: CCAC Central West
199 County Court Blvd., 3rd Fl., Brampton, ON L6W 4P3
905-796-0040 Fax: 905-796-5620 1-800-733-1177
www.ccac-ont.ca
David Lehtovaara, Board Chair

Brantford: CCAC Hamilton Niagara Haldimand Brant - Brant Branch Office
274 Colborne St., Brantford, ON N3T 2H5
519-759-7752 Fax: 519-759-7130 1-866-759-7752
www.ccac-ont.ca
Note: Head office for the region
Melody Miles, Executive Director

Burlington: CCAC Hamilton Niagara Haldimand Brant - Burlington Branch Office
440 Elizabeth St., 4th Fl., Burlington, ON L7R 2M1
905-639-5228 Fax: 905-639-5320 1-800-810-0000
www.ccac-ont.ca
Melody Miles, Executive Director

Cambridge: Langs Farm Village Association
#1, 887 Langs Dr., Cambridge, ON N3H 5K4
519-653-1470 Fax: 519-653-1285
billd@langs.org
William Davidson, Executive Director

Chatham: CCAC Erie St. Clair
PO Box 306, 712 Richmond St., Chatham, ON N7M 5K4
519-436-2222 888-447-4468 www.ccac-ont.ca
Note: Head Office located at the Chatham-Kent branch, with other branch offices located in Sarnia & Windsor. Provides access to in-home health & personal support services to help individuals live independently at home, & assists with the transition to long term care when living at home is no longer possible
Rose Scott, Board Chair

Cornwall: CCAC for Eastern Counties
709 Cotton Mill St., Cornwall, ON K6H 7K7
613-936-1171 800-267-0852 www.ec.ccac-ont.ca
David Marshall, Executive Director

Cornwall: Centre de santé communautaire de l'Estrie
#6, 841, rue Sydney, Cornwall, ON K6H 3J7
613-937-2683 Fax: 613-937-2698
info@cscestrie.on.ca
www.cscestrie.on.ca
Marc Bisson

Emo: Emo Health Centre
PO Box 390, 260 Front St., Emo, ON P0W 1E0
807-482-2881 Fax: 807-482-2493 www.riversidehealthcare.ca
Parent: Riverside Health Care Facilities Inc.
Number of Beds: 12 long-term, 3 acute care beds
Wayne Woods

Forest: North Lambton Community Health Centre
PO Box 1120, 59 King St. West, Forest, ON N0N 1J0
519-786-4545 Fax: 519-786-6318
ninfo@nlchc.com
www.nlchc.com
Parent: Erie St. Clair Local Health Integration Network
Mac Redmond, Executive Director

Grand Bend: Grand Bend Area Community Health Centre
PO Box 1269, 29 Gill Rd., Grand Bend, ON N0M 1T0
519-238-2362 Fax: 519-238-6478 www.gbachc.ca
Dan Steinwald, Executive Director

Guelph: CCAC Waterloo Wellington - Guelph Branch Office
#201, 450 Speedvale Ave. West, Guelph, ON N1H 7G7
519-823-2550 Fax: 519-823-8682 1-800-265-8338
information@ww.ccac-ont.ca
www.ccac-ont.ca
Note: Long-term care placement services; information & referral to other community services; in-home health services; school health support services; access to long-term care facilities; access to adult day programs; mental health & palliative care services
Helene Ireton, Executive Assistant

Hamilton: CCAC Hamilton Niagara Haldimand Brant - Hamilton Branch Office
310 Limeridge Rd. West, Hamilton, ON L9C 2V2
905-523-8600 Fax: 905-528-1883 1-800-450-8002
www.ccac-ont.ca
Melody Miles, Executive Director

Hamilton: Centre de santé communautaire Hamilton/Niagara
460, rue Main est, 2e étage, Hamilton, ON L8N 1K4
905-528-0163 Fax: 905-528-9196
cschwn@iaw.on.ca
www.centredesantecommunautaire.com
Robert Bisson, Directeur général

Hamilton: Hamilton Urban Core Community Health Centre
71 Rebecca St., Hamilton, ON L8R 1B6
905-522-3233 Fax: 905-522-3433
dbrooks@hucchc.com
www.hucchc.com
Denise Brooks, Executive Director
dbrooks@hucchc.com

Hamilton: North Hamilton Community Health Centre
554 John St. North, Hamilton, ON L8L 4S1
905-523-6611 Fax: 905-523-5173 www.northhamiltonchc.org
Year Founded: 1987
Note: Offers a variety of services and programs, including programs for men and women living with HIV/AIDS and programs for new immigrants/refugees
Beth Beader, Executive Director

Huntsville: Muskoka-East Parry Sound CCAC
100 Frank Miller Dr., Huntsville, ON P1H 1H7
705-789-6451 Fax: 705-789-1982
ccac@muskoka.ccac-ont.ca
www.mahc.ca
Vaughn Adamson, Executive Director

Ignace: Mary Berglund Community Health Centre/MBCHC
PO Box 450, Ignace, ON P0T 1T0
807-934-6719 Fax: 807-934-6552
mbchced@bellnet.ca
www.maryberglundchc.com
Note: Specialties: Primary care; Public health nursing; Physiotherapy; Chronic disease follow-up; Health promotion; Men's & women's wellness clinics; Blood sugar & blood pressure screening programs; Chiropractic services; Massage therapy
Lillian Napierala, Executive Director

Kenora: CCAC North West - Kenora Branch Office
21 Wolsley St., 2nd Fl., Kenora, ON P9N 3W7
807-467-4757 Fax: 807-468-1437 1-877-661-6621
www.ccac-ont.ca
Tuija Puiras, Executive Director
tuija.puiras@nw.ccac-ont.ca

Kingston: CCAC South East - Kingston Head Office
#300, 1471 John Counter Blvd., Kingston, ON K7M 8S8
613-544-8200 Fax: 613-544-3888 www.ccac-ont.ca
John Hill, Board Chair

Kingston: North Kingston Community Health Centre
400 Elliot Ave., Kingston, ON K7K 6M9
613-542-2949 Fax: 613-542-3872
info@nkchc.kchc.ca
www.kchc.ca/nkchc
Hersh Sehdev, Executive Director

Kirkland Lake: CCAC Timiskaming
PO Box 520, Kirkland Lake, ON P2N 3J5
705-567-2222 Fax: 705-567-9407 www.timisk.ccac-ont.ca
Denis Labelle, Executive Director
denis.labelle@timisk.ccac-ont.ca

Kitchener: CCAC Waterloo Wellington
800 King St. West, Kitchener, ON N2G 1E8
519-748-2222 Fax: 519-883-5555 1-888-883-3313
information@ww.ccac-ont.ca
www.ccac-ont.ca
Note: Head office for the region
Helene Ireton, Executive Assistant

Kitchener: Kitchener Downtown Community Health Centre
59 Frederick St., Kitchener, ON N2H 2L3
519-745-4404 Fax: 519-745-3709
mail@kdchc.org
www.kdchc.org
Sheila Braidek, Executive Director

Lanark: North Lanark County Community Health Centre
207 Robertson Dr., Lanark, ON K0G 1K0
613-259-2182 Fax: 613-259-5235 866-762-0496
info@northlanarkchc.on.ca
northlanarkchc.on.ca
Wanda MacDonald

Lindsay: CCAC Central East - Lindsay Branch Office
370 Kent St. W, Lindsay, ON K9V 6G8
705-324-9165 Fax: 705-324-0884 1-800-347-0285
www.cacc-ont.ca
William N. Botshka, Board Chair

London: CCAC London & Eastern Middlesex
356 Oxford St. West, London, ON N6H 1T3
519-473-2222 Fax: 519-472-4045 1-800-811-5146
info-london@sw.ccac-ont.ca
www.ccac-ont.ca

Note: Head office for the South West CCAC & regional office for London & E. Middlesex
Sandra Coleman, Executive Director, South West CCAC

London: London InterCommunity Health Centre
659 Dundas St. East, London, ON N5W 2Z1
519-660-0874 Fax: 519-642-1532
mail@lihc.on.ca (General); orders@lihc.on.ca (Resources)
www.lihc.on.ca
Year Founded: 1989
Note: Specialties: Inclusive & equitable health & social services to persons who experience barriers to care; Mental health care; Diabetes program; Options clinic HIV anonymous testing; Health & youth outreach services. Number of employees: 70
Michelle Hurtubise

Longlac: NorWest Community Health Centre - Longlac Site
PO Box 910, 99 Skinner Ave., Longlac, ON P0T 1T0
807-876-2271 Fax: 807-876-2473
www.norwestchc.org/longlac.htm

Merrickville: Merrickville District Community Health Centre
PO Box 550, 354 Read St., Merrickville, ON K0G 1N0
613-269-3400 Fax: 613-269-4958
info@mdchc.on.ca
www.mdchc.on.ca
Note: Specialties: Social work; Dietitian services; Health education; Individual & family counselling; Case management, such as asthma; Foot care services; Flu clinics; Immunizations
Peter McKenna, Executive Director

New Liskeard: Centre de santé communautaire du Témiskaming
CP 38, 83, av Whitewood, New Liskeard, ON P0J 1P0
705-647-5775 Fax: 705-647-6011
jocelydg@csctim.on.ca
Jocelyne Maxwell, Directrice générale

Newmarket: CCAC Central - Newmarket Head Office
#1, 1100 Gorham St., Newmarket, ON L3Y 8Y8
905-895-1240
info@central.ccac-ont.ca
www.ccac-ont.ca
Old Name: Etobicoke & York CCAC
Vikram Gulati, Board Chair

North Bay: Near North CCAC
1164 Devonshire Ave., North Bay, ON P1B 6X5
705-476-2222 Fax: 705-476-6719 888-533-2222
nnccac@nnccac.on.ca
www.nearnorth.ccac-ont.ca
Lloy Schindeler, Executive Director

Oshawa: Oshawa Community Health Centre
Dr. Bryce A. Brown Wellness Centre, 115 Grassmere Ave., Oshawa, ON L1H 3X7
905-723-0036 Fax: 905-432-3902
info@ochc.ca; help@ochc.ca (Volunteering & support
www.ochc.ca
Note: Specialties: Child development; Youth recreation; Women's wellness; Health promotion; Fmaily community outreach; Education services, such as the diabetes education program; Counselling; Parenting groups; Regular check-ups; Rehabilitation
Lee Kierstead, Executive Director

Ottawa: Bruyère Continuing Care
Soins continus Bruyère
43 Bruyère St., Ottawa, ON K1N 5C8
613-562-0050 Fax: 613-562-6367
communications@bruyere.org
www.bruyere.org
Old Name: Sisters of Charity of Ottawa Health Service, Elisa
Year Founded: 1993
Number of Beds: 757 beds
Note: hospital with complex continuing care, rehabilitation, palliative care & long term care services; includes Elisabeth-Bruyere Health Centre, Saint-Vincent Hospital, Résidence Saint-Louis & Villa Marguerite
Jean Bartkowiak, President; CEO

Ottawa: Carlington Community & Health Services
900 Merivale Rd., Ottawa, ON K1Z 5Z8
613-722-4000 Fax: 613-761-1805
mbirming@carlington.ochc.org
www.carlington.ochc.org
Michael Birmingham, Executive Director

Ottawa: CCAC Champlain
#100, 4200 Labelle St., Ottawa, ON K1J 1J8
613-745-5525 Fax: 613-745-6984 1-800-538-0520
information@champlain.ccac-on.ca
www.ccac-ont.ca
Note: Health & personal support services for individuals living independently at home or recuperating from a hospital stay; advocacy for seniors; support for caregivers & families; assistance with transition to new care settings; information & referral. Serving communities of Renfrew County, Ottawa, & the Eastern Counties
Lynn Graham, Board Chair

Ottawa: Centretown Community Health Centre
420 Cooper St., Ottawa, ON K2P 2N6
613-233-4443 Fax: 613-233-3987
info@centretownchc.org
www.centretownchc.org
Marguarite Keeley, Executive Director

Ottawa: Ottawa Community Care Access Centre/CCAC
Centre d'accès aux soins communautaires
#100, 4200 Labelle St., Ottawa, ON K1J 1J8
613-745-5525 Fax: 613-745-6984 800-538-0520 **TDD:** 613-745-0049
information@champlain.ccac-ont.ca
www.ottawa.ccac-ont.ca
Note: Specialties: Home care; Coordination of community care; Information about long-term care options
Sandra Golding, Executive Director

Ottawa: Pinecrest-Queensway Health & Community Services
1365 Richmond Rd., 2nd Fl., Ottawa, ON K2B 6R7
613-820-4922 Fax: 613-820-2006
general@pqhcs.com
www.pqhcs.com
Wanda MacDonald, Executive Director

Ottawa: Sandy Hill Community Health Centre
211 Nelson St., Ottawa, ON K1N 1C7
613-789-1500 Fax: 613-789-7962
info@sandyhillchc.on.ca
www.sandyhillchc.on.ca
Note: Provides a variety of Health and Social Services in the Eastern Ottawa region
Karen Patzer, Executive Director

Ottawa: Somerset West Community Health Centre
55 Eccles St., Ottawa, ON K1R 6S3
613-238-8210 Fax: 613-238-7595
jmccarth@swchc.on.ca
www.swchc.on.ca
Jack McCarthy, Executive Director

Ottawa: South-East Ottawa Centre for a Healthy Community
#600, 1355 Bank St., Ottawa, ON K1H 8K7
613-737-5115 Fax: 613-739-8199
office@seochc.on.ca

Owen Sound: CCAC North Bruce & Grey Counties
255 - 18th St. West, Owen Sound, ON N4K 6Y1
519-371-2112 Fax: 519-371-5612 1-888-371-2112
info-owensound@sw.ccac-ont.ca
www.ccac-ont.ca
Sandra Coleman, Executive Director, South West CCAC

Parry Sound: West Parry Sound Health Centre
6 Albert St., Parry Sound, ON P2A 3A4
705-746-9321 www.wpshc.com
Year Founded: 1897
Number of Beds: 49 beds
Note: Acute & complex continuing care, rehabilitation, on-site Lakeland Long Term Care Facility (90 beds), Community Care Access Centre, emergency services, surgery, diagnostic imaging, chemotherapy, sleep disorder clinic, lab, telehealth, Base Hospital Program & nursing stations in Britt, Pointe au Baril, Rosseau, Whitestone, Argyle & Moosedeer, specialist clinics
Norm Maciver, CEO

Peterborough: CCAC Central East - Peterborough Branch Office
#202, 700 Clonsilla Ave., Peterborough, ON K9J 5Y3
705-743-2212 Fax: 705-743-9559 1-888-235-7222
www.ccac-ont.ca
William N. Botshka, Board Chair

Portland: Country Roads Community Health Centre
PO Box 58, 4319 Cove Rd., Portland, ON K0G 1V0
613-272-3443 Fax: 613-272-3463
schant@crchc.on.ca
Sandra Chant, Executive Director

Richmond Hill: CCAC Central - Richmond Hill Site
#400, 9050 Yonge St., Richmond Hill, ON L4C 9S6
905-763-9928
info@central.ccac-ont.ca
www.ccac-ont.ca
Old Name: York Region CCAC
Vikram Gulati, Board Chair

Sault Ste Marie: Algoma Community Care Access Centre
390 Bay St. 2nd Fl., Sault Ste Marie, ON P6A 1X2
705-949-1650 Fax: 705-949-1663 800-668-7705
marjo.keranen@algoma.ccac-ont.ca
www.ccac-ont.ca
Jim Dalgliesh, Executive Director

Sault Ste Marie: Group Health Centre Sault Ste. Marie
240 McNabb St., Sault Ste Marie, ON P6B 1Y5
705-759-1234 Fax: 705-759-7469 800-461-2407
inquiries@ghc.on.ca
www.ghc.on.ca
Note: GHC is a progressive, multidisciplinary, consumer-sponsored health care facility, built by private funds donated by local union members. A partnership of the Sault Ste. Marie & District Group Health Association & the Algoma District Medical Group. Number of staff: 300+
Tom Bonell, Chairman, Group Health Association

Seaforth: CCAC Huron County
PO Box 580, 32 Centennial Dr., Seaforth, ON N0K 1W0
519-527-0000 Fax: 519-527-1255 1-800-267-0535
info-seaforth@sw.ccac-ont.ca
www.ccac-ont.ca
Sandra Coleman, Executive Director, South West CCAC

Simcoe: CCAC Hamilton Niagara Haldimand Brant - Haldimand-Norfolk Branch Office
76 Victoria St., Simcoe, ON N3Y 1L5
519-426-7400 Fax: 519-426-4384 1-800-265-8068
www.ccac-ont.ca
Melody Miles, Executive Director

Smiths Falls: CCAC South East - Smith Falls Branch Office
#1, 52 Abbott St. North, Smiths Falls, ON K7A 1W3
613-283-8012 Fax: 613-283-0308 1-800-267-6041
www.ccac-ont.ca
John Hill, Board Chair

St Catharines: CCAC Hamilton Niagara Haldimand Brant - Niagara Branch Office
149 Hartzel Rd., St Catharines, ON L2P 1N6
905-684-9441 Fax: 905-684-8463 1-800-263-5480
www.ccac-ont.ca
Melody Miles, Executive Director

St Jacobs: Woolwich Community Health Centre
10 Parkside Dr., St Jacobs, ON N0B 2N0
519-664-3794 Fax: 519-664-2182
genmail@wchc.on.ca
www.wchc.on.ca
Denise Squire, Executive Director

St Thomas: CCAC Elgin County
294 Talbot St., St Thomas, ON N5P 4E3
519-631-9907 Fax: 519-631-2236 1-800-563-3098
info-stthomas@sw.ccac-ont.ca
www.ccac-ont.ca
Sandra Coleman, Executive Director, South West CCAC

Stratford: CCAC Perth County
65 Lorne Ave. East, Stratford, ON N5A 6S4
519-273-2222 Fax: 519-273-2139 1-800-269-3683
info-stratford@sw.ccac-ont.ca
www.ccac-ont.ca
Old Name: Perth County Community Care Access Centre
Sandra Coleman, Executive Director, South West CCAC

Sudbury: Centre de santé communautaire de Sudbury
19 Frood Rd., Sudbury, ON P3C 4Y9
705-670-2274 Fax: 705-670-2277
gelinasf@csc.sudbury.com
www.csc.sudbury.com
France Gélinas, Executive Director

Sudbury: Manitoulin-Sudbury CCAC
1760 Regent St. South, Sudbury, ON P3E 3Z8
705-522-3461 Fax: 705-522-8018 800-461-2919
info@ms.ccac-ont.ca
www.ms.ccac-ont.ca
Nancy Mongeon, Executive Director

***Thunder Bay:* CCAC of The District of Thunder Bay**
#200, 1159 Alloy Dr., Thunder Bay, ON P7B 6M8
807-345-7339 Fax: 807-345-8868 800-626-5406
www.tb.ccac-ont.ca
Tuija Puiras, Executive Director

***Thunder Bay:* NorWest Community Health Centre - Thunder Bay Site**
525 Simpson St., Thunder Bay, ON P7C 3J6
807-622-8235 Fax: 807-622-7637
execdirector@norwestchc.org
www.norwestchc.org/thunder_bay.htm
Wendy Talbot, Executive Director

***Timmins:* Cochrane District CCAC**
#101, 330 Second Ave., Timmins, ON P4N 8A4
705-267-7766 Fax: 705-267-7795 888-668-2222
inquiries-cdccac@cochrane.ccac-ont.ca
www.cdccac.com
Joy Galloway, Executive Director

***Timmins:* Misiway Milopemahtesewin Community Health Centre**
130 Wilson Ave., Timmins, ON P4N 2S9
705-264-2200 Fax: 705-264-2243
misiwayoa@vianet.ca
www.misiway.ca
Cah-Ling Lew, Executive Director

***Tobermory:* Grey Bruce Health Services**
7275 Hwy. 6, Tobermory, ON N0H 2T0
519-793-3445 www.gbhs.on.ca/tobermory.php
Division of: Tobermory Clinic
Note: Specialties: Family health; Community care; Minor day surgery; Mental health counselling. Number of Employees: 4 physicians + 1 nurse practitioner + 1 social worker + several clinic nurses

***Toronto:* Access Alliance Multicultural Community Health Centre**
#500, 340 College St., Toronto, ON M5T 3A9
416-324-8677 Fax: 416-324-9074
mail@accessalliance.ca
www.accessalliance.ca
Note: Provides community health services to refugees & immigrants
Axelle Janczur, Executive Director

***Toronto:* Anishnawbe Health Toronto**
225 Queen St. East, Toronto, ON M5A 1S4
416-360-0486 Fax: 416-365-1083 www.aht.ca
Year Founded: 1984
Note: An accredited community health centre, utilizing traditional healing approaches. A range of services is available, including fetal alcohol spectrum disorder services, diabetic care, HIV testing, mental health services & psychiatry, counselling, naturopathy, chiropody, women's services, massage therapy, & dental services. Other centres located at: 179 Gerrard St. E., 416-920-2605; and 22 Vaughan Rd., 416-657-0379. Mental Health Crisis Management Service: 416-891-8606.
Joe Hester, Executive Director

***Toronto:* Anne Johnston Health Station**
2398 Yonge St., Toronto, ON M4P 2H4
416-486-8666 Fax: 416-486-8660
Catherine Brookman, Executive Director

***Toronto:* Bernard Betel Centre for Creative Living**
1003 Steeles Ave. West, Toronto, ON M2R 3T6
416-225-2112 Fax: 416-225-2097
reception@betelcentre.org
www.betelcentre.org
Note: provide education, recreation, arts, fitness and health services
Esta Wall, Executive Director

***Toronto:* Black Creek Community Health Centre**
#5, 2202 Jane St., Toronto, ON M3M 1A4
416-249-8000 Fax: 416-249-4594
patrizia@bcchc.com
www.bcchc.com
Cary Milner, Executive Director

***Toronto:* CCAC Central - Sheppard Site**
#700, 45 Sheppard Ave. East, Toronto, ON M2N 5W9
416-222-2241
info@central.ccac-ont.ca
www.ccac-ont.ca
Vikram Gulati, Board Chair

***Toronto:* CCAC Central East - Scarborough Branch Office**
1940 Eglinton Ave. East, 3rd Fl., Toronto, ON M1L 4R1
416-750-2444 Fax: 416-750-4117 1-866-779-1931
www.ccac-ont.ca
William N. Botshka, Board Chair

***Toronto:* CCAC Toronto Central**
#305, 250 Dundas St. West, Toronto, ON M5T 2Z5
416-506-9888 Fax: 416-506-0374 1-866-243-0061
toronto_ccac@toronto.ccac-ont.ca
www.ccac-ont.ca
Judith Hayward, Board Chair

***Toronto:* CCAC Toronto Central - Leaside Park Drive Site-East York**
#1, 1 Leaside Park Dr., Toronto, ON M4H 1R1
416-423-3559 Fax: 416-423-9800
toronto_ccac@toronto.ccac-ont.ca
www.ccac-ont.ca
Old Name: East York Access Centre
Judith Hayward, Executive Director

***Toronto:* Central Toronto Community Health Centres**
168 Bathurst St., Toronto, ON M5V 2R4
416-703-8482 Fax: 416-703-8479
info@ctchc.com
www.ctchc.com
Division of: Queen West Community Health Centre
Note: Medical services (with specialized services for the homeless), psychiatric & mental health services, individual & group counselling, harm reduction program (safer sex, safer drug use, Hepatitis C & HIV prevention), needle exchange, diabetes education program, chiropody, perinatal nursing, dental clinic.
Hal DeLair, Executive Director

***Toronto:* Central Toronto Community Health Centres**
467 Jarvis St., Toronto, ON M4Y 2G8
416-927-8553 Fax: 416-927-9365
info@ctchc.com
www.ctchc.com
Division of: Shout Clinic
Year Founded: 1992
Note: Walk-in medical clinic providing comprehensive health care services to homeless & street involved youth, 16-24 years of age.
Hal DeLair, Executive Director

***Toronto:* Centre francophone de Toronto**
22 College St., 1st Fl., Toronto, ON M5G 1K3
416-922-2672 Fax: 416-922-6624
jg@cmsctoronto.org
Old Name: Centre médico-social communautaire
Jean-Gilles Pelletier, Executive Director

***Toronto:* Davenport Perth Neighbourhood Centre**
1900 Davenport Rd., Toronto, ON M6N 1B7
416-658-6812 Fax: 416-656-1264
Keith McNair, Executive Director

***Toronto:* East End Community Health Centre**
343 Coxwell Ave., Toronto, ON M4L 3B5
416-778-5858 Fax: 416-778-5855
Joyce Kalsen, Executive Director

***Toronto:* Flemingdon Health Centre**
10 Gateway Blvd., Toronto, ON M3C 3A1
416-429-4991 Fax: 416-422-3573
fhcinfo@fhc-chc.com
Peter Yue, Executive Director

***Toronto:* Four Villages Community Health Centre**
1700 Bloor St. West, Toronto, ON M6P 4C3
416-604-3361 Fax: 416-604-3367
Almerinda Rebelo, Executive Director

***Toronto:* Lawrence Heights Community Health Centre**
12 Flemington Rd., Toronto, ON M6A 2N4
416-787-1661 Fax: 416-787-3761
achohen@lhchc.com
www.lhchc.com
Andrea Cohen, Executive Director

***Toronto:* Parkdale Community Health Centre**
1229 Queen St. West, Toronto, ON M6K 1L2
416-537-2455 Fax: 416-537-5133
Note: Specialties: Service in several languages; Primary care; Educational programs, such as pre- and post-natal classes; Support groups; Counselling; Mental health support; HIV testing
Simone Hammond, Executive Director

***Toronto:* Regent Park Community Health Centre**
465 Dundas St. East, Toronto, ON M5A 2B2
416-364-2261 Fax: 416-364-0822
rpchc@regentparkchc.org
www.regentparkchc.org
Year Founded: 1973
Note: Emphasis on an integrated approach: health promotion, disease prevention, social services. A community-founded & operated facility, with a focus on comprehensive, accessible care. Services in English, Cantonese, Mandarin, Vietnames, Somali & Spanish. The Pathways to Education Program for youth at risk, created & first implemented in Regent Park, has been adopted by communities across Canada
Carolyn Acker, Executive Director

***Toronto:* South Riverdale Community Health Centre**
955 Queen St. East, Toronto, ON M4M 3P3
416-461-1925 Fax: 416-461-3578
srchc@srchc.com
Lynne Raskin, Executive Director

***Toronto:* Stonegate Community Health Centre**
150 Berry Rd., Toronto, ON M8Y 1W3
416-231-7070 Fax: 416-231-2663
info@stonegatechc.org
www.stonegatechc.org
Note: Specialties: Asthma care program research; Pre & post natal programs; Early years programs; Women's programs; Seniors' programs; Housing support & case management
Lucia Furgivele, Executive Director

***Toronto:* Toronto East General Hospital**
840 Coxwell Ave., Toronto, ON M4C 5T2
416-469-6464 Fax: 416-469-6164
ptrep@tegh.on.ca (Patients); community@tegh.on.ca (Community)
www.tegh.on.ca
Division of: Family Health Centre
Year Founded: 2002
Note: Specialties: Low-risk obstetrics; Psychotherapy; Telephone health advisory service

***Toronto:* West Hill Community Services**
3545 Kingston Rd., Toronto, ON M1M 1R6
416-284-5931 Fax: 416-724-5205
westhill@westhill-cs.on.ca
www.westhill-cs.on.ca
Pat Jensen, Executive Director

***Toronto:* Women's Health in Women's Hands**
#500, 2 Carlton St., Toronto, ON M5B 1J3
416-593-7655 Fax: 416-593-5867
whiwh@web.net
www.whiwh.com
Notisha Massaquoi, Executive Director

***Tweed:* Gateway Community Health Centre**
PO Box 99, 41 McClellan St., Tweed, ON K0K 3J0
613-478-1211 Fax: 613-478-6692
Jeanne Goodhand, Executive Director

***West Lorne:* West Elgin Community Health Centre**
PO Box 761, 168 Main St., West Lorne, ON N0L 2P0
519-768-1715 Fax: 519-768-2548
info@wechc.on.ca
www.wechc.on.ca
Note: Provides health services and community programs to residents of the western Elgin area

***Whitby:* CCAC Central East - Whitby Head Office**
Whitby Corporate Centre, 209 Dundas St. East, 5th Fl., Whitby, ON L1N 7H8
905-430-3308 Fax: 905-430-3297 1-800-263-3877
www.ccac-ont.ca
Old Name: Durham Access to Care
William N. Botshka, Board Chair

***Windsor:* CCAC Windsor/Essex**
5415 Tecumseh Rd. East, 2nd Fl., Windsor, ON N8T 1C5
519-258-8211 Fax: 519-258-2004
ccac.reception@we.ccac-ont.ca
www.we.ccac-ont.ca
Mary Wilson, Executive Director

***Windsor:* Sandwich Community Health Centre**
PO Box 7391, 749 Felix Ave., Windsor, ON N9C 4E9
519-258-6002 Fax: 519-528-3693
mailbox@sandwichchc.org
www.sandwichchc.org
Year Founded: 1982

***Windsor:* Teen Health Centre**
Head Office, 1585 Ouellette Ave., Windsor, ON N8X 1K5
519-253-8481 Fax: 519-253-4362 www.teenhealthcentre.com
Note: Specialties: Counselling; Primary care; Special Additions, a prenatal program; Diabetes In Action, a community based

diabetes program; Street Health Homeless Initiative Program, a program to serve homeless or at-risk persons in Windsor & Essex County
Sheila Gordon, Executive Director

Woodstock: CCAC Oxford County
1147 Dundas St., Woodstock, ON N4S 8W3
519-539-1284 Fax: 519-539-0065 1-800-561-5490
info-woodstock@sw.ccac-ont.ca
www.ccac-ont.ca
Sandra Coleman, Executive Director, South West CCAC

Special Treatment Centre

Barrie: Royal Victoria Hospital of Barrie Community Care Centre for Substance Abuse
70 Wellington St. West, Barrie, ON L4N 1K4
705-728-4226 Fax: 705-728-7308 www.rvh.on.ca
Number of Beds: 17 beds
Note: Intoxification management, withdrawal management, assessments, family education, discharge planning
Jack Vandenberg, Director

Brantford: Lansdowne Children's Centre
39 Mount Pleasant St., Brantford, ON N3T 1S7
519-753-3153 Fax: 519-753-5927
lansdowne.children@sympatico.ca
Martin McIntyre, Director

Cambridge: KidsAbility - Centre for Child Development
c/o Chaplin Family YMCA, 250 Hespeler Rd., Cambridge, ON N1R 3H3
519-621-7580 Fax: 519-621-4651 www.kidsability.ca
Old Name: Rotary Children's Centre
Division of: Cambridge Site
Year Founded: 1957
Note: Specialty: Services for children & young adults with physical, developmental, & communication disabilities

Chatham: Prism Centre for Audiology & Children's Rehabilitation
355 Lark St., Chatham, ON N7L 5B2
519-354-0520 Fax: 519-354-7355 http://www.prismcentre.com/
Old Name: Kent County Children's Treatment Centre
Mary Anne McLean, Executive Director
Donna Litwin-Makey, Executive Director
519-354-0520, dlitwinmakey@prismcentre.com

Cornwall: Cornwall Withdrawal Management Centre
35 Second St. East, Cornwall, ON K6H 1Y2
613-938-8506 Fax: 613-938-2867
Number of Beds: 16 beds
Note: detoxification hospital
Christine Penney, Manager

Fergus: KidsAbility - Centre for Child Development
160 St. David St. South, Fergus, ON N1M 2L3
519-787-2612 Fax: 519-843-7597 www.kidsability.ca
Old Name: Rotary Children's Centre
Division of: Fergus Site
Year Founded: 1957
Note: Specialty: Services for children & young adults with physical, developmental, & communication disabilities

Guelph: KidsAbility - Centre for Child Development
c/o West End Community Centre, 21 Imperial Rd. South, Guelph, ON N1K 1X3
519-780-0186 Fax: 519-780-0470 www.kidsability.ca
Old Name: Rotary Children's Centre
Division of: Guelph Site
Year Founded: 1957
Note: Specialty: Services for children & young adults with physical, developmental, & communication disabilities

Hamilton: Hamilton Regional Cancer Centre
699 Concession St., Hamilton, ON L8V 5C2
905-387-9495 Fax: 905-575-6323 www.hrcc.on.ca
George Browman, CEO

Kingston: Cancer Centre of Southeastern Ontario
25 King St. West, Kingston, ON K7L 5P9
613-544-2630 Fax: 613-544-9708 800-567-5722 www.krcc.on.ca

Kingston: Child Development Centre
c/o Hotel Dieu Hospital, 166 Brock St., Kingston, ON K7L 5G2
613-544-3400 Fax: 613-545-3557
www.hoteldieu.com/cdcopen.html
Robin L. Jones, Director

Kingston: Hotel Dieu Hospital Kingston Detoxification Centre
240 Brock St., Kingston, ON K7L 5G2
613-549-6461 Fax: 613-546-4254 www.hoteldieu.com
Note: detoxification hospital
Gerry Gregory, Director

Kitchener: Waterloo Regional Withdrawal Management Centre
52 Glasgow St., Kitchener, ON N2G 1N6
519-749-4300 Fax: 519-749-4328
Number of Beds: 21 beds

London: London Health Sciences Centre
PO Box 5165, 790 Commissioners Rd. East, London, ON N6A 4L6
519-685-8600
LRCPEducation@lhsc.on.ca (Patient education)
www.lhsc.on.ca
Division of: London Regional Cancer Program
Note: Specialties: Inpatient & outpatient cancer care; Radiation therapy; Chemotherapy; Syooirt services, such as social work & diet & nutrition counselling
Michael Sherar, Vice-President

London: Thames Valley Children's Centre
779 Baseline Rd. East, London, ON N6C 5Y6
519-685-8680 Fax: 519-685-8689
tvcc@tvcc.on.ca; innovations@tvcc.on.ca (Innovative products/books)
www.tvcc.on.ca
Year Founded: 1949
Note: Specialties: Rehabilitation services for children with physical disabilities, developmental delays, & communication disorders; Assessment & diagnosis services; Autism intervention program; Intensive behavioural intervention; Physiotherapy; Occupational therapy; Research; School support program. Number of Employees: 350+ + 500 volunteers + 55 students
John A. LaPorta, Exec. Director/CEO

Mississauga: Erinoak Kids
2277 South Millway, Mississauga, ON L5L 2M5
905-820-7111 Fax: 905-820-1333
Note: Outpatient services only
Diana Thomson, Executive Director

Mount Brydges: Southwest Middlesex Health Centre
22262 Mill Rd., RR#5, Mount Brydges, ON N0L 1W0
519-264-2800
A. Lamont, Administrator

Orillia: Huronia Regional Centre
PO Box 1000, 700 Memorial Ave., Orillia, ON L3V 6L2
Number of Beds: 584 beds
Note: rehabilitation hospital
James Duncan, Administrator

Oshawa: Grandview Children's Centre
600 Townline Rd. South, Oshawa, ON L1H 7K6
905-728-1673 Fax: 905-728-2961 800-304-6180 www.grtc.ca
Old Name: Grandview Rehabilitation & Treatment Centre of Dur
Vicky Earle, Executive Director

Ottawa: The Morgentaler Clinic
65 Bank St., Ottawa, ON K1P 5N2
613-567-8300 Fax: 613-567-9128
info@yenott.com
www.morgentaler.ca
Division of: Ottawa Site
Note: Specialty: Abortion services; Counselling

Ottawa: The Ottawa Children's Treatment Centre/OCTC
Le Centre de traitement pour enfants d'Ottawa
395 Smyth Rd., Ottawa, ON K1H 8L2
613-737-0871 Fax: 613-523-5167 800-565-4839 www.octc.ca
Note: From several locations in Ottawa & area, The Centre provides specialized care for children with multiple physical, developmental & behavioural needs. Services in English & French
Kathleen Stokely, Executive Director

Ottawa: The Ottawa Hospital/TRC
505 Smyth Rd., Ottawa, ON K1H 8M2
613-737-7350
patientrelations@ottawahospital.on.ca
www.ottawahospital.on.ca
Division of: Rehabilitation Centre
Note: Specialties: Rehabilitation of persons with a disabling physical illness or injury; Prosthetics & orthotics; Physiotherapy; Occupational therapy; Respiratory therapy; Speech-language pathology; Psychological services; Vocational rehabilitation counselling; Social work; Research
Cathy Danbrook, CEO

Ottawa: Ottawa Regional Cancer Centre
General Campus, 501 Smyth Rd., Ottawa, ON K1H 1C4
613-737-7700
patientlibrary@ottawahospital.on.ca
www.ottawahospital.on.ca/sc/cancer/index-e.asp
Note: Specialties: Screening; Early Detection; Diagnosis; Treatment; Supportive Care; Palliative Care; Research
William K. Evans, CEO

Ottawa: Sisters of Charity of Ottawa Health Services Detoxification Centre
62 Bruyère St., Ottawa, ON K1N 5C5
613-241-1525 Fax: 613-241-2172
Virginia Hamilton, Director

Peterborough: Five Counties Children's Centre
872 Dutton Rd., Peterborough, ON K9H 7G1
705-748-2221 Fax: 705-748-3526 888-779-9916
info@fivecounties.on.ca
www.fivecounties.on.ca
Note: children with special needs 0-19 years of age
Diane Pick, CEO

Sarnia: Pathways Health Centre for Children
1240 Murphy Rd., Sarnia, ON N7S 2Y6
519-542-3471 Fax: 519-542-4115
info@pathwayscentre.org
www.pathwayscentre.org
Note: children's treatment centre
Jenny Greensmith, Executive Director

Sault Ste Marie: Children's Rehabiliation Centre - Algoma
74 Johnson Ave., Sault Ste Marie, ON P6C 2V5
705-759-1131 Fax: 705-759-0783
Note: outpatient health services centre
Donna Morrison, Executive Director

Sault Ste Marie: Sault Ste. Marie Detoxification Unit
911 Queen St. East, Sault Ste Marie, ON P6A 2B6
705-942-1872 Fax: 705-759-6369
Number of Beds: 15 beds
Note: detox centre
Raimo Viitala, Manager

St Agatha: kidsLINK (NDSA)
PO Box 190, 1855 Notre Dame Dr., St Agatha, ON N0B 2L0
519-746-5437 Fax: 519-746-3055
Number of Beds: 26 beds
Note: Children's mental health residential & day treatment services; outpatient services, respite, prevention & early intervention for children & families
Sonia Pouyat, CEO

St Catharines: Hôtel Dieu Shaver Health & Rehabilitation Centre
541 Glenridge Ave., St Catharines, ON L2T 4C2
905-685-1381 Fax: 905-687-3232
info@hoteldieushaver.org
www.hoteldieushaver.org
Old Name: Hôtel-Dieu Health Sciences Hospital - Niagara
Parent: Hamilton Niagara Haldimand Brant Local Health Integration Network
Number of Beds: 124 beds
Note: Complex Continuing Care & Rehabilitation
Jane Rufrano, CEO

St Catharines: Niagara Peninsula Children's Centre
567 Glenridge Ave., St Catharines, ON L2T 4C2
905-688-3550 Fax: 905-688-1055 800-896-5496
info@npcc.on.ca
www.npcc.on.ca
Note: children's rehabilitation centre
John TeBrake, Executive Director

St Catharines: St Catharines Detoxification (Men's) Unit
10 Adams St., St Catharines, ON L2R 2V8
905-682-7211 Fax: 905-687-9768
Number of Beds: 22 beds
Note: men's detox
Norma Medulun, Director

St Catharines: St Catharines Detoxification (Women's) Unit
6 Adams St., St Catharines, ON L2R 2V8
905-687-9721 Fax: 905-687-9768
Number of Beds: 14 beds
Norma Medulun, Director

Sudbury: Children's Treatment Centre
c/o Laurentian Hospital, 1204 St Jerome St., Sudbury, ON P3A 2V9
705-560-8000 Fax: 705-560-4273

Note: outpatient, community-based rehabilitation centre
Sally Spence, Coordinator
Pat Tessier, Environmental Services

Sudbury: Women's Withdrawal Management Service
336 Pine St., Sudbury, ON P3C 1X8
705-671-7167 Fax: 705-675-5730
Number of Beds: 13 beds
Note: non-medical withdrawal management service
Lise Chamberland, Manager

Thunder Bay: George Jeffrey Children's Treatment Centre
507 North Lillie St., Thunder Bay, ON P7C 4V8
807-623-4381 Fax: 807-623-6626 www.georgejeffrey.com
Note: special needs children
Eiji Tsubouchi, CEO

Timmins: Cochrane Temiskaming Children's Treatment Centre
#1, 733 Ross Ave. East, Timmins, ON P4N 8S8
705-264-4700 Fax: 705-268-3585 800-575-3210
Mary MacKay, Executive Director

Toronto: Bloorview Kids Rehab
150 Kilgour Road, Toronto, ON M4G 1R8
416-425-6220 Fax: 416-425-6591 1-800-363-2440
info@bloorview.ca
www.bloorview.ca
Old Name: Bloorview Children's Hospital
Division of: Bloorview Site
Number of Beds: 75
Note: pediatric rehabilitation & continuing care complex
Valerie McMurty, President/CEO

Toronto: Bob Rumball Centre for the Deaf
2395 Bayview Ave., Toronto, ON M2L 1A2
416-449-9651 Fax: 416-449-8881
info@bobrumball.org
www.bobrumball.org
Number of Beds: 56 beds
Note: long-term care facility for the deaf
Bob Rumball, Executive Director
Robert Ray, Director, Physical Plant

Toronto: Bridgepoint Hospital
14 St. Matthews Rd., Toronto, ON M4M 2B5
416-461-8252 Fax: 416-461-5696 www.bridgepointhealth.ca
Old Name: The Riverdale Hospital
Number of Beds: 547 beds
Note: chronic care & rehabilitation hospital
Marian Walsh, President/CEO
Bill Grant, Director, Engineering
416/461-2190
Joseph Mancuso, Director, Environmental Services & Facilities Planning
Robert Carman, Chair

Toronto: Cabbagetown Women's Clinic
302 Gerrard St. East, Toronto, ON M5A 2G7
416-323-0642 Fax: 416-323-3099 800-399-1592
www.cabbagetownwomensclinic.com
Year Founded: 1989
Note: Licensed as and Independent Health facility funded by the Ontario Min. of Health & Long Term Care, the clinic provides medical services to women seeking a legal & safe abortion.

Toronto: Casey House Hospice
9 Huntley St., Toronto, ON M4Y 2K8
416-962-7600 Fax: 416-962-5147
info@caseyhouse.on.ca
www.caseyhouse.com
Number of Beds: 13 beds; 120 home care clients
Note: hospice; home care office
Catherine Adam, Interim CEO

Toronto: Centre for Addiction & Mental Health
33 Russell St., Toronto, ON M5S 2S1
416-595-6000 Fax: 416-595-9997 800-463-6273
webmaster@camh.net
www.camh.net
Old Name: Addiction Research Foundation
Division of: ARF Site
Number of Beds: 614 beds
Note: drug rehabilitation centre
Paul Garfinkel, President; CEO

Toronto: Centre for Addiction & Mental Health
175 Brentcliffe Rd., Toronto, ON M4G 3Z1
416-425-8501
Division of: Brentcliffe Rd. Site
Number of Beds: 47 beds

Toronto: Centre for Addiction & Mental Health (Corporate Office)
33 Russell St., Toronto, ON M5S 2S1
416-595-6878
webmaster@camh.net
www.camh.net
Number of Beds: 614 beds
Note: addiction treatment
Paul Garfinkel, President/CEO

Toronto: Choice in Health Clinic
#301, 1678 Bloor St. West, Toronto, ON M4X 1W3
416-975-9300 Fax: 416-975-0314 www.choiceinhealth.ca
Note: abortion clinic
Michelle Joseph, Executive Director

Toronto: Eye Bank of Canada
c/o Dept. of Ophthalmology, University of Toronto, 1 Spadina Cres., Toronto, ON M5S 2J5
416-978-7355 Fax: 416-978-1522
eye.bank@utoronto.ca
www.eyebank.utoronto.ca
Division of: Ontario Division
David Rootman, Medical Director
William Dixon, Medical Co-director

Toronto: Marvelle Koffler Breast Centre
J. & W. Lebovic Health Complex, Mount Sinai Hospit, 600 University Ave., 12th Fl., Toronto, ON M5G 1X5
416-586-8799 www.mountsinai.on.ca/care/mkbc
Year Founded: 1995
Note: Specialties: Outpatient facility for breast health & disease; Mammography / Breast imaging; Pathology; Surgery; Psychiatry; Nutrition; Boutique addressing the needs of women who have experienced breast cancer; Palliative medicine
P. Goodwin, Director

Toronto: The Morgentaler Clinic
727 Hillsdale Ave. East, Toronto, ON M4S 1V4
416-932-0446 Fax: 416-932-0837 800-556-6835
mclinic@passport.ca
www.morgentaler.ca
Note: Specialties: Abortion services; Counselling; Contraceptive education; Testing for sexually transmitted infections
Henry Morgentaler, Director

Toronto: Runnymede Healthcare Centre
625 Runnymede Rd., Toronto, ON M6P 3A3
416-762-7316 Fax: 416-762-3836 www.runnymedehc.ca
Year Founded: 1945
Note: Specialties: Complex continuing care for persons with long-term disorders, such as neurological disorders; Occupational therapy; Physiotherapy; Speech-language pathology; Social work
Normand A. Allaire, President; CEO

Toronto: St. John's Rehabilitation Hospital
285 Cummer Ave., Toronto, ON M2M 2G1
416-226-6780 Fax: 416-226-6265
info@stjohnsrehab.com
www.stjohnsrehab.com
Number of Beds: 160 beds
Note: Ontario's only hospital dedicated to specialized rehabilitation services & care: burn injuries, organ transplant rehabilitation, cancer, cardiovascular surgery, strokes & other neurological conditions, traumatic injuries & complex medical conditions. Teaching site for the University of Toronto & a leading research facility. A multicultural & multifaith environment dedicated to the values of care of the Sisters of St. John the Divine
Malcolm Moffat, President; CEO
Joyce Bailey, Board Chair

Toronto: St. Michael's Hospital Detoxification Centre
314 Adelaide St. East, Toronto, ON M5A 1N1
416-864-5078 Fax: 416-864-5146
Number of Beds: 22 beds
Note: detoxification hospital
John Rutledge, Director

Toronto: Sunnybrook Health Sciences Centre - Holland Orthopaedic & Arthritic Centre
43 Wellesley St. East, Toronto, ON M4Y 1H1
416-967-8500 Fax: 416-967-8521 www.sunnybrook.ca
Note: Care for complex injuries of the musculoskeletal system, with a focus on traumatic injury management, joint reconstruction & replacement, surgery, sports & activity-related injury management, rehabilitation, rheumatology. The Clinic has a second location at the main Sunnybrook site, 2075 Bayview Ave., Toronto
Barry A. McLellan, President/CEO

Toronto: Sunnybrook Health Sciences Centre - The Odette Cancer Centre
2075 Bayview Ave., Toronto, ON M4N 3M5
416-480-5000 Fax: 416-217-1338 www.sunnybrook.ca
Note: Comprehensive cancer care, multidisciplinary, evidence-based approach; research, education & community outreach
Barry A. McLellan, President/CEO

Toronto: Toronto East General Hospital
985 Danforth Ave., Toronto, ON M4J 1M1
416-461-2010 Fax: 416-461-1164
ptrep@tegh.on.ca (Patients); community@tegh.on.ca (Community)
www.tegh.on.ca
Division of: Withdrawal Management Centre
Number of Beds: 22 beds
Note: Specialties: Crisis intervention for adult males, Physical care for males in acute states of intoxication; Withdrawal from alcohol & other addictive substances; Addictions assessments; Counselling; Rehabilitation services; Education on substance abuse to family members
D. Smith, Manager

Toronto: Toronto Rehabilitation Institute
550 University Ave., Toronto, ON M5G 2A2
416-597-3422 Fax: 416-597-1977
communications@torontorehab.on.ca
www.torontorehab.com
Also Known As: Toronto Rehab
Number of Beds: 541 beds
Note: Rehabilitation & complex continuing care; includes Hillcrest Centre; Lakeside Long-Term Care Centre; Lyndhurst Centre; E.W. Bickle Centre; Rumsey Centre, & University Centre
Mark Rochon, President/CEO

Toronto: Toronto Western Hospital - Addiction Outpatient/Aftercare Clinic
399 Bathurst St., Toronto, ON M5T 2S8
416-603-5735 Fax: 0
Note: Assessment & referral, individual & group therapy, counseling, psychiatric consultation, education. Services in English, French, Portuguese, Polish

Toronto: University Health Network - Princess Margaret Hospital
610 University Ave., Toronto, ON M5G 2M9
416-946-2000
uhn.info@uhn.on.ca
www.uhn.ca/PMH/
Year Founded: 1952
Number of Beds: 130 inpatient beds
Note: A teaching hospital of the University of Toronto, PMH is a global leader in the fight against cancer & one of the top cancer treatment & research centres in the world. Specialties include: surgical oncology, chemotherapy, psychosocial oncology, radiation therapy, bone marrow transplantation, radiation oncology, hematology, & medical imaging. The Ontario Cancer Institute comprises the research wing of the hospital. Staff: 139+ oncologists, 400 RN's, 1,178 support staff
Sarah Downey, Executive Director; Site Lead

Toronto: West End Creche Child & Family Clinic
197 Euclid Ave., Toronto, ON M6J 2J8
416-868-1827 Fax: 416-868-1827
Tony Diniz, Executive Director

Toronto: West Park Healthcare Centre
82 Buttonwood Ave., Toronto, ON M6M 2J5
416-243-3600 Fax: 416-243-8947
feedback@westpark.org
www.westpark.org
Old Name: West Park Hospital
Number of Beds: 477 beds
Note: rehabilitation & chronic care facility
Anne-Marie Malek, President/CEO
Mike Bonnah, Director, Facilities & Materials Management

Waterloo: KidsAbility - Centre for Child Development
500 Hallmark Dr., Waterloo, ON N2K 3P5
519-886-8886 Fax: 519-886-7292 888.372.2259
www.kidsability.ca
Old Name: Rotary Children's Centre
Year Founded: 1957
Note: Specialties: Services for children & young adults with physical, developmental, & communication disabilities; Autism intervention; Occupational therapy; Physiotherapy; Speech-language therapy; Augmentative communication; Therapeutic recreation; Social work. Number of Employees: 200 + 300 volunteers
Stephen Swatridge, Executive Director

Windsor: **Children's Rehabilitation Centre of Essex County**
3945 Matchette Rd., Windsor, ON N9C 4C2
519-252-7281 Fax: 519-252-5873
info@childrensrehab.com
www.childrensrehab.com
Elaine M. Whitmore, CEO

Windsor: **Windsor Regional Hospital Withdrawal Management**
393 Mill St., Windsor, ON N9C 2R3
519-257-5225 Fax: 519-257-5175
Number of Beds: 20 beds
Note: detoxification hospital
William Marcotte, Director, Operations

Nursing Homes

Ailsa Craig: **Craigholme Nursing Home**
221 Main St. East, RR#1, Ailsa Craig, ON N0M 1A0
519-293-3215 Fax: 519-293-3941 www.craigwielgardens.on.ca
Number of Beds: 83 beds
Heather Beauregard, Adm.

Alexandria: **Community Nursing Home**
PO Box 300, 92 Centre St., Alexandria, ON K0C 1A0
613-525-2022 Fax: 613-525-2023
Number of Beds: 70 beds
Terry A. Dubé

Almonte: **Almonte Country Haven**
333 Country St., Almonte, ON K0A 1A0
613-256-3095 Fax: 613-256-3096
rgourlie@omniway.ca
www.omni-way.com/ourhomes/almonte.htm
Number of Beds: 82 beds
Rick Gourlie, Administrator

Almonte: **Fairview Manor**
PO Box 1360, 95 Spring St., Almonte, ON K0A 1A0
613-256-3113 Fax: 613-256-5780
Number of Beds: 100 beds
Helen James, Director, Housekeeping
Linda Chaplin, Administrator

Aurora: **Willows Estate**
13837 Yonge St., Aurora, ON L4G 3G8
905-727-0128 Fax: 905-841-0454 www.omni-way.com
Number of Beds: 84 beds
Note: Specialties: Long-term care; Care for persons with Alzheimer's disease & dementia; Life enrichment program
Susan Bean, Administrator
Ray Strevez, Supervisor, Environmental Services

Aylmer: **Chateau Gardens Nursing Home**
465 Talbot St. West, Aylmer, ON N5H 1K8
519-773-3423 Fax: 519-765-2573 www.chateaugardens.com
Number of Beds: 60 beds
Mary Vergeer, Administrator

Aylmer: **Terrace Lodge**
475 Talbot St. East, 49462 Talbot Line, Aylmer, ON N5H 3A5
519-773-9205 Fax: 519-765-2627 www.elginhomes.ca
Number of Beds: 100 beds
Note: Specialties: Long-term care; Secure unit; Physiotherapy; Activity program; Adult day program, including a specialized program for Alzheimer's patients; Respite care; Palliative care
Helen Notte, Administrator

Bancroft: **Hastings Centennial Manor**
PO Box 758, 1 Manor Lane, Bancroft, ON K0L 1C0
613-332-2070 Fax: 613-332-2837
Number of Beds: 110 beds
B. White, Supervisor, Maintenance
Claudette Dignard-Remillard, Administrator

Barrie: **Coleman Care Centre**
140 Cundles Rd. West, RR#2, Barrie, ON L4M 4S4
705-726-8691 Fax: 705-726-5085
Number of Beds: 112 beds
Ralph Spracklin, Maintenance
Françoise Bouchard, Administrator

Barrie: **Grove Park Home for Senior Citizens**
234 Cook St., Barrie, ON L4M 4H5
705-726-1003 Fax: 705-726-1076 www.groveparkhome.on.ca
Number of Beds: 143 beds
Robert Dixon, Director, Physical Plant
Terry Codling, Administrator

Barrie: **Leisureworld Caregiving Centre - Barrie**
130 Owen St., Barrie, ON L4M 3H7
705-726-8621 Fax: 705-726-0821
adm.barrie@leisureworld.ca
www.leisureworld.ca/barrie.html
Number of Beds: 57 beds
Mary LaChapelle, Administrator

Barrys Bay: **Valley Manor Nursing Home**
PO Box 880, 88 Mintha St., Barrys Bay, ON K0J 1B0
613-756-2643 Fax: 613-756-7601 www.valleymanor.org
Number of Beds: 90 beds
Note: Adult Day Program
Ron Coulas, Director, Physical Plant
Linda Shulist, Administrator

Beamsville: **Albright Manor**
5035 Mountain St., Beamsville, ON L0R 1B2
905-563-8252 Fax: 905-563-5223
Number of Beds: 231 beds
John E. Buma, CEO

Beeton: **Simcoe Manor Home for the Aged**
PO Box 100, Beeton, ON L0G 1A0
905-729-2267 Fax: 905-729-4350
Number of Beds: 126 beds
Earl Gray, Supervisor

Belleville: **Bellmont Long-Term Care Facility**
250 Bridge St. West, Belleville, ON K8P 5N3
613-968-8835 Fax: 613-968-3207
Old Name: Montgomery Lodge Nursing Home.
Number of Beds: 128 beds
David Clegg, Administrator

Belleville: **Belmont Long Term Care Facility**
250 Bridge St. West, Belleville, ON K8P 1B6
613-968-4434 Fax: 613-968-3207
Number of Beds: 60 beds
James A. Clegg, Administrator

Belleville: **Hastings Manor**
PO Box 458, 476 Dundas St. West, Belleville, ON K8N 5B2
613-968-6467 Fax: 613-967-0128
info@hastingsmanorfoundation.ca
www.hastingsmanorfoundation.ca
Year Founded: 1908
Number of Beds: 253 beds
Claudette Dignard-Remillard, Administrator

Belleville: **Westgate Lodge**
37 Wilkie St., Belleville, ON K8P 4E4
613-966-1323 Fax: 613-966-5126
admin@westgatelodge.ca
Number of Beds: 88 beds
Elizabeth McGrath, Administrator

Bobcaygeon: **Pinecrest Nursing Home**
3418 County Rd. 36, RR#2, Bobcaygeon, ON K0M 1A0
705-738-2366 Fax: 705-738-9414
Number of Beds: 65 beds
Note: Specialties: Activation program
Maryliz Mitchell, Administrator

Bolton: **King Nursing Home**
49 Sterne St., Bolton, ON L7E 5T1
905-857-4117 Fax: 905-857-5181
kingnh@on.aibn.com
Year Founded: 1966
Number of Beds: 86 beds
Janice L. King, Administrator

Bolton: **Vera M. Davis Community Care Centre**
80 Allan Dr., Bolton, ON L7E 1P7
905-857-0975 Fax: 905-857-7872
Number of Beds: 64 beds
Wendy Beattie, Administrator

Bradford: **Bradford Place Nursing Home**
2656 6th Line, RR#1, Bradford, ON L3Z 2A4
905-952-2270 Fax: 905-775-0263
olivia.schmitz@specialty-care.com
www.specialty-care.com
Number of Beds: 150 beds
Olivia Schmitz, Administrator
olivia.schmitz@specialty-care.com

Brampton: **Extendicare - Brampton**
7891 McLaughlin Rd., Brampton, ON L6Y 5H8
905-459-4904 Fax: 905-459-5625
cnh_brampton@extendicare.com
www.extendicarecanada.com/brampton/
Number of Beds: 150 beds

Brampton: **Leisureworld Caregiving Centre - Brampton Meadows**
215 Sunny Meadows Blvd., Brampton, ON L6R 3B5
905-458-7604
adm.bm@leisureworld.ca
www.leisureworld.ca/brampton_meadows.html
Number of Beds: 160 beds
Angie Heinze, Administrator

Brampton: **Leisureworld Caregiving Centre - Brampton Woods**
9257 Goreway Dr., Brampton, ON L6T 3Y7
905-799-7502
susan.wendt@leisureworld.ca
www.leisureworld.ca/brampton_woods.html
Number of Beds: 160 beds
Susan Wendt, Administrator

Brampton: **Peel Manor**
525 Main St. North, Brampton, ON L6X 1N9
905-453-4140 Fax: 905-453-9140
Number of Beds: 177 beds
Note: Long-term care centre
Carolyn Clubine, Administrator

Brantford: **Hardy Terrace Long Term Care**
612 Mount Pleasant Rd., RR#2, Brantford, ON N3T 5L5
519-484-2431 Fax: 519-484-2590
Number of Beds: 69 beds
Lloyd Smith, Administrator

Brantford: **Leisureworld Caregiving Centre - Brantford**
389 West St., Brantford, ON N3R 3V9
519-759-4666 Fax: 519-759-0200
adm.brantford@leisureworld.ca
www.leisureworld.ca/brantford.html
Number of Beds: 120 permanent, 2 short stay beds
Christy Whiddet, Director of Care
Barbara Naykalyk-Hunt, Administrator

Brockville: **St. Lawrence Lodge**
PO Box 1130, 1803 Prescott Rd. East, Brockville, ON K6V 5W2
613-345-0255 Fax: 613-345-1029
info@stll.org
www.stll.org
Number of Beds: 240 beds
Note: Long-term care home
Gary Blair, Purchasing Agent
William R. Luker, Administrator

Brockville: **Sherwood Park Manor**
1814 Hwy. 2 East, Brockville, ON K6V 5T1
613-342-5531 Fax: 613-342-3767
Number of Beds: 107 beds
Joan Bennett, Administrator
J. Vanderwal, Director, Physical Plant

Brunner: **Country Meadows Retirement & Living Centre**
Ana St., Lot 16, Brunner, ON N0K 1C0
519-595-8903 Fax: 519-595-8272
brunner@perth.net
Number of Beds: 43 beds
Elinor Morley, Administrator

Brussels: **Huronlea Home for the Aged**
820 Turnberry St. South, Brussels, ON N0G 1H0
519-887-9267 Fax: 519-482-5263
Number of Beds: 64 beds; 2 respite beds
Barb Springhall, Administrator

Burlington: **Cama Woodlands Nursing Home**
159 Panin Rd., Burlington, ON L7P 5A6
905-681-6441 Fax: 905-681-2678
a.lawlor@bellnet.ca
www.camawoodlands.com
Number of Beds: 64 beds
Allene Lawlor, Administrator

Burlington: **Maple Villa Long Term Care Centre**
441 Maple Ave., Burlington, ON L7S 1L8
905-639-2264 Fax: 905-639-3034
maplevilla@maplevilla.ca
www.maplevilla.ca
Number of Beds: 93 beds
Barbara Goetz, Administrator

Cambridge: **Fairview Mennonite Home**
515 Langs Dr., Cambridge, ON N3H 5E4
519-653-5719 Fax: 519-650-1242
Number of Beds: 84 beds
Earl Gerber, Director, Maintenance
T. Kennel, Exec. Dir.

***Cambridge:* Golden Years Nursing Home**
PO Box 3277, 704 Eagle St. North, Cambridge, ON N3H 4T3
519-653-5493 Fax: 519-650-1495
nancy@goldenyearscambridge.com
www.goldenyearscambridge.com
Number of Beds: 88 beds
Nancy Kauffman-Lambert, Administrator

***Campbellford:* Burnbrae Gardens**
320 Burnbrae Road East, RR#3, Campbellford, ON K0L 1L0
705-653-4100 Fax: 705-653-2598
scymbaluk@omniway.com
www.onmi-way.com/ourhomes/burnbrae.htm
Number of Beds: 43 beds
Susan Cymbaluk, Administrator/Director of Care
scymbaluk@omniway.com
Rosie Coppens, Office Manager

***Cannifton:* E.J. McQuigge Lodge**
PO Box 68, Black Diamond Rd. & Hwy. 37, Cannifton, ON K0K 1K0
613-966-7717 Fax: 613-966-7646
agarland@mcquiggelodge.com
www.mcquiggelodge.com
Number of Beds: 56 beds
Anita Garland, Administrator
agarland@mcquiggelodge.com

***Cannington:* Bon-Air Nursing Home**
131 Laidlaw St. South, Cannington, ON L0E 1E0
705-432-2385 Fax: 705-432-3331
bonair@chartwellreit.ca
Number of Beds: 55 units
Lynne Disik, Administrator

***Chapleau:* Bignucolo Residence**
PO Box 757, 6 Broomhead Rd., Chapleau, ON P0M 1K0
705-864-1520 Fax: 705-864-0449
Year Founded: 1998
Number of Beds: 25 beds
Note: Specialties: Long-term care; Chronic care; Respite care; Pet therapy

***Chatham:* St. Andrews Residence**
99 Park St., Chatham, ON N7M 3R5
519-354-8103 Fax: 519-351-2407
info@standrewsresidence.com
www.standrewsresidence.com
Number of Beds: 95 beds
W.L. Alexander, Administrator/CEO

***Chatham:* Victoria Residence**
190 Stanley Ave., Chatham, ON N7M 3J9
519-354-0610 Fax: 519-354-7741
Number of Beds: 90 beds
Note: home for the aged
Patricia Cuncic, Administrator

***Chesley:* Elgin Abbey Nursing & Retirement Home**
PO Box 7, 380 First Ave. North, Chesley, ON N0G 1L0
519-363-3195 Fax: 519-363-0375
elginabb@log.on.ca
Number of Beds: 41 beds; 27 long-term-care, 14 retirement home
Jennifer Soper, Program Manager
Tracee Givens, Administrator

***Clinton:* Huronview Home for the Aged**
77722A London Rd. Hwy 4 S, RR#5, Clinton, ON N0M 1L0
519-482-3451
Number of Beds: 119 beds
Barb Springall, Administrator

***Cobourg:* Extendicare - Cobourg**
130 New Densmore Rd., Cobourg, ON K9A 5W2
905-372-0377 Fax: 905-372-0477
cnh_cobourg@extendicare.com
www.extendicarecanada.com
Number of Beds: 69 beds

***Collingwood:* Collingwood Nursing Home Limited**
250 Campbell St., Collingwood, ON L9Y 4J9
705-445-3991 Fax: 705-445-5060
cnh@collingwoodnursinghome.com
www.collingwoodnursinghome.com
Number of Beds: 60 beds
Peter Zober, Administrator

***Corbeil:* Nipissing Manor Nursing Care Centre**
1202 Hwy. 94, RR#1, Corbeil, ON P0H 1K0
705-752-1100 Fax: 705-752-2570
Number of Beds: 143 beds
W.E. Graham, Administrator

***Cornwall:* Glen-Stor-Dun Lodge**
1900 Montréal Rd., Cornwall, ON K6H 7L1
613-933-3384 Fax: 613-933-7214 www.glenstordunlodge.com
Number of Beds: 132 beds
D. Seller, Director, Housekeeping/Physical Plant
Donna Derouchie, Administrator

***Cornwall:* Parisien Manor**
439 Second St. East, Cornwall, ON K6H 1Z2
613-933-2592 Fax: 613-933-3839 www.parisienmanor.ca
Year Founded: 1982
Note: Specialties: Long-term care; Activation programs; Counselling; Social services; Dental services; Music therapy; Physiotherapy; Occupational therapy; Foot care
Norman Quenneville, Administrator

***Cornwall:* St. Joseph's Villa (Cornwall)**
14 York St., Cornwall, ON K6J 5T2
613-933-6040 Fax: 613-933-9429
executiveoffices@stjosephscentre.ca
www.stjosephscentre.ca
Number of Beds: 150 beds
Jeanette Despatie, Executive Director
Allan Greg, Director, Physical Plant

***Cornwall Island:* Tsi ion kwa nonh so:te**
RR#3, Cornwall Island, ON K6H 5R7
613-932-1409 Fax: 613-932-8845
Old Name: Akwesasne Adult Care Facility
Number of Beds: 30 beds
Note: Specialties: Geriatric residential health care; Water therapy; Palliative care
Bonnie Cole, Administrator

***Creemore:* Creedan Valley Nursing Home**
PO Box 309, 143 Mary St., Creemore, ON L0M 1G0
705-466-3437 Fax: 705-466-3063
Number of Beds: 96 beds
Debbie Fleming, Administrator

***Creemore:* Leisureworld Caregiving Centre - Creedan Valley**
143 Mary St., Creemore, ON L0M 1G0
705-466-3437
adm.creedan@leisureworld.ca
www.leisureworld.ca/creedan.html
Number of Beds: 95 beds
Paula Rentner, Administrator

***Deep River:* North Renfrew Long-Term Care Centre**
PO Box 1988, 47 Ridge Rd., Deep River, ON K0J 1P0
613-584-1900 Fax: 613-584-9183
nrltcsin@magma.ca
www.magma.ca/~nrltcsin
Number of Beds: 20 long-term care; 9 supportive care; 1 respite
Ann Aikens, Administrator

***Delhi:* Delhi Long Term Care Centre**
750 Gibraltar St., Delhi, ON N4B 3B3
519-582-3400 Fax: 519-582-0300
delhinh@kwic.com
Number of Beds: 60 beds
Janet Krolouski, Administrator

***Deseronto:* Friendly Manor Nursing Home**
PO Box 305, Hwy. 2, Deseronto, ON K0K 1X0
613-396-3438 Fax: 613-396-2729
judy_manor@hotmail.com
Number of Beds: 60 beds
Judith Norlock, Manager

***Elmira:* Leisureworld Caregiving Centre - Elmira**
120 Barnswallow Dr., Elmira, ON N3B 2Y9
519-669-5777
angie.heinz@leisureworld.ca
www.leisureworld.ca/elmira.html
Number of Beds: 92 permanent, 2 short stay beds
Cathy Holland, Administrator

***Elora:* Wellington County Terrace Home for the Aged**
PO Box 70, Wellington Dr., Elora, ON N0B 1S0
519-846-5359 Fax: 519-846-9192
Number of Beds: 176 beds
Peter M. Barnes, Administrator
R. Granger, Purchasing Director
Don Giles, Director, Housekeeping

***Englehart:* Northview Nursing Home**
PO Box 1139, 77 River Rd., Englehart, ON P0J 1H0
705-544-8191 Fax: 705-544-8255
northview@ntl.sympatico.ca
Number of Beds: 48 beds
Ruth Sulis, Administrator/DOC

A. Saunders, Director, Physical Plant

***Espanola:* Espanola Nursing Home**
799 Queensway Ave., Espanola, ON P5E 1R3
705-869-1420 Fax: 705-869-2608
Number of Beds: 30 beds
Paul L. Davies, Administrator
Diane Mokohonuk, Environmental Manager

***Essex:* Iler Lodge**
111 Iler Ave., Essex, ON N8M 1T6
519-776-9482 Fax: 519-776-4292
ilerlodge@reveraliving.com
www.reveraliving.com/homes/exr/
Old Name: Essex Health Care Centre
Number of Beds: 104 beds
Cheryl Labute, Administrator

***Forest:* North Lambton Rest Home**
PO Box 640, 39 Morris St., Forest, ON N0N 1J0
519-786-2151 Fax: 519-786-2156
Number of Beds: 87 beds
Jeffrey J. Harvey, Assistant Administrator
George Tomlinson, Environmental Services Supervisor

***Fort Erie:* Crescent Park Lodge**
4 Hagey Ave., Fort Erie, ON L2A 5M5
905-871-8330 Fax: 905-871-9212
Number of Beds: 68 beds
Rose Turner, Administrator

***Gananoque:* Carveth Care Centre**
375 James St., Gananoque, ON K7G 2Z1
613-382-4752 Fax: 613-382-8514
Number of Beds: 94 beds
Tim Gibson, Vice-President, Administration & Finance
Ray Gentile, Supervisor, Plant Maintenance

***Georgetown:* Bennett Health Care Centre**
1 Princess Anne Dr., Georgetown, ON L7G 2B8
905-873-0115 Fax: 905-873-1403
info@bennetthealthcarecentre.ca
www.bennetthealthcarecentre.ca
Number of Beds: 66 beds
Mark Ewer, Administrator

***Gloucester:* Extendicare - Laurier Manor**
1715 Montréal Rd., Gloucester, ON K1J 6N4
613-741-5122 Fax: 613-741-8432
Number of Beds: 240 beds
Norm Slatter, Administrator

***Goderich:* Maitland Manor**
290 South St., Goderich, ON N7A 4G6
519-524-7324 Fax: 519-524-8739
maitland@reveraliving.com
www.reveraliving.com
Number of Beds: 91 beds
Note: Specialties: Long-term care; Restorative care programs; Foot care; Specialized skin & wound care program; Physiotherapy; Music therapy; Respite care
Angie Dunn, Acting Administrator

***Gravenhurst:* Leisureworld Caregiving Centre - Muskoka**
200 Kelly Dr., Gravenhurst, ON P1P 1P3
705-687-3444 Fax: 705-687-9094
marion.barton@leisureworld.ca
www.leisureworld.ca/muskoka.html
Year Founded: 1999
Number of Beds: 180 long-term care, 2 short term beds, 28 retirement suites
Marion Barton, Administrator
Denise Ward, Director, Care

***Grimsby:* Kilean Lodge**
83 Main St. East, Grimsby, ON L3M 1N6
905-945-9243 Fax: 905-945-1126
kileanlodge@reveraliving.com
www.reveraliving.com/homes/70
Number of Beds: 50 beds
Sonja Jonescu, Executive Director

***Grimsby:* Shalom Manor**
12 Bartlett Ave., Grimsby, ON L3M 4N5
905-945-9631 Fax: 905-945-1211
info@shalommanor.ca
www.shalommanor.ca
Year Founded: 1966
Number of Beds: 144 beds
Note: Home for the aged affiliated with the Christian Reformed Church
Chris Rynberk, CEO
Rita Fluit, Director, Nursing

Yettie Termorshuizen, Director, Environmental Services

Guelph: Eden House Nursing Home
Country Rd. 29, RR#2, Guelph, ON N1H 6H8
519-856-4622 Fax: 519-856-1274
admin@edenhousecarehome.ca
www.edenhousecarehome.ca
Parent: Waterloo Wellington Local Health Integration Network
Number of Beds: 58 nursing home, 21 retirement home
John Bouwmeester, Administrator

Guelph: Lapointe-Fisher Nursing Home
271 Metcalfe St., Guelph, ON N1E 4Y8
519-821-9030 Fax: 519-821-6021
guelph@lapointefisher.ca
guelph.lapointefisher.ca
Number of Beds: 92 beds
Tom Hudson, Administrator
Reg Carreor, Environmental Services Supervisor

Haileybury: Extendicare - Tri-Town
PO Box 999, 143 Bruce St., Haileybury, ON P0J 1K0
705-672-2151 Fax: 705-672-5348
gjulien@extendicare.com
Number of Beds: 60 beds
Ghislaine Julien, Administrator

Haliburton: Extendicare - Haliburton
PO Box 780, 167 Park St., Haliburton, ON K0M 1S0
705-457-1722 Fax: 705-457-3914
cnh_halibruton@extendicare.com
www.extendicarecanada.com/haliburton/
Number of Beds: 60 beds
Jane Rosenberg, Administrator
Doug Holmes, Maintenance Supervisor

Halton Hills: Extendicare - Halton Hills
9 Lindsay Court, Halton Hills, ON L7G 6G9
905-702-8760 Fax: 905-702-7430 www.extendicare.com
Number of Beds: 130 beds
André Spekkens, Administrator

Hamilton: Arbour Creek Long Term Care Centre
2717 King St. East, Hamilton, ON L8G 1J3
905-573-4900
info.arbourcreek@thomashealthcare.com
Number of Beds: 128 beds
Shirley Thomas Weir

Hamilton: Extendicare - Hamilton
90 Chedmac Dr., Hamilton, ON L9C 7S6
905-318-4472 Fax: 905-318-1162
cnh_hamilton@extendicare.com
www.extendicarecanada.com/hamilton/
Number of Beds: 160 beds

Hamilton: Hamilton Continuing Care
125 Wentworth St. South, Hamilton, ON L8N 2Z1
905-527-1482 Fax: 905-527-0679
lorraine_preston_orchard@hotmail.com
Number of Beds: 64 beds
Lorraine Preston-Orchard, Administrator

Hamilton: Macassa Lodge
701 Upper Sherman Ave., Hamilton, ON L8V 3M7
905-546-2800 Fax: 905-546-4989
saphsweb@hamilton.ca
www.hamilton.ca/phcs/macassa
Number of Beds: 270 beds
Note: Specialties: Long term care; Adult day program; Social work
Mark Ewer, Administrator

Hamilton: Parkview Nursing Centre
545 King St. West, Hamilton, ON L8P 1C1
905-525-5903 Fax: 905-525-8717
www.parkviewnursingcentre.com
Number of Beds: 126 beds
Andrea Pohl, Administrator
Tom Sachade, Manager, Maintenance/Physical Plant

Hamilton: Victoria Nursing Home
176 Victoria Ave. North, Hamilton, ON L8L 5G1
905-527-9111 Fax: 905-526-1871 www.victoriagardens.ca
Number of Beds: 76 beds
Ranka Stipancic, Administrator

Hanover: Hanover Care Centre
700 - 19 Ave., Hanover, ON N4N 3S6
519-364-3700 Fax: 519-364-7194
hcc@bmts.com
Number of Beds: 41 beds
Dennis Laver, Director, Physical Plant
Bill Garcia, Administrator

Hearst: Foyer des Pionniers
PO Box 1538, 1317 Edward St., Hearst, ON P0L 1N0
705-372-2820 Fax: 705-372-2826
Number of Beds: 61 beds
Joëlle Lacroix, Director of Care

Ingersoll: Leisureworld Caregiving Centre - Oxford
263 Wonham St. South, Ingersoll, ON N5C 3P6
519-485-3920
adm.oxford@leisureworld.ca
www.leisureworld.ca
Year Founded: 1975
Number of Beds: 80 long-term care beds
Note: Specialties: Restorative care; Physiotherapy program; Pet therapy; Palliative care
Carolee Milliner, Administrator
Ted Cripps, Environmental Services Supervisor

Iroquois Falls: South Centennial Manor
240 Fyfe St., Iroquois Falls, ON P0K 1E0
705-258-3836 Fax: 705-258-3694
Number of Beds: 68 beds
Dan O'Mara, CEO
Richard Hadley, Director, Physical Plant

Kapuskasing: Extendicare - Kapuskasing
PO Box 460, 45 Ontario St., Kapuskasing, ON P5N 2Y5
705-335-8337 Fax: 705-337-6051
cnh_kapuskasing@extendicare.com
www.extendicarecanada.com/kapuskasing/
Number of Beds: 60 beds
Jacynthe Ouellette, Administrator

Kapuskasing: North Centennial Manor
2 Kimberley Dr., Kapuskasing, ON P5N 1L5
705-335-6125 Fax: 705-337-1091
Number of Beds: 71 beds
Note: non-profit charitable home for the aged
Gil M. Dionne, Administrator
Jean-Claude Lauzon, Supervisor, Plant Maintenance

Kemptville: Bayfield Manor Nursing & Retirement Home
PO Box 300, 100 Elvira St., Kemptville, ON K0G 1J0
613-258-7484 Fax: 613-258-3838
bayfield@bayfieldmanor.on.ca
www.bayfieldmanor.on.ca
Number of Beds: 66 bed nursing home + 46 suite retirement home
Michael J. Hall, Administrator

Kenora: Birchwood Terrace Central Park Lodge
PO Box 2630, 237 Lakeview Drive, R.R. #1, Kenora, ON P9N 3X8
807-468-9532 Fax: 807-468-4060
birchwoodterrace@reveraliving.com
Number of Beds: 94 beds
Soili Helppi, Executive Director
soili.helppi@reveraliving.com

Kenora: Pinecrest Home for the Aged
1220 Valley Dr., Kenora, ON P9N 2W7
807-468-3165 Fax: 807-468-6346
Kevin L. Queen, Administrator

King City: King City Lodge Nursing Home
146 Fog Rd., King City, ON L7B 1A3
905-833-5037 Fax: 905-833-5925 www.kingcitylodge.com
Number of Beds: 36 beds
Kelly Graham, Administrator; Director, Nursing

Kingston: Extendicare - Kingston
309 Queen Mary Rd., Kingston, ON K7M 6P4
613-549-5010 Fax: 613-549-7347
cnh_kingston@extendicare.com
www.extendicarecanada.com/kingston/
Number of Beds: 150 beds
Marilyn C. Benn, Administrator

Kingston: Rideaucrest Home
175 Rideau St., Kingston, ON K7K 3H6
613-530-2818 Fax: 613-531-9107
Number of Beds: 170 beds
Note: municipal home for the aged
John D. Smith, Administrator

Kirkland Lake: Extendicare - Kirkland Lake
PO Box 3900, 155 Government Rd. East, Kirkland Lake, ON P2N 3P4
705-567-3268 Fax: 705-567-4638
cnh_kirklandlake@extendicare.com
www.extendicarecanada.com/kirklandlake/
Number of Beds: 100 beds
Susan Enouy, Administrator

Kirkland Lake: Teck Pioneer Residence
145A Government Rd. East, Kirkland Lake, ON P2N 3P4
705-567-3264 www.teckpioneerresidence.com
Year Founded: 1965
Note: Specialties: Nursing services for long-term care residents; Dementia care; Activity program; Restorative care
Nancy Allick, Administrator
Donna LeGros, Director, Nursing
Phil Sullivan, Environmental Services Supervisor

Kitchener: A.R. Goudie Eventide Home (Salvation Army)
369 Frederick St., Kitchener, ON N2H 2P1
519-744-5182 Fax: 519-744-3887
info@argoudieeventide.ca
www.argoudieeventide.ca
Number of Beds: 80 beds
Gary Butt, Executive Director
gbutt@argoudieeventide.ca
Anabela Henriques, Manager, Resident Care Services
ahenriques@argoudieeventide.ca
Alison Westman, Manager, Dietary & Environmental Services
awestman@argoudieeventide.ca

Kitchener: Forest Heights Long Term Care Centre
60 Westheights Dr., Kitchener, ON N2N 2A8
519-576-3320 Fax: 519-745-3227
Number of Beds: 240 beds
Michelle Vermeeren, Administrator

Kitchener: Trinity Village Care Centre/TVCC
2727 Kingsway Dr., Kitchener, ON N2C 1A7
519-893-6320 Fax: 519-893-3432
cverleyen@trinityvillage.com
www.trinityvillage.com
Number of Beds: 150 residential capacity
Note: Specialties: Eden Alternative Philosophy of Care; Long-term care; Therapeutic services; Recreation programming; Palliative care
Debby Riepert, Administrator
Elizabeth Barnes, Supervisor, Environmental Health

Kitchener: Village of Winston Park
695 Blockline Rd., Kitchener, ON N2E 3K1
519-576-2430 Fax: 519-576-8990
info@winstonpark.net
www.winstonpark.net
Number of Beds: 271 beds
Michael Schmidt, Administrator

L'Orignal: Résidence Champlain
428 Front Rd. Wesst, L'Orignal, ON K0B 1K0
613-675-4617 Fax: 613-675-1374
champlain@chartwellreit.ca
www.chartwellreit.ca
Old Name: CHS pleasant Rest Inc; Pleasant Rest Nursing Home
Number of Beds: 60 beds
Jacinthe Loiselle, Administrator

Lakefield: Extendicare - Lakefield
19 Fraser St., Lakefield, ON K0L 2H0
705-652-7112 Fax: 705-652-7733
cnh_lakefield@extendicare.com
www.extendicarecanada.com/lakefield/
Number of Beds: 100 beds

Leamington: Leamington Nursing Home
24 Franklin Rd., Leamington, ON N8H 4B7
519-326-3289 Fax: 519-326-0102
Number of Beds: 120 beds
Roxanne Belli, Administrator

Leamington: Leamington United Mennonite Home
35 Pickwick Dr., Leamington, ON N8H 2P2
519-326-6109 Fax: 519-326-3595
Number of Beds: 82 beds
Linda Tiessen, Administrator

Leamington: Sun Parlor Home for Senior Citizens
175 Talbot St. East, Leamington, ON N8H 1L9
519-326-5731 Fax: 519-326-8952
www.countyofessex.on.ca/countyservices/sunparlor_home.asp
Year Founded: 1900
Number of Beds: 206 beds
Note: Specialties: Long-term care; Mental health services; Physiotherapy; Restorative care programs; Speech therapy; Occupational therapy; Audiology screening; Life enrichment services
Bill MacDonald, Administrator

Lindsay: Extendicare - Kawartha Lakes
125 Colborne St. East, Lindsay, ON K9V 4R3

705-878-5392 Fax: 705-878-7910
cnh_kawarthalakes@extendicare.com
www.extendicarecanada.com/lindsaykawartha/
Number of Beds: 64 beds

***Lions Head:* Golden Dawn Nursing Home**
PO Box 129, 80 Main St., Lions Head, ON N0H 1W0
519-793-3433 Fax: 519-793-4503
Number of Beds: 45 beds
Frank Walker, Administrator
Bruce Haksins, Maintenance Supervisor

***Little Current:* Manitoulin Centennial Manor**
PO Box 460, 70 Robinson St. West, Little Current, ON P0P 1K0
705-368-2710 Fax: 705-368-2694
Number of Beds: 60 beds
Cathy Deacon, Administrator; Director, Residential Services

***London:* Chateau Gardens (Queens) Nursing Home**
518 Queens Ave., London, ON N6B 1Y7
519-434-2727 Fax: 519-679-3482
Number of Beds: 63 beds
Donna Heffron, Administrator

***London:* Chelsey Park (Oxford) Nursing Home**
310 Oxford St. West, London, ON N6H 4N6
519-432-1855 Fax: 519-679-7324 www.chelseypark.com
Number of Beds: 243 beds
Note: retirement community
Rhonda Roberts, Administrator

***London:* Extendicare - London**
860 Waterloo St., London, ON N6A 3W6
519-433-6658 Fax: 519-642-1711
cnh_london@extendicare.com
Number of Beds: 170 beds
Charles Marczinski, Administrator
John Plachta, Supervisor, Maintenance

***London:* McCormick Home**
2022 Kains Rd., London, ON N6K 0A8
519-432-2648 Fax: 519-645-6982 www.mccormickhome.on.ca
Number of Beds: 160 beds
Note: Specialties: Long-term care; Ddementia care; Alzheimer outreach services day program; Social work
Michael P. Boucher, Executive Director
Roy Langille, Director, Physical Operations

***Long Sault:* Woodland Villa**
30 Mille Roches Rd., Long Sault, ON K0C 1P0
613-534-2276 Fax: 613-534-8559
mrasenberg@omniway.ca
www.omni-way.com/ourhomes/woodland.htm
Number of Beds: 112 beds
Michael Rasenberg, Administrator

***Markdale:* Grey Gables Home for the Aged**
PO Box 380, 206 Toronto St. South, Markdale, ON N0C 1H0
519-986-3010 Fax: 519-986-4644
sperson@greycounty.ca
Old Name: Grey Owen Lodge
Number of Beds: 66 beds
Shirley Person, Administrator

***Markham:* Markhaven, Home for Seniors**
54 Parkway Ave., Markham, ON L3P 2G4
905-294-2233 Fax: 905-294-6521
markhaven@markhaven.ca
www.markhaven.ca
Note: Specialties: Medical care; Nursing care; Physiotherapy; Special needs activities. Number of Employees: 149
Don Jennings, Maintenance Supervisor
Noreen Kallai, Executive Director

***Maryhill:* Twin Oaks of Maryhill Inc.**
1360 Maryhill Rd., Maryhill, ON N0B 2B0
519-648-2117 www.twinoaksmaryhill.com
Number of Beds: 31 beds
Note: Specialties: Secured area
Ralph Link, Administrator

***Mattawa:* Algonquin Nursing Home**
PO Box 270, 231 Tenth St., Mattawa, ON P0H 1V0
705-744-2202 Fax: 705-744-2787 800-579-4284
vala@anh.ca
www.anh.ca
Number of Beds: 72 beds
Leonard Simpson, Maintenance
Zena Monestime, Administrator

***Meaford:* Meaford Long Term Care Centre**
135 William St., Meaford, ON N4L 1T4
519-538-1010 Fax: 519-538-5699
businessoffice@meafordlongtermcare.com
www.meafordlongtermcare.com
Number of Beds: 77 beds
Note: Specialties; Restorative care program; Psychogeriatric outreach; Life enrichment programs; Services of a wound care specialist; Services of a pain specialist; Palliative care
Doris Bilitz, Administrator
Randy Turner, Environmental Services

***Merrickville:* Hilltop Manor**
1005 St Lawrence St., Merrickville, ON K0G 1N0
613-269-4707 Fax: 613-269-3534
elizabeth@hilltopmanor.ca
www.hilltopmanor.ca
Number of Beds: 89 beds

***Merrickville:* Hilltop Manor Nursing Home Ltd.**
PO Box 430, 1005 St. Lawrence St., Merrickville, ON K0G 1N0
613-269-4707 Fax: 613-269-3534
hilltop@alphainter.net
Number of Beds: 60 beds
Bernard Bouchard, Administrator
Wayne Pierce, Environmental Supervisor

***Metcalfe:* Township of Osgoode Care Centre**
7650 Snake Island Rd., Metcalfe, ON K0A 2P0
613-821-1034 Fax: 613-821-0388
osgoodecare@virtualwave.com
Number of Beds: 55 units
Note: Specialties: Long-term nursing care; Organized leisure activities
Murray B. Munro, Administrator
Deborah Nixon, Director, Nursing
Blaine Wright, General Service Supervisor

***Milverton:* Knollcrest Lodge**
50 William St., Milverton, ON N0K 1M0
519-595-8121 Fax: 519-595-8199
srae@knollcrestlodge.com
Number of Beds: 77 beds
Susan Rae, Administrator

***Minden:* Hyland Crest Senior Citizens' Home**
PO Box 30, 6 McPherson St., Minden, ON K0M 2K0
705-286-2140 Fax: 705-286-6384
hylandcrest@interhop.net
Number of Beds: 62 beds
Foster Loucks, Administrator
Peter Fearrey, Maintenance Supervisor
Peter Fearrey, Director, Environmental Services

***Mississauga:* Carmel Heights Seniors' Residence**
1720 Sherwood Forest Circle, Mississauga, ON L5K 1R1
905-822-5298 Fax: 905-822-7386
carmelheights@rogers.com
www.carmelheights.ca
Old Name: Carmel Heights Home for the Aged
Number of Beds: 48 beds
Note: home for the aged residential care
M. Veronica, Administrator

***Mississauga:* Chelsey Park (Streetsville) Nursing Home**
1742 Bristol Rd. West, Mississauga, ON L5M 1X9
905-826-3045 Fax: 905-826-9978 www.diversicare.ca
Number of Beds: 118 beds
Wendy Shelley, Administrator
George Holland, Coordinator, Environmental Services

***Mississauga:* Chelsey Park Nursing Home**
2250 Hurontario St., Mississauga, ON L5B 1M8
905-270-0411 Fax: 905-270-1749
Number of Beds: 237 beds
Alice Grzesiak, Administrator

***Mississauga:* Extendicare - Mississauga**
855 John Watt Blvd., Mississauga, ON L5W 1G2
905-696-0719
cnh_mississauga@extendicare.com
Number of Beds: 140 beds

***Mississauga:* Mississauga Lifecare Centre**
55 The Queensway West, Mississauga, ON L5B 1B5
905-270-0170 Fax: 905-270-8465
Number of Beds: 26 respite; 166 long-term care
Ina Reynolds, Administrator
Bill Cody, Director, Maintenance

***Mississauga:* Mississauga Long Term Care Facility**
26 Peter St. North, Mississauga, ON L5H 2G7
905-278-2213 www.mltcfacility.com
Old Name: Mississauga Nursing Home Inc.
Number of Beds: 55 beds
Novak Bajin, Administrator

***Mississauga:* Sheridan Villa**
2460 Truscott Dr., Mississauga, ON L5J 3Z8
905-791-8668 Fax: 905-823-7971
Number of Beds: 236 beds
Inga Mazuryk, Administrator
John Squire, Environmental Services

***Mississauga:* Tyndall Nursing Home Ltd.**
1060 Eglinton Ave. East, Mississauga, ON L4W 1K3
905-624-1511 Fax: 905-629-9346
info@tyndallnursinghome.com
www.tyndallestates.net
Number of Beds: 151 residents
Note: Specialties: Long-term care; Restorative feeding program
B.D. Jolly, Administrator
Alisea Vernon, Health; Safety Committee

***Mitchell:* Mitchell Nursing Home Ltd.**
184 Napier St., Mitchell, ON N0K 1N0
519-348-8861 Fax: 519-348-4214
Parent: Ritz Lutheran Villa
Year Founded: 1969
Number of Beds: 48 beds
Cathy Wight, Administrator

***New Hamburg:* Nithview Home and Seniors Village**
200-218 Boullee St., New Hamburg, ON N0B 2G0
519-662-2280 Fax: 519-662-1090
Year Founded: 1972
Number of Beds: 96 beds
Note: Mennonite nursing home
Brent Martin, Administrator

***Newcastle:* Fosterbrooke Long Term Care Facility**
330 King St. West, Newcastle, ON L1B 1G9
905-987-4702 Fax: 905-987-3621
fosterbrooke@cplreit.com
Number of Beds: 88 beds
Barbara Tomaszewski, Acting Administrator

***Newcastle:* Fosterbrooke Long Term Care Facility**
330 King St. West, Newcastle, ON L1B 1G9
905-987-4702 Fax: 905-987-3621
Number of Beds: 88 beds
Christine Nidd, Administrator

***Newmarket:* Central Care Corporation - Mackenzie Place**
52 George St., Newmarket, ON L3Y 4V3
905-853-3242 Fax: 905-895-5139 www.cplcanada.com
Number of Beds: 93 beds
Anne Deelstra, Administrator

***Newmarket:* Eagle Terrace**
329 Eagle St., Newmarket, ON L3Y 1K3
905-895-5187 Fax: 905-895-2645
eagleterrace@cplreit.com
Number of Beds: 70 beds
Michael Griffin, Administrator
Elizabeth Laur, Director

***Newmarket:* Eagle Terrace**
329 Eagle St., Newmarket, ON L3Y 1K3
905-895-5187 Fax: 905-895-2645
eagleterrace@reveraliving.com
retirementresidencesreit.com/homes/07/
Number of Beds: 70 beds
Michael Griffin, Administrator

***Newmarket:* Maple Health Centre - York Region Long-Term Care & Seniors Branch**
194 Eagle St., Newmarket, ON L3Y 1J6
905-895-3628 Fax: 905-895-5843
Number of Beds: 100 beds
Lynn Parsons, Assistant Administrator; Director, Care

***Newmarket:* Newmarket Health Centre-York Region Long-Term Care & Seniors Branch**
194 Eagle St., Newmarket, ON L3Y 1J6
905-895-3628 Fax: 905-895-5843
Number of Beds: 132 beds
Marlene Parsons, Assistant Administrator; Director, Care

***Niagara Falls:* Oakwood Park Lodge**
6747 Oakwood Dr., Niagara Falls, ON L2E 7E3
905-356-8732 Fax: 905-356-2122
oakwoodparklodge@cogeco.net
www.conmedhealth.com
Year Founded: 1975
Number of Beds: 153 beds
Paul Taylor, Administrator

***Niagara Falls:* The Salvation Army Honorable Ray & Helen Lawson Eventide Home**
5050 Jepson St., Niagara Falls, ON L2E 1K5
905-356-1221 Fax: 905-356-9609
info@niagaraeventide.ca
www.niagaraeventide.ca
Note: Specialties: Long-term care for senior; Activity program
Grace Herber, Administrator
Harold Barwes, Head, Maintenance

***Niagara Falls:* Valley Park Lodge**
6400 Valley Way, Niagara Falls, ON L2E 7E3
905-358-3277 Fax: 905-358-3012
Number of Beds: 65 beds
Jennifer Kennedy, Administrator
Ron Jones, Maintenance Supervisor

***North Bay:* Leisureworld Caregiving Centre - North Bay**
401 William St., North Bay, ON P1A 1X5
705-476-2602 Fax: 705-476-1624
ruth.gauthier@leisureworld.ca
www.leisureworld.ca/northbay.html
Number of Beds: 147 suites, 1 short stay bed; 6 convalescent care
Ruth Gauthier, Administrator
Carol Passmore, Director, Nursing

***Northbrook:* Pine Meadow Nursing Home**
PO Box 100, 124 Lloyd St., Northbrook, ON K0H 2G0
613-336-9120 Fax: 613-336-9144
Year Founded: 1993
Number of Beds: 60 beds
Note: Specialties: Residential nursing care for seniors
Kim Harvey, Administrator

***Norwich:* Norvilla Nursing Home**
11 Elgin St. East, Norwich, ON N0J 1P0
519-863-2717 Fax: 519-863-3955
Number of Beds: 40 beds

***Ohsweken:* Iroquois Lodge**
PO Box 309, 1755 Chiefswood Rd, Ohsweken, ON N0A 1M0
519-445-2224 Fax: 519-445-4180
iroquoislodge@on.aibn.com
Number of Beds: 50 beds
Wanda Green, Administrator
Patti Powless, Nursing Supervisor

***Orillia:* Oak Terrace**
291 Mississauga St. West, Orillia, ON L3V 3B9
705-325-2289 Fax: 705-325-7178
oakterrace@reveraliving.com
Note: Specialties: Foot care; Physiotherapy programs; Restorative care programs; Dental services; Music therapy; Pet therapy
Marianne Williams, Administrator

***Orleans:* St. Louis Residence**
879, ch Parc Hiawatha, Orleans, ON K1C 2Z6
613-562-6262 Fax: 613-683-5001
rslinfo@bruyere.org
Number of Beds: 198 beds
Note: charitable home for the aged
Hélène Tassé, Administrator

***Oshawa:* Extendicare - Oshawa**
82 Park Rd. North, Oshawa, ON L1J 4L1
905-579-0011 Fax: 905-579-1733 www.extendicare.com
Number of Beds: 175 beds
Linda Grills, Administrator

***Ottawa:* Extendicare - Medex**
1865 Baseline Rd., Ottawa, ON K2C 3K6
613-225-5650 Fax: 613-225-0960
cnh_medex@extendicare.com
Number of Beds: 193 beds
William Smith, Administrator
T. de Kemp, Supervisor, Maintenance

***Ottawa:* Extendicare - New Orchard Lodge**
99 New Orchard Ave., Ottawa, ON K2B 5E6
613-820-2110 Fax: 613-820-6380
cnh_neworchardlodge@extendicare.com
Number of Beds: 111 beds
Susan Reed, Administrator
William Kirk, Director, Phyical Plant

***Ottawa:* Extendicare - Starwood**
114 Starwood Rd., Ottawa, ON K2G 3N5
613-224-3960
Number of Beds: 192 beds

***Ottawa:* Extendicare - West End Villa**
2179 Elmira Dr., Ottawa, ON K2C 3S1
613-829-3501 Fax: 613-829-3504
cnh_westendvilla@extendicare.com
Number of Beds: 240 beds
Note: nursing home
Lynda Welch, Administrator

***Ottawa:* Glebe Centre Inc.**
950 Bank St., Ottawa, ON K1S 5G6
613-238-2727 Fax: 613-238-4759
info@glebecentre.ca
www.glebecentre.ca
Old Name: Bronson Place
Janice Bridgewater, Senior Centre Director
jbridgewater@glebecentre.ca

***Ottawa:* Island Lodge**
1 Porter's Island, Ottawa, ON K1N 5M2
613-789-5100 Fax: 613-789-3704
Number of Beds: 165 beds
Diane Officer, Executive Director
Ray Duffy, Environmental Services

***Ottawa:* Perley & Rideau Veterans' Health Centre**
1750 Russell Rd., Ottawa, ON K1G 5Z6
613-526-7170 Fax: 613-526-7172 www.prvhc.com
Year Founded: 1995
Number of Beds: 450 residential capacity
Note: Specialties: Geriatric care; Recreation services; Dementia programming; Respite care for people in the mid-stages of dementia; Convalescent care
Greg Fougère, Executive Director
Bob Paré, Manager, Plant Services
Kerry Kelly, Manager, Housekeeping Linen Servs. & Materials Managemen

***Ottawa:* Villa Marconi**
1026 Baseline Rd., Ottawa, ON K2C 0A6
613-727-6201 Fax: 613-727-9352
villamarconi@villamarconi.com
www.villamarconi.com
Number of Beds: 125 beds
Walter Cibischino, President

***Owen Sound:* Lee Manor**
875 - 6 St. East, Owen Sound, ON N4K 5W5
519-376-4420 Fax: 519-371-5406 www.greycounty.on.ca
Number of Beds: 150 beds
Note: Municipal home for aged
Marjorie McNeil, Administrator

***Parkhill:* Chateau Gardens Parkhill**
PO Box 129, 250 Tain St., Parkhill, ON N0M 2K0
519-294-6342 Fax: 519-294-0107
Number of Beds: 59 beds
Brenda Nethercott, Administrator

***Parry Sound:* Belvedere Heights**
21 Belvedere Ave., Parry Sound, ON P2A 2A2
705-746-5871 Fax: 705-774-7300
bh@zeuter.com
www.belvedereheights.com
Number of Beds: 101 beds
Bev Preuss, CEO

***Pembroke:* Miramichi Lodge**
725 Pembrooke St. W, Pembroke, ON K8A 8S9
613-735-0175 Fax: 613-735-8061
Number of Beds: 166 beds
Shelley Sheedy, Administrator

***Perth:* Lanark Lodge**
115 Christie Lake Rd., Perth, ON K7H 3C6
613-267-4225 Fax: 613-264-2668
lanarklodge@county.lanark.on.ca
Number of Beds: 163 beds
Whynn Turner, Administrator

***Perth:* Perth Community Care Centre**
101 Christie Lake Rd., RR#4, Perth, ON K7H 3C6
613-267-2506 Fax: 613-267-7060
adm.perth@diversicare.ca
www.diversicare.ca
Number of Beds: 121 residential capacity
Note: Specialties: Long-term care; Activity program; Restorative care program; Physiotherapy
Joyce Firlotte, Administrator

***Peterborough:* Extendicare - Peterborough**
80 Alexander Ave., Peterborough, ON K9J 6B4
705-743-7552 Fax: 705-742-9664
Number of Beds: 172 beds
Margaret Lazure, Administrator

***Peterborough:* St. Joseph's at Fleming**
659 Brealey Dr., Peterborough, ON K9K 2R8
705-743-4744 Fax: 705-743-7532 www.stjosephsatfleming.com
Old Name: Marycrest Home of the Aged; Anson House
Year Founded: 2004
Debra Cooper Burger, Administrator

***Petrolia:* Fiddick's Nursing Home**
PO Box 340, 437 First Ave., Petrolia, ON N0N 1R0
519-882-0370 Fax: 519-882-0375
fiddicks@xcelco.on.ca
Number of Beds: 128 beds
Michael Fiddick, Administrator
Todd Fiddick, Supervisor, Plant Maintenance

***Picton:* H.J. MacFarland Memorial Home**
603 Hwy 49, RR#2, Picton, ON K0K 2T0
613-476-2138 Fax: 613-476-6952
egervais@pecounty.on.ca
Number of Beds: 84 beds
Ellen Gervais, Administrator
egervais@pecounty.on.ca

***Picton:* Kentwood Park**
PO Box 1298, 2 Ontario St., Picton, ON K0K 2T0
613-476-5671 Fax: 613-476-3986
www.omni-way.com/ourhomes/kentwood.htm
Number of Beds: 48 beds
Tina Cole, Administrator/Nursing Administrative Services Manager
tcole@omniway.ca

***Picton:* Picton Manor Nursing Home**
9 Hill St. West, Picton, ON K0K 2T0
613-476-6140 Fax: 613-476-5240 www.pictonmanor.com
Number of Beds: 78 beds
Note: Specialties: Nursing care; Restorative care; Activity program; Life enrichment progran; Palliative care
Norma Bongard, Administrator

***Picton:* West Lake Terrace**
PO Box 2229, R.R. #1, 1673 County Rd. #12, Picton, ON K0K 2T0
613-393-2055 Fax: 613-393-2057
Number of Beds: 47 beds
Mary Lynn Lester, Administrator

***Plantagenet:* Pinecrest Nursing Home Ltd.**
PO Box 250, 101 Parent St., RR#1, Plantagenet, ON K0B 1L0
613-673-4835 Fax: 613-673-2675
Note: Specialties: Long-term care; Activity program
Marcel Parent, Administrator

***Port Dover:* Dover Cliffs Long Term Care Centre, Port Dover**
PO Box 430, 501 St. George St., Port Dover, ON N0A 1N0
519-583-1422 Fax: 519-583-3197
pailinelyne@cplodges.com
www.cplcanada.com
Old Name: Versa-Care Centre, Port Dover
Number of Beds: 70 beds
Pauline Lyne, Executive Director
Shelly Desgagne, Office Manager
shellydesgagne@cplodges.com

***Port Hope:* Community Nursing Home**
20 Hope St. South, Port Hope, ON L1A 2M8
905-885-6367 Fax: 905-885-6368
Number of Beds: 97 beds
Nancy Jordan, Administrator

***Port Hope:* Extendicare - Port Hope**
360 Croft St., Port Hope, ON L1A 4K8
905-885-1266 Fax: 905-885-5328
cnh_porthope@extendicare.com
www.extendicare.com
Number of Beds: 128 beds

***Port Perry:* Community Nursing Home**
PO Box 660, 15941 Simcoe St. North, Port Perry, ON L9L 1A6
905-985-3205 Fax: 905-985-3721
Number of Beds: 107 beds
Kim Mitchell, Administrator

***Powassan:* Eastholme Home for the Aged**
PO Box 400, 62 Big Bend Ave., Powassan, ON P0H 1Z0
705-724-2005 Fax: 705-724-5429
easthome@onlink.net
www.eastholme.ca
Number of Beds: 104 beds
Steven Piekarski, Administrator
Stephen Pierarski, Administrator

***Prescott:* Wellington House**
PO Box 401, 990 Edward St. North, Prescott, ON K0E 1T0
613-925-2834 Fax: 613-925-5425
Number of Beds: 60 beds
Note: Long-term care facility
Bernadette Timco, Administrator
Diana Gaudet, Supervisor, Environmental Services

***Puslinch:* Morriston Park Nursing Home Inc.**
7363 Calfass Rd., RR#2, Puslinch, ON N0B 2J0
519-822-9179 Fax: 519-822-4459
Number of Beds: 28 beds
Alfred Urfey, Administrator

***Red Lake:* Northwood Lodge**
PO Box 420, Hwy 105, Red Lake, ON P0V 2M0
807-727-2323 Fax: 807-727-3546
northwood.lodge@kenoradistricthomes.ca
Number of Beds: 32 beds
Note: home for the aged
Doris Coghill, Administrator

***Renfrew:* Bonnechere Manor**
470 Albert St., Renfrew, ON K7V 4L5
613-432-4873 Fax: 613-432-7138
Year Founded: 1958
Number of Beds: 177 beds
Shayne Hoelke, Admintstrator

***Renfrew:* Groves Park Lodge Long Term Care Facility**
470 Raglan St. North, Renfrew, ON K7V 1P5
613-432-5823 Fax: 613-432-5287
carrol.haywood@gemhealth.com
www.gemhealth.com/gem_health_care_group_groves_park.html
Old Name: Groves Park Lodge Nursing Home
Number of Beds: 75 beds
Carrol Haywood, Administrator

***Richmond Hill:* Leisureworld Caregiving Centre - Richmond Hill**
170 Red Maple Rd., Richmond Hill, ON L4B 4T8
905-731-2273
jodi.macisaac@leisureworld.ca
www.leisureworld.ca/richmondhill.html
Number of Beds: 160 beds
Jodi MacIsaac, Administrator

***Richmond Hill:* Mariann Home**
9915 Yonge St., Richmond Hill, ON L4C 1V1
905-884-9276 Fax: 905-884-1800
mariann.home@rogers.com
Number of Beds: 64 beds
Note: Specialties: Peritoneal dialysis; Care for seniors with cognitive or psychiatric impairment; Palliative care. Number of employees: 80
Mary William Verhoeven, Administrator

***Rockland:* St. Joseph Nursing Home**
1615 Laurier St., Rockland, ON K4K 1C8
613-446-5126 Fax: 613-446-1516
Number of Beds: 64 beds
Ginette Whittingham, Administrator

***Sarnia:* Vision Nursing Home**
229 Wellington St., Sarnia, ON N7T 1G9
519-336-6551 Fax: 519-336-5878
recpt@vision74.com
Number of Beds: 108 permanent beds, 2 respite
Note: Christian-based nursing home
Bernard Bax, Administrator
Neil Whittle, Supervisor, Maintenance

***Sault Ste Marie:* Extendicare - Tendercare**
770 Great Northern Rd., Sault Ste Marie, ON P6A 5K7
705-949-3611 Fax: 705-945-6303
cnh_tendercare@extendicare.com
Number of Beds: 120 beds
Janice Dupuis, Administrator

***Sault Ste Marie:* Extendicare - Van Daele**
39 Van Daele St., Sault Ste Marie, ON P6B 4V3
705-949-7934 Fax: 705-945-0968
cnh_vandaele@extendicare.com
Number of Beds: 150 beds
Janice Hodgson, Administrator

***Sault Ste Marie:* F.J. Davey Home**
860 Great Northern Rd., Sault Ste Marie, ON P6A 5K7
705-942-2204 Fax: 705-942-2234
Number of Beds: 184 beds
Peter J. MacLean, Administrator

***Sault Ste Marie:* Mauno Kaihla Koti**
723 North St., Sault Ste Marie, ON P6B 6G8
705-945-9987 Fax: 705-945-1217
Number of Beds: 60 beds
Lewis Massad, Executive Director

***Scarborough:* Kennedy Lodge Nursing Home**
1400 Kennedy Rd., Scarborough, ON M1P 4V6
416-752-8282 Fax: 416-752-0645
kennedylodge@reveraliving.com
Number of Beds: 289 beds
Note: long term care facility
Donna Michaels, Administrator

***Schumacher:* Extendicare - Timmins**
PO Box 817, 15 Hollinger Lane, Schumacher, ON P0N 1G0
705-360-1913 Fax: 705-268-3975
cnh_timmins@extendicare.com
Parent: North East Local Health Integration Network
Number of Beds: 121 beds
Claude Roy, Administrator

***Selby:* Village Green Long Term Care Facility**
PO Box 94, Selby, ON K0K 2Z0
613-388-2693 Fax: 613-388-2694
Number of Beds: 66 beds
Linda Pierce, Administrator

***Simcoe:* Cedarwood Village**
500 Queensway West, Simcoe, ON N3Y 4R4
519-426-8305 Fax: 519-426-2511
cedarwood@kwic.com
Number of Beds: 91 beds
Tanna Day, Administrator

***Simcoe:* Norfolk Hospital Nursing Home/NHNH**
365 West St., Simcoe, ON N3Y 1T7
519-426-0130 Fax: 519-429-6988
residents@ngh.on.ca (Residents' e-mail)
www.ngh.on.ca
Year Founded: 1975
Number of Beds: 80 beds
Note: Specialties: Long-term nursing care; Activation program; Wound care; Physiotherapy; Occupational therapy; Speech Therapy; Restorative care; Pet therapy; Social work; Psychogeriatics; Palliative care
William C. Lewis, Executive Director
J.J. Knott, Director, Physical Plant

***Sioux Lookout:* William A. (Bill) George Extended Care Facility**
75 Fifth Ave., Sioux Lookout, ON P8T 1K9
807-737-1364 Fax: 807-737-2449
Number of Beds: 20 beds
Debra Harris, Executive Director
Ed Patterson, Environmental Services

***Smiths Falls:* Broadview Nursing Centre**
210 Brockville St., Smiths Falls, ON K7A 3Z4
613-283-1845 Fax: 613-283-7073
bnc@on.aibn.com
Number of Beds: 75 beds
Sandra Sheridan, Director of Care

***St Catharines:* Extendicare - St. Catharines**
283 Pelham Rd., St Catharines, ON L2S 1X7
905-688-3311 Fax: 905-688-5774
cnh_stcatharines@extendicare.com
Number of Beds: 152 beds
Jane Freeman, Acting Administrator

***St Catharines:* Heidehof Home for the Aged**
600 Lake St., St Catharines, ON L2N 4J4
905-935-3344 Fax: 905-935-0081 www.heidehof.com
Number of Beds: 106 beds
Elena Caddis, Administrator
ecaddis@heidehof.com
Erika Ledwez, Manager, Resident & Community Relations
eledwez@heidehof.com

***St Catharines:* Tabor Manor**
1 Tabor Dr., St Catharines, ON L2N 1V9
905-934-2548
office@tabormanor.net
www.tabormanor.net/site
Number of Beds: 82 residential capacity
Note: Specialties: Accommodation & nursing care to senior citizens, especially those of the Mennonite constituency in Niagara; Activity program; Foot care
Ben Wohlgemut, Administrator
Tony Carrière, Director, Physical Plant

***St Catharines:* West Park Health Centre**
103 Pelham Rd., St Catharines, ON L2S 1S9
905-688-1031 Fax: 905-688-9646
Number of Beds: 93 beds
Natalie Foster, Administrator

***St Jacobs:* Derbecker's Heritage House Ltd.**
54 Eby St., St Jacobs, ON N0B 2N0
519-664-2921 Fax: 519-664-2380
Number of Beds: 72 beds
Pamela Derbecker, Administrator

***Stoney Creek:* Pine Villa Nursing Home**
490 Hwy. #8, Stoney Creek, ON L8G 1G6
905-662-5033
info.pinevilla@thomashealthcare.com
www.thomashealthcare.com
Year Founded: 1967
Number of Beds: 38 beds
Note: Specialties: Nursing care; Enhanced restorative care program; Physiotherapy; Foot care; Massage therapy; Activity program
Conrad Thomas, Administrator

***Stouffville:* Green Gables Manor Inc.**
9th Line Rd., RR#2, Stouffville, ON L4A 7X3
905-640-1310 Fax: 905-640-2231
Number of Beds: 69 beds
Gerald Harquail, President

***Stouffville:* Parkview Home for the Aged**
123 Weldon Rd., Stouffville, ON L4A 0G8
905-640-1911 Fax: 905-640-4051
admin@parkviewhome.ca
www.parkviewhome.ca
Number of Beds: 109 beds
Note: Long-term care facility
Wallace Kribs, Home Administrator
Michael MacDonald, Director, Environmental Services

***Stratford:* Hillside Manor**
5066 Perth East Line 34, RR#5, Stratford, ON N5A 6S6
519-393-5132 Fax: 519-393-5130
hillsidemanor@reveraliving.com
www.reveraliving.com/homes/19/
Number of Beds: 90 beds
Sylvie Ledermueller, Administrator
Mary Anne Weller, Director of Care

***Stratford:* PeopleCare Stratford**
198 Mornington St., Stratford, ON N5A 5G3
519-271-4440 Fax: 519-271-4446 www.peoplecare.ca
Year Founded: 1980
Number of Beds: 60 residents
Note: Specialties: Long-term care; Activity program; Restorative care
Patricia Kelly, Administrator

***Stratford:* Spruce Lodge Senior Citizens Residence**
643 West Gore St., Stratford, ON N5A 1L4
519-271-4090 Fax: 519-271-5862
Number of Beds: 128 beds
Peter L. Bolland, Administrator

***Strathroy:* Strathmere Lodge**
PO Box 5000, 599 Albert St., Strathroy, ON N7G 3J3
519-245-2520 Fax: 519-245-5711
www.county.middlesex.on.ca/strathmerelodge
Year Founded: 1880
Note: Specialties: Special care area for Alzheimer residents; Respite care & short stays
Larry Hills, Administrator
Terry Meservia, Supervisor, Maintenance

***Sturgeon Falls:* Au Château Home for the Aged**
100 Michaud St., PO Bag 110, Sturgeon Falls, ON P2B 2Z4
705-753-1550 Fax: 705-753-3135
Number of Beds: 162 beds
Wayne M. Foisey, Administrator
Simone Brazeau, Coordinator, Environmental Services

***Sudbury:* Extendicare - Falconbridge**
281 Falconbridge Rd., Sudbury, ON P3A 5K4
705-566-7980 Fax: 705-566-2997
cnh_falconbridge@extendicare.com
www.extendicarecanada.com/sudburyfalconbridge/
Number of Beds: 234 beds
James Foreman, Administrator
J. Kovacs, Director, Physical Plant

***Sudbury:* Extendicare - York**
333 York St., Sudbury, ON P3E 5J3
705-674-4221 Fax: 705-674-4281
cnh_york@extendicare.com
Number of Beds: 288 beds
Nancy Foreman, Administrator

***Tavistock:* Bonnie Brae Health Care Centre**
PO Box 489, 55 Woodstock St. North, Tavistock, ON N0B 2R0
519-655-2420 Fax: 519-655-3432
bonniebrae@reveraliving.com
www.reveraliving.com/homes/51
Number of Beds: 80 beds
Joyce Penney, Administrator
joycepenney@reveraliving.com

***Tecumseh:* Banwell Gardens**
3000 Banwell Rd., Tecumseh, ON N8N 2M4
519-735-3204 Fax: 519-735-1836
vctecumseh@cplreit.com
Number of Beds: 142 beds
Sharell Polk, Administrator
James Ashton, Manager, Environmental Services

***Tecumseh:* Brouillette Manor**
11900 Brouillette Ct., Tecumseh, ON N8N 4X8
519-735-9810 Fax: 519-735-8569
Number of Beds: 60 beds
Nancy Comiskey, Administrator

***Tecumseh:* Extendicare - Tecumseh**
2475 St. Alphonse St., Tecumseh, ON N8N 2X2
519-739-2998
Number of Beds: 128 beds

***Thessalon:* Algoma Manor**
135 Dawson St., Thessalon, ON P0R 1L0
705-842-2840 Fax: 705-842-2650
csmith@adhfa.org
www.adsab.on.ca/algomamanor/index.htm
Number of Beds: 106 beds
Peter MacLean, Administrator
Mark Heller, Coordinator, Environmental Services

***Thornbury:* Errinrung Residence**
PO Box 69, 67 Bruce St., Thornbury, ON N0H 2P0
519-599-2737 Fax: 519-599-3410
Old Name: Errinrung Nursing & Retirement Home
Number of Beds: 74 beds
Note: Total Employees: 38 f-t; 30 p-t
Yvonne Taylor, Director of Retirement Home
Deb Hughson, Director of Care

***Thunder Bay:* Bethammi Nursing Home, St. Joseph's Heritage**
63 Carrie St., Thunder Bay, ON P7A 4J2
807-768-4400 Fax: 807-768-8820
Number of Beds: 110 beds
Carl White, President
Victor Carlson, Director, Environmental Services

***Thunder Bay:* Dawson Court Home for the Aged**
523 North Algoma St., Thunder Bay, ON P7A 5C2
807-684-2926 Fax: 807-345-8854
Number of Beds: 150 beds
Michael Kennedy, Administrator
mkennedy@thunderbay.ca

***Thunder Bay:* Grandview Lodge/Thunder Bay**
200 Lillie St. North, Thunder Bay, ON P7C 5Y2
807-625-2923 Fax: 807-623-4075
Number of Beds: 150 beds
Wendy Kirkpatrick

***Thunder Bay:* Pioneer Ridge**
750 Tungsten St., Thunder Bay, ON P7B 6R1
807-684-3910 Fax: 807-684-3916 www.thunderbay.ca
Number of Beds: 150 beds
Note: Specialties: Long-term nursing care for older persons; Restorative care; Rehabilitation; Units for persons with cognitive challenges, Alzheimer's disease, & other dementias; Secure therapeutic parks; Life enrichment program
Joyce Greene, Administrator

***Tillsonburg:* Maple Manor Nursing Home**
73 Bidwell St., Tillsonburg, ON N4G 3T8
519-842-3563 Fax: 519-842-3038
Number of Beds: 102 beds
George Kaniuk, Administrator

***Timmins:* Golden Manor Home for the Aged**
481 Melrose Blvd., Timmins, ON P4N 5H3
705-360-2664 Fax: 705-360-2683
golden_manor@timmins.ca
Number of Beds: 174 beds
Heather Bozzer, Administrator
Claude Bruneau, Supervisor, Maintenance

***Toronto:* Apotex Centre - Jewish Home for the Aged**
3560 Bathurst St., Toronto, ON M6A 2E1
416-785-2500 Fax: 416-785-2464
Number of Beds: 372 beds

***Toronto:* Barton Place Long Term Care Facility**
914 Bathurst St., Toronto, ON M5R 3G5
416-533-9473 Fax: 416-538-2685 www.bartonplace.ca
Number of Beds: 130 beds
Réjane Jones, Administrator

***Toronto:* Bendale Acres**
2920 Lawrence Ave. East, Toronto, ON M1P 2T8
416-397-7000 Fax: 416-397-7067
Number of Beds: 302 beds
Margaret Aerola, Administrator
Richard Doberstein, Supervisor, Maintenance
Russ Persons, Manager, Building Services

***Toronto:* Casa Verde Health Centre**
3595 Keele St., Toronto, ON M3J 1M7
416-633-3431 Fax: 416-633-6736
Number of Beds: 252 beds
Haren Kapadia, Administrator

***Toronto:* Castleview Wychwood Towers**
351 Christie St., Toronto, ON M6G 3C3
416-392-5700 Fax: 416-392-4157
Number of Beds: 490 beds
Vija Mallia, Administrator
Steven Hughes, Manager, Building Services

***Toronto:* Cheltenham Nursing Home**
5935 Bathurst St., Toronto, ON M2R 1Y8
416-223-4050 Fax: 416-223-4159
Number of Beds: 170 beds
Marlene Van Ham, Administrator

***Toronto:* Christie Gardens**
600 Melita Cres., Toronto, ON M6G 3Z4
416-530-1330 Fax: 416-530-1686
cbelmore@christiegardens.org
www.christiegardens.org
Number of Beds: 88 beds
Catherine Belmore, Administrator

***Toronto:* Craiglee Nursing Home**
102 Craiglee Dr., Toronto, ON M1N 2M7
416-264-2260
Number of Beds: 94 beds
Doris McDougall, Administrator

***Toronto:* Cummer Lodge Home for the Aged**
205 Cummer Ave., Toronto, ON M2M 2E8
416-392-9500 Fax: 416-392-9499
Number of Beds: 391 beds
Leah Walters, Administrator
George Abiad, Manager, Building Services

***Toronto:* Drs. Paul & John Rekai Centre**
345 Sherbourne St., Toronto, ON M5A 2S3
416-964-1599 Fax: 416-969-3907
Also Known As: Rekai Centre
Number of Beds: 129 beds
Linda Joyal, Director of Resident Programs

***Toronto:* Ehatare Nursing Home**
40 Old Kingston Rd., Toronto, ON M1E 3J5
416-284-0828 Fax: 416-284-5595
ehatare@on.aibn.com
Number of Beds: 32 beds
Ruth McFarlane, Administrator
Enno Pflug, Director, Physical Plant

***Toronto:* Extendicare - Bayview**
550 Cummer Ave., Toronto, ON M2K 2M2
416-226-1331 Fax: 416-226-2745
cnh_bayview@extendicare.com
www.extendicarecanada.com/willowdale/
Number of Beds: 203 beds
Susan Schendel, Administrator

***Toronto:* Extendicare - Guildwood**
60 Guildwood Pkwy., Toronto, ON M1E 1N9
416-266-7711 Fax: 416-269-5123
cnh_guildwood@extendicare.com
www.extendicarecanada.com/westhill/
Number of Beds: 169 beds
Dwayne Wyrwas, Administrator

***Toronto:* Extendicare - Rouge Valley**
551 Conlins Rd., Toronto, ON M1B 5S1
416-282-6768 www.extendicare.com
Number of Beds: 192 beds

***Toronto:* Extendicare - Scarborough**
3830 Lawrence Ave. East, Toronto, ON M1G 1R6
416-439-1243 Fax: 416-439-4818 www.extendicare.com
Number of Beds: 155 beds

***Toronto:* Fairview Nursing Home**
14 Cross St., Toronto, ON M6J 1S8
416-534-8829 Fax: 416-538-1658
Number of Beds: 108 beds
Herbert Chambers, Administrator

***Toronto:* Fudger House**
439 Sherbourne St., Toronto, ON M4X 1K6
416-392-5252 Fax: 416-392-4174
Number of Beds: 249 beds
Lorraine Siu, Administrator
Derek Bloomfield, Coordinator, Environmental Services

***Toronto:* Garden Court Nursing Home**
1 Sand Beach Rd., Toronto, ON M8V 2W2
416-259-6172 Fax: 416-259-7925
Number of Beds: 45 beds
Dean Davey, Administrator
P. Collins, Supervisor, Plant Maintenance

***Toronto:* Hellenic Care for Seniors**
33 Winona Dr., Toronto, ON M6G 3Z7
416-654-3904 Fax: 416-654-1080
hcare@hellenichome.org
www.hellenichome.org
Number of Beds: 81 beds
Dorothy Godbold, Administrator

***Toronto:* Heritage Nursing Home**
1195 Queen St. East, Toronto, ON M4M 1L6
416-461-8185 Fax: 416-461-5472
administrator@heritagenursinghome.com
www.heritagenursinghome.com
Number of Beds: 201 beds
Note: Specialties: Long-term nursing care; Supervision & security for residents with Alzheimer's Disease or dementia; Restorative care, including physiotherapy; Activation & recreation program; Chinese programs
Melba Graham, Administrator

***Toronto:* Highbourne Lifecare Centre**
420 The East Mall, Toronto, ON M9B 3Z9
416-621-8000 Fax: 416-621-8003
www.ourhomeyourhome.eycan.com
Number of Beds: 250 beds
Evelyn McDonald, Administrator

***Toronto:* Ivan Franko Ukrainian Home (Etobicoke)**
767 Royal York Rd., Toronto, ON M8Y 2T3
416-239-7364
Number of Beds: 85 beds
Maria Kiebalo, Administrator

***Toronto:* Kipling Acres**
2233 Kipling Ave., Toronto, ON M9W 4L3
416-392-2300 Fax: 416-392-3360
Year Founded: 1959
Number of Beds: 337 beds
Lianne Neumann, Administrator
lneumann@toronto.ca

***Toronto:* Lakeshore Lodge**
3197 Lakeshore Blvd. West, Toronto, ON M8V 3X5
416-392-9400 Fax: 416-392-9401
hfa-ll@toronto.ca
www.toronto.ca/homesfortheaged/lakeshore.htm
Number of Beds: 150 beds
Robert Price, Administrator

***Toronto:* Leisureworld Caregiving Centre - Ellesmere**
1000 Ellesmere Rd., Toronto, ON M1P 5G2
416-291-0222
adm.ellesmere@leisureworld.ca
www.leisureworld.ca/ellesmere.html
Number of Beds: 224 beds
Michael Aikins, Administrator

***Toronto:* Leisureworld Caregiving Centre - Etobicoke**
70 Humberline Dr., Toronto, ON M9W 7H3
416-213-7300
lora.palmer@leisureworld.ca
www.leisureworld.ca/etobicoke.html
Number of Beds: 160 beds
Lora Palmer, Administrator
Caterina Ierino, Director of Care

***Toronto:* Leisureworld Caregiving Centre - Lawrence**
2005 Lawrence Ave. West, Toronto, ON M9N 3V4

416-243-8879
adm.lawrence@leisureworld.ca
www.leisureworld.ca/lawrence.html
Year Founded: 2002
Number of Beds: 224 beds; 2 respite
Gary Bowers, Administrator
Amo Nandlall, Director of Care

Toronto: Leisureworld Caregiving Centre - Norfinch
22 Norfinch Dr., Toronto, ON M3N 1X1
416-623-1120 Fax: 416-623-1121
anne.deelstramcnara@leisureworld.ca
www.leisureworld.ca/norfinch.html
Year Founded: 2003
Number of Beds: 160 beds
Anne Deelstra McNamara, Administrator
Jane Pristach, Director of Nursing

Toronto: Leisureworld Caregiving Centre - O'Connor
1800 O'Connor Dr., Toronto, ON M4A 1W7
416-285-2000
jeanette.sanichar@leisureworld.ca
www.leisureworld.ca/oc_gate.html
Year Founded: 2001
Number of Beds: 318 beds
Jeanette Sanichar, Administrator
Stacey Gamble, Assistant Director of Nursing

Toronto: Leisureworld Caregiving Centre - Rockcliffe
3015 Lawrence Ave. East, Toronto, ON M1P 2V7
416-264-3201 Fax: 416-264-2914
adm.rockcliffe@leisureworld.ca
www.leisureworld.ca/rockcliffe.html
Old Name: Rockcliffe Long Term Care Facility
Year Founded: 1972
Number of Beds: 204 beds
Andrea E. Boswell, Administrator
Nelson Urbe, Maintenance Technician

Toronto: Leisureworld Caregiving Centre - St. George
225 St. George St., Toronto, ON M5R 2M2
416-967-3985 Fax: 416-967-3951
jane.noble@leisureworld.ca
www.leisureworld.ca/stgeorge.html
Number of Beds: 238 beds
Barbara Beecroft, Director of Nursing
Jane Noble, Administrator

Toronto: Leisureworld Caregiving Centre - Scarborough
130 Midland Ave., Toronto, ON M1N 4B2
416-264-2301 Fax: 416-264-3704
terry.teare@leisureworld.ca
www.leisureworld.ca/scarborough.html
Number of Beds: 299 long-term care, 53 retirement beds
Note: Retirement beds in adjoining Midland Gardens
Terry Teare, Administrator
Kathy Metcalfe, Director of Care

Toronto: Lincoln Place Nursing Home
429 Walmer Rd., Toronto, ON M5P 2X9
416-967-6949 Fax: 416-928-1965
Number of Beds: 248 beds
Celeste Blocker, Administrator
Kim Weece, Director, Environmental Services

Toronto: Mon Sheong Home for the Aged
36 D'Arcy St., Toronto, ON M5T 1J7
416-977-3762 Fax: 416-977-3231
msf@monsheong.org
www.monsheong.org
Number of Beds: 105 beds
Ricky Kwan, Administrator
Joseph Wong, Supervisor, Housekeeping/Maintenance

Toronto: North Park Nursing Home
450 Rustic Rd., Toronto, ON M6L 1W9
416-247-0531 Fax: 416-247-6159
northparknursinghome@rogers.com
Number of Beds: 75 beds
Alayne Twaddle, Director, Residential Care

Toronto: Norwood Nursing Home Ltd.
122 Tyndall Ave., Toronto, ON M6K 2E2
416-535-3011
administration@norwoodcare.ca
Year Founded: 1957
Number of Beds: 60 beds
Note: Specialties: Long-term care; Rehabilitative care; Palliative care room
Horst Sebald, Administrator

Toronto: Thompson House
1 Overland Dr., Toronto, ON M3C 2C3
416-447-7244 Fax: 416-447-6364
info@betterlivinghealth.org
www.betterlivinghealth.org
Number of Beds: 136 beds
Note: Specialties: Long-term care; Nursing care; Physiotherapy; Rehabilitative services; Recreation program; Restorative care; Social work; Palliative care
Bernita Borgh, Vice-President, Residential Services

Toronto: True Davidson Acres
200 Dawes Rd., Toronto, ON M4C 5M8
416-397-0400
Year Founded: 1973
Note: Specialties: Nursing care; Rehabilitation; Recreation program; Music & art therapy
Sylvia Moreland, Administrator

Toronto: Ukrainian Canadian Care Centre
60 Richview Rd., Toronto, ON M9A 5E4
416-243-7653 Fax: 416-243-7452 www.stdemetrius.ca
Number of Beds: 152 beds
Note: Specialties: Long-term care; Therapeutic recreation; Social work
Sandy Lomaszewycz, Executive Director
Natalie Popowich, Coordinator, Environmental Services

Toronto: Wesburn Manor
400 The West Mall, Toronto, ON M9C 5S1
416-394-3600 Fax: 416-394-3606
Number of Beds: 192 beds
Elaine Russell, Administrator

Toronto: The Wexford Residence Inc.
1860 Lawrence Ave. East, Toronto, ON M1R 5B1
416-752-8877 Fax: 416-752-8414 1-877-807-0810
information@thewexford.org
www.thewexford.org
Year Founded: 1978
Number of Beds: 166 long-term care residents
Note: Specialties: Long-term care & apartment accommodation for seniors; Secure units for persons with cognitive impairments; Physiotherapy; Podiatry; Life enrichment therapy
Nicholas J. Manherz, Executive Director
Alan Pitts, Coordinator, Environmental Services

Toronto: Yee Hong Centre for Geriatric Care
2311 McNicoll Ave., Toronto, ON M1V 5L3
416-321-6333 Fax: 416-321-6313
centre@yeehong.com
www.yeehong.com
Number of Beds: 250 beds
Florence Wong, CEO

Toronto: Yorkview Lifecare Centre
2045 Finch Ave. West, Toronto, ON M3N 1M9
416-745-0811 Fax: 416-745-0568
Number of Beds: 276 beds
Marce Fulford, Administrator

Trenton: Trent Valley Lodge
195 Bay St., Trenton, ON K8V 1H9
613-392-9235 Fax: 613-392-0688
tvl@bellnet.ca
Year Founded: 1970
Number of Beds: 70 beds
Note: Specialties: Restorative care; Activation services; Long-term stroke care
Bill Weaver, Administrator

Trout Creek: Lady Isabelle Nursing Home
PO Box 10, 102 Corkery St., Trout Creek, ON P0H 2L0
705-723-5232 Fax: 705-723-5794
main@ladyisabelle.ca
www.ladyisabelle.ca
Number of Beds: 66 beds
Sadie Newman, Administrator
George Newman, Manager, Physical Plant/Material Management

Unionville: Bethany Lodge
23 Second St., Unionville, ON L3R 2C2
905-477-3838 Fax: 905-477-2888 www.bethanylodge.org
Number of Beds: 128 beds
Basil Tambakis, Administrator

Vineland: United Mennonite Home/UMH
4024 Twenty-Third St., Vineland, ON L0R 2C0
905-562-7385 Fax: 905-562-3711
thehome@umh.ca
www.umh.ca
Old Name: United Mennonite Home for the Aged
Year Founded: 1955
Number of Beds: 128 beds
Note: Specialties: Activity program; Physiotherapy; Pet therapy
Art Sieb, Administrator

Virgil: Heritage Place
1743 Four Mile Creek Rd., Virgil, ON L0S 1T0
905-468-1111
Number of Beds: 36 beds
Tim Siemens, CEO

Walkerton: Brucelea Haven
PO Box 1600, 41 McGivern St. West, Walkerton, ON N0G 2V0
519-881-1570 Fax: 519-881-0231
bcgil@brucecounty.on.ca
www.brucecounty.on.ca/bruceleahaven.php
Year Founded: 1898
Number of Beds: 144 beds
Elanor McEwen, Administrator
Lesley Borth, Director of Care

Wardsville: Babcock Community Care Centre
196 Wellington St., Wardsville, ON N0L 2N0
519-693-4415 Fax: 519-693-4876
jbabcock@mnsi.net
www.babcockonline.com
Old Name: Babcock Nursing Home
Number of Beds: 60 beds
J.C. Babcock, Administrator/Owner

Warkworth: Community Nursing Home
PO Box 68, 97 Mill St., Warkworth, ON K0K 3K0
705-924-2311 Fax: 705-924-1711
cnhwarakworth@communitylifecare.on.ca
Number of Beds: 60 beds
Myrna Ogden, Administrator
Linda Black, Environmental Contact

Waterdown: Alexander Place
329 Parkside Dr., Waterdown, ON L0K 2H0
905-689-2662
alexanderplace@jarlette.com
www.hamiltonltc.org/facilities/alexander.htm
Number of Beds: 128 beds

Waterloo: Parkwood Mennonite Home Inc.
726 New Hampshire St., Waterloo, ON N2K 4M1
519-885-4810 Fax: 519-885-6720
info@parkwoodmennonitehome.com
www.fairviewmennonitehomes.com/parkwood
Number of Beds: 96 beds
Gloria Dirks, Administrator
John McCutchen, Manager, Environmental Services

Welland: Foyer Richelieu Welland Inc.
655 Tanguay Ave., Welland, ON L3B 6A1
905-734-1400 Fax: 905-734-1386
Number of Beds: 61 beds
André Tremblay, Administrator

Welland: Woodlands of Sunset
920 Pelham St., Welland, ON L3C 1Y5
905-892-3845 Fax: 905-892-5882 www.regional.niagara.on.ca
Parent: Hamilton Niagara Haldimand Brant Local Health Integration Network
Number of Beds: 120 beds
Tom Hunter, Administrator
G. Meek, Manager, Purchasing

Whitby: Fairview Lodge
PO Box 300, 632 Dundas St. West, Whitby, ON L1N 5S3
905-668-5851 Fax: 905-668-8934
Number of Beds: 198 beds
Laura MacDermaid, Administrator

Wiarton: Gateway Haven
PO Box 10, 671 Frank St., Wiarton, ON N0H 2T0
519-534-1113 Fax: 519-534-4733
bcgwh@brucecounty.on.ca
Number of Beds: 100 beds
Bob Moreton, Administrator
Doug Buckland, Environmental Services

Wikwemikong: Wikwemikong Nursing Home
PO Box 114, 2281 Wikwemikong Way, Wikwemikong, ON P0P 2J0
705-859-3107 Fax: 705-859-2245
Number of Beds: 60 beds
Mark Manitowabi, Administrator
David Fox, Manager, Purchasing

Winchester: Dundas Manor Nursing Home
PO Box 970, 533 Clarence St., Winchester, ON K0C 2K0

613-774-2293 Fax: 613-774-4015
dunman@istar.ca
Number of Beds: 98 beds
Note: seniors home
Jill M. Alguire, Administrator
Daniel Dorey, Maintenance Supervisor

Windsor: Chateau Park Nursing Home
2990B Riverside Dr. West, Windsor, ON N9C 1A2
519-254-4341 Fax: 519-254-7931
Number of Beds: 59 beds
Mary Butler, Administrator

Windsor: Extendicare - Southwood Lakes
1255 North Talbot Rd., Windsor, ON N9G 3A4
519-945-7249
cnh_southwoodlakes@extendicare.com
Number of Beds: 150 beds

Windsor: Malden Park Continuing Care Centre
1453 Prince Rd., Windsor, ON N9C 3Z4
519-257-5451 Fax: 519-257-5444
Number of Beds: 145 beds
Note: Long-term Care Facility
Al Grundner, Administrator

Windsor: Villa Maria Home for the Aged
2856 Riverside Dr. West, Windsor, ON N9C 1A2
519-254-3763 Fax: 519-254-7657
Number of Beds: 120 beds
Note: home for the aged
Ken Deane, President/CEO

Woodbridge: Pine Grove Lodge
8403 Islington Ave. West, Woodbridge, ON L4L 1X3
905-850-3605
pinegrovelodge@chartwellreit.ca
www.chartwellreit.ca
Year Founded: 1959
Number of Beds: 40 suites
Note: Specialties; Long-term care; Medication administration; Wellness monitoring; Cultural & activity program, catering to Italian & Canadian cultures; Recreation therapy; Occupational therapy; Physiotherapy; Podiatry; Respite care

Woodslee: Country Village Health Care Centre
County Rd. 8, RR#2, Woodslee, ON N0R 1V0
519-839-4812 Fax: 519-839-4813
Number of Beds: 104 beds
Jane Brooks Keller, Administrator
Doug Ferguson, Manager, Maintenance

Zurich: Blue Water Rest Home
37792 Zurich-Hensall Road, RR 3, Zurich, ON N0M 2T0
519-236-4373 Fax: 519-236-7685
bluewaterhome@hay.net
Number of Beds: 65 beds
Martha Craig, Administrator

Long Term/Retirement Care

Long Term Care Facility

Alliston: Good Samaritan Nursing Home
481 Victoria St. East, Alliston, ON L9R 1J8
705-435-5722 Fax: 705-435-0235
gsnh@csolve.net
Number of Beds: 64 beds
Don Stymeist, Supervisor, Physical Plant
Lynda Weaver, Administrator

Amherstburg: Richmond Terrace
89 Rankin Ave., Amherstburg, ON N9V 1E7
519-736-5571 Fax: 519-736-2995 www.richmondterrace.ca
Number of Beds: 115 beds
Victoria Iler, Administrator
viler@richmondterrace.ca

Ancaster: The Willowgrove Long Term Care Residence
1217 Old Mohawk Rd., Ancaster, ON L9K 1P6
905-304-6781
willowgroveltc@chartwellreit.ca
www.chartwellreit.ca
Parent: Chartwell Seniors Housing REIT
Number of Beds: 168 units
Stephen Suske, CEO, Chartwell Seniors Housing REIT

Athens: Maple View Lodge
PO Box 100, 746 County Rd. 42 E, Athens, ON K0E 1B0
613-924-2696 Fax: 613-924-2123
Number of Beds: 60 beds
Note: home for the aged
Faye Barkley, Acting Administrator

Aurora: Aurora Resthaven
32 Mill St., Aurora, ON L4G 2R9
905-727-1939 Fax: 905-727-6299
auroreresthaven@chartwellreit.ca
www.chartwellreit.ca/home_locations/aurora_rest.htm
Number of Beds: 176 beds
Sheila Hoinkes, Administrator

Aurora: Blue Hills Child & Family Service
402 Bloomington Rd. West, Aurora, ON L4G 3G8
905-773-4323 Fax: 905-773-8133 1-866-536-4323
gendeliv@bluehillschildandfamily.ca
www.bluehillschildandfamily.ca
Number of Beds: 9 beds
Note: children's mental health centre; special care home; outpatient services; family therapy
Sylvia Pivko, Executive Director
spivko@bluehillschildandfamily.ca

Aylmer: Chateau Gardens Aylmer
465 Talbot St. West, Aylmer, ON N5H 1K8
519-773-3423 Fax: 519-765-2573
aylmer@chateaugardens.com
www.chateaugardens.com
Number of Beds: 60 beds
Mary Vergeer, Administrator

Barrie: Heritage Place
20 Brooks St., Barrie, ON L4N 7X2
705-728-2389 Fax: 705-728-6049 www.ioof.com/?page_id=13
Doreen M. Saunders, CEO
dsaunders@ioof.com

Barrie: I.O.O.F. Senior Citizen Homes Inc.
Heritage Place, 10 Brooks St., Barrie, ON L4N 5L3
705-728-2364 Fax: 705-728-6024
Number of Beds: 155 beds long-term care; 80 units supportive housing; 20 uni
Note: long-term care & seniors housing
Doreen M. Saunders, CEO

Barrie: Victoria Village Manor
78 Ross St., Barrie, ON L4N 1G3
705-728-3456 Fax: 705-728-4057 www.victoriavillage.ca
Number of Beds: 128 long-term care beds, 57 life-lease housing units

Beaverton: Lakeview Manor
133 Main St. West, Beaverton, ON L0K 1A0
705-426-7388 Fax: 705-426-4218
pearle.perez@region.durhamon.ca
Number of Beds: 149 beds
Note: home for the aged
Pearle Perez, Administrator
Warren Manning, Manager, Support Services

Belleville: Plainfield Community Homes
9 Millennium Pkwy., Belleville, ON K8N 4Z5
613-969-7407 Fax: 613-969-7775
Number of Beds: 80 beds
Note: community residences for those with developmental disabilites
John B. Klassen, Executive Director

Blind River: Golden Birches Terrace
525 Causley St., Blind River, ON P0R 1B0
705-356-2265 Fax: 705-356-1220
Number of Beds: 42 beds
Gaston Lavigne, CEO

Bracebridge: The Pines
98 Pine St., Bracebridge, ON P1L 1N5
705-645-4488 Fax: 705-645-6857
www.muskoka.on.ca/community/the_pines.htm
Number of Beds: 160 beds
Note: Long term care residence
Janice Fox, Administrator
jfox@muskoka.on.ca

Bradford: Specialty Care Bradford Valley
2656 Line 6, Bradford, ON L3Z 3H5
905-952-2270 Fax: 905-775-0263
olivia.schmitz@specialty-care.com
www.specialty-care.com
Olivia Schmitz, Administrator

Brampton: Leisureworld Caregiving Centre - Tullamore
133 Kennedy Rd. South, Brampton, ON L6W 3G3
905-459-2324
adm.tullamore@leisureworld.ca
www.leisureworld.ca
Year Founded: 1965
Number of Beds: 159 beds
Note: Specialties: Long-term care; Restorative care; Occupational therapy; Physiotherapy; Care for persons with Alzheimer's disease; Respite care; Pet therapy; Palliative care
Wendy Shelley, Administrator

Brampton: Rosedale Retirement Residence
12 William St., Brampton, ON L6V 1L2
905-454-3788 Fax: 905-846-0447
Number of Beds: 12 beds
Rose Hamilton, Administrator

Brampton: Specialty Care Woodhall Park
10260 Kennedy Rd. North, Brampton, ON L6T 3S1
905-495-4695 Fax: 905-495-4693
david.wilson@specialty-care.com
www.specialty-care.com
Number of Beds: 147 beds
David Wilson, Administrator

Brantford: Brantwood Residential Development Centre
25 Bell Lane, Brantford, ON N3T 1E1
519-753-2658 Fax: 519-753-5639
info@brantwood.ca
www.brantwood.ca
Number of Beds: 67 beds
Dianne Belliveau, Executive Director

Brantford: John Noble Home
97 Mount Pleasant St., Brantford, ON N3T 1T5
519-756-2920 Fax: 519-754-1521
jnhuser@on.aibn.com
www.jnh.ca
Number of Beds: 156 beds
Eleanor Maslin, Administrator

Brantford: St. Joseph's Lifecare Centre
99 Wayne Gretzky Pkwy., Brantford, ON N3S 6T6
519-751-7096 Fax: 519-753-7996 www.sjlc.ca
Old Name: St. Joseph's Hospital
Romeo Cercone, Administrator

Brighton: Maplewood
PO Box 249, 12 Maplewood Ave., Brighton, ON K0K 1H0
613-475-2442 Fax: 613-475-4445
Number of Beds: 49 beds
Note: Long-term care residence
Arlene Lawlor, Administrator; Director, Nursing

Burlington: Billings Court Manor
3700 Billings Court, Burlington, ON L7N 3N6
905-333-4006 Fax: 905-333-4416 888-274-6445
Number of Beds: 160 units
Ann Chartier, Administrator

Burlington: Participation House - Hamilton & District
1022 Waterdown Rd., Burlington, ON L7T 1N3
905-527-7949 Fax: 905-333-8711
info@participationhouse.hamilton.on.ca
www.participationhouse.hamilton.on.ca
Number of Beds: 39 beds
Note: Provides services designed to enhance the quality of life of adults with disabilities
Cindy Kinnon, Executive Director

Caledon: Charlestown Residential School
19646 Kennedy Rd., RR#1, Caledon, ON L0N 1C0
519-941-8472 Fax: 519-941-0824
Number of Beds: 20 beds
Note: special care home, group home, treatment centre (behaviour)
Wayne Dunster, Executive Director

Chatham: Copper Terrace Long Term Care Facility
91 Tecumseh Rd., Chatham, ON N7M 1B3
519-354-5442 Fax: 519-354-0362 www.copperterrace.ca
Number of Beds: 151 beds
Kathy Morningstar, Administrator
kmorningstar@ckha.on.ca

Chatham: Meadow Park Care Centre - Chatham
110 Sandys St., Chatham, ON N7L 4X3
519-351-1330 Fax: 519-351-7933 www.jarlette.com
Number of Beds: 97 beds
Anne Marie Rumble, Administrator
amrumble@jarlette.com
Joanne Wytinck, Director of Care
jwytinck@jarlette.com

Chatham: Riverview Gardens
519 King St. West, Chatham, ON N7M 1G8
519-352-4823 Fax: 519-352-2891
CKseniors@chatham-kent.ca
www.chatham-kent.ca

Old Name: Thamesview Lodge
Number of Beds: 320 beds
Colleen Wilson, Director, Senior Services
Donna Cottingham, Manager, Resident Care Services

Chatsworth: Country Lane Long Term Care Centre
RR#3, Chatsworth, ON N0H 1G0
519-794-2244 Fax: 519-794-2597
countrylane@reveraliving.com
www.reveraliving.com
Number of Beds: 34 beds
Lynn Jamieson, Administrator

Chesley: Parkview Manor
98 - 3rd St. SE, Chesley, ON N0G 1L0
519-363-2416 Fax: 519-363-2171
parkviewmanor@reveraliving.com
www.reveraliving.com
Number of Beds: 34 beds
Carole Woods, Administrator

Clarence Creek: Centre d'accueil Roger-Séguin
435 Lemay St., Clarence Creek, ON K0A 1N0
613-488-2053 Fax: 613-488-2274
Number of Beds: 110 beds
Note: charitable
Charles Lefebvre, Administrator

Cobourg: Golden Plough Lodge
983 Burnham St., Cobourg, ON K9A 5J6
905-372-8759 Fax: 905-372-8525
hassanja@county.northumberland.on.ca
Number of Beds: 162 beds
John Hassan, Administrator

Cochrane: Villa Minto
PO Box 280, 241 - 8 St., Cochrane, ON P0L 1C0
705-272-7200 Fax: 705-272-4155
Number of Beds: 33 beds
Note: Villa Minto is an independent LTC facility housed in the chronic care wing of The Lady Minto Hospital
Dan O'Mara, Administrator

Cornwall: Sandfield Place
220 Emma St., Cornwall, ON K6J 5V8
613-933-6972 Fax: 613-938-2261
sandfield@bellnet.ca
www.sandfieldplace.ca
Also Known As: 458422 Ontario Limited
Number of Beds: 53 long term care beds, 34 retirement beds
Note: Long term care & retirement living
Bill Kinnear, Administrator
bill,kinnear@bellnet.ca

Delaware: Middlesex Terrace
2094 Gideon Dr., R.R.#1, Delaware, ON N0L 1E0
519-652-3483 Fax: 519-652-8733 www.middlesexterrace.ca
Number of Beds: 105 beds
Tanya Pol, Administrator
tpol@middlesexterrace.ca

Dundas: St. Joseph's Villa (Dundas)
56 Governor's Rd., Dundas, ON L9H 5G7
905-627-3541 Fax: 905-628-0825
pokrafka@sjv.on.ca
www.sjv.on.ca
Parent: Hamilton Niagara Haldimand Brant Local Health Integration Network
Number of Beds: 378 beds
Paul O'Krafka, Executive Director
Jerry Vajsar, Supervisor, Maintenance

Dundas: Wentworth Lodge
41 South St. West, Dundas, ON L9H 4C4
905-546-2618 Fax: 905-546-2854
saphsweb@hamilton.ca
www.hamilton.ca/phcs/wentworth
Number of Beds: 160 beds
Note: home for the aged
Lynda Secord, Administrator

Dunnville: Grandview Lodge
657 Lock St. West, Dunnville, ON N1A 1V9
905-774-7547 Fax: 905-774-1440
grandview@haldimandcounty.on.ca
www.haldimandcounty.on.ca
Number of Beds: 128 beds
Joanne McGuire, Administrator
Harold Winger, Supervisor, Maintenance

Durham: Rockwood Terrace
PO Box 660, 575 Sadler St. East, Durham, ON N0G 1R0
519-369-6035 Fax: 519-369-6736 www.greycounty.ca
Number of Beds: 100 beds
Note: Long term care
Karen Kraus, Administrator
kkraus@greycounty.ca

Elmira: Chateau Gardens (Elmira) Nursing Home
11 Herbert St., Elmira, ON N3B 2B8
519-669-2921 Fax: 519-669-3027
Number of Beds: 48 beds
Joan Norris, Administrator
Allison Westman, Environmental Services Supervisor

Elmvale: Sara-Vista Long Term Care Facility
27 Simcoe St., Elmvale, ON L0L 1P0
705-322-2182 Fax: 705-322-8326
saravista@reveraliving.com
www.reveraliving.com
Number of Beds: 60 beds
Karen Jones, Administrator

Fort Erie: Gilmore Lodge
50 Gilmore Rd., Fort Erie, ON L2A 2M1
905-871-6160 Fax: 905-871-0435
Number of Beds: 79 beds
Bev Goodman, Administrator

Fort Erie: Maple Park Lodge
6 Hagey Ave., Fort Erie, ON L2A 5M5
905-994-0224 Fax: 905-994-8628
Number of Beds: 96 units
Note: Nursing home

Fort Frances: Rainycrest Home for the Aged
550 Osborne St., Fort Frances, ON P9A 3T2
807-274-9858 Fax: 807-274-7368
Number of Beds: 147 beds
Note: home for the aged
Jill Colquhoun, Administrator
Allan Johnstone, Coordinator, Environmental Services

Glenburnie: Fairmount Home for the Aged
2069 Battersea Rd., RR#1, Glenburnie, ON K0H 1S0
613-546-4264 Fax: 613-546-0489
jshillington@frontenaccounty.ca
www.frontenaccounty.ca/?q=fairmount_home
Number of Beds: 128 beds
Note: home for the aged
Julie Shillington, Administrator

Gore Bay: Manitoulin Lodge
3 Main St., Gore Bay, ON P0P 1H0
705-282-2007 Fax: 705-282-3422 www.jarlette.com
Number of Beds: 61 beds
Lorna Fogg, Administrator
lfogg@jarlette.com

Grimsby: Deer Park Villa
150 Central Ave., Grimsby, ON L3M 4Z3
905-945-4164 Fax: 905-945-1239 877-945-4764
kim.eros@regional.niagara.on.ca
Number of Beds: 39 beds
Kim Eros, Administrator/Director of Resident Care
kim.eros@regional.niagara.on.ca

Guelph: The Elliott Community
170 Metcalfe St., Guelph, ON N1E 4Y3
519-822-0491 Fax: 519-822-5658
info@elliottcommunity.org
www.elliottcommunity.org
Number of Beds: 270 beds
Note: Retirement suites & long term care
Trevor Lee, CEO

Haileybury: Temiskaming Lodge
100 Bruce St., Haileybury, ON P0J 1K0
705-672-2123 Fax: 705-672-5734 www.jarlette.com
Number of Beds: 82 beds
Francine Gosselin, Administrator
fgosselin@jarlette.com

Hamilton: Grace Villa Hamilton
45 Lockton Cres., Hamilton, ON L8V 4V5
905-387-4812 Fax: 905-387-4814
jzomer@gracevilla.ca
www.gracevilla.ca
Number of Beds: 184 beds
JoAnn Zomer, Administrator
jzomer@gracevilla.ca

Hamilton: Idlewyld Manor
449 Sanatorium Rd., Hamilton, ON L9C 2A7
905-574-2000 Fax: 905-574-0482
office@idlewyldmanor.com
www.idlewyldmanor.com
Number of Beds: 101 beds
Robert J. Malloy, Executive Director

Hamilton: St. Elizabeth Villa
391 Rymal Rd. West, Hamilton, ON L9B 1V2
905-388-9691 Fax: 905-388-9953
stelizabeth.villa@bellnet.ca
www.stelizabethhomesociety.org
Note: assisted living
Maria Szucs, Administrator

Hamilton: St. Peter's Residence at Chedoke
125 Redfern Ave., Hamilton, ON L9C 7W9
905-777-3837 Fax: 905-383-1099
residence@stpetes.ca
www.stpetes.ca
Number of Beds: 210 beds
Donna Cripps, President/CEO

Hamilton: Shalom Village
70 Macklin St. North, Hamilton, ON L8S 3S1
905-529-1613 Fax: 905-529-7542
info@shalomvillage.on.ca
www.shalomvillage.on.ca
Number of Beds: 60 beds
Note: Long term care & assisted living, day program; kosher meals provided; Jewish & ecumenical services. Shalom Village Too with 64 beds & 30 apartments is located adjacent
Patricia Morden, Chief Executive Coach

Hamilton: Townsview Lifecare Centre
39 Mary St., Hamilton, ON L8R 3L8
905-523-6427 Fax: 905-528-0610
eyi_townsview_complex@extendicare.com
www.hamiltonltc.org
Number of Beds: 219 beds
Andrew Adamyk, Administrator
aadamyk@extendicare.com

Hamilton: The Wellington
1430 Upper Wellington St., Hamilton, ON L9A 5H3
905-385-2111 Fax: 905-385-2110 www.thewellington.ca
Number of Beds: 102 long term care beds, 80 retirement beds
Note: Long term care & retirement community
Tanya Macdonald, Administrator
Doretta Skidmore, Contact, Residence Information
dskidmore@thewellington.ca

Huntsville: Muskoka Landing
65 Rogers Cove Dr., Huntsville, ON P1H 2L9
705-788-7713 Fax: 705-788-1424 www.jarlette.com
Number of Beds: 94 long-term care beds
Bill Thurlow, Administrator
bthurlow@jarlette.com

Jacksons Point: Cedar Lane Lodge
895 Lake Dr. East, Jacksons Point, ON L0E 1L0
905-722-8928
Number of Beds: 17 beds
Note: supported independant living
Jeff Smith, Administrator

Jasper: Rosebridge Manor
131 Roses Bridge Rd., RR#2, Jasper, ON K0G 1G0
613-283-5471 Fax: 613-283-9012 www.omniway.com
Number of Beds: 78 beds
Dorothy Broeders-Morin, Administrator
dmorin@omniway.ca
Gary Foster, Director, Housekeeping/Physical Plant

Kincardine: Trillium Court Seniors Community
550 Phillip Pl., Kincardine, ON N2Z 3A6
519-396-4400 Fax: 519-366-9092
trillium@reveraliving.com
www.reveraliving.com
Number of Beds: 40 beds + 60 retirement suites
Note: Independent & assisted living, retirement lodge, long-term care, respite & convalescent options
Pam Campbell, Administrator
M. Furnvale, Supervisor, Environmental Services

Kingston: Providence Care - St. Mary's of the Lake Hospital Site
340 Union St., Kingston, ON K7L 5A2
613-544-5220 Fax: 613-544-8558
bonuttim@providencecare.ca
www.pccchealth.org
Number of Beds: 144 beds
Note: Acute care, complex continuing care, geriatric medicine, rehabilitation, palliative care, respite care
Michele Bonutti, Site Administrator/CFO

Kingston: Providence Manor
275 Sydenham St., Kingston, ON K7K 1G7

613-549-4164 Fax: 613-549-7472
nowlans@providencecare.ca
www.pccchealth.org

Number of Beds: 243 beds
Note: Long-term care
Shelagh Nowlan, Site Administrator

Kingston: Specialty Care Trillium Centre
800 Edgar St., Kingston, ON K7M 8S4
613-547-0040 Fax: 613-547-3734
jennifer.powley@specialty-care.com
www.specialty-care.com

Number of Beds: 234 units
Note: Comprehensive long-term care services. Trillium Ridge Retirement Community located adjacent
Jennifer Powley, Administrator

Kitchener: Lanark Heights Long-Term Care
46 Lanark Cres., Kitchener, ON N2N 2Z8
519-743-4200 Fax: 519-743-4225
info@lanarkcare.com
www.lanarkcare.com

Number of Beds: 107 units

Kitchener: Sunnyside Home
247 Franklin St. North, Kitchener, ON N2A 1Y5
519-893-8482 Fax: 519-893-4450 www.region.waterloo.on.ca
Number of Beds: 251 residential capacity
Note: Specialty: Long-term care
Gail Carlin, Administrator
Wendy Reid, Chair, Health & Safety Committee
Reg Weber, Supervisor, Maintenance

Kitchener: The Westmount Long Term Care Residence
200 David Bergey Dr., Kitchener, ON N2E 3Y4
519-570-2115 Fax: 519-579-9770
westmountltc@chartwellreit.ca
www.chartwellreit.ca

Parent: Chartwell Seniors Housing REIT
Number of Beds: 160 units
Stephen Suske, CEO, Chartwell Seniors Housing REIT

Komoka: Country Terrace Long Term Care Home
10072 Oxbow Dr., RR#3, Komoka, ON N0L 1R0
519-657-2955 Fax: 519-657-8516
mraithby@countryterrace.ca
www.countryterrace.ca

Old Name: Country Terrace Nursing Home
Parent: South West Local Health Integration Network
Number of Beds: 120 beds
Mary Raithby, Executive Director

L'Orignal: Résidence Champlain
428 Front Rd. West, L'Orignal, ON K0B 1K0
613-675-4617
champlain@chartwellreit.ca
www.chartwellreit.ca

Parent: Chartwell Seniors Housing REIT
Number of Beds: 60 beds
Stephen Suske, CEO, Chartwell Seniors Housing REIT

Lancaster: Chateau Gardens (Lancaster)
PO Box 429, 105 Military Rd. North, Lancaster, ON K0C 1N0
613-347-3016 Fax: 613-347-1680

Number of Beds: 60 beds
Ron Gingrich, Administrator

Limoges: Résidence Limoges
131-133 Ottawa St., Limoges, ON K0A 2M0
613-443-5303 Fax: 613-443-1943

Number of Beds: 25 lits
François Grégoire, Administrateur

Limoges: St. Viateur Nursing Home
1003 Limoges Rd. South, Limoges, ON K0A 2M0
613-443-5751 Fax: 613-443-5950

Number of Beds: 64 beds
Richard R. Marleau, Administrator

Lindsay: Chimo Youth & Family Services, Inc.
#3, 2 Kent St. West, Lindsay, ON K9V 2Y1
705-324-3300 Fax: 705-324-3304

Number of Beds: 16 beds
Note: children's residential mental health residence
Margaret Rose Jackson, Executive Director

Lindsay: Frost Manor
225 Mary St. West, Lindsay, ON K9V 5K3
705-324-8333 Fax: 705-878-5840 www.omni-way.com
Number of Beds: 62 beds
Linda Burr, Administrator

London: Anago Resources Inc.
371 Princess Ave., London, ON N6B 2A7
519-435-1099 Fax: 519-435-0062
info@anago.on.ca
www.anago.on.ca

Number of Beds: 63 beds
Note: young offenders; developmental handicap group home; child & family intervention treatment
Mandy L. Bennett, Executive Director

London: Chateau Gardens London
2000 Blackwater Rd., London, ON N5X 4K6
519-434-2727

Number of Beds: 95 beds

London: Chelsey Park Retirement Community
310 Oxford St. West, London, ON N6H 4N6
519-432-1855 www.chelseypark.com
Number of Beds: 247 beds

London: Dearness Services
710 Southdale Rd., London, ON N6E 1R8
519-661-0400 Fax: 519-661-0446
Number of Beds: 348 beds
L. Hignett, Administrator

London: Longworth Long Term Care
590 Longworth Rd., London, ON N6K 4X9
519-472-6424 Fax: 519-472-8852
info@longworthcare.com
www.longworthcare.com

Number of Beds: 160 beds
Note: Specialties: Long term care; Restorative care program; Massage therapy; Physiotherapy; Family & personal counseling services

London: Meadow Park Care Centre & Retirement Lodge - London
1210 Southdale Rd. East, London, ON N6E 1B4
519-686-0484 Fax: 519-686-9932 www.jarlette.com
Note: Long term care facility & retirement lodge
Terri Daly, Administrator, Care Centre
tdaly@jarlette.com
Michelle Gatt, General Manager, Retirement Lodge
mgatt@jarlette.com

London: St. Joseph's Health Care, London Mount Hope Centre for Long Term Care
21 Grosvenor St., London, ON N6A 1Y1
519-646-6000 Fax: 519-646-6054
Communications.Department@sjhc.london.on.ca
www.sjhc.london.on.ca

Number of Beds: 390 beds
Jane Boudreau-Bailey, Director

Markham: The Woodhaven Long Term Care Residence
380 Church St., Markham, ON L6B 1E1
905-472-3320
woodhavenltc@chartwellreit.ca
www.chartwellreit.ca

Parent: Chartwell Seniors Housing REIT
Number of Beds: 192 units
Stephen Suske, CEO, Chartwell Seniors Housing REIT

Maxville: Maxville Manor
80 Mechanic St. West, Maxville, ON K0C 1T0
613-527-2170 Fax: 613-527-3103 www.maxvillemanor.ca
Year Founded: 1968
Number of Beds: 120 beds + 2 respite beds
Note: Specialties: Long-term care services; Therapy services; The Seniors' Centre, providing outreach services to persons in the community with physical disabilities & special needs; Adult day program; Seniors' clinics, such as hearing, optometry, & foot care. Number of Employees: 130
R.E.C. Munro, Executive Director
Sally Bennett, Director, Nursing
Neil McCormick, Director, Environmental Services

Midland: Hillcrest Village Care Centre
255 Russell St., Midland, ON L4R 5L6
705-526-3781 Fax: 705-526-5656
information@hvcc.ca
www.hvcc.ca

Old Name: St. Andrew's Centennial Manor
Number of Beds: 100 beds
Walter Ens, Administrator

Milton: Allendale
185 Ontario St. South, Milton, ON L9T 2M4
905-878-4141 Fax: 905-878-8797 866-442-5866
johnstoi@halton.ca
www.halton.ca/scs/seniors/ltc/allendale.htm
Number of Beds: 300 beds
Ingrid Johnston, Administrator

Milton: Mount Nemo Christian Nursing Home
4486 Guelph Line, RR#2, Milton, ON L9T 2X6
905-335-3636 Fax: 905-335-3699
mountnemonursinghome@cogeco.net
www.mountnemochristiannh.on.ca

Number of Beds: 60 beds
Note: long term care home
Lynette Royeppen, Administrator

Mississauga: Cawthra Gardens
590 Lolita Gardens, Mississauga, ON L5A 4N8
905-306-9984

Number of Beds: 192 beds

Mississauga: Chelsey Park Mississauga Long-Term Care Facility
2250 Hurontario St., Mississauga, ON L5B 1M8
905-270-0411

Number of Beds: 237 beds

Mississauga: Chelsey Park Streetsville Long-Term Care Facility
1742 Bristol Rd. West, Mississauga, ON L5M 1X9
905-826-3045

Mississauga: Heritage House Retirement Home
73 King St. West, Mississauga, ON L5B 1H1
905-279-4800 Fax: 905-615-8141
theheritagehouse@rogers.com
www.heritagehouseonline.com

Note: Specialties: Physiotherapy; Occupational therapy; Specialized rehabilitative care; Recovery from surgery; Cardiac care program; Orthopedic care; Acitvity program; Respite or short stays
Janice MacInnis, Administrator
Angus MacInnis, Administrator

Mississauga: Specialty Care Mississauga Road
4350 Mississauga Rd., Mississauga, ON L5M 7C8
905-812-1175 Fax: 905-812-1173
gayle.stuart@specialty-care.com
www.specialty-care.com

Number of Beds: 160 beds
Gayle Stuart, Administrator

Mississauga: Villa Forum
175 Forum Dr., Mississauga, ON L4Z 4E5
905-501-1443 Fax: 905-501-0094
Number of Beds: 160 units
Note: Long-term care facility

Mississauga: The Wenleigh Long Term Care Residence
2065 Leanne Blvd., Mississauga, ON L5K 2L6
905-822-4663
wenleighltc@chartwellreit.ca
www.chartwellreit.ca

Parent: Chartwell Seniors Housing REIT
Number of Beds: 161 units
Stephen Suske, CEO, Chartwell Seniors Housing REIT

Mitchell: Ritz Lutheran Villa
Rd. 164 - 4118A, RR#5, Mitchell, ON N0K 1N0
519-348-8612 Fax: 519-348-4420
info@ritzlutheranvilla.com
www.ritzlutheranvilla.com

Number of Beds: 83 beds
Note: charitable home for the aged, retirement community with rental apartments & life lease town homes
Brent E. Nafziger, Administrator
Randy Satchell, Building Services Supervisor

Napanee: The John M. Parrott Centre
309 Bridge St. West, Napanee, ON K7R 2G4
613-354-3306 Fax: 613-354-7387
bsmith@lennox-addington.on.ca
www.lennox-addington.on.ca

Old Name: Lenadco Home
Number of Beds: 168 beds
Note: Long term care
Brian Smith, Director

Nepean: Carleton Lodge
55 Lodge Rd., Nepean, ON K2C 3H1
613-825-3763 Fax: 613-825-0245
hanora.mcgrath@ottawa.ca

Number of Beds: 160 beds
Hanora McGrath, Administrator

Newmarket: Southlake Residential Care Village
640 Grace St., Newmarket, ON L3Y 2L1

905-895-7661 Fax: 905-895-9806
www.southlakeregional.org/southlakeresidentialcarevillage.html
Year Founded: 2004
Number of Beds: 192 beds
Note: Number of staff: 200
Terry Collins, Executive Director
tcollins@extendicare.com

Niagara Falls: Bella Senior Care Residence
8720 Willoughby Dr., Niagara Falls, ON L2G 7X3
905-295-2727
info@bellaseniorcare.com
www.bellaseniorcare.com
Number of Beds: 160 units

Niagara on the Lake: Chateau Gardens - Niagara
PO Box 985, 120 Wellington St., Niagara on the Lake, ON L0S 1J0
905-468-2111 Fax: 905-468-4463
niagara@chateaugardens.com
www.chateaugardens.com
Number of Beds: 124 beds
Susan Norton, Administrator

Niagara on the Lake: Upper Canada Lodge
272 Wellington St., Niagara on the Lake, ON L0S 1J0
905-468-4208 Fax: 905-468-0520
uppercanada@niagararegion.ca
Year Founded: 1988
Number of Beds: 80 beds
Colleen Johnson, Administrator
Dave Shedden, Supervisor, Maintenance

North Bay: Cassellholme
400 Olive St., North Bay, ON P1B 6J4
705-474-4250 Fax: 705-474-6129
bethcamph@on.aibn.com
www.cassellholme.on.ca
Number of Beds: 240 beds
Note: home for the aged
Beth Campbell, Administrator

Oakville: The Waterford Long Term Care Residence
2140 Baronwood Dr., Oakville, ON L6M 4V6
Parent: Chartwell Seniors Housing REIT
Year Founded: 2003
Number of Beds: 168 units
Stephen Suske, CEO, Chartwell Seniors Housing REIT

Oakville: Wyndham Manor
291 Reynolds St., Oakville, ON L6J 3L5
905-849-7766
Number of Beds: 128 beds

Orillia: The Leacock Care Centre
25 Museum Dr., Orillia, ON L3V 7T9
705-325-9181 Fax: 705-325-5179 www.jarlette.com
Number of Beds: 145 long-term care beds
Marilyn Hauser, Administrator
mhauser@jarlette.com

Orleans: Kingsway Arms at St. Joseph Manor
1510 St. Joseph Blvd., Orleans, ON K1C 7L1
613-830-4000 Fax: 613-830-7607
manoirstjoseph@on.aibn.com
www.kingswayarms.com/stjoseph.php
Number of Beds: 80 beds
Jeannine Zacconi, Director of Care

Orleans: Madonna Long Term Care Facility
1541 St. Joseph Blvd., Orleans, ON K1C 1S9
613-824-2040
sallibhai@chartwellreit.ca
www.chartwellreit.ca
Note: Specialties: Restorative care; Palliative care

Orleans: Résidence Saint-Louis
879, ch Hiawatha Park, Orleans, ON K1C 2Z6
613-824-1720 Fax: 613-824-8064
rslinfo@scohs.on.ca
www.scohs.on.ca
Number of Beds: 198 lits
Note: Établissement francophone de soins de longue durée
Jean Bartkowiak, President-directeur général, Service de santé SCO Health Service

Oshawa: Hillsdale Estates
590 Oshawa Blvd. North, Oshawa, ON L1G 5T9
905-579-1777 Fax: 905-579-3911
Year Founded: 2003
Number of Beds: 435 beds
Len Cserhati, Administrator
Linda Doherty, Director, Resident Care

Oshawa: Thorntonview
186 Thornton Rd. South, Oshawa, ON L1J 5Y2
905-576-5181 Fax: 905-576-0078
thorntonview@reveraliving.com
www.reveraliving.com
Number of Beds: 154 beds
Note: Long-term care, palliative care, services for physically challenged adults
Arlene Inkster, Administrator

Oshawa: The Wynfield Long Term Care Residence
451 Woodmount Dr., Oshawa, ON L1G 8E3
905-571-0065 Fax: 905-579-4902
wynfieldltc@chartwellreit.ca
www.chartwellreit.ca
Number of Beds: 172 beds
Katherine Jackson, Administrator
Stephen Suske, CEO, Chartwell Seniors Housing REIT

Ottawa: Carlingview Manor
2330 Carling Ave., Ottawa, ON K2B 7H1
613-820-9328 Fax: 613-820-9774
carlingviewmanor@cplodges.com
Number of Beds: 320 beds
Lori Norris, Administrator

Ottawa: Hillel Lodge
10 Nadolny Sachs Private, Ottawa, ON K2A 4G7
613-728-3900 Fax: 613-728-6550
Also Known As: The Bess & Moe Greenberg Family Hillel Lodge
Number of Beds: 100 beds
Stephen Schneiderman, Executive Director

Ottawa: Hillel Lodge (The Bess & Moe Greenberg Family)
10 Nadolny Sachs Pvt., Ottawa, ON K2A 4G7
613-728-3900 Fax: 613-728-6550
sss@hillel-ltc.com
Number of Beds: 100 beds
Note: Charitable home for the aged
Stephen Schneiderman, Executive Director

Ottawa: St. Patrick's Home of Ottawa Inc.
2865 Riverside Dr., Ottawa, ON K1V 8N5
613-731-4660 Fax: 613-731-4056
here@stpats.ca
www.stpats.ca
Number of Beds: 202 beds
Note: home for the aged
Mona Martin, Executive Director

Ottawa: The Salvation Army Ottawa Booth Centre
171 George St., Ottawa, ON K1N 5W5
613-241-1573 Fax: 613-241-2818 www.ottawaboothcentre.org
Old Name: Metropole & Salvage Depot
Year Founded: 1908
Note: Specialties: Anchorage Program, an addiction treatment program; Street outreach
Carson Durdle, Executive Director

Ottawa: Wymering Manor Ltd.
845 Kirkwood Ave., Ottawa, ON K1Z 5Y1
613-722-8811 Fax: 613-722-0795
Number of Beds: 28 beds
Note: long-term psychiatric care home for women
Mary Calerone, Manager

Owen Sound: Versa-Care Summit Place
850 - 4th St. East, Owen Sound, ON N4K 6A3
519-376-3212 Fax: 519-371-0923
summitplace@reveraliving.com
www.reveraliving.com
Number of Beds: 159 beds
Renate Cowan, Executive Director
renate.cowan@reveraliving.com

Palmerston: Royal Terrace
600 Whites Rd., Palmerston, ON N0G 2P0
519-343-2611 Fax: 519-343-2860
royalter@wightman.ca
www.royalterracepalmerston.ca
Number of Beds: 121 beds
Note: Long-term & residential care
Kash Ramchandani, Administrator

Paris: Park Lane Terrace
295 Grand River St. North, Paris, ON N3L 2N9
519-442-2753 Fax: 519-442-6176 www.parklaneterrace.ca
Number of Beds: 132 beds
Debora Saville, Administrator
dsaville@parklaneterrace.ca

Parry Sound: Lakeland Long Term Care Facility
6 Albert St., Parry Sound, ON P2A 3A4
705-746-9667 Fax: 0 1-866-959-9005
swhite@lakelandltc.ca
www.chartwellreit.ca or www.wpshc.com
Note: Located within the West Parry Sound Health Centre complex
Norman Maciver, CEO

Pembroke: Marianhill
600 Cecelia St., Pembroke, ON K8A 7Z3
613-735-6838 Fax: 613-732-3934 www.marianhill.ca
Number of Beds: 200 beds
Note: Catholic long-term and chronic care facility
Terry McBurney, Executive Director

Penetanguishene: Georgian Manor
7 Harriett St., Penetanguishene, ON L9M 1K8
705-549-3166 Fax: 705-549-6062
djackson@county.simcoe.on.ca
Number of Beds: 107 beds
Note: home for the aged
Jane Sinclair, Senior Administrator

Penetanguishene: Ruth Haarer Home for Special Care
PO Box 1067, 2 Water St., Penetanguishene, ON L9M 1V6
705-549-7296
Old Name: Ruth Haarer Residence
Number of Beds: 18 beds
Ruth Haarer, Administrator

Peterborough: Fairhaven Home
881 Dutton Rd., Peterborough, ON K9H 7S4
705-743-4265 Fax: 705-743-6292
Number of Beds: 253 beds
Note: home for the aged
Deborah Hammons, Executive Director

Peterborough: Riverview Manor
1155 Water St., Peterborough, ON K9H 3P8
705-748-6706 Fax: 705-748-5407
magreco@omniway.ca
www.omni-way.com
Number of Beds: 124 beds
Sue Matwey, Administrator

Peterborough: Springdale Country Manor
2698 Clifford Line, Peterborough, ON K9J 6X6
705-742-8811 Fax: 705-742-8812
www.omni-way.com/ourhomes/springdale.htm
Number of Beds: 65 beds
Maureen Imamovic, Administrator
mimamovic@omniway.ca

Petrolia: Lambton Meadowview Villa
3958 Petrolia Line, RR#4, Petrolia, ON N0N 1R0
519-882-1470 Fax: 519-882-1633
Number of Beds: 123 beds, 2 short stay beds
Note: home for the aged
Marlene Jackson, Acting Resident Manager

Port Colborne: Northland Manor
Northland Pointe, 2 Fielder Ave., Port Colborne, ON L3K 6G4
905-835-9335 Fax: 905-835-6518
northland@niagararegion.ca
Number of Beds: 150 beds
Note: Long-term care facility
Maureen Shantz, Administrator

Port Stanley: Extendicare - Port Stanley
4551 East Rd., Port Stanley, ON N5L 1J6
519-782-3339 Fax: 519-782-4756
cnh_portstanley@extendicare.com
www.extendicare.com
Number of Beds: 60 beds
Bahime Charania, Administrator; Director, Nursing

Ridgetown: The Village Retirement Residence
9 Myrtle St., Ridgetown, ON N0P 2C0
519-674-5427 Fax: 519-674-2422
thevillageretirementresidence@reveraliving.com
www.reveraliving.com
Number of Beds: 160 beds
Donna Kingelin

Rockland: St. Joseph Long-Term Care Facility
1615 Laurier St., Rockland, ON K4K 1C8
613-446-5126
Number of Beds: 64 units

Sarnia: Sumac Lodge
1464 Blackwell Rd., Sarnia, ON N7S 5M4

519-542-3421 Fax: 519-542-3604
sumaclodge@reveraliving.com
www.reveraliving.com
Number of Beds: 100 beds
Ann Currie, Executive Director
ann.currie@reveraliving.com

***Sarnia:* Twin Lakes Terrace**
1310 Murphy Rd., Sarnia, ON N7S 6K5
519-542-2939 Fax: 519-542-0879
kim_vandam@srgroup.ca
www.srgroup.ca
Parent: Steeves & Rozema Group
Number of Beds: 56 beds; 60 long-term care beds
Note: Independent & assisted living, convalescent & respite options
Kim Van Dam, Managing Director

***Sarsfield:* Sarsfield Colonial Home**
PO Box 130, 2861 Colonial Rd., Sarsfield, ON K0A 3E0
613-835-2977 Fax: 613-835-2982
Number of Beds: 46 beds
Chantal Crispin, Administrator
chantalcrispin@rogers.com

***Shelburne:* Dufferin Oaks Home for Senior Citizens**
151 Centre St., Shelburne, ON L0N 1S4
519-925-2140 Fax: 519-925-5067
duffoaks@dufferincounty.on.ca
www.dufferincounty.on.ca
Number of Beds: 160 beds
Note: non-profit municipal long-term care facility
Brenda Urbanski, Administrator
Gerald Black, Supervisor, Maintenance

***Simcoe:* Norview Lodge**
PO Box 604, 44 Rob Blake Way, Simcoe, ON N3Y 4L8
519-426-0902 Fax: 519-426-9867 www.norfolkcounty.on.ca
Number of Beds: 179 beds
Note: home for the aged
Kim Jenereaux, Administrator
Brian Koncir, Supervisor, Maintenance

***St Catharines:* Henley House Limited**
20 Earnest St., St Catharines, ON L2N 7T2
905-937-9703 www.chartwellreit.ca
Number of Beds: 160 beds
Note: Specialties: Long-term nursing & personal care; Therapeutic programs; Physiotherapy; Restorative care; Palliative care

***St Catharines:* Linhaven**
403 Ontario St., St Catharines, ON L2N 1L5
905-934-3364 Fax: 905-934-6975
Number of Beds: 248 beds
Note: Specialties: Long term care; Alzheimer's disease, memory loss, & related dementias; Respite services; Adult day service
Dan Oettinger, Administrator

***St Catharines:* Niagara Ina Grafton Gage Home**
413 Linwell Rd., St Catharines, ON L2M 7Y2
905-935-6822 Fax: 905-935-6847
poneill@niggv.on.ca
www.niggv.on.ca
Number of Beds: 40 beds
Note: supportive housing for seniors
Patrick O'Neill, CEO

***St Thomas:* Barton Residence**
31 Southwick St., St Thomas, ON N5R 3R7
519-633-3413
Number of Beds: 16 lits
Sheila Barton, Proprietor

***St Thomas:* Kettle Creek Residence**
58 St. George St., St Thomas, ON N5P 2L1
519-633-7647 Fax: 519-633-9312
kettlecreek@execulink.com
Old Name: Kettle Creek Gardens
Note: HSC needs
Dana Lawrence, Administrator

***St Thomas:* Valleyview Home for the Aged**
350 Burwell Rd., St Thomas, ON N5P 0A3
519-631-1030 Fax: 519-631-3462
mccarroll@valleyview.st-thomas.on.ca
Number of Beds: 136 beds
Note: home for the aged
Michael Carroll, Administrator

***St. Thomas:* Elgin Manor Home for the Aged**
39232 Fingal Line, St. Thomas, ON N5P 3S5
519-631-0620 Fax: 519-631-2307 www.elginhomes.ca
Number of Beds: 90 beds
Pat Vendevenne, Director, Homes & Senior Services
pvandevenne@elgin-county.on.ca

***Stittsville:* Specialty Care Granite Ridge**
5501 Abbott St., Stittsville, ON K2S 2C5
613-836-0331 Fax: 613-241-1986
norm.slatter@specialty-care.com
www.specialty-care.com
Number of Beds: 224 beds
Norm Slatter, Administrator

***Stoney Creek:* Clarion Nursing Home**
337 Hwy. 8, Stoney Creek, ON L8G 1E7
905-664-2281 Fax: 905-664-2966
info@clarionnursinghome.on.ca
www.clarionnursinghome.on.ca
Number of Beds: 100 beds
Michael Janjic, Administrator

***Stoney Creek:* Heritage Green Nursing Home**
353 Isaac Brock Dr., Stoney Creek, ON L8J 2J3
905-573-7177 Fax: 905-573-7151
hgnh@bellnet.ca
www.hamiltonltc.org/facilities/heritage.htm
Number of Beds: 167 beds
Rosemary Okimi, Administrator
Reg Charles, Manager, Maintenance

***Stoney Creek:* Stoney Creek Lifecare Centre**
199 Glover Rd., Stoney Creek, ON L8E 5J2
905-643-1795
eyi_stoneycreek_lc@extendicare.com
www.hamiltonltc.org
Number of Beds: 45 beds
Stephanie Zajczenko-Opdam, Administrator
sopdam@extendicare.com

***Stouffville:* Specialty Care Bloomington Cove**
13621 Ninth Line, Stouffville, ON L4A 7X3
905-640-1310 Fax: 905-640-0995
bernard.boreland@specialty-care.com
www.specialty-care.com
Number of Beds: 112 beds
Bernard Boreland, Administrator

***Stratford:* L'Arche Stratford**
PO Box 522 Main Street, Stratford, ON N5A 6T7
519-271-9751 Fax: 519-271-1861
info@larche.stratford.on.ca
www.larche.ca/en/communities/stratford/
Number of Beds: 24 beds

***Stratford:* Greenwood Court**
90 Greenwood Dr., Stratford, ON N5A 7W5
519-273-4662 Fax: 519-273-1458
Number of Beds: 45 beds
Fred Zehr, Administrator

***Thunder Bay:* Harper Residence**
42 Lake St., Thunder Bay, ON P7B 2V6
807-345-7625 Fax: 807-346-8733
harper@tbaytel.net
Number of Beds: 10 beds
Note: Group home
Sheila Harper

***Thunder Bay:* OPTIONS Northwest Personal Support Services**
95 Cumberland St. North, Thunder Bay, ON P7A 4M1
807-344-4994 Fax: 807-346-5811 www.optionsnorthwest.com
Year Founded: 1965
Note: Specialty: Personal & residential support for persons with developmental challenges, physical disabilities, chronic behaviour problems, & mental health challenges; Counselling; Support groups
Bernard Travis, Executive Director

***Thunder Bay:* Roseview Manor**
99 Shuniah St., Thunder Bay, ON P7A 2Z2
807-344-6929 Fax: 807-344-7132
roseviewmanor@reveraliving.com
www.reveraliving.com
Old Name: Central Park Lodge
Number of Beds: 157 beds
Gail Gallant, Executive Director

***Tilbury:* Tilbury Manor Long-Term Care Home**
PO Box 160, 16 Fort St., Tilbury, ON N0P 2L0
519-682-0243 Fax: 519-682-2358
adm.tilbury@diversicare.ca
www.diversicare.ca
Number of Beds: 75 beds
Jennifer Middleton, Administrator

***Toronto:* Altamont Long-Term Care Facility**
92 Island Rd., Toronto, ON M1C 2P5
416-284-4781 Fax: 416-284-3634
adm.altamont@diversicare.ca
Number of Beds: 159 beds

***Toronto:* Baycrest Centre for Geriatric Care**
3560 Bathurst St., Toronto, ON M6A 2E1
416-785-2500 Fax: 416-785-2464 www.baycrest.org
Number of Beds: 300 beds
Note: group home

***Toronto:* Carefree Lodge**
306 Finch Ave. East, Toronto, ON M2N 4S5
416-397-1500 Fax: 416-397-1501
Number of Beds: 126 beds
Note: home for the aged
Debbie Araujo, Administrator

***Toronto:* Central Park Lodge West Side**
1145 Albion Rd., Toronto, ON M9V 4J7
416-745-4800 Fax: 416-745-0445
westside@reveraliving.com
www.reveraliving.com
Number of Beds: 290 beds
Soo Wong, Administrator
S. Amadeo, Supervisor, Environmental Services

***Toronto:* Cheltenham Long-Term Care Facility**
5935 Bathurst St., Toronto, ON M2R 1Y8
416-223-4050
Number of Beds: 170 beds

***Toronto:* Chester Village**
717 Broadview Ave., Toronto, ON M4K 2P5
416-466-2173 Fax: 416-466-6781
Number of Beds: 174 beds
Note: home for the aged
Henriette Koning, CEO
Richard Dreja, Director, Physical Plant

***Toronto:* Copernicus Lodge**
66 Roncesvalles Ave., Toronto, ON M6R 3A7
416-536-7122 Fax: 416-536-8242
Number of Beds: 108 beds
Note: home for the aged
Gisela Styka, Executive Director

***Toronto:* Dom Lipa Nursing Home & Seniors Centre**
52 Neilson Dr., Toronto, ON M9C 1V7
416-621-3820 Fax: 416-621-9773
info@domlipa.ca; t.macdermid@domlipa.ca
www.domlipa.ca
Number of Beds: 66 nursing home, 30 retirement beds
Theresa MacDermid, Administrator

***Toronto:* The Gibson Long Term Care Centre**
1925 Steeles Ave. East, Toronto, ON M2H 2H3
416-493-4666 Fax: 416-493-4886
gibsonltc@chartwellreit.ca
www.chartwellreit.ca
Old Name: Extendicare - North York
Parent: Chartwell Seniors Housing REIT
Number of Beds: 202 beds
Stephen Suske, CEO, Chartwell Seniors Housing REIT

***Toronto:* Ina Grafton Gage Home (Toronto)**
2 O'Connor Dr., Toronto, ON M4K 2K1
416-422-4890 Fax: 416-422-1613
info@iggh.org
www.iggh.org
Number of Beds: 110 beds
Gordon Blowes, Administrator
Hernando Zorilla, Director, Physical Plant

***Toronto:* Kingsway Arms at McCowan**
2881 Eglinton Ave. East, Toronto, ON M4G 2K3
416-266-4445 Fax: 416-264-8377
mccowan.kams@rogers.com
www.kingswayarms.com/mccowan.php
Gina Cook, Executive Director
Tim Valyear, Director, Marketing
marketingoffice.kams@rogers.com

***Toronto:* Lakeside Long-Term Care Centre**
150 Dunn Ave., Toronto, ON M6K 2R6
416-533-2828
www.torontorehab.com/patient/longterm/index.htm
Number of Beds: 128 Beds

***Toronto:* Maynard Nursing Home**
28 Halton St., Toronto, ON M6J 1R3
416-533-5198 Fax: 416-533-3531
www.maynardnursinghome.com

Year Founded: 1961
Number of Beds: 77 beds
Note: Specialties: Service to residents of Portuguese origin; Recreational & social activities
Rosemary Mifsud, Administrator

Toronto: Nisbet Lodge
740 Pape Ave., Toronto, ON M4K 3S7
416-469-1105 Fax: 416-469-2996
info@nisbetlodge.com
www.nisbetlodge.com
Number of Beds: 103 beds
Note: Christian long-term care home
Glen Moorhouse, Executive Director

Toronto: North York General Hospital - Seniors' Health Centre
2 Buchan Ct., Toronto, ON M2J 5A3
416-756-0066 Fax: 416-495-9738 www.nygh.on.ca
Number of Beds: 192 beds
Note: Long term care facility, ambulatory geriatric services
Bonnie Adamson, CEO

Toronto: The O'Neill Centre
33 Christie St., Toronto, ON M6G 3B1
416-536-1116 Fax: 416-536-6941
adminassist@oneillcentre.ca
www.oneillcentre.ca
Number of Beds: 172 beds
Note: Resident care & retirement living
Christine Dalglish, Administrator

Toronto: Oakdale Child & Family Service Ltd.
291 Chisholm Ave., Toronto, ON M4C 4W5
416-699-5600 Fax: 416-699-6547
tor-oakdale@on.aibn.com
www.oakdaleservices.com
Note: Specialties: Long & short term care for children with special needs; Teaching independence in life skills, social & community awareness, & appropriate communication methods
Lisa Bache, Administrator

Toronto: Providence Healthcare
3276 St. Clair Ave. East, Toronto, ON M1L 1W1
416-285-3666 Fax: 416-285-3758
info@providence.on.ca
www.providence.on.ca
Old Name: Providence Centre Home for the Aged, Chronic Care
Number of Beds: 288 long-term care, 347 hospital beds
Note: Comprised of Providence Hospital, the Cardinal Ambrozic Houses of Providence, & Providence Community Centre; long-term care, rehabilitation & complex continuing care, community clinics, Alzheimer Day Program, caregiver support services, Tamil Caregiver Project. Focus is on the mission & values of the founding Sisters of St. Joseph
Neil McEvoy, President/CEO
Josie Walsh, Vice President, Programs; Chief Nurse Executive
Peter Nord, Vice President, Medical Affairs; Chief of Staff

Toronto: La Salle Manor
61 Fairfax Cres., Toronto, ON M1L 1Z7
416-752-3932 Fax: 416-752-4047
Number of Beds: 28 beds
Note: supportive housing
Francis McCrea, Administrator

Toronto: Shepherd Lodge
3760 Sheppard Ave. East, Toronto, ON M1T 3K9
416-609-5700 Fax: 416-609-8329
info@shepherdvillage.org
www.shepherdvillage.org
Year Founded: 1961
Number of Beds: 252 beds
Brock Hall, Vice President, Client Care Services

Toronto: Suomi-Koti Toronto
795 Eglinton Ave. East, Toronto, ON M4G 4E4
416-425-4134 Fax: 416-425-6319
seniorscentre@suomikoti.ca
www.suomikoti.ca
Also Known As: Toronto Finnish Cdn Srs Centre & Nursing Home
Number of Beds: 88 apartment units, 34 nursing beds
Juha Mynttinen, Administrator
Leila Carnegie, Director of Care

Toronto: Villa Colombo Homes for the Aged Inc.
40 Playfair Ave., Toronto, ON M6B 2P9
416-789-2113 Fax: 416-789-5435
general@villacolombo.on.ca
www.villacharities.com
Number of Beds: 391 beds
Pat Stoddart, Administrator
Mac Brett, Director, Housekeeping/Maintenance

Toronto: West Park Long-Term Care Centre
82 Buttonwood Ave., Toronto, ON M6M 2J5
416-243-3600 Fax: 416-243-8947
feedback@westpark.org
www.westpark.org
Note: Rehabilitation, complex continuing care, and long-term care facility

Toronto: The Westbury Long Term Care Centre
495 The West Mall, Toronto, ON M9C 5S3
416-622-7094
westburyltc@chartwellreit.ca
www.chartwellreit.ca
Note: Specialties: Nursing & personal care; Restorative care; Social, recreational, & physical activity programs; Specialized neighbourhood for persons with dementia; Palliative care

Trenton: Crown Ridge Place Nursing Home
106 Crown St., Trenton, ON K8V 6R3
613-392-1289 Fax: 613-392-6360
gfreeman@crownridgehealth.ca
Number of Beds: 84 beds
Greg Freeman, Administrator

Unionville: Union Villa
Unionville Home Society, 4300 Hwy. #7 East, Unionville, ON L3R 1L8
905-477-2839
customerservice@uhs.on.ca
www.uhs.on.ca/uhs_unionvilla.php
Year Founded: 1970
Number of Beds: 160 residential capacity
Note: Specialties: Long-term nursing care; Activation program; Therapeutic mental & physical stimulation; Respite care; Day guest program
Graham Constantine, President/CEO

Val Caron: Elizabeth Centre
Centre Elizabeth
2100 Main St., Val Caron, ON P3N 1S7
705-897-7695 Fax: 705-897-0181 www.jarlette.com
Number of Beds: 128 beds
Shelly Murphy, Administrator
smurphy@jarlette.com

Vanier: Centre d'accueil Champlain
275 Perrier Ave., Vanier, ON K1L 5C6
613-746-3543 Fax: 613-746-5572
Number of Beds: 160 beds
Note: home for the aged
Pierre Arsenault, Administrator

Wallaceburg: Fairfield Park
1934 Dufferin Ave., Wallaceburg, ON N8A 4M2
519-627-1663 Fax: 519-627-9920
Number of Beds: 99 beds
Tracey Maxim, Administrator
Shona Outridge, Director of Operations

Watford: Watford Quality Care Centre
PO Box 400, 344 Victoria St., Watford, ON N0M 2S0
519-876-2928 Fax: 519-876-3930 www.watfordqualitycare.ca
Number of Beds: 62 beds
Lynne-Anne Gallaway, Administrator
lgallaway@watfordqualitycare.ca

Windsor: Huron Lodge
1881 Cabana Rd. W, Windsor, ON N9G 1C7
519-253-6060 Fax: 519-977-8027
www.citywindsor.ca/000278.asp
Number of Beds: 256 beds
Note: Number of Employees: 160
Lucie B. Lombardo, Administrator
Linda Larsh, Manager, Environmental Services

Windsor: Regency Park Nursing Home
567 Victoria Ave., Windsor, ON N9A 4N1
519-254-1141 Fax: 519-254-3759
Number of Beds: 72 beds
Annemarie White, Administrator

Woodbridge: Friuli Long-Term Care
40 Friuli Ct., Woodbridge, ON
416-443-0409
Number of Beds: 168 beds

Woodbridge: Kristus Darzs Latvian Home
11290 Pine Valley Dr., Woodbridge, ON L4L 1A6
905-832-3300 Fax: 905-832-2029
kristusdarzs@kdlatvianhome.com
www.kdlatvianhome.com
Number of Beds: 100 beds
Jolanta Linde, Director of Operations

Woodstock: Woodingford Lodge
PO Box 308, 423 Devonshire Ave., Woodstock, ON N4S 7X9
519-539-1245 Fax: 519-539-8937 www.county.oxford.on.ca
Number of Beds: 228 beds
Beth Martin, Administrator

Nursing Homes

Ajax: Ballycliffe Lodge Ltd.
70 Station Rd., Ajax, ON L1S 1R9
905-683-7321 Fax: 905-427-5846
ballycliffelodge@chartwellreit.ca
www.chartwellreit.ca
Number of Beds: 100 beds; 65 retirement lodge beds
Christine Langton, Administrator

Amherstview: Helen Henderson Care Centre
343 Amherst Dr., Amherstview, ON K7N 1X3
613-384-4585 Fax: 613-384-9407
Number of Beds: 70 retirement home beds; 102 nursing home beds
Larry Gibson, Administrator

Arnprior: The Grove Arnprior & District Nursing Home
275 Ida St. North, Arnprior, ON K7S 3M7
613-623-6547 Fax: 613-623-4554
arnprior.hospital@arnprior.com
www.arnpriorhospital.com
Number of Beds: 60 beds
Marlene McRoberts, Chair
David Moore, Vice Chair

Arthur: Caressant Care Nursing and Retirement Homes Limited
PO Box 700, 215 Eliza St., Arthur, ON N0G 1A0
519-848-3795 Fax: 519-848-2273 www.caressantcare.com
Division of: Caressant Care Arthur
Number of Beds: 80 beds
Lara Riehl, Administrator

Blenheim: Blenheim Community Village
PO Box 220, 10 Mary Ave., Blenheim, ON N0P 1A0
519-676-8119 Fax: 519-676-0610
blenheim@reveraliving.com
www.reveraliving.com/homes/bl
Number of Beds: 101 beds
Note: nursing home & retirement lodge
Barbara Ferren, Executive Director

Bobcaygeon: Specialty Care Case Manor
28 Boyd St., Bobcaygeon, ON K0M 1A0
705-738-2374 Fax: 705-738-3821
margaret.misetic@specialty-care.com
www.specialty-care.com
Old Name: Case Manor Nursing Home
Number of Beds: 96 beds
Margaret Misetic, Administrator

Bourget: Caressant Care Nursing and Retirement Homes Limited
PO Box 99, 2279 Laval St., Bourget, ON K0A 1E0
613-487-2331 Fax: 613-487-3464 www.caressantcare.com
Division of: Caressant Care Bourget
Number of Beds: 50 beds
Louise Dion, Administrator

Bowmanville: Marnwood Life Care Centre
26 Elgin St., Bowmanville, ON L1C 3C8
905-623-5731 Fax: 905-623-4497
Number of Beds: 60 beds
Note: Specialties: Social work; Physiotherapy
Tracey Werheid, Administrator

Bowmanville: Strathaven Life Care Centre
264 King St. East, Bowmanville, ON L1C 1P9
905-623-2553 Fax: 905-623-1374
eyi_strathaven_lc@extendicare.com
www.ourhomeyourhome.eycan.com
Number of Beds: 199 beds
Patrick Brown, Administrator
pjbrown@extendicare.com

Brampton: Holland Christian Homes Inc.
7900 McLaughlin Rd. South, Brampton, ON L6V 3N2
905-459-3333 Fax: 905-459-8667
fronre@hch.ca
www.hch.ca
Old Name: Faith Manor Nursing Home
Number of Beds: 120 beds
Note: Dutch Heritage
John Kalverda, Executive Director
johnka@hch.ca

Peter Dykstra, Administrator, Grace Manor
petedy@hch.ca

Brantford: Versa-Care Centre - Brantford
425 Park Rd. North, Brantford, ON N3R 7G5
519-759-1040 Fax: 519-759-5343
vcbrantford@reveraliving.com
www.reveraliving.com
Number of Beds: 167 beds
Debbie Bonney, Administrator

Burlington: The Brant Centre Long Term Care Residence
1230 Northshore Blvd. East, Burlington, ON L7S 1C5
905-639-2848 Fax: 0
brantcentreltc@chartwellreit.ca
www.chartwellreit.ca
Parent: Chartwell Seniors Housing REIT
Year Founded: 2003
Number of Beds: 175 beds
Adam Banks, Administrator
Barbara Murphy, Director of Care
Stephen Suske, CEO, Chartwell Seniors Housing REIT

Cambridge: Caressant Care Nursing and Retirement Homes Limited
3680 Speedsville Rd., Cambridge, ON N3H 4R6
519-650-0100 Fax: 519-650-1697
Division of: Cambridge Country Manor
Number of Beds: 79 beds
Brenda Nadeau, Administrator

Cambridge: Riverbend Place Retirement Community
650 Coronation Blvd., Cambridge, ON N1R 7S6
519-740-3820 Fax: 519-740-0961
riverbendplace@reveraliving.com
www.reveraliving.com
Number of Beds: 146 beds
Note: Assisted living & independent living programs; short term, respite & convalescent options; community includes nursing home, retirement lodge, apartments
Margaret Dykeman, Administrator

Cambridge: Saint Luke's Place
1624 Franklin Blvd., Cambridge, ON N3C 3P4
519-658-5183 Fax: 519-658-2991 www.saintlukesplace.ca
Number of Beds: 150 beds
Note: home for the aged; provides long term care, retirement home & apartments
Bev Preuss, Administrator

Carleton Place: Stoneridge Manor
256 High St., Carleton Place, ON K7C 1X1
613-257-4355 Fax: 613-253-2190
stoneridgemanor@reveraliving.com
www.reveraliving.com
Number of Beds: 60 beds
Michelle Ferguson, Administrator
michelle.ferguson@reveraliving.com

Cobden: Caressant Care Nursing and Retirement Homes Limited
12 Wren Dr., Cobden, ON K0J 1K0
613-646-2109 Fax: 613-646-2182 www.caressantcare.com
Division of: Caressant Care Cobden
Year Founded: 2000
Number of Beds: 60 beds
Linda Tracey, Administrator

Cobourg: Streamway Villa Nursing Home
19 James St. West, Cobourg, ON K9A 2J8
905-372-0163 Fax: 905-372-0581 www.omni-way.com
Number of Beds: 59 beds
Robin Holland, Administrator
rholland@omniway.ca

Collingwood: Bay Haven Nursing Home Inc.
499 Hume St., Collingwood, ON L9Y 4H8
705-445-6501 Fax: 705-445-6506
bayhaven@georgian.net
www.bayhaven.com
Number of Beds: 60 beds
Karen Milligan, Administrator

Collingwood: Sunset Manor & Village
49 Raglan St., Collingwood, ON L9Y 4X1
705-445-4499 Fax: 705-445-9742
www.county.simcoe.on.ca/healthsocialservices/longtermcare/sunsetmanor/
Year Founded: 1968
Number of Beds: 148 beds
Note: Nursing & convalescent home
Erin Evans, Site Administrator; Director, Resident Care

Cornwall: Versa-Care - Cornwall
201 - 11 St. East, Cornwall, ON K6H 2Y6
613-933-7420 Fax: 613-933-2759
vccornwall@reveraliving.com
www.reveraliving.com
Number of Beds: 118 beds
Donna Derouchie, Administrator

Courtland: Caressant Care Nursing and Retirement Homes Limited
PO Box 279, 4850 County Rd. 59, Courtland, ON N0J 1E0
519-688-0710 Fax: 519-688-0052
Old Name: Sacred Heart Villa
Division of: Caressant Care Courtland
Number of Beds: 54 beds
Linda Hare, Administrator
Gilbert Dooms, Supervisor, Maintenance

Embrun: St. Jacques Nursing Home
Foyer St-Jacques
PO Box 870, 915 Notre Dame St., Embrun, ON K0A 1W0
613-443-3442 Fax: 613-443-1716
info@stjacques.ca
www.stjacques.ca
Number of Beds: 60 beds
Ginette Beaudin, Administrator
gbeaudin@stjacques.ca

Exeter: Exeter Villa Nursing & Retirement Home
155 John St. East, Exeter, ON N0M 1S1
519-235-1581 Fax: 519-235-3219
exevilla@cabletv.on.ca
www.atkcareinc.ca/exeterservices
Parent: ATK Care Inc.
Number of Beds: 57 nursing care beds, 66 retirement beds
Nancy Tweddle, Administrator

Fergus: Caressant Care Nursing and Retirement Homes Limited
450 Queen St. East, Fergus, ON N1M 2Y7
519-843-2400 www.caressantcare.com
Division of: Caressant Care Fergus
Year Founded: 1986
Number of Beds: 87 beds
Shannon Brinkman, Administrator
Marion Douglas, Director, Nursing

Fordwich: Fordwich Village Nursing Home
3063 Adelaide St., Fordwich, ON N0G 1V0
519-335-3168 Fax: 519-335-3825
fordwichadmin@tnt21.com
www.atkcareinc.ca/fordwhichservices
Parent: ATK Care Inc.
Number of Beds: 33 beds
Note: Long term care facility
Catherine Weber, Administrator

Hagersville: Norcliffe LifeCare Centre
85 Main St. North, Hagersville, ON N0A 1H0
905-768-1641 Fax: 905-768-1685
Number of Beds: 60 units
Note: Retirement home
Marilyn Tone, Acting Administrator

Hamilton: St. Olga's Lifecare Centre
570 King St. West, Hamilton, ON L8P 1C2
905-522-8572 Fax: 905-522-1553
eyi_st.olgas_LC@extendicare.com
www.hamiltonltc.org/facilities/st_olgas.htm
Number of Beds: 93 beds
Judy Peck, Administrator
jpeck@extendicare.com

Hamilton: Versa-Care Centre - Hamilton
330 Main St. East, Hamilton, ON L8N 3T9
905-523-7134 Fax: 905-523-7137
vchamilton@reveraliving.com
www.reveraliving.com
Number of Beds: 128 beds
Walter Sguazzin, Administrator

Harriston: Caressant Care Nursing and Retirement Homes Limited
PO Box 520, 24 Louise St., Harriston, ON N0G 1Z0
519-338-3700 Fax: 519-338-2744 www.caressantcare.com
Division of: Caressant Care Harriston
Number of Beds: 89 beds
Note: Long term care facility, with secure unit for residents with dementia, & adjacent retirement home.
Mary-Therese Haid, Administrator
Eleanor MacEwen, Infection Control

Hawkesbury: Résidence Prescott et Russell
Prescott & Russell Residence
1020, boul Cartier, Hawkesbury, ON K6A 1W7
613-632-2755 Fax: 613-632-4056 www.prescott-russell.on.ca
Number of Beds: 146 lits
Note: Maison de soins de longue durée. Employés: 171
Louise Lalonde, Administratrice
François Martineau, Directeur des soins infirmiers
Danielle Duval, Coordonnatrice, Admissions; Services financiers

Hensall: Queensway Nursing & Retirement Home
PO Box 369, 100 Queen St. East, Hensall, ON N0M 1X0
519-262-2830 Fax: 519-262-3403
queensway.admin@tcc.on.ca
Number of Beds: 60 beds nursing home & 57 beds retirement home
Note: retirement home
Kathy Holdsworth, Administrator

Huntsville: Fairvern Nursing Home Inc.
14 Mill St., Huntsville, ON P1H 2A4
705-789-4476 Fax: 705-789-1371
fairvernmail@mahc.ca
www.mahc.ca & www.fairvernnursinghome.ca
Parent: Muskoka Algonquin Healthcare
Number of Beds: 76 beds
Barry Lockhart, CEO
Christopher Thomas, Chair

Keswick: Specialty Care Cedarvale Lodge
121 Morton Dr., Keswick, ON L4P 2M5
905-476-2656 Fax: 905-476-5689 www.specialty-care.com
Number of Beds: 100 beds
Note: Nursing home with 40-bed retirement home attached
Donna Taylor, Administrator
donna.taylor@specialty-care.com

Kitchener: Forest Heights Long Term Care Centre
60 Westheights Dr., Kitchener, ON N2N 2A8
519-576-3320 Fax: 519-745-3227
Number of Beds: 240 beds
Michelle Vermeeren, Administrator
Dolly LaBelle, Health; Safety Committee
Lynne Jones, Purchasing Agent

Listowel: Caressant Care Nursing and Retirement Homes Limited
710 Reserve Ave., Listowel, ON N4W 2L1
519-291-1041 Fax: 519-291-5420 www.caressantcare.com
Division of: Caressant Care Listowel
Number of Beds: 52 beds
Lara Martinez, Administrator

London: Versa-Care Elmwood Place
46 Elmwood Pl. West, London, ON N6J 1J2
519-433-7259 Fax: 519-660-0158
elmwoodpl@reveraliving.com
www.reveraliving.com/homes/lo/
Old Name: Elmwood Place
Number of Beds: 97 beds
Lorell Jones, Administrator

Marmora: Caressant Care Nursing and Retirement Homes Limited
58 Burstall St., Marmora, ON K0K 2M0
613-472-3130 Fax: 613-472-5388 www.caressantcare.com
Division of: Caressant Care Marmora
Number of Beds: 84 beds
Linda Merkley, Administrator

Matheson: Rosedale Centre
507 - 8th Ave., Matheson, ON P0K 1N0
Year Founded: 1989
Number of Beds: 20 beds
Note: Specialty: Long term nursing & supportive care; Foot care; Therapy; Number of Employees: 72 (Bingham Memorial Hospital & adjoined Rosedale Centre)
Daniel O'Mara, Chief Executive Officer
705-273-2424, mailto:micsceo@puc.net

Mount Forest: Saugeen Valley Nursing Centre Ltd.
465 Dublin St., Mount Forest, ON N0G 2L3
519-323-2140 Fax: 519-323-3540
svnc@wightman.ca
Number of Beds: 87 beds
Note: Nursing & respite care
Andrea Parsons, Administrator

Norwood: Pleasant Meadow Manor
99 Alma St., Norwood, ON K0L 2V0
705-639-5308 Fax: 705-639-5309
www.omni-way.com/ourhomes/pleasant.htm
Parent: OMNI

Number of Beds: 61 beds
Note: Long term care
Fraser Wilson, CEO
Sandra Brow, Administrator; Director of Care, Care

Orangeville: Avalon Care Centre & Retirement Lodge
355 Broadway Ave., Orangeville, ON L9W 3Y3
519-941-3351 Fax: 519-941-9532 www.jarlette.com
Number of Beds: 137 long term care beds, 77 retirement lodge beds
Note: Long term care centre & retirement residence
Chan Sooklal, Administrator, Care Centre
csooklal@jarlette.com
Debbie Rydall, General Manager, Retirement Lodge
drydall@jarlette.com

Orillia: Trillium Manor Home for the Aged
12 Grace Ave., Orillia, ON L3V 2K2
705-325-1504 Fax: 705-325-7661
Year Founded: 1969
Number of Beds: 122 beds
Janice McQuaig, Site Administrator
Jane Sinclair, General Manager, Health & Cultural Services

Ottawa: La Villa Marguerite
75 Bruyere St., Ottawa, ON K1N 5C8
613-562-4262 Fax: 613-562-4223
villa-marguerite@scohs.on.ca
www.scohs.on.ca
Number of Beds: 71 beds
Note: Long-term care
Jean Bartkowiak, President/CEO, Service de santé SCO Health Service

Owen Sound: Versa-Care Georgian Heights
1115 - 10 St. East, Owen Sound, ON N4K 6B1
519-371-1441 Fax: 519-371-1092
georgianheights@reveraliving.com
www.reveraliving.com
Number of Beds: 40 beds
Joanne Porter, Administrator

Owen Sound: Versa-Care Maple View
1029 - 4th Ave. West, Owen Sound, ON N4K 4W1
519-376-2522 Fax: 519-376-3110
mapleview@reveraliving.com
www.reveraliving.com
Number of Beds: 29 beds
Andrea Hodgkins, Acting Administrator

Paris: Telfer Place Retirement Residence
245 Grand River St. North, Paris, ON N3L 3V8
519-442-4411 Fax: 519-442-6724
telferplaceretirementresidence@reveraliving.com
www.reveraliving.com
Number of Beds: 45 beds
Note: Independent living program; retirement lodge, apartments; long-term care; convalescent & respite options
Kathy Le Gresley, Administrator
Henry Filetstra, Supervisor, Maintenance

Picton: Versa-Care Hallowell House
PO Box 800, RR#1, Picton, ON K0K 2T0
613-476-4444 Fax: 613-476-1566
hallowellhouse@reveraliving.com
www.reveraliving.com
Number of Beds: 97 beds
Janice F. Wilkes, Administrator
Carl Markland, Supervisor, Maintenance

Port Hope: Regency Manor Retirement & Nursing Home
66 Dorset St. East, Port Hope, ON L1A 1E3
905-885-4558 Fax: 905-885-7386
regencymanor@bellnet.ca
Number of Beds: 101 beds
Charlene Smith, Administrator

Sarnia: Trillium Villa
1221 Michigan Ave., Sarnia, ON N7S 3Y3
519-542-5529 Fax: 519-542-5953
trillium_villa@snr.on.ca
www.ltc.snr.on.ca
Year Founded: 1970
Number of Beds: 152 beds
Joyce Haneca, Administrator

Sault Ste Marie: Great Northern Retirement Home
760 Great Northern Rd., Sault Ste Marie, ON P6A 5K7
705-945-9405 Fax: 705-945-6303
Number of Beds: 120 retirement, 34 interim nursing home beds
Nadia Longo, Administrator

Seaforth: Seaforth Manor Nursing Home
100 James St., Seaforth, ON N0K 1W0
519-527-0030 Fax: 519-527-2862
seaforth.admin@tcc.on.ca
Number of Beds: 118 beds
Note: Nursing & retirement home
Catherine Schalk, Administrator

Shelburne: Shelburne Residence
200 Robert St., Shelburne, ON L0N 1S1
519-925-3746 Fax: 519-925-1476
shelburne.admin@bellnet.ca
Number of Beds: 60 nursing beds, 28 retirement rooms
Note: Combined nursing home & retirement facility
Mike Dickin, Administrator

St Catharines: Tufford Nursing Home
312 Queenston St., St Catharines, ON L2P 2X4
905-682-0503 www.hamptontufford.com
Year Founded: 1960
Number of Beds: 64 residential capacity
Note: Specialties: Long-term nursing care; Social work; Physiotherapy; Podiatry; Activation program; Palliative care

St Catharines: Versa-Care Centre - St. Catharines
168 Scott St., St Catharines, ON L2N 1H2
905-934-3321 Fax: 905-934-9011
vcstcatharines@reveraliving.com
www.reveraliving.com
Number of Beds: 200 beds
Sandra A. Fredericks, Administrator

St Marys: Kingsway Lodge
310 Queen St. East, RR #6, St Marys, ON N4X 1C8
519-284-2921 Fax: 519-284-4468
info@kingswaylodge.com
www.kingswaylodge.com
Number of Beds: 89 beds, 52 units
Scott A. Mackay, Administrator
smackay@on.aibn.com

St Marys: Wildwood Care Centre Inc.
PO Box 2200, 100 Ann St., St Marys, ON N4X 1A1
519-284-3628 Fax: 519-284-0575 www.wildwoodcarecentre.com
Number of Beds: 82 beds
Lynn Walsh, Administrator

St Thomas: Caressant Care Nursing and Retirement Homes Limited
4 Mary Bucke St., St Thomas, ON N5R 5J6
519-633-3164 Fax: 519-631-8362 www.caressantcare.com
Division of: Caressant Care St. Thomas - Mary Bucke St. Facility
Number of Beds: 60 beds
Ann Starswell, Administrator

St. Thomas: Caressant Care Nursing and Retirement Homes Limited
15 Bonnie Pl., St. Thomas, ON N5R 5T8
519-633-6493 Fax: 519-633-9329 www.caressantcare.com
Division of: Caressant Care St. Thomas - Bonnie Place Facility
Number of Beds: 182 beds
Note: Long term care facility, with secure unit for residents with dementia.
Vicki Martinez, Administrator

Stayner: Stayner Nursing Home
PO Box 350, 244 Main St. East, Stayner, ON L0M 1S0
705-428-3614 Fax: 705-428-0537
Number of Beds: 49 beds
Lorraine Baker, Administrator

Stirling: Stirling Manor Nursing Home
PO Box 220, 218 Edward St., Stirling, ON K0K 3E0
613-395-2596 Fax: 613-395-0930 www.stirling-rawdon.com
Number of Beds: 75 beds
Judith Norlock, Administrator
judy_manor@hotmail.com
Linda Phillips, Acting Director, Nursing
Cheryl Campbell, Office Manager

Strathroy: Sprucedale Care Centre Inc.
96 Kittridge Ave. East, Strathroy, ON N7G 2A8
519-245-2808 Fax: 519-245-1767
Number of Beds: 62 beds
Darren Micallef, Administrator
darren@sprucedale.ca

Sutton: River Glen Haven Nursing Home
160 High St., Sutton, ON L0E 1R0
905-722-3631 Fax: 905-722-8638
rghadmin@bellnet.ca
www.atkcareinc.ca/suttonservices.htm
Parent: ATK Care Inc.
Number of Beds: 109 beds
Note: Long term & secured care
Karen Ryan, Administrator

Tavistock: Caressant Care Nursing and Retirement Homes Limited
94 William St., Tavistock, ON N0B 2R0
519-655-2344 Fax: 519-655-2162
Division of: The Maples Home for Seniors
Number of Beds: 43 beds
Lois Riehl, Administrator

Thunder Bay: Pinewood Court
2625 East Walsh St., Thunder Bay, ON P7E 2E5
807-577-1127 Fax: 0
pinewoodcourt@reveraliving.com
www.reveraliving.com
Number of Beds: 75 beds
Note: Long term care
Cheryl Grant, Administrator
Ron Campbell, Director, Environmental Services

Thunder Bay: Versa-Care Centre - Thunder Bay
135 South Vickers St., Thunder Bay, ON P7E 1J2
807-623-9511 Fax: 807-623-6992
vcthunderbay@reveraliving.com
www.reveraliving.com
Number of Beds: 161 beds
Joanne Lent, Executive Director

Toronto: St. Clair O'Connor Community Nursing Home
2701 St. Clair Ave. East, Toronto, ON M4B 3M3
416-757-8757 Fax: 416-751-7315
Number of Beds: 25 beds
Susan Gallant, Administrator
s.gallant@scoc.ca

Toronto: Seven Oaks
9 Neilson Rd., Toronto, ON M1E 5E1
416-392-3500 Fax: 416-392-3579
www.toronto.ca/ltc/sevenoaks.htm/
Year Founded: 1989
Number of Beds: 249 beds
Note: Services for long term care, including adult day programs, services to the Armenian & Tamil communities, & an on-site child care centre
Karen Wallace, Administrator

Toronto: Tendercare Living Centre
1020 McNicoll Ave., Toronto, ON M1W 2J6
416-499-2020 Fax: 416-499-3379
peggyli@tendercare.ca
www.tendercare.ca
Number of Beds: 254 beds
Note: Nursing home & retirement community
Francis Martis, Administrator

Toronto: Tony Stacey Centre for Veterans Care
59 Lawson Rd., Toronto, ON M1C 2J1
416-284-9235 Fax: 416-284-7169
info@tonystaceycentre.ca
www.tonystaceycentre.ca
Year Founded: 1977
Number of Beds: 100 beds
Catherine Hilge, Administrator
chilge@bellnet.ca

Toronto: Versa-Care Centre - Rexdale
95 Humber College Blvd., Toronto, ON M9V 5B5
416-746-7466 Fax: 416-740-5812
vcrexdale@reveraliving.com
www.reveraliving.com
Number of Beds: 94 beds
Andrew Shinder, Administrator
Glen Elliott, Director, Physical Plant

Toronto: White Eagle Residence
138 Dowling Ave., Toronto, ON M6K 3A6
416-533-7935 Fax: 416-533-5154
whiteeagleresidence@chartwellreit.ca
www.chartwellreit.ca
Parent: Chartwell Seniors Housing REIT
Number of Beds: 56 beds
Stephen Suske, CEO, Chartwell Seniors Housing REIT

Uxbridge: ReachView Village
130 Reach St., Uxbridge, ON L9P 1L3
905-852-5281 Fax: 905-852-0117
reachviewvillage@reveraliving.com
www.reveraliving.com
Old Name: Versa-Care Centre, Uxbridge
Number of Beds: 100 beds

***Waterloo:* Pinehaven Nursing Home & Retirement Residence**
229 Lexington Rd., Waterloo, ON N2K 2E1
519-885-0255 Fax: 519-885-4216
jross@thecaringnetwork.ca
www.pinehaven.ca
Number of Beds: 85 beds
Note: Specialty: long term care
Joanne Ross, Administrator

***Whitby:* Sunnycrest Nursing Home**
1635 Dundas St. East, Whitby, ON L1N 2K9
905-576-0111 Fax: 905-576-4712
info@sunnycrest.ca
www.sunnycrest.ca
Number of Beds: 136 beds
Jane Smith, Administrator
jsmith@sunnycrest.ca

***Windsor:* Riverside Place**
3181 Meadowbrook Lane, Windsor, ON N8T 0A4
519-974-0148 Fax: 519-974-7305
riversideplace@reveraliving.com
www.reveraliving.com

***Windsor:* Versa-Care Windsor Place**
350 Dougall Ave., Windsor, ON N9A 4P4
519-256-7868 Fax: 519-256-1991
vcwindsorplace@reveraliving.com
www.reveraliving
Number of Beds: 244 beds
Bonnie Spry, Administrator

***Woodbridge:* Devonshire Pine Grove Inc.**
c/o Pine Grove Lodge, 8403 Islington Ave. North, Woodbridge, ON L4L 1X3
905-850-3605 Fax: 905-850-3832
smrpinelodge@rogers.com
chartwellcare.com
Number of Beds: 100 nursing home beds & 40 retirement residence suites
Sonia Ryerson, Administrator

***Woodstock:* Caressant Care Nursing and Retirement Homes Limited**
81 Fyfe Ave., Woodstock, ON N4S 8Y3
519-539-6461 Fax: 519-539-7467 www.caressantcare.com
Division of: Caressant Care Woodstock
Number of Beds: 240 beds
Judy Peck, Administrator

Retirement Residences

***Amherstburg:* Victoria Street Manor**
184 Victoria St. South, Amherstburg, ON N9V 2K5
519-736-2525 Fax: 519-736-8587 www.countyofessex.on.ca
Number of Beds: 14 beds
Note: Specialties: Residential care for seniors; Medication administration
Della Dyck, Manager

***Amherstview:* Briargate Retirement Living Centre**
4567 Bath Rd., Amherstview, ON K7N 1A8
613-384-9333 Fax: 613-384-4443
briargate@reveraliving.com
Number of Beds: 95 beds
Leanne Weir, Executive Director

***Ancaster:* Carrington Place Retirement Residence**
75 Dunham Dr., Ancaster, ON L9G 1X7
905-648-0343 Fax: 905-648-9581

***Ancaster:* Highgate Retirement Residence**
325 Fiddlers Green Rd., Ancaster, ON L9G 1W9
905-648-8399 Fax: 905-648-3350
Number of Beds: 40 beds
Clare Aiken, Administrator

***Arnprior:* Arnprior Villa Retirement Residence**
15 Arthur St., Arnprior, ON K7S 1A1
613-623-0414 Fax: 613-623-0947
arnprior@reveraliving.com
www.reveraliving.com
Number of Beds: 81 beds
Becky Hollingsworth, Executive Director

***Aurora:* Aurora Retirement Centre**
145 Murray Dr., Aurora, ON L4G 2C7
905-841-2777 Fax: 905-841-1562
auroraretirement@chartwellreit.ca
www.chartwellreit.ca/home_locations/aurora_ret.htm
Number of Beds: 58 units
Avril Davies, Administrator

***Aurora:* Park Place Manor**
15055 Yonge St., Aurora, ON L4G 6T4
905-727-2952 Fax: 905-727-5435
parkplacemanor@chartwellreit.ca
www.chartwellreit.ca
Number of Beds: 93 suites
Note: Specialties: Recreational activities; Wellness monitoring; Foot care; Respite, trial, seasonal, & convalescent stay
John Jeffs, Administrator

***Barrie:* Barrie Manor**
340 Blake St., Barrie, ON L4M 1L3
705-722-3611 Fax: 705-722-4530
barriemanor@home.com
www.simcoecounty.net/barriemanor.htm
Number of Beds: 113 beds
Sylvia Ward, Administrator

***Barrie:* Mulcaster Mews**
130 Mulcaster St., Barrie, ON L4M 3M9
705-725-9119 Fax: 705-725-8848
enquires@mulcastermews.ca
www.geocities.com/mulcastermews
Number of Beds: 52 beds
Maggie Rae, Administrator

***Barrie:* Roberta Place**
489 Essa Rd., Barrie, ON L4N 9E4
705-728-2900 Fax: 705-728-8535 www.jarlette.com
Number of Beds: 138 bed retirement lodge, 139 long term care beds
Note: Roberta Place long term care facility is located at 503 Essa Rd.
Carolyn McLeod, Administrator
cmcleod@jarlette.com
Sandra Fernandez, General Manager, Retirement Lodge
sfernandez@jarlette.com

***Barrie:* Simcoe Terrace Retirement Centre**
44 Donald St., Barrie, ON L4N 1E3
705-722-5750 Fax: 705-722-7041
info@simcoeterrace.com
www.simcoeterrace.com
Number of Beds: 98 beds
Anne Ollikainen, Administrator

***Barrie:* Woods Park Care Centre**
110 Lillian Cres., Barrie, ON L4N 5H7
705-739-6881 Fax: 705-739-0638
cathy.cotton@specialty-care.com
Number of Beds: 67 units
Note: nursing home/retirement home
Cathy Cotton, Administrator

***Beachburg:* Country Haven Retirement Home**
1387 Beachburg Rd., RR#1, Beachburg, ON K0J 1C0
613-582-7021 Fax: 613-582-7075
chrh@nrtco.net
www.countryhavenretirementhome.com
Number of Beds: 75 beds
R. Legault, Manager

***Belleville:* Bayview Retirement Home**
435 Dundas St. West, Belleville, ON K8P 1B6
613-966-6268 Fax: 613-966-6675
bayview@chartwellreit.ca
www.chartwellreit.ca
Number of Beds: 60 beds
Patricia Tooze, Administrator

***Belleville:* The Richmond Retirement Residence**
175 North Front St., Belleville, ON K8P 4Y8
613-966-4407 www.richmondretirement.ca
Note: Specialties: Medication management; Wellness program; Social & therapeutic programs; Respite stays
Andrea E. McLister, Administrator

***Bracebridge:* Bracebridge Villa Retirement Lodge**
690 Hwy. 118 West, Bracebridge, ON P1L 1W8
705-645-6364 Fax: 705-645-1684
interest@bracebridgevilla.ca
www.bracebridgevilla.ca
Number of Beds: 82 units
Corrine Hall, Manager

***Bracebridge:* James Street Place**
148 James St., Bracebridge, ON P1L 1S7
705-645-1431 Fax: 705-645-5415
jamesstreet@chartwellreit.ca
www.chartwellreit.ca/home_locations/james_street.htm
Number of Beds: 73 suites
Rosalid Taylor, Administrator

***Brampton:* Woodhall Park Retirement Village**
10250 Kennedy Rd., RR#4, Brampton, ON L6T 3S1
905-846-1441
postmaster@woodhallpark.ca
www.woodhallpark.ca
Number of Beds: 80 suites
Andrew Post, Administrator

***Brantford:* Amber Lea Place**
384 St. Paul Ave., Brantford, ON N3R 4N4
519-754-0000 Fax: 519-759-1401
info@amberleaplace.com
www.amberleaplace.com
Parent: Mundi Holdings Ltd.
Number of Beds: 50 beds
Dev Mundi, Administrator

***Brantford:* Charlotte Villa Retirement Residence**
120 Darling St., Brantford, ON N3T 5W6
519-759-5250 Fax: 519-759-8403
charlotte@reveraliving.com
www.reveraliving.com
Number of Beds: 80 beds
Note: Independent & assisted living, secured living for dementia care
Carol Sterkenburg, Administrator/Care Coordinator

***Brantford:* Tranquility Place**
PO Box 3000, 436 Powerline Rd., Brantford, ON N3T 6G5
519-759-2222 www.allegroresidences.ca
Year Founded: 1988
Note: Specialties: Physiotherapy; Foot care clinic; Physical activities
Paul Rade, General Manager

***Brighton:* Applefest Lodge**
PO Box 850, 120 Elizabeth St., Brighton, ON K0K 1H0
613-475-3510 Fax: 613-475-3431
info@applefestlodge.ca
www.applefestlodge.ca
Number of Beds: 50 beds
Marilyn McLeod, Manager
interest@applefestlodge.com

***Brockville:* Bridlewood Manor**
1026 Bridlewood Dr., Brockville, ON K6V 7J8
613-345-2477 Fax: 613-345-4188
bridlewood@reveraliving.com
www.reveraliving.com/homes/207
Number of Beds: 67 units
Dennis Daoust, Executive Director

***Brockville:* Rosedale Retirement Centre**
1813 County Rd. 2E, RR#1, Brockville, ON K6V 5T1
613-342-0200 Fax: 613-342-8729
rosedale@chartwellreit.ca
www.chartwellreit.ca
Parent: Chartwell Seniors Housing REIT
Number of Beds: 69 suites
Stephen Suske, CEO, Chartwell Seniors Housing REIT

***Burlington:* Appleby Place**
500 Appleby Line, Burlington, ON L7L 5Z6
905-333-1611 Fax: 905-333-0596
applebyplace@lrc.ca
www.reveraliving.com/homes/8001/
Number of Beds: 90 units
Mary Turnbull, General Manager

***Burlington:* Bethany Residence**
2387 Industrial St., Burlington, ON L7P 3A1
905-335-3463 Fax: 905-335-1202
Number of Beds: 121 beds
Sheri Levy-Abraham, Manager

***Burlington:* Brantwood Lifecare Centre**
802 Hager Ave., Burlington, ON L7S 1X2
905-637-3481 Fax: 905-637-7514
www.ourhomeyourhome.eycan.com
Number of Beds: 178 beds
Kevin Baglole, Administrator
kbaglole@extendicare.com

***Burlington:* Christopher Court Retirement Home**
392 Pearl St., Burlington, ON L7R 2M9
905-639-4055 Fax: 905-639-9171
reynolds@residencesallegro.com
www.residencesallegro.com
Number of Beds: 50 beds
Lorie Tokola, General Manager

***Burlington:* Christopher Terrace Retirement Home**
3131 New St., Burlington, ON L7N 3P8
905-632-5072 Fax: 905-632-5074

Number of Beds: 80 beds
Laurie Johnston, Manager

Burlington: Lakeshore Place Retirement Residence
5314 Lakeshore Rd., Burlington, ON L7L 6L8
905-333-0009 Fax: 905-333-3103
info@caregard.ca
www.lakeshoreplace.ca/lakeshore.htm
Number of Beds: 156 beds (residential care, assisted & daily living)
Note: assisted living retirement residence
Nancy Fischer, Administrator

Burlington: Park Avenue Manor
924 Park Ave. West, Burlington, ON L7T 1N7
905-333-3323
parkavenuegm@cogeco.net
www.chartwellreit.ca
Number of Beds: 69 suites
Note: Specialties: Recreational activities; Medication administration; Wellness monitoring; Respite care; Convalescent, seasonal, & trial stays
Carrie T. Campbell, General Manager

Cambridge: Avonlea Place
611 Dunbar Rd., Cambridge, ON N3H 2T4
519-650-1102 Fax: 519-650-3382
avonleaplace@rogers.com
Number of Beds: 32 beds
Jason Rumph

Cambridge: Queen's Square Terrace
10 Melville St. North, Cambridge, ON N1S 1H5
519-621-2777 Fax: 519-622-1299
queenssquare@chartwellreit.ca
www.chartwellreit.ca
Parent: Chartwell Seniors Housing REIT
Number of Beds: 80 suites
Stephen Suske, CEO, Chartwell Seniors Housing REIT

Carleton Place: Carleton Place Manor
6 Arthur St., Carleton Place, ON K7C 4S4
613-253-7360 Fax: 613-253-5048
Number of Beds: 115 rooms
Corrie Berryman, Executive Director

Chatham: Maple City Retirement Residence
97 McFarlane Ave., Chatham, ON N7L 4V6
519-354-7111 Fax: 519-351-5780
adm.maplecity@diversicare.ca
www.diversicare.ca
Number of Beds: 75 beds
Hilda Michielsen, Administrator

Chatham: Residence on The Thames
850 Grand Ave. West, Chatham, ON N7L 5H5
519-351-7220 Fax: 519-436-0360
crystal_houle@srgroup.ca
www.srgroup.ca
Parent: Steeves & Rozema Group
Number of Beds: 75 beds
Note: Independent living
Liddy Krieger, Executive Director
Crystal Houle, Office Manager

Codrington: Dorland House Retirement Residence
387 Goodrich Rd., Codrington, ON K0K 1R0
613-475-4846 Fax: 613-475-4961
dorlandhouse@sympatico.ca
www.orca-homes.com
Number of Beds: 28 beds
Joan Dorland, Administrator

Cornwall: Chateau Cornwall
41 Amelia St., Cornwall, ON K6H 7E5
613-937-4700 Fax: 613-932-6407
chateaucornwall@chartwellreit.ca
Number of Beds: 105 suites
Denis Carr, Manager

Delhi: Delrose Retirement Residence
725 Gibraltar St., Delhi, ON N4B 3C7
519-582-4072 Fax: 519-582-2273
Number of Beds: 53 beds
Annemarie Barker, Administrator

Dresden: Park Street Place Retirement Residence
650 Park St., Dresden, ON N0P 1M0
519-683-4474 Fax: 519-683-4555 www.diversicare.ca
Year Founded: 1987
Note: Specialties: Foot care; Physiotherapy; Medication management; Recreational activities; Respite & convalescent stays
Hilda Michielsen, Administrator

Dundas: The Georgian Retirement Residence
255 Governor's Rd., Dundas, ON L9H 3K4
905-627-8444 Fax: 905-627-9820
georgian@chartwellreit.ca
www.chartwellreit.ca
Parent: Chartwell Seniors Housing REIT
Number of Beds: 60 suites
Stephen Suske, CEO, Chartwell Seniors Housing REIT

Fort Erie: Garrison Place Retirement Residence
373 Garrison Rd., Fort Erie, ON L2A 1N1
905-871-6410 Fax: 905-871-5422
garrisonplace@reveraliving.com
www.reveraliving.com
Number of Beds: 80 beds
Note: Secured living for dementia care residents; respite & convalescent options
Judy Gibson, Manager

Georgetown: Mountainview Residence
222 Mountainview Rd. North, Georgetown, ON L7G 3R2
905-877-1800 Fax: 905-873-9083
info@mountainviewresidence.com
www.mountainviewresidence.com
Number of Beds: 82 suites
Christopher Summer, Manager

Gloucester: Camilla Gardens
1119 Bathgate Dr., Gloucester, ON K1J 9N4
613-747-7000 Fax: 613-747-1804
camillagardens@bellnet.ca
www.camillaresidence.yp.ca
Number of Beds: 54 beds
Lyne Bellefeuille, Administrator

Gloucester: Elmsmere Retirement Residence
889 Elmsmere St., Gloucester, ON K1J 8G4
613-745-2409 Fax: 613-745-4955
elmsmereplace@reveraliving.com
Number of Beds: 57 units
Pierre Lefebvre, Manager

Gloucester: Ogilvie Villa
1345 Ogilvie Rd., Gloucester, ON K1J 7P5
613-742-6524 Fax: 613-742-7380
ogilvie@reveraliving.com
www.reveraliving.com
Year Founded: 1995
Number of Beds: 64 residential capacity
Note: Specialties: Recreation program; Short term stays
Bob Lemay, Manager

Goderich: Goderich Place Retirement Residence
30 Balvina Dr. East, Goderich, ON N7A 4L5
519-524-4243 Fax: 519-524-8173
goderichplace@on.aibn.com
Number of Beds: 68 beds
Valerie Posadas, Administrator

Goderich: Maple Grove Lodge
45 Nelson St. East, Goderich, ON N7A 1R7
519-524-8610
Number of Beds: 25 beds
Note: Nursing home

Gravenhurst: Gravenhurst Manor
300 Muskoka Rd. North, Gravenhurst, ON P1P 1N8
705-687-3356 Fax: 705-687-5685
gravenhurstmanor@chartwellreit.ca
www.chartwellreit.ca/home_locations/gravenhurst.htm
Number of Beds: 50 suites
Gay Pengilly, Administrator

Grimsby: Maplecrest Village Retirement Residence
85 Main St. East, Grimsby, ON L3M 1N6
905-945-7044 Fax: 905-945-6187
maplecrest@reveraliving.com
Number of Beds: 80 beds
Leanne Dabbs, Administrator

Guelph: College Place Retirement Residence
166 College Ave. West, Guelph, ON N1G 1S4
519-822-0090 Fax: 519-822-2310
college@reveraliving.com
www.reveraliving.com
Old Name: Meadowcroft Place Retirement Centre
Number of Beds: 57 residential capacity
Note: Specialties: Assisted living program; Podiatry services; Recreation program; Short term stays
Alice Johnstone, Executive Director

Guelph: Norfolk Manor
128 Norfolk St., Guelph, ON N1H 4J8
519-837-1100 Fax: 519-836-4003
david@norfolkmanor.ca
www.norfolkmanor.ca
Number of Beds: 67 beds
David Ing, Manager

Guelph: Stone Lodge Retirement Residence
165 Cole Rd., Guelph, ON N1G 4N9
519-767-0880 Fax: 519-767-1690
stonelodge@reveraliving.com
www.reveraliving.com
Number of Beds: 130 units
Note: Independent & assisted living; convalescent & respite options
E. Lyn Fisher, Administrator

Guelph: Village of Riverside Glen
60 Woodlawn Rd. East, Guelph, ON N1H 8M8
519-822-5272 Fax: 519-822-5520
www.oakwoodretirement.com/riverside.html
Number of Beds: 196 beds
Michell Vermeeren, Manager

Hamilton: Atrium Villa
467 Main St. East, Hamilton, ON L8M 1K1
905-521-4442 Fax: 905-521-8247
atriumvilla@chartwellreit.ca
chartwellreit.ca/home_locations/atrium_villa.htm
Number of Beds: 67 units
Margaret Coulter, Manager

Hamilton: Central Park Lodges - Hamilton
35 Arkledun Ave., Hamilton, ON L8N 2H5
905-522-2471 Fax: 905-570-0032
Number of Beds: 76 beds
Carol Sterkenburg, Administrator

Hamilton: Good Shepherd Centre
PO Box 1003, 135 Mary St., Hamilton, ON L8N 3R1
905-528-9109 Fax: 905-546-1743
Number of Beds: 24 beds
Richard McPhee, Executive Director

Hamilton: Proctor Manor Retirement Home
81 Proctor Blvd., Hamilton, ON L8M 2M5
905-545-2427 Fax: 905-547-7195
Old Name: Proctor Manor Nursing Home
Number of Beds: 23 beds
Joyce Carey, Manager

Hamilton: Stinson Manor
112 Stinson St., Hamilton, ON L8N 1S5
905-521-9112 Fax: 905-521-9106

Hamilton: Townsview Retirement Residence
52 Catherine St. North, Hamilton, ON L8R 1J1
905-527-1200 www.ourhomeyourhomecanada.ca
Number of Beds: 57 residential capacity
Note: Specialties: Personal nursing care; Catheter care; Colostomy care; Diabetes care; Oxygen care; Wellness program; Medication administration; Activity program
Derrick Bernardo, Administrator

Hanover: The Village Seniors Community
101 Tenth St., Hanover, ON N4N 1M9
519-364-4320 Fax: 519-364-6953
thevillageseniors'community@reveraliving.com
www.reveraliving.com
Number of Beds: 70 long-term, 95 retirement beds, 100 seniors' apartments
Karen Kraus, Administrator

Harrow: Harrowood Seniors Community
1 Pollard Dr., Harrow, ON N0R 1G0
519-738-2286 Fax: 519-738-2700
Old Name: Harrowood Rest Home
Number of Beds: 105 beds
Note: seniors community
Carol Chisholm, Administrator

Hawkesbury: Place Mont Roc
100 Industrial Blvd., Hawkesbury, ON K6A 3M8
613-632-2900
pmr@hawk.igs.net
Number of Beds: 95 beds
Heather Sheffield, Administrator

Huntsville: Rogers Cove Retirement Residence
4 Coveside Dr., Huntsville, ON P1H 2J9
705-789-1600 Fax: 705-789-8781
rogerscove@chartwellreit.ca
www.chartwellreit.ca
Parent: Chartwell Seniors Housing REIT
Number of Beds: 55 suites

Stephen Suske, CEO, Chartwell Seniors Housing REIT

Ingersoll: Oxford Manor Retirement Home
276 Oxford St., Ingersoll, ON N5G 2W1
519-485-0350 Fax: 519-485-7254
oxfordmanor@chartwellreit.ca
www.chartwellreit.ca
Number of Beds: 46 units
Note: Specialties: Activity program; Medication administration; Wellness monitoring; Respite care; Trial stays
Diance Nant, Administrator

Kanata: Chartwell House Kanata
20 Shirley's Brook Dr., Kanata, ON K2K 2W8
613-591-8939 Fax: 613-591-1933
Number of Beds: 84 beds
Johanne Laframboise, General Manager
jlaframboise@chartwellreit.ca
Lisa Giles, Community Relations Manager
lgiles@chartwellreit.ca

Kanata: Fairfield Manor Retirement Home
17 Lombardo Dr., Kanata, ON K2L 4E8
613-592-5772 Fax: 613-592-8928
info@fairfieldmanor.ca
www.fairfieldmanor.ca
Number of Beds: 46 Beds
Lisa Knopp, Administrator

Kanata: Kanata Retirement Residence
145 Castlefrank Rd. South, Kanata, ON K2L 3X9
613-831-3333 Fax: 613-831-0153
kanataplace@reveraliving.com
Number of Beds: 66 units
Robyn Bosik, Executive Director

Kanata: Walden Retirement Residence
27 Weaver Cres., Kanata, ON K2K 2Z8
613-591-3991 Fax: 613-591-9647
Number of Beds: 93 beds
Heidi Eichenberger, General Manager

Kincardine: Malcolm Place
PO Box 100, 255 Durham St., Kincardine, ON N2Z 2Y6
519-396-5800 Fax: 519-396-5236
home@malcolmplace.on.ca
www.malcolmplace.ca
Number of Beds: 41 beds
Note: Retirement Residence
Dorinda Bowers, Administrator

Kingston: The Rosewood
833 Sutton Mills Ct., Kingston, ON K7P 2N9
613-384-7131 Fax: 613-634-3247
debbie.helferty@specialty-care.com
www.speciality-care.com
Number of Beds: 70 units
Note: Independent living
Debbie Helferty, General Manager

Kingston: St. Lawrence Place
181 Ontario St., Kingston, ON K7L 5M1
613-544-5900 Fax: 613-544-9971
st.lawrence@reveraliving.com
www.reveraliving.com
Number of Beds: 71 units
Margaret Bennett, Executive Director

Kingston: Trillium Ridge Retirement Community
800 Edgar St., Kingston, ON K7M 8S4
613-547-0040 Fax: 613-547-3734
taimi.post@specialty-care.com
www.specialty-care.com
Note: Independent living. Specialty Care Trillium Centre long-term care residence located adjacent
Taimi Post, Director, Marketing & Resident Services

Kingsville: Kings Manor Residence
31 Pearl St. West, Kingsville, ON N9Y 1V3
519-733-5378 Fax: 519-733-8552
mmayhew@mnsi.net
Number of Beds: 9 beds
Marie Mayhew, Manager

Kitchener: Bankside Terrace
71 Bankside Dr., Kitchener, ON N2N 3L1
519-749-9999 Fax: 519-749-1947
bankside@chartwellreit.ca
www.chartwellreit.ca/home_locations/bankside_terrace.htm
Number of Beds: 86 units
Brad Lawrence, Manager

Kitchener: Conestoga Lodge Retirement Residence
55 Hugo Cres., Kitchener, ON N2M 5J1
519-576-2140 Fax: 519-576-1790 www.conestogalodge.com
Number of Beds: 88 beds
Betty Cushing, Manager

Kitchener: Conestoga Towers - Trillium Retirement Apartments
221 Queen St. South, Kitchener, ON N2G 1W5
519-578-9280 Fax: 519-578-9626
Number of Beds: 36 beds
Barbara Sutcliffe, Administrator

Kitchener: Fergus Place Retirement Residence
164 Fergus Ave., Kitchener, ON N2A 2H2
519-894-9600 Fax: 519-894-3383
fergus@reveraliving.com
www.reveraliving.com
Old Name: Meadowcroft Place
Number of Beds: 76 residential capacity
Note: Specialty: Short term stays
Jane Hagelberg, Administrator

Kitchener: Lafontaine Terrace
169 Borden Ave. North, Kitchener, ON N2H 3J5
519-576-2800 Fax: 519-742-4242
lafontaine@on.aibn.com
Jeff Edwards, Administrator

Kitchener: Lanark Place Retirement Residence
44 Lanark Cres., Kitchener, ON N2N 2Z8
519-743-0121 Fax: 519-743-8901
info@lanarkcare.com
www.lanarkcare.com
Number of Beds: 107 units
Nancy Douglas, Manager

Kitchener: Victoria Place Retirement Residence
290 Queen St. South, Kitchener, ON N2G 1W3
519-576-1300 Fax: 519-744-7097
victoriaplace@reveraliving.com
www.reveraliving.com
Number of Beds: 73 beds
Note: Independent & assisted living
Deb Gemmell, Executive Director

Leamington: Erie Glen Manor Retirement Residence
119 Robson Rd., Leamington, ON N8H 3V4
519-322-2384 Fax: 519-322-1411
Number of Beds: 81 beds
Shelley Gould, Administrator

Leamington: Leamington Lodge Residential Care Centre Ltd.
PO Box 353, 24 Russell St., Leamington, ON N8H 3W3
519-326-3591 Fax: 519-326-8787
Number of Beds: 40 beds
Jane Lee, Administrator

London: Ashwood Manor Ltd.
79 David St., London, ON N6P 1B4
519-652-9006 Fax: 519-652-2592
info@ashwoodmanor.com
www.ashwoodmanor.com
Number of Beds: 72 units
Kathleen Hobden, Administrator

London: Central Park Lodge - London
279 Horton St., London, ON N6B 1L3
519-434-4544 Fax: 519-673-4971
cplondon@reveraliving.com
www.reveraliving.com
Number of Beds: 87 units
Note: Assisted living
Susan O'Neill, Administrator

London: Horizon Place Retirement Residence
760 Horizon Dr., London, ON N6H 5G3
519-641-6330 Fax: 519-641-0570
horizon@reveraliving.com
www.reveraliving.com
Old Name: Meadowcroft Place
Number of Beds: 84 residential capacity
Note: Specialties: Assisted living program; Recreation therapy; Podiatry; Short term stays
Marilyn Weekley, Manager

London: Kensington Village
1340 Huron St., London, ON N5V 3R3
519-455-3910 Fax: 519-455-1570
sbrooks@kensingtonvillage.org
www.kensingtonvillage.org
Year Founded: 1984
Number of Beds: 139 suites
Peter Schlegel, Administrator
519/455-3910, pschlegel@kensingtonvillage.org
Wendy Harrison, Director, Retirement Care
519/455-3910, wharrison@kensingtonvillage.org

London: Longworth Retirement Residence
600 Longworth Rd., London, ON N6K 4X9
519-472-1115 Fax: 519-472-1134
info@longworthcare.com
www.longworthcare.com
Number of Beds: 126 suites
Note: Specialty: Retirement / assisted living; Physiotherapy; Massage therapy; Reiki; Reflexology

London: Waverley Mansion Retirement Residence
10 Grand Ave., London, ON N5C 1K9
519-667-1381 Fax: 519-667-9601
gm.waverley@diversicare.ca
www.diversicare.ca
Year Founded: 1987
Number of Beds: 65 beds
Note: Specialties: Supported care services for older adults; Medication administration & supervision; Physiotherapy; Foot care; Recreational program; Respite care; Convalescent stays
Suzi McArthur, Administrator

Midland: King Place Retirement Residence
750 King St., Midland, ON L4R 4K5
705-526-0514 Fax: 705-526-8769
kingplace@reveraliving.com
www.reveraliving.com
Number of Beds: 80 beds
Note: Independent & assisted living; secured living for dementia care residents; respite & convalescent options
Sharon Penrose, Manager

Midland: The Villa Care Centre & Retirement Lodge
689 Yonge St., Midland, ON L4R 2E1
705-526-4238 Fax: 705-526-5080 www.jarlette.com
Number of Beds: 158 beds
Edith Robitaille, Administrator
erobitaille@jarlette.com
Tanya Wilfling, General Manager
twilfling@jarlette.com
Michelle Lloyd, Customer Service Coordinator
mlloyd@jarlette.com

Mississauga: Beechwood Place
1500 Rathburn Rd. East, Mississauga, ON L4W 4L7
905-238-0800 Fax: 905-238-4926
beechwoodplace@lrc.ca
Number of Beds: 137 suites
Deborah Rushton, Executive Director
Julie Shuster, Director of Marketing

Mississauga: Bough Beeches Place Retirement Residence
1130 Bough Beeches Blvd., Mississauga, ON L4W 4G3
905-625-2022 Fax: 905-238-3052
boughbeeches@reveraliving.com
www.reveraliving.com
Old Name: Meadowcroft Place
Year Founded: 1984
Number of Beds: 109 residential capacity
Note: Specialties: Assisted living program; Secured living program, for persons with dementia & Alzheimers disease; Short term stays; Fitness program; Podiatry services
Karen Douglas, Administrator

Mississauga: Erin Mills Lodge
2132 Dundas St. West, Mississauga, ON L5K 2K7
905-823-6700 Fax: 905-823-2410
info@erinmillscare.com
www.erinmillscare.com
Number of Beds: 141 retirement units, 86 long-term care beds
Mary Whalen, Administrator

Mississauga: King Gardens Retirement Residence
85 King St. East, Mississauga, ON L5A 4G6
905-566-4545 Fax: 905-566-0327
kinggardens@reveraliving.com
www.reveraliving.com/homes/226
Number of Beds: 147 beds
Agnes Kupny, Executive Director

Morrisburg: Hartford Retirement Centre
3 Fifth St. West, Morrisburg, ON K0C 1X0
613-543-3984 Fax: 613-543-4262
hartford@chartwellreit.ca
www.chartwellreit.ca
Number of Beds: 67 suites
Lynn Hill, Administrator

Mount Forest: Birmingham Lodge
356A Birmingham St. East, Mount Forest, ON N0G 2L2
519-323-4019 Fax: 519-323-3005 www.diversicare.ca

Number of Beds: 95 units
Ilonka van Willigen, Administrator

Napanee: The Riverine Independent & Retirement Living
328 Dundas St. West, Napanee, ON K7R 4B5
613-354-8188 Fax: 613-354-8186 866-387-2217
Number of Beds: 42 beds
Note: Specialties: Medication administration; Social & recreational program
Greg Freeman, Manager

Nepean: Riverpark Place Retirement Residence
1 Corkstown Rd., Nepean, ON K2H 1B6
613-828-8882 Fax: 613-828-8908
info@caregard.ca
www.riverparkplace.ca
Number of Beds: 173 beds (residential care, assisted & daily living)
Cathy Arthurs-Hall, Administrator

Nepean: Stillwater Creek Retirement Community
18 Robertson Rd., Nepean, ON K2H 1C6
613-828-7575 Fax: 613-828-7524
info@caregard.ca
www.stillwatercreek.ca
Year Founded: 2001
Number of Beds: 204 units
Note: Specialties: Independent living; Assisted living; Recreation programs
Mike Traub, Administrator

Newmarket: Alexander Muir Retirement Residence
197 Prospect St., Newmarket, ON L3Y 3T7
905-836-8399 Fax: 905-836-9322
mayers@residencesallegro.com
www.residencesallegro.com/en/
Number of Beds: 96 units
Michael Ayers, General Manager

Niagara Falls: Cavendish Manor Retirement Residence
5781 Dunn St., Niagara Falls, ON L2G 2N9
905-354-2733 Fax: 905-354-4164 www.cavendishmanor.com
Number of Beds: 69 units
Janice Amos, Manager

Niagara Falls: Chippawa Place
4118 Main St., Niagara Falls, ON L2G 6C2
905-295-6744 Fax: 905-295-6306
Number of Beds: 26 beds
Mark Budic, Administrator
Susan Budic, Administrator

Niagara Falls: Lundy Manor Retirement Residence
7860 Lundy's Lane, Niagara Falls, ON L2H 1H1
905-356-1511 Fax: 905-356-1736
lundy@reveraliving.com
www.reveraliving.com
Number of Beds: 95 capacity
Note: Specialties: Assisted living program; Short term stays; Podiatry services
Art Derbernardi, Manager

Niagara Falls: Willoughby Manor
3584 Bridgewater St., Niagara Falls, ON L2G 6H1
905-295-6288 Fax: 905-295-4767
willoughbymanor@chartwellreit.ca
www.chartwellreit.ca
Parent: Chartwell Seniors Housing REIT
Number of Beds: 52 suites
Note: Retirement residence, with convalescent, respite & seasonal stay options
Stephen Suske, CEO, Chartwell Seniors Housing REIT

North Bay: Barclay House Retirement Residence
600 Chippewa St. West, North Bay, ON P1B 9E7
705-476-6585 Fax: 705-476-6542
barclay@chartwellreit.ca
www.chartwellreit.ca
Parent: Chartwell Seniors Housing REIT
Number of Beds: 64 suites
Stephen Suske, CEO, Chartwell Seniors Housing REIT

Norwood: Maple View Retirement Centre
90 Victoria St., RR#2, Norwood, ON K0L 2V0
705-639-5374 Fax: 705-639-1793
Number of Beds: 60 beds
Kim Ward, Administrator

Oakville: Churchill Place
345 Church St., Oakville, ON L6J 7G4
905-338-3311 Fax: 905-338-7117
churchillplace@lrc.ca
www.reveraliving.com
Number of Beds: 69 suites
Note: Independent living, convalescent & respite options
Carole Huppenthal, General Manager

Oakville: The Kensington
25 Lakeshore Rd. West, Oakville, ON L6K 3X8
905-844-4000 Fax: 905-842-9229
thekensingtonon@lrc.ca
www.reveraliving.com
Number of Beds: 120 suites
Note: Independent living
Judy Martin, General Manager

Oakville: Oakville Senior Citizens Residence
#2220, 2222 Lakeshore Rd. West, Oakville, ON L6L 5G5
905-827-4139 Fax: 905-827-8047
oscr@oakvilleseniors.com
www.oakvilleseniors.com
Number of Beds: 164 apartment tower units + 172 residential tower rooms

Oakville: Trafalgar Lodge Retirement Residence
299 Randall St., Oakville, ON L6J 6B4
905-842-8408 Fax: 905-842-8410
trafalgar@reveraliving.com
www.reveraliving.com
Number of Beds: 75 units
Note: Independent & assisted living; convalescent & respite options
Eileen Brajovic, Executive Director

Orangeville: Lord Dufferin Centre
32 First St., Orangeville, ON L9W 2E1
519-941-8433 Fax: 519-941-2615 www.lorddufferincentre.ca
Number of Beds: 78 private suites
Note: Specialties: Physiotherapy; Foot care
Donna Holwell, Manager

Orillia: Atrium Retirement Residence
230 Coldwater Rd. West, Orillia, ON L3V 3M2
705-325-7300 Fax: 705-325-9078
atrium@chartwellreit.ca
chartwellreit.ca/home_locations/atrium.htm
Number of Beds: 50 units
Miriam Leduc, Manager

Orillia: Birchmere Retirement Residence
234 Bay St., Orillia, ON L3V 3W8
705-326-8520 Fax: 705-326-5273
birchmere@on.aibn.com
Number of Beds: 77 beds
Jackie Payne, Administrator

Orillia: Champlain Manor
65 Fittons Rd. West, Orillia, ON L3V 3V2
705-326-8597 Fax: 705-326-9831
champlainmanor@on.aibn.com
www.retireorillia.com
Number of Beds: 65 beds
Jackie Payne, Administrator

Oshawa: Cedarcroft Place (Oshawa)
649 King St. East, Oshawa, ON L1H 8P9
905-723-9490
cedarcroft-oshawa@cplodges.com
Number of Beds: 102 units
Marjorie Beattie, Administrator

Ottawa: Amica at Bearbrook Court
2645 Innes Rd., Ottawa, ON K1B 3J7
613-837-8720 Fax: 613-837-8107
bearbrook@amica.ca
www.amica.ca/bearbrook/
Number of Beds: 122 suites
Luke Goulette, General Manager

Ottawa: Billings Lodge
1180 Bélanger Ave., Ottawa, ON K1H 8A2
613-737-7877 Fax: 613-737-7886
Number of Beds: 100 beds
Alain Brunet, Administrator

Ottawa: Blackburn Lodge Seniors Residence Inc.
2412 Cléroux Cres., Ottawa, ON K1W 1A3
613-837-7467 Fax: 613-837-0250
agraham@blackburnlodge.com
www.blackburnlodge.com
Number of Beds: 53 beds
Alyson Graham, Assistant Manager
David Porter, Manager

Ottawa: Central Park Lodges - Ottawa 1
2374 Carling Ave., Ottawa, ON K2B 7G5
613-820-7333 Fax: 613-820-6815
ottawa1@reveraliving.com
www.reveraliving.com
Number of Beds: 135 units
Note: Independent & assisted living, respite & convalescent options. Central Park Lodge Ottawa 2 located at 2370 Carling Ave.
Ray Hould, General Manager

Ottawa: Colonel By Retirement Residence
43 Aylmer St., Ottawa, ON K1S 4R5
613-730-2002
colonelby@cplodges.com
Number of Beds: 122 units

Ottawa: The Edinburgh Retirement Residence
10 Vaughan St., Ottawa, ON K1M 2H6
613-747-2233 Fax: 613-747-6741
edinburgh@reveraliving.com
www.reveraliving.com
Number of Beds: 66 beds
Note: Independent & assisted living programs
Mary Albota, Administrator

Ottawa: Hunt Club Manor
1351 Hunt Club Rd., Ottawa, ON K1V 1A6
613-733-4776 Fax: 613-733-0496
huntclubmanor@reveraliving.com
www.retirementresidences.com/homes/8018/
Number of Beds: 78 beds
Tracy Fowers, General Manager

Ottawa: Manoir Gallien
162 Murray St., Ottawa, ON K1N 5M8
613-241-1331 Fax: 613-241-2693
info@manoirgalleon.com
Number of Beds: 75 units
Note: Senior's residence
Sandra Sullivan, Administrator

Ottawa: New Edinburgh Square
420 Mackay St., Ottawa, ON K1M 2C4
613-744-0901 Fax: 613-742-3039
newedinburghsquare@chartwellreit.ca
www.chartwellreit.ca
Number of Beds: 111 suites
Jacqueline Brown, General Manager

Ottawa: Parklane Residence
1095 Merivale Rd., Ottawa, ON K1Z 6A9
613-725-1064 Fax: 613-728-3533
Number of Beds: 107 beds
Note: Retirement residence
Claude Desforges, Manager

Ottawa: Presland Residence
198 Presland Rd., Ottawa, ON K1K 2B8
613-745-0089
Serge Grégoire, Administrator

Ottawa: Rideau Place On-The-River
550 Wilbrod St., Ottawa, ON K1N 9M3
613-234-6003 Fax: 613-234-9498
rideauplace@chartwellreit.ca
www.chartwellreit.ca; www.rideauplace.com
Parent: Chartwell Seniors Housing REIT
Number of Beds: 98 suites
Note: Retirement residence; short-term respite & convalescent care
Stephen Suske, CEO, Chartwell Seniors Housing REIT
Brian Kimberley, Marketing Manager

Ottawa: Rothwell Heights Retirement Residence
1735 Montréal Rd., Ottawa, ON K1J 6N4
613-744-2322
Number of Beds: 114 units
Anita Hurtubise, Administrator

Ottawa: Sandy Hill Retirement Residence
353 Friel St., Ottawa, ON K1N 7W7
613-234-3838 Fax: 613-234-5472
sandyhill@reveraliving.com
www.reveraliving.com
Number of Beds: 71 beds
Note: Independent & assisting living programs; respite, convalescent options
Mélanie Lefebvre, Executive Director

Ottawa: Sterling Place Retirement Residence
2716 Richmond Rd., Ottawa, ON K2B 8M3

613-829-6527 Fax: 613-829-6201
sterling@reveraliving.com
www.reveraliving.com
Number of Beds: 116 beds
Note: Independent & assisted living programs; dementia care; respite & convalescent options
Rosemary Rowley, Manager

Ottawa: Stittsville Retirement Community
1354 Stittsville Main St., Ottawa, ON K2S 1V4
613-836-2216 Fax: 613-836-1903
stittville@reveraliving.com
www.reveraliving.com
Number of Beds: 75 beds
Note: Independent living
Pat Leishman, Manager

Ottawa: Thorncliffe Place Retirement Home
1 Thorncliffe Pl., Ottawa, ON K2H 9N9
613-596-3853 Fax: 613-596-6225
info@thorncliffeplace.com
www.thorncliffeplace.com
Year Founded: 1989
Number of Beds: 81 suites
Note: Specialties: Activity program; Supervision of medications; Memory support; Elderobics; Convalescent stays
Don Francis, Administrator

Ottawa: Watford House Residence
75 Powell Ave., Ottawa, ON K1S 1Z9
613-230-7423 Fax: 613-230-9194
Number of Beds: 22 beds
Anatoli Brouchkov, Administrator

Owen Sound: Central Place
855 - 3 Ave. East, Owen Sound, ON N4K 2K6
519-371-1968 Fax: 519-371-5357
Number of Beds: 90 beds
John Landen, President

Owen Sound: Hannah Walker Place
832 - 2 Ave. West, Owen Sound, ON N4K 4M5
519-371-1664 Fax: 519-371-5286
Number of Beds: 57 beds
John F. Landen, President

Owen Sound: John Joseph Place
854 - 2 Ave. West, Owen Sound, ON N4K 4M5
519-371-3240 Fax: 519-371-6441
Number of Beds: 45 beds
Linda Crigger, Facility Manager

Pakenham: Country View Lodge
4676 Darks Side Rd., Pakenham, ON K0A 2X0
613-624-5714 Fax: 613-624-5715
info@countryviewlodge.ca
www.countryviewlodge.ca
Number of Beds: 34 beds
Note: retirement home with assisted living/nursing service
Abdullah Al Hussain, Administrator

Paris: Penmarvian Retirement Home
185 Grand River St. North, Paris, ON N3L 2N2
519-442-7140 Fax: 519-442-7156
info@penmarvian.com
www.penmarvian.com
Year Founded: 1980
Number of Beds: 38 beds
Note: Specialties: Nursing care; Activity program
Maria Toncic, Administrator

Perth: Rideau Ferry Country Home
1333, Rideau Ferry Rd., RR#5, Perth, ON K7H 3C7
613-267-6213 Fax: 613-267-6261
Number of Beds: 45 units
Note: Offers both retirement residences and assisted daily living services
Mary Ross, Administrator

Peterborough: Empress Gardens Retirement Residence
131 Charlotte St., Peterborough, ON K9J 2T6
705-876-1314 Fax: 705-876-1908
thegardens@aoninc.com
www.gardensofpeterborough.ca
Number of Beds: 88 beds
Joanne Stone, Executive Director

Peterborough: Peterborough Manor
1039 Water St., Peterborough, ON K9H 3P5
705-748-5343 Fax: 705-876-4741
peterboroughmanor@chartwellreit.ca
www.chartwellreit.ca
Number of Beds: 101 suites
Note: Specialties: Medication administration; Wellness monitoring; Assistance to persons with oxygen, catheters, & ostomies; Activity program; Podiatry; Respite care; Convalescent stays
Martha Creally, Administrator

Peterborough: Princess Gardens Retirement Residence
100 Charlotte St., Peterborough, ON L9J 7L4
705-750-1234 Fax: 705-750-0711 1-866-741-6036
www.princessgardens.ca
Number of Beds: 132 beds
Note: Independent retirement amenities; assisted living/enriched care options; respite & convalescent care
Juris Taurins, Manager

Pickering: Community Nursing Home
1955 Valley Farm Rd., Pickering, ON L1V 1X6
905-831-2522 Fax: 905-420-6030
jbrantonwallace@clmi.ca
Number of Beds: 233 long-term care beds, 61 retirement suites
Joan Branton Wallace, Administrator

Port Hope: Port Hope Villa
65 Ward St., Port Hope, ON L1A 1L8
905-885-2915 Fax: 905-885-2921
ldukes@communitylifecare.on.ca
Number of Beds: 33 beds
Leslie Dukes, Administrator

Port Hope: The Tower of Port Hope Retirement Residence
164 Peter St., Port Hope, ON L1A 1C6
905-885-7261 Fax: 905-885-1519
towerofporthope@chartwellreit.ca
www.chartwellreit.ca
Parent: Chartwell Seniors Housing REIT
Number of Beds: 44 suites
Stephen Suske, CEO, Chartwell Seniors Housing REIT
Julie Inglis, Administrator

Port Perry: West Shore Village
293 Perry St., Port Perry, ON L9L 1S6
905-985-8660 Fax: 905-985-1881 1-800-248-0848
info@westshorevillage.ca
www.westshorevillage.ca
Number of Beds: 71 suites
Note: Specialties: Supported living for seniors; Foot care; Reflexology; Massage therapy; Recreational program; Respite care
Karen Arbuckle, Manager

Renfrew: Quail Creek Retirement Centre
450 Albert St., Renfrew, ON K7V 4K4
613-432-9502 Fax: 613-432-9533
quailcreek@chartwellreit.ca
www.chartwellreit.ca
Number of Beds: 58 beds
Bev Powell, Administrator

Richmond: Richmond Lodge Ltd.
PO Box 1030, 6197 Perth St., Richmond, ON K0A 2Z0
613-838-5016 Fax: 613-838-5017
info@richmondlodge.ca
www.richmondlodge.ca
Number of Beds: 42 beds
Note: Retirement residence
Claudette Richel, Administrator

Richmond Hill: Brookside/Hilltop Retirement Residence
980 Elgin Mills Rd. East, Richmond Hill, ON L4S 1M4
905-884-9248 Fax: 905-884-9745
brooksideplace@reveraliving.com
www.retirementresidences.com/homes/208
Number of Beds: 140 units
Sandra Fernandez, Executive Director

Rockland: Résidence Jardins Bellerive
2950 Laurier St., Rockland, ON K4K 1T3
613-446-7122 Fax: 613-446-7343
Number of Beds: 80 Units
Youri Brouchkov, Administrator

Rockland: Résidence Simon Inc.
845, rue St-Jean, Rockland, ON K4K 1K5
613-446-7023 Fax: 613-446-4867
Number of Beds: 46 lits
Albert Bourdeau, Propriétaire

Sarnia: Marshall Gowland Manor
749 Devine St., Sarnia, ON N7T 1X3
519-336-3720 Fax: 519-336-3734 www.lambtononline.com
Year Founded: 2004
Number of Beds: 126 beds
Note: Specialties: Long-term care; Day programs
Jackie Miller, Resident Manager

Sarnia: Residence on The St. Clair
170 Front St. South, Sarnia, ON N7T 2M5
519-336-1455 Fax: 519-336-8966
cathy_mcintosh@srgroup.ca
www.srgroup.ca
Parent: Steeves & Rozema Group
Number of Beds: 73 beds
Note: Independent living, convalescent & respite options
Cathy McIntosh, Managing Director

Sarnia: Rosewood Manor
711 Indian Rd. North, Sarnia, ON N7T 7Z5
519-332-8877 Fax: 519-332-5047
heather_taylor@srgroup.ca
www.srgroup.ca
Parent: Steeves & Rozema Group
Number of Beds: 55 beds
Note: Independent & assisted living
Heather Taylor, Executive Director

Sault Ste Marie: Pathways Retirement Residence
375 Trunk Rd., Sault Ste Marie, ON P6A 6T5
705-759-1079 Fax: 705-759-1211
info@pathwaysret.com
www.pathwaysret.com
Old Name: Pathways Seniors Residence
Number of Beds: 133 beds
Elaine Robertson, Administrator

Sault Ste Marie: Windsor Park Retirement Residence
617 Queen St. East, Sault Ste Marie, ON P6A 2A6
705-949-2273 Fax: 705-949-2279
Number of Beds: 75 beds
Nat Cicchelli, Administrator

Seaforth: Maplewood Manor
13 Church St., Seaforth, ON N0K 1W0
519-527-1440

Simcoe: Heritage Lodge
182 Norfolk St. South, Simcoe, ON N3Y 2W4
519-428-0930 Fax: 519-428-9103
Annemarie Barker, Administrator

Smiths Falls: Willowdale Retirement Centre
9 Armstrong Dr., Smiths Falls, ON K7A 5H7
613-283-0691 Fax: 613-283-0350
willowdale@chartwellreit.ca
www.chartwellreit.ca
Parent: Chartwell Seniors Housing REIT
Number of Beds: 59 suites
Stephen Suske, CEO, Chartwell Seniors Housing REIT

St Catharines: The Loyalist Retirement Residence
190 King St., St Catharines, ON L2R 3J7
905-641-4422 Fax: 905-641-4989
loyalist@reveraliving.com
www.retirementresidences.com
Number of Beds: 118 residential capacity
Note: Specialties: Assisted living; Nursing supervision; Medication administration; Podiatry services; Recreation & fitness program; Respite care; Convalescent stays
Lydia Tarasiuk, Administrator

St Catharines: Mount Carmel Home
78 Yates St., St Catharines, ON L2R 5R9
905-685-9155
Year Founded: 1920
Number of Beds: 69 beds
Note: seniors residence
M. Anne, Administrator

St Catharines: Tufford Manor Retirement Home
312 Queenston Rd., St Catharines, ON L2P 2X4
905-682-0411 Fax: 905-682-2770 www.hamptontufford.com
Note: Specialties: Short term stays Medication administration
Mike Walter, Administrator
Maria Soares, Director, Housekeeping/Maintenance

St Thomas: Metcalfe Gardens Retirement Residence
45 Metcalfe St., St Thomas, ON N5R 5Y1
519-631-9393 Fax: 519-631-2563 www.diversicare.ca
Year Founded: 1988
Number of Beds: 97 suites
Note: Specialties: Foot care; Physiotherapy; Recreation programs; Respite care
Deborah Geerlinks, Administrator

***St. Joachim:* St. Joachim Manor**
2718 County Rd. 42, St. Joachim, ON N0R 1S0
519-728-1215 Fax: 519-728-0113
Number of Beds: 23 beds
Zlatko Horvat, Owner
Nada Horvat, Owner

***Stoney Creek:* Stoney Creek Retirement Residence**
199 Glover Rd., Stoney Creek, ON L8E 5J2
905-643-1795 Fax: 905-643-1085
www.ourhomeyourhomecanada.ca
Year Founded: 1994
Number of Beds: 39 units
Note: Specialties: Activity program; Catheter care; Colostomy care; Oxygen care; Diabetes care; Medication administration; Wellness program
Genny Lourenco, Retirement Manager

***Stratford:* Anne Hathaway Residence**
480 Downie St., Stratford, ON N5A 7Y5
519-275-2125 Fax: 519-275-2126
annehathaway@chartwellreit.ca
Old Name: The Griffin Residence
Number of Beds: 68 beds
Dianne Roth, Administrator

***Stratford:* Cedarcroft Place Retirement Home**
260 Church St., Stratford, ON N5A 2R6
519-275-0030 Fax: 519-273-0373
cedarcroft-stratford@cplodges.com
Number of Beds: 110 units
Daniel Vito, Administrator

***Sudbury:* Hillside Park Retirement Residence**
82 Ignatius St., Sudbury, ON P3C 5G3
705-675-1999 Fax: 705-675-8233
Number of Beds: 69 beds
Anil Pabani, Administrator

***Sudbury:* Westmount Retirement Residence**
599 William Ave., Sudbury, ON P3A 5W3
705-566-6221 Fax: 705-566-0808
westmount@chartwellreit.ca
www.chartwellreit.ca
Parent: Chartwell Seniors Housing REIT
Number of Beds: 84 suites
Stephen Suske, CEO, Chartwell Seniors Housing REIT

***Temiskaming Shores:* Northdale Manor**
PO Box 370, 142-130 Lakeshore Rd., Temiskaming Shores, ON P0J 1P0
705-647-6541 Fax: 705-647-8284
nordale@ntl.sympatico.ca
www.northdalemanor.ca
Number of Beds: 70 suites
Note: Retirement home
Jan Edwards, Administrator

***Thornhill:* Glynnwood Retirement Residence**
7700 Bayview Ave., Thornhill, ON L3T 5W1
905-881-9475 Fax: 905-881-9490
glynnwood@on.aibn.com
Number of Beds: 143 units
Paul Mitchell, Administrator

***Thorold:* Chestnut Court Retirement Home**
10 Ormond St. North, Thorold, ON L2V 1Y7
905-227-5550 Fax: 905-227-5575
info@chestnuthome.com
www.chestnuthome.com
Number of Beds: 50 beds
Elizabeth Dumoulin, Administrator

***Tilbury:* Hudson Manor**
PO Box 1150, 36 Lawson St., Tilbury, ON N0P 2L0
519-682-3366 Fax: 519-682-0688
douellette.hm@diversicare.ca
Number of Beds: 50 beds
Debbie Ouellette, Administrator

***Tillsonburg:* Tillsonburg Retirement Centre**
183 Rolph St., Tillsonburg, ON N4G 3Y9
519-688-0347 Fax: 519-688-2471
tillsonburgretirement@chartwellreit.ca
www.chartwellreit.ca
Parent: Chartwell Seniors Housing REIT
Number of Beds: 51 suites
Stephen Suske, CEO, Chartwell Seniors Housing REIT

***Timmins:* Chateau Georgian Retirement Residence**
455 Cedar St. North, Timmins, ON P4N 8K4
705-267-7935
chateaugeorgian@chartwellreit.ca
www.chartwellreit.ca
Number of Beds: 63 suites
Note: Specialties: Wellness monitoring; Physical therapy; Recreation therapy; Podiatry; Respite care; Convalescent stays
Lynn Budd, Manager

***Toronto:* The Annex Retirement Residence**
123 Spadina Rd., Toronto, ON M5R 2T1
416-961-6446 Fax: 416-961-3299
theannex@reveraliving.com
www.reveraliving.com
Number of Beds: 102 beds
Note: Independent & assisted living, secured living for dementia care
Maria Silva, General Manager

***Toronto:* The Balmoral Club**
155 Balmoral Ave., Toronto, ON M4V 1J5
416-927-0055 Fax: 416-927-0925
balmoralclub@amica.ca
www.amica.ca
Number of Beds: 66 beds
Monica Byrne, Administrator

***Toronto:* Baycrest Centre for Geriatric Care**
55 Ameer Ave., Toronto, ON M6A 2Z1
416-785-2500 Fax: 416-785-2496
mjacobson@baycrest.org
www.baycrest.org
Division of: Terraces of Baycrest
Number of Beds: 199 Apartments
Note: supportive living
Sheila Smyth, Director

***Toronto:* Baycrest Centre for Geriatric Care**
3560 Bathurst St., Toronto, ON M6A 2E1
416-785-2500 Fax: 416-785-2464
swherbert@baycrest.org
www.baycrest.org
Number of Beds: 300 beds
Stephen W. Herbert, President/CEO

***Toronto:* Beach Arms Retirement Residence**
505 Kingston Rd., Toronto, ON M4L 1V5
416-698-0414 Fax: 416-698-9839
info@beacharms.com
www.beacharms.com
Number of Beds: 80 beds
Susan Turner, Administrator

***Toronto:* Belmont House**
55 Belmont St., Toronto, ON M5R 1R1
416-964-9231 Fax: 416-964-1448
information@belmonthouse.com
www.belmonthouse.com
Number of Beds: 55 apartments, 26 retirement suites; 140 long-term care beds
Note: Total employees: 28
Maria Elias, Chief Executive Officer
melias@belmonthouse.com

***Toronto:* Centennial Park Place Retirement Residence**
25 Centennial Park Rd., Toronto, ON M9C 5H1
416-621-2139 Fax: 416-621-9801
centennial@reveraliving.com
www.reveraliving.com
Old Name: Meadowcroft Place Retirement Residence
Number of Beds: 48 residential capacity
Note: Specialty: Podiatry services; Fitness program
Naida McKechnie, Manager

***Toronto:* Central Park Lodges - Queens Drive 1**
265 Queens Dr., Toronto, ON M6L 3C6
416-241-1113 Fax: 416-241-1801
queensdr2@reveraliving.com
www.reveraliving.com
Number of Beds: 113 beds
Note: Independent & assisted living, respite & convalescent options. Central Park Lodge Queens Drive 2 located at 303 Queens Drive
Brenda MacCallum, General Manager

***Toronto:* Central Park Lodges - Queens Drive 2**
303 Queens Dr., Toronto, ON M6L 3C1
416-241-1113 Fax: 416-241-1801
queensdr2@reveraliving.com
www.reveraliving.com
Number of Beds: 156 units
Note: Independent & assisted living. Central Park Lodge Queens Drive 1 located at 265 Queens Drive
L. Kabot, Administrator

***Toronto:* Don Mills Seniors' Apartments**
1055-1057 Don Mills Rd., Toronto, ON M3C 1W9
416-445-7555 Fax: 416-445-0417
donmillsseniorsapts@lrc.ca
www.reveraliving.com/homes/8005/
Number of Beds: 143 suites
Erik Smith, General Manager

***Toronto:* Donway Place**
8 The Donway East, Toronto, ON M3C 3R7
416-445-7555 Fax: 416-445-0417
donway.place@lrc.ca
www.reveraliving.com/homes/8006/
Number of Beds: 245 suites
Erik Smith, Administrator

***Toronto:* Eden Manor**
251 St George St., Toronto, ON M5R 2M2
416-515-1136 Fax: 416-515-1137
edenmanor@bellnet.ca
www.edenmanor.ca
Number of Beds: 25 beds
W. Boggs, Administrator

***Toronto:* Fellowship Towers**
877 Yonge St., Toronto, ON M4W 3M2
416-923-8887 Fax: 416-923-1343
inquiries@fellowshiptowers.com
www.fellowshiptowers.com
Number of Beds: 284 beds
Marilyn Burton, Administrator
mburton@fellowshiptowers.com

***Toronto:* Forest Hill Place**
645 Castlefield Ave., Toronto, ON M5N 3A5
416-785-1511 Fax: 416-785-6228
fh.mkg@lrc.ca
www.lrc.ca
Number of Beds: 125 suites

***Toronto:* Glebe Manor Retirement Residence**
17 Glebe Rd. West, Toronto, ON M5P 1C8
416-485-1150 Fax: 416-485-6378
J.T. Whitebread, Administrator

***Toronto:* Grenadier Retirement Residence**
2100 Bloor St. West, Toronto, ON M6S 1M7
416-769-2885 Fax: 416-769-7238 www.thegrenadier.com
Note: Specialties: Physiotherapy; Wellness program; Activity program; Medication administration; Short-term stays
Dwight Mountney, Administrator

***Toronto:* Harold & Grace Baker Centre**
1 Northwestern Ave., Toronto, ON M6M 2J7
416-654-2889 Fax: 416-654-0217
bakercentre@reveraliving.com
www.reveraliving.com
Number of Beds: 233 beds
Milena Sujer, Administrator
Owen Shaw, Manager, Environmental Services

***Toronto:* Hazelton Place**
111 Avenue Rd., Toronto, ON M5R 3J8
416-928-0111 Fax: 416-928-0118 www.hazeltonplace.ca
Number of Beds: 130 units
Lillian Russell, General Manager

***Toronto:* Lansing Retirement Residence**
10 Senlac Rd., Toronto, ON M2N 6P8
416-250-7029 Fax: 416-250-7853
Number of Beds: 110 beds
Jill Estioko, Manager

***Toronto:* Leaside Retirement Residence**
10 William Morgan Dr., Toronto, ON M4H 1E7
416-425-3722 Fax: 416-425-3946
leaside@reveraliving.com
www.reveraliving.com
Number of Beds: 211 beds
Note: Secured living for dementia care
P. Lemdal, General Manager

***Toronto:* Livingston Lodge Retirement Residence**
65 Livingston Rd., Toronto, ON M1E 1L1
416-264-4348 Fax: 416-264-4340 www.residencesallegro.com
Number of Beds: 103 capacity
Note: Specialities: Physiotherapy; Foot care
Janet Iwaszozenko, Executive Director

***Toronto:* McNicoll Manor**
1020 McNicoll Ave., Toronto, ON M1W 2J6
416-499-3313 Fax: 416-499-3379 www.tendercare.ca
Note: Specialties: Physiotherapy
Maureen McAlaster, Coordinator

***Toronto:* New Horizons Tower**
1140 Bloor St. West, Toronto, ON M6H 4E6

416-536-6111 Fax: 416-536-6748
welcome@newhorizonstower.com
www.newhorizonstower.com

Number of Beds: 197 beds
Note: Christian nursing home
Ian C. Logan, Administrator

Toronto: Pine Villa Retirement Residence
1035 Eglinton Ave. West, Toronto, ON M6C 2C8
416-787-5626 Fax: 416-787-3441
pinevilla@reveraliving.com
www.reveraliving.com

Number of Beds: 71 units
Note: Specialties: Medication administration; Assistance for residents who require oxygen, catheters, & ostomies; Physiotherapy; Podiatry; Recreation therapy
Sharon Rosenblum, Executive Director

Toronto: Rayoak Place Retirement Residence
1340 York Mills Rd., Toronto, ON M3A 3R1
416-391-0633 Fax: 416-391-3320
rayoakplace@reveraliving.com
www.reveraliving.com

Also Known As: Meadowcroft Place
Number of Beds: 66 beds
Note: Independent & assisted living
Linda Mullins, Manager

Toronto: Shepherd Terrace Retirement Suites
3758 Sheppard Ave. East, Toronto, ON M1T 3K9
416-609-5700 Fax: 416-293-6229 www.shepherdvillage.org
Number of Beds: 144 units, including 112 assisted living suites
Brock Hall, Administrator

Toronto: Spencer House
36 Spencer Rd., Toronto, ON M6K 2J6
416-531-5737 Fax: 416-531-4722
dsquires@leisureworld.ca
www.leisureworld.ca
Number of Beds: 120 long-term care; 58 retirement beds
Donald Squires, Administrator

Toronto: Terrace Gardens Retirement Residence
3705 Bathurst St., Toronto, ON M6A 2E8
416-789-7670 Fax: 416-789-3372
terrace@reveraliving.com
www.reveraliving.com
Note: Jewish retirement residence; independent & assisted living, secured living for dementia care, convalescent & respite options; COR supervised, mashgiach on site

Utterson: Rowanwood Retirement Residence
81 Rowanwood Rd., Utterson, ON P0B 1M0
705-789-6424 Fax: 705-789-1821
rowanwood@cplodges.com

Number of Beds: 86 beds
Gail Sargeant, Manager

Vankleek Hill: Heritage Lodge Retirement Residence
48 Wall St., Vankleek Hill, ON K0B 1R0
613-678-2690 Fax: 613-678-6760
vankleek@reveraliving.com
Old Name: Vankleek Residence
Number of Beds: 72 beds
Sandra McCormick, Executive Director

Varry's Bay: Water Tower Lodge
9 Stafford St., Varry's Bay, ON K0J 1B0
613-756-9086
watertowerlodge@nrtco.net
www.watertowerlodge.com
Number of Beds: 44 units

Vineland: The Orchards Retirement Residence
Heritage Village, 3421 Frederick Ave., Vineland, ON L0R 2C0
905-562-7357 Fax: 905-562-3051 800-263-4957
www.residencesallegro.com
Year Founded: 1999
Note: Specialties: Medication management; Personal care assistance; Activities program; Physiotherapy; Respite & convalescence care
Bonnie Magwood, Administrator

Walkerton: Maple Court Villa
5 Fourth St., Walkerton, ON N0G 2V0
519-881-2233 Fax: 519-881-0336
maplecourt@chartwellreit.ca
Number of Beds: 47 Suites
Note: Nursing home
JoAnn Todd, Administrator

Waterloo: Lutherwood
139 Father David Bauer Dr., Waterloo, ON N2L 6L1
519-747-4413 www.luthervillage.org
Division of: Luther Village on the Park
Note: Specialties: Assisted living

Waterloo: Terrace on the Square
100 Caroline St. South, Waterloo, ON N2L 1X5
519-749-2888 Fax: 519-749-1674
terraceonthesquare@chartwellreit.ca
www.chartwellreit.ca
Parent: Chartwell Seniors Housing REIT
Number of Beds: 88 suites
Stephen Suske, CEO, Chartwell Seniors Housing REIT

Windsor: Central Park Lodge - Windsor
3387 Riverside Dr. East, Windsor, ON N8Y 1A8
519-948-5293 Fax: 519-948-7513
windsor@reveraliving.com
www.reveraliving.com
Number of Beds: 141 units
Note: Independent & assisted living, secured living for dementia care, respite & convalescent options
Jean Piccinato, General Manager
Marc St. Pierre, Manager, Physical Plant

Windsor: Devonshire Seniors' Residence
901 Riverside Dr. West, Windsor, ON N9A 7J6
519-252-2273 Fax: 519-252-2324 877-521-5686
info@devonshireseniors.com
www.orca-homes.com
Number of Beds: 259 beds
Sharon Woodward, General Manager

Wingham: Braemar Retirement Centre
719 Josephine St. North, Wingham, ON N0G 2W0
519-357-3430 Fax: 519-357-2303 1-888-817-5828
info@braemar-rc.com
www.braemar-rc.com
Number of Beds: 25 beds
Archie Macgowan, Administrator
519/357-3430, macgowana@hurontel.on.ca
M.C. MacGowan, President/CEO
519/357-3430, mcmacgowan@braemar-rc.com

Mental Health Facilities

Mental Health Hospital/Clinic/Facility

Aurora: Southdown Institute
1335 St. John's Rd. East, Aurora, ON L4G 3G8
905-727-4214 Fax: 905-727-4214
administration@southdown.on.ca;
assessment@southdown.on.ca
www.southdown.on.ca
Number of Beds: 44 beds
Note: Specialties: Residential & outpatient psychological treatment to clergy & religious; Psychodynamic group therapy; Individual & group addiction counselling; 12-step groups; Specialized group treatment for persons who have violated sexual boundaries; Art therapy; Health education
Raymond Dlugos, CEO

Blenheim: Southwestern Regional Centre
RR#1, Blenheim, ON N0P 1A0
519-676-6001 Fax: 519-676-5836
Number of Beds: 496 beds
Poul Christensen, Administrator

Brockville: Brockville Mental Health Centre
PO Box 1050, 1804 Hwy. 2 East, Brockville, ON K6V 5W7
613-345-1461 Fax: 613-342-6194 www.rohcg.on.ca
Old Name: Brockville Psychiatric Hospital
Number of Beds: 200 beds
George Weber, President/CEO

Fergus: Community Mental Health Clinic
234 St. Patrick St. East, Fergus, ON N1M 1M6
519-843-6191 Fax: 519-265-7723
V. Lediett, Executive Director

Guelph: Homewood Health Centre
150 Delhi St., Guelph, ON N1E 6K9
519-824-1010 Fax: 519-824-8751
www.homewood.org/healthcentre/main.php
Year Founded: 1883
Number of Beds: 312 beds
Note: Number of Employees: 650; Specialty: Behavioural, addiction & psychiatric services
W. Sheppard, Director, Environmental Services
Edgardo L. Pérez, CEO; Chief of Staff

Hamilton: St. Joseph's Centre for Mountain Health Services
PO Box 585, 100 - 5 St. West, Hamilton, ON L8N 3K7
905-388-2511 Fax: 905-575-6038 www.stjosham.on.ca
Number of Beds: 165 beds
Darlene Barnes, Vice-President
Al Manente, Director, Plant Services
Zenek J. Dybka, Assistant, Hospital Services

Kingston: Ongwanada Hospital
191 Portsmouth Ave., Kingston, ON K7M 8A6
613-548-4417 Fax: 613-548-8135 www.ongwanada.com
Year Founded: 1948
Number of Beds: 227 beds
Note: Specialties: Support for persons with developmental disabilities; Day support; Medical services; Vocational & life skills training; Occupational therapy; Physiotherapy; Hydrotherapy; Snoezelen rRoom; Community behavioural services; Respite care; Research. Number of employees: 494
Robert W. Seaby, Executive Director

Kingston: Providence Care - Mental Health Services
PO Box 603, 752 King St., Kingston, ON K7L 4X3
613-546-1101 Fax: 613-548-5588
prowsea@providencecare.ca
www.pccchealth.org
Old Name: Kingston Psychiatric Hospital
Number of Beds: 198 beds
Note: Adult Treatment & Rehabilitation, Geriatric Psychiatry, Forensic Psychiatry
Allen Prowse, Vice President, Mental Health; Administrator

London: Child & Parent Resource Institute
600 Sanatorium Rd., London, ON N6H 3W7
519-858-2774 Fax: 519-858-3913
Number of Beds: 75 beds
Anne Stark, Administrator

London: Regional Mental Healthcare, London
PO Box 5532 B, 850 Highbury Ave., London, ON N6A 4H1
519-455-5110 Fax: 519-455-9986
Communications.Department@sjhc.london.on.ca
www.sjhc.london.on.ca
Parent: St. Joseph's Health Care, London
Number of Beds: 385 beds

North Bay: Northeast Mental Health Centre
PO Box 3010, 4700 Hwy. 11 North, North Bay, ON P1B 8L1
705-474-1200 Fax: 705-472-1694 www.nemhc.on.ca
Old Name: North Bay Psychiatric Hospital
W. Duguette, Chief Engineer/Maintenance Supervisor

Oakville: Central West Specialized Developmental Services
53 Bond St., Oakville, ON L6K 1L8
905-844-7864 Fax: 905-844-3545
sbadali@cwsds.ca
Old Name: Oaklands Regional Centre
Year Founded: 2006
Note: Specialties: Care & support to persons with multiple developmental disabilities; Basic life skill development; Psychiatry; Behaviour therapy; Occupational therapy; Speech therapy; Respite care
Jim Preston, Director

Ottawa: Royal Ottawa Health Care Group
1145 Carling Ave., Ottawa, ON K1Z 7K4
613-722-6521 Fax: 613-722-4577 www.rohcg.on.ca
Number of Beds: 199 beds (Royal Ottawa Hospital)
Bruce Swan, CEO
Jerry Rogers, Director, Environmental Services

Penetanguishene: Penetanguishene Mental Health Centre
500 Church St., Penetanguishene, ON L9M 1G3
705-549-3181 Fax: 705-549-1549 www.mhcva.on.ca
W. Gregoire, Manager, Plant Services

St Thomas: Regional Mental Health Care, St. Thomas
PO Box 2004, 467 Sunset Dr., St Thomas, ON N5P 3V9
519-631-8510 Fax: 519-633-0852
Communications.Department@sjhc.london.on.ca
www.sjhc.london.on.ca
Parent: St. Joseph's Health Care, London
Number of Beds: 145 beds

Sudbury: Northeast Mental Health Centre
680 Kirkwood Dr., Sudbury, ON P3E 1X3
705-675-9193 Fax: 705-675-6817
dchateauvert@nemhc.on.ca
www.nemhc.on.ca
Division of: Sudbury Campus
Number of Beds: 12 children's beds
Robert Cunningham, CEO

***Sudbury:* Sudbury Regional Hospital - Kirkwood Site Hôpital régional de Sudbury - Emplacement Kirkwood**
680 Kirkwood Dr., Sudbury, ON P3E 1X3
705-675-9193 1-866-469-0822
communications@hrsrh.on.ca
www.hrsrh.on.ca
Note: Acute inpatient psychiatry services
Vickie Kaminiski, CEO
Chris McKibbon, Chief of Staff

***Thunder Bay:* Lakehead Psychiatric Hospital**
PO Box 2930, 580 Algoma St. North, Thunder Bay, ON P7B 5G4
807-343-4300 Fax: 807-343-4387 800-209-9034
www.sjcg.net/services/mentalhealth/lph/
Dawn Eccles, Coordinator, Environmental Services

***Toronto:* Bellwood Health Services Inc.**
1020 McNicoll Ave., Toronto, ON M1W 2J6
416-495-0926 Fax: 416-495-7943 800-387-6198
info@bellwood.ca
www.bellwood.ca
Note: Specialties: Treatment & education for persons who struggle with addictions, such as alcohol & drugs, eating disorders, post traumatic stress disorder, problem gambling, & problematic sexual behaviour; Assessment; Withdrawal management services; Residential treatment program for persons with alcohol addiction; 12-step education & support groups; Life skills coaching; Stress management; Group therapy; Nutritional education & counselling
M. Linda Bell, Chief Executive Officer
Laura Bhoi, President
Janet Lansche, Vice-President, Finance & Administration
Susan McGrail, Director, Clinical Services
Mark Weiss, Medical Director
Mani Alcaide, Manager, Nursing
Michael Hartmann, Manager, Continuing Care & Volunteer Services
Penny Lawson, Manager, Family Services & Special Programs

***Toronto:* Thistletown Regional Centre for Children & Adolescents**
51 Panorama Ct., Toronto, ON M9V 4L8
416-326-0600 Fax: 416-326-9078
Note: Specialties: Counselling for children & youth up to 19 years of age; Family assessment & therapy; Treatment & education for youth with autism & developmental disorders; Sexual abuse treatment & family education; Home support; Outpatient services
Gail Gonda, Administrator

***Toronto:* Toronto East General Hospital/COS**
#203, 177 Danforth Ave., Toronto, ON M4K 1N2
416-461-2000 Fax: 416-461-2222
ptrep@tegh.on.ca (Patients); community@tegh.on.ca (Community)
www.tegh.on.ca
Division of: Community Outreach Services
Note: Specialties: Community based mental health services; Counselling to adults; Supported housing; Psychiatric treatment; Psycho-social rehabilitation; Family support program; Community & school outreach program

***Whitby:* Whitby Mental Health Centre**
700 Gordon St., Whitby, ON L1N 5S9
905-668-5881 Fax: 905-430-4032 1-800-341-6323
communications@wmhc.ca
www.whitbymentalhealthcentre.ca
Note: Specialized, tertiary mental health care on an inpatien/outpatient basis. Residences in Stouffville, Oshawa; community service sites in Newmarket, Georgina, Maple, Uxbridge, Port Perry, Bowmanville, Lindsay & Whitby. Number of staff: 1,200
Glenna Raymond, President/CEO

Special Care Home

***Aurora:* Kerry's Place Autism Services**
#190, 34 Berczy St., Aurora, ON L4G 1W9
905-841-6611 Fax: 905-841-1461 www.kerrysplace.com
Year Founded: 1974
Note: autistic adults home
Glenn Rampton, Executive Director
grampton@kerrysplace.org

***Belleville:* Cheshire Homes - Hastings-Prince Edward**
246 John St., Belleville, ON K8N 3G1
613-966-2941 Fax: 613-966-2461
cheshirehomes@on.aibn.com
T. Wylie-Meyers, Director

***Brantford:* Participation House Brantford**
PO Box 2048, 10 Bell Lane, Brantford, ON N3T 5W5
519-756-1430 Fax: 519-756-0795
www.participationhousebrantford.org
Number of Beds: 30 beds
Note: Non-for-profit organization serving the needs of adults with physical disabilities
Steve Leighfield, Executive Director

***Campbellford:* Wingfield**
RR#3, Campbellford, ON K0L 1L0
705-653-3127
wingfieldhome@sympatico.ca
www.wingfieldhome.com
Number of Beds: 24 beds
Note: private home for developmentally handicapped adults
W. Klompmaker, Administrator
J. Shelley, Administrator

***Cochrane:* Cochrane Community Living**
PO Box 2330, Cochrane, ON P0L 1C0
705-272-5365 Fax: 705-272-4983
icccl@msicafe.com
Number of Beds: 12 beds in 3 facilities
Mac Hiltz, Interim Executive Director

***Collingwood:* Canford House**
695 St. Marie St., Collingwood, ON L9Y 3L4
705-445-5203 Fax: 705-445-7357
Number of Beds: 32 beds
Wayne Canning, Administrator

***Cornwall:* Mains Ouvertes/Open Hands**
123 Pick St., Cornwall, ON K6J 3P5
613-933-0012 Fax: 613-932-5134
Number of Beds: 27 beds
Gerry Miller, Executive Director

***Dryden:* Patricia Gardens Care Home**
#100, 35 Van Horne Ave., Dryden, ON P8N 3B4
807-223-5278

***Gravenhurst:* Val-Glo Home for Special Care**
Doe Lake Rd., RR#3, Gravenhurst, ON P1P 1R3
705-687-6285
Number of Beds: 14 beds
Dianne Rivers, Administrator

***Hamilton:* Lynwood Hall Child & Family Centre**
526 Upper Paradise Rd., Hamilton, ON L9C 5E3
905-389-1361 Fax: 905-389-8765 www.lynwoodhall.com
Note: Specialties: Mental health services, including day treatment, home-based services, & residential services
Alex Thomson, Executive Director

***Hanmer:* Kingsley Residential Home**
PO Box 118, 36 Oscar St., Hanmer, ON P3P 1X6
705-969-5538
Number of Beds: 6 beds
Jeannine Kingsley, Proprietor

***Hanover:* HARC Inc.**
521 - 11th Ave., Hanover, ON N4N 2J3
519-364-6100 Fax: 519-364-7488
harcinc@bmts.com
Number of Beds: 15 beds
Charlie Caudle, Executive Director

***Holland Landing:* Cedar Lane Residential Home Inc.**
19704 Holland Landing Rd., Holland Landing, ON L9N 1M8
905-836-4272

***Keswick:* Pipe & Slipper Home**
2926 Old Homestead Rd., Keswick, ON L4P 3E9
905-476-3601

***Kilworthy:* Trentview House**
1647 Kilworthy Rd., RR#1, Kilworthy, ON P0E 1G0
705-689-5685 Fax: 705-689-5844
trentviewhouse@encode.com
Year Founded: 1979
Number of Beds: 25 beds
Note: Specialties: Services for adults with mental health disabilities

***Kirkfield:* Silver Hills Residential Home**
PO Box 63, Kirkfield, ON K0M 2B0
705-438-3556 Fax: 705-438-3556
Number of Beds: 12 beds
Barbara Brown, Administrator

***Kitchener:* Beattie Residential Home**
251 Queen St. South, Kitchener, ON N2G 1W4
519-743-0047
Number of Beds: 20 beds
Kathy Beattie, Administrator

***Kitchener:* Smith Residential Home**
226 Queen St. South, Kitchener, ON N2P 2P7
519-743-5117
jvos@sunbeamlodge.com
Number of Beds: 26 beds
Pat Smith, Executive Director

***Kitchener:* Sunbeam Lodge**
389 Pinnacle Dr., Kitchener, ON N2G 3W5
519-896-6718
teena@sunbeamlodge.com
www.sunbeamlodge.com
Number of Beds: 22 beds
Note: Specialties: Lont-term residential care & treatment for children with special needs; Day program; Physiotherapy treatment; Kinesiology; Communications programs; Independent living skills program. Number of Employees: 9 Registered Nurses & Registered Practical Nurses + 2 Kinessiologists + 1 Program Coordinator + 21 Child Care Attendants + 1 Dietician + 2 Housekeepers + 1 Executive Secretary
John Vos, Administrator
Shabnam Vos, Administrator

***Kitchener:* Sunbeam Residential Development Centre**
2749 Kingsway Dr., Kitchener, ON N2C 1A7
519-893-6200 Fax: 519-893-9034
postmaster@sunbeamcentre.com
www.sunbeamcentre.com
Year Founded: 1956
Note: Specialties: Care for individuals with diverse & complex developmental challenges; Long-term & short-term support; Activation; Sensory stimulation
Shaune Lawton, Executive Director

***Lindsay:* Keast Residence**
RR#6, Lindsay, ON K9V 4R6
705-328-0631
Number of Beds: 12 beds
M. Keast, Administrator

***Lucan:* Crest Support Services**
13570 Elginfield Rd., RR#1, Lucan, ON N0M 2J0
519-227-6766 Fax: 519-227-6768 www.crestsupportservices.ca
Note: Specialties: Services for adults with mental health or developmental disabilities; Accommodation services; Operation of three small businesses to provide training & employment opportunities
David Ragobar, Executive Director
david@thecrestcentre.com

***Markham:* Participation House**
9 Butternut Lane, Markham, ON L3P 3M1
905-294-0944 Fax: 905-294-7834
postmaster@participationhouse.net
www.participationhouse.net
Number of Beds: 52 beds
Note: Provides services designed to enhance the qualify of life of people with disabilities
Sharon M. Lawlor, Executive Director

***Nepean:* Total Communication Environment/TCE**
#5, 203 Colonnade Rd. South, Nepean, ON K2E 7K3
613-228-0999 Fax: 613-228-1402
tceadmin@tceottawa.org; tcehr@tceottawa.org (Human Resources)
www.tceottawa.org
Year Founded: 1979
Note: Specialties: Services for adults with multiple disabilities & special communication needs; Respite care; Day services; Outreach to long-term care homes
Karen Anderson, Executive Director

***Newmarket:* Brigitta's Residential Home Inc.**
128 Arden Ave., Newmarket, ON L3Y 4H6
905-895-5890
Number of Beds: 22 beds
Brigitta Miller, Administrator

***Newmarket:* Brookside Lodge**
542 Wellington St., Newmarket, ON L3Y 2C6
905-853-7342
Number of Beds: 29 beds
Dave Sedore, Proprietor

***Newmarket:* Brown's Residential Home**
399 Queen St., Newmarket, ON L3Y 2G9
905-898-1955

***Newmarket:* Heritage Lodge**
508 College St., Newmarket, ON L3Y 1C6

905-853-1587 Fax: 905-764-1360
johngas@learned.com
Number of Beds: 21 beds
John Gaspar, Director

Newmarket: Lakeview Place Home for Special Care
#223, 16715-12 Yonge St., Newmarket, ON L3X 1X4
905-898-1015 Fax: 905-898-6414
info@tshyr.ca
www.tshyr.ca
Number of Beds: 19 beds
Monica Auerbach, Executive Director

Newmarket: Parkview Manor
683 Gorham St., Newmarket, ON L3Y 1L5
905-895-9064 Fax: 905-895-9064
parkview@caringplaces.com
www.caringplaces.com
Number of Beds: 23 beds
Note: Home for special care
John Gaspar, Director

North Bay: North Bay & District Association for Community Living
161 Main St. East, North Bay, ON P1B 1A9
705-476-3288 Fax: 705-476-4788 www.nbdacl.org
Number of Beds: 35 beds
Rheal Thorn, Executive Director

Orangeville: Dufferin Association for Community Living
#10, 29 Centennial Rd., Orangeville, ON L9W 1R1
519-941-8971 Fax: 519-941-9121
Number of Beds: 44 beds
Starr Olsen, Executive Director

Ottawa: Roberts/Smart Centre
1199 Carling Ave., Ottawa, ON K1Z 8N8
613-728-1946 Fax: 613-728-4986 800-279-9941
info@rsc-crs.com
www.robertssmartcentre.com
Number of Beds: 47 beds
Cameron Macleod, Executive Director

Owen Sound: Kent Residential Home
1065 - 9 Ave. West, Owen Sound, ON N4K 5R8
519-371-5029 Fax: 519-371-3237
kenthome@bellnet.ca
Old Name: Tucker's Residential Home
Number of Beds: 18 beds
Note: residential home for people with mental illness
Yvonne Kent

Oxford Mills: Old Mill Guest Home
PO Box 218, 12 Bridge St., Oxford Mills, ON K0G 1S0
613-258-3366 Fax: 613-258-3130
Number of Beds: 22 beds
Note: Specialties: Residential services for post-psychiatric patients; Social programs

Peterborough: Community Living Peterborough
223 Aylmer St., Peterborough, ON K9J 3K3
705-743-2411 Fax: 705-743-3722
Number of Beds: 32 beds
Dianne M. Austin, Manager

Peterborough: Kinark Child & Family Services
380 Armour Rd., Peterborough, ON K9H 7L7
705-742-3803 Fax: 705-743-4144
kinzz@sympatico.ca
Number of Beds: 12 beds
Note: children's mental health centre
Alan Vallillee, Area Program Director

Petrolia: Lambton County Developmental Services
PO Box 1210, 339 Centre St., Petrolia, ON N0N 1R0
519-882-0933 Fax: 519-882-3386
administration@lcds.on.ca
www.lcds.on.ca
Old Name: Lambton County Association for Mentally Handicappe
Number of Beds: 68 beds
Note: Provides services to persons with intellectual disabilities
Don Seymour, Executive Director

Powassan: Eide's Residential Home
495 Main St., Powassan, ON P0H 1Z0
705-724-2748

Saint-Pascal-Baylon: St. Pascal Residential Home
2454 du Lac Rd., RR#1, Saint-Pascal-Baylon, ON K0A 3N0
613-488-2626

St Catharines: Montebello Place
1 Montebello Pl., St Catharines, ON L2R 6B5
905-984-6506 Fax: 905-984-6504
Old Name: Horvath Residence
Year Founded: 1973
Number of Beds: 15 beds
Sharon Okum, Co-Owner
David Okum, Co-Owner

St Thomas: Tara Hall Residential Care Home
38 Chester St., St Thomas, ON N5R 1V2
519-631-4937 Fax: 519-631-1526
tarahall@rogers.com
Year Founded: 1988
Number of Beds: 36 beds
Note: Specialties: Assisted living for adults with an intellectual disability, brain injury, or mental illness
James Akey, Manager

Thunder Bay: Marcinowsky Residential Home
601 Alice Ave., RR#14, Thunder Bay, ON P7G 1X1
807-767-6199
Number of Beds: 10 beds
Stephanie Marcinowsky, Administrator/Owner

Toronto: Community Head Injury Resource Services of Toronto
62 Finch Ave. West, Toronto, ON M2N 7G1
416-240-8000 Fax: 416-240-1149
hedyc@chirs.com
www.chirs.com/CHIRS/
Number of Beds: 27 beds
Hedy Chandler, Executive Director

Toronto: Griffin Centre
24 Silverview Dr., Toronto, ON M2M 2B3
416-222-1153 Fax: 416-222-1321
contact@griffin-centre.org
www.griffin-centre.org
Number of Beds: 10 beds
Laurie Dart, Executive Director

Toronto: Hincks-Dellcrest Treatment Centre
440 Jarvis St., Toronto, ON M4Y 2H4
416-924-1164 Fax: 416-924-8208
info@hincksdellcrest.org
www.hincksdellcrest.org
Note: Children's mental health
John Spekkens, Executive Director

Toronto: Salvation Army Broadview Village
1132 Broadview Ave., Toronto, ON M4K 2S5
416-425-1052 Fax: 416-425-6579
Number of Beds: 61 beds
Note: Facility for adults with developmental disabilities
Glenda Davis, Director

Toronto: Youthdale Treatment Centres Ltd.
227 Victoria St., Toronto, ON M5B 1T8
416-368-4896 Fax: 416-368-3192
Number of Beds: 70 beds
Dan Hagler, Executive Director

Vars: Pine Rest Residence
PO Box 109, 5876 Bearbrook Rd., Vars, ON K0A 3H0
613-835-2849 Fax: 613-835-9335
Number of Beds: 33 residential capacity
Note: Specialties: Residential care for persons with developmental disabilities, psychiatric disabilities, or those who suffer from alcoholism; Medication supervision; Respite care
Raymond Meloche, Administrator

Vars: Résidence Ste-Marie
Ste-Marie Residence
PO Box 73, 5855, ch Buckland, Vars, ON K0H 3H0
613-835-2525
Number of Beds: 40 lits
Note: Spécialisée à la prestation des soins aux personnes atteintes de maladie mentale grave; soins infirmiers, activités hebdomadaires
Gaëtan Brisson, Propriétaire
Suzanne Brisson, Propriétaire

Vineland: Amber Lodge
4024 Martin Rd., RR#1, Vineland, ON L0R 2C0
905-562-7272 Fax: 905-892-9700
William Ram, Administrator/Owner

Vineland: Bethesda Home for the Mentally Handicapped Inc.
PO Box 1000, Vineland, ON L0R 2C0
905-562-4184 Fax: 905-562-4621
Number of Beds: 42 beds
Donald Boese, Executive Director

Waterloo: Lutherwood
Administrative Office, 139 Father David Bauer Dr., Waterloo, ON N2L 6L1
519-884-7755 Fax: 519-884-9071
admin@lutherwood.ca
www.lutherwood.ca
Note: Specialties: Mental health services for children & families, including assessment, a youth shelter, housing support services, residential treatment, family crisis & prevention counselling, a community services program, & school-based interventions; Senior services, including independent & supported living resources
John Colangeli, CEO

Waterloo: Lutherwood
285 Benjamin Rd., Waterloo, ON N2J 3Z4
519-884-1470 Fax: 519-886-8479 www.lutherwood.ca
Division of: Children's Mental Health Services
Number of Beds: 6 beds (Bridgelands program); 10 beds (Woodlands program)
Note: Specialties: Day treatment program; Residential treatment program; Group & individual skills training; Individual & family counselling; Home support; Community integration; Crisis support

Waterloo: Underhill Residential Home
127 Erb St. West, Waterloo, ON N2L 1T7
519-884-7160 Fax: 519-884-5936
Note: Specialties: Residential & personal care services for seniors & persons with mental health concerns

Prince Edward Island

Government Departments in Charge

PRINCE EDWARD ISLAND: Department of Community Services, Seniors & Labour
Jones Bldg., PO Box 2000, 11 Kent St., 2nd Fl., Charlottetown, PE C1A 7N8
902-620-3777 Fax: 902-368-4740 1-866-594-3777
www.gov.pe.ca/sss
Janice Sherry, Minister, Community Services, Seniors & Labour
902-368-4930, Fax: 902-368-4974, jasherry@gov.pe.ca
Sharon Cameron, Deputy Minister
902-368-6520, Fax: 902-368-4740, secameron@gov.pe.ca
Rona M. Brown, Director, Child & Family Services

902-368-5396, Fax: 902-368-4258, rmbrown@gov.pe.ca
W. Lorne Clow, Director, Corporate & Financial Services
902-368-6109, Fax: 902-894-0242, wlclow@gov.pe.ca
Bob D. Creed, Director, Social Programs
902-368-6446, Fax: 902-620-3553, bdcreed@gov.pe.ca
Faye M. Martin, Director, Pharmacy, Housing, Dentistry & Seniors
902-569-0545, Fax: 902-894-0242, fmmartin@gov.pe.ca
Laura Steeves, Communications Officer
902-620-3409, Fax: 902-894-0242

PRINCE EDWARD ISLAND: Department of Health & Wellness
PO Box 2000, 16 Garfield St., 1st Fl., Charlottetown, PE C1A 7N8
902-368-6130 Fax: 902-368-6136 www.gov.pe.ca/health
Carolyn
Bertram, Minister, Health & Wellness
902-368-5250, Fax: 902-368-4121, cibertran@gov.pe.ca
Tracey
Cutcliffe, Deputy Minister
902-368-5290, Fax: 902-368-4121, tdcutcliffe@gov.pe.ca
Kevin Barnes, Director, Policy & Administration

902-368-4865, Fax: 902-368-4224, kcbarnes@gov.pe.ca
Thelma Johnston, Director, Vital Statistics

902-838-0884, Fax: 902-838-0883
Mark Triantafillou, Director, Mental Health
902-368-5411, Fax: 902-620-3077
Autumn Tremere, Communications Officer
902-368-5610, Fax: 902-368-4224, agtremere@gov.pe.ca

Regional Health Authorities

Alberton: West Prince Health Region
PO Box 10, Alberton, PE C0B 1B0
902-853-8660 Fax: 902-853-8658
pajost@ihis.org
Number of Beds: 40 acute care, 72 long-term care beds
Phil Jost, CEO

Charlottetown: Health PEI
PO Box 2000, Charlottetown, PE C1A 7N8

902-368-6130 Fax: 902-368-6136
healthinput@gov.pe.ca
www.oneislandhealthsystem.ca
Year Founded: 2010
Note: Population Served: 140,985. Area Covered: The Province of Prince Edward Island
Leo Steven, Chair
Richard Wedge, Executive Director, Medical Affairs
Darlene Gillis, Manager, Communications
902-368-6172, dgillis@gov.pe.ca
Keith Dewar, President; Chief Executive Officer
Rick Adams, Executive Director, Queen Elizabeth Hospital
Deborah Bradley, Executive Director, Community Hospitals & Primary Health Care
Arlene Gallant-Bernard, Executive Director, Prince County Hospital
Terry Keefe, Executive Director, Financial Services
Pamela Trainor, Executive Director, Corporate Development & Innovation
Dale Vandenborre, Executive Director, Health Information Management
Cecil Villard, Executive Director, Home Based & Long Term Care

Charlottetown: Provincial Health Services Authority
PO Box 6600, Charlottetown, PE C1A 8T5
902-894-0141 Fax: 902-894-0138
Year Founded: 2002
Note: Responsible for planning & delivering specialized acute & secondary health care services
Keith Dewar, CEO

Charlottetown: Queens Health Region
PO Box 2000, 161 St. Peters Rd., Charlottetown, PE C1A 7N8
902-368-6160 Fax: 902-368-6169
Old Name: Queens Region Health Authority
Note: Child & family services, community services, continuing care, social support
Susan Howard, CEO
Sylvia Poirier, Chair

Montague: Kings Health Region
PO Box 3000, 35 Douses Rd., Montague, PE C0A 1R0
902-838-0945 Fax: 902-838-0940
Betty Fraser, CEO

Summerside: East Prince Health Board
243 Harbour Dr., Summerside, PE C1N 3G6
902-888-8028 Fax: 902-888-8458
Katherine Kelly, CEO

Hospitals

Hospitals - General

Alberton: Western Hospital Corporation
PO Box 10, Alberton, PE C0B 1B0
902-853-8650 Fax: 902-853-8651
mgbolger@ihis.org
Number of Beds: 25 beds
Marlene Bolger, Administrator

Charlottetown: Queen Elizabeth Hospital Inc.
PO Box 6600, 60 Riverside Dr., Charlottetown, PE C1A 8T5
902-894-2111 Fax: 902-894-2416 www.gov.pe.ca
Number of Beds: 274 beds
Note: Acute care hospital, with burn care services, coronary care, psychiatry, physiotherapy, occupational therapy, orthpedic & specialized gynecological surgery, eye surgery, plastic surgery, neonatal intensive care, cancer care, diagnostic imaging
Rick Adams, Executive Director
Kelly Rayner, Director, Hospital Services

Montague: King's County Memorial Hospital
409 McIntyre Ave., Montague, PE C0A 1R0
902-838-0777 Fax: 902-838-0770
njfallis@ihis.org
Number of Beds: 30 beds
Jean Fallis, Administrator
njfallis@ihis.org

O'Leary: Community Hospital O'Leary
PO Box 160, 14 MacKinnon Dr., O'Leary, PE C0B 1V0
902-859-8700 Fax: 902-859-8774
Year Founded: 1957
Number of Beds: 13 acute care beds + 24 long-term care beds + 1 respite bed
Note: Specialties: Acute care; Immunization program; Lifeline emergency response system; Long-term care (Phone: 902-859-8750, Fax: 902-859-8756); Respite care
Phil Jost, CEO

Souris: Souris Hospital
PO Box 640, 17 Knights Ave., Souris, PE C0A 2B0
902-687-7150 Fax: 902-687-7175
www.gov.pe.ca/health/index.php3?number=1020338&lang=E#SHContact
Number of Beds: 17 beds
Note: An acute care, rural facility with services including ambulatory care, x-ray, physiotherapy, occupational therapy, pharmacy, nutrition counseling, private dental clinic, provincial & seniors housing program, immunization program
Betty Fraser, CEO, KHR
Terry Campbell, Site Administrator

Summerside: Prince County Hospital
PO Box 3000, 65 Roy Boates Ave., Summerside, PE C1N 2A9
902-432-2500 Fax: 902-438-4511
gmmartin@ihis.org
www.pchcare.com
Number of Beds: 102 beds
Note: Specialties: Emergency, surgery, internal medicine, obstetrics, pediatrics, psychiatry, radiology, rehabilitation, oncology
Arlene Gallant-Bernard, Executive Director

Tyne Valley: Stewart Memorial Hospital
PO Box 10, Tyne Valley, PE C0B 2C0
902-831-7900 Fax: 902-831-7901
Number of Beds: 23 beds
Note: Specialties: Acute care; Long-term care, Respite care; Palliative care
Aleah MacLennan, Nursing Coordinator

Community Health Centres

Community Health Care Centres

Charlottetown: Home Care Support
PO Box 2000, 115 Murchison Lane., Charlottetown, PE C1A 7N5
902-368-4790 Fax: 902-368-4858
Nora McCabe

Montague: Home Care Support
PO Box 820, Montague, PE C0A 1R0
902-838-0950 Fax: 902-838-0774
Sandy MacLean, Home Care Nursing Supervisor

O'Leary: Home Care Support
PO Box 160, O'Leary, PE C0B 1V0
902-859-8730 Fax: 902-859-8701
Paula Caulien

Special Treatment Centre

Charlottetown: Euston Street Group Home
190 Euston St., Charlottetown, PE C1A 1W8
902-566-2964
Note: adolescent group home
Donnie Campbell, Manager

Charlottetown: Maple Street Group Home
14 Vail Dr., Charlottetown, PE C1A 2L5
902-368-1699
Number of Beds: 12 beds; one 72-hour emergency care bed
Note: adolescent group home
Donnie Campbell, Manager

Charlottetown: Provincial Addictions Treatment Facility
PO Box 2000, Charlottetown, PE C1A 7N8
902-368-4120 Fax: 902-368-6229 1-888-299-8399
www.gov.pe.ca/hirc
Number of Beds: 41 beds
Note: To provide safe, medically supervised detoxification
Jim Good, Family Counselor

Charlottetown: Provincial Adolescent Group Home
PO Box 2000, 185 Beach Grove Rd., Charlottetown, PE C1E 1Z7
902-368-6420 Fax: 902-368-6428
mamacmillan@ihis.org
Number of Beds: 9 beds; 1 emergency 72-hour bed
Note: adolescent residential treatment
John MacMillan, Manager, Adolescent Services

Nursing Homes

Alberton: Maplewood Manor
PO Box 400, 400 Church St., Alberton, PE C0B 1B0
902-853-8610 Fax: 902-853-8616
Number of Beds: 47 beds
Note: government-run
Phil Jost, CEO

Charlottetown: Beach Grove Home
200 Beach Grove Rd., Charlottetown, PE C1E 1L3
902-368-6750 Fax: 902-368-6764
Number of Beds: 131 beds
Note: government-run
Cecil Villard, Director

Charlottetown: Garden Home
310 North River Rd., Charlottetown, PE C1A 3M4
902-892-4131 Fax: 902-892-7326
Number of Beds: 112 beds
Note: private
Kirk DeBoer, Administrator

Charlottetown: Lennox Nursing Home
140 Water St., Charlottetown, PE C1A 1A7
902-894-4968 Fax: 902-368-2004
Number of Beds: 25 beds
Note: private
Tamara Casford, Administrator

Charlottetown: MacMillan Lodge Ltd.
PO Box 1861, 230 Richmond St., Charlottetown, PE C1A 1J5
902-894-7173 Fax: 902-894-3818
Year Founded: 1999
Claudette MacMillan, Owner/Operator

Charlottetown: Park West Lodge
22 Richmond St., Charlottetown, PE C1A 1H4
902-566-2260 Fax: 902-894-7818
Kevin Gauthier

Charlottetown: PEI Atlantic Baptist Homes Inc.
16 Centennial Dr., Charlottetown, PE C1A 5C5
902-566-5975 Fax: 902-368-3760
altbaptist@eastlink.ca
Number of Beds: 101 beds
Note: Specialty: Long-term care by an interdisciplinary team
Enid Dollar, Administrator

Charlottetown: The Prince Edward Home
5 Brighton Rd., Charlottetown, PE C1A 8T6
902-368-5946 Fax: 902-368-5646
Number of Beds: 131 beds
Note: Palliative care, convalescent, respite care; long-term care; day program for seniors; meals-on-wheels program
Don Gorveatt, Director

Montague: Riverview Manor
PO Box 820, 82 Main St. South, Montague, PE C0A 1R0
902-838-0772 Fax: 902-838-0774
jlfraser@ihis.org
Number of Beds: 50 beds
Note: Long-term & palliative care
Judy Fraser, Administrator

Souris: Colville Manor
PO Box 640, 44 Chapel Ave., Souris, PE C0A 2B0
902-687-7090 Fax: 902-687-7103
Number of Beds: 51 beds
Note: government-run
Marilyn Barrett, Acting Director, Acute & Continuing Care

Summerside: Summerset Manor
205 Lefurgey Ave., Summerside, PE C1N 2L9
902-888-8310 Fax: 902-888-8338
Number of Beds: 82 beds
Note: Specialties: Long-term care; Operation of the Chapman Centre, a day program that provides therapeutic services to seniors who live in their own home; Physiotherapy; Occupational therapy; Foot care; Respite care
Faye Feener, Manager

Summerside: Wedgewood Manor
310 Brophy St., Summerside, PE C1N 5N4
902-888-8340 Fax: 902-888-8369
Faye Feener, Manager

Long Term/Retirement Care

Long Term Care Facility

Alberton: Rev. W.J. Phillips Residence
Alberton, PE C0B 1B0
902-853-3109 Fax: 902-853-2485 www.phillipsresidence.com
Number of Beds: 14 beds; 14 independent living units
Note: community care & beds
Garth MacKinnon

Belfast: Dr. John Gillis Memorial Lodge
Eldon Belfast PO, Belfast, PE C0A 1A0
902-659-2337 Fax: 902-659-2865
douglas@gillislodge.com

Number of Beds: 62 beds
Douglas MacKenzie

Charlottetown: Andrews of Charlottetown
73 Malpeque Rd., Charlottetown, PE C1A 7J9
902-368-2790 Fax: 902-894-3464
info@andrewsofpei.com
andrewsofpei.com/andrews_of_charlottetown.php
Number of Beds: 72 beds
Note: community care beds

Charlottetown: Champion Lodge
48 Green St., Charlottetown, PE C1A 2E8
902-894-8968 Fax: 902-894-3878
Number of Beds: 8 beds
Colleen MacDonald

Charlottetown: Charlotte Residence
39 All Souls Lane, Charlottetown, PE C1A 1P9
902-894-8134
Number of Beds: 26 beds
Joyce Pickles, Administrator

Charlottetown: Corrigan Home
22 Hemlock Ct., Charlottetown, PE C1A 8E3
902-894-9686 Fax: 902-894-3686
Number of Beds: 28 beds
Note: community care beds

Charlottetown: Corrigan Lodge
8 Ellis Rd., Charlottetown, PE C1A 8N4
902-894-5858
Number of Beds: 16 beds
Note: community care beds

Charlottetown: Elm Crest Lodge
267 Richmond St., Charlottetown, PE C1A 1J7
902-566-5996 Fax: 902-368-8382
Number of Beds: 14 beds
Note: community care beds

Charlottetown: Langille House
214 Kent St., Charlottetown, PE C1A 1P2
902-628-8228 Fax: 902-628-6656
Number of Beds: 33 beds
Note: community care beds
Shirley Keenan

Charlottetown: McQuaid Lodge
36 Kent St., Charlottetown, PE C1A 1M8
902-892-0791
Gerard Arsenault

Charlottetown: Old Rose Lodge
319 Queen St., Charlottetown, PE C1A 4C4
902-368-8313
theoldroselodge@pei.aibn.com
Helen Roberts

Charlottetown: Stamper Residence
29 Fitzroy St., Charlottetown, PE C1A 1R2
902-894-3815
Number of Beds: 20 beds
Joyce Pickles, Administrator

Charlottetown: Tenderwood Lodge Inc.
15 Hawthorne Ave., Charlottetown, PE C1A 5X8
902-566-5174

Charlottetown: Whisperwood Villa
160 St. Peters Rd., Charlottetown, PE C1A 5P8
902-566-5556 Fax: 902-566-5222
Number of Beds: 88 beds + 36 nursing home beds
Note: community care facility; private nursing home
Ray Brow, Administrator

Crapaud: South Shore Villa
PO Box 111, 159 Sherwwod Forest Dr., Crapaud, PE C0A 1J0
902-658-2228 Fax: 902-658-2576
Number of Beds: 52 beds
Note: Parent ID changed only, 08/10 — Not a complete update
Lynn Dawson

Georgetown: Carroll's Lodge
PO Box 133, 110 Gordon St., Georgetown, PE C0A 1L0
902-652-2369
Number of Beds: 7 beds
Barb Carroll

Hunter River: Rosewood Residence
PO Box 97, 4260 Hopedale Rd., Route 13, Hunter River, PE C0A 1N0
902-964-2436 Fax: 902-964-2436
info@rosewoodresidence.ca
www.rosewoodresidence.ca
Number of Beds: 41 beds
Note: community care beds
Lori E. Weeks, Director

Kensington: Clinton View Lodge
RR#6, Kensington, PE C0B 1M0
902-866-2276 Fax: 902-886-2073
Number of Beds: 43 beds (25 nursing home beds)
Note: private nursing home; community care facility
Tracy Perrin

Kensington: MacEwen Mews Seniors Residence
RR#6, Kensington, PE C0B 1M0
902-836-4678

Lower Montague: Shady Rest Convalescent Home
RR#2, Lower Montague, PE C0A 1R0
902-838-4298 Fax: 902-838-4298
Number of Beds: 37 beds
Note: community care beds
Jackie MacKay, Owner/Operator

Miscouche: Miscouche Villa
PO Box 40, 20 Lady Slipper Dr., Miscouche, PE C0B 1T0
902-436-1946 Fax: 902-436-3215
johnd@pei.sympatico.ca
Number of Beds: 35 beds
Note: community care beds
Barbara Perry, Manager

Montague: MacKinnon Pines Community Care Facility
PO Box 298, 505 Campbellton St., Montague, PE C0A 1R0
902-838-2656 Fax: 902-838-3542

Montague: Queens Gardens
394 Queens Rd., Montague, PE C0A 1R0
902-838-8440
Number of Beds: 7 beds

New Glasgow: River View Home
RR#2, New Glasgow, PE C0A 1N0
902-964-2795 Fax: 902-621-0453
Number of Beds: 20 beds
Note: community care beds for seniors & the mentally challenged
Kathy Dutton, Proprietor
Martin Dutton

O'Leary: Lady Slipper Villa
PO Box 40, 490 Main St., O'Leary, PE C0B 1V0
902-859-3544 Fax: 902-859-3255
info@ladyslippervilla.com
ladyslippervilla.com
Number of Beds: 47 beds
Note: community care beds
Karen Cook, Administrator

Souris: Bayview Lodge
22 Washington St., Souris, PE C0A 2B0
902-687-3122 Fax: 902-687-3512
Number of Beds: 32 beds
Note: community care beds
Gerard Arsenault

Summerside: Andrews of Summerside
317 Pope Rd., Summerside, PE C1N 6G4
902-436-0859 Fax: 902-436-1565
info@andrewsofpei.com
www.andrewsofpei.com/andrews_of_summerside.php
Number of Beds: 58 beds
Note: community care facility
Erroll Andrews, Administrator

Summerside: MacDonald's Community Care Home Inc.
197 Cambridge St., Summerside, PE C1N 1N1
902-436-7359

Tignish: Tignish Seniors Home Care Cooperative Limited
116 MacLeod Lane, Tignish, PE C0B 2B0
902-882-4663
Year Founded: 2002
Note: Specialty: Assisted living
Leslie VanHee, Administrator

Tyne Valley: Murphy's Country Lodge
Tyne Valley, PE C0B 2C0
902-831-2213 Fax: 902-831-2309
Number of Beds: 11 beds
Note: community care beds
Earlene Murphy

Wellington: Chez Nous
PO Box 88, 64 Sunset Dr., Wellington, PE C0B 2E0
902-854-3426 Fax: 902-854-3055
cheznous@isn.net
Number of Beds: 25 beds
Note: community care beds
Antoine Richard

Mental Health Facilities

Mental Health Hospital/Clinic/Facility

Charlottetown: Hillsborough Hospital & Special Care Centre
PO Box 1929, 115 Murchison Lane, Charlottetown, PE C1A 7N5
902-368-5400 Fax: 902-368-5467 www.gov.pe.ca/health
Number of Beds: 75 beds
Note: Specialties: Psychiatry; Medical services for persons with acute or long-term mental illnesses or mental handicaps, & psychogeriatric patients; Day services for former patients; Assessment; Behavioural management
Cecil Villard, Administrator
Don Hughes, Director, Environmental Services

Charlottetown: Sherwood Home
PO Box 1929, Charlottetown, PE C1A 7N8
902-368-4141 Fax: 902-368-4931
Number of Beds: 14 beds
Elaine Blanchard, Administrator

Québec

Département gouvernemental responsable

QUéBEC: Ministère de la Santé et des services sociaux
1075, ch Ste-Foy, Québec, QC G1S 2M1
418-266-8900 Fax: 418-644-4574 800-707-3380
info@msss.gouv.qc.ca
www.msss.gouv.qc.ca

Agences de développement de réseaux locaux de service de santé et de services sociaux

Baie-Comeau: Agence de la santé et des services sociaux de la C"te-Nord
691, rue Jalbert, Baie-Comeau, QC G5C 2A1
418-589-9845 Fax: 418-295-2703
www.agencesante09.gouv.qc.ca
Nicole Demers, Présidente-directrice générale

Chibougamau: Centre régional de la santé et des services sociaux de la Baie-James
312, 3e rue, Chibougamau, QC G8P 1N5
418-748-3575 Fax: 418-748-2021
Old Name: Régie régionale de la santé et des services sociau
Diane Laboissonnière, Présidente-directrice-gen. (intérim)

Chicoutimi: Agence de la santé et des services sociaux du Saguenay-Lac-St-Jean
930, rue Jacques-Cartier est, Chicoutimi, QC G7H 7K9
418-545-4980 Fax: 418-545-8791
info@santesaglac.gouv.qc.ca
www.santesaglac.gouv.qc.ca
Martine Couture, Présidente-directrice générale

Chisasibi: Conseil cri de la santé et des services sociaux de la Baie-James
CP 250, Chisasibi, QC J0M 1E0
819-855-2844 Fax: 819-855-2098
Joanne Bezzubetz, Directrice générale

Gaspé: Agence de la santé et des services sociaux de la Gaspésie-Iles-de-la-Madeleine
144, boul Gaspé, Gaspé, QC G4X 1A9
418-368-2349 Fax: 418-368-4942
agence11@ssss.gouv.qc.ca
www.agencessgim.ca
Pierre Michaud, Président-directeur général

Gatineau: Agence de la santé et des services sociaux de l'Outaouais
104, rue Lois, Gatineau, QC J8Y 3R7
819-770-7747 Fax: 819-770-3891 www.santeoutaouais.qc.ca
Also Known As: Santé Outaouais
Roch Martel, Président-directeur général

Joliette: **Agence de la santé et des services sociaux de Lanaudière**
245, rue du Curé-Majeau, Joliette, QC J6E 8S8
450-759-1157 Fax: 450-759-0023
chetu@ssss.gouv.qc.ca
www.santelanaudiere.qc.ca
Jean-François Foisy, Président-directeur général

Kuujjuaq: **Régie régionale de la santé et des services sociaux du Nunavik**
CP 900, Kuujjuaq, QC J0M 1C0
819-964-2222 Fax: 819-964-2888
information_rrsss17@ssss.gouv.qc.ca
www.rrsss17.gouv.qc.ca
Gilles Boulet, Dir. gen. (intérim)

Laval: **Agence de la santé et des services sociaux de Laval**
Tour A, 800, boul Chomedey, 2e étage, Laval, QC H7N 3Y4
450-978-2000 Fax: 450-978-2100
regie-laval@ssss.gouv.qc.ca
www.sssslaval.gouv.qc.ca
Claude Desjardins, Président-directeur général (intérim)

Longueuil: **Agence de la santé et des services sociaux de la Montérégie**
1255, rue Beauregard, Longueuil, QC J4K 2M3
450-928-6777 Fax: 450-679-6443
agencemonteregie@ssss.gouv.qc.ca
www.santemonteregie.qc.ca/agence
Luc Boileau, Président-directeur général

Montréal: **Agence de la santé et des services sociaux de Montréal**
3725, rue St-Denis, Montréal, QC H2X 3L9
514-286-6500 Fax: 514-286-5669 www.santemontreal.qc.ca
David Levine, Président-directeur général

Québec: **Agence de la santé et des services sociaux de la Capitale-Nationale**
555, boul Wilfrid-Hamel est, Québec, QC G1M 3X7
418-525-1500 Fax: 418-529-4463
03rrsss@ssss.gouv.qc.ca
www.rrsss03.gouv.qc.ca
Michel Fontaine, Président-directeur général

Rimouski: **Agence de la santé et des services sociaux du Bas-St-Laurent**
#115, 288, rue Pierre-Saindon, Rimouski, QC G5L 9A8
418-724-5231 Fax: 418-723-1597 www.agencesssbsl.gouv.qc.ca
Note: L'Agence regroupe des établissements de santé et de services sociaux des régions suivantes: Kamouraska, Rivière-du-Loup, Témiscouata, Les Basques, Rimouski-Neigette, La Mitis, La Matapédia, et Matane.
Claude Lévesque, Président-directeur général

Rouyn-Noranda: **Agence de la santé et des services sociaux de l'Abitibi-Témiscamingue**
1, 9e rue, Rouyn-Noranda, QC J9X 2A9
819-764-3264 Fax: 819-797-1947
www.sante-abitibi-temiscamingue.gouv.qc.ca
Lise St-Amour, Présidente-Directrice générale

Saint-Jér"me: **Agence de la santé et des services sociaux des Laurentides**
#210, 1000, rue Labelle, Saint-Jér"me, QC J7Z 5N6
450-436-8622 Fax: 450-432-8712
information.rr15@ssss.gouv.qc.ca
www.rrsss15.gouv.qc.ca
Micheline Vallières-Joly, Présidente-directrice générale
Miriam David, Responsable des achats en commun

Sainte-Marie: **Agence de la santé et des services sociaux de Chaudière-Appalaches**
363, rte Cameron, Sainte-Marie, QC G6E 3E2
418-386-3363 Fax: 418-389-1500
reception.rr12@ssss.gouv.qc.ca
www.agencesss12.gouv.qc.ca
Marc Tanguay, Président-directeur général

Sherbrooke: **Agence de la santé et des services sociaux de l'Estrie**
#300, 300, rue King est, Sherbrooke, QC J1G 1B1
819-566-7861 Fax: 819-569-8894
information.agence05@ssss.gouv.qc.ca
www.santeestrie.qc.ca
Michel Baron, Président-directeur général

Trois-Rivières: **Agence de la santé et des services sociaux de la Mauricie et du Centre-du-Québec**
550, rue Bonaventure, Trois-Rivières, QC G9A 2B5
819-693-3636 Fax: 819-373-1627
commissaires.plaintes04@ssss.gouv.qc.ca
www.agencesss04.qc.ca
Michèle Laroche, Présidente-directrice générale

Centres hospitaliers

Amos: **Centre de santé et de services sociaux Les Eskers de l'Abitibi**
622, 4e rue ouest, Amos, QC J9T 2S2
819-732-3341 Fax: 819-732-7054
www.sante-abitibi-temiscamingue.gouv.qc.ca
Parent: Agence de la santé et des services sociaux de l'Abitibi-Témiscamingue
Number of Beds: 96 lits hospitaliers; 103 lits de soins de longue durée
Note: Le CSSS regroupe le Centre hospitalier Hôtel-Dieu d'Amos, un centre d'hébergement, et 4 points de service CLSC.
Michel Michaud, Directeur général
michel_michaud@ssss.gouv.qc.ca
Jean McGuire, Président, Conseil d'administration

Amqui: **Centre de santé et de services sociaux de La Matapédia**
135, av Gaétan-Archambault, Amqui, QC G5J 2K5
418-629-2211 Fax: 418-629-4498 www.csssmatapedia.qc.ca; www.chamqui.qc.com
Parent: Agence de la santé et des services sociaux du Bas-St-Laurent
Number of Beds: 40 lits hospitaliers; 96 lits de soins de longue durée
Note: Le CSSS regroupe l'Hôpital d'Amqui, le centre d'hébergement Marie-Anne Ouellet, et 3 points de service CLSC (Causapscal,Sayabec, et St-Moïse).
Alain Paquet, Directeur général

Baie-Saint-Paul: **Centre de santé et de services sociaux de Charlevoix**
a/s Hôpital de Baie-Saint-Paul, 74, rue Ambroise-Fafard, Baie-Saint-Paul, QC G3Z 2J6
418-435-5150 www.cssscharlevoix.qc.ca
Parent: Agence de la santé et des services sociaux de la Capitale-Nationale
Note: Le CSSS de Charlevoix regroupe 2 hôpitaux (Baie-Saint-Paul, et La Malbaie); 5 points de service CLSC; 4 centres d'hébergement; et 8 points de service CRDI.
Micheline Tremblay, Directrice générale
micheline.tremblay@ssss.gouv.qc.ca

Candiac: **Centre de santé et de services sociaux Jardins-Roussillon**
90, boul Marie-Victorin, Candiac, QC J5R 1C1
450-659-7661 Fax: 450-444-6260
www.santemonteregie.qc.ca/jardins-roussillon
Parent: Agence de la santé et des services sociaux de la Montérégie
Note: Le CSSS regroupe l'Hôpital Anna-Laberge, 3 centres d'hébergement, et 3 points de service CLSC.
Paul Moreau, Directeur général

Dolbeau-Mistassini: **CSSS Maria-Chapdelaine**
2000, boul Sacré-Coeur, Dolbeau-Mistassini, QC G8L 2R5
418-276-1234 Fax: 418-276-4355
www.csssmariachapdelaine.com
Parent: Agence de la santé et des services sociaux du Saguenay-Lac-St-Jean
Number of Beds: 59 lits hospitaliers; 119 lits de soins de longue durée
Note: Centre administratif du CSSS, et l'Hôpital de Dolbeau-Mistassini. Le CSSS regroupe 2 centres d'hébergement (L'Oasis, et Centre d'hébergement Normandin), 2 points de service CLSC (Normandin, et Les Jardins du Monastère), et l'Hôpital.
Normand Brassard, Directeur général

Drummondville: **Centre de santé et de services sociaux Drummond**
570, rue Heriot, Drummondville, QC J2B 1C1
819-478-6464
csssdrummond@ssss.gouv.qc.ca
www.csssdrummond.qc.ca
Parent: Agence de la santé et des services sociaux de la Mauricie et du Centre-du-Québec
Year Founded: 2004
Number of Beds: 191 lits hospitaliers; 474 lits de soins de longue durée
Note: Le CSSS regroupe l'Hôpital Sainte-Croix, le CLSC Drummond, 3 centres d'hébergement, et 5 autres points de service; il est affilié à l'Université de Sherbrooke pour les activités d'enseignement médical.
Nagui Habashi, Directeur général

La Sarre: **Centre de santé et de services sociaux des Aurores-Boréales**
679, 2e Rue est, La Sarre, QC J9Z 2X7
819-333-2311 Fax: 819-333-4316
www.sante-abitibi-temiscamingue.gouv.qc.ca
Parent: Agence de la santé et des services sociaux de l'Abitibi-Témiscamingue
Number of Beds: 71 lits hospitaliers (courte durée); 182 lits de soins de longue durée
Note: Le CSSS regroupe un centre de soins de courte durée (La Sarre), 3 centres d'hébergement (La Sarre, Macamic, et Palmarolle), et 6 points de service CLSC (Beaucanton, Duparquet, Dupuy, Gallichan, Normétal, et Taschereau).
Paul Fortin, Directeur général
paul_fortin@ssss.gouv.qc.ca
Ghislain Godbout, Président, Conseil d'administration

Lac-Mégantic: **CSSS du Granit**
3569, rue Laval, Lac-Mégantic, QC G6B 1A5
819-583-0330 Fax: 819-583-5239 800-827-2572
info.granit@ssss.gouv.qc.ca
www.csssgranit.qc.ca
Parent: Agence de la santé et des services sociaux de l'Estrie
Number of Beds: 35 lits hospitaliers; 122 lits de soins de longue durée (3 points de service)
Note: Le CSSS regroupe un centre hospitalier, 2 centres et 1 unité d'hébergement, 2 centres de jour, et 4 points de services CLSC.
Pierre Latulippe, Directeur général

Lachute: **Centre de santé et de services sociaux d'Argenteuil**
145, av de la Providence, Lachute, QC J8H 4C7
450-562-3761 Fax: 450-566-3316 www.csssargenteuil.qc.ca
Parent: Agence de la santé et des services sociaux des Laurentides
Number of Beds: 49 lits hospitaliers; 131 lits de soins de longue durée
Note: Le CSSS offre des services de santé physique et services aux personnes en perte d'autonomie; point de service de Grenville: 93, rue des Érables, 819-242-0778.
Raymond Roberge, Directeur général

Laval: **Centre de santé et de services sociaux de Laval**
1515, boul Chomedey, Laval, QC H7V 3Y7
450-978-8300 www.cssslaval.qc.ca
Parent: Agence de la santé et des services sociaux de Laval
Number of Beds: 532 lits hospitaliers; 777 lits de soins de longue durée
Note: Le CSSS, le plus gros au Québec, regroupe l'Hôpital de la Cité-de-la-Santé, 5 centres d'hébergement, et 7 points de service CLSC; services hospitaliers de courte durée; services ambulatoires; services d'hébergement et de soins de longue durée; services de première ligne.
Luc Lepage, Directeur général
Alain Goudreau, Directeur, Services professionnels et hospitaliers/Affaires mé
Lucie Gagnon, Directrice, Soins infirmiers

Longueuil: **Centre de santé et de services sociaux Pierre-Boucher**
1333, boul Jacques-Cartier est, Longueuil, QC J4M 2A5
450-468-8111 www.santemonteregie.qc.ca/cssspierreboucher
Parent: Agence de la santé et des services sociaux de la Montérégie
Number of Beds: 340 lits hospitaliers; 916 lits de soins de longue durée
Note: Le CSSS regroupe l'Hôpital Pierre-Boucher, 7 points de service CLSC, 7 centres d'hébergement, et un centre d'hébergement privé non conventionné.
Caroline Barbir, Directrice générale

Magog: **Centre de santé et de services sociaux de Memphrémagog**
50, rue Saint-Patrice est, Magog, QC J1X 3X3
819-843-2572 Fax: 819-868-3240 800-268-2572
csssm.santeestrie.qc.ca
Parent: Agence de la santé et des services sociaux de l'Estrie
Number of Beds: 36 lits hospitaliers; 132 lits de soins de longue durée
Note: Le CSSS regroupe l'Hôpital de Memphrémagog, et 2 points de service CLSC; soins de longue durée, et services aux personnes en perte d'autonomie.
Monique Corbeil, Directrice générale
Jules Racine, Coordonnateur, Services techniques

Matane: **Centre de santé et de services sociaux de Matane**
333, rue Thibault, Matane, QC G4W 2W5
418-562-3135 Fax: 418-562-9374
www.agence.sssbsl.gouv.qc.ca

Number of Beds: 45 lits hospitaliers; 152 lits de soins de longue durée
Note: Le CSSS regroupe l'Hôpital de Matane, le centre d'hébergement de Matane, et 3 points de service CLSC.
Nicole Morin, Directrice générale

Mont-Laurier: Centre de santé et de services sociaux d'Antoine-Labelle
515, boul Dr Albiny-Paquette, Mont-Laurier, QC J9L 1K8
819-623-6127 Fax: 819-623-9451 www.cssssal.org
Parent: Agence de la santé et des services sociaux des Laurentides
Year Founded: 2004
Number of Beds: 473 lits
Note: Le CSSS regroupe l'Hôpital de Mont-Laurier, le Centre de services de Rivière-Rouge, le Centre d'hébergement Sainte-Anne, et 3 points de service CLSC.
Jean-Pierre Urbain, Directeur général

Montréal: CSSS de Saint-Léonard et Saint-Michel
3130, rue Jarry est, Montréal, QC H1Z 4N8
514-722-3000 csss-stleonardstmichel.qc.ca
Parent: Agence de la santé et des services sociaux de Montréal
Note: Centre administratif du CSSS; 3 centres d'hébergement: Quatre-Temps, Quatre-Saisons, et Saint-Michel; 2 CLSCs: Saint-Léonard, et Saint-Michel.
Suzanne Hébert, Directrice générale

Montréal: CSSS Jeanne-Mance
155, boul Saint-Joseph est, Montréal, QC H2T 1H4
514-842-7180 Fax: 514-380-5152 www.csssjeannemance.ca
Parent: Agence de la santé et des services sociaux de Montréal
Note: Le CSSS Jeanne-Mance regroupe 5 CLSCs: Faubourgs/Parthenais, Faubourgs/Sanguinet, Faubourgs/Visitation, Plateau-Mont-Royal, et Saint-Louis-du-Parc; 7 CHSLDs: Armand-Lavergne, Bruchési, Centre-Ville-de-Montréal, Manoire-de-l'Age-d'Or, Émilie-Gamelin, Ernest-Routhier, et Jean-De La Lande; et 1 clinique de médecine familiale: Notre-Dame.
Ron Rayside, Président du Conseil d'administration
Sylvie Simard, Directrice générale intérimaire

Notre-Dame-du-Lac: Centre de santé et de services sociaux de Témiscouata
58, rue de l'Église, Notre-Dame-du-Lac, QC G0L 1X0
418-899-6751 Fax: 418-899-2809
marie.noelle.bosse.csssstemis@ssss.gouv.qc.ca
www.cssstemiscouata.com
Parent: Agence de la santé et des services sociaux du Bas-St-Laurent
Number of Beds: 35 lits hospitaliers (courte durée); 111 lits de soins de longue durée
Note: Le CSSS regroupe l'Hôpital de Notre-Dame-du-Lac, 5 points de service CLSC, 3 centres d'hébergement, et 9 autres points de service.
Camil Dion, Directeur général

Rimouski: Centre régional de santé et de services sociaux de Rimouski-Neigette
150, av Rouleau, Rimouski, QC G5L 5T1
418-723-7851 Fax: 418-724-8632
courrierweb.crsssr@ssss.gouv.qc.ca
www.chrr.qc.ca
Parent: Agence de la santé et des services sociaux du Bas-St-Laurent
Number of Beds: 255 lits hospitaliers; 246 lits de soins de longue durée
Note: Le CSSS regroupe l'Hôpital régional de Rimouski, le centre d'hébergement de Rimouski, et 4 points de service CLSC; soins généraux et spécialisés (néonatalogie, psychiatrie, santé physique).
Raymond Coulombe, Directeur général

Rivière-du-Loup: Centre de santé et de services sociaux de Rivière-du-Loup
75, rue St-Henri, Rivière-du-Loup, QC G5R 2A4
418-868-1010 Fax: 418-868-1035 www.csssriviereduloup.qc.ca
Parent: Agence de la santé et des services sociaux du Bas-St-Laurent
Number of Beds: 145 lits hospitaliers; 207 lits de soins de longue durée
Note: Le CSSS regroupe le Centre hospitalier régional du Grand-Portage, 3 centres d'hébergement, et 3 points de service CLSC.
Raymond April, Directeur général
Alyre Bois, Président, Conseil d'administration
Julie Roy, Secrétaire

Roberval: Centre de santé et de services sociaux Domaine-du-Roy
450, rue Brassard, Roberval, QC G8H 1B9
418-275-0110 Fax: 418-275-6202
hdr@ssss.gouv.qc.ca; info@cmdp-roberval.com
www.cmdp-roberval.com
Parent: Agence de la santé et des services sociaux du Saguenay-Lac-St-Jean
Number of Beds: 135 lits hospitaliers; 201 lits de soins de longue durée; 15 lits traitement spécialisés
Note: Le CSSS regroupe l'hôpital (Hôtel-Dieu de Roberval), le CLSC et le centre de réadaptation en alcoolisme et autres toxicomanies (Pavillon Gérard-Tremblay), et le Centre d'hébergement Roberval; 2 autres points de service CLSC; et 2 autres centres d'hébergement.
Jacques Dubois, Directeur général

Rouyn-Noranda: Centre de santé et de services sociaux de Rouyn-Noranda
4, 9e Rue, Rouyn-Noranda, QC J9X 2B2
819-764-5131 Fax: 819-764-2948
diane_cote@ssss.gouv.qc.ca
www.sante-abitibi-temiscamingue.gouv.qc.ca; www.csssrn.qc.ca
Parent: Agence de la santé et des services sociaux de l'Abitibi-Témiscamingue
Number of Beds: 123 lits hospitaliers; 172 lits de soins de longue durée
Note: Le CSSS regroupe l'Hôpital de Rouyn-Noranda, le Centre d'hébergement Rouyn-Noranda, le Centre d'hébergement Ressource du Sourire, et 8 points de service CLSC.
Huguette Lemay, Directrice générale
Luc Blanchette, Président, Conseil d'administration
Martine Humbert, Directrice, Santé physique

Saint-Hyacinthe: Centre de santé et de services sociaux Richelieu-Yamaska
2750, boul Laframboise, Saint-Hyacinthe, QC J2S 4Y8
450-771-3333 Fax: 450-771-3748
info@lesommetavotreportee.qc.ca
www.lesommetavotreportee.qc.ca;
www.santemonteregie.qc.ca/richelieu-yamaska
Parent: Agence de la santé et des services sociaux de la Montérégie
Note: Centre administratif du CSSS; Hôpital Honoré-Mercier; 3 points de service CLSC: des Maskoutains (Saint-Hyacinthe), MRC-d'Acton, et des Patriotes (Beloeil); 5 centres d'hébergement: Andrée-Perrault, l'Hôtel-Dieu-de-Saint-Hyacinthe, MRC-d'Acton, Marguerite-Adam, et Montarville; 1 clinique de médecine familiale.
Daniel Castonguay, Directeur général

Saint-Jean-sur-Richelieu: CSSS Haut-Richelieu-Rouville
978, boul du Séminaire nord, Saint-Jean-sur-Richelieu, QC J3A 1E5
450-358-2572 Fax: 450-349-4115
www.santemonteregie.qc.ca/haut-richelieu-rouville
Parent: Agence de la santé et des services sociaux de la Montérégie
Note: 15 installations, y compris L'Hôpital du Haut-Richelieu; 4 points de service CLSC; 6 centres d'hébergement; une clinique jeunesse; et services de consultation externe (psychiatrie, réadaptation pédiatrique, clinique d'évaluation TED).
Christine Lessard, Directrice générale

Saint-Pascal: Centre de santé et de services sociaux de Kamouraska
575, av Martin, Saint-Pascal, QC G0L 3Y0
418-856-7000 Fax: 418-492-1793 www.agencesssbsl.gouv.qc.ca
Number of Beds: 49 lits hospitaliers; 181 lits de soins de longue durée
Note: Le CSSS regroupe le Centre Notre-Dame-de-Fatima (centre hospitalier), 3 centres d'hébergement, et 3 points de service CLSC.
Michel Beaulieu, Directeur général

Sainte-Agathe-des-Monts: Centre de santé et de services sociaux des Sommets
Pavillon administratif Jacques-Duquette, 234, rue Saint-Vincent, Sainte-Agathe-des-Monts, QC J8C 2B8
819-324-4000 Fax: 819-324-4010 www.csss-sommets.com
Parent: Agence de la santé et des services sociaux des Laurentides
Number of Beds: 104 lits hospitaliers; 219 lits de soins de longue durée
Note: Le CSSS regroupe un hôpital, 3 centres d'hébergement, et 3 points de service CLSC.
Jacques Morin, Président, Conseil d'administration

Sainte-Thérèse: Centre de santé et de services sociaux de Thérèse-De Blainville
125, rue Duquet, Sainte-Thérèse, QC J7E 0A5
450-430-4553 www.cssstheresedeblainville.qc.ca
Parent: Agence de la santé et des services sociaux des Laurentides
Number of Beds: 377 lits de soins de longue durée
Note: Le CSSS regroupe un centre de services médicaux, 2 centres d'hébergement, un centre de prélèvement, et un point de service à Sainte-Anne-des-Plaines.
André Poirier, Directeur général

Sherbrooke: CSSS-Institut universitaire de gériatrie de Sherbrooke
375, rue Argyll, Sherbrooke, QC J1J 3H5
819-780-2220 www.csss-iugs.ca
Parent: Agence de la santé et des services sociaux de l'Estrie
Number of Beds: 64 lits hospitaliers; 765 lits de soins de longue durée
Note: Centre de la direction générale du CSSS, et l'Hôpital et Centre d'hébergement Argyll; le CSSS regroupe 4 centres d'hébergement: Argyll, D'Youville, St-Joseph, et St-Vincent; 2 hôpitaux: Argyll, et D'Youville; 5 points de service CLSC; et un centre de maternité; 2 500 employé(e)s.
Carol Fillion, Directeur général
Michel Levesque, Directeur, Soins infirmiers
Suzanne Gosselin, Directrice, Services professionnels et du partenariat médical
Marie Trousdell, Directrice, Services et programmes aux personnes âgées ou en pe

Témiscaming: Centre de santé et de services sociaux de Témiscaming-et-de-Kipawa
CP 760, 180, rue Anvik, Témiscaming, QC J0Z 3R0
819-627-3385 Fax: 819-327-3629 www.temiscaming.et/csss;
www.sante-abitibi-temiscamingue.gouv.qc.ca
Parent: Agence de la santé et des services sociaux de l'Abitibi-Témiscamingue
Number of Beds: 6 lits hospitaliers; 14 lits de soins de longue durée
Note: Le CSSS regroupe un hôpital, un centre d'hébergement, et un point de service CLSC.
Jean-Philippe Legault, Directeur général
jean-philippe_legault@ssss.gouv.qc.c

Trois-Pistoles: Centre de santé et de services sociaux des Basques
550, rue Notre-Dame est, Trois-Pistoles, QC G0L 4K0
418-851-3700 Fax: 418-851-2934 www.agencesssbsl.gouv.qc.ca
Parent: Agence de la santé et des services sociaux du Bas-St-Laurent
Number of Beds: 60 lits hospitaliers; 26 lits de soins de longue durée
Note: Le CSSS regroupe le Centre hospitalier de Trois-Pistoles, le centre d'hébergement Villa Dubé, et un point de service CLSC.
Line Moisan, Directrice générale
Roberto Dionne, Président, Conseil d'administration

Trois-Rivières: Centre de santé et de services sociaux de Trois-Rivières
155, rue Toupin, Trois-Rivières, QC G8T 3Z8
819-370-2100 Fax: 819-379-9644 www.cssstr.qc.ca
Parent: Agence de la santé et des services sociaux de la Mauricie et du Centre-du-Québec
Number of Beds: 10 lits hospitaliers; 660 lits de soins de longue durée
Note: Le CSSS regroupe le Centre Cloutier-du Rivage (hôpital); le Centre de services ambulatoires de gériatrie; les points de service CLSC de l'Horloge, Les Forges, Marguerite-Bourgeois, et Ste-Geneviève; Résidence Cooke, Résidence Joseph-Denys, le Centre St-Joseph et Résidence La Providence, et Résidence Louis-Denoncourt.
Jacques Longval, Directeur général

Val-d'Or: Centre de santé et de services sociaux de la Vallée-de-l'Or
725, 6e rue, Val-d'Or, QC J9P 3Y1
819-825-6711 Fax: 819-825-7909
marie-clair_c"té@ssss.gouv.qc.ca
www.sante-abitibi-temiscamingue.gouv.qc.ca; www.csssvo.qc.ca
Parent: Agence de la santé et des services sociaux de l'Abitibi-Témiscamingue
Number of Beds: 145 lits hospitaliers; 185 lits de soins de longue durée
Note: Le CSSS regroupe l'Hôpital et le CLSC de Val-d'Or, 2 autres points de service CLSC, 2 centres d'hébergement, et l'Hôpital psychiatrique de Malartic.
Jérôme Lamont, Directeur général
André Tessier, Directeur intérimaire, Services hospitaliers

Victoriaville: Centre de santé et de services sociaux d'Arthabaska-et-de-l'Érable
5, rue des Hospitalières, Victoriaville, QC G6P 6N2
819-357-2030 Fax: 819-357-4314 www.csssae.qc.ca
Parent: Agence de la santé et des services sociaux de la Mauricie et du Centre-du-Québec
Number of Beds: 199 lits hospitaliers; 451 lits de soins de longue durée

Note: Le CSSS regroupe l'Hôtel-Dieu d'Arthabaska, 4 points de service CLSC, et 8 centres d'hébergement.
Marcel Dubois, Président, Conseil d'administration

Ville-Marie: Centre de santé et de services sociaux du Lac-Témiscamingue
22, rue Notre-Dame nord, Ville-Marie, QC J9V 1W8
819-622-2773 Fax: 819-629-3257
www.sante-abitibi-temiscamingue.gouv.qc.ca; www.cssslt.qc.ca
Parent: Agence de la santé et des services sociaux de l'Abitibi-Témiscamingue
Number of Beds: 31 lits hospitaliers; 69 lits de soins de longue durée
Note: Le CSSS regroupe un hôpital (Pavillon Sainte-Famille), un centre d'hébergement (Pavillon Duhamel), et 8 points de service CLSC.
Jacynthe Bérubé, Directrice générale
jacynthe_berube@ssss.gouv.qc.ca

Windsor: Centre de santé et de services sociaux du Val-Saint-François
79, rue Allen, Windsor, QC J1S 2P8
819-542-2777 Fax: 819-845-5521 vsf,santeestrie.qc.ca
Parent: Agence de la santé et des services sociaux de l'Estrie
Number of Beds: 135 lits de soins de longue durée
Note: Le CSSS regroupe 3 points de service CLSC (Urgence mineure de Windsor, Richmond, et Valcourt); et 3 centres d'hébergement (Windsor, Richmond, et Valcourt).
Pierre Lalande, Directeur général

Maria: Centre de santé et de services sociaux de la Baie-des-Chaleurs
419, boul Perron, Maria, QC G0C 1Y0
418-759-3443 Fax: 418-759-5063 888-311-3451
csssbc@csssbc.qc.ca
www.csssbc.qc.ca
Parent: Agence de la santé et des services sociaux de la Gaspésie-Iles-de-la-Madeleine
Number of Beds: 77 lits hospitaliers; 214 lits de soins de longue durée
Note: Le CSSS regroupe l'Hôpital de Maria; 3 centres d'hébergement (Maria, New Carlisle, et Matapédia); 5 points de service CLSC (Malauze de Matapédia, Saint-Omer, Pointe-à-la-Croix, Paspébiac, et Caplan); et un centre de médecine familiale.
Bernard Nadeau, Directeur général

Centre de traitments spécialisés

Mont-Joli: Centre de santé et de services sociaux de La Mitis
800, av du Sanatorium, Mont-Joli, QC G5H 3L6
418-775-7261 Fax: 418-775-8551 www.centremitissien.net
Number of Beds: 24 lits; 175 lits de soins de longue durée
Note: Le CSSS regroupe un centre de santé, un centre d'hébergement, un point de service CLSC, un centre de réadaptation en déficience physique, et la Maison des naissances Colette-Julien.
Isabelle Malo, Directrice générale
cmssc_dg@centremitissien.net

Hôpitaux

Centres hospitaliers

Alma: Centre de santé et de services sociaux de Lac-Saint-Jean-Est
300, boul Champlain sud, Alma, QC G8B 3N8
418-669-2000 Fax: 418-668-9695
Old Name: Centre le Jeannois
Parent: Agence de la santé et des services sociaux du Saguenay-Lac-St-Jean
Number of Beds: 260 lits
Bertin Riverin, Directeur général

Amos: Centre hospitalier Hôtel-Dieu d'Amos
622, 4e rue ouest, Amos, QC J9T 2S2
819-732-3341 Fax: 819-732-7054
www.sante-abitibi-temiscamingue.gouv.qc.ca
Division of: CSSS Les Eskers de l'Abitibi
Number of Beds: 96 lits
Note: Services diagnostiques; urgence et traumatologie; othopédie; rhumatologie; ophtalmologie; chirurgie plastique/reconstructive/maxillo-faciale; gynécologie; obstétrique; gériatrie; physiotherapie; réadaptation cardio-respiratoire.
Michel Michaud, Directeur général, CSSS Les Eskers de l'Abitibi
michel_michaud@ssss.gouv.qc.ca

Asbestos: Centre de santé et de services sociaux des sources
475, 3e av, Asbestos, QC J1T 1X6
819-879-7151 Fax: 819-879-7433
Old Name: Centre de santé de la MRC d'Asbestos
Parent: Agence de la santé et des services sociaux de l'Estrie
Number of Beds: 17 lits, 88 lits longue durée
Mario Morand, Directeur général

Baie-Comeau: Centre de santé et de services sociaux de Manicouagan
635, boul Joliet, Baie-Comeau, QC G5C 1P1
418-589-3701 Fax: 418-589-9654 877-484-3701
jean_marc_arsenault@ssss.gouv.qc.ca
Parent: Agence de la santé et des services sociaux de la C"te-Nord
Number of Beds: 106 lits
Daniel Côté, Directeur général

Baie-Saint-Paul: Hôpital de Baie-Saint-Paul
74, rue Ambroise-Fafard, Baie-Saint-Paul, QC G3Z 2J6
418-435-5150 www.csscharlevoix.qc.ca
Division of: CSSS de Charlevoix
Parent: Agence de la santé et des services sociaux de la Capitale-Nationale
Number of Beds: 40 lits hospitaliers; 56 lits de soins de longue durée
Note: Services: anesthésie, chirurgie, gériatrie, psychiatrie, radiologie, ophtalmologie, urologie; soins généraux et spécialisés; urgence.
Micheline Tremblay, Directrice générale, CSSS de Charlevoix
micheline.tremblay@ssss.gouv.qc.ca

Beauceville: Centre de santé et de services sociaux de Beauce
253, 108e rue, Beauceville, QC G5X 2Z3
418-228-2031 Fax: 418-227-3825
csssbeauce@ssss.gouv.qc.ca
www.csssbeauce.qc.ca
Division of: Centre administratif
Parent: Agence de la santé et des services sociaux de Chaudière-Appalaches
Number of Beds: 117 lits en santé physique; 25 lits en santé mentale
Note: Installations: Centre hospitalier Beauce-Etchemin (Saint-Georges); les CLSCs: Saint-Joseph, Beauceville, La Guadeloupe, Saint-Georges, & Saint-Gédéon; les Centres d'hébergement: Beauceville, Saint-Georges (ouest), & Saint-Georges (est).

Beaupré: Hôpital Sainte-Anne-de-Beaupré
11000, rue des Montagnards, Beaupré, QC G0A 1E0
418-827-3738 www.csssqn.qc.ca
Division of: CSSS de Québec-Nord
Parent: Agence de la santé et des services sociaux de la Capitale-Nationale
Number of Beds: 172 lits
Note: Services infirmiers, médicaux, et psychosociaux.
Lucie Lacroix, Directrice générale, CSSS de Québec-Nord

Bedford: Centre hospitalier de Bedford
CP 1140, 34, rue St-Joseph, Bedford, QC J0J 1A0
450-248-3339
Parent: Agence de la santé et des services sociaux de la Montérégie
Number of Beds: 42 lits

C"te Saint-Luc: Hôpital Mont-Sinai
5690, boul Cavendish, C"te Saint-Luc, QC H4W 1S7
514-369-2222 Fax: 514-369-2225 www.sinaimontreal.ca
Parent: Agence de la santé et des services sociaux de Montréal
Number of Beds: 57 lits
Joseph Rothbart, Directeur général

Chandler: Centre de santé et de services sociaux du Rocher-Percé
CP 3300, 451, rue Mgr Ross est, Chandler, QC G0C 1K0
418-689-2261 Fax: 418-689-5945 www.agencesssgim.ca
Also Known As: Hôpital de Chandler
Division of: Centre hospitalier de Chandler
Parent: Agence de la santé et des services sociaux de la Gaspésie-Iles-de-la-Madeleine
Number of Beds: 113 lits
Note: Soins hospitaliers; soins de longue durée; a fusionné avec le CLSC-CHSLD Pabok en 2004.
Chantal Duguay, Directrice générale

Châteauguay: Hôpital Anna-Laberge
200, boul Brisebois, Châteauguay, QC J6K 4W8
450-699-2425 800-700-0621
www.santemonteregie.qc.ca/jardins-roussillons
Division of: CSSS Jardins-Roussillon
Parent: Agence de la santé et des services sociaux de la Montérégie
Number of Beds: 226 lits hospitaliers
Paul Moreau, Directeur général, CSSS Jardins-Roussillon

Chibougamau: Centre régional de santé et services sociaux Baie-James
312, 3e rue, Chibougamau, QC G8P 1N5
418-748-3575 Fax: 418-748-6391
Parent: Centre régional de la santé et des services sociaux de la Baie-James
Number of Beds: 32
Diane Laboissonnière, Directrice générale

Chicoutimi: Centre de santé et de services sociaux de Chicoutimi
CP 5006, 305, av Saint-Vallier, Chicoutimi, QC G7H 5H6
418-541-1000 Fax: 418-541-1144
Parent: Agence de la santé et des services sociaux du Saguenay-Lac-St-Jean
Number of Beds: 432 lits hospitaliers, 275 lits longue durée
Richard Lemieux, Directeur général

Coaticook: Centre de santé et de services sociaux de la MRC de Coaticook
138, rue Jeanne-Mance, Coaticook, QC J1A 1W3
819-849-9102 Fax: 819-849-6735
rlavigne.coaticook@ssss.gouv.qc.ca
Old Name: Centre de santé de la MRC de Coaticook
Parent: Agence de la santé et des services sociaux de l'Estrie
Pierre-André Rainville, Directeur général

Coteau-du-Lac: Centre de santé et de services sociaux du Suroit
341, ch du Fleuve, Coteau-du-Lac, QC J0P 1B0
450-371-9925 Fax: 450-377-1372
Number of Beds: 391 lits
François Rabeau, Directeur général

Donnacona: Centre hospitalier Portneuf
250, boul Gaudreau, Donnacona, QC G3M 1L7
418-285-3025 Fax: 418-285-3508
lucie_gagnon@ssss.gouv.qc.ca
Number of Beds: 369 lits
Lucie Gagnon, Directrice générale
Philippe Leboeuf, Président du conseil d'administration

Drummondville: Hôpital Sainte-Croix
570, rue Heriot, Drummondville, QC J2B 1C1
819-478-6464
csssdrummond@ssss.gouv.qc.ca
www.csssdrummond.qc.ca
Division of: CSSS Drummond
Parent: Agence de la santé et des services sociaux de la Mauricie et du Centre-du-Québec
Number of Beds: 191 lits
Note: Anatomopathologie, chirurgie générale, gynécologie-obstétrique, pédiatrie, médecine familiale/interne/nucléaire, ophtalmologie, orthopédie, psychiatrie, radiologie, urologie.
Nagui Habashi, Directeur général, CSSS Drummond

Fermont: Centre de santé et de services sociaux de l'Hématite
CP 550, 1, rue Aquilon, Fermont, QC G0G 1J0
418-287-5461 Fax: 418-287-5281
Parent: Agence de la santé et des services sociaux de la C"te-Nord
Number of Beds: 5 lits
Normand Ducharme, Directeur général

Gaspé: Centre de santé et de services sociaux de la C"te-de-Gaspé
215, boul de York ouest, Gaspé, QC G4X 2W2
418-368-3301 Fax: 418-368-7150 www.cssscotedegaspe.ca
Division of: Hôpital Hôtel-Dieu
Parent: Agence de la santé et des services sociaux de la Gaspésie-Iles-de-la-Madeleine
Number of Beds: 56 lits hospitaliers
Jean-Pierre Tremblay, Directeur général

Gatineau: Centre de santé et de services sociaux de Gatineau
Centre administratif, 257, rue Laurier, Gatineau, QC J8X 3W8
819-966-6420 www.csssgatineau.qc.ca
Also Known As: CSSS de Gatineau
Parent: Agence de la santé et de services sociaux de l'Outaouais
Year Founded: 2004
Number of Beds: 508 lits
Note: Le CSSS de Gatineau regroupe les hôpitaux de Gatineau et de Hull, 8 sites de CLSC, 4 centres d'hébergement, la Maison de naissance de l'Outaouais, 3 hôpitaux de jours gériatriques, et un centre de médicine familiale; 425 médecins; 8 sages-femmes; 5 000 employé(e)s.
André O. Rodier, Directeur général
819-966-6560

***Gatineau:* CSSS de Papineau - Centre administratif**
578, rue MacLaren est, Gatineau, QC J8L 2W1
819-986-3359 Fax: 819-986-5671
csss_papineau@ssss.gouv.qc.ca
www.cssspapineau.qc.ca
Parent: Agence de la santé et de services sociaux de l'Outaouais
Gilles Clavel, Directeur général (par intérim)

***Gatineau:* CSSS de Papineau - Hôpital de Papineau**
155, rue Maclaren est, Gatineau, QC J8L 0C2
819-986-3341 Fax: 819-986-4000
csss_papineau@ssss.gouv.qc.ca
www.cssspapineau.qc.ca
Parent: Agence de la santé et de services sociaux de l'Outaouais
Number of Beds: 63 lits hospitaliers; 55 lits soins longue durée
Gilles Clavel, Directeur général (par intérim), CSSS de Papineau

***Gatineau:* Hôpital de Gatineau**
909, boul de La Vérendrye, Gatineau, QC J8P 7H2
819-966-6100 www.csssgatineau.qc.ca
Division of: CSSS de Gatineau
Parent: Agence de la santé et de services sociaux de l'Outaouais
Number of Beds: 243 lits
André O. Rodier, Directeur général, CSSS de Gatineau
819-966-6560
André Moreau, Directeur, Services professionels/Affaires médicales
819-966-6104
Gilles Coulombe, Directeur, Soins infirmiers/Pratiques professionnelles
819-966-6540

***Gatineau:* Hôpital de Hull**
116, boul Lionel-Émond, Gatineau, QC J8Y 1W7
819-966-6200 Fax: 819-966-6306 www.csssgatineau.qc.ca
Division of: CSSS de Gatineau
Parent: Agence de la santé et de services sociaux de l'Outaouais
Number of Beds: 265 lits
André O. Rodier, Directeur général, CSSS de Gatineau
819-966-6560

***Granby:* Centre de santé et de services sociaux de la Haute Yamaska**
205, boul Leclerc Ouest, Granby, QC J2G 1T7
450-375-8000 Fax: 450-375-8032
Parent: Agence de la santé et des services sociaux de la Montérégie
Number of Beds: 303 lits
Claude Vézina, Directeur général

***Greenfield Park:* Hôpital Charles LeMoyne**
3120, boul Taschereau, Greenfield Park, QC J4V 2H1
450-466-5000 Fax: 450-466-8887
www.santemonteregie.qc.ca/hclm
Parent: Agence de la santé et des services sociaux de la Montérégie
Number of Beds: 571 lits
Note: L'Hôpital est le centre hospitalier régional et universitaire de la Montérégie; affilié à l'Université de Sherbrooke; soins et services de court durée en santé physique, santé mentale, réadaptation; recherche; enseignement universitaire.
Yvan Gendron, Directeur général
Alphonse Montminy, Directeur, Services professionnels et hospitaliers
Ginette Brunelle, Directrice, Soins infirmiers

***Hâvre-Saint-Pierre:* Centre de santé et de services sociaux de La Minganie**
1035, Promenade des Anciens, Hâvre-Saint-Pierre, QC G0G 1P0
418-538-2212 Fax: 418-538-2365
Parent: Agence de la santé et des services sociaux de la C"te-Nord
Number of Beds: 13 lits hospitaliers, 60 lits longue durée
Danièle Limoges, Directrice générale
Richard Thibeault, Contremaître

***Joliette:* Les entreprises Symel inc.**
600, rue Saint-Louis, Joliette, QC J6E 9C9
450-756-4282 Fax: 450-755-4959
Parent: Agences de développement de réseaux locaux de services de santé et de services sociaux
Number of Beds: 28 lits
Cynthia Lapointe, Directrice générale

***Jonquière:* Centre de santé et de services sociaux de Jonquière**
2230, rue de l'Hôpital, Jonquière, QC G7X 4H6
418-695-7700 Fax: 418-695-7729
info@carrefoursante.qc.ca
www.carrefoursante.qc.ca
Old Name: Centre hospitalier Jonquière
Parent: Agence de la santé et des services sociaux du Saguenay-Lac-St-Jean
Number of Beds: 70 lits hospitaliers, 299 lits de longue durée
Note: Centre hospitalier, centre local de services communautaires, centre d'hébergement, centre de réadaptation (alcoolisme/toxicomanie; déficience physique).
Lucille Dauphin, Directrice générale

***Kahnawake:* Conseil des Mohawks de Kahnawake**
CP 720, Kahnawake, QC J0L 1B0
450-638-3930 Fax: 450-638-4634
Number of Beds: 10 lits hospitaliers, 33 lits longue durée
Suzanne Horn, Directrice générale

***La Baie:* Centre de santé et de services sociaux Cléophas-Claveau**
CP 38, 1000, rue Docteur-Desgagné, La Baie, QC G7B 3P9
418-544-3381 Fax: 418-544-0770 www.santesaglac.gouv.qc.ca
Parent: Agence de la santé et des services sociaux du Saguenay-Lac-St-Jean
Number of Beds: 25 lits hospitaliers, 114 lits de longue durée
Note: Centre hospitalier: Hôpital de La Baie; centre local de services communautaires; et centres d'hébergement: Foyer de Bagotville, Foyer Saint-Joseph de la Baie.
Martine Nepton, Directrice générale

***La Malbaie:* Hôpital de La Malbaie**
CP 340, 303, rue St-Étienne, La Malbaie, QC G5A 1T1
418-665-1700 www.cssscharlevoix.qc.ca
Also Known As: Centre hospitalier de St-Joseph de La Malbaie
Division of: CSSS de Charlevoix
Parent: Agence de la santé et des services sociaux de la Capitale-Nationale
Number of Beds: 56 lits hospitaliers
Micheline Tremblay, Directrice générale, CSSS de Charlevoix
micheline.tremblay@ssss.gouv.qc.ca

***La Tuque:* Centre de santé et de services sociaux du Haut-Saint-Maurice**
885, boul Ducharme, La Tuque, QC G9X 3C1
819-523-4581 Fax: 819-523-7992
Parent: Agence de la santé et des services sociaux de la Mauricie et du Centre-du-Québec
Number of Beds: 82 lits
Michèle Ouellet, Directrice générale (intérim)

***LaSalle:* Centre hospitalier de LaSalle**
8585, Terrasse Champlain, LaSalle, QC H8P 1C1
514-362-8000 www.santemontreal.qc.ca
Also Known As: l'Hôpital de LaSalle
Parent: Agence de la santé et de services sociaux de Montréal
Number of Beds: 110 lits hospitaliers, 123 lits longue durée

***Lac-Etchemin:* Centre de santé et de services sociaux des Etchemins**
331, place du Sanatorium, Lac-Etchemin, QC G0R 1S0
418-625-3101 Fax: 418-625-3109
csssetchemins@ssss.gouv.qc.ca
www.csssetchemins.qc.ca
Division of: Centre administratif
Parent: Agence de la santé et des services sociaux de Chaudière-Appalaches
Number of Beds: 206 lits
Note: Installations: l'Hôpital; le CLSC Saint-Prosper, et Centre d'hébergement Pavillon de l'Hospitalité; pour la clientèle en santé mentale: L'Équinoxe, L'Intemporel, & L'Intermédiaire; pour la clientèle en déficience physique: Résidence Le Tremplin; & L'Atelier du Lac (réadaptation travail socioprofessionnel).
France Laplante Theberge, Directrice générale (intérim)

***Laval:* Hôpital de la Cité-de-la-Santé**
1755, boul René-Laennec, Laval, QC H7M 3L9
450-668-1010 www.cssslaval.qc.ca
Division of: CSSS de Laval
Number of Beds: 414 lits hospitaliers; 38 lits de psychiatrie
Luc Lepage, Directeur général, CSSS de Laval
Alain Goudreau, Directeur, Services professionnels et hospitaliers/Affaires mé

***Laval:* Jewish Rehabilitation Hospital Hôpital juif de réadaptation**
3205, Place Alton-Goldbloom, Laval, QC H7V 1R2
450-688-9550 Fax: 450-688-3673 www.hjr-jrh.qc.ca
Parent: Agence de la santé et de services sociaux de Laval
Year Founded: 1962
Number of Beds: 120
André Ibghy, Executive Director
450/688-9550, Fax: 450/688-4401, aibghy_hjr@ssss.gouv.qc.ca

***Laval:* Santé Courville inc.**
5200, 80e rue, Laval, QC H7R 5T6
450-627-7990 Fax: 450-627-7993
Parent: Agence de la santé et de services sociaux de Laval
Number of Beds: 120 lits
Christine Durocher, Directrice générale

***Les Escoumins:* Centre de santé et de services sociaux de la Haute-C"te-Nord**
CP 1000, 4, rue de l'Hôpital, Les Escoumins, QC G0T 1K0
418-233-2931 Fax: 418-233-2608
Parent: Agence de la santé et des services sociaux de la C"te-Nord
Number of Beds: 20 lits hospitaliers, 76 lits longue durée
Micheline Anctil, Directrice générale
Katleen Dion, Directeur, soins infirmiers

***Lévis:* Hôtel-Dieu de Lévis**
143, rue Wolfe, Lévis, QC G6V 3Z1
418-835-7121 Fax: 418-835-7143
info@hdl.qc.ca
www.hdl.qc.ca
Division of: Centre administratif
Parent: Agence de la santé et des services sociaux de Chaudière-Appalaches
Number of Beds: 343 lits
Hervé Moysan, Directeur général
Robert Amyot, Directeur, Services techniques
Diana Lancup, Responsable des services sanitaires et lingerie

***Longueuil:* Hôpital Pierre-Boucher**
1333, boul Jacques-Cartier est, Longueuil, QC J4M 2A5
450-468-8111 www.santemonteregie.qc.ca/cssspierreboucher
Division of: CSSS Pierre-Boucher
Number of Beds: 340 lits
Note: Urgence; soins intensifs; soins palliatifs; services médicaux; chirurgie; psychiatrie.
Caroline Barbir, Directrice générale, CSSS Pierre-Boucher

***Loretteville:* Centre hospitalier Chauveau**
29, rue de l'Hôpital, Loretteville, QC G2A 2T7
418-842-3651 Fax: 418-842-8931
Parent: Agence de la santé et des services sociaux de la Capitale-Nationale
Number of Beds: 154 lits + service ambulatoire
Reynald Gagnon, Directeur général

***Louiseville:* Centre de santé et de services sociaux de Maskinongé**
41, boul Comtois, Louiseville, QC J5V 2H8
819-228-2731 Fax: 819-228-2973
yves_martin@ssss.gouv.qc.ca
Number of Beds: 151 lits
Yves Martin, Directeur général

***Lourdes-de-Blanc-Sablon:* Centre de santé et de services sociaux de la Basse-C"te-Nord**
CP 130, 1070, boul Dr Camille Marcoux, Lourdes-de-Blanc-Sablon, QC G0G 1W0
418-461-2144 Fax: 418-461-2731
Parent: Agence de la santé et des services sociaux de la C"te-Nord
Number of Beds: 22 lits hospitaliers, 28 lits longue durée
André Racine, Directeur général (intérim)

***Maniwaki:* CSSS de la Vallée-de-La-Gatineau**
309, boul Desjardins, Maniwaki, QC J9E 2E7
819-449-2300 Fax: 819-449-6137 www.csvg.qc.ca
Parent: Agence de la santé et de services sociaux de l'Outaouais
Number of Beds: 40 lits hospitaliers, 101 lits longue durée
Michel Leger, Directeur général

***Mansfield et Pontefract:* Centre de santé et de services sociaux du Pontiac**
CP 430, 160, ch de la Chute, Mansfield et Pontefract, QC J0X 1V0
819-683-3000 Fax: 819-683-3682 800-567-9625
www.santepontiac.qc.ca
Parent: Agence de la santé et de services sociaux de l'Outaouais
Number of Beds: 39 lits hospitaliers, 115 lits longue durée
Richard Grimard, Directeur général

***Maria:* Hôpital de Maria**
419, boul Perron, Maria, QC G0C 1Y0
418-759-3443 Fax: 418-759-5063
csssbc@csssbc.qc.ca
www.csssbc.qc.ca
Division of: CSSS de la Baie-des-Chaleurs
Parent: Agence de la santé et des services sociaux de la Gaspésie-Iles-de-la-Madeleine

Number of Beds: 77 lits
Note: Unité de médecine familiale Baie-des-Chaleurs: 418-759-1336, poste 2811.
Bernard Nadeau, Directeur général, CSSS de la Baie-des-Chaleurs

***Mont-Laurier:* Hôpital de Mont-Laurier**
2561, ch de la Lièvre sud, Mont-Laurier, QC J9L 3G3
819-623-1234 Fax: 819-440-4376
Division of: CSSS d'Antoine-Labelle
Parent: Agence de la santé et des services sociaux des Laurentides
Number of Beds: 62 lits
Jean-Pierre Urbain, Directeur général, CSSS d'Antoine-Labelle

***Montmagny:* Centre de santé et de services sociaux de Montmagny-L'Islet**
350, boul Taché ouest, Montmagny, QC G5V 3R8
418-248-0630 Fax: 418-248-6838 www.csssml.qc.ca
Division of: Centre administratif
Parent: Agence de la santé et des services sociaux de Chaudière-Appalaches
Number of Beds: 71 lits hospitaliers
Note: Installations: Hôtel-Dieu de Montmagny (l'hôpital); les CLSCs: Saint-Jean Port-Joli, Saint-Pamphile, Saint-Fabien-de-Panet, Montmagny, & l'Isle-aux-Grues; les Centres d'hébergement: Sainte-Perpétue, Saint-Eugène, Cap-Saint-Ignace, Saint-Fabien-de-Panet, Saint-Jean Port-Joli, & Montmagny.
Marie-Claude Ouellet, Directeur général

***Montréal:* Centre de santé et de services sociaux du coeur de l'île**
1385, rue Jean-Talon est, Montréal, QC H2E 1S6
514-495-6754 Fax: 514-495-6734 www.hopitaljean-talon.qc.ca
Parent: Agence de la santé et des services sociaux de Montréal
Number of Beds: 320 lits
Francine Lortie, Directrice générale

***Montréal:* Centre de santé et de services sociaux du Sud-Ouest-Verdun**
6161, rue Laurendeau, Montréal, QC H4E 3X6
514-766-0546 Fax: 514-732-5107
Old Name: CSSS de Verdun/C. St-Paul, St-Henri et P. St-Charl
Parent: Agence de la santé et des services sociaux de Montréal
Number of Beds: 1,309 lits
Danielle McCann, Directrice génerale

***Montréal:* Centre hospitalier de l'Université de Montréal**
3840, rue St-Urbain, Montréal, QC H2W 1T8
514-890-8000 Fax: 514-412-7224
Parent: Agence de la santé et des services sociaux de Montréal
Number of Beds: 1217 lits hospitaliers, 170 lits longue durée
Denis R. Roy, Directeur général

***Montréal:* Centre hospitalier de St. Mary**
3830, av Lacombe, Montréal, QC H3T 1M5
514-345-3511 Fax: 514-345-3836 www.smhc.qc.ca
Parent: Agence de la santé et des services sociaux de Montréal
Number of Beds: 251 lits hospitaliers, 65 lits longue durée
Arvind K. Joshi, Directeur général

***Montréal:* Centre hospitalier Fleury**
2180, rue Fleury est, Montréal, QC H2B 1K3
514-381-9311 Fax: 514-383-5086
bruno.lheureux.chfleury@ssss.gouv.qc.ca
Parent: Agence de la santé et des services sociaux de Montréal
Number of Beds: 149 lits hospitaliers, 25 lits longue durée
Bruno J. L'Heureux, Directeur général associé

***Montréal:* Centre hospitalier Jacques-Viger**
1051, rue St-Hubert, Montréal, QC H2L 3Y5
514-842-7181
Parent: Agence de la santé et des services sociaux de Montréal
Number of Beds: 447 lits

***Montréal:* Centre hospitalier Richardson/Centre Henri Bradet**
5425, rue Bessborough, Montréal, QC H4V 2S7
514-483-1380 Fax: 514-483-4596
Parent: Agence de la santé et des services sociaux de Montréal
Number of Beds: 42 lits hospitaliers, 125 lits longue durée
Francine Dupuis, Directrice générale (par intérim)

***Montréal:* Centre hospitalier universitaire Sainte-Justine**
3175, ch de la C"te Ste-Catherine, Montréal, QC H3T 1C5
514-345-4931 Fax: 514-345-4808
Parent: Agence de la santé et des services sociaux de Montréal
Number of Beds: 434 lits hospitaliers, 55 lits longue durée
Khiem Dao, Directeur général

***Montréal:* Centre universitaire de santé McGill - Hôpital neurologique de Montréal Montréal Neurological Hospital**
3801, University, Montréal, QC H3A 2B4
514-934-1934 Fax: 514-398-3338 www.muhc.mcgill.ca
Parent: Agence de la santé et des services sociaux de Montréal
Number of Beds: 1,193 lits, 173 lits longue durée
Arthur T. Porter, Directeur général
Jean Pierre Bertrand, Directeur, Services techniques
Stephen Black, Manager, Environmental Services

***Montréal:* Hôpital Catherine Booth de l'Armée du Salut**
4375, av Montclair, Montréal, QC H4B 2J5
514-481-0431 Fax: 514-481-0029
s.bourdeau@ssss.gouv.qc.ca
Parent: Agence de la santé et des services sociaux de Montréal
Number of Beds: 84 lits
Note: réadaptation
Edith Verstege, Directrice générale (intérim)

***Montréal:* Hôpital de réadaptation Lindsay**
6363, ch Hudson, Montréal, QC H3S 1M9
514-737-3661 Fax: 514-737-0592
hrl@ssss.gouv.qc.ca
www.hopital-lindsay.qc.ca
Parent: Agence de la santé et des services sociaux de Montréal
Number of Beds: 155 lits
Note: hôpital spécialisé de courte-durée
Réjean Plante, Directeur général

***Montréal:* Hôpital du Sacré-Coeur de Montréal**
5400, boul Gouin ouest, Montréal, QC H4J 1C5
514-338-2222 Fax: 514-338-2384
www.crhsc.umontreal.ca/hscm/
Parent: Agence de la santé et des services sociaux de Montréal
Number of Beds: 554 lits hospitaliers
Note: outpatient services & trauma centre
Michel Larivière, Directeur général
Julien Ricard, Chef de service de la salubrité
514/338-2214

***Montréal:* Hôpital général de Montréal The Montréal General Hospital**
1650, av Cedar, Montréal, QC H3G 1A4
514-934-1934 Fax: 514-934-8200 www.muhc.ca
Parent: Agence de la santé et des services sociaux de Montréal
Number of Beds: 417 beds
Arthur T. Porter, Directeur général

***Montréal:* Hôpital général juif Sir Mortimer B. Davis Sir Mortimer B. Davis Jewish General Hospital**
3755, ch C"te Ste-Catherine, Montréal, QC H3T 1E2
514-340-8222 Fax: 514-340-7510
Parent: Agence de la santé et des services sociaux de Montréal
Number of Beds: 571 lits hospitaliers, 100 lits longue durée
Henri Elbaz, Directeur général
Jacques Benzaquen, Directeur, Services techniques

***Montréal:* Hôpital Maisonneuve-Rosemont**
5415, boul de l'Assomption, Montréal, QC H1T 2M4
514-252-3400 Fax: 514-252-3408
www.maisonneuve-rosemont.org
Parent: Agence de la santé et des services sociaux de Montréal
Number of Beds: 617 lits hospitaliers, 183 lits longue durée
Carole Deschambeault, Directrice générale

***Montréal:* Hôpital Santa Cabrini**
5655, rue St-Zotique est, Montréal, QC H1T 1P7
514-252-6000 Fax: 514-252-6453
Parent: Agence de la santé et des services sociaux de Montréal
Number of Beds: 141 lits hospitaliers
Irène Giannetti, Directrice générale

***Montréal:* Hopital Shriners pour enfants (Quebec) inc.**
1529, av Cedar, Montréal, QC H3G 1A6
514-842-4464 Fax: 514-842-7553
Parent: Agence de la santé et des services sociaux de Montréal
Number of Beds: 40 lits
Maureen Brennan, Directrice générale

***Montréal:* Institut de cardiologie de Montréal**
5000, rue Bélanger est, Montréal, QC H1T 1C8
514-376-3330 Fax: 514-593-2540 www.icm-mhi.org
Parent: Agence de la santé et des services sociaux de Montréal
Number of Beds: 153 lits
Robert Busilacchi, Directeur général

***Montréal:* Institut Philippe Pinel de Montréal**
10905, boul Henri-Bourassa est, Montréal, QC H1C 1H1
514-648-8461 Fax: 514-494-4406 www.pinel.qc.ca/
Parent: Agence de la santé et des services sociaux de Montréal
Number of Beds: 295 lits
Paul-André Lafleur, Directeur général
Paul-Emile Trudeau, Directeur, Services techniques

***Montréal:* Institut universitaire de gériatrie de Montréal**
4565, ch Queen Mary, Montréal, QC H3W 1W5
514-340-1424 Fax: 514-340-3500
Parent: Agence de la santé et des services sociaux de Montréal
Number of Beds: 379 lits
Céline Crowe, Directrice générale (intérim)

***Nicolet:* Centre de santé et de services sociaux de Bécancour-Nicolet-Yamaska**
675, rue St-Jean-Baptiste, Nicolet, QC J3T 1S4
819-293-2071 Fax: 819-293-6160
Old Name: Centre de santé Nicolet-Yamaska
Parent: Agence de la santé et des services sociaux de la Mauricie et du Centre-du-Québec
Number of Beds: 10 lits de courte durée gériatrique, 303 lits longue durée
Raynald Beaupré, Directeur général
André Melançon, Chef, Services techniques

***Ormstown:* Hôpital Barrie Memorial**
Centre de santé et services sociaux du Haut-Sai, CP 200, 28, rue Gale, Ormstown, QC J0S 1K0
450-829-2321 Fax: 450-829-3582
Parent: Agence de la santé et des services sociaux de la Montérégie
Number of Beds: 49 lits hospitaliers
Francine Lortie, Directrice générale
francine.lotrie@rrsss16.gouv.qc.ca

***Pointe-Claire:* Hôpital général du Lakeshore**
160, ch Stillview, Pointe-Claire, QC H9R 2Y2
514-630-2225 Fax: 514-630-3302
Parent: Agence de la santé et des services sociaux de la Montérégie
Number of Beds: 227 lits hospitaliers, 30 lits longue durée
Luc Lepage, Directeur général

***Québec:* Centre de santé et de services sociaux de Québec-Nord**
7150, boul Cloutier, Québec, QC G1H 5V5
418-651-2572 Fax: 418-628-8668
Number of Beds: 959 lits
Lucie Lacroix, Directrice générale

***Québec:* Le Centre de santé et de services sociaux de Québec-Nord/CSSSQN**
2915, av. du Bourg-Royal, 4e étage, Québec, QC G1C 3S2
418-661-5666 Fax: 418-780-8726
Number of Beds: 18 lits hospitaliers, 144 lits longue durée
Reynald Gagnon, Directeur général

***Québec:* Centre hospitalier affilié universitaire de Québec**
1401, 18e rue, Québec, QC G1J 1Z4
418-649-0252 Fax: 418-649-5557 www.cha.quebec.qc.ca
Division of: Hôpital de l'Enfant-Jésus - Hôpital du Saint-Sacrement
Parent: Agence de la santé et des services sociaux de la Capitale-Nationale
Number of Beds: 668 lits
Marie Girard, Directeur général

***Québec:* Centre hospitalier universitaire de Québec/CHUQ**
11, C"te du Palais, Québec, QC G1R 2J6
418-525-4444 Fax: 418-691-5205
Parent: Agence de la santé et des services sociaux de la Capitale-Nationale
Number of Beds: 187 lits hospitaliers; 946 lits (courte durée et pouponnière); 100 lits (hébergement et soins de longue durée); 54 lits (néonatalogie)
René Rouleau, Directeur général

***Québec:* Hôpital Jeffery Hale**
1250, ch Ste-Foy, Québec, QC G1S 2M6
418-683-4471 Fax: 418-683-8980
dg.jhale@sympatico.ca
Parent: Agence de la santé et des services sociaux de la Capitale-Nationale
Number of Beds: 12 lits hospitaliers, 100 lits longue durée
Louis Hanrahan, Directeur général
Réné Corriveau, Coordonnateur, services techniques

***Rimouski:* Hôpital régional de Rimouski**
150, av Rouleau, Rimouski, QC G5L 5T1
418-723-7851 Fax: 418-724-8632
courrierweb.crsssr@ssss.gouv.qc.ca
www.chrr.qc.ca
Division of: CSSS de Rimouski-Neigette

Number of Beds: 255 lits
Raymond Coulombe, Directeur général, CSSS de Rimouski-Neigette

***Rivière-Rouge:* Centre de services de Rivière-Rouge**
1525, rue L'Annonciation nord, Rivière-Rouge, QC J0T 1T0
819-275-2118 Fax: 819-275-2464 www.csssal.org
Division of: CSSS d'Antoine-Labelle
Jean-Pierre Urbain, Directeur général, CSSS d'Antoine-Labelle

***Roberval:* Hôtel-Dieu de Roberval/Centre d'hébergement Roberval**
450, rue Brassard, Roberval, QC G8H 1B9
418-275-0110 Fax: 418-275-6202
hdr@ssss.gouv.qc.ca
www.cmdp-roberval.com
Division of: CSSS Domaine-du-Roy
Number of Beds: 135 lits hospitaliers; 100 lits de soins de longue durée
Note: L'hôpital offre service d'urgence, médecine générale/interne/nucléaire, ophtalmologie, obstétrique, orthopédie, pédiatrie, chirurgie, psychiatrie, urologie, réadaptation physique.
Jacques Dubois, Directeur général, CSSS Domaine-du-Roy

***Saint-Charles-Borromée:* Centre de santé et de services sociaux du Nord de Lanaudière**
1000, boul Sainte-Anne, Saint-Charles-Borromée, QC J6E 6J2
450-759-8222 Fax: 450-759-7969
Parent: Agences de développement de réseaux locaux de services de santé et de services sociaux
Number of Beds: 996 lits
Note: Centre hospitalier à vocations multiples
Caroline Barbir, Directrice générale

***Saint-Eustache:* CSSS du Lac-des-Deux-Montagnes**
520, boul Arthur-Sauvé, Saint-Eustache, QC J7R 5B1
450-473-6811 Fax: 450-473-6966 www.moncsss.com
Parent: Agence de la santé et des services sociaux des Laurentides
Year Founded: 2004
Number of Beds: 221 lits hospitaliers; 258 lits d'hébergement/SLD
Note: Réseau local de services de santé et de services sociaux; 4 installations: CH de Saint-Benoît, CH de Saint-Eustache, CLSC Jean-Olivier-Chénier, et Hôpital de Saint-Eustache; 2 400 employés/employées et médecins, et 180 bénévoles.
Roch Martel, Directeur général

***Saint-Eustache:* Manoir Saint-Eustache**
CP 850, 55, rue Chenier, Saint-Eustache, QC J7R 4Y8
450-472-0013 Fax: 450-472-3104
Parent: Agence de la santé et des services sociaux des Laurentides
Number of Beds: 194 lits

***Saint-Hyacinthe:* Hôpital Honoré-Mercier**
2750, boul Laframboise, Saint-Hyacinthe, QC J2S 4Y8
450-771-3333 Fax: 450-771-3748
info@lesommetavotreportee.qc.ca
www.lesommetavotreportee.qc.ca;
www.santemonteregie.qc.ca/richelieu-yamaska
Division of: CSSS Richelieu-Yamaska
Parent: Agence de la santé et des services sociaux de la Montérégie
Number of Beds: 273 lits
Note: Centre mère-enfant-famille; Pédiatrie; Soins intensifs; Chirurgie.
Daniel Castonguay, Directeur général, CSSS Richelieu-Yamaska
Diane Poirier, Directrice, Affaires médicales
Carmen Messier, Directrice, Soins infirmiers/Pratiques professionnelles

***Saint-Jean-sur-Richelieu:* Hôpital du Haut-Richelieu**
978, boul du Séminaire nord, Saint-Jean-sur-Richelieu, QC J3A 1B7
450-359-5000 Fax: 450-359-5251
Division of: CSSS Haut-Richelieu-Rouville
Parent: Agence de la santé et des services sociaux de la Montérégie
Number of Beds: 307 lits
Note: L'Hôpital, et le centre administratif du CSSS Haut-Richelieu-Rouville.
Christine Lessard, Directrice générale, CSSS Haut-Richelieu-Rouville
Krystyna Pecko, Directrice générale adjointe/Directrice des affaires mé

***Saint-Marc-des-Carrières:* Centre de santé et de services sociaux de Portneuf**
CP 400, 1045, boul Bona-Dussault, Saint-Marc-des-Carrières, QC G0A 4B0
418-285-3025 Fax: 418-285-3508
Parent: Agence de la santé et des services sociaux de la Capitale-Nationale
Number of Beds: 14 lits hospitaliers, 347 lits longue durée
Note: hébergement et soins de longue durée: Centre d'hébergement Donnaconna, Centre d'hébergement Saint-Casimir, Centre d'hébergement Saint-Marc-des-Carrières, Centre d'hébergement Saint-Raymond, Centre hospitalier Portneuf
Lucie Gagnon, Directrice générale

***Saint-Romuald:* Centre de santé et de services sociaux du Grand Littoral**
975, rue de la Concorde, Saint-Romuald, QC G6W 8A7
418-380-8991 Fax: 418-832-9041
info-directiongenerale-csssgrandlittoral@ssss.gouv.qc.ca
www.csssgrandlittoral.qc.ca
Division of: Centre administratif
Parent: Agence de la santé et des services sociaux de Chaudière-Appalaches
Note: Installations: CLSC & Unité de médecine familiale Saint-Romuald; les autres CLSCs: Saint-Lazare, Sainte-Marie, Laurier-Station, Lévis, & Centre Paul-Gilbert; les Centres d'hébergement: Saint-Gervais, Saint-Raphaël, Saint-Anselme, Sainte-Claire, Lévis, Hébergement Ilot Desjardins, Résidence Louis Édouard-Couture, Saint-Apollinaire, Saint-Flavien, Sainte-Croix, Saint-Sylvestre, Sainte-Marie, Saint-Isidore, & Sainte-Hénédine.

***Saint-Tite:* Centre de santé et de services sociaux de la Vallée-de-la-Batiscan**
CP 430, 750, rue du Couvent, Saint-Tite, QC G0X 3H0
418-365-7555 Fax: 418-365-6009
Number of Beds: 171 lits
Alain Lampron, Directeur général

***Sainte-Adèle:* Centre de santé et de services sociaux des Pays-d'en-Haut**
1390, boul de Sainte-Adèle, Sainte-Adèle, QC J8B 2N5
450-229-6601 Fax: 450-229-7220
Parent: Agence de la santé et des services sociaux des Laurentides
Number of Beds: 91 lits
Jacqueline Gagnon, Directrice générale

***Sainte-Anne-de-Bellevue:* Hôpital Sainte-Anne**
Le ministère des affaires des anciens combattants, 305, boul des Anciens-Combattants, Sainte-Anne-de-Bellevue, QC H9X 1Y9
514-457-3440 800-361-9287
steanne@vac-acc.gc.ca
www.vac-acc.gc.ca
Parent: Agence de la santé et des services sociaux de Montréal
Number of Beds: 590 lits
Rachel Corneille-Gravel, Directrice générale

***Salaberry-de-Valleyfield:* Centre de santé et de services sociaux du Suroît**
150, rue St-Thomas, Salaberry-de-Valleyfield, QC J6T 6C1
450-371-9920 www.chsuroit.qc.ca
Parent: Agence de la santé et des services sociaux de la Montérégie
Number of Beds: 384 lits
François Rabeau, Directeur général

***Sept-Iles:* Centre de santé et de services sociaux de Sept-Iles**
45, rue Père Divet, Sept-Iles, QC G4R 3N7
418-962-9761 Fax: 418-962-2701
Parent: Agence de la santé et des services sociaux de la C"te-Nord
Number of Beds: 117 lits hospitaliers, 96 lits longue durée
Jean-René Blouin, Directeur général
Claude Lantaigne, Chef, Services d'entretien sanitaire

***Shawinigan:* Centre de santé et de services sociaux de l'énergie**
1705, av Georges, Shawinigan, QC G9N 2N1
819-536-7500 Fax: 819-536-7658
Parent: Agence de la santé et des services sociaux de la Mauricie et du Centre-du-Québec
Number of Beds: 404 lits
Guy Lemieux, Directeur général

***Shawinigan-Sud:* Hôpital du Centre-de-la Mauricie**
50, 119e rue, Shawinigan-Sud, QC G9P 5K1
819-536-7500
Parent: Agence de la santé et des services sociaux de la Mauricie et du Centre-du-Québec
Number of Beds: 178 lits hospitaliers, 45 lits longue durée

***Shawville:* Centre hospitalier du Pontiac**
200, rue Argue, Shawville, QC J0X 2Y0
819-647-2211 Fax: 819-647-2409 santepontiac.qc.ca/
Parent: Agence de la santé et de services sociaux de l'Outaouais
Number of Beds: 71 lits
Richard Grimard, Directeur général
Jacques Boissonneault, Chef de service, Biologie médicale

***Sherbrooke:* Centre hospitalier universitaire de Sherbrooke**
555, rue Murray, Sherbrooke, QC J1G 2K8
819-346-1110 Fax: 819-822-6789 www.chus.qc.ca
Number of Beds: 682 lits
Patricia Gauthier, Directrice générale

***Sorel-Tracy:* Centre de santé et de services sociaux de Sorel-Tracy**
400, av Hôtel-Dieu, Sorel-Tracy, QC J3P 1N5
450-746-5555 Fax: 450-746-4897
Parent: Agence de la santé et des services sociaux de la Montérégie
Number of Beds: 260 lits
Benoît Marchessault, Directeur général

***Ste-Anne-des-Monts:* Centre de santé et de services sociaux de la Haute-Gaspésie**
50, rue du Belvédère, Ste-Anne-des-Monts, QC G4V 1X4
418-763-2261 Fax: 418-763-7460 www.agencesssgim.ca;
www.cssshautegaspesie.qc.ca
Also Known As: Hôpital de Sainte-Anne-des-Monts
Division of: Hôpital des Monts
Parent: Agence de la santé et des services sociaux de la Gaspésie-Iles-de-la-Madeleine
Year Founded: 1972
Number of Beds: 35 lits hospitaliers
Robert Deschênes, Directeur général
Pierre Roger, Directeur, Services techniques
René Ouellet, Chef, Entretien ménager, buanderie, lingerie

***Terrebonne:* Centre de santé et de services sociaux du Sud de Lanaudière**
911, montée des Pionniers, Terrebonne, QC J6V 2H2
450-654-7525 Fax: 450-470-2640
Parent: Agences de développement de réseaux locaux de services de santé et de services sociaux
Number of Beds: 347 lits
Michel Bouffard, Directeur général

***Terrebonne:* Centre hospitalier Pierre-Le Gardeur**
911, montée des Pionniers, Terrebonne, QC J6V 2H2
450-654-7525 www.chpierrelegardeur.ca
Parent: Agences de développement de réseaux locaux de services de santé et de services sociaux
Number of Beds: 273 lits

***Thetford Mines:* Centre de santé et de services sociaux de la région de Thetford**
1717, rue Notre-Dame est, Thetford Mines, QC G6G 2V4
418-338-7777 Fax: 418-335-7616
chra@ssss.gouv.qc.ca
www.centresantethetford.ca
Division of: Centre administratif
Parent: Agence de la santé et des services sociaux de Chaudière-Appalaches
Number of Beds: 336 lits
Note: Installations: l'Hôpital; les CLSCs: Thetford Mines, Adstock, Disraeli, & East Broughton; les Centres d'hébergement: Denis-Marcotte, Lac-Noir, Marc-André-Jacques, St-Joseph, René-Lavoie, & Valin.
François Chauvette, Directeur des activités, CLSC
Denis Martin, Directeur de l'hébergement
Normand Baker, Directeur général, CSSSRT

***Trois-Pistoles:* Centre hospitalier Trois-Pistoles**
550, rue Notre-Dame est, Trois-Pistoles, QC G0L 4K0
418-851-1111 Fax: 418-851-2934 www.agencesssbsl.gouv.qc.ca
Division of: CSSS des Basques
Number of Beds: 60 lits
Line Moisan, Directrice générale, CSSS des Basques

***Trois-Rivières:* Centre St-Joseph/Résidence La Providence**
731, rue Sainte-Julie, Trois-Rivières, QC G9A 1Y1
819-370-2100 www.cssstr.qc.ca
Division of: CSSS de Trois-Rivières
Parent: Agence de la santé et des services sociaux de la Mauricie et du Centre-du-Québec
Number of Beds: 198 lits hospitaliers; 100 lits de soins de longue durée

Note: Centre St-Joseph: services hospitaliers; Résidence La Providence: hébergement 819-370-2200, poste 43104.
Jacques Longval, Directeur général, CSSS de Trois-Rivières

***Verdun:* Hôpital Douglas**
6875, boul Lasalle, Verdun, QC H4H 1R3
514-761-6131 Fax: 514-761-4816
dredea@douglas.mcgill.ca
Parent: Agence de la santé et des services sociaux de Montréal
Number of Beds: 210 lits hospitaliers, 192 lits longue durée
Note: mental hospital affiliated with McGill University; also community services, outpatient services, housing, social rehabilitation, specialized services (eating disorders, alcoholism & drug abuse, schizophrenia, aging, dementia & Alzheimer dementia)
Jacques Hendlisz, Directeur général

***Verdun:* Pavillon Manoir**
5500, boul Lasalle, Verdun, QC H4H 1N9
514-769-8801
Old Name: CHSLD Champlain - Manoir de Verdun
Parent: Agence de la santé et des services sociaux de Montréal
Number of Beds: 220 lits

***Victoriaville:* Hôtel-Dieu d'Arthabaska**
5, rue des Hospitalières, Victoriaville, QC G6P 6N2
819-357-2030 Fax: 819-357-7406 www.csssae.qc.ca
Division of: CSSS d'Arthabaska-et-de-l'Érable
Parent: Agence de la santé et des services sociaux de la Mauricie et du Centre-du-Québec
Number of Beds: 199 lits
Marcel Dubois, Président, Conseil d'administration, CSSS d'Arthabaska-et-de-l

***Wakefield:* Centre de santé et de services sociaux des Collines**
PO Box 160 Wakefield, 101, ch Burnside, Wakefield, QC J0X 3G0
819-459-1112 Fax: 819-459-1894 877-459-1112
www.santedescollines.qc.ca
Also Known As: CSSS des Collines
Parent: Agence de la santé et de services sociaux de l'Outaouais
Number of Beds: 16 lits hospitaliers; 10 lits de soins de longue durée
Note: Le CSSS: l'Hôpital Mémorial de Wakefield (services bilingues); Centre d'hébergement La Pêche; le CLSC des Collines et ses 4 points de services de Cantley, Chelsea, La Pêche, et Val-des-Monts; 18 médecins et 8 médecins conseils; 275 employés/employées.
Pierre Rochon, Directeur général

***Weedon:* Centre de santé et de services sociaux du Haut-St-François**
460, 2e av, Weedon, QC J0B 3J0
819-877-3434 Fax: 819-877-3714
Old Name: CLSC-CHSLD du Haut-St-François
Parent: Agence de la santé et des services sociaux de l'Estrie
Number of Beds: 108 lits
Louisette Gosselin, Directrice générale

Hôpitaux privés

***Kahnawake:* Kateri Memorial Hospital Centre Centre hospitalier Kateri Memorial**
PO Box 10, Kahnawake, QC J0L 1B0
450-638-3930 Fax: 450-638-4634
admin@kmhc.ca
www.kmhc.ca; www.santemonteregie.qc.ca/jardins-roussillon
Also Known As: Tehsakotitsén:tha
Division of: CSSS Jardins-Roussillon
Parent: Agence de la santé et des services sociaux de la Montérégie
Number of Beds: 43 beds/lits
Note: Family medicine, home care, community health, infection prevention and control, nutrition services, occupational therapy, physiotherapy, speech therapy, social services.
Susan Horne, Executive Director

***Montréal:* Centre métropolitain de Chirurgie Plastique Inc.**
999, rue de Salaberry, Montréal, QC H3L 1L2
514-332-7091 Fax: 514-332-7095
Parent: Agence de la santé et des services sociaux de Montréal
Number of Beds: 17 lits
Pierre Brassard, Directeur général

***Montréal:* Hôpital Marie-Clarac**
3530, boul Gouin est, Montréal, QC H1H 1B7
514-321-8800 Fax: 514-321-9626
www.hopitalmarie-clarac.qc.ca/
Parent: Agence de la santé et des services sociaux de Montréal
Number of Beds: 204 lits
Pierre-Anne Mandato, Directrice générale

***Montréal:* Hôpital Shriners pour enfants (Québec) inc.**
Shriners Hospital for Children
1529, av Cedar, Montréal, QC H3G 1A6
514-842-4464 Fax: 514-842-7553
Parent: Agence de la santé et des services sociaux de Montréal
Number of Beds: 40 lits
Maureen Brennan, Directrice générale
John Krisa, Superviseur, Installations matériels

***Sillery:* La Maison Michel Sarrazin**
2101, ch St-Louis, Sillery, QC G1T 2P5
418-688-0878 Fax: 418-681-8636
info@michel-sarrazin.ca
www.michel-sarrazin.ca
Parent: Agence de la santé et des services sociaux de la Capitale-Nationale
Number of Beds: 15 lits
Michel L'Heureux, Directeur général

Centres locaux des services communautaires (CLSC)

***Alma:* CLSC Le Norois**
Édifice complexe J.-Gagnon, 100, rue Saint-Joseph sud, Alma, QC G8B 7A6
418-668-4563 Fax: 418-668-6462
monette.desbiens@ssss.gouv.qc.ca
Parent: Agence de la santé et des services sociaux du Saguenay-Lac-St-Jean
Bertin Riverin, Directeur général

***Aupaluk:* Dispensaire d'Aupaluk**
Aupaluk, QC J0M 1X0
819-491-9090 Fax: 819-491-7020
clsc.aupaluk@ssss.gouv.qc.ca
Number of Beds: 1 lit
Madge Pomerleau, Directrice générale

***Barachois:* CLSC Mer et Montagnes**
1070, rte 132, Barachois, QC G0C 1A0
418-645-2572 Fax: 418-645-2106 www.cssscotedegaspe.ca
Division of: Point de service Barachois
Parent: Agence de la santé et des services sociaux de la Gaspésie-Iles-de-la-Madeleine
Note: CSSS Côte-de-Gaspé.

***Bassin:* Centre de santé et de services sociaux des Iles**
CP 57, 702, ch du Bassin, Bassin, QC G4T 0C8
418-937-2572 Fax: 418-937-5381 www.agencesssgim.ca; www.csssdesiles.qc.ca
Division of: CLSC de Bassin
Parent: Agence de la santé et des services sociaux de la Gaspésie-Iles-de-la-Madeleine

***Beloeil:* CLSC La Vallée des Patriotes**
347, rue Duvernay, Beloeil, QC J3G 5S8
514-536-2572
Parent: Agence de la santé et des services sociaux de la Montérégie
Number of Beds: 225 lits

***Berthierville:* CLSC d'Autray**
761, rue Notre-Dame, Berthierville, QC J0K 1A0
450-836-7011
Parent: Agences de développement de réseaux locaux de services de santé et de services sociaux
Number of Beds: 237 lits
Norman Blackburn, Directeur général

***Boucherville:* CLSC des Seigneuries de Boucherville**
160, boul De Montarville, Boucherville, QC J4B 6S2
450-655-3630 Fax: 450-655-8530
www.santemonteregie.qc.ca/cssspierreboucher
Division of: CSSS Pierre-Boucher
Parent: Agence de la santé et des services sociaux de la Montérégie
Caroline Barbir, Directrice générale, CSSS Pierre-Boucher

***Brossard:* Centre de santé et de services sociaux Champlain**
Complexe Taschereau, #100, 5811, boul Taschereau, Brossard, QC J4Z 1A5
450-445-4452 Fax: 450-445-5535
Parent: Agence de la santé et des services sociaux de la Montérégie
Suzanne Beauchamp, Directrice générale

***C"te Saint-Luc:* Centre local de services communautaires René-Cassin**
#600, 5800, boul Cavendish, C"te Saint-Luc, QC H4W 2T5
514-488-9163 Fax: 514-485-1612
dkobernick@ssss.gouv.qc.ca
www.geronto.org
Parent: Agence de la santé et des services sociaux de Montréal
Note: local health & social service centre
Joëlle Khalfa, Directeur général

***C"te Saint-Luc:* Hôpital Mont-Sinai**
5690, boul Cavendish, C"te Saint-Luc, QC H4W 1S7
514-369-2222 Fax: 514-369-2225
Parent: Agence de la santé et des services sociaux de Montréal
Number of Beds: 57 lits
Joseph Rothbart, Directeur général

***Candiac:* CLSC Kateri**
90, boul Marie-Victorin, Candiac, QC J5R 1C1
450-659-7661 Fax: 450-444-6260
www.santemonteregie.qc.ca/jardins-roussillon
Division of: CSSS Jardins-Roussillon
Parent: Agence de la santé et des services sociaux de la Montérégie
Number of Beds: 340 lits
Paul Moreau, Directeur général, CSSS Jardins-Roussillon

***Cantley:* Centre de santé et de services sociaux des Collines - CLSC Cantley**
850, Montée de la Source, Cantley, QC J8V 3H4
819-459-1112 Fax: 819-827-5818 877-459-1112
www.santedescollines.qc.ca
Also Known As: CSSS-CLSC des Collines
Parent: Agence de la santé et de services sociaux de l'Outaouais
Pierre Rochon, Directeur général, CSSS des Collines

***Cap-Chat:* Centre de santé et de services sociaux de la Haute-Gaspésie**
49, rue Notre-Dame, Cap-Chat, QC G0E 1E0
418-786-5594 Fax: 418-786-2638 www.agencesssgim.ca; www.cssshautegaspesie.qc.ca
Division of: CLSC de Cap-Chat
Parent: Agence de la santé et des services sociaux de la Gaspésie-Iles-de-la-Madeleine
Robert Deschênes, Directeur général

***Cap-aux-Meules:* Centre de santé et de services sociaux des Iles**
420, ch Principal, Cap-aux-Meules, QC G4T 1S1
418-986-2572 Fax: 418-986-4911 www.agencesssgim.ca; www.csssdesiles.qc.ca
Division of: CLSC de Cap-aux-Meules
Parent: Agence de la santé et des services sociaux de la Gaspésie-Iles-de-la-Madeleine

***Caplan:* CLSC de Caplan**
96, rte 132, Caplan, QC G0C 1H0
418-388-2572 Fax: 418-388-2645
csssbc@csssbc.qc.ca
www.csssbc.qc.ca
Division of: CSSS de la Baie-des-Chaleurs
Parent: Agence de la santé et des services sociaux de la Gaspésie-Iles-de-la-Madeleine
Bernard Nadeau, Directeur général, CSSS de la Baie-des-Chaleurs

***Châteauguay:* CLSC Châteauguay**
101, rue Lauzon, Châteauguay, QC J6K 1C7
450-699-3333 Fax: 450-691-6202
www.santemonteregie.qc.ca/jardins-roussillon
Division of: CSSS Jardins-Roussillon
Parent: Agence de la santé et des services sociaux de la Montérégie
Paul Moreau, Directeur général, CSSS Jardins-Roussillon

***Chertsey:* CLSC de Matawinie**
485, rue Dupuis, Chertsey, QC J0K 3K0
450-882-2488
Parent: Agences de développement de réseaux locaux de services de santé et de services sociaux

***Chicoutimi:* Centre de santé et de services sociaux de Chicoutimi**
CP 5006, 305, St Vallier, Chicoutimi, QC G7H 5H6
418-541-1000 Fax: 418-541-1144
Richard Lehieux, Directeur général

***Drummondville:* CLSC Drummond**
350, rue Saint-Jean, Drummondville, QC J2B 5L4
819-474-2572
csssdrummond@ssss.gouv.qc.ca
www.csssdrummond.qc.ca
Division of: CSSS Drummond
Parent: Agence de la santé et des services sociaux de la Mauricie et du Centre-du-Québec
Note: Santé au travail: 819-474-8428

Nagui Habashi, Directeur général, CSSS Drummond

Forestville: Centre de santé et de services sociaux de la Haute-C"te-Nord - Pavillon Forestvi
CP 790, 2, 7e rue, Forestville, QC G0T 1E0
418-587-2212 Fax: 418-587-2865
Parent: Agence de la santé et des services sociaux de la C"te-Nord
Number of Beds: 20 lits
Micheline Anctil, Directrice générale

Gascons: CLSC de Gascons
CP 28, 63, rte 132, Gascons, QC G0C 1P0
418-396-2572 Fax: 418-396-2367 www.agencesssgim.ca
Parent: Agence de la santé et des services sociaux de la Gaspésie-Iles-de-la-Madeleine
Note: CSSS du Rocher-Percé.

Gaspé: CLSC Mer et Montagnes
CP 6397, 205, boul de York ouest, 2e étage, Gaspé, QC G4X 2R8
418-368-2572 Fax: 418-368-1532 www.cssscotedegaspe.ca
Division of: Point de service Gaspé
Parent: Agence de la santé et des services sociaux de la Gaspésie-Iles-de-la-Madeleine
Note: CSSS Côte-de-Gaspé.

Gatineau: CLSC de Gatineau - Point de service de la Gappe
777, boul de la Gappe, Gatineau, QC J8T 8R2
819-966-6550 Fax: 819-966-6552 www.csssgatineau.qc.ca
Division of: CSSS de Gatineau
Parent: Agence de la santé et de services sociaux de l'Outaouais
Note: Services généraux santé; soins infirmiers et ambulatoires; consulation médicale pour les clientèles vulnérables.
André O. Rodier, Directeur général, CSSS de Gatineau
Micheline Malette, Directrice, Services généraux/Santé publique 819-966-6510

Gatineau: CLSC de Gatineau - Point de service Gatineau
80, av Gatineau, Gatineau, QC J8T 4J3
819-966-6550 Fax: 819-966-6572 www.csssgatineau.qc.ca
Division of: CSSS de Gatineau
Parent: Agence de la santé et de services sociaux de l'Outaouais
Note: Centre local de services communautaires.
André O. Rodier, Directeur général, CSSS de Gatineau

Gatineau: CLSC de Gatineau - Point de service LeGuerrier
425, rue LeGuerrier, Gatineau, QC J9H 6N8
819-966-6540 Fax: 819-966-6541 www.csssdegatineau.qc.ca
Division of: CSSS de Gatineau
Parent: Agence de la santé et de services sociaux de l'Outaouais
André O. Rodier, Directeur général, CSSS de Gatineau 819-966-6560
Micheline Malette, Directrice, Services généraux/Santé publique

Gatineau: CLSC Vallée-de-la-Lievre
578, rue Maclaren est, Gatineau, QC J8L 2W1
819-986-3359 Fax: 819-986-5671
csss_papineau@ssss.gouv.qc.ca
www.cssspapineau.qc.ca
Parent: Agence de la santé et de services sociaux de l'Outaouais
Gilles Clavel, Directeur général (par intérim), CSSS de Papineau

Grande-Entrée: Centre de santé et de services sociaux des Iles
CP 2, site 5, rte 199, Grande-Entrée, QC G4T 7B3
418-985-2572 Fax: 418-985-2862 www.agencesssgim.ca; www.csssdesiles.qc.ca
Division of: CLSC d'Old Harry
Parent: Agence de la santé et des services sociaux de la Gaspésie-Iles-de-la-Madeleine
Germain Chevarie, Directeur général

Grande-Vallée: CLSC Mer et Montagnes
71, rue St-François-Xavier est, Grande-Vallée, QC G0E 1K0
418-393-2572 Fax: 418-393-2952 www.cssscotedegaspe.ca
Division of: Point de service Grande-Vallée
Parent: Agence de la santé et des services sociaux de la Gaspésie-Iles-de-la-Madeleine
Note: CSSS Côte-de-Gaspé.

Grosse-Ile: Centre des santé et de services des Iles
773, ch Principal, Grosse-Ile, QC G4T 6B5
418-985-2572 Fax: 418-985-2862 www.agencesssgim.ca; www.csssdesiles.qc.ca
Division of: CLSC de l'Est
Parent: Agence de la santé et des services sociaux de la Gaspésie-Iles-de-la-Madeleine

Huntingdon: CLSC Huntingdon
#200, 10, rue King, Huntingdon, QC J0S 1H0
450-264-6108 Fax: 450-264-6801
Parent: Agence de la santé et des services sociaux de la Montérégie
Guy Deschenes, Directeur général

Ile d'Entrée: Centre de santé et de services sociaux des Iles
Ile d'Entrée, QC G4T 1Z1
418-986-4299 Fax: 418-986-4094 www.agencesssgim.ca; www.csssdesiles.qc.ca
Division of: CLSC de l'Ile d'Entrée
Parent: Agence de la santé et des services sociaux de la Gaspésie-Iles-de-la-Madeleine

Joliette: CLSC de Joliette
380, boul Base-de-Roc, Joliette, QC J6E 9J6
450-755-2111 Fax: 450-755-4896
Jean-François Foisy, Directeur général adjoint

Jonquière: CLSC de la Jonquière
CP 580, 3667, boul Harvey, Jonquière, QC G7X 7W4
418-695-2572
Parent: Agence de la santé et des services sociaux du Saguenay-Lac-St-Jean
Lucille Dumont, Directrice générale

Kawawachikamach: CLSC Naskapi
CP 5154, 9, rue Naskapi, Kawawachikamach, QC G0G 2Z0
418-585-2897 Fax: 418-585-3126 866-585-2110
Parent: Agence de la santé et des services sociaux de la C"te-Nord
Luc Guènette, Directeur général (intérim)

Kipawa: Health Centre of Eagle Village
3 Ogima, Eagle Village First Nation, Kipawa, QC J0Z 2H0
819-627-9060 Fax: 819-627-1885
davem@eaglevillagefirstnation.ca
www.eaglevillagefirstnation.ca
David McLaren, Health Director
davidm@eaglevillagefirstnation.ca

Kuujjuaq: Centre de santé Tulattavik de l'Ungava
PO Box 149, Kuujjuaq, QC J0M 1C0
819-964-2905 Fax: 819-964-6353
information_rrsss17@ssss.gouv.qc.ca
www.rrsss17.gouv.qc.ca; www.ungava.info
Parent: Régie régionale de la santé et des services sociaux du Nunavik
Number of Beds: 15 lits hospitaliers; 10 lits de soins de longue durée
Note: Urgence; soins médicaux; soins infirmiers; maternité; radiologie; pharmacie; électrocardiographie; laboratoire; physiothérapie.
Madge Pomerleau, Directrice générale
madge.pomerleau@ssss.gouv.qc.ca

La Malbaie: CLSC de La Malbaie
535, boul de Comporté, La Malbaie, QC G5A 1S8
418-665-6413 www.cssscharlevoix.qc.ca
Division of: CSSS de Charlevoix
Micheline Tremblay, Directrice générale, CSSS de Charlevoix
micheline.tremblay@ssss.gouv.qc.ca

La Tuque: CLSC du Haunt Saint-Maurice
350, av Brown, La Tuque, QC G9X 2W4
819-523-6171 Fax: 819-523-6176
Guy Lemieux, Directeur général

LaSalle: CLSC de LaSalle
8550, boul Newman, LaSalle, QC H8N 1Y5
514-364-2572 Fax: 514-364-6365 www.santemontreal.qc.ca
Parent: Agence de la santé et des services sociaux de Montréal
Jean-Paul Bouchard, Directeur général

Lachine: Centre de santé et de services sociaux de Dorval-Lachine-LaSalle
1900, rue Notre-Dame, Lachine, QC H8S 2G2
514-364-2572 www.santemontreal.qc.ca
Division of: Centre administratif
Parent: Agence de la santé et des services sociaux de Montréal
Note: Installations: l'Hôpital de LaSalle (110 lits de courte durée, 123 lits de longue durée); les CLSCs: LaSalle, & Dorval-Lachine; les Centres d'hébergement: LaSalle (202 lits), Dorval (111 lits), Lachine (200 lits), & Nazaire-Piché (Lachine; 100 lits).
Jean-Paul Bouchard, Directeur général

Lachine: CLSC de Dorval-Lachine
1900, rue Notre-Dame, Lachine, QC H8S 2G2
514-639-0650 Fax: 514-639-0666 www.santemontreal.qc.ca
Parent: Agence de la santé et des services sociaux de Montréal
Note: Services de santé; services sociaux curatifs et préventifs.
Paul Perreault, Directeur général

Lachute: Centre de santé et de services sociaux d'Argenteuil
145, av de la Providence, Lachute, QC J8H 4C7
450-562-3761 Fax: 450-566-3316
Number of Beds: 49 lits
Jocelyn Ouellet, Directeur général

Laval: CLSC des Mille-Iles
4731, boul Levesque est, Laval, QC H7C 1M9
450-661-2572 Fax: 450-661-6177 www.cssslaval.qc.ca
Division of: CSSS de Laval
Note: Les autres points de service CLSC: Marigot (2 sites), Mille-Iles (304, boul Cartier ouest), Ruisseau-Papineau (2 sites), et Sainte-Rose.
Luc Lepage, Directeur général, CSSS de Laval

Longueuil: CLSC de Longueuil-Ouest
201, boul Curé-Poirier, Longueuil, QC J4J 2G4
450-651-9830 Fax: 450-651-4606
www.santemonteregie.qc.ca/cssspierreboucher
Division of: CSSS Pierre-Boucher
Parent: Agence de la santé et des services sociaux de la Montérégie
Caroline Barbir, Directrice générale, CSSS Pierre-Boucher

Longueuil: CLSC Simonne-Monet-Chartrand
1303, boul Jacques-Cartier est, Longueuil, QC J4M 2Y8
450-463-2850 Fax: 450-646-7552
www.santemonteregie.qc.ca/cssspierreboucher
Division of: CSSS Pierre-Boucher
Parent: Agence de la santé et des services sociaux de la Montérégie
Caroline Barbir, Directrice générale, CSSS Pierre-Boucher

Low: CLSC Low - Centre de Santé Vallée-de-la-Gatineau
CP 130, 334, rte 105, Low, QC J0X 2C0
819-422-3548 Fax: 819-422-3568
Parent: Agence de la santé et de services sociaux de l'Outaouais
André Marcoux, Directeur général

Marsoui: Centre de santé et de services sociaux de la Haute-Gaspésie
CP 154, 1, rue du Quai, Marsoui, QC G0E 1S0
418-288-5511 Fax: 418-288-2572 www.agencesssgim.ca; www.cssshautegaspesie.qc.ca
Division of: CLSC de Marsoui
Parent: Agence de la santé et des services sociaux de la Gaspésie-Iles-de-la-Madeleine

Matapédia: CLSC Malauze de Matapédia/Centre d'hébergement de Matapédia
14, rue Perron est, Matapédia, QC G0J 1V0
418-865-2221 Fax: 418-865-2317
csssbc@csssbc.qc.ca
www.csssbc.qc.ca
Division of: CSSS de la Baie-des-Chaleurs
Parent: Agence de la santé et des services sociaux de la Gaspésie-Iles-de-la-Madeleine
Note: Services sociaux; programme petite enfance; clinique de vaccination et dépistage; programme de santé mentale; services aux personnes handicapées; soutien à domicile; service dentaire. Le centre d'hébergement est situé au deuxième étage du CLSC.
Bernard Nadeau, Directeur général, CSSS de la Baie-des-Chaleurs

Mont-Laurier: CLSC des Hautes-Laurentides
515, boul Albiny-Paquette, Mont-Laurier, QC J9L 1K8
819-623-1228
Parent: Agence de la santé et des services sociaux des Laurentides

Mont-Louis: Centre de santé et de services sociaux de la Haute-Gaspésie
CP 100, 19, 1er av ouest, Mont-Louis, QC G0E 1T0
418-797-2744 Fax: 418-797-5173 www.agencesssgim.ca; www.cssshautegaspesie.qc.ca
Division of: CLSC de Mont-Louis
Parent: Agence de la santé et des services sociaux de la Gaspésie-Iles-de-la-Madeleine

Montréal: Centre de santé et de services sociaux Cavendish
5425, av Bessborough, Montréal, QC H4V 2S7
514-483-1380 Fax: 514-483-4596 www.santemontreal.qc.ca
Parent: Agence de la santé et des services sociaux de Montréal

Number of Beds: 125 lits
Note: Installations: l'Hôpital Richardson (125 lits); les CLSCs: Notre-Dame-de-Grâce-Montréal-Ouest, & René-Cassin (Côte St-Luc); le Centre d'hébergement Henri-Bradet.
Francine Dupuis, Directrice générale

Montréal: Centre de santé et de services sociaux d'Ahuntsic et Montréal-Nord
1725, boul Gouin est, Montréal, QC H2C 3H6
514-384-2000 Fax: 514-384-4245 www.santemontreal.qc.ca
Parent: Agence de la santé et des services sociaux de Montréal
Note: Installations: l'Hôpital Fleury (194 lits); les CLSCs: Ahuntsic, & Montréal-Nord; les Centres d'hébergement: Paul-Lizotte, Laurendeau, Légaré, & Louvain.
Mac Fortin, Directeur général

Montréal: Centre de santé et de services sociaux d'Ahuntsic et Montréal-Nord (Hôpital Fleu
2180 est, rue Fleury, Montréal, QC H2BH2C 3H6
514-381-9311 Fax: 514-383-5249
Parent: Agence de la santé et des services sociaux de Montréal
Bruno L'Heureux, Directeur exécutif, Hôpital Fleury et Services professionnels et hospit

Montréal: Centre de santé et de services sociaux de la Montagne
5700, ch de la C"te-des-Neiges, Montréal, QC H3T 2A8
514-731-8531 Fax: 514-731-9600 www.santemontreal.qc.ca
Parent: Agence de la santé et des services sociaux de Montréal
Note: Installations: les CLSCs: Côte-des-Neiges (Outremont), Métro, & Parc-Extension; Maison de naissance Côte-des-Neiges; Programme régional d'acceuil & d'intégration des demandeurs d'asile.
Marc Sougavinski, Dir. gen.

Montréal: Centre de santé et de services sociaux de la Pointe-de-l'Ile
9503, rue Sherbrooke est, Montréal, QC H1L 6P2
514-356-2572 Fax: 514-356-2571
Parent: Agence de la santé et des services sociaux de Montréal
Andre Gagnière, Directeur général

Montréal: Centre de santé et de services sociaux du coeur-de-l'île
1385, rue Jean-Talon est, Montréal, QC H2E 1S6
514-495-6754 Fax: 514-495-6734
Old Name: CSSS de la Petite Patrie et Villeray
Parent: Agence de la santé et des services sociaux de Montréal
Number of Beds: 320 lits
Manon Boily, Directrice générale

Montréal: Centre de santé et de services sociaux du Sud-Ouest-Verdun
6161, rue Laurendeau, Montréal, QC H4E 3X6
514-766-0546 Fax: 514-732-5107
www.cssssudouestverdun.qc.ca
Parent: Agence de la santé et des services sociaux de Montréal
Number of Beds: 1550 lits (permanent, temporaire, courte durée, gériatrique)
Danielle McCann, Directeur général

Montréal: Centre de santé et de services sociaux Lucille-Teasdale
3095, rue Sherbrooke est, Montréal, QC H1W 1B2
514-523-1173 Fax: 514-528-2706
Parent: Agence de la santé et des services sociaux de Montréal
Number of Beds: 1,223 lits
Gary Furlong, Directeur général

Montréal: Centre local de services communautaires Métro
#500, 1801, boul de Maisonneuve ouest, Montréal, QC H3H 1J9
514-934-0354 Fax: 514-934-3776
Parent: Agence de la santé et des services sociaux de Montréal
Gary Furlong, Directeur général

Montréal: Centre local de services communautaires Saint-Henri
3833, rue Notre-Dame ouest, Montréal, QC H4C 1P8
514-933-7541 Fax: 514-933-1740
Parent: Agence de la santé et des services sociaux de Montréal
Louis-Paul Thauvette, Directeur général

Montréal: Clinique communautaire de Pointe St-Charles
500, av Ash, Montréal, QC H3K 2R4
514-937-9251 Fax: 514-937-3492
Parent: Agence de la santé et des services sociaux de Montréal
Clermont Racine, Directeur général

Montréal: CLSC Ahuntsic
1165, boul Henri-Bourassa est, Montréal, QC H2C 3K2
514-381-4221
Parent: Agence de la santé et des services sociaux de Montréal
Daniel Corbeil, Directeur général

Montréal: CLSC C"te-des-Neiges
5700, ch de la C"te-des-Neiges, Montréal, QC H3T 2A8
514-731-8531 Fax: 514-731-9600 www.santemontreal.qc.ca; www.clsccote-des-neiges.qc.ca
Parent: Agence de la santé et des services sociaux de Montréal
Marc Sougavinski, Directeur général

Montréal: CLSC de Bordeaux-Cartierville
11822, av du Bois-de-Boulogne, Montréal, QC H3M 2X6
514-331-2572 Fax: 514-331-5827 www.santemontreal.qc.ca
Parent: Agence de la santé et des services sociaux de Montréal

Montréal: CLSC de Rosemont du CSSS Lucille-Teasdale
3311, boul Saint-Joseph est, Montréal, QC H1X 1W3
514-524-3541 Fax: 514-524-2624
www.santemontreal.qc.ca/csss/teasdale
Parent: Agence de la santé et des services sociaux de Montréal
Number of Beds: 1215 lits dans le CSSS
Gary Furlong, Directeur général du CSSS

Montréal: CLSC des Faubourgs - Visitation
1705, rue de la Visitation, Montréal, QC H2L 3C3
514-527-2361 Fax: 514-598-7754 www.csssjeannemance.ca
Division of: CSSS Jeanne-Mance
Parent: Agence de la santé et des services sociaux de Montréal
Ron Rayside, Président du Conseil d'administration, CSSS Jeanne-Mance
Sylvie Simard, Directrice générale intérimaire, CSSS Jeanne-Mance

Montréal: CLSC du Plateau Mont-Royal
4689, av Papineau, Montréal, QC H2H 1V4
514-521-7663 Fax: 514-521-1886
www.clsc-du-plateau-mt-royal.qc.ca
Parent: Agence de la santé et des services sociaux de Montréal
Nicole Corbin, Directrice générale

Montréal: CLSC du Plateau Mont-Royal
4689, av Papineau, Montréal, QC H2H 1V4
514-521-0645
Parent: Agence de la santé et des services sociaux de Montréal

Montréal: CLSC Hochelaga-Maisonneuve
4201, rue Ontario est, Montréal, QC H1V 1K2
514-253-2181 Fax: 514-253-1239
jean.pierre.perreault@ssss.gouv.qc.ca
www.clsc-hochelaga-maisonneuve.qc.ca
Parent: Agence de la santé et des services sociaux de Montréal
André Desilets, Directeur général

Montréal: CLSC la Petite Patrie
6520, rue de Saint-Vallier, Montréal, QC H2S 2P7
514-273-4508 Fax: 514-272-6278
Parent: Agence de la santé et des services sociaux de Montréal

Montréal: CLSC Mercier-Est/Anjou
9403, rue Sherbooke est, Montréal, QC H1L 6P2
514-356-2572 Fax: 514-356-2571
meadg@microtec.net
Parent: Agence de la santé et des services sociaux de Montréal
André Lemelin, Directeur général

Montréal: CLSC Notre-Dame-de-Grâce/Montréal-Ouest
2525, boul Cavendish, Montréal, QC H4B 2Y4
514-485-1670 Fax: 514-485-6406
clscndg@clsc-ndg.qc.ca
clsc-ndg.qc.ca
Parent: Agence de la santé et des services sociaux de Montréal
Terry Kaufman, Directeur général

Montréal: CLSC Parc Extension
445, rue Jean-Talon ouest, Montréal, QC H3N 1R1
514-273-9591 Fax: 514-273-8954
Parent: Agence de la santé et des services sociaux de Montréal

Montréal: CLSC Pointe-aux-Trembles/Montréal-Est
13926, rue Notre-Dame est, Montréal, QC H1A 1T5
514-642-4050 Fax: 514-498-7505
Parent: Agence de la santé et des services sociaux de Montréal

Montréal: CLSC Rivière-des-Prairies
CSSS de la Pointe-de-l'Ile, 8655, boul Perras, Montréal, QC H1E 4M7
514-494-4924 Fax: 514-494-8182
Parent: Agence de la santé et des services sociaux de Montréal
Gaétan Mercure, Directeur général

Montréal: CLSC Saint-Louis-du-Parc
#100, 15, av du Mont-Royal ouest, Montréal, QC H2T 2R9
514-286-9657 Fax: 514-286-9706 www.csssjeannemance.ca
Division of: CSSS Jeanne-Mance
Parent: Agence de la santé et des services sociaux de Montréal
Ron Rayside, Président du Conseil d'administration, CSSS Jeanne-Mance
Sylvie Simard, Directrice générale intérimaire, CSSS Jeanne-Mance

Montréal: CLSC Saint-Michel
7950, boul Saint-Michel, Montréal, QC H1Z 3E1
514-374-8223 Fax: 514-374-9180
Parent: Agence de la santé et des services sociaux de Montréal
Manon Boily, Directrice générale

Montréal: CLSC Villeray
1425, rue Jarry est, Montréal, QC H2E 1A7
514-376-4141
Parent: Agence de la santé et des services sociaux de Montréal
Nicole Clouâtre, Directrice générale

Montréal: CLSC-CHSLD Olivier-Guimond
5810, rue Sherbrooke est, Montréal, QC H1N 1B2
514-255-2365 Fax: 514-255-1443
Old Name: CLSC Olivier-Guimond
Parent: Agence de la santé et des services sociaux de Montréal
Alain Lemay, Directeur général (intérim)

Montréal: Santé au travail
#430, 75, rue de Port-Royal, Montréal, QC H3L 3T1
514-858-2460 Fax: 514-858-6568

Montréal-Nord: CLSC Montréal-nord
11441, boul Lacordaire, Montréal-Nord, QC H1G 4J9
514-327-0400 Fax: 514-327-1275
Parent: Agence de la santé et des services sociaux de Montréal
Pierre Latry, Directeur général

Murdochville: CLSC Mer et Montagnes
600, rue Dr William-May, Murdochville, QC G0E 1W0
418-784-2572 Fax: 418-784-3629 www.cssscotedegaspe.ca
Division of: Point de service Murdochville
Parent: Agence de la santé et des services sociaux de la Gaspésie-Iles-de-la-Madeleine
Note: CSSS Côte-de-Gaspé.

New Carlisle: Centre de santé Le Rivage
CP 208, 96, rte 132, New Carlisle, QC G0C 1H0
418-388-2572 Fax: 418-388-2645
Division of: Le CLSC
Parent: Agence de la santé et des services sociaux de la Gaspésie-Iles-de-la-Madeleine

Paspébiac: CLSC de Paspébiac
273, boul Gérard-D.-Lévesque ouest, Paspébiac, QC G0C 2K0
418-752-2572 Fax: 418-752-6734
csssbc@csssbc.qc.ca
www.csssbc.qc.ca
Division of: CSSS de la Baie-des-Chaleurs
Parent: Agence de la santé et des services sociaux de la Gaspésie-Iles-de-la-Madeleine
Bernard Nadeau, Directeur général, CSSS de la Baie-des-Chaleurs

Percé: CLSC de Percé
CP 269, 98, rte 132, Percé, QC G0C 2L0
418-782-2572 Fax: 418-782-5501 www.agencesssgim.ca
Parent: Agence de la santé et des services sociaux de la Gaspésie-Iles-de-la-Madeleine
Note: CSSS du Rocher-Percé.

Pierrefonds: Centre de santé et de services sociaux de l'Ouest-de-l'Ile
West Island Health and Social Services Centre
13800, boul Gouin ouest, Pierrefonds, QC H8Z 3H6
514-626-2572 Fax: 514-626-6514 www.santemontreal.qc.ca
Parent: Agence de la santé et des services sociaux de Montréal
Note: Installations: l'Hôpital général du Lakeshore; les CLSCs: Pierrefonds, Lac-Saint-Louis (Pointe-Claire); et le Centre d'hébergement Denis-Benjamin-Viger (L'Ile-Bizard).
Luc LePage, Dir. gen.

Plessisville: CLSC-CHSLD de l'Érable
1331, rue Saint-Calixte, Plessisville, QC G6L 1P4
819-362-6301 Fax: 819-362-6300 www.csssae.qc.ca
Division of: CSSS d'Arthabaska-et-de-l'Érable
Parent: Agence de la santé et des services sociaux de la Mauricie et du Centre-du-Québec
Number of Beds: 40 lits de soins de longue durée
Note: CLSC de l'Érable, et l'Unité de soins longue durée de l'Érable.
Marcel Dubois, Président, Conseil d'administration, CSSS d'Arthabaska-et-de-l

***Pohénégamook:* CLSC de Pohénégamook**
1922, rue St-Vallier, Pohénégamook, QC G0L 2T0
418-859-2450 Fax: 418-859-1285 www.cssstemiscouata.com
Division of: CSSS de Témiscouata
Parent: Agence de la santé et des services sociaux du Bas-St-Laurent
Number of Beds: 25 lits
Camil Dion, Directeur général, CSSS de Témiscouata

***Pointe-...-la-Croix:* CLSC de Pointe-...-la-Croix**
48, boul Interprovincial, Pointe-...-la-Croix, QC G0C 1L0
418-788-5454 Fax: 418-788-2510
csssbc@csssbc.qc.ca
www.csssbc.qc.ca
Division of: CSSS de la Baie-des-Chaleurs
Parent: Agence de la santé et des services sociaux de la Gaspésie-Iles-de-la-Madeleine
Bernard Nadeau, Directeur général, CSSS de la Baie-des-Chaleurs

***Pointe-Claire:* CLSC Lac St-Louis**
180, av Cartier, Pointe-Claire, QC H9S 4S1
514-697-4110 Fax: 514-697-6341
rbresnen@ssss.gouv.qc.ca
Parent: Agence de la santé et des services sociaux de Montréal
Ruth Bresnen, Directrice générale adjointe interimaire

***Port-Cartier:* Centre de santé et de services sociaux de Port-Cartier**
3, rue de Shelter Bay, Port-Cartier, QC G5B 2W9
418-766-2572 Fax: 418-766-5229
Parent: Agence de la santé et des services sociaux de la C"te-Nord
Daniel Camire, Directeur général

***Puvirnituq:* Centre de santé Inuulitsivik**
ch Baie d'Hudson, Puvirnituq, QC J0M 1P0
819-988-2957 Fax: 819-988-2796
inuulitsivik@ssss.gouv.qc.ca
www.inuulitsivik.ca
Parent: Régie régionale de la santé et des services sociaux du Nunavik
Number of Beds: 17 lits hospitaliers; 8 lits de soins de longue durée
Note: Soins médicaux, soins dentaires; sages-femmes; services en santé mentale; télémedicine; laboratoire; points de service: Akulivik, Inukjuak, Ivujivik, Kuujjuarapik, Puvirnituq, Salluit et Umiujuaq.
Jane Beaudoin, Directrice générale

***Quaqtaq:* Dispensaire de Quaqtaq**
General Delivery, Quaqtaq, QC J0M 1J0
819-492-9977 Fax: 819-492-9004
clsc.quaqtaq@ssss.gouv.qc.ca
Parent: Régie régionale de la santé et des services sociaux du Nunavik
Madge Pomerleau, Directrice générale

***Québec:* Centre de santé et de services sociaux de la vieille-capitale**
1, av du Sacré-Coeur, Québec, QC G1N 2W1
418-529-4777 Fax: 418-691-0711
Parent: Agence de la santé et des services sociaux de la Capitale-Nationale
Sylvain Gagnon, Directeur général

***Québec:* CLSC Haute-Ville**
55, ch Ste-Foy, Québec, QC G1R 1S9
418-641-2572 Fax: 418-691-0711
Parent: Agence de la santé et des services sociaux de la Capitale-Nationale
Gaétan Garon, Directeur général

***Québec:* CLSC Haute-Ville-des-Rivières**
1720, boul Père-Lelièvre, Québec, QC G1M 3J6
418-688-9212

***Richelieu:* CLSC du Richelieu**
700, rue Martel, Richelieu, QC J3L 5R6
450-658-7561 Fax: 450-460-3544
Parent: Agence de la santé et des services sociaux de la Montérégie
Danielle McCann, Directrice générale

***Richmond:* CLSC de Richmond**
110, rue Barlow, Richmond, QC J0B 2H0
819-542-2777 Fax: 819-826-3867 vsf.santeestrie.qc.ca
Division of: CSSS du Val-Saint-François
Pierre Lalande, Directeur général, CSSS du Val-Saint-François

***Rimouski:* CLSC Rimouski-Neigette**
165, rue des Gouverneurs, Rimouski, QC G5L 7R2
418-724-7204 Fax: 418-724-5494
courrierweb.crsssr@ssss.gouv.qc.ca
www.chrr.qc.ca
Division of: CSSS de Rimouski-Neigette
Parent: Agence de la santé et des services sociaux du Bas-St-Laurent
Note: 3 autres points de service: Saint-Fabien, Saint-Marcellin, et Saint-Narcisse
Raymond Coulombe, Directeur général, CSSS de Rimouski-Neigette

***Rivière-au-Renard:* CLSC Mer et Montagnes**
154, boul Renard est, Rivière-au-Renard, QC G4X 5R5
418-269-2572 Fax: 418-269-5294 www.cssscotedegaspe.ca
Division of: Point de service Rivière-au-Renard
Parent: Agence de la santé et des services sociaux de la Gaspésie-Iles-de-la-Madeleine
Number of Beds: 3 lits
Note: CSSS Côte-de-Gaspé.
Jean-Pierre Tremblay, Directeur général

***Rivière-du-Loup:* CLSC de Rivière-du-Loup**
22, rue Saint-Laurent, Rivière-du-Loup, QC G5R 4W5
418-867-2642 Fax: 418-867-4713 www.csssriviereduloup.qc.ca
Division of: CSSS de Rivière-du-Loup
Parent: Agence de la santé et des services sociaux du Bas-St-Laurent
Raymond April, Directeur général, CSSS Rivière-du-Loup

***Rouyn-Noranda:* CLSC - l'Hôpital de Rouyn-Noranda**
3, 9e rue, Rouyn-Noranda, QC J9X 2A9
819-764-5131 Fax: 819-764-2948
www.sante-abitibi-temiscamingue.gouv.qc.ca; www.csssrn.qc.ca
Division of: CSSS de Rouyn-Noranda
Parent: Agence de la santé et des services sociaux de l'Abitibi-Témiscamingue
Note: Point de service CLSC, et consultations externes CHSGS.
Huguette Lemay, Directrice générale, CSSS de Rouyn-Noranda

***Saint-André-Avellin:* CLSC et Centre d'hébergement Petite-Nation**
14, rue Saint-André, Saint-André-Avellin, QC J0V 1W0
819-983-7341 Fax: 819-983-7812
clsc-chsld_petite-nation@ssss.gouv.qc.ca
www.cssspapineau.qc.ca; www.santeautravail.net
Parent: Agence de la santé et de services sociaux de l'Outaouais
Gilles Clavel, Directeur général (par intérim), CSSS de Papineau

***Saint-Esprit:* CLSC Montcalm**
102, rue St-Isidore, Saint-Esprit, QC J0K 2L0
450-839-3676 Fax: 450-839-7811
Parent: Agences de développement de réseaux locaux de services de santé et de services sociaux
Paul-Yvon de Billy, Directeur général

***Saint-Eustache:* Centre de santé et de services sociaux Deux-Montagnes et Sud de Mirabel**
29, ch Oka, Saint-Eustache, QC J7R 1K6
450-491-1233 Fax: 450-491-3424 www.monclsc.com
Division of: CLSC Jean-Olivier-Chenier
Parent: Agence de la santé et des services sociaux des Laurentides
Christiane Arbour, Directrice générale

***Saint-Félicien:* Centre local de services communautaires des Prés-Bleus**
CP 10, 1228, boul Sacre-Coeur, Saint-Félicien, QC G8K 2R2
418-679-5270 Fax: 418-679-3510
Parent: Agence de la santé et des services sociaux du Saguenay-Lac-St-Jean
Jean-Guy Lamothe, Directeur général (par intérim)

***Saint-Hubert:* CLSC Saint-Hubert**
6800, boul Cousineau, Saint-Hubert, QC J3Y 8Z4
450-443-7400 Fax: 450-676-4645
16_clsc_sainthubert@rrsss16.gouv.qc.ca
Parent: Agence de la santé et des services sociaux de la Montérégie
Suzanne Beauchamp, Directrice générale

***Saint-Jean-sur-Richelieu:* CLSC de la Vallée-des-Forts**
978, boul du Séminaire nord, Saint-Jean-sur-Richelieu, QC J3A 1E5
450-358-2572 Fax: 450-349-0724
www.santemonteregie.qc.ca/haut-richelieu-rouville
Division of: CSSS Haut-Richelieu-Rouville
Christine Lessard, Directrice générale, CSSS Haut-Richelieu-Rouville

***Saint-Jérome:* CLSC Arthur-Buies**
430, rue Labelle, Saint-Jérome, QC J7Z 5L3
450-431-2221
Parent: Agence de la santé et des services sociaux des Laurentides

***Saint-Léonard:* CLSC de Saint-Léonard**
5540, rue Jarry est, Saint-Léonard, QC H1P 1T9
514-328-3460 csss-stleonardstmichel.qc.ca
Division of: CSSS de Saint-Léonard et Saint-Michel
Parent: Agence de la santé et des services sociaux de Montréal
Suzanne Hébert, Directrice générale, CSSS de Saint-Léonard et Saint-Michel

***Saint-Ludger:* CSSS du Granit - CLSC Saint-Ludger**
210-A, rue La Salle, Saint-Ludger, QC G0M 1W0
819-548-0330 Fax: 819-548-5553 www.csssgranit.qc.ca
Parent: Agence de la santé et des services sociaux de l'Estrie
Pierre Latulippe, Directeur général, CSSS du Granit

***Saint-Omer:* CLSC de Saint-Omer**
107, rte 132 ouest, Saint-Omer, QC G0C 2Z0
418-364-7064 Fax: 418-364-7119
csssbc@csssbc.qc.ca
www.csssbc.qc.ca
Division of: CSSS de la Baie-des-Chaleurs
Parent: Agence de la santé et des services sociaux de la Gaspésie-Iles-de-la-Madeleine
Bernard Nadeau, Directeur général, CSSS de la Baie-des-Chaleurs

***Saint-Paulin:* CLSC de St-Paulin**
2841, rue Laflèche, Saint-Paulin, QC J0K 3G0
819-268-2572 Fax: 819-268-2505

***Saint-Rémi:* CLSC Jardin-du-Québec**
2, rue Sainte-Famille, Saint-Rémi, QC J0L 2L0
450-454-4671 Fax: 450-454-4538
www.santemonteregie.qc.ca/jardins-roussillon
Division of: CSSS Jardins-Roussillon
Paul Moreau, Directeur général, CSSS Jardins-Roussillon

***Sainte-Geneviève-de-Batis:* CLSC des Chenaux**
90, rte Rivière-...-Veillette, RR#4, Sainte-Geneviève-de-Batis, QC G0X 2R0
418-362-2727
Parent: Agence de la santé et des services sociaux de la Mauricie et du Centre-du-Québec
Gaétan Lebel, Directeur général

***Salaberry-de-Valleyfield:* CLSC Seigneurie de Beauharnois**
#200, 71, rue Maden, Salaberry-de-Valleyfield, QC J6S 3V4
514-371-0143 Fax: 514-371-7682
Parent: Agence de la santé et des services sociaux de la Montérégie
François Rabeau, Directeur général

***Sherbrooke:* CLSC de Sherbrooke - Point de service 50 rue Camirand**
50, rue Camirand, Sherbrooke, QC J1H 4J5
819-780-2222 www.csss-iugs.ca
Division of: CSSS-Institut universitaire de gériatrie de Sherbrooke
Parent: Agence de la santé et des services sociaux de l'Estrie
Note: Autres points de service: 95, rue Camirand; 356, rue King ouest; 1200, rue King est; et 8, rue Speid.
Carol Fillion, Directeur général, CSSS-Institut universitaire de gériatrie de Sherbro

***Sorel-Tracy:* Hôpital Richelieu/CLSC du Havre**
30, rue Ferland, Sorel-Tracy, QC J3P 3C7
450-743-5569 Fax: 450-743-1803
Parent: Agence de la santé et des services sociaux de la Montérégie
Ginette Rhealt, Manager

***Ste-Anne-des-Monts:* Centre de santé et de services sociaux de la Haute-Gaspésie**
52, rue Belvédère, Ste-Anne-des-Monts, QC G4V 1X4
418-763-7771 Fax: 418-763-7176 www.agencesssgim.ca; www.cssshautegaspesie.qc.ca
Division of: CLSC de Ste-Anne-des-Monts
Parent: Agence de la santé et des services sociaux de la Gaspésie-Iles-de-la-Madeleine

***Terrebonne:* CLSC Lamater**
1317, boul des Seigneurs, Terrebonne, QC J6W 5B1
450-471-2881
Parent: Agences de développement de réseaux locaux de services de santé et de services sociaux
François Lamarre, Directeur général

***Trois-Rivières:* Centre de service Les Forges**
500, rue Saint-Georges, Trois-Rivières, QC G9A 2K8
819-379-7131 Fax: 819-373-7726

Parent: Agence de la santé et des services sociaux de la Mauricie et du Centre-du-Québec
Gilles Tétu, Directeur général

Val-Bélair: **CLSC de la Jacques-Cartier**
1465, rue de l'Etna, Val-Bélair, QC G3K 2S2
418-843-2572 Fax: 418-842-4662
Parent: Agence de la santé et des services sociaux de la Capitale-Nationale
Reynald Gagnon, Directeur général

Vaudreuil-Dorion: **Centre de santé et de services sociaux de Vaudreuil-Soulanges**
490, boul Harwood, Vaudreuil-Dorion, QC J7V 7H4
450-455-6171 Fax: 450-455-9086
Parent: Agence de la santé et des services sociaux de la Montérégie
Diane Boileau Seperich, Directrice générale

Victoriaville: **CLSC Suzor-C"té**
100, rue de l'Ermitage, Victoriaville, QC G6P 9N2
819-758-7281 www.csssae.qc.ca
Division of: CSSS d'Arthabaska-et-de-l'Érable
Parent: Agence de la santé et des services sociaux de la Mauricie et du Centre-du-Québec
Marcel Dubois, Président, Conseil d'administration, CSSS d'Arthabaska-et-de-l

Centre de traitments spécialisés

Amos: **Centre Normand**
621, rue Harricana, Amos, QC J9T 2P9
819-732-8241 Fax: 819-727-2210
www.sante-abitibi-temiscamingue.gouv.qc.ca; www.centrenormand.org
Number of Beds: 10 lits
Note: Offre des services de réadaptation aux personnes qui présentent une dépendance - à l'alcool, drogues illicites, médicaments, jeu; services de support psychosocial.
Pierre Michel Guay, Directeur général
pierremichel_guay@ssss.gouv.qc.ca

Amos: **CRDI Abitibi-Témiscamingue Clair-Foyer**
841, 3e rue ouest, Amos, QC J9T 2T4
819-732-6511 Fax: 819-732-0922
www.sante-abitibi-temiscamingue.gouv.qc.ca
Number of Beds: 31 lits
Note: Centre de réadaptation (déficience intellectuelle); services de support.
Denis Plourde, Directeur général
danplo@ssss.gouv.qc.ca

Baie-Comeau: **Centre de protection et de réadaptation de la C"te-Nord**
835, boul Joliet, Baie-Comeau, QC G5C 1P5
418-589-9927 Fax: 418-589-4304
Parent: Agence de la santé et des services sociaux de la C"te-Nord
Note: et centre jeunesse
Claude Montigny, Directeur général

Baie-Comeau: **Centre de protection et de réadaptation de la C"te-Nord**
836, boul Joliet, Baie-Comeau, QC G5C 1P5
418-589-9927 Fax: 418-589-4304
Number of Beds: 225 lits
Claude Montigny, Directeur général

Beauceville: **Centre de réadaptation en alcoolisme et toxicomanie de Chaudière-Appalaches**
253, rte 108, Beauceville, QC G5X 2Z3
418-774-3304 Fax: 418-774-4423
alto_beauce@ssss.gouv.qc.ca
www.agencesss12.gouv.qc.ca
Parent: Agence de la santé et des services sociaux de Chaudière-Appalaches
Number of Beds: 14 lits
Huguette Giroux, Directrice générale

Beauport: **Centre de réadaptation Ubald-Villeneuve**
2525, ch de la Canardière, 2e étage, Beauport, QC G1J 2G3
418-663-5008 Fax: 418-663-6575
Old Name: Centre de réadaptation en toxicomanie de Québec
Number of Beds: 22 lits
Note: toxicomanie
Dominique Paquette, Directrice générale

Bonaventure: **Centre de réadaptation de la Gaspésie**
CP 667, 238, av Port-Royal, Bonaventure, QC G0C 1E0
418-534-4243 Fax: 418-534-2411 www.agencesssgim.ca
Division of: Point de service MRC de Bonaventure
Parent: Agence de la santé et des services sociaux de la Gaspésie-Iles-de-la-Madeleine
Note: Déficiences physiques et intellectuelles.

Bonaventure: **Centre jeunesse Gaspésie/Les Iles**
CP 308, 193, av Port Royal, Bonaventure, QC G0C 1E0
418-534-3283 Fax: 418-534-4024 www.agencesssgim.ca
Division of: Point de service Unité La Balise
Parent: Agence de la santé et des services sociaux de la Gaspésie-Iles-de-la-Madeleine
Number of Beds: 12 lits
Note: Pour mésadaptées socio-affectifs.

Bonaventure: **Centre jeunesse Gaspésie/Les Iles**
CP 308, 106, av Port-Royal, Bonaventure, QC G0C 1E0
418-534-2272 Fax: 418-534-4278 www.agencesssgim.ca
Division of: Point de service Succursale Bonaventure-Avignon
Parent: Agence de la santé et des services sociaux de la Gaspésie-Iles-de-la-Madeleine

Cap-aux-Meules: **Centre jeunesse Gaspésie/Les Iles**
CP 268, 539-2, ch Principal, Cap-aux-Meules, QC G4T 1E7
418-986-2230 Fax: 418-986-5445 www.agencesssgim.ca
Division of: Point de service Succursale des Iles
Parent: Agence de la santé et des services sociaux de la Gaspésie-Iles-de-la-Madeleine

Carleton: **Centre de réadaptation de la Gaspésie**
CP 26, 314, boul Perron ouest, Carleton, QC G0C 1J0
418-364-6037 Fax: 418-364-7040 www.agencesssgim.ca
Division of: Point de service MRC d'Avignon - Carleton
Parent: Agence de la santé et des services sociaux de la Gaspésie-Iles-de-la-Madeleine
Note: Déficience intellectuelle.

Chandler: **Centre de réadaptation de la Gaspésie**
CP 2168, 328, boul René-Lévesque ouest, Chandler, QC G0C 1K0
418-689-4286 Fax: 418-689-7155 www.agencesssgim.ca
Division of: Point de service MRC du Rocher-Percé
Parent: Agence de la santé et des services sociaux de la Gaspésie-Iles-de-la-Madeleine
Note: Déficiences physiques et intellectuelles.

Chandler: **Centre jeunesse Gaspésie/Les Iles**
CP 280, 105, rue Commerciale ouest, Chandler, QC G0C 1K0
418-689-2286 Fax: 418-689-4643 www.agencesssgim.ca
Division of: Point de service Succursale Rocher-Percé
Parent: Agence de la santé et des services sociaux de la Gaspésie-Iles-de-la-Madeleine

Charlesbourg: **Centre de réadaptation La Maisonnée**
855, boul Louis XIV, Charlesbourg, QC G1H 1A6
418-628-0662 Fax: 418-628-5440
celine.auclair@ssss.gouv.qc.ca
Number of Beds: 11 lits
Note: centre de réadaptation
Lucie Lacroix, Directrice générale

Chicoutimi: **Le Centre jeunesse du Saguenay-Lac-Saint-Jean**
520, rue Jacques-Cartier est, Chicoutimi, QC G7H 8A2
418-549-4853 Fax: 418-693-0768 800-463-9188
www.cjsaglac.qc.ca
Number of Beds: 116 lits
Note: centre de réadaptation
Daniele Riverin, Directrice générale

Fatima: **Centre de réadaptation de la Gaspésie**
CP 549, 695, ch des Caps, Fatima, QC G4T 2S9
418-986-4870 Fax: 418-986-2623 www.agencesssgim.ca
Division of: Point de service MRC des Iles-de-la-Madeleine
Parent: Agence de la santé et des services sociaux de la Gaspésie-Iles-de-la-Madeleine
Note: Déficience physique.

Gaspé: **Centre de réadaptation de la Gaspésie**
CP 6320, 150, rue Mgr Ross, aile 550, Gaspé, QC G4X 2R8
418-368-2306 Fax: 418-368-7761 www.agencesssgim.ca
Division of: Point de service MRC de La C"te-de-Gaspé
Parent: Agence de la santé et des services sociaux de la Gaspésie-Iles-de-la-Madeleine
Note: Déficiences physiques et intellectuelles.

Gaspé: **Centre jeunesse Gaspésie/Les Iles**
418, montée Wakeham, Gaspé, QC G4X 2V7
418-368-1803 Fax: 418-368-8744 www.agencesssgim.ca
Division of: Point de service Unité La Vigie
Parent: Agence de la santé et des services sociaux de la Gaspésie-Iles-de-la-Madeleine
Number of Beds: 14 places
Note: Centre de réadaptation.

Gaspé: **Centre jeunesse Gaspésie/Les Iles**
#100, 205, boul de York ouest, Gaspé, QC G4X 2V7
418-368-1803 Fax: 418-368-5478 www.agencesssgim.ca
Parent: Agence de la santé et des services sociaux de la Gaspésie-Iles-de-la-Madeleine
Number of Beds: 55 lits

Gaspé: **Centre jeunesse Gaspésie/Les Iles**
#100, 205, boul de York ouest, Gaspé, QC G4X 2V7
418-368-1803 Fax: 418-368-6303 www.agencesssgim.ca
Division of: Point de service Unité La Rade
Parent: Agence de la santé et des services sociaux de la Gaspésie-Iles-de-la-Madeleine

Gaspé: **Centre jeunesse Gaspésie/Les Iles**
#100, 205, boul de York ouest, Gaspé, QC G4X 2V7
418-368-3381 Fax: 418-368-5101 www.agencesssgim.ca
Division of: Point de service Succursale C"te-de-Gaspé
Parent: Agence de la santé et des services sociaux de la Gaspésie-Iles-de-la-Madeleine

Gatineau: **Centre Jellinek**
25, rue Saint-François, Gatineau, QC J9A 1B1
819-776-5584 Fax: 819-776-0255 866-776-5585
jellinek@jellinek.org
www.jellinek.org
Old Name: Pavillon Jelinek
Number of Beds: 33 places
Note: centre de réadaptation des drogues, de l'alcool ou du jeu
Raymond Rochon, Directeur général

Gatineau: **Centre régional de réadaptation La Ressource**
135, boul Saint-Raymond, Gatineau, QC J8Y 6X7
819-777-6261 Fax: 819-777-0701
Number of Beds: 37 lits
Note: centre de réadaptation (déficience auditive, visuelle, & motrice)
Jean-Pierre Blais, Directeur général

Gatineau: **Les Centres jeunesse de l'Outaouais**
105, boul Sacré-Coeur, Gatineau, QC J8X 1C5
819-771-6631
Number of Beds: 149 lits
Note: centre jeunesse, protection
Gilles Clavel, Directeur général

Gatineau: **Pavillon du Parc inc.**
768, boul St-Joseph, Gatineau, QC J8Y 4B8
819-684-1022 Fax: 819-684-1023
info@pavillonduparc.qc.ca
www.pavillonduparc.qc.ca
Number of Beds: 92 lits
Note: centre de réadaptation
Thierry Boyer, Directeur général

Joliette: **Centre de réadaptation La Myriade**
339, boul Base-de-Roc, Joliette, QC J6E 5P3
450-753-9600 Fax: 450-753-1930
Number of Beds: 38 lits
Robert Lasalle, Directeur général

Joliette: **Les Centres jeunesse de Lanaudière**
260, rue Lavaltrie sud, Joliette, QC J6E 5X7
450-756-4555 Fax: 450-756-0814
Number of Beds: 135 lits
Pierre Racette, Directeur général

Jonquière: **Centre de santé et de services sociaux de Jonquière**
2230, rue de l'Hôpital, Jonquière, QC G7X 4H6
418-695-7700 Fax: 418-695-7729
Number of Beds: 40 lits
Lucie Dauphin, Directrice générale

Kuujjuaq: **Centre de santé Tulattavik de l'Ungava**
CP 149, Kuujjuaq, Kuujjuaq, QC J0M 1C0
819-964-2905 Fax: 819-964-2653
Number of Beds: 23 lits
Madge Pomerleau, Directrice générale

Lachine: **Centre de réadaptation de l'Ouest de Montréal**
8000, rue Notre-Dame, Lachine, QC H8R 1H2
514-363-3025 Fax: 514-364-5997
Parent: Agence de la santé et des services sociaux de Montréal
Number of Beds: 186 lits
Note: centre de réadaptation en déficience intellectuelle
John Aung-Thwin, Directeur général

Lachine: **Centre de réadaptation Lisette-Dupras**
8000, rue Notre-Dame, Lachine, QC H8R 1H2
514-364-2280 Fax: 514-364-0608 www.lisette-dupras.ca.
Number of Beds: 524 lits
Note: centre de réadaptation
John Aung-Thwin, Directeur général

Laval: **Centre Jeunesse de Laval**
308, boul Cartier ouest, Laval, QC H7N 2J2
450-975-4150 Fax: 450-975-4276
Number of Beds: 269 lits
Note: Centre de la protection de la jeunesse/centre de réadaptation
Pierre Patenaude, Directeur général

Laval: **CRDI Normand-Laramée**
304, boul Cartier ouest, 2e étage, Laval, QC H7N 2J2
450-972-2099 Fax: 450-972-2020
Number of Beds: 95 lits
Note: centre de réadaptation
Claude Belley, Directeur général

Lennoxville: **Centre d'accueil Dixville inc.**
CP 150, 155, rue Belvidere, Lennoxville, QC J1M 1Z4
819-821-2928 Fax: 819-821-2920
Number of Beds: 100 lits
Note: centre de réadaptation
Francine Caron, Directrice générale

Lennoxville: **Centre Notre-Dame de l'Enfant (Sherbrooke) Inc.**
CP 150, 155, rue Belvidere, Lennoxville, QC J1M 1Z4
819-821-2928 Fax: 819-821-2920
Number of Beds: 178 lits
Note: centre de réadaptation en déficience intellectuelle
Francine Caron, Directrice générale

Lévis: **Centre de réadaptation en déficience intellectuelle de Chaudière-Appalaches**
55, rue du Mont-Marie, Lévis, QC G6V 0B8
418-833-3218 Fax: 418-833-9849 866-333-3218
crdi@chaudiere.appalaches@ssss.gouv.qc.ca
www.crditedca.com
Division of: Centre administratif
Parent: Agence de la santé et des services sociaux de Chaudière-Appalaches
Number of Beds: 674 lits
Dominique Paquette, Directeur général

Lévis: **Les Centres jeunesse Chaudière-Appalaches**
#300, 100, rue Monseigneur-Bourget, Lévis, QC G6V 2Y9
418-837-9331 Fax: 418-838-8860 www.cj12.qc.ca
Division of: Centre administratif
Number of Beds: 146 lits
Note: Services de la protection de la jeunesse; service aux jeunes contrevenants; service d'adoption; services de réadaptation. Installations: Lévis, Saint-Romuald, Montmagny, Sainte-Marie, Saint-Joseph, Saint-Georges & Thetford Mines.
Pierre Morin, Directeur général

Longueuil: **Centre de réadaptation en déficience intellectuelle Montérégie-est**
1255, rue Beauregard, Longueuil, QC J4K 2M3
450-679-6511 Fax: 450-928-3655
16_crdime_information@ssss.gouv.qc.ca
www.crdime.qc.ca
Number of Beds: 1157 lits
Johanne Gauthier, Directrice générale

Longueuil: **Centre jeunesse de la Montérégie**
25, boul Lafayette, Longueuil, QC J4K 5C8
450-928-5125 Fax: 450-679-3731
Number of Beds: 398 lits
Camil Picard, Directeur général

Mont-Laurier: **Centre de santé et de services sociaux d'Antoine-Labelle**
515, boul Albiny-Paquette, Mont-Laurier, QC J9L 1K8
819-623-6127 Fax: 819-623-9451
Number of Beds: 138 lits
Pierre Gfeller, Directeur général

Mont-Royal: **Centre Miriam**
8160, ch Royden, Mont-Royal, QC H4P 2T2
514-345-0210 Fax: 514-345-8965 www.centremiriam.ca
Number of Beds: 241 lits
Note: centre de réadaptation
Jean-Pierre Aumont, Directeur général (intérim)

Montréal: **Association montréalaise pour les aveugles**
Montréal Association for the Blind
7000, rue Sherbrooke ouest, Montréal, QC H4B 1R3
514-489-8201 Fax: 514-489-3477
mabinfo@mab.ca
www.mab.ca
Number of Beds: 8 lits
Note: centre de réadaptation (déficience visuelle) et CHSLD
Paul Gareau, Directeur général

Montréal: **Atelier le Fil d'Ariane inc.**
#100, 4837, rue Boyer, Montréal, QC H2J 3E6
514-842-5592 Fax: 514-842-8343
lisette.clauveau.ariane@ssss.gouv.qc.ca
www.atelierlefildariane.org
Number of Beds: 20 places
Note: Un atelier de travail pour des adultes ayant des limitations fonctionnelles sur le plan intellectuel; l'atelier favorise l'intégration sociale & communautaire & l'autonomie personnelle & professionnelle des artisans.
Lisette Claveau, Directrice générale

Montréal: **Centre d'accueil le programme de Portage inc.**
865, carré Richmond, Montréal, QC H3J 1V8
514-939-0202 Fax: 514-939-3929
Number of Beds: 231 lits
Note: centre de réadaptation des drogues
Peter Vamos, Directeur général

Montréal: **Centre de réadaptation Constance-Lethbridge**
7005, boul de Maisonneuve ouest, Montréal, QC H4B 1T3
514-487-1770 Fax: 514-487-5494
Parent: Agence de la santé et des services sociaux de Montréal
Note: déficience motrice
Ghislaine Prata, Directrice générale

Montréal: **Centre Dollard-Cormier**
950, rue de Louvain est, Montréal, QC H2M 2E8
514-385-0046 Fax: 514-385-5728
www.centredollardcormier.qc.ca
Number of Beds: 55 lits
Madeleine Roy, Directrice générale

Montréal: **Centre hospitalier universitaire Sainte-Justine**
3175, ch de la C"te Sainte-Catherine, Montréal, QC H3T 1C5
514-345-4931 Fax: 514-345-4808
Number of Beds: 55 lits
Khiem Dao, Directeur général

Montréal: **Centre jeunesse de Montréal - Institut universitaire**
4675, rue Bélanger, Montréal, QC H1T 1C2
514-593-3979 Fax: 514-593-3982
institut.universitaire@cjm-iu.qc.ca
www.centrejeunessedemontreal.qc.ca
Number of Beds: 826 admissions
Note: services psychosociaux et de réadaptation
Jean-Pierre Duplantie, Directeur général

Montréal: **La Corporation du centre de réadaptation Lucie-Bruneau**
2275, av Laurier est, Montréal, QC H2H 2N8
514-527-4521 Fax: 514-527-0979
Parent: Agence de la santé et des services sociaux de Montréal
Number of Beds: 50 lits
Note: centre de réadaptation (déficience motrice)
Alain Lefebvre, Directeur général

Montréal: **CSSS de Bordeaux-Cartierville-Saint Laurent**
555, boul Gouin ouest, Montréal, QC H3L 1K5
514-331-3020 Fax: 514-331-0874 www.santemontreal.qc.ca
Division of: Centre administratif
Parent: Agence de la santé et des services sociaux de Montréal
Note: Installations: les CLSCs: Bordeaux-Cartierville, & Saint-Laurent; les Centres d'hébergement: Notre-Dame-de-la-Merci, Saint-Joseph-de-la-Providence, Saint-Laurent, & Cartierville.
Daniel Corbeil, Directeur général

Montréal: **Hôpital de réadaptation Villa Medica**
225, rue Sherbrooke est, Montréal, QC H2X 1C9
514-288-8201 www.villamedica.ca
Parent: Agence de la santé et des services sociaux de Montréal
Number of Beds: 150 lits
Note: centre hospitalier de réadaptation
Michel Duchesne, Directeur général

Montréal: **L'institut de réadaptation de Montréal**
6300, av Darlington, Montréal, QC H3S 2J4
514-340-2085 Fax: 514-340-2091 www.irm.qc.ca
Parent: Agence de la santé et des services sociaux de Montréal
Number of Beds: 102 lits
Note: centre de réadaptation
Jacques R. Nolet, Directeur général

Montréal: **Institut Raymond-Dewar**
3600, rue Berri, Montréal, QC H2L 4G9
514-284-2581 Fax: 514-284-5086
ird@raymond-dewar.gouv.qc.ca
www.raymond-dewar.qc.ca
Parent: Agence de la santé et des services sociaux de Montréal
Note: centre de réadaptation (déficience auditive et de la parole et du language)
Pierre-Paul Lachapelle, Directeur général

Montréal: **Maison Elisabeth**
2131, av de Marlowe, Montréal, QC H4A 3L4
514-482-2488 Fax: 514-482-9467
Number of Beds: 18 lits
Linda Schachtler, Directrice générale

Montréal: **The Morgentaler Clinic**
Clinique Morgentaler
#710, 30, boul St Joseph est, Montréal, QC H2T 1G9
514-844-4844 Fax: 514-844-7883 888-401-4844
cliniquem@bellnet.ca
www.morgentalermontreal.ca
Division of: Montreal Site
Year Founded: 1968
Note: Specialties: Pregnancy termination services; Post-abortion service

Montréal: **Services de réadaptation L'Intégrale**
#110, 75, rue de Port-Royal est, Montréal, QC H3L 3T1
514-387-1234 Fax: 514-387-5013 www.integrale.org
Old Name: Centre de réadaptation l'Intégrale
Number of Beds: 31 lits
Jean-Pierre Aumont, Directeur général

Puvirnituq: **Centre de santé Inuulitsivik**
ch Baie d'Hudson, Puvirnituq, QC J0M 1P0
819-988-2957 Fax: 819-988-2796
Number of Beds: 8

Québec: **Centre de réadaptation en déficience intellectuelle de Québec**
110, rue de Courcelette, Québec, QC G1N 4T4
418-683-2511 Fax: 418-683-9735
Number of Beds: 530 lits
Renaud Cloutier, Directeur général (intérim)

Québec: **Institut de réadaptation en déficience physique de Québec**
525, boul Wilfrid Hamel, Québec, QC G1M 2S8
418-529-9141 Fax: 418-529-7318
communications@irdpq.qc.ca
www.irdpq.qc.ca
Parent: Agence de la santé et des services sociaux de la Capitale-Nationale
Number of Beds: 165 lits
Note: centre de réadaptation (déficience physique)
Richard Brousseau, Directeur général

Restigouche: **Centre jeunesse Gaspésie/Les Iles**
CP 193, 4, ch Pacific, Restigouche, QC G0C 2R0
418-788-5605 Fax: 418-788-2751 www.agencesssgim.ca
Division of: Point de service Unité Gignu
Parent: Agence de la santé et des services sociaux de la Gaspésie-Iles-de-la-Madeleine

Rimouski: **Centre de réadaptation en déficience intellectuelle du Bas St-Laurent**
274, rue Potvin, Rimouski, QC G5L 7P5
418-723-4425 Fax: 418-722-6113
Old Name: Centre de réadaptation intellectuelle du Bas St-La
Number of Beds: 348 lits
Guylaine Côté, Directrice générale

Rimouski: **Centre jeunesse du Bas-St-Laurent**
CP 3500, 287, rue Pierre-Saindon, 3e étage, Rimouski, QC G5L 8V5
418-723-1255 Fax: 418-722-0620 www.agencesssbsl.gouv.qc.ca
Number of Beds: 73 lits
Marie-Sylvie Bêche, Directrice générale

Roberval: **Centre de réadaptation en déficience intellectuelle du Saguenay-Lac-Saint-Jean**
835, rue Roland, Roberval, QC G8H 3J5
418-275-1360 Fax: 418-275-6595
Number of Beds: 617 lits
Note: Centre de réadaptation pour personnes présentant une déficience intellectuelle
Laurent Bouillon, Directeur général

Roberval: **CLSC-CRAT de Roberval**
Pavillon Gérard-Tremblay, 400, av Bergeron, aile A, Roberval, QC G8H 1K8
418-275-0634 Fax: 418-275-0423
hdr@ssss.gouv.qc.ca
www.cmdp-roberval.com
Division of: CSSS Domaine-du-Roy

Number of Beds: CRAT: 15 lits
Note: Le CLSC offre des services de santé et Info-Santé (811), services sociaux généraux, et services spécifiques; le CRAT offre des services d'adaptation ou réadaptation en alcoolisme et autres toxicomanies.
Jacques Dubois, Directeur général, CSSS Domaine-du-Roy

***Rouyn-Noranda:* Centre de réadaptation La Maison**
CP 1055, 100, ch Docteur-Lemay, Rouyn-Noranda, QC J9X 5C8
819-762-6592 Fax: 819-762-2049
www.sante-abitibi-temiscamingue.gouv.qc.ca; www.crlm.qc.ca
Number of Beds: 55 lits
Note: Centre de réadaptation (déficience physique, troubles envahissants du développement).
Line St-Amour, Directrice générale
Line_St-Amour@ssss.gouv.qc.ca

***Saint-Jean-sur-Richelieu:* Les services de réadaptation du Sud-Ouest et du Renfort**
#105, 315, rue MacDonald, Saint-Jean-sur-Richelieu, QC J3B 8J3
450-348-6121 Fax: 450-348-8440
Number of Beds: 581 lits
Gilles Bertrand, Directeur général

***Saint-Jérome:* Centre du Florès**
500, boul des Laurentides, Saint-Jérome, QC J7Z 4M2
450-569-2970 Fax: 450-569-2961 877-569-2970
Number of Beds: 0
Note: centre de réadaptation
Cathy Lévesque, Attachée de direction
cathy_levesque@ssss.gouv.qc.ca
Lucie Leduc, Directrice générale

***Saint-Jérome:* Centre jeunesse des Laurentides**
#241, 500, boul des Laurentides, Saint-Jérome, QC J7Z 4M2
450-436-7607 Fax: 450-436-4811
Number of Beds: 160 lits
Bernard Fortin, Directeur général

***Saint-Jérome:* Pavillon Ste-Marie inc.**
45, rue du Pavillon, Saint-Jérome, QC J7Y 3R6
450-438-3583 Fax: 450-438-7481
Parent: Agence de la santé et des services sociaux des Laurentides
Number of Beds: 100 lits
Francyne Jolicoeur, Directrice générale

***Saint-Philippe:* Pavillon Foster**
CP 119, 6, rue Foucreault, Saint-Philippe, QC J0L 2K0
450-659-8911 Fax: 450-659-7173 www.pavillonfoster.org
Number of Beds: 20 lits
Note: alcohol/drug rehabilitation
John Topp, Directeur général

***Saint-Romuald:* Centre de réadaptation en déficience physique Chaudière-Appalaches**
2055, boul de la Rive-Sud, Saint-Romuald, QC G6W 2S5
418-834-5888 Fax: 418-834-0018 www.rrss12.gouv.qc.ca
Parent: Agence de la santé et des services sociaux de Chaudière-Appalaches
Number of Beds: 48 lits
Note: Programmes: Déficience auditive, Déficience du langage, Déficience motrice (enfant, adulte), Clinique de sclérose en plaques, Programme d'évaluation & de réadaptation en conduite automobile, Neurotraumatisme, Dépistage du traumatisme craniocérébral léger, Programme intensif de gestion autonome de la douleur, et Programme de suppléance à la communication. Points de service: Beauce-Etchemin (Beauceville), Montmagny-L'Islet (Montmagny), l'Amiante (Thetford Mines), et Littoral (Charny).

***Sept-Iles:* Bande indienne des montagnes de Sept-Iles/Maliotenam**
1089, rue Dequen, Sept-Iles, QC G4R 4L9
418-962-0222 Fax: 418-968-0935
Number of Beds: 29 lits
Jean-Marie Caron, Directeur général

***Sherbrooke:* Centre de réadaptation Estrie inc.**
1930, rue King ouest, Sherbrooke, QC J1J 2E2
819-346-8411 Fax: 819-564-7670
Parent: Agence de la santé et des services sociaux de l'Estrie
Number of Beds: 117 lits
Note: centre de réadaptation (déficience motrice)
Lucie Dumas, Directrice générale

***Sherbrooke:* Centre Jean-Patrice Chaisson/Maison St-Georges**
1930, rue King ouest, Sherbrooke, QC J1J 2E2
819-821-2500 Fax: 819-563-8322
Parent: Agence de la santé et des services sociaux de l'Estrie
Number of Beds: 45 lits
Note: centre de réadaptation des drogues
Denis Bougie, Directeur général

***Sherbrooke:* Centre jeunesse de l'Estrie**
594, boul Queen nord, Sherbrooke, QC J1H 3R7
819-564-7100 Fax: 819-564-7109
Number of Beds: 121 lits
Note: centre jeunesse
Carol Fillion, Directrice générale (intérim)

***Sherbrooke:* Villa Marie-Claire inc.**
470, rue Victoria, Sherbrooke, QC J1H 3J2
819-563-1622 Fax: 819-563-6990
Number of Beds: 15 lits
Louisette Breton, Directrice générale

***St-Léonard:* Centre de réadaptation en déficience intellectuelle Gabrielle Major**
6455, rue Jean Talon est, 6e étage, St-Léonard, QC H1S 3E8
514-259-2245 Fax: 514-259-5906
Old Name: Centre d'accueil Charleroi.
Parent: Agence de la santé et des services sociaux de Montréal
Number of Beds: 221 lits
Ginette Bissonnette, Directrice générale (intérim)

***Ste-Anne-des-Monts:* Centre de réadaptation de la Gaspésie**
CP 370, 230, rte du Parc, Ste-Anne-des-Monts, QC G4V 2C4
418-763-3325 Fax: 418-763-5631 www.agencesssgim.ca
Parent: Agence de la santé et des services sociaux de la Gaspésie-Iles-de-la-Madeleine
Number of Beds: 131 lits
Jacques Tremblay, Directeur général

***Ste-Anne-des-Monts:* Centre de réadaptation de la Gaspésie**
230, rte du Parc, Ste-Anne-des-Monts, QC G4V 2C4
418-763-3325 Fax: 418-763-5631 www.agencesssgim.ca
Division of: Point de service MRC de la Haute-Gaspésie
Parent: Agence de la santé et des services sociaux de la Gaspésie-Iles-de-la-Madeleine
Note: Déficiences physiques et intellectuelles.

***Ste-Anne-des-Monts:* Centre de santé et de services sociaux de la Haute-Gaspésie**
50, rue Belvédère, Ste-Anne-des-Monts, QC G4V 1X4
418-763-5000 Fax: 418-763-9024 www.agencesssgim.ca; www.cssshautegaspesie.qc.ca
Division of: Centre de réadaptation L'Escale
Parent: Agence de la santé et des services sociaux de la Gaspésie-Iles-de-la-Madeleine
Note: Pour personnes toxicomanes. Le Centre se relocalisera en 2010. Les nouvelles installations seront adjacentes à l'Hôpital des Monts.

***Ste-Anne-des-Monts:* Centre jeunesse Gaspésie/Les Iles**
#EB-132, 230, rte du Parc, Ste-Anne-des-Monts, QC G4V 2C4
418-763-2251 Fax: 418-763-2538 www.agencesssgim.ca
Division of: Point de service Succursale Haute-Gaspésie
Parent: Agence de la santé et des services sociaux de la Gaspésie-Iles-de-la-Madeleine

***Ste-Anne-des-Monts:* Hôpital des Monts**
50 rue Belvedere, Ste-Anne-des-Monts, QC G4V 1X4
418-763-5000 Fax: 418-763-9024 www.agencesssgim.ca; www.cssshautegaspesie.qc.ca
Division of: Centre de réadaptation L'Escale
Parent: Agence de la santé et des services sociaux de la Gaspésie-Iles-de-la-Madeleine
Note: Pour personnes toxicomanes. Le Centre relocalisera en 2010. Les nouvelles installations seront adjacentes à l'Hôpital des Monts.

***Trois-Rivières:* Centre de réadaptation Interval**
20, rue Notre-Dame est, Trois-Rivières, QC G8T 9J1
819-693-0041 Fax: 819-693-0045 www.centreinterval.qc.ca
Parent: Agence de la santé et des services sociaux de la Mauricie et du Centre-du-Québec
Number of Beds: 40 lits
Note: centre de réadaptation (déficience motrice)
Serge Lemieux, Directeur général

***Trois-Rivières:* Centre de services en déficience intellectuelle Mauricie-Centre-du-Québec**
3255, rue Foucher, Trois-Rivières, QC G8Z 1M6
819-379-6868 Fax: 819-379-5155
Parent: Agence de la santé et des services sociaux de la Mauricie et du Centre-du-Québec
Number of Beds: 523 lits
Michel Boutet, Directeur général

***Trois-Rivières:* Le Centre jeunesse de la Mauricie et Centre-du-Québec**
1455, boul du Carmel, Trois-Rivières, QC G8Z 3R7
819-378-5481 Fax: 819-378-6857
Number of Beds: 142 lits
Note: centre de réadaptation
Richard Desrochers, Directeur général

***Trois-Rivières:* Domremy Mauricie-Centre-du-Québec**
440, rue des Forges, Trois-Rivières, QC G9A 2H5
819-374-4744 Fax: 819-374-4502
Number of Beds: 30 lits
Note: centre de réadaptation des drogues
Pierre Bourassa, Directeur général

***Val-d'Or:* Centre jeunesse de l'Abitibi-Témiscamingue**
700, boul Forest, Val-d'Or, QC J9P 2L3
819-825-0002 Fax: 819-825-5132
Number of Beds: 57 lits
Regean Bergeron, Directrice générale

***Verdun:* Havre-Jeunesse**
4360, boul Lasalle, Verdun, QC H4G 2A8
514-769-5050 Fax: 514-769-3510
Number of Beds: 15 lits
Wallace B. Johnson, Directeur général

***Wemotaci:* Conseil de la Nation Atikamekw**
Wemotaci, QC G0X 3R0
418-523-6153 Fax: 418-676-8965
Number of Beds: 9
Clément St-Cyr, Directeur général

***Westmount:* Centre de jeunesse Mont Saint-Patrick Inc.**
5, Weredale Park, Westmount, QC H3Z 1Y5
514-989-1885
Number of Beds: 9 lits
Note: centre de réadaptation (déficience visuelle)
Michael Udy, Directeur général

***Westmount:* Les Centres de jeunesse Shawbridge**
5 Weredale Park, Westmount, QC H3Z 1Y5
514-989-1885
Number of Beds: 138 lits
Note: centre de réadaptation (déficience motrice)
Michael Udy, Directeur général

***Westmount:* Les centres de la jeunesse et de la famille Saint-Georges**
5, Weredale Park, Westmount, QC H3Z 1Y5
514-932-7161
Old Name: Centre d'accueil Horizons de la Jeunesse
Number of Beds: 243 lits
Note: centre de réadaptation (déficience motrice) + déficience sensorielle
Michael Udy, Directeur général

Centres d'hébergement et des soins delongue durée (CHSLD)

***Buckingham:* Centre d'accueil de Buckingham**
111, rue Lucerne, Buckingham, QC J8L 2M4
819-986-1043 Fax: 819-986-9602
Parent: Agence de la santé et de services sociaux de l'Outaouais
Number of Beds: 79 lits
Jacques Prud'Homme, Directeur général

***Dorval:* Le Strathmore**
2400, ch Herron, Dorval, QC H9S 5W3
514-631-7288 Fax: 514-631-9208
lestrathmore@chartwellreit.ca
www.chartwellreit.ca/home_locations/lestrathmore.htm
Number of Beds: 70 lits
Barbara Lee, Directrice générale

***Gatineau:* Résidence Ste-Marie**
156, boul Lorrain, Gatineau, QC J8P 2G2
819-663-5736 Fax: 819-643-1358
Number of Beds: 23 lits
Palmyra Séguin, Directrice générale

***Granby:* Centre Howard Enr.**
237, boul Montcalm, Granby, QC J2G 5C2
514-372-7678
Number of Beds: 66 lits
Marcel Rémillard, Directeur général

***Grandes-Bergeronnes:* Centre de santé et de services sociaux de la Haute-C"te-Nord - Pavillon Bergeron**
CP 68, 450, rue de la Mer, Grandes-Bergeronnes, QC G0T 1G0
418-232-6224 Fax: 418-232-6771
Parent: Agence de la santé et des services sociaux de la C"te-Nord
Number of Beds: 32 lits
Micheline Anctil, Directeur général

***Ham-Nord:* Foyer Saints-Anges de Ham-Nord inc.**
CP 269, 493, rue Principale, Ham-Nord, QC G0P 1A0
819-344-2940 Fax: 819-344-2584
Parent: Agence de la santé et des services sociaux de la Mauricie et du Centre-du-Québec
Number of Beds: 38 lits
Alain Lavertu, Directeur général

***Iberville:* Pavillon Iberville Enr.**
135, 8e av, Iberville, QC J2X 1K8
514-346-9292
Number of Beds: 15 lits
Rachèle Dorval, Propriétaire

***Joliette:* Centre d'accueil Saint-Eusèbe**
585, boul Manseau, Joliette, QC J6E 3E5
450-759-8222 Fax: 450-759-1579
Parent: Agences de développement de réseaux locaux de services de santé et de services sociaux
Number of Beds: 159 lits
Jean-Claude Berlinguet, Directeur général

***Montréal:* Centre d'accueil Judith Jasmin**
8850, rue Bisaillon, Montréal, QC H1K 4N2
514-354-5990 Fax: 514-354-4916
Parent: Agence de la santé et des services sociaux de Montréal
Number of Beds: 75 lits

***Montréal:* Centre de coordination des services Dandurand**
3958, rue Dandurand, 3e étage, Montréal, QC H1X 1P7
514-723-2003 Fax: 514-729-9697
Parent: Agence de la santé et des services sociaux de Montréal

***Montréal:* Centre hospitalier Gériatrique Maimonides**
5795, av Caldwell, Montréal, QC H4W 1W3
514-483-2121 Fax: 514-483-1561
maimonides@ssss.gouv.qc.ca
Parent: Agence de la santé et des services sociaux de Montréal
Number of Beds: 387 lits
Barbra Gold, Directrice générale

***Montréal:* Résidence Pie IX**
4090, rue Martial, Montréal, QC H1H 1X4
514-327-2333 Fax: 514-327-3276
Parent: Agence de la santé et des services sociaux de Montréal
Number of Beds: 42 lits
Note: Centre de réadaptation
Serge Beauchamp, Directeur général

***Montréal-Nord:* Pavillon de la Détente 1993 Enr.**
6880, boul Gouin est, Montréal-Nord, QC H1G 6L8
514-321-5107 Fax: 514-328-8987
Number of Beds: 55 lits
Irène Sirois, Administratrice

***Pierrefonds:* Manoir Ile de l'Ouest**
17725, boul Pierrefonds, Pierrefonds, QC H9J 3L1
514-620-9850 Fax: 514-620-3196
Parent: Agence de la santé et des services sociaux de Montréal
Number of Beds: 63 lits
Heather Karakas, Directrice générale

***Rawdon:* Heather Hospital Inc.**
Hôpital Heather inc.
3462, 3e av, Rawdon, QC J0K 1S0
450-834-2512 Fax: 450-834-5798
Parent: Agences de développement de réseaux locaux de services de santé et de services sociaux
Number of Beds: 85 lits
Paul Arbec, Directeur général

***Roberval:* Résidence des Érables**
992, boul Saint-Joseph, Roberval, QC G8H 2L9
418-275-4376
Number of Beds: 23 lits
Note: déficience intellectuelle

***Saint-Benoît-Labre:* Pavillon Baillargeon inc.**
357, rte 271, Saint-Benoît-Labre, QC G0M 1P0
418-228-9141 Fax: 418-226-3772
Number of Beds: 35 places
Richard Busque, Directeur général

***Saint-Eustache:* Domaine des Trois Pignons**
112, 25e av, Saint-Eustache, QC J7P 2V2
450-473-5961 Fax: 450-491-1847
Number of Beds: 92 lits
Suzanne Clavet, Directrice générale

***Saint-Fabien:* Pavillon St-Fabien**
CP 520, 142, 1re rue, Saint-Fabien, QC G0L 2Z0
418-869-2709
Number of Beds: 27 lits
Sylvain Paquet, Directeur général

***Saint-Pierre-de-l'Ile-d'O:* Centre d'hébergement Alphonse-Bonenfant**
1199, ch Royal, Saint-Pierre-de-l'Ile-d'O, QC G0A 4E0
418-828-9114 Fax: 418-828-1127
Parent: Agence de la santé et des services sociaux de la Capitale-Nationale
Number of Beds: 50 lits
Aline Prémont, Directeur général

***Saint-Zacharie:* Résidence l'Eden**
668, 12e av, Saint-Zacharie, QC G0M 2C0
418-593-5200 Fax: 418-593-5200
Year Founded: 1964
Number of Beds: 30 lits
Linda L. Lacroix

***Sainte-Geneviève:* Château sur le Lac**
16289, boul Gouin ouest, Sainte-Geneviève, QC H9H 1E2
514-620-9794 Fax: 514-696-3196
Parent: Agence de la santé et des services sociaux de Montréal
Number of Beds: 50 lits
B.S. Kachra, Directeur général

***Verdun:* Manoir des Floralies Verdun**
1050, rue Gordon, Verdun, QC H4G 2S2
514-766-2858 Fax: 514-766-8701
Parent: Agence de la santé et des services sociaux de Montréal
Number of Beds: 103 lits
Louise Fontaine, Directrice générale

***Victoriaville:* Pavillon Familial des Bois-Francs inc.**
21, rue Marchand, Victoriaville, QC G6P 4J5
819-752-9920

***Acton Vale:* Centre d'hébergement de la MRC-d'Acton**
1268, rue Ricard, Acton Vale, QC J0H 1A0
450-546-3234 Fax: 450-546-4811
info@lesommetavotreportee.qc.ca
www.lesommetavotreportee.qc.ca;
www.santemonteregie.qc.ca/richelieu-yamaska
Division of: CSSS Richelieu-Yamaska
Parent: Agence de la santé et des services sociaux de la Montérégie
Number of Beds: 81 lits
Daniel Castonguay, Directeur général, CSSS Richelieu-Yamaska
Réjeanne Boudreau, Directrice du Programme hébergement-milieu de vie, CSSS Richelieu-Yamaska

***Akwesasne:* Conseil Mohawk d'Akwesasne**
CP 40, Akwesasne, QC H0M 1A0
613-575-2507
Number of Beds: 30 lits
Bonnie Cole, Directrice générale

***Anjou:* CHSLD Le Royer**
7351, rue Jean-Desprez, Anjou, QC H1K 5A6
514-493-9397 Fax: 514-493-9103
Parent: Agence de la santé et des services sociaux de Montréal
Number of Beds: 96 lits
Guy Joly, Directeur général

***Baie-Saint-Paul:* Centre d'accueil Pierre-Dupré**
CP 1779, 10, rue Boivin, Baie-Saint-Paul, QC G3Z 1B0
418-435-5562 Fax: 418-435-4049
Number of Beds: 60 lits
Robert Vallières, Directeur général

***Beaconsfield:* Manoir Beaconsfield**
34, av Woodland, Beaconsfield, QC H9W 4V9
514-694-2000 Fax: 514-694-5000
Parent: Agence de la santé et des services sociaux de Montréal
Number of Beds: 23 lits
Annie Maffre, Directrice générale

***Beauharnois:* Centre d'accueil le Vaisseau d'Or**
55, rue Saint-André, Beauharnois, QC J6N 3G7
450-429-6403 Fax: 450-429-6602
Number of Beds: 88 lits
Lise Bélisle-Bélanger, Directrice générale

***Beauport:* Centre d'hébergement du Fargy**
700, boul des Chutes, Beauport, QC G1E 2B7
418-663-9934
Parent: Agence de la santé et des services sociaux de la Capitale-Nationale
Number of Beds: 60 lits, 4 lits d'hébergement temporaires

***Beauport:* Centre d'hébergement Saint-Augustin.**
2135, rue Terrasse-Cadieux, Beauport, QC G1C 1Z2
418-667-3910 www.cha.quebec.qc.ca
Parent: Agence de la santé et des services sociaux de la Capitale-Nationale
Number of Beds: 34 lits de gériatrie

***Beauport:* Centre de santé Orléans (Yvonne Sylvain)**
3365, rue Guimont, Beauport, QC G1E 2H1
418-663-8171 Fax: 418-663-0602
Number of Beds: 116 lits
Lucie Lacroix, Directrice général

***Beloeil:* Centre d'hébergement Champlain-Beloeil**
221, rue Brunelle, Beloeil, QC J3G 2M9
514-467-3356
Parent: Agence de la santé et des services sociaux de la Montérégie
Number of Beds: 53 lits

***Beloeil:* Centre d'hébergement Marguerite-Adam**
425, rue Hubert, Beloeil, QC J3G 2T1
450-467-1631 Fax: 450-467-4210
info@lesommetavotreportee.qc.ca
www.lesommetavotreportee.qc.ca;
www.santemonteregie.qc.ca/richelieu-yamaska
Division of: CSSS Richelieu-Yamaska
Parent: Agence de la santé et des services sociaux de la Montérégie
Number of Beds: 70 lits
Daniel Castonguay, Directeur général, CSSS Richelieu-Yamaska
Réjeanne Boudreau, Directrice du Programme hébergement-milieu de vie, CSSS Richelieu-Yamaska

***Berthierville:* CHSLD Le Château inc.**
1231, rue Dr Olivier-M.-Gendron, Berthierville, QC J0K 1A0
450-836-6241 Fax: 450-836-4013
Number of Beds: 64 lits
Guy Ducharme, Directeur général

***Boucherville:* Centre d'hébergement Jeanne-Crevier**
151, rue De Muy, Boucherville, QC J4B 4W7
450-641-0595 Fax: 450-641-3082
www.santemonteregie.qc.ca/cssspierreboucher
Division of: CSSS Pierre-Boucher
Number of Beds: 93 lits
Caroline Barbir, Directrice générale, CSSS Pierre-Boucher

***Bromptonville:* Centre Brompton**
15, rue de la Croix sud, Bromptonville, QC J0B 1H0
819-846-2708 Fax: 819-846-4328
Parent: Agence de la santé et des services sociaux de l'Estrie

***Brossard:* Centre d'accueil Marcelle Ferron inc.**
8600, boul Marie Victorin, Brossard, QC J4X 1A1
450-923-1430 Fax: 450-923-1805
camf@dsuper.net
Parent: Agence de la santé et des services sociaux de la Montérégie
Number of Beds: 175 lits
Zefferino Guiducci, Directeur général

***Brossard:* CHSLD Vigi Brossard**
5955, boul Grande-Allée, Brossard, QC J4Z 3G4
450-656-8500 Fax: 450-656-8586 www.vigisante.com
Parent: Vigi Santé Ltée
Number of Beds: 66 lits
Note: Agence/région administrative: Agence de la santé et des services sociaux de Montérégie.

***C"te Saint-Luc:* Centre d'hébergement Waldorf inc.**
7400, ch de la C"te-Saint-Luc, C"te Saint-Luc, QC H4W 3J4
514-369-1000 Fax: 514-489-3968
lewaldorf@reveraliving.com
www.reveraliving.com
Number of Beds: 20 lits
Aileen Rabinovitch, Directrice générale

***C"te Saint-Luc:* Centre hospitalier gériatrique Maimonides**
5795, av Caldwell, C"te Saint-Luc, QC H4W 1W3
514-483-2121
Parent: Agence de la santé et des services sociaux de Montréal
Number of Beds: 387 lits
Barbra Gold, Directrice générale

C"te Saint-Luc: Les résidences montréalaises de l'église unie pour personnes agées
5790, av Parkhaven, C"te Saint-Luc, QC H4W 1Y1
514-482-0590 Fax: 514-482-2643
Number of Beds: 216 beds
Annette Rudy, Dir. gen.

Cap-aux-Meules: Centre hospitalier de l'Archipel
596, ch Principal, Cap-aux-Meules, QC G4T 1G1
418-986-3658 www.agencesssgim.ca; www.csssdesiles.qc.ca
Division of: CHSLD Villa Plaisance
Parent: Agence de la santé et des services sociaux de la Gaspésie-Iles-de-la-Madeleine
Number of Beds: 50 lits
Note: CSSS des Iles.
Germain Chevarie, Directeur général

Chambly: Manoir Soleil inc.
125, rue Daigneault, Chambly, QC J3L 1G7
450-658-4441 Fax: 450-658-6521
Number of Beds: 68 lits
Nancy Gaudet, Directrice générale

Chandler: Centre de santé et de services sociaux du Rocher-Percé
CP 1090, 633, av Daignault, Chandler, QC G0C 1K0
418-689-2572 Fax: 418-689-4707 www.agencesssgim.ca
Also Known As: CLSC de Chandler
Division of: CLSC-CHSLD Pabok
Parent: Agence de la santé et des services sociaux de la Gaspésie-Iles-de-la-Madeleine
Number of Beds: 62 lits
Note: A fusionné avec le Centre hospitalier de Chandler en 2004.
Chantal Duguay, Directrice générale

Chandler: CLSC-CHSLD Pabok
75, rue des Cèdres, Chandler, QC G0C 1K0
418-689-6621 Fax: 418-689-4860 www.agencesssgim.ca
Also Known As: CLSC de Chandler
Division of: Point de service Le CHSLD - Villa Pabos
Parent: Agence de la santé et des services sociaux de la Gaspésie-Iles-de-la-Madeleine
Note: CSSS du Rocher-Percé.

Charlesbourg: Centre d'hébergement de Charlesbourg
7150, boul Cloutier, Charlesbourg, QC G1H 5V5
418-628-0456 Fax: 418-622-8676
Parent: Agence de la santé et des services sociaux de la Capitale-Nationale
Number of Beds: 64 lits
Note: Hébergement permanent, centre de jour

Charlesbourg: Centre d'hébergement St-Jean-Eudes
6000, 3e av ouest, Charlesbourg, QC G1H 7J5
418-627-1124 Fax: 418-627-4995
Number of Beds: 141 lits
Clémence Boucher, Directrice générale

Charlesbourg: Centre d'hébergement St-Joseph inc.
1430, av Notre-Dame, Charlesbourg, QC G2N 1S1
418-849-1891 Fax: 418-849-1892
Parent: Agence de la santé et des services sociaux de la Capitale-Nationale
Number of Beds: 30 lits
Yvonnette Côté-Létourneau, Directrice générale

Châteauguay: Centre d'hébergement Champlain Châteauguay
210, rue Salaberry sud, Châteauguay, QC J6K 3M9
450-632-4451 Fax: 450-699-1696
www.santemonteregie.qc.ca/jardins-roussillon
Division of: CSSS Jardins-Roussillon
Parent: Agence de la santé et des services sociaux de la Montérégie
Number of Beds: 96 lits
Paul Moreau, Directeur général, CSSS Jardins-Roussillon

Chicoutimi: Centre d'hébergement Mgr-Victor-Tremblay
1236, rue D'Angoulême, Chicoutimi, QC G7H 6P9
418-698-3911
Parent: Agence de la santé et des services sociaux du Saguenay-Lac-St-Jean
Number of Beds: 50 lits

Chicoutimi: CHSLD de Chicoutimi
904, rue Jacques-Cartier est, Chicoutimi, QC G7H 2A9
418-698-3900 Fax: 418-543-6285
Number of Beds: 104 lits
Benoît Duplessis, Directeur général

Chicoutimi: Foyer St-François inc.
912, rue Jacques-Cartier est, Chicoutimi, QC G7H 2A9
418-549-3727 Fax: 418-543-2038
sonia.bergeron@ssss.gouv.qc.ca
Number of Beds: 64 lits
Sonia Bergeron, Directrice générale

Clermont: Foyer de Clermont inc.
CP 520, 6, rue du Foyer, Clermont, QC G4A 1G8
418-439-4684
Parent: Agence de la santé et des services sociaux de la Capitale-Nationale
Number of Beds: 42 lits

Cleveland: Foyer Wales
506, rte 243, Cleveland, QC J0B 2H0
819-826-3266 Fax: 819-826-2549
Number of Beds: 222 lits
Simms Stuart, Directeur général

Contrecoeur: CLSC-CHSLD de Contrecoeur
4700, rte Marie-Victorin, Contrecoeur, QC J0L 1C0
450-587-5025 Fax: 450-587-8411
www.santemonteregie.qc.ca/cssspierreboucher
Division of: CSSS Pierre-Boucher
Parent: Agence de la santé et des services sociaux de la Montérégie
Number of Beds: 52 lits
Note: Centre d'hébergement, et le point de service CLSC des Seigneuries de Contrecoeur (450-652-2917).
Caroline Barbir, Directrice générale, CSSS Pierre-Boucher

Coteau-du-Lac: Pavillon Laura Ferguson
CP 909, 60, ch du Fleuve, Coteau-du-Lac, QC J0P 1B0
514-267-3379
Number of Beds: 15 places
Paul-Henri Boutin, Directeur général

Cowansville: Centre de santé et de services sociaux La Pommeraie
950, rue Principale, Cowansville, QC J2K 1K3
450-266-5522
Number of Beds: 251 lits
Diane Daigle, Directrice générale

Cowansville: Résidence Manoir Beaumont (1988) Inc.
430, rue Beaumont, Cowansville, QC J2K 1W1
514-263-6235 Fax: 514-263-8598
Number of Beds: 36 lits
Note: Hébergement et soins de longue durée
Monique Fréchette, Directrice générale

Deux-Montagnes: CHSLD Vigi Deux-Montagnes inc.
580, 20e av, Deux-Montagnes, QC J7R 7E9
450-473-5111 Fax: 450-491-4686 www.vigisante.com
Parent: Vigi Santé Ltée
Number of Beds: 76 lits
Note: Agence/région administrative: Agence de la santé et des services sociaux des Laurentides.
Robert Fournier, Directeur général

Disraéli: Résidence René-Lavoie
CP 698, 260, av Champlain, Disraéli, QC G0N 1E0
418-449-2020 Fax: 418-449-4006
csssrt@ssss.gouv.qc.ca
www.centresantethetford.ca/sante-quebec/
Parent: Agence de la santé et des services sociaux de Chaudière-Appalaches
Number of Beds: 47 lits

Dolbeau: Pavillon Maison du Bel Age
2020, rue Provencher, Dolbeau, QC G8L 3E6
418-276-1866 Fax: 418-276-1866
Number of Beds: 53 places
Note: Maison d'hébergement pour personnes agées autonomes
Gisèle Laroche, Directrice générale

Dollard-des-Ormeaux: Vigi Santé Ltée
197, rue Thornhill, Dollard-des-Ormeaux, QC H9B 3H8
514-684-0930 Fax: 514-684-0179 www.vigisante.com
Number of Beds: 1,500 lits
Note: Propriétaire et administrateur de 15 centres d'hébergement, présente dans plusieurs régions du Québec. Le siège du CHSLD Vigi Dollard-des-Ormeaux, avec 160 lits.
Vincenzo Simonetta, Directeur général

Dorval: Centre d'hébergement Chartwell inc.
2400, ch Herron, Dorval, QC H9S 5W3
514-631-7288 Fax: 514-631-9208
Number of Beds: 325 lits
Claudette Cloutier, Directrice générale

Drummondville: Centre d'hébergement Frederick-George-Heriot
75, rue St-Georges, Drummondville, QC J2C 4G6
819-477-0544
csssdrummond@ssss.gouv.qc.ca
www.csssdrummond.qc.ca
Division of: CSSS Drummond
Number of Beds: 354 lits
Nagui Habashi, Directeur général, CSSS Drummond
Lyse Garant, Directrice du Programme, Personnes en perte d'autonomie

Farnham: Foyers Farnham inc.
800, rue Saint-Paul nord, Farnham, QC J2N 2K6
450-293-3168 Fax: 450-293-7878
Parent: Agence de la santé et des services sociaux de la Montérégie
Number of Beds: 61 lits

Gaspé: CHSLD Mgr Ross
150, rue Mgr Ross, Gaspé, QC G4X 2S7
418-368-3301 Fax: 418-368-6730 www.cssscotedegaspe.ca
Parent: Agence de la santé et des services sociaux de la Gaspésie-Iles-de-la-Madeleine
Number of Beds: 129 lits
Note: CSSS Côte-de-Gaspé.

Gatineau: CHSLD de Hull - Centre d'hébergement Foyer du Bonheur
125, boul Lionel-Émond, Gatineau, QC J8Y 5S8
819-966-6410 Fax: 819-966-6414 www.csssgatineau.qc.ca; www.santeoutaouais.qc.ca
Division of: CSSS de Gatineau
Parent: Agence de la santé et de services sociaux de l'Outaouais
Number of Beds: 263 lits
Nancy Bergeron, Directrice adjointe en hébergement, Soutien à l'autonomie
819-966-6440

Gatineau: CHSLD de Hull - Centre d'hébergement La Piet...
273, rue Laurier, Gatineau, QC J8X 3W8
819-966-6420 Fax: 819-966-6421 www.csssgatineau.qc.ca; www.santeoutaouais.qc.ca
Division of: CSSS de Gatineau
Parent: Agence de la santé et de services sociaux de l'Outaouais
Number of Beds: 158 lits
Nancy Bergeron, Directrice adjointe en hébergement, Soutien à l'autonomie
819-966-6440

Gatineau: CLSC-CHSLD de Gatineau - Centre d'hébergement Maison Bon Séjour
134, rue Jean-René Monette, Gatineau, QC J8P 7C3
819-966-6450 Fax: 819-966-6453 www.csssgatineau.qc.ca
Division of: CSSS de Gatineau
Parent: Agence de la santé et de services sociaux de l'Outaouais
Number of Beds: 100 lits
Nancy Bergeron, Directrice adjointe en hébergement, Soutien à l'autonomie
819-966-6440

Gracefield: CHSLD Gracefield
CP 317, 1, rue du Foyer, Gracefield, QC J0X 1W0
819-463-2100 Fax: 819-463-4721
Parent: Agence de la santé et de services sociaux de l'Outaouais
Number of Beds: 31 lits
Bruno Larivière, Coordonateur, Hébergement

Granby: Centre Villa Bonheur
71, rue Court, Granby, QC J2G 4Y7
450-776-5222 Fax: 450-372-7617
Parent: Agence de la santé et des services sociaux de la Montérégie
Number of Beds: 108 lits

Grand-Mère: CHSLD du Centre Mauricie
1650, 6e av, Grand-Mère, QC G9T 2K4
819-533-2500 Fax: 819-538-7640
Parent: Agence de la santé et des services sociaux de la Mauricie et du Centre-du-Québec
Number of Beds: 406 lits
Guy D'Anjou, Directeur général

Huntingdon: Centre hospitalier du Comté de Huntingdon
CP 6000, 198, rue Châteaugauy, Huntingdon, QC J0S 1H0
450-264-6111 Fax: 450-264-4923
Number of Beds: 60 lits

Guy Deschenes, Directeur général

Ile-Bizard: Centre d'accueil Denis-Benjamin Viger
3292, rue Cherrier, Ile-Bizard, QC H9C 1E4
514-620-6310 Fax: 514-620-6553
Parent: Agence de la santé et des services sociaux de Montréal
Number of Beds: 125 lits

Ile-Perrot: Centre d'accueil Laurent-Bergevin
200, boul Perrot, Ile-Perrot, QC J7V 7M7
514-453-5860 Fax: 514-453-8939
Parent: Agence de la santé et des services sociaux de la Montérégie
Number of Beds: 82 lits

Irlande: Pavillon Morisset Huppé Inc.
CP 2060, 290, rte 165, Irlande, QC G6H 2N7
418-428-3568 Fax: 418-428-3021
lucy.morisset.info@globetrotter.net
Number of Beds: 14 places
Note: Pavillon d'hébergement pour adultes handicapés physiques intellectuels lourds
Lucie Morisset-Huppé, Directrice générale

Jonquière: Centre d'hébergement Georges-Hébert
2841, rue Faraday, Jonquière, QC G7S 5C8
418-695-7727 Fax: 418-695-7737 wpp01.msss.gouv.gc.ca
Parent: Agence de la santé et des services sociaux du Saguenay-Lac-St-Jean
Number of Beds: 75 lits

Jonquière: Centre d'hébergement Sainte-Marie
2184, rue Perrier, Jonquière, QC G7X 9C9
418-695-7800 Fax: 418-695-7738
Number of Beds: 66 lits
Note: Hébergement permanent et temporaire

Jonquière: Pavillon Arvida
CP 1200, 1841, rue Deschênes, Jonquière, QC G7S 4K6
418-548-8231 Fax: 418-548-6875
Parent: Agence de la santé et des services sociaux du Saguenay-Lac-St-Jean
Number of Beds: 60 lits

La Baie: Foyer de Bagotville
562, rue Victoria, La Baie, QC G7B 3M6
418-544-2853 Fax: 418-544-6012
Parent: Agence de la santé et des services sociaux du Saguenay-Lac-St-Jean
Number of Beds: 33 lits

La Baie: Foyer St-Joseph de La Baie inc.
1893, rue Alexis-Simard, La Baie, QC G7B 2K9
418-544-2865 Fax: 418-544-8936
Parent: Agence de la santé et des services sociaux du Saguenay-Lac-St-Jean
Number of Beds: 48 lits

La Guadeloupe: Pavillon Notre-Dame
CP 490, 437, 15e rue ouest, La Guadeloupe, QC G0M 1G0
418-459-3476 Fax: 418-459-6428
Number of Beds: 50 lits
Richard Busque, Directeur général

LaSalle: Centre d'hébergement de LaSalle
8686, rue Centrale, LaSalle, QC H8P 3N4
514-364-6700 www.santemontreal.qc.ca
Parent: Agence de la santé et des services sociaux de Montréal
Number of Beds: 202 lits
Léonard Vincent, Directeur général

LaSalle: Hôpital Ste-Thérèse inc.
9307, boul LaSalle, LaSalle, QC H8R 2M7
514-366-3556 Fax: 514-367-3718
Parent: Agence de la santé et des services sociaux de Montréal
Number of Beds: 47 lits

Labelle: CHSLD de Labelle
CP 38, 50, rue de l'Église, Labelle, QC J0T 1H0
819-686-2372 Fax: 819-686-1950 www.csss-sommets
Division of: CSSS des Sommets
Number of Beds: 46 lits
Jacques Morin, Président, Conseil d'administration, CSSS des Sommets

Lac-Bouchette: Centre d'hébergement de Lac-Bouchette inc.
Édifice Foyer de Lac-Bouchette, CP 39, 99, rte de l'Ermitage, Lac-Bouchette, QC G0W 1V0
418-348-6313 Fax: 418-348-6342
Division of: CSSS Domaine-du-Roy
Number of Beds: 14 lits
Jacques Dubois, Directeur général, CSSS Domaine-du-Roy

Lac-Mégantic: CSSS du Granit - CHSLD/Centre de jour Lac-Mégantic
3675, rue du Foyer, Lac-Mégantic, QC G6B 2K2
819-583-0330 Fax: 819-583-0900
Parent: Agence de la santé et des services sociaux de l'Estrie
Number of Beds: 46 lits
Pierre Latulippe, Directeur général, CSSS du Granit

Lac-au-Saumon: Centre d'hébergement Marie-Anne Ouellet
6, rue Turbide, Lac-au-Saumon, QC G0J 1M0
418-778-5816 Fax: 418-778-3391 www.csssmatapedia.qc.ca
Division of: CSSS de La Matapédia
Number of Beds: 96 lits
Alain Paquet, Directeur général, CSSS de La Matapédia

Lachenaie: Centre hospitalier Pierre-Le Gardeur
911, montée des Pionniers, Lachenaie, QC J6V 2H2
450-654-7525
communications-chlg@chpierrelegardeur.ca
www.chpierrelegardeur.ca/
Number of Beds: 20 lits
Gisèle Boyer, Directrice générale

Lachine: Centre d'hébergement de Lachine
650, place d'Accueil, Lachine, QC H8S 3Z5
514-634-7161 www.santemontreal.qc.ca
Parent: Agence de la santé et des services sociaux de Montréal
Number of Beds: 217 lits

Lachine: CHSLD Nazaire-Piché
150, 15e av, Lachine, QC H8S 3L9
514-637-1780 www.santemontreal.qc.ca
Parent: Agence de la santé et des services sociaux de Montréal
Number of Beds: 100 lits
Marie-Hélène Girard, Directrice générale

Lambton: CSSS du Granit - CLSC/CHSLD de Lambton
310-A, rue Principale, Lambton, QC G0M 1H0
418-486-7441 Fax: 418-486-2172 www.csssgrant.qc.ca
Also Known As: La Maison Paternelle
Number of Beds: 32 lits
Note: Le point de service Lambton regroupe un centre local de services communautaire (CLSC), un centre d'hébergement, et un centre de jour.
Pierre Latulippe, Directeur général, CSSS du Granit

Laval: Centre d'hébergement de la Rive
4605, boul Sainte-Rose, Laval, QC H7R 5S9
450-627-5599 Fax: 450-627-5107 www.sssslaval.gouv.qc.ca
Division of: Prodimax inc.
Parent: Agence de la santé et de services sociaux de Laval
Number of Beds: 79 lits
Note: Centre privé non-conventionné.
Jacques Le Guern, Directeur général

Laval: Centre d'hébergement de la Villa-des-Tilleuls inc.
5590, boul des Laurentides, Laval, QC H7K 2K2
450-628-0322 Fax: 450-622-3674 msss.gouv.qc.ca; www,sssslaval.gouv.qc.ca
Parent: Agence de la santé et de services sociaux de Laval
Number of Beds: 68 lits
Note: Centre privé non-conventioné.
Réginald Ratle, Directeur général

Laval: Centre d'hébergement l'Eden de Laval inc
8528, boul Lévesque est, Laval, QC H7A 1W6
450-665-6283 msss.qc.ca; www.sssslaval.gouv.qc.ca
Parent: Agence de la santé et des services sociaux de Laval
Number of Beds: 43 lits
Note: Centre privé non-conventioné.
Alain Fafard, Directeur général

Laval: Centre d'hébergement St-François inc.
4105, Montée Masson, Laval, QC H7B 1B6
450-666-6541 Fax: 450-666-1601
Number of Beds: 53 lits
Marie-Christine Moulin, Directrice générale

Laval: CHSLD Saint-Jude inc.
4410, boul St-Martin ouest, Laval, QC H7T 1C3
450-687-7714 Fax: 450-682-0330
Parent: Agence de la santé et des services sociaux de Laval
Number of Beds: 204 lits
Daniel Leclair, Directeur général

Laval: Manoir St-Patrice inc.
3615, boul Perron, Laval, QC H7V 1P4
450-681-1621 Fax: 450-681-6120
Number of Beds: 132 lits
Ann Carey, Directrice générale

Laval: La Résidence du Bonheur
5855, rue Boulard, Laval, QC H7B 1A3
450-666-1567 Fax: 450-666-6387
info@residencedubonheur.com
www.residencedubonheur.com; www.sssslaval.gouv.qc.ca
Parent: Agence de la santé et de services sociaux de Laval
Number of Beds: 50 lits
Note: Centre privé non-conventionné.
John Pakis, Directeur général
john.pakis@residencedubonheur.com

Laval: Résidence Riviera inc.
2999, boul Notre-Dame, Laval, QC H7V 4C4
450-682-0111 Fax: 450-682-0154
www.chsldresidenceriviera.com
Number of Beds: 128 lits
Jean Nadon, Directeur général
Michel Samson, Directeur, Services techniques

Lévis: Centre d'accueil Saint-Joseph de Lévis inc
107, rue Saint-Louis, Lévis, QC G6V 6R9
418-833-3414 Fax: 418-833-3417
Parent: Agence de la santé et des services sociaux de Chaudière-Appalaches

Lévis: Centre d'accueil Saint-Joseph de Lévis inc.
107, rue Saint-Louis, Lévis, QC G6V 4G9
418-833-3414 Fax: 418-833-3417
www.casaintjosephdelevis.qc.ca
Number of Beds: 158 lits
Gervais Morissette, Directeur général

Lévis: CLSC-CHSLD de la MRC Desjardins
15, rue de l'Arsenal, Lévis, QC G6V 4P6
418-835-3400
Number of Beds: 95 lits
Renée Lachance-Auger, Directrice générale

Lévis: Pavillon Bellevue inc.
99, rue Monseigneur-Bourget, Lévis, QC G6V 9V2
418-833-3490 Fax: 418-833-6874
Parent: Agence de la santé et des services sociaux de Chaudière-Appalaches
Number of Beds: 50 lits
Claude Talbot, Directeur général

Lévis: Villa Mon Domaine inc.
109, av Mont-Marie, Lévis, QC G6V 8B4
418-837-6408 Fax: 418-837-2626
Parent: Agence de la santé et des services sociaux de Chaudière-Appalaches
Number of Beds: 57 lits
Jean-Noël Begin, Directeur général

Longueuil: Centre d'accueil St-Laurent inc.
480, rue LeMoyne ouest, Longueuil, QC J4H 1X1
450-670-5480 Fax: 450-670-9874
www.santemonteregie.qc.ca/cssspierreboucher
Division of: CSSS Pierre-Boucher
Number of Beds: 32 lits
Note: CHSLD privé non conventionné
Caroline Barbir, Directrice générale, CSSS Pierre-Boucher

Longueuil: CHSLD de Mgr-Coderre
2761, rue Beauvais, Longueuil, QC J4M 2A4
450-448-3607 Fax: 450-448-4322
www.santemonteregie.qc.ca/cssspierreboucher
Division of: CSSS Pierre-Boucher
Parent: Agence de la santé et des services sociaux de la Montérégie
Number of Beds: 154 lits
Caroline Barbir, Directrice générale, CSSS Pierre-Boucher

Longueuil: CHSLD du Chevalier-De Lévis
40, rue Lévis, Longueuil, QC J4H 1S5
450-670-5391 Fax: 450-670-7292
www.santemonteregie.qc.ca/cssspierreboucher
Old Name: CHSLD de Longueuil
Division of: CSSS Pierre-Boucher
Number of Beds: 142 lits
Caroline Barbir, Directrice générale, CSSS Pierre-Boucher

Longueuil: CHSLD René-Lévesque
1901, rue Claude, Longueuil, QC J4G 1Y5
450-651-4609 Fax: 450-670-7731
www.santemonteregie.qc.ca/cssspierreboucher
Division of: CSSS Pierre-Boucher
Number of Beds: 224 lits
Caroline Barbir, Directrice générale, CSSS Pierre-Boucher

Loretteville: Foyer de Loretteville inc.
165, rue Lessard, Loretteville, QC G2B 2V9
418-842-9191 Fax: 418-842-4472

Parent: Agence de la santé et des services sociaux de la Capitale-Nationale
Number of Beds: 74 lits

Lyster: Centre d'hébergement des Quatre-Vents
2180, rue Bécancour, Lyster, QC G0S 1V0
819-389-5923 Fax: 819-389-5969
Old Name: Foyer de Lyster
Division of: CSSS d'Arthabaska-et-de-l'Érable
Parent: Agence de la santé et des services sociaux de la Mauricie et du Centre-du-Québec
Number of Beds: 26 lits
Marcel Dubois, Président, Conseil d'administration, CSSS d'Arthabaska-et-de-l

Magog: Gestion SGH Inc.
64, rue St-Pierre, Magog, QC J1X 3A2
819-843-0202 Fax: 819-843-9518
Old Name: Résidence Ste-Marguerite Marie
Number of Beds: 27 lits
Carine Thuin, Directeur général

Malartic: Centre d'hébergement Saint-Martin de Malartic
CP 639, 701, rue de la Paix, Malartic, QC J0Y 1Z0
819-757-3663 Fax: 819-757-3309
www.sante-abitibi-temiscamingue.gouv.qc.ca; www.csssvo.qc.ca
Division of: CSSS de la Vallée-de-l'Or
Parent: Agence de la santé et des services sociaux de l'Abitibi-Témiscamingue
Number of Beds: 57 lits
Note: Centre d'hébergement/centre de jour.
Jérôme Lamont, Directeur général, CSSS de la Vallée-de-l'Or
Marie Cloutier, Directrice, Programme personnes en perte d'autonomie

Maria: Centre d'hébergement de Maria
491, boul Perron, Maria, QC G0C 1Y0
418-759-3458 Fax: 418-759-5103
csssbc@csssbc.qc.ca
www.csssbc.qc.ca
Old Name: Résidence Saint-Joseph
Division of: CSSS de la Baie-des-Chaleurs
Parent: Agence de la santé et des services sociaux de la Gaspésie-Iles-de-la-Madeleine
Number of Beds: 91 lits
Bernard Nadeau, Directeur général, CSSS de la Baie-des-Chaleurs

Marieville: Centre d'hébergement Sainte-Croix
300, rue Docteur-Poulin, Marieville, QC J3M 1L7
450-460-4475 Fax: 450-460-4104
www.santemonteregie.qc.ca/haut-richelieu-rouville
Division of: CSSS Haut-Richelieu-Rouville
Parent: Agence de la santé et des services sociaux de la Montérégie
Number of Beds: 128 lits
Note: Hébergement permanent et temporaire, centre de jour, réadaptation fonctionnelle intensive.
Lucie Tétreault, Directrice, Personnes en perte d'autonomie liée au vieillisemen

Matane: Centre d'hébergement de Matane
150, av Saint-Jér"me, Matane, QC G4W 3A2
418-562-4154 Fax: 418-562-9281 www.agencesssbsl.gouv.qc.ca
Division of: CSSS de Mataine
Parent: Agence de la santé et des services sociaux du Bas-St-Laurent
Number of Beds: 106 lits
Nicole Morin, Directrice générale, CSSS de Matane

Métabetchouan-Lac-a-la-Cr: Pavillon de Métabetchouan et point de service sud (CLSC)
1895, rte 169, Métabetchouan-Lac-a-la-Cr, QC G8G 1B4
418-349-2861 Fax: 418-349-8774
Parent: Agence de la santé et des services sociaux du Saguenay-Lac-St-Jean
Number of Beds: 168 lits

Mirabel: Centre de santé et de services sociaux Deux-Montagnes et Sud de Mirabel
9100, rue Dumouchel, Mirabel, QC J7N 5A1
450-258-2481 Fax: 450-258-4980
Division of: Centre d'accueil de St-Benoît
Number of Beds: 75 lits
Christiane Arbour, Directrice générale

Mont-Joli: CHSLD de La Mitis
800, av du Sanatorium, Mont-Joli, QC G5H 3L6
418-775-7261 Fax: 418-775-1241 www.centremitissien.net
Division of: CSSS de La Mitis
Parent: Agence de la santé et des services sociaux du Bas-St-Laurent
Number of Beds: 175 lits
Isabelle Malo, Directrice générale, CSSS de La Mitis
cmssc_dg@centremitissien.net

Mont-Laurier: CHSLD Sainte-Anne
411, rue de la Madone, Mont-Laurier, QC J9L 1S1
819-623-5940 Fax: 819-623-7347 www.csssal.org
Old Name: CHSLD Sainte-Anne et C"me Cartier
Division of: CSSS d'Antoine-Labelle
Parent: Agence de la santé et des services sociaux des Laurentides
Number of Beds: 128 lits
Jean-Pierre Urbaine, Directeur général, CSSS d'Antoine-Labelle
Jean-Pierre St-Louis, Coordonnateur des unités de vie, CHSA

Mont-Royal: CHSLD Vigi Mont-Royal
275, av Brittany, Mont-Royal, QC H3P 3C2
514-739-5593 Fax: 514-733-7973 www.vigisante.com
Parent: Vigi Santé Ltée
Number of Beds: 273 lits
Note: Agence/région administrative: Agence de la santé et des services sociaux de Montréal.
Vincent Simonetta, Directeur général

Montréal: Centre Biermans
7905, rue Sherbrooke est, Montréal, QC H1L 1A4
514-351-9891 Fax: 514-351-1556
Old Name: CHSLD Biermans-Triest
Parent: Agence de la santé et des services sociaux de Montréal
Number of Beds: 197 lits
Note: centre de réadaptation

Montréal: Centre d'accueil Father Dowd Father Dowd Home
6565, ch Hudson, Montréal, QC H3S 2T7
514-341-1007 Fax: 514-341-8988
Parent: Agence de la santé et des services sociaux de Montréal
Number of Beds: 134 lits
Carole McDonough, Directrice générale

Montréal: Centre d'accueil Heritage Inc.
5716, ch de la C"te-Saint-Antoine, Montréal, QC H4A 1R9
514-484-2645
Number of Beds: 16 lits
Ron Marolia, Directeur général

Montréal: Centre d'accueil Louis Riel
2120, rue Augustin-Cantin, Montréal, QC H3K 3G3
514-931-2263 Fax: 514-931-2299
Parent: Agence de la santé et des services sociaux de Montréal
Number of Beds: 100 lits
Germain Harvey, Directeur général

Montréal: Centre d'hébergement Armand-Lavergne
3500, rue Chapleau, Montréal, QC H2K 4N3
514-527-8921 www.csssjeannemance.ca; www.santemontreal.qc.ca
Division of: CSSS Jeanne-Mance
Parent: Agence de la santé et des services sociaux de Montréal
Number of Beds: 182 lits
Note: Centre de jour; centre d'hébergement permanent.
Ron Rayside, Président du Conseil d'administration, CSSS Jeanne-Mance
Sylvie Simard, Directrice générale intérimaire, CSSS Jeanne-Mance

Montréal: Centre d'hébergement de Louvain
9600, rue St-Denis, Montréal, QC H2M 1P2
514-381-7256 Fax: 514-381-6486
Parent: Agence de la santé et des services sociaux de Montréal
Number of Beds: 155 lits
Richard Jean, Directeur général

Montréal: Centre d'hébergement de Saint-Michel
3130, rue Jarry est, Montréal, QC H1Z 4N8
514-722-3000 csss-stleonardstmichel.qc.ca
Division of: CSSS de Saint-Léonard et Saint-Michel
Number of Beds: 192 lits
Note: Centre administratif du CSSS, et centre d'hébergement.
Suzanne Hébert, Directrice générale, CSSS de Saint-Léonard et Saint-Michel
Johanne Maître, Directrice de l'hébergement, CSSS de Saint-Léonard et Saint-Michel

Montréal: Centre d'hébergement des Quatre-Temps
7400, boul Saint-Michel, Montréal, QC H2A 2Z8
514-270-9271 Fax: 514-270-6779 csss-stleonardstmichel.qc.ca
Old Name: CHSLD les Havres
Division of: CSSS de Saint-Léonard et Saint-Michel
Parent: Agence de la santé et des services sociaux de Montréal
Number of Beds: 192 lits
Suzanne Hébert, Directrice générale, CSSS de Saint-Léonard et Saint-Michel
Johanne Maître, Directrice de l'hébergement, CSSS de Saint-Léonard et Saint-Michel

Montréal: Centre d'hébergement Légaré
1615, av Émile-Journault, Montréal, QC H2M 2G3
514-384-5490 www.santemontreal.qc.ca
Parent: Agence de la santé et des services sociaux de Montréal
Number of Beds: 105 lits
Daniel Corbeil, Directeur général

Montréal: Centre d'hebergement Marie-Rollet
5003, rue Saint-Zotique est, Montréal, QC H1T 1N6
514-729-5281 Fax: 514-593-5568
Parent: Agence de la santé et des services sociaux de Montréal
Number of Beds: 110 lits
Note: Hébergement et soins de longue durée
Renée Pettigrew, Directrice

Montréal: Centre de soins prolongés Grace Dart
5155, rue Ste-Catherine est, Montréal, QC H1V 2A5
514-255-2833 Fax: 514-255-6275
Parent: Agence de la santé et des services sociaux de Montréal
Number of Beds: 381 lits
Léon Gilbert, Directeur général (intérim)

Montréal: Centre Le Cardinal inc.
12900, rue Notre-Dame est, Montréal, QC H1A 1R9
514-645-2766 Fax: 514-640-6267
Parent: Agence de la santé et des services sociaux de Montréal
Number of Beds: 204 lits
Léonard Chevarie, Directeur général

Montréal: CHSLD Bourget inc.
11570, rue Notre-Dame est, Montréal, QC H1B 2X4
514-645-1673 Fax: 514-645-1673
Parent: Agence de la santé et des services sociaux de Montréal
Number of Beds: 112 lits
Note: Un établissement privé.
Diane Girard, Directrice générale

Montréal: CHSLD Centre-Ville-de-Montréal
66, boul René-Lévesque est, Montréal, QC H2X 1N3
514-861-9331 Fax: 514-861-8385
Division of: CSSS Jeanne-Mance
Parent: Agence de la santé et des services sociaux de Montréal
Number of Beds: 196 lits
Ron Rayside, Président du Conseil d'administration, CSSS Jeanne-Mance
Sylvie Simard, Directrice générale intérimaire, CSSS Jeanne-Mance

Montréal: Les CHSLD de mon quartier
7445, rue Hochelaga, Montréal, QC H1N 3V2
514-251-6000 Fax: 514-251-9826
Old Name: gentre-hospitalier -Centre d'accueil Gouin-Rosemon
Parent: Agence de la santé et des services sociaux de Montréal
Number of Beds: 351 lits
France Mailhot, Directrice générale

Montréal: CHSLD de St-Andrew, de Father-Dowd et de St-Margaret
50 av Hillside, Montréal, QC H3Z 1V9
514-932-3630 Fax: 514-932-4379
Number of Beds: 300 lits
Note: Résidence Father Dowd: 134 lits, 6565 ch Hudson; Résidence St-Andres: 70 lits, 3350 boul Cavendish; Résidence St-Margaret: 96 lits, 50 av Hillside.
Carole McDonough, Directeur général

Montréal: CHSLD du Manoir-de-l'Age-d'Or
3430, rue Jeanne-Mance, Montréal, QC H2X 2J9
514-842-1147 Fax: 514-842-1146 www.csssjeannemance.ca
Division of: CSSS Jeanne-Mance
Number of Beds: 189 lits
Ron Rayside, Président du Conseil d'administration, CSSS Jeanne-Mance
Sylvie Simard, Directrice générale intérimaire, CSSS Jeanne-Mance

Montréal: CHSLD Émilie-Gamelin
1440, rue Dufresne, Montréal, QC H2K 3J3
514-527-8921 Fax: 514-527-3587 www.csssjeannemance.ca
Division of: CSSS Jeanne-Mance
Parent: Agence de la santé et des services sociaux de Montréal
Number of Beds: 184 lits
Ron Rayside, Président du Conseil d'administration, CSSS Jeanne-Mance
Sylvie Simard, Directrice générale intérimaire, CSSS Jeanne-Mance

Montréal: CHSLD Jean XXIII inc.
6900, 15e av, Montréal, QC H1X 2V9
514-725-2190 Fax: 514-728-5901
Parent: Agence de la santé et des services sociaux de Montréal
Number of Beds: 24 lits
Marie-Claire Lamontagne, Directrice générale

Montréal: CHSLD Jeanne-LeBer
7445, rue Hochelaga, Montréal, QC H1N 3V2
514-251-6000
Parent: Agence de la santé et des services sociaux de Montréal
Number of Beds: 351 lits

Montréal: CHSLD juif de Montréal
5725, av Victoria, Montréal, QC H3W 3H6
514-738-4500 Fax: 514-738-2611
Parent: Agence de la santé et des services sociaux de Montréal
Number of Beds: 160 beds
Barbara Gold, Dir. gén. (intérim)

Montréal: CHSLD les Cèdres
95, boul Gouin est, Montréal, QC H3L 1A6
514-389-1023 Fax: 514-389-0581
cedars@istar.ca
Number of Beds: 22 lits
Diane Chaunt, Directrice générale

Montréal: CHSLD Manoir Fleury inc.
2145, rue Fleury est, Montréal, QC H2B 1J8
514-388-1553 Fax: 514-388-4161
Parent: Agence de la santé et des services sociaux de Montréal
Number of Beds: 25 lits
Rose Renzo, Directrice générale

Montréal: CHSLD Marie-Claret inc.
3345, boul Henri-Bourassa est, Montréal, QC H1H 1H6
514-322-4380 Fax: 514-326-8811 www.vigisante.com
Parent: Vigi Santé Ltée
Number of Beds: 78 lits
Note: Agence/région administrative: Agence de la santé et des services sociaux de Montréal.
Jean-Guy Laplante, Directeur général

Montréal: CHSLD Paul Gouin
5900, rue St-Vallier, Montréal, QC H2S 2P3
514-273-3681 Fax: 514-273-7645
Parent: Agence de la santé et des services sociaux de Montréal
Number of Beds: 100 lits

Montréal: CHSLD Providence Notre-Dame-de-Lourdes
1870, boul Pie-IX, Montréal, QC H1V 2C6
514-527-4595 Fax: 514-527-4475
Parent: Agence de la santé et des services sociaux de Montréal
Number of Beds: 162 lits
Robert St-Pierre, Directeur général

Montréal: Foyer Rousselot
5655, rue Sherbrooke est, Montréal, QC H1N 1A4
514-254-9421 Fax: 514-254-3967
Parent: Agence de la santé et des services sociaux de Montréal
Number of Beds: 157 lits
Robert Boucher, Directeur général

Montréal: Groupe Champlain inc.
7150, rue Marie-Victorin, Montréal, QC H1G 2J5
514-324-2044 Fax: 514-324-5900 www.groupechamplain.qc.ca
Parent: Groupe Santé Sedna inc.
Year Founded: 1966
Number of Beds: 1443 lits
Note: 15 établissements
André Brunelle, Directeur général

Montréal: L'Hôpital Chinois de Montréal (1963)
189, av Viger est, Montréal, QC H2X 3Y9
514-871-0961 Fax: 514-871-0966
Parent: Agence de la santé et des services sociaux de Montréal
Number of Beds: 128 lits
Anthony Shao, Directeur général

Montréal: Institut Canadien-Polonais du Bien-Etre inc.
5655, rue Bélanger, Montréal, QC H1T 1G2
514-259-2551 Fax: 514-259-9948
Parent: Agence de la santé et des services sociaux de Montréal
Number of Beds: 126 lits
Anna Brychcy, Directrice générale

Montréal: Manoir Cartierville
12235, rue Grenet, Montréal, QC H4J 2N9
514-337-7300 Fax: 514-337-4188
manoircartierville@ssss.gouv.qc.ca
Parent: Agence de la santé et des services sociaux de Montréal
Number of Beds: 285 lits
Eveline Lyrette, Directrice générale

Montréal: Petites Soeurs des Pauvres - Ma Maison St-Joseph
5605, rue Beaubien est, Montréal, QC H1T 1X4
514-254-4991 Fax: 514-257-1742
Parent: Agence de la santé et des services sociaux de Montréal
Number of Beds: 80 lits
Cécile de L'Enfant-Jésus, Directrice générale

Montréal: Résidence Berthiaume-du Tremblay
1635, boul Gouin est, Montréal, QC H2C 1C2
514-381-1841 Fax: 514-381-1090
www.berthiaume-du-tremblay.com
Parent: Agence de la santé et des services sociaux de Montréal
Number of Beds: 246 lits
Nicole Ouellet, Directrice générale

Montréal: La Résidence Fulford
1221, rue Guy, Montréal, QC H3H 2K8
514-935-5933 Fax: 514-933-3773
Parent: Agence de la santé et des services sociaux de Montréal
Number of Beds: 6 lits
Note: residence for women
Laurie Kirkpatrick, Directrice générale

Montréal: Résidence Rive Soleil inc.
15150, rue Notre-Dame est, Montréal, QC H1A 1W6
514-642-5509 Fax: 514-642-8320
Parent: Agence de la santé et des services sociaux de Montréal
Number of Beds: 50 lits
Christiane Chaussé, Directrice général

Montréal: Résidence Sainte-Claire inc.
8950, rue Sainte-Claire est, Montréal, QC H1L 1Z1
514-351-3877 Fax: 514-352-5956
Parent: Agence de la santé et des services sociaux de Montréal
Number of Beds: 38 lits
Yvan Daniel, Directeur général

Montréal: Résidence St-Jacques
8712, rue St-Hubert, Montréal, QC H2M 1Y5
514-389-5800 Fax: 514-389-8399
Parent: Agence de la santé et des services sociaux de Montréal
Year Founded: 1989
Number of Beds: 25 lits
Paulette Théodore, Directrice générale

Montréal: Résidence Yvon-Brunet
6250, av Newman, Montréal, QC H4E 4K4
514-765-8000 Fax: 514-765-8064
Parent: Agence de la santé et des services sociaux de Montréal
Year Founded: 1982
Number of Beds: 185 lits
Daniel Chartrand, Directeur du programme hébergement
Danielle McCann, Directrice générale
danielle.mccann@ssss.gouv.qc.ca

Montréal: Résidences Mance-Décary (CHSLD)
1800, rue St-Jacques, Montréal, QC H3J 2R5
514-935-4681 Fax: 514-935-6189
Parent: Agence de la santé et des services sociaux de Montréal
Number of Beds: 580 lits
André Paquette, Directeur général

Montréal-Nord: CHSLD Gouin inc.
4445, boul Henri-Bourassa est, Montréal-Nord, QC H1H 5M4
514-324-2044 www.groupechamplain.qc.ca
Parent: Groupe Champlain inc.
Number of Beds: 93 lits
Note: Agence/région administrative: Agence de la santé et des services sociaux de Montréal.
André Brunelle, Directeur général

Montréal-Nord: Résidence Angelica inc.
3435, boul Gouin est, Montréal-Nord, QC H1H 1B1
514-324-6110 Fax: 514-324-9332
Parent: Agence de la santé et des services sociaux de Montréal
Number of Beds: 400 lits
Anne-Marie Marolo, Directrice générale

Montréal-Nord: Villa Belle Rive inc.
5320, boul Gouin est, Montréal-Nord, QC H1G 1B4
514-321-1367 Fax: 514-322-4211
Parent: Agence de la santé et des services sociaux de Montréal
Number of Beds: 27 lits
Louis-René Lanctôt, Directeur général

New Carlisle: Centre d'hébergement de New Carlisle
108, rue Principale, New Carlisle, QC G0C 1Z0
418-752-3386 Fax: 418-752-6483
csssbc@csssbc.qc.ca
www.csssbc.qc.ca
Division of: CSSS de la Baie-des-Chaleurs
Parent: Agence de la santé et des services sociaux de la Gaspésie-Iles-de-la-Madeleine
Number of Beds: 75 lits
Bernard Nadeau, Directeur général, CSSS de la Baie-des-Chaleurs

Normandin: CLSC-CHSLD de Normandin
1205, rue St-Cyrille, Normandin, QC G8M 4K1
418-274-1234 Fax: 418-274-6970
www,csssmariachapdelaine.com
Division of: CSSS Maria Chapdelaine
Parent: Agence de la santé et des services sociaux du Saguenay-Lac-St-Jean
Number of Beds: 35 lits de soins de longue durée
Note: Centre d'hébergement; point de service CLSC; centre de jour.
Normand Brassard, Directeur général, CSSS Maria Chapdelaine

North Hatley: Connaught Home
77 Main St., North Hatley, QC J0B 2C0
819-842-2164 Fax: 819-842-2667
massawippi@videotron.ca
Number of Beds: 41 lits
Richard F. Tracy, Executive Director

North Hatley: La Maison Blanche de North Hatley inc.
CP 298, 977, rue Massawippi, North Hatley, QC J0B 2C0
819-842-2478 Fax: 819-842-2470
Number of Beds: 60 lits
Serge Croteau, Directeur général

Notre-Dame-du-Bon-Conseil: CLSC-CHSLD L'Accueil Bon-Conseil
91, rue Saint-Thomas, Notre-Dame-du-Bon-Conseil, QC J0C 1A0
819-336-2122
csssdrummond@ssss.gouv.qc.ca
www.csssdrummond.qc.ca
Division of: CSSS Drummond
Parent: Agence de la santé et des services sociaux de la Mauricie et du Centre-du-Québec
Number of Beds: 52 lits
Note: Centre d'hébergement; le point de service CLSC: 819-474-2572.
Nagui Habashi, Directeur général, CSSS Drummond

Notre-Dame-du-Nord: CHSLD des premières nations du Timiskaming
20, av Algonquin, Notre-Dame-du-Nord, QC J0Z 3B0
819-723-2225 Fax: 819-723-2112
www.sante-abitibi-temiscamingue.gouv.qc.ca; wpp01.msss.gouv.qc.ca
Division of: CSSS du Lac-Témiscamingue
Parent: Agence de la santé et des services sociaux de l'Abitibi-Témiscamingue
Number of Beds: 20 lits
Note: Établissement privé non conventionné
Estelle St-Cyr Perreault, Directrice générale

Oka: Manoir Oka inc.
CP 567, 2083, ch Oka, Oka, QC J0N 1E0
450-479-6447 Fax: 450-479-6447
Parent: Agence de la santé et des services sociaux des Laurentides
Number of Beds: 34 lits
Robert Fournier, Directeur général

Pierrefonds: Manoir Pierrefonds inc. - 9130-9377QC.inc.
18465, boul Gouin ouest, Pierrefonds, QC H9K 1A6
514-626-6651 Fax: 514-626-6415
Parent: Agence de la santé et des services sociaux de Montréal
Number of Beds: 183 unités
Lorraine Lincourt, Directrice générale

Pierreville: Foyer Lucien Shooner inc.
CP 220, 50, rue Lt-Gouv.-Paul-Comtois, Pierreville, QC J0G 1J0
450-568-2712 Fax: 450-568-3658
Parent: Agence de la santé et des services sociaux de la Mauricie et du Centre-du-Québec
Number of Beds: 38 lits
Marcel Nolet, Directeur général

Plessisville: Foyer des Bois-Francs
1450, av Trudelle, Plessisville, QC G6L 3K4
819-362-3558 Fax: 819-362-9266
Parent: Agence de la santé et des services sociaux de la Mauricie et du Centre-du-Québec
Number of Beds: 40 lits
Michel Lauzon, Directeur général

Pointe-Claire: CHSLD Bayview inc.
27, ch Lakeshore, Pointe-Claire, QC H9S 4H1
514-695-9384 Fax: 514-695-5723 www.chsldbayview.com
Also Known As: Centre Bayview
Parent: Agence de la santé et des services sociaux de Montréal

Number of Beds: 128 lits
Note: Un établissement privé de soins de longue durée.
George Guillon, Directeur général

Princeville: Centre d'hébergement de Saint-Eusèbe
CP 610, 435, rue Saint-Jacques, Princeville, QC G6L 5C5
819-364-2355 Fax: 819-364-7824 www.csssae.qc.ca
Also Known As: Foyer St-Eusèbe
Division of: CSSS d'Arthabaska-et-de-l'Érable
Parent: Agence de la santé et des services sociaux de la Mauricie et du Centre-du-Québec
Number of Beds: 26 lits
Marcel Dubois, Président, Conseil d'administration, CSSS d'Arthabaska-et-de-l

Québec: Centre d'accueil Nazareth inc.
715, rue des Glacis, Québec, QC G1R 3P8
418-694-0492 Fax: 418-694-9452
Parent: Agence de la santé et des services sociaux de la Capitale-Nationale
Number of Beds: 75 lits
Louise Gaudreault, Directrice générale

Québec: Centre d'hébergement Saint-Antoine
1451, boul Père-Lelièvre, Québec, QC G1M 1N8
418-683-2516 Fax: 418-683-4031 www.csssvc.qc.ca
Parent: Agence de la santé et des services sociaux de la Capitale-Nationale
Number of Beds: 284 lits
Note: Hébergement et soins de longue durée
Gerard Roy, Directeur général

Québec: Centre hospitalier N"tre-Dame du Chemin inc.
510, ch Ste-Foy, Québec, QC G1S 2J5
418-681-7882 Fax: 418-681-5387
Number of Beds: 50 lits
Antoine Pichette, Directeur général

Québec: Centre hospitalier St-François inc
1604, 1e av, Québec, QC G1L 3L6
418-524-6033 Fax: 418-524-9542
Number of Beds: 29 lits
Yvan Girard, Directeur général

Québec: Centre hospitalier St-Sacrement ltée
1165, ch Ste-Foy, Québec, QC G1S 2M8
418-527-4836 Fax: 418-527-1743
stephan.pichette@ssss.gouv.qc.ca
Parent: Agence de la santé et des services sociaux de la Capitale-Nationale
Number of Beds: 63 lits
Stéphan Pichette, Directeur général

Québec: CLSC-CHSLD Basse-Ville - Limoilou - Vanier
260, boul Langelier, Québec, QC G1K 5N1
418-529-0931 Fax: 418-521-5801 msss.gouv.qc.ca
Parent: Agence de la santé et des services sociaux de la Capitale-Nationale
Number of Beds: 99 lits
André Métivier, Directeur général

Québec: La Corporation Notre-Dame de Bon-Secours
990, rue Gérard-Morisset, Québec, QC G1S 1X6
418-681-4637
Number of Beds: 20 lits
Michel Bilodrau, Directeur général

Québec: Foyer Ste-Marie-des-Anges Résidence
2390, boul Masson, Québec, QC G1P 1J4
418-871-5365 www.cmafhaiti.org/foyer.htm
Number of Beds: 14 chambres
Note: Pour personnes retraitées autonomes et en perte d'autonomie
Gisèle Boivin, Directrice générale

Québec: Hôpital Ste-Monique inc.
4805, boul Wilfrid Hamel, Québec, QC G1P 2J7
418-871-8701 Fax: 418-871-0105
Number of Beds: 58 lits
Andrée Begin, Directrice générale
Edith Tassé, Directrice, Soins infirmiers et du personnel

Québec: Habitation Grande-Allée
1175, av Turnbull, Québec, QC G1R 5L5
418-522-3979 Fax: 418-522-7870
Number of Beds: 30 lits
Lyse Gauthier, Directrice générale

Québec: Résidence Louis-Hebert
1550, rue Pointe-aux-Lièvres nord, Québec, QC G1L 4M8
418-529-5511 Fax: 418-524-1143
Parent: Agence de la santé et des services sociaux de la Capitale-Nationale
Number of Beds: 52 lits
Richard Rousseau, Directeur général par intérim

Rawdon: CHSLD Heather I
3931, ch Lakeshore, Rawdon, QC J0K 1S0
450-834-3070 Fax: 450-834-5805
info@manoirheather.com
www.manoirheather.com
Also Known As: Manoir Heather/Heather Lodge
Number of Beds: 76 lits
Note: CHSLD Heather II: 3462, 3e av, Rawdon, QC J0K 1S0, 450-834-2512.
Paul Arbec, Directeur général

Rawdon: Monsieur Rémy Landry
3567, rue Church, Rawdon, QC J0K 1S0
450-834-2794 Fax: 450-834-8286
Old Name: Centre d'Accueil Bouleaux Argentés
Parent: Agences de développement de réseaux locaux de services de santé et de services sociaux
Number of Beds: 16 lits
Rémy Landry, Directeur général

Richmond: Centre d'hébergement de Richmond
980, rue McGauran, Richmond, QC J0B 2H0
819-542-2777 Fax: 819-826-5724 vsf.santeestrie.qc.ca
Division of: CSSS du Val-Saint-François
Parent: Agence de la santé et des services sociaux de l'Estrie
Number of Beds: 54 lits
Pierre Lalande, Directeur général, CSSS du Val-Saint-François

Richmond: Wales Home
Foyer Wales
506, rte 243 nord, Richmond, QC J0B 2H0
819-826-3266 Fax: 819-826-2549 www.waleshome.ca
Parent: Agence de la santé et des services sociaux de l'Estrie
Number of Beds: 190 lits
Stuart Simms, Directeur général

Rimouski: Centre d'hébergement de Rimouski
645, boul Saint-Germain ouest, Rimouski, QC G5L 3S2
418-724-4111 Fax: 418-724-0604
courrierweb.crsssr@ssss.gouv.qc.ca
www.chrr.qc.ca
Division of: CSSS de Rimouski-Neigette
Parent: Agence de la santé et des services sociaux du Bas-St-Laurent
Number of Beds: 246 lits
Raymond Coulombe, Directeur général, CSSS de Rimouski-Neigette

Rimouski: Foyer Ste-Bernadette inc.
280, av Belzile, Rimouski, QC G5L 8K7
418-723-0040 Fax: 418-723-0615
Number of Beds: 24 lits
Claude Talbot, Directeur général

Rimouski: Manoir de Caroline inc.
280, rue Belzile, Rimouski, QC G5L 8K7
418-723-0611 Fax: 418-723-0615
Number of Beds: 85 lits
Claude Talbot, Directeur général

Rivière-Bleue: Centre d'hébergement Rivière-Bleue
45, rue du Foyer sud, Rivière-Bleue, QC G0L 2B0
418-893-5511 Fax: 418-893-7151 www.cssstemiscouata.com
Division of: CSSS de Témiscouata
Parent: Agence de la santé et des services sociaux du Bas-St-Laurent
Number of Beds: 44 lits
Monique Dumas, Directrice, Services des personnes en perte d'autonomie, CSSS d

Rivière-Ouelle: Centre Thérèse-Martin
100, ch de la Petite-Anse, Rivière-Ouelle, QC G0L 2C0
418-856-7000 Fax: 418-856-4381 www.agencesssbsl.gouv.qc.ca
Division of: CSSS de Kamouraska
Parent: Agence de la santé et des services sociaux du Bas-St-Laurent
Number of Beds: 48 lits
Michel Beaulieu, Directeur général, CSSS de Kamouraska

Rivière-du-Loup: Centre d'hébergement Saint-Joseph
28, rue Joly, Rivière-du-Loup, QC G5R 3H2
418-862-6385 Fax: 418-862-1986 www.csssriviereduloup.qc.ca
Division of: CSSS de Rivière-du-Loup
Parent: Agence de la santé et des services sociaux du Bas-St-Laurent
Number of Beds: 145 lits
Note: Hébergement permanent et centre de jour.
Raymond April, Directeur général, CSSS de Rivière-du-Loup

Rouyn-Noranda: Centre d'hébergement de Rouyn-Noranda
512, av Richard, Rouyn-Noranda, QC J9X 4M1
819-762-0908 Fax: 819-764-5036
www.sante-abitibi-temiscamingue.gouv.qc.ca; www.csssrn.qc.ca
Old Name: Maison Pie XII
Division of: CSSS de Rouyn-Noranda
Parent: Agence de la santé et des services sociaux de l'Abitibi-Témiscamingue
Number of Beds: 157 lits
Note: Centre d'hébergement, centre de jour, hôpital de jour.
Huguette Lemay, Directrice générale, CSSS de Rouyn-Noranda
Annie Audet, Directrice, Programme des personnes en perte d'autonomie

Saint-Alexandre-de-Kamour: Centre Villa Maria
404, av du Foyer, Saint-Alexandre-de-Kamour, QC G0L 2G0
418-856-7000 Fax: 418-495-2829
Division of: CSSS de Kamouraska
Parent: Agence de la santé et des services sociaux du Bas-St-Laurent
Number of Beds: 46 lits
Michel Beaulieu, Directeur général, CSSS de Kamouraska

Saint-Antoine-sur-Richeli: Accueil du Rivage inc.
1008, ch du Rivage, Saint-Antoine-sur-Richeli, QC J0L 1R0
450-787-3436 Fax: 450-787-1156
communication.csssry@rrsss16.gouv.qc.ca
www.santemonteregie.qc.ca
Number of Beds: 36 lits
Jean Bergeron, Directeur général

Saint-Antonin: Centre d'hébergement de Saint-Antonin
CP 430, 286, rue Principale, Saint-Antonin, QC G0L 2J0
418-862-7993 Fax: 418-862-5278 www.csssriviereduloup.qc.ca
Division of: CSSS de Rivière-du-Loup
Parent: Agence de la santé et des services sociaux du Bas-St-Laurent
Number of Beds: 42 lits
Raymond April, Directeur général, CSSS de Rivière-du-Loup

Saint-Augustin-de-Desmaur: Jardins du Haut Saint-Laurent (1992) inc.
4770, rue Saint-Felix, Saint-Augustin-de-Desmaur, QC G3A 1B1
418-872-4936 Fax: 418-872-4245
jhsl1990@hardins-hsl.com
www.jardins-hsl.com
Number of Beds: 140 lits
Nathalie Côté, Directrice générale

Saint-Bernard-de-Lacolle: Florence Groulx inc.
7, rang Saint-Louis, Saint-Bernard-de-Lacolle, QC J0J 1V0
450-246-3879 Fax: 450-246-4111
Number of Beds: 50 lits
Daniel Gaudette, Directeur général

Saint-Bruno-de-Montarvill: Centre d'hébergement de Montarville
265, boul Seigneurial ouest, Saint-Bruno-de-Montarvill, QC J3V 2H4
450-461-2650 Fax: 450-461-2968
info@lesommetavotreportee.qc.ca
www.lesommetavotreportee.qc.ca;
www.santemonteregie.qc.ca/richelieu-yamaska
Division of: CSSS Richelieu-Yamaska
Parent: Agence de la santé et des services sociaux de la Montérégie
Number of Beds: 155 lits
Daniel Castonguay, Directeur général, CSSS Richelieu-Yamaska
Réjeanne Boudreau, Directrice du Programme hébergement-milieu de vie, CSSS Richelieu-Yamaska

Saint-Casimir: Centre d'hébergement Saint-Casimir
CP 10, 605, rue Fleury, Saint-Casimir, QC G0A 3L0
418-339-2861 Fax: 418-339-2875
Parent: Agence de la santé et des services sociaux de la Capitale-Nationale
Number of Beds: 64 lits
Fernand Morasse, Directeur général

Saint-Célestin: Centre Saint-Célestin
CP 90, 475, rue Houde, Saint-Célestin, QC J0C 1G0
819-229-3617 Fax: 819-229-1165
Parent: Agence de la santé et des services sociaux de la Mauricie et du Centre-du-Québec
Number of Beds: 52 lits
Marcel Nolet, Directeur général

Saint-Constant: **Centre d'hébergement Jean-Louis-Lapierre**
199, rue St-Pierre, Saint-Constant, QC J5A 2N8
450-632-4451 Fax: 450-632-2004
www.santemonteregie.qc.ca/jardins-roussillon
Division of: CSSS Jardins-Roussillon
Number of Beds: 76 lits
Paul Moreau, Directeur général, CSSS Jardins-Roussillon

Saint-Cyprien: **Centre d'hébergement de Saint-Cyprien**
101-C, rue Collin, Saint-Cyprien, QC G0L 2P0
418-963-2272 www.csssriviereduloup.qc.ca
Number of Beds: 20 lits
Raymond April, Directeur général, CSSS de Rivière-du-Loup

Saint-Eustache: **Société en commandite centre d'accueil l'Ermitage**
112, 25e av, Saint-Eustache, QC J7P 2V2
450-473-5961 Fax: 450-491-1847
Number of Beds: 78 lits
Kevin Shemie, Directeur général

Saint-Félicien: **Centre d'hébergement de Saint-Félicien**
Édifice Foyer de la Paix, 1229, boul Sacré-Coeur, Saint-Félicien, QC G8K 1A5
418-679-1585 Fax: 418-679-2376
hdr@ssss.gouv.qc.ca
www.cmdp-roberval.com
Division of: CSSS Domaine-du-Roy
Parent: Agence de la santé et des services sociaux du Saguenay-Lac-St-Jean
Number of Beds: 46 lits
Note: Hébergement permanent et temporaire; centre de jour.
Jacques Dubois, Directeur général, CSSS Domaine-du-Roy

Saint-Gabriel-de-Brandon: **Centre d'accueil Desy**
CP 840, 90, rue Maskinonge, Saint-Gabriel-de-Brandon, QC J0K 2N0
450-835-4712 Fax: 450-835-7606
Parent: Agences de développement de réseaux locaux de services de santé et de services sociaux
Number of Beds: 54 lits
Jacques Morin, Comptable

Saint-Georges: **Centre hospitalier de l'Assomption**
16750, boul Lacroix, Saint-Georges, QC G5Y 2G4
416-228-2041 Fax: 416-226-4117
Parent: Agence de la santé et des services sociaux de Chaudière-Appalaches

Saint-Hubert: **Centre Henriette Céré**
6435, ch de Chambly, Saint-Hubert, QC J3Y 3R6
514-678-3291 Fax: 514-443-1360
Parent: Agence de la santé et des services sociaux de la Montérégie
Number of Beds: 99 lits
Jean-Denis Godbout, Directeur général

Saint-Hubert: **Centre hospitalier Rive-sud inc.**
5300, ch Chambly, Saint-Hubert, QC J3Y 3N7
450-445-0123 Fax: 450-445-1175
Number of Beds: 34 lits
André Brunelle, Directeur général

Saint-Hubert: **Pavillon Résidence Saint-Hubert**
5160, montée Saint-Hubert, Saint-Hubert, QC J3Y 1V7
450-676-8411
Number of Beds: 38
Note: ressource intermédiaire en santé mentale

Saint-Hubert: **Pavillon St-Hubert**
3823, rue Grand Boulevard, Saint-Hubert, QC J4T 2M3
450-445-3598 Fax: 450-462-3767

Saint-Hyacinthe: **Centre d'hébergement Andrée-Perrault**
1955, av Pratte, Saint-Hyacinthe, QC J2S 7W5
514-771-4536 Fax: 450-771-5499
info@lesommetavotreportee.qc.ca
www.lesommetavotreportee.qc.ca;
www.santemonteregie.qc.ca/richelieu-yamaska
Division of: CSSS Richelieu-Yamaska
Parent: Agence de la santé et des services sociaux de la Montérégie
Number of Beds: 70 lits
Daniel Castonguay, Directeur général, CSSS Richelieu-Yamaska
Réjeanne Boudreau, Directrice du Programme hébergement-milieu de vie, CSSS Richelieu-Yamaska

Saint-Hyacinthe: **CHSLD Résidence Bourg-Joli inc.**
2915, boul Laframboise, Saint-Hyacinthe, QC J2S 4Z3
450-773-4197 Fax: 450-773-6545
Parent: Agence de la santé et des services sociaux de la Montérégie
Number of Beds: 24 lits
Marc Breton, Directeur général

Saint-Jean-sur-Richelieu: **Centre d'hébergement Georges-Phaneuf**
230, rue Jacques-Cartier nord, Saint-Jean-sur-Richelieu, QC J3B 6T4
450-346-1133 Fax: 450-346-2199
www.santemonteregie.qc.ca/haut-richelieu-rouville
Division of: CSSS Haut-Richelieu-Rouville
Parent: Agence de la santé et des services sociaux de la Montérégie
Number of Beds: 124 lits
Lucie Tétreault, Directrice, Personnes en perte d'autonomie liée au vieillisseme

Saint-Jean-sur-Richelieu: **Centre d'hébergement Gertrude-Lafrance**
150, boul Saint-Luc, Saint-Jean-sur-Richelieu, QC J3A 1G2
450-349-5555 Fax: 450-348-7693
www.santemonteregie.qc.ca/haut-richelieu-rouville
Division of: CSSS Haut-Richelieu-Rouville
Parent: Agence de la santé et des services sociaux de la Montérégie
Number of Beds: 174 lits
Lucie Tétreault, Directrice, Personnes en perte d'autonomie liée au vieillisseme

Saint-Jérome: **L'Auberge St-Jér"me Inc.**
66, rue Danis, Saint-Jérome, QC J7Y 2R3
514-436-3131
Parent: Agence de la santé et des services sociaux des Laurentides
Number of Beds: 92 lits

Saint-Jérome: **CHSLD de la Rivière du Nord**
531, rue Laviolette, Saint-Jérome, QC J7Y 2T8
450-436-3061 Fax: 450-436-8328
Parent: Agence de la santé et des services sociaux des Laurentides
Number of Beds: 305 lits
Note: Centres d'hébergement: Youville, l'Auberge, et Lucien G. Rolland.
Jean-Pierre Perreault, Directeur général

Saint-Lambert: **CHSLD de la MRC de Champlain**
831, av Notre-Dame, Saint-Lambert, QC J4R 1S1
450-672-3320 Fax: 450-672-3370
andree.ouellette@rrsss16.gouv.qc.ca
Number of Beds: 313 lits
Gisèle Lacoste, Directrice générale
Real Guilbert, Directeur, Services techniques

Saint-Lambert: **Résidence du Parc**
33, av Argyle, Saint-Lambert, QC J4P 3P5
450-878-3081 Fax: 450-465-4369
residenceduparc@reveraliving.com
www.reveraliving.com
Number of Beds: 105 lits
Denyse Saey, Directrice générale

Saint-Laurent: **Les Cèdres - Centre d'accueil pour personnes âgées**
#200, 1275, boul de la C"te-Vertu, Saint-Laurent, QC H4L 4V2
514-389-1023 Fax: 514-389-0581
Number of Beds: 25 lits
Rose Khoury, Directrice générale

Saint-Laurent: **Centre d'hébergement St-Vincent-Marie inc.**
1175, boul de la C"te-Vertu, Saint-Laurent, QC H4L 5J1
514-744-1175
Parent: Agence de la santé et des services sociaux de Montréal
Number of Beds: 66 lits
Danny Macdonald, Directeur général

Saint-Laurent: **CHSLD-CLSC Saint-Laurent**
1055, av Ste-Croix, Saint-Laurent, QC H4L 3Z2
514-748-6400 Fax: 514-748-6449
Parent: Agence de la santé et des services sociaux de Montréal
Number of Beds: 154 lits

Saint-Liguori: **Foyer Saint-Liguori**
771, rue Principale, Saint-Liguori, QC J0K 2X0
450-753-7062 Fax: 450-753-3208
Parent: Agences de développement de réseaux locaux de services de santé et de services sociaux
Number of Beds: 48 lits
Paul-Yvon de Billy, Directeur général

Saint-Louis-du-Ha!-Ha!: **Centre d'hébergement St-Louis**
25, rue Saint-Philippe, Saint-Louis-du-Ha!-Ha!, QC G0L 3S0
418-854-2631 Fax: 418-854-0430 www.cssstemiscouata.com
Division of: CSSS de Témiscouata
Parent: Agence de la santé et des services sociaux du Bas-St-Laurent
Number of Beds: 43 lits
Monique Dumas, Directrice, Services des personnes en perte d'autonomie, CSSS d

Saint-Michel-de-Bellechas: **CHSLD Vigi Notre-Dame de Lourdes**
CP 10, 80, rue Principale, Saint-Michel-de-Bellechas, QC G0R 3S0
418-884-2811 Fax: 418-884-3714 www.vigisante.com
Parent: Vigi Santé Ltée
Number of Beds: 40 lits
Note: Agence/région administrative: Agence de la santé et des services sociaux de Chaudière-Appalaches.
Vincent Simonetta, Directeur général
Michelle Harvey, Directeur adjointe, Services techniques

Saint-Michel-des-Saints: **Centre d'accueil Brassard**
CP 309, 390, rue Brassard, Saint-Michel-des-Saints, QC J0K 3B0
514-833-6331 Fax: 514-833-6093
Parent: Agences de développement de réseaux locaux de services de santé et de services sociaux
Number of Beds: 35 lits
Jean-Jacques Lamarche, Directeur général par intérim

Saint-Michel-du-Squatec: **CHSLD de Squatec**
10, rue Saint-André, Saint-Michel-du-Squatec, QC G0L 4H0
418-855-2442 Fax: 418-855-2357 www.cssstemiscouata.com
Old Name: Domaine du Sommet
Division of: CSSS de Témiscouata
Number of Beds: 24 lits
Monique Dumas, Directrice, Services des personnes en perte d'autonomie, CSSS d

Saint-Narcisse: **Centre multiservice - Centre d'accueil de St-Narcisse**
361, rue du College, Saint-Narcisse, QC G0X 2Y0
418-328-3351 Fax: 418-328-4140
Parent: Agence de la santé et des services sociaux de la Mauricie et du Centre-du-Québec
Number of Beds: 31 lits
Gilles Cossette, Directeur général

Saint-Pac"me: **Centre d'Anjou**
127, rue Galarneau, Saint-Pac"me, QC G0L 3X0
418-856-7000 Fax: 418-852-3230 www.agencesssbsl.gouv.qc.ca
Division of: CSSS de Kamouraska
Parent: Agence de la santé et des services sociaux du Bas-St-Laurent
Number of Beds: 60 lits
Michel Beaulieu, Directeur général, CSSS de Kamouraska

Saint-Pierre-les-Becquets: **Centre d'hébergement Romain-Becquet**
255, rte Marie-Victorin, Saint-Pierre-les-Becquets, QC G0X 2Z0
819-263-2245 Fax: 819-263-2636
Parent: Agence de la santé et des services sociaux de la Mauricie et du Centre-du-Québec
Number of Beds: 35 lits
Note: Hébergement permanent et temporaire
Jacqueline Côté, Chef, Administration

Saint-Raymond: **Centre hébergement Saint-Raymond**
324, rue Saint-Joseph, Saint-Raymond, QC G3L 1J7
418-337-4611 Fax: 418-337-4808
Parent: Agence de la santé et des services sociaux de la Capitale-Nationale
Number of Beds: 64 lits
Fernand Morasse, Directeur général

Saint-Rémi: **Centre d'hébergement de Saint-Rémi**
CP 820, 110, rue du Collège, Saint-Rémi, QC J0L 2L0
450-454-4694 Fax: 450-454-3614
www.santemonteregie.qc.ca/jardins-roussillon
Division of: CSSS Jardins-Roussillon
Parent: Agence de la santé et des services sociaux de la Montérégie
Number of Beds: 58 lits
Paul Moreau, Directeur général, CSSS Jardins-Roussillon

Saint-Romuald: **CHSLD Chanoine-Audet inc.**
2155, ch du Sault, Saint-Romuald, QC G6W 2K7
418-834-5322 Fax: 418-834-5754 www.groupechamplain.qc.ca
Parent: Groupe Champlain inc.

Number of Beds: 96 lits
Note: Agence/région administrative: Agence de la santé et des services sociaux de Chaudière-Appalaches.
Julie Gendreau, Directeur général

***Saint-Siméon:* CLSC-CHSLD de Saint-Siméon**
CP 7, 371, rue Saint-Laurent, Saint-Siméon, QC G0T 1X0
418-638-2414 www.cssscharlevoix.qc.ca
Division of: CSSS de Charlevoix
Parent: Agence de la santé et des services sociaux de la Capitale-Nationale
Number of Beds: 18 lits
Note: Centre local de services communautaires (418-638-2369); centre d'hébergement et centre de jour.
Micheline Tremblay, Directrice générale, CSSS de Charlevoix
micheline.tremblay@ssss.gouv.qc.ca

***Saint-Timothée:* La Maison des Aîne(e)s**
1, rue des Aînes, Saint-Timothée, QC J6S 6M8
450-377-3925 Fax: 450-377-3490
Parent: Agence de la santé et des services sociaux de la Montérégie
Number of Beds: 38 lits
Denis Charland, Directeur général

***Saint-Tite:* Centre multiservice Foyer Mgr Paquin**
CP 400, 580, rue du Couvent, Saint-Tite, QC G0X 3H0
418-365-5107 Fax: 418-365-7914
Parent: Agence de la santé et des services sociaux de la Mauricie et du Centre-du-Québec
Number of Beds: 55 lits
Gilles Cossette, Directeur général

***Sainte-Anne-de-la-Pérade:* Centre multiservice Foyer de la Pérade**
CP 217, 60, rue de la Fabrique, Sainte-Anne-de-la-Pérade, QC G0X 2J0
418-325-2313 Fax: 418-325-3233
Parent: Agence de la santé et des services sociaux de la Mauricie et du Centre-du-Québec
Number of Beds: 42 lits
Gilles Cossette, Directeur général

***Sainte-Cécile:* Pavillon Ste-Cécile**
4581, rue Principale, Sainte-Cécile, QC G0Y 1J0
819-583-0400 Fax: 819-583-0983
Number of Beds: 15 lits
Alain Hinse, Directeur général

***Sainte-Foy:* Résidence Paul Triquet**
789, rue de Belmont, Sainte-Foy, QC G1V 4V2
418-657-6890 Fax: 418-657-6894
maisonpaultriquet@mail.chuq.qc.ca
www.chuq.qc.ca/maisonpaultriquet
Also Known As: La Maison Paul-Triquet
Parent: Agence de la santé et des services sociaux de la Capitale-Nationale; CHUQ
Year Founded: 1987
Number of Beds: 64 lits
Note: Centre d'hébergement de soins de longue durée pour anciens combattants
René Rouleau, Directeur général

***Sainte-Sophie:* Centre d'hébergement Jaclo Inc.**
CP 129, 2319, rue Sainte-Marie, Sainte-Sophie, QC J0R 1S0
450-436-5627 Fax: 450-436-6663
Number of Beds: 31 lits
Claude Brière, Directeur général

***Sainte-Thérèse:* Centre d'hébergement Drapeau-Deschambault**
100, rue du Chanoine Lionel-Groulx, Sainte-Thérèse, QC J7E 5E1
450-437-4267 Fax: 450-437-0788
www.csssthereseblainville.qc.ca
Division of: CSSS de Thérèse-De Blainville
Parent: Agence de la santé et des services sociaux des Laurentides
Number of Beds: 223 lits
André Poirier, Directeur général, CSSS de Thérèse-De Blainville

***Sainte-Thérèse:* CHSLD Boise Ste-Thérèse Inc.**
179, Place Fabien-Drapeau, Sainte-Thérèse, QC J7E 5W6
450-430-6767 Fax: 450-430-6965
boisesteterese@darkshell.com
Number of Beds: 41 CHSLD privé; 60 autonomes
Stephanie Drolet, Directrice générale

***Saint-Éphrem-de-Beauce:* Résidence St-Éphrem inc.**
CP 310, 1, rue Plante, Saint-Éphrem-de-Beauce, QC G0M 1R0
418-484-2121 Fax: 418-484-2144
restep@telstep.net
Number of Beds: 40 lits
Lynda Roy, Directrice générale

***Salaberry-de-Valleyfield:* Les Centres du Haut St-Laurent (CHSLD) Valleyfield**
80, rue de Marche, Salaberry-de-Valleyfield, QC J6T 1P5
450-373-4013 Fax: 450-373-0325
chsl@rocler.qc.ca
www.rocler.qc.ca/chsl
Parent: Agence de la santé et des services sociaux de la Montérégie
Number of Beds: 177 lits
Claude Chayer, Directeur général

***Shawinigan:* CHSLD Vigi Les Chutes**
5000, av Albert-Tessier, Shawinigan, QC G9N 8P9
819-539-5408 Fax: 819-539-5400 www.vigisante.com
Parent: Vigi Santé Ltée
Number of Beds: 64 lits
Note: Agence/région administrative: Agence de la santé et des services sociaux de la Mauricie.
Vincent Simonetta, Directeur général

***Shawville:* Pavillon Pontiac**
CP 2001, 290, rue Marion, Shawville, QC J0X 2Y0
819-647-5755 Fax: 819-647-2453
Old Name: CHSLD Shawville
Parent: Agence de la santé et de services sociaux de l'Outaouais
Number of Beds: 50 lits
Joan Brown, Manager

***Sherbrooke:* Centre d'hébergement St-Joseph**
611, boul Queen-Victoria nord, Sherbrooke, QC J1H 3R6
819-780-2222 www,csss-iugs.ca
Division of: CSSS-Institut universitaire de gériatrie de Sherbrooke
Parent: Agence de la santé et des services sociaux de l'Estrie
Number of Beds: 144 lits
Carol Fillion, Directeur général, CSSS-Institut universitaire de gériatrie de Sherbro

***Sherbrooke:* CHSLD Vigi Shermont inc.**
3220, 12e av nord, Sherbrooke, QC J1H 5H3
819-820-8900 Fax: 819-820-8902 www.vigisante.com
Parent: Vigi Santé Ltée
Number of Beds: 52 lits
Note: Agence/région administrative: Agence de la santé et des services sociaux de l'Estrie.
Jean Sevigny, Directeur général

***Sherbrooke:* Les Dominicaines des saints anges gardiens**
361, rue Moore, Sherbrooke, QC J1H 1C1
819-346-5512 Fax: 819-563-5023
Old Name: Mont St-Dominique
Number of Beds: 50 lits
Nevenka Skrindar, Directrice générale

***Sillery:* Pavillon Saint-Dominique**
1045, boul René-Lévesque ouest, Sillery, QC G1S 1V3
418-681-3561 Fax: 418-687-9196
info@pavstdom.org
www.pavstdom.org
Number of Beds: 152 lits
Jeannine Nadeau, Directrice générale

***Sillery:* Saint Brigid's Home Inc.**
1645, ch Saint-Louis, Sillery, QC G1S 4M3
418-681-4687 Fax: 418-527-6862
Parent: Agence de la santé et des services sociaux de la Capitale-Nationale
Number of Beds: 162 lits
Louis Hanrahan, Directeur général

***Sorel-Tracy:* CHSLD du Bas-Richelieu**
151, rue George, Sorel-Tracy, QC J3P 1C8
450-746-5555 Fax: 450-746-4897
Number of Beds: 261 lits
René Legault, Directeur général (intérim)

***Sorel-Tracy:* Foyer Richelieu**
40, rue de Ramesay, Sorel-Tracy, QC J3P 3Y7
514-742-5936 Fax: 514-742-1613
Parent: Agence de la santé et des services sociaux de la Montérégie
Number of Beds: 60 lits
Jacques Blais, Directeur général

***Sorel-Tracy:* Hôpital Richelieu/CLSC Du Havre**
30, rue Ferland, Sorel-Tracy, QC J3P 3C7
514-743-5569 Fax: 514-743-1803
Parent: Agence de la santé et des services sociaux de la Montérégie
Number of Beds: 18 lits
Jacques Blais, Directeur général
Jeanine Larosée, Chef, Entretient sanitaire

***Sorel-Tracy:* Résidence Sorel-Tracy inc.**
4025, rue Frontenac, Sorel-Tracy, QC J3R 4G8
450-742-9428 Fax: 450-742-9668
Number of Beds: 64 lits
Julie Bien-Aimé, Directrice générale

***St-Charles-de-Bellechasse:* Résidence Charles Couillard Inc.**
20, av St-Georges, St-Charles-de-Bellechasse, QC G0R 2T0
418-887-6455 Fax: 418-887-1316
Number of Beds: 35 lits
Gerard Dion, Directeur général

***St-Georges:* Centre hospitalier de l'Assomption Inc.**
16750, boul Lacroix, St-Georges, QC G5Y 2G4
418-228-2041 Fax: 418-228-9366
Number of Beds: 96 lits
Gérard Gendreau, Directeur général

***St-Georges-de-Beauce:* CHSLD L'Assomption**
16750, boul Lacroix, St-Georges-de-Beauce, QC G5Y 2G4
418-228-2041 Fax: 418-228-9366 www.groupechamplain.qc.ca
Parent: Groupe Champlain inc.
Number of Beds: 96 lits
Note: Agence/région administrative: Agence de la santé et des services sociaux de Lanaudière.

***St-Jovite:* CLSC-CHSLD des Trois Vallées - Résidence St-Jovite**
CP 910, 925, rue Ouimet, St-Jovite, QC J0T 2H0
819-425-2793 Fax: 819-425-8857
Number of Beds: 69 lits
Christine Lessard, Directrice générale

***St-Sauveur-des-Monts:* CHSLD Villa du Vieux Sapin Inc.**
55, rue Hochar, St-Sauveur-des-Monts, QC J0R 1R6
450-227-2241 Fax: 450-227-6186
Old Name: Les Residences Desjardins
Number of Beds: 34 lits
Colette Desjardins, Directrice générale

***Ste-Cécile-de-Masham:* CLSC-CHSLD des Collines**
9, ch Passe-Partout, Ste-Cécile-de-Masham, QC J0X 2W0
819-456-1112 Fax: 819-456-4531 877-459-1112
www.santedescollines.qc.ca
Number of Beds: Centre d'hébergement La Pêche: 32 lits.
Note: Y compris le Centre d'hébergement La Pêche et le CLSC Masham.
Pierre Rochon, Directeur général, CSSS des Collines
Jean-Paul Racine, Président, Conseil d'administration

***Ste-Marguerite-du-Lac-Mas:* Manoir de la Pointe Bleue (1978)**
428, rue du Baron-Louis-Empain, Ste-Marguerite-du-Lac-Mas, QC J0T 1L0
450-228-2503 Fax: 450-228-3312
Parent: Agence de la santé et des services sociaux des Laurentides
Number of Beds: 91 lits
Jacqueline Gagnon, Directrice générale

***Sutton:* Foyer Sutton**
CP 719, 50, rue Western, Sutton, QC J0E 2K0
514-538-3332 Fax: 514-538-0514
Parent: Agence de la santé et des services sociaux de la Montérégie
Number of Beds: 74 lits
Michel Asselin, Directeur général

***Terrebonne:* CHSLD de La C"te Boisée inc.**
4300, rue d'Angora, Terrebonne, QC J6X 4P1
450-471-5877 Fax: 450-471-7511
Number of Beds: 140 lits
Gerald Asselin, Directeur général

***Thetford Mines:* Résidence La Rosée d'Or**
736, boul Ouellet ouest, Thetford Mines, QC G6G 4X5
418-335-7681 Fax: 418-338-3774
Number of Beds: 9 lits
Laurent Chartier

***Trois-Rivières:* Résidence Cooke**
3450, rue Ste-Marguerite, Trois-Rivières, QC G8Z 1X3
819-375-7713 www.csssstr.qc.ca
Division of: CSSS de Trois-Rivières
Parent: Agence de santé et des services sociaux de la Mauricie et du Centre-du-Québec
Number of Beds: 190 lits
Jacques Longval, Directeur général, CSSS de Trois-Rivières

***Trois-Rivières:* Résidence Joseph-Denys**
1274, rue Laviolette, Trois-Rivières, QC G9A 1W4
819-378-4837 Fax: 819-374-6697 www.cssstr.qc.ca
Division of: CSSS de Trois-Rivières
Parent: Agence de la santé et des services sociaux de la Mauricie et du Centre-du-Québec
Number of Beds: 119 lits
Note: Hébergement permanent et temporaire.
Jacques Longval, Directeur général, CSSS de Trois-Rivières

***Trois-Rivières:* Résidence Louis-Denoncourt**
435, rue Saint-Roch, Trois-Rivières, QC G9A 2L9
819-376-2566 Fax: 819-376-5620 www.cssstr.qc.ca
Division of: CSSS de Trois-Rivières
Parent: Agence de la santé et des services sociaux de la Mauricie et du Centre-du-Québec
Number of Beds: 75 lits
Note: Hébergement permanent
Jacques Longval, Directeur général, CSSS de Trois-Rivières

***Upton:* Domaine du Bel Age**
CP 89, 906, rue Lanoie, Upton, QC J0H 2E0
514-549-4405
Number of Beds: 9 lits
Jacqueline Gosslin, Directrice générale

***Vanier:* Résidence Christ-Roi**
300, boul Wilfrid-Hamel, Vanier, QC G1M 2R9
418-682-1711 Fax: 418-682-1770
Parent: Agence de la santé et des services sociaux de la Capitale-Nationale
Number of Beds: 142 lits
Note: Hébergement permanent/soins de longue durée, hôpital de jour, hébergement temporaire, consultations externes
Gaétan Garon, Directeur général
Lucien Jobin, Directeur, Services techniques
Francine Smith, Chef du service d'entretien sanitaire

***Varennes:* CHSLD du Littoral**
60, rue d'Youville, Varennes, QC J3X 1T6
450-652-2995 Fax: 450-652-4755
Old Name: Foyer Lajemmerais
Number of Beds: 261 lits
Bernard Lamy, Directeur général (par intérim)

***Vaudreuil-Dorion:* Le Regroupement des CHSLD des Trois Rives**
408, av St-Charles, Vaudreuil-Dorion, QC J7V 7M9
450-453-5860 Fax: 450-455-1998
Parent: Agence de la santé et des services sociaux de la Montérégie
Number of Beds: 341 lits
Lise Bélisle, Directeur général

***Vaudreuil-Dorion:* 2863-9839 Québec inc.**
170, rue Boileau, Vaudreuil-Dorion, QC J7V 8A3
450-424-6458
Parent: Agence de la santé et des services sociaux de la Montérégie
Number of Beds: 51 lits
Denis Charland, Directeur général

***Verdun:* Centre d'accueil Real Morel**
3500, rue Wellington, Verdun, QC H4G 1T3
514-761-5874 Fax: 514-761-7264
Parent: Agence de la santé et des services sociaux de Montréal
Number of Beds: 148 lits

***Victoriaville:* Centre d'hébergement du Chêne**
61, rue de l'Ermitage, Victoriaville, QC G6P 6X4
819-758-7511 Fax: 819-758-2398 www.csssae.qc.ca
Division of: CSSS d'Arthabaska-et-de-l'Érable
Parent: Agence de la santé et des services sociaux de la Mauricie et du Centre-du-Québec
Number of Beds: 122 lits
Note: Les autres centres d'hébergement: Quatre-Vents, Saint-Eusèbe, Sacré-Coeur, Étoiles-d'Or, et Roseau.
Marcel Dubois, Président, Conseil d'administration, CSSS d'Arthabaska-et-de-l

***Waterloo:* Centre de Waterloo**
5300, av Courville, Waterloo, QC J0E 2N0
450-539-5512 Fax: 450-375-5655
Parent: Agence de la santé et des services sociaux de la Montérégie
Number of Beds: 41 lits longue durée

***Waterloo:* Centre gériatrique Courville**
CP 580, 5305, av Courville, Waterloo, QC J0E 2N0
450-539-1821 Fax: 450-539-1937
ecourville@belage.qc.ca
Parent: Agence de la santé et des services sociaux de la Montérégie
Number of Beds: 52 lits
Evelyn Courville, Directrice générale

***Waterville:* Foyer de Waterville**
265, rue Compton est, Waterville, QC J0B 3H0
819-837-2454 Fax: 819-837-2916
Number of Beds: 20 lits
Jeannette Delage, Directrice générale

***Weedon:* Site Foyer de Weedon**
245, rue Saint-Janvier, Weedon, QC J0B 3J0
819-877-2500 Fax: 819-877-3089
Parent: Agence de la santé et des services sociaux de l'Estrie
Number of Beds: 53 lits
Colette Maynard, Directrice, Soins Infirmiers

***Westmount:* Centre d'accueil St-Margaret St. Margaret's Home**
50, av Hillside, Westmount, QC H3Z 1V9
514-932-3630 Fax: 514-932-4379
Number of Beds: 96 lits
Carole McDonough, Directeur général

***Westmount:* Chateau Westmount inc.**
4860, boul de Maisonneuve ouest, Westmount, QC H3Z 3G2
514-369-3000 Fax: 514-369-0014
info@chateauwestmount.ca
Parent: Agence de la santé et des services sociaux de Montréal
Number of Beds: 112 lits
Ginette Villeneuve, Directrice générale

***Wotton:* Le Centre d'accueil de Wotton**
CP 270, 666, rue Saint-Jean, Wotton, QC J0A 1N0
819-828-2251 Fax: 819-828-3555
Parent: Agence de la santé et des services sociaux de l'Estrie
Number of Beds: 23 lits
Mario Morand, Directeur général

Centres d'hébergement et des soins delongue durée (CHSLD)

***La Doré:* Ressource intermédiaire de La Doré**
CP 190, 4921, rue des Peupliers, La Doré, QC G0W 2J0
418-256-3851 Fax: 418-256-3608
hdr@ssss.gouv.qc.ca
www.cmdp-roberval.com
Also Known As: Résidence La Doré
Division of: CSSS Domaine-du-Roy
Number of Beds: 21 lits
Guy Dufour, Directeur général

***Laval:* Centre d'hébergement de Sainte-Dorothée**
350, boul Samson ouest, Laval, QC H7X 1J4
514-689-0933 Fax: 514-689-3147
Division of: CSSS de Laval
Number of Beds: 277 lits
Note: Les autres centres d'hébergement: Fernand-Larocque, Idola-Saint-Jean, La Pinière, et Rose-de-Lima.
Luc Lepage, Directeur général, CSSS de Laval

***Baie-d'Urfé:* Maxwell Residence**
678, rue Surrey, Baie-d'Urfé, QC H9X 3S1
514-457-3111 Fax: 514-457-7909 www.maxwellresidence.com
Note: Specialties: Fitness center & health programs
R.W. Maxwell, Administrator

***Laval:* Les Loggias et Villa Val des Arbres**
3245, boul St-Martin est, Laval, QC H7E 4T6
450-661-0911 Fax: 450-661-9820
info@villavaldesarbres.com
www.chartwellreit.ca; www.villavaldesarbres.com
Division of: Chartwell Seniors Housing REIT
Parent: Agence de la santé et des services sociaux de Laval
Note: Centre privé non-conventionné; 163 unités, 48 appartements, 115 chambres.
Denis Lagueux, Président, Chartwell-Québec

Hôpitaux psychiatriques et assistance communautaire

***Beauport:* Centre hospitalier Robert Giffard**
2601, rue de la Canardière, Beauport, QC G1J 2G3
418-663-5321 Fax: 418-663-9774 www.rgiffard.qc.ca
Parent: Agence de la santé et des services sociaux de la Capitale-Nationale
Number of Beds: 503 lits
Michel Gervais, Directeur général

***Fatima:* Centre de réadaptation en déficience intellectuelle-TED**
695, ch des Caps, Fatima, QC G4T 2S9
418-986-3590 Fax: 418-986-5778 www.agencesssgim.ca; www.csssdesiles.qc.ca
Parent: Agence de la santé et des services sociaux de la Gaspésie-Iles-de-la-Madeleine

***Gatineau:* Centre hospitalier Pierre-Janet**
20, rue Pharand, Gatineau, QC J9A 1K7
819-771-7761 Fax: 819-771-2908
www.pierre-janet.qc.ca/bienvenue.htm
Parent: Agence de la santé et de services sociaux de l'Outaouais
Number of Beds: 87 lits
Pierre Gagnon, Directeur général
Michel Thivierge, Chef, Services techniques
819/776-8096

***Malartic:* Hôpital psychiatrique de Malartic**
CP 800, 1141, rue Royale, Malartic, QC J0Y 1Z0
819-757-4342 Fax: 819-757-4330
www.sante-abitibi-temiscamingue-gouv.qc.ca; www.csssvo.qc.ca
Division of: CSSS de la Vallée-de-l'Or
Parent: Agence de la santé et des services sociaux de l'Abitibi-Témiscamingue
Number of Beds: 34 lits
Note: Services de santé mentale et psychiatrie; soins aigus; soins de longue durée.
Jérôme Lamont, Directeur général, CSSS de la Vallée-de-l'Or
Alain Beaucage, Directeur, Programme santé mentale/psychiatrie

***Montréal:* Hôpital Louis-H. Lafontaine**
7401, rue Hochelaga, Montréal, QC H1N 3M5
514-251-4000 Fax: 514-251-0856 www.hlhl.qc.ca
Parent: Agence de la santé et des services sociaux de Montréal
Number of Beds: 606 lits
André Lemieux, Directeur général

***Montréal:* Hôpital Rivière-des-Prairies**
7070, boul Perras, Montréal, QC H1E 1A4
514-323-7260 Fax: 514-323-8622 www.hrdp.qc.ca
Parent: Agence de la santé et des services sociaux de Montréal
Number of Beds: 125 lits
Michel Lapointe, Directeur général

***Québec:* Centre de réadaptation en déficience intellectuelle de Québec**
110, rue de Courcelette, Québec, QC G1M 2S8
418-529-9141 Fax: 418-529-7318
Parent: Agence de la santé et des services sociaux de la Capitale-Nationale
Renaud Turmel, Directeur général (intérim)

***Saint-Wenceslas:* Centre l'Aubier inc.**
CP 27, 1170, rue Sainte-Thérèse, Saint-Wenceslas, QC G0Z 1J0
819-224-7669
Number of Beds: 50 lits
Francine P. Lampron, Directrice générale

Saskatchewan

Government Departments in Charge

SASKATCHEWAN: Saskatchewan Health
T.C. Douglas Building, 3475 Albert St., Regina, SK S4S 6X6
306-787-0146 Fax: 306-787-8310
info@health.gov.sk.ca
www.health.gov.sk.ca
Note: Establishes policy & standards, provides funding, supports regional health authorities, & ensures the provision of essential health services. Branches: acute & emergency services, communications, community care branch, Deputy Minister's Office, drug plan & extended benefits, financial services, Health Information Solutions Centre, health registration & vital statistics, human resources, medical services, policy & planning branch, population health, primary health services, regional accountability, regional policy, Saskatchewan Disease Control Laboratory, & workforce planning
Ernie Craig, Senior Information Consultant

Regional Health Authorities

***Black Lake:* Athabasca Health Authority**
PO Box 124, Black Lake, SK S0J 0H0
306-439-2200 Fax: 306-439-2211
vrobillard@athabascahealth.ca
www.athabascahealth.ca
Note: Provides health care services to the First Nations communities of Black Lake, & Fond du Lac; Stony Rapids; Uranium City; & Camsell Portage.
Georgina Macdonald, CEO

***Buffalo Narrows:* Keewatin Yatthé Regional Health Authority**
Metis Society Bldg., PO Box 40, Pederson Ave., Buffalo Narrows, SK S0M 0J0

306-235-2220 Fax: 306-235-2229 866-274-8506
richard.petit@kyrha.sk.ca
www.kyrha.ca
Number of Beds: 58 beds
Carol Gillis, CEO

***La Ronge:* Mamawetan Churchill River Health Region**
PO Box 6000, La Ronge, SK S0J 1L0
306-425-2422 Fax: 306-425-5513
information@mcrrha.sk.ca
www.mcrrha.sk.ca
Note: Regional health authority serving over 22,000 people
Kathy Chisholm, CEO

***Moose Jaw:* Five Hills Health Region**
455 Fairford St. East, Moose Jaw, SK S6H 1H3
306-694-0296 Fax: 306-694-0282 1-888-425-1111
inquiries@fhhr.ca
www.fhhr.ca
Note: Facilities: In-patient acute care hospitals in Assiniboia, Central Butte, Gravelbourg, & Moose Jaw; Health & wellness centres in Craik, Kincaid, Lafleche, Rockglen, Mossbank, & Willow Bunch. Number of Employees: 1,700. Population Served: 55,246. Area Served: South-central Saskatchewan
Cheryl Craig, Chief Executive Officer
Velma Geddes, Chair
Craig Beesley, Executive Director, Strategy & Communications
306-694-0300

***North Battleford:* Prairie North Health Region**
1092 - 107 St., North Battleford, SK S9A 1Z1
306-446-6606 Fax: 306-446-4114
cora.r@pnrha.ca
www.pnrha.ca
David Fan, CEO

***Prince Albert:* Prince Albert Parkland Health Region**
PO Box 5700, 2345 - 10 Ave. West, Prince Albert, SK S6V 7V6
306-765-6100 Fax: 306-763-6096 800-922-1834
kholmgren@paphr.sk.ca
www.paphr.sk.ca
Cecile Hunt, CEO

***Regina:* Regina Qu'Appelle Health Region**
2180 - 23 Ave., Regina, SK S4S 0A5
306-766-5279 Fax: 306-766-5222 888-354-8111
publicaffairs@rqhealth.ca
www.rqhealth.ca
Number of Beds: 1,504 beds
Note: Offers health services and programs to over 245,000 people across 120 communities
Dwight Nelson, President; CEO

***Rosetown:* Heartland Regional Health Authority**
PO Box 2110, 100 Hwy. #4 South, Rosetown, SK S0L 2V0
306-882-4111 Fax: 306-882-1389
heartland@hrha.sk.ca
www.hrha.sk.ca
Number of Beds: 499 long term care beds; 67 acute care; 50 other
Note: Facilities in 16 communities, including a district hospital in Kindersley. Services include primary & acute health care, emergency services, telehealth, public health, dental health, counselling, addictions services, occupation therapy, speech & language therapy, nutrition.
Ken Wersch, CEO/President

***Saskatoon:* Saskatoon Regional Health Authority**
Saskatoon Square, 410 - 22nd St. East, 3rd Fl., Saskatoon, SK S7K 5T6
306-655-3300 Fax: 306-655-3394
general.inquiries@saskatoonhealthregion.ca
www.saskatoonhealthregion.ca
Number of Beds: 830 beds
Note: Provides health services to over 290,000 people across over 100 communities
Maura Davies, CEO/President

***Swift Current:* Cypress Health Region**
429 - 4th Ave. NE, Swift Current, SK S9H 2J9
306-778-5100 Fax: 306-773-9513 1-888-461-7443
info@cypressrha.ca
www.cypresshealth.ca
Note: Facilities: 20 hospitals, long term care facilities, & health centres. Number of Employees: 1,650. Population Served: 44,000. Area Served: Southwest Saskatchewan
Tyler Bragg, Chair
Ivo Radevski, Senior Medical Officer
Beth Adashynski, Executive Director, Quality & Privacy
Larry Allsen, Executive Director, Finance
Bryce Martin, Executive Director, Communications
Brenda Schwan, Executive Director, Human Resources
Beth Vachon, Executive Director, Community Health Services
Kim Kruse, Director, Executive & Board Support

***Tisdale:* Kelsey Trail Regional Health Authority**
PO Box 1780, 901 - 108 Ave. Wet, Tisdale, SK S0E 1T0
306-873-3898 Fax: 306-873-3224
ddobson@kthr@shin.sk.ca
www.kelseytrailhealth.ca
Number of Beds: 61 beds
Joe Kirwan, Interim President; CEO

***Weyburn:* Sun Country Health Region**
PO Box 2003, Weyburn, SK S4H 2Z9
306-842-8718 Fax: 306-842-8738
info@schr.sk.ca
www.suncountry.sk.ca
Number of Beds: 461 beds
Calvin Tant, CEO

***Yorkton:* Sunrise Regional Health Authority**
270 Bradbrooke Dr., Yorkton, SK S3N 2K6
306-786-0103 Fax: 306-786-0122
www.sunrisehealthregion.sk.ca
Number of Beds: 561 beds
Joe Kirwan, CEO

Hospitals

Hospitals - General

***Arcola:* Arcola Health Centre**
PO Box 419, 607 Prairie Ave., Arcola, SK S0C 0G0
306-455-2771 Fax: 306-455-2397 www.suncountry.sk.ca
Parent: Sun Country Regional Health Authority
Note: Hospital Specialties: Emergency; Inpatient services

***Assiniboia:* Assiniboia Union Hospital**
501 - 6 Ave., Assiniboia, SK S0H 0B0
306-642-3351 www.fhhr.ca
Parent: Five Hills Regional Health Authority
Number of Beds: 12 acute care beds; 4 respite / palliative care beds
Note: Hospital specialties: Emergency service; Acute care; Laboratory service; Respite care; Palliative care

***Balcarres:* Balcarres Integrated Care Centre/BICC**
PO Box 340, 100 South Elgin St., Balcarres, SK S0G 0C0
306-334-2634 Fax: 306-334-2674 www.rqhealth.ca
Parent: Regina Qu'Appelle Health Region
Year Founded: 1999
Number of Beds: 9 acute care beds; 42 long term beds; 2 respite beds
Note: Hospital Specialties: Emergency services; Acute care; Physiotherapy; Diabetes education; Mental health & drug & alcohol counselling; Respite services; Day care services; Home care nursing; Long term care Number of Employees: 90
Lorraine Mazerall, Facility Manager
lorraine.mazerall@rqhealth.ca
Elaine Stefanick, Coordinator, Care

***Big River:* Big River Health Centre**
PO Box 100, 220 - 1st Ave. North, Big River, SK S0J 0E0
306-469-2220 www.paphr.sk.ca
Parent: Prince Albert Parkland Regional Health Authority
Number of Beds: 9 acute care beds; 28 long term care beds; 2 respite care beds; 1 palliative care bed
Note: Specialties: Emergency services; Acute care; Laboratory services; Public health services; Physiotherapy; Occupational therapy; Long term care; Home care; Respite care; Palliative care

***Biggar:* Biggar Union Hospital**
PO Box 130, 501 - 1 Ave. West, Biggar, SK S0K 0M0
306-948-3323 Fax: 306-948-2011 www.hrha.sk.ca
Parent: Heartland Regional Health Authority
Number of Beds: 13 acute care beds, 2 other
Note: Acute care.
Marian Fritz, Facility Manager

***Broadview:* Broadview Hospital**
PO Box 100, 901 Nina St., Broadview, SK S0G 0K0
306-696-2441 Fax: 306-696-2611 www.rqhealth.ca
Parent: Regina Qu'Appelle Health Region
Number of Beds: 16 acute care beds
Note: Hospital Specialties: Emergency services; Diagnostic services; Ambulatory care; Native liaison work; Respite care; Palliative care
Jacqui Fawcett-Kennett, Manager

jacqui.fawcett-kennett@rqhealth.ca

***Canora:* Canora Hospital**
PO Box 749, 1219 Main St., Canora, SK S0A 0L0
306-563-5621 Fax: 306-563-5571
www.sunrisehealthregion.sk.ca
Parent: Sunrise Regional Health Authority
Year Founded: 1968
Number of Beds: 16 acute care beds; 10 long term care beds; 2 respite beds
Note: Hospital Specialties: Emergency services; Laboratory services; Radiology; Acute care; Occupational therapy; Respite care; Long term care
Karen Kraynick, Administrator

***Central Butte:* Central Butte Regency Hospital**
PO Box 40, Central Butte, SK S0H 0T0
306-796-2190
inquiries@fhhr.ca
www.fhhr.ca
Parent: Five Hills Regional Health Authority
Number of Beds: 5 acute care beds; 22 residents at special care home
Note: Hospital Specialties: Acute care; Special care home

***Davidson:* Davidson & District Health Centre**
PO Box 758, 900 Government Rd., Davidson, SK S0G 1A0
306-567-2801 Fax: 306-567-2073 www.hrha.sk.ca;
www.townofdavidson.com/services/healthservices.php
Parent: Heartland Regional Health Authority
Number of Beds: 30 long term care beds, 2 acute care, 6 other
Note: Acute care, long term care.
Cathy Hinther, Care Team Manager

***Esterhazy:* St. Anthony's Hospital**
PO Box 280, 216 Ancona St., Esterhazy, SK S0A 0X0
306-745-3973 Fax: 306-745-3245
www.sunrisehealthregion.sk.ca/default.aspx?page=15
Parent: Sunrise Regional Health Authority
Year Founded: 1940
Number of Beds: 22 acute care beds
Note: Emergency & outpatient services, visiting primary care services & dietition, x-ray
Joe Kirwan, CEO, SRHA
306-786-0103, Fax: 306-786-0122
Sharon Tropin, Director, Communication, SRHA
306- 786-014
Carol Unchulenko, Facility Administrator
carol.unchulenko@shr.sk.ca

***Estevan:* St. Joseph's Hospital**
PO Box 5000, 1174 Nicholson Rd., Estevan, SK S4A 2V6
306-637-2400 Fax: 306-637-2490
Parent: Sun Country Regional Health Authority
Number of Beds: 93 beds
Darwin Giem, Executive Director
Emile Wilvers, Maintenance Manager
306/634-0418

***Fort Qu'Appelle:* All Nations Healing Hospital/ANHH**
PO Box 300, 450 - 8th St., Fort Qu'Appelle, SK S0G 1S0
306-332-5611 Fax: 306-332-5033
gboehme@fhqtc.com (Director of ANHH & Health Services)
www.fortquappelle.com/anhh.html
Parent: Regina Qu'Appelle Health Region
Number of Beds: 13 acute care beds + 1 palliative care bed
Note: Hospital Specialties: First Nations health services; Acute care; Emergency services; Women's health (306-332-2673); Mental health; Diabetes education; Nutrition education; Number of Employees: 100
Lorna Breitkreuz, Director, Client Services
306-332-2440, lbreitkreuz@fhqtc.com

***Gravelbourg:* St. Joseph's Hospital/Foyer d'Youville**
PO Box 50, 216 Bettez St., Gravelbourg, SK S0H 1X0
306-648-3185 Fax: 306-648-3440
thinks_stjoes@sasktel.net
www.stjosephshospital-gravelbourg.com
Parent: Five Hills Regional Health Authority
Number of Beds: 9 hospital beds, 50 nursing home beds

***Hafford:* Hafford Hospital & Special Care Centre**
PO Box 130, 213 South Ave. East, Hafford, SK S0J 1A0
306-549-4266 Fax: 306-549-4660
Parent: Prince Albert Parkland Regional Health Authority
Number of Beds: 18 beds
Linda E. Fendelet, Director of Care

***Herbert:* Herbert Morse Hospital**
PO Box 220, 303 Brownlee St., Herbert, SK S0H 2A0
306-784-2202 Fax: 306-784-3452
Parent: Cypress Regional Health Authority

***Hudson Bay:* Hudson Bay Health Care Facility**
PO Box 940, 614 Prince St., Hudson Bay, SK S0E 0Y0
306-865-2219 Fax: 306-865-2429

Parent: Kelsey Trail Regional Health Authority
Number of Beds: 15 beds
Note: integrated facility with acute, long-term care & respite & daycare
Sharon Wood, Director, Health Services

Humboldt: Humboldt District Hospital
PO Box 10, 1210 - 9 St. North, Humboldt, SK S0K 2A0
306-682-2603 Fax: 306-682-4046
www.saskatoonhealthregion.ca/your_health/ch_humbolt.htm
Old Name: St. Elizabeth's Hospital
Parent: Saskatoon Regional Health Authority
Number of Beds: 42 beds
Rick Schindel, Executive Director

Ile-a-la-Crosse: St. Joseph's Hospital
PO Bag 500, Ile-a-la-Crosse, SK S0M 1C0
306-833-2016 Fax: 306-833-2556
Parent: Keewatin Yatthé Regional Health Authority
Number of Beds: 31 beds, including 12 longterm care beds
Lorraine Roy, Administrator

Indian Head: Indian Head Union Hospital
PO Box 340, 300 Hospital St., Indian Head, SK S0G 2K0
306-695-2272 Fax: 306-695-2525
Parent: Regina Qu'Appelle Health Region
Number of Beds: 15 beds
Peter Fell, Supervisor, Plant Maintenance
Karen Earnshaw, Manager

Kamsack: Kamsack Hospital/Kamsack Nursing Home
PO Box 429, 341 Stewart St., Kamsack, SK S0A 1S0
306-542-2635 Fax: 306-542-4360
Parent: Sunrise Regional Health Authority
Number of Beds: 20 acute care, 63 long-term care, 2 respite beds
Chris Meyer, Hospital Administrator

Kelvington: Kelvington Hospital
PO Box 70, 512 - 1 Ave. South, Kelvington, SK S0A 1W0
306-327-4711 Fax: 306-327-5115
Parent: Kelsey Trail Regional Health Authority
Number of Beds: 18 beds
Denise Geck, Director, Health Services

Kerrobert: Kerrobert Integrated Health Care Facility
PO Box 320, 635 Alberta Ave., Kerrobert, SK S0L 1R0
306-834-2646 Fax: 306-834-1007 www.hrha.sk.ca
Parent: Heartland Health Region
Number of Beds: 26 long term care beds, 24 acute/program/long term care
Note: Long term care facility + health centre.
Fenton Yeo, Facility Manager
B. Roszell, Supervisor, Physical Plant

Kindersley: Kindersley Integrated Health Care Facility
1003 - 1 St. West, Kindersley, SK S0L 1S2
306-463-2611 Fax: 306-463-4550 www.hrha.sk.ca
Parent: Heartland Regional Health Authority
Number of Beds: 21 acute care beds, 5 other; 80 long term care beds
Note: Long term care; acute care.
Wanda Desrosiers, Facility Manager
Harvey Penner, Chief Engineer

Kipling: Kipling Memorial Health Centre
PO Box 420, 803 - 1 St., Kipling, SK S0G 2S0
306-736-2552 Fax: 306-736-8407
Parent: Sun Country Health Region
Number of Beds: 14 beds
Colleen Easton, Manager, Health Services
A. Gall, Supervisor, Physical Plant

La Loche: La Loche Health Centre
Bag 1, La Loche, SK S0M 1G0
306-822-6333 Fax: 306-822-2112 888-688-7072
Parent: Keewatin Yatthé Regional Health Authority
Number of Beds: 27 beds
Mary Bradstreet-Metali, Director, Primary Care

Lanigan: Lanigan Hospital
PO Box 609, 306 Downing Dr., Lanigan, SK S0K 2M0
306-365-1400 Fax: 306-365-3354
www.saskatoonhealthregion.ca/your_health/ch_lanigan.htm
Parent: Saskatoon Regional Health Authority
Number of Beds: 10 beds
Janet Lees, Manager

Leader: Leader Hospital
423 Main St. East, Leader, SK S0N 1H0
306-628-3845 Fax: 306-628-3320
www.cypresshealth.ca/leader.htm
Parent: Cypress Regional Health Authority
Number of Beds: 24

Lestock: St. Joseph's Integrated Care Centre
PO Box 280, 505 Westmoor St., Lestock, SK S0A 2G0
306-274-2215 Fax: 306-274-2045
Parent: Regina Qu'Appelle Health Region
Number of Beds: 16 beds
F. Ricci, Manager, Plant Maintenance
Kate Beattie, Manager

Lloydminster: Lloydminster Hospital
3820 - 43 Ave., Lloydminster, SK S9V 1Y5
306-820-6000 Fax: 306-825-6516
Parent: Prairie North Health Region
Number of Beds: 58 acute care beds
Note: Hospital Specialties: Cancer treatment & Care-Alberta Community Cancer Centres; Hemodialysis - Northern Alberta Renal Program; Surgical services & recovery; Obstetrics; Paediatrics; Special care unit. Number of Employees: 664
Lois Sonnega, Director, Acute Care

Loon Lake: Loon Lake Hospital & Special Care Home
PO Box 69, 510 - 2nd Ave., Loon Lake, SK S0M 1L0
306-837-2114 Fax: 306-837-2268
Parent: Prairie North Health Region
Neal Sylvestre, Director, Rural Health Facilities

Maidstone: Maidstone Health Complex
PO Box 160, 214 - 5th Ave. East, Maidstone, SK S0M 1M0
306-893-2622 Fax: 306-893-2922
Parent: Prairie North Health Region
Number of Beds: 11 acute beds + 24 long-term care beds + 2 respite beds
Note: Specialties: Community health services, including home care & counselling; Acute care; Long-term care wing; Respite care; Palliative care
Emily Hardy, Facility Manager

Maple Creek: Maple Creek Hospital
PO Box 1330, Hwy. 21 South, Maple Creek, SK S0N 1N0
306-662-2611 Fax: 306-662-3210
www.cypresshealth.ca/maplecreek.htm
Parent: Cypress Regional Health Authority
Number of Beds: 20

Meadow Lake: Northwest Health Facility
#2, 711 Centre St., Meadow Lake, SK S9X 1E6
306-236-1500 Fax: 306-236-3244
Also Known As: Meadow Lake Hospital
Parent: Prairie North Health Region
Note: Specialty: Acute care; Diagnostic imaging
Debbie Carey, Director, Acute Care Services

Melfort: Melfort Hospital
PO Box 1480, 510 Broadway Ave., Melfort, SK S0E 1A0
306-752-8700 Fax: 306-752-8711 www.kelseytrailhealth.ca
Parent: Kelsey Trail Regional Health Authority
Note: Specialties: Acute care; General Surgery; Radiology services; Chemotherapy; Mental health & addiction services; Diabetes & Heart Health Centre; Palliative care
Judy Blair, Director, Health Services

Melville: St. Peter's Hospital
PO Box 1810, 200 Heritage Dr., Melville, SK S0A 2P0
306-728-5407 Fax: 306-728-4870
www.sunrisehealthregion.sk.ca/default.aspx?page=21
Parent: Sunrise Regional Health Authority
Year Founded: 1942
Number of Beds: 30 acute care beds
Note: Emergency services, obstetrics, general surgery, outpatient services, physiotherapy, social work, Lifeline Response Centre, chemotherapy outreach program, pharmacy
Joe Kirwan, CEO, SRHA
306-786-0103, Fax: 306-786-0122
Sharon Tropin, Director, Communications, SRHA
306- 786-014
Kim Bucsis, Site Manager
Fax: 306-728-1859, kim.bucsis@shr.sk.ca

Moose Jaw: Moose Jaw Union Hospital
455 Fairford St. East, Moose Jaw, SK S6H 1H3
306-694-0200 Fax: 306-694-5596
Parent: Five Hills Regional Health Authority
Number of Beds: 120 beds
Dan Florizone, CEO
John Borody, President; CEO

Moosomin: Southeast Integrated Care Centre - Moosomin
PO Box 1, 320 Gertie St., Moosomin, SK S0G 3N0
306-435-3303 Fax: 306-435-3211
Old Name: Moosomin Union Hospital
Parent: Regina Qu'Appelle Health Region
Number of Beds: 27 in-patient; 58 long-term
Dan Ireland, Supervisor, Physical Plant
Sharon Ann Wood, Manager

Nipawin: Nipawin Hospital
PO Box 389, 800 - 6 St. East, Nipawin, SK S0E 1E0
306-862-4643 Fax: 306-862-9310
Parent: Kelsey Trail Regional Health Authority
Number of Beds: 36 beds
Marg Currie, Director, Health Services

North Battleford: Battlefords Union Hospital
1092 - 107 St., North Battleford, SK S9A 1Z1
306-446-6600 Fax: 306-446-6561 www.pnrha.ca
Parent: Prairie North Health Region
Number of Beds: 200 beds
Note: Hospital specialties: Emergency services; Acute care; Day patient clinic
Shelly Horsman, Nurse Manager
Shelly.Horsman@pnrha.ca
Sharon Jaindl, Health Information Services
Sharon.Jaindl@pnrha.ca
Pam Nyholt, Supervisor, Laboratory
Pam.Nyholt@pnrha.ca

Outlook: Outlook & District Health Centre
PO Box 309, 609 Pangman St., Outlook, SK S0L 2N0
306-867-8676 Fax: 306-867-9449
Parent: Heartland Regional Health Authority
Year Founded: 2008
Number of Beds: 11 acute care beds + 45 continuing care beds
Note: Specialties: Acute care; Diagnostic services; Therapies; Community health; Public health inspecitions; Mental health services; Home care; Long-term care; Respite care; Adult day care; Palliative care
Thelma McPherson, Facility Manager

Porcupine Plain: Porcupine Carragana Hospital
PO Box 70, Windsor Ave., Porcupine Plain, SK S0E 1H0
306-278-2211 Fax: 306-278-3088
Parent: Kelsey Trail Regional Health Authority
Number of Beds: 13 beds
Christine Pohl, Director, Heatlh Services
Keith Butler, Supervisor, Physical Plant

Preeceville: Preeceville & District Integrated Health Centre
PO Box 469, 712 - 7 St. NE, Preeceville, SK S0A 3B0
306-547-2102 Fax: 306-547-2223
Old Name: Preeceville Hospital; Preeceville & District Integ
Parent: Sunrise Regional Health Authority
Number of Beds: 10 acute care, 38 long-term care beds
Note: Doctors' medical clinic, acute & long-term care
G. Jolson, Director, Physical Plant
Joanne Bodnar, Nurse Administrator

Prince Albert: Victoria Hospital
1200 - 24 St. West, Prince Albert, SK S6V 5T4
306-764-1551 Fax: 306-763-5322
Parent: Prince Albert Parkland Regional Health Authority
Number of Beds: 147 beds
Tom Graham, Director, Housekeeping
John Piggott, Director, Operations

Redvers: Redvers Health Centre
PO Box 30, 18 Eichhorst St., Redvers, SK S0C 2H0
306-452-3553 Fax: 306-452-3556
Parent: Sun Country Regional Health Authority
Number of Beds: 12 beds
Myrna Petersen, Manager, Health Services
Joe Chicione, Maintenance

Regina: Pasqua Hospital
4101 Dewdney Ave., Regina, SK S4T 1A5
306-766-2222 Fax: 306-766-2745
Parent: Regina Qu'Appelle Health Region
Number of Beds: 179 beds
Dwight Nelson, President; CEO
Darrell Tunstead, Director, Property Management Services
306/766-2314

Regina: Regina General Hospital
1440 - 14 Ave., Regina, SK S4P 0W5
306-766-4444 Fax: 306-766-4723
Parent: Regina Qu'Appelle Health Region
Number of Beds: 404 beds
Note: Offers full-range acute care services; home to the Wasakaw Pisim Native Health Centre, Sleep Disorders Centre, and 50-bed mental health facility
Dwight Nelson, President; CEO

Darrell Tunstead, Director, Property Management Services
306/766-2314

Rosetown: **Rosetown & District Health Centre**
PO Box 850, Hwy. 4 North, Rosetown, SK S0L 2V0
306-882-2672 Fax: 306-882-3335
Parent: Heartland Health Region
Year Founded: 1964
Number of Beds: 22 beds
Gail Adamowski, Facility Manager

Rosthern: **Rosthern Hospital**
PO Box 309, 2016 - 2 St., Rosthern, SK S0K 3R0
306-232-4811 Fax: 306-232-4887
Parent: Saskatoon Regional Health Authority
Year Founded: 1950
Number of Beds: 30 beds
Note: Acute care facility with six physicians on-staff, plus 60 employees
Henry Zacharias, Supervisor
Robert Hogel, Administrator

Saskatoon: **Royal University Hospital**
103 Hospital Dr., Saskatoon, SK S7N 0W8
306-655-1000 Fax: 306-655-1037
Parent: Saskatoon Regional Health Authority
Year Founded: 1955
Number of Beds: 377 beds
Jim Fergusson, President
Clarence Clotter, MHO; General Manager, Public Health Services
306/655-4338, Fax: 306/655-4414

Saskatoon: **St. Paul's Hospital**
1702 - 20 St. West, Saskatoon, SK S7M 0Z9
306-655-5800 Fax: 306-655-5555 www.stpaulshospital.org
Parent: Saskatoon Regional Health Authority
Number of Beds: 213 beds
Brenda FizGerald, CEO
Jerri Taman, Manager, Housekeeping
David Loveridge, Manager, Powerhouse

Saskatoon: **Saskatoon City Hospital**
701 Queen St., Saskatoon, SK S7K 0M7
306-655-8000 Fax: 306-655-8269
Parent: Saskatoon Regional Health Authority
Year Founded: 1909
Number of Beds: 280 beds
John Malcolm, President
Richard Rodda, Vice-President, Support Services & Operations

Shellbrook: **Shellbrook & District Hospital**
PO Box 70, 211 - 2nd Ave. W, Shellbrook, SK S0J 2E0
306-747-2603 Fax: 306-747-3004
Parent: Prince Albert Parkland Regional Health Authority
Number of Beds: 20 beds
Mansford Kennedy, Supervisor, Physical Plant
Clifford E. Skange, Administrator

Spiritwood: **Spiritwood & District Health Complex**
PO Box 159, 400 - 1 St. East, Spiritwood, SK S0J 2M0
306-883-2133 Fax: 306-883-4446 800-887-6251
Parent: Prince Albert Parkland Regional Health Authority
Number of Beds: 36 beds
Cecile Hunt, CEO, PAPRHA
306-765-6405, Fax: 306-765-6401
Carroll Joyes, Director, Long Term Care, PAPRHA
Doug Dahl, Communication Officer, PAPRHA
306-765-6409

Swift Current: **Cypress Regional Hospital**
2004 Saskatchewan Dr., Swift Current, SK S9H 5M8
306-778-9400 Fax: 306-773-9431
http://www.cypressrha.ca/facilities_sc_page.htm
Old Name: Swift Current Regional Hospital
Parent: Cypress Regional Health Authority
Year Founded: 1951
Note: Services include intensive care, long-term care, palliative care, inpatient and outpatient surgery, renal dialysis, pediatric care, CT scans, obstetrics/gynecology, midwifery and general medical care.
Beth Vachon, interim CEO, CRHA
Bryce Martin, Executive Director, Communications, CRHA

Tisdale: **Tisdale Hospital**
PO Box 1630, 2010 - 110th Ave. West, Tisdale, SK S0E 1T0
306-873-2621 Fax: 306-873-5994 www.kelseytrailhealth.ca
Parent: Kelsey Trail Regional Health Authority
Note: Specialties: Acute care; Diabetes & Heart Health Centre; Hemodialysis satellite unit; Mental health & addiction services; Home care; Palliative care
Anne Haley-Callaghan, Manager, Community Health

Unity: **Unity & District Health Centre**
PO Box 741, Hwy. 14 North, Unity, SK S0K 4L0
306-228-2666 Fax: 306-228-2292
Old Name: Unity Hospital
Year Founded: 2001
Note: Specialties: Acute care; Diagnostic services; Maternity services; Community health services; Public health nursing; Mental health services; Counselling; Physiotherapy; Occupational therapy; Home care; Long-term care; Respite care; Palliative care
Kim Halter, Facility Manager
Randy Scherr, Supervisor, Plant Maintenance

Uranium City: **Uranium City Health Centre**
PO Box 360, Baska Rd., Uranium City, SK S0J 2W0
306-498-2412 Fax: 306-498-2577
Parent: Athabasca Health Authority

Wadena: **Wadena Hospital**
PO Box 10, 533 - 5 St. NE, Wadena, SK S0A 4J0
306-338-2515 Fax: 306-338-2720
Parent: Saskatoon Regional Health Authority
Year Founded: 1989
Number of Beds: 18 beds
Note: Provides acute, respite, and long-term care
Dayle Maryniak, Site Manager

Wakaw: **Wakaw Hospital**
PO Box 309, 301 - 1 St. North, Wakaw, SK S0K 4P0
306-233-4611 Fax: 306-233-5990
Parent: Saskatoon Regional Health Authority
Number of Beds: 22 beds
Note: Acute care facility
Pat Taciuk, Manager

Watrous: **Watrous Hospital**
PO Box 130, 702 - 4 St. East, Watrous, SK S0K 4T0
306-946-1200 Fax: 306-946-2369
Parent: Saskatoon Regional Health Authority
Number of Beds: 14 beds
J. Reichert, Supervisor, Physical Plant
Wendy Crouch, Manager

Wawota: **Wawota Memorial Health Centre**
PO Box 60, 609 Choo Foo Cres., Wawota, SK S0G 5A0
306-739-2244 Fax: 306-739-2479
Parent: Sun Country Regional Health Authority
Number of Beds: 6 beds
Laurel Charles, Manager, Health Services

Weyburn: **Weyburn General Hospital**
PO Box 2003, 201 - 1 Ave. NE, Weyburn, SK S4H 2Z9
306-842-8400 Fax: 306-842-0737
Parent: Sun Country Regional Health Authority
Number of Beds: 50 beds
Lee Spencer, CEO
Gene Schmidt, Director, Materials Management
Don Rose, Director, Physical Plant

Wolseley: **Wolseley Memorial Union Hospital**
PO Box 458, 801 Ouimet St., Wolseley, SK S0G 5H0
306-698-2213 Fax: 306-698-2988
Parent: Regina Qu'Appelle Health Region
Number of Beds: 15 beds
Jeanette Switzer, Facilities Manager

Wynyard: **Wynyard Integrated Facility**
PO Box 670, 400 - 1st St. West, Wynyard, SK S0A 4T0
306-554-6126 Fax: 306-554-2765
Parent: Saskatoon Regional Health Authority
Number of Beds: 58 beds
J. Skilinick, Supervisor, Physical Plant
Lara Prystai, Manager, Client Services

Yorkton: **Yorkton Regional Health Centre**
270 Bradbrooke Dr., Yorkton, SK S3N 2K6
306-782-2401 Fax: 306-786-6295
www.shr.sk.ca/default.aspx?page=27
Parent: Sunrise Regional Health Authority
Number of Beds: 87 beds; 6 ICU; 12 Pediatrics; 15 maternity; 21 surgery
Donna Milbrandt, Director, Client Services

Federal

Saskatoon: **Regional Psychiatric Centre (Prairies)**
c/o Correctional Service Canada, 2520 Central Ave., Saskatoon, SK S7K 3X5
306-975-5400 Fax: 306-975-6024
Number of Beds: 210 beds
Peter Guenter, Executive Director

Community Health Centres

Community Health Care Centres

Arborfield: **Arborfield & District Health Care Centre**
PO Box 160, 5 Ave., Arborfield, SK S0E 0A0
306-769-8757 Fax: 306-769-8759
Parent: Kelsey Trail Regional Health Authority
Number of Beds: 36 beds
Sharon Frisky, Director, Health Services

Beauval: **Beauval Health Centre**
PO Box 68, Beauval, SK S0M 0G0
306-288-4800 Fax: 306-288-2225
Parent: Keewatin Yatthé Regional Health Authority
Robin Wallace, Nurse, Primary Care

Beechy: **Beechy Health Centre**
PO Box 68, 226 1st Ave. North, Beechy, SK S0L 0C0
306-859-2118 Fax: 306-859-2206 www.hrha.sk.ca; www.beechysask.ca/healthcare.htm
Parent: Heartland Regional Health Authority
Note: Primary health care, lab/radiology services, visiting community health services: public health, counselling, occupational health, nutrition.
Donna Sutherland, Primary Health

Bengough: **Bengough Health Centre**
PO Box 399, 400 - 2 St. West, Bengough, SK S0C 0K0
306-268-2048 Fax: 306-268-4339
bhc@sk.sympatico.ca
Parent: Sun Country Health Region
Number of Beds: 28 long-term care beds, 1 palliative, 1 respite, 2 observato
Madonna L. Unterresner, Community Health Services Manager

Birch Hills: **Birch Hills Medical Centre**
PO Box 578, 7 Wilson St., Birch Hills, SK S0J 0G0
306-749-3331 Fax: 306-749-2440
Parent: Prince Albert Parkland Regional Health Authority
Karl Humeniuk, CEO

Black Lake: **Athabasca Health Facility**
PO Box 124, Black Lake, SK S0J 0H0
306-439-2200 Fax: 306-439-2210
Parent: Athabasca Health Authority
Year Founded: 2003
Number of Beds: 14 beds
Note: Located on the Chicken Indian Reserve. Services include acute care, birthing services, long term care, emergency & ambulatory care, public health, mental health, addictions therapy, traditional healing, radiology & lab services.

Borden: **Borden Community Health Centre**
PO Box 90, Borden, SK S0K 0N0
306-997-2110 Fax: 306-997-2114
Parent: Saskatoon Regional Health Authority
Monica Kohlhammer, Administrator

Buffalo Narrows: **Buffalo Narrows Health Centre**
PO Box 40, Buffalo Narrows, SK S0M 0J0
306-235-5800 Fax: 306-235-4500
Parent: Keewatin Yatthé Regional Health Authority
Kate Cote, Nurse, Primary Care

Cabri: **Prairie Health Care Centre**
PO Box 79, 517 - 1 St. North, Cabri, SK S0N 0J0
306-587-2623 Fax: 306-587-2751
Parent: Cypress Regional Health Authority
Number of Beds: 22 beds
Dean Scott, Supervisor, Maintenance

Carrot River: **Carrot River Health Centre**
PO Box 10, 4101 - 1 Ave. West, Carrot River, SK S0E 0L0
306-768-2725 Fax: 306-768-3233
Parent: Kelsey Trail Regional Health Authority
Number of Beds: 38 beds
Bessie Lefebvre, Director, Health Services

Climax: **Border Health Centre**
PO Box 60, 301 - 1 St. West, Climax, SK S0N 0N0
306-293-2222 Fax: 306-293-2860 www.cypresshealth.ca/climax
Parent: Cypress Regional Health Authority
Number of Beds: 4 beds

Coronach: **Coronach Health Centre**
PO Box 150, 240 South Ave. East, Coronach, SK S0H 0Z0
306-267-2022 Fax: 306-267-2324
Parent: Sun Country Health Region
Number of Beds: 15 beds
Judy Ludtke, Manager, Community Health Services
306/267-2123

Craik: **Craik & District Health Centre**
PO Box 208, 620 Mary St., Craik, SK S0G 0V0
306-734-2288 Fax: 306-734-2248
Parent: Five Hills Regional Health Authority
Number of Beds: 16 beds

Creighton: **Creighton Health Centre**
PO Box 219, Creighton, SK S0P 0A0
306-688-8620 Fax: 306-688-8629
Parent: Mamawetan Churchill River Health Region

Cudworth: **Cudworth Nursing Home/Health Centre**
PO Box 190, 607 - 4 Ave., Cudworth, SK S0K 1B0
306-256-3423 Fax: 306-256-3343
Parent: Saskatoon Regional Health Authority
Number of Beds: 32 beds
Rose Normand, Site Manager

Cumberland House: **Cumberland House Health Centre**
PO Box 8, 2 Ave., Cumberland House, SK S0E 0S0
306-888-2244 Fax: 306-884-2269
Parent: Kelsey Trail Regional Health Authority

Cupar: **Cupar Health Centre**
PO Box 100, Cupar, SK S0G 0Y0
306-723-4300 Fax: 306-723-4416
Parent: Regina Qu'Appelle Health Region
Betty Smith, Acting Manager

Cut Knife: **Cut Knife Health Complex**
PO Box 220, Cut Knife, SK S0M 0N0
306-398-4718 Fax: 306-398-2206
Parent: Prairie North Health Region
Number of Beds: 33 beds
Note: attached Special Care Home
Louise Blais, Facility Manager

Delisle: **Delisle Community Health & Social Centre**
305 First St. West, Delisle, SK S0L 0P0
306-493-2810 Fax: 306-493-2812
Parent: Saskatoon Regional Health Authority
M. Shostal, CEO

Dinsmore: **Dinsmore Health Care Centre**
PO Box 219, 1 St. East, Dinsmore, SK S0L 0T0
306-846-2222 Fax: 306-846-2225
Parent: Heartland Regional Health Authority
Number of Beds: 18 long term care beds, 4 other
Note: Long term care; visiting care services include physiotherapy, occupational therapy, mental health consultation, nutrition, child health.
Anne Rankin, Facility Manager
Jim Cheyne, Supervisor, Plant Maintenance

Dodsland: **Dodsland Clinic**
4 Ave., Dodsland, SK S0L 0V0
306-356-2172
Old Name: Dodsland Health Centre
Note: community-owned clinic

Eastend: **Eastend Wolf Willow Health Centre**
PO Box 490, 555 Redcoat Dr., Eastend, SK S0N 0T0
306-295-3534 Fax: 306-295-3223
Parent: Cypress Regional Health Authority
Number of Beds: 24 beds

Eatonia: **Eatonia Health Centre**
205 - 2nd Ave. West, Eatonia, SK S0L 0Y0
306-967-2591 Fax: 306-967-2373 www.hrha.sk.ca; www.townofeatonia.com/services/healthcare.html
Parent: Heartland Regional Health Authority
Note: Physician services; wellness program; lab/radiology; home care services; emergency services; occupational therapy; pharmacy deliveries.
Faye Hofer, Facility Manager

Edam: **Lady Minto Health Care Center**
PO Box 330, Edam, SK S0M 0V0
306-397-2222 Fax: 306-397-2225
caroll.s@pnrha.ca
Parent: Prairie North Health Region
Number of Beds: 2 convalescent, 3 respite, 1 palliative, 14 long-term care b
Note: integrated facility
Caroll Spence, Facility Manager

Elrose: **Elrose Health Centre**
PO Box 100, 505 Main St., Elrose, SK S0L 0Z0
306-378-2882 Fax: 306-378-2812 www.hrha.sk.ca
Parent: Heartland Regional Health Authority
Number of Beds: 30 long term care beds, 3 other
Note: Long term care; respite/palliative & convalescent.
Wendy Smith, Care Team Manager

Eston: **Eston Health Centre**
PO Box 667, 800 Main St., Eston, SK S0L 1A0
306-962-3667 Fax: 306-962-3900 www.hrha.sk.ca
Parent: Heartland Regional Health Authority
Number of Beds: 32 long term care beds, 4 other
Ruth Miller, Facility Manager, Care
R. Hartsook, Supervisor, Plant Maintenance

Fillmore: **Fillmore Union Health Centre**
PO Box 246, 100 Main St., Fillmore, SK S0G 1N0
306-722-3315 Fax: 306-722-3877
Old Name: Fillmore Health Centre
Parent: Sun Country Health Region
Number of Beds: 25 beds
Reg Fisher, Manager, Physical Plant Maintenance
Linda Wilson, Director, Community Services

Foam Lake: **Foam Lake Health Centre**
PO Box 190, 715 Saskatchewan Ave. East, Foam Lake, SK S0A 1A0
306-272-3325 Fax: 306-272-4449
Parent: Sunrise Regional Health Authority
Brianna Arneson, Manager, Health Services

Gainsborough: **Gainsborough & Area Health Centre**
PO Box 420, 312 Stephens St., Gainsborough, SK S0G 1S0
306-685-2277 Fax: 306-685-4636
Parent: Sun Country Health Region
Number of Beds: 19 beds
R. Spencer, Supervisor, Physical Plant
Laurie Cole, Administrator

Goodsoil: **L. Gervais Memorial Health Centre**
PO Box 100, Main St., Goodsoil, SK S0M 1A0
306-238-2100 Fax: 306-238-4449
Parent: Prairie North Health Region
Number of Beds: 18 beds
Note: health centre with a nursing home & attached special care home
Louise Roth, Facility Manager

Grenfell: **Grenfell Health Centre**
PO Box 243, 721 Stella St., Grenfell, SK S0G 2B0
306-697-2853 Fax: 306-697-3459
Parent: Regina Qu'Appelle Health Region
Diana Lerner, Manager

Gull Lake: **Gull Lake Special Care Centre**
PO Box 539, 751 Grey St., Gull Lake, SK S0N 1A0
306-672-4700 Fax: 306-672-4133
Parent: Cypress Regional Health Authority
Number of Beds: 37 beds

Hodgeville: **Hodgeville Health Centre**
PO Box 232, 105 Main St., Hodgeville, SK S0H 2B0
306-677-2292 Fax: 306-677-2584
Parent: Cypress Regional Health Authority

Imperial: **Long Lake Valley Integrated Facility**
PO Box 180, Imperial, SK S0G 2J0
306-963-2210 Fax: 306-963-2518
publicaffairs@rqhealth.ca (Regina Qu'Appelle Health Region)
Parent: Regina Qu'Appelle Health Region
Year Founded: 1992
Number of Beds: 15 long term care beds; 3 respite or palliative beds
Note: Specialties: Short-term & long-term care; Respite & day care services; Well baby clinics; Foot Care clinics; Outreach programs; Education programs
Wanda Gustafson, Administrator

Invermay: **Invermay Health Centre/Gateway Lodge**
PO Box 160, 303 - 4 Ave. North, Invermay, SK S0A 1M0
306-593-2133 Fax: 306-593-4566
Parent: Sunrise Regional Health Authority
Number of Beds: 26 beds
Oney Pollock, Manager, Health Services

Ituna: **Ituna Pioneer Health Care Centre**
PO Box 130, 320 - 5 Ave. East, Ituna, SK S0A 1N0
306-795-2622 Fax: 306-795-3592
Parent: Sunrise Regional Health Authority
Number of Beds: 38 beds
Shelley Cherney, Administrator, Health Services

Kincaid: **Kincaid Health Centre**
PO Box 179, Municipal Rd., Kincaid, SK S0H 2J0
306-264-3233 Fax: 306-264-3878
Parent: Five Hills Regional Health Authority
Pat Williamson, Sec.-Treas.

Kinistino: **Kinistino Health Centre**
111 Meyers Ave., Kinistino, SK S0J 1H0
306-864-2292
Parent: Prince Albert Parkland Regional Health Authority
Number of Beds: 10 beds

Kyle: **Kyle & District Health Centre**
PO Box 70, 208 - 3 Ave. East, Kyle, SK S0L 1T0
306-375-2251 Fax: 306-375-2422
Parent: Heartland Health Region
Number of Beds: 19 beds
Wendy Gunderson, Facility Manager

La Ronge: **La Ronge Health Centre**
PO Box 6000, 227 Backlund St., La Ronge, SK S0J 1L0
306-425-2422 Fax: 306-425-5432
information@mcrrha.sk.ca
www.mcrrha.sk.ca
Parent: Mamawetan Churchill River Health Region
Number of Beds: 18 acute, 14 longterm, 8 detox, 8 pediatric, 2 respite
Kathy Chisholm, CEO

Lafleche: **LaFleche & District Health Centre**
PO Box 159, 315 Main St., Lafleche, SK S0H 2K0
306-472-5230 Fax: 306-472-5405
Parent: Five Hills Regional Health Authority
Number of Beds: 16 beds

Lampman: **Lampman Community Health Centre**
PO Box 100, 309 - 2 Ave. East, Lampman, SK S0C 1N0
306-487-2561 Fax: 306-487-3103
Parent: Sun Country Health Region
Number of Beds: 22 beds
Bernadette Wright, Community Coordinator
G. Neumier, Manager, Plant Maintenance

Langenburg: **Langenburg Health Centre**
200 Heritage Dr., Langenburg, SK S0A 2A0
306-743-2661 Fax: 306-743-5025
Parent: Sunrise Regional Health Authority
Number of Beds: 48 beds

Leoville: **Evergreen Health Centre**
PO Box 160, 238 - 2nd St., Leoville, SK S0J 1N0
306-984-2136 Fax: 306-984-2046
Parent: Prince Albert Parkland Regional Health Authority
Number of Beds: 17 beds
Note: Nursing home
Terri Kirushelniski, Director of Care

Leroy: **Leroy Community Health & Social Centre**
PO Box 7, 211 - 1 Ave. NE, Leroy, SK S0K 2P0
306-286-3347 Fax: 306-286-3888
Parent: Saskatoon Regional Health Authority

Lloydminster: **Lloydminster & District Co-operative Health Services Ltd.**
PO Box 530, Lloydminster, SK S9V 0Y6
306-825-4427

Lucky Lake: **Lucky Lake Health Centre**
First Ave., Lucky Lake, SK S0L 1Z0
306-858-2133 Fax: 306-858-2312
Parent: Heartland Health Region
Bruce Iverarity, Maintenance
Betty Ann Trumbley, Facility Manager

Macklin: **St. Joseph's Health Centre**
PO Box 190, Hwy. 31 North, Macklin, SK S0L 2C0
306-753-2115 Fax: 306-753-2181
Parent: Heartland Health Region
Number of Beds: 3 acute care; 23 long term care
Fenton Yeo, Executive Director

Maryfield: **Maryfield Health Centre**
PO Box 164, 233 Main St., Maryfield, SK S0G 3K0
306-646-2133 Fax: 306-646-2088
Parent: Sun Country Regional Health Authority

Midale: **Mainprize Manor & Health Centre**
PO Box 239, 206 South St., Midale, SK S0C 1S0
306-458-2300 Fax: 306-458-2764
Parent: Sun Country Health Region
Note: Specialties: Doctor clinics; Outpatient service; Day respite care; Long-term care
Bernadette Wright, Director, Community Services

Montmartre: **Montmartre Health Centre**
PO Box 206, 237 - 2 Ave. East, Montmartre, SK S0G 3M0
306-424-2222 Fax: 306-424-2227
Parent: Regina Qu'Appelle Health Region
Number of Beds: 16 beds
Marg Hayes, Facility Manager

Mossbank: **Mossbank Health Centre**
General Delivery, Mossbank, SK S0H 3G0
306-354-2300 Fax: 306-354-2819

Parent: Five Hills Regional Health Authority

***Neilburg:* Manitou Health Centre**
PO Box 190, 105 - 2nd Ave. W, Neilburg, SK S0M 2C0
306-823-4262 Fax: 306-823-4590
Parent: Prairie North Health Region
Louise Blais, Coordinator, Health Services

***Neudorf:* Neudorf Health & Social Centre**
420 Main St., Neudorf, SK S0A 2T0
306-748-2566 Fax: 306-748-2868
Note: Senior centre

***Nokomis:* Nokomis Health Centre (Puffer Special Care Home Corp.).**
PO Box 98, 103 - 2 Ave. East, Nokomis, SK S0G 3R0
306-528-2114 Fax: 306-528-4655
Parent: Saskatoon Regional Health Authority
Number of Beds: 17 beds
Wendy Renwick, Manager, Client Services

***Oxbow:* Galloway Health Centre**
PO Box 268, 917 Tupper St., Oxbow, SK S0C 2B0
306-483-2956 Fax: 306-483-5178
Parent: Sun Country Health Region
Number of Beds: 14 beds
Bill Cannon, Community Coordinator

***Pangman:* Pangman Health Centre**
PO Box 90, 211 Keeler St., Pangman, SK S0C 2C0
306-442-2044 Fax: 306-442-4227 www.suncountry.sk.ca
Parent: Sun Country Regional Health Authority
Note: Specialties: Rehabilitation services; Public health inspection; Mental health services; Diabetes program; Ambulance services; Home care; Palliative care
Pat Kessler, Community Health Services Manager

***Paradise Hill:* Paradise Hill Health Centre**
PO Box 179, 1st Ave., Paradise Hill, SK S0M 2G0
306-344-2255 Fax: 306-344-2277 www.pnrha.ca
Parent: Prairie North Health Region
Neal Sylvestre, Director, Rural Facilities

***Pinehouse:* Pinehouse Health Centre**
PO Box 70, Pinehouse, SK S0J 2B0
306-884-5670 Fax: 306-884-5689 www.mcrrha.sk.ca
Parent: Mamawetan Churchill River Health Region
Note: Specialties: Public health; Health education; Primary care; Addiction services; Mental health services; Home care services

***Ponteix:* Ponteix Health Centre**
PO Box 600, 428 - 2 Ave., Ponteix, SK S0N 1Z0
306-625-3382 Fax: 306-625-3764 1-877-800-0002
www.cypresshealth.ca/ponteix.htm/
Parent: Cypress Health Region
Note: Specialties: Radiology, Laboratory Services, Home Care, Nutrition, Mental Health, Baby Clinic, Public Health, Foyer St. Joseph Nursing Home, Ambulance Service

***Prince Albert:* Prince Albert Co-Operative Health Centre**
110 - 8 St. East, Prince Albert, SK S6V 0V7
306-763-6464 Fax: 306-763-2101
Parent: Prince Albert Parkland Regional Health Authority
E. Calder, Administrator

***Quill Lake:* Quill Lake Community Health & Social Centre**
PO Box 126, 50 Main St., Quill Lake, SK S0A 3E0
306-383-2266 Fax: 306-383-2290
Parent: Saskatoon Regional Health Authority

***Radville:* Radville Marian Health Centre**
217 Warren St., Radville, SK S0C 2G0
306-869-2224 Fax: 306-869-2653
Parent: Sun Country Health Region
Number of Beds: 51 beds
Robert Shaw, Administrator

***Raymore:* Raymore Community Health & Social Centre**
PO Box 134, 806 - 2 Ave., Raymore, SK S0A 3J0
306-746-2231 Fax: 306-746-4639
Parent: Regina Qu'Appelle Health Region
Year Founded: 1981
Andrea Sebastian, Contact

***Regina:* Al Ritchie Health Action Centre**
325 Victoria Ave., Regina, SK S4N 0P5
306-766-7660 Fax: 306-766-7409 www.rqhealth.ca
Parent: Regina Qu'Appelle Health Region
Note: Provides GED exam support services, skills registry, job search support, prenatal nutrition advice, community computer, Dad's Group, family crafts, quit smoking program, seniors' potluck lunch, community kitchen, foot care, primary care nurse (by appt), food bank referrals, video lending library.
D. Lemon, Supervisor

***Regina:* Four Directions Community Health Centre**
3510 - 5 Ave., Regina, SK S4T 0M2
306-766-7540 Fax: 306-766-7534
Parent: Regina Qu'Appelle Health Region
Sharon Banning, Supervisor

***Rockglen:* Grasslands Health Centre**
PO Box 219, 1006 Hwy. 2, Rockglen, SK S0H 3R0
306-476-2030 Fax: 306-476-2534
Parent: Five Hills Regional Health Authority
Number of Beds: 17 beds

***Rose Valley:* Rose Valley Health Centre**
PO Box 310, 119 McCallum St., Rose Valley, SK S0E 1M0
306-322-2115 Fax: 306-322-2037
Parent: Kelsey Trail Regional Health Authority
Judy Moen, Community Health Manager

***Sandy Bay:* Sandy Bay Health Centre**
PO Box 39, Sandy Bay, SK S0P 0G0
306-754-5400 Fax: 306-754-5429
Parent: Mamawetan Churchill River Health Region
Note: Provides Primary Care, Public Health, Health Education, Telehealth, and Home Care services

***Saskatoon:* Community Health Services (Saskatoon) Association Ltd.**
455 - 2 Ave. North, Saskatoon, SK S7K 2C2
306-664-4241 Fax: 306-644-4120
Parent: Saskatoon Regional Health Authority

***Smeaton:* Smeaton & District Health Centre**
PO Box 158, Smeaton, SK S0J 2J0
306-426-2051 Fax: 306-426-2229
Parent: Kelsey Trail Regional Health Authority
Margo Marshall, Community Coordinator

***Southey:* Southey Health Action Centre**
PO Box 519, Southey, SK S0G 4P0
306-726-2239 Fax: 306-726-4472
southeyhealth@sasktel.net
www.rqhealth.ca
Parent: Regina Qu'Appelle Health Region
Rosemary Flaman, Contact

***Spalding:* Spalding Community Health Centre**
PO Box 220, 133 Centre St., Spalding, SK S0K 4C0
306-872-2011 Fax: 306-872-2186
Parent: Saskatoon Regional Health Authority
Jan Berger, Manager

***St Walburg:* St Walburg Health Complex**
PO Box 339, St Walburg, SK S0M 2T0
306-248-6719 Fax: 306-248-3413
Parent: Prairie North Health Region
Number of Beds: 31 beds
Note: attached special care home
Chris Thiele, Facility Manager

***Strasbourg:* Strasbourg & District Health Centre**
303 Edward St., Strasbourg, SK S0G 4V0
306-725-3220 Fax: 306-725-4060 www.townofstrasbourg.ca
Parent: Saskatoon Regional Health Authority
Year Founded: 1974
Note: Specialties: Physiotherapy; Counselling; Public health services
Tracy Hastings, Manager

***Turtleford:* Riverside Health Complex**
PO Box 10, 1 St. South, Hwy. 303, Turtleford, SK S0M 2Y0
306-845-2195 Fax: 306-845-2772 www.pnrha.ca
Parent: Prairie North Health Region
Number of Beds: 31 beds
Note: Attached special care home
Neal Sylvestre, Director, Rural Health Facilities

***Vanguard:* Vanguard Health Care Centre**
PO Box 190, Division St., Vanguard, SK S0N 2V0
306-582-2044 Fax: 306-582-4833
Parent: Cypress Regional Health Authority
Note: Weekly clinic, nurse practitioner on staff, lab & x-ray services twice a week, visiting health professionals
Suresh Kassett, Family Physician

***Weyakwin:* Weyakwin Health Centre**
General Delivery, Weyakwin, SK S0J 1W0
306-663-6100 Fax: 306-663-6165
Parent: Mamawetan Churchill River Health Region

***Whitewood:* Whitewood Community Health Centre**
PO Box 669, 921 Gambetta St., Whitewood, SK S0G 5C0
306-735-2688 Fax: 306-735-2512
Parent: Regina Qu'Appelle Health Region
Number of Beds: 30 beds
Muriel Beutler, Manager

***Wilkie:* Wilkie & District Health Centre/Poplar Courts**
PO Box 459, 304 - 7 Ave. East, Wilkie, SK S0K 4W0
306-843-2644 Fax: 306-843-3222
Parent: Heartland Regional Health Authority
Number of Beds: 4 acute care, 37 long-term care beds
Carrien Glassford, Care Team Manager

***Willow Bunch:* Willow Bunch Wellness Centre**
PO Box 6, 17 - 3 St. East, Willow Bunch, SK S0H 4K0
306-473-2310 Fax: 306-473-2677
Parent: Five Hills Regional Health Authority

***Wynyard:* Community Health Services Association**
PO Box 1539, 315 Bosworth St., Wynyard, SK S0A 4T0
306-554-3363 Fax: 306-554-2994
Parent: Saskatoon Regional Health Authority
Sharon Armstrong

Nursing Stations

***Stony Rapids:* Black Lake Nursing Station**
General Delivery, Stony Rapids, SK S0J 2R0
306-284-2124 Fax: 306-264-2090

Special Treatment Centre

***Melville:* Saul Cohen Family Resource Centre**
PO Box 164, 720 Manitoba St., Melville, SK S0A 2P0
306-728-2629 Fax: 306-728-5569
saulcohencentre@hotmail.com
www.geocities.com/HotSprings/Resort/9900/
Parent: Sunrise Regional Health Authority
Note: Outpatient counseling & support individuals & families affected by addictions
Sherry Shumay

***North Battleford:* Saskatchewan Hospital**
PO Box 39, North Battleford, SK S9A 2X8
306-446-6800 Fax: 306-445-5392
Parent: Prairie North Health Region
Number of Beds: 156 beds
Note: psychiatric rehabilitation hospital
Linda Shynkaruk, Director

***Regina:* Wascana Rehabilitation Centre**
2180 - 23 Ave., Regina, SK S4S 0A5
306-766-5100 Fax: 306-766-5244
Parent: Regina Qu'Appelle Health Region
Number of Beds: 307 inpatient
Note: rehabilitation centre, long term care centre
Dwight Nelson, President; CEO

Nursing Homes

***Assiniboia:* Assiniboia Pioneer Lodge**
PO Box 1120, 800 - 1 St. West, Assiniboia, SK S0H 0B0
306-642-3311 Fax: 306-642-3099
Parent: Five Hills Regional Health Authority
Number of Beds: 128 beds
Jim Larson, Administrator

***Assiniboia:* Ross Payant Centennial Home**
PO Box 1120, 300 Jubilee Place, Assiniboia, SK S0H 0B0
306-642-3330 Fax: 306-642-3243
Old Name: Ross Payant Centennial Home
Parent: Five Hills Regional Health Authority
Number of Beds: 38 beds

***Big River:* Lakewood Lodge**
PO Box 760, Big River, SK S0J 0E0
306-469-2333 Fax: 306-469-2193
Number of Beds: 29 beds
Helen Donald, Director, Care

***Biggar:* Diamond Lodge Co. Ltd.**
PO Box 340, 402 - 2 St. West, Biggar, SK S0K 0M0
306-948-3385 Fax: 306-948-5421
Parent: Heartland Regional Health Authority
Number of Beds: 60 beds
Jo Angelopoulos, Facility Manager

***Birch Hills:* Birchview Nursing Home**
PO Box 578, 7 Wilson St., Birch Hills, SK S0J 1J0
306-749-2288 Fax: 306-749-2440
Old Name: Birchview Lodge
Parent: Prince Albert Parkland Regional Health Authority
Number of Beds: 30 beds

***Broadview:* Broadview & District Centennial Lodge Inc.**
PO Box 670, 310 Calgary St., Broadview, SK S0G 0K0
306-696-2459 Fax: 306-696-2577
Parent: Regina Qu'Appelle Health Region
Number of Beds: 36 beds
Linda Zinkhan, Manager

***Canwood:* Whispering Pine Place Inc.**
PO Box 418, 300 - 1st Ave., Canwood, SK S0J 0K0
306-468-2900 Fax: 306-468-2199
Parent: Prince Albert Parkland Regional Health Authority
Number of Beds: 30 beds
Brenda Person, Administrator

***Carlyle:* Moose Mountain Lodge**
PO Box 729, 6 St. West, Carlyle, SK S0C 0R0
306-453-2434 Fax: 306-453-2726
Parent: Sun Country Health Region
Number of Beds: 52 beds
Joanne Hollingshead, Manager
Harold Smith, Maintenance

***Carnduff:* Sunset Haven**
PO Box 250, 415 Spencer St., Carnduff, SK S0C 0S0
306-482-3424 Fax: 306-482-5233 www.suncountry.sk.ca
Parent: Sun Country Health Region
Note: Specialties: Long-term care; Home care; Palliative care
Cathy Stephenson, Sec.-Treas.
Shirley Wright, Director of Care

***Central Butte:* Central Butte Regency Hospital**
PO Box 430, Central Butte, SK S0H 0T0
306-796-4338 Fax: 306-796-4407
Parent: Five Hills Regional Health Authority
Number of Beds: 22 beds
Debbie Bauck, Program Coordinator

***Cupar:* Cupar & District Nursing Home Inc.**
PO Box 310, 213 Mills St., Cupar, SK S0G 0Y0
306-723-4228 Fax: 306-723-4248
Parent: Regina Qu'Appelle Health Region
Number of Beds: 48 beds
Betty Smith, Interim Administrator

***Duck Lake:* Duck Lake & District Nursing Home Inc.**
PO Box 370, Victoria Ave., Duck Lake, SK S0K 1J0
306-467-4440 Fax: 306-467-2220
Division of: Goodwill Manor
Parent: Saskatoon Regional Health Authority
Number of Beds: 30 beds
Jean-Marie Allard, Facility Coordinator

***Estevan:* Estevan Regional Nursing Home**
PO Box 5000, 1921 Wallock Rd., Estevan, SK S4A 2V6
306-634-2689 Fax: 306-634-7906
Parent: Sun Country Health Region
Number of Beds: 76 beds
Brenda Rabman, Administrator

***Eston:* Jubilee Lodge Inc.**
822 Main St., Eston, SK S0L 1A0
306-962-3667 Fax: 306-962-3900
ruth.miller@hrha.sk.ca
www.hrha.sk.ca
Parent: Heartland Health Region
Number of Beds: 37 beds
Ruth Miller, Administrator
W. Turner, Director, Physical Plant

***Foam Lake:* Foam Lake Jubilee Home**
PO Box 460, 421 Alberta Ave. East, Foam Lake, SK S0A 1A0
306-272-4141 Fax: 306-272-4973
Parent: Sunrise Regional Health Authority
Number of Beds: 51 beds
Arlene Scratton, Manager, Health Services

***Fort Qu'appelle:* Echo Lodge**
PO Box 1790, 560 Broadway St. West, Fort Qu'appelle, SK S0G 1S0
306-332-4300 Fax: 306-332-5708
Parent: Regina Qu'Appelle Health Region
Number of Beds: 51 beds
Darlene Demoskoff

***Grenfell:* Grenfell & District Pioneer Home**
PO Box 760, 710 Regina Ave., Grenfell, SK S0G 2B0
306-697-2842 Fax: 306-697-2280
Parent: Regina Qu'Appelle Health Region
Number of Beds: 34 beds
Diana Lerner, Manager
Rick Gerhardt, Maintenance

***Indian Head:* Golden Prairie Home**
PO Box 250, 916 Eden St., Indian Head, SK S0G 2K0
306-695-3636 Fax: 306-695-2698
Parent: Regina Qu'Appelle Health Region
Number of Beds: 38 beds
Karen Earnshaw, Manager

***Kelvington:* Kelvindell Lodge**
PO Box 280, 701 - 6 Ave. West, Kelvington, SK S0A 1W0
306-327-5151 Fax: 306-327-4504
Parent: Kelsey Trail Regional Health Authority
Number of Beds: 46 beds
Shelley Rutherford, Asst. Manager, Community Health
Kevin O'Neil, Maintenance

***Kerrobert:* Buena Vista Lodge**
645 Columbia Ave., Kerrobert, SK S0L 1R0
306-834-2646 Fax: 306-834-1007
Parent: Heartland Regional Health Authority
Number of Beds: 28 beds
Fenton Yeo, Facility Manager
L. Menssa, Director, Physical Plant

***Kindersley:* Heritage Manor**
1003 - 1st St. West, Kindersley, SK S0L 1S2
306-463-2611 Fax: 306-465-4550
Parent: Heartland Health Region
Number of Beds: 80 beds
Wanda Desrosiers, Facility Manager
Peter Whiteman, Director, Physical Plant

***Kinistino:* Jubilee Lodge**
PO Box 370, 410 Myers Ave., Kinistino, SK S0J 1H0
306-864-2851 Fax: 306-864-2440
Parent: Prince Albert Parkland Regional Health Authority
Number of Beds: 36 beds
Carol Pryznyk, Administrator

***Kipling:* Willowdale Lodge**
PO Box 537, 128 - 4 St. South, Kipling, SK S0G 2S0
306-736-2218 Fax: 306-736-2986
Parent: Sun Country Health Region
Number of Beds: 28 beds
Kelly Bru, Facility Manager
Linus Blacstock, Maintenance

***Langham:* Langham Senior Citizens Home**
PO Box 287, 140 Main St., Langham, SK S0K 2L0
306-283-4210 Fax: 306-283-4212
Parent: Saskatoon Regional Health Authority
Number of Beds: 17 beds
Margaret Balzer, Administrator

***Leader:* Western Senior Citizens Home**
PO Box 69, 400 - 1 St. West, Leader, SK S0N 1H0
306-628-3565 Fax: 306-628-3733
Parent: Cypress Regional Health Authority
Number of Beds: 36 beds
Note: Level 3 & 4

***Leask:* Wheatland Lodge Inc.**
PO Box 130, Hwy. 40, Leask, SK S0J 1M0
306-466-4949 Fax: 306-466-2209
Parent: Prince Albert Parkland Regional Health Authority
Number of Beds: 30 beds
Darlene Batty, Director, Care

***Lumsden:* Lumsden & District Heritage Home Inc.**
PO Box 479, 10 Aspen Bay, Lumsden, SK S0G 3C0
306-731-2247 Fax: 306731-3307
heritagehome@rqhealth.ca
Parent: Regina Qu'Appelle Health Region
Number of Beds: 30 long-term care beds
Note: Specialties: Assisted living services for seniors; Adult day support program
Wilf Frey, Maintenance
Shirley Wright, Executive Director

***Maple Creek:* Cypress Lodge Nursing Home**
PO Box 878, Hwy. 21 South, Maple Creek, SK S0N 1N0
306-662-2671 Fax: 306-662-2501
Old Name: Cypress Lodge Corp
Parent: Cypress Regional Health Authority
Number of Beds: 48 beds

***Melfort:* Nirvana Pioneer Villa**
PO Box 1480, Melfort, SK S0E 1A0
306-752-8827 Fax: 306-752-8822
Sandy Weseen, Coordinator, Care

***Melfort:* Parkland Place**
PO Box 2260, 402 Bemister Ave. East, Melfort, SK S0E 1A0
306-752-1777 Fax: 306-752-1776 www.kelseytrailhealth.ca
Old Name: Parkland Care Centre
Parent: Kelsey Trail Regional Health Authority
Number of Beds: 103 long-term care beds; 2 respite beds
Note: Specialty: Acquired brain injury program
Melanie Woods, Coordinator, Care

***Melville:* St. Paul Lutheran Home**
PO Box 1390, 100 Heritage Dr., Melville, SK S0A 2P0
306-728-7340 Fax: 306-728-5471
Parent: Sunrise Regional Health Authority
Number of Beds: 143 beds
Note: Long-term care facility affiliated with the Evangelical Lutheran Church in Canada
Gord Wyatt, Director, Long-term Care

***Moose Jaw:* Extendicare - Moose Jaw**
1151 Coteau St. West, Moose Jaw, SK S6H 5G5
306-693-5191 Fax: 306-692-1770
cnh_moosejaw@extendicare.com
Parent: Five Hills Regional Health Authority
Number of Beds: 127 beds

***Moose Jaw:* Providence Place**
100 - 2nd Ave. NE, Moose Jaw, SK S6H 1B8
306-694-8081 Fax: 306-694-8804
rmul@fhhr.ca
Parent: Five Hills Regional Health Authority
Number of Beds: 188 beds
Note: Geriatric long-term care, assessment & rehabilitation
Raymond E. Mullire

***Moosomin:* Eastern Saskatchewan Pioneer Lodge Nursing Home**
405 Windover Ave., Bag #3, Moosomin, SK S0G 3N0
306-435-2100 Fax: 306-435-4295
Parent: Regina Qu'Appelle Health Region
Number of Beds: 57 beds
Sharon Ann Wood, Interim Manager

***Nipawin:* Pineview Lodge**
PO Box 2105, 400 - 6th Ave. East, Nipawin, SK S0E 1E0
306-862-9828 Fax: 306-862-2400 www.kelseytrailhealth.ca
Parent: Kelsey Trail Regional Health Authority
Number of Beds: 96 beds
Note: Specialties: Long-term care; Dementia care unit; Day care services; Respite care

***North Battleford:* River Heights Lodge**
2001 - 99 St., North Battleford, SK S9A 0S3
306-446-6950 Fax: 306-445-6032
Parent: Prairie North Health Region
Number of Beds: 106 beds
Note: Special care home
Kelly Day, Facility Manager

***Ponteix:* Foyer St-Joseph Nursing Home**
PO Box 450, 428 - 2 Ave., Ponteix, SK S0N 1Z0
306-625-3366 Fax: 306-625-3918
Parent: Cypress Regional Health Authority
Number of Beds: 33 beds
Larry Piché, Director, Physical Plant

***Porcupine Plain:* Red Deer Nursing Home**
PO Box 70, 330 Oak St., Porcupine Plain, SK S0E 1H0
306-278-2469 Fax: 306-278-3088
Parent: Kelsey Trail Regional Health Authority
Number of Beds: 36 long-term care beds; 2 respite beds
Chris Pohl, Community Health Manager

***Preeceville:* Preeceville Lions Housing Corp. Ltd.**
PO Box 348, 26 - 3 Ave. NW, Preeceville, SK S0A 3B0
306-547-3112 Fax: 306-547-3215
Parent: Sunrise Regional Health Authority
Number of Beds: 28 beds; 1 respite
N. Babiuk, Physical Plant
Joanne Bodnar, Manager, Health Services

***Redvers:* Redvers Centennial Haven**
PO Box 399, 18 Eichhorst St., Redvers, SK S0C 2H0
306-452-3331 Fax: 306-452-3556
Parent: Sun Country Health Region
Number of Beds: 24 beds
Myrna Peterson, Manager, Health Services

***Regina:* Extendicare - Elmview**
4125 Rae St., Regina, SK S4S 3A5
306-586-1787 Fax: 306-585-0255
Parent: Regina Qu'Appelle Health Region
Number of Beds: 62 beds
Cathy Hauck, Administrator

***Regina:* Extendicare - Parkside**
4540 Rae St., Regina, SK S4S 3B4
306-586-0220 Fax: 306-585-0622

Parent: Regina Qu'Appelle Health Region
Number of Beds: 228 beds
Lloyd Wood, Maintenance Supervisor
Dona Jones, Administrator

Regina: Extendicare - Sunset
260 Sunset Dr., Regina, SK S4S 2S3
306-586-3355 Fax: 306-584-8082
Parent: Regina Qu'Appelle Health Region
Number of Beds: 152 beds
Sandra Callan, Administrator

Regina: Qu'Appelle House
1425 College Ave., Regina, SK S4P 1B4
306-522-0335 Fax: 306-522-4800
Parent: Regina Qu'Appelle Health Region
Number of Beds: 34 beds
Diane Serban, Executive Director

Regina: Regina Lutheran Home
1925 - 5 Ave. North, Regina, SK S4R 7W1
306-543-4055 Fax: 306-543-4094
Parent: Regina Qu'Appelle Health Region
Number of Beds: 91 beds
Note: Nursing home
Glenn Knapp, Director, Maintenance
Allan Hoffman, Executive Director

Regina: Regina Pioneer Village Ltd.
430 Pioneer Dr., Regina, SK S4T 6L8
306-757-5646 Fax: 306-757-5001
Parent: Regina Qu'Appelle Health Region
Number of Beds: 390 beds
Arnold Evancio, Manager, Maintenance
Dick Chinn, CEO

Regina: Santa Maria Senior Citizens Home
4215 Regina Ave., Regina, SK S4S 0J5
306-766-7100 Fax: 306-766-7115
Parent: Regina Qu'Appelle Health Region
Number of Beds: 147 beds
Bill Wilson, Manager, Maintenance
Beverly Olineck, Administrator

Rosetown: Wheatbelt Centennial Lodge Inc.
PO Box 250, 301 Centennial Dr., Rosetown, SK S0L 2V0
306-882-5210 Fax: 306-882-6696
Parent: Heartland Regional Health Authority
Number of Beds: 28 beds
B. Madden, Director, Physical Plant
Gail Adamowski, Facility Manager

Rosthern: Mennonite Nursing Home Inc.
PO Box 370, Hwy. 11 South, Rosthern, SK S0K 3R0
306-232-4861 Fax: 306-232-5611
www.saskatoonhealthregion.ca
Parent: Saskatoon Regional Health Authority
Year Founded: 1963
Note: Specialties: Long-term care; Adult Day Program
Joan Lemauviel, CEO

Saltcoats: Lakeside Manor Care Home Inc.
PO Box 340, 101 Crescent Lake Rd., Saltcoats, SK S0A 3R0
306-744-2305 Fax: 306-744-2414
Parent: Sunrise Regional Health Authority
Number of Beds: 28 beds, 2 respite
Shirley Pachal, Facility Manager

Saskatoon: Jubilee Residences Inc. (Porteous)
833 Ave. P North, Saskatoon, SK S7L 2W5
306-382-2626 Fax: 306-382-2633
yvonne.morgan@saskatoonhealthregion.ca
www.jubileeresicences.ca/
Parent: Saskatoon Regional Health Authority
Number of Beds: 95 beds
Yvonne Morgan, Administrator
306/382-2626, Fax: 306/382-2633

Saskatoon: Jubilee Residences Inc. (Stensrud)
2202 McEown Ave., Saskatoon, SK S7L 3L6
306-373-5580 Fax: 306-477-0308
handerson@jubilee.sk.ca
Parent: Saskatoon Regional Health Authority
Number of Beds: 95 beds
Heather Anderson, Administrator

Saskatoon: Oliver Lodge Special Care Home
1405 Faulkner Cres., Saskatoon, SK S7L 3R5
306-382-4111 Fax: 306-382-9822
Parent: Saskatoon Regional Health Authority
Year Founded: 1949
Number of Beds: 139 beds
Note: Specialties: Specialized services for persons with dementia; Day program for seniors; Respite care
Morley Mitchell, Administrator

Saskatoon: Parkridge Centre
110 Gropper Cres., Saskatoon, SK S7M 5N9
306-655-3800 Fax: 306-655-3801
www.parkridgequalityoflife.com
Parent: Saskatoon Regional Health Authority
Number of Beds: 217 beds
Karen Knelsen, Resident Care Services
Dale Gagnon, Manager, Plant Operation

Saskatoon: St. Ann's Senior Citizens Village Corp.
2910 Louise St., Saskatoon, SK S7J 3L8
306-374-8900 Fax: 306-477-2623
Parent: Saskatoon Regional Health Authority
Number of Beds: 80 beds
Note: Affiliated with the Catholic Health Ministry of Saskatchewan
R.A. Svoinbjornson, Administrator

Saskatoon: St. Joseph's Home
33 Valens Dr., Saskatoon, SK S7L 3S2
306-382-6306 Fax: 306-384-0140
Parent: Saskatoon Regional Health Authority
Number of Beds: 85 beds
Theodosia, Administrator

Saskatoon: Saskatoon Convalescent Home
101 - 31 St. West, Saskatoon, SK S7L 0P6
306-244-7155 Fax: 306-244-2066
www.saskatoonconvalescenthome.com
Parent: Saskatoon Regional Health Authority
Number of Beds: 59 beds
Patricia Jarvis, Administrator

Saskatoon: Sherbrooke Community Centre
401 Acadia Dr., Saskatoon, SK S7H 2E7
306-655-3600 Fax: 306-655-3727
www.sherbrookecommunitycentre.ca
Parent: Saskatoon Regional Health Authority
Number of Beds: 270 beds
Note: Long-term care home. Also provides a Community Day Program for 100 local residents
Bruce Pyett, Director, Maintenance
Suellen Beatty, CEO

Saskatoon: Sunnyside Adventist Care Centre
2200 St. Henry Ave., Saskatoon, SK S7M 0P5
306-653-1267 Fax: 306-653-7223
admin@sunnysidecare.ca
www.sunnysidecare.ca
Old Name: Sunnyside Nursing Home
Parent: Saskatoon Regional Health Authority
Year Founded: 1964
Note: Specialties: Nursing care; Physiotherapy; Activity program; Palliative care
Collin Akre, Administrator

Spiritwood: Idylwild Lodge
PO Box 159, Spiritwood, SK S0J 2M0
306-883-2267 Fax: 306-883-3121
Number of Beds: 35 beds
Carroll Joyes, Director, Care
Louis Willick, Director, Maintenance

Stoughton: Newhope Pioneer Lodge Inc.
PO Box 38, 123 Government Rd. North, Stoughton, SK S0G 4T0
306-457-2552 Fax: 306-457-3732
Parent: Sun Country Health Region
Number of Beds: 30 beds
Linda Wilson, Director, Community Services

Swift Current: Palliser Regional Care Centre
440 Central Ave. South, Swift Current, SK S9H 3G6
306-778-5160 www.cypresshealth.ca
Parent: Cypress Regional Health Authority
Number of Beds: 94 beds

Swift Current: Prairie Pioneers Lodge
302 Central Ave. South, Swift Current, SK S9H 3G3
306-778-5192 Fax: 306-773-1635
Parent: Cypress Regional Health Authority
Number of Beds: 41 beds

Swift Current: Swift Current Care Centre/SCCC
700 Aberdeen St. SE, Swift Current, SK S9H 3E3
306-773-9371 Fax: 306-773-1353 www.cypresshealth.ca
Parent: Cypress Regional Health Authority
Number of Beds: 63 beds
Note: Specialties: Nursing care from Registered Nurses, Registered Psychiatric Nurses, & Licensed Practical Nurses; Social work; Activity program; Respite care program

Tisdale: Newmarket Manor
PO Box 2620, 2001 Newmarket Dr., Tisdale, SK S0E 1T0
306-873-5828 Fax: 306-873-4822
Parent: Kelsey Trail Regional Health Authority
Number of Beds: 40 beds
Ann Boxall, Director, Care

Tisdale: Sasko Park Lodge
PO Box 1330, 806 - 97 Ave., Tisdale, SK S0E 1T0
306-873-4585 Fax: 306-873-2404
Parent: Kelsey Trail Regional Health Authority
Number of Beds: 33 beds, 15 suites
Ann Boxall, Director, Care

Turtleford: Riverside Health Complex Integrated Facility
PO Box 10, 1st St. S, Turtleford, SK S0M 2Y0
306-845-2195 Fax: 306-845-2772
Old Name: Turtle River Nusing Home
Number of Beds: 27 beds
Patrick Blais, Coordinator, Health Services

Wakaw: Lakeview Pioneer Lodge Inc.
PO Box 189, 400 First St. North, Wakaw, SK S0K 4P0
306-233-4621 Fax: 306-233-5225
Parent: Saskatoon Regional Health Authority
Number of Beds: 46 beds
Gracie Kungle, Administrator

Waldheim: Menno Homes of Saskatchewan Inc.
PO Box 130, Waldheim, SK S0K 4R0
306-945-2070 Fax: 306-945-4641
menno.homes@sasktel.net
Year Founded: 1963
Number of Beds: 105 residential capacity
Note: Number of Employees: 105
Marlin J. Roth, Executive Director

Watrous: Manitou Lodge
PO Box 130, 404 - 1 St., Watrous, SK S0K 4T0
306-946-3718 Fax: 306-946-2296
Parent: Saskatoon Regional Health Authority
Number of Beds: 35 beds
Debbie Okrainetz, Manager, Client Services

Wawota: Deer View Lodge
PO Box 240, 201 Wilfred St., Wawota, SK S0G 5A0
306-739-2400 Fax: 306-739-2802
Parent: Sun Country Health Region
Number of Beds: 34 beds

Wolseley: Lakeside Home
PO Box 10, 710 Quimet, Wolseley, SK S0G 5H0
306-698-2573 Fax: 306-698-2975
Parent: Regina Qu'Appelle Health Region
Number of Beds: 78 beds
Ruth Platt, Purchasing Agent
Jim Bonner, Maintenance Supervisor
Maggie Petrychyn, Manager

Yorkton: Yorkton & District Nursing Home Corporation
200 Bradbrooke Dr., Yorkton, SK S3N 2K5
306-786-0800 Fax: 306-786-0808
www.sunrisehealthregion.sk.ca
Parent: Sunrise Regional Health Authority
Number of Beds: 243 beds
Lynn Wrishko, Manager, Health Services
Brenda Walsh, Manager, Health Services

Long Term/Retirement Care

Nursing Homes

Moose Jaw: Pioneer Housing Lodge & Village
1000 Albert St., Moose Jaw, SK S6H 2Y2
306-693-4616
Parent: Five Hills Regional Health Authority

Personal Care Homes

Avonlea: Coteau Range Manor
PO Box 239, 210 New Warren Pl., Avonlea, SK S0H 0C0
306-868-2033
Parent: Five Hills Regional Health Authority
Number of Beds: 40 beds

Bangor: Morris Lodge Society Inc.
PO Box 54, Lots 4-12, Block 6, Main St., Bangor, SK S0A 0E0
306-728-5322 Fax: 306-728-2048
Number of Beds: 20 beds

Beechy: Beechy Community Care Home
205 Railway Ave., Beechy, SK S0L 0C0
306-859-4470
Number of Beds: 10 beds
Noël Taylor, Genevieve Fleuter

Biggar: Beaulah's Care Home
320 - 2 Ave. East, Biggar, SK S0K 0M0
306-948-5648 Fax: 306-948-2860
Number of Beds: 10 beds
Beaulah Oystryk

Codette: Serenity Lane
PO Box 152, Codette, SK S0E 0P0
306-862-2579
Parent: Kelsey Trail Regional Health Authority
Number of Beds: 10 beds
Debbie Karlee

Eatonia: Eatonia Oasis Living Inc.
PO Box 217, 205, 2nd Ave. W, Eatonia, SK S0L 0Y0
306-967-2447 Fax: 306-967-2373 eatoniaoasisliving.com
Old Name: Eatonia Personal Care Home
Number of Beds: 23 beds
Lorraine Bews, Chairperson

Estevan: Creighton Lodge
1028 Hillcrest Dr., Estevan, SK S4A 1Y7
306-634-4154

Herbert: Herbert Heritage Manor
PO Box 10, Herbert, SK S0H 2A0
306-784-3167 Fax: 306-784-3564
hhm@sasktel.net
Number of Beds: 40 beds
Note: personal care home level 1 & 2
Brian D. Penner, Administrator

Kamsack: Eaglestone Lodge Personal Care Home Inc.
PO Box 1330, Kamsack, SK S0A 1S0
306-542-2620 Fax: 306-542-4342
Number of Beds: 42 beds
Kim Fullawka, Manager; Director, Care

Lanigan: Central Parkland Lodge
PO Box 609, 36 Downing Dr. East, Lanigan, SK S0K 2M0
306-365-1400 Fax: 306-365-3354
Parent: Saskatoon Regional Health Authority
Number of Beds: 35 beds
Darla Washington, Manager, Client Services

Moose Jaw: Capilano Court
1236 - 3rd Ave. NW, Moose Jaw, SK S6H 3V3
306-693-4518
Parent: Five Hills Regional Health Authority

Moose Jaw: Chez Nous
1101 Grafton Ave., Moose Jaw, SK S6H 3S4
306-693-4371 Fax: 306-693-5300
Parent: Five Hills Regional Health Authority
Number of Beds: 60 beds

Moose Jaw: Evergreen's Personal Care Home
1033 Main St. North, Moose Jaw, SK S6H 0X1
306-692-7410
Parent: Five Hills Regional Health Authority
Number of Beds: 10 beds
Leland Agar
Lois Agar

Moose Jaw: Ina Grafton Gage Home
200 Iroquois St. East, Moose Jaw, SK S6H 4T3
306-692-4882 Fax: 306-692-3433
Parent: Five Hills Regional Health Authority
Brenda Deobald, Administrator; Director, Care

Moose Jaw: Oxford Place Inc.
1007 Main St. North, Moose Jaw, SK S6H 0X1
306-692-2837 Fax: 306-692-3837
oxfordplace@sasktel.net
Parent: Five Hills Regional Health Authority

Moose Jaw: Valley View Centre
PO Box 1300, Moose Jaw, SK S6H 4R2
306-694-3000 Fax: 306-694-3003
Number of Beds: 348 beds
Terry Hardy, Director

Oxbow: Bow Valley Villa Corp.
319 Wylie Ave., Oxbow, SK S0C 2B0
306-483-2744 Fax: 306-483-2915

Pangman: Deep South Personal Care Home
PO Box 150, 211 Keeler St., Pangman, SK S0C 2C0
306-442-2043 Fax: 306-442-4261
dspch@sasktel.net
Parent: Sun Country Regional Health Authority
Connie Lozinsky, Administrator

Ponteix: Rolling Hills Villa Ltd.
PO Box 148, 332 - 2 St. West, Ponteix, SK S0N 1Z0
306-625-3511

Prince Albert: Hillside Care Home
231 - 21 St. East, Prince Albert, SK S6V 1L9
306-764-5039
Parent: Prince Albert Parkland Regional Health Authority
Number of Beds: 10 beds
Angie Kopera, Owner
Nettie Mitchell, Owner

Prince Albert: Nelson Care Home Ltd.
1336 - 7th St. East, Prince Albert, SK S6V 0V1
306-922-9506
Parent: Prince Albert Parkland Regional Health Authority

Rosthern: Rosthern Mennonite Home for the Aged
PO Box 790, 510 - 4 Ave., Rosthern, SK S0K 3R0
306-232-4822
Number of Beds: 20 beds
Jacob Loewen, Chair

Saskatoon: Arbor Villa Care Home
315 Kenderdine Rd., Saskatoon, SK S7N 3S9
306-249-3317
Parent: Saskatoon Regional Health Authority
Number of Beds: 13 beds

Saskatoon: Ashton Care Home
438 Ave. Y North, Saskatoon, SK S7L 3L2
306-382-8975 Fax: 306-283-4142
Parent: Saskatoon Regional Health Authority
Number of Beds: 10 beds
Bernice Obnokon

Saskatoon: Balicanta Personal Care Home
510 Spencer Cres., Saskatoon, SK S7K 7T4
306-934-5903
Parent: Saskatoon Regional Health Authority
Number of Beds: 12 beds
Marino Balicanta

Saskatoon: Bergman's Private Home Care
333 LaRonge Rd., Saskatoon, SK S7K 4S1
306-934-2031 Fax: 306-934-2031
Parent: Saskatoon Regional Health Authority

Saskatoon: Betty Sandulak's Personal Care Home
122 Adilman Dr., Saskatoon, SK S7K 7S5
306-931-7859
Old Name: Betty's Private Care Home
Parent: Saskatoon Regional Health Authority
Number of Beds: 10 beds

Saskatoon: Fairhaven Personal Care Home
139 Olmstead Rd., Saskatoon, SK S7M 4L9
306-382-7800
Parent: Saskatoon Regional Health Authority

Saskatoon: M & M Private Care Home
518/520 Russell Rd., Saskatoon, SK S7K 6L6
306-242-6501 Fax: 306-934-8027
Parent: Saskatoon Regional Health Authority
Number of Beds: 12 beds
Note: Specialties: Diabetic care; Respite care
Marionela Cabello

Saskatoon: Marg's Care Home Ltd.
310 Adilman Dr., Saskatoon, SK S7K 7K5
306-975-1189
Parent: Saskatoon Regional Health Authority

Shellbrook: T.L.C. Personal Care Home
308 - 3rd Ave. East, Shellbrook, SK S0J 2E0
306-747-3123
Year Founded: 1997

Speers: Oasis Personal Care Home
PO Box 26, Speers, SK S0M 2V0
306-246-2067 Fax: 306-246-2028
info@oasiscarehome.ca
www.oasiscarehome.ca
Parent: Prince Albert Parkland Regional Health Authority
Year Founded: 1993
Delbert Miller, Co-Owner; Operator
Sheila Miller, Co-Owner; Operator

St Louis: Regnier Personal Care Home Inc.
457 River Rd., St Louis, SK S0J 2C0
306-422-8223
Lynn Regnier

Theodore: Theodore Health Centre
PO Box 70, 615 Anderson Ave., Theodore, SK S0A 4C0
306-647-2115 Fax: 306-647-2238
www.sunrisehealthregion.sk.ca
Parent: Sunrise Regional Health Authority
Number of Beds: 20 beds
Note: Specialties: Long-term care; Nursing services; Phlebotomy service; Respite care; Palliative care
Donna Gawryliuk, Head Nurse

Wadena: Pleasant View Care Home
PO Box 10, 533 - 5 St. NE, Wadena, SK S0A 4J0
306-338-2412 Fax: 306-338-2720
Parent: Saskatoon Regional Health Authority
Number of Beds: 46 beds
Bayle Maryniak, Site Manager

Watson: Quill Plains Centennial Lodge/Watson Health Complex
PO Box 220, 402 - 2 St. NE, Watson, SK S0K 4V0
306-287-3791 Fax: 306-287-3386
Parent: Saskatoon Regional Health Authority
Number of Beds: 54 beds

Weyburn: Crocus Plains Villa Ltd.
1135 Park Ave., Weyburn, SK S4H 0K6
306-842-0616
Parent: Sun Country Regional Health Authority
Carole Krieger, President

Weyburn: Parkway Lodge Personal Care Home
420 - 8 Ave. SE, Weyburn, SK S4H 3N2
306-842-7868
Parent: Sun Country Regional Health Authority

Weyburn: Tatagwa View
PO Box 2003, 808 Souris Valley Rd., Weyburn, SK S4H 2Z9
306-842-8398 Fax: 306-842-8341 www.suncountry.sk.ca
Old Name: Souris Valley Extended Care Centre
Parent: Sun Country Regional Health Authority
Year Founded: 2005
Number of Beds: 123 beds
Note: Specialties: Long-term care; Mental health services (10 beds); Acquired brain injury services; Diabetes program; Rehabilitation services; Day care centre; Palliative care
Marnell Cornish, Administrator

Special Care Home

Saskatoon: LutherCare Communities
Main Corporate Office, 1212 Osler St., Saskatoon, SK S7N 0T9
306-664-0300 Fax: 306-664-0311
luthercare@shaw.ca
www.luthercare.com
Old Name: Lutheran Sunset Home
Parent: Saskatoon Regional Health Authority
Year Founded: 1955
Note: Specialties: Group living for young adults; Community day programs for adults; Home support; Intermediate care; Seniors' housing; Long-term nursing care
Bernard McCallion, CEO

Saskatoon: LutherCare Communities
1800 Alexandra Ave., Saskatoon, SK S7K 3C7
306-664-0366 Fax: 306-664-0395
lsc@luthercare.com
www.luthercare.com
Division of: Luther Seniors' Centre
Year Founded: 1985
Note: Specialties: Day program for adults with irreversible dementia; Social services; Nursing; Personal care; Sensory stimulation

Saskatoon: LutherCare Communities
1212 Osler St., Saskatoon, SK S7N 0T9
306-664-0300
luthercare@shaw.ca
www.luthercare.com
Division of: Luther Special Care Home
Year Founded: 1955
Number of Beds: 129 beds, including 49 special needs beds & 2 respite beds
Note: Specialties: Secure special needs unit for residents with cognitive impairment; Nursing care; Physio, occupational, & recreational therapy; Community day program for seniors at risk; Respite care

Mental Health Facilities

Mental Health Hospital/Clinic/Facility

Weyburn: Community Health Services
PO Box 2003, Weyburn, SK S4H 2Z9
306-842-8718 Fax: 306-842-8738
DSchultz@schd.sk.ca
Number of Beds: 10 beds
Note: community health centre
Joan Panteluk, Manager, Community Health Services

Special Care Home

Arborfield: Arborfield Special Care Lodge
PO Box 160, Arborfield, SK S0E 0A0
306-769-8757 Fax: 306-769-8759
Parent: Kelsey Trail Regional Health Authority
Number of Beds: 36 beds
Sharon Frisky, Community Coordinator

Battleford: Battlefords District Care Centre
PO Box 69, 1308 Winnipeg St., Battleford, SK S0M 0E0
306-446-6900 Fax: 306-937-2258
hccc@bathd.sk.ca
Parent: Prairie North Health Region
Number of Beds: 124 beds
Carol Dyck, Facility Manager

Canora: Canora Gateway Lodge
PO Box 1387, 212 Centre Ave. East, Canora, SK S0A 0L0
306-563-5685 Fax: 306-563-5711
Parent: Sunrise Regional Health Authority
Number of Beds: 78 beds
Oney Pollock, Manager, Health Services

Carrot River: Pasquia Special Care Home
PO Box 250, 4101 - 1 Ave West, Carrot River, SK S0E 0L0
306-862-2725 Fax: 306-768-3233
Parent: Kelsey Trail Regional Health Authority
Number of Beds: 35 long-term care beds
Andrew Will

Dalmeny: Spruce Manor Special Care Home
PO Box 190, 701 First St., Dalmeny, SK S0K 1E0
306-254-2101 Fax: 306-254-2178
Parent: Saskatoon Regional Health Authority
Number of Beds: 36 beds
Tom Nicholls, Administrator
Jonathan Redekop, Maintenance

Esterhazy: Centennial Special Care Home
PO Box 310, 300 James St., Esterhazy, SK S0A 0X0
306-745-6444 Fax: 306-745-2741
Parent: Sunrise Regional Health Authority
Number of Beds: 46 beds
Doreen Strong, Manager, Health Services

Herbert: Herbert Nursing Home Inc.
PO Box 520, 405 Herbert Ave., Herbert, SK S0H 2A0
306-784-2466 Fax: 306-784-2449
Parent: Cypress Regional Health Authority
Number of Beds: 55 beds
Gordon Milton, Administrator
Lyle Zacharias, Director, Plant Maintenance

Humboldt: St. Mary's Villa
PO Box 1360, 1109 - 13 St. North, Humboldt, SK S0K 2A0
306-682-2628 Fax: 306-682-3211
Parent: Saskatoon Regional Health Authority
Number of Beds: 101 beds
Jan Berger, Site Manager

Langenberg: Centennial Special Care Home
PO Box 9, 200 Heritage Dr, Langenberg, SK S0A 2A0
306-743-2232 Fax: 306-743-5025
Parent: Sunrise Regional Health Authority
Number of Beds: 48 beds

Lloydminster: Jubilee Home
3902 - 45 Ave., Lloydminster, SK S9V 1Z1
306-820-5950 Fax: 306-825-9869 www.pacha.ca
Parent: Prairie North Health Region
Number of Beds: 50 beds
Bobbie Stevenson, Facility Manager

Mankota: Prairie View Health Centre
PO Box 390, 241 - 1 Ave., Mankota, SK S0H 2W0
306-628-3565 Fax: 306-628-3733
Parent: Cypress Regional Health Authority
Number of Beds: 20 beds

Meadow Lake: Northland Pioneers Lodge Inc.
515 - 3 St. West, Meadow Lake, SK S9X 1L1
306-236-1500 Fax: 306-236-3244
Parent: Prairie North Health Region
Number of Beds: 55 beds
Shelley Wasyliw, Facility Manager

Melville: Centennial Special Care Home
PO Box 1390, 200 Heritage Rd., Melville, SK S0A 2P0
306-743-2232 Fax: 306-743-5025

Middle Lake: Bethany Pioneer Village Inc.
PO Box 8, Middle Lake, SK S0K 2X0
306-367-2033 Fax: 306-367-2155
Parent: Saskatoon Regional Health Authority
Number of Beds: 36 beds
Glenn McDougall, Administrator

Moosomin: Eastern Saskatchewan Pioneer Lodge
506 Windover Ave., Bag 3, Moosomin, SK S0G 3N0
306-435-2326 Fax: 306-435-3335
Parent: Regina Qu'Appelle Health Region
Number of Beds: 57 beds
Sharon Ann Wood

Nipawin: Nipawin District Nursing Home
PO Box 2105, 400 - 6th Ave. East, Nipawin, SK S0E 1E0
306-862-9828 Fax: 306-862-2400
Parent: Kelsey Trail Regional Health Authority
Number of Beds: 96 beds

North Battleford: Société Joseph Breton Inc. (Villa Pascal)
1301 - 113 St., North Battleford, SK S9A 3K1
306-445-8465 Fax: 306-445-5117
Parent: Prairie North Health Region
Number of Beds: 40 beds
Thérèse Michaud, Administrator

Prince Albert: Herb Bassett Home
1220 - 25 St. West, Prince Albert, SK S6V 7P7
306-765-6000 Fax: 306-765-6207
Parent: Prince Albert Parkland Regional Health Authority
Number of Beds: 144 beds
John Piggott

Prince Albert: Mont St. Joseph Home Inc.
777 - 28 St. East, Prince Albert, SK S6V 8C2
306-953-4500 Fax: 306-953-4550
Parent: Prince Albert Parkland Regional Health Authority
Number of Beds: 120 beds
Note: Special care home
Brian Martin, Executive Director

Raymore: Silver Heights Special Care Home
PO Box 549, 402 McLean St., Raymore, SK S0A 3J0
306-746-5744 Fax: 306-746-5747
Parent: Regina Qu'Appelle Health Region
Number of Beds: 31 beds
Kate Beattie, Facility Manager

Regina: Salvation Army William Booth Special Care Home
50 Angus Rd., Regina, SK S4R 8P6
306-543-0655 Fax: 306-543-1292
Parent: Regina Qu'Appelle Health Region
Number of Beds: 83 beds
Graham Brown, Executive Director

Saskatoon: Circle Drive Special Care Home Inc.
PO Box 60020, 3055 Preston Ave. South, Saskatoon, SK S7T 1C3
306-955-4800 Fax: 306-955-2376
Parent: Saskatoon Regional Health Authority
Number of Beds: 50 beds
Blair MacPherson, Supervisor, Physical Plant
Leonard Enns, Administrator

Saskatoon: Convent of Sion
#114, 3104 Louise Pl., Saskatoon, SK S7J 5J8
306-373-0335
macdonaldkay@shaw.ca
Parent: Saskatoon Regional Health Authority
Number of Beds: 6 beds
Kay MacDonald, Director

Saskatoon: Extendicare - Preston
2225 Preston Ave., Saskatoon, SK S7J 2E7
306-374-2242 Fax: 306-373-2203
Parent: Saskatoon Regional Health Authority
Number of Beds: 82 beds
Patricia Amos, Administrator

Saskatoon: Senior Sisters of Sion Residence
333 Acadia Dr., Saskatoon, SK S7H 3V5
306-374-9566 Fax: 306-374-6648
kaymac@sasktel.net
Parent: Saskatoon Regional Health Authority
Number of Beds: 27 beds
Katherine MacDonald, Director

Saskatoon: Ursuline Sisters of St Angela's Convent (St Angela's)
1212 College Dr., Saskatoon, SK S7N 0W4
306-242-5566 Fax: 306-975-7046
Parent: Saskatoon Regional Health Authority
Number of Beds: 5 beds

Strasbourg: Last Mountain Pioneer Home
PO Box 549, 700 Prospect Ave., Strasbourg, SK S0G 4V0
306-725-3342 Fax: 306-725-3404
cfuessel.lshd@shin.sk.ca
Parent: Saskatoon Regional Health Authority
Number of Beds: 43 beds
Connie Fuessel, Manager

Warman: Warman Mennonite Special Care Home
PO Box 100, 201 - 3 Ave. North, Warman, SK S0K 4S0
306-933-2011 Fax: 306-933-2782
Parent: Saskatoon Regional Health Authority
Number of Beds: 31 beds
John Friesen, Administrator

Weyburn: Weyburn Special Care Home
PO Box 2003, 704 - 5 St. NE, Weyburn, SK S4H 2Z9
306-842-4455 Fax: 306-842-3084
Parent: Sun Country Health Region
Number of Beds: 90 beds

Yukon Territory

Government Departments in Charge

YUKON TERRITORY: Health & Social Services
PO Box 2703, Whitehorse, YT Y1A 2C6
867-667-5770 Fax: 867-667-3096 www.hss.gov.yk.ca

Hospitals

Hospitals - General

Watson Lake: Watson Lake Hospital
PO Box 500, Watson Lake, YT Y0A 1C0
867-536-4444 Fax: 867-536-7302
Number of Beds: 10 beds
Note: Number of staff: 1 nurse-in-charge, 7 additional nurses
Sue Rudd, Nurse in Charge

Whitehorse: Whitehorse General Hospital
5 Hospital Rd., Whitehorse, YT Y1A 3H7
867-393-8700 Fax: 867-393-8771 www.whitehorsehospital.ca
Number of Beds: 49 beds
Ron Browne, CEO

Community Health Centres

Community Health Care Centres

Beaver Creek: Beaver Creek Health Centre
General Delivery, Beaver Creek, YT Y0B 1A0
867-862-4444 Fax: 867-862-7909

Carcross: Carcross Health Centre
General Delivery, Carcross, YT Y0A 1B0
867-821-4444 Fax: 867-821-3909
hc.carcross@gov.yk.ca

Carmacks: Carmacks Health Centre
PO Box 230, Carmacks, YT Y0B 1C0
867-863-4444 Fax: 867-863-6612
carmacks.nic@gov.yk.ca
Number of Beds: 2 beds
Jocelyn Rhode, Acting Nurse Practitioner in Charge

Dawson: Dawson City Health Centre
PO Box 10, Dawson, YT Y0B 1G0
867-993-4444 Fax: 867-993-5811

Destruction Bay: Destruction Bay Health Centre
General Delivery, Destruction Bay, YT Y0B 1H0
867-841-4444 Fax: 867-841-5274

Faro: Faro Health Centre
PO Box 99, Faro, YT Y0B 1K0
867-994-4444 Fax: 867-994-3457

Haines Junction: Haines Junction Health Centre
PO Box 5334, Haines Junction, YT Y0B 1L0

867-634-4444 Fax: 867-634-2733

***Mayo:* Mayo Nursing Station**
PO Box 98, Mayo, YT Y0B 1M0
867-996-4444 Fax: 867-996-2018
hc.mayo@gov.yk.ca
Note: Specialties: Public health services; Health promotion services; Home care services. Number of Employees: 1 doctor + 3 community nurse practitioners

***Old Crow:* Old Crow Health Centre**
General Delivery, Old Crow, YT Y0B 1N0
867-996-4444 Fax: 867-966-3614 www.oldcrow.ca/nursing
Year Founded: 1960
Note: Specialties: Nursing care; Health promotion; Home & community care

***Pelly Crossing:* Pelly Crossing Health Centre**
General Delivery, Pelly Crossing, YT Y0B 1P0
867-537-4444 Fax: 867-537-3611
hc.pelly-crossing@gov.yk.ca

***Ross River:* Ross River Health Centre**
General Delivery, Ross River, YT Y0B 1S0
867-969-4444 Fax: 867-969-2014

***Teslin:* Teslin Health Centre**
General Delivery, Teslin, YT Y0A 1B0
867-390-4444
Note: Specialties: Public health services; Health promotion; Clinical care by community nurses; Home care

***Watson Lake:* Watson Lake Health Centre**
PO Box 500, Watson Lake, YT Y0A 1C0
867-536-7483 Fax: 867-536-7011
Sue Rudd

Long Term/Retirement Care

Long Term Care Facility

***Dawson City:* McDonald Lodge for Seniors**
PO Box 310, 636 - 5th Ave., Dawson City, YT Y0B 1G0
867-993-5345 Fax: 867-993-5849 1-800-661-0408
Number of Beds: 11 residential beds, including 2 respite beds
Note: 0pecialties: Residential care for seniors & physically challenged persons who require moderate assistance; Recreational & therapeutic activities; Respite care; Home support services; Palliative care
Adeline Griffin-Viney, Manager

***Whitehorse:* Copper Ridge Place**
60 Lazulite Dr., Whitehorse, YT Y1A 6S9
867-393-7500 Fax: 867-393-7510
bev.oyler@gov.yk.ca
Number of Beds: 96 beds

***Whitehorse:* Norman D. Macaulay Lodge**
2 Klondike Rd., Whitehorse, YT Y1A 3L5
867-667-5955 Fax: 867-393-6237
bev.oyler@gov.yk.ca
Number of Beds: 44 beds

SECTION 11
LAW FIRMS

Major Law Firms

Bennett Jones LLP
#4500, Bankers Hall East Tower 855 - 2nd St. SW, Calgary AB T2P 4K7
403-298-3100 403-265-7219 Telex: 038-24524
firmwatch@bennettjones.ca
www.bennettjones.ca
Profile: 6 Offices, 159 Lawyers, Founded in: 1922
Bennett Jones' Financial Services & Banking Practice Group has broad experience in all types of Canadian debt financing transactions; in addition this group has had frequent involvement in cross-border debt financings; our lawyers are used to working with sophisticated finance executives from many of Canada's largest corporations as well as finance professionals from North America's leading banks & investment dealers; Bennett Jones has extensive expertise in all aspects of financing for companies involved in the oil & gas, power & telecommunications industries; our group's services include: syndicated bank lending transactions; subordinated debt transactions; public & private debt offerings; cross-border public & private debt offerings; leasing & other asset-based structured financings; project finance; hedging agreements; debt restructuring; insolvency & litigation
Senior and Managing Partners:
James G. Smeltzer, Managing Partner
403-298-3168
smeltzerj@bennettjones.ca
Farouk S. Adatia, Partner
403-298-3342
adatiaf@bennettjones.ca
Philip D. Backman, Partner
403-298-3366
backmanp@bennettjones.ca
Darryl J. Barber, Partner
403-298-3001
barberd@bennettjones.ca

Blake, Cassels & Graydon LLP
#2800, Commerce Court West 199 Bay St., Toronto ON M5L 1A9
416-863-2400 416-863-2653 Telex: 06-219687
toronto@blakes.com
www.blakes.com
Profile: 5 Offices, 410 Lawyers, Founded in: 1856
Financial Services; Mergers & Acquisitions; Structured Finance; Securities; Business; Commodity Tax & Trade; Corporate Governance; E-commerce; Restructuring & Insolvency; Taxation; Pension & Employee Benefits
Senior and Managing Partners:
Robert M. Granatstein, Managing Partner
416-863-2748
robert.granatstein@blakes.com
Simon A. Finch, Partner
416-863-2159
simon.finch@blakes.com
James J. Shanks, Senior Partner
416-863-3845
james.shanks@blakes.com
Frank P. Arnone, Partner
416-863-4295
frank.arnone@blakes.com
Stephen R. Ashbourne, Partner
416-863-3086
stephen.ashbourne@blakes.com
J. Alan Aucoin, Partner
416-863-2635
jaa@blakes.com
Barbara J. Austin, Partner
416-863-3893
barbara.austin@blakes.com
Bryan C. Bailey, Partner
416-863-2297
bryan.bailey@blakes.com
Nigel Campbell, Partner
416-863-2429
nigel.campbell@blakes.com
Anoop Dogra, Partner
416-863-3052
anoop.dogra@blakes.com

Davies Ward Phillips & Vineberg LLP
#4400, 1 First Canadian Place, Toronto ON M5X 1B1
416-863-0900 416-863-0871
info@dwpv.com
www.dwpv.com
Profile: 4 Offices, 235 Lawyers, Founded in: 1961
Business transactions & business operations including acquisitions, divestitures, financing, securities, real estate & land development
Senior and Managing Partners:
Ed Babin, Senior Partner
416-863-5503
ebabin@dwpv.com
Robert T. Bauer, Senior Partner
416-863-5552
rbauer@dwpv.com
Carol Hansell, Senior Partner
416-863-5592
chansell@dwpv.com
Stephen Ruby, Senior Partner
416-863-5515
sruby@dwpv.com
Conrad Druzeta, Partner
416-367-7442
cdruzeta@dwpv.com
K.A. Siobhan Monaghan, Partner
416-863-5558
smonaghan@dwpv.com

Davis LLP
#2800, Park Place 666 Burrard St., Vancouver BC V6C 2Z7
604-687-9444 604-687-1612
www.davis.ca
Profile: 8 Offices, Founded in: 1892
As a full-service law firm, Davis LLP provides a comprehensive range of legal services to clients around the world, through offices across Canada & in Japan. The firm has 88 partners worldwide, & 134 other lawyers around the world. Business can be conducted in English, French, Japanese, Spanish, Mandarin, Cantonese, Korean, German, Italian, Dutch, Estonian, & Polish. Established in Vancouver in 1892, the firm has more than 220 lawyers working in integrated practice groups that focus on client service & specialization. Davis strives to help clients achieve their business objectives & resolve business problems quickly & effectively. The firm is strong in all the traditional areas of legal practice. Across the firm, lawyers continuously cultivate commercial & government relationships to both facilitate the conduct of business & to identify new business opportunities for clients. Davis & its lawyers are recognized as leaders in numerous domestic & international ratings publications.
Senior and Managing Partners:
Brian F. Hiebert, Managing Partner
604-643-2917
bhiebert@davis.ca

Fraser Milner Casgrain LLP
1 First Canadian Place P.O Box 100 100 King St. West, Toronto ON M5X 1B2
416-863-4511 416-863-4592
webmaster@fmc-law.com
www.fmc-law.com
Profile: 7 Offices, 500 Lawyers, Founded in: 1839
Senior and Managing Partners:
Christopher E. Pinnington, Managing Partner
416-863-4409
chris.pinnington@fmc-law.com
Frank E.P. Bowman, Senior Partner
416-367-6820
frank.bowman@fmc-law.com
Ronald A. Goldenberg, Senior Partner
416-863-4724
ronald.goldenberg@fmc-law.com
Michael G. Horan, Senior Partner
416-367-6773
michael.horan@fmc-law.com
Thomas J. Hunter, Senior Partner
416-863-4555
tom.hunter@fmc-law.com
Steve Watson, Senior Partner
416-863-4686
steve.watson@fmc-law.com

Heenan Blaikie S.E.N.C.R.L/SRL
#2500, 1250, boul René-Lévesque ouest, Montréal QC H3B 4Y1
514-846-1212 514-846-3427
www.heenanblaikie.com
Profile: 9 Offices, 500 Lawyers, Founded in: 1973
Heenan Blaikie LLP business law practitioners provide a full range of services to some of Canada's largest corporations & financial institutions, as well as to many smaller, growth-oriented companies in all types of transactions & corporate governance issues: mergers & acquisitions, international & domestic joint ventures, reorganizations, regulatory matters, venture capital investment, financing arrangements with commercial & private lenders, directors' & officers' liabilities, trademark & copyright matters; software licensing & outsourcing contracts
Senior and Managing Partners:
Guy Tremblay, Managing Partner
514-846-2271
gtremblay@heenan.ca
Claudette Bellemare, Partner
514-846-2248
cbellemare@heenan.ca
Peter M. Blaikie, Founding Partner
514-846-2328
pblaikie@heenan.ca
Roy L. Heenan, Founding Partner
514-846-2264
rheenan@heenan.ca
Donald J. Johnston, Founding Partner
514-846-2280
djohnston@heenan.ca
Bernard Amyot, Partner
514-846-2321
bamyot@heenan.ca
Stuart S. Aronovitch, Partner
514-846-2339
saronovitch@heenan.ca
Marcel Aubut, Partner
514-846-2326
maubut@heenan.ca
Christine Baudouin, Partner
514-846-2323
cbaudouin@heenan.ca
Carl Bélanger, Partner
514-846-2212
cbelanger@heenan.ca

Lang Michener LLP
#2500, Brookfield Place 181 Bay St., Toronto ON M5J 2T7
416-360-8600 416-365-1719
rrcranston@langmichener.ca (Office Managing Partner)
www.langmichener.ca
Profile: 3 Offices, 90 Lawyers, Founded in: 1927
Financial services include insurance law, banking & project finance, business law, mergers & acquisitions, business restructuring & insolvency, franchising & distribution, real estate law, securities, & tax law.
Senior and Managing Partners:

McCarthy Tétrault LLP
#5300, Toronto-Dominion Bank Tower, Toronto ON M5K 1E6
416-362-1812 416-868-0673
toronto@mccarthy.ca
www.mccarthy.ca
Profile: 7 Offices, 319 Lawyers, Founded in: 1855
One of our largest practice areas is in corporate finance, where we represent public issuers & underwriters in corporate finance matters involving the preparation of prospectuses & other offering documents for public & private offerings; we have extensive experience in dealing with mergers & acquisitions & corporate reorganizations; our practice has involved us in many significant takeovers, as well as the development & implementation of defensive strategies in hostile bid situations to improve shareholder values
Senior and Managing Partners:
Thomas B. Akin, Senior Partner
416-601-7934
takin@mccarthy.ca
Steven Baum, Partner
416-601-8120
sbaum@mccarthy.ca
Anthony M.C. Alexander, Partner
416-601-7705
aalexand@mccarthy.ca
Lorraine Allard, Partner
416-601-7948
lallard@mccarthy.ca
James H. Archer, Partner
416-601-7931
jarcher@mccarthy.ca
Ian Arellano, Partner
416-601-7520
iarellan@mccarthy.ca
Andrew Armstrong, Partner
416-601-8310
aarmstro@mccarthy.ca
Gordon D. Baird, Partner
416-601-7892
gbaird@mccarthy.ca
Michael E. Barrack, Partner
416-601-7894
mbarrack@mccarthy.ca
Sarit E. Batner, Partner
416-601-7756
sbatner@mccarthy.ca

McMillan Binch Mendelsohn
#4400, BCE Place, Bay Wellington Tower 181 Bay St., Toronto ON M5J 2T3

416-865-7000 416-865-7048 888-622-4624
info@mcmillan.ca
www.mcmillan.ca
Profile: 2 Offices, 145 Lawyers, Founded in: 1903
Senior and Managing Partners:
Paul J. Avis, Senior Partner
416-865-7006
paul.avis@mcmbm.com
John W. Craig, Senior Partner
416-865-7128
john.craig@mcmbm.com
John A. Paterson, Senior Partner
416-865-7021
john.paterson@mcmbm.com
Graham W.S. Scott, Senior Partner
416-865-7247
graham.scott@mcmbm.com
Richard B. Thomas, Senior Partner
416-865-7179
richard.thomas@mcmbm.com
Michael P. Whitcombe, Senior Partner
416-865-7126
michael.whitcombe@mcmbm.com

Miller Thomson LLP

#5800, Scotia Plaza P.O Box 1011 40 King St. West, Toronto ON M5H 3S1
416-595-8500 416-595-8695 888-762-5559
toronto@millerthomson.com
www.millerthomson.com
Profile: 9 Offices, 500 Lawyers, Founded in: 1957
Bankruptcy; Corporate Commercial; E-Commerce; Estates/Pensions; Financial Services; Franchising; Insolvency & Insurance; Mergers & Acquisitions; Securities; Tax Law
Senior and Managing Partners:
Bryan J. Buttigieg, Partner
416-595-8172
bbuttigieg@millerthomson.com
Gerald D. Chipeur, Partner
403-298-2434
gchipeur@millerthomson.com
Louis Coallier, Partner
514-871-5488
lcoallier@millerthomsonpouliot.com
Eric Couture, Partner
519-871-5489
ecouture@millerthomsonpouliot.com
Tony Crossman, Partner
604-643-1244
tcrossman@millerthomson.com
Debra Curcio Lister, Partner
780-429-9763
dcurciolister@millerthomson.com
Tamara Farber, Partner
416-595-8520
tfarber@millerthomson.com
Sandra A. Gogal, Partner
416-595-8574
sgogal@millerthomson.com
Luc Gratton, Partner
514-871-5482
lgratton@millerthomsonpouliot.com
Daniel L. Kiselbach, Partner
604-643-1263
dkiselbach@millerthomson.com
Rosanne M. Kyle, Partner
604-643-1235
rkyle@millerthomson.com
Bruce J. McMeekin, Partner
905-415-6791
bmcmeekin@millerthomson.com
Brent J. Muir, Partner
514-871-5478
bmuir@millerthomsonpouliot.com
Robin-Lee A. Norris, Partner
519-780-4638
rnorris@millerthomson.com
Pierre Paquet, Partner
514-871-5427
ppaquet@millerthomsonpouliot.com
John R. Tidball, Partner
905-415-6710
jtidball@millerthomson.com
Louise Tremblay, Partner
514-871-5476
ltremblay@millerthomsonpouliot.com
Darin J. Hannaford, Partner
780-429-9714
dhannaford@millerthomson.ca
Sandra L. Hawes, Partner
G. James Thorlakson, Partner
780-429-9721
jthorlakson@millerthomson.ca
Wendi P. Crowe, Partner
Kent H. Davidson, Partner
780-429-9790
kdavidson@millerthomson.com
Debra Curcio Lister, Partner
780-429-9763
dcurciolister@millerthomson.com
Brian J. Curial, Partner
James M. Kalyta, Partner
Bryan J. Kickham, Q.C., Partner
Kevin D. Trumpour, Partner
780-429-9707
ktrumpour@millerthomson.com
Robert L. Falby, Partner
416-595-8173
rfalby@millerthomson.com
Aaron E. Atcheson, Partner
519-931-3526
aatcheson@millerthomson.com
James A. Duke, Q.C., Partner
780-429-9750
jduke@millerthomson.ca
Joseph W. Yurkovich, Q.C., Partner
780-429-9716
jyurkovich@millerthomson.ca
Robert J. Fuller, Partner
416-595-8514
rfuller@millerthomson.com
Constance I. Taylor, Partner
Scott J. Hammel, Partner
780-429-9726
shammel@millerthomson.ca
Terrence M. Warner, Partner
780-429-9727
twarner@millerthomson.com
Eugene J.A. Gierczak, Partner
416-596-2132
egierczak@millerthomson.com
Bruce N. Geiger, Partner
780-429-9774
bgeiger@millerthomson.com
Charles J. Schwartz, Partner
416-595-7904
cschwartz@millerthomson.com
John N. Turner, Partner
416-595-8607
jturner@millerthomson.com
Brian W.L. Tod, Q.C., Partner
780-429-9723
btod@millerthomson.ca
Michael J. Wren, Partner
416-595-8184
mwren@millerthomson.com
William J. Kenny, Q.C., Partner
Daniel C.P. Stachnik, Q.C., Partner
780-429-9761
dstachnik@millerthomson.ca
John A. Cross, Q.C., Partner
780-429-9745
jcross@millerthomson.com

Ogilvy Renault LLP/S.E.N.C.R.L., s.r.l.

#1100, 1981, av McGill College, Montréal QC H3A 3C1
514-847-4747 514-286-5474
montreal@ogilvyrenault.com
www.ogilvyrenault.com
Profile: 6 Offices, 176 Lawyers, Founded in: 1879
Asset-based Lending; Banking & Financial Products; Corporate & Commercial Law; Insolvency & Restructuring; Mergers & Acquisitions; Projects & Project Finance; Securities; Tax
Senior and Managing Partners:
Christian J. Beaudry, Senior Partner
514-847-4416
cbeaudry@ogilvyrenault.com
Louis J. Gouin, Senior Partner
514-847-4425
lgouin@ogilvyrenault.com
Pierre Hébert, Senior Partner
514-847-4474
phebert@ogilvyrenault.com
William Hesler, Senior Partner
514-847-4510
whesler@ogilvyrenault.com
Olivier F. Kott, Senior Partner
514-847-4445
okott@ogilvyrenault.com
Daniel I. Lack, Senior Partner
514-847-4471
dlack@ogilvyrenault.com
Lise Bergeron, Senior Partner
514-847-4506
lbergeron@ogilvyrenault.com
Claude Brunet, Senior Partner
514-847-4726
cbrunet@ogilvyrenault.com
Christine A. Carron, Senior Partner
514-847-4404
ccarron@ogilvyrenault.com
Jules Charette, Senior Partner
514-847-4450
jcharette@ogilvyrenault.com
Robert P. Charlton, Senior Partner
514-847-4459
rcharlton@ogilvyrenault.com
John A. Coleman, Senior Partner
514-847-4503
jcoleman@ogilvyrenault.com
Marc Duquette, Senior Partner
514-847-4508
mduquette@ogilvyrenault.com
L. Yves Fortier, Senior Partner
514-847-4740
yfortier@ogilvyrenault.com

Osler, Hoskin & Harcourt LLP

#6100, P.O Box 50 One First Canadian Place, Toronto ON M5X 1B8
416-362-2111 416-862-6666
counsel@osler.com
www.osler.com
Profile: 5 Offices, 450 Lawyers,
Advises many of Canada's corporate leaders as well as U.S. & international parties with extensive interests in Canada; third-party research confirms the firm's preeminent position in the marketplace; with over 400 lawyers based in Toronto, Montréal, Ottawa, Calgary & New York, our critical mass of experience with the largest domestic & cross-border business combinations enables us to exercise acknowledged strengths in mergers & acquisitions, tax, competition & litigation, & leverage our specialty expertise in fields like commercial property & infrastructure projects, IP & IT, among many others
Senior and Managing Partners:
Dale R. Ponder, Managing Partner
416-862-6500
dponder@osler.com
Harvey Kirsh, Senior Partner
416-862-6844
hkirsh@osler.com
Stephen P. Sigurdson, Managing Partner
416-862-4261
ssigurdson@osler.com
Ronald G. Atkey, Senior Partner
416-862-6421
ratkey@osler.com
Lyndon A.J. Barner, Senior Partner
416-862-6679
lbarnes@osler.com
Laurie Barrett, Senior Partner
416-862-6599
lbarrett@osler.com
Terrence R. Burgoyne, Senior Partner
416-862-6601
tburgoyne@osler.com
Jean M. Fraser, Senior Partner
416-862-6537
jfraser@osler.com
Judith E. Harris, Senior Partner
416-862-4609
jharris@osler.com
Andrew H. Kingissepp, Senior Partner
416-862-6507
akingissepp@osler.com

Stewart McKelvey Stirling Scales

#900, Purdy's Wharf Tower One P.O Box 997 Central1959 Upper Water St., Halifax NS B3J 2X2
902-420-3200 902-420-1417
halifax@smss.com
www.smss.com
Profile: 7 Offices, 91 Lawyers, Founded in: 1867
Senior and Managing Partners:
John Rogers, Managing Partner
902-420-3340
jrogers@smss.com
T. Arthur Barry, Partner
902-420-3364
abarry@smss.com
Lydia S. Bugden, Partner
902-420-3372
lbugden@smss.com

Douglas J. Mathews, Partner
902-420-3320
dmathews@smss.com
John D. Plowman, Partner
902-420-3322
jplowman@smss.com
Richard F. Southcott, Partner
902-420-3304
rsouthcott@smss.com
Lawrence J. Stordy, Partner
902-420-3347
lstordy@smss.com

Stikeman Elliott LLP
#5300, Commerce Court West 199 Bay St., Toronto ON M5L 1B9
416-869-5500 416-947-0866 877-973-5500 Telex: 06-22536
info@stikeman.com
www.stikeman.com
Profile: 8 Offices, 200 Lawyers, Founded in: 1952
As a full-service business law firm, we advise on a wide range of matters including securities, structured financial products, investment activity, mergers & acquisitions, joint ventures, public-private partnerships & government advisory mandates; our particular strength lies in developing innovative, workable solutions to complex legal concerns; our success in building an international profile is reflected in our consistent inclusion in international "league tables" in such areas as project finance, privatizations & international securities transactions
Senior and Managing Partners:
Roderick F. Barrett, Managing Partner
416-869-5524
rbarrett@stikeman.com
William J. Braithwaite, Senior Partner
416-869-5654
wbraithwaite@stikeman.com
Edward J. Waitzer, Senior Partner
416-869-5587
ewaitzer@stikeman.com
Jeffrey M. Singer, Partner
416-869-5656
jsinger@stikeman.com

Torys LLP
#3000, Toronto-Dominion Centre P.O Box 270 79 Wellington St. West, Toronto ON M5K 1N2
416-865-0040 416-865-7380
info@torys.com
www.torys.com
Profile: 1 Offices, 202 Lawyers,
An international business law firm with more than 330 lawyers in its Toronto & New York offices; the firm acts for all types of financial institutions, including banks, life insurance companies, property & casualty insurance companies, trust & loan companies & securities dealers; we act as corporate counsel to a number of Canada's largest life insurance companies; our banking involvement includes work for Canada's five largest banks, as well as for numerous foreign banks; we are frequently retained to act on special projects, regulatory matters, merchant banking, secured transactions, institutional lending, & investment funds & management matters; Torys has also acted for a number of major foreign banks that have invested in Canadian entities & established Canadian banking subsidiaries, branches & other business vehicles in Canada
Senior and Managing Partners:
Les Viner, Managing Partner
416-865-8107
lviner@torys.com
Philip J. Brown, Partner
416-865-8238
pbrown@torys.com
Michael F.E. Akkawi, Partner
416-865-8122
makkawi@torys.com
Michael D. Amm, Partner
416-865-8140
mdamm@torys.com
Rose Bailey, Partner
416-865-7380
rbailey@torys.com
Amanda C. Balasubramanian, Partner
416-865-8137
abalasubramanian@torys.com
Richard J. Balfour, Partner
416-865-7339
rbalfour@torys.com
Peter D. Ballantyne, Partner
416-865-7521
pballantyne@torys.com
Sheila R. Block, Partner
416-865-7319
sblock@torys.com
Scott A. Bomhof, Partner
416-865-7370
sbomhof@torys.com

Provincial Law Firms

Alberta

** indicates # of lawyers*

***Banff*: Karras Rathbone - *2**
P.O Box 899 Main205 Bear St., Banff AB T1L 1A9
403-762-2770 403-762-5961
karalaw@telus.net

***Barrhead*: Driessen Law Office - *1**
P.O Box 4220 Main5017 - 50 Ave., Barrhead AB T7N 1A2
780-674-2276 780-674-4592
solutions@drlessenlaw.ca

***Bonnyville*: Fraser, Allan Wayne, Professional Corporation - *1**
CP 6710 Main4816 - 50 Ave., Bonnyville AB T9N 2H2
780-826-3355 780-826-6132
awfraser@telusplanet.net

***Bonnyville*: Wood & Wiebe - *2**
#101, CP 8060 Main5001 - 49 Ave., Bonnyville AB T9N 2J3
780-826-5767 780-826-4654
woodwieb@telusplanet.net

***Brooks*: Bell Law Office - *1**
CP 670 Main, Brooks AB T1R 1B6
403-362-3447 403-362-4379
dhb@telus.net

***Calgary*: Anderson Law Firm - *1**
14 Strathridge Grove SW, Calgary AB T3H 4M1
403-253-4597 403-253-4599
latitude@telus.net

***Calgary*: Barron, Deborah L. - *1**
#200, 2120 - 4th St. West, Calgary AB T2S 1W7
403-238-0000 403-238-2255
deborahbarron@shaw.ca

***Calgary*: Beattie, Alan V.M., Q.C. - *1**
3621 - 1A St. SW, Calgary AB T2S 1R4
403-245-5255 403-228-0254
beattiea@shaw.ca

***Calgary*: Borden Ladner Gervais LLP - *103**
#1000, Canterra Tower 400 - 3rd Ave. SW, Calgary AB T2P 4H2
403-232-9500 403-266-1395
info@blgcanada.com
www.blgcanada.com

***Calgary*: Bruni & Company - *2**
707 - 15th Ave. SW, Calgary AB T2R 0R8
403-266-5664 403-262-6343
brunicorp@shaw.ca

***Calgary*: Burnet, Duckworth & Palmer LLP - *125**
#1400, First Canadian Centre 350 - 7th Ave. SW, Calgary AB T2P 3N9
403-260-0100 403-260-0332
counsel@bdplaw.com
www.bdplaw.com

***Calgary*: Burstall Winger LLP - *26**
#1600, Dome Tower 333 - 7th Ave. SW, Calgary AB T2P 2Z1
403-264-1915 403-266-6016
info@burstall.com
www.burstall.com

***Calgary*: Butlin Oke Roberts & Nobles - *5**
#100, 1501 - 1 St. SW, Calgary AB T2R 0W1
403-543-7750 403-543-7759

***Calgary*: Cairns, Richard, Q.C. - *1**
#210, The Burns Bldg. 237 - 8 Ave. SE, Calgary AB T2G 5C3
403-205-3155 403-546-0034
counsel@echambers.ca
www.echambers.ca

***Calgary*: Caron & Partners LLP, Barristers & Solicitors - *16**
#2100, Scotia Centre 700 - 2 St. SW, 21st Fl., Calgary AB T2P 2W1
403-262-3000 403-237-0111
legalservices@caronpartners.com
www.caronpartners.com

***Calgary*: Carscallen Leitch LLP - *29**
#1500, 407 - 2 St. SW, Calgary AB T2P 2Y3
403-262-3775 403-262-2952
info@cllawyers.com
www.cllawyers.com

***Calgary*: Castle & Associates, Barristers & Solicitors - *7**
#302, 221 - 10th Ave. SE, Calgary AB T2G 0V9
403-265-3403 403-269-3217
mailbox@castleandassociates.ca
www.castleandassociates.ca

***Calgary*: Clark & Associates - *2**
#203, 136 - 17 Ave. NE, Calgary AB T2E 1L6
403-520-2011 403-230-3509
bclark@clarkandassociates.ca
www.clarkandassociates.ca

***Calgary*: Clark Dymond McCaffery O'Brien-Kelly - *3**
#300, 1122 - 4 St. SW, Calgary AB T2R 1M1
403-265-7070 403-232-6750
lawcdmg@telusplanet.net

***Calgary*: Cuming, Gillespie & Raymaker - Alberta Injury Lawyers - *5**
#1130, 396 - 11th Ave. SW, Calgary AB T2R 0C5
403-571-0555 403-232-8818 800-682-2480
jcuming@cuminggillespie.com; cgillespie@cuminggillespie.com
www.cuminggillespie.com

***Calgary*: Daniel J. Aberle Professional Corporation - *1**
#305, 602 - 11 Ave. SW, Calgary AB T2R 1J8
403-229-1129 403-245-9660

***Calgary*: Dartnell & Lutz - *2**
#840, 840 - 6 Ave. SW, Calgary AB T2P 3E5
403-264-8484 403-263-9110
dartnell-lutz@shaw.ca

***Calgary*: Davison, Worden LLP - *6**
#1710, 540 - 5 Ave. SW, Calgary AB T2P 0M2
403-262-7745 403-262-7011

***Calgary*: Demiantschuk, Milley, Burke & Hoffinger - *10**
#1200, 1015 - 4th St. SW, Calgary AB T2R 1J4
403-252-9937 403-263-8529
assistance@legalsolutions.ca
www.legalsolutions.ca

***Calgary*: Dunphy Best Blocksom LLP, Barristers & Solicitors - *20**
#2100, 777 - 8th Ave. SW, Calgary AB T2P 3R5
403-265-7777 403-269-8911
info@dbblaw.com
www.dbblaw.com

***Calgary*: Ellert Law - *2**
#510, 706 - 7 Ave. SW, Calgary AB T2P 0Z1
403-269-3315 403-269-3329
dale.ellert@ellertlaw.com

***Calgary*: Everard Kubitz & Mueller - *3**
#308, 2116 - 27 Ave. NE, Calgary AB T2E 7A6
403-250-7100 403-291-5473
lawyers@ekmlawyers.com

***Calgary*: Faber Bickman Leon - *7**
#350, 603 - 7 Ave. SW, Calgary AB T2P 2T5
403-263-1540 403-269-2653
lfaber@fbllaw.ca; dbickman@fbllaw.ca; lleon@fbllaw.ca
www.fbllaw.ca

***Calgary*: Fagan & Chow - *2**
#375, 926 - 5th Ave. SW, Calgary AB T2P 0N7
403-517-1777 403-517-1776
davidg_chow@yahoo.ca
www.patrickfagan.com

***Calgary*: Fasken Martineau - *24**
#3400, First Canadian Centre 350 - 7th Ave. SW, Calgary AB T2P 3N9
403-261-5350 403-261-5351
calgary@fasken.com
www.fasken.com

***Calgary*: Felesky Flynn LLP - *33**
#5000, Petro Canada Centre 150 - 6th Ave. SW, Calgary AB T2P 3Y7
403-260-3300 403-263-9649
felesky@felesky.com
www.felesky.com

Calgary: **Fric, Lowenstein & Co. LLP - *4**
#310, 2891 Sunridge Way, Calgary AB T1Y 7K7
403-291-2594 403-291-2668
friclow@telusplanet.net

Calgary: **German Fong Albus, Barristers & Solicitors - *3**
#418, Hewlett Packard Bldg. 715 - 5 Ave. SW, Calgary AB T2P 2X6
403-263-7880 403-237-7075
mjfong@gfal-law.com; sfalbus@gfal-law.com
www.gfal-law.com

Calgary: **Gorman, Gorman, Burns & Watson - *2**
#500, 1135 - 17 Ave. SW, Calgary AB T2T 0B6
403-244-5515 403-244-5605

Calgary: **Gottlieb, David M., Law Office - *1**
#8, 5602 - 4 St. NW, Calgary AB T2K 1B2
403-275-4881 403-274-0367
gottlieb.david@telusplanet.net

Calgary: **Hadley & Davis - *2**
#311, 1711 - 4 St. SW, Calgary AB T2S 1V8
403-264-1234 403-264-0999
info@hadleydavis.com
www.hadleydavis.com

Calgary: **Hansen & Company - *2**
538 - 9 Ave. SE, Calgary AB T2G 0S1
403-261-6890 403-263-1632 800-523-6162
info@hansen-company.com
www.hansen-company.com

Calgary: **Heinz, Stephen Graham - *1**
#2900, 350 - 7 Ave. SW, Calgary AB T2P 3N9
403-262-4462 403-265-4496
stephen.heinz@3web.net

Calgary: **Jamison, Michael M. - *1**
2503 - 22 St. SW, Calgary AB T2T 5G3
403-217-1250 403-287-1968
mmjlaw2@shaw.ca

Calgary: **Kelly & Kelly - *4**
#220, 3505 - 32nd St. NE, Calgary AB T1Y 5Y9
403-266-6296 403-264-2954
kellykp@telusplanet.net; tjolliff@telusplanet.net

Calgary: **Kerr, Robert D. - *1**
#300, 840 - 6 Ave. SW, Calgary AB T2P 3E5
403-265-1331 403-265-1332
bkerr@shaw.ca

Calgary: **King, Jack A., Q.C. - *1**
10 Forest Grove Pl. SE, Calgary AB T2A 7G6
403-235-4600

Calgary: **Lee & Kong - *2**
#330, 1324 - 17 Ave. SW, Calgary AB T2T 5S8
403-233-9432 403-237-9614
leekong@canada.com

Calgary: **Lehan, Menzies, Walters & Abdi - *6**
9937 Fairmount Dr. SE, Calgary AB T2J 0S2
403-261-4010 403-261-4040

Calgary: **Lirenman, Peterson - *3**
#300, Notre Dame Place 255 - 17 Ave. SW, Calgary AB T2S 2T8
403-245-0111 403-245-0115

Calgary: **Lord Russell - *6**
410 - 6th St. SW, Calgary AB T2P 1X2
403-262-7722 403-262-5991
simonl@telus.net; vicruss@telus.net

Calgary: **Low, Glenn & Card - *6**
#120, 3636 - 23 St. NE, Calgary AB T2E 8Z5
403-291-2532 403-291-2534
lawyer@lgc-law.com

Calgary: **Macleod Dixon LLP - *167**
#3700, Canterra Tower 400 Third Ave. SW, Calgary AB T2P 4H2
403-267-8222 403-264-5973
Bill.Tuer@macleoddixon.com; Anne.Derby@macleoddixon.com
www.macleoddixon.com

Calgary: **McCaffery Mudry Pritchard LLP, Barristers & Solicitors - *7**
#2200, 736 - 6 Ave. SW, Calgary AB T2P 3T7
403-260-1400 403-260-1444
postmaster@mccafferylaw.ca
www.mccafferylaw.ca

Calgary: **McConnell MacInnes - *7**
1245 - 70 Ave. SE, Calgary AB T2H 2X8
403-278-7001 403-271-2826
kfm@mcmaclaw.com; jrm@mcmaclaw.com

Calgary: **McGown Johnson - *4**
#110, 7260 - 12th St. SE, Calgary AB T2H 2S5
403-255-5114 403-258-3840
mjlaw@mcgownjohnson.com

Calgary: **McKenna Law Office - *1**
1505 - 5 St. SW, Calgary AB T2R 1P2
403-716-2092 403-234-7911
paul@mckennalegal.com

Calgary: **McLeod & Company LLP - *37**
14505 Bannister Rd. SE, 3rd Fl., Calgary AB T2X 3J3
403-278-9411 403-271-1769
pnbreen@mcleod-law.com; tmcarswell@mcleod-law.com
www.mcleod-law.com

Calgary: **McTavish, Anne E. - *1**
7410E - 5th St. SE, Calgary AB T2H 2L9
403-252-4965 403-253-7743
anne.mctavish@telusplanet.net

Calgary: **Miles, Davison LLP - *23**
#1600, Bow Valley Square II 205 - 5th Ave. SW, Calgary AB T2P 2V7
403-298-0333 403-263-6840
thefirm@milesdavison.com; jed@milesdavison.com
www.milesdavison.com

Calgary: **Millar Smith & Associates, Barristers, Solicitors, Notaries - *1**
#300, 1130 Kensington Rd. NW, Calgary AB T2N 3P3
403-283-1925 403-270-8033
millar.associates@shaw.ca
www.wes-law.com

Calgary: **Milne, Davis & Young - *2**
#850, 933 - 17th Ave. SW, Calgary AB T2T 5R6
403-229-3000 403-229-3282
milnedavisyoung@shaw.ca; r.a.young@shaw.ca

Calgary: **Moore Wittman Phillips - *6**
#850, 1015 - 4 St. SW, Calgary AB T2R 1J4
403-269-8500 403-269-8515
mwp@nucleus.com

Calgary: **North Hill Law Office - *1**
P.O Box 32053 RPO Bankview2619 - 14 St. SW, Calgary AB T2T 5X6
403-282-1515 403-220-1575
oldmanncuba@hotmail.com

Calgary: **O'Brien, Devlin, Markey & Macleod, Barristers & Solicitors - *3**
#1310, Watermark Tower 530 - 8th Ave. SW, Calgary AB T2P 3S8
403-265-5616 403-264-8146
nobrien@obriendevlin.com; bdevlin@obriendevlin.com
www.obriendevlin.com

Calgary: **Parlee McLaws LLP - *32**
#3400, Petro Canada Centre 150 - 6th Ave. SW, Calgary AB T2P 3Y7
403-294-7000 403-265-8263
lawyers@parlee.com
www.parlee.com

Calgary: **Peterson, Shields, & Galbraith - *6**
#204, 755 Lake Bonavista Dr. SE, Calgary AB T2J 0N3
403-271-9710 403-271-3942
info@petersonshields.com; rmp@petersonshields.com

Calgary: **Pittman MacIsaac & Roy - *4**
#2600, West Tower, Sun Life Plaza 144 - 4th Ave. SW, Calgary AB T2P 3N4
403-237-6566 403-237-6594
gwp@pmrlaw.ca; stm@pmrlaw.ca; rfr@pmrlaw.ca;
makn@pmrlaw.ca
www.pmrlaw.ca

Calgary: **Pomerance & Company - *3**
#1430, 1122 - 4th St. SW, Calgary AB T2R 1M1
403-278-5840 403-271-6929 866-278-5840
pomeranc@telus.net
www.pomerancelaw.ca

Calgary: **Purdy & Purdy - *2**
#801, 1015 - 4th St. SW, Calgary AB T2R 1J4
403-777-4850 403-777-4855

Calgary: **Rogers & Company, Barristers & Solicitors - *5**
#200, 815 - 10 Ave. SW, Calgary AB T2R 0B4
403-263-6805 403-263-6800
reception@rogcolaw.com
www.rogcolaw.com

Calgary: **Ruff, A. Charles - *1**
#202, 1409 Edmonton Trail NE, Calgary AB T2E 3K8
403-230-0999 403-230-0991
chasruff@shaw.ca

Calgary: **Salmon & Company - *2**
#1100, 707 - 7 Ave. SW, Calgary AB T2P 3H6
403-231-2705 403-705-1214
david@salmonco.ca

Calgary: **Schwartzberg Law Office - *1**
3923 - 17 Ave. SW, Calgary AB T3E 0C3
403-232-1302 403-249-6655
schwartzberglaw@shawcable.com

Calgary: **Shachnowich, William J. - *1**
1700 Varsity Estates Dr. NW, Calgary AB T3B 2W9
403-269-1313 403-210-0106
shachnow@telus.net

Calgary: **Smith & Smith - *2**
#503, 1300 - 8 St. SW, Calgary AB T2R 1B2
403-229-1727 403-229-1730

Calgary: **Smith Law Office - *1**
348 - 14 St. NW, Calgary AB T2N 1Z7
403-283-8018 403-270-3065
j.smith@smithlawoffice.ca

Calgary: **Smith Mack Lamarsh - *3**
#450, United Place 808 - 4 Ave. SW, Calgary AB T2P 3E8
403-234-7779 403-263-7897
cmsmith@telusplanet.net; slamarsh@telusplanet.net

Calgary: **Spier Harben - *11**
#1400, Iveagh House 707 - 7th St. SW, Calgary AB T2P 3H6
403-263-5130 403-264-9600
asattin@spierharben.com

Calgary: **Stewart & McCullough - *4**
#307, 1228 Kensington Rd. NW, Calgary AB T2N 3P7
403-270-2641 403-670-7025
martin.meronek@shaw.ca

Calgary: **Stones Carbert Waite LLP, Barristers & Solicitors - *9**
#1600, 635 - 8th Ave. SW, Calgary AB T2P 3M3
403-263-5656 403-263-5553
info@scwlawyers.com; stones@scwlawyers.com
www.scwlawyers.com

Calgary: **Story Law Office - *1**
#240, 3015 - 12 St. NE, Calgary AB T2E 7J2
403-250-1918 403-250-3287

Calgary: **Sugimoto & Company - *5**
#204, 2635 - 37 Ave. NE, Calgary AB T1Y 5Z6
403-291-4650 403-291-4099
sugimoto@sugimotolaw.com

Calgary: **Thompson, Ball & McMahon - *2**
#534, 11012 Macleod Trail SE, Calgary AB T2J 6A5
403-271-5050 403-271-5298
thompsonball@telus.net; jpmcm@telus.net

Calgary: **Thornborough, Smeltz - *4**
#630, Southcentre Executive Tower 11012 Macleod Trail SE, Calgary AB T2J 6A5
403-271-3221 403-271-6684
tammy@thornsmeltz.com

Calgary: **Walsh Wilkins Creighton LLP - *17**
#2800, 801 - 6 Ave. SW, Calgary AB T2P 4A3
403-267-8400 403-264-9400
mail@wwclawyers.com
www.wwclawyers.com

Calgary: **Ward, Peter M. - *1**
#300, 400 - 5th Ave. SW, Calgary AB T2P 0L6
403-263-1158 403-264-9218

Calgary: **Warren Tettensor Amantea LLP, Barristers & Solicitors - *10**
1413 - 2 St. SW, Calgary AB T2R 0W7
403-228-7007 403-244-1948
info@warren.ab.ca
www.warren.ab.ca

Calgary: **White & Company - *2**
#204, 3716 - 61 Ave. SE, Calgary AB T2C 1Z4
403-236-2110 403-279-4842

Calgary: **Wolfman & Company - *2**
#700, 640 - 8th Ave. SW, Calgary AB T2P 1G7
403-263-6710 403-266-1896
info@wolfmanlaw.com

Calgary: **Zenith Hookenson LLP - *3**
#218, Mayfair Place 6707 Elbow Dr. SW, Calgary AB T2V 0E4
403-259-5041 403-258-0719
zenithco@telusplanet.net

Camrose: **Andreassen Borth, Barristers, Solicitors, Notaries, Mediators - *4**
#200, 4870 - 51 St., Camrose AB T4V 1S1
780-672-3181 780-672-0682
aob@telusplanet.net
www.andreassenolsonborth.com

Camrose: **Farnham West Stolee LLP - *3**
5016 - 52 St., Camrose AB T4V 1V7
780-679-0444 780-679-0958
camlaw@telusplanet.net

Camrose: **Fielding & Company LLP - *4**
#100, 4918 - 51 St., Camrose AB T4V 1S3
780-672-8851 780-672-4707
lawyers@camroselaw.com
www.camroselaw.com

Camrose: **Knaut, Johnson - *2**
4925 - 51 St., Camrose AB T4V 1S4
780-672-5561 780-672-5565

Coaldale: **Fast, Leonard D. - *1**
P.O Box 1360 Main1709 - 20 Ave., Coaldale AB T1M 1N2
403-345-4415 403-345-2719
lfastlaw@telusplanet.net

Coaldale: **Lammi Law - *1**
P.O Box 1329 Main1910 - 18 St., Coaldale AB T1M 1N1
403-345-3922 403-345-2172
lammilaw@telusplanet.net

Cold Lake: **Todd, Drake, Williams, Findlater LLP - *5**
P.O Box 908 4807 - 51 St., Cold Lake AB T9M 1P2
780-594-7151 780-594-7155
rmtodd@tdlaw.ca; ldrake@tdlaw.ca

Coronation: **Spady, E. Roger - *1**
P.O Box 328 5015 Victoria Ave., Coronation AB T0C 1C0
403-578-3131 403-578-2660

Drumheller: **Ross, Todd & Company - *3**
P.O Box 970 98 - 3 Ave. West, Drumheller AB T0J 0Y0
403-823-5186 403-823-6407
reception@drumhellerlaw.com; sharon.clark@drumhellerlaw.com

Drumheller: **Schumacher, Gough & Company - *2**
P.O Box 2800 196 - 3rd Ave. West, Drumheller AB T0J 0Y0
403-823-2424 403-823-6984 866-923-2424
sgp_law@telus.net; sgp_harry@telus.net

Edmonton: **Abbey Hunter Davison - *3**
9636 - 102A Ave., Edmonton AB T5H 0G5
780-421-8585 780-425-0472
dhabbey@shaw.ca

Edmonton: **Abbey, David R. - *1**
#780, TransAlta Place 10150 - 100 St. NW, Edmonton AB T5J 0P6
780-423-2793 780-423-2750
dabbey@telus.net

Edmonton: **Ackroyd LLP Barristers & Solicitors - *17**
#1500, First Edmonton Place 10665 Jasper Ave., Edmonton AB T5J 3S9
780-423-8905 780-423-8946
aprd@ackroydlaw.com
www.ackroydlaw.com

Edmonton: **Agrios, Jack N., Q.C., LL.B, O.C. - *1**
#1325, Manulife Place 10180 - 101 St., Edmonton AB T5J 3S4
780-696-6915 780-969-6901
jack@jackagrios.com

Edmonton: **Andrew, March & Oake - *9**
#300, 10020 - 101A Ave. NW, Edmonton AB T5J 3G2
780-429-3391 780-424-8483

Edmonton: **Ares Law - *1**
LeMarchand Tower 11507 - 100 Ave., Edmonton AB T5K 2R2
780-488-1951 780-482-6048

Edmonton: **Baker Purdon Caskenette - *2**
10263 - 178 St., Edmonton AB T5S 1M3
780-489-5566 780-486-7735
bpurdon@planet.eon.net

Edmonton: **Beresh Cunningham Aloneissi O'Neill Hurley - *10**
#300, MacLean Block Box 300 10110 - 107 St., Edmonton AB T5J 1J4
780-421-4766 780-429-0346 877-277-4766
bdc@bdc.ca

Edmonton: **Berndt, Helmut - *1**
#1780, 10020 - 101A Ave. NW, Edmonton AB T5J 3G2
780-439-6643 780-439-6696

Edmonton: **Biamonte Cairo & Shortreed LLP - *13**
#1600, 10025 - 102A Ave., Edmonton AB T5J 2Z2
780-425-5800 780-426-1600 888-425-2620
biamonte@biamonte.com

Edmonton: **Bishop & McKenzie LLP - *29**
#2500, 10104 - 103 Ave., Edmonton AB T5J 1V3
780-426-5550 780-426-1305
edmonton@bishopmckenzie.com
www.bishopmckenzie.com

Edmonton: **Braithwaite Boyle - *5**
Braithwaite Boyle Bldg. 11816 - 124 St. NW, Edmonton AB T5L 0M3
780-451-9191 780-451-9198 800-661-4902
ken.braithwaite@accidentinjurylawyer.com
www.accidentinjurylawyer.com

Edmonton: **Braul McEvoy & Gee - *3**
#2170, Sun Life Place 10123 - 99 St., Edmonton AB T5J 3H1
780-423-2481 780-423-2474
lawyers@braullaw.ab.ca

Edmonton: **Broda & Company - *1**
13723 - 93 St., Edmonton AB T5E 5V6
780-456-9330 780-456-9339

Edmonton: **Brosseau & Associates - *2**
#1955, Commerce Place 10155 - 102 St. NW, Edmonton AB T5J 4G8
780-426-4000 780-424-4616

Edmonton: **Brownlee LLP - *59**
#2200, Commerce Place 10155 - 102 St., Edmonton AB T5J 4G8
780-497-4800 780-424-3254
e-mail@brownleelaw.com
www.brownleelaw.com

Edmonton: **Bryan & Company LLP - *38**
#2600, Manulife Place Box 2600 10180 - 101 St., Edmonton AB T5J 3Y2
780-423-5730 780-428-6324 800-357-9265
info@bryanco.com; djcorrigan@bryanco.com (Advocacy)
www.bryanco.com

Edmonton: **Campbell & Company - *5**
#100, 4208 - 97 St. NW, Edmonton AB T6E 5Z9
780-434-6565 780-434-1692

Edmonton: **Campbell & Van Doesburg - *2**
#300, 10230 - 142 St., Edmonton AB T5N 3Y6
780-451-2661 780-452-1051
charles@campbellvandoesburg.com

Edmonton: **Campbell, A.F. - *1**
#2410, Oxford Tower 10235 - 101 St. NW, Edmonton AB T5J 3G1
780-428-8882 780-421-0818
pgl31416@telusplanet.ca

Edmonton: **Chatwin Cox & Michalyshyn - *6**
#1000, 10060 Jasper Ave. NW, Edmonton AB T5J 3R8
780-421-7667 780-424-7231
lawyers@chatwin.ab.ca

Edmonton: **Chomicki Baril Mah LLP - *19**
#1201, TD Tower 10088 - 102 Ave., Edmonton AB T5J 4K2
780-423-3441 780-420-1763
office_admin@cbmllp.com
www.cbmllp.com

Edmonton: **Chopra, Chopra & Chopra - *1**
#517, 12111 - 51 St., Edmonton AB T6H 6A3
780-429-4961 780-426-3512
manichopra.msn@attcanada.net

Edmonton: **Clancy, Michael H. - *1**
9844 - 106 St. NW, Edmonton AB T5K 1B8
780-424-9014 780-424-9023 800-647-7723

Edmonton: **Cleall Barristers Solicitors - *12**
#2500, Commerce Place 10155 - 102nd St., Edmonton AB T5J 4G8
780-425-2500 780-425-1222
main@cleall.ca
www.cleall.ca

Edmonton: **Cochard Johnson - *2**
#305, Empire Bldg. 10800 Jasper Ave., Edmonton AB T5J 1V9
780-429-9929 780-429-9981

Edmonton: **Coley, Hennessy & Cassis - *3**
#212, 3132 Parsons Rd., Edmonton AB T6N 1L6
780-468-2551 780-466-8006
chc@connect.ab.ca

Edmonton: **Coulter & Power - *2**
#2200, Metropolitan Pl. 10303 Jasper Ave., Edmonton AB T5J 3N6
780-413-2300 780-420-0049

Edmonton: **Cousineau, C.D. - *1**
#215, 11098 - 156 St. SW, Edmonton AB T5P 4M8
780-455-0485 780-447-5853

Edmonton: **Cox Trofimuk Campbell - *4**
#2400, 10303 Jasper Ave., Edmonton AB T5J 3T8
780-422-6242 780-428-1137

Edmonton: **Croll, Ted R. - *1**
#1300, 10665 Jasper Ave., Edmonton AB T5J 3S9
780-420-9903 780-424-3631
trcroll@shaw.ca

Edmonton: **Cummings Andrews Mackay LLP - *8**
#500, 10150 - 100 St. NW, Edmonton AB T5J 0P6
780-428-8222 780-426-2670 800-565-5745
cam@cummings.ab.ca
www.cummings.ab.ca

Edmonton: **Davidson Gregory Danyliuk - *3**
110 Place 10008 - 110 St., Edmonton AB T5K 1J6
780-482-5496 780-482-1930 866-887-8868
crimlaw@telusplanet.net

Edmonton: **Dawson, Stevens, Duckett & Shaigec - *9**
#300, Dawson Bldg. 9924 - 106 St., Edmonton AB T5K 1C4
780-424-9058 780-425-0172 800-661-3176
www.dsscrimlaw.com

Edmonton: **de Villars Jones - *4**
#300, Noble Bldg. 8540 - 109 St., Edmonton AB T6G 1E6
780-433-9000 780-433-9780
adev@sagecounsel.com

Edmonton: **Dlin, Gary A. - *1**
7904 Gateway Blvd., Edmonton AB T6E 6C3
780-438-4972 780-435-1037

Edmonton: **Duncan & Craig LLP, Lawyers & Mediators - *46**
#2800, Scotia Place 10060 Jasper Ave., Edmonton AB T5J 3V9
780-428-6036 780-428-9683 800-782-9409
edmonton@dcllp.com
www.dcllp.com

Edmonton: **Durocher Simpson - *6**
Old Strathcona Law Office 7904 Gateway Blvd., Edmonton AB T6E 6C3
780-420-6850 780-425-9185
mail@dursim.com
www.dursim.com

Edmonton: **Eccleston, E.L. - *1**
235 North Town Mall, Edmonton AB T5E 6C1
780-478-6635 780-476-8587
eccl@telusplanet.net

Edmonton: **Embury & McFayden - *1**
#602, Centre 104 5241 Calgary Trail NW, Edmonton AB T6H 5G8
780-439-7302 780-433-6510
emburymc@telus.net

Edmonton: **Emery Jamieson LLP - *26**
#1700, Oxford Tower 10235 - 101st St., Edmonton AB T5J 3G1

780-426-5220 780-420-6277 866-212-5220
general@emeryjamieson.com
www.emeryjamieson.com

Edmonton: **Feehan Law Office - *2**
#1740, Sun Life Place 10123 - 99 St., Edmonton AB T5J 3H1
780-424-6425 780-424-6477

Edmonton: **Field Law - *59**
#2000, Oxford Tower 10235 - 101st St., Edmonton AB T5J 3G1
780-423-3003 780-428-9329 800-222-6479
wbrown@fieldlaw.com; lturner@fieldlaw.com
www.fieldlaw.com

Edmonton: **Gariepy, Richard - *1**
10039 - 117 St., Edmonton AB T5K 1W7
780-482-7370 780-482-2553

Edmonton: **Gawlinski & Parkatti, Barristers & Solicitors - *2**
Sun Life Pl. #990, 10123 - 99th St., Edmonton AB T5J 3H1
780-428-6645 780-428-6649
sjgawlinski@gp-law.ca; dtparkatti@gp-law.ca
www.gp-law.ca

Edmonton: **Gledhill Larocque - *8**
#1950, 10205 - 101 St., Edmonton AB T5J 2Z2
780-425-3511 780-426-5919

Edmonton: **Gunn Prithipaul & Hatch - *5**
#100, 9924 - 106th St. NW, Edmonton AB T5K 1C4
780-488-4460 780-488-4783
info@gplegal.ca
www.gplegal.ca

Edmonton: **Hall & Van Campenhout - *2**
12026 - 102 Ave. NW, Edmonton AB T5K 0R9
780-482-5732 780-482-5736

Edmonton: **Hansma Bristow & Finlay LLP, Barristers, Solicitors & Notaries Public - *7**
13815 - 127 St. NW, 2nd Fl., Edmonton AB T6V 1A8
780-456-3661 780-457-9381
info@hblaw.ca; hansma@hblaw.ca; r.finlay@hblaw.ca

Edmonton: **Henning Byrne - *7**
#1450, Standard Life Centre 10405 Jasper Ave. NW, Edmonton AB T5J 3N4
780-421-1707 780-425-9438 888-702-1707
general@henningbyrne.com
www.henningbyrne.com

Edmonton: **Heritage Law Offices - *5**
#108, 284 - 109 St., Edmonton AB T6J 6B7
780-436-0011 780-436-7000

Edmonton: **Herring, B.J. - *1**
10402 - 155 St., Edmonton AB T5P 2M3
780-469-2609

Edmonton: **Hladun & Company - *4**
#100, 10187 - 104 St. NW, Edmonton AB T5J 0Z9
780-423-1888 780-424-0934
inquiries@hladun.com

Edmonton: **Horwitz, William K. - *1**
#140, 17010 - 103 Ave., Edmonton AB T5S 1K7
780-486-3100 780-489-9671

Edmonton: **Hustwick Wetsch Moffat & McCrae - *9**
#600, Capital Pl. 9707 - 110 St. NW, Edmonton AB T5K 2L9
780-482-6555 780-482-6613
advocacy@planet.eon.net

Edmonton: **Kiss, Robert A. - *1**
17393 - 108 Ave, Edmonton AB T5S 1G2
780-447-7205 780-481-6258

Edmonton: **Kravinchuk, I. Samuel - *1**
#800, 10310 Jasper Ave. NW, Edmonton AB T5J 2W4
780-426-4884 780-425-9359

Edmonton: **Kuckertz Law Office - *2**
#202, 8003 - 102 St., Edmonton AB T6E 4A2
780-432-9308 780-439-9950
h.kuckertz@kuckertzlaw.com

Edmonton: **Leslie, Keith M. - *1**
1612 - 89 St. NW, Edmonton AB T6K 2A9
780-463-4019 780-468-2976
kleslie@agt.net

Edmonton: **Lister, Philip G. - *1**
#2410, Oxford Tower 10235 - 101 St., Edmonton AB T5J 3G1
780-422-6114 780-421-0818
phil@listerlaw.com

Edmonton: **Lyons Albert & Cook - *2**
#306, 10328 - 81 Ave. NW, Edmonton AB T6E 1X2
780-437-0743 780-438-6695
laclaw@telusplanet.net

Edmonton: **Malhotra & Company - *1**
#315, 10909 Jasper Ave., Edmonton AB T5J 3L9
780-423-5792 780-426-0081

Edmonton: **Marcovitch, M.B. - *1**
#1300, 10665 Jasper Ave. NW, Edmonton AB T5J 3S9
780-453-4390 780-424-3631

Edmonton: **Matheson & Company LLP - *6**
10410 - 81 Ave., Edmonton AB T6E 1X5
780-433-5881 780-432-9453
general@mathesonlaw.com

Edmonton: **McGee Richard - *3**
#1155, Weber Centre 5555 Calgary Trail NW, Edmonton AB T6H 5P9
780-437-2240 780-438-5788
trichard@mcgeerichard.com
www.mcgeerichard.com

Edmonton: **McKee & Company - *2**
#281, 11717 - 42 St. NW, Edmonton AB T5W 4V8
780-471-1100 780-471-1150
mckee.co@shaw.ca

Edmonton: **Mckenzie House Law Group - *2**
#8603, 104 St. NW, Edmonton AB T6E 4G6
780-424-3558 780-424-5515

Edmonton: **McLennan Ross LLP - *46**
#600, West Chambers 12220 Stony Plain Rd., Edmonton AB T5N 3Y4
780-482-9200 780-482-9100 800-567-9200
info@mross.com
www.mross.com

Edmonton: **McPhail, R. - *1**
#150, 12225 - 105 Ave., Edmonton AB T5N 0Y3
780-482-5947 780-482-2429

Edmonton: **McPike Johnston Barristers & Solicitors - *2**
11914 - 129 Ave., Edmonton AB T5E 0N3
780-455-6678 780-453-1093
mcpike@4lawyer.ca

Edmonton: **Melnyk & Co. - *3**
#200, 9939 Jasper Ave., Edmonton AB T5J 2W8
780-428-8900 780-429-8889
melnykco@telusplanet.net

Edmonton: **Michaels, Joseph J. - *1**
#1985 Sun Life Place 10123 - 99 St. NW, Edmonton AB T5J 3H1
780-424-0354

Edmonton: **Mintz & Chow - *6**
#400, 10357 - 109 St. NW, Edmonton AB T5J 1N3
780-425-2041 780-425-2195
mincho@telusplanet.net

Edmonton: **Mitchell, W. Robert - *1**
#405, 10408 - 124 St., Edmonton AB T5N 1R5
780-482-5791 780-488-0965

Edmonton: **Murray, Chilibeck & Horne - *3**
10605 - 172nd St. NW, Edmonton AB T5S 1P1
780-484-2323 780-486-4289

Edmonton: **Neuman Thompson - *6**
#200, 12220 Stony Plain Rd. NW, Edmonton AB T5N 3Y4
780-482-7645 780-488-0026

Edmonton: **Nicholl & Akers - *7**
#200, 10187 - 104 St. NW, Edmonton AB T5J 0Z9
780-429-2771 780-425-1665

Edmonton: **Nickerson Roberts Holinski & Mercer - *9**
#100, 7712 - 104 St., Edmonton AB T6E 4C5
780-428-0041 780-425-0272
reception@nrhmlaw.com
www.nrhmlaw.com

Edmonton: **Ogilvie LLP - *26**
#1400, 10303 Jasper Ave., Edmonton AB T5J 3N6
780-421-1818 780-429-4453
info@ogilvielaw.com
www.ogilvielaw.com

Edmonton: **Parker, Phillip G. - *1**
10704 - 108 St., 2nd Fl., Edmonton AB T5H 3A3
780-424-3200 780-424-2369

Edmonton: **Patrick & Patrick - *1**
#800, 10310 Jasper Ave. NW, Edmonton AB T5J 2W4
780-426-4884 780-425-9358

Edmonton: **Phelan, Patrick J. - *1**
#1550, Sun Life Pl. 10123 - 99 St., Edmonton AB T5J 3H1
780-424-7730 780-428-4484
patrick.phelan@telus.net

Edmonton: **Philion, Roy A. - *1**
#880, 10020 - 101 Ave. NW, Edmonton AB T5J 3G2
780-423-2977 780-424-8098

Edmonton: **Poitras, Ronald W. - *1**
#300, 10209 - 97 St., Edmonton AB T5J 0L6
780-424-3270 780-429-2615

Edmonton: **Polack, Meindersma, Liddell - *3**
#300, High Park Corner 14925 - 111 Ave., Edmonton AB T5M 2P6
780-486-0926 780-444-1393

Edmonton: **Pundit & Chotalia - *2**
#1506, Edmonton City Centre 10025 - 102A Ave., Edmonton AB T5J 2Z2
780-421-0861 780-425-6048
shirish@chotalia.com

Edmonton: **Rand Kiss Turner - *3**
#1600, 10020 - 101A Ave. NW, Edmonton AB T5J 3G2
780-423-1984 780-423-1969

Edmonton: **Recto, Peter E. - *1**
#903, 10060 Jasper Ave., Edmonton AB T5J 3R8
780-423-1283 780-473-8324
recto2000@hotmail.com

Edmonton: **Reich, H.M. - *1**
#1550, Sun Life Place 10123 - 99 St., Edmonton AB T5J 3H1
780-424-7732 780-428-4484
reichlaw@telus.net

Edmonton: **Reynolds, Mirth, Richards & Farmer LLP - *36**
#3200, Manulife Place 10180 - 101 St., Edmonton AB T5J 3W8
780-425-9510 780-429-3044 800-661-7673
mail@rmrf.com
www.rmrf.com

Edmonton: **Richard D. Rennick Professional Corporation - *1**
#2200, 10123 - 99 St. NW, Edmonton AB T5J 3H1
780-426-5510 780-420-1645
lawfirm@rennicklaw.ca

Edmonton: **Ritchie Mill Law Office - *5**
#102, 10171 Saskatchewan Dr. NW, Edmonton AB T6E 4R5
780-431-1444 780-431-1499 888-333-8818
office@rmlo.com

Edmonton: **Ross, James D. - *1**
#1003, Highfield Place 10010 - 106 St., Edmonton AB T5J 3L8
780-482-3144 780-424-7379

Edmonton: **Savaryn & Savaryn - *1**
P.O Box 45083 Landsdowne, Edmonton AB T6H 5Y1
780-422-7548
savaryn@telusplanet.net

Edmonton: **Savich Law Office - *1**
#200, 10350 - 172 St., Edmonton AB T5S 1G9
780-486-7300 780-489-0682
don@savichlaw.ca
www.savichlaw.ca

Edmonton: **Schwab, Schwab & Schwab - *3**
9908 - 106 St., Edmonton AB T5K 1C4
780-426-6715 780-426-2301
schwab@telusplanet.net

Edmonton: **Schwartz, D.L. - *1**
#324, 10909 Jasper Ave. NW, Edmonton AB T5J 3L9
780-424-0259 780-424-0299
thebigkahuna@interbaun.com

Edmonton: **Shtabsky & Tussman LLP - *7**
#1400, 10025 - 102A Ave., Edmonton AB T5J 2Z2
780-429-4671 780-424-3580
st400@stlaw.com
www.stlaw.com

Edmonton: Shymko, W.J. - *1
#200, 10105 - 108 Ave., Edmonton AB T5H 1A7
780-425-6414 780-425-6416

Edmonton: Sitko, Larry A. - *1
#201, 12907 - 97 St. NW, Edmonton AB T5E 4C2
780-476-7686 780-476-7688

Edmonton: Stewart Law Offices - *2
11724 - 103 Ave. NW, Edmonton AB T5K 0S7
780-482-3800 780-482-5600
stwlaw@telusplanet.net

Edmonton: Taylor & Jewell - *2
#215, Millbourner Mall 38 Ave. NW, Edmonton AB T6K 3L6
780-450-5761 780-468-4524

Edmonton: Tennant, R.I. - *1
#712, 10010 - 106 St., Edmonton AB T5J 3L8
780-425-2289

Edmonton: Tkachuk & Patterson - *2
#1260, First Edmonton Place 10665 Jasper Ave. NW, Edmonton AB T5J 3S9
780-428-1593 780-426-6679
tkalaw@alberta.com

Edmonton: Tymoczko, Helen S. - *1
#106, 10108 - 125 St., Edmonton AB T5N 4B6
780-472-1758 780-476-4085

Edmonton: Welsh & Company - *1
#888, 4445 Calgary Trail South, Edmonton AB T6H 5R7
780-438-3500 780-438-3129

Edmonton: Wheatley Sadownik - *4
#2000, 10123 - 99 St., Edmonton AB T5J 3H1
780-423-6671 780-420-6327
mail@wheatleysadownik.com
www.wheatleysadownik.com

Edmonton: Worton, Hunter & Callaghan - *3
#1270, 5555 Calgary Trail NW, Edmonton AB T6H 5P9
780-436-8554 780-436-8566
main@wortonhunter.com

Edmonton: Young, Ronald J. - *1
#204, 10265 - 107 St., Edmonton AB T5J 5G2
780-424-3311 780-425-9609

Edson: Anderson, Robert W. - *1
P.O Box 6748 202B - 50 St., Edson AB T7E 1V1
780-723-3245 780-723-5443
rwandlaw@telus.net

Edson: Calvert, Dennis C. - *1
P.O Box 6658 Main107 - 50 St., Edson AB T7E 1V1
780-723-6047 780-723-3602

Fairview: Byers, H.A. - *1
P.O Box 2200, Fairview AB T0H 1L0
780-835-4100 780-835-4171

Fort McMurray: Campbell & Cooper - *4
#212, 9714 Main St., Fort McMurray AB T9H 1T6
780-791-7787 780-791-0750
laywers@mcmurraylaw.com

Fort McMurray: Gorsalitz Law Office - *1
9912 Manning Ave., Fort McMurray AB T9H 2B9
780-791-4115 780-743-0040

Fort McMurray: Mason, Samuel N. - *1
#104, 10012 Franklin Ave., Fort McMurray AB T9H 2K6
780-743-5002 780-743-4150

Fort Saskatchewan: Fotty & Torok-Both - *4
10509 - 100 Ave., Fort Saskatchewan AB T8L 1Z5
780-998-4841 780-998-4821

Fort Saskatchewan: Jenkins & Jenkins - *2
#200, 9906 - 102 St., Fort Saskatchewan AB T8L 2C3
780-998-4200 780-998-4370
cjenkins@jenkins-law.com

Grande Cache: Arnesen, Harry - *1
P.O Box 385 2502 Pine Plaza, Grande Cache AB T0E 0Y0
780-827-2458 780-827-3734

Grande Prairie: Gurevitch Headon & Associates - *4
9931 - 106 Ave., Grande Prairie AB T8V 1J4
780-539-3710 780-532-2788 866-720-3710
gplaw@telus.net
www.grandeprairielaw.ca

Grande Prairie: Howey, Angela L. - *1
201 Professional Bldg. 9905 - 101 Ave., Grande Prairie AB T8V 0X7
780-539-0690 780-539-3813

Grande Prairie: Kay, McVey, Smith & Carlstrom LLP - *11
#600, Windsor Ct. 9835 - 101st Ave., Grande Prairie AB T8V 5V4
780-532-7771 780-532-1158 888-531-7771
ksms@kayship.com
www.kayship.com

Grande Prairie: Pollick, Robert S. Professional Corporation, Barristers & Solicit - *1
#200, 10006 - 101 Ave., Grande Prairie AB T8V 0Y1
780-538-8290 780-538-4515
enniski@telusplanet.net

Grande Prairie: Walisser Shavers LLP - *2
#202, 10027 - 101 Ave., Grande Prairie AB T8V 0X9
780-532-0315 780-532-3369
loganw@telusplanet.net

Hanna: Ross, Todd & Company - *3
P.O Box 1330 124 - 2 Ave. West, Hanna AB T0J 1P0
403-854-4431 403-854-2561
reception@drumhellerlaw.com

High Prairie: Jong, Harry J. - *2
P.O Box 1379, High Prairie AB T0G 1E0
780-523-4554 780-523-5550
hjlaw@cablecomet.com

High River: Dearing, A. George Professional Corp. - *1
#103, 14 - 2 Ave. SE, High River AB T1V 1G4
403-652-2771 403-652-2699
gdearing@telus.net

Hinton: Johnson McClelland Murdoch - *4
213 Pembina Ave., Hinton AB T7V 2B3
780-865-2222 780-865-8857
lawyer@jmmlaw.ca

Hinton: Woods & Robson - *2
110 Brewster Dr., Hinton AB T7V 1B4
780-865-3086 780-865-7149
woodsrob@telusplanet.net

Hobbema: Littlechild, J. Wilton - *1
P.O Box 370, Hobbema AB T0C 1N0
780-585-3038 780-585-2025
jwlittle@incentre.net

Innisfail: Tulloch Law Office - *1
P.O Box 6099 5030 - 50 St., Innisfail AB T4G 1S7
403-227-5591 403-227-1230
carolyntulloch@telus.net

Leduc: Elgert & Company - *1
5206 - 50 St., Leduc AB T9E 6Z6
780-986-3487 780-986-2040
herbelgert@shaw.ca

Leduc: Jackie, Handerek & Forester, Barristers & Solicitors - *4
4710 - 50 St., Leduc AB T9E 6W2
780-986-5081 780-986-8807
jhf@leduclawyers.ab.ca
www.leduclawyers.ab.ca

Leduc: Kahlke, E. - *1
5102 - 50 Ave., Leduc AB T9E 6V4
780-986-8427 780-986-3108

Leduc: Zalapski & Pahl - *4
#1, 5304 - 50 St., Leduc AB T9E 6Z6
780-986-8428 780-986-2552

Lethbridge: Davidson & Williams LLP - *11
P.O Box 518 501 - 4 St. South, Lethbridge AB T1J 4X2
403-328-1766 403-320-5434
lethbridge@davidsonandwilliams.com
www.davidsonandwilliams.com

Lethbridge: de Walle, Frank - *1
323 - 7 St. South, Lethbridge AB T1J 2G4
403-328-8800 403-328-8502
dewalle@telusplanet.net

Lethbridge: Dodic Toone Maclean - *4
416B Stafford Dr. South, Lethbridge AB T1J 2L2
403-329-1330 403-329-1311

Lethbridge: Huckvale Wilde Harvie MacLennan LLP - *7
P.O Box 1028 410 - 6th St. South, Lethbridge AB T1J 4A2
403-328-8856 403-380-4050
mad@huckvale.ca

Lethbridge: MacLachlan McNab Hembroff - *6
1003 - 4th Ave. South, Lethbridge AB T1J 0P7
403-381-4966 403-329-9300
mmh@mmhlawyers.com
www.mmhlawyers.com

Lethbridge: Millar & Keith LLP - *2
200 - 3rd St. South, Lethbridge AB T1J 1Y7
403-327-5716 403-329-4063
mtklaw@telusplanet.net

Lethbridge: Milne Pritchard Law Office - *2
#807, 400 - 4 Ave. South, Lethbridge AB T1J 4E1
403-329-1133 403-329-0395

Lethbridge: Moodie, Harold N. - *1
P.O Box 9 Main212 - 5 St. South, 2nd Fl., Lethbridge AB T1J 3Y3
403-328-0005 403-329-0945

Lethbridge: Peterson & Purvis LLP - *8
P.O Box 1165 537 - 7th St. South, Lethbridge AB T1J 4A4
403-328-9667 403-320-1393
p-plaw@telusplanet.net

Lethbridge: Pollock & Company - *3
#200, 434 - 7th St. South, Lethbridge AB T1J 4K1
403-329-6900 403-327-9790 800-262-4857
dlplaw@lawpollock.com
www.lawpollock.com

Lethbridge: Ruston, Q.C, Rhonda - *1
501 - 4 St. South, Lethbridge AB T1J 4K2
403-328-4483 403-206-7435
rkruston@telusplanet.net

Lethbridge: Shapiro & Company - *1
#200, 427 - 5 St. South., Lethbridge AB T1J 2B6
403-328-9300 403-328-9307
shapco@telusplanet.net

Lethbridge: Stringam Denecky Law Office - *9
P.O Box 757 Main314 - 3 St. South, Lethbridge AB T1J 3Z6
403-328-5577 403-327-1141
results@stringam.ca; sdenecky@stringam.ca
www.stringam.ca

Lloydminster: Kindrachuk Law Office - *1
5014 - 48 St., Lloydminster AB T9V 0H8
780-875-6600 780-875-6601
kindrachuklaw@shaw.ca

Medicine Hat: Biddell Law Office - *3
735 - 2 St. SE, Medicine Hat AB T1A 0E2
403-527-7737 403-528-8907
kbiddell@monarch.net

Medicine Hat: Gordon, Smith & Company - *3
P.O Box 490 378 - 1 St. SE, Medicine Hat AB T1A 7G2
403-527-5506 403-527-0577
gsco@shockware.com

Medicine Hat: MacLean Wiedemann - *3
525 - 2 St. SE, Medicine Hat AB T1A 0C5
403-527-3343 403-526-0473

Medicine Hat: Pritchard & Company LLP - *7
#204, P.O Box 100 430 - 6th Ave. SE, Medicine Hat AB T1A 7E8
403-527-4411 403-527-9806
lawyers@pritchardandcompany.com
www.pritchardandcompany.com

Medicine Hat: Rombough, Yarshenko & Rath - *2
#106, 579 - 3 St. SE, Medicine Hat AB T1A 0H2
403-527-3030 403-526-0151

Medicine Hat: Schindel, D.G. - *1
#1, 3295 Dunmore Rd. SE, Medicine Hat AB T1B 3R2
403-529-5548 403-529-2694
daryl@millerlaw.ca

Medicine Hat: Sihvon Carter Fisher & Berger LLP - *8
499 - 1st St. SE, Medicine Hat AB T1A 0A7
403-526-2600 403-526-3217
scfb@scfb.ca
www.scfb.ca

Nanton: **Roddie, Robert G. Q.C. - *1**
P.O Box 100 2113 - 20 St., Nanton AB T0L 1R0
403-646-2211 403-646-3159
rodmclaw@telusplanet.net

Okotoks: **Dixon, Charles A. - *1**
P.O Box 1169 51 Riverside Gate, Okotoks AB T1S 1B2
403-938-8131 403-938-6365

Okotoks: **Simper, Edward D. - *1**
P.O Box 1117 Main84 Elizabeth St., Okotoks AB T1S 1B2
403-938-2101 403-938-6020
simpered@fclc.com

Peace River: **Mathieu Hryniuk LLP - *6**
P.O Box 6210 10012 - 101 St., Peace River AB T8S 1S2
780-624-2565 780-624-5766
mhse@telusplanet.net
mathieuhryniuk.com

Peace River: **Thietke, Murphy & Harcourt - *5**
P.O Box 6778 9910 - 97 Ave., Peace River AB T8S 1S5
780-624-1122 780-624-4443 800-353-6270

Pincher Creek: **Jasman & Evans - *1**
P.O Box 2530 985 East Ave., Pincher Creek AB T0K 1W0
403-627-2877 403-627-4495
jasman_evans@shaw.ca

Ponoka: **Noble & Kidd - *1**
P.O Box 4278 5024 - 51 Ave., Ponoka AB T4J 1R7
403-783-3325 403-783-5080
noblekid@telus.net

Ponoka: **Wyrozub, Richard D. - *1**
P.O Box 4338 Main, Ponoka AB T4J 1R7
403-783-5521 403-783-2012

Red Deer: **Duhamel Manning Feehan Warrender Glass LLP - *13**
5233 - 49 Ave., Red Deer AB T4N 6G5
403-343-0812 403-340-3545
altalaw@reddeeraltalaw.com
www.reddeeraltalaw.com

Red Deer: **Flanagan Sully - *2**
#202, 4825 - 47 St., Red Deer AB T4N 1R3
403-342-7715 403-347-5955
fslaw@telusplanet.net

Red Deer: **Gerig Hamilton Neeland - *5**
#501, 4901 - 48 St., Red Deer AB T4N 6M4
403-343-2444 403-343-6522
info@ghnh.net

Red Deer: **Gross, Donald A. - *1**
#274, 4919 - 59 St., Red Deer AB T4N 6C9
403-343-3715 403-343-7435

Red Deer: **Johnston Ming Manning LLP - *13**
Royal Bank Bldg. 4943 - 50th St., 3rd & 4th Fl., Red Deer AB T4N 1Y1
403-346-5591 403-346-5599
info@jmmlawrd.ca
www.johnstonmingmanning.com

Red Deer: **Lee & Short - *4**
4801 - 49 St., Red Deer AB T4N 1T8
403-343-1212 403-341-3066
galbrecht@leeshort.com

Red Deer: **Loney, Harold - *1**
#201, 4702 - 49 Ave., Red Deer AB T4N 6L5
403-343-0122 403-309-1969

Red Deer: **MacSween, P.E.B. - *1**
4824 - 51 St., Red Deer AB T4N 2A5
403-342-5595 403-341-3130

Red Deer: **Penny, Patrick A. - *1**
#290, 4819C - 48 Ave., Red Deer AB T4N 3T2
403-342-9595 403-346-9778

Red Deer: **Schnell Hardy Jones LLP - *8**
#504, 4909 - 49th St., Red Deer AB T4N 1V1
403-342-7400 403-340-0520 800-342-7405
lawyers@schnell-law.com
www.schnell-law.com

Red Deer: **Sisson Warren Sinclair - *9**
#600, First Red Deer Place 4911 - 51 St., Red Deer AB T4N 6V4
403-343-3320 403-343-6069
email@swslawyers.com

Redwater: **McCallum, D.L. - *1**
PO Box 396, Redwater AB T0A 2W0
780-942-3040 780-942-2003 800-390-2257

Rimbey: **Pfau, David R. - *1**
P.O Box 1009 5001 - 50th Ave., Rimbey AB T0C 2J0
403-843-2296 403-843-2344

Rocky Mountain House: **Crossley, Peter Law Office - *1**
P.O Box 1108 4616 - 47 Ave., Rocky Mountain House AB T4T 1A8
403-845-2828 403-845-4630

Rocky Mountain House: **Dunsford & Scott - *3**
P.O Box 370 5135 - 48 Ave., Rocky Mountain House AB T4T 1A3
403-845-7112 403-845-4670
reception@dunsfordandscott.com

Rocky Mountain House: **Woollard Hopkins & Company - *2**
5133 - 49 St., Rocky Mountain House AB T4T 1B8
403-845-2545 403-845-2285
wooll@woollardhopkins.com

Sherwood Park: **Nigro & Company - *1**
282 Kaska Rd., Sherwood Park AB T8A 4G7
780-467-9559 780-467-0720

Sherwood Park: **Spratlin, Thomas E. - *1**
#14B, 363 Sioux Rd., Sherwood Park AB T8A 4W7
780-464-5404 780-417-1759
spratlin@telus.net

Slave Lake: **McMillan, Allan G. - *1**
#2, 221 - 3 Ave. NW, Slave Lake AB T0G 2A1
780-849-2227 780-849-2143
mcmillan@telusplanet.net

Slave Lake: **Twinn Barristers & Solicitors - *1**
P.O Box 1460 810 Caribou Trail NE, Slave Lake AB T0G 2A0
780-849-4319 780-805-3274
ctwinn@twinnlaw.com

Spruce Grove: **Heil, Randall C. - *1**
#201, Cumbria Centre 93 McLeod Ave., Spruce Grove AB T7X 2Z9
780-962-9700 780-962-9329
rheil@telus.net

Spruce Grove: **Joly, Robert A. - *1**
#4, 20 McLeod Ave., Spruce Grove AB T7X 3Y1
780-962-4447 780-962-3638
bbjoly@shaw.ca

St Albert: **Goldsman, Ritzen, Shadlyn - *5**
#609, Grandin Park Tower 22 Sir Winston Churchill Ave., St Albert AB T8N 1B4
780-458-0500 780-459-2472

St Albert: **Rowand, Thomas A. Professional Corp. - *1**
#208, Summit Centre 200 Boudreau Rd., St Albert AB T8N 6B9
780-458-9440 780-458-9442
trowand@telusplanet.net

St Albert: **Weary & Company - *2**
#400, 30 Green Grove Dr., St Albert AB T8N 5H6
780-459-5596 780-459-6572

Stony Plain: **Birdsell Grant Gardner Morck - *6**
#102, 5300 - 50 St., Stony Plain AB T7Z 1T8
780-963-8181 780-963-9618
admin@bgglaw.com

Stony Plain: **Stone, M.P. - *1**
#300, P.O Box 56 MainRR#3, Stony Plain AB T7Z 1X3

Sylvan Lake: **Vanden Brink Law Office - *1**
P.O Box 9613 Main, Sylvan Lake AB T4S 1S8
403-885-2222 403-885-2226
benbrink@direcway.com

Taber: **Baldry Sugden - *2**
5401 - 50 Ave., Taber AB T1G 1V2
403-223-3585 403-223-1732
balsug@telusplanet.net

Turner Valley: **Broadhurst, Beverly A.B. - *1**
#2, P.O Box 501 101 Sunset Blvd. SW, Turner Valley AB T0L 2A0
403-933-3255 403-933-4104

Vermilion: **Reynolds & Flemke - *2**
#11, 5125 - 50 Ave., Vermilion AB T9X 1A8
780-853-5339 780-853-4200

Vermilion: **Wheat Law Office - *2**
5042 - 49 Ave., Vermilion AB T9X 1B7
780-853-4707 780-853-4499
wheatlaw@telusplanet.net

Wainwright: **Van Winssen, Peter. - *1**
1013 - 5 Ave., Wainwright AB T9W 1L6
780-842-5140 780-842-3830

Westlock: **Tims & Company - *2**
#2, P.O Box 490 9831 - 107th St., Westlock AB T7P 1R9
780-349-5366 780-349-6510

Wetaskiwin: **Deckert Allen Cymbaluk Genest - *4**
#301, P.O Box 6060 5201 - 51st Ave., Wetaskiwin AB T9A 2E8
780-352-3301 780-352-5976

Wetaskiwin: **McDonald Street Law Office - *1**
4408 - 51 St., Wetaskiwin AB T9A 1K5
780-352-0369 780-352-0393

Wetaskiwin: **Schumacher & Associates - *4**
5118 - 50 Ave., Wetaskiwin AB T9A 0S6
780-352-6691 780-352-0599
schumacher@incentre.net

Whitecourt: **McConnell Law Office - *1**
P.O Box 1795 Main5115 Highway St., Whitecourt AB T7S 1P5
780-778-4945 780-778-3851

British Columbia

** indicates # of lawyers*

100 Mile House: **Centennial Law Corporation - *3**
P.O Box 819, 100 Mile House BC V0K 2E0
250-395-3881 250-395-2644
centenniallaw@bcinternet.net

Abbotsford: **Fast Welwood & Wiens - *4**
#305, 2692 Clearbrook Rd., Abbotsford BC V2T 2Y8
604-850-6640 604-857-1833
info@faswel.com

Abbotsford: **Goddard, Larry W. - *1**
#105, 2955 Gladwin Rd., Abbotsford BC V2T 5T4
604-853-3535 604-853-9033

Abbotsford: **Linley, Duignan & Company - *5**
#200, P.O Box 2040 Clearbrook2548 Clearbrook Rd, Abbotsford BC V2T 3T8
604-859-7134 604-859-0843
thefirm@linleyduignan.com

Abbotsford: **Robertson, Downe & Mullally - *20**
33695 South Fraser Way, Abbotsford BC V2S 2C1
604-853-0774 604-852-3829 888-853-0774
info@rdmlawyers
www.rdmlawyers.com

Abbotsford: **Wilson, Lloyd H. - *1**
2644 Montrose Ave., Abbotsford BC V2S 3T6
604-853-3355 604-853-2644
lloydhwilson_company@hotmail.com

Armstrong: **Blakely & Co. - *1**
#201, P.O Box 357 2595 Pleasant Valley Blvd., Armstrong BC V0E 1B0
250-546-3188 250-546-2677
blakely@junction.net

Brentwood Bay: **Stevenson Jenko - *2**
P.O Box 425 7105A West Saanich Rd., Brentwood Bay BC V8M 1R3
250-652-5151 250-652-9687
stevensonjenko@telus.net

Burnaby: **Bergen Legal Services - *1**
5816 Sherban Ct., Burnaby BC V5B 4P2
604-291-9291 604-291-9335

Burnaby: **Bergmann, W.E. - *1**
4550 East Hastings St., Burnaby BC V5C 2K4
604-298-8211 604-298-8216

Burnaby: **Cobbett & Cotton - *7**
4259 East Hastings St., Burnaby BC V5C 2J5
604-299-6251 604-299-6627
mail@cobett-cotton.com

Burnaby: Dorman, Kenneth H. - *1
#1507, 4330 Kingsway, Burnaby BC V5H 4G7
604-430-3421 604-430-0636

Burnaby: Edwards, Edwards & Edwards - *3
#510, 5021 Kingsway, Burnaby BC V5H 4A5
604-433-2445 604-433-8209

Burnaby: Fitzsimmons, James K. - *1
#200, 6960 Royal Oak Ave., Burnaby BC V5J 4J2
604-298-8939 604-298-8956

Burnaby: Foran, Robert A. - *1
#275, c/o UMA Group Ltd. 3001 Wayburne Dr., Burnaby BC V5G 4W3
604-631-6232 604-685-1035
bob.foran@uma.aecom.com
www.umagroup.com

Burnaby: Fraser, James K. Law Corporation - *1
#200, 4603 Kingsway, Burnaby BC V5H 4M4
604-433-0010 604-435-0269
jkf@jkf.ca

Burnaby: Greenbank Murdoch & Company - *2
#2109, 4710 Kingsway, Burnaby BC V5H 4M2
604-437-6611 604-437-3065
info@bmgm.com

Burnaby: Hawthorne, Piggott & Company - *7
#208, 1899 Willingdon Ave., Burnaby BC V5C 5T1
604-299-8371 604-299-1523
lawyers@hawthornelaw.com

Burnaby: O'Neill, Rozenberg - *2
#201, 4547 Hastings St., Burnaby BC V5C 2K3
604-294-8311 604-294-5278 800-354-1888

Burnaby: Pihl & Company - *1
#205, 5481 Kingsway, Burnaby BC V5H 2G1
604-437-8837 604-437-3529

Burnaby: Russell Kuhl & Co. - *2
#220, 4411 Hastings St., Burnaby BC V5C 2K1
604-298-1038 604-298-1037
russellradio@telus.net; mail@jeffkuhl.com

Burnaby: Starr & Company - *2
#205, 5481 Kingsway, Burnaby BC V5H 2G1
604-435-5588 604-435-5588
gbstarr@telus.net

Burnaby: Warren, Eder - *2
#216, 3989 Henning Dr., Burnaby BC V5C 6P8
604-687-0134 604-687-5176 800-461-3455
warren&eder@shawbiz.ca

Burnaby: Wesley, Maureen J. - *1
4270 McGill St., Burnaby BC V5C 1M9
604-298-6555 604-298-6540

Burnaby: Yaremovich, Patricia - *1
#105, 6540 East Hastings St., Burnaby BC V5B 4Z5
604-320-0688 604-320-0007
pyaremovich@shaw.ca

Campbell River: Shook, Wickham, Bishop & Field - *8
906 Island Hwy., Campbell River BC V9W 2C3
250-287-8355 250-287-8112
info@crlawyers.ca
www.crlawyers.ca

Campbell River: Tees Kiddle Spencer - *4
#200, 1260 Shoppers Row, Campbell River BC V9W 2C8
250-287-7755 250-287-3999 800-224-7755
tks@tkslaw.com
www.tkslaw.com

Castlegar: Polonicoff & Perehudoff - *2
1115 - 3 St., Castlegar BC V1N 2A1
250-365-3343 250-365-6307
polper@netidea.com

Chilliwack: Kaye Thome Toews & Hansford - *7
CP 372 9202 Young Rd., Chilliwack BC V2P 6J4
604-792-1977 604-792-7077 888-792-1977
ktc@ktclawoffice.com
www.ktthlawyers.com

Clearbrook: Kuzminski Neufeld Rebane, Valley Law Group - *3
#201, 2890 Garden St., Clearbrook BC V2T 4W7
604-853-5401 604-853-8358

Clearwater: Kurta, John - *1
P.O Box 5171 32 East Old North Thompson Hwy., Clearwater BC V0E 1N0
250-674-2126 250-674-3493

Coquitlam: Spagnuolo & Company Real Estate Lawyers - *10
#300, 906 Roderick Ave., Coquitlam BC V3K 1R1
604-527-4242 604-527-8976 888-873-2829
info@bcrealestatelawyers.com
www.bcrealestatelawyers.com

Coquitlam: Spraggs & Company - *1
#202, 1030 Westwood St., Coquitlam BC V3C 4E4
604-464-3333

Coquitlam: Taylor Bardal - *3
#220, 1024 Ridgeway Ave., Coquitlam BC V3J 1S5
604 931 3477 604 931 1277

Coquitlam: Zipp & Company - *2
820 Henderson Ave., Coquitlam BC V3K 1P2
604-936-7743

Courtenay: Dow, James E. - *1
#7, 625 Cliffe Ave., Courtenay BC V9N 2J6
250-338-7701 250-338-6641
jamesdow@shaw.ca

Courtenay: Ives Burger, Barristers & Solicitors - *3
505 - 5 St., Courtenay BC V9N 1K2
250-334-2416 250-334-3198
info@ivesburgerlaw.com
www.ivesburgerlaw.com

Courtenay: Morris, C.H.L. - *1
949 Fitzgerald Ave., Courtenay BC V9N 2R6
250-338-5311 250-338-1818
crispinmorris@shaw.ca

Courtenay: Pouss, Roy William - *1
243 - 4th St., Courtenay BC V9N 1G7
250-334-3188 250-334-3174

Courtenay: Swift Datoo Law Corporation - *8
#201, 467 Cumberland Rd., Courtenay BC V9N 2C5
250-334-4461 250-334-2335 877-334-4461
lawyers@swiftdatoo.com
www.swiftdatoo.com

Cranbrook: Rella & Paolini - *2
#6, 10 Ave. South, 2nd Fl., Cranbrook BC V1C 2M8
250-426-8981 250-426-8987 866-426-8981
rellaco@shaw.ca

Cranbrook: Robertson & Co. - *1
#200, 135 - 10 Ave. South, Cranbrook BC V1C 2N1
250-489-4346 250-489-1899
robertson@cranbrooklaw.com
www.cranbrooklaw.com

Cranbrook: Steidl, Kambeitz - *2
#201, 907 Baker St., Cranbrook BC V1C 1A4
250-426-7211 250-426-6100
sk@steidlco.com

Dawson Creek: Higson Apps - *3
#201, 1136 - 103 Ave., Dawson Creek BC V1G 2G7
250-782-9134 250-782-9135 888-782-9134
rapps@plenerthigson.com

Dawson Creek: Mitchell Schuller - *3
#2, 933 - 103 Ave., Dawson Creek BC V1G 2G4
250-782-8155 250-782-4525
mitchellschuller@shawcable.com

Delta: Broad, James - *1
9337 - 120 St., Delta BC V4C 6R8
604-585-3422 604-585-3613

Delta: Buckley Hogan - *3
9453 - 120 St., Delta BC V4C 6S2
604-588-0431 604-588-0062
lawyers@buckho.com

Delta: Deschamps-Carlson, Danielle D. - *3
#201, 5155 Trunk Rd., Delta BC V4K 1W4
604-940-8182 604-940-9892
info@severidelawgroup.com

Delta: McPhillips, David C. - *1
4924 - 2A Ave., Delta BC V4M 3V1
604-943-6750 604-943-6350

Delta: Stasiuk & Rose - *2
#203, 1205 - 56 St., Delta BC V4L 2A6
604-943-8272 604-943-8416
r.stasiuk@stasiuk-rose.com

Delta: TNT Lawyers - *3
7929 - 120 St., Delta BC V4C 6P6
604-502-5615 604-591-8722 800-750-5122
info@icbcinjurylawyers.ca
www.icbcinjurylawyers.ca

Delta: Valair, Dell C. - *1
10 - 5900 Ferry Rd., Delta BC V4K 5C3
604-940-3318 604-940-3324
dell@lightspeed.ca

Duncan: Coleman Fraser Parcells - *4
#202, 58 Station St., Duncan BC V9L 1M4
250-748-1013 250-743-8318 888-748-1013

Duncan: Ridgway & Company - *5
#200, 44 Queens Rd., Duncan BC V9L 2W4
250-746-7121 250-746-4070
info@ridgco.com
www.ridgco.com

Duncan: Whittaker, J.B. - *1
Main7334 Waltons Mountain Rd., RR#1, Duncan BC V9L 5W8
250-748-6674

Fernie: Bentley, R.W. - *1
P.O Box 2038, Fernie BC V0B 1M0
250-423-9241 250-423-6440
bentleylaw@elkvalley.net

Fort St John: Earmme & Associates - *3
10740 - 101st Ave., Fort St John BC V1J 2B4
250-785-6961 250-785-6967

Gibsons: Rowe, J. Wayne - *1
758 School Rd., Gibsons BC V0N 1V0
604-886-2029 604-886-9191

Hope: Kennedy, Jensen - *2
CP 1719 400 Park St., Hope BC V0X 1L0
604-869-9981 604-869-7640
www.kennedyjensen.com

Hornby Island: Campbell, Sally - *1
4505 Roburn Rd., Hornby Island BC V0R 1Z0
250-335-2272 250-335-0895
scampbel@island.net
www.island.net/~scampbell

Hornby Island: Kelly, Sue M. - *1
P.O Box 14 Anderson, Hornby Island BC V0R 1Z0
250-335-0735 250-335-0732 Telex: 04-354613
smkelly@telus.net

Kamloops: Cundari & Company Law Corporation - *4
#810, 175 - 2 Ave., Kamloops BC V2C 5W1
250-372-3368 250-372-5554
cundari@cundarilaw.com
www.cundarilaw.com

Kamloops: Gibraltar Law Group - *3
#102, 418 St. Paul St., Kamloops BC V2C 2J6
250-374-3737 250-374-0035 877-374-3737
mail@gibraltarlawgroup.com
www.gibraltarlawgroup.com

Kamloops: Gillespie Renkema Barnett Broadway LLP - *1
#200, 121 St. Paul St., Kamloops BC V2C 3K8
250-374-4463 250-374-5250

Kamloops: Horne Marr Zak - *5
#600, 175 Second Ave., Kamloops BC V2C 5W1
250-372-1221 250-372-8339 800-558-1933
hmz@hmzlaw.com
www.hmzlaw.com

Kamloops: Jensen Carroll Watt - *7
#300, Old Firehall #1 125 - 4 Ave., Kamloops BC V2C 3N3
250-372-8811 250-828-6697 800-949-3362
jmc@jmc.bc.ca

Kamloops: Mair Jensen Blair Lawyers LLP - *15
#700, 275 Lansdowne St., Kamloops BC V2C 6H6
250-374-3161 250-374-6992
info@mjblaw.com
www.mjblaw.com

Kamloops: Morelli Chertkow LLP, Lawyers - *11
#300 180 Seymour St., Kamloops BC V2C 2E3

250-374-3344 250-374-1144 888-374-3350
info@morellichertkow.com
www.morellichertkow.com

Kamloops: Nixon, Craig Law Corp. - *1
#880, 175 - 2nd Ave., Kamloops BC V2C 5W1
250-374-1555 250-374-9992
onlc@direct.ca

Kamloops: Taylor Epp & Dolder - *3
#300, 153 Seymour St., Kamloops BC V2C 2C8
250-374-3456 250-828-6808
taylor_epp_dolder@telus.net

Kamloops: Wozniak & Walker - *2
533 Nicola St., Kamloops BC V2C 2P9
250-374-6226 250-374-4485

Kelowna: Beairsto Sabey - *2
#201, 401 Glenmore Rd., Kelowna BC V1V 1Z6
250-762-6111 250-762-6480 866-268-6383
lawyers@beairstosabey.com

Kelowna: Christiansen, Drummond - *2
#207, 389 Queensway Ave., Kelowna BC V1Y 8E6
250-862-2332 250-862-2353
cnklaw@telus.net

Kelowna: Doak Shirreff LLP - *14
#200, Chancery Place 537 Leon Ave., Kelowna BC V1Y 2A9
250-763-4323 250-763-4780 800-661-4959
thefirm@doakshirreff.com
www.doakshirreff.com

Kelowna: Fraser Murray Huck - *3
#200, 1449 St Paul St., Kelowna BC V1Y 7S5
250-868-8306 250-868-8301
cfraser@frasermurraylaw.com

Kelowna: Glazier Polley - *4
1674 Bertram St., 2nd Fl., Kelowna BC V1Y 9G4
250-763-3343 250-763-9524

Kelowna: Pihl & Associates Law Corporation - *6
#300, 1465 Ellis St., Kelowna BC V1Y 2A3
250-762-5434 250-762-5450
lawyers@pihl.bc.ca
www.okanaganlawyers.com

Kelowna: Porter Ramsay LLP - *8
#200, 1465 Ellis St., Kelowna BC V1Y 2A3
250-763-7646 250-762-9960 888-933-4411
lawyers@porterramsay.com
www.porterramsay.com

Kelowna: Pushor Mitchell LLP, Lawyers & Trade-Mark Agents - *31
1665 Ellis St., 3rd Fl., Kelowna BC V1Y 2B3
250-762-2108 250-762-9115 800-558-1155
lawyers@pushormitchell.com
www.pushormitchell.com

Kelowna: Schlosser & Co. - *1
3017 Tutt St., Kelowna BC V1Y 2H4
250-763-1393

Kelowna: Thomas Butler LLP - *4
#700, 1708 Dolphin Ave., Kelowna BC V1Y 9S4
250-763-0200 250-762-8848
www.thomasbutlerllp.com

Kelowna: Tinker, Churchill, Rule - *3
1573 Ellis St., Kelowna BC V1Y 2A7
250-763-7333 250-763-5507
tinkerchurchillrule@shawlink.ca

Kitimat: Wozney & Company - *2
366 City Centre, Kitimat BC V8C 1T6
250-632-7151 250-632-7100
rwozney@telus.net

Langley: Bryenton, Rosberg & Company - *4
#300, 20689 Fraser Hwy., Langley BC V3A 4G4
604-530-7135 604-530-7118
bryros@telus.net

Langley: Campbell, Burton & McMullan LLP - *11
#200, 4769 - 222 St., Langley BC V2Z 3C1
604-533-3821 604-533-5521
info@cbmlawyers.com
www.cbmlawyers.com

Langley: Fleming, Olson & Taneda - *3
4038 - 200B St., Langley BC V3A 1N9
604-533-3411 604-533-8749
fotlawyers@aol.com

Langley: MacDonald, Boyle & Jeffery - *1
20450 Fraser Hwy., Langley BC V3A 4G2
604-530-3141 604-530-9573

Langley: Waterstone Law Group LLP - *4
#304, 20338 - 65th Ave., Langley BC V2Y 2K3
604-533-2300 604-533-2387 800-880-1667
info@waterstonelaw.com
www.waterstonelaw.com

Lillooet: Kaser, R. Kendel - *1
P.O Box 1449 416 Main St., Lillooet BC V0K 1V0
250-256-7519 250-256-7554

Maple Ridge: Vernon & Thompson Law Group - *4
22311 - 119 Ave., Maple Ridge BC V2X 2Z2
604-463-6281 604-463-7497
law@vernon-thompson.com

Matsqui Village: Miner, John Andrew - *1
CP 219 34033 Lougheed Hwy., Matsqui Village BC V2V 5X8
604-826-3930 604-826-4172

Mill Bay: Hicks & Co. - *1
#24, P.O Box 83 2720 Mill Bay Rd., Mill Bay BC V0R 2P0
250-743-3245 250-743-3756

Mission: Taylor, Tait, Ruley & Company - *5
33066 First Ave., Mission BC V2V 1G3
604-826-1266 604-826-4288
info@taylortait.com
www.taylortait.com

Nanaimo: Carlson & Company - *3
669 Terminal Ave. North, Nanaimo BC V9S 4K1
250-753-7582 250-753-7583
lawyers@carlson-law.com

Nanaimo: Heath & Company - *7
#200, 1808 Bowen Rd., Nanaimo BC V9S 5W4
250-753-2202 250-753-3949 866-753-2202
consult@nanaimolaw.com
www.nanaimolaw.com

Nanaimo: Hobbs Hargrave - *2
301 Franklyn St., Nanaimo BC V9R 2X5
250-753-3477 250-753-7927
bhobbs@hobbslaw.com
www.hobbslaw.com

Nanaimo: Mont & Walker Law Corporation - *4
201 Selby St., Nanaimo BC V9R 2R2
250-753-6435 250-753-5285 877-753-6453
mont@islandlaw.ca
www.islandlaw.ca

Nanaimo: Ramsay Lampman Rhodes - *15
111 Wallace St., Nanaimo BC V9R 5B2
250-754-3321 250-754-1148
info@rlr-law.com
www.rlr-law.com

Nelson: Nasmyth, Morrow & Bogusz - *2
#105, 465 Ward St., Nelson BC V1L 1S7
250-352-3171 250-352-1777
nmgb@telus.net

Nelson: Terry Napora Law Office - *1
608 Baker St., Nelson BC V1L 4J4
250-352-3321 250-354-4547 800-579-5338
tnapora@napwood.ca

Nelson: Wallach, Susan E. - *1
#4, 577 Baker St., Nelson BC V1L 4J1
250-352-6124 250-352-3460

New Westminster: Bondoreff, Gordon J. - *1
#202, 713 Columbia St., New Westminster BC V3M 1B2
604-526-4491 604-526-5979
gbondoreff@telus.net

New Westminster: Dickey, Browning, Ray, Soga, Dunne - *5
#203, 668 Carnarvon St., New Westminster BC V3M 5Y6
604-526-4525 604-526-8595
info@triallawyers.ca
www.triallawyers.ca

New Westminster: Drabik, Raymond E. Law Corp. - *1
#217, 713 Columbia St., New Westminster BC V3M 1B2
604-526-4875 604-526-4879
red_law@telus.net

New Westminster: Goodwin & Mark - *6
#217, 713 Columbia St., New Westminster BC V3M 1B2
604-522-9884 604-526-8044
gm@goodmark.ca
www.goodmark.ca

New Westminster: Kinman Mulholland - *2
#400, 628 Sixth Ave., New Westminster BC V3M 6Z1
604-526-1805 604-526-8056
info@kamlawyers.com
www.kamlawyers.com

North Vancouver: Ardagh Hunter - *2
#300, 1401 Lonsdale Ave., North Vancouver BC V7M 2H9
604-986-4366 604-986-9286
account@ahtlaw.com

North Vancouver: Bjurman, Trevors R. - *1
#205, 1433 Lonsdale Ave., North Vancouver BC V7M 2H9
604-983-3728 604-983-0148
bjurman@smartt.com

North Vancouver: Forrest, Gray, Lewis & Gillett - *1
#201, 145 - 15th St. East, North Vancouver BC V7L 2P7
604-988-5244 604-988-0093
fglg@dowco.com

North Vancouver: Hollander, M. - *1
#320, 145 West 17 St., North Vancouver BC V7M 1V5
604-986-4354 604-986-9183
marjon@intergate.ca

North Vancouver: Jabour, Sudeyko - *1
#603, 145 East 13th St., North Vancouver BC V7L 2L4
604-986-8600 604-986-4872 877-860-7575
dsudeyko@telus.net
www.jaboursudeyko.com

North Vancouver: Johnson, Robert W. - *1
#300, 1401 Lonsdale Ave., North Vancouver BC V7M 2H9
604-984-0305 604-984-0304
robert.johnson@ahtlaw.com

North Vancouver: Kroon, E.B. - *1
#100, 132 East 14 St., North Vancouver BC V7L 2N3
604-980-7021 604-980-7426

North Vancouver: Lakes, Straith & Whyte LLP - *4
#301, 145 - West 15th St. West, North Vancouver BC V7M 1R9
604-984-3646 604-984-8573 800-488-7788
www.lakes-straith.com

North Vancouver: Lynn Valley Law - *1
#40, 1199 Lynn Valley Rd., North Vancouver BC V7J 3H2
604-985-8000 604-985-5999
admin@lynnlaw.ca
www.lynnlaw.ca

North Vancouver: North Shore Law LLP - *15
171 West Esplanade, 6th Floor, North Vancouver BC V7M 3J9
604-980-8571 604-980-4019 877-980-8571
inquiries@northshorelaw.com
www.northshorelaw.com

North Vancouver: Perrick, Ron Law Corp. - *2
#480, 145 West 17 St., North Vancouver BC V7M 1V5
604-984-9521 604-984-9104

North Vancouver: Poyner Baxter LLP - *3
#408, 145 Chadwick Ct., North Vancouver BC V7M 3K1
604-988-6321 604-988-3632
info@poynerbaxter.com
www.poynerbaxter.com

North Vancouver: Reid, Robert C. - *1
#233, 1433 Lonsdale Ave., North Vancouver BC V7M 2H9
604-984-4357 604-984-4326
robertcreid@hotmail.com

North Vancouver: Roper, D.A. - *1
334 West 15th St., North Vancouver BC V7M 1S5
604-986-0488 604-984-3463
roperlaw@shawbiz.ca

Oliver: Gordon & Young - *3
P.O Box 1800 36011 - 97th St., Oliver BC V0H 1T0
250-498-4941 250-498-4100

Osoyoos: Gordon & Company - *2
#202, 8309 Main St., Osoyoos BC V0H 1V0
250-495-6508 250-495-6404
gordonco@telus.net
www.sunnyosoyoos.com/webpages/gordon_company.htm

Parksville: Davis & Avis - *2
#201, CP 1600 156 Morison Ave., Parksville BC V9P 2H5

250-248-5731 250-248-5730
law@davis-avis.com
www.davis-avis.com

***Parksville*: Hossack, John A., & Company - *1**
CP 1486 311 McKinnon St., Parksville BC V9P 2H4
250-248-9241 250-248-8375
john@hossack-law.com
www.hossack-law.com

***Parksville*: Lebedovich, Patricia E. - *1**
P.O Box 214, Parksville BC V9P 2G4
866-711-3084
lebedovich@shaw.ca

***Penticton*: Boyle & Company - *10**
#3201, 100 Front St., Penticton BC V2A 1H1
250-492-6100 250-492-4877 800-665-8244
www.boyleco.bc.ca

***Penticton*: Gilchrist & Company - *4**
#101, 123 Martin St., Penticton BC V2A 7X6
250-492-3033 250-492-6162
info@gilchristlaw.com
www.gilchristlaw.com

***Penticton*: Ginther, Kathryn J. - *1**
#301, 301 Main St., Penticton BC V2A 5B7
250-487-4355 250-487-4356
kjg@kgintherlaw.com

***Penticton*: Halbauer & McAndrews - *2**
445 Ellis St., Penticton BC V2A 4M1
250-492-7225 250-492-7395
www.pentictonlawyers.com

***Port Alberni*: Badovinac, Scoffield & Mosley - *3**
3290 - 3 Ave., Port Alberni BC V9Y 4E1
250-724-1275 250-724-7200
bsm@albernilaw.com
www.albernilaw.com

***Port Alberni*: Beckingham & Co. - *2**
5029 Argyle St., Port Alberni BC V9Y 1V5
250-724-0111 250-724-4422
beck@port.island.net

***Port Coquitlam*: Darychuk Deane-Cloutier - *2**
#310, 2755 Lougheed Hwy., Port Coquitlam BC V3B 5Y9
604-464-2644 604-464-2533

***Port Coquitlam*: Sarava, Henry - *1**
#2300, 2850 Shaughnessy St., Port Coquitlam BC V3C 6K5
604-944-2114 604-552-7709
henrysarava@hotmail.com
www.lawyers.com/saravacriminaldefence

***Port Hardy*: Nowosad & Company - *1**
CP 1289 8700 Market St., Port Hardy BC V0N 2P0
250-949-6031 250-949-2633
info@macisaacgroup.com
www.macisaacgroup.com

***Port Moody*: Burke Tomchenko Morrison - *5**
#301, 2502 St. Johns St., Port Moody BC V3H 2B4
604-937-1166 604-937-5577
firm@btmlawyers.com
www.btmlawyers.com

***Prince George*: Davis, John A. - *1**
#1, 1515 - 2 Ave., Prince George BC V2L 3B8
250-564-5544 250-562-9427
jdlaw@shawcable.com

***Prince George*: Fletcher Repstock - *5**
440 Brunswick St., Prince George BC V2L 2B6
250-564-1313 250-563-4362 877-690-1110
repstock@netbistro.com

***Prince George*: Gibbs, Richard C. - *1**
1134 - 3rd Ave., Prince George BC V2L 3E5
250-564-6460 250-562-0671
rcgibbs@telus.net

***Prince George*: Heather Sadler Jenkins LLP - *16**
#700, Royal Bank Bldg. P.O Box 4500 550 Victoria St., Prince George BC V2L 2K1
250-565-8000 250-565-8001 866-565-8777
hsj@hsjlawyers.com
www.hsjlawyers.com

***Prince George*: Hope Heinrich, Barristers & Solicitors - *9**
1598 - 6th Ave., Prince George BC V2L 5G7
250-563-0681 250-562-3761 800-663-8230
www.hh.bc.ca

***Prince George*: Leverman & Company - *1**
Courtyard Lane 1057 - 3rd Ave., Prince George BC V2L 3E3
250-564-1212 250-756-1588

***Prince George*: Madill, Ronald W. - *1**
1033 - 3rd Ave., Prince George BC V2L 3E3
250-562-5000 250-562-5105

***Prince George*: Mooney, J.A. - *1**
1033 - 3rd Ave., Prince George BC V2L 3B3
250-562-3324 250-562-9444
jim@jamesmooney.com

***Prince George*: Traxler Haines - *6**
#614, 1488 - 4 Ave., Prince George BC V2L 4Y2
250-563-7741 250-563-2953

***Prince George*: Wilbur & Company - *1**
1057 - 3rd Ave., Prince George BC V2L 3E3
250-564-1444 250-563-2842
dwilbur@shaw.ca

***Prince George*: Wilson King LLP - *10**
#1000, 299 Victoria St., Prince George BC V2L 5B8
250-960-3200 250-562-7777 800-365-4566
www.wilsonking.com

***Prince Rupert*: Kan, Marina C-K - *1**
P.O Box 722, Prince Rupert BC V8J 3S1
250-624-6060 250-624-6451

***Prince Rupert*: Peters, Irene G. Law Corp. - *2**
#304, 1488 - 14 Ave., Prince Rupert BC V2L 4Y2
250-627-7771 250-624-2191

***Prince Rupert*: Punnett & Johnston - *2**
#7, 222 - 3rd Ave. West, Prince Rupert BC V8J 1L1
250-624-2106 250-627-8805
pj@citytel.net

***Prince Rupert*: Silversides, Merrick & McLean - *4**
P.O Box 188 217 - 3rd Ave. West, Prince Rupert BC V8J 3P7
250-624-2116 250-627-7786
reception@silverco.ca

***Qualicum Beach*: Rodway & Perry - *2**
#1, CP 138 699 Beach Rd., Qualicum Beach BC V9K 1S7
250-752-9526 250-752-9521
rodwayandperry@shaw.ca
www.macisaacgroup.com

***Qualicum Beach*: Walker & Wilson, Barristers & Solicitors - *2**
#2, 707 Primrose St., Qualicum Beach BC V9K 2K1
250-752-6951 250-752-6022
kwalker@qblaw.ca
www.qblaw.ca

***Quesnel*: Schmitz, John B. - *1**
633 Clark St., Quesnel BC V2J 1L3
250-992-6793 250-992-6795

***Revelstoke*: Lavallée, Bernard C. - *1**
P.O Box 244 109 Connaught Ave., Revelstoke BC V0E 2S0
250-837-5168 250-837-5178
bcl59lawyer@rctvonline.net

***Revelstoke*: Lundberg, R.A. - *1**
119 Campbell Ave., Revelstoke BC V0E 2S0
250-837-5196 250-837-4746
robertlundberg@rctvonline.net

***Richmond*: Ash, O'Donnell, Hibbert - *4**
#1, 11575 Bridgeport Rd., Richmond BC V6X 1T5
604-273-9111 604-273-1117
aohlaw2007@gmail.com
www.ashodonnellhibbert.ca

***Richmond*: Carvalho, V.N. - *1**
13811 Gilbert Rd., Richmond BC V7E 2H8
604-274-5636 604- -
vncarvalho@shaw.ca

***Richmond*: Cohen, Buchan, Edwards - *9**
#208, 4940 No. 3 Rd., Richmond BC V6X 3A5
604-273-6411 604-273-4512
gary@cbelaw.com
www.cbelaw.com

***Richmond*: Graves, Douglas B. - *1**
#317, 8055 Anderson Rd., Richmond BC V6Y 1S2
604-276-0069

***Richmond*: Henderson Livingston Stewart LLP - *4**
Old Steveston Courthouse 12011 - 3rd Ave., Richmond BC V7E 3K1
604-241-2855 604-241-2866
office@hlslawyers.com
www.steveston.bc.ca

***Richmond*: Hoodekoff, Bernard - *1**
#206, 5811 Cooney Rd., Richmond BC V6X 3M1
604-278-8451 604-278-8453

***Richmond*: Humphry Paterson - *2**
#205, 8171 Park Rd., Richmond BC V6Y 1S9
604-278-3031 604-278-3021
humpat@telus.net

***Richmond*: INC Business Lawyers - *2**
#1201, 11871 Horseshoe Way, Richmond BC V7A 5H5
604-272-6960 604-272-6959 888-272-7771
info@incorporate.ca
www.incorporate.ca

***Richmond*: Jang Cheung Lee Chu Law Corporation - *7**
#700, London Plaza 5951 No. 3 Rd., Richmond BC V6X 2E3
604-276-8300 604-276-8309
office@jclclawcorp.com
www.jclclawcorp.com

***Richmond*: Kahn Zack Ehrlich Lithwick - *10**
#270, 10711 Cambie Rd., Richmond BC V6X 3G5
604-270-9571 604-270-8282 888-529-6368
general@kzellaw.com
www.kzellaw.com

***Richmond*: Krag, Kenneth B. - *1**
#228, 8055 Anderson Rd., Richmond BC V6Y 1S2
604-270-8702 604-270-6708

***Richmond*: Kuchta, Theodore - *1**
8480 Rosebank Cres., Richmond BC V7A 2K6
604-274-4513 604-276-2800
tedkuch@aol.com

***Richmond*: Label, Susan - *1**
#250, 11590 Cambie Rd., Richmond BC V6X 3Z5
604-273-6448 604-273-6998
www.susanlabel.com

***Richmond*: Phillips Paul - *2**
#215, 4800 No. 3 Rd., Richmond BC V6X 3A6
604-273-5297 604-273-1643
philpaul@direct.ca

***Richmond*: Wong & Tsang - *4**
#310, 8120 Granville Ave., Richmond BC V6Y 1P3
604-279-9023 604-279-9025

***Saanichton*: Wilson, C.J. Kip - *1**
#6, 7855 East Saanich Rd., Saanichton BC V8M 2B4
250-544-0727 250-544-0728
kipwilson@home.com

***Salmon Arm*: Brooke, Jackson, Downs - *4**
Centennial Building CP 67 51 - 3rd St. NE, Salmon Arm BC V1E 4N2
250-832-9311 250-832-3801 Telex: 048-8397
bjdlaw@sunwave.net
www.bjdlaw.com

***Salmon Arm*: Seale Law Corp. - *1**
CP 3248 450 Lakeshore Dr. NE, Salmon Arm BC V1E 4S1
250-832-9301 250-832-9300

***Salmon Arm*: Sivertz, Kiehlbauch & Zachernuk - *3**
#320, P.O Box 190 351 Hudson Ave. NE, Salmon Arm BC V1E 4N3
250-832-8031 250-832-6177

***Salt Spring Island*: Clement, Ian H. - *1**
#1, 105 Rainbow Rd., Salt Spring Island BC V8K 2V5
250-537-5505 250-537-5099

***Salt Spring Island*: McEwen, J. Anthony - *1**
1860 Fulford-Ganges Rd., Salt Spring Island BC V8K 2A5
250-653-4979 250-653-9212

***Sechelt*: Prowse, William C. - *1**
6866 Island View Rd., Sechelt BC V0N 3A8
604-740-0303 604-740-0306
transmed@telus.net

***Sidney*: Finall, Alice E. - *1**
2412B Beacon Ave., 2nd Fl., Sidney BC V8L 1X4
250-656-6668 250-656-9366
final@telus.net

Sidney: Henley & Walden - *3
#201, 2377 Bevan Ave., Sidney BC V8L 4M9
250-656-7231 250-656-0937 800-656-7231
inquiries@henleywalden.com
www.henleywalden.com

Sidney: McKimm & Lott - *7
9830 - 4th St., Sidney BC V8L 2Z3
250-656-3961 250-655-3329
reception@mclott.com
www.mclott.com

Smithers: Perry & Company - *4
CP 790 1081 Main St., Smithers BC V0J 2N0
250-847-4341 250-847-5634
mail@perryco.ca
www.perryco.ca

Smithers: Toews, G. Ronald, Q.C. - *1
P.O Box 970 3835 - 10th Ave., Smithers BC V0J 2N0
250-847-2187 250-847-2183
grt@buckley.net

Sooke: Hallgren & Faulkner - *2
P.O Box 939 6595 Sooke Rd., Sooke BC V0S 1N0
250-642-5271 250-642-6006 800-358-5271
hallgrenfaulkner@shaw.ca

Squamish: Race & Company - *6
#201, CP 1850 1365 Pemberton Ave., Squamish BC V0N 3G0
604-892-5254 604-892-5461
d.race@racesq.com
www.raceandcompany.com

Summerland: Bell, Jacoe & Company, Barristers & Solicitors - *2
P.O Box 520 13211 Victoria Rd. North, Summerland BC V0H 1Z0
250-494-6621 250-494-8055 800-663-0392
belljacoe@shaw.ca
www.bell-jacoe.com

Surrey: Benson, Alan J. - *1
#106, 15585 - 24 Ave., Surrey BC V4A 2J4
604-538-4911 604-538-5754

Surrey: Bowers, Spencer A. - *1
8893 - 160 St., Surrey BC V4N 2X8
604-951-9224 604-951-9224
sabowers@axionet.com

Surrey: Brawn, Karras & Sanderson - *3
#340, 5620 - 152nd St., Surrey BC V3A 3K2
604-588-5344 604-588-2331
infodesk@bkslaw.com
www.bkslaw.com

Surrey: Davidson, James L. & Company - *3
#403, P.O Box 271 16033 - 108 Ave., Surrey BC V4N 1P2
604-951-2990 604-951-2991
jld@look.ca

Surrey: Egolf, G. - *1
14135 - 60 Ave., Surrey BC V3X 2N2
604-594-4166

Surrey: Guildford Law Group - *3
#200, 10330 - 152 St., Surrey BC V3R 4G8
604-585-1196 604-585-3293
www.guildfordlaw.com

Surrey: Janeson, Sharen - *1
#456, 15355 - 24 Ave., Surrey BC V4A 2H9
604-536-6884 604-618-9500
sjaneson@shaw.ca

Surrey: Kaminsky & Company - *4
#220, 7525 King George Hwy., Surrey BC V3W 5A8
604-591-7877 604-591-1978
kaminsky@zis.net

Surrey: Kane, Shannon & Weiler - *22
#220, 7565 - 132nd St., Surrey BC V3W 1K5
604-591-7321 604-591-7149
info@ksw.bc.ca
www.ksw.bc.ca

Surrey: MacMillan, Tucker, & Mackay - *3
5690 - 176A St., Surrey BC V3S 4H1
604-574-7431 604-574-3021

Surrey: Maier & Co. - *1
#310, 10524 King George Hwy., Surrey BC V3S 2X2
604-582-5951 604-588-0779
maier@telus.net

Surrey: McAndrew, A.L. - *1
#240, 13711 - 72 Ave., Surrey BC V3W 2P2
604-591-2288 604-591-7366

Surrey: McQuarrie Hunter LLP - *26
#200, 13889 - 104th Ave., Surrey BC V3T 1W8
604-581-0461 604-581-7110
www.mcquarrie.com

Surrey: McRae, Allan D. - *1
#309, 1656 Martin Dr., Surrey BC V4A 6E7
604-538-1511

Surrey: Nyack & Persad - *2
#201, 9380 - 120 St., Surrey BC V3V 4B9
604-588-9933 604-588-2731
nyackpersad@hotmail.com

Surrey: Richards & Richards - *3
10325 - 150 St., Surrey BC V3R 4B1
604-588-6844 604-588-8800
richard.george@richardslaw.com

Surrey: Swedahl, E.R. - *1
#11, 15243 - 91 Ave., Surrey BC V3R 8P8
604-581-3232 604-589-3741

Surrey: Taylor, Bjorge & Company - *2
#205, 1676 Martin Dr., Surrey BC V4A 6E7
604-536-1117 604-536-0445

Surrey: Whaites, P. Barry - *1
#200, 5746 - 176A St., Surrey BC V3S 4H2
604-574-0770 604-574-0107

Terrace: Crampton Personal Law Corporation - *2
4623 Park Ave., Terrace BC V8G 1V5
250-635-6330 250-635-4795 800-667-0080
Gordon_Crampton@telus.net; bryan_crampton@telus.net

Terrace: Talstra & Company - *3
#101, 3219 Eby St., Terrace BC V8G 4R3
250-638-1137 250-638-1306 877-998-4222

Terrace: Warner Bandstra Brown - *5
#200, 4630 Lazelle Ave., Terrace BC V8G 1S6
250-635-2622 250-635-4998

Trail: Ghilarducci & Cromarty - *2
1309 Bay Ave., Trail BC V1R 4A7
250-368-6455 250-368-6107

Trail: McEwan Harrison & Co. - *6
1432 Bay Ave., Trail BC V1R 4B1
250-368-8211 250-368-9401
www.mcewanharrison.com

Trail: Westcott Simpkin & Co. - *1
1402 Bay Ave., Trail BC V1R 4B1
250-358-9171 250-368-3369
westcottlaw@shawbiz.ca

Tsawwassen: Millichamp & Company - *1
#210, 1530 - 56 St., Tsawwassen BC V4L 2A8
604-943-7401 604-943-7402
millichamplaw@dccnet.com

Vancouver: Access Law Group - *7
#1700, 1185 Georgia St. West, Vancouver BC V6E 4E6
604-689-8000 604-689-8835
reception@accesslaw.ca
www.accesslaw.ca

Vancouver: Alexander Holburn Beaudin & Lang, LLP - *75
#2700, P.O Box 10057 700 West Georgia St., Vancouver BC V7Y 1B8
604-484-1700 604-484-9700 877-688-1351
info@ahbl.ca
www.ahbl.ca

Vancouver: Alexander, William J. - *1
#167, 1917 - 4th Ave. West, Vancouver BC V6J 1M7
604-831-3743 604-831-6273

Vancouver: Andersen, Paul - *2
1662 - 8th Ave. West, Vancouver BC V6J 4R8
604-734-8411 604-734-8511
andersen_paul@telus.net

Vancouver: Anderson, Brian W., Law Corporation - *1
835 Granville St., 2nd Fl., Vancouver BC V6Z 1K7
604-684-5367

Vancouver: Anfield Sujir Kennedy & Durno - *6
#1600, Pacific Centre P.O Box 10068 609 Granville St., Vancouver BC V7Y 1C3
604-669-1322 604-669-3877
mailbox@askdlaw.com

Vancouver: Armstrong Simpson - *4
#2080, 777 Hornby St., Vancouver BC V6Z 1S4
604-683-7361 604-662-3231

Vancouver: Aydin Bird - *4
#530, North Office Tower 650 - 41 Ave. West, Vancouver BC V5Z 2M9
604-266-5828 604-266-3929
aydin@aydinco.com
www.aydinco.com

Vancouver: Barbeau, Evans, Goldstein - *4
#280, 666 Burrard St., Vancouver BC V6C 2X8
604-688-4900 604-688-0649
info@beg-law.com
www.beg-law.com

Vancouver: Barnes, Gail - *1
149 Main St., Vancouver BC V6A 2S5
604-684-1124 604-684-1122
egray@sprint.ca

Vancouver: Beck, Robinson & Company - *4
#700, 686 West Broadway, Vancouver BC V5Z 1G1
604-874-0204 604-874-0820
lawyers@beckrobinson.com
www.beckrobinson.com

Vancouver: Bellows, Robert W. - *1
#620, 1385 West 8 Ave., Vancouver BC V6H 3V9
604-736-5500 604-736-5522
rbellows@telus.net

Vancouver: Bennett, Parkes - *2
#460, 2609 Granville St., Vancouver BC V6H 3H3
604-734-6838 604-738-6789

Vancouver: Bernard, Shoni Lee - *1
5052 Victoria Dr., Vancouver BC V5P 3T8
604-473-9330 604-323-0093

Vancouver: Bianchin, Raymond J. - *1
#410, 2609 Granville St., Vancouver BC V6H 3H3
604-683-8111 604-685-0194

Vancouver: Birnie & Company - *2
#2433, Three Bentall Centre P.O Box 49116 Bentall595 Burrard St., Vancouver BC V7X 1G4
604-688-4511 604-688-0511
dbirnie@birnieco.com

Vancouver: Bolton & Muldoon - *4
#360, 1122 Mainland St., Vancouver BC V6B 5L1
604-687-7078 604-687-3022

Vancouver: Boughton Law Corporation - *50
#700, P.O Box 49290 595 Burrard St., Vancouver BC V7X 1S8
604-687-6789 604-683-5317
lawyers@boughton.ca
www.boughton.ca

Vancouver: Bradley, Joyce W. - *1
P.O Box 45565 Westside, Vancouver BC V6S 2N5
604-732-3886 604-732-3781
jwbmediate@telus.net

Vancouver: Brown, H.K. - *1
#1504, 100 West Pender St., 15th Fl., Vancouver BC V6B 1R8
604-684-1021 604-688-6243
henrykbrownlawcorporation@telus.net

Vancouver: Buchanan, J.G. - *1
#788, 601 West Broadway, Vancouver BC V5Z 4C2
604-876-0343 604-876-9035

Vancouver: Bull, Housser & Tupper LLP - *100
#3000, Royal Centre P.O Box 11130 1055 West Georgia St., Vancouver BC V6E 3R3
604-687-6575 604-641-4949 888-687-6575 Telex: 04-53395
mailbox@bht.com
www.bht.com

Vancouver: Burns, Fitzpatrick, Rogers & Schwartz - *8
#1400, 510 Burrard St., Vancouver BC V6C 3A8
604-685-0121 604-685-2104
bfrs@bfrs.ca
www.bfrs.ca

Vancouver: Caldwell, Bradley M. - *1
#401, 815 Hornby St., Vancouver BC V6Z 2E6
604-689-8894 604-689-5739

Vancouver: Chalke & Company - *1
708-1155 W. Pender St., Vancouver BC V6E 2P4
604-980-4855 604-980-6469

Vancouver: Chan Yue & Lee - *1
#212, 475 Main St., Vancouver BC V6A 2T7
604-687-4576 604-683-3258
canyua@intergate.ca

Vancouver: Chen & Leung - *9
#728, North Tower, Oakridge Centre 650 - 41st Ave. West, Vancouver BC V5Z 2M9
604-264-8331 604-264-8387
info@cllawyers.ca
www.cllawyers.ca

Vancouver: Clark Wilson LLP - *80
#800, 885 Georgia St. West, Vancouver BC V6C 3H1
604-687-5700 604-687-6314
agb@cwilson.com
www.cwilson.com

Vancouver: Cofman, Morley E. Law Corp. - *1
#1500, 701 West Georgia St., Vancouver BC V7Y 1C6
604-696-6674 604-801-5911
mcofman@shaw.ca

Vancouver: Collins & Cullen - *2
#750, 999 West Broadway, Vancouver BC V5Z 1K5
604-730-2678 604-730-2628

Vancouver: Comparelli, James - *2
#704, 510 West Hastings St., Vancouver BC V6B 1L8
604-683-6888 604-683-4497
james@comparelli.com
www.comparelli.com

Vancouver: Crestani, F.S. - *1
5052 Victoria Dr., Vancouver BC V5P 3T8
604-251-1168 604-253-7726

Vancouver: Cristall, Kenneth - *1
#610, P.O Box 12110 808 Nelson St., Vancouver BC V6Z 2H2
604-654-2250 604-682-8879

Vancouver: Crosby, Harry - *1
5052 Victoria Dr., Vancouver BC V5P 3T8
604-321-6922 604-323-0093

Vancouver: Dallas & Company - *1
852 Seymour St., Vancouver BC V6B 3L6
604-681-6171 604-683-1000
dallas&co@telus.net

Vancouver: Dangerfield, A. Kenneth - *1
#1000, P.O Box 49290 Bentall595 Burrard St., Vancouver BC V7X 1S8
604-687-6789 604-683-5317
kdangerfield@boughton.ca

Vancouver: DeMeulemeester, A.J. - *1
#202, 119 Pender St. West, Vancouver BC V6B 1S5
604-685-6610 604-682-5687

Vancouver: Derpak, White & Company - *3
#901, 1788 Broadway West, Vancouver BC V6J 1Y1
604-736-9791 604-736-7197
derpakwhite@telus.net

Vancouver: Dobbin, J.W. - *1
123 Main St., Vancouver BC V6A 2S5
604-669-6045 604-669-6041
jwd@jwdobbin.com

Vancouver: Donaldson Jetté - *4
#490, 1090 Hornby St., Vancouver BC V6B 2W9
604-681-5232 604-681-1331
hrusso@donaldsonjette.ca

Vancouver: Donna L. Kydd Law Corporation - *1
#250, 1501 West Broadway, Vancouver BC V6J 4Z6
604-732-5031 604-732-5071
dlkydd@kyddlaw.ca; sthomas@kyddlaw.ca
www.kyddlaw.ca

Vancouver: DuMoulin, Boskovich - *16
#1800, Manulife Place Box 52 1095 West Pender St., Vancouver BC V6E 2M6
604-669-5500 604-688-8491 800-288-9893
info@dubo.com
www.dubo.com

Vancouver: Edwards, Kenny & Bray LLP - *23
#1900, The Grosvenor Bldg. 1040 West Georgia St., Vancouver BC V6E 4H3
604-689-1811 604-689-5177
inquiry@ekb.com
www.ekb.com

Vancouver: Ellis, Nauss & Jones - *2
#600, 1665 West Broadway, Vancouver BC V6J 1X1
604-731-9276 604-734-0206

Vancouver: Ellis, Roadburg - *2
#200, 853 Richards St., Vancouver BC V6B 3B4
604-669-7131 604-669-7684

Vancouver: Epstein Wood - *8
#650, 1500 West Georgia St., Vancouver BC V6G 2Z6
604-685-4321 604-685-7901

Vancouver: Falconer, Robert J., Q.C. - *1
#400, 409 Granville St., Vancouver BC V6C 1T2
604-683-5674 604-682-8417
robert.falconer@axion.net

Vancouver: Fan & Co. - *3
#601, 609 Gore Ave., Vancouver BC V6A 2Z8
604-683-0471 604-683-8748
hfan@telus.net

Vancouver: Farris, Vaughan, Wills & Murphy LLP - *87
700 West Georgia St., 25th Floor, Vancouver BC V7Y 1B3
604-684-9151 604-661-9349 Telex: 04-507819
info@farris.com
www.farris.com

Vancouver: Fayers & Company - *2
#380, 5740 Cambie St., Vancouver BC V5Z 3A6
604-325-1246 604-325-1261

Vancouver: Flader, Larry C. - *1
4244 Doncaster Way, Vancouver BC V6S 2L6
604-224-7225

Vancouver: Fogal, Constance C. - *1
3570 Hull St., Vancouver BC V5N 4R9
604-872-2128

Vancouver: Fraser & Company - *9
#1200, 999 Hastings St. West, Vancouver BC V6C 2W2
604-669-5244 604-669-5791
securities@fraserlaw.com

Vancouver: Friesen & Epp - *4
5660 Yew St., Vancouver BC V6M 3Y3
604-264-8386 604-264-8815
erwinepp@stargate.ca

Vancouver: Ganapathi & Company - *2
#302, 1224 Hamilton St., Vancouver BC V6B 2S8
604-689-9222 604-689-4888 866-689-9222
nathan@ganapathico.com; info@ganapathico.com
www.ganapathico.com

Vancouver: Gavin, Gayle D. - *1
4168 - 11th Ave., Vancouver BC V6R 2L6
604-222-2827

Vancouver: Gibbons Fowler Nathanson - *6
#440, The Marine Building 355 Burrard St., Vancouver BC V6C 2G8
604-684-0778 604-684-0799
reception@gibbonsfowler.com
www.gibbonsfowler.com

Vancouver: Glasner Q.C., Kenneth Law Corp. - *1
#1414, P.O Box 12158 808 Nelson St., Vancouver BC V6Z 2H2
604-683-4181 604-683-0226
glasnerqc@telus.net

Vancouver: Gordon, C.H.J. - *1
#115, 2025 - 1st Ave. West, Vancouver BC V6J 1H1
604-730-8838

Vancouver: Gornall, P.D. - *1
#1820, 355 Burrard St., Vancouver BC V6C 2G8
604-681-7932 604-775-8555
pdg@telus.net

Vancouver: Grant, Murray H. - *1
#2020, P.O Box 11547 650 West Georgia St., Vancouver BC V6B 4N7
604-683-9621 604-683-5084

Vancouver: Granville Law Group - *2
#200, 835 Granville St., Vancouver BC V6Z 1K7
604-669-6580 604-688-7291

Vancouver: Grossman & Stanley, Business Lawyers - *4
#800, Box 55 1090 West Georgia St., Vancouver BC V6E 3V7
604-683-7454 604-683-8602
info@grossmanstanley.com
www.grossmanstanley.com

Vancouver: Guinn, W.F. - *1
671G Market Hill, Vancouver BC V5Z 4B5
604-872-6658 604-876-3304

Vancouver: Guy & Company - *1
#100, 190 Alexander St., Vancouver BC V6A 1B5
604-681-6164 604-681-7420
guy_and_company@telus.net

Vancouver: Hara & Company - *3
#301, 460 Nanaimo St., Vancouver BC V5L 4W3
604-255-4800 604-255-8111
haraco@telus.net

Vancouver: Harper Grey LLP - *53
#3200, Vancouver Centre 650 West Georgia St., Vancouver BC V6B 4P7
604-687-0411 604-669-9385
info@harpergrey.com
www.harpergrey.com

Vancouver: Harris & Brun - *6
555 West Georgia St., Vancouver BC V6B 1Z5
604-683-2466 604-683-4541

Vancouver: Harris & Company LLP - *33
Bentall 5 550 Burrard St., 14th Floor, Vancouver BC V6C 2B5
604-684-6633 604-684-6632
info@harrisco.com
www.harrisco.com

Vancouver: Helsing, John E. - *1
#347, 1275 West 6th Ave., Vancouver BC V6H 1A6
604-739-7731 604-738-7134

Vancouver: Hemsworth, Schmidt - *2
#430, 580 Hornby St., Vancouver BC V6C 3B6
604-687-4456 604-687-0586

Vancouver: Hogan & Company - *1
#900, 850 Hastings St. West, Vancouver BC V6C 1E1
604-687-8806 604-687-7089

Vancouver: Holmes & Company - *2
#1880, 1066 Hastings St. West, Vancouver BC V6E 3X1
604-688-7861 604-688-0426
sdh@holmescompany.com
www.holmescompany.com

Vancouver: Hordo & Bennett - *8
#1801, Nelson Sq. P.O Box 12146 808 Nelson St., Vancouver BC V6Z 2H2
604-682-5250 604-682-7872
general@hrb.bc.ca

Vancouver: Hull, Peter J. - *1
869 West 20 Ave., Vancouver BC V5Z 1Y3
604-874-0200

Vancouver: Hutchins Caron & Associates, Barristers & Solicitors
#400, 601 West Broadway, Office 5, Vancouver BC V5Z 4C2
604-871-4327 604-871-4336
www.hutchinslegal.ca

Vancouver: Ishkanian, Vahan A. - *1
#1100, 1200 - 73rd Ave. West, Vancouver BC V6P 6G5
604-267-3033 604-264-6133
vishkanian@pepito.ca

Vancouver: Jeffery & Calder - *4
#601 815 Hornby St., Vancouver BC V6Z 2E6
604-669-5534 604-669-7563
contact@jefferycalder.com
www.jefferycalder.com

Vancouver: Jenkins Marzban Logan LLP - *13
#900, Nelson Square 808 Nelson St., Vancouver BC V6Z 2H2
604-681-6564 604-681-0766
info@jml.ca
www.jml.ca

Vancouver: Jussa, R.N. - *1
#204, 4676 Main St., Vancouver BC V5V 3R7
604-872-8191 604-872-8217

Vancouver: Kaplan & Waddell - *3
#102, 2590 Granville St., Vancouver BC V6H 3H1
604-736-8021 604-736-3845

Vancouver: Katz & Company - *1
#1018, Nelson Square P.O Box 12135 808 Nelson St., Vancouver BC V6Z 2H2
604-669-6226 604-669-6752

Vancouver: Kennedy, C. Robert - *1
#206, 190 Alexander St., Vancouver BC V6A 1B5
604-684-3927 604-684-3228

Vancouver: Kerfoot & Company - *4
#300, 5687 Yew St., Vancouver BC V6M 3Y2
604-263-2565 604-263-2737
bbk@kerfootandco.com
www.kerfootandco.com

Vancouver: Killam Cordell Murray - *4
#2000, 401 Georgia St. West, Vancouver BC V6B 5A1
604-622-5252 604-622-5244
sgc@killamcordel.com

Vancouver: King, William N. - *1
#400, United Kingdom Bldg. 409 Granville St., Vancouver BC V6C 1T2
604-682-1245 604-682-8417
janice.s@shaw.ca

Vancouver: Klein, Lyons - *9
#1100, 1333 Broadway West, Vancouver BC V6H 4C1
604-874-7171 604-874-7180
info@kleinlyons.com
www.kleinlyons.com

Vancouver: Kontou, Dimitri A. - *1
#1550, 355 Burrard St., Vancouver BC V6G 2C8
604-662-7244 604-687-3097
dkontou@telus.net

Vancouver: Kornfeld & Company - *2
#310, 698 Seymour St., Vancouver BC V6B 3K6
604-689-3838 604-689-0526

Vancouver: Lam, Yoke - *1
#328, 88 East Pender St., Vancouver BC V6A 1T1
604-689-1123 604-689-2003

Vancouver: Lando & Company - *6
#2010, Royal Centre P.O Box 11140 1055 Georgia St. West, Vancouver BC V6E 3P3
604-682-6821 604-662-8293
info@lando.ca
www.lando.ca

Vancouver: Laughton & Company - *2
#1090, 1090 Georgia St. West, Vancouver BC V6E 3V7
604-683-6665 604-683-6622

Vancouver: Law Office of David J. MacFarlane, Barrister & Solicitor
#490, 99 West Broadway, Vancouver BC V5Z 1K5
604-732-7481 604-732-3205
macper@telus.net

Vancouver: Lawson Lundell LLP - *100
#1600, Cathedral Place 925 West Georgia St., Vancouver BC V6C 3L2
604-685-3456 604-669-1620
jsmith@lawsonlundell.com
www.lawsonlundell.com

Vancouver: Laxton & Company - *3
1285 West Pender St., 10th Fl., Vancouver BC V6E 4B1
604-682-3871 604-682-3704

Vancouver: Lecovin & Company - *2
#560, P.O Box 193 1125 Howe St., Vancouver BC V6Z 2K8
604-687-1721 604-687-1799
lecovin@intergate.ca

Vancouver: Lee, Jack L. - *1
127 East Pender St., 3rd Fl., Vancouver BC V6A 1T6
604-683-7241 604-683-3279

Vancouver: Lew & Lee - *3
#108, 329 Main St., Vancouver BC V6A 2S9
604-685-8331 604-685-8334

Vancouver: Lew, Chuck - *1
#1010, 207 Hastings St. West, Vancouver BC V6B 1H7
604-688-3601 604-688-7866
lewlaw@uniserve.com

Vancouver: Lew, H.H., & Company - *1
22 - 10th Ave. West, Vancouver BC V5Y 1R6
604-879-3151 604-879-3707
hhlew@shaw.ca

Vancouver: Lindsay Kenney LLP - *55
#1800, 401 West Georgia St., Vancouver BC V6B 5A1
604-687-1323 604-687-2347 866-687-1323
info@lklaw.ca
www.lklaw.ca

Vancouver: Lipetz & Company - *1
#202, 2902 West Broadway, Vancouver BC V6K 2G8
604-733-5611 604-738-5611

Vancouver: Lo, Keith A. - *2
#338, 237 Keefer St., Vancouver BC V6A 1X6
604-687-4315 604-681-2289

Vancouver: Long, R.H. & Co. - *1
865 - 46th Ave. West, Vancouver BC V5Z 2R4
604-876-0492 604-876-3219
rhlong@shaw.ca

Vancouver: Macaulay McColl LLP - *9
#1575, P.O Box 11635 650 West Georgia St., Vancouver BC V6B 4N9
604-687-9811 604-687-8716 800-233-4405
lawyers@macaulay.com
www.macaulay.com

Vancouver: MacKenzie Fujisawa LLP - *19
#1600, 1095 West Pender St., Vancouver BC V6E 2M6
604-689-3281 604-685-6494
lawyers@maclaw.bc.ca
www.mackenziefujisawa.com

Vancouver: MacKinlay Woodson Diebel - *2
#1170, 1040 West Georgia St., Vancouver BC V6E 4H1
604-669-1511 604-669-1566
corp@woodsonlaw.bc.ca

Vancouver: MacLean Family Law Group - *4
#3103, 1077 Cordova St. West, Vancouver BC V6C 2C6
604-602-9000 604-682-0556
info@bcfamilylaw.ca

Vancouver: MacLeod, Morag M.J. - *1
#800, 555 West Georgia St., Vancouver BC V6B 1Z6
604-430-8444 604-430-1164
celtlaw@telus.net

Vancouver: Maitland & Company - *5
#700, 625 Howe St., Vancouver BC V6C 2T6
604-681-7474 604-681-3896
maitco@maitland.com
www.maitland.com/Newindex

Vancouver: Maxwell Bulmer Hopman - *4
900 Helmcken St., Vancouver BC V6Z 1B3
604-669-4912 604-662-3975

Vancouver: McClusky, Joanne S. - *1
#810, 675 Hastings St. West, Vancouver BC V6B 1N2
604-689-4010 604-684-2349
jmcclusky@telus.net

Vancouver: McCrea & Associates - *4
#102, 1012 Beach Ave., Vancouver BC V6E 1T7
604-662-8200 604-662-8225
lawyers@mccrealaw.ca
www.mccrealaw.ca

Vancouver: McKenzie & Company - *2
891 Helmcken St., Vancouver BC V6Z 1B1
604-687-7811 604-685-4358

Vancouver: McLachlan Brown Anderson - *9
938 Howe St., 10th Fl., Vancouver BC V6Z 1N9
604-331-6000 604-331-6008

Vancouver: McNeney & McNeney - *5
#300, 195 Alexander St., Vancouver BC V6A 1N8
604-867-1766 604-687-0181 800-535-6565
bikerlaw@kwik.net

Vancouver: McPhee, Richard A. - *1
#1025, 1185 West Georgia St., Vancouver BC V6E 4E6
604-682-0926 604-688-8615 Telex: 04-508813 VICMA
vml@pro.net

Vancouver: Mickelson, Brian E. - *1
100 West Pender St., 2nd Fl., Vancouver BC V6B 1R8
604-688-8588 604-681-0652

Vancouver: Mickelson, J.L. - *2
#302, 1110 Hamilton St., Vancouver BC V6B 2S2
604-684-0040 604-684-0048
dajones@telus.net

Vancouver: Morrison, Don - *2
#1109, 207 West Hastings St., Vancouver BC V6B 1H7
604-685-7097 604-662-7511
don.morrison@telus.net
www.donmorrisonlaw.com

Vancouver: Mortimer & Rose - *2
#920, 777 Hornby St., Vancouver BC V6Z 1S4
604-669-0440 604-669-0228

Vancouver: Murdy & McAllister - *7
#1155, Two Bentall Centre P.O Box 49059 Bentall555 Burrard St., Vancouver BC V7X 1C4
604-689-5263 604-689-9029

Vancouver: Myers, Waddell, McMurdo & Karp - *10
195 Alexander St., 5th Fl., Vancouver BC V6A 1B8
604-688-8331 604-688-8350 888-244-9995
lm@myersco.ca
www.myersco.ca or www.vancouverdefencelawyer.com

Vancouver: Nelson & Vanderkruyk - *3
#440, 355 Burrard St., Vancouver BC V6C 2G8
604-684-1311 604-684-6402
nelsonvanderkruyk@nvlaw.ca

Vancouver: Nelson, B.J. - *1
#103, 1012 Beach Ave., Vancouver BC V6E 1T7
604-685-7317 604-682-3965

Vancouver: Nordlinger, K.F., Q.C. & Associates - *4
#109, 1008 Beach Ave., Vancouver BC V6E 1T7
604-689-5134 604-689-5323
katherine@nordlinger.net

Vancouver: Northwest Law Group - *6
#1880, 1055 West Georgia St., Vancouver BC V6E 3P3
604-687-5792 604-687-6650

Vancouver: Norton Stewart Business Lawyers - *5
#1600, P.O Box 11104 1055 West Georgia St., Vancouver BC V6E 3P3
604-687-0555 604-689-1248

Vancouver: Oland & Company - *2
#2020, Vancouver Centre P.O Box 11547 650 West Georgia St., Vancouver BC V6B 4N7
604-683-9621 604-669-4556
shiplaw@aboland.com

Vancouver: Osten & Osten - *1
#356, P.O Box 11113 5740 Cambie St., Vancouver BC V6E 3A6
604-683-9104 604-688-0034

Vancouver: Owen Bird Law Corporation - *33
#2900, Three Bentall Centre CP 49130 595 Burrard St., Vancouver BC V7X 1J5
604-688-0401 604-688-2827
inquiries@owenbird.com
www.owenbird.com

Vancouver: Paine Edmonds LLP - *15
#1100, 510 Burrard St., Vancouver BC V6C 3A8
604-683-1211 604-681-5084 800-669-8599
law@paine-edmonds.com
www.paine-edmonds.com

Vancouver: Pape Salter Teillet - *3
#460, 220 Cambie St., Vancouver BC V6B 2M9
604-681-3002 604-681-3050
admin@pstlaw.ca

Vancouver: Paquette, Al - *1
#5, 8431 Granville St., Vancouver BC V6P 4Z9
604-261-3211 604-261-5382

Vancouver: Peterson Stark Scott - *11
#500, 1195 West Broadway, Vancouver BC V6H 3X5
604-736-9811 604-736-2859 800-555-3288
van@petersonstark.bc.ca
www.petersonstark.bc.ca

Vancouver: Polsky Shamash, Susan L. - *1
#150, 4600 Jacombs Rd., Vancouver BC V6V 3B1
604-664-7800 604-664-7898 800-663-2782

Vancouver: Poulsen & Co. - *4
#1800, 999 West Hastings St., Vancouver BC V6C 2W2

604-681-0123 604-683-1375
pchapman@poulsenlaw.com
www.poulsenlaw.com

Vancouver: **Quorum Business Lawyers - *7**
#1450, 1075 West Georgia St., Vancouver BC V6E 3C9
604-682-0701 604-682-7359
www.quorumlaw.com

Vancouver: **Raibmon, Richard - *1**
#1535, Nelson Sq. P.O Box 12134 808 Nelson St., Vancouver BC V6Z 2H2
604-688-8551 604-687-1799
rlrlaw@uniserve.com

Vancouver: **Rankin, Bond - *2**
#200, 157 Alexander St., Vancouver BC V6A 1B8
604-682-3621 604-682-3919

Vancouver: **Raphanel, Gayle M. - *1**
#501, 815 Hornby St., Vancouver BC V6Z 2E6
604-682-2200 604-682-2246
gmr@dowco.com

Vancouver: **Richards Buell Sutton LLP - *36**
#700, 401 West Georgia St., Vancouver BC V6B 5A1
604-682-3664 604-688-3830
info@rbs.ca
www.rbs.ca

Vancouver: **Roberts & Stahl - *5**
#500, 220 Cambie St., Vancouver BC V6B 2M9
604-684-6377 604-684-6387
cbarthe@robertsstahl.com
www.robertsstahl.com

Vancouver: **Rogers Law Office - *2**
#1210, 1140 Pender St. West, Vancouver BC V6E 4G1
604-681-5600 604-681-1475
dan@shorttco.com

Vancouver: **Roper Greyell LLP, Employment & Labour Lawyers - *24**
#800, Park Place 666 Burrard St., Vancouver BC V6C 3P3
604-806-0922 604-806-0933
info@ropergreyell.com
www.greyell.com

Vancouver: **Rosenberg & Rosenberg - *3**
671D Market Hill, Vancouver BC V5Z 4B5
604-879-4505 604-879-4934
rosenberg_law@telus.net

Vancouver: **Rosenbloom & Aldridge - *3**
#440, 355 Burrard St., Vancouver BC V6C 2G8
604-605-5555 604-684-6402
rosenbloom_aldridge@telus.net

Vancouver: **Rosner, J.H. - *1**
#770, 475 Georgia St. West, Vancouver BC V6B 4M9
604-687-6638 604-682-2481
roslaw@telus.net

Vancouver: **Ross, R.D. Q.C. - *1**
4741 West 2 Ave., Vancouver BC V6T 1C1
604-228-9701 604-228-9055

Vancouver: **Rubin, Howard Law Corp. - *1**
405E - 4 St., Vancouver BC V7L 1J4
604-984-2030 604-988-0068
howard@howard-rubin.com

Vancouver: **Sacks, Morrie Law Corporation - *1**
#207, 1525 - 8th Ave. West, Vancouver BC V6T 1T5
604-685-7629 604-685-7630
morrie@collaborativedivorce.ca
www.nocourtdivorce.ca

Vancouver: **Sandberg, Charles A. - *1**
#108, 2786 - 16 Ave. West, Vancouver BC V6K 4M1
604-734-7768 604-733-1229

Vancouver: **Scarisbrick, P.N. - *1**
234 Abbott St., Vancouver BC V6B 2K8
604-688-0495 604-688-0201

Vancouver: **Schwartz, David A. - *1**
#600, 890 West Pender St., Vancouver BC V6C 1J9
604-687-0811 604-687-1327
schwartzdav@gmail.com

Vancouver: **Serka, A.P. - *1**
#788, 601 West Broadway, Vancouver BC V5Z 4C2
604-876-8761 604-876-9035

Vancouver: **Shapiro, Murray H. - *1**
694 West 19th Ave., Vancouver BC V5Z 1X1
604-879-6777 604-879-6728

Vancouver: **Shelton, S.S. - *1**
3469 Commercial St., Vancouver BC V5N 4E8
604-251-2144 604-251-2781

Vancouver: **Shimizu, George - *1**
#718, P.O Box 50959 808 Nelson St., Vancouver BC V6Z 2H2
604-685-4467 604-685-4408
geoshimizu@telus.net

Vancouver: **Silbernagel & Company - *2**
#700, 595 Howe St., Vancouver BC V6C 2T5
604-687-9621 604-687-5960
stephen@silbernagellaw.com

Vancouver: **Simon Wener - *2**
#620, 1385 - 8 Ave. West, Vancouver BC V6H 3V9
604-736-5500 604-736-5522
info@simonwener.com
www.simonwener.com

Vancouver: **Sisett & Co. - *2**
#603, 601 West Broadway, Vancouver BC V5Z 4C2
604-879-8811 604-879-7346 800-446-5879
sisett@sisettlaw.com
www.sisettlaw.com

Vancouver: **Smith & Hughes - *2**
#102, 4088 Cambie St., Vancouver BC V5Z 2X8
604-683-4176 604-683-2621
rhughes@smithhughes.com
www.smith-hughes.com

Vancouver: **Spearing, Michael P.S. - *1**
#501, 1949 Beach Ave., Vancouver BC V6G 1Z2
604-681-0699
michaelspearing@telus.net

Vancouver: **Spring Brammall - *1**
2774 Granville St., Vancouver BC V6H 3J3
604-732-3881 604-732-3883

Vancouver: **Stephens & Holman - *6**
#500, 1200 - 33 St. West, Vancouver BC V6P 6Z6
604-730-4100 604-736-2867
simon.holman@stephenandhelman.com
www.stephensandholman.com

Vancouver: **Te Hennepe, G.J. - *1**
#203, 4545 West 10th Ave., Vancouver BC V6R 4N2
604-228-1433 604-228-9822
tehennepe@telus.net

Vancouver: **Thompson & Elliott - *4**
1285 West Broadway, 8th Fl., Vancouver BC V6H 3X8
604-731-1161 604-731-6527

Vancouver: **Thorpe, Bonnie L. - *1**
6909 Cambie St., Vancouver BC V6P 3H1
604-325-0020 604-325-0020

Vancouver: **Timothy J. Vondette Law Corporation - *1**
#506, 1128 Hornby St., Vancouver BC V6Z 2L4
604-669-6990 604-669-6944
tvondette@aol.com

Vancouver: **Toews & Company - *2**
#1488, 777 Hornby St., Vancouver BC V6Z 1S4
604-601-5365 604-681-3019
info@toewsco.net

Vancouver: **Tupper, Jonsson & Yeadon - *6**
#1710, 1177 Hastings St. West, Vancouver BC V6E 2L3
604-683-9262 604-681-0139
tupjon@globalserve.net

Vancouver: **La Van & Company - *3**
#704, 1478 West Hastings St., Vancouver BC V6G 3J6
604-669-1411 604-669-9080
jack@lavanco.com

Vancouver: **Van Twest, C.J. - *1**
#405, 1160 Burrard St., Vancouver BC V6Z 2E8
604-683-8874 604-683-8841
twest@interchange.ubc.ca

Vancouver: **Varty & Company - *2**
#900, 555 Burrard St., Vancouver BC V7X 1M8
604-684-5356 604-443-5001
www.vartylaw.ca

Vancouver: **Von Dehn & Company - *3**
#700, 595 Howe St., Vancouver BC V6C 2T5
604-688-4541 604-687-5960
vondehnco@telus.net

Vancouver: **Wai, T. Wing - *1**
#205, 475 Main St., Vancouver BC V6A 2T7
604-688-2291 604-688-8983

Vancouver: **Wasko, Gregory A. - *1**
1306 Bidwell St., #D, Vancouver BC V6G 2L1
604-662-3038

Vancouver: **Watts, Richard H. Law Corp. - *1**
1776 - 29th Av. West, Vancouver BC V6J 2Z5
604-682-2671 604-648-8142

Vancouver: **Westlake, K.S. - *1**
#1720, 355 Burrard St., Vancouver BC V6C 2G8
604-687-9831 604-687-7089
kenwestlake@telus.net

Vancouver: **Wilson, P.J. - *1**
#400, 744 West Hastings St., Vancouver BC V6C 1A5
604-684-4751 604-684-8319

Vancouver: **Wizinsky, David J. - *1**
#450, 800 Pender St. West, Vancouver BC V6C 2V6
604-805-6114 604-689-5528
wiz@uniserve.com

Vancouver: **Wong, P.L. - *1**
#407, 1541 West Broadway, Vancouver BC V6J 1W7
604-731-5301 604-731-1266

Vancouver: **Wong, W.G. - *1**
145 Keefer St., 2nd Fl., Vancouver BC V6A 1X3
604-685-9361 604-684-1299
wwong@radiant.net

Vancouver: **Wooster, A.K. - *1**
#570, 999 West Broadway, Vancouver BC V5Z 1K5
604-684-1204 604-684-1206
akwoods@aol.com

Vancouver: **Yerxa, D.W.H. - *1**
#1200, 805 West Broadway, Vancouver BC V5Z 1K1
604-873-5225

Vancouver: **Young, Anderson - *19**
#1616, Nelson Square CP 12147 808 Nelson St., Vancouver BC V6Z 2H2
604-689-7400 604-689-3444 800-665-3540
reception@lya.bc.ca
www.lya.bc.ca

Vancouver: **Youngson, David L. - *1**
#10, 1656 - 11th Ave. West, Vancouver BC V6J 2B9
604-266-6588 604-266-6393
saluspopuli@shaw.ca

Vanderhoof: **Peleshok, Steven F. - *1**
P.O Box 1128 2608 Burrard Ave., Vanderhoof BC V0J 3A0
250-567-9277 250-567-2657

Vernon: **Cancade Crosby - *2**
2608 - 48 Ave., Vernon BC V1T 8K8
250-549-1999 250-558-3910 877-646-1999
cancadelaw@hotmail.com

Vernon: **Danyliu & Company - *1**
9055 Binns Rd., Vernon BC V1B 3B7
250-549-3111 250-549-4135 888-549-3186
danyliu@shaw.ca

Vernon: **Fiddes, Kenneth R. - *1**
#2, 2908 - 31 Ave., Vernon BC V1T 2G4
250-542-5391 250-542-4199
fiddes@shaw.ca

Vernon: **Kidston & Company - *4**
#200, 3005 - 30th St., Vernon BC V1T 2M1
250-545-0711 250-545-4776
tmm@kidston.ca
www.kidston.ca

Vernon: **Maguire, John S. Barrister & Solicitor - *1**
3018 - 29 St., Vernon BC V1T 5A7
250-545-6054 250-545-7227
jsmag@sigmag.com

Vernon: **Steiner & Company - *1**
3107A - 31 Ave., Vernon BC V1T 2G9
250-545-1371 250-542-5630 800-661-2600

Victoria: **Acheson Whitley - *5**
535 Yates St., 4th Fl., Victoria BC V8W 2Z6
250-384-6262 250-384-5353 877-275-8766
info@achesonwhitley.com
www.achesonwhitley.com

Victoria: **Adair, Robert D. - *1**
#201, 4430 Chatterton Way, Victoria BC V8X 5J2
250-479-9367 250-479-8316
adair@adairlaw.ca

Victoria: **Anniko, Hunter - *2**
#201, 300 Gorge Rd. West, Victoria BC V9A 1M8
250-385-1233 250-385-4078
ah@annikohunter-law.com

Victoria: **Berge, Hart & Cassels - *3**
1207 Quadra St., Victoria BC V8W 2K8
250-388-9477 250-388-9470
admin@bergehart.ca

Victoria: **Brennan, Christopher - *1**
1027 Pandora Ave., Victoria BC V8V 3P6
250-388-9024 250-388-9060
chrisbrennan@shaw.ca

Victoria: **Carr Buchan & Co. - *5**
520 Comerford St., Victoria BC V9A 6K8
250-388-7571 250-388-7327 888-313-7571
carrbuchan@esquimaltlaw.com;fhughes@esquimaltlaw.com

Victoria: **Clapp & Company - *1**
4599 Chatterton Way, Victoria BC V8X 4Y7
250-479-1422 250-479-1667

Victoria: **Clay & Company. Lawyers & Mediators - *7**
837 Burdett Ave., Main Fl., Victoria BC V8W 1B3
250-386-2261 250-389-1336 877-688-9634
lawyers@clay.bc.ca
www.clay.bc.ca

Victoria: **Considine & Company, Barristers & Solicitors - *1**
30 Dallas Rd., Victoria BC V8V 0A2
250-381-7788 250-381-1042
www.considinelaw.com

Victoria: **Cook Roberts LLP - *20**
1175 Douglas St., 7th Fl., Victoria BC V8W 2E1
250-385-1411 250-413-3300
lawmark@cookroberts.bc.ca
www.cookroberts.bc.ca

Victoria: **Cox, Taylor - *9**
Burnes House 26 Bastion Sq., 3rd Fl., Victoria BC V8W 1H9
250-388-4457 250-382-4236
mailbox@coxtaylor.bc.ca

Victoria: **Crease Harman & Company - *14**
#800, 1070 Douglas St., Victoria BC V8W 2S8
250-388-5421 250-388-4294
creaseharman@creaseharman.com
www.creaseharman.com

Victoria: **Dinning Hunter Lambert & Jackson - *10**
1192 Fort St., Victoria BC V8V 3K8
250-381-2151 250-386-2123
info@dinninghunter.com
www.dinninghunter.com

Victoria: **Easdon & Company - *1**
#500, 645 Fort St., Victoria BC V8W 1G2
250-386-3544 250-380-7299
easdonlaw@pacificcoast.net

Victoria: **Finnegan, P.S. - *1**
#6, 1140 Fort St., Victoria BC V8V 3K8
250-384-4252 250-384-4252
psfinnegan@shaw.ca

Victoria: **Goult & Company - *1**
2185 Theatre Lane, Victoria BC V8R 6T1
250-595-1621 250-595-5888
goultco@shaw.ca

Victoria: **Green & Helme - *4**
1161 Fort St., Victoria BC V8V 3K9
250-361-9600 250-361-9181
greenandhelme@greenclaus.com

Victoria: **Harlton, Lenore B. - *1**
#105, 230 Menzie St., Victoria BC V8V 2G7
250-382-5161 250-382-5160

Victoria: **Hatter, Thompson, Shumka & McDonagh - *4**
#201, 919 Fort St., Victoria BC V8V 3K3
250-388-4931 250-386-8088 800-667-0705

Victoria: **Holmes & Isherwood - *1**
1190 Fort St., Victoria BC V8V 3K8
250-383-7157 250-383-1535

Victoria: **Horne Coupar - *7**
612 View St., 3rd Fl., Victoria BC V8W 1J5
250-388-6631 250-388-5974
answers@hc-law.com

Victoria: **Hutchison Oss-Cech Marlatt, Barristers & Solicitors - *5**
#1 505 Fisgard St., Victoria BC V8W 1R3
250-360-2500
info@hom-law.com
www.hom-law.com

Victoria: **Jawl & Bundon - *8**
1007 Fort St., 4th Fl., Victoria BC V8V 3K5
250-385-5787 250-385-4364
info@jawlandbundon.com

Victoria: **Johnson, W.S. Law Corp. - *1**
#309, 895 Fort St., Victoria BC V8W 1H7
250-382-2404 250-382-2426

Victoria: **Jones Emery Hargreaves Swan - *12**
#1212, 1175 Douglas St., Victoria BC V8W 2E1
250-382-7222 250-382-5436
lawyers@jonesemery.com

Victoria: **MacIsaac & Company - *6**
CP 933 1117 Wharf St., 3rd Fl., Victoria BC V8W 1T7
250-381-5353 250-380-7272 800-663-6299
info@macisaacgroup.com
www.macisaacgroup.com

Victoria: **Main, David A. - *1**
#330, 702 Fort St., Victoria BC V8W 1H2
250-383-4541 250-382-5160

Victoria: **McConnan, Bion, O'Connor & Peterson - *14**
#420, 880 Douglas St., Victoria BC V8W 2B7
250-385-1383 250-385-2841 888-385-1383
info@mcbop.com
www.mcbop.com

Victoria: **McMicken & Bennett - *2**
303 - 1111 Blanshard St., Victoria BC V8W 2H7
250-385-9555 250-385-9841
lawyer@mcmickenbennett.bc.ca

Victoria: **Milton, Johnson - *2**
#204, 947 Fort St., Victoria BC V8V 3K3
250-385-5523 250-385-7420

Victoria: **Moore-Stewart, Robert - *1**
#616, 620 View St., Victoria BC V8W 1J6
250-380-1887 250-380-9134
rmoorest@telus.net

Victoria: **Mulroney, David & Company - *6**
#701, 1803 Douglas St., Victoria BC V8T 5C3
250-389-6022 250-389-6033

Victoria: **Neighbourhood Law Centre - *1**
207 Menzies St., Victoria BC V8V 2G6
250-383-5012 250-385-1174
amicus@islandnet.com
www.islandnet.com/~amicus

Victoria: **Pearlman Lindholm - *14**
#201, 19 Dallas Rd., Victoria BC V8V 5A6
250-388-4433 250-388-5856
nphilpott@pearlmanlindholm.com
www.pearlmanlindholm.com

Victoria: **Randall & Company - *3**
#103, 1006 Fort St., Victoria BC V8V 3K4
250-382-9282 250-382-0366
randall@randallco.com

Victoria: **Salmond, Ashurst - *3**
1620 Cedar Hill Cross Rd., Victoria BC V8P 2P6
250-477-4143 250-477-4451
derekgsalmon@ashurst.com

Victoria: **Skillings & Company - *2**
B 777 Blanshard St., Victoria BC V8W 2G9
250-388-5136 250-388-5195
skillco@shawcable.com

Victoria: **Smith Hutchison - *2**
#301, 1640 Oak Bay Ave., Victoria BC V8W 1E5
250-388-6666 250-389-0400
mhutchqc@bclawfirm.com
www.bclawfirm.com

Victoria: **Stevenson, Doell & Company - *4**
999 Fort St., Victoria BC V8V 3K3
250-388-7881 250-388-7324

Victoria: **Straith & Company - *3**
#704, 880 Douglas St., Victoria BC V8W 2B7
250-386-1434 250-386-1421 877-636-1434
inquiries@straithlaw.ca

Victoria: **Stretton, Christine A. - *1**
#204, 947 Fort St., Victoria BC V8V 3K3
250-388-5333 250-382-8644
castretton@pacificcoast.net

Victoria: **Turnham Woodland, Barristers & Solicitors - *4**
1002 Wharf St., Victoria BC V8W 1T4
250-385-1122 250-385-6522
hturnham@turnwood.bc.ca
www.turnhamwoodland.ca

Victoria: **Wilson Marshall - *5**
#200, 911 Yates St., Victoria BC V8V 4X3
250-385-8741 250-385-0433 877-385-8741
reception@wilsonmarshall.com

West Vancouver: **Andree, Alan Stewart, Esq. - *1**
#21, 285 - 17th St., West Vancouver BC V7V 3S6
604-922-6999 604-922-6912
stewart@alansr.com

West Vancouver: **Brister, Yeager Law Corporation - *2**
#202, 1555 Marine Dr., West Vancouver BC V7V 1N9
604-921-1295 604-921-1297
ryeager@dimissal.ca
www.dismissal.ca

West Vancouver: **Fowle, Wm. Randall - *3**
#1003, 100 Park Royal South, West Vancouver BC V7T 1A2
604-922-6310 604-922-6302 800-663-8996
fowle@axion.net

West Vancouver: **Geraghty, G.C. - *1**
#200, 100 Park Royal South, West Vancouver BC V7T 1A2
604-921-9221 604-921-9125
geraghty@gglawcorp.com
www.gglawcorp.com

West Vancouver: **Goluboff & Mazzei, Barristers & Solicitors - *3**
#201, 585 - 16th St., West Vancouver BC V7V 3R8
604-925-6900 604-926-7817
rgoluboff@goluboffmazzei.com
www.goluboffmazzei.com

West Vancouver: **McCrea & Company - *1**
#101, 2221 Folkestone Way, West Vancouver BC V7S 2Y6
604-926-4524 604-926-0222

West Vancouver: **McMahon, E. Michael - *1**
#204, 2408 Haywood Ave., West Vancouver BC V7V 1Y1
604-926-1076 604-926-1023
www.taxlitigate.com

West Vancouver: **Sweeney, Ann Marie - *1**
#104, 1590 Bellevue Ave., West Vancouver BC V7V 1A7
604-922-0131 604-922-0171

Westbank: **Bassett & Company - *5**
#260, 2300 Carrington Rd., Westbank BC V4T 2N6
250-768-5152 250-768-3003
info@okanaganlaw.com
www.okanaganlaw.com

Whistler: **Mountain Law Corporation - *1**
#200, 1410 Alpha Lake Rd., Whistler BC V0N 1B1
604-938-4947 604-938-0471
shrimpco@direct.ca

White Rock: **Cleveland & Doan - *3**
1321 Johnston Rd., White Rock BC V4B 3Z3
604-536-5002 604-536-7002
lawyers@cleveland-doan.com
www.cleveland-doan.com

White Rock: Mark, E.G. - *1
15252 Thrift Ave., White Rock BC V4B 2L2
604-542-0202 604-542-0203

White Rock: Medland & Company - *1
14582 - 18th Ave., White Rock BC V4A 5V5
604-230-8476 604-535-4145
medlandco@shaw.ca

White Rock: Prodor, Joseph M. - *1
15260 Thrift Ave., White Rock BC V4B 2L1
604-536-4676 877-577-6367
jprodor@axionet.com

Manitoba

** indicates # of lawyers*

Altona: Wiens & Cole LLP - *3
P.O Box 1120 111 Centre Ave. East, Altona MB R0G 0B0
204-324-6451 204-324-1275

Beausejour: Bellan Wasylin & Associates - *5
P.O Box 520 527 Park Ave., Beausejour MB R0E 0C0
204-268-2000 204-268-3519

Brandon: Carroll, Henry N., Q.C. - *3
1331 Princess Ave., Brandon MB R7A 0R4
204-727-2266 204-727-0548

Brandon: Deller, Terri E. Law Office - *1
801 Princess Ave., Brandon MB R7A 0P5
204-726-0128
dellerlaw@westman.wave.ca

Brandon: Hunt, Miller & Co. LLP - *7
148 - 8 St., Brandon MB R7A 3X1
204-727-8491 204-727-4350
hmc@westman.wave.ca

Brandon: Meighen, Haddad & Company - *15
P.O Box 22105 110 - 11 St., Brandon MB R7A 6Y9
204-727-8461 204-726-1948
mail@mhlaw.ca
www.mhlaw.ca

Brandon: Paterson Patterson Wyman & Abel - *7
#1, Carriage House 1040 Princess Ave., Brandon MB R7A 0P8
204-727-2424 204-728-4670
patersons@mts.net
www.patersons.ca

Brandon: Potter, James W. - *1
1202 Princess Ave., Brandon MB R7A 0R3
204-727-6431 204-727-2818

Brandon: Roy, Johnston & Company - *8
363 - 10 St., Brandon MB R7A 4E9
204-727-0761 204-726-1339
royjohnstonco@westman.wave.ca

Carman: Lee & Lee - *2
5 Centre Ave. West, Carman MB R0G 0J0
204-745-6751 204-745-3481

Carman: McCarthy & Brown - *2
71 Main St., Carman MB R0G 0J0
204-745-2028 204-745-3513
mcbr@mts.net

Dauphin: Dawson Law Office - *1
34 - 1 Ave. NW, Dauphin MB R7N 1G7
204-638-4101 204-638-8541

Dauphin: Hawkins & Sanderson - *1
20 - 2nd Ave. NW, Dauphin MB R7N 1H2
204-638-4121 204-638-5942

Dauphin: Irwin Law Office - *2
122 Main St. North, Dauphin MB R7N 1C2
204-638-9249 204-638-3647
irwinlaw@mts.net

Dauphin: Johnston & Company - *7
P.O Box 551 18 - 3 Ave. NW, Dauphin MB R7N 2V4
204-638-3211 204-638-9646
irwinlaw@mts.net

Deloraine: Lanchbery, Sheldon - *1
P.O Box 489, Deloraine MB R0M 0M0
204-747-2082 204-747-2180
slanchbery@escape.ca

Flin Flon: Ginnell, Bauman, Watt - *2
P.O Box 697 47 Main St., Flin Flon MB R8A 1N5
204-687-3431 204-687-5219

Manitou: Selby Law Office - *2
P.O Box 279 351 Main St., Manitou MB R0G 1G0
204-242-2801 204-242-2723
selbylaw@mts.net

Minnedosa: Sims & Company - *2
P.O Box 460 76 Main St. South, Minnedosa MB R0J 1E0
204-867-2717 204-867-2434
minnedosa@simsco.mb.ca
www.simsco.mb.ca

Morden: Hoeschen & Sloane
326 Stephen St., Morden MB R6M 1T5
204-822-4463 204-822-6416
hslaw@mts.net

Neepawa: Taylor Law Office - *2
P.O Box 309 294 Hamilton St, Neepawa MB R0J 1H0
204-476-2336 204-476-5783
taylaw@mts.net

Portage la Prairie: Greenberg & Greenberg - *2
P.O Box 157 231 Saskatchewan Ave. East, Portage la Prairie MB R1N 3B2
204-857-6878 204-857-3011
greenlaw@mts.net

Portage la Prairie: Miller Pressey Selinger - *1
P.O Box 368 103 Saskatchewan Ave. East, Portage la Prairie MB R1N 3B7
204-857-3436 204-857-9238
mpslaw@mts.net

Roblin: Gregoire, Marcel J.J.R. - *1
P.O Box 1630 158 Main St., Roblin MB R0L 1P0
204-937-2117 204-937-4576
mgreg@mb.sympatico.ca

Selkirk: Kitchen, W. Douglas - *1
1202 River Rd., Selkirk MB R1A 2E1
204-482-8929

Selkirk: Kohaykewych & Associates - *1
413 Main St., Selkirk MB R1A 1V2
204-482-7925 204-482-7099
kohaykewych@mts.net

Selkirk: Moore, David L. & Assoc. - *2
407 Main St., Selkirk MB R1A 1T9
204-482-3921 204-482-5564 877-482-3921
d.moore.law@mts.net

Souris: Forrest & Forrest - *1
P.O Box 276 4 Crescent Ave., Souris MB R0K 2C0
204-483-2171 204-483-3389
fforrest@mts.net

Steinbach: Loewen Henderson Banman Legault LLP - *4
#200, 250 Main St., Steinbach MB R5G 1Y8
204-326-6454 204-326-6917

Steinbach: Smith Neufeld Jodoin - *14
P.O Box 1267, Steinbach MB R5G 1M9
204-326-3442 204-326-2154
lawyers@snj.mb.ca
www.snj.mb.ca

Stonewall: Grantham Law Offices - *1
Westside Plaza P.O Box 1400 #1, 333 Main St., Stonewall MB R0C 2Z0
204-467-5527 204-467-5550

Swan River: Burnside & Company - *2
P.O Box 340 509 Main St. East, Swan River MB R0L 1Z0
204-734-3485 204-734-2872
ggb@burnsideferris.com

Swan River: Palsson Law Office - *2
P.O Box 1238 114 - 5th Ave. North, Swan River MB R0L 1Z0
204-734-4528 204-734-5085

The Pas: Bjornsson & Wight Law Office - *2
#3, P.O Box 1769 314 Edwards Ave., The Pas MB R9A 1L5
204-627-1200 204-627-1210
dblwlaw@mailme.ca

The Pas: Watkins Law Office - *1
P.O Box 1349 Main114 - 3rd St., The Pas MB R9A 1L3
204-623-6472 204-623-6486

Thompson: Mayer, Dearman & Pellizzaro - *3
7 Selkirk Ave., Thompson MB R8N 0M4
204-677-2393 204-778-8125

Thompson: McDonald, Huberdeau - *3
Westwood Mall 436 Thompson Dr. North, Thompson MB R8N 0C6
204-677-2366 204-677-3249

Winkler: Hoeschen & Stewart
#6, 720 Norquay Dr., Winkler MB R6W 4A6
204-325-4233 204-325-9889
hslaw@mts.net

Winnipeg: Abrams George Tweed Wawrykow - *4
#4, 549 Regent Ave. West, Winnipeg MB R2C 1R9
204-949-3080 204-949-3089
btweed@atwlaw.ca

Winnipeg: Agrawal Law Office - *1
B 83 Sherbrook St., Winnipeg MB R3C 2B2
204-779-7265 204-779-6334

Winnipeg: Aikins, MacAulay & Thorvaldson LLP - *93
Commodity Exchange Tower 360 Main St., 30th Fl., Winnipeg MB R3C 4G1
204-957-0050 204-957-0840
amt@aikins.com
www.aikins.com

Winnipeg: Bernstein & Hirsch - *3
#508, 283 Portage Ave., Winnipeg MB R3B 2B5
204-942-0706 204-957-1345

Winnipeg: Booth, Dennehy LLP - *15
387 Broadway Ave., Winnipeg MB R3C 0V5
204-957-1717 204-943-6199
general@dek-law.com

Winnipeg: Campbell Marr - *13
10 Donald St., Winnipeg MB R3C 1L5
204-942-3311 204-943-7997
dimarr@campbellmarr.com
www.campbellmarr.com

Winnipeg: Cassidy Ramsay - *7
385 St. Mary Ave., 2nd Fl., Winnipeg MB R3C 0N1
204-943-7454 204-943-9563
kwan@cassidyramsay.com

Winnipeg: Chapman Goddard Kagan - *8
1864 Portage Ave., Winnipeg MB R3J 0H2
204-888-7973 204-832-3461 800-665-6119
info@cgklaw.ca
www.cgklaw.ca

Winnipeg: Cherniack Smith - *7
#200, 100 Osborne St., Winnipeg MB R3L 1Y5
204-452-4000 204-477-1856

Winnipeg: D'Arcy & Deacon LLP - *34
330 St. Mary Ave., 12th Fl., Winnipeg MB R3C 4E1
204-942-2271 204-943-4242
inquiries@darcydeacon.com
www.darcydeacon.com

Winnipeg: Dowhan & Dowhan - *2
61 Albert St., Winnipeg MB R3B 1G3
204-942-4235 204-956-4560

Winnipeg: Duboff Edwards Haight & Schachter - *10
#1900, 155 Carlton St., Winnipeg MB R3C 3H8
204-942-3361 204-942-3362
duboff@dehslaw.com

Winnipeg: Edmond & Associates - *4
#204, 1120 Grant Ave., Winnipeg MB R3M 2A6
204-452-5314 204-452-5989
gedmond@edmond.ca

Winnipeg: Einarson & Einarson - *3
#1105, 444 St. Mary Ave., Winnipeg MB R3C 3T1
204-942-2419

Winnipeg: Friesen, David, Q.C. & Associates - *1
#711, 213 Notre Dame Ave., Winnipeg MB R3B 1N3
204-942-2171

Winnipeg: Garber, Zachary I. - *1
385 St. Mary Ave., 2nd Fl., Winnipeg MB R3C 0N1
204-943-7454 204-943-9563

Winnipeg: George, J. David & Associates - *2
108 Regent Ave. East, Winnipeg MB R2C 0C1
204-982-7503 204-222-4761
david-dg@shaw.ca

Winnipeg: Habing Law - *3
2643 Portage Ave., Winnipeg MB R3J 0P9

204-832-8322 204-832-3906
ron@habinglaw.com

Winnipeg: Hogue, ALain J. Law Office - *1
194 Provencher Blvd., Winnipeg MB R2H 0G3
204-237-9600 204-233-2689

Winnipeg: Hook & Smith - *4
#201, 3111 Portage Ave., Winnipeg MB R3K 0W4
204-885-4520 204-837-9846
general@hookandsmith.com

Winnipeg: Inkster Christie Hughes LLP, Barristers & Solicitors - *13
#700, 444 St. Mary Ave., Winnipeg MB R3C 3T1
204-947-6801
info@inksterchristie.ca
www.inksterchristie.ca

Winnipeg: Ironquil Meadmore, Marion - *1
1187 Fleet Ave., Winnipeg MB R3M 1K9
204-947-1509

Winnipeg: Karasevich Windsor Jenion Hedley LLP - *4
#440, 5 Donald St. South, Winnipeg MB R3L 2T4
204-477-0285 204-453-8876
jgk@escape.ca

Winnipeg: Knight, D.R. Law Office - *1
#101, 900 Harrow St. East, Winnipeg MB R3M 3Y7
204-948-0400 204-948-0401
ruteyj@mts.net

Winnipeg: Krawchuk & Company - *2
#2250, 360 Main St., Winnipeg MB R3C 3Z3
204-943-4561 204-947-5724
krawchukandco@mts.net

Winnipeg: Lehman, Victoria E., Law Offices - *1
412 Wardlaw Ave., Winnipeg MB R3L 0L7
204-453-6416 204-477-1379

Winnipeg: Loewen & Martens, Barristers & Solicitors - *5
1101 Henderson Hwy., Winnipeg MB R2G 1L4
204-338-9364 204-338-8379
lmlaw@shawbiz.ca

Winnipeg: MacInnes, Burbidge - *2
#500, 177 Lombard Ave., Winnipeg MB R3B 0W5
204-942-5256 204-942-5259

Winnipeg: McJannet Rich - *5
#1710, Newport Centre 330 Portage Ave., Winnipeg MB R3C 0C4
204-957-0951 204-989-0688

Winnipeg: McRoberts Law Office LLP - *13
#200, Madison Square 1630 Ness Ave., Winnipeg MB R3J 3X1
204-944-7907 204-772-1684
consult@mcrobertslawoffice.com
www.mcrobertslawoffice.com

Winnipeg: Michaels & Stern - *2
#300, 326 Broadway Ave., Winnipeg MB R3C 0S5
204-989-5500 204-989-5508
michaelsandstern@mts.net

Winnipeg: Moss, Peter J. - *5
1002 Pembina Hwy., Winnipeg MB R3T 1Z5
204-284-3221 204-284-7960
mosslaw@shaw.ca

Winnipeg: Murray & Kovnats - *2
#100, 1600 Ness Ave., Winnipeg MB R3J 3W7
204-957-1700 204-942-2325
brmk1@aol.com

Winnipeg: Myers Weinberg LLP - *25
#724, Cargill Bldg. 240 Graham Ave., Winnipeg MB R3C 0J7
204-942-0501 204-956-0625
info@myersfirm.com

Winnipeg: Nozick, Stanley S. - *1
#605, 386 Broadway, Winnipeg MB R3C 3R6
204-944-8227 204-944-9246
snozick@escape.ca

Winnipeg: Orle, Davidson, Giesbrecht, Bargen - *10
280 Stradbrook Ave., Winnipeg MB R3L 0J6
204-989-2760 204-989-2774
general@odgb.mb.ca
www.odgb.mb.ca

Winnipeg: Parashin Law Office - *1
404 McGregor St., Winnipeg MB R2W 4X5
204-582-3558

Winnipeg: Perlov Stewart LLP - *5
#610, One Lombard Place, Winnipeg MB R3B 3G5
204-944-9295 204-956-4270
www.pslfirm.ca

Winnipeg: Pitblado LLP - *57
#2500, Commodity Exchange Tower 360 Main St., Winnipeg MB R3C 4H6
204-956-0560 204-957-0227
firm@pitblado.com
www.pitblado.com

Winnipeg: Pollock, Gordon C. - *1
841 Brock St., Winnipeg MB R3N 0Z7
204-489-4945 204-489-5071
gpollock7@shaw.ca

Winnipeg: Prober, Jay C. - *1
#208, 387 Broadway Ave., Winnipeg MB R3C 0V5
204-957-1205 204-943-6199

Winnipeg: Pullan Kammerloch Frohlinger - *10
#300, 240 Kennedy St., Winnipeg MB R3C 1T1
204-956-0490 204-947-3747
firm@pkf-law.com
www.pkflawyers.com

Winnipeg: Radchuk & Company - *1
10 Salvia Bay, Winnipeg MB R2V 2L8
204-338-8880 204-334-5241

Winnipeg: Restall & Restall - *4
295 Broadway, Winnipeg MB R3C 0R9
204-925-2525 204-949-9331
restall@escape.ca

Winnipeg: Ridd, Russell - *1
405 Broadway, 6th Fl., Winnipeg MB R3C 3L6
204-945-2871 204-945-1260
rridd@gov.mb.ca

Winnipeg: Robertson Shypit Soble Wood - *5
#202, 1555 St. Mary's Rd., Winnipeg MB R2M 5L9
204-257-6061 204-254-7183

Winnipeg: Rose, James F.C. - *1
582 Bruce Ave., Winnipeg MB R3J 0W5
204-889-3885 204-889-3885 800-414-8091
jamesrose@shaw.ca
www.members.shaw.ca/jamesrose/baddebt.htm

Winnipeg: Rosenbaum & Company - *4
#201, 2211 McPhillips St., Winnipeg MB R2V 3M5
204-338-4663 204-338-4667

Winnipeg: Rutledge Law Office - *2
#310, 3025 Portage Ave., Winnipeg MB R3K 2E2
204-987-7575 204-837-3638
rutlaw@mts.net

Winnipeg: Shewchuk & Associates - *2
2645 Portage Ave., Winnipeg MB R3J 0P9
204-889-4595

Winnipeg: Slusky & Slusky - *1
#1028, 363 Broadway, Winnipeg MB R3C 3N9
204-943-5455 204-942-4301

Winnipeg: Sukhan, J.S. - *1
1158 Clarence Ave., Winnipeg MB R3T 1S9
204-284-0728

Winnipeg: Tapper Cuddy LLP - *23
#1000, 330 St. Mary Ave., Winnipeg MB R3C 3Z5
204-944-8777 204-947-2593
tc@tcwpg.com
www.tcwpg.com

Winnipeg: Taylor McCaffrey LLP - *62
400 St. Mary Ave., 9th Fl., Winnipeg MB R3C 4K5
204-949-1312 204-957-0945
www.tmlawyers.com

Winnipeg: Tepley Law Office - *1
#401, 460 Main St., Winnipeg MB R3B 1B6
204-942-7218

Winnipeg: Teskey Legal & ADR Services - *1
1905 One Evergreen Pl., Winnipeg MB R3L 0E9
204-943-8395 204-943-1288
teskey@mb.sympatico.ca

Winnipeg: Thompson Dorfman Sweatman LLP - *68
#2200, CanWest Global Place 201 Portage Ave., Winnipeg MB R3B 3L3
204-957-1930 204-934-0570
tds@tdslaw.com
www.tdslaw.com

Winnipeg: Thullner, John F. - *1
#102, 2200 McPhillips St., Winnipeg MB R2V 3P4
204-694-0161

Winnipeg: Tupper & Adams - *8
200 Portage Ave., 4th Fl., Winnipeg MB R3C 3X2
204-942-0161 204-943-2385
general@tupper-adams.mb.ca
www.tupper-adams.mb.ca

Winnipeg: Van Walleghem, W.R. - *1
#206, 1120 Grant Ave., Winnipeg MB R3M 2A6
204-477-0210 204-452-9746

Winnipeg: Warkentin & Calver - *1
3651 Roblin Blvd., Winnipeg MB R3R 0E2
204-949-3230 204-949-3249
pcalver@warkcal.ca
www.warkcal.ca

Winnipeg: Waskiw, E. - *1
441 Perth Ave., Winnipeg MB R2V 0T9
204-334-7372

Winnipeg: Werier, Arthur M. - *1
905 Corydon Ave., Winnipeg MB R3M 0W8
204-475-7923

Winnipeg: Wilder Wilder & Langtry - *9
#1500, Richardson Bldg. 1 Lombard Pl., Winnipeg MB R3B 0X3
204-947-1456 204-957-1368 888-420-0847
admin@wilderwilder.com
www.wilderwilder.com

New Brunswick

** indicates # of lawyers*

Atholville: Gauvin, Roger G. - *1
65 Fairview St., Atholville NB E3N 4N3
506-753-4545 506-753-2006

Bathurst: Hazen, John Douglas - *1
132 Main St., Bathurst NB E2A 1A4
506-545-9220 506-545-9224

Bathurst: Robichaud, Theriault, Riordon, Arseneault - *5
#300, Keystone Place P.O Box 506 270 Douglas Ave., Bathurst NB E2A 3Z4
506-548-8822 506-548-5297

Bouctouche: LeBlanc, Yvon J.G. - *2
25, boul Irving, Bouctouche NB E4S 3J5
506-743-2427 506-743-8314
lebbell@nbnet.nb.ca

Campbellton: Delaney, Terrance H., Q.C. - *2
#206, P.O Box 490 123 Water St., Campbellton NB E3N 3G9
506-753-7618 506-759-7315
terra1@nb.sympatico.ca

Caraquet: LeBouthillier, Alie A. - *1
CP 5661 295, boul St-Pierre ouest, Caraquet NB E1W 1B7
506-727-3484 506-727-3484
alie@nb.aira.com

Chipman: Lockwood, Sharon R. - *1
28 Northrup Dr., Chipman NB E4A 2P7
506-339-6632 506-339-5130
sharon.lockwood@nb.aibn.com

Dalhousie: Dubé & Associate - *2
P.O Box 1900 390 William St., Dalhousie NB E0K 1B0
506-684-5661 506-684-5011

Edmundston: Poitras, Roger D. - *1
87, ch Canada, Edmundston NB E3V 1V6
506-739-7335 506-735-4139

Fredericton: Allen Dixon Smith - *13
#340, P.O Box 190 AWestmorland St., Fredericton NB E3B 4Y9
506-453-0900 506-453-0907
www.allendixonsmith.ca

Fredericton: Atkinson & Atkinson - *1
P.O Box 700 108 Queen St., Fredericton NB E3B 5B4

506-451-7777 506-451-1029
fealaw@nb.aibn.com

***Fredericton*: Campbell, B.H. - *1**
P.O Box 295 A334 Saint John St., Fredericton NB E3B 4B6
506-458-8140 506-450-6186
bhclaw@nb.aibn.com

***Fredericton*: D'Arcy, Leycester D. - *1**
P.O Box 93 A, Fredericton NB E3B 4Y2
506-454-2552

***Fredericton*: Dean & McMath - *2**
406 Regent St., Fredericton NB E3B 3X7
506-458-8555 506-444-0920
dwmcmath@deanmcmath.ca

***Fredericton*: Gaffney & Burke - *2**
466 Bowlen St., Fredericton NB E3A 2T4
506-458-8124 506-458-2652
gaffneyburke@nb.aibn.com

***Fredericton*: Gordon F. Gregory Law Office - *1**
#2, 110 Queen St., Fredericton NB E3B 1A5
506-458-8060 506-459-8288

***Fredericton*: Hughes, Yeamans, Campbell - *2**
P.O Box 295 551 Charlotte St., Fredericton NB E3B 4Y9
506-458-8140 506-450-6186

***Fredericton*: Kenny & Murray - *5**
P.O Box 1572 A228 Brunswick St., Fredericton NB E3B 5G2
506-458-1108 506-458-2645
kenny@nbnet.nb.ca

***Fredericton*: Matthews McCrea Elliott - *7**
197 Main St., Fredericton NB E3A 1E1
506-458-5959 506-460-5934
office@matthewsmccreaelliott.com
www.matthewsmccreaelliott.com

***Fredericton*: McAllister, Charles S. - *1**
68 London Ct., Fredericton NB E3B 6K9
506-454-6852

***Fredericton*: Paul-Elias, Mark C. - *1**
#5, Pepper Creek Plaza 336, Rte. 10, Richibucto Rd., Fredericton NB E3A 7E1
506-458-1880 506-458-9868
peppercreek@brunnet.net

***Fredericton*: Pugh, Gerald R. - *1**
57 Carleton St., 4th Fl., Fredericton NB E3B 3T2
506-450-2666 506-457-4295
drwp@nb.aibn.com

***Fredericton*: Yerxa, Stephenson - *3**
#208, P.O Box 175 A403 Regent St., Fredericton NB E3B 4Y9
506-459-1450 506-459-2301
lawoffice@yerstep.com
www.yerstep.com

***Grand Falls*: Duffie, DesChênes - *2**
Box 7336 346 Chapel St., Grand Falls NB E3Z 2M4
506-473-2221 506-473-3253
peduffie@nbnet.nb.ca

***Grand Falls*: Pichette, Gilles A. - *1**
P.O Box 7128 257 Broadway, Grand Falls NB E3Z 2K1
506-473-4776 506-473-6493
gillespichette@nb.aibn.com

***Grand Falls*: Seheult, Peter - *1**
#7248, 275 Sheriff St., Grand Falls NB E3Z 3A1
506-473-2164 506-473-5543
seheult@nbnet.nb.ca

***Lamèque*: Noël, Roger A., Etude Legale - *2**
CP 2038 Main5120E, rte 113, Lamèque NB E8T 3N4
506-344-2217 506-344-5380
info@eteudelegalenoel.com

***Memramcook*: Gauthier, Jacques - *1**
835, rue Principale, Memramcook NB E4K 2R9
506-758-9002 506-758-2400
acadian22@hotmail.com

***Minto*: Thorne, Sheila R. - *1**
24 Queen St., Minto NB E4B 3P2
506-327-6120

***Miramichi*: Losier, Rosemary - *1**
P.O Box 112 Main173 Wellington St., Miramichi NB E1N 3A5
506-773-6817

***Miramichi*: Maynes, Mahoney & Tremblay - *4**
P.O Box 518 1723 Water St., Miramichi NB E1N 3A8
506-778-8336 506-778-2103

***Moncton*: Arsenault, Michel C. - *1**
1255 Main St., Moncton NB E1C 1H9
506-857-8008 506-857-8885
mcalaw@nb.aibn.com

***Moncton*: Bingham Robinson McLennan Ehrhardt & Teed - *18**
#300, Heritage Court 95 Foundry St., Moncton NB E1C 5H7
506-857-8856 506-857-2017

***Moncton*: Delehanty Rinzler Druckham - *3**
#101, P.O Box 1083 720 Main St., Moncton NB E1C 8P6
506-857-3030 506-857-0085
www.drdlaw.ca

***Moncton*: Forbes Roth Basque - *7**
P.O Box 480, Moncton NB E1C 8L9
506-857-4880 506-857-0151

***Moncton*: Fowler & Fowler - *2**
69 Waterloo St., Moncton NB E1C 0E1
506-857-8811 506-857-9297

***Moncton*: Hughes, John D.**
P.O Box 29072 98 Bonaccord St., Moncton NB E1G 4R3
506-382-9072

***Moncton*: LeBlanc Boucher Rodger Bourque - *3**
740 Main St., Moncton NB E1C 1E6
506-858-0110 506-858-9497
lbrb@nbnet.nb.ca

***Moncton*: LeBlanc, Martin, Sweet & Cormier - *5**
P.O Box 1285 51 Highfield St., Moncton NB E1C 8P9
506-859-1212 506-859-7309

***Moncton*: Letcher & Murray - *3**
76 Albert St., Moncton NB E1C 1B1
506-857-2070 506-859-9195

***Moncton*: Maxwell - Matheson - *2**
Assumption Place 770 Main St., 10th Fl., Moncton NB E1C 1E7
506-857-8470 506-857-4031

***Moncton*: Murphy Collette Murphy - *7**
250 Lutz St., Moncton NB E1C 5G3
506-856-8560 506-856-8579
manager@murco.nb.ca
www.murco.nb.ca

***Moncton*: Murphy, Murphy & Mollins - *3**
89 Church St., Moncton NB E1C 4Z4
506-857-9120 506-857-9129
mmmlaw@nb.aibn.com

***Moncton*: Schelew, Alan D. - *1**
#100, P.O Box 182 803 Main St., Moncton NB E1C 8K9
506-857-2272 506-857-2276
schelew@nb.aibn.com
www.monctonlawyer.com

***Oromocto*: McKay, Blair W. - *1**
#3, 291 Restigouche Rd., Oromocto NB E2V 2H2
506-446-3000 506-446-9010

***Perth-Andover*: Johnson, Mark C. - *2**
1143 West Riverside Dr., Perth-Andover NB E7H 5G5
506-273-6818 506-273-6590
mjlaw@nbnet.nb.ca

***Perth-Andover*: Paul, Stewart C., Law Office - *1**
P.O Box 2981 Main, Perth-Andover NB E7H 5M2
506-273-4445 506-273-4491

***Petit-Rocher*: Boudreau, Robert M. - *1**
561 rue Principale, Petit-Rocher NB E8J 1J4
506-783-4246 506-783-2354
rboudro@nbnet.nb.ca

***Riverview*: Wilbur & Wilbur - *2**
706B Coverdale Rd., Riverview NB E1B 3L1
506-387-7715 506-387-5875
swilbur@wilburandwilbur.com
www.wilburandwilbur.com

***Sackville*: Meldrum Law - *2**
7 Bridge St., Sackville NB E4L 3N6
506-536-3870 506-536-2131 866-792-1416
meldrumk@nbnet.nb.ca

***Sackville*: Samuelsen, Ove B. - *1**
1 Squire St., Sackville NB E4L 4K8
506-536-0511 506-536-1169
ovesam@nbnet.nb.ca

***Saint John*: Barry Spalding - *20**
#710, Mercantine Centre P.O Box 6010 A55 Union Street, Saint John NB E2L 4R5
506-633-4226 506-633-4206 888-743-4226
info@barryspalding.com
www.barryspalding.com

***Saint John*: Boyle, Dennis - *1**
345 Lancaster Ave. West, Saint John NB E2M 2L3
506-634-7575 506-634-8237

***Saint John*: Clark Drummie - *22**
P.O Box 6850 40 Wellington Row, Saint John NB E2L 4S3
506-633-3800 506-633-3811
cd@clarkdrummie.ca
www.clarkdrummie.ca

***Saint John*: Correia & Collins - *3**
1 Market Sq. PO Box 6969, RPO Brunswick Sq., Saint John NB E2L 4S4
506-648-1700 506-648-1701

***Saint John*: Farrell, Lynda D. - *4**
City Hall P.O Box 1971 Main15 Market Sq., 8th Fl., Saint John NB E2L 4L1
506-658-2860 506-658-2802

***Saint John*: Gilbert McGloan Gillis - *15**
P.O Box 7174 22 King St., Saint John NB E2L 1G3
506-634-3600 506-634-3612 888-246-4529
gmg@gmglaw.com
www.gmglaw.com

***Saint John*: Gorman Nason - *10**
P.O Box 7286 A121 Germain St., Saint John NB E2L 4S6
506-634-8600 506-634-8685
info@GormanNason.com
www.gormannason.com

***Saint John*: Henderson, John M. - *1**
#410, 40 Charlotte St., Saint John NB E2L 2H6
506-652-5502 506-634-1795
jmhlaw@nbnet.nb.ca

***Saint John*: Macdonald, W. Rodney - *1**
108 Prince William St., Saint John NB E2L 2B3
506-632-8999 506-634-1532

***Saint John*: MacLeod, A. Wilber Q.C. - *1**
108 Prince William St., Saint John NB E2L 2B3
506-632-8999

***Saint John*: Mosher Chedore**
#300, 33 Charlotte St., 3rd Fl., Saint John NB E2L 2H3
506-634-1600 506-634-0740
lawfirm@nb.sympatico.ca

***Saint John*: Northrup, Richard A. - *1**
#420, 40 Charlotte St., Saint John NB E2L 2H6
506-634-8134 506-693-3473
nbrick@nb.aibn.com

***Saint John*: Riley, John G. - *1**
#410, 40 Charlotte St., Saint John NB E2L 2H6
506-634-1188 506-634-1795
jgrileylaw@nb.aibn.com

***Saint John*: Teed & Teed, Barristers & Solicitors - *1**
P.O Box 6639 A127 Prince William St., Saint John NB E2L 4S1
506-634-7320 506-634-7423
info@teedandteed.com
www.teedandteed.com

***Saint John*: Whelly & Kelly - *4**
122 Carleton St., Saint John NB E2L 2Z7
506-634-1193 506-693-9040
partner@nb.aibn.com

***Saint John*: Wilson, Theodore E. - *1**
10 Prince Edward St., Saint John NB E2L 4M5
506-633-8788 506-632-2023

***Shediac*: Leger, Michel C. - *2**
CP 1900 5, rue Mill, Shediac NB E4P 2H8
506-532-0100 506-532-6332
mike0100@nbnet.nb.ca

***Shippagan*: Godin, Lizotte, Robichaud, Guignard - *4**
246, boul J.D.Gauthier, Shippagan NB E8S 1P9

506-336-0400 506-336-0409
glrg@nbnet.nb.ca

Shippagan: Theriault, Larocque, Boudreau - *3
P.O Box 160 283 J.D. Gauthier Blvd., Shippagan NB E8S 1N6
506-336-4726 506-336-1159
tla@nbnet.nb.ca

St Andrews: Bartlett, David A. - *1
239 Water St., St Andrews NB E5B 1B3
506-529-9000 506-529-9003
bartllaw@nb.aibn.com

St Stephen: Sutherland, Ronald W. - *1
P.O Box 427 71 King St., St Stephen NB E3L 2X3
506-466-5330 506-466-3692

Sussex: Gerrish, D. James - *1
#1, 480 Main St., Sussex NB E4S 2S4
506-433-4234 506-432-1814
gersmi@nbnet.nb.ca

Sussex: Palmer & Palmer - *2
17 Queen St., Sussex NB E4E 2A4
506-433-2168 506-433-4740

Sussex: Purnell & Fulton - *1
30 Church Ave., Sussex NB E4E 1Y7
506-433-4215 506-433-4216
lawyers@nbnet.nb.ca

Tracadie-Sheila: Doiron, Lebouthillier, Boudreau, Allain - *4
CP 3010 Bureau3674, rue Principale, Tracadie-Sheila NB E1X 1G5
506-395-0044 506-395-0050
dllb@nbnet.nb.ca

Woodstock: McCue Brewer Dickinson - *3
179 Broadway St., Woodstock NB E7M 1B7
506-325-2835 506-328-6248
mblaw@nbnet.nb.ca

Woodstock: Wilson, Stephen L. - *1
#1, 733 Main St., Woodstock NB E7M 2E6
506-325-1100 506-328-4873
stepwil@nbnet.nb.ca

Newfoundland & Labrador

** indicates # of lawyers*

Bay Roberts: Morrow & Morrow - *2
P.O Box 870 344 Conception Bay Hwy., Bay Roberts NL A0A 1G0
709-786-9207 709-786-9507
morrow@nf.aibn.com

Carbonear: Finn, J. William - *1
66 Powell Dr., Carbonear NL A1Y 1A5
709-596-5143 709-596-3208

Channel-Port-aux-Basques: Marks & Parsons - *4
#3, P.O Box 640 9 Barhaven Dr., Channel-Port-aux-Basques NL A0M 1C0
709-695-7341 709-695-3944
b.marks@mplaw.com

Corner Brook: Monaghan, Murphy & Watton - *4
Mercantile Trust Bldg. Box 815 Main17 West St., Corner Brook NL A2H 6H9
709-634-3231 709-634-8889
contacts@monmar.nf.net

Corner Brook: Poole Althouse, Barristers & Solicitors - *10
Western Trust Bldg. P.O Box 812 49 - 51 Park St., Corner Brook NL A2H 6H7
709-634-3136 709-634-8247 877-634-3136
info@pa-law.ca
www.poolealthouse.ca

Corner Brook: Watton, Graham, Law Office - *1
Noton Bldg. P.O Box 188 133 Riverside Dr., Corner Brook NL A2H 6C7
709-639-7490 709-634-7229
watton@nf.aibn.com

Gander: Easton Hillier Lawrence Preston - *8
Polaris Bldg. P.O Box 408 61 Elizabeth Dr., Gander NL A1V 1G4
709-256-4006 709-651-2850
gander.law@nf.sympatico.ca

Labrador City: Miller & Hearn - *2
P.O Box 129 Main, Labrador City NL A2V 2K3
709-944-3666 709-944-5494
miller&hearn@crrstv.net

St. John's: Benson Myles - *21
#900, Atlantic Place P.O Box 1538 215 Water St., St. John's NL A1C 5N8
709-579-2081 709-579-2647
info@bensonmyles.com
www.bensonmyles.com

St. John's: Cox and Palmer - *43
#1000, Scotia Centre 235 Water St., St. John's NL A1C 1B6
709-738-7800 709-738-7999
stjohns@coxandpalmer.com
www.coxandpalmer.com

St. John's: Crosbie, Ches Barristers - *5
169 Water St., St. John's NL A1C 1B1
709-579-4000 709-579-9671 888-579-3262
ccb@chescrosbie.nf.net

St. John's: Dodd, Michael W. - *2
#301, P.O Box 578 C291 Water St., St. John's NL A1C 5K8
709-754-4098 709-754-3223
mdodd@mdoddlaw.com

St. John's: Fraize Law Offices - *2
P.O Box 5217, St. John's NL A1C 5W1
709-726-7978 709-726-8201
tfraize@fraizelawoffices.nf.net

St. John's: French, Noseworthy & Associates - *5
#122, Elizabeth Towers 100 Elizabeth Ave., St. John's NL A1B 1S1
709-754-1800 709-754-2701
jbfrench@nf.aibn.com

St. John's: Lewis, Day - *2
A 84 Airport Rd., 1st Fl., St. John's NL A1A 4Y3
709-753-2545 709-753-2266 877-553-2545
kellyhall@lewisday.ca
www.lewisday.com

St. John's: Lewis, Sinnott, Shortall, Hurley - *4
#300, TD Place P.O Box 884 C140 Water St., St. John's NL A1C 5L7
709-753-7810 709-738-2965
lssh@nf.aibn.com

St. John's: Martin Whalen Hennebury Stamp - *11
P.O Box 5910 15 Church Hill, St. John's NL A1C 5X4
709-754-1400 709-754-0915
info@mwhslaw.com
www.mwhslaw.com

St. John's: McGrath, John W. - *2
18 Argyle St., St. John's NL A1A 1V3
709-726-5250 709-738-0614
jwmcgrath@nf.aibn.com

St. John's: Noonan, Oakley - *2
P.O Box 5303, St. John's NL A1C 5W1
709-726-9598 709-726-9614
joakley@nfld.net

St. John's: O'Dea, Earle - *15
P.O Box 5955 323 Duckworth St., St. John's NL A1C 5X4
709-726-3524 709-726-9600
odeaearle@odeaearle.nf.ca
www.odeaearle.nf.ca

St. John's: Roebothan, McKay & Marshall - *13
P.O Box 5236 209 Duckworth St., St. John's NL A1C 5W1
709-753-5805 709-753-5221 800-563-5563
wrmm@wrmm.nf.net

St. John's: White, Ottenheimer & Baker - *20
Baine Johnson Centre P.O Box 5457 10 Fort William Pl., St. John's NL A1C 5W4
709-722-7584 709-722-9210
wob@wob.nf.ca
www.wob.nf.ca

Northwest Territories

** indicates # of lawyers*

Hay River: Shabala, Stephen M. - *1
#205, 31 Capital Dr., Hay River NT X0E 1G2
867-874-3365 867-874-6955

Yellowknife: Fuglsang, Peter C. & Associates - *1
P.O Box 2459 Main4912 - 49 St., Yellowknife NT X1A 2P8
867-920-4344 867-873-3386

Yellowknife: Peterson, Stang & Malakoe - *7
P.O Box 939 4902 - 49 St., Yellowknife NT X1A 2N7
867-669-8450 867-873-6543
lawyers@norlaw.nt.ca
www.norlaw.nt.ca

Nova Scotia

** indicates # of lawyers*

Amherst: Archibald, Morley - *2
P.O Box 548, Amherst NS B4H 4A1
902-667-3856 902-667-0104
aml@ns.sympatico.ca

Amherst: Fairbanks Law Office - *1
P.O Box 103, Amherst NS B4H 3Y6
902-667-7579 902-667-0644
william.fairbanks@ns.aliantzinc.ca
www.fairbankslawoffice.com

Amherst: Hicks, LeMoine - *3
P.O Box 279 15 Princess St., Amherst NS B4H 3Z2
902-667-7214 902-667-5886
info@hickslemoine.ca
www.hickslemonie.ca

Annapolis Royal: Armstrong & Armstrong - *1
P.O Box 575, Annapolis Royal NS B0S 1A0
902-532-2155 902-532-7211
armstrong@ns.aliantzinc.ca

Antigonish: MacIsaac, Daniel J. - *1
P.O Box 1478 Main30 Church St., Antigonish NS B2G 2L7
902-863-5398 902-863-9440

Antigonish: MacPherson MacNeil Macdonald - *2
188 Main St., Antigonish NS B2G 2B9
902-863-2925 902-863-2925
mthree@eastlink.com

Antigonish: Meehan, William F., Q.C. - *1
P.O Box 1803 Main195 Main St., Antigonish NS B2G 2M5
902-863-3136 902-863-6270
wmeehan@hotmail.com

Barrington: Eldridge, G. David - *1
P.O Box 157 2459 Hwy. 3, Barrington NS B0W 1E0
902-637-2878 902-637-2025
eldridgeqc@eastlink.ca

Bedford: Cameron Rhindress - *1
1394 Bedford Hwy., Bedford NS B4A 1E2
902-835-7444 902-835-3819
crhindross@accesscable.net

Bedford: Gillis Associates, Barristers & Solicitors - *2
#310, Sun Tower 1550 Bedford Hwy., Bedford NS B4A 1E6
902-835-6174 902-835-1486 866-277-3863
admin@gillisassociates.ca
www.gillisassociates.ca

Bedford: Melnick, Doll, Condran - *3
#302, 1160 Bedford Hwy., Bedford NS B4A 1C1
902-835-2300 902-835-2303
melnick.doll.condran@ns.sympatico.ca

Berwick: Stewart & Turner - *2
P.O Box 208 196 Cottage St., Berwick NS B0P 1E0
902-538-3123 902-538-7933

Berwick: Waterbury Newton - *2
P.O Box 475 188 Commercial St., Berwick NS B0P 1E0
902-538-3168 902-538-8680
mailberwick@waterburynewton.ns.ca
www.nslawyers.com

Bridgewater: Morris, J. Patrick - *1
344 King St., Bridgewater NS B4V 1A9
902-543-6661 902-543-6639
morris@eastlink.ca

Bridgewater: Power, Dempsey, Cooper & Leefe - *5
84 Dufferin St., Bridgewater NS B4V 2G3
902-543-7815 902-543-3196
pdclaw@ns.sympatico.ca

Bridgewater: Romneylaw Inc. - *2
P.O Box 368 136 Aberdeen Rd., Bridgewater NS B4V 2W9
902-543-4444 902-543-0232
romneylaw1@eastlink.ca

Dartmouth: Boyne Clarke - *39
#700, Belmont House P.O Box 876 33 Alderney Dr., Dartmouth NS B2Y 3Z5

902-469-9500 902-463-7500 800-207-6589
info@boyneclarke.ns.ca
www.boyneclarke.ns.ca

Dartmouth: Grant, David A. - *1
63 Tacoma Dr., Dartmouth NS B2W 3E7
902-463-6300 902-435-7910
davidgrant@ns.sympatico.ca

Dartmouth: Landry McGillivray, Barristers, Solicitors, Notaries - *10
#300, Quaker Landing P.O Box 1200 Main33 Ochterloney St., Dartmouth NS B2Y 4B8
902-463-8800 902-463-0590
slg@landrymcgillivray.ns.ca
www.landrymcgillivray.ca

Dartmouth: Langille & Associates - *1
#201, P.O Box 767 56 Portland St., Dartmouth NS B2Y 3Z3
902-463-5200 902-465-5200
ken.langille@ns.aliantzinc.ca

Dartmouth: Pyne, Lester - *1
194 Caledonia Rd., Dartmouth NS B2X 1L4
902-434-6167 902-434-5448

Dartmouth: Wolfson, Schelew, Zatzman - *4
#500, Bank of Commerce Bldg. P.O Box 2308 73 Tacoma Dr., Dartmouth NS B2W 3Y4
902-435-7000 902-435-4085 888-990-5263
wszlaw@wsz.ns.ca

Digby: Outhouse, James L. Q.C. - *1
P.O Box 1567 78 Water St., Digby NS B0V 1A0
902-245-2551 902-245-6622
jamesouthouse@ns.aliantzinc.ca

Enfield: Blackburn English - *3
287 Hwy. 2, Enfield NS B2T 1C9
902-883-2264 902-883-8744
blackburn.english@ns.sympatico.ca

Glace Bay: Crosby, Burke & Macrury
P.O Box 86 Main38 Union St., Glace Bay NS B1A 5V1
902-849-3971 902-849-7009

Glace Bay: McIntyre, Gillis & O'Leary - *2
P.O Box 187 Main65 Minto St., Glace Bay NS B1A 5V2
902-849-6507 902-849-0555
gblaw@auracom.com

Glace Bay: Raniseth, David H. - *1
P.O Box 249 34 McKeen St., Glace Bay NS B1A 5B9
902-849-0960 902-849-6512

Halifax: Angus, Frederick - *1
#935, 5991 Spring Garden Rd., Halifax NS B3H 1Y6
902-420-9595 902-423-8040
fred.angus@ns.sympatico.ca

Halifax: Barss, Hare & Turner - *1
#137, Roy Bldg. Central1657 Barrington St., Halifax NS B3J 2A1
902-423-1249

Halifax: Beaton Derrick - *2
1345 Hollis St., Halifax NS B3J 1T8
902-474-7482 902-474-8115

Halifax: Beveridge, MacPherson & Duncan - *3
P.O Box 547 Central1684 Barrington St., 4th Fl., Halifax NS B3J 2R7
902-423-9143 902-422-7837

Halifax: Block, Marven C., Q.C. - *1
#305, Coburg Pl. 6389 Coburg Rd., Halifax NS B3H 2A5
902-425-5077 902-429-5198
lomar@istar.ca

Halifax: Blois, Nickerson & Bryson - *17
#500, P.O Box 2147 1568 Hollis St., Halifax NS B3J 3B7
902-425-6000 902-429-7347
info@bloisnickerson.com
www.bloisnickerson.com

Halifax: Burchell Hayman Parish - *23
#1800, 1801 Hollis St., Halifax NS B3J 3N4
902-423-6361 902-420-9326
firm@burchells.ca
www.burchells.ca

Halifax: Christie Cuffari Law Office - *1
#310, 1657 Barrington St., Halifax NS B3J 2A1
902-422-2297 902-422-2162
cclo@ca.inter.net

Halifax: Coady Filliter - *7
#208, 880 Spring Garden Rd., Halifax NS B3H 1Y1
902-429-6264 902-423-3044
wroy@coadyfilliter.com

Halifax: Cooper & McDonald - *6
Old Auction House 1669 Granville St., Halifax NS B3J 1X2
902-429-2191 902-425-3217

Halifax: Cragg & Weir - *3
6452 Quinpool Rd., Halifax NS B3L 1A8
902-422-1776 902-429-0016
bob.cragg@ns.sympatico.ca

Halifax: Crowe Dillon Robinson - *8
#2000, 7075 Bayers Rd., Halifax NS B3L 2C1
902-453-1732 902-454-9948

Halifax: Garson, Knox & MacDonald - *3
1741 Brunswick St., Halifax NS B3J 3X8
902-425-0222 902-423-4690

Halifax: Gaudet, Gilbert L. - *1
6156 Quinpool Rd., Halifax NS B3L 1A3
902-422-1243

Halifax: Gaum, Simon L., Q.C. - *1
#206, Tower One, Halifax Shopping Centre 7001 Mumford Rd., Halifax NS B3L 4N9
902-423-6391 902-455-0974

Halifax: Goldberg Thompson - *8
#400, Sentry Place 1559 Brunswick St., Halifax NS B3J 2G1
902-421-1161 902-425-0266
inquiries@uncommonlaw.com
www.goldbergthompson.com

Halifax: Hopkins, Walter E. - *1
#105, 276 Bedford Hwy., Halifax NS B3M 2K6
902-445-2984 902-445-4333

Halifax: Medjuck & Medjuck - *1
P.O Box 1074 1601 Lower Water St., Halifax NS B3J 2X1
902-429-4061 902-422-7639
medjuck@ns.sympatico.ca

Halifax: Metcalf & Company - *6
Benjamin Wier House 1459 Hollis St., Halifax NS B3J 1V1
902-420-1990 902-429-1171
metcalf&company@metcalf.ns.ca
www.metcalf.ns.ca

Halifax: Moore & Associates - *4
P.O Box 1537 Central1475 Hollis St., Halifax NS B3J 2Y3
902-420-1066 902-420-1938
mcm.ma@ns.sympatico.ca

Halifax: Paton & Paton MacDonald Law Office - *1
12 Robert Allen Dr., Halifax NS B3M 3G8
902-457-5111 902-457-5113
act@istar.com

Halifax: Paul, Clyde A. & Associates - *4
349 Herring Cove Rd., Halifax NS B3R 1V9
902-477-2518 902-479-1482
capaul@ns.sympatico.ca

Halifax: Quackenbush, Thomson & Robbins - *5
2571 Windsor St., Halifax NS B3K 5C4
902-492-1655 902-492-1697
qtr@qtrlaw.com

Halifax: Ritch Durnford, Lawyers - *16
#1200, CIBC Bldg. 1809 Barrington St., Halifax NS B3J 3K8
902-429-3400 902-422-4713
info@ritchdurnford.com; library@ritchdurnford.com
www.ritchdurnford.com

Halifax: Walker, Dunlop - *6
PO Box 36057, RPO Spring Garden, Halifax NS B3J 3J1
902-423-8121 902-429-0621
walker.dunlop@ns.sympatico.ca

Halifax: Wickwire Holm - *22
#2100, P.O Box 1054 1801 Hollis St., Halifax NS B3J 2X6
902-429-4111 902-429-8215 866-429-4111
wh@wickwireholm.com
www.wickwireholm.com

Kentville: Forse, Nathanson - *2
P.O Box 655 325 Main St., Kentville NS B4N 3X7
902-678-1616 902-678-1615 800-667-3879

Kentville: Fraser, Donald C. - *1
P.O Box 668 Main35R Webster St., Kentville NS B4N 3X9
902-678-4006 902-678-2999
fraser.law@ns.aliantzinc.ca

Liverpool: Tutty & DiPersio - *2
#167, P.O Box 760 171 Main St., Liverpool NS B0T 1K0
902-354-5756 902-354-7395

Lower Sackville: Farwell, David F. - *1
#206, Vogue Optical Plaza 405 Sackville Dr., Lower Sackville NS B4C 2R9
902-865-5537 902-865-4354
davidfarwell@ns.sympatico.ca

Lunenburg: Burke & Macdonald - *2
P.O Box 549 28 King St., Lunenburg NS B0J 2C0
902-634-8354 902-634-4226

Middleton: Dowell, C. Hanson Q.C. - *1
P.O Box 910, Middleton NS B0S 1P0
902-825-3059 902-825-3154
lawdow@ns.sympatico.ca

Middleton: Durland, Gillis & Schumacher, Associates - *2
P.O Box 700 74 Commercial St., Middleton NS B0S 1P0
902-825-3415 902-825-2522

New Glasgow: Goodman MacDonald & Patterson - *3
P.O Box 697 Main47 Riverside Dr., New Glasgow NS B2H 5G2
902-752-5090 902-755-3545

New Glasgow: MacIntosh, MacDonnell & MacDonald - *10
#260, Aberdeen Business Centre P.O Box 368 Main610 East River Rd., 2nd Fl., New Glasgow NS B2H 5E5
902-752-8441 902-752-7810 888-752-8441
office@macmacmac.ns.ca

New Waterford: Broderick, Charles - *1
P.O Box 151 3316 Plummer Ave., New Waterford NS B1H 4K4
902-862-6471 902-862-9513
cblaw@istar.ca

New Waterford: Hinchey, M. Sweeney - *1
3383 Plummer Ave., New Waterford NS B1H 1Z1
902-862-2368 902-862-9581
hinchems@yahoo.com

Pictou: MacLean & MacDonald - *2
P.O Box 730 90 Coleraine St., Pictou NS B0K 1H0
902-485-4347 902-485-8887
law@macleanmacdonald.com

Port Hawkesbury: Pickup & MacDowell - *2
#2, 308 Philpott St., Port Hawkesbury NS B9A 2B8
902-625-2500 902-625-0500
pkpmd@auracom.com

Pubnico: d'Entremont & Boudreau - *2
P.O Box 118, Pubnico NS B0W 2W0
902-762-3119 902-762-3124
rjboudreau@klis.com

Shelburne: Miller, Donald R. - *1
6767 Shore Rd. RR#3, Shelburne NS B0T 1W0
902-637-2527 902-637-2165

Shubenacadie: Carruthers & MacDonell Law Office Inc. - *3
Chubenacadie Professional Centre P.O Box 280 #204, 5 Mill Village Rd., Shubenacadie NS B0N 2H0
902-758-2591 902-758-4022

Stellarton: O'Blenis, R.E. - *1
P.O Box 1500 179 Foord St., Stellarton NS B0K 1S0
902-752-1575

Stellarton: Skoke & Company
P.O Box 850 Foord St., Stellarton NS B0K 1S0
902-755-5711 902-752-6561

Sydney: Cusack Law Office - *1
205 Charlotte St., Sydney NS B1P 1C4
902-564-8396 902-564-0030
cusacklaw@ns.sympatico.ca

Sydney: Khattar & Khattar - *6
P.O Box 387 378 Charlotte St., Sydney NS B1P 6H2
902-539-9696 902-562-7147 888-542-8827
elaine@khattar.ca

Sydney: Lorway MacEachern - *4
112 Charlotte St., Sydney NS B1P 1B9

902-539-4447 902-564-9844
northlaw@cbnet.ns.ca

Sydney: MacDonald & MacLennan - *1
P.O Box 1148 275 Charlotte St., Sydney NS B1P 6J7
902-564-4429 902-539-2303

Sydney: McLeod, Hugh R. - *1
P.O Box 306 275 Charlotte St., Sydney NS B1P 6H2
902-539-2261 902-539-3386
hugh.mcleod@ns.sympatico.ca

Truro: Archibald Lederman - *2
P.O Box 1100 Main43 Walker St., Truro NS B2N 5G9
902-895-0524 902-893-7608
plederman@archibaldlederman.ca

Truro: Curtis, David F. Q.C. - *1
#202, P.O Box 458 640 Prince St., Truro NS B2N 1G4
902-895-0528 902-893-1158
dcurtislaw@ns.aliantzinc.ca

Truro: MacLean, Melinda J., Q.C. - *1
P.O Box 126 Main188 Queen St., Truro NS B2N 5B6
902-895-2866 902-893-1455

Truro: McLellan, Richards & Bégin - *2
P.O Box 1064 779 Prince St., Truro NS B2N 5G9
902-895-4417 902-897-9890 866-600-0011
www.truro-law.com

Truro: Scanlan, Gerard P. - *1
P.O Box 1228 Main640 Prince St., Truro NS B2N 5N2
902-895-9249 902-893-3078
scanpayn@tru.eastlink.ca

Upper Tantallon: Smith-Camp & Associates - *1
#203, 5209 St. Margaret's Bay Rd., Upper Tantallon NS B3Z 1E3
902-826-2193 902-826-1043
smithcamplaw@hotmail.com

Westville: Facey, S. Charles, Q.C. - *1
P.O Box 610 1912 Drummond Rd., Westville NS B0K 2A0
902-396-4191 902-396-3606
charles.facey@ns.sympatico.ca

Windsor: Adams & Company - *2
P.O Box 2379 189 Gerrish St., Windsor NS B0N 2T0
902-798-8384 902-798-0432
hadams.adamsco@ns.sympatico.ca

Windsor: Nelson Law - *2
P.O Box 2018 258 King St., Windsor NS B0N 2T0
902-798-5797 902-798-2332
nelson.law@ns.sympatico.ca

Windsor: Romans, John D. - *1
P.O Box 1024 140 King St., Windsor NS B0N 2T0
902-798-8311

Wolfville: Kimball Brogan Law Office - *4
121 Front St., Wolfville NS B4P 1A6
902-542-5757 902-542-5759 800-294-7851
info@kimballbrogan.ca
www.kimballbrogan.ca

Wolfville: Thompson-Sheppard Q.C., Dianne E. - *1
80 Kent Ave., Wolfville NS B4P 1V1
902-542-2388 902-542-0794
paddles@ns.sympatico.ca

Ontario

** indicates # of lawyers*

Ajax: Greening & Bucknam - *1
#202, 50 Commercial Ave., Ajax ON L1S 2H5
905-683-7037 905-683-7627
bucknam@rogers.com

Alexandria: Lefebvre, Jean-Marc, Q.C. - *2
P.O Box 519 32 Main St. North, Alexandria ON K0C 1A0
613-525-1358 613-525-3411
lefebvre@bellnet.ca

Alliston: Galbraith, Mary L. - *1
22 Church St. South, Alliston ON L9R 1V9
705-435-4324 705-435-2628

Alliston: Gilmore & Gilmore - *2
P.O Box 250 458 Victoria St. East, Alliston ON L9R 1V5
705-435-4339 705-435-6520 877-855-3425
info@gilmoreandgilmore.com
www.gilmoreandgilmore.com

Almonte: Chapman, L.G. William, Barrister, Solicitor, & Notary Public - *1
P.O Box 362 77 Little Bridge St., Almonte ON K0A 1A0
613-256-3072 613-256-5164
lgwilliamchapman@bellnet.ca
www.lgwilliamchapman.com

Almonte: Wheeler, Evelyn - *1
P.O Box 1540 38 Mill St., Almonte ON K0A 1A0
613-256-4148 613-256-4708
www.evelynwheeler.com

Amherstburg: Baker Busch - *2
41 Sandwich St. South, Amherstburg ON N9V 1Z5
519-736-2154 519-736-2466

Amherstview: Vince, William E.M. - *1
6 Speers Blvd., #J-1, Amherstview ON K7N 1Z6
613-389-6727 613-389-6256
wvince@cogeco.ca

Angus: MacKenzie, Gordon R. - *1
P.O Box 600 Unit A, 189 Mill St., Angus ON L0M 1B2
705-424-1331 705-424-6441
gmackenzie@on.aibn.com
www.yourlocallawyer.com

Aurora: Di Cecco, Jones - *2
#205, 15171 Yonge St., Aurora ON L4G 1M1
905-751-1517 905-751-1518
dicecco.jones@diceccojones.com

Aurora: Switzer, Barry W. - *1
P.O Box 246 15187 Yonge St., Aurora ON L4G 1L8
905-727-9488 905-841-8647

Aurora: Thomas McPherson & Associates - *2
P.O Box 338 15220 Yonge St., Aurora ON L4G 3H4
905-727-3151 905-841-2164
mcpherson@auroralaw.net
www.mcphersonassoc.yp.ca

Aylmer: Doyle & Prendergast - *2
10 Sydenham St. East, Aylmer ON N5H 1L2
519-773-3105 519-765-1728

Aylmer: Gloin, Hall & Shields - *4
139 Talbot St. East, Aylmer ON N5H 1H3
519-773-9221 519-765-1885
ghsaylaw@amtelecom.net

Bancroft: Plater, L.C. - *1
P.O Box 1150 129 Hastings St. North, Bancroft ON K0L 1C0
613-332-1605 613-332-2619

Barrie: Allison, Nancy Lee - *1
P.O Box 308 285 Grove Street East, Barrie ON L4M 2R2
705-737-5702 705-737-1614
nlalliso@csolve.net

Barrie: Bryson, Thomas - *1
11 Sophia St. West, Barrie ON L4N 1H9
705-728-2232 705-728-7525
tbrysonlaw@bellnet.ca

Barrie: Burgar, Rowe - *18
P.O Box 758 90 Mulcaster St., Barrie ON L4M 4Y5
705-721-3377 705-721-4025
burgarrowe@burgarrowe.com
www.burgarrowe.com

Barrie: Card, Peter C. - *1
111 Toronto St., Barrie ON L4N 1V1
705-739-9111 705-739-8111

Barrie: Carroll Heyd Chown - *5
#20, P.O Box 548 556 Bryne Dr., Barrie ON L4M 4T7
705-722-4400 705-722-0704
admin@chcbarristers.com

Barrie: Cowan & Carter - *1
P.O Box 722 107 Collier St., Barrie ON L4M 4Y5
705-728-4521 705-728-8744

Barrie: Cugelman & Eisen - *2
#201, 28 Owen St., Barrie ON L4M 3G7
705-721-1888 705-721-7755
cugelman@cugelmaneisen.com
www.cugelmaneisen.com

Barrie: Graham Wilson & Green, Barristers & Solicitors, Notaries, Mediators - *12
#107, 190 Cundles Rd. East, Barrie ON L4M 4S5
705-737-1811 705-737-5390
gwg@gwg.on.ca
www.gwg.on.ca

Barrie: Jacoby, Klaus N. - *1
P.O Box 350 34 Clapperton St., Barrie ON L4M 4T5
705-726-0238 705-726-9197
jaco@jacobylaw.ca

Barrie: Menzies, J. Marvin - *1
#104, P.O Box 1175 Main89 Dunlop St. East, Barrie ON L4M 5E2
705-722-5432 705-722-0218
marvinmenzies@on.aibn.com

Barrie: Mitchell, R. John - *1
P.O Box 1 40 Clapperton St., Barrie ON L4M 4S9
705-726-8855 705-721-0782

Barrie: Norman, Gerald E. - *1
P.O Box 732 99 Bayfield St., Barrie ON L4M 4Y5
705-726-2772 705-734-1942
geraldnorman@normanlawoffice.ca
www.normanlawoffice.ca

Barrie: Oatley, Vigmond, Personal Injury Lawyers LLP - *14
151 Ferris Lane, Barrie ON L4M 6C1
705-726-9021 705-726-2132 888-662-2481
info@oatleyvigmond.com
www.oatleyvigmond.com

Barrie: Owen, Harris-Lowe - *4
P.O Box 848 26 Owen St., Barrie ON L4M 4Y6
705-726-1181 705-726-1463
odlaw@owendickey.com
www.owendickey.com

Barrie: Ruttan, Charles F. - *1
23 Owen St., Barrie ON L4M 3G8
705-737-0688 705-722-4749
chuckruttan@ruttanlaw.ca

Barrie: Scharf, Mark - *1
103 Collier St., Barrie ON L4M 1H2
705-728-0555 705-722-3741

Beamsville: Vandeyar, M.G. - *1
#7, Lincoln Kingsway Plaza P.O Box 489 5041 King St., Beamsville ON L0R 1B0
905-563-8818 905-563-7750

Beaverton: Woodcock & Tomlinson - *1
P.O Box 512 402 Simcoe St., Beaverton ON L0K 1A0
705-426-7317 705-426-5740

Belle River: Deziel, J.L. - *1
P.O Box 909 531 Notre Dame, Belle River ON N0R 1A0
519-728-2000 519-728-4599 800-501-3494
jldeziel@cogeco.net

Belleville: Kafka, Edward J. - *3
P.O Box 243 309 Front St., Belleville ON K8N 5A2
613-968-3416 613-968-3417
elkafka.barr@bellnet.ca

Belleville: O'Flynn Weese LLP - *10
65 Bridge St. East, Belleville ON K8N 1L8
613-966-5222 613-966-7991
info@owtlaw.com
www.owtlaw.com

Belleville: Reynolds O'Brien LLP - *8
P.O Box 1327 183 Front St., Belleville ON K8N 5J1
613-966-3031 613-966-2390
mail@reynoldsobrien.com
www.reynoldsobrien.com

Belleville: Rolston, C. Roderick - *1
#202, 175 Front St., Belleville ON K8N 2Y9
613-962-9154 613-962-8109 800-361-4437
rrolston@reach.net

Belleville: Templeman Menninga LLP - *18
#200, P.O Box 234 205 Dundas St. East, Belleville ON K8N 5A2
613-966-2620 613-966-2866
info@tmlegal.com
www.tmlegal.com

Belleville: Van Huizen, Berend - *1
210 Church St., Belleville ON K8N 3C3
613-962-8645 613-962-7689
berend@berendvanhuizenlaw.com
www.berendvanhuizenlaw.com

Blenheim: Kerr & Wood - *1
P.O Box 1150 15 George St., Blenheim ON N0P 1A0

519-676-5465 519-676-3918
kerrwood@ciaccess.com

***Bobcaygeon*: Walker, Robert J. - *1**
P.O Box 243 4 King St. West, Bobcaygeon ON K0M 1A0
705-738-3588 705-738-4252

***Bolton*: Carberry, Jean P. - *1**
34 Queen St., Bolton ON L4E 1B3
905-857-2332 905-857-2367
jpclaw@jpclaw.ca

***Bolton*: Neiman, Callegari - *4**
Unit K-1, 18 King St. East, Bolton ON L7E 1E8
905-857-0095 905-857-0488
info@neimancallegari.ca
www.neimancallegari.ca

***Bolton*: Penfold, Mark E. - *2**
P.O Box 225 49 Queen St. North, Bolton ON L7E 5T2
905-857-2835 905-857-0091 800-954-4054
mark.penfold@boltonlaw.ca

***Bowmanville*: Brown, William - *1**
P.O Box 1 71 Mearns Court, Bowmanville ON L1C 4N4
905-623-3305 905-623-3287

***Bowmanville*: Kelly, Mervyn B., Barrister & Solicitor - *1**
42 Prince St., Bowmanville ON L1C 1G6
905-623-4444
merv@claringtonlawyers.com
www.claringtonlawyers.com

***Bracebridge*: Jacques, Brian G. - *1**
#103, P.O Box 1227 145 Ontario Street, Bracebridge ON P1L 2A7
705-645-8743 705-645-8895
brianjacqueslaw@bellnet.ca

***Bracebridge*: Lee, Roche & Kelly - *4**
P.O Box 990 6 Dominion St., Bracebridge ON P1L 1V2
705-645-2286 705-645-5541 866-331-1100
nickroche@lrklaw.ca

***Bracebridge*: Sugg, Fitton & Taylor LLP - *2**
5 Chancery Lane 1, Bracebridge ON P1L 2E3
705-645-5211 705-645-8021
chancerylane@cogeco.net

***Bradford*: Evans & Evans - *2**
P.O Box 190 21 Holland St. West, Bradford ON L3Z 2A8
905-775-3381 905-775-8835
law@evansevans.ca

***Brampton*: Acri, MacPherson - *7**
#200, 134 Queen St. East, Brampton ON L6V 1B2
905-459-6160 905-459-4606 877-468-8494
general.inquiry@acrimacpherson.com
www.acrimacpherson.com

***Brampton*: Brown, Edmond O'Donoghue - *1**
#100, 205 County Court Blvd., Brampton ON L6W 4R6
905-454-4141 905-454-4463
edbrown@bellnet.ca

***Brampton*: Dale, Streiman & Kurz - *6**
480 Main St. North, Brampton ON L6V 1P8
905-455-7300 905-455-5848 866-219-8109
mail@dsklaw.com
www.dsklaw.com

***Brampton*: Dalzell & Waite - *2**
#19, 1 Bartley Bull Pkwy., Brampton ON L6W 3T7
905-454-2288 905-454-2297

***Brampton*: Davis Webb LLP - *7**
#800, 24 Queen St. East, Brampton ON L6V 1A3
905-451-6714 905-454-1876
info@daviswebb.ca
www.daviswebb.com

***Brampton*: Hillier & Hillier - *1**
165 Main St. North, Brampton ON L6X 1N1
905-453-8636 905-453-6267
ava@avahillier.ca

***Brampton*: Hope & Henderson Law Office - *2**
253 Main St. North, Brampton ON L6X 1N3
905-451-7700 905-451-6620
henlaw@sympatico.ca

***Brampton*: Lawrence, Lawrence, Stevenson - *14**
43 Queen St. West, Brampton ON L6Y 1L9
905-451-3040 905-451-5058
lls@lawrences.com
www.lawrences.com

***Brampton*: Lent, D.R. - *1**
38 Queen St. West, Brampton ON L6X 1A1
905-457-4215 905-457-6454

***Brampton*: Linton, R.J. - *1**
21 John St., Brampton ON L6W 1Z1
905-453-3145 905-454-2270

***Brampton*: Matheson, Holmes A. - *1**
#301, 134 Queen St. East, Brampton ON L6V 1B2
905-451-6504 905-451-0288
hamatheson@on.aibn.com

***Brampton*: McClelland Law, A Professional Corporation, Lawyers - *2**
202 Main St. North, Brampton ON L6V 1P1
905-793-3026 905-793-2446
info@mcclellandlaw.com
www.mcclellandlaw.com

***Brampton*: McCulligh, W. John - *1**
#301, 197 County Court Blvd., Brampton ON L6W 4P6
905-459-1545 905-459-2826
wmcculligh@bellnet.ca

***Brampton*: North Peel & Dufferin Community Legal Services - *4**
#601, 24 Queen St. East, Brampton ON L6V 1A3
905-455-0160 905-455-0832 866-455-0160

***Brampton*: Prouse, Dash & Crouch - *11**
50 Queen St. West, Brampton ON L6X 4H3
905-451-6610 905-451-1549 877-217-4732
pdc@pdclawyers.ca
www.prousedash.ca

***Brampton*: Richardson, Schnall & Sanderson - *1**
#402, 134 Queen St. East, Brampton ON L6V 1B2
905-451-1593 905-451-3132

***Brampton*: Simmons, Da Silva & Sinton - *11**
#200, 201 County Court Blvd., Brampton ON L6W 4L2
905-457-1660 905-457-5641
www.sdslawfirm.com

***Brampton*: Smith, George Paul - *1**
280 Main St. North, Brampton ON L6V 1P6
905-457-9791 905-457-9798
gpsmith@pathcom.com
www.peelbarristers.com

***Brampton*: Speigel Nichols Fox - *7**
#400, 44 Peel Centre Dr., Brampton ON L6T 4B5
905-791-6262 905-791-6446
snf1@ontlaw.com
www.ontlaw.com

***Brampton*: Szumlanski, Victor E. - *1**
9610 McLaughlin Rd. North, Brampton ON L6X 0B8
905-456-1673 905-456-1201

***Brampton*: Wainwright, Alan - *1**
#102, 197 County Court Blvd., Brampton ON L6W 4P6
905-453-9520 905-450-7842
awainwright@bellnet.ca
www.peelbarristers.com/wainwright

***Brampton*: Walsh, Michael J. - *1**
280 Main St. North, Brampton ON L6V 1P6
905-453-4105 905-457-3075
walaw@on.aibn.com

***Brampton*: Wiley, J.T. - *1**
#100, 205 County Court Blvd., Brampton ON L6W 4R6
905-454-5600 905-454-4463

***Brantford*: Ainsworth, Douglas C. - *1**
Main120B Market St., Brantford ON N3T 3A1
519-756-4220 519-756-3462

***Brantford*: Boddy, Ryerson - *6**
#101, P.O Box 1265 172 Dalhousie St., Brantford ON N3T 5T3
519-753-8417 519-753-7421

***Brantford*: Calder, Donald C. - *1**
40 Nelson St., Brantford ON N3T 2M8
519-759-1910 519-759-2881

***Brantford*: Frost, S. - *1**
101 Wellington St., Brantford ON N3T 2M1
519-753-4113

***Brantford*: Hospodar, Davies & Goold - *3**
120 Market St., Brantford ON N3T 3A1
519-759-0082 519-759-8490

***Brantford*: Lefebvre & Lefebvre LLP - *7**
P.O Box 488 75 Chatham St., Brantford ON N3T 5N9
519-756-3350 519-756-4727
info@lefebvrelawyers.ca
www.lefebvrelawyers.ca

***Brantford*: Miller, Miller & Maltby - *2**
11 Nelson St., Brantford ON N3T 2M6
519-753-4118 519-753-2596

***Brantford*: Staats, Newton - *3**
P.O Box 1417 188 Mohawk St., Brantford ON N3S 2X2
519-756-5217 519-756-4783
staatsnewton@on.aibn.com

***Brantford*: Trepanier Verity - *6**
P.O Box 144 Main63 Charlotte St., Brantford ON N3T 2W6
519-756-8700 519-756-5454
info@trepanierverity.com

***Brantford*: Underwood & Ion - *2**
Main442 Grey St., Unit B, Brantford ON N3S 7N3
519-759-0920 519-759-2122
uisp@sympatico.ca

***Brantford*: Vandervet, Paul - *1**
P.O Box 1495 107 Wellington St., Brantford ON N3T 5V6
519-759-4240 519-759-4863
vonkor@bellnet.ca

***Brantford*: Waterous, Holden, Amey, Hitchon LLP - *19**
P.O Box 1510 20 Wellington St., Brantford ON N3T 5V6
519-759-6220 519-759-8360
law@waterousholden.com
www.waterousholden.com

***Brantford*: Wyatt, Purcell, Stillman & Karkkainen - *3**
P.O Box 1115 Main442 Grey St., Brantford ON N3S 7N3
519-756-5800 519-756-3861
wyattpurcell@wyatturcell.com

***Brigden*: Tennyson, W.E. - *1**
P.O Box 232 3015 Brigden Rd., Brigden ON N0N 1B0
519-864-1189 519-864-1966
tennysonlaw@bellnet.ca

***Brockville*: Fitzpatrick & Culic - *1**
21 Pine St., Brockville ON K6V 1E9
613-342-6693 613-342-8449
culiclaw@ripnet.com

***Brockville*: Flood, R.W. - *1**
13 Hartley St., Brockville ON K6V 3N2
613-345-0087 613-342-5294

***Brockville*: Fraser & Bickerton - *1**
#100, P.O Box 692 36 Broad St., Brockville ON K6V 5V8
613-345-3377 613-345-3372
www.fraserbickerton.ca

***Brockville*: Hain, David A. - *1**
P.O Box 757 58 King St. East, Brockville ON K6V 5W1
613-342-5577 613-342-1773
david@hainlaw.com
www.hainlaw.com

***Brockville*: Henderson Johnston Fournier - *2**
61 King St. East, Brockville ON K6V 5V4
613-345-5613 613-345-6473
info@hendersonjohnstonfournier.com
www.hendersonjohnstonfournier.com

***Brockville*: Macintosh, Q.C., John H. - *1**
P.O Box 451 2 Court House Ave., Brockville ON K6V 5V6
613-345-5653 613-345-6022
jmacintosh@ripnet.com

***Brockville*: Preston, Harry R. - *1**
#201, P.O Box 1814 Main68 King St. West, Brockville ON K6V 3P9
613-342-1866 613-342-1634
preslaw@bellnet.ca

***Brockville*: Wilson Evely - *1**
P.O Box 1 3 Court Terrace, Brockville ON K6V 4T4
613-345-1907 613-345-4604
wilson-evely@bellnet.ca

***Burlington*: Cleaver Crawford LLP - *2**
2019 Caroline St., Burlington ON L7R 1L1

905-634-5581 905-634-1563
eldon.hunt@cleavercrawford.ca

Burlington: **Green Germann - *3**
P.O Box 400 411 Guelph Line, Burlington ON L7R 3Y3
905-639-1222 905-632-6977
info@greengermann.ca
www.greengermann.ca

Burlington: **Hastings, Charlebois - *2**
3513 Mainway Dr., Burlington ON L7M 1A9
905-332-1888 905-332-0021
mail@hclawyers.ca

Burlington: **Kosterski, Richard R. - *1**
394 Guelph Line, Burlington ON L7R 3L4
905-637-8249 905-637-6015
richard@kosterskilaw.ca

Burlington: **Simpson & Rich - *1**
#12, 460 Brant St., Burlington ON L7R 4B6
905-681-1521 905-333-5075
gdrlaw@worldchat.com

Burlington: **Simpson, Wigle LLP - *27**
#501, Sims Square Bldg. 390 Brant St., Burlington ON L7R 4J4
905-639-1052 905-333-3960
matthewsl@simpsonwigle.com
www.simpsonwigle.com

Burlington: **Sutherland, Thomas R., Q.C. - *1**
3310 South Service Road, Burlington ON L7N 3M6
905-634-5521 905-631-7914

Burlington: **Thatcher & Wands - *2**
1457 Ontario St., Burlington ON L7S 1G6
905-681-0444 905-681-2937
office@thatcherandwands.com
www.thatcherandwands.com

Caledon East: **Jenney, George W. - *1**
15891 Airport Rd., Caledon East ON L7C 1J3
905-584-9300 905-584-9233

Caledonia: **Arrell Law LLP - *3**
2 Caithness St. West, Caledonia ON N3W 2J2
905-765-5414 905-765-5144
www.arrellplacelaw.com

Caledonia: **Benedict & Ferguson - *2**
322 Argyle St. South, Caledonia ON N3W 1K8
905-765-4004 905-765-3001

Caledonia: **Humenik, L.S. - *1**
P.O Box 2112 19 Argyle St. North, Caledonia ON N3W 1B6
905-765-3162 905-765-4313
larman@mountaincable.net

Callander: **Olah, George D. - *1**
492 Main Street, Callander ON P0H 1H0
705-752-1323 705-752-1283
georgeolah@bellnet.ca

Cambridge: **Bond & Brownell - *3**
P.O Box 1148 57 Ainslie Street North, Cambridge ON N1R 3J7
519-623-2311 519-623-6957
info@bondbrownell.ca
www.bondbrownell.ca

Cambridge: **Hauser, Gary E.J. - *1**
1666 King St. East, Cambridge ON N3H 3R7
519-653-1521 519-650-1466
ghauser@golden.net

Cambridge: **Loker, George E. - *1**
P.O Box 1723 Galt108 Myers Rd., Cambridge ON N1R 2Z8
519-621-4300 519-621-4300
eloker@golden.net

Cambridge: **Mann, Paul M. Professional Corp. - *1**
25 George St. South, Cambridge ON N1S 2N3
519-623-0700 519-622-4091
info@paulmann.ca
www.paulmann.ca

Cambridge: **McSevney Law Offices - *2**
708 Duke St., Cambridge ON N3H 3T6
519-653-3217 519-653-3702
www.mcsevneylaw.com

Cambridge: **Pettitt, Schwarz - *2**
#403, 73 Water St. North, Cambridge ON N1R 7L6
519-621-2450 519-621-5750
bob@pettittschwarz.com
www.pettittschwarz.com

Cambridge: **Wilson, J. Craig - *1**
P.O Box 1297 2 Water St. North, Cambridge ON N1R 3B1
519-622-0192

Cambridge: **Wraight, W.C. - *1**
P.O Box 22103 15 Main St., Cambridge ON N1R 8E3
519-623-3330 519-621-0136

Carleton Place: **Bennett, Kenneth J. - *1**
32 Beckwith Street, Carleton Place ON K7C 2T2
613-257-1655 613-257-8837

Carleton Place: **Courtice, P.D. - *1**
P.O Box 29 164 Bridge St., Carleton Place ON K7C 2V7
613-257-5001 613-257-8797
pdclaw@on.aibn.com

Carleton Place: **Jones, N. Alan - *1**
92 Bridge St., Carleton Place ON K7C 2V3
613-257-3811 613-253-0479
ajones@bellnet.ca

Chatham: **Benoit, Van Raay, Spisani, Fuerth & Quaglia - *5**
P.O Box 1087 Main124 Thames St., Chatham ON N7L 2Y8
519-352-8580 519-352-4114

Chesley: **McLean, Ross C. - *2**
P.O Box 118 27 1st Ave. South, Chesley ON N0G 1L0
519-363-3190 519-363-2213
rossmclean@bmts.com

Clinton: **Hiltz, D. Gerald - *1**
P.O Box 1087 52 Huron St., Clinton ON N0M 1L0
519-482-3414 519-482-7525

Cobourg: **Cooper, Rodger F. - *1**
253 Division St., #102, Cobourg ON K9A 3P9
905-372-8728 905-372-0720 888-251-1945
cooper@eagle.ca

Cobourg: **SMM Law Professional Corp. - *3**
#205, The Fleming Bldg. 1005 Elgin St., Cobourg ON K9A 5J4
905-372-3395 905-372-1695
smmlaw@smmlaw.com
www.smmlaw.com

Colborne: **Carter, J.A. - *1**
P.O Box 699 26 King St. East, Colborne ON K9A 1K7
905-355-3322 905-355-3104 877-399-3322
jcarter@bellnet.ca

Collingwood: **Baulke Augaitis Stahr LLP - *4**
P.O Box 100 150 Hurontario St., Collingwood ON L9Y 3Z4
705-445-4930 705-445-1871 866-230-9993
info@collingwoodlaw.com
www.collingwoodlaw.com

Collingwood: **Bulmer, J.D., Q.C. - *1**
Main126 Hurontario St., Collingwood ON L9Y 2L9
705-445-9244 705-444-5741

Collingwood: **Greasley, Brian - *1**
P.O Box 490 33 Ste. Marie St., Collingwood ON L9Y 3J9
705-429-5199 705-445-2269

Collingwood: **Lant, Larry E. - *1**
P.O Box 248 Main217 Minnesota St., Collingwood ON L9Y 3S4
705-445-2886 705-444-5837
lantlaw@on.aibn.com

Concord: **DiMonte, Patrick - *1**
#211, 3100 Steeles Ave. West, Concord ON L4K 3R1
905-738-2101 905-738-1168
patdimonte@on.aibn.com

Concord: **Okell & Weisman - *2**
#407, 1600 Steeles Ave. West, Concord ON L4K 4M2
905-761-8711 905-761-8633

Concord: **Silverstein, Alan G. - *1**
#318, 1600 Steeles Ave. West, Concord ON L4K 4M2
905-761-1600 905-761-0948
alan.silverstein@rogers.com

Cornwall: **Adams, Sherwood, Swabey & Follon - *4**
305 - 2 St. East, Cornwall ON K6H 1Y8
613-938-3330 613-938-7885
adams@adamssherwood.ca
www.adamssherwoof.ca

Cornwall: **Bergeron Filion - *2**
103 Sydney St., Cornwall ON K6H 3H1
613-932-2911 613-932-2356
bobbergeron@pppoe.ca

Cornwall: **Giovanniello, Bellefeuille - *2**
340 - 2nd St. East, Cornwall ON K6H 1Y9
613-938-0294 613-932-2374
law@gblawfirm.ca
www.gblawfirm.ca

Cornwall: **Guindon, MacLean & Castle - *3**
50 - 2 St. East, Cornwall ON K6H 1Y3
613-933-3931 613-933-6123
info@g-m-c.on.ca

Cornwall: **White, Donald J. - *1**
700 Montreal Rd., Cornwall ON K6H 1C4
613-933-6443 613-933-6453
nwhite10@cogeco.ca

Cornwall: **Wilson, Poirier, Byrne - *2**
132 - 2nd St. West, Cornwall ON K6J 1G5
613-938-2224 613-938-8005
apoirier@bellnet.ca; tombyrne@bellnet.ca

Deep River: **Roche & Dakin - *2**
P.O Box 1240 11 Champlain St., Deep River ON K0J 1P0
613-584-3392 613-584-4922
rochdaki@bellnet.ca

Delhi: **Hanselman, John R. - *1**
138 Eagle St., Delhi ON N4B 1S5
519-582-0770 519-582-1876

Dresden: **Mathany, Timothy D. - *1**
P.O Box 568 347 St. George St. South, Dresden ON N0P 1M0
519-683-6219 519-683-6548

Dryden: **McAuley & Partners - *4**
P.O Box 159 4 Whyte Ave., Dryden ON P8N 2Y8
807-223-2254 807-223-3794
www.mcauleylaw.com

Dryden: **Vermeer & Van Walleghem - *2**
P.O Box 938 Main65 King St., 2nd Fl., Dryden ON P8N 2Z5
807-223-3311 807-223-4133
lawweb@vermeerlaw.com
www.vermeerlaw.com

Dunnville: **Chambers, G. Donald - *1**
110 Lock St. East, Dunnville ON N1A 1J7
905-744-7485 905-774-7486

Elmira: **Rudavsky, Cynthia M. - *1**
9 Church St. West, Elmira ON N3B 1M2
519-669-2200 519-669-4349
rudavsky@sentex.net

Elmira: **Woods, Clemens & Fletcher Professional Corporation - *3**
P.O Box 216 9 Memorial Ave., Elmira ON N3B 2R1
519-669-5101 519-669-5618
lawoffice@woodsclemens.ca

Elora: **Morris, J.E. - *1**
149 Geddes Street, Elora ON N0B 1S0
519-846-5366 519-846-8170
john@johnmorrislaw.ca

Essex: **Hickey, Bryne - *2**
14 Centre St., Essex ON N8M 1N9
519-776-7349 519-776-8161
byrnelaw@bellnet.ca

Etobicoke: **Bailey, John H. - *1**
#901, 701 Evans Ave., Etobicoke ON M9C 1A3
416-622-2725 416-622-8952
jhblaw@aol.com

Etobicoke: **Birks, Langdon & Elliott - *2**
#329, 4195 Dundas St. West, Etobicoke ON M8X 1Y4
416-239-3431 416-239-8259

Etobicoke: **Christie & Associates - *4**
750 Scarlett Road, Etobicoke ON M9P 2V1
416-249-8300 416-249-1480

Etobicoke: **Derry, P.G. - *1**
1 Eva Road, Etobicoke ON M9C 4Z5
416-868-6483 416-364-1697

Exeter: **Raymond & McLean - *1**
P.O Box 100 387 Main St. South, Exeter ON N0M 1S0
519-235-2234 519-235-2671
raymclea@quadro.net

***Fenelon Falls*: Gowanlock, David J. - *1**
P.O Box 607 14 Oak St., Fenelon Falls ON K0M 1N0
705-887-2582 705-887-1871

***Fergus*: Grant & Acheson - *4**
P.O Box 128 265 Bridge St., Fergus ON N1M 2W7
519-843-1960 519-843-6888
www.grant-acheson.com

***Fort Erie*: Hagan & McDowell - *2**
P.O Box 68 29 Jarvis St., Fort Erie ON L2A 5M6
905-871-4440 905-871-9266
rmcdowell@computan.com

***Fort Erie*: Jacobi, D.J. - *1**
P.O Box 1028 1321 Garrison Rd., Fort Erie ON L2A 1P3
905-871-4244

***Fort Frances*: Brunetta, Clare Allan - *1**
P.O Box 656 420 Victoria Ave., Fort Frances ON P9A 3M9
807-274-9809 807-274-8760
cbrunetta@nwonet.net

***Fort Frances*: Eustace, Lawrence A. - *1**
510 Portage Ave., Fort Frances ON P9A 2A3
807-274-3247 807-274-6447
larry@eustace-law.com

***Fort Frances*: Phillips, Lawrence G. - *1**
237 Church St., Fort Frances ON P9A 1C7
807-274-8525 807-274-5758
phillaw19@hotmail.com

***Fort Frances*: Taylor, Donald A. - *1**
504 Armit Ave., Fort Frances ON P9A 2H7
807-274-7811 807-274-8485
dalaw@shaw.ca

***Gananoque*: Steacy & Delaney - *2**
P.O Box 70 Main110 Stone St., Gananoque ON K7G 2T6
613-382-2137 613-382-7794
stacey.delaney@cogeco.net
www.gananoque.com/steacyanddelaney

***Georgetown*: Eason, Jeffrey L. - *1**
P.O Box 159 Main116 Guelph St., Georgetown ON L7G 4T1
905-877-6961 905-877-9725
jeffreyleason@bellnet.ca

***Georgetown*: Helson Kogon Ashbee Schaljo & Associates LLP - *5**
132 Mill St., Georgetown ON L7G 2C6
905-877-5206 905-877-3948
helsonkogon.general@cogeco.net

***Georgetown*: How, W. Glen & Associates**
P.O Box 40, Georgetown ON L7G 4T1
905-873-4545 905-873-4522
wghow@wghow.ca

***Georgetown*: Howitt, R.T., Q.C. - *1**
#301, 83 Mill St., Georgetown ON M9C 1X6
905-877-5139 905-877-1155

***Georgetown*: Manderson, William H. - *1**
#1004, 83 Mill Street, Georgetown ON L7G 5E9
905-873-0121
billmanderson@on.aibn.com

***Georgetown*: Sopinka & Kort - *2**
145 Mill St., Georgetown ON L7G 2C2
905-877-0196 905-877-0604
wsopinka@sopinka-kort.com

***Gloucester*: MacQuarrie Whyte Killoran - *3**
#208, 1980 Ogilvie Rd., Gloucester ON K1J 9L3
613-748-1600 613-748-0800
info@mwklaw.ca
www.ottawaorleanslawyers.com; www.mwklaw.ca

***Goderich*: Donnelly & Murphy - *7**
18 Court House Square, Goderich ON N7A 3Y7
519-524-2154 519-524-8550
admin@dmlaw.on.ca

***Goderich*: Pickell, Norman, B. - *1**
58 South Street, Goderich ON N7A 3L5
519-524-8335 519-524-1530
pickell@normanpickell.com
www.normanpickell.com

***Goderich*: Troyan & Fincher - *2**
44 North St., Goderich ON N7A 2T4
519-524-2115 519-524-4481
troyanfincher@cabletv.on.ca

***Gore Bay*: Land, Terence E. - *1**
P.O Box 90 4 Eleanor St., Gore Bay ON P0P 1H0
705-282-2710 705-282-2205

***Gore Bay*: Weppler, James E. - *1**
P.O Box 222 65 Meredith St., Gore Bay ON P0P 1H0
705-282-3354 705-282-3211

***Grand Bend*: Forrester, Michael G. - *1**
General Delivery 82 Ontario St. South, Grand Bend ON N0M 1T0
519-238-5297 519-238-5234

***Gravenhurst*: Stuart & Cruickshank - *2**
P.O Box 1270 195 Church St., Gravenhurst ON P1P 1V4
705-687-3441 705-687-5405
s.c@bellnet.ca

***Gravenhurst*: Sullivan, Lyle A. - *1**
225 Muskoka Rd. South, Gravenhurst ON P1P 1H6
705-687-2219 705-687-7951
lyleasullivan@bellnet.ca

***Grimsby*: Sinclair, Murakami, Loney & Van Velzen - *2**
55 Main St. East, Grimsby ON L3M 1R3
905-945-9271 905-945-3066 800-363-5073

***Guelph*: Hugh Guthrie Q.C. Professional Corporation - *2**
P.O Box 187 59 Woolwich St., Guelph ON N1H 3V1
519-824-2020 519-824-2023

***Guelph*: Jackman & Rowles - *2**
P.O Box 37 Main17 Cork St. West, Guelph ON N1H 2W9
519-824-4883 519-821-2910
mmjr@on.aibn.com

***Guelph*: Maiocco & DiGravio - *2**
230 Speedvale Ave. West, Guelph ON N1H 1C4
519-836-2710 519-836-7312

***Guelph*: McElderry, Morris - *5**
P.O Box 875 84 Woolwich St., Guelph ON N1H 3T9
519-822-8150 519-822-1921

***Guelph*: Moon Heath LLP - *3**
P.O Box 180 Main164 Norfolk St., Guelph ON N1H 6J9
519-824-2540 519-763-6785
info@moonheath.com
www.moonheath.com

***Guelph*: Nicholson & Doney - *3**
P.O Box 1505 137 Norfolk St., Guelph ON N1H 6N9
519-837-3000 519-837-1758 888-839-1898
ron@nicholsondoney.ca
www.nicholsondoney.ca

***Guelph*: Sorbara, Schumacher, McCann LLP - *18**
457 Woolwish Street, Guelph ON N1H 3X6
519-836-1510 519-836-9215
firm@sorbaralaw.com
www.sorbaralaw.com

***Guelph*: Vorvis, Anderson, Gray, Armstrong LLP - *4**
353 Elizabeth Street, Guelph ON N1H 2X9
519-824-7400 519-824-7521
vaga@vaga.ca
www.vaga.ca

***Hagersville*: Baxter, James R. - *1**
P.O Box 490 19 King St. West, Hagersville ON N0A 1H0
905-768-3363 905-768-1550
jrbaxter@mountaincable.net

***Haliburton*: Selbie, R.G. - *1**
P.O Box 186, Haliburton ON K0M 1S0
705-457-2435 705-457-3074

***Hamilton*: Agro, Zaffiro - *19**
P.O Box 2069 LCD 11 James St. South, Hamilton ON L8N 3G6
905-527-6877 905-527-6843
mail@agrozaffiro.com
www.agrozaffiro.com

***Hamilton*: Barrs, R.B. - *1**
#204, 640 Upper James St., Hamilton ON L9C 2Z2
905-387-9212 905-387-6109

***Hamilton*: Bartolini, Berlingieri, Barrafato; Fortino LLP - *5**
#101, 154 Main St. East, Hamilton ON L8N 1G9
905-577-6833 905-577-6839
lawfirm@bbb-lawyers.on.ca

***Hamilton*: Borkovich, Peter - *1**
46 Jackson St. East, Hamilton ON L8N 1L1
905-527-0990 905-521-1976

***Hamilton*: Brock Howard Bedford - *1**
166 John St. South, Hamilton ON L8N 2C4
905-527-3867 905-527-3860

***Hamilton*: Burns, Vasan & Associates - *6**
#305, 21 King St. West, Hamilton ON L8P 4W9
905-522-1381 905-522-0855
douglasburns@bvlvlaw.ca

***Hamilton*: Chertkoff, Gary, Q.C. - *1**
#412, 20 Jackson St. West, Hamilton ON L8P 1L2
905-522-2439 905-522-9198

***Hamilton*: Clyde Halford - *1**
336 Sanatorium Rd., Hamilton ON L9C 2A4
905-388-0973 905-388-2797

***Hamilton*: Connor, Connor, Guyer & Araiche - *2**
#210, 1104 Fennell Ave. East, Hamilton ON L8T 1R9
905-385-3229 905-385-6182
ccga@mountaincable.net

***Hamilton*: Dudzic, Barristers & Solicitors - *2**
#1014, P.O Box 988 LCD1105 Main St. East, Hamilton ON L8N 3R1
905-528-4251 905-528-5325
dudziclaw@dudziclaw.com

***Hamilton*: Ennis, Paul H. - *1**
#502, 105 Main St. East, Hamilton ON L8N 1G6
905-525-9335 905-525-9988

***Hamilton*: Evans, Philp - *23**
P.O Box 930 A, Hamilton ON L8N 3P9
905-525-1200 905-525-7897
info@evansphilp.com
www.evansphilp.com

***Hamilton*: Foreman Rosenblatt & Lewis - *3**
425 York Blvd., Hamilton ON L8R 3M3
905-525-3570 905-523-0363
ylcinfo@yorklawcentre.com

***Hamilton*: Frankel Law Offices - *1**
#1201, 105 Main St. East, Hamilton ON L8N 1G6
905-522-3972 905-528-2767
stephan@frankelaw.ca

***Hamilton*: Genesee & Clarke - *3**
#2225, 25 Main St. West, Hamilton ON L8P 1H1
905-527-6666 905-522-7085
frank@geneseeclarke.com

***Hamilton*: Gerald Swaye & Associates - *6**
#901, 105 Main St. East, Hamilton ON L8N 1G6
905-524-2861 905-524-2313
gswaye@swaye.ca

***Hamilton*: Gordon, Robbie D. - *1**
P.O Box 490 488 Ferguson Ave., Hamilton ON L8L 4Z5
705-672-3338 705-672-2451

***Hamilton*: Guyatt, Grasznbeek & Millikin - *1**
#401, 20 Jackson St. West, Hamilton ON L8P 1L2
905-528-8369 905-528-8066
keith.millikin@bellnet.ca

***Hamilton*: Harper, Jaskot - *5**
#200, 1 James St. South, Hamilton ON L8P 4R5
905-522-3517 905-522-3555 800-522-3517
www.jaskotfamilylaw.ca

***Hamilton*: Harvey Katz & Associates, Barristers, Solicitors, & Notaries Public - *3**
14 Hess St. South, Hamilton ON L8P 3M8
905-523-1442 905-525-3817
harvey@hjklaw.on.ca
www.hjklaw.on.ca

***Hamilton*: Inch Hammond Professional Corporation - *10**
#1500, 1 King St. West, Hamilton ON L8P 4X8
905-525-4481 905-525-0031
ies@inchlaw.com

***Hamilton*: Jaskula, Sherk - *2**
#915, 135 James St. South, Hamilton ON L8P 2Z6
905-577-1040 905-577-7775
csherk@jaskulasherk.com

***Hamilton*: Katz, H.E. - *1**
15 Bold St., Hamilton ON L8P 1T3

905-522-0040 905-522-2981
call@howardkatzlaw.com

Hamilton: Landeg, Spitale - *2
#806, 20 Hughson St. South, Hamilton ON L8N 2A1
905-529-7462 905-528-6787

Hamilton: Lazier Hickey Langs O'Neal - *10
25 Main St. West, 15th Fl., Hamilton ON L8P 1H1
905-525-3652 905-525-6278
lawfirm@lazierhickey.com
www.lazierhickey.com

Hamilton: Lees & Lees - *1
#2225, 25 Main St. West, Hamilton ON L8P 1H1
905-523-7830 905-523-4677
leeslaw@leesandlees.ca

Hamilton: Malcolm, W.J.I. - *1
#709, 20 Hughson St. South, Hamilton ON L8N 2A1
905-528-4291 905-528-4292

Hamilton: McCusker, Anthony E. - *2
#101, 200 Aberdeen Avenue, Hamilton ON L8P 2P9
905-523-0593 905-522-0988 877-523-3909
mccusker@on.aibn.com

Hamilton: McHugh Mowat Whitmore Ionico MacPherson LLP - *6
337 Queenston Rd., Hamilton ON L8K 1H7
905-549-4676 905-549-5819
www.mmwimlawfirm.ca

Hamilton: McLelland & Dean - *1
1 King St. West, 7th Fl., Hamilton ON L8P 1A4
905-546-0393 905-527-6286

Hamilton: Millar, Alexander - *2
#830, 120 King St. West, Hamilton ON L8P 4V2
905-528-1186

Hamilton: Milligan Gresko Brown Vitulli Limberis LLP, Barristers & Solicitors - *4
#1060, 120 King St. West, Hamilton ON L8P 4V2
905-522-7700 905-528-6543
gjg@mgblawyers.ca
www.mgbvllaw.com

Hamilton: Morwick, E.Y. - *1
97 John St. South, Hamilton ON L8N 2C2
905-529-2343 905-528-0070

Hamilton: Nolan Law Offices - *3
1 King St. West, 7th Fl., Hamilton ON L8P 1A4
905-522-9261 905-525-5836
info@nolanlaw.ca
www.nolalnaw.ca

Hamilton: Olenski, J.Z. - *1
#200, 845 Upper James St., Hamilton ON L9C 3A3
905-387-3922 905-387-0291
johnlenski@netscape.net

Hamilton: Parker, George J. - *1
142 James St. South, Lower Level, Hamilton ON L8P 3A2
905-523-5636 905-523-4910

Hamilton: Pazaratz, A. - *1
117 Hunter St. East, Hamilton ON L8N 1M5
905-523-5850 905-528-0722

Hamilton: Read, Geoffrey M. - *1
172 Main St. East, Hamilton ON L8N 1G9
905-684-3187 905-522-6677

Hamilton: Robinson, McCallum, McKerracher, Graham - *1
#300, 69 John St. South, Hamilton ON L8N 2B9
905-528-1435 905-529-1570
m.graham@on.aibn.com

Hamilton: Ross & McBride - *30
P.O Box 907 LCD11 King St. West, Hamilton ON L8N 3P6
905-526-9800 905-526-0732
www.rossmcbride.com

Hamilton: Ross & McBride LLP - *39
Commerce Place 1 King Street West, 10th floor, Hamilton ON L8N 3P6
905-526-9800 905-526-0732
contact@rossmcbride.com
www.rossmcbride.com

Hamilton: Rubenstein, Michael N. - *1
#200, 242 James St. South, Hamilton ON L8P 3B3

905-525-9636 905-521-0690
smerz@primus.ca

Hamilton: Sapiano, L.I. - *1
#1500, 105 Main St. East, Hamilton ON L8N 1G6
905-523-1665 905-523-4436
lsapiano@gta.igs.net

Hamilton: Scarfone Hawkins LLP - *15
P.O Box 926 Depot 11 James St. South, Hamilton ON L8N 3P9
905-523-1333 905-523-5878
hmartin@shlaw.ca
www.scarfonehawkinsllp.com

Hamilton: Schreiber & Smurlick - *1
1219 Main St. East, Hamilton ON L8K 1A5
905-545-1107

Hamilton: Simpson & Watson - *3
950 King St. West, Hamilton ON L8S 1K8
905-527-1174 905-577-0661
5271174@bellnet.ca

Hamilton: Smith & Smith - *1
1416 King St. East, Hamilton ON L8M 1H8
905-544-6034

Hamilton: Sondola, F.P. - *1
#204, 131 John St. South, Hamilton ON L8N 2C3
905-523-1970 905-523-1971

Hamilton: Steadman, J.J. - *1
124 MacNab St. South, Hamilton ON L8P 3C3
905-529-6400 905-521-1924

Hamilton: Sullivan, Festeryga, Lawlor & Arrell - *17
1 James St. South, 11th Fl., Hamilton ON L8P 4R5
905-528-7963 905-577-0077
general@sullivanfesteryga.com
www.sullivanfesteryga.com

Hamilton: Szpiech, Ellis, Skibinski, Shipton - *4
414 Main St. East, Hamilton ON L8N 1J9
905-524-2454 905-523-1733
sess@on.aibn.com

Hamilton: Tharen, Edward - *1
1243 Barton St. East, Hamilton ON L8H 2V8
905-547-1618 905-549-5654

Hamilton: Thoman Soule LLP, Lawyers - *6
P.O Box 187 LCD 146 Jackson St. East, Hamilton ON L8N 3C5
905-529-8195 905-529-7906
info@thomansoule.com
www.thomansoule.com

Hamilton: Tkach & Tokiwa - *1
#71, Mountain Plaza Mall 651 Upper James St., Hamilton ON L9C 5R8
905-383-3545 905-574-3020
tkachlaw@mountaincable.net

Hamilton: Wasserman & Associates - *1
#6, 105 Main St. East, Hamilton ON L8N 1G6
905-522-4242 905-521-0052

Hamilton: Weisz, Rocchi & Scholes - *6
#200, Effort Trust Bldg. 242 Main St. East, Hamilton ON L8N 1H5
905-523-1842 905-528-9254
tweisz@wrs.on.ca
www.wrs.on.ca

Hamilton: White, Nicholas - *1
120 Jackson St. East, Hamilton ON L8N 1L3
905-521-8901 905-521-9564
nwhite@netaccess.on.ca

Hamilton: Yachetti, Lanza & Restivo - *6
#100, 154 Main St. East, Hamilton ON L8N 1G9
905-528-7534 905-528-5275
info@ylrlawyers.com
www.ylrlawyers.com

Hanover: Duffy, Kenneth P. - *1
414 - 10 St., Hanover ON N4N 1P6
519-364-1440 519-364-6023
kduffy@wightman.ca

Hanover: Garcia, Robert W. - *2
P.O Box 37, Hanover ON N4N 3C3
519-364-3643 519-364-6594
rgarcia@garcia-law.com

Harrow: Melinz, Karl G. - *1
P.O Box 880 41A Centre St. West, Harrow ON N0R 1G0
519-738-2232 519-738-9080
kgmelinz@msni.net

Hawkesbury: Gerald E.Langlois & Associates - *2
471 McGill St., Hawkesbury ON K6A 1R1
613-632-8600 613-632-5274
langlois@hawk.igs.net

Hawkesbury: Julien & Cormier Professional Corporation - *2
132 Race St., Hawkesbury ON K6A 1V2
613-632-0148 613-632-1810

Hawkesbury: Pilon Professional Corporation - *1
280 Main St. West, Hawkesbury ON K6A 2H7
613-632-0103 613-632-2800
pilons@bellnet.ca

Hawkesbury: Woods Parisien - *2
#200, 115 Main St. East, Hawkesbury ON K6A 1A1
613-632-8557 613-632-8559
parisien@on.aibn.com

Hillsburgh: Harper, Robert P. - *1
P.O Box 10 115 Main St., Hillsburgh ON N0B 1Z0
519-855-4961 519-855-4029
robertharper@bellnet.ca

Huntsville: Anderson, James S.
#5, 133 Hwy. 60, Huntsville ON P1H 1C2
705-789-8823 705-789-1272
jamesanderson@sympatico.ca

Huntsville: Cochran, A.B. - *1
#5, 133 Hwy. 60, Huntsville ON P1H 1C2
705-789-5538 705-789-1272
acochran@vianet.ca

Huntsville: Smith, G.A. - *1
#1, 3 Fairy Ave., Huntsville ON P1H 1G7
705-789-8829 705-789-2984
glensmith@bellnet.ca

Ingersoll: Nesbitt Coulter LLP - *1
183 Thames St. South, Ingersoll ON N5C 2T6
519-485-5651 519-485-6582
mborndahl@nesbittlaw.com

Innisfil: Gibson & Adams LLP - *4
8000 Yonge St., Innisfil ON L9S 1L5
705-436-1701 705-436-1710
ganda@gibsonandadams.ca

Iroquois Falls: Alexander, J. Kenneth - *1
P.O Box 290 A283 Main St., Iroquois Falls ON P0K 1G0
705-232-4309 705-232-5274

Iroquois Falls: McGrath, Susan T. - *1
P.O Box 700, Iroquois Falls ON P0K 1G0
705-232-4055 705-232-6301
mcgrath@nt.net

Jarvis: Kelly, W.E. - *1
P.O Box 430 32 Main St. North, Jarvis ON N0A 1J0
519-587-4561 519-587-5052

Kapuskasing: Bourgeault Brunelle Dumais Boucher - *4
P.O Box 446 7 Cain Ave., Kapuskasing ON P5N 1S8
705-335-6121 705-335-8127

Kapuskasing: Wainwright, Guy A. - *1
19 Cain Ave., Kapuskasing ON P5N 1T2
705-335-8501 705-337-1474
gwainrt@ntl.sympatico.ca

Kenora: Carten Law Office - *2
#201, P.O Box 2050 Main344 Second St. South, Kenora ON P9N 3X8
807-468-3036 807-468-7576
cartenlaw@gokenora.com

Kenora: Elliott, David James - *1
Stone House 225 Main St. South, Kenora ON P9N 1T3
807-468-3355 807-468-7858

Kenora: Gibson & Wexler - *2
P.O Box 2450 111 Main St. South, Kenora ON P9N 3X8
807-468-3061 807-468-7940

Kenora: Hook, Seller & Lundin - *4
#204, Bannister Centre 301 - 1 Ave. South, Kenora ON P9N 1W2

807-468-9831 807-468-8384
jthook@hsllawyers.com
www.hsllawyers.com

Kenora: Shewchuk, MacDonell, Ormiston, Richardt & Fregeau LLP - *6
P.O Box 1970 214 Main St. South, Kenora ON P9N 1T2
807-468-9828 807-468-5504
www.kenoralaw.com

Keswick: Pollock, R.E. - *1
#300, 449 The Queensway South, Keswick ON L4P 2C9
905-476-0021 905-476-0134

Kincardine: Mahood, Graham E. Professional Corporation - *2
313 Lambton St., Kincardine ON N2Z 2Y8
519-396-8144 519-396-9446
mahood&darcy@tnt2.com

Kincardine: Mathers, William S. - *1
226 Queen St., Kincardine ON N2Z 2S5
519-396-4147 519-396-1872
wwmlawyer@bmts.com

Kingston: Bishop, Wm. J.F. - *2
P.O Box 1403 338 Montreal St., Kingston ON K7L 5C6
613-544-0644 613-544-2197
bill.bishop@on.aibn.com

Kingston: Black, Lloyd, Caron - *2
P.O Box 247 249 Brock St., Kingston ON K7L 4V8
613-546-3286 613-549-1193
blcm@adan.kingston.net

Kingston: Caldwell & Moore - *2
260 Barrie St., Kingston ON K7L 3K7
613-545-1860 613-545-1862
caldwell-moore@cogeco.ca

Kingston: Cooper, Robert K. - *1
11 Carruthers St., Kingston ON K7L 1L9
613-544-3634

Kingston: Cunningham, Swan, Carty, Little & Bonham LLP - *18
#201, City Place II 1473 John Counter Blvd., Kingston ON K7M 8Z6
613-544-0211 613-542-9814
info@cswan.com
www.cswan.com

Kingston: Gale, John R. - *1
238 Wellington St., 1st Fl., Kingston ON K7K 2Y8
613-546-4283 613-546-9861
info@galeforlaw.ca
www.galeforlaw.ca

Kingston: Gay, Wayne C., & Associate - *2
P.O Box 370 Main275 Ontario St., Kingston ON K7L 4W2
613-549-4300 613-549-6948
waynegay@waynegay.com

Kingston: Good & Elliott Hawkins LLP - *3
P.O Box 1253 Main153 Brock St., Kingston ON K7L 4Y8
613-544-1330 613-547-4538

Kingston: Headrick, Wayne R.J. - *1
1770 Bath Rd., Kingston ON K7M 4Y2
613-384-4403 613-384-7056
wheadrik@kos.net

Kingston: Hickey & Hickey - *2
P.O Box 110 93 Clarence St., Kingston ON K7L 4V6
613-548-3191 613-548-8195
hickeym@on.aibn.com

Kingston: Higgs, Mary Ann - *1
#206, P.O Box 700 275 Ontario St., Kingston ON K7L 4X1
613-548-7399 613-548-1862
maryannhiggs@on.aibn.com

Kingston: Jacob Macpherson Menard - *2
#102, 780 Midpark Dr., Kingston ON K7M 7P6
613-389-1999 613-384-8777
macpherson@kingston-lawyers.ca

Kingston: McCue, M.A. - *1
#201A, 837 Princess St., Kingston ON K7L 1G8
613-542-3700 613-542-5700
mamccue@kingston.net

Kingston: McDiarmid, G.Y. - *1
P.O Box 1010 Main3 Rideau St., Kingston ON K7L 4X8
613-546-3274 613-546-1493
gmcdiarmid@on.aibn.com

Kingston: Morley Law Office - *1
211 Division St., Kingston ON K7K 3Z2
613-542-2192 613-542-2393
info@lesmorley.com
www.lesmorley.com

Kingston: O'Connor, Fergus J. (Chip) - *1
P.O Box 1959 104 Johnson St., Kingston ON K7L 5J7
613-546-5581 613-546-5540
oconnor@kos.net

Kingston: Slack, Douglas M. - *1
#1, 817 Blackburn Mews, Kingston ON K7P 2N6
613-384-7260 613-384-7262
dm.slack@utoronto.ca

Kingston: Steele, Letitia M. - *1
P.O Box 29013 Portsmouth, Kingston ON K7M 8W6
613-542-1795 613-542-2471

Kingston: Tepper Law Office - *1
P.O Box 1265 Main461 Princess St., Kingston ON K7L 4Y8
613-546-1169 613-546-6992
gtepper@kingston.net

Kingston: Thomson, A.G. - *1
232 Brock St., Kingston ON K7L 1S4
613-549-5111 613-549-4074
thomson@kingston.net

Kingston: Troughton, Thomas W. - *1
#103, P.O Box 668 Main780 Midpark Dr., Kingston ON K7L 4X1
613-634-0302 613-384-8777
troughton@frontenaclaw.on.ca

Kingston: Trousdale & Trousdale - *2
#200, 184 Wellington St., Kingston ON K7L 3E4
613-546-2231 613-546-9001

Kingsville: Dunnion & Dunmore - *1
59 Main St. East, Kingsville ON N9Y 1A1
519-733-6573 519-733-3172
pdunmore@cogeco.net

Kirkland Lake: Munn, Judith L. - *1
P.O Box 970 11 Station Rd. South, Kirkland Lake ON P2N 3L2
705-567-9224 705-567-9227
judmunn@ntl.aibn.com

Kirkland Lake: Shorrock, G. - *1
P.O Box 490, Kirkland Lake ON P2N 3J5
705-567-5213 705-567-3987
shorlaw@ntl.sympatico.ca

Kitchener: Amos, G.C. - *1
276 Frederick St., Kitchener ON N2H 2N4
519-576-8480 519-579-3042

Kitchener: Babcock, Derek K. - *1
28 Weber St. West, Kitchener ON N2H 3Z2
519-742-3570 519-576-7451
dbabcock@on.aibn.com

Kitchener: Chris Lawyers - *1
194 Weber St. East, Kitchener ON N2H 1E4
519-570-4400 519-570-4242 888-570-9697
contactus@chrislawyers.com
www.chrislawyers.com

Kitchener: Coffey, J. Mark - *1
#705, Corporation Square 30 Duke St. West, Kitchener ON N2H 3W5
519-742-5100 519-742-5229

Kitchener: Cox, H.J. - *1
#610, 50 Queen St. North, Kitchener ON N2H 6P4
519-744-6551 519-744-9885
hjcox@golden.net

Kitchener: Crawford, N.A. - *1
1444 King St. East, Kitchener ON N2G 2N7
519-743-3615 519-743-2212

Kitchener: Dietrich Law Office - *2
141 Duke St. East, Kitchener ON N2H 1A6
519-749-0770 519-749-0288
george.deitrich@sympatico.ca

Kitchener: Giffen LLP - *12
#500, Commerce House P.O Box 2396 50 Queen St. North, Kitchener ON N2H 6M3
519-578-4150 519-578-8740 866-688-4150
info@giffenlawyers.com
www.giffenlawyers.com

Kitchener: Haalboom, R. Q.C. - *1
7 Duke St. West, Kitchener ON N2H 6N7
519-579-2920 519-576-0471
richard@haalboom.ca

Kitchener: Hare, R.J. - *1
741 King St. West, Kitchener ON N2G 1E3
519-576-6710

Kitchener: Hertzberger & Associates, Barristers & Solicitors - *2
Penthouse, Corporation Square 30 Duke St. West, Kitchener ON N2H 3W5
519-570-1944 519-570-0989
reception@hertzbergerlaw.com
www.hertzbergerlaw.com

Kitchener: Kay Professional Corporation - *4
177 Victoria St. North, Kitchener ON N2H 5C5
519-579-1220 519-743-8063
law@kaylaw.ca
www.kaylaw.ca

Kitchener: Kelly & Co. - *3
#903, 50 Queen St. North, Kitchener ON N2H 6P4
519-579-3360 519-579-2556
bkelly@kellylaw.com
www.kellylaw.com

Kitchener: Kosky, Sheldon - *1
71 Weber St. East, Kitchener ON N2H 1C6
519-578-1480 519-579-2537

Kitchener: Lawrence, R.G.R., Q.C. - *1
18 Irvin St., Kitchener ON N2H 1K8
519-742-4443 519-578-4201

Kitchener: Ludwig, Lichtenheldt & Eby - *3
P.O Box 1463 C97 Frederick St., Kitchener ON N2G 4H6
519-579-3000 519-579-5660

Kitchener: Madorin, Snyder LLP - *18
P.O Box 1234 C55 King St. West, Kitchener ON N2G 4G9
519-744-4491 519-741-8060
reception@kw-law.com
www.kw-law.com

Kitchener: Mollison, McCormick - *6
P.O Box 2307 B71 Weber St. East, Kitchener ON N2H 6L2
519-579-1040 519-579-2537
mmollison@mollisonlaw.com

Kitchener: Roetsch & Schaffer - *2
284 Frederick St., Kitchener ON N2H 2N4
519-576-5310 519-576-2797

Kitchener: Shannon, John D. E. - *1
30 Spetz St., Kitchener ON N2H 1K1
519-743-3654 519-578-9521
jdeslaw@bellnet.ca

Kitchener: Smith, Hunt, Buck - *2
P.O Box 2008 C, Kitchener ON N2H 6L1
519-579-3400 519-741-9041
office@smithhuntbuck.com

Kitchener: Smyth, Hobson - *1
#206, 7 Duke St. West, Kitchener ON N2H 6N7
519-578-9400 519-578-7482

Kitchener: Tummillo-Goy, Teresa - *1
228 Frederick St., Kitchener ON N2H 2M8
519-888-9440 519-888-9750
teresa@ttglaw.ca

Kitchener: Voll & Santos - *2
30 Spetz St., Kitchener ON N2H 1K1
519-578-3400 519-578-9521

Kitchener: Walters Gubler - *2
#604, 30 Duke St. West, Kitchener ON N2H 3W5
519-578-8010 519-578-9395
inquiries@wglaw.org

Kitchener: Zalman, W.R. - *1
#102, 684 Belmont Ave. West, Kitchener ON N2M 1N6
519-579-6170 519-579-6171

Kleinburg: Black & Associates - *3
#1, 10472 Islington Ave., Kleinburg ON L0J 1C0
905-939-8050 905-939-8025
blackm@bellnet.ca
www.blackandassociates.ca

Lakefield: Baker & Cole - *2
8 Bridge St., Lakefield ON K0L 2H0

705-652-8161 705-652-7088
thomas.cole@nexicom.net

Lakefield: Booth, G.A. - *1
P.O Box 116 34 Bridge St., Lakefield ON K0L 2H0
705-652-3378 705-652-6823
gary@boothlawoffice.org

Lancaster: Syrduk, Paul D. - *1
P.O Box 9 10 Oak St., Lancaster ON K0C 1N0
613-347-2423 613-347-7118
syruduk@glen-net.ca

Leamington: Owen Spettigue Professional Corporation - *1
P.O Box 327 57 Talbot St. East, Leamington ON N8H 3W3
519-326-2687 519-326-1344
cowenspettiguelaw@bellnet.ca

Leamington: Reid, Collins, Ricci, Enns & Rollier - *5
60 Talbot St. West, Leamington ON N8H 1M4
519-326-3237 519-326-8139
rrcre@mnsi.net

Lindsay: Cornell, Mortlock & Sillberg - *1
P.O Box 536 Main272 Kent St. West, Lindsay ON K9V 4S5
705-324-4312 705-324-7525

Lindsay: Evans, J.W. - *1
P.O Box 427 Main219 Kent St. West, Lindsay ON K9V 4S5
705-324-3207 705-328-1128

Lindsay: Frost, Frost & Gorwill - *1
#217, 189 Kent St. West, Lindsay ON K9V 5G6
705-324-2193 705-324-9879

Lindsay: McLeod, J. Scott - *1
#7, 1 William St. South, Lindsay ON K9V 3A3
705-324-6711 705-324-5723

Lindsay: Scott & Scott - *1
#219, P.O Box 660 189 Kent St. West, Lindsay ON K9V 4S5
705-324-5181 705-324-8077

Listowel: Pratt & Pratt - *1
P.O Box 10 280 Inkerman St. West, Listowel ON N4W 3H2
519-291-3612 519-291-3613
dwpratt@prattlawoffice.ca

London: Ambrogio & Ambrogio - *2
#611, 200 Queens Ave., London ON N6A 1J3
519-438-7219 519-438-5919

London: Arvai, Karl Professional Corp. - *4
#1508, 140 Fullarton St., London ON N6A 5P2
519-672-0911 519-642-1272
k.arvai@karlarvai.com

London: Bangarth, Daniel S.J. - *1
#209, 1069 Wellington Rd. South, London ON N6E 2H6
519-472-2340 519-657-8173
darlene.howard@sympatico.ca

London: Bates Law Office - *1
#1, 151 Pine Valley Blvd., London ON N6K 3T6
519-472-0330 519-472-1814
tabates@rogers.com

London: Beechie, Madison, Sawchuk LLP - *3
439 Waterloo St., London ON N6B 2P1
519-673-1070 519-439-4363

London: Behr Law Firm - *3
#1105, 383 Richmond St., London ON N6M 3C4
519-438-4530 519-679-6576

London: Belanger, Cassino, Coulston & Gallagher - *4
#153, 759 Hyde Park Rd., London ON N6H 3S2
519-472-6310 519-657-5189

London: Belch, G.P.
P.O Box 5035 B300 Dufferin Ave., London ON N6A 4L9
519-661-4708 519-661-5530
gbelch@london.ca

London: Belecky & Belecky - *2
95 Dufferin Ave., London ON N6A 1K3
519-673-5630 519-667-4836
aj@belecky.ca; jf@belecky.ca

London: Brown, Beattie, O'Donovan LLP - *24
City Centre Tower 380 Wellington St., 16th Fl., London ON N6A 5B5
519-679-0400 519-679-6350
bboinfo@bbo.on.ca
www.bbo.on.ca

London: Burgard Q.C., Mervin F. - *1
#203, 219 Oxford St. West, London ON N6H 1S5
519-679-9900 519-679-8546

London: Campbell M. Dockstader - *1
36 Chapple Hill Rd., London ON N6G 2H3
519-657-4080 519-657-2516

London: Circelli, Luigi E. - *1
557 Talbot St., London ON N6A 2S9
519-673-1850 519-673-4966
lcircelli@bellnet.ca

London: Cohen Highley LLP - *22
One London Pl. 255 Queens Ave., 11th Fl., London ON N6A 5R8
519-672-9330 519-672-5960
hall@cohenhighley.com
www.cohenhighley.com

London: Cram & Associates - *6
#514, 200 Queens Ave., London ON N6A 1J3
519-673-1670 519-439-5011
pbosch@cramassociates.com

London: Dewar, William L. - *1
479 Talbot St., London ON N6A 2S4
519-672-1830 519-661-0095
wildew@on.aibn.com

London: Dickie, Ronald W. - *1
#3237, 450 Talbot St., London ON N6A 4K3
519-679-9660 519-667-3362
rwdickielaw@on.aibn.com

London: Duggan, Kenneth - *1
#203, 111 Waterloo St., London ON N6B 2M4
519-672-5360 519-433-6975
kvduggan@bellnet.ca

London: Foster, Townsend, Graham & Associates - *15
551 Waterloo St., London ON N6B 2R1
519-672-5272 519-672-9313 888-354-0448
firm@ftgalaw.com
www.ftgalaw.com

London: Frauts, Dobbie - *3
585 Talbot St., London ON N6A 2T2
519-679-4000 519-679-7700
info@frautsdobbie.ca

London: Fryday, Murphy, Brown - *2
#201, 145 Wharncliffe Rd. South, London ON N6J 2K4
519-679-8800 519-673-3632
kfryday@londonlawyers.com

London: Giffen & Partners - *4
465 Waterloo St., London ON N6B 2P4
519-679-4700 519-432-8003
office@giffens.com

London: Harding, J.G. - *1
635 Wellington St., London ON N6A 3R8
519-439-0641 519-439-0643
j.harding@bmts.com

London: Harrison Pensa LLP - *51
P.O Box 3237 450 Talbot St., London ON N6A 4K3
519-679-9660 519-667-3362
info@harrisonpensa.com
www.harrisonpensa.com

London: Lepine, Paul F. - *1
570 Queens Ave., London ON N6B 1Y8
519-432-4155 519-432-6861
pflepine@mnsi.net

London: Lerners LLP - *64
P.O Box 2335 80 Dufferin Ave., London ON N6A 4G4
519-672-4510 519-672-2044
lerner.london@lerners.ca
www.lerners.ca

London: Libis, V. - *1
93 Dufferin Ave., London ON N6A 1K3
519-434-6821 519-434-9515
valdis.libis@odyssey.on.ca

London: Lisowski, John R. - *1
607 Queens Ave., London ON N6B 1Y9
519-679-5000 519-673-1717

London: Little & Jarrett - *5
P.O Box 2757 412 King St., London ON N6A 4H4
519-672-8121 519-432-0784

London: MacKewn, Winder, Kirwin LLP - *4
#300, 376 Richmond St., London ON N6A 3C7
519-672-2040 519-672-6583
mwk@mwk.on.ca

London: Mann, Edward J. - *1
#605, 137 Dundas St., London ON N6A 1E9
519-672-8707 519-660-4678
ejmann@on.aibn.com

London: McKenzie Lake Lawyers LLP - *35
300 Dundas St., London ON N6B 1T6
519-672-5666 519-672-2674
info@mckenzielake.com
www.mckenzielake.com

London: McNamara, Pizzale - *3
#220, 200 Queens Ave., London ON N6A 1J3
519-434-2174 519-642-7654
mcpizz@execulink.com

London: Menear Worrad & Associates - *7
100 Fullarton St., London ON N6A 1K1
519-672-7370 519-663-1165
mmenear@menearlaw.com

London: Morris, Brian K. - *1
#36, 14 Cadeau Terrace, London ON N6K 4X5
519-461-4684
brian.morris@sympatico.ca

London: Morrow, Armand - *1
42 Hampton Cres., London ON N6H 2N8
519-471-7607 519-471-9121

London: Mueller, Frederick A. - *1
141 Wortley Rd., London ON N6C 3P4
519-673-1300 519-673-1728
fred_mueller@rogers.com

London: Nelligan, Barry F. - *1
#202, 145 Wharncliffe Rd. South, London ON N6J 2K4
519-438-1709 519-438-1700

London: O'Donnell, James R. - *1
#16, 440 Wellington St., London ON N6A 3P2
519-673-0600 519-439-3468
james@jamesodonnell.ca

London: Patton Cormier & Associates - *4
#1512, 140 Fullarton St., London ON N6A 5P2
519-432-8282 519-432-7285
apatton@pattoncormier.ca

London: Robertson, S. Michael - *1
#105, 186 Albert St., London ON N6A 1M1
519-660-1147 519-660-0840
smrobertson.lawyer@bellnet.ca

London: Siskind, Cromarty, Ivey & Dowler LLP - *65
P.O Box 2520 680 Waterloo St., London ON N6A 3V8
519-672-2121 519-672-6065 877-672-2121
info@siskinds.com
www.siskinds.com

London: Stambler & Mills - *1
#1511, 148 Fullarton St., London ON N6A 5P3
519-672-6240 519-433-9593

London: Thomas, L. Kent - *1
11 Stanley St., London ON N6C 1A9
519-438-4181 519-433-5557

London: Thomson Mahoney Dobson Delorey - *6
#200, 145 Wharncliffe Rd., London ON N6J 2K4
519-673-1151 519-673-3632
tmdd@londonlawyers.com

London: Underhill Joles - *1
607 Princess Ave., London ON N6B 2C1
519-432-4644 519-438-3936

London: Valassis, Despina S. - *1
579 Talbot St., London ON N6A 2T2
519-439-2768

London: Walker & Wood - *1
60 Barons Ct., London ON N6C 5J3
519-672-3500 519-672-2420
walkerwood@rogers.com

***Manotick*: Wilson Law Partners LLP - *3**
P.O Box 429 5542 Main St., Manotick ON K4M 1A4
613-692-3547 613-692-0826
andrew@wilsonlawpartners.com
www.wilsonlawpartners.com

***Maple*: Newman, M.D. - *1**
62 Lancer Dr., Maple ON L6A 1C9
905-832-5602 905-832-5446
mdnewman@rogers.com

***Markdale*: Dunlop, Johnson & Pust - *2**
P.O Box 433 21 Main St. East, Markdale ON N0C 1H0
519-986-2100 519-986-2904
johnslaw@on.aibn.com; pustlaw@on.aibn.com

***Markdale*: Harris, Willis - *1**
P.O Box 466 45 Main St. West, Markdale ON N0C 1H0
519-900-2740 519-986-4205
ewillis@bmts.com

***Markham*: Bongard, Marvin B. - *1**
P.O Box 509 10 Washington St., Markham ON L3P 3R2
905-294-7555 905-294-8360
marvin@mbongard.com

***Markham*: Burstein & Greenglass LLP - *4**
#200, Royal Bank Bldg. 7481 Woodbine Ave., Markham ON L3R 2W1
905-475-1266 905-475-7851
office@bglaw.ca

***Markham*: Cattanach Hindson Sutton VanVeldhuizen - *7**
52 Main St. North, Markham ON L3P 1X5
905-294-0666 905-294-5688

***Markham*: Dicker, Ernest, Q.C. - *1**
10 Fairway Heights Cres., Markham ON L3T 1K2
905-889-5556 905-889-3306

***Markham*: Gangbar, Sydney, Q.C. - *1**
#303, 80 Tiverton Ct., Markham ON L3R 0G4
905-470-0272 905-470-8365
sydneygangbar@rogers.com

***Markham*: Garbe, E. Alan - *1**
7507 Kennedy Rd., Markham ON L3R 0L8
905-415-9100 905-479-3625
eagarbe@garbe-law.com

***Markham*: Jozefacki, Fielding - *2**
#200, 4961 Hwy. 7 East, Markham ON L3R 1N1
905-940-3141 905-940-3139
jozefackilaw@hotmail.com

***Markham*: Kaufman, Barry M. - *1**
#308, 3950 - 14th Ave., Markham ON L3R 0A9
905-477-8848 905-477-8489
barrykaufman@rogers.com

***Markham*: Luftspring, Alan J. - *1**
#236, 7181 Woodbine Ave., Markham ON L3R 1A3
905-479-1200 905-479-9769
alanluftspring@rogers.com
www.gtalawyer.com

***Markham*: Matthews, Irene L. - *1**
#104, 7225 Woodbine Ave., Markham ON L3R 1A3
905-475-9716 905-475-9142

***Markham*: Mingay & Vereshchak - *3**
81 Main St. North, Markham ON L3P 1X7
905-294-0550 905-294-9141
info@mvlaw.net

***Markham*: Moad, G. Arthur - *1**
#206, 5762 Hwy. 7, Markham ON L3P 1A8
905-294-6446 905-294-4436
gamoad@on.aibn.com

***Markham*: Parnes, R. - *1**
Markham Industrial Park P.O Box 3249 4701 Hwy. 7., Markham ON L3R 6G6
905-477-5151 905-477-6778

***Markham*: Rotenberg, Theodore B. - *1**
#303, 80 Tiverton Ct., Markham ON L3R 0G4
905-479-3331 905-479-5017
general@rogerlaw.com

***Markham*: Seltzer, Barry - *1**
#205, 80 Tiverton Ct., Markham ON L3R 0G4
905-475-9001 905-475-9004
barry@barryseltzer.com

***Markham*: Smith, Paul F. - *1**
#202, 5762 Hwy. 7, Markham ON L3P 1A8
905-294-9955 905-294-4004

***Markham*: Sokolsky, A. Melvin - *1**
#3, 200 Riviera Dr., Markham ON L3R 5M1
905-944-9427 905-479-7025

***Markham*: Solomon, E. Bruce - *1**
7507 Kennedy Rd., Markham ON L3R 0L8
905-479-1900 905-479-9793
ebs@markhamlaw.ca

***Markham*: Starzynski, D.M., Q.C. - *1**
#205, 16th Ave. Shopping Centre 9275 Hwy. 48 North, Markham ON L6E 1A3
905-294-3891 905-471-2550 877-411-0902
starzynski@sympatico.ca

***Markham*: Thomas & Pelman**
4701 Hwy. 7 East, Markham ON L3R 1M7
905-477-2233 905-477-7668
thomasandpelman@thomasandpelman.com

***Markham*: Zwicker, Jack - *1**
#306, 7100 Woodbine Ave., Markham ON L3R 5J2
905-470-2544 905-470-2571
jackzwicker@rogers.com

***Marmora*: Philpot, A.L. - *1**
P.O Box 430 65 Forsyth St., Marmora ON K0K 2M0
613-472-2245 613-472-3310
bcomeau@countrylawyer.on.ca
www.countrylawyer.on.ca

***Meaford*: Kopperud Hamilton - *1**
76 Sykes St. North, Meaford ON N4L 1R2
519-538-2044 519-538-5323 877-593-1938
kopperudlaw@bmts.com
www.bluemountainlawyers.com

***Meaford*: Scheifele, Erskine & Renken - *4**
P.O Box 3395 39 Nelson St. West, Meaford ON N4L 1A5
519-538-2510 519-538-1843
info@meafordlawyers.com

***Midland*: Deacon Taws - *2**
P.O Box 247 476 Elizabeth St., Midland ON L4R 4K8
705-526-3791 705-526-2688
admin@deacontaws.com
www.deacontaws.com

***Midland*: Hacker Gignac Rice - *16**
518 Yonge St., Midland ON L4R 2C5
705-526-2231 705-526-0313 800-205-4052
hgr@hgr.ca
www.hgr.ca

***Midland*: Prost Associates - *2**
P.O Box 96 323 Midland Ave., Midland ON L4R 4K6
705-526-9328 705-526-1209
prostlaw@bellnet.ca

***Midland*: Warren, Wanda L. - *2**
512 Dominion Ave., Midland ON L4R 1P8
705-528-1665 705-526-3238 800-838-8706

***Milton*: Hutchinson, Thompson, Henderson & Mott - *2**
264 Main St., Milton ON L9T 1P2
905-878-2841 905-878-3937
lawoffice@lawmilton.com

***Milton*: Malcolm, D.I. - *1**
6439 Hwy. 25 South, RR#1, Milton ON L9T 2X5
905-876-3033 905-876-3448

***Milverton*: Kenny, W. Stirling Law Office - *1**
11 Main St. North, Milverton ON N0K 1M0
519-595-8171 519-271-7397

***Mississauga*: Bannon, J. Paul - *2**
#360, 33 City Centre Dr., Mississauga ON L5B 2N5
905-272-3412

***Mississauga*: Bartels, N. - *1**
#304, 470 Hensall Circle, Mississauga ON L5A 1X7
905-276-8286

***Mississauga*: Bennett, Richard T. - *2**
82 Queen St. South., Mississauga ON L5M 1K6
905-826-1453 905-826-7185
richardbennett@sprint.ca

***Mississauga*: Bhattacharya, Eugene J. - *1**
295 Matheson Blvd. East, Mississauga ON L4Z 1X8
905-507-3796 905-507-6011

***Mississauga*: Bukovac, Michael J. - *1**
1325 Burnhamthorpe Rd. East, Mississauga ON L4Y 3V8
905-238-1411 905-629-9277
michaelbukovac@on.aibn.com

***Mississauga*: Burych Lawyers - *3**
#204, 89 Queensway West, Mississauga ON L5B 2V2
905-896-8600 905-896-9757
burychlawyers@bellnet.ca

***Mississauga*: Carey, Thomas - *1**
1325 Burnhamthorpe Rd. East, Mississauga ON L4Y 3V8
905-624-1149 905-624-0522
tomcarey@bellnet.ca

***Mississauga*: Chojnacki, Richard C. - *1**
#301, 29 Tannery St., Mississauga ON L5N 1V1
905-821-3644 905-821-8355

***Mississauga*: David, Arthur H. - *1**
#6 & #12, 2145 Dunwin Dr., Mississauga ON L5L 4L9
905-828-2300 905-828-4602
a.david@bellnet.ca

***Mississauga*: Davidson, Douglas M. - *1**
#200, 1552 Dundas St. West, Mississauga ON L5C 1E4
905-279-3330 905-279-2735

***Mississauga*: Day, Michael J. - *1**
93 Queen St. South, Mississauga ON L5M 1K7
905-826-5670 905-826-5673
mday@michaeljday.com

***Mississauga*: Eades Law Office - *1**
7229 Pacific Circle, Mississauga ON L5T 1S9
905-795-4040 905-564-2315

***Mississauga*: Fellman, Richard Alan - *1**
#100, 46 Village Centre Pl., Mississauga ON L4Z 1V9
905-275-2231 905-275-8323
rfellman@on.aibn.com

***Mississauga*: Fram, David A. - *1**
810 Meadow Wood Road, Mississauga ON L5J 2S6
905-916-0130 905-916-1600
david@davidfram.com
www.davidfram.com

***Mississauga*: Garvey & Garvey LLP - *3**
972 Clarkson Rd. South, Mississauga ON L5J 2V7
905-823-4400 905-823-5153

***Mississauga*: Ghalioungui, J.M.P. - *1**
#11, 4040 Creditview Rd.., Mississauga ON L5C 3Y8
905-820-4442 905-820-4442

***Mississauga*: Gora, John L.Z. - *1**
893 Beechwood Ave., Mississauga ON L5G 4E3
905-278-7678 905-271-5568

***Mississauga*: Kain & Ball - *3**
#240, 1900 Dundas St. West, Mississauga ON L5K 1P9
905-855-4888 905-855-3760
kainandball@on.aibn.com

***Mississauga*: Keller, Julian B. - *1**
#301, 25 Watline Ave., Mississauga ON L4Z 2Z1
905-890-2211 905-890-2246
juliankeller@rogers.com

***Mississauga*: Kerba, Sami N. - *1**
1093 Lakeshore Rd. East, Mississauga ON L5E 1E8
905-274-6073 905-274-9876
samikerba@nskerba.com

***Mississauga*: Keyser Mason Ball LLP, Barristers & Solicitors - *24**
#1600, 4 Robert Speck Pkwy., Mississauga ON L4Z 1S1
905-276-9111 905-276-2298
kmb@kmblaw.com
www.kmblaw.com

***Mississauga*: Klein Law, Barristers, Mediators, Notaries - *3**
#38, 1100 Central Pkwy. West, Mississauga ON L5C 4E5
905-272-2540 905-272-2100
contact@kleinlaw.ca
www.kleinlaw.ca

***Mississauga*: Kostyniuk & Bruggeman - *3**
#213, 1515 Matheson Blvd. East, Mississauga ON L4W 2P5
905-602-5551 905-602-9775
rkostyniuk@rogers.com

Mississauga: Malicki & Malicki - *1
3020 Kirwin Ave., Mississauga ON L5A 2K6
905-279-6250 905-279-3878
marek@malicki.ca

Mississauga: Marks & Ciraco - *2
#303, 4310 Sherwoodtowne Blvd., Mississauga ON L4Z 4C4
905-712-8300 905-712-8559
www.marksandciraco.com

Mississauga: McIntyre, Robert D., Q.C. - *1
#410, 30 Eglinton Ave. West, Mississauga ON L5B 3E7
905-366-9700 905-366-9707
rdm@ontlaw.com
www.ontlaw.com

Mississauga: Nathwani, D.M. - *1
#129, 1250 Mississauga Valley Blvd., Mississauga ON L5A 3R6
905-273-7887

Mississauga: Newbury, R. Geoffrey - *1
#106, 150 Lakeshore Rd. West, Mississauga ON L5H 3R2
905-271-9600 905-271-1638
newbury@mandamus.org

Mississauga: Osmak, O.J. - *1
#126, Central Parkway Mall 377 Burnhamthorpe Rd. East, Mississauga ON L5A 3Y1
905-277-0229 905-277-4966
osmak@on.aibn.com

Mississauga: Ovenden & Ovenden - *2
#204, 130 Dundas St. East, Mississauga ON L5A 3V8
905-270-8544 905-273-7386

Mississauga: Pallett Valo LLP - *27
#1600, 90 Burnhamthorpe Rd. West, Mississauga ON L5B 3C3
905-273-3300 905-273-6920 800-323-3781
marketing@pallettvalo.com
www.pallettvalo.com

Mississauga: Plener, Larry R. - *1
2564 Confederation Pkwy., Mississauga ON L5B 1S2
905-897-8611 905-897-8807
lplener@sympatico.ca

Mississauga: Polla, F. - *1
#100, 3643 Cawthra Rd., Mississauga ON L5A 2Y4
905-566-8640

Mississauga: Rawding, Lindsay - *2
#201, 3415 Dixie Rd., Mississauga ON L4Y 2B1
905-625-4442 905-624-0184

Mississauga: Richardson, Terry D. - *1
18 Mississauga Rd. North, Mississauga ON L5H 2H4
905-891-0011 905-891-1410

Mississauga: Saltzman, J.
#15, 7205 Goreway Dr., Mississauga ON L4T 2T9
905-671-1178 905-671-8030
jerry_westwood@hotmail.com

Mississauga: Shulman, Allan - *1
2225 Erin Mills Pkwy., Mississauga ON L5K 1T9
905-822-3563 905-822-6342
ashulman@on.aibn.com

Mississauga: Tannahill, Lockhart and Clark Law - *3
#10, 5805 Whittl Blvd., Mississauga ON L4Z 2J1
905-502-5770 905-502-5009
www.tlcl.ca

Mississauga: Thompson, MacColl & Stacy - *9
#5, 1020 Matheson Blvd. East, Mississauga ON L4W 4J9
905-625-5591 905-238-3313

Mississauga: Watson, Brian M. - *1
#105, 3034 Palston Rd., Mississauga ON L4Y 2Z6
905-272-0942 905-272-1682
watsonlaw@sympatico.ca

Mitchell: Wilson, William E. - *1
102 Ontario Rd., Mitchell ON N0K 1N0
519-348-8488 519-348-4226
wewilson@ezlink.ca

Moosonee: Keewaytinok Native Legal Services - *2
P.O Box 218 40 Revillon Rd. North, Moosonee ON P0L 1Y0
705-336-2981 705-336-2577
lantzp@lao.on.ca; khangkd@lao.on.ca
www.keewaytinok.org

Morrisburg: Gorrell, Grenkie, Leroy & Rémillard - *4
P.O Box 820, Morrisburg ON K0C 1X0
613-543-2922 613-543-4228
info@gglrlaw.ca

Morrisburg: McInnis, MacEwen, Horner & Pietersma - *2
P.O Box 733, Morrisburg ON K0C 1X0
613-543-2946 613-543-3867

Mount Forest: Fallis, Fallis & McMillan - *2
150 Main St. South, Mount Forest ON N0G 2L0
519-323-2800 519-323-4115
ffmlaw@wightman.ca

Mount Forest: Grant, Deverell & Lemaich LLP - *3
166 Main St. South, Mount Forest ON N0G 2L0
519-323-1600 519-323-3877
info@northwellington-law.ca

Napanee: Doreleyers, C. F. - *2
P.O Box 398 Main35 Dundas St. East, Napanee ON K7R 3P5
613-354-3375 613-354-5641

Nepean: Chiarelli Cramer Witteveen - *3
Centrepointe Chambers 92 Centrepointe Dr., Nepean ON K2G 6B1
613-723-9100 613-723-9105
ccw@centrepointelaw.com

Nepean: Clermont Clausi Gardiner & Associates - *5
1447 Woodroffe Ave., Nepean ON K2G 1W1
613-225-0037 613-225-0921

Nepean: Cohen, E. Max, Q.C. - *1
24 Kitimat Cres., Nepean ON K2H 7G5
613-828-5855 613-237-0510

Nepean: Doraty & Ferris
28 Northside Rd., Nepean ON K2H 5Z3
613-829-7171 613-829-0244
inquiries@doratyferris.com

Nepean: MacKay & Sanderson - *2
#201, 1580 Merivale Rd., Nepean ON K2G 4B5
613-238-6180 613-238-3288

Nepean: Ward, Jo-Anne E. - *1
17 Scout St., Nepean ON K2C 4B9
613-729-7667 613- -

Newmarket: Dunsmuir Advocates - *2
P.O Box 2003 Main17070 Yonge St., Newmarket ON L3Y 6W4
905-895-7741 905-853-5851
www.dunsmuiradvocates.com

Newmarket: Hill Hunter Losell Law Firm LLP - *7
#200, P.O Box 324 Main17360 Yonge St., Newmarket ON L3Y 4X7
905-895-1007 905-895-4064

Newmarket: Schneider, A. - *1
291 Davis Dr., Newmarket ON L3Y 2N6
905-898-1342 905-898-1344

Newmarket: Stiver Vale - *7
195 Main St. South, Newmarket ON L3Y 3Y9
905-895-4571 905-853-2958

Niagara Falls: Broderick & Partners - *7
P.O Box 897 4625 Ontario Ave., Niagara Falls ON L2E 6V6
905-356-2621 905-356-6904

Niagara Falls: Galloway, Charles A. - *1
5146 Victoria Ave., Niagara Falls ON L2E 4E3
905-356-2512 905-356-2513

Niagara Falls: Knight, S. James, Q.C. - *1
4683 Queen St., Niagara Falls ON L2E 2L9
905-356-1524 905-357-9686

Niagara Falls: Lucas, Patricia - *1
4056 Dorchester Rd., Niagara Falls ON L2E 6M9
905-357-4510 905-357-9757

Niagara Falls: McDonald, D.J. - *1
P.O Box 726 Main4683 Queen St., Niagara Falls ON L2E 6V5
905-356-1524 905-357-9686
danielmcdonald@bellnet.ca

Niagara Falls: McKay, Heath - *2
#102, 4701 St. Clair Ave., Niagara Falls ON L2E 3S9
905-357-0660 905-357-5680

Niagara Falls: McNab, G.F., Q.C. - *1
4056 Dorchester Rd., Niagara Falls ON L2E 6M9
905-357-4510 905-357-9757
mcnablucas@on.aibn.com

Niagara Falls: Minov, N. - *1
2455 Lepp Ave., Niagara Falls ON L2J 2B9
905-356-4420 905-356-0333

Niagara Falls: Rocca, James - *1
4056 Dorchester Rd., Niagara Falls ON L2E 6M9
905-357-3730 905-356-6185
jamesrocca@bellnet.com

Niagara Falls: Sharpe, Beresh & Gnys - *4
Elgin Block 4673 Ontario Ave., 3rd Fl., Niagara Falls ON L2E 3R1
905-357-5555 905-357-5760
sharpe@sbglawfirm.com

Niagara Falls: Slovak, William, Q.C. - *1
5627 Main St., Niagara Falls ON L2G 5Z3
905-374-6000 905-374-9410 877-231-0011
mjs5627@hotmail.com

Niagara Falls: Ungaro, Guy - *1
#101, 3486 Portage Rd., Niagara Falls ON L2J 2K4
905-357-5310 905-357-9677
guyungaro@hotmail.com

Niagara on the Lake: King, W.R. - *1
P.O Box 900 431 Mississauga St., Niagara on the Lake ON L0S 1J0
905-468-3272 905-468-5441
kinglaw@bellnet.ca

Niagara Falls: Martin Sheppard Fraser LLP - *13
P.O Box 900 4701 St. Clair Ave., 2nd Fl., Niagara Falls ON L2E 6V7
905-354-1611 905-354-5540 800-263-2502
lawyers@martinshep.com
www.martinshep.com

North Bay: Birnie Associates - *1
P.O Box 100 Main116 McIntyre St. West, North Bay ON P1B 8G8
705-497-1900 705-497-1700
m.c.b@sympatico.ca

North Bay: Bowness & Murray - *2
348 Fraser St., North Bay ON P1B 3W7
705-474-9680 705-474-4218

North Bay: Clements, Barrister & Solicitor - *1
477 Sherbrooke St., North Bay ON P1B 2C2
705-472-4890 705-472-9612

North Bay: Colvin & Colvin Professional Corporation - *2
P.O Box 657 Main577 Main St. West, North Bay ON P1B 8J5
705-476-5161 705-476-9902 877-268-8566
colvinlaw@cogeco.net

North Bay: Gorman Barristers - *1
Thompson Building 101 McIntyre St. West, North Bay ON P1B 2Y5
705-476-0500 705-476-8054

North Bay: Lucenti, Orlando & Ellies Professional Corporation - *4
P.O Box 358 373 Main St. West, North Bay ON P1B 8H5
705-472-9500 705-472-4814
info@loellp.ca

North Bay: McIntosh, James R. - *1
325 Main St. West, North Bay ON P1B 2T9
705-476-2500 705-476-9347
maclaw@efni.com

North Bay: McLachlan Froud LLP - *2
#202, 373 Main St. West, North Bay ON P1B 2T9
705-476-6333 705-476-4397
hughmclachlan@sympatico.ca; jeffrey.froud@sympatico.ca

North Bay: Wallace Klein Partners in Law LLP - *7
P.O Box 37 225 McIntyre St. West, North Bay ON P1B 8G8
705-474-2920 705-474-1758
info@partnersinlaw.net

Oakville: Baggs, Douglas D. - *1
P.O Box 100 Main233 Robinson St., Oakville ON L6J 4Z5
905-842-8600 905-842-8242
doug@dougbaggs.com
dougbaggs.com

Oakville: **Day, Richard B. - *1**
164 Trafalgar Rd., Oakville ON L6J 3G6
905-844-8581 905-842-6166
rick@daylaw.ca

Oakville: **Gardner, J.B. - *1**
P.O Box 249 228 Lakeshore Rd. East, Oakville ON L6J 5A2
905-844-3218 905-844-3699
jbg@quixnet.net

Oakville: **King, Brian W., Q.C. - *1**
#34, Hopedale Mall 1515 Rebecca St., Oakville ON L6L 5G8
905-827-0808 905-827-8380
bking@briankinglaw.com
www.briankinglaw.com

Oakville: **Lush, Bowker Aird - *4**
P.O Box 734 261 Lakeshore Rd. East, Oakville ON L6J 1H9
905-844-0381 905-849-4540 877-844-0381
lawyers@lushbowkeraird.on.ca

Oakville: **Marshall, Thomas H., Q.C., Barristers & Solicitors - *2**
#209, 1540 Cornwall Rd., Oakville ON L6J 7W5
905-844-0464 905-844-3983
sanderson@oakvillefamilylawyer.ca
www.oakvillefamilylawyer.ca

Oakville: **Naumetz, Kathryn S., Law Office - *1**
263 Church St., Oakville ON L6J 1N7
905-845-2241 905-845-0193

Oakville: **O'Connor MacLeod Hanna LLP - *20**
700 Kerr St., Oakville ON L6K 3W5
905-842-8030 905-842-2460
info@omh.ca
www.omh.ca

Oakville: **Ryrie, Kerr, Davidson - *2**
P.O Box 100 Main233 Robinson St., Oakville ON L6J 4Z5
905-842-8600 905-842-4774

Orangeville: **Mullin, Thwaites & Ward LLP - *4**
25 First St., Orangeville ON L9W 2Z5
519-941-4559 519-941-4806
psprouleward@mtwlawoffice.com
www.mtwlawoffice.com

Orangeville: **Parkinson & Parkinson - *1**
145 Broadway St., Orangeville ON L9W 1K2
519-941-3627 519-941-3444
pp@parkinsonparkinson.ca

Orangeville: **Peterson & Peterson**
P.O Box 1607 18 Lawton St., Orangeville ON L9W 4X4
705-356-9877 705-356-7498
larryd.peterson@sympatico.ca

Orillia: **Barlow, H. Robert, Q.C. - *1**
Main5 McLean Cr., RR#1, Orillia ON L3V 6H1
705-326-6881 705-326-3063

Orillia: **Crawford, McKenzie, McLean, Anderson & Duncan LLP - *7**
P.O Box 520 Orillia40 Coldwater St. East, Orillia ON L3V 6K4
705-325-2753 705-325-4913
mclaw@mclaw.ca

Orillia: **Kinnear, Brian D. - *1**
#108, P.O Box 656 17 Colborne St. East, Orillia ON L3V 6K7
705-323-9386 705-323-9388
bkinnearlaw@on.aibn.com

Orillia: **Parslow, Allan C. - *1**
212 John St., Orillia ON L3V 3H7
705-329-2223 705-329-0433

Orillia: **Russell Christie LLP - *7**
P.O Box 158 505 Memorial Ave., Orillia ON L3V 6J3
705-325-1326 705-327-1811
rcmkw@russellchristie.com

Orleans: **Dust Evans Professional Corporation - *4**
2589 St. Joseph Blvd., Orleans ON K1C 1G4
613-837-1010 613-837-9670 800-379-6668
info@dustevans.com
www.dustevans.com

Orleans: **Trudel, Roger P. - *1**
2828 St. Joseph Blvd., Orleans ON K1C 1G7
613-837-2641 613-830-5613
roger.trudel@on.aibn.com

Orono: **Lycett, W.K., Q.C. - *1**
P.O Box 87 5301 Main St., Orono ON L0B 1M0
905-983-5007 905-983-9022
wklycett@look.ca

Oshawa: **Bolotenko, Aleksandr G. - *1**
#303, 17 King St. East, Oshawa ON L1H 1A8
905-433-1176 905-433-0283
abolotenko@agblaw.com

Oshawa: **Boychyn & Boychyn - *1**
#1E, 57 Simcoe St. South, Oshawa ON L1H 4G4
905-576-2670 905-576-0915
dboychyn@rogers.com

Oshawa: **Creighton Victor Alexander Hayward Morison & Hall LLP - *5**
P.O Box 26010 235 King St. East, Oshawa ON L1H 8R4
905-723-3446 905-432-2323
inquire@durhamlawyers.ca
www.durhamlawyers.ca

Oshawa: **Diamond, Fischman & Pushman - *2**
P.O Box 26008 206179 King St. East, Oshawa ON L1H 8R4
905-723-5243 905-436-6041
office@dflplaw.com

Oshawa: **Elliott & Hughes - *2**
106 Stevenson Rd. South, Oshawa ON L1J 5M1
905-571-1774 905-571-7706 877-272-5220

Oshawa: **Kelly Greenway Bruce - *8**
P.O Box 886 114 King St. East, Oshawa ON L1H 7N1
905-723-2278 905-432-2663
mail@oshawalawyers.com
www.oshawalawyers.com

Oshawa: **Kitchen Kitchen Simeson McFarlane - *7**
P.O Box 428 86 Simcoe St. South, Oshawa ON L1H 7L5
905-579-5302 905-579-6073 888-669-6446
mail@kksm.com

Oshawa: **Lancaster, K.L. - *1**
52 Division St., Oshawa ON L1G 5L9
905-571-3901 905-571-4241

Oshawa: **Laskowsky & Laskowsky - *1**
73 Centre St. South, Oshawa ON L1H 4A1
905-579-0777 905-576-9918

Oshawa: **Mack, Kisbee & Greer - *3**
146 Simcoe St. North, Oshawa ON L1G 4S7
905-571-1400 905-571-0735

Oshawa: **Marks & Marks - *1**
#304, 17 King St. East, Oshawa ON L1H 1A8
905-728-5151 905-433-4018

Oshawa: **McCallum, Elaine M.F. - *1**
P.O Box 1098 B174 Athol St. East, Oshawa ON L1J 5Y9
905-579-8866 905-579-8913 888-579-5252
elainemfmccallum@on.aibn.com

Oshawa: **Stolwyk, Frank H.M. - *1**
57 Simcoe St. South, Unit 1-F, Oshawa ON L1H 4G4
905-576-8100 905-579-6762
franks4950@aol.com

Oshawa: **Strike, Salmers & Furlong - *3**
P.O Box 2096 A55 William St. East, Oshawa ON L1H 7V4
905-723-1101 905-723-1157
allanfurlong@ssf-oshawa.com

Oshawa: **Swartz, Ronald L. - *1**
231 Simcoe St. North, Oshawa ON L1G 4T1
905-576-3392 905-576-3397
rlswatrz@interlinks.net

Oshawa: **Thomas, David B. - *1**
28B Albert St., Oshawa ON L1H 8S5
905-576-5666 905-576-5289

Oshawa: **Worboy, Ronald F. - *1**
153 Simcoe St. North, Oshawa ON L1G 4S6
905-723-2288 905-576-1355

Oshawa: **Yanch & Yanch - *1**
#1D, P.O Box 154 57 Simcoe St. South, Oshawa ON L1H 7L1
905-728-9495 905-721-8044
yanchfirm@hotmail.com

Ottawa: **Adams, Douglas R. - *1**
#1502, 222 Queen St., Ottawa ON K1P 5V9
613-238-8076 613-238-5519

Ottawa: **Anders, Young, Strong & Jonah - *4**
#401, 1580 Merivale Rd., Ottawa ON K2G 4B5
613-224-1621 613-224-8827

Ottawa: **Barnes, Gary R. - *3**
#500, 200 Elgin St., Ottawa ON K2P 1L5
613-225-2529 613-225-3930
barnesgary@rogers.com

Ottawa: **Beament Green - *6**
979 Wellington Ave., Ottawa ON K1Y 2X7
613-241-3400 613-241-8555
info@beament.com
www.beament.com

Ottawa: **Bell, Baker LLP - *12**
#500, 116 Lisgar St., Ottawa ON K2P 0C2
613-237-3444 613-237-1413

Ottawa: **Bogue, John E. - *1**
#802, 200 Elgin St., Ottawa ON K2P 1L5
613-234-4901 613-236-8906

Ottawa: **Bosada & Associates - *1**
#222, 280 Metcalfe St., Ottawa ON K2P 1R7
613-563-1001 613-563-1031
richard@bosada.ca

Ottawa: **Bulger, Young - *3**
#310, 411 Roosevelt Ave., Ottawa ON K2A 3X9
613-728-5881 613-728-6158
bulgeryoung@on.aibn.com

Ottawa: **Callan, Honeywell LLP - *2**
#420, 875 Carling Ave., Ottawa ON K1S 5P1
613-729-2460 613-729-1710

Ottawa: **Carroll & Wallace - *3**
#502, 66 Slater St., Ottawa ON K1P 5H1
613-236-5494 613-232-7322
cwmlaw@cyberus.ca

Ottawa: **Chiasson, Paul-Emile - *1**
#600, 116 Lisgar St., Ottawa ON K2P 0C2
613-230-8800 613-236-3136
pechiasson@sympatico.ca

Ottawa: **Conlin & McAlpin - *2**
1678 Bank St., Ottawa ON K1V 7Y6
613-737-4140 613-737-7903
pconlin@conlinlaw.com

Ottawa: **DioGuardi & Company LLP - *3**
#300, 100 Gloucester St., Ottawa ON K2P 0A4
613-237-2222 613-594-9092
pd@dioguardiandco.com

Ottawa: **Edelson, Michael D. & Associates - *5**
#600, 200 Elgin St., Ottawa ON K2P 1L5
613-237-2290 613-237-0071
mail@edelsonlaw.ca
www.edelsonlaw.ca

Ottawa: **Edwards, J.J. Mark - *1**
96 Helena St., Ottawa ON K1Y 3N1
613-722-2613 613-722-9484
medwards@edwardslaw.ca

Ottawa: **Farber & Robillard - *2**
330 Churchill Ave. North, Ottawa ON K1Z 5B9
613-722-9418 613-722-5981

Ottawa: **Fernandez-Davila, Pablo - *1**
162 Laurier Ave. West, Ottawa ON K1P 5J4
613-565-8686 613-565-8989
info@fernandez-davila.com

Ottawa: **Finlayson & Singlehurst - *3**
70 Gloucester St., 4th Fl., Ottawa ON K2P 0A2
613-232-0227 613-232-0542 Telex: 0636900-25
fands@attglobal.net

Ottawa: **Flint, Ann L. - *1**
#203, 190 Somerset St. West, Ottawa ON K2P 0J4
613-594-5461 613-594-5468

Ottawa: **Goldberg Wiseman Stroud & Hollingsworth LLP, Barristers & Solicitors - *4**
486 Gladstone Ave., Ottawa ON K1R 5N8
613-237-4922 613-237-2920
info@gwshlaw.com
www.gsklaw.com

Ottawa: **Good, Donald R. - *2**
Merivale Depot P.O Box 5118, Ottawa ON K2C 3H4
613-228-9676 613-228-7404 800-661-8837
farmlaw@on.aibn.com

Ottawa: **Goss, McCorriston, Stel - *3**
#203, 2430 Bank St., Ottawa ON K1V 0T7

613-738-0023 613-738-1294

Ottawa: Hewitt, Hewitt, Nesbitt, Reid - *7
#604, Fuller Bldg. 75 Albert St., Ottawa ON K1P 5E7
613-563-0202 613-563-0445
info@hewitts-law.com

Ottawa: Honey/MacMillan - *3
146 Richmond Rd., Ottawa ON K1Z 6W2
613-722-2493 613-722-2773
honeymac@rogers.com

Ottawa: Karam Greenspon - *4
301 Elgin St., Ottawa ON K2P 2N9
613-232-9911 613-232-5979

Ottawa: Kerr, J.K., Q.C. - *1
#404, 71 Bank St., Ottawa ON K1P 5N2
613-232-7902 613-563-8067

Ottawa: Laird, Sheena - *2
#110, 261 Cooper St., Ottawa ON K2P 0G3
613-232-3575 613-232-6622
asselin7@bellnet.ca
www.asselinlaird.com

Ottawa: Langevin Morris LLP - *14
190 O'Connor St., 9th Fl., Ottawa ON K2P 2R3
613-230-5787 613-230-8563
general@langevinmorris.com
www.langevinmorris.com

Ottawa: Low, Murchison, LLP - *17
#200, 441 Maclaren St., Ottawa ON K2P 2H3
613-236-9442 613-236-7942
lawyer@lowmurchison.com
www.lowmurchison.com

Ottawa: MacKay & Sanderson - *2
#201, 1580 Merivale Rd., Ottawa ON K2G 4B5
613-238-6180 613-238-3288

Ottawa: MacKinnon & Phillips - *8
#802, 200 Elgin St., Ottawa ON K2P 1L5
613-236-0662 613-236-8906

Ottawa: Maclaren, Corlett - *8
#1625, 50 O'Connor St., Ottawa ON K1P 6L2
613-233-1146 613-233-7190
mail@macorlaw.com
www.macorlaw.com

Ottawa: Marcus McNamara & Wilson - *4
#305, 185 Somerset St. West, Ottawa ON K2P 0J2
613-233-4083 613-233-3132
marpar@sympatico.ca

Ottawa: McCann Law Offices - *4
#605, 200 Elgin St., Ottawa ON K2P 1L5
613-236-1410 613-563-1367

Ottawa: McCloskey McCloskey - *2
#202, 5307 Canotek Rd., Ottawa ON K1J 9M2
613-745-0395 613-745-8007
law@mccloskey.net

Ottawa: McGuinty & McGuinty - *3
1801 Kilborn Ave., Ottawa ON K1H 6N1
613-526-3858 613-526-3187
reception@mcguintylaw.ca

Ottawa: Merovitz Potechin LLP - *8
#301, 200 Catherine St., Ottawa ON K2P 2K9
613-563-7544 613-563-4577
mplaw@mpottawa.com

Ottawa: Mirsky, Pascoe - *3
#300, 39 Robertson Rd., Ottawa ON K2H 8R2
613-828-2120 613-596-0881

Ottawa: Moffat & Co., Macera & Jarzyna - *24
D427 Laurier Ave. West, 12th Fl., Ottawa ON K1R 7Y2
613-238-8173 613-235-2508 Telex: 053-3273
mail@macerajarzyna.com
www.macerajarzyna.com

Ottawa: More & McLeod - *1
#212, 2249 Carling Ave., Ottawa ON K2B 7E9
613-820-7888 613-820-3044
morelaw@bellnet.ca

Ottawa: Mount Clark Yemensky - *3
#208, 1400 Clyde Ave., Ottawa ON K2G 3J2
613-226-8817 613-224-8943

Ottawa: Nelligan O'Brien Payne - *42
#1500, 50 O'Connor, Ottawa ON K1P 6L2
613-238-8080 613-238-2098
info@nelligan.ca
www.nelligan.ca

Ottawa: Nicol & Lazier - *2
#400, 331 Cooper St., Ottawa ON K2P 0G5
613-232-4241 613-236-9325

Ottawa: O'Connor, Claire B. - *1
#101, 745B Montréal Rd., Ottawa ON K1K 0T1
613-745-9446 613-745-0800
cboc@bellnet.ca

Ottawa: Paradis, Jones, Horwitz, Bowles Associates - *4
#900, 200 Elgin St., Ottawa ON K2P 1L5
613-238-5074 613-230-3250

Ottawa: Perley-Robertson, Hill & McDougall LLP - *36
#1400, 340 Albert St., Ottawa ON K1R 0A5
613-238-2022 613-238-8775 800-268-8292
lawyers@perlaw.ca
www.perlaw.ca

Ottawa: Piazza, Brooks - *2
#202, 309 Cooper St., Ottawa ON K2P 0G5
613-238-2244 613-238-3382
ph@piazzalaw.com

Ottawa: Plant Quinn Thiele - *7
#700, 200 Elgin St., Ottawa ON K2P 1L5
613-563-1131 613-230-8297
mquinn@pqtlaw.com
www.pqtlaw.com

Ottawa: Puccini, Helene Bruce - *1
#307, 150 Isabella St., Ottawa ON K1S 1V7
613-230-6295 613-567-3559
helene@puccini.ca

Ottawa: Radnoff, Pearl LLP - *12
100 Gloucester St., Ottawa ON K2P 0A4
613-594-8844 613-594-9092
www.radnoffpearl.com

Ottawa: Ranger & Associés - *1
#1000, 141 Laurier Ave. West, Ottawa ON K1P 5J3
613-234-2255 613-234-2301

Ottawa: Roine, Larry A. - *1
#200, 2650 Queensview Dr., Ottawa ON K2B 8H6
613-820-8888 613-820-8818

Ottawa: Schwartz, Macey - *1
#1006, 75 Albert St., Ottawa ON K1P 5E7
613-236-1872 613-236-8639
macey@bellnet.ca

Ottawa: Scott & Coulson - *2
#420, 1335 Carling Ave., Ottawa ON K1Z 8N8
613-725-3723 613-729-8613

Ottawa: Segal, Talarico, Habib, Molot LLP - *6
#200, 2650 Queensview Dr., Ottawa ON K2B 8H6
613-820-8888 613-820-8818
www.legal-team.com

Ottawa: Shapiro, Cohen - *6
P.O Box 3440 D112 Kent St., Ottawa ON K1P 6P1
613-232-5300 613-563-9231 800-563-9390

Ottawa: Soloway, Wright LLP - *21
#900, 427 Laurier Ave. West, Ottawa ON K1R 7Y2
613-236-0111 613-238-8507 800-207-5880
info@solowaywright.com
www.solowaywright.com

Ottawa: Sundin, Anna E. - *1
276 Sunnyside Ave., Ottawa ON K1S 0R8
613-445-3183 613-730-7484
asundin@storm.ca

Ottawa: Tierney Stauffer - *11
#510, 1600 Carling Ave., Ottawa ON K1Z 0A1
613-728-8057 613-728-9866
www.tierneystauffer.com

Ottawa: Vered, Gilad - *1
1801 Woodward Dr., Ottawa ON K2C 0R3
613-226-2000 613-225-0391
gvered@arnon.ca

Ottawa: Victor Ages Vallance LLP, Barristers & Solicitors - *8
112 Lisgar St., Ottawa ON K2P 0C2
613-238-1333 613-238-8949
rfurtado@vavlawyers.com
www.vavlawyers.com

Ottawa: Vincent Dagenais Gibson LLP/S.R.L. - *11
#600, 325 Dalhousie St., Ottawa ON K1N 7G2
613-241-2701 613-241-2599
susan.emmett@vdgjustice.ca

Ottawa: Whillans, Robert A. - *1
540 Courtenay Ave., Ottawa ON K2A 3B3
613-238-1515 613-238-1323

Ottawa: Williams McEnery - *8
169 Gilmour St., Ottawa ON K2P 0N8
613-237-0520 613-237-3163
www.williamsmcenery.com

Owen Sound: Boyce, Herbert E. - *1
#103, Dominion Place P.O Box 968 887 Third Ave. East, Owen Sound ON N4K 6H6
519-371-4160 519-371-1604

Owen Sound: Grace, D.A. - *1
P.O Box 952 Main949 - 2 Ave. West, Owen Sound ON N4K 4M8
519-371-9370 519-371-5747
dougrace@bmts.com

Owen Sound: Greenfield & Barrie - *2
P.O Box 665 142 - 10 St. West, Owen Sound ON N4K 5R4
519-376-4930 519-376-4010
gblaw@btms.com

Owen Sound: Kirby, Robinson, Treslan & Conlan - *6
P.O Box 730 930 -1 Ave. West, Owen Sound ON N4K 5W9
519-376-7450 519-376-8288
info@owensoundlawyers.com

Owen Sound: Laing, Catherine A. - *1
P.O Box 664 935 - 2 Ave. West, Owen Sound ON N4K 5R4
519-371-2202 519-376-4683
calaing@bellnet.ca

Owen Sound: Middlebro' & Stevens LLP - *6
P.O Box 100 1030 - 2 Ave. East, Owen Sound ON N4K 5P1
519-376-8730 519-376-7135
ms@mslaw.ca
www.mslaw.ca

Owen Sound: Murray & Thomson - *2
P.O Box 1060 912 - 2 Ave. West, Owen Sound ON N4K 6K6
519-376-6350 519-376-0835
message@mtlaw.ca
www.mtlaw.ca

Parry Sound: Douglas, Larry W. - *1
22 Miller St., Parry Sound ON P2A 1S8
705-746-9471 705-746-9606

Parry Sound: Holmes, David A. - *1
2 William St., Parry Sound ON P2A 1V1
705-746-4223 705-746-6368
daholmes@cogeco.ca

Parry Sound: Lund, Lisa M. Barrister & Solicitor - *1
34 Mary St., Parry Sound ON P2A 1E4
705-746-4215 705-746-5357
lisa.lund@lisalund.ca

Parry Sound: Piddington & Newman - *2
97 James St., Parry Sound ON P2A 1T7
705-746-9365 705-746-7159
newmanps@vianet.ca

Pembroke: Felhaber, B. Lynne - *1
#100, 77 Mary St., Pembroke ON K8A 5V4
613-735-6866 613-735-6641

Pembroke: Garretto & Price - *1
P.O Box 697 Main141A Lake St., Pembroke ON K8A 6X9
613-732-2883 613-732-3436
gprice@bellnet.ca

Pembroke: Huckabone, O'Brien, Instance. Bradley, Lyle - *6
P.O Box 487 284 Pembroke St. East, Pembroke ON K8A 6X7
613-735-2341 613-735-0920
admin@hsolawyers.com
www.hsolawyers.com

Pembroke: Johnson, Fraser & March - *3
P.O Box 366 Main259 Pembroke St. East, Pembroke ON K8A 6X6
613-735-0624 613-735-0625
jfmlawyers@nrtco.net

Perth: Anderson, Greg W.. Barrister, Solicitor, Notary - *1
10 Market Sq., Perth ON K7H 1V7
613-267-9898 613-267-2741
greg@greganderson.ca
www.greganderson.ca

Perth: Reid, Michael P. - *1
#202, Code's Mill 53 Herriott St., Perth ON K7H 1T5
613-267-7280 613-267-7285
mike@reidlaw.ca
www.reidlaw.ca

Perth: Rubino & Chaplin - *1
P.O Box 338 10A Gore St. West, Perth ON K7H 3E4
613-267-5227 613-267-3951
admin@rubinoandchaplin.ca

Perth: Smith, Kenneth W., Barrister & Solicitor - *1
P.O Box 157 27 Foster St., Perth ON K7H 3E3
613-267-5910 613-264-0789
kenwsmith@on.aibn.com
www.kennethwsmith.com

Peterborough: Aitken, Richard - *1
P.O Box 2126 Main364 Water St., Peterborough ON K9J 7Y4
705-742-0440 705-742-0889
raitkens@cgocable.net

Peterborough: Crook, John S. - *1
#5, P.O Box 1539 Main261 George St. North, Peterborough ON K9J 7H7
705-742-5415 705-742-1867

Peterborough: Devitt, H. Girvin - *1
P.O Box 1449 Main858 Chemong Rd., Peterborough ON K9J 7H6
705-742-5471
devitt@nexicom.net

Peterborough: Douglas F. Walker Professional Corporation - *2
243 Hunter St. W., Peterborough ON K9H 2L4
705-748-3012 705-748-2746
www.dfwalker.com

Peterborough: Dunn & Dunn - *1
469 Water St., Peterborough ON K9H 3M2
705-743-6460 705-748-2675

Peterborough: Farquharson Daly - *1
161 Hunter St. West, Peterborough ON K9H 2L1
705-742-9241 705-741-1601

Peterborough: Galvin, P. Douglas - *1
P.O Box 1118 Main#1, 182 McDonnel St., Peterborough ON K9J 7H4
705-743-7500 705-743-2336

Peterborough: Gowland, Boriss - *4
P.O Box 1629 371 Reid St., Peterborough ON K9H 4G4
705-743-7252 705-743-1850

Peterborough: Guerin, Joan M. - *1
#4, P.O Box 1420 Main193 Simcoe St., Peterborough ON K9J 7H6
705-743-9087 705-743-8528

Peterborough: Hauraney, James S. - *1
305 Reid St., Peterborough ON K9J 3R2
705-748-2333 705-748-2618

Peterborough: Howell Fleming LLP - *10
P.O Box 148 415 Water St., Peterborough ON K9J 6Y5
705-745-1361 705-745-6220
lkulatungam@howellfleming.com
www.howellfleming.com

Peterborough: Johnston, Rod E. - *1
P.O Box 29 521 George St. North, Peterborough ON K9J 6Y5
705-748-2244 705-743-3128

Peterborough: Lech, Lightbody & O'Brien - *2
116 Hunter St. West, Peterborough ON K9H 2K6
705-742-3844 705-742-0121
maryruth@hunterstreetlaw.com

Peterborough: Lillico Bazuk Kent Galloway - *4
P.O Box 568 163 Hunter St. West, Peterborough ON K9J 6Z6
705-743-3577 705-743-0013
lbkg@lbkglaw.com

Peterborough: Linda Willcox Whetung Professional Corporation - *1
521 George St. North, Peterborough ON K9J 6Y5
705-743-6470 705-743-3128
linda@lindawhetung.com

Peterborough: Lockington Lawless Fitzpatrick - *11
P.O Box 1146 332 Aylmer St. North, Peterborough ON K9J 7H4
705-742-1674 705-742-4677
info@locklaw.ca

Peterborough: McGarrity, John E. - *1
Main343 Stewart St., Peterborough ON K9H 4A7
705-743-1822 705-743-4870
mcgarrity@trytel.net

Peterborough: McMichael, Davidson - *1
418A Sheridan St., Peterborough ON K9H 3J9
705-745-0571 705-745-0411
lawoffice@mcmichaeldavidson.com

Peterborough: Moldaver & McFadden - *2
121 George St. North, Peterborough ON K9J 7H6
705-743-1801 705-743-0397

Peterborough: Stocker, Robert A. - *1
174 Wallis Dr., Peterborough ON K9J 6C3
705-745-5786
raslaw@cogeco.ca

Peterborough: Usher, G.H. - *1
P.O Box 327 359 Aylmer St. North, Peterborough ON K9J 6Z3
705-743-4221 705-743-8692

Petrolia: Lang, Wallace B. - *1
P.O Box 700 4245 Petrolia Lane, Petrolia ON N0N 1R0
519-882-0770 519-882-3144

Pickering: Edmiston, G.W. - *1
1281 Commerce St., Pickering ON L1W 1C7
905-839-8270

Pickering: Fletcher, J. Paul - *1
P.O Box 667 Main, Pickering ON L1V 3T3
905-922-2027
jpaulfletcherlaw@aol.com

Pickering: Storm, Harvey - *1
#8B, 1400 Bayly St., Pickering ON L1W 3R2
905-839-5121 905-420-4062 888-876-5529
harvey@harveystorm.com
www.harveystorm.com

Pickering: Stroud, Murray - *1
356 Kingston Rd., Pickering ON L1V 1A2
905-509-1353 905-509-2370
mstroud@stroudlaw.ca
www.stroudlaw.ca

Pickering: Wakefield, G.R. - *1
1 Evelyn Ave., Pickering ON L1V 1N3
905-509-5267 905-509-5270
grwakefield@rogers.com

Pickering: Walker, Head - *8
#800, Corporate Centre 1315 Pickering Pkwy., Pickering ON L1V 7G5
905-839-4484 905-420-1073
wlkhd@walkerhead.com
www.walkerhead.com

Picton: Campbell, Bruce F. - *1
P.O Box 1260 194 Main St., Picton ON K0K 2T0
613-476-2366 613-476-9821
bcampbl@kos.net

Picton: Martin, William M. - *1
P.O Box 2160 316 Main St., Picton ON K0K 2T0
613-476-2116 613-476-8143

Picton: Mowat, Donald T. - *1
P.O Box 2290 165 Main St., Picton ON K0K 2T0
613-476-3261 613-476-4417

Picton: Walmsley & Walmsley - *1
P.O Box 1500 340 Main St., Picton ON K0K 2T0
613-476-5516 613-476-5725
walaw@kos.net

Picton: Ward, Jack H. - *1
P.O Box 530 51 Mary St., Picton ON K0K 2T0
613-476-3640 613-476-3435

Port Colborne: Lambie, Brian N. - *1
109 Adelaide St., Port Colborne ON L3K 2W4
905-835-8455 905-835-5966

Port Colborne: Tuck, John D. - *1
P.O Box 334 84 West St., Port Colborne ON L3K 5W1
905-834-4525 905-834-3254
pclaw@bellnet.ca

Port Colborne: Wilson, Opatovsky - *2
P.O Box 99 190 Elm St., Port Colborne ON L3K 5V7
905-835-1163 905-835-2171 888-288-8338

Port Dover: Driscoll & Gaunt - *1
P.O Box 580 110 St. Andrew St., Port Dover ON N0A 1N0
519-583-1411 519-583-1110

Port Elgin: Gruetzner, George D. - *1
P.O Box 10 667 Goderich St., Port Elgin ON N0H 2C0
519-832-2482 519-389-4617

Port Hope: Day, Wilfred, A. - *1
P.O Box 65 Main111 Ontario St., Port Hope ON L1A 3V9
905-885-8118 905-885-7470
dayphope@on.aibn.com

Port Perry: Fowler, Michael L. - *2
175 North St., Port Perry ON L9L 1B7
905-985-8411 905-985-0029
mfowler@fowlerlaw.ca

Prescott: Tobin, Richard M. - *1
257 King St. West, PO Box 760, Prescott ON K0E 1T0
613-925-2853 613-925-5741

Rama: Nahwegahbow, Corbiere - *3
P.O Box 46 7410 Benson Side Rd., Rama ON L0K 1T0
705-325-0520 705-325-7204
mail@nncfirm.ca

Renfrew: Chown & Smith - *2
297 Raglan St. South, Renfrew ON K7V 1R6
613-432-3669 613-432-2874
chown.smith@bellnet.ca

Renfrew: Gallagher, Lawrence E. - *1
33 Renfrew Ave. East, Renfrew ON K7V 2W6
613-432-8537 613-432-8538
legallagher@nrtco.net

Renfrew: McNab, Stewart & Prince - *2
117 Raglan St. South, Renfrew ON K7V 1P8
613-432-5844 613-432-7832
dstewart@mcnablaw.com; tprince@mcnablaw.com
www.mcnablaw.com

Richmond Hill: Bouroukis, Peter D. - *1
#411, 15 Wertheim Ct., Richmond Hill ON L4B 3H7
905-771-7030 905-771-7027
pbouroukis@rogers.com

Richmond Hill: Chauhan, Jay - *1
#309, 330 Hwy. 7 East, Richmond Hill ON L4B 3P8
905-771-1235 905-771-1237
jayadvocate@yahoo.ca
www.jaychauhan.com

Richmond Hill: Lawlor, John J. Q.C. - *1
#102, 10211 Yonge St., Richmond Hill ON L4C 3B3
905-884-9133 905-884-9507
johnlawlor@on.aibn.com

Richmond Hill: Levine, Garry E. - *1
16 O'Connor Cres., Richmond Hill ON L4C 7P3
905-709-9444 905-770-3782
glevine@rogers.com

Richmond Hill: Malach & Fidler - *11
#6, 30 Wertheim Ct., Richmond Hill ON L4B 1B9
905-889-1667 905-889-1139
mf@netcom.ca

Richmond Hill: Parker Garber & Chesney - *1
250 West Beaver Creek Rd., Richmond Hill ON L4B 1C7
905-764-0404 905-764-0320

Richmond Hill: Virgilio, Vumbaca - *2
#500, 1 Pearce St. West, Richmond Hill ON L4B 3K3
905-882-8666 905-882-1082
jvirgilio@virgiliolaw.com

Ridgetown: Nicol, Daniel B. - *1
P.O Box 700 64 Main St. East, Ridgetown ON N0P 2C0

519-674-3372 519-674-3352
dbnicol@pppoe.ca

Ripley: Crawford, Mill & Davies
P.O Box 100 38 Queen St., Ripley ON N0G 2R0
519-395-2633 519-395-4947
cmdripley@hurontel.ca

Sarnia: Beaudet, Paul R. - *1
P.O Box 2162 251 Exmouth St., Sarnia ON N7T 7L7
519-337-1529 519-336-2569
beaudet@ebtech.net
www.sarnia.com/beaudet

Sarnia: Brown, Roderick, Q.C. - *1
555 Exmouth St., Sarnia ON N7T 5P6
519-336-7880 519-336-6584
re_brown2927@hotmail.com

Sarnia: Carpeneto, James J. - *1
316 Christina St. North, Sarnia ON N7T 5V5
519-336-6955 519-336-8401

Sarnia: Elliott & Porter - *2
#101, St. Clair Corporate Centre 265 Front St. North, Sarnia ON N7T 7X1
519-336-4600 519-336-4640

Sarnia: George Murray Shipley Bell, LLP - *9
P.O Box 2196 2 Ferry Dock Hill, Sarnia ON N7T 7L8
519-336-8770 519-336-1811

Sarnia: Gray, Bruce, Kowalyshyn, Cimetta - *5
P.O Box 2259 1166 London Rd., Sarnia ON N7T 7L7
519-336-9700 519-336-3289

Sarnia: McLeod, Pamela J. - *1
1350 L'Heritage Dr., Sarnia ON N7S 6H8
519-542-7714 519-542-5577
mcleodlaw@ebtech.net

Sarnia: Robbins, Henderson & Davis - *4
#201, 208 North Christina St., Sarnia ON N7V 1X6
519-344-5265 519-344-1558

Sarnia: Westfall, Peter - *1
#104, 805 Christina St. North, Point Edward, Sarnia ON N7V 1X6
519-344-1155 519-344-1842
pwestfall@bellnet.ca

Sarnia: Whitnall, Raymond A. - *1
345 Christina St. North, Sarnia ON N7T 5V6
519-336-9460 519-336-8366

Sarnia: Wyrzykowski & Robb - *2
P.O Box 2200 Main, Sarnia ON N7T 7L7
519-336-6118 519-336-9550
orw@ebtech.net

Sault Ste Marie: Allemano & Fitzgerald - *2
P.O Box 10, Sault Ste Marie ON P6A 5L2
705-942-0142 705-942-7188

Sault Ste Marie: Bisceglia Dumanski Rasaiah LLP - *3
747 Queen St. East, 2nd Fl., Sault Ste Marie ON P6A 2A8
705-942-5856 705-942-6493
bdrlawfirm@bellnet.ca
www.bdlawfirm.ca

Sault Ste Marie: Ferranti & Chorney - *2
189 East St., Sault Ste Marie ON P6A 3C8
705-949-6200 705-949-6208

Sault Ste Marie: Hamilton, Nixon - *2
P.O Box 249 67 Elgin St., Sault Ste Marie ON P6A 5L8
705-759-8498 705-759-8781

Sault Ste Marie: Laidlaw, Paciocco, Melville - *3
#604, 421 Bay St., Sault Ste Marie ON P6A 1X3
705-949-7790 705-949-5816
paciocco@vianet.ca

Sault Ste Marie: Lawson, O. Kennedy - *1
#104, 473 Queen St. East, Sault Ste Marie ON P6A 1Z5
705-759-5030 705-942-5309

Sault Ste Marie: McLeod, Baxter, Tremblay-Hall - *3
494 Albert St. East, Sault Ste Marie ON P6A 2K2
705-759-0948 705-759-2042

Sault Ste Marie: O'Neill DeLorenzi Cresswell Ostroski - *6
116 Spring St., Sault Ste Marie ON P6A 3A1
705-949-6901 705-949-0618
info@saultlawyers.com
www.saultlawyers.com

Sault Ste Marie: Peres, R.C., Q.C. - *1
#104, 212 Queen St. East, Sault Ste Marie ON P6A 5X8
705-949-9411 705-949-3759

Sault Ste Marie: Scott, William R. - *1
#202, 629A Queen St. East, Sault Ste Marie ON P6A 2A6
705-949-4333 705-945-0958
wmrscottlaw@yahoo.com

Sault Ste Marie: Shamess, Carol A. - *1
181 March St., Sault Ste Marie ON P6A 2Z6
705-942-2580 705-942-5048

Sault Ste Marie: Walker, Thompson - *1
#506, P.O Box 428 123 March St., Sault Ste Marie ON P6A 5M1
705-949-7806 705-759-0457
walkerlaw@sympatico.ca

Sault Ste Marie: Wishart Law Firm LLP - *6
#500, 390 Bay St., Sault Ste Marie ON P6A 1X2
705-949-6700 705-949-2465
wishart@wishartlaw.com
www.wishartlaw.com

Scarborough: Antflyck, Mazin Aulis LLP - *3
1501 Ellesmere Rd., Scarborough ON M1P 4T6
416-431-1500 416-431-1912
antflyckmazin@on.aibn.com

Schomberg: Smith, Clarke G. - *1
Brownsville Junction Plaza #10, 17250 Hwy. 27, Schomberg ON L0G 1T0
905-939-2344 905-727-7096
cgsmith@aci.on.ca

Seaforth: Devereaux Murray LLP - *2
P.O Box 220 77 Main St. South, Seaforth ON N0K 1W0
519-527-0850 519-527-2324
c4thlaw@devereauxmurray.ca

Seeleys Bay: Atkinson, D.J. - *1
RR#1, Seeleys Bay ON K0H 2N0
613-382-2692

Shelburne: Timmerman & Haskell - *2
P.O Box 216 305 Owen Sound St., Shelburne ON L0N 1S0
519-925-2608 519-925-2268

Simcoe: Brimage, Tyrrell, Van Severen & Homeniuk - *10
21 Norfolk St. North, Simcoe ON N3Y 4L1
519-426-5840 519-426-7515
law@brimage.com
www.brimage.com

Simcoe: Cline, Backus, Nightingale & McArthur, LLP - *8
P.O Box 528 Main39 Colborne St. North, Simcoe ON N3Y 4N5
519-426-6763 519-426-2055
cbnmlaw@kwic.com
www.clinebackus.com

Simcoe: Cobb & Jones LLP - *7
P.O Box 548 23 Argyle St., Simcoe ON N3Y 4N5
519-428-0170 519-428-3105
cobblaw@cobbjones.ca
www.cobbjones.ca

Simcoe: Sheppard, MacIntosh, Lados - *5
P.O Box 677 58 Peel St., Simcoe ON N3Y 4T2
519-426-1382 519-426-1392
lawyers@sheppardmacintosh.com

Simcoe: Smelko Law Office - *1
25 Norfolk St. North, Simcoe ON N3Y 3N6
519-426-1711 519-426-7863 866-684-8527
smelkolaw@on.aibn.com

Smiths Falls: Fournier, G.W. - *1
P.O Box 752 35 Daniel St., Smiths Falls ON K7A 4W6
613-283-8818 613-283-8951

Smiths Falls: Howard Ryan Kelford Knott & Dixon, Barristers & Solicitors - *5
2 Main St. East, Smiths Falls ON K7A 1A2
613-283-6772 613-283-8840 888-852-5175
lthompson@smithsfallslaw.ca
www.smithsfallslaw.ca

Smiths Falls: Kirkland & Murphy Professional Corporation - *3
P.O Box 220 15 Russell St. East, Smiths Falls ON K7A 4T1
613-283-0515 613-283-8557
reception@smithsfallslawyers.com

Smiths Falls: Ross Cliffen & Morrison - *3
P.O Box 804 30 Russell St. East, Smiths Falls ON K7A 4W6
613-283-7331 613-283-6792
rosslaw@ripnet.com
www.rossandcliffen.com

Southampton: Forsyth, Robert E. - *1
P.O Box 420 243 High St., Southampton ON N0H 2L0
519-797-3223 519-797-3192
forsyth3@bmts.com

St Catharines: Chown, Cairns LLP - *17
P.O Box 760 80 King St., St Catharines ON L2R 6Y8
905-688-4500 905-688-0015
lawyers@chowlaw.com
www.chownlaw.com

St Catharines: Coy, Barch - *1
46 Ontario St., St Catharines ON L2R 5J4
905-641-1146 905-641-1148

St Catharines: Crossingham, Brady - *2
P.O Box 307 63 Ontario St., St Catharines ON L2R 6V2
905-641-1621 905-685-1461
cbm@vaxxine.com

St Catharines: Daniel & Partners LLP - *9
Dominion Bldg. P.O Box 24022 39 Queen St., St Catharines ON L2R 7P7
905-688-9411 905-688-5747 800-263-3650
lawyers@niagaralaw.ca

St Catharines: Forster, Lewandowski & Cords - *2
P.O Box 1180 Main82 Lake St., St Catharines ON L2R 7A7
905-688-9110 905-688-0901 866-715-9380
f.l.c@on.aibn.com

St Catharines: Frayne, Ralph H. - *1
9 Raymond St., St Catharines ON L2R 2S9
905-684-1147 905-684-7147

St Catharines: Hanna, John B. - *1
P.O Box 24044 Main, St Catharines ON L2R 7P7
905-687-9347 905-687-3939

St Catharines: Heelis, Williams, Little & Almas LLP, Barristers & Solicitors - *6
P.O Box 1056 14 Church St., St Catharines ON L2R 7A3
905-687-8200 905-684-4844
rwilliam@14churchstlawoffice.com
www.14churchstlawoffice.com

St Catharines: Lancaster, Brooks & Welch LLP - *17
P.O Box 790 80 King St., St Catharines ON L2R 6Z1
905-641-1551 905-641-1830
www.lbwlawyers.com

St Catharines: Marotta, Frank M. - *1
21 Duke St., St Catharines ON L2R 5W1
905-688-5401 905-688-6204
fmarotta@vaxxine.com

St Catharines: Martens, Lingard LLP - *7
195 King St., St Catharines ON L2R 3J6
905-687-6551 905-687-6553
lawyers@martenslingard.ca

St Catharines: O'Neill & Radford - *1
154 James St., St Catharines ON L2R 7A3
905-641-2633 905-682-0264
bmradford@bellnet.ca

St Catharines: Sullivan, Mahoney LLP - *27
P.O Box 1360 40 Queen St., St Catharines ON L2R 6Z2
905-688-6655 905-688-5814
lawyers@sullivan-mahoney.com
www.sullivan-mahoney.com

St Thomas: Glover, W.J., Law Office - *1
P.O Box 575 Main458 Talbot St., St Thomas ON N5P 3V6
519-633-2300 519-633-0964
gloverlawyer@aol.com

St Thomas: Gunn & Associates - *5
108 Centre St., St Thomas ON N5R 2Z7
519-631-0700 519-631-1468
lawyers@gunn.on.ca

St Thomas: Upsdell, Robert J. - *1
59 Metcalfe St., St Thomas ON N5R 3K4

519-633-7100 519-633-8984

***St Thomas*: Walker, Arnold B. - *1**
4 Elgin St., St Thomas ON N5R 3L6
519-633-3273 519-633-8585

***Stoney Creek*: Coombs & Lutz - *1**
6 Lake Ave. South, Stoney Creek ON L8G 1P3
905-664-6341 905-664-8966
lutz@bellnet.ca

***Stoney Creek*: Mazza, Murray R. - *1**
426 Hwy. 8, Stoney Creek ON L8G 1G2
905-561-1444
idseast@cogeco.net

***Stoney Creek*: O'Brien & Skrtich - *1**
26 King St. East, Stoney Creek ON L8G 1J8
905-662-2855 905-662-8881

***Stouffville*: Button, Armstrong & Ness - *3**
P.O Box 220 Main6361 Main St., Stouffville ON L4A 7Z5
905-640-3530 905-640-7027
banlaw@rogers.com

***Stratford*: Buechler, W. John - *1**
488 Erie St., Stratford ON N5A 2N6
519-271-3520 519-271-0097

***Stratford*: Fair, Michael F. - *1**
24 Downie St., 2nd Fl., Stratford ON N5A 6W3
519-271-2912 519-271-2732

***Stratford*: Mountain Mitchell LLP - *7**
P.O Box 846 56 Albert St., Stratford ON N5A 6W3
519-271-6770 519-271-9261
main@mountainmitchell.com
www.mountainmitchell.com

***Stratford*: Skinner, Dunphy & Bantle LLP - *4**
P.O Box 542 1 Ontario St., Stratford ON N5A 6T7
519-271-7330 519-271-1762
thefirm@stratfordlaw.com

***Stratford*: Waller, L. Ray - *1**
#103, P.O Box 813 Main386 Cambria St., Stratford ON N5A 6W1
519-271-4420 519-271-7833

***Strathroy*: Dack, Robert J. - *1**
16 Front St. East, Strathroy ON N7G 1Y4
519-245-0370 519-245-0523

***Strathroy*: Jones, Gibbons & Reis - *2**
39 Front St. West, Strathroy ON N7G 1X5
519-245-1110 519-245-5859
jmr@webgate.net

***Strathroy*: Quinlan & Somerville - *2**
18 Front St. East, Strathroy ON N7G 1Y4
519-245-0342 519-245-0108
lawyers@quinlansomerville.com

***Strathroy*: Ramkelawan, H.P. - *1**
P.O Box 254 MainRR#5, Strathroy ON N7G 3J2
519-245-6074

***Strathroy*: Sinker, George E. - *2**
53 Front St. West, Strathroy ON N7G 1X6
519-245-1144 519-245-6090
gsinker@bellnet.ca

***Sudbury*: Barnett, Michael G. - *1**
264 Elm St., Sudbury ON P3C 1V4
705-674-3210 705-674-1265

***Sudbury*: Beach, William G. - *1**
224 Applegrove St., Sudbury ON P3C 1N3
705-675-5685 705-675-6601

***Sudbury*: Conroy Trebb Scott Hurtubise LLP, Barristers, Solicitors - *6**
164 Elm St., Sudbury ON P3C 1T7
705-674-6441 705-673-9567 800-627-1825
info@sudburylegal.com
www.sudburylegal.com

***Sudbury*: DeDiana, Eloranta & Longstreet - *1**
219 Pine St., Sudbury ON P3C 1X4
705-674-4289 705-671-1047

***Sudbury*: Desmarais, Keenan LLP - *10**
#201, 62 Frood Rd., Sudbury ON P3C 4Z3
705-675-7521 705-675-7390 800-290-5465
www.desmaraiskeenan.com

***Sudbury*: Doig, Hugh A., Q.C. - *1**
296 Larch St., Sudbury ON P3B 1M2
705-674-4213 705-671-1652
doig@on.aibn.com

***Sudbury*: Fabbro, Robert L. - *1**
#1, 54 Elgin St., Sudbury ON P3E 3N2
705-675-6620 705-675-6655
robertfabbro@on.aibn.com

***Sudbury*: Howe, Brian N. - *1**
235 Elm St. West, Sudbury ON P3C 1T8
705-674-8317 705-674-2952

***Sudbury*: Kuyek, Donald - *1**
229 Elm St. West, Sudbury ON P3C 1T8
705-675-1227 705-675-5350 877-414-0311

***Sudbury*: Lacroix, Forest LLP/s.r.l. - *10**
Place Balmoral 36 Elgin St., Sudbury ON P3C 5B4
705-674-1976 705-674-6978
office@sudburylaw.com
www.sudburylaw.com

***Sudbury*: Mensour & Mensour - *2**
#101, 238 Elm St., Sudbury ON P3C 1V3
705-673-6787 705-673-1418

***Sudbury*: Miller, Maki - *14**
176 Elm St., Sudbury ON P3C 1T7
705-675-7503 705-675-8669
oharam@millermaki.com

***Sudbury*: Paquette & Renzini - *3**
#200, 1188 St. Jerome St., Sudbury ON P3A 2V9
705-560-2121 705-560-8072
mail@paquette-renzini.ca

***Sudbury*: Parisé Law Office - *2**
58 Lisgar St., 2nd Fl., Sudbury ON P3E 3L7
705-674-4042 705-674-4242
pariselaw@unitz.ca

***Sudbury*: Stoner, Norman G. - *1**
#202, 124 Cedar St., Sudbury ON P3E 1B4
705-675-8307 705-675-7245
ngslaw@bellnet.ca

***Sudbury*: Thomas, Stanley J. - *1**
111 Durham St., Sudbury ON P3E 3M9
705-674-8306 705-675-8466

***Sudbury*: Treherne, Serge F. - *1**
P.O Box 1269 144 Elm St. West, Sudbury ON P3C 1T7
705-670-9689 705-670-9141 877-550-5616

***Sudbury*: Wilkins & Wilkins - *2**
P.O Box 490 B176 Elm St., Sudbury ON P3E 4P6
705-675-1200

***Sundridge*: Hardy & Associates, Michael A. - *2**
P.O Box 1060 105 Main St. East, Sundridge ON P0A 1Z0
705-384-5770 705-384-5771
sunlaw@bellnet.ca

***Sutton*: Fahey, Patrick J. Law Office - *2**
P.O Box 487 100 High St., Sutton ON L0E 1R0
905-722-3771 905-722-9852
pat.pjf@rogers.com

***Thornhill*: Arrigo, Augustine M., Q.C. - *1**
48 Guardsman Rd., Thornhill ON L3T 6L4
905-889-6131

***Thornhill*: Crupi, Cosimo A. Law Office Barrister & Solicitor - *1**
#302, 305 Renfrew Dr., Thornhill ON L3R 9S7
905-415-8900 905-415-8902
cacrupi@crupilaw.ca
www.crupilaw.ca

***Thornhill*: Cunningham, Iain Stewart - *1**
20 Cypress Point Ct., Thornhill ON L3T 1V7
905-764-7376 905-707-5818

***Thornhill*: Fish & Associates Professional Corporation - *3**
7951 Yonge St., Thornhill ON L3T 2C4
905-881-1500 905-881-6535
bfish@bfishandassociates.com
www.familyfight.com

***Thornhill*: Flisfeder, A.M. - *1**
45 Janesville Rd., Thornhill ON L4J 6Z9
416-469-0375 416-469-0375

***Thornhill*: Gaglione, Gregory J. - *1**
#202, 7368 Yonge St., Thornhill ON L4J 8H9
416-882-0066 416-882-2550

***Thornhill*: Greenberg, Barry S. - *1**
7626A Yonge St., Thornhill ON L4J 1V9
905-886-9535 905-886-9540
bsgreenberg@rogers.com

***Thornhill*: Iseman, Seymour - *1**
#216, 2900 Steeles Ave. East, Thornhill ON L3T 4X1
905-881-8800 905-881-7391
siseman@allstream.net

***Thornhill*: MacDougall, Janet - *1**
#202, 8108 Yonge St., Thornhill ON L4J 1W4
905-886-4907 905-886-8070

***Thornhill*: Merritt, R.G. - *1**
#205, 7089 Yonge St., Thornhill ON L3T 2A7
905-889-3430 905-889-7290
rgmerritt@home.com

***Thornhill*: Morganstein, D. Todd - *1**
#110, 8111 Yonge St., Thornhill ON L3T 4V9
905-881-8289 905-881-2696

***Thornhill*: Raphael Barristers - *4**
#202, 1137 Centre St., Thornhill ON L4J 3M6
416-594-1812 416-594-0868
braphael@raphaelbar.com

***Thornhill*: Seltzer, Erwin S. - *1**
9 MacArthur Dr., Thornhill ON L4J 7T6
905-731-7131

***Thornhill*: Weinstein, Ben - *1**
#203, 1 Clark Ave. West, Thornhill ON L4J 7Y6
905-889-5364 905-889-3231

***Thorold*: Simon, John J. - *1**
P.O Box 505 Thorold7 Front St. North, Thorold ON L2V 4W1
905-227-9191 905-227-7234
john_smith@hotmail.com

***Thorold*: Young, McNamara - *2**
18 Albert St. East, Thorold ON L2V 1P1
905-227-3777 905-227-5988

***Thunder Bay*: Atwood Labine Arnone McCartney LLP - *5**
501 Donald St. East, Thunder Bay ON P7E 6N6
807-623-4342 807-623-2098
asl@asl-law.com
www.alamlaw.ca

***Thunder Bay*: Buset & Partners LLP - *12**
1121 Barton St., Thunder Bay ON P7B 5N3
807-623-2500 807-622-7808
law@buset-partners.com
www.buset-partners.com

***Thunder Bay*: Carrel+Partners LLP - *13**
1136 Alloy Dr., Thunder Bay ON P7B 6M9
807-346-3000 807-346-3600 800-263-0578
info@carrel.com
www.carrel.com

***Thunder Bay*: Cheadles LLP - *8**
#2000, P.O Box 10429 715 Hewitson St., Thunder Bay ON P7B 6T8
807-622-6821 807-623-3892

***Thunder Bay*: Christie Potestio Freitag - *3**
#203, 920 Tungsten St., Thunder Bay ON P7B 5Z6
807-344-6651 807-345-1105
potestio@chrpot.on.ca

***Thunder Bay*: Colborne, Donald R. - *1**
Site 14, Comp 67, RR#13, Thunder Bay ON P7B 5E4
807-344-6628 807-983-3079
colborne@microage-tb.com

***Thunder Bay*: Erickson & Partners - *8**
291 South Court St., Thunder Bay ON P7B 2Y1
807-345-1213 807-345-2526 800-465-3912

***Thunder Bay*: Filipovic, Brothers & Conway - *5**
#20, Tomlinson Block 8A North Cumberland St., Thunder Bay ON P7A 4L1
807-343-9090 807-345-1397 800-760-8694

***Thunder Bay*: Lauder, Rick E. - *1**
217 Van Norman St., Thunder Bay ON P7A 4B6

807-683-4444 807-345-0337
rick.lauder@shawbiz.ca
www.ricklauder.shawbiz.ca

***Thunder Bay*: Martin Scrimshaw Scott - *4**
Cumberland Park 1 Cumberland St. South, Thunder Bay ON P7B 2T1
807-345-3600 807-344-8152
msslaw@tbaytel.net

***Thunder Bay*: Mitton, Thomas C. - *1**
123 South Brodie St., Thunder Bay ON P7E 1B8
807-623-4320 807-622-8038
tcmitton@tbaytel.net

***Thunder Bay*: Mullen, Robert D. - *1**
395 Fort William Rd., Thunder Bay ON P7B 2Z3
807-344-5848 807-344-5877
rmullen@shawbiz.ca

***Thunder Bay*: Petrone Hornak Garofalo Mauro - *7**
76 Algoma St. North, Thunder Bay ON P7A 4Z4
807-344-9191 807-345-8391 800-465-3988

***Thunder Bay*: Stewart, A.D. - *1**
#112, 105 May St. North, Thunder Bay ON P7C 3N9
807-623-7852 807-623-0014
astewart@807-city.on.ca

***Thunder Bay*: Watkinson, Thomas G. - *1**
123 Brodie St. South, Thunder Bay ON P7E 1B8
807-624-5605 807-623-6096

***Thunder Bay*: Weiler, Maloney, Nelson - *11**
#201, 1001 William St., Thunder Bay ON P7B 6M1
807-623-1111 807-623-4947
weilers@wmnlaw.com
www.weilers.ca

***Tilbury*: Jutras, R.M. - *1**
P.O Box 417 50 Queen St. South, Tilbury ON N0P 2L0
519-682-3100 519-682-3622

***Tilbury*: Taylor & Delrue - *3**
P.O Box 459 40 Queen St. South, Tilbury ON N0P 2L0
519-682-0164 519-682-2777
taydel@cogeco.net

***Tillsonburg*: Battin, James G. - *1**
25 Bidwell St., Tillsonburg ON N4G 3T4
519-688-9033 519-688-9036
bidlaw@kwic.com

***Tillsonburg*: Gibson, Linton, Toth, Campbell & Bennett - *3**
P.O Box 5 Main36 Broadway, Tillsonburg ON N4G 4H3
519-842-3658 519-842-5001
gltcb@kwic.com

***Tillsonburg*: Groom & Szorenyi - *1**
36 Broadway, Tillsonburg ON N4G 4H3
519-842-4205 519-842-4261

***Tillsonburg*: Mandryk, Stewart & Morgan - *3**
65 Bidwell St., Tillsonburg ON N4G 3T8
519-842-4228 519-842-7659
mhlaw@oxford.net

***Tillsonburg*: Morris, Jenkins & Gilvesy - *2**
P.O Box 280 Main19 Ridout St. East, Tillsonburg ON N4G 4H8
519-842-9017 519-842-3394
lisa@morris-jenkins.com

***Timmins*: Brooks, Sydney - *1**
81 Balsam St. South, Timmins ON P4N 2C9
705-264-5341 705-264-2550

***Timmins*: Carlesso Barazzutti - *2**
#204, Scotiabank Bldg. 3 Pine St. South, Timmins ON P4N 2J9
705-264-1374 705-264-1450

***Timmins*: Desrosiers, Suzanne - *1**
92 Spruce St. North, Timmins ON P4N 6M8
705-268-6492 705-264-1940
sdesrosiers@peroonainternet.com

***Timmins*: Evans, Bragagnolo & Sullivan - *8**
120 Pine St. South, Timmins ON P4N 2K4
705-264-1285 705-264-7424
ebslawyers@ebslawyers.com

***Timmins*: Huot, J.P. - *1**
P.O Box 1065 36 Maple St. South, Timmins ON P4N 7H9
705-267-6464 705-264-3260

***Timmins*: Racicot, Maisonneuve, Labelle, Cooper - *6**
15 Balsam St. South, Timmins ON P4N 2C7
705-264-2385 705-268-3949
mlclaw@ntl.sympatico.ca

***Timmins*: Riopelle Griener Professional Corporation - *6**
#202, 85 Pine St. South, Timmins ON P4N 2K1
705-264-9591 705-264-1393 866-624-1614
www.rglaw.ca

***Toronto*: Aaron & Aaron - *1**
#1400, 10 King St. East, Toronto ON M5C 1C3
416-364-9366 416-364-3818
bob@aaron.ca
www.aaron.ca

***Toronto*: Adams, G. Chalmers - *1**
#100, 1255 Yonge St., Toronto ON M4T 1W6
416-929-7232 416-929-7225
chalmers@bellnet.ca

***Toronto*: Advocate Placement Ltd. - *4**
#200, 1200 Bay St., Toronto ON M5R 2A5
416-927-9222 416-927-8772 800-461-1275
resume@advocateplacement.com
www.advocateplacement.com

***Toronto*: Agnew, Gladstone LLP - *2**
215 Carlton St., Toronto ON M5A 2K9
416-964-0021 416-964-0744
yagnew@agnewgladstone.com
www.agnewgladstone.com

***Toronto*: Aiken, Irving J. - *1**
#1105, 65 Queen St. West, Toronto ON M5H 2M5
416-947-0199 416-947-0379

***Toronto*: Alpert Law Firm - *2**
#900, 1 St. Clair Ave. East, Toronto ON M4T 2V7
416-923-0809 416-923-1549
halpert@alpertlawfirm.ca
www.alpertlawfirm.ca

***Toronto*: Altman, Harriet - *1**
68 Garnier Court, Toronto ON M2M 4C9
416-224-5240 416-224-0360 877-224-5229

***Toronto*: Altman, Sheldon L. - *1**
264B Adelaide St. East, Toronto ON M5A 1N1
416-929-1313 416-929-1316
altmansheldon@aol.com
www.sheldonaltman.com

***Toronto*: Altwerger, Baker, Weinberg - *3**
#2901, P.O Box 2450 2300 Yonge St., Toronto ON M4P 1E4
416-480-1662 416-480-0017
stevea@lexpertor.com

***Toronto*: Amourgis, Julie Evelyn - *1**
#800, 439 University Ave., Toronto ON M5G 1Y8
416-504-5844 416-369-1723

***Toronto*: Anderson Bourdon Burgess**
#116, 295 The West Mall, Toronto ON M9C 4Z4
416-621-9644 416-621-9668
anderson@andersonbb.com
www.andersonbb.com

***Toronto*: Applebaum, Jerry - *1**
36 Covington Rd., Toronto ON M6A 1G1
416-785-1140

***Toronto*: Armel, Gray LLP - *5**
#500, 390 Bay St., Toronto ON M5H 2Y2
416-362-1400 416-362-1404

***Toronto*: Arn, D.W. - *1**
380 Bathurst St., Toronto ON M5T 2S6
416-603-3658 416-603-1144

***Toronto*: Ash, William - *1**
#801, 55 Eglinton Ave. East, Toronto ON M4P 1G8
416-486-8751 416-486-8789
willash@bellnet.ca

***Toronto*: Ashbourne & Caskey - *1**
2077 Lawrence Ave. West, Toronto ON M9N 1H7
416-247-6677 416-247-3519

***Toronto*: AvRuskin, S.J. - *1**
66 Charles St. East., Toronto ON M4Y 2R3
416-922-4147 416-922-8022

***Toronto*: Aylesworth LLP - *33**
Ernst & Young Tower, TD Centre P.O Box 124 222 Bay St., 18th Fl., Toronto ON M5K 1H1
416-777-0101 416-865-1398
ekay@aylaw.com
www.aylesworth.com

***Toronto*: Baerg, J. Waldo - *1**
#506, 372 Bay St., Toronto ON M5H 2W9
416-366-3705 416-366-0157
waldobaerg@on.aibn.com

***Toronto*: Baker & McKenzie LLP - *51**
#2100, Brookfield Place P.O Box 874 181 Bay St., Toronto ON M5J 2T3
416-863-1221 416-863-6275
www.bakernet.com

***Toronto*: Baker Schneider Ruggiero LLP - *8**
#1000, 120 Adelaide St. West, Toronto ON M5H 3V1
416-363-2211 416-363-0645

***Toronto*: Baker, J. Anthony - *1**
500 Danforth Ave., Toronto ON M4K 1P6
416-463-4411 416-463-4562
baker@tonybakerlaw.com
www.tonybakerlaw.com

***Toronto*: Baksh, Ahmad N. - *1**
#307, 1280 Finch Ave. West, Toronto ON M3J 3K6
416-667-1922 416-667-0304
anbaksh@bellnet.ca

***Toronto*: Banks & Starkman - *2**
#310, 200 Ronson Dr., Toronto ON M9W 5Z9
416-243-3394 416-243-9692
lbanks@banksandstarkman.com
www.banksandstarkman.com

***Toronto*: Barrs, J.R. - *1**
23 Bedford Road, Toronto ON M5R 2J9
416-366-6466 416-364-2308

***Toronto*: Bart, Jacqueline R. - *1**
#2200, Law Chambers, ING Tower 181 University Ave., Toronto ON M5H 3M7
416-601-1346 416-601-1357
jbart@canadianrelocationlaw.com
www.canadianrelocationlaw.com

***Toronto*: Basman, Smith - *19**
111 Richmond St. West, 8th Floor, Toronto ON M5H 2G4
416-365-0300 416-365-9276 877-262-0001 Telex: 06-980391
info@basmansmith.com
www.basmansmith.com

***Toronto*: Batcher, Wasserman & Associates - *2**
#500, 718 Wilson Ave., Toronto ON M3K 1E2
416-635-6300 416-635-6376 877-813-0820

***Toronto*: Beach, Hepburn - *4**
#1000, 36 Toronto St., Toronto ON M5C 2C5
416-350-3500 416-350-3510
gpiper@beachlaw.com
www.beachlaw.com

***Toronto*: Beard, Winter - *47**
#701 130 Adelaide St. West, Toronto ON M5H 2K4
416-593-5555 416-593-7760
info@beardwinter.com
www.beardwinter.com

***Toronto*: Bellissimo, Steven - *1**
#1200, 439 University Ave., Toronto ON M5G 1Y8
416-362-6437 416-972-9940
steve@sblaw.ca

***Toronto*: Benson Percival Brown - *17**
#800, 250 Dundas St. West, Toronto ON M5T 2Z6
416-977-9777 416-977-1241
www.bensonpercival.com

***Toronto*: Bereskin & Parr - *55**
Scotia Plaza 40 King St. West, 40th Fl., Toronto ON M5H 3Y2
416-364-7311 416-361-1398 888-364-7311
info@bereskinparr.com
www.bereskinparr.com

***Toronto*: Bergel & Edson - *7**
#501, 1018 Finch Ave. West, Toronto ON M3J 3L5
416-663-2211 416-663-2348 866-492-3743
www.bergeledson.com

***Toronto*: Betel, Myer - *1**
7 Farrington Dr., Toronto ON M2L 2B4

416-447-4333 416-447-3773
mbctel@rogers.com

Toronto: **Bigelow, Hendy - *6**
#200, 789 Don Mills Rd., Toronto ON M3C 1T5
416-429-3110 416-429-3057
bigelows@on.aibn.com
www.bigelowhendy.com

Toronto: **Birenbaum & Bernstein - *2**
#101, 3042 Keele St., Toronto ON M3M 2H5
416-633-3720 416-633-4546

Toronto: **Birenbaum, Steinberg, Landau, Savin & Colraine LLP - *9**
#1000, 33 Bloor St. East, Toronto ON M4W 3H1
416-961-4100 416-961-2531
birenbaum@bslsc.com
www.bslsc.com

Toronto: **Black, Sutherland LLP - *11**
#3425, P.O Box 34 130 Adelaide St. West, Toronto ON M5H 3P5
416-361-1500 416-361-1674 866-902-7557
info@blacksutherland.com
www.blacksutherland.com

Toronto: **Blaier, Harry - *1**
#1800, Madison Centre 4950 Yonge St., Toronto ON M2N 6K1
416-224-0200 416-224-0758
hblaier@torlaw.com

Toronto: **Blaney McMurtry LLP - *108**
#1500, 2 Queen St. East, Toronto ON M5C 3G5
416-593-1221 416-593-5437 Telex: 06-22326
info@blaney.com
www.blaney.com

Toronto: **Bliss, Jonathan A. - *1**
370 Bloor St. East, Toronto ON M4W 3M6
416-927-9000 416-927-9069
jonbliss@sympatico.ca

Toronto: **Bloom & Lanys - *1**
#100, 250 Roehampton Ave., Toronto ON M4P 1R9
416-486-9913 416-485-6054 877-835-7658
barb@bloom-lanys.com

Toronto: **Bloomenfeld, Joseph L. - *1**
#2110, 120 Adelaide St. West, Toronto ON M5H 2C9
416-363-7315 416-363-7697

Toronto: **Blumberg Segal LLP - *6**
#1202, 390 Bay St., Toronto ON M5H 2Y2
416-361-1982 416-363-8451
info@blumbergs.ca
www.blumbergs.ca

Toronto: **Bodnaruk & Capone - *2**
#416, P.O Box 49 370 King St. West, Toronto ON M5V 1J9
416-593-7000 416-593-5359

Toronto: **Bomza, G.H. - *1**
#2303, 180 Dundas St. West, Toronto ON M5G 1Z8
416-598-2244 416-598-3830
rosehallmgmt@bellnet.ca

Toronto: **Book, Ira E. - *1**
#200, 85 Scarsdale Rd., Toronto ON M3B 2R2
416-447-2665 416-447-0066
ira@irabook.com

Toronto: **Borski, Norman H.R., Q.C. - *1**
#201, 2256B Bloor St. West, Toronto ON M6S 1N6
416-766-2441

Toronto: **Botiuk, Y.R., Q.C. - *2**
#212, 2323 Bloor St. West, Toronto ON M6S 4W1
416-763-4333 416-763-0613

Toronto: **Boyce, Mary E.E. - *1**
69 Elm St., Toronto ON M5G 1H2
416-591-7588 416-971-9092

Toronto: **Bradley, P.G. - *1**
1051 Tapscott Rd., Toronto ON M1X 1A1
416-298-0066 416-299-8008
patrick@runnymede-dev.com

Toronto: **Braithwaite, L.A., C.M., O.Ont., Q.C. - *1**
250 Wincott Dr., Toronto ON M9R 2R5
416-249-2288 416-249-2280

Toronto: **Braund, G.K.C., Q.C. - *1**
#204, 3333 Bayview Ave., Toronto ON M2K 1G4
416-223-0862 416-223-4073

Toronto: **Brent, Philip E. - *1**
#1160, 36 Toronto St., Toronto ON M5C 2C5
416-203-1449 416-203-1772
brentayr@allstream.net

Toronto: **Bresver, Grossman, Scheininger & Chapman - *5**
#2800, 390 Bay St., Toronto ON M5H 2Y2
416-869-0366 416-869-0321

Toronto: **Brown & Burnes - *6**
#1400, 390 Bay St., Toronto ON M5H 2Y2
416-366-7927 416-363-9602
info@brownburnes.com
www.brownburnes.com

Toronto: **Brown & Korte Barristers - *12**
130 Adelaide St. West, 31st Fl., Toronto ON M5H 3P5
416-869-0123 416-869-0271
lawyers@brownandkorte.ca
www.brownandkorte.com

Toronto: **Brown, Kenneth J. - *1**
45 Mogul Dr., Toronto ON M2H 2M8
416-499-8005 416-499-8048
k.j.brown@sympatico.ca

Toronto: **Brown, M.H. - *1**
38 Berwick Ave., Toronto ON M5P 1H1
416-487-5122 416-487-5168
mel@browngroup.net

Toronto: **Brown, Peck & Lubelsky - *4**
5287 Yonge St., Toronto ON M2N 5R3
416-223-8811 416-223-8485

Toronto: **Brudner, Jack - *1**
301 Donlands Avenue, Toronto ON M4J 3R8
416-267-1148 416-267-4741

Toronto: **Bruner, G.J. - *1**
167 Danforth Ave., Toronto ON M4K 1N2
416-461-0983 416-462-3347

Toronto: **Bryant, Anthony G. - *1**
#1706, 51 York Mills Road, Toronto ON M2P 1B6
416-927-7441 416-413-0230
tbryant@istar.ca

Toronto: **Burke, J.J. - *1**
#302, 2405 Lakeshore Blvd. West, Toronto ON M8V 1C6
416-252-9101
jjburke@bellnet.ca

Toronto: **Burkman, Harry R. - *1**
#2810, P.O Box 129 1 First Canadian Pl., Toronto ON M5X 1A4
416-364-3831 416-364-3832
hburkman@burkman.com
www.burkman.com

Toronto: **Burnett & Jacobson - *3**
48 St. Clair Ave. West, Toronto ON M4V 3C9
416-922-8710 416-964-5840

Toronto: **Bussin & Bussin - *3**
#1822, 181 University Ave., Toronto ON M5H 3M7
416-364-4925 416-868-1818
bruce@bussinlaw.com

Toronto: **CaleyWray - *10**
#1205, 111 Richmond St. West, Toronto ON M5H 2G4
416-366-3763 416-366-3293
mail@caleywray.com
www.caleywray.com

Toronto: **Campbell, John R., Q.C. - *2**
5 Douglas Crescent, Toronto ON M4W 2E6
416-924-9066 416-961-0510
hkljrc@pathcom.com

Toronto: **Cancilla, G.H. - *1**
#506, 372 Bay St., Toronto ON M5H 2W9
416-366-9504 416-628-6628
ghc@cancillaw.com

Toronto: **Cannings, John - *5**
#400, 425 University Ave., Toronto ON M5G 1T6
416-591-0703 416-591-0710
info@jcannings.com
www.jcannings.com/

Toronto: **Canton, Ruth - *1**
2489 Bloor St. West, Toronto ON M6S 1R6
416-769-5759 416-769-3132 888-838-7432

Toronto: **Cappell Parker LLP, Barristers & Solicitors - *2**
#1200, Toronto-Dominion Centre 95 Wellington St. West, Toronto ON M5J 2Z9
416-367-0900 416-367-0901
fecappell@cappell.com
www.cappell.com

Toronto: **Caroline, Michael W. - *1**
#803, Waterpark Place 10 Bay St., Toronto ON M5J 2R8
416-203-2250 416-203-2280
mwcaroline@bellnet.ca

Toronto: **Carroll, C. Anthony - *1**
#1807, 8 King St. East, Toronto ON M5C 1B5
416-361-0522 416-361-0248
carrollt@istar.ca

Toronto: **Cass, G.M. - *1**
#401, 265 Yorkland Blvd., Toronto ON M2J 1S5
416-767-2277 416-491-0273

Toronto: **Cassels Brock & Blackwell LLP - *203**
#2100, Scotia Plaza 40 King St. West, Toronto ON M5H 3C2
416-869-5386 416-350-6912 Telex: 06-23415
lsaltman@casselsbrock.com
www.casselsbrock.com

Toronto: **Ceresney, Weisberg Associates - *2**
#202, 4651 Sheppard Ave. East, Toronto ON M1S 3V4
416-291-7701 416-291-1766

Toronto: **Chaitons LLP - *20**
185 Sheppard Ave. West, Toronto ON M2N 1M9
416-222-8888 416-222-8402
info@chaitons.com
www.chaiton.com

Toronto: **Chapin-Hill, Beverly C. - *1**
16 Neville Park Blvd., Toronto ON M4E 3P6
416-690-1832 416-698-6041
bev@chapinandchapin.ca
www.chapinandchapin.com

Toronto: **Chapnick & Associates - *4**
228 Carlton St., Toronto ON M5A 2L1
416-968-2160 416-975-9338
www.chapnickassociates.com

Toronto: **Chop, Christopher E. - *1**
#2000, 1 Queen St. East, Toronto ON M5C 2W5
416-601-4159 416-601-0206
chop@allstream.net

Toronto: **Christies - *8**
#301, Confederation Sq. 20 Richmond St. East, Toronto ON M5C 2R9
416-367-0680 416-367-0429
information@christie-lawyers.com
www.christie-lawyers.com

Toronto: **Christoff, B.N. - *1**
#304, 3335 Yonge St., Toronto ON M4N 2M1
416-482-0990 416-482-6511

Toronto: **Cirone, Dino J. - *1**
#2, 2084 Danforth Ave., Toronto ON M4C 1J9
416-423-8515 416-423-4971

Toronto: **Clapp, S.G. - *1**
18 Erskine Ave., Toronto ON M4P 1Y2
416-484-4840 416-484-0821
stanleyclapp@on.aibn.com

Toronto: **Clark, Farb, Fiksel - *6**
188 Avenue Rd., Toronto ON M5J 2J1
416-599-7761 416-324-4220
www.cfflaw.com

Toronto: **Clarke, Freeman, Miller & Ryan - *1**
1863 Danforth Ave., Toronto ON M4C 1J3
416-698-9323 416-698-9110

Toronto: **Clyne, L. Peter - *1**
#1709, 5650 Yonge St., Toronto ON M2M 4G3
416-922-0864 416-922-6856
clynelaw@on.aibn.com

Toronto: **Coates, Robert G. - *1**
#307, 120 Carlton St., Toronto ON M5A 4K2
416-925-6490 416-925-4492
robert@rgcoates.com
www.rgcoates.com

Toronto: Cohen, M.V. - *1
111 Richmond Street West, Toronto ON M5H 2G4
416-363-8366
mvcohen2002@yahoo.ca

Toronto: Collins, John - *1
#400, 357 Bay St., Toronto ON M5H 2R7
416-364-9006 416-862-7911
john.collins@on.aibn.com

Toronto: Cooper & Cooper - *1
#208, 133 Richmond St. West, Toronto ON M5H 2L3
416-362-6459 416-362-3139

Toronto: Cooper, Kleinman - *2
3 Rowanwood Ave., Toronto ON M4W 1Y5
416-867-1400 416-867-1873
gwcooper@cooperkleinman.ca

Toronto: Cooper, Morris - *1
99 Yorkville Ave., Toronto ON M5R 3K5
416-961-2626 416-961-4000
cooper@cooperlaw.ca

Toronto: Copeland Duncan - *2
31 Prince Arthur Ave., Toronto ON M5R 1B2
416-964-8126 416-960-5456
paulcope9@yahoo.com

Toronto: Copelovici, Jack - *1
#204, 1220 Sheppard Ave. East, Toronto ON M2K 2S5
416-494-0910 416-494-5480
jack@copel-law.com

Toronto: Costa, Fernando D. - *1
#200, 1112 Dundas St. West, Toronto ON M6J 1X2
416-534-6357 416-534-6219
fd.costa@bellnet.ca

Toronto: Costigan Horgan - *2
#410, 120 Carlton St., Toronto ON M5A 4K2
416-922-8611 416-922-1963
acostigan@chmlegal.com

Toronto: Cousins, D.B. - *1
#203, 425 University Ave., Toronto ON M5G 1T6
416-977-8871 416-599-8075
david.b.cousins@bellnet.ca

Toronto: Coutts, Crane, Ingram - *7
#700, 480 University Ave., Toronto ON M5G 1V2
416-977-0956 416-977-5331
info@couttscrane.com
www.couttscrane.com

Toronto: Cowitz, Ronald - *1
#308, 344 Bloor St. West, Toronto ON M5S 3A7
416-944-9594

Toronto: Cox, Christopher G. - *1
#209, 1711 McCowan Rd., Toronto ON M1S 2Y3
416-447-4274 416-823-3215
cgcoxlaw@hotmail.com

Toronto: Cozen O'Connor - *8
#2000, 1 Queen St. East, Toronto ON M5C 2W5
416-361-3200 416-361-1405 Telex: 06-986391

Toronto: Cremer, F.H. - *1
#201, 1593 Wilson Ave., Toronto ON M3L 1A5
416-244-5575 416-247-3844

Toronto: Crosse, Leroy A. - *1
#203, 705 Lawrence Ave. West, Toronto ON M6A 1B4
416-785-8338 416-785-9369

Toronto: Crowe, Paul J. - *1
#220, 4950 Yonge St., Toronto ON M2N 6K1
416-733-0255 416-221-9965 877-649-9999
pauljcrowe@hotmail.com

Toronto: Crum-Ewing & Poliacik - *2
56 Sheppard Ave. West, Toronto ON M2N 1M2
416-733-9292 416-733-9654
poliacik@ceplaw.ca

Toronto: Cundari, Gino A.J. - *1
1179 St. Clair Ave. West, Toronto ON M6E 1B5
416-654-9000 416-654-6688

Toronto: Cusmariu, J. Jerome - *1
1310 Dundas St. West, Toronto ON M6J 1Y1
416-533-1173 416-533-0761
jcusmariu@on.aibn.com

Toronto: Cutler, E.H. - *1
#18A, 156 Duncan Mill Rd., Toronto ON M3B 3N2
416-449-4962 416-449-5107
ernestcutler@bellnet.ca

Toronto: Czuma, Ritter - *2
410 - 120 Carlton St., Toronto ON M5A 4K2
416-599-5799 416-599-9981
michael@michaelczuma.com
www.michaelczuma.com

Toronto: D'Alimonte, E.L. - *1
#203, 1111 Albion Rd., Toronto ON M9V 1A9
416-741-5373

Toronto: Danson, Recht, Voudouris LLP - *5
#2000, 700 Bay St., Toronto ON M5G 1Z6
416-929-2200 416-929-2192
www.drv-law.com

Toronto: Danson, Zucker & Connelly - *3
#500, 70 Bond St., Toronto ON M5B 1X3
416-863-9955 416-863-4896

Toronto: Daris, James - *1
#101, 8 Irwin Ave., Toronto ON M4Y 1K9
416-465-4973 416-465-6042

Toronto: David Charles Barristers Professional Corp. - *4
#800, 1200 Bay St., Toronto ON M5R 2A5
416-923-7407 416-923-6070

Toronto: Davies McLean Zweig Associates - *3
1035 McNicoll Ave., Toronto ON M1W 3W6
416-756-7500 416-512-1212

Toronto: Davison, Marie - *1
327 Eglinton Ave. East, Toronto ON M4P 1L7
416-486-9701 416-483-1397

Toronto: de Zoysa, Tilaka - *1
#207, 2131 Lawrence Ave. East, Toronto ON M1R 5G4
416-752-2253 416-752-6356

Toronto: Deacon, Spears, Fedson & Montizambert - *7
#2900, 2300 Yonge St., Toronto ON M4P 1E4
416-489-5677 416-489-7794
info@condolaw.to
www.condolaw.to

Toronto: DelZotto, Zorzi LLP - *12
4810 Dufferin St., #D, Toronto ON M3H 5S8
416-665-5555 416-665-9653
info@dzlaw.com
www.dzlaw.com

Toronto: Dempsey, A.M., Q.C. - *1
533 Queen St. East, Toronto ON M5A 1V1
416-364-6755 416-364-7049

Toronto: Devenney, Donald W. - *1
#1106, 66 Spadina Rd., Toronto ON M5R 2T4
416-964-2687

Toronto: Devlin, Jane H. - *1
#701, 100 Adelaide St. West, Toronto ON M5H 1S3
416-366-3091 416-366-0879
arbserv@istar.ca

Toronto: Devry, Smith & Frank - *27
#100, 95 Barber Greene Rd., Toronto ON M3C 3E9
416-449-1400 416-449-7071
info@devrylaw.ca
www.devrylaw.ca

Toronto: Dewji, Iqbal I. - *1
#810, 255 Duncan Mill Road, Toronto ON M3B 2H9
416-449-9600 416-449-9348
iimd@rogers.com

Toronto: Diamond, Michael R. - *1
#200, 111 Eglinton Ave. East, Toronto ON M4P 1H4
416-482-2666 416-482-4165
sndicator@sympatico.ca

Toronto: Dickson MacGregor Appell LLP - *9
#306, 10 Alcorn Ave., Toronto ON M4V 3A9
416-927-0891 416-927-0385
ellis@dicksonlawyers.com
www.dicksonlawyers.com

Toronto: Doan, H.J. Barrister & Solicitor - *1
18 Wild Briarway, Toronto ON M2J 2L2
416-491-2700 416-502-9373

Toronto: Dolman, C.H., Q.C. - *1
#102, 10 Milner Business Ct., Toronto ON M1B 3C6
416-754-8177 416-754-8337
cdolman@rogers.com

Toronto: Donnelly, Brian P. - *1
#1509, 180 Dundas St. West, Toronto ON M5G 1Z8
416-597-2191 416-597-9808

Toronto: Donnelly, J. Brian - *1
#201, 1165A St. Clair Ave. West, Toronto ON M6E 1B2
416-653-0311 416-653-6653
jbd@jbdonnelly.com

Toronto: Downtown Legal Services - *3
655 Spadina Ave., Toronto ON M5S 2H9
416-934-4535 416-934-4536
law.dls@utoronto.ca
www.dls.utoronto.ca

Toronto: Draimin, William C. - *1
#101, 45 St. Clair Ave. West, Toronto ON M4V 1K9
416-920-4605 416-960-0698
wdraimin@draiminlaw.com

Toronto: Dranoff & Huddart - *2
#314, 1033 Bay St., Toronto ON M5S 3A5
416-925-4500 416-925-5197
info@dranoffhuddart.com
www.dranoffhuddart.com

Toronto: Drummie, J. Blair - *1
326 Richmond St. West, Toronto ON M5V 1X2
416-921-0915 416-925-6181

Toronto: Dungey, Thomas S. - *1
46 Fairview Blvd., Toronto ON M4K 1L9
416-469-3088 416-469-6739
tsdungey@rogers.com

Toronto: Durbin, Norman L.. - *1
2530 Jane St., Toronto ON M3L 1S1
416-743-2345 416-743-0645

Toronto: Dutton Brock LLP - *31
#1700, 438 University Ave., Toronto ON M5G 2L9
416-593-4411 416-593-5922
info@duttonbrock.com
www.duttonbrock.com

Toronto: Dzwiekowski, Diana C. - *1
260 Willard Ave., Toronto ON M6S 3R2
416-762-7251 416-762-7252

Toronto: Ecclestone, Hamer, Poisson & Neuwald & Freeman - *5
#900, 372 Bay St., Toronto ON M5C 1J3
416-365-7135 416-365-2189
ecclchyk@idirect.com

Toronto: Edgar, John M. - *1
2901 Bloor St. West, Toronto ON M8X 1B3
416-231-3261 416-231-8352

Toronto: Elkind, Lipton & Jacobs LLP - *8
#1900, 1 Queen St. East, Toronto ON M5C 2W6
416-367-0871 416-367-9388
info@elkindlipton.com
www.eljlaw.com

Toronto: Epstein Cole LLP - *25
#2200, 393 University Ave., Toronto ON M5G 1E6
416-862-9888 416-862-2142
www.epsteincole.com

Toronto: Epstein, Norman - *1
281 Eglinton Ave. East, Toronto ON M4P 1L3
416-225-5577 416-483-5541

Toronto: Ermacora, J.A. - *1
75 Lowther Ave., Toronto ON M5R 1C9
416-961-5500 416-961-9905
jermac@sympatico.ca

Toronto: Field, Brown - *3
5140 Yonge Street, Toronto ON M7A 2K2
416-595-1111 416-595-7312 Telex: 06-983639

Toronto: Filion Wakely Thorup Angeletti LLP - *26
#2601, P.O Box 32 150 King St. West, Toronto ON M5H 4B6
416-408-3221 416-408-4814
toronto@filion.on.ca
www.filion.on.ca

Toronto: Fine, Andrew - *1
#306, 1000 Finch Ave. West, Toronto ON M3J 2V5

416-785-9499

Toronto: **Fisch & Antonette - *1**
419 College St., Toronto ON M5T 1T1
416-920-6312 416-920-1780
josephyfisch@hotmail.com

Toronto: **Fisch, Joseph Y. - *2**
#1, 394 College St., Toronto ON M5T 1S7
416-920-6312 416-920-1780
josephyfisch@hotmail.com

Toronto: **Fishbayn, Steven M. - *1**
#400, 100 Richmond St. West, Toronto ON M5H 3K6
416-361-9555 416-862-7602

Toronto: **Fisher, R.A. - *1**
#309, 95 Barber Greene Rd., Toronto ON M3C 3E9
416-449-3004 416-441-6898
royfisher@hotmail.com

Toronto: **Fiske, Donald R. - *1**
#665, West Tower, Clarica Centre 3300 Bloor St. West, Toronto ON M8X 2X8
416-234-2177 416-234-9039
fiske@bellnet.ca

Toronto: **Fleischer & Kochberg - *1**
#203, 77 Finch Ave. West, Toronto ON M2N 2H5
416-223-8102 416-223-9502
thefirm@relo-law.com
www.relo-law.com

Toronto: **Fleming, White & Burgess - *2**
#1000, 2 Bloor St. West, Toronto ON M4W 3E2
416-961-2868 416-961-2964
flemingwhite@bellnet.ca

Toronto: **Fleury, Comery LLP - *4**
#104, 215 Morrish Rd., Toronto ON M1C 1E9
416-282-5754 416-282-9906
thefirm@fleurcom.on.ca
www.fleurcom.on.ca

Toronto: **Flom, Ronald - *2**
#712, 2345 Yonge St., Toronto ON M4P 2E5
416-482-2777 416-482-2599

Toronto: **Fogler, Rubinoff LLP - *94**
#1200, Toronto-Dominion Centre 95 Wellington St. West, Toronto ON M5J 2Z9
416-864-9700 416-941-8852 866-861-9700
thefirm@foglers.com
www.foglers.com

Toronto: **Fraser, Simms and Reid - *1**
#2, 15 John St., Toronto ON M9N 1J2
416-241-0111 416-241-1911

Toronto: **Freedman, Harvey - *3**
#100, 79 Shuter St., Toronto ON M5B 1B3
416-363-1737 416-861-9919
hfreedman@freedmans.ca

Toronto: **Freedman, Joel P. - *1**
#303, 3200 Dufferin St., Toronto ON M6A 2T3
416-248-6231 416-241-0080
joelpfreedman@hotmail.com

Toronto: **Freedman, Norman J., Q.C.**
#2150, 121 King St. West, Toronto ON M5H 3T9
416-815-7767 416-815-7722

Toronto: **Friedman, J., Q.C. - *1**
#202, 30 St. Clair Ave. West, Toronto ON M4V 3A1
416-515-0575 416-515-0454
jack.friedman@bellnet.ca

Toronto: **Friend, David G., Q.C. - *1**
#202, 3459 Sheppard Ave. East, Toronto ON M1T 3K5
416-754-0333 416-292-0473
dfriend@bellnet.ca

Toronto: **Frymer, Harry - *1**
#320, 100 Richmond St. West, Toronto ON M5H 3K6
416-869-1073 416-869-1840

Toronto: **Fyshe McMahon LLP - *9**
#2000, 393 University Ave., Toronto ON M5G 1E6
416-977-1525 416-977-1526

Toronto: **Gabriel, F.A. - *1**
#203, 425 University Ave., Toronto ON M5G 1T6
416-593-6621 416-599-8075
fgabriel@bellnet.ca

Toronto: **Garbig, Douglas Gordon, A Professional Corporation - *1**
#3101, P.O Box 52 401 Bay St., Toronto ON M5H 2Y4
416-862-7822 416-862-2568
garbig@garbig.com

Toronto: **Gardiner, Roberts LLP - *67**
#3100, Scotia Plaza 40 King St. West, Toronto ON M5H 3Y2
416-865-6600 416-865-6636
www.gardiner-roberts.com

Toronto: **Garfin Zeidenberg LLP - *13**
#800, Yonge Norton Centre 5255 Yonge St., Toronto ON M2N 6P4
416-512-8000 416-512-9992 877-529-9910
gzinfo@gzlegal.com
www.gzlegal.com

Toronto: **Garfinkle, Biderman - *19**
#801, One Financial Place 1 Adelaide St. East, Toronto ON M5C 2V9
416-869-1234 416-869-0547
www.garfinkle.com

Toronto: **Gasee, Cohen & Youngman, Barrister & Solicitor - *6**
#200, 65 Queen St. West, Toronto ON M5H 2M5
416-363-3351 416-363-0252
info@gcylaw.com
www.gcylaw.com

Toronto: **Geffen, L.B. - *1**
#205, 2907 Kennedy Rd., Toronto ON M1V 1S8
416-292-6688 416-292-6649
lgeffen@idirect.com

Toronto: **Gelfand & Co. - *2**
519 King Street West, Toronto ON M5V 1K4
416-929-4949 416-929-1996 877-286-4296
lgelfand@gelfandandco.com

Toronto: **Georgieff, Basil L. - *1**
3543A St. Clair Ave. East, Toronto ON M1K 1L6
416-464-6888 416-267-1452
basgeo@msn.com

Toronto: **Gershuny, Lorne - *1**
1577 Bloor St. West, Toronto ON M6P 1A6
416-539-0989 416-536-3618
lgershuny@hotmail.com

Toronto: **Gilbert, Wright & Kirby LLP - *9**
#2302, P.O Box 103 401 Bay St., Toronto ON M5H 2Y4
416-363-3100 416-363-1379
info@gwklaw.com
www.gwklaw.com

Toronto: **Gilbertson Davis Emerson LLP - *8**
#2020, 20 Queen St. West, Toronto ON M5H 3R3
416-979-2020 416-979-1285
office@gilbertsondavis.com
www.gilbertsondavis.com

Toronto: **Giroday, Leslie M. - *1**
190 Sixth St., Toronto ON M8V 3A5
416-255-1063 416-251-8699
lmgiroday@sympatico.ca

Toronto: **Glasner, Earl - *1**
#320, 100 Richmond St. West, Toronto ON M5H 3K6
416-869-1076
earlglasner@rogers.com

Toronto: **Glass, Alan A. - *1**
#500, 1000 Finch Ave. West, Toronto ON M3J 2V5
416-667-9796 416-667-8048

Toronto: **Glass, Murray, Bianchi - *4**
50 Richmond St. East, 5th Fl., Toronto ON M5C 1N7
416-363-9295 416-363-7659
lglass@glassassoc.com

Toronto: **Glatt, Louis - *1**
2354 Danforth Ave., Toronto ON M4C 1K7
416-422-2107 416-422-2606

Toronto: **Glober & Cohen, Associates - *3**
114 Scollard St., Toronto ON M5R 1G2
416-324-9994 416-324-0966

Toronto: **Gluckstein & Associates LLP - *7**
#301, P.O Box 53 595 Bay St., Toronto ON M5G 2C2
416-408-4252 416-408-4235 866-308-7722
info@gluckstein.com
www.gluckstein.com

Toronto: **Godfrey & Corcoran - *1**
#702, 55 Queen St. East, Toronto ON M5C 1R6
416-363-0484 416-363-0485
ccorcoran@idirect.com

Toronto: **Goldhar & Nemoy - *2**
#214, 120 Carlton St., Toronto ON M5A 4K2
416-928-1488 416-924-7166

Toronto: **Goldkind, H.A. - *1**
#320, 100 Richmond St. West, Toronto ON M5H 3K6
416-366-5280

Toronto: **Goldman, Jeffrey W. - *1**
#300, 3500 Dufferin St., Toronto ON M3K 1N2
416-787-1818 416-787-1810
jeffreygoldman@goldmanlawoffice.com

Toronto: **Goldman, R.M. - *1**
#301, 481 Univeristy Ave., Toronto ON M5G 2E9
416-977-8008 416-364-2308
rgoldman@defender.ca

Toronto: **Goldman, Spring, Kichler & Sanders - *7**
#700, 40 Sheppard Ave. West, Toronto ON M2N 6K9
416-225-9400 416-225-4805

Toronto: **Goldstein & Grubner LLP - *2**
#212, 3459 Sheppard Ave. East, Toronto ON M1T 3K5
416-292-0414 416-292-4508
k.goldstein@rogers.com; igrubner@rogers.com

Toronto: **Goldstein, H.S. - *1**
#1202, P.O Box 159 4950 Yonge St., Toronto ON M2N 6K1
416-223-0600

Toronto: **Goldstein, Rosen & Rassos LLP - *2**
#102, 1648 Victoria Park Ave., Toronto ON M1R 1P7
416-757-4156 416-757-9318
trassos@grrlaw.ca

Toronto: **Golish & Golish - *2**
21 Fairholme Avenue, Toronto ON M6B 2W4
416-789-2438 416-789-2438

Toronto: **Goodman and Carr LLP - *90**
#2300, 200 King St. West, Toronto ON M5H 3W5
416-595-2300 416-595-0567 800-890-7319
mail@goodmancarr.com
www.goodmancarr.com

Toronto: **Goodman, Solomon & Gold - *3**
#1500, 439 University Ave., Toronto ON M5G 1Y8
416-595-5555 416-595-7020

Toronto: **Goodman, Stanley, Q.C. - *1**
#1800, 4950 Yonge St., Toronto ON M2N 6K1
416-224-0224 416-224-0758
stangoodman@torlaw.com

Toronto: **Goose, Martin Z. - *1**
#504, 555 Burnhamthorpe Rd., Toronto ON M9C 2Y3
416-239-4811 416-239-1707
martingoose@bellnet.ca

Toronto: **Gotlieb, Nathan - *1**
#1800, Madison Centre 4950 Yonge St., Toronto ON M2N 6K1
416-224-0200 416-224-0758
ngotlieb@torlaw.com

Toronto: **Gottlieb, G.L., Q.C. - *1**
#309, 600 Bay St., Toronto ON M5G 1M6
416-977-3835 416-977-3807
glgqc@interlog.com
www.glgqc.com

Toronto: **Gould, Max A. - *1**
#1000, 30 St. Clair Ave. West, Toronto ON M4V 3A1
416-964-0290 416-964-7102

Toronto: **Gould, Michael J. - *1**
75 Bannatyne Dr., Toronto ON M2L 2P2
416-510-3030

Toronto: **Graham Tobe - *1**
#202, 1 Yorkdale Rd., Toronto ON M6A 3A1
416-256-1555 416-256-0918

Toronto: **Grant, D.J. - *1**
#412, 1220 Sheppard Ave. East, Toronto ON M2K 2S5
416-490-9206 416-490-9949

Toronto: **Green & Chercover - *15**
30 St. Clair Ave. West, 10th Fl., Toronto ON M4V 3A1

416-968-3333 416-968-0325
inquiry@greenchercover.ca
www.greenchercover.ca

Toronto: **Green & Spiegel - *12**
#2800, 390 Bay St., Toronto ON M5H 2Y2
416-862-7880 416-862-1698 Telex: 06 218815 G AND

Toronto: **Green, David J. - *1**
#1, 399 Spadina Ave., Toronto ON M5T 2G6
416-979-2333 416-597-8966

Toronto: **Green, Weldon F., Q.C. - *1**
P.O Box 151 6 Portneuf Ct., Toronto ON M5A 4E4
416-364-4465 416-364-3657
wfgreenco@on.aibn.com

Toronto: **Greenbaum, Donald M., Q.C. - *1**
258 Wilson Ave., Toronto ON M3H 1S6
416-631-7504 416-631-9895
baum@globility.com

Toronto: **Greenberg & Levine - *2**
2223 Kennedy Rd., Toronto ON M1T 3G5
416-292-6500 416-292-6559
reception@greenbergandlevine.com
www.greenbergandlevine.com

Toronto: **Greenberg, Jack - *1**
#204, 181 Eglinton Ave. East, Toronto ON M4P 1J4
416-485-8833 416-485-3246
jackgreenberg@greenberglawyers.ca

Toronto: **Greenspan, White - *7**
144 King St. East, Toronto ON M5C 1G8
416-366-3961 416-366-7994
www.greenspanwhite.com

Toronto: **Gresik, E.J. - *1**
101 Scollard St., Toronto ON M5R 1G4
416-924-0781 416-960-9650

Toronto: **Grimanis, C. - *1**
799 Carlaw Avenue, Toronto ON M4K 3E4
416-469-1176 416-469-4252

Toronto: **Grosberg, C.H. - *1**
#205, 2907 Kennedy Rd., Toronto ON M1V 1S8
416-752-9745 416-292-6649

Toronto: **Guberman Garson Bush - *7**
#1920, 130 Adelaide St. West, Toronto ON M5H 3P5
416-363-1234 416-363-8760
immlaw@ggbilaw.com
www.gubermangarson.com

Toronto: **Guoba, J.M. - *2**
#211, 2425 Eglinton Ave. East, Toronto ON M1K 5G8
416-759-4500 416-759-4510

Toronto: **Hadbavny, Lawrence - *1**
Law Society of Upper Canada 130 Queen St. West, Toronto ON M5H 2N6
416-947-3906 416-644-4880
lhadbavn@lsuc.on.ca

Toronto: **Hahn & Maian - *2**
664 Mount Pleasant Rd., Toronto ON M4S 2N3
416-486-9445 416-486-1174
johnhahn@idirect.com

Toronto: **Hahn, Kenneth A. - *1**
1078 Kipling Ave., Toronto ON M9B 3M2
416-231-3353 416-231-6773

Toronto: **Halpert, Allan S. - *2**
37 Maitland St., Toronto ON M4Y 1C8
416-968-7733 416-968-7192
allan@halpertlaw.com

Toronto: **Hans & Hans - *1**
17 Wembley Rd., Toronto ON M6C 2E8
416-960-5445 416-924-7541
hansoff10@rogers.com

Toronto: **Haque, Zakaul - *1**
#205, 1058A Albion Rd., Toronto ON M9V 1A7
416-743-6302 416-743-4783

Toronto: **Harasymowycz, George M. - *1**
#200, 2311 Bloor St. West, Toronto ON M6S 1P1
416-766-2472 416-766-3297
george@haraslaw.com

Toronto: **Harrington, Murray P. - *1**
285 Pitfield Rd., Toronto ON M1S 1Z2
416-299-0477 416-299-7570

Toronto: **Harris, David E. - *1**
#1900, 439 University Ave., Toronto ON M5G 1Y8
416-585-9329 416-408-2372
delih@inforamp.net

Toronto: **Hartmann, Klaus - *1**
391 Willowdale Ave., Toronto ON M2N 5A8
416-590-0311 416-590-0312

Toronto: **Hebb, Marian D. - *2**
250 Merton Street, Toronto ON M4S 1B1
416-971-6618 416-971-4144
mhebb@sympatico.ca

Toronto: **Heiber, E.S. - *1**
#200, 70 Bond St., Toronto ON M5B 1X3
416-362-2768 416-865-5328
esheiber@hvllp.com

Toronto: **Heifetz, Crozier, Law - *5**
#600, 10 King St. East, Toronto ON M5C 1C3
416-863-1717 416-368-3133
dcrozier@hclaw.com
www.hclaw.com

Toronto: **Heller, Rubel - *9**
#1902, 120 Adelaide St. West, Toronto ON M5H 1T1
416-863-9311 416-863-9465
mshore@hellerrubel.com

Toronto: **Hicks Morley Hamilton Stewart Storie LLP - *75**
TD Tower, TD Centre Box 371 P.O Box 371 TD Centre66 Wellington St., 30th Fl., Toronto ON M5K 1K8
416-362-1011 416-362-9680
www.hicksmorley.com

Toronto: **Hiltz Szigeti LLP - *2**
#906, 94 Cumberland St., Toronto ON M5R 1A3
416-968-6575 416-968-3424
lawyers@hslaw.ca

Toronto: **Holder, Gerri C. - *1**
#901, 701 Evans Ave., Toronto ON M9C 1A3
416-626-3069 416-622-8952
gholder@rogers.com

Toronto: **Holoboff, Christopher - *1**
#500, 27 Queen St. East, Toronto ON M5C 2M6
416-868-0878 416-868-0879
choloboff@aol.com

Toronto: **Hornstein, E.R. - *1**
19 Relmore Rd., Toronto ON M5P 2Y4
416-901-7949

Toronto: **Houser, Henry & Syron - *6**
#2000, 145 King St. West, Toronto ON M5H 2B6
416-362-3411 416-362-3757
inquiries@houserhenry.com
www.houserhenry.com

Toronto: **Howie, Sacks & Henry LLP - *12**
#2800, P.O Box 4 401 Bay St., Toronto ON M5H 2Y4
416-361-5990 416-361-0083 877-474-5997
hsh@hshlawyers.com
www.hshlawyers.com

Toronto: **Hughes, Amys LLP - *27**
#200, 48 Yonge St., Toronto ON M5E 1G6
416-367-1608 416-367-8821 800-565-1713
info@hughesamys.com
www.hughesamys.com

Toronto: **Hughes, Dorsch, Garland, Coles LLP - *5**
#400, 365 Bay St., Toronto ON M5H 2V1
416-868-1300 416-861-1147

Toronto: **Hung, Edward F. - *2**
#319, 1033 Bay St., Toronto ON M5S 3A5
416-926-8777 416-926-1799
edhung@best-litigate.com
www.lawyersintoronto.com

Toronto: **Hutchinson, P.N.J. - *1**
#302, P.O Box 68 70 Dixfield Dr., Toronto ON M9C 4J4
416-621-4430

Toronto: **Hynes, David L. - *1**
#2200, 181 University Ave., Toronto ON M5H 3M7
416-601-9299 416-601-9311
dlh@davidlhynes.com

Toronto: **Iler, Campbell - *8**
#700, 890 Yonge St., Toronto ON M4W 3P4
416-598-0103 416-598-3484
www.ilercampbell.com

Toronto: **Isenberg, Alvin - *2**
#804, 5075 Yonge St., Toronto ON M2N 6C6
416-225-5136 416-225-6877
alvinisenberg@alvinisenberg.com

Toronto: **Jackman, Waldman & Associates - *6**
281 Eglinton Ave. East, Toronto ON M4P 1L3
416-482-6501 416-489-9618

Toronto: **Jacobson & Jacobson - *2**
#222, 3089 Bathurst St., Toronto ON M6A 2A4
416-787-0611 416-787-4873

Toronto: **James, Siddall & Derzko - *4**
#1305, 55 Queen St. East, Toronto ON M5C 1R6
416-860-0166 416-860-0041

Toronto: **Jeffery, Robertson, Watson & Pendrith - *2**
#1812, 2 Carlton St., Toronto ON M5B 1J3
416-977-7700 416-977-8570
nwatson@sympatico.ca

Toronto: **Johnson, John A. - *1**
697 The Queensway, Toronto ON M8V 1L2
416-503-4418

Toronto: **Johnston, Daphne - *1**
#2000, 393 University Ave., Toronto ON M5G 1E6
416-599-9635 416-599-6043 800-364-5793
daphnejohnston@rogers.com

Toronto: **Jones, Rogers LLP - *5**
#1600, 155 University Ave., Toronto ON M5H 3B7
416-361-0626 416-361-6303
law@jonesrogers.ca

Toronto: **Joseph, Mary K.E. - *1**
113 Riverdale Ave., Toronto ON M4K 1C2
416-363-8048 416-406-0038
mary@maryjoseph.ca

Toronto: **Kacaba & Associates - *2**
#440, 100 Richmond St. West, Toronto ON M5H 3K6
416-361-1777 416-361-1776

Toronto: **Kalen Group, The - *1**
262 Avenue Rd., Toronto ON M4V 2G7
416-929-7781 416-929-7784
kalen@mrgeenjeans.ca

Toronto: **Kang, Chan Yeung - *1**
#210, 280 Sheppard Ave. East, Toronto ON M2N 3B1
416-221-1417 416-221-1732
cykanglaw@hotmail.com

Toronto: **Kasman, Sheldon L. & Associate - *2**
#201, 1622 Eglinton Ave. West, Toronto ON M6E 2G8
416-789-1888 416-789-5928
law@kasman.com
www.kasman.com

Toronto: **Kavanagh Bateman & Baek LLP - *4**
#550, 141 Adelaide St. West, Toronto ON M5H 3L5
416-304-0600 416-304-0669

Toronto: **Kavanagh, J.M., Q.C. - *1**
#340, 100 Cowdray Ct., Toronto ON M1S 5C8
416-265-3560 416-265-1944

Toronto: **Kay, Robert C. - *1**
161 Bay Street, Toronto ON M5J 2S1
416-362-9999

Toronto: **Kayfetz, D.H. - *1**
99 South Dr., Toronto ON M4W 1R7
416-364-8131 416-964-9009

Toronto: **Keith & Kramer - *2**
#404, 1200 Bay St., Toronto ON M5R 2A5
416-922-4417 416-922-9328
tkeith@interlog.com

Toronto: **Kerbel, M.L. - *1**
#1001, 65 Queen St. West, Toronto ON M5H 2M5
416-364-9532
mlkerbel@sympatico.ca

Toronto: **Kestenberg Siegal Lipkus - *8**
65 Granby St., Toronto ON M5B 1H8

416-597-0000 416-597-6567
postmaster@ksllaw.com
www.ksllaw.com

Toronto: **Kimel, R.S. - *1**
444 Adelaide St. West, Toronto ON M5V 1S7
416-703-1877 416-504-9216

Toronto: **King & King - *1**
#2, 823 Millwood Rd., Toronto ON M4G 1W3
416-368-4678 416-368-7234
aek@kingandking.net

Toronto: **Kirsh, Sheila - *1**
#1812, 181 University Ave., Toronto ON M5H 3M7
416-367-1765 416-594-0868
sheila@kirsh-law.com
www.kirsh-law.com

Toronto: **Kopolovic, Strigberger - *1**
#300, 69 Elm St., Toronto ON M5G 1H2
416-971-7272 416-971-9092

Toronto: **Koroloff & Huckins - *2**
#304, 1110 Sheppard Ave. East, Toronto ON M2K 2W2
416-229-6226 416-229-6517

Toronto: **Koskie Minsky - *36**
#900, P.O Box 52 20 Queen St. West, Toronto ON M5H 3R3
416-977-8353 416-977-3316
www.koskieminsky.com

Toronto: **Kostyniuk & Greenside - *8**
2481 Bloor St. West, Toronto ON M6S 1P7
416-762-8238 416-762-5042

Toronto: **Koziebrocki, Irwin - *1**
#400, 100 Richmond St. West, Toronto ON M5H 3K6
416-364-7292 416-364-7473
thekozman@aol.com

Toronto: **Krauss, Weinryb - *2**
#1540, 5140 Yonge St., Toronto ON M2N 6L7
416-222-4446 416-222-9788

Toronto: **Kroll, Gerald, Q.C. - *1**
#1800, 4950 Yonge St., Toronto ON M2N 6K1
416-224-0200 416-224-0758
kroll@torlaw.com

Toronto: **Kuretzky Vassos - *9**
#1404, 151 Yonge St., Toronto ON M5C 2W7
416-865-0504 416-865-9567
info@kuretzkyvassos.com
www.kuretzkyvassos.com

Toronto: **Kwan, Grace F. - *1**
90A Isabella St., 3rd Fl., Toronto ON M4Y 1N4
416-968-2014 416-968-2054
gkwan@295.ca

Toronto: **Kyser, Wolfgang H. - *1**
#310, 401 Queen's Quay West, Toronto ON M5V 2Y2
416-863-1053 416-861-0191

Toronto: **Lalla, Tikam K. - *1**
1203 Bloor St. West, Toronto ON M6H 1N4
416-532-2801 416-532-4942

Toronto: **Lalonde, D. Wayne, Barrister & Solicitor - *1**
#2000, The Law Chambers 393 University Ave., 20th Fl., Toronto ON M5G 1E6
416-585-2868 416-593-4446
dwaynelalonde@lawchambers.com
www.lawchambers.com

Toronto: **Lamourie, Garry E. J. - *1**
#2104, 180 Dundas St. West, Toronto ON M5G 1Z8
416-597-9828 416-597-9808

Toronto: **Langdon, C. Robert, Q.C. - *1**
140 Dinnick Cres., Toronto ON M4N 1L8
416-483-2887 416-484-4306
c.robert.langdon@sympatico.ca

Toronto: **Laufer, Sam - *1**
#3902, 44 Charles St. West, Toronto ON M4Y 1R8
416-922-9455 416-923-8870
legitlaw@yahoo.com.au

Toronto: **Lawer, John V., Q.C. - *1**
#306, 40 St. Clair Ave. East, Toronto ON M4T 1M9
416-922-0737 416-922-1896
johnv@johnvlawer.on.ca

Toronto: **Laxton Glass LLP - *11**
#200, 390 Bay St., Toronto ON M5H 2Y2
416-363-2353 416-363-7112

Toronto: **Lemire, J.C. - *1**
#500, 70 Bond St., Toronto ON M5B 1X3
416-363-1097 416-863-4896

Toronto: **Leroy, Thomas J. - *1**
#304, 375 University Ave., Toronto ON M5G 2G1
416-979-2352 416-979-8562
leroyt@lao.on.ca

Toronto: **Lévesque, Gérard - *1**
184 Lake Promenade, Toronto ON M8W 1A8
416-253-0129 416-253-4737

Toronto: **Levitt, Lightman, Dewar & Graham LLP - *3**
#1, 16 Four Seasons Pl., Toronto ON M9B 6E5
416-620-0362 416-620-5158
flevitt@lldg.ca

Toronto: **Levy, Alan D. - *1**
75 Robert St., Toronto ON M5S 2K4
416-929-8282 416-929-9895
alan@alanlevy.ca
www.alanlevy.ca

Toronto: **Levy, E.J., Q.C. - *1**
#400, 100 Richmond St. West, Toronto ON M5H 3K6
416-364-7292 416-364-7473

Toronto: **Lindenberg & Lindenberg - *2**
#100, 287 Eglinton Ave. East, Toronto ON M4P 1L3
416-484-8177 416-322-0807

Toronto: **Lofranco Chagpar Barristers - *6**
#1300, 5255 Yonge St., Toronto ON M2N 6P4
416-223-8333 416-223-3404
info@lofrancobarristers.com

Toronto: **Lomer, Frost - Barristers - *2**
#1515, 180 Dundas St. West, Toronto ON M5G 1Z8
416-923-1900 416-847-2564

Toronto: **Loopstra Nixon LLP - *18**
#600, Woodbine Place 135 Queens Plate Dr., Toronto ON M9W 6V7
416-746-4710 416-746-8319
TheStraightAnswer@loonix.com
www.loopstranixon.com

Toronto: **Lynch, Michael M., Q.C. - *1**
#414, Richmond Tower 100 Richmond St. West, Toronto ON M5H 3K6
416-972-9828 416-964-0823

Toronto: **MacLeod, Paul A. - *1**
32 Elm St., Toronto ON L3M 1H3
905-945-9659 905-945-0838
office@macleod-barr.com

Toronto: **MacMaster, Poolman Law Office - *1**
#203, 150 Eglinton Ave. East, Toronto ON M4P 1E8
416-250-8387 416-250-6233
info@macmasterpoolman.com
www.macmasterpoolman.com

Toronto: **MacMillan Rooke Boeckle - *5**
#3005, P.O Box 96 401 Bay St., Toronto ON M5H 2Y4
416-360-1194 416-360-8469 800-661-7606
info@macmillanrooke.com

Toronto: **Malamet, Dan - *1**
10 Audubon Ct., Toronto ON M2N 1T9
416-865-6952 416-863-6275
dan.malamet@bakernet.com

Toronto: **Malcolm, T.R. Anthony - *1**
#601, 8 King St. East, Toronto ON M5C 1B5
416-864-1608 416-864-1549
tram@tramalcolm.com

Toronto: **Malo, Pilley & Lehman - *3**
1067 Bloor St. West, Toronto ON M6H 1M5
416-534-3555 416-534-7625

Toronto: **Mandel, Harvey - *1**
#203, 55 Queen St. East, Toronto ON M5C 1R6
416-364-7717 416-364-4813

Toronto: **Marchildon, Pierre F. - *1**
#308, Dundas-Lambton Centre 4195 Dundas St. West, Toronto ON M8X 1Y4
416-236-0686 416-236-0650 866-236-0686
pfmlaw@on.aibn.com

Toronto: **Markle, May, Phibbs - *8**
#300, 500 Sheppard Ave. East, Toronto ON M2N 6H7
416-593-4385 416-593-4478

Toronto: **Marks, H. David, Q.C. - *1**
#2150, 1 Queen St. East, Toronto ON M5C 2W5
416-863-1550 416-863-9670
david.marks@waldin.ca

Toronto: **Marszewski, Eva E. - *1**
13 Maple Ave., Toronto ON M4W 2T5
416-927-1820 416-967-4549
marszewski@aol.com

Toronto: **Martin, Malcolm H. - *1**
#310, 49 The Donway West, Toronto ON M3C 3M9
416-449-4111 416-449-7879
mmartin@malcolmmartin.com

Toronto: **Martynowicz, Alexander - *1**
#300, 940 The East Mall, Toronto ON M9B 6J7
416-622-9222 416-622-0333

Toronto: **Masters & Masters - *2**
#440, 65 Queen St. West, Toronto ON M5H 2M5
416-361-1399 416-361-6181
masterslaw@sympatico.ca
www.masterslaw.com

Toronto: **McBride Wallace Laurent & Cord LLP - *8**
#200, 5464 Dundas St. West, Toronto ON M9B 1B4
416-231-6555 416-231-6630

Toronto: **McCarthy, D.V. - *1**
#302, 885 Progress Ave., Toronto ON M1H 3G3
416-289-9620 416-439-9553

Toronto: **McComb Dockrill - *2**
#2707, T-D Bank Tower, Toronto-Dominion Centre P.O Box 17 T-D Centre, Toronto ON M5K 1A1
416-366-1881 416-366-0608
mccombdockrill@on.aibn.com

Toronto: **McGregor, David R. - *1**
#316, 18 Wynford Dr., Toronto ON M3C 3S2
416-485-1123 416-485-8742
dmseus@yahoo.ca

Toronto: **McInnis, Nicoll - *2**
#507, 330 Bay St., Toronto ON M5H 2S8
416-362-1354 416-362-1465

Toronto: **McIver & McIver - *2**
#700, 1 Richmond St. West, Toronto ON M5H 3W4
416-864-9000 416-864-9190

Toronto: **McLachlan Winter - *4**
#1500, 123 Edward St., Toronto ON M5G 1E2
416-596-7077 416-596-7629

Toronto: **McLean & Kerr LLP - *23**
#2800, 130 Adelaide St. West, Toronto ON M5H 3P5
416-364-5371 416-366-8571
mail@mcleankerr.com
www.mcleankerr.com

Toronto: **McMaster, McIntyre & Smyth LLP, Barristers & Solicitors - *5**
2777 Dundas St. West, Toronto ON M6P 1Y4
416-769-4188 416-769-4147 888-769-4188
mail@mmslawyers.com
www.mmslawyers.com

Toronto: **Menzies, von Bogen - *2**
1071B Bloor St. West, Toronto ON M6H 1M5
416-532-2833 416-532-6553 877-218-0084
menzies2@on.aibn.com

Toronto: **Merifield, E.H. - *1**
#2200, 4950 Yonge St., Toronto ON M2N 6K1
416-218-8381 416-218-8384

Toronto: **Midanik, David M. - *1**
34 Shaflesbury Ave., Toronto ON M4T 1A1
416-967-1603 416-967-1604
dmm@rogers.com

Toronto: **Mikitchook, Yaroslav - *1**
#509, 80 Richmond St. West, Toronto ON M5H 2A4
416-361-1668 416-361-6140

Toronto: **Miller & Miller - *2**
1577 Bloor St. West, Toronto ON M6P 1A6
416-536-1159 416-536-3618

Toronto: Miller, Helen - *1
#914, 1110 Finch Ave. West, Toronto ON M3J 2T2
416-665-4343 416-665-0110

Toronto: Mills & Mills LLP - *25
#700, 2 St. Clair Ave. West, Toronto ON M4V 1L5
416-863-0125 416-863-3997
mills@millsandmills.ca
www.millsandmills.ca

Toronto: Minden Gross Grafstein & Greenstein LLP - *50
#2200, 145 King St. West, Toronto ON M5H 4G2
416-362-3711 416-864-9223
dcarty@mindengross.com
www.mindengross.com

Toronto: Minz, Paul - *1
#1, 3520 Pharmacy Ave., Toronto ON M1W 2T8
416-499-9350 416-499-1463

Toronto: Mircheff & Mircheff - *1
#2B, 3030 Midland Ave., Toronto ON M1S 5C9
416-321-2885 416-321-3345
mircheff@on.aibn.com

Toronto: Miskin Flancman & Frisch - *2
1286 Kennedy Rd., Toronto ON M1P 2L5
416-752-2221 416-752-8434 877-468-1120
miskflan@hotmail.com

Toronto: Mitchell, Bardyn & Zalucky LLP - *10
#200, 3029 Bloor St. West, Toronto ON M8X 1C5
416-234-9111 416-234-9114
info@mbzlaw.com

Toronto: Mitchell, Heather - *1
#300, 165 Avenue Rd., Toronto ON M5R 3S4
416-927-6565 416-975-3999
hhmitchell@heathermitchelllaw.com

Toronto: Mitchell, M.J., Q.C. - *1
#403, 1 Yorkdale Rd., Toronto ON M6A 3A1
416-362-0901 416-781-3110
purlex@bellnet.ca

Toronto: Mitz, L.R. - *1
#100, 185 King St. East, Toronto ON M5A 1J4
416-365-7979 416-361-0229

Toronto: Mogil, M.S. - *1
#610, 4211 Yonge St., Toronto ON M2P 2A9
416-590-7999 416-590-9998

Toronto: Monaghan, Bernard J. - *1
#4084, 3080 Yonge St., Toronto ON M4N 3N1
416-486-9919 416-486-1885

Toronto: Morgan, Barbara - *1
#216, 4195 Dundas St. West, Toronto ON M8X 1Y4
416-234-8248 416-234-8252

Toronto: Morris & Morris LLP - *7
#920, 390 Bay St., Toronto ON M5H 2Y2
416-366-2291 416-366-5988

Toronto: Morris, D.S. - *1
129 John St., Toronto ON M5V 2E2
416-977-4799 416-977-4472

Toronto: Morris, L.J. - *1
101 Scollard St., Toronto ON M5R 1G4
416-924-0711 416-960-9650

Toronto: Morrison Brown Sosnovitch - *12
#910, P.O Box 28 1 Toronto St., Toronto ON M5C 2V6
416-368-0600 416-368-6068
bizlaw@businesslawyers.com
www.businesslawyers.com

Toronto: Moskowitz, S.S. - *1
740 Spadina Ave., Toronto ON M5S 2J2
416-961-8864 416-961-7654

Toronto: Mostyn & Mostyn - *4
845 St. Clair Ave. West, 4th Fl., Toronto ON M6C 1C3
416-653-3819 416-653-3891
info@mostyn.ca
www.mostyn.ca

Toronto: Murray & Gregory - *2
160 John St., 3rd Fl., Toronto ON M5V 2E5
416-598-1643 416-598-9520

Toronto: Naumovich, J.
#101, 813 Broadview Ave., Toronto ON M4K 2P8
416-466-2119 416-466-2581

Toronto: Naylor, W.E.M. - *1
#203, 637 College St., Toronto ON M6G 1B5
416-532-9940 416-532-9983
naylor-william@on.aibn.com

Toronto: Neal and Smith - *2
#300, 3443 Finch Ave. East, Toronto ON M1W 2S1
416-494-4545 416-494-4660
nealsmith@bellnet.ca
www.nealandsmith.com

Toronto: Newman Weinstock - *1
#201, 3625 Dufferin St., Toronto ON M3K 1Z2
416-630-3220 416-630-7632
rawein@on.aibn.com

Toronto: Ngan, Alexandra - *1
#306, 1033 Bay St., Toronto ON M5S 3A5
416-925-3333 416-925-3339

Toronto: Nicol, Alexander R. - *1
175 Rumsey Rd., Toronto ON M4G 1P4
416-467-7652 416-425-4217

Toronto: Nightingale, Howard - *1
#302, 4580 Dufferin St., Toronto ON M3H 5Y2
416-663-4423 416-663-4424 877-224-8225
info@howardnightingale.com

Toronto: O'Donohue & O'Donohue - *3
#210, 330 Bay St., Toronto ON M5H 2S8
416-361-3231 416-361-3472
mail@odonohue.ca

Toronto: O'Neill, Browning, Pineau - *2
#302, 372 Bay St., Toronto ON M5H 2W9
416-868-0544 416-868-0724
browninglaw@rigers

Toronto: O'Reilly, Moll - *1
300 Main St., Toronto ON M4C 4X5
416-690-3324 416-690-3330

Toronto: Oiye, Henderson - *2
#1812, 2 Carlton St., Toronto ON M5B 1J3
416-977-7700 416-977-8570
alex@oiyehenderson.com

Toronto: Olch, Torgov, Cohen LLP - *2
#901, 111 Richmond St. West, Toronto ON M5H 2G4
416-363-8366 416-363-0783
otc@otclaw.ca

Toronto: Orbach, Katzman & Herschorn - *3
#1001, 317 Adelaide St. West, Toronto ON M5V 1P9
416-967-6777 416-967-1506
sender@okhlaw.ca

Toronto: Orkin, Mark M., Q.C. - *1
#1401, 111 Richmond St. West, Toronto ON M5H 2G4
416-363-4108 416-365-9276
mmorkin@look.ca

Toronto: Osak, Samuel - *1
6 Bitteroot Rd., Toronto ON M3H 4J4
416-630-1041 416-630-1043
sosak@sympatico.ca

Toronto: Osborne, M.A. - *1
#201, 100 Sheppard Ave. West, Toronto ON M2N 1M6
416-225-1145 416-225-0832

Toronto: Oster Wolfman LLP - *4
#200, 133 Berkeley St., Toronto ON M5A 2X1
416-365-7163 416-365-1270
kow@kow.on.ca

Toronto: Ouanounou, Samy - *1
#352, 1111 Finch Ave. West, Toronto ON M3J 2E5
416-222-3434 416-222-3629
solaw@on.aibn.com

Toronto: Owens, Wright - *12
#300, 20 Holly St., Toronto ON M4S 3B1
416-486-9800 416-486-3309
owenswright@owenswright.com

Toronto: Pace Law Firm - *12
295 The West Mall, 6th Fl., Toronto ON M9C 4Z4
416-236-3060 416-236-1809 877-236-3060
lawyers@pacelawfirm.com
www.pacelawfirm.com

Toronto: Pantazis, Demetrius - *1
870 Danforth Ave., Toronto ON M4J 1L7
416-469-5355 416-469-8136
dpantazis@on.aibn.com

Toronto: Pape Barristers Professional Corporation - *4
#1910, P.O Box 69 1 Queen St. East, Toronto ON M5C 2W5
416-364-8765 416-364-8855
pjp@papebarristers.com

Toronto: Papernick & Papernick - *1
60 Purdon Dr., Toronto ON M3H 4X1
416-633-0043 416-633-9488

Toronto: Papernick, Allan, Q.C. - *1
#203, 1200 Eglinton Ave. East, Toronto ON M3C 1H9
416-445-1273 416-445-1678
apapernick@bellnet.ca

Toronto: Parker, Mary Lou - *1
#800, 2 St. Clair Ave. East, Toronto ON M4T 2T5
416-920-4708 416-920-3819
mlparker@tor.axxent.ca

Toronto: Paterson, MacDougall LLP, Barristers, Solicitors - *13
#900, P.O Box 100 1 Queen St. East, Toronto ON M5C 2W5
416-366-9607 416-366-3743
bmacdoug@pmlaw.com
www.pmlaw.com

Toronto: Patterson, Philip - *1
#305, 1033 Bay St., Toronto ON M5S 3A5
416-968-9188 416-925-2860
ppaterson@on.aibn.com

Toronto: Paul & Paul - *2
39 Hayden St., Toronto ON M4Y 2P2
416-968-1777 416-968-1211
npaul@bellnet.ca

Toronto: Paul, J.G. - *1
#5, 1778 Bloor St. West, Toronto ON M6P 3K4
416-767-9919 416-767-6272

Toronto: Payne, Murray E. - *1
3329 Bloor St. West, Toronto ON M8X 1E7
416-232-1242 416-231-1280

Toronto: Peace, Burns, Halkiw & Manning LLP - *2
#100, 25 Morrow Ave., Toronto ON M6R 2H9
416-533-1025 416-516-5305

Toronto: Peirce, McNeely Associates - *3
25 Lesmill Rd., Toronto ON M3B 2T3
416-449-2060 416-449-2068

Toronto: Pelensky, Michael - *1
#300, 2 Toronto St., Toronto ON M5C 2B6
416-863-1300 416-863-4942

Toronto: Penman & Penman - *1
4168 Dundas St. West, Toronto ON M8X 1X3
416-231-5696 416-231-5697
wrjp@penman.ca

Toronto: Peters & Kestelman - *1
245 Coxwell Ave., Toronto ON M4L 3B4
416-465-3561 416-465-3563

Toronto: Phillips & Phillips - *1
#2200, 181 University Ave., Toronto ON M5H 3M7
416-601-6802 416-601-9590
brucenorth@phillipsandphillipslaw.com

Toronto: Picov & Kleinberg - *2
#100, 110 Eglinton Ave. West, Toronto ON M4R 1A3
416-488-2100 416-488-2794
kpicov@bellnet.ca

Toronto: Piller, L.A. - *1
#2200, 181 University Ave., Toronto ON M5H 3M7
416-601-1622 416-363-7239
lpiller@pillerross.com
www.pillerross.com

Toronto: Pivnick, Jillian M. - *1
#410, 350 Lonsdale Rd., Toronto ON M5P 1R6
416-484-6306

Toronto: Polten & Hodder, Barristers & Solicitors - *6
#2200 DBRS Tower, Adelaide Place 181 University Ave., Toronto ON M5H 3M7

416-601-6766 416-947-0909
epolten@poltenhodder.com (Eric P. Polten)
www.poltenhodder.com

Toronto: Posen, E.G. - *1
101 Brookview Dr., Toronto ON M6A 2K5
416-782-5344
posen@pathcom.com

Toronto: Posesorski, Gary M. - *1
5 Wembley Rd., Toronto ON M6C 2E8
416-780-9655 416-783-4574

Toronto: Posthumus, Wietse G. - *1
#2700, West Tower 55 Avenue Rd., Toronto ON M5R 3L2
416-929-3030 416-961-9898

Toronto: Potts, Weisberg & Musil - *3
#206, 90 Eglinton Ave. East, Toronto ON M4P 2Y3
416-485-7366 416-485-7300
pwmlaw@interlog.com

Toronto: Powell Weir, Barristers & Solicitors - *2
#506, 50 Gervais Dr., Toronto ON M3C 1Z3
416-441-6840 416-441-0330
mike@powellweir.com; gordon@powellweir.com
www.powellweir.com

Toronto: Preobrazenski, C.G. - *1
#414, The Richmond Tower 100 Richmond St. West, Toronto ON M5H 3K6
416-964-1717 416-964-0823
marie@interware.com

Toronto: Price, Stephen & Associates - *1
#1708, 5000 Yonge St., Toronto ON M2N 7E9
416-365-0766 416-365-0866

Toronto: Proctor, D.R., Q.C. - *1
#8A, 1921 Eglinton Ave. East, Toronto ON M1L 2L6
416-751-3958 416-751-3770

Toronto: Prousky, Victor - *1
#220, 2040 Yonge St., Toronto ON M4S 1Z9
416-482-3611 416-486-3325

Toronto: Purcell, V.E., Q.C. - *1
6 Silverdale Cres., Toronto ON M3A 3H1
416-445-7600 416-425-4310

Toronto: Pyne, R.G. - *1
3329 Bloor St. West, Toronto ON M8X 1E7
416-231-3339 416-231-1280

Toronto: Quirk, McGillicuddy & Sutton - *1
1604 Dufferin St., Toronto ON M6H 3L7
416-652-3543 416-652-2730
fran@qmsutton.ca

Toronto: Rachlin & Wolfson LLP - *10
#1500, 390 Bay St., Toronto ON M5H 2Y2
416-367-0202 416-367-1820
enquiry@rachlinlaw.com
www.rachlinlaw.com

Toronto: Radomski, Danuta H. - *1
351 Castlefield Ave., Toronto ON M5N 1L4
416-322-6134 416-489-1462
dradomski@on.aibn.com

Toronto: Rawana & Rawana Barristers & Solicitors - *2
11721 Sheppard Ave. East, 2nd Fl., Toronto ON M1B 1G3
416-281-8505 416-286-4353

Toronto: Reble, John H. - *1
277 Glengrove Ave. West, Toronto ON M5N 1W3
416-485-9123
jreble@istar.ca

Toronto: Regan Desjardins LLP - *10
#1502, P.O Box 2069 20 Eglinton Ave. West, Toronto ON M4R 1K8
416-601-1000 416-601-9255
reception@rkdlaw.com
www.regandesjardins.com

Toronto: Reiber, T.S., Professional Corporation - *1
#211, 1110 Sheppard Ave. East, Toronto ON M2K 2W2
416-927-9841 416-975-1531
terry@reiber.ca

Toronto: Reid, McLean & Scott - *1
2938 Danforth Ave., Toronto ON M4C 1M5
416-699-1131 416-699-1958

Toronto: Reilly, Mary P. - *2
701 Coxwell Ave., Toronto ON M4C 3C1
416-461-7553 416-461-2679

Toronto: Reingold & Reingold - *1
#4068, P.O Box 17 3080 Yonge St., Toronto ON M4N 3N1
416-483-3364 416-440-1942
jrqc58@bellnet.ca

Toronto: Reisler, A.C.J. - *1
161 Bridgeland Ave., Toronto ON M6A 1Z1
416-781-4002 416-781-7797
areisler@wastecogroup.com

Toronto: Reisman, Stanley - *1
#308, 360 Bloor St. West, Toronto ON M5S 1X1
416-961-8864 416-961-7654

Toronto: Rekai Frankel LLP - *6
33 Bloor St. East, 16th Fl., Toronto ON M4W 3H1
416-960-8876 416-924-2371
eleanor@mobilitylaw.com
www.mobilitylaw.com

Toronto: Richardson, Lewis J. - *1
#2000, 393 University Ave., Toronto ON M5G 1E6
416-599-1226 416-962-9997

Toronto: Richman & Richman - *1
#404, 255 Duncan Mill Rd., Toronto ON M3B 3H9
416-510-1575 416-510-1580
richman.richman@on.aibn.com

Toronto: Rickerd, D.S., Q.C. - *1
21 Elm Ave., Toronto ON M4W 1M9
416-929-5177 416-921-8322
drickerd@yorku.ca

Toronto: Ricketts, Harris LLP - *12
#816, Guardian of Canada Tower 181 University Ave., Toronto ON M5H 2X7
416-364-6211 416-364-1697
mail@rickettsharris.com
www.rickettsharris.com

Toronto: Riley, McGivney - *3
#2300, 439 University Ave., Toronto ON M5G 1Y8
416-364-7611 416-596-7562
mailbox@rileymclaw.ca

Toronto: Roach, Schwartz & Associates, Barristers & Solicitors - *7
688 St. Clair Ave. West, Toronto ON M6C 1B1
416-657-1465 416-657-1511
www.roachschwartz.com

Toronto: Robertson & Keith - *1
3464 Kingston Rd., Toronto ON M1M 1R5
416-261-1220 416-261-1716

Toronto: Robins, Appleby & Taub LLP - *20
#2600, 120 Adelaide St. West, Toronto ON M5H 1T1
416-868-1080 416-868-0306
www.robinsapplebyandtaub.com

Toronto: Rochester, Lawlor - *1
#800, 141 Adelaide St. West, Toronto ON M5H 3L5
416-366-2267 416-368-3467
bb@glaholt.com
www.glaholt.com

Toronto: Rogers & Rowland - *2
#700, 4 King St. West, Toronto ON M5H 1B6
416-214-2089 416-864-0271
rogersrow@aol.com

Toronto: Roland, Nelson - *1
333 Adelaide St. West, 3rd Fl., Toronto ON M5V 1R5
416-351-1591 416-340-9250
nroland@allstream.net

Toronto: Rose & Rose - *2
#300, 230 Sheppard Ave. West, Toronto ON M2N 1N1
416-590-9990 416-590-9991

Toronto: Rose, Persiko, Rakowsky, Melvin LLP - *2
#600, 390 Bay St., Toronto ON M5H 2Y2
416-868-1900 416-868-1708

Toronto: Rosen, Allan C. - *1
#904, 27 Queen St. East, Toronto ON M5C 2M6
416-363-1601 416-363-5620
acrosenlaw@rogers.com

Toronto: Rosen, Solomon L. - *1
#1, 2933 Dufferin St., Toronto ON M6B 3S7
416-789-7133 416-782-3507

Toronto: Rosenberg, Elliot F. - *1
#201, 4949 Bathurst St., Toronto ON M2R 1Y1
416-512-7373 416-512-7374
tlpress@patncom.com

Toronto: Rosenfarb, Stanley - *1
#800, 2001 Sheppard Ave. East, Toronto ON M2J 4Z8
416-494-4899 416-494-3024
stan@srlaw.com

Toronto: Ross, Larry H. - *1
#200, 609 Bloor St. West, Toronto ON M6G 1K5
416-535-6211 416-535-7698

Toronto: Ross, R.M. - *1
181 University Ave., 22nd Fl., Toronto ON M5H 3M7
416-601-1563 416-363-7239
rross@pillerross.com

Toronto: Rossman, A.M. - *1
#216, 801 York Mills Rd., Toronto ON M3B 1X7
416-444-2201 416-444-0571

Toronto: Rotenberg, Cecil L. - *3
#900, 1000 Finch Ave. West, Toronto ON M3J 2V5
416-449-8866 416-510-9090 Telex: 06-966797 LOYAN
immigration@clrqc.com
www.clrqc.com

Toronto: Roth, Frank L. - *1
#500, 70 Bond St., Toronto ON M5B 1X3
416-963-8776 416-863-4896
flr@bondlaw.net

Toronto: Roth, Neal H. - *1
#401, 60 St. Clair Ave. West, Toronto ON M4T 1N5
416-351-7706 416-351-7684
nealroth@on.aibn.com

Toronto: Rubenstein, Siegel - *2
#402, 1200 Sheppard Ave. East, Toronto ON M2K 2S5
416-499-5252 416-499-2290

Toronto: Ruby & Edwardh - *7
11 Prince Arthur Ave., Toronto ON M5R 1B2
416-964-9664 416-964-8305

Toronto: Rudnik, George A. - *1
#1901, 260 Queens Quay West, Toronto ON M5J 2N3
416-927-7788 416-925-9963

Toronto: Rumack, Martin K.I. - *1
#202, 2 St. Clair Ave. East, Toronto ON M4T 2T5
416-961-3441 416-961-1045
martin@martinrumack.com
www.martinrumack.com

Toronto: Rumanek, Brian A. - *1
#204, 200 Evans Ave., Toronto ON M8Z 1J7
416-252-9115 416-253-0494
thelawman@rogers.com

Toronto: Rusek, Richard E. - *1
1623 Bloor St. West, Toronto ON M6P 1A6
416-533-8563

Toronto: Rush, G.C.
2970 Lake Shore Blvd. West, Toronto ON M8V 1J7
416-251-2291

Toronto: Rutherford, C.H. - *1
#500, 1000 Finch Ave. West, Toronto ON M3J 2V5
416-667-9796

Toronto: Rye & Partners - *3
#1200, 65 Queen St. West, Toronto ON M5H 2M5
416-362-4901 416-362-8291
partners@ryeandpartners.com
www.ryeandpartners.com

Toronto: Saginur, Howard - *1
#1205, 25 Sheppard Ave. West, Toronto ON M2N 6S6
416-512-1912 416-221-8372
howard@saginur.com
www.saginur.com

Toronto: Salehmohamed, F.G. - *1
#202, 747 Don Mills Rd., Toronto ON M3C 1T2
416-421-7000 416-421-5388

Toronto: Saltman, M. Arbitrations Ltd. - *1
#107, 100 Adelaide St. West, Toronto ON M5H 2G4
416-366-3091 416-366-0879
arbserve@aol.com

Toronto: **Sanderson Entertainment Law - *2**
#201, 326 Richmond St. West, Toronto ON M5V 1X2
416-971-6616 416-971-4144
info@sandersonlaw.ca
www.sandersonlaw.ca

Toronto: **Sandler, Gordon - *2**
#260, 1027 Yonge St., Toronto ON M4W 2K9
416-971-5102 416-971-5305

Toronto: **Sanwalka, Shil K., Q.C. - *1**
#602, 18 Wynford Dr., Toronto ON M3C 3S2
416-449-7755 416-449-6969
skslaw@sanwalka.org

Toronto: **Scandiffio, J.F. - *1**
533 Queen St. East, Toronto ON M5A 1V1
416-364-6755 416-364-7049

Toronto: **Scandiffio, P.M., Q.C. - *1**
#308, 344 Bloor St. West, Toronto ON M5S 3A7
416-515-1660 416-515-1526

Toronto: **Schipper, Lionel H., Q.C. - *1**
#1010, 22 St. Clair Ave. East, Toronto ON M4T 2S3
416-923-7755 416-961-7011

Toronto: **Schwartz, Cecil - *1**
#2108, Madison Centre P.O Box 130 4950 Yonge St., Toronto ON M2N 6K1
416-250-0083 416-512-8275
cecil@cecilschwartz.com

Toronto: **Scully, B.M. Barrister & Solicitor - *1**
31 Prince Arthur Ave., Toronto ON M5R 1B2
416-968-2456 416-960-5456

Toronto: **Scully, Peter B. - *1**
42 Heath St. West., Toronto ON M4V 1T3
416-929-2909 416-929-2909
scullylaw@sympatico.ca

Toronto: **Segal, Gary L. - *1**
#1000, 60 St. Clair Ave. West, Toronto ON M4T 1N5
416-967-5400 416-967-7877
immigration@garysegal.com

Toronto: **Seon Gutstadt Lash LLP - *6**
#1800, 4950 Yonge St., Toronto ON M2N 6K1
416-224-0224 416-224-0758
boblash@torlaw.com
www.torlaw.com

Toronto: **Sera Associates - *2**
#1800, 4950 Yonge St., Toronto ON M2N 6K1
416-222-7668 416-224-0758

Toronto: **Shapiro, Lawrence N. - *1**
#800, 2001 Sheppard Ave. East, Toronto ON M2J 4Z8
416-494-4899 416-494-3024
lshapiro@tpg.to

Toronto: **Sharma & Sharma - *2**
942 Gerrard St. East, Toronto ON M4M 1Z2
416-461-0467 416-461-5817

Toronto: **Sheppard Shalinksy Brown - *3**
488 Huron St., Toronto ON M5R 2R3
416-966-6885 416-966-6837
Ysheppard@sfmlaw.com

Toronto: **Sherman, S.L. - *1**
2645 Eglinton Ave. East, Toronto ON M1K 2S2
416-261-7161 416-261-7163

Toronto: **Shibley Righton LLP - *32**
#700, 250 University Ave., Toronto ON M5H 3E5
416-214-5200 416-214-5400 877-214-5200
torontoinfo@shibleyrighton.com
www.shibleyrighton.com

Toronto: **Shier, Bernard S. - *1**
219 Carlton St., Toronto ON M5A 2L2
416-923-8997 416-923-8380

Toronto: **Shier, Stanley I., Q.C. - *1**
65 Queen St. West, 17th Fl., Toronto ON M5H 2M5
416-366-9591 416-366-2107
stanleyshier@shierlaw.com

Toronto: **Shime, O.B., Q.C. - *1**
#200, 70 Bond St., Toronto ON M5B 1X3
416-366-8009 416-365-7702
disputeservices@bellnet.ca

Toronto: **Shoihet, E.I. - *1**
9 Cortleigh Blvd., Toronto ON M4R 1K5
416-863-9594

Toronto: **Shorser, Geary B. - *1**
#2000, 393 University Ave., Toronto ON M5G 1E6
416-977-7749 416-593-1352

Toronto: **Shour, Robert - *1**
#2000, 393 University Ave., Toronto ON M5G 1E6
416-977-4492 416-977-4971
ralshour@on.aibn.com

Toronto: **Silver, Louis D., Q.C. - *1**
15 Silvergrove Rd., Toronto ON M2L 2N5
416-445-2795 416-445-7243
louisdsilverqc@rogers.com

Toronto: **Silver, Martin I. - *1**
#403, 1 Yorkdale Rd., Toronto ON M6A 3A1
416-781-5224 416-781-3110
trilex@interlog.com

Toronto: **Silverman, Sheldon N. - *1**
#638, 121 Richmond St. West, Toronto ON M5H 2K1
416-363-6295 416-363-3047
ssilverman@sympatico.ca

Toronto: **Sim, Hughes, Ashton & McKay LLP - *9**
330 University Ave., 6th Fl., Toronto ON M5G 1R7
416-595-1155 416-595-1163 Telex: 065-2467 Simbas
mailsim@sim-mcburney.com
www.sim-mcburney.com

Toronto: **Simmonds, Monty M., Q.C. - *1**
#1000, 2 St. Clair Ave. West, Toronto ON M4V 1L5
416-967-6706 416-967-9483
services@medshire.com

Toronto: **Singer, Isaac - *1**
2424 Bloor St. West, Toronto ON M6S 1P9
416-766-1135 416-769-5365
isinger@bellnet.ca

Toronto: **Singer, Keyfetz, Crackower & Saltzman - *2**
532 Eglinton Ave. East, Toronto ON M4P 1N6
416-488-6900 416-488-7530

Toronto: **Singer, Kwinter LLP - *8**
#214, Polo Centre 1033 Bay St., Toronto ON M5S 3A5
416-961-2882 416-961-6760 866-285-6927
info@singerkwinter.com
www.singerkwinter.com

Toronto: **Sitzer, Michael - *1**
255 Lesmill Rd., Toronto ON M3B 2V1
416-391-2500 416-391-3165
msitzer@sitzergroup.com

Toronto: **Sklar, Stewart Floyd - *1**
#5, 1267A St. Clair Ave. West, 2nd Fl., Toronto ON M6E 1B8
416-654-6111 416-654-6100

Toronto: **Skolnik, S.H. - *1**
#318, 4002 Sheppard Ave. East, Toronto ON M1S 4R5
416-297-7300 416-298-7142

Toronto: **Skurka, Steven Allen - *2**
#205, 970 Lawrence Ave. West, Toronto ON M6A 3B6
416-787-6529 416-787-7788
sskurka@ssclawyers.com

Toronto: **Slater & Wells - *2**
644 Evans Ave., Toronto ON M8W 2W6
416-259-4293 416-259-1286

Toronto: **Slocombe, Paul - *1**
387A Jane St., Toronto ON M6S 3Z3
416-762-0725 416-762-6350

Toronto: **Smith, K.D. - *1**
#500, 70 Bond St., Toronto ON M5B 1X3
416-361-0232 416-863-4896

Toronto: **Smith, Raymond I. - *1**
#1507, 8 King St. East., Toronto ON M5C 1B5
416-861-8695 416-861-9074
raylaw@on.aibn.com

Toronto: **Smither, Stanley - *1**
B1 309 Mt. Pleasant Rd., Toronto ON M4T 2C2
416-485-7511 416-488-9028

Toronto: **Snider, D.B. - *1**
978 Kingston Rd., Toronto ON M4E 1S9
416-699-0424 416-699-0285

Toronto: **Snitman, Irving - *1**
554 Annette St., Toronto ON M6S 2C2
416-767-0805 416-767-4619
irv@irvingsnitman.com

Toronto: **Solnik & Solnik Professional Corp. - *2**
2991 Dundas St. West, Toronto ON M6P 1Z4
416-767-7506 416-767-4738
manny@solnikandsolnik.com
www.solnikandsolnik.com

Toronto: **Solomon, Grosberg LLP - *6**
#1704, 55 University Ave., Toronto ON M5J 2H7
416-366-7828 416-366-3513
lawyers@solgro.com

Toronto: **Somjen, J.J. - *2**
#810, 1240 Bay St., Toronto ON M5R 2A7
416-922-8083 416-922-4234
somjen@somjen.com

Toronto: **Sonenberg, Larry S. - *1**
1123 Albion Rd., Toronto ON M9V 1A9
416-749-6000 416-749-6004 877-388-5962
lssonenberg@on.aibn.com

Toronto: **Sotos LLP - *11**
#1250, 180 Dundas St. West, Toronto ON M5G 1Z8
416-977-0007 416-977-0717
info@sotosllp.com
www.sotosllp.com

Toronto: **Spencer Law Firm - *1**
#300, 162 Cumberland St., Toronto ON M5R 3N5
416-967-1571 416-966-1161

Toronto: **Spiro, Michael - *1**
#207, 3625 Dufferin St., Toronto ON M3K 1Z2
416-630-1370 416-633-2229

Toronto: **Spring, Harvey - *1**
#488, 22 College St., Toronto ON M5G 1K2
416-967-0800 416-967-2783
harveyspring@bellnet.ca

Toronto: **Stafford, C.A. - *1**
1036 Coxwell Ave., Toronto ON M4C 3G5
416-421-3211

Toronto: **Stefoff, James - *1**
#1505, 80 Richmond St. West, Toronto ON M5H 2A4
416-366-7984

Toronto: **Steidman, Maxwell, Q.C. - *1**
#201, 1013 Wilson Ave., Toronto ON M3K 1G1
416-366-7661 416-360-6868

Toronto: **Stein, Larry C. - *1**
#203, 2 Tippett Rd., Toronto ON M3H 2V2
416-636-8100 416-636-6545

Toronto: **Steinberg Morton Frymer - *14**
#1100, 5255 Yonge St., Toronto ON M2N 6P4
416-225-2777 416-225-7112
smf@smflaw.com
www.smflaw.com

Toronto: **Stephenson, James A., Q.C. - *1**
3 Daleberry Pl., Toronto ON M3B 2A5
416-383-1488

Toronto: **Stern & Landesman - *3**
#1724, 390 Bay St., Toronto ON M5H 2Y2
416-869-3422 416-869-3449

Toronto: **Stewart, Deborah L. - *1**
106 Glencairn Ave., Toronto ON M4R 1M9
416-226-9340 416-226-5341

Toronto: **Stikeman Keeley Spiegel Pasternack LLP - *4**
220 Bay St., 7th Fl., Toronto ON M5J 2W4
416-367-1930 416-365-1813
info@stikeman.to
www.stikeman.to

Toronto: **Stone & Osborne - *2**
#201, 100 Sheppard Ave. West, Toronto ON M2N 1M6
416-225-1145 416-225-0832

Toronto: **Stone & Wenus - *2**
330 Broadview Ave., Toronto ON M4M 2G9
416-469-4125 416-469-2877

Toronto: **Stortini Lee-Whiting - *2**
#1704, 80 Richmond St. West, Toronto ON M5H 2C6

416-368-1091 416-368-7234

Toronto: Strashin, David S. - *1
#702, 55 Eglinton Ave. East, Toronto ON M4P 1G8
416-482-8171 416-485-4174

Toronto: Strathman, Michael - *1
219 Carlton St., Toronto ON M5A 2L2
416-922-2424 416-923-8380
michael@strathmanlaw.ca

Toronto: Stringer, Brisbin, Humphrey Management Lawyers - *11
#1100, 110 Yonge St., Toronto ON M5C 1T4
416-862-1616 416-363-7358 866-821-7306
chumphrey@sbhlawyers.com
www.sbhlawyers.com

Toronto: Stroz, John F., Q.C. - *1
2275 Dundas St. West, Toronto ON M6R 1X6
416-536-2131 416-536-5451

Toronto: Struyk, J.A.F. - *1
1144 Queen St. East, Toronto ON M4M 1L1
416-463-1188 416-463-9020
strike@tcn.net

Toronto: Suppa, S. - *1
#10, 927 The Queensway, Toronto ON M8Z 5Z7
416-252-5688 416-252-4511

Toronto: Sutton, Ralph A. - *1
#1800, 4950 Yonge St., Toronto ON M2N 6K1
416-224-0200 416-224-0758
rsutton@torlaw.com

Toronto: Swadron Associates - *6
115 Berkeley St., Toronto ON M5A 2W8
416-362-1234 416-362-1232
mail@swadron.com
www.swadron.com

Toronto: Swartz, H.A - *2
#106, 1120 Finch Ave. West, Toronto ON M3J 3H7
416-665-0600 416-665-2848

Toronto: Tang, Mimi - *1
#202, 1210 Sheppard Ave. East, Toronto ON M2K 1E3
416-491-2929 416-491-0990

Toronto: Tanner & Guiney - *1
#3425, Box 34 130 Adelaide St. West, Toronto ON M5H 3P5
416-862-7745 416-862-7874
rgtanner@tannerguiney.com
www.tannerguiney.com

Toronto: Tatham, Pearson - *3
5524 Lawrence Ave. East, Toronto ON M1C 3B2
416-284-4749 416-284-3086 800-970-5670
info@tathampearson.com

Toronto: Taube, Stanley - *1
#503, 33 Jackes Ave., Toronto ON M4T 1E2
416-513-1233

Toronto: Taveroff & Associates - *2
#900, 2 Sheppard Ave. East, Toronto ON M2N 5Y7
416-221-9343 416-221-8928

Toronto: Thom, Stephen - *1
#500, 70 Bond St., Toronto ON M5B 1X3
416-364-3371 416-863-4896

Toronto: Thomson, Rogers - *26
#3100, 390 Bay St., Toronto ON M5H 1W2
416-868-3100 416-868-3134 888-223-0448
info@thomsonrogers.com
www.thomsonrogers.com

Toronto: Tick, Lorne B. - *1
36 Elkpath Ave., Toronto ON M2L 2W1
416-444-9146 416-444-9146
ltick@rogers.com

Toronto: Tikal's - *1
178 St. George St., Toronto ON M5R 2M7
416-968-7070 416-968-1876

Toronto: Tinianov, Philip - *1
#1800, 4950 Yonge St., Toronto ON M2N 6K1
416-363-0866 416-224-0758
ptinianov@torlaw.com

Toronto: Titherington, M.K. - *1
46 Northcliffe Blvd., Toronto ON M6H 3H2
416-656-6465

Toronto: Tkatch & Associates - *2
#488, 22 College St., Toronto ON M5G 1K2
416-968-0333 416-968-0232
tkatchlaw@aol.com

Toronto: Tomas, Norman W. - *1
954A Royal York Rd., Toronto ON M8X 2E5
416-233-5567 416-233-9779
ntomas@bellnet.ca

Toronto: Toomath & Associates - *1
133 Berkeley St., 3rd Fl., Toronto ON M5A 2X1
416-869-0900 416-366-4711

Toronto: Torkin Manes Cohen Arbus LLP - *68
#1500, 151 Yonge St., Toronto ON M5C 2W7
416-863-1188 416-863-0305 800-665-1555
info@torkinmanes.com
www.torkinmanes.com

Toronto: Torrie, Paul G. - *2
45 Saint Nicholas St., Toronto ON M4Y 1W6
416-964-9530 416-925-8122
paul@global-adr.com

Toronto: Traub Moldaver - *5
#1801, 4 King St. West, Toronto ON M5H 1B6
416-214-6500 416-214-7275 877-727-6500

Toronto: Traversy, Philip J. - *1
#900, 2 Sheppard Ave. East, Toronto ON M2N 5Y7
416-221-9343 416-221-8928
p.traversy@rogers.com

Toronto: Treloar, T.J. - *1
#401, 302 The East Mall, Toronto ON M9B 6C7
416-232-2919 416-232-9201

Toronto: Tsantis, Constantine - *1
69 Elm St., Toronto ON M5G 1H2
416-599-6689 416-971-9092

Toronto: Tucker, Maureen L. - *1
43 Madawaska Ave., Toronto ON M2M 2R1
416-221-5122 416-226-9737 877-580-2049
mltlaw@on.aibn.com

Toronto: Urquhart, Urquhart, Aiken & Medcof - *1
#1505, 5140 Yonge St., Toronto ON M2N 6L7
416-595-1111 416-595-7312 Telex: 06-983639
fieldbrown@bellnet.ca

Toronto: Vine, David R. - *1
#1604, 80 Richmond St. West, Toronto ON M5H 2A4
416-863-9341 416-863-9342

Toronto: Wagman, Sherkin - *2
#200, 756A Queen St. East, Toronto ON M4M 1H4
416-465-1102 416-465-3941
charles_wagman@wagmansherkin.ca

Toronto: Waldin, de Kenedy - *3
#2150, 1 Queen St. East, Toronto ON M5C 2W5
416-364-6761 416-364-3866
waldin@waldin.ca

Toronto: Walker Poole Nixon LLP - *6
#515, 5160 Yonge St., Toronto ON M2N 6L9
416-225-5160 416-225-0072
info@wpnlaw.com
www.wpnlaw.com

Toronto: Walker, Ellis - *2
390 Bay St., 30th Fl., Toronto ON M5H 1W2
416-363-2144 416-363-1541

Toronto: Wallace, J.H.G. - *1
551 Gerrard St. East, Toronto ON M4M 1X7
416-463-6666 416-463-8259

Toronto: Walton, Brigham & Kelly - *2
301 Donlands Ave., Toronto ON M4J 3R8
416-425-4300 416-425-4310
tkelly@bellnet.ca

Toronto: Wappel, Toome, Babits, Laar & Bell LLP - *6
#1801, 400 University Ave., Toronto ON M5G 1S5
416-598-1333 416-598-5024

Toronto: Warren Bergman Associates - *2
2925 Bathurst St., Toronto ON M6S 3B1
416-763-4183 416-763-1310 877-763-4183
dwarren@warrenbergman.com

Toronto: Warren, Howard E. - *1
#802, 2 Sheppard Ave. East, Toronto ON M2N 5Y7
416-598-4777 416-598-4316
hwarren@askhoward.com

Toronto: Watson, M.O. - *1
27 Whitehorn Cres., Toronto ON M2J 3B1
416-493-8541 416-493-9042
barwat@rogers.com

Toronto: Weatherhead, Weatherhead - *2
#500, 27 Queen St. East, Toronto ON M5C 2M6
416-362-1369 416-362-5013
weatherhead@bellnet.ca

Toronto: Webster, J.H. - *2
2600 Danforth Ave., Toronto ON M4C 1L3
416-699-9644 416-699-8905

Toronto: Webster, John David, Q.C. - *1
290 Lytton Blvd., Toronto ON M5N 1R6
416-489-6255

Toronto: Weingust, John, Q.C. - *1
Penthouse 481 University Ave., 10th Fl., Toronto ON M5G 2E9
416-977-7786 416-340-0064

Toronto: Weinles, F. Sheldon - *1
104 Caribou Rd., Toronto ON M5N 2A9
416-780-1330 416-780-1331

Toronto: Weinstock, Gilbert - *1
#401, 1850 Victoria Park Ave., Toronto ON M1R 1T1
416-759-1354 416-759-3256

Toronto: WeirFoulds LLP - *78
#1600, Exchange Tower P.O Box 480 130 King St. West, Toronto ON M5X 1J5
416-365-1110 416-365-1876
firm@weirfoulds.com
www.weirfoulds.com

Toronto: Wenus, Irwin - *1
27 Acton Ave., Toronto ON M3H 4G6
416-633-5830

Toronto: Wigdor, Robin J. - *1
#901, 159 Frederick St., Toronto ON M5A 4P1
416-504-7237
robin@wigdor.com
www.wigdor.com/robin/

Toronto: Willard & Devitt - *1
155 Roncesvalles Ave., Toronto ON M6R 2L3
416-531-1136 416-531-4096
robert@robertbeaumont.ca

Toronto: Willms & Shier Environmental Lawyers LLP - *11
#900. 4 King St. West, Toronto ON M5H 1B6
416-863-0711 416-863-1938
info@willmsshier.com
www.willmsshier.com

Toronto: Wilson, David S. - *1
#2000, 393 University Ave., Toronto ON M5G 1E6
416-943-1223 416-943-1049
dswilson@davidswilsonlaw.com

Toronto: Winter, Norman H. - *1
#801, 1 St. Clair Ave. East, Toronto ON M4T 2V7
416-964-0325 416-964-2494
nw@nwinlaw.com

Toronto: Wise, G.R. - *1
3329 Bloor St. West, Toronto ON M8X 1E7
416-231-7399 416-231-1280

Toronto: Wise, Roy - *2
#201, 40 Scollard St., Toronto ON M5R 3S1
416-866-4144 416-866-7946
roy.wise@wiseandassociates.com

Toronto: Wong, Wing H - *1
#202, 4433 Sheppard Ave. East, Toronto ON M1S 1V3
416-298-6767 416-298-3844 Telex: 16986391 TOR

Toronto: Wootten, George A., Q.C. - *1
#901, 701 Evans Ave., Toronto ON M9C 1A3
416-621-7470 416-621-6838

Toronto: Wright & Associates - *5
897 Kipling Ave., Toronto ON M8Z 5H3
416-236-7905 416-236-5644
wright.associates@wnalaw.com

Toronto: Wright, K.E. - *1
#1001, 65 Queen St. West, Toronto ON M5H 2M5
416-364-1157

Toronto: Yaremko, John, Q.C. - *1
1 Connable Dr., Toronto ON M5R 1Z7
416-921-7158

Toronto: Yee & Lee - *2
#1506, 180 Dundas St. West, Toronto ON M5G 1Z8
416-977-0091 416-977-6335
yeelee@ipoline.com

Toronto: Yoannou, Theodore C. - *1
#600, 1000 Finch Ave. West, Toronto ON M3J 2V5
416-650-1011 416-650-1980
tedyoannou@hotmail.com

Toronto: Zadorozny, D.R. - *1
#216, 4195 Dundas St. West, Toronto ON M8X 1Y4
416-239-2333 416-239-1752 866-396-7251
drz@drzlaw.com

Toronto: Zaldin & Fine - *3
#1012, 111 Richmond St. West, Toronto ON M5H 2G4
416-868-1431 416-868-6381
zalfin@ca.inter.net

Toronto: Zaldin, Lawrence - *1
#424, 3600 Yonge St., Toronto ON M4N 3R8
416-488-1766 416-488-3555
lzaldin@sympatico.ca

Toronto: Zammit Semple LLP - *4
#601, 130 Bloor St. West, Toronto ON M5S 1N5
416-923-2601 416-923-1391

Toronto: Zapf, C. - *1
2424 Bloor St. West, 2nd Fl., Toronto ON M6S 1P9
416-766-4208 416-769-5365

Toronto: Zeldin, Collin - *2
23 Bedford Rd., Toronto ON M5R 2J9
416-964-7914 416-964-8067
collin@zecol.com

Toronto: Zifkin, David L. - *1
90A Isabella St., 1st Fl., Toronto ON M4Y 1N4
416-927-7720 416-964-9348
dzifkin@zifkin.com
www.zifkin.com

Toronto: Zisman, R.
#307, 120 Carlton St., Toronto ON M5A 4K2
416-925-6490 416-925-4492
rzisman@rgcoates.com

Toronton: Jemmott, M.M., Q.C. - *1
344 Dupont Street, Toronto ON M5R 1V9
416-975-0787
marvajemmott@bellnet.ca

Tottenham: Feehely, Gastaldi - *4
P.O Box 370 5 Mill St. East, Tottenham ON L0G 1W0
905-936-4262 905-936-5102
fg@feehelygastaldi.com

Tottenham: Smith & Associates - *2
P.O Box 970 23 Queen St. South, Tottenham ON L0G 1W0
905-936-4221 905-936-4223

Trenton: Bonn Law Office - *4
80 Division St., Trenton ON K8V 5S5
613-392-9207 613-392-6367
georgebonn@bonnlaw.com

Trenton: Fleming Garrett Sioui - *5
P.O Box 397 Main21 Quinte St., Trenton ON K8V 5R6
613-965-6430 613-965-6400
fgs@reach.net

Tweed: Bryan, L.G. - *1
P.O Box 669 325 Victoria St. North, Tweed ON K0K 3J0
613-478-6100 613-478-3485
lbryan@intranet.ca

Tweed: Lackie, Bart F. - *1
2718 Mallbank Rd., RR#4, Tweed ON K0K 3J0
613-478-9940 613-478-6061
bart@linesat.com

Unionville: Wood, M.T.P. - *1
10050 Warden Ave., Unionville ON L6C 1N3
905-887-5999 905-887-5826

Uxbridge: Bailey & Sedore - *2
11 Brock St. East, Uxbridge ON L9P 1M4
905-852-3363 905-852-3480

Uxbridge: Hoban, Randall B. - *1
20 Bascom St., Uxbridge ON L9P 1J3
905-852-3666

Uxbridge: Turner, P.D., Q.C. - *1
P.O Box 760 63 Albert St., Uxbridge ON L9P 1E5
905-852-6196 905-852-6197
doug@pdturner.com

Vaughan: Bratty & Partners LLP - *14
#200, 7501 Keele St., Vaughan ON L4K 1Y2
905-760-2600 905-760-2900
info@bratty.com
www.bratty.com

Vaughan: Fine & Deo - *7
#300, 3100 Steeles Ave. West, Vaughan ON L4K 3R1
905-760-1800 905-760-0050 888-346-3336
info@finedeo.com

Vaughan: Gambin RDQ LLP - *7
#400, 3901 Hwy. 7, Vaughan ON L4L 8L5
905-264-7800 905-264-7808

Vaughan: Salvatori, Enzo - *1
#4, 161 Pennsylvania Ave., Vaughan ON L4K 1C3
416-745-1777 416-745-2220

Vaughan: Shiner Kent LLP - *3
#203, 3800 Steeles Ave. West, Vaughan ON L4L 4G9
905-798-2929 905-850-3397

Walkerton: Farr, D.A. - *1
P.O Box 518 229 Durham St. East, Walkerton ON N0G 2V0
519-881-1611 519-881-1733
dfarr@wightman.ca

Walkerton: Magwood, Van De Vyvere, Thompson, & Grove-McClement LLP - *4
#8280, P.O Box 880 215 Durham St., Walkerton ON N0G 2V0
519-881-3230 519-881-3595
wmvt@bmts.com

Wallaceburg: Carscallen, Reinhart, Mathany, Maslak
P.O Box 409 Main619 James St., Wallaceburg ON N8A 4X1
519-627-2261 519-627-1030

Wallaceburg: Hyde, Hyde & McGregor - *2
233 Creek St., Wallaceburg ON N8A 4C3
519-627-2081 519-627-1615

Wasaga Beach: Loton, Maurice - *1
P.O Box 500 802 Mosley St., Wasaga Beach ON L9Z 2H4
705-429-4332 705-429-4683

Waterford: Birnie & Gaunt - *2
P.O Box 429 70 Alice St., Waterford ON N0E 1Y0
519-443-8676 519-443-5596

Waterford: Brennan, C.A. - *1
P.O Box 1229 19 Main St. South, Waterford ON N0E 1Y0
905-443-8643 905-443-4489
neilbrennan@bellnet.ca

Waterloo: Amy, Appleby & Brennan - *3
372 Erb St. West, Waterloo ON N2L 1W6
519-884-7330 519-884-7390
aab-lawoffice@rogers.com

Waterloo: Bigg, Richard C. - *1
#206, 50 Westmount Rd. North, Waterloo ON N2L 2R5
519-886-1678 519-886-1791
biggslaw@bellnet.ca

Waterloo: Chris & Volpini - *2
375 University Ave. East, Waterloo ON N2K 3M7
519-888-0999 519-888-0995
cvlaw@chrisvolpinilawyers.com

Waterloo: Dueck, Sauer, Jutzi & Noll - *8
403 Albert St., Waterloo ON N2L 3V2
519-884-2620 519-884-0254
tedd@dsjnlaw.com
www.dsjnlaw.com

Waterloo: Fitzpatrick, W. Marlene - *1
420 Weber St. North, Waterloo ON N2L 4E7
519-725-9500 519-725-2379
marlenefitzpatrick@on.aibn.com

Waterloo: Haney, Haney & Kendall - *5
P.O Box 185 41 Erb St. East, Waterloo ON N2J 3Z9
519-747-1010 519-747-9323
hhk@haneylaw.com

Waterloo: Heimbecker, Fred J. - *1
295 Weber St. North, Waterloo ON N2J 3H8
519-886-1750 519-886-0503
heim@bellnet.ca

Waterloo: Hoskinson, William C. - *1
P.O Box 22103 50 Westmount Rd. North, Waterloo ON N2L 6J7
519-571-1022 519-743-0490

Waterloo: John E. Lang - *1
21 Posthorn Place, Waterloo ON N2L 5E8
519-578-3330 519-578-3337
johnelang@rogers.com

Waterloo: Kominek, Gladstone - *1
#311, 55 Erb St. East., Waterloo ON N2J 4K8
519-886-1050 519-747-9565
glynne.gladstone2@sympatico.ca

Waterloo: Kraushaar, Eric M. - *1
#5, 620 Davenport Rd., Waterloo ON N2V 2C2
519-886-0088 519-746-1122
eric@churchill-homes.com

Waterloo: Miller, P.M. - *1
15 Westmount Rd. South, Waterloo ON N2L 2K2
519-884-1332 519-884-1161

Waterloo: Oldfield, Greaves, D'Agostino & Billo - *6
P.O Box 16580 172 King St. South, Waterloo ON N2J 4X8
519-576-7200 519-576-0131
watlaw@watlaw.com

Waterloo: Shortt, Hanbidge, Richardson & Welch - *4
P.O Box 550 Waterloo7 Union St. East, Waterloo ON N2J 4B8
519-579-5600 519-579-2725
shs@shslaw.com

Waterloo: Sloan Strype LLP - *2
P.O Box 547 92 Erb St. East, Waterloo ON N2J 4B8
519-886-1590 519-886-8545
jsloan@sloanstrypelaw.com
www.sloanstrypelaw.com

Waterloo: Weir & Fedy - *2
#105, 109 Erb St. West, Waterloo ON N2L 1T4
519-883-1844 519-883-1845
jweir@weirfedy.com

Waterloo: White, Duncan & Linton LLP - *6
P.O Box 457 45 Erb St. East, Waterloo ON N2J 4B5
519-886-3340 519-886-8651

Welland: Banks, George C.M. - *1
P.O Box 127 Main191 Division St., Welland ON L3B 5P2
905-735-1770 905-735-7031
george.banks@bellnet.ca

Welland: Blackadder Green Marion Halinda & Wood LLP - *5
P.O Box 580 136 East Main St., Welland ON L3B 5R3
905-735-3620 905-735-1577

Welland: Flett Beccario, Barristers & Solicitors - *7
P.O Box 340 Main190 Division St., Welland ON L3B 5P9
905-732-4481 905-732-2020
flett@flettbeccario.com

Welland: Houghton, Sloniowski & Stengel - *3
170 Division St., Welland ON L3B 4A2
905-734-4577 905-732-3765 888-483-9770

Welland: Kajan, Rodney J. - *1
#102, P.O Box 130 60 King St., Welland ON L3B 5P2
905-732-1352 905-732-0531

Welland: Kormos & Evans Law Office - *1
14 Niagara St., Welland ON L3C 1H9
905-732-4424 905-732-7574
markevans@on.aibn.com
www.markevanslaw.com

Welland: Pylypuk, Anthony W. - *1
P.O Box 605 80 King St., Welland ON L3B 5R4
905-735-2300 905-735-9230
awpylypuk@pylypuk.com

Welland: Swayze & Swayze - *1
P.O Box 667 Main131 Division St., Welland ON L3B 5R4
905-734-4553 905-734-8015
swayze@bellnet.ca

Welland: Talmage & DiFiore - *2
P.O Box 97 221 Division St., Welland ON L3B 5P2
905-732-4477 905-732-4718
talstradi@iaw.on.ca

Westport: Barker Willson Professional Corporation - *1
P.O Box 309 30 Main St., Westport ON K0G 1X0
613-273-3166 613-273-3676
bwoffice@barkerwillson.com
www.barkerwillson.com

Wheatley: Eaton, J.H. - *1
26 Erie St. South, Wheatley ON N0P 2P0
519-825-7032 519-825-9570
joyce.eaton@3web.net

Whitby: Babbs, Donna C. Family Law Professional Corporation - *1
P.O Box 358 Main117 King St., Whitby ON L1N 5S4
905-668-7704 905-665-9229

Whitby: Johnston, Montgomery, Barristers & Solicitors - *3
201 Byron St. South, Whitby ON L1N 4P7
905-666-2252 905-430-0878
gmb@lawhitby.com (Office Manager)
www.lawhitby.com

Whitby: Michaels & Michaels - *1
#201, 1450 Hopkins St., Whitby ON L1N 2C3
905-665-7711 905-430-9100
michaels_michaels@on.aibn.com

Whitby: Schein, Edward P. - *1
107 Kent St., Whitby ON L1N 4Y1
905-666-1266 905-668-2023

Whitby: Schneider, Howard - *1
107 Kent St., Whitby ON L1N 4Y1
905-668-1677 905-668-2023

Whitby: Stelmach, B.P. - *1
#5, 11 Stanely Ct., Whitby ON L1N 8P9
905-430-6611 905-430-6828
stelmach@bellnet.ca

Wiarton: Pegg, Peter - *1
P.O Box 569 647 Berford St., Wiarton ON N0H 2T0
519-534-2011 519-534-4494

Winchester: Barnhart, David J. - *1
P.O Box 730 489 Main St., Winchester ON K0C 2K0
613-774-2808 613-774-5731

Windsor: Barat, Farlam, Millson - *5
#510, 251 Goyeau St., Windsor ON N9A 6V2
519-258-2424 519-258-2451
bfm@bellnet.ca

Windsor: Bartlet & Richardes LLP - *13
#1000, Canada Bldg. 374 Ouellette Ave., Windsor ON N9A 1A9
519-253-7461 519-253-2321
mail@bartlet.com
www.bartlet.com

Windsor: Berecz, Anita M. - *1
#304, 267 Pelissier St., Windsor ON N9A 5N8
519-258-8306 519-258-4184
amberecz law@bellnet.ca

Windsor: Bondy, Riley, Koski - *2
#310, 176 University Ave. West, Windsor ON N9A 5P1
519-258-1641 519-258-1725
info@bondyriley.com

Windsor: Branoff, Danny - *1
912 Wyandotte St. East, Windsor ON N9A 3J8
519-258-4244 519-258-4247

Windsor: Carroccia, Maria - *1
#602, Canada Bldg. 374 Ouellette Ave., Windsor ON N9A 1A8
519-258-0905 519-258-8755 888-959-9917

Windsor: Cervi, F. Michael - *1
#400, 1500 Ouellette Ave., Windsor ON N8X 1K7
519-258-9494 519-258-9985

Windsor: Chodola Reynolds Binder - *5
720 Walker Rd., Windsor ON N8Y 2N3
519-254-6433 519-254-7990
info@crblaw.ca

Windsor: Corrent & Macri - *8
110 Tecumseh Rd. East, Windsor ON N8X 2P8
519-255-7332 519-255-9123
mail@correntmacri.com

Windsor: Donaldson, Donaldson, Greenaway - *5
547 Devonshire Rd., Windsor ON N8Y 2L6
519-255-7333 519-255-7173
ddglaw@on.aibn.com

Windsor: Fazio & Associates - *4
333 Wyandotte St. East, Windsor ON N9A 3H7
519-258-5030 519-971-9051

Windsor: Fodor, Julie - *1
642 Windermere Rd., Windsor ON N8Y 3E1
519-256-8238 519-258-5780

Windsor: Gatti Law Professional Corporation - *2
#400, 267 Pelissier St., Windsor ON N9A 4K4
519-258-1010 519-258-0163
arg@argatti.com

Windsor: Goldstein DeBiase Manzocco, The Personal Injury Law Firm - *5
#900, HSBC Bank Tower 176 University Ave. West, Windsor ON N9A 5P1
519-253-5242 519-253-0218
gdm@thepersonalinjurylawfirm.net
www.thepersonalinjurylawfirm.net

Windsor: Goulin & Patrick - *2
500 Windsor Ave., Windsor ON N9A 6Y5
519-258-8073 519-977-0694
goulinpa@wincom.net

Windsor: Kamin, Fisher, Burnett, Ziriada & Robertson - *5
#200, 176 University Ave. West, Windsor ON N9A 5P1
519-252-1123 519-977-6503
info@kaminlaw.ca

Windsor: Kirwin Partners LLP, Lawyers - *10
423 Pelissier St., Windsor ON N9A 4L2
519-255-9840 519-255-1413
www.kirwinpartners.com

Windsor: Legal Assistance of Windsor - *3
85 Pitt St. East, Windsor ON N9A 2V3
519-256-7831 519-256-1387

Windsor: Maleyko, D'hondt - *3
#260, 2109 Ottawa St., Windsor ON N8Y 1R8
519-258-8220 519-258-7788

Windsor: Mariotti, A.R. - *1
#202, 176 University Ave. West, Windsor ON N9A 5P1
519-258-1931 519-973-7575
arm.law@sympatico.ca

Windsor: McTague Law Firm LLP - *21
455 Pelissier St., Windsor ON N9A 6Z9
519-255-4300 519-255-4360
info@mctague.net
www.mctague.net

Windsor: McWilliams & McWilliams - *1
#710, 100 Ouellette Ave., Windsor ON N9A 6T3
519-258-1100 519-258-7384
mjmcwilliams@winlaw.ca

Windsor: Meconi, Tullio - *1
349 Wyandotte St. East, Windsor ON N9A 3H7
519-252-7274

Windsor: Miller Canfield Paddock & Stone LLP - *21
#300, P.O Box 1390 443 Ouellette Ave., Windsor ON N9A 6R4
519-977-1555 519-977-1566
www.millercanfield.com

Windsor: Mousseau DeLuca McPherson Prince LLP - *11
#500, 251 Goyeau, Windsor ON N9A 6V2
519-258-0615 519-258-6833
lawyers@mousseaulaw.com

Windsor: Ohler, John G. - *2
101 Tecumseh Rd. West, Windsor ON N8X 1E8
519-256-5496 519-256-1492
ohlerlawfirm@bellnet.ca

Windsor: Oxley, James W.
1854 Kildare Rd., Windsor ON N8W 2W7
519-258-7211

Windsor: Revait, D.R. - *1
#209, Royal Windsor Terrace 380 Pelissier, Windsor ON N9A 6W8
519-258-7030 519-258-2629
derek.revait@bellnet.ca

Windsor: Salem & McCullough - *2
2828 Howard Ave., Windsor ON N8X 3Y3
519-966-3633 519-972-7788

Windsor: Shanfield, Stephen L. - *1
#333, 880 Ouellette Ave., Windsor ON N9A 1C7
519-258-3338 519-258-3335
ssh@mnsi.net
www.shanfieldlaw.com

Windsor: Sherwell, Brian - *1
827 Pillette Rd., Windsor ON N8Y 3B4
519-945-1109 519-948-0003

Windsor: Stipic Arpino - *3
1574 Ouellette Ave., Windsor ON N8X 1K7
519-258-3201 519-258-2665
msa@mnsi.net

Windsor: Sutts, Strosberg LLP - *20
#600, Westcourt Place 251 Goyeau St., Windsor ON N9A 6V4
519-258-9333 519-186-6613
www.strosbergco.com

Windsor: Watters, Michael V. - *1
P.O Box 7292 Sandwich, Windsor ON N9C 3Z1
519-253-6877 519-253-9277

Windsor: Wortley, G.V. - *1
2490 Talbot Rd., Windsor ON N9H 1A6
519-967-9410 519-967-9431
wortley@jet2.net

Windsor: Wunder, Martin, Q.C. - *1
#908, 100 Ouellette Ave., Windsor ON N9A 6T3
519-252-1121

Woodbridge: Borgatti, F. - *1
7135 Islington Ave., 2nd Fl., Woodbridge ON L4L 1V9
905-851-2883 905-851-2887

Woodbridge: Bourque, Roger - *1
#301D, 3800 Steeles Ave. West, Woodbridge ON L4L 4G9
905-856-7101 905-856-1524
rogerbourque@bellnet.ca

Woodbridge: Capo, Sgro, Dilena, Hemsworth, Mendicino - *7
#400, 7050 Weston Rd., Woodbridge ON L4L 8G7
905-850-7000 905-850-7050

Woodbridge: Ciccia, Ralph - *1
#400, 7050 Weston Rd., Woodbridge ON L4L 8G7
905-850-6408 905-850-7050
rciccia@ciccia.ca

Woodbridge: Cosman, Gray LLP - *3
#104, 8 Director Ct., Woodbridge ON L4L 3Z5
905-850-3110 905-850-3123
mark.cosman@cosmangray.com

Woodbridge: Mancini Associates LLP - *3
#505, 7050 Weston Rd., Woodbridge ON L4L 8G7
905-851-7717 905-851-7718

Woodbridge: Paradiso & Associates - *1
#504, 216 Chrislea Rd., Woodbridge ON L4L 8S5
905-850-6006 905-850-5616 800-429-735
mail@paradisolaw.com
www.paradisolaw.com

Woodbridge: Piccin, Bottos - *5
#201, 4370 Steeles Ave. West, Woodbridge ON L4L 4Y4
905-850-0155 905-850-0498

Woodbridge: Rocca, Felix - *1
#302, 7050 Weston Rd., Woodbridge ON L4L 8G7
905-851-7747 905-851-7834
felixrocca@rogers.com

Woodbridge: Rosati, Jack - *1
#206, 4550 Hwy. 7, Woodbridge ON L4L 4Y6
905-264-7566 905-264-4054

Woodbridge: Stabile Professional Corporation - *2
#905, 3700 Steeles Ave. West, Woodbridge ON L4L 8K8
905-851-6711 905-851-5773
vista@stablaw.com

Woodbridge: Tanzola & Sorbara - *5
#101, 10 Director Ct., Woodbridge ON L4L 7E8
905-265-2252 905-265-0667

Woodbridge: Turner, Brooks - *1
#15, 4220 Steeles Ave. West, Woodbridge ON L4L 3S8
905-851-7110 905-851-4229
sturner.barrister@bellnet.ca

Woodbridge: Valenti, P.M. - *1
#300, West Bldg. 3800 Steeles Ave., Woodbridge ON L4L 4G9
905-850-8550 905-850-9998

Woodstock: Brown, Debra A. - *1
94 Graham St., Woodstock ON N4S 6J7
519-539-9870 519-539-9248
debra@dabrownlaw.com

Woodstock: Kratzmann, Peter H. - *1
48 Vansittart Ave., Woodstock ON N4S 6E2
519-537-2221 519-537-5150
phklaw@primus.ca

Woodstock: Lemon, Gordon - *3
P.O Box 336 487 Princess St., Woodstock ON N4S 7X6
519-537-6629 519-539-2459
info@beattylaw.on.ca

Woodstock: White Coad LLP - *5
P.O Box 1059 5 Wellington St. North, Woodstock ON N4S 8A4
519-421-1500 519-539-6926
rcoad@whitecoad.com

Woodstock: Wolyniuk, R.B. - *3
P.O Box 1233 19 Riddell St., Woodstock ON N4S 8R2
519-539-7431 519-539-4975

Prince Edward Island

** indicates # of lawyers*

Charlottetown: Campbell Lea - *9
P.O Box 429 15 Queen St., Charlottetown PE C1A 7K7
902-566-3400 902-566-9266
office@campbelllea.com
www.campbelllea.com

Charlottetown: Carr, Stevenson & MacKay - *9
Peake House P.O Box 522 50 Water St., Charlottetown PE C1A 7L1
902-892-4156 902-566-1377
csm@csmlaw.com
www.csmlaw.com/

Charlottetown: Foster Hennessey MacKenzie - *3
P.O Box 38 Central129 Water St., Charlottetown PE C1A 7K2
902-892-3406 902-368-8239

Charlottetown: Macnutt & Dumont - *4
P.O Box 965 57 Water St., Charlottetown PE C1A 7M4
902-894-5003 902-368-3782
info@macnuttdumont.ca

Charlottetown: Matheson & Murray - *8
#202, Queen Square 119 Queen St., Charlottetown PE C1A 4B3 Canada
902-894-7051 902-368-3762
info@mathesonandmurray.com
www.mathesonandmurray.com

Charlottetown: Mullally, Philip - *1
P.O Box 2560 Central51 University Ave., Charlottetown PE C1A 8C2
902-892-5452 902-892-7013
pmullally@philipmullallylawoffice.com

Charlottetown: Reagh, Elizabeth S., Q.C. - *1
17 West St., Charlottetown PE C1A 3S3
902-892-7667 902-368-8629
reagh@isn.net

Montague: Fraser, Alfred K., Q.C. - *2
P.O Box 516 554 Main St. North, Montague PE C0A 1R0
902-838-2041 902-838-2754
pearle@akfraserlaw.com

Summerside: Hammond Q.C., David R. - *1
740A Water St. East, Summerside PE C1N 5X1
902-436-4267 902-436-4268
dhammond@pei.aibn.com

Summerside: Lyle & McCabe - *2
P.O Box 300 290 Water St., Summerside PE C1N 4Y8
902-436-4296 902-436-4072
www.lylemccabelawoffice.com

Québec

** indicates # of lawyers*

Alma: Larouche, Lalancette, Pilote & Bouchard - *7
723, ch du Pont-Taché nord, Alma QC G8B 5B7
418-662-6475 418-662-9239
www.llpb.ca

Amos: Ayotte Martineau McGuire Boyer - *2
39A, av 1re ouest, Amos QC J9T 1T7
819-732-5258 819-732-0394

Amos: Bigué, avocats - *6
91, Première ave ouest, Amos QC J9T 1T7
819-732-8911 819-732-1470

Amos: Geoffroy, Matte, Kélada & Associés - *4
4, rue Principale, Amos QC J9T 2K6
819-732-1698 819-732-7513
geoffroy.matte@sympatico.ca

Asbestos: Beaubien, Denis - *1
601, boul Simoneau, Asbestos QC J1T 4G7
819-879-7177 819-879-2962
denis.beaubien@cgocable.ca

Beauport: Blouin & Associés - *3
1217, av Royal, Beauport QC G1E 2B2
418-663-2931 418-663-3792
blouin@blouinetassocies.com
www.blouinetassocies.com

Bedford: Lévesque, François - *1
16, rue Dutch, Bedford QC J0J 1A0
450-248-3353 450-248-4462

Beloeil: Bastien, Morand, Blanchette - *6
201, boul Laurier, Beloeil QC J3G 4G8
450-467-5849 450-467-3152 877-467-5849
rbastien@avocatsbmb.com

Berthierville: Sylvestre, André
1300, rue Notre Dame, Berthierville QC J0K 1A0
450-836-6213 450-836-7712
andre_sylvestre@bellnet.ca

Brossard: Hargreaves, Louis D. - *1
5480, croissant Beaumanoir, Brossard QC J4Z 2G4
450-462-3142 450-462-5881
louishargreaves@hotmail.com

Buckingham: Montreuil, Denis - *1
143, rue Joseph, Buckingham QC J8L 1G3
819-986-2701

Chandler: Gaul & Associes - *1
CP 757, Chandler QC G0C 1K0
418-689-2241

Chicoutimi: Côté, Martin - *1
CP 1475 Racine106, rue Garon, Chicoutimi QC G7H 3C1
418-543-3111 418-543-0753

Chicoutimi: Girard Allard Guimond Avocats - *3
#202, 200, rue Racine est, Chicoutimi QC G7H 1S1
418-543-0725 418-543-1765
girardallardguimond@bellnet.ca

Dolbeau-Mistassini: Bouchard Voyer Boily - *3
1273, boul Wallberg, Dolbeau-Mistassini QC G8L 1H3
418-276-2234 418-276-3582
bvb@bellnet.ca

Dolbeau-Mistassini: Simard, Boivin, Lemieux - *4
112, av de l'Église, Dolbeau-Mistassini QC G8L 4W4
418-276-2570 418-276-8797 877-276-2570
blh@blh.ca
www.sblavocats.com

Donnacona: Dussault, Claude - *1
299, rue Notre-Dame, Donnacona QC G3M 1H1

Dorval: Amaron, Viberg & Pecho - *3
#200, 280, av Dorval, Dorval QC H9S 3H4
514-636-4992 514-636-8122

Dorval: Gagnon, Francine - *1
545A, prom Lakeshore, Dorval QC H9S 2B1
514-631-6429 514-631-5606

Drummondville: Biron, Paul - *1
#202, 150, rue Marchand, Drummondville QC J2C 4N1
819-477-8741 819-477-7166

Drummondville: Blais, Roger avocat inc - *2
215, rue Lindsay, Drummondville QC J2C 1N8
819-477-2235 819-477-8674
blaisavocats@bellnet.ca

Drummondville: Jutras et Associés - *5
449, rue Hériot, Drummondville QC J2B 1B4
819-477-6321 819-474-5691
info@jutras.qc.ca
www.jutras.qc.ca

Gatineau: Beaudry, Bertrand Avocats - *10
Maison du Citoyen 25, rue Laurier, 4e étage, Gatineau QC J8X 4C8
819-770-4880 819-595-4979
avocats@beaudry-bertrand.com

Gatineau: Bélanger, Robert - *1
307, boul Saint-Joseph, Gatineau QC J8Y 3Y6
819-771-6679 819-771-9675
robert.belanger.avocat@sympatico.ca

Gatineau: Boivin, Françoise - *1
#104, 160, boul de l'Hôpital, Gatineau QC J8T 8J1
819-243-7293 819-243-5913
francoiseboivin@videotron.ca

Gatineau: Fontaine, Pierre - *1
25, rue Bernier, Gatineau QC J8Z 1E7
819-771-6578

Gatineau: Gaudreau - *2
167, rue Notre-Dame-de-l'Ile, Gatineau QC J8X 3T3
819-770-7928 819-770-1424
bergeron.gaudreau@qc.aira.com

Gatineau: Kehoe, Blais, Major - Avocats - *3
#200, 344, boul Maloney est, Gatineau QC J8P 7A6
819-663-2439 819-663-4816
kbm@bellnet.ca

Gatineau: Lapointe, Cayen - *3
#200, 370, boul Gréber, Gatineau QC J8T 5R6
819-568-0663 819-568-0226
lapointecayen@videotron.ca

Gatineau: Letellier & Associés - *7
#127, 139, boul de l'Hôpital, Gatineau QC J8T 8A3
819-243-1336 819-243-9425
info@letellier.com
www.letellier.com

Gatineau: Lora, E. Wayne - *3
175, rue Champlain, Gatineau QC J8X 3R3
819-778-6511 819-770-5703
wlora@mac.com

Gatineau: Pharand Joyal - *5
166, rue Wellington, Gatineau QC J8X 2J4
819-771-7781 819-771-0608
pharand.joyal@qc.aira.com

Gatineau: Ste-Marie & Lacombe - *2
175, rue Champlain, Gatineau QC J8X 3R3
819-770-7800 819-770-5703

Gatineau: Sarrazin & Charlebois - *2
162, rue Wellington, Gatineau QC J8X 2J4
819-770-4888 819-770-0712
sarrazin-charlebois@videotron.ca

Gracefield: Major, Louise - *1
40, rue Principale, Gracefield QC J0X 1W0
819-463-3477 819-463-4603
lmajor@notarius.net

Granby: Gaudet Galipeau Parcel - Avocats - *5
18, rue Court, Granby QC J2G 4Y5
450-777-1070 450-777-5960
gaudav@bellnet.ca

Granby: Laflamme, Daniel - *1
#200, 328, rue Principale, Granby QC J2G 2W4
450-372-3545

Hampstead: Lifshitz, Judith - *1
30, ch Belsize, Hampstead QC H3X 3J8
514-488-8561 514-488-0121

Joliette: Asselin & Asselin - Avocats - *4
569, rue Archambault, Joliette QC J6E 2W7
450-755-5050 450-755-5111

Joliette: Ferland & Bélair - *3
#150, 430, rue de Lanaudière, Joliette QC J6E 7X1
450-759-7412 450-759-5366 888-759-7412
avocats@ferlandbelair.ca

Jonquière: Turcotte Fortin Cantin Marceau & Gagnon - *6
CP 2040 Kenogami2106 Sainte-Famille, Jonquière QC G7X 7X6
418-547-2108 418-547-9519
tfcmg@bellnet.ca

La Malbaie: Dallaire, Marie-Claude - *1
#220, CP 237 251, rue John-Nairne, La Malbaie QC G5A 1T7
418-665-6417 418-665-6174
marieclaude.dallaire@ccjg.qc.ca

Lac-Mégantic: Drouin, Daniel - *1
4927, rue Laval, Lac-Mégantic QC G6B 1E2
819-583-0787 819-583-4631
ddrouin@notarius.net

Lachine: Laurier, Cêré & Couturier - *3
356, 90e av, Lachine QC H8R 2Z7
514-363-0220 514-363-9495
laurierj@videotron.ca

Lachine: Saint-Amour, Louise - *1
#3, 1375, rue Notre-Dame, Lachine QC H8S 2C9
514-634-8243 514-634-3044
saintamourlouise@yahoo.ca

Lachute: Steeves, William M.C. - *1
18, boul de la Providence, Lachute QC J8H 3K9
450-562-2465 450-562-2467

Lasalle: Pillarella, Pascal - *1
#202, 7925, boul Newman, Lasalle QC H8N 2N9
514-364-3100 514-364-1604

Laval: Alepin Gauthier, Avocats - *13
#601, 3080, boul Le Carrefour, Laval QC H7T 2R5
450-681-3080 450-681-1476
info@alepin.com
www.alepin.com

Laval: Allaire & Associés - *17
#202, CP 422 St-Martin1333, boul Chomedey, Laval QC H7V 3Z4
450-978-5866 450-978-5871

Laval: Bertrand, Guerard & Bleau - *3
134, boul. des Laurentides, Laval QC H7G 2T3
450-663-0851

Laval: Dagenais, Poupart - *5
#650, 2550, boul Daniel-Johnson, Laval QC H7T 2L1
450-978-2442 450-973-4010

Laval: Dupuis, Robert - *1
509, rue Lartigue, Laval QC H7N 3T6
450-663-5280 450-663-5281 866-663-5280
merobertdupuis_avocat@msn.com

Laval: Fournier, Diamond - *2
#1102, 2500, boul Daniel-Johnson, Laval QC H7T 2P6
450-682-7011 450-686-8566

Laval: Lamarche, Pierre - *1
237A, boul des Prairies, Laval QC H7N 2T8
450-667-9802 450-667-5740
plamarche@g1bonavocat.com
www.g1bonavocat.com

Laval: Mignault, Jean - *1
#2020, 400 Armand-Frapier, Laval QC H7V 4B4
514-332-4110 514-334-6043
jean.mignault@2020.net

Laval: Turcotte, Nolet - *5
#470, 500, boul St. Martin ouest, Laval QC H7M 3Y2
450-901-0151 450-901-0152
turcotte.nolet@qc.aira.com

Longueuil: Allard, Raymond - *1
1150, boul Marie-Victorin, Longueuil QC J4G 2M4
450-442-8600 450-463-1043
rallard@strsm.qc.ca

Longueuil: Bernard, Brassard - Avocats - *13
#200, 101, boul Roland-Therrien, Longueuil QC J4H 4B9
450-670-7900 450-670-0673 888-670-7900
commitment@bernard-brassard.com
www.bernard-brassard.com

Longueuil: Dubois et Associés - *3
#97, 45, Place Charles-Lemoyne, Longueuil QC J4K 5G5
450-646-2613 450-646-4225
duboisetassocies@videotron.ca

Lorraine: Courtemanche, André J. - *1
107, boul Val D'Ajol, Lorraine QC J6Z 4G4
450-582-4242 450-965-6958
acourtemanche@muridal.ca

Lévis: Gosselin, Lagueux, Roy - *4
CP 1247 Lévis67, Côte-du-Passage, Lévis QC G6V 6R8
418-833-0311 418-833-1749
glrnotaires@notarius.net

Matane: Deschenes & Doiron, Avocats, s.e.n.c. - *2
352, av St-Jérôme, Matane QC G4W 3B1
418-562-2097 418-562-2926
dedoiron@globetrotter.qc.ca

Mont-Joli: Pelletier, Yvan - *1
CP 333 BureauChef1555, boul Jacques-Cartier, Mont-Joli QC G5H 3L2
418-775-4306

Mont-Laurier: Rancourt, Roger - *1
673, Carré Laurier, Mont-Laurier QC J9L 2W4
819-623-4485

Montmagny: Daveluy, Robert, Q.C. - *1
#22, 46, rue St-Jean-Baptiste est, Montmagny QC G5V 1J8
418-248-1072

Montréal: Allen, Joseph W. - *1
#203, 6855, av de l'Epée, Montréal QC H3N 2C7
514-274-9393 514-274-5614
jwallenimmlaw@bellnet.ca

Montréal: Archambault, Claude F. - *3
50, rue Le Royer ouest, Montréal QC H2Y 1W7
514-845-4234 514-845-4236
www.claudefarchambault.pj.ca

Montréal: Baron Abrams - *9
#200, 4141, rue Sherbrooke ouest, Montréal QC H3Z 1B8
514-935-7783 514-989-1811
info@baronabrams.com

Montréal: Barza, Howard A. - *1
#450, 2015, rue Peel, Montréal QC H3A 1T8
514-288-9322 514-288-2562

Montréal: Beaudry Dessurealt - *3
#304, 480, boul St-Laurent, Montréal QC H2Y 3Y7
514-282-0727 514-282-9363

Montréal: Bélanger, Sauvé - *73
#1700, 1, Place Ville Marie, Montréal QC H3B 2C1
514-878-3081 514-878-3053
info@belangersauve.com
www.belangersauve.com

Montréal: Belliardo, Edouard J. - *1
#701, 4, rue Notre-Dame est, Montréal QC H2Y 188
514-845-6253 514-845-8056

Montréal: Berger & Winston - *2
#1150, 615, boul René-Lévesque ouest, Montréal QC H3B 1P5
514-288-4177 514-876-1090
martin@bergerandwinston.com

Montréal: Bernier, Jean - *1
560, boul St Joseph est, Montréal QC H2J 1J9
514-849-2301 514-849-2309

Montréal: Blank, Harry - *1
#1416, 1255, rue University, Montréal QC H3B 3X1
514-866-1125 514-866-6898
hablank@videotron.ca

Montréal: Bloomfield, Harry J.F. - *1
#1720, 1080, Côte du Beaver Hall Hill, Montréal QC H2Z 1S8
514-871-9571 514-397-0816
hbloomfield@fieldbloom.com
www.bloomfieldandassociates.ca

Montréal: Boyer, Gariépy - *4
#200, 417, rue St-Nicolas, Montréal QC H2Y 2P4
514-287-9585 514-844-5243
boga@bellnet.ca

Montréal: Brisebois, Sarto - *2
#710, 10, rue St-Jacques, Montréal QC H2Y 1L3
514-849-9444 514-849-0119

Montréal: Brisset Bishop -Avocats - *6
#2020, 2020, rue University, Montréal QC H3A 2A5
514-393-3700 514-393-1211
general@brissetbishop.com
www.brissetbishop.com

Montréal: Brodeur, Yvan - *1
#401, 31, rue St-Jacques, Montréal QC H2Y 1K9
514-849-5659 514-849-3633

Montréal: Brunet, Jacques - *1
#103, 3714, rue Ontario est, Montréal QC H1W 1R9
514-524-6638

Montréal: Caisse, Daniel - *3
33, St-Jacques, 4e étage, Montréal QC H2Y 1L3
514-288-2250
caisseetrichard@qc.aira.com

Montréal: Campbell, Cohen, Leveille - *4
#1802, 2, Place Alexis Nihon 3500, boul de Maisonneuve ouest, Montréal QC H3Z 3C1
514-937-9445 514-937-2618

Montréal: Cazelais, Pauline, Q.C. - *1
2339, Terrasse Guindon, Montréal QC H1H 1L7
514-522-5427

Montréal: Cerundolo & Maiorino - *2
1807, rue Jean-Talon est, Montréal QC H1E 1T4
514-376-0335 514-376-6334

Montréal: Chaikelson, Morris - *1
4950, av Ponsard, Montréal QC H3W 2A5
514-482-1896 514-482-0359
chaimor@videotron.ca

Montréal: Chalifoux, Montpetit, Vaillancourt & Associés - *12
#200, 28, rue Notre-Dame est, Montréal QC H2Y 1B9
514-842-1006 514-842-1811

Montréal: Chapados, François - *1
#2400, 1010, rue Sherbrooke ouest, Montréal QC H3A 2T2
514-844-2234 514-844-2087

Montréal: Charbonneau & Archambault - *2
#2420, 500, place d'Armes, Montréal QC H2Y 2W2
514-842-0754

Montréal: Charness, Charness & Charness - *3
#1100, 440, boul René-Lévesque ouest, Montréal QC H2Z 1V7
514-878-1808 514-871-1149
char3law@bellnet.ca

Montréal: Chevalier, Maurice - *1
#1407, 3555, rue Berri, Montréal QC H2L 4G4
514-845-5551

Montréal: Choquette Beaupré Rheaume - *4
#200, 5316, av du Parc, Montréal QC H2V 4G7
514-270-3192 514-270-8876

Montréal: Colby, Monet, Demers, Delage & Crevier - *16
#2900, Tour McGill College 1501, av McGill College, Montréal QC H3A 3M8
514-284-3663 514-284-1961
cmddc@colby-monet.com
www.colby-monet.com

Montréal: Côté, Benoit - *1
1252, rue Beaubien est, Montréal QC H2S 1T9
514-272-5755
benoit.cote@bellnet.ca

Montréal: Cyr, Hamel, Bégin - *3
#300, 13301, rue Sherbrooke est, Montréal QC H1A 1C2
514-642-2676 514-642-1663
jacquescyr@vocat.com
www.chbavocats.ca

Montréal: Daunais, Jean-Louis - *1
#100, 10550, rue Iberville, Montréal QC H2B 2V1
514-385-1601

Montréal: De Grandpré Chait SENCRL-LLP - *62
#2900, 1000, rue de la Gauchetière ouest, Montréal QC H3B 4W5
514-878-4311 514-878-4333
info@degrandpre.com
www.degrandpre.com

Montréal: de la Madeleine, Claude - *1
3600, boul Henri-Bourassa est, Montréal QC H1H 1J4

514-323-2112

Montréal: Derome, Charles - *1
5064, av du Parc, Montréal QC H2V 4G1
514-271-4700 514-271-4708
charles.derome@videotron.net

Montréal: Des Marais, Claude - *1
1206, boul St. Joseph, Montréal QC H2J 1L6
514-521-0047

Montréal: Desjardins, Lapointe, Mousseau, Bélanger - *9
#2185, 600, rue de la Gauchetière ouest, Montréal QC H3B 4L8
514-875-5404 514-875-5647
notaire@dlmb.ca
www.dlmb.ca

Montréal: Desjardins, Robert - *1
4515, rue Notre-Dame ouest, Montréal QC H4C 1S3
514-932-0819

Montréal: Desrosiers, Turcotte, Vanclair, Massicotte - *6
#503, 480, boul St. Laurent, Montréal QC H2Y 3Y7
514-387-9284 514-397-9922

Montréal: Di Tullio, Donato - *1
7647, boul Gouin est, Montréal QC H1E 1A7
514-648-1048 514-648-3288
ditullio@odyssee.net

Montréal: Doyon Izzi Nivoix - *6
#501, 6455, rue Jean-Talon est, Montréal QC H1S 3E8
514-253-3338 514-251-0560
info@dinlex.com

Montréal: Druker Zilbert Schwartz - *5
#605, 1255, carré Phillips, Montréal QC H3B 3G5
514-871-1300 514-871-1304

Montréal: Du Mesnil, Mario - *2
1595, rue St-Hubert, 4e étage, Montréal QC H2L 3Z2
514-526-6625 514-524-4341

Montréal: Duceppe, Théoret & Associés - *3
1595, rue St-Hubert, 4e étage, Montréal QC H2L 3Z2
514-526-6621 514-524-4341

Montréal: Fattal, Emile J. - *1
#705, 1134, rue Ste-Catherine ouest, Montréal QC H3B 1H4
514-861-4545 514-874-1639
occidental@europe.com

Montréal: Fishman Flanz Meland Paquin SENCRL/LLP - *11
#4100, 1250, boul René-Lévesque ouest, Montréal QC H3B 4W8
514-932-4100 514-932-4170
info@ffmp.ca
www.ffmp.ca

Montréal: Fitzwilliam, C.A. - *1
#2821, 1, Place Ville Marie, Montréal QC H3B 4R4
514-940-5353
cf@fitzwilliamlegal.com

Montréal: Frankel & Spina - *2
#401, 60, rue St-Jacques, Montréal QC H2Y 1L5
514-849-3544 514-849-4457
plvspina@frankelspina.ca

Montréal: Franklin & Franklin - *2
#545, 4141, rue Sherbrooke ouest, Montréal QC H3Z 1B8
514-935-3576 514-935-6862
info@franklinlegal.com

Montréal: Frumkin, Feldman & Glazman - *3
#2270, Place du Canada 1010, rue de la Gauchetière ouest, Montréal QC H3B 2N2
514-861-2812 514-861-6062

Montréal: Garceau Pasquin Pagé Viens - *15
204, Place d'Youville, Montréal QC H2Y 2B4
514-845-5171 514-845-5578
lesavocats@procassur.com

Montréal: Gasco Goodhue - *15
#2100, 1080, côte du Beaver Hall, Montréal QC H2Z 1S8
514-397-0066 514-397-0393
lawyers@gasco.qc.ca
www.gasco.qc.ca

Montréal: Gautier, Ulrich - *1
#2350, 500, place D'Armes, Montréal QC H2Y 2W2
514-288-3344 514-288-3344
ugautier@videotron.ca

Montréal: Gendron, Carpentier, S.E.N.C - *2
#300, 615, boul René-Lévesque ouest, Montréal QC H3B 1P5
514-395-4527 514-395-6031
cargen@bellnet.ca

Montréal: Gervais & Gervais - *1
#2100, 500, place d'Armes, Montréal QC H2Y 2W2
514-288-4241 514-849-9984

Montréal: Gingras Ouellet - *2
4141, av Pierre-de-Coubertin, Montréal QC H1V 3N7
514-252-4638 514-252-6906

Montréal: Goldwater, Dubé, Family Law - *4
#2310, 3500, de Maisonneuve ouest, Montréal QC H3Z 3C1
514-861-4367 514-861-7601
inquiries@goldwaterdube.com
www.goldwaterdube.com

Montréal: Gottlieb & Pearson - *9
#1920, 2020, rue University, Montréal QC H3A 2A5
514-288-1744 514-288-6629 Telex: 05-267600
thibault@gottliebpearson.com

Montréal: Gross, Pinsky - *11
2, Place Alexis Nihon 3500, boul de Maisonneuve ouest, Montréal QC H3Z 3C1
514-934-1333 514-933-0810
gropin@grosspinsky.com

Montréal: Gurman, Crevier Inc. - *2
#700, 125, rue Chabanel ouest, Montréal QC H2N 1E4
514-858-1118 514-858-1121
agurman@gurman-crevier.com

Montréal: Hadjis & Hadjis - *2
#707, 1117, rue Ste-Catherine ouest, Montréal QC H3B 1H9
514-849-3526 514-849-1595

Montréal: Handelman, Handelman & Schiller - *3
#1610, 1255, rue Université, Montréal QC H3B 3X3
514-866-5071 514-866-4210
re@hhslaw.ca

Montréal: Hanna Glasz & Sher - *5
#1750, 770, rue Sherbrooke ouest, Montréal QC H3A 1G1
514-284-9551 514-284-3419
briansher@qc.aibn.com

Montréal: Hébert, Downs, Lepage, Soulière & Carette - *6
#2830, 500, place d'Armes, Montréal QC H2Y 2W2
514-284-2351 514-284-2354
edowns@hdavocates.com
www.hdavocats.com

Montréal: Hussey, Brent K. - *1
#200, 280, av Droval, Montréal QC H9S 3H4
514-636-4992 514-636-8122
bkhussey@videotron.ca

Montréal: Iacono, Michel A. - *1
#2000, 300, rue Léo-Pariseau, Montréal QC H2X 4B3
514-288-1414

Montréal: Kaufman, I.H. - *1
#711, 1117, rue Ste-Catherine ouest, Montréal QC H3B 1H9
514-282-7401 514-282-9209

Montréal: Kierans & Guay - *2
#440, 606, rue Cathcart, Montréal QC H3B 1K9
514-866-3394 514-866-3398

Montréal: Kliger & Kliger - *2
#808, 1255, carré Phillips, Montréal QC H3B 3G1
514-281-1720 514-281-0678

Montréal: Kounadis Perreault - *3
#2000, 300, av Leo-Pariseau, Montréal QC H2X 4B3
514-844-8631 514-844-6691

Montréal: Lachapelle, Lucien - *1
5971, rue St-Hubert, Montréal QC H2S 2L8
514-277-2164

Montréal: Lagarde, Gaetan - *2
#201, 1554, boul Mont-Royal est, Montréal QC H2J 1Z2
514-521-2442 514-525-5561
gaela@videotron.ca

Montréal: Lamarre Perron Lambert Vincent - *6
#200, 480, boul St-Laurent, Montréal QC H2Y 3Y7
514-798-1515 514-798-5599

Montréal: Lapointe Rosenstein - *56
#1400, 1250, boul René-Lévesque ouest, Montréal QC H3B 5E9
514-925-6300 514-925-9001
general@lapointerosenstein.com
www.lapointerosenstein.com

Montréal: LaTraverse Avocats - *4
#1510, 1010, rue Sherbrooke ouest, Montréal QC H3A 2R7
514-938-1313 514-938-3691
latraverse@latraverse.ca
www.latraverse.ca

Montréal: Lavery, de Billy - *116
#4000, 1, Place Ville-Marie, Montréal QC H3B 4M4
514-871-1522 514-871-8977
info@lavery.qc.ca
www.laverydebilly.com

Montréal: Lazare & Altschuler - *2
#2210, 1010, rue Sherbrooke ouest, Montréal QC H3A 2R7
514-878-3341 514-878-3314
lazare@lazalt.com

Montréal: Lebrun-Sylvestre, Micheline - *1
#305, 10500, boul de l'Acadie, Montréal QC H4N 2V4

Montréal: Lechter, John, E. - *1
#202, 2015, rue Drummond, Montréal QC H3G 1W7
514-845-4287 514-845-1803

Montréal: Liebman & Associés
#1500, 1, carré Westmount, Montréal QC H3Z 2P9
514-846-0666 514-935-2314
info@liebman.org
www.liebman.org

Montréal: Lord & Associes - *6
#210, 1010, rue Ste-Catherine est, Montréal QC H2L 2G3
514-864-7313 514-864-7329

Montréal: Loulou, Robert - *1
#1, 7924, rue St-Denis, Montréal QC H2R 2G1
514-388-3511 514-388-3211

Montréal: Lozeau Gonthier Masse Richard - *8
#1900, 1010, rue de la Gauchetière ouest, Montréal QC H3B 2N2
514-981-5600 514-981-5601
lgmr@ican.net

Montréal: Marchand, Melançon, Forget - *36
#1900, 1, Place Ville-Marie, Montréal QC H3B 2C3
514-393-1155 514-861-0727 800-270-3881
info@mmflegal.com
www.mmflegal.com

Montréal: Marchi, Bellemare - *5
#200, 400, ave McGill, Montréal QC H2Y 2G1
514-288-5753 514-284-6606
marchibellemare.com

Montréal: Maynard & Zaor - *3
#1101, 507, Place d'Armes, Montréal QC H2Y 2W8
514-288-1101 514-499-8548

Montréal: McConomy, Narvey, Green - *3
#1500, 1255, rue University, Montréal QC H3B 3X2
514-866-4466 514-866-4467

Montréal: McGilton Johnston Hodess - *3
#1210, 2045, rue Stanley, Montréal QC H3A 2V4
514-842-1714 514-842-1718

Montréal: Melançon, Marceau, Grenier & Sciortino - *15
#300, 1717, boul René-Lévesque est, Montréal QC H2L 4T3
514-525-3414 514-525-2803
www.mmgs.qc.ca

Montréal: Mercier, Jean - *1
#203, 4059, rue Hochelaga, Montréal QC H1W 1K4
514-252-0888

Montréal: Miller & Khazzam - *2
#525, 4150, Ste-Catherine ouest, Montréal QC H3Z 2Y5
514-875-8040 514-875-8044

Montréal: Miller, Adel & Associés - *3
#1210, 507, Place d'Armes, Montréal QC H2Y 2W8
514-845-4151 514-845-0306
aadel@adellaw.net

Montréal: Moisan Lasalle Perreault - *2
#280, 450, rue Sherbrooke est, Montréal QC H2L 1J8

514-844-3077 514-844-1018
raymondelasalle@qc.aira.com

Montréal: Mondor, Rougeau, Lambert, Le Borgne - *6
#200, 402, rue Notre-Dame est, Montréal QC H2Y 1C8
514-840-9119 514-840-0177

Montréal: Monette Barakett, Avocats S.E.N.C. - *25
#2100, 1010, rue de la Gauchetière ouest, Montréal QC H3B 2R8
514-878-9381 514-878-3957
monette@monette-barakett.com
www.monette-barakett.com

Montréal: Morabito, Carmelo - *1
#3001, 5095, rue Jean-Talon est, Montréal QC H1S 3G4
514-727-0332 514-727-9315
carmorab@total.net

Montréal: Myszka & Tepner - *2
#204, 4781, av Van Horne, Montréal QC H3W 1J1
514-737-4069

Montréal: Nudleman Lamontagne - *2
#458, 1981, ave McGill College, Montréal QC H3A 2W9
514-866-6674 514-866-9822
info@nlglegal.ca

Montréal: Oligny & Jacques - *2
#107, 1394, du Mont-Royal est, Montréal QC H2J 1Y7
514-871-2240 514-871-0874
oligny@generation.net

Montréal: Pateras & Iezzoni - *5
#2314, 500, place d'Armes, Montréal QC H2Y 2W2
514-284-0860 514-843-7990
fgill@pateras-iezzoni.com

Montréal: Pearl & Associates - *3
1170, Place du Frère André, 4e étage, Montréal QC H3B 3C6
514-861-1170 514-861-0850 866-710-1170
lawyers@pearlandassociates.com

Montréal: Phillips, Frederick R. - *1
5511, place Bradford, Montréal QC H3W 2M6
514-733-8469

Montréal: Phillips, Friedman, Kotler - *18
#900, Place du Canada 1010, rue de la Gauchetière ouest, Montréal QC H3B 2P8
514-878-3371 514-878-3691
info@pfklaw.com
www.pfklaw.com/

Montréal: Plante, Marcel - *1
6984, rue St-Denis, Montréal QC H2S 2S4
514-272-8217

Montréal: Polak, Therrien, Turcotte - *1
#1500, 1, carré Westmount, Montréal QC H3Z 2P9
514-935-6226 514-935-2314

Montréal: Polisuk Lord - *2
#2650, 1155, boul René-Lévesque ouest, Montréal QC H3B 4S5
514-861-8546 514-861-1298
rwlord@polisuklord.com

Montréal: Pollack, Kravitz & Teitelbaum - *3
#1810, 1, carre Westmount, Montréal QC H3Z 2P9
514-905-1373 514-905-1377

Montréal: Ranger, Jacques - *1
5694, av Laurendeau, Montréal QC H4E 3W4
514-766-0756

Montréal: Robinson Sheppard Shapiro - *61
#4600, 800, Place Victoria, Montréal QC H4Z 1H6
514-878-2631 514-878-1865 Telex: 05-27343
info@rsslex.com
www.rsslex.com

Montréal: Rousseau, Gaudry - *3
12675, rue Sherbrooke est, 2e étage, Montréal QC H1A 3W7
514-875-8243 514-875-9903 888-875-8243
rrousseau@rousseaugaudry.com
www.rousseaugaudry.com

Montréal: Sabloff, Leonard I. & Associates - *1
6600, route Trans-Canada, Montréal QC H9R 4S2
514-426-4626 514-426-3977
sabloff@hotmail.com

Montréal: St. Pierre, Johanne - *1
#101, 1395, rue Fleury est, Montréal QC H2C 1R7

Montréal: Saulnier, Jean - *1
7190, rue St-Denis, Montréal QC H2R 2E2
514-273-1525

Montréal: Schneider, Bernard K. - *1
#3, 6175, av d'Esplanade, Montréal QC H2T 3A2
514-277-6540 514-277-6554

Montréal: Schratz, Anthony N. - *1
#400, 630, rue Sherbrooke ouest, Montréal QC H3A 1E4
514-289-9362 514-289-9312
aschratz@bellnet.ca

Montréal: Seal Seidman G.P. - *4
#1050, 2015, rue Drummond, Montréal QC H3G 1W7
514-842-8861 514-288-1708
lseidman@sealseidman.qc.ca

Montréal: Sergio Tucci & Associés - *4
201, rue St-Zotique est, Montréal QC H2S 1L2
514-271-0650 514-270-2164

Montréal: Sirota, Laizer - *1
#305, 10, rue St-Jacques, Montréal QC H2Y 1L3
514-844-1123 514-844-4071

Montréal: Spiegel Sohmer Inc.
#1203, 5, place Ville Marie, Montréal QC H3B 2G2
514-875-2100 514-875-8237
www.spiegelsohmer.com

Montréal: Steckler, Arthur H. - *1
#120, 5115, av de Gaspé, Montréal QC H2T 3B7
514-273-8891 514-273-1576

Montréal: Stein Monast, S.E.N.C.R.L.
#2400, Tour de la Banque Nationale 600, rue de la Gauchetière ouest, Montréal QC H3B 4L8
514-878-9411 514-878-4800 800-670-0102
www.desjardinsducharme.ca

Montréal: Stern & Blumer - *2
#1825, CP 983 300, av Leo-Pariseau, Montréal QC H2W 2N1
514-842-1133 514-842-3105

Montréal: Sternthal Katznelson Montigny - *9
#1020, Place du Canada 1010, rue de la Gauchetière ouest, Montréal QC H3B 2N2
514-878-1011 514-878-9195
info@skm.ca
www.skm.ca

Montréal: Sumbulian, Mark, Avocat / Advocate - *1
#1610, 1350, rue Sherbrooke ouest, Montréal QC H3G 1J1
514-281-1955 514-281-1956
sumbulian@bellnet.ca

Montréal: Talbot & Avocats - *2
4519, rue St-Denis, Montréal QC H2J 2L4
514-849-2930 514-982-0716
liber-t@vigie.net

Montréal: Tassé & Vescio - *2
2421, rue Allard, Montréal QC H4E 2L3
514-769-9654 514-769-7363

Montréal: Tiger Goldman - *2
#716, 1010, rue Sherbrooke ouest, Montréal QC H3A 2R7
514-284-8401 514-284-8408

Montréal: Toulch, Harvey - *1
#406, 1117, rue Ste-Catherine ouest, Montréal QC H3B 1H9
514-849-1289 514-849-3101
hm@info-internet.net

Montréal: Toupin, Robert - *1
1344, rue Jean-Talon est, Montréal QC H2E 1S1
514-278-5400 514-278-7584

Montréal: Trudel Nadeau Avocats S.E.N.C.R.L. - *20
#2500, Place du Parc 300, av Léo-Pariseau, Montréal QC H2X 4B7
514-849-5754 514-499-0312
info@trudelnadeau.com
www.trudelnadeau.com

Montréal: Turner, H. Peter - *1
256, rue Devon, Montréal QC H3R 1B9
514-731-3544 514-737-3770

Montréal: Unterberg, Carisse, Labelle, Dessureault, Lebeau & Petit - *4
#700, 1980, rue Sherbrooke ouest, Montréal QC H3H 1E8

514-934-0841 514-937-6547
contact@utlnet.com

Montréal: Zimmerman, Blitt - *2
#410, 345, av Victoria, Montréal QC H3Z 2N2
514-483-2444 514-483-2477

New Carlisle: Grenier, Grenier, Grenier - *3
CP 519, New Carlisle QC G0C 1Z0
418-752-3308 418-752-6935
grenier1@globetrotter.qc.ca

New Carlisle: St-Onge & Assels - *2
CP 727 100A, boul Gérard-D.-Levesque, New Carlisle QC G0C 1Z0
418-752-3351 418-752-2740
stonge_assels@globetrotter.net

Paspébiac: Moulin, Gilles - *1
CP 880, Paspébiac QC G0C 2K0
418-752-2244

Pointe-Claire: Gelfand, Stanley - *1
#306, 189, boul Hymus, Pointe-Claire QC H9R 1E9
514-695-4542 514-695-7975

Québec: Bedard, Herman - *2
#206, 51, rue des Jardins, Québec QC G1R 4L6
418-692-2425 418-692-2528

Québec: Bernatchez, André - *1
#220, 157, rue des Chênes ouest, Québec QC G1L 1K6
418-628-4575

Québec: Cote, Roland - *1
1445, rue Maine, Québec QC G1G 2J6

Québec: Dussault Lemieux Larochelle sencrl - *14
#450, 2795, boul Laurier, Québec QC G1V 4M7
418-657-2424 418-657-1793
avocats@dllavocats.com

Québec: Garneau, Verdon, Michaud, Samson, La Société d'Avocats - *10
67, rue Ste-Ursule, Québec QC G1R 4E7
418-692-3010 418-692-1742
gvm@qc.aira.com

Québec: Giasson et Associés - *29
#551, 2, rue des Jardins, Québec QC G1R 4S9
418-641-6156 418-641-6353
serge.giasson@ville.quebec.qc.ca

Québec: Gosselin, Bussières, Bedard, Ouellet - *4
#315, 400, boul Jean-Lesage, Québec QC G1K 8W1
418-529-9968 418-524-5243

Québec: Grondin, Poudrier, Bernier - *36
#900, 500, Grande Allée est, Québec QC G1R 2J7
418-683-3000 418-683-8784 800-463-5172
gpb@grondinpoudrier.com
www.grondinpoudrier.com

Québec: Joli-Cour Lacasse Avocats - *26
#600, 1134, Grande Allée Ouest, Québec QC G1S 1E5
418-681-7007 418-681-7100
communications@jolicoeurlacasse.com
www.jolicoeurlacasse.com

Québec: Montreuil, Micheline Anne - *1
1050, rue François-Blondeau, Québec QC G1H 2H2
418-621-5032 418-621-5092
micheline@micheline.ca
www.micheline.ca

Québec: Morency Avocats - *31
#400, 3075, ch des Quatre-Bourgeois, Québec QC G1W 4X5
418-651-9900 418-651-5184
avocats@morencyavocats.com
www.morencyavocats.com

Québec: O'Brien, Avocats - *10
#600, 140, Grande Allée est, Québec QC G1R 5M8
418-648-1511 418-648-9335
obrien@obrienavocats.qc.ca

Québec: Siskinds Desmeules Avocats - *5
#320, 43, rue Buade, Québec QC G1R 4A2
418-694-2009 418-694-0281
claude.desmeules@siskindsdesmeules.com

Québec: Tremblay, Bois, Mignault & Lemay - *34
#200, 1195, av Lavigerie, Québec QC G1V 4N3
418-658-9966 418-658-6100 800-807-9966 Telex: 051-3786QBC

avocats@tremblaybois.qc.ca
www.tremblaybois.qc.ca

Repentigny: Duval, Brochu, Tremblay & Associées - *2
#201, 275B, rue Paradis, Repentigny QC J6A 8H2
450-581-2777 450-585-7565

Rimouski: Blouin, Jean - *1
216, av de la Cathedrale, Rimouski QC G5L 5J2

Rimouski: Dumais, Norman - *1
#200, CP 998 Bureau-Chef97, rue St-Germain ouest, Rimouski QC G5L 7E1
418-723-3179 418-723-3195
dumais.avocat@globetrotter.net

Rimouski: Laprise, Lacroix & Associes - *4
R0901 9, rue Jules-A. Brillant, Rimouski QC G5L 7E4
418-722-5587 418-722-5949
raymond.lacroix@telus.com

Rivière-du-Loup: Aide Juridique - *3
#200, 37, rue de la Cour, Rivière-du-Loup QC G5R 3Z5
418-862-1522 418-862-4528
bajrdl@ccjbslg.qc.ca

Rivière-du-Loup: Rioux Bossé Massé Moreau - *6
CP 487 12, rue de la Cour, Rivière-du-Loup QC G5R 3Z1
418-862-3565 418-862-4408
rbmm@qc.aira.com
www.rbmm.qc.ca

Saint-Georges: Lessard, Raymond - *1
12285, av 1re, Saint-Georges QC G5Y 2E2

Saint-Hyacinthe: Brodeur, Boileau - *3
1700, rue Girouard ouest, Saint-Hyacinthe QC J2S 3A1
450-773-8566 450-778-3749

Saint-Hyacinthe: Sylvestre & Associés Avocats S.E.N.C. - *9
#236, 1600, rue Girouard ouest, Saint-Hyacinthe QC J2S 2Z8
450-773-8445 450-773-2112
etude@avocatssylvestre.ca

Saint-Jean-sur-Richelieu: Gingras, Paul Barry - *2
229, rue Jacques-Cartier nord, Saint-Jean-sur-Richelieu QC J3B 6T3
450-347-0433 450-346-0099
gingras@qc.aira.com

Saint-Jean-sur-Richelieu: Lachance & Morin - *2
108, rue St-Charles, Saint-Jean-sur-Richelieu QC J3B 2C1
450-346-4464

Saint-Jean-sur-Richelieu: Lauzon, Claude - *1
160, rue Longueuil, Saint-Jean-sur-Richelieu QC J3B 6P1
450-347-2344 450-347-4132

Saint-Joseph-de-Beauce: Cliche, Laflamme & Loubier - *6
CP 160 109, rue Verreault, Saint-Joseph-de-Beauce QC G0S 2V0
418-397-5264 418-397-5269
cliclafl@globetrotter.qc.ca

Saint-Joseph-de-Beauce: Giroux & Binette - *2
#100, 700, av Robert-Cliche, Saint-Joseph-de-Beauce QC G0S 2V0
418-397-7288 418-397-7283

Saint-Jérôme: Lalonde Geraghty Riendeau Lapierre - *8
44, rue De Martigny ouest, Saint-Jérôme QC J7Z 2E9
450-436-8022 450-436-5185
lalondegeraghty@lgrl.ca
www.lgrl.ca

Saint-Jérôme: Prévost Fortin D'Aoust - *30
#400, 55, rue Castonguay, Saint-Jérôme QC J7Y 2H9
450-436-8244 450-436-9735
info@pfdlex.com
www.pfdlex.com

Saint-Lambert: Demers, André - *1
439, av Notre-Dame, Saint-Lambert QC J4P 2K5
514-875-2007 514-466-7315

Saint-Lambert: Sullivan, William - *1
147, ch Tiffin, Saint-Lambert QC J4P 3E8
514-397-1504 514-397-1505
wslaw@qc.aibn.com

Saint-Laurent: Kravitz & Kravitz - *3
#350, 750, boul Marcel-Laurin, Saint-Laurent QC H4M 2M4
514-748-2889 514-748-5191
kravitz@centra.ca

Sainte-Julie: Boyer, Roland - *1
69, av Mont Bruno, RR#3, Sainte-Julie QC J3E 3A1
450-649-3772 450-649-0101
rolandboyer@yahoo.com

Sainte-Marie: Sylvain, Parent, Gobeil - *4
CP 40 225, rue du College, Sainte-Marie QC G6E 3B4
418-387-2727 418-387-7070
spgs@globetrotter.net

Salaberry-de-Valleyfield: Les Avocats Rancourt, Legault & St-Onge - *7
175, rue Salaberry, Salaberry-de-Valleyfield QC J6T 2J1
450-371-2221 450-371-2094
courrier@rancourtlegault.com
www.rancourtlegault.com

Sept-Iles: Besnier, Dion & Rondeau - *6
865, boul Laure, Sept-Iles QC G4R 1Y6
418-962-9775 418-968-6806
besnier.avocats@cgocable.ca

Sept-Iles: Desrosiers & Associés - *3
#201, 440, av Brochu, Sept-Iles QC G4R 2W8
418-962-7392 418-962-6100
desricar@globetrotter.qc.ca

Shawinigan: Dugré, Pierre - *1
305, 7e rue, Shawinigan QC G9N 1C6
819-537-8902 819-537-0267 877-744-0090
pierredugre@cgocable.ca

Sherbrooke: Beauchamp, Claude R. - *1
#101, 380, rue King ouest, Sherbrooke QC J1H 1R4
819-563-7733 819-563-7734

Sherbrooke: Belhumeur, Pierre - *1
#101, 380, rue King ouest, Sherbrooke QC J1H 1R4
819-566-1676 819-563-7734
pilul@interlinx.qc.ca

Sherbrooke: Boudreau, Gerard G. - *1
2571, boul Portland, Sherbrooke QC J1J 1V6
819-562-0848 819-569-3580

Sherbrooke: Boutin, Jean-Claude - *1
#100, 75, rue Wellington nord, Sherbrooke QC J1H 5A9
819-569-9933 819-822-0041

Sherbrooke: Delorme, LeBel, Bureau, s.e.n.c. - *7
#100, 2355, rue King ouest, Sherbrooke QC J1J 2G6
819-566-6222 819-566-4221
dlb@dlbavocats.com

Sherbrooke: Drouin Lemieux - *2
18, rue Wellington nord, Sherbrooke QC J1H 5B7
819-566-3939
drouinlemieux@qc.aira.com

Sherbrooke: Fontaine, Panneton & Associes - *8
#220, 2050, rue King ouest, Sherbrooke QC J1J 2E8
819-564-1222 819-822-2180
louis.panneton1@qc.aira.com

Sherbrooke: Gérin Custeau Francoeur - *3
100, rue Richmond, Sherbrooke QC J1H 6E1
819-348-0274

Sherbrooke: Hackett, Campbell, Bouchard - *4
80, rue Peel, Sherbrooke QC J1H 4K1
819-565-7885 819-566-0888
info@hcblegal.com

Sillery: Hickson, Martin, Blanchard - *3
1170, ch St-Louis, Sillery QC G1S 1E5
418-681-9671 418-527-6938
hickson.martin.blanchard@qc.aira.com

Sorel: Ally & Ally - *1
53, rue George, Sorel QC J3P 1B9
450-743-7979 450-743-9821

Sorel: Lepage, Carole - *1
96, rue George, Sorel QC J3P 1C3
450-742-3766 450-742-1133
avocate@carolelepage.qc.ca

St-Georges-de-Beauce: Poirier, Jérôme - *1
11720, 1re av, St-Georges-de-Beauce QC G5Y 2C8
418-228-3123 418-228-0494
jerome.poirier@globetrotter.net

St-Léonard: DiPace, Mercadente - *6
#202, 5450, rue Jarry est, St-Léonard QC H1P 1T9
514-326-3300 514-326-4706
mercadante@videotron.net

St-Romuald-d'Etchemin: Gagnon, Huguette - *1
CP 2096, St-Romuald-d'Etchemin QC G6W 5M3
418-839-2045 418-839-2061
gagnonh@videotron.ca

Ste-Thérèse-De-Blainville: Brazeau, Grégoire & Cliche - *3
72, rue Blainville ouest, Ste-Thérèse-De-Blainville QC J7E 1X3
514-430-1530 514-430-3607

Trois-Rivières: Biron, Spain & Associés - *3
CP 444 154, rue Radisson, Trois-Rivières QC G9A 5G4
819-375-4187 819-375-7395

Trois-Rivières: Hénaire, Louis - *1
CP 1745 983, rue Hart, Trois-Rivières QC G9A 5M4
819-379-3355 819-379-1227

Val-d'Or: Cain Lamarre Casgrain Wells - *5
#202, 855, 3e av, Val-d'Or QC J9P 1T2
819-825-4153 819-825-9769
info@clcw.ca
www.clcw.qc.ca

Val-d'Or: Cossette & DuFour - *1
795, 3e av, Val-d'Or QC J9P 1S8
819-825-2787 819-874-4160

Valleyfield: Droiun, Gingras, Robert & Toulouse - *4
#200A, 30, av de Centenaire, Valleyfield QC J6S 5X4
450-370-3064 450-370-3068
ccjers.valleyfield@sympatico.ca

Valleyfield: Vachon, Martin & Besner - *3
72, rue Montcalm, Valleyfield QC J6T 2C9
514-371-7771 514-371-2438
vachon@rocler.qc.ca

Varennes: Desjardins, Lessard - *2
#203 1950, boul René Gaultier, Varennes QC J3X 1P5
450-652-1830 450-652-3484

Verdun: Beaudet, Robert - *2
5331, rue Bannantyne, Verdun QC H4H 1E8
514-769-8527 514-769-7466

Victoriaville: Caron, Garneau, Bellavance - *3
268, boul Bois Francs nord, Victoriaville QC G6P 1G5
819-758-8251 819-752-4520
avocatscg@bellnet.ca

Westmount: Aster & Aster - *2
#410, 345, av Victoria, Westmount QC H3Z 2N2
514-483-2445 514-483-0009
asterma@asterlaw.com
www.asterlaw.com

Westmount: Cohen, Paul B. - *1
#809, 4000, boul de Maisonneuve ouest, Westmount QC H3Z 1J9
514-931-3691 514-931-3637
paulcohen@bellnet.ca

Westmount: Coleman, A. Barry - *1
#660, 4141, rue Sherbrooke ouest, Westmount QC H3Z 1B8
514-935-5030 514-935-3559

Westmount: Crestohl & Associates - *1
#1200, 1, Carré Westmount, Westmount QC H3Z 2P4
514-932-7392 514-932-0990

Westmount: David & Touchette - *2
#1800, 1 Westmount Sq., Westmount QC H3Z 2P9
514-871-8174 514-871-8052
mdavid@davidtouchette.com
www.davidtouchette.com

Westmount: Diamond, M. & Associates Inc. - *3
#400, 345, av Victoria, Westmount QC H3Z 2N2
514-483-2303 514-483-2373

Westmount: Dorais, André R. Avocats - *3
#2000, 1, carré Westmount, Westmount QC H3Z 2P9
514-938-0808 514-938-8888
adorais@ardavocats.com

Westmount: Szewczuk, Rosalie - *1
4420, rue Ste-Catherine ouest, Westmount QC H3Z 1R2
514-933-4453 514-934-3134
rosiesz@videotron.ca

Saskatchewan
** indicates # of lawyers*

Assiniboia: Lewans & Ford - *2
P.O Box 759 228 Centre St., Assiniboia SK S0H 0B0
306-642-3543 306-642-5777

Assiniboia: Marlin Law Office - *1
P.O Box 1088 200 Centre St., Assiniboia SK S0H 0B0
306-642-3933 306-642-5399
gmarlin@sk.sympatico.ca

Assiniboia: Mountain & Mountain - *2
P.O Box 459 101 - 4 Ave. West, Assiniboia SK S0H 0B0
306-642-3866 306-642-5848
lee.mountain@sasktel.net
mounl.sasktelwebsite.net/

Biggar: Busse Law Professional Corporation - *1
Credit Union Bldg. P.O Box 669 302 Main St., Biggar SK S0K 0M0
306-948-3346 306-948-3366
busselaw@sasktel.net

Broadview: Moore, Gary G. - *1
P.O Box 610 616 Main St., Broadview SK S0G 0K0
306-696-2454 306-696-3105

Brownlee: Rawlings, Frederick R.C. - *1
P.O Box 70, Brownlee SK S0H 0M0
306-759-2621

Estevan: Kohaly & Elash - *2
P.O Box 580 1312 - 4th St., Estevan SK S4A 0X2
306-634-3631 306-634-6901
paulelash@kemlaw.sk.ca

Estevan: Komarnicki Trobert - *2
#305, P.O Box 725 1133 - 4 St., Estevan SK S4A 2A6
306-634-2616 306-634-9881
ktlaw@sasktel.net

Eston: Hughes Law Office - *1
P.O Box 729 204 Main St. South, Eston SK S0L 1A0
306-962-4111 306-962-3302

Fort Qu'appelle: Halford Law Office - *1
122 Boundary Avenue North, Fort Qu'appelle SK S0G 1S0
306-332-5661 306-332-4293

Gravelbourg: Anderson & Company - *2
P.O Box 1016 209 Main St, Gravelbourg SK S0H 1X0
306-648-2582 306-648-2501

Humboldt: Behiel, Will & Biemans - *4
P.O Box 878 602 - 9 St., Humboldt SK S0K 2A0
306-682-2642 306-682-5165
office_bmwlaw@sasktel.net
www.behielwill.com

Indian Head: KMP Law - *2
523 Grand Ave., Indian Head SK S0G 2K0
306-695-2704
kmplaw.com

Kindersley: Ard Law Office - *1
P.O Box 1898 111 1 Avenue West, Kindersley SK S0L 1S0
306-463-2626 306-463-4917
ard.law@sasktel.net

Kindersley: Sheppard & Millar - *2
P.O Box 1510 113 - 1 Ave. East., Kindersley SK S0L 1S0
306-463-4647 306-463-6133

La Ronge: Buckle Law Office - *1
#1B, 1603 Bedford Dr., La Ronge SK S0J 1L0
306-425-5959 306-425-2840

Lloydminster: Fox Wakefield - *2
P.O Box 50 5105 - 49 St., Lloydminster SK S9V 0Y6
780-875-9105 780-875-6748

Lloydminster: Lonsdale Law Office - *2
102 Professional Bldg. P.O Box 1248 5117 - 48 St., Lloydminster SK S9V 1G1
780-875-5185 780-875-6547
jagman@telusplanet.net

Melfort: Annand Law Office - *2
P.O Box 69 208 Main St., Melfort SK S0E 1A0
306-752-2707 306-752-4484
www.annandlawoffice.com

Melfort: Kapoor Selnes Klimm & Brown - *3
417 Main St., Melfort SK S0E 1A0
306-752-5777 306-752-2712

Melfort: Price-Jones, Ronald - *1
P.O Box 129 #3 Hwy. East, Melfort SK S0E 1A0
306-752-5701 306-752-2444
ronp-j@sasktel.net

Melville: Bell, Kreklewich & Company - *3
P.O Box 2000 147 - 3 Ave. East, Melville SK S0A 2P0
306-728-5468 306-728-4444
bell.kreklewich_bkc@sasktel.net

Melville: Schmidt Law Office - *1
P.O Box 160 126 - 2nd Ave., Melville SK S0A 2P0
306-728-5481 306-728-4201
s.lo@sasktel.net

Moose Jaw: Acton, Murray D. - *1
330 Main St. North, Moose Jaw SK S6H 3J9
306-694-0052 306-691-0445
actonlaw@shaw.ca

Moose Jaw: Curran & Fielding - *2
#108, 54 Ominica St. West, Moose Jaw SK S6H 1W9
306-693-7181 306-691-0187

Moose Jaw: Grayson & Company - *7
P.O Box 908 350 Langdon Cres., Moose Jaw SK S6H 4P6
306-693-6176 306-693-1515
grayson@sasknet.net

Moose Jaw: Ocrane, Terrance Law Office - *1
#1, 53 Stadacona St. West, Moose Jaw SK S6H 1Z2
306-694-4922 306-692-6386
ocranelawoffice@sasktel.net

Moose Jaw: Walper-Bossence, B.A. Q.C - *1
84 Athabasca St. W, Moose Jaw SK S6H 2B5
306-693-7288 306-692-6760
brendawalperlaw@shaw.ca
www.walperlaw.ca

Moose Jaw: Whittaker, Craik, MacLowich & Hughes - *2
P.O Box 1178 109 Ominica St. West, Moose Jaw SK S6H 4P9
306-694-4677 306-694-5747

Moosomin: Osman, Gordon & Co. - *6
P.O Box 280 626 Carleton St., Moosomin SK S0G 3N0
306-435-3851 306-435-3962

Nipawin: Carson Law Office - *1
P.O Box 1983, Nipawin SK S0E 1E0
306-862-5554

Nipawin: Eremko & Eremko - *1
P.O Box 250, Nipawin SK S0E 1E0
306-862-4477

Nipawin: Taylor & Co. - *3
P.O Box 850 117 - 1 Ave. East, Nipawin SK S0E 1E0
306-873-1865
j.taylor_lawoffice@sasktel.net

North Battleford: Cawood Walker Demmans Baldwin - *4
#201, P.O Box 905 1291 - 102 St., North Battleford SK S9A 2Z3
306-445-6177 306-445-7076
cawood.et.al@sasktel.net

North Battleford: Conroy, David - *1
#101, 1351 - 101 St., North Battleford SK S9A 0Z9
306-445-3613 306-445-9088
conroylaw@sasktel.net

North Battleford: Jones & Hudec - *6
P.O Box 1179 10211 - 12 Ave., North Battleford SK S9A 3K2
306-446-2211 306-446-3022
jhlaw@sasktel.net
www.joneshudec.com

North Battleford: Lindgren, Blais, Frank & Illingworth - *4
P.O Box 940 1301 - 101 St., North Battleford SK S9A 2Z3
306-445-2422 306-445-2313
mlbfh@sasktel.net
www.lbfilaw.com

North Battleford: Migneault Greenwood - *4
1391 101st Street, North Battleford SK S9A 2Y8
306-445-4436 306-445-6444
kevan@mglawoffice.com

Prince Albert: Balon Krishan - *3
1335B - 2nd Ave. West, Prince Albert SK S6V 5B2
306-922-5151 306-763-1755
bkm.law@sasktel.net

Prince Albert: Eggum, Abrametz, Eggum - *4
#101, 88 - 13th St. East, Prince Albert SK S6V 1C6
306-763-7441 306-764-2882
klleggum@inet2000.com; petervabrametz@inet2000.com

Prince Albert: Holash Logue McCullagh Law Office - *4
P.O Box 2080 1102 - 1 Ave. West, Prince Albert SK S6V 6V4
306-764-4244 306-764-4949

Prince Albert: Loewen & Klassen Law Office - *2
1100 1st Avenue East, Prince Albert SK S6V 2A7
306-922-0212 306-922-2422

Prince Albert: Sanderson Balicki Popescul - *7
#200, 110 - 11 St. East, Prince Albert SK S6V 1A1
306-764-2222 306-764-2221

Prince Albert: West, Siwak - *2
1109 Central Ave., Prince Albert SK S6V 4V7
306-763-7467 306-763-7469
west.siwak@sasktel.net

Prince Albert: Wilcox Zuk Law Office - *6
20 - 12 St. West, Prince Albert SK S6V 3B3
306-922-4700 306-922-0633
princealbert@mwzlaw.com

Prince Albert: Zatlyn Law Office - *4
2531 - 11th St. East, Prince Albert SK S6V 0Z8
306-922-1444 306-922-5848
zatlyn@sasktel.net

Regina: Bertram Scrivens MacLeod - *6
#1730, Avord Tower 2002 Victoria Ave., Regina SK S4P 0R7
306-525-2737 306-565-3244
office@bertramlaw.ca
www.bsmlaw.ca

Regina: Dahlem, Findlay - *2
2100 Smith St., Regina SK S4P 2P2
306-522-3631 306-565-2616
don.findlay@sasktel.net
www.donfindlay.ca

Regina: Duchin, Bayda & Kroczynski - *4
2515 Victoria Ave., Regina SK S4P 0T2
306-359-3131 306-359-3372

Regina: Gates & Company - *5
3132 Avonhurst Dr., Regina SK S4R 3J7
306-949-5544 306-775-2995
office@gateslaw.ca

Regina: Germain, Elaine - *1
2269 Hamilton St., Regina SK S4P 2E7
306-525-8311 306-565-2766

Regina: Gerrand Rath Johnson - *13
#700, Toronto Dominion Bank Bldg. 1914 Hamilton St., Regina SK S4P 3N6
306-522-3030 306-522-3555
grj@grj.ca
www.grj.ca

Regina: Griffin Toews Maddigan Brabant - *6
1530 Angus St., Regina SK S4T 1Z1
306-525-6125 306-525-5226
griffin.toews@sasktel.net

Regina: Kanuka Thuringer LLP, Barristers & Solicitors - *28
#1400, 2500 Victoria Ave., Regina SK S4P 3X2
306-525-7200 306-359-0590
firm@kanukathuringer.com
www.kanukathuringer.com

Regina: KMP Law - *5
2600 Victoria Ave., Regina SK S4T 1K2
306-761-6200 306-761-6222
kmplaw.com

Regina: MacKay & McLean - *3
2042 Cornwall St., Regina SK S4P 2K5
306-569-1301 306-569-8560
dgmackay@sasktel.net
www.mackaymclean.com/index

Regina: MacLean Keith - *4
Nicol Ct. 2398 Scarth St., Regina SK S4P 2J7
306-757-1611 306-757-0712

Regina: MacPherson Leslie & Tyerman LLP - *34
#1500, Hill Centre I 1874 Scarth St., Regina SK S4P 4E9
306-347-8000 306-352-5250
www.mlt.com

Regina: **McCrank Stewart Johnson - *9**
#208, 2208 Scarth St., Regina SK S4P 2J6
306-525-2191 306-757-8138
vrm@sasktel.net

Regina: **McDougall Gauley - *30**
1500 - 1881 Scarth St., Regina SK S4P 4K9
306-757-1641 306-359-0785
mramsay@mcdougallgauley.com
www.mcdougallgauley.com

Regina: **Merchant Law Group LLP - *7**
#100, Saskatchewan Drive Plaza 2401 Saskatchewan Dr., Regina SK S4P 4H8
306-359-7777 306-522-3299 888-567-7777
gbh@sk.sympatico.ca
www.merchantlaw.com

Regina: **Morgan, Khaladkar & Skinner - *2**
2510 - 13 Ave., Regina SK S4P 0W2
306-525-9191 306-525-0006

Regina: **Olive, Waller, Zinkhan & Waller - *18**
#1000, 2002 Victoria Ave., Regina SK S4P 0R7
306-359-1888 306-352-0771
owzw@owzw.com
www.owzw.com

Regina: **Phillips & Co. - *3**
Holdane House 2100 Scarth St., Regina SK S4P 2H6
306-569-0811 306-565-3434
phillips.co@sasktel.net

Regina: **Sheppard, Braun, Muma - *2**
#204, 3988 Albert St., Regina SK S4S 3R1
306-586-6020 306-586-8525
sbmlaw@sasktel.net

Regina: **Silversides & Cox - *2**
180 Saskatchewan Pl. 1870 Albert St., Regina SK S4P 4B7
306-337-4560 306-337-4568

Regina: **Walker, Singer & McCannell - *3**
1872 Angus St., Regina SK S4T 1Z4
306-352-8109 306-352-7339

Regina: **Willows Tulloch - *1**
533 Victoria Avenue, Regina SK S4N 0P4
306-924-8600 306-924-8601
ntulloch@accesscom.ca

Regina: **Wilson, Garrett Q.C. - *1**
2237 Smith St., Regina SK S4P 2P5
306-352-1641 306-525-8884

Rosetown: **Aseltine Skelton & Turner - *2**
P.O Box 1120 314 Main St., Rosetown SK S0L 2V0
306-882-4244 306-882-3969

Saskatoon: **Agnew & Company - *3**
279 - 3rd Avenue North, Saskatoon SK S7K 2H8
306-244-7966 306-244-8010
agnewco@sasktel.net

Saskatoon: **Balfour Moss - *5**
#600, Princeton Tower 123 - 2nd Ave. South, Saskatoon SK S7K 7E6
306-665-7844 306-652-1586
balfourmoss.saskatoon@balfourmoss.com
www.balfourmoss.com

Saskatoon: **Bodnar Campbell - *2**
#100, 200 - 3 Ave. South, Saskatoon SK S7K 1M1
306-664-3314 306-664-3354
office@bwclaw.ca

Saskatoon: **Brayford Shapiro - *2**
311 - 21 St. East., Saskatoon SK S7K 0C1
306-244-5656 306-244-5644
www.shapirolaw.ca

Saskatoon: **Brent & Greenhorn - *2**
3026 Taylor St. East, Saskatoon SK S7H 4J2
306-955-9544 306-955-2656
bandg@sasktel.net
www.lynnegreenhorn.com

Saskatoon: **Burlingham Cuelenaere Legal Prof. Corp. - *4**
1043 - 8 St. East, Saskatoon SK S7H 0S2
306-343-9581 306-343-1947
burlinghamcuelenaere@sasktel.net

Saskatoon: **Campbell, William J. - *1**
#100, 220 - 3 Ave. South, Saskatoon SK S7K 1M1
306-664-3314 306-664-3354
wjcampbell@sasktel.net

Saskatoon: **Dufour Scott Phelps & Mason - *5**
#400, 135 - 21st St. East, Saskatoon SK S7K 0B4
306-244-2201 306-244-2420
www.dufourlaw.com

Saskatoon: **Halyk Kennedy Knox - *3**
321 - 6 Ave. North, Saskatoon SK S7K 2S3
306-665-3434 306-652-1915
halyk@sasktel.net

Saskatoon: **Hnatyshyn Gough - *7**
#601, 402 - 21st St. East, Saskatoon SK S7K 0C3
306-653-5150 306-652-5859
hglaw@hglaw.ca
www.hglaw.ca

Saskatoon: **Kloppenburg & Kloppenburg - *2**
#603, Princeton Tower 123 - 2nd Ave. South, Saskatoon SK S7K 7E6
306-665-7600 306-665-7800
juristen@kloppenburg.ca
www.kloppenburg.ca

Saskatoon: **Koskie Helms - *2**
#3, 501 Gray Ave., Saskatoon SK S7N 2H8
306-242-8478 306-653-2120
firm@koskie.com
www.koskie.com

Saskatoon: **Leland Kimpinski LLP - *7**
#800, 230 - 22nd St. East, Saskatoon SK S7K 0E9
306-244-6686 306-653-7008
info@lelandlaw.ca
www.lelandlaw.ca

Saskatoon: **MacDermid Lamarsh - *13**
#320, 728 Spadina Cres. East, Saskatoon SK S7K 3H2
306-652-9422 306-242-1554
macmarsh@macmarsh.com
www.macdermidlamarsh.com

Saskatoon: **MacLean Keith - *2**
#1300, 410 - 22 St. East, Saskatoon SK S7K 5T6
306-664-9200 306-664-1960
maxleankeith@sk.sympatico.ca

Saskatoon: **Martel, Louis E. - *1**
811 Bayview Cres., Saskatoon SK S7V 1B7
306-652-6830 306-652-6836
martellawoffice@sasktel.net
www.martellawoffice.ca

Saskatoon: **Mathiason, Valkenburg - *1**
#705, 230 - 22nd St. East, Saskatoon SK S7K 0E9
306-242-1202 306-244-4423
mvm@sasktel.net

Saskatoon: **Nussbaum & Company - *2**
#204, 2102 - 8 St. East, Saskatoon SK S7H 0V1
306-955-8890 306-955-1293
nussbaum@sasktel.net

Saskatoon: **Plaxton Gillies Barristers & Solicitors - *2**
#200, 402 - 21 St. East, Saskatoon SK S7K 0C3
306-653-1500 306-664-6659
contactus@plaxtonlaw.com

Saskatoon: **Quon Ferguson - *2**
#704, 224 - 4th Ave. South, Saskatoon SK S7K 5M5
306-665-8828 306-665-8835

Saskatoon: **Robertson Stromberg Pedersen LLP - *21**
#600, Canada Building 105 - 21st St. East, Saskatoon SK S7K 0B3
306-652-7575 306-652-2445
rs.stoon@thinkrsplaw.com
www.thinkrsplaw.com

Saskatoon: **Roe & Company - *6**
#313, 220 - 3 Ave. South, Saskatoon SK S7K 1M1
306-244-9865 306-934-6827
smurray@sasktel.net
http://www.roeandcompany.ca/

Saskatoon: **Scharfstein Gibbings Walen & Fisher LLP - *12**
#500, Scotiabank Bldg. 111 - 2 Ave. South, Saskatoon SK S7K 1K6
306-653-2838 306-652-4747
lawyers@scharfsteinlaw.com
www.scharfsteinlaw.com

Saskatoon: **Sonnenschein Law Office - *1**
Lincoln's Inn 313 - 20 St. East, Saskatoon SK S7K 0A9
306-652-4730 306-653-5760
sonnenschein@sasktel.net

Saskatoon: **Stevenson Hood Thornton Beaubier LLP - *14**
#500, 123 - 2nd Ave. South, Saskatoon SK S7K 7E6
306-244-0132 306-653-1118
info@shtb-law.com
www.shtb-law.com

Shaunavon: **Geving, Coralie O. - *1**
23 - 3 Ave. East, Shaunavon SK S0N 2M0
306-297-2205 306-297-2411

Swift Current: **Anderson & Company - *6**
P.O Box 610 51 - 1st Ave. NW, Swift Current SK S9H 3W4
306-773-2891 306-778-3364
anderson.company@sasktel.net

Swift Current: **Holland Law Office - *1**
P.O Box 97 262 - 2 Ave. NE, Swift Current SK S9H 3V5
306-773-0661 306-773-9630

Swift Current: **MacBean Tessem - *6**
Box 550 P.O Box 550 151 First Ave. NE, Swift Current SK S9H 2B1
306-773-9343 306-778-3828
macbeantessem@macbeantessem.com
www.macbeantessem.com

Swift Current: **McLaughlin, Forrester, Heinrichs - *3**
#9, P.O Box 100 244 - 1 Ave. NE, Swift Current SK S9H 2B4
306-773-7205 306-773-9715
mfh.law@sasktel.net

Turtleford: **Wooff, D.S. - *1**
P.O Box 99, Turtleford SK S0M 2Y0
306-845-2599

Unity: **Hepting Neil & Jeanson - *3**
P.O Box 600 206 - 2nd Ave. West, Unity SK S0K 4L0
306-228-2631 306-228-4449
hepting.neil@sasktel.net

Wadena: **Marquette Law Firm - *1**
P.O Box 699 234 Main St., Wadena SK S0A 4J0
306-338-2554 306-338-3131
marqlaw@sasktel.net

Weyburn: **Nimegeers, Schuck, Wormsbecker & Bobbitt - *5**
P.O Box 8 319 Souris Ave. NE, Weyburn SK S4H 2J8
306-842-4654 306-842-0522
law@nswb.com
www.nswb.com

Wynyard: **Klebeck Law Office - *1**
P.O Box 1120 115 Ave. B East, Wynyard SK S0A 4T0
306-554-2523 306-554-2099
klebeck.law.office@sasktel.net

Wynyard: **Paulson & Ferraton - *1**
P.O Box 460 106 Main St., Wynyard SK S0A 4T0
306-554-2134 306-554-2342
paulson.ferraton@sasktel.net

Yorkton: **Stanatinos, Leland & Campbell LLP - *9**
P.O Box 188 36 - 4 Ave. North, Yorkton SK S3N 2V7
306-783-8541 306-786-7484

Yukon Territory

** indicates # of lawyers*

Whitehorse: **Austring, Fendrick, Fairman & Parkkari - *8**
The Drury Bldg. 3081 - 3rd Ave., Whitehorse YT Y1A 4Z7
867-668-4405 867-668-3710 800-661-0533
info@lawyukon.com
www.lawyukon.com

Whitehorse: **Lackowicz, Shier & Hoffman - *8**
#300, 204 Black St., Whitehorse YT Y1A 2M9
867-668-5252 867-668-5251
lackowicz.shier@yukonlaw.com

Whitehorse: **Macdonald & Company - *3**
#200, 204 Lambert St., Whitehorse YT Y1A 3T2
867-667-7885 867-667-7600
gmacdonald@anton.yk.ca

SECTION 12
LIBRARIES

Library & Archives Canada: 1333

Government Departments in Charge of Libraries: 1333

Library listings are arranged by Province. Each Province includes the following categories:

Regional Systems

Public Libraries

Archives

Library & Archives Canada
395 Wellington St., Ottawa ON K1A 0N4
613/996-5115; Fax: 613/995-6274
URL: www.collectionscanada.ca
Librarian & Archivist of Canada, Daniel J. Caron

Canadian Book Exchange Centre (CBEC): 613/952-8902; Fax: 613/954-9891; Email: cbecccel@lacbac.gc.ca; URL: www.collectionscanada.ca/cbecccel/; Symbol: OONL; OOA-Chief, Bill Murphy

Canadian Cataloguing in Publications Program (CIP): 819/994-6881; Fax: 819/997-7517; Email: cip@lacbac.gc.ca; URL:www.collectionscanada.ca/cip; Symbol: OONL; OOA-CIP Coordinator, Luc Simard

Canadian ISBN/ISMN Agency: 819/994-6872; Fax: 819/997-7517; Email: isbn@lac-bac.gc.ca; URL:www.collectionscanada.ca/isbn; Symbol: OONL; OOA

Database Networks (Union Catalogue): 819/997-7990; Fax: 819/994-4388; Email: union.catalogue@lacbac.gc.ca; URL: www.collectionscanada.ca/6/21/; Symbol: OONL; OOA-Chief, Emilie Lowenberg

Jacob M. Lowy Collection: 613/995-7960; Fax: 613/943-1112; Email: lowy@lac-bac.gc.ca; URL:www.collectionscanada.ca/6/26/s26-400-e.html; Symbol: OONL-Curator, Cheryl Jaffee

Legal Deposit: 819/997-9565; Fax: 819/953-8508; Email: legal.deposit@lac-bac.gc.ca; URL: www.collectionscanada.ca/6/25/index-e.html; Symbol: OONL; OOA-Chief, John Stegenga

Reference & Genealogy Division: 613/996-5115; Fax:613/995-6274; Email: reference@lac-bac.gc.ca; URL: www.collectionscanada.ca/services/005-220-e.html; www.genealogy.gc.ca/index_e.html; Symbol: OONL; OOA-Director, Antonio Lechasseur

Government Departments in Charge of Libraries

ALBERTA: Alberta Community Development, Community & Citizenship Services, Libraries, Community & Voluntary Sector Services Branch, Libraries Section, #803, Standard Life Centre, 10405 Jasper Ave., Edmonton, AB T5J 4R7, 780/427-6315; Fax: 780/415-8594, Email: libraries@gov.ab.ca, URL: www.cd.gov.ab.ca - Director, Punch Jackson

BRITISH COLUMBIA: Ministry of Education, Public Library Services Branch, 65 Humbold St., 5th Fl., PO Box 9831, Stn Prov Govt, Victoria BC V8V 4W8, 250/356-1791; Fax: 250/953-3225; Toll Free: 800-663-7051, Email: plsb@gov.bc.ca, URL: www.bced.gov.bc.ca/pls - Director of Library Services, Maureen Wood

MANITOBA: Culture, Heritage & Tourism Public Library Services Branch, #200, 1525 - 1st St. South, Brandon MB R7A 7A1, 204/726-6590, Fax: 204/726-6868, Email: pls@gov.mb.ca, URL: www.gov.mb.ca/chc/maplin - Director, Maureen Cubberley

NEW BRUNSWICK: New Brunswick Public Library Service, Place 2000, Provincial Office, 250 King St., Fredericton NB E3B 9M9, 506/453-2354, Fax: 506/444-4064, Email: sylvie.nadeau@gnb.ca, URL: www.gnb.ca/003/index-e.asp - Executive Director, Sylvie Nadeau

NEWFOUNDLAND & LABRADOR: Provincial Information & Library Resources Board, 48 St. George's Ave., Stephenville NL A2N 1K9, 709/643-0900, Fax: 709/643-0925, Email: shawntetford@nlpubliclibraries.ca, URL: www.nlpubliclibraries.ca - Executive Director, Shawn Tetford

NORTHWEST TERRITORIES: Northwest Territories Public Library Services, 75 Woodland Dr., Hay River NT X0E 1G1, 867/874-6531, Fax: 867/874-3321, Toll Free: 866-297-0232, Email: alison_hopkins@gov.nt.ca, URL: www.nwtpls.gov.nt.ca -Territorial Librarian, Alison Hopkins

NOVA SCOTIA: Nova Scotia Provincial Library, 770 Kempt Rd., Halifax NS B3K 4X8, 902/ 424-2457, Fax: 902/424-0633, Email: admin@nshpl.library.ns.ca, URL: www.library.ns.ca - Provincial Librarian, Jennifer Evans

NUNAVUT: Nunavut Public Library Services, PO Box 270, Baker Lake NU X0C 0A0, 867/793-3327, Fax: 867/793-3332, URL: www.gov.nu.ca/cley/home/english/libraries.html - Manager, Library Services, Petra Mauerhoff

ONTARIO: Ministry of Culture, Heritage & Libraries Branch, 400 University Ave., 4th Fl., Toronto ON M7A 2R9, 416/314-7342: Fax: 416/314-7635, Email: suzanne.roweknight@mcl.gov.on.ca; rita.scagnetti@mcl.gov.on.ca, URL: www.culture.gov.on.ca/english/culdiv/library - Manager of Libraries: Suzanne Rowe-Knight, Director, Heritage & Libraries Branch: Rita Scagnetti

PRINCE EDWARD ISLAND: Provincial Library Service, 89 Redhead Rd., PO Box 7500, Morell PE C0A 1S0, 902/961-7320, Fax: 902/961-7322, Email: ajgroen@gov.pe.ca, URL: www.library.pe.ca - Provincial Librarian, Allan J. Groen

QUÉBEC: Ministère de la Culture et des Communications, Lecture et Livre, Bibliothèques - Direction de la coordination et du soutien à la gestion des programmes, Édifice Guy-Frégault, 225, Grande Allée est, Bloc C, RC, Québec QC G1R 5G5, 418/380-2304, Télécopieur: 418/380-2324, Courriel: jacques.morrier@mcc.gouv.qc.ca, URL: www.mcc.gouv.qc.ca - Responsable: Jacques Morrier

SASKATCHEWAN: Provincial Library, 1945 Hamilton St., 8th Fl., Regina SK S4P 2C8, 306/787-2976, Fax: 306/787-2029, Email: jcampbell@library.gov.sk.ca, URL: www.learning.gov.sk.ca/branches/prov_library/index.shtml - Provincial Librarian: Joylene Campbell

YUKON: Yukon Public Libraries, Public Library Services, Government of Yukon, Community Libraries, PO Box 2703, Whitehorse YT Y1A 2C6, 867/667-5239, Fax: 867/393-6333, Toll Free (in Yukon): 800-661-0408, local 5239, Email: whitehorse.library@gov.yk.ca, URL: www.community.gov.yk.ca/libraries - Manager: Julie Ourom

Alberta

Regional Systems

Chinook Arch Regional Library System
2902 - 7th Ave. North, Lethbridge AB T1H 5C6
403-380-1500, Fax: 403-380-3550
arch@chinookarch.ab.ca
www.chinookarch.ab.ca
Maggie Macdonald, CEO
mmacdonald@chinookarch.ab.ca

Marigold Library System
710 - 2nd St., Strathmore AB T1P 1K4
403-934-5334, Fax: 403-934-5331
admin@marigold.ab.ca
www.marigold.ab.ca
Rowena Lunn, Director
rfl@marigold.ab.ca

Northern Lights Library System
5615 - 48 St., Elk Point AB T0A 1A0
780-724-2596, Fax: 780-724-2597
info@nlls.ab.ca
www.nlls.ab.ca
Mircea Panciuk, Director
director@nlls.ab.ca

Parkland Regional Library System (Alberta)
5404 - 56th Ave., Lacombe AB T4L 1G1
403-782-3850, Fax: 403-782-4650
rsheppard@prl.ab.ca
www.prl.ab.ca
Ronald Sheppard, Director

Peace Library System
8301 - 110 St., Grande Prairie AB T8W 6T2
780-538-4656, Fax: 780-539-5285
peacelib@peacelibrarysystem.ab.ca
www.peacelibrarysystem.ab.ca
Linda Duplessis, Director
lduplessis@peacelibrarysystem.ab.ca

Shortgrass Library System
2375 - 10th Ave. SW, Medicine Hat AB T1A 8G2
403-529-0550, Fax: 403-528-2473
director@shortgrass-lib.ab.ca
www.shortgrass-lib.ab.ca
Harold Storlien, Director

Yellowhead Regional Library
433 King St., Spruce Grove AB T7X 2Y1
780-962-2003, Fax: 780-962-2770
yrlquery@yrl.ab.ca
www.yrl.ab.ca
Clive Maishment, Director

Public Libraries

Acadia Valley: Acadia Municipal Library
Warren Peers School, PO Box 6, Acadia Valley AB T0J 0A0
403-972-3744, Fax: 403-972-2000
aavalibrary@marigold.ab.ca
www.marigold.ab.ca/about/memberlibs/acadia.html
Maxine Booker, Chair

Acme: Acme Municipal Library
610 Walsh Ave., Acme AB T0M 0A0
403-546-3879, Fax: 403-546-2248
aamlibrary@marigold.ab.ca
www.marigold.ab.ca/about/memberlibs/acme.html
Colleen Herrara, Library Manager
aamlibrary@marigold.ab.ca

Airdrie: Airdrie Public Library
#111, 304 Main St. South, Airdrie AB T4B 3C3
403-948-0600, Fax: 403-912-4002
info@airdriepubliclibrary.ca
www.airdriepubliclibrary.ca
Janine Jevne, Director
janine.jevne@airdriepubliclibrary.ca

Alberta Beach: Alberta Beach Public Library
4811 - 50th Ave., Alberta Beach AB T0E 0A0
780-924-3491, Fax: 780-924-3491
ablibrary@yrl.ab.caa
www.albertabeachlibrary.ca
Leann Knysh, Chair

Alder Flats: Alder Flats Public Library
Hwy. 13, Alder Flats AB T0C 0A0
780-388-3881, Fax: 780-388-3887
afpl@wrps.ab.ca
www.alderflatslibrary.ab.ca
Judy Miners, Library Director
780-388-3881

Alix: Alix Public Library
4928 - 50th St., Alix AB T0C 0B0
403-747-3233
alixpublic@libs.prl.ab.ca
alixpublic.prl.ab.ca
Beth Richardson, Librarian

Alliance: Alliance Community Library
101 - 1st Ave. East, Alliance AB T0B 0A0
780-879-3733
alliancelibrary@libs.prl.ab.ca
alliance.prl.ab.ca/index.htm
Tracy Rombough, Libary Manager
aplen7@telusplanet.net

Amisk: Amisk Municipal Library
5005 - 50 St., Amisk AB T0B 0B0
780-628-5457, Fax: 780-856-3980
amisklibrary@libs.prl.ab.ca
Carmen Toma, Library Manager

Andrew: Andrew Municipal Public Library
c/o Andrew School, 4922 - 50th Ave., Andrew AB T0B 0C0
780-365-3501, Fax: 780-365-3734
public@mcsnet.ca
www.andrewschool.ca
Denise Dorland, Librarian

Arrowwood: Arrowwood Municipal Library
22 Main St., Arrowwood AB T0L 0B0
403-534-3932, Fax: 403-534-3932, 866-941-4177
help@arrowwoodlibrary.ca
www.arrowwoodlibrary.ca/client/arrowwood
Dorothy Way, Library Manager

Ashmont: Ashmont Community Library
Ashmont School, Main St., Ashmont AB T0A 0C0
780-726-3877, Fax: 780-726-3777
www.ashmontlibrary.ab.ca
Karen Duperron, Librarian

Athabasca: Alice B. Donahue Library & Archives
4716 - 48th St., Athabasca AB T9S 2B6
780-675-2735
aathpublib@telusplanet.net
www.athabascalibrary.ab.ca
Cynthia Graefe, Library Manager & Resource Sharing Contact
librarian@athabascalibrary.ab.ca

Banff: Banff Public Library
101 Bear St., Banff AB T1L 1H3
403-762-2661, Fax: 403-762-3805
banff_library@telusplanet.net
www.banfflibrary.ab.ca
Holly Nguyen, Librarian

Barnwell: Barnwell Municipal Library
490 Cottonwood St., Barnwell AB T0K 0B0
403-223-3626, 866-941-4177
libbar@barnwelllibrary.ca
www.barnwelllibrary.ca/client/barnwell

Cindy Evanson, Library Manager
cevanson@barnwelllibrary.ca
403-223-3626

Barrhead: Barrhead Public Library
5103 - 53 Ave., Barrhead AB T7N 1N9
780-674-8519, Fax: 780-674-8520
plibrary@barrheadpubliclibrary.ca
www.barrheadpubliclibrary.ca
Elaine Dickie, Library Director

Bashaw: Bashaw Municipal Library
5112 - 52nd St., Bashaw AB T0B 0H0
780-372-4055, Fax: 780-372-4055
bashawlibrary@libs.prl.ab.ca
bashawlibrary.prl.ab.ca/
Cindy Hunter, Library Manager
780-372-4055

Bassano: Bassano Memorial Library
522 - 2nd Ave., Bassano AB T0J 0B0
403-641-4065
bmlcapic@eidnet.org
www.shortgrass-lib.ab.ca/bml

Bawlf: David Knipe Memorial Library
203 Hanson St., PO Box 116, Bawlf AB T0B 0J0
780-373-3882, Fax: 780-373-3882
bawlflibrary@libs.prl.ab.ca
bawlflibrary.prl.ab.ca
Fern Reinke, Library Manager

Bear Canyon: Bear Point Community Library
PO Box 43, Bear Canyon AB T0H 0B0
780-595-3771, Fax: 780-595-3762
librarian@bearpointlibrary.ab.ca
www.bearpointlibrary.ab.ca
Tannis Bigam, Librarian

Beaumont: Bibliothèque de Beaumont Library
5700 - 49th St., Beaumont AB T4X 1S7
780-929-2665, Fax: 780-929-1291
val@beaumontlibrary.com
www.beaumontlibrary.com
Tracey Allan, Librarian
Tracey@beaumontlibrary.com
780-929-2665

Beaverlodge: Beaverlodge RCMP Centennial Library
406 - 10th St., Beaverlodge AB T0H 0C0
780-354-2569, Fax: 780-354-3078
abarlibrary@telusplanet.net
www.beaverlodgelibrary.ab.ca
Shelly Longson, Library Manager

Beiseker: Beiseker Municipal Library
Old Railway Station, 601 - 1st Ave., Beiseker AB T0M 0G0
403-947-3230, Fax: 403-947-2146
abemlibrary@marigold.ab.ca
www.beisekerlibrary.com
Tracy Bell, Library Manager

Bellevue: Bellevue Municipal Library
2802 - 222nd St., Bellevue AB T0K 0C0
403-564-5201, Fax: 403-564-5201
libbel@chinookarch.ab.ca
Doreen Glavin, Librarian
403-564-5201

Bentley: Bentley Municipal Library
5014 - 49 Ave., Bentley AB T0C 0J0
403-748-4626, Fax: 403-748-4627
bentleylibrary@libs.prl.ab.ca
bentleylibrary.prl.ab.ca
Tina Whitfield, Library Manager

Berwyn: Berwyn W.I. Municipal Library
5105 - 51st St., Berwyn AB T0H 0E0
780-338-3616, Fax: 780-338-3616
librarian@berwynlibrary.ab.ca
Kim Byard, Library Manager

Big Valley: Big Valley Municipal Library
29 - 1st Ave. South, Big Valley AB T0J 0G0
403-876-2642, Fax: 403-876-2401
bigvalleylibrary@prl.ab.ca
bvlibrary.prl.ab.ca
Janice E. Hermus, Librarian

Black Diamond: Sheep River Community Library
301 Center Ave., Black Diamond AB T0L 0H0
403-933-3278, Fax: 403-933-3278
abdsrclibrary@marigold.ab.ca
Muhammad Zia-Ul-Haque, Librarian

Blackfalds: Blackfalds Public Library
5018 Waghorn St., Blackfalds AB T0M 0J0
403-885-2343, Fax: 403-885-4353
library@blackfaldslibrary.com
www.blackfaldslibrary.com
Carley Binder, Librarian

Blairmore: Crowsnest Pass Municipal Library - Blairmore
2114 - 127 St., Blairmore AB T0K 0E0
403-562-8393, Fax: 403-562-8397
libbla@chinookarch.ab.ca
Judy Bradley, Librarian

Blue Ridge: Blue Ridge Community Library
24A Main St., Blue Ridge AB T0E 0B0
780-648-7323, Fax: 780-648-2348
www.yrl.ab.ca/about/lib/abrc.html
Mary Anne Lehman, Chair

Bodo: Bodo Public Library
PO Box 93, Bodo AB T0B 0M0
780-753-6079, Fax: 780-753-8195
bodolibrary@libs.prl.ab.ca
www.prl.ab.ca/ABOD
Roxanna Wotschell, Library Manager

Bon Accord: Bon Accord Public Library
PO Box 749, Bon Accord AB T0A 0K0
780-921-2540, Fax: 780-921-2580
director@bonaccordlibrary.ab.ca
www.bonaccordlibrary.ab.ca
Dyvonna Inkster, Chair

Bonnyville: Bonnyville Municipal Library
4804 - 49th Ave., Bonnyville AB T9N 2J3
780-826-3071, Fax: 780-826-2058
librarian@bonnyvillelibrary.ab.ca
www.bonnyvillelibrary.ab.ca
Ina Smith, Library Director

Bow Island: Bow Island Municipal Library
510 Centre St., Bow Island AB T0K 0G0
403-545-2828, Fax: 403-545-6642
bowlib@shortgrass.ca
www.shortgrass.ca/bowisland/
Susan Andersen, Library Manager

Bowden: Bowden Public Library
1700 - 23rd St., Bowden AB T0M 0K0
403-224-3688, Fax: 403-224-2244
bowdenlibrary@libs.prl.ab.ca
www.town.bowden.ab.ca/library.html
Roy Middleton, President

Boyle: Boyle Public Library
5002 - 3 St., Boyle AB T0A 0M0
780-689-4161, Fax: 780-689-5660
librarian@boylepublib.ab.ca
www.boylepublib.ab.ca
Katherine Bulmer, Library Manager

Breton: Breton Public Library
4916 - 50th Ave., Breton AB T0C 0P0
780-696-3740, Fax: 780-696-3590
bretonlibrary@yrl.ab.ca
www.bretonlibrary.ab.ca
Diane Shave, Library Director

Brocket: Oldman River Cultural Centre Library
PO Box 70, Brocket AB T0K 0H0
403-965-3939, Fax: 403-965-2289
oldmancc@telusplanet.net
Reg Crow Shoe, Director

Brooks: Berry Creek Community School Library
RR#2, Brooks AB T1R 1E2
403-566-3743, Fax: 403-566-3736
acclibrary@marigold.ab.ca
www.marigold.ab.ca/about/memberlibs/berrycreek.html
Susan Conners, Library Manager

Brooks: Brooks Public Library
420 - 1st Ave. West, Brooks AB T1R 1B9
403-362-2947, Fax: 403-362-8111
brolib@shortgrass.ca
www.shortgrass-lib.ab.ca/bpl
Dino Champlone, Head Librarian

Brownfield: Brownfield Community Library
PO Box 63, Brownfield AB T0C 0R0
403-578-2247, Fax: 403-578-4208
brownfieldlibrary@libs.prl.ab.ca
www.prl.ab.ca/ABROW

Pat Martin, Chair

Brownvale: Brownvale Community Library
PO Box 178, Brownvale AB T0H 0L0
780-597-2250
Maureen Osowetski, Library Manager

Bruderheim: Metro Kalyn Community Library
5017 - 49th St., Bruderheim AB T0B 0S0
780-796-3032, Fax: 780-796-3032
librarian@bruderheimpl.ab.ca
Diana Mack, Community Librarian

Cadogan: Cadogan Public Library
304 - 2nd St., General Delivery, Cadogan AB T0B 0T0
780-753-6933, Fax: 780-753-3155
cadoganlibrary@libs.prl.ab.ca
Deb Prediger, Library Manager

Calgary: Alberta Association of College Librarians Newsletter
SAIT, 1301 - 16th Ave. NW, Calgary AB T2M 0L4
780-497-5141
dave.weber@sait.ca
www.nait.ca/libresources/aacl/news.htm
Dave Weber, Editor

Calgary: Calgary Public Library
616 MacLeod Trail SE, Calgary AB T2G 2M2
403-260-2600
dear.library@calgarypubliclibrary.com
calgarypubliclibrary.com
Gerry Meek, CEO

Calgary: Letter of the LAA
80 Baker Cres. NW, Calgary AB T2L 1R4
403-284-5818, Fax: 403-282-6646
christine.sheppard@shaw.ca
www.laa.ab.ca
Christine Sheppard, Editor

Calmar: Calmar Public Library
4705 - 50th Ave., PO Box 238, Calmar AB T0C 0V0
780-985-3472, Fax: 780-985-2859
library3@telusplanet.net
www.calmarpubliclibrary.ca
Carol Nystrom, Library Director

Camrose: Camrose Public Library
4710 - 50th Ave., Camrose AB T4V 0R8
780-672-4214, Fax: 780-672-9165
cpldir@libs.prl.ab.ca
www.library.camrose.ab.ca
Donna Watson, Chair

Canmore: Canmore Public Library
950 - 8 Ave., Canmore AB T1W 2T1
403-678-2468, Fax: 403-678-2165
info@canmorelibrary.ab.ca
www.canmorelibrary.ab.ca
Don Pickard, Chair

Carbon: Carbon Municipal Library
Community Centre, PO Box 70, Carbon AB T0M 0L0
403-572-3440
acarmlibrary@marigold.ab.ca
Steve Nedoshytko, Chair

Cardston: Jim & Mary Kearl Library
25 - 3rd Ave. West, Cardston AB T0K 0K0
403-653-4775, Fax: 403-653-4716
libcard@chinookarch.ab.ca
Donna Beazer, Library Manager
dbeazer@cardstonlibrary.ca
403-653-4707

Carmangay: Carmangay & District Municipal Library
414 Grand Ave., Carmangay AB T0L 0N0
403-643-3777, Fax: 403-643-3777
help@carmangaylibrary.ca
www.carmangaylibrary.ca/client/carmangay
Marian Schibbelhute, Library Manager

Caroline: Caroline Municipal Library Board
5023 - 50 Ave., Caroline AB T0M 0M0
403-722-4060, Fax: 403-722-4070
carolinelibrary@libs.prl.ab.ca
carolinelibrary.prl.ab.ca
Iris Stevens, Chair

Carstairs: Carstairs Public Library
1402 Scarlett Ranch Rd., Carstairs AB T0M 0N0
403-337-3943, Fax: 403-337-3943
carstairs@libs.prl.ab.ca
www.carstairspublic.prl.ab.ca

Anne Strilchuk, Librarian

***Castor:* Castor Public Library**
5103 - 51 St., Castor AB T0C 0X0
403-882-3999
castorlibrary@libs.prl.ab.ca
www.prl.ab.ca/ACAST
Wendy Bozek, Library Manager

***Cereal:* Cereal & District Municipal Library**
415 Main St., Cereal AB T0J 0N0
403-326-3883
acermlibrary@marigold.ab.ca
Denise Reider, Library Manager

***Champion:* Champion Municipal Library**
2 Ave. South, Champion AB T0L 0R0
403 897-3099, Fax: 403-897-3098
help@championlibrary.ca
www.championlibrary.ca
Patty Abel, Librarian

***Chauvin:* Chauvin Municipal Library**
5200 - 4th Ave. North, Chauvin AB T0B 0V0
780-858-3744, Fax: 780-858-2392
drfolkins@telusplanet.net

***Claresholm:* Claresholm Municipal Library**
211 - 49 Ave. West, Claresholm AB T0L 0T0
403-625-4168, Fax: 403-625-2939
libcla@chinookarch.ab.ca
Kathy Davies, Library Manager
kdavies@chinookarch.ab.ca

***Cleardale:* Menno Simons Public Library**
PO Bag 100, Cleardale AB T0H 3Y0
780-685-3623, Fax: 780-685-3665
gulas@prsd.ab.ca
Sylvia Gula, Librarian

***Clive:* Clive Public Library**
Clive Village Office, 5115 - 50 St., Clive AB T0C 0Y0
403-784-3131, Fax: 403-784-3131
clivelibrary@libs.prl.ab.ca
www.clivepublib.prl.ab.ca
Sue Giesbrecht, Chair

***Coaldale:* Coaldale Public Library**
2014 - 18 St., Coaldale AB T1M 1E9
403-345-1340, Fax: 403-345-1342
help@coaldalelibrary.ca
www.coaldalelibrary.ca
Jane Franz, Librarian

***Cochrane:* Nan Boothby Memorial Library**
405 Railway St. West, Cochrane AB T4C 2E2
403-932-4353, Fax: 403-932-4385
nanboothby@home.com
www.cochranepubliclibrary.ca
Adrian Dalwood, Librarian

***Cold Lake:* Cold Lake Public Library**
5513B - 48 Ave., Cold Lake AB T9M 1X9
780-594-8828, Fax: 780-594-7787
ill@library.coldlake.ab.ca (Resource sharing)
www.library.coldlake.ab.ca
Kellie Bellew Martin, Chair

***Consort:* Consort Municipal Library**
Consort School, PO Box 456, Consort AB T0C 1B0
403-577-2501, Fax: 403-577-2112
aconmlibrary@marigold.ab.ca
Lisa Myers-Sortland, Chair

***Coronation:* Coronation Memorial Library**
5001 Royal St., PO Box 453, Coronation AB T0C 1C0
403-578-3445, Fax: 403-578-3020
coronationlibrary@libs.prl.ab.ca
Val Cornell, Chair

***Coutts:* Coutts Municipal Library**
218 - 1st Ave. South, Coutts AB T0K 0N0
403-344-3804, Fax: 403-344-3815
Sharon Wollersheim, Librarian
sharon.wollersheim@horizon.ab.ca

***Cremona:* Cremona Municipal Library**
Village of Cremona Municipal Bldg., 205 - 1 St. East, Cremona AB T0M 0R0
403-637-3100
cremonalibrary@libs.prl.ab.ca
www.prl.ab.ca
Sandra Herbert, Library Manager

***La Crete:* La Crete Community Library**
10001 - 99 Ave., La Crete AB T0H 2H0
780-928-3166, Fax: 780-928-3166
helenw@fvsd.ab.ca
Helen Wiebe, Librarian
helenw@fvsd.ab.ca

***Crossfield:* Crossfield Municipal Library**
1026 Chisholm Ave., Crossfield AB T0M 0S0
403-946-4232, Fax: 403-946-4212
crossfield.library@telus.net
www.crossfieldlibrary.org
Barbara Code, Librarian

***Czar:* Czar Municipal Library**
PO Box 127, Czar AB T0B 0Z0
780-857-3740, Fax: 780-857-2224
czarlibrary@libs.prl.ab.ca
Jackie Almberg, Library Manager

***Darwell:* Darwell Public Library**
Darwell Community Hall, 54225B Hwy. 765, Darwell AB T0E 0L0
780-892-3746, Fax: 780-892-3743
www.darwellpubliclibrary.ab.ca
Diana Richardson, Library Director

***Daysland:* Daysland Public Library**
5130 - 50th St., Daysland AB T0B 1A0
780-679-7263
dayslandlibrary@libs.prl.ab.ca
www.prl.ab.ca
Mickey Miller, Library Manager

***Debolt:* Debolt Public Library**
PO Box 480, Debolt AB T0H 1B0
780-957-3770
librarian@deboltlibrary.ab.ca
Yvonne McIntyre, Library Manager

***Delburne:* Delburne Municipal Library**
2210 Main St., Delburne AB T0M 0V0
403-749-3848, Fax: 403-749-3848
delburnelibrary@libs.prl.ab.ca
delburnelibrary.prl.ab.ca/
Relda Chambers, Librarian

***Delia:* Delia Municipal Library**
Delia School, Delia AB T0J 0W0
403-364-3777, Fax: 403-364-3805
admlibrary@marigold.ab.ca
Barb Marshall, Chair

***Derwent:* Derwent Municipal Library**
PO Box 210, Derwent AB T0B 1C0
780-741-3744, Fax: 780-741-3792
Leona Bielech, Librarian

***Devon:* Devon Public Library**
Devon Shopping Center, #101, 17 Athabasca Ave., Devon AB T9G 1G5
780-987-3720
www.devonpubliclibrary.ca
Barry Fildes, Chair

***Didsbury:* Didsbury Municipal Library**
2033 - 19 Ave., Didsbury AB T0M 0W0
403-335-3142, Fax: 403-335-3141
didsburylibrary@libs.prl.ab.ca
dml.prl.ab.ca
Inez Kosinski, Librarian
403-335-3142

***Donalda:* Donalda Municipal Library**
5001 Main St., Donalda AB T0B 1H0
403-883-2345, Fax: 403-883-2022
donaldalibrary@libs.prl.ab.ca
donaldalibrary.prl.ab.ca
Susan Dahl, Library Manager

***Drayton Valley:* Drayton Valley Municipal Library**
5120 - 52 St., Drayton Valley AB T7A 1R7
780-514-2228, Fax: 780-542-5753
dvml@incentre.net
www.draytonvalleylibrary.ca
Nesan Naidoo, Librarian
nnaidoo@incentre.net

***Drumheller:* Drumheller Public Library**
224 Centre St., Drumheller AB T0J 0Y0
403-823-5382, Fax: 403-823-3651
drumlib@magtech.ca
www.drumhellerlibrary.ca
Linde Turner, Head Librarian

***Duchess:* Duchess Public Library**
PO Box 88, Duchess AB T0J 0Z0
403-378-4369, Fax: 403-378-4369
manager@duchesspubliclibrary.ca
www.duchesspubliclibrary.ca
Shannon Vanderloh, Library Manager

***Duffield:* Duffield Community Library**
1 Main St., Duffield AB T0E 0N0
780-892-2644, Fax: 780-892-3344
www.duffieldcommunitylibrary.ab.ca
Sandy Cornell, Chair

***Duffield:* Keephills Community Library**
RR#1, Duffield AB T0E 0N0
780-731-0000, Fax: 780-731-2433
www.keephillslibrary.ab.ca
Debbie Ramsay, Library Director
dramsay@psd70.ab.ca

***Eaglesham:* Eaglesham Public Library**
PO Box 206, Eaglesham AB T0H 1H0
780-359-3792, Fax: 780-359-3745
aeaglibrary@telusplanet.net
Norma Bolster, Contact

***Eckville:* Eckville Public Library**
PO Box 492, Eckville AB T0M 0X0
403-746-3240, Fax: 403-746-2900
eckvillelibrary@libs.prl.ab.ca
www.prl.ab.ca/AECK
Judith Thompson, Library Manager

***Edberg:* Edberg Municipal Library**
48 First Ave. West, PO Box 93, Edberg AB T0B 1J0
780-678-5606, Fax: 780-678-5606
edberglibrary@libs.prl.ab.ca
www.edberglibrary.prl.ab.ca/index.html
Colleen Wack, Library Manager

***Edgerton:* Edgerton Public Library**
5037 - 50 Ave., Edgerton AB T0B 1K0
780-755-2666, Fax: 780-755-2667
aedgpublib@telusplanet.net
www.edgertonlibrary.ab.ca
Mary Ann Sparks, Librarian
780-758-2666

***Edmonton:* Edmonton Public Library**
7 Sir Winston Churchill Sq., Edmonton AB T5J 2V4
780-496-7000, Fax: 780-496-1885
webmaster@epl.ca
www.epl.ca
Linda C. Cook, Chief Executive Officer
lcook@epl.ca
780-496-7050

***Edmonton:* The AALT Technician: Journal of the Alberta Association of Library Technicians**
PO Box 700, Edmonton AB T5J 2L4
, 866-350-2258
journal@aalt.org
www.aalt.org/about/journal/index.html
Crystal Friars, Editor

***Edson:* Edson Public Library**
4726 - 8th Ave., Edson AB T7E 1S8
780-723-6691, Fax: 780-723-9728
info@edsonlibrary.org
www.edsonlibrary.org
JoAnn Hooper, Librarian
hooperj@edsonlibrary.org

***Elk Point:* Elk Point Public Library**
5123 - 50 Ave., Elk Point AB T0A 1A0
780-724-3737, Fax: 780-724-3739
www.elkpointlibrary.ab.ca
Daphne Schnurer, Librarian

***Elnora:* Elnora Public Library**
210 Main St., Elnora AB T0M 0Y0
403-773-3966, Fax: 403-773-3922
elnoralibrary@libs.prl.ab.ca
elnoralibrary.prl.ab.ca/
Wanda Strandquist, Library Manager

***Empress:* Empress Municipal Library**
PO Box 188, Empress AB T0J 1E0
403-565-3936, Fax: 403-565-2010
aemlibrary@marigold.ab.ca
Charl Vincent, Library Manager

***Enchant:* Enchant Community Library**
PO Box 3000, Enchant AB T0K 0V0

403-739-3835, Fax: 403-739-2585
book1@telus.net
Sharon Hagen, Librarian

Entwistle: **Entwistle Municipal Library**
PO Box 323, Entwistle AB T0E 0S0
780-727-3811, Fax: 780-727-2440
kgibb@psd70.ab.ca
Karen Gibb, Librarian

Evansburg: **Evansburg & District Municipal Library**
PO Box 339, Evansburg AB T0E 0T0
780-727-2030, Fax: 780-727-2437
heatnutb@gryd.ab.ca
Heather Nutbrown, Library Manager
heatnutb@gryd.ab.ca

Exshaw: **Bighorn Library**
2 Heart Mt. Dr., Exshaw AB T0L 2C0
403-673-3571, Fax: 403-673-3571
aexclibrary@marigold.ab.ca
Rose Reid, Librarian

Fairview: **Fairview Public Library**
PO Box 248, Fairview AB T0H 1L0
780-835-2613, Fax: 780-835-2613
afvlibrary@telusplanet.net
Chris Burkholder, Librarian
librarian@fairviewlibrary.ab.ca
780-835-2613

Falher: **Bibliothèque Dentinger/ Dentinger Library**
CP 60, Falher AB T0H 1M0
780-837-2776, Fax: 780-837-8755
www.peacelibrarysystem.ab.ca/Falher.html
Maureen Carter, Responsable

Fawcett: **M. Alice Frose Library**
PO Box 150, Fawcett AB T0G 0Y0
780-954-3827, Fax: 780-954-3934
mmeyn@phrd.ab.ca
www.fawcettlibrary.ab.ca
Marie Meyn, Library Clerk

Flatbush: **Flatbush Community Library**
General Delivery, Flatbush AB T0G 0Z0
780-681-3756, Fax: 780-681-3940
librarian@flatbushlibrary.ab.ca
www.flatbushlibrary.ab.ca
Rose Herdman, Librarian

Foremost: **Foremost Municipal Library**
103 - 1st Ave., Foremost AB T0K 0X0
403-867-3855
forlib@shortgrass-lib.ab.ca
www.shortgrass-lib.ab.ca/foremost/
Joanne Harty, Library Manager

Forestburg: **Forestburg Municipal Library**
4901 - 50th St., Forestburg AB T0B 1N0
780-582-4110, Fax: 780-582-4127
forestburglibrary@libs.prl.ab.ca
www.forestburg.ca/home/community_services/library
Judy Oberg, Librarian

Fort Assiniboine: **Fort Assiniboine Public Library**
Fort Assiniboine School, 35 State Ave., Fort Assiniboine AB T0G 1A0
780-584-2227, Fax: 780-674-8575
www.fortassiniboinelibrary.ab.ca
Irene Olson, Board Chair

Fort MacLeod: **Fort MacLeod Municipal Library**
PO Box 1479, Fort MacLeod AB T0L 0Z0
403-553-3880, Fax: 403-553-2643
libfor@chinookarch.ab.ca
Sharon Edwards, Librarian

Fort McMurray: **Fort McMurray Public Library**
151 MacDonald Dr., Fort McMurray AB T9H 5C5
780-743-7800, Fax: 780-743-5952
fmpl.ca
Craig Shufelt, Director

Fort Saskatchewan: **Fort Saskatchewan Public Library**
10011 - 102 St., Fort Saskatchewan AB T8L 2C5
780-998-4275, Fax: 780-992-3255
fsasklib@fspl.ca
www.fspl.ca
Debbie Saranchuk, Chair

Fort Vermilion: **Fort Vermilion Community Library**
5103 River Rd., Fort Vermilion AB T0H 1N0
780-927-4279, Fax: 780-927-4746
afvclibrary@platinum.ca
www.fortvermilioncommunitylibrary.com
Dina Clark, President

Fox Creek: **Fox Creek Municipal - School Library**
501 - 8 St., Fox Creek AB T0H 1P0
780-622-2343, Fax: 780-622-4160
foxcreeklibrary@yahoo.com
www.foxcreeklibrary.ca
Leslie Ann Sharkey, Head Librarian

Galahad: **Galahad Municipal Library**
PO Box 25, Galahad AB T0B 1R0
780-583-3917, Fax: 780-583-3957
gallib@libs.prl.ab.ca
galahadpublic.prl.ab.ca/
Lori Wegenast, Librarian

Gem: **Gem Jubilee Library**
PO Box 6, Gem AB T0J 1M0
403-641-3245

La Glace: **La Glace Community Library**
PO Box 209, La Glace AB T0H 2J0
780-568-4696, Fax: 780-568-4707
librarian@laglacelibrary.ab.ca
Evelyn Siebert, Head of Library

Gleichen: **Gleichen & District Library Society**
404 Main St., Gleichen AB T0J 1N0
403-734-2390, Fax: 403-734-2390
agmlibrary@marigold.ab.ca
www.marigold.ab.ca/about/memberlibs/gleichen.html
Amanda Gendron, President

Glenwood: **Glenwood Municipal Library**
PO Box 1156, Glenwood AB T0K 2R0
403-626-3660, Fax: 403-626-3660
toviatt@glenwoodlibrary.ca
Twylla Oviatt, Librarian
toviatt@glenwoodlibrary.ca
403-626-3660

Grande Cache: **Grande Cache Municipal Library**
10601 Shand Ave., Grande Cache AB T0E 0Y0
780-827-2081, Fax: 780-827-3112
www.grandecachelibrary.ab.ca
Laurel A. Kelsch, Library Director
laurkels@gyrd.ab.ca

Grande Prairie: **Grande Prairie Public Library**
#101, 9839 - 103 Ave., Grande Prairie AB T8V 6M7
780-532-3580, Fax: 780-538-4983
gplib@gppl.ab.ca
www.gppl.ab.ca
Laurie Harrison, Library Director
lharrison@gppl.ab.ca
780—35-7-74

Granum: **Granum Public Library**
310 Railway Ave., Granum AB T0L 1A0
403-687-3912, Fax: 403-687-3912
help@granumpubliclibrary.ca
www.granumpubliclibrary.ca

Grassland: **Grassland Public Library**
Hwy. 63, Grassland AB T0A 1V0
780-525-3733, Fax: 780-525-3750
librarian@grasslandlibrary.ab.ca
www.grasslandlibrary.ab.ca
Lori Zachkewich, Library Manager

Grassy Lake: **Grassy Lake Public Library**
PO Box 690, Grassy Lake AB T0K 0Z0
403-655-2232, Fax: 403-655-2259
help@grassylakelibrary.ca
www.grassylakelibrary.ca

Grimshaw: **Grimshaw Municipal Library**
5007 - 47 Ave., Grimshaw AB T0H 1W0
780-332-4553, Fax: 780-332-1250
www.grimshawlibrary.ab.ca
Linda Chmilar, Library Manager
lchmilar@grimshawlibrary.ab.ca

Gunn: **Rich Valley Public Library**
RR#1, Gunn AB T0E 1A0
780-967-3525
rvpublib@yrl.ab.ca
www.richvalleylibrary.ab.ca
Betti-Ann Laporte, Librarian

Hanna: **Hanna Municipal Library**
202 - 1st Ave. West, Hanna AB T0J 1P0
403-854-3865, Fax: 403-854-2772
library@hanna.ca
www.hanna.ca/library
Mary McKay, Library Director

Hardisty: **Hardisty & District Public Library**
5027 - 50 St., Hardisty AB T0B 1V0
780-888-3947, Fax: 780-888-3947
hardistylibrary@libs.prl.ab.ca
hardistylib.prl.ab.ca
Billi-Jo Wildeboer, Library Manager

Hay Lakes: **Hay Lakes Municipal Library**
106 Main St., Hay Lakes AB T0B 1W0
780-878-2665
haylakescontact@prl.ab.ca
haylakeslibrary.prl.ab.ca
Belinda Wegner, Library Manager

Hays: **Hays Public Library**
PO Box 36, Hays AB T0K 1B0
403-725-3744, Fax: 403-725-3744
help@hayslibrary.ca
www.hayslibrary.ca
Diane Wickenheiser, Library Manager

Heinsburg: **Heinsburg Community Library**
General Delivery, Heinsburg AB T0A 1X0
780-943-3913, Fax: 780-943-3773
heinsburglibrary@netscape.net
www.heinsburgcapsite.8k.com
Kelly Hovdestad, Library Clerk
kelly_hovdestad@sperd.ca

Heisler: **Heisler Municipal Library**
100 Haultain Ave., Heisler AB T0B 2A0
780-889-3999, Fax: 780-889-3999
heislerlibrary@libs.prl.ab.ca
www.prl.ab.ca/AHEI
Marvis Zimmer, Library Manager

High Level: **High Level Municipal Library**
10601 - 103 St., High Level AB T0H 1Z0
780-926-2097, Fax: 780-926-4268
librarian@highlevellibrary.ab.ca
www.highlevellibrary.ab.ca
Jennilyn Boire, Library Director

High Prairie: **High Prairie Municipal Library**
4723 - 53 Ave., High Prairie AB T0G 1E0
780-523-3838, Fax: 780-523-3838
librarian@highprairielibrary.ab.ca
www.highprairielibrary.ab.ca
Janet Lemay, Library Manager

High River: **High River Centennial Library**
909 - 1st St. West, High River AB T1V 1A5
403-652-2917, Fax: 403-652-7203
hrlibrary@highriver.net
www.marigold.ab.ca/about/memberlibs/highriver.html
Deb Gardiner, Librarian

Hines Creek: **Hines Creek Municipal Library**
PO Box 750, Hines Creek AB T0H 2A0
780-494-3879, Fax: 780-494-3605
librarian@hinescreeklibrary.ab.ca
Sharon Nazarko, Librarian
librarian@hinescreeklibrary.ab.ca
780-494-3879

Hinton: **Hinton Municipal Library**
803 Switzer Dr., Hinton AB T7V 1V1
780-865-2363, Fax: 780-865-4292
hettwild@hintonlibrary.org
www.hintonlibrary.org
Hetty Wilderdijk, Director, Library Arts & Culture
780-865-6051

Holden: **Holden Municipal Library**
4912 - 50 St., Holden AB T0B 2C0
780-688-3838, Fax: 780-688-3838
librarian@holdenlibrary.ab.ca
www.holdenlibrary.ab.ca
Julianne Foster, Chair

Hughenden: **Hughenden Public Library**
PO Box 36, Hughenden AB T0B 2E0
780-856-2435, Fax: 780-856-2435
hughendenlibrary@libs.prl.ab.ca
Patricia Mackie, Library Manager
hughendenlibrary@libs.prl.ab.ca

Hussar: **Hussar Municipal Library**
102 - 2 St. NW, Hussar AB T0J 1S0

403-787-3788, Fax: 403-787-3922
ahumlibrary@marigold.ab.ca
www.marigold.ab.ca/about/memberlibs/hussar.html
Gay V. Harms, Library Manager

Hythe: **Hythe Public Library**
10013 - 100 St., Hythe AB T0H 2C0
780-356-3014, Fax: 780-356-2009
staff@hythelibrary.ab.ca
www.hythelibrary.ab.ca
Karen Bass, Library Manager

Innisfail: **Innisfail Public Library**
4949 - 49th St., Innisfail AB T4G 1A5
403-227-4407, Fax: 403-227-3122
innisfail@libs.prl.ab.ca
ipl.prl.ab.ca
Colleen Hayden, Librarian
chayden@libs.prl.ab.ca

Irma: **Irma Community Library**
5012 - 51st Ave., Irma AB T0B 2H0
780-754-3746, Fax: 780-754-3802
www.irmalibrary.ca
Leah Larson, Library Manager
leah.larson@btps.ca

Irvine: **Irvine Library**
78 South Railway St., Irvine AB T0J 1V0
403-834-3758
Joan L. Côté, Chair
403-834-3820

Jarvie: **Jarvie Public Library**
PO Box 119, Jarvie AB T0G 1H0
780-954-3935, Fax: 780-954-3885
kklein@phrd.ab.ca
Kim Klein, Librarian
kklein@phrd.ab.ca

Keg River: **Keg River Community Library**
PO Box 3, Keg River AB T0H 2G0
780-981-2128, Fax: 780-981-2262
kegrlib@telus.net
www.kegriverlibrary.ab.ca
Janice Freeman, Library Manager

Killam: **Killam Community Library**
5017 - 49th Ave., Killam AB T0B 2L0
780-385-3032, Fax: 780-385-3698
killamlibrary@libs.prl.ab.ca
Karen Auburn, Librarian
780-376-2197

Kinuso: **Kinuso Municipal Library**
PO Box 60, Kinuso AB T0G 1K0
780-775-3694, Fax: 780-775-3650
librarian@kinusolibrary.ab.ca
Susan Moody, Librarian

Kitscoty: **Kitscoty Municipal Library**
4910 - 51 St., Kitscoty AB T0B 2P0
780-846-2822, Fax: 780-846-2215
peggdavi@kes.btps.ca
Peggy Davies, Librarian

Lac La Biche: **Stuart MacPherson Library**
McArthur Place, Lower Level, 10307 - 100 St., Lac La Biche AB T0A 2C0
780-623-7467, Fax: 780-623-7499
headlibrarian@stuartmacphersonlibrary.ca
Maureen Penn, Librarian

Lacombe: **Lacombe Public Library**
#101, 5214 - 50 Ave., Lacombe AB T4L 0B6
403-782-3433, Fax: 403-782-3329
christinap@libs.prl.ab.ca
www.lacombelibrary.org
Christina Petrisor, Head Librarian
christinap@libs.prl.ab.ca

Lafond: **Lafond Public Library**
PO Box 20, Lafond AB T0A 2G0
780-645-2432, Fax: 780-645-2432
librarian@lafondlibrary.ab.ca
Romona Logozar, Librarian
librarian@lafondlibrary.ab.ca

Lamont: **Lamont Municipal Library**
PO Box 180, Lamont AB T0B 2R0
780-895-2228, Fax: 780-895-2600
lamontpublib@telusplanet.net
Joanne Flaman, Public Librarian

Leduc: **Leduc Public Library**
2 Alexandra Park, Leduc AB T9E 4C4
780-986-2637, Fax: 780-986-3462
www.library.leduc.ab.ca
Christine Brown, Head Librarian
cbrown@library.leduc.ab.ca

Lethbridge: **Lethbridge Public Library**
810 - 5th Ave. South, Lethbridge AB T1J 4C4
403-380-7310, Fax: 403-329-1478
lpl@lethbridgepubliclibrary.ca
www.lethbridgepubliclibrary.ca
Elizabeth Rossnagel, Director
lrossnagel@lethbridgepubliclibrary.ca
403-380-7340

Linden: **Linden Municipal Library**
215 - 1st. SE, Linden AB T0M 1J0
403-546-3757, Fax: 403-546-4220
almlibrary@marigold.ab.ca
www.marigold.ab.ca/about/memberlibs/linden.html
Debbie Martin, Librarian

Lloydminster: **Lloydminster Public Library**
5010 - 49th St., Lloydminster AB T9V 0K2
780-875-0850, Fax: 780-875-6523
info@lloydminster.info
www.lloydminster.info
Ronald Gillies, Head Librarian
hlib@lloydminster.info

Lomond: **Lomond Community Library**
PO Box 290, Lomond AB T0L 1G0
403-792-3934, Fax: 403-792-3934
liblom@chinookarch.a.ca
Mary McNamara, Librarian
liblom@chinookarch.ab.ca
403-792-3934

Longview: **Longview Municipal Library**
128 Morrison Place, Longview AB T0L 1H0
403-558-3927, Fax: 403-558-3927
alomlibrary@telusplanet.net
Elizabeth Perry, Librarian
ALOMlibrary@telusplanet.net
403-558-3927

Lougheed: **Lougheed Public Library**
5004 - 50 St., Lougheed AB T0B 2V0
780-386-2498, Fax: 780-386-2136
lougheedlibrary@libs.prl.ab.ca
Lorraine Greenlee, Librarian
780-888-1278

Magrath: **Magrath Municipal Library**
6N - 1 St. W., Magrath AB T0K 1J0
403-758-6498, Fax: 403-758-6442
libmag@chinookarch.ab.ca
Charlotte Lester, Librarian

Manning: **Manning Municipal Library**
311 - 4th Ave. SE, Manning AB T0H 2M0
780-836-3054, Fax: 780-836-3054
librarian@manninglibrary.ab.ca
www.manninglibrary.ab.ca
Lesley Spry-Shandro, Head Librarian
780-836-3054

Mannville: **Mannville Municipal Library**
5029, 50 St. - PO Box 186, Mannville AB T0B 2W0
780-763-3611, Fax: 780-763-3611
librarian@mannvillelibrary.ab.ca
www.mannvillelibrary.ab.ca
Theresa Myroniuk, Library Head

Marwayne: **Marwayne Public Library**
105 - 2nd St. South, Marwayne AB T0B 2X0
780-847-3930, Fax: 780-847-3796
librarian@marwaynelibrary.ab.ca
www.marwaynelibrary.ab.ca
Riley Sleeman, Collections/Education Co-ordinator

Mayerthorpe: **Mayerthorpe Public Library**
4909 - 52nd St., Mayerthorpe AB T0E 1N0
780-786-2404, Fax: 780-786-4590
mayep@telusplanet.net
www.mayerthorpelibrary.ab.ca
Eleanor Mitchell, Librarian

McLennan: **McLennan Municipal Library**
19 - 1st Ave. NW, McLennan AB T0H 2L0
780-324-3767, Fax: 780-324-2288
librarian@mclennanlibrary.ab.ca
Carole Laboucan, Librarian

Medicine Hat: **Medicine Hat Public Library**
414 First St. SE, Medicine Hat AB T1A 0A8
403-502-8527, Fax: 403-502-8529
library@medicinehat.ca
www.shortgrass-lib.ab.ca/mhpl
Rachel Sarjeant-Jenkins, Chief Librarian
403-502-8528

Milk River: **Milk River Municipal Library**
321 - 3rd Ave. NE, Milk River AB T0K 1M0
403-647-3793
mkrlib@chinookarch.ab.ca
www.chinookarch.ab.ca/chinookarch/
Lynn Bouldry, Librarian
lbouldry@milkriverlibrary.ca

Millarville: **Millarville Community Library**
Box 59, Millarville AB T0L 1K0
403 931-3919, Fax: 403-931-2475
amclibrary@marigold.ab.ca
Norma Dawson, Librarian

Millet: **Millet Public Library**
PO Box 30, Millet AB T0C 1Z0
780-387-5222
millet@yrl.ab.ca
www.milletlibrary.ab.ca
Kristin Litke, Library Manager

Milo: **Milo Municipal Library**
#220-1st St. South, Milo AB T0L 1L0
403-599-3850, Fax: 403-599-3850
help@milolibrary.ca
eps.chinookarch.ca/rooms/portal/page/21975_Milo
Joanne Monner, Head Librarian

Mirror: **Mirror Public Library**
5202 - 50 Ave., Mirror AB T0B 3C0
403-788-3044
mirrorlibrary@gmail.com
Heather Beamish, Librarian

Morrin: **Morrin Municipal Library**
Main St., PO Box 284, Morrin AB T0J 2B0
403-772-3922, Fax: 403-772-3707
AMOMlibrary@telusplanet.net
Susan Woodford, Librarian

Myrnam: **Myrnam Community Library**
New Myrnam School, 5105 - 50 St., Myrnam AB T0B 3K0
780-366-3801, Fax: 780-366-2332
librarian@myrnamlibrary.ab.ca
www.myrnamlibrary.ab.ca
Ann Godziuk, Librarian
librarian@myrnamlibrary.ab.ca
780-366-3801

Nampa: **Nampa Municipal Library**
PO Box 509, Nampa AB T0H 2R0
780-322-3805, Fax: 780-322-3955
nlibrary@nampalibrary.ab.ca
Cathy Rasmussen, Librarian

Nanton: **Nanton Municipal Library/Thelma Fanning Memorial Library**
1907 - 21 Ave., Nanton AB T0L 1R0
403-646-5535, Fax: 403-646-2653
nantlibr@chinookarch.ab.ca
Judi McMasters, Library Manager
jmcmasters@chinookarch.ab.ca

Neerlandia: **Neerlandia Public Library**
PO Box 10, Neerlandia AB T0G 1R0
780-674-5384, Fax: 780-674-2927
solthuis@phrd.ab.ca
Sandra Olthuis, Librarian

New Sarepta: **New Sarepta Community Library**
c/o New Sarepta Community High School, 5150 Center St., PO Box 147, New Sarepta AB T0B 3M0
780-941-2432, Fax: 780-941-2224
newsareptalibrary@yrl.ab.ca
www.newsareptalibrary.ca
Willow Schnell, Library Director

Newbrook: **Newbrook Public Library**
Main St., PO Box 208, Newbrook AB T0A 2P0
780-576-3772, Fax: 780-576-2115
librarian@newbrooklibrary.ab.ca
www.newbrooklibrary.ab.ca
Rose Alexander, Library Manager

Niton Junction: **Green Grove Public Library**
53521A Range Rd. 130, Niton Junction AB T0E 1S0

780-795-2474, Fax: 780-795-3933
www.greengrovelibrary.ab.ca
Toni Ice, Library Manager
toniice@gyrd.ab.ca

***Nordegg:* Nordegg Public Library**
General Delivery, Nordegg AB T0M 2H0
403-721-2339
nordegglibrary@libs.prl.ab.ca
Heather Clement, Librarian

***Okotoks:* Okotoks Public Library**
7 Riverside Dr. West, Okotoks AB T1S 1A6
403-938-2220, Fax: 403-938-4317
okotokslibrary@okotoks.net
www.okotokslibrary.ca
Tessa Nettleton, Director
okotokslibrary@okotoks.net
403-938-2220

***Olds:* Olds & District Municipal Library**
5217 - 52 St., Olds AB T4H 1H7
403-556-6460, Fax: 403-556-6692
oml2@libs.prl.ab.ca
oml.prl.ab.ca
Lesley Winfield, Head Librarian
oml2libs.prl.ab.ca
403-556-6460

***Onoway:* Onoway Public Library**
4808 - 51 St., Onoway AB T0E 1V0
780-967-2445, Fax: 780-967-2445
onowaylibrary@yrl.ab.ca
www.onowaylibrary.ab.ca
Kelly Huxley, Librarian
onowaylibrary@yrl.ab.ca

***Oyen:* Oyen Municipal Library**
105 - 3rd Ave. West, Oyen AB T0J 2J0
403-664-3580, Fax: 403-664-2520
aoymlibrary@marigold.ab.ca
Tricia Fischbuch, Librarian

***Paradise Valley:* Three Cities Municipal Library**
PO Box 60, Paradise Valley AB T0B 3R0
780-745-2277, Fax: 780-745-2641
sbabcock@paradisevalleylibrary.ab.ca
Sandra Babcock, Librarian
780-745-2541

***Peace River:* Peace River Municipal Library**
9807 - 97 Ave., Peace River AB T8S 1H6
780-624-4076, Fax: 780-624-4086
aprml@prmlibrary.ab.ca
www.prmlibrary.ab.ca
Chantal Patterson, Librarian

***Penhold:* Penhold & District Public Library**
1013 Aberdeen St., Penhold AB T0M 1R0
403-886-2636, Fax: 403-886-2638
penholdlibrary@libs.prl.ab.ca
penholdlibrary.prl.ab.ca
Myra Binnendyk, Head of Library

***Picture Butte:* Picture Butte Municipal Library**
120 - 4th St. South, Picture Butte AB T0K 1V0
403-732-4141
lbexte@picturebuttelibrary.ca
Linda Bexte, Library Manager

***Pincher Creek:* Pincher Creek Municipal Library**
899 Main St., Pincher Creek AB T0K 1W0
403-627-3813, Fax: 403-627-2847
help@pinchercreeklibrary.ca
Janice Day, Acting Librarian
403-627-3813

***Plamondon:* Plamondon Municipal Library**
PO Box 630, Plamondon AB T0A 2T0
780-798-3852, Fax: 780-798-3860
headlibrarian@stuartmacphersonlibrary.ca
www.plamondonlibrary.ab.ca
Maureen Penn, Director, Library Services

***Ponoka:* Ponoka Jubilee Library**
5110 - 48 Ave., Ponoka AB T4J 1J3
403-783-3843, Fax: 403-783-3973
jubilee@rttinc.com
Norma-Jean Colquhoun, Librarian

***Provost:* Provost Municipal Library**
PO Box 449, Provost AB T0B 3S0
780-753-2801
provostlibrary@libs.prl.ab.ca
Colleen Vaughn, Library Supervisor

***Radway:* Radway Public Library**
PO Box 220, Radway AB T0A 2V0
780-736-3548, Fax: 780-736-3858
aradpublib@telusplanet.net
Terrie-Lynne Rosa, Librarian

***Rainbow Lake:* Rainbow Lake Municipal Library**
1 Atco Rd., Rainbow Lake AB T0H 2Y0
780-956-3656, Fax: 780-956-3858
librarian@rainbowlakelibrary.ab.ca
Cheryl Edwards, Librarian

***Rainier:* Alcoma Public Library**
c/o Alcoma School, General Delivery, Rainier AB T0J 2M0
403-362-3741, Fax: 403-362-8897
aplcapic@eidnet.org
www.shortgrass-lib.ab.ca/acl

***Ralston:* Graham Community Library**
R35 Dugway Dr., Community Centre, Ralston AB T0J 2N0
403-544-3670, Fax: 403-544-3814
grahamlib@yahoo.ca
www.grahamcommunitylibrary.ca
Stefanie Schranz, Librarian Manager
grahamlib@yahoo.ca

***Raymond:* Raymond Public Library**
15 Broadway South, Raymond AB T0K 2S0
403-752-4785, Fax: 403-752-4785
rlibrary@chinookarch.ab.ca
Faye Geddes, Librarian

***Red Deer:* Red Deer Public Library**
4818 - 49th St., Red Deer AB T4N 1T9
403-346-4576
www.rdpl.org
Mike Todd, Chair
miket@aipins.ca

***Redcliff:* Redcliff Public Library**
131 Main St. South, Redcliff AB T0J 2P0
403-548-3335
redlib@shortgrass-lib.ab.ca
www.shortgrass.ca/rpl/
Reita Wilson, Library Manager
403-548-3335

***Redwater:* Redwater Public Library**
4915 - 48th St., Redwater AB T0A 2W0
780-942-3464, Fax: 780-942-2013
director@redwaterlibrary.ab.ca
www.redwaterlibrary.ab.ca
Judy Dewald, Director of Library Services
director@redwaterlibrary.ab.ca

***Rimbey:* Rimbey Municipal Library**
4938 - 50 Ave., Rimbey AB T0C 2J0
403-843-2841, Fax: 403-843-2841
rimbeylibrarian@libs.prl.ab.ca
rimbeylibrary.prl.ab.ca
Jean Keetch, Librarian

***Rochester:* Rochester Community Library**
PO Box 309, Rochester AB T0G 1Z0
780-698-3970, Fax: 780-698-2290
tammy.morey@aspenview.org
www.rochesterlibrary.ab.ca
Tammy Morey, Librarian

***Rocky Mountain House:* Rocky Mountain House Public Library**
4922 - 52 St., Rocky Mountain House AB T4T 1B1
403-845-2042, Fax: 403-845-5633
armh@telusplanet.net
rmhlibrary.prl.ab.ca
Karen Paquette, Library Manager

***Rockyford:* Rockyford Municipal & District Library**
PO Box 277, Rockyford AB T0J 2R0
403-533-3964
armlibrary@marigold.ab.ca
Frances Garriott, Head Librarian

***Rolling Hills:* Rolling Hills Public Library**
302 - 4th St., Rolling Hills AB T0J 2S0
403-964-2186, Fax: 403-964-3659
rhlcapic@eidnet.org
Johnene Amulung, Library Volunteer

***Rosemary:* Rosemary Community Library**
Rosemary Academic School, Block 6, Dahlia St., PO, Box 210, Rosemary AB T0J 2W0
403-378-4493, Fax: 403-378-4388
donnaj@grasslands.ab.ca
www.shortgrass-lib.ab.ca/rml
Donna Janzen, Library Technician
donnaj@grasslands.ab.ca

***Rumsey:* Rumsey Community Library**
PO Box 113, Rumsey AB T0J 2Y0
403-368-3939, Fax: 403-368-2207
arumlibrary@marigold.ab.ca
Patty Steen, Librarian

***Rycroft:* Rycroft Municipal Library**
PO Box 248, Rycroft AB T0H 3A0
780-765-3973, Fax: 780-765-2002
Kimberley Bawkowy, Librarian

***Ryley:* McPherson Public Library**
PO Box 139, Ryley AB T0B 4A0
780-663-3999, Fax: 780-663-3909
librarian@mcphersonlibrary.ab.ca
www.mcphersonlibrary.ab.ca
Andrea Mendoza, Chair

***St Albert:* St Albert Public Library**
5 St Anne St., St Albert AB T8N 3Z9
780-459-1530, Fax: 780-458-5772
sapl@sapl.ab.ca
www.sapl.ab.ca
Pamela Forsyth, Director
pforsyth@sapl.ab.ca
780-459-1681

***St Isidore:* St Isidore Community Library/ Bibliothèque de St Isidore**
PO Box 1168, St Isidore AB T0H 3B0
780-624-8182, Fax: 780-624-9182
marielavoie@bibliothequestisidore.ab.ca
Marie Lavoie, Chair & Librarian

***St Paul:* St Paul Municipal Library**
4802 - 53 St., St Paul AB T0A 3A0
780-645-4904, Fax: 780-645-5198
librarian@stpaullibrary.ab.ca
www.stpaullibrary.ab.ca

***Sangudo:* Sangudo Public Library**
PO Box 524, Sangudo AB T0E 2A0
780-785-3431, Fax: 780-785-3179
sangudo.library@yrl.ab.ca
Jana Branston, Library Manager

***Seba Beach:* Seba Beach Public Library**
PO Box 159, Seba Beach AB T0E 2B0
780-797-3940
sebap@telusplanet.net
www.sebabeachlibrary.ab.ca
Cathy Lillico, Library Manager

***Sedgewick:* Sedgewick Municipal Library**
5011 - 51 Ave., Sedgewick AB T0B 4C0
780-384-3003, Fax: 780-384-3003
sedgewicklibrary@libs.prl.ab.ca
sedgpublib.prl.ab.ca
Judy Ferrier, Librarian

***Sexsmith:* Sexsmith Shannon Library**
9917 - 99 Ave., Sexsmith AB T0H 3C0
780-568-4333, Fax: 780-568-4333
librarian@shannonlibrary.ab.ca
www.shannonlibrary.ab.ca
Sheryl Pelletier, Library Manager

***Sherwood Park:* Strathcona County Library**
#300, 2020 Sherwood Dr., Sherwood Park AB T8A 5P7
780-449-5801, Fax: 780-467-6861
ssiga@sclibrary.ab.ca
www.sclibrary.ab.ca
Sharon Siga, Library Director
ssiga@sclibrary.ab.ca
780-449-5814

***Silver Valley:* Savanna Community Library**
PO Box 49, Silver Valley AB T0H 3E0
780-351-3808, Fax: 780-353-2405

***Slave Lake:* Slave Lake Municipal Library**
320 - 2nd St. NE, Slave Lake AB T0G 2A0
780-849-5250, Fax: 780-849-3275
librarian@slavelakelibrary.ab.ca
www.slavelakelibrary.ab.ca
Lori Herdzik, Librarian

***Smith:* Smith Community Library**
924 - 9th St., Smith AB T0G 2B0

780-829-2389, Fax: 780-829-2389
librarian@smithlibrary.ab.ca
www.smithlibrary.ab.ca
Mary Hastie, Librarian
780-829-3882

Smoky Lake: Smoky Lake Municipal Public Library
5010 - 50th St., Smoky Lake AB T0A 3C0
780-656-4212, Fax: 780-656-4212
librarian@smokylakelibrary.ab.ca
www.smokylakelibrary.ab.ca
Melody Kaban, Library Manager

Spirit River: Spirit River Municipal Library
4812 - 44th Ave., Spirit River AB T0H 3G0
780-864-4038, Fax: 780-864-3006
tracy@spiritriverlibrary.ab.ca
Tracy Skoworodko, Librarian

Spruce Grove: Spruce Grove Public Library
35 - 5th Ave., Spruce Grove AB T7X 2C5
780-962-4423, Fax: 780-962-4826
library@sprucegrovelibrary.org
www.sprucegrovelibrary.org
Tammy Svenningsen
tammy@sprucegrovelibrary.org

Standard: Standard Municipal Library
822 The Broadway, Standard AB T0J 3G0
403-644-3995
astmlibrary@marigold.ab.cat
Sophie MacMullen, Librarian

Stavely: Stavely Municipal Library
4823 - 49th St., Stavely AB T0L 1Z0
403-549-2190, Fax: 403-549-2190
help@stavelylibrary.ca
Jean Cochlan, Librarian

Stettler: Stettler Public Library
6202 - 44th Ave., Stettler AB T0C 2L1
403-742-2292, Fax: 403-742-5481
spl@libs.prl.ab.ca
spl.prl.ab.ca
Deborah Cryderman, Librarian

Stirling: Stirling Municipal Library
229 - 4th Ave., Stirling AB T0K 2E0
403-756-3665
libstir@chinookarch.ab.ca
Charlene Fletcher, Director, Library Services
libstir@chinookarch.ab.ca

Stony Plain: Stony Plain Public Library
#112, 4613 - 52nd Ave., Stony Plain AB T7Z 1E7
780-963-5440, Fax: 780-963-1746
info@stonyplainlibrary.org
www.stonyplainlibrary.org
Linda Naccarato, Director
lindan@stonyplainlibrary.org
780-968-5709

Strathmore: Strathmore Municipal Library
85 Lakeside Blvd., Strathmore AB T1P 1A1
403-934-5440, Fax: 403-934-1908
asmlibmgr@marigold.ab.ca
Margie Lavoie, Librarian

Sundre: Sundre Municipal Library
#2, 310 Centre St. N, Sundre AB T0M 1X0
403-638-4000, Fax: 403-638-5755
sundrelibrary@libs.prl.ab.ca
www.sundre.prl.ab.ca
Michael Baird, Library Director
403-638-4000

Swan Hills: Swan Hills Public Library
5536 Main St., Swan Hills AB T0G 2C0
780-333-4505, Fax: 780-333-4551
nkeough@yrl.ab.ca
www.swanhillslibrary.ab.ca
Nancy Keough, Head Librarian

Sylvan Lake: Sylvan Lake Public Library
4715 - 50 Ave., Sylvan Lake AB T4S 1C5
403-887-2130, Fax: 403-887-0537
sylvan.library@shawbiz.ca
sylvanlibrary.prl.ab.ca/sylvan.htm
Barbara Bulat, Director
barbara.bulat@shawbiz.ca
403-887-2130

Taber: Taber Public Library
5415 - 50 Ave., Taber AB T1G 1V2
403-223-4343, Fax: 403-223-4314
help@taberlibrary.ca
Helen Jury, Head Librarian
403-223-4343

Thorhild: Thorhild & District Municipal Library
210 - 7 Ave., Thorhild AB T0A 3J0
780-398-3502, Fax: 780-398-2100
librarian@thorhildlibrary.ab.ca
thorhildlibrary.ab.ca
Rose Alexander, Library Manager

Thorsby: Thorsby Municipal Library
PO Box 319, Thorsby AB T0C 2P0
780-789-3808, Fax: 780-789-3805
thorsbypublib@telusplanet.net
Louise Normandeau, Librarian

Three Hills: Three Hills Municipal Library
122 - 3rd Ave. South, Three Hills AB T0M 2A0
403-443-2360
athmlibrary@marigold.ab.ca
www.3hillslibrary.com
Wendy Cuffe, Head Librarian

Tilley: Tilley Public Library
PO Box 177, Tilley AB T0J 3K0
403-377-2233, Fax: 403-377-2097
tillib@shortgrass.ca
Brenda Arnold, Librarian
brendaa@grasslands.ab.ca

Tofield: Tofield Municipal Library
5407 - 50 St., Tofield AB T0B 4J0
780-662-3838, Fax: 780-662-3929
librarian@tofieldlibrary.ca
library.tofieldalberta.ca
Connie Forst, Library Manager

Tomahawk: Tomahawk Public Library
PO Box 69, Tomahawk AB T0E 2H0
780-339-3935, Fax: 780-339-2121
Chris Goerz, Librarian

Trochu: Trochu Municipal Library
317 Main St., Trochu AB T0M 2C0
403-442-2458
atrmlibrary@marigold.ab.ca
Sherie Campbell, Librarian

Two Hills: Alice Melnyk Public Library
5009 Diefenbaker (50th) Ave., Two Hills AB T0B 4K0
780-657-3553, Fax: 780-657-3553
www.twohillslibrary.ab.ca
Elizabeth Wells, Library Manager & Resource Sharing Contact
librarian@twohillslibrary.ab.ca

Valhalla Centre: Valhalla Community Library
PO Box 68, Valhalla Centre AB T0H 3M0
780-356-3834, Fax: 780-356-3834
librarian@valhallalibrary.ab.ca
Gail Perry, Librarian
780-356-2382

Valleyview: Valleyview Municipal Library
4804 - 50 Ave., Valleyview AB T0H 3N0
780-524-3033, Fax: 780-524-4563
library@valleyviewlibrary.ab.ca
www.valleyviewlibrary.ab.ca
Yvonne Mury, Library Manager
yvonne@valleyview.ab.ca

Vauxhall: Vauxhall Public Library
314 - 2nd Ave. North, Vauxhall AB T0K 2K0
403-654-2370, Fax: 403-654-2370
libvau@chinookarch.ab.ca
Carol Bell, Librarian
403-654-2037

Vegreville: Vegreville Public Library
4709 - 50 St., Vegreville AB T9C 1L2
780-632-3491, Fax: 780-603-2338
library@vegreville.com
www.vegrevillelibrary.ab.ca
Amber Zary, Director
780-632-3491

Vermilion: Vermilion Public Library
5001 - 49th Ave., Vermilion AB T9X 1B8
780-853-4288, Fax: 780-853-1783
admin@vermilionpubliclibrary.ca
www.vermilionpubliclibrary.ca
Donna Jones, Library Manager

Veteran: Veteran Municipal Library
PO Box 527, Veteran AB T0C 2S0
403-575-3915, Fax: 403-575-3870
Nicole Larson, Librarian

Viking: Viking Municipal Library
4920, 53 Ave., Viking AB T0B 4N0
780-336-4992, Fax: 780-336-4992
librarian@vikinglibrary.ab.ca
www.vikinglibrary.ab.ca
Marayann Wolosinka, Librarian

Vimy: Vimy Community/School Library
PO Box 29, Vimy AB T0G 2J0
780-961-3014, Fax: 780-961-2094
pdespins@phrd.ab.ca
Pauline Despins, Librarian

Vulcan: Vulcan Municipal Library
303 Centre St., Vulcan AB T0L 2B0
403-485-2571, Fax: 403-485-2571
help@vulcanlibrary.ca
eps.chinookarch.ca/rooms/portal/page/22161_Vulcan
Linda Lambert, Librarian

Wabamun: Wabamun Public Library
5132 - 53 Ave., Wabamun AB T0E 2K0
780-892-2713, Fax: 780-892-7294
bettyl@wabamunlibrary.ca
www.wabamunlibrary.ca
Betty Lalonde, Head Librarian

Wainwright: Wainwright Public Library
921 - 3rd Ave., Wainwright AB T9W 1C5
780-842-2673, Fax: 780-842-2340
librarian@wainwrightlibrary.ab.ca
www.wainwrightlibrary.ab.ca
Jodi Dahlgren, Librarian

Wandering River: Wandering River Women's Institute Community Library
PO Box 8, Wandering River AB T0A 3M0
780-771-3939, Fax: 780-774-2117
librarian@wanderingriverlibrary.ab.ca
Gerda Rebkowich, Chairperson

Warburg: Warburg Public Library
PO Box 299, Warburg AB T0C 2T0
780-848-2391, Fax: 780-848-2296
warburglibrary@yrl.ab.ca
Gail O'Neil, Library Manager

Warner: Warner Memorial Municipal Library
206 - 3rd Ave., Warner AB T0K 2L0
403-642-3988, Fax: 403-642-3988
help@warnerlibrary.ca
eps.chinookarch.ca/rooms/portal/page/22182_Warner
Andrea Tapp, Librarian

Water Valley: Water Valley Public Library
PO Box 250, Water Valley AB T0M 2E0
403-637-3899
watervalleylibrary@libs.prl.ab.ca
www.watervalleycommunity.ca/library.html
Jaymee Shea, Librarian

Westlock: Westlock Municipal Library
#1, 10007 - 100 Ave., Westlock AB T7P 2H5
780-349-3060, Fax: 780-349-5291
ljbooth@westlocklibrary.ca
Lisbeth J. Booth, Librarian

Wetaskiwin: Wetaskiwin Public Library
5002 - 51st Ave., Wetaskiwin AB T9A 0V1
780-361-4446, Fax: 780-352-3266
library@wetaskiwin.ca
www2.wetaskiwin.ca/library

Whitecourt: Whitecourt & District Public Library
5201 - 49 St., Whitecourt AB T7S 1N3
780-778-2900, Fax: 780-778-2827
whitep@telusplanet.net
Thyra Verbaas, Librarian

Wildwood: Wildwood Public Library
5112 - 50th St., Wildwood AB T0E 2M0
780-325-3882, Fax: 780-325-3920
librarian@wildwoodlibrary.ab.ca
www.wildwoodlibrary.ab.ca
Tammy Kalzan, Board Chair

Winfield: Winfield Community Library
PO Box 360, Winfield AB T0C 2X0
780-682-2423, Fax: 780-682-2490
winfieldlibrary@yrl.ab.ca

Pat Thoreson, Librarian

***Worsley:* Worsley & District Library**
216 Alberta Ave., Worsley AB T0H 3W0
780-685-3842, Fax: 780-685-3766
rookc@prsd.ab.ca
www.geocities.com/worsleyanddistrictlibrary
Colleen Rook, Librarian

***Wrentham:* Wrentham Library**
PO Box 111, Wrentham AB T0K 2P0
403-222-2485, Fax: 403-222-2101
libwren@chinookarch.ab.ca
Alice Cook, Library Supervisor

***Youngstown:* Youngstown Municipal Library**
Main St., PO Box 39, Youngstown AB T0J 3P0
403-779-3864, Fax: 403-779-3828
aymlibrary@telusplanet.net
Annette Lupuliak, Librarian

***Zama City:* Zama Community Library**
PO Box 14, Zama City AB T0H 4E0
780-683-2888, Fax: 780-683-2889
www.zamacity.ca
Janet Forrest, Librarian

Archives

Karen Langley, Document & Records Coordinator/University Archivist
karenl@athabascau.ca
780-675-6268

***Athabasca:* Thomas A. Edge Archives & Special Collections**
Athabasca University, 1 University Dr., Athabasca AB T9S 3A3
780-675-6268, Fax: 780-675-6950, 800-788-9041
karenl@athabascau.ca
www.athabascau.ca/archives

***Banff:* Alpine Club of Canada**
PO Box 160, Banff AB T1L 1A3
403-762-2291, Fax: 403-762-2339
archives@whyte.org
Ruth Oltmann, Librarian, Alpine Club

***Banff:* Banff Centre for Continuing Education**
107 Tunnel Mountain Dr., Banff AB T1L 1H5
403-762-6265, Fax: 403-762-6266
library@banffcentre.ca
www.banffcentre.ca/library
James Rout, Managing Librarian
james_rout@banffcentre.ca
403-762-6658

***Banff:* Whyte Museum of the Canadian Rockies**
PO Box 160, Banff AB T1L 1A3
403-762-2291, Fax: 403-762-2339
archives@whyte.org
whyte.org
Elizabeth Kundert-Cameron, Librarian
403-762-2291 ext. 332

***Brooks:* Eastern Irrigation District**
550 Industrial Rd., Brooks AB T1R 1B2
403-362-1400, Fax: 403-362-6206
archive@eid.ab.ca
www.eid.ab.ca/general_information.htm
Darlene Fisher, Records Manager Specialist
403-362-1439
H.D. (Sandy) Ayer, Archivist
sayer@auc-nuc.ca
403-410-2947

***Calgary:* Archibald-Thomson Archives**
#630, 833 - 4th Ave. SW, Calgary AB T2P 3T5
403-410-2000
sayer@auc-nuc.ca

***Calgary:* Calgary Highlanders Museum & Archives**
4520 Crowchild Trail SW, Calgary AB T3E 1T8
403-974-2855
Mike Henry, Archvist

***Calgary:* Calgary Police Service**
316 - 7th Ave. SE, Calgary AB T2G 4Z1
403-206-4566
pol11014@calgarypolice.ca
www.youthlinkcalgary.com
Janet Pieschel, Executive Director
Linda Fraser, Curator
lmfraser@ucalgary.ca

***Calgary:* Canadian Architectural Archives**
2500 University Dr. NW, Mackimmie Library, 12th, Fl., Calgary AB T2N 1N4
403-220-7420, Fax: 403-284-2109
lmfraser@ucalgary.ca
Apollonia Steele, Special Collections Librarian
asteele@ucalgary.ca

***Calgary:* Diocese of Calgary, Archives**
c/o University of Calgary, Special Collections, 2500 University Dr. NW, Calgary AB T2N 1N4
403-220-5972, Fax: 403-284-2109
diocese@calgary.anglican.ca
www.ucalgary.ca/library/SpecColl/anglican.htm

***Calgary:* Glenbow - Alberta Institute/Glenbow Museum**
130 - 9th Ave. SE, Calgary AB T2G 0P3
403-268-4204, Fax: 403-232-6569
glenbow@glenbow.org
www.glenbow.org
Douglas E. Cass, Director, Library & Archives
dcass@glenbow.org
403-268-4203

***Calgary:* Heritage Park Society**
1900 Heritage Dr. SW, Calgary AB T2V 2X3
403-268-8500, Fax: 403-268-8501
reception@heritagepark.ab.ca
www.heritagepark.ca
Sylvia Harnden, Curator
403-268-8536

***Calgary:* Legal Archives Society of Alberta**
#510, 919 - 11th Ave. SW, Calgary AB T2R 1P3
403-244-5510, Fax: 403-541-9102
legalarc@legalarchivessociety.ab.ca
www.legalarchivessociety.ab.ca
Graham Price, President
legalarc@legalarchivessociety.ab.ca

***Calgary:* Lord Strathcona's Horse Regimental Museum**
4520 Crowchild Trail SW, Calgary AB T2T 5J4
403-974-2854, Fax: 403-974-2858
archives@strathconas.ca
www.strathconas.ca
Lee Ramsden, Archivist
403-974-2854

***Calgary:* Naval Museum of Alberta**
1820 - 24 St. SW, Calgary AB T2T 0G6
403-242-0002, Fax: 403-240-1966
curator@navalmuseum.ab.ca
www.navalmuseum.ab.ca
Cal Annis, General Manager

***Calgary:* Sisters Faithful Companions of Jesus**
219 - 19th Ave. SW, Calgary AB T2S 0C8
403-228-3623, Fax: 403-541-9297
shc@fcjsisters.ca
www.fcjsisters.org
Elizabeth Fitzgerald, Archivist

***Calgary:* The City of Calgary**
Admin Bldg., 313 - 7th Ave. SE, Main Fl., Calgary AB T2P 2M5
403-268-8180, Fax: 403-268-6731
archives@calgary.ca
www.calgary.ca
Lisa Atkinson, Archives Program Manager
lisa.atkinson@ucalgary.ca
403-220-3024

***Calgary:* University of Calgary Archives**
Library Tower, 2500 University Dr. NW, 12th Fl., Calgary AB T2N 1N4
403-220-7271, Fax: 403-210-3075
uarc@ucalgary.ca
archives.ucalgary.ca

***Cardston:* Cardston & District Historical Society**
89 - 3rd Ave. West, Cardston AB T0K 0K0
403-653-4002
dalowry@shaw.ca
H. Dale Lowry, Director
dalowry@shaw.ca
Jane Bowe-McCarthy, Conference Archivist
780-427-8687

***Edmonton:* Alberta & Northwest Conference, Archives**
c/o Provincial Archives of Alberta, 8555 Roper Rd., Edmonton AB T6E 5W1
780-427-8687, Fax: 780-427-4646
Jane.Bowe-McCarthy@gov.ab.ca
www.united-church.ca/archives/alberta/home.shtm

***Edmonton:* Alberta Council, Archives & Museum**
11055 - 107th St., Edmonton AB T5H 2Z6
780-424-5510
data@albertagirlguides.com
www.girlguides.ca

***Edmonton:* Canadian Moravian Archives**
2304 - 38 St., Edmonton AB T6L 4K9
780-440-3050, Fax: 780-463-2143
William G. Brese, President
wbrese@interbaun.com

***Edmonton:* City of Edmonton Archives**
10440 - 108 Ave., Edmonton AB T5H 3Z9
780-496-8710, Fax: 780-496-8732
cms.archives@edmonton.ca
www.edmonton.ca/archives

***Edmonton:* Edmonton Public Schools**
10425 - 99th Ave., Edmonton AB T5K 0E5
780-422-1970, Fax: 780-426-0192
archives@epsb.ca
archives.epsb.net
Catherine D. Luck, Supervisor
catherine.luck@epsb.ca

***Edmonton:* Provincial Archives of Alberta**
8555 Roper Rd., Edmonton AB T6E 5W1
780-427-1750, Fax: 780-427-4646
paa@gov.ab.ca
www.archivesalberta.org/walls/paa.htm
Jonathan Davidson, Reference Archivist, Library & Access Services
jonathan.davidson@gov.ab.ca
780-427-1056

***Edmonton:* Ukrainian Canadian Archives & Museum of Alberta**
9543 - 110th Ave., Edmonton AB T5H 1H3
780-424-7580, Fax: 780-420-0562
ucama@shaw.ca
www.ucama.com
Alexander Makar, Director
Bryan Corbett, University Archivist
bryan.corbett@ualberta.ca
780-466-6123

***Edmonton:* University of Alberta Archives**
#100, 8170 - 50th St., Edmonton AB T6B 2E6
780-466-6118, Fax: 780-466-5210
archives@ualberta.ca
www.ualberta.ca/archives/

***Jasper:* Jasper-Yellowhead Museum & Archives**
PO Box 42, Jasper AB T0E 1E0
780-852-3013, Fax: 780-852-3240
archives@jaspermuseum.org
www.jaspermuseum.org
Meghan Power, Archivist

***Lethbridge:* Sir Alexander Galt Museum & Archives**
502 - 1st St. South, Lethbridge AB T1J 1Y4
403-329-7302, Fax: 403-329-4958, 866-320-3898
archives@galtmuseum.com
www.galtmuseum.com/index.htm
Greg Ellis, City Archivist
Michael Perry, University Archivist
mike.perry@uleth.ca
403-329-2714

***Lethbridge:* University of Lethbridge Archives**
Library Bldg., Level 11, 4401 University Dr., Lethbridge AB T1K 3M4
403-329-2714, Fax: 403-329-2022
archives@uleth.ca
www.uleth.ca/lib/archives/

***Medicine Hat:* Esplanade Arts & Heritage Centre**
401 - 1st St. SE, Medicine Hat AB T1A 8W2
403-502-8582, Fax: 403-502-8589
phipype@medicinehat.ca
www.esplanade.ca/archives/archives.html
Philip Pype, Archivist
403-502-8585

***Millet:* Millet & District Historical Society**
c/o Millet & District Museum & Archives Room,, 5120 - 50 St., Millet AB T0C 1Z0

780-387-5558, Fax: 780-387-5548
info@milletmuseum.ca
home.cablerocket.com/~milletmuseum
Tracey Leavitt, Museum/Archives Coordinator

Morley: **Nakoda Institute**
PO Box 120, Morley AB T0L 1N0
403-881-3949, Fax: 403-881-4250
Ian Getty, Contact

Olds: **Mountain View Museum - Olds Historical Society**
PO Box 3882, Olds AB T4H 1P6
403-556-8464
mvmuseum@oldsmuseum.ca
www.oldsmuseum.ca
Geraldine Wiper, Archivist

Red Deer: **Red Deer & District Archives**
4525 - 47A Ave., Red Deer AB T4N 6Z6
403-309-8403, Fax: 403-342-6644
archives@city.red-deer.ab.ca
Michael Dawe, City Archivist

St Albert: **Musée Héritage Museum**
5 St Anne St., St Albert AB T8N 3Z9
780-459-1528, Fax: 780-459-1546
museum@compusmart.ab.ca
www.compusmart.ab.ca/museum
Ann Ramsden, Director of Heritage

Stony Plain: **The Multicultural Heritage Centre**
5411 - 51 St., Stony Plain AB T7Z 1X7
780-963-2777, Fax: 780-963-0233
margit@multicentre.org
www.multicentre.org
Margit Knupp, Historical Resources Coordinator
margit@multicentre.org
780-963-2777

Taber: **Taber & District Museum Society**
4702 - 50th St., Taber AB T1G 2B6
403-223-5708, Fax: 403-223-0529
tiimchin@teusplanet.net
Ruby Danforth, Contact

Wetaskiwin: **City of Wetaskiwin**
4904 - 51 St., Wetaskiwin AB T9A 1L2
780-361-4423, Fax: 780-352-0930
archives@wetaskiwin.ca
www2.wetaskiwin.ca/Archives/
Carolyn Hill, Archivist
archives@wetaskiwin.ca

British Columbia

Regional Systems

Cariboo Regional District Library
108 - 3rd Ave. North, #A, Williams Lake BC V2J 2A4
250-392-3630, 800-665-1636
colleens@cariboord.bc.ca
www.cln.bc.ca
Colleen Swift, Manager, Library Services

Fraser Valley Regional Library
34589 Delair Rd., Abbotsford BC V2S 5Y1
604-859-7141, Fax: 604-852-5701, 888-668-4141
www.fvrl.bc.ca
Peter Fassbender, Chair

Okanagan Regional Library Headquarters
1430 KLO Rd., Kelowna BC V1W 3P6
250-860-4033, Fax: 250-861-8696
www.orl.bc.ca
Ted Bacigalupo, Chair

Peace River Associated Libraries
c/o Hudson's Hope Public Library, 30 Dudley Dr., Hudson's Hope BC V0C 1V0
250-783-9414, Fax: 250-783-9414
hh.ill@pris.bc.ca
www.pris.bc.ca/pral/main.htm
Mariann Field Hill, Chair

Public Library InterLINK
c/o Burnaby Public Library, Kingsway Branch, 7252, Kingsway, Burnaby BC V5E 1G3
604-517-8441, Fax: 604-517-8410
info@interlinklibraries.ca
www.interlinklibraries.ca
Rita Avigdor, Manager of Operations
rita.avigdor@interlinklibraries.ca

Thompson-Nicola Regional District Library System
#300, 465 Victoria St., Kamloops BC V2C 2A9
250-374-8866, Fax: 250-374-8355
postmaster@tnrdlib.bc.ca
www.tnrdlib.bc.ca

Vancouver Island Regional Library
6250 Hammond Bay Rd., Nanaimo BC V9T 6M9
250-758-4697, Fax: 250-758-2482
info@virl.bc.ca
www.virl.bc.ca
Rosemary Bonanno, Executive Director

Public Libraries

Alert Bay: **Alert Bay Public Library**
118 Fir St., Alert Bay BC V0N 1A0
250-974-5721, Fax: 250-974-5026
abplb@island.net
www.alertbay.com/library/
Sheila Jolliffe, Community Librarian

Atlin: **Atlin Library**
Courthouse Bldg., 2nd St., Atlin BC V0W 1A0
library@atlin.net
Linda Brown, Contact

Bowen Island: **Bowen Island Public Library**
430 Bowen Trunk Rd., Bowen Island BC V0N 1G0
604-947-9788, Fax: 604-947-9788
info@bowenlibrary.ca
www.bowenlibrary.ca
Tina Nielsen, Librarian
tnielsen@bowenlibrary.ca

Burnaby: **Burnaby Public Library**
6100 Willingdon Ave., Burnaby BC V5H 4N5
604-436-5427, Fax: 604-436-2961
bpl@bpl.bc.ca
www.bpl.bc.ca
Edel Toner-Rogala, Chief Librarian
604-436-5427

Burnaby: **Rare Bird**
c/o Anne Grainger, 7464 Rosewood St., Burnaby BC V5E 2G5
604-990-0507
www.cablelan.net/frose/CLABCnews.html

Burns Lake: **Burns Lake Public Library**
585 Government St., Burns Lake BC V0J 1E0
250-692-3192, Fax: 250-692-7488
libraryn@burnslakelibrary.com
burnslake.bclibrary.ca
Linda L. Palmer, Head Librarian

Castlegar: **Castlegar & District Public Library**
1005 - 3rd St., Castlegar BC V1N 2A2
250-365-6611, Fax: 250-365-7765
info@castlegarlibrary.com
www.castlegarlibrary.com
Heather Maisel, Library Director
heather@castlegarlibrary.com

Chetwynd: **Chetwynd Public Library**
5012 - 46th St., Chetwynd BC V0C 1J0
250-788-2559, Fax: 250-788-2186
fasleson@pris.bc.ca
www.chetwyndpubliclibrary.com
Fay Asleson, Librarian

Coquitlam: **Coquitlam Public Library**
575 Poirier St., Coquitlam BC V3J 6A9
604-937-4144, Fax: 604-937-4145
director@library.coquitlam.bc.ca
www.library.coquitlam.bc.ca
Rhian Piprell, Director
rpiprell@library.coquitlam.bc.ca
604-937-4132

Cranbrook: **Cranbrook Public Library**
1212 2nd St. N, Cranbrook BC V1C 4T6
250-426-4063, Fax: 250-426-2098
staff@cranbrookpubliclibrary.ca
www.cranbrookpubliclibrary.ca
Ursula Brigl, Library Director
ubrigl@cranbrookpubliclibrary.ca
250-426-4063 ext. 101

Crawford Bay: **Eastshore Community Library (Reading Centre)**
16234 King St., Crawford Bay BC V0B 1E0
250-227-6960

Dawson Creek: **Dawson Creek Municipal Public Library**
1001 McKellar Ave., Dawson Creek BC V1G 4W7
250-782-4661, Fax: 250-782-4667
dclib@pris.ca
dawsoncreek.bclibrary.ca
Jenny Snyder, Head Librarian

Dease Lake: **Dease Lake Reading Centre**
PO Box 237, Dease Lake BC V0C 1L0
250-771-3636
Carolyn Moore, Librarian

Edgewater: **Edgewater Reading Centre**
PO Box 129, Edgewater BC V0A 1E0
250-347-9558

Edgewood: **Inonoaklin Valley Reading Centre**
409 Monashee Ave., Edgewood BC V0G 1J0
250-269-7212, Fax: 250-269-7633
sbampton@hotmail.com
Susan Bampton, Librarian
sbampton@hotmail.com

Elkford: **Elkford Public Library**
816 Michel Rd., Elkford BC V0B 1H0
250-865-2912, Fax: 250-865-2460
elklib1@telus.net
www.elkfordlibrary.org
Sharon Gumowsky, Head Librarian
elklib1@telus.net

Fauquier: **Fauquier Reading Centre**
519 Willow St., Fauquier BC V0G 1K0
250-269-7348
Frank Poirier, Librarian

Fernie: **Fernie Heritage Library**
492 - 3rd Ave., Fernie BC V0B 1M0
250-423-4458, Fax: 250-423-7906
library@elkvalley.net
www.fernieheritagelibrary.com
Emma Dressler, Librarian

Fort Nelson: **Fort Nelson Public Library**
Town Square, 5315 - 50th Ave. South, Fort Nelson BC V0C 1R0
250-774-6777, Fax: 250-774-6777
fnpl@fortnelson.bclibrary.ca
www.fortnelson.bclibrary.ca
Ramona Allan, Chair

Fort St James: **Fort St James Public Library**
425 Manson St., Fort St James BC V0J 1P0
250-996-7431, Fax: 250-996-7484
fortlib@fsjames.com
fortstjames.bclibrary.ca
Diana Uhrich, Librarian

Fort St John: **Fort St John Public Library**
10015 - 100th Ave., Fort St John BC V1J 1Y7
250-785-3731, Fax: 250-785-7982
fsjlibrary@fsjlibrary.ca
fortstjohn.bclibrary.ca
Kimberly Partanen, Head

Fraser Lake: **Fraser Lake Public Library**
228 Endako Ave., Fraser Lake BC V0J 1S0
250-699-8888, Fax: 250-699-8899
fllibrarian@bcgroup.net
fraserlake.bclibrary.ca/
Audrey Fennema, Chief Librarian

Fruitvale: **Beaver Valley Public Library**
1847 - 1st St., Fruitvale BC V0G 1L0
250-367-7114, Fax: 250-367-7130
bvpublic@telus.net
beavervalley.bclibrary.ca
Marie Onyett, Head Librarian

Gibsons: **Gibsons District Public Library**
470 South Fletcher Rd., Gibsons BC V0N 1V0
604-886-2130, Fax: 604-886-2689
www.gibsons.bclibrary.ca
Ms Michelle Southam, Chief Librarian
michelle.southam@gdpl.scrd.bc.ca

Grand Forks: **Grand Forks & District Public Library**
7342 - 5th St., Grand Forks BC V0H 1H0
250-442-3944, Fax: 250-442-2645
gflibrary@grandforkslibrary.com
grandforks.bclibrary.ca
Heather Buzzell, Library Director

***Granisle:* Granisle Public Library**
#2 Village Sq., McDonald Ave., Granisle BC V0J 1W0
250-697-2713
library@granisle.net
granisle.bclibrary.ca
Sherry Smith, Chief Librarian

***Grasmere:* Grasmere Reading Centre**
PO Box 75, Grasmere BC V0B 1R0
250-887-3412, Fax: 250-887-3274
Bonnie Crosson, Head of Library

***Greenwood:* Greenwood Public Library**
346 South Copper St., Greenwood BC V0H 1J0
250-445-6111, Fax: 250-445-6111
greenlib@shaw.ca
greenwood.bclibrary.ca
Judy Foucher, Community Librarian

***Hazelton:* Hazelton District Public Library**
4255 Government St., Hazelton BC V0J 1Y0
250-842-5961, Fax: 250-842-2176
hazlib@bulkley.net
www.hazeltonlibrary.bc.ca
Eve Hope, Librarian

***Houston:* Houston Public Library**
3150 - 14th St., Houston BC V0J 1Z0
250-845-2256, Fax: 250-845-2088
hlibrary@telus.net
library.houston.ca
Toni McKilligan, Chief Librarian

***Invermere:* Invermere Public Library**
201 - 7th Ave., Invermere BC V0A 1K0
250-342-6416, Fax: 250-342-6416
invlibrary@cyberlink.bc.ca
invermere.bclibrary.ca
Elizabeth Robinson, Head Librarian

***Kimberley:* Kimberley Public Library**
115 Spokane St., Kimberley BC V1A 2E5
250-427-3112, Fax: 250-427-7157
staff@kimberleylibrary.net
kimberley.bclibrary.ca
Karin von Wittgenstein, Director

***Kitwanga:* Gitanyow Independent School Reading Centre**
PO Box 369, Kitwanga BC V0J 2A0
250-849-5528, Fax: 250-849-5870
Bernadette McLean, Chair

***Lions Bay:* Lions Bay Library (Reading Centre)**
400 Centre Rd., Lions Bay BC V0N 2E0
604-921-6944

***Mackenzie:* Mackenzie Public Library**
400 Skeena Dr., Mackenzie BC V0J 2C0
250-997-6343, Fax: 250-997-5792
macklib@mackbc.com
mackenzie.bclibrary.ca
Wanda Davis, Librarian

***Madeira Park:* Pender Harbour Reading Centre**
12952 Madeira Park Rd., Madeira Park BC V0N 2H0
604-883-2983

***McBride:* McBride & District Public Library**
241 Dominion St., McBride BC V0J 2E0
250-569-2411, Fax: 250-569-2411
library@mcbridebc.org
www.mcbridebc.org/library
Margaret Griffiths, Community Librarian

***Midway:* Midway Public Library**
612 - 6th Ave., Midway BC V0H 1M0
250-449-2620, Fax: 250-449-2389
info@midwaylibrary.bc.ca
midway.bclibrary.ca
Stephanie Boltz, Librarian
info@midwaylibrary.bc.ca

***Nelson:* Nelson Municipal Library**
602 Stanley St., Nelson BC V1L 1N4
250-352-6333, Fax: 250-354-1799
jstockdale@nelson.ca
nelson.bclibrary.ca
June Stockdale, Chief Librarian

***New Denver:* New Denver Reading Centre**
PO Box 38, New Denver BC V0G 1S0
250-358-2221
Agnes Emary, Chair

***New Westminster:* New Westminster Public Library**
716 - 6th Ave., New Westminster BC V3M 2B3
604-527-4660, Fax: 604-527-4674
listener@nwpl.ca
www.nwpl.ca
Julie Spurrell, Chief Librarian
spurrell@nwpl.ca
604-527-4675

***North Vancouver:* North Vancouver City Library**
120 West 14th St., North Vancouver BC V7M 1N9
604-998-3450, Fax: 604-983-3624
nvcl@cnv.org
www.cnv.org/nvcl
Jane Watkins, Chief Librarian
jwatkins@cnb.org
604-990-4226

***North Vancouver:* North Vancouver District Public Library**
1277 Lynn Valley Rd., North Vancouver BC V7J 2A1
604-990-5800, Fax: 604-984-7600
www.nvdpl.ca
Areef Abraham, Chair
scoularh@nvdpl.ca

***Pender Island:* Pender Island Public Library**
4407 Bedwell Harbour Rd., Pender Island BC V0N 2M0
250-629-3722, Fax: 250-629-3788
pilibrary@cablelan.net
www.penderislandlibrary.ca
Jean MacDonald, Chief Librarian

***Penticton:* Penticton Public Library**
785 Main St, Penticton BC V2A 5E3
250-770-7781
library@summer.com
www.library.penticton.bc.ca
Larry R. Little, Chief Librarian

***Port Moody:* Port Moody Public Library**
100 Newport Dr., Port Moody BC V3H 5C3
604-469-4575, Fax: 604-469-4576
askthelibrary@cityofportmoody.com
library.portmoody.ca
Heather Scoular, Library Director
heather.scoular@cityofportmoody.com

***Pouce Coupe:* Pouce Coupe Public Library**
5000 - 49 Ave., Pouce Coupe BC V0C 2C0
250-786-5765
bpoc.ill@pris.bc.ca
www.poucecoupe.bclibrary.ca
Courtenay Johnston, Community Librarian

***Powell River:* Powell River Municipal Library**
4411 Michigan Ave., Powell River BC V8A 2S3
604-485-4796, Fax: 604-485-5320
powellriverlibrary@shaw.ca
www.powellriverlibrary.ca
Stephanie Hall, Head Librarian

***Prince George:* Prince George Public Library**
887 Dominion St., Prince George BC V2L 5L1
250-563-9251, Fax: 250-563-0892
www.lib.pg.bc.ca
Allan Wilson, Chief Librarian

***Prince Rupert:* Prince Rupert Public Library**
101 - 6th Ave. West, Prince Rupert BC V8J 1Y9
250-627-1345, Fax: 250-627-7743
info@princerupertlibrary.ca
www.princerupertlibrary.ca
Denise St. Arnaud, Chief Librarian
chieflib@citytel.net

***Radium Hot Springs:* Radium Hot Springs Public Library**
4863 Stanley St., Radium Hot Springs BC V0A 1M0
250-347-2434
radiumpubliclibrary@hotmail.com

***Richmond:* Richmond Public Library**
#100, 7700 Minoru Gate, Richmond BC V6Y 1R9
604-231-6405, Fax: 604-273-0459
www.yourlibrary.ca/aboutus/contactus.cfm
www.yourlibrary.ca
Gregory Buss, Chief Librarian
greg.buss@yourlibrary.ca
604-231-6418

***Riondel:* Riondel Reading Centre**
PO Box 29, Riondel BC V0B 2B0
250-225-3570
Muriel Paquette, Chair

***Roberts Creek:* Roberts Creek Community Library**
General Delivery, Roberts Creek BC V0N 2W0
604-886-2130

***Rossland:* Rossland Public Library**
2180 Columbia Ave., Rossland BC V0G 1Y0
250-362-7611, Fax: 250-362-7138
rosslib@telus.net
rosslib.kics.bc.ca
Indira Wickremasinghe, Head Librarian

***Sechelt:* Sechelt Public Library**
5797 Cowrie St., Sechelt BC V0N 3A0
604-885-3260, Fax: 604-885-5183
info@sechelt.bclibrary.ca
www.sechelt.bclibrary.ca
Iris Loewen, Chief Librarian
iris.loewen@sechelt.bclibrary.ca

***Smithers:* Smithers Public Library**
3817 Alfred Ave., Smithers BC V0J 2N0
250-847-3043, Fax: 250-847-1533
info@smitherslibrary.ca
www.smitherslibrary.ca
Iva Allen, Library Director

***Stewart:* Stewart Public Library**
824 Main St., Stewart BC V0T 1W0
250-636-2380, Fax: 250-636-2380
bsp_ill@mountainharbour.ca
www.stewart.bclibrary.ca
Galina Dyrant, Librarian

***Surrey:* Surrey Public Library**
13742 - 72nd Ave., Surrey BC V3W 2P4
604-598-7300, Fax: 604-598-7310
bsur@surrey.ca
www.spl.surrey.bc.ca
Beth Barlow, Chief Librarian
babarlow@surrey.ca
604-598-7304

***Taylor:* Taylor Public Library**
PO Box 730, Taylor BC V0C 2K0
250-789-9878, Fax: 250-789-3543
library@districtoftaylor.com

***Trail:* Trail & District Public Library**
1051 Victoria St., Trail BC V1R 3T3
250-364-1731, Fax: 250-364-2176
director@traillibrary.com
www.traillibrary.com
Helen Graham, Director
director@traillibrary.com

***Tumbler Ridge:* Tumbler Ridge Public Library**
340 Front St., Tumbler Ridge BC V0C 2W0
250-242-4778, Fax: 250-242-4707
mburton@tumblerridgelibrary.org
www.tumblerridge.bclibrary.ca
Michele Burton, Library Manager

***Valemount:* Valemount Public Library**
1090A Main St., Valemount BC V0E 2Z0
250-566-4367, Fax: 250-566-4278
library@valemount.com
valemount.bclibrary.ca
Wendy Smith, Chief Librarian

***Vancouver:* Archives Association of British Columbia Newsletter**
PO Box 78530, University Post Office, Vancouver BC V6T 1Z4
604-666-9699
aabc@aabc.bc.ca
aabc.bc.ca/aabc/newsletter

***Vancouver:* BCLA Reporter**
#150, 900 Howe St., Vancouver BC V6Z 2M4
604-683-5354, Fax: 604-609-0707
office@bcla.bc.ca
www.bcla.bc.ca
Ted Benson, Editor

***Vancouver:* Isaac Waldman Jewish Public Library**
950 West 41st Ave., Jewish Community Centre of Greater Vancouver, Vancouver BC V5Z 2N7
604-257-5111, Fax: 604-257-5119
library@jccgv.bc.ca
www.jccgv.com/home/library.htm
Karen Corrin, Librarian

Vancouver: Teacher Librarian: the Journal for School Library Professionals K-12
#343, 100 - 1001 West Broadway, Vancouver BC V6H 4E4
604-925-0266, Fax: 604-925-0566
admin@teacherlibrarian.com
www.teacherlibrarian.com
Ken Haycock, Editor

Vancouver: The Bookmark
c/o BC Teachers' Federation, #100, 550 West 6th Ave., Vancouver BC V5Z 4P2
604-871-2283
www.bctf.ca/BCTLA/bookmark.html
Heather Daly, Editor

Vancouver: Vancouver Public Library
350 West Georgia St., Vancouver BC V6B 6B1
604-331-4000, Fax: 604-331-4080
info@vpl.ca
www.vpl.vancouver.bc.ca
Paul Whitney, City Librarian
paulwhi@vpl.ca
604-331-4007

Vancouver: Yaacing
#150, 900 Howe St., Vancouver BC V6Z 2M4
604-683-5354, Fax: 604-609-0707
office@bcla.bc.ca
www.bcla.bc.ca/yaacs
Phillippa Brown, Editor

Vanderhoof: Vanderhoof Public Library
PO Bag 6000, Vanderhoof BC V0J 3A0
250-567-4060, Fax: 250-567-4458
vhpl@telus.net
www.vanderhoofpubliclibrary.com
Jane Gray, Librarian

Victoria: Greater Victoria Public Library
735 Broughton St., Victoria BC V8W 3H2
250-384-5222, Fax: 250-385-5971
www.gvpl.ca
Lee Teal, interim CEO
lteal@gvpl.ca
250—41-3-03

Victoria: View Royal Public Library
45B View Royal Ave., Victoria BC V9B 1A6
250-479-2723, Fax: 250-479-2723
vivr.ill@shaw.ca
members.shaw.ca/vivr.ill
Jim Powell, Chair

West Vancouver: West Vancouver Memorial Library
1950 Marine Dr., West Vancouver BC V7V 1J8
604-925-7400, Fax: 604-925-5933
info@westvanlibrary.ca
www.westvanlibrary.ca
Ann Goodhart, Chief Librarian
agoodhart@westvanlibrary.ca
604-925-7424

Whistler: Whistler Public Library
4329 Main St., Whistler BC V0N 1B4
604-935-8433, Fax: 604-935-8434
info@whistlerlibrary.ca
www.whistlerlibrary.ca
Lauren Stara, Library Director
lstara@whistlerlibrary.ca
604-935-8438

Archives

Abbotsford: Matsqui-Sumas-Abbotsford Museum Archives
1B, 32320 George Ferguson Way, Abbotsford BC V2T 6N4
604-853-3722, Fax: 604-853-3726
msaarchives@shaw.ca
www.abbotsford.net/msamuseum
Lynne Wright, Executive Director
mail@msa.museum.bc.ca
604-853-0313

Alert Bay: U'Mista Cultural Centre
Front St., PO Box 253, Alert Bay BC V0N 1A0
250-974-5403, Fax: 250-974-5499
info@umista.ca
umista.org
Andrea Sanborn, Contact

Ashcroft: Ashcroft Museum
402 Brink St., Ashcroft BC V0K 1A0
250-453-9232, Fax: 250-453-9664
Kathy Paulos, Curator
250-453-9232

Barkerville: Barkerville Historic Town
PO Box 19, Barkerville BC V0K 1B0
604-994-3302
W.G. Quackenbush, Curator
bill.quackenbush@bakrerville.ca
888-994-3332 ext. 25

Burnaby: Japanese Canadian National Museum
6688 Southoaks Cres., Burnaby BC V5E 4M7
604-777-7000, Fax: 604-777-7001
jcnm@nikkeiplace.org
www.jcnm.ca
Timothy Savage, Archivist
tsavage@nikkeiplace.org
Ian Forsyth, University Archivist
ian_forsyth@sfu.ca
604-291-3262

Burnaby: Simon Fraser University Archives
#0400, Maggie Benston Student Services Centre,, 8888 University Dr., Simon Fraser University, Burnaby BC V5A 1S6
778-782-5433
britt@sfu.ca
www.sfu.ca/archives/

Campbell River: Campbell River Museum & Archives
470 Ocean Island Hwy., Campbell River BC V9W 4Z9
250-287-3103, Fax: 250-286-0109
general.inquiries@crmuseum.ca
www.crmuseum.ca
Linda Hogarth, Curator & Education Manager
linda.hogarth@crmuseum.ca
Judy Deon, College Librarian
jdeon@selkirk.ca

Castlegar: Selkirk College Archives
301 Frank Beinder Way, Castlegar BC V1N 3J1
250-365-1229, Fax: 250-365-7259, 888-953-1133
bcs@selkirk.ca
library.selkirk.bc.ca

Chilliwack: Chilliwack Archives
9291 Corbould St., Chilliwack BC V2P 4A6
604-795-9255, Fax: 604-795-5291
cm-chin@dowco.com
www.chilliwack.museum.bc.ca/cm
Ron Denman, Director
604-795-5210
Ron Denman, Director

Chilliwack: Chilliwack Museum
45820 Spadina Ave., Chilliwack BC V2P 1T3
604-795-5210, Fax: 604-795-5291
cm_chin@dowco.com
chilliwack.museum.bc.ca/cm

Cranbrook: Canadian Museum of Rail Travel - Cranbrook Archives, Museum Landmark Foundation
One Van Horne St. North, Box 400, Cranbrook BC V1C 4H9
604-489-3918
archives@trainsdeluxe.com
www.trainsdeluxe.com
Garry Anderson, Executive Director/Archivist
mail@trainsdeluxe.com
250-489-3918

Cumberland: Cumberland Museum & Archives
2680 Dunsmuir Ave., PO Box 258, Cumberland BC V0R 1S0
250-336-2445, Fax: 250-336-2321
barb@cumberlandmuseum.ca
www.cumberlandmuseum.ca
Barbara Lemky, Contact

Delta: Delta Museum & Archives
4858 Delta St., Delta BC V4K 2T8
604-946-9322, Fax: 604-946-5791
Kathy Bossort, Archivist

Delta: Parent Finders of Canada
19 English Bluff Rd., Delta BC V4M 2M4
604-948-1069, Fax: 604-948-2036
jvanstone@dccnet.com
www.parentfinders.org
Joan E. Vanstone, National Director
jvanstone@dccnet.com
604-948-1069

Duncan: Cowichan Valley Museum & Archives
Duncan Train Station, Canada Ave., PO Box 1014, Duncan BC V9L 3Y2
250-746-6612, Fax: 250-746-6612
cvmuseum.archives@shaw.ca
cowichanvalleymuseum.bc.ca
Kathryn Gagnon, Contact

Fort Langley: Langley Centennial Museum & National Exhibition Centre
9135 King St., Fort Langley BC V1M 2S2
604-888-3922, Fax: 604-888-7291
information@langleymuseum.org
www.langleymuseum.org
Sue Morhun, Manager, Community & Heritage Services

Fort St John: North Peace Historical Society
9323 - 100th St., Fort St John BC V1J 4N4
250-787-0430, Fax: 250-787-0405
fsjnpmuseum@solarwinds.com
collections.ic.gc.ca/north_peace/
Garth A. Sager, Museum Manager

Fort Steele: Fort Steele Heritage Town
9851 Hwy. 93/95, Fort Steele BC V0B 1N0
250-417-6000, Fax: 250-489-2624
Info@FortSteele.bc.ca
www.fortsteele.bc.ca
Kristin Schachtel, Head

Harrison Mills: Kilby Store & Farm
215 Kilby Rd., Harrison Mills BC V0M 1L0
604-796-9576, Fax: 604-796-9592
info@kilby.ca
www.kilby.ca
Bob Parliament, Area Manager
604-796-3859

Hazelton: 'Ksan Historical Village & Museum
PO Box 326, Hazelton BC V0J 1Y0
250-842-5544, Fax: 250-842-6533, 877-842-5518
ksan@ksan.org
www.ksan.org
Laurel Smith Wilson, Executive Director
kwan@ksan.org
250-842-5544

Kamloops: Kamloops Museum & Archives
207 Seymour St., Kamloops BC V2C 2E7
250-828-3576, Fax: 250-828-3760
museum@kamloops.ca
www.kamloops.ca/museum/index.shtml
Elisabeth Duckworth

Kamloops: Secwepemc Cultural Education Society
#311, 355 Yellowhead Hwy., Kamloops BC V2H 1H1
250-828-9749, Fax: 250-372-8833
museum@secwepemc.org
www.secwepemc.org
Daniel Saul, Museum Manager

Kaslo: Kootenay Lake Archives
312 - 4th St., Kaslo BC V0G 1M0
250-353-9633
archives@klhs.bc.ca
www.klhs.bc.ca/archives.htm
Elizabeth Scarlett, Archivist
Howard Hisdal, Diocesan Archivist
kootenay_archives@telus.net
250-762-3306

Kelowna: Diocese of Kootenay, Archives
1876 Richter St., Kelowna BC V1Y 2M9
250-762-3306, Fax: 250-762-4150
diocese_of_kootenay@telus.net

Kelowna: Kelowna Public Archives
470 Queensway Ave., Kelowna BC V1Y 6S7
250-763-2417, Fax: 250-763-5722
archives@kelownamuseums.ca
www.kelownamuseums.ca/kelowna-public-archives.html
Donna Johnson, Archivist

Kitimat: Kitimat Centennial Museum
293 City Centre, Kitimat BC V8C 1T6
250-632-8950, Fax: 250-632-7429
kitimatmuseum@telus.net
www.kitimatmuseum.ca
Louise Avery, Curator

Lake Cowichan: Kaatza Historical Society
125 South Shore Rd., Lake Cowichan BC V0R 2G0
250-749-6142, Fax: 250-749-3900
khs@island.net
www.kaatzamuseum.ca
Barbara Simkins, Curator/Manager
Sylvia Stepforth, Head, Archives

***Langley:* Trinity Western University Archives**
7600 Glover Rd., Langley BC V2Y 1Y1
604-513-2121, Fax: 604-513-2063
archives.twu.ca:8080/

***Maple Ridge:* Corporation of the District of Maple Ridge**
11995 Haney Pl., Maple Ridge BC V2X 6A9
604-463-5221, Fax: 604-467-7329
Irene Gauld, Contact

***Merritt:* Nicola Valley Museum & Archives**
2201 Coldwater Ave., Merritt BC V1K 1B8
250-378-4145, Fax: 250-378-4145
nvma@uniserve.com
www.nicolavalleymuseum.org
Barb Watson, Office Administrator
nvma@uniserve.com
250-378-4145

***Mission:* Mission Community Archives**
33215 - 2nd Ave., Mission BC V2V 4L1
604-820-2621
mca@missionarchives.com
www.missionarchives.com
Valerie Billesberger, Archivist/Records Manager
604-820-2621

***Nakusp:* Arrow Lakes Historical Society**
92B - 7th Ave. NW, Nakusp BC V0G 1R0
250-265-0110, Fax: 250-265-0110
alhs@netidea.com
Rosemarie Parent, President
miltrose@telus.net
250-265-3323

***Nanaimo:* Nanaimo District Museum**
100 Museum Way, Nanaimo BC V9R 5S8
250-753-1821, Fax: 250-740-0125
info@nanaimomuseum.ca
www.nanaimomuseum.ca
David Hill-Turner, Curator

***Nelson:* Nelson & District Museum, Art Gallery, Archives & Historical Society**
502 Vernon St., Nelson BC V1L 4E7
250-352-9813, Fax: 250-352-9810
nmchin@direct.ca
www.touchstonesnelson.ca/archives/index.php
Shawn F. Lamb, Collections Manager and Archivist
collections@touchstonesnelson.ca

***Nelson:* Roman Catholic Diocese of Nelson**
402 West Richards St., Nelson BC V1L 3K3
250-352-6921, Fax: 250-352-1737
nelson.diocese@telus.net
www.diocese.nelson.bc.ca
R.J. (Ron) Welwood, Contact
r-fwelwood@shaw.ca
Joan Wenman, Archivist/Monographs & Govt Documents Collections Librarian
604-527-5181

***New Westminster:* Archives**
100 Royal Ave., New Westminster BC V3L 5B2
wenmanj@douglas.bc.ca

***New Westminster:* New Westminster Museum/Archives**
302 Royal Ave., New Westminster BC V3L 1H7
604-527-4640, Fax: 604-527-4641
bdykes@newwestcity.ca
www.nwpr.bc.ca
Barry Dykes, Archivist
bdykes@newwestcity.ca
604-527-4642

***North Vancouver:* North Vancouver Museum & Archives**
3203 Institute Rd., North Vancouver BC V7K 3E5
604-990-3700, Fax: 604-987-5688
nvmac@dnv.org
www.dnv.org/nvma
Janet Turner, Archivist
turnerj@dnv.org

***Penticton:* Penticton (R.N. Atkinson) Museum & Archives**
785 Main St., Penticton BC V2A 5E3
250-490-2451, Fax: 250-492-0440
museum@city.penticton.bc.ca
penticton.ca/museum/default.asp
Peter Ord, Director & Curator
museum@city.penticton.bc.ca
250-490-2451

***Port Alberni:* Alberni District Historical Society**
255 Wallace St., Port Alberni BC V9Y 3Y6
250-723-2181, Fax: 250-723-1035
adhs@uniserve.com
Anne W. Holt, Volunteer Archivist
cah@uniserve.com
250-723-3006

***Port Clements:* Port Clements Historical Society**
PO Box 417, Port Clements BC V0T 1R0
250-557-4576

***Prince George:* Exploration Place**
333 Becott Pl., Prince George BC V2L 4V7
250-562-1612, Fax: 250-562-6395, 866-562-1612
archive@theexplorationplace.com
www.theexplorationplace.com
Bob Campbell, Manager, Curatorial Services
bob@theexplorationplace.com
250-562-1612 ext. 230
Cliff Armstrong, Contact
calarch@citytel.net

***Prince Rupert:* Diocese of Caledonia, Archives**
200 - 4th Ave. West, Prince Rupert BC V8J 1P3
250-624-6013, Fax: 250-624-4299
calarch@citytel.net
www.caledonia.anglican.org

***Prince Rupert:* Prince Rupert City & Regional Archives**
100 - 1st Ave, East, Prince Rupert BC V8J 1A6
250-624-3326, Fax: 250-624-3706
archives@citytel.net
www.princerupertlibrary.ca/archives/
Jean Eiers-Page, Archivist

***Quesnel:* Quesnel & District Museum & Archives**
705 Carson Ave., Quesnel BC V2J 2B6
250-992-9580, Fax: 250-992-9680
ehunter@city.quesnel.bc.ca
www.quesnelmuseum.ca
E Hunter, Curator
ehunter@city.quesnel.bc.ca

***Revelstoke:* Revelstoke Museum & Archives**
PO Box 1908, Revelstoke BC V0E 2S0
250-837-3067, Fax: 250-837-3094
rm_chin@revelstoke.net
www.revelstokemuseum.ca
Cathy English, Curator
250-837-3067

***Richmond:* City of Richmond Archives**
7700 Minoru Gate, Richmond BC V6Y 1R9
604-247-8305, Fax: 604-231-6464
archives@richmond.ca
www.richmond.ca/cityhall/archives/about/about.htm
Lynne Waller, Archivist
lwaller@richmond.ca
604-231-6430

***Sooke:* Sooke Region Museum**
2070 Phillips Rd., Sooke BC V0S 1N0
250-642-6351, Fax: 250-642-7089, 866-888-4748
info@sookeregionmuseum.com
www.sookeregionmuseum.com
Joyce Linell, Contact

***Summerland:* Summerland Museum & Heritage Society**
PO Box 1491, Summerland BC V0H 1Z0
250-494-9395, Fax: 250-494-9326
info@summerlandmuseum.org
www.summerlandmuseum.org
Sherril Foster, Curator

***Surrey:* City of Surrey Archives**
6022 - 176th St., Surrey BC V3S 4E8
604-502-6459, Fax: 604-502-6457
rgallagher@surrey.ca
Bev Sommer, Manager of Heritage Services
bsommer@surrey.ca
604-502-6460

***Trail:* Trail City Archives**
1394 Pine Ave., Trail BC V1R 4E6
250-364-0829, Fax: 250-364-0830
history@trail.ca
www.trailhistory.com
Jamie Forbes, Corporate Administrator
jforbes@trail.ca
250-364-0800
Bob Stewart, Archivist

***Vancouver:* B.C. Conference**
6000 Iona Dr., Vancouver BC V6T 1L4
604-822-9589, Fax: 604-822-9212
united-archives@vst.edu
bc.united-church.ca/archives/
Jean Reeve, Archives

***Vancouver:* BC Council Archives**
1476 West 8th Ave., Vancouver BC V6H 1E1
604-734-4877, Fax: 604-714-6645
info@bc-girlguides.org
www.girlguides.ca

***Vancouver:* British Columbia Sports Hall of Fame & Museum**
Gate A, BC Place Stadium, Beatty & Robson Sts., Vancouver BC V6B 4Y8
604-687-5520, Fax: 604-687-5510
info@bcsportshalloffame.com
www.bcsportshalloffame.com
Jason Beck, Curator
jason.beck@bssportshalloffame.com
604-687-5520

***Vancouver:* City of Vancouver Archives**
1150 Chestnut St., Vancouver BC V6J 3J9
604-736-8561, Fax: 604-736-0626
archives@vancouver.ca
www.vancouver.ca/archives
Leslie Mobbs, City Archivist & Director, Records & Archives Division
leslie.mobbs@vancouver.ca
Melanie Wallace, Archivist
anglican-archives@vst.edu
604-822-9583

***Vancouver:* Diocese of New Westminster, Archives**
6000 Iona Dr., Vancouver BC V6T 1L4
604-822-9583, Fax: 604-822-9212
anglican-archives@vst.edu
www.vancouver.anglican.ca

***Vancouver:* Institute of Indigenous Government / Union of BC Indian Chiefs**
342 Water St., 5th Fl., Vancouver BC V6B 1B6
604-684-0231, Fax: 604-684-5726
library@ubcic.bc.ca
www.ubcic.bc.ca/department/library.htm
Kim Lawson, Archivist/Librarian
library@ubcic.bc.ca
604-684-0241

***Vancouver:* Jewish Historical Society of BC**
#206, 950 West 41st Ave., Vancouver BC V5Z 2N7
604-257-5199
jhsofbc@direct.ca
www.jewishmuseum.ca
Diane Rodgers, Archivist

***Vancouver:* Roman Catholic Archdiocese of Vancouver**
150 Robson St., Vancouver BC V6B 2A7
604-683-0281, Fax: 604-683-4288
aseles@rcav.bc.ca
www.rcav.org/Archives/index.htm
Anthea Seles, Records Manager/Archivist
aseles@rcav.bc.ca
604-683-0281 ext. 302

***Vancouver:* Satellite Video Exchange Society**
1965 Main St., Vancouver BC V5T 3C1
604-872-8449, Fax: 604-876-1185
videoout@telus.net
www.videoinstudios.com
Lauren Howes, Distribution Coordinator
Christopher Hives, University Archivist
chives@interchange.ubc.ca
604-822-5877

***Vancouver:* University Archives**
1961 East Mall, Vancouver BC V6T 1Z1
604-822-5877, Fax: 604-822-3242
www.library.ubc.ca/archives

***Vancouver:* Vancouver Ballet Society**
677 Davie St., 6th Fl., Vancouver BC V6B 2G6
604-681-1425
archives@vancouverballetsociety.ca
www.vancouverballetsociety.ca/archives.html

Leslie Nadon, Administrator
vbs@telus.net

Vancouver: **Vancouver Holocaust Education Centre**
#50, 950 West 41st Ave., Vancouver BC V5Z 2N7
604-264-0499, Fax: 604-264-0497
library@vhec.org
www.vhec.org
Roberta Kremer, Executive Director
rkremer@vhec.org

Vernon: **Greater Vernon Museum & Archives**
3009 - 32nd Ave., Vernon BC V1T 2L8
250-542-3142, Fax: 250-542-5358
archives@vernonmuseum.ca
www.vernonmuseum.ca
Barbara Bell, Archivist

Victoria: **City of Victoria Archives**
8 Centenial Sq., Victoria BC V8W 1P7
250-361-0375, Fax: 250-361-0394
archives@victoria.ca
www.victoria.ca/archives/archives.shtml
Trevor Livelton, Archivist
Debra Barr, Diocesan Archivist

Victoria: **Diocese of British Columbia, Archives**
900 Vancouver St., Victoria BC V8V 3V7
250-386-7781, Fax: 250-386-4013, 800-582-8627
darchives@bc.anglican.ca
www.bc.anglican.ca

Victoria: **Esquimalt Municipal Archives**
1149-A Esquimalt Rd., Victoria BC V9A 3N6
250-412-8540, Fax: 250-412-8541
parkerd@esquimalt.ca
Dave Parker, Archivist
parkerd@esquimalt.ca

Victoria: **Roman Catholic Diocese of Victoria**
#1, 4044 Nelthorpe St., Victoria BC V8X 2A1
250-479-1331, Fax: 250-479-5423
chancery@rcdvictoria.org
www.rcdvictoria.org
Michael Lapierre, Vicar-General

Victoria: **Saanich Municipal Archives**
3100 Tillicum Rd., Victoria BC V9A 6T2
250-475-1775, Fax: 250-388-7819
caroline.duncan@saanich.ca
www.saanicharchives.ca
Caroline Duncan, Municipal Archivist
caroline.duncan@saanich.ca
250-475-1775

Victoria: **Sisters of St Ann**
1550 Begbie St., Victoria BC V8R 1K8
250-592-0685, Fax: 250-592-0234
archives@ssabc.ca
Michaeleen King, Archivist

Waglisla: **Heiltsuk Cultural Education Centre**
PO Box 880, Waglisla BC V0T 1Z0
250-957-2626, Fax: 250-957-2780
treid@hcec.ca
Terri Reid, Resource Centre Assistant

West Vancouver: **West Vancouver Archives**
680 - 17th St., West Vancouver BC V7V 3T2
604-925-7298
archives@westvancouver.ca
www.wvma.net
Shaunna Moore, District Archivist
smoore@westvancouver.ca
604-925-7298

White Rock: **White Rock Museum & Archives**
14970 Marine Dr., White Rock BC V4B 1C4
604-541-2222, Fax: 604-541-2223
whiterockmuseum@telus.net
Hugh Ellenwood, Community Historian

Manitoba

Regional Systems

Border Regional Library
312 - 7th Ave., Virden MB R0M 2C0
204-748-3862, Fax: 204-748-3862
brlibrary.cimnet.ca
Linda Grant-Braybrook, Librarian

Evergreen Regional Library
65 First Ave., Gimli MB R0C 1B0
204-642-7912, Fax: 204-642-8319
exec@mts.net
www.townofarborg.com/library.default.asp
Valerie Eyolfson, Head Librarian
exec@mts.net
204-642-7912

Lac du Bonnet Regional Library
PO Box 216, Lac du Bonnet MB R0E 1A0
204-345-2653, Fax: 204-345-6827
mldb@mts.net
Vickie Short, Head Librarian

Lakeland Regional Library (Manitoba)
318 Williams Ave., Killarney MB R0K 1G0
204-523-4949
lrl@mb.sympatico.ca
Gloria Kinsley, Librarian

Parkland Regional Library (Manitoba)
504 Main St. North, Dauphin MB R7N 1C9
204-638-6410, Fax: 204-638-9483
prlhq@parklandlib.mb.ca
www.parklandlib.mb.ca
Glenn Butchart, Director
GButchart@parklandlib.mb.ca

South Central Regional Library
160 Main St., Winkler MB R6W 4B4
204-325-7174, Fax: 204-331-1847
headlib@scrlibrary.mb.ca
www.scrlibrary.mb.ca
Mary Toma, Head Librarian
headlib@srclibrary.mb.ca
204-325-5864

Southwestern Manitoba Regional Library
149 Main St., Melita MB R0M 1L0
204-522-3923
swmblib@mail.techplus.com
www.mts.net/~swmblib/
Valorie Wray, Librarian

Western Manitoba Regional Library
#1, 710 Rosser Ave., Brandon MB R7A 0K9
204-727-6648, Fax: 204-727-4447
wmrlibrary@wmrlibrary.mb.ca
www.wmrlibrary.mb.ca
Kathy Thornborough, Chief Librarian
thornborough@wmrlibrary.mb.ca

Public Libraries

Baldur: **Regional Municipality of Argyle Public Library**
627 Elizabeth St. East, Baldur MB R0K 0B0
204-535-2314, Fax: 204-535-2242
rmargyle@gmail.com
Cheri McLaren

Beausejour: **Brokenhead River Regional Library**
427 Park Ave., Beausejour MB R0E 0C0
204-268-7570, Fax: 204-268-7570
brrlibr@mts.net
www.efree.mb.ca/brrl/home.html
Debbie Winnicki, Head Librarian

Boissevain: **Boissevain & Morton Regional Library**
436 South Railway St., Boissevain MB R0K 0E0
204-534-6478, Fax: 204-534-3710
mbom@mts.net
www.bmlibrary.ca

Brandon: **Public Library Services newsletter / Le Bulletin d'information des services de bibliothèques publiques**
#200, 1525 First St. South, Brandon MB R7A 7A1
204-726-6590
pls@gov.mb.ca
maplin.gov.mb.ca/cgi-bin/about.cgi

La Broquerie: **Bibliothèque Saint-Joachim Library**
29, Baie Normandeau, La Broquerie MB R0A 0W0
204-424-9533, Fax: 204-424-5610
bstjl@bsjl.ca
www.bsjl.ca
Yolande Tétrault, Présidente, Conseil d'administration

Carman: **Boyne Regional Library**
15 - 1st Ave. SW, Carman MB R0G 0J0
204-745-3504
boynereg@mts.net
Sandra Yeo, Head Librarian
204-745-3504

Cartwright: **Cartwright Branch Library**
483 North Railway St., Cartwright MB R0K 0L0
204-529-2261
cartlib@mts.net
www.lakelandregionallibrary.ca
Andrea Trembath, Branch Librarian

Churchill: **Churchill Public Library**
Town Centre Complex, PO Box 730, Churchill MB R0B 0E0
204-675-2731, Fax: 204-675-2934
Bonnie Allen, Librarian

Deloraine: **Bren Del Win Centennial Library**
311 North Railway Ave. West, PO Box 584, Deloraine MB R0M 0M0
204-747-2415, Fax: 204-747-3446
bdwlib@mts.net
Helen Schoenbaert, Chair

Eriksdale: **Eriksdale Public Library**
PO Box 219, Eriksdale MB R0C 0W0
204-739-2668, Fax: 204-739-2668
epl1@mts.net
Rita L. Cushnie, Librarian
epl1@mts.net

Flin Flon: **Flin Flon Public Library**
58 Main St., Flin Flon MB R8A 1J8
204-687-3397, Fax: 204-687-4233
ffpl@mts.net
www.flinflonpubliclibrary.ca
Phyllis Stadnick, Library Administrator
ffpladmin@mts.net
204-687-3397

Gillam: **Bette Winner Public Library**
PO Box 400, Gillam MB R0B 0L0
204-652-2617, Fax: 204-652-2617
bwinner@gillamnet.com
Ricci Bangle, Head Librarian

Headingley: **Headingley Public Library**
49 Alboro St., Headingley MB R4J 1A3
204-888-5410, Fax: 204-831-7207
hml@mts.net
www.headingleylibrary.ca
Joan Spice, Head Librarian

Holland: **Victoria Municipal Library**
PO Box 371, Holland MB R0G 0X0
204-526-2011
victlib@goinet.ca
Ivan Bruneay, Chair

Ile-des-Chênes: **Bibliothèque Ritchot - Ile-des-Chênes**
École Gabrielle-Roy, CP 581, Ile-des-Chênes MB R0A 0T0
204-878-2147, Fax: 204-878-3495
ritchot@atrium.ca
www.richot.com/libraries.htm
Louise Durand, Bibliothécaire

Lundar: **Pauline Johnson Library**
23 Main St., Lundar MB R0C 1Y0
204-762-5367
mlpj@mts.net
Kristin Jobling, Assistant Librarian

Lynn Lake: **Lynn Lake Centennial Library**
PO Box 1127, Lynn Lake MB R0B 0W0
204-356-8222
Margaret Thomson, Librarian

MacGregor: **North Norfolk MacGregor Regional Library**
35 Hampton St. East, MacGregor MB R0H 0R0
204-685-2796, Fax: 204-685-2478
macllib@mts.net
Antoinette Blankvoort, Head Librarian

Minnedosa: **Minnedosa Regional Library**
45 - 1st Ave. SE, Minnedosa MB R0J 1E0
204-867-2585, Fax: 204-867-6140
mmr@mts.net
Linda Cook, Librarian

Morris: **Valley Regional Library**
141 Main St. South, Morris MB R0G 1K0
204-746-2136
valleylib@mts.net
www.town.morris.mb.ca/library.html
Dinne DeKezel, Librarian
204-746-2136

Norway House: **Ayamiscikawikamik Public Library**
General Delivery, Norway House MB R0B 1B0
204-359-6047, Fax: 204-359-6262
sam@yahoo.ca
Violet Ouellette, Librarian

Notre-Dame-de-Lourdes: **Bibliothèque Père Champagne/ Père Champagne Library**
44, rue Rodgers, CP 399, Notre-Dame-de-Lourdes MB R0G 1M0
204-248-2386
ndbiblio@yahoo.ca
Gisèle Théroux, Responsable

The Pas: **The Pas Regional Library**
53 Edwards Ave., The Pas MB R9A 1R2
204-623-2023, Fax: 204-623-4594
library@mts.net
www.thepasregionallibrary.com
Carol Ham, Library Administrator

Pilot Mound: **Pilot Mound Library**
219 Broadway Ave. West, Pilot Mound MB R0G 1P0
204-825-2035, Fax: 204-825-2784
pmlibrary@mts.net
www.pilotmoundlibrary.ca
Allison MacAulay, Librarian

Pinawa: **Pinawa Public Library**
Vanier Dr., General Delivery, Pinawa MB R0E 1L0
204-753-2496, Fax: 204-753-2770
email@pinawapubliclibrary.com
Marg Stokes, Head Librarian
plibrary@sdwhiteshell.mb.ca
204-753-2496

Portage la Prairie: **Portage la Prairie Regional Library**
40B Royal Rd. North, Portage la Prairie MB R1N 1V1
204-857-4271, Fax: 204-239-4387
portlib@portagelibrary.com
Percy Gregoire-Voskamp, Head Librarian
pvoskamp@portagelibrary.com

Rapid City: **Rapid City Regional Library**
PO Box 8, Rapid City MB R0K 1W0
204-826-2732
rcreglib@mts.net
Shirley Martin, Head Librarian

Reston: **Reston District Library**
220 - 4th St., Reston MB R0M 1X0
204-877-3673
restonlb@mb.sympatico.ca

Rivers: **Prairie Crocus Regional Library**
137 Main St., Rivers MB R0K 1X0
204-328-7613
pcrl@mts.net
www.prairiecrocuslibrary.ca
Dora M. Irvine, Librarian

Rossburn: **Rossburn Regional Library**
53 Main St. North, Rossburn MB R0J 1V0
204-859-2687, Fax: 204-859-2687
rrl@mts.net
Stephanie Parkinson, Librarian/Book-Keeper
rrl@mts.net

Russell: **Russell & District Regional Library**
339 Main St., Russell MB R0J 1W0
204-773-3127
ruslib@mts.net
Louise Sidoryk, Library Technician

Saint-Claude: **Bibliothèque Saint-Claude/ St. Claude Library**
50 - 1st St., Saint-Claude MB R0G 1Z0
204-379-2524
stclib@mts.net
Lynn Gobin, Librarian

Ste-Anne-des-Chênes: **Bibliothèque Ste-Anne Library**
16, rue de l'Eglise, Ste-Anne-des-Chênes MB R5H 1H8
204-422-9958, Fax: 204-422-9958
steannelib@steannemb.ca
bibliosteannelib.8m.com/cac_en.html
Monica Ball, Bibliothécaire

Ste Rose du Lac: **Ste Rose Regional Library**
General Delivery, Ste Rose du Lac MB R0L 1S0
204-447-2527
sroselib@mts.net
www.steroseregionallibrary.info
Elaine Chaput, Head Librarian

St Georges: **Allard Library/ Bibliothèque Allard**
14 Caron Bay, St Georges MB R0E 1V0
204-367-8443, Fax: 204-367-8443

St Jean Baptiste: **Bibliothèque Montcalm Library**
113B - 2nd Ave., St Jean Baptiste MB R0G 2B0
204-758-3137, Fax: 204-758-3574
biblio@atrium.ca
www.rmofmontcalm.com/bibliothequemontcalmlibrary
Diane Bérard, Bibliothécaire
dmtberard@hotmail.com

St Pierre Jolys: **Jolys Regional Library/ Bibliothèque régionale Jolys**
505 Hébert Ave., St Pierre Jolys MB R0A 1V0
204-433-7729
stplibrary@jrlibrary.mb.ca
www.jrlibrary.mb.ca
Janet Banfield, CEO

Selkirk: **Red River North Regional Library**
303 Main St., Selkirk MB R1A 1S7
204-482-3522, Fax: 204-482-6166
library@ssarl.org
www.ssarl.org
Ken Kuryliw, Director, Library Services
kkuryliw@ssarl.org

Shilo: **Shilo Community Library**
Bldg. T 100, Notre Dame & French, Box 177, Shilo MB R0K 2A0
204-765-2590
shilolib@mb.sympatico.ca

Snow Lake: **Snow Lake Community Library**
Joseph H. Kerr School, 201 Cherry Ave., Snow Lake MB R0B 1M0
204-358-2322, Fax: 204-358-2116
clibrary@mail.josephhkerrsnowlake.mb.ca
Vivian Bennett, Librarian
204-358-2833

Somerset: **Somerset Library/ Bibliothèque Somerset**
289 Carlton Ave., Somerset MB R0G 2L0
204-744-2170
somlib@mts.net
Lucille Labossiere, Librarian
204-744-2860

Souris: **Glenwood & Souris Regional Library**
#18, 114 - 2nd St. South, Souris MB R0K 2C0
204-483-2757
gsrl@mts.net
Margaret Greaves, Library Supervisor

Steinbach: **Jake Epp Library**
255 Elmdale St., Steinbach MB R6G 1N6
204-326-6841, Fax: 204-326-6859
jakeepplibrary@yahoo.com
www.jakeepplibrary.com
Loraine Trudeau, Head Librarian
jakeepplibrary@yahoo.com
204-326-6841

Stonewall: **South Interlake Regional Library**
419 Main St., Stonewall MB R0C 2Z0
204-467-8415, Fax: 204-467-9809
sirl@mts.net
www.sirlibrary.com
Darlene Dallman, Chief Administation Officer
sirl@mts.net
204-467-5767

Swan River: **North-West Regional Library**
610 - 1st St. North, Swan River MB R0L 1Z0
204-734-3880, Fax: 204-734-3880
nwrl@mts.net
www.swanriverlibrary.ca
June McKenzie, Head Librarian

Thompson: **Thompson Public Library**
81 Thompson Dr. North, Thompson MB R8N 0C3
204-677-3717, Fax: 204-778-5844
info@thompsonlibrary.com
www.thompsonlibrary.com
Cheryl Davies, Administrator
admin@thompsonlibrary.com

Winnipeg: **Archinews / Archinouvelles**
PO Box 26005 Stn Maryland, Winnipeg MB R3G 3R3
204-942-3491, Fax: 204-942-3492
ama1@mts.net
www.mbarchives.mb.ca
Carole Pelchat, Chair, Information & Outreach Committee

Winnipeg: **MFL Occupational Health Centre**
#102, 275 Broadway, Winnipeg MB R3C 4M6
204-949-0811, Fax: 204-956-0848, 888-843-1229
mflohc@mflohc.mb.ca
www.mflohc.mb.ca/mflohc_folder/information_&_resources.html
Tiffany Pau, Library Coordinator
204-949-7909

Winnipeg: **MLA Newsline**
#606, 100 Arthur St., Winnipeg MB R3B 1H3
204-943-4567, Fax: 204-942-1555
mla@uwinnipeg.ca
www.mla.mb.ca
Liane Patterson, Director, Communications & Publications

Winnipeg: **Winnipeg Public Library**
251 Donald St., Winnipeg MB R3C 3P5
204-986-6472, Fax: 204-942-5671
wpl-info@winnipeg.ca
wpl.city.winnipeg.mb.ca/library/
Rick Walker, Manager of Library Services
rwalker@winnipeg.ca

Archives

Boissevain: **Boissevain Community Archives**
436 South Railway St., Boissevain MB R0K 0E0
204-534-6478, Fax: 204-534-3710
mbom@mts.net
www.boissevain.ca/archives_library/archives_resources.html
Michelle Scott, Archivist

Brandon: **City of Brandon**
410 - 9th St., Brandon MB R7A 6A2
204-729-2289, Fax: 204-729-8244
www.city.brandon.mb.ca
Donna Phillips, Classification Clerk
Maxine Sobkow, Diocesan Secretary & Archivist
diobran@mts.net
204-727-7550

Brandon: **Diocese of Brandon, Archives**
PO Box 21009, W.E.P.O., Brandon MB R7B 3W8
204-727-7550, Fax: 204-727-4135
diobran@mts.net
www.dioceseofbrandon.org

Brandon: **Magnacca Research Centre**
122 - 18th St., Brandon MB R7A 5A4
204-727-1722, Fax: 204-727-1722
dalymus@mts.net
www.mts.net/~dalymus/archives.htm
Eileen Trott, Archivist

Brandon: **26th Field Regiment RCA/12th Manitoba Dragoons Museum**
1116 Victoria Ave., Brandon MB R7A 1B2
204-728-2559, Fax: 204-725-1766
museum@12mbdragoons.com
www.12mbdragoons.com
Ross Neale, Curator
museum@12mbdragoons.com

Carberry: **Carberry Plains Archives**
115 Main St., Carberry MB R0K 0H0
204-834-6614, Fax: 204-834-6604
cparchives@mts.net
www.mts.net/~archives/
Penny Shaw, Archivist
cparchives@mts.net

Churchill: **Diocese of Churchill Hudson Bay**
Eskimo Museum, 242 La Verendrye Ave., Churchill MB R0B 0E0
204-675-2030, Fax: 204-675-2140
Lorraine Brandson, Curator

Flin Flon: **Flin Flon Community Archives**
58 Main St., Flin Flon MB R8A 1J8
204-687-3397, Fax: 204-687-4233
ffpl@mts.net
Phyllis Stadnick, Administrator

Killarney: **J.A.V. David Museum**
414 Williams Ave., Killarney MB R0K 1G0
204-523-7325
Donna Wilkins, Archivist

Leaf Rapids: **Leaf Rapids Community Archives**
PO Box 190, Leaf Rapids MB R0B 1W0
204-473-2742, Fax: 204-473-2566
Lisa Everton, Archivist
lrpl@mts.net
204-473-2742

MacGregor: **North Norfolk MacGregor Archives**
PO Box 435, MacGregor MB R0H 0R0
204-685-2805
Lorraine Chant, Contact

Shilo: **Royal Canadian Artillery Museum**
Canadian Forces Base Shilo, Shilo MB R0K 2A0
204-765-3000, Fax: 204-765-5289
rcamuseum@techplus.ca
Rick Sanderson, Director

Steinbach: **Mennonite Heritage Village**
231 PTH 12 North, Steinbach MB R5G 1T8
204-326-9661, Fax: 204-326-5046, 800-280-8741
info@mennoniteheritagevillage.com
www.mennoniteheritagevillage.com
Roland Sawatzky, Senior Curator
rms@mennoniteheritagevillage.com
204-326-9661

Thompson: **Heritage North Museum**
162 Princeton Dr., Thompson MB R8N 2A4
204-677-2216, Fax: 204-677-8953
hnmuseum@mts.net
www.thompson.heritage.north.museum/600archives.htm
Paul Legault, Contact

Winnipeg: **Archevêché de St-Boniface**
151 de la Cathédrale Ave., Winnipeg MB R2H 0H6
204-237-9851, Fax: 204-231-2652
Yolande Comeau, Secrétaire de la chancelerie

Winnipeg: **Archives des Soeurs Grises, St Boniface/ Grey Nun Archives, St-Boniface**
151 Despins St., Winnipeg MB R2H 0L7
204-237-8941, Fax: 204-237-3466
archsgm@mts.net
Carole Boily, Archiviste
cboily@sgm.mb.ca

Winnipeg: **Archives of Manitoba/ Archives du Manitoba**
#130, 200 Vaughan St., Winnipeg MB R3C 1T5
204-945-3971, Fax: 204-948-2008, 800-617-3588
archives@gov.mb.ca
www.gov.mb.ca/chc/archives/
Gordon Dodds, Archivist of Manitoba
204-945-6140

Winnipeg: **Centre for Mennonite Brethren Studies**
1310 Taylor Ave., Winnipeg MB R3M 3Z6
204-669-6575, Fax: 204-654-1865, 888-669-6575
kreddig@mbconf.ca
www.mbconf.ca/mbstudies/index.en.html

Winnipeg: **City of Winnipeg**
380 William Ave., Winnipeg MB R3A 0J1
204-986-5325, Fax: 204-986-7133
www.winnipeg.ca/clerks/docs/archives/archives.stm
Gerry Berkowski, City Records Manager & Archivist
Diane Haglund, Conference Archivist

Winnipeg: **Conference of Manitoba & Northwestern Ontario**
Library, University of Winnipeg, 515 Portage Ave., Winnipeg MB R3B 2E3
204-783-0708, Fax: 204-786-1824
d.haglund@uwinnipeg.ca
www.united-church.ca/archives/mnwo/

Winnipeg: **Costume Museum of Canada**
109 Pacific Ave., Winnipeg MB R3B 0M1
204-989-0072, Fax: 204-989-0074
info@costumemuseum.com
www.costumemuseum.com
Brenda Hamer, Collections Coordinator
info@costumemuseum.com
Myrna Brownlie, Archivist
archives@rupertsland.ca
204-992-4203

Winnipeg: **Diocese of Rupert's Land, Archives**
935 Nesbitt Bay, Winnipeg MB R3T 1W6
204-992-4203, Fax: 204-992-4219, 866-693-4418
archives@rupertsland.ca
rupertsland.ca

Winnipeg: **Fire Fighters Historical Society of Winnipeg**
56 Maple St., Winnipeg MB R3B 0Y8
204-942-4817, Fax: 204-885-1306
firemuseum@gatewest.net
www.winnipegfiremuseum.ca
Barbara Kuryluk, Curator
kuryluk@gatewest.net
204-942-4817

Winnipeg: **Fort Garry Horse Museum & Archives**
551 Machray Ave., Winnipeg MB R2W 1A8
204-586-6298, Fax: 204-582-0370
museum12006@fortgarryhorse.ca
www.fortgarryhorse.ca
Larry Lajeunesse, Head, Library
llajeunesse@mb.sympatico.ca
204-582-0370

Winnipeg: **Grand Lodge of Manitoba**
420 Corydon Ave., Winnipeg MB R3L 0N8
204-832-6062, Fax: 204-284-3527
rkiv@shaw.ca
www.grandlodge.mb.ca/masonic_archives.html

Winnipeg: **Jewish Heritage Centre of Western Canada**
#C116, 123 Doncaster St., Winnipeg MB R3N 2B2
204-477-7461, Fax: 204-477-7465
heritage@jhcwc.org
www.jhcwc.org/archives.htm
Vanesa Harari, Archivist
vharari@jhcwc.org

Winnipeg: **Manitoba Council**
#213, 530 Century St., Winnipeg MB R3H 0Y4
204-774-1939, Fax: 204-774-9271
info@girlguides.mb.ca
www.girlguides.ca

Winnipeg: **Manitoba Gay/Lesbian Archive**
#1, 222 Osborne St. South, Winnipeg MB R3C 1Z3
204-284-5208, Fax: 204-478-1160, 888-399-0005
info@rainbowresourcecentre.org
www.rainbowresourcecentre.org
Lindsay Butt, Librarian
info@rainbowresourcecentre.org
204-284-5208

Winnipeg: **Manitoba Museum**
190 Rupert Ave., Winnipeg MB R3B 0N2
204-988-0662, Fax: 204-942-3679
csteffan@manitobamuseum.ca
www.manitobamuseum.ca
Patricia Henry, Library Technician

Winnipeg: **Mennonite Heritage Centre**
600 Shaftesbury Blvd., Winnipeg MB R3P 0M4
204-888-6781, Fax: 204-831-5675, 866-888-6785
archives@mennonitechurch.ca
www.mennonitechurch.ca/programs/archives/
Alf Redekopp, Director
aredekopp@mennonitechurch.ca
Carole Pelchat, Archiviste
204-233-0210 ext. 398

Winnipeg: **Service des archives**
200, av de la Cathédrale, Winnipeg MB R2H 0H7
204-233-0210, Fax: 204-233-9472
cperlchat@ustboniface.mb.ca
www.ustboniface.mb.ca/cusb/archives

Winnipeg: **Sisters of Our Lady of the Missions/ Religieuses de Notre Dame des Missions**
St Edward's Convent, Provincial Office, 800 Adele Ave, Winnipeg MB R3E 0K6
204-774-5067
rndms@mb.sympatico.ca

Winnipeg: **Soeurs Missionnaires Oblates du Sacré-Coeur et de Marie Immaculée**
Maison généraliste, 601 Aulneau St., Winnipeg MB R2H 2V5
204-233-7287, Fax: 204-235-7418
missobladmgen@shaw.ca
Thérèse Bilodeau, Archiviste

Winnipeg: **Transcona Historical Museum**
141 Regent Ave. West, Winnipeg MB R2C 1R1
204-222-0423
transon@istar.ca
www.transconamuseum.mb.ca

Winnipeg: **Ukrainian Catholic Church**
Archbishop's Chancery, 233 Scotia St., Winnipeg MB R2V 1V7
204-338-7801, Fax: 204-339-4006
archepar@escape.ca
www.archeparchy.ca
Gloria Romaniuk, Archivist
Gloria Romaniuk, Archivist

Winnipeg: **Ukrainian Cultural & Educational Centre Archives**
184 Alexander Ave. East, Winnipeg MB R3B 0L6
204-942-0218, Fax: 204-943-2857

Winnipeg: **Western Canada Aviation Museum**
Hangar T-2, 958 Ferry Rd., Winnipeg MB R3H 0Y8
204-786-5503, Fax: 204-775-4761
info@wcam.mb.ca
www.wcam.mb.ca
Brian Watson, Coordinator

New Brunswick

Regional Systems

AWK Library Regional Office/ Région de bibliothèques AWK
#201, 644 Main St., Moncton NB E1C 1E2
506-869-6032, Fax: 506-869-6022
annette.selmes@gnb.ca
www.gnb.ca
Tina Bourgeois, Regional Director
tina.bourgeois@gnb.ca

Chaleur Library Region/ Région de bibliothèques Chaleur
113A Roseberry St., Campbellton NB E3N 2G6
506-789-6599, Fax: 506-789-7318
tina.bourgeois@gnb.ca
www1.gnb.ca
Sarah Kilfoil, Regional Director
sarah.kilfoil@gnb.ca

Fundy Library Regional Office/ Région de bibliothèques de Fundy
1 Market Sq., Saint John NB E2L 4Z6
506-643-7222, Fax: 506-643-7225
lucy.harrigan@gnb.ca
www.gnb.ca
Ian A. Wilson, Regional Director
ian.wilson@gnb.ca
506-643-7242

Haut-Saint-Jean Library Regional Office/ Région de bibliothèques Haut-Saint-Jean
540 Principale St., Saint-Basile NB E7C 1J5
506-263-3423, Fax: 506-263-3425
www.gnb.ca
Johanne Jacob, Regional Director
johanne.jacob@gnb.ca

York Library Region/ Région de bibliothèques York
4 Carleton St., Fredericton NB E3B 5P4
506-453-5380, Fax: 506-457-4878
www.gnb.ca
Jill Foster, Regional Director
jill.foster@gnb.ca

Public Libraries

Atholville: **Bibliothèque publique d'Atholville/ Atholville Public Library**
275, rue Notre-Dame, Atholville NB E3N 4T1
506-789-2914, Fax: 506-789-2056
biblioda@gnb.ca
www1.gnb.ca
Nicole Richard, Gestionnaire
nicole.r.richard@gnb.ca
506-789-2914

Bas-Caraquet: **Bibliothèque publique de Bas-Caraquet/ Bas-Caraquet Public Library**
8185-2, rue St-Paul, Bas-Caraquet NB E1W 6C4
506-726-2775, Fax: 506-726-2770
bibliobc@gnb.ca
www1.gnb.ca
Mylène May Gionet, Gestionnaire (par intérim)

Bathurst: **Bibliothèque publique Smurfit-Stone/ Smurfit-Stone Public Library**
#1, 150, rue St. George, Bathurst NB E2A 1B5

506-548-0706, Fax: 506-548-0708
bibliocn@gnb.ca
www1.gnb.ca

Julie Lefrançois, Directrice
julie.lefrancois@gnb.ca

***Beresford:* Bibliothèque publique Mgr-Robichaud/ Mgr. Robichaud Public Library**
#3, 855, rue Principale, Beresford NB E8K 1T3
506-542-2704, Fax: 506-542-2714
bibliomr@gnb.ca
www1.gnb.ca

Tanya Eindiguer, Gestionnaire par intérim
tanya.eindiguer@gnb.ca

***Boiestown:* Boiestown Community - School Library**
Upper Miramichi Regional High School, #1, 3466 Rte. 625, Boiestown NB E6A 1C8
506-369-2022, Fax: 506-369-2023
boiestown.library@gnb.ca
www.gnb.ca

Gail Ross, Library Manager

***Bouctouche:* Bibliothèque publique Gérald-Leblanc/ Gérald Leblanc Public Library**
#100, 84, boul Irving, Bouctouche NB E4S 3L4
506-743-7263, Fax: 506-743-7263
bibliopb@gnb.ca
www1.gnb.ca

Michele-Ann Goguen, Responsable

***Campbellton:* Bookmobile**
113A Roseberry St., Campbellton NB E3N 2G6
506-789-6599, Fax: 506-789-7318
chaleurbm@gnb.ca
www1.gnb.ca

Darlene MacLean, Supervisor
darlene.maclean@gnb.ca
506-789-7339

***Campbellton:* Campbellton Centennial Library/ Bibliothèque du Centenaire de Campbellton**
2 Aberdeen St., Campbellton NB E3N 2J4
506-753-5253, Fax: 506-753-3803
bibliocc@gov.nb.ca
www1.gnb.ca

Jocelyn Paquette, Library Director
jocelyn.paquette@gnb.ca

***Caraquet:* Bibliothèque publique Mgr-Paquet/ Mgr. Paquet Public Library**
10A, du rue Colisée, Caraquet NB E1W 1A5
506-726-2681, Fax: 506-726-2685
bibliock@gnb.ca
www1.gnb.ca

Carole Hébert, Gestionnaire
carole.hebert@gnb.ca
506-726-2681

***Chipman:* Chipman Public Library**
8 King St., Chipman NB E4A 2H3
506-339-5852, Fax: 506-339-9804
chipman.publiclibrary@gnb.ca
www.gnb.ca

Krista Blyth, Library Manager

***Dalhousie:* Bibliothèque du centenaire de Dalhousie/ Dalhousie Centennial Library**
403, rue Adelaide, Dalhousie NB E8C 1B6
506-684-7370, Fax: 506-684-7374
bibliocd@gnb.ca
www1.gnb.ca

Sandra Babin, Gestionnaire
sandra.babin@gnb.ca

***Dieppe:* Bibliothèque publique de Dieppe/ Dieppe Public Library**
333, av Acadie, Dieppe NB E1A 1G9
506-877-7945, Fax: 506-877-7910
bibliopd@gnb.ca
www.gnb.ca

Emanuela Chiriac, Directrice

***Doaktown:* Doaktown Community - School Library**
Doaktown Consolidated High School, 430 Main St., Doaktown NB E9C 1E8
506-365-2018, Fax: 506-365-2019
dtcslib@gnb.ca
www.gnb.ca

Belva Brown, Library Manager

***Dorchester:* Dorchester Public Library**
3516 Cape Rd., Dorchester NB E4K 2X5
506-379-3032
DorchPL@gnb.ca
www1.gnb.ca

Krista Johansen, Library Manager

***Edmundston:* Mgr. W.J. Conway Public Library/ Bibliothèque publique Mgr-W.-J. Conway**
33, Irène St., Edmundston NB E3V 1B7
506-735-4713, Fax: 506-737-6848
biblioed@gnb.ca
www.gnb.ca

Robert Daigle, Library Director

***Florenceville:* Andrew & Laura McCain Public Library/ Bibliothèque publique Andrew-et-Laura-McCain**
8 McCain St., Florenceville NB E7L 3H6
506-392-5294, Fax: 506-392-8108
florenpl@gnb.ca
www.gnb.ca

Julie Craig, Library Manager

***Fredericton:* Dr. Marguerite Michaud Library/ Bibliothèque Dr Marguerite Michaud**
Centre communautaire Sainte-Anne, 715 Priestman St., Fredericton NB E3B 5W7
506-453-7100, Fax: 506-453-3958
BiblioDMM@gnb.ca
www.franco-fredericton.com/bibliomm

Françoise Caron, Librarian

***Fredericton:* Fredericton - Nashwaaksis Public - School Library**
324 Fulton Ave., Fredericton NB E3A 5J4
506-453-3241, Fax: 506-444-4129
nashwaaksis.library@gnb.ca
www.gnb.ca

***Fredericton:* Fredericton Public Library**
12 Carleton St., Fredericton NB E3B 5P4
506-460-2800, Fax: 506-460-2801
FtonPub@gnb.ca
www.gnb.ca

Brian R. Steeves, Library Director

***Fredericton:* York Bookmobile**
4 Carleton St., Fredericton NB E3B 5P4
506-453-5380, Fax: 506-457-4878
york.bookmobile@gnb.ca
www.gnb.ca

Maria Whitlock, Supervisor, Bookmobile

***Grand Falls:* Grand Falls Public Library/ Bibliothèque publique de Grand-Sault**
Town Hall, #201, 131 Pleasant St., Grand Falls NB E3Z 1G6
506-475-7781, Fax: 506-475-7783
gfplib@gnb.ca
www.gnb.ca

Émilie Lefrançois, Library Director

***Grand Manan:* Grand Manan Library**
1144 Rte. 776, Grand Manan NB E5G 4E8
506-662-7099, Fax: 506-662-7094
GrandMananLibrary@gnb.ca
www1.gnb.ca/0003/library.asp?Code=FG

Kendra Neves, Manager

***Hartland:* Dr. Walter Chestnut Public Library/ Bibliothèque publique Dr-Walter-Chestnut**
#1, 395 Main St., Hartland NB E7P 2N3
506-375-4876, Fax: 506-375-6816
hartlandl@gnb.ca
www.gnb.ca

Jean Haywood, Library Manager

***Harvey:* Harvey Community Library**
Harvey High School, 2055 Rte. 3, Harvey NB E6K 3W9
506-366-2206, Fax: 506-366-2210
harvey.library@gnb.ca
www.gnb.ca

Joanne Cole, Library Manager

***Hillsborough:* Hillsborough Public Library**
#2, 2849 Main St., Hillsborough NB E4H 2X7
506-734-3722, Fax: 506-734-3711
Hillsborough.publiclibrary@gnb.ca
www1.gnb.ca

Barbara Alcorn, Library Manager
Hillsborough.publiclibrary@gnb.ca
506-734-3722

***Kedgwick:* Kedgwick Public Library/ Bibliothèque publique de Kedgwick**
116 Notre-Dame St., #P, Kedgwick NB E8B 1H8
506-284-2757, Fax: 506-284-4557
bibliopk@gnb.ca
www.gnb.ca

Louise Lang-Levesque, Library Manager

***Lamèque:* Bibliothèque publique de Lamèque/ Lamèque Public Library**
46, rue du Pêcheur nord, Lamèque NB E8T 1J3
506-344-3262, Fax: 506-344-3263
bibliopl@gnb.ca
www1.gnb.ca

Jeanne-Mance Noël, Gestionnaire
jeanne.mance@gnb.ca
506-344-3262

***McAdam:* McAdam Public Library**
Municipal Bldg., 146 Saunders Rd., McAdam NB E6J 1L2
506-784-1403, Fax: 506-784-1402
mcadam.library@gnb.ca
www.gnb.ca

Anthony Dickinson, Library Manager

***Memramcook:* Bibliothèque publique de Memramcook/ Memramcook Public Library**
#1, 540, rue Centrale, Memramcook NB E4K 3S6
506-758-4029, Fax: 506-758-4030
bibliopm@gnb.ca
www1.gnb.ca

Jocelyne LeBlanc, Responsable
bibliopm@gnb.ca
506-758-4029

***Minto:* Minto Public Library**
Municipal Bldg., #2, 420 Pleasant Dr., Minto NB E4B 2T3
506-327-3220, Fax: 506-327-3041
minto.publiclibrary@gnb.ca
www.gnb.ca

Mary Lambropoulos, Library Manager

***Miramichi:* Miramichi - Médiathèque Père-Louis-Lamontagne**
Centre communautaire Carrefour Beausoleil, 300 Beaverbrook Rd., Miramichi NB E1V 1A1
506-627-4084, Fax: 506-627-4592
mediathequeP@gnb.ca
www.mpll.nb.ca

Geneviève Thériault, Library Director

***Miramichi:* Miramichi - Newcastle Public Library**
100 Fountain Head Lane, Miramichi NB E1V 4A1
506-623-2450, Fax: 506-623-2335
Npublib@gnb.ca
www.gnb.ca

Catherine Reid, Library Director

***Mirimichi:* Miramichi - Chatham Public Library**
24 King St., Mirimichi NB E1N 2N1
506-773-6274, Fax: 506-773-6963
chathmpl@gnb.ca
www.gnb.ca

Jennifer Wilcox, Library Director

***Moncton:* Moncton Public Library/ Bibliothèque publique de Moncton**
#101, 644 Main St., Moncton NB E1C 1E2
506-869-6000, Fax: 506-869-6040
mplib@gnb.ca
www.monctonpubliclibrary.ca

Chantale Bellemare, Library Director
mplib@gnb.ca
506-869-6000

***Nackawic:* Nackawic Public - School Library/ Bibliothèque publique-scolaire de Nackawic**
30 Landegger Dr., Nackawic NB E6G 1E9
506-572-2136, Fax: 506-575-2336
nackawic.library@gnb.ca
www.gnb.ca

Paulette Tonner, Library Manager

***Oromocto:* Oromocto Public Library**
54 Miramichi Rd., Oromocto NB E2V 1S2
506-357-3329, Fax: 506-357-5161
oromocto.publiclibrary@gnb.ca
www.gnb.ca

Muriel M. Morton, Library Director

***Perth-Andover:* Perth-Andover Public Library/ Bibliothèque publique de Perth-Andover**
642 East Riverside Dr., Perth-Andover NB E7H 1Z6
506-273-2843, Fax: 506-273-1913
paplib@gnb.ca
www.gnb.ca

Tammie Wright, Library Manager

Petitcodiac: **Petitcodiac Public Library**
#101, 6 Kay St., Petitcodiac NB E4Z 4K6
506-756-3144, Fax: 506-756-3142
Petitcodiac.PublicLibrary@gnb.ca
www1.gnb.ca/publiclibraries
Cathy MacDonald, Library Manager
Petitcodiac.PublicLibrary@gnbcca
506-756-3144

Petit-Rocher: **Bibliothèque publique de Petit-Rocher/ Petit-Rocher Public Library**
#110, 702, rue Principale, Petit-Rocher NB E8J 1V1
506-542-2744, Fax: 506-542-2745
bibliopr@gnb.ca
www1.gnb.ca
Sonia Frenette, Gestionnaire
sonia.frenette@gnb.ca

Plaster Rock: **Plaster Rock Public - School Library/ Bibliothèque publique-scolaire de Plaster Rock**
290A Main St., Plaster Rock NB E7G 2C6
506-356-6018, Fax: 506-356-6019
prplib@gnb.ca
www.gnb.ca
Carolyn Knowlton, Branch Manager

Port Elgin: **Port Elgin Public Library**
1 Station St., Port Elgin NB E4M 1C6
506-538-2118, Fax: 506-538-2126
PortEPL@gnb.ca
www1.gnb.ca
Kathleen Grigg, Library Manager
PortEPL@gnb.ca
506-538-2118

Quispamsis: **Kennebecasis Public Library**
1 Landing Ct., Quispamsis NB E2E 4R2
506-849-5314, Fax: 506-849-5318
info@kvlibrary.org
www.kvlibrary.org
Leslye McVicar, Director

Richibucto: **Bibliothèque publique de Richibucto/ Richibucto Public Library**
9376, rue Main, Richibucto NB E4W 4C9
506-523-7851, Fax: 506-523-7851
bibliori@gnb.ca
www1.gnb.ca
Chantale Robichaud, Responsable (par intérim)
bibliori@gnb.ca
506-523-7851

Richibucto: **Subheadquarters**
9239 Main St., Richibucto NB E4W 5P5
506-523-7666, Fax: 506-523-7648
imelda.collette@gnb.ca
www1.gnb.ca
Imelda Collette, Supervisor

Riverview: **Riverview Public Library**
34 Honour House Ct., Riverview NB E1B 3Y9
506-387-2108, Fax: 506-387-4970
riverview.publiclibrary@gnb.ca
www.townofriverview.ca/web?service=vpage/2947
Lynn Cormier, Librarian
lynn.cormier@gnb.ca
506-387-2108

Sackville: **Sackville Public Library**
66 Main St., Sackville NB E4L 4A7
506-364-4915, Fax: 506-364-4915
spublib@gnb.ca
www.geocities.com/sacklib/SKLIB.html
Allan J. Alward, Library Manager
spublib@gnb.ca
506-364-4915

Saint John: **Le Cormoran Library**
67 Ragged Point Rd., Saint John NB E2K 5C3
506-658-4610, Fax: 506-658-3984
BiblioLC@gnb.ca
Mireille Mercure, Director
mireille.mercure@gnb.ca

Saint John: **Saint John Free Public Library, East Branch**
#2, 545 Westmorland Pl., Saint John NB E2J 2G5
506-643-7250, Fax: 506-696-5354
EastBranch.PublicLibrary@gnb.ca
Emily King, Branch Manager

Saint John: **Saint John Free Public Library, Main Branch**
1 Market Sq., Saint John NB E2L 4Z6
506-643-7220, Fax: 506-643-7225
sjfpl@gnb.ca
www.gnb.ca/0003/regions/saint_john_main_branch.asp
Joann Hamilton-Barry, City Librarian

Saint John: **Saint John Free Public Library, West Branch**
621 Fairville Blvd., Saint John NB E2M 4X5
506-643-7260, Fax: 506-672-1752
westbranch.publiclibrary@gnb.ca
Robin Sexton-Mayes, Branch Manager

St Andrews: **Ross Memorial Library**
110 King St., St Andrews NB E5B 1Y6
506-529-5125, Fax: 506-529-5129
standrpl@gnb.ca
www.rossmemlibrary.org
Lesley Wells, Library Manager

Saint-Antoine: **Bibliothèque publique de Saint-Antoine/ St Antoine Public Library**
11, av Jeanne d'Arc, Saint-Antoine NB E4V 1H2
506-525-4028, Fax: 506-525-4199
bibliosa@gnb.ca
www1.gnb.ca
Paulette Léger, Responsable

Saint-Basile: **Haut Saint-Jean-Bookmobile**
540 Principale St., Saint-Basile NB E7C 1J5
506-263-3426, Fax: 506-263-3437
bibliobus-hsj@gnb.ca
www.gnb.ca
Andrée Boutot-Cyr, Supervisor, Bookmobile

Saint-François-de-Madawaska: **Mgr. Plourde Public Library/ Bibliothèque publique Mgr-Plourde**
15 Bellevue St., Saint-François-de-Madawaska NB E7A 1A4
506-992-6052, Fax: 506-992-6047
stfplib@gnb.ca
www.gnb.ca
Bertin Nadeau, Library Manager

Saint-Léonard: **Dr. Lorne J. Violette Public Library/ Bibliothèque publique Dr.-Lorne-J.-Violette**
180 St-Jean St., Saint-Léonard NB E7E 2B9
506-423-3025, Fax: 506-423-3026
stlplib@gnb.ca
www.gnb.ca
Nathalie Nadeau-Plourde, Library Manager

Saint-Quentin: **La Moisson Public Library/ Bibliothèque publique La Moisson de Saint-Quentin**
Municipal Bldg., 206 Canada St., Saint-Quentin NB E8A 1H1
506-235-1955, Fax: 506-235-1957
bibliolm@gnb.ca
www.bibliothequesaint-quentin.com
Hélène DuRepos Thériault, Library Manager

St Stephen: **St Croix Public Library**
11 King St., St Stephen NB E3L 2C1
506-466-7529, Fax: 506-466-7574
ststeppl@gnb.ca
www.gnb.ca/publiclibraries
Elva Hatt, Library Manager

Salisbury: **Salisbury Public Library**
3215 Main St., Salisbury NB E4J 2K7
506-372-3240, Fax: 506-372-3261
salisbury.publiclibrary@gnb.ca
www1.gnb.ca
Margaret Crosthwaite, Library Manager
salisbury.publiclibrary@gnb.ca
506-372-3240

Shediac: **Bibliothèque publique de Shediac/ Shediac Public Library**
#100, 290, rue Main, Shediac NB E4P 2E3
506-532-7014, Fax: 506-532-8400
bibliosh@gnb.ca
www1.gnb.ca
Gabrielle LeBlanc, Responsable
bibliosh@gnb.ca
506-532-7014

Shippagan: **Bibliothèque publique Laval-Goupil/ Laval-Goupil Public Library**
128, rue Mgr-Chiasson, Shippagan NB E8S 1X7
506-336-3920, Fax: 506-336-3921
bibliops@gnb.ca
www1.gnb.ca
Pauline Godin, Gestionnaire
pauline.godin@gnb.ca

Stanley: **Stanley Community Library**
#2, 28 Bridge St., Stanley NB E6B 1B2
506-367-2492, Fax: 506-367-2764
stanley.library@gnb.ca
www.gnb.ca
Kelly Dickinson, Library Manager

Sussex: **Sussex Regional Library**
46 Magnolia Ave., Sussex NB E4E 2H2
506-432-4585, Fax: 506-432-4583
sussexpl@gnb.ca

Tracadie-Sheila: **Bibliothèque publique de Tracadie-Sheila/ Tracadie-Sheila Public Library**
3620, rue Principale, Tracadie-Sheila NB E1X 1C9
506-394-4005, Fax: 506-394-4009
bibliots@gnb.ca
www1.gnb.ca
Hager Braham, Directrice
hager.braham@gnb.ca

Welshpool: **Campobello Public Library**
3 Welshpool St., Welshpool NB E5E 1G3
506-752-7082, Fax: 506-752-7083
campbopl@nb.ca
Stephanie Milbury, Library Manager
506-752-1013

Woodstock: **L.P. Fisher Public Library/ Bibliothèque publique L.-P.-Fisher**
679 Main St., Woodstock NB E7M 2E1
506-325-4777, Fax: 506-325-4811
lpfisher.library@gnb.ca
www.gnb.ca
Jonathan Tait, Library Manager

Archives

Bathurst: **Herman J. Good, VC, Canadian Legion**
575 St Peters Ave., Bathurst NB E2A 2Y5
506-546-3135, Fax: 506-546-1011
Michael White, Curator
506-546-4751

Bouctouche: **Musée de Kent**
150, ch du Couvent, Bouctouche NB E4S 3C1
506-743-5005
Pierre Cormier, Directeur

Caraquet: **Fédération des caisses populaires acadiennes**
295, boul St-Pierre ouest, Caraquet NB E1W 1A4
506-726-4000, Fax: 506-726-4001
edna.blanchard@acadie.com
Edna Blanchard, Commis aux archives
edna.blanchard@acadie.com

Dalhousie: **Restigouche Regional Museum**
115 George St., Dalhousie NB E8C 1R6
506-684-7490, Fax: 506-684-7613
gurrm@nbnet.nb.ca
Bill Clarke, Contact

Edmundston: **Centre de documentation et d'études Madawaskayennes**
165, boul Hébert, Edmundston NB E3V 2S8
506-737-5058, Fax: 506-737-5373
mtheriau@umce.ca
www.umce.ca/biblio/cdem/
Guy Lefrançois, Responsable
glefranc@umce.ca
Frank Morehouse, Diocesan Archivist
frankm@nbet.nb.ca

Fredericton: **Diocesan Archives, Anglican Diocese of Fredericton**
c/o Provincial Archives of New Brunswick, PO Box 6000, Fredericton NB E3B 5H1
506-453-2122, Fax: 506-453-3288
fredericton.anglican.org/buildings/archives.html

Fredericton: **Provincial Archives of New Brunswick/ Archives provinciales du Nouveau-Brunswick**
23 Dineen Dr., University of New Brunswick Campus, Fredericton NB E3B 5H1
506-453-2122, Fax: 506-453-3288
provincial.archives@gnb.ca
www.gnb.ca/Archives
Marion Beyea, Provincial Archivist
Marion.Beyea@gnb.ca
506-444-4021

Patricia Belier, Librarian/Head, Archives & Special Collections
belier@unb.ca
506-447-3263

Fredericton: University of New Brunswick Archives & Special Collections Dept
Harriet Irving Library, 5 Macaulay Lane, Fredericton NB E3B 5H5
506-453-4748, Fax: 506-453-4595
archives@unb.ca
www.lib.unb.ca/archives/

Grand Falls: Grand Falls Museum/ Musée de Grand-Sault
#100, 68 Madawaska Rd., Grand Falls NB E3Y 1C6
506-473-5265
Anne Rideout Côté, President, Grand Falls Historical Society

Grand Manan: Grand Manan Museum
1141 Rte. 776, Grand Manan NB E5G 4E9
506-662-3424
gmadmin@grandmananmuseum.ca
www.grandmananmuseum.ca
Ava Sturgeon, Archivist
ava@nb.sympatico.ca

Hampton: King's County Museum
27 Centennial Rd., Hampton NB E5N 6N3
506-832-6009, Fax: 506-832-6409
kingscm@nbnet.nb.ca
personal.nbnet.nb.ca/kingscm
A. Faye Pearson, Museum Director
506-832-6009

Miramichi: St Michael's Museum & Genealogical Centre
10 Howard St., Miramichi NB E1N 3A7
506-778-5152, Fax: 506-778-5156
mmuseum@nbnet.nb.ca
www.saintmichaelsmuseum.com
Theresa Flynn, Head Librarian
Judith Colwell, Archivist
ucarchiv@nb.sympatico.ca
506-536-0998

Sackville: Maritime Conference, Archives
32 York St., Sackville NB E4L 4R4
506-536-0998, Fax: 506-536-2900
ucarchiv@nb.sympatico.ca
www.marconf.ca/archives.htm
Rhianna Edwards, University Archivist
redwards@mta.ca
506-364-2563

Sackville: Mount Allison University Archives
Ralph Pickard Bell Library, 49 York St., Sackville NB E4L 1C6
506-364-2563, Fax: 506-364-2617
archives@mta.ca
www.mta.ca/library/archives/index.htm

Saint John: New Brunswick Museum
277 Douglas Ave., Saint John NB E2K 1E5
506-643-2322, Fax: 506-643-2360
archives@nmb-mnb.ca
www.nbm-mnb.ca
Felicity Osepchook, Head
506-643-2324

Saint John: Roman Catholic Diocese of Saint John
1 Bayard Dr., Saint John NB E2L 3L5
506-653-6807, Fax: 506-653-6812
archives@dioceseofsaintjohn.org
Mary McDevitt, Archivist

Saint John: Saint John Jewish Historical Museum
29 Wellington Row, Saint John NB E2L 3H4
506-633-1833, Fax: 506-642-9926
sjjhm@nbnet.nb.ca
personal.nbnet.nb.ca/sjjhm
Katherine Biggs-Craft, Head

St Andrews: Charlotte County Archives
123 Frederick St., St Andrews NB E5B 1Z1
506-529-4248, Fax: 506-529-4248
contact@ccarchives.ca
www.ccarchives.ca
Faye Marks, Genealogist

St Martins: Quaco Museum Archives
236 Main St., St Martins NB E5R 1B8
506-833-4740
archives@quaco.ca

Shippagan: Société historique Nicolas Denys
218, boul J.D. Gauthier, Shippagan NB E8S 1P6
506-336-3461, Fax: 506-336-3434
shnd@umcs.ca
Ivan Robichaud, Président

Woodstock: Carleton County Historical Society
128 Connell St., Woodstock NB E7M 1L5
506-328-9706, Fax: 506-328-2942
cchs@nb.aibn.com
www.cchs-nb.ca

Newfoundland & Labrador

Regional Systems

Newfoundland & Labrador Public Libraries - Central Division
6 Bell Pl., Gander NL A1V 2T4
709-651-5351, Fax: 709-256-2194
Patricia Parsons, Central Division Manager
patriciaparsons@nlpubliclibraries.ca

Newfoundland & Labrador Public Libraries - West Newfoundland-Labrador Division
5 Union St., Corner Brook NL A2H 5M7
709-634-7333, Fax: 709-634-7313
sandychilcote@nlpubliclibraries.ca
www.nlpubliclibraries.ca
Sanford Chilcote, Manager
sandychilcote@nlpubliclibraries.ca

Provincial Information & Library Resources Board - Eastern Division
Arts & Culture Centre, St. John's NL A1B 3A3
709-737-3508, Fax: 709-737-3571
johnwhite@nlpl.ca
www.nlpl.ca
John White, Division Manager
johnwhite@nlpubliclibraries.ca
709-737-3508

Public Libraries

L'Anse au Loup: Labrador South Public Library
L'Anse au Loup NL A0K 3L0
709-927-5542
podell@nlpl.ca
www.nlpl.ca
Pauline O'Dell, Library Technician

Arnold's Cove: Arnold's Cove Public Library
5 Highliner Dr., Arnold's Cove NL A0B 1A0
709-463-8707
gsmith@nlpl.ca
www.nlpl.ca
Gwen Smith, Librarian

Baie Verte: Baie Verte Public Library
PO Box 178, Baie Verte NL A0K 1B0
709-532-8361
ecooper@nlpl.ca
www.nlpl.ca
Eileen Cooper, Library Technician

Bay Roberts: Bay Roberts Public Library
76 Cross Rd., Bay Roberts NL A0A 1G0
709-786-9629
mclarke@nlpl.ca
www.nlpl.ca
Marilyn Clarke, Librarian

Bell Island: Bell Island Public Library
Provincial Government Bldg., 20 Bennett St., Bell Island NL A0A 4H0
709-488-2413
www.nlpl.ca
John White, Manager, Easter Division
johnwhite@nlpl.ca
709—73-7-35

Bishop's Falls: Bishop's Falls Public Library
PO Box 329, Bishop's Falls NL A0H 1C0
709-258-6244
cstanley@nlpl.ca
www.nlpl.ca
Cora Stanley, Librarian

Bonavista: Bonavista Memorial Public Library
PO Box 400, Bonavista NL A0C 1B0
709-468-2185
bwilton@nlpl.ca
www.nlpl.ca
Brenda Wilton, Librarian

Botwood: Botwood Kinsmen Public Library
240 Water St., Botwood NL A0H 1E0
709-257-2091
pcoates@nlpl.ca
www.nlpl.ca
Phyllis Coates, Library Technician

Brigus: Brigus Public Library
General Delivery, Brigus NL A0A 1K0
709-528-3156
epercey@nlpl.ca
www.nlpl.ca
Elsie Percey, Library Technician

Buchans: Buchans Public Library
Lakeside Academy, Buchans Hwy., Lakeside Academy, Buchans NL A0H 1G0
709-672-3859
dpennell@nlpl.ca
www.nlpl.ca
Dawn Pennell, Librarian

Burgeo: Burgeo Public Library
PO Box 370, Burgeo NL A0M 1A0
709-886-2673
fmacdonald@nlpl.ca
www.nlpl.ca.ca
Freda MacDonald, Library Technician

Burin: Burin Public Library
PO Box 219, Burin NL A0E 1G0
709-891-1924
ppeddle@nlpl.ca
www.nlpl.ca
Patricia Peddle, Librarian

Cape St George: Cape St George Public Library
879 Oceanview Dr., Cape St George NL A0N 1T1
709-644-2852, Fax: 709-664-2852
ecornect@nlpl.ca
www.nlpl.ca
Elizabeth Cornect, Library Technician

Carbonear: Carbonear Public Library
PO Box 928, Carbonear NL A1Y 1C4
709-596-3382
msnow@nlpl.ca
www.nlpl.ca
Maureen Snow, Librarian

Carmanville: Carmanville Public Library
Phoenix Academy, 95-97 Main St., PO Box 105, Carmanville NL A0G 1N0
709-534-2370
kbutt@nlpl.ca
www.nlpl.ca
Kay Butt, Librarian

Cartwright: Cartwright Public Library
PO Box 330, Cartwright NL A0K 1V0
709-938-7219
hclark@nlpl.ca
www.nlpl.ca
Hilda Clark, Library Technician

Catalina: Catalina (Joseph E. Clouter) Public Library
PO Box 69, Catalina NL A0C 1J0
709-469-3045
kjohnson@nlpl.ca
www.nlpl.ca
Kimberley Johnson, Librarian

Centreville: Intertown Public Library
c/o Centreville Academy, 2 Memory Lane, PO Box 100, Centreville NL A0G 4P0
709-678-2700
vrogers@nlpl.ca
www.nlpl.ca
Veronica Rogers, Librarian

Change Islands: Change Islands Public Library
c/o A.R. Scammell Academy, Main St. North, PO Box 129, Change Islands NL A0G 1R0
709-621-5566
choffe@nlpl.ca
www.nlpl.ca
Christine Hoffe, Librarian

***Channel-Port-aux-Basques:* Port aux Basques Public Library**
PO Box 790, Channel-Port-aux-Basques NL A0M 1C0
709-695-3471, Fax: 709-695-3471
bingram@nlpl.ca
www.nlpl.ca
Brenda Ingram, Library Technician

***Churchill Falls:* Churchill Falls Public Library**
PO Box 160, Churchill Falls NL A0R 1A0
709-925-3281, Fax: 709-925-3487
lbryant@nlpl.ca
www.nlpl.ca
Loretta Bryant, Library Technician

***Clarenville:* Clarenville Public Library**
98 Manitoba Dr., Clarenville NL A5A 1K7
709-466-7634
tmaclean@nlpl.ca
www.nlpl.ca
Tanya MacLean, Librarian

***Conception Bay South:* Conception Bay South Public Library**
110 Conception Bay Hwy., Conception Bay South NL A1W 3A5
709-834-4241
brideout@nlpl.ca
www.nlpl.ca
Bertha Rideout, Library Technician

***Cormack:* Cormack Public Library**
280A Veterans Dr., Cormack NL A8A 2R4
709-635-7022, Fax: 709-635-7022
mmorris@nlpl.ca
www.nlpl.ca
Marie Morris, Library Technician

***Corner Brook:* Corner Brook Public Library**
Sir Richard Squires Bldg., Mt Bernard Ave., Corner Brook NL A2H 6J8
709-634-0013, Fax: 709-634-0200
mfeaver@nlpl.ca
www.cornerbrooklibrary.org
Melissa Feaver, Librarian
mfeaver@nlpl.ca

***Cow Head:* Cow Head Public Library**
PO Box 130, Cow Head NL A0K 2A0
709-243-2467
nshears@nlpl.ca
www.nlpl.ca
Nora Shears, Library Technician

***Daniels Harbour:* Daniels Harbour Public Library**
15 Church Lane, Daniels Harbour NL A0K 2C0
709-898-2283
shumber@nlpl.ca
www.nlpl.ca
Sharon Humber, Library Technician

***Deer Lake:* Deer Lake Public Library**
4 Poplar Rd., Deer Lake NL A8A 1Z4
709-635-3671, Fax: 709-635-3671
wcramm@nlpl.ca
www.nlpl.ca
Worneta Cramm, Library Technician

***Doyles:* Codroy Valley Public Library**
General Delivery, Doyles NL A0N 1J0
709-955-3158, Fax: 709-955-2620
jgillis@nlpl.ca
www.nlpl.ca
Judy Gillis, Library Technician

***Fogo:* Fogo Island Public Library**
Fogo NL A0G 2B0
709-266-2210, Fax: 709-266-2384
mfoley@nlpl.ca
www.nlpl.ca
Marion Foley, Library Technician

***Fortune:* Fortune Public Library**
PO Box 400, Fortune NL A0E 1P0
709-832-0232
fherridge@nlpl.ca
www.nlpl.ca
Fay Herridge, Library Technician

***Fox Harbour PB:* Fox Harbour Public Library**
PO Box 74, Fox Harbour PB NL A0B 1V0
709-227-2135
cmurray@nlpl.ca
www.nlpl.ca
Catherine Murray, Library Technician

***Gambo:* Gambo Public Library**
6 Centennial Rd., Gambo NL A0G 1T0
709-674-5052
scollins@nlpl.ca
www.nlpl.ca
Sylvia Collins, Library Technician

***Gander:* Gander Public & Resource Library**
6 Bell Pl., Gander NL A1V 1X2
709-651-5356
mstuckless@nlpl.ca
www.nlpl.ca
Michelle Stuckless, Library Technician

***Garnish:* Garnish (Greta Hollett) Memorial Library**
PO Box 40, Garnish NL A0E 1T0
709-826-2371
lnolan@nlpl.ca
www.nlpl.ca
Linda Nolan, Library Technician

***Gaultois:* Gaultois Public Library**
PO Box 100, Gaultois NL A0H 1N0
709-841-3311
www.nlpl.ca

***Glenwood:* Glenwood Public Library**
26 Main St., Glenwood NL A0G 2K0
709-679-5700
kgillingham@nlpl.ca
www.nlpl.ca
Kelly Gillingham, Librarian

***Glovertown:* Alexander Bay Public Library**
Glovertown Academy, Penney's Brook Rd., Glovertown NL A0G 2L0
709-533-6688
rsweetapple@nlpl.ca
www.nlpl.ca
Rose Sweetapple, Librarian

***Grand Bank:* Grand Bank Public Library**
PO Box 1000, Grand Bank NL A0E 1W0
709-832-0310
jfox@nlpl.ca
www.nlpl.ca
Jane Fox, Library Technician

***Grand Falls-Windsor:* Harmsworth Public Library**
Gordon Pinsent Centre for the Arts, 1 Cromer Ave., Grand Falls-Windsor NL A2A 1W9
709-489-2303, Fax: 709-489-9328
mcrant@nlpl.ca
www.nlpl.ca
Madonna Crant, Librarian

***Greenspond:* Greenspond Memorial Library**
PO Box 70, Greenspond NL A0G 2N0
709-269-3434
cblackwood@nlpl.ca
www.nlpl.ca
Cindy Blackwood, Librarian

***Happy Valley-Goose Bay:* Melville Public Library**
Elizabeth Goudie Bldg., 141 Hamilton River Rd., Happy Valley-Goose Bay NL A0P 1E0
709-896-8045
hskoglund@nlpl.ca
www.nlpl.ca
Hyra Skoglund, Library Tecnician

***Harbour Breton:* Harbour Breton Public Library**
PO Box 569, Harbour Breton NL A0H 1P0
709-885-2165
vbennett@nlpl.ca
www.nlpl.ca
Vivian Bennett, Library Technician

***Harbour Grace:* Harbour Grace Public Library**
PO Box 40, Harbour Grace NL A0A 2M0
709-596-3894
dquinn@nlpl.ca
www.nlpl.ca
Doreen Quinn, Library Technician

***Hare Bay:* Hare Bay/Dover Public Library**
Jane Collins Academy, 22 Anstey's Rd., Hare Bay NL A0G 2P0
709-537-2391, Fax: 709-537-2374
rcollins@nlpl.ca
www.nlpl.ca
Robin Collins, Librarian

***Harry's Harbour:* Harry's Harbour Public Library**
PO Box 65, Harry's Harbour NL A0J 1E0
709-624-5464
eking@nlpl.ca
www.nlpl.ca
Ellen King, Librarian

***Hermitage:* Hermitage Public Library**
John Watkins Academy, PO Box 159, Hermitage NL A0H 1S0
709-883-2421
bwillmott@nlpl.ca
www.nlpl.ca
Bernice Willmott, Library Technician

***Holyrood:* Holyrood Public Library**
PO Box 263, Holyrood NL A0A 2R0
709-229-7852
dcarr@nlpl.ca
www.nlpl.ca
Dianne Carr, Library Technician

***Kings Point:* Tilley Memorial Public Library**
PO Box 100, Kings Point NL A0J 1J0
709-268-2282
pbowers@nlpl.ca
www.nlpl.ca
Patsy Bowers, Library Technician

***Labrador City:* Margaret Butt Memorial Public Library**
306 Hudson Dr., Labrador City NL A2V 1L5
709-944-2190, Fax: 709-944-3674
tandrews@nlpl.ca
www.nlpl.ca
Trudy Andrews, Library Technician

***Lark Harbour:* Lark Harbour (Blow-Me-Down) Public/School Library**
PO Box 120, Lark Harbour NL A0L 1H0
709-681-2147, Fax: 709-681-2147
lsheppard@nlpl.ca
www.nlpl.ca
Lesley Sheppard, Library Technician

***Lewisporte:* Lewisporte Public Library**
PO Box 1179, Lewisporte NL A0G 3A0
709-535-2519
jsnow@nlpl.ca
www.nlpl.ca
Judy Snow, Librarian

***Lourdes:* Lourdes Public/School Library**
82 Main St., Lourdes NL A0N 1R0
709-642-5388
pwoodrow@nlpl.ca
www.nlpl.ca
Patricia Woodrow, Library Technician

***Lumsden:* Lumsden Public Library**
Lumsden School Complex, PO Box 119, Lumsden NL A0G 3E0
709-530-2617
kstagg@nlpl.ca
www.nlpl.ca
Kay Stagg, Librarian

***Marystown:* Marystown Public Library**
PO Box 1270, Marystown NL A0E 2M0
709-279-1507
pmayo@nlpl.ca
www.nlpl.ca
Patricia Mayo, Library Technician

***Mount Pearl:* Mount Pearl (Ross King) Memorial Public Library**
65 Olympic Dr., Mount Pearl NL A1N 5H6
709-368-3603
ygillard@nlpl.ca
www.nlpl.ca
Yvonne Gillard, Library Technician

***Musgrave Harbour:* John B. Wheeler Public Library**
PO Box 130, Musgrave Harbour NL A0G 3J0
709-655-2730
eabbott@nlpl.ca
www.nlpl.ca
Eunice Abbott, Library Technician

***Norris Arm:* Norris Arm Public Library**
65 Norris Ave., PO Box 100, Norris Arm NL A0G 3M0
709-653-2531
lrowsell@nlpl.ca
www.nlpl.ca
Leona Rowsell, Librarian

***Norris Point:* Norris Point Public Library**
PO Box 129, Norris Point NL A0K 3V0
709-458-3368
jsamms@nlpl.ca
www.nlpl.ca
Judy Samms, Library Technician

***North West River:* North West River Library & Info Centre**
PO Box 410, North West River NL A0P 1M0
709-497-8705, Fax: 709-497-8705
nwrvollibrary@hotmail.com
www.nlpubliclibraries.ca
Isobel Watts, Volunteer Coordinator
isowatts@labcoll.goose.nf.ca
709-497-8217

***Old Perlican:* Old Perlican Public Library**
PO Box 265, Old Perlican NL A0A 3G0
709-587-2028
etuttle@nlpl.ca
www.nlpl.ca
Elizabeth Tuttle, Library Technician

***Pasadena:* Pasadena Public Library**
16 - 10th Ave., Pasadena NL A0L 1K0
709-686-2792
amenchion@nlpl.ca
www.nlpl.ca
Angela Menchion, Library Technician

***Placentia:* Placentia Public Library**
PO Box 119, Placentia NL A0B 2Y0
709-227-3621
dbowering@nlpl.ca
www.nlpl.ca
Doris Bowring, Library Technician

***Point Leamington:* Point Leamington Public Library**
PO Box 78, Point Leamington NL A0H 1Z0
709-484-3541
bwarford@nlpl.ca
www.nlpl.ca
Beverley Warford, Librarian

***Port au Port:* Port au Port Public Library**
PO Box 220, Port au Port NL A0N 1T0
709-648-2472, Fax: 709-648-9512
jclarke@nlpl.ca
www.nlpl.ca
Janice Clarke, Library Technician

***Port Saunders:* Port Saunders (Ingornachoix) Public Library**
PO Box 59, Port Saunders NL A0K 4H0
709-861-3690
ebiggin@nlpl.ca
www.nlpl.ca
Evelyn Biggin, Library Technician

***Pouch Cove:* Pouch Cove Public Library**
PO Box 40, Pouch Cove NL A0A 3L0
709-335-2652
lbragg@nlpl.ca
www.nlpl.ca
Laura Bragg, Library Technician

***Pouch Cove:* Resource Links**
PO Box 9, Pouch Cove NL A0A 3L0
709-335-2394, Fax: 709-335-2978
resourcelinks@nfld.com
www.resourcelinks.ca
Victoria Pennell, Editor

***Ramea:* Ramea Public Library**
PO Box 59, Ramea NL A0N 2J0
709-625-2344
flushman@nlpl.ca
www.nlpl.ca
Frances Lushman, Library Technician

***Robert's Arm:* Robert's Arm Public Library**
PO Box 119, Robert's Arm NL A0J 1R0
709-652-3100
hsuley@nlpl.ca
www.nlpl.ca
Helen Suley, Librarian

***Rocky Harbour:* Rocky Harbour Public Library**
PO Box 40, Rocky Harbour NL A0K 4N0
709-458-2900
jsamms@nlpl.ca
www.nlpl.ca
Judy Samms, Library Technician

***St Alban's:* St Alban's Public Library**
PO Box 70, St Alban's NL A0H 2E0
709-538-3034
www.nlpl.ca
Kerri-Ann Snook, Librarian

***St Anthony:* St Anthony Public Library**
PO Box 129, St Anthony NL A0K 4S0
709-454-3025
jelliott@nlpl.ca
www.nlpl.ca
Jocelyn Elliott, Library Technician

***St Bride's:* Cape Shore Public Library**
General Delivery, St Bride's NL A0B 2Z0
709-337-2360
jnash@nlpl.ca
www.nlpl.ca
Jacqueline Nash, Library Technician

***St Fintans:* St Fintan's (Bay St George South) Public/School Library**
PO Box 70, St Fintans NL A0N 1Y0
709-645-2186, Fax: 709-645-2780
amacinnis@nlpl.ca
www.nlpl.ca
Anita MacInnis, Library Technician

***St George's:* St George's Public Library**
PO Box 249, St George's NL A0N 1Z0
709-647-3808, Fax: 709-647-3108
jdowney@nlpl.ca
www.nlpl.ca
Joan Downey, Library Technician

***St. John's:* ANLA Bulletin/ Association of Newfoundland & Labrador Archives**
RPO Churchill Sq., PO Box 23155, St. John's NL A1B 4J9
709-726-2867, Fax: 709-729-0578
anla@nf.sympatico.ca
www.anla.nf.ca
Jessie Chisholm, Editor

***St. John's:* APLA Bulletin**
Queen Elizabeth II Library, Memorial University, St. John's NL A1B 3Y1
709-737-2080, Fax: 709-737-2153
igibson@mun.ca
www.apla.ca/bulletin
Ian Gibson, Editor

***St. John's:* St John's Public Libraries**
Arts & Culture Centre, 125 Allendale Rd., St. John's NL A1B 3A3
709-737-2133, Fax: 709-737-2660
reference@nlpl.ca
www.nlpl.ca
Michelle Walters, Manager
michellewalters@nlpubliclibraries.ca
709-737-3946

***St Lawrence:* St Lawrence Public Library**
PO Box 366, St Lawrence NL A0E 2V0
709-873-2650
vlockyer@nlpl.ca
www.nlpl.ca
Vicki Etechegary-Lockyer, Library Technician

***St Lunaire-Griquet:* St Lunaire-Griquet Public Library**
General Delivery, St Lunaire-Griquet NL A0K 2X0
709-623-2904
mbussey@nlpl.ca
www.nlpl.ca
Mae Bussey, Library Technician

***La Scie:* La Scie Public Library**
PO Box 285, La Scie NL A0K 3M0
709-675-2004
ktilley@nlpl.ca
www.nlpl.ca
Karen Tilley, Library Technician

***Seal Cove WB:* Seal Cove Public Library**
PO Box 70, Seal Cove WB NL A0K 5E0
709-531-2505
kpinksen@nlpl.ca
www.nlpl.ca
Karen Pinksen, Librarian

***Sop's Arm:* Sop's Arm Public Library**
Main St., General Delivery, Sop's Arm NL A0K 5K0
709-482-2225
dwhite@nlpl.ca
www.nlpl.ca
Diane White, Library Technician

***Southern Harbour:* Southern Harbour Public Library**
PO Box 167, Southern Harbour NL A0B 3H0
709-463-8814
bwhiffen@nlpl.ca
www.nlpl.ca
Bride Whiffen, Library Technician

***Springdale:* Springdale Public Library**
Indian River High School, PO Box 1414, Springdale NL A0J 1T0
709-673-4169
jhamilton@nlpl.ca
www.nlpl.ca
Judy Hamilton, Librarian

***Stephenville:* Newfoundland & Labrador Public Libraries**
48 St George's Ave., Stephenville NL A2N 1K9
709-643-0900, Fax: 709-643-0925
illstaff@nlpl.ca
www.nlpl.ca
Shawn Tetford, Executive Director
stetford@nlpl.ca
709-643-0902

***Stephenville:* Stephenville (Kindale) Public Library**
45 Carolina Ave., Stephenville NL A2N 3P8
709-643-4262, Fax: 709-643-5781
mwhite@nlpl.ca
www.nlpl.ca
Monica White, Library Technician

***Stephenville Crossing:* Stephenville Crossing Public Library**
PO Box 610, Stephenville Crossing NL A0N 2C0
709-646-2173, Fax: 709-646-2065
jdowney@nlpl.ca
www.nlpl.ca
Joan Downey, Library Technician

***Summerford:* Summerford Public Library**
1 Main St., Summerford NL A0G 4E0
709-629-3244
mboyd@nlpl.ca
www.nlpl.ca
Mavis Boyd, Librarian

***Torbay:* Torbay Public Library**
1288A Torbay Rd., Torbay NL A1K 1B2
709-437-6571
mdeibel@nlpl.ca
www.nlpl.ca
Marcia Deibel, Library Technician

***Trepassey:* Trepassey Public Library**
PO Box 183, Trepassey NL A0A 4B0
709-438-2224
pmccormack@nlpl.ca
www.nlpl.ca
Patricia McCormack, Library Technician

***Twillingate:* Twillingate Public Library**
PO Box 338, Twillingate NL A0G 4M0
709-884-2353
dhayward@nlpl.ca
www.nlpl.ca
Deborah Hayward, Librarian

***Victoria:* Victoria Memorial Public Library**
PO Box 190, Victoria NL A0A 4G0
709-596-3682
scolbourne@nlpl.ca
www.nlpl.ca
Shona Colbourne, Library Technician

***Wabush:* Wabush Public Library**
PO Box 179, Wabush NL A0R 1B0
709-282-3479, Fax: 709-282-3479
pstrickland@nlpl.ca
www.nlpl.ca
Paulette Strickland, Library Technician

***Wesleyville:* Wesleyville Public Library**
Lester Pearson High School, PO Box 70, Wesleyville NL A0G 4R0
709-536-5777
bhounsell@nlpl.ca
www.nlpl.ca
Beverley Hounsell, Librarian

Whitbourne: **Whitbourne Public Library**
PO Box 400, Whitbourne NL A0B 3K0
709-759-2461
gsomerton@nlpl.ca
www.nlpl.ca
Gloria Somerton, Library Technician

Winterton: **Winterton Public Library**
PO Box 119, Winterton NL A0B 3M0
709-583-2119
bpitcher@nlpl.ca
www.nlpl.ca
Betty Pitcher, Library Technician

Woody Point: **Woody Point (Edgar L. Roberts Memorial) Library**
PO Box 179, Woody Point NL A0K 1P0
709-453-2556
mharris@nlpl.ca
www.nlpl.ca
Michelle Harris, Library Technician

Archives

Bonavista: **Bonavista Historical Society**
102 Church St., Bonavista NL A0C 1B0
709-468-2880
www.anla.nf.ca/bvista.htm
Gordon Bradley, President

Botwood: **Botwood Heritage Society Archive**
PO Box 490, Botwood NL A0H 1E0
709-257-2071, Fax: 709-257-3330
Everett Elliott, Contact
John Edgar, Archivist
jedgar@nf.sympatico.ca
709-639-8712

Corner Brook: **Diocesan Synod of Western Newfoundland, Archives**
25 Main St., Corner Brook NL A2H 1C2
709-639-8712, Fax: 709-639-1636
dsown@nf.aibn.com
westernnewfoundland.anglican.org/

Happy Valley-Goose Bay: **Them Days Labrador Archives**
3 Courte Manche St., Happy Valley-Goose Bay NL A0P 1E0
709-896-8531, Fax: 709-896-4970
them.days@nf.aibn.com
www.themdays.com
Aimee Chaulk, Editor

Harbour Grace: **Conception Bay Museum**
PO Box 298, Harbour Grace NL A0A 2M0
709-596-5465, Fax: 709-596-5465
pfahey@conceptionbaymuseum.nf.ca
www.baccalieutourism.com
Peggy Fahey, Curator

Musgrave Harbour: **Fisherman's Museum**
4 Marine Dr., PO Box 159, Musgrave Harbour NL A0G 3J0
709-655-2162
Sophie Mercer, Town Clerk
709-655-2119

St. John's: **City of St John's Archives**
495 Water St., 3rd Fl., St. John's NL A1C 5M2
709-576-8167, Fax: 709-576-8254
archives@stjohns.ca
www.stjohns.ca/cityservices/archives/index.jsp
Helen Miller, Archivist

St. John's: **Congregation of Sisters of Mercy**
Waterford Bridge Rd., St. John's NL A1C 5P5
709-726-7320, Fax: 709-726-4414
mmpower@sistersofmercynf.org
Marie Michael Power, Archivist
Julia Mathison, Diocesan Archivist

St. John's: **Diocese of Eastern Newfoundland & Labrador, Archives**
19 King's Bridge Rd., St. John's NL A1C 3K4
709-576-6697, Fax: 709-576-7122
archives@anglicanenl.nf.net
anglican.nfol.ca
Martin Lovelace, Director
martinl@mun.ca
709-737-8601

St. John's: **Folklore & Language Archive**
Memorial University, St. John's NL A1B 3X8
709-737-8401, Fax: 709-737-4718
munfla@mun.ca
www.mun.ca/folklore
Heather Wareham, Archivist
mha@mun.ca

St. John's: **Maritime History Archive**
Henrietta Harvey Bldg., Memorial University, St. John's NL A1C 5S7
709-737-8428, Fax: 709-737-3123
mha@mun.ca
www.mun.ca/mha/
Alison Piercey, Conference Archivist

St. John's: **Newfoundland & Labrador Conference, Archives**
320 Elizabeth Ave., St. John's NL A1B 1T9
709-754-0386, Fax: 709-754-8336
unitedchurch@nfld.net
www.newlabconf.com/

St. John's: **Newfoundland Historical Society/ Archival & Library Collection**
Colonial Bldg., Military Rd., PO Box 23154,, Churchill Sq., St. John's NL A1B 4J9
709-722-3191, Fax: 709-729-0578
nhs@nf.aibn.com
www.infonet.st-johns.nf.ca/providers/nfldhist
Allan Byrne, Office Manager

St. John's: **Presentation Congregation Archives**
Cathedral Sq., Presentation Convent, PO Box 758, St. John's NL A1C 5L4
709-753-7291, Fax: 709-753-1578
prescong@nf.aibn.com
Mary Perpetua Kennedy, Archivist
perpetuakennedy@hotmail.com

St. John's: **Provincial Archives of Newfoundland & Labrador**
9 Bonaventure Ave., St. John's NL A1C 5P9
709-757-8030, Fax: 709-757-8031
archives@therooms.ca
www.therooms.ca/archives/
Greg Walsh, Director/Provincial Archivist
709-757-8032

St. John's: **Queen's College**
#3000, 210 Prince Philip Dr., St. John's NL A1B 3R6
709-753-0116, Fax: 709-753-1214, 877-753-0116
queens@mun.ca
www.mun.ca/queens
John Mellis, Contact

St. John's: **Roman Catholic Archdiocese of St John's**
200 Military Rd., St. John's NL A1C 5N5
709-726-3660, Fax: 709-739-6458
ldohey@nf.aibn.com
www.stjohnsarchdiocese.nf.ca/archives.asp
Larry Dohey, Archivist
ldohey@nf.aibn.com

St. John's: **Sport Archives of Newfoundland and Labrador**
The Rooms Provincial Archives, Rm. 18 Colonial Bldg., Military Rd., St. John's NL A1B 4J6
709-729-0591
sanl@mail.gov.nl.ca
www.tcr.gov.nl.ca/panl/sanl/
Linda Murphy, Volunteer Archivist

Trinity TB: **Trinity Historical Society Archives**
Lester-Garland House, West St., 3rd Fl., PO Box 8, Trinity TB NL A0C 2S0
709-464-3599, Fax: 709-464-3599
info@trinityhistoricalsociety.com
www.trinityhistoricalsociety.com
Clarence Dewling, Archivist

Wesleyville: **Bonavista North Regional Museum & Gallery**
PO Box 257, Wesleyville NL A0G 4R0
709-536-2110, Fax: 709-536-3039
museum@nf.aibn.com
Duke Kelloway, Chair

Northwest Territories

Regional Systems

NWT Public Library Services
75 Woodland Dr., Hay River NT X0E 1G1
867-874-6531, Fax: 867-874-3321
kevin_lafferty@gov.nt.ca
www.nwtpls.gov.nt.ca
Alison Hopkins, Territorial Librarian
alison_hopkins@gov.nt.ca
867-874-3531

Public Libraries

Fort Simpson: **John Tsetso Memorial Library**
PO Box 258, Fort Simpson NT X0E 0N0
867-695-3276, Fax: 867-695-3276
si_library@gov.nt.ca
www.ece.gov.nt.ca/Public_Library_Services/CommunityLibraries.h
Lorraine Ocko, Librarian
867—69-5-32

Fort Smith: **Mary Kaeser Library**
170 McDougal Rd., Fort Smith NT X0E 0P0
867-872-2296, Fax: 867-872-5303
mkl@gov.nt.ca
Jeri Miltenberger, Local Librarian
jeri_miltenberger@gov.nt.ca

Hay River: **Northwest Territories Centennial Library**
75 Woodland Dr., Hay River NT X0E 1G1
867-874-6486, Fax: 867-874-3834
www.nwtpls.gov.nt.ca
Christine Gyapay, Local Librarian
christine_gyapay@gov.nt.ca

Inuvik: **Inuvik Centennial Library**
100 MacKenzie Rd., Inuvik NT X0E 0T0
867-777-8620, Fax: 867-777-8621
IK_Library@gov.nt.ca
www.inuvik.ca/townhall/library.html
Beverly Garven, Head Librarian

Norman Wells: **Norman Wells Community Library**
PO Box 97, Norman Wells NT X0E 0V0
867-587-2956, Fax: 867-587-2193
normanwells_library@gov.nt.ca
Lori Shapansky, Local Librarian

Tulita: **Tulita Community Library**
General Delivery, Tulita NT X0E 0K0
867-588-4471, Fax: 867-588-4908
Darlene Etchinelle, Librarian

Yellowknife: **Yellowknife Public Library**
Centre Square Mall, 5022 - 49th St., 2nd Fl., Yellowknife NT X1A 3R8
867-920-5642, Fax: 867-920-5671
library@yellowknife.ca
www.yellowknife.ca
Deborah Bruser, Library Manager
dbruser@yellowknife.ca
867-669-3401

Archives

Fort Smith: **Northern Life Museum National Exhibition Centre**
110 King St., Fort Smith NT X0E 0P0
867-872-2859, Fax: 867-872-5808
nlm@auroranet.nt.ca
Kevin Brunt, Curator of Collections
curator@auroranet.net.ca

Yellowknife: **Northwest Territories Dept. of Education, Culture & Employment**
Prince of Wales Northern Heritage Centre, PO Box, 1320, Yellowknife NT X1A 2L9
867-873-7698, Fax: 867-873-0660
nwtarchives@ece.learnnet.nt.ca
www.pwnhc.ca
D. Richard Valpy, Territorial Archivist
richard_valpy@ece.learnnet.nt.ca
867-873-7657

Nova Scotia

Regional Systems

Annapolis Valley Regional Library
26 Bay Rd., Bridgetown NS B0S 1C0
902-665-2995, Fax: 902-665-4899, 866-922-0229
www.valleylibrary.ca
Shirley Pineo, Chair

Cape Breton Regional Library
50 Falmouth St., Sydney NS B1P 6X9
402-562-3279, Fax: 902-564-0765
inssc@nssc.library.ns.ca
www.cbrl.ca
Rod MacArthur, Chair

Colchester-East Hants Public Library
754 Prince St., Truro NS B2N 1G9
902-895-0235, Fax: 902-895-7149, 888-632-9088
anstc@nstc.library.ns.ca
cehlibrary.ednet.ns.ca
Janet D. Pelley, Library Director
jpelley@nstc.library.ns.ca

Eastern Counties Regional Library
390 Murray St., Mulgrave NS B0E 2G0
902-747-2597, Fax: 902-747-2500
info@nsme.library.ns.ca
www.ecrl.library.ns.ca
Shirley McNamara, Chair

Halifax Public Libraries
60 Alderney Dr., Dartmouth NS B2Y 4P8
902-490-5744, Fax: 902-490-5889
www.halifaxpubliclibraries.ca
Leo McKenna, Chair

Pictou-Antigonish Regional Library
PO Box 276, New Glasgow NS B2H 5E3
902-755-6031, Fax: 902-755-6775, 866-779-7761
info@parl.ns.ca
www.parl.ns.ca
Eric Stackhouse, Chief Librarian, Systems Librarian, & Board Secretary

Western Counties Regional Library
405 Main St., Yarmouth NS B5A 1G3
902-742-2486, Fax: 902-742-6920
insy@nsy.library.ns.ca (Interlibrary loans)
www.westerncounties.ca
Gary Archibald, Chair
ansy@nsy.library.ns.ca

Public Libraries

***Amherst:* Cumberland Regional Library**
PO Box 220, Amherst NS B4H 3Z2
902-667-2135, Fax: 902-667-1360
crl@nsamc.library.ns.ca
www.crl.library.ns.ca
Robert Angel, Chair

***Halifax:* Épilogue**
c/o Faculty of Management, Dalhousie University, Halifax NS B3H 3J5
902-494-3656, Fax: 902-494-2451
macdonal@is.dal.ca
sim.management.dal.ca/Research_and_Publications/Publications
Bertrum H. MacDonald, Editor

***Halifax:* Occasional Papers Series**
c/o Faculty of Management, Dalhousie University, Halifax NS B3H 3J5
902-494-3656, Fax: 902-494-2451
sim@dal.ca
www.sim.management.dal.ca/Research_and_Publications/Descripti
Fiona Black, Editor
fiona.black@dal.ca

***Halifax:* Y-A Hotline**
c/o Faculty of Management, Dalhousie University, Halifax NS B3H 3J5
902-494-3656, Fax: 902-494-2451
howardv@dal.ca
www.mgmt.dal.ca/slis/Publications/YAHotline.html
Vivian Howard, Editor

***Hebbville:* South Shore Regional Library**
Bldg. 15442, Hwy. #3, PO Box 34, Hebbville NS B4V 2W3
902-543-2548, Fax: 902-543-8191, 877-455-2548
info@southshorepubliclibraries.ca
www.southshorepubliclibraries.ca
Cheryl Stenström, Chief Librarian

Archives

***Amherst:* Cumberland County Museum**
150 Church St., Amherst NS B4H 3C4
902-667-2561, Fax: 902-667-0996
ccmuseum@ns.aliantzinc.ca
www.cumberlandcountymuseum.com
Shirley Nickerson, Manager/Curator

***Annapolis Royal:* Historic Restoration Society of Annapolis County**
136 St. George St., Annapolis Royal NS B0S 1A0
902-532-7754, Fax: 902-532-0700
Ryan Scranton, Executive Director
scrantrg@gov.ns.ca

***Antigonish:* Antigonish Heritage Museum**
20 East Main St., Antigonish NS B2G 2E9
902-863-6160
antheritage@parl.ns.ca
www.parl.ns.ca/aheritage
Jocelyn Gillis, Manager
Kathleen MacKenzie, Archivist
kmackenz@stfx.ca

***Antigonish:* St Francis-Xavier University Archives**
Angus L. MacDonald Library, PO Box 5000, Antigonish NS B2G 2W5
902-867-2201, Fax: 902-867-5153
archives@stfx.ca
libmain.stfx.ca/newlib/collections/archives

***Baddeck:* Alexander Graham Bell National Historic Site/ Lieu Historique National Alexander Graham Bell**
559 Chebucto St., Baddeck NS B0E 1B0
902-295-2069, Fax: 902-295-3496
aynsley.macfarlane@pc.gc.ca
bell.uccb.ns.ca
Aynsley MacFarlane, Site Manager

***Barrington:* Cape Sable Historical Society Centre**
2402 Hwy. 3, Barrington NS B0W 1E0
902-637-2185, Fax: 902-637-2185
Brenda Maxwell, Archives Manager
maxwelbm@gov.ns.ca

***Barss Corners:* Parkdale-Maplewood Community Museum**
3005 Barss Corner Rd., Barss Corners NS B0R 1A0
902-644-2893, Fax: 902-644-3422
p-mcm@hotmail.com
parkdale.ednet.ns.ca
Barbara Gail Wentzell, Curator
p-mcm@hotmail.com

***Bridgetown:* Bridgetown & Area Historical Society**
12 Queen St., PO Box 645, Bridgetown NS B0S 1C0
902-665-4530
fm.lourie@ns.sympatico.ca
Frances Nixon, Museum Administrator

***Bridgewater:* DesBrisay Museum**
130 Jubilee Rd., Bridgewater NS B4V 3X9
902-543-4033, Fax: 902-543-4713
museum@bridgewater.ca
www.desbrisaymuseum.ca
Linda Bedford, Curator
lbedford@bridgewater.ca

***Canso:* Canso Historical Society**
c/o Whitman House Museum, 1297 Union St., Canso NS B0H 1H0
902-366-2170, Fax: 902-366-3093
cansotouristbureau@ns.sympatico.ca

***Centreville:* Archelaus Smith Museum**
915 Hwy. 330, Centreville NS B0W 1P0
902-745-3361
westhome@eastlink.ca
Bryant Newell, Secretary/Treasurer

***Church Point:* St Mary's Museum/ Le Musée Sainte Marie**
PO Box 28, RR#1, Church Point NS B0W 1M0
902-769-2832, Fax: 902-769-0048
stmarysmuseum@hotmail.com
www.geocities.com/st_marys_church2001/st.html
Blanche Forrest, Secretary, Museum Committee

***Dartmouth:* Black Cultural Centre for Nova Scotia**
1149 Main St., Dartmouth NS B2Z 1A8
902-434-6223, Fax: 902-434-2306, 800-465-0767
mail@bccns.com
www.bccns.com
Henry Bishop, Chief Curator

***Dartmouth:* Cole Harbour Rural Heritage Society**
471 Poplar Dr., Dartmouth NS B2W 4L2
905-434-0222
farmmuseum@ns.sympatico.ca
www3.ns.sympatico.ca/farmmuseum

***Dartmouth:* Dartmouth Heritage Museum**
Evergreen House, 26 Newcastle St., Dartmouth NS B2Y 3M5
902-464-2300, Fax: 902-464-8210
dhmuseum@ednet.ns.ca
www.dartmouthheritagemuseum.ns.ca
Anita Price, Curator

***Halifax:* Canadian Broadcasting Corporation (Halifax)/ Société Radio-Canada (Halifax)**
PO Box 3000, Halifax NS B3J 3E9
902-420-4160, Fax: 902-420-4281
doug.kirby@cbc.ca
www.novascotia.cbc.ca
Doug Kirby, Media Library Coordinator
doug_kirby@cbc.ca
902-420-4160
Lorraine Slopek, Diocesan Archivist
archives@nspeidiocese.ca
905-420-0717 ext. 231

***Halifax:* Diocese of Nova Scotia & Prince Edward Island, Archives**
5732 College St., Halifax NS B3H 1X3
902-420-0717, Fax: 902-425-0717
archives@nspeidiocese.ca
www.nspeidiocese.ca

***Halifax:* Nova Scotia Archives & Records Management**
6016 University Ave., Halifax NS B3H 1W4
902-424-6060, Fax: 902-424-0628
nsarm@gov.ns.ca
www.gov.ns.ca/nsarm
W. Brian Speirs, Provincial Archivist

***Halifax:* Nova Scotia Sport Hall of Fame**
#446, 1800 Argyle St., Halifax NS B3J 3N8
902-421-1266, Fax: 902-425-1148
sporthalloffame@eastlink.ca
www.novascotiasporthalloffame.com
Bill Robinson, Executive Director
billr@eastlink.ca

***Halifax:* Pier 21**
1055 Marginal Rd., Halifax NS B3H 4P6
902-425-7770, Fax: 902-423-4045
library@pier21.ca
www.pier21.ca
Carrie-Ann Smith, Research Librarian
Madeleine Lefebvre, University Librarian
madeleine.lefebvre@smu.ca

***Halifax:* St Mary's University Archives**
5946 Inglis St., Halifax NS B3H 3C3
902-420-5508, Fax: 902-420-5561
www.smu.ca/library

***Halifax:* Sisters of Charity of St Vincent de Paul (Halifax)**
Mount St. Vincent Motherhouse, 150 Bedford Hwy., Halifax NS B3M 4K9
902-457-3500, Fax: 902-457-3506
archives@schalifax.ca
www.schalifax.ca/sub/06roots/03archive.html
Marie Gillen, Director of Heritage

***Halifax:* The Shambhala Archives**
1084 Tower Rd., Halifax NS B3H 2Y5
902-420-1118, Fax: 902-423-2750
archives@shambhala.org
www.shambhala.org/archives
Michael Moosberger, University Archivist & Manager, Archives & Special Collections
Michael.Moosberger@dal.ca
902-494-5176

***Halifax:* University Archives & Special Collections**
c/o Killam Memorial Library, 6225 University Ave., Halifax NS B3H 4H8
902-494-3615, Fax: 902-494-2062
archives@dal.ca
www.library.dal.ca/archives/index.htm

***Liverpool:* The Thomas Raddall Research Centre**
109 Main St., Liverpool NS B0T 1K0
902-354-4058, Fax: 902-354-2050
rafusela@gov.ns.ca
queensmuseum.netfirms.com/archives.html

Linda Rafuse, Director
Judith Romard, Librarian

***Louisbourg:* Fortress of Louisbourg Library**
259 Park Service Rd., Louisbourg NS B1C 2L2
902-733-3534, Fax: 902-733-2423
LHS.library@pc.gc.ca
fortress.uccb.ns.ca

***Middleton:* Macdonald Museum**
21 School St., Middleton NS B0S 1P0
902-825-6116, Fax: 902-825-0531
macdonald.museum@ns.sympatico.ca
www.macdonaldmuseum.ca
Sarah Carswell, Librarian

***Parrsboro:* Parrsborough Shore Historical Society**
PO Box 98, Parrsboro NS B0M 1S0
902-254-2899
Susan Clarke, Manager
ottawa.house@ns.sympatico.ca

***Pictou:* Hector Exhibit Centre**
86 Haliburton Rd., Pictou NS B0K 1H0
902-485-4563, Fax: 902-485-5213
pcghs@gov.ns.ca
www.rootsweb.com/~nspcghs/
Marlene Chisholm, Researcher
marlene.chisholm@ns.sympatico.ca

***Port Hastings:* Port Hastings Historical Museum & Archives**
9 Church St., Port Hastings NS B9A 1N5
902-625-1295
gutofcanso@ns.sympatico.ca
Beryl MacDonald-MacLeod, Curator

***Shearwater:* Shearwater Aviation Museum**
12 Wing Shearwater, PO Box 5000, Stn Main, Shearwater NS B0J 3A0
902-720-2165, Fax: 902-720-2037
awmuseum@ns.sympatio.ca
www.shearwateraviationmuseum.ns.ca
Christine Dunphy, Librarian/Archivist
awmuseum@ns.sympatico.ca
902-720-2165

***Shelburne:* Shelburne County Museum**
20 Dock St., Shelburne NS B0T 1W0
902-875-3219, Fax: 902-875-4141
shelburne.museum@ns.sympatico.ca
www.historicshelburne.com
Finn Bower, Curator

***Sydney:* Beaton Institute**
1250 Grand Lake Rd., Sydney NS B1M 1A2
902-563-1329, Fax: 902-562-8899
beaton@cbu.ca
beaton.capebretonu.ca

***Truro:* Colchester Historical Museum**
29 Young St., Truro NS B2N 3W3
902-895-6284, Fax: 902-895-9530
colchesterarchives@ns.aliantzinc.ca
www.genealogynet.com/Colchester/
Nan D. Harvey, Archivist

***Tusket:* Argyle Township Court House Archives**
8162 Hwy. 3, PO Box 101, Tusket NS B0W 3M0
902-648-2493, Fax: 902-648-2537
atcha@ns.alianzinc.ca
www.argylecourthouse.com
Peter Crowell, Municipal Records Manager & Archivist
atcha@ns.aliantzinc.ca

***Windsor:* West Hants Historical Society**
281 King St., Windsor NS B0N 2T0
902-798-4706, Fax: 902-798-8535
whhs@glinx.com
www.glinx.com/users/whhs
Lilla Siderius, Head
Patricia Townsend, University Archivist
pat.townsend@acadiau.ca
902-585-1549

***Wolfville:* Esther Clark Wright Archives (Atlantic Baptist Archives)**
PO Box 4, Wolfville NS B4P 2R6
902-585-1011, Fax: 902-585-1748
archives@acadiau.ca
library.acadiau.ca/archives/

***Yarmouth:* Yarmouth County Museum Research Library & Archives**
22 Collins St., Yarmouth NS B5A 3C8
902-742-5539, Fax: 902-749-1120
ycarchives@eastlink.ca
yarmouthcountymuseum.ednet.ns.ca
Jamie Serran, Archivist

Nunavut

Regional Systems

Nunavut Public Library Services
PO Box 270, Baker Lake NU X0C 0A0
867-793-3327, Fax: 867-793-3332
Robin Brown, Acting Manager, Library Policy
rbrown2@gov.nu.ca
867-793-3327

Public Libraries

***Arviat:* Donald Suluk Library**
PO Bag 4000, Arviat NU X0C 0E0
867-857-2579, Fax: 867-857-4048
dsigurdson@publiclibraries.nu.ca
Diane Sigurdson, Local Librarian

***Baker Lake:* Thomas Tapatai Library**
PO Box 150, Baker Lake NU X0C 0A0
867-793-4657, Fax: 867-793-4659
ttlbaker@yahoo.ca
Sally Aaruaq, Local Librarian

***Cambridge Bay:* May Hakongak Community Library**
PO Box 1106, Cambridge Bay NU X0B 0C0
867-983-2163, Fax: 867-983-2614
mhcbl@hotmail.com
Sandra Dionne, Local Librarian

***Clyde River:* Clyde River Community Library**
c/o Ilisaqsivik Family Resource Centre, Ilisaqsivik Society, PO Box 150, Clyde River NU X0A 0E0
867-924-6565, Fax: 867-924-6570
www.ilisaqsivik.ca
Raygee Atsiqtaq, Local Librarian
ratsiqtaq@publiclibraries.nu.ca

***Igloolik:* Igloolik Amitturmiut Library**
PO Box 30, Igloolik NU X0A 0L0
867-934-8812, Fax: 867-934-8779
nubnp@gov.nu.ca
Nancy Kadlutsika, Local Librarian
nkadlutsiak@publiclibraries.nu.ca

***Iqaluit:* Iqaluit Centennial Library**
Unikkaarvik Bldg., PO Bag 189A, Iqaluit NU X0A 0H0
867-979-5400, Fax: 867-979-1373
nuic@gov.nu.ca
www.publiclibraries.nu.ca/communities.html
Madeleine Cornthwaite, Librarian
mcornthwaite@gov.nu.ca

***Kugluktuk:* Kugluktuk Community Library**
PO Box 190, Kugluktuk NU X0B 0E0
867-982-3098, Fax: 867-982-3060
kugluktuklibrary@hotmail.com
Lucy Nivingalok, Local Librarian

***Nanisivik:* Nanisivik Community Library**
PO Box 115, Nanisivik NU X0A 0X0
867-436-7445, Fax: 867-436-7235
leycheverie@hotmail.com
Ley Cheverie, Librarian
leycheverie@hotmail.com
867-436-7445

***Pangnirtung:* Qimiruvik Library**
Angmarlik Centre, PO Box 403, Pangnirtung NU X0A 0R0
867-473-8678, Fax: 867-473-8685
lnauyuq@publiclibraries.nu.ca
Lorna Nauyuq, Local Librarian
867-473-8678

***Pond Inlet:* Rebecca P. Idlout Library**
Bldg. 215, Pond Inlet NU X0A 0S0
867-899-8972, Fax: 867-899-8175
pondinletlibrary@yahoo.ca
Ezrah Kasarnak, Librarian

***Rankin Inlet:* John Ayaruaq Library**
PO Bag 002, Rankin Inlet NU X0C 0G0
867-645-8081, Fax: 867-645-8082
ftheytaz@publiclibraries.nu.ca
Fabienne Theyez, Local Librarian
library@artic.ca
867-645-8081

Archives

***Iqaluit:* Nunatta Sunakkutangit Museum**
Bldg. 212, PO Box 1900, Iqaluit NU X0A 0H0
867-979-5537, Fax: 867-979-4533
museum@nunanet.com
Brian Lunger, Manager/Curator
museum@nunanet.com

***Iqaluit:* Nunavut Dept. of Culture, Language, Elders & Youth**
Bldg. 917, 2nd Fl. PO Box 1000, Stn 800, Iqaluit NU X0A 0H0
867-975-5500, Fax: 867-975-5504
cley@gov.nu.ca
www.gov.nu.ca/cley/home/english/archives.html
Edward Atkinson, Territorial Archivist & Historian

Ontario

Regional Systems

Ontario Library Service North/ Service des bibliothèques de l'Ontario nord
334 Regent St., Sudbury ON P3C 4E2
705-675-6467, Fax: 705-675-2285, 800-461-6348
www.olsn.ca
S. Leanne Clendening, CEO
lclendening@olsn.ca
705-675-6467 ext. 209

Southern Ontario Library Service (SOLS)
#902, 111 Peter St., Toronto ON M5H 2H1
416-961-1669, Fax: 416-961-5122, 800-387-5765
www.sols.org
Laurey Gillies, CEO
lgillies@sols.org

Public Libraries

***Addison:* Elizabethtown/Kitley Twp Public Library**
6544 New Dublin Rd., RR#2, Addison ON K0E 1A0
613-345-7480, Fax: 613-345-7235, 800-492-3175
mail@elizabethtown-kitley.on.ca
www.elizabethtown-kitley.on.ca/library.htm
Ruth Blanchard, Librarian

***Ajax:* Ajax Public Library**
55 Harwood Ave. South, Ajax ON L1S 2H8
905-683-4000, Fax: 905-683-6960
libraryinfo@townofajax.com
www.townofajax.com/library
Geoffrey Nie, Chief Librarian
geoff.nie@townofajax.com
905-683-4000 ext. 8825

***Alban:* French River Public Library/ Bibliothèque publique de la Rivière-des-français**
796 Chemin/Hwy 64, Alban ON P0M 1A0
705-857-1771, Fax: 705-857-1392
anceo@on.aibn.com
www.frenchriverlibrary.ca
Suzanne Duval, Librarian
anceo@on.aibn.com
705-898-2965

***Alliston:* New Tecumseth Public Library**
17 Victoria St. East, Alliston ON L9R 1T3
705-435-0250, Fax: 705-435-0750
www.ntpl.ca
Paula Coutts, CEO
pcoutts@ntpl.ca

***Almonte:* Mississippi Mills Public Library**
155 High St., Almonte ON K0A 1A0
613-256-1037
pnelson@mississippimills.ca
www.mississippimills.com/library
Peter Nelson, Chief Librarian

***Angus:* Essa Centennial Library**
18 King St., Angus ON L0M 1B2
705-424-6531, Fax: 705-424-5512
essalib@essa.library.on.ca
www.essa.library.on.ca
Janine Harris-Wheatley, CEO
ceoadmin@essa.library.on.ca
705-424-2679

Apsley: **North Kawartha Public Library & Life Long Learning Centre**
175 Burleigh St., PO Box 335, Apsley ON K0L 1A0
705-656-4333, Fax: 705-656-2538
library@northkawartha.on.ca
www.northkawarthalibrary.com
Shannon Hunter, CEO

Arnprior: **Arnprior Public Library**
21 Madawaska St., Arnprior ON K7S 1R6
613-623-2279, Fax: 613-623-0281
library@arncap.com
www.arncap.com/library/index.htm
Neil Salminen, Chair

Astorville: **East Ferris Public Library/ Bibliothèque publique d'East Ferris**
1257 Village Rd., PO Box 160, Astorville ON P0H 1B0
705-752-2042, Fax: 705-752-2042
efpl@onlink.net
www.olsn.ca/east_ferrispl
Christine Joly, Co-Chair

Athens: **Township of Athens Public Library**
5 Central St., Athens ON K0E 1B0
613-924-2048
athenspl@bellnet.ca
Freda Schaafsma, Head Librarian
613-924-9036

Atikokan: **Atikokan Public Library**
Civic Centre, Atikokan ON P0T 1C0
807-597-4406, Fax: 807-597-1514
jlewis@aplibrary.org
www.aplibrary.org
Jonathan Lewis, CEO/Librarian
jlewis@aplibrary.org
807-594-4406

Aurora: **Aurora Public Library**
15145 Yonge St., Aurora ON L4G 1M1
905-727-9493, Fax: 905-727-9374
www.library.aurora.on.ca
Louise Procter Maio, CEO
lproctermaio@library.aurora.on.ca
905-727-9494 ext. 221

Bala: **Wahta Mohawks Public Library**
2664, Muskoka Rd. #38, Bala ON P0C 1A0
705-756-2354, Fax: 705-756-2376
www.wahta.ca/programs.htm
Shirley Sahanatien, CEO

Bancroft: **Bancroft Public Library**
14 Flint St., Bancroft ON K0L 1C0
613-332-3380, Fax: 613-332-5473
bancroftlibrary@bellnet.ca
www.bancroftpubliclibrary.ca
Kimberly McMunn, CEO

Barrie: **Barrie Public Library**
60 Worsley St., Barrie ON L4M 1L6
705-728-1010, Fax: 705-728-4322
barlib@barrie.ca
www.library.barrie.on.ca
Al Davis, Director of Library Services
adavis@barrie.ca
705-728-1010 ext. 7500

Barry's Bay: **Barry's Bay & Area Public Library**
19474 Opeongo Line, Barry's Bay ON K0J 1B0
613-756-2000, Fax: 613-756-2000
bblibry@bellnet.ca
library.barrys-bay.ca
Angela E. Lorbetskie, Librarian

Baysville: **Lake of Bays Public Library**
Community Centre, 10 University Ave., Baysville ON P0B 1A0
705-767-2361, Fax: 705-767-2361
www.lakeofbayslibrary.ca
David Johnstone, Chair
lakeofbaysboard@vianet.ca

Beamsville: **Lincoln Public Library**
4996 Beam St., Beamsville ON L0R 1B0
905-563-7014, Fax: 905-563-1810
info@lincoln.library.on.ca
www.lincoln.library.on.ca
Jill Nicholson, CEO
nicholson@lincoln.library.on.ca

Bear Island: **Temagami First Nation Public Library/ Bibliothèque publique de Tribu Temagami**
General Delivery, Bear Island ON P0H 1C0
705-237-8876, Fax: 705-237-8959
tfnpl@onlink.net
www.temagamifirstnation.ca/PublicLibrary.htm
Virginia Mackenzie, CEO
tfnl@onlink.net
705-237-8876

Bearskin Lake: **Bearskin Lake Public Library/ Bibliotheque Publique de Bearskin**
Bearskin Lake ON P0V 1E0
807-363-2518, Fax: 807-363-1066
Robert Mickenack, Councillor

Beaverton: **Brock Township Public Libraries**
401 Simcoe St., PO Box 310, Beaverton ON L0K 1A0
705-426-9283, Fax: 705-426-9353
info@brocklibraries.ca
www.brocklibraries.ca
Karen Enss, Chair
karenenss@brocklibraries.ca
705—43-2-32

Belleville: **Belleville Public Library**
254 Pinnacle St., Belleville ON K8N 3A1
613-968-6731, Fax: 613-968-6841
www.bellevillelibrary.com
Lesley Bell, CEO
lbell@bellevillelibrary.com
613-968-6731 ext. 2222

Birch Island: **Whitefish River First Nation Public Library**
46 Bay of Islands Rd., Birch Island ON P0P 1A0
705-285-0028, Fax: 705-285-4532
whitefishriverfirstnationlibrary@hotmail.com
www.whitefishriver.ca/admin/public_library.htm
Gregor Jocko, CEO/Librarian
705-285-0028

Blenheim: **Caldwell First Nation Library**
RR#2, 10297 Talbot Rd., Blenheim ON N0P 1A0
519-676-5499
caldwell@ciaccess.com
Larry Johnson, Chief

Blind River: **Blind River Public Library/ Bibliothèque de Blind River**
8 Woodward Ave., Blind River ON P0R 1B0
705-356-7616
brpl@onlink.net
www.onlink.net/~brpl

Blind River: **Mississauga First Nation Library**
148 Village Rd., Blind River ON P0R 1B0
705-356-5335, Fax: 705-356-4206
mfnlibrary@onlink.net
www.onlink.net/~mfnlib/library.htm
Sherry Caibaiosai, Librarian

Bonfield: **Bonfield Public Library**
365 Hwy. 531, Bonfield ON P0H 1E0
705-776-2396, Fax: 705-776-1154
bpl@ontera.net
www.ontera.net/~bpl
Greg Boxwell, Chair

Borden: **Borden Public & Military Library/ Bibliothèque publique et militaire de Borden**
Bldg. E-102, 41 Kapyong Rd., Borden ON L0M 1C0
705-424-1200
bordenlibrary@interhop.net
home.interhop.net/bordenlibrary/
Donald Allen, Chief Librarian

Bowmanville: **Clarington Public Library**
163 Church St., Bowmanville ON L1C 1T7
905-623-7322
info@clarington-library.on.ca
www.clarington-library.on.ca
Edith Hopkins, Chief Executive Officer

Bracebridge: **Bracebridge Public Library**
94 Manitoba St., Bracebridge ON P1L 2B5
705-645-4171, Fax: 705-645-6551
bracelib@vianet.on.ca
www.bracebridge.library.on.ca
Cathryn Rodney, CEO/Chief Librarian
crodney@vianet.ca

Bradford: **Bradford West Gwillimbury Public Library**
100 Holland Ct., Bradford ON L3Z 2A7
905-775-3328, Fax: 905-775-1236
bwgmailbox@bradford.library.on.ca
www.bradford.library.on.ca
Gary Lamb, Chair

Brampton: **Brampton Library**
65 Queen St. East, Brampton ON L6W 3L6
905-793-4636
info@bramlib.on.ca
www.bramlib.on.ca
Adele Kostiak, Chief Executive Officer
akostiak@bramlib.on.ca
905—79-3-46 ext. 4311

Brantford: **Brantford Public Library**
173 Colborne St., Brantford ON N3T 2G8
519-756-2220, Fax: 519-756-4979
info@brantford.library.on.ca
www.brantford.library.on.ca
Geoff Wilson, Chair

Bridgenorth: **Smith-Ennismore-Lakefield Public Library**
826 Ward St., Bridgenorth ON K0L 1H0
705-292-5065, Fax: 705-292-6695
www.mypubliclibrary.ca
Joan MacDonald, Librarian
jmacdonald@mypubliclibrary.ca

Brighton: **Brighton Public Library**
35 Alice St., Brighton ON K0K 1H0
613-475-2511, Fax: 613-475-3453
brightonpl@gmail.com
www.brighton.library.on.ca
Peter Gysbers, Chair

Britt: **Britt Public Library**
841 Riverside Dr., Britt ON P0G 1A0
705-383-2292, Fax: 705-383-0077
britt.lib@hotmail.com
www.olsn.ca/BrittPL
Barbara Wohleber, Chief Executive Officer

Britt: **Magnetawan First Nation Public Library/ Bibliothèque publique de Prèmiere Nation de Magnetawan**
Box 15, RR#1, Britt ON P0G 1A0
705-383-2477, Fax: 705-383-2566
mfnlibrary@hotmail.com
Wanda Noganosh, Librarian

Brockville: **Augusta Township Public Library**
4500 County Rd. 15, RR#2, Brockville ON K6V 5T2
613-926-2449, Fax: 613-926-0440
augusta@augustalibrary.com
www.augustalibrary.com
Jacquie Kelly, Chair

Brockville: **Brockville Public Library**
23 Buell St., Brockville ON K6V 5T7
613-342-3936, Fax: 613-342-9598
info@brockvillelibrary.ca
www.brockvillelibrary.ca
Margaret Wicklum, Chair

Bruce Mines: **Bruce Mines & Plummer Additional Union Public Library**
33 Desbarats St., Bruce Mines ON P0R 1C0
705-785-3370, Fax: 705-785-3370
bmpa@ontera.net
www.bruceminesandplummerlibrary.ca
Lorelee Gordon, CEO/Librarian

Buckhorn: **Galway-Cavendish & Harvey Twp Public Library**
5 George St., Buckhorn ON K0L 1J0
705-657-3695, Fax: 705-657-3695
library@galwaycavendishharveylibrary.ca
www.galwaycavendishharveylibrary.ca/
Maria Bradburn, CEO

Burks Falls: **Burks Falls, Armour & Ryerson Union Public Library**
39 Copeland St., Burks Falls ON P0A 1C0
705-382-3327, Fax: 705-382-3327
bflib1@surenet.net
www.surenet.net/~bflib1
Sandy Henshall, CEO

Burlington: **Burlington Public Library**
2331 New St., Burlington ON L7R 1J4
905-639-3611, Fax: 905-681-7277
askalibrarian@bpl.on.ca
www.bpl.on.ca

Maureen Barry, CEO
barrym@bpl.on.ca
905-639-3611 ext. 100

***Burlington:* The Courier**
c/o AIC Investment Services Inc., 1375 Kerns Rd., Burlington ON L7R 4X8
905-331-4242, Fax: 905-331-4309
sblundell@aic.com
www.sla.org/chapter/ctor/newsletter/courierinfo.asp
Elizabeth Malak-McMullan, Editor

***Calabogie:* Greater Madawaska Public Library**
4984 Calabogie Rd., Calabogie ON K0J 1H0
613-752-2317, Fax: 613-752-2617
mjhale@bellnet.ca
www.townshipofgreatermadawaska.com/library.htm
Mary-Joan Hale, CEO/Librarian
mjhale@bellnet.ca
613-752-2317

***Caledon East:* Caledon Public Library**
6500 Old Church Rd., Caledon East ON L7C 0H3
905-584-1456, Fax: 905-584-1374
www.caledon.library.on.ca
Bill Manson, Chief Executive Officer
bmanson@caledon.library.on.ca
519—92-7-56

***Callander:* Callander Public Library**
30 Catherine St., Callander ON P0H 1H0
705-752-2544, Fax: 705-752-2819
apeden@ontera.net
www.mycallander.ca/library/library-home/
Alison Peden, CEO
705-752-2544

***Calstock:* Constance Lake First Nation Public Library**
2 Musko St., PO Box 5000, Calstock ON P0L 1B0
705-463-1199, Fax: 705-463-2077
suthliz@clfn.on.ca
Lizzie Sutherland, CEO
suthliz@clfn.on.ca

***Cambridge:* Cambridge Libraries & Galleries**
1 North Sq., Cambridge ON N1S 2K6
519-621-0460, Fax: 519-621-2080
www.cambridgelibraries.ca
Marilyn Scott, Board Chair

***Campbellford:* Trent Hills Public Library**
98 Bridge St. East, Campbellford ON K0L 1L0
705-653-3611, Fax: 705-653-4611
trenthillslibrary@trenthills.ca
www.trenthillslibrary.ca
Donna Wilson, CEO

***Carleton Place:* Carleton Place Public Library**
101 Beckwith St., Carleton Place ON K7C 2T3
613-257-2702
carletonlibdsl@vianet.ca
www.carletonplace.ca
Janet Baril, Librarian

***Cartier:* Cartier Public Library/ Bibliothèque publique de Cartier**
Lansdowne St., PO Box 1000, Cartier ON P0M 1J0
705-965-2481
Joanne Ederer, Chief Executive Officer

***Casselman:* Bibliothèque publique de Casselman/ Casselman Public Library**
675, rue Dollard, Casselman ON K0A 1M0
613-764-5505, Fax: 613-764-5507
bibliotheque@bibliocasselman.ca
www.bibliocasselman.ca
Aline Gareau, Bibliothécaire

***Castleton:* Township of Cramahe Public Library**
Town Hall, 1780 Percy St., Castleton ON K0K 1M0
905-344-7320, Fax: 905-344-7320
Sue La Berge, CEO

***Chapleau:* Chapleau Public Library**
20 Pine St. East, Chapleau ON P0M 1K0
705-864-0852, Fax: 705-864-0295
plchapleau@post.library.on.ca
www.chapleaucapsite.zoomshare.com
Maureen Travis, Chief Librarian

***Chatham:* Chatham-Kent Public Library**
120 Queen St., Chatham ON N7M 2G6
519-354-2940, Fax: 519-354-2602
CKlibrary@chatham-kent.ca
www.chatham-kent.ca/community+services/library
Diane Daly, Chair
cklibraryboard@chatham-kent.ca

***Christian Island:* Beausoleil First Nation Library**
80 Kate Kegwin St., Christian Island ON L0K 1C0
705-247-2255, Fax: 705-247-2239
bfnlibrary@hotmail.com
Kathy Peters, Librarian

***Clinton:* Huron County Library**
77722B London Rd., RR#5, Clinton ON N0M 1L0
519-482-5457, Fax: 519-482-7820
libraryadmin@huroncounty.ca
www.huroncounty.ca/library
Dorothy Kelly, Chair

***Cobalt:* Cobalt Public Library/ Bibliothèque publique du Cobalt**
30 Lang St., Cobalt ON P0J 1C0
705-679-8120, Fax: 705-679-8120
cobaltlibrary@ontera.net
ca.geocities.com/cobaltlibrary/
Margaret Leaper, Chief Executive Officer

***Cobden:* Township of Whitewater Region**
12 Wren Dr., Cobden ON K0J 1K0
613-646-7592
www.whitewaterregion.ca/departments/library.htm
Heather Steege, Librarian
coblib@nrtco.net
613-646-7592

***Cobourg:* Cobourg Public Library**
200 Ontario St., Cobourg ON K9A 5P4
905-372-9271, Fax: 905-372-4538
info@cobourg.library.on.ca
www.cobourg.library.on.ca
Charmaine Lindsay, CEO
clindsay@cobourg.library.on.ca
905-372-9271 ext. 6200

***Cochrane:* Cochrane Public Library/ Bibliothèque publique Cochrane**
178 - 4th Ave., Cochrane ON P0L 1C0
705-272-4178, Fax: 705-272-4165
cochranelib@puc.net
Carole-Ann Churcher, Acting CEO

***Coe Hill:* Wollaston & Limerick Public Library**
2149 Hwy. 620, Coe Hill ON K0L 1P0
613-337-5183, Fax: 613-337-5183
coehilllibrary@bellnet.ca
www.wolaston-limericklibrary.ca
Bonnie Weise, Head Librarian

***Coldwater:* Coldwater Memorial Public Library**
31 Coldwater Rd., Coldwater ON L0K 1E0
705-686-3601, Fax: 705-686-3741
library@coldwater.library.on.ca
www.coldwater.library.on.ca
Adah Silk, Chair

***Collingwood:* Collingwood Public Library**
100 Second St., Collingwood ON L9Y 1E5
705-445-1571
clib@collingwoodpubliclibrary.ca
www.collingwoodpubliclibrary.ca
Donna Mansfield, Chair

***Cornwall:* Akwesasne Library & Museum**
c/o Mohawk Council of Akwesasne, PO Box 579, Cornwall ON K6H 5T3
518-358-2240, Fax: 518-358-2649
info@akwesasneculturalcenter.org
www.akwesasneculturalcenter.org
Glory Cole, Director
coleg@northnet.org

***Cornwall:* Cornwall Public Library (Ontario)/ Bibliothèque publique de Cornwall**
45 Second St. East, PO Box 939, Cornwall ON K6H 5V1
613-932-4796, Fax: 613-932-2715
generalmail@library.cornwall.on.ca
www.library.cornwall.on.ca
Jacqueline Houde, Chair

***Cornwall:* Stormont, Dundas & Glengarry County Library/ Bibliothèque des comtés unis Stormont, Dundas et Glengarry**
26 Pitt St., Cornwall ON K6J 3P2
613-936-8777, Fax: 613-936-2532
generalinfo@sdglibrary.ca
www.sdglibrary.ca
Bill McGimpsey, Chair

***Curve Lake:* Curve Lake First Nation Public Library**
22 Winooleeda St., Curve Lake ON K0L 1R0
705-657-3217, Fax: 705-657-8708
curvelakepl@hotmail.com
Susie V. Taylor, CEO
705-657-8045 ext. 217

***Cutler:* Serpent River First Nation Public Library**
49 Village Rd., Cutler ON P0P 1B0
705-844-2009, Fax: 705-844-2736
ljones.srfn@ontera.net
Patricia Squires, Librarian

***Deep River:* Deep River Public Library**
55 Ridge Rd., Deep River ON K0J 1P0
613-584-4244
www.deepriverlibrary.ca
Tom Wiwcharuk, Chief Executive Officer

***Deep River:* Laurentian Hills Public Library**
34465 Hwy. 17, RR#1, Deep River ON K0J 1P0
613-584-2714, Fax: 613-584-9145
library@town.laurentianhills.on.ca
town.laurentianhills.on.ca/Library/
Maureen L. Bakewell, Librarian

***Deseronto:* Deseronto Public Library**
358 Main St., Deseronto ON K0K 1X0
613-396-2744, Fax: 613-396-3466
deserontopubliclibrary@yahoo.ca
www.deserontopubliclibrary.ca
Don Simpson, Chair

***Deseronto:* Ka:nhiote/Tyendinaga Territory Public Library**
1644 York Rd., RR#1, Deseronto ON K0K 1X0
613-967-6264, Fax: 613-396-3627
karenl@tyendinaga.net
www.tyendinaga.net/volunteer/kanhiote
Karen Lewis, CEO
karenl@tyendinaga.net

***Devlin:* Naicatchewenin Indian Band Library**
Rainy Lake Indian Reserve, RR#1, Devlin ON P0W 1C0
807-486-3407, Fax: 807-486-3704
Darlene Smith, Librarian

***Dobie:* Dobie Public Library**
92 McPherson St., Dobie ON P0K 1B0
705-568-8951, Fax: 705-568-8951
publib@nt.net
Dianne Quinn, CEO

***Dokis:* Dokis First Nation Public Library**
129 Loop St., Dokis ON P0M 2K0
705-763-2511, Fax: 705-763-2765
dokislibrary@hotmail.com
Angeline Dokis, Librarian
dokislibrary@hotmail.com

***Dorion:* Dorion Public Library**
170 Dorion Loop Rd., Dorion ON P0T 1K0
807-857-2318, Fax: 807-857-2203
dorlib@tbaytel.net
www.dorionpubliclibrary.ca
Betty Chambers, Head Librarian

***Douglas:* Admaston-Bromley Public Library**
PO Box 130, Hwy. 60, Douglas ON K0J 1S0
613-649-2576, Fax: 613-649-2676
info@admastonbromleylibrary.com
www.admastonbromleylibrary.com
Anne English, Head Librarian

***Douro:* Douro-Dummer Public Library/ Bibiothèque publique de Douro-Dummer**
435 - 4th Line, General Delivery, Douro ON K0L 1S0
705-652-8599
douro_dummer_library@pcpostal.com
www.dourodummer.on.ca/departmentlibrary.php
Edna Latone, Librarian

***Dryden:* Dryden Public Library**
36 Van Horne Ave., Dryden ON P8N 2A7
807-223-1475, Fax: 807-223-4312
library@dryden.ca
www.dryden.ca/city_services/library
Sandra Weitzel, CEO

***Dubreuilville:* Bibliothèque publique de Dubreuilville/ Dubreuilville Public Library**
120 Magpie St., Dubreuilville ON P0S 1B0
705-884-1435, Fax: 705-884-1437, 877-637-8010
dpl@dubreuilville.ca
Mélanie Plourde, Directrice

***Dunchurch:* Whitestone Hagerman Memorial Public Library**
2206 Hwy. 124, Dunchurch ON P0A 1G0
705-389-3311, Fax: 705-389-3311
whitestonelibrary@vianet.ca
www.dunchurchlibrary.org
Lori Guillemette, Library Administrator

***Dundalk:* Southgate Public Library**
90 Main St. East, Dundalk ON N0C 1B0
519-923-3248, Fax: - - 8
southgatepl@bmts.com
www.southgate-library.com
Dianne Dean, CEO
southgatepl@bmts.com

***Dunnville:* Haldimand County Public Library**
111 Broad St. East, Dunnville ON N1A 1E8
905-774-7595, Fax: 905-774-4294
djackson@haldimandcounty.on.ca
www.haldimandcounty.on.ca
Debra Jackson, CEO
djackson@haldimandcounty.on.ca
905-318-3272 ext. 15

***Durham:* West Grey Library System**
240 Garafraxa St. North, Durham ON N0G 1R0
519-369-2107, Fax: 519-369-9966
westgreylibrary@yahoo.ca
www.westgreylibraries.com
Marlaine Elvidge, Chief Executive Officer, West Grey Library System

***Eabamet Lake:* Fort Hope First Nation Public Library**
PO Box 297, Eabamet Lake ON P0T 1L0
807-242-8421, Fax: 807-242-1592

***Ear Falls:* Ear Falls Public Library**
50 Balsam Ave., Ear Falls ON P0V 1T0
807-222-3209, Fax: 807-222-3432
efpl@goearfalls.com
www.olsn.ca/earfallspl
Becky Bergman, Librarian

***Earlton:* Township of Armstrong Public Library/ Bibliothèque publique Canton Earlton**
35 - 10th St., Earlton ON P0J 1E0
705-563-2717, Fax: 705-563-2093
earltonlibrary@ntl.sympatico.ca
Chantal Lavergne, CEO
earltonlibrary@ntl.sympatico.ca

***Eganville:* Bonnechere Union Public Library**
74A Maple St., Eganville ON K0J 1T0
613-628-2400, Fax: 613-628-5377
info@bonnechereupl.com
www.bonnechereupl.com
Jennifer Coleman-Davidson, CEO/CFO
ceo@bonnechereupl.com

***Elgin:* Rideau Lakes Public Library**
26 Halladay St., PO Box 189, Elgin ON K0G 1E0
613-359-5334, Fax: 613-359-5418
elginlibrary@ripnet.com
www.rideaulakeslibrary.ca
Rita Purcell, Library Chair
purcell.rita@sympatico.ca

***Elk Lake:* Elk Lake Public Library**
PO Box 218, Elk Lake ON P0J 1G0
705-678-2340, Fax: 705-678-2340
elklake@ontera.net
Peggy Verrier, CEO
elklake@ontera.net
705-678-2340

***Elliot Lake:* Elliot Lake Public Library**
Algo Centre Mall, 151 Ontario Ave., Elliot Lake ON P5A 2T2
705-461-7204, Fax: 705-461-9464
www.elliotlakelibrary.com
Pat McGurk, Interim CEO
705-461-7204 ext. 2801

***Embrun:* Bibliothèque publique du Canton de Russell/ Russell Township Public Library**
#2, 717 Notre Dame St., Embrun ON K0A 1W1
613-443-3636, Fax: 613-443-0668
mylibrary@russellbiblio.com
www.russellbiblio.on.ca
Claire Dionne, Directrice générale
claire.dionne@russellbiblio.com

***Emo:* Emo Public Library**
Jessie St., PO Box 490, Emo ON P0W 1E0
807-482-2575, Fax: 807-482-2575
emolib@bellnet.ca
www.twspemo.on.ca
Shirley Sheppard, Librarian

***Emsdale:* Perry Twp (Emsdale) Public Library**
25 Joseph St., Emsdale ON P0A 1J0
705-636-5454, Fax: 705-636-5454
perrylib@ontera.net
www.olsn.ca/library/perry/index.htm
Patricia Aitchison, Head Librarian
705-636-5454

***Englehart:* Englehart Public Library/ Bibliothèque publique d'Englehart**
#809, 71 - 4th Ave., Englehart ON P0J 1H0
705-544-2100, Fax: 705-544-2238
techepl@ontera.net
www.englehartpubliclibrary.ca
Munroe Burton, Chair

***Espanola:* Espanola Public Library**
245 Avery Dr., Espanola ON P5E 1S4
705-869-2940, Fax: 705-869-6463
library@town.espanola.on.ca
www.town.espanola.on.ca
Charles Grayson, Librarian

***Essex:* Essex County Library**
#101, 360 Fairview Ave. West, Essex ON N8M 1Y3
519-776-5241, Fax: 519-776-6851
www.essexcountylibrary.ca
William (Bill) Varga, Chair

***Fauquier:* Bibliothèque publique de Fauquier-Strickland/ Fauquier-Strickland Public Library**
25, rue Grzela, Fauquier ON P0L 1G0
705-339-2521, Fax: 705-339-2421
biblioff@vianet.ca
www.olsn.ca
Jocelyne Ratté, Directrice générale

***Fergus:* Wellington County Library**
552 Wellington Rd. 18, RR#1, Fergus ON N1M 2W3
519-846-0918, Fax: 519-846-2066
www.county.wellington.on.ca
Janice Hindley, Chief Librarian
janiceh@wellington.ca
519—84-6-09 ext. 224

***Flesherton:* Grey Highlands Public Library**
10 Elizabeth St., Flesherton ON N0C 1E0
519-924-2241, Fax: 519-924-2562
flepub@bmts.com
www.greyhighlandspubliclibrary.com/index.htm
Wilda Allen, CEO/Chief Librarian
pallen@bmts.com

***Flinton:* Addington-Highlands Public Library**
927 Flinton Rd., Flinton ON K0H 1P0
613-333-1091
FlintonLibraryCAP@addingtonhighlandspubliclibr
www.addingtonhighlandspubliclibrary.ca
June Phillips, CEO & Had Librarian

***Fonthill:* Pelham Public Library**
43 Pelham Town Sq., Fonthill ON L0S 1E0
905-892-6443, Fax: 905-892-3392
pelhampl@post.library.on.ca
www.pelhamlibrary.on.ca
Stephanie Stowe, CEO
905-892-6443

***Forest:* Chippewas of Kettle & Stony Point Library**
RR#2, 6218 Indian Lane, Forest ON N0N 1J0
519-786-2955, Fax: 519-786-6904
ksplibrary@xcelco.on.ca
Beverly Bresette, CEO
bevb@xcelco.ca

***Fort Erie:* Fort Erie Public Library**
136 Gilmore Rd., Fort Erie ON L2A 2M1
905-871-2546, Fax: 905-871-2191
information@forterie.library.on.ca
www.forterie.library.on.ca
Gordon Thomson, CEO
gthomson@forterie.library.on.ca

***Fort Frances:* Fort Frances Public Library**
363 Church St., Fort Frances ON P9A 1C9
807-274-9879, Fax: 807-274-4496
msedgwick@fort-frances.com
library.fort-frances.com
Margaret Sedgwick, Librarian

***Gananoque:* Gananoque Public Library**
100 Park St., Gananoque ON K7G 2Y5
613-382-2436
gplp@bellnet.ca
John Love, Librarian

***Garden River:* Garden River First Nation Public Library**
14 Syrette Lake Rd., Garden River ON P6A 5K9
705-946-3933, Fax: 705-945-1415
Irene Gray, CEO
irene.gray@gardendriver.ca

***Garden Village:* Nipissing First Nation Public Library**
36 Semo Rd., Garden Village ON P2B 3K2
705-753-2050, Fax: 705-753-0571
glennab@nfn.ca
Glenna Beaucage, CEO

***Georgetown:* Halton Hills Public Library**
9 Church St., Georgetown ON L7G 2A3
905-873-2681, Fax: 905-873-6118
www.library.hhpl.on.ca
Jane Diamanti, Director
diamantij@hhpl.on.ca
905-873-2681 ext. 2501

***Geraldton:* Greenstone Public Library**
405 Second St. West, Geraldton ON P0T 1M0
807-854-2421, Fax: 807-854-2421
greenstonepl@hotmail.com
www.olsn.ca/greenstone/
Mari Mannisto, CEO

***Gilmour:* Tudor & Cashel Baverstock Memorial Public Library**
371 Weslemkoon Lake Rd., Gilmour ON K0L 1W0
613-473-5032, Fax: 613-474-0664
library@tudorandcashel.com
Mary Hawkins, CEO/Librarian

***Gogama:* Gogama Public Library/ Bibliothèque publique de Gogama**
Low Ave., PO Box 238, Gogama ON P0M 1W0
705-894-2448
glibrary@onlink.net
Sue Primeau, Volunteer Head Librarian

***Gogama:* Mattagami First Nation Public Library**
PO Box 99, Gogama ON P0M 1W0
705-894-2003, Fax: 705-894-2386
msh@onlink.net
www.olsn.ca
Patsy Mckay, CEO
msh@onlink.net
705-894-2003

***Golden Lake:* Algonquins of Pikwakanagan Library**
c/o 1657A Mishomis Inamo, Golden Lake ON K0J 1X0
613-625-2402
library@pikwakanagan.ca
Estelle Amikons, CEO

***Gore Bay:* Gore Bay Union Public Library**
15 Water St., Gore Bay ON P0P 1H0
705-282-2221, Fax: 705-282-2221
gorebaylibrary@gorebaycable.com
Johanna Allison, CEO
gblibrary@onlink.net

***Grafton:* Alnwick - Haldimand Public Libraries**
10836 County Rd. #2, Grafton ON K0K 2G0
905-349-2822
hallibhq@eagle.ca
www.alnwickhaldimand.ca
Carol Dempsey, Chief Executive Officer

***Grand Valley:* Grand Valley Public Library**
4 Amaranth St. East, Grand Valley ON L0N 1G0
519-928-5622, Fax: 519-928-2586
grandvalleylibrary@primus.ca
www.grandvalley.org
Shann Leighton, CEO
shannleighton@primus.ca

Gravenhurst: **Gravenhurst Public Library**
180 Sharpe St. West, Gravenhurst ON P1P 1J1
705-687-3382, Fax: 705-687-7016
illo@gravenhurst.ca
www.gravenhurst.ca/library
Edward Reece, CEO
ereece@gravenhurst.ca

Grimsby: **Grimsby Public Library**
18 Carnegie Lane, Grimsby ON L3M 1Y1
905-945-5142, Fax: 905-945-4442
Barry Church, Chief Librarian

Guelph: **Guelph Public Library**
100 Norfolk St., Guelph ON N1H 4J6
519-824-6220
www.library.guelph.on.ca
Randall Wilson, Chair

Hagersville: **Mississaugas of the New Credit First Nation Public Library**
RR#6, Hagersville ON N0A 1H0
905-768-5686, Fax: 905-768-1225
nclib@netrover.com
Veronica Jamieson, CEO

Haileybury: **Temiskaming Shores Public Library**
545 Lakeshore Rd., Haileybury ON P0J 1K0
705-672-3707, Fax: 705-672-5966
haillib@ontera.net
www.temisklibrary.com
Roger Oblin, Chair

Haliburton: **Haliburton County Public Library**
739 Mountain St., Haliburton ON K0M 1S0
705-457-2241
www.libris.ca/hali
Cheryl Murdoch, Chair

Hamilton: **Hamilton Public Library**
55 York Blvd., Hamilton ON L8R 3K1
905-546-3200, Fax: 905-546-3202
askhpl@hpl.ca
www.hpl.ca
Ken Roberts, Chief Librarian
kroberts@hpl.ca
905—54-6-32

Hanover: **Hanover Public Library**
451 - 10th Ave., Hanover ON N4N 2P1
519-364-1420, Fax: 519-364-1747
hanpub@hanover.ca
Agnes Rivers-Moore, Chief Librarian

Havelock: **Havelock-Belmont-Methuen Twp Public Library**
13 Quebec St., Havelock ON K0L 1Z0
705-778-2621, Fax: 705-778-2621
habellib@nexicom.net
www.hbmlibrary.on.ca
Sandra Harris, Head Librarian/CEO
habellib@nexicom.net

Hawkesbury: **Bibliothèque publique de Hawkesbury/ Hawkesbury Public Library**
550, Higginson St., Hawkesbury ON K6A 1H1
613-632-0106, Fax: 613-636-2097
marthes@bibliotheque.hawkesbury.on.ca
www.bibliotheque.hawkesbury.on.ca
Marie-Josée Fortier, Directrice générale
fortierm@bibliotheque.hawkesbury.on.ca
613-632-0106 ext. 2251

Hearst: **Bibliothèque publique de Hearst/ Hearst Public Library**
801, rue George, Hearst ON P0L 1N0
705-372-2843, Fax: 705-372-2833
hearstpl@ontera.net
www.bibliohearst.on.ca
Francine Daigle, CEO
hearstpl@ontera.net
705-372-2843

Hilton Beach: **Hilton Union Public Library**
3048 Marks St., Hilton Beach ON P0R 1G0
705-246-2557
diane.gerhart@sympatico.ca
Diane Gerhart, Librarian
diane.gerhart@sympatico.ca

Holland Landing: **East Gwillimbury Public Library**
19513 Yonge St., Holland Landing ON L9N 1L8
905-836-6492, Fax: 905-836-6499
infoegpl@primus.ca
www.eastgwillimbury.ca/library
Greg Gulas, CEO
ggulas@primus.ca
905-836-6492

Hornepayne: **Hornepayne Township Public Library**
200 Front St., Hornepayne ON P0M 1Z0
807-868-2332, Fax: 807-868-3111
lkahara@ontera.net
Lynda Kahara, CEO

Huntsville: **Huntsville Public Library**
7 Minerva St., Huntsville ON P1H 1W4
705-789-5232
library@huntsvillelibrary.net
www.huntsvillelibrary.net
Ana Mackenzie, Chief Librarian

Ignace: **Ignace Public Library**
36 Main St., Ignace ON P0T 1T0
807-934-2280, Fax: 807-934-6452
ipl-catherine@nwconx.net
www.olsn.ca/ignace
Pam Greenwood, Contact

Innisfil: **Innisfil Public Library**
967 Innisfil Beach Rd., Innisfil ON L9S 1V3
705-431-7410
lakeshore@innisfil.library.on.ca
www.innisfil.library.on.ca
Susan Downs, Chief Librarian & CEO
sdowns@innisfil.library.on.ca

Iron Bridge: **Huron Shores Public Library**
10 John St., Iron Bridge ON P0R 1H0
705-843-2192, Fax: 705-843-2035
huronshores@onlink.net
www.olsn.ca/huronshores
Terri Beharriell, CEO/Librarian

Iroquois Falls: **Bibliothèque publique d'Iroquois Falls Public Library**
725 Synagogue St., Iroquois Falls ON P0K 1G0
705-232-5722, Fax: 705-232-7166
Lina Tremblay-Joseph, CEO
ifpl@onlink.net

Kagawong: **Billings Twp Public Library**
18 Upper St., Kagawong ON P0P 1J0
705-282-2944
billings@xplornet.com
Beth Gordon, CEO

Kakabeka Falls: **Conmee Public Library**
Conmee Community Centre, 19 Holland Rd. West, RR#1, Kakabeka Falls ON P0T 1W0
807-475-5229
conmeelibrary@msn.com
www.conmee.com/library.html
Selly Pajamaki, Chief Executive Officer
spajamaki@aidsthunderbay.org

Kapuskasing: **Kapuskasing Public Library/ Bibliothèque publique de Kapuskasing**
24 Mundy Ave., Kapuskasing ON P5N 1P9
705-335-3363, Fax: 705-335-2464
kaplibrary@ntl.sympatico.ca
Cecile Langlois, Librarian

Kearney: **Kearney & Area Public Library**
8 Main St., Kearney ON P0A 1M0
705-636-5849, Fax: 705-636-7060
kearneylibrary@hotmail.com
www.olsn.ca/kearney
Brandi Nolan, CEO/Librarian

Keene: **Otonabee-South Monaghan Public Library**
3252 County Rd. 2, Keene ON K0L 2G0
705-295-6814
keene_library@nexicom.net
www.otosoumon.library.on.ca
Carolanne Nadeau, CEO

Kemptville: **North Grenville Public Library**
669 South Gower Dr., Kemptville ON K0G 1J0
613-258-4711, Fax: 613-258-4134
info@ngpl.ca
www.ngpl.ca
Susan Higgins, Manager, Library Services
shiggins@ripnet.com

Kenora: **City of Kenora Public Library**
24 Main St. South, Kenora ON P9N 1S7
807-467-2081, Fax: 807-467-2085
maeisler@kenora.ca
www.kenorapubliclibrary.org
Erin Roussin, Head Librarian
eroussin@kenora.ca

Keswick: **Georgina Public Libraries**
90 Wexford Dr., Keswick ON L4P 3P7
905-476-7233, Fax: 905-476-8724
www.georgina-library.com
Mary Baxter, CEO/Director, Library Services
mbaxter@georgina.ca
905—47-6-72 ext. 101

Killaloe: **Killaloe & District Public Library**
1 John St., Killaloe ON K0J 2A0
613-757-2211, Fax: 613-757-3634
killaloelibrary@vcip.ca

King City: **King Township Public Library**
1970 King Rd., King City ON L7B 1A6
905-833-5101, Fax: 905-833-0824
www.king-library.on.ca
Murray McCabe, CEO & Chief Librarian
m.mccabe@king-library.on.ca

Kingfisher Lake: **Kingfisher Lake First Nation Public Library**
General Delivery, Kingfisher Lake ON P0V 1Z0
807-532-0067

Kingston: **Canadian Law Library Review / Bibliothèques de droit canadiennes**
#310, 4 Cataraqui St., Kingston ON K7L 5C8
613-531-9339, Fax: 613-531-0626
office@callacbd.ca
www.callacbd.ca/cll-jour.html
Lenore Rapkin, Editor

Kingston: **Kingston Frontenac Public Library**
130 Johnson St., Kingston ON K7L 1X8
613-549-8888, Fax: 613-549-8476
www.kfpl.ca
Claudette Richardson, Chair

Kirkland Lake: **Teck Centennial Library**
10 Kirkland St. East, Kirkland Lake ON P2N 1P1
705-567-7966, Fax: 705-568-6303
library@tkl.ca
www.olsn.ca/kirklandlakepl/
Cheryl Lafreniere, Chief Librarian

Kitchener: **Kitchener Public Library**
85 Queen St. North, Kitchener ON N2H 2H1
519-743-0271, Fax: 519-743-1261
askus@kpl.org
www.kpl.org
Sonia Lewis, CEO
sonia.lewis@kpl.org

Lanark: **Lanark Highlands Public Library**
75 George St., Lanark ON K0G 1K0
613-259-3068
lanarklib@perth.igs.net
www.lanarkhighlands.ca/MunicipalServices/Library.htm
Wanda Proulx, CEO

Lansdowne: **Leeds & the Thousand Islands Public Library**
1B Jessie St., Lansdowne ON K0E 1L0
613-659-3885, Fax: 613-659-4192
leedsti@ltipl.net
www.ltipl.net
Linda Chadwick, Librarian

Larder Lake: **Larder Lake Public Library/ Bibliothèque publique de Larder Lake**
29 Godfrey St., Larder Lake ON P0K 1L0
705-643-2222, Fax: 705-643-2222
llpublib@onlink.net
Patricia Bodick, Library Technician/CEO

Latchford: **Latchford Public Library**
66 Main St., Latchford ON P0J 1N0
705-676-2030
lpl@ontera.net
Edith Robillard, CEO

Limoges: **Bibliothèque publique de la municipalité de la Nation**
205, ch Limoges, Limoges ON K0A 2M0

613-443-1630, Fax: 613-524-2545
nationlibrary@bellnet.ca
Helena Morgan, Directrice générale

Lindsay: City of Kawartha Lakes Public Library
190 Kent St. West, Lindsay ON K9V 2Y6
705-324-9411, Fax: 705-878-1859, 888-822-2225
libraryadministration@city.kawarthalakes.on.ca
www.city.kawarthalakes.on.ca\library
Peter Cowie, Chair

Listowel: North Perth Public Library
260 Main St. West, Listowel ON N4W 1A1
519-291-4621, Fax: 519-291-2235
npl@northperth.library.on.ca
www.northperth.library.on.ca
Sheila Durand, CEO
sdurand@northperth.library.on.ca

Little Current: Aundeck Omni Kaning First Nation Public Library
13 Hill St., Little Current ON P0P 1K0
705-368-3696, Fax: 705-368-3563
aokpubliclibrary@hotmail.com
Norma McGraw, Librarian
705-368-3696

Little Current: Northeastern Manitoulin & the Islands Public Library
50 Meredith St. West, Little Current ON P0P 1K0
705-368-2444, Fax: 705-368-0708
nemilib@vianet.on.ca
www.nemilib.vianet.ca
Judith Kift, Librarian & CEO

London: London Public Library
251 Dundas St., London ON N6A 6H9
519-661-4600, Fax: 519-663-9013
info@lpl.london.on.ca
www.londonpubliclibrary.ca
Susanna Hubbard Krimmer, CEO
519-661-5143

M'Chigeeng: M'Chigeeng First Nation Public Library
18 Lakeview Dr., M'Chigeeng ON P0P 1G0
705-377-5540, Fax: 705-377-5080
bookwormsandy@yahoo.com
Sandra Bayer, CEO
705-377-5540

MacTier: Township of Georgian Bay Public Library
2 Muskoka Rd., MacTier ON P0C 1H0
705-375-5430, Fax: 705-375-5430
mactier1@interhop.net
www.olsn.ca/georgianbaypl/
Barbara Swyers, CEO

Madoc: Madoc Public Library
20 Davidson St., Madoc ON K0K 2K0
613-473-4456
madoc_public_library@bellnet.ca
www.madocpubliclibrary.com
Susan Smith, CEO
susansmith@bellnet.ca

Magnetawan: Magnetawan Public Library
4304 North Sparks St., Magnetawan ON P0A 1P0
705-387-4411, Fax: 705-387-0636
magcap@ontera.net
www.magnetawanlibrary.ca
Erin Phillips, CEO/Librarian

Manitouwadge: Manitouwadge Public Library
Community Centre, Manitouwadge ON P0T 2C0
807-826-3913, Fax: 807-826-4640
library-man@nwconx.net
Janis Lamothe, Librarian/CEO

Manitowaning: Assiginack Public Library
25 Spragge St., Manitowaning ON P0P 1N0
705-859-2110, Fax: 705-859-3010
aplgoodtomes@email.com
www.assiginacklibrary.org
Debbie Robinson, CEO/Librarian

Marathon: Marathon Public Library
22 Peninsula Rd., Marathon ON P0T 2E0
807-229-0740, Fax: 807-229-3336
tneedham@tbaytel.net
Tamara Needham, Librarian

Markham: Markham Public Libraries
6031 Highway 7, Markham ON L3P 3A7
905-513-7977, Fax: 905-471-6015
comments@markham.library.on.ca
www.markham.ca/mpl
Catherine Biss, CEO
cbiss@markham.library.on.ca

Markstay: Markstay-Warren Public Library/ Bibliothèque publique de Markstay-Warren
7 Pioneer St. East, Markstay ON P0M 2G0
705-853-0635, Fax: 705-721-9924
www.olsn.ca/markstay-warrenpl
Donna Smith, CEO/Librarian
donna061@sympatico.ca
705-853-0635

Marmora: Marmora & Lake Public Library
37 Forsyth St., Marmora ON K0K 2M0
613-472-3122
marmoralibrary@gmail.com
www.marmora.info/library
Sheryl Price, CEO

Massey: Sables-Spanish River Public Library Board
185 Grove St., Massey ON P0P 1P0
705-865-2641, Fax: 705-865-2641
masseylibrary@etown.net
massey.etown.net/
Lilliane Richer, CEO
info@masseylibrary.comt
705-865-2641

Massey: Sagamok Anishnawbek Public Library
PO Box 610, Massey ON P0P 1P0
705-865-2970, Fax: 705-865-3411
Colleen Eshkakogan, Librarian

Matheson: Black River-Matheson Public Library
PO Box 450, Matheson ON P0K 1N0
705-273-2760, Fax: 705-273-1755
brmlibrary@hotmail.com
www.blackriver-matheson.com
Karen Ukrainetz, CEO/Librarian

Mattawa: Mattawa (John Dixon) Public Library
370 Pine St., Mattawa ON P0H 1V0
705-744-5550, Fax: 705-744-1714
mplibrary@efni.com
users.efni.com/~mplibrary/
Lise Moore Asselin, CEO

Maynooth: Hastings Highlands Public Library
33011 Hwy 62 North, Maynooth ON K0L 2S0
613-338-2262, Fax: 613-338-3292
info@hastingshighlandspubliclibrary.ca
www.hastingshighlandspubliclibrary.ca
Julie Andrews-Jotham, CEO/Librarian

McKellar: McKellar Twp Public Library
701 Hwy. 124, McKellar ON P0G 1C0
705-389-2611, Fax: 705-389-2611
mckellarlib@vianet.ca
www.mckellarpubliclibrary.ca
Joan Ward, Librarian
jward@post.library.on.ca

Meaford: Meaford Public Library
15 Trowbridge St. West, Meaford ON N4L 1V4
519-538-1060, Fax: 519-538-1808
info@meafordlibrary.on.ca
www.meafordlibrary.on.ca
Rita Orr, CEO
rita@meaford.com

Merrickville: Merrickville Public Library
446 Main St. East, Merrickville ON K0G 1N0
613-269-3326
merrickville_ill@bellnet.ca
www.village.merrickville-wolford.on.ca/mpl/library.htm
Mary Kate Laphen, Librarian

Midhurst: Simcoe County Library Co-Operative
County Administration Centre, 1110 Hwy. 26, Midhurst ON L0L 1X0
705-726-9300, Fax: 705-726-3991
gayle.hall@simcoe.ca
www.geocities.com/Athens/Forum/9021/
Gayle Hall, Chief Librarian
gayle.hall@simcoe.ca
705-726-4300 ext. 1258

Midhurst: Springwater Township Public Library
12 Finlay Mill Rd., Midhurst ON L0L 1X0
705-737-5650, Fax: 705-737-3594
midhurst.library@springwater.ca
www.springwater.ca/thingstodo/libraries
Lynn Patkau, Chief Librarian

Midland: Midland Public Library
320 King St., Midland ON L4R 3M6
705-526-4216, Fax: 705-526-1474
midlibrary@town.midland.on.ca
www.midlandlibrary.com
Bill Molesworth, Chief Librarian
bmolesworth@town.midland.on.ca

Millbrook: Cavan Monaghan Libraries
1 Dufferin St., Millbrook ON L0A 1G0
705-932-2919, Fax: 705-932-4019
www.cavanmonaghanlibraries.ca
Margot Loucks, Chief Executive Librarian & Librarian

Milton: Milton Public Library
45 Bruce St., Milton ON L9T 2L5
905-875-2665, Fax: 905-875-4324
www.mpl.on.ca
Leslie Fitch, CEO
leslie.fitch@mpl.on.ca
905-875-2665 ext. 3252

Milverton: Perth East Public Library
27 Main St. South, Milverton ON N0K 1M0
519-595-8395, Fax: 519-595-2943
pel@pcin.on.ca
www.pertheast.library.on.ca
Patti Henhoeffer, CEO
phenhoeffer@pcin.on.ca

Mindemoya: Central Manitoulin Public Libraries
6020 King St., Mindemoya ON P0P 1S0
705-377-5334, Fax: 705-377-5585
bookworm@amtelecom.net
Claire Cline, CEO/Chief Librarian

Mine Centre: Seine River First Nation Public Library
PO Box 129, Mine Centre ON P0W 1H0
807-599-2870, Fax: 807-599-2871
srlibrary@bellnet.com
Glenda Potson, Librarian
gpotson@fort-frances.lakeheadu.ca

Mississauga: Mississauga Library System
301 Burnhamthorpe Rd. West, Mississauga ON L5B 3Y3
905-615-3500, Fax: 905-615-3625
library.info@mississauga.ca
www.mississauga.ca/portal/residents/library
Don Mills, Director of Library Services
don.mills@mississauga.ca
905-615-3200 ext. 3601

Mitchell: West Perth Public Library
105 St. Andrew St., Mitchell ON N0K 1N0
519-348-9234, Fax: 519-348-4540
wpl@pcin.on.ca
www.westperth.library.on.ca
Caroline Shewburg, Librarian

Mobert: Pic Mobert First Nation Public Library
General Delivery, Mobert ON P0M 2J0
807-822-1594, Fax: 807-822-1578
principal@picmobert.ca

Moonbeam: Bibliothèque publique de Moonbeam/ Moonbeam Public Library
53, av St-Aubin, Moonbeam ON P0L 1V0
705-367-2462, Fax: 705-367-2120
biblio@village.moonbeam.on.ca
www.moonbeam.ca/bibliotheque.htm
Gisèle Belisle, Directrice-Responsable
705-367-2462

Morson: Big Grassy First Nation Public Library
PO Box 453, Morson ON P0W 1J0
807-488-5916, Fax: 807-488-5345
bglibrary@bgfn.on.ca
www.bgfn.on.ca/library.htm
Kitty Gale, Librarian

Muncey: Chippewas of the Thames
RR#1, 328 Chippewa Rd., Muncey ON N0L 1Y0
519-289-2176, Fax: 519-289-2230
cfnbooks@mnsi.net
Arlene Elm, Librarian

Muncey: Munsee-Delaware First Nation Public Library
RR#1, Muncey ON N0L 1Y0

519-289-5396, Fax: 519-289-5156
Rose Snake, CEO

Murillo: Oliver Paipoonge Public Library
1 Baxendale Rd., Murillo ON P0T 2G0
807-935-2729
www.olsn.ca/OliverPaipoonge
Maxine McCulloch, CEO
mmcculloch@post.library.on.ca

Napanee: Lennox & Addington County Library
97 Thomas St. East, Napanee ON K7R 4B9
613-354-4883, Fax: 613-354-3112
www.lennox-addington.on.ca
Mary Anne Evans, Director, Information Services
mevans@lennox-addington.on.ca

Naughton: Whitefish Lake First Nation Public Library
c/o Band Offices, 25 Reserve Rd., Naughton ON P0M 2M0
705-692-1102, Fax: 705-692-5010
library@wlfn.com
www.wlfn.com
Mary Fraser, Librarian

Nepean: Nepean Public Library/ Bibliothèque publique de Nepean
101 Centrepointe Dr., Nepean ON K2G 5K7
613-727-6637, Fax: 613-727-6677
www.biblioottawalibrary.ca/explore/branches/nc_e.cfm
George Skarzynski, Executive Director
george.skarzynski@library.on.ca
613-727-6637

Nestor Falls: Ojibways of Onigaming First Nation Public Library
School Rd., Nestor Falls ON P0X 1K0
807-484-2612, Fax: 807-484-2352
onigamingfn@yahoo.com
Geraldine Kelly, CEO

Newmarket: Newmarket Public Library
438 Park Ave., Newmarket ON L3Y 1W1
905-953-5110, Fax: 905-953-5104
npl@newmarketpl.ca
www.newmarketpl.ca
Patricia G. Wilson, CEO
pwilson@newmarketpl.ca
905-953-5110 ext. 467

Niagara Falls: Niagara Falls Public Library
4848 Victoria Ave., Niagara Falls ON L2E 4C5
905-356-8080, Fax: 905-356-7004
nfpl@nflibrary.ca
www.nflibrary.ca
Joseph Longo, Chief Librarian
jlongo@nflibrary.ca

Niagara on the Lake: Niagara Historical Research Centre
c/o Niagara on the Lake Public Library, 10, Anderson Lane, Niagara on the Lake ON L0S 1J0
905-468-2023, Fax: 905-468-3334
historylinda@yahoo.ca
vaxxine.com/fa/notlpl/
Greg Smith, CEO

Niagara on the Lake: Niagara on the Lake Public Library
10 Anderson Lane, Niagara on the Lake ON L0S 1J0
905-468-2023, Fax: 905-468-3334
kmcgrath@niagara.com
www.notlpubliclibrary.org
Greg Smith, CEO

Nipigon: Nipigon Public Library
25 Third St., Nipigon ON P0T 2J0
807-887-3142, Fax: 807-887-3142
niplib@nwconx.net
www.nwconx.net/~niplib/nnpl.html
Sumiye Sugawara, Library Technician/CEO

Nobel: Shawanaga First Nation Public Library
2 Church St., Nobel ON P0G 1G0
705-366-2526, Fax: 705-366-2740
csousa_20@hotmail.com
Chelsie Sousa, CEO
csousa_20@hotmail.com

North Bay: North Bay Public Library
271 Worthington St. East, North Bay ON P1B 1H1
705-474-4830
library@cityofnorthbay.ca
www.cityofnorthbay.ca/library

Paul Walker, CEO

Norwood: Asphodel-Norwood Public Library
2363 County Rd. 45, Norwood ON K0L 2V0
705-639-2228
norwest@asphodelnorwood.com
www.anpl.org

Oakville: Oakville Public Library
120 Navy St., Oakville ON L6J 2Z4
905-815-2042, Fax: 905-815-2024
interloan@oakville.ca
www.opl.on.ca
Lori Sims, CEO
lsims@oakville.ca

Ohsweken: Six Nations Public Library
PO Box 149, Ohsweken ON N0A 1M0
519-445-2954, Fax: 519-445-2873
saunders@snpl.ca
www.snpl.ca
Sabrina Saunders, Director, Library Services
saunders@snpl.ca
519-445-2954

Opasatika: La Bibliothèque d'Opasatika/ Opasatika Public Library
6, rue St. Antione, CP 100, Opasatika ON P0L 1Z0
705-369-3421, Fax: 705-369-2002
twpopas@ntl.sympatico.ca
www.geocities.com/bibliotheque_opasatika/
Diane Lambert, Bibliothécaire
librairi@ntl.sympatico.ca
705-369-3346

Orangeville: Orangeville Public Library
1 Mill St., Orangeville ON L9W 2M2
519-941-0610, Fax: 519-941-4698
info@orangeville.ca
www.orangeville.library.on.ca
Cindy Weir, CEO
cweir@orangeville.ca
519-941-0610 ext. 222

Orillia: Orillia Public Library
36 Mississaga St. West, Orillia ON L3V 3A6
705-325-2338, Fax: 705-327-1744
info@orilliapubliclibrary.ca
www.orilliapubliclibrary.ca/
Dawn Silver, CEO
dsilver@orilliapubliclibrary.ca

Orillia: Ramara Public Library
5482 Hwy. 12 South, Orillia ON L3V 6H7
705-325-5776, Fax: 705-325-8176
info@ramarapubliclibrary.org
www.ramarapubliclibrary.org
Janet Banfield, CEO

Oshawa: Oshawa Public Library
65 Bagot St., Oshawa ON L1H 1N2
905-579-6111, Fax: 905-433-8107
khaley@oshawalibrary.on.ca
www.oshawalibrary.on.ca
Ian Heckford, CEO
iheckford@oshawalibrary.on.ca
905-579-6111 ext. 212

Oshawa: United Way - Oshawa, Whitby, Clarington, Brock & Scugog
345 Simcoe St. South, Oshawa ON L1H 4J2
905-436-7377, Fax: 905-436-6414, 866-436-6910
informdurham@bellnet.ca
www.informdurham.com
Cathy Gowland, Manager, Information Services

Ottawa: ACA Bulletin
PO Box 2596, Stn D, Ottawa ON K1P 5W6
613-234-6977, Fax: 613-234-8500
aca@archivists.ca
archivists.ca/publications/bulletin.aspx
Larry Dohey, Editor
ldohey@nf.aibn.com

Ottawa: Archivaria
PO Box 2596, Stn D, Ottawa ON K1P 5W6
613-234-6977, Fax: 613-234-8500
aca@archivists.ca
archivists.ca/publications/archivaria.aspx
Catherine Bailey, Editor

Ottawa: Bulletin
Communications, Library & Archives Canada, 395 Wellington St, Ottawa ON K1A 0N4
613-995-7969, Fax: 613-991-9871
publications@lac-bac.gc.ca
www.collectionscanada.ca/publications/bulletin/index-e.html
Jean-Marie Brière, Editor

Ottawa: CAML Review
c/o Music Division, 395 Wellington St., Ottawa ON K1A 0N4
613-996-7519, Fax: 613-952-2895
dmaley@laurentian.ca
www.yorku.ca/caml
Desmond Maley, Editor

Ottawa: Feliciter
328 Frank St., Ottawa ON K2P 0X8
613-232-9625, Fax: 613-563-9895
jgreen@cla.ca
www.cla.ca/AM/Template.cfm?Section=Feliciter1
Mary-Lu Brennan, Convenor, Member Communications Advisory Committee

Ottawa: Impact
328 Frank St., Ottawa ON K2P 0X8
613-232-9625, Fax: 613-563-9895
vpennell@nfld.com
www.caslibraries.ca/newsletter
Victoria Pennell, Editor

Ottawa: Ottawa Public Library/ Bibliothèque publique d'Ottawa
120 Metcalfe St., Ottawa ON K1P 5M2
613-580-2945, Fax: 613-567-8815
www.biblioottawalibrary.ca
Barbara Clubb, City Librarian and CEO
barbara.clubb@biblioottawalibrary.ca

Ottawa: School Libraries in Canada
328 Frank St., Ottawa ON K2P 0X8
613-232-9625, Fax: 613-563-9895
jbranch@ualberta.ca
www.schoollibraries.ca
Jennifer Branch, Editor

Ottawa: Special Issues
328 Frank St., Ottawa ON K2P 0X8
613-232-9625, Fax: 613-563-9895
info@cla.ca
www.cla.ca/caslis/special_issues.htm
Rebecca Beausejour, Editor

Owen Sound: Owen Sound & North Grey Union Public Library
824 - 1st Ave. West, Owen Sound ON N4K 4K4
519-376-6623, Fax: 519-376-7170
library@owensound.library.on.ca
www.owensound.library.on.ca
Judy Armstrong, Library Director/CEO
jbarms@owensound.library.on.ca
519-376-6623 ext. 201

Paris: County of Brant Public Library
12 William St., Paris ON N3L 1K7
519-442-2433, Fax: 519-442-7582
paris.library@county.brant.on.ca
www.brant.library.on.ca
Gay Kozak Selby, Chief Librarian
gay.kozakselby@brant.ca

Parry Sound: Parry Sound Public Library
29 Mary St., Parry Sound ON P2A 1E3
705-746-9601, Fax: 705-746-9601
pslib@zeuter.com
www.pspl.on.ca
Laurine Tremaine, CEO

Parry Sound: Wasauksing First Nation Public Library
1508 Geewadin Rd., Parry Sound ON P2A 2X4
705-746-2531, Fax: 705-746-5984
wpl@vianet.on.ca
Carol M. Pegahmagabow, CEO

Pawitik: Whitefish Bay First Nation Public Library
General Delivery, Pawitik ON P0X 1L0
807-226-5698, Fax: 807-226-1089
naotkamegwanning_public_library@hotmail.com
Roberta Crow, CEO

Pelee Island: Pelee Island Public Library
1073 West Shore Rd., Pelee Island ON N0R 1M0
519-724-2028
Lynn Tiessen, Chair

Pembroke: Pembroke Public Library
237 Victoria St., Pembroke ON K8A 4K5

613-732-8844, Fax: 613-732-1116
askus@pembroke.library.on.ca
www.pembroke.library.on.ca
Margaret Mau, CEO

***Penetanguishene:* Penetanguishene Public Library**
24 Simcoe St., Penetanguishene ON L9M 1R6
705-549-7164, Fax: 705-549-3932
rmarchand@penetanguishene.library.on.ca
www.penetanguishene.library.on.ca
Rosemary Marchand, CEO

***Perth:* Perth Union Library**
30 Herriott St., Perth ON K7H 1T2
613-267-1224, Fax: 613-267-7899
perthlibrary@vianet.ca
www.perthunionlibrary.ca
Faye Cunningham, Head Librarian
fcunningham@vianet.ca

***Petawawa:* Petawawa Public Library**
16 Civic Centre Rd., Petawawa ON K8H 3H5
613-687-2227, Fax: 613-687-2527
info@petawawapubliclibrary.ca
www.petawawapubliclibrary.ca
C.M. Goldsmith, Librarian

***Peterborough:* Library Lines**
520 Weller St., Peterborough ON K9H 2N6
705-743-5998
gwjwthexton@nexicom.net
www.churchlibraries.ca/publications.htm
June Wilson Thexton, Editor

***Peterborough:* Peterborough Public Library**
345 Aylmer St. North, Peterborough ON K9H 3V7
705-745-5382, Fax: 705-745-8958
comments@city.peterborough.on.ca
www.peterborough.library.on.ca
Becky Rogers, CEO
brogers@city.peterborough.on.ca
705-745-5382 ext. 2380

***Philipsburg:* Region of Waterloo Library**
2017 Nafziger Rd., RR#2, Philipsburg ON N3A 3H4
519-575-4590, Fax: 519-634-5371
libhq@region.waterloo.on.ca
www.rwl.library.on.ca
Lucille Bish, Director, Community Services
blucille@region.waterloo.on.ca

***Pickering:* Pickering Public Library**
1 The Esplanade, Pickering ON L1V 6K7
905-831-6265, Fax: 905-831-6927, 888-831-6266
help@picnet.org
www.picnet.org
Cathy Grant, CEO

***Picton:* County of Prince Edward Public Library**
208 Main St., Picton ON K0K 2T0
613-476-5962, Fax: 613-476-3325
frdesk@peclibrary.org
www.peclibrary.org
Barbara Sweet, CEO

***Port Carling:* Township of Muskoka Lakes Library Board**
69 Joseph St., Port Carling ON P0B 1J0
705-765-5650, Fax: 705-765-0422
pclib@muskoka.com
www.muskoka.com/library
Elizabeth H. Glen, CEO/Librarian
pclib@muskoka.com
705-765-5650

***Port Colborne:* Port Colborne Public Library**
310 King St., Port Colborne ON L3K 4H1
905-834-6512, Fax: 905-835-5775
www.portcolbornelibrary.org
Jennifer R. Parry, Director of Library Services

***Port Elgin:* Bruce County Public Library**
1243 McKenzie Rd., Port Elgin ON N0H 2C6
519-832-6935, Fax: 519-832-9000
bruce2@brucecounty.on.ca
library.brucecounty.on.ca
Marzio Apolloni, CEO
mapolloni@brucecounty.on.ca

***Port Hope:* Port Hope Public Library**
31 Queen St., Port Hope ON L1A 2Y8
905-885-4712, Fax: 905-885-4181
library@porthope.ca
www.phpl.ca
Barbara Stephenson, Chief Librarian
bstephenson@porthpe.ca

***Port Loring:* Port Loring & District (Argyle) Public Library**
11767 Hwy. 522, Port Loring ON P0H 1Y0
705-475-2316, Fax: 705-757-3284
ArgyleCommunityLibrary@hotmail.com
Patti O'Handley, Chief Executive Officer

***Port McNicoll:* Tay Township Public Libraries**
715 - 4th Ave., Port McNicoll ON L0K 1R0
705-534-3511, Fax: 705-534-3511
pmlibrary@tay.township.on.ca
www.tay.library.on.ca
Heather Walker, Head Librarian
hwalker@tay.township.on.ca
705-534-3511

***Port Perry:* Mississaugas of Scugog Island First Nation Library**
22600 Island Rd., Port Perry ON L9L 1B6
905-985-1826, Fax: 905-985-7958
library@scugogfirstnation.com
Joan Wood, Librarian
jwood@scugogfirstnation.com
905-985-1826 ext. 222

***Port Perry:* Scugog Memorial Public Library**
231 Water St., Port Perry ON L9L 1A8
905-985-7686, Fax: 905-985-7210
info@scugoglibrary.ca
www.scugoglibrary.ca
Amy Caughlin, CEO
acaughlin@scugoglibrary.ca

***Port Rowan:* Port Rowan Public Library**
1034 Main St., Port Rowan ON N0E 1M0
519-586-3201, Fax: 519-586-3297
prpl@kwic.com
Marsha Johnstone, Librarian

***Powassan:* Powassan & District Union Public Library**
324 Clark St., Powassan ON P0H 1Z0
705-724-3618, Fax: 705-724-5525
hmcdonnell@ontera.net
powlib.www2.onlink.net
Helen McDonnell, CEO
hmcdonnell@post.library.on.ca

***Prescott:* Prescott Public Library**
360 Dibble St. West, Prescott ON K0E 1T0
613-925-4340, Fax: 613-925-0100
library@prescott.ca
www.prescott.ca/library/index.asp
Jane McGuire, Chief Librarian/CEO

***Rainy River:* Rainy River Public Library**
202 - 4th St., Rainy River ON P0W 1L0
807-852-3375, Fax: 807-852-3375
librr@tbaytel.net
my.tbaytel.net/librr/
Sheila McIntosh, Librarian/CEO

***Rama:* Mnjikaning First Nation Public Library**
6147 Rama Rd., Rama ON L0K 1T0
705-325-3611, Fax: 705-326-2146
barbara.lewis@mnjikaning.ca
Barbara Lewis, Libary Coordinator
barbara.lewis@mnjikaning.ca
705-325-3611 ext. 1407

***Red Lake:* Red Lake Public Library**
117 Howey St., Red Lake ON P0V 2M0
807-727-2230, Fax: 807-727-2230
rllib212@yahoo.com
www.nwconx.net/~rllib
Arlene Johnson, CEO

***Red Rock:* Red Rock Public Library**
42 Salls St., Red Rock ON P0T 2P0
807-886-2558, Fax: 807-886-2558
rrocklib@gmail.com
www.nextlibrary.com/redrock
Sandra Parker, Librarian

***Redbridge:* Phelps Public Library**
42 Old Mill Rd., RR#1, Redbridge ON P0H 2A0
705-663-2720
Beverly Reynolds, Librarian

***Renfrew:* Renfrew Public Library**
13 Railway Ave. East, Renfrew ON K7V 3A9
613-432-8151, Fax: 613-432-7680
renlib@renfrew.library.on.ca
www.renfrew.library.on.ca
Bettijane O'Neill, Chief Librarian

***Richards Landing:* St Joseph Twp Public Library**
PO Box 9, Richards Landing ON P0R 1J0
705-246-2353, Fax: 705-246-2353
sjtlibrary@ontera.net
stjosephisland.net
Sharon Thomas, Librarian/Treasurer/CEO

***Richmond Hill:* Richmond Hill Public Library**
1 Atkinson St., Richmond Hill ON L4C 0H5
905-884-9288, Fax: 905-884-6544
www.rhpl.richmondhill.on.ca
Jane Horrocks, CEO

***Rockland:* Bibliothèque publique de Clarence-Rockland/ Clarence-Rockland Public Library**
1560, rue Laurier, Rockland ON K4K 1P7
613-446-5680, Fax: 613-446-1518
llapalme@clarence-rockland.com
Lyne Lapalme, Directrice
llapalme@clarence-rockland.com

***Roseneath:* Alderville Learning Centre & Library**
11696 Second Line Rd., Roseneath ON K0K 2X0
905-352-2488, Fax: 905-352-1080
aldervillelearningcentre@eagle.ca
www.aldervillelearningcentre.com
Dona Wigmore, Librarian

***St Catharines:* St Catharines Public Library**
54 Church St., St Catharines ON L2R 7K2
905-688-6103, Fax: 905-688-6292
admin@stcatharines.library.on.ca
www.stcatharines.library.on.ca
Lilita Stripnieks, CEO
lstripnieks@stcatharines.library.on.ca
905-688-6103 ext. 235

***St Charles:* St Charles Public Library**
22 Ste. Anne St., St Charles ON P0M 2W0
705-867-5332, Fax: 705-867-2511
stcharles.library@yahoo.ca
cap-pac.8m.com
Lorraine Dubé, Chief Librarian
705-867-5332

***Saint-Isidore:* Bibliothèque publique de la municipalité de La Nation**
25, rue de L'Arena, Saint-Isidore ON K0C 2B0
613-524-2252, Fax: 613-524-2545
nationlibrary@bellnet.ca
www.nationmun.ca
Helena Morgan, CEO
nationlibrary@bellnet.ca
613-524-2252

***St Marys:* St Marys Public Library**
15 Church St. North, St Marys ON N4X 1B4
519-284-3346
tpope@postlibrary.on.ca
www.stmarys.library.on.ca
Terri Pope, Librarian/CEO
tpope@stmaryspubliclibrary.ca

***St Thomas:* Elgin County Library**
450 Sunset Dr., St Thomas ON N5R 5V1
519-631-1460, Fax: 519-631-9209
sloponen@elgin-county.on.ca
www.elgincounty.ca/ElginCounty/CulturalServices/Library
Sandi Loponen, Library Coordinator
sloponen@elgin-county.on.ca

***St Thomas:* St Thomas Public Library**
153 Curtis St., St Thomas ON N5P 3Z7
519-631-6050, Fax: 519-631-1987
rdenham@st-thomas.library.on.ca
www.st-thomas.library.on.ca
Rudi Denham, CEO

***Sandy Lake:* Deer Lake Indian Band Library**
c/o Band Offices via Favourable Lake PO, Sandy Lake ON P0V 1V0
L. Stoney, Librarian

***Saugeen:* Saugeen First Nation Library**
812 French Bay Rd., Saugeen ON N0H 2L0
519-797-5986, Fax: 519-797-5987
sfnlibrary@bmts.com

Theresa Gill, CEO

Sault Ste Marie: **Batchewana First Nation**
236 Frontenac St., RR#4, Sault Ste Marie ON P6A 5K9
705-759-0914, Fax: 705-759-9171
bfn.library@adss.on.ca
www.batchewana.ca
Darlene Syrette, Librarian

Sault Ste Marie: **Prince Township Library/ Bibliothèque publique du Canton Prince**
3042 Second Line, RR#6, Sault Ste Marie ON P6A 6K4
705-779-3653, Fax: 705-779-2725
ptpl@twp.prince.on.ca
www.twp.prince.on.ca
Marguerite LaHaye, CEO
ptpl@twp-rince.on.ca
705-779-3653

Sault Ste Marie: **Sault Ste Marie Public Library**
50 East St., Sault Ste Marie ON P6A 3C3
705-759-5236
www.ssmpl.ca
Christopher Rous, Chair

Savant Lake: **Savant Lake Community Library**
General Delivery, Savant Lake ON P0V 2S0
807-584-2242, Fax: 807-584-2272
Barbara Smith, Principal

Schreiber: **Schreiber Public Library**
314 Scotia St., Schreiber ON P0T 2S0
807-824-2477, Fax: 807-824-2996
schlib@nwconx.net
www.schreiberlibrary.ca
Donna Mikeluk, Head Librarian
schlib@nwconx.net
807-824-2477

Shannonville: **Tyendinaga Township Public Library**
852 Melrose Rd., RR#1, Shannonville ON K0K 3A0
613-967-0606, Fax: 613-396-2080
librarian@ttpl.ca
www.ttpl.ca
Frances Smith, Librarian/CEO

Sheguiandah: **Sheguiandah First Nation Public Library**
142 O'Ogemah Miilcan Rd., Sheguiandah ON P0P 1W0
705-368-2198, Fax: 705-368-3697
sheg1stnationpl@yahoo.com
Tammi Assinewai, Librarian

Shelburne: **Shelburne Public Library**
PO Box 127, Shelburne ON L0N 1S0
519-925-2168, Fax: 519-925-2168
spl1@bellnet.ca
Mary Lynne Armstrong, CEO

Sheshegwaning: **Sheshegwaning Public Library**
Sheshegwaning St., PO Box 1, Sheshegwaning ON P0P 1X0
705-283-3014, Fax: 705-283-4038
debracada@hotmail.com
www.olsn.ca/sheshegwaning
Debra Cada, CEO
debracada@hotmail.com

Shoal Lake: **Iskutewisakaggun #39 First Nation Community Public Library**
PO Box 5, Kejick Post Office, Shoal Lake ON P0X 1E0
807-733-3621, Fax: 807-733-3635
i_ross38@hotmail.com
Irene Ross, CEO
i_ross38@hotmail.com

Simcoe: **Norfolk County Public Library**
46 Colborne St. South, Simcoe ON N3Y 4H3
519-426-3506, Fax: 519-426-0657
library@norfolkcounty.on.ca
www.norfolk.library.on.ca
Bill Hett, CEO

Sioux Lookout: **Sioux Lookout Public Library**
21 5th Ave., Sioux Lookout ON P8T 1B3
807-737-3660, Fax: 807-737-4046
info@slpl.on.ca
www.slpl.on.ca
Wendy MacDonald, CEO/Chief Librarian
slpl@nwconw.net
807-737-3660

Sioux Narrows: **Sioux Narrows Public Library**
Sioux Narrows Public School, PO Box 119, Sioux Narrows ON P0X 1N0
807-226-5204, Fax: 807-226-5712
library@kmts.ca
Alice Motlong, Head Librarian
807-226-5204

Smiths Falls: **Smiths Falls Public Library**
81 Beckwith St. North, Smiths Falls ON K7A 2B9
613-283-2911, Fax: 613-283-9834
smithsfallslibrary@vianet.ca
Karen Schecter, Chief Librarian

Smithville: **West Lincoln Public Library**
Town Hall Complex, 318 Canboro St., Smithville ON L0R 2A0
905-957-3756
westlincolnlibrary.tripod.com

Smooth Rock Falls: **Smooth Rock Falls Public Library/ Bibliothèque publique de Smooth Rock Falls**
120 Ross Rd., Smooth Rock Falls ON P0L 2B0
705-338-2318, Fax: 705-338-2330
smooth@ntl.sympatico.ca
Lise Gagnon, CEO

South River: **South River-Machar Union Library**
22 Marie St., PO Box 190, South River ON P0A 1X0
705-386-0222, Fax: 705-386-0222
osrmlibrary@hotmail.com
www.oisn.ca/srmupl
Jan Heinonen, CEO
osrmlibrary@hotmail.com

Southwold: **Oneida Community Library**
2315 Keystone Pl., Southwold ON N0L 2G0
519-652-3271
librarian@oneida.on.ca
Corey Nicholas, CEO

Spanish: **Spanish Public Library/ Bibliothèque publique du Spanish**
8 Trunk Rd., Spanish ON P0P 2A0
705-844-2555, Fax: 705-844-2555
library@town.spanish.on.ca
www.town.spanish.on.ca/pages/library.asp
Hanne Sauvé, Chief Librarian
library@town.spanish.on.ca
705-844-2555

Spencerville: **Edwardsburgh / Cardinal Public Library**
5 Henderson St., Spencerville ON K0E 1X0
613-658-5575
cardinallibrary@bellnet.ca
www.cardinallibrary.ca
Marva Sothmann, Head Librarian

Stayner: **Clearview Public Library**
201 Huron St., Stayner ON L0M 1S0
705-428-3595
jlachap@clearviewtwp.on.ca
www.clearview.library.on.ca
Joyce Smith, Chair

Stirling: **Stirling-Rawdon Public Library**
43 Front St., Stirling ON K0K 3E0
613-395-2837
suew@stirlingrawdonpubliclibrary.ca
www.stirlingrawdonpubliclibrary.ca
Sue Winfield, CEO/Head Librarian

Stonecliffe: **Head, Clara & Maria Township Public Library**
15 Township Hall Rd., Stonecliffe ON K0J 2K0
613-586-2526, Fax: 613-586-2596
hcmlibra@xplornet.com
Gayle Watters, CEO

Stouffville: **Whitchurch-Stouffville Public Library**
30 Burkholder St., Stouffville ON L4A 4K1
905-642-7323, Fax: 905-640-1384, 888-603-4292
cnordheimerjames@whitchurch-library.on.ca
www.whitchurch-library.on.ca
Carolyn Nordheimer James, CEO
cnordheimer@whitchurch-library.on.ca
905-642-7323 ext. 223

Stratford: **Stratford Public Library**
19 St Andrew St., Stratford ON N5A 1A2
519-271-0220, Fax: 519-271-3843
spl@pcin.on.ca
www.stratford.library.on.ca
Sam Coghlan, CEO

Strathroy: **Middlesex County Library**
34B Frank St., Strathroy ON N7G 2R4
519-245-8237, Fax: 519-245-8238
www.middlesex.library.on.ca
Lindsay Brock, Reference Librarian
519—24-5-12

Stratton: **Stratton Community Library**
11605 Hwy. 11, Stratton ON P0W 1N0
807-483-5455, Fax: 807-483-5882
morley@nwonet.net
Anna H.M. Boily, Clerk-Treasurer

Sturgeon Falls: **West Nipissing Public Library/ Bibliothèque publique de Nipissing Ouest**
#107, 225 Holditch St., Sturgeon Falls ON P2B 1T1
705-753-2620, Fax: 705-753-2131
mail@wnpl.ca
www.wnpl.ca
Carole Marion, Chief Executive Officer
cmarion@wnpl.ca

Sudbury: **Greater Sudbury Public Library/ Bibliothèque publique du grand Sudbury**
74 Mackenzie St., Sudbury ON P3C 4X8
705-673-1155, Fax: 705-673-0554
infoser@sudbury.library.on.ca
www.sudbury.library.on.ca
Fern Cormier, Chair

Sundridge: **Sundridge-Strong Union Public Library**
110 Main St., Sundridge ON P0A 1Z0
705-384-7311, Fax: 705-384-7311
sslibrary@hotmail.com
www.olsn.ca/sundridgestronglibrary
Denise Rogers, Librarian

Sutton West: **Chippewas of Georgina Island First Nation Public Library**
Joseph Snake Rd., RR#2, Sutton West ON L0E 1R0
705-437-4328, Fax: 705-437-4597
gifnlib@ils.net
Karen Foster, CEO
karenfoster@knet.ca
705-437-4327

Tehkummah: **Tehkummah Township Public Library**
Municipal Offices Bldg., RR#1, Tehkummah ON P0P 2C0
705-859-3301, Fax: 705-859-2605
tehklib@yahoo.ca
Judy McDermid, Librarian

Temagami: **Temagami Public Library**
Welcome Centre, 7 Lakeshore Dr., Temagami ON P0H 2H0
705-569-2945, Fax: 705-569-2834
library@temagami.ca
www.temagami.ca/htm/library.htm
Shelley Rowland, CEO/Librarian

Terrace Bay: **Terrace Bay Public Library**
1010B Hwy. 17, Terrace Bay ON P0T 2W0
807-825-3315, Fax: 807-825-1249
terracebaypl@hotmail.com
www.nwconx.net/~terpl/
Mary Deschatelets, CEO

Thamesville: **Delaware Nation Public Library**
RR#3, Thamesville ON N0P 2K0
519-692-3411, Fax: 519-692-5522
dkstonefi@yahoo.ca
Darryl Stonefish, CEO

Thessalon: **Thessalon First Nation Public Library**
RR#2, PO Box 9, Thessalon ON P0R 1L0
705-842-1258, Fax: 705-842-2332
tfn_library@hotmail.com
Sherry Richards, Librarian

Thessalon: **Thessalon Union Public Library**
187 Main St., Thessalon ON P0R 1L0
705-842-2306, Fax: 705-842-5690
library@thesslibcap.com
www.thesslibcap.com
Mary D. Bockman, CEO

Thornbury: **The Blue Mountains Public Library**
PO Box 580, Thornbury ON N0H 2P0
519-599-3681, Fax: 519-599-7951
info@thebluemountainslibrary.ca
www.thebluemountainslibrary.ca
Carol Cooley, CEO
ccooley@thebluemountainslibrary.ca

Thornhill: **Vaughan Public Libraries**
900 Clark Ave. West, Thornhill ON L4J 8C1
905-653-7323, Fax: 905-709-1530
www.vaughanpl.com
Margie Singleton, Chief Executive Officer
margie.singleton@vaughan.ca

Thorold: **Thorold Public Library**
14 Ormond St. North, Thorold ON L2V 1Y8
905-227-2581, Fax: 905-227-2311
thoroldpubliclibrary@cogeco.net
www.thoroldpubliclibrary.ca
Patricia Bronson, CEO
pbronson@cogeco.net
905-227-2581

Thunder Bay: **Thunder Bay Public Library**
285 Red River Rd., Thunder Bay ON P7B 1A9
807-345-8275, Fax: 807-344-5119
adults@tbpl.ca (Adult services)
www.tbpl.ca
George Saarinen, Chair
gsaarinen@tbpl.ca

Tillsonburg: **Tillsonburg Public Library**
2 Library Lane, Tillsonburg ON N4G 4S7
519-842-5571, Fax: 519-842-2941
publiclibrary@tillsonburg.ca
Matthew Scholtz, Librarian
mscholtz@web.ocl.net

Timmins: **Timmins Public Library/ Bibliothèque municipale de Timmins**
320 Second Ave., Timmins ON P4N 8A4
705-360-2623, Fax: 705-360-2688
tpl_2@timmins.ca
tpl.timmins.ca
Judith Heinzen, CEO
tpl_4@timmins.ca
705-360-8520

Toronto: **ACCESS**
#303, 100 Lombard St., Toronto ON M5C 1M3
416-363-3388, Fax: 416-941-9581, 866-873-9867
info@accessola.com
www.accessola.com
Larry Moore, Editor

Toronto: **Cross Cultural Communication Centre**
2909 Dundas St. West, Toronto ON M6P 1Z1
416-760-7855, Fax: 416-760-7911
Carmen Alcalde, Librarian

Toronto: **Informed**
c/o Claude T. Bissell Bldg., 140 St George St., Toronto ON M5S 3G6
416-978-3034, Fax: 416-978-5762
alumni@fis.utoronto.ca
www.fis.utoronto.ca/people/fisaa/FISnewsletter/
Judy Donnelly, Editor

Toronto: **Jewish Public Library of Toronto**
4600 Bathurst St., 4th Fl., Toronto ON M2R 3V3
416-635-2996
jewishpubliclibrary@ujafed.org
Susan Jackson, Executive Director, Latner Centre for Jewish Knowledge & Heritage
416-635-2996

Toronto: **Off the Record**
#301, 258 Adelaide St. East, Toronto ON M5A 1N1
416-533-9592, Fax: 416-533-1481
aao@aao.fis.utoronto.ca
aao.fis.utoronto.ca/aa/otr.html
Marianne Henskens, Executive Director

Toronto: **Papers of the Bibliographical Society of Canada / Cahiers de la Société bibliographique du canada**
42 Belmont St., Toronto ON M5R 1P8
416-487-6729
slatham@gbrownc.on.ca
www.library.utoronto.ca/bsc/paperseng.html
Sheila Latham, Editor

Toronto: **Shelf Life**
789 Yonge St., Toronto ON M4W 2G8
416-393-7215
www.torontopubliclibrary.ca/new_she_index.jsp
Nancy Marshall, Library Board Contact

Toronto: **The Bibliographical Society of Canada Bulletin / La Société bibliographique du canada. Bulletin**
c/o Anne McGaughey, PO Box 575, Stn P, Toronto ON M5S 2T1
416-487-6729
mcgaughe@yorku.ca
www.library.utoronto.ca/bsc
Patricia Belier, Editor

Toronto: **The Teaching Librarian**
#303, 100 Lombard St., Toronto ON M5C 1M3
416-363-3388, Fax: 416-941-9581, 866-873-9867
membership@accessola.com
www.accessola.com/osla/about/magazine.htm

Toronto: **Toronto Public Library**
789 Yonge St., Toronto ON M4W 2G8
416-393-7000, Fax: 416-393-7083
www.torontopubliclibrary.ca
Josephine Bryant, City Librarian (retiring July, 2008)
jbryant@torontopubliclibrary.ca
416-393-7032

Trenton: **Quinte West Public Library**
7 Creswell Dr., Trenton ON K8V 6X5
613-394-3381, Fax: 613-394-2079
info.qwpl@city.quintewest.on.ca
www.library.quintewest.com
Craig Desjardins, Chair

Tweed: **Municipality of Tweed Public Library**
255 Metcalf St., Tweed ON K0K 3J0
613-478-1066, Fax: 613-478-6457
tweedlibrary@vianet.ca
tweedlibrary.ca
Catherine Anderson, CEO

Uxbridge: **Uxbridge Twp Public Library**
9 Toronto St. South, Uxbridge ON L9P 1P3
905-852-9747
uxlib@powergate.ca
www.uxlib.com
Alexandra Hartmann, Chief Librarian

Val Rita: **Val Rita-Harty Public Library/ Bibliothèque municipale de Val Rita-Harty**
106, rue Gouvernement, Val Rita ON P0L 2G0
705-335-8700, Fax: 705-335-8700
bibliovalrita@hotmail.com
www.valharty.ca
Cecile Lamontagne, Présidente du conseil bibliothèque

Vankleek Hill: **Champlain Township Public Library/ Bibliothèque Champlain**
94 Main St. East, PO Box 520, Vankleek Hill ON K0B 1R0
613-678-2216, Fax: 613-678-2216
library@champlaintwplibrary.ca
www.champlaintwplibrary.ca
Lise Béliveau, Chair

Virginiatown: **McGarry Twp Public Library/ Bibliothèque publique de McGarry**
1 - 27 St., Virginiatown ON P0K 1X0
705-634-2312, Fax: 705-634-2312
mcgarry@onlink.net
www.mcgarrypubliclibrary.8m.com/main_en.html
Leah Collins, CEO/Librarian

Wainfleet: **Wainfleet Twp Public Library**
19M9 Park St., PO Box 118, Wainfleet ON L0S 1V0
905-899-1277, Fax: 905-899-2495
www.wainfleetlibrary.ca
Lorrie Atkinson, CEO
latkinson@wainfleetlibrary.ca

Wallaceburg: **Bkejwanong First Nation Public Library**
RR#3, Wallaceburg ON N8A 4K9
519-627-7034, Fax: 519-627-7035
bkejlib@mail.com
Lynda Lou Classens, Librarian/CEO
library@wifn.org
519-627-7034

Wasaga Beach: **Wasaga Beach Public Library**
120 Glenwood Dr., Wasaga Beach ON L9Z 2K5
705-429-5481, Fax: 705-429-5481
wblibrary@georgian.net
www.wasagabeach.library.on.ca
Jackie Beaudin, CEO

Waterloo: **Waterloo Public Library**
35 Albert St., Waterloo ON N2L 5E2
519-886-1310, Fax: 519-886-7936
cbrown@wpl.ca
www.wpl.ca
Cathy Matyas, Chief Librarian
cmatyas@wpl.ca
519-886-1310 ext. 123

Wawa: **Michipicoten Twp Public Library**
40 Broadway Ave., Wawa ON P0S 1K0
705-856-2062, Fax: 705-856-1488
mtpl@wawa.cc
www.mtpl.on.ca
Jayne Griffith, CEO/Head Librarian

Weagamow Lake: **North Caribou First Nation Public Library**
PO Box 158, Weagamow Lake ON P0V 2Y0
807-469-1288, Fax: 807-469-1132
beatricekanate@knet.ca
Beatrice Kanate, CEO

Welland: **Welland Public Library**
50 The Boardwalk, Welland ON L3B 6J1
905-734-6210, Fax: 905-734-8955
ref@welland.library.on.ca
www.welland.library.on.ca
Janet C. Booth, CEO
jbooth@welland.library.on.ca

Wendover: **Bibliothèque publique du Canton d'Alfred et Plantagenet/ Alfred & Plantagenet Public Library**
3104 av du Quai, Wendover ON K0A 3K0
613-673-2923
bibliowend@yahoo.ca
www.alfred-platagenet.com/en/Libraries_42.html
Catherine Bélisle, Directrice

Westport: **Westport Public Library**
3 Spring St., Westport ON K0G 1X0
613-273-3223, Fax: 613-273-3223
library@rideau.net
Pamela Stuffles, Librarian

Whitby: **Whitby Public Library**
405 Dundas St. West, Whitby ON L1N 6A1
905-668-6531, Fax: 905-668-7445
admin@whitbylibrary.on.ca
www.whitbylibrary.on.ca
Ian Ross, Chief Librarian

White River: **White River Public Library**
123 Superior St., White River ON P0M 3G0
807-822-1113
wrlib@nwconx.net
www.whiteriverlibrary.com
Jan Ramage, CEO

Whitedog: **Wabaseemoong First Nation Public Library**
General Delivery, Whitedog ON P0X 1P0
807-927-2000

Whitney: **South Algonquin Public Library**
PO Box 208, Whitney ON K0J 2M0
613-637-5471, Fax: 613-637-5471
whitlib@northcom.net
www.olsn.ca/southalgonquin
Charlene Alexander, CEO
613-637-5471

Wiarton: **Ninda Kikaendjigae Wigammik First Nation Public Library**
RR#5, Wiarton ON N0H 2T0
519-534-1508, Fax: 519-534-2130
liz.taylor@bmts.com
Daphne Johnston, CEO/Librarian

Wikwemikong: **Wikwemikong First Nation Public Library**
34-A Henry St., Wikwemikong ON P0P 2J0
705-859-2692, Fax: 705-859-3851
smish@amtelecom.net
www.wiky.net
Sheri Mishibinijima, Librarian
smish@amtelecom.net

Windsor: **Windsor Public Library**
850 Ouellette Ave., Windsor ON N9A 4M9
519-255-6770, Fax: 519-255-7207
wpl@city.windsor.on.ca
www.windsorpubliclibrary.com

Nancy Peel, Manager
npeel@windsorpubliclibrary.com
519-255-6770

***Woodstock:* Oxford County Library**
Oxford County Administration Bldg., 21 Reeve St., Woodstock ON N4S 7Y3
519-539-9800, Fax: 519-485-4028
www.ocl.net
Don McKay, Chair

***Woodstock:* Woodstock Public Library**
445 Hunter St., Woodstock ON N4S 4G7
519-539-4801, Fax: 519-539-5246
gbaumbach@woodstock.library.on.ca
www.woodstock.library.on.ca
Gary Baumbach, Chief Librarian
gbaumbach@woodstock.library.on.ca

***Wyoming:* Lambton County Library Headquarters**
787 Broadway St., Wyoming ON N0N 1T0
519-845-3324, Fax: 519-845-0700, 866-324-6912
library.headquarters@county-lambton.on.ca
www.lclmg.org
April James, Manager, Libraries, Museums, & Cultural Services
april.james@county-lambton.on.ca

Archives

***Ameliasburgh:* Quinte Educational Museum & Archives**
13 Coleman St., Ameliasburgh ON K0K 1A0
613-966-5501
qema@bellnet.ca
www.pec.on.ca/victoriaschoolhouse
Dan Rainey, President

***Amherstburg:* Marsh Collection Society**
235A Dalhousie St., Amherstburg ON N9V 1W6
519-736-9191, Fax: 519-736-7166
mcschin@mnsi.net
www.mnsi.net/~mcschin
Jennifer MacLeod, Archivist
mcschin@mnsi.net
519-736-9191

***Amherstburg:* North American Black Historical Museum**
277 King St., Amherstburg ON N9V 2C7
519-736-5433, 800-713-6336
nabhm@mnsi.net
www.blackhistoricalmuseum.com
Elise Harding-Davis, Curator/Administrator

***Aylmer:* Aylmer & District Museum Association**
14 East St., Aylmer ON N5H 1W2
519-773-9723, Fax: 519-773-9723
aylmermuseum@amtelecom.net
www.amtelecom.net/~aymlermuseum/
Pat Zimmer, Curator

***Bayfield:* Bayfield Archives Room**
20 Main St. North, Bayfield ON N0M 1G0
519-565-2376
bayarchives@tcc.on.ca
www.bayfieldhistorical.ca
Elaine Sturgeon, Archivist
519-565-2376

***Beachville:* County of Oxford Archives**
12 Vine St., Beachville ON N0J 1A0
519-423-1928, Fax: 519-423-1964
archives@county.oxford.on.ca
www.county.oxford.on.ca/archives
Mary Gladwin, Archivist
mgladwin@ocl.net
519-426-1928 ext. 210

***Brampton:* Region of Peel Archives**
Peel Heritage Complex, 9 Wellington St. East, Brampton ON L6W 1Y1
905-791-4055, Fax: 905-451-4931
diane.allengame@peelregion.ca
www.region.peel.on.ca/heritage/archives.htm
Diane Allengame, Collections Registrar/Regional Archivist
diane.allengame@peelregion.ca
905-791-4055

***Brantford:* Brant Museum Archives**
57 Charlotte St., Brantford ON N3T 2W6
519-752-2483, Fax: 519-752-1931
information@brantmuseum.ca
brantmuseum.ca
Joan Kanigan-Fairen, Executive Director

***Bridgenorth:* Smith Ennismore Historical Society**
826 Ward St., Bridgenorth ON K0L 1H0
705-292-9430, Fax: 705-742-4136
feedback@sehs.on.ca
sehs.on.ca
Bernice Harris, Contact
m.bharris@cogeco.ca

***Brockville:* Brockville Museum**
5 Henry St., Brockville ON K6V 6M4
613-342-4397, Fax: 613-342-7345
info@brockvillemuseum.com
www.brockvillemuseum.com
Bonnie Burke, Curator/Director
bburke@brockville.com
613-342-4397

***Burlington:* Joseph Brant Museum**
1240 North Shore Blvd. East, Burlington ON L7S 1C5
905-634-3556, Fax: 905-634-4498, 888-748-5386
jbm@on.aibn.com
Barbara E. Teatero, Director

***Cambridge:* Cambridge Archives**
46 Dickson St., 2nd Fl., Cambridge ON N1R 1T7
519-740-4680, Fax: 519-623-0058
archives@city.cambridge.on.ca
www.city.cambridge.on.ca
Jim Quantrell, Archivist
quantrellj@city.cambridge.on.ca
519-740-4680 ext. 4610

***Cannington:* Cannington & Area Historical Society**
PO Box 196, Cannington ON L0E 1E0
705-432-2430, Fax: 705-432-2909

***Chatham:* Chatham-Kent Museum**
75 William St. North, Chatham ON N7M 4L4
519-360-1998, Fax: 519-354-4170
CKccc@chatham-kent.ca
Stephanie Suitor, Curator
stephanies@chatham-kent.ca

***Combermere:* Madonna House Archives**
2888 Dafoe Rd. RR#2, Combermere ON K0J 1L0
613-756-1766, Fax: 613-756-0211
archives@madonnahouse.org
www.madonnahouse.org
Mary Rowland, Contact

***Delhi:* Delhi Tobacco Museum & Heritage Centre**
200 Talbot Rd., Delhi ON N4B 2A2
519-582-0278, Fax: 519-582-0122
tobacco.museum@norfolkcounty.ca
Judy A. Livingstone, Curator/Director

***Fergus:* Wellington County Museum & Archives**
0536 Wellington Rd. 18, RR#1, Fergus ON N1M 2W3
519-846-0916, Fax: 519-846-9630
karen@wcm.on.ca
www.wcm.on.ca
Bonnie Callen, Museum Administrator

***Fort Frances:* Fort Frances Museum & Cultural Centre**
259 Scott St., Fort Frances ON P9A 1G8
807-274-7891, Fax: 807-274-4103
phawley@fort-frances.com
www.fort-frances.com/museum
Pam Hawley, Director-Curator

***Georgetown:* Esquesing Historical Society**
9 Church St., Georgetown ON L7G 2A3
905-877-9510
mrowe6@cogeco.ca
www.esquesinghistoricalsociety.ca
Stephen Blake, President, Esquesing Historical Society

***Goderich:* Huron County Museum Archives**
110 North St., Goderich ON N7A 2T8
519-524-2686, Fax: 519-524-1922
www.huroncounty.ca/museum
Beth Ross, Director
bross@huroncounty.ca
519-524-2686

***Gravenhurst:* Gravenhurst Archives**
Gravenhurst Public Library, 180 Sharpe St. West, Gravenhurst ON P1P 1J1
705-687-3382, Fax: 705-687-7016
rkirton@gravenhurst.ca
Marion Fry, Volunteer Archivist

***Guelph:* Guelph Museums**
6 Dublin St. South, Guelph ON N1H 4L5
519-836-1221, Fax: 519-836-5280
museum@guelph.ca
www.guelph.ca/museum
Bev Dietrich, Curator
519-836-1221 ext. 224

***Haliburton:* Haliburton Highlands Museum**
PO Box 535, Haliburton ON K0M 1S0
705-457-2760
haliburtonmuseum@halhinet.on.ca
www.haliburtonhighlands.com/museum
Thomas Ballantine, Director

***Hamilton:* Canadian Baptist Archives/ Archives baptistes canadiennes**
c/o McMaster Divinity College, 1280 Main St. West, Hamilton ON L8S 4K1
905-525-9140, Fax: 905-577-4782
cbarch@mcmaster.ca
www.macdiv.ca/students/baptistarchives.php
Gordon Heath, Director
gheath@mcmaster.ca
905-525-9140 ext. 26409
Carl Spadoni, Research Collections Librarian

***Hamilton:* Diocese of Niagara, Archives**
Division of Archives, McMaster University Library,, 1280 Main St. West, Hamilton ON L8S 4L6
905-525-9140, Fax: 905-546-0625
archives@mcmaster.ca
library.mcmaster.ca/archives/anglican/anhome.html
Darcy Glidden, Manager
dglidden@hpl.ca
905-546-3200 ext. 6343

***Hamilton:* Local History & Archives Department**
55 York Blvd., Hamilton ON L8N 4E4
905-546-3408
hpl.hwcn.org/comment.html
www.hpl.ca
Sherry Wykes, Archivist

***Keewatin:* Diocese of Keewatin, Archives**
915 Ottawa St., Keewatin ON P0X 1C0
807-547-3353, Fax: 807-547-3356
dioceseofkeewatin@gokenora.com

***Kenora:* Lake of the Woods Museum**
300 Main St. South, Kenora ON P9N 1T2
807-467-2105, Fax: 807-467-2109
museum@kmts.ca
www.lakeofthewoodsmuseum.ca
Lori Nelson, Director
Paul Banfield, Diocesan Archivist
banfield@post.queens.ca

***Kingston:* Anglican Diocese of Ontario, Archives**
90 Johnston St., Kingston ON K7L 1X7
613-544-4774, Fax: 613-547-3745
archives@ontario.anglican.ca
www.ontario.anglican.ca/archives

***Kingston:* Fort Henry**
PO Box 213, Kingston ON K7L 4V8
613-542-7388, Fax: 613-542-3054
getaway@parks.on.ca .
www.forthenry.com
Ron Ridley, Curator
ron.ridley@forthenry.com

***Kingston:* Marine Museum of the Great Lakes at Kingston**
55 Ontario St., Kingston ON K7L 2Y2
613-542-2261, Fax: 613-542-0043
marmuseum@marmuseum.ca
www.marmuseum.ca
Maurice Smith, Curator Emeritus
Paul Banfield, Acting University Archivist
banfield@post.queensu.ca
613-533-6000 ext. 74460

***Kingston:* Queen's University Archives**
Kathleen Ryan Hall, 11 Medical Quadrangle, Kingston ON K7L 3N6
613-533-2378, Fax: 613-533-6403
archives@post.queensu.ca
archives.queensu.ca

***Kingston:* Religious Hospitallers of St. Joseph, St Joseph Province**
16 Manitou Cres. East, Kingston ON K7N 1B2

613-389-0275, Fax: 613-384-6978
reg.archives@bellnet.ca
Rodney Carter, Archivist

Kingston: Roman Catholic Archdiocese of Kingston
390 Palace Rd., Kingston ON K7L 4T3
613-548-4461, Fax: 613-548-4744
www.romancatholic.kingston.on.ca/index.html

Kingston: Sisters of Providence of St. Vincent de Paul
1200 Princess St., Kingston ON K7M 3C9
613-544-4525, Fax: 613-531-9805
archives@providence.ca
Gayle Desarmia, Head, Information & Heritage Services
archives@providence.ca
613-544-4525

Kingston: The International Hockey Hall of Fame & Museum
277 York St., Kingston ON K7K 1R7
613-544-2355, Fax: 613-544-2844
info@ihhof.com
www.ihhof.com
Mark Potter, President

Kitchener: Doon Heritage Crossroads
10 Huron Rd., Kitchener ON N2P 2R7
519-748-1914, Fax: 519-748-0009
hliz@region.waterloo.on.ca
www.region.waterloo.on.ca/doon/
Elizabeth Hardin, Registrar/Researcher
hliz@region.waterloo.on.ca
Karen Ball-Pyatt, Local History Librarian
519-743-0271 ext. 252

Kitchener: Grace Schmidt Room of Local History
85 Queen St. North, Kitchener ON N2H 2H1
519-743-0271
karen.ball-pyatt@kpl.org
Elaine Baldwin, Medical Librarian
ebaldwin@smgh.ca
519-749-6549

Kitchener: St Mary's General Hospital (Kitchener) Archives
911 Queen's Blvd., Kitchener ON N2M 1B2
519-749-6549, Fax: 519-749-6526

Kitchener: Schneider Corporation
321 Courtland Ave. East, Kitchener ON N2G 2W1
519-741-5000
Karen Trussler, Communication Editor/Archivist

Kleinburg: McMichael Canadian Art Collection/ Collection McMichael d'Art Canadien
10365 Islington Ave., Kleinburg ON L0J 1C0
905-893-1121, Fax: 905-893-2588
lmorita@mcmichael.com
Linda Morita, Librarian/Archivist
lmorita@mcmichael.com

Listowel: Listowel & Area Division
260 Main St. West, Listowel ON N4W 1A1
519-291-1598, Fax: 519-291-5611
listowelarchives@pcin.on.ca
www.stratfordpertharchives.on.ca
James R. Broadfoot, Archivist
archives@huron.anglican.ca

London: Diocese of Huron Archives
Huron University College, 1349 Western Rd., London ON N6G 1H3
519-645-7956, Fax: 519-645-8669
archives@huron.anglican.ca
www.archives.diohuron.org
John H. Lutman, Head, Talman Collection
jlutman@lib.uwo.ca
519-661-2111

London: J.J. Talman Regional Collection
D.B. Weldon Library, University of Western Ontario, 1151 Richmond St., London ON N6A 3K7
519-661-2111
www.lib.uwo.ca/weldon/docs/regional.html
Arthur McClelland, London Room Librarian
arthur.mcclelland@lpl.london.on.ca

London: London Room
251 Dundas St., London ON N6A 6H9
519-661-4600
info@lpl.london.on.ca
www.londonpubliclibrary.ca

London: Museum London
421 Ridout St. North, London ON N6A 5H4
519-661-0330, Fax: 519-661-2559
jcwean@museumlondon.ca
Janette Cousins Ewan, Art Registrar

London: The Royal Canadian Regiment Museum
Wolseley Barracks, 750 Elizabeth St., London ON N5Y 4T7
519-660-5102, Fax: 519-660-5344
breede.c@forces.gc.ca
thercr.ca
Claus Breede, Curator
519-660-5102
Robin Keirstead, University Archivist
rkeirste@uwo.ca
519-661-2111 ext. 87289

London: University of Western Ontario Archives
Archives & Research Collections Centre, University of Western Ontario, 1151 Richmond St., London ON N6A 3K7
519-661-2111, Fax: 519-850-2979
archiveservices@uwo.ca
www.lib.uwo.ca/archives

Midland: Huronia Museum
549 Little Lake Park, Midland ON L4R 4P4
705-526-2844, Fax: 705-527-6622
director@huroniamuseum.com
www.huroniamuseum.com
Jamie Hunter, Curator

Milton: Halton Region Museum
5181 Kelso Rd., Milton ON L9T 2X7
905-875-2200, Fax: 905-876-4322, 866-442-5866
museum@halton.ca
www.region.halton.on.ca/museum
Linda Twitchell, Curator

Minesing: Simcoe County Archives
1149 Hwy. 26, RR#2, Minesing ON L0L 1Y2
705-726-9331, Fax: 705-725-5341
archives@simcoe.ca
www.county.simcoe.on.ca/cultureinformation/archives/
Bruce Beacock, County Archivist

Mississauga: Pentecostal Assemblies of Canada
2450 Milltower Ct., Mississauga ON L5N 5Z6
905-542-7400, Fax: 905-542-7313
archives@paoc.org
www.paoc.org/about/archives
Marilyn Stroud, Assistant Archivist
mstroud@paoc.org
905-842-7400 ext. 5282
Lynda Jones, Archives Clerk

Mitchell: Mitchell Division
7D Frances St., Mitchell ON N0K 1N0
519-348-8817, Fax: 519-348-9805
mitchellarchives@pcin.on.ca
www.stratfordpertharchives.on.ca

Morrisburg: Upper Canada Village
13740 County Rd. 2, Morrisburg ON K0C 1X0
613-543-3704, Fax: 613-543-4098
www.uppercanadavillage.com
Jan Omond, Contact

Napanee: Lennox & Addington County Museum & Archives
97 Thomas St. East, Napanee ON K7R 4B9
613-354-3027
archives@lennox-addington.on.ca
lennox-addington.on.ca
Jane Foster, Manager
613-354-3027

Niagara on the Lake: Shaw Festival Theatre Foundation Library
PO Box 774, Niagara on the Lake ON L0S 1J0
905-468-7140, Fax: 905-468-5438
www.shawfest.com
Nancy Butler, Head

North Bay: Nipissing Archives
Discovery North Bay, 100 Ferguson St., North Bay ON P1B 1W8
705-476-2323, Fax: 705-476-9300
info@heritagenorthbay.com
www.city.north-bay.on.ca/museum
Jennifer Bell, Director
education@heritagenorthbay.com

Norwich: Norwich & District Historical Society
91 Stover St. North, RR#3, Norwich ON N0J 1P0
519-863-3638, Fax: 519-863-2343
norwichdhs@execulink.com
www.norwichdhs.ca
Mary Beth Start, Curator/Archivist

Oil Springs: Oil Museum of Canada
2324 Kelly Rd., Oil Springs ON N0N 1P0
519-834-2840, Fax: 519-834-2840
omcchin@ebtech.net
Connie Bell, Manager
connie.bell@county-lambton.on.ca

Orillia: Mariposa Folk Foundation
37 Mississauga St. W, Orillia ON L3V 3A5
705-329-2333, Fax: 705-329-4099
www.mariposafolk.com
Paulette Kirkey, President

Orillia: Stephen Leacock Museum/Archives
50 Museum Dr., Orillia ON L3V 7T9
705-329-1908, Fax: 705-326-5578
leacock@transdata.ca
www.leacockmuseum.com
Craig Metcalf, Director

Orono: Clarke Museum & Archives
7086 Old Kirby School Rd., RR#1, Orono ON L0B 1M0
905-983-9243
cma-chin@durham.net

Oshawa: Oshawa Community Museum & Archives
1450 Simcoe St. South, Lakeview Park, Oshawa ON L1H 8S8
905-436-7624, Fax: 905-436-7625
archivist@oshawamuseum.org
www.oshawamuseum.org/archives.html
Amber Nowak, Contact

Oshawa: Robert McLaughlin Gallery
Civic Centre, 72 Queen St., Oshawa ON L1H 3Z3
905-576-3000, Fax: 905-576-9774
communications@rmg.on.ca
www.rmg.on.ca
Barb Duff, Library Services Coordinator
bduff@rmg.on.ca
905-576-3000 ext. 102
Glenn J. Lockwood, Diocesan Archivist

Ottawa: Anglican Diocese of Ottawa
420 Sparks St., Ottawa ON
613-232-7124, Fax: 613-232-7088
archives@ottawa.anglican.ca
www.ottawa.anglican.ca/archives.shtml
Jane Boyko, Archivist
jboyko@bankofcanada.ca
613-782-8673

Ottawa: Bank of Canada Archives
234 Wellington St., Ottawa ON K1A 0G9
613-782-8673, Fax: 613-782-7387
jboyko@bankofcanada.ca

Ottawa: Bytown Railway Society
PO Box 141, Stn A, Ottawa ON K1N 8V1
613-745-1201
info@bytownrailwaysociety.ca
www.bytownrailwaysociety.ca
Paul Bown, Archivist

Ottawa: C. Robert Craig Memorial Library
Ottawa City Archives, 110 Laurier Ave. West, Ottawa ON K1P 1J1
613-580-2424, Fax: 613-580-2614
KennethHealy@cs.com
www.ovar.ca/CraigLibrary/craiglib.htm
Dave Knowles, President & Librarian
knowles@istar.ca
613-722-4473

Ottawa: Canadian Institute of Geomatics/ Association canadienne des sciences géomatiques
#400, 1390 Prince of Wales Dr., Ottawa ON K2C 3N6
613-224-9851, Fax: 613-224-9577
editgeo@magma.ca
www.cig-acsg.ca
Carol Railer, Production & Advertising Manager

Ottawa: Canadian Intergovernmental Conference Secretariat/ Secrétariat des conférences intergouvernementales Canadiennes
222 Queen St., 10th Fl., Ottawa ON K1P 5V9
613-995-4310, Fax: 613-947-4336
info@scics.gc.ca
www.scics.gc.ca
Jane Dubé, Head, Information Management

***Ottawa:* Canadian Museum of Nature/ Musée canadien de la nature**
PO Box 3443, Stn D, Ottawa ON K1P 6P4
613-364-4042, Fax: 613-364-4026
cmnlib@mus-nature.ca
www.nature.ca
Patrice Stevenson, Librarian
pstevenson@mus-nature.ca
613-364-4045

***Ottawa:* Canadian Ski Museum/ Le Musée canadien du ski**
1960 Scott St., Ottawa ON K1Z 8L8
613-722-3584, Fax: 613-722-2914
info@skimuseum.ca
www.skimuseum.ca

***Ottawa:* Canadian Women's Movement Archives/ Archives canadiennes du mouvement des femmes**
Morisset Library, University of Ottawa, #603, 65 University Pvt, Ottawa ON K1N 6N5
613-562-5910, Fax: 613-562-5133
arcs@uottawa.ca
www.biblio.uottawa.ca/
Lucie Desjardins, Archivist
lucie.desjardins@uottawa.ca

***Ottawa:* Centre de recherche en histoire religieuse du Canada/ Research Centre in Religious History of Canada**
223 Main St., Ottawa ON K1S 1C4
613-236-1393, Fax: 613-782-3005
crh-rc-rhc@ustpaul.ca
www.ustpaul.ca/RCRHC/index_e.asp
Pierre Hurtubise, Directeur

***Ottawa:* City of Ottawa Archives/ Archives municipales d'Ottawa**
Bytown Pavilion, 111 Sussex Dr., 1st Fl., Ottawa ON K1N 1J1
613-580-2424, Fax: 613-580-2614
archives@ottawa.ca
ottawa.ca/residents/heritage/archives/index_en.html
David Bullock, City Archivist
david.bullock@ottawa.ca
613-580-2424 ext. 13787

***Ottawa:* Friends of Library & Archives Canada**
395 Wellington St., Ottawa ON K1A 0N4
613-992-8304, Fax: 613-943-2343
friends.amis@lac-bac.gc.ca
www.collectionscanada.ca/friends/index-e.html
Ron Cohan, President
Christina Tessier, Director

***Ottawa:* Historical Society of Ottawa, Bytown Museum Archives**
PO Box 523, Stn B, Ottawa ON K1P 5P6
613-234-4570, Fax: 613-234-4846
bytownmuseum@storm.ca
www.bytownmuseum.com
Doug Robinson, Deputy Conference Archivist

***Ottawa:* Montréal & Ottawa Conference Archives - Ottawa & Seaway Valley Presbyteries**
City of Ottawa Archives, 111 Sussex Dr., 1st Floor, Bytown Pavillion, Ottawa ON K1N 1J1
613-580-2424, Fax: 613-580-2614
archives@ottawa.ca
www.united-church.ca/archives/mo/ottawa.shtm

***Ottawa:* National Archival Appraisal Board/ Conseil national d'évaluation des archives**
c/o CCA, #501, 130 Albert St., Ottawa ON K1P 5G4
613-565-1222, Fax: 613-565-5445
info@naab.ca
www.naab.ca
Louise Pilon, Administrator
lpilon@archives.ca

***Ottawa:* Oblats de Marie-Immaculée**
175, rue Main, Ottawa ON K1S 1C3
613-237-0580, Fax: 613-232-4064
archives@ustpaul.ca
A. Dubois, Directeur

***Ottawa:* Ottawa Jewish Archives**
21 Nadolny Sachs Private Lane, Ottawa ON K2A 1R9
613-798-4696, Fax: 613-798-4695
archives@jccottawa.com
www.ottawajewisharchives.ca
Dawn Logan, Archivist

***Ottawa:* Roman Catholic Archdiocese of Ottawa/ Corporation Episcopale Catholique Romaine d'Ottawa**
1247 Kilborn Pl., Ottawa ON K1H 6K9
613-738-5025, Fax: 613-738-0130
psabourin@ecclesia-ottawa.org
P. Sabourin, Archivist
psabourin@ecclesia-ottawa.org
Roland Leclaire, Archivist
613-237-0580

***Ottawa:* St Paul University Archives**
175, rue Main, Ottawa ON K1S 1C3
613-237-0580

***Ottawa:* Scouts Canada**
1345 Baseline Rd., Ottawa ON K2C 0A7
613-224-5131, Fax: 613-224-3571, 888-726-8876
mailbox@scouts.ca
www.scouts.ca

***Ottawa:* Soeurs du Sacré-Coeur de Jésus, Saint-Hubert**
15 Oblate Ave., Ottawa ON K1S 0E6
613-237-6607
Hélène Beaulieu, Responsable

***Ottawa:* The Royal College of Physicians & Surgeons of Canada**
774 Echo Dr., Ottawa ON K1S 5N8
613-730-8177, Fax: 613-730-2410, 800-668-3740
barbara.woodward@rcpsc.edu
rcpsc.medical.org/membership/roddick_e.php
Michel Prévost, Archiviste en chef
michel.provost@uottawa.ca
613-562-5825

***Ottawa:* University of Ottawa Archives and Special Collections**
#603, 65 University, Ottawa ON K1N 6N5
613-562-5910, Fax: 613-562-5133
arcs@uottawa.ca
Glenn J. Lockwood, Archivist

***Ottawa:* Wilfred H. Bradley Reference Library**
71 Bronson Ave., Ottawa ON K1R 6G6
613-232-7124, Fax: 613-232-7088
archives@ottawa.anglican.ca
www.ottawa.anglican.ca/archives.shtml

***Owen Sound:* Grey Roots Museum & Archives**
102599 Grey Rd. 18, RR#4, Owen Sound ON N4K 5N6
519-376-3690, Fax: 519-376-4654, 877-473-9766
kfoster@greycounty.on.ca
www.greyroots.com
Karin Foster, Archivist
kfoster@greycounty.on.ca

***Pembroke:* Grey Sisters of the Immaculate Conception**
Marguerite Centre, 700 MacKay St., Pembroke ON K8A 1G6
613-732-9916, Fax: 613-735-2048
jacquie@margueritecentre.com
Jacquelyn Wolgemuth, Head Librarian

***Perth:* The Perth Museum & Archives**
11 Gore St. East, Perth ON K7H 1H4
613-267-1947, Fax: 613-267-5635
perthmuseum@town.perth.on.ca
www.perthcanada.com
Susan McNichol, Curator
perthmuseum@town.perth.on.ca

***Peterborough:* Peterborough Centennial Museum & Archives**
Armour Hill, 300 Hunter St. East, Peterborough ON K9H 2L8
705-743-5180, Fax: 705-743-2614
mcharles@city.peterborough.on.ca
www.pcma.ca/archives_about.htm
Mary Charles, City Archivist
Bernadine Dodge, Special Collections
bdodge@trentu.ca

***Peterborough:* Trent University Archives**
Bata Library, Trent University, Peterborough ON K9J 7B8
705-748-1011
archives@trentu.ca
www.trentu.ca/archives

***Picton:* County of Prince Edward Archives**
44 Union St., Picton ON K0K 2T0
613-476-6100
archives@pecounty.on.ca
www.pecounty.on.ca/archives.html
Pamela Noxon, Chair
613-393-2204

***Prescott:* Grenville County Historical Society**
500 Railway Ave., Prescott ON K0E 1T0
613-925-0489
gchs@ripnet.com
web.ripnet.com/~gchs
Bonnie Gaylord, Research Chair

***Richmond Hill:* Sculptors Society of Canada/ La Société des sculpteurs du Canada**
273 Richmond St., Richmond Hill ON L4C 3Z2
416-214-0389, Fax: 416-214-0389
gallery@cansculpt.org
www.cansculpt.org
Karen Stoskopf Harding, Archivist

***St Catharines:* Ontario Genealogical Society**
PO Box 2224, St Catharines ON L2M 7R8
nbogs@becon.org
www.ogs.on.ca/niagara/default.htm
Cheryl Bowman, Contact
bowcarr@hotmail.com
905-685-6900

***St Catharines:* St Catharines Museum at Lock 3**
1932 Welland Canals Pkwy., St Catharines ON L2R 7K6
905-984-8880, Fax: 905-984-6910
museuminfo@stcatharines.ca
www.stcatharineslock3museum.ca
Arden Phair, Curator of Collections
aphair@stcatharines.ca
905-984-880 ext. 231
David Sharron, Head, Special Collections and University Archivist
d.sharron@brocku.ca
905-688-5550 ext. 3264

***St Catharines:* Special Collections & Archives**
James A. Gibson Library, Brock University, 500 Glenridge Ave., 10th Fl., St Catharines ON L2S 3A1
905-688-5550, Fax: 905-988-5490
d.sharron@brocku.ca
www.brocku.ca/library/spcl/index.htm

***Sault Ste Marie:* Sault Ste Marie & 49th Field Regiment RCA Historical Society**
690 Queen St. East, Sault Ste Marie ON P6A 2A4
a05-256-7278, Fax: 705-759-3058
heritage@saultmuseum.com
www.saultmuseum.com
Kim Forbes, Director/Curator

***Simcoe:* Norfolk Heritage Centre**
109 Norfolk St. South, Simcoe ON N3Y 2W3
519-426-1583, Fax: 519-426-1584
office@norfolklore.com
www.norfolklore.com
William R. Yeager, Curator
curator@norfolklore.com
519-426-1583

***Southampton:* Bruce County Museum & Cultural Centre**
33 Victoria St. North, Southampton ON N0H 2L0
519-797-2080, Fax: 519-797-2191, 866-318-8889
archives@brucecounty.on.ca
www.brucemuseum.ca
Barbara Ribey, Director/Curator
bribey@brucecounty.on.ca

***Stratford:* Stratford-Perth Archives**
24 St Andrew St., Stratford ON N5A 1A3
519-271-0531, Fax: 519-273-5746
sparchives@perthcounty.ca
www.stratfordpertharchives.on.ca
Betty Jo Belton, Acting Archivist
519-271-0531 ext. 256

***Stratford:* The Stratford Shakespeare Festival Archives**
423 Brunswick St., Stratford ON N5A 7Z8
519-271-0055, Fax: 519-271-1040
jedmonds@stratfordshakespearefestival.com
www.stratfordshakespearefestival.com
Jane Edmonds, Archives Manager
jedmonds@stratfordfestival.ca
Marthe Brown, Archivist

***Sudbury:* Diocese of Algoma, Archives**
c/o J.N. Desmarais Library, Laurentian University, Sudbury ON P3E 2C6

705-675-1151, Fax: 705-675-4877
archives@laurentian.ca
www.laurentian.ca/library/archives
Julie Bisaillon, Archives Technician

Sudbury: **Diocese of Moosonee, Archives**
J.N. Desmarais Library, Laurentian University, Sudbury ON P3E 2C6
705-675-1151, Fax: 705-675-4877
archives@laurentian.ca
www.laurentian.ca/library/archives/archives_e.php

Teeterville: **Teeterville Pioneer Museum**
194 Teeter St., Teeterville ON N0E 1S0
519-582-0278, Fax: 519-582-0122
teeterville.museum@norfolkcounty.on.ca
Judy A. Livingstone, Curator/Director

Thunder Bay: **City of Thunder Bay**
235 Vickers St. North, Thunder Bay ON P7E 1J5
807-625-2270, Fax: 807-622-4212
msybalski@thunderbay.ca
Matt Szybalski, Manager, Corporate Records & Archivist
807-625-3390
Jeremy Mohr, Archivist

Thunder Bay: **Lakehead University Archives**
955 Oliver Rd., Thunder Bay ON P7B 5E1
807-343-8302, Fax: 807-343-8007

Thunder Bay: **Northwestern Ontario Sports Hall of Fame**
219 May St. South, Thunder Bay ON P7E 1B5
807-622-2852, Fax: 807-622-2736
nwosport@tbaytel.net
www.nwosportshalloffame.com
Kathryn Dwyer, Curator
807-622-2852

Thunder Bay: **Thunder Bay Historical Museum**
425 Donald St. East, Thunder Bay ON P7E 5V1
807-623-0801, Fax: 807-622-6880
info@thunderbaymuseum.com
www.thunderbaymuseum.com
Thorold Tronrud, Curator
807-623-0801

Toronto: **Archives of Ontario**
134 Ian Macdonald Blvd., Toronto ON M7A 2C5
416-327-1600, Fax: 416-327-1999, 800-668-9933
reference@ontario.ca
www.archives.gov.on.ca
Miriam McTiernan, Archivist of Ontario
miriam.mctiernan@ontario.ca
416-327-1602

Toronto: **Art Gallery of Ontario/ Musée des beaux-arts de l'Ontario**
317 Dundas St. West, Toronto ON M5T 1G4
416-979-6642, Fax: 416-979-6602
library_archives@ago.net
www.ago.net
Karen McKenzie, Chief Librarian
karen_mckenzie@ago.net
416-979-6660

Toronto: **Arts & Letters Club**
14 Elm St., Toronto ON M5G 1G7
416-597-0223
info@artsandlettersclub.ca
www.artsandlettersclub.ca
Margaret Spence, Chair, Library Committee

Toronto: **Bergendal Collection of Mediaeval Manuscripts**
15 Duncan St., Toronto ON M5H 3P9
416-925-8044, Fax: 416-925-3631
bergendalcoll@sympatico.ca
www3.sympatico.ca/bergendalcoll
Joseph Pope, Curator
joepope@sympatico.ca
416-925-8044

Toronto: **Brothers of the Christian Schools Archives**
131 Farnham Ave., Toronto ON M4V 1H7
416-929-7878, Fax: 416-929-1277
wfarrell@rogers.com
Walter Farrell, F.S.C., Archivist
wfarrell@rogers.com

Toronto: **Burgee Data Archives**
117 Airdrie Rd., Toronto ON M4G 1M6
416-423-9979, Fax: 416-423-9979
peter_edwards@etel.tdsb.on.ca
Peter B. Edwards, Director

Toronto: **Canadian Lesbian & Gay Archives**
50 Charles St East, Toronto ON M4Y 2N6
416-777-2755
queeries@clga.ca
www.clga.ca/archives/
Mary MacDonald, President

Toronto: **Canadian Opera Company/ La compagnie d'opéra canadienne**
227 Front St. East, Toronto ON M5A 1E8
416-306-2328, Fax: 416-363-5584
birthej@coc.ca
Birthe Joergensen, Archivist

Toronto: **Canadian Royal Heritage Trust**
#206A, 3050 Yonge St., Toronto ON M4N 2K4
416-482-4909, Fax: 416-544-8082
kg3library@crht.cam
Claudia Willetts, Librarian
kg3library@crht.ca
416-482-4909

Toronto: **City of Toronto Archives**
255 Spadina Rd., Toronto ON M5R 2V3
416-397-0778, Fax: 416-392-9685
archives@toronto.ca
www.toronto.ca/archives
Daphne Gaby Donaldson, Director of Corporate Records & Archives
ddonald@toronto.ca
416-392-9673

Toronto: **College of Physicians & Surgeons of Ontario**
80 College St., Toronto ON M5G 2E2
416-967-2600, Fax: 416-961-3330, 800-268-7096
rma@cpso.on.ca
www.cpso.on.ca
Joseph Travers, Contact
416-967-2600 ext. 227
Mary-Anne Nicholls, Archivist/Records Officer
manicholls@toronto.anglican.ca
416-363-7678 ext. 219

Toronto: **Diocese of Toronto, Archives**
135 Adelaide St. East, Toronto ON M5C 1L8
416-363-6021, Fax: 416-363-7678, 800-668-8932
manicholls@toronto.anglican.ca
www.toronto.anglican.ca
Nancy Mallett, Chair, Archives & Museum Committee
archives@stgamescathedral.on.ca
416-364-7865 ext. 233

Toronto: **Diocese of Toronto, St James' Cathedral Archives**
65 Church St., Toronto ON M5C 2E9
416-364-7865
archives@stjamescathedral.on.ca
www.stjamescathedral.on.ca/archives.asp#10

Toronto: **Etobicoke Historical Society**
c/o Montgomery's Inn, 4709 Dundas St. West, Toronto ON M9A 1A8
dorans@idirect.com
www.etobicokehistorical.com
Gregory Wowchuk, President
dorans@idirect.com

Toronto: **Exhibition Place**
2 Manitoba Dr., Toronto ON M6K 3C3
416-263-3658, Fax: 416-263-3681
LCobon@explace.on.ca
www.explace.on.ca
Linda Cobon, Manager, Records & Archives

Toronto: **General Archives of the Basilian Fathers**
95 St Joseph St., Toronto ON M5S 2R9
416-921-7861, Fax: 416-921-8357
archives@basilian.org
www.basilian.org
James E. Rent, CSB, Archivist
John L. Hardy, College Archivist
jhardy@gbrownc.on.ca
416-415-5000 ext. 2676

Toronto: **George Brown College of Applied Arts & Technology Archives**
#103, 500 Macpherson Ave., Toronto ON M5R 1X1
416-415-5000, Fax: 416-415-4772, 800-265-2002
rmacaula@georgebrown.ca

Toronto: **Heritage Scarborough**
24 Collins Rd., Toronto ON M1C 1C3
416-396-6930
Richard Schofield, Heritage Consultant & Scarborough Archivist

Toronto: **Hockey Hall of Fame**
BCE Place, 30 Yonge St., Toronto ON M5E 1X8
416-360-7735, Fax: 416-360-1316
acquisitions@hhof.com
www.hhof.com/html/rc00.shtml
Miragh Addis, Archivist & Collections Registrar
maddis@hhof.com

Toronto: **Holy Blossom Temple**
1950 Bathurst St., Toronto ON M5P 3K9
416-789-3291
www.holyblossom.org
David Hart, Archivist

Toronto: **Institute of the Blessed Virgin Mary in North America (Loretto Sisters)**
101 Mason Blvd., Toronto ON M5M 3E2
416-487-5543, Fax: 416-485-9884
canpro.archives@bellnet.ca
Juliana Dusel, IBVM, Archivist

Toronto: **Jesuits in English Canada**
1325 Bay St., Toronto ON M5R 2C4
416-962-4500, Fax: 416-962-4501
Jacques Monet, Archivist
Helen McNeil, Archivist
archives@crht.ca

Toronto: **King Louis XIV Memorial Archives**
Fealty Heritage Centre, #206A, 3050 Yonge St., Toronto ON M4N 2K4
416-482-4909, Fax: 416-544-8082
archives@crht.ca
www.crht.ca/Resources

Toronto: **Montgomery's Inn Museum**
4709 Dundas St. West, Toronto ON M9A 1A8
416-394-8113, Fax: 416-394-6027
rreid@toronto.ca
Randall Reid, Programmes Officer
416-394-6025

Toronto: **National Ballet of Canada/ Ballet national du Canada**
470 Queens Quay West, Toronto ON M5V 3K4
416-345-9686, Fax: 416-345-8323
anevile@national.ballet.ca
www.national.ballet.ca/thecompany/archives/
Adrienne Nevile, Archives Coordinator
Nancy Hurn, General Synod Archives
nhurn@national.anglican.ca

Toronto: **National Office - General Synod Archives**
80 Hayden St., Toronto ON M4Y 3G2
416-924-9199, Fax: 416-968-7983
archives@national.anglican.ca

Toronto: **Ontario Genealogical Society**
#102, 40 Orchard View Blvd., Toronto ON M4R 1B9
416-489-0734, Fax: 416-489-9803
lchester@ogs.on.ca
www.ogs.on.ca
L.A. Chester, Chair

Toronto: **Queen's Own Rifles of Canada Regimental Museum**
c/o Casa Loma, 1 Austin Terrace, Toronto ON M5R 1X8
416-923-1171, Fax: 416-923-5734
info@casaloma.org
P. Sigmundson, Curator

Toronto: **Queen's York Rangers (1st American Regiment) Museum**
CFA Fort York, 660 Fleet St. West, Toronto ON M5V 1A9
416-203-4600
qyrang@connection.com
Gail Donald, Manager
gail_donald@cbc.ca
416-205-5880

Toronto: **Radio Archives**
205 Wellington St. West, Toronto ON M5V 3G7
416-205-8602
archives.cbc.ca/info/281g_en23shtml
Dorion Liebgott, Curator

Toronto: **Reuben & Helene Dennis Museum**
1700 Bathurst St., Toronto ON M5P 3K3

416-781-3514, Fax: 416-781-0150
museum@beth-tzedic.org

Toronto: Roman Catholic Archdiocese of Toronto
#505, 1155 Yonge St., Toronto ON M4T 1W2
416-934-3400, Fax: 416-934-3444
archives@archtoronto.org
www.archtoronto.org/archives
Marc Lerman, Diocesan Archivist
416-934-3400 ext. 505

Toronto: St John's Convent
233 Cummer Ave., Toronto ON M2M 2E8
416-226-2201, Fax: 416-222-4442
convent@ssjd.ca
www.ssjd.ca/convent.html
Joyce Bodley, Librarian
416-226-2201 ext. 309

Toronto: St John's Rehabilitation Hospital Archives
c/o Administration, 285 Cummer Ave., Toronto ON M2M 2G1
416-226-6780
info@stjohnsrehab.com.

Toronto: St Joseph's Health Centre (Toronto) Archives
30 The Queensway, Toronto ON M6R 1B5
416-530-6389, Fax: 416-530-6836

Toronto: Scarboro Mission Society
2685 Kingston Rd., Toronto ON M1M 1M4
416-261-7135, Fax: 416-261-0820, 800-260-4815
info@scarboromissions.ca
www.scarboromissions.ca
John Carten, Councillor
jcarten@scarboromissions.ca

Toronto: Scarborough Historical Society
6282 Kingston Rd., Toronto ON M1C 1K9
416-396-6930, Fax: 416-282-9482
info@scarboroughhistorical.com
Richard Schofield, Archivist
Jane E. Nokes, Corporate Archivist
jane.nokes@scotiabank.com

Toronto: Scotiabank Archives
44 King St. West, 19th Fl. East, Toronto ON M5H 1H1
416-866-6207, Fax: 416-933-2363
jane.nokes@scotiabank.com
Greg McKinnon, Manager/Archivist

Toronto: Sesquicentennial Museum & Archives
263 McCaul St., Toronto ON M5T 1W7
416-397-3680, Fax: 416-397-3685
greg.mckinnon@tdsb.on.ca

Toronto: Sisters of St Joseph of Toronto
3377 Bayview Ave., Toronto ON M2M 3S4
416-222-1101, Fax: 416-222-9816
lwicks@csj-to.ca
www.csj-to.ca
Linda Wicks, Archivist

Toronto: Sisters Servants of Mary Immaculate
5 Austin Terrace, Toronto ON M5R 1Y1
416-924-7422, Fax: 416-928-9261
ssmi.org@rogers.com
www.ssmi.org
Frances Byblow, Contact

Toronto: Tartu Institute
300 Bloor St. W, Toronto ON M5B 1W4
416-925-9405, Fax: 416-925-2295
rweiler7@cogeco.ca
Roland Weller, Archivist
rweller7@cogeco.ca
905-627-3856

Toronto: The Canadian Children's Book Centre
#101, 40 Orchard View Blvd., Toronto ON M4R 1B9
416-975-0010, Fax: 416-975-8970
info@bookcentre.ca
www.bookcentre.ca
Naseem Hrab, Librarian
naseem@bookcentre.ca

Toronto: The Film Reference Library
2 Carlton St., East Mezzanine, Toronto ON M5B 1J3
416-967-1517, Fax: 416-967-0628
www.filmreferencelibrary.ca
Sylvia Frank, Director

Toronto: The Ontario Jewish Archives
4600 Bathurst St., Toronto ON M2R 3V2
416-635-2883, Fax: 416-635-1408
ojal@ujafed.org
www.ontariojewisharchives.org
Ellen Scheinberg, Director
escheinberg@ujafed.org
416-635-2883

Toronto: The Presbyterian Church in Canada
50 Wynford Dr., Toronto ON M3C 1J7
416-441-1111, Fax: 416-441-2825, 800-619-7301
karnold@presbyterian.ca
www.presbyterianarchives.ca
Kim Arnold, Archivist/Records Administrator
karnold@presbyterian.ca

Toronto: The Royal Canadian Yacht Club
141 St George St., Toronto ON M5R 2L8
416-967-7245, Fax: 416-967-5710
heritage@rcyc.ca
www.rcyc.ca
Diane Blake, Staff Archivist
416-967-7245 ext. 351

Toronto: The Salvation Army
26 Howden Rd., Toronto ON M1R 3E4
416-285-4344, Fax: 416-285-7763
heritage_centre@can.salvationarmy.org
www.salvationist.ca/heritage
John E. Carew, Director
john_carew@can.salvationarmy.org

Toronto: Todmorden Mills Heritage Museum & Art Centre
850 Coxwell Ave., Toronto ON M4C 5R1
416-396-2819
todmorden@toronto.ca
Rita Russell, Acting Curator
416-396-2819
Shaaron Grogan-Sheahan, Assistant Superintendent of Education
shaaron.grogan-sheahan02@tcdsb.org
416-222-8282 ext. 2162

Toronto: Toronto Catholic District School Board Archives
80 Sheppard Ave. East, Toronto ON M2N 6E8
416-222-8282, Fax: 416-229-5345
shaaron.grogan-sheahan02@tcdsb.org
www.tcdsb.org

Toronto: Toronto Port Authority
60 Harbour St., Toronto ON M5J 1B7
416-863-2011, Fax: 416-863-4830
btokawa@torontoport.com
www.torontoport.com/corporate_archives.asp?id=37
Beth Tokawa, Records Administrator/Archivist
btokawa@torontoport.com

Toronto: Toronto Symphony Orchestra
60 Simcoe St., Toronto ON M5J 2H5
416-593-0976, Fax: 416-593-6788
gcorrin@tso.ca
John Dunn, Volunteer Archivist

Toronto: Toronto-Dominion Bank Archives Department
#1704, 110 Yonge St., Toronto ON M5C 1T4
416-982-8848, Fax: 416-499-6609
Hugh Rendle, Head
hrendle@tyndale.ca
416-226-6620 ext. 6716

Toronto: Tyndale University College & Seminary Archives
25 Ballyconnor Ct., Toronto ON M2M 4B3
416-226-6380, Fax: 416-226-6746

Toronto: United Church of Canada Archives
3250 Bloor St. West, Toronto ON M8X 2Y4
416-231-5931, Fax: 416-231-3103
archives@united-church.ca
www.united-church.ca
Sharon P. Larade, Chief Archivist
Garron Wells, University Archivist
garron.wells@utoronto.ca

Toronto: University of Toronto Archives & Records Management Services
Thomas Fisher Rare Book Library, 120 St George St., 4th Fl., Toronto ON M5S 1A5
416-978-5344, Fax: 416-946-5343
garron.wells@utoronto.ca
content.library.utoronto.ca/utarms/
Evelyn Collins, Archivist
evelyn.collins@utoronto.ca
416-926-2348

Toronto: University of Toronto St Michael's College Archives
#304, 113 St Joseph St., Toronto ON M5S 1J4
416-926-1300, Fax: 416-926-7262
nouwen.archives@utoronto.ca
www.utoronto.ca/stmikes/
Henri Pilon, Archivist

Toronto: University of Toronto Trinity College Archives
6 Hoskin Ave., Toronto ON M5S 1H8
416-978-2019, Fax: 416-978-2797
archives@trinity.utoronto.ca
www.trinity.utoronto.ca/archives

Toronto: University of Toronto University College Archives
15 King's College Circle, Toronto ON M5S 3H7
416-978-8154, Fax: 416-971-2059

Toronto: Upper Canada College Archives
200 Lonsdale Rd., Toronto ON M4V 1W6
416-488-1125, Fax: 416-484-8613
mspence@ucc.on.ca
www.ucc.on.ca/podium/default.aspx?t=6617
Marian Spence, Archivist
John Tagg, Librarian
jtagg@westpark.org
416-243-3600 ext. 2048

Toronto: West Park Healthcare Centre Archives
82 Buttonwood Ave., Toronto ON M6M 2J5
416-243-3600

Toronto: Weston Historical Society
1901 Weston Rd., Toronto ON M9N 3P1
416-249-6663
westonhistoricalsociety@rogers.com
www.welcometoweston.ca/whs
Eva Ferguson, Project Manager
416-487-0049 ext. 10

Toronto: York Pioneer & Historical Society
2482 Yonge St., Toronto ON M4P 2H5
416-483-0907
mrsh638@aol.com
John Marshall, Archivist
416-961-4420
Michael Moir, University Archivist & Head, Special Collections

Toronto: York University Archives & Special Collections
#305, Scott Library, 4700 Keele St., Toronto ON M3J 1P3
416-736-5442, Fax: 416-650-8039
archives@yorku.ca
www.library.yorku.ca/ccm/ArchivesSpecialCollections/index.htm

Tweed: Tweed & Area Heritage Centre
40 Victoria St. North, Tweed ON K0K 3J0
613-478-3989, Fax: 613-478-6457
tweedheritageinfo@on.aibn.com
Evan Morton, Curator
613-478-3989

Uxbridge: Uxbridge Historical Centre
7239 Concession 6, Uxbridge ON L9P 1R2
905-852-5854, Fax: 905-852-5854
museum@town.uxbridge.on.ca
www.uxlib.com/museum
Allan McGillivray, Curator
museum@town.uxbridge.on.ca
905-852-5854

Vaughan: City of Vaughan Archives
10401 Dufferin St., Vaughan ON L6A 1S2
905-832-2281
archives@city.vaughan.on.ca
www.city.vaughan.on.ca/culture_recreation/archives/index.cfm

Vernon: Osgoode Township Historical Society
7814 Lawrence St., Vernon ON K0A 3J0
613-821-4062
oths@magma.ca
www.magma.ca/~oths/
James Stevenson, Curator/Archivist
oths@magma.ca

Waterford: The Waterford & Townsend Historical Society
Spruce Row Museum, 159 Nichol St., Waterford ON N0E 1Y0

519-443-4211, Fax: 519-443-5640
sprucerow.museum@norfolkcounty.on.ca
Glen Bell, Contact

Waterloo: Evangelical Lutheran Church in Canada
#1502, 6 Willow St., Waterloo ON N2J 4S3
519-884-1970
erichrwschultz@aol.com
www.easternsynod.org
Erich R.W. Schultz, Archivist
erichrwschultz@aol.com

Waterloo: Mennonite Archives of Ontario
Conrad Grebel University College, 140 Westmount, Rd. North, Waterloo ON N2L 3G6
519-885-0220, Fax: 519-885-0014
marchive@uwaterloo.ca
grebel.uwaterloo.ca/mao/index.html
Sam Steiner, Librarian & Archivist
steiner@library.uwaterloo.ca

Waterloo: Museum & Archive of Games
University of Waterloo, Burt Mathews Hall, Waterloo ON N2L 3G1
519-888-4424, Fax: 519-746-6776
museum@healthy.uwaterloo.ca
www.gamesmuseum.uwaterloo.ca
Brian Smale, Director
smale@healthy.uwaterloo.ca
Jane Britton, Operations manager
519-888-4567 ext. 32445

Waterloo: Special Collections & Archives
Dana Porter Library, 200 University Ave. West, Waterloo ON N2L 3G1
519-888-4567, Fax: 519-888-4322
www.lib.uwaterloo.ca/discipline/SpecColl/Special1.html
Joan Mitchell, Archives Librarian
jmmitchell@wlu.ca
519-884-0710 ext. 3825

Waterloo: Wilfrid Laurier University Archives
75 University Ave. West, 1st Fl., Waterloo ON N2L 3C5
519-884-0710, Fax: 519-884-8023
www.library.wlu.ca/libinfo/dept/spar.html

Whitby: Town of Whitby Archives
Whitby Public Library, 405 Dundas St., Whitby ON L1N 6A1
905-668-6531, Fax: 905-668-7445
b.winter@sympatico.ca
Brian Winter, Archivist
Brian Walker, Town Archivist

Whitby: Whitby Archives
405 Dundas St.West, Whitby ON L1N 6A1
905-668-6531, Fax: 905-668-7445
admin@whitbylibrary.on.ca
www.whitbylibrary.on.ca

Williamstown: Glengarry Historical Society
Bethune-Thompson House, 19730 John St., Williamstown ON K0C 2J0
613-347-3006
David G. Anderson, Contact
anderson@glen-net.ca

Windsor: Assumption University Archives
400 Huron Church Rd., Windsor ON N9C 2J9
519-973-7033, Fax: 519-973-7089
cbertrand@assumptionu.ca
www.assumptionu.ca

Windsor: Serbian Heritage Museum
6770 Tecumseh Rd. East, Windsor ON N8T 1E6
519-944-4884, Fax: 519-974-3963
members.tripod.com/swo_heritage/serbian.htm
Deanna Pavlov, Curator

Windsor: Windsor's Community Museum/ Le Musée communautaire de Windsor
254 Pitt St. West, Windsor ON N9A 5L5
519-253-1812, Fax: 519-253-0919
wmuseum@city.windsor.on.ca
www.windsorpubliclibrary.com/branches/museum/hours.php

Prince Edward Island

Regional Systems

Prince Edward Island Public Library Service
89 Red Head Rd., Morell PE C0A 1S0
902-961-7320, Fax: 902-961-7322
plshq@gov.pe.ca
www.library.pe.ca
Kathleen Eaton, Provincial Librarian
keeaton@gov.pe.ca

Public Libraries

Abram-Village: Bibliothèque publique d'Abram-Village
a/s École Évangéline, RR#3, Abram-Village PE C0B 2E0
902-854-7268, Fax: 902-854-2981
abram@gov.pe.ca
www.library.pe.ca
Doris Arsenault, Branch Library Technician

Alberton: Alberton Public Library
460 Main St., PO Box 449, Alberton PE C0B 1B0
902-853-3049
alberton@gov.pe.ca
www.library.pe.ca
Kelly Gillis, Branch Library Technician

Borden: Borden-Carleton Public Library
244 Borden Ave., Borden PE C0B 1X0
902-437-6492
borden-carleton@gov.pe.ca
www.library.pe.ca
Sharon Leard, Branch Library Technician

Breadalbane: Breadalbane Public Library
4023 Dixon Rd., Breadalbane PE C0A 1E0
902-964-2520
breadalbane@gov.pe.ca
www.library.pe.ca
Joan Sutton, Branch Library Technician

Charlottetown: Bibliothèque Dr. J. Edmond Arsenault
5 rue Acadienne Hillsborough Pkwy., Charlottetown PE C1C 1M2
902-368-6092
carrefour@gov.pe.ca
www.library.pe.ca
Lyne Cadieux, Responsable

Charlottetown: Confederation Centre Public Library
PO Box 7000, Charlottetown PE C1A 8G8
902-368-4642, Fax: 902-368-4652
ccpl@gov.pe.ca
www.library.pe.ca
Trina O'Brien Leggott, Chief Librarian

Cornwall: Cornwall Public Library (PEI)
39 Lowther Dr., Cornwall PE C0A 1H0
902-629-8415
cornwall@gov.pe.ca
www.library.pe.ca
Wheatley Pam, Branch Library Technician

Crapaud: Crapaud Public Library
20424 Trans Canada Hwy., Crapaud PE C0A 1J0
902-658-2297
crapaud@gov.pe.ca
www.library.pe.ca
Luann Molyneaux, Branch Library Technician

Georgetown: Georgetown Genevieve Soloman Memorial Library
36 Kent St., Georgetown PE C0A 1L0
902-652-2832
georgetown@gov.pe.ca
www.library.pe.ca
Mary Cameron, Branch Library Technician

Hunter River: Hunter River Public Library
19816 Rte. 2, Hunter River PE C0A 1N0
902-964-2800
hunter_river@gov.pe.ca
www.library.pe.ca
Elisa Brown-Martel, Branch Library Technician

Kensington: Kensington Public Library
55 Victoria St., Kensington PE C0B 1M0
902-836-3721
kensington@gov.pe.ca
www.library.pe.ca
Stephanie Campbell, Branch Library Technician

Kinkora: Kinkora Public Library
45 Anderson St., Kinkora PE C0B 1N0
902-887-2172
kinkora@gov.pe.ca
www.library.pe.ca
Catherine Arsenault, Branch Library Technician

Montague: Montague Public Library
273 Queen's Rd., Montague PE C0A 1R0
902-838-2928
montague@gov.pe.ca
www.library.pe.ca
Swarna Chandrasekera, Branch Library Technician

Morell: Morell Public Library
89 Red Head Rd., Morell PE C0A 1S0
902-961-3389
morell@gov.pe.ca
www.library.pe.ca
Maria Van De Cappelle, Branch Library Technician

Mount Stewart: Mount Stewart Public Library
104 Main St., Mount Stewart PE C0A 1T0
902-676-2050
mtstewart@gov.pe.ca
www.library.pe.ca
Maria Van De Cappelle, Branch Library Technician

Murray Harbour: Murray Harbour Public Library
1381 Main St., Murray Harbour PE C0A 1V0
902-962-3875
murray_harbour@gov.pe.ca
www.library.pe.ca
Kaye MacLean, Branch Library Technician

Murray River: Murray River Leona Giddings Memorial Library
1066 McInnis Rd., Murray River PE C0A 1V0
902-962-2667
murray_river@gov.pe.ca
www.library.pe.ca
Kaye MacLean, Branch Library Technician

O'Leary: O'Leary Public Library
18 Community St., O'Leary PE C0B 1V0
902-859-8788
o'leary@gov.pe.ca
www.library.pe.ca
Nancy McNally, Branch Library Technician

St. Peters: St. Peters Public Library
1968 Cardigan Rd., St. Peters PE C0A 2A0
902-961-3415
st_peter's@gov.pe.ca
www.library.pe.ca
Ann MacInnis, Branch Library Technician

Souris: Souris Public Library
75 Main St., Souris PE C0A 2B0
902-687-2157, Fax: 902-687-4426
souris@gov.pe.ca
www.library.pe.ca
Kathy MacEwen, Branch Library Technician

Stratford: Stratford Public Library (PEI)
57 Bunbury Rd., Stratford PE C1B 1T8
902-569-7441
stratford@edu.pe.ca
www.library.pe.ca
Jane McKinney, Branch Library Technician

Summerside: Bibliothèque J.-Henri-Blanchard
5, av Maris Stella, Summerside PE C1N 3Y5
902-432-2748, Fax: 902-888-1686
blanchard@gov.pe.ca
www.library.pe.ca
Juanita Lewis, Branch Library Technician

Summerside: School Library Advocate
c/o Wendy Doucette, Elm St. School, 256 Elm St., Summerside PE C1N 3V5
902-368-6085
wodoucette@edu.pe.ca
www.edu.pe.ca/peitla/sla.htm
Wendy Doucette, President

Summerside: Summerside Rotary Library
192 Water St., Summerside PE C1N 1B1
902-436-7323, Fax: 902-888-8055
summerside@gov.pe.ca
www.library.pe.ca
Jean-François Savaria, Branch Librarian

Tignish: Tignish Public Library
103 School St., Tignish PE C0B 2B0
902-882-7363
tignish@gov.pe.ca
www.library.pe.ca
Diane McCue, Branch Library Technician

Tyne Valley: **Tyne Valley Public Library**
19 Allen Rd., Tyne Valley PE C0B 2C0
902-831-2928
tyne_valley@gov.pe.ca
www.library.pe.ca
Carolyn Millar, Branch Library Technician

Archives

Charlottetown: **Prince Edward Island Public Archives & Records Office**
Hon. George Coles Bldg., 4th Fl., 175 Richmond St., PO Box 1000, Charlottetown PE C1A 7M4
902-368-4290, Fax: 902-368-6327
archives@gov.pe.ca
www.gov.pe.ca/cca/index.php3?number=1004626&lang=E
Jill MacMicken Wilson, Provincial Archivist
jswilson@gov.pe.ca
902-368-4351
Simon Lloyd, Librarian, Special Collections
slloyd@upei.ca
902-566-0536

Charlottetown: **University of Prince Edward Island Archives**
Robertson Library, 550 University Ave., Charlottetown PE C1A 4P3
902-894-2802, Fax: 902-628-4305
www.upei.ca/library

Québec

Regional Systems

Réseau BIBLIO de l'Abitibi-Témiscamingue-Nord-du-Québec
20, av Québec, Rouyn-Noranda QC J9X 2E6
819-762-4305, Fax: 819-762-5309
info@crsbpat.qc.ca
Louis Dallaire, Directeur général
louis.dallaire@reseaubiblioatnq.qc.ca

Réseau BIBLIO de l'Estrie
4155, rue Brodeur, Sherbrooke QC J1L 1K4
819-565-9744, Fax: 819-565-9157
crsbpe@reseaubiblioestrie.qc.ca
www.reseaubiblioestrie.qc.ca
Joelle Thivierge, Directrice générale
jthivierge@reseaubiblioestrie.qc.ca
819-565-9744 ext. 102

Réseau BIBLIO de l'Outaouais
2295, rue Saint-Louis, Gatineau QC J8T 5L8
819-561-6008, Fax: 819-561-6767
biblio@crsbpo.qc.ca
Sylvie Thibault, Directrice générale
sylvie.thibault@crsbpo.qc.ca

Réseau BIBLIO de la Capitale-Nationale et de la Chaudière-Appalaches
3189, rue Albert-Demers, Charny QC G6X 3A1
418-832-6166, Fax: 418-832-6168, 866-446-6166
info@reseaubibliocnca.qc.ca
Lucie Gobeil, Directrice générale
lgobeil@reseaubibliocnca.qc.ca
418-832-6166

Réseau BIBLIO de la Côte-Nord
59, rue Napoléon, Sept-Iles QC G4R 5C5
418-962-1020, Fax: 418-962-5124
info@crsbpcn.qc.ca
Jean-Roch Gagnon, Directeur général
jrgagnon@crsbpcn.qc.ca
418-962-1020

Réseau BIBLIO de la Gaspésie-Iles-de-la-Madeleine
31, rue des Écoliers, Cap-Chat QC G0J 1E0
418-786-5597, Fax: 418-786-2024
info@reseaubibliogim.qc.ca
www.reseaubiblioduquebec.qc.ca/portail/index.aspx?page=2&RID=4
Aurélien Bisson, Directeur général
aurelien.bisson@reseaubibliogim.qc.ca

Réseau BIBLIO de la Montérégie
275, rue Conrad-Pelletier, La Prairie QC J5R 4V1
450-444-5433, Fax: 450-659-3364
jlabelle@reseaubibliomonteregie.qc.ca
www.reseaubibliomonteregie.qc.ca
Jacqueline Labelle, Directrice générale
jlabelle@reseaubibliomonteregie.qc.ca

Réseau BIBLIO des Laurentides
29, rue Brissette, Sainte-Agathe-des-Monts QC J8C 3L1
819-326-6440, Fax: 819-326-0885
jturnbull@crsbpl.qc.ca
JoAnne Turnbull, Directrice générale

Réseau BIBLIO du Bas-Saint-Laurent
465, rue St-Pierre, Rivière-du-Loup QC G5R 4T6
418-867-1682, Fax: 418-867-3434
crsbp@crsbp.net
www.reseaubibliobsl.qc.ca
Jacques Côté, Directeur général

Réseau BIBLIO du Centre-du-Québec, de Lanaudière et de la Mauricie
3125, rue Girard, Trois-Rivières QC G8Z 2M4
819-375-9623, Fax: 819-375-0132, 877-324-2546
crsbp@reseaubibliocqlm.qc.ca
www.reseaubibliocqlm.qc.ca
Hélène Arseneau, Directrice générale
helene.arseneau@reseaubibliocqlm.qc.ca
819-375-9623

Réseau BIBLIO du Saguenay-Lac-Saint-Jean
100, rue Price ouest, Alma QC G8B 4S1
418-662-6425, Fax: 418-662-7593, 800-563-6425
sbolduc@reseaubiblioslsj.qc.ca
www.reseaubiblioslsj.qc.ca
Johanne Belley, Directrice générale
jbelley@reseaubiblioslsj.qc.ca

Public Libraries

Acton Vale: **Bibliothèque Acton Vale**
1093A, rue Saint-André, Acton Vale QC J0H 1A0
450-546-2703, Fax: 450-642-1165
acton.vale@reseaubibliomonteregie.qc.ca
Sophia Bédard, Responsable

Aguanish: **Bibliothèque d'Aguanish**
106, rue Jacques-Cartier, Aguanish QC G0G 1A0
418-533-2323, Fax: 418-533-2012
aguanib@globetrotter.net
www.reseaubiblioduquebec.qc.ca
Normande Blais, Responsable
418-533-2352

Albanel: **Bibliothèque publique d'Albanel**
153A, Principale, Albanel QC G8M 3J3
613-679-2663
albanel@crsbpslsj.biblio.qc.ca
Marguerite Dubeau, Responsable
613-279-5800

Albertville: **Bibliothèque d'Albertville**
1058, rue Principale, Albertville QC G0J 1A0
418-756-6015
biblio.albert@crsbp.net
www.reseaubiblioduquebec.qc.ca
Danielle Berger, Responsable

Alma: **Bibliothèque municipale d'Alma**
500, rue Collard ouest, Alma QC G8B 1N2
418-669-5140, Fax: 418-669-5089
martin.bouchard@alma.biblio.qc.ca
www.ville.alma.qc.ca/mini_site.php?idMini=175
Martin Bouchard, Responsable

Alma: **Bibliothèque publique de Delisle**
221, rue des Bruyères, Alma QC G8E 1J9
418-668-2697
delisle@reseaubiblioslsj.qc.ca
Ghislain Girard, Responsable
418-480-3396

Alma: **Bibliothèque publique de Saint-Coeur-de-Marie**
5791, av du Pont nord, Alma QC G8E 1X1
418-347-3729, Fax: 418-347-3697
stcoeur@reseaubiblioslsj.qc.ca
www.crsbpslsj.biblio.qc.ca/st-coeur-de-marie
Martine Gobeil, Responsable

Amherst: **Bibliothèque de Saint-Rémi**
124, rue St-Louis, Amherst QC J0T 2L0
819-687-3372, Fax: 819-687-8430
stremi@crsbpl.qc.ca
www.reseaubiblioduquebec.qc.ca
Hélène Dion, Responsable

Amqui: **Bibliothèque Madeleine-Gagnon**
24, promenade de l'Hôtel de Ville, Amqui QC G5J 3E1
418-629-4242, Fax: 418-629-4090
bibliotheque@ville.amqui.qc.ca
Marie Côté, Responsable

Ange-Gardien: **Bibliothèque municipale d'Ange-Gardien**
249, rue Saint-Joseph, Ange-Gardien QC J0E 1E0
450-293-3987
ange.gardien@reseaubibliomonteregie
Sylvie Raymond, Responsable

Angliers: **Bibliothèque d'Angliers**
14, rue Baie Miller, Angliers QC J0Z 1A0
819-949-4351, Fax: 819-949-4321
angliers@reseaubibliotnq.qc.ca
www.reseaubiblioduquebec.qc.ca
Manon Corbin, Responsable

L'Anse-Saint-Jean: **Bibliothèque publique de L'Anse-St-Jean**
3, rue du Couvent, L'Anse-Saint-Jean QC G0V 1J0
418-549-7196
anse@reseaubiblioslsj.qc.ca
www.reseaubiblioduquebec.qc.ca
Germaine Boudreault, Responsable

Armagh: **Bibliothèque municipale d'Armagh**
9, rue de la Salle, Armagh QC G0R 1A0
418-466-3004, Fax: 418-466-2409
armabib@globetrotter.qc.ca
www.reseaubiblioduquebec.qc.ca/armagh
Sylvie Chabot, Responsable

Arntfield: **Bibliothèque de Arntfield**
15, rue Fugère, Arntfield QC J0Z 1B0
819-279-2241, Fax: 819-279-2481
arntfield@reseaubibliotnq.qc.ca
www.reseaubiblioduquebec.qc.ca
Jeannine Drouin, Responsable
819-279-2329

Arundel: **Bibliothèque d'Arundel/ Arundel Library**
2, rue du Village, Arundel QC J0T 1A0
819-687-8246, Fax: 819-687-8760
arundel@crsbpl.qc.ca
www.reseaubiblioduquebec.qc.ca
Fran Jones, Responsable

Asbestos: **Bibliothèque municipale d'Asbestos**
351, boul Saint-Luc, Asbestos QC J1T 2W4
819-879-4363, Fax: 819-879-0608
bibliasbestos@ville.asbestos.qc.ca
www.ville.asbestos.qc.ca/biblio/index.html
Julie Fontaine, Responsable

L'Ascension: **Bibliothèque de l'Ascension**
4, rue Principale ouest, L'Ascension QC J0T 1W0
819-275-1546, Fax: 819-275-1546
bibliotheque@municipalite-lascension.qc.ca
www.reseaubiblioduquebec.qc.ca/l'ascension
Monique Turpin, Responsable

L'Ascension: **Bibliothèque publique de L'Ascension**
900, 4e av est, L'Ascension QC G0W 1Y0
418-347-3482, Fax: 418-347-4253
ascens@reseaubiblioslsj.qc.ca
Diane Tremblay, Coordonnatrice

L'Assomption: **Bibliothèque Christian-Roy**
375, rue St-Pierre, L'Assomption QC J5W 2B6
450-589-5671, Fax: 450-589-6882
bibliotheque@ville.lassomption.qc.ca
www.ville.lassomption.qc.ca/cbiblio.html
Marjolaine Bertrand, Bibliothécaire
450-589-5671 ext. 237

L'Assomption: **Les Bibliothèques publiques de Laval-Laurentides-Lanaudière**
399, rue Dorval, L'Assomption QC J5W 1A1
450-589-5671, Fax: 450-589-6882
bibliotheque@ville.lassomption.qc.ca
www.bplll.qc.ca
Stéphane Legault, Président
bibliotheque@ville.lassomption.qc.ca
450-589-5671 ext. 237

Aston-Jonction: **Bibliothèque d'Aston-Jonction**
210, rue Lemire, Aston-Jonction QC G0Z 1A0
, Fax: 819-226-3459
biblio070@reseaubibliocqlm.qc.ca
www.reseaubiblioduquebec.qc.ca
Léa Houle, Responsable

Auclair: **Bibliothèque Auclair**
777, rue du Clocher, Auclair QC G0L 1A0

418-899-0417
biblio.auclair@crsbp.net
www.reseaubiblioduquebec.qc.ca
Cécile Castonguay, Responsable

Aumond: **Bibliothèque de Aumond**
679, rue Principale, Aumond QC J0W 1W0
819-449-4006, Fax: 819-449-7448
admaumond@crsbpo.qc.ca
www.reseaubiblioduquebec.qc.ca/Aumond/
Diane Guénette, Responsable

Aylmer Sound: **Bibliothèque d'Aylmer Sound**
Aylmer Sound QC G0G 1N0
418-242-2105, Fax: 418-787-2241
Patsy Anderson, Responsable

La Baie: **Bibliothèque de La Baie**
1911, 6e av, La Baie QC G7B 1S1
418-698-5350, Fax: 418-697-5087
webbiblio@ville.saguenay.qc.ca
www.ville.saguenay.qc.ca
Anne Lebel, Chef de division, Bibliothèques de Saguenay
anne.lebel@ville.saguenay.qc.ca

Baie-Comeau: **Bibliothèque municipale Alice-Lane**
6, av Radisson, Baie-Comeau QC G4Z 1W4
418-296-8304, Fax: 418-296-8328
vbc@ville.baie-comeau.qc.ca
Yvon Grondin, Superviseur responsable
ygrondin@ville.baie-comeau.qc.ca
418-396-8361

Baie-des-Sables: **Bibliothèque de Baie-des-Sables**
20, rue du Couvent, Baie-des-Sables QC G0J 1C0
418-772-6704
biblio.sables@crsbp.net
www.reseaubiblioduquebec.qc.ca
Monique Roy, Responsable

Baie-du-Febvre: **Bibliothèque de Baie-du-Febvre**
23, rue de l'Église, Baie-du-Febvre QC J0G 1A0
450-783-6484, Fax: 450-783-2235
biblio032@reseaubibliocqlm.qc.ca
www.reseaubiblioduquebec.qc.ca
Lise Laforce, Responsable

Baie-Sainte-Catherine: **Bibliothèque municipale de Baie-Sainte-Catherine**
308, rue Leclerc, Baie-Sainte-Catherine QC G0T 1A0
418-237-4241, Fax: 418-237-4223
www.reseaubiblioduquebec.qc.ca/baie-sainte-catherine
Patricia Ouellet, Responsable

Baie-Saint-Paul: **Bibliothèque René-Richard**
9, rue Forget, Baie-Saint-Paul QC G3Z 1T4
418-435-5858, Fax: 418-435-0010
bibliobsp@charlevoix.net
www.baiestpaul.com/bibliotheque/
Denise Ouellet, Responsable

Baie-Trinité: **Bibliothèque de Baie-Trinité**
3, rue St-Joseph, Baie-Trinité QC G0H 1A0
418-939-2231, Fax: 418-939-2616
cacibt@globetrotter.net
www.reseaubiblioduquebec.qc.ca
Ghislaine Harvey, Responsable
ghislhar@hotmail.com
418-939-2535

Barraute: **Bibliothèque Barraute**
600, 1re Rue, Barraute QC J0Y 1A0
819-734-6762, Fax: 819-734-6762
barraute@reseaubiblioatnq.qc.ca
Claire Voyer, Responsable

Bassin: **Bibliothèque de L'Ile-du-Havre-Aubert**
#104, 280, ch de Bassin, Bassin QC G4T 0B5
418-937-2279, Fax: 418-937-5558
bibliohavre@muniles.ca
www.reseaubiblioduquebec.qc.ca
Christiane Turbide, Responsable

Batiscan: **Bibliothèque municipale de Batiscan**
791-2, place de la Solidarité, Batiscan QC G0X 1A0
819-840-0600, Fax: 819-362-3174
biblio025@reseaubibliocqlm.qc.ca
www.reseaubiblioduquebec.qc.ca
Caroline Pelletier, Responsable

Béarn: **Bibliothèque de Béarn**
38, rue Principale nord, Béarn QC J0Z 1G0
819-726-2251, Fax: 819-726-2121
bearn@reseaubiblioatnq.qc.ca
www.reseaubiblioduquebec.qc.ca

Linda Gaudet, Responsable

Beaucanton: **Bibliothèque Beaucanton**
2709, boul McDuff, #C, Beaucanton QC J0Z 1H0
819-941-2686, Fax: 819-941-2686
beaucanton@reseaubiblioatnq.qc.ca
www.reseaubiblioduquebec.qc.ca
Célyne Beauchamp, Responsable

Beauceville: **Bibliothèque Madeleine-Doyon**
100, Place de l'Église, Beauceville QC G5X 1X3
418-774-2466, Fax: 418-774-2499
biblio@ville.beauceville.qc.ca
www.reseaubiblioduquebec.qc.ca/beauceville
Marie-Andrée Giroux, Responsable

Beauharnois: **Bibliothèque Dominique-Julien**
#100, 600, rue Ellice, Beauharnois QC J6N 3P7
450-429-3546, Fax: 450-429-3820
Marielle Vinet, Responsable

Beaulac-Garthby: **Bibliothèque de Saints-Martyrs-Canadiens**
13, ch du Village, Beaulac-Garthby QC G0Y 1B0
819-344-5171
biblio157@reseaubibliocqlm.qc.ca
www.reseaubiblioduquebec.qc.ca
Pierre L. Ramsay, Responsable

Beaumont: **Bibliothèque Luc-Lacourcière**
64, ch du Domaine, Beaumont QC G0R 1C0
418-837-2658, Fax: 418-837-2658
bibl.l.lacourciere@videotron.ca
www.reseaubiblioduquebec.qc.ca/beaumont/
Nicole Maheu, Responsable

Beaupré: **Bibliothèque La Plume d'oie**
11298, rue de La Salle, Beaupré QC G0A 1E0
418-827-8483, Fax: 418-827-3818
bibliotheque@ville.beaupre.qc.ca
www.reseaubiblioduquebec.qc.ca/beaupre/
Charlotte Bouchard, Responsable

Bécancour: **Bibliothèque publique de Bécancour**
1295, av Nicolas-Perrot, Bécancour QC G9H 1A1
819-294-4455
biblio.becancour@tr.cgocable.ca
www.bibliomcq.qc.ca/becancour/info_general/

Bedford: **Bibliothèque Léon-Maurice-Côté**
52, rue Du Pont, Bedford QC J0J 1A0
450-248-4625
bedford@reseaubibliomonteregie.qc.ca
Renée Dallaire, Responsable

Bégin: **Bibliothèque publique de Bégin**
120B, rue Tremblay, Bégin QC G0V 1B0
418-672-4503
begin@reseaubibliosIsj.qc.ca
Marie-Joseph Thérriault, Responsable

Belcourt: **Bibliothèque de Belcourt**
219, rue Communautaire, Belcourt QC J0Y 2M0
819-737-8894, Fax: 819-737-4084
belcourt@reseaubiblioatnq.qc.ca
www.reseaubiblioduquebec.qc.ca
Christine Labbée, Responsable

Bellecombe: **Bibliothèque de Bellecombe**
1161, rte des Pionniers, Bellecombe QC J0Z 1K0
819-797-8302, Fax: 819-797-6585
bellecombe@reseaubiblioatnq.qc.ca
www.reseaubiblioduquebec.qc.ca
Gaétane Morrissette, Responsable

Belleterre: **Bibliothèque de Belleterre**
265, 1e av, Belleterre QC J0Z 1L0
819-722-2052, Fax: 819-722-2527
belleterre@reseaubiblioatnq.qc.ca
www.reseaubiblioduquebec.qc.ca
Claudette Rioux Gauthier, Responsable

Beloeil: **Bibliothèque municipale de Beloeil**
620, rue Richelieu, Beloeil QC J3G 5E8
450-467-7872, Fax: 450-467-3257
biblio@ville.beloeil.qc.ca
Johanne Guèvremont, Directrice
biblio@ville.beloeil.qc.ca
450-467-7872

Berthier-sur-Mer: **Bibliothèque Camille-Roy**
5, rue du Couvent, Berthier-sur-Mer QC G0R 1E0
418-259-2353, Fax: 418-259-2038
biblcamr@globetrotter.qc.ca
www.reseaubiblioduquebec.qc.ca

Jocelyne Guimont, Responsable
418-259-2622

Le Bic: **Bibliothèque de Le Bic**
149, rue Sainte-Cécile, Le Bic QC G0L 1B0
418-736-5325
biblio.lebic@crsbp.net
www.reseaubiblioduquebec.qc.ca
Martine Fournier, Bibliothécaire

Biencourt: **Bibliothèque de Biencourt**
#1, 2, rue Saint-Marc, Biencourt QC G0K 1T0
418-499-2423
biblio.biencourt@crsbp.net
www.reseaubiblioduquebec.qc.ca
Marthe Aubry Leduc, Responsable

Blainville: **Bibliothèque municipale de Blainville**
1000, ch du Plan-Bouchard, Blainville QC J7C 3S9
450-434-5370, Fax: 450-434-5378
bibliotheque@ville.blainville.qc.ca
www.ville.blainville.qc.ca
Patrick Toupin, Directeur, Loisirs et développement communautaire

Blue Sea: **Bibliothèque Blue Sea**
2, ch Blue Sea, Blue Sea QC J0X 1C0
819-463-2261, Fax: 819-463-4345
admbluesea@crsbpo.qc.ca
www.reseaubiblioduquebec.qc.ca/bluesea
Isabelle Gauthier, Responsable

Boisbriand: **Bibliothèque municipale de Boisbriand**
901, boul. de la Grande-Allée, Boisbriand QC J7G 1W6
450-435-7466, Fax: 450-435-0627
glauzon@ville.boisbriand.qc.ca
Stéphane Legault, Directeur

Bois-Franc: **Bibliothèque de Bois-Franc**
466, rte 105, Bois-Franc QC J9E 3A9
819-441-0645, Fax: 819-449-4407
admboisfranc@crsbpo.qc.ca
www.reseaubiblioduquebec.qc.ca/BoisFranc
Francine Marenger, Bibliothécaire

Bonaventure: **Bibliothèque Françoise-Bujold**
95A, av Port-Royal, Bonaventure QC G0C 1E0
418-534-4238, Fax: 418-534-4336
bonapret@globetrotter.net
Thérèse Arsenault, Responsable

Boucherville: **Bibliothèque Montarville-Boucher-De la Bruère**
501, ch du Lac, Boucherville QC J4B 6V6
450-449-8650, Fax: 450-449-6865
bibliotheque@ville.boucherville.qc.ca
www.ville.boucherville.qc.ca
Sylvie Provost, Directrice

Bouchette: **Bibliothèque de Bouchette**
36, rue Principale, Bouchette QC J0X 1E0
819-465-2555, Fax: 819-465-2318
admbouchette@crsbpo.qc.ca
www.reseaubiblioduquebec.qc.ca/Bouchette
Pierre Carrière, Responsable

Boulanger: **Bibliothèque publique de Sainte-Jeanne-d'Arc**
400, rue Verreault, Boulanger QC G0W 1E0
418-276-1189
jeanne@reseaubibliosIsj.qc.ca
www.reseaubiblioduquebec.qc.ca
Madelaine Tremblay, Responsable

Brébeuf: **Bibliothèque de Brébeuf**
#2, 217, rte 323, Brébeuf QC J0T 1B0
819-425-9833, Fax: 819-425-6611
brebeuf@crsbpl.qc.ca
www.reseaubiblioduquebe.qc.ca
Ginette Bernard, Responsable

Brigham: **Bibliothèque municipale de Brigham**
118, av des Cèdres, Brigham QC J2K 4J4
450-266-0500
brigham@reseaubibliomonteregie.qc.ca
Céline Vaillancourt, Responsable
rbcv@endirect.qc.ca
450-263-6677

Bristol: **Bibliothèque de Bristol/ Bristol Library**
32, ch Aylmer, Bristol QC J0X 1G0
819-647-5555, Fax: 819-647-2424
admbristol@crsbpo.qc.ca
www.reseaubiblioduquebec.qc.ca/Bristol

Kelly Dowe, Responsable

***Brossard:* Bibliothèque de Brossard (Georgette-Lepage)**
7855, av San-Francisco, Brossard QC J4X 2A4
450-923-6300, Fax: 450-923-7042
bibliotheque@ville.brossard.qc.ca
www.ville.brossard.qc.ca/biblio
Suzanne Payette, Directrice
suzanne.payette@ville.brossard.qc.ca
450-923-6300 ext. 291

***Brownsburg-Chatham:* Bibliothèque de Brownsburg-Chatham**
200, rue MacVicar, Brownsburg-Chatham QC J8G 2Z6
450-533-5355
biblio@brownsburgchatham.ca
www.reseaubiblioduquebec.qc.ca
Brigitte Bowen, Responsable

***Bryson:* Bibliothèque de Bryson**
833, rue Principale, Bryson QC J0X 1H0
819-648-2543, Fax: 819-648-5297
admbryson@crsbpo.qc.ca
www.reseaubiblioduquebec.qc.ca/Bryson
Charlotte Miljour, Responsable

***Buckingham:* Bibliothèque municipale de Buckingham**
181, rue Joseph, Buckingham QC J8L 1G6
819-595-7461
clarocqu@ville.buckingham.qc.ca
Lise Robitaille, Responsable
819-986-4211

***Buckland:* Bibliothèque Biblio Buck**
4340, rue Principale, Buckland QC G0R 1G0
418-789-3119, Fax: 418-789-3119
www.reseaubiblioduquebec.qc.ca/buckland
Claude Gignac, Responsable
418-789-119

***Cabano:* Bibliothèque Cabano**
14A, du Vieux Chemin, Cabano QC G0L 1E0
418-845-5568, Fax: 418-854-0118
biblio.cabano@crsbp.net
Huguette Nadeau, Responsable
biblio.cabano@crsbp.net
418-854-5568 ext. 200

***Cacouna:* Bibliothèque de Cacouna**
420, rue du Couvent, Cacouna QC G0L 1G0
418-860-2651
biblio.cacouna@crsbp.net
www3.sympatico.ca/bibkakou
Louise Létourneau, Responsable

***Cadillac:* Bibliothèque Cadillac**
15, 1ère av est, Cadillac QC J0Y 1C0
819-759-3606, Fax: 819-759-3607
cadillac@reseaubiblioatnq.qc.ca
www.crsbpat.qc.ca/cadillac/
Rita Maranda, Responsable

***Calixa-Lavallée:* Bibliothèque municipale de Calixa-Lavallée**
771, rang Beauce, Calixa-Lavallée QC J0L 1A0
450-583-5417
calixa.lavallee@reseaubibliomonteregie.qc.ca
www.reseaubiblioduquebec.qc.ca
Nicole Jacques, Responsable

***Campbell's Bay:* Bibliothèque de Campbell's Bay/Litchfield**
4, rue Patterson, Campbell's Bay QC J0X 1K0
819-648-5676, Fax: 819-648-2045
admcampbell@crsbpo.qc.ca
www.reseaubiblioduquebec.qc.ca/CampbellsBay
Lucille Lacourse, Responsable

***Candiac:* Bibliothèque municipale de Candiac**
59, ch Haendel, Candiac QC J5R 1R7
450-635-6032, Fax: 450-635-0900
biblio@ville.candiac.qc.ca
www.ville.candiac.qc.ca
Patricia Lemieux, Responsable

***Cantley:* Bibliothèque municipale de Cantley**
8, ch River, Cantley QC J8V 2Z9
819-827-3434, Fax: 819-827-4328
biblio@bibliocantley.qc.ca
www.bibliocantley.qc.ca
Bibiane Rondeau, Coordonnatrice

***Cap-aux-Meules:* Bibliothèque de Cap-aux-Meules**
#3, 315, ch Principal, Cap-aux-Meules QC G4T 1E2
418-986-6821, Fax: 418-986-5446
bibliocamiles@hotmail.com
Suzanne Chevrier, Responsable

***Cap-Chat:* Bibliothèque La ruche littéraire**
27, des Écoliers, Cap-Chat QC G0J 1E0
418-786-2068
bbocchat@globetrotter.qc.ca
Carmeline Langlais, Responsable
418-786-2149

***Cap-d'Espoir:* Bibliothèque de Cap-d'Espoir**
52, rue du Curé-Poirier, Cap-d'Espoir QC G0C 1G0
418-782-2921, Fax: 418-782-2590
bbocesp@globetrotter.net
Marie-Lise Rail, Responsable

***Caplan:* Bibliothèque Jeanne-Ferlatte**
17, boul Perron est, Caplan QC G0C 1H0
418-388-2545, Fax: 418-388-2429
bibliocaplan@hotmail.com
Colette Bertrand, Responsable

***Cap-Saint-Ignace:* Bibliothèque Léo-Pol-Morin**
100, Place de l'Église, Cap-Saint-Ignace QC G0R 1H0
418-246-3037, Fax: 418-246-5663
biblicap@globetrotter.qc.ca
www.reseaubiblioduquebec.qc.ca/cap-saint-ignace
Lyne Gobeil, Responsable

***Cap-Santé:* Bibliothèque municipale de Cap-Santé**
15, rue Marie-Fitzbach, Cap-Santé QC G0A 1L0
418-285-6891, Fax: 418-285-0009
capsante@globetrotter.qc.ca
www.reseaubiblioduquebec.qc.ca/cap-sante
Francine Germain, Responsable
418-285-2374

***Capucins:* Bibliothèque de Capucins**
294, rte du Village, Capucins QC G0J 1H0
418-786-2013
bbocapu@globetrotter.net
www.reseaubiblioduquebec.qc.ca
Jeannine Harrisson, Responsable

***Carleton-sur-Mer:* Bibliothèque Gabrielle-Bernard-Dubé**
774, boul Perron, Carleton-sur-Mer QC G0C 1J0
418-364-7103
livre1@globetrotter.net
Julie Poulin, Responsable

***Causapscal:* Bibliothèque de Causapscal**
3, Place de la Fabrique, Causapscal QC G0J 1J0
418-756-3522
biblio.causap@crsbp.net
www.reseaubiblioduquebec.qc.ca
Thérèse Audit, Responsable

***Les Cèdres:* Bibliothèque municipale de Les Cèdres**
1060, ch du Fleuve, Les Cèdres QC J7T 1A1
450-452-4363
cedres@reseaubibliomonteregie.qc.ca
Odette Marois, Responsable
omarois@ville.lescedres.qc.ca

***Chambly:* Bibliothèque municipale de Chambly**
1691, rue Bourgogne, Chambly QC J3L 1Y8
450-658-2711, Fax: 450-447-4525
biblio@ville.chambly.qc.ca
www.ville.chambly.qc.ca/biblio
Carole Mainville-Bériault, Directrice
cmberiault@ville.chambly.qc.ca
450-658-0674

***Chambord:* Bibliothèque publique de Chambord**
72-1, boul de la Montagne, Chambord QC G0W 1G0
418-342-8295
chambord@crsbpslsj.biblio.qc.ca
Andrée Chiasson, Responsable

***Champlain:* Bibliothèque de Champlain**
963, rue Notre-Dame, Champlain QC G0X 1C0
819-840-0407, Fax: 819-295-3032
biblio005@crsbpcqlm.qc.ca
www.reseaubiblioduquebec.qc.ca
Isabelle Vézina, Responsable

***Chandler:* Bibliothèque municipale-scolaire de Chandler**
131, boul René-Lévesque, Chandler QC G0C 1K0
418-689-3808, Fax: 418-689-3639
giselec@globetrotter.net
Gisele Cyr, Directeur

***Chapais:* Bibliothèque publique de Chapais**
28, 1e av, Chapais QC G0W 1H0
418-745-3244
chapais@reseaubiblioslsj.qc.ca
www.reseaubiblioduquebec.qc.ca
Line Lambert, Responsable

***Charette:* Bibliothèque de Charette (Armance-Samson)**
390, rue Saint-Édouard, Charette QC G0X 1E0
819-221-2095
biblio023@reseaubiblioqclm.qc.ca
www.reseaubiblioduquebec.qc.ca
Louise Gélinas, Responsable

***Charlemagne:* Bibliothèque Camille-Laurin de Charlemagne**
84, rue du Sacré-Coeur, Charlemagne QC J5Z 1W8
450-581-7243, Fax: 450-581-0597
biblio@ville.charlemagne.qc.ca
www.ville.charlemagne.qc.ca/biblio.htm
Christine Arel, Responsable
biblio@ville.charlemagne.qc.ca
450-581-7243 ext. 36

***Châteauguay:* Bibliothèque municipale de Châteauguay**
25, boul Maple, Châteauguay QC J6J 3P7
450-698-3080, Fax: 450-698-3077
biblio@ville.chateauguay.qc.ca
www.ville.chateauguay.qc.ca
Céline Lussier, Chef, Division bibliothèque
celine-lussier@ville.chateauguay.qc.ca
450-698-3095

***Chazel:* Bibliothèque municipale de Chazel**
343, rue Principale, Chazel QC J0Z 1N0
819-333-3262
chazel.ao.ca
Hélène Charrois, Coordonnatrice

***Chelsea:* Bibliothèque de Chelsea/ Chelsea Library**
100, ch Old Chelsea, Chelsea QC J9B 1C1
819-827-4019
bibliotheque@chelsea.ca
www.chelsea.ca
Béatrice O'Byrne, Bibliothécaire

***Chelsea:* Bibliothèque de Chelsea, succursale Farm Point/ Chelsea Library, Farm Point Branch**
331, ch de la Rivière, Chelsea QC J9B 2M6
819-459-3158, Fax: 819-827-2642
bibliotheque@chelsea.ca
www.chelsea.ca
Christine Léger, Responsable

***Chénéville:* Bibliothèque Chénéville/Lac-Simon**
77, rue Hôtel-de-Ville, Chénéville QC J0V 1E0
819-428-3583, Fax: 819-428-4838
biblio.cheneville@mrcpapineau.com
www.reseaubiblioduquebec.qc.ca/Cheneville
Madeleine Tremblay, Responsable

***Chertsey:* Bibliothèque de Chertsey**
333, av de l'Amitié, Chertsey QC J0K 3K0
450-882-4738
mpicard@municipalite.chertsey.qc.ca
www.reseaubiblioduquebec.qc.ca
Monique Picard, Responsable
mpicard@municipalite.chertsey.qc.ca

***Chester-Est:* Bibliothèque de Chester-Est**
3456, rue Principale, Chester-Est QC G0P 1H0
819-382-2862
biblio148@reseaubiblioqclm.qc.ca
Émilie Brown-Pothitos, Responsable

***Chesterville:* Bibliothèque de Chesterville**
474, rue de l'Acceuil, Chesterville QC G0P 1J0
819-382-2997
biblio146@reseaubiblioqclm.qc.ca
www.reseaubiblioduquebec.qc.ca
Louise Lefebvre, Responsable

***Chevery:* Bibliothèque de Chevery**
CP 92, Chevery QC G0G 1G0
418-787-2244, Fax: 418-787-2241
biblioch@globetrotter.net
Ana Osborne, Responsable

Chibougamau: **Bibliothèque municipale de Chibougamau**
601, 3e rue, Chibougamau QC G8P 3A2
418-748-2497, Fax: 418-748-2980
bibliotheque@ville.chibougamau.qc.ca
www.ville.chibougamau.qc.ca
Lise Matte, Bibliotechnicienne
lisematte@ville.chibougamau.qc.ca
418-748-2497

Chicoutimi: **Bibliothèque de Chicoutimi**
155, rue Racine est, Chicoutimi QC G7H 1R5
418-698-5350, Fax: 418-698-5359
webbiblio@ville.saguenay.qc.ca
www.ville.saguenay.qc.ca
Anne Lebel, Chef de division, Bibliothèques de Saguenay
anne.lebel@ville.saguenay.qc.ca

Chicoutimi: **Bibliothèque de Rivière-du-Moulin**
1410, rue des Cèdres, Chicoutimi QC G8A 2E6
418-698-3226
webbiblio@ville.saguenay.qc.ca
www.ville.saguenay.qc.ca
Anne Lebel, Chef de division, Bibliothèques de Saguenay
anne.lebel@ville.saguenay.qc.ca

Chute-aux-Outardes: **Bibliothèque de Chute-aux-Outardes**
4, rue de l'École, Chute-aux-Outardes QC G0H 1C0
418-567-2535, Fax: 418-567-4478
bibliotheque.desjardins@csestuaire.qc.ca
www.reseaubiblioduquebec.qc.ca
Manon Finn, Responsable

Chute-Saint-Philippe: **Bibliothèque de Chute-Saint-Philippe**
592, ch du Progrès, Chute-Saint-Philippe QC J0W 1A0
819-585-3397, Fax: 819-585-4949
bibliotheque@chute-saint-philippe.qc.ca
www.reseaubiblioduquebec.qc.ca/chute-saint-philippe
Françoise St-Amour, Responsable

Clarenceville: **Bibliothèque municipale de Saint-Georges-de-Clarenceville**
1340, ch Middle, Clarenceville QC J0J 1B0
450-294-3200
clarenceville@reseaubibliomonteregie.qc.ca
Nestor Rassart, Responsable

Cléricy: **Bibliothèque de Cléricy**
931, rue du Souvenir, Cléricy QC J0Z 1P0
819-637-2131, Fax: 819-637-2133
clericy@reseaubiblioatnq.qc.ca
www.reseaubiblioduquebe.qc.ca
Lise Robin Boucher, Responsable

Clermont: **Bibliothèque municipale de Clermont**
11, rue Jean Talon, Clermont QC G4A 1A4
418-439-2903, Fax: 418-439-4889
biblioc@cite.net
www.reseaubiblioduquebec.qc.ca/clermont
Ginette Simard, Responsable

Clerval: **Bibliothèque de Clerval**
579, rue du Village, Clerval QC J0Z 1R0
819-783-2640, Fax: 819-783-2640
clerval@crsbpat.qc.ca
www.crsbpat.qc.ca/clerval
Germaine Thibault-Riopel, Responsable

Cloridorme: **Bibliothèque de Cloridorme**
472, rte 132, Cloridorme QC G0E 1G0
418-395-2609, Fax: 418-395-2228
munclori@globetrotter.qc.ca
www.reseaubiblioduquebec.qc.ca
Marie Dufresne, Responsable

Cloutier: **Bibliothèque de Cloutier**
531, rte 391 sud, Cloutier QC J0Z 1S0
819-797-8613, Fax: 819-797-1299
cloutier@reseaubiblioatnq.qc.ca
www.reseaubiblioduquebec.qc.ca
Rachel Jutras, Responsable

Coaticook: **Bibliothèque Françoise-Maurice**
34, rue Main est, Coaticook QC J1A 1N2
819-849-4013, Fax: 819-849-0479
biblcoat@bibliotheque.coaticook.qc.ca
www.bibliotheque.coaticook.qc.ca
Patrick Falardeau, Directeur, Conseil d'administration

Colombier: **Bibliothèque de Colombier**
570, rue Principale, Colombier QC G0H 1P0
418-565-3013, Fax: 418-565-3289
bibliocolombier@hotmail.com
Isabelle Maltais, Responsable

La Conception: **Bibliothèque de La Conception**
1373, boul du Centenaire, La Conception QC J0T 1M0
819-686-3016, Fax: 819-686-5808
biblio69@crsbpl.qc.ca
www.reseaubiblioduquebec.qc.ca
Manuela Brassard-Erba, Responsable

La Corne: **Bibliothèque de La Corne**
380A, rte 111, La Corne QC J0Y 1R0
819-799-2365, Fax: 819-799-3571
lacorne@reseaubiblioatnq.qc.ca
www.reseaubiblioduquebec.qc.ca
Paméla Dumais, Responsable

Coteau-du-Lac: **Bibliothèque Jules-Fournier**
3, rue du Parc, Coteau-du-Lac QC J0P 1B0
450-763-2763, Fax: 450-763-2495
bibliotheque@coteau-du-lac.com
Louise Laventure, Régisseur
louiselaventure@coteau-du-lac.ca

Les Coteaux: **Bibliothèque municipale Des Coteaux**
65, rte 338, Les Coteaux QC J7X 1A2
450-267-1414, Fax: 450-267-3532
coteaux@reseaubibliomonteregie.qc.ca
Lucie Hamel, Responsable

Cowansville: **Bibliothèque Gabrielle-Giroux-Bertrand**
171, rue Principale, Cowansville QC J2K 3L9
450-263-4071, Fax: 450-263-7477
biblio129@reseaubibliomonteregie.qc.ca
www.reseaubiblioduquebec.qc.ca; www.cowansville.org
Brigitte Messier, Responsable

Crabtree: **Bibliothèque de Crabtree**
59, 16e rue, Crabtree QC J0K 1B0
450-754-4332
biblio114@reseaubibliocqlm.qc.ca
www.reseaubiblioduquebec.qc.ca
Marjolaine Bertrand, Responsable
450-754-4332

Dalmas: **Bibliothèque publique de St-Augustin**
710, rue Principale, Dalmas QC G0W 1K0
418-374-1084
augustin@reseaubiblioslsj.qc.ca
Rosette Savard, Responsable

Dalquier: **Bibliothèque Saint-Félix-de-Dalquier**
20, rue Principale nord, Dalquier QC J0Y 1G0
819-732-2424
Francine Briand, Responsable
819-732-2424

Danville: **Bibliothèque municipale de Danville**
Hôtel de Ville, Danville QC J0A 1A0
819-839-3236, Fax: 819-839-2918
biblio053@reseaubiblioestrie.qc.ca
www.reseaubiblioduquebec.qc.ca
Daniel Hinse, Responsable

Daveluyville: **Bibliothèque de Daveluyville**
436, 5e Rue, Daveluyville QC G0Z 1C0
819-367-3645, Fax: 819-367-3550
biblio057@reseaubibliocqlm.qc.ca
www.reseaubiblioduquebec.qc.ca
Jacqueline B. Pépin, Responsable

Dégelis: **Bibliothèque Élisabeth-Turgeon**
663, 6e rue ouest, Dégelis QC G5T 1Y3
418-853-2380
biblio.degelis@crsbp.net
www.reseaubiblioduquebec.qc.ca
Gertrude Leclerc, Responsable

Delson: **Bibliothèque municipale de Delson**
1, 1e av, Delson QC J5B 1M9
450-632-1050
delson@reseaubibliomonteregie.qc.ca
www.reseaubiblioduquebec.qc.ca
Lyne Croussette, Responsable

Desbiens: **Bibliothèque publique de Desbiens**
1058, rue Marcellin, Desbiens QC G0W 1N0
418-346-5739
desbiens@reseaubiblioslsj.qc.ca
Pâquerette Fortin, Responsable

Deschaillons-sur-St-Laurent: **Bibliothèque de Deschaillons-sur-Saint-Laurent**
1042A, rue Marie-Victorin, Deschaillons-sur-St-Laurent QC G0S 1G0
819-292-2483, Fax: 819-292-3194
biblio101@reseaubibliocqlm.qc.ca
www.reseaubiblioduquebec.qc.ca
Odette Gilbert, Responsable

Deschambault-Grondines: **Bibliothèque Du Bord de l'Eau**
115, rue de l'Église, Deschambault-Grondines QC G0A 1S0
418-286-6938, Fax: 418-286-6511
bibdesch@globetrotter.qc.ca
www.reseaubiblioduquebec.qc.ca/deschambault/
Jacqueline Gignac, Responsable

Destor: **Bibliothèque Destor**
945B, ch du Parc, Destor QC J9X 5A3
819-637-2279, Fax: 819-637-2095
destor@reseaubiblioatnq.qc.ca
Rita Tremblay, Responsable

Deux-Montagnes: **Bibliothèque de Deux-Montagnes/ Deux-Montagnes Libary**
200, rue Henri-Dunant, Deux-Montagnes QC J7R 4W6
450-473-2702, Fax: 450-473-2816
jchaput@ville.deux-montagnes.qc.ca
www.ville.deux-montagnes.qc.ca/bibliotheque/
Johanne Chaput, Responsable, Activités culturelles
450-473-2702

Dolbeau-Mistassini: **Bibliothèque de Dolbeau-Mistassini**
175, 4e av, Dolbeau-Mistassini QC G8L 1W6
418-276-1317, Fax: 418-276-8188
www.dolbeau.biblio.qc.ca
Pauline Lapointe, Responsable
lapointe@biblio-dolbeau.qc.ca

La Doré: **Bibliothèque publique de la Doré**
4450, des Peupliers, La Doré QC G8J 1E5
418-256-3992, Fax: 418-256-3992
ladore@crsbpslsj.biblio.qc.ca
Jacynthe Harvey, Responsable et présidente
418-256-3287

Dosquet: **Bibliothèque La Bouquinerie/Dosquet**
1, rue Viger, Dosquet QC G0S 1H0
418-728-3994
octaved@globetrotter.net
www.reseaubiblioduquebec.qc.ca/dosquet/
Nathalie Lachance, Responsable

Drummondville: **Bibliothèque municipale Côme-Saint-Germain**
545, rue des Écoles, Drummondville QC J2B 1J6
819-478-6573, Fax: 819-478-0399
biblio@ville.drummondville.qc.ca
www.ville.drummondville.qc.ca
Joceline-Andrée Turcotte, Chef de division
jturcotte@ville.drummondville.qc.ca
819-478-6588

Duhamel: **Bibliothèque Duhamel**
1899, rue Principale, Duhamel QC J0V 1G0
819-428-7100, Fax: 819-428-1941
admduhamel@crsbpo.qc.ca
www.reseaubiblioduquebec.qc.ca/Duhamel/
Roselyne Bernard, Responsable

Dunham: **Bibliothèque municipale de Dunham/ Dunham Municipal Library**
3638, rue Principale, Dunham QC J0E 1M0
450-295-2621
dunham@reseaubibliomonteregie.qc.ca
www.reseaubiblioduquebec.qc.ca
Marie Bonneville, Responsable

Duparquet: **Bibliothèque Duparquet**
54, rue Principale, Duparquet QC J0Z 1W0
819-948-2455, Fax: 819-948-2266
duparquet@reseaubiblioatnq.qc.ca
www.crsbpat.qc.ca/duparquet/
Lise Baron, Responsable

Dupuy: **Bibliothèque de Dupuy**
63, av du Chemin de Fer, Dupuy QC J0Z 1X0
819-783-2147, Fax: 819-783-2147
dupuy@reseaubiblioatnq.qc.ca
www.reseaubiblioduquebec.qc.ca
Huguette Huot, Responsable

***Durham-Sud:* Bibliothèque de Durham-Sud**
77, rue de l'Église, Durham-Sud QC J0H 2C0
819-858-1156, Fax: 819-858-2044
biblio153@reseaubibliocqlm.qc.ca
Jacques Boyer, Responsable

***East Broughton:* Bibliothèque La Bouquinerie/East Broughton/Sacré-Coeur-de-Jésus**
372A, av du Collège, East Broughton QC G0N 1G0
418-427-4900, Fax: 418-427-3514
bouquinerie@eastbroughton.com
www.reseaubiblioduquebec.qc.ca/eastbroughton/
Lynda Laplante, Responsable

***Les Éboulements:* Bibliothèque Félix-Antoine-Savard**
248B, rue du Village, Les Éboulements QC G0A 2M0
418-489-2990, Fax: 418-635-2520
bibliotheque@leseboulements.com
www.reseaubiblioduquebec.qc.ca/leseboulements/
Philippe Naud, Responsable

***Entrelacs:* Bibliothèque d'Entrelacs**
2351, ch Entrelacs, Entrelacs QC J0T 2E0
450-228-3931, Fax: 450-228-4866
biblient@entrelacs.com
www.entrelacs.com/biblio_frame.htm
Suzanne Larivière, Responsable

***L'Épiphanie:* Bibliothèque de L'Épiphanie**
83, rue Amireault, L'Épiphanie QC J5X 1A1
450-588-4470
biblio061@reseaubibliocqlm.qc.ca
www.reseaubiblioduquebec.qc.ca
Nathalie L'Espérance, Responsable

***Les Escoumins:* Bibliothèque municipale des Escoumins**
12, rue Boily, Les Escoumins QC G0T 1K0
418-233-3097, Fax: 418-233-3273
escobiblio@globetrotter.qc.ca
Odile Boisvert, Responsable

***Esprit-Saint:* Bibliothèque d'Esprit-Saint**
121, rue Principale, Esprit-Saint QC G0K 1A0
418-779-2716
biblio.esprit@crsbp.net
www.reseaubiblioduquebec.qc.ca
Sylvie Boucher, Responsable

***L'Étang-du-Nord:* Bibliothèque de l'Étang-du-Nord**
1589, ch Étang-du-Nord, L'Étang-du-Nord QC G4T 3C1
418-986-3321, Fax: 418-986-6231
georgettenoelchev@hotmail.com
Georgette Chevarie, Responsable

***Fabre:* Bibliothèque Le Coquelicot**
620, av de l'Église, Fabre QC J0Z 1Z0
819-634-2745, Fax: 819-634-2646
fabre@reseaubiblioatnq.qc.ca
www.reseaubiblioduquebec.qc.ca
Jacinthe Breton Desrochers, Responsable

***Farnham:* Bibliothèque de Farnham inc.**
479, rue de l'Hôtel de Ville, Farnham QC J2N 2H3
450-293-3375, Fax: 450-293-2989
bibliofarnham@bellnet.ca
bibliofarnham.ca
Dino Coudé, Responsable

***Fassett:* Bibliothèque Fassett/Notre-Dame-de-Bonsecours**
19, rue Gendron, Fassett QC J0V 1H0
819-423-6943, Fax: 819-423-5388
admfassett@crsbpo.qc.ca
www.reseaubiblioduquebec.qc.ca/Fassett/
Nathalie Frenière, Responsable

***Fatima:* Bibliothèque de Fatima**
#2, 730, ch des Caps, Fatima QC G4T 2T3
418-986-4736
biblio.fatima@hotmail.com
www.reseaubiblioduquebec.qc.ca
Thérèse Harvie, Responsable

***Ferland-et-Boilleau:* Bibliothèque publique de Ferland-Boileau**
466, rte 381, Ferland-et-Boilleau QC G0V 1H0
418-676-2547, Fax: 418-676-2506
ferland@reseaubiblioslsj.qc.ca
www.reseaubiblioduquebec.qc.ca
Isabelle Lavoie, Responsable

***Ferme-Neuve:* Bibliothèque de Ferme-Neuve**
144, 12e rue, Ferme-Neuve QC J0W 1C0
819-587-3102, Fax: 819-587-4820
bibfn@tlb.sympatico.ca
www.reseaubiblioduquebec.qc.ca
Andrée Quevillon, Responsable

***Fermont:* Bibliothèque publique de Fermont**
130, Le Carrefour, Fermont QC G0G 1J0
418-287-3227, Fax: 418-287-3274
biblio.fermont@sympatico.ca
www3.sympatico.ca/biblio.fermont
Aline Martel, Technicienne en documentation
bibliofermont@diffusionfermont.ca
418-287-3227

***Forestville:* Bibliothèque municipale de Forestville**
10, 10e rue, Forestville QC G0T 1E0
418-587-4483, Fax: 418-587-2458
biblioforestville@globetrotter.net
www.reseaubiblioduquebec.qc.ca
Roger Dumont, Responsable

***Fort-Coulonge:* Bibliothèque de Fort-Coulonge**
134, rue Principale, Fort-Coulonge QC J0X 1V0
819-683-3421, Fax: 819-683-3627
biblio.fc@fortcoulonge.qc.ca
www.fortcoulonge.qc.ca
Pierrette Lafrenière, Responsable

***Fortierville:* Bibliothèque de Fortierville**
198A, rue de la Fabrique, Fortierville QC G0S 1J0
819-287-4309, Fax: 819-287-5922
biblio015@reseaubibliocqlm.qc.ca
Denise Lemay, Responsable

***Fossambault-sur-le-Lac:* Bibliothèque municipale de Fossambault-sur-le-Lac (La Source)**
145, boul Gingras, Fossambault-sur-le-Lac QC G0A 3M0
418-875-3133, Fax: 418-875-3544
fossam@coopcscf.com
www.fossambault-sur-le-lac.com
Monique Blouin, Responsable
418-875-2876

***Franquelin:* Bibliothèque municipale de Franquelin**
27, rue des Érables, Franquelin QC G0H 1E0
418-296-1406, Fax: 418-296-6946
bibli.munic.franquelin@globetrotter.net
www.reseaubiblioduquebec.qc.ca
Diane Jourdain, Responsable

***Fugèreville:* Bibliothèque de Fugèreville**
33A, rue Principale, Fugèreville QC J0Z 2A0
819-748-2276, Fax: 819-748-2422
fugereville@reseaubiblioatnq.qc.ca
www.reseaubiblioduquebec.qc.ca
Gaétane Falardeau, Responsable

***Gallichan:* Bibliothèque La Gallithèque**
207, ch de la Rivière ouest, Gallichan QC J0Z 2B0
819-787-6301
gallichan@mrcao.qc.ca
gallichan.ao.ca
Brigitte Rivard, Responsable

***Gallix:* Bibliothèque municipale de Gallix**
524, av Lapierre, Gallix QC G0G 1L0
418-766-3264
www.reseaubiblioduquebec.qc.ca
Lyne Porlier, Responsable

***Gaspé:* Bibliothèque Alma-Bourget-Costisella**
10, côte Cartier, Gaspé QC G4X 1V2
418-368-2104, Fax: 418-368-8532
biblio.gaspe@globetrotter.net
Adrienne Bisson, Responsable

***Gaspé:* Bibliothèque de Cap-aux-Os**
1826, boul Forillon, Gaspé QC G4X 6L4
418-368-2104, Fax: 418-368-6810
capauxos@globetrotter.net
www.reseaubiblioduquebec.qc.ca
Rita Beaudin, Responsable

***Gaspé:* Bibliothèque de Douglastown**
28, rue St-Patrick, Gaspé QC G4X 2Y2
418-368-2104, Fax: 418-368-0284
biblio.douglastown.globetrotter.net
www.reseaubiblioduquebec.qc.ca
Maria Griffith, Responsable

***Gaspé:* Bibliothèque de L'Anse-au-Griffon**
465, boul du Griffon, Gaspé QC G4X 6A3
418-368-2104, Fax: 418-368-6837
bboaag@globetrotter.qc.ca
www.reseaubiblioduquebec.qc.ca
Camille Malouin, Responsable

***Gaspé:* Bibliothèque de L'Anse-à-Valleau**
9, rue Mathurin, Gaspé QC G4X 4A8
418-368-2104
www.reseaubiblioduquebec.qc.ca
Priscillia Poirier, Responsable
priscillia.poirier@globetrotter.qc.ca

***Gaspé:* Bibliothèque de Petit-Cap**
439, boul Petit-Cap, Gaspé QC G4X 4L1
418-368-2104
bibliopetitcap@globetrotter.net
www.reseaubiblioduquebec.qc.ca
Philomène Cloutier, Responsable

***Gaspé:* Bibliothèque de Saint-Majorique**
3-1, Montée de Corte-Réal, Gaspé QC G4X 6R7
418-368-2104
biblio.stmajorique@globetrotter.net
www.reseaubiblioduquebec.qc.ca
Gracia Cabot, Responsable

***Gatineau:* Bibliothèque municipale de Gatineau**
#317, 144, boul de l'Hôpital, Gatineau QC J8T 7S7
819-595-7460, Fax: 819-243-2399, 800-299-2002
bibliotheque@gatineau.ca
www.ville.gatineau.qc.ca/gatineau/bibliotheque.htm
Carole Laguë, Chef de division
lague.carole@gatineau.qc.ca
819-243-2548

***Gethsémani:* Bibliothèque de La Romaine**
École Marie-Sarah, Poste Restante, Gethsémani QC G0G 1M0
418-787-2241
www.reseaubiblioduquebec.qc.ca

***Girardville:* Bibliothèque publique de Girardville**
180, rue Principale, Girardville QC G0W 1R0
418-258-3222, Fax: 418-258-3473
girardv@reseaubiblioslsj.qc.ca
Francine Lambert, Responsable
418-258-3222

***Godbout:* Bibliothèque municipale de Godbout**
102B, rue Alexandre, Godbout QC G0H 1G0
418-568-7702, Fax: 418-568-7356
biblio.godbout@hotmail.com
www.reseaubiblioduquebec.qc.ca
Caroline Morin, Responsable
curbymorin@globetrotter.net
418-568-7420

***Gracefield:* Bibliothèque de Gracefield**
3, rue de la Polyvalente, Gracefield QC J0X 1W0
819-463-1180, Fax: 819-463-4236
admgracefield@crsbpo.qc.ca
www.reseaubiblioduquebec.qc.ca/Gracefield
Denise Pelletier Rochon, Responsable

***Granby:* Bibliothèque Paul-O.-Trépanier**
11, rue Dufferin, Granby QC J2G 2T8
450-776-8320, Fax: 450-776-8313
bibliotheque@ville.granby.qc.ca
www.biblio.ville.granby.qc.ca/bibliotheque/
Linda Laberge, Responsable
llaberge@ville.granby.qc.ca

***Grande-Entrée:* Bibliothèque de Grande-Entrée**
214, rte 199, Grande-Entrée QC G4T 7A4
418-985-2288, Fax: 418-985-2149
biblioge@muniles.ca
www.reseaubiblioduquebec.qc.ca
Raoul Cyr, Responsable

***Grande-Rivière:* Bibliothèque La Détente/Grande-Rivière**
210, rue du Carrefour, Grande-Rivière QC G0C 1V0
418-385-3833, Fax: 418-385-2290
geber@globetrotter.qc.ca
Marie-Paule Berger, Responsable

***Grandes-Bergeronnes:* Bibliothèque Les Bergeronnes**
514, rue du Boisé, Grandes-Bergeronnes QC G0T 1G0
418-232-1134, Fax: 418-232-6602
info@batture.ca
www.reseaubibliquebec.qc.ca
Ninon Marty, Responsable

Grandes-Piles: **Bibliothèque de Grandes-Piles**
650, 4e av, Grandes-Piles QC G0X 1H0
819-533-3697, Fax: 819-538-6947
biblio030@reseaubibliocqlm.qc.ca
www.reseaubiblioduquebec.qc.ca
Line Blanchard, Responsable

Grande-Vallée: **Bibliothèque de Grande-Vallée**
3, rue St-François-Xavier est, Grande-Vallée QC G0E 1K0
418-393-2166, Fax: 418-393-2274
bbogrval@globetrotter.net
www.reseaubiblioduquebec.qc.ca
Gaétanne Normand, Responsable
normandg@hotmail.com

Grand-Mère: **Bibliothèque Hélène-B. Beauséjour**
650, 8e rue, Grand-Mère QC G9T 6K1
819-538-5555
bibliotheque@ville.shawinigan.qc.ca
www.shawinigan.ca
Charlotte Lecours, Responsable des bibliothèques
819-536-7211 ext. 501

Grand-Remous: **Bibliothèque de Grand-Remous**
1508, rte Transcanadienne, Grand-Remous QC J0W 1E0
819-438-2168, Fax: 418-438-2364
admgrandremous@crsbpo.qc.ca
www.reseaubiblioduquebec.qc.ca/Grand-Remous
Lise Fraser, Responsable

Greenfield Park: **Bibliothèque de Greenfield Park**
225, rue Empire, Greenfield Park QC J4V 1T9
450-463-7140, Fax: 450-466-8112
www.longueuil.ca/bibliotheques/
Lise Lafleur, Responsable
lise.lafleur@ville.longueuil.qc.ca

Grenville: **Bibliothèque de Grenville**
18, rue Tri-Jean, Grenville QC J0V 1J0
819-242-2585, Fax: 819-242-5891
grenville@crsbpl.qca
www.reseaubiblioduquebec.qc.ca
Céline Joly, Responsable

Grenville-sur-la-Rouge: **Bibliothèque de Calumet**
130, rue Principale, Grenville-sur-la-Rouge QC J0V 1B0
819-242-8088, Fax: 819-242-1232
biblio5@crsbpl.qc.ca
www.reseaubiblioduquebec.qc.ca
Judy Smith, Responsable

Grenville-sur-la-Rouge: **Bibliothèque de Pointe-au-Chêne**
2714, rte 148, Grenville-sur-la-Rouge QC J0V 1B0
819-242-0298
biblio12@crsbpl.qc.ca
www.reseaubiblioduquebec.qc.ca
Johanne Nantel, Responsable

Grondines: **Bibliothèque L'Ardoise**
525, ch Sir-Lomer-Gouin, Grondines QC G0A 1W0
418-268-8359, Fax: 418-268-5553
bibligron@csportneuf.qc.ca
www.reseaubiblioduquebec.qc.ca/grondines/
Guylaine Rivard, Responsable

Gros-Morne: **Bibliothèque de Gros-Morne**
1, rue de l'Église ouest, Gros-Morne QC G0E 1L0
418-797-2610
www.reseaubiblioduquebec.qc.ca
Albertine Laflamme, Responsable

Grosse-Ile: **Bibliothèque de Grosse-Ile**
448, ch Principal, Grosse-Ile QC G4T 6A8
418-986-2885, Fax: 418-985-2955
hwood@easternshores.qc.ca
Natasha Joncas, Responsable

Guérin: **Bibliothèque de Guérin**
516A, rue St-Gabriel, Guérin QC J0Z 2E0
819-784-7024, Fax: 819-784-7026
guerin@reseaubiblioatnq.qc.ca
www.reseaubiblioduquebec.qc.ca
Sylvie Laverdière, Responsable

Guyenne: **Bibliothèque de Guyenne**
1255-F, rang 5, Guyenne QC J0Y 1L0
819-732-9128, Fax: 819-732-0904
guyenne@reseaubiblioatnq.qc.ca
www.reseaubiblioduquebec.qc.ca
Francine Simard, Responsable

Ham-Nord: **Bibliothèque de Ham-Nord**
474, rue Principale, Ham-Nord QC G0P 1A0
819-344-2805, Fax: 819-344-2805
biblio150@reseaubibliocqlm.qc.ca
www.reseaubiblioduquebec.qc.ca
Joanne Lacasse, Responsable

Harrington Harbour: **Bibliothèque de Harrington Harbour**
CP 7, Harrington Harbour QC G0G 1N0
418-787-2244, Fax: 418-787-2241
bibliohh@globetrotter.net
www.reseaubiblioduquebec.qc.ca
Judi Ransom, Responsable

Havre-aux-Maisons: **Bibliothèque de Havre-aux-Maisons**
37, ch Central, Havre-aux-Maisons QC G4T 5H1
418-969-2100
biblioham@muniles.ca
www.reseaubiblioduquebec.qc.ca
Marcel Thériault, Responsable

Havre-Saint-Pierre: **Bibliothèque municipale de Havre-St-Pierre**
1045, rue Dulcinée, Havre-Saint-Pierre QC G0G 1P0
418-538-3301, Fax: 418-538-3439
biblio.havrest-pierre@globetrotter.net
www.reseaubiblioduquebec.qc.ca
Nicole Cormier, Responsable

Hemmingford: **Bibliothèque municipale d'Hemmingford/ Hemmingford Community Library**
552, av Goyette, Hemmingford QC J0L 1H0
450-247-0010
hemmingford@reseaubibliomonteregie.qc.ca
www.reseaubiblioduquebec.qc.ca
Elizabeth Nicholls, Responsable

Henryville: **Bibliothèque municipale d'Henryville**
#104, 854, rue St-Jean-Baptiste, Henryville QC J0J 1E0
450-299-1165
henryville@reseaubibliomonteregie.qc.ca
www.reseaubiblioduquebec.qc.ca
Mathieu Fortin, Responsable

Hérouxville: **Bibliothèque de Hérouxville**
1060, rue Saint-Pierre, Hérouxville QC G0X 1J0
418-365-7337, Fax: 418-365-7041
biblio090@reseaubibliocqlm.qc.ca
www.reseaubiblioduquebec.qc.ca
Julie L'Heureux, Responsable

Honfleur: **Bibliothèque La Livrothèque**
320, rue Saint-Jean, Honfleur QC G0R 1N0
418-885-8212, Fax: 418-885-9195
livro@globetrotter.qc.ca
www.reseaubiblioduquebec.qc.ca/honfleur/
Isabelle Roussy, Responsable

Hope Town: **Bibliothèque de Hope Town**
224, rte 132, Hope Town QC G0C 2K0
418-752-3848, Fax: 418-752-2434
hopelibrary@globetrotter.net
www.reseaubiblioduquebec.qc.ca
Lynda McWhirter, Responsable

Huberdeau: **Bibliothèque d'Huberdeau**
101, rue Du Pont, Huberdeau QC J0T 1G0
819-687-1164, Fax: 819-687-8808
huberdeau@crsbpl.qc.ca
www.reseaubiblioduquebec.qc.ca
Suzanne Fortin, Responsable

Huntingdon: **Little Green Library/ La Petite Bibliothèque Verte**
6 Hunter St., Huntingdon QC J0S 1H0
450-264-4872
Laura Smith, President

Ile-du-Grand-Calumet: **Bibliothèque Ile-du-Grand-Calumet**
2, rue Brizard, Ile-du-Grand-Calumet QC J0X 1J0
819-648-5966, Fax: 819-648-2659
admcalumet@crsbpo.qc.ca
www.reseaubiblioduquebec.qc.ca/Grand-Calument/
Chantal Corriveau, Responsable

Inverness: **Bibliothèque de Inverness (L'Inverthèque)**
1801, rue Dublin, Inverness QC G0S 1K0
418-453-2867, Fax: 418-453-2554
biblio145@reseaubibliocqlm.qc.ca
www.reseaubiblioduquebec.qc.ca
Hélène Laplante, Responsable

L'Isle-aux-Coudres: **Bibliothèque 'Pour la suite du monde'**
1026, ch des Coudriers, L'Isle-aux-Coudres QC G0A 3J0
418-438-2602, Fax: 418-438-2750
iacsdm@charlevoix.net
www.reseaubiblioduquebec.qc.ca/coudres
Claudine Hovington, Responsable
418-438-2602

L'Isle-aux-Grues: **Bibliothèque La Rose des Vents/L'Isle-aux-Grues**
107, ch de la Volière, L'Isle-aux-Grues QC G0R 1P0
418-248-8060, Fax: 418-248-4680
Lisette Painchaud, Responsable
418-248-4687

L'Islet: **Bibliothèque Jean-Paul-Bourque/L'Islet-sur-Mer**
16, rte des Pionniers est, L'Islet QC G0R 2B0
418-247-7576, Fax: 418-247-5009
www.reseaubiblioduquebec.qc.ca/l'islet-sur-mer/
Jacqueline C. Kirouac, Responsable

L'Islet: **Bibliothèque Léon-Laberge**
#1, 284, boul Nilus-Leclerc, L'Islet QC G0R 2C0
418-247-5345, Fax: 418-247-5085
bleonl@globetrotter.qc.ca
www.reseaubiblioduquebec.qc.ca/l'islet/
Madeleine Gagnon, Responsable

L'Isle-Verte: **Bibliothèque de Notre-Dame-des-Sept-Douleurs**
ch de l'Ile, L'Isle-Verte QC G0L 1K0
418-898-3451
biblio.douleurs@crsbp.net
www.reseaubiblioduquebec.qc.ca
Maryse Dickner, Responsable

Issoudun: **Bibliothèque La Rêverie/Notre-Dame-de-Sacré-Coeur-d'Issoudun**
268, rue Principale, Issoudun QC G0S 1L0
418-728-9061, Fax: 418-728-2303
biblisso@globetrotter.net
www.reseaubiblioduquebec.qc.ca/issoudun
Carole Couture, Responsable

Joliette: **Maison de la culture Bonsecours de Joliette inc.**
585, rue Archambault, Joliette QC J6E 2W7
450-755-6400, Fax: 450-755-6426
biblio@bibliojoliette.qc.ca
www.bibliojoliette.qc.ca
Suzie Charbonneau, Directrice générale
biblio@bibliojoliette.qc.ca
450-755-6400

Jonquière: **Bibliothèque d'Arvida**
2850, Place Davis, Jonquière QC G7X 7W7
418-698-5350, Fax: 418-699-6046
webbiblio@ville.saguenay.qc.ca
www.ville.saguenay.qc.ca
Anne Lebel, Chef de division, Bibliothèques de Saguenay
anne.lebel@ville.saguenay.qc.ca

Jonquière: **Bibliothèque de Kénogami**
3750, boul du Royaume, Jonquière QC G7X 9S4
418-698-5350
webbiblio@ville.saguenay.qc.ca
www.ville.saguenay.qc.ca
Anne Lebel, Chef de division, Bibliothèques de Saguenay
anne.lebel@ville.saguenay.qc.ca

Jonquière: **Bibliothèque St-Michel**
3885, boul Harvey, Jonquière QC G7X 9B1
418-698-5350
webbiblio@ville.saguenay.qc.ca
www.ville.saguenay.qc.ca
Anne Lebel, Chef de division, Bibliothèques de Saguenay
anne.lebel@ville.saguenay.qc.ca

Kégaska: **Bibliothèque municipale de Kégaska**
Poste Restante, Kégaska QC G0G 1S0
418-787-2244, Fax: 418-787-2241
www.reseaubiblioduquebec.qc.ca

Kiamika: **Bibliothèque de Kiamika**
3, ch Valiquette, Kiamika QC J0W 1G0
819-585-3225, Fax: 819-585-3992
kiamika@sympatico.ca
Nanette Sirois, Responsable

Kingsey Falls: **Bibliothèque de Kingsey Falls**
13, rue Caron, Kingsey Falls QC J0A 1B0

819-363-3818
biblio040@reseaubibliocqlm.qc.ca
Suzanne Boulet, Responsable

Kinnear's Mills: Bibliothèque La Boukinnerie
120, rue des Églises, Kinnear's Mills QC G0N 1K0
418-424-0082, Fax: 418-424-3015
biblikin@gabskycom.com
www.reseaubiblioduquebec.qc.ca
Michelle Bernier-Pageau, Responsable

Knowlton: Bibliothèque Commémorative Pettes/ Pettes Memorial Library
276, ch Knowlton, Knowlton QC J0E 1V0
450-243-6128, Fax: 450-243-5272
Pettes@endirect.qc.ca
pettes.ca

Labelle: Bibliothèque de Labelle
7393, boul du Curé-Labelle, Labelle QC J0T 1H0
819-681-3371, Fax: 819-686-3820
labelle@crsbpl.qc.ca
www.reseaubiblioduquebec.qc.ca
Nathalie Robson, Responsable
labelle@crspbl.qc.ca

Labrecque: Bibliothèque publique de Labrecque
3425, rue Ambroise, Labrecque QC G0W 2S0
418-481-1618, Fax: 418-481-2022
Denise Villeneuve, Responsable
418-481-1327

Lac-a-la-Croix: Bibliothèque publique de Lac-à-la-Croix
#002, 335, de Rouillac, Lac-a-la-Croix QC G8G 2B5
418-349-8133
lac.croix@reseaubibliosIsj.qc.ca
Guylaine Dufour, Responsable

Lac-à-la-Tortue: Bibliothèque de Lac-à-la-Tortue
1082, 37e av, Lac-à-la-Tortue QC G0X 1L0
819-538-5882
bibliotheque@ville.shawinigan.qc.ca
www.shawinigan.ca
Charlotte Lecours, Responsable des bibliothèques

Lac-au-Saumon: Bibliothèque Bertrand-Leblanc
20, Place de la Municipalité, Lac-au-Saumon QC G0J 1M0
418-778-3008
biblio.saumon@crsbp.net
www.reseaubiblioduquebec.qc.ca
France Lee, Responsable

Lac-aux-Sables: Bibliothèque de Lac-aux-Sables
820, rue Saint-Alphonse, Lac-aux-Sables QC G0X 1M0
418-336-3238, Fax: 418-336-2500
biblio045@reseaubibliocqlm.qc.ca
www.reseaubiblioduquebec.qc.ca
Louise Veillette, Responsable

Lac-Beauport: Bibliothèque L'Écrin
46, ch du Village, Lac-Beauport QC G0A 2C0
418-849-6133, Fax: 418-849-0361
ecrin@ccapcable.com
www.reseaubiblioduquebec.qc.ca/lac-beauport
Claudette Robillard, Responsable

Lac-Bouchette: Bibliothèque publique de Lac-Bouchette
#110, 258, Principale, Lac-Bouchette QC G0W 1V0
418-348-9302
lac.bouchett@reseaubibliosIsj.qc.ca
Lucie Paradis, Responsable

Lac-Cayamant: Bibliothèque municipale de Cayamant
5, ch Lachapelle, Lac-Cayamant QC J0X 1Y0
819-463-4171, Fax: 819-463-4020
admcayamant@crsbpo.qc.ca
www.reseaubiblioduquebec.qc.ca/Cayamant
Suzanne Vallières, Responsable

Lac-des-Aigles: Bibliothèque Lac-des-Aigles
75A, rue Principale, Lac-des-Aigles QC G0K 1V0
418-779-2300
biblio.aigles@crsbp.net
Lise Leblanc, Responsable
418-779-2330

Lac-des-Écorces: Bibliothèque de Lac-des-Écorces
570, boul St-François, Lac-des-Écorces QC J0W 1H0
819-585-2555
bibliolde@lacdesecorces.ca
www.reseaubiblioduquebec.qc.ca
Nicole Thériault, Responsable

Lac-des-Iles: Bibliothèque de Saint-Aimé-du-Lac-des-Iles
877, ch Diotte, Lac-des-Iles QC J0W 1J0
819-597-4174, Fax: 819-597-2554
biblio59@crsbpl.qc.ca
www.reseaubiblioduquebec.qc.ca
Pierrette D. Pilotte, Responsable

Lac-des-Loups: Bibliothèque Lac-des-Loups (La Pêche)
275, rue Pontbriand, Lac-des-Loups QC J0X 3K0
819-456-3222, Fax: 819-456-4534
admlac-des-loups@crsbpo.qc.ca
www.reseaubiblioduquebec.qc.ca/Lac-Des-Loups
Michelle Archambault, Responsable

Lac-des-Plages: Bibliothèque Lac-des-Plages
2053, ch Tour-du-Lac, Lac-des-Plages QC J0T 1K0
819-426-2391, Fax: 819-426-2085
admdesplages@crsbpo.qc.ca
www.reseaubiblioduquebec.qc.ca/Lac-Des-Plages
Micheline Tessier, Responsable

Lac-des-Seize-Iles: Bibliothèque de Lac-des-Seize-Iles
47, de l'Église, Lac-des-Seize-Iles QC J0T 2M0
450-226-9942
biblio@xplornet.com
www.reseaubiblioduquebec.qc.ca/lac-des-seize-iles
Anne Bates, Responsable

Lac-du-Cerf: Bibliothèque de Lac-du-Cerf
15, rue Émard, Lac-du-Cerf QC J0W 1S0
819-597-2249, Fax: 819-597-4163
biblio@lac-du-cerf.ca
www.reseaubiblioduquebec.qc.ca
Francine Boismenu-St-Louis, Responsable

Lac-Édouard: Bibliothèque de Lac-Édouard
195, rue Principale, Lac-Édouard QC G0X 3N0
819-653-2238, Fax: 819-653-2238
biblo024@reseaubibliocqlm.qc.ca
www.reseaubiblioduquebec.qc.ca
Sonia Cloutier, Responsable

Lac-Etchemin: Bibliothèque L'Élan
208A, 2e av, Lac-Etchemin QC G0R 1S0
418-625-5325, Fax: 418-625-3175
biblio@sogetel.net
www.reseaubiblioduquebec.qc.ca/lac-etchemin/
Jacques Gagnon, Responsable

Lachute: Bibliothèque Jean-Marc-Belzile
378, rue Principale, Lachute QC J8H 1Y2
450-562-3781, Fax: 450-562-1431
biblio@ville.lachute.qc.ca
Émilie Paquin, Chef de service de la bibliothèque et des activités culturelles
epaquin@ville.lachute.qc.ca
450-562-3781 ext. 255

Lac-Kénogami: Bibliothèque de Lac-Kénogami
3000, ch de l'Église, Lac-Kénogami QC G7X 7V6
418-695-4717, Fax: 418-547-6158
webbiblio@ville.saguenay.qc.ca
www.ville.saguenay.qc.ca
Caroline Tremblay, Responsable

Lac-Mégantic: Bibliothèque municipale de Lac-Mégantic
5086, rue Frontenac, Lac-Mégantic QC G6B 1H3
819-583-0876, Fax: 819-583-0878
www.bibliomegantic.qc.ca
Daniel Lavoie, Directeur/Bibliothécaire
direction@bibliomegantic.qc.ca

Lacolle: Bibliothèque municipale de Lacolle
3, rue de Collège, Lacolle QC J0J 1J0
450-515-8050
www.lacolle.com/services.html
Linda Corbière, Responsable

Lac-Saguay: Bibliothèque de Lac-Saguay
257A, rte 117, Lac-Saguay QC J0W 1L0
819-278-3972, Fax: 819-278-0260
info@lacsaguay.qc.ca
www.reseaubiblioduquebec.qc.ca
Micheline Bouliane, Responsable

Lac-Sainte-Marie: Bibliothèque municipale de Lac-Sainte-Marie
8, rue Laramée, Lac-Sainte-Marie QC J0X 1Z0
819-467-3779, Fax: 819-467-4826
admstemarie@crsbpo.qc.ca
www.reseaubiblioduquebec.qc.ca/Lac-Ste-Marie
Marie-Paule Bertrand, Bibliothécaire

Lac-Saint-Paul: Bibliothèque de Lac-Saint-Paul
384, rue Principale, Lac-Saint-Paul QC J0W 1K0
819-587-4283, Fax: 819-587-4892
biblio52@crsbpl.qc.ca
www.reseaubiblioduquebec.qc.ca/lac-saint-paul
Charlaine Miller, Responsable
819-587-4379

Lac-Supérieur: Bibliothèque de Lac-Supérieur
1277, ch du Lac-Supérieur, Lac-Supérieur QC J0T 1J0
819-681-3370, Fax: 819-688-3010
biblio@muni.lacsuperieur.qc.ca
www.reseaubiblioduquebec.qc.ca
Thérèse Gaucher, Responsable

Laforce: Bibliothèque Laforce
703, rue Principale, Laforce QC J0Z 2J0
819-722-2461, Fax: 819-722-2462
laforce@reseaubiblioatnq.qc.ca
Lise Bray, Responsable

Lamarche: Bibliothèque publique de Lamarche
102, rue Principale, Lamarche QC G0W 1X0
418-481-2713
lamarche@reseaubibliosIsj.qc.ca
www.reseaubiblioduquebec.qc.ca
Rose Perron-Tremblay, Responsable

Landrienne: Bibliothèque Landrienne
158, rue Principale est, Landrienne QC J0Y 1V0
819-732-4357, Fax: 819-732-3866
landrienne@reseaubiblioatnq.qc.ca
Linda Perron, Responsable

Lanoraie: Bibliothèque de Lanoraie (Ginette-Rivard-Tremblay)
#100, 12, rue Louis-Joseph-Doucet, Lanoraie QC J0K 1E0
450-887-1100, Fax: 450-836-5229
biblio060@reseaubibliocqlm.qc.ca
Jacques Gagné, Responsable

Larouche: Bibliothèque publique de Larouche
709, rue Gauthier, Larouche QC G0W 1Z0
418-695-2201
larouche@reseaubibliosIsj.qc.ca
Lucette Douillard, Directrice
lo7.frang@symptico.ca

Laterrière: Bibliothèque de Laterrière
6167, rue Notre-Dame, Laterrière QC G7N 1A1
418-698-5350, Fax: 418-678-2647
webbiblio@ville.saguenay.qc.ca
www.ville.saguenay.qc.ca
Anne Lebel, Chef de division, Bibliothèques de Saguenay
anne.lebel@ville.saguenay.qc.ca

Laurier-Station: Bibliothèque Wilfrid Laurier
147, rue Saint-Denis, Laurier-Station QC G0S 1N0
418-728-5939
bwlaurier@globetrotter.net
www.reseaubiblioduquebec.qc.ca
Nancy Dubois, Responsable

Laurierville: Bibliothèque de Laurierville
148A, rue Grenier, Laurierville QC G0S 1P0
819-365-4913, Fax: 819-365-4936
biblio122@reseaubibliocqlm.qc.ca
Aline Desrochers, Responsable

Laval: Bibliothèques de Laval. Service de la vie communautaire, de la culture et des communications
1535, boul Chomedey, Laval QC H7V 3Z4
450-662-4343, Fax: 450-978-5833
adm-biblio@ville.laval.qc.ca
www.ville.laval.qc.ca
Paul Lemay, Dir. Serv. de vie communautaire, culture et communications
p.lemay@ville.laval.qc.ca

Lavaltrie: Bibliothèque de Lavaltrie
241, Saint-Antoine-Nord, Lavaltrie QC J5T 2G7
450-586-2921, Fax: 450-586-0124
biblio011@reseaubibliocqlm.qc.ca
Brigitte Richer, Directrice

Laverlochère: Bibliothèque de Laverlochère
3, rue Principale sud, Laverlochère QC J0Z 2P0

819-765-2549, Fax: 819-765-2089
laverlochere@reseaubiblioatnq.qc.ca
Maryse Gervais, Responsable

***Lebel-sur-Quévillon:* Bibliothèque Lebel-sur-Quévillon**
500, Place Quévillon, Lebel-sur-Quévillon QC J0Y 1X0
819-755-4826, Fax: 819-755-8124
lebel@reseaubiblioatnq.qc.ca
Mona Savard, Responsable

***Leclercville:* Bibliothèque Aux Rayons d'Or**
166, rue de l'Église, Leclercville QC G0S 2K0
819-292-2331, Fax: 819-292-2639
leclercville@bellnet.ca
Jeannine Beaudet, Responsable

***Lefebvre:* Bibliothèque de Lefebvre**
193, 10e rang, Lefebvre QC J0H 2C0
819-394-3354, Fax: 819-394-2782
biblio081@reseaubibliocqlm.qc.ca
www.reseaubiblioduquebec.qc.ca
France Gagnon Noël, Responsable

***Lejeune:* Bibliothèque de Lejeune**
69, rue de la Grande-Coulée, Lejeune QC G0L 1S0
418-855-2428
biblio.lejeune@crsbp.net
www.reseaubiblioduquebec.qc.ca
Pauline Gilbert, Responsable

***Lemieux:* Bibliothèque de Lemieux**
526, rue de l'Eglise, Lemieux QC G0X 1S0
819-283-2506
biblio138@reseaubibliocqlm.qc.ca
www.reseaubiblioduquebec.qc.ca
Lucie Blanchette, Responsable

***Lennoxville:* Bibliothèque publique de Lennoxville/ Lennoxville Public Library**
101, rue Queen, Lennoxville QC J1M 1J7
819-562-4949, Fax: 819-563-3705
bibliolen@gmail.com
www.lennoxvillelibrary.ca
Barbara Gosselin, Responsable

***Longue-Pointe-de-Mingan:* Bibliothèque de Longue-Pointe-de-Mingan**
878, ch du Roi, Longue-Pointe-de-Mingan QC G0G 1V0
418-949-2053, Fax: 418-949-2166
biblipte@globetrotter.qc.ca
Andrée Legault, Responsable

***Longueuil:* Bibliothèques publiques de Longueuil**
1100, rue Beauregard, Longueuil QC J4K 2L1
450-463-7180, Fax: 450-646-8874
www.longueuil.ca/bibliotheques/
Micheline Perreault, Chef du Service des bibliothèques
micheline.perreault@ville.longueuil.qc.ca
450-463-7100 ext. 7244

***Lorraine:* Bibliothèque municipale de Lorraine**
31, boul de Gaulle, Lorraine QC J6Z 3W9
450-621-1071
bibliotheque@ville.lorraine.qc.ca
www.ville.lorraine.qc.ca
Paulette Gouroff, Directrice
450-621-1071

***Lorrainville:* Bibliothèque Lorrainville**
2, rue St-Jean-Baptiste est, Lorrainville QC J0Z 2R0
819-625-2464, Fax: 819-625-2380
lorrainville@reseaubiblioatnq.qc.ca
www.lorrainville.ca
Alain Guimond, Responsable

***Lotbinière:* Bibliothèque 'Au fil des pages'**
30, rue Joly, local 100, Lotbinière QC G0S 1S0
418-796-2912, Fax: 418-796-2198
biblotbi@globetrotter.qc.ca
Lucille Beaudet, Responsable

***Lourdes-de-Blanc-Sablon:* Bibliothèque de Blanc-Sablon**
20, rue Mgr Scheffer, Lourdes-de-Blanc-Sablon QC G0G 1W0
418-461-2030, Fax: 418-461-2529
scheffer@globetrotter.net
Vincent Joncas, Responsable

***Low:* Bibliothèque municipale de Low**
4A, ch D'Amour, Low QC J0X 2C0
819-422-3218, Fax: 819-422-3796
admlow@crsbpo.qc.ca
www.reseaubiblioduquebec.qc.ca/Low
Lise Legros, Responsable

***Luskville-Pontiac:* Bibliothèque de Luskville**
2024, rte 148, Luskville-Pontiac QC J0X 2G0
819-455-2370, Fax: 819-455-9756
admluskville@crsbpo.qc.ca
www.reseaubiblioduquebec.qc.ca/Luskville
Louise Ramsay, Responsable

***Lyster:* Bibliothèque de Lyster (Graziella-Ouellet)**
2375, rue Bécancour, Lyster QC G0S 1V0
819-389-5787, Fax: 819-389-5981
biblio144@reseaubibliocqlm.qc.ca
Pierrette Fradette, Responsable

***Macamic:* Bibliothèque de Colombourg**
705, Rang 2-3 ouest, Macamic QC J0Z 2S0
819-333-5783, Fax: 819-333-1075
colombourg@reseaubiblioatnq.qc.ca
www.reseaubiblioduquebec.qc.ca
Noëlla Royer, Responsable

***Macamic:* Bibliothèque de Macamic**
34A, 6e av ouest, Macamic QC J0Z 2S0
819-782-4604, Fax: 819-782-4464
macamic@reseaubiblioatnq.qc.ca
www.reseaubiblioduquebec.qc.ca
Ginette Labbé, Responsable

***La Macaza:* Bibliothèque de La Macaza**
53, rue des Pionniers, La Macaza QC J0T 1R0
819-275-2077, Fax: 819-275-2337
biblio-lamacaza@bellnet.ca
www.reseaubiblioduquebec.qc.ca
Nicole Ayotte, Responsable
nicoleayotte1@hotmail.com

***Madeleine-Centre:* Bibliothèque Jacques-Ferron**
104, rue Principale, Madeleine-Centre QC G0E 1P0
418-393-3269, Fax: 418-393-2869
bbostema@globetrotter.qc.ca
Carole Giroux, Responsable

***Magog:* Bibliothèque municipale d'Omerville**
65, rue St-Jacques ouest, Magog QC J1X 4H4
819-868-6679
biblio078@reseaubiblioestrie.qc.ca
www.reseaubiblioduquebec.qc.ca
Monique Saint-Onge, Responsable

***Magog:* Bibliothèque municipale Memphrémagog**
61, rue Merry nord, Magog QC J1X 2E7
819-843-1330, Fax: 819-843-1594
biblio@ville.magog.qc.ca
www.ville.magog.qc.ca
Diane Boulé, Responsable/Bibliothécaire
dianeb@abacom.com

***Malartic:* Bibliothèque Malartic**
621, De la Paix, Malartic QC J0Y 1Z0
819-757-4449, Fax: 819-757-3084
malartic@reseaubiblioatnq.qc.ca
Maurice Bélanger, Responsable

***La Malbaie:* Bibliothèque Laure-Conan**
395, rue St-Etienne, La Malbaie QC G5A 1S8
418-665-6027, Fax: 418-665-6481
bibli.malbaie@qc.aira.com
ville.lamalbaie.qc.ca/bibliotheques/
Marie-Claire Fortin, Responsable

***La Malbaie:* Bibliothèque municipale de Cap-à-l'Aigle**
768, rue Saint-Raphaël, La Malbaie QC G5A 2P2
418-665-7596, Fax: 418-665-7597
biblioca@cite.net
www.reseaubiblioduquebec.qc.ca/cap-a-l'aigle/
Louise Belley, Responsable

***Manawan:* Bibliothèque de Manawan**
470, rue Otapi, Manawan QC J0K 1M0
819-971-1379, Fax: 819-971-1266
biblio067@reseaubibliocqlm.qc.ca
Janette Ottawa, Responsable

***Mandeville:* Bibliothèque municipale de Mandeville**
162A, rue Desjardins, Mandeville QC J0K 1L0
514-835-2055
bibliomandeville@intermonde.net
municipalite.mandeville.qc.ca
Monique Bessette, Coordonnatrice

***Maniwaki:* Bibliothèque de Maniwaki/Déléage/Egan-Sud**
14, rue Comeau, Maniwaki QC J9E 2R8
819-449-2738, Fax: 819-449-7626
admmaniwaki@crsbpo.qc.ca
www.reseaubiblioduquebec.qc.ca/Maniwaki/
Colette Archambault, Responsable

***Manseau:* Bibliothèque de Manseau**
200A, rue Roux, Manseau QC G0X 1V0
819-356-2450, Fax: 819-356-2721
biblio084@reseaubibliocqlm.qc.ca
www.reseaubiblioduquebec.qc.ca
Denise Bernier, Responsable

***Mansfield:* Bibliothèque Mansfield-et-Pontefract**
314, rue Principale, Mansfield QC J0X 1V0
819-683-3491, Fax: 819-683-3590
admmansfield@crsbpo.qc.ca
www.reseaubiblioduquebec.cq.ca/Mansfield/
Martine Laroche, Responsable

***Maria:* Bibliothèque Noël-Audet**
475, rue des Chardonnerets, Maria QC G0C 1Y0
418-759-3832, Fax: 418-759-5035
bbomaria@globetrotter.qc.ca
www.reseaubiblioduquebec.qc.ca
Sylvie Boudreau, Responsable

***Marieville:* Bibliothèque Commémorative Desautels**
1801, rue du Pont, Marieville QC J3M 1J7
450-460-4444, Fax: 450-460-3526
biblio126@reseaubibliomonteregie.qc.ca
www.ville.marieville.qc.ca/bibliotheque/
Daniel Lalonde, Responsable
d.lalonde@ville.marieville.qc.ca

***Marsoui:* Bibliothèque de Marsoui**
2, rue des Écoliers, Marsoui QC G0E 1S0
418-288-5508
michelle.cote@globetrotter.net
www.reseaubiblioduquebec.qc.ca
Michelle Côté, Responsable

***Mascouche:* Bibliothèque municipale de Mascouche**
3015, ave des Ancêtres, Mascouche QC J7K 1X6
450-474-4159, Fax: 450-474-3410
biblio@ville.mascouche.qc.ca
www.ville.mascouche.qc.ca
Sarah Germain, Bibliothécaire professionnelle

***Mashteuiatsh:* Bibliothèque publique de Mashteuiatsh**
1743, rue Amishk, Mashteuiatsh QC G0W 2H0
418-275-2473, Fax: 418-275-0097
caci@mashteuiatsh.ca
Louise Langlais, Bibliotechnicienne

***Maskinongé:* Bibliothèque de Maskinongé**
11, rue Marcel, Maskinongé QC J0K 1N0
819-227-4656
biblio059@reseaubibliocqlm.qc.ca
www.reseaubiblioduquebec.qc.ca
Andrée Livernoche, Responsable

***Massueville:* Bibliothèque municipale de Massueville/St-Aimé**
846A, rue de l'Église, Massueville QC J0G 1K0
450-788-3120
aime@reseaubibliomonteregie.qc.ca
www.reseaubiblioduquebec.qc.ca
Claire Berger, Responsable

***Matane:* Bibliothèque municipale de Matane (Fonds de Solidarité FTQ)**
Complexe culturel Joseph-Rouleau, #2, 520, av Saint-Jérôme, Matane QC G4W 3B5
418-562-9233, Fax: 418-566-2064
biblio@ville.matane.qc.ca
www.ville.matane.qc.ca/bibliotheque_municipale.html
Lise Whittom Grenier, Responsable
l.grenier@ville.matane.qc.ca

***Matapédia:* Bibliothèque de Matapédia**
5, rue Hôtel-de-Ville, Matapédia QC G0J 1V0
418-865-2917, Fax: 418-865-2828
bbomatap@globetrotter.net
www.reseaubiblioduquebec.qc.ca
Julie Michaud, Responsable
418-865-2135

***Les Méchins:* Bibliothèque municipale de Les Méchins**
164, rue Principale, Les Méchins QC G0J 1T0

418-729-1346, Fax: 418-729-3585
biblio.mechins@mrcdematane.qc.ca
www.lesmechins.com
Louise Farand, Responsable

***Mercier:* Bibliothèque municipale de Mercier**
16, rue du Parc, Mercier QC J6R 1E5
450-692-6780, Fax: 450-691-6529
danielmorin@bibliothequedemercier.qc.ca
Daniel Morin, Responsable
daniel.morin@bibliothequedemercier.qc.ca

***Messines:* Bibliothèque de Messines**
3, ch de la Ferme, Messines QC J0X 2J0
819-465-2637, Fax: 819-465-2943
admmessines@crsbpo.qc.ca
www.reseaubiblioduquebec.qc.ca/Messines
Claire Lacroix, Responsable

***Métabetchouan:* Bibliothèque publique de Métabetchouan**
87, rue Saint-André, Métabetchouan QC G8G 1Z2
418-349-2838
metabet@crsbpslsj.biblio.qc.ca
www.reseaubiblioduquebec.qc.ca
Hélène Lachance, Responsable
418-349-3517

***Middle Bay:* Bibliothèque de Middle Bay**
Middle Bay QC G0G 1Z0
418-379-2911, Fax: 418-379-2959
Louise Buckle, Responsable

***La Minerve:* Bibliothèque de La Minerve**
8, rue Mailloux, La Minerve QC J0T 1S0
819-274-2313, Fax: 819-274-2031
laminerve@crsbpl.qc.ca
www.reseaubiblioduquebec.qc.ca
Marcelle Grégoire, Responsable

***Mirabel:* Bibliothèque municipale de Mirabel**
17710, rue du Val-d'Espoir, Mirabel QC J7J 1A1
450-475-2082, Fax: 450-430-2868
www.ville.mirabel.qc.ca/bibliotheque.asp
France Genest, Chef bibliothécaire
f.genest@ville.mirabel.qc.ca

***Moisie:* Bibliothèque de Moisie**
250, ch des Forges, Moisie QC G0G 2B0
418-927-2279
bimoisie@globetrotter.net
Nancy Malenfant, Personne-ressource

***Montbeillard:* Bibliothèque Montbeillard**
551, rue du Village, Montbeillard QC J0Z 2X0
819-797-7110, Fax: 819-797-2390
montbeillard@reseaubiblioatnq.qc.ca
Diane St-Onge, Responsable

***Mont-Brun:* Bibliothèque Mont-Brun**
955, rue Principale, Mont-Brun QC J0Z 2Y0
819-637-7101, Fax: 819-637-2374
montbrun@reseaubiblioatnq.qc.ca
www.crsbpat.qc.ca/montbrun/
Noëlla Thibault, Responsable

***Montcalm:* Bibliothèque de Montcalm**
30, rte du Lac-Rond Nord, Montcalm QC J0T 2V0
819-687-2575, Fax: 819-687-2374
biblio@municipalite.montcalm.qc.ca
www.reseaubiblioduquebec.qc.ca/montcalm
Pierre Nadeau, Responsable

***Mont-Carmel:* Bibliothèque Odile-Boucher**
22, rue de la Fabrique, Mont-Carmel QC G0L 1W0
418-498-3500
biblio.carmel@crsbp.net
Denise Chamberland, Responsable
418-498-3492

***Montcerf-Lytton:* Bibliothèque Montcerf-Lytton**
16, rue Principale nord, 2e étage, Montcerf-Lytton QC J0W 1N0
819-449-2065, Fax: 819-449-7310
admmontcerf@crsbpo.qc.ca
www.reseaubiblioduquebec.qc.ca/Montcerf/
Christine Ménard, Responsable

***Montebello:* Bibliothèque de Montebello**
240A, rue Bonsecours, Montebello QC J0V 1L0
819-423-6213, Fax: 819-423-5703
admmontebello@crsbpo.qc.ca
www.reseaubiblioduquebec.qc.ca/Montebello/
Mariette Côté, Responsable

***Mont-Joli:* Bibliothèque Jean-Louis-Desrosiers**
1477, boul Jacques-Cartier, Mont-Joli QC G5H 2V5
418-775-4106, Fax: 418-775-4037
julie.belanger@ville.mont-joli.qc.ca
Julie Bélanger, Responsable

***Mont-Laurier:* Bibliothèque de Des Ruisseaux**
1269, boul Des Ruisseaux, Mont-Laurier QC J9L 3G6
819-623-6748, Fax: 819-623-6810
desruisseaux@crsbpl.qc.ca
www.reseaubiblioduquebec.qc.ca
Louise Paquette, Responsable

***Mont-Laurier:* Bibliothèque de Mont-Laurier**
385, rue Du Pont, Mont-Laurier QC J9L 2R5
819-623-1833, Fax: 819-623-7079
bibliotheque.mont-laurier@tlb.sympatico.ca
www.reseaubiblioduquebec.qc.ca
Edith Whear, Responsable

***Mont-Laurier:* Bibliothèque de Val-Limoges**
3620, ch Val-Limoges, Mont-Laurier QC J9L 3G6
819-623-9124
vallimoges@crsbpl.qc.ca
www.reseaubiblioduquebec.qc.ca
Louise Paquette, Responsable

***Mont-Louis:* La Bibliothèque Liratou de Mont-Louis**
1, 1e av ouest, Mont-Louis QC G0E 1T0
418-797-2310, Fax: 418-797-2928
biblioliratou@globetrotter.net
Brigitte Lapointe, Responsable
418-797-2337

***Montpellier:* Bibliothèque de Montpellier**
4B, rue du Bosquet, Montpellier QC J0V 1M0
819-428-3663, Fax: 819-428-1221
admmontpellier@crsbpo.qc.ca
www.reseaubiblioduquebec.qc.ca/Montpellier/
Claudette Riopel, Responsable

***Montréal:* A rayons ouverts**
475, boul de Maisonneuve est, Montréal QC H2L 5C4
514-873-1101, Fax: 514-873-9312
info@bnquebec.ca
www.banq.qc.ca

***Montréal:* ARGUS**
#103, 353, rue St-Nicolas, Montréal QC H2Y 2P1
514-845-3327, Fax: 514-845-1618
admin@cbpq.qc.ca
URL: www.cbpq.qc.ca
Robert Garon, Directeur

***Montréal:* Atwater Library/ Bibliothèque Atwater**
1200, av Atwater, Montréal QC H3Z 1X4
514-935-7344, Fax: 514-935-1960
info@atwaterlibrary.ca
www.atwaterlibrary.ca
Lynn Verge, Executive Director
lverge@atwaterlibrary.ca
514-935-7344

***Montréal:* Bibliothèque Reginald J.P. Dawson**
1967, boul Graham, Montréal QC H3R 1G9
514-734-2966, Fax: 514-734-3089
denis.chouinard@ville.mont-royal.qc.ca
Denis Chouinard, Responsable

***Montréal:* Corpo Clip**
#103, 353, rue St-Nicolas, Montréal QC H2Y 2P1
514-845-3327, Fax: 514-845-1618
info@cbpq.qc.ca
www.cbpq.qc.ca
Michel Claveau, Éditeur

***Montréal:* Documentation et bibliothèques**
#202, 3414, av du Parc, Montréal QC H2X 2H5
514-281-5012, Fax: 514-281-8219
Gilles Deschatelets, Éditeur

***Montréal:* En direct de l'EBSI**
CP 6128, Succ Centre-Ville, Montréal QC H3C 3J7
514-343-2244, Fax: 514-343-5753
ebsiinfo@ebsi.umontreal.ca
www.fas.umontreal.ca/EBSI

***Montréal:* Jewish Public Library (Montréal)/ La Bibliothèque publique juive (Montréal)**
1, carré Cummings Sq., 5151, Côte Ste-Catherine Rd., Montréal QC H3W 1M6
514-345-2627, Fax: 514-345-6477
info_@jplmontreal.org
www.jewishpubliclibrary.org
Eva Raby, Executive Director

***Montréal:* La bibliographie du Québec**
2275, rue Holt, Montréal QC H2G 3H1
514-873-1100, Fax: 514-873-4310
bibliographie@banq.qc.ca

***Montréal:* Nouvelles de l'ASTED**
#202, 3414, av du Parc, Montréal QC H2X 2H5
514-281-5012, Fax: 514-281-8219
info@asted.org
www.asted.org

***Montréal:* Réseau des bibliothèques publiques de Montréal**
801, rue Brennan (Pavillon Prince), 5e étage, Montréal QC H2C 0G4
514-872-5923, Fax: 514-872-4911
www.ville.montreal.qc.ca/biblio
Louise Guillemette-Labory, Directrice-associée
lglabory@ville.montreal.qc.ca

***Montréal:* The Fraser-Hickson Institute/ Institut Fraser-Hickson**
4855, av Kensington, Montréal QC H3X 3S6
514-489-5301, Fax: 514-489-5302
webmaster@fraserhickson.qc.ca
www.fraserhickson.qc.ca
Frances Ackerman, Librarian

***Mont-Saint-Hilaire:* Bibliothèque Armand-Cardinal**
150, rue du Centre Civique, Mont-Saint-Hilaire QC J3H 3M8
450-467-2854, Fax: 450-446-5879
bibliotheque@villemsh.ca
www.ville.mont-saint-hilaire.qc.ca
Francine Ledoux-Nadeau, Bibliothécaire
francine.ledoux.nadeau@ville.mont-saint-hila

***Mont-Saint-Michel:* Bibliothèque de Mont-Saint-Michel**
94, rue de l'Église, Mont-Saint-Michel QC J0W 1P0
819-587-3093
biblio55@lino.com
www.reseaubiblioduquebec.qc.ca
Lucette Castonguay, Responsable

***Mont-Saint-Pierre:* Bibliothèque Kevin Pouliot-Bernatchez**
102, rue Cloutier, Mont-Saint-Pierre QC G0E 1V0
418-797-2898, Fax: 418-797-2307
bbomtsp@globetrotter.net
Karine Sergerie, Responsable

***Mont-Tremblant:* Bibliothèque Samuel-Ouimet**
1147, rue de St-Jovite, Mont-Tremblant QC J8E 1V1
819-425-8614, Fax: 819-425-1391
biblio.samuel-o@villedemont-tremblant.qc.ca
www.reseaubiblioduquebec.qc.ca
Gabriel Lemelin, Responsable

***Morin-Heights:* Bibliothèque de Morin-Heights**
823, ch du Village, Morin-Heights QC J0R 1H0
450-226-3232, Fax: 450-226-8786
bibliomh@cgocable.ca
www.reseaubiblioduquebec.qc.ca
Audrey Gibeault, Responsable

***La Motte:* Bibliothèque de La Motte**
349, ch St-Luc, La Motte QC J0Y 1T0
819-732-0505, Fax: 819-727-4248
lamotte@reseaubiblioatnq.qc.ca
www.reseaubiblioduquebec.qc.ca
Nicole Richard, Responsable

***Murdochville:* Bibliothèque de Murdochville**
635, 5e rue, Murdochville QC G0E 1W0
418-784-2866, Fax: 418-784-2607
bbomurd@globetrotter.net
www.reseaubiblioduquebec.qc.ca
Sonia Dunn, Responsable

***Mutton Bay:* Bibliothèque municipale de Mutton Bay**
École St-Lawrence, PR, Mutton Bay QC G0G 2C0
418-733-2263, Fax: 418-773-2696
Darlene Gallichon, Responsable

***Namur:* Bibliothèque Namur/ Namur Library**
331, rue Hôtel-de-Ville, Namur QC J0V 1N0
819-426-2457, Fax: 819-426-3074
admnamur@crsbpo.qc.ca
www.reseaubiblioduquebec.qc.ca/Namur/
Tammie Leggett, Responsable

***Napierville:* Bibliothèque municipale de Napierville**
290, rue St-Alexandre, Napierville QC J0J 1L0

450-245-0030, Fax: 450-245-3777
napierville@reseaubibliomonteregie.qc.ca
www.reseaubiblioduquebec.qc.ca
Viviane Leroux, Responsable

***Natashquan:* Bibliothèque de Natashquan**
29, ch d'en Haut, Natashquan QC G0G 2E0
418-726-3362, Fax: 418-726-3698
natashb@globetrotter.net
www.reseaubiblioduquebec.qc.ca
Cindy Carbonneau, Responsable

***Nédélec:* Bibliothèque de Nédélec**
68, rue Principale, Nédélec QC J0Z 2Z0
819-784-2297, Fax: 819-784-2126
nedelec@reseaubiblioatnq.qc.ca
www.reseaubiblioduquebec.qc.ca
Jacqueline Aylwin, Responsable

***Neuville:* Bibliothèque Félicité-Angers**
760, rte 138, Neuville QC G0A 2R0
418-876-2023, Fax: 418-876-3349
f.-angers@videotron.ca
www.reseaubiblioduquebec.qc.ca/neuville
Diane Forgues-Michaud, Responsable

***New Richmond:* Bibliothèque du Vieux-Couvent**
99, Place Suzanne-Guité, New Richmond QC G0C 2B0
418-392-7070, Fax: 418-392-5331
biblio@villenewrichmond.com
www.reseaubiblioduquebec.qc.ca
Chantal Cormier, Responsable

***Newport:* Bibliothèque de Newport**
208, rte 132, Newport QC G0C 2A0
418-777-2523, Fax: 418-689-3639
bbonewpt@globetrotter.qc.ca
www.reseaubiblioduquebec.qc.ca
Dolores Bouchard, Responsable

***Nicolet:* Bibliothèque de Nicolet**
116, rue Evariste-Lecompte, Nicolet QC J3T 1E6
819-293-6007, Fax: 819-293-6767
biblio072@reseaubibliocqlm.qc.ca
www.reseaubiblioduquebec.qc.ca
Serge Rousseau, Responsable

***Nominingue:* Bibliothèque de Nominingue**
2112, ch du Tour du Lac, Nominingue QC J0W 1R0
819-278-3384, Fax: 819-278-4967
biblio51@crsbpl.qc.ca
www.reseaubiblioduquebec.qc.ca/nominingue
Nicole Jorg, Responsable

***Normandin:* Bibliothèque municipale de Normandin**
1156, rue Valois, Normandin QC G8M 3Z8
418-274-2241, Fax: 418-274-2241
bibliotheque@ville.normandin.qc.ca
Diane Bernier, Technicienne en documentation
bibliotheque@ville.normandin.qc.ca

***Normétal:* Bibliothèque Normétal**
36A, rue Principale, Normétal QC J0Z 3A0
819-788-2505, Fax: 819-788-2730
normetal@reseaubiblioatnq.qc.ca
www.crsbpat.qc.ca/normetal/
Annie Lamoureux, Responsable

***North Hatley:* Bibliothèque de North Hatley/ North Hatley Library**
165, rue Main, North Hatley QC J0B 2C0
819-842-2110
biblio@nhlibrary.qc.ca
www.nhlibrary.qc.ca
Susan Gwyn, Responsable

***Notre-Dame-de-Ham:* Bibliothèque de Notre-Dame-de-Ham**
25, rue de l'Église, Notre-Dame-de-Ham QC G0P 1C0
819-344-5010
biblio149@reseaubibliocqlm.qc.ca
France McSween, Responsable

***Notre-Dame-de-la-Merci:* Bibliothèque de Notre-Dame-de-la-Merci**
1900, Montée de la Réserve, Notre-Dame-de-la-Merci QC J0T 2A0
819-424-2152, Fax: 819-424-7347
biblio42@crsbpl.qc.ca
www.reseaubiblioduquebec.qc.ca
Célina Riopel, Responsable

***Notre-Dame-de-la-Paix:* Bibliothèque Notre-Dame-de-la-Paix**
10, rue Saint-Jean-Baptiste, Notre-Dame-de-la-Paix QC J0V 1P0
819-522-6610, Fax: 819-522-6710
admpaix@crsbpo.qc.ca
www.reseaubiblioduquebec.qc.ca/Notre-Dame-de-la-Paix
Suzon Côté, Responsable

***Notre-Dame-de-la-Salette:* Bibliothèque de Notre-Dame-de-la-Salette**
68, rue des Saules, Notre-Dame-de-la-Salette QC J0X 2L0
819-766-2872, Fax: 819-766-2983
admsalette@crsbpo.qc.ca
www.reseaubiblioduquebec.qc.ca/Notre-Dame-de-la-Salette
Christine Rose Boucher, Responsable

***Notre-Dame-de-Lorette:* Bibliothèque publique de Notre-Dame-de-Lorette**
22, rue Principale, Notre-Dame-de-Lorette QC G0W 1B0
418-276-3941
Georgette Bouchard, Responsable

***Notre-Dame-de-Lourdes:* Bibliothèque Notre-Dame-de-Lourdes**
3971, rue Principale, Notre-Dame-de-Lourdes QC J0K 1K0
450-759-7864
bibliondl@pandore.qc.ca
www.notredamedelourdes.ca

***Notre-Dame-de-Montauban:* Bibliothèque de Notre-Dame-de-Montauban**
421, rue Principale, Notre-Dame-de-Montauban QC G0X 1W0
418-336-2353
biblio058@reseaubibliocqlm.qc.ca
www.reseaubiblioduquebec.qc.ca
Denise Villemure, Responsable

***Notre-Dame-de-Pontmain:* Bibliothèque de Notre-Dame-de-Pontmain**
15, rue Notre-Dame, Notre-Dame-de-Pontmain QC J0W 1S0
819-597-2382
bibliotheque@mun-pontmain.qc.ca
www.reseaubiblioduquebec.qc.ca
Francine Leclair, Responsable

***Notre-Dame-de-Portneuf:* Bibliothèque La Découverte/Notre-Dame-de-Portneuf**
500A, rue Notre-Dame, Notre-Dame-de-Portneuf QC G0A 2Z0
418-286-4452, Fax: 418-286-8150
bptavocats@globetrotter.net
www.reseaubiblioduquebec.qc.ca/portneuf
Johanne Savard, Responsable
johannesavard@hotmail.ca
418-286-3509

***Notre-Dame-des-Monts:* Bibliothèque La Girouette**
87, rue Notre-Dame, Notre-Dame-des-Monts QC G0T 1L0
, Fax: 418-439-0883
www.reseaubiblioduquebec.qc.ca/monts/
Marie-Paule Boudreault, Responsable

***Notre-Dame-des-Pins:* Bibliothèque Le Signet/Notre-Dame-des-Pins**
2755, 1e av, Notre-Dame-des-Pins QC G0M 1K0
418-774-9454
biblnddp@sogetel.net
www.reseaubiblioduquebec.qc.ca/pins/
Lyette Roy, Responsable

***Notre-Dame-du-Bon-Conseil:* Bibliothèque de Notre-Dame-du-Bon-Conseil**
541, rue Notre-Dame, Notre-Dame-du-Bon-Conseil QC J0C 1A0
819-336-2967
biblio096@reseaubibliocqlm.qc.ca
www.reseaubiblioduquebec.qc.ca
Véronique Montesinos, Responsable

***Notre-Dame-du-Lac:* Bibliothèque Notre-Dame-du-Lac**
681, rue Commerciale, Notre-Dame-du-Lac QC G0L 1X0
418-899-6004
biblio.ndlac@crsbp.net
Judith Pellerin, Responsable
418-899-6045

***Notre-Dame-du-Laus:* Bibliothèque de Notre-Dame-du-Laus**
4, rue de l'Église, Notre-Dame-du-Laus QC J0X 2M0
819-767-2772
biblio057@crsbpl.qc.ca
www.reseaubiblioduquebec.qc.ca
Francine Boisvert, Responsable

***Notre-Dame-du-Nord:* Bibliothèque Notre-Dame-du-Nord**
15, rue Desjardins, Notre-Dame-du-Nord QC J0Z 3B0
819-723-2695, Fax: 819-723-2483
nord@reseaubiblioatnq.qc.ca
Carmen Laliberté, Responsable

***Notre-Dame-du-Portage:* Bibliothèque de Notre-Dame-du-Portage**
539, rte du Fleuve, Notre-Dame-du-Portage QC G0L 1Y0
418-862-9163
biblio.portage@crsbp.net
www.reseaubiblioduquebec.qc.ca
Jacinthe Leblanc, Responsable

***Nouvelle:* Bibliothèque de Nouvelle**
470, rue Francoeur, Nouvelle QC G0C 2E0
418-794-2253, Fax: 418-794-2254
bbonouv@globetrotter.net
www.reseaubiblioduquebec.qc.ca
Louise Leblanc, Responsable

***Noyan:* Bibliothèque municipale de Noyan/ Noyan Public Library**
1312, ch de la Petite-France, Noyan QC J0J 1B0
450-294-2175
noyan@reseaubibliomonteregie.qc.ca
Claude Jeunehomme, Responsable

***Obedjiwan:* Bibliothèque d'Obedjiwan**
92, rue Tcikatnaw, Obedjiwan QC G0W 3B0
819-974-1221, Fax: 819-974-1224
biblio065@reseaubibliocqlm.qc.ca
www.reseaubiblioduquebec.qc.ca
Rachelle Chachai, Responsable

***Odanak:* Bibliothèque de Odanak**
58, rue Waban-Aki, Odanak QC J0G 1H0
514-568-0107, Fax: 514-568-0107
biblio139@reseaubibliocqlm.qc.ca
www.reseaubiblioduquebec.qc.ca/Portail/index.aspx?page=3&BID=1
Marie-Chantal Bouchard, Responsable

***Old Fort Bay:* Bibliothèque de Old Fort**
Old Fort Bay QC G0G 2G0
418-379-2911, Fax: 418-379-2959
René Fequet, Responsable

***Ormstown:* Bibliothèque municipale d'Ormstown**
85, rue Roy, Ormstown QC J0S 1K0
450-829-3249
ormstown@reseaubibliomonteregie.qc.ca
Madeleine Robidoux, Responsable

***Otter Lake:* Bibliothèque Otter Lake**
340, av Martineau, Otter Lake QC J0X 2P0
819-453-7344, Fax: 819-453-7311
admotterlake@crsbpo.qc.ca
www.reseaubiblioduquebec.qc.ca/OtterLake/
Esther Dubeau, Responsable

***Packington:* Bibliothèque Packington**
115, rue Soucy, Packington QC G0L 1Z0
418-853-5362, Fax: 418-853-6427
biblio.packing@crsbp.net
Denis Moreau, Responsable

***Padoue:* Bibliothèque de Padoue**
215, rue Beaulieu, Padoue QC G0J 1X0
418-775-8188
biblio.padoue@crsbp.net
Cécile Ouellet Caron, Responsable

***Palmarolle:* Bibliothèque Palmarolle**
115, rue Principale, Palmarolle QC J0Z 3C0
819-787-3459, Fax: 819-787-2412
palmarolle@reseaubiblioatnq.qc.ca
Ghislaine Bégin, Responsable

***Papineauville:* Bibliothèque de Papineauville**
294, rue Papineau, Papineauville QC J0V 1R0
819-427-5511, Fax: 819-427-8318
admpapineau@crsbpo.qc.ca
www.reseaubiblioduquebec.qc.ca/Papineauville
Suzanne Gauthier, Responsable

***Parisville:* Bibliothèque de Parisville**
1260, rue St-Jacques, Parisville QC G0S 1X0

819-292-2644, Fax: 819-292-2214
biblio103@reseaubibliocqlm.qc.ca
Jeannine Boucher, Responsable

***Paspébiac:* Bibliothèque de Paspébiac**
95, boul Gérard-D.-Levesque Ouest, Paspébiac QC G0C 2K0
418-752-2277, Fax: 418-752-6747
pretpas@globetrotter.qc.ca
www.reseaubiblioduquebec.qc.ca
Noula Castilloux, Responsable

***Percé:* Bibliothèque de Percé**
137, rte 132, Percé QC G0C 2L0
418-782-5305, Fax: 418-782-5487
bboperce@globetrotter.qc.ca
www.reseaubiblioduquebec.qc.ca
Pierrette Cloutier, Responsable

***Péribonka:* Bibliothèque publique de Péribonka**
296A, Édouard-Niquet, Péribonka QC G0W 2G0
418-374-2890, Fax: 418-374-2491
Cynthia Gauthier, Responsable
418-374-2831

***Petite-Rivière-St-François:* Bibliothèque Gabrielle-Roy/Petite-Rivière-Saint-François**
1069, rue Principale, Petite-Rivière-St-François QC G0A 2L0
418-632-5895, Fax: 418-632-5886
biblioprsf@hotmail.com
www.reseaubiblioduquebec.qc.ca/petite-riviere
Suzanne Lapointe, Responsable

***Petite-Vallée:* Bibliothèque de Petite-Vallée**
45, rue Principale, Petite-Vallée QC G0E 1Y0
418-393-2949, Fax: 418-393-2949
bibliopv@globetrotter.net
www.reseaubiblioduquebec.qc.ca
Lorraine Lachance, Responsable

***Petit-Saguenay:* Bibliothèque publique de Petit-Saguenay**
46, rue Tremblay, Petit-Saguenay QC G0V 1N0
418-272-3083
petitsag@reseaubiblioslsj.qc.ca
Aurore Gagné, Responsable

***Pierreville:* Bibliothèque de Notre-Dame-de-Pierreville**
48, rue Principale, Pierreville QC J0G 1J0
450-568-2087
biblio142@reseaubibliocqlm.qc.ca
www.reseaubiblioduquebec.qc.ca
Maryse Boisvert, Responsable
450-568-2090

***Pierreville:* Bibliothèque de Pierreville (Jean-Luc-Précourt)**
26, rue Ally, Pierreville QC J0G 1J0
450-568-3500, Fax: 450-568-0689
biblio051@reseaubibliocqlm.qc.ca
www.reseaubiblioduquebec.qc.ca
Chantale Bellamy, Responsable

***Pike River:* Bibliothèque Saint-Pierre-de-Véronne-à-Pike-River**
548, rte 202, Pike River QC J0J 1P0
450-248-7689, Fax: 450-248-2120
pike.river@reseaubibliomonteregie.qc.ca
www.pikeriver.com/_pikeriver/biblio.htm
Stéphane Dulude, Bénévole

***Pincourt:* Bibliothèque de Pincourt/ Pincourt Library**
225, boul Pincourt, Pincourt QC J7V 9T2
514-425-1104, Fax: 514-425-6668
bibliopincourt@videotron.ca
pages.infinit.net/biblipin
Sylvie de Repentigny, Régisseure

***Plaisance:* Bibliothèque de Plaisance**
281, rue Desjardins, Plaisance QC J0V 1S0
819-427-1189, Fax: 819-427-5015
admplaisance@crsbpo.qc.ca
www.reseaubiblioduquebec.qc.ca/Plaisance
Martine Prud'homme, Responsable

***Plessisville:* Bibliothèque municipale de la Ville de Plessisville**
1800, rue Saint-Calixte, Plessisville QC G6L 1R6
819-362-6628, Fax: 819-362-6421
bibliotheque@ville.plessisville.qc.ca
www.ville.plessisville.qc.ca/fr/content/heures_biblio.aspx
Suzanne Bédard, Responsable
sbedard@ville.plessisville.qc.ca
819-362-6628

***La Pocatière:* Bibliothèque municipale de La Pocatière**
#4, 900, 6e av, La Pocatière QC G0R 1Z0
418-856-3459
biblio.pocati@crsbp.net
www.reseaubiblioduquebec.qc.ca
Sylvie Dionne, Responsable

***Pointe-à-la-Croix:* Bibliothèque de La Petite-Rochelle**
44A, rue Lasalle, Pointe-à-la-Croix QC G0C 1L0
418-788-1305
biblio.41@hotmail.com
www.reseaubiblioduquebec.qc.ca
Lise P. Young, Responsable

***Pointe-aux-Outardes:* Bibliothèque de Pointe-aux-Outardes**
481, ch Principale, Pointe-aux-Outardes QC G0H 1H0
418-567-9529, Fax: 418-567-4409
biblipao@globetrotter.net
Guylaine Chouinard, Responsable

***Pointe-Calumet:* Bibliothèque La Sablière**
190, 41e Av, Pointe-Calumet QC J0N 1G2
450-473-6991, Fax: 450-473-6571
www.reseaubiblioduquebec.qc.ca
Brigitte Lessard, Responsable
b.lessard@municipalite.point-calumet.qc.ca

***Pointe-Claire:* ABQLA Bulletin**
PO Box 1095, Pointe-Claire QC H9S 4H9
514-697-0146
abqla@abqla.qc.ca
www.abqla.qc.ca/bulletin.html
Meg Sinclair, Editor

***Pointe-des-Cascades:* Bibliothèque Adrienne Demontigny-Clément**
52, ch du Fleuve, Pointe-des-Cascades QC J0P 1M0
450-455-5310
pointe.cascades@reseaubibliomonteregie.qc.ca
Camille St-Marseille, Responsable

***Pointe-Lebel:* Bibliothèque de Pointe-Lebel**
255, rue Granier, Pointe-Lebel QC G0H 1N0
418-589-2424, Fax: 418-589-6154
bpteleb@globetrotter.net
Lise Therrien, Responsable
418-589-2424

***Pont-Rouge:* Bibliothèque Auguste-Honoré-Gosselin**
41, rue du Collège, Pont-Rouge QC G3H 3A4
418-873-4067, Fax: 418-873-4141
bibliopontrouge@hotmail.com
www.reseaubiblioduquebec.qc.ca/pont-rouge
Denyse Simard, Responsable

***Port-Cartier:* Bibliothèque municipale de Port-Cartier (Le Manuscrit)**
21, rue des Cèdres, Port-Cartier QC G5B 2W5
418-766-3366, Fax: 418-766-3561
bportcar@globetrotter.qc.ca
www.villeport-cartier.com
Stéphan Harvey, Régisseur culturel
418-766-3854

***Port-Menier:* Bibliothèque municipale de l'Ile d'Anticosti**
38, ch des Forestiers, Port-Menier QC G0G 2Y0
418-535-0381
biblioanticosti@xplornet.com
Wendy Tremblay, Responsable
418-535-0250

***Portneuf-sur-Mer:* Bibliothèque de Portneuf-sur-Mer**
170, rue Principale, Portneuf-sur-Mer QC G0T 1P0
418-238-5303, Fax: 418-238-5319
annie.morin@bellnet.ca
Annie Morin, Sec.-trés., Portneuf-sur-Mer

***Poularies:* Bibliothèque Poularies**
990, rue Principale, Poularies QC J0Z 3E0
819-782-5159, Fax: 819-782-5063
poularies@reseaubiblioatnq.qc.ca
Sophie Dallaire, Responsable

***La Prairie:* Bibliothèque Léo-Lecavalier**
500, rue Saint-Laurent, La Prairie QC J5R 5X2
450-444-6710, Fax: 450-444-6708
biblio@ville.laprairie.qc.ca
www.ville.laprairie.qc.ca/bibliotheque/acces.asp
Brigitte Tremblay, Responsable

***Préissac Nord:* Bibliothèque de Préissac-des-Rapides**
6, rue Des Rapides, Préissac Nord QC J0Y 2E0
819-732-4938, Fax: 819-732-4909
preissacn@reseaubiblioatnq.qc.ca
www.reseaubiblioduquebec.qc.ca
Huguette Béland, Responsable

***Préissac Sud:* Bibliothèque de Preissac Sud**
186, av du Lac, Préissac Sud QC J0Y 2E0
819-759-4138, Fax: 819-759-4138
preissacs@reseaubiblioatnq.qc.ca
www.reseaubiblioduquebec.qc.ca
Yolande P. Gagné, Responsable

***Prévost:* Bibliothèque Jean-Charles-Des Roches**
2945, boul du Curé-Labelle, Prévost QC J0R 1T0
450-224-5231, Fax: 450-224-3024
prevost@crsbpl.qc.ca
www.reseaubiblioduquebec.qc.ca
Christian Schryburt, Responsable

***Price:* Bibliothèque de Price**
1, rue du Centre, Price QC G0J 1Z0
418-775-5596
biblio.price@crsbp.net
www.reseaubiblioduquebec.qc.ca
Lise Roy, Responsable

***Princeville:* Bibliothèque de Princeville (Madeleine-Bélanger)**
140, rue Saint-Jean-Baptiste sud, Princeville QC G6L 5A5
819-364-5071
biblio079@reseaubibliocqlm.qc.ca
Madeleine Beaudoin, Responsable

***Proulxville:* Bibliothèque de Saint-Séverin**
1986, Place du Centre, Proulxville QC G0X 2B0
418-365-5844, Fax: 418-365-7544
biblio008@reseaubibliocqlm.qc.ca
www.reseaubiblioduquebec.qc.ca
Sylvie Brouillette, Responsable

***Québec:* Archives: La revue de l'Association des archivistes du Québec**
CP 423, Québec QC G1R 4R2
418-652-2357, Fax: 418-646-0868
infoaaq@archivistes.qc.ca
www.archivistes.qc.ca/revuearchives/revuearchives.html

***Québec:* Bulletin de la Bibliothèque de l'Assemblée nationale**
Édifice Pamphile-Le May, 1035, rue des Parlementaires, Québec QC G1A 1A3
418-643-7596, Fax: 418-641-2636
bulletin@assnat.qc.ca
www.assnat.qc.ca/fra/Bibliotheque/publications/Bulletin
Carmen Gosselin, Éditeur

***Québec:* La chronique**
CP 423, Québec QC G1R 4R2
418-652-2357, Fax: 418-646-0868
infoaaq@archivistes.qc.ca
www.archivistes.qc.ca

***Québec:* Réseau des bibliothèques de la Ville de Québec**
350, rue Saint-Joseph est, Québec QC G1K 3B2
418-641-6789, Fax: 418-641-6787
courrier@institutcanadien.qc.ca
www.bibliothequesdequebec.qc.ca
Marie Goyette, Directrice

***Quyon:* Quyon Library**
12, rue Saint-John, Quyon QC J0X 2V0
819-458-1227, Fax: 819-458-9756
admquyon@crsbpo.qc.ca
www.reseaubiblioduquebec.qc.ca/Quyon
Bernadette Milks, Coordonnateur

***Ragueneau:* Bibliothèque municipale Amaury-Tremblay**
13, rue des Loisirs, Ragueneau QC G0H 1S0
418-567-8453, Fax: 418-567-2344
biblirag@globetrotter.net
www.reseaubiblioduquebec.qc.ca
Édith Martel, Responsable

***Ravignan:* Bibliothèque Liratu**
108A, rue de l'Église, Ravignan QC G0R 2L0
, Fax: 418-267-5930
www.reseaubiblioduquebec.qc.ca/saint-louis-de-gonzague/
Yollande Rancourt-Bilodeau, Responsable

***Rawdon:* Bibliothèque de Rawdon (Alice-Quintal)**
3643, rue Queen, Rawdon QC J0X 1S0
450-834-2596
biblio076@reseaubibliocqlm.qc.ca
www.reseaubiblioduquebec.qc.ca
Renée Lalonde, Responsable

***La Reine:* Bibliothèque La Reine**
1, 3e av ouest, La Reine QC J0Z 2L0
819-947-5271, Fax: 819-947-5271
lareine@reseaubiblioatnq.qc.ca
Angèle Thouin, Responsable

***Rémigny:* Bibliothèque de Rémigny**
1304, ch de l'Église, Rémigny QC J0Z 3H0
819-761-2331, Fax: 819-761-2421
remigny@reseaubiblioatnq.qc.ca
www.reseaubiblioduquebec.qc.ca
Jocelyne Savignac, Responsable

***Repentigny:* Bibliothèque municipale de Repentigny**
1, Place d'Evry, Repentigny QC J6A 8H7
450-470-3420, Fax: 450-470-3079
bibliotheque@ville.repentigny.qc.ca
www.ville.repentigny.qc.ca/bibliotheque
Chantal Brodeur, Chef de division
brodeurc@ville.repentigny.qc.ca
450-470-3001 ext. 3427

***Richelieu:* Bibliothèque municipale Simonne-Monet-Chartrand**
200, boul Richelieu, Richelieu QC J3L 3R4
450-658-1157
richelieu@reseaubibliomonteregie.qc.ca
www.villederichelieu.org
Claude Monast, Responsable

***Richmond:* Bibliothèque municipale de Richmond-Cleveland**
820, rue Gouin, Richmond QC J0B 2H0
819-826-5814, Fax: 819-826-5547
bibliothequercm@ville.richmond.qc.ca
www.ville.richmond.qc.ca
Suzanne Nault, Responsable

***Rigaud:* Bibliothèque municipale de Rigaud**
102, St Pierre, Rigaud QC J0P 1P0
450-451-8841, Fax: 450-451-8845
Sonya Baron, Coordonnatrice
biblio@ville.rigaud.qc.ca
450-451-8841

***Rimouski:* Bibliothèque de Sainte-Blandine**
22, rue Lévesque, Rimouski QC G5N 5S6
418-735-5055
biblio.blandine@crsbp.net
www.reseaubiblioduquebec.qc.ca
Nicole Testa, Responsable

***Rimouski:* Bibliothèque Lisette-Morin**
110, rue de l'Évêché, Rimouski QC G5L 7C7
418-724-3164
bibliotheque.lisette-morin@ville.rimouski.qc.c
www.ville.rimouski.qc.ca/citoyens/bibliotheques/lisettemorin.a
Nicole Gagnon, Responsable

***Rimouski:* Bibliothèque Pointe-au-Père**
315, av Thomas-Dionne, Rimouski QC G5M 1M7
418-722-4748
biblio.pere@crsbp.net
Ginette Ménard, Responsable

***Ripon:* Bibliothèque de Ripon**
31, rue Coursol, Ripon QC J0V 1V0
819-983-2000, Fax: 819-983-1327
admripon@crsbpo.qc.ca
www.reseaubiblioduquebec.qc.ca/Ripon
Céline Derouin, Responsable

***Rivière-à-Claude:* Bibliothèque de Rivière-à-Claude**
520, rue Principale est, Rivière-à-Claude QC G0E 1Z0
418-797-2455
mcrioux@globetrotter.net
www.reseaubiblioduquebec.qc.ca
Marie-Claude Rioux, Responsable

***Rivière-au-Tonnerre:* Bibliothèque de Rivière-au-Tonnerre**
473, rue Jacques-Cartier, Rivière-au-Tonnerre QC G0G 2L0
418-465-2255, Fax: 418-465-2956
crsbp@globetrotter.net
Marie-Josée Lapierre, Responsable

***Rivière-du-Loup:* Bibliothèque municipale Françoise-Bédard**
67, rue du Rocher, Rivière-du-Loup QC G5R 1J8
418-862-4252, Fax: 418-862-3478
yves.savard@ville.riviere-du-loup.qc.ca
www.ville.riviere-du-loup.qc.ca/biblio
Sylvie Michaud, Directrice
sylvie.michaud@ville.riviere-du-loup.qc.ca

***Rivière-Éternite:* Bibliothèque publique de Rivière Eternité**
404, rue Principale, Rivière-Éternite QC G0V 1P0
418-272-1052
eternite@crsbpslsj.biblio.qc.ca
Lucie Gagné, Responsable

***Rivière-Héva:* Bibliothèque Rivière-Héva**
15A, rue du Parc, Rivière-Héva QC J0Y 2H0
819-735-2306, Fax: 819-735-4251
heva@reseaubiblioatnq.qc.ca.
www.crsbpat.qc.ca/riviereheva/
Nicole Turcotte, Responsable

***Rivière-Pentecôte:* Bibliothèque de Rivière-Pentecôte**
4344, rue Jacques-Cartier, Rivière-Pentecôte QC G0H 1R0
418-799-2143, Fax: 418-799-2263
www.reseaubiblioduquebec.qc.ca
Hélène Jean, Responsable

***Rivière-Rouge:* Bibliothèque de Sainte-Véronique**
2167, boul Fernand-Lafontaine, Rivière-Rouge QC J0T 1T0
819-275-3759, Fax: 819-275-3759
bibliovero@riviere-rouge.ca
www.reseaubiblioduquebec.qc.ca
Claire Cochet, Responsable

***Roberval:* Bibliothèque Georges-Henri-Lévesque**
829, boul St-Joseph, Roberval QC G8H 2L6
418-275-2333, Fax: 418-275-7045
jaudette@ville.roberval.qc.ca
www.roberval.biblio.qc.ca
Jacques Audette, Responsable

***Rock Forest:* Bibliothèque du secteur de Rock Forest**
968, rue du Haut-Bois sud, Rock Forest QC J1N 2C8
819-823-8676, Fax: 819-823-8345
bibliotheque.rockforest@ville.sherbrooke.qc.ca
www.ville.sherbrooke.qc.ca

***Rollet:* Bibliothèque Rollet**
761, rue Principale, Rollet QC J0Z 3J0
819-797-7110, Fax: 819-493-1210
rollet@reseaubiblioatnq.qc.ca
www.crsbpat.qc.ca/rollet/
Liliane Monderie, Responsable

***Rosemère:* Bibliothèque municipale H J Hemens de Rosemère**
339, rue Grande-Côte, Rosemère QC J7A 1K2
450-621-6132, Fax: 450-621-6131
biblio@ville.rosemere.qc.ca
ville.rosemere.qc.ca/biblio
Marc Bineault, Bibliothécaire - Chef de service
mbineault@ville.rosemere.qc.ca
514-621-6132

***Rougemont:* Bibliothèque municipale de Rougemont**
839, rue Principale, Rougemont QC J0L 1M0
450-469-3213
rougemont@reseaubibliomonteregie.qc.ca
Simone Tétrault, Responsable
450-469-3452

***Rouyn-Noranda:* Bibliothèque de Beaudry**
6884, boul Témiscamingue, Rouyn-Noranda QC J9Y 1N1
819-797-2543, Fax: 819-797-2108
beaudry@reseaubiblioatnq.qc.ca
Marguerite Petit, Responsable

***Rouyn-Noranda:* Bibliothèque municipale de Rouyn-Noranda**
201, av Dallaire, Rouyn-Noranda QC J9X 4T5
819-762-0944, Fax: 819-797-7136
info@biblrn.qc.ca
www.biblrn.qc.ca
Joël Lacoursière, Directeur général
joel.lacoursiere@biblrn.qc.ca

***Rouyn-Noranda:* L'échange**
20, av Québec, Rouyn-Noranda QC J9X 2E6
819-762-4305, Fax: 819-762-5309
info@crsbpat.qc.ca
www.reseaubiblioatnq.qc
Rosianne Avoine, Éditeur

***Roxton Pond:* Bibliothèque municipale de Roxton Pond**
905, rue Saint-Jean, Roxton Pond QC J0E 1Z0
450-372-6991
roxton.pond@reseaubibliomonteregie.qc.ca
www.reseaubiblioduquebec.qc.ca
Diane Blanchard, Responsable

***Sabrevois:* Bibliothèque municipale de Sainte-Anne-de-Sabrevois**
1218, rte 133, Sabrevois QC J0J 2G0
450-346-0899
sabrevois@reseaubibliomonteregie.qc.ca
Guylaine Marchand, Responsable

***Sacré-Coeur-Saguenay:* Bibliothèque de Sacré-Coeur**
89-A, Principale nord, Sacré-Coeur-Saguenay QC G0T 1Y0
418-236-4621, Fax: 418-236-9144
www.reseaubiblioduquebec.qc.ca
Vanessa Deschênes, Responsable
vandeschenes@hotmail.com

***Saint-Adelphe:* Bibliothèque de Saint-Adelphe (Roger-Fontaine)**
150, rue Baillargeon, Saint-Adelphe QC G0X 2G0
418-322-6634, Fax: 418-322-5434
biblio004@reseaubibliocqlm.qc.ca
www.reseaubiblioduquebec.qc.ca
Lyne Deshaies, Responsable

***Saint-Adolphe-d'Howard:* Bibliothèque de Saint-Adolphe-d'Howard**
1881, ch du Village, Saint-Adolphe-d'Howard QC J0T 2B0
819-327-2117, Fax: 819-327-2282
biblio24@crsbpl.qc.ca
www.reseaubiblioduquebec.qc.ca
Vickie Vandal, Responsable

***Saint-Aimé-des-Lacs:* Bibliothèque La Plume d'Or**
123B, rue Principale, Saint-Aimé-des-Lacs QC G0T 1S0
418-439-2229
www.reseaubiblioduquebec.qc.ca/lacs
Hélène Perron, Responsable

***Saint-Alban:* Bibliothèque Biblio-Chut!/Saint-Alban**
179, rue Principale, Saint-Alban QC G0A 3B0
418-268-3557, Fax: 418-268-5073
www.reseaubiblioduquebec.qc.ca/saint-alban
Monette Perreault, Responsable

***Saint-Alexis-de-Matapédia:* Bibliothèque de Saint-Alexis-de-Matapédia**
190, rue Principale, Saint-Alexis-de-Matapédia QC G0J 2E0
418-299-2520, Fax: 418-299-3011
Rachel Lebrun, Responsable

***Saint-Alexis-de-Montcalm:* Bibliothèque de Saint-Alexis**
232, rue Principale, Saint-Alexis-de-Montcalm QC J0K 1T0
450-839-7277, Fax: 450-831-2108
biblio110@reseaubibliocqlm.qc.ca
France Parent, Responsable

***Saint-Alexis-des-Monts:* Bibliothèque de Saint-Alexis-des-Monts (Léopold-Bellemare)**
105, rue Hôtel-de-Ville, Saint-Alexis-des-Monts QC J0K 1V0
819-265-3598
biblio028@reseaubibliocqlm.qc.ca
Danielle Gagnon, Responsable

***Saint-Alphonse-de-Caplan:* Bibliothèque de A B C du savoir**
134A, rue Principale ouest, Saint-Alphonse-de-Caplan QC G0C 2V0
418-388-5577, Fax: 418-388-2435
bbostal@globetrotter.net
www.reseaubiblioduquebec.qc.ca
Roselyn Onraet, Responsable

***Saint-Alphonse-de-Granby:* Bibliothèque municipale de Saint-Alphonse-de-Granby**
360, rue Principale, Saint-Alphonse-de-Granby QC J0E 2A0
450-375-7229, Fax: 450-375-4570
alphonse@reseaubibliomonteregie.qc.ca
Julie Fortin, Responsable

Saint-Alphonse-Rodriguez: **Bibliothèque de Saint-Alphonse-Rodriguez (Docteur-Jacques-Olivier)**
20, rue de la Plage, Saint-Alphonse-Rodriguez QC J0K 1W0
450-883-2264, Fax: 450-883-3959
biblio062@reseaubibliocqlm.qc.ca
Lina Laforest, Responsable

Saint-Amable: **Maison de la culture Jacqueline Gemme**
446, rue Daniel, Saint-Amable QC J0L 1N0
450-649-1524
amable@reseaubibliomonteregie.qc.ca
www.reseaubiblioduquebec.qc.ca
France Therrien, Responsable

Saint-Ambroise: **Bibliothèque publique de Saint-Ambroise**
156, rue Gaudreault, Saint-Ambroise QC G7P 2J9
418-672-2253
stambro@crsbpslsj.biblio.qc.ca
www.reseaubiblioduquebec.qc.ca
Carole Gagné, Responsable

Saint-André-Avellin: **Bibliothèque de Saint-André-Avellin**
532, rue Charles-Auguste Montreuil, Saint-André-Avellin QC J0V 1W0
819-983-2840, Fax: 819-983-2344
admavellin@crsbpo.qc.ca
www.reseaubiblioduquebec.qc.ca/St-Andre-Avellin
Adéodat Bernard, Responsable

Saint-André-d'Argenteuil: **Bibliothèque 'Au fil des mots'**
1, rte des Seigneurs, Saint-André-d'Argenteuil QC J0V 1X0
450-537-2022
Andréanne Legault, Responsable

Saint-André-de-Kamouraska: **Bibliothèque de Saint-André**
126, rue Principale, Saint-André-de-Kamouraska QC G0L 2H0
418-493-2150
biblio.andre@crsbp.net
www.reseaubiblioduquebec.qc.ca
Micheline Saint-André, Responsable

Saint-André-de-Restigouche: **Bibliothèque de Saint-André-de-Restigouche**
163, rue Principale, Saint-André-de-Restigouche QC G0J 1G0
418-865-2234, Fax: 418-865-1393
m.st.and.restigouche@globetrotter.net
www.reseaubiblioduquebec.qc.ca
Blandine Parent, Responsable

Saint-Anicet: **Bibliothèque municipale de Saint-Anicet**
1547, rte 132, Saint-Anicet QC J0S 1M0
450-264-9431, Fax: 450-264-3544
anicet@reseaubibliomonteregie.qc.ca
Carmen Bourgoyne, Responsable

Saint-Antoine-de-Tilly: **Bibliothèque La Corne de brume**
943, rte de L'Église, Saint-Antoine-de-Tilly QC G0S 2C0
418-886-2603
www.reseaubiblioduquebec.qc.ca/tilly
Hughes Lansac, Responsable

Saint-Antoine-sur-Richelieu: **Bibliothèque Hélène-Dupuis-Marion**
#2, 1060, rue du Moulin Payet, Saint-Antoine-sur-Richelieu QC J0L 1R0
450-787-3140, Fax: 450-787-2852
antoine@reseaubibliomonteregie.qc.ca
Nicole Villiard, Responsable

Saint-Antonin: **Bibliothèque Paradis du Livre**
261, rue Principale, Saint-Antonin QC G0L 2J0
418-867-2353, Fax: 418-862-3268
biblio.antonin@crsbp.net
Hélène Léveillé, Responsable

Saint-Apollinaire: **Bibliothèque Au Jardin des livres/Saint-Apollinaire**
#102, 94, rue Principale, Saint-Apollinaire QC G0S 2E0
418-881-2447, Fax: 418-881-4152
bibliotheque@s-apollinaire.com
www.reseaubiblioduquebec.qc.ca/saint-apollinaire
Denise Olivier, Responsable

Saint-Arsène: **Bibliothèque Saint-Arsène**
49, rue de l'Église, Saint-Arsène QC G0L 2K0
418-867-2205
biblio.arsene@crsbp.net
Suzanne Michaud, Responsable

Saint-Athanase: **Bibliothèque Saint-Athanase**
6081, ch de l'Église, Saint-Athanase QC G0L 2L0
418-859-1143
biblio.athanase@crsbp.net
Diane Dumont, Responsable

Saint-Aubert: **Bibliothèque Charles-E.-Harpe**
14, rue des Loisirs, Saint-Aubert QC G0R 2R0
418-598-3623, Fax: 418-598-3369
bibliaub@videotron.qc.ca
www.reseaubiblioduquebec.qc.ca/saint-aubert/
Céline Bélanger, Responsable

Saint-Augustin-de-Desmaures: **Bibliothèque Alain-Grandbois**
160, rue Jean-Juneau, Saint-Augustin-de-Desmaures QC G3A 2P1
418-878-5473, Fax: 418-878-1300
bibliotheque.alain-grandbois@ville.st-augustin
www.ville.st-augustin.qc.ca/biblio
Martine Lirette, Directrice de la bibliothèque
Martine.Lirette@ville.st-augustin.qc.ca

Saint-Augustin-Saguenay: **Bibliothèque de Saint-Augustin**
École de Saint-Augustin, 710, rue Principale, Saint-Augustin-Saguenay QC G0W 1K0
418-947-2404, Fax: 418-947-2533
jgalliboismsa@globetrotter.net
Wendy Keogh, Responsable

Saint-Barthélemy: **Bibliothèque de Saint-Barthélemy**
1980, rue Bonin, Local 105, Saint-Barthélemy QC J0K 1X0
450-885-3511, Fax: 450-885-2165
biblio046@reseaubibliocqlm.qc.ca
Louise Belhumeur, Responsable

Saint-Basile: **Bibliothèque Au fil des mots/Saint-Basile**
41, rue Caron, Saint-Basile QC G0A 3G0
418-329-2858, Fax: 418-329-3743
bibli0@saintbasile.qc.ca
www.reseaubiblioduquebec.qc.ca/saint-basile
Lise Bélanger, Responsable

Saint-Basile-le-Grand: **Bibliothèque Roland Leblanc**
40, rue Savaria, Saint-Basile-le-Grand QC J3N 1L8
450-461-8085, Fax: 450-461-8089
bibliotheque@ville.saint-basile-le-grand.qc.ca
www.biblothequesaintbasile.qc.ca
France Goyette, Directrice

Saint-Benjamin: **Bibliothèque La Détente/Saint-Benjamin**
440, rue du Collège, Saint-Benjamin QC G0M 1N0
418-594-8189, Fax: 418-594-6068
www.reseaubiblioduquebec.qc.ca/saint-benjamin
Régine Perras, Responsable
418-594-5635

Saint-Benoît-Labre: **Bibliothèque L'Envolume**
216, rte 271, Saint-Benoît-Labre QC G0M 1P0
418-228-9250, Fax: 418-228-0518
biblstbe@globetrotter.qc.ca
www.reseaubiblioduquebec.qc.ca/saint-benoit-labre/
Josette Labbé, Responsable

Saint-Bernard: **Bibliothèque Liratout/Saint-Bernard**
540, rue Vaillancourt, Saint-Bernard QC G0S 2G0
418-475-4669, Fax: 418-475-4602
bibliost-bernard@nouvellebeauce.com
www.reseaubiblioduquebec.qc.ca/saint-bernard
Carolle Larochelle, Responsable

Saint-Bernard-de-Michaudvil: **Bibliothèque municipale de Saint-Bernard-de-Michaudville**
390, rue Principale, Saint-Bernard-de-Michaudvil QC J0H 1C0
450-792-3190, Fax: 450-792-3591
bernard.sud@reseaubibliomonteregie.qc.ca
Marie-Sylvie Lavallée, Responsable

Saint-Blaise-sur-Richelieu: **Bibliothèque municipale de Saint-Blaise-sur-Richelieu**
#6, 795, rue des Loisirs, Saint-Blaise-sur-Richelieu QC J0J 1W0
450-291-5944, Fax: 450-291-5095
blaise@reseaubibliomonteregie.qc.ca

Laure Desrochers, Responsable

Saint-Bonaventure: **Bibliothèque de Saint-Bonaventure**
110, rue Cyr, Saint-Bonaventure QC J0C 1C0
819-396-1676, Fax: 819-396-2335
biblio120@reseaubibliocqlm.qc.ca
www.reseaubiblioduquebec.qc.ca
Gisèle Corbin, Responsable
819-396-1676

Saint-Bruno-de-Guigues: **Bibliothèque de Saint-Bruno-de-Guigues**
23B, rue Principale nord, Saint-Bruno-de-Guigues QC J0Z 2G0
819-728-2910, Fax: 819-728-2404
guigues@reseaubiblioatnq.qc.ca
www.reseaubiblioduquebec.qc.ca
Louise Gagnon, Responsable

Saint-Bruno-de-Kamouraska: **Bibliothèque des Brulots**
6, rue Du Couvent, Saint-Bruno-de-Kamouraska QC G0L 2M0
418-492-5281
biblio.bruno@crsbp.net
www.reseaubiblioduquebec.qc.ca
Ginette Beaulieu, Responsable

Saint-Bruno-de-Montarville: **Bibliothèque municipale de Saint-Bruno-de-Montarville**
82, boul Seigneurial ouest, Saint-Bruno-de-Montarville QC J3V 5N7
450-645-2950, Fax: 450-441-8485
bibliotheque@stbruno.ca
Jean-Marc Lynch, Bibliothécaire en chef
jean-marc.lynch@ville.stbruno.qc.ca
450-653-2443 ext. 2850

Saint-Bruno-Lac-Saint-Jean: **Bibliothèque publique de Saint-Bruno**
550, rue 4H, Saint-Bruno-Lac-Saint-Jean QC G0W 2L0
418-343-2007
stbruno@reseaubiblioslsj.qc.ca
Denise Martel, Responsable
418-343-3488

Saint-Calixte: **Bibliothèque de Saint-Calixte**
6250, rue Hôtel-de-Ville, Saint-Calixte QC J0K 1Z0
450-222-2782, Fax: 450-222-2789
biblio@mscalixte.qc.ca
www.reseaubiblioduquebec.qc.ca/saint-calixte
Madeleine Vézina, Responsable

Saint-Casimir: **Bibliothèque Jean-Charles-Magnan**
510, boul de la Montagne, Saint-Casimir QC G0A 3L0
418-339-2909, Fax: 418-339-3105
jcmagnan@csportneuf.qc.ca
www.reseaubiblioduquebec.qc.ca/saint-casimir/
Ange-Aimée Asselin, Responsable

Saint-Célestin: **Bibliothèque de Saint-Célestin (Claude-Bouchard)**
450B, rue Marquis, Saint-Célestin QC J0C 1G0
819-229-3403
biblio130@reseaubibliocqlm.qc.ca
www.reseaubiblioduquebec.qc.ca
Nicole Cameron, Responsable

Saint-Charles-de-Bourget: **Bibliothèque publique de Saint-Charles-de-Bourget**
362, rue Principale, Saint-Charles-de-Bourget QC G0V 1G0
418-672-1082, Fax: 418-672-4403
stcharle@crsbpslsj.biblio.qc.ca
Isabelle Néron, Responsable
418-672-1082

Saint-Charles-de-Drummond: **Club de Lecture Centre Réal-Rochefort/Saint-Charles-de-Drummond**
565, rue Victorin, Saint-Charles-de-Drummond QC J2C 1C1
819-477-2326, Fax: 819-477-0697
ccsc@ville.drummondville.qc.ca
Guylslaine Dion-Daneault, Responsable

Saint-Charles-Garnier: **Bibliothèque de Saint-Charles-Garnier**
38, de Saint-Charles-Garnier, Saint-Charles-Garnier QC G0K 1K0
418-798-4305
biblio.garnier@crsbp.net
www.reseaubiblioduquebec.qc.ca
Brigitte Gagnon, Responsable

Saint-Clément: **Bibliothèque de Saint-Clément**
25A, rue Saint-Pierre, Saint-Clément QC G0L 2N0
418-963-2258, Fax: 418-963-2619
biblio.clement@crsbp.net
www.reseaubiblioduquebec.qc.ca
Thérèse Saint-Pierre, Responsable

Saint-Cléophas: **Bibliothèque de Saint-Cléophas**
356, rue Principale, Saint-Cléophas QC G0J 3N0
418-536-3215
biblio.cleophas@crsbp.net
www.reseaubiblioduquebec.qc.ca
Gina Poirier, Responsable
418-536-3031

Saint-Cléophas-de-Brandon: **Bibliothèque de Saint-Cléophas-de-Brandon**
750, rue Principale, Saint-Cléophas-de-Brandon QC J0K 2A0
450-889-5683, Fax: 450-889-8007
biblio107@reseaubibliocqlm.qc.ca
www.reseaubiblioduquebec.qc.ca
Marie-Line Gingras, Responsable

Saint-Clet: **Bibliothèque municipale de Saint-Clet**
25, rue Piché, Saint-Clet QC J0P 1S0
450-465-3175
clet@reseaubibliomonteregie.qc.ca
www.reseaubiblioduquebec.qc.ca
Brigitte Lalonde, Responsable

Saint-Colomban: **Bibliothèque de Saint-Colomban**
326, montée de l'Église, Saint-Colomban QC J5K 1B1
450-436-1453, Fax: 450-432-1863
biblio@st-colomban.qc.ca
www.reseaubiblioduquebec.qc.ca
Lucie Jubinville, Responsable

Saint-Côme: **Bibliothèque de Saint-Côme**
1677, 55e rue, Saint-Côme QC J0K 2B0
450-883-3911, Fax: 450-883-6431
biblio054@reseaubibliocqlm.qc.ca
Josée Blanchard, Responsable

Saint-Côme-Linière: **Bibliothèque municipale de Saint-Côme-Linière**
1375, 18e rue, Saint-Côme-Linière QC G0M 1J0
418-685-3825, Fax: 418-685-2566
bibliostcome@hotmail.com
www.reseaubiblioduquebec.qc.ca/saint-come
Chantal Poulin, Responsable

Saint-Constant: **Bibliothèque municipale de Saint-Constant**
85, Mtée Saint-Régis, Saint-Constant QC J5A 1X8
450-632-8732, Fax: 450-632-9399
bibliotheque@ville.saint-constant.qc.ca
Nathalie Groulx, Responsable

Saint-Cuthbert: **Bibliothèque de Saint-Cuthbert**
1891, rue Principale, Saint-Cuthbert QC J0K 2C0
450-836-4852, Fax: 450-836-4833
biblio126@reseaubibliocqlm.qc.ca
Pierre-Yvon Laporte, Responsable

Saint-Cyprien: **Bibliothèque de Saint-Cyprien (Alphonse-Desjardins)**
187, rue Principale, Saint-Cyprien QC G0L 2P0
418-963-1887
biblio.cyprien@crsbp.net
www.reseaubiblioduquebec.qc.ca
Ginette Gagné, Responsable

Saint-Cyprien-des-Etchemins: **Bibliothèque municipale de Saint-Cyprien**
399, rue Principale, Saint-Cyprien-des-Etchemins QC G0R 1B0
418-383-3476, Fax: 418-383-5269
Sandy DeBlois, Responsable

Saint-Damase: **Bibliothèque municipale de Saint-Damase**
113, rue St-Étienne, Saint-Damase QC J0H 1J0
418-797-3341
damase@reseaubibliomonteregie.qc.ca
Hélène Simard, Responsable

Saint-Damase-de-l'Islet: **Bibliothèque municipale de Saint-Damase-de-l'Islet**
28, rue de Village est, Saint-Damase-de-l'Islet QC G0R 2X0
418-598-9370, Fax: 418-598-9370
Sylvie Cloutier, Responsable
syclou@globetotter.net
418-598-9264

Saint-Damase-de-Matapédia: **Bibliothèque de Saint-Damase-de-Matapédia**
18, av du Centenaire, Saint-Damase-de-Matapédia QC G0J 2J0
418-776-2103
biblio.damase@crsbp.net
www.reseaubiblioduquebec.qc.ca
Edith Deschênes, Responsable

Saint-Damien: **Bibliothèque de Saint-Damien**
6960, rue Principale, Saint-Damien QC J0K 2E0
450-835-7519
biblio041@reseaubibliocqlm.qc.ca
www.reseaubiblioduquebec.qc.ca
Josée St-Martin, Responsable

Saint-Damien-de-Buckland: **Bibliothèque Le Bouquin d'Or/Saint-Damien-de-Buckland**
75, rue Saint-Gérard, Saint-Damien-de-Buckland QC G0R 2Y0
418-789-2127, Fax: 418-789-2125
www.reseaubiblioduquebec.qc.ca/saint-damien
Marielle Dion-Jobin, Responsable de la bibliothèque
418-789-2125

Saint-Denis: **Bibliothèque de Saint-Denis**
2, A rte de l'Église, Saint-Denis QC G0L 2R0
418-867-8883
biblio.denis@crsbp.net
www.reseaubiblioduquebec.qc.ca
Doris Rivard, Responsable

Saint-Didace: **Bibliothèque de Saint-Didace**
530A, rue Principale, Saint-Didace QC J0K 2G0
450-835-3933, Fax: 450-835-0602
biblio128@reseaubibliocqlm.qc.ca
www.reseaubiblioduquebec.qc.ca
Isabel Lamoureux, Responsable

Saint-Dominique: **Bibliothèque municipale de Saint-Dominique**
488, Saint-Dominique, Saint-Dominique QC J0H 1L0
450-771-0256
dominique@reseaubibliomonteregie.qc.ca
Manon Denault, Responsable

Saint-Donat: **Bibliothèque de Saint-Donat**
510, rue Desrochers, Saint-Donat QC J0T 2C0
819-424-3044, Fax: 819-424-5020
biblio@saintdonat.ca
www.reseaubiblioduquebec.qc.ca/saint-donat
Anita Desmeules, Responsable

Saint-Donat: **Bibliothèque de Saint-Donat**
101, rue Bérubé, Saint-Donat QC G0K 1L0
418-739-3368
biblio.donat@crsbp.net
www.reseaubiblioduquebec.qc.ca
Madeleine Leclerc, Responsable

Sainte-Adèle: **Bibliothèque Claude-Henri-Grignon**
170, rue Morin, Sainte-Adèle QC J8B 2P7
450-229-2921, Fax: 450-229-2283
Stéphanie Lachaine, Responsable
slachaine@ville.sainte-adele.qc.ca

Sainte-Adèle: **Bibliothèque Jean-Baptiste-Rolland**
1200, rue Claude-Grégoire, Sainte-Adèle QC J8B 1E9
450-229-2921, Fax: 450-229-2283
Stéphanie Lachaine, Responsable
slachaine@ville.sainte-adele.qc.ca

Sainte-Agathe-de-Lotbinière: **Bibliothèque municipale Rayons d'Art**
402A, rue Gosford ouest, Sainte-Agathe-de-Lotbinière QC G0S 2A0
418-599-2830, Fax: 418-599-2905
rayons@coopsteagathe.com
www.reseaubiblioduquebec.qc.ca/sainte-agathe
Denise Allard-Martineau, Responsable

Sainte-Agathe-des-Monts: **Bibliothèque municipale de Sainte-Agathe-des-Monts**
10, rue St-Donat, Sainte-Agathe-des-Monts QC J8C 1P5
819-326-2848
biblio49@crsbpl.qc.ca
France Bélanger, Responsable

Sainte-Angèle-de-Méríci: **Bibliothèque de Sainte-Angèle-de-Mérici**
23, rue de la Fabrique, Sainte-Angèle-de-Mérici QC G0J 2H0
418-775-6436
biblio.merici@crsbp.net
www.reseaubiblioduquebec.qc.ca
Guylaine Hudon, Responsable

Sainte-Angèle-de-Monnoir: **Bibliothèque Sainte-Angèle-de-Monnoir**
1, rue des Loisirs, Sainte-Angèle-de-Monnoir QC J0L 1P0
450-460-3590
angele@monteregie.crsbp.qc.ca

Sainte-Angèle-de-Prémont: **Bibliothèque de Sainte-Angèle-de-Prémont**
2451, rue Camirand, Sainte-Angèle-de-Prémont QC J0K 1R0
819-268-5079, Fax: 819-268-5536
biblio124@reseaubibliocqlm.qc.ca
www.reseaubiblioduquebec.qc.ca
Denis Beauregard, Responsable

Sainte-Anne-de-la-Pérade: **Bibliothèque de Sainte-Anne-de-la-Pérade (Armand-Goulet)**
100, rue de la Fabrique, Sainte-Anne-de-la-Pérade QC G0X 2J0
418-325-2216, Fax: 418-325-3070
biblio014@reseaubibliocqlm.qc.ca
www.reseaubiblioduquebec.qc.ca
Cécile Fortier, Responsable

Sainte-Anne-des-Monts: **Bibliothèque municipale Blanche-Lamontagne**
120, 7e rue ouest, Sainte-Anne-des-Monts QC G4V 2L2
418-763-3811, Fax: 418-763-3842
bbosadm@globetrotter.qc.ca
Francis Pelletier, Directeur
418-763-3810

Sainte-Anne-des-Plaines: **Bibliothèque publique de Sainte-Anne-des-Plaines**
155, rue des Cèdres, Sainte-Anne-des-Plaines QC J0N 1H0
450-478-4337
biblio.sadp@videotron.ca
www.ville.ste-anne-des-plaines.qc.ca/biblio/
Danielle Labelle, Directrice

Sainte-Anne-du-Lac: **Bibliothèque de Sainte-Anne-du-Lac**
1B, rue St-François-Xavier, Sainte-Anne-du-Lac QC J0W 1V0
819-586-2161, Fax: 819-586-2203
bibsadl@tlb.sympatico.ca
www.reseaubiblioduquebec.qc.ca
Lida Touchette, Responsable
819-586-2856

Sainte-Aurélie: **Bibliothèque Le Maillon**
151B, ch des Bois-Francs, Sainte-Aurélie QC G0M 1M0
418-593-3021, Fax: 418-593-3961
maillon@sogetel.net
www.reseaubiblioduquebec.qc.ca/sainte-aurelie/
JoAnne Leclerc, Responsable

Sainte-Barbe: **Bibliothèque municipale Lucie Benoît**
468, ch de l'Église, Sainte-Barbe QC J0S 1P0
450-371-2424
barbe@reseaubibliomonteregie.qc.ca
Lucie Benoît, Responsable

Sainte-Béatrix: **Bibliothèque de Sainte-Béatrix**
Pavillon du Village, Sainte-Béatrix QC J0K 1Y0
450-883-2245, Fax: 450-883-1772
administration@stebeatrix.com
www.sainte-beatrix.com
Micheline Thibault, Responsable

Sainte-Brigide-d'Iberville: **Bibliothèque de Sainte-Brigide-d'Iberville**
#100, 509, 9e rang, Sainte-Brigide-d'Iberville QC J0J 1X0
450-293-4363, Fax: 450-293-1243
administration@sainte-brigide.qc.ca
www.sainte-brigide.qc.ca
Francine Belzile, Responsable
450-293-7358

Sainte-Brigitte-de-Laval: **Bibliothèque Le Trivent**
3, rue du Couvent, Sainte-Brigitte-de-Laval QC G0A 3K0
418-666-4666, Fax: 418-825-3114
trivent.bibli@csdps.qc.ca
www.reseaubiblioduquebec.qc.ca/sainte-brigitte/
Marie-Ôve Joubert, Responsable

Sainte-Brigitte-des-Saults: **Bibliothèque de Sainte-Brigitte-des-Saults**
400, rue Principale, Sainte-Brigitte-des-Saults QC J0C 1E0
819-336-4460, Fax: 819-336-4410
biblio043@reseaubibliocqlm.qc.ca
www.reseaubiblioduquebec.qc.ca
Jocelyne Guérin, Responsable

***Sainte-Catherine:* Bibliothèque publique de Sainte-Catherine**
5365, boul St-Laurent, Sainte-Catherine QC J5C 1A6
450-632-0590, Fax: 450-632-9908
bibliotheque@ville.sainte-catherine.qc.ca
www.ville.sainte-catherine.qc.ca/francais/biblio_accueil.html
Lise Forcier, Directrice

***Ste-Catherine-de-la-J-Carti:* Bibliothèque Anne-Hébert**
22, rue Louis-Jolliet, Ste-Catherine-de-la-J-Carti QC G3N 2V3
418-875-2171, Fax: 418-875-2699
bibliotheque@villescjc.com
www.reseaubiblioduquebec.qc.ca/cartier
Geneviève Roger, Responsable

***Sainte-Cécile-de-Lévrard:* Bibliothèque de Sainte-Cécile-de-Lévrard**
234, rue Principale, Sainte-Cécile-de-Lévrard QC G0X 2M0
819-263-0368, Fax: 819-263-2104
biblio113@reseaubibliocqlm.qc.ca
www.reseaubiblioduquebec.qc.ca
Yvette Demers, Responsable

***Sainte-Cécile-de-Masham:* Bibliothèque de Sainte-Cécile-de-Masham (La Pêche)**
5, rue Principale ouest, Sainte-Cécile-de-Masham QC J0X 2W0
819-456-2627, Fax: 819-456-4228
admmasham@crsbpo.qc.ca
www.reseaubiblioduquebec.qc.ca/Masham
Gisèle Duguay, Responsable

***Sainte-Christine:* Bibliothèque municipale de Sainte-Christine**
629, rue des Loisirs, Sainte-Christine QC J0H 1H0
819-858-2828
christine@reseaubibliomonteregie.qc.ca
www.reseaubiblioduquebec.qc.ca
Rosalie Proulx, Responsable

***Sainte-Claire:* Bibliothèque municipale de Sainte-Claire**
135, rue Principale, Sainte-Claire QC G0R 2V0
418-883-3314, Fax: 418-883-3845
msclaire@globetrotter.qc.ca
Serge Gagnon, Directeur général et secrétaire-trésorier
sgagn@globetrotter.net
418-883-3314

***Sainte-Clotilde-de-Beauce:* Bibliothèque municipale de Sainte-Clotilde-de-Beauce**
307, rue du Couvent, Sainte-Clotilde-de-Beauce QC G0N 1C0
418-427-2018, Fax: 418-427-2637
pp307@hotmail.com
Paulette Pomerleau, Responsable
418-427-2181

***Saint-Edmond-les-Plaines:* Bibliothèque publique de Saint-Edmond**
561, rue Principale, Saint-Edmond-les-Plaines QC G0W 2M0
418-274-3069, Fax: 418-274-5629
stedmond@crsbpslsj.biblio.qc.ca
Lucie Coté, Responsable

***Saint-Édouard:* Bibliothèque municipale de Saint-Édouard**
405B, Montée Lussier, Saint-Édouard QC J0L 1Y0
450-454-2056
edouard@reseaubibliomonteregie.qc.ca
www.reseaubiblioduquebec.qc.ca
Fleurette Michaud, Responsable

***Saint-Edouard-de-Lotbinière:* Bibliothèque municipale de Saint-Édouard-de-Lotbinière**
105, rue de L'École, Saint-Edouard-de-Lotbinière QC G0S 1Y0
418-796-2433, Fax: 418-796-2228
biblsted@globetrotter.qc.ca
Martha Blanchet, Responsable

***Saint-Édouard-de-Maskinongé:* Bibliothèque de Saint-Édouard-de-Maskinongé**
3851, rue Notre-Dame, Saint-Édouard-de-Maskinongé QC J0K 2H0
819-268-2883
biblio123@reseaubibliocqlm.qc.ca
www.reseaubiblioduquebec.qc.ca
Hélène Robert, Responsable

***Sainte-Elisabeth-de-Proulx:* Bibliothèque publique de Sainte-Elisabeth-de-Proulx**
1254, rue Principale, Sainte-Elisabeth-de-Proulx QC G8M 4V2
418-276-9494
elisabeth@reseaubibliosIsj.qc.ca
Rosanne Carrier-Simard, Responsable

***Sainte-Elizabeth:* Bibliothèque de Sainte-Elisabeth (Françoise-Allard-Bérard)**
2270, rue Principale, Sainte-Elizabeth QC J0K 2J0
450-759-2875
biblio068@reseaubibliocqlm.qc.ca
www.reseaubiblioduquebec.qc.ca
Josette Lamontagne, Responsable

***Sainte-Élizabeth-de-Warwick:* Bibliothèque de Sainte-Élizabeth-de-Warwick**
228, rue Principale, Sainte-Élizabeth-de-Warwick QC J0A 1M0
819-358-2429, Fax: 819-358-9192
biblio141@reseaubibliocqlm.qc.ca
www.reseaubiblioduquebec.qc.ca
Christiane Luscher, Responsable
819-358-6980

***Sainte-Émélie-de-l'Énergie:* Bibliothèque de Sainte-Émélie-de-l'Énergie**
241, rue Coutu, Sainte-Émélie-de-l'Énergie QC J0K 2K0
450-886-3823, Fax: 450-886-9175
biblio053@reseaubibliocqlm.qc.ca
www.reseaubiblioduquebec.qc.ca
Diane Durand, Responsable

***Sainte-Eulalie:* Bibliothèque de Sainte-Eulalie**
757A, rue des Bouleaux, Sainte-Eulalie QC G0Z 1E0
819-225-8069, Fax: 819-225-4078
biblio074@reseaubibliocqlm.qc.ca
www.reseaubiblioduquebec.qc.ca
Marjolaine Rheault, Responsable
819-225-4434

***Sainte-Famille:* Bibliothèque municipale de Sainte-Famille**
3912-1, ch Royal, Sainte-Famille QC G0A 3P0
418-666-4666, Fax: 418-829-2513
biblisfa@csdps.qc.ca
www.reseaubiblioduquebec.qc.ca/sainte-famille
Ernest Labranche, Responsable

***Sainte-Flavie:* Bibliothèque Olivar-Asselin**
505, rte de la Mer, Sainte-Flavie QC G0J 2L0
418-775-7050
biblio.flavie@crsbp.net
www.reseaubiblioduquebec.qc.ca
Liz Fortin, Responsable

***Sainte-Florence:* Bibliothèque de Sainte-Florence**
29, rue des Loisirs, Sainte-Florence QC G0J 2M0
418-756-5079
biblio.florence@crsbp.net
www.reseaubiblioduquebec.qc.ca
Gaétane Morin, Responsable

***Sainte-Françoise:* Bibliothèque de Sainte-Françoise (Bas-Saint-Laurent)**
31, rue Principale, Sainte-Françoise QC G0L 3B0
418-851-3878
biblio.francoise@crsbp.net
www.reseaubiblioduquebec.qc.ca
Édith Rioux, Responsable

***Sainte-Françoise:* Bibliothèque de Sainte-Françoise (Centre-du-Québec)**
563, rue Principale, Sainte-Françoise QC G0S 2N0
819-287-5838
biblio104@reseaubibliocqlm.qc.ca
www.reseaubiblioduquebec.qc.ca
Diane Bélanger, Responsable

***Ste-Geneviève-de-Batiscan:* Bibliothèque de Sainte-Geneviève-de-Batiscan (Clément-Marchand)**
2, rue du Centre, Ste-Geneviève-de-Batiscan QC G0X 2R0
418-363-2261
biblio036@reseaubibliocqlm.qc.ca
www.reseaubiblioduquebec.qc.ca
Nicole Lahaie, Responsable

***Ste-Geneviève-de-Berthier:* Bibliothèque de Sainte-Geneviève-de-Berthier (Léo-Paul-Desrosiers)**
391, rang de la Rivière-Bayonne sud, Ste-Geneviève-de-Berthier QC J0K 1A0
450-836-4333, Fax: 450-836-7260
biblio066@reseaubibliocqlm.qc.ca
www.reseaubiblioduquebec.qc.ca
Gabrielle Desjardins, Responsable

***Sainte-Germaine-Boulé:* Bibliothèque de Sainte-Germaine-Boulé**
240, rue Roy, Sainte-Germaine-Boulé QC J0Z 1M0
819-787-6477, Fax: 819-787-6477
boule@reseaubiblioatnq.qc.ca
www.reseaubiblioduquebec.qc.ca
Odette Rancourt Audet, Responsable

***Ste-Gertrude-Mannville:* Bibliothèque de Sainte-Gertrude**
391, rte 395, Ste-Gertrude-Mannville QC J0Y 2L0
819-727-2244, Fax: 819-727-2244
gertrude@crsbpat.qc.ca
Geneviève Michaud, Responsable

***Sainte-Hedwidge-de-Roberval:* Bibliothèque publique de Sainte-Hedwidge**
1090, rue Principale, Sainte-Hedwidge-de-Roberval QC G0W 2R0
418-275-3020
hedwidge@crsbpslsj.biblio.qc.ca
www.reseaubiblioduquebec.qc.ca
Michelle Morin, Responsable
418-275-4963

***Sainte-Hélène:* Bibliothèque de Sainte-Hélène**
707, rue du Couvent, Sainte-Hélène QC G0L 3J0
418-492-3819
biblio.helene@crsbp.net
www.reseaubiblioduquebec.qc.ca
Lucie Bérubé, Responsable
lucieberube42@hotmail.com
418-492-3324

***Sainte-Hélène-de-Bagot:* Bibliothèque municipale de Sainte-Hélène-de-Bagot**
384, 6e av, Sainte-Hélène-de-Bagot QC J0H 1M0
450-791-2618
helene@reseaubibliomonteregie.qc.ca
www.reseaubiblioduquebec.qc.ca
France Vachon, Responsable

***Ste-Hélène-de-Mancebourg:* Bibliothèque de Sainte-Hélène-de-Mancebourg**
459, ch Rangs 2 et 3, Ste-Hélène-de-Mancebourg QC J0Z 2T0
819-333-4609, Fax: 819-333-9591
mancebourg@reseaubiblioatnq.qc.ca
www.reseaubiblioduquebec.qc.ca
Émilienne Jérôme, Responsable
819-333-5766

***Sainte-Hénédine:* Bibliothèque La Détente/Sainte-Hénédine**
111, rue Principale, Sainte-Hénédine QC G0S 2R0
418-935-3993, Fax: 418-935-3113
biblsthe@globetrotter.qc.ca
www.reseaubiblioduquebec.qc.ca/sainte-henedine/
Doris Drouin-Dubreuil, Responsable

***Sainte-Irène:* Bibliothèque de Sainte-Irène**
362, rue de la Fabrique, Sainte-Irène QC G0J 1P0
418-629-5705
biblio.irene@crsbp.net
www.reseaubiblioduquebec.qc.ca
Sylvie Chenel, Responsable

***Ste-Jeanne-d'Arc-de-Matane:* Bibliothèque de Sainte-Jeanne-d'Arc-de-Matane**
205, rue Principale, Ste-Jeanne-d'Arc-de-Matane QC G0J 2T0
418-776-5814
biblio.jeanne@crsbp.net
www.reseaubiblioduquebec.qc.ca
Pauline Proulx, Responsable

***Sainte-Julie:* Bibliothèque municipale de Sainte-Julie**
1600, ch du Fer-à-Cheval, Sainte-Julie QC J3E 2M1
450-922-7070, Fax: 450-922-7077
biblio@ville.sainte-julie.qc.ca
Marie-Hélène Parent, Bibliothécaire en chef
mhparent@ville.sainte-julie.qc.ca
450-922-7115 ext. 7071

***Sainte-Julienne:* Bibliothèque Gisèle-Paré**
2550, rue Marcel-Masse, Sainte-Julienne QC J0K 2T0

450-831-3811, Fax: 450-831-4433
biblio43@crsbpl.qc.ca
www.reseaubiblioduquebec.qc.ca/sainte-julienne
Marielle Rompré, Responsable

Saint-Élie-de-Caxton: **Bibliothèque de Saint-Élie-de-Caxton**
50, ch des Loisirs, Saint-Élie-de-Caxton QC G0X 2N0
819-221-4095
biblio115@reseaubibliocqlm.qc.ca
www.reseaubiblioduquebec.qc.ca
Charline Plante, Responsable

Saint-Éloi: **Bibliothèque de Saint-Éloi**
456, rue Principale, Saint-Éloi QC G0L 2V0
biblio.eloi@crsbp.net
www.reseaubiblioduquebec.qc.ca
Rachel Tardif, Responsable

Sainte-Louise: **Bibliothèque Idée-Lire**
506, rue Principale, Sainte-Louise QC G0R 3K0
418-354-7730
www.reseaubiblioduquebec.qc.ca/sainte-louise
Jacqueline Lizotte, Responsable

Saint-Elphège: **Bibliothèque de Saint-Elphège (La Bouquinerie)**
227A, rue de l'Église, Saint-Elphège QC J0G 1J0
450-568-7339, Fax: 450-568-0288
biblio007@reseaubibliocqlm.qc.ca
www.reseaubiblioduquebec.qc.ca
Monique Champagne Lemire, Responsable

Sainte-Luce: **Bibliothèque de Luceville**
67, rue Saint-Pierre est, Sainte-Luce QC G0K 1P0
418-739-3534
biblio.luceville@crsbp.net
www.reseaubiblioduquebec.qc.ca
Sylvanne Saint-Laurent, Responsable

Sainte-Luce: **Bibliothèque de Sainte-Luce**
1, rue Langlois, Sainte-Luce QC G0K 1P0
418-739-3393
biblio.luce@crsbp.net
www.reseaubiblioduquebec.qc.ca
Luc Bourassa, Responsable

Sainte-Lucie-de-Beauregard: **Bibliothèque A la Bouquinerie**
21, rte des Chutes, Sainte-Lucie-de-Beauregard QC G0R 3L0
418-223-3122, Fax: 418-223-3121
www.reseaubiblioduquebec.qc.ca/sainte-lucie
Huguette Rouillard, Responsable
418-223-3613

Ste-Lucie-des-Laurentides: **Bibliothèque de Sainte-Lucie-des-Laurentides**
2057, ch des Hauteurs, Ste-Lucie-des-Laurentides QC J0T 2J0
819-326-3228, Fax: 819-326-0592
biblio041@crsbpl.qc.ca
www.municipalite.sainte-lucie-des-laurentides.qc.ca
Lorraine Beauchamp, Responsable

Saint-Elzéar: **Bibliothèque de Saint-Elzéar**
144, ch Principal, Saint-Elzéar QC G0C 2W0
418-534-4314, Fax: 418-534-2626
bbostelz@globetrotter.net
www.reseaubiblioduquebec.qc.ca
Lucille Ferlatte, Responsable

Saint-Elzéar-de-Témiscouata: **Bibliothèque de Saint-Elzéar (Saint-Elzéar-de-Témiscouata)**
320, rue Principale, Saint-Elzéar-de-Témiscouata QC G0L 2W0
418-534-3513
biblio.elzear@crsbp.net
www.reseaubiblioduquebec.qc.ca
Thérèse Sirois, Responsable

Sainte-Madeleine: **Bibliothèque municipale de Sainte-Madeleine**
1040A, rue Saint-Simon, Sainte-Madeleine QC J0H 1S0
450-795-3959, Fax: 450-795-3736
madeleine@reseaubibliomonteregie.ca
www.reseaubiblioduquebec.qc.ca
Cathy Collins, Responsable

Ste-Marcelline-de-Kildare: **Bibliothèque de Sainte-Marcelline-de-Kildare**
435, 1ère av Pied-de-la-Montagne, Ste-Marcelline-de-Kildare QC J0K 2Y0
450-883-2241, Fax: 450-883-2242
biblio135@reseaubibliocqlm.qc.ca
www.reseaubiblioduquebec.qc.ca
Gisèle Labine, Responsable

Sainte-Marguerite: **Biblio La Bouquine**
235, rue Saint-Jacques, Sainte-Marguerite QC G0S 2X0
418-935-7089, Fax: 418-935-3709
www.reseaubiblioduquebec.qc.ca/sainte-marguerite/
Adrienne Gagné, Responsable

Sainte-Marguerite: **Bibliothèque de Sainte-Marguerite**
15, rue de la Vérendrye, Sainte-Marguerite QC G0J 2Y0
418-756-3364
biblio.margot@crsbp.net
www.reseaubiblioduquebec.qc.ca
Colette Marquis, Responsable

Ste-Marguerite-du-Lac-Masso: **Bibliothèque de Sainte-Marguerite-Estérel**
4, rue des Lilas, Ste-Marguerite-du-Lac-Masso QC J0T 1L0
450-228-4442, Fax: 450-228-4442
biblio031@crsbpl.qc.ca
www.reseaubiblioduquebec.qc.ca/sainte-marguerite-esterel
Joane Grandmaison, Responsable

Sainte-Marie: **Bibliothèque Honorius-Provost**
80, rue St-Antoine, Sainte-Marie QC G6E 4B8
418-387-2240, Fax: 418-387-2454
jacques.filiatrault@ville.sainte-marie.qc.ca
www.ville.sainte-marie.qc.ca
Jacques Filiatrault, Responsable

Sainte-Marie-de-Blandford: **Bibliothèque de Sainte-Marie-de-Blandford**
492, rue des Bosquets, Sainte-Marie-de-Blandford QC G0X 2W0
819-283-2127, Fax: 819-283-2169
biblio108@reseaubibliocqlm.qc.ca
www.reseaubiblioduquebec.qc.ca
Carmen Bilodeau, Responsable

Sainte-Marie-Salomé: **Bibliothèque de Sainte-Marie-Salomé**
121, rue Viger, Sainte-Marie-Salomé QC J0K 2Z0
450-839-6212, Fax: 450-753-5236
biblio050@reseaubibliocqlm.qc.ca
www.reseaubiblioduquebec.qc.ca
Diane Éthier, Responsable

Sainte-Marthe-sur-le-Lac: **Bibliothèque municipale de Sainte-Marthe-sur-le-Lac**
3003, ch Oka, Sainte-Marthe-sur-le-Lac QC J0N 1P0
450-974-7111, Fax: 450-974-7110
biblio.stemarthe@videotron.ca
Micheline Aloi, Commis senior
biblio.stemarthe@videotron.ca
450-947-7111

Sainte-Mélanie: **Bibliothèque de Sainte-Mélanie (Louise-Amélie-Panet)**
940, rue Principale, Sainte-Mélanie QC J0K 3A0
450-889-5871
biblio111@reseaubibliocqlm.qc.ca
www.reseaubiblioduquebec.qc.ca
Martin Alarie, Responsable

Saint-Émile-de-Suffolk: **Bibliothèque de Saint-Émile-de-Suffolk**
299, route des Cantons, Saint-Émile-de-Suffolk QC J0V 1Y0
819-426-3447, Fax: 819-426-3447
bibblio.stemile@mrcpapineau.com
www.reseaubiblioduquebec.qc.ca
Georgette Haineault, Responsable

Sainte-Monique: **Bibliothèque de Sainte-Monique**
247, rue Principale, Sainte-Monique QC J0G 1N0
819-289-2051, Fax: 819-289-2344
biblio052@reseaubibliocqlm.qc.ca
www.reseaubiblioduquebec.qc.ca
Pierrette Beauchemin, Responsable

Sainte-Monique-Lac-St-Jean: **Bibliothèque publique de Sainte-Monique**
138, rue Honfleur, Sainte-Monique-Lac-St-Jean QC G0W 2T0
418-347-4391
monique@reseaubiblioslsj.qc.ca
Normande Gauthier, Directrice

Sainte-Paule: **Bibliothèque de Sainte-Paule**
102, rue Banville, Sainte-Paule QC G0J 3C0
418-737-1378
biblio.paule@crsbp.net
www.reseaubiblioduquebec.qc.ca
Carmen Côté-D'Amour, Responsable

Sainte-Perpétue: **Bibliothèque de Sainte-Perpétue**
2504, rang St-Joseph, Sainte-Perpétue QC J0C 1R0
819-336-6275
biblio094@reseaubibliocqlm.qc.ca
www.reseaubiblioduquebec.qc.ca
Colette Laplante, Responsable

Sainte-Pétronille: **Bibliothèque municipale de Sainte-Pétronille**
3, ch de l'Église, Sainte-Pétronille QC G0A 4C0
418-828-2270, Fax: 418-828-1364
bibliospetro@qc.aira.com
Lise Paquet, Responsable

Saint-Épiphane: **Bibliothèque de Saint-Épiphane**
216, rue du Couvent, Saint-Épiphane QC G0L 2X0
418-867-3225
biblio.epiphane@crsbp.net
www.reseaubiblioduquebec.qc.ca
Jacqueline Jalbert, Responsable

Sainte-Rita: **Bibliothèque Sainte-Rita**
23, rue de L'Église est, Sainte-Rita QC G0L 4G0
418-963-2967
biblio.rita@crsbp.net
www.reseaubiblioduquebec.qc.ca
Lucille Turcotte, Responsable

Sainte-Rose-de-Watford: **Bibliothèque municipale de Sainte-Rose-de-Watford**
693, rue Carrier, Sainte-Rose-de-Watford QC G0R 4G0
418-267-5264, Fax: 418-267-5812
biblioste-rose@sogetel.net
www.reseaubiblioduquebec.qc.ca/sainte-rose
Lisette Gagnon, Responsable
jlcya@sogetel.net
418-267-5721

Sainte-Rose-du-Nord: **Bibliothèque publique de Ste-Rose-du-Nord**
126, rue Descente-des-Femmes, Sainte-Rose-du-Nord QC G0V 1T0
418-675-2250
ste-rose@reseaubiblioslsj.qc.ca
www.crsbpslsj.biblio.qc.ca/ste-rose-du-nord
Lise Clairmont, Responsable

Sainte-Sabine: **Bibliothèque Sabithèque**
#203, 4, rue St-Charles, Sainte-Sabine QC G0R 4H0
418-383-5788, Fax: 418-383-5488
ste-sabine@globetrotter.qc.ca
www.reseaubiblioduquebec.qc.ca/sainte-sabine/
Lorraine Mercier, Responsable

Ste-Séraphine: **Bibliothèque de Sainte-Séraphine**
2660, rue Centre communautaire, Ste-Séraphine QC J0A 1E0
819-336-3222, Fax: 819-336-3800
biblio085@reseaubibliocqlm.qc.ca
www.reseaubiblioduquebec.qc.ca
Monique Raîche, Responsable

Sainte-Sophie-de-Lévrard: **Bibliothèque de Sainte-Sophie-de-Lévrard**
184A, rue St-Antoine, Sainte-Sophie-de-Lévrard QC G0X 3C0
819-288-0334, Fax: 819-288-5804
biblio102@reseaubibliocqlm.qc.ca
www.reseaubiblioduquebec.qc.ca
Daniel Désilets, Responsable

Saint-Esprit: **Bibliothèque de Saint-Esprit (Alice-Parizeau)**
45, rue des Écoles, Saint-Esprit QC J0K 2L0
450-831-2274, Fax: 450-839-6070
biblio125@reseaubibliocqlm.qc.ca
Diane Lamarre, Responsable

Sainte-Thècle: **Bibliothèque de Sainte-Thècle**
301, rue St-Jacques, Sainte-Thècle QC G0X 3G0
418-289-3717, Fax: 418-289-3014
biblio016@reseaubibliocqlm.qc.ca
www.reseaubiblioduquebec.qc.ca
Thérèse Lemelin, Responsable

Sainte-Thérèse: **Bibliothèque municipale de Sainte-Thérèse**
150, boul du Séminaire, Sainte-Thérèse QC J7E 1Z2

450-434-1442, Fax: 450-434-6070
ltheriault@ville.sainte-therese.qc.ca
ville.sainte-therese.qc.ca
Lise Thériault, Directrice

***Ste-Thérèse-de-la-Gatineau:* Bibliothèque municipale de Sainte-Thérèse-de-la-Gatineau**
29, rue Principale, Ste-Thérèse-de-la-Gatineau QC J0X 2X0
819-449-7964, Fax: 819-449-2194
admtherese@crsbpo.qc.ca
Josée Riel, Coordonnatrice

***Saint-Étienne-de-Beauharnoi:* Bibliothèque municipale de Saint-Étienne-de-Beauharnois**
430, rue de l'Église, Saint-Étienne-de-Beauharnoi QC J0S 1S0
450-429-6384, Fax: 450-429-6384
etienne@reseaubibliomonteregie.qc.ca
Carole Lalande, Responsable

***Saint-Étienne-des-Grès:* Bibliothèque de Saint-Étienne-des-Grès**
#300, 190, rue Saint-Honoré, Saint-Étienne-des-Grès QC G0X 2P0
819-535-5192
biblio019@reseaubibliocqlm.qc.ca
www.reseaubiblioduquebec.qc.ca
Denis Boisvert, Responsable

***Saint-Étienne-des-Grès:* Bibliothèque de Saint-Thomas-de-Caxton**
332, rue des Loisirs, Saint-Étienne-des-Grès QC G0X 2P0
819-296-3004
biblio105@reseaubibliocqlm.qc.ca
www.reseaubiblioduquebec.qc.ca
France Bournival, Responsable

***Saint-Eugène:* Bibliothèque publique de Saint-Eugène**
469, rue Principale, Saint-Eugène QC G0W 1B0
418-276-7790
steugene@reseaubiblioslsj.qc.ca
www.reseaubiblioduquebec.qc.ca
Lise Lavoie, Responsable

***Saint-Eugène-de-Guigues:* Bibliothèque de Saint-Eugène-de-Guigues**
4, 1ère av ouest, Saint-Eugène-de-Guigues QC J0Z 3L0
819-785-4441, Fax: 819-785-2301
eugene@reseaubiblioatnq.qc.ca
www.reseaubiblioduquebec.qc.ca
Lorraine Falardeau, Responsable

***Sainte-Ursule:* Bibliothèque de Sainte-Ursule (C.-J. Magnan)**
215, rue Lessard, Sainte-Ursule QC J0K 3M0
819-228-0735, Fax: 819-228-8326
biblio031@reseaubibliocqlm.qc.ca
Suzanne Pilon, Responsable

***Saint-Eusèbe:* Bibliothèque de Saint-Eusèbe**
222B, rue Principale, Saint-Eusèbe QC G0L 2Y0
418-899-0150
biblio.eusebe@crsbp.net
www.reseaubiblioduquebec.qc.ca
Gisèle Lebrun Bolduc, Responsable

***Saint-Eustache:* Bibliothèque municipale Guy-Bélisle**
80, boul Arthur-Sauvé, Saint-Eustache QC J7R 2H7
450-974-5035, Fax: 450-974-5054
ngrimard@ville.saint-eustache.qc.ca
biblio.ville.saint-eustache.qc.ca
Nicole Grimard, Responsable
ngrimard@ville.saint-eustache.qc.ca

***Sainte-Victoire-de-Sorel:* Bibliothèque municipale de Sainte-Victoire-de-Sorel**
519, ch Ste-Victoire, Sainte-Victoire-de-Sorel QC J0G 1T0
450-782-3111
victoire@reseaubibliomonteregie.qc.ca
Micheline Lamoureux, Responsable

***Saint-Fabien:* Bibliothèque de Saint-Fabien**
10, 7e Avenue, Saint-Fabien QC G0L 2Z0
418-869-2602
biblio.fabien@crsbp.net
www.reseaubiblioduquebec.qc.ca
Raynald Beaulieu, Responsable

***Saint-Fabien-de-Panet:* Bibliothèque Fabiothèque/Saint-Fabien-de-Panet**
199, rue Bilodeau, Saint-Fabien-de-Panet QC G0R 2J0
418-249-4417, Fax: 418-249-2507
fabiot@globetrotter.qc.ca
www.reseaubiblioduquebec.qc.ca/saint-fabien-de-panet
Michèle Thibodeau, Responsable
418-249-2732

***Saint-Faustin-Lac-Carré:* Bibliothèque du Lac**
64, rue de la Culture, Saint-Faustin-Lac-Carré QC J0T 1J1
819-688-5434, Fax: 819-688-5644
bibliodulac@municipalite.stfaustin.qc.ca
www.crsbpl.qc.ca/bibliotheques/Saint-Faustin-Lac-Carre.html
Marielle Jacques, Responsable

***Saint-Félicien:* Bibliothèque municipale de Saint-Félicien**
#200, 1209, boul Sacré Coeur, Saint-Félicien QC G8K 2R5
418-679-2100, Fax: 418-679-1449
biblio@ville.stfelicien.qc.ca
www.stfelicien.biblio.qc.ca
Johanne Laprise, Responsable

***Saint-Félicien:* Bibliothèque publique de Saint-Méthode**
3159, rue Saint-Méthode, Saint-Félicien QC G8K 3C2
418-679-0757
stmethode@reseaubiblioslsj.qc.ca
Thérèse Fortin, Responsable

***Saint-Félix-d'Otis:* Bibliothèque publique de Saint-Félix-d'Otis**
455, rue Principale, Saint-Félix-d'Otis QC G0V 1M0
418-544-1144
stfelix@reseaubiblioslsj.qc.ca
Nathalie Simard, Responsable

***Saint-Félix-de-Kingsey:* Bibliothèque de Saint-Félix-de-Kingsey**
6105-B, rue Principale, Saint-Félix-de-Kingsey QC J0B 2T0
819-848-1400
biblio152@reseaubibliocqlm.qc.ca
www.reseaubiblioduquebec.qc.ca
Pauline Roy, Responsable

***Saint-Félix-de-Valois:* Bibliothèque de Saint-Félix-de-Valois**
4863, rue Principale, Saint-Félix-de-Valois QC J0K 2M0
450-889-5589, Fax: 450-889-7911
biblio010@reseaubibliocqlm.qc.ca
Suzie Thériault, Responsable

***Saint-Ferdinand:* Bibliothèque de Saint-Ferdinand (Onil-Garneau)**
620, rue Notre-Dame, Saint-Ferdinand QC G0N 1N0
418-428-9607
biblio049@reseaubibliocqlm.qc.ca
Lucie Lamontagne, Responsable

***Saint-Ferréol-les-Neiges:* Bibliothèque Aux Sources/Saint-Ferréol-les-Neiges**
33, rue de l'Église, Saint-Ferréol-les-Neiges QC G0A 3R0
418-826-3540, Fax: 418-826-0489
www.reseaubiblioduquebec.qc.ca/saint-ferreol
Lucie Bédard, Responsable

***Saint-Flavien:* Bibliothèque La Flaviethèque/Saint-Flavien**
6, rue Caux, Saint-Flavien QC G0S 2M0
418-728-0025, Fax: 418-728-4190
biblifla@globetrotter.qc.ca
www.reseaubiblioduquebec.qc.ca/saint-flavien
Carole Turgeon, Responsable

***Saint-Fortunat:* Bibliothèque municipale de Saint-Fortunat**
173, rue Principale, Saint-Fortunat QC G0P 1G0
418-344-5399
www.reseaubiblioduquebec.qc.ca/saint-fortunat
Huguette Garneau, Responsable

***Saint-François-d'Assise:* Bibliothèque de Saint-François-d'Assise**
457, ch Central, Saint-François-d'Assise QC G0J 2N0
418-299-2099, Fax: 418-299-3037
munstfrs@globetrotter.net
Monelle Gallant, Responsable

***Saint-François-de-Sales:* Bibliothèque publique de Saint-François-de-Sales**
255, rue de l'Église, Saint-François-de-Sales QC G0W 1M0
418-348-9444
franco@reseaubiblioslsj.qc.ca
Myriam Simard, Responsable
418-348-6736

***Saint-François-du-Lac:* Bibliothèque de Saint-François-du-Lac**
480, rue Notre-Dame, Saint-François-du-Lac QC J0G 1M0
450-568-1130, Fax: 450-568-7465
biblio158@reseaubibliocqlm.qc.ca
www.reseaubiblioduquebec.qc.ca
Ghislaine Lachapelle, Responsable

***Saint-Fulgence:* Bibliothèque publique de Saint-Fulgence**
251, Saguenay, Saint-Fulgence QC G0V 1S0
418-674-2588
bibliostfulgence@videotron.ca
Lina Tremblay, Responsable
bibliostfulgence@videotron.ca
418-674-2440

***Saint-Gabriel-de-Brandon:* Bibliothèque de Saint-Gabriel (Au fil des pages)**
53, rue Beausoleil, Saint-Gabriel-de-Brandon QC J0K 2N0
450-835-2212, Fax: 450-835-1493
biblio013@reseaubibliocqlm.qc.ca
Noëlla Ganley, Responsable

***Saint-Gabriel-de-Rimouski:* Bibliothèque Le Bouquinier**
103, rue Leblanc, Saint-Gabriel-de-Rimouski QC G0K 1M0
418-798-8310, Fax: 418-798-4108
biblio.gabriel@crsbp.net
www.reseaubiblioduquebec.qc.ca
Hélène Thibeault, Responsable

***Saint-Gédéon:* Bibliothèque publique de Saint-Gédéon**
208, Dequen, Saint-Gédéon QC G0W 2P0
418-345-8798
stgedeon@reseaubiblioslsj.qc.ca
www.crsbpslsj.biblio.qc.ca
Carole Gagnon, Responsable

***Saint-Germain:* Bibliothèque de Saint-Germain**
506, rue de la Fabrique, Saint-Germain QC G0L 3G0
418-492-5767
biblio.germain@crsbp.net
www.reseaubiblioduquebec.qc.ca
Simone Lévesque, Responsable

***Saint-Germain-de-Grantham:* Bibliothèque de Saint-Germain-de-Grantham (Le Signet)**
299, rue Notre-Dame, Saint-Germain-de-Grantham QC J0C 1K0
819-395-2644
biblio100@reseaubibliocqlm.qc.ca
www.reseaubiblioduquebec.qc.ca
Louise Gaillard-Simoneau, Responsable
819-395-4463

***Saint-Gervais:* Bibliothèque Faubourg de la Cadie**
36A, rue de la Fabrique est, Saint-Gervais QC G0R 3C0
418-887-3628, Fax: 418-887-3628
bibliger@globetrotter.qc.ca
www.reseaubiblioduquebec.qc.ca/saint-gervais/
Micheline Trudel, Responsable

***Saint-Gilles:* Bibliothèque Le Signet/Saint-Gilles**
1540, rue du Couvent, Saint-Gilles QC G0S 2P0
418-888-5178, Fax: 418-888-5486
bibliosg@globetrotter.qc.ca
www.reseaubiblioduquebec.qc.ca/saint-gilles/
Pascale Bélanger, Responsable

***Saint-Guillaume:* Bibliothèque de Saint-Guillaume**
106, rue Saint-Jean-Baptiste, Saint-Guillaume QC J0C 1L0
819-396-3754, Fax: 819-396-0184
biblio087@reseaubibliocqlm.qc.ca
www.reseaubiblioduquebec.qc.ca
Jocelyne Taillon, Responsable

***Saint-Guy:* Bibliothèque de Saint-Guy**
54, ch Principal, Saint-Guy QC G0K 1W0
418-963-1490
biblio.guy@crsbp.net
Nathalie Belisle, Responsable

***Saint-Henri-de-Lévis:* Bibliothèque La Reliure/Saint-Henri**
123, rue Belleau, Saint-Henri-de-Lévis QC G0R 3E0
418-882-0694, Fax: 418-882-0302
bibhenri@globetrotter.qc.ca
www.reseaubiblioduquebec.qc.ca/saint-henri
Céline Labrecque, Responsable

Saint-Henri-de-Taillon: **Bibliothèque publique de Saint-Henri-de-Taillon**
504, rue Principale, Saint-Henri-de-Taillon QC G0W 2X0
418-347-3243, Fax: 418-347-1138
sthenri@reseaubibliosls j.qc.ca
www.crsbpslsj.biblio.qc.ca/st-henri-de-taillon
Chantale Fortin, Responsable
418-347-1513

Saint-Hippolyte: **Bibliothèque de Saint-Hippolyte**
871, ch des Hauteurs, Saint-Hippolyte QC J8A 1J2
450-224-4137, Fax: 450-224-9927
bibliosthip@bellnet.ca
Élise Chaumont, Responsable

Saint-Honoré-de-Chicoutimi: **Bibliothèque publique de Saint-Honoré**
100, Paul-Aimé Hudon, Saint-Honoré-de-Chicoutimi QC G0V 1L0
418-673-3790
sthonore@qc.aira.com
Hélène Chaput, Coordonnatrice
beauh211156@hotmail.com

Saint-Honoré-de-Témiscouata: **Bibliothèque Les Moussaillons**
6B, rue de l'Église, Saint-Honoré-de-Témiscouata QC G0L 3K0
418-497-3996
biblio.honore@crsbp.net
www.reseaubiblioduquebec.qc.ca
Hélène Paradis, Responsable
418-497-2316

Saint-Hugues: **Bibliothèque municipale de Saint-Hugues**
207, rue Saint-Germain, Saint-Hugues QC J0H 1N0
450-794-2630, Fax: 450-794-2630
hugues@reseaumonteregie.qc.ca
www.reseaubiblioduquebec.qc.ca
Marie Bernier Lavigne, Responsable

Saint-Hyacinthe: **Médiathèque maskoutaine**
2720, rue Dessaulles, Saint-Hyacinthe QC J2S 2V7
450-773-1830, Fax: 450-773-3398
info@mediatheque.qc.ca
www.mediatheque.qc.ca
Yves Tanguay, Directeur
tanguayy@mediatheque.qc.ca
450-773-1830 ext. 23

Saint-Ignace-de-Loyola: **Bibliothèque de Saint-Ignace-de-Loyola**
621, rue de l'Église, Saint-Ignace-de-Loyola QC J0K 2P0
450-836-1831, Fax: 450-836-1400
biblio156@reseaubibliocqlm.qc.ca
www.reseaubiblioduquebec.qc.ca
Andrée Bergeron, Responsable

Saint-Irénée: **Bibliothèque Adolphe-Basile-Routhier**
136, rue Principale, Saint-Irénée QC G0T 1V0
, Fax: 418-452-8221
www.reseaubiblioduquebec.qc.ca/saint-irenee
Micheline Mongrain, Responsable

Saint-Isidore: **Bibliothèque municipale de Saint-Isidore**
5, rue Boyer, Saint-Isidore QC J0L 2A0
450-454-9871
isidore@reseaubibliomonteregie.qc.ca
Ginette Goyette, Responsable

Saint-Isidore: **Bibliothèque municipale La Livrerie/Saint-Isidore**
126, rte Coulombe, Saint-Isidore QC G0S 2S0
418-882-5670, Fax: 418-882-5902
lalivrerie@globetrotter.net
www.reseaubiblioduquebec.qc.ca/saint-isidore
Catherine-Émilie Martel, Responsable

Saint-Jacques: **Bibliothèque municipale Marcel-Dugas**
16, rue Maréchal, Saint-Jacques QC J0K 2R0
450-839-3926, Fax: 450-839-2387
biblio@st-jacques.org
www.st-jacques.org/bibli/index.html
Francine Roy-Gaudet, Responsable

Saint-Jacques-de-Leeds: **Bibliothèque La Ressource**
425, rue Principale, Saint-Jacques-de-Leeds QC G0N 1J0
418-424-3181, Fax: 418-424-0126
biblio.leeds@minfo.net
www.reseaubiblioduquebec.qc.ca/leeds/
Louise Dionne, Responsable

Saint-Jacques-le-Mineur: **Bibliothèque municipale de Saint-Jacques-le-Mineur**
89, rue Principale, Saint-Jacques-le-Mineur QC J0J 1Z0
450-347-1888, Fax: 450-347-5754
jacques@reseaubibliomonteregie.qc.ca
Benoît D'Avignon, Responsable

Saint-Janvier-de-Joly: **Bibliothèque Adrien-Lambert/Saint-Janvier-de-Joly**
729, rue des Loisirs, Saint-Janvier-de-Joly QC G0S 1M0
418-728-2984, Fax: 418-728-2984
adrienlambert1936@hotmail.com
www.reseaubiblioduquebec.qc.ca/joly
Marielle Sylvain, Responsable
marieboufffonsylvain@hotmail.com

Saint-Jean-Baptiste: **Bibliothèque municipale de Saint-Jean-Baptiste**
3090, rue Principale, Saint-Jean-Baptiste QC J0L 2B0
450-467-1786
jean.baptiste@reseaubibliomonteregie.qc.ca
Sylvie Sweeney, Responsable

Saint-Jean-Chrysostome: **Bibliothèques Lévis**
959, rue de l'Hôtel-de-Ville, Saint-Jean-Chrysostome QC G6Z 2N8
418-835-4982, Fax: 418-839-2640
bibliolevis@ville.levis.qc.ca
bibliotheques.ville.levis.qc.ca
Suzanne Rochefort, Chef du service des bibliothèques
srochefort@ville.levis.qc.ca

Saint-Jean-de-Brébeuf: **Bibliothèque Bibliomagie/Saint-Jean-de-Brébeuf**
844, rue de l'Église, Saint-Jean-de-Brébeuf QC G6G 0A1
418-453-2571, Fax: 418-453-2339
www.reseaubiblioduquebec.qc.ca/saint-jean-de-brebeuf
Solange Bolduc, Responsable

Saint-Jean-de-Dieu: **Bibliothèque de Saint-Jean-de-Dieu**
32, rue Principale sud, Saint-Jean-de-Dieu QC G0L 3M0
418-963-3529
biblio.jeandieu@crsbp.net
www.reseaubiblioduquebec.qc.ca
Francine Rioux, Responsable

Saint-Jean-de-Matha: **Bibliothèque de Saint-Jean-de-Matha**
81, rue Sainte-Louise, Saint-Jean-de-Matha QC J0K 2S0
450-886-5855
biblio047@reseaubibliocqlm.qc.ca
www.reseaubiblioduquebec.qc.ca
Nicole Léonard, Responsable
450-886-5855

Saint-Jean-Port-Joli: **Bibliothèque Marie-Bonenfant/Saint-Jean-Port-Joli**
7B, place de l'Église, Saint-Jean-Port-Joli QC G0R 3G0
418-598-3187, Fax: 418-598-3085
biblio.stjean@globetrotter.net
www.reseaubiblioduquebec.qc.ca/joli
Gilberte Picard, Responsable

Saint-Jean-sur-Richelieu: **Bibliothèques municipales de Saint-Jean-sur-Richelieu**
180, rue Laurier, Saint-Jean-sur-Richelieu QC J3B 7B2
450-357-2111, Fax: 450-357-2055
biblio@ville.saint-jean-sur-richelieu.qc.ca
www.ville.saint-jean-sur-richelieu.qc.ca
Camille Bricault, Chef, Division bibliothèques

Saint-Jérôme: **Bibliothèque Marie-Antoinette-Foucher**
101, place du Curé-Labelle, Saint-Jérôme QC J7Z 1X6
450-432-0569, Fax: 450-436-1211
www.ville.saint-jerome.qc.ca/pages/
Chantal Paquin, Bibliothécaire
cpaquin@villesaint-jerome.qc.ca
450-436-1512 ext. 3350

Saint-Joseph-de-Beauce: **Bibliothèque de Saint-Joseph-de-Beauce**
139-100, rue Sainte-Christine, Saint-Joseph-de-Beauce QC G0S 2V0
418-397-6160, Fax: 418-397-5715
bibjoseph@globetrotter.net
www.reseaubiblioduquebec.qc.ca/saint-joseph-de-beauce
Gilberte Doyon, Responsable

Saint-Joseph-de-Kamouraska: **Bibliothèque de Saint-Joseph-de-Kamouraska**
298-B, rue Principale, Saint-Joseph-de-Kamouraska QC G0L 3P0
418-493-2658
biblio.joseph@crsbp.net
www.reseaubiblioduquebec.qc.ca
Anita Toner, Responsable
418-493-2658

Saint-Joseph-de-Lepage: **Bibliothèque de Saint-Joseph-de-Lepage**
70, rue de la Rivière, Saint-Joseph-de-Lepage QC G5H 3N8
418-775-4607, Fax: 418-775-3004
biblio.lepage@crsbp.net
www.reseaubiblioduquebec.qc.ca
Noëlla Dupont, Responsable

Saint-Joseph-du-Lac: **Bibliothèque de Saint-Joseph-du-Lac**
70, Montée du Village, Saint-Joseph-du-Lac QC J0N 1M0
450-623-7833, Fax: 450-623-2889
biblio64@crsbpl.qc.ca
www.reseaubiblioduquebec.qc.ca
Hélène Caron, Responsable
hcaron@ssdl.qc.ca
450-623-1072 ext. 4

Saint-Jude: **Bibliothèque St-Jude**
940, rue de Centre, Saint-Jude QC J0H 1P0
450-792-2164
jude@monteregie.crsbp.qc.ca
Daniele Boulanger, Responsable

Saint-Julien: **Bibliothèque municipale de Saint-Julien**
794, ch Saint-Julien, Saint-Julien QC G0N 1B0
418-423-3410, Fax: 418-423-3410
bibliotheque@st-julien.ca
www.reseaubiblioduquebec.qc.ca/saint-julien
Yolande Poirier, Responsable

Saint-Juste-du-Lac: **Bibliothèque de Saint-Juste-du-Lac**
37, ch Principal, Saint-Juste-du-Lac QC G0L 3R0
418-899-0374
biblio.juste@crsbp.net
Jeanne Benoist, Responsable

Saint-Juste-du-Lac: **Bibliothèque Lots-Renversés**
Route 295, Saint-Juste-du-Lac QC G0L 1V0
418-899-0375
biblio.lotsren@crsbp.net
Leslie Bingham, Responsable

Saint-Justin: **Bibliothèque de Saint-Justin**
1281, rue Gérin, Saint-Justin QC J0K 2V0
819-227-1110, Fax: 819-227-4876
biblio056@reseaubibliocqlm.qc.ca
www.reseaubiblioduquebec.qc.ca
Josianne Messier, Responsable

Saint-Lambert: **Bibliothèque municipale de Saint-Lambert**
490, av Mercille, Saint-Lambert QC J4P 2L5
450-466-3910, Fax: 450-923-6512
bibliotheque@saint-lambert.ca
Guylaine Pellerin, Directrice
guylaine.pellerin@ville.saint-lambert.qc.ca
405-466-3889 ext. poste

Saint-Lazare: **Bibliothèque Biblio-Culture**
116B, rue de la Fabrique, Saint-Lazare QC G0R 3J0
418-883-2551, Fax: 418-883-2551
biblio.st-lazare@globetrotter.net
www.reseaubiblioduquebec.qc.ca/saint-lazare
Raoul Laflamme, Responsable
laflammer@globetrotter.net
418-883-3005

Saint-Léonard-d'Aston: **Bibliothèque de Saint-Léonard-d'Aston (Lucille-M.-Desmarais)**
146, rue des Écoles, Saint-Léonard-d'Aston QC J0C 1M0
819-399-3368
biblio089@reseaubibliocqlm.qc.ca
Sylvie Turmel, Responsable

Saint-Léonard-de-Portneuf: **Bibliothèque Biblio 'Fleur de lin'**
260, rue Pettigrew, Saint-Léonard-de-Portneuf QC G0A 4A0
418-337-3961, Fax: 418-337-6742
bibliofleurdelin@hotmail.com
www.reseaubiblioduquebec.qc.ca/saint-leonard
Ginette Paquet, Responsable

***Saint-Léon-le-Grand:* Bibliothèque de Saint-Léon-le-Grand (Bas-Saint-Laurent)**
241, rue Gendron, Saint-Léon-le-Grand QC G0J 2W0
418-743-2914
biblio.granleon@crsbp.net
www.reseaubiblioduquebec.qc.ca
Lise Fournier, Responsable

***Saint-Léon-le-Grand:* Bibliothèque de Saint-Léon-le-Grand (Mauricie)**
44, rue de la Fabrique, Saint-Léon-le-Grand QC J0K 2W0
819-228-3236, Fax: 819-228-8088
biblio029@reseaubibliocqlm.qc.ca
www.reseaubiblioduquebec.qc.ca
Diane Lavergne, Responsable

***Saint-Liboire:* Bibliothèque municipale de Saint-Liboire**
21, Place Mauriac, Saint-Liboire QC J0H 1R0
450-793-4751
liboire@reseaubibliomonteregie.qc.ca
Julie Girouard, Responsable

***Saint-Liguori:* Bibliothèque de Saint-Liguori**
741, rue Principale, Saint-Liguori QC J0K 2X0
450-753-4446, Fax: 450-753-4638
biblio006@reseaubibliocqlm.qc.ca
www.reseaubiblioduquebec.qc.ca
Jeanne Gagné-Richard, Responsable
450-753-4446

***Saint-Lin-Laurentides:* Bibliothèque de Saint-Lin-Laurentides**
920, 12e av, Saint-Lin-Laurentides QC J5M 2W2
450-439-2486, Fax: 450-439-1525
biblio@saint-lin-laurentides.com
www.reseaubiblioduquebec.qc.ca/saint-lin-laurentides
Jocelyne Dufort, Responsable

***Saint-Louis-de-Blandford:* Bibliothèque de Saint-Louis-de-Blandford**
80, rue Principale, Saint-Louis-de-Blandford QC G0Z 1B0
819-364-7007, Fax: 819-364-2781
biblio116@reseaubibliocqlm.qc.ca
www.reseaubiblioduquebec.qc.ca
Françoise Lafond, Responsable

***Saint-Louis-de-Gonzague:* Bibliothèque municipale de Saint-Louis-de-Gonzague**
140, rue Principale, Saint-Louis-de-Gonzague QC J0S 1T0
450-371-9411, Fax: 450-371-7428
louis.gonzague@reseaubibliomonteregie.qc.ca
www.reseaubiblioduquebec.qc.ca
Marie-Andrée Demers, Responsable

***Saint-Louis-du-Ha!Ha!:* Bibliothèque de Saint-Louis-du-Ha!Ha!**
234, rue Commerciale, Saint-Louis-du-Ha!Ha! QC G0L 3S0
418-854-4031
biblio.louis@crsbp.net
www.reseaubiblioduquebec.qc.ca
Laurette Lavoie, Responsable

***Saint-Luc-de-Bellechasse:* Bibliothèque L'Éveil/Saint-Luc-de-Bellechasse**
115, rue de la Fabrique, Saint-Luc-de-Bellechasse QC G0R 1L0
418-636-2776, Fax: 418-636-2776
bibliotheque@sogetel.net
www.reseaubiblioduquebec.qc.ca/saint-luc
Lisette Bilodeau, Responsable

***Saint-Luc-de-Vincennes:* Bibliothèque de Saint-Luc-de-Vincennes**
660, rue Principale, Saint-Luc-de-Vincennes QC G0X 3K0
819-295-3608, Fax: 819-295-3782
biblio097@reseaubibliocqlm.qc.ca
www.reseaubiblioduquebec.qc.ca
Louise Lemire, Responsable
819-295-3603

***Saint-Ludger-de-Milot:* Bibliothèque publique de Saint-Ludger-de-Milot**
739, Gaudreault, Saint-Ludger-de-Milot QC G0W 2B0
418-373-2489, Fax: 418-373-2554
stludger@reseaubiblioslsj.qc.ca
Johanne Godin, Responsable

***Saint-Malachie:* Bibliothèque J.-A.-Kirouac**
1184, rue Principale, Saint-Malachie QC G0R 3N0
418-642-5127, Fax: 418-642-2231
jakir@globetrotter.qc.ca
www.reseaubibliodequebec.qc.ca/saint-malachie/

Louise Guénette, Responsable

***Saint-Marc-du-Lac-Long:* Bibliothèque Saint-Marc-du-Lac-Long**
14A, rue de l'Église, Saint-Marc-du-Lac-Long QC G0L 1T0
418-893-1075, Fax: 418-893-1339
biblio.laclong@crsbp.net
Jeanne-D'Arc Poliquin, Responsable

***Saint-Marcel-de-Richelieu:* Bibliothèque Saint-Marcel-de-Richelieu**
#2, 1060, rue des Ormes, Saint-Marcel-de-Richelieu QC J0L 1R0
450-787-3140, Fax: 450-794-1140
antoine@monteregie.crsbp.qc.ca
Nicole Beauchamp, Responsable
450-794-2706

***Saint-Marcellin:* Fautoulire**
336, rte 234, Saint-Marcellin QC G0K 1R0
418-798-8164
biblio.marcellin@crsbp.net
www.reseaubiblioduquebec.qc.ca
Mélanie Labbé, Responsable

***Saint-Marc-sur-Richelieu:* Bibliothèque municipale Archambault-Trépanier/Saint-Marc-sur-Richelieu**
102, rue de la Fabrique, Saint-Marc-sur-Richelieu QC J0L 2E0
450-584-2258
marc@reseaubibliomonteregie.qc.ca
www.reseaubiblioduquebec.qc.ca
Nancy Bélanger, Responsable

***Saint-Mathias-sur-Richelieu:* Bibliothèque municipale de Saint-Mathias-sur-Richelieu**
50, rue Lussier, Saint-Mathias-sur-Richelieu QC J3L 6A4
450-447-0679
mathias@reseaubibliomonteregie.qc.ca
www.reseaubiblioduquebec.qc.ca
France Desautels, Responsable

***Saint-Mathieu:* Bibliothèque municipale de Saint-Mathieu**
299, ch Saint-Édouard, Saint-Mathieu QC J0L 2H0
450-659-9528
mathieu@reseaubibliomonteregie.qc.ca
Danielle Routhier, Responsable

***Saint-Mathieu-de-Beloeil:* Bibliothèque municipale Ryane-Provost**
5000, rue des Loisirs, Saint-Mathieu-de-Beloeil QC J3G 2C9
450-467-7490
mathieu.beloeil@reseaubibliomonteregie.qc.ca
www.reseaubiblioduquebec.qc.ca
Claude Monast, Responsable

***Saint-Mathieu-de-Rioux:* Bibliothèque de Saint-Mathieu-de-Rioux**
41, rue de l'Église, Saint-Mathieu-de-Rioux QC G0L 3T0
418-738-3057
biblio.mathieu@crsbp.net
www.reseaubiblioduquebec.qc.ca
Peggy Dufaut, Responsable

***Saint-Mathieu-du-Parc:* Bibliothèque de Saint-Mathieu-du-Parc (Micheline H.- Gélinas)**
600, ch Saint-Marc, Saint-Mathieu-du-Parc QC G0X 1N0
819-532-2345
biblio093@reseaubibliocqlm.qc.ca
www.reseaubiblioduquebec.qc.ca
Suzie Parent, Responsable

***Saint-Maurice:* Bibliothèque de Saint-Maurice**
1380, rue Notre-Dame, Saint-Maurice QC G0X 2X0
819-378-7315
biblio026@reseaubibliocqlm.qc.ca
www.reseaubiblioduquebec.qc.ca
Aline Harnois, Responsable

***Saint-Médard:* Bibliothèque de Saint-Médard**
1, rue Principale est, Saint-Médard QC G0L 3V0
418-963-1588
biblio.medard@crsbp.net
www.reseaubiblioduquebec.qc.ca
Andrée Beaulieu, Responsable
andreeobeaulieu@hotmail.com

***Saint-Michel:* Bibliothèque municipale Claire-Lazure**
440, place Saint-Michel, Saint-Michel QC J0L 2J0
450-454-7995
michel@reseaubibliomonteregie.qc.ca
www.reseaubiblioduquebec.qc.ca
Lucie Longtin, Responsable

***Saint-Michel-de-Bellechasse:* Bibliothèque Benoît-Lacroix**
8, av Saint-Charles, Saint-Michel-de-Bellechasse QC G0R 3S0
418-884-2766, Fax: 418-884-2866
biblistmic@globetrotter.net
www.reseaubiblioduquebec.qc.ca/saint-michel
Gilbert Théberge, Responsable

***Saint-Michel-des-Saints:* Bibliothèque de Saint-Michel-des-Saints (Antonio-Saint-Georges)**
390B, rue Matawin, Saint-Michel-des-Saints QC J0K 3B0
450-833-5471
biblio044@reseaubibliocqlm.qc.ca
www.reseaubiblioduquebec.qc.ca
Cécile Baudouard, Responsable

***Saint-Michel-du-Squatec:* Bibliothèque Alma-Durand**
149, rue St-Joseph, CP 104, Saint-Michel-du-Squatec QC G0L 4H0
418-855-2708, Fax: 418-855-5228
biblio.squatec@crsbp.net
Céline Morin, Responsable

***Saint-Modeste:* Bibliothèque de Saint-Modeste**
312, rue Principale, Saint-Modeste QC G0L 3W0
418-867-2352
biblio.modeste@crsbp.net
www.reseaubiblioduquebec.qc.ca
Solange Chouinard, Responsable

***Saint-Narcisse:* Bibliothèque de Saint-Narcisse (Gérard-Desrosiers)**
509, rue Massicotte, Saint-Narcisse QC G0X 2Y0
418-328-4430, Fax: 418-328-4348
biblio001@reseaubibliocqlm.qc.ca
www.reseaubiblioduquebec.qc.ca
Rose-Alice Lafontaine, Responsable

***Saint-Narcisse-de-Beaurivag:* Bibliothèque municipale de Saint-Narcisse-de-Beaurivage**
510, rue de l'École, Saint-Narcisse-de-Beaurivag QC G0S 1W0
418-475-6464, Fax: 418-475-6880
biblio.st-narcisse@globetrotter.net
www.reseaubiblioduquebec.qc.ca/saint-narcisse
Monique Arlen, Responsable
418-475-6750

***Saint-Nazaire-d'Acton:* Bibliothèque municipale de Saint-Nazaire-d'Acton**
715, rue des Loisirs, Saint-Nazaire-d'Acton QC J0H 1V0
819-392-2090
nazaire@reseaubibliomonteregie.qc.ca
Maryse Pelland, Responsable

***Saint-Nérée:* Bibliothèque Biblio Du Centenaire**
2139, route Principale, Saint-Nérée QC G0R 3V0
418-243-3649, Fax: 418-243-2136
www.reseaubiblioduquebec.qc.ca/saint-neree
Francine Nadeau, Responsable

***Saint-Noël:* Bibliothèque de Saint-Noël**
12, rue Saint-Joseph est, Saint-Noël QC G0J 3A0
418-776-2549
biblio.noel@crsbp.net
www.reseaubiblioduquebec.qc.ca
Diane Leclerc, Responsable

***Saint-Odilon:* Bibliothèque L'Intello/Saint-Odilon-de-Cranbourne**
111, rue de l'Hôtel-de-Ville, Saint-Odilon QC G0S 3A0
418-464-4803, Fax: 418-464-4800
lintello@globetrotter.qc.ca
www.reseaubiblioduquebec.qc.ca/saint-odilon
Mariette Vachon, Responsable
418-464-2463

***Saint-Omer:* Bibliothèque de Saint-Omer**
106B, rte 132 est, Saint-Omer QC G0C 2Z0
418-364-6485
bibliostomer@globetrotter.net
www.reseaubiblioduquebec.qc.ca
Line Arsenault, Responsable

***Saint-Ours:* Bibliothèque municipale de Saint-Ours**
2636, rue de l'Immaculée-Conception, Saint-Ours QC J0G 1P0
450-785-2779
ours@reseaubibliomonteregie.qc.ca
www.reseaubiblioduquebec.qc.ca
Lucie Grenier, Responsable

Saint-Pacôme: **Bibliothèque de Saint-Pacôme**
27, rue Saint-Louis, Saint-Pacôme QC G0L 3X0
418-852-2356
biblio.pacome@crsbp.net
www.reseaubiblioduquebec.qc.ca
Marc Bélanger, Responsable

Saint-Pamphile: **Bibliothèque Marie-Louise-Gagnon/Saint-Pamphile**
3, rue Elgin sud, Saint-Pamphile QC G0R 3X0
418-356-5403, Fax: 418-356-5502
pamphile@globetrotter.net
www.saintpamphile.ca
Micheline Leclerc, Responsable

Saint-Pascal: **Bibliothèque de Saint-Pascal**
470, rue Notre-Dame, Saint-Pascal QC G0L 3Y0
418-492-2312
biblio.pascal@crsbp.net
www.reseaubiblioduquebec.qc.ca
Jeannine Desjardins, Responsable

Saint-Patrice-de-Beaurivage: **Bibliothèque Florence-Guay/Saint-Patrice-de-Beaurivage**
470, du Manoir, Saint-Patrice-de-Beaurivage QC G0S 1B0
418-596-2439, Fax: 418-596-2430
borivage@globetrotter.qc.ca
www.reseaubiblioduquebe.qc.ca/saint-patrice
Claire Béland, Responsable
450-596-3074

Saint-Paul de l'île-aux-Noi: **Bibliothèque municipale Lucile-Langlois-Éthier**
959C, rue Principale, Saint-Paul de l'île-aux-Noi QC J0J 1G0
450-291-5585
paul.ile.noix@reseaubibliomonteregie.qc.ca
www.reseaubiblioduquebec.qc.ca
Roger Langlois, Responsable

Saint-Paul-d'Industrie: **Bibliothèque de Saint-Paul**
18, boul Brassard, Saint-Paul-d'Industrie QC J0K 3E0
450-759-3333, Fax: 450-759-6396
biblio071@reseaubibliocqlm.qc.ca
www.reseaubiblioduquebec.qc.ca
Isabelle Plouffe, Responsable

Saint-Paul-de-la-Croix: **Bibliothèque de Saint-Paul-de-la-Croix**
1-B, rue du Parc, Saint-Paul-de-la-Croix QC G0L 3Z0
418-898-3095, Fax: 418-898-2322
biblio.croix@crsbp.net
www.reseaubiblioduquebec.qc.ca
Johanne Lagacé, Responsable
418-898-2568

Saint-Paulin: **Bibliothèque de Saint-Paulin (Jeannine-Julien)**
3051, rue Bergeron, C.P. 39, Saint-Paulin QC J0K 3G0
819-268-2425, Fax: 819-268-2890
biblio118@reseaubibliocqlm.qc.ca
www.reseaubiblioduquebec.qc.ca
Lucie Marcouiller, Responsable

Saint-Philippe: **Bibliothèque Saint-Philippe/Le Vaisseau d'Or**
2223, rte Édouard VII, Saint-Philippe QC J0L 2K0
450-659-7701, Fax: 450-659-5354
bibliotheque@municipalite.saint-philippe.qc.ca
www.municipalite.saint-philippe.qc.ca
Line Thibodeau, Responsable

Saint-Philippe-de-Néri: **Bibliothèque de Saint-Philippe-de-Néri**
11, rue de l'Église, Saint-Philippe-de-Néri QC G0L 4A0
418-498-3843
biblio.philip@crsbp.net
www.reseaubiblioduquebec.qc.ca
Mariette Dumais, Responsable

Saint-Pie: **Bibliothèque municipale de Saint-Pie**
309, rue Notre-Dame, Saint-Pie QC J0H 1W0
450-772-2332, Fax: 450-772-2332
pie@reseaubibliomonteregie.qc.ca
Danielle Massé, Responsable

Saint-Pie-de-Guire: **Bibliothèque de Saint-Pie-de-Guire**
445C, rue Principal, Saint-Pie-de-Guire QC J0G 1R0
450-784-0232
biblio132@reseaubibliocqlm.qc.ca
www.reseaubiblioduquebec.qc.ca
Sylvie Courchesne, Responsable

Saint-Pierre-de-Broughton: **Bibliothèque Maurice-Couture/Saint-Pierre-de-Broughton**
6, du Couvent, Saint-Pierre-de-Broughton QC G0N 1T0
418-424-3450, Fax: 418-424-0389
biblio.m.couture@minfo.net
www.reseaubiblioduquebec.qc.ca/broughton
Brigitte Routhier, Responsable

Saint-Pierre-de-l'Ile-d'Orl: **Bibliothèque Oscar-Ferland**
515, rte des Prêtres, Saint-Pierre-de-l'Ile-d'Orl QC G0A 4E0
418-828-2962, Fax: 418-828-2855
www.reseaubiblioduquebec.qc.ca/saint-pierre/
Lisette Grégoire, Responsable

Saint-Pierre-les-Becquets: **Bibliothèque de Saint-Pierre-les-Becquets**
108, rue des Loisirs, Saint-Pierre-les-Becquets QC G0X 2Z0
819-263-0797, Fax: 819-263-2622
biblio086@reseaubibliocqlm.qc.ca
Francine Bergeron, Responsable

Saint-Placide: **Bibliothèque de Saint-Placide**
73, rue de l'Église, Saint-Placide QC J0V 2B0
450-258-1780, Fax: 450-258-0364
biblio@municipalite.saint-placide.qc.ca
www.reseaubiblioduquebec.qc.ca
Danielle Le Moëligou, Responsable
450-258-42

Saint-Polycarpe: **Bibliothèque municipale de Saint-Polycarpe**
7, rue Ste-Catherine, Saint-Polycarpe QC J0P 1X0
450-265-3444, Fax: 450-265-3010
polycarpe@reseaubibliomonteregie.qc.ca
www.reseaubiblioduquebec.qc.ca
Suzanne Poirier, Responsable
450-265-3043

Saint-Prime: **Bibliothèque publique de Saint-Prime**
616, rue Principale, Saint-Prime QC G8J 1T4
418-251-4976
stprime@reseaubiblioslsj.qc.ca
Claudette Tremblay, Responsable

Saint-Prosper: **Bibliothèque de Saint-Prosper (Livresque)**
371, rue de l'Église, Saint-Prosper QC G0X 3A0
418-328-4219, Fax: 418-328-4219
biblio012@reseaubibliocqlm.qc.ca
www.reseaubiblioduquebec.qc.ca
Christiane Couture, Responsable

Saint-Raphaël: **Bibliothèque Jeannine-Marquis-Garant**
88, rue du Foyer, Saint-Raphaël QC G0R 4C0
418-243-3437, Fax: 418-243-2605
www.reseaubiblioduquebec.qc.ca/saint-raphael/
René Bouchard, Responsable

Saint-Rémi: **Bibliothèque municipale de Saint-Rémi**
25, Saint-Sauveur, Saint-Rémi QC J0L 2L0
450-454-2418, Fax: 450-454-4083
bibliotheque@ville.saint-remi.qc.ca
Patrick Thibert, Responsable
450-454-9227

Saint-René-de-Matane: **Bibliothèque de Saint-René-de-Matane**
178, av Saint-René, Saint-René-de-Matane QC G0J 3E0
418-224-1339
www.municipalite.st-rene-matane.qc.ca
Paulette Dugas, Responsable
418-224-1339

Saint-Robert: **Bibliothèque municipale de Saint-Robert**
1, Aggée-Pelletier, Saint-Robert QC J0G 1S0
450-782-2562
robert@reseaubibliomonteregie.qc.ca
Mariette Latour, Responsable

Saint-Roch-de-l'Achigan: **Bibliothèque de Saint-Roch-de-l'Achigan**
30, rue Dr Wilfrid-Locat nord, Saint-Roch-de-l'Achigan QC J0K 3H0
450-588-5838, Fax: 450-588-4478
biblio109@reseaubibliocqlm.qc.ca
www.reseaubiblioduquebec.qc.ca
Jocelyne Allard, Responsable

Saint-Roch-de-Mékinac: **Bibliothèque de Saint-Roch-de-Mékinac**
1216, rue Principale, Saint-Roch-de-Mékinac QC G0X 2E0
819-646-5635
biblio033@reseaubibliocqlm.qc.ca
www.reseaubiblioduquebec.qc.ca
Claudia Klaus, Responsable

Saint-Roch-de-Richelieu: **Bibliothèque municipale de Saint-Roch-de-Richelieu**
1111, rue du Parc, Saint-Roch-de-Richelieu QC J0L 2M0
450-785-2755
roch@reseaubibliomonteregie.qc.ca
Hélène Jackson, Responsable

Saint-Roch-des-Aulnaies: **Bibliothèque Bibli-Aulnaies/Saint-Roch-des-Aulnaies**
1028, de la Seigneurie, Saint-Roch-des-Aulnaies QC G0R 4E0
418-354-2566, Fax: 418-354-2059
stroch@globetrotter.qc.ca
www.reseaubiblioduquebec.qc.ca/aulnaies
Louise Filion, Responsable
louloufilion@hotmail.com
418-354-2233

Saint-Rosaire: **Bibliothèque de Saint-Rosaire**
9, rue St-Pierre, Saint-Rosaire QC G0Z 1K0
819-795-4861, Fax: 819-795-4861
biblio088@reseaubibliocqlm.qc.ca
www.reseaubiblioduquebec.qc.ca
Jacques Dubois, Responsable

Saint-Samuel: **Bibliothèque de Saint-Samuel**
143, rue de l'Église, Saint-Samuel QC G0Z 1G0
819-353-1242, Fax: 819-353-1499
biblio137@reseaubibliocqlm.qc.ca
www.reseaubiblioduquebec.qc.ca
Noëlla Grondin, Responsable

Saint-Sauveur: **Bibliothèque de Saint-Sauveur**
33, av de l'Église, Saint-Sauveur QC J0R 1R0
450-227-2669, Fax: 450-227-3362
biblio.st-sauveur@cgocable.ca
www.reseaubiblioduquebec.qc.ca
Claudette St-Jacques, Responsable

Saint-Sébastien: **Bibliothèque municipale de Saint-Sébastien**
595, rue de La Fabrique, Saint-Sébastien QC G0Y 1M0
819-652-2727
biblio092@reseaubiblioestrie.qc.ca
www.st-sebastien.com
Eric Bernier, Responsable

Saint-Sévère: **Bibliothèque de Saint-Sévère (Denise L. Noël)**
47, rue Principale, Saint-Sévère QC G0X 3B0
819-264-5656
biblio119@reseaubibliocqlm.qc.ca
www.reseaubiblioduquebec.qc.ca
Jocelyne Lavigne, Responsable

Saint-Séverin-de-Beauce: **Bibliothèque municipale de Saint-Séverin**
900, rue des Lacs, Saint-Séverin-de-Beauce QC G0N 1V0
418-426-2423, Fax: 418-426-1274
bibcle@oricom.ca
www.reseaubiblioduquebec.qc.ca/saint-severin
Cécile Couture, Responsable

Saint-Siméon: **Bibliothèque municipale de Saint-Siméon**
505A, rue Saint-Laurent, Saint-Siméon QC G0T 1X0
418-638-2691, Fax: 418-638-5145
www.reseaubiblioduquebec.qc.ca/saint-simeon
Lyse Leblond, Responsable

Saint-Siméon-de-Bonaventure: **Bibliothèque de Saint-Siméon**
116, rue Bélanger, Saint-Siméon-de-Bonaventure QC G0C 3A0
418-534-2606, Fax: 418-534-3830
bbostsim@globetrotter.net
www.reseaubiblioduquebec.qc.ca
Huguette Lepage, Responsable
hlepage@globetrotter.net
418-534-3928

Saint-Simon: **Bibliothèque de Saint-Simon**
39, rue de l'Église, Saint-Simon QC G0L 4C0
biblio.simon@crsbp.net
www.reseaubiblioduquebec.qc.ca
France Beauchesne, Responsable
418-738-2517

***Saint-Simon:* Bibliothèque municipale Lise-Bourque-St-Pierre**
46, rue des Loisirs, Saint-Simon QC J0H 1Y0
450-798-2276
simon@reseaubibliomonteregie.qc.ca
Claire Bousquet, Responsable
450-798-2624

***Saint-Stanislas:* Bibliothèque publique de Saint-Stanislas**
955, rue Principale, Saint-Stanislas QC G8M 4W8
418-276-4476
stanisla@reseaubiblioslsj.qc.ca
Line Laprise, Responsable

***Saint-Stanislas-de-Kostka:* Bibliothèque Saint-Stanislas-de-Kostka**
117, rue Centrale, Saint-Stanislas-de-Kostka QC J0S 1W0
450-370-4650
stanislas@monteregie.crsbp.qc.ca
Christiane Blanchard, Responsable

***Saint-Sulpice:* Bibliothèque de Saint-Sulpice**
215, rue des Loisirs, Saint-Sulpice QC J5W 6C9
450-589-7816
biblio133@reseaubibliocqlm.qc.ca
www.reseaubiblioduquebec.qc.ca
Julie Parent, Responsable

***Saint-Sylvère:* Bibliothèque de Saint-Sylvère**
260, rte de l'École, Saint-Sylvère QC G0Z 1H0
819-285-2699, Fax: 819-285-2075
biblio037@reseaubibliocqlm.qc.ca
www.reseaubiblioduquebec.qc.ca
Linda Searles, Responsable

***Saint-Sylvestre:* Bibliothèque municipale de Saint-Sylvestre**
824, rue Principale, Saint-Sylvestre QC G0S 3C0
418-596-2427, Fax: 418-596-2384
sylve@globetrotter.qc.ca
Isabelle Gagnon, Responsable
munisylvestre@globetrotter.net
418-596-3400

***Saint-Télesphore:* Bibliothèque municipale de Saint-Télesphore**
1421, rte 340, Saint-Télesphore QC J0P 1Y0
450-269-2364
telesphore@reseaubibliomonteregie.qc.ca
Lisa Longtin, Responsable

***Saint-Tharcisius:* Bibliothèque de Saint-Tharcisius**
55, rue Principale, Saint-Tharcisius QC G0J 3G0
418-629-4727
biblio.tharci@crsbp.net
www.reseaubiblioduquebec.qc.ca
Maryse Rioux, Responsable

***Saint-Théodore-d-Acton:* Bibliothèque autonome de Saint-Théodore-d'Acton**
1803, rue Principale, Saint-Théodore-d-Acton QC J0H 1Z0
450-546-5643
www.st-theodore.com

***Saint-Thomas-de-Joliette:* Bibliothèque de Saint-Thomas (Jacqueline-Plante)**
#941, 10, rue Principale, Saint-Thomas-de-Joliette QC J0K 3L0
450-759-8173, Fax: 450-759-2530
biblio117@crsbpcqlm.qc.ca
www.reseaubiblioduquebec.qc.ca
Brigitte Brunet, Responsable

***Saint-Thomas-Didyme:* Bibliothèque publique de Saint-Thomas-de-Didyme**
31-1, av du Moulin, Saint-Thomas-Didyme QC G0W 1P0
418-274-4034
thomas@reseaubiblioslsj.qc.ca
Denise Bergeron, Responsable

***Saint-Tite:* Bibliothèque de Saint-Tite (Marielle-Brouillette)**
330, rue du Moulin, Saint-Tite QC G0X 3H0
418-365-6203
biblio017@researubibliocqlm.qc.ca
www.reseaubiblioduquebec.qc.ca
Noëlla Gauthier, Responsable

***Saint-Ubalde:* Bibliothèque Guy-Laviolette**
400, rue de l'Aréna, Saint-Ubalde QC G0A 4L0
418-277-2124, Fax: 418-277-2055
www.reseaubiblioduquebec.qc.ca/saint-ubalde/
Odile Tessier, Responsable

***Saint-Valentin:* Bibliothèque municipale de Saint-Valentin**
790, 4e Ligne, Saint-Valentin QC J0J 2E0
450-291-3948
valentin@reseaubibliomonteregie.qc.ca
www.reseaubiblioduquebec.qc.ca/valentin/
Réjane Hébert Olivier, Responsable

***Saint-Valère:* Bibliothèque de Saint-Valère**
2A, rue du Parc, Saint-Valère QC G0P 1M0
819-353-3464, Fax: 819-353-3465
biblio127@reseaubibliocqlm.qc.ca
www.reseaubiblioduquebec.qc.ca
Hélène Provencher-Hébert, Responsable

***Saint-Valérien:* Bibliothèque de Saint-Valérien**
159, rue Principale, Saint-Valérien QC G0L 4E0
418-736-8170
biblio.valerien@crsbp.net
www.reseaubiblioduquebec.qc.ca
Chantal Paquet, Responsable

***Saint-Vallier:* Bibliothèque Marie-Josephte-Corrivaux**
365, av de l'Église, Saint-Vallier QC G0R 4J0
418-884-3190, Fax: 418-884-2454
biblstva@globetrotter.qc.ca
www.reseaubiblioduquebec.qc.ca/saint-vallier/
Monique Rochefort, Responsable

***Saint-Vianney:* Bibliothèque de Saint-Vianney**
170-B, av Centrale, Saint-Vianney QC G0J 3J0
418-629-4082
biblio.vianney@crsbp.net
Estelle Allaire, Responsable

***Saint-Victor:* Bibliothèque Biblio Luc-Lacourcière**
287, rue Marchand, Saint-Victor QC G0M 2B0
418-588-6689, Fax: 418-588-6855
lacours@globetrotter.qc.ca
www.reseaubiblioduquebec.qc.ca/saint-victor/
Marc Bélanger, Responsable

***Saint-Wenceslas:* Bibliothèque de Saint-Wenceslas**
1240, rue Principale, Saint-Wenceslas QC G0Z 1J0
819-224-4055
biblio073@reseaubibliocqlm.qc.ca
www.reseaubiblioduquebec.qc.ca
Jeanne Champagne, Responsable

***Saint-Zénon:* Bibliothèque de Saint-Zénon (Danièle-Bruneau)**
6191, rue Principale, Saint-Zénon QC J0K 3N0
450-884-0328, Fax: 450-884-5285
biblio048@reseaubibliocqlm.qc.ca
www.reseaubiblioduquebec.qc.ca
Simone L. Boisvert, Responsable

***Saint-Zéphirin-de-Courval:* Bibliothèque de Saint-Zéphirin-de-Courval**
950, rue des Loisirs, Saint-Zéphirin-de-Courval QC J0G 1V0
450-564-2401, Fax: 450-564-2339
biblio092@reseaubibliocqlm.qc.ca
www.reseaubiblioduquebec.qc.ca
Angèle Lefebvre, Responsable

***Saint-Zotique:* Bibliothèque municipale de Saint-Zotique**
1250, rue Principale, Saint-Zotique QC J0P 1Z0
450-267-3689
dg@st-zotique.com
www.st-zotique.com
Ginette Léger, Responsable

***La Sarre:* Bibliothèque municipale Richelieu de La Sarre**
Maison de la culture, 195, rue Principale, La Sarre QC J9Z 1Y3
819-333-2294, Fax: 819-333-2296
www.biblrn.qc.ca/biblls
Lise Gaignard, Directrice

***Sayabec:* Bibliothèque Quilit**
8B, rue Keable, Sayabec QC G0J 3K0
418-536-5431
biblio.sayabec@crsbp.net
www.reseaubiblioduquebec.qc.ca
Thérèse Arsenault, Responsable

***Scott:* Bibliothèque municipale de Scott**
1070, rte Kennedy, Scott QC G0S 3G0
418-387-1837
munscott@globetrotter.net
www.reseaubiblioduquebec.qc.ca/scott
Roger Pigeon, Responsable

***Senneterre:* Bibliothèque de Senneterre**
121, 1e rue Est, Senneterre QC J0Y 2M0
819-737-8829, Fax: 819-737-4215
senneterre@reseaubiblioatnq.qc.ca
www.reseaubiblioduquebec.qc.ca
Denise Dufour, Responsable
819-737-8322

***Sept-Iles:* Bibliothèque Louis-Ange-Santerre**
500, av Jolliet, Sept-Iles QC G4R 2B4
418-964-3355, Fax: 418-964-3353
www.ville.sept-iles.qc.ca
Sylvie Pelletier, Superviseure
sylvie.pelletier@ville.sept-iles.qc.ca

***Shannon:* Bibliothèque municipale de Shannon**
50, rue St-Patrick, Shannon QC G0A 4N0
418-844-1622, Fax: 418-844-2111
biblio@cableshannon.com
www.reseaubiblioduquebec.qc.ca/shannon/
Brigitte Olivier, Responsable

***Shawinigan:* Bibliothèque Fabien-LaRochelle**
550, av de l'Hôtel-de-Ville, Shawinigan QC G9N 6V3
819-536-7218, Fax: 819-536-0808
bibliotheque@ville.shawinigan.qc.ca
www.shawinigan.ca
Charlotte Lecours, Responsable des bibliothèques

***Shawville:* Bibliothèque Shawville/Clarendon/Thorne/ Shawville/Clarendon/Thorne Library**
356, rue Main, Shawville QC J0X 2Y0
819-647-3732, Fax: 819-647-3732
admshawville@crsbpo.qc.ca
www.reseaubiblioduquebec.qc.ca/ShawvilleClarendon
Jennifer Davies, Responsable

***Sherbrooke:* Bibliothèque municipale Éva-Senécal**
450, rue Marquette, Sherbrooke QC J1H 1M4
819-821-5860, Fax: 819-822-6110
bibliotheque@ville.sherbrooke.qc.ca
www.ville.sherbrooke.qc.ca
Linda Travis, Chef, Section bibliothèque
819-821-5862

***Shipshaw:* Bibliothèque de Shipshaw (Rivage)**
3760, rte Saint-Léonard, Shipshaw QC G7P 1H5
418-695-7135, Fax: 418-542-6173
webbiblio@ville.saguenay.qc.ca
www.ville.saguenay.qc.ca
Lyne Racine, Responsable

***Shipshaw:* Bibliothèque de Shipshaw (Rivière)**
4281-A, rue des Pins, Shipshaw QC G7P 1L8
418-542-3982, Fax: 418-542-6231
webbiblio@ville.saguenay.qc.ca
www.ville.saguenay.qc.ca
Ginette Tremblay, Responsable

***Sorel-Tracy:* Bibliothèque municipale de Sorel-Tracy**
3015, Place des loisirs, Sorel-Tracy QC J3R 5S5
450-780-5600
www.ville.sorel-tracy.qc.ca
Guy Desjardins, Régisseur, Culture & Bibliothèque

***Sorel-Tracy:* Bibliothèque municipale de Sorel-Tracy**
145, rue George, Sorel-Tracy QC J3P 1C7
450-780-5600
www.ville.sorel-tracy.qc.ca
Guy Desjardins, Régisseur, Culture & Bibliothèque

***St-Alexandre-de-Kamouraska:* Bibliothèque Saint-Alexandre**
480, av de l'École, St-Alexandre-de-Kamouraska QC G0L 2G0
418-495-3123
biblio.alexi@crsbp.net
Hélène Therrien, Responsable

***Stanbridge East:* Bibliothèque Denise-Larocque-Duhamel/ Denise Larocque Duhamel Library**
12A, rue Maple, Stanbridge East QC J0J 2H0
450-248-4662
stanbridge@reseaubibliomonteregie.qc.ca
Nicole L'Heureux, Responsable

***Standon:* Bibliothèque l'Étincelle**
514B, rue Principale, Standon QC G0R 4L0

418-642-2708, Fax: 418-642-2570
etincel@globetrotter.qc.ca
www.reseaubiblioduquebec.qc.ca/saint-leon
Mario Grenier, Responsable

***Stanstead:* Haskell Free Library Inc.**
1 Church St., Stanstead QC J0B 3E2
819-876-2471, Fax: 802-873-3634
info@haskellopera.org
www.haskellopera.org
Nancy Rumery, Librarian

***St-Barnabé-Nord:* Bibliothèque de Saint-Barnabé**
70, rue Duguay, St-Barnabé-Nord QC G0X 2K0
819-264-2085, Fax: 819-264-2079
biblio027@reseaubibliocqlm.qc.ca
www.reseaubiblioduquebec.qc.ca
Luc Gélinas, Responsable

***St-Boniface-de-Shawinigan:* Bibliothèque de Saint-Boniface**
155, rue Langevin, St-Boniface-de-Shawinigan QC G0X 2L0
819-535-3330, Fax: 819-535-1242
biblio021@reseaubibliocqlm.qc.ca
www.reseaubiblioduquebec.qc.ca
Chantal Gélinas, Responsable

***St-Charles-de-Bellechasse:* Bibliothèque Jacques-Labrie/Saint-Charles-de-Bellechasse**
2829A, av Royale, St-Charles-de-Bellechasse QC G0R 2T0
418-887-6561, Fax: 418-887-6779
biblstch@globetrotter.qc.ca
www.reseaubiblioduquebec.qc.ca/saint-charles
Manon Larochelle, Responsable

***St-David-de-Falardeau:* Bibliothèque publique Saint-David-de-Falardeau**
124, boul St-David, St-David-de-Falardeau QC G0V 1C0
418-673-6395
stdavid@reseaubiblioslsj.qc.ca
www.reseaubiblioduquebec.qc.ca
Francine Allard, Responsable

***St-Dominique-du-Rosaire:* Bibliothèque de St-Dominique-du-Rosaire**
235, rue Principale, St-Dominique-du-Rosaire QC J0Y 2K0
819-727-4144, Fax: 819-727-4344
dominique@reseaubiblioatnq.qc.ca
www.reseaubiblioduquebec.qc.ca
Marcelle Gravelle, Responsable

***St-François-Xavier-de-Viger:* Bibliothèque de Saint-François-Xavier-de-Viger**
125, rue Principale, St-François-Xavier-de-Viger QC G0L 3C0
418-497-2430, Fax: 418-497-2302
biblio.xavier@crsbp.net
www.reseaubiblioduquebec.qc.ca
Diana Morin, Responsable

***St-Jean-de-l'Ile-d'Orléans:* Bibliothèque municipale de Saint-Jean-de-l'Ile-d'Orléans**
10, ch des Côtes, St-Jean-de-l'Ile-d'Orléans QC G0A 3W0
418-829-3336, Fax: 418-829-0997
biblio.vm@sympatico.ca
Françoise Laberge, Responsable

***St-Lambert-Desmeloizes:* Bibliothèque de St-Lambert**
509B, rte du 5e & 8e rang, St-Lambert-Desmeloizes QC J0Z 1V0
819-788-2491, Fax: 819-788-2491
lambert@reseaubiblioatnq.qc.ca
www.reseaubiblioduquebec.qc.ca
Jeanne D'Arc Fluet, Responsable

***St-Laurent-de-l'Ile-d'Orléa:* Bibliothèque David-Gosselin/Saint-Laurent-de-l'Ile-d'Orléans**
#1, 1330, ch Royal, St-Laurent-de-l'Ile-d'Orléa QC G0A 3Z0
418-828-2529, Fax: 418-828-2170
bibliosaintlaurentiledorleans@gmail.com
www.reseaubiblioduquebec.qc.ca/saint-laurent
Guy Delisle, Responsable
guy.delisle2@gmail.com

***St-Marcel-de-L'Islet:* Bibliothèque municipale de Saint-Marcel**
46, rue Taché est, St-Marcel-de-L'Islet QC G0R 3R0
418-356-2691, Fax: 418-356-2820
Rita Avoine, Responsable

***St-Nazaire-de-Buckland:* Bibliothèque municipale de St-Nazaire**
PR, St-Nazaire-de-Buckland QC G0R 3T0
418-642-2945
René Blais, Responsable

***St-Nazaire-du-Lac-St-Jean:* Bibliothèque publique de St-Nazaire**
220, rue Principale, St-Nazaire-du-Lac-St-Jean QC G0W 2V0
418-662-1422
nazaire@reseaubiblioslsj.qc.ca
Peggy Vézina, Responsable

***St-Norbert-d'Arthabaska:* Bibliothèque de Norbertville**
42, rue Landry, St-Norbert-d'Arthabaska QC G0P 1B0
819-260-0560
biblio147@reseaubibliocqlm.qc.ca
www.reseaubiblioduquebec.qc.ca
Suzie Leblanc, Responsable

***Stoneham:* Bibliothèque Jean-Luc-Grondin**
325, ch du Hibou, Stoneham QC G0A 4P0
418-848-3399, Fax: 418-848-1748
jlgrondin@sympatico.ca
www.reseaubiblioduquebec.qc.ca/stoneham/
Gaétane St-Laurent, Responsable

***St-Pierre-de-la-Riv.-du-Sud:* Bibliothèque municipale de Saint-Pierre-de-la-Rivière-du-Sud**
620, rue Principale, St-Pierre-de-la-Riv.-du-Sud QC G0R 4B0
418-248-8031, Fax: 418-241-1477
biblstpi@globetrotter.qc.ca
www.reseaubiblioduquebec.qc.ca/saint-pierre-r-s
Georgette Roy, Responsable
groy45@globetrotter.net
418-248-2319

***St-Stanislas-de-Champlain:* Bibliothèque Émile-Bordeleau/Saint-Stanislas**
33A, rue du Pont, St-Stanislas-de-Champlain QC G0X 3E0
418-328-4556, Fax: 418-328-4121
biblio002@reseaubibliocqlm.qc.ca
www.reseaubiblioduquebec.qc.ca
Ghislaine B. Asselin, Responsable

***Sutton:* Bibliothèque municipale de Sutton**
19, rue Highland, Sutton QC J0E 2K0
450-538-5843, Fax: 450-538-4286
sutton@reseaubibliomonteregie.qc.ca
Lisa Charbonneau, Responsable

***Tadoussac:* Bibliothèque municipale de Tadoussac**
162, des Jésuites, Tadoussac QC G0T 2A0
418-235-4446, Fax: 418-235-4433
ville@tadoussac.com
www.tadoussac.com
Johanne Hovington, Responsable
418-235-4512

***Taschereau:* Bibliothèque de Taschereau**
50, rue Morin, Taschereau QC J0Z 3N0
819-796-2219
taschereau@reseaubiblioatnq.qc.ca
www.reseaubiblioduquebec.qc.ca
Hélène Pelletier, Responsable

***Témiscamingue:* Bibliothèque de Témiscamingue**
40, rue Boucher, Témiscamingue QC J0Z 3R0
819-627-9778, Fax: 819-627-3019
biblioTEM@hotmail.com
Suzelle Plante, Responsable

***Terrasse-Vaudreuil:* Bibliothèque Terrasse-Vaudreuil**
74, 7e av, Terrasse-Vaudreuil QC J7V 3M9
514-425-0430
terrasse.vaudreuil@monteregie.crsbp.qc.ca
Huguette Noël, Responsable

***Terrebonne:* Bibliothèque publique de Terrebonne**
3424, rue Camus, Terrebonne QC J6W 4N7
450-470-0933
www.ville.terrebonne.qc.ca/loisirs_bibliotheques-publiques.php
Céline Paquette, Coordonnatrice aux bibliothèques
celine.paquette@ville.terrebonne.qc.ca

***Tête-à-la-Baleine:* Bibliothèque municipale de Tête-à-la-Baleine**
Centre Communautaire, Municipalité de la Côte-Nord-du-Golfe-du-Saint-Laurent, Tête-à-la-Baleine QC G0G 2W0
418-787-2244, Fax: 418-787-2241
bibliotb@globetrotter.net
Olive Marcoux, Responsable

***Thetford Mines:* Bibliothèque publique de Black Lake**
Polyvalente de Black Lake, 499, St-Désiré, Thetford Mines QC G6H 1L7
418-423-4291, Fax: 418-423-4909
Carmen Poulin, Agente de bureau

***Thurso:* Bibliothèque de Thurso/Lochaber-Partie-Ouest/Lochaber**
341A, rue Victoria, Thurso QC J0X 3B0
819-985-3479, Fax: 819-386-0134
admthurso@crsbpo.qc.ca
www.reseaubiblioduquebec.qc.ca/Thurso
Lysette Boyer, Responsable

***Tingwick:* Bibliothèque de Tingwick**
1266, rue St-Joseph, Tingwick QC J0A 1L0
819-359-3225, Fax: 819-359-2233
biblio083@reseaubibliocqlm.qc.ca
www.reseaubiblioduquebec.qc.ca
Lyse Brochu, Responsable

***Tourville:* Bibliothèque municipale de Tourville**
946, Principale, Tourville QC G0R 4M0
418-359-2106, Fax: 418-359-3671
municipal.tourville@globetrotter.net
Ghislaine Legros, Responsable
418-359-2192

***Très-Saint-Rédempteur:* Bibliothèque municipale de Très-Saint-Rédempteur**
769, rte Principale, Très-Saint-Rédempteur QC J0P 1P0
450-451-5203
redempteur@reseaubibliomonteregie.qc.ca
Carolle Lalonde, Responsable

***La Trinité-des-Monts:* Bibliothèque de La Trinité-des-Monts**
12, rue Principale ouest, La Trinité-des-Monts QC G0K 1B0
418-779-2272
biblio.trinite@crsbp.net
www.reseaubiblioduquebec.qc.ca
Léonie Morin, Responsable

***Trois-Pistoles:* Bibliothèque Anne-Marie-D'Amours**
145, rue de l'Aréna, Trois-Pistoles QC G0L 4K0
418-851-2374, Fax: 418-851-3567
biblio.pistoles@crsbp.net
www.reseaubiblioduquebec.qc.ca
Karen Dionne, Directrice
k.dionne@ville-trois-pistoles.ca

***Trois-Rives:* Bibliothèque de Saint-Joseph-de-Mékinac**
258, rue St-Joseph, Trois-Rives QC G0X 2C0
819-646-5686, Fax: 819-646-5686
biblio034@reseaubibliocqlm.qc.ca
www.reseaubiblioduquebec.qc.ca
Georgette Doucet, Responsable

***Trois-Rivières:* Bibliothèques de Trois-Rivières**
1425, place de l'Hôtel-de-Ville, Trois-Rivières QC G9A 5L9
819-372-4615
bibliotheques@v3r.net
www.biblio.v3r.net
Michel Lacoursière, Chef de service, Bibliothèques de Trois-Rivières
mlacoursiere@v3r.net
819-372-4645

***La Tuque:* Bibliothèque municipale de la Tuque**
575, rue St-Eugène, La Tuque QC G9X 2T5
819-523-3100, Fax: 819-523-4487
bibliotheque@ville.latuque.qc.ca
Alain Michaud, Bibliothécaire

***Upton:* Bibliothèque municipale d'Upton**
784, rue Saint-Éphrem, Upton QC J0H 2E0
450-549-4537
Francine Savoie, Responsable
450—54-9-45

***Val-Alain:* Bibliothèque L'Hiboucou**
1198, rue de l'Église, Val-Alain QC G0S 3H0
418-744-3313, Fax: 418-744-3222
hiboucou@globetrotter.qc.ca
www.reseaubiblioduquebec.qc.ca/val-alain/
Karine Fleury, Responsable

***Val-Barrette:* Bibliothèque de Val-Barrette**
135, rue St-Joseph, Val-Barrette QC J0W 1Y0
819-585-3131, Fax: 819-585-4915
val-barrette@sympatico.ca
www.crsbpl.qc.ca/bibliotheques/Val-Barrette.html

Nicole Thériault, Responsable
ntheriault001@hotmail.com
819-585-2490

Val-Brillant: Bibliothèque Val-Brillant
11, rue Saint-Pierre ouest, Val-Brillant QC G0J 3L0
418-742-3711
biblio.brillant@crsbp.net
Adrienne Aubut, Responsable

Valcourt: Bibliothèque publique Yvonne L. Bombardier
1002, rue J.A. Bombardier, Valcourt QC J0E 2L0
450-532-2250, Fax: 450-532-5807
bylb@fjab.qc.ca
Karine Corbeil, Responsable
k.corbeil@fjab.qc.ca

Val-d'Espoir: Bibliothèque de Val-d'Espoir
1240, 5e Rang est, Val-d'Espoir QC G0C 3G0
bbovesp@globetrotter.qc.ca
www.reseaubiblioduquebec.qc.ca
Lorraine Dallaire, Responsable

Val-d'Or: Bibliothèque municipale de Val-d'Or
600, 7e rue, Val-d'Or QC J9P 3P3
819-824-2666, Fax: 819-825-3062
bibliotheque@ville.valdor.qc.ca
www.ville.valdor.qc.ca
Olivier Barrette, Responsable
barretto@ville.valdor.qc.ca

Val-David: Bibliothèque de Val-David
1355, rue de l'Académie, Val-David QC J0T 2N0
819-322-2900, Fax: 819-322-1307
bibliotheque@valdavid.com
www.reseaubiblioduquebec.qc.ca
Michel Usal, Responsable

Val-des-Bois: Bibliothèque de Val-des-Bois/Bowman
593, rte 309, Val-des-Bois QC J0X 3C0
819-454-2280, Fax: 819-454-2211
admvaldesbois@crsbpo.qc.ca
www.reseaubiblioduquebec.qc.ca/Val-des-Bois
Denise Dubois, Responsable

Val-des-Monts: Bibliothèque de Perkins (Val-des-Monts)
17, ch du Manoir, Val-des-Monts QC J8N 7E8
819-671-1476, Fax: 819-457-4141
admperkins@crsbpo.qc.ca
www.reseaubiblioduquebec.qc.ca/Perkins
Denise Cécyre, Responsable

Val-des-Monts: Bibliothèque de Poltimore/Denholm (Val-des-Monts)
2720, rte Principale, Val-des-Monts QC J8N 3B6
819-457-4467, Fax: 819-457-4141
bibliopoltimore@crsbpo.qc.ca
www.reseaubiblioduquebec.qc.ca/Poltimore
Gabriel Ewen, Responsable

Val-des-Monts: Bibliothèque de Saint-Pierre-de-Wakefield (Val-des-Monts)
24, ch du Parc, Val-des-Monts QC J8N 4H8
819-457-1911, Fax: 819-457-9113
admstpierre@crsbpo.qc.ca
www.reseaubiblioduquebec.qc.ca
Colette Prud'Homme, Responsable

Val-Morin: Bibliothèque Francine Paquette
6160, rue Morin, Val-Morin QC J0T 2R0
819-324-5672
valmorin@crsbpl.qc.ca
www.reseaubiblioduquebec.qc.ca
Jacqueline Leonard, Responsable

Val-Paradis: Bibliothèque de Val-Paradis
1865-A, ch des Rangs 1 et 10, Val-Paradis QC J0Z 3S0
819-941-2046, Fax: 819-941-2485
paradis@reseaubiblioatnq.qc.ca
www.reseaubiblioduquebec.qc.ca
Renée Bégin, Responsable

Val-Saint-Gilles: Bibliothèque de Val-Saint-Gilles
801, rue Principale, Val-Saint-Gilles QC J0Z 3T0
819-333-5676, Fax: 819-333-3116
gilles@reseaubiblioatnq.qc.ca
www.reseaubiblioduquebec.qc.ca
Nicole Richer, Responsable

Varennes: Bibliothèque Jacques-Lemoyne-de-Sainte-Marie
2221, boul René-Gaultier, Varennes QC J3X 1E3
450-652-3949
m.lamoureux@ville.varennes.qc.ca
www.ville.varennes.qc.ca/biblio/
Michèle Lamoureux, Bibliothécaire

Vaudreuil-Dorion: Bibliothèque municipale de Vaudreuil-Dorion
51, rue Jeannotte, Vaudreuil-Dorion QC J7V 6E6
450-455-5588, Fax: 450-455-5653
biblio@ville.vaudreuil-dorion.qc.ca
www.ville.vaudreuil-dorion.qc.ca
Michelle Dupuy, Directrice, Arts et Culture

Vendée: Bibliothèque de Vendée
1816, ch du Village, Vendée QC J0T 2T0
819-681-3372
vendee@crsbpl.qc.ca
www.reseaubiblioduquebec.qc.ca
Jeannine Dallaire, Responsable

Verchères: Bibliothèque municipale-scolaire Dansereau-Larose
36, rue Dalpé, Verchères QC J0L 2R0
450-583-3309, Fax: 450-583-3637
vercheres@reseaubibliomonteregie.qc.ca
Sylvie Bissonnette, Responsable

Victoriaville: Bibliothèque Charles-Édouard-Mailhot
2, rue de l'Ermitage, Victoriaville QC G6P 6T2
819-758-8441, Fax: 819-758-9432
www.bibliomcq.qc.ca/victoriaville
Louise Grondines, Directrice
louise.grondines@ville.victoriaville.qc.ca

Villebois: Bibliothèque de Villebois
3889, rue de l'Église, Villebois QC J0Z 3V0
819-941-2684, Fax: 819-941-2685
villebois@reseaubiblioatnq.qc.ca
www.reseaubiblioduquebec.qc.ca
Marie Vézina, Responsable

Ville-Marie: Bibliothèque Ville-Marie 'La Bouquine'
50, rue Notre-Dame de Lourdes, Ville-Marie QC J9V 1X9
819-629-2881
villemarie@reseaubiblioatnq.qc.ca
www.reseaubiblioatnq.qc.ca/villemarie/
Cécile Boily, Responsable

Wakefield: Wakefield Library/ Bibliothèque de Wakefield (La Pêche)
20 Valley Dr., Wakefield QC J0X 3G0
819-459-3266, Fax: 819-459-8832
bibliwakefield@cyberus.ca
www.bibliowakefieldlibrary.ca
Sue Graham, Coordinator

Warwick: Bibliothèque de Warwick (P.-Rodolphe-Baril)
181, rue St-Louis, Warwick QC J0A 1M0
819-358-4325, Fax: 819-358-4326
bibliowarwick@cablevision.com
www.reseaubiblioduquebec.qc.ca
France Gendron, Responsable
819-358-4325

Waterloo: Bibliothèque publique de Waterloo/ Waterloo Public Library
650, rue de la Cour, Waterloo QC J0E 2N0
450-539-2268
biblio@cacwaterloo.qc.ca
Gisèle Dupuis, Responsable

Wemotaci: Bibliothèque de Wemotaci
CP 222, Wemotaci QC G0X 3R0
819-666-2232, Fax: 819-666-2233
biblio064@reseaubibliocqlm.qc.ca
www.reseaubiblioduquebec.qc.ca
Yvette Niquay, Responsable

Wickham: Bibliothèque de Wickham
893, rue Moreau, Wickham QC J0C 1S0
819-398-6878, Fax: 819-398-7166
biblio154@reseaubibliocqlm.qc.ca
www.reseaubiblioduquebec.qc.ca
Pierrette Courchesne, Responsable

Windsor: Bibliothèque municipale Patrick-Dignan de Windsor
52, rue St-Georges, Windsor QC J1S 1J5
819-845-7115, Fax: 819-845-5516
bibliwin@abacom.com
www.bibliotheque.windsor.qc.ca

Yamachiche: Bibliothèque de Yamachiche (J.-Alide-Pellerin)
440, rue Sainte-Anne, Yamachiche QC G0X 3L0
819-296-3580, Fax: 819-296-3542
biblio020@reseaubibliocqlm.qc.ca
www.reseaubiblioduquebec.qc.ca
Hélène Larose, Responsable

Archives

Alma: Société d'histoire du Lac-Saint-Jean
1671, Du Pont, Alma QC G8B 5G2
418-668-2606, Fax: 418-668-5851
info@shlsj.org
www.sagamie.org/shlsj/
Gaston Martel, Archiviste

Amos: Société d'histoire d'Amos
222, 1e av est, Amos QC J9T 1H3
819-732-6070, Fax: 819-732-3242
societe.histoire@cableamos.com
www.societehistoireamos.com
Pierrette Blais, Archiviste

Baie-Comeau: Société historique de la Côte-Nord
9, av Marquette, Baie-Comeau QC G4Z 1K4
418-296-8228, Fax: 418-294-4187
shcn@globetrotter.net
Danielle Saucier, Archiviste

Baie-Comeau: Ville de Baie-Comeau
19, av Marquette, Baie-Comeau QC G4Z 1K5
418-296-8108, Fax: 418-296-3759
souellet@ville.baie-comeau.qc.ca
Sylvain Ouellet, Greffier
souellet@ville.baie-comeau.qc.ca

Cap-de-la-Madeleine: Sanctuaire Notre-Dame du Cap
626, rue Notre-Dame, Cap-de-la-Madeleine QC G8T 4G9
819-374-2441, Fax: 819-374-2441
André Boucher, Responsable

Chambly: Société d'histoire de la Seigneurie de Chambly
2445, rue Bourgogne, Chambly QC J3L 2A5
450-658-2666
shsc@societehistoirechambly.org
Paul-Henri Hudon, 1er vice-président
Régis Guérin, Archiviste régional

Chicoutimi: Centre de Saguenay-Lac-St-Jean
#C103-930, rue Jacques Cartier est, Chicoutimi QC G7H 7K9
418-698-3516, Fax: 418-698-3758, 800-363-9028
anq.chicoutimi@banq.qc.ca

Chicoutimi: Evêché de Chicoutimi
602, rue Racine est, Chicoutimi QC G7H 1V1
418-543-0783, Fax: 418-543-2141
diocese.chicoutimi@videotron.net
Marie B. Demers, Chancelière
dmarieberthedio@hotmail.com
418-543-0783 ext. 252

Chicoutimi: Séminaire de Chicoutimi
679, rue Chabanel, Chicoutimi QC G7H 1Z7
418-543-8645
seminairedechicoutimi@hotmail.com
Clément Jacques Simard, Archiviste

Chicoutimi: Société historique du Saguenay
930, rue Jacques Cartier est, Chicoutimi QC G7H 7K9
418-549-2805
shs@cybernaute.com
www.shistoriquesaguenay.com
Louise Bouchard, Directrice générale

Gaspé: Centre d'archives de la Gaspésie/Musée de la Gaspésie
80, boul Gaspé, Gaspé QC G4X 1A9
418-368-1534, Fax: 418-368-1535
archives@museedelagaspesie.ca
www.museedelagaspesie.ca/cag/french/index.htm
Carlos Suich, Directeur général
direction.musee@globetrotter.net
418-368-1534

Gatineau: Archives municipales de la Ville de Gatineau
855, boul de la Gappe, Gatineau QC J8T 8H9

819-243-2329, Fax: 819-243-2341
archives@ville.gatineau.qc.ca
www.ville.gatineau.qc.ca/archives/
Bernard Savoie, Responsable, Chef, Section gestion des documents et des archives
Hélène Cadieux, Archiviste régionale

Gatineau: Centre de l'Outaouais
855, boul de la Gappe, Gatineau QC J8T 8H9
819-568-8798, Fax: 819-568-5933
anq.gatineau@banq.qc.ca
Brian Beaven, Contact
Brian.Beaven@lac-bac.gc.ca

Gatineau: Eastern Ontario Chapter (EOC)
550, boul de la Cité, Gatineau QC J8T 0A7
819-934-7333, Fax: 819-934-7333
Brian.Beaven@lac-bac.gc.ca

Gatineau: Western Québec School Board
170, rue Principale, Gatineau QC J9H 6K1
819-864-2336, Fax: 819-684-1328, 800-363-9111
wqsb@wqsb.qc.ca
www.wqsb.qc.ca
Ann Bilodeau, Contact

Granby: Société d'histoire de la Haute-Yamaska
135, rue Principale, Granby QC J2G 2V1
450-372-4500
info@shhy.org
www.shhy.org
Richard Racine, Responsable des archives

Jonquière: La Commission scolaire de la Jonquière
3644, rue Saint-Jules, Jonquière QC G7X 2K9
418-542-7551, Fax: 418-542-1505
sgeneral@csjonquiere.qc.ca
Christian St-Gelais, Secrétaire général
Christine Otis, Responsable
christine.otis@cjonquiere.qc.ca

Jonquière: Service de gestion des documents et des archives
2505, rue St-Hubert, Jonquière QC G7X 7W2
418-547-2191, Fax: 418-547-6965
christine.otis@cjonqiere.qc.ca

Knowlton: Brome County Historical Society/ Société historie du comté de Brome
130 Lakeside, Knowlton QC J0E 1V0
450-243-6782
bchs@endirect.qc.ca
Marion L. Phelps, Archivist

Lac-aux-Sables: Société d'histoire de Lac-aux-Sables et d'Hervey-Jonction
40, rue Bourassa, Lac-aux-Sables QC G0X 1M0
418-336-2918
shlashj@hotmail.com
www.rabaska.com/histoire/lacauxsables.htm
Annie Gauthier, Responsable
anik3@globetrotter.net

Lac-Etchemin: Société du patrimoine de Sainte-Justine-de-Langevin
212E, 2e av, Lac-Etchemin QC G0R 1S0
418-625-1231, Fax: 418-625-5980
etchemin@eccetera.com
Ghislain Royer, Archiviste
geobec@belin.qc.ca
418-625-1231

Lachine: Musée de Lachine
1, ch du Musée, Lachine QC H8S 4L9
514-634-3478, Fax: 514-637-6784
museedelachine@lachine.ca
www.lachine.ville.montreal.qc.ca/musee

Lac-Mégantic: Société d'histoire et du patrimoine de la région de Mégantic
5086, rue Frontenac, Lac-Mégantic QC G6B 1H3
819-583-0876, Fax: 819-583-0878
bibliomegantic@hotmail.com
www.bibliomegantic.qc.ca
Julie Bourque, Directrice
directeur@bibliotheque.lac-megantic.qc.ca

Laval: Frères des écoles chrétiennes, Montréal
300, ch du Bord-de-l'Eau, Laval QC H7X 1S9
450-689-4151, Fax: 450-689-6260
archives@delasalle.qc.ca
Louis-Marie Côté, Archiviste
archives@delasalle.qc.ca

Laval: Société d'histoire et de généalogie de l'Ile Jésus
4290, boul Samson, Laval QC H7W 2G9
450-681-9096, Fax: 450-686-8270
shgij@bellnet.ca
www.genealogie.org/club/shgij
Nicole Boyer, Directrice générale

Lennoxville: Lennoxville-Ascot Historical & Museum Society
9 Speid St., Lennoxville QC J1M 1Z3
819-564-0409, Fax: 819-564-8951
lrider@uplands.ca
www.uplands.ca/eng/lenn-ascot.html
Lillian Rider, Head of Archives
Sophie Morel, Contact

Lennoxville: Montréal & Ottawa Conference Archives - Quebec-Sherbrooke Presbytery (Eastern Townships)
c/o Archives, Eastern Townships Research Centre,, Bishop's University, Lennoxville QC J1M 1Z7
819-822-9600, Fax: 819-822-9661
etrc2@ubishops.ca
www.united-church.ca/archives/mo/eastern.shtm

Longueuil: Soeurs des Saints Noms de Jésus et de Marie, Longueuil
80, rue Saint-Charles est, Longueuil QC J4H 1A9
450-651-8104, Fax: 450-651-8636
archivessnjm@videotron.ca
Yvonne Painchaud, Archiviste

Magog: Société d'histoire du Lac Memphrémagog
525, Verchères, Magog QC J1X 3K9
memphre@cgocable.ca
www.memphre.com
Jacques Boisvert, Président

Montréal: Archevêché de Montréal
2000, rue Sherbrooke ouest, Montréal QC H3H 1G4
514-931-7311, Fax: 514-931-3432
chancellerie@diocesemontreal.org
www.diocesemontreal.org
Mgr. Michel Parent, Archiviste
awalhin@diocesemontreal.org

Montréal: Archives de Montréal
#108R, 275, rue Notre-Dame est, Montréal QC H2Y 1C6
514-872-1173, Fax: 514-872-3475
consultation_archives@ville.montreal.qc.ca
www.ville.montreal.qc.ca/archives
Denys Chouinard, Chef de section des archives
dchouinard@ville.montreal.qc.ca
514-872-3496

Montréal: Archives provinciales des Capucins et Bibliothèque franciscaine provinciale des Capucins
3650, boul de la Rousselière, Montréal QC H1A 2X9
514-642-5391, Fax: 514-642-5033
franceguilbert@hotmail.com
Godefroy-C. Dévost, Bibliothécaire-Archiviste
514-642-5391 ext. 345

Montréal: Bank of Montreal
105, rue Saint-Jacques, 1e étage, Montréal QC H2Y 1L6
514-877-6810, Fax: 514-877-7341
yolaine.toussaint@bmo.com
Yolaine Toussaint, Archivist
Robert Desaulniers, Archivist

Montréal: Canadian Centre for Architecture Archives
1920, rue Baile, Montréal QC H3H 2S6
514-939-7011, Fax: 514-939-7020
ref@cca.qc.ca
www.cca.qc.ca

Montréal: Canadian Jewish Congress/ Congrès Juif Canadien
1590, av Docteur Penfield, Montréal QC H3G 1C5
514-931-7531, Fax: 514-931-0548
archives@cjccc.ca
www.cjccc.ca/national_archives
Janice Rosen, Archives Director
archives@cjccc.ca
Bob Kennell, Manager, Heritage Marketing

Montréal: Canadian Pacific Archives/ Archives chemin de fer Canadien Pacifique
910, rue Peel, Montréal QC H3C 3E4
514-395-5132, Fax: 514-395-5135
archives@cpr.ca
www.cprheritage.com
Christiane Huot, Directrice
huot.christiane@uqam.ca

Montréal: Centre de documentation (gestion)
Pavillion Hubert-Aquin, local A-R175, 400, rue St-Catherine Est, Montréal QC H2X 3J8
514-987-6136, Fax: 514-987-8487
Jean-François Chartrand, Bibliothécaire
jean-francois.chartrand@banq.qc.ca
514-873-3065

Montréal: Centre de Montréal, Laval, Laurentides, Lanaudière, Montérégie
535, av Viger est, Montréal QC H2L 2P3
514-873-6000, Fax: 514-873-2980
anq.montreal@mcc.gouv.qc.ca
Daniel Picot, Directeur

Montréal: Centre de recherche de l'Oratoire Saint-Joseph
3800, ch Queen Mary, Montréal QC H3V 1H6
514-733-8211, Fax: 514-733-9735
crdosj@iquebec.com

Montréal: Concordia University Archives
#1015, Hall Bldg., 1455, boul de Maisonneuve ouest, Montréal QC H3G 1M8
514-848-2424, Fax: 514-848-2857
nancy.marrelli@concordia.ca
archives3.concordia.ca
Nancy Marrelli, Director of Archives
nancy.marrelli@concordia.ca
514-848-2424 ext. 7776

Montréal: Congrégation de Notre-Dame de Montréal
2330, rue Sherbrooke ouest, Montréal QC H3H 1G8
514-931-5891, Fax: 514-931-2915
cndarchives@cnd-m.com
Richard Virr, Diocesan Archivist
archives@montreal.anglican.ca
514-843-6577

Montréal: Diocese of Montréal, Archives
1444, av Union, Montréal QC H3A 2B8
514-843-6577, Fax: 514-843-6344
archives@montreal.anglican.ca
montreal.anglican.ca
Claude Minotto, Directeur
claude.minotto@umontreal.ca
514-343-6022

Montréal: Division des Archives
Université de Montréal - Pavillon Roger-Gaudry, #615, 2900, boul Édouard-Montpetit, Montréal QC H3T 1J4
514-343-6023, Fax: 514-343-6577
archives@archiv.umontreal.ca
www.archiv.umontreal.ca

Montréal: Frères de St Gabriel, Province de Montréal
1601, boul Gouin est, Montréal QC H2C 1C2
514-387-7337, Fax: 514-387-0735
fsgarchives@bellnet.ca
André Forget, Archiviste
Stephanie L. Sykes, Director

Montréal: Historical Collection/ Le Service de la documentation historique
6055 Monkland Ave., Montréal QC H4A 1H3
514-870-5214, Fax: 514-484-4429

Montréal: McCord Museum
690, rue Sherbrooke ouest, Montréal QC H3A 1E9
514-398-7100, Fax: 514-398-5045
francois.cartier@mccord.mcgill.ca
www.musee-mccord.qc.ca
Nicole Vallières, Director, Collection Management
514-398-7100 ext. 282
Johanne Pelletier, University Archivist
johanne.pelletier@mcgill.ca

Montréal: McGill University Archives
3459, rue McTavish, Montréal QC H3A 1Y1
514-398-3772, Fax: 514-398-8456
johanne.pelletier@mcgill.ca
www.archives.mcgill.ca
Beverly Anderson-Levine, Conference Archivist

Montréal: Montréal & Ottawa Conference Archives - Montréal, Lauren & Ottawa Presbyteries
c/o Centre de Montréal, Archives nationales du, Québec, 535, av Viger est, Montréal QC H2L 2P3
514-873-6000, Fax: 514-873-2980
archives.mo@istar.ca
www.united-church.ca/archives/mo/montreal.shtm

***Montréal:* Montréal Holocaust Memorial Centre/ Centre commémoratif de l'holocauste à Montréal**
5151, ch Côte Sainte-Catherine, Montréal QC H3W 1M6
514-345-2605, Fax: 514-344-2651
info@mhmc.ca
www.mhmc.ca
Bill Surkis, Executive Director
Anne-Marie Zeppetelli, Archiviste des collections
azeppetelli@macm.org

***Montréal:* Musée d'art contemporain de Montréal Archives des collections**
185, rue Sainte-Catherine ouest, Montréal QC H2X 3X5
514-847-6267, Fax: 514-874-6293
azepetelli@macm.org

***Montréal:* Oblats de Marie Immaculée, Montréal**
3456, av du Musée, Montréal QC H3G 2C7
514-844-1924, Fax: 514-285-2248
arcomi@videotron.ca
Jean-Paul Demers, Archiviste

***Montréal:* Oratoire St-Joseph**
3800, ch Queen-Mary, Montréal QC H3V 1H6
514-733-8211, Fax: 514-733-5269
recherche@saint-joseph.org
Daniel Picot, Directeur du centre de recherche et documentation OSJ
514-733-8211 ext. 2331

***Montréal:* Pères de Ste-Croix, Montréal**
4994, ch Côte-des-Neiges, Montréal QC H3V 1A4
514-735-1526, Fax: 514-735-7813
archivescsc@perescsc-qc.com
Hélène Fortier, Archiviste
514-735-1526 ext. 420

***Montréal:* Pères Dominicains, Montréal**
2715, ch Côte Ste-Catherine, Montréal QC H3T 1B6
514-341-2244, Fax: 514-341-3233
archives@opmontreal.net
Luc Aubin, Archiviste provincial

***Montréal:* Port de Montréal**
Édifice Port de Montréal Aile, 1, Cité du, Havre, Montréal QC H3C 3R5
514-283-3098, Fax: 514-283-6981
duguayd@port-montreal.com
www.port-montreal.com
Denise Duguay, Archiviste/Superviseur, Gestion des documents
duguayd@port-montreal.com
514-283-7009

***Montréal:* Séminaire de Saint-Sulpice de Montréal**
116, rue Notre-Dame ouest, Montréal QC H2Y 1T2
514-849-6561, Fax: 514-286-9021
Rolland Litalien, p.s.s, Responsable

***Montréal:* Soeurs Grises de Montréal**
138, rue Saint-Pierre, Montréal QC H2Y 2L7
514-842-9411, Fax: 514-842-0142
mmyarch1@csgm.qc.ca
Suzanne Morin, Responsable des archives

***Montréal:* The Gazette (Montréal)**
200, 1010, rue Ste-Catherine ouest, Montréal QC H3B 5L1
514-987-2412, Fax: 514-987-2433
library@thegazette.canwest.com
www.canada.com/montreal/montrealgazette
Michael Porritt, Library Administrator
mporritt@thegazette.canwest.com

***Montréal:* Vidéographe inc**
#504, 460, rue Sainte-Catherine ouest, Montréal QC H3B 1A7
514-866-4727, Fax: 514-866-4725
info@videographe.qc.ca
www.videographe.qc.ca

***Nicolet:* Les Soeurs de l'Assomption de la Sainte-Vierge**
251, rue Saint-Jean Baptiste, Nicolet QC J3T 1X9
819-293-2011, Fax: 819-293-8315
archives@sasv.ca
Nathallie Savard, Bibliotechnicienne
archives@sasv.ca

***Nicolet:* Séminaire de Nicolet**
#110, 900, boul Louis-Fréchette, Nicolet QC J3T 1V5
819-293-4838, Fax: 819-293-4543
seminairedenicolet@sogetel.net
Marie Pelletier, Archiviste

***Oka:* Société d'histoire d'Oka**
2017, ch d'Oka, Oka QC J0N 1E0
450-479-8556, Fax: 450-479-8556
Pierre Bernard, Responsable, Documentation
prbernard@videotron.ca

***Oka:* Tsi Ronterihwanonhnha ne Kanienkeha/ Kanehsatake Resource Centre**
407 St Michel, Oka QC J0N 1E0
450-479-1651, Fax: 450-479-8587
konokwe@generation.net
www.schoolnet.ca/aboriginal/oka/index-e.html
Hilda Nicholas, Director

***Outremont:* Fondation Lionel-Groulx**
#257, 261, av Bloomfield, Outremont QC H2V 3R6
514-271-4759, Fax: 514-271-6369
crlq@cam.org
Robert Boily, Directeur général

***Pierrefonds:* Montréal Arrondissement Pierrefonds / Senneville**
13665, boul Pierrefonds, Pierrefonds QC H9A 2Z4
514-624-1124, Fax: 514-624-1300
aallaire@pierrefond-senneville.qc.ca
Anne-Marie Allaire, Archiviste
aallaire@pierrefond-senneville.qc.ca
514-624-1011

***La Pocatière:* Evêché de Sainte-Anne-de-la-Pocatière**
#1200, 4, av Painchaud, La Pocatière QC G0R 1Z0
418-856-1811, Fax: 418-856-5863
diocesesap@bellnet.ca
Céline Hudon, Archiviste
819-856-1811 ext. 131

***La Pocatière:* Société historique de la Côte-du-Sud**
100, 4e av Painchaud, La Pocatière QC G0R 1Z0
418-856-2104, Fax: 418-856-2104
archsud@bellnet.ca
www.shcds.org
François Taillon, Directeur, centre des archives

***La Prairie:* Archives des Frères de l'Instruction chrétienne**
870, ch de Saint-Jean, La Prairie QC J5R 2L5
450-659-1922, Fax: 450-659-3717
archivesfic@mail.com
Jean Laprotte, Responsable
jlaprotte@mail.com

***La Prairie:* Société d'histoire de La Prairie de la Magdeleine**
249, rue Sainte-Marie, La Prairie QC J5R 1G1
514-659-1393, Fax: 514-569-1393
histoire@laprairieshlm.com
Edith Gagnon, secrétaire-coordonnatrice

***Québec:* Archives des Augustines du Monastère de l'Hôpital Général de Québec**
260, boul Langelier, Québec QC G1K 5N1
418-692-0461, Fax: 418-692-2668
denisrobitaille@augustines.ca
www.augustines.ca
Colette Huit, Responsable
Danielle Aubin, Directrice
416-643-2158

***Québec:* Archives du Séminaire de Québec**
9, rue de l'Université, Québec QC G1R 5K1
418-643-2158, Fax: 418-692-5206, 866-710-8031
archives@mcq.org
www.mcq.org

***Québec:* Centrale des syndicats du Québec**
#100, 320, rue St-Joseph est, Québec QC G1K 9E7
418-649-8888, Fax: 418-649-8800
documentation@csq.qc.net
www.csq.qc.net
François Gagnon, Conseiller
gagnon.francois@csq.qc.net
Guy Dinel, Chef, Division des archives
guy.dinel@sg.ulaval.ca
418-656-3428

***Québec:* Division des Archives**
#5489, Pavillon Jean-Charles Bonenfant, Québec QC G1K 7P4
418-656-3722, Fax: 418-656-3826
division.archives@sg.ulaval.ca
www.archives.ulaval.ca

***Québec:* Église catholique de Québec**
1073, boul René-Lévesque ouest, Québec QC G1S 4R5
418-688-1211, Fax: 418-688-1399
diocese@diocesequebec.qc.ca
Abbé Armand Gagné, Directeur
Danielle Aubin, Directrice

***Québec:* Fonds Ancien, Bibliothèque du Séminaire de Québec**
9, rue de l'Université, Québec QC G1R 5K1
418-643-2158, Fax: 418-692-5206, 866-710-8031
archives@mcq.org
www.mcq.org

***Québec:* Les Archives de la Ville de Québec**
350, rue St-Joseph est, 4e étage, Québec QC G1K 3B2
418-641-6214
greffearchives@ville.quebec.qc.ca
Jacques Dorais, Directeur de la Division du service au public et des archives

***Québec:* Monastère des Augustines de l'Hôtel-Dieu de Québec**
75, rue des Remparts, Québec QC G1R 3R9
418-692-0461, Fax: 418-692-2668
www.augustines.ca
Claire Gagnon, Archiviste

***Québec:* Musée de la Civilisation**
16, rue de la Barricade, Québec QC G1K 8W9
418-643-2158, Fax: 418-646-8779, 866-710-8031
documentation@mcq.org
www.mcq.org
Danielle Aubin, Responsable

***Québec:* Musée du Royal 22e Régiment/ Museum of the Royal 22e Régiment**
La Citadelle, Québec QC G1R 4V7
418-694-2800, Fax: 418-694-2853
information@lacitadelle.qc.ca
www.lacitadelle.qc.ca
Jocelyne Milot, Directrice du musée
information@lacitadell.qc.ca
418-694-2800 ext. 2840

***Québec:* Pères Eudistes**
6125, av 1 est, Québec QC G1H 2V9
418-626-6494, Fax: 418-628-8774
cjmeudes@sympatico.ca
www.eudistes.org/archives.htm
André Samson, Responsable
cjmeudes@sympatico.ca
418-626-6494

***Québec:* Religieux de St-Vincent-de-Paul (Canada)**
2555, ch Ste-Foy, Québec QC G1V 1T8
418-650-3441, Fax: 418-650-5459
noel.b@relsv.qc.ca
www.relsv.qc.ca
Noël Béland, Archiviste
noel.b@relsv.qc.ca

***Québec:* Société d'histoire de Sainte-Foy**
CP 8586, Québec QC G1V 4N5
418-654-4275
Michel Germain, Vice-Président
418-653-3215

***Québec:* Soeurs de Saint-Joseph-de-Saint-Vallier, Québec**
560, ch Sainte-Foy, Québec QC G1S 2J6
418-681-7361, Fax: 418-683-4440
archives.st-joseph@sympatico.ca
Marie-Ange Boily, Archiviste

***Québec:* Soeurs Servantes du Saint-Coeur-de-Marie, Beauport**
37, rue des Cascades, Québec QC G1E 2K1
418-661-3766, Fax: 418-661-3766

***Québec:* Soeurs Servantes du Saint-Coeur-de-Marie, Québec**
598, 8e av, Québec QC G1J 3L7
418-529-0672, Fax: 418-529-0332
Madeleine Lamothe, Archiviste

***Québec:* Soeurs Ursulines de Québec**
2, rue du Parloir, Québec QC G1R 4M5
418-692-2523, Fax: 418-692-1356
archurs.qc@bellnet.ca
Marie Marchand, Responsable, Archives
archurs.qc@bellnet.com
418-695-2523 ext. 254

Repentigny: **Commission scolaire des Affluents, Affaires corporatives et gestion de l'information**
80, rue Jean-Baptiste-Meilleur, Repentigny QC J6A 6C5
450-492-9400, Fax: 450-492-3721
alain.proulx@sg.csaffluents.qc.ca
www.csaffluents.qc.ca
Jacques Dufour, Secrétaire général et directeur des communications
Robert Marcil, Responsable

Rigaud: **Archives Collège Bourget**
65, rue St-Pierre, Rigaud QC J0P 1P0
450-451-0815, Fax: 450-451-4171

Rimouski: **Archevêché de Rimouski**
CP 730, Rimouski QC G5L 7C7
418-723-3320, Fax: 418-722-8978
Sylvain Gosselin, Archiviste
418-723-3320

Rimouski: **Bibliothèque**
#J-330, 300, Allée des Ursulines, Rimouski QC G5L 3A1
418-723-1986, Fax: 418-724-1621
Pierre_Collins@uqar.uquebec.ca
Donald O'Farrell, Archiviste

Rimouski: **Centre du Bas St-Laurent, Gaspésie-Iles-de-la-Madeleine**
Édifice Louis-Joseph-Moreault, 337, rue Moreault, Rimouski QC G5L 1P4
418-727-3500, Fax: 418-727-3739
anq.rimouski@banq.qc.ca
www.banq.qc.ca

Rivière-du-Loup: **Commission scolaire de Kamouraska - Rivière du Loup**
464, rue Lafontaine, Rivière-du-Loup QC G5R 3Z5
418-868-2422, Fax: 418-867-1704
charesig@oskamloup.qc.ca
Ghislaine Charest, Agente d'administration à la gestion documentaire
charesig@oskamloup.qc.ca
Marthe Begin, Technicienne en documentation
Marthe.Begin@banq.qc.ca

Rouyn-Noranda: **Centre d'Abitibi-Témiscamingue et Nord-du-Québec**
27, rue du Terminus ouest, Rouyn-Noranda QC J9X 2P3
819-763-3484, Fax: 819-763-3480
anq.rouyn@banq.qc.ca

Sainte-Agathe-des-Monts: **Commission scolaire des Laurentides**
13, rue Sainte-Antoine, Sainte-Agathe-des-Monts QC J8C 2C3
819-326-0333, Fax: 819-326-2121
archives@cslaurentides.qc.ca
www.cslaurentides.qc.ca
André Bouchard, Directeur Général
boucharda@cslaurentides.qc.ca
819-326-0333 ext. 2004

Sainte-Anne-de-Beaupré: **Pères rédemptoristes, Sainte-Anne-de Beaupré**
10018, av Royale, Sainte-Anne-de-Beaupré QC G0A 3C0
418-827-3781, Fax: 418-827-8227
Samuel Baillargeon, Archiviste

Saint-Hyacinthe: **Centre d'histoire de Saint-Hyacinthe**
650, rue Girouard est, Saint-Hyacinthe QC J2S 2W2
450-774-0203, Fax: 450-774-7101
infos@chsth.com
Jean-Noël Dion, Archiviste

Saint-Jean-sur-Richelieu: **Société d'histoire du Haut-Richelieu**
203, rue Jacques Cartier nord, CP 212, Saint-Jean-sur-Richelieu QC J3B 6Z4
450-358-5220
shhr@qc.aira.com
www.genealogie.org
Nicole Poulin, Responsable

Saint-Jérome: **Commission scolaire de la Rivière-du-Nord**
995, rue Labelle, Saint-Jérome QC J7Z 5N7
450-436-5040
tremblayr@csrdn.qc.ca
Rémi Tremblay, Responsable

Saint-Jérome: **La Compagnie de Jésus**
175, boul des Hauteurs, Saint-Jérome QC J7Z 5E7
450-438-3593, Fax: 450-438-6617
jesuitebibliostj@videotron.ca
Andre Gendron, Bibliothécaire

Saint-Joseph-de-Beauce: **Société du patrimoine des Beaucerons**
#400, 139, rue Sainte-Christine, Saint-Joseph-de-Beauce QC G0S 2V0
418-397-6379, Fax: 418-397-6379
beaucero@globetrotter.qc.ca
www.culture-quebec.qc.ca/patrimoine-beauce
Daniel Carrier, Directeur général

Saint-Laurent: **Arrondissement de Saint-Laurent**
777, boul Marcel Laurin, Saint-Laurent QC H4M 2M7
514-855-6000, Fax: 514-855-4121
chevrier.josee@ville.saint-laurent.qc.ca
Josée Chevrier, Coordonnatrice, Gestion de documents
chevrier.josee@ville.saint-laurent.qc.ca

Saint-Laurent: **Soeurs de Sainte-Croix, Saint-Laurent**
Pavillon Saint-Joseph, 900, ch. Côté Vertu, Saint-Laurent QC H4L 4T9
514-747-6132
Suzanne Gratton, Archiviste

Sept-Iles: **Centre de la Côte-Nord**
#190-2, 700, boul Laure, Sept-Iles QC G4R 1Y1
418-964-8434, Fax: 418-964-8500
anq.sept-iles@mcc.gouv.qc.ca

Shawinigan: **Commission scolaire de l'Énergie**
2072, rue Gignac, Shawinigan QC G9N 6V7
819-539-6971, Fax: 819-539-7797, 888-711-0013
abadeaux@csenergie.qc.ca
www.csenergie.qc.ca
Aline Badeaux, Responsable

Sherbrooke: **Archevêché de Sherbrooke**
130, rue de la Cathédrale, Sherbrooke QC J1H 4M1
819-563-9934, Fax: 819-562-0125
bibliotheque@diocesedesherbrooke.org
Roger Roy, Vicaire général
vicgeneral@diocesedessherbrooke.org
Gilles Durand, Archivist
gilles.durand@mcc.gouv.qc.ca

Sherbrooke: **Centre de l'Estrie**
#401, 225, rue Frontenac, Sherbrooke QC J1H 1K1
819-820-3010, Fax: 819-820-3146
anq.sherbrooke@mcc.gouv.qc.ca

Sherbrooke: **Commission scolaire de la Région-de-Sherbrooke**
2955, boul de l'Université, Sherbrooke QC J1K 2Y3
819-822-5540, Fax: 819-822-5530
www.csrs.qc.ca
Diane Boivin, Analyste en gestion documentaire
819-843-9266
Hélène Liard, Archiviste
helene.liard@societehistoire.com

Sherbrooke: **Département des archives**
275, rue Dufferin, Sherbrooke QC J1H 4M5
819-821-5406, Fax: 819-821-5417
societehistoire@societehistoire.com
shs.ville.sherbrooke.qc.ca
James Sweeny, Archivist
jsweeny@ubishops.ca
819-822-9600 ext. 2567

Sherbrooke: **Diocese of Quebec, Archives**
Library, Bishop's University, 2600, rue College, Sherbrooke QC J1M 0C8
819-822-9600, Fax: 819-822-9661
jsweeny@ubishops.ca
www.ubishops.ca/library_info/lib-old.htm
Julie Roy, Archivist

Sherbrooke: **Montréal & Ottawa Conference Archives - Quebec-Sherbrooke Presbytery**
c/o Centre régional de l'Estrie, Archives, nationales du Québec, #401, 225, rue Frontenac, Sherbrooke QC J1H 1K1
819-820-3010, Fax: 819-820-3146
anq.sherbrooke@banq.qc.cq
www.united-church.ca/archives/mo/quebec.shtm
Huguette Pinard-Lachance, Directrice
archive@seminaire-sherbrooke.qc.ca
819-563-2050 ext. 262

Sherbrooke: **Service des archives du séminaire de Sherbrooke**
195, rue Marquette, Sherbrooke QC J1H 1L6
819-563-2050, Fax: 819-562-8261
archive@seminaire-sherbrooke.qc.ca

Sherbrooke: **Société d'histoire de Sherbrooke**
275, rue Dufferin, Sherbrooke QC J1H 4M5
819-821-5406, Fax: 819-821-5417
societehistoire@societehistoire.com
Hélène Liard, Archiviste
helene.liard@societehistoire.com
819-821-5406

Sorel-Tracy: **Société historique Pierre-de-Saurel inc**
6-A, rue St-Pierre, Sorel-Tracy QC J3P 3S2
450-780-5739, Fax: 450-746-1655
shps@loginnovation.com
Catherine Objois, Directrice

Stanbridge East: **Missisquoi Historical Society**
2, rue River, Stanbridge East QC J0J 2H0
450-248-3153, Fax: 450-248-0420
jantle@museemissisquoi.ca
www.museemissisquoi.ca
Judy Antle, Archivist
jantle@museemissisquoi.ca
450-248-3153

Stanstead: **Stanstead Historical Society/ Société historique de Stanstead**
535, rue Dufferin, Stanstead QC J0B 3E0
819-876-7322, Fax: 819-876-7936
archives@colbycurtis.ca
www.colbycurtis.ca/eng/archives.html
Aileen Desbarats, Archivist
info@colbycurtis.ca

Thetford Mines: **Société des archives historiques de la région de l'Amiante**
671, boul Frontenac ouest, Thetford Mines QC G6G 1N1
418-338-8591, Fax: 418-338-3498
sahra@ccgepth.qc.ca
www.sahra.qc.ca
Stéphane Hamann, Directeur - Archiviste

Trois-Rivières: **Centre de la Mauricie et Centre-du-Québec**
#208, 225, rue des Forges, Trois-Rivières QC G9A 2G7
819-371-6015, Fax: 819-371-6158
anq.trois-rivieres@banq.qc.ca

Trois-Rivières: **Evêché de Trois-Rivières**
362, Bonaventure, Trois-Rivières QC G9A 2B3
819-374-7022, Fax: 819-375-6382
archives@evechetr.org
Denise Maltais, Archiviste diocésaine
819-378-8321
Suzanne Girard, Directrice des archives
suzanne.girard@ssj.qc.ca
819-376-4459 ext. 73

Trois-Rivières: **Service des archives**
858, rue Laviolette, Trois-Rivières QC G9A 5S3
819-376-4459, Fax: 819-378-0607
astr@ssj.qc.ca
Etienne Audet, Responsable
etienne.audet@uqtr.ca
819-376-5005 ext. 2254

Trois-Rivières: **Service des archives et des collections**
3351, boul des Forges, Trois-Rivières QC G8Z 1T7
819-376-5030
mario.audet@uqtr.ca

Trois-Rivières: **Soeurs Ursulines, Trois-Rivières**
784, rue des Ursulines, Trois-Rivières QC G9A 5B5
819-375-6039, Fax: 819-691-0490
urstr.archives@cgocable.ca
Claude Jutras, Archiviste responsable

Trois-Rivières: **Ville de Trois-Rivières**
370, rue des Forges, Trois-Rivières QC G9A 2H1
819-372-4647, Fax: 819-374-9872
archives@v3r.net
Céline Lamy, Archiviste

Val-d'Or: **Société d'histoire de Val d'Or**
600, 7e rue, Val-d'Or QC J9P 3P3
819-825-6352, Fax: 819-825-3062
Louiselle Alain, Présidente

Victoriaville: **Commission scolaire des Bois-Francs**
40, boul Bois-Francs, Victoriaville QC G6P 6S5
819-758-6453, Fax: 819-758-5827
mprovencher@csbf.qc.ca

Michael Provencher, Secrétaire général

Westmount: **Avataq Cultural Institute**
#400, 215 Redfern Ave., Westmount QC H3Z 3L5
514-989-9031, Fax: 514-989-8789, 800-361-5029
avataq@avataq.qc.ca
www.avataq.qc.ca
Christelle Cuillert, Archivist
christelle@avataq.qc.ca
514-989-9031 ext. 241

Saskatchewan

Regional Systems

Chinook Regional Library
1240 Chaplin St. West, Swift Current SK S9H 0G8
306-773-3186, Fax: 306-773-0434
chinook@chinook.lib.sk.ca
www.chinooklibrary.ca/chinook.htm
Michael J. Keaschuk, Director

Lakeland Library Region (Saskatchewan)
1302 - 100th St., North Battleford SK S9A 0V8
306-445-6108, Fax: 306-445-5717
info@lakeland.lib.sk.ca
www.lakeland.lib.sk.ca
Annmarie Hillson, Regional Librarian

Palliser Regional Library
366 Coteau St. West, Moose Jaw SK S6H 5C9
306-693-3669, Fax: 306-692-5657
webmaster@palliser.lib.sk.ca
www.palliserlibrary.ca
Janet Smith, Director
jsmith@palliser.lib.sk.ca

Parkland Regional Library (Saskatchewan)
PO Box 5049, Yorkton SK S3N 3Z4
306-783-7022, Fax: 306-782-2844
office@parkland.lib.sk.ca
www.parkland.lib.sk.ca
Deirdre Crichton, Regional Library Director
dcrichton@parkland.lib.sk.ca

Southeast Regional LIbrary
49 Bison Ave., Weyburn SK S4H 0H9
306-848-3100, Fax: 306-842-2665
library.srl@southeast.lib.sk.ca
www.southeast.lib.sk.ca
Allan Johnson, CEO & Library Director

Wapiti Regional Library
145 - 12th St. East, Prince Albert SK S6V 1B7
306-764-0712, Fax: 306-922-1516
wapiti@panet.pa.sk.ca
www.panet.pa.sk.ca
Kevin Phillip, Acting Regional Director

Wheatland Regional Library
806 Duchess St., Saskatoon SK S7K 0R3
306-652-5077, Fax: 306-931-7611
admin@wheatland.sk.ca
www.wheatland.sk.ca
Rena Bartsch, Director
rbartsch@wheatland.sk.ca
306-652-4182

Public Libraries

Abbey: **Abbey Branch Library**
133 Main St., PO Box 185, Abbey SK S0N 0A0
306-689-2202
abbey@chinook.lib.sk.ca
www.chinooklibrary.ca/abbey.htm
Marilyn Turgeon, Librarian

Aberdeen: **Aberdeen Library**
Aberdeen Recreational Complex, 2nd Fl., Aberdeen SK S0K 0A0
306-253-4349
aberdeen.library@wheatland.sk.ca
www.wheatland.sk.ca/branches_aberdeen.html

Admiral: **Admiral Branch Library**
PO Box 152, Admiral SK S0N 0B0
306-297-4040
www.chinooklibrary.ca/admiral.htm
Shannon Wallis, Librarian

Air Ronge: **Senator Myles Venne School Public Library**
Box 268, Air Ronge SK S0J 3G0
306-425-2478, Fax: 306-425-2815
emirasty.slk@pnls.sk.ca
Edna Mirasty, Librarian
smvs09@sk.sympatico.ca
306-425-2478

Alameda: **Alameda Branch Library**
200 - 5th St., Alameda SK S0C 0A0
306-489-2066
alameda@southeast.lib.sk.ca
hip.southeast.lib.sk.ca/Southeast/Docs/alameda.html
Dee Anne Schiestel, Chair

Allan: **Allan Library**
216 Main St., Allan SK S0K 0C0
306-257-4222
allan.library@sasktel.net
www.wheatland.sk.ca
Sandra Wilson, Library Contact

Alvena: **Alvena Public Library**
Business / Commerce Complex, 101 Main St., Alvena SK S0K 0E0
306-943-2003
alvcirc@panet.pa.sk.ca
www.panet.pa.sk.ca
Donna Leschinski, Chair

Arborfield: **Arborfield Public Library**
Town Office, 201 Main St., PO Box 223, Arborfield SK S0E 0A0
306-276-9330
arbcirc@panet.pa.sk.ca
Irene Lindsay, Chair

Archerwill: **Archerwill Public Library**
1st Ave., Archerwill SK S0E 0B0
306-323-2128
arccirc@panet.pa.sk.ca
Genene Kimber-Zinger, Chair

Arcola: **Arcola Branch Library**
127 Main St., Arcola SK S0C 0G0
306-455-2321
arcola@southeast.lib.sk.ca
hip.southeast.lib.sk.ca/Southeast/Docs/arcola.html
Shauna Forester, Librarian

Assiniboia: **Assiniboia & District Public Library**
201 - 3rd Ave. West, Assiniboia SK S0H 0B0
306-642-3631, Fax: 306-642-5622
assiniboia@palliser.lib.sk.ca
www.palliserlibrary.ca
Carol Munro, Branch Librarian

Avonlea: **Avonlea Branch Library**
201 Main St. West, Avonlea SK S0H 0C0
306-868-2076, Fax: 306-868-2221
avonlea@palliser.lib.sk.ca
www.palliserlibrary.ca
Sheryl Ursu, Librarian

Balgonie: **Balgonie Branch Library**
129 Railway St., Balgonie SK S0G 0E0
306-771-2332
balgonie@southeast.lib.sk.ca
Dawn Grad, Librarian

Battleford: **Battleford Branch Library**
201 - 22nd St., Battleford SK S0M 0E0
306-937-2646, Fax: 306-937-6631
battleford.lib@lakeland.lib.sk.ca
www.lakeland.lib.sk.ca
Rita Kuntz, Branch Librarian

Beauval: **Beauval Public Library**
PO Bag 9000, Beauval SK S0M 0G0
306-288-2022, Fax: 306-288-2202
sb@pnls.lib.sk.ca
Carol Edguist, Librarian

Beechy: **Beechy Library**
PO Box 154, Beechy SK S0L 0C0
306-859-2032
beechy.library@sasktel.net
Lois Meaden, Branch Library Staff Contact

Bengough: **Bengough Branch Library**
301 Main St., Bengough SK S0C 0K0
306-268-2022
bengough@southeast.lib.sk.ca
www.southeast.lib.sk.ca/branches.html
Fay Adam, Branch Librarian

Bethune: **Bethune Branch Library**
Community Hall, 524 East St., Bethune SK S0G 0H0
306-638-3046, Fax: 306-638-3102
bethune@palliser.lib.sk.ca
www.palliserlibrary.ca
Robbie Curtis, Librarian

Bienfait: **Bienfait Branch Library**
414 Main St., Bienfait SK S0C 0M0
306-388-2995, Fax: 306-388-2223
bienfait@southeast.lib.sk.ca
www.southeast.lib.sk.ca
Bonnie Gibson, Librarian

Big River: **Big River Branch Library**
PO Box 154, Big River SK S0J 0E0
306-469-2152
bigcirc@panet.pa.sk.ca
www.panet.pa.sk.ca
Joan Holbrook, Librarian

Biggar: **Biggar Lionel A. Jones Library**
202 - 3rd Ave. West, Biggar SK S0K 0M0
306-948-3911
biggar.library@wheatland.sk.ca
Darlene Stainbrook, Community Librarian

Birch Hills: **Birch Hills Branch Library**
PO Box 396, Birch Hills SK S0J 0G0
306-749-3281
bircirc@panet.pa.sk.ca
Joanne Bzdel, Branch Librarian

Bjorkdale: **Bjorkdale Public Library**
PO Box 210, Bjorkdale SK S0E 0E0
306-886-2119
bjocirc@panet.pa.sk.ca
Janice Willerton, Chair

Blaine Lake: **Blaine Lake Branch Library**
General Delivery, Blaine Lake SK S0J 0J0
306-497-3130
blacirc@panet.pa.sk.ca
Lorraine Kouznitsoff, Chair

Borden: **Borden Library**
303 - 1st Ave., Borden SK S0K 0N0
306-997-2220
borden.lib@lakeland.llb.sk.ca
Diane Sylvester, Branch Librarian

Briercrest: **Briercrest Branch Library**
Community Center, Main St. PO Box 97, Briercrest SK S0H 0K0
306-799-2137
briercrest@palliser.lib.sk.ca
www.palliserlibrary.ca
Eleanor Anderson, Chair

Broadview: **Broadview Branch Library**
515 Main St., PO Box 590, Broadview SK S0G 0K0
306-696-2414
broadview@southeast.lib.sk.ca
www.southeast.lib.sk.ca
Sandra Charbonneau, Chair

Bruno: **Bruno Branch Library**
522 Main St., Bruno SK S0K 0S0
306-369-2353
bruno.library@wheatland.sk.ca
Donna Olchowski, Branch Head

Buffalo Narrows: **Wisewood Public Library**
PO Box 309, Buffalo Narrows SK S0M 0J0
306-235-4240, Fax: 306-235-4452
wisewoodlibrary@NLSD113.net
Darlene Petit, Librarian

Burstall: **Burstall Branch Library**
PO Box 309, Burstall SK S0N 0H0
306-679-2177
burstall@chinook.lib.sk.ca
www.chinooklibrary.ca/burstall.htm
Janet Albrecht, Chair

Cabri: **Cabri Branch Library**
Town Hall Complex, Centre St., PO Box 18, Cabri SK S0N 0J0
306-587-2911
cabri.chinook@sasktel.net
www.chinooklibrary.ca/cabri.htm
Liz Gossard, Chair

Candle Lake: **Candle Lake Public Library- Paperback Deposit**
PO Box 136, Candle Lake SK S0J 3E0
306-929-3121
Donna Hawrylak, Librarian

Canwood: **Canwood Branch Library**
PO Box 23, Canwood SK S0J 0K0
306-468-2501
cancirc@panet.pa.sk.ca
Doris Wideen, Chair

Carlyle: **Carlyle Branch Library**
119 Souris Ave. West, Carlyle SK S0C 0R0
306-453-6120
carlyle@southeast.lib.sk.ca
hip.southeast.lib.sk.ca/Southeast/Docs/carlyle.html
Kathy Homer, Chair
306—45-3-62

Carnduff: **Carnduff Branch Library**
Carnduff Education Complex, 506 Anderson Rd., Carnduff SK S0C 0S0
306-482-3255
carnduff@southeast.lib.sk.ca
Elizabeth Henger, Chair
306—48-2-32

Carrot River: **Carrot River Branch Library**
Town Office / Library Complex, Main St., PO Box 1001, Carrot River SK S0E 0L0
306-768-2501
carcirc@panet.pa.sk.ca
Carol Stewart, Chair

Central Butte: **Central Butte Branch Library**
271 Butte St., PO Box 276, Central Butte SK S0H 0T0
306-796-2222
cent_chinook@hotmail.com
www.chinooklibrary.ca/central
Sylvia Lindquist, Chair

Chaplin: **Chaplin Branch Library**
Hall Complex, 2nd Ave., PO Box 225, Chaplin SK S0H 0V0
306-395-2524
chaplin@chinook.lib.sk.ca
www.chinooklibrary.ca/chaplin
Duane Farnel, Chair

Choiceland: **Choiceland Branch Library**
Town Office, 116 - 1st St. East, Choiceland SK S0J 0M0
306-428-2216, Fax: 306-428-2071
chocirc@panet.pa.sk.ca
Elaine McLean, Chair

Christopher Lake: **Christopher Lake Branch Library**
Village Office, Hwy. 263, PO Box 27, Christopher Lake SK S0J 0N0
306-982-4763
chrcirc@panet.pa.ck.ca
Gwen Collee, Chair

Climax: **Climax Branch Library**
Village Complex, 120 Main St., PO Box 323, Climax SK S0N 0N0
306-293-2229
climax@chinook.lib.sk.ca
www.chinooklibrary.ca/climax
Michelle Smith, Chair

Cochin: **Cochin Book Depository**
Hwy. 4, PO Box 190, Cochin SK S0M 0L0
306-386-1148, Fax: 306-386-2305
cochinlibrary@sasktel.net
Judy Smith, Contact

Coleville: **Coleville Library**
R.M. Bldg., PO Box 45, Coleville SK S0L 0K0
306-965-2551
coleville.library@sasktel.net
Wendy Bahm, Branch Library Staff Contact

Colonsay: **Colonsay Library**
RM Bldg., PO Box 172, Colonsay SK S0K 0Z0
306-255-2232
colonsay.library@wheatland.sk.ca
Val Pidlisney, Branch Library Staff Contact

Conquest: **Conquest Branch Library**
Conquest Community Centre, PO Box 130, Conquest SK S0L 0L0
306-856-4555
conquestlibrary@wheatland.sk.ca
www.wheatland.sk.ca/branches_conquest.html

Consul: **Consul Branch Library**
Prescod St., PO Box 121, Consul SK S0N 0P0
306-299-2118
consul@chinook.lib.sk.ca
www.chinooklibrary.ca/consul.htm
Jolene Gershon, Chair

Coronach: **Coronach Branch Library**
111A Center St., Coronach SK S0H 0Z0
306-267-3260
coronach@palliser.lib.sk.ca
www.palliserlibrary.ca
Colleen Christopherson-Coe, Chair

Craik: **Craik Branch Library**
611 - 1st Ave., PO Box 339, Craik SK S0G 0V0
306-734-2388, Fax: 306-734-2688
craik@palliser.lib.sk.ca
www.palliserlibrary.ca
Wanda Paradis, Chair

Crystal Springs: **Crystal Springs Paperback Deposit**
PO Box 28, Crystal Springs SK S0K 1A0
306-749-2632
Brenda Fisher, Branch Librarian

Cudworth: **Cudworth Branch Library**
Cudworth Town Complex, 426 - 2nd Ave., PO Box 321, Cudworth SK S0K 1B0
306-256-3530, Fax: 306-256-3515
cudcirc@panet.pa.sk.ca
Regina Bantle, Chair

Cut Knife: **Cut Knife Community Branch Library**
115 Broad St., PO Box 595, Cut Knife SK S0M 0N0
306-398-2342
cutknife.lib@lakeland.lib.sk.ca
www.lakeland.lib.sk.ca

Cut Knife: **Poundmaker School Library**
PO Box 640, Cut Knife SK S0M 0N0
306-398-4966, Fax: 306-398-4058
Corinne Weenie, Librarian

Dalmeny: **Dalmeny Branch Library**
301 Railway Ave., PO Box 850, Dalmeny SK S0K 1E0
306-254-2119
dalmeny.library@wheatland.sk.ca
www.wheatland.sk.ca
Dana Perkins, Librarian

Davidson: **Davidson Branch Library**
314 Washington Ave., PO Box 754, Davidson SK S0G 1A0
306-567-2022, Fax: 306-567-2081
davidson@palliser.lib.sk.ca
www.palliserlibrary.ca
Angela Shaw, Chair

Debden: **Debden Public Library**
Village Office, #3, 204 - 2nd Ave. East, Debden SK S0J 0S0
306-724-2240
debcirc@panet.pa.sk.ca
Linda Berscheid, Chair

Delisle: **Delisle Library**
201 - 1st St. West, Delisle SK S0L 0P0
306-493-8288
delisle.library@wheatland.sk.ca

Denzil: **Denzil Branch Library**
Brooks Ave., PO Box 188, Denzil SK S0L 0S0
306-358-2118, Fax: 306-358-4828
denzil.lib@lakeland.lib.sk.ca
www.lakeland.lib.sk.ca

Dinsmore: **Dinsmore Branch Library**
Town Office, 100 Main St., PO Box 369, Dinsmore SK S0L 0T0
306-846-2011
dinsmore.library@wheatland.sk.ca
www.wheatland.sk.ca
Mary McBain, Community Librarian

Dodsland: **Dodsland Branch Library**
135 Second Ave., PO Box 100, Dodsland SK S0L 0V0
306-356-2180
dodsland.library@sasktel.net
www.wheatland.sk.ca

Drake: **Drake Library**
Francis St., Drake SK S0K 1H0
306-363-2101
drake.library@wheatland.sk.ca
www.wheatland.sk.ca/branches_drake.html

Duck Lake: **Duck Lake Public Library**
410 Victoria Ave., Duck Lake SK S0K 1J0
306-467-2016
duccirc@panet.pa.sk.ca
Diane Perrin, Branch Librarian

Dundurn: **Dundurn Branch Library**
300 - 3rd Ave., PO Box 626, Dundurn SK S0K 1K0
306-492-2366
dundurn.library@wheatland.sk.ca
www.wheatland.sk.ca
Candace Myers, Branch Head

Eastend: **Eastend Branch Library**
Pottery St., PO Box 91, Eastend SK S0N 0T0
306-295-3788
eastend@chinook.lib.sk.ca
www.chinooklibrary.ca/eastend.htm
Gail Bock, Librarian

Eatonia: **Eatonia Branch Library**
PO Box 100, Eatonia SK S0L 0Y0
306-967-2224
eatonia.library@wheatland.sk.ca
www.townofeatonia.com/services/library.html
Sandy Guidinger, Chair

Edam: **Edam Library**
1000 Main St., Edam SK S0M 0V0
306-397-2223, Fax: 306-397-2626
edam.lib@lakeland.lib.sk.ca
Trudy McMurphy, Librarian

Elbow: **Elbow Branch Library**
402 Minto St., Elbow SK S0H 1J0
306-854-2220
elbow@palliser.lib.sk.ca
www.palliserlibrary.ca
Janice Scrimbitt, Branch Librarian

Elrose: **Elrose Branch Library**
Town Office, PO Box 185, Elrose SK S0L 0Z0
306-378-2808
elrose.library@wheatland.sk.ca
www.wheatland.sk.ca

Estevan: **Estevan Public Library**
701 Souris Ave. North, Estevan SK S4A 2T1
306-636-1620, Fax: 306-634-5830
estevan@southeast.lib.sk.ca
www.cap.estevan.sk.ca/library
Gregory Salmers, Head Librarian
greg@southeast.lib.sk.ca

Eston: **Eston Branch Library**
218 Main St., Eston SK S0L 1A0
306-962-3513
eston.library@wheatland.sk.ca
www.wheatland.sk.ca

Fillmore: **Fillmore Branch Library**
51 Main St., Fillmore SK S0G 1N0
306-722-3369
fillmore@southeast.lib.sk.ca
Joy Pollock, Librarian

Fort Qu'appelle: **Fort Qu'Appelle Branch Library**
140 Company Ave. South, Fort Qu'appelle SK S0G 1S0
306-332-6411
fort.quappelle@southeast.lib.sk.ca
www.fortquappelle.com/library
Holly Smith, Librarian
306-332-6411

Fort Qu'appelle: **Standing Buffalo Branch Library**
PO Box 248, Fort Qu'appelle SK S0G 1S0
306-332-4414
Eleice Bear, Librarian

Fox Valley: **Fox Valley Branch Library**
PO Box 145, Fox Valley SK S0N 0V0
306-666-2045
foxvalley@chinook.lib.sk.ca
www.chinooklibrary.ca/fox.htm
Valerie Reinboldt, Librarian

Frontier: **Frontier Branch Library**
211 - 1st St. West, Frontier SK S0N 0W0
306-296-4667
fron.chinook@sasktel.net
www.chinooklibrary.ca/frontier.htm
Holly Johnson, Librarian

Gainsborough: **Gainsborough Branch Library**
401 Railway, Gainsborough SK S0C 0Z0

306-685-2229
gainsborough@southeast.lib.sk.ca
Marjorie Johnson, Librarian

***Glaslyn:* Glaslyn Library**
182 Main St., Glaslyn SK S0M 0Y0
306-342-4748, Fax: 306-342-4748
glaslyn.lib@lakeland.lib.sk.ca
www.lakeland.lib.sk.ca
Jody Seifert, Librarian

***Glenavon:* Glenavon Branch Library**
311 Railway Ave., Glenavon SK S0G 1Y0
306-429-2180
glenavon@southeast.lib.sk.ca
hip.southeast.lib.sk.ca/Southeast/Docs/glenavon.html
Heather Wozniak, Librarian

***Glentworth:* Glentworth Branch Library**
PO Box 200, Glentworth SK S0H 1V0
306-266-4804
glentworth@chinook.lib.sk.ca
www.chinooklibrary.ca/glent.htm
Meryle Iwanicki, Librarian

***Goodsoil:* Goodsoil Library**
301 Main St. North, Goodsoil SK S0M 1A0
306-238-2155, Fax: 306-238-2155
goodsoil.lib@lakeland.lib.sk.ca
www.lakeland.lib.sk.ca
Jolynn Berlinger, Librarian
306-238-2155

***Gravelbourg:* Gravelbourg Branch Library**
PO Box 568, Gravelbourg SK S0H 1X0
306-648-3177
gravelbourg@chinook.lib.sk.ca
www.chinooklibrary.ca/gravel.htm
Valerie Alix, Librarian

***Green Lake:* Dore Lake Book Deposit**
c/o Hamlet of Dore Lake, General Delivery, Green Lake SK S0M 1B0
306-832-4528

***Grenfell:* Grenfell Branch Library**
1109 Wolseley Ave., Grenfell SK S0G 2B0
306-697-2455
grenfell@southeast.lib.sk.ca
hip.southeast.lib.sk.ca/Southeast/Docs/grenfell.html
Ann Neuls, Librarian

***Gronlid:* Gronlid Branch Library**
PO Box 192, Gronlid SK S0E 0W0
306-277-4633
grocirc@panet.pa.sk.ca
www.panet.pa.sk.ca/branchweb/gronlid/public.htm
Norma Lovell, Librarian

***Gull Lake:* Gull Lake Branch Library**
1377 Conrad Ave., Gull Lake SK S0N 1A0
306-672-3277
gull@chinook.lib.sk.ca
www.city.swift-current.sk.ca/chinook/gull.htm
Sandra Kettner, Librarian

***Hafford:* Hafford Library**
17 Main St., Hafford SK S0J 1A0
306-549-2373, Fax: 306-549-2333
haffordlibrary@hotmail.com
Carol Herman, Librarian

***Hague:* Hague Library**
210 Railway St., Hague SK S0K 1X0
306-225-4326
hague.library@sasktel.net
www.wheatland.sk.ca/branches_hague.html
Lynn Williamson, Branch Librarian
hague.library@sasktel.net

***Hanley:* Hanley Branch Library**
112A Lincoln St., Hanley SK S0G 2E0
306-544-2546
hanley.library@wheatland.sk.ca
www.wheatland.sk.ca/branches_hanley.html
Ann Rogers, Branch Librarian

***Hazlet:* Hazlet Branch Library**
PO Box 73, Hazlet SK S0N 1E0
306-678-2155
hazlet@chinook.lib.sk.ca
www.chinooklibrary.ca/hazlet.htm
Elaine Little, Librarian

***Herbert:* Herbert Branch Library**
517 Herbert Ave., Herbert SK S0H 2A0
306-784-2484
herbert@chinook.lib.sk.ca
www.chinooklibrary.ca/herbert.htm
Jane Epp, Librarian

***Hodgeville:* Hodgeville Branch Library**
PO Box 68, Hodgeville SK S0H 2B0
306-677-2223
hodgeville@chinook.lib.sk.ca
www.chinooklibrary.ca/hodge.htm
Elizabeth Haubrich, Librarian

***Holdfast:* Holdfast Branch Library**
PO Box 205, Holdfast SK S0G 2H0
306-488-2000
holdfast@palliser.lib.sk.ca
www.palliserlibrary.ca
Janet Couture, Branch Librarian

***Hudson Bay:* Hudson Bay Public Library**
130 Main St., Hudson Bay SK S0E 0Y0
306-865-3110, Fax: 306-865-2800
hudcirc@panet.pa.sk.ca
Glennys Shewchuk, Librarian

***Humboldt:* Humboldt Reid-Thompson Public Library**
705 Main St., Humboldt SK S0K 2A0
306-682-2034, Fax: 306-682-2035
humcirc@panet.pa.sk.ca
www.panet.pa.sk.ca/BranchDir_list.asp
Rose Ward, Branch Librarian

***Ile-a-la-Crosse:* Ile a la Crosse Elementary School**
PO Box 70, Ile-a-la-Crosse SK S0M 1C0
306-833-2010, Fax: 306-833-2322
Valerie Gardiner, School Librarian
vgardiner@icsd.ca
306-833-2010

***Imperial:* Imperial Branch Library**
PO Box 238, 310 Royal St., Imperial SK S0G 2J0
306-963-2272, Fax: 306-963-2445
imperial@palliser.lib.sk.ca
www.palliserlibrary.ca
Donalda MacLellan, Branch Librarian

***Indian Head:* Indian Head Branch Library**
419 Grand Ave., Indian Head SK S0G 2K0
306-695-3922
indian.head@southeast.lib.sk.ca
Colleen Reynard, Librarian

***Island Lake:* Island Lake Library**
Island Lake First Nations School, Island Lake SK S0M 3G0
306-837-4868, Fax: 306-837-4558
sli.ill@lakeland.lib.sk.ca
Helen Kowal, Librarian

***Kenaston:* Kenaston Library**
PO Box 309, Kenaston SK S0G 2N0
306-252-2130
kenaston.library@wheatland.sk.ca
www.wheatland.sk.ca/branches_kenaston.html
Faye McVeigh, Branch Librarian

***Kennedy:* Kennedy Branch Library**
235 Scott St., Kennedy SK S0G 2R0
306-538-2020
kennedy@southeast.lib.sk.ca
Amy Hewson, Librarian

***Kerrobert:* Kerrobert Library**
PO Box 618, Kerrobert SK S0L 1R0
306-834-5211, Fax: 306-834-2633
kerrobert.library@wheatland.sk.ca
Heather Wack, Branch Library Staff Contact

***Kincaid:* Kincaid Branch Library**
PO Box 146, Kincaid SK S0H 2J0
306-264-3910
kinc.chinook@sasktel.net
www.chinooklibrary.ca/kincaid.htm
Trudy Turgeon, Librarian

***Kindersley:* Kindersley Library**
104 Princess St., Kindersley SK S0L 1S2
306-463-4141, Fax: 306-463-6834
kindersley.library@wheatland.sk.ca
Marilyn Shea, Librarian

***Kinistino:* Kinistino Branch Library**
PO Box 774, Kinistino SK S0J 1H0
306-864-2537
kincirc@panet.pa.sk.ca
Joanne Jansen, Librarian
circ1@sk.sympatico.ca

***Kipling:* Kipling Branch Library**
207 - 6th Ave., Kipling SK S0G 2S0
306-736-2911
kipling@southeast.lib.sk.ca
Jody Levey, Head Librarian

***Kyle:* Kyle Public Library**
116 Centre St., Kyle SK S0L 1T0
306-375-2566
kyle.library@wheatland.sk.ca
Elva Akister, Community Librarian

***Lafleche:* Lafleche Branch Library**
157 Main St., PO Box 132, Lafleche SK S0H 2K0
306-472-5466
lafleche@chinook.lib.sk.ca
www.chinooklibrary.ca/lafleche.htm
Gloria McIvor, Librarian

***Lake Alma:* Lake Alma Branch Library**
Hwy. 18, PO Box 216, Lake Alma SK S0C 1M0
306-447-2061
lake.alma@southeast.lib.sk.ca
Bernice Bloor, Librarian

***Lampman:* Lampman Branch Library**
302 Main St., Lampman SK S0C 1N0
306-487-2202
lampman@southeast.lib.sk.ca
Martha Engel, Librarian

***Landis:* Landis Library**
PO Box 124, Landis SK S0K 2K0
306-658-2177
landis.library@wheatland.sk.ca
www.wheatland.sk.ca/branches_landis.html
Vera Halter, Branch Librarian

***Langham:* Langham Library**
PO Box 697, Langham SK S0K 2L0
306-283-4362
langham.library@sasktel.net
www.wheatland.sk.ca
Dean Buhr, Community Librarian

***Lanigan:* Lanigan Library**
PO Box 70, Lanigan SK S0K 2M0
306-365-2472
lanigan.library@wheatkabd.sk.ca
www.wheatland.sk.ca/branches_lanigan.html
Fran Nugent, Branch Library Staff Contact

***Lashburn:* Lashburn Branch Library**
95 Main St., Box 160, Lashburn SK S0M 1H0
306-285-4144
lashburn.lib@lakeland.lib.sk.ca
Bernadette Evans, Librarian

***Leader:* Leader Branch Library**
151 - 1st St. West, Leader SK S0N 1H0
306-628-3830
leader@chinook.lib.sk.ca
www.chinooklibrary.ca/leader.htm
Lois Smith, Librarian

***Leask:* Leask Branch Library**
PO Box 117, Leask SK S0J 1M0
306-466-4577, Fax: 306-466-2000
leacirc@panet.pa.sk.ca
Connie Peake, Librarian

***Leoville:* Leoville Branch Library**
22 Main St., Leoville SK S0J 1N0
306-984-2057, Fax: 306-984-2337
leocirc@panet.pa.sk.ca
Judy Wandler, Branch Librarian
306-984-2057

***Livelong:* Livelong Branch Library**
PO Box 161, Livelong SK S0M 1J0
306-845-3395
livelong.lib@lakeland.lib.sk.ca
Inga Sample, Librarian

***Loon Lake:* Loon Lake Branch Library**
PO Box 216, Loon Lake SK S0M 1L0
306-837-2186
loonlake.lib@lakeland.lib.sk.ca
www.lakeland.lib.sk.ca

Gwen Lindstrom, Librarian
loonlake.lib@lakeland.lib.sk.ca

Loreburn: **Loreburn Branch Library**
Village Office, Loreburn SK S0H 2S0
306-644-2026
loreburn@palliser.lib.sk.ca
www.palliserlibrary.ca
Janice Scrimbitt, Branch Librarian

Lucky Lake: **Lucky Lake Library**
101 - 1st Ave. South, Lucky Lake SK S0L 1Z0
306-858-2246
luckylake.library@wheatland.sk.ca
www.wheatlandlibrary.sk.ca
Elaine Ylioja, Community Librarian

Lumsden: **Lumsden Branch Library**
Centennial Hall, 40 - 3rd Ave., Lumsden SK S0G 3C0
306-731-2433
lumsden@southeast.lib.sk.ca
Sheila Felix, Librarian

Luseland: **Luseland Library**
510 Grand Ave., Luseland SK S0L 2A0
306-372-4808
luseland.library@sasktel.net
Diane Hurford, Branch Library Staff Contact

Macklin: **Macklin Branch Library**
5001 Press Ave., Macklin SK S0L 2C0
306-753-2933, Fax: 306-753-3234
macklin.lib@lakeland.lib.sk.ca
Linda Engele, Librarian

Maidstone: **Maidstone Branch Library**
#102B, 108 - 1st Ave. West, Maidstone SK S0M 1M0
306-893-4153, Fax: 306-893-4153
maidstone.lib@lakeland.lib.sk.ca
Lorna Foster, Librarian

Makwa: **Makwa Branch Library**
Box 10, General Delivery, Makwa SK S0M 1N0
306-236-3995
makwa.lib@sk.sympatico.ca
Michelle Boehler, Branch Librarian
306-236-3995

Mankota: **Mankota Branch Library**
PO Box 373, Mankota SK S0H 2W0
306-478-2331
mank.chinook@sasktel.net
www.chinooklibrary.ca/mankota.htm
Maggie Brown, Librarian

Manor: **Manor Branch Library**
45 Main St., Manor SK S0C 1R0
306-448-2266, Fax: 306-448-2266
manor@southeast.lib.sk.ca
www.southeast.lib.sk.ca
Rita Kyle, Librarian

Maple Creek: **Maple Creek Branch Library**
205 Jasper St., Maple Creek SK S0N 1N0
306-662-3522
maplecreek@chinook.lib.sk.ca
www.chinooklibrary.ca/maple.htm
Evelyn Southwood, Librarian

Marcelin: **Marcelin Branch Library**
Town Office, 1st Ave. South, Marcelin SK S0J 1R0
306-226-2110
marcirc@panet.pa.sk.ca
Peggy Brad, Librarian

Marsden: **Marsden Branch Library**
#104 Centre St., Marsden SK S0M 1P0
306-826-5666, Fax: 306-826-5666
marsden.lib@lakeland.lib.sk.ca
Denise Polkinghorne, Librarian

Marshall: **Marshall Branch Library**
13 Main St., Marshall SK S0M 1R0
306-387-6155, Fax: 306-387-6555
marshall.lib@lakeland.lib.sk.ca
Donna Ferguson, Librarian

Martensville: **Martensville Library**
PO Box 1180, Martensville SK S0K 2T0
306-956-7311
martensville.library@wheatland.sk.ca
Marla Skomar, Head Librarian

Maryfield: **Maryfield Branch Library**
PO Box 160, Maryfield SK S0G 3K0
306-646-2148
maryfield@southeast.lib.sk.ca
Doreen Jurkovich, Librarian

Mayfair: **Mayfair Branch Library**
Mayfair Central School, PO Box 70, Mayfair SK S0M 1S0
306-246-4465
mayfair.lib@lakeland.lib.sk.ca
Janet Cherwinski, Librarian

Maymont: **Maymont Library**
PO Box 102, Maymont SK S0M 1T0
306-389-2006
maymont.lib@sk.sympatico.ca
Mary Scott, Librarian

Meadow Lake: **Meadow Lake Library**
320 Centre St., PO Box 9000, SPMC Mailroom, Meadow Lake SK S9X 1V8
306-236-5396, Fax: 306-236-6282
meadowlake.lib@lakeland.lib.sk.ca
Tara Million, Librarian

Meath Park: **Meath Park Branch Library**
PO Box 122, Meath Park SK S0J 1T0
306-929-2133, Fax: 306-929-2401
meacirc@panet.pa.sk.ca
Ruth Holodniuk, Librarian

Medstead: **Medstead Branch Library**
209 - 2nd Ave., Medstead SK S0M 1W0
306-342-4609
medstead.lib@lakeland.lib.sk.ca
Nissa Shields, Librarian

Melfort: **Melfort Public Library**
106 Crawford Ave. West, Melfort SK S0E 1A0
306-752-2022, Fax: 306-752-2022
melcirc@panet.pa.sk.ca
Penny Markland, Librarian

Meota: **Meota Library**
PO Box 214, Meota SK S0M 1X0
306-892-2113
meota.library@sasktel.net
Deborah Pearce, Librarian

Mervin: **Mervin Branch Library**
11 Main St., Mervin SK S0M 1Y0
306-845-2784, Fax: 306-845-3563
mervin.lib@sk.sympatico.ca
Dawn Simkins, Librarian
306-845-2784

Meskanaw: **Meskanaw Paperback Deposit**
General Delivery, Meskanaw SK S0K 2W0
306-864-3730

Midale: **Midale Branch Library**
PO Box 185, Midale SK S0C 1S0
306-458-2263
midale@southeast.lib.sk.ca
Lydia Duncan, Librarian

Milden: **Milden Library**
PO Box 7, Milden SK S0L 2L0
306-935-4600
milden.library@sasktel.net
www.wheatland.sk.ca/branches_milden.html
Sandra Frey, Library Assistant

Milestone: **Milestone Library**
112 Main St., Milestone SK S0G 3L0
306-436-2112
milestone@southeast.lib.sk.ca
Diana Cook, Librarian

Mistatim: **Mistatim Branch Library**
Railway Ave., Mistatim SK S0E 1B0
306-889-2008
miscirc@panet.pa.sk.ca
Theresa McHugh, Librarian

Montmartre: **Montmartre Regional Library**
136 Central, Montmartre SK S0G 3M0
306-424-2029
montmartre@southeast.lib.sk.ca
Lillian Ripplinger, Librarian

Montreal Lake: **Montreal Lake Community Library**
PO Box 150, Montreal Lake SK S0J 1Y0
306-663-5602, Fax: 306-663-5652
sml@pnls.lib.sk.ca
Blanche Bird, Librarian

Moose Jaw: **Moose Jaw Public Library**
461 Langdon Cres., Moose Jaw SK S6H 0X6
306-692-2787, Fax: 306-692-3368
reference.smj@sasktel.net
www.moosejawlibrary.ca
Anne Warriner, Head Librarian
librarian.smj@sasktel.net

Moosomin: **Moosomin Branch Library**
701 Main St., Moosomin SK S0G 3N0
306-435-2107
moosomin@southeast.lib.sk.ca
Christie McGonigal, Librarian

Morse: **Morse Branch Library**
PO Box 64, Morse SK S0H 3C0
306-629-3335
morse@chinook.lib.sk.ca
www.chinooklibrary.ca/morse.htm
Donna Fafard, Librarian

Mortlach: **Mortlach Branch Library**
Main St., Mortlach SK S0H 3E0
306-355-2202
mortlach@palliser.lib.sk.ca
www.palliserlibrary.ca
Linda Locke, Branch Librarian

Mossbank: **Mossbank Branch Library**
310 Main St., Mossbank SK S0H 3G0
306-354-2474
mossbank@palliser.lib.sk.ca
www.palliserlibrary.ca
Debbie Sullivan, Branch Librarian

Naicam: **Naicam Branch Library**
109 Center St., Naicam SK S0K 2Z0
306-874-2156
naicirc@panet.pa.sk.ca
Darla Christianson, Librarian
naicirc@panet.pa.sk.ca

Neilburg: **Neilburg Branch Library**
108 Centre St., Neilburg SK S0M 2C0
306-823-4234
neilburg.lib@lakeland.lib.sk.ca
Sharon Schempp, Librarian

Nipawin: **Nipawin Branch Library**
214 - 2nd Ave. East, Nipawin SK S0E 1E0
306-862-4867
nipcirc@panet.pa.sk.ca
www.nipawinlibrary.ca
Nancy Budd, Branch Librarian

Nokomis: **Nokomis Library**
PO Box 38, Nokomis SK S0G 3R0
306-528-2251
nokomis.library@wheatland.sk.ca
Teresda Strachan, Librarian

North Battleford: **North Battleford Library**
1392 - 101st St., North Battleford SK S9A 1A2
306-445-3206, Fax: 306-445-6454
www.northbattlefordlibrary.com
R. Raeber, Librarian
rraeber@lakeland.lib.sk.ca
306-445-3206

North Battleford: **Saskatchewan Hospital Branch Library**
PO Box 39, North Battleford SK S9A 2X8
306-446-6863, Fax: 306-446-6810
saskhospital.lib@lakeland.lib.sk.ca
Rita Kuntz, Branch Librarian

Odessa: **Odessa Branch Library**
PO Box 91, Odessa SK S0G 3S0
306-957-2020
odessa@southeast.lib.sk.ca
Sheila Leurer, Librarian

Ogema: **Ogema Branch Library**
117 Main St., Ogema SK S0C 1Y0
306-459-2985
ogema@southeast.lib.sk.ca
hip.southeast.lib.sk.ca/Southeast/Docs/ogema.html
Valerie Dunn, Librarian

Osler: **Osler Library**
228 Willow Dr., Osler SK S0K 3A0
306-239-4774, Fax: 306-239-2194
osler.library@yourlink.ca
www.wheatland.sk.ca/branches_osler.html

Laura Hildebrand, Librarian

Oungre: **Oungre Branch Library**
PO Box 88, Oungre SK S0C 1Z0
306-456-2662
oungre@southeast.lib.sk.ca
Rozann Graefer, Librarian

Outlook: **Outlook Library**
505 Franklin St. South, Outlook SK S0L 2N0
306-867-8823, Fax: 306-867-1831
outlook.library@wheatland.sk.ca
Elaine Nadeau, Librarian

Oxbow: **Oxbow Branch Library/Ada Staples Library**
516 Prospect Ave., Oxbow SK S0C 2B0
306-483-5175, Fax: 306-483-2276
oxbow@southeast.lib.sk.ca
Marty James, Librarian

Paddockwood: **Paddockwood Library**
PO Box 178, Paddockwood SK S0J 1Z0
306-989-2124, Fax: 306-989-2123
padcirc@panet.pa.sk.ca
Joan Carriere, Librarian

Pangman: **Pangman Library**
PO Box 113, Pangman SK S0C 2C0
306-442-2119
pangman@southeast.lib.sk.ca
Carolyn Colbow, Librarian

Paradise Hill: **Paradise Hill Branch Library**
2nd Ave., Paradise Hill SK S0M 2G0
306-344-4741
paradisehill.lib@lakeland.lib.sk.ca
Dianne Palsich, Branch Librarian

Paynton: **Paynton Branch Library**
General Delivery, Paynton SK S0M 2J0
306-895-2175
paynton.lib@lakeland.lib.sk.ca
Linda Peterson, Librarian

Pelican Narrows: **Tawowikamik Public Library**
PO Box 100, Pelican Narrows SK S0P 0E0
306-632-2022, Fax: 306-632-2022
spn@pnis.lib.sk.ca
Margaret Brass, Head Librarian
306-632-2161

Pennant Station: **Pennant Branch Library**
General Delivery, Pennant Station SK S0N 1X0
306-626-3316
pennant@chinook.lib.sk.ca
www.chinooklibrary.ca/pennant.htm
Sharon Windsor, Librarian

Perdue: **Perdue Library**
PO Box 253, Perdue SK S0K 3C0
306-237-4227
perdue.library@sasktel.net
Mary Lee Sapsford, Librarian

Pierceland: **Pierceland Library**
Main St., Pierceland SK S0M 2K0
306-839-2166
pierceland.lib@lakeland.lib.sk.ca
Ann Hill, Librarian

Pilger: **Pilger Library**
PO Box 116, Pilger SK S0K 3G0
306-367-4809
pilcirc@panet.pa.sk.ca
Delores Pomedli, Head Librarian

Pilot Butte: **Pilot Butte Branch Library**
PO Box 668, Pilot Butte SK S0G 3Z0
306-781-3403
pilot.butte@southeast.lib.sk.ca
Sharon Millie, Librarian

Plenty: **Plenty Library**
PO Box 70, Plenty SK S0L 2R0
306-932-4455
plenty.library@sasktel.net
Lynn Halter, Branch Library Staff Contact

Ponteix: **Ponteix Branch Library**
130 - 1st Ave. East, PO Box 700, Ponteix SK S0N 1Z0
306-625-3353
ponteix@chinook.lib.sk.ca
www.chinooklibrary.ca/ponteix.htm
Marie Kouri, Librarian

Porcupine Plain: **Porcupine Plain Library**
PO Box 162, Porcupine Plain SK S0E 1H0
306-278-2488
porcirc@panet.pa.sk.ca
Joanne Yacyshyn, Librarian

Prairie River: **Prairie River Branch Library**
General Delivery, Prairie River SK S0E 1J0
306-889-4521
pracirc@panet.pa.sk.ca
Pat Danku, Librarian

Prelate: **Prelate Branch Library**
Drawer 40, Prelate SK S0N 2B0
306-673-2340
prelate@chinook.lib.sk.ca
www.chinooklibrary.ca/prelate.htm
Darlene Wagner, Librarian

Prince Albert: **John M. Cuelenaere Public Library**
125 - 12th St. East, Prince Albert SK S6V 1B7
306-763-8496, Fax: 306-763-3816, 888-975-8165
library@jmcpl.ca
www.jmcpl.ca
Sharon Karr, Acting Director
skarr@jmcpl.ca
306—76-3-85

Prud'Homme: **Prud'Homme Public Library**
45 Government Rd., Prud'Homme SK S0K 3K0
306-654-2221
prucirc@panet.pa.sk.ca
Jennifer Wesdyk, Librarian

Qu'Appelle: **Qu'Appelle Branch Library**
PO Box 450, Qu'Appelle SK S0G 4A0
306-699-2902
quappelle@southeast.lib.sk.ca
Elizabeth Fries, Librarian

Rabbit Lake: **Rabbit Lake Branch Library**
PO Box 146, Rabbit Lake SK S0M 2L0
306-824-2089
rabbitlake.lib@lakeland.lib.sk.ca
Marlene Martens, Librarian

Radisson: **Radisson Branch Library**
PO Box 161, Radisson SK S0K 3L0
306-827-4521
radisson.lib@lakeland.lib.sk.ca
Shirley Hosegood, Branch Librarian

Radville: **Radville Branch Library**
420 Floren St., Radville SK S0C 2G0
306-869-2742
radville@southeast.lib.sk.ca
Shannon Bourassa, Librarian

Redvers: **Redvers Library**
53B Railway Ave., Redvers SK S0C 2H0
306-452-3255
redvers@southeast.lib.sk.ca
Janet Dauvin, Librarian

Regina: **Forum**
#15, 2010 - 7th Ave., Regina SK S4R 1C2
306-780-9413, Fax: 306-780-9447
slaforum@sasktel.net
www.lib.sk.ca/sla/newsletter.html

Regina: **Regina Public Library**
2311 - 12th Ave., Regina SK S4P 0N3
306-777-6000, Fax: 306-949-7260
www.reginalibrary.ca
Jeff Barber, Library Director
jbarber@reginalibrary.ca
306—77-7-60

Regina: **The Medium**
3142 Athol St., Regina SK S4S 1Y7
306-373-1660, Fax: 306-374-1122
bmcneil@rbe.sk.ca
www.stf.sk.ca/prof_growth/ssc/ssla/medium.html
Barb McNeil, Editor

Regina Beach: **Regina Beach Branch Library**
133 Donovel Cres., Regina Beach SK S0G 4C0
306-729-2062
regina.beach@southeast.lib.sk.ca
www.southeast.lib.sk.ca
Lorie Gejdos, Acting Librarian

Riverhurst: **Riverhurst Branch Library**
The Village Square, Box 37, Riverhurst SK S0H 3P0
306-353-2130
riverhurst@palliser.lib.sk.ca
www.palliserlibrary.ca
Donna Miner, Librarian

Rocanville: **Rocanville Branch Library**
218 Ellice St., Rocanville SK S0A 3L0
306-645-2088
rocanville@southeast.lib.sk.ca
www.southeast.lib.sk.ca
Catherine Stanhope, Librarian

Rockglen: **Rockglen Branch Library**
Main St., Rockglen SK S0H 3R0
306-476-2350, Fax: 306-476-2339
rockglen@palliser.lib.sk.ca
www.palliserlibrary.ca
Claudette Schnell, Branch Librarian

La Ronge: **La Ronge Public Library**
1222 Hildebrand Dr., La Ronge SK S0J 1L0
306-425-2160, Fax: 306-425-3883
sla@pnls.lib.sk.ca
www.pnls.lib.sk.ca/laronge/
Rosemary Loeffler, Library Administrator
r.loeffler.sla@pnls.lib.sk.ca

La Ronge: **Pahkisimon Nuye,ah Library System**
118 Avro Pl., La Ronge SK S0J 1L0
306-425-4525, Fax: 306-425-4572
pnlshq@pnls.lib.sk.ca
www.pnls.lib.sk.ca
Audrey Mark, Director

Rosetown: **Rosetown Library**
#201, 5 Ave. East, Rosetown SK S0L 2V0
306-882-3566
rosetown.library@wheatland.sk.ca
Lydia Hare, Manager

Rosthern: **Rosthern Library**
PO Box 27, Rosthern SK S0K 3R0
306-232-5377
rosthern.library@wheatland.sk.ca
Agnes Epp, Librarian

Rouleau: **Rouleau Branch Library**
204 Main St., Rouleau SK S0G 4H0
306-776-2322
rouleau@palliser.lib.sk.ca
www.palliserlibrary.ca
Dee Colibaba, Branch Librarian

St Benedict: **St Benedict Library**
Centre St., PO Box Box 10, St Benedict SK S0K 3T0
306-289-2072
sbencirc@panet.pa.sk.ca
Lee Ann Hannotte, Librarian

St Brieux: **St Brieux Branch Library**
PO Box 70, St Brieux SK S0K 3V0
306-275-2133, Fax: 306-275-4907
sbricirc@panet.pa.sk.ca
Kim Ells, Librarian

St Louis: **St Louis Branch Library**
PO Box 70, St Louis SK S0J 2C0
306-422-8511
sloucirc@panet.pa.sk.ca
Birgit Raduenz, Librarian

St Walburg: **St Walburg Library**
124 Main St., St Walburg SK S0M 2T0
306-248-3250, Fax: 306-248-3278
stwalburg.lib@lakeland.lib.sk.ca
www.stwalburglibrary.ca
Valerie L'Heureux, Librarian

Saskatoon: **Saskatoon Public Library**
311 - 23rd St. East, Saskatoon SK S7K 0J6
306-975-7558, Fax: 306-975-7542
illreps@saskatoonlibrary.ca
www.saskatoonlibrary.ca
Zenon Zuzak, Director of Libraries
z.zuzak@saskatoonlibrary.ca

Sceptre: **Sceptre Branch Library**
PO Box 128, Sceptre SK S0N 2H0
306-623-4244
sceptre@chinook.lig.sk.ca
www.chinooklibrary.ca/sceptre.htm
Sherry Egeland, Librarian

Sedley: **Sedley Branch Library**
224 Broadway, Sedley SK S0G 4K0

306-885-4506
sedley@southeast.lib.sk.ca
Jocelyn Weinberger, Librarian

Shaunavon: **Shaunavon Branch Library**
440 Center St., Shaunavon SK S0N 2M0
306-297-3844
shaunavon@chinook.lib.sk.ca
www.chinooklibrary.ca/shaunavn.htm
Lorie Gronhovd, Librarian

Shell Lake: **Shell Lake Branch Library**
PO Box 310, Shell Lake SK S0J 2G0
306-427-2272, Fax: 306-427-2272
shllcirc@panet.pa.sk.ca
Pat Pelchat, Librarian

Shellbrook: **Shellbrook Branch Library**
105 Railway Ave. West, Shellbrook SK S0J 2E0
306-747-3419
shbrcinc@panet.pa.sk.ca
Alanna Carswell, Librarian

Shellbrook: **Sturgeon Lake Branch Library**
Sturgeon Lake Central School, PO Box 24, Shellbrook SK S0J 2E0
306-764-5506
Sharon Daniels, Librarian

Simmie: **Simmie Branch Library**
PO Box 66, Simmie SK S0N 2N0
306-297-6217
www.chinooklibrary.ca/simmie.htm
Grace Olson, Librarian

Smeaton: **Smeaton Branch Library**
PO Box 149, Smeaton SK S0J 2J0
306-426-2049, Fax: 306-426-2291
smecirc@panet.pa.sk.ca
Gayle Olson, Librarian

Sonningdale: **Sonningdale Library**
PO Box 40, Sonningdale SK S0K 4B0
306-237-9533
sonlib@sasktel.net
Connie Guiness, Branch Library Staff Contact

Speers: **Speers Branch Library**
Main St., Speers SK S0M 2V0
306-246-4866
speers.lib@lakeland.lib.sk.ca
Maureen Kachmarski, Branch Librarian

Spiritwood: **Spiritwood Branch Library**
Box 177, Spiritwood SK S0J 2M0
306-883-2337
spicirc@panet.pa.sk.ca
Joyce Carriere, Librarian

Spruce Home: **Spruce Home Branch Library**
General Delivery, Spruce Home SK S0J 2N0
306-764-8377
sprucehomewapiti@yahoo.com
Julie Czychowski, Branch Librarian

Stanley Mission: **Keethanow Public Library**
PO Box 70, Stanley Mission SK S0J 2P0
306-635-2104, Fax: 306-635-2050
l.ratt.ssk@pnls.lib.sk.ca
Lucy Ratt, Branch Librarian

Star City: **Star City Branch Library**
PO Box 371, Star City SK S0E 1P0
306-863-4364
stacirc@panet.pa.sk.ca
Dena MacKenzie, Librarian

Stewart Valley: **Stewart Valley Branch Library**
Box 1, Stewart Valley SK S0N 2P0
svlibrary@t2.net
www.chinooklibrary.ca/stewart.htm
Kathy King, Librarian

Stoughton: **Stoughton Branch Library**
232 Main St., Stoughton SK S0G 4T0
306-457-2484
stoughton@southeast.lib.sk.ca
Laura Lee Knibbs, Librarian

Stranraer: **Stranraer Book Deposit**
PO Box 130, Stranraer SK S0L 3B0
306-237-7603
stranraer.library@wheatland.sk.ca
Charlene Bradley, Branch Library Staff

Swift Current: **Swift Current Branch Library**
411 Herbert St. East, Swift Current SK S9H 1M5
306-778-2752, Fax: 306-773-8769
sclibrary@sasktel.net
www.city.swift-current.sk.ca/library
Manisha Khetarpal, Librarian

Tisdale: **Tisdale Public Library**
800 - 101st ST., Tisdale SK S0E 1T0
306-873-4767
tiscirc@panet.pa.sk.ca
Isabel Hankins-Wilk, Librarian
tisdale_lib@yahoo.com

Tompkins: **Tompkins Library**
PO Box 203, Tompkins SK S0N 2S0
306-622-2255
tompkins@chinook.lib.sk.ca
www.chinooklibrary.ca/tompkins.htm
Lynne Baumann, Librarian

Tugaske: **Tugaske Branch Library**
Main St., PO Box 10, Tugaske SK S0H 4B0
306-759-2215, Fax: 306-759-2253
tugaske@palliser.lib.sk.ca
www.palliserlibrary.ca/tugaske/tugaske.htm
Kathy Russell, Branch Librarian

Turtleford: **Thunderchild Branch Library**
PO Box 600, Turtleford SK S0M 2Y0
306-845-4325, Fax: 306-845-3339
Susan Wapass, Librarian

Turtleford: **Turtleford Branch Library**
PO Box 146, Turtleford SK S0M 2Y0
306-845-2074
turtleford.lib@lakeland.lib.sk.ca
Hilma Copeland, Branch Librarian

Unity: **Unity Library**
General Delivery, Unity SK S0K 4L0
306-228-2802
unity.library@wheatland.sk.ca
Michelle Schumack, Branch Library Staff Contact

Val Marie: **Val Marie Branch Library**
Box 93, Val Marie SK S0N 2T0
306-298-2133
valmarie@chinook.lib.sk.ca
www.chinooklibrary.ca/valmarie.htm
Judy Gunter, Librarian

Vanguard: **Vanguard Branch Library**
PO Box 85, Vanguard SK S0N 2V0
306-582-2244
vanguard@chinook.lib.sk.ca
www.chinooklibrary.ca/vanguard.htm
Melanie Clark, Librarian

Vibank: **Vibank Branch Library**
101 - 2nd Ave., Vibank SK S0G 4Y0
306-762-2270
vibank@southeast.lib.sk.ca
www.southeast.lib.sk.ca
Betty Kuntz, Librarian
vibank@southeast.lib.sk.ca
306-762-2270

Viscount: **Viscount Library**
PO Box 117, Viscount SK S0K 4M0
306-944-2155
viscount.library@sasktel.net
Carol Brown, Librarian

Vonda: **Vonda Public Library**
316 Main St., Vonda SK S0K 4N0
306-258-2035
voncirc@panet.pa.sk.ca
Jennifer Wesdyk, Librarian

Wakaw: **Wakaw Branch Library**
PO Box 464, Wakaw SK S0K 4P0
306-233-5552
wakcirc@panet.pa.sk.ca
Lee Ann Hannotte, Librarian

Waldheim: **Waldheim Branch Library**
PO Box 446, Waldheim SK S0K 4R0
306-945-2221
waldheim.library@sasktel.net
Irene Balman, Librarian

Wapella: **Wapella Branch Library**
519 South Railway St., Wapella SK S0G 4Z0
306-532-4419
wapella@southeast.lib.sk.ca
Sharon Matheson, Librarian

Warman: **Warman Library**
101 Klassen St., Warman SK S0K 4S0
306-933-4387
warman.library@wheatland.sk.ca
Margaret-Ann Janzen, Community Librarian

Waskesiu Lake: **Waskesiu Lake Library**
PO Box 202, Waskesiu Lake SK S0J 2Y0
306-663-5999
Marilyn Hegel, Librarian

Watrous: **Watrous Library**
306 Main St., Watrous SK S0K 4T0
306-946-2244
watrous.library@wheatland.sk.ca
Kathleen Kimmig, Community Librarian

Wawota: **Wawota Branch Library**
308 Railway, Wawota SK S0G 5A0
306-739-2375
wawota@southeast.lib.sk.ca
Maureen Jensen, Librarian

Weldon: **Weldon Branch Library**
PO Box 55, Weldon SK S0J 3A0
306-887-4466
welcirc@panet.pa.sk.ca
Terry Coldevin, Librarian

Weyburn: **Weyburn Public Library**
45 Bison Ave. NE, Weyburn SK S4H 0H9
306-842-4352, Fax: 306-842-1255
weyburn@southeast.lib.sk.ca
wcapqlx.sasktelwebhosting.com/wpl
Kam Teo, City Librarian

White City: **White City Branch Library**
12 Ramm Ave., White City Community Centre, PO Box 308, White City SK S0G 5B0
306-781-2118
white.city@southeast.lib.sk.ca
Lori Lee Harris, Branch Librarian

White Fox: **White Fox Branch Library**
301 Elinor St., White Fox SK S0J 3B0
306-276-5800
whicirc@panet.pa.sk.ca
Debbie Woods, Librarian

Whitewood: **Whitewood Library**
731 Lalonde St., Whitewood SK S0G 5C0
306-735-4233
whitewood@southeast.lib.sk.ca
Irene Blyth, Librarian

Wilkie: **Wilkie Library**
202 - 2nd Ave. East, Wilkie SK S0K 4W0
306-843-2616
wilkie.library@wheatland.sk.ca
Terri Dueck, Branch Library Staff Contact

Willow Bunch: **Willow Bunch Branch Library**
Main St., PO Box 280, Willow Bunch SK S0H 4K0
306-473-2405
willowbunch@palliser.lib.sk.ca
www.palliserlibrary.ca
Cindy Philippon, Branch Librarian

Windthorst: **Windthorst Branch Library**
202 Angus St., Windthorst SK S0G 5G0
306-224-2159
windthorst@southeast.lib.sk.ca
Jill Taylor, Librarian

Wolseley: **Wolseley Branch Library**
#5, 101 Sherbrooke St., Wolseley SK S0G 5H0
306-698-2221
wolseley@southeast.lib.sk.ca
www.southeast.lib.sk.ca
Sharon Jeeves, Librarian
wolseley@southeast.lib.sk.ca
306-698-2221

Wood Mountain: **Wood Mountain Branch Library**
2nd Ave. West, Wood Mountain SK S0H 4L0
306-266-2110
woodmountain@palliser.lib.sk.ca
www.palliserlibrary.ca
Edie Klein, Branch Librarian

Yellow Creek: **Yellow Creek Branch Library**
General Delivery, Yellow Creek SK S0K 4X0
306-279-2191
yelcirc@panet.pa.sk.ca
Eileen Orenchuk, Librarian

Yellow Grass: **Yellow Grass Branch Library**
213 Souris St., Yellow Grass SK S0G 5J0
306-465-2574
yellow.grass@southeast.lib.sk.ca
Betty Guest, Librarian

Young: **Young Library**
114 Main St., Young SK S0K 4Y0
306-259-2227
young.library@sasktel.net
Gisele Camber, Branch Library Staff Contact

Zenon Park: **Zenon Park Paperback Deposit**
920 Park Rd., Zenon Park SK S0E 1W0
306-767-2451, Fax: 306-767-2548
wapiti@panet.pa.sk.ca
www.panet.pa.sk.ca
Michelle Le Blanc, Librarian

Archives

Duck Lake: **Duck Lake Historical Museum**
5 Anderson Ave., Duck Lake SK S0K 1J0
306-467-2057, 866-467-2057
duckmuf@sk.sympatico.ca
www.dlric.org/museum.html
Céline Perillat, Curator
Rae Benson, Archivist
306-764-2041

Prince Albert: **Diocese of Saskatchewan**
1308 - 5th Ave. East, Prince Albert SK S6V 2H7
306-763-2455, Fax: 306-764-5172
www.skdiocese.com/archives/
Rae Benson, Archivist
306-763-2455

Prince Albert: **Orra Sheldon Resource Centre**
1308 - 5th Ave. East, Prince Albert SK S6V 2H7
306-763-2455, Fax: 306-764-5172
diocres@sasktel.net
www.skdiocese.com/archives

Prince Albert: **Prince Albert Historical Society/Museum**
10 River St. East, Prince Albert SK S6V 8A9
306-764-2992
historypa@citypa.com
historypa.com
William D. Smiley, Archivist
historypa@citypa.com
Trevor Powell, Archivist & Registrar
tm.powell@sasktel.net

Regina: **Diocese of Qu'Appelle, Archives**
Saskatchewan Archives Board, University of Regina, 303 Hillsdale St., Regina SK S4P 1B8
306-787-4068, Fax: 306-787-1197
quappelle@sasktel.net
diocse.sasktelwebsite.net/

Regina: **Regina Firefighters' Museum**
1205 Ross Ave., Regina SK S4P 3C8
306-777-7830, Fax: 306-777-6807
Jim Kerr, Contact

Regina: **Royal Canadian Mounted Police Museum/ Musée de la Gendarmerie royale du Canada**
PO Box 6500, Regina SK S4P 3J7
306-780-5838, Fax: 306-780-6349
W.A.F. MacKay, Director
306-780-5836

Regina: **Saskatchewan Archives Board**
3303 Hillsdale St., Regina SK S4S 6W9
306-787-4068, Fax: 306-787-1197
info.regina@archives.gov.sk.ca
www.saskarchives.com
Trevor J.D. Powell, Provincial Archivist
306-787-4066

Regina: **Saskatchewan Genealogical Society**
#110, 1514 - 11th Ave., Regina SK S4P 0H2
306-780-9207, Fax: 306-780-3615
sgslibrary@sasktel.net
www.saskgenealogy.com
Celeste Rider, Librarian
Carol Hixson, University Librarian
carol.hixson@uregina.ca
306-585-4132

Regina: **University Archives & Special Collections**
3737 Wascana Pkwy., Regina SK S4S 0A2
306-585-4014, Fax: 306-585-4493
archives@uregina.ca

Saskatoon: **City of Saskatoon Archives**
88 - 24th St. East, Saskatoon SK S7K 0K4
306-975-7811, Fax: 306-975-2612
www.saskatoon.ca/org/clerks_office/archives/index.asp
J. Jeffrey O'Brien, City Archivist
jeff.obrien@sasktoon.ca

Saskatoon: **Diocese of Saskatoon, Archives**
PO Box 1965, Saskatoon SK S7K 3S5
306-244-5651, Fax: 306-933-4606
anglicansynod@sasktel.net
www.saskatoon.anglican.org
Dorothea Funk, Local History Coordinator
d.funk@saskatoonlibrary.ca

Saskatoon: **Local History Room**
311 - 23rd St. East, Saskatoon SK S7K 0J6
306-975-7578, Fax: 306-975-7542
www.saskatoonlibrary.ca

Saskatoon: **Mohyla Institute**
1240 Temperance St., Saskatoon SK S7N 0P1
306-653-1944, Fax: 306-653-1902
mohyla@sasktel.net
www.mohyla.ca
Jeannette Brandell, Archivist

Saskatoon: **Saskatchewan Synod, Archives**
114 Seminary Cres., Saskatoon SK S7N 0X3
306-249-1119, Fax: 306-966-7852
sharonm@sk.sympatico.sk
www.sasksynod.elcic.ca
Nadine Charabin, Chief Archivist
info.saskatoon@archives.gov.sk.ca
306-933-5832

Saskatoon: **Saskatoon Office**
Murray Bldg., 3 Campus Dr., Saskatoon SK S7N 5A4
306-933-5832, Fax: 306-933-7305
info.saskatoon@archives.gov.sk.ca
www.saskarchives.com
Tim Hutchinson, University Archivist

Saskatoon: **University Archives**
#301 Main Library, 3 Campus Dr., University of, Saskatchewan, Saskatoon SK S7N 5A4
306-966-6028, Fax: 306-966-6040
university.archives@usask.ca
www.usask.ca/archives

Verigin: **National Doukhobour Heritage Village Inc.**
PO Box 99, Verigin SK S0A 4H0
306-542-4441
ndhv@yourlink.ca
Philip Perepelkin, Archivist

Weyburn: **Soo Line Historical Society**
411 Industrial Lane, Weyburn SK S4H 1W3
306-842-2922, Fax: 306-842-2922
slhm@sasktel.net

Yukon Territory

Public Libraries

Destruction Bay: **Destruction Bay Volunteer Branch Library**
General Delivery, Destruction Bay YT Y0B 1H0
867-841-5161

Mayo: **Keno City Volunteer Branch Library**
Site 1, Box 17, Mayo YT Y0B 1M0
867-995-2394

Whitehorse: **Yukon Public Libraries**
2071 - 2nd Ave., Whitehorse YT Y1A 2C6
867-667-5239, Fax: 867-393-6333, 800-661-0408
whitehorse.library@gov.yk.ca
www.ypl.gov.yk.ca
Hans Ott, Chair
wplboard@yahoo.ca

Archives

Dawson: **Dawson City Museum**
595 Fifth Ave., Dawson YT Y0B 1G0
867-993-5291, Fax: 867-993-5839
dcmuseum@northwestel.net
Cheryl Thompson, Museum Director/Administration
867-993-5291

Whitehorse: **Yukon Tourism & Culture**
400 College Dr., Whitehorse YT Y1A 2C6
867-667-5321, Fax: 867-393-6253
yukon.archives@gov.yk.ca
www.yukonarchives.ca
Ian Burnett, Territorial Archivist
Ian.Burnett@gov.yk.ca
867-667-5321

SECTION 13
PUBLISHING

Publishers

Book Publishers

Aardvark Enterprises (Div. of Speers Investments Ltd.)
204 Millbank Dr. SW, Calgary, AB T2Y 2H9
403-256-4639,
ISBNs: ISBN: 0-921057; ISSN: 0831-1919
Publishers of poems, short stories & how-to books
J. Alvin Speers, President

AB collector publishing
5835 Grant St., Halifax, NS B3H 1C9
902-425-6935, Fax: 506-385-1981, 888-748-5514
darklady@nbnet.nb.ca
www.abcollectorpublishing.ca

Publisher of poetry, short stories, biography, drama, works relating to photography, ceramics, art & history, in English, French, German
Astrid Brunner, Publisher

Abbeyfield Publishers
 # 304, 160 Balmoral Ave., Toronto, ON M4V 1J7
416-925-6458, Fax: 416-925-4165, 866-370-9407
info@whiteknightbooks.ca
www.whiteknightbooks.ca
Bill Belfontaine, Publisher

ABC Publishing
80 Hayden St., Toronto, ON M4Y 3G2
416-924-1332, Fax: 416-924-2760, 800-265-6397
customerservice@afcanada.com
www.afcanada.com
ISBNs: 0-919030, 0-919891, 0-921846
The premier source for Anglican prayer & hymn books, Path books, & parish programming materials & other resources for Church leaders, the Anglican Book Centre & its publishing unit, ABC Publishing, merged with Augsburg Fortress Canada in 2007. Customers may take advantage of shared ordering & distribution channels

Academic Printing & Publishing
#403, 9-3151 Lakeshore Rd., Kelowna, BC V1W 3S9
250-764-6427, Fax: 250-764-6428
academicpublishing@shaw.ca
www.academicprintingandpublishing.com
ISBNs: ISSNs: 0003-6390; 1206-5269; 1206-3696
Publishers of scholarly books & journals, with emphasis on Philosophy
Roger A. Shiner, Director

Acadiensis Press
Campus House, University of New Brunswick, PO Box 4400, Fredericton, NB E3B 5A3
506-453-4978, Fax: 506-453-5068
acadnsis@unb.ca
www.lib.unb.ca/Texts/Acadiensis
ISBNs: ISSN: 0044-5871
Publisher of ACADIENSIS: The Journal of the History of the Atlantic Region, & books on the culture & history of Atlantic Canada
Dr. David Frank, Managing Editor

Acorn Press
PO Box 22024, Charlottetown, PE C1A 9J2
902-892-8151, Fax: 902-566-0756
info@acornpresscanada.com
www.acornpresscanada.com
ISBNs: 1-894838014-9; 1-894838-16-5-64
Publishing books about Prince Edward Island, with emphasis on Prince Edward Island authors, Acorn Press lists works of fiction, poetry, folklore, history & literature for children
Laurie Brinklow, Publisher

Addison-Wesley Publishers Ltd.
PO Box 580, 26 Prince Andrew Pl., Toronto, ON M3C 2T8
416-447-5101, Fax: 416-443-0948, 800-387-8028
www.pearsoncanada.ca
ISBNs: 9780321531193; 9780321510105
Addison-Wesley, a Pearson imprint, is a key publisher of technical resources of particular interest to computer programmers, engineers & system administrators. Academic titles include astronomy, mathematics & statistics, economics & finance
MR Allan T. Reynolds, President & CEO, Pearson Canada

Aero Training Products Inc.
#105, 6080 Russ Baker Way, Richmond, BC V7B 1B4
604-278-0432, Fax: 604-278-4255, 800-567-3221
www.aerotraining.com
Training materials for pilots & technicians

Aggie Blinkhorn Organization Inc.
PO Box 88549, #101, 13753 - 72nd Ave., Surrey, BC V3W 0X1
604-594-7607, Fax: 604-594-7289
blinkhorn@estacom.com
ISBNs: ISBN: 0-9696248; SAN: 118-5039

Agogic Publishing
#406, 109 - 10 St., New Westminster, BC V3M 3X7
604-290-2692, Fax: 604-540-4419
agogic@iglide.net
www.agogic.biz
ISBNs: ISBN: 1-896595
Publishers of learner's guides for guitar

Alexander Press
2875, av Douglas, Montréal, QC H3R 2C7
514-738-5517, Fax: 514-738-4718, 866-303-5517
alexanderpress@gmail.com
www.alexanderpress.com
ISBNs: ISBN: 1-896800
Publishes Christian Orthodox books & media in Greek, English & French

Alpel Publishing
CP 203, Chambly, QC J3L 4B3
450-658-6205, Fax: 450-658-3514
alpel@videotron.ca
ISBNs: ISBN: 0-9691932, 0-921993
Elie Albala, President

Alpine Book Peddlers
#140, 405 Bow Meadows Cres., Canmore, AB T1W 2W8
403-678-2280, Fax: 403-678-2840
alpinebk@aeontech.ca
ISBNs: ISBN: 0-9699368, 0-9692631, 0-919934, 0-9692457; SAN: 1187546
John Blum

Alter Ego Editions
5922, rue Jeanne-Mance, Montréal, QC H2V 458
514-276-7429, Fax: 514-276-7429
books@alterego.montreal.qc.ca
www.alterego.montreal.qc.ca
ISBNs: ISBN: 1-896743
Small independent French-Language publisher

The Alternate Press
#508, 264 Queens Quay West, Toronto, ON M5J 1B5
416-260-0303, 800-215-9574
altpress@lifemedia.ca
www.lifemedia.ca/altpress
ISBNs: 0-920118-04-6; 978-0-920118-15-3;0-920118-00-3
An imprint of Life Media, The Alternate Press publishes materials promoting home schooling & natural learning, natural parenting, natural business (home-based & green), & poetry
MS Wendy Priesnitz, Publisher

The Althouse Press
Faculty of Education, University of Western Ontario, 1137 Western Rd., London, ON N6G 1G7
519-661-2096, Fax: 519-661-3833
press@uwo.ca
www.edu.uwo.ca/althousepress
ISBNs: ISBN: 0-920354; SAN: 115-1142
Dr. Greg Dickinson, Director

Annick Press Ltd.
15 Patricia Ave., Toronto, ON M2M 1H9
416-221-4802, Fax: 416-221-8400
annickpress@annickpress.com
www.annickpress.com
ISBNs: ISBN: 0-920236, 920303, 1-55037; SAN: 115-0065
Publishers of books for children & young adults; Publishers of Robert Munsch & Loris Lesynski; Publishes approximately 30 books a year
Rick Wilks

Anvil Press
PO Box 3008 MPO, Vancouver, BC V6B 3X5
604-876-8710, Fax: 604-879-2667
info@anvilpress.com
www.anvilpress.com
ISBNs: ISBN: 1-895636
Brian Kaufman, Publisher

Apple Press Publishing
810 Landresse Ct., Newmarket, ON L3X 1M6
905-853-7979, Fax: 905-853-1175, 866-222-8883
info@applepressbooks.com
ISBNs: ISBN: 0-919972
Publishes educational books & resources
George Quinn, President

Aquila Communications Ltd.
2642, rue Diab, Saint-Laurent, QC H4S 1E8
514-338-1065, Fax: 514-338-1948, 800-667-7071
aquila@aquilacommunications.com
www.aquilacommunications.com
ISBNs: ISBN: 0-88510, 2-89054; SAN: 115-2483, 115-8295
Publishes French as a Second Language reading materials from grades 4 through college
Mike Kelada, Vice-President & General Manager
Sami Kelada, President/CEO

Arbeiter Ring Publishing
#201E, 121 Osborne St., Winnipeg, MB R3L 1Y4
204-942-7058, Fax: 204-944-9198
info@arbeiterring.com
www.arbeiterring.com
ISBNs: ISBN: 1-894037
Publishers of books on contemporary politics, culture, and social issues.

Argenta Friends Press
Press Rd., Naksup, BC V0G 1R0
250-366-4314, Fax: 250-366-4314
afp@look.ca
ISBNs: ISBN: 0-920367
Pat Cattermole

Ariane Editions Inc.
#110, 1209, rue Bernard ouest, Outremont, QC H2V 1V7
514-276-2949, Fax: 514-279-4121
info@ariane.qc.ca
www.ariane.qc.ca
ISBNs: ISBN: 2-920987
Martine Vallée
Marc Vallée

Armdale Publications
#203, 10544 - 106 St. NW, Edmonton, AB T5J 2M4
780-429-1073, Fax: 780-425-5844
armadale@global-serve.net
Winston Mohabir
Haloshini Naideo, Manager

Arsenal Pulp Press Ltd.
#200, 341 Water St., Vancouver, BC V6B 1B8
604-687-4233, Fax: 604-687-4283
info@arsenalpulp.com
www.arsenalpulp.com
ISBNs: ISBN: 0-88978, 1-55152; SAN: 115-0847
Publisher with over 200 titles in print, including literary fiction & non-fiction; cultural & gender studies; gay, lesbian & multicultural literature; cookbooks & guidebooks.
Robert Ballantyne, Associate Publisher
Brian Lam, Publisher
Janice Beley, Marketing Director

Art Global
384, av Laurier ouest, Montréal, QC H2V 2K7
514-272-6111, Fax: 514-272-8609
kermoyan@edirom.com
ISBNs: ISBN: 2-920718
Ara Kermoyan

Art Metropole
788 King St. West, Toronto, ON M5V 1N6
416-703-4400, Fax: 416-703-4404
info@artmetropole.com
www.artmetropole.com
ISBNs: ISBN: 0-920956; SAN: 156-9902
Publishers of art books & publications
A.A. Bronson, Director

Artel Educational Resources Ltd.
5528 Kingsway, Burnaby, BC V5H 2G2
604-435-4949, Fax: 604-435-1955, 800-665-9255
info@arteleducational.ca
www.arteleducational.ca
ISBNs: SAN: 116-029X
Publishes educational resources for schools, institutions, home schoolers & the general public; Includes material for all levels of education, ESL & Special Education
Vern Milani, President

Artery Enterprises Ltd.
PO Box 3302, Langley, BC V3A 4R6
604-534-8122, Fax: 604-534-8124, 888-333-1006
info@artery.ca
www.artery.ca
ISBNs: ISBN: 0-920431; SAN: 117-0198

Artextes Éditions / Centre d'information Artexte
#508, 460, rue Sainte-Catherine ouest, Montréal, QC H3B 1A7
514-874-0049, Fax: 514-874-0316
info@artexte.ca
www.artexte.ca

ISBNs: ISBN:
Publishes critical anthologies, monographs & references dealing with visual, media & interdisciplinary art
François Dion, Director

Asquith House Limited/Michael Preston Associates
94 Asquith Ave., Toronto, ON M4W 1J8
416-925-3577, Fax: 416-925-8823, 800-646-6858
m.preston@sympatico.ca

ISBNs: SAN: 115-4915
Publishes educational books, reading programs, maps & globes
M. Preston
P. Preston

Athabasca University
Copyright Office, 1 University Dr., Athabasca, AB T9S 3A3
780-675-6204, Fax: 780-675-6338, 800-788-9041
copyright@athabascau.ca
www.athabascau.ca

ISBNs: ISBN: 0-919737
Lori-Ann Claerhout, Copyright Officer

Athena Books
47 Sarrazin Way, Ottawa, ON K2J 4A5
613-825-6986
athena@magma.ca
www.magma.ca/~athena

ISBNs: ISBN: 1-895520
Robert Allan Stewart, President

Atlantic Book Ltd.
PO Box 1910, 35 Cobequid Dr., Truro, NS B2N 5R1
902-893-1057, Fax: 902-893-1464, 888-773-7727
atlantic.book@ns.sympatico.ca

ISBNs: SAN: 111-0608

Augsburg Fortress Publishers
500 Trillium Dr., Kitchener, ON N2G 4Y4
519-748-2200, Fax: 519-748-9835, 800-265-6397
info@afcanada.com
www.afcanada.com

The publishing wing of the Evangelical Lutheran Church in America, Augsburg Fortress also services the Evangelical Lutheran Church in Canada & publishes Bibles, Bible study resources, multicultural materials, music, & seasonal & special occasion books.
Larry N. Willard, Canadian Operations Director

Aviation Publishers Co. Ltd.
PO Box 1361 B, Ottawa, ON K1P 5R4
613-244-8280, Fax: 613-244-8281
info@aviationpublishers.com
www.aviationpublishers.com

ISBNs: ISBN: 0-9690054
Publishers of the ground school flight training manual "From the Ground Up" as well as other books on flight training & aeronautical theory.
William N. Peppler, President
Graeme Peppler, General Manager

Backroad Mapbooks
#106, 1500 Hartley Ave., Coquitlam, BC V3K 7A1
604-521-6277, Fax: 604-521-6260, 877-520-5670
info@backroadmapbooks.com; hr@backroadmapbooks.com
www.backroadmapbooks.com
Other information: GPS Maps, E-mail: gps@backroadmapbooks.com

Backroad Mapbooks produces up-to-date outdoor recreation Canadian maps & guidebooks.
Russell Mussio, President, rmussio@backroadmapbooks.com
Chris Taylor, Vice-President & Manager, National Sales, ctaylor@backroadmapbooks.com
Andrew Allen, Contact, Mapping Department, aallen@backroadmapbooks.com

Bacon & Hughes Limited
#30, 81 Auriga Dr., Ottawa, ON K2E 7Y5
613-226-8136, Fax: 613-226-8121, 800-563-2468
sales@baconandhughes.ca
www.baconandhughes.ca

Bacon & Hughes Limited provides learning resources from early childhood to the secondary level. Teacher resources & French literature are also available.

Bahá'¡ Distribution Service
#9, 945 Middlefield Rd., Toronto, ON M1V 5E1
416-609-9900, Fax: 416-609-9600, 800-465-3287
orders@bahaibooksonline.com
www.bahaibooksonline.com

Banff Centre Press
The Banff Centre, PO Box 1020, 107 Tunnel Mountain Dr., Banff, AB T1L 1H5
403-762-6410, Fax: 403-762-6277, 800-565-9989
press@banffcentre.ca
www.banffcentre.ca/press

The Banff Centre Press publishes books of contemporary art, culture, & literature.
Mary E. Hofstetter, President & Chief Executive Officer
J.A. (Art) Nutt, Vice-President & Chief Finanacial Officer

The Battered Silicon Dispatch Box
PO Box 204, Shelburne, ON L0N 1S0
519-925-3027, Fax: 519-925-3482
gav@bmts.com
www.batteredbox.com

ISBNs: ISBN: 1-55246
Publishers of Sherlock Holmes and other out-of-print works by Canadian & international authors
George A. Vanderhurgh

Battle Street Books
175 Battle St., Kamloops, BC V2C 2L1
250-372-1119, Fax: 250-372-1830
info@battlestreetbooks.com
www.battlestreetbooks.com

Battle Street Books publishes the novels, plays, & short stories of British Columbia writer, Ernest Langford.

BC Decker Inc.
PO Box 620 LCD 1, #310, 69 John St. South, Hamilton, ON L8N 3K7
905-522-7017, 800-568-7281
customercare@bcdecker.com
www.bcdecker.com

BC Decker publishes the ACP Medicine & ACS Surgery book products in both print & digital editions, as well as ten specialty medical journals, to serve the informational needs of health care professionals & students.

Béliveau Éditeur
5090, rue de Bellechasse, Montréal, QC H1T 2A2
514-253-0403, Fax: 514-256-5078
admin@beliveaueditеur.com
www.beliveaueditеur.com

ISBNs: ISBN: 2-89092
Spécialités: Affaires, finances, biographies, psychologie et sciences humaines, religion, mathématiques, physique, chimie
Mathieu Béliveau, Président-directeur général

Bendall Books Educational Publishers
PO Box 115, Mill Bay, BC V0R 2P0
250-743-2946, Fax: 250-743-2910
admin@bendallbooks.com
www.bendallbooks.com

Bendall Books is a publisher & distributor of educational materials for the college & university sector.
Raymond Bendall, Publisher

The Best of Bridge Publishing Ltd.
#800, 120 Eglington Ave. E, Toronto, ON M4P 1E2
416-322-6552, Fax: 416-322-6936
bestofbridge@robertrose.ca
www.bestofbridge.com

ISBNs: ISBN: 0-9690425
Publishers of cookbooks
Joan Wilson, President

Betelgeuse Books
#516, 3044 Bloor St. West, Toronto, ON M8X 2Y8
Betelgeuse@sympatico.ca
www.maxpages.com/betelgeuse

Betelgeuse Books publishes books about northern Canada.

Between the Lines (BTL)
#404, 720 Bathurst St., Toronto, ON M5S 2R4
416-535-9914, Fax: 416-535-1484, 800-718-7201
info@btlbooks.com; editor@btlbooks.com
www.btlbooks.com

Between the Lines provides books with critical perspectives on culture, economics, & society.
Amanda Crocker, Editorial Coordinator
Paula Brill, Marketing & Promotion Coordinator, Marketing & Promotion
Voula Kraniou, Financial Coordinator
Jennifer Tiberio, Design & Production Coordinator

Bibliothèque nationale du Québec
2275, rue Holt, Montréal, QC H2G 3H1
514-873-1100, Fax: 514-873-9312, 800-363-9028
info@bnquebec.ca
www.bnquebec.ca

ISBNs: ISBN: 2-550, 2-551
Lise Bissonnette, Présidente et directrice générale

Black Moss Press
2450 Byng Rd., Windsor, ON N8W 3E8
519-252-2551, Fax: 519-253-7809
www.blackmosspress.com/pages/2OurBooks.html

The literary press publishes Canadian literature, including poetry & short story anthologies.
Marty Gervais, President

Black Rose Books
CP 1258 Place du Parc, Montréal, QC H2W 2R3
800-565-9523
info@blackrosebooks.net
www.blackrosebooks.net

Black Rose Books publishes critical writing on topics such as philosophy, politics, history, sociology, & hte environment.
Robert Dollins, Editorial Administrator

Blue Heron Press
160 Greenlees Dr., Kingston, ON K7K 6P4
613-549-4334
info@blueheronpress.ca
www.blueheronpress.ca

The literary press specializes in Canadian literature.

Bodhi Publishing
PO Box 144, Kinmount, ON K0M 2A0
705-488-3248, Fax: 705-488-2455
dana@bodhipublishing.org
www.bodhipublishing.netfirms.com

The charitable organization publishes books by Venerable Namgyal Rinpoche.

The Books Collective
#214-21, 10405 Jasper Ave., Edmonton, AB T5J 3S2
780-448-0590, Fax: 780-448-0640
admin@bookscollective.com
www.bookscollective.com

ISBNs: ISBN: 1-895836, 0-88878
Candas Jane Dorsey, Contact

Boomerang Éditeur Jeunesse inc.
33, rue de Chenonceau, Blainville, QC J7B 1P6
450-430-3259, Fax: 450-430-4607
info@boomerangjeunesse.com
www.boomerangjeunesse.com

Resources for children

Borealis Book Publishers
8 Mohawk Cres., Nepean, ON K2H 7G6
613-829-0150, Fax: 613-829-7783, 877-696-2585
drt@borealispress.com
www.borealispress.com

Borealis Book Publishers consists of Borealis Books, Tecumseh Books, Publishing Advisors Inc., Journal of Canadian Poetry, Canadian Critical Editions, & the Parliamentary Handbook / Répertoire Parlementaire Canadien.

Boston Mills Press
c/o Firefly Books, 66 Leek Cres., Richmond Hill, ON L4B 1H1
416-499-8412, Fax: 416-499-8313, 800-387-6192
service@fireflybooks.com

ISBNs: 0-919783; 0-919822
Boston Mills Press publishes nonfiction books for adults, including nature, history, travel, & transportation titles. It is a client publisher of Firefly Books.

Bradley Publications
2352 Smith St., Regina, SK S4P 2P6
306-525-3305, Fax: 306-757-1810

Breakwater Books Ltd.
PO Box 2188, 100 Water St., St. John's, NL A1C 6E6

709-722-6680, Fax: 709-753-0708, 800-563-3333
info@breakwater.nf.net
www.breakwaterbooks.com
ISBNs: ISBN: 0-919519, 0-920911, 1-55081; SAN 115-0154
Newfoundland's first publishing house; specializing in educational & curriculum materials, and resources with an emphasis on the history & unique culture of Newfoundland & Labrador
Clyde Rose, President

Brendan Kelly Publishing Inc.
2122 Highview Dr., Burlington, ON L7R 3X4
905-335-3359, Fax: 905-335-5104
mail@brendankellypublishing.com
www.brendankellypublishing.com
ISBNs: ISBN: 1-895997, 0-9695244
Specialists in the subject areas of mathematics, business, sports & psychology
Brendan Kelly, President

Breton Books & Music
RR#1, Wreck Cove, NS B0C 1H0
902-539-5140, Fax: 902-539-9117, 800-565-5140
bretonbooks@ns.sympatico.ca
www.capebretonbooks.com
ISBNs: ISBN: 1-895415
Showcasing Cape Breton authors
Ronald Caplan, President

Brick Books
PO Box 20081, 431 Boler Rd., London, ON N6K 4G6
519-657-8579
brick.books@sympatico.ca
www.brickbooks.ca
ISBNs: ISBN: 0-919626, 1-894078; SAN: 115-0162
Small literary press devoted to the work of Canadian poets
Kitty Lewis, General Manager

Brindle & Glass Publishing Ltd.
6 - 356 Simcoe St., Victoria, BC V8V 1L1
250-360-0829
info@brindleandglass.com
www.brindleandglass.com
Ruth Linka, Publisher

Broadview Press
PO Box 1243, #5, 280 Perry St., Peterborough, ON K9J 7H5
705-743-8990, Fax: 705-743-8353
customerservice@broadviewpress.com
www.broadviewpress.com
ISBNs: ISBN: 0-921149, 1-55111; SAN: 115-6772
With additional offices in Guelph, Halifax & Calgary; specializing in English Studies & Philosopy
Don LePan, President

Broken Jaw Press Inc. (MAPP)
PO Box 596 A, Fredericton, NB E3B 5A6
506-454-5127, Fax: 506-454-5127
editors@brokenjaw.com
www.brokenjaw.com
ISBNs: ISBN: 0-921411, 1-896647, 1-55391; SAN: 117-1437
Joe Blades, Publisher

Broquet inc. / Broquet Publishing Company Inc.
97-B, Montee des Bouleaux, Saint-Constant, QC J5A 1A9
450-638-3338, Fax: 450-638-4338
info@broquet.qc.ca
www.broquet.qc.ca
ISBNs: ISBN: 2-89000
Antoine Broquet, Éditeur

The Brucedale Press
PO Box 2259, Port Elgin, ON N0H 2C0
519-832-6025
brucedale@bmts.com
www.bmts.com/~brucedale
ISBNs: ISBN: 0-9698716, 1-896922
Specializing in Bruce Peninsula & Queen's Bush writers, artists & photographers
Anne Duke Judd, Contact

Bungalo Books
#100, 17 Elk Ct., Kingston, ON K7M 7A4
613-374-2494, Fax: 613-389-2351
bungalo@pokeweed.com; bungalo@cgocable.net
www.bungalobooks.com
ISBNs: ISBN: 0-921285
Books for children
John Bianchi, President, john@johnbianchi.com
Frank B. Edwards, Publisher

Bunker to Bunker Books
PO Box 914 T, Calgary, AB T2H 2H4
403-512-2123
bunkertobunkerbooks@yahoo.com
www.bunkertobunkerbooks.com
ISBNs: ISBN: 0-9699039
Military firearms books, British & Canadian military collectible books, WW II history
Geoff Todd, Contact

Burgher Books
#504, 555 Richmond St. West, Toronto, ON M5V 3B1
416-504-3471, Fax: 416-504-6604
info@burgher.com

BuschekBooks
PO Box 74053, 5 Beechwood Ave., Ottawa, ON K1M 2H9
613-744-2589, Fax: 613-744-2967
contact@buschekbooks.com
www.buschekbooks.com
ISBNs: ISBN: 0-9699904, 1-894543
John Buschek, Publisher

Butterfly Books Ltd.
PO Box 294, Maple Creek, SK S0N 1N0
W.P. Stewart, President

Butterworths Canada Ltd.
#700, 123 Commerce Valley Dr. East, Markham, ON L3T 7W8
905-479-2665, 800-668-6481
media@lexisnexis.ca; customerservice@lexisnexis.ca
www.butterworths.ca
ISBNs: ISBN: 0-409
Now a part of LexisNexis Canada, Butterworths' catalogue focuses on Canadian law. Vancouver Office: #920, 355 Burrard St., Vancouver, BC, V6C 2G8, Tel.: 604-684-1462. Ottawa Office: #700, 112 Kent St., Ottawa, ON, K1P 5P2, Tel.: 613-238-3499. Toronto Office: #400, 905 King St. West, Toronto, ON, M6K 3G9, Tel.: 416-862-7656. Montréal Office: #111, 215 rue St. Jacques, Montréal, QC, H2Y 1M6.

Caitlin Press Inc.
8100 Alderwood Rd., Halfmoon Bay, BC V0N 1Y1
604-885-9194, 877-964-4953
www.caitlin-press.com
ISBNs: ISBN: 1-894759, 0-920576; SAN: 115-2793
Specializing in BC authors, poetry, stories of the Central Interior and in works by and about BC women.
Vici Johnstone, Publisher & Owner, vici@caitlin-press.com

Callawind Publications Inc. / Publications Callawind inc.
#179, 3551, boul St. Charles, Kirkland, QC H9H 3C4
514-685-9109, Fax: 514-685-7952
info@callawind.com
www.callawind.com
ISBNs: ISBN: 1-896511
Specializing in cookbooks & children's books; also available in the U.S. from #200, 4501 Forbes Blvd., Lanham, MD, 20706, Tel: 800-462-6420, www.bibliodistribution.com.
Marcy Claman, President

Cambridge University Press
66 Pine St. South, Port Hope, ON L1A 3G1
905-885-9315, Fax: 905-885-9332, 877-406-5248
toronto@cambridge.org
www.cambridge.org
ISBNs: ISBN: 0-521; SAN: 281-3769
Cambridge U. Press publishes academic & educational writing from arouns the world, currently over 2500 titles and 200 journals per year. Vancouver office: c/o Curriculum Plus, 40407 Ayr Dr., Box 2319, Vancouver, BC, V0N 3G0, Tel: 800-660-1244, Email: ian.sutherland@shaw.ca
Pamela Robinson, Sales Representative, probinson@cambridge.org

Canada Law Book Inc.
240 Edward St., Aurora, ON L4G 3S9
905-841-6472, Fax: 905-841-5085, 800-263-2037
www.canadalawbook.ca
ISBNs: ISBN: 0-88804
Specializing in legal resources (print & online), & current awareness services
Stuart Morrison, President, The Cartwright Group Ltd.
Ruth Epstein, VP, Canada Law Book LL.B.

Canadian Bible Society
10 Carnforth Rd., Toronto, ON M4A 2S4
416-757-4171, Fax: 416-757-3376, 800-465-2425
info@biblesociety.ca
www.biblesociety.ca
ISBNs: ISBN: 0-88834; SAN: 112-5559
The Society translates, publishes & distributes the Bible throughout Canada
Rev. Ted Seres, National Director, tseres@biblesociety.ca
Dennis Hillia, Director, Operations, dhillis@biblesociety.ca

Canadian Centre for Community Renewal (CCCR)
PO Box 1161 A, Port Alberni, BC V9Y 7M1
250-752-4710, Fax: 250-752-4718, 888-255-6779
www.cedworks.com
ISBNs: 1-895818
CCCR publishes information on the principles of community economic development. The on-line catalogue carries nearly 600 articles, papers, and books available in portable document format (PDF).
Mike Lewis, Executive Director, 250-723-1139, mlewis@cedworks.com
Don McNair, Editor & Publisher, mcnair@cedworks.com

Canadian Circumpolar Institute
1 - 42 Pembina Hall, University of Alberta, Edmonton, AB T6G 2H8
403-492-4512, Fax: 403-492-1153
ccinst@gpu.srv.ualberta.ca
www.uofaweb.ualberta.ca/polar/
ISBNs: ISBN: 1-896445, 0-919058
Elaine Maloney, Managing Editor, elaine.maloney@ualberta.ca
Cindy S. Mason, Business Manager, 780-492-4512, cindy.mason@ualberta.ca

Canadian Council on Social Development
#100, 190 O'Connor St., Ottawa, ON K2P 2R3
613-236-8977, Fax: 613-236-2750
council@ccsd.ca.
www.ccsd.ca
ISBNs: ISBN: 0-88810; SAN: 115-284X
CCSD is a non-governmental, not-for-profit publisher in the social development field, with titles covering economic security & poverty, employment & labour market issues, social policies & programs.
Peggy Taillon, President & CEO, ext. 253, taillon@ccsd.ca
Katherine Scott, VP, Research, ext. 245, scott@ccsd.ca

Canadian Educators' Press
1230 White Clover Way, Mississauga, ON L5V 1K7
905-826-0578
cepress@sympatico.ca
ISBNs: ISBN: 1-896191
CEP publishes titles related to Canadian law and law enformcement.
Silma Deonarine, Manager

Canadian Government Publishing
350 Albert St., 4th Floor, Ottawa, ON K1A 0S5
613-941-5995, Fax: 613-998-1450, 800-635-7943
publications@pwgsc.gc.ca
publications.gc.ca
ISBNs: ISBN: 0-660, 0-662; SAN: 115-2882
The official publisher for the Government of Canada, CGP publishes priced documents in print, Braille, and large-print formats and on a variety of subjects, such as health, finance, science and education, among others. These publications include books, serials, monographs, maps, pamphlets, and information kits. Formats also include online publishing and electronic publications.

The Canadian Institute for Law, Theology & Public Policy
89 Douglasview Rise SE, Calgary, AB T2Z 2P5
403-720-8714, Fax: 403-720-8746
ciltpp@cs.com
www.ciltpp.com
ISBNs: ISBN: 1-896363
Publishes books and taps which seek to integrate in depth the Christian faith with public policy issues
Will Moore, President

Canadian Institute of Chartered Accountants (CICA)
277 Wellington St. West, Toronto, ON M5V 3H2
416-977-3222, Fax: 416-977-8585
www.cica.ca
ISBNs: 1-55385, 0-88800
Published material includes resources for accountants & accounting students.
Doug Baker, Chair FCA
Kevin Dancey, President & CEO FCA, 416-204-3333, Fax: 416-204-3405, kevin.dancey@cica.ca
Peter Hoult, Director, Information & Productivity, 416-204-3330, peter.hoult@cica.ca

Canadian Institute of Resources Law
#3353 MFH, University of Calgary, 2500 University Dr. NW, Calgary, AB T2N 1N4
403-220-3200, Fax: 403-282-6182
cirl@ucalgary.ca
www.cirl.ca
ISBNs: ISBN: 0-919269; SAN: 115-2904
The Institute publishes the results of its research & proceedings

of conferences that it sponsors, on the topic of Natural Resources Law. Titles include, "Canada Energy Law Service."
Richard Neufeld, Chair
J. Owens Saunders, Executive Director, 403-220-3975, josaunde@ucalgary.ca

Canadian Institute of Strategic Studies
#702, 165 University Ave., Toronto, ON M5H 3B8
416-322-8128, Fax: 416-322-8129
info@ciss.ca
www.ciss.ca

ISBNs: 1-894736, 0-919769; SAN: 115-2912
The Institute publishes books, papers & journals devoted to the research & analysis of Canadian Military Affairs, security affairs & international relations in general.
Sen. Hugh Segal, Chair
Alex Morrison, President

Canadian Institute of Ukrainian Studies Press (CIUS Press)
University of Toronto, Rm. 308, 256 McCaul St., Toronto, ON M5T 1W5
416-978-6934, Fax: 416-978-2672
cius@chass.utoronto.ca
www.ciuspress.com
ISBNs: 0-920862, 1-895571, 1-894301, 1-894865; SAN: 115-2920
The Institute is the publishing arm of the Canadian Institute of Ukranian Studies. It focuses on original research in English on Ukrainian history, language, literature, contemporary Ukraine, and Ukrainians in Canada. It also publishes English translations of Ukrainian monographs and memoirs.
Dr. Zenon Kohut, Director, CIUS

Canadian International Council (CIC)
#210, 45 Willcocks St., Toronto, ON M5S 1C7
416-946-7209, Fax: 416-946-7319, 800-668-2442
info@onlinecic.org
www.onlinecic.org
ISBNs: 0-9866175; SAN: 115-2890
CIC is a non-partisan, nationwide research council which publishes content on Canada's foreign policy.
Jim Balsillie, Chair
Jennifer Jeffs, President
Laura Sunderland, Communications Officer, lsunderland@onlinecic.org

Canadian Museum of Civilization
100 Laurier St., Gatineau, QC K1A 0M8
819-776-8387, Fax: 819-776-8535, 800-555-5621
publications@civilization.ca
www.civilization.ca
ISBNs: ISBN: 0-660; SAN: 115-4532
Together with the Canadian War Museum, the CMC publishes a range of books, papers, essays, journals and reports with a focus on Canadian history, prehistory & civilization for both adults and children.
Victor Rabinovitch, President & CEO, 819-776-7116, victor.rabinovitch@civilization.ca
Chantal Schryer, VP, Public Affairs & Publishing, 819-776-8499, chantal.schryer@civilization.ca
Stéphanie Verner, Media Relations Officer, 819-776-7169, stephanie.verner@civilization.ca

Canadian Paperbacks Publishing Ltd.
17 Gwynne Ave., Ottawa, ON K1Y 1X1
613-722-1171,
ISBNs: ISBN: 0-919554
This is the publisher of "A Dictionary of Canadian Artists," a resource of biographies. The copyright of this 8-volume series however was sold to the National Gallery of Canada (www.gallery.ca) in 2007, where the project continues online.
Colin S. MacDonald, President

Canadian Plains Research Center Press (CPRCP Press)
University of Regina, 3737 Wascana Parkway, Regina, SK S4S 0A2
306-585-4758, Fax: 306-585-4699, 866-874-2257
canadian.plains@uregina.ca
www.cprcpress.ca
ISBNs: ISBN: 0-88977; SAN: 115-0278
The CPRCP Press is publishing arm of the University of Regina. It publishes scholarly manuscripts on aspects of life in the Prairie region, as well as non-fiction trade titles concerning the Prairies.
Harry Diaz, Executive Director, harry.diaz@uregina.ca
Brian Mlazgar, Publications Manager, 306-585-4795, brian.mlazgar@uregina.ca

Canadian Scholars' Press Inc. (CSPI)
#801, 180 Bloor St. West, Toronto, ON M5S 2V6
416-929-2774, Fax: 416-929-1926
info@cspi.org
www.cspi.org
ISBNs: 1-55130, 0-921627, 1-894184
CSPI is an independent publisher of texts, scholarly works, and titles that present themes and issues of interest to the general Canadian market. It also imprints Women's Press and Sumach Press, both with a focus on feminist work which contributes to the social identity of Canada, and also Kellom Books which carries poetry, fiction and non-fiction by men.
Andrew Wayne, President, awayne@cspi.org
Rick Walker, VP, Book Publishing, rick.walker@cspi.org
Drew Hawkins, VP, Custom Publishing, dhawkins@cspi.org

Canadian Urban Institute / Institut urbain du Canada
PO Box 612, #402, 555 Richmond St. W, Toronto, ON M5V 3B1
416-365-0816, Fax: 416-365-0650
cui@canurb.com
www.canurb.com
ISBNs: 1-895446
Terry Cooke, Chair
Michael Fenn, Interim President & CEO, 416-365-0816, X-233, mfenn@canurb.com

Canadian Water Resources Association (CWRA) / Association canadienne des ressources hydriques
1401 - 14th St., Lethbridge, AB T1H 2W6
403-317-0017
www.cwra.org
ISBNs: 1-896513, 0-9694535
CWRA publishes journals, books & reports on water resources in Canada. Titles include the quarterly publication, Canadian Water Resources Journal, the newsletter, Water News.
Rick Ross, Executive Director, fjross@telusplanet.net

CANAV Books
51 Balsam Ave., Toronto, ON M4E 3B6
416-698-7559, Fax: 416-693-4344
www.canavbooks.com
ISBNs: ISBN: 0-9690703, 0-91022; SAN: 115-3021
Publishers of books on aviation history
Larry Milberry, Publisher, larry@canavbooks.com

Can-Ed Media Ltd.
43 Moccasin Trail, Toronto, ON M3C 1Y5
416-445-3900, Fax: 416-445-9976
canedmedia@sympatico.ca
ISBNs: ISBN: 0-920102; SAN: 170-0073
Specializes in dance & fitness recordings & instruction books

Cape Breton University Press
PO Box 5300, 1250 Grand Lake Rd., Sydney, NS B1P 6L2
902-563-1955, Fax: 902-563-1177
cbu_press@cbu.ca
www.cbu.ca/press
ISBNs: 0-920336, 1-897009; SAN: 115-5458
Publishing arm of Cape Breton University.
Mike R. Hunter, Editor-in-Chief, 902-563-1955, mike_hunter@cbu.ca

Capemara Communications Inc.
4623 William Head Rd., Victoria, BC V9C 3Y7
250-474-3935, Fax: 250-478-3979, 800-661-0368
info@capamara.com
capamara.com

This publisher offers specialty magazines and trade newspapers for various industries in Canada and around the world. Titles include: Aquaculture, Hatchery International, Small Farm Canada, Crane & Hoist Canada.

Captus Press
 # 14-15, 1600 Steeles Ave. West, Concord, ON L4K 4M2
416-736-5537, Fax: 416-736-5793
info@captus.com
www.captus.com
ISBNs: 0-921801, 1-895712, 1-896691, 1-55322
Captus is a publisher of textbooks which provide a Canadian context for university and college courses in the subjects of business, law, disability studies, and Aboriginal economic development.
Randy Hoffman, President

Carraig Books / Livres Carraig
CP 8733, Sainte-Foy, QC G1V 4N6
418-651-5918
carraigbooks@sympatico.ca
ISBNs: 0-9690805, 0-9698581
The company specializes in books on Quebec-Irish history with titles including, "Eyewitness - Grosse Ile - 1847," "The Shamrock Trail, Tracing the Irish in Quebec City."
Marianna O'Gallagher, m.ogallagher@sympatico.ca

Carswell
One Corporate Plaza, 2075 Kennedy Rd., Toronto, ON M1T 3V4
416-609-8000, Fax: 416-298-5094, 800-387-5351
carswell.comments@thomson.com
www.carswell.com
ISBNs: 0-459, 0-7798, 0-88820; SAN: 115-0316
Carswell publishes directories, including the Lexpert Legal Directory, Tax & Accounting, Business, Compliance & International.
Don Van Meer, President/CEO

CBC Learning
PO Box 500 A, 205 Wellington St. West, Toronto, ON M5W 1E6
416-205-6384, Fax: 416-205-2376, 866-999-3072
cbclearning@cbc.ca
www.cbceds.ca
ISBNs: ISBN: 0-660; SAN: 115-2777
Publishes resources related to CBC programs & programming

CCH Canadian Limited
#300, 90 Sheppard Ave. East, Toronto, ON M2N 3A1
416-224-2224, Fax: 416-224-2243, 800-268-4522
cservice@cch.ca; support@cch.ca
www.cch.ca
ISBNs: ISBN: 1-55367, 1-55141, 0-88796, 1-55496; SAN: 115-2785
Publishers of professional information products involving tax, accounting, law, financial planning & human resources
Ian Rhind, President/CEO
Allan Orr, VP, Finance & Administration, aorr@cch.ca

Cedar Cave Books
PO Box 180, Newmarket, ON L3Y 4X1
Fax: 905-895-7613, 866-895-9296
info@cedarcave.com
www.cedarcave.com/

Cedar Cave Books are self-publishers of a number of non-fiction books, with titles including "Yoga for Cats," and "Florida, Eh?"

Centax Books & Distribution
1150 - 8th Ave., Regina, SK S4R 1C9
306-359-7580, Fax: 800-823-6829, 800-667-5595
centax@printwest.com
www.centaxbooks.com
ISBNs: 0-919845, 1-895292, 1-894022, 1-897010
Together with its sister company, Publishing Solutions, Centax produces and markets cookbooks, RCMP history books, business and family management books, family lifestyle, gardening, self-help and sports books.
Dan Marce, General Manager, d.marce@printwest.com
Tracy Wilson, Office Manager, t.wilson@printwest.com
Margo Embury, Director, Operations, m.embury@printwest.com

Centre for Addiction & Mental Health (CAMH)
33 Russell St., Toronto, ON M5S 2S1
416-595-6059, Fax: 416-593-4694, 800-661-1111
publications@camh.net
www.camh.net
Other information: 1-800-463-627
ISBNs: 0-88868, 1-77052; SAN 115-0081
CAMH publishes resources for therapists, doctors, nurses, front-line workers, and other professionals in the fields of addictions & mental health. Materials include research papers, pamphlets, newsletters and journals.

Centre for the Grief Journey Inc.
PO Box 201, 2 - 3415 Dixie Rd., Mississauga, ON L4Y 4J6
905-624-8080, Fax: 905-624-6742
info@griefjourney.com
www.griefjourney.com
ISBNs: 0-9697841
The company publishes books & other resources to support the grieving process.
Dr. Bill Webster, bwebster@griefjourney.com

Le Centre FORA
432, av Westmount, unité H, Sudbury, ON P3A 5Z8
705-524-3672, Fax: 705-524-8535, 888-814-4422
info@centrefora.on.ca
www.centrefora.on.ca
ISBNs: ISBN: 2-921706
Centre francophone d'édition en éducation de base des adultes, et de diffusion de matériel éducatif pour tout âge. Service d'édition: coordination de projects, production, impression, rédaction, etc. Service de diffusion. Bureaux: Sudbury, North Bay.
Yolande Clément, Directrice générale, yclement@centrefora.on.ca

Centre franco-ontarien de ressources pédagogiques
435, rue Donald, Ottawa, ON K1K 4X5
613-747-8000, Fax: 613-747-2808, 877-742-3677
cforp@cforp.on.ca
www.cforp.on.ca

Centre multiservices en éducation; développement, édition; production multimedia; programmation; formation professionnelle; imprimerie
Gilles Leroux, Directeur général, x253, robert.arseneault@cforp.on.ca

Céthial Books for Children (Canada) Inc.
PO Box 252 Mount Royal, Montréal, QC H3P 3C5
514-278-3333, 800-238-4425
cethial@cethial.com; info@cethial.com
www.cethial.com
ISBNs: ISBN: 1-55274, 1-896933

CGS Communications, Inc.
2521 Nicklaus Ct., Burlington, ON L7M 4V1
905-332-0083, Fax: 905-319-1641
info@cgscommunications.com
www.cgscommunications.com
ISBNs: ISBN: 0-929079
Published materials include books on career/educational planning and scholarship informaton.

CHA Press
17 York St., Ottawa, ON K1N 9L6
613-241-8005, Fax: 613-241-5055
custserv@cha.ca
www.cha.ca/cart/catalog/cha-publications.html
ISBNs: ISBN: 0-919100, 1-896151
Pamela C. Fralick, President & CEO

The Charlton Press
PO Box 820 Willowdale B, Toronto, ON M2K 2R1
416-488-1418, Fax: 416-488-4656, 800-442-6042
chpress@charltonpress.com
www.charltonpress.com
ISBNs: ISBN: 0-88968: SAN: 115-0235
Publishers of catalogues on 20th century collectables including coins, bank notes & others
W.K. Cross, Publisher

Chenelière Éducation
7001, boul St-Laurent, Montréal, QC H2S 3E3
514-273-1066, Fax: 514-276-0324, 800-565-5531
info@cheneliere-education.ca
www.cheneliere.ca
ISBNs: ISBN: 2-89310, 2-89461
Y compris Groupe Beauchemin, Gaëtan Morin Éditeur, et les Publications Graficor
Jacques Rochefort, Président-directeur général, jrochefort@cheneliere.ca
Michel Carl Perron, Vice-président, Production, mcperron@cheneliere.ca

Chestnut Publishing Group
#610, 4005 Bayview Ave, Toronto, ON M2M 3Z9
416-224-5824, Fax: 416-224-0595
sharkstark@sympatico.ca
www.chestnutpublishing.com
ISBNs: ISBN: 1-894601, 0-9731237, 0-9689552, 0-9688946
CPG publishes educational material for both adult & children, ESL materials, as well as novels & teacher's guides targeted at reluctant readers. It has 4 imprints: Chestnut Publishing, High Interest Publishing (HIP), Lynx Publishing and Patnor Books with its New Start Suspense Series.
Stanley Starkman

Clifford Ford Publications
#15, 120 Walnut Ct., Ottawa, ON K1R 7W2
613-237-0550
crford@cliffordfordpublications.ca
www.cliffordfordpublications.ca
ISBNs: ISBN: 0-919883
This is a publisher of a wide range of sheet music, including Canadian historical anthologies, choral collections and pedagogical music, as well as those works composed by Clifford Ford.

CNIB
1929 Bayview Ave., Toronto, ON M4G 3E8
416-486-2500, Fax: 416-480-7700, 800-563-2642
info@cnib.ca
www.cnib.ca
ISBNs: 0-616, 0-921122
CNIB reproduces materials in alternative formats, including DAISY audio, Braille

Coach House Books
401 Huron St., Toronto, ON M5S 2G5
416-979-2217, Fax: 416-977-1158, 800-367-6360
mail@chbooks.com
www.chbooks.com
ISBNs: 1-55245, 1-897439, 1-77056
Coach House Books publishes Canadian content across a variety of fields: fiction, poetry, art & architecture, drama & performing arts, children's, social science & travel, including a series of books about Toronto. It has been nominated for a slew of literary awards, such as Griffin Poetry Prizes, Governor General's Awards, Trillium Book Awards, and the Ontario Premier's Award for Excellence in the Arts.
Stan Bevington, Publisher, stan@chbooks.com
Alana Wilcox, Editorial Director, alana@chbooks.com

Codasat Canada Ltd.
3122 Blenheim St., Vancouver, BC V6K 4J7
604-228-9952, Fax: 604-228-4733
www.codasat.com

In addition to inventory management services, Codasat offers sales & distribution services to small & medium-sized publishers wishing to sell books in the Canadian market.
Sandra Hargreaves, Co-owner

Colombo & Company
42 Dell Park Ave., Toronto, ON M6B 2T6
416-782-6853, Fax: 416-782-0285
jrc@ca.inter.net
www.colombo.ca
ISBNs: 1-894540, 0-9695092, 1-896308
This is the publishing imprint for books by John Robert Colombo & colleagues, including poetry & poetry anthologies, Canadiana, reference works & quotation collections, mysteries, humour, & translations.
John Robert Colombo, Publisher

Commoners' Publishing Society Inc.
631 Tubman Cres., Ottawa, ON K1V 8L5
613-523-2444, Fax: 613-260-0401, 866-890-9489
cheriton@on.aibn.com
www.commonerspublishing.com
ISBNs: 0-88970; SAN: 115-0243
Although by no means limited to men's issues, Commoners' publishes books on parenting, marriage and divorce policy from a male perspecitive.
Glenn Cheriton, President

The Communication Project
9 Lobraico Lane, Whitchurch-Stouffville, ON L4A 7X5
905-640-8914, Fax: 905-640-2922, 800-772-7765
tcp@tcpnow.com
www.tcppress.com
ISBNs: ISBN: 1-896232
A research & education group, with an independent press, dedicated to quality books for children & adults in the areas of literacy, science education, life course, & intergenerational relationships

Community Legal Education Ontario (CLEO) / Éducation juridique communautaire Ontario
#600, 119 Spadina Ave., Toronto, ON M5V 2L1
416-408-4420, Fax: 416-408-4424
cleo@cleo.on.ca
www.cleo.on.ca
ISBNs: 0-88903; SAN: 115-3110
CLEO is a community legal clinic specializing in public legal education and publishing booklets, pamphlets, fact sheets & manuals, all written in clear language for people with low incomes, immigrants & refugees, seniors, injured workers, & women. Topics include workers' rights, landlord & tenant law, immigration law, family law, consumer rights, & women's rights. Most publications are available in French, and some are available in other languages. MOst are free of charge.
Julie Mathews, Chief Privacy Officer, privacyofficer@cleonet.ca

Company's Coming Publishing Limited
2311 - 96 St., Edmonton, AB T6N 1G3
780-450-6223, Fax: 780-450-1857
info@companyscoming.com
www.companyscoming.com
ISBNs: 1-896891, 1-897069, 1-895455, 0-9690695, 0-9693322, 1-897477
This is the publisher of an extensive array of cookbooks, including a selection of series, with Kids Cooking, Pint Size, and Focus as examples. In addition, Company's Coming publishes a series of craft books.
Grant Lovig, President & Publisher
Gail Lovig, Vice-President, Marketing & Distribution
Kim Hamilton, Marketing Coordinator, 780-450-6223, X-264, kimh@companyscoming.com

Continental Records Company Ltd.
PO Box 7, Streetsville, ON L5M 2B7
905-813-9544, Fax: 905-812-4993, 800-494-6129
conrecs@gocontinental.com
www.gocontinental.com
ISBNs: 0-920325
In addition to selling 45 RPM records & unique oldies on CD, Continental Records publishes chart books and music books. Titles include The Record & CD Collector's Directory. The company also offers The Directory of Canadian Recruiters, a compilation of employment firms & organizations.
Neil Patte, President

Continuing Legal Education Society of British Columbia (CLEBC)
#300, 845 Cambie St., Vancouver, BC V6B 5T2
604-669-3544, Fax: 604-669-9260, 800-663-0437
custserv@cle.bc.ca
www.cle.bc.ca
ISBNs: 1-55258, 0-86504, SAN. 115-3153
CLEBC specializes in books, papers, case digests & manuals for the legal profession, covering a variety of practice areas including aboriginal law, administrative law, criminal law, family law, labour, real estate, tax and more. An online subscription service is also available.
Susan Munro, Director of Publications, 604-893-2106, smunro@cle.bc

Copp Clark Professional
#1, 1675 Sismet Rd., Mississauga, ON L4W 4K8
905-238-2882, Fax: 905-238-3413, 877-389-3378
info@coppclark.com
www.coppclark.com
ISBNs: 0-7730, 0-273
The oldest, continuously active publisher in Canada, Copp Clark publishes resources for the financial trading community, authoritative reference data on holiday observances.
Ronald S. Marr, President & Publisher
Grace D'Alfonso, Editorial Director

Cordillera Books
PO Box 46, 8415 Granville St., Vancouver, BC V6P 4Z9
604-261-1695, Fax: 604-266-4469
richbook@shaw.ca
ISBNs: 1-895590
Publishers of naval, maritime history and shipping books
S.C. Heal

Cormorant Books Inc.
#230, 215 Spadina Ave., Toronto, ON M5T 2C7
416-929-4957, Fax: 416-929-3596, 800-565-9523
www.cormorantbooks.com
ISBNs: 0-920953, 1-896951, 1-897151; SAN: 115-4176
Cormorant Books specializes in fiction emerging Canadian writers, reissues of Canadian literary classics, and English translations of works by Quebec writers. There is a selection of gay & lesbian literature, as well as non-fiction titles, including historical biographies and memoirs.
J. Marc Coté, President & Publisher

Coteau Books
2517 Victoria Ave., Regina, SK S4P 0T2
306-777-0170, Fax: 306-522-5152, 800-440-4471
coteau@coteaubooks.com
www.coteaubooks.com
ISBNs: 0-919926, 1-55050
Coteau Books is a not-for-profit, cooperatively run press specializing in fiction, poetry, drama & fiction for young readers, with some emphasis on Saskatchewan writers.
Nik L. Burton, Managing Editor

Crabtree Publishing Company
616 Welland Ave., St. Catharines, ON L2M 5V6
905-682-5221, Fax: 800-355-7166, 800-387-7650
custserv@crabtreebooks.com
www.crabtreebooks.com
ISBNs: 0-7787, 0-86505, 1-4271; SAN: 115-1436
With offices in the U.S., Canada, the U.K. and Australia, Crabtreespecializes in children's non-fiction work & educational products on many curriculum subjects. Material is published in an audio format and in several languages, including Spanish and French. Imprints include: A Bobbie Kalman Book; Leaps and Bounds Books; and Look, Listen, & Learn.
Lisa Antonsen, National Account Manager
Peter Crabtree, President

Cranberry Tree Press
#173, 5060 Tecumseh Rd. East, Windsor, ON N8T 1C1
Fax: 519-945-6207
mail@cranberrytreepress.com
www.cranberrytreepress.com

ISBNs: 0-9681325, 0-9684218, 1-894668
Cranberry Tree Press is a contract, co-operative publishing service with editors & designers on staff.
Lenore Langs, Publisher & Editor

Creative Book Publishing Ltd.
PO Box 8660 A, St. John's, NL A1B 3T7
709-748-0813, Fax: 709-579-6511
nlbooks@transcontinental.ca
www.creativebookpublishing.ca
ISBNs: 0-920021, 1-895387, 1-894294, 1-897174, 0-920884
Creative Book Publishing specializes in works by Newfoundland & Labrador authors, promoting them to national & international markets. Genres include fiction, poetry, memoirs, history, women's studies and more. Books are published under 3 imprints: Creative Publishers, Killick Press, & Tuckamore Books.
Russell Wangersky, General Manager, rwanger@thetelegram.com
Donna Francis, Editor & Marketing Manager, donna.francis@transcontinental.ca

Crisp Learning Canada
60 Briarwood Ave., Mississauga, ON L5G 3N6
905-274-5678, Fax: 905-278-2801, 800-446-4797
info@crisplearning.ca
www.crisplearning.ca
ISBNs: 0-921601; SAN: 116-0478
Crisp Learning publishes a library of books & training manuals specializing in: communication, conflict resolution, presentation skills, telephone skills, sales & marketing, customer service, managing, organizational development, and personal improvement.
Stephen Connolly, President, steveconnolly@homeroom.ca

Cross Canada Books
354 Wellesley St. East, Toronto, ON M4X 1H3
416-925-7807, Fax: 416-925-9946, 800-473-4078
doug.fisher@sympatico.ca
ISBNs: 0-920400
Book distributor

Crown Publications Inc.
PO Box 9452 Prov Govt, 563 Superior St., Victoria, BC V8W 9V7
250-387-6409, Fax: 250-387-1120, 800-663-6105
crownpub@gov.bc.ca
www.crownpub.bc.ca
ISBNs: ISBN: 0-9696417
Crown Publications is the authorized distributor of British Columbia acts, regulations & related legislative publications, and an authorized agent for Canadian Federal Government publications.
Sherry Brown, Director, 250-356-6876, sherry.brown@gov.bc.ca
Wendy Pope, Manager, 250-356-5392, wendy.pope@gov.bc.ca

Culture Concepts Books
69 Ashmount Cres., Toronto, ON M9R 1C9
416-245-8119, Fax: 416-245-3383
cultureconcepts@rogers.com
www.cultureconceptsbooks.ca
ISBNs: 0-921472
Culture Concepts Books publishes fiction titles and academic titles in adult education, food, nutrition and culture. Also offered are professional editing services & manuscript evaluation, selected literary agency & book production.
Thelma Barer-Stein, President

Cyclops Press
#1, 164 Browning Ave., Toronto, ON M4K 1W5
mail@cyclopspress.com
www.cyclopspress.com
ISBNs: 1-894177
An independent, artist-run, multimedia, literary micro- publisher specializing in poetry, novels, feature films & videos, CDs, interdisciplinary art projects. Material is distributed through Signature Editions, www.signature-editions.com.
Clive Holden
Alissa York

Dance Collection Danse Publishing
145 George St., Toronto, ON M5A 2M6
416-365-3233, Fax: 416-365-3169, 800-665-5320
talk@dcd.ca
www.dcd.ca
ISBNs: ISBN: 0-929003
Publisher of DANCE COLLECTION DANSE MAGAZINE, and books on dance
Miriam Adams, Co-director

Database Directories
588 Dufferin St., London, ON N6B 2A4
519-433-1666, Fax: 519-430-1131
mail@databasedirectory.com
www.databasedirectory.com
ISBNs: ISBN: 1-896537
Publisher of current contact information on Canadian schools, libraries, book retailers & municipalities
Lesley Classic, CEO

David C. Cook Distribution Canada
PO Box 98, 55 Woodslee Ave., Paris, ON N3L 3E5
800-263-2664, Fax: 800-461-8575, 000-000-0000
custserv@davidccook.ca
www.davidccook.ca
ISBNs: SAN: 170-0197
Distribution wing of David C. Cook Publishing, Colorado Springs, CO. Specializing in Christian literature & communication resources

Davus Publishing
150 Norfolk St. South, Simcoe, ON N3Y 2W2
519-426-2027, Fax: 519-426-0105
davuspub@sympatico.ca
www.kwic.com/davus/
ISBNs: ISBN: 0-915317
Featuring the works of David Beasley, and Major John Richardson, Canada's first novelist
Dr. David Beasley, Publisher

DC Books
PO Box 666 St. Laurent, 950, rue Décarie, Montréal, QC H4L 4V9
514-843-8130, Fax: 514-939-0569, 800-591-6250
dcbooks@videotron.ca
www.dcbooks.ca
ISBNs: 0-919688, 1-897190; SAN: 115-8988
DC Books publishes poetry & prose with innovative Canadian emphasis, histories, memoirs, & drama. Also offered are Railfare DC Books about railways & Moosehead Anthology. The house is a Member of the Association of English Editors of Quebec, & the Literary Press Group.
Keith Henderson, Managing Editor
Steve Luxton, Editor-in-chief

Detselig Enterprises Ltd.
c/o Temeron Books Inc., #210, 1220 Kensington Rd. NW, Calgary, AB T2N 3P5
403-283-0900, Fax: 403-283-6947
temeron@telusplanet.net
www.temerondetselig.com
ISBNs: ISBN: 0-920490, 1-55059; SAN: 115-0324
Specializing in general trade & academic books written by authors from Canada, the U.S., Austria and The Netherlands
T.E. Giles, President

Diffusion Dimedia inc.
539, boul Lebeau, Saint-Laurent, QC H4N 1S2
514-336-3941, Fax: 514-331-3916
general@dimedia.qc.ca
www.dimedia.qc.ca

Diffuse & distribue des livres de langue française au Canada
Johanne Paquette, Contact

Diffusion du Livre Mirabel
5757, rue Cypihot, Saint-Laurent, QC H4S 1R3
514-334-2690, Fax: 514-334-4720, 800-263-3678
erpidlm@erpi.com
www.erpi.com
ISBNs: ISBN: 0-88527
Division d'Éditions du Renouveau Pédagogique Inc.; livres jeunesse & imagerie, informatique, littérature, livres de cuisine, bandes dessinées
Normand Cleroux, Président

Diffusion Inter-Livres
1703, rue Belleville, Lemoyne, QC J4P 3M2
450-465-0037, Fax: 450-923-8966
liguegc@cam.org
www.inter-livres.ca
Joël Coppieter

Doubleday Canada Ltd.
c/o Random House of Canada Limited, One Toronto St., Unit 300, Toronto, ON M5C 2V6
416-364-4449, Fax: 416-364-6863, 000-000-0000
www.randomhouse.ca
ISBNs: ISBN: 0-385; SAN: 115-0340
Doubleday Canada is an imprint of Random House of Canada, publishing high quality Canadian literary & commercial fiction from new & established writers, memoirs, history, business, & social & political journalism
John Neale, President
Evaughn Moffat, Vice-President, Sales & Marketing

Douglas & McIntyre Publishing Group
#201, 2323 Quebec St., Vancouver, BC V5T 4S7
604-254-7191, Fax: 604-254-9099, 800-387-0117
dm@douglas-mcintyre.com
www.douglas-mcintyre.com
ISBNs: ISBN: 0-88894, 1-55054, 1-55365; SAN: 115-1886, 115-026X
Specializing in high quality Canadian fiction & non-fiction.
Imprints: Douglas & McIntyre, Greystone Books
Mark Scott, President
Scott McIntyre, Publisher, Douglas & McIntyre
Rob Sanders, Publisher, Greystone Books

Dovehouse Editions Inc.
1890 Fairmeadow Cres., Ottawa, ON K1H 7B9
613-731-7601, Fax: 613-731-7601
www.dovehouse.ca
ISBNs: ISBN: 0-919473, 1-895537
Publishers of The Carleton Renaissance Plays in Translation Series, as well as other works in Renaissance Studies; Publications of the Barnabe Riche Society; University of Toronto Italian Studies; and Ottawa Hispanic Studies
Dr. Donald Beecher, Editor

Dragon Hill Publishing Ltd.
5474 Thibault Wynd NW, Edmonton, AB T6R 3P9
780-239-4996
info@dragonhillpublishing.com
www.dragonhillpublishing.com
ISBNs: ISBN: 1-896124
Publishing for the popular adult and youth markets, in the subject areas of self-help, biography, success guides, and traditional cultures
Gary Whyte, Publisher

Drawn & Quarterly
PO Box 48056, Montréal, QC H2V 4S8
514-279-2221, Fax: 514-279-2221
info@drawnandquarterly.com
www.drawnandquarterly.com
ISBNs: ISBN: 1-896597
Publisher of comic books & graphic novels
Chris Oliveros, Publisher

DreamCatcher Publishing Inc.
55 Canterbury St., Saint John, NB E2L 2C6
506-632-4008, Fax: 506-632-4009, 877-631-7323
elizabeth.margaris@dreamcatcherpublishing.ca
www.dreamcatcherpublishing. ca
ISBNs: ISBN: 1-894372
Specializing in Maritime writers, fiction & non-fiction for children & adults
Elizabeth Margaris, Publisher

The Dundurn Group
#500, 3 Church St., Toronto, ON M5E 1M2
416-214-5544, Fax: 416-214-5556
info@dundurn.com
www.dundurn.com
ISBNs: ISBN: 0-919670, 1-55002, 0-88924, 1-895681, 0-88882, 0-88866,
Specializing in Canadian content in a number of subject areas, including adult & juvenile fiction & non-fiction, history, literature & literary criticism, health, music, travel & business
Kirk Howard, President

Duval Education / Duval Éducation
#100, 233 Dunbar Ave., Montreal, QC H3P 2H4
514-932-8229, Fax: 514-932-9175, 888-932-8229
duvalhouse@duvalhouse.com
www.duvalhouse.com
ISBNs: ISBN: 1-55220, 1-895850
Educational resources in English & French, ESL materials, Aboriginal resources
Simon de Jocas, Vice President, simon.dejocas@nelson.com

eastendbooks
45 Fernwood Park Ave., Toronto, ON M4E 3E9
416-691-6816, Fax: 416-691-2414
info@eastendbooks.com
www.eastendbooks.com
ISBNs: ISBN: 1-896973
A small-press with an Ontario focus, publishing material in a range of subjects, including fiction, travel, current events, modern jazz
Jeanne MacDonald

Écrits des Forges
992-A, rue Royale, Trois-Rivières, QC G9A 4H9
819-840-8492
ecritsdesforges.com
ISBNs: ISBN: 2-89046
Poésie, et essais en poésie

Stéphane Despatie, Director général

ECW Press
#200, 2120 Queen St. East, Toronto, ON M4E IE2
416-694-3348, Fax: 416-698-9906
info@ecwpress.com
www.ecwpress.com
ISBNs: ISBN: 1-55022, 0-920802, 1-920763; SAN: 115-1274
Publishers of Essays on Canadian Writing, & a diverse selection of contemporary poetry, fiction, writings on culture & politics, biography
Jack David, Co-publisher
Crissy Boylan, Managing Editor

EDIMAG inc.
CP 325 Rosemont, Montréal, QC H1X 3B8
514-522-2244, Fax: 514-522-6301
info@edimag.com
www.edimag.com
ISBNs: ISBN: 2-921735, 2-89542
Santé, alimentation & recettes, environnement, connaissances pratiques, jeux & sport, loisirs
Pierre Nadeau, Éditeur

Éditions Actualisation
Place du Parc, #2200, 300, rue Léo-Pariseau, Montréal, QC H2X 4B3
514-284-2622, Fax: 514-284-2625, 877-688-0101
admin@actualisation.com
www.actualisation.com
Matériel pour animer des formations, destiné aux formateurs, éducateurs et conseillers en ressources humaines: guides, manuels, questionnaires. Québec: Centre de la technologie, 1995, rue Frank Carrel, bureau 102, 418-688-0100.
Louis Fortin, Président MBA, louis.fortin@actualisation.com

Éditions Anne Sigier inc.
a/s Éditions Médiaspaul, 3965, boul Henri-Bourassa est, Montréal, QC H1H 1L1
514-322-7341, Fax: 514-322-4281
mediaspaul@mediaspaul.qc.ca
www.annesigier.qc.ca
ISBNs: ISBN: 2-89129
Bibles, livres de spiritualité chrétienne, beaux-livres
Anne Sigier
Jacques Sigier

Éditions Arts, Lettres et Techniques inc.
12, rue Northcote, Hampstead, QC H3X 1P5
514-747-4784,
ISBNs: ISBN: 0-921137
Droit, médecine, techniques, sciences, arts
Jacqueline Irali, Présidente

Les Éditions Behaviora inc.
CP 91, 151, ch Bellevue, Eastman, QC J0E 1P0
450-297-0515, Fax: 450-297-0516
behaviora@sympatico.ca
www.behaviora.qc.ca
ISBNs: ISBN: 2-7629
Ouvrages de psychologie, de pédagogie, & de sciences sociales
Dr. Rodrigue Otis

Éditions Bellarmin
a/s Éditions Fides, 306, rue Saint-Zotique est, Montréal, QC H2S 1L6
514-745-4290, Fax: 514-745-4299
editions@fides.qc.ca
www.fides.qc.ca
ISBNs: ISBN: 0-88502, 2-89007
Michel Maillé, Directeur général

Les Éditions Brault et Bouthillier / Brault & Bouthillier Publishing
4823, rue Sherbrooke ouest, Montréal, QC H3Z 1G7
514-932-9466, Fax: 514-932-5929, 866-750-9466
editions@ebbp.ca
www.ebbp.ca
ISBNs: ISBN: 0-88537, 2-7615
Manuels scolaires, ouvrages pédagogiques/parascolaires; français et anglais
Jean Brault, Président
Yves Brault, Vice-président
Paul Beullac, Éditeur

Les Éditions CEC inc.
9001, boul Louis-H.-La Fontaine, Anjou, QC H1J 2C5
514-351-6010, Fax: 514-351-3534, 800-363-0494
infoped@ceceditions.com
www.editionscec.com
ISBNs: ISBN: 0-7751, 2-7617
Ouvrages pour tous les ordres d'enseignement - manuels scolaires, ouvrages de référence, grammaires, anthologies littéraires

Éditions CERES
CP 1089 B, Montréal, QC H5B 3K9
514-937-7138, Fax: 514-937-9875
editionsceres@gmail.ca
www.editionsceres.ca
ISBNs: ISBN: 0-919089
Les éditions CERES publient exclusivement des livres érudits
C. Stéfane

Les Éditions Chouette
#B-238, 1001, rue Lenoir, Montréal, QC H4C 2Z6
514-925-3325, Fax: 514-925-3323
info@editions-chouette.com
www.chouettepublishing.com
Livres Caillou
Christine L'Heureux, Présidente fondatrice

Les Éditions Cornac
5, rue Sainte-Ursule, Québec, QC G1R 4C7
418-692-0377, Fax: 418-692-0605
editionscornac.com
ISBNs: ISBN: 2-921310, 2-89529
Livres jeunesse; poésie; essais; albums illustrés; a pour mission d'encourager l'expression des Premières Nations
Michel Brûlé, Éditeur, michel@editionscornac.com

Les Éditions de l'Hexagone
1010, rue de la Gauchetière est, Montréal, QC H2L 2N5
514-523-7993, Fax: 514-282-7530
adpcommandes@messageries-adp.com
www.edhexagone.com
ISBNs: ISBN: 2-89006, 2-89295
Littérature québécoise
Danielle Fournier, Directrice

Les Éditions de l'Homme
955, rue Amherst, Montréal, QC H2L 3K4
514-523-1182, Fax: 514-597-0370
adpcommandes@messagies-adp.com
www.editions-homme.com
ISBNs: ISBN: 2-7619, 2-89005, 2-89006
Livres de sciences humaines
Pierre Lespérance, Président
Pierre Bourdon, Vice-président à l'édition

Éditions de l'Instant même
865, av Moncton, Québec, QC G1S 2Y4
418-527-8690, Fax: 418-681-6780
info@instantmeme.com
www.instantmeme.com
ISBNs: ISBN: 2-921197, 2-9800635, 2-89502
Romans, essais, nouvelles
Marie Taillon, Directrice générale

Les Éditions de L'IQRC/Les Presses de l'Université Laval
Pavillon Maurice-Pollack, #3103, 2305, rue de l'Université, Québec, QC G1V 0A6
418-656-2803, Fax: 418-656-3305, 800-859-7474
presses@pul.ulaval.ca
www.pulaval.com
ISBNs: ISBN: 2-89224
Américana, bioéthique critique, cinéma et société, culture québécoise, éducation, géographie, histoire sociale, lectures, politique
Denis Dion, Directeur général

Les Éditions de la courte échelle
5243, boul Saint-Laurent, Montréal, QC H2T 1S4
514-274-2004, Fax: 514-270-4160
info@courteechelle.com
www.courteechelle.com
ISBNs: ISBN: 2-89021; SAN: 116-0249
Un leader de la littérature jeunesse francophone - livres pour les trois à six ans; collection adulte
Hélène Derome, Présidente/Éditrice

Éditions de la Paix
127, rue Lussier, Saint-Alphonse-de-Granby, QC J0E 2A0
450-375-4765, Fax: 450-375-4765
info@editpaix.qc.ca
www.editpaix.qc.ca
Jeunesse, patrimoine, romans, poésie, spiritualité
Jean-Paul Tessier, Président-directeur général

Les Éditions de la Pleine Lune
223, 34e av, Lachine, QC H8T 1Z4
514-637-6366, Fax: 514-637-6366
editpllune@videotron.ca
www.pleinelune.qc.ca
ISBNs: ISBN: 2-89024
Ouvrages québécois et canadiens
Marie-Madeleine Raoult, Directrice

Éditions de Mortagne
CP 116, Boucherville, QC J4B 5E6
450-641-2387, Fax: 450-655-6092
info@editionsdemortagne.com
www.editionsdemortagne.com
ISBNs: ISBN: 2-89074
Biographies, romans, collection 'Lime et citron', guides pratiques, santé, psychologie, astrologie, motivation
Max Permingeat, Président

Les Éditions des Plaines
CP 123, Saint-Boniface, MB R2H 3B4
204-235-0078, Fax: 204-233-7741
admin@plaines.mb.ca
www.plaines.mb.ca
ISBNs: ISBN: 0-920944, 2-921353, 2-89611
La maison s'applique à donner la parole aux écrivains de l'Ouest canadien
Doris Touchette, Adjointe administrative

Les Éditions du Blé
340, boul Provencher, Saint-Boniface, MB R3H 0G7
204-237-8200, Fax: 204-233-8182
direction@editionsduble.ca
www.livres-disques.ca/editions_ble/home/index.cfm
ISBNs: ISBN: 0-920640, 2-921347
La première maison d'édition francophone de l'Ouest canadien; ouvrages des auteurs de la région - poésie, romans, essais, théâtre, livres pour enfants & adolescents
Lucien Chaput

Éditions du Bois-de-Coulonge
1140, av De Montigny, Sillery, QC G1S 3T7
418-683-6332, Fax: 418-683-6332
www.ebc.qc.ca
ISBNs: ISBN: 2-9801397
Services aux collectivités & vente directe au grand public
Richard Leclerc, Propriétaire Ph.D.

Éditions du Boréal
4447, rue Saint-Denis, Montréal, QC H2J 2L2
514-287-7401, Fax: 514-287-7664
boreal@editionsboreal.qc.ca
www.editionsboreal.qc.ca
ISBNs: ISBN: 2-89052, 0-7646
Fiction, poésie, essais, histoire, biographies, livres pratiques, collections jeunesse
Pascal Assathiany, Directeur général

Éditions du Nordir
Dép des lettres française, Université d'Ottawa, 60, rue Université, Ottawa, ON K1N 6N5
819-243-1253, Fax: 819-243-6201
lenordir@sympatico.ca
www.livres-disques.ca/editions_nordir
ISBNs: ISBN: 0-921272
Biographies, études littéraires, poésie, réflexions sociales

Les Éditions du Noroît
#202, 4609, rue d'Iberville, Montréal, QC H2H 2L9
450-727-0005, Fax: 450-723-6660
lenoroit@lenoroit.com
www.lenoroit.com
ISBNs: ISBN: 2-89018
Livres de poésie
Karine Hubert

Les Éditions du Remue-Ménage inc.
#501, 110, rue Ste-Thérèse, Montréal, QC H2Y 1E6
514-876-0097, Fax: 514-876-7951
info@editions-remuemenage.qc.ca
www.editions-remuemenage.qc.ca
ISBNs: ISBN: 2-89091
Livres sur les femmes: biographie, culture, développement international, éducation, études féministes, poésie, politique, santé
Rachel Bédard, Éditrice

Éditions du Renouveau Pédagogique inc.
5757, rue Cypihot, Saint-Laurent, QC H4S 1R3
514-334-2690, Fax: 514-334-4720, 800-263-3678
info@erpi.com
www.erpi.com
ISBNs: ISBN: 2-7613
Maison d'édition scolaire; matériel didactique pour tous les niveaux d'enseignement
Normand Cléroux, Président

Les Éditions du Septentrion
1300, av Maguire, Québec, QC G1T 1Z3
418-688-3556, Fax: 418-527-4978
sept@septentrion.qc.ca
www.septentrion.qc.ca

Spécialisée en histoire, archéologie, science politique, ethnographie, et aux sciences humaines
Denis Vaugeois, Président

Les Éditions du Trécarré
La Tourelle, #800, 1055, boul René-Lévesque est, Montréal, QC H2L 4S5
514-849-5259, Fax: 514-849-1388
adpcommandes@messageries-adp.com
www.edtrecarre.com
ISBNs: ISBN: 2-89249, 2-89568
Livres pratiques (cuisine, santé); cahiers d'exercices; littérature jeunesse
Marc Laberge, Président
Colette Laberge, Redactrice en chef

Éditions du Vermillon
305, rue Saint-Patrick, Ottawa, ON K1N 5K4
613-241-4032, Fax: 613-241-3109
leseditionsduvermillon@rogers.com
www.leseditionsduvermillion.ca
ISBNs: ISBN: 0-919925, 1-895873, 1-894547, 1-897058
Romans, poésie, bandes dessinées, guides pédagogiques, essais
Monique Bertoli, Directrice générale

Éditions Fides
306, rue Saint-Zotique est, Montréal, QC H2S 1L6
514-745-4290, Fax: 514-745-4299
editions@fides.qc.ca
www.fides.qc.ca
ISBNs: ISBN: 2-7621
Littérature (collection de poche 'Bibliothèque québécoise'), essais, livres religieux, ouvrages de référence, beaux livres; collection Éditions Bellarmin
Michel Maillé, Directeur général

Les Éditions Flammarion Ltée
375, av Laurier ouest, Montréal, QC H2V 2K3
514-277-8807, Fax: 514-278-2085
info@flammarion.qc.ca
www.flammarion.qc.ca
ISBNs: ISBN: 2-89077
Une maison d'édition généraliste
Jean-Michel Sivry, Président

Éditions Ganesha
CP 484 Youville, Montréal, QC H2P 2W1
450-641-2395, Fax: 450-641-2989
courriel@editions-ganesha.qc.ca
www.editions-ganesha.qc.ca

Ouvrages diverses: philosophie, religion/cultes, psychologie
André Beaudoin
Lucie Cournoyer

Les Éditions Héritage
300, rue Arran, Saint-Lambert, QC J4R 1K5
514-875-0327, Fax: 514-672-1481, 888-228-1498
ISBNs: ISBN: 2-7625, 0-7773
Luc Payette, Président

Éditions Hurtubise inc
1815, av De Lorimier, Montréal, QC H2K 3W6
514-523-1523, Fax: 514-523-9969, 800-361-1664
www.editionshurtubise.com
ISBNs: ISBN: 2-89045, 2-89428
Littérature, beaux livres, jeunesse, éducation
Hervé Foulon, Président-directeur général

Les Éditions JCL inc.
930, rue Jacques-Cartier est, Chicoutimi, QC G7H 7K9
418-696-0536, Fax: 418-696-3132
jcl@jcl.qc.ca
www.jcl.qc.ca
ISBNs: ISBN: 2-89431, 2-920176
Éditeur généraliste: romans, histoire, culture, jeunesse
Jean-Claude Larouche, Président

Les Éditions JML inc.
1150, ch des Patriotes nord, Mont-St-Hilaire, QC J3G 4S6
450-536-1565, Fax: 450-536-2565
infos@editionsjml.com
www.editionsjml.com
ISBNs: ISBN: 2-89234
Cahiers de préparation de cours, cahiers de titulariat, relevés de notes, relevés d'absences

Éditions l'Artichaut inc.
355, rue Dubé, Rimouski, QC G5L 4W6
418-723-1554, Fax: 418-725-4828
artichaut@editionslartichaut.com
www.editionslartichaut.com
ISBNs: ISBN: 2-921288; 2-922998
Matériel didactique axé sur le développement des compétences en langue française (niveaux primaire, secondaire)
Ginette Tremblay, Propriétaire

Les Éditions La Pensée Inc.
4370, rue de l'Hôtel de Ville, Montréal, QC H2W 2H5
514-848-9042, Fax: 514-848-9836, 800-667-5442
administration@editions-lapensee.qc.ca
www.editions-lapensee.qc.ca
Marc-Aimé Guérin, President

Les Éditions le Griffon d'argile
7649, boul Wilfrid-Hamel, Sainte-Foy, QC G2G 1C3
418-871-6898, Fax: 418-871-6818, 800-268-6898
admin@griffondargile.com
www.griffondargile.com
ISBNs: ISBN: 2-920210, 2-920922, 2-89443
André Gosselin

Les Éditions le Renouveau Charlesbourg inc.
CP 87605 Charlesbourg, 870, carré de Tracy est, Québec, QC G1G 5W6
418-628-3445, Fax: 418-624-2277, 877-628-3445
info@editionslerenouveau.com
www.editionslerenouveau.com

Guide de lecture de la Bible, ouvrages du domaine religieux, musique, objets religieux
Jacques Roy, Responsable

Éditions Les 400 Coups
#B550, 1001, rue Lenoir, Montréal, QC H4C 2Z6
514-381-1422, Fax: 514-487-8811
info@editions400coups.com
www.editions400coups.ca
ISBNs: ISBN: 2-920993, 2-89540
Albums jeunesse, livres d'art, bandes dessinées. Publient également sous les noms de Mille-Iles, de Zone convective, et de Mécanique générale
Myriam Comtois, Responsable, Communications, m.comtois@editions400coups.com

Éditions Liber
2318, rue Bélanger, Montréal, QC H2G 1C8
514-522-3227, Fax: 514-522-2007
info@editionsliber.org
www.editionsliber.org
ISBNs: ISBN: 2-921569, 2-89578
Études & essais en philosophie, sciences humaines, littérature
Giovanni Calabrese, Directeur

Éditions Libre Expression
La Tourelle, #800, 1055, boul. René-Lévesque E, Montréal, QC H2L 4S5
514-849-5259, Fax: 514-849-1388
www.edlibreexpression.com
ISBNs: ISBN: 2-89111, 2-7648
Fiction, biographie, essais, histoire, culture, guides, beaux livres, livres de poche

Les Éditions Logiques
La Tourelle, #800, 1055, boul René-Lévesque est, Montréal, QC H2L 4S5
514-849-5259, Fax: 514-849-1388
adpcommandes@messageries-adp.com
www.edlogiques.com
ISBNs: ISBN: 2-89381
Gestion des affaires, économie, pédagogie, psychologie populaire, philosophie, sociologie

Éditions Marie-France ltée
9900, av des Laurentides, Montréal, QC H1H 4V1
514-329-3700, Fax: 514-329-0630, 800-563-6644
editions@marie-france.qc.ca
www.marie-france.qc.ca
ISBNs: ISBN: 2-89168
Informatique, littérature, mathématique, français, français immersion
Jean H. Lachapelle, Président

Éditions MultiMondes
930, rue Pouliot, Québec, QC G1V 3N9
418-651-3885, Fax: 418-651-6822, 800-840-3029
multimondes@multim.com
www.multim.com
ISBNs: ISBN: 2-921146, 2-89544
Environnement, santé, jeunesse, muséologie, pédagogie, science et technologie
Jean-Marc Gagnon, Président, jmgagnon@multim.com
Lise Morin, Vice-présidente, lmorin@multim.com

Éditions Paulines
5610, rue Beaubien est, Montréal, QC H1T 1X5
514-253-5610, Fax: 514-253-1907
editions@paulines.qc.ca
www.paulines.qc.ca
ISBNs: ISBN: 0-920912
Ouvrages de spiritualité

Les Éditions Perce-Neige ltée
#22, 140 Botsford St., Moncton, NB E1C 4X4
506-383-4446, Fax: 506-857-2064
perceneige@nb.aibn.com
perceneige.recf.ca
ISBNs: ISBN: 2-920221
Essaies historiques, études littéraires, contes traditionnels et récits, poésie, romans
Paul Bourque, Directeur général

Éditions Phidal inc./Phidal Publishing Inc.
5740, rue Ferrier, Montréal, QC H4P 1M7
514-738-0202, Fax: 514-738-5102, 800-738-7349
customer@phidal.com
www.phidal.com
ISBNs: ISBN: 2-89393, 2-7643
Ouvrages pour enfants
Albert Soussan, Président

Éditions Prise de Parole
#205, 109, rue Elm, Sudbury, ON P3C 1T4
705-675-6491, Fax: 705-673-1817
prisedeparole@bellnet.ca
www.livres-disques.ca/prise_parole/
ISBNs: ISBN: 0-920814, 0-921573, 2-89423
Bandes dessinées, beaux livres, contes traditionnels, enfants, ados, études littéraires, poésie, revues, romans
Denise Truax, Directrice générale, prisedeparole@bellnet.ca
Sylvie Lessard, Agente de commercialisation, pdpcommercialisation@bellnet.ca
Alain Mayotte, Directeur administratif, pdpadministration@bellnet.ca

Les Éditions Québec Amérique
329, rue de la Commune ouest, 3e étage, Montréal, QC H2Y 2E1
514-499-3000, Fax: 514-499-3010
courrier@quebec-amerique.com
www.quebec-amerique.com
ISBNs: ISBN: 0-88552, 2-89037, 2-7644
Ouvrages de référence, littérature, jeunesse
Jacques Fortin, CEO

Les Éditions Quebecor
7, ch Bates, Montréal, QC H2V 4V7
514-270-1746, Fax: 514-270-5313
simard.jacques@quebecoreditions.com
www.quebecoreditions.com
ISBNs: ISBN: 0-88617, 2-89089, 2-9801107
Affaires, alimentation, astrologie, biographie, guides pratiques, littérature, santé, sports, nouvel âge
Jacques Simard, Éditeur

Les Éditions Reynald Goulet inc.
40, rue Mireault, Repentigny, QC J6A 1M1
450-654-2626, Fax: 450-654-5433, 800-663-3021
info@goulet.ca
www.goulet.ca
ISBNs: ISBN: 2-89377
Ouvrages de bureautique, d'informatique, de dessin assisté par ordinateur, et l'autoformation au niveau post-secondaire
Reyald Goulet, Président & Dir. général

Éditions Saint-Martin
#501, 7333, place des Roseraies, Anjou, QC H1M 2X6
514-529-0920, Fax: 514-352-1764
info@stmartin-decarie.com
www.stmartin-decarie.com
ISBNs: ISBN: 2-89035
Ouvrages grand public; manuels collégials et universitaires. Éditions Saint-Martin a fait l'acquisition de deux autres maisons d'éditions: Décarie éditeur, et Éditions Carcajou.
Stéphane Lavoie, Directeur général

Les Éditions SMG inc.
#203, 5365, boul Jean XXIII, Trois-Rivières, QC G8Z 4A6
819-376-5650, Fax: 819-373-2904
ISBNs: ISBN: 2-89094

Les Éditions Stanké
La Tourelle, #800, 1055, boul René-Lévesque Est, Montréal, QC H2L 4S5

514-849-5259, Fax: 514-849-1388
info@groupelibrex.com
www.edstanke.com
ISBNs: ISBN: 2-7604, 0-88566
Ouvrages grand public: romans, essais, récits
Alain Stanké, Président & Dir.-gén.
Patrick Leimgruber, Directeur commercial

Les Éditions Thémis
Faculté de droit, Université de Montréal, CP 6128 Centre-Ville, Montréal, QC H3C 3J7
514-343-6627, Fax: 514-343-6779
info@editionsthemis.com
www.themis.umontreal.ca
ISBNs: ISBN: 2-920376, 2-89400; SAN: 115-8252
Livres juridiques; Revue juridique Thémis
Stéphane Rousseau, Président et Dir. général

Les Éditions Un Monde différent ltée
#101, 3905, rue Isabelle, Brossard, QC J4Y 2R2
450-656-2660, Fax: 450-659-9328, 800-443-2582
info@umd.ca
www.umd.ca
ISBNs: ISBN: 2-89225, 2-92000
Traductions et adaptations de best-sellers américains, ouvrages d'auteurs canadiens et internationaux
Michel Ferron, Éditeur

Les Éditions Vents d'Ouest
185, rue Eddy, Gatineau, QC J8X 2X2
819-770-6377, Fax: 819-770-0559
info@ventsdouest.ca
www.ventsdouest.ca
Ado, histoire, romans, essais, nouvelles
Melvin Jomphe, Président

Les Éditions XYZ inc. / XYZ Publishing
1815, av De Lorimier, Montréal, QC H2K 3W6
514-525-2170, Fax: 514-525-7537
info@editionsxyz.com
www.editionsxyz.com
ISBNs: ISBN: 2-89261 French; 0-9683601 Eng.
Dominique Lemay, Directrice générale, dominique.lemay@editionsxyz.com
André Vanasse, Conseiller littéraire, andre.vanasse@editionsxyz.com

Éditions Yvon Blais
CP 180, Cowansville, QC J2K 3H6
450-266-1086, Fax: 450-263-9256, 800-363-3047
editionsyvonblais.professeurs@thomsonreuters.com
www.editionsyvonblais.c om
ISBNs: ISBN: 2-89451
Éditeur juridique; textes des conférences des formations continues du Barreau du Québec; fiscalité; ressources humaines
Yvon Blais, Président

EDU Reference Publishers Direct Inc.
#3, 109 Woodbine Downs Blvd., Toronto, ON M9W 1Y6
416-674-8622, Fax: 416-674-6215
eduref@edureference.com
www.edureference.com
ISBNs: ISBN: 0-86596, 0-04150
A distributor - bringing publishers & buyers in the Canadian education community together
Orland Kirkness, President

Educa Books
PO Box 2694 D, Ottawa, ON K1P 5W6
613-738-2163, Fax: 613-247-0256
educa2@yahoo.com
educa0.tripod.com/edu/
ISBNs: ISBN: 1-895959, 1-55394
Specialists in dictionaries, reference books, language learning resources
L. Martin

EGS Press
#118, 283 Danforth Ave., Toronto, ON M4K 1N2
416-829-8014
info@egspress.com
www.egspress.com
ISBNs: ISBN: 0-9685330
Publisher of research material in the fields of media, the arts & therapy from the European Graduate School, Switzerland, and the annual journal POIESIS: A JOURNAL OF THE ARTS & COMMUNICATION
Stephen K. Levine, Editor-in-Chief

Ekstasis Editions
PO Box 8474 Main, Victoria, BC V8W 3S1
250-361-9941, Fax: 250-385-3378, 866-961-9951
ekstasis@islandnet.com
www.ekstasiseditions.com
ISBNs: ISBN: 0-921215, 1-896860, 0-9691289, 1-894800
Literary publisher, with focus on poetry, fiction & criticism; Cherubim Books imprint for Children's & Young Adult books
Richard Olafson

Elsevier Canada
1 Goldthorne Ave., Toronto, ON M8Z 5S7
416-253-3640, Fax: 416-255-5456, 800-665-1148
cs.canada@elsevier.com
www.elsevier.ca; www.lb.ca
ISBNs: ISBN: 0-3230, 0-3974, 0-3998, 0-4430, 0-4160, 1-5566, 1-5605,
Robert Dingee

Emond Montgomery Publications Limited
60 Shaftesbury Ave., Toronto, ON M4T 1A3
416-975-3925, Fax: 416-975-3924, 888-837-0815
info@emp.ca; orders@emp.ca
www.emp.ca
ISBNs: ISBN: 0-920722, 1-55239
Specialists in legal publishing & textbooks
D. Paul Emond, President/CEO

Empyreal Press
PO Box 1708, Champlain, NY
skarwood@videotron.ca
www.skarwood.com
ISBNs: ISBN: 0-921852
An independent literary press, specializing in new & established Canadian writers of poetry, prose & non-fiction
Geoffrey Isherwood, CEO

Environmental Law Centre
#800, 10025 - 106 St., Edmonton, AB T5J 1G4
780-424-5099, Fax: 780-424-5133, 800-661-4238
elc@elc.ab.ca
www.elc.ab.ca
ISBNs: ISBN: 0-921503
Publishing objective information about environmental & natural resources law & policy
Cindy Chiasson, Executive Director

Ergo Books
PO Box 1439 B, London, ON N6A 5M2
519-432-4357
ergopro@ergobooks.com
www.ergobooks.com
ISBNs: ISBN: 0-920516; SAN: 115-3374
Specializing in fiction, poetry, humour, local history & memoirs by Southwestern Ontario writers
Winston G. Schell, Publisher

Essence Publishing
20 Hanna Ct., Belleville, ON K8P 5J2
613-962-0234, Fax: 613-962-3055, 800-238-6376
info@essence-publishing.com
www.essencegroup.com
ISBNs: ISBN: 1-896400, 1-894169, 1-55306
Specializing in short-run publishing, with emphasis on Christian themes & perspectives

Everyday Publications Inc.
310 Killaly St. West, Port Colborne, ON L3K 6A6
905-834-5552, Fax: 905-834-8045
books@everydaypubications.org
www.everydaypublications.or g
ISBNs: ISBN: 0-88873, 0-919586; SAN: 115-3398
Specializing in books about the Bible, in English, French, Spanish, Portuguese, Swahili & Chinese
R.E. Harlow, Publisher

Exile Editions Ltd.
134 Eastbourne Ave., Toronto, ON M5P 2G6
Fax: 416-969-9556
info@exileeditions.com
www.exileeditions.com
ISBNs: ISBN: 1-550960, 0-920428; SAN: 115-3404
Specializing in fiction, poetry, drama, non-fiction & translations, from established and new writers
Michael Callaghan, Publisher

Exportlivre
289, boul Desaulniers, Saint-Lambert, QC J4P 1M8
450-671-3888, Fax: 450-671-2121
order@exportlivre.com
www.exportlivre.com
Book export agency, handling orders for books in English & French in the areas of trade & non-trade publications, children's fiction & non-fiction, scientific & technical books, textbooks, scholarly publications & government publications
Thomas Déri, Directeur

Fairmount Books Inc.
120 Duffield Dr., Markham, ON L6G 1B5
905-475-0988, Fax: 905-475-1072
sales@fairmountbooks.ca
www.fairmountbooks.ca
ISBNs: ISBN: 0-921372; SAN: 106-7886
Wholesaler of remaindered books
Marty Cutler, President

Federation of Ontario Naturalists (FON)
#201, 366 Adelaide St. W., Toronto, ON M5V 1R9
416-444-8419, Fax: 416-444-9866, 800-440-2366
info@ontarionature.org
www.ontarionature.org
Publisher of ON Nature; other resources available through the online Shop
Caroline Schultz, Executive Director

Fernwood Publishing Co. Ltd.
PO Box 5, 32 Oceanvista Lane, Site 2A, Black Point, NS B0J 1B0
902-857-1388, Fax: 902-857-1328
info@fernpub.ca
www.fernwoodpublishing.ca
ISBNs: ISBN: 1-895686, 1-55266
Errol Sharpe, Publisher
Cynthia Martin, Promotions

Fifth House Publishers
#1511, 1800 - 4 St. SW, Calgary, AB T2S 2S5
403-571-5230, Fax: 403-571-5235, 800-387-9776
charlene@fitzhenry.ca
www.fitzhenry.ca
ISBNs: ISBN: 0-920079, 1-894004, 1-894856, 1-895618; SAN: 115-1134
Specializing in non-fiction with a Western Canadian emphasis
Charlene Dobmeier, Publisher

Firefly Books Ltd.
66 Leek Cres., Richmond Hill, ON L4B 1H1
416-499-8412, Fax: 416-499-8313, 800-387-6192
service@fireflybooks.com
www.fireflybooks.com
Other information: Toll-Free Fax: 800-450-0391
Firefly Books publishes non-fiction books & distributes non-fiction & children's books.
Rob Lidstone, Contact, Sales Operations, Data Export, & Website, rlidstone@fireflybooks.com
Parisa Michailidis, Contact, Special & Corporate Sales, parisa@fireflybooks.com
Ann Quinn, Contact, Schools & Libraries, annq@fireflybooks.com
Diane Vanderkooy, Contact, Rights, dianevan@fireflybooks.com

Fisher House Publishers
10907 - 34A Ave., Edmonton, AB T5J 2T9
780-435-2320, Fax: 780-468-2058
fisherhousejohn@hotmail.com
www.fisherhouse.com
ISBNs: ISBN: 1-896255
John R. Fisher Ph.D

Fitzhenry & Whiteside Limited
195 Allstate Pkwy., Markham, ON L3R 4T8
905-477-9700, Fax: 800-260-9777, 800-387-9776
godwit@fitzhenry.ca
www.fitzhenry.ca
ISBNs: ISBN: 0-55041, 0-88902, 1-55005, 1-894004, 1-895618, 0-7737, 0
Specializing in history, biography, poety, sports, photography, reference resources, and children's and young adult material. Owner of Red Deer Press Inc., and Fifth House Publishers
Sharon Fitzhenry, President

Flanker Press Ltd.
PO Box 2522 C, St. John's, NL A1C 6K1
709-739-4477, Fax: 709-739-4420, 866-739-4420
info@flankerpress.com
www.flankerpress.com
ISBNs: ISBN: 0-9698767, 1-894463
Specializing in regional Newfoundland & Labrador historical fiction & non-fiction titles; imprints include Pennywell Books, & Brazen Books

Fleurbec
198, ch de la Grande-Grillade, Saint-Henri-de-Lévis, QC G0R 3E0

418-882-0843, Fax: 418-882-6133
melilot@sympatico.ca
www.fleurbec.com

ISBNs: ISBN: 2-920174
Guides d'identification, ouvrages scientifiques, guide culinaire - plantes sauvages, flore
Gisèle Lamoureux, Dirigeante

Formac Publishing Company Limited
5502 Atlantic St., Halifax, NS B3H 1G4
902-421-7022, Fax: 902-425-0166, 800-565-1975
orderdesk@formac.ca
www.formac.ca
ISBNs: ISBN: 0-88780, 0-921921; SAN: 115-1371
Publishers & distributors
James Lorimer, Publisher

49th Avenue Press
100 West 49th Ave., Vancouver, BC V5Y 2Z6
604-323-5374, Fax: 604-323-5597
lholmes@langara.bc.ca
www.bendallbooks.com
ISBNs: ISBN: 1-896661
Linda Holmes, President

The Fraser Institute
1770 Burrard St., 4th Fl., Vancouver, BC V6J 3G7
604-688-0221, Fax: 604-688-8539, 800-665-3558
info@fraserinstitute.ca
www.fraserinstitute.ca
ISBNs: ISBN: 0-88975; SAN: 115-3498
Offices in Vancouver, Calgary, Toronto, Montreal; engaged in research & publication with emphasis on economics, public policy and other issues that affect Canadians
Mark Mullins, Executive Director

Frederick Harris Music Co. Ltd.
#1, 5865 McLaughlin Rd., Mississauga, ON L5R 1B8
905-501-1595, Fax: 905-501-0929, 800-387-4013
fhmc@frederickharris.com
www.frederickharris.com
Darlene Dunn, Customer Service Representative

Friday 501
PO Box 31599, Whitehorse, YT Y1A 6L2
867-668-3501, Fax: 867-668-4472
info@friday501.com
www.friday501.com

Friday Circle
Dept. of English, University of Ottawa, Ottawa, ON K1N 6N5
613-562-5800, Fax: 613-562-5990
fridaycircle@uottawa.ca
www.fridaycircle.uottawa.ca
ISBNs: ISBN: 1-896362, 1-9697391
Publishing works by faculty, students & alumni of the Creative Writing Program, University of Ottawa
Seymour Mayne, Co-editor

Full Blast Productions
70 Allan Dr., St. Catherines, ON L2N 1E9
Fax: 905-937-2657, 877-355-2578
fbp@cogeco.ca
www.fullblastproductions.mybisi.com
ISBNs: ISBN: 1-895451
Publisher of English & Spanish language teaching resources

Fundy Guild Inc.
Fundy National Park, #2, 8642, RR#114, Fundy National Park, NB E4H 4V2
506-887-6094, Fax: 506-887-6008
info@fundyguild.ca
www.fundyguild.ca
ISBNs: ISBN: 0-920383
Publishes books related to the bay of Fundy & Fundy National Park
Beulah Michelin

Gaspereau Press
47 Church Ave., Kentville, NS B4N 2M7
902-678-6002, Fax: 902-678-7845, 877-230-8232
info@gaspereau.com
www.gaspereau.com
ISBNs: ISBN: 1-894031
Specializing in contemporary literature by emerging & established Canadian authors, with publishing & printing under one roof
Gary Dunfield, Co-publisher
Andrew Steeves, Co-publisher

General Store Publishing House
PO Box 415, 499 O'Brien Rd., Renfrew, ON K7A 4A6
613-432-7697, Fax: 613-432-7184, 800-465-6072
submissions@gsph.com
www.gsph.com
ISBNs: ISBN: 0-919431, 1-896182, 1-894263, 1-897113 SAN: 115-6853
Tim Gordon, President

Georgetown Publications Inc.
34 Armstrong Ave., Georgetown, ON L7G 4R9
905-873-8498, Fax: 888-595-3009, 888-595-3008
info@gtwcanada.com
www.georgetownpublications.com
ISBNs: ISBN: 0-9731994, 0-9733149
Distributor for Allison & Busby, American Girl Pubishing, Hampton Roads Publishing, & Large Print Press, among others

Gilpin Publishing
PO Box 597, Alliston, ON L9R 1V7
705-424-6507, Fax: 705-424-6507
mail@gilpin.ca
www.gilpin.ca
ISBNs: ISBN: 0-921046; SAN: 119-6162
Music publishing - MP3s, CDs, piano methods, instrumental & choral arrangements, sheet music
Wayne Gilpin, Publisher

The Ginger Press
848 - 2 Ave. East, Owen Sound, ON N4K 2H3
519-376-4233, Fax: 519-376-9871, 800-463-9937
maryann@gingerpress.com
www.gingerpress.com
ISBNs: ISBN: 0-921773
A bookshop, café, & publishing house, specializing in Owen Sound & area writers & subjects
Maryann Thomas, Publisher

Godwin Books
1212 Hampshire Rd., Victoria, BC V8S 4T1
250-414-0215, Fax: 250-414-0216
rthomson@islandnet.com
www.godwinbooks.com
ISBNs: ISBN: 0-9696774
Featuring books by Robert Thomson & George Godwin
Robert Stuart Thomson, Editor

Good Medicine Books
PO Box 844, Skookumchuck, BC V0B 2E0
canadiancaboose@yahoo.com
goodmedicinefoundation.com
ISBNs: ISBN: 0-920698
Good Medicine Cutural Foundation publishes a collection of material on a theme of trains, as well documentation & accounts on First Nations People, in particular, the Pikunni.
Adolf Hungry Wolf, Publisher

Goose Lane Editions
#330, 500 Beaverbrook Ct., Fredericton, NB E3B 5X4
506-450-4251, Fax: 506-459-4991, 888-926-8377
info@gooselane.com
www.gooselane.com
ISBNs: ISBN: 0-919197, 0-86492, 0-920110; SAN: 115-3420
Small independent publisher of high-quality, award-winning books.
Susanne Alexander, Publisher

Gordon Soules Book Publishers Ltd.
1354-B Marine Dr., West Vancouver, BC V7T 1B5
604-922-6588, Fax: 604-688-5442
books@gordonsoules.com
www.gordonsoules.com
ISBNs: ISBN: 0-919574, 1-894661, 0-920045; SAN: 115-0987
Publisher of self-help, health, fitness & natural medicine books; cookbooks; tarot decks & tarot books; travel books & maps
Gordon Soules, President

Granville Island Publishing
#212, 1656 Duranleau St., Vancouver, BC V6H 3S4
604-688-0320, Fax: 604-668-0132, 877-688-0320
info@granvilleislandpublishing.com
www.granvilleislandpublishing.com
ISBNs: ISBN: 1-894694; SAN: 118-7953
Services for self-published authors
Jo Blackmore, Publisher

Grass Roots Press
6520 - 82 Avenue, Main Floor, Edmonton, AB T6B 0E7
780-413-6491, Fax: 780-413-6582, 888-303-3213
info@grassrootsbooks.net
www.literacyservices.com

Specializing in adult literacy resources
DR Pat Campbell, President

Great Plains Publications Ltd.
#420, 70 Arthur St., Winnipeg, MB R3B 1G7
204-475-6799, Fax: 204-475-0138
info@greatplains.mb.ca
www.greatplains.mb.ca
ISBNs: ISBN: 0-9697804, 1-894283
Specializing in the best books from the Prairies & authors from across Canada
Gregg Shilliday, Publisher

Green Dragon Press
#1009, 2267 Lakeshore Blvd. West, Toronto, ON M8V 3X2
416-251-6366, Fax: 416-251-6365
www3.sympatico.ca/equity.greendragonpress
ISBNs: ISBN: 1-896781
Publishes books & materials on women's equity

Grey House Publishing Canada
#301 - 555 Richmond St. West, Toronto, ON M5V 3B1
416-644-6479, Fax: 416-644-1904, 866-433-4739
info@greyhouse.ca
www.greyhouse.ca
ISBNs: ISBN: 978-1-59237
Publishers of a number of comprehensive Canadian directories including the Canadian Almanac & Directory, Associations Canada, Libraries Canada & the Canadian Parliamentary Guide.
Bryon Moore, General Manager
Robert Lang, Editorial Manager

Grolier
#570, 1700, boul Laval, Laval, QC H7S 2N6
450-667-5497, Fax: 450-667-7694, 800-563-3231
customerservice@grolier.qc.ca
www.grolier.ca
ISBNs: ISBN: 0-7172; SAN 115-3668
Publisher of children's books

Groundwood Books
#801, 110 Spadina Ave., Toronto, ON M5V 2K4
416-363-4343, Fax: 416-363-1017
www.groundwoodbooks.com
ISBNs: ISBN: 0-88899; SAN 115-0391
Publisher of children's books in English & Spanish
Patricia Aldana, Publisher

Groupe Éducalivres inc. - Éditions Études Vivantes
955, rue Bergar, Laval, QC H7L 4Z6
514-334-8466, Fax: 514-334-8387, 800-567-3671
commentaires@educalivres.com
www.educalivres.com
ISBNs: ISBN: 2-7607, 0-88586, 0-289022, 0-03-92

Groupe Modulo
#300, 233, av Dunbar, Montréal, QC H3P 2H4
514-738-9818, Fax: 514-738-5838, 888-738-9818
www.moduloediteur.com
ISBNs: ISBN: 2-89113, 2-920210, 2-920922, 2-89443, 2-920190, 2-921363
Éditeur au préscolaire et au primaire
Jean Bouchard, Directeur général

GTK Press
#109, 18 Wynford Dr., Toronto, ON M3C 3S2
416-385-1313, Fax: 416-385-1919, 866-485-7737
info@gtkpress.com
www.gtkpress.com
ISBNs: ISBN: 1-894318, 1-55137
Publisher of curriculum resources, notably science, technology, mathematics
K.L. Kwong, President & CEO

Guérin éditeur ltée
4501, rue Drolet, Montréal, QC H2T 2G2
514-842-3481, Fax: 514-842-4923, 800-398-8337
france.larochelle@guerin-editeur.qc.ca
www.guerin-editeur.qc.ca
ISBNs: ISBN: 2-7601
L'éditeur des écoles. Groupe Guérin: Guérin, éditeur limitée, Les Éditions La Pensée Inc., et LIDEC Inc.
Marc-Aimé Guérin, President

Guernica Editions Inc.
PO Box 117 P, Toronto, ON M5S 2S6
416-658-9888, Fax: 416-657-8885, 800-565-9523
guernicaeditions@cs.com
www.guernicaeditions.com
ISBNs: ISBN: 0-919349, 2-89135, 0-920717, 1-55071; SAN: 115-0421
Antonio D'Alfonso, Editor in Chief

Guy Saint-Jean Éditeur
3154, boul Industriel, Laval, QC H7X 4P7

450-663-1777, Fax: 450-663-6666
info@saint-jeanediteur.com
www.saint-jeanediteur.com

ISBNs: ISBN: 2-920340, 2-89455
Guides pratiques sur la santé, la psychologie populaire, le sport, le jardinage; beaux-livres; littérature; Green Frog Publishing (www.greenfrogpublishing.com) et MarieGray (www.mariegray.com)
Nicole Saint-Jean

GWEV Publishing Inc.
PO Box 565, Stittsville, ON K2S 1A6
613-831-9154, Fax: 613-831-4291, 866-747-3797
Sylvia@gwevpublishing.com
www.gwevpublishing.com

ISBNs: ISBN: 0-9681414, 0-9731300
Publisher of children's books
Sylvia Vincent, Publisher

H.B. Fenn & Company Ltd.
34 Nixon Rd., Bolton, ON L7E 1W2
905-951-6600, Fax: 905-951-6601, 800-267-3366
sales@hbfenn.com
www.hbfenn.com

ISBNs: ISBN: 0-919768, 1-55168; SAN: 115-1746
Book distributor
Harold B. Fenn, President

Hades Publications, Inc.
PO Box 1414 M, Calgary, AB T2P 2L6
403-254-0160, Fax: 403-254-0456
admin@hadespublications.com
www.trickster.com

ISBNs: ISBN: 0-919230, 0-921298
Publishes books and other materials on Magic, Illusion, Conjuring & Variety Arts
Brian Hades, Publisher

Hancock House Publishers Ltd.
19313 Zero Ave., Surrey, BC V3S 9R9
604-538-1114, Fax: 604-538-2262, 800-938-1114
sales@hancockhouse.com
www.hancockhouse.com

ISBNs: ISBN: 0-88839, 0-91954; SAN: 115-3730
Publishers of wildlife & nature books
David Hancock, President

Hans Schafler & Co. Ltd.
#2, 1184 Speers Rd., Oakville, ON L6L 2X4
905-827-2949, Fax: 905-827-2524, 877-646-9323
info@schafler.com
www.schafler.com

Publishes curriculum books for schools
Lisbeth Schafler

Happy Landings
851 Heritage Dr., RR#4, Merrickville, ON K0G 1N0
613-269-2552, Fax: 613-269-3962
books@happylandings.com
www.happylandings.com

ISBNs: ISBN: 0-9697322
Publisher of aviation books by Garth Wallace
Liz Wallace, Publisher

Harbour Publishing Co. Ltd.
PO Box 219, Madeira Park, BC V0N 2H0
604-883-2730, Fax: 604-883-9451, 800-667-2988
info@harbourpublishing.com
www.harbourpublishing.com

ISBNs: ISBN: 0-920080, 1-55017
Specializing in BC authors & books of the Pacific Northwest
Howard White, President

Harlequin Enterprises Limited
225 Duncan Mill Rd., Toronto, ON M3B 3K9
416-445-5860, Fax: 416-445-8655, 800-387-0112
customer_ecare@harlequin.ca
www.eharlequin.com

ISBNs: ISBN: 0-373, 1-55166, 0-778; SAN: 115-3749
Specializing in series romance & fiction for women
Katherine Orr, Vice President, Public Relations

HarperCollins Canada Ltd.
2 Bloor St. East, Toronto, ON M4W 1A8
416-975-9334, Fax: 416-975-5223, 800-387-0117
hcorder@harpercollins.com
www.harpercollins.ca

ISBNs: SAN: 150-026X
Canadian imprints include Avon, Greenwillow Books, HarperAudio, HarperBusiness, HarperLargePrint, William Morrow, among many others; specializing in Canadian fiction & non-fiction, for adults & children

Hartley & Marks Publishers
3661 Broadway West, Vancouver, BC V6R 2B8
800-277-5887, Fax: 800-707-5887
info@hartleyandmarks.com
www.hartleyandmarks.com

ISBNs: ISBN: 0-88179; SAN: 115-3757

Herald Press
#C8, 490 Dutton Dr., Waterloo, ON N2L 6H7
519-747-5722, Fax: 519-747-5721, 800-245-7894
hpcan@mph.org
www.heraldpress.com

ISBNs: ISBN: 0-8361; SAN: 116-0931
The trade publishing division of Mennonite Publishing Network; specializing in resources with emphasis on the Anabaptist perspective, biblical studies, mission, family & church life
Ron Rempel, Publisher, Canadian Branch

Heritage House Publishing Co. Ltd.
#108, 17665 - 66A Ave., Surrey, BC V3S 2A7
604-574-7067, Fax: 604-574-9942, 800-665-3302
distribution@heritagehouse.ca
www.heritagehouse.ca

ISBNs: ISBN: 0-919214, 1-895811, 1-894384; SAN: 115-8287
Specializing in Western Canadian non-fiction subjects & authors
Rodger Touchie, President

HikingCamping.com
PO Box 8563, Canmore, AB T1W 2V3
Fax: 403-678-3343
nomads@hikingcamping.com
www.hikingcamping.com

Specializing in guidebooks for hikers & campers, works of inspiration, insight & philosophy, & photography

Historical Trails West/Historical Research Centre
1115 - 8th Ave. South, Lethbridge, AB T1J 1P7
403-328-3824
hrc@ourheritage.net
www.ourheritage.net

Specializing in books & resources of Western Canadian interest
Bruce A. Haig, Director

Hogrefe & Huber Publishers
1543 Bayview Ave., Toronto, ON M4G 3B5
416-482-6339, Fax: 416-617-354, 800-228-3749
hhpub@hogrefe.com
www.hogrefe.com

ISBNs: ISBN: 0-88937, 0-920887; SAN: 115-379X
Specializing in resources in the areas of applied & experimental psychology, health, pharmacology, psychiatry & neurosciences
DR G.-J. Hogrefe, Publisher

House of Anansi Press
#801, 110 Spadina Ave., Toronto, ON M5V 2K4
416-363-4343, Fax: 416-363-1017, 800-663-5714
info@anansi.ca
www.anansi.ca

ISBNs: ISBN: 0-88784; SAN: 115-0391
Specializing in new & established Canadian writers of fiction, non-fiction & poetry, & French-Canadian works in translation
Sarah MacLachlan, President
Lynn Henry, Publisher

Human Kinetics Canada
#100, 475 Devonshire Rd., Windsor, ON N8Y 2L5
519-971-9500, Fax: 519-971-9797, 800-465-7301
info@khcanada.com
www.humankinetics.com

Humanitas
228, de la Lande, Rosemère, QC J4A 4J1
450-965-6624, Fax: 450-965-8839
humanitas@cyberglobe.net
www.editionshumanitas.com

ISBNs: ISBN: 2-89396, 2-9800950
Art, poésie, romans, essais, théâtre
Constantin Stoiciv

Hyperion Press Limited
300 Wales Ave., Winnipeg, MB R2M 2S9
204-256-9204, Fax: 204-255-7845
tamos@mts.net

ISBNs: ISBN: 0-920534, 1-895340, 1-895569; SAN: 115-124X
Dr. Marvis Tutiah, President
Arlene Osen, Vice President

Imago Press
30 Laws St., Toronto, ON M6P 2Y7
416-604-9741
imagorediron@rogers.com
http://pages.interlog.com/~imago/

ISBNs: ISBN: 0-920489, 0-9697555
Marshall Hryciuk

Inclusion Press International
47 Indian Trail, Toronto, ON M6R 1Z8
416-658-5363, Fax: 416-658-5067
inclusionpress@inclusion.com
www.inclusion.com

ISBNs: ISBN: 1-895418
Resource materials with emphasis on diversity, inclusion & community, for educational institutions, government agencies, human service agencies, First Nations organizations
Jack Pearpoint, Co-publisher
Marsha Forest, Co-publisher

Inner City Books
PO Box 1271 Q, Toronto, ON M4T 2P4
416-927-0355, Fax: 416-924-1814
info@innercitybooks.net
www.innercitybooks.net

ISBNs: ISBN: 0-919123, 1-894574; SAN: 115-3870
Publishers of studies in Jungian Psychology by Jungian Analysts
Daryl Sharp, President

Insomniac Press
#403, 192 Spadina Ave., Toronto, ON M5T 2C2
416-504-6270, Fax: 416-504-9313
mike@insomniacpress.com
www.insomniacpress.com

ISBNs: ISBN: 1-895837, 1-894663
Independent press that publishes non-fiction, poetry & fiction
Mike O'Connor, Publisher, mike@insomniacpress.com
Dan Varrette, Managing Editor, dan@insomniacpress.com

Institut de recherches psychologiques, inc. / Institute of Psychological Research Inc.
34, rue Fleury ouest, Montréal, QC H3L 1S9
514-382-3000, Fax: 514-382-3007, 800-363-7800
info@i-r-p.ca
www.i-r-p.ca

ISBNs: ISBN: 0-88509, 2-89109
Robert Chevrier

The Institute for Research on Public Policy / L'Institut de recherche en politiques publiques
#200, 1470, rue Peel, Montréal, QC H3A 1T1
514-985-2461, Fax: 514-985-2559
irpp@irpp.org
www.irpp.org

ISBNs: ISBN: 0-920380, 0-88645; SAN: 115-3889, 115-0537
Specializing in research & publication with emphasis on Canadian public policy, Canadian federalism, economic policy, international relations; publisher of POLICY OPTIONS journal
Suzanne Ostiguy McIntyre, Vice President, Operations
Mel Cappe, President

Institute for Risk Research
University of Waterloo, 200 University Ave. West, Waterloo, ON N2L 3G1
519-888-4567, Fax: 519-725-4834
irr-neram@uwaterloo.ca
www.irr-neram.ca

ISBNs: ISBN: 0-88898, 0-9696747, 0-9684982
Along with The Network for Environmental Risk Assessment and Management (NERAM), the Institute for Risk Research specializes in research & publications in the areas of risk, risk management for the environment, human health, industrial safety & transportation
Dr. John Shortreed, Executive Committee

Institute of Intergovernmental Relations
Room 301, School of Policy Studies, Queen's University, Kingston, ON K7L 3N6
613-533-2080, Fax: 613-533-6868
iigr@iigr.ca
www.iigr.ca

ISBNs: ISBN: 0-88911, 1-55339
Specializing in research & publication, with emphasis on Canadian federalism, intergovernmental relations, constitutional reform & social union
Thomas J. Courchene, Director

International Development Research Centre (IDRC) / Le Centre de recherches pour le développement international
PO Box 8500, 150 Kent St., Ottawa, ON K1G 3H9
613-236-6163, Fax: 613-563-2476
pub@idrc.ca
www.idrc.ca

ISBNs: ISBN: 0-88936, 1-55250
Publishers of IDRC Bulletin, & resources with emphasis on

international development, sustainable development, food, health, social issues
Bill Carman, Senior Communications Advisor, Publishing

International Institute for Sustainable Development
161 Portage Ave. East, 6th Floor, Winnipeg, MB R3B 0Y4
204-958-7700, Fax: 204-958-7710
info@iisd.org
www.iisd.org
ISBNs: ISBN: 1-895536
Specializing in books & other materials with emphasis on the IISD's institutional & research history. Offices in Ottawa, New York & Geneva
David Runnalls, President & CEO
Stuart Slayen, Manager, Publishing & Communications

International Press Publications Inc.
#21, 90 Nolan Ct., Markham, ON L3R 4L9
905-946-9588, Fax: 905-946-9590
sales@ippbooks.com
www.ippbooks.com
ISBNs: SAN: 170-0049
"Specialists in directories on all subjects from all over the world; largest distributors of books on career guidance, general reference, research, text books, dictionaries; free search for rare & out-of-print books from any country"
Bali Sethi, President

Irwin Law Inc.
#206, 14 Duncan St., Toronto, ON M5H 3G8
416-862-7690, Fax: 416-862-9236, 888-314-9014
www.irwinlaw.com
ISBNs: ISBN: 1-55221
Jeffrey Miller, Publisher

Is Five Press
#200, 161 Eglinton Ave. East, Toronto, ON M4P 1J5
416-480-2408, Fax: 416-480-2546
tom@isfive.com
www.isfive.com
ISBNs: ISBN: 0-920934; SAN: 115-3943
Specializing in books, manuals & curriculum resources in social & environmental subject areas; other services include writing, design, translation & editing

ISER Books
Facilities Management Building, Room FM-2005A, Memorial University, St. John's, NL A1C 5S7
709-737-3453, Fax: 709-737-4342
iser-books@mun.ca
www.mun.ca/iser
ISBNs: ISBN: 1-894725, 0-919666; SAN: 115-3897
Al Potter, Manager

Island Studies Press
University of Prince Edward Island, 550 University Ave., Charlottetown, PE C1A 4P3
902-566-0386, Fax: 902-566-0756
iis@upei.ca
www.upei.ca
ISBNs: ISBN: 0-919013
Publisher of books on the history, literature, culture and environment of Prince Edward Island

ITMB Publishing Ltd.
530 West Broadway, Vancouver, BC V5Z 1E9
604-879-3621, Fax: 604-879-4521
itmb@itmb.com
www.itmb.com
ISBNs: ISBN: 0-921463, 1-895907, 1-55341; SAN: 112-6997
Publisher of travel maps
Jack Joyce, President

J & L Macpherson Educational Services Ltd.
3030 Collens Hill Rd., Kelowna, BC V1Z 1P5
250-769-4321, Fax: 250-769-3045
jlmltd@fichtner.com
W. John Macpherson
Lydia Macpherson

J. Gordon Shillingford Publishing Inc.
PO Box 86 Corydon Ave., Winnipeg, MB R3M 3S3
204-779-6967, Fax: 204-779-6970
jgshill@allstream.net
jgshillingford.com
ISBNs: ISBN: 1-896239, 0-919754, 0-969761, 0-920486, 0-968942
Primarily a literary publisher; publishes on average 14 titles/year.
J. Gordon Shillingford, President
Karen Green, Marketing Director
Glenda MacFarlane, Drama Editor
Catherine Hunter, Poetry Editor

J.C. George Enterprises
577 Mount Pleasant Rd., Toronto, ON M4S 2M5
416-483-4353, Fax: 416-791-8586
mgfa@interlog.com
ISBNs: ISBN: 0-921369
Publishes educational materials & books

J.E.S.L. Educational Products
58 Glen Park Ave., Toronto, ON M6B 2C2
416-785-7941, Fax: 416-785-7941
jesl@rogers.com
www.interlog.com/~jesl
ISBNs: ISBN: 0-9691264, 0-9684362
Publishes Jewish educational materials
Edmond Y. Lipsitz

J.P. Delf Companies
13020 Delf Pl., Richmond, BC V6V 2A2
604-278-4600, Fax: 604-276-0118
delf@helix.net
ISBNs: ISBN: 1-55056, 0-969-6208

Jack The Bookman Ltd.
#4, 1150 Kerrisdale Blvd., Newmarket, ON L3Y 8Z9
905-836-5999, Fax: 905-836-1152, 800-563-5168
jackthebookman@sympatico.ca
www.jackthebookman.com
Library wholesalers
Scott Davey, Vice-President

James Lorimer & Co. Ltd., Publishers
#1002, 317 Adelaide St. W, Toronto, ON M5V 1P9
416-362-4762, Fax: 416-362-3939
info@lorimer.ca
www.lorimer.ca
ISBNs: ISBN: 0-88862, 1-55028; SAN: 115-1134
Lynn Schellenberg, Acquisitions Editor, acquisitions@lorimer.ca
Faye Smailes, Children's Book Editor, childrenseditor@lorimer.ca
James Lorimer, Publisher, publisher@lorimer.ca
Allison McDonald, Editorial & Marketing Coordinator, promotion@lorimer.ca

Jesperson Publishing
See Breakwater Books,
ISBNs: ISBN: 1-894377, 0-921692, 0-920502
Clyde Rose, Publisher

John Markham & Associates
11210 Elderberry Way, Sidney, BC V8L 5J6
250-655-1823, Fax: 250-655-1826, 800-865-1826
jma@jamtags.com

John Wiley & Sons Canada Ltd.
#400, 5353 Dundas St. W, Toronto, ON M9B 6H8
416-236-4433, Fax: 416-236-4447, 800-567-4797
canada@wiley.com
www.wiley.com
ISBNs: ISBN: 0-471; SAN: 115-1185
William J. Pesce, President & CEO
Timothy B. King, Sr. Vice-President, Planning & Development
Bill Zerter, Chief Operating Officer, John Wiley & Sons Canada, Ltd.

John Wiley & Sons Inc.
111 River St., Hoboken, NJ
201-748-6000, Fax: 201-748-6088
info@wiley.com
www.wiley.com
Ellis E. Cousens, Executive Vice President, Chief Financial & Operations Officer
William J. Arlington, Sr. Vice President, Human Resources
Gary M. Rinck, Sr. Vice President, Human Resources

Johnson Gorman Publishers
2003 - 35 Ave. SW, Calgary, AB T2T 2E2
403-246-7956, Fax: 403-246-8926
ISBNs: ISBN: 0-921835; SAN: 115-0871
Dennis Johnson

Johnstone Training & Consultation (JTC) Inc.
PO Box 1927, Kemptville, ON K0G 1J0
613-258-3092, Fax: 613-258-9971, 888-408-6647
jtcinc@jtcinc.ca
www.jtcinc.ca
ISBNs: ISBN: 1-895271
Resource materials for not-for-profits & charities
Laura Kelly

Jordan Music Productions
PO Box 160 M, Toronto, ON M6S 4T3
905-938-5050, Fax: 905-938-9970, 800-567-7733
sjordan@sara-jordan.com
www.sara-jordan.com
ISBNs: ISBN: 1-895523, 1-894262, 1-533860; SAN: 118-959X
Publisher & producer of educational songs & music

Juris Analytica Publishing Inc.
604 - 10080 Jasper Ave., Edmonton, AB T5J 1V9
780-420-9010, Fax: 780-420-9030
ISBNs: ISBN: 0-9698958

The Kashtan Press
22 Gretna Green, Kingston, ON K7M 3J2
613-546-8364
luciuk@luciuk.ca
luciuk.ca/kashtanpress.html
ISBNs: ISBN: 1-896354
Primarily Ukranian & Ukranian/Canadian History
Dr. Lubomyr Luciuk

Ken Haycock & Associates Inc
#343, 101-1001 West Broadway, Vancouver, BC V6H 4E4
604-925-0266, Fax: 604-925-0566
admin@kenhaycock.com
www.kenhaycock.com
ISBNs: ISBN: 0-920175
Ken Haycock, Publisher
Michelle Rudert, Director, Client Services

Keng Seng Enterprises Inc.
#103, 4000, rue St-Ambroise, Montréal, QC H4C 2C7
514-939-3971, Fax: 514-989-1922
canada@kengseng.com
www.kengseng.com
ISBNs: ISBN: 1-895494
David Chen, President

Kerrwil Publications Ltd.
#800, 2 St. Clair Ave. E, Toronto, ON M4T 2T5
416-622-6736, Fax: 416-695-0453
www.kerrwil.com

Key Porter Books Limited
6 Adelaide St. E, 10th Fl., Toronto, ON M5C 1H6
416-862-7777, Fax: 416-862-2304
info@keyporter.com
www.keyporter.com
ISBNs: ISBN: 0-88619, 1-55013, 1-89555, 1-55228, 1-5263, 1-5536
Publishes about 100 titles per year; covering politics, fiction, history, environment, children's, health, sports, cookbooks & photography
Jordan Fenn, Vice President & Publisher, jordan.fenn@keyporter.com
Paula Sloss, Special & Corporate Sales, 416-862-7777 x222, paula.sloss@keyporter.com
Sandra Homer, Manager, International Rights & Co-editions, 416-862-7777 x260, sandra.homer@keyporter.com
Louise Ward, Production Manager, 416-862-7777 x247, lward@keyporter.com
Rob Howard, Sales & Marketing, 416-862-7777 x235, rob.howard@keyporter.com

Kids Can Press Ltd.
29 Birch Ave., Toronto, ON M4V 1E2
416-925-5437, Fax: 416-960-5437, 800-265-0884
info@kidscan.com
www.kidscanpress.com
ISBNs: ISBN: 0-919964, 0-55337, 1-55074; SAN: 115-4001
Specializes in children's literature & children's books
Lisa Lyons, President

Kinbridge Publications
PO Box 89065, RPO Westdale, Hamilton, ON L8S 4R5
Fax: 905-627-0431
ISBNs: ISBN 0-9693233
M.A. Major, Manager

Kindred Productions
1310 Taylor Ave., Winnipeg, MB R3M 3Z6
204-669-6575, Fax: 204-654-1865, 800-545-7322
kindred@mbconf.ca
www.kindredproductions.com
ISBNs: ISBN: 0-919797, 0-921788, 1-894791
Publishing & distribution arm of the Mennonite Bretheren Churches in North America.
Marilyn Hudson, Director

Kirkton Press Ltd.
396 Grills Rd., RR#1, Baltimore, ON K0K 1C0
905-349-3443, Fax: 905-349-3420, 800-332-3663
kirkton@eagle.ca
www.breakingtheviciouscycle.info

ISBNs: ISBN: 0-9692768
Publishers of *The Vicious Cyclei series of diet/health books.*
Elaine Gottschall, President
Herbert Gottschall, Vice-President

Kitchener News Company Ltd.
PO Box 274 Waterloo, 455 Dutton Dr., Waterloo, ON N2J 4A4
519-884-3710, Fax: 519-885-4640, 800-265-8839
www.kitnews.com
ISBNs: ISBN 0-394
Educational books & mass market paperbacks

Knopf Canada
#210, 33 Yonge St., Toronto, ON M5E 1G4
416-777-9477, Fax: 416-777-9470
ISBNs: ISBN: 0-394, 0-676
Louise Dennys, Publisher

Koala Books of Canada Ltd.
14327 - 95A Ave., Edmonton, AB T5N 0B6
780-452-5149, Fax: 780-452-5149
jcarolan@nucleus.com
ISBNs: SAN: 169-9385
John Carolan, General Manager

Kosoy Travel Guides
112 Fairholme Ave., Toronto, ON M6B 2W9
416-256-0974, Fax: 416-256-0974
torcan22@yahoo.com
ISBNs: ISBN: 0-919632; SAN: 115-8724
Ted Kosoy

Kugh Enterprises
PO Box 31821, Whitehorse, YT Y1A 6L3
867-633-2118, Fax: 867-633-3307
gkarpes@northwestel.net
www.yukonweb.com/tourism/kugh
ISBNs: ISBN: 1-896
Publisher of Wilderness books about the Yukon.
Gus Karpes

Lambrecht Publications
1763 Maple Bay Rd., Duncan, BC V9L 5N6
250-748-8722, Fax: 250-748-8722, 877-774-4372
ISBNs: ISBN: 0-919383; SAN: 115-057X
H. Lambrecht, Publisher

Lancaster House
#200, 17 Dundonald St., Toronto, ON M4Y 1K3
416-977-6618, Fax: 416-977-5873, 888-298-8841
lan@lancasterhouse.com
www.lancasterhouse.com
ISBNs: ISBN: 0-920450
Publishes information & hosts conferences in the areas of labour & employment law.
Paul Wollaston, General Manager
Vanessa Scott, Editorial Coordinator
Cristina Santos, Production Coordinator/Database Administrator
Norma Nixon, Manager, Customer Service & Database

LandOwner Resource Centre
PO Box 599, 5524 Dickinson St., Manotick, ON K4M 1A5
613-692-3571, Fax: 613-692-0831
info@lrconline.com
www.lrconline.com
ISBNs: 0-9680992
Publishes information on forestry, agriculture, wildlife, water, soil and other land management issues.

Largy Books
PO Box 6023, Fort McMurray, AB T9H 4W1
403-791-1750, Fax: 403-791-1750
madame_faucon@hotmail.com
ISBNs: ISBN: 0-9698203

Laurier Books Ltd.
PO Box 2694 D, Ottawa, ON K1P 5W6
613-738-2163, Fax: 613-247-0256
educa2@yahoo.com
educa0.tripod.com/edu
ISBNs: ISBN: 1-895959, 1-55394; SAN: 168-2806
Publishers of Educational Books, Foreign Language Dictionaries; French Language Dictionaries; Native American Books & Native Languages; Asian Studies books
Marthe Lalwani

Lazara Press
PO Box 2269 Main, Vancouver, BC V6B 3W2
604-872-1134, Fax: 604-874-6661
www.lazarapress.ca
ISBNs: ISBN: 0-920999
Small, progressive publishing house located in Vancouver. Publishers of poetry, literature, broadsides & chapbooks.
Committed to publishing & distributing works that might not otherwise be available.
Penny Goldsmith, Owner/Founder

Learnxs Press
5050 Yonge St., Toronto, ON M2N 5N8
416-397-3911
learnxs.foundation@tbsb.on.ca
ISBNs: ISBN: 0-920020; SAN: 115-4060
Publishing house for the production & sale of innovative learning materials in conjunction with the Toronto District School Board.
Ross Richardson, Production Manager

Leméac Éditeur
4609, rue d'Iberville, 1er étage, Montréal, QC H2H 2L9
514-524-5558, Fax: 514-524-3145
lemeac@lemeac.com
www.lemeac.com
ISBNs: ISBN: 2-7609, 0-7761
Notre politique éditoriale essentiellement à caractère littéraire s'inscrit surtout dans les domaines du roman, du théâtre contemporain, de l'essai, de la biographie de personalités ayant marqué le secteur culturel.
Lise P. Bergevin, Directrice générale

LexisNexis Canada Inc.
#700, 123 Commerce Valley Drive E, Markham, ON L3T 7W8
905-479-2665, Fax: 905-479-2826, 800-668-6481
info@lexisnexis.ca
www.lexisnexis.ca
ISBNs: ISBN: 0-409, 0-433; SAN: 115-2750
Provider of invormation & services to law professionals, corporations, government & academic institutions through online products.
Michael Pilmer, President & CEO

Libra Information Services
PO Box 353 A, 18 Eastern Ave. Lower Level, Toronto, ON M5W 1C2
416-364-0050, Fax: 416-364-0606
libra@web.ca
www.web.ca/~libra
Publishers of material on Innovative Health Care methods, and for Social Investors & Conscious Consumers

Librairie Gallimard de Montréal
3700, boul Saint-Laurent, Montréal, QC H2X 2V4
514-499-2012, Fax: 514-499-1535
info@gallimardmontreal.com
www.gallimardmontreal.com

Librairie Wilson & Lafleur Ltée
40, rue Notre-Dame est, Montréal, QC H2Y 1B9
514-875-6326, Fax: 514-875-8356, 800-363-2327
libraire@wilsonlafleur.com
www.wilsonlafleur.com
ISBNs: ISBN: 2-89127
Éditeur en droit et législation
Claude Wilson

Library Bound
#6-7, 75 Rankin Ave., Waterloo, ON N2V 1W2
519-885-3233, Fax: 519-885-2662, 800-363-4728
lbi@librarybound.com
www.librarybound.com
ISBNs: SAN: 116-9203
Also provide services for shelf-ready materials
Heather Bindseil, President, 5198853233 ext.28, heatherb@librarybound.com
Lisa Bendig, Accounting Department, lisab@librarybound.com
Ron Stadnik, Print Collections Development, 5198853233 ext.26, ron@librarybound.com

Lidec Inc.
4350, av de l'Hôtel-de-Ville, Montréal, QC H2W 2H5
514-843-5991, Fax: 514-843-5252, 800-350-5991
lidec@lidec.qc.ca
www.lidec.qc.ca
ISBNs: ISBN: 2-7608, 0-7762
La maison Lidec fut fondée par les Frères des écoles chrétiennes pour répondre aux besoins de l'éducation, puis achetée en 1985 par le Groupe Guérin. Lidec se spécialise dans le matériel scolaire de tous les niveaux et de toutes les disciplines. La maison publie des manuels de base et du matériel complémentaire pour l'enseignement primaire, secondaire, collégial et universitaire adaptés aux différents programmes du Ministère de l'Éducation du Québec et des autres provinces canadiennes.
Marc-Aimé Guérin, President

Life Cycle Books Ltd.
#20, 1149 Bellamy Rd. N, Toronto, ON M1H 1H7
Fax: 866-690-8532, 800-880-5860
canorders@lifecyclebooks.com
www.lifecyclebooks.com
ISBNs: ISBN: 0-919225; SAN: 115-8417
Publisher of pro-life & abstinence books and other educational materials.

Lifestyle Books
PO Box 42, Grand Falls, NL A2A 2J3
709-489-6796, Fax: 709-489-6796
c.coish@nf.sympatico.ca
ISBNs: ISBN: 0-9691126, 0-9699031
Cal Coish, President

Lingo Media Inc.
#703, 151 Bloor St. West, Toronto, ON M5S 1S4
416-927-7000, Fax: 416-927-1222, 866-927-7011
mkraft@lingomedia.com
www.lingomedia.com
Develops and publishes English Language Learning materials for use in China.
Michael Kraft, mkraft@lingomedia.com
Khurram Qureshi, kqureshi@lingomedia.com

Linguatech éditeur inc.
CP 26026 Salaberry, Montréal, QC H3M 1L0
514-336-5207, Fax: 514-336-4736
linguatechediteur@bellnet.ca
home.ican.net/~lingua
ISBNs: ISBN: 2-920342
Publications: dictionnaires et vocabulaires; Actes de congrès; Ouvrages didactiques; Langues de spécialité
André Dubuc, Président
Robert Dubuc, Vice-Président
Odette Dubuc, Secrétaire

Little Brick Schoolhouse Inc.
PO Box 84001, 1235 Trafalgar Rd., Oakville, ON L6H 3J0
905-844-4669, Fax: 905-690-3400
schoolhouse@cogeco.ca
www.littlebrick.com
ISBNs: ISBN: 0-919788
Publisher of Educational entertainment products dealing with Canadian & American History.
Robert Livesey, President

Lobster Press Limited
1620, rue Sherbrooke ouest, #C & D, Montréal, QC H3H 1C9
514-904-1100, Fax: 514-904-1101
marketing@lobsterpress.com
www.lobsterpress.com
ISBNs: ISBN: 1-894222, 1-897073, 2-922435
Publisher of children's books
Alison Fripp, President & Publisher
Meghan Nolan, Editor
Stephanie Hindley, Director, Marketing
Ruth Joseph, Office Manager

Lone Pine Publishing
10145 - 81 Ave., Edmonton, AB T6E 1W9
780-433-9333, Fax: 780-433-9646, 800-661-9017
info@lonepinepublishing.com
www.lonepinepublishing.com
ISBNs: ISBN: 0-919433, 1-55105; SAN: 115-4125
Focus as a regional publisher in the Rocky Mountains, West Coast & Great Lakes. Focus on nature, outdoor recreation & popular history.
Shane Kennedy, President
Nancy Foulds, Senior Editor
David Cleary, Director of Sales & Marketing

Lorraine Greey Publications Limited
#303, 56 The Esplanade, Toronto, ON M5E 1A7
416-366-9729, Fax: 416-367-3998
Lorraine Durham Greey, President

Louise Courteau, éditrice inc.
481, Lac St-Louis est, Saint-Zénon, QC J0K 3N0
450-884-5958, Fax: 450-884-5913
presse@louisdecourteau.com
www.louisdecorteau.com
Louise Courteau, Éditrice

Loyal Colonies Press
304 Olympus Ave., Kingston, ON K7M 4T9
613-389-0866
tvincent@can.rogers.com
www.bibliofiles.ca/lc_index.cfm
ISBNs: ISBN: 0-929832
Publishers of history books, largely biographies of Canadians; Publishes roughly 2 books per year.
Thomas B. Vincent, Proprietor

Lugus Publications Ltd.
48 Falcon St., Toronto, ON M4S 2P5
416-322-5113, Fax: 416-484-9512
gethin@la-rampa.com
ISBNs: ISBN: 0-921633, 1-896266
Publishes Children's books and other books & pamphlets.
Annual sales of $200,000 - $350,000
Gethin James, Manager

Lyalta Publishing
4903 Benson Rd. West, Calgary, AB T2L 1R9
403-233-2558, Fax: 403-266-7078, 888-322-2558
lyle@lyaltapublishing.com
www.lyaltapublishing.com
ISBNs: ISBN: 0-9699101, 0-9681761
Assists individuals and small organizations in self-publishing
Lyle Manery, Founder

Lynx Images Inc.
PO Box 5961 A, Toronto, ON M5W 1P4
416-925-8422, Fax: 416-925-8352
website@lynximages.com
www.lynximages.com
ISBNs: ISBN: 0-9698427, 1-894073
Documentary Film production company & publisher. Publishes books dealing with Canadian History & companion books to documentaries.
Russell Floren, President
Barbara Chisolm, Vice-President, Publishing

MacKenzie Art Gallery
3475 Albert St., Regina, SK S4S 6X6
306-584-4285, Fax: 306-569-8191
sandra.nixon@uregina.ca
www.mackenzieartgallery.ca
ISBNs: ISBN: 1-896470
Publishes books about visual arts and Canadian & local artists

Madison Press Books
#200, 1000 Yonge St., Toronto, ON M4Y 2K2
416-923-5027, Fax: 416-923-9708
info@madisonpressbooks.com
www.madisonpressbooks.com

Independent publishers of illustrated non-fiction titles; Catalog includes a number of international best-sellers including Robert D. Ballard's 'Discovery of the Titanic'; Also publish children's books & custom publishing programs for corporate clients
Oliver Salzmann, Publisher, 4169235027 ext. 223, osalzmann@madisonpressbooks.com
Alison Maclean, Associate Publisher, amaclean@madisonpressbooks.com

Madonna House Publications
Madonna House, 2888 Dafoe Rd., Combermere, ON K0J 1L0
613-756-3728, Fax: 613-756-0103, 888-703-7110
publications@madonnahouse.org
www.madonnahouse.org/publications
ISBNs: ISBN: 0-921440
Non-profic Catholic Christian publisher of religious books, audiobooks, videos, music & cards.
Linda Lambeth

Malcolm Lester & Associates
22 St. Clair Ave. E, 14th Fl., Toronto, ON M4T 2S3
416-928-2637, Fax: 416-944-3122
malcolm@malcolmlester.com
www.malcolmlester.com
ISBNs: ISBN: 1-9659415
Publisher & publishing consultant; Develop books for other publishers; Develops custom books for corporate clients, individuals & organizations.
Malcolm Lester, malcolm@malcolmlester.com
Andrea Knight, andrea@malcolmlester.com

Map Art
70 Bloor St. East, Oshawa, ON L1H 3M2
905-436-2525, 877-231-6277
info@mapart.com
www.mapart.com

Leading publishers of Maps, Atlases, Wall Maps & Street Guides.

Maple Tree Press Inc.
#200, 51 Front St. East, Toronto, ON M5E 1B3
416-304-0702, Fax: 416-304-0525
info@mapletreepress.com
www.mapletreepress.com
ISBNs: ISBN: 0-919872, 0-920775, 1-895688, 1-897066, 1-894379; SAN: 1
Publishers of non-fiction books for children covering a wide variety of topics including Sports, Humor, Science, Crafts, Canada, History & Culture.
Sheba Meland

Marcus Books
301 Petheram Pl., Newmarket, ON L3X 1J8
905-478-2201
thomas.rieder@sympatico.ca
ISBNs: ISBN: 0-919951; SAN: 115-4249
Thomas Rieder, President

Marshall Cavendish
#3, 109 Woodbine Downs Rd., Toronto, ON M9W 6Y1
416-674-8622, Fax: 416-674-6215
info@edureference.com
www.marshallcavendish.com
ISBNs: ISBN: 0-7614
Publishes educational, home & library reference & non-fiction titles.
Orland Kirkness

Marvin Melnyk Associates Ltd
PO Box 220, Queenston, ON L0S 1L0
905-262-4964, Fax: 905-262-4974, 800-682-0029
meljack@niagara.com
ISBNs: ISBN: 0-919803; SAN: 115-4281
John O. Fritz, Vice-President
Marvin Melnyk, President

Master Point Press
331 Douglas Ave., Toronto, ON M5M 1H2
416-781-0351, Fax: 416-781-1831
info@masterpointpress.com
www.masterpointpress.com
ISBNs: ISBN: 0-9698461, 1-894154, 1-897106
Publisher of a variety of books on the topic of the card game Bridge; also publishes books on other games, as well as software
Ray Lee, President
Linda Lee, Co-owner

MasterAthlete Book Publishing Group Ltd.
75 Main St., Mount Albert, ON L0G 1M0
905-473-9714, Fax: 905-473-9715
ISBNs: ISBN: 0-921016; SAN: 118-3613
Liz Roach, President

McArthur & Company
#402, 322 King St. West, Toronto, ON M5V 1J2
416-408-4007, Fax: 416-408-4081
info@mcarthur-co.com
www.mcarthur-co.com
ISBNs: ISBN: 1-55278; SAN: 117-9713
Publisher & distributor of Canadian & international fiction & non-fiction; Publisher of 63 best-sellers & 21 #1 bestsellers.
Kim McArthur, President, Publisher
Jim Palmeieri, Director, Finance
Jessica Scott, Production & Rights

McClelland & Stewart Ltd. (M&S)
5th Fl., 75 Sherbourne St., Toronto, ON M5A 2P9
416-598-1114, Fax: 416-598-7764, 800-788-1074
mail@mcclelland.com
www.mcclelland.com
ISBNs: ISBN: 0-7710; SAN: 115-4192
Publisher of over 100 titles annually, both fiction & non-fiction. Publishers of authors such as Margaret Atwood, Alistair MacLeod, Rohinton Mistry & Jane Urquhart. Publishers of political memoirs, including Pierre Elliott Trudeau's.
Douglas J. Pepper

McGilligan Books
PO Box 16024, 1260 Dundas St. West, Toronto, ON M6J 3W2
416-538-0945
info@mcgilliganbooks.com
www.mcgilliganbooks.com
ISBNs: ISBN: 0-9698064, 1-894692
Publishers of fiction & non-fiction, emphasizing multiracial & multicultural books.
Ann Decter, Publisher

McGill-Queen's University Press
Marketing Dept., McGill-Queen's University Press, 3430 McTavish St., Montréal, QC H3A 1X9
514-398-3750, Fax: 514-398-4333, 877-864-8477
mqup@mqup.ca
www.mqup.mcgill.ca
ISBNs: ISBN: 0-88629, 0-7735, 0-88911, 1-55339; SAN: 106-4206
Publisher of non-fiction books, with over 1800 books in print and numerous awards & bestsellers.
Philip Cercone, Executive Director & Senior Editor, 514-398-3750, philip.cercone@mcgill.ca
John Zucchi, Deputy Senior Editor, 514-398-2056, john.zucchi@mcgill.ca
Joan McGilvray, Coordinating Editor, 514-398-3922, joan.mcgilvray@mcgill.ca
Joanne Pisano, Permissions & Rights Coordinator, 514-398-2068, joanne.pisano@mcgill.ca

McGill-Queen's University Press
Queen's University, 144 Barrie St., Kingston, ON K7L 3N6
613-533-2155, Fax: 613-533-6822
mqup@post.queensu.ca
www.mqup.mcgill.ca
ISBNs: ISBN: 0-7735
Donald H. Akenson, Senior Editor
Kyla Madden, Deputy Senior Editor, 6kmm3@queensu.ca

McGraw-Hill Ryerson Limited
300 Water St., Whitby, ON L1N 9B6
905-430-5000, Fax: 905-430-5020, 800-565-5758
cs_queries@mcgrawhill.ca
www.mcgrawhill.ca
ISBNs: ISBN: 0-07; SAN: 115-060X
Publishers of a large quantity of education materials, including textbooks
John Dill, President/CEO

MDAG Publishing
8035 Redtail Ct., Surrey, BC V3W 0N4
604-502-0796
contact@mdag.com
www.mdag.com/publishing
ISBNs: 0-9682039
Released tools & publications produced by the Minesite Drainage Assessment Group

Mediacorp Canada Inc.
21 New St., Toronto, ON M5R 1P7
416-964-6069, Fax: 416-964-3202
info@mediacorp.ca
www.mediacorp.ca
ISBNs: ISBN: 0-9681447, 1-894450
Publishers of data & publications regarding employment, employers & labour

Megamy Publishing Ltd.
PO Box 3507, Spruce Grove, AB T7X 3A7
780-960-3539, Fax: 780-960-3539
megamy@compusmart.ab.ca
ISBNs: ISBN: 0-9681916

The Mercury Press
PO Box 672 P, Toronto, ON M5S 2Y4
416-531-4338, Fax: 416-531-0765, 800-591-6250
contact@themercurypress.ca
www.themercurypress.ca
ISBNs: ISBN: 0-920544, 1-55128; SAN: 115-009X
Publishers of poetry, fiction, murder mysteries & non-fiction by Canadian authors

Messageries ADP inc.
955, rue Amherst, Montréal, QC H2L 3K4
514-523-1182, Fax: 514-521-4434, 800-361-4806
www.messageries-adp.com

Diffuseur et distributeur de livres francophones au Canada; partenaire de 139 maisons d'édition québécoises, françaises, belges et suisses

Michelin North America (Canada) Inc.
Travel Publications, #510, 2540, boul Daniel Johnson, Laval, QC H7T 2T9
800-361-8236
ISBNs: ISBN: 2-06; SAN: 115-0618
Publishes maps & travel guides
Jack Haugh

Michi-Mook Enterprises
817 Queen St. East, Sault Ste Marie, ON P6A 2A4
705-946-5746, Fax: 705-946-3577
ISBNs: ISBN: 1-896579, 0-9698326
Publishes personalized childrens books
Lou Mangone

Mile Oak Publishing Inc.
#81, 20 Mineola Rd. East, Mississauga, ON L5G 4N9
905-274-4356
mile_oak@compuserve.com
www.i75online.com
ISBNs: ISBN: 1-896819
Publishers of the "Along Interstate-75" travel guide.
Dave Hunter, Publisher

Mini Mocho Press
PO Box 57424 Jackson, Hamilton, ON L8P 4X2

905-523-1518
jamesstrecker@sympatico.ca
ISBNs: ISBN: 0-921980
Publishes a catalog of 26 titles featuring primarily authors from Southern Ontario
James Strecker

Misthorn Press
Comp. 11, Site 660, RR#6, Courtenay, BC V9N 8H9
250-335-2237, Fax: 250-338-8469
ISBNs: ISBN: 0-9680159

MLR Editions Canada
Dept. of English & Film Studies, Wilfrid Laurier Univ, Waterloo, ON N2L 3C5
519-884-0710, Fax: 519-886-9351
ptiessen@wlu.ca
ISBNs: ISBN: 0-9692539
Paul Tiessen, Publisher

MOD Publishing
4 Fairview Blvd., Toronto, ON M4K 1L9
416-466-9275, Fax: 416-466-7493
jean.weihs@rogers.com
www.modpublishing.com
ISBNs: ISBN: 0-9684559, 0-9683974, 1-894461
Publishes supplemental educational aids that covers material not covered within current cirriculum

Modus Vivendi
55 rue Jean-Talon Ouest, Montréal, QC H2R 2W8
514-272-0433, Fax: 514-272-7234
info@modusaventure.com
www.modusaventure.com
ISBNs: ISBN: 2-921556, 2-92155, 2-89523, 2-922148 (Presses Aventure)
Publishers of non-fiction books covering topics such as arts & crafts, cooking, food & wine, diet & health, games & activities, home renovations and others.
Jean Poitras, Editeur

Monarch Books of Canada
5000 Dufferin St., Toronto, ON M3H 5T5
416-663-8231, Fax: 416-736-1702, 800-404-7404
customer_service@monarchbooks.ca
www.monarchbooks.ca

Specializes in distributing Children's books, Teacher Resources, Special Needs, Sports, Reference and more, from a wide range of publishers, as well as bestselling audiobook titles.

Mondia éditeurs inc.
105, rue de Martigny ouest, Saint-Jérome, QC J7Y 2G2
514-438-8479, Fax: 514-884-8307
ISBNs: ISBN: 0-88556, 2-89114, 0-9861676

Money Jar Publishing
#2021, 642 Sheppard Ave. East, Toronto, ON M2K 1B9
416-223-7312
millyard@rogers.com
ISBNs: ISBN: 0-9695889
John Millyard, Owner

Montréal Museum of Fine Arts / Musée des beaux-arts de Montréal
PO Box 3000 H, Montréal, QC H3G 2T9
514-285-2000
flavoie@mbamtl.org
www.mbamtl.org; www.mmfa.qc.ca
ISBNs: ISBN: 2-89192
Francine Lavoie, Head, Publishing, flavoie@mbamtl.org

Moonprint Press
PO Box 293, Winnipeg, MB R3C 2G9
204-237-5504,
Diane Driedger, Co-Publisher
Cecile Guillemot, Co-Publisher

Moose Enterprise Book & Theatre Play Publishing
684 Walls Side Rd., Sault Ste Marie, ON P6A 5K6
705-779-3331, Fax: 705-779-3331, 888-826-6698
mooseenterprises@on.aibn.com
www.moosehidebooks.com
ISBNs: ISBN: 0-9698319, 0-9681852, 0-9684909, 0-9686086, 1-894650
Local publishers of plays, children's short stories, non-fiction & fiction works.
Richard Mousseau, Publisher, rmousseau@moosehidebooks.com

Mosaic Press
#1, 1252 Speers Rd., Oakville, ON L6L 5N9
905-825-2130, Fax: 905-825-2130
info@mosaic-press.com
www.mosaic-press.com
ISBNs: ISBN: 0-88962; SAN: 115-4362, 115-4370
Publishes over 20 original titles each year, with a back catalog of over 500 books covering all genres. Literature; The Arts; Social Studies & INternational Studies
Howard Aster, Publisher

Mother Tongue Publishing Ltd.
290 Fulford-Ganges Rd., Salt Spring Island, BC V8K 2K6
250-537-4155, Fax: 250-537-4725
info@mothertonguepress.com
www.mothertonguepress.com
ISBNs: ISBN: 1-896949, 0-9698904
Publishers of local authors as well as books on British Columbia art history, art & literature.

Moving to Magazines Ltd.
178 Main St., Unionville, ON L3R 2G9
905-479-0641, Fax: 905-479-1286
info@movingto.com
www.movingto.com
ISBNs: ISBN: 1-895020
Publishers of the "Moving to" series of publications geared towards people moving to new cities in Canada.
Anita Wood, President/Publisher

Multicultural Books
Richmond Gardens, #307, 6311 Gilbert Rd., Richmond, BC V7C 3V7
604-277-3894
jrmbooks@hotmail.com
ISBNs: ISBN: 0-9694933
Joe M. Ruggier

Multicultural History Society of Ontario
43 Queen's Park Cres. East, Toronto, ON M5S 2C3
416-979-2973, Fax: 416-979-7947
ISBNs: ISBN: 0-919045
Publishers of a number of journals and non-fiction books dealing with Multicultural History in Ontario

Munsey Music
PO Box 511, Richmond Hill, ON L4C 4Y8
905-737-0208, Fax: 905-737-0208
info@MunseyMusic.com
www.MunseyMusic.com
ISBNs: ISBN: 0-9697066, 0-9685152; SAN: 116-967X
Terence Munsey, President

Napoleon Publishing/Rendezvous Press
#201, 178 Willowdale Ave., Toronto, ON M2N 4Y8
416-730-9052, Fax: 416-730-8096, 877-730-9052
napoleon@napoleonandcompany.com
www.napoleonandcompany.com
ISBNs: ISBN: 0-929141, 1-894917; SAN: 115-0022
Publishers of Children's picture books, novels, biographies & educational resources under the Napoleon Imprint. Rendezvous Press imprint covers general fiction & general interest books.
Sylvia McConnell, President

Native Law Centre
University of Saskatchewan, Rm. 160, Law Bldg. 15 Campus Drive., Saskatoon, SK S7N 5A6
306-966-6189, Fax: 306-966-6207
native.law@usask.ca
www.usask.ca/nativelaw/
ISBNs: ISBN: 0-88880; SAN: 115-4540
Publishers of materials relating to First Nations & Aboriginal Law in Canada.
Zandra Wilson, Publications Editor, 3069666192, zandra.wilson@usask.ca

NDE Publishing
#15, 30 Wertheim Ct., Richmond Hill, ON L4B 1B9
905-727-8580, Fax: 905-229-0448
info@ndepublishing.com
www.ndepublishing.com
ISBNs: ISBN: 1-55321, 1-55375

Nelson Education Ltd.
1120 Birchmount Rd., Toronto, ON M1K 5G4
416-752-9100, Fax: 416-752-8101, 800-668-0671
inquire@nelson.com
www.nelson.com
ISBNs: ISBN: 0-176; SAN: 115-0669
Canada's leading Educational Publisher. Publishes K-12 textbooks and educational products, as well as higher education, professional learning & business education publications
William D. Rieders, Acting President
Michael Andrews, CFO
Beverly Buxton, Vice-President, School Division
James Reeve, Vice-President, Higher Education Division

New Orphic Publishers
706 Mill St., Nelson, BC V1L 4S5
250-354-0494, Fax: 250-352-0743
ISBNs: ISBN: 0-9699162, 0-9682800, 1-9687317; 1-894842-04-9
Ernest Hekkanen, President

New Society Publishers
PO Box 189, Gabriola, BC V0R 1X0
250-247-9737, Fax: 250-247-7471, 800-567-6772
info@newsociety.com
www.newsociety.com
ISBNs: ISBN: 1-55092, 0-86571
Progressive publishing company that specializes in books about activism & ecological sustainability
Judith Plant

New Star Books Ltd.
#107, 3477 Commercial St., Vancouver, BC V5N 4E8
604-738-9429, Fax: 604-738-9332
info@newstarbooks.com
www.newstarbooks.com
ISBNs: ISBN: 0-919573, 0-921586, 1-55420; SAN: 115-1908
Publishes 6-10 titles annually covering politically- and socially-based non-fiction as well as fiction, poetry and books on local history & culture.
Rolf Maurer, President/Publisher

New World Publishing
PO Box 36075, Halifax, NS B3J 3S9
902-576-2055, Fax: 902-576-2095, 877-211-3334
nwp1@eastlink.ca
www.newworldpublishing.com
ISBNs: ISBN: 1-895814
Francis Mitchell, Managing Editor

NeWest Publishers Ltd.
#201, 8540 - 109 St., Edmonton, AB T6G 1E6
780-432-9427, Fax: 780-433-3179, 866-796-5473
info@newestpress.com
www.newestpress.com
ISBNs: ISBN: 0-920316, 0-920897, 1-896300
Western regional press publishing 10-12 books annually
Ruth Linka, General Manager

Newport Bay Publishing Limited
356 Cyril Owen Pl., Victoria, BC V9E 2B6
250-479-4616, Fax: 250-479-3836
info@newportbay.ca
www.newportbay.ca/publishing
ISBNs: ISBN: 0-921513
Publishers of a small number of books covering the following subjects: biography, world governance, alternative economics, alternative health and medicine, home and garden, media/journalism, Native peoples, nature/environment, philosophy, social sciences, and women/feminism.
Donna Lindenberg

Nightwood Editions
3692 Beach Ave., RR#2, Roberts Creek, BC V0N 2W2
604-885-0212, Fax: 604-885-0212
info@nightwoodeditions.com
www.nightwoodeditions.com
ISBNs: ISBN: 0-88971; SAN: 115-2661
Publishers of new poetry & fiction by Canadian writers; Also publishes non-fiction works

Nimbus Publishing Ltd.
PO Box 9166, 3731 MacKintosh St., Halifax, NS B3K 5M8
902-454-7404, Fax: 902-455-5440, 800-646-2879
info@nimbus.ns.ca
www.nimbus.ns.ca
ISBNs: ISBN: 0-920852, 0-921054, 1-55109; SAN: 115-0685
Terrilee Bulger, Sales & Marketing Manager, tbulger@nimbus.ns.ca
John S. Marshall, President

North Shore Publishing Inc.
2351 Sinclair Circle, Burlington, ON L7P 3C1
905-336-2364, Fax: 905-336-5110
info@canadianheritagebooks.com
www.canadianheritagebooks. com
ISBNs: ISBN: 1-896899
Publishers of local heritage books in Southern Ontario

Northern Canada Mission Distributors
PO Box 3030, Prince Albert, SK S6V 7V4
306-764-3388, Fax: 306-764-3390
ncmd@ncem.ca
www.ncem.ca
ISBNs: ISBN: 0-920731, 1-896968
William Dyck

The North-South Institute / L'Institut Nord-Sud
#200, 55 Murray St., Ottawa, ON K1N 5M3
613-241-3535, Fax: 613-241-7435
nsi@nsi-ins.ca
www.nsi-ins.ca

ISBNs: ISBN: 1-896770; SAN: 115-4605
Publishers of findings made by the North-South Institute
Roy Culpepper, President, rculpepper@nsi-ins.ca
Ann Weston, Vice-President & Coordinator of Research, aweston@nsi-ins.ca

Novalis Publishing
Saint Paul University, 223 Main St., Ottawa, ON K1S 1C4
613-236-1393, Fax: 613-782-3004, 800-313-3020
tradebooks@novalis.ca
www.novalis.ca

ISBNs: ISBN: 2-89088, 2-89507; SAN: 115-4621
Religious publishing house in the Catholic Tradition; Publishes in the areas of liturgy, prayer, spirituality, sacramental practice, catechetics, religious education and personal growth.
Michael O'Hearn, Director, mohearn@ustpaul.ca
Kevin Burns, Editorial Director, kburns@ustpaul.ca

NRC Research Press
National Research Council of Canada, 1200 Montreal Rd., Bldg. M-55, Ottawa, ON K1A 0R6
613-993-9084, Fax: 613-952-7656
pubs@nrc-cnrc.gc.ca.
pubs.nrc-cnrc.gc.ca

Publishes research findings conducted by the National Research Council of Canada
Cameron Macdonald, Director, Publishing

Oasis Press
38 Nina St., Toronto, ON M5R 1Z4
416-534-5124, Fax: 416-537-8421
allenmorgan@sympatico.ca
oasispress.allenmorgan.com

ISBNs: ISBN: 1-895092
Publishers of story collections for children
Allen Morgan

Oberon Press
#205, 145 Spruce St., Ottawa, ON K1R 6P1
613-238-3275, Fax: 613-238-3275
oberon@sympatico.ca
www3.sympatico.ca/oberon

ISBNs: ISBN: 0-88750, 0-7780; SAN: 115-0723
Publishers of fiction by Canadian Authors. Publishes 10 new titles annually, and has 650 titles in print.
Nicholas Macklem, President

OCAPT Business Books
27 Donna Marie Dr., Welland, ON L3C 2X7
905-735-2967, Fax: 905-788-0839, 888-579-3013
ocapt@iaw.on.ca
www.ocapt.com

ISBNs: ISBN: 0-915299, 1-56327, 0-527, 0-9667843
Publishes books & visual learning products for the manufacturing & service industries
Gail Grimaldi

Ontario Outdoor Publications
PO Box 1414 C, 1431 Stavebank Rd., Mississauga, ON L5G 2V5
905-891-1714, Fax: 905-891-2352

ISBNs: ISBN: 0-9690474; SAN: 115-4672
K. Duncliffe, President

Oolichan Books
PO Box 10, Lantzville, BC V0R 2H0
250-390-4839, Fax: 866-299-0026, 877-390-4839
oolichan@island.net
www.oolichan.com

ISBNs: ISBN: 0-88982; SAN: 115-4680
Publishes poetry, fiction & non-fiction titles including literary criticism, memoirs & books on regional history
Ron Smith, Publisher
Hiro Boga, Managing Editor
Pat Smith, Consulting Editor

Optimum Publishing International Inc.
PO Box 524, Maxville, ON K0C 1T0
613-527-2222, Fax: 613-527-3333
info@optimumbooks.com
optimumbooks.com

ISBNs: ISBN: 0-88890
Publishers of non-fiction books covering true crime, politics & history

Orca Book Publishers Ltd.
PO Box 5626 B, Victoria, BC V8R 6S4
250-380-1229, Fax: 250-380-1892, 800-210-5277
orca@orcabook.com
www.orcabook.com

ISBNs: ISBN: 0-920501, 1-55143; SAN: 115-7485
Publishers of children's books; with ovr 350 titles in print & 60 new titles per year. Picturebooks, Early chapter books, teen novels
Bob Tyrrell, Publisher
Andrew Wooldridge, Associate Publisher
Dayle Sutherland, Marketing Director
Melanie Jeffs, Office Manager

Organisation for Economic Cooperation and Development (OECD)
#650, 2001 L St. NW, Washington, DC
202-785-6323, Fax: 202-785-0350, 800-456-6323
washington.contact@oecd.org
www.oecdwash.org

ISBNs: ISBN: 92-64
Sandra Wilson, Head, Center for Public Affairs

Our Schools/Our Selves
107 Earl Grey Rd., Toronto, ON M4J 3L6
416-463-6978, Fax: 416-463-6978, 800-565-1975
satu.repo@utoronto.ca

ISBNs: ISBN: 0-921908
Satu Repo

Owl's Head Press
8500 Main St., Alma, NB E4H 1M7
506-887-2073,

ISBNs: ISBN: 0-920635

Oxford University Press - Canada
70 Wynford Dr., Toronto, ON M3C 1J9
416-441-2941, Fax: 416-444-0427, 800-387-8020
customer.service@oup.com
www.oupcanada.com

ISBNs: ISBN: 0-19; SAN: 115-731
One of the oldest publishing companies in the world; Publishers of non-fiction & educational material
David Stover, President
Wendy Moran, Associate Vice-President/Director, Creative Services
David Steele, Vice-President/Director, School Division

P.D. Meany Publishers
145 Westminster Ave., Toronto, ON M6R 1N8
416-516-2903, Fax: 416-516-7632
info@pdmeany.com
www.pdmeany.com

ISBNs: ISBN: 0-88835; SAN: 115-4273
Publishers of a variety of fiction & non-fiction titles
Pierrek L'Abbé

Pacific Edge Publishing Ltd.
1773 El Verano Dr., Gabriola, BC V0R 1X6
250-247-9093, Fax: 250-247-9083, 800-668-8806
info@pacificedgepublishing.com
www.pacificedgepublishing.com

ISBNs: ISBN: 1-895110
Publisher & distributor of educational resources for K-12 teachers.
Chris Sherwood

Pacific Educational Press
Faculty of Education, University of British Columbia, 6365 Biological Sciences Rd., Vancouver, BC V6T 1Z4
604-822-5385, Fax: 604-822-6603
pep@interchange.ubc.ca
www.pep.educ.ubc.ca

ISBNs: ISBN: 0-88865, 1-895766; SAN: 115-1266
Publishing house of the Faculty of Education at the University of British Columbia; Publishes educational resources
Catherine Edwards, Director

Paideia Press Ltd.
2318 Regional Rd. 81, Jordan Station, ON L0R 1S0
905-562-5719, Fax: 905-562-7828

ISBNs: ISBN: 0-88815; SAN: 115-4761
John Hultink

Pandora Press
33 Kent Ave., Kitchener, ON N2G 3R2
519-578-2381, Fax: 519-578-1826, 866-696-1678
judith@pandorapress.com
www.pandorapress.com

ISBNs: ISBN: 0-9698762, 0-9685543, 1-894710
Judith Jutzi, Manager, judith@pandorapress.com

Paperplates Books
19 Kenwood Ave., Toronto, ON M6C 2RB
416-651-2551, Fax: 416-651-2910
paper@perkolator.com
www.paperplates.org

Small Publishing House; Publishes short fiction & personal essays
Bernard Kelly
Cary Fagan

Parkland Publishing
501 Mount Allison Pl., Saskatoon, SK S7H 4A9
306-242-7731
info@parklandpublishing.com
www.parklandpublishing.com

Publishes non-fiction books about Saskatchewan, hiking in Saskatchewan & trivia about Saskatchewan
Robin Kaplan, Co-founder
Arlene Kaplan, Co-founder

Pathway Publishers
RR#4, Aylmer, ON N5H 2R3

ISBNs: ISBN: 0-919374
Amish & Anabaptist Publishing House

Pearson Education Canada Inc.
26 Prince Andrew Pl., Toronto, ON M3C 2T8
416-447-5101, Fax: 416-443-0948, 800-263-9965
www.pearsoncanada.ca

ISBNs: 9780131113497; 9780131228436; 9780131280397
A Pearson Canada imprint, Pearson Education Canada Inc. is the largest publisher of print & electronic curriculum materials in Canada
MR Allan T. Reynolds, President & CEO, Pearson Canada

Pedlar Press
PO Box 26 P, 191 Madison Ave., Toronto, ON M5S 2S6
416-534-2011, Fax: 416-535-9677

ISBNs: ISBN: 0-9681884, 0-9686522, 0-9732140

Pegasus Publishing
PO Box 26, Causeway Rd., Site 19, Seaforth, NS B0J 1N0
902-827-3204
jenniblackmore@eastlink.ca

ISBNs: ISBN: 0-9692552
Jenni Blackmore

Pembroke Publishers Limited
538 Hood Rd., Markham, ON L3R 3K9
905-477-0650, Fax: 905-477-3691
mary@pembrokepublishers.com
www.pembrokepublishers.com

ISBNs: ISBN: 0-921217, 1-55138
Publisher of educational resources for parents & teachers covering: Reading & Writing; Grammar & Speaking; Thinking & drama; Classroom management & major issues in education
Claudia Connolly, General Manager
Mary Macchiusi, President

Pemmican Publications Inc.
150 Henry Ave., Winnipeg, MB R3B 0J7
204-589-6346, Fax: 204-589-2063
pemmican@pemmican.mb.ca
www.pemmican.mb.ca

ISBNs: ISBN: 0-91943, 0-921827; SAN: 115-1657
Publishers of children's books, fiction & non-fiction related to Metis culture & heritage.
Andreen Hourie, Managing Editor

Pendas Productions
525 Canterbury Rd., London, ON N6G 2N5
519-434-8555
pendas@pennkemp.ca
www.pennkemp.ca

ISBNs: ISBN: 0-920820
Gavin Stairs

Penguin Books Canada Ltd.
#700, 90 Eglinton Ave. East, Toronto, ON M4P 2Y3
416-925-2249, Fax: 416-925-0068
info@penguin.ca
www.penguin.ca

ISBNs: 9781592403691; 9780140260670; 9780142004272
Penguin Books Canada is a division of Pearson Canada, & publishes paperback & hardcover books in a range of subjects, for adults & children. Winner of the 2008 Canadian Booksellers Association Publisher of the Year Award
MR David Davidar, President
MS Yvonne Hunter, Director, Publicity & Marketing

Penumbra Press
PO Box 940, Manotick, ON K4M 1A8

613-692-5590, Fax: 613-692-5589
john@penumbrapress.ca
www.penumbrapress.com
ISBNs: ISBN: 0-921254, 0-929806, 1-894131; SAN: 115-0774
Small fine-art & literary publishing house; Publishes Northern and Native literatures; children's literature; poetry; translations of Scandinavian literature; history; mythology; art books
John Flood, President

Phaidon Press Inc.
14 Glenwood Ave., Toronto, ON M6P 3C6
416-761-1755, Fax: 416-761-9316
enquiries@phaidon.com
www.phaidon.com
Publisher of books on the visual arts

Picasso Publications Inc.
#3904, 10080 Jasper Ave., Edmonton, AB T5J 1V9
780-420-1070, Fax: 780-420-0475
sales@picassopublications.com
ISBNs: ISBN: 1-55279

Pippin Publishing Corp.
PO Box 242 Don Mills, Toronto, ON M3C 2S2
416-510-2918, Fax: 416-510-3359
jld@pippinpub.com
www.pippinpub.com
ISBNs: ISBN: 0-88751; SAN: 115-3293
Jonathan Lovat Dickson

Playwrights Canada Press
#230, 215 Spadina Ave., Toronto, ON M5T 2C7
416-703-0013, Fax: 416-408-3402
publisher@playwrightscanada.com
www.playwrightscanada.com
ISBNs: ISBN: 0-88754, 0-919834
Publishes roughly 32 books of plays, theatre history & criticism annually
Angela Rebeiro, Project Coordinator, editor@playwrightscanada.com
Annie Gibson, Publisher

Pokeweed Press
#337, 829 Norwest Rd., Kingston, ON K7P 2N3
613-374-2494
publisher@pokeweed.com
www.pokeweed.com
ISBNs: ISBN: 1-894323
Frank B. Edwards, Publisher

Polar Bear Press
35 Price Andrew Pl., Toronto, ON M3C 2H2
416-449-4000, Fax: 416-449-9924, 800-490-4049
north49@idirect.com
ISBNs: ISBN: 1-896757

Polestar Book Publishers
An Imprint of Raincoast Books, 9050 Shaughnessy St., Vancouver, BC V6P 6E5
604-323-7100, Fax: 604-323-2600, 800-663-5714
info@raincoast.com
www.raincoast.com
ISBNs: ISBN: 0-919591, 1-896095
Michelle Benjamin, Publisher

Pontifical Institute of Mediaeval Studies, Dept. of Publications
59 Queen's Park Cres. East, Toronto, ON M5S 2C4
416-926-7142, Fax: 416-926-7258
pontifex@chass.utoronto.ca
www.pims.ca
ISBNs: ISBN: 0-88844; SAN: 115-0804
Small University Press publishing the results of research carried out by all medievalists
Rev. James K. McConica, President CSB, OC

Porcupine's Quill Inc.
68 Main St., Erin, ON N0B 1T0
519-833-9158, Fax: 519-833-9845
pql@sentex.net
www.sentex.net/~pql
ISBNs: ISBN: 0-88984; SAN: 115-0820
Small publishing house, Publishers of Canadian poetry & literature
Tim Inkster, Publisher
Elke Inkster, Publisher

Portage & Main Press
#100, 318 McDermot Ave., Winnipeg, MB R3A 0A2
204-987-3500, Fax: 866-734-8477, 800-667-9673
books@pandmpress.com
www.portageandmainpress.com
ISBNs: ISBN: 0-919566, 1-89110, 1-895411, 1-55379
Publishers of educational books & resources for teachers
Catherine Gerbosi, President

Potlatch Publications Limited
30 Berryhill Ave., Waterdown, ON L0R 2H4
905-689-2104, Fax: 905-689-1632
robtnielsen@aol.com
www.angelfire.com/on3/potlatch
ISBNs: ISBN: 0-919676; SAN: 115-1355
Robert Nielsen, President

Pottersfield Press
83 Leslie Rd., East Lawrencetown, NS B2Z 1P8
902-827-4517, Fax: 902-455-3652, 800-646-2879
www.pottersfieldpress.com
ISBNs: ISBN: 0-919001, 1-895900; SAN: 115-0790
Publishers of a number of non-fiction books, including local history & geography; memoirs; & biographies
Lesley Choyce

Power Engineering Books Ltd.
7 Perron St., St Albert, AB T8N 1E3
780-458-3155, Fax: 780-460-2530, 800-667-3155
sales@powerengbooks.com
www.powerengbooks.com
ISBNs: SAN: 115-4850
Andrew Benko

Prairie House Books
PO Box 84007 Market Mall, Calgary, AB T3A 5C4
403-202-5438, Fax: 403-202-5437
phbooks@telusplanet.net
ISBNs: ISBN: 1-895012
Wayne Magnuson, Editor/Publisher

Prentice-Hall Canada Inc.
26 Prince Andrew Place, Don Mills, ON M3C 2T8
416-447-5101, Fax: 416-443-0948
cdn_ordr@prenhall.com
www.pearsoncanada.ca
ISBNs: 9780137149445; 9780205608171
A Pearson Canada (Pearson Education) imprint.
MR Allan T. Reynolds, President & CEO, Pearson Canada

The Press of the Nova Scotia College of Art & Design
5163 Duke St., Halifax, NS B3J 3J6
902-444-9600, Fax: 902-425-2420
thepress@nscad.ns.ca
www.nscad.ns.ca/press/press_relaunched.php
ISBNs: ISBN: 0-919616
Publishers of scholarly works in the fields of contemporary art, craft & design
Susan McEachern, Editorial Director

Les Presses de l'Université de Montréal
306, rue Saint-Zotique est, Montréal, QC H2S 1L6
514-343-6933, Fax: 514-343-2232
pum@umontreal.ca
www.pum.umontreal.ca
ISBNs: ISBN: 2-7606
A pour mandat le diffusion des résultats de la recherche universitaire (livres, revues, édition électronique); la transférence des connaissances scientifiques à un large public; participation à la vie de la Cité; et contribution au rayonnement national et international de l'Université de Montréal
Antoine Del Busso, Directeur général, delbussa@pum.umontreal.ca

Presses de l'Université du Québec
Édifice Le Delta 1, #450, 2875, boul Laurier, Sainte-Foy, QC G1V 2M2
418-657-4399, Fax: 418-657-2096, 800-859-7474
puq@puq.ca
www.puq.ca
ISBNs: ISBN: 0-7770, 2-7605, 2-920073
Céline Fournier, Directrice générale, 4186574399
Micheline Auger, Secrétaire de direction, 4186574399
Bianca Drapeau, Directrice du marketing, 4186574075 x.224, bianca.drapeau@puq.ca

Les Presses de l'Université Laval
#3103, Pavillon Maurice-Pollack, 2305, rue de l'Université, Québec, QC G1V 0A6
418-656-2803, Fax: 418-656-3305, 800-859-7474
presses@pul.ulaval.ca
www.pulaval.com
ISBNs: ISBN: 2-7637, 2-89224
Ouvrages didactiques, manuels, travaux savants; diffuseur et distributeur
Denis Dion, Directeur général, denis.dion@pul.ulaval.ca
Louise Saint-Michel, Secrétaire, louise.saint-michel@pul.ulaval.ca

Presses Inter Universitaires
PO Box 36, Cap-Rouge, QC G1Y 3C6
418-657-6050, Fax: 418-657-7630
ISBNs: ISBN: 2-89441

The Prince Edward Island Museum & Heritage Foundation
2 Kent St., Charlottetown, PE C1A 1M6
902-368-6600, Fax: 902-368-6608
mhpei@gov.pe.ca
www.peimuseum.com
ISBNs: ISBN: 0-920434

Probe International
225 Brunswick Ave., Toronto, ON M5S 2M6
416-964-9223, Fax: 416-964-8239
www.probeinternational.org
ISBNs: ISBN: 0-919849, 1-85383, 0-7656

Productive Publications
#1210, 1930 Yonge St., Toronto, ON M4S 1Z4
416-483-0634, Fax: 416-322-7434
productivepublications@rogers.com
www.productivepublications.ca
ISBNs: ISBN: 0-920847, 1-896210, 1-55270; SAN: 117-1712
Iain Williamson, Owner

Prosveta Inc.
3950 Albert Mines, North Hatley, QC J0B 2C0
819-564-8212, Fax: 819-564-1823, 800-854-8212
prosveta@prosveta-canada.com
www.prosveta-canada.com
ISBNs: ISBN: 1-895978
Publishers of books related to philosophy & meditation authored by Omraam Mikhael Aivanhov
Huguette Paquin, Vice-Presidente

Psycan Corporation
#12, 120 West Beaver Creek Rd., Richmond Hill, ON L4B 1L2
905-731-8795, Fax: 905-731-5029, 800-263-3558
mail@psycan.com
www.psycan.com
Family-owned & operated publisher of eductional & clinical resources

Ptarmigan Press
1372 - 16th Ave., Campbell River, BC V9W 2E1
250-286-0878, Fax: 250-286-9749
info@kaskgraphics.com
www.kaskgraphics.com/ptarmigan/
ISBNs: ISBN: 0-919537; SAN: 116-0281
Small publishing house; Publisher of non-fiction covering Fishing; Hiking; Local history; Autobiography; Cooking; How To; Health; Sexual Abuse
Ann Kask

Public Works & Government Services Canada - Depository Services Program / Travaux public et services gouvernement aux Canada - Progra
350 Albert St., 4th Fl., Ottawa, ON K1A 0S5
613-993-1695, Fax: 613-941-2410
dsp-psd@pwgsc.gc.ca
dsp-psd.pwgsc.gc.ca
ISBNs: ISBN: 0-662, 0-660; SAN: 115-2882
Publishes federal government publications and distribute them to oublic & academic libraries.
Christine Leduc, Director, 6139965959

Publications Ontario
50 Grosvenor St., Toronto, ON M7A 1N8
416-326-5300, Fax: 416-613-566, 800-668-9938
www.publications.serviceontario.ca
ISBNs: ISBN: 0-7743, 0-7729, 0-7778
Publishers of government publications, including driver's handbook, fire codes, building codes, agricultural publications, employment standards & occupational health & safety
Marg Munro, Manager
Eric Steeves, Director

Publishers Group Canada
#402, 559 College St., Toronto, ON M6G 1A9
416-934-9900, Fax: 416-934-1410, 800-747-8147
graham@pgcbooks.ca
www.pgcbooks.ca
ISBNs: SAN: 117-0171
Distributors of a large number of non-fiction, fiction & children's books for a large number of publishers.
Graham Fidler, Exec. Vice-President, ext. 203, graham@pgcbooks.ca
Suzanne Wice, Director, Sales & Marketing, ext. 207, suzanne@pgcbooks.ca

Purich Publishing Ltd.
PO Box 23032 Market Mall, Saskatoon, SK S7J 5H3
306-373-5311, Fax: 306-373-5315
purich@sasktel.net
www.purichpublishing.com
ISBNs: ISBN: 1-895830
Publishers of books dealing with Aboriginal & Social Justice Issues; Law & Western Canadian History; Focus on the university, college & reference market
K. Bolstad
D. Purich

Quarry Press
20 Hatter St., Kingston, ON K7M 2L5
613-548-8429, Fax: 613-548-1556
ISBNs: ISBN: 0-919627, 1-55082; SAN: 115-4958
Bob Hilderley, Publisher

Québec dans le Monde
CP 8503 Sainte-Foy, #404, 1001, route de l'Eglise, Québec, QC G1V 4N5
418-659-5540, Fax: 418-659-4143
info@quebecmonde.com
www.quebecmonde.com
ISBNs: ISBN: 2-921309, 2-89525, 2-9801130; SAN: 116-8657
Denis Turcotte, Directeur général

Québec Science Éditeur
#300, 4388, rue St-Denis, Montréal, QC H2J 2L1
514-843-6888, Fax: 514-843-4897
courrier@quebecscience.qc.ca
www.cybersciences.com
ISBNs: ISBN: 2-920073
Jean-Yves Poirier, jypoirier@velo.qc.ca
Raymond Lemieux, Rédacteur en chef

Quill & Quire
111 Queen St. East, Toronto, ON M5C 1S2
416-364-3333, Fax: 416-595-5415
www.quillandquire.com

Publishers of directories of publishers

Quintin Publishers / Éditions Michel Quintin
PO Box 340, 4770, rue Foster, Waterloo, QC J0E 2N0
450-539-3774, Fax: 450-539-4905
info@editionsmichelquintin.ca
www.editionsmichelquintin.c a
ISBNs: ISBN: 2-920438, 2-89435; SAN: 116-5356
Michel Quintin, Président-directeur général
Johanne Ménard, Édition scientifique, jmenard@editionsmichelquintin.ca
Mélanie Roy, Coordonnatrice, production, info@editionsmichelquintin.ca

R.G. Mitchell Family Books Inc.
565 Gordon Baker Rd., Toronto, ON M2H 2W2
416-499-4615, Fax: 416-499-6340, 800-268-3445
info@rgm.ca
www.rgm.ca
ISBNs: SAN: 168-4604
David Freeland, President
Keith Chesire, Chair

Rainbird Press
4890 Mackenzie St., Vancouver, BC V6L 2R6
604-224-4756, Fax: 604-224-4740
michaelbullock@hotmail.com
m_bullock.tripod.com
ISBNs: ISBN: 0-9690504, 0-9684894
Publishers of the poetry of Michael Bullock.
Lori-Ann Latremouille

Raincoast Books Distribution Ltd.
9050 Shaughnessy St., Vancouver, BC V6P 6E5
604-323-7100, Fax: 604-323-2600, 800-663-5714
info@raincoast.com
www.raincoast.com
ISBNs: ISBN: 0-920417, 1-895714, 1-55192, 1-896095, 0-919591; SAN 115
Full-service book distributor and former publisher (Publishing operations closed in January of 2008).
Allan MacDougall, President/CEO

Rand McNally Canada Inc.
90A Royal Crest Ct., Markham, ON L3R 9X6
905-477-8480, Fax: 905-477-7408, 800-205-6277
customerservicecanada@randmcnally.com
www.randmcnally.ca
ISBNs: ISBN: 0-88640
Publishers of maps and atlases

Random House of Canada Ltd.
#300, 1 Toronto St., Toronto, ON M5C 2V6
416-364-4449, Fax: 416-364-6863
ISBNs: ISBN: 0-394, 0-679; SAN: 115-088X
Louise Dennys, Vice-President

Random House of Canada Ltd.
2775 Matheson Blvd. East, Mississauga, ON L4W 4P7
905-624-0672, Fax: 905-624-6217, 800-668-4247
www.randomhouse.com
ISBNs: ISBN: 0-394, 0-679 0-449, 0-553 0-385 0-7704, 0-676; SAN: 201-
Large publisher of best-selling & award-winning books; distributor of many international authors
Brad Martin, President & COO
David Kent, Publisher
Katheleen Bain, Vice-President, Sales & Marketing

Reach for Unbleached!
Attn. D. Broten, PO Box 39, Whaletown, BC V0P 1Z0
250-935-6992
dbroten@rfu.org
www.rfu.org
ISBNs: 0-9680431
Publishers of environmental education material about paper & pulp mill monitoring

Reader's Digest Association (Canada) Ltd.
1100, boul René Levesque ouest, Montréal, QC H3B 5H5
514-940-0751, Fax: 514-940-3637, 866-736-3382
trade@readersdigest.ca
www.readersdigest.ca
ISBNs: ISBN: 0-88850; SAN 115-0898, 115-4974
Andrea C. Martin, President/CEO

Red Deer Press
#1512, 1800 - 4th St. SW, Calgary, AB T2S 2S5
403-509-0800, Fax: 403-228-6503
rdp@reddeerpress.com
www.reddeerpress.com
ISBNs: ISBN: 0-88995; SAN: 115-0871
Publishes picture books, junior, juvenile, Young Adult fiction and non-fiction and adult non-fiction titles
Richard Dionne, Publisher, 4035090804, dionne@reddeerpress.com
Peter Carver, Children's Editor

Reference Press
PO Box 70, Teeswater, ON N0G 2S0
519-392-6634, Fax: 519-392-6634
refpress@wcl.on.ca
www.libris.ca/refpress
ISBNs: ISBN: 0-919981; SAN: 115-687X
Publisher of Canadian reference materials & software for use in school & public libraries
Gordon Ripley

Reflections
PO Box 178, Gabriola, BC V0R 1X0
250-247-8685,
ISBNs: ISBN: 0-9692570

Renouf Publishing Co. Ltd. / Éditions Renouf limitées
#1, 5369 Canotek Rd., Ottawa, ON K1J 9J3
613-745-2665, Fax: 613-745-7660, 866-767-6766
orders@renoufbooks.com
www.renoufbooks.com
ISBNs: ISBN: 0-88852; SAN: 170-8066
Publishers of over 35 international organizations' publiations & documents
Gordon Grahame, President
Avrum Kerzner, Comptroller
Brigid Grahame, General Manager

Repository Press
Comp. 8, Site 29, RR#7, Prince George, BC V2N 2J5
250-562-7074, Fax: 250-561-7094
harris@cnc.bc.ca
ISBNs: ISBN: 0-920104; SAN: 115-5016
John Harris, Publisher/Editor
Joanne Armstrong, Marketing

The Resource Centre Inc.
PO Box 190, Waterloo, ON N2J 3Z9
519-885-0826, Fax: 519-747-5629, 800-923-0330
sales@theresourcecentre.com
www.theresourcecentre.com
ISBNs: ISBN: 0-920701; SAN: 115-5032
Publishers of educational resources, including books on ESL, Language & Writing among other subjects
N. Gridgeman, President

Revue Cap-aux-Diamants
CP 26 Haute-Ville, #2113, 1, côte de la Fabrique, Québec, QC G1R 4M8
418-656-5040, Fax: 418-656-7282
revue.cap-aux-diamants@hst.ulaval.ca
www.capauxdiamants.org
ISBNs: ISBN: 2-920069
Yves Beauregard

River City Press
PO Box 752, Sarnia, ON N7T 7J7
519-344-5284, Fax: 519-344-5284
ISBNs: ISBN: 0-920940
Mel Cameron

Riverwood Publishers Ltd.
471 Eagle St., Newmarket, ON L3Y 1K7
905-853-8887, Fax: 905-853-3330, 800-561-2674
info@riverwoodpub.com
www.riverwoodpub.com
ISBNs: ISBN: 1-895121; SAN: 116-1288
Publishers of children's books & Canadian distributors of Usborne Books, a respected children's book publisher.
Ron Charlesworth, President

Robert Davies Multimedia Publishing / Éditions multimedia Robert Davies inc.
9 Parkside Pl., Montréal, QC H3Z 1T3
514-934-5433, Fax: 514-937-8765, 800-481-2440
rdppub@rdppub.com
www.rdppub.com
ISBNs: ISBN: 1-895854, 1-55207, 2-89019, 2-89462
Robert Davies, Publisher

Robert Rose Inc.
120 Eglington Ave. E, Toronto, ON M4P 1E2
416-322-6552, Fax: 416-322-6936
www.fireflybooks.com/RR.html
ISBNs: ISBN: 1-896503, 0-7788
Publishers of cookbooks; Distributed by Firefly Books
Robert J. Dees

Robin Brass Studio Inc.
PO Box 335 R, Montréal, QC H2S 2R0
514-272-7463, Fax: 514-272-7971
rbrass@sympatico.ca
www.rbstudiobooks.com
ISBNs: ISBN: 1-896941; SAN: 115-5040
Small publishing house producing primarily non-fiction, especially within the area of military history & other Canadian history; Also designs and produces books under contract for other publishers & organizations

Rocky Mountain Books
#108, 17665 - 66A Ave., Surrey, BC V3S 2A7
604-574-7067, 800-665-3302
distribution@heritagehouse.ca
www.rmbooks.com
ISBNs: ISBN: 0-921102; SAN: 115-5040
Publisher of outdoor activity guidebooks, historical accounts of Canadian mountaineering and other adventures, biographies & related non-fiction
Tony Daffern, Publisher

Ronsdale Press
3350 West 21st Ave., Vancouver, BC V6S 1G7
604-738-4688, Fax: 604-731-4548
ronsdale@shaw.ca
www.ronsdalepress.com
ISBNs: ISBN: 0-921870, 1-55380; SAN: 116-2454
Publishers of fiction, poetry, regional history, biography and autobiography, books of ideas about Canada, as well as children's books; Presently has roughly 140 books in print.
Ronald B. Hatch, Director

Roseway Publishing Co. Ltd.
32 Oceanvista Lane, Site 2A, Box 5, Black Point, NS B0T 1B0
902-857-1388, Fax: 902-857-1328
info@rosewaypublishing.ca
www.rosewaypublishing.com,
www.selfpublishingspecialists.com
ISBNs: ISBN: 0-9694180, 1-896496
Small publishing house; Publishes plays & fiction & non-fiction books of local interest
Kathleen K. Tudor, Owner/Manager

Routledge/Taylor & Francis Books
#2102, 110 Erskine Ave., Toronto, ON M4P 1Y4
416-482-4562, Fax: 416-482-3043
probinson@taylorandfrancis.com
www.routledge-ny.com
ISBNs: ISBN: 0-415, 0-87830
Publishers of educational & academic resources for the college/university market
Colin Jones, President

Rowland & Jacob Inc.
52 Hazelton Ave., Toronto, ON M5R 2E2
416-921-9557, Fax: 416-921-0408
ISBNs: ISBN: 0-921430
Publishers of travel guides for major Canadian cities

The Rowman & Littlefield Publishing Group
Canadian Sales Office, 10 Cushendun Rd., Toronto, ON M1E 2B3
416-282-3592
donmacivor@rogers.com
www.rowmanlittlefield.com

Canadian sales office for large international publisher focusing on non-fiction books for the academic market

The Royal Astronomical Society of Canada
136 Dupont St., Toronto, ON M5R 1V2
416-924-7973, Fax: 416-924-2911, 844-626-2665
mempub10001@rasc.ca
www.rasc.ca

Publishes journals and guides to astronomy
Jo Taylor, Membership & Publications Clerk

Rubicon Publishing Inc.
PO Box 69596, Oakville, ON L6J 7R4
905-849-8777, Fax: 905-849-7579
contact@rubiconpublishing.com
www.rubiconpublishing.com
ISBNs: ISBN: 0-921156; SAN: 115-432X
Publisher of educational resources for students and educators for grades K-12.
Kimberley Wulf
Maggie Goh

Safety Sense Enterprises
PO Box 9512 T, Ottawa, ON K1G 3V2
613-830-9342, Fax: 613-830-4284
ISBNs: ISBN: 0-9695568
Hon. Heward Graffley, President/CEO

Salal Press
PO Box 36060, Victoria, BC V9A 7J5
250-384-0305, Fax: 250-384-0351
salal@horizon.bc.ca
ISBNs: ISBN: 1-894012
Small publisher of novels and non-fiction books
Clare Thorbes

Sandhill Publishing
#4, 3308 Appaloosa Rd., Kelowna, BC V1V 2G9
250-491-1446, Fax: 250-491-4066, 800-667-3848
info@sandhillbooks.com
www.sandhillbooks.com
ISBNs: ISBN: 0-920923; SAN: 115-2181
Distributor for Small Press & Independent Publishers
Nancy Wise

Saunders Book Company
PO Box 308, 199 Campbell St., Collingwood, ON L9Y 3Z7
705-445-4777, Fax: 705-445-9569, 800-461-9120
info@saundersbook.ca
www.saundersbook.ca
ISBNs: SAN: 169-9768
Publishers of books for educational books & fiction for K-12 schools & libraries
John Saunders, President
James Saunders, Sales, james.saunders@saundersbook.ca

Saxon House Canada
PO Box 6947 A, Toronto, ON M5W 1X6
416-488-7171, Fax: 416-488-2989
ISBNs: ISBN: 0-9693934
Publishers of history books
W.H. Wallace, General Manager

Scholar's Choice
PO Box 7214, 2323 Trafalgar St., London, ON N5Y 5S7
519-453-7470, Fax: 519-455-2853, 800-265-1095
sales@scholarschoice.ca
www.scholarschoice.ca
ISBNs: ISBN: 0-88809; SAN: 170-0014
Publisher & retailer of educational materials
Scott Webster, President
Cindy Webster, Executive Vice-President

Scholastic Canada Ltd. / Éditions Scholastic
175 Hillmount Rd., Markham, ON L6C 1Z7
905-887-7323, Fax: 905-887-1131
custsev@scholastic.ca
www.scholastic.ca
ISBNs: ISBN: 0-590; SAN: 115-5164
Leading publishers & distributors of children's books & educational materials in French & English
Iole Lucchese, Co-President
Linda Goswell, Co-President

School Book Fairs Limited
2201 Dunwin Dr., Mississauga, ON L5L 1X2
905-828-6620, Fax: 905-828-2761, 800-268-4557
sbf@sbfmedia.com
www.sbfmedia.com
ISBNs: ISBN: 0-921932; SAN 115-5083
Publisher & distributor of mass market & trade paperbacks for schools; Also publish educational resource books

Script Publishing Inc.
#200, 839 - 5th Ave. SW, Calgary, AB T2P 3C8
403-547-3400, Fax: 403-241-8575
ISBNs: ISBN: 0-9694287, 1-896015
Publishers of scripts & plays
P. Douglas McArthur, President

Second Story Press
#401, 20 Maud St., Toronto, ON M5S 2R4
416-537-7850, Fax: 416-537-0588
info@secondstorypress.ca
www.secondstorypress.on.ca
ISBNs: ISBN: 0-929005, 1-896764; SAN: 115-1134
Publishers of roughly 8 titles per sesaon, spanning adult fiction & non-fiction; children's fiction, non-fiction & picture books; Young Adult fiction & non-fiction. Special interest areas include Judaica, Ability Issues, Coping with Cancer & Queer rights
Margie Wolf, President

Self-Counsel Press Ltd.
1481 Charlotte Rd., North Vancouver, BC V7J 1H1
604-986-3366, Fax: 604-986-3947, 800-663-3007
www.self-counsel.com
ISBNs: ISBN: 0-88908, 1-55180; SAN: 115-0545
Publisher of self-help law books & books for small business
Diana R. Douglas, President

September Dreams Publishing
PO Box 44085 Southcentre PO, 9419 Fairmount Dr. SE, Calgary, AB T2J 7C5
403-519-7418
viktor@septemberdreams.com
www.septemberdreams.com
ISBNs: ISBN: 0-9695763
Publishers of four books covering business, computer, humour & lifestyle
Viktor E. Oey
Rudy W. Oey

Septembre éditeur inc.
CP 9425 Sainte-Foy, 2825, ch des Quatre-Bourgeois, Québec, QC G1V 4B8
418-658-7272, Fax: 418-652-0986, 800-361-7755
serviceclientele@septembre.com
www.septembre.com
ISBNs: ISBN: 2-930433, 2-89471
Matériel didactique; éducation; emplois; formation; littérature jeunesse; management; ressources humaines; métiers; orientation; outils pédagogiques
Martin Rochette, Président-directeur général

Services documentaires multimedia inc.
#620, 5650, rue d'Iberville, Montréal, QC H2GH3L 3T1
514-382-0895, Fax: 514-384-9139
informations@sdm.qc.ca
www.sdm.qc.ca
ISBNs: ISBN: 2-89059, 0-88523
Denis Lévesque, Directeur Général
Claude Jourdain, Direction de l'info. et du dév. tech.
Diane Dallaire-Talbot, Directrice, l'Exploration

Servidec
50 Main St., Ottawa, ON K1S 1B2
613-237-5577, Fax: 613-230-1762, 800-265-0375

Shard Press
102 Garnet Ave., Toronto, ON M6G 1V7
416-538-2679, Fax: 416-538-2679
kyril@shard.com
www.shard.com
ISBNs: ISBN: 0-9696455
Cyril Chen

Sheltus & Picard Inc.
CP 1321, Bedford, QC J0J 1A0
450-248-7319, Fax: 450-248-2057
cp.jas.rm@acbm.net
ISBNs: ISBN: 0-9696296
Small publisher specializing in local history
J.A. Sheltus, President/CEO
C. Picard, Vice-President & Editor

Shoreline Press
23, rue Sainte-Anne, Sainte-Anne-de-Bellevue, QC H9X 1L1
514-457-5733, Fax: 514-457-5733
shoreline@sympatico.ca
www.shorelinepress.ca
ISBNs: ISBN: 0-9695180, 0-9698752, 1-896754; SAN 116-9564
Independent press publishing specializing in memoirs & titles of local interest
Judy Isherwood, Owner & Publisher

Sierra Club Books
85 Second St., 2nd Fl., San Francisco, CA
415-977-5500, Fax: 415-977-5799
booksinfo@sierraclub.org
www.sc.org/books/

Signature Editions
PO Box 206 Corydon, Winnipeg, MB R3M 3S7
204-779-7803, Fax: 204-779-6970
signature@allstream.net
www.signature-editions.com
ISBNs: ISBN: 0-921833, 1-897109; SAN: 115-0723
Karen Haughian, Publisher

Simon & Schuster Canada
#600, 625 Cochrane Dr., Markham, ON L3R 9R9
905-943-9942, Fax: 905-943-9026, 800-268-3216
info@simonandschuster.ca
www.simonsayscanada.com
ISBNs: ISBN: 1-55525, 0-38224, 0-945299; SAN: 115-4788
Publishers of a large catalog of books covering all aspects of fiction & non-fiction
Deborah Woods, President
Susan Stoddart, Chair

Simply Read Books Inc.
#501, 5525 West Blvd., Vancouver, BC V6M 3W6
604-727-2960, Fax: 604-263-5707
info@simplyreadbooks.com
www.simplyreadbooks.com

Publishers of fiction for children & young adults

Sinai Multi-lingual Books
7356 Ontario St., Vancouver, BC V5X 3B8
604-327-6694, Fax: 604-327-6694
info@booksm.com
www.booksm.com
ISBNs: ISBN: 1-896277
Publishes books in English, French, Arabic, Chinese, German, Russian & Spanish
Cynthia Wong

Singing Shield Productions
104 Ray Blvd., Thunder Bay, ON P7B 4C4
807-344-8355, Fax: 807-344-8355
pebarr@tbaytel.net
ISBNs: ISBN: 0-9691717; SAN: 115-5784
Elinor Barr

Sister Vision Press
101 Dewson St., Toronto, ON M6H 1H4
416-533-9353,
ISBNs: ISBN: 0-920813, 1-896705
Stephanie Martin
Makeda Silvera

Snowapple Press
PO Box 66024 Heritage, Edmonton, AB T6J 6T4
403-437-0191, Fax: 403-437-0191
ISBNs: ISBN: 1-895592
Guy Tessier, Publisher

Socadis Inc.
420, rue Stinson, Ville Saint-Laurent, QC H4N 3L7
514-331-3300, Fax: 514-745-3282, 800-361-2847
socinfo@socadis.com
www.socadis.com

Society to Overcome Pollution
716 St. Ferdinand, Montréal, QC H4C 2T2
514-932-7267,

Sound & Vision Publishing Ltd.
#103, 109 Beech Ave., Toronto, ON M4E 3H5
www.soundandvision.com
ISBNs: ISBN: 0-920151; SAN: 115-0979
Publishers of books about contemporary music & music history
Geoff Savage, Publisher

Southwest Québec Publishing
PO Box 539, 27, rue Prince, 2e étage, Huntingdon, QC J0S 1H0
450-264-6200, Fax: 450-264-5387
ISBNs: ISBN: 1-895656
Maurice J. King, President
Janet Hicks, Editor

Spindrift Publishing
PO Box 50, Barrington, NS B0W 1E0
902-637-2569, Fax: 902-637-2324
ISBNs: ISBN: 0-9691458
Hattie Perry, Publisher

Statistics Canada
c/o Circulation Management, 120 Parkdale Ave., Ottawa, ON K1A 0T6
613-951-7277, Fax: 613-951-1584, 800-700-1033
order@statcan.ca
www.statcan.ca
ISBNs: ISBN: 0-660, 0-662
Publishes research and information conducted by Statistics Canada

Steller Press Ltd.
#13, 4335 West 10 Ave., Vancouver, BC V6R 2H6
604-222-2955, Fax: 604-222-2965
info@stellerpress.com
www.stellerpress.com
ISBNs: ISBN: 1-894143
Regional publisher; focusing on books for the Pacific Northwest & Lower Mainland
Steve Paton

Stoneycroft Publishing
PO Box 1710, RR#1, Yarmouth, NS B5A 4A5
902-742-2667
stuarttrask@eastlink.ca
ISBNs: ISBN: 1-896269
Gwen G. Trask

Studio Word
228 Park Ridge Cl., Camrose, AB T4V 4P1
780-672-2551, Fax: 780-672-5887
studioword@studioword.com
www.studioword.com
ISBNs: ISBN: 0-969, 0-968, 1-894361
Publishes training manuals for popular software applications
Lois Larson, Owner

Subway Books Ltd.
#203, 1819 Pendrell St., Vancouver, BC V6G 1T3
604-488-1388,
ISBNs: ISBN: 0-9681660
Publishes books on social issues, non-fiction topics, biographies & poetry

Sumach Press
#202, 1415 Bathurst St., Toronto, ON M5R 3H8
416-531-6250, Fax: 416-531-3892
info@sumachpress.com
www.sumachpress.com
ISBNs: ISBN: 1-894549, 1-896764, 0-929005; SAN: 115-1134
Publishers of feminist writing
Lois Pike

Summerthought Publishing
PO Box 2309, Banff, AB T1L 1C1
403-762-0531, Fax: 403-762-3095
info@summerthought.com
www.summerthought.com
ISBNs: ISBN: 0-919934; SAN: 115-2149
Publisher of the Canadian Rockies Trail Guide
Andrew Hempstead, Publisher

Summit Educational Services
PO Box 149, Richmond Hill, ON L4C 4X9
905-883-9427, Fax: 905-770-8576, 800-741-5956
admin@summit-ed.com
www.summit-ed.com
ISBNs: ISBN: 1-895187
Arlene Marks, President

Sun-Scape Enterprises Ltd.
290 Healey Rd., Bolton, ON L7E 1C9
905-951-3155, Fax: 905-951-9712
ISBNs: ISBN: 0-919842
Kenneth George Mills

Talon Books Ltd.
PO Box 2076, 278 East 1st Ave., Vancouver, BC V6B 3S3
604-444-4889, Fax: 604-444-4119
info@talonbooks.com
www.talonbooks.com
ISBNs: ISBN: 0-88922; SAN: 115-5334; Telebook: S1150391
Publishers specializing in poetry, drama & literary criticism. Also publishes fiction & non-fiction
Karl Siegler, President
Christy Siegler, Marketing & Promotion
Kevin Williams, Sales & Marketing Coordinator, kevin@talonbooks.com
Gregory Gibson, Production Coordinator, production@talonbooks.com

Tanager Press
145 Troy St., Mississauga, ON L5G 1S8
contact@tanagerpress.com
www.tanagerpress.com
ISBNs: ISBN: 1-895410
Publishes resources for those learning guitar & musical theory
N. Ledwidge
J. Neveleff

Tangled Web Audio
#133, 1063 King St. West, Hamilton, ON L8S 1L8
905-522-5349, Fax: 905-522-0711
ISBNs: ISBN: 1-896552

Tantalas Books
PO Box 255, 10 Towers Ave., Gander, NL A1V 1W6
709-656-8833, Fax: 709-651-3849
ISBNs: ISBN: 0-9695519

Taylor & Francis
325 Chestnut St., 8th Fl., Philadelphia, PA
215-625-8900, Fax: 215-625-2940

TechnoKids Inc.
1282A Cornwall Rd., Oakville, ON L6J 7W5
905-631-9112, Fax: 905-631-9113, 800-221-7921
information@technokids.com
www.technokids.com
ISBNs: ISBN: 1-894995
Publisher of technology cirriculum for schools

Temeron Books Inc.
#210, 1220 Kensington Rd. NW, Calgary, AB T2N 3P5
403-283-0900, Fax: 403-283-6947
temeron@telusplanet.net
www.temerondetselig.com
ISBNs: ISBN: 1-895510, 1-55059, 0-920490; SAN: 115-0324
Publishers of educational resources in the fields of psychology, social & political science; history, biography & memoirs; Health; K9 Training & Information; Living & Social Interaction
T.E. Giles, President

Ten Speed Press
c/o Hornblower Books, #1202, 200 Woolner Ave., Toronto, ON M6N 1Y4
416-461-7973, Fax: 416-461-0365, 800-404-4446
alan@tenspeed.ca
www.tenspeed.com/canada.htm
ISBNs: ISBN: 0-89815, 1-58008, 0-89087, 1-883672, 1-58246, 1-58761

Terrific Titles for Young Readers
52 Hazelton Ave, Toronto, ON M5R 2E2
416-921-9557,

Theytus Books
Green Mountain Rd., Lot 45, RR#2, Comp. 8, Site 50, Penticton, BC V2A 6J7
250-493-7181, Fax: 250-493-5302
info@thaytusbooks.ca
www.theytusbooks.ca
ISBNs: ISBN: 0-919441, 1-894778; SAN: 115-1517
Aboriginal-owned & operated publishing house; Focus is on publishing books of Aboriginal literature, children's books, history, culture, politics & educational materials
Anita Large, Publishing Manager

Thistledown Press Ltd.
633 Main St., Saskatoon, SK S7H 0J8
306-244-1722, Fax: 306-244-1762
tdpress@thistledownpress.com
www.thistledownpress.com/
ISBNs: ISBN: 0-920066, 1-894345, 0-920633, 1-895449
Publishes poetry & fiction for adults & young adults by Canadian writers; Also publishes resources for teachers
Allan Forrie, Publisher, editorial@thistledownpress.com
Jackie Forrie, Publishing & Production Manager, tdpress@thistledownpress.com
Taylor Leedahl, Promotions Manager, taylor.leedahl@thistledownpress.com
Kathy Painchaud, Marketing, marketing@thistledownpress.com

Thomas Allen & Son Ltd.
390 Steelcase Rd. East, Markham, ON L3R 1G2
905-475-9126, Fax: 905-475-4255, 800-458-5504
info@t-allen.com
www.thomas-allen.com
ISBNs: ISBN: 0-919028, 088762; SAN: 115-1762
Publishers of award-winning bestsellers; Publish a small, highly-focused list of no more than 10-12 books a year, both fiction & non-fiction
T.J. Allen

Thompson Educational Publishing, Inc.
20 Ripley Ave., Toronto, ON M6S 3N9
416-766-2763, Fax: 416-766-0398, 877-366-2763
publisher@thompsonbooks.com
www.thompsonbooks.com
ISBNs: ISBN: 1-55077; SAN: 115-0391
Publishes educational texts in the social sciences & humanities
Keith Thompson, President

Tikka Books
PO Box 203, Chambly, QC J3L 4B3
450-658-6205
leila@tikkabooks.com
www.tikkabooks.com
ISBNs: ISBN: 1-896106; 0-921993
Independent publishing house
Leila Pelposaari, Publisher

Timeless Books
#423, 215 Spadina Ave., Toronto, ON M5T 2C7
416-644-1030, Fax: 416-644-0116
contact@timeless.org
www.timeless.org
ISBNs: ISBN: 0-931454, 2-9044616
Publishers of teachings on yoga, including poetry & spiritual biography; Also publishes classic books & audio
Andrew Wedman, Publisher, andrew@timeless.org
Clea McDougall, Editor, clea@timeless.org
Kendra Ward, Managing Editor, kendra@timeless.org

Times Mirror Professional Publishing
130 Flaska Dr., Markham, ON L6G 1B8
905-470-6739, Fax: 905-470-0050
ISBNs: ISBN: 0-8016; SAN: 115-4389

TouchWood Editions Ltd.
Editorial & Marketing, #6, 356 Simcoe St., Victoria, BC V8V 1L1
250-360-0829, Fax: 250-385-0829
info@touchwoodeditions.com
www.touchwoodeditions.com
ISBNs: ISBN: 0-920663, 1-894898
Publishes books with a focus on history, historical fiction, biography, food, nautical subjects, mysteries & art/architecture
Pat Touchie, President

Tradewind Books
#202, 1807 Maritime Mews, Vancouver, BC V6H 3W7
604-662-4405, Fax: 604-730-0454
tradewindbooks@eudoramail.com
www.tradewindbooks.com
ISBNs: ISBN: 1-896580
Publishers of children's literature recognized internationally
Michael Katz

Tralco Educational Services Inc.
#101, 1030 Upper James St., Hamilton, ON L9C 6X6
905-575-5717, Fax: 905-575-1783, 888-487-2526
sales@tralco.com
www.tralco.com
ISBNs: ISBN: 0-921376, 1-894738, 1-55409
Publishes supplementary materials for second-language education; Publishes in French, German, Spanish, ESL & Italian. Also produces activity books, videos, audio cassettes, games & software
Karen Traynor, President

Tree Frog Press Ltd.
10144 - 89 St., Edmonton, AB T5H 1P7
780-429-1947
www.bookpublishers.ab.ca/members/treefrog.html
ISBNs: ISBN: 0-88967; SAN: 115-1053
Involved in custom book production for self-publishers & organizations & families
Allan Shute, Editor & Publisher

Tree House Press Inc.
#2, 110 Lansing Dr., Hamilton, ON L8W 3A1
Fax: 905-574-0228, 800-776-8733
contact@treehousepress.com
www.treehousepress.com

ISBNs: ISBN: 1-895165
Publishes educational resources specifically made for each province's educational standards

Trent University. Academic Skills Centre
Trent University, PO Box 4800, 1600 West Bank Dr., Peterborough, ON K9J 7B8
705-748-1720, Fax: 705-748-1830
acdskills@trentu.ca
www.trentu.ca/academicskills
ISBNs: ISBN: 0-9693668, 1-894674

Tri-Fold Books (Distributor)
141 King St., Guelph, ON N1E 4P7
519-821-9901, Fax: 519-821-5333, 800-572-2300
info@trifoldbooks.com
ISBNs: SAN: 106-4320
Douglas N. Cass, Owner

Trifolium Books Inc.
A Fitzhenry & Whiteside Company, 195 Allstate Pkwy., Markham, ON L3R 4T8
905-477-9700, Fax: 905-477-9179, 800-387-9776
bookinfo@fitzhenry.ca
www.fitzhenrty.ca
ISBNs: ISBN: 1-895579, 1-55244
Publishes practical resources in science, technology, information technology, mathematics, careers, general business and life skills, for schools (elementary and secondary), trade professional and reference and library markets.
Sharon Fitzhenry

Trout Lily Press
940 Holly Ave., Winnipeg, MB R3T 1W5
www.sju.ca/troutlily/
Very small independent publisher of poetry & prose

TSAR Publications
PO Box 6996 A, Toronto, ON M5W 1X7
416-483-7191, Fax: 416-486-0706
inquiries@tsarbooks.com
www.tsarbooks.com
ISBNs: ISBN: 0-929661, 1-894770
Publishes 6-8 titles of fiction, poetry & non-fictoin (literary criticism, history) annually.

Tumbleweed Press
#4, 1853A Avenue Rd., Toronto, ON M5M 2G3
416-781-4010, Fax: 416-781-2764
info@tumblebooks.com
www.tumbleweed-press.com
ISBNs: ISBN: 0-9683303, 0-9680678
Custom publishers of children's books to be used for marketing purposes

TUNS Press
Faculty of Architecture & Planning, Dalhousie University, PO Box 1000, Halifax, NS B3J 2X4
902-494-3925, Fax: 902-423-6672
tuns.press@dal.ca
tunspress.dal.ca
ISBNs: ISBN: 0-929112
Publishing arm of the Faculty of Architecture & Planning at Dalhousie University

Turnstone Press
#018, 100 Arthur St., Winnipeg, MB R3B 1H3
204-947-1555, Fax: 204-942-1555
editor@turnstonepress.com
www.turnstonepress.com
ISBNs: ISBN: 0-88801; SAN: 115-1096
Publishers of fiction, literary criticism, poetry & non-fiction; Imprints include Turnstone Press which publishes mysteries, thrillers & noir fiction
Manuela David, Managing Editor
Patrick Gunter, Marketing Director

Ulverscroft Large Print (Canada) Ltd.
PO Box 80038, Burlington, ON L7L 6B1
905-637-8734, Fax: 905-333-6788, 888-860-3365
ulpbcan@worldchat.com
www.ulverscroft.com
ISBNs: ISBN: 0-7089
Publishers of large print books, producing 84 large print books monthly.
Diane van Veen

Ulysses Travel Guides / Éditions Ulysse
4176, rue Saint-Denis, Montréal, QC H2W 2M5
514-843-9447, Fax: 514-843-9448
info@ulysses.ca
www.ulyssesguides.com
ISBNs: ISBN: 2-921444, 2-89464; SAN: 115-7167
Publishers of Canadian travel guides covering all areas of the country with a focus on Québec
Daniel Desjardins

Umberto Press
PO Box 42086, 2300 Oak Bay Ave., Victoria, BC V8R 6T4
250-721-7239, Fax: 250-592-6463

United Church Publishing House
#300, 3250 Bloor St. West, Toronto, ON M8X 2Y4
416-231-5931, Fax: 416-231-3103, 800-288-7365
bookpub@united-church.ca
www.united-church.ca/ucph
ISBNs: ISBN: 0-919000, 1-55134; SAN: 111-6002
Rebekah Chevalier, Director, Publishing P, 4162317680 ext 4034, rchevali@united-church.ca

University Extension Press
#237 Williams Bldg., University of Saskatchewan, 221 Cumberland Ave. N, Saskatoon, SK S7N 1M3
306-966-5558, Fax: 306-966-5567
extension.press@usask.ca
www.extension.usask.ca
Perry Millar, Managing Editor
Bertram Wolfe, Director

University of Alberta Press
Ring House 2, University of Alberta, Edmonton, AB T6G 2E1
780-492-3662, Fax: 780-492-0719
www.uap.ualberta.ca
ISBNs: ISBN: 0-88864; SAN: 118-9794
Linda D. Cameron, Director, 7804920717, linda.cameron@ualberta.ca

University of British Columbia Press
2029 West Mall, Vancouver, BC V6T 1Z2
604-822-5959, Fax: 604-822-6083, 877-377-9378
frontdesk@ubcpress.ca
www.ubcpress.ca
ISBNs: ISBN: 0-7748; SAN: 115-1118
Publishing branch of the University of British Columbia; Largest scholarly press in Western Canada; Publishes 50-60 books annually with over 800 published since establishment; Specialties include political science, native studies, forestry, Asian studies, Canadian history, environmental studies, planning & urban studies.
R. Peter Milroy, Director

University of Calgary Press
2500 University Dr. NW, Calgary, AB T2N 1N4
403-220-7578, Fax: 403-282-0085, 800-663-5714
ucpress@ucalgary.ca
www.uofcpress.com
ISBNs: ISBN: 0-919813, 1-895176, 1-55238; SAN: 115-0871
Publishing arm of the University of Calgary
Donna Livingstone, Director, 4032203511, livingsd@ucalgary.ca
Karen Buttner, Editorial Secretary, 4032203979, kbuttner@ucalgary.ca
John King, Senior Editor, 4032204208, jking@ucalgary.ca
Peter Enman, Editor, 4032202606, enman@ucalgary.ca

University of Manitoba Press
301 St. John's College, University of Manitoba, Winnipeg, MB R3T 2M5
204-474-6465, Fax: 204-474-7566
uofm_press@umanitoba.ca
www.umanitoba.ca/publications/uofmpress
ISBNs: ISBN: 0-88755; SAN: 115-5474
Publishing arm of the University of Manitoba; Publishes 6-8 scholarly works annually; Best known for Native History, Canadian History, Native Studies & Canadian literary studies.
David Carr, Director, 2044749242, carr@cc.umanitoba.ca
Cheryl Miki, Marketing Coordinator, 2044749495, miki@cc.umanitoba.ca
Pat Sanders, Managing Editor, 2044747338, sandersp@cc.umanitoba.ca

University of Ottawa Press (UOP/PUO) / Presses de l'Université d'Ottawa
542 King Edward St., Ottawa, ON K1N 6N5
613-562-5246, Fax: 613-562-5247, 800-565-9523
press@uottawa.ca
www.uopress.uottawa.ca
ISBNs: ISBN: 0-7766, 2-7603
Canada's oldest French Language university press & the only Bilingual University press in North America
Marie Clausén, Managing Editor, 6135625800 ext 3064, msec@uottawa.ca
Eric Nelson, Editor, Acquisitions, 6135625800 ext 3065, enelson@uottawa.ca
Heidi Laing, Editor, Livres Français, 6135625800 ext 1562, hlaing@uottawa.ca

University of Toronto Centre of Criminology
14 Queen's Park Cres. W., Toronto, ON M5S 3K9
416-978-7124, Fax: 416-978-4195
criminology.publications@utoronto.ca
www.criminology.utoronto.ca
ISBNs: ISBN: 0-919584
In-house publishing facility to showcase research of Centre faculty & graduate students
Rita Donelan, Assistant to the Director

University of Toronto Press
#700, 10 St. Mary St., Toronto, ON M4Y 2W8
416-978-2239, Fax: 416-978-4738, 800-565-9523
publishing@utpress.utoronto.ca
www.utpress.utoronto.ca
ISBNs: ISBN: 0-8020; SAN: 115-1134, 115-3234
Publishing arm of the University of Toronto
Anne Laughlin, Managing Editor, 4169782239 ext236, alaughlin@utpress.utoronto.ca
Charley LaRose, Publications Co-ordinator, 4169782239 ext237, clarose@utpress.utoronto.ca

Up Here Publishing
#800, 4920 - 52th St., Yellowknife, NT X1A 3T1
867-766-6710, Fax: 867-873-9876, 800-661-0861
www.uphere.ca
Ronne Heming, Vice-President, ronne@outcrop.com

Véhicule Press
PO Box 125 Place du Parc, Montréal, QC H2W 4A3
514-844-6073, Fax: 514-844-7543
vp@vehiculepress.com
www.vehiculepress.com
ISBNs: ISBN: 0-919890, 1-55065; SAN: 115-1150
Simon Dardick, Co-Publisher
Nancy Marrelli, Co-Publisher

Vesta Publications Ltd.
PO Box 1641, Cornwall, ON K6H 5R9
613-932-7735
vesta@primus.ca
ISBNs: ISBN: 0-919806, 1-55065; SAN: 115-5520
Stephen Gill, Editor

Visual Arts Ontario
#225, 215 Spadina Ave., Toronto, ON M5T 2C7
416-591-8883, Fax: 416-591-2432
info@vao.org
www.vao.org
ISBNs: ISBN: 0-920708; SAN: 115-5539
Publishes materials that address the interests of visual artists in Ontario
Hennie L. Wolff

VLB Éditeur
1010, rue de la Gauchetière est, Montréal, QC H2L 2N5
514-523-7993, Fax: 514-282-7530
adpcommandes@messageries-adp.com
www.edvlb.com
ISBNs: ISBN: 2-89005
Martin Balthazar, Éditeur

Voyageur Publishing
1474 Clayton Rd., RR1, Almonte, ON K0A 1A0
613-256-9435, Fax: 613-256-9435
info@voyageurpublishing.ca
www.voyageurpublishing.ca/
ISBNs: ISBN: 0-921842
Publishers of Canadian History books with a Christian Perspective
Liz Jefferson, Promotions Contact

Wall & Emerson, Inc.
205 Bethune College, 4700 Keele St., Toronto, ON M3J 1P3
416-467-8685, Fax: 416-352-5368, 877-409-4601
wall@wallbooks.com
www.wallbooks.com
ISBNs: ISBN: 1-895131, 0-921332; SAN: 116-0486
Client publisher of the University of Toronto Press; Publishes textbooks for universities & colleges, primarily in adult education, science, history of science, mathematics, English as a second language, and industrial engineering
Byron E. Wall, President

Warwick Publishing
#200, 161 Frederick St., Toronto, ON M5A 4P3
416-596-1555, Fax: 416-596-1520
nick@warrickgp.com
www.warwickgp.com
ISBNs: ISBN: 1-895629, 1-894020, 1-894622
Publishes daily interest, non-fiction trade books with a focus on sports, food & drink, and personal finance.
Nick Pitt

Waterloo Music Co. Ltd.
3 Regina St. North, Waterloo, ON N2J 4A5
519-886-4990, Fax: 519-886-4999
ISBNs: ISBN: 0-88909, 0-88797; SAN: 157-9363
William Brubacher, President

Weigl Educational Publishers Ltd.
6325 - 10 St. SE, Calgary, AB T2H 2Z9
403-233-7747, Fax: 403-233-7769
info@weigl.com
www.weigl.com
ISBNs: ISBN: 0-9690637, 0-919879, 1-896990; SAN: 115-1312, 115-5536
Publishers of educational resources & books
Linda Weigl, President & Publisher

West Coast Paradise Publishing
PO Box 2093 Main, Sardis, BC V2R 1A5
604-824-9528, Fax: 604-824-9541
rya@shaw.ca
rg.anstey.ca
ISBNs: ISBN: 0-9697494, 1-896779, 1-897031
Self-publishers of over 50 books by Robert G. Anstey
Yvonne Anstey

White Knight Books
#304, 160 Balmoral Ave., Toronto, ON M4V 1J7
416-925-6548, Fax: 416-925-4165
info@whiteknightbooks.ca
www.whiteknightbooks.ca
ISBNs: 978-1-89745-603-3
Publisher of books in a range of subject areas, including Biography; Business; Canadian History; Education; Health & Medicine; Humour; Personal Finance; Poetry; Self-Help; Travel. For White Knight Book Distribution Services Ltd., consult www.whiteknightbookdistribution.com
Bill Belfontaine, Publisher
Karen Thomas, Creative Director, White Knight Books, design@whiteknightbooks.ca
Bill Husion, Sales Consultant, White Knight Distribution Services Lt
Jody Hronek, Special Sales, White Knight Book Distribution Services

Whitecap Books Ltd.
351 Lynn Ave., North Vancouver, BC V7J 2C4
604-980-9852, Fax: 604-980-8197
whitecap@whitecap.ca
www.whitecap.ca
ISBNs: ISBN: 1-895099, 1-55110, 1-55285; SAN: 115-1290
Currently publishes more than 300 Canadian & foreign titles; Primary emphasis is in the areas of food & wine, but also publish children's fiction & non-fiction; travel sports & transportation.
Michael Burch, President
Nick Rundall, Vice-President
Robert McCullogh, Publisher
Meghan Spong, Production Manager

Whitecap Books Ltd.
#306, 20 Maud St., Toronto, ON M5V 2M5
416-469-1555, Fax: 416-504-3376
customerservice@whitecap.ca
www.whitecap.ca/
Michael E. Burch, President

Whitlands Publishing Ltd.
4444 Tremblay Dr., Victoria, BC V8N 4W5
250-477-0192
info@whitlands.com
www.whitlands.com
ISBNs: ISBN: 0-9685061, 0-9734383
Publishers of novels by J. Robert Whittle

Wildlife Conservation
2300 Southam Blvd., Bronx, NY
718-220-6876, Fax: 718-584-2625
subscribe@wcs.org
www.wildlifeconservation.org

Wilfrid Laurier University Press
75 University Ave. West, Waterloo, ON N2L 3C5
519-884-0710, Fax: 519-725-1399
press@wlu.ca
www.wlupress.wlu.ca
ISBNs: ISBN: 0-88920; SAN: 115-1525
Publishing arm of Wilfrid Laurier University; Publishes 28-30 titles annually in the fields of history, literature, sociology, social work, life writing, film and media studies, aboriginal studies, women's studies, philosophy, & religious studies
Brian Henderson, Director, x6123, brian@press.wlu.ca
Lisa Quinn, Acquisitions Editor, x2843, quinn@press.wlu.ca
Rob Kohlmeier, Managing Editor, x6119, rob@press.wlu.ca

Wilson et Lafleur
40, rue Notre-Dame, Montréal, QC H2Y 1B9
514-875-6326, Fax: 514-875-8356
librarie@wilsonlafleur.com
www.wilsonlafleur.com
ISBNs: ISBN: 2-89127
Claude Wilson, Président

Windflower Communications
67 Flett Ave., Winnipeg, MB R2K 3N3
204-668-7475, Fax: 204-661-8530, 800-465-6564
windflower@brandtfamily.com
ISBNs: ISBN: 1-895308
Publishes 2-4 books annually
Gilbert G. Brandt, President
Susan Brandt, Vice-President
SuAnn Brandt Goertzen, Manager, Wholesale Division

Winslow Publishing
PO Box 38012, 550 Eglinton Ave. West, Toronto, ON M5N 3A8
416-789-4733
winslow@interlog.com
www.winslowpublishing.com
ISBNs: ISBN: 0-921199
Michelle West

Wolsak & Wynn Publishers Ltd.
#102, 69 Hughson St. N, Hamilton, ON L8R 1G5
905-972-9885, Fax: 905-972-8589
info@wolsakandwynn.ca
www.wolsakandwynn.ca
ISBNs: ISBN: 0-919897
Publishers of award-winning poetry; 122 titles in all

Women's Press
#801, 180 Bloor St. West, Toronto, ON M5S 2V6
416-929-2774, Fax: 416-929-1926
info@womenspress.ca
www.womenspress.ca
ISBNs: ISBN: 0-88961, 0-921881, 0-7737, 0-921556; SAN: 115-5628
Publishes high-quality feminist writing
Jack Wayne, President, jwayne@cspi.org
Megan Mueller, Editorial Director, meganmueller@cspi.org

Wood Lake Publishing
9025 Jim Bailey Rd., Kelowna, BC V4V 1R2
250-766-2778, Fax: 250-766-2736, 800-299-2926
info@woodlake.com
www.woodlakebooks.com
ISBNs: ISBN: 1-55145, 1-896836; SAN: 117-7436
Publishers of religious books and religious education tools
Lois Huey Heck, Marketing Manager
Bonnie Schlosser, Publisher

Word of Mouth Production
299 Booth Ave., Toronto, ON M4M 2M7
416-462-0670, Fax: 416-462-0682
mail@torontofunplaces.com
www.torontofunplaces.com
ISBNs: ISBN: 0-9684432
Publishes a directory of recreation activities to do in the GTA and southern Ontario
Nathalie Prézeau

Wordwrights Canada
PO Box 456 O, Toronto, ON M4A 2P1
416-752-0689, Fax: 416-752-0689
wordwrights@sympatico.ca
www.wordwrights.ca
ISBNs: ISBN: 0-920835
Self-publishers of poetry
Susan Ioannou

Work 4 Projects Ltd.
CP 400, Succ Victoria, Westmount, QC H3Z 2V8
514-489-4941, Fax: 514-489-5505

Wuerz Publishing Ltd.
895 McMillan Ave., Winnipeg, MB R3M 0T2
204-956-0308, Fax: 204-956-5053
ISBNs: ISBN: 0-929963
Steve Wuerz

YYZ Books
#140, 401 Richmond St. West, Toronto, ON M5V 3A8
416-598-4546, Fax: 416-598-2282
yyz@yyzartistsoutlet.org
www.yyzartistsoutlet.org
ISBNs: ISBN: 0-920397
Publishes a variety of current writing focusing on art & culture

Magazine & Newspaper Publishers

AgMedia Inc.
58 Teal Dr., Guelph, ON N1C 1G4
519-763-4044, Fax: 519-763-4482
publisher@betterfarming.com

Agricultural Publishing Co Ltd.
#1504, One Yonge St., Toronto, ON M5E 1E5
416-364-5324, Fax: 416-364-5857

Alberta Business Research Ltd
200-10621 100 Ave. NW, Edmonton, AB T5J 0B3
780-429-1610, Fax: 780-421-7677

Andrew John Publishing
#220, 115 King St. West, Dundas, ON L9H 1V1
905-628-4309, Fax: 905-628-6847
info@andrewjohnpublishing.com
www.andrewjohnpublishing.co m
Andrew John Publishing Inc. is a trade oriented publishing house with a focus on health sciences and specializing in association and society publishing. They publish, for example, "Wavelength", "Caslpo", "Canadian Hearing Report", "College Contact" and "Listen Ecoute".

Annex Publishing & Printing Inc.
#220, 6200 Dixie Rd., Mississauga, ON L5T 2E1
905-795-0110, Fax: 905-795-2967
bookstore@annexweb.com
A variety of publications including Bakers Journgal, Canadian Pizza Magazine, Canadian Florist, and Canadian Poultry.

Annex Publishing & Printing Inc.
PO Box 530, 105 Donly Dr. South, Simcoe, ON N3Y 4N5
519-429-3966, Fax: 519-429-3112, 800-265-2827
mfredericks@annexweb.com
www.annexweb.com
Michael Fredericks, President, Magazine division, mfredericks@annexweb.com

Annex Publishing & Printing Inc.
PO Box 530, 105 Donly Dr. South, Simcoe, ON N3Y 4N5
519-429-3966, Fax: 519-429-3112, 888-404-1129
amatthews@annexweb.com (A.Matthews: Pro. Manager)
www.annexweb.com
AnnexWeb publishes publications such as "Bakers Journal", "Canadian Chiropractor", "Canadian Florist", "Canadian Firefighter", "Canadian Pizza", "Wings", and "Helicopter". They also publish books on a variety of topics such as baking, horticulture, pizza, and horses.
Fredericks Michael, President and CEO, mfredericks@annexweb.com
Diane Kleer, VP/Group Publisher (Annex Publishing Divison), dkleer@annexweb.com

Armadale Publications Inc.
PO Box 1193 Main PO, 203 10544 106SE, Edmonton, AB T5H 2X6
780-429-1073, Fax: 780-425-5844
armadale@global-serve.net
ww.albertaoilandgas.com
Cal Kelly, Editor

August Communications Ltd.
2151 Portage Ave., #A, Winnipeg, MB R3J 0L4
204-957-0265, Fax: 204-957-0217, 888-573-1136
Gladwyn D. Nickel, Publisher

Bale Communications Inc.
#1463, 1011 Upper Middle Rd. East, Oakville, ON L6H 5Z9
416-252-9400, Fax: 416-252-8002
info@adnews.com
www.adnews.com
Bale Communications publishes Adnews, A Canadian publication which offers daily advertising & marketing news.
Rob Bale, Publisher
Derek Winkler, Editor

Battlefords Publishing Ltd.
892 - 104th St., North Battleford, SK S9A 1M9
306-445-7261, Fax: 306-445-3223, 866-549-9979
battlefords.publishing@sasktel.net
Battlefords Publishing Ltd. is a newspaper & web printing company.
Alana Schweitzer, Publisher

Baum Publications Ltd.
#201, 2323 Boundary Rd., Vancouver, BC V5M 4V8

604-291-9900, Fax: 604-291-1906
circulation@baumpub.com
www.baumpub.com

Baum Publications Ltd. publishes specialty trade publications, such as Contractors Magazine, Heavy Equipment Guide, Oil & Gas Product News, & Recycling Product News.
Engelbert J. Baum, President, ebaum@baumpub.com
Ken Singer, Publisher & Vice-President, ksinger@baumpub.com
Melvin Date Chong, Controller & Vice-President, mdatechong@baumpub.com
Tina Anderson, Manager, Production, tanderson@baumpub.com

Baxter Publications Inc.
310 Dupont St., Toronto, ON M5R 1V9
416-968-7252, Fax: 416-968-2377
baxgroup@baxter.net; humanres@baxter.net
www.baxter.net

Baxter Publications is the publisher of education products & travel industry products. Services include web design & development, web hosting, & digital publishing.

Bayard Presse Canada Inc.
4475, rue Frontenac, Montréal, QC H2H 2S2
514-522-3936, Fax: 514-522-1761

Becker Associates
#202, 10 Morrow Ave., Toronto, ON M6R 2J1
416-538-1650, Fax: 416-489-1713
info@beckerassociates.ca
www.beckerassociates.ca
Other information: Montréal Phone: 514-274-0742

Becker Associates offers services such as editorial management, production management, & web-based publishing for publications & scholarly journals.
Adam Becker, President, Publications & Web, abecker@beckerassociates.ca

Bowes Publishers Ltd.
PO Box 1620, Kenora, ON P9N 3X7
807-468-5555, Fax: 807-468-1060
mail@kenoraenterprise.com
www.lotwenterprise.com

ISBN: 0-9782505

Bowes Publishers Ltd.
1540 North Routledge Pk, London, ON N6H 5L6
780-986-2271, Fax: 780-986-6397
bowes@bowesnet.com
www.bowesnet.com

Newspaper network, online resources, company directory.
Margaret Choja, Office Manager, 519-657-5510, mchoja@bowes.com

Breton Communications Inc.
#202, 495 boul. St-Martin ouest, Laval, QC H7M 1Y9
450-629-6005, Fax: 450-629-6044
breton.com@bretoncom.com
www.bretoncom.com
Martine Breton, President, martine@bretoncom.com

Brunico Communications Ltd.
#100, 366 Adelaide St. West, Toronto, ON M5V 1R9
416-408-2300, Fax: 416-408-0870
brunico@magic.ca
www.brunico.com

Through print, electronic publications and industry events, Brunico connects indicIduals and organizations, building communities specializing in the entertainment and marketing sectors. Brunico Marketing Inc., the California subsidiary of Brunico Communications Ltd., produces Brunico's entertainment and marketing conferences in New York, Washington, Los Angeles and other U.S. cities.

Bryarhouse Publishing Ltd.
10893 Old River Rd., Komoka, ON N0L 1R0
519-657-2088, Fax: 519-657-2796

Business Information Group
#800, 12 Concorde Pl., Toronto, ON M3C 4J2
416-442-5600, Fax: 416-442-2191, 800-668-2374
www.businessinformationgroup.ca
ISBNs: 1-55257, 0-919217, 0-919378, 0-9693221, 0-911448
Trade & technical magazines
Bruce Creighton, President

Business Information Group
#705, East Tower, 1, rue Holiday est, Pointe-Claire, QC H9R 5N3

Byrne Publishing Group Inc
#10 - 1753 Dolphin Ave., Kelowna, BC V1Y 8A6
250-861-5399, Fax: 250-868-3040, 888-311-1119
info@okanaganlife.com
www.okanaganlife.com

Cameron Publications Ltd.
42 Borden Ave., Dartmouth, NS B3B 1C8
902-468-1635, Fax: 902-468-1623

Campbell Communications Inc.
PO Box 5310, 1218 Langley St., 3rd Fl., Victoria, BC V8R 6S4
250-388-7231, Fax: 250-385-3563
focusadmin@shaw.ca
www.focusonline.ca

ISBNs: ISBN: 1-895297
Publisher of FOCUS Magazine
Leslie Campbell, Publisher & Editor

Canada Wide Media Limited
4180 Lougheed Hwy., 4th Fl., Burnaby, BC V5C 6A7
604-299-7311, Fax: 604-299-9188
cwm@canadawide.com
www.canadawide.com

Canada Wide Media provides a range of media services and products, in printed publications and digital media.
Peter Legge, President & Publisher LL.D, plegge@canadawide.com
Heather Parker, Senior Vice-President CGA, hparker@canadawide.com
Samantha Legge, Vice-President, Marketing, slegge@canadawide.com
Corinne Smith, Vice-President, Production, csmith@canadawide.com

Canadian Arctic Resources Committee
488 Gladstone Ave, Ottawa, ON K1N 8V4
613-759-4284, Fax: 613-237-3845, 866-949-9006
www.carc.org
ISBNs: ISSN: 0380-5522
Publisher of Northern Perspectives journal, & other publications dealing with the long-term environmental and social wellbeing of northern Canada and its peoples. Yellowknife office: 5003 - 48 St., P.O. Box 1705, Yellowknife, NT, X1A 2P3, Email: davidg@carc.org.
Charles Birchall, Chair
Jan Glyde, Contact, janglyde@carc.org

Canadian Committee on Labour History
Peace Hills Trust Tower, Athabasca University, 1200, 10011 - 109 St., Edmonton, AB T5J 3S8

cclh@athabascau.ca
www.cclh.ca
ISBNs: ISBN: 0-9692060, 0-9695835, 1-894000; SAN: 115-4168
Publisher of Labour/Le Travail: Journal of Canadian Labour Studies, as well as books & bulletins around the subject of labour history.
Alvin Finkel, President, alvinf@athabascau.ca
Rhonda Hinther, Vice-President, rhonda.hinther@civilization.ca
Gregory S. Kealey, Treasurer, gkealey@unb.ca

Canadian Controlled Media Communications
#101, 5397 Eglinton Ave. West, Toronto, ON M9C 5K6
416-928-2909, Fax: 416-966-1181, 800-320-6420
www.ccmc.ca

CCMC is a sports and entertainment marketing company with ventures in publishing, radio and television, internet, event production and media creation. Published products include SCOREGolf and CFL Illustrated.

Canadian Energy Research Institute
#150, 3512 - 33rd St. NW, Calgary, AB T2L 2A6
403-282-1231, Fax: 403-284-4181
ceri@ceri.ca
www.ceri.ca

ISBNs: 0-920522, 1-896091; SAN: 115-2866
CERI is an independent, not-for-profit research establishment created through a partnership of industry, academia, and government. It aims to provide relevant, objective economic research in energy and related environmental issues. CERI's publications are categorized into Studies and Periodicals. Studies are reports published by the Institute on completion of study projects.
Peter Howard, Interim President & CEO, 403-220-2379, phoward@ceri.ca

Canadian Government Publishing
350 Albert St., 4th Floor, Ottawa, ON K1A 0S5

613-941-5995, Fax: 613-954-5779, 800-635-7943
publications@pwgsc.gc.ca
publications.gc.ca

The Government of Canada's official publisher, CGP publishes priced documents in print, Braille, and large-print formats and on a variety of subjects, such as health, finance, science and education, among others. These publications include books, serials, monographs, maps, pamphlets, and information kits.Formats also include online publishing and electronic publications. Hours M-F 8am-5pm.

Canadian Home Publishers
#120, 511 King St. West, Toronto, ON M5V 2Z4
416-593-0204, Fax: 416-591-1630
chheditorial@canhomepub.com
www.houseandhome.com
Lynn Reeves, President & Publisher
Kirby Miller, VP & General Manager

Canadian Institute of Mining, Metallurgy & Petroleum (CIM) / Institut canadien des mines, de la métallurgie et du pétrol
#1250, 3500 boul de Maisonneuve ouest, Westmount, QC H3Z 3C1
514-939-2710, Fax: 514-939-2714
cim@cim.org
www.cim.org
ISBNs: 1-894475, 0-919086, 1-926872
Chris Twigge-Molecey, President, 905-403-3926, Fax: 905-855-7629, ctwigge-molecey@hatch.ca
Jean Vavrek, Executive Director, ext. 1301, Fax: 514-939-2714, jvavrek@cim.org
Angela Hamlyn, Dir., Media & Communications, ext. 1303, ahamlyn@cim.org

Canadian Medical Association
1867 Alta Vista Dr., Ottawa, ON K1G 5W8
613-731-9331, Fax: 613-565-5471, 866-971-9171
pubs@cmaj.ca
www.cmaj.ca; www.cma.ca
ISBNs: 1-894391, 0-920169, 1-897490
The Association publishes the Canadian Medical Association Journal (CMAJ) in print and online. CMAJ showcases innovative research and ideas aimed at improving health. It publishes original clinical research, analyses and reviews, news and editorials.

Canstar Community News Ltd.
1355 Mountain Ave., Winnipeg, MB R2X 3B6
204-697-7000,

Published titles include such community newspapers as The Herald, The Lance, The Metro and The Times.

Carswell
One Corporate Plaza, 2075 Kennedy Rd., Toronto, ON M1T 3V4
416-609-8000, Fax: 416-298-5094
carswell.customerrelations@thomson.com
www.carswell.com
ISBNs: 0-459, 0-7798, 0-88820
Carswell publishes information and electronic research solutions to the legal, tax, finance, accounting and human resources markets. Its material is integrated information available in a range of formats, including books, looseleaf services, journals, newsletters, CD-ROMS and online.
Don Van Meer, President & CEO

CHMM Inc.
#4, 951 Denison St., Markham, ON L3R 3W9
905-305-6155, Fax: 905-305-6255
comments@solidwastemag.com
http://www.solidwastemag.com

The company publishes Solid Waste & Recycling Magazine, providing environmental information to industry and government. Topics include: Recycling, Diversion, Composting, The Haulers Page, Landfill Technology, Equipment, Regulation Roundup, and Final Analysis. The publication is available to qualified Canadians for free.

Chronicle Information Resources Ltd.
#306, 555 Burnhamthorpe Rd., Toronto, ON M9C 2Y3
416-916-2476, Fax: 800-865-1632, 866-632-4766
health@chronicle.org
www.chronicle.ca
ISBNs: 0-9685848
This is a privately-held independent producer of periodicals, newsletters, websites and information for medical practitioners, and for the pharmaceutical and biotech industries. Publications include, "The Chronicle of Cancer Therapy," "The Chronicle Neurology Network," and "The Skin Book."

R.Allan Ryan, Editorial Director, allan.ryan@chronicle.ca

CLB Media Inc.
240 Edward St., Aurora, ON L4G 3S9
905-727-0077, Fax: 905-727-0017
www.clbmedia.ca

CLB Media properties include more than 26 business-to-business publications and web sites in such fields as industrial/manufacturing, logging/milling, workplace management, security and automotive.

CMP Publications
PO Box 34097, Halifax, NS B3J 3S1
902-425-1320, Fax: 902-425-1325
cmp@cmppublications.com
www.cmppublications.com

ISBNs: 0-9693595, 0-9739494
The company is dedicated to researching, publishing and / or distributing information and books related to the natural and social sciences. Titles include themes on fisheries, agriculture, construction, environment, recycling and more.

Cottage Life Books
54 St. Patrick St., Toronto, ON M5T 1V1
416-599-2000, Fax: 416-599-0500, 877-874-5253
clmag@cottagelife.com
www.cottagelife.com

ISBNs: 0-9696922
In addition to keeping a website with a plethora of information about cottage lifestyle, the company publishes Cottage Life magazine and distributes a small selection of cottage-related books.
Al Zikovitz, Publisher, zikovitz@cottagelife.com
Stacie Smith, Media Contact, 416-910-8112, smithcommunications@sympatico.ca

Craig Kelman & Associates Ltd.
2020 Portage Ave., 3rd Fl., Winnipeg, MB R3J 0K4
204-985-9780, Fax: 204-985-9799
info@kelman.ca
www.kelman.ca

ISBNs: 0-9694013
CK&A is a full-service contract publisher of magazines, newsletters & directories. Staff includes writers, editors & designers.
Chris Kelman, 866-985-9791, chris@kelman.ca

CTC Communications Corp.
#102, 155A Matheson Blvd. West, Mississauga, ON L5R 3L5
905-712-3636, Fax: 905-712-2935
info@ctccomm.com
www.ctccomm.com

Dakota Design & Advertising Ltd.
Bay 114, 3907 - 3A St. NE, Calgary, AB T2E 6S7
403-250-1128, Fax: 403-250-1194

Directories International Limited
PO Box 84021, 1235 Trafalgar Rd., Oakville, ON L6H 1A1
905-337-3030, Fax: 905-452-8133
mansoor@emanon.com

Newspaper manufacturers

Les Éditions Apex inc. / Apex Publications Inc.
185, rue Saint-Paul, Québec, QC G1K 3W2
418-692-2110, Fax: 800-664-2739, 800-905-7468
info@photolife.com
www.photolife.com

Éditeur de périodiques: "Photo Life", et "Photo Solution"
Valérie Racine, Rédactrice en chef, editor@photolife.com

Les Editions du Journal de l'Assurance
#100, 321, rue de la Commune ouest, Montréal, QC H2Y 2E1
514-289-9595, Fax: 514-289-9527
reception@journal-assurance.ca
www.journal-assurance.ca

Publications: "FlashFinance.ca", "Le Journal de l'assurance", "CarrièresAssurance.ca", "Le Congrès de l'assurance et de l'investissement", "QuébecInc.", et "The Insurance & Investment Journal".
Serge Therrien, Président et éditeur, serge.therrien@journal-assurance.ca

Les Éditions du Monde alimentaire inc.
#102, 200, rue MacDonald, Saint-Jean-sur-Richelieu, QC J3B 8J6
450-349-0107, Fax: 450-349-6923

Les Éditions forestières
#203, 1175, rue Lavigerie, Québec, QC G1V 4P1
418-877-4583, Fax: 418-877-6449
www.lemondeforestier.ca

Publication: Le journal "Le Monde forestier"
Guy Lavoie, Directeur général, direction@lemondeforestier.ca

Les Éditions Héritage
300, rue Arran, Saint-Lambert, QC J4R 1K5
514-875-9012, Fax: 514-672-5448
Luc Payette, Président

Éditions Infopresse inc.
4310, boul St-Laurent, Montréal, QC H2W 1Z3
514-842-5873, Fax: 514-842-2422
redaction@infopresse.com
www.infopresse.com

"Le Portail du marketing, de la publicité et des communications."
Bruno Gautier, Président et éditeur
Sandrine Archambault, Directrice générale, frederic.bruniquel@infopresse.com

Les Éditions Rogers limitée
#800, 1200, av McGill College, Montréal, QC H3B 4G7
514-845-5141, Fax: 514-845-7503
www.leseditionsrogers.ca
Brian Segal, Président/Chef de la direction

Editions Versicolores inc.
1320 Saint-Joseph Blvd., Québec, QC G2K 1G2
418-628-8690, Fax: 418-628-0524

Egress Enterprises Inc
PO Box 1094 A, 1476 Latta Rd., Kelowna, BC V1P 1B4
250-765-6065, Fax: 250-765-7346

English Literary Studies (ELS)
Dept. of English, University of Victoria, PO Box 3070, Victoria, BC V8W 3W1
250-721-7237, Fax: 250-721-6498
hedyt@uvic.ca
www.engl.uvic.ca

ISBNs: ISBN: 0-920604; SAN: 115-3366
Hedy Miller

L'Escale Nautique
175, rue Saint-Paul, Québec, QC G1K 3W2
418-692-3779, Fax: 418-694-6904
production@escalenautique.qc.ca
www.escalenautique.qc.ca

Le leader de la presse nautique au Québec; publications y compris le journal "L'Escale nautique", et "Guide du tourisme nautique"
Michel Veilleux, Directeur général

Family Communications Inc.
65 The East Mall, Toronto, ON M8Z 5W3
416-537-2604, Fax: 416-538-1794
sales@canadianbride.com
www.canadianbride.com

Family Communications is Canada's largest privately-held, independent publisher of women's magazines, holding a leading position in Canada's bridal, new parent and home buying markets through its flagship titles: "Today's Bride", "Best Wishes", "Mon Bébé", "Expecting", "C'est Pour Quand", etc..

Family Communications Inc./Communications Famille inc.
#1, 37 Hanna Ave., Toronto, ON M6K 1X1
450-622-0091, Fax: 450-622-0099
Manon Le Moyne, Editeur

Farm Business Communications
PO Box 9800, Winnipeg, MB R3C 3K7
204-944-5760, Fax: 204-942-8463
Bob Willcox, 204-944-5751, bob.willcox@fbcpublishing.com
John Morriss, 204-944-5754, john.morriss@fbcpublishing.com

Farm Papers Ltd.
#105B, 9547 - 152 St., Surrey, BC V3R 5Y5
604-585-3131, Fax: 604-585-1504

Formula Publications Ltd.
4-447 Speers Rd., Oakville, ON L6K 3S7
905-842-6591, Fax: 905-842-6843
www.carguidemagazine.com

Manufactor / Distributor

Giroux Publishing
102 Ellis St., Penticton, BC V2A 4L5
250-493-0942, Fax: 250-493-7526, 800-361-7526
cgiroux@awinc.com

Globe Interactive
444 Front St. West, Toronto, ON M5V 2S9
416-585-5250, Fax: 416-585-5249, 800-268-9128
www.theglobeandmail.com

ISBNs: ISBN: 0-921925
Publisher of The Globe & Mail daily newspaper, in print & online
Jim Sheppard, Executive Editor, Online News

Groupe Bomart
#204, 905 Michèle-Bohec, Blainville, QC J7C 5J6
450-435-3131, Fax: 450-435-3884
www.bomartgroup.com

Spécialisée dans l'édition de magazines dans le domaine du camionnage, de transport, de la logistique et des affaires

Groupe Constructo
#200, 1500, boul Jules-Poitras, Saint-Laurent, QC H4N 1X7
514-745-5720, Fax: 514-339-2267, 800-363-0910
www.constructo.ca

Constructo is a divison of Transcontinental and a partner of CGI for SEAO.
Manon Bouchard, Marketing contact, 514-856-6609, manon.bouchard@trancontinental.ca

Groupe Magazines S.A. Inc.
#300, 275, boul des Braves, Terrebonne, QC J6W 3H6
450-964-7590, Fax: 450-964-2327

Groupe Ro-na Dismat
#100, 1570, ch Ampere, Boucherville, QC J4B 7L4
405-641-7526, Fax: 405-641-6688

GSA Publishing Group
#200, 1104 Hornby St., Vancouver, BC V6Z 1V8
604-689-2909, Fax: 604-689-2989
sales@gsapublishing.com
www.gsapublishing.com

Travel magazine for travel agents.

Helpard Publishing Inc.
#401, rte 7575 Trans Canada, Saint-Laurent, QC H4T 1V6
514-956-1361, Fax: 514-956-1461

Herald Publishing Co.
PO Box 280, Dundalk, ON N0C 1B0
519-923-2203, Fax: 519-923-2747
www.herald-publishing.com

Homes for Sale Magazine Ltd.
178 Main St., Unionville, ON L3R 2G9
905-479-4663, Fax: 905-479-4482, 800-363-4663
info@homesmag.com
www.homesmag.com/

Various publications including Homes Magazine, Active Adult Magazine, Condo Life Magazine, Moving To Magazines, Ontario Design Trade Sourcebook, and Renovation and Decor Magazine.
Michael Rosset, Publisher
Risë Levy, Editor
Natalie Armstrong, Circulation Manager

Homes Publishing Group
178 Main St., Unionville, ON L3R 2G9
905-479-4663, Fax: 905-479-1286, 800-363-4663
info@homesmag.com
www.homesmag.com/

HOMES Publishing Group publishes titles such as "Homes Magazines", "Active Adult Magazine", "Condo Life Magazine", and "Moving To Magazines".
Liz Bonser, Director of Sales

Horse Publications Group
PO Box 670, 225 Industrial Pkwy. South, Aurora, ON L4G 4J9
905-727-0107, Fax: 905-841-1530, 800-505-7428
editor@horse-canada.com
www.horse-canada.com

Publications includes Horse Sport, Horse-Canada & Canadian Thoroughbred, and Horsepower.
Jennifer Anstey, Publisher, Staff, janstey@horse-canada.com
Susan Stafford, Mangaging Editor (Horse Sport), Staff, editor@horse-canada.com
Lee Benson, Mangaging Editor (Horse-Canada), Staff, info@horse-canada.com
Jennifer Morrison, Mangaging Editor (Canadian Thoroughbred), Staff, teditor@horse-canada.com

IG Publications Ltd.
PO Box 3090, 101 Owl St., Banff, AB T1L 1C7
403-760-3484, Fax: 403-760-2341
igpub@telusplanet.net
www.igpublications.com

Publishes travel information for B.C.

Insurancewest Media Ltd.
PO Box 3311 Terminal, Vancouver, BC V6B 3Y3
604-874-1001, Fax: 604-874-3922
manager@insurancewest.ca
www.insurancewest.ca

Publishes a variety of publications such as "The BC Broker", "Insurancewest", "Alberta Insurance Directory", and "British Columbia Insurance Directory".

Investment Executive Inc.
100 - 25 Sheppard Ave. W., Toronto, ON M2N 6S7
416-227-8266, Fax: 416-218-3544, 888-366-4200
support@investmentexecutive.com
www.investmentexecutive.com

Ishcom Publications Ltd.
#201, 2065 Dundas St. East, Mississauga, ON L4X 2W1
905-206-0150, Fax: 905-206-9972, 800-201-8596

JCFT Forest Communications Inc.
#14, rue 90 Morgan, Baie-d'Urfé, QC H9X 3A8
514-457-2211, Fax: 514-457-2558
jcft@qc.aira.com; info@forestcommunications.com
www.forestcommunications.com

Publishes "Canadian Wood Products", Canadian Forest Industries", and "Opérations Forestieres".

Journal la Nouvelle Édition
2030 boul Pie-IX, Montréal, QC H1V 2C8
514-257-1000, Fax: 514-257-7505
www.journaledition.com

"Journal des gens d'affaires de Montréal"; actualités économiques
Alain Dulong, Président/Éditeur, a.dulong@journaledition.com

JuneWarren Publishing Ltd.
#300, 5735 - 7 St. NE, Calgary, AB T2E 8V3
780-944-9333, Fax: 780-944-9500, 800-563-2946
marketing@junewarren.com
www.junewarren.com
Bill Whitelaw, Publisher

Kenilworth Publishing
#710, 15 Wertheim Ct., Richmond Hill, ON L4B 3H7
905-771-7333, Fax: 905-771-7336

Kerrwil Publications Ltd.
2 St.Clair Ave.E, Suite 800, Toronto, ON M4T 2T5
416-703-7167, Fax: 416-531-0348
peter@kerrwil.com

Key Publishers
59 Front St. East, 2nd Fl., Toronto, ON M5E 1B3
416-364-3333, Fax: 416-594-3374

Kingston Publications
PO Box 1352, 11 Princess St., Kingston, ON K7L 1A1
613-549-8442, Fax: 613-549-4333

Koocanusa Publications Inc.
100-100 7th Ave. South, Cranbrook, BC V1C 2J4
250-426-7253, Fax: 250-426-4125, 800-665-2382
koocanusa@cintek.com
www.koocanusapublications.com

Magazine and directory publishing.

Kostuch Publications Ltd.
101-23 Lesmill Rd., Toronto, ON M3B 3P6
416-447-0888, Fax: 416-447-5333
mlima@foodservice.ca
www.foodserviceworld.com

Publisher serving the foodservice and hospitality markets in Canada such as "Foodservice and Hospitality" and "Hotelier".
Kostuch Mitch, President and Group Publisher, mkostuch@foodservice.ca
Rosanna Caira, Editor and Publisher, rcaira@foodservice.ca

Kylix Media Inc
5165 Sherbrooke St., Montréal, QC H4A 1T6
514-481-5892, Fax: 514-481-9699

Landscape Ontario Horticultural Trades Association
7856 - 5th Line South, RR#4, Milton, ON L9T 2X8
905-875-1805, Fax: 905-875-0183, 800-265-5656
LANDSCAPEONTARIO@SPECTRANET.CA
www.HORT-TRADES.COM
Crispin Co, Circulation Manager
Rita Weedenburg, Publisher
Linda Erskine, Editor

Laurentian Technomedia Inc. (LTI)
501 Oakdale Rd., Toronto, ON M3N 1W7
416-746-7360, Fax: 416-746-1421
www.lti.on.ca

LexisNexis Canada Ltd.
#700, 123 Commerce Valley Dr. East, Markham, ON L3T 7W8
905-479-2665, Fax: 905-479-3758, 800-668-6481
sales@lexisnexis.ca
www.lexisnexis.ca

Lighthouse Publishing Ltd
353 York St., Bridgewater, NS B4V 3K2
902-543-2457, Fax: 902-543-2228
lighthse@fox.nstn.ca
fox.nstn.ca/~lighthse/

Malcolm Média
3650, boul Pitfield, Pierrefonds, QC H8Y 3L4
514-327-4464, Fax: 514-327-0514

Malcolm Publishing Inc.
3100 de la Concorde East Blvd. Suite 213, Laval, QC H7E 2B8
450-665-0271, Fax: 450-665-2974
hclmag.media@videotron.ca
www.harrowsmithcountrylife.ca

Publishes Harrowsmith Country Life.

Martin Charlton Communications
#300, 1914 Hamilton St., Regina, SK S4N 3N6
306-584-1000, Fax: 306-352-4110
www.martincharlton.ca

This is a public relations consultant with services including writing, graphic design, media training, communications planning, among others.

McLeish Communications Inc.
1, rue Pacifique, Sainte-Anne-de-Bellevue, QC H9X 1C5
514-457-2423, Fax: 514-457-2577

MediaEdge Communications Inc.
#1000, 5255 Yonge St., Toronto, ON M2N 6P4
416-512-8186, Fax: 416-512-8344, 866-216-0860
www.mediaedge.ca

Publications including Building Strategies, Canadian Apartment Magazine, CondoBusiness, Construction Business, and Design Quarterly.
Kevin Brown, President

Mediconcept Inc.
#300, 3333, boul Cote-Vertu, Saint-Laurent, QC H4R 2N1
514-331-4561, Fax: 514-336-1129
medicopea@netaxis.qc.ca

Mercury Publications Ltd.
1740 Wellington Ave., Winnipeg, MB R3H 0E8
204-954-2085, Fax: 204-954-2057

Metro Guide Publishing
1300 Hollis St., Halifax, NS B3J 1T6
902-420-9943, Fax: 902-429-9058
publishers@metroguide.ca
Sheila Blair, Publisher

Moorshead Magazines Ltd.
#500, 505 Consumers Rd., Toronto, ON M2J 4V8
416-491-3699, Fax: 416-491-3996
www.moorshead.com

Publications include Family Chronicle; Internet-genealogy; History Magazine.

Multi-Vision Publishing Inc.
#1100, 655 Bay St., Toronto, ON M5G 2K4
416-595-9944, Fax: 416-595-7217

National Research Council of Canada - NRC Research Press
Bldg. M-55, Montréal Rd., Ottawa, ON K1A 0R6
613-993-0362, Fax: 613-952-7656
pubs@nrc-cnrc.gc.ca
www.nrc.ca/cisti/journals/rj.html

Publisher of scholarly journals since 1929. They are part of the Canada Institute for Scientific and Technical Information and publish 16 journals, monographs, conference proceedings, and allied publications.
Bruce P. Dancik, Editor-in-Chief, pubs@nrc-cnrc.gc.ca

Naylor Communications Ltd.
100 Sutherland Ave., Winnipeg, MB R2W 3C7
204-947-0222, Fax: 204-947-2047, 800-665-5456
cpopper@naylor.com
www.naylor.com

Provides customized association marketing communications, including magazines, member directories, online buyers' guides, e-newsletters, digital magazines, show guides, and event marketing and promotion materials. Their products are to "build IMAGE" and generate significant non-dues revenue for our association partners. Publications includes "Icon", "The Clarifier", "Who's Who", "Connections", "Pace", and "Association Leadership".
Robert Thompson, Publisher

NCC Specialty Publications
11 Thornhill Dr., Dartmouth, NS B3B 1R9
902-468-8027, Fax: 902-468-2425

New Age Times Ink.
356 Dupont St., Toronto, ON M5R 1V9
416-964-0528,

News Canada Inc.
#810, 111 Peter St., Toronto, ON M5V 2H1
416-599-9900, Fax: 416-599-9700, 888-855-6397
www.newscanada.com

*Provides print editors with feature news stories of interest to their readers.

Norris-Whitney Communications Inc.
#7, 23 Hannover Dr., St Catharines, ON L2W 1A3
905-641-3471, Fax: 905-641-1648, 877-746-4692
info@nor.com
www.nor.com

Norris-Whitney Communications Inc. is an international communications company specializing in the music, audio, and lighting fields.

North Huron Publishing Inc.
PO Box 429, 404 Queen St., Blyth, ON N0M 1H0
519-523-4311, Fax: 519-523-9140

Publications include; The Citizen, The Rural Voice, and Stops Along the Way.

North Island Publishing Ltd.
#8, 1606 Sedlescomb Dr., Mississauga, ON L4X 1M6
905-625-7070, Fax: 905-625-4856
www.mastheadonline.ca
Bill Shields, Editor (The Magazine About Magazines), 905-625-7070

North Superior Publishing Inc.
1145 Barton St., Thunder Bay, ON P7B 5N3
807-623-2348, Fax: 807-623-7515
nspinc@tbaytel.net
www.northsuperiorpublishing.com

Publishes "Golfing News", "Business", and "Snowmobile News".
Sylvia Gomez, Sales Rep, 807-623-2348, sylvia@northsuperiorpublishing.com

Northern Star Communications Ltd.
900 - 6 Ave. SW, 5th Fl., Calgary, AB T2P 3K2
403-263-6881, Fax: 403-263-6886, 800-052-6417
editor@northernstar.ab.ca
www.northernstar.ab.ca

Four oilpatch magazines- "The Roughneck", "Energy Processing Canada", "Propane Canada" and "The Roughneck Buy and Sell", as well as the annual "Alberta Gas Plant Directory" and volume one of the "Roughneck Joke Book".
Scott, Publisher, scott@northernstar.ab.ca

Nytek Publishing Inc., Division of New Communications Group Ltd.
451 Attwell Dr., Toronto, ON M9W 5C4
416-242-8088, Fax: 416-242-8085
rshuker@nytek.ca
Simon Blake, Editor
Jim Gillen, National Sales Manager
Bill Begin, Publisher
Ron Shuker, Executive Editor

Pat Glionna, Circulation Manager

Omnicom Publications Inc.
#300, 512 King St. East, Toronto, ON M5A 1M1
416-955-1550, Fax: 416-955-1391

Ontario Association of Certified Engineering Technicians & Technologists
#404, 10 Four Seasons Pl., Toronto, ON M6B 6H7
416-621-9621, Fax: 416-621-8694
info@oacett.org
www.oacett.org

OACETT will be the foremost organization for advancing the engineering and applied science technology profession. They are dedicated to excellence in the engineering and applied science technology profession in a manner that serves and protects the public interest.

The Ontario Historical Society
34 Parkview Ave., Toronto, ON M2N 3Y2
416-226-9011, Fax: 416-226-2740
ohs@historicalsociety.ca
www.ontariohistoricalsociety.ca

OP Publishing Ltd.
#900, 1080 Howe St., Vancouver, BC V6Z 2T1
604-606-4644, Fax: 604-687-1925, 800-816-0747
info@oppublishing.com
www.oppublishing.com

Publishes magazines such as "Fishing", "Cottage", "Pacific Yachting", "Western Sportsman", "Outdoor Edge", "Canadian Aviator", "BC Marine Parks Guide", and "BC Fishing".
Mark Yelic, Publisher

OT Communications
1025-101 Sixth Ave. SW, Calgary, AB T2P 3P4
403-264-3270, Fax: 403-264-3276, 800-465-0322
info@otcommunications.com
www.otcommunications.com

Ottawa News Publishing
#3B, 15 Antares Dr., Nepean, ON K2E 7Y9
613-723-5970, Fax: 613-723-1862

Newspapers

Our Kids Publications Ltd.
4242 Rockwood Rd., Mississauga, ON L4W 1L8
905-272-1843, Fax: 905-272-0474
agatha@ourkids.net
www.ourkids.net

Magazine "Our Kids Go to Camp" is devoted to helping parents find the right camp for their children and "Our Kids Go To School" is devoted to helping parents find the "best education for their kids".
Agatha Stawicki, Director, Marketing & Advertising

Pacific Island Publishers Co. Ltd.
818 Broughton St., Victoria, BC V8W 1E4
250-383-3633, Fax: 250-480-3233
info@wheremagazine.com

Parkhurst Publishing
400 McGill St., 3rd Fl., Montréal, QC H2Y 2G1
514-397-8833, Fax: 514-397-0228
www.parkpub.com

ISBNs: 0-9688648, 0-9698972, 0-9732870
Parkhurst is a medical publishing house providing a wide range of medical media journals and educational communications to physicians and patients. Toronto office: 416-489-8045.

Perks Publications Inc.
3 Kennett Dr., Whitby, ON L1P 1L5
905-430-7267, Fax: 905-430-6418, 877-880-4877
admin@perkspub.com
www.perkspub.com

Publishes Trade Magazines, Journals, Periodicals, and News Letter for Associations across the county.
Tanja Nowotny, Editor/Art Director, 905-697-8905, Fax: 905-697-2596, tanja@perkspub.com

Pilot Press Ltd.
#213, 3347 Oak St., Victoria, BC V8X 1R2
250-658-6575, Fax: 250-658-6576, 800-656-7598
pilotpress@shaw.ca

Plesman Communications Inc.
400-2005 Sheppard Ave. East, Toronto, ON M2N 6S7
416-467-9562, Fax: 416-497-6022

Plesman Communications Inc.
Tour B, #305, 1470, rue Peel, Montréal, QC H3A 1T1

Polyscience Publications Inc.
PO Box 148, 44 Seize Arpents, Morin-Heights, QC J0R 1H0
450-226-5870, Fax: 450-226-5866
polysc@ietc.com

Post Newspapers Inc.
340 Sheppard Ave. East, Toronto, ON M2N 3B4
416-250-7979, Fax: 416-250-1737
postnews@idirect.com

Postmedia Network Inc.
1450 Don Mills Rd., Toronto, ON M3B 3R5
416-383-2300
www.postmedia.com

The company is a publisher by circulation of paid English-language daily newspapers. Titles include: National Post, Vancouver Sun, Edmonton Journal, Calgary Herald, Star Phoenix, Ottawa Citizen, (Montréal) Gazette. Online titles include Canada.com and Dose.ca.
Ron Osborne, Chair
Paul Godfrey, President & CEO
Doug Lamb, Executive VP & CFO
Gillian Akai, VP, Legal Affairs, 416-383-2550, gakai@postmedia.com

Progress Publishing Co Ltd.
#510, 1489 Marine Dr., West Vancouver, BC V7T 1B8
604-922-6717, Fax: 604-922-1739

Publicom inc.
CP 365, #400, 1055, côte du Beaver Hall, Montréal, QC H2Y 3H1
514-274-0004, Fax: 514-274-5884

Publicor
7, ch Bates, Outremont, QC H2V 4V7
514-270-1100, Fax: 514-270-6900
Andre Vilder, Editor

Publiédition inc.
620, boul Industriel, Saint-Jean-sur-Richelieu, QC J3B 7X4
514-856-7821, Fax: 514-359-0836

Pulsus Group Inc.
2902 South Sheridan Way, Oakville, ON L6J 7L6
905-829-4770, Fax: 905-829-4799
pulsus@pulsus.com
www.pulsus.com

Privately owned Canadian company which publishes "The Canadian Journal of Cardiology", "The Canadian Journal of Gastroenterology", "The Canadian Journal of Infectious Diseases & Medical Microbiology", "The Canadian Journal of Plastic Surgery", "Canadian Respiratory Journal", "Pain Research & Management", "Paediatrics & Child Health", and "Experimental & Clinical Cardiology".
LeBlanc Ann, Vice-President, 905-829-4770 ext 124
Lisa Robb, Director of Advertising Sales, 905-829-4770 ext 143

Reed Construction Data
4285 Canada Way, Burnaby, BC V5G 1H2
604-433-8164, Fax: 604-433-9549, 800-465-6475

Rive-nord medias inc.
896, rue de Puyjalon, Baie-Comeau, QC G5C 1N1
418-589-5900, Fax: 418-589-5263

Robins Southern Printing (1990) Ltd.
1320 - 36 St. North, Lethbridge, AB T1H 5H8
403-328-5114, Fax: 403-328-5443

Rodar International Inc.
84 Hymus Blvd., Pointe-Claire, QC H9R 1E4
514-697-7738, Fax: 514-697-4114
cjo.cancer.ctrl@sympatico.ca

Rogers Media Inc.
1 Mount Pleasant Rd., Toronto, ON M4Y 2Y5
416-764-2000,

Rogers Publishing Ltd.
1 Mount Pleasant Rd., Toronto, ON M4Y 2Y5
416-764-2000,

Publications include "Canadian Business", "Chatelaine", "Flare", "Todays' Parents", "Macleans", "Money Sense", "Profit", "Marketing", "Lou Lou" and "Ontario Out of Doors" as well as Quebec magazines "L'actualité", "Le Bulletin", "Châtelaine", et "Lou Lou".
John H. Tory, President & CEO

Salon Communications Inc.
#1902, 365 Bloor St. East, Toronto, ON M4W 3L4
416-869-3131, Fax: 416-869-3008

Sawmill Creek Communications
PO Box 1800, #11, 4040 Creditview Rd., Mississauga, ON L5C 3Y8
905-569-1800, Fax: 905-569-1818

Solstice Publishing Inc.
47 Soho Sq., Toronto, ON M5T 2Z2
416-595-1252, Fax: 416-595-7255, 800-263-5295

Southam Information & Technology Group Inc.
280 Yorkland Blvd., Willowdale, ON M2J 4Z6
www.southam.com

STA Communications Inc.
#306, 955, boul St-Jean, Pointe-Claire, QC H9R 5K3
514-695-7623, Fax: 514-695-8554
cme@sta.ca
www.stacommunications.com

Journals include "Diagnosis", "CME", "Clinicien", Cardiology", and"Pharmaceutical".
Paul Brand, Contact (Montreal office), 541-695-8393 ext.220, paulb@sta.ca

Stitches: the Journal of Medical Humour
CLB Media Inc., 240 Edward St., Aurora, ON L4G 3S9
905-727-0077, Fax: 905-727-0017
stiches@stichesmagaine.com; knuenhuis@cllbmedia.ca
www.stitchesmagazine.com

Medical humor magazine.
Simon Hally, Associate Publisher & Editor

Stone & Cox Ltd.
500-111 Peter St., Toronto, ON M5V 2H1
416-599-0772, Fax: 416-599-0867
cathysp@cdnins.com
Cathy St Pierre, Contact, 416-599-0772 ext 103, Fax: 416-599-0867, cathysp@cdnins.com

Suggitt Publishing Ltd.
950 Bell Tower, 10104 103 Ave., Edmonton, AB T5J 0H8
780-413-6163, Fax: 780-413-6185, 877-784-4488

Consumer magazines.

Sundance Publications Ltd.
PO Box 939, 423 Mountain Ave., Neepawa, MB ROJ 1HO
204-476-2309, Fax: 204-476-5802
neepress@mts.net
www.neepawapress.com

Publications such as the Neepawa Press.
Jack Gibson, Publisher, gibson@neepawapress.com

Sunrise Publishing
2213B Hanselman Ct., Saskatoon, SK S7L 6A8
306-244-5668, Fax: 306-244-5679, 800-247-5743
http://sunrisepublish.com

Swan Erickson Publishing Inc.
#1235, 1011 Upper Middle Rd. East, Oakville, ON L6H 5Z9
905-475-4231, Fax: 905-475-3512

Synergistic Publications
132 Adrian Cres., Markham, ON L3P 7B3
905-472-2801, Fax: 905-472-3091
www.canadiandefencereview.ca

Thomson Healthcare Communications
#200, 1120 Birchmount Rd., Scarborough, ON M1K 5G4
416-750-8900, Fax: 416-751-8126

Thornhill Publications Ltd.
#16, 7780 Woodbine Ave., Markham, ON L3R 2N7
905-475-1743,

Today's Parent Group
269 Richmond St. West, Toronto, ON M5V 1X1
416-596-8680, Fax: 416-596-1991

Toro Communications
#224, 2560 Matheson Blvd. East, Mississauga, ON L4W 4Y9
905-238-5625, Fax: 905-000-0000

Periodical publishers

Town Media Inc., a division of Osprey Media Group
1074 Cooke Blvd., Burlington, ON L7T 4A8

905-634-8003, Fax: 905-634-7661
info@townmedia.ca
www.townmedia.ca

Trajan Publishing Corp.
PO Box 28103 Lakeport, #10, 600 Ontario St., St Catharines, ON L2N 7P8
905-646-7744, Fax: 905-646-0995, 800-408-0352
office@tranjan.ca
www.trajan.com

Produces "Antique & Collectibles Showcase" and "Canadian Coin News& Canadian Stamp News".
Judy Sheluk, Editor (Antique and Collectibles Showcase), acseditor@rogers.com

Transcontinental ITBusiness Group
#100, 25 Sheppard Ave. West, Toronto, ON M2N 6S7
416-733-7600,

Transcontinental Media Inc.
1100, boul René-Lévesque ouest, 24e étage, Montréal, QC H3B 4X9
514-392-9000, Fax: 514-392-1489, 800-361-5479
www.transcontinental-media.com

Publishes a variety of magazines, newspapers, and books. Magazines include Canadian Living, Coup de pouce, Elle Canada and Sytle at home. They also publish a variety of books and educational materials.

Transcontinental Publications G.T. Inc.
#500, 2608 Granville St., Vancouver, BC V6H 3V3

Transcontinental Specialty Publications/Holiday Media
Suite 609, 1888 Brunswick Ave., Halifax, NS B3J 3J8
902-425-8255, Fax: 902-425-8118, 800-537-5507
jnearing@holidaymedia.ca, dhillier@holidaymedia.ca
www.holidaymedia.ca
Dan Hillier, Account Exec (Toronto & Area; Lake Country and Northlan, dhillier@holidaymedia.ca
Studley Serena, Account Executive (Kitchener; Hamilton; W & E Ontario), sstudley@holidaymedia.ca

Tribute Publishing Inc.
71 Barber Greene Rd., Toronto, ON M3C 2A2
416-445-0544, Fax: 416-445-2894
generalinfo@tribute.ca
www.tribute.ca

Entertainment magazine

Turbopress Inc.
4105, boul Matte, Brossard, QC J4Y 2P4
450-444-1103, Fax: 514-738-4929, 800-561-0318
www.turbopress.net

TVA Publications
7, ch Bates, Outremont, QC H2V 4V7
514-270-1100, Fax: 514-270-6900, 800-663-4984

Periodicals, publishing.

University of Calgary Press
2500 University Dr. NW, Calgary, AB T2N 1N4
403-220-7578, Fax: 403-282-0085
ucomail@ucalgary.ca
www.ucalgary.ca/UofC/departments/UP
Dr. Geoffrey Simmins, 403-220-3511, simmins@ucalgary.ca

University of Toronto Press Inc.
5201 Dufferin St., Toronto, ON M3H 5T8
416-667-7838, Fax: 416-667-7881
journals@utpress.utoronto.ca
www.utpjournals.com

Publishes a variety of journals including "Bookbird: a journal of international children's literature", "The Canadian Journal on Aging", "The Canadian Journal of Information and Library Sciences", "Eighteenth Century Fiction","SIMILE: Studies in Media and Information Literacy Education", and "Ulimate Reality and Meaning".
Anne Marie Corrigan, Vice-President (Journals), 416-667-7777 ext7838, acorrigan@utpress.utoronto.ca

Velo Québec Éditions
1251, rue Rachel est, Montréal, QC H2J 2J9
514-521-8356, Fax: 514-521-5711

Westcoast Publishing Ltd
1496 West 72nd Ave., Vancouver, BC V6P 3C8
604-266-7433, Fax: 604-263-8620
fish@west_coast.com

Wood Mountain Post Provincial Park
#530, 3211 Albert St., Regina, SK S4S 5W6
306-787-9572, Fax: 306-787-7000, 800-205-7070

Sioux First Nations & NWMP arifacts; open June-Sept

Youngblood Publishing
Suite 404, 4580 Dufferin St., North York, ON M3H 5Y2
416-665-7333, Fax: 416-665-7226

Youth Culture Inc.
#245, 401 Richmond St. West, Toronto, ON M5V 1X3
416-595-1313, Fax: 416-595-1312
info@youthculture.com
www.youthculture.com

Magazines are directed and marketed towards teens and "tweens".
Kaaren Whitney-Vernon, President, CEO, and Group Publisher, karen@youthculture.com
Sarah Graham, Associate Editor (Vervegirl, Fuel, Desperado & Bangzone, sara@youthculture.com

Zanny Ltd.
11966 Woodbine Ave., Gormley, ON L0H 1G0
905-887-5048, Fax: 905-887-0764

Newspapers

Alberta

Daily Newspapers in Alberta

***Calgary:* Calgary Herald**
PO Box 2400 M, 215 - 16 St. SE, Calgary, AB T2P 0W8
403-235-7100, Fax: 403-235-7379, 800-327-9219
www.calgaryherald.com
Circulation: 140,000 *Frequency: Morning*
Peter Menzies, General Manager
Brendan T. Hughes, Vice-President, Advertising
Malcolm Kirk, Editor-in-chief

***Calgary:* The Calgary Sun**
2615 - 12 St. NE, Calgary, AB T2E 7W9
403-410-1010, Fax: 403-250-4258
www.calgarysun.com
Circulation: 66,394, Mon.-Sat.; 97,050, Sun. *Frequency: Morning*
Guy Huntingford, Publisher
Chris Nelson, Editor-in-chief

***Edmonton:* The Edmonton Journal**
PO Box 2421, 10006 - 101 St., Edmonton, AB T5J 2S6
780-429-5100, Fax: 780-429-5604
www.edmontonjournal.com
Circulation: Mon.-Thu./Sat. 131,306, Fri. 148,701, Sun., 128,306 *Frequency: Morning*
Linda Hughes, President & Publisher
Heather Boyd, City Editor

***Edmonton:* The Edmonton Sun**
#250, 4990 - 92 Ave., Edmonton, AB T6B 3A1
780-468-0100, Fax: 780-468-0139
mailbag@edmontonsun.com
www.edmontonsun.com
Circulation: 74,173, Mon.-Sat.; 113,092, Sun. *Frequency: Morning*
Gordon Norrie, Publisher & CEO
Graham Dalziel, Editor-in-chief

***Fort McMurray:* Fort McMurray Today**
c/o Sun Media Inc., PO Box 4008, 8550 Franklin Ave., Fort McMurray, AB T9H 3G1
780-743-8186, Fax: 780-715-3820
today@fortmcmurraytoday.com
www.fortmcmurraytoday.com
Circulation: 6,043, Mon.-Thu.; 7,248, Fri. *Frequency: Afternoon/evening, Mon.-Fri.*
Tim O'Rouke, Publisher
Michael Hall, Managing Editor

***Grande Prairie:* Daily Herald-Tribune**
PO Box 3000, 10604 - 100 St., Grande Prairie, AB T8V 6V4
780-532-1110, Fax: 780-532-2120
dht@bowesnet.com
www.dailyheraldtribune.com
Circulation: 8,384, Mon.-Thu.; 12,830, Fri. *Frequency: Mon.-Fri.; Afternoon*
Doug Hare, Asst. Publisher
Fred Rinne, Managing Editor
Kent Keebaugh, Publisher

***Lethbridge:* The Lethbridge Herald**
Southern Alberta Newspapers, PO Box 670, 504 - 7th St. South, Lethbridge, AB T1J 3Z7
403-328-4411, Fax: 403-328-4536
www.lethbridgeherald.com
Circulation: 18,950, Sun.-Thu.; 23,213, Fri., 20,386, Sat. *Frequency: Morning*
Bob Carey, General Manager & Vice-President
Doyle MacKinnon, Managing Editor

***Medicine Hat:* Medicine Hat News**
Southern Alberta Newspapers, PO Box 10, 3257 Dunmore Rd. SE, Medicine Hat, AB T1A 7E6
403-527-1101, Fax: 403-527-1244, 800-682-2476
www.medicinehatnews.com
Mike Hertz, Publisher

***Red Deer:* Red Deer Advocate**
PO Box 5200, 2950 Bremner Ave., Red Deer, AB T4N 5G3
403-343-2400, Fax: 403-341-6560
editorial@reddeeradvocate.com
www.reddeeradvocate.com
Circulation: 17,440 *Frequency: Afternoon*
Joe McLaughlin, Editor
Fred Gorman, Publisher

Other Newspapers in Alberta

***Airdrie:* Airdrie City View**
PO Box 5368, Bay 5, 213 Main St. North, Airdrie, AB T4B 2T9
403-948-1885, Fax: 403-948-2554
production@airdriecityview.com
www.airdriecityview.com
Circulation: 11,997 *Frequency: Fri.*
Cam Christianson, Publisher
Nathan Anderson, Editor

***Airdrie:* Airdrie Echo**
PO Box 3820, 112 First Ave. NE, Airdrie, AB T4B 2B9
403-948-7280, Fax: 403-912-2341
airdrieprod@bowesnet.com
www.airdrieecho.com
Other information: Editorial Email: airdrie.echo@shaw.ca
Circulation: 13,725 *Frequency: Wed.*
Don Scotten, Publisher

***Athabasca:* Athabasca Advocate**
4917B - 49th St., Athabasca, AB T9S 1C5
780-675-9222, Fax: 780-675-3143
Circulation: 3,612 *Frequency: Tue.*
Ross Hunter, Publisher

***Banff:* The Banff Crag & Canyon**
PO Box 129, 201 Bear St., 2nd Fl., Banff, AB T1L 1H2
403-762-2453, Fax: 403-762-5274
www.banffcragandcanyon.com
Circulation: 6,970 *Frequency: Tues.*
Kim Oliver, Publisher
Dave Husdal, Editor

***Banff:* Summit UP**
PO Box 129, 201 Bear St., 2nd Fl., Banff, AB T0L 0C0
403-762-2453, Fax: 403-762-5274
editor@banffcragandcanyon.com
Circulation: 16,280 *Frequency: Weekly*
Candis Zell, Circulation/Subscription
Al Guthrow, Publisher
Dave Husdal, Editor

***Barrhead:* Barrhead Leader**
PO Box 4520, Barrhead, AB T7N 1A4
780-674-3823, Fax: 780-674-6337
leader@barrhead.greatwest.ca
www.greatwest.ca
Circulation: 3,841 *Frequency: Tue.*
Carol Farnalls, Publisher
Ray Wangen, Editor

***Bashaw:* Bashaw Star**
PO Box 188, 4909 - 50th St., Bashaw, AB T0B 0H0
780-372-3608, Fax: 780-372-4445
stetnews@telusplanet.net
Circulation: 564 *Frequency: Tue.*
Audrey Brown, Publisher

***Bassano:* Bassano Times**
PO Box 780, 216 - 3rd St., Bassano, AB T0J 0B0
403-641-3636, Fax: 403-641-3952
btimes@telusplanet.net
Circulation: 568 *Frequency: Tue.*
Mary Lou Brooks, Publisher & Editor-in-chief

Beaumont: **La Nouvelle Beaumont News**
5021B - 52nd Ave., Beaumont, AB T4X 1E5
780-929-6632, Fax: 780-929-6634
beaunews@telusplanet.net
dispatchnews.ca
Circulation: 4,999 *Frequency: Fri.*
Mary Ann Johnston, Publisher
George Brown, Editor

Beaverlodge: **Beaverlodge Advertiser**
PO Box 300, 920 First Ave., Beaverlodge, AB T0H 0C0
780-354-2460, Fax: 780-354-2460
Circulation: 1,180 *Frequency: Wed.*
Trevor Harris, Publisher

Blairmore: **The Crowsnest Pass Promoter**
PO Box 1019, 13343 - 20 Ave., Blairmore, AB T0K 0E0
403-562-8884, Fax: 403-562-2242
publisher@crowsnestpasspromoter.com
www.crowsnestpasspromoter.com
Circulation: 1,576 *Frequency: Fri.*
Kathy Taylor, Editor & Publisher

Blairmore: **The Pass Herald**
Crowsnest Mall, PO Box 960, Blairmore, AB T0K 0E0
403-562-2248, Fax: 403-562-8379
passherald@shaw.ca
www.passherald.net
Circulation: 2,220 *Frequency: Tue.*
Gail Sygutek, Publisher

Bonnyville: **Bonnyville Nouvelle**
5304 - 50 Ave., Bonnyville, AB T9N 1Y4
780-826-3876, Fax: 780-826-7062
nouvelle@greatwest.com
www.greatwest.ca
Circulation: 3,626 *Frequency: Mon.; English & French*
Dave Hutton, Publisher

Bow Island: **County Commentator & Cypress Courier**
PO Box 580, 147 - 5th Ave., Bow Island, AB T0K 0G0
403-545-2258, Fax: 403-545-6886
dpilon@my403.com
www.bowislandcommentator.com
Circulation: 5,842
Coleen Campbell, Publisher

Brooks: **Brooks & County Chronicle**
PO Box 1568 Main, Brooks, AB T1R 1C4
403-793-2252
www.brooksinthenews.com
Circulation: 11,712 *Frequency: Mon.*
M. Joan Brees, Publisher

Brooks: **Brooks Bulletin**
PO Box 1450, 124 - 3rd St. West, Brooks, AB T1R 1C3
403-362-5571, Fax: 403-362-5080
editor@brooksbulletin.com
www.brooksbulletin.com
Circulation: 4,569 *Frequency: Tue.*
James Nesbitt, Sr., Publisher

Calgary: **Calgary Community Digest**
#453, 3545 - 32nd Ave. NE, Calgary, AB T1Y 6M6
403-271-8275, Fax: 604-875-0336
digestnews@yahoo.ca
Circulation: 25,000 *Frequency: Tue.*
N. Ebrahim, Manager, Advertisements

Calgary: **Calgary Herald Your City**
PO Box 2400 M, 215 - 16th St. SE, Calgary, AB T2P 0W8
403-235-7538, Fax: 403-235-7379
Circulation: 115,000 *Frequency: Thur.; 2 city area editions*
Dan Gaynor, Publisher

Calgary: **Le Chinook**
6415 Larkspur Way, Calgary, AB T3E 5P9
403-232-5488, Fax: 403-232-5489
lechinook@shaw.ca
Circulation: 10 000 *Frequency: Mensuel; français*
Agathe Fillion

Camrose: **Camrose Booster**
4925 - 48 St., Camrose, AB T4V 1L7
780-672-3142, Fax: 780-672-2518
ads@camrosebooster.com
camrosebooster.com
Circulation: 12,941 *Frequency: Tue.*
Blain Fowler, Publisher
Berdie Fowler, Editor

Camrose: **Camrose Canadian**
4903 - 49 Ave., Camrose, AB T4V 0M9
780-672-4421, Fax: 780-672-5323
production@camrosecanadian.com
www.camrosecanadian.com
Circulation: 12,948 *Frequency: Sun.*
Lynne Chernin, Publisher
Elaine Pennington, Editor

Canmore: **Canmore Leader**
#100, 50 Lincoln Park, Canmore, AB T1W 1N8
403-678-2365, Fax: 403-678-2996
info@canmoreleader.com
www.canmoreleader.com
Circulation: 6,856 *Frequency: Wed.*
Kim Oliver, Publisher

Canmore: **Rocky Mountain Outlook**
PO Box 8610, Canmore, AB T1W 2V3
403-609-0220
www.rockymountainoutlook.ca
Circulation: 12,404 *Frequency: Thu.*
Carol Picard, Editor

Cardston: **Temple City Star**
PO Box 2060, 80 - 2nd Ave. West, Cardston, AB T0K 0K0
403-653-4664, Fax: 403-653-4006
tempcity@telusplanet.net
www.templecitystar.com
Circulation: 3,000 *Frequency: Thurs.*
Robert Smith, Publisher

Castor: **Castor Advance**
PO Box 120, Castor, AB T0C 0X0
403-882-4044, Fax: 403-882-2010
Circulation: 873 *Frequency: Thu.*
Aubrey Brown, Publisher
Stewart Brown, Editor

Claresholm: **Claresholm Local Press**
PO Box 520, 4913 - 2nd St. West, Claresholm, AB T0L 0T0
403-625-4474, Fax: 403-625-2828
www.claresholmlocalpress.ca
Circulation: 1,839 *Frequency: Wed.*
Rob Vogt, Editor
Roxanne Thompson, General Manager

Coaldale: **Sunny South News**
PO Box 30, Coaldale, AB T1M 1M2
403-345-3081
www.sunnysouthnews.com
Circulation: 3,576 *Frequency: Tue.*
Coleen Campbell, Publisher

Cochrane: **Calgary Country**
Bay 8, 206 - 5th Ave. West, Cochrane, AB T4C 1X3
403-932-3500, Fax: 403-932-3935
www.calgarycountry.com
Darryl Mills, Editor
Bob Doornenbal, Publisher

Cochrane: **Cochrane Eagle**
126A River Ave., Cochrane, AB T4C 2C2
403-932-6588, Fax: 403-851-6520
www.cochraneeagle.com
Circulation: 12,200 *Frequency: Weekly*
Jack Tennant, Publisher
Ian Tennant, Editor

Cochrane: **Rocky View Times/Cochrane Times**
206 - 5th Ave. West, Bay 8, Cochrane, AB T4C 1X3
403-932-3500, Fax: 403-932-3935
www.cochranetimes.com
Circulation: 10,000 *Frequency: Wed.*
Bob Doornenbal, Publisher

Cold Lake: **Cold Lake Sun**
PO Box 268, 5517 - 55 St., Cold Lake, AB T9M 1P1
780-594-5881, Fax: 780-594-2120
gcclsun@telusplanet.net
www.coldlakesun.com
Circulation: 5,849 *Frequency: Tue.*
Raymon Picco, Publisher

Cold Lake: **The Courier**
Centennial Bldg. #67, PO Box 6190 Forces, Cold Lake, AB T9M 2C5
780-594-5206, Fax: 780-594-2139
thecourier@telus.net
www.thecouriernewspaper.ca
Circulation: 3,000 *Frequency: Tue.*
Joy Smith, Editor
Diana Warbeck, Manager

Consort: **Consort Enterprise**
PO Box 129, 5008 - 52nd St., Consort, AB T0C 1B0
403-577-3337, Fax: 403-577-3611
consort_enterprise@awnet.net
consortenterprise.awna.com
Circulation: 1,285 *Frequency: Wed.*
Carol Bruha, Publisher

Coronation: **Coronation Review**
PO Box 70, 4923 Victoria Ave., Coronation, AB T0C 1C0
403-578-4111, Fax: 403-578-2088
coronews@wildroseinternet.ca
www.coronationreview.com
Circulation: 1,140 *Frequency: Mon.*
Joyce Webster, Publisher
Joyce Webster, Editor

Didsbury: **Didsbury Review**
PO Box 760, 2017 - 19th Ave., Didsbury, AB T0M 0W0
403-335-3301, Fax: 403-335-8143
mereview@airenet.com
www.didsburyreview.ca/
Circulation: 3,001 *Frequency: Tue.*
Murray Elliott, Publisher

Drayton Valley: **Drayton Valley Western Review**
PO Box 6960, 4905 - 52nd Ave., Drayton Valley, AB T7A 1S3
780-542-5380, Fax: 780-542-9200
dvwr@incentre.net
www.draytonvalleywesternreview.com
Circulation: 4,301 *Frequency: Tue.*
Kelly Stone, Publisher
Graham Long, Editor

Drumheller: **Drumheller Mail**
PO Box 1629, Drumheller, AB T0J 0Y0
403-823-2580, Fax: 403-823-3864
information@drumhellermail.com
www.drumhellermail.com
Circulation: 4,826 *Frequency: Wed.*
Ossie Sheddy

Drumheller: **The Drumheller Valley Times**
PO Box 1627, 110 - 3 Ave. West, Drumheller, AB T0Y 0Y0
403-823-6397, Fax: 403-823-6813
info@valleytimes.ca
www.valleytimes.ca
Circulation: 5,549 *Frequency: Tue.*
Isabell Fooks, Publisher

Edmonton: **Beverly Page**
PO Box 51034, Highland Post Office, Edmonton, AB T5W 5G5
780-479-3959,
Circulation: 15,000
Marcel Dalton, Publisher

Edmonton: **Edmonton Examiner**
#250, 4990 - 92 Ave., Edmonton, AB T6B 3A1
780-444-5450, Fax: 780-451-1421
www.edmontonexaminer.com
Circulation: 136,477 *Frequency: Wed.*
Barry Hanson, Editor
John Caputo, Publisher

Edmonton: **Journal Le Franco**
#201, 8627 - 91 St., Edmonton, AB T6C 3N1
780-465-6581, Fax: 780-469-1129
journal@lefranco.ab.ca
www.lefranco.ab.ca
Circulation: 3,500 *Frequency: Vendredi; français*
Éric Batalla, Directeur

Edson: **Edson Leader**
PO Box 6330, 4820 - 3rd Ave., Edson, AB T7E 1T8
780-723-3301, Fax: 780-723-5171
leadernews@telusplanet.net
www.edsonleader.com
Circulation: 2,824 *Frequency: Mon.*
Derek Pyne, Publisher
Chandra Lye, Editor

Edson: **The Weekly Anchor**
PO Box 6870, 420 - 50 St., Edson, AB T7E 1V2
780-723-5787, Fax: 780-723-5725
anchor@yellowhead.com
www.weeklyanchor.com
Circulation: 6,100 *Frequency: Every other Mon.*
Craig McArthur, Publisher

Elk Point: **Elk Point Review**
PO Box 309, 4809 - 50 Ave., Elk Point, AB T0A 1A0
780-724-4087,
Circulation: 602 *Frequency: Tue.*
Clare Gauvreau, Publisher

***Fairview:* Fairview Post**
PO Box 1900, 10118 - 110 St., Fairview, AB T0H 1L0
780-835-4925, Fax: 780-835-4227
info@fairviewpost.com
www.fairviewpost.com
Circulation: 2,256 *Frequency: Tue.*
Scott Fitzpatrick, Publisher
Natasha Botha, Editor

***Falher:* Smoky River Express**
PO Box 644, 217 Main St. SW, Falher, AB T0H 1M0
780-837-2585, Fax: 780-837-2102
srexpress@telus.net
www.smokyriverexpress.com
Circulation: 2,166 *Frequency: Wed.*
Kevin Laliberte, Editor
Jeff Burgar, Publisher

***Fort MacLeod:* Macleod Gazette**
PO Box 720, 310 - 24th St., Fort MacLeod, AB T0L 0Z0
403-553-3391, Fax: 403-553-2961
ftmgazet@telusplanet.net
www.fortmacleodgazette.com
Circulation: 1,309 *Frequency: Wed.*
Frank McTighe, Publisher

***Fort Saskatchewan:* Fort Saskatchewan Record**
#155, 10420 - 98 Ave., Fort Saskatchewan, AB T8L 2N6
780-998-7070, Fax: 780-998-5515
fortsaskrecord@telusplanet.net
www.fortsaskatchewanrecord .com
Circulation: 16,780 *Frequency: Tue., Fri.*
Wayne Jobb, Publisher

***Grande Cache:* Grande Cache Mountaineer**
2702 Pine Plaza, PO Box 660, Grande Cache, AB T0E 0Y0
780-827-3539, Fax: 780-827-3530
gcnews@telus.net
grandecachenews.awna.com
Circulation: 1,296 *Frequency: Tue.*
Noel Edey, Publisher
Arthur Veitch, Editor

***Grande Prairie:* Peace Country Sun**
PO Box 3000, 10604 - 100 St., Grande Prairie, AB T8V 6V4
780-532-1110, Fax: 780-532-2120
www.peacecountrysun.com
Circulation: 19,721 *Frequency: bi-weekly; also Peace Country Farmer (circ. 29,190)*
Kent Keebaugh, Publisher

***Grimshaw:* The Mile Zero News**
PO Box 1010, Grimshaw, AB T0H 1W0
780-332-2215, Fax: 780-332-4380
milezeronews@mackreport.ab.ca
Circulation: 1,292 *Frequency: Wed.*

***Hanna:* Hanna Herald**
PO Box 790, Hanna, AB T0J 1P0
403-854-3366, Fax: 403-854-3256
haherald@telusplanet.net
www.hannaherald.com
Circulation: 2,455 *Frequency: Tue.*
Mario Prusina, Publisher

***Hardisty:* The Hardisty World**
PO Box 419, 5135 - 50 St., Hardisty, AB T0B 1V0
780-888-3836, Fax: 780-888-3850
hworld@telusplanet.net
www.hardistyworld.awna.com/
Rob Rondeau, Publisher

***High Level:* High Level Echo**
PO Box 1018, 10006 - 97 St., High Level, AB T0H 1Z0
780-926-2000, Fax: 780-926-2001
Circulation: 1,599 *Frequency: Wed.*
Tom Mihaly, Publisher

***High Prairie:* South Peace News**
c/o South Peace News, PO Box 1000, 4901 - 51 Ave., High Prairie, AB T0G 1E0
780-523-4484, Fax: 780-523-3039
spn@inetnorth.net
www.southpeacenews.com
Circulation: 1,813 *Frequency: Wed.*
May Burgar, Publisher

***High River:* High River Times**
618 Centre St. South, High River, AB T1V 1E9
403-652-2034, Fax: 403-652-3962
info@highrivertimes.com
www.highrivertimes.com
Circulation: 12,930 *Frequency: Wed., Fri.*
Nancy Middleton, Publisher

***Hinton:* Hinton Parklander**
104 McLeod Ave., Hinton, AB T7V 2A9
780-865-3115, Fax: 780-865-1252
bbentt@telusplanet.net
www.hintonparklander.com
Circulation: 2,569 *Frequency: Mon.*
Tyler Waugh, Publisher
Bradley Fehr, Editor

***Hythe:* Hythe Headliner**
Hythe Family & Community Support Services, PO Box 622, 10011A - 100 St., Hythe, AB T0H 2C0
780-356-2004, Fax: 780-356-2009
headliner@telus.net
www.hythe.ca
Circulation: 1,000 *Frequency: Bi-weekly*
Monica Shaw, Director
Gisela Everton, Manager, Advertisements

***Innisfail:* Innisfail Province**
4932 - 49th St., Innisfail, AB T4G 1N2
403-227-3477, Fax: 403-227-3330
rbrinson@innisfail.greatwest.ca
www.innisfailprovince.com
Circulation: 8,425 *Frequency: Tue.*
Ray Brinson, Publisher

***Irricana:* Carstairs Courier**
PO Box 40, Irricana, AB T0M 1B0
403-337-2806, Fax: 403-337-3160
www.carrstairscourier.awna.com
Circulation: 2,951 *Frequency: Tue.*
Jackie Taylor, Publisher

***Irricana:* Crossfield Five Village Weekly**
c/o Tall Taylor Publishing Ltd., PO Box 40, 2nd Ave. & 2nd St., Irricana, AB T0M 1B0
403-935-4221, Fax: 403-935-4981
deal@wheel-deal.com
www.wheel-deal.com
Circulation: 14,555

***Jasper:* Jasper Booster**
PO Box 940, 622 Connaught, Jasper, AB T0E 1E0
780-852-3620, Fax: 780-852-3384
jbooster@incentre.net
www.jasperbooster.com
Circulation: 797 *Frequency: Wed.*
Mary-Ann Kostiuk, Publisher

***La Crete:* Northern Pioneer**
PO Box 571, La Crete, AB T0H 2H0
780-928-4000,
Circulation: 999

***Lac La Biche:* Lac La Biche Post**
PO Box 508, 10211 - 101 St., Lac La Biche, AB T0A 2C0
780-623-4221, Fax: 780-623-4230
Circulation: 2,832 *Frequency: Tue.*
Rob McKinley, Publisher

***Lacombe:* Lacombe Globe**
5022 - 50th St., Lacombe, AB T4L 1W8
403-782-3498, Fax: 403-782-5850
publisher@lacombglobe.com
www.lacombeglobe.com
Circulation: 2,911 *Frequency: Tue.*
Mary-Ann Kostiuk, Publisher
Lisa Joy, Editor

***Lamont:* Lamont Farm 'N' Friends**
PO Box 800, Lamont, AB T0B 2R0
780-421-9715, Fax: 780-942-2515
redwater@shaw.ca
Circulation: 21,922 *Frequency: Tue.*
Ed Cowley, Publisher/Editor

***Leduc:* Leduc Representative**
4504 - 61 Ave., Leduc, AB T9E 3Z1
780-986-2271, Fax: 780-986-6397
editor-rep@webcoleduc.com
www.leducrep.com
Circulation: 12,881 *Frequency: Fri.*
Neil Sutcliffe, Publisher

***Lethbridge:* Lethbridge Shopper**
234 - 12th St. B North, Lethbridge, AB T1H 2K7
403-329-8225, Fax: 403-329-8211
www.theshoppergroup.com
Circulation: 35,500 *Frequency: Sat.*
Brian Legoff, Manager

***Lloydminster:* Lloydminster Meridian Booster**
5714 - 44th St., Lloydminster, AB T9V 0B6
780-875-3362, Fax: 780-875-3423
booster@telusplanet.net
www.meridianbooster.com
Circulation: 43,041 *Frequency: Mon., Wed., Fri.*
Shaun Jessome, Publisher
Dana Smith, Managing Editor

***Manning:* Manning Banner Post**
PO Box 686, Manning, AB T0H 2M0
780-836-3588, Fax: 780-836-2820
bannerpost@mackreport.ab.ca
Circulation: 1,200 *Frequency: Wed.*
Tim Mihlay, Publisher

***Mayerthorpe:* The Freelancer**
PO Box 599, Mayerthorpe, AB T0E 1N0
780-786-2602, Fax: 780-786-2663
may-free@telusplanet.net
www.mayerthorpefreelancer.com
Circulation: 1,254 *Frequency: Wed.*
Jim Gray, Publisher

***Medicine Hat:* Medicine Hat Shopper**
922 Allowance Ave. SE, Medicine Hat, AB T1A 3G7
403-527-5777, Fax: 403-526-7352
rheizelman@ac403.com
www.shoppergroup.com
Circulation: 23,688 *Frequency: Sat.*
Ron Heizelman, General Manager

***Medicine Hat:* Prairie Post**
3257 Dunmore Rd. SE, Medicine Hat, AB T1B 3R2
403-527-1101, Fax: 403-528-2276, 800-682-2476
jtennant@prairie-post.com
www.prairie-post.com
Circulation: 24,500 *Frequency: Fri.*
Jim Tennant, General Manager
Mike Hertz, Group Publisher

***Morinville:* The Free Press**
PO Box 3005, Morinville, AB T8R 1P7
780-939-3309, Fax: 780-939-3093
redwater@shaw.ca
Circulation: 9,452 *Frequency: Tue.*
Ed Cowley, Publisher

***Morinville:* The Morinville Free Press**
PO Box 3005, Morinville, AB T8R 2P7
780-939-3309, Fax: 780-939-3093
redwater@shaw.ca
Circulation: 9,452 *Frequency: Tue.*
Ed Cowley, Editor

***Morinville:* Morinville Mirror**
10205 - 100 Ave., Morinville, AB T8R 1P9
780-939-2133, Fax: 780-939-2425
mirror1@telusplanet.net
www.morinvillemirror.com
Circulation: 10,048 *Frequency: Wed.*
Sonia Fedorus, Publisher
Lawrence Gleason, Editor

***Morinville:* Redwater Tribune**
10205 - 100 Ave., Morinville, AB T8R 1P9
780-460-8868, Fax: 780-939-2425
tribnews@bowesnet.com
www.redwatertribune.com
Circulation: 3,701 *Frequency: Wed.*
Sonia Fedorus, Publisher

***Nanton:* Nanton News**
PO Box 429, 2129 - 20 St., Nanton, AB T0L 1R0
403-646-2023, Fax: 403-646-2848
natnnews@telusplanet.net
www.nantonnews.com
Circulation: 1,012 *Frequency: Wed.*
Nancy Middleton, Publisher

***Okotoks:* The Western Wheel**
PO Box 150, 9 McRae St., Okotoks, AB T1S 2A2
403-938-6397, Fax: 403-938-2518
info@westernwheel.com
www.westernwheel.com
Circulation: 14,370 *Frequency: Wed.*
Paul Rockley, Publisher

***Olds:* Mountain View County News**
6102 - 46 St., Olds, AB T4H 1M5
403-556-3351, Fax: 403-556-3464
oldsgaz@telusplanet.net
Circulation: 14,465 *Frequency: Every other Fri.*

***Olds:* The Olds Albertan**
PO Box 3910, 5021 - 51 St., Olds, AB T4H 1P6

403-556-7510, Fax: 403-556-7515
albertan@olds.greatwest.ca
www.oldsalbertan.awna.com
Circulation: 6,675 *Frequency: Tues.*
Murray Elliott, Publisher

Olds: Olds Albertan
PO Box 3910, 6102 - 46 St., Olds, AB T4H 1P6
403-556-7510, Fax: 403-556-3464
oldsgaz@telusplanet.net
oldsalbertan.awna.com
Circulation: 6,675 *Frequency: Tue.*
Murray Elliott, Publisher

Onoway: The Lac Ste. Anne Bulletin
PO Box 822, Onoway, AB T0E 1V0
780-967-4754, Fax: 780-967-4756
tbulletin@icrossroads.com
Frequency: Fri.

Oyen: Oyen Echo
109 - 6th Ave. East, Oyen, AB T0J 2J0
403-664-3622, Fax: 403-664-3622
oyenecho@telusplanet.net
oyenecho.awna.com
Circulation: 1,446 *Frequency: Tue.*
Ronald Holmes, Publisher

Peace River: Peace River Record-Gazette
PO Box 6870, 10009 - 100 Ave., Peace River, AB T8S 1S6
780-624-2591, Fax: 780-624-8600
news@prrecordgazette.com
www.prrecordgazette.com
Circulation: 2,834 *Frequency: Tue.*
Scott Fitzpatrick, Publisher

Pincher Creek: Pincher Creek Echo
PO Box 1000, 714 Main St., Pincher Creek, AB T0K 1W0
403-627-3252, Fax: 403-627-3949
www.pinchercreekecho.com
Circulation: 2,432 *Frequency: Fri.*
Kathy Taylor, Publisher

Ponoka: Ponoka News & Advertiser
PO Box 4217, 5010 - 50th Ave., Ponoka, AB T4J 1R6
403-783-3311, Fax: 403-783-6300
publisher@ponokanews.com
www.ponokanews.com/
Circulation: 6,257 *Frequency: Wed.*
Tiffany Williams, Editor

Provost: Provost News
PO Box 180, 5111 - 50th St., Provost, AB T0B 3S0
780-753-2564, Fax: 780-753-6117
www.provostnews.ca
Circulation: 1,981 *Frequency: Wed.*
Richard Holmes, Publisher

Red Deer: Red Deer Express
#121, 5301 - 43 St., Red Deer, AB T4N 1C8
403-346-3356, Fax: 403-347-6620
adviser@reddeer.greatwest.ca
www.reddeerexpress.com
Circulation: 39,104 *Frequency: Wed.*
Graham Schofield, Publisher
Sean McCann, Editor

Red Deer: Red Deer Life
2950 Bremner Ave., PO Bag 5200, Red Deer, AB T4N 5G3
Frequency: Sun.

Redwater: The Review
PO Box 850, Redwater, AB T0A 2W0
780-942-2023, Fax: 780-942-2515
redwater@shaw.ca
Circulation: 7,742 *Frequency: Tue.*
Wanda Cowley, Publisher
Edwin Cowley, Editor

Rimbey: Rimbey Review
PO Box 244, 5001 - 50 Ave., Rimbey, AB T0C 2J0
403-843-4909, Fax: 403-843-4907
publisher@rimbeyreview.com
www.rimbeyreview.com
Circulation: 5,419 *Frequency: Tues.*
Doug Wyrostok, Publisher

Rocky Mountain House: The Mountaineer
4814 - 49 St., Rocky Mountain House, AB T4T 1S8
403-845-3334, Fax: 403-845-5570
editor@rmh-mountaineer.com
rmh-mountaineer.awna.com
Circulation: 4,301 *Frequency: Tue.*
Glen Mazza, Publisher
Brian Mazza, Editor

Rycroft: The Central Peace Signal
PO Box 250, Rycroft, AB T0H 3A0
780-765-3604, Fax: 780-765-2188
admin@cpsignal.com
www.centralpeacesignal.com
Circulation: 2,389 *Frequency: Tue.*
Dan Zahara, Publisher

Sedgewick: The Community Press
PO Box 99, Sedgewick, AB T0B 4C0
780-384-3641, Fax: 780-384-2244
info@thecommunitypress.com
www.thecommunitypress.com
Circulation: 2,722 *Frequency: Tue.*
Kerry Anderson, Publisher

Sherwood Park: The News
168 Kaska Rd., Sherwood Park, AB T8A 4G7
780-464-0033, Fax: 780-464-8512
parknews@telusplanet.net
www.sherwoodparknews.com
Circulation: 21,386 *Frequency: Wed.*
David Clarke, Editor
B. Wayne Jobb, Publisher

Sherwood Park: Strathcona County This Week
#154A, 150 Chippewa Rd., Sherwood Park, AB T8A 6A2
780-464-5176, Fax: 780-467-4125
thisweek@telusplanet.net
www.strathconathisweek.com
Circulation: 24,435 *Frequency: Fri.*
Andreas Morse, Senior Reporter
Mike Ivanik, Sales Coordinator

Slave Lake: Lakeside Leader
PO Box 849, 103 - 3rd St. NE, Slave Lake, AB T0G 2A0
780-849-4380, Fax: 780-849-3903
www.lakesideleader.com
Circulation: 3,544 *Frequency: Wed.*
Mary Burgar, Publisher

Slave Lake: Slave Lake Scope
PO Box 1130, Slave Lake, AB T0G 2A0
780-849-4350, Fax: 780-849-2433
Circulation: 1,018 *Frequency: Sat.*
Bruce Thomas, Publisher

Smoky Lake: Smoky Lake Signal
PO Box 328, Smoky Lake, AB T0A 3C0
780-656-4114, Fax: 780-656-4361
www.smokylake.com/index.php
Circulation: 1,639 *Frequency: Wed.*
Lorne Taylor, Publisher

Spruce Grove: Calmar Community Voice
PO Box 3595, Spruce Grove, AB T7X 3A8
780-962-9228, Fax: 780-962-1021
comvoice@telusplanet.net
www.com-voice.com
Circulation: 3,000 *Frequency: Every other Tue.*
Elaine Lewchuck, Publisher

Spruce Grove: The Examiner
PO Box 4206, 322 McLeod Ave., Spruce Grove, AB T7X 2K5
780-962-4257, Fax: 780-962-0658
ritas@bowesnet.com
www.sprucegroveexaminer.com
Circulation: 9,342 *Frequency: Fri.*
Rita Sharek, Publisher

Spruce Grove: Onoway Community Voice
PO Box 3595, 15A Alberta Ave., Spruce Grove, AB T7X 3A8
780-962-9228, Fax: 780-962-1021
comvoice@telusplanet.net
www.com-voice.com
Circulation: 5,000 *Frequency: Every other Tue.*
Elaine Lewchuck, Publisher

Spruce Grove: Wabamun Community Voice
PO Box 3595, 15A Alberta Ave., Spruce Grove, AB T7X 3A8
780-962-9228, Fax: 780-962-1021
sales@com-voice.com
com-voice.com
Circulation: Zone 1 6,000; Zone 2 5,000; Zone 3 3,500; Total 14,500 *Frequency: Every other Tue.*
Elaine Lewchuck, Publisher

St Albert: Saint City News
#145, 44 Riel Dr., St Albert, AB T8N 5C4
780-460-8000, Fax: 780-460-2437
www.saintcitynews.com
Circulation: 24,397 *Frequency: Fri.*
John Roberts, Publisher

St Albert: St. Albert Gazette
PO Box 263 Main, St Albert, AB T8N 1N3
780-460-5500, Fax: 780-460-8220
www.stalbertgazette.com
Circulation: 44,142 *Frequency: Wed., Sat.*
Duff Jamison, Publisher
Sue Gawlak, Managing Editor

St Michael: Elk Island Triangle
PO Box 170, St Michael, AB T0B 4B0
780-896-2223, Fax: 780-896-2281, 866-896-2333
trinews@telusplanet.net
Circulation: 1,600 *Frequency: 1st & 3rd Fri./mth.*
Joanne Paltzat, Publisher

St Paul: St. Paul Journal
PO Box 159, 4813 - 50th Ave., St Paul, AB T0A 3A0
780-645-3342, Fax: 780-645-2346
www.spjournal.com
Circulation: 4,171 *Frequency: Tue.*
Claire Gauvreau, Publisher

Stettler: Stettler Independent
PO Box 310, 4810 - 50th Ave., Stettler, AB T0C 2L0
403-742-2395, Fax: 403-742-8050
stetnews@telusplanet.net
stetnews.awna.com
Circulation: 3,323 *Frequency: Wed.*
Marlene Conibear, Publisher

Stony Plain: Stony Plain Reporter
5006 - 50 St., Stony Plain, AB T7Z 1T3
780-963-2291, Fax: 780-963-9716
stony_plain_reporter@awnet.net
www.stonyplainreporter.com
Circulation: 9,636 *Frequency: Fri.*
Inez Scheideman, Publisher

Strathmore: Strathmore Standard
PO Box 2250, 136 - 2nd Ave., Strathmore, AB T1P 1K2
403-934-3021, Fax: 403-934-5011
editorial@strathmorestandard.com
www.strathmorestandard.com
Circulation: 5,512 *Frequency: Thurs.*
Gary Hickling, Editor

Sundre: Sundre Round-Up
PO Box 599, Sundre, AB T0M 1X0
403-638-3577, Fax: 403-638-3077
roundup@sundre.greatwest.ca
sundreroundup.com
Circulation: 2,308 *Frequency: Tues.*
Ray Lachambre, Publisher

Swan Hills: Swan Hills Grizzly Gazette
PO Box 1000, 4924 Plaza Ave., Swan Hills, AB T0G 2C0
780-333-2100, Fax: 780-333-2111
sgazette@telusplanet.net
shgazette.awna.com
Circulation: 500 *Frequency: Tue.*
Carol Webster, Publisher

Sylvan Lake: Eckville Echo
#103, 5020 - 50A St., Sylvan Lake, AB T4S 1R2
403-887-2331, Fax: 403-887-2081
echo@sylvanlakenews.com
www.eckvilleecho.com
Circulation: 2,293 *Frequency: Fri.*
Barry Hibbert, Publisher

Sylvan Lake: Sylvan Lake News
#103, 5020 - 50A St., Sylvan Lake, AB T4S 1R2
403-887-2331, Fax: 403-887-2081
production@sylvanlakenews.com
www.sylvanlakenews.com
Circulation: 7,500 *Frequency: Fri.*
Barry Hibbert, Publisher

Taber: Taber Times
4822 - 53 St., Taber, AB T1G 1W4
403-223-2266, Fax: 403-223-1408
tabads@my403.com
www.tabertimes.com
Circulation: 2,870 *Frequency: Wed.*
Garrett Simmons, Editor
Coleen Campbell, Publisher

Three Hills: The Capital
PO Box 158, 411 Main St., Three Hills, AB T0M 2A0
403-443-5331, Fax: 403-443-7331
three_hills_capital@awna.com
threehillscapital.awna.com
Circulation: 4,133 *Frequency: Wed.*
Timothy J. Shearlaw, Publisher

Tofield: **Tofield Mercury**
PO Box 150, 5312 - 50 St., Tofield, AB T0B 4J0
780-662-4046, Fax: 780-662-3735
tofmerc@telusplanet.net
Circulation: 1,457 *Frequency: Tue.*
Kerry Anderson, Publisher

Two Hills: **Two Hills & County Chronicle**
PO Box 668, 4708-50 Street, Two Hills, AB T0B 4K0
780-657-2524, Fax: 780-657-2534
chroni2h@telus.net
Circulation: 1,604 *Frequency: Tue.*
Ruven Rajoo, Publisher

Valleyview: **Valley Views**
PO Box 787, 4713 - 50th St., Valleyview, AB T0H 3N0
780-524-3490, Fax: 780-524-4545
valley_views@awna.com
valleyviewspub.awna.com
Circulation: 1,270 *Frequency: Wed.*
Joan Plaxton, Publisher

Vauxhall: **Vauxhall Advance**
PO Box 302, 516 - 2nd Ave. North, Vauxhall, AB T0K 2K0
403-654-2122
www.vauxhalladvance.com
Circulation: 673 *Frequency: Thu.*
Coleen Campbell, Publisher

Vegreville: **Vegreville News Advertiser**
PO Box 810, Vegreville, AB T9C 1R9
780-632-2861, Fax: 780-632-7981, 800-522-4127
editor@newsadvertiser.com
www.newsadvertiser.com
Circulation: 10,700 *Frequency: Mon.*
Arthur Beaudrette, General Manager
Dan Beaudrette, Publisher

Vegreville: **Vegreville Observer**
PO Box 489, Vegreville, AB T9C 1R6
780-632-2353, Fax: 780-632-3235
news@vegobserver.ca
Circulation: 7,426 *Frequency: Wed.*
Daniel Beaudette, Publisher, Editor, and Advertising Manager
Arthur Beaudette, General Manager

Vermilion: **Vermilion Standard**
4917 - 50 Ave., Vermilion, AB T9X 1A6
780-853-5344, Fax: 780-853-5203
news@vermilionstandard.com
www.vermilionstandard.com
Circulation: 2,722 *Frequency: Tue.*
Dan Macpherson, Publisher and General Manager

Veteran: **Veteran Eagle**
PO Box 462, Veteran, AB T0C 2S0
403-575-3892, Fax: 403-575-3938
veagle@agt.net
www.geocities.com/veteraneagle
Circulation: 525 *Frequency: Thu.*
Les Hainer, Publisher

Viking: **The Weekly Review**
PO Box 240, 5311 - 50th St., Viking, AB T0B 4N0
780-336-3422, Fax: 780-336-3223
wrnews@telusplanet.net
www.vikingweeklyreview.com
Circulation: 1,252 *Frequency: Tue.*
Patricia Harcourt, Editor

Vulcan: **Vulcan Advocate**
PO Box 389, 211 Centre St., Vulcan, AB T0L 2B0
403-485-2036, Fax: 403-485-6938
publisher@vulcanadvocate.com
www.vulcanadvocate.com
Circulation: 2,095 *Frequency: Wed.*
Nancy Middleton, Publisher
Catherine Pooley, Editor, Pooley

Wainwright: **Wainwright Review**
414 - 10th St., Wainwright, AB T9W 1P5
780-842-4465, Fax: 780-842-2760
kelly@starnews.ca
www.starnews.ca
Circulation: 2,014 *Frequency: Wed.*
Roger Holmes, Publisher, roger@starpress.ca
Derek Kilbourn, Associate Editor, derek@starnews.ca

Wainwright: **Wainwright Star Regional**
414 - 10 St., Wainwright, AB T9W 1P5
780-842-4465, Fax: 780-842-2760
starnews@telusplanet.net
starnews.ca
Circulation: 8,800 *Frequency: Wed.; also Wainwright Star Chronicle (circ: 1,937)*
Rogers Holmes, Publisher

Westlock: **Westlock News**
9871 - 107th St., Westlock, AB T7P 1R9
780-349-3033, Fax: 780-349-3677
news@westlock.greatwest.ca
Circulation: 3,889 *Frequency: Mon.*
George Blais, Publisher
Brian Bachynski, General Manager

Wetaskiwin: **Wetaskiwin Times Advertiser**
PO Box 6900, 5104 - 53rd Ave., Wetaskiwin, AB T9A 2G5
780-352-2231, Fax: 780-352-4333
editor@wetaskiwintimes.com
www.wetaskiwintimes.com
Circulation: 10,316 *Frequency: Mon.*
Brian Bentt, Publisher

Whitecourt: **Whitecourt Star**
PO Box 630, 4732 - 50th Ave., Whitecourt, AB T7S 1N7
780-778-3977, Fax: 780-778-6459
general@whitecourtstar.com
www.whitecourtstar.com
Circulation: 2,844 *Frequency: Wed.*
Pam Allain, Publisher

British Columbia

Daily Newspapers in British Columbia

Dawson Creek: **Peace River Block News**
Hollinger Canadian Newspapers L.P., 901 - 100th Ave., Dawson Creek, BC V1G 1W2
250-782-4888, Fax: 250-782-6770
prbsales@pris.bc.ca
Circulation: 2,177 *Frequency: Mon.-Fri; also Peace River Block News Sunday Regional (Sun., circ. 10,000)*
Jamie Durham, Managing Editor
Susan Rand, Publisher

Fort St John: **Alaska Highway News**
Hollinger Canadian Newspapers L.P., 9916 - 98th St., Fort St John, BC V1J 3T8
250-785-5631, Fax: 250-785-3522
ahnews@awink.com
www.canada.com/cityguides/fortstjohn/index.html
Circulation: 3,844 *Frequency: Mon.-Fri.*
Ginette Graves, Associate Publisher
Dustin Walker, Managing Editor
William Julian, Publisher

Kamloops: **The Daily News, Kamloops**
Hollinger Canadian Newspapers L.P., 393 Seymour St., Kamloops, BC V2C 6P6
250-372-2331, Fax: 250-372-0823
www.kamloopsnews.ca
Circulation: 13,643 *Frequency: Morning*
Don Herron, Publisher

Kelowna: **Capital News**
2495 Enterprise Way, Kelowna, BC V1X 7K2
250-763-3212, Fax: 250-862-5275
nlark@kelownacapnews.com
www.kelownacapnews.com
Circulation: 157,854 *Frequency: Wed., Fri., Sun.*
Nigel Lark, Publisher

Kelowna: **Daily Courier**
550 Doyle Ave., Kelowna, BC V1Y 7V1
250-762-4445, Fax: 250-762-3866
www.kelownadailycourier.ca
Circulation: 17,000 *Frequency: Morning*
Alison Yesilcimen, Publisher

Kimberley: **The Daily Bulletin**
335 Spokane St., Kimberley, BC V1A 1Y9
250-427-5333, Fax: 250-427-5336
bulletin@cyberlink.bc.ca
www.dailytownsman.com
Circulation: 1,800 *Frequency: Afternoon*

Nanaimo: **Nanaimo Harbour City Star**
B1-2575 McCullough Rd., Nanaimo, BC V9S 5W5
250-729-4200, Fax: 250-729-4256
cduddy@nanaimodailynews.com
www.nanaimodailynews.com
Circulation: 91,931 *Frequency: Wed., Sat.*
Cale Cowan, Managing Editor
Curt Duddy, Publisher

Nelson: **Daily News**
266 Baker St., Nelson, BC V1L 4H3
250-352-3552, Fax: 250-352-2418
ndnews@netidea.com
www.nelsondailynews.com
Circulation: 4,347 *Frequency: Afternoon*

Penticton: **Herald**
186 Nanaimo Ave. West, Penticton, BC V2A 1N4
250-492-4002, Fax: 250-492-2403
www.pentictonherald.ca
Circulation: 8,235 *Frequency: Morning, Mon.-Sat.*
André Martin, General Manager

Port Alberni: **Alberni Valley Times**
4918 Napier St., Port Alberni, BC V9Y 3H5
250-723-8171, Fax: 250-723-0586
www.avtimes.net
Circulation: 6,100 *Frequency: Mon.-Fri.*
Rick Methot, Publisher
Karen Boden, Managing Editor

Prince George: **Prince George Citizen**
PO Box 5700, 150 Brunswick St., Prince George, BC V2L 5K9
250-562-2441, Fax: 250-562-7453
news@princegeorgecitizen.com
www.princegeorgecitizen.com
Circulation: 16,011 *Frequency: Mon.*
Del Laverdure, Publisher

Prince Rupert: **Daily News**
801 - 2nd Ave. West, Prince Rupert, BC V8J 1H6
250-624-6781, Fax: 250-624-2851, 800-343-0022
prdnews@citytel.net
www.canada.com/cityguides/princerupert/index.html
Frequency: Evening, Mon.-Fri.
Rodney Venis, Managing Editor
Lynda Lafleur, Publisher

Trail: **Trail Daily Times**
Hollinger Canadian Newspapers L.P., 1163 Cedar Ave., Trail, BC V1R 4B8
250-368-8551, Fax: 250-368-8550
sales@trailtimes.ca
Circulation: 5,490 *Frequency: Afternoon; also West Kootenay Weekender (23,000), Fri.*
Tracy Gilchrist, Editor
Barbara Blatchford, Publisher

Vancouver: **Metro Vancouver**
#250, 1190 Homer St., Vancouver, BC V6B 2X6
604-602-1002, Fax: 866-254-6504
www.metronews.ca
Frequency: 145,000
Mary Kemmis, Publisher/Managing Director

Vancouver: **The Province**
#1, 200 Granville St., Vancouver, BC V6C 3N3
604-605-2000, Fax: 604-605-2720
www.canada.com/vancouver/theprovince/index.html
Circulation: 216,074 *Frequency: Morning, Sun.-Fri.*
Wayne Moriarty, Editor-in-chief

Vancouver: **The Vancouver Sun**
Pacific Newspaper Group Inc., #1, 200 Granville St., Vancouver, BC V6C 3N3
604-605-2000, Fax: 604-605-2308
info@png.canwest.com
www.canada.com/vancouversun/info/index.html
Circulation: 196,903 Mon.-Thu., 252,000 Fri., 253,900 Sat.
Frequency: Morning
Dennis Skulsky, Publisher
Patricia Graham, Editor-in-chief

Victoria: **Times Colonist**
PO Box 300, 2621 Douglas St., Victoria, BC V8T 4M2
250-380-5211, Fax: 250-380-5353
www.canada.com/victoriatimescolonist/index.html
Circulation: 77,000 *Frequency: Morning*

Other Newspapers in British Columbia

100 Mile House: **The 100 Mile House Advisor**
PO Box 490, 351A South Birch Ave., 100 Mile House, BC V0K 2E0
250-395-1053, Fax: 250-395-1057
editor@100milehouseadvisor.com
Circulation: 6,084 *Frequency: Wed.*
Tari Meade, Publisher

100 Mile House: **100 Mile House Free Press**
PO Box 459, #3, 536 Horse Lake Rd., 100 Mile House, BC V0K 2E0

250-395-2219, Fax: 250-395-3939
100milefreepress@bcnewsgroup.com
www.100milefreepress.net
Circulation: 3,631 *Frequency: Wed.*
Iris Phillips, Editor

Abbotsford: **Abbotsford News**
34375 Gladys Ave., Abbotsford, BC V2S 2H5
604-853-1144, Fax: 604-850-5426
editor@abbynews.com
www.abbynews.com
Circulation: 124,288 *Frequency: Tue., Thu., Sat.*
Josh O'Connor, Publisher
Rick Rake, Editor

Abbotsford: **Abbotsford Times**
#1, 30887 Peardonville Rd., Abbotsford, BC V2T 6K2
604-854-5244, Fax: 604-854-1140
editorial@abbotsfordtimes.com
www.abbotsfordtimes.com
Circulation: 88,281 *Frequency: Tue., Fri.*
Rod Thomson, Publisher

Agassiz: **Agassiz-Harrison Observer**
PO Box 129, Agassiz, BC V0M 1A0
604-796-4300, Fax: 604-796-2081
observer@uniserve.com
www.agassizharrisonobserver.com
Circulation: 4,349 *Frequency: Wed.*
Andrew Franklin, Publisher
Darla Dickinson, Editor

Aldergrove: **Aldergrove Star**
27106 Fraser Hwy., Aldergrove, BC V4W 3P6
604-856-8303, Fax: 604-856-5212
www.aldergrovestar.com
Circulation: 10,700 *Frequency: Thu.*
Dwayne Weldendorf, Publisher
Kurt Langmann, Editor

Armstrong: **Armstrong Advertiser**
PO Box 610, 3400 Okanagan St., Armstrong, BC V0E 1B0
250-546-3121, Fax: 250-546-3636
armadver@telus.net
www.northokanagan.net
Circulation: 2,500 *Frequency: Wed.*
J.H. Jamieson

Ashcroft: **Ashcroft-Cache Creek Journal**
PO Box 190, 128 - 4th St., Ashcroft, BC V0K 1A0
250-453-2261, Fax: 250-453-9625
journal@uniserve.com
www.ash-cache-journal.com
Circulation: 1,179 *Frequency: Tue.*
Tuula Opheim, Publisher

Barriere: **North Thompson Star/Journal**
PO Box 1020, Barriere, BC V0E 1E0
250-672-5611
advertising@starjournal.net
www.starjournal.net
Circulation: 836 *Frequency: Mon.*
Al Kirkwood, Publisher
Jill Hayward, Editor

Bowen Island: **Bowen Island Undercurrent**
PO Box 130, Government Rd., Bowen Island, BC V0N 1G0
publisher@northshoreoutlook.com
www.bowenislandundercurrent.com
Frequency: Fri.
Linda Stewart, Publisher

Bowen Island: **Undercurrent**
PO Box 130, Bowen Island, BC V0N 1G0
604-947-2442, Fax: 604-947-0148
undercurrent@bcnewsgroup.com
www.bowenislandundercurrent. com
Circulation: 1,400 *Frequency: Fri.*
Edythe Hanen, Editor
Dave McCullough, Publisher

Burnaby: **Burnaby Now**
#201A, 3430 Brighton Ave., Burnaby, BC V5A 3H4
604-444-3451, Fax: 604-444-3460
www.burnabynow.com
Circulation: 98,155 *Frequency: Sat., Wed.*
Brad Alden, Publisher
Pat Tracy, Editor

Burnaby: **Burnaby/New Westminster News Leader**
6569 Kingsway, Burnaby, BC V5E 1E1
604-438-6397
publisher@burnabynewsleader.com
www.burnabynewsleader.com
Circulation: 61,463 *Frequency: Thu., Sat.*
Tracy Keenan, Publisher

Burnaby: **New Westminster Record**
#201A, 3430 Brighton Ave., Burnaby, BC V5A 3H4
604-444-3451, Fax: 604-444-3460
editorial@royalcityrecord.com
www.royalcityrecord.com
Circulation: 32,821 *Frequency: Sat., Wed.*
Pat Tracy, Editor
Brad Alden, Publisher

Burns Lake: **Lakes District News**
PO Box 309, 23 - 3rd Ave., Burns Lake, BC V0J 1E0
250-692-7526, Fax: 250-692-3685
newsroom@ldnews.net
www.ldnews.net
Circulation: 1,864 *Frequency: Wed.*
Laura Blackwell, Publisher

Campbell River: **Campbell River Courier-Islander**
PO Box 310, 1040 Cedar St., Campbell River, BC V9W 5B5
250-287-7464, Fax: 250-287-8891
editor@island.net
Circulation: 15,470 *Frequency: Wed.*
Neil Cameron, Publisher

Campbell River: **Campbell River Mirror**
#104, 250 Dogwood St., Campbell River, BC V9W 2X9
250-287-9227, Fax: 250-287-3238
mirror@island.net
www.campbellrivermirror.com
Circulation: 31,765 *Frequency: Wed., Fri.*
Zena Williams, Publisher
Alistair Taylor, Editor

Campbell River: **Campbell River North Islander**
PO Box 310, 1040 Cedar St., Campbell River, BC V9W 5B5
250-287-7464, Fax: 250-287-8891
editor@island.net
Circulation: 21,142 *Frequency: Fri.*
Neil Cameron, Publisher

Campbell River: **North Islander**
1040 Cedar St., Campbell River, BC V9W 5B5
250-287-7464
www.northislandmidweek.com
Circulation: 21,142 *Frequency: Fri.*
Neil Cameron, Publisher
Paul Rudan, Editor

Castlegar: **Castlegar News**
#1, 425 Columbia Ave., Castlegar, BC V1N 1G8
250-365-6397, Fax: 250-365-6390
publisher@castlegarnews.com
www.castlegarnews.com
Circulation: 6,600 *Frequency: Wed.*
Ken Alexander, Editor
Mike Johnstone, Publisher

Chetwynd: **Chetwynd Echo**
5208 North Access Rd., Chetwynd, BC V0C 1J0
250-788-2246
echo@chetwyndecho.com
chetwyndecho.com
Circulation: 1,300 *Frequency: Tue.*

Chilliwack: **Chilliwack Progress**
45860 Spadina Ave., Chilliwack, BC V2P 6H9
604-702-5550
editor@theprogress.com
www.theprogress.com
Circulation: 65,614 *Frequency: Tue., Fri., Sat.*
Andrew Franklin, Publisher
Gregg Knill, Editor

Chilliwack: **Chilliwack Times**
45951 Tretheway Ave., Chilliwack, BC V2P 1K4
604-792-9117, Fax: 604-792-9300
editorial@chilliwacktimes.com
www.chilliwacktimes.com
Circulation: 27,000 *Frequency: Tue., Fri.*
Ken Goudswaard, Editor

Clearwater: **North Thompson Times**
Brookfield Mall, PO Box 2592, RR#2, Clearwater, BC V0E 1N0
250-674-3343
newsroom@clearwatertimes.com
www.clearwatertimes.com
Circulation: 1,334 *Frequency: Mon.*
Al Kirkwood, Publisher

Coquitlam: **The Now**
#1, 2700 Barnet Hwy., Coquitlam, BC V3B 1B8
604-942-4192
publisher@theonnews.com
www.thenownews.com
Circulation: 54,525 *Frequency: Wed., Fri.*
Bob Moody, Publisher

Courtenay: **Comox Valley Echo**
407D - 5th St., Courtenay, BC V9N 1J7
250-334-4722, Fax: 250-334-3172
echo@mars.ark.com
www.canada.com/vancouverisland/comoxvalleyecho/index.html
Circulation: 22,776 *Frequency: Tue.*
Sean Doran, Contact

Courtenay: **Comox Valley Record**
PO Box 3729, 765 McPhee Ave., Courtenay, BC V9N 7P1
250-338-5811, Fax: 250-338-5568
editor@comoxvalleyrecord.com
www.comoxvalleyrecord.com
Circulation: 44,124 *Frequency: Wed., Fri.*
Mark Allen, Editor
Grant Lawrence, Publisher

Cranbrook: **Cranbrook Daily Townsman**
822 Cranbrook St. North, Cranbrook, BC V1C 3R9
250-426-5201, Fax: 250-426-5003
accounting@dailytownsman.com
www.dailytownsman.com
Circulation: 3,800 *Frequency: Mon.-Fri.*
Steen Jorgensen, Publisher

Cranbrook: **The Kootenay Advertiser**
1510 - 2nd St. North, Cranbrook, BC V1C 3L2
250-489-3455, Fax: 250-489-3743, 800-665-2382
advertising@kootenayadvertiser.com
www.kootenayadvertiser.com
Circulation: 28,090 *Frequency: Mon., Fri.; TV listing supplement, 7 Days Magazine (Mon.)*
Darcy Wiebe, Publisher
Kerstin Renner, Editor

Creston: **Creston Valley Advance**
PO Box 1279, 1018 Canyon St., Creston, BC V0B 1G0
250-428-2266, Fax: 250-428-3320
advance@kootenay.com
www.crestonvalley.com/advance
Circulation: 3,141 *Frequency: Thu.*
Steen Jorgenson, General Manager
Brian Lawrence, Editor

Dawson Creek: **Dawson Creek Mirror**
1316 Alaska Ave., Dawson Creek, BC V1G 1Z3
250-782-9424, Fax: 250-782-9454
Circulation: 8,200 *Frequency: Fri.*

Dawson Creek: **Tumbler Ridge Observer**
PO Box 620, 901 - 100 Ave., Dawson Creek, BC V0C 2W0
250-242-5343, Fax: 250-782-6770
prbsales@pris.bc.ca
www.tumblerridgenews.com
Circulation: 1,500 *Frequency: Wed.*
Loraine Funk, Publisher
Susan Rand, Publisher

Delta: **Delta Optimist**
207-4840 Delta St., Delta, BC V4K 2T6
604-946-4451, Fax: 604-946-5680
editor@delta-optimist.com
www.delta-optimist.com
Circulation: 33,754 *Frequency: Wed., Sat.*
Ted Murphy, Editor

Delta: **South Delta Leader**
#7, 1363 - 56 St., Delta, BC V4L 2P7
604-948-3640, Fax: 604-943-8619
newsroom@southdeltaleader.com
www.southdeltaleader.com
Circulation: 15,827 *Frequency: Fri.*
Lisa Farquharson, Publisher
Chris Bryan, Editor

Duncan: **Cowichan News Leader**
#2, 5380 Trans Canada Hwy., Duncan, BC V9L 6W4
250-746-4471
publisher@cowichannewsleader.com
www.cowichannewsleader.com
Circulation: 20,595 *Frequency: Wed.*
Jim Parker, Publisher
John McKinley, Editor

Duncan: **The Pictorial**
#2, 5380 Trans Canada Hwy., Duncan, BC V9L 6W4
250-746-4471, Fax: 250-746-8529
www.cowichannewsleader.com/
Circulation: 23,153 *Frequency: Sun.*
John McKinley, Editor
Bill Macadam, Editor

Fernie: **Fernie Free Press**
342 - 2nd Ave., PO Bag 5000, Fernie, BC V0B 1M0
250-423-4666, Fax: 250-423-3110, 866-337-6437
freepres@shawcable.com
www.thefreepress.ca
Circulation: 1,851 *Frequency: Wed.*
Cina Wales-Green, Publisher

Fort Nelson: **Fort Nelson News**
PO Box 600, #3, 4448 - 50th Ave. North, Fort Nelson, BC V0C 1R0
250-774-2357, Fax: 250-774-3612
editorial@fortnelsonnews.ca
www.fortnelsonnews.ca
Circulation: 2,238 *Frequency: Wed.*
Judith Kenyon, Editor

Fort St James: **Fort St. James Caledonia Courier**
PO Box 1298, 366 Stuart Dr., Fort St James, BC V0J 1P0
250-996-8482, Fax: 250-996-7973
www.caledoniacourier.com
Circulation: 825 *Frequency: Wed.*
Scott Farmer, Publisher

Fort St John: **North Peace Express**
9909 100 Ave., Fort St John, BC V1J 1Y4
250-787-7030
abnews@awink.com
www.nenews.ca
Circulation: 25,000 *Frequency: Wed.*
Bruce Lantz, Publisher

Fort St John: **The Northerner**
9916 - 98A Ave., Fort St John, BC V1J 1S2
250-785-5631, Fax: 250-785-3522
graphicsnorth@awink.com
www.thenortherner.ca
Circulation: 7,500 *Frequency: Wed.*
Dustin Walker, Editor
William Julian, Publisher

Gabriola: **Gabriola Sounder**
1001 Pat Burns Ave., Gabriola, BC V0R 1X2
250-247-9337, Fax: 250-247-8147
sounder@island.net
www.soundernews.com
Circulation: 3,580 *Frequency: Mon.*
Sue de Carteret, Editor
Bill de Carteret, Publisher

Gold River: **The Record**
PO Box 279, Gold River, BC V0P 1G0
250-283-2324
record@island.net
www.island.net/~record
Circulation: 1,300 *Frequency: Twice monthly*
Lynne West, Associate Publisher
Jerry West, Editor

Grand Forks: **Boundary Weekender**
7255 Riverside Drive, Grand Forks, BC V0H 1H0
250-442-2191, Fax: 250-442-3336
gfgazedt@sunshinecable.com
www.canwestmediaworks.com
Circulation: 4,208 *Frequency: Fri.*
Sandra Watts, Publisher
Richard Finnigan, Editor

Grand Forks: **Grand Forks Gazette**
PO Box 700, 7330 - 2nd St., Grand Forks, BC V0H 1H0
250-442-2191, Fax: 250-442-3336
gfgazedt@sunshinecable.com
Circulation: 2,807 *Frequency: Wed.*
Sandra Barron, Publisher
Jason Harshenin, Editor

Greenwood: **Big White Mountaineer**
PO Box 99, Greenwood, BC V0H 1J0
250-445-2233, Fax: 250-445-2243
Circulation: 5,000

Greenwood: **Boundary Creek Times Mountaineer**
PO Box 99, Greenwood, BC V0H 1J0
250-445-2233, Fax: 250-445-2243
bctimes@direct.ca
Circulation: 1,894 *Frequency: Fri.*

Reed Turcotte, Publisher

Hagensborg: **Coast Mountain News**
PO Box 250, 1290 Hwy. 20, Hagensborg, BC V0T 1H0
250-982-2696, Fax: 250-982-2512
cmnews@belco.bc.ca
Circulation: 1,150 *Frequency: Every other Thu.*

Hope: **Hope Standard**
PO Box 1090, 540 Wallace St., Hope, BC V0X 1L0
604-869-2421, Fax: 604-869-7351
www.hopestandard.com
Circulation: 2,062 *Frequency: Thu.*
Simone Rolph, Editor
Andrew Franklin, Publisher

Houston: **Houston Today Newspaper**
PO Box 899, 3232 Hwy. 6, Houston, BC V0J 1Z0
250-845-2890, Fax: 250-845-7893
www.houston-today.com
Circulation: 1,076 *Frequency: Wed.*
Mary Ann Ruiter, Publisher

Invermere: **The Valley Echo**
PO Box 70, 530 - 13th St., Invermere, BC V0A 1K0
250-342-9216, Fax: 250-342-3930
www.invermerevalleyecho.com
Circulation: 2,971 *Frequency: Wed.*
Sheila Tutty, Publisher
Ian Cobb, Editor

Kamloops: **Kamloops This Week**
1365B Dalhousie Dr., Kamloops, BC V2C 5P6
250-374-7467
ktw@bcnewsgroup.com
www.kamloopsthisweek.com
Circulation: 88,680 *Frequency: Wed., Fri., Sun.*
Kelly Hall, Publisher
Christopher Foulds, Managing Editor

Keremeos: **Keremeos Review**
PO Box 130, 613 - 7 Ave., Keremeos, BC V0X 1N0
250-499-2653, Fax: 250-499-2645
review@nethop.net
www.keremeosreview.com
Circulation: 1,344 *Frequency: Thu.*
Chuck Bennett, Publisher

Keremeos: **The Review**
PO Box 220, 613 7th Ave., Keremeos, BC V0X 1N0
250-499-2653, Fax: 250-499-2645
reviewads@nethop.net
www.keremosreview.com
Frequency: Thu.
Chuck Bennett, Publisher

Kitimat: **Northern Sentinel**
626 Enterprise Ave., Kitimat, BC V8C 2E4
250-632-6144, Fax: 250-639-9373
advertising@northernsentinel.com
www.northernsentinel.com
Circulation: 1,655 *Frequency: Wed; also Weekend Advertiser (Sat., circ. 15,650)*
Sandra Dugdale, Publisher

Kitimat: **Weekend Advertiser**
626 Enterprise Ave., Kitimat, BC V8C 2G4
250-632-6144, Fax: 250-639-9373
advertising@northernsentinel.com
www.northernsentinel.com
Circulation: 15,800
Sandra Dugdale, Publisher, publisher@northernsentinel.com

Ladysmith: **Ladysmith-Chemainus Chronicle**
PO Box 400, 341 - 1st Ave., Ladysmith, BC V9G 1A3
250-245-2277, Fax: 250-245-2260
lccedit@vinewsgroup.com
www.ladysmithchronicle.com
Circulation: 2,640 *Frequency: Tue.*
Richard Dutka, Publisher
Jason Youmans, Editor

Lake Country: **Lake Country Calendar**
#3 3370 Beaver Lake Rd., Lake Country, BC V4V 1S7
250-766-4688, Fax: 250-766-4645
calendar@cablelan.net
www.lakecountrynews.net
Circulation: 6,758 *Frequency: Wed., Sat.*
Jack McCarthy, Publisher

Lake Cowichan: **Lake Cowichan Gazette**
PO Box 10, 170E Cowichan Lake Rd., Lake Cowichan, BC V0R 2G0
250-749-4383, Fax: 250-749-4385
www.lakecowichangazette.com

Circulation: 936 *Frequency: Wed.*
Dennis Skalicky, Publisher

Lake Errock: **Valley Express**
PO Box 84, Lake Errock, BC V0M 1N0
604-820-1930,
Circulation: 4,000
Joanne Taylor, Publisher

Langley: **Langley Advance News**
#112, 6375 - 202nd St., Langley, BC V2Y 1N1
604-534-8641, Fax: 604-534-3383
editorial@langleyadvance.com
www.langleyadvance.com
Circulation: 81,580 *Frequency: Tue., Fri.*
Bob Groeneveld, Editor
Liz Lynch, General Manager

Langley: **Langley Times**
PO Box 3097, 20258 Fraser Hwy., Langley, BC V3A 4R3
604-533-4157, Fax: 604-533-0219
www.langleytimes.com
Circulation: 117,264 *Frequency: Wed., Fri., Sun.*
Dwane Weidendorf, Publisher
Frank Bucholtz, Editor

Lantzville: **The Lantzville Log**
Lantzville Log Society, PO Box 268, 6958 Jacks Rd., Lantzville, BC V0R 2H0
250-390-2847, Fax: 250-390-2847
info@thelog.ca
www.thelog.ca
Circulation: 3,626 *Frequency: Ist Mon. of month*
Wanda Cullen, Contact

Lazo: **Comox Totem Times**
PO Box 1000 Main, 19 Wing, CFB Comox, Lazo, BC V0R 2K0
250-339-2541, Fax: 250-339-5209
Circulation: 2,000 *Frequency: Monthly*

Lillooet: **Bridge River-Lillooet News**
PO Box 709, Lillooet, BC V0K 1V0
250-256-4219, Fax: 250-256-4210, 877-300-8569
lillooetnews@cablelan.net
www.lillooetnews.net
Circulation: 1,581 *Frequency: Wed.*
Bain Gair, Publisher

Lumby: **Lumby Valley Times**
PO Box 408, 2062 Park Ave., Lumby, BC V0E 2G0
250-547-6990, Fax: 250-547-6992
lvt@telus.net
Circulation: 2,600 *Frequency: Wed.*
Rod Neufeld, Publisher

Mackenzie: **The Times**
PO Box 609, 540 Mackenzie Blvd., Mackenzie, BC V0J 2C0
250-997-6675, Fax: 250-997-4747
thetimes@mackbc.com
Circulation: 1,500 *Frequency: Tue.*
Jackie Benton, Editor

Maple Ridge: **The Maple Ridge- Pitt Meadows News**
22328 - 119th Ave., Maple Ridge, BC V2X 2Z3
604-467-1122, Fax: 604-463-4731
editor@mapleridgenews.com
www.mapleridgenews.com
Circulation: 59,724 *Frequency: Wed., Sat.*
Michael Hall, Editor
Jim Coulter, Publisher

Maple Ridge: **Maple Ridge-Pitt Meadows Times**
Unit 2, 22345 North Ave., Maple Ridge, BC V2X 8T2
604-463-2281, Fax: 604-463-9943
www.mrtimes.com
Circulation: 27,400 *Frequency: Tue. & Fri.*
Fred Armstrong, Publisher

Merritt: **Merritt Herald**
PO Box 9, 2090 Granite Ave., Merritt, BC V1K 1B8
250-378-4241, Fax: 250-378-6818
newsroom@merrittherald.com
www.merrittherald.com
Circulation: 1,404 *Frequency: Wed.*
Rick Proznick, Publisher

Merritt: **The Merritt News**
PO Box 939, Merritt, BC V1K 1B8
250-378-8876,
Circulation: 5,094 *Frequency: Fri.*
Tracy McCall, Publisher

Merritt: **Valley Express**
PO Box 9, 2090 Granite Ave., Merritt, BC V1K 1B8

250-378-4241, Fax: 250-378-6818
mvherald@uniserve.com

Circulation: 5,442 *Frequency: Sat.*
Rick Proznick, Publisher

Mission: Mission City Record
33047 - 1st Ave., Mission, BC V2V 1G2
604-826-6221, Fax: 604-826-8266
mcrecord@uniserve.com
www.missioncityrecord.com
Circulation: 10,780 *Frequency: Thu.*
Josh O'Connor, Publisher
Jason Roessle, Editor

Nakusp: Arrow Lakes News
PO Box 189, 203 Broadway Ave., Nakusp, BC V0G 1R0
250-265-3823
newsroom@arrowlakesnews.com
www.arrowlakesnews.com
Circulation: 1,040 *Frequency: Wed.*
Lynda Lafleur, Publisher

Nanaimo: Harbour City Star
B1-2575 McCullough Rd., #B1, Nanaimo, BC V9S 5W5
250-729-4200
www.nanaimodailynews.com
Circulation: 91,931 *Frequency: Wed., Sat.*
Curt Duddy, Publisher, wking@island.net

Nanaimo: Nanaimo News Bulletin
777 Poplar St., Nanaimo, BC V9S 2H7
250-753-3707
publisher@nanaimobulletin.com
www.nanaimobulletin.com
Circulation: 98,079 *Frequency: Tues., Thurs., Sat.*
Roy Linder, Publisher

Nelson: Kootenay Weekly Express
554 Ward St., Nelson, BC V1L 1S9
250-354-3910, Fax: 250-352-5075, 800-665-3288
express@expressnews.bc.ca
www.expressnews.ca
Circulation: 11,801 *Frequency: Wed.*
Nelson Becker, Publisher

Nelson: West Kootenay Weekender
266 Baker St., Nelson, BC V1L 4H3
250-352-3552, Fax: 250-352-2418
weekender@nelsondailynews.com
Circulation: 26,646 *Frequency: Fri; supplement to Nelson Daily News, Trail Daily Times*
John A. Smith, Publisher

North Vancouver: North Shore News
100 - 126 East 15th St., North Vancouver, BC V7L 2P9
604-985-2131, Fax: 604-985-2104
editor@nsnews.com
www.nsnews.com
Circulation: 192,584 *Frequency: Wed., Fri., Sun.*
Doug Foot, General Manager
Terry Peters, Managing Editor

North Vancouver: North Shore Outlook
#104, 980 West 1st St., North Vancouver, BC V7P 3N4
604-903-1000, Fax: 604-903-1001
www.northshoreoutlook.com
Circulation: 58,183 *Frequency: Thu.*
Linda Stewart, Publisher
Andrew McCredie, Editor

Oliver: Oliver Chronicle
PO Box 880, 36083 - 97th St., Oliver, BC V0H 1T0
250-498-3711, Fax: 250-498-3966
olivernews@img.net
www.oliverchronicle.com
Other information: Advertising Email: ads@oliverchronicle.com
Circulation: 2,393 *Frequency: Wed.*
Michael Newman, Publisher

Osoyoos: Osoyoos Times
PO Box 359, 8712 Main St., Osoyoos, BC V0H 1V0
250-495-7225, Fax: 250-495-6616
news@osoyoostimes.com
www.osoyoostimes.com
Circulation: 2,340 *Frequency: Wed.*
Chuck Bennett, Editor-in-chief
Chris Stodola, Publisher & General Manager

Parksville: Parksville Qualicum News
PO Box 1180, #4, 154 Middleton Ave., Parksville, BC V9P 2H2
250-248-4341, Fax: 250-248-4655
www.pqbnews.com
Circulation: 33,562 *Frequency: Tues., Fri.*
Julie Chambers, Publisher

Peachland: The Peachland Signal
PO Box 1300, 4478 - 3rd St., RR# 7, Peachland, BC V0H 1X7
250-767-2004, Fax: 250-767-3306, 877-867-7977
signal@shawcable.com
Circulation: 1,491 *Frequency: Thu.*
Darren Bayrack, Publisher

Peachland: Peachland View
#102A, 4200 Beach Ave., Peachland, BC V0H 1X6
250-767-7771, Fax: 250-767-3337
peachlandview@shaw.ca
Circulation: 3,500
Kathie McClinton

Pender Island: Gulf Islands, Island Tides
PO Box 55, Pender Island, BC V0N 2M0
250-629-3660, Fax: 250-629-3838
news@islandtides.com
www.islandtides.com
Circulation: 17,500
Christa Grace-Warrick, Publisher

Penticton: Penticton Western News
2250 Camrose St., Penticton, BC V2A 8R1
250-492-3636, Fax: 250-492-9843
western@img.net
www.pentictonwesternnews.com
Circulation: 61,316 *Frequency: Wed., Fri., Sun.*
Dan Ebanal, Editor
Mark Walker, Publisher

Port Alberni: Pennyworth
4656 Margaret St., Port Alberni, BC V9Y 6H2
250-723-3709
pennywth@uniserve.com
Circulation: 10,885 *Frequency: Wed.*
Linda Patterson

Port Coquitlam: The Tri-City News
1405 Broadway St., Port Coquitlam, BC V3C 6L6
604-525-6397
brian@tricitynews.com
www.tricitynews.com
Circulation: 161,637 *Frequency: Wed., Fri., Sun.*
Brian McCristall, Publisher

Port Hardy: North Island Gazette
PO Box 458, 7305 Market St., Port Hardy, BC V0N 2P0
250-949-6225, Fax: 250-949-7655
publisher@northislandgazette.com
northislandgazette.com
Circulation: 2,228 *Frequency: Wed.*
Teresa Bird, Publisher

Powell River: Powell River Peak
4400 Marine Ave., Powell River, BC V8A 2K1
604-485-5313, Fax: 604-485-5007
publisher@prpeak.com
www.prpeak.com
Circulation: 11,680 *Frequency: Wed., Fri.*
Joyce Carlson, Publisher
Laura Walz, Editor

Prince George: Prince George Free Press
1773 South Lyon St., Prince George, BC V2N 1T3
250-564-0005, Fax: 250-562-0025
editor@pgfreepress.com
pgfreepress.com
Circulation: 59,590 *Frequency: Wed., Fri.*
Dennis Chapman, Publisher
Darlene Osborne, General Manager
Bill Phillips, Editor

Prince George: Prince George This Week
145 Brunswick St., Prince George, BC V2L 2B2
250-563-9988, Fax: 250-562-5012
Circulation: 32,500 *Frequency: Sun.; also Central Interior Buy & Sell (Wed. 8,000)*
Christine Skorepa, Editor

Princeton: Similkameen News Leader
PO Box 956, 226A Bridge St., Princeton, BC V0X 1W0
250-295-4149, Fax: 250-295-4103, 888-350-9969
george@thenewsleader.ca
www.thenewsleader.ca
Circulation: 1,400
W. George Elliott, Publisher/Owner

Princeton: Similkameen Spotlight
PO Box 340, Princeton, BC V0X 1W0
250-295-3535, Fax: 250-295-7322
editor@similkameenspotlight.com
www.similkameenspotlight.com
Circulation: 1,372 *Frequency: Wed.*
Geri Swanson, Publisher
Richard MacKenzie, Editor

Queen Charlotte: Queen Charlotte Islands Observer
PO Box 205, 623 - 7th St., Queen Charlotte, BC V0T 1S0
250-559-4680, Fax: 250-559-8433
observer@qcislands.net
www.qciobserver.com
Circulation: 1,444 *Frequency: Thu.*

Quesnel: Cariboo Observer
188 Carson Ave., Quesnel, BC V2J 2A8
250-992-2121
advertising@quesnelobserver.com
www.quesnelobserver.com
Circulation: 14,162 *Frequency: Wed., Sun.*
Darcy Wiebe, Publisher
Andrea Johnston, Editor

Quesnel: The Quesnel Advisor
369C Anderson Dr., Quesnel, BC V2J 2G1
250-992-5572, Fax: 250-992-6044
editorial@quesneladvisor.com
www.quesneladvisor.com
Circulation: 7,546 *Frequency: Wed.*
Kim Saunders, Publishers

Revelstoke: Revelstoke Times Review
PO Box 20, Revelstoke, BC V0E 2S0
250-837-4667
www.revelstoketimesreview.com
Circulation: 2,040 *Frequency: Wed.*
Mavis Cann, Publisher
David F. Rooney, Editor

Richmond: Richmond Review
#140, 5671 No. 3 Rd., Richmond, BC V6X 2C7
604-247-3700
www.richmondreview.com
Circulation: 94,215 *Frequency: Thu., Sat.*
Josh O'Connor, Publisher

Salmon Arm: Salmon Arm Observer
PO Box 550, 51 Hudson Ave., Salmon Arm, BC V1E 4N7
250-832-2131, Fax: 250-832-5140
newsroom@saobserver.net
www.saobserver.net
Other information: Ad Email: advertising@saobserver.net
Circulation: 3,687 *Frequency: Wed.*
Tracy Hughes, Editor
Ron Lovestone, Publisher

Salmon Arm: The Shuswap Market News
PO Box 550, Salmon Arm, BC V1E 4N7
250-832-2131, Fax: 250-832-5140
newsroom@saobserver.net
www.saobserver.net
Other information: Ad Email: advertising@saobserver.net
Circulation: 14,786 *Frequency: Fri.*
Ron Lovestone, Publisher
Tracy Hughes, Editor

Salt Spring Island: Gulf Islands Driftwood
Driftwood Publishing Ltd., 328 Lower Ganges Rd., Salt Spring Island, BC V8K 2V3
250-537-9933, Fax: 250-537-2613, 877-537-9933
driftwood@gulfislands.net
www.gulfislands.net
Circulation: 4,311 *Frequency: Wed.*
Penny Sakamoto, Publisher

Sechelt: Coast Reporter
PO Box 1388, 5485 Warf Rd., Sechelt, BC V0N 3A0
604-885-4811, Fax: 604-885-4818
classified@coastreporter.net
www.coastreporter.net
Circulation: 13,123 *Frequency: Fri.*
Peter Kvarnstrom, Publisher

Sicamous: Eagle Valley News
PO Box 113, 1133 Parksville St., Sicamous, BC V0E 2V0
250-836-2570, Fax: 250-836-2661
evnews@bcnewsgroup.com
Circulation: 942 *Frequency: Wed.*
Ron Lovestone, Publisher
Tracy Hughes, Editor

Sidney: Peninsula News Review
9726 First St., Sidney, BC V8L 3C9
250-656-1151, Fax: 250-656-5526
penreview@vinewsgroup.com
www.peninsulanewsreview.com
Circulation: 13,796 *Frequency: Wed.*

Susan Hodgson, Publisher
Judy Reimche, Editor

***Smithers:* Interior News**
PO Box 2560, Smithers, BC V0J 2N0
250-847-3266, Fax: 250-847-2995
advertising@interior-news.com
www.interior-news.com
Circulation: 3,838 *Frequency: Wed.*
Vic Swan, Publisher

***Sooke:* Sooke News Mirror**
PO Box 339, 6711 Eustace Rd., Sooke, BC V0S 1N0
250-642-5752, Fax: 250-642-4767
rod@vinewsgroup.com
www.sookenewsmirror.com
Circulation: 5,394 *Frequency: Wed.*
Rod Sluggett, Publisher

***Squamish:* Squamish Chief**
PO Box 3500, 38117 - 2nd Ave., Squamish, BC V8B 0B9
604-892-9161, Fax: 604-892-8483
www.squamishchief.com
Circulation: 3,866 *Frequency: Fri.*
Cathryn Atkinson, Editor
Tim Shoults, Publisher

***Summerland:* Summerland Review**
PO Box 309, 13224 Victoria Rd., Summerland, BC V0H 1Z0
250-494-5406
www.summerlandreview.com/
Circulation: 2,327 *Frequency: Thurs.*
Mark Walker, Publisher
John Arendt, Editor

***Surrey:* Apna Roots**
#103, 12414 - 82nd Ave., Surrey, BC V3W 3E9
604-599-5021, Fax: 604-599-5415
staff@apnaroots.com
www.apnaroots.com
Circulation: 15,000 *Frequency: Weekly*
Rue Hayer Bains, Publisher

***Surrey:* Cloverdale Reporter News & Traveling Times**
17586 - 56A Ave., Surrey, BC V3S 1G3
604-575-2405, Fax: 604-575-2406
crnews@shaw.ca
www.cloverdalereporter.com
Circulation: 20,000
Ursula Maxwell, Publisher/Managing Editor

***Surrey:* Indo-Canadian Times**
#103, 12414 - 82nd Ave., Surrey, BC V3W 3E9
604-599-5408, Fax: 604-599-5415
indo@direct.ca, indo@telus.net
www.indo-canadiantimes.com
Circulation: 32,000 *Frequency: Weekly; Punjabi*
Rupinder Hayer, Publisher

***Surrey:* The Indo-Canadian Voice**
#200, 12732 - 80th Ave., Surrey, BC V3W 3A7
604-502-6100, Fax: 604-502-6111
ads@voiceonline.com
www.voiceonline.com/voice/thisweek/
Circulation: 15,000 *Frequency: Weekly*
Vinnie Combow, Editor

***Surrey:* The Leader**
#205, 5450 - 152nd St., Surrey, BC V3S 5J9
604-575-2744
newsroom@surreyleader.com
www.surreyleader.com
Circulation: 259,235 *Frequency: Wed., Fri., Sun.*
Bruce McAuliffe, Publisher, publisher@surreyleader.com
Andrew Holota, Editor

***Surrey:* The Link**
#101, 13463 - 78th Ave., Surrey, BC V3W 0A8
604-591-5160, Fax: 604-591-2113
linknews@smartt.com
www.thelinkpaper.ca
Circulation: 17,000 *Frequency: Sat.*
Rakesh Puri, General Manager

***Surrey:* Surrey Now**
#201, 7889 - 132nd St., Surrey, BC V3W 4N2
604-572-0064, Fax: 604-572-6438
ghollick@thenownewspaper.com
www.thenownewspaper.com
Circulation: 115,000 *Frequency: Tues., Fri.*
Gary Hollick, Publisher

***Terrace:* The Terrace Standard**
3210 Clinton Ave., Terrace, BC V8G 5R2
250-638-7283, Fax: 250-638-8432
newsroom@terracestandard.com
www.terracestandard.com
Circulation: 7,963 *Frequency: Wed.; also The Skeena Marketplace (Sat., circ. 10,200)*
Rod Link, Publisher

***Ucluelet:* The Westerly News**
PO Box 317, 1701 Peninsula Rd., Ucluelet, BC V0R 3A0
250-726-7029, Fax: 250-726-4282
westnews@ukeecable.net
home.ukeecable.net/%7Ewestnews
Circulation: 1,108 *Frequency: Wed.*
Susan McIntyre, Publisher

***Valemount:* The Valley Sentinel**
PO Box 688, 1012 Commercial Dr., Valemount, BC V0E 2Z0
250-566-4425, Fax: 250-566-4528
sentinel@valemount.com
www.thevalleysentinel.com
Circulation: 1,013 *Frequency: Wed.*
William J. Mahoney, Publisher

***Vancouver:* East Side Revue**
1574 West 6th Ave., Vancouver, BC V6J 1R2
604-738-1411
www.vancourier.com
Circulation: 118,802 *Frequency: Wed., Fri.*
Rod Raglin, Publisher

***Vancouver:* L'Express du Pacifique**
#227A, 1555, 7e av ouest, Vancouver, BC V6J 1S1
604-736-3734, Fax: 604-736-3740
administration@lexpress.org
www.lexpress.org
Circulation: 1 800 *Frequency: Lundi; aux deux semaines*
Stéphanie Descôteaux
Raphael Perdrau, directeur de la publication
Cécil Lepage, journaliste

***Vancouver:* The False Creek News**
661A Market Hill, Vancouver, BC V5Z 4B5
604-875-9626, Fax: 604-875-0336
fcnews@hotmail.com
Circulation: 25,000 *Frequency: Fri.*
A. Juma, Publisher

***Vancouver:* Jewish Independent**
#200, 291 East 2nd Ave., Vancouver, BC V5T 1B8
604-689-1520
editor@jewishindependent.ca
www.jewishbulletin.ca
Circulation: 5,000 *Frequency: Weekly*

***Vancouver:* The Vancouver Courier**
1574 - West 6th Ave., Vancouver, BC V6J 1R2
604-738-1411
www.vancourier.com
Circulation: 24,358 *Frequency: Fri.*
Peter Ballard, Publisher

***Vancouver:* West Side Revue**
1736A - 33rd Ave. East, Vancouver, BC V5N 3E2
604-327-1665,
Circulation: 7,700 *Frequency: Sun.*
Rod Raglin, Publisher

***Vancouver:* WestEnder**
200-1490 W. Broadway, Vancouver, BC V6H 4E8
604-606-8686
www.westender.com
Circulation: 56,064 *Frequency: Thu.*
James Craig, Publisher
Michael White, Editor

***Vanderhoof:* Omineca Express**
PO Box 1007, 150 West Columbia, Vanderhoof, BC V0J 3A0
250-567-9258, Fax: 250-567-2070
www.ominecaexpress.com
Circulation: 1,460 *Frequency: Wed.*
Scot Farmer, Publisher
Allan Wishart, Editor

***Vernon:* The Morning Star**
4407 - 25th Ave., Vernon, BC V1T 1P5
250-545-3322, Fax: 250-542-1510
morningstarads@bcnewsgroup.com
www.vernonmorningstar.com
Circulation: 101,536 *Frequency: Wed., Fri., Sun.*
Karen Hill, Publisher
Glenn Mitchell, Editor

***Victoria:* Country Life in B.C.**
3917 Mildred St., Victoria, BC V8Z 7A2
250-708-0085, Fax: 250-708-0095
countrylifeinbc@shaw.ca
www.countrylifeinbc.com
Circulation: 8,900 *Frequency: Monthly*
Peter Wilding, Publisher & Editor

***Victoria:* Esquimalt News**
818 Broughton St., Victoria, BC V8W 1E4
250-381-5664, Fax: 250-386-2624
wporter@vinewsgroup.com
www.esquimaltnews.com
Circulation: 14,071 *Frequency: Wed., Fri.*
Vern Faulkner, Editor
Kirk Freeman, Publisher

***Victoria:* Goldstream News Gazette**
PO Box 7310 D, #117, 777 Goldstream Ave., Victoria, BC V9B 2X4
250-478-9552, Fax: 250-478-6545
www.goldstreamgazette.com
Circulation: 33,123 *Frequency: Wed., Fri.*
Andrew Topf, Editor
Penny Sakamoto, Publisher

***Victoria:* Lookout**
c/o CFB Esquimalt, PO Box 17000 Forces, 1522 Esquimalt Rd., Victoria, BC V9A 7N2
250-363-3014, Fax: 250-363-3015
frontoffice@lookoutnewspaper.com
www.lookoutnewspaper.com
Circulation: 4,021 *Frequency: Mon.; English & French*
Melissa Atkinson, Publisher

***Victoria:* Oak Bay News**
818 Broughton St., Victoria, BC V8W 1E4
250-598-4123, Fax: 250-386-2624
www.oakbaynews.com
Circulation: 14,114 *Frequency: Wed., Fri.*
Kirk Freeman, Publisher
Jim Zeeben, Editor

***Victoria:* Saanich News**
818 Broughton St., Victoria, BC V8W 1E4
250-920-2090
saanichnews@pinc.com
www.saanichnews.com
Circulation: 65,904 *Frequency: Wed., Fri.*
Penny Sakamoto, Publisher
Jim Zeeben, Editor

***Victoria:* Victoria News**
818 Broughton St., Victoria, BC V8W 1E4
250-386-3484, Fax: 250-386-2624
www.vicnews.com
Circulation: Wed. 23,165; Fri. 23,500; Total 46,665 *Frequency: Wed., Fri.*
Kirk Freeman, Publisher
Keith Norbury, Editor

***Westbank:* Westside Weekly**
550 Doyle Ave., Westbank, BC V1Y 7V1
250-470-0748
www.kelownadailycourier.ca
Circulation: 18,316 *Frequency: Wed.*
Alison Yesilcimen, Publisher

***Whistler:* The Whistler Question**
#238, 4370 Lorimer Rd., Whistler, BC V0N 1B4
604-932-5131, Fax: 604-932-2862
general@whistlerquestiom.com
www.whistlerquestion.com
Circulation: 10,000 *Frequency: Thurs.*
Stephanie Matches, Publisher
David Burke, Editor

***White Rock:* The Peace Arch News**
1545 Johnston Rd., White Rock, BC V4B 3Z6
604-531-1711, Fax: 604-531-7977
publisher@peacearchnews.com
www.peacearchnews.com
Circulation: 63,067
Rob Demone, Editor
Linda Hooton, Publisher

***Williams Lake:* The Cariboo Advisor**
68 North Broadway, Williams Lake, BC V2G 1C1
250-398-5516, Fax: 250-398-5855
writeus@caribooadvisor.com
www.caribooadvisor.com
Circulation: 12,004 *Frequency: Wed.*

***Williams Lake:* Tribune Weekend**
188 - 1st Ave. North, Williams Lake, BC V2G 1Y8
250-392-2331
www.wltribune.com
Circulation: 6,196 *Frequency: Tue., Thu.; also the Weekender (circ. 10,300)*
Lorne Doerkson, Publisher
Bill Phillips, Editor

Manitoba

Daily Newspapers in Manitoba

***Brandon:* Brandon Sun**
501 Rosser Ave., Brandon, MB R7A 0K4
204-727-2451
www.brandonsun.com
Circulation: 16,470; Sat. 22,358 *Frequency: Evening*
Ewan Pow, Publisher
William E. Chester, General Manager

***Flin Flon:* The Reminder**
10 North Ave., Flin Flon, MB R8A 0T2
204-687-3454, Fax: 204-687-4473
online@ffdailyreminder.com
www.r-online.ca
Circulation: 3,800 *Frequency: Afternoon*

***Portage la Prairie:* Portage Daily Graphic**
PO Box 130, 1941 Saskatchewan Ave. West, Portage la Prairie, MB R1N 3B4
204-857-3427, Fax: 204-239-1270
ads.dailygraphic@shawcable.com
www.portagedailygraphic.co m
Circulation: 4,300
Barry Clayton, Publisher

***Winnipeg:* Winnipeg Free Press**
1355 Mountain Ave., Winnipeg, MB R2X 3B6
204-697-7122, Fax: 204-697-7370
letters@freepress.mb.ca
www.winnipegfreepress.com
Circulation: 119,738 Mon.-Fri., 166,422 Sat., 115,652 Sun.
Frequency: Morning
Murdoch Davis, Publisher
Bob Cox, Editor
John Sullivan, Associate Editor, 204-697-7293

***Winnipeg:* The Winnipeg Sun**
1700 Church Ave., Winnipeg, MB R2X 3A2
204-694-2022, Fax: 204-697-0759
wpgsun@wpgsun.com
www.winnipegsun.com
Circulation: 45,407 Mon.-Sat., 58,712 Sun. *Frequency: Morning*
Ed Huculak, Publisher

Other Newspapers in Manitoba

***Altona:* Altona Red River Valley Echo**
PO Box 700, Altona, MB R0G 0B0
204-324-5001, Fax: 204-324-1402
altona.echo@mts.net
www.altonaecho.com
Circulation: 6,400 *Frequency: Fri.*
Rick Reimer, General Manager

***Baldur:* Baldur-Glenboro Gazette**
PO Box 280, Baldur, MB R0K 0B0
204-535-2127, Fax: 204-827-2207
gazette@mts.net
www.baldur-glenborogazette.ca
Circulation: 1,866 *Frequency: Tue.*
Travis Johnson, Publisher
Mike Johnson, Publisher

***Beausejour:* The Clipper Weekly**
PO Box 2033, 27A - 3rd St. South, Beausejour, MB R0E 0C0
204-268-4700, Fax: 204-268-3858
mail@clipper.mb.ca
www.clipper.mb.ca
Circulation: 11,407 *Frequency: Mon.*
Kimberley MacAulay, Publisher

***Beausejour:* The Review**
726 Park Ave., Beausejour, MB R0E 0C0
204-467-2421, Fax: 204-268-4570
info@valleytimes.ca
www.beausejourreview.com
Circulation: 6,904 *Frequency: Fri.*
Lana Meier, Publisher

***Bladur:* Glenboro Gazette**
PO Box 280, Bladur, MB R0K 0B0
204-535-2127, Fax: 204-827-2207
www.baldur-glenborogazette.ca
Circulation: 1,866 *Frequency: Tue.*
Michael Johnson, Co-Publisher
Travis Johnson, Co-Publisher

***Boissevain:* Boissevain Recorder**
PO Box 220, 561 Stephen St., Boissevain, MB R0K 0E0
204-534-6479, Fax: 204-534-2977
brecorder@mts.net
www.boissevainrecorder.mb.ca
Circulation: 1,351 *Frequency: Sat.*
Lorraine Houston, Publisher & Editor

***Brandon:* Westman Review**
501 Rosser Ave., Brandon, MB R7A 0K4
204-727-2451, Fax: 204-727-0385
Circulation: 20,000 *Frequency: Sun.*

***Brandon:* Wheat City Journal**
800 Rosser Ave., Brandon, MB R7A 6N5
204-725-0209, Fax: 204-725-3021
info@wheatcityjournal.ca
www.wheatcityjournal.ca
Circulation: 20,962 *Frequency: Thursday (Weekly).*
Kyla Henderson, Editor

***Carberry:* Carberry News-Express**
PO Box 220, Carberry, MB R0K 0H0
204-834-2153, Fax: 204-834-2714
letters@carberrynews.ca
www.carberrynews.ca
Circulation: 1,146 *Frequency: Mon.*
Angie Reynolds, Advertising Manager
John Lupton, Editor & Publisher

***Carman:* The Valley Leader**
70 Main St. South, Carman, MB R0G 0J0
204-745-2051, Fax: 204-745-3976
www.carmanvalleyleader.com
Circulation: 5,852 *Frequency: Fri.*
Rick Reimer, Publisher

***Cartwright:* Southern Manitoba Review**
PO Box 249, Cartwright, MB R0K 0L0
204-529-2342, Fax: 204-529-2029
www.southernmanitobareview.com
Circulation: 867 *Frequency: Thu.*
Vicky M. Wallace, Publisher

***Darlingford:* The Southern Shopper & Review**
RR#2, Darlingford, MB R0G 0L0
Frequency: Fri.

***Dauphin:* Dauphin Herald**
PO Box 548, 120 - 1st Ave., NE, Dauphin, MB R7N 2V4
204-638-4420, Fax: 204-638-8760
dherald@mts.net
www.dauphinherald.com
Circulation: 5,426 *Frequency: Tue.*
Robert Gilroy, Publisher

***Emerson:* The Southeast Journal**
PO Box 68, Emerson, MB R0A 0L0
204-373-2493, Fax: 204-373-2084
www.connecta.com
Circulation: 2,984 *Frequency: Sat.*
Brenda Piett, Publisher

***Grandview:* Grandview Exponent**
PO Box 39, Grandview, MB R0L 0Y0
204-546-2555, Fax: 204-546-3081
expos@mts.net
www.grandviewexponent.com
Circulation: 1,178 *Frequency: Tue.*
Clayton Chaloner, Publisher & Editor

***Killarney:* Killarney Guide**
PO Box 670, 417 William Ave., Killarney, MB R0K 1G0
204-523-4611, Fax: 204-523-4445
Circulation: 2,396 *Frequency: Fri.*
Garry Struth, Publisher

***Lac du Bonnet:* Lac du Bonnet Leader**
83 - 3 St., Lac du Bonnet, MB R0E 1A0
204-467-2421, Fax: 204-345-6344
leader@mts.net
www.lacdubonnetleader.com
Circulation: 5,013 *Frequency: Fri.*
Lana Meier, Publisher

***Manitou:* Manitou Western Canadian**
PO Box 190, 424 Ellis Ave. East, Manitou, MB R0G 1G0
204-242-2555, Fax: 204-242-3137
Circulation: 1,516 *Frequency: Tue.*
Grant Howatt, Co-Publisher

***Melita:* Deloraine Times & Star**
PO Box 820, Melita, MB R0M 1L0
204-747-2249, Fax: 204-747-3999
deltimes@mb.sympatico.ca
Circulation: 1,278 *Frequency: Sat.*
Bruce Schwanke, Publisher

***Melita:* Melita New Era**
PO Box 820, 128 Main St., Melita, MB R0M 1L0
204-522-3491, Fax: 204-522-3648
newera@mts.net
Circulation: 1,713 *Frequency: Sat.*
Bruce Schwanke, Publisher

***Minnedosa:* Minnedosa Tribune**
PO Box 930, 14 - 3rd Ave., SW, Minnedosa, MB R0J 1E0
204-867-3816, Fax: 204-867-5171
trib@minnedosatribune.com
www.minnedosatribune.com
Circulation: 2,894 *Frequency: Mon.*
Jennifer Muth, Publisher

***Morden:* The Morden Times**
104 - 8th St., Morden, MB R6M 1Y7
204-822-4421, Fax: 204-822-4079
news@mordentimes.com
www.mordentimes.com
Circulation: 6,798 *Frequency: Fri.*
Rick Reimer, Publisher

***Neepawa:* Neepawa Banner**
PO Box 699, 423 Mountain Ave., Neepawa, MB R0J 1H0
204-476-2309, Fax: 204-476-5802
gibson@neepawapress.com
www.neepawabanner.com
Circulation: 11,171 *Frequency: Mon.*
Ken Waddell, Publisher & Editor

***Neepawa:* Neepawa Press**
PO Box 939, 423 Mountain Ave., Neepawa, MB R0J 1H0
204-476-2309, Fax: 204-476-5802
neepress@mts.net
www.neepawapress.com
Circulation: 8,676 *Frequency: Mon.*
Jack Gibson, Publisher

***Pilot Mound:* The Sentinel Courier**
PO Box 179, 13 Railway Ave., Pilot Mound, MB R0G 1P0
204-825-2772, Fax: 204-825-2439
sentinel@mts.net
Circulation: 1,010 *Frequency: Tue.*
Sheila Howell, Publisher

***Portage la Prairie:* Central Manitoba Shopper & News**
1943 Saskatchewan Ave. West, Portage la Prairie, MB R1N 3B4
Frequency: Tues.

***Portage la Prairie:* Central Plains Herald-Leader**
PO Box 130, 1941 Saskatchewan Ave. West, Portage la Prairie, MB R1N 3B4
204-857-3427, Fax: 204-239-1270
www.cpheraldleader.com
Circulation: 10,577 *Frequency: Sat.*
Berry Clayton, Publisher

***Reston:* Reston Recorder**
PO Box 10, Reston, MB R0M 1X0
204-877-3321, Fax: 204-877-3115
recorder@mb.sympatico.ca
www.rmofpipestone.com/recorder/advertise.htm
Circulation: 893 *Frequency: Sat.*
Bruce Schwanke, Publisher

***Rivers:* Rivers Banner**
PO Box 70, Rivers, MB R0K 1X0
204-328-7494, Fax: 204-328-5212
riversbanner@inetlink.ca
www.riversbanner.com
Circulation: 1,862 *Frequency: Sat.*
Ken Waddell, Publisher
Sheila Runions, General Manager

***Roblin:* Roblin Review**
PO Box 938, 119 - 1st Ave. NW, Roblin, MB R0L 1P0
204-937-8377, Fax: 204-937-8212
roblinreview@mts.net
Circulation: 1,731 *Frequency: Tue.*
Brent Wright, Publisher

Russell: **Russell Banner**
PO Box 100, Russell, MB R0J 1W0
204-773-2069, Fax: 204-773-2645
rbanner@mts.net
www.russellbanner.com
Circulation: 1,534 *Frequency: Tue.*
R.I. Gilroy, Publisher

Saint-Boniface: **La Liberté**
CP 190, 383 Provencher Blvd., Saint-Boniface, MB R2H 3B4
204-237-4823, Fax: 204-231-1998
la-liberte@la-liberte.mb.ca
www.journaux.apf.ca/laliberte
Circulation: 6 000 *Frequency: Vendredi; français*
Sylviane Lanthier, Directrice générale

Selkirk: **Selkirk Journal**
PO Box 190, 217 Clandeboye Ave., Selkirk, MB R1A 0X2
204-482-7402, Fax: 204-482-3336
sjournal@mts.net
www.selkirkjournal.com
Circulation: 18,363 *Frequency: Fri.*
Lana Meier, Publisher

Shilo: **Shilo Stag**
T-114 Community Centre, CFB Shilo, Shilo, MB R0K 2A0
204-765-3000, Fax: 204-765-3014
stag@escape.ca
Circulation: 3,000 *Frequency: Thurs., Bi-weekly*
Janine Avery, Editor

Shoal Lake: **Crossroads This Week**
PO Box 160, 353 Station Rd., Shoal Lake, MB R0J 1Z0
204-759-2644, Fax: 204-759-2521
gnesbitt@mts.net
www.crossroadsthisweek.com
Circulation: 2,943 *Frequency: Sat.*
Greg Nesbitt, Publisher

Souris: **Souris Plaindealer**
PO Box 488, 2 Crescent Ave. East, Souris, MB R0K 2C0
204-483-2070, Fax: 204-483-3866
Circulation: 1,425 *Frequency: Sat.*
Bruce Schwanke, Publisher

Steinbach: **The Carillon**
PO Box 1290, 377 Main St., Steinbach, MB R5G 1A5
204-326-3421, Fax: 204-326-4860, 800-442-0463
info@thecarillon.com
www.thecarillon.com
Circulation: 10,651 *Frequency: Thu.*
Rick Derksen, Publisher

Stonewall: **The Interlake Spectator**
PO Box 190, Stonewall, MB R0C 2Z0
204-642-2421, Fax: 204-642-8275
ispec@mts.net
www.interlakespectator.com
Circulation: 14,341 *Frequency: Fri.*
Lana Meier, Publisher

Stonewall: **Stonewall Argus & Teulon Times**
PO Box 190, 410 Main St., Stonewall, MB R0C 2Z0
204-467-2421, Fax: 204-467-5967
interlakepublishing@shaw.ca
stonewallargusteulontimes.com
Circulation: 3,731 *Frequency: Fri.*
Lana Meier, Publisher

Swan River: **Swan Valley Star & Times**
PO Box 670, 704 Main St., Swan River, MB R0L 1Z0
204-734-3858, Fax: 204-734-4935
info@starandtimes.ca
www.starandtimes.ca
Circulation: 3,746 *Frequency: Tue.*
Brian Gilroy, General Manager

The Pas: **Opasquia Times**
PO Box 750, 148 Fischer Ave., The Pas, MB R9A 1K8
204-623-3435, Fax: 204-623-5601
Circulation: 4,111 *Frequency: Wed., Fri.*
Brian Gilroy, Publisher

Thompson: **Nickel Belt News**
PO Box 887, 141 Commercial Pl., Thompson, MB R8N 1N8
204-677-4534, Fax: 204-677-3681
Circulation: 5,125 *Frequency: Mon.*

Thompson: **Thompson Citizen**
PO Box 887, 141 Commercial Pl., Thompson, MB R8N 1N8
204-677-4534, Fax: 204-677-3681
precambrian@mts.net
www.thompsoncitizen.net
Circulation: 2,770 *Frequency: Mon., Wed., Fri.*

John Barker, Editor
Diana Hiscock, General Manager

Treherne: **The Times**
PO Box 50, Treherne, MB R0G 2V0
204-723-2542, Fax: 204-723-2754
trehernetimes@mts.net
Circulation: 2,788 *Frequency: Mon.*
Gary Lodwick, Publisher

Virden: **Virden Empire Advance**
PO Box 250, 300 Nelson St. West, Virden, MB R0M 2C0
204-748-3931, Fax: 204-748-1816
empire12@mts.net
Circulation: 2,585 *Frequency: Sat.*
Grant/Marlain Shoemaker, Publisher
Brent Fitzpatrick, Editor

Winkler: **The Winkler Times**
PO Box 1356, Winkler, MB R6W 4B3
204-325-4771, Fax: 204-325-5059
www.winklertimes.com
Circulation: 6,531 *Frequency: Fri.*
Rick Reimer, Publisher

Winnipeg: **Farmers' Independent Weekly**
PO Box 1846 Main, Winnipeg, MB R3C 3R1
204-254-7253, Fax: 204-257-4263
info@fiwonline.com
www.fiwonline.com
John Morriss, Publisher & Editor

Winnipeg: **Headingley Headliner**
1465 St. James St., Winnipeg, MB R3H 0W9
204-798-0800, Fax: 204-953-4300
headliner@man.net
www.canstarnews.com
Circulation: 5,320 *Frequency: Fri.*
Bob Verge, Publisher

Winnipeg: **The Herald**
1465 St. James St., Winnipeg, MB R3H 0W9
204-789-0800, Fax: 204-953-4300
www.canstarnews.com
Circulation: 36,692 *Frequency: Thu.*
Bryan Metcalfe, Publisher

Winnipeg: **The Jewish Post & News**
113 Hutchings St., Winnipeg, MB R2X 2V4
204-694-3332, Fax: 204-694-3916
jewishp@mts.net
www.jewishpostandnews.com
Circulation: 2,600 *Frequency: Wed.; supplement, Lifestyles (3 times a year; circ. 30,000)*
Matt Bellan, Editor
Bernie Bellan, Business Manager

Winnipeg: **The Lance**
1465 St. James St., Winnipeg, MB R3H 0W9
204-789-0800, Fax: 204-953-4300
www.canstarnews.com
Circulation: 55,665 *Frequency: Thu.*
Bryan Metcalfe, Publisher

Winnipeg: **The Metro**
1465 St. James St., Winnipeg, MB R3H 0W9
204-789-0800, Fax: 204-953-4300
www.canstarnews.com
Circulation: 52,944 *Frequency: Thu.*
Bryan Metcalfe, Publisher

Winnipeg: **the Times**
1465 St. James St., Winnipeg, MB R3H 0W9
204-789-0800, Fax: 204-953-4300
tcweeklies@transcontinental.ca
www.canstarnews.com
Circulation: 34,736 *Frequency: Wed.*
Dale Penner, Publisher & General Manager

Winnipeg: **Voxair**
PO Box 17000 Forces, 17 Wing Winnipeg, Winnipeg, MB R3J 3Y5
204-833-2500, Fax: 204-833-2809
voxair@mts.net
www.voxair.ca
Circulation: 4,000 *Frequency: Every other Wed.; English & French*
Lt.Col. P. Conway, Editor-in-chief

New Brunswick

Daily Newspapers in New Brunswick

Caraquet: **L'Acadie Nouvelle**
CP 5536, 476, boul St-Pierre ouest, Caraquet, NB E1W 1B7
506-727-4444, Fax: 506-727-7620
infos@acadienouvelle.com
www.acadienouvelle.com/acadienouvelle/index.cfm
Circulation: 16 800 *Frequency: Matin; français*

Fredericton: **Daily Gleaner**
984 Prospect St. West, Fredericton, NB E3B 5A2
506-452-6670
info@canadaeast.com
www.canadaeast.com/dg/
Circulation: 30,200 *Frequency: Mon.-Sat.*

Moncton: **The Times-Transcript**
PO Box 1001, 939 Main St., Moncton, NB E1C 8P3
506-859-4900, Fax: 506-859-4904
news@timestranscript.com
www.canadaeast.com/tt/
Circulation: 38,394 *Frequency: Mon.-Fri.*

Saint John: **The New Brunswick Telegraph Journal**
PO Box 2350, 210 Crown St., Saint John, NB E2L 3V8
506-632-8888, Fax: 506-633-6758, 877-389-6397
newsroom@nbpub.com
www.canadaeast.com/tp/
Circulation: 41,362 *Frequency: Mon.-Sat.*

Other Newspapers in New Brunswick

Bathurst: **Northern Light**
PO Box 416, Bathurst, NB E2A 1P4
506-546-4491, Fax: 506-546-1491
Circulation: 5,516 *Frequency: Tue.*
Maurice Aube, Publisher

Campbellton: **L'Aviron**
#406, 113, rue Robeberry, Campbellton, NB E3N 2G6
506-753-7637, Fax: 506-753-3628
atelier.campbellton@hebdosquebecor.com
hebdosquebecor.com
Circulation: 6,100 *Frequency: Vendredi*
Louise Decary, Rédactrice-en-chef

Campbellton: **The Tribune**
PO Box 486, 6 Shannon St., Campbellton, NB E3N 3G9
506-753-4413, Fax: 506-759-9595
tribune@tribpub.nb.ca
www.tribpub.nb.ca
Circulation: 4,066 *Frequency: Wed.; English & French*
Nancy Cook, Publisher

Campbellton: **La Voix du Restigouche**
6 Shannon St., Campbellton, NB E3N 2Y2
506-753-4413, Fax: 506-759-9595
nouvelles@tribunenb.ca
www.tribpub.nb.ca
Circulation: 15,073 *Frequency: Sat.*
Nancy Cook, Publisher

Dieppe: **Journal Dieppe Journal**
988, rue Champlain, Dieppe, NB E1A 1P8
506-388-8200, Fax: 506-388-8201
journaldieppejournal@nb.aibn.com
www.dieppejournal.ca
Circulation: 6,178 *Frequency: Fri.*

Edmundston: **Le Madawaska**
20, rue St. François, Edmundston, NB E3V 1E3
506-735-5575, Fax: 506-735-8086
grondin.paul@brunswicknews.com
apf.ca/lemadawaska
Circulation: 9 000 *Frequency: Mercredi; bilingue*
Paul Grondin

Edmundston: **La République**
20, rue St. François, Edmundston, NB
506-735-5575,

Grand Falls: **Victoria County Star**
PO Box 7363, 229 Broadway Blvd., Grand Falls, NB E3Z 2K1
506-473-3083, Fax: 506-473-3105
rickard.mark@victoriastar.ca
Circulation: 2,549 *Frequency: Wed.*
Hermel Volpe, Publisher

Grand Sault: **La Cataracte**
CP 7363, 229, boul Broadway, Grand Sault, NB E3Z 2K1
506-473-3083,
Circulation: 5 300 *Frequency: Wed.*
Don Calhoun, Publisher

Hampton: **The Hampton Herald**
242 Main St., Hampton, NB E5N 6B8
506-832-5613, Fax: 506-832-3353
tnherald@nbnet.nb.ca
www.ossekeag.ca/hampton-herald

Hampton: **The Sussex Herald**
242 Main St., Hampton, NB E5N 6B8
506-832-5613, Fax: 506-832-3353
www.ossekeag.ca/sussex.htm

Miramichi: **Miramichi Leader**
PO Box 500, Miramichi, NB E1V 3M6
506-773-5853, Fax: 506-622-7422
news@miramichileader.com
www.miramichileader.com
Circulation: 10,506 *Frequency: Mon., Wed.*
Bill MacIntosh, Publisher
Nick Stephens, Editor

Miramichi: **Miramichi Weekend**
PO Box 500, 175 General Manson Way, Miramichi, NB E1V 3M6
506-773-5853
news@miramichileader.com
www.miramichileader.com
Circulation: 7,105 *Frequency: Fri.*
Bill MacIntosh, Publisher
Cathy Carnahan, Editor

Oromocto: **Oromocto Post-Gazette**
281 Restigouche Rd., Oromocto, NB E2V 2H5
506-357-9813,
Circulation: 15,533 *Frequency: Sat.*
Eric Lawson, Publisher

Richibucto: **L'Étoile de Kent**
#2, 9406, rue Principale, Richibucto, NB E4W 4E1
506-523-6231, Fax: 506-523-6520
redaction@journaletoile.com
Frequency: Samedi
Mario Tardiff

Riverview: **The County Chronicle**
75 Canusa Dr., Riverview, NB E1B 2W6
506-387-4085, Fax: 506-387-9096
ctychron@nbnet.nb.ca
Circulation: 8,500
David Singer, Publisher

Sackville: **Sackville Tribune-Post**
80 Main St., Sackville, NB E4L 4A7
506-536-2500, Fax: 506-536-4024
tribune@nbnet.nb.ca
Circulation: 2,603 *Frequency: Wed.*
Paul Ramsay, Publisher
Scott Doherty, Editor

Shediac: **Le Moniteur Acadien**
CP 5191, 817, Boudreau Ouest, Shediac, NB E4P 8T9
506-532-6680, Fax: 506-532-6681
moniteur@rogers.com
www.capacadie.com/moniteuracadien
Circulation: 5 132 *Frequency: Mercredi, français*
Carole Landry, Rédactrice en chef

St Stephen: **International Money Saver**
179A King St., St Stephen, NB E3L 2E4
506-466-5072, Fax: 506-466-5717
moneysav@nbnet.nb.ca
Circulation: 15,000 *Frequency: Sat.*

St Stephen: **St. Croix Courier**
PO Box 250, St Stephen, NB E3L 2X2
506-466-3220, Fax: 506-466-9950
jim@stcroixcourier.ca
www.stcroixcourier.com
Circulation: 4,019 *Frequency: Tue.; also: Courier Weekend, Atlantic Coast Guide*
Leith Orr, Publisher

Sussex: **Kings County Record**
593 Main St., Sussex, NB E4E 7H5
506-433-1070, Fax: 506-432-3532
news@kingscorecord.com
Circulation: 4,795 *Frequency: Tue.*
Beverly Gauvreau, Publisher
Gisele McKnight, Editor

Woodstock: **The Bugle**
110 Carleton St., Woodstock, NB E7M 1E4
506-328-8863, Fax: 506-328-3208
Circulation: 4,341 *Frequency: Tues.*
Ken Langdon, Publisher
Jim Dumville, Editor

Woodstock: **Bugle Observer**
110 Carleton St., Woodstock, NB E7M 1E4
506-328-8863, Fax: 506-328-3208
Circulation: 5,341 *Frequency: Tue.*
Ken Langdon, Publisher

Newfoundland & Labrador

Daily Newspapers in Newfoundland & Labrador

Corner Brook: **The Western Star**
PO Box 460, 160 West St., Corner Brook, NL A2H 6E7
709-634-4348, Fax: 709-637-4675, 800-454-4348
newsroom@thewesternstar.com
www.thewesternstar.com
Circulation: 52,500 *Frequency: Daily; Morning, Mon.- Sat.*
Robert Verge, Publisher
Richard Williams, Editor

St. John's: **The Telegram**
PO Box 5970, Columbus Dr., St. John's, NL A1C 5X7
709-364-6300, Fax: 709-364-9333
telegram@thetelegram.com
www.thetelegram.com
Circulation: 33,065 Mon.-Fri., 58,887 Sat., 33,693 Sun.
Frequency: Mon.-Fri. pm; Sat.-Sun. am
Miller H. Ayre, Publisher
Russell Wangersky, Managing Editor

Other Newspapers in Newfoundland & Labrador

Carbonear: **The Compass**
PO Box 760, 176 Water St., Carbonear, NL A1Y 1C3
709-596-6458
www.cbncompass.ca
Circulation: 4,776 *Frequency: Tue.*
Scott Courage, Publisher

Clarenville: **The Packet**
8B Thompson St., Clarenville, NL A5A 1Y9
709-466-2243
www.thepacket.ca
Circulation: 4,979 *Frequency: Mon.*
Scott Courage, Publisher

Gander: **Beacon**
PO Box 420, Gander, NL A1V 1W8
709-256-4371, Fax: 709-256-3826
info@beaconnl.ca
www.ganderbeacon.ca
Circulation: 4,585 *Frequency: Mon.*
Paul Banks, Manager/Editor

Grand Falls-Windsor: **Advertiser**
PO Box 129, Grand Falls-Windsor, NL A2A 2J4
709-489-2162
www.gfwadvertiser.ca
Circulation: 5,819 *Frequency: Mon., Thu.*
Scott Courage, Publisher

Happy Valley-Goose Bay: **The Labradorian**
PO Box 39 B, Happy Valley-Goose Bay, NL A0P 1E0
709-896-3341
www.thelabradorian.ca
Circulation: 2,019 *Frequency: Mon.*
Shawn Woodford, Publisher

Harbour Breton: **The Coaster**
PO Box 188, Harbour Breton, NL A0G 1P0
709-489-2162
www.thecoaster.ca
Circulation: 1,702 *Frequency: Tue.*
Scott Courage, Publisher

Labrador City: **The Aurora**
PO Box 423, Labrador City, NL A2V 2K7
709-944-2957
www.theaurora.ca
Circulation: 1,869 *Frequency: Mon.*
Shawn Woodford, Publisher

Lewisporte: **The Pilot**
PO Box 1210, Lewisporte, NL A0G 3A0
709-535-6910, Fax: 709-535-8640
www.lportepilot.ca
Circulation: 3,686 *Frequency: Wed.*
Scott Courage, Publisher

Lumsden: **Kittiwake Commentary**
PO Box 130, Lumsden, NL A0G 3E0
709-530-2111, Fax: 709-530-2221
Circulation: 4,500 *Frequency: Monthly*
James Combden, Editor
Audrey Manning, Publisher

Marystown: **The Southern Gazette**
PO Box 1116, Marystown, NL A0E 2M0
709-279-3188, Fax: 709-279-2628
www.southerngazette.ca
Circulation: 3,816 *Frequency: Tue.*
Scott Courage, Publisher

Paradise: **The Shoreline News**
PO Box 3065, Paradise, NL A1L 3W2
709-834-2169, Fax: 709-834-4364
tsnews@avint.net
Circulation: 14,800 *Frequency: Sun.*
Franklin Petten, Publisher

Placentia: **The Charter**
PO Box 450, Placentia, NL A0B 2Y0
709-227-5240
www.thecharter.ca
Circulation: 1,011 *Frequency: Mon.*
Scott Courage, Publisher

Port Aux Basques: **The Gulf News**
PO Box 1090, Port Aux Basques, NL A0M 1C0
709-695-3671
www.gulfnews.ca
Circulation: 2,720 *Frequency: Mon.*
Shawn Woodford, Publisher

Springdale: **The Nor-Wester**
PO Box 28, Springdale, NL A0J 1T0
709-673-3721, Fax: 709-673-4171
www.thenorwester.ca
Circulation: 3,239 *Frequency: Wed.*
Scott Courage, Publisher

St Anthony: **The Northern Pen**
PO Box 520, St Anthony, NL A0K 4S0
709-454-2191, Fax: 709-454-3718
northernpen@nf.sympatico.ca
www.northernpen.ca
Circulation: 5,186 *Frequency: Mon.*
Shawn Woodford, Publisher
Allan Bock, Editor

St. John's: **The Express**
PO Box 8660 A, St. John's, NL A1B 3T7
709-722-8500, Fax: 709-579-7745
express@optipress.ca
www.theexpress.ca
Circulation: 41,386 *Frequency: Wed.*
Scott Courage, Publisher

St. John's: **Le Gaboteur**
65 chemin Ridge, St. John's, NL A1B 4P5
709-753-9585, Fax: 709-753-9586
gaboteur@nf.sympatico.ca
www.gaboteur.ca
Circulation: 1 000 *Frequency: Bi-mensuel; français*

Stephenville: **The Georgian**
PO Box 283, Stephenville, NL A2N 2Z4
709-643-4531, Fax: 709-643-5041
georgian@optipress.ca
www.thegeorgian.ca
Circulation: 2,029 *Frequency: Tue.*
Shawn Woodford, Publisher

Northwest Territories

Other Newspapers in Northwest Territories

Fort Smith: **Slave River Journal**
PO Box 990, 207 McDougall Rd., Fort Smith, NT X0E 0P0
867-872-2784, Fax: 867-872-2754, 888-355-6729
editor.srj@auroranet.nt.ca
www.srji.com
Circulation: 1,346 *Frequency: Wed.*
Don Jaque, Publisher
Sandra Jaque, Managing Editor

Hay River: **The Hub**
8-4 Courtoreille St., Hay River, NT X0E 1G2
867-874-6577, Fax: 867-874-2679
editor@hayriverhub.com
www.hayriverhub.com
Circulation: 2,322 *Frequency: Wed.*
Chris Brodeur, Publisher

Yellowknife: **L'Aquilon**
CP 1325, Yellowknife, NT X1A 2N9

867-873-6603, Fax: 867-873-2158
aquilon@internorth.com
www.aquilon.nt.ca
Circulation: 1,000 *Frequency: Vendredi; français*
Alain Bessette, Publisher

***Yellowknife:* Deh Cho Drum**
PO Box 2820, Yellowknife, NT X1A 2R1
867-873-4031
advertising@nnsl.com
www.nnsl.com
Circulation: 1,458 *Frequency: Thu.*
Petra Ehrke, Manager, National/Territorial Advertising

***Yellowknife:* Den Cho Drum**
PO Box 2820, Yellowknife, NT X1A 2R1
867-873-4031
nnsl@nnsl.com
www.nnsl.com
Circulation: 1,450 *Frequency: Thu.*
J.W. Sigvaldson, Publisher
Michael Scott, General Manager

***Yellowknife:* Nunavut News North**
PO Box 2820, 5108 - 50th St., Yellowknife, NT X1A 2R1
867-873-4031, Fax: 867-873-8507
advertising@nnsl.com
www.nnsl.com
Circulation: 6,592 *Frequency: Mon.*
Jack Sigvaldason, Publisher

***Yellowknife:* NWT News North**
PO Box 2820, 5108 - 50th St., Yellowknife, NT X1A 2R1
867-873-4031, Fax: 867-873-8507
nnsl@nnsl.com
www.nnsl.com
Circulation: 9,158 *Frequency: Mon.*
Sig Sigvaldason, Publisher
Bruce Valpy, Managing Editor

***Yellowknife:* Yellowknifer**
PO Box 2820, 5108 - 50th St., Yellowknife, NT X1A 2R1
867-873-4031, Fax: 867-873-8507
nnsl@nnsl.com
www.nnsl.com
Circulation: Wed 5,220; Fri 5,875; Total 11,095. *Frequency: Wed., Fri.*
J.W. Sigvaldason, Publisher

Nova Scotia

Daily Newspapers in Nova Scotia

***Amherst:* Daily News**
PO Box 280, 147 South Albion St., Town Square, Amherst, NS B4H 3Z2
902-667-5102, Fax: 902-667-0419
dcole@amherstdaily.com
www.amherstdaily.com
Circulation: 3,700 *Frequency: Mon.-Sat.*
Darrell Cole, Managing Editor

***Halifax:* The Chronicle Herald, The Sunday Herald**
PO Box 610, Halifax, NS B3J 2T2
902-426-2811, Fax: 902-426-1158
newsroom@herald.ca
www.herald.ns.ca
Circulation: 114,000

***Halifax:* The Daily News**
1601 Lower Water St., Halifax, NS B3P 3J6
902-444-4444
info@hfxnews.ca
www.hfxnews.ca
Circulation: 55,000 *Frequency: Mon.-Sun.*
Jamie Thomson, Publisher

***New Glasgow:* The News**
PO Box 159, 352 East River Rd., New Glasgow, NS B2H 5E2
902-928-3500, Fax: 902-752-1945
news@ngnews.ca
www.newglasgownews.com
Circulation: 8,086 *Frequency: Evening*
Richard Russell, Publisher
Dave Glenen, Managing Editor

***Sydney:* Cape Breton Post**
PO Box 1500, 255 George St., Sydney, NS B1P 6K6
902-564-5451, Fax: 902-562-7077
news@cbpost.com
www.cbpost.com
Circulation: 27,300 *Frequency: Morning*
Fred Jackson, Managing Editor

***Truro:* Truro Daily News**
PO Box 220, 6 Louise St., Truro, NS B2N 5C3
902-893-9405, Fax: 902-893-0518
news@trurodaily.com
www.trurodaily.com
Circulation: 7,200 *Frequency: Mon.-Sat.*

Other Newspapers in Nova Scotia

***Amherst:* The Citizen**
PO Box 280, 10 Lawrence St., Amherst, NS B4H 3Z2
902-667-5102, Fax: 902-667-0419
www.amherstdaily.com
Circulation: 3,262 *Frequency: Sat.*
Richard Russell, Publisher

***Antigonish:* The Casket**
PO Box 1300, 88 College St., Antigonish, NS B2G 2L7
902-863-4370, Fax: 902-863-1943
editor@thecasket.ca
www.thecasket.ca
Circulation: 5,097 *Frequency: Wed.*
Brian Lazzuri, Editor
Ken Sims, Publisher

***Bass River:* The Shoreline Journal**
RR#1, Bass River, NS B0M 1B0
902-647-2968, Fax: 902-647-2194, 800-406-1426
shoreline@ns.sympatico.ca
Frequency: last Thu. of every month
Donna Benoit, Contact

***Berwick:* Berwick Register**
227 Commercial St., Berwick, NS B0P1E0
902-538-3180, Fax: 902-538-8583
www.berwickregister.ca
Circulation: 2,186 *Frequency: Wed.*

***Bridgewater:* Bridgewater Bulletin**
353 York St., Bridgewater, NS B4V 3K2
902-543-2457, Fax: 902-543-2228
mail@lighthouse.ns.ca
www.lighthouse.ns.ca
Circulation: 7,108 *Frequency: Wed.*
Lynn Hennigar, President

***Bridgewater:* Progress Enterprise**
353 York St., Bridgewater, NS B4V 3K2
902-634-8863, Fax: 902-634-3572
www.lighthouse.ns.ca
Circulation: 3,038 *Frequency: Wed.*
Lynn Hennigar, Publisher

***Enfield:* The Laker**
287 Hwy. 2, Enfield, NS B2T 1C9
902-883-3181, Fax: 902-883-3180
leith@advocatemediainc.com
Circulation: 5,151 *Frequency: Monthly*
Leith Orr

***Enfield:* The Weekly Press**
287 Hwy. 2, Enfield, NS B2T 1C9
902-883-3181, Fax: 902-420-0524
leith@advocatemediainc.com
www.enfieldweeklypress.com
Circulation: 1,877 *Frequency: Wed.*
Leith Orr, Publisher

***Greenwood:* The Aurora**
PO Box 99, CFB Greenwood, Greenwood, NS B0P 1N0
902-765-1494, Fax: 902-765-1717
aurora@auroranewspaper.com
www.auroranewspaper.com
Circulation: 5,900 *Frequency: Mon.; English & French*
Stephen Boates, Manager, Publisher

***Guysborough:* Guysborough Journal**
PO Box 210, 48 Main St., Guysborough, NS B0H 1N0
902-533-2851, Fax: 902-533-2750
advertising@guysboroughjournal.ca
www.guysboroughjournal.com
Circulation: 2,018 *Frequency: Wed.*
Allan Murphy, Owner
Helen Murphy, Owner

***Halifax:* The Coast, Halifax's Weekly**
5435 Portland Pl., Halifax, NS B3K 6R7
902-422-6278, Fax: 902-425-0013
coast@thecoast.ns.ca
www.thecoast.ca
Circulation: 20,000 *Frequency: Weekly*
Christine Oreskovich, Publisher
Kyle Shaw, Editor
Catherine Salisbury, President

***Inverness:* The Oran**
PO Box 100, 15767 Central Ave., Inverness, NS B0E 1N0
902-258-3400, Fax: 902-258-2632
oran@ns.aliantzinc.ca
www.oran.ca
Circulation: 4,509 *Frequency: Wed.*
Rankin MacDonald, Editor
Frank MacDonald, Publisher

***Kentville:* The Advertiser**
PO Box 430, Kentville, NS B4N 3X4
902-681-2121, Fax: 902-681-0830
nsclassified@kentvilleadvertiser.ca
www.novanewsnow.com
Circulation: 5,508 *Frequency: Tue.*
Caroline Andrews, Publisher

***Kentville:* Digby Courier**
PO Box 430, 9185 Commercial St., Kentville, NS B4N 3X4
902-245-4715, Fax: 902-245-6136
editor@digbycourier.ca
www.digbycourier.ca
Circulation: 1,801 *Frequency: Thurs.*
John DeMings, Editor

***Kentville:* Hants Journal**
PO Box 430, 9185 Commercial St., Kentville, NS B4N 3X4
902-681-2121, Fax: 902-798-5451
journal.optipresspublishing.com
Circulation: 3,154 *Frequency: Thurs.*
Caroline Andrews, Publisher

***La Butte:* Le Courrier de la Nouvelle-Écosse**
9250, Route 1, La Butte, NS B0W 2L0
902-769-3078, Fax: 902-769-3869
abonnements@lecourrier.com
www.lecourrier.com
Circulation: 1,546 *Frequency: Vendredi; français*
Marie-Claude Dion, Editor-in-chief

***Liverpool:* Liverpool Advance**
PO Box 10, 271 Main St., Liverpool, NS B0T 1K0
902-354-3441, Fax: 902-354-2455
info@theadvance.ca
www.atlanticnewsnet.ca
Circulation: 2,620 *Frequency: Tues.*
Caroline Andrews, Publisher

***Middleton:* The Annapolis County Spectator**
PO Box 880, 87 Commercial St., Middleton, NS B0S 1P0
902-825-3457
www.annapolisspectator.ca
Circulation: 3,090 *Frequency: Thurs.*
Caroline Andrews, Publisher

***Middleton:* Bridgetown Monitor**
PO Box 880, 87 Commercial St., Middleton, NS B0S 1P0
902-665-4441, Fax: 902-665-4014
Circulation: 1,445 *Frequency: Tue.; also Mirror-Examiner (Wed.)*
Kirk Cross, Publisher

***Middleton:* The Mirror-Examiner**
PO Box 880, Middleton, NS B0S 1P0
902-825-3457, Fax: 902-825-6707
Circulation: 2,411 *Frequency: Wed.*
Garnet Austen, Publisher
Lawrence Powell, Editor

***Oxford:* Oxford Journal**
PO Box 10, Oxford, NS B0M 1P0
902-447-2051, Fax: 902-447-2055
thejournal@ns.sympatico.ca
Circulation: 2,460 *Frequency: Wed.*
Charlie Weeks, Editor
Paul Marchant, Publisher

***Pictou:* Pictou Advocate**
PO Box 1000, 21 George St., Pictou, NS B0K 1H0
902-485-8014, Fax: 902-752-4816
leith@advocatemediainc.com
www.pictouadvocate.com
Circulation: 3,173 *Frequency: Wed.*
Leith Orr, Publisher
Jason Warren, Editor

***Pictou:* The Tatamagouche Light**
PO Box 1000, Pictou, NS B0K 1H0
902-485-8014,
Circulation: 4,015 *Frequency: Mon.*
Leith Orr, Publisher

***Port Hawkesbury:* The Reporter**
2 MacLean Ct., Port Hawkesbury, NS B9A 3K2

902-625-3300, Fax: 902-625-1701
Circulation: 4,390 *Frequency: Tue., Fri.*
Rick Cluett, Publisher

Shelburne: The Coast Guard
PO Box 100, 164 Water St., Shelburne, NS B0T 1W0
902-875-3244, Fax: 902-875-3454
www.novanewsnow.com
Circulation: 4,058 *Frequency: Tue.*
Caroline Andrews, Publisher

Springhill: Springhill & Parrsboro Record
PO Box 670, 72 Main St., Springhill, NS B0M 1X0
902-597-3731, Fax: 902-667-1402
www.springhillrecord.com
Circulation: 1,673 *Frequency: Wed.*
Kevin Cummings, General Manager

Yarmouth: The Vanguard
PO Box 128, 2 Second St., Yarmouth, NS B5A 4B1
902-742-7111, Fax: 902-742-2311
www.novanews.com
Circulation: 5,242 *Frequency: Tue.*
Caroline Andrews, Publisher

Nunavut

Other Newspapers in Nunavut

Iqaluit: Nunatsiaq News
PO Box 8, Iqaluit, NU X0A 0H0
867-979-5357, Fax: 867-979-4763
editor@nunatsiaq.com
www.nunatsiaq.com
Circulation: 5,916 *Frequency: Fri.; English & Inuktitut*
Steven Roberts, Publisher

Yellowknife: Kivalliq News
PO Box 2820, Yellowknife, NU X1A 2R1
867-873-4031, Fax: 867-873-8507
advertising@nnsl.com
www.nnsl.com
Circulation: 1,746 *Frequency: Wed.*
Petra Ehrke, Advertising Manager

Ontario

Daily Newspapers in Ontario

Barrie: Barrie Examiner
Osprey Media Group, 571 Bayfield St. North, Barrie, ON L4M 4Z9
705-726-6537, Fax: 705-728-7717
news@thebarrieexaminer.com
www.thebarrieexaminer.com
Circulation: 10,558 *Frequency: Evening, Mon.-Sat.*
Mike Beaudin, Managing Editor
Mike Power, Publisher

Belleville: The Intelligencer
45 Bridge St. East, Belleville, ON K8N 5C7
613-962-9171, Fax: 613-962-9652
newsroom@intelligencer.ca
www.intelligencer.ca/webapp/sitepages/
Circulation: Mon.-Fri., Sun. 16,998; Sat. 18,000 *Frequency: Afternoon*
Roger Cazabon, Managing Editor

Brantford: The Expositor
Southam Publications, PO Box 965, 53 Dalhousie St., Brantford, ON N3T 5S8
519-756-2020, Fax: 519-756-4911
www.brantfordexpositor.ca
Circulation: 22,082 *Frequency: Morning*
Michael Pearce, Publisher

Brockville: Recorder & Times
PO Box 10, 1600 California Ave., Brockville, ON K6V 5T8
613-342-4441, Fax: 613-342-4456, 800-267-4434
editor@recorder.ca
www.recorder.ca
Circulation: 13,500 *Frequency: Evening, Mon.-Sat.*
Jeff Lawson, Manager, Advertising
Bob Pearce, Publisher

Chatham: Chatham Daily News
Osprey Media Group, PO Box 2007, 45 - 4th St., Chatham, ON N7M 5M6
519-354-2000, Fax: 519-354-9489
news@chathamdailynews.ca
www.chathamdailynews.ca/webapp/sitepages
Circulation: 13,373 *Frequency: Evening*
Bruce Corcoran, Managing Editor

Cobourg: Cobourg Daily Star
Northumberland Publishers, PO Box 400, 99 King St. West, Cobourg, ON K9A 4L1
905-372-0131, Fax: 905-372-4966
cdsletters@northumberlandtoday.com
www.northumberlandtoday.com
Circulation: 4,503 *Frequency: Evening*
Darren J. Murphy, Publisher
Mandy Martin, Managing Editor

Cornwall: Standard-Freeholder
44 Pitt St., Cornwall, ON K6J 3P3
613-933-3160, Fax: 613-933-7521
www.standard-freeholder.com
Circulation: 14,800 *Frequency: Morning, Mon.-Sat.*
Milton Ellis, Publisher

Fort Frances: Daily Bulletin
PO Box 339, 116 - 1st St. East, Fort Frances, ON P9A 3M7
807-274-5373, Fax: 807-274-7286, 800-465-8508
news@fortfrances.com
www.fftimes.com
Circulation: 2,500 *Frequency: Afternoon*
J.R. Cumming, Publisher
Mike Behan, Editor

Guelph: The Guelph Mercury
#8, 14 Macdonell St., Guelph, ON N1H 6P7
519-822-4310, 866-871-9868
editor@guelphmercury.com
www.guelphmercury.com/
Circulation: 40,578 *Frequency: Evening*
Phil Andrews, Managing Editor

Hamilton: The Hamilton Spectator
PO Box 300, 44 Frid St., Hamilton, ON L8N 3G3
905-526-3333, Fax: 905-526-1395, 800-263-6902
www.thespec.com
Circulation: 103,664 Mon.-Fri., 118,606 Sat. *Frequency: Evening*
Pat Collins, Publisher, pcollins@thespec.com
MarkGary Goodale, Director, Circulation & Marketing, mgoodale@thespec.com

Kenora: Daily Miner & News
PO Box 1620, 33 Main St. South, Kenora, ON P9N 3X7
807-468-5555, Fax: 807-468-4318
minerandnews@norcomcable.com
www.kenoradailyminerandnews. com
Circulation: 4,000 *Frequency: Evening*
Mitch Wolfe, Publisher

Kingston: The Kingston Whig-Standard
PO Box 2300, 6 Cataraqui St., Kingston, ON K7L 4Z7
613-544-5000, Fax: 613-530-4122
kinwhig@thewhig.com
www.thewhig.com
Circulation: 27,695 Mon.-Fri., 38,822 Sat. *Frequency: Morning & evening*
Fred Laflamme, Publisher
Christina Spencer, Editor

Kirkland Lake: Northern Daily News
Osprey Media Group, PO Box 1030, 8 Duncan Ave., Kirkland Lake, ON P2N 3L4
705-567-5321, Fax: 705-567-6162
news@northernnews.ca
www.northernnews.ca/webapp/sitepages/
Circulation: 5,800 *Frequency: Evening*
Joe O'Grady, Managing Editor

Kitchener: The Record
160 King St. East, Kitchener, ON N2G 4E5
519-894-2231, Fax: 519-894-3829
recordlibrary@therecord.com
www.therecord.com
Circulation: 81,702 *Frequency: Morning, 6 days a week*
Lynn Haddrall, Editor

Lindsay: The Lindsay Daily Post
17 William St. North, Lindsay, ON K9V 3A3
705-324-2113, Fax: 705-324-0174
linretail@thepost.ca
www.thepost.ca
Circulation: 5,500 *Frequency: Morning*
Andy Wheeler, Publisher
Andrew Carroll, Editor

London: The London Free Press
PO Box 2280, 369 York St., London, ON N6A 4G1
519-679-6666, Fax: 519-667-4523, 800-265-4105
letters@lfpress.com
www.lfpress.com
Circulation: 91,716 Sun.-Fri., 110,223 Sat. *Frequency: Morning*
Paul Berton, Editor-in-chief
Susan Muszak, Publisher & CEO

Niagara Falls: Review
Niagara Newspaper Group, PO Box 270, 4801 Valley Way, Niagara Falls, ON L2E 6T6
905-358-5711, Fax: 905-356-0785
citydesk@nfreview.com
www.niagarafallsreview.ca
Circulation: 17,000 *Frequency: Morning*
David A. Beattie, Publisher
Joe Wallace, Editor

North Bay: North Bay Nugget
Osprey Media Group, 259 Worthington St. West, North Bay, ON P1B 8J6
705-472-3200, Fax: 705-472-1438
nugget@nugget.ca
www.nugget.ca
Circulation: 29,000 *Frequency: Evening, Mon.-Fri.; morning, Sat.*
Paul McCuaig, Publisher
John Size, Managing Editor

Orillia: Packet & Times
Osprey Media Group, 31 Colborne St. East, Orillia, ON L3V 1T4
705-325-1355, Fax: 705-325-7691
www.orilliapacket.com
Circulation: 13,092
Andrea Demeer, Publisher
Casandra Bellefeuille, Editor

Ottawa: Le Droit
CP 8860 T, #222, 47 Clarence St., Ottawa, ON K1N 3J9
613-562-0111, Fax: 613-562-7572
ledroit@ledroit.com
www.cyberpresse.ca/droit
Circulation: 33 281 lun.-ven., 40 638 sam. *Frequency: Matin; français*
Jacques Pronovost, Editeur/Président
Andre Larocque, Rédacteur

Ottawa: Metro Ottawa
#402, 116 Albert St., Ottawa, ON K1P 5G3
613-236-5058, Fax: 866-253-2024
ottawalistings@metronews.ca
www.metronews.ca
Other information: Toll Free Fax: 1-866-253-2024
Circulation: 60,000
Dara Mottahed, Publisher

Ottawa: The Ottawa Citizen
PO Box 5020, 1101 Baxter Rd., Ottawa, ON K2C 3M4
613-829-9100, Fax: 613-726-1198, 800-267-6100
www.ottawacitizen.com
Circulation: 129,852 Mon.-Fri., 161,901 Sat., 129,749 Sun.
Jim Orban, Publisher & General Manager
Scott Anderson, Editor

Ottawa: The Ottawa Sun
6 Antares Dr., Ottawa, ON K1G 5H7
613-739-7000, Fax: 613-739-8041
oped@sunpub.com
www.ottawasun.com
Circulation: 25,176 Mon.-Fri., 55,197 Sun., 47,710 Sat. *Frequency: Morning*
Mike Therien, Editor-in-chief
Rick Gibbons, Publisher

Owen Sound: Sun Times
Osprey Media Group, PO Box 200, 290 - 9th St. East, Owen Sound, ON N4K 3P2
519-376-2250, Fax: 519-376-7190
cmcmenemy@thesuntimes.ca
www.owensoundsuntimes.com
Circulation: 24,198 *Frequency: Evening*

Pembroke: The Daily Observer
Osprey Media Group, 186 Alexander St., Pembroke, ON K8A 4L9
613-732-3691, Fax: 613-732-2226
editor@thedailyobserver.ca
www.thedailyobserver.ca
Circulation: 5,950 *Frequency: Evening*
Peter Lapinskie, Managing Editor

Peterborough: Examiner
Osprey Media Group, PO Box 3890, 730 Kingsway, Peterborough, ON K9J 8L4
705-745-4641, Fax: 705-741-3217
news1@ptbo.igs.net
www.thepeterboroughexaminer.com
Circulation: 25,453 Mon.-Sat., 23,367 Sun. *Frequency: Morning*

Jim Ambrose, Publisher
Ed Arnold, Managing Editor

Port Hope: Port Hope Evening Guide
Osprey Media Group, 97 Walton St., Port Hope, ON L1A 1N4
905-885-2471, Fax: 905-885-7442
www.northumberlandtoday.com
Francis Baker, Managing Editor
Rob Forbes, Publisher & General Manager

Sarnia: Observer
Osprey Media Group, 140 South Front St., Sarnia, ON N7T 7M8
519-344-3641, Fax: 519-332-2951, 800-668-0564
editorial@theobserver.ca
www.theobserver.ca
Circulation: 22,415 *Frequency: Mon.-Fri., Evening; Sat., morning*
Daryl Smith, Publisher
Rod Hilts, Managing Editor

Sault Ste Marie: Sault Star
145 Old Garden River Rd., Sault Ste Marie, ON P6A 5M5
705-759-3030, Fax: 705-759-0102
ssmstar@saultstar.com
www.saultstar.com
Circulation: 20,003, Mon. - Sat. *Frequency: Evening (morning Sat.)*

Simcoe: Tuesday Times Reformer
PO Box 370, 50 Gilberston Dr., Simcoe, ON N3Y 4L2
519-426-5710, Fax: 519-426-9255
refedit@bowesnet.com
www.simcoereformer.ca
Circulation: 19,630 *Frequency: Tues.*
Kim Novak, Managing Editor

St Catharines: The St Catharines Standard
17 Queen St., St Catharines, ON L2R 5G5
905-684-7251, Fax: 905-684-6032
standard@stcatharinesstandard.ca
www.scstandard.com
Circulation: 33,000 Mon.-Fri., 47,000 Sat. *Frequency: Afternoon*
Andrea Krilluck, Managing Editor
Paul McCuaig, Publisher

St Thomas: The St. Thomas Times-Journal
16 Hincks St., St Thomas, ON N5R 5Z2
519-631-2790, Fax: 519-631-5653, 800-663-3410
www.stthomastimesjournal.com
Circulation: 7,971 *Frequency: Evening*
Bev Ponton, Publisher
Ross Porter, Managing Editor

Stratford: The Beacon-Herald
PO Box 430, 16 Packham Rd., Stratford, ON N5A 6T6
519-271-2220, Fax: 519-271-1031, 800-265-8577
bhadvertising@bowesnet.com
www.stratfordbeaconherald.com
Circulation: 11,457 *Frequency: Daily*
Amber Olgilvie, Publisher
Larke Turnbull, City Editor

Sudbury: The Sudbury Star
33 MacKenzie St., Sudbury, ON P3C 4Y1
705-674-5271, Fax: 705-674-6834
thesudburystar@thesudburystar.com
www.thesudburystar.com/webapp/sitepage s/
Circulation: 26,333 Mon.-Sat., 23,960 Sun. *Frequency: Morning*
Roger Cazebon, Managing Editor
Dan Johnson, Publisher

Thunder Bay: The Chronicle-Journal
Horizon Operations (Canada) Ltd., 75 South Cumberland St., Thunder Bay, ON P7B 1A3
807-343-6200, Fax: 807-345-3582
editor@chroniclejournal.com
www.chroniclejournal.com
Frequency: 29,110 Mon.-Fri.; 31,764 Sat.; 26,513 Sun.
Brian Dryden, Managing Editor
Colin Bruce, Publisher

Timmins: Daily Press
c/o Osprey Media Group Inc., 187 Cedar St. South, Timmins, ON P4N 7G1
705-268-5050, Fax: 705-268-7373
news@thedailypress.ca
www.timminspress.com
Circulation: 13,541 *Frequency: Morning*
Bruce Cowan, Publisher & General Manager
David McGee, Managing Editor

Toronto: Daily Racing Form
47 Voyageur Ct. North, Toronto, ON M9W 4Y2
416-798-1911, Fax: 416-798-1919
Circulation: 3,570 Mon., 5,529 Tue.-Fri. 9,558 Sat., 8,465 Sun.
Frequency: Morning
Bill Tallon, Editor

Toronto: The Globe and Mail
444 Front St. West, Toronto, ON M5V 2S9
416-585-5600, Fax: 416- -
www.globeandmail.com
Circulation: 316,428 *Frequency: Morning, Mon. to Sat.; also Report on Business Magazine, Globe Television*
Isabella Cattelan, CFO
Phillip Crawley, Publisher & CEO
Edward Greenspon, Editor-in-chief

Toronto: Metro Toronto
703, 1 Concorde Gate, Toronto, ON M3C 3N6
416-486-4900, Fax: 416-482-8097
www.metronews.ca
Circulation: 220,000
Greg Lutes, Publisher

Toronto: National Post
300-1450 Don Mills Rd., Toronto, ON M3B 3R5
416-383-2300, Fax: 416-383-2305
www.nationalpost.com
Frequency: Mon.-Fri. (175,238); Sat. (217,115)
Gordon Fisher, President
Douglas Kelly, Publisher
Mark Spencer, Vice-President, Advertising Sales
Jonathan Harris, Vice-President, Digital Media
Santina Zito, Vice-President, Operations
Stephen Meurice, Editor-in-chief

Toronto: Toronto 24 hours
333 King St. East, Toronto, ON M5A 3X5
416-350-6400, Fax: 416-350-6523
Circulation: 238,612
Bob Harris, Publisher

Toronto: The Toronto Star
One Yonge St., Toronto, ON M5E 1E6
416-367-4500, Fax: 416-869-4328
city@thestar.ca
www.thestar.com
Circulation: 390,163 Mon.-Fri., 566,706 Sat., 347,790 Sun.
Frequency: Morning, 2 editions
John D. Cruickshank, Publisher
Michael Cooke, Editor, lettertoed@thestar.ca

Toronto: The Toronto Sun
Sun Media Corp., 333 King St. East, Toronto, ON M5A 3X5
416-947-2222, Fax: 416-368-0374
www.torontosun.com
Circulation: 179,004, Mon.-Fri., 151,101, Sat., 311,689, Sun.
Frequency: Morning
Mike Power, Publisher
James Wallace, Editor-in-chief, james.wallace@sunmedia.ca

Welland: The Tribune
PO Box 278, 228 East Main St., Welland, ON L3B 5P5
905-732-2411, Fax: 905-732-3660
tribune@wellandtribune.ca
www.wellandtribune.ca
Circulation: 14,260
Mike Walsh, Publisher & General Manager
George Duma, Managing Editor

Windsor: The Windsor Star
167 Ferry St., Windsor, ON N9A 4M5
519-255-5768, Fax: 519-255-5520
letters@win.southam.ca
www.canada.com/windsorstar
Circulation: 72,514 Mon.-Fri., 82,127 Sat. *Frequency: Morning*
Marty Beneteau, Editor
Jim McCormack, Publisher

Woodstock: Sentinel-Review
16 Brock St., Woodstock, ON N4S 8A5
519-537-2341, Fax: 519-537-3049
osn@annexweb.com
www.woodstocksentinelreview.com
Circulation: 9,600 *Frequency: Evening; supplement - CoverStory (weekly, circ. 15,200)*
Pat Logan, Group Publisher

Other Newspapers in Ontario

20 Hanna Court: Stirling Shield
20 Hanna Court, ON K8P 5J2
613-962-0234
www.shieldmedia.ca
Circulation: 2,872 *Frequency: Fri.*
Earl Jones, Publisher

Ailsa Craig: Middlesex Banner
PO Box 433, 175 Main St., Ailsa Craig, ON N0M 1A0
519-293-1095
www.banner.on.ca
Circulation: 1,170 *Frequency: Wed.*
Brad Harness, Publisher

Ajax: Ajax/Pickering News Advertiser
130 Commercial Ave., Ajax, ON L1S 2H5
905-683-5110, Fax: 905-683-7363
www.durhamregion.com
Circulation: 142,337 *Frequency: Wed., Fri., Sun.*
Tim Whittaker, Publisher
Tony Doyle, Editor

Alexandria: Glengarry News
PO Box 10, 3 Main St., Alexandria, ON K0C 1A0
613-525-2020, Fax: 613-525-3824
gnews@glengarrynews.ca
www.glengarrynews.ca
Circulation: 6,242 *Frequency: Wed.*
J. T. Grossmith, Publisher

Alliston: Alliston Herald
PO Box 280, #22, 169 Dufferin St. South, Alliston, ON L9R 1E6
705-435-6228, Fax: 705-435-3342
www.simcoe.com
Circulation: 23,475 *Frequency: Wed., Fri.*
Joe Anderson, Publisher

Amherstburg: The Amherstburg Echo
238 Dalhousie St., Amherstburg, ON N9V 1W4
519-736-2147, Fax: 519-736-8384
echooffice@bowesnet.com
www.amherstburgecho.com
Circulation: 8,283 *Frequency: Tue.*

Arnprior: Arnprior Chronicle-Guide
116 John St. North, Arnprior, ON K7S 2N6
613-623-6571, Fax: 613-623-7518
dwalter@runge.net
www.runge.net
Circulation: 2,400 *Frequency: Tue.*
Bryan Wiltsie, Publisher

Arthur: Arthur Enterprise-News
PO Box 310, 106 Charles St. East, Arthur, ON N0G 1A0
519-848-2410, Fax: 519-848-3665
enterprise@wellingtonnorth.com
www.wellingtonnorth.com
Circulation: 748 *Frequency: Fri.*
Lynne Pinnegar, Publisher

Atikokan: Atikokan Progress
PO Box 220, 109 Main St. East, Atikokan, ON P0T 1C0
807-597-2731, Fax: 807-597-6103
progress@nwon.com
Circulation: 1,513 *Frequency: Mon.*
Eve Shine, Publisher
Michael P. McKinnon, Editor

Aurora: The Auroran
#3, 75 Mary St., Aurora, ON L4G 1G3
www.auroran.com
Rosemary Schumaker, Publisher
Ron W. Wallace, Editor

Aylmer: Aylmer Express
PO Box 160, Aylmer, ON N5H 2R9
519-773-3126, Fax: 519-773-3147
Circulation: 3,886 *Frequency: Wed.*
John Hueston, Publisher

Ayr: Ayr News
PO Box 1173, Ayr, ON N0B 1E0
519-632-7432, Fax: 519-632-7743
Circulation: 3,588 *Frequency: Wed.*
James W. Schmidt, Publisher
John P. Schmidt, Editor

Bancroft: Bancroft Times
PO Box 1894, 93 Hastings St. North, Bancroft, ON K0L 1C0
613-332-2300, Fax: 613-332-4887
bancroft-times@sympatico.ca
Circulation: 4,971 *Frequency: Thurs.*
David Walker, Publisher

Barrie: Barrie Advance
21 Patterson Rd., Barrie, ON L4N 7W6
705-726-0573, Fax: 705-726-9350
www.simcoe.com
Circulation: 112,078 *Frequency: Wed., Fri.*

Joe Anderson, Publisher

***Barrie:* Super Shopper, Buy, Trade & Sell**
124 Brock St., Barrie, ON L4N 2M2
705-726-6015, Fax: 705-726-6015, 800-461-7585
ads@supershopper.com
www.supershopper.com
Circulation: 13,271 *Frequency: Thu.*
Laurie Crosson

***Barrys Bay:* Barry's Bay This Week**
PO Box 220, 41 Bay St., Barrys Bay, ON K0J 1B0
613-756-2944, Fax: 613-756-2994
bsummers@barrysbaythisweek.com
www.barrysbaythisweek.com
Circulation: 2,642 *Frequency: Wed.*
David Zilstra, General Manager
Douglas Gloin, Editor

***Beamsville:* Grimsby/West Lincoln Independent**
PO Box 400, 4309 Central Ave., Beamsville, ON L0R 1B0
905-563-5393, Fax: 905-563-7977
twilkins@rannie.com
west.niagaracommunitynewspapers.com
Circulation: 45,526 *Frequency: Wed., Fri.*
Tom Wilkinson, Editor

***Beamsville:* Lincoln Post Express**
PO Box 400, 4991 King St., Beamsville, ON L0R 1B0
905-563-5393, Fax: 905-563-7977
Circulation: 2,260

***Beeton:* Beeton/New Tecumseth Times**
PO Box 310, Beeton, ON L0G 1A0
905-729-2287, Fax: 905-729-2541
admin.syp@rogers.com
Circulation: 2,490 *Frequency: Wed.*
John Archibald, Publisher
Bruce Haire, Publisher

***Beeton:* Caledon Citizen**
PO Box 310, 34 Main St. West, Beeton, ON L0G 1A0
905-857-6626, Fax: 905-857-6363
editor@caledoncitizen.com
www.caledoncitizen.com
Circulation: 9, 814 *Frequency: Wed.*
Bruce Haire, Publisher
Mark Pavilons, Editor

***Beeton:* Innisfil Scope**
PO Box 310, 34 Main St. West, Beeton, ON L0G 1A0
905-729-2287, Fax: 905-729-2541
admin.syp@rogers.com
www.innisfilscope.com
Circulation: 11,755 *Frequency: Wed.*
John Archibald, General Manager
Bruce Haire, Publisher

***Beeton:* King Township Sentinel**
PO Box 310, Beeton, ON L0G 1A0
905-729-2287, Fax: 905-729-2541
admin.syp@rogers.com
www.kingsentinel.com
Circulation: 6,499 *Frequency: Wed.*
John Archibald, Publisher
Bruce Haire, Publisher

***Beeton:* Woodbridge Advertiser**
PO Box 379, 2 Main St. West, Beeton, ON L0G 1A0
905-729-4501, Fax: 905-729-3961, 888-285-4501
info@ontariosauctionpaper.com
Circulation: 5,500 *Frequency: Thu.*
Karl Mallette, Publisher

***Belle Ewart:* The Innisfil Enterprise**
PO Box 222, Belle Ewart, ON L0L 1C0
705-456-2424, Fax: 705-456-8249
innisfilenterprise.ca
Carol McPherson, Publisher

***Belle River:* Lakeshore News**
PO Box 429, Belle River, ON N0R 1A0
519-728-1082, Fax: 519-728-4551
www.windsoressexnews.com
Circulation: 1,759 *Frequency: Wed.*
William Harris, Editor
Gary Baxter, Publisher

***Belleville:* Belleville Shopper's Market**
PO Box 446, 365 North Front St., Belleville, ON K8N 5A5
613-962-3422, Fax: 613-962-1353
www.shoppersmarket.on.ca
Circulation: 42,800 *Frequency: Sat.*
Charles Parker, General Manager

***Belleville:* Campbellford Shield**
20 Hanna Court, Belleville, ON K8P 5J2
613-962-0234
www.shieldmedia.ca
Circulation: 4,920 *Frequency: Fri.*
Earl Jones, Publisher

***Belleville:* Hastings Shield**
20 Hanna Court, Belleville, ON K8P 5J2
613-962-0234, Fax: 613-472-5026
www.shieldmedia.ca
Circulation: 2,534 *Frequency: Fri.*
Earl Jones, Publisher

***Belleville:* Madoc Shield**
20 Hanna Court, Belleville, ON K8P 5J2
613-962-0234
www.shieldmedia.ca
Circulation: 2,885 *Frequency: Fri.*
Earl Jones, Publisher

***Belleville:* Marmora Shield**
20 Hanna Court, Belleville, ON K8P 5J2
613-962-0234
www.shieldmedia.ca
Circulation: 2,117 *Frequency: Fri.*
Nancy Derrer, Editor

***Belleville:* Norwood Shield**
20 Hanna Court, Belleville, ON K8P 5J2
613-962-0234
www.shieldmedia.ca
Circulation: 2,469 *Frequency: Fri.*
Earl Jones, Piblisher

***Belleville:* Prince Edward Free Press**
PO Box 7500, RR#7, Belleville, ON K8N 4Z7
Frequency: Tue.

***Blenheim:* Blenheim News-Tribune**
PO Box 160, 62 Talbot St. West, Blenheim, ON N0P 1A0
519-676-3321, Fax: 519-676-3454
Circulation: 2,548 *Frequency: Wed.*
Peter Laurie, Publisher

***Blyth:* The Citizen**
PO Box 429, 404 Queen St., Blyth, ON N0M 1H0
519-523-4792, Fax: 519-523-9140
norhuron@scsinternet.com
www.northhuron.on.ca
Circulation: 1,976 *Frequency: Thu.*
Keith Roulston, Publisher
Bonnie Gropp, Editor

***Bolton:* Caledon Enterprise**
PO Box 99, #4A, 12612 Hwy. 50, Bolton, ON L7E 5T1
905-857-3433, Fax: 905-857-5002
www.metroland.com
Circulation: 28, 054 *Frequency: Wed. 13,193; Sat. 14,861*
Bill Anderson, General Manager

***Borden:* The Borden Citizen**
S-138, PO Box 1000 Main, Rafah Cres., Borden, ON L0M 1C0
705-423-2496, Fax: 705-423-3452
Circulation: 6,000 *Frequency: Wed., English & French*
Col. W. Reid, Publisher

***Bothwell:* The Spirit of Bothwell**
261 Main St., Bothwell, ON N0P 1C0
519-695-2508, Fax: 519-695-5078
spirit@ciaccess.com
www.spiritofbothwell.com
Circulation: 725 *Frequency: Wed.*
Dean Muharrem, Publisher

***Bracebridge:* Bracebridge Examiner**
PO Box 1049, 16 Manitoba St., Bracebridge, ON P1L 1V2
705-645-8771, Fax: 705-645-1718
exanews@muskoka.com
www.bracebridgeexaminer.com
Circulation: 5,463 *Frequency: Wed.*
Joe Anderson, Publisher

***Bracebridge:* Muskoka Sun**
PO Box 1600, #203, 175 Manitoba St., Bracebridge, ON P1L 1V6
705-645-4463, Fax: 705-645-3928
sun@muskoka.com
Circulation: 24,500 *Frequency: Thu.; also Muskoka Life (annually)*

***Bracebridge:* The Muskokan**
PO Box 1049, 16 Manitoba St., Bracebridge, ON P1L 1V2
705-645-8771, Fax: 705-645-1718
muskokan@muskoka.com
www.muskokan.com
Circulation: 25,000 *Frequency: Thu.*
Andrew Wagner-Chazalon, Editor
Ted Britton, Publisher

***Bradford:* Bradford West Gwillimbury Times**
PO Box 1570, 74 John St. West, Bradford, ON L3Z 2B8
905-775-4471, Fax: 905-775-4489
info@times.net
www.times.net
Circulation: 11,000 *Frequency: Sat.*
Miriam King, Editor
Richard Fonger, Publisher

***Brampton:* Brampton Pennysaver**
#1, 56 Bramsteele Rd., Brampton, ON L6W 3M7
905-454-0854, Fax: 905-450-5792
pennysaver_production@wwwdc.com
www.torontowestpennysaver.com
Circulation: 177,367 *Frequency: Sun.; also publish: Caledon Pennysaver, Malton Pennysaver, Mississauga Pennysaver & Rexdale Pennysaver*
Dale Davis, General Manager

***Brampton:* Le Régional**
99 Professors Lake Pkwy., Brampton, ON L6S 4P8
905-790-3229, Fax: 905-790-9127, 800-525-6752
info@leregional.com
www.leregional.com
Circulation: 10,000 *Frequency: Mercredi*
Christiane Beaupré, Rédactrice en chef

***Brighton:* The Independent**
PO Box 1030, 1 Young St., Brighton, ON K0K 1H0
613-475-0255, Fax: 613-475-4546
newsroom@eastnorthumberland.com
www.indynews.ca
Circulation: 18,505 *Frequency: Wed.*
Stasha Conolly, Publisher

***Brockville:* St. Lawrence EMC**
7712 Kent Blvd., Brockville, ON K6V 7H6
613-342-0305, Fax: 613-498-0307
stlemc@storm.com
www.perfprint.ca
Frequency: Fri.
Duncan Weir, Publisher

***Burford:* Burford Times**
PO Box 100, 115 King St., Burford, ON N0E 1A0
519-449-5478, Fax: 519-449-5478
burfordtimes@brant.net
www.burfordtimes.com
Circulation: 2,000 *Frequency: Wed.*
Bill Johnston, Publisher & Editor

***Burks Falls:* Almaguin News**
PO Box 518, 185 Ontario St., Burks Falls, ON P0A 1C0
705-382-9996, Fax: 705-382-3440, 800-731-6397
news@almaguinnews.com
www.almaguinnews.com
Circulation: 3,783 *Frequency: Wed.*
Joe Anderson, Publisher
Bruce Hickey, Editor

***Burks Falls:* Burks Falls Marketplace**
PO Box 518, 183 Ontario St., Burks Falls, ON P0A 1C0
705-382-3843, Fax: 705-382-3440, 800-731-6397
news@almaguinnews.com
www.almaguinnews.com
Circulation: 12,600; Almaguin News 6,200 *Frequency: Fri.*
Peter Barr, Publisher
Allan Dennis, Editor

***Burlington:* Burlington Post**
#1, 5040 Mainway, Burlington, ON L7L 7G5
905-632-4444
www.haltonsearch.com
Circulation: 46,777 Wed., 57,619 Fri., 46,781 Sun. *Frequency: Wed., Fri., Sun.*
Niel Oliver, Publisher

***Burlington:* Cityscope**
1343 Headen Rd., Burlington, ON L7M 1X4
905-637-2900, Fax: 905- -
Circulation: 53,000
Dave de Jong, Publisher

***Caledonia:* Grand River Sachem**
3 Sutherland St. West, Caledonia, ON N3W 1C1

905-765-4441, Fax: 905-765-3651
sachem@sachem.on.ca
www.sachem.on.ca
Circulation: 18,110 *Frequency: Fri.*
Neil Dring, Publisher
Neil Dring, Editor

***Caledonia:* The Regional News This Week**
345 Argyle St. South, Caledonia, ON N3W 1L8
905-765-4210, Fax: 905-765-3563
Circulation: 21,200 *Frequency: Wed.*
Christine Pickup, Publisher

***Caleton Place:* Almonte Gazette**
PO Box 430, 53 Bridge St., Caleton Place, ON K7C 3P5
613-257-1303, Fax: 613-257-7373
cpcedit@runge.net
www.runge.net
Circulation: 1,988 *Frequency: Wed.*
Diane Pinder-Moss, Editor
Derek Walter, Publisher

***Cambridge:* Cambridge Times**
1460 Bishop St., Cambridge, ON N1R 7N6
519-623-7395
www.cambridgetimes.ca
Circulation: 127,025 *Frequency: Tue., Thu., Fri.*
Peter Winkler, Publisher

***Cannington:* Brock Citizen**
30 Cameron St. East, Cannington, ON L0E 1E0
705-432-8842, Fax: 705-324-5694
showard@mykawartha.com
www.mykawartha.com
Circulation: 7,110 *Frequency: Fri.*
Bruce Danford, Publisher
Scott Howard, Editor

***Carleton Place:* The Canadian**
PO Box 430, 53 Bridge St., Carleton Place, ON K7C 3P5
613-257-1303, Fax: 613-257-7373
dpindermoss@runge.net
www.runge.net
Circulation: 2,561 *Frequency: Tue.*
Diane Pinder-Moss, Editor
Derek Walter, Publisher, Sales

***Cayuga:* The Haldimand Press**
PO Box 100, Cayuga, ON N0A 1E0
905-768-3111, Fax: 905-772-5465
press.c@news-net.ca
Circulation: 4,307 *Frequency: Wed.*
Robert Hall, Publisher

***Chatham:* Chatham This Week**
#7, 930 Richmond St., Chatham, ON N7M 5J5
519-351-7331, Fax: 519-351-7774
www.chathamthisweek.com
Circulation: 18,550 *Frequency: Wed.*
Peter Epp, Editor

***Chatham:* Chatham-Kent Pennysaver**
#7, 930 Richmond St., Chatham, ON N7M 5L1
519-351-4362, Fax: 519-351-2452, 877-351-7331
chathampennysaver@bowesnet.com
www.chathampennysaver.com
Circulation: 30,000 *Frequency: Fri.*
Ken Oliver, Publisher

***Chesterville:* Chesterville Record**
PO Box 368, Chesterville, ON K0C 1H0
613-448-2321, Fax: 613-448-3260
www.agrinews.ca
Circulation: 1,941 *Frequency: Wed.*
Robin Morris, Publisher

***Clinton:* Clinton News-Record**
PO Box 39, 53 Albert St., Clinton, ON N0M 1L0
519-482-3443, Fax: 519-482-7341
clinton.news@bowesnet.com
www.clintonnewsrecord.com
Circulation: 2,438 *Frequency: Wed.*
Tom Williscraft, Publisher

***Cobden:* Cobden Sun**
PO Box 100, 36 Crawford St., Cobden, ON K0J 1K0
613-646-2380, Fax: 613-628-3291
cobdensun@nrtco.net
Circulation: 1,374 *Frequency: Wed.*
Ron Tracey, Publisher

***Cobourg:* Northumberland News**
#212, 884 Division St., Cobourg, ON K9A 5V6
905-373-7355, Fax: 905-373-4719
www.northumberlandnews.com
Circulation: 44,954 *Frequency: Wed., Fri.*
Tim Whittaker, Publisher

***Cochrane:* Cochrane Times-Post**
PO Box 10, 171 - 6th Ave., Cochrane, ON P0L 1C0
705-272-3344, Fax: 705-272-3434
www.cochranetimespost.com
Circulation: 2,200 *Frequency: Fri.*
Wayne Major, Publisher

***Colborne:* Colborne Chronicle**
PO Box 208, 11 King St. East, Colborne, ON K0K 1S0
905-355-2843, Fax: 905-355-1639
cchronicle@rol.ca
www.northumberlandtoday.com
Circulation: 913 *Frequency: Thu.*
Mike Walsh, Publisher

***Collingwood:* Collingwood Enterprise-Bulletin**
PO Box 98, 77 St. Marie St., Collingwood, ON L9Y 3Z4
705-445-4611, Fax: 705-444-6477
editorial@theenterprisebulletin.com
www.theenterprisebulletin.com
Circulation: 18,591 *Frequency: Wed., Fri.; also Enterprise-Bulletin This Week (Fri., circ. 13,652)*
Doreen Sykes, Publisher
Morgan Ian Adams, Editor

***Collingwood:* Collingwood/Wasaga Beach Connection**
4-155 First St., Collingwood, ON L9Y 1A4
705-444-1875, Fax: 705-444-1876
connection@simcoe.com
www.collingwoodconnection.com
Circulation: 19,640 *Frequency: Fri.*
Joe Anderson, Publisher
Larry Culham, Editor

***Cornwall:* Le Journal**
113 Montréal Rd., Cornwall, ON K6H 1B2
613-938-1433, Fax: 613-938-2798
rlduplan@glen-net.ca
Circulation: 2,300 *Frequency: Jeudi; français*
Roger Duplantie, President

***Cornwall:* Seaway News**
29 - 2nd St. East, Cornwall, ON K6H 1Y2
613-933-0014, Fax: 613-933-0024
info@cornwallseawaynews.com
www.cornwallseawaynews.com
Circulation: 34,964 *Frequency: Fri.*
Rick Shaver, Editor & General Manager
R.N. Aubry, Publisher

***Deep River:* North Renfrew Times**
PO Box 310, 11 Champlain St., Deep River, ON K0J 1P0
613-584-4161, Fax: 613-584-1062
drcanrt@magma.ca
www.northrenfrewtimes.com
Circulation: 2,226 *Frequency: Wed.*
Terry Myers, Editor
Terry Myers, Editor-in-chief

***Delhi:* Delhi News-Record**
237 Main St., Delhi, ON N4B 2M4
519-582-2510, Fax: 519-582-4040
www.delhinewsrecord.com
Circulation: 1,447 *Frequency: Wed.*
Cam McKnight, Publisher
Greg MacLachlin, Editor

***Dorchester:* Dorchester Signpost**
15 Bridge St., Dorchester, ON N0L 1G2
519-268-7337, Fax: 519-268-3260
Circulation: 2,370 *Frequency: Wed.*
Fred Huxley, Publisher

***Drayton:* The Community News**
PO Box 189, 41 Wellington St. North, Drayton, ON N0G 1P0
519-638-3066, Fax: 519-638-3066, 800-708-9555
www.wellingtonadviser.com
Circulation: 4,689 *Frequency: Fri.*
W.H. Adsett, Publisher

***Dresden:* North Kent Leader**
PO Box 490, 254 Main St., Dresden, ON N0P 1M0
519-683-4485, Fax: 519-683-4355
www.northkentleader.com
Circulation: 929 *Frequency: Wed.*
Jim Blake, Publisher

***Dryden:* Dryden Observer**
PO Box 3009, Dryden, ON P8N 2Y9
807-223-2390, Fax: 807-223-2907, 800-465-7230
lauriep@drydenobserver.ca
www.drydenobserver.ca
Circulation: 3,945 *Frequency: Wed.*
Warner Bloomfield, Editor
Roy Wilson, President & Publisher

***Dundalk:* Dundalk Herald**
PO Box 280, Dundalk, ON N0C 1B0
519-923-2203, Fax: 519-923-2747
Circulation: 2,053 *Frequency: Wed.*
Matthew Walls, Publisher
Mary Fowler, Editor

***Dundalk:* Flesherton Advance**
PO Box 280, Dundalk, ON N0C 1B0
519-923-2203, Fax: 519-923-2747
Circulation: 1,634 *Frequency: Wed.*
Matt Walls, Publisher
Cathy Walls, General Manager

***Dundas:* Ancaster News**
47 Cootes Dr., Dundas, ON L9H 1B5
905-628-6313, Fax: 905-628-6313
www.ancasternews.com
Circulation: 12,591 *Frequency: Fri.*
Neil Oliver, Publisher

***Dundas:* Dundas Star News**
47 Cootes Dr., Dundas, ON L9H 1B5
905-628-6313, Fax: 905-628-5485
www.dundasstarnews.com
Circulation: 18,047 *Frequency: Fri.*
Neil Oliver, Publisher

***Dundas:* Hamilton Mountain News**
47 Cootes Dr., Dundas, ON L9H 1B5
905-628-6313
www.hamiltonmountainnews.com
Circulation: 48,883 *Frequency: Fri.*
John Rousseau, Associate Publisher

***Dundas:* Stoney Creek News**
47 Cootes Dr., Dundas, ON L9H 1B5
905-628-6313
www.stoneycreeknews.com
Circulation: 29,791 *Frequency: Fri.*
Neil Oliver, Publisher

***Dunnville:* Dunnville Chronicle**
131 Lock St. East, Dunnville, ON N1A 1J6
905-774-7632, Fax: 905-774-5744
www.dunnvillechronicle.ca
Circulation: 2,642 *Frequency: Wed.; also CoverStory (Sat.)*
Mike Walsh, Publisher

***Eganville:* Eganville Leader**
PO Box 310, 154 John St., Eganville, ON K0J 1T0
613-628-2332, Fax: 613-628-3291
leader@nrtco.net
www.eganvilleleader.com
Circulation: 4,931 *Frequency: Wed.*
Ron Tracey, Co-Publisher
Gerald Tracey, Editor & Co-Publisher

***Elliot Lake:* Elliot Lake Standard**
14 Hillside Dr. South, Elliot Lake, ON P5A 1M6
705-848-7195, Fax: 705-848-0249, 800-463-6408
standard@elliottlakestandard.ca
www.elliotlakestandard.ca
Circulation: 4,564 *Frequency: Wed.*
Ray Ethelston, Publisher

***Elmira:* Elmira Independent**
PO Box 128, 24 Church St. West, Elmira, ON N3B 2Z5
519-669-5155, Fax: 519-669-5928
editor@elmiraindependent.com
www.elmiraindependent.com
Circulation: 3,320 *Frequency: Fri.*
Gail Martin, Editor

***Elmira:* Woolwich Observer**
20B Arthur St., North, Elmira, ON N3B 1Z9
519-669-5790, Fax: 519-669-5753
info@woolwichobserver.com
www.woolwichobserver.com
Circulation: 12,689 *Frequency: Sat.*
Joe Merlihan, Publisher

***Erin:* Erin Advocate**
#5, 8 Thompson Cres., Erin, ON N0B 1T0
519-833-9603, Fax: 519-833-9605
editorial@erinadvocate.com
www.metroland.com
Circulation: 2,200 *Frequency: Wed.*

Ken Nugent, Publisher

***Espanola:* Mid-North Monitor**
#15, 417 - 2nd Ave., Espanola, ON P5E 1L1
705-869-0588, Fax: 705-869-0587
ads@midnorthmonitor.com
www.midnorthmonitor.com
Circulation: 3,492 *Frequency: Wed.*
Ray Ethleston, Publisher

***Essex:* Essex Free Press**
16 Centre St., Essex, ON N8M 1N9
519-776-4268, Fax: 519-776-4014
essexfreepress@on.aibn.com
essexfreepress.reinvented.net
Circulation: 3,460 *Frequency: Wed.*
Laurie Brett, Publisher

***Etobicoke:* Bloor West Villager**
307 Humberline Dr., Etobicoke, ON M9W 5V1
416-767-3644, Fax: 416-767-4880
www.insidetoronto.ca
Circulation: 38,571 *Frequency: Fri.*
Betty Carr, Publisher
Deborah Bodine, Editor-in-chief

***Exeter:* Exeter Times-Advocate**
PO Box 850, 424 Main St., Exeter, ON N0M 1S0
519-235-1331, Fax: 519-235-0766
www.southhuron.com
Circulation: 3,775 *Frequency: Wed.*
Jim Beckett, Publisher

***Fergus:* Fergus-Elora News-Express**
PO Box 130, 390 Tower St. South, Fergus, ON N1M 2W7
519-843-1310, Fax: 519-843-1334
editor@centrewellington.com
www.centrewellington.com
Circulation: 3,587 *Frequency: Wed.*
John Roberts, General Manager

***Fergus:* The Wellington Advertiser**
PO Box 252, 180 St. Andrew St. East, Fergus, ON N1M 2W8
519-843-5410, Fax: 519-843-7607
info@wellingtonadvertiser.com
www.wellingtonadvertiser.co m
Circulation: 39,071 *Frequency: Fri.*
W.H. Adsett, Publisher

***Fonthill:* The Voice of Pelham**
PO Box 40, 111 Regional Rd. 20, Fonthill, ON L0S 1E0
905-892-8690, Fax: 905-892-0823
thevoice@vaxxine.com
www.thevoiceofpelham.ca
Circulation: 8,528 *Frequency: Wed.*
Shawn Taylor, Editor

***Fort Erie:* The Times**
PO Box 1219, #1, 450 Garrison Rd., Fort Erie, ON L2A 1N2
905-871-3100, Fax: 905-871-5243
feeditor@cogeco.net
times.niagaracommunitynewspapers.com
Circulation: 12,043 *Frequency: Sat.*
Tim Dundas, Publisher

***Fort Frances:* Fort Frances Times**
PO Box 339, 116 - 1st St. East, Fort Frances, ON P9A 3M7
807-274-5373, Fax: 807-274-7286, 800-465-8508
www.fortfrances.com
Circulation: 5,240 *Frequency: Wed.*
Jim Cumming, Publisher
Mike Behan, Editor

***Gananoque:* Gananoque Reporter**
79 King St. East, Gananoque, ON K7G 1E8
613-382-2156, Fax: 613-382-3010
reporter@tipgananoque.com
www.gananoquereporter.com
Circulation: 3,616 *Frequency: Wed.*
Ken Koyama, Publisher

***Georgetown:* Georgetown Independent/Free Press**
#29, 280 Guelph St., Georgetown, ON L7G 4B1
905-873-0301, Fax: 905-873-0398
www.independentfreepress.com
Circulation: 42,299 *Frequency: Wed., Fri.*
John McGhie, Editor
Ken Nugent, Publisher

***Geraldton:* Times Star**
PO Box 490, 414 Main St., Geraldton, ON P0T 1M0
807-854-1919, Fax: 807-854-1682
tstar@astrocom-on.com
www.timestar.ca
Circulation: 1,293 *Frequency: Wed.*

Stephane Parent, Publisher

***Glencoe:* Transcript & Free Press**
PO Box 400, 243 Main St., Glencoe, ON N0L 1M0
519-287-2615, Fax: 519-287-2408
tranfree@excelco.on.ca
Circulation: 2,069 *Frequency: Wed.*
Dale Hayter, Publisher
Marie Williams-Gagnon, Editor

***Gloucester:* L'Express d'Orléans / Orleans Express**
#30, 5300 Canotek Rd., Gloucester, ON K1J 8R7
613-744-4800, Fax: 613-744-8232
production_orleans@transcontinental.ca
journaux.apf.ca/expressorleans
Circulation: 36,500 *Frequency: Mardi; français*
Madeleine Joanisse, Éditeur
Florence Bolduc, Rédacteur en chef

***Goderich:* Goderich Signal-Star**
PO Box 220, 120 Huckins St., Goderich, ON N7A 4B6
519-524-2614, Fax: 519-524-5145
gssads@bowesnet.com
www.goderichsignalstar.com
Circulation: 5,530 *Frequency: Wed; also Focus (every other Fri.)*
Dave Sykes, Publisher
Ron Bunoy, Editor

***Gore Bay:* The Manitoulin West Recorder**
PO Box 235, Meredith St., Gore Bay, ON P0P 1H0
705-282-2003, Fax: 705-282-2432
therecorder@bellnet.ca
www.manitoulin.ca/recorder_etc/recorder.html
Circulation: 1,961 *Frequency: Fri.*
Rick McCutcheon, Publisher

***Grand Bend:* The Lakeshore Advance**
PO Box 1195, 58 Ontario St. North, Grand Bend, ON N0M 1T0
519-238-5383, Fax: 519-238-5131
ladvance@bowesnet.com
www.lakeshoreadvance.com
Circulation: 1,587 *Frequency: Wed.*
Neil Clifford, General Manager
Linda Hillman-Rapley, Editor

***Gravenhurst:* Gravenhurst Banner**
PO Box 849, 140 Muskoka Rd. South, Gravenhurst, ON P1P 1X2
705-687-6674, Fax: 705-687-7213
Circulation: 3,043 *Frequency: Wed.*
Joe Anderson, Publisher

***Gravenhurst:* Muskoka Today**
140 - 1st St. South, Gravenhurst, ON P1P 1H5
705-687-5777, Fax: 705-687-1009, 800-240-2329
news@muskokatoday.com
www.muskokatoday.com
Circulation: 10,000
Lois Cooper, Editor
Mark Clairmont, Publisher

***Grimsby:* Grimsby Lincoln News**
32 Main St. West, Grimsby, ON L3M 1R4
905-945-8392, Fax: 905-945-3916
info@thegrimsbylincolnnews.com
www.thegrimsbylincolnnews. com
Circulation: 22,093 *Frequency: Wed.*
Ian Oliver, Publisher

***Guelph:* Guelph Pennysaver**
86 Dawson Rd., Guelph, ON N1H 1A8
519-823-5070, Fax: 519-823-2161
classifieds@guelphpennysaver.com
www.guelphpennysaver.com
Circulation: 47,300 *Frequency: Fri.*
Rocky Nash, General Manager

***Guelph:* The Guelph Tribune**
#1, 27 Woodlawn Rd. West, Guelph, ON N1H 1G8
519-763-3333, Fax: 519-763-4814
gtribune@sentex.net
www.guelphtribune.ca
Circulation: 84,356 *Frequency: Tue. 39,808, Fri. 44,548*
Dwayne Weidendorf, Publisher

***Haliburton:* Haliburton County Echo**
PO Box 360, 146 Highland St., Haliburton, ON K0M 1S0
705-457-1037, Fax: 705-457-3275
info@haliburtonecho.on.ca
www.haliburtonecho.ca
Circulation: 4,302 *Frequency: Tue.*
Don Smith, Publisher

Martha Perkins, Editor

***Hamilton:* Dundas-Ancaster Recorder**
PO Box 68041 Blakely, Hamilton, ON L8M 3M7
905-385-7192, Fax: 905- -
Circulation: 13,000 *Frequency: Tue.*
Margaret Casey, Publisher

***Hamilton:* Hamilton Recorder**
PO Box 68041 Blakely, Hamilton, ON L8M 3M7
905-385-7192, Fax: 905- -
Circulation: 20,000 *Frequency: Wed.*
Margaret Casey, Publisher

***Hanover:* The Post**
413 - 18th Ave., Hanover, ON N4N 3S5
519-364-2001, Fax: 519-364-6950
postads@thepost.on.ca
www.thepost.on.ca
Lori Gillespie, Managing Editor
Marie David, Publisher

***Harcourt:* The Highlands Courier**
PO Box 88, Harcourt, ON K0L 1X0
705-448-1388, Fax: 705-448-1394
hillo@sympatico.ca
Circulation: 1,000 *Frequency: Monthly*
Andrea Hillo, Publisher/Owner

***Harrow:* Harrow News**
PO Box 310, 563 Queen St., Harrow, ON N0R 1G0
519-738-2542, Fax: 519-738-3874
harnews@mnsi.net
Circulation: 1,360 *Frequency: Tue.*
Cecil MacKenzie, Publisher

***Hawkesbury:* Le Carillon**
CP 1000, Hawkesbury, ON K6A 3H1
613-632-4155, Fax: 613-632-6122
nouvelles@eap.on.ca
www.lecarillon.ca
Circulation: 19,587 *Frequency: Mercredi; français*
Bertrand Castonguay, Publisher

***Hawkesbury:* Hawkesbury Tribune/Express**
PO Box 1000, 299, rue Principale est, Hawkesbury, ON K6A 3H1
613-632-4155, Fax: 613-632-8601
pub@eap.on.ca
Circulation: 23,750 *Frequency: Fri., English & French*
Roger Duplantie

***Hawkesbury:* Le/The Regional**
124, rue Principale est, Hawkesbury, ON K6A 1A3
613-632-0112, Fax: 613-632-0277, 888-477-3566
regional@hawk.igs.net
Circulation: 32,800 *Frequency: Fri.; English & French*
André Cayer
Sylvain Roy

***Hearst:* Le Nord**
CP 2320, 813, rue Georges, Hearst, ON P0L 1N0
705-372-1233, Fax: 705-362-5954
lenord@lenord.on.ca
www.lenord.on.ca
Circulation: 3 500 *Frequency: Mercredi; français et anglais*
André Bolduc, Rédacteur-en-chef
Omer Cantin, Éditeur/Publisher

***Huntsville:* Huntsville Forester**
11 Main St. West, Huntsville, ON P1H 2C6
705-789-5541, Fax: 705-789-9381
news@huntsvilleforester.com
www.huntsvilleforester.com
Circulation: 6,305 *Frequency: Wed.*
Joe Anderson, Publisher

***Huntsville:* Muskoka Advance**
11 Main St. West, Huntsville, ON P1H 2C5
705-645-8771, Fax: 705-645-1718
Circulation: 23,509 *Frequency: Sun.*

***Ignace:* Ignace Driftwood**
PO Box 989, 153 Balsam St., Ignace, ON P0T 1T0
807-934-6482, Fax: 807-934-6667
driftwood@bellnet.ca
Circulation: 445 *Frequency: Wed.*
Dennis Smyk, Publisher

***Ingersoll:* Ingersoll Times**
19 King St. West, Ingersoll, ON N5C 2J2
519-485-3631, Fax: 519-485-6652
ingersoll@bowesnet.com
www.ingersolltimes.com
Circulation: 2,235 *Frequency: Wed.*

Pat Logan, Publisher

Iroquois Falls: The Enterprise
PO Box 834, 727 Synagogue St., Iroquois Falls, ON P0K 1G0
705-232-4081, Fax: 705-232-4235
Circulation: 2,345 *Frequency: Thurs.*
W.C. Cavell, Publisher

Kanata: Kanata Kourier-Standard
#202, 240 Terrence Matthews Cres., Kanata, ON K2M 2C4
613-591-3060, Fax: 613-591-8503
www.runge.net
Circulation: 24,430 *Frequency: Fri.*
Brian Wiltsie, Publisher

Kanata: Stittsville News
#202, 240 Terrence Matthews Cres., Kanata, ON K2M 2C4
613-836-1357, Fax: 613-836-5621
www.runge.net
Circulation: 1,935 *Frequency: Tues.*
Bryan Wiltsie, Publisher

Kapuskasing: L'Horizon
2 Queen St., Kapuskasing, ON P5N 1G6
705-335-5850, Fax: 705-335-5958
horizon@nt.net
Frequency: Vendredi; aussi Le/The Weekender (Vendredi)

Kapuskasing: Kapuskasing Northern Times
51 Riverside Dr., Kapuskasing, ON P5N 1A7
705-335-2283, Fax: 705-337-1222
kaptimes@bowesnet.com
www.kapuskasingtimes.com
Circulation: 2,912 *Frequency: Wed.; English & French*
Wayne Major, Publisher

Kemptville: The Chieftain
PO Box 529, 29 Plaza Dr., Kemptville, ON K0E 1K0
613-652-4395, Fax: 613-652-2508
comnew@magmacom.com
www.runge.net
Circulation: 648 *Frequency: Wed.*
Fred Runge, Publisher

Kemptville: Kemptville Advance
PO Box 1420, Kemptville, ON K0G 1J0
613-258-3451, Fax: 613-258-7734
news@comnews.ca
www.runge.net
Circulation: 2,031 *Frequency: Wed.*
Chris Webb, Publisher
Ashley Kulp, Editor

Kenora: Kenora Lake of the Woods Enterprise
PO Box 1620, 33 Main St., Kenora, ON P9N 3X7
807-468-6397, Fax: 807-468-1060
info@kenoraenterprise.com
www.lotwenterprise.com
Circulation: 9,400 *Frequency: Sat.*
Jim Blight

Keswick: Georgina Advocate
461 The Queensway South, Keswick, ON L4P 2C9
905-476-7753, Fax: 905-476-5785
www.yorkregion.com
Circulation: 16,757 *Frequency: Thurs.*
Ian Proudfoot, Publisher

Kincardine: The Independent
PO Box 1240, 840 Queen St., Kincardine, ON N2Z 2Z4
519-396-3111, Fax: 519-396-3899
indepen@bmts.com
www.independent.on.ca
Circulation: 2,203 *Frequency: Wed.*
Eric Howald, Publisher

Kincardine: Kincardine News
719 Queen St., Kincardine, ON N2Z 1Z9
519-396-2963, Fax: 519-396-3790
kincardine@bowesnet.com
www.kincardinenews.com
Circulation: 3,736 *Frequency: Wed.*
Carol McKnight, Publisher
Troy Patterson, Editor

Kingston: Frontenac Gazette
1748 Bath Rd., Kingston, ON K7M 4Y2
613-389-8884, Fax: 613-389-1870
heritagenewspaper@bellnet.ca
Circulation: 10,045 *Frequency: Tue.*
Darryl Cembal, President

Kingston: The Heritage Newspaper
1784 Bath Rd., Kingston, ON K7M 4Y2
613-389-8884, Fax: 613-389-1870
heritagenewspaper@bellnet.ca
www.whatsonkingston.com/heri tage/
Circulation: 26,596 *Frequency: Fri.*
Darryl Cembal, President

Kingston: Kingston This Week
607 Gardiners Rd., Kingston, ON K7M 3Y4
613-389-7400
news@kingstonthisweek.com
www.kingstonthisweek.com
Circulation: 97,444 *Frequency: Tue., Fri.*
Ken Koyama, Publisher

Kingsville: Kingsville Reporter
17 Chestnut St., Kingsville, ON N9Y 1J9
519-733-2211, Fax: 519-733-6464
www.kingsreporter.emporium.on.ca
Circulation: 2,350 *Frequency: Tue.*
Greg Sims, Publisher

Kitchener: Pennysaver
685 Wabanaki Dr., Kitchener, ON N2C 2G3
519-894-1400, Fax: 519-894-5401
www.kitchenerpennysaver.com
Frequency: Sat.

Lakefield: Lakefield Herald
PO Box 1000, 74 Bridge St., Lakefield, ON K0L 2H0
705-652-5114, Fax: 705-652-6912, 877-652-6594
info@lakefieldherald.com
www.lakefieldherald.com
Circulation: 1,036 *Frequency: Fri.*
Simon Conolly, Publisher

Lasalle: LaSalle Post
1775 Sprucewood Ave., Lasalle, ON N9J 1X7
519-250-2880, Fax: 519-250-2881
lapost@windsoressexnews.com
www.windsoressexnews.com
Circulation: 9,768 *Frequency: Wed.*
Gary Baxter, Publisher

Leamington: Leamington Post & Shopper
27 Princess St., Leamington, ON N8H 2X8
519-326-4434, Fax: 519-326-2171
leampost@wincom.net
www.leamingtonpostandshopper.com
Circulation: 5,000 *Frequency: Wed.; also Leamington Shopper (Sat., circ. 17,000)*
Linda Gage, Manager, Sales
Don Gage, Publisher
Mike Thibodeau, Editor

Lindsay: Bobcaygeon Independent
96 Albert St. South, Lindsay, ON K9V 3H7
705-324-8600, Fax: 705-324-5694
Circulation: 1,700 *Frequency: Wed.*
Lois Tuffin, Editor-in-chief

Lindsay: Fenelon Falls Gazette
c/o Lindsay This Week, 96 Albert St. South, Lindsay, ON K9V 3H7
Frequency: Tue.
Bruce Danford, Publisher

Listowel: Listowel Banner
PO Box 97, 185 Wallace Ave. North, Listowel, ON N4W 3H2
519-291-1660, Fax: 519-291-3771
gbisch@northperth.com
www.northperth.com
Circulation: 3,480 *Frequency: Wed.; also Independent & Independent Plus (Fri.)*
Bill Huether, General Manager
Patrick Raftis, Editor

Little Current: The Manitoulin Expositor
PO Box 369, One Manitowaning Rd., Little Current, ON P0P 1K0
705-368-2744, Fax: 705-368-3822
theexpositor@etown.net
www.manitoulin.ca
Circulation: 5,703 *Frequency: Wed.*
R.L. McCutcheon, Publisher
Jim Moodie, Editor

London: London Pennysaver
369 York St., London, ON N6A 4G1
519-667-5486, Fax: 519-667-4573
pennyreaderads@londonpennysaver.com
www.londonpennysaver.com
Circulation: 144,000 *Frequency: Fri.*
Marj Bastow, General Manager

London: The Londoner
PO Box 7400, London, ON N5Y 4X3
519-673-5005, Fax: 519-673-4624
www.thelondoner.ca
Circulation: 107,623 *Frequency: Wed.*
Alan Glaser, Publisher
Philip McLeod, Editor

Lucknow: Lucknow Sentinel
PO Box 400, 619 Campbell St., Lucknow, ON N0G 2H0
519-528-2822, Fax: 519-528-3529
lucksent@bowesnet.com
www.lucknowsentinel.com
Circulation: 1,639 *Frequency: Wed.*
Pat Livingston, Publisher
Sara Bender, Editor

Manitouwadge: Echo
PO Box 550, #8, Hallmark Sq., Manitouwadge, ON P0T 2C0
807-826-3788, Fax: 807-826-3910
echo_manitouwadge@hotmail.com
Circulation: 610 *Frequency: Wed.*
B.J. Schermann, Publisher

Manotick: Manotick Messenger
PO Box 567, 1165 Beaverwood Rd., Manotick, ON K4M 1A5
613-692-6000, Fax: 613-692-3758
newsfile@bellnet.ca
www.storm.ca/~newsfile/
Circulation: 955 *Frequency: Wed.*
Jeff Morris, Publisher

Manotick: The Manotick Review
PO Box 102, 1142 Tighe St., Manotick, ON K4M 1A2
613-432-3655, Fax: 613-692-2456
comnews@magmacom.com
www.runge.net/mercury
Circulation: 342 *Frequency: Wed.*
Bryan Wiltsie, Publishing

Manotick: Ottawa-South This Month
PO Box 102, 1142 Tighe St., Manotick, ON K4M 1A2
613-692-3211, Fax: 613-692-2456
comnews@magma.ca
Circulation: 17,063
Peter Peers, Manager, Sales
Brian Crawford, Publisher
Joe Morin, Editor

Marathon: Marathon Mercury
PO Box 369, 14 Peninsula Rd., Marathon, ON P0T 2E0
807-229-1520, Fax: 807-229-1595
marathonmercury@shaw.ca
Circulation: 1,341 *Frequency: Tue.*
Garry R. McInnes, Publisher

Markham: Markham Economist & Sun
9 Heritage Rd., Markham, ON L3P 1M3
905-294-2200, Fax: 905-294-1538
www.yorkregion.com
Circulation: 179,476 *Frequency: Tues., Thurs. & Sat.*
Ian Proudfoot, Publisher
Dave Teetzel, Editor

Marmora: Land O'Lakes Sun
PO Box 250, Marmora, ON K0K 2M0
613-472-2431, Fax: 613-472-5026
zoo@kos.net
Circulation: 5,565 *Frequency: Sat.*
Brian Dunning, Editor

Mattawa: Mattawa Recorder
PO Box 67, 341 McConnell St., Mattawa, ON P0H 1V0
705-744-5361, Fax: 705-744-5361
Circulation: 1,050 *Frequency: Sun.*
Heather Edwards, Contact

Meaford: Express
68 Sykes St. North, Meaford, ON N4L 1R2
519-538-1421, Fax: 519-538-5028, 866-771-6235
themeafordexpress@rogers.com
Circulation: 2,544 *Frequency: Wed.*
Doug Rowe, Publisher

Midland: Free Press
PO Box 37, Midland, ON L4R 4K6
705-526-5431, Fax: 705-526-1771
freepress@midlandfreepress.com
www.midlandfreepress.com
Circulation: 5,429 *Frequency: Wed., Fri.*
Sandy Coghlan, Publisher

Midland: Midland/Penetanguishene Mirror
PO Box 77, 488 Dominion Ave., Midland, ON L4R 1P6

705-527-5500, Fax: 705-527-5467
themirror@simcoe.com
www.midlandmirror.com
Circulation: 14,026 Wed., 19,404 Fri. *Frequency: Wed., Fri.*
Joe Anderson, Publisher

Midland: **Penetanguishene Free Press**
PO Box 37, 845 King St., Unit 4, Midland, ON L4R 4K3
705-526-5431, Fax: 705-526-1771
freepress@midlandfreepress.com
www.midlandfreepress.com
Circulation: 6,657 *Frequency: Tue., Fri.*
Sandy Coghlan, General Manager

Mildmay: **Mildmay Town Crier Weekly**
PO Box 190, 100 Elora St., Mildmay, ON N0G 2J0
519-367-2681, Fax: 519-367-5417
thecrier@wightman.ca
Circulation: 1,800 *Frequency: Wed.*
John H. Hafermehl, Publisher

Millbrook: **The Green Hills Gazette**
69 King St. East, Millbrook, ON L0A 1G0
Frequency: Thurs.

Millbrook: **Millbrook Times**
PO Box 285, 5 Lisa Court, Millbrook, ON L0A 1G0
705-932-3001,
Circulation: 1,816 *Frequency: Thu.*
Beverley Martin, Publisher

Milton: **Milton Canadian Champion**
PO Box 248, 191 Main St, Milton, ON L9T 4N9
905-878-2341, Fax: 905-878-4943
www.haltonsearch.com
Circulation: 38,934 *Frequency: Tues., Fri.*
Karen Smith, Editor

Minden: **The Times**
PO Box 97, 134 Bobcaygeon Rd., Minden, ON K0M 2K0
705-286-1288, Fax: 705-286-4768
editor@mindentimes.ca.ca
www.mindentimes.ca
Circulation: 2,891 *Frequency: Wed.*
Martha Perkins, Editor
David Zilstra, Publisher
Don Smith, Publisher

Mississauga: **Mississauga Booster**
5650 Keaton Cres., Unit A, Mississauga, ON L5R 3G3
905-890-4606, Fax: 905-890-3999
http://webhome.idirect.com/~booster/start.html
Circulation: 120,000 *Frequency: Every other Fri.*
Paul McCallion, Publisher
Ron Lenyk, Publisher

Mississauga: **Mississauga News**
3145 Wolfedale Rd., Mississauga, ON L5C 3A9
905-273-8111, Fax: 905-273-9119
www.mississauganews.com
Circulation: 367,941 *Frequency: Wed., Fri., Sun; supplement, Community News (Wed.)*
Ron Lenyk, Publisher

Mississauga: **The Weekly Voice**
#212, 6705 Tomken Rd., Mississauga, ON L5T 2J6
905-795-8282, Fax: 905-795-9801
info@weeklyvoice.com
www.weeklyvoice.com
Circulation: 30,000 (English); 20,000 (Punjabi) *Frequency: Fri.*
Jazz Samra, Publisher

Mitchell: **Mitchell Advocate**
PO Box 669, 42 Montreal St., Mitchell, ON N0K 1N0
519-348-8431, Fax: 519-348-8836
abader@bowesnet.com
www.mitchelladvocate.com
Circulation: 2,479 *Frequency: Wed.*
Andy Bader, Publisher

Morrisburg: **Morrisburg Leader**
PO Box 891, 41 Main St., Morrisburg, ON K0C 1X0
613-543-2987, Fax: 613-543-3643
Circulation: 2,111 *Frequency: Wed.*
Sam Laurin, Publisher & Editor
Bonnie McNairn, Managing Editor

Mount Forest: **Mount Forest Confederate**
PO Box 130, 277 Main St. South, Mount Forest, ON N0G 2L0
519-323-1550, Fax: 519-323-4548
editor@mountforest.com
www.mountforest.com
Circulation: 2,649 *Frequency: Wed.*
Lynne Pinnegar, Publisher

Napanee: **Napanee Beaver**
72 Dundas St. East, Napanee, ON K7R 1H9
613-354-6641, Fax: 613-354-2622
beaver@bellnet.ca
www.napaneebeaver.com
Circulation: 2,385 *Frequency: Wed.*
Seth DuChene, Editor
Jean Morrison, Publisher

Napanee: **The Napanee Guide**
#11, 2 Dairy Ave., Napanee, ON K7R 3T1
613-354-6648, Fax: 613-354-6708
www.napaneeguide.com
Circulation: 14,101 *Frequency: Fri.*
Ken Koyama, Publisher

Nepean: **Alta Vista Canterbury News**
#3B, 15 Antares Dr., Nepean, ON K2E 7Y9
613-723-5970, Fax: 613-723-1862
ottnews@ottnews.ca
Circulation: 36,000 *Frequency: Every other Thu.; also Britannia/Lincoln Heights News, Carlingwood/Baseline News, Glebe & Ottawa South News, Westboro/Hampton Park News*
Michael Wollock, Publisher
Tom Collins, Editor

Nepean: **Barrhaven Independent**
PO Box 29011, Nepean, ON K2J 4A9
613-825-9858, Fax: 613-692-3758
newsfile@bellnet.ca
www.barrhavenindependent.on.ca
Circulation: 17,445 *Frequency: Fri.*
Derek Dunn, Editor

Nepean: **Nepean This Week**
#200, 9 Camelot Dr., Nepean, ON K2G 5W6
613-723-7951, Fax: 613-723-9589
publisher@nepeanthisweek.com
www.nepeanthisweek.com
Circulation: 44,757 *Frequency: Fri.*
Chris Webb, Publisher

New Hamburg: **New Hamburg Independent**
PO Box 670, 77 Peel St., New Hamburg, ON N3A 1E7
519-662-1240, Fax: 519-662-3521, 800-563-3578
editor@newhamburgindependent.ca
www.newhamburgindependent.ca
Circulation: 3,060 *Frequency: Wed.*
Neil Oliver, Publisher
Cal Bosveld, Publisher

New Liskeard: **Journal O'Courant**
CP 1358, New Liskeard, ON P0J 1P0
705-647-9898,
Frequency: Wed.

New Liskeard: **The Temiskaming Speaker**
PO Box 580, 18 Wellington St., New Liskeard, ON P0J 1P0
705-647-6791
www.northernontario.ca
Circulation: 4,840 *Frequency: Wed.*
Dave Armstrong, Publisher

Newmarket: **Newmarket Era Banner**
PO Box 236, 580 Steven Ct., Newmarket, ON L3Y 4X1
905-773-7627, Fax: 905-773-7626
www.yorkregion.com
Circulation: 174,637 *Frequency: Tues., Thur., Sun.*
Ian Proudfoot, Publisher

Niagara Falls: **Niagara Falls News**
4949 Victoria Ave., Niagara Falls, ON L2E 4C7
905-357-2440, Fax: 905-357-1620
twilkinson@niagaracommunitynewspapers.com
falls.niagaracommunitynewspape rs.com

Niagara Falls: **Niagara Shopping News**
4949 Victoria Ave., Niagara Falls, ON L2E 4C7
905-357-2440, Fax: 905- -
Circulation: 29,650 *Frequency: Fri.*

Nipigon: **Nipigon-Red Rock Gazette**
PO Box 1057, 145 Railway St., Nipigon, ON P0T 2J0
807-887-3583, Fax: 807- -
Circulation: 1,008 *Frequency: Tue.*
Linda Harbison, Publisher

North York: **Canadian Jewish News**
 # 205, 1500 Don Mills Rd., North York, ON M3B 3K4
416-391-1836
www.cjnews.com
Circulation: 41,302 *Frequency: Thur.*
Vera Gillman, Advertising Manager
Mordechai Ben-Dat, Editor

Norwich: **Norwich Gazette**
PO Box 459, 4 Washington St., Norwich, ON N0J 1P0
519-863-2262, Fax: 519-863-3229
norwich@bowesnet.com
www.norwichgazette.ca
Circulation: 1,433 *Frequency: Wed.*
Pat Logan, Publisher
Jennifer Vandermeer, Editor

Oakville: **Milton Shopping News**
1158 South Service Rd. West, Oakville, ON L6L 5T7
905-827-2244, Fax: 905-827-2308
Circulation: 18,700 *Frequency: Tues., Fri.*
Bill Whitaker Sr.

Oakville: **Oakville Beaver**
467 Speers Rd., Oakville, ON L6K 3S4
905-845-3824
www.insidehalton.com; www.metroland.com
Circulation: 139,631 *Frequency: Wed., Fri., Sun.; also North News (Fri.), & Oakville Marketplace (Tue.)*
Oakville's community newspaper; print and online editions
Neil Oliver, Publisher
Jill David, Editor-in-Chief

Oakville: **Oakville Shopping News**
1158 South Service Rd. West, Oakville, ON L6L 5T7
905-827-2244, Fax: 905-827-2308
Circulation: 46,500 *Frequency: Wed., Fri.*
Bill Whitaker Sr.

Oakville: **Oakville Today**
#10, 2526 Speers Rd., Oakville, ON L6L 5M2
905-825-2229, Fax: 905-825-8315
newsroom@oakvilletoday.ca
www.oakvilletoday.ca
Circulation: 26,800 *Frequency: Thu.*
Lars Melander, Publisher

Ohsweken: **Tekawennake - Six Nations & New Credit**
PO Box 130, Ohsweken, ON N0A 1M0
519-753-0077, Fax: 519-753-0011
teka@tekanews.com
www.tekanews.com
Circulation: 2,500 *Frequency: Wed.*
Scott Smith

Orangeville: **Orangeville Banner**
37 Mill St., Orangeville, ON L9W 2M4
519-941-1350, Fax: 519-941-9600
banner@orangevillebanner.com
www.orangeville.com
Circulation: 19,115 Tue.; 23,055 Fri. *Frequency: Tue., Fri.*
Keith Poole, Publisher

Orangeville: **Orangeville Citizen**
10 - 1st St., Orangeville, ON L9W 2C4
519-941-2230, Fax: 519-941-9361
mail@citizen.on.ca
www.citizen.on.ca
Circulation: 11,983 *Frequency: Thurs.*
Tom Claridge, Editor
Alan Claridge, Publisher

Orillia: **Orillia Today**
25 Ontario St., Unit 1, Orillia, ON L3V 6H1
705-329-2058, Fax: 705-329-2059
www.orilliatoday.com
Circulation: 41,430 *Frequency: Wed., Fri.*
Joe Anderson, Publisher

Orono: **Orono Weekly Times**
PO Box 209, 5310 Main St., Orono, ON L0B 1M0
905-983-5301
oronotimes@speedline.ca
Circulation: 1,067 *Frequency: Wed.*
Margaret Zwart, Publisher

Oshawa: **Oshawa/Whitby This Week, Clarington This Week, Canadian Statesman**
PO Box 481, 865 Farewell Ave., Oshawa, ON L1H 7L5
905-579-4400, Fax: 905-579-2238
www.durhamregion.com
Circulation: 147,467 *Frequency: Wed., Fri., Sun.*
Tim Whittaker, Publisher
Chris Bovie, Editor-in-chief

Ottawa: **Centretown News**
c/o St. Patrick's Bldg., Carleton University School of Journ, #531, 1125 Colonel By Dr., Ottawa, ON K1S 5B6
613-520-7410, Fax: 613-520-4068
ctown@carleton.ca
www.carleton.ca/ctown/home/homeNew.htm
Circulation: 16,000 *Frequency: Every other Fri.*

Klaus Pohle, Publisher

Ottawa: Greenboro Hunt Club Park News
#3B, 15 Antares Dr., Ottawa, ON K2E 7Y9
613-723-5970, Fax: 613-723-1862
ottnews@ottnews.ca
Circulation: 36,000 *Frequency: Every other Thu.*
Mike Wollock, Publisher

Ottawa: The Hill Times
69 Sparks St., Ottawa, ON K1P 5A5
613-232-5952, Fax: 613-232-9055
www.thehilltimes.ca
Circulation: 12,947 *Frequency: Mon.*
Jim Creskey, Publisher
Kate Malloy, Editor

Ottawa: Hunt Club Riverside News
#3B, 15 Antares Dr., Ottawa, ON K2E 7Y9
613-723-5970, Fax: 613-723-1862
ottnews@ottnews.ca
Circulation: 36,000 *Frequency: Thu.*
Mike Wollock, Publisher

Ottawa: Ottawa Pennysaver
PO Box 9729 T, 6 Antares Dr., Phase III, Ottawa, ON K1G 5H7
613-733-4099, Fax: 613-733-7107
www.ottawapennysaver.com
Frequency: Sat.

Ottawa: The Spectrum
Boyd McRubie Communications Inc., PO Box 16130 F, Ottawa, ON K2C 3S9
613-226-2738
thespectrum@hotmail.com
Circulation: 6,000 *Frequency: Monthly, except July & August*
Ewart Walters

Ottawa: The Star
#30, 5300 Canotek Rd., Ottawa, ON K1J 8R7
613-744-4800, Fax: 613-744-1976
thestar@transcontinental.ca
www.neighbourhoodnews.ca
Circulation: 35,000 *Frequency: Tues.*
Terry Tyo, Publisher

Owen Sound: Markdale Standard
209 9th St. East, Owen Sound, ON N4K 5P2
519-376-2250
themarkdalestandard@bmts.com
www.markdalestandard.com
Circulation: 648 *Frequency: Wed.*
Cheryl McMenemy, Publisher & General Manager

Palmerston: Minto Express
PO Box 757, 171 William St., Palmerston, ON N0G 2P0
519-343-2440, Fax: 519-343-2267
www.mintoexpress.com
Circulation: 1,260 *Frequency: Tue.*
Paul Teahen, General Manager
Patrick Raftis, Editor

Paris: Paris Star
59 Grand River St. North, Paris, ON N3L 2N9
519-442-7866, Fax: 519-442-3100
parisstar@bowesnet.com
www.parisstaronline.com
Circulation: 1,638 *Frequency: Wed.*
Andrea DeMeer, Publisher

Parkhill: Forest Standard
PO Box 400, Parkhill, ON N0M 2K0
519-786-5242, Fax: 519-786-4884
standard@xcelco.on.ca
www.foreststandard.com
Circulation: 2,481 *Frequency: Thurs.*
Dale Hayter, Publisher

Parkhill: Parkhill Gazette
PO Box 400, 165 King St., Parkhill, ON N0M 2K0
519-294-6264, Fax: 519-294-6391
Circulation: 1,177 *Frequency: Thurs.*
Dale Hayter, Publisher

Parry Sound: Parry Sound Beacon Star
PO Box 370, 67 James St., Parry Sound, ON P2A 1T6
705-746-2104, Fax: 705-746-8369
www.parrysoundbeaconstar.com
Circulation: 3,688 *Frequency: Sat.*
Fred Heidman, General Manager

Parry Sound: Parry Sound North Star
PO Box 370, 67 James St., Parry Sound, ON P2A 2X4
705-746-2105, Fax: 705-746-8369
www.parrysoundnorthstar.com
Circulation: 4,101 *Frequency: Wed.*
Fred Heidman, General Manager

Penetanguishene: Le Goût de Vivre
343, av Lafontaine, RR#3, Penetanguishene, ON L9M 1R3
705-533-3349, Fax: 705-533-3422
legout-de-vivre@sympatico.ca
www.journaux.apf.ca/legoutde vivre
Circulation: 1 000 *Frequency: 1er et 3e jeudi du mois; français*

Perth: Perth Courier
PO Box 156, 39 Gore St. East, Perth, ON K7H 3E3
613-267-1100, Fax: 613-267-3986
courier@perth.igs.net
www.perthcourier.com
Circulation: 4,836 *Frequency: Wed.*
John W. Clement, Publisher
Ian Gray, Editor

Petawawa: Petawawa Post
Bldg. P-106, Petawawa, ON K8H 2X3
613-687-5511
petawawapost@bellnet.ca
www.psppetawawa.com/petawawapost.cfm
Circulation: 7,700 *Frequency: Tue.*
Carol Bullied, Editor

Peterborough: Peterborough This Week
884 Ford St., Peterborough, ON K9J 5V3
705-749-3383, Fax: 705-749-0074
www.mykawartha.com
Circulation: 96,277 *Frequency: Wed., Fri.*
Bruce Danford, Publisher

Petrolia: The Petrolia Topic
PO Box 40, 4182 Petrolia Line, Petrolia, ON N0N 1R0
519-882-1770, Fax: 519-882-3212
www.petroliatopic.com
Circulation: 2,422 *Frequency: Wed.*
Daryl Smith, Publisher

Picton: Picton Gazette
PO Box 80, Picton, ON K0K 2T0
613-476-3201, Fax: 613-476-3464
gazette@connect.reach.net
www.pictongazette.com
Circulation: 2,170 *Frequency: Wed.; The Picton Gazette Regional (Sat., circ. 10,602)*
Jean M. Morrison, Publisher

Port Colborne: In Port
149 King St., Port Colborne, ON L3K 4G3
905-834-4521, Fax: 905-834-5422
itait@wellandtribune.ca
www.wellandtribune.ca
Circulation: 5,300 *Frequency: Wed.*
Mike Walsh, Publisher

Port Dover: Port Dover Maple Leaf
PO Box 70, 351 Main St., Port Dover, ON N0A 1N0
519-583-0112, Fax: 519-583-3200
info@inportdover.com
www.inportdover.com
Circulation: 3,163 *Frequency: Wed.*
Stan Morris, Publisher

Port Elgin: Shoreline Beacon
PO Box 539, 694 Goderich St., Port Elgin, ON N0H 2C0
519-832-9001, Fax: 519-389-4793
shoreline@bmts.com
www.shorelinebeacon.com
Circulation: 4,510 *Frequency: Wed.*
Carol McKnight, Publisher

Port Perry: Port Perry Star
180 Mary St, #11, Port Perry, ON L9L 1C4
905-985-7383, Fax: 905-985-3708
advertising@portperrystar.com
www.ducharmregion.com
Circulation: 23,400 *Frequency: Wed., Fri.*
Tim Whittaker, Publisher

Prescott: Prescott Journal
PO Box 549, 231 King St. West, Prescott, ON K0E 1T0
613-925-4265, Fax: 613-925-3472
slp@ripnet.com
www.prescottjournal.com
Circulation: 2,441 *Frequency: Wed.*
Lisa D. Taylor, Publisher

Rainy River: Rainy River Record
PO Box 280, 312 - 3rd St., Rainy River, ON P0W 1L0
807-852-3366, Fax: 807-852-4434
info@rainyriverrecord.com
www.rainyriverrecord.com
Circulation: 788 *Frequency: Tue.*
J.R. Cumming, Publisher
Ken Johnston, Editor

Rainy River: The Westend Weekly
PO Box 66, Rainy River, ON P0W 1L0
807-852-3815, Fax: 807-852-4011
Circulation: 8,600 *Frequency: Wed.*
Ron McAllister, Publisher
Jacquie Dufresne, Editor-in-chief

Renfrew: Renfrew Mercury
PO Box 400, 35 Opeongo Rd., Renfrew, ON K7V 1A8
613-432-3655, Fax: 613-432-6689
rmedit@runge.net
www.runge.net
Circulation: 4,006 *Frequency: Tue.*
Fred Runge, Publisher
Lucy Hass, Editor

Renfrew: Renfrew Weekender
PO Box 400, 35 Opeongo Rd., Renfrew, ON K7V 4A8
613-432-3655, Fax: 613-432-6689
rmedit@runge.net
www.runge.net
Circulation: 14,795 *Frequency: Fri.*
Lucy Hass, Editor
Fred Runge, Publisher
Derek Walter, General Manager

Richmond Hill: The Liberal
PO Box 390, 1550 16th Ave., Richmond Hill, ON L4B 3K9
905-881-3373, Fax: 905-881-9924
www.yorkregion.com
Circulation: 197,459 *Frequency: Tue., 45,443; Thur. 76,048; Sun., 75,968*
Ian Proudfoot, Publisher
Debora Kelly, Editor-in-chief

Richmond Hill: Vaughan Citizen
Suite 100, 1550 16th Avenue Bld.F, Richmond Hill, ON L4B 3K9
905-881-3373, Fax: 905-660-3118
www.yorkregion.com
Other information: Toronto Line: 416/661-0047
Circulation: Sun. 42,000 and Thurs. 42,924; Total: 84, 924.
Frequency: Sunday and Thursday.
Ian Proudfoot, Publisher

Ridgetown: The Ridgetown Independent News
PO Box 609, 1 Main St., Ridgetown, ON N0P 2C0
519-674-5205, Fax: 519-674-2573
Circulation: 2,200 *Frequency: Wed.*
Jim Brown, Publisher

Rockland: Journal Vision Prescott/Russell
PO Box 897, 1579 Laurier, Rockland, ON K4K 1L5
613-446-6456, Fax: 613-446-1381
vision@eap.on.ca
Circulation: 18,100

Russell: Russell Villager
PO Box 550, 191 Castor St., Russell, ON K4R 1E1
613-445-3804, Fax: 613-445-3843
villager@magma.ca
Circulation: 989 *Frequency: Wed.*
Robin Morris, Managing Publisher

Sarnia: Lambton-Sarnia Pennysaver
1383 Confederation St., Sarnia, ON N75 5P1
519-336-1100, Fax: 519-336-1833
info@sarniamedia.com
www.sarniamedia.com
Circulation: 45,700 *Frequency: Sat.*

Sarnia: Sarnia This Week
1383 Confederation St., Sarnia, ON N7S 5P1
519-336-1100, Fax: 519-336-1833
www.sarniamedia.com
Circulation: 24,026 *Frequency: Wed.*
Linda Leblanc, Publisher

Sault Ste Marie: Sault Ste Marie This Week
PO Box 188, 2 Towers St., Sault Ste Marie, ON P6A 5L6
705-949-6111, Fax: 705-942-8596
stwnews@saultthisweek.com
www.saultthisweek.com/webapp/sitepages/
Circulation: 34,047 *Frequency: Wed.*
Fred Bright, Publisher

Schreiber: Terrace Bay Schreiber News
PO Box 720, 303 Scotia St., Schreiber, ON P0T 2S0
807-824-2021,
Circulation: 481 *Frequency: Tue.*
Linda Harbison, Publisher

Seaforth: **Seaforth Huron Expositor**
PO Box 69, 11 Main St., Seaforth, ON N0K 1W0
519-527-0240, Fax: 519-527-2858
seaforth@bowesnet.com
www.seaforthhuronexpositor.com
Circulation: 2,020 *Frequency: Wed.*
Tom Williscraft, Publisher
Susan Hundertmark, Editor

Shelburne: **Shelburne Free Press & Economist**
PO Box 100, Shelburne, ON L0N 1S0
519-925-2832, Fax: 519-925-5500
www.citizen.on.ca
Circulation: 2,108 *Frequency: Thurs.*
Thomas Claridge, Publisher

Simcoe: **Tuesday Times-Reformer**
PO Box 370, 50 Gilbertson Dr., Simcoe, ON N3Y 4L2
519-426-5710, Fax: 519-426-9255
www.simcoereformer.ca
Circulation: 19,630 *Frequency: Tue.*
Cam McKnight, Publisher

Sioux Lookout: **Sioux Lookout Bulletin**
PO Box 1389, 40 Front St., Sioux Lookout, ON P8T 1B9
807-737-3209, Fax: 807-737-3084
office@siouxbulletin.com
www.siouxbulletin.com
Circulation: 4,444 *Frequency: Wed.*
Dick MacKenzie, Publisher

Sioux Lookout: **Wawatay News**
Wawatay Native Communications Society, PO Box 1180, Sioux Lookout, ON P8T 1B7
807-737-2951, Fax: 807-737-3224
bryanp@wawatay.on.ca
www.wawatay.on.ca
Circulation: 9,050 *Frequency: Every other Thu.; English, Ojibwe & Cree*
Bryan Phelan, Publisher and General Manager

Smiths Falls: **Perth Record News EMC**
PO Box 158, 65 Lorne St. South, Smiths Falls, ON K7A 4T1

Smiths Falls: **Smiths Falls Record News**
PO Box 158, 65 Lorne St., Smiths Falls, ON K7A 4T1
613-283-3182, Fax: 613-283-7480
Circulation: 11,000 *Frequency: Tues.*
Duncan Weir, Publisher

St Catharines: **Thorold News**
PO Box 86, 140 Welland Ave. North, St Catharines, ON L2R 2N6
905-688-4332, Fax: 905-688-6313
stcatharinesnews@bellnet.ca
www.thorold.niagaracommunityn ewspapers.com
Circulation: 6,827 *Frequency: Wed.*
Tim Dundas, Publisher

St George: **The Paris Chronicle**
PO Box 354, St George, ON N0E 1N0
519-837-4187
cmparafenko@hotmail.com
Circulation: 3,800 *Frequency: Monthly, last Fri.*
Carol Parafenko

St Marys: **St Marys Journal-Argus**
PO Box 1030, 115 Queen St. East, St Marys, ON N4X 1B7
519-284-2440, Fax: 519-284-3650
editor@stmarys.com
www.stmarys.com
Circulation: 2,621 *Frequency: Wed.*
Laura Payton, Editor

St Thomas: **Elgin County Market**
16 Hincks St., St Thomas, ON N5R 5Z2
519-631-3782, Fax: 519-631-3759
www.elgincountymarket.com
Circulation: 30,600
Linda Axelson, Publisher

Stayner: **Angus-Borden Sun**
PO Box 80, 250 Main St. East, Stayner, ON L0M 1S0
705-428-2638, Fax: 705-428-6909
schalsun@bmts.com
www.simcoe.com
Circulation: 5,000 *Frequency: Wed.*
Joe Anderson, Publisher
John Devine, Editor-in-chief

Stirling: **The Belleville-Quinte Community Press**
PO Box 88, 14 Demerest Rd., Stirling, ON K0K 3E0
613-967-8467, Fax: 613-395-2992
general@communitypress-online.com
www.communitypress-online.com
Circulation: 38,211 *Frequency: Fri.*
Dan Kennedy, Publisher

Stirling: **The Community Press**
PO Box 88, Stirling, ON K0K 3E0
613-395-3015, Fax: 613-395-2992
general@communitypress-online.com
www.communitypress-online.com
Circulation: 10,494 *Frequency: Fri.*
Alan Coxwell, Publisher

Stirling: **The Community Press (East Ed.)**
PO Box 88, Stirling, ON K0K 3E0
613-395-3015, Fax: 613-395-2992
general@communitypress-online.com
www.communitypress-online.com
Circulation: 10,000 *Frequency: Fri.*

Stouffville: **Stouffville Sun-Tribune**
34 Civic Ave., Stouffville, ON L4A 1H2
905-640-2612, Fax: 905-640-8778
www.yorkregion.com
Circulation: 18,374 *Frequency: Thu., Sat.*
Ian Proudfoot, Publisher
Debora Kelly, Editor-in-chief

Stratford: **Inside Stratford/Perth**
PO Box 23016, #4, 285 Lorne Ave., Stratford, ON N5A 7V8
519-272-0051, Fax: 519-272-0067
inside@primus.ca
www.insidestratfordperth.com
Circulation: 24,086 *Frequency: Fri.*
Nancy Johnson, Publisher
Richard Johnson, Editor

Stratford: **Marketplace**
PO Box 430, 16 Packham Rd., Stratford, ON N5A 6T6
519-271-2220, Fax: 519-271-1026, 800-265-8577
beaconherald@bowesnet.com
www.stratfordbeaconherald.com
Circulation: 16,000 *Frequency: weekly*
Dave Carter, Publisher

Stratford: **Stratford City Gazette**
413 Hibernia St., Stratford, ON N5A 5W2
519-271-8002
www.southwesternontario.ca/sw/news/stratford/
Circulation: 13,490 *Frequency: Fri.*
Kevin McCann, General Manager
Jim Hagarty, Editor

Strathroy: **Strathroy Age-Dispatch**
8 Front St. East, Strathroy, ON N7G 1Y4
519-245-2370, Fax: 519-245-1647
agedispatch@strathroyonline.com
www.strathroyagedispatch.com
Circulation: 4,070 *Frequency: Wed.*
Denise Armstrong, Manager, Advertising
Steve Down, Publisher
Dave Cameron, Editor

Sturgeon Falls: **Sturgeon Falls Tribune**
206 King St., Sturgeon Falls, ON P2B 1R7
705-753-2930, Fax: 705-753-5231
tribune@westnipissing.com
Circulation: 2,661 *Frequency: Tue.; English & French*
Suzanne Gammon, Publisher

Sudbury: **Journal Le Voyageur**
525, av Notre-Dame, Sudbury, ON P3C 5L1
705-673-3377, Fax: 705-673-5854, 866-688-7027
levoyageur@levoyageur.ca
www.levoyageur.ca
Circulation: 8 700 *Frequency: Mercredi; français*
Gouled Hassan, Administration
Réjean Grenier, Éditeur
Yves Nadeau, Directeur, Marketing
William Levasseur, Rédacteur

Sudbury: **Northern Life**
158 Elgin St., Sudbury, ON P3E 3N5
705-673-5667, Fax: 705-673-4652
resource@northernlife.ca
www.northernlife.ca
Circulation: 90,727 *Frequency: Wed., Fri.*
Abbas Homayed, Publisher

Sudbury: **South Side Story**
#204, 469 Bouchard St., Sudbury, ON P3E 2K8
705-523-2339, Fax: 705-523-8499
Circulation: 47,100
Colin Firth, Contact

Tavistock: **Tavistock Gazette**
PO Box 70, 119 Woodstock South, Tavistock, ON N0B 2R0
519-655-2341, Fax: 519-655-3070
gazette@tavistock.on.ca
www.tavistock.on.ca
Circulation: 1,323 *Frequency: Wed.*
William Gladding, Publisher

Tecumseh: **Shoreline Week**
1614 Lesperance Rd., Tecumseh, ON N8N 1Y2
519-735-2080, Fax: 519-735-2082
shoreline@windsoressexnews.com
www.windsoressexnews.com
Circulation: 15,024 *Frequency: Wed.*
Gary Baxter, Publisher

Thamesville: **Thamesville Herald**
PO Box 580, 65 London Rd., Thamesville, ON N0P 2K0
519-692-3825, Fax: 519- -
Circulation: 772 *Frequency: Wed.*
Allison Humphrey, Publisher

Thessalon: **The North Shore Sentinel**
PO Box 640, 155 Main St., Thessalon, ON P0R 1L0
705-842-2504, Fax: 705-842-2679
Circulation: 2,315 *Frequency: Wed.*
Randy Rankin, Publisher

Thornbury: **The Courier Herald**
PO Box 190, 51 Bruce St. S, Thornbury, ON N0H 2P0
519-599-3760, Fax: 519-599-3214
www.bluemountainschamber.ca/courier
Circulation: 1,100 *Frequency: Wed.; also Meaford Express (Wed., circ. 2,521)*
Kathy Taylor, Publisher

Thorold: **Niagara This Week**
#1, 3550 Schmon Pkwy., Thorold, ON L2V 4Y6
905-688-2444
www.niagarathisweek.com
Circulation: 342,000 *Frequency: Wed., Fri.*
Mike Williscraft, Director of Editorial

Thunder Bay: **Thunder Bay's Source**
87 North Hill St., Thunder Bay, ON P7A 5V6
807-346-2600, Fax: 807-345-9923
ldunick@dougallmedia.com
www.tbsource.com
Circulation: 48,000 *Frequency: Fri.*
Leith Dunick, Publisher

Tilbury: **Tilbury Times**
PO Box 490, Tilbury, ON N0P 2L0
519-682-0411, Fax: 519-682-3633
tiltimes@ciaccess.com
www.windsoressexnews.com
Circulation: 1,962 *Frequency: Wed.*
Gary Baxter, Publisher
Bob Odette, Associate Editor

Tillsonburg: **Tillsonburg Independent**
PO Box 190, 25 Townline Rd., Tillsonburg, ON N4G 4H6
519-688-6397, Fax: 519- -
www.tillsonburgnews.ca
Circulation: 10,201 *Frequency: Wed.*
Cam McKnight, Publisher

Tillsonburg: **Tillsonburg News**
PO Box 190, 25 Townline Rd., Tillsonburg, ON N4G 4H6
519-688-4400, Fax: 519-842-3511
www.tillsonburgnews.ca
Circulation: 8,019 *Frequency: Mon., Fri.*
Cam McKnight, Publisher

Timmins: **Les Nouvelles**
187, rue Cedar, Timmins, ON P4N 7G1
705-268-2955, Fax: 705-268-3614
lesnouv@vianet.ca
www.apf.ca/lesnouvelles
Frequency: Mercredi; français
Doris Bouchard, Editor
Bruce Cowan, Publisher

Timmins: **Timmins Times**
815 Pine St. South, Timmins, ON P4N 8S3
705-268-6252, Fax: 705-268-2255
times@timminstimes.com
www.timminstimes.com
Circulation: 37,416 *Frequency: Wed., Fri.*
Heather Duhns, Managing Editor
Linda Leblanc, Publisher

Tobermory: **The Bruce Peninsula Press**
PO Box 89, 39 Legion St., Tobermory, ON N0H 2R0
519-596-2658, Fax: 519-596-8030, 800-794-4480
info@tobermorypress.com
Circulation: 3,000 *Frequency: 16 times a year*
John Francis, Publisher
Holly Dunham, Editor

Toronto: **The Annex Gleaner**
154 Harbord St., Toronto, ON M5S 1H2
416-504-6987, Fax: 416-504-8792
editor@gleaner.on.ca
Circulation: 33,500 *Frequency: also The Liberty Gleaner, Village Gleaner*
Brian Burchell, Publisher
Anne Marie Brissenden, Editor-in-chief

Toronto: **The Bay Street Times**
#514, 5334 Yonge St., Toronto, ON M2N 6V1
416-949-6332, Fax: 416-997-6697
editor@baystreettimes.com
www.baystreettimes.com
Frequency: Monthly

Toronto: **Bayview Post**
30 Lesmill Rd., Toronto, ON M3B 2T6
416-250-7979, Fax: 416-250-1737
info@postcitymagazines.com
www.postcitymagazines.com
Circulation: 30,000 *Frequency: also North Toronto Post, North York Post, Richmond Hill Post*
Lorne London, Publisher

Toronto: **Beach Metro Community News**
2196 Gerrard St. East, Toronto, ON M4E 2C7
416-698-1164, Fax: 416-698-1253
admin@beachmetro.com
www.beachmetro.com
Circulation: 30,000 *Frequency: Tue.*
Sheila Blinoff, General Manager
Carole Stimmell, Editor

Toronto: **Beach Riverdale Mirror**
100 Tempo Ave., Toronto, ON M2H 2N8
416-493-4400, Fax: 416-493-6190
www.insidetoronto.ca
Circulation: 21,228 *Frequency: Fri.*
Betty Carr, Publisher

Toronto: **Downtown Bulletin**
#121, 260 Adelaide St. East, Toronto, ON M5A 1N1
416-929-0011
info@communitybulletin.ca
www.thebulletin.ca
Circulation: 60,000 *Frequency: Mon., Monthly*
Frank Touby, Editor
Paulette Touby, Publisher

Toronto: **East York Mirror**
100 Tempo Ave., Toronto, ON M2H 3S5
416-493-4400, Fax: 416-493-6190
www.insidetoronto.ca/to/eastyork/
Circulation: 35,302 *Frequency: Fri.*
Betty Carr, Publisher
Deborah Bodine, Editor-in-chief

Toronto: **Etc...News**
201 Leslie St., Toronto, ON M4M 3C6
416-465-7554, Fax: 416-778-7540
etcnews@sympatico.ca
www.etcnews.ca
Circulation: 25,000 *Frequency: 16 times a year; every 3rd Thurs.*
Bruce Brackett, Publisher, brackett@sympatico.ca
Terry Brackett, Editor

Toronto: **Etobicoke Guardian**
307 Humberline Dr., Toronto, ON M9W 5V1
416-675-4390, Fax: 416-675-9296
etg@mirror-guardian.com
www.insidetoronto.ca
Circulation: 138,838 *Frequency: Wed., Fri.*
Tony Poland, Editor-in-chief
Betty Carr, Publisher

Toronto: **European Reporter**
PO Box 6039, Toronto, ON L5P 1B2
647-274-8689, Fax: 905-281-9436
mail@europeanreporter.com
www.europeanreporter.com
Frequency: Bi-weekly

Toronto: **L'Express**
17 Carlaw Ave., Toronto, ON M4M 2R6
416-465-2107, Fax: 416-465-3778
express@lexpress.to
www.lexpress.to
Circulation: 20,000 *Frequency: Mardi; français; et: L'Observateur, London; L'Information, Hamilton/Burlington & Le Courrier d'Oshawa, Métro Courrier*
D.P. Mazare

Toronto: **Hi-Rise**
#121, 95 Leeward Glenway, Toronto, ON M3C 2Z6
416-424-1393, Fax: 416-467-8262
sec.valdunn@vif.com
www.hi-risenews.com
Circulation: 60,000 *Frequency: Monthly*
Valerie Dunn

Toronto: **New Canada**
#500, 120 Eglinton Ave. East, Toronto, ON M4P 1E2
416-481-7793, Fax: 416- -, 888-667-5877
humanrights@sympatico.ca
www.hrrc.ca
Circulation: 10,000 *Frequency: Fri.; English, Urdu & Panjabi*
Hasanat Ahmad Syed, Editor-in-chief

Toronto: **The New Canadian**
524 Front St. West, Toronto, ON M5V 1B8
416-593-1583, Fax: 416-593-1871
newcdn@japancominc.com
Circulation: 10,000 *Frequency: Thu.; English & Japanese*
Shin Kawai, Publisher

Toronto: **North York Mirror**
100 Tempo Ave., Toronto, ON M2H 3S5
416-493-4400, Fax: 416-493-6190
www.insidetoronto.ca/to/northyork/
Circulation: 193,559 *Frequency: Wed., Fri.*
Betty Carr, Publisher
David Harvey, Editor-in-chief

Toronto: **Our Toronto Free Press**
#200, 49 Elm St., Toronto, ON M5G 1H1
416-977-0183, Fax: 416-977-1322
www.canadafreepress.com
Frequency: Tue.
Judi McLeod, Editor & Owner

Toronto: **Scarborough Mirror**
100 Tempo Ave., Toronto, ON M2H 3S5
416-493-4400, Fax: 416-493-6190
scm@torontocommunitynews.com
www.insidetoronto.ca/to/scar borough/
Circulation: 227,965 *Frequency: Wed., Fri.*
Betty Carr, Publisher
Alan Shackleton, Editor-in-chief

Toronto: **Share**
658 Vaughan Rd., Toronto, ON M6E 2Y5
416-656-3400, Fax: 416-656-0691
share@interlog.com
www.sharenews.com
Circulation: 50,000
Arnold A. Auguste, Publisher

Toronto: **Thornhill Post**
30 Lesmill Rd., Toronto, ON M2N 3B4
416-250-7979, Fax: 416-250-1737
admin@postcitymagazines.com
www.postcitymagazines.com
Circulation: 30,000 *Frequency: Fri.*
Lorne London, Publisher

Toronto: **Toronto Street News**
c/0 LoveCry, 1024 Queen St. East, Toronto, ON M4M 1K4
416-406-0099
debramoon-ivil.tripod.com/thetorontostreetnews/id1.html
Circulation: 3,000 *Frequency: Weekly*
Victor Fletcher, Publisher

Toronto: **Town Crier**
101 Wingold Ave., Toronto, ON M6B 1P8
416-785-4300, Fax: 416-488-4918
info@towncrieronline.ca
www.towncrieronline.ca
Frequency: Monthly; nine separate newspapers: Bayview Mills TC, Bloor-Annex TC (circ. 30,000); Beach Riverdale TC (circ. 30,000); Leaside-Rosedale TC (circ. 25,000); North Toronto TC (circ. 30,000) Forest Hill T
Eric McMillan, Managing Editor
Lori Abittan, President & Publisher

Toronto: **The Village Post**
30 Lesmill Rd., Toronto, ON M3B 2T6
416-250-7979, Fax: 416-250-1737
postnews@idirect.com
Circulation: 27,000
Lorne London, Publisher

Toronto: **The Villager**
#206, 2323 Bloor St. West, Toronto, ON M8X 1B6
416-239-3029, Fax: 416-767-4880
www.thevillager.ca
Circulation: 42,351 *Frequency: Fri.*
Dave Harvey, Contact

Toronto: **The Women's Post**
#804, 2 Carlton St., Toronto, ON M5B 1J3
416-964-5850, Fax: 416-964-6142
www.womenspost.ca
Circulation: 71,818 *Frequency: Bi-monthly*
Sarah Whatmough-Thomson, Editor

Toronto: **York Guardian**
100 Tempo Ave., Toronto, ON M2H 3S5
416-493-4400, Fax: 416-493-6190
www.insidetoronto.com/news/york?thePub=york
Circulation: 30,000 *Frequency: Fri.*
Betty Carr, Publisher
Deborah Bodine, Editor-in-chief

Trenton: **Trentonian**
41 Quinte St., Trenton, ON K8V 5R3
613-392-6501, Fax: 613-392-0505
newsroom@trentonian.ca
www.trentonian.ca
Circulation: 6,642 *Frequency: Mon., Wed., Fri.*

Tweed: **Tweed News**
PO Box 550, Tweed, ON K0K 3J0
613-478-2017, Fax: 613-478-2749
thenews@magma.ca
Circulation: 1,111 *Frequency: Wed.*
Rodger Hanna, Publisher & Editor
Roseann Trudeau, Circulation Manager

Uxbridge: **Times-Journal**
PO Box 459, 16 Bascom St., Uxbridge, ON L9P 1M9
905-852-9141, Fax: 905-852-9341
jpirone@durhamregion.com
www.durhamregion.com
Circulation: 16,941 *Frequency: Wed, Fri.*
Tim Whittaker, Publisher, jpirone@durhamregion.com

Vankleek Hill: **Vankleek Hill Review**
PO Box 160, 76 Main St. East, Vankleek Hill, ON K0B 1R0
613-678-3327, Fax: 613-678-2700, 877-678-3327
review@thereview.on.ca
www.thereview.on.ca
Circulation: 3,662 *Frequency: Wed.; English & French*
Louise Sproule, Publisher
Richard Mahoney, Editor

Virgil: **Niagara Advance**
PO Box 430, Virgil, ON L0S 1T0
905-468-3283, Fax: 905-468-3137
notleditorial@cogeco.net
Circulation: 7,331 *Frequency: Sat.*
Tim Dundas, Publisher
Penny Coles, Editor

Walkerton: **Walkerton Herald-Times**
PO Box 190, 10 Victoria St., Walkerton, ON N0G 2V0
519-881-1600, Fax: 519-881-0276
www.walkerton.com
Circulation: 2,200 *Frequency: Wed.*
John McPhee, General Manager

Wallaceburg: **Wallaceburg Courier Press**
1542 Dufferin Ave., Wallaceburg, ON N8A 2W9
519-627-1488, Fax: 519-627-0640
couriernews@kent.net
www.wallaceburgcourierpress.com
Circulation: 11,168 *Frequency: Wed.*
Dean Muharrem, Publisher

Wallaceburg: **Wallaceburg News**
538 James St., Wallaceburg, ON N8A 2N9
519-627-2557, Fax: 519-627-1261
www.thewallaceburgnews.ca
Frequency: Wed.
Wayne Snider, Managing Editor
Daryl Smith, Publisher

Wasaga Beach: **Stayner Sun**
1456B Mosley St., Wasaga Beach, ON L9Z 2B9
705-428-2638, Fax: 705-422-2446
www.staynersun.ca
Circulation: 1,128 *Frequency: Wed.*
Joe Anderson, Publisher

Wasaga Beach: **The Wasaga Sun**
1456B Mosley St., Wasaga Beach, ON L9Z 2B9
705-428-2638, Fax: 705-422-2446
www.wasagasun.ca
Circulation: 7,457 *Frequency: Wed.*
Joe Anderson, Publisher

Waterdown: **Flamborough Review**
PO Box 20, 30 Main St. North, Waterdown, ON L0R 2H0
905-689-4841, Fax: 905-689-3110
www.haltonsearch.com
Circulation: 13,662 *Frequency: Fri.*

Waterloo: **Waterloo Chronicle**
#20, 279 Weber St. North, Waterloo, ON N2J 3H8
519-886-2830, Fax: 519-886-9383
www.waterloochronicle.ca
Circulation: 31,564 *Frequency: Wednesday (weekly)*
Neil Oliver, Publisher

Watford: **Watford Guide-Advocate**
PO Box 99, 5292 Nauvoo Rd., Watford, ON N0M 2S0
519-876-2809, Fax: 519-876-2322
guideadvocate@execulink.com
Circulation: 1,160 *Frequency: Thursday (weekly).*
Dale Hayter, Publisher

Wawa: **Wawa/Algoma News Review**
PO Box 528, 37 Ste-Marie St., Wawa, ON P0S 1K0
705-856-2267, Fax: 705-856-4952, 800-461-9209
waprint2@ontera.net
Circulation: 1,060 *Frequency: Wed.*
W. Robert Avis, Publisher & Editor
Krystal Gignac, Advertising Manager

West Lorne: **The Chronicle**
PO Box 100, 167 Main St., West Lorne, ON N0L 2P0
519-768-2220, Fax: 519-768-2221
chronicle@bowesnet.com
www.thechronicle-online.com
Frequency: Thu.

Westport: **The Review-Mirror**
PO Box 130, 15 Church St., Westport, ON K0G 1X0
613-273-8000, Fax: 613-273-8001
revmir@rideau.net
www.review-mirror.com
Circulation: 1,929 *Frequency: Thur.*
Howard Crichton, Publisher

Wheatley: **Wheatley Journal**
PO Box 10, 14 Talbot West, Wheatley, ON N0P 2P0
519-825-4541, Fax: 519-825-4546
Circulation: 946 *Frequency: Wed.*
Rick Epplett, Publisher

Wiarton: **Wiarton Echo**
PO Box 220, 573 Berford St., Wiarton, ON N0H 2T0
519-534-1560, Fax: 519-534-4616
wiartonecho@bmts.com
www.wiartonecho.com
Circulation: 2,593 *Frequency: Wed.*
Keith Gilbert, Publisher

Winchester: **Winchester Press**
c/o 2woMor Publications Inc., PO Box 399, Winchester, ON K0C 2K0
613-774-2524, Fax: 613-774-3967
news@winchesterpress.on.ca
www.winchesterpress.on.ca
Circulation: 9,964 *Frequency: Wed.*
Donna Rushford, Publisher/Advertising Manager
Allen VanBridger, Co-Publisher/Managing Editor

Windsor: **Journal Le Rempart**
7515, chemin Forest Glade, Windsor, ON N8T 3P5
519-948-4139, Fax: 519-948-0628
info@lerempart.ca
www.lerempart.ca
Circulation: 1 000 *Frequency: Mercredi; français*
Denis Poirier, Publisher

Windsor: **Windsor Pennysaver**
#400, 4525 Rhodes Dr., Windsor, ON N8W 5R8
519-966-4500, Fax: 519-966-3660
classified@windsorpennysaver.com
www.windsorpennysaver.com
Circulation: 119,000 *Frequency: Fri.*

Wingham: **Wingham Advance-Times**
PO Box 390, 5 Diagonal Rd., Wingham, ON N0G 2W0
519-357-2320, Fax: 519-357-2900
editor@wingham.com
www.wingham.com
Circulation: 1,988 *Frequency: Wed.*
Kathy Steele, Publisher and General Manager

Woodstock: **Oxford Shopping News**
16 Brock St., Woodstock, ON N4S 3B4
519-537-6657, Fax: 519-537-8542
www.oxfordshoppingnews.com
Circulation: 28,284 *Frequency: Tue.*
Pat Logan, Publisher

Prince Edward Island

Daily Newspapers in Prince Edward Island

Charlottetown: **The Guardian**
PO Box 760, 165 Prince St., Charlottetown, PE C1A 7L8
902-629-6000, 800-267-6397
comments@theguardian.pe.ca
www.theguardian.pe.ca
Circulation: 21,023 *Frequency: Morning*
Don Brander, Publisher
Gary MacDougall, Managing Editor

Summerside: **Journal Pioneer**
PO Box 2480, 4 Queen St., Summerside, PE C1N 4K5
902-436-2125, Fax: 902-436-3027
info@journalpioneer.com
www.journalpioneer.com
Circulation: 10,257 *Frequency: Evening*
Darlene Shea, Managing Editor
Sandy Rundle, Publisher

Other Newspapers in Prince Edward Island

Alberton: **West Prince Graphic**
PO Box 339, 4 Railway St., Alberton, PE C0B 1B0
902-853-3320, Fax: 902-853-3071
jean.kenny@westprince.com
www.peicanada.com
Circulation: 6,016 *Frequency: Wed.*
Paul MacNeill, Publisher and General Manager

Montague: **The Eastern Graphic**
PO Box 790, 567 Main St. South, Montague, PE C0A 1R0
902-838-2515, Fax: 902-838-4392, 800-806-5443
www.peicanada.com
Circulation: 5,396 *Frequency: Wed.*
Paul MacNeill, Publisher

Summerside: **La Voix Acadienne**
5, av Maris Stella, Summerside, PE C1N 6M9
902-436-6005, Fax: 902-888-3976
pub@lavoixacadienne.com
www.lavoixacadienne.com
Circulation: 1 100 *Frequency: Mercredi; français*
Marcia Enman, Directrice général

Québec

Daily Newspapers in Québec

Chicoutimi: **Le Quotidien du Saguenay-Lac-St-Jean**
1051, boul Talbot, Chicoutimi, QC G7H 5C1
418-545-4474, Fax: 418-690-8824
www.cyberpresse.ca/quotidien
Circulation: 29 131 *Frequency: Matin; français*
Guy Granger, Président & Editeur
Michel Simard, Rédacteur-en-chef

Granby: **La Voix de L'Est**
76, rue Dufferin, Granby, QC J2G 9L4
450-375-4555, Fax: 450-777-7221
www.cyberpresse.ca/vde/
Circulation: 14 955 lun.-ven., 18,563 sam. *Frequency: Matin; français*
Jacques Pronovost, Président & Éditeur

Montréal: **Le Devoir**
2050, rue de Bleury, 9e étage, Montréal, QC H3A 3M9
514-985-3333, Fax: 514-985-3390
redaction@ledevoir.com
www.ledevoir.com
Circulation: 24 582 lun.-ven., 39 084 sam. *Frequency: Matin; français*
Josée Boileau, Rédactrice-en-chef

Montréal: **Le Journal de Montréal**
4545, rue Frontenac, Montréal, QC H2H 2R7
514-521-4545, Fax: 514-525-5442
http://lejournaldemontreal.canoe.ca
Circulation: 265 573 lun.-ven., 316 457 sam., 265 610 dim.
Frequency: Matin; français
Lyne Robitaille, Présidente et Éditrice

Montréal: **Metro**
#700, 625, av du President Kennedy, Montréal, QC H3A 1K2
514-286-1066, Fax: 514-286-9310

Montréal: **The Montréal Gazette**
#200, 1010 St. Catherine St. West, Montréal, QC H3B 5L1
514-987-2222, Fax: 514-987-2399
www.montrealgazette.com
Circulation: 148,000 Mon.-Fri.; 217,000 Sat.; 138,000 Sun.
Raymond Brassard, Managing Editor, 514-987-2508

Montréal: **La Presse**
7, rue St-Jacques, Montréal, QC H2Y 1K9
514-285-7000, Fax: 514-285-6808
www.cyberpresse.ca
Circulation: 185 609 lun.-ven., 268 236 sam., 194 012 dim.
Frequency: Matin; français
Guy Crevier, Président et éditeur
Éric Trottier, Vice-président et éditeur adjoint

Montréal: **Quotidien 24 heures Montréal**
465 McGill St., 3rd Fl., Montréal, QC H2Y 4B4
514-373-2424, Fax: 514-373-2400
information@24-heures.ca
toronto.24hrs.ca
Circulation: 134,691
Serge Gosselin, Editor

Québec: **Le Soleil**
CP 1547 Terminus, 410, boul Charest est, Québec, QC G1K 7J6
418-686-3394, Fax: 418-686-3374
redaction@lesoleil.com
www.cyberpresse.ca/le-soleil
Circulation: 181 380 *Frequency: Matin; français*
Claude Gagnon, Président & éditeur
Raymond Tardif, Éditeur adjoint

Sherbrooke: **The Record**
PO Box 1200, 1195 Galt East, Sherbrooke, QC J1K 1A1
819-569-9525, Fax: 819-569-3945, 800-463-9525
www.sherbrookerecord.com
Circulation: 25,135 *Frequency: Mon.-Fri.*
Randy Kinnear, Publisher
Sharon McCully, Editor-in-chief

Sherbrooke: **La Tribune**
1950, rue Roy, Sherbrooke, QC J1K 2X8
819-564-5450, Fax: 819-564-8098, 800-567-6955
redaction@latribune.qc.ca
www.cyberpresse.ca
Circulation: 32 000 lun.-ven., 42 000 sam. *Frequency: Matin; français*
Louise Boisvert, President and editor
Louise Boisvert, Présidente et éditrice

Trois-Rivières: **Le Nouvelliste**
CP 668, 1920, rue Bellefeuille, Trois-Rivières, QC G9A 3Y2
819-376-2501, Fax: 819-691-4356
noured@lenouvelliste.qc.ca
www.cyberpresse.ca/nouvelliste
Circulation: 45 000 lun.-ven., 48 000 sam. *Frequency: Matin; français*
Alain Turcotte, Rédactrice-en-chef
Raymond Tardif, Éditeur

Vanier: **Le Journal de Québec**
450, rue Bechard, Vanier, QC G1M 2E9
418-683-1573, Fax: 418-683-8886
commentaires@journaldequebec.com
www.journaldequebec.com
Circulation: 98 490 lun.-ven., 121 943 sam., 100 575304 dim.
Frequency: Matin; français
Jean-Claude L'Abbée, Éditeur et Chef de la direction
Serge Côté, Rédacteur en chef

Other Newspapers in Québec

Acton Vale: **La Pensée de Bagot**
962, rue St-André, Acton Vale, QC J0H 1A0
450-546-3271, Fax: 450-546-3491
publicite@lapensee.qc.ca
www.lapensee.qc.ca
Circulation: 13 660 *Frequency: Dimanche*
Michel Dorais, Directeur

Alma: **Le Lac Saint-Jean**
100 rue St-Joseph sud local #01, Alma, QC G8B 7A4
418-668-4545, Fax: 418-668-8522
redaction_alma@transcontinental.ca
www.lelacstjean.com
Circulation: 19 716 *Frequency: Samedi*
Gaston Martin

Amqui: **L'Avant-poste**
59, St-Benoît ouest, Amqui, QC G5J 2E4
418-629-3443, Fax: 418-629-2919
avantposte@globetrotter.net
www.hebdosquebecor.com/avp/in dex_avp.asp
Circulation: 8 815 *Frequency: Samedi*
Michèle Bérubé, Rédactrice-en-chef

Asbestos: **Les Actualités**
78, rue St-Jean, Asbestos, QC J1T 3R3
819-879-6681, Fax: 819-879-2355
fernand.lallier@hebdesquebecor.com
www.hebdosquebecor.com/aca/index_aca. asp
Circulation: 14 800 *Frequency: Samedi*
Fernand Lallier, Éditeur
Louise Jutras, Rédactrice-en-chef

Baie-Comeau: **Baie-Comeau-Objectif Plein Jour**
#309, 625, boul Laflèche, Baie-Comeau, QC G5C 1C5
418-589-5900, Fax: 418-589-5263
Circulation: 16 366 *Frequency: Vendredi, aussi Plein Jour sur la Manicouagan (mercredi, tirage 15 866)*

Baie-Comeau: **Journal Haute Côte Nord Est**
965, Parfondeval, Baie-Comeau, QC G5C 2W8
418-589-2090, Fax: 418-589-9989
journalhcn.baiecomeau@globetrotter.net
Circulation: 15 378

Baie-Comeau: **Le Plein-Jour en Haute Côte-Nord**
#309, 625, boul Laflèche, Baie-Comeau, QC G5C 1C5
418-589-5900, Fax: 418-589-5263
objectif@globetrotter.net
www.hebdosquebecor.com/pjh/index_pjh.asp
Circulation: 6 468 *Frequency: Vendredi*
Claude Mercier, Directeur général

Baie-Saint-Paul: **L'Hebdo Charlevoisien**
45, Raymond Mailloux, Baie-Saint-Paul, QC G3Z 1W2
418-665-1299, Fax: 418-665-2051
lhebdo.charlevoisien@sympatico.ca
www.journalhebdocharlevoisien.com
Circulation: 13 033 *Frequency: Samedi*
Guy Charlebois, Directeur de production
Charles Warren, Directeur

Beaulac-Garthby: **Le Contact de Beaulac-Garthby**
CP 58, 9, rue de la Chapelle, Beaulac-Garthby, QC G0Y 1BO
418-458-2737, Fax: 418-458-2737
contactbg2002@yahoo.ca
Circulation: 355
Andree Sautier, Redactrice-en-chef
Serge Frederick, President

Beloeil: **L'Oeil Régional**
393, boul Laurier, Beloeil, QC J3G 4H6
450-467-1821, Fax: 450-467-3087
journal@oeilregional.com
www.oeilregional.com
Circulation: 30 000 *Frequency: Samedi*
Guy Gilbert, Éditeur
Bernard Blanchard, Rédacteur-en-chef

Boucherville: **Journal La Relève Inc.**
528, rue St-Charles, Boucherville, QC J4B 3M5
450-641-4844, Fax: 450-641-4849
lareleve@lareleve.qc.ca
www.lareleve.qc.ca
Circulation: 54 650 *Frequency: Jeudi et Vendredi*
Charles Desmarteau, Directeur général

Boucherville: **La Seigneurie**
391, boul de Montagne, Boucherville, QC J4B 1B7
450-641-3360, Fax: 450-655-9752
info@la-seigneurie.qc.ca
www.hebdos.net/lsb
Circulation: 29 421 *Frequency: Samedi*
Serge Landry, Éditeur

Brossard: **Brossard-Eclair**
#A105, 7900, boul Taschereau, Brossard, QC J4X 1C2
450-466-3344, Fax: 450-466-9019
infos@brossardeclair.qc.ca
www.hebdosquebecor.com/bre/index_bre.asp
Circulation: 23 880 *Frequency: Mardi; French & English*
Léo Gagnon, Rédacteur-en-chef

Brossard: **Le Journal de St-Hubert**
#A105, 7900, boul Taschereau, Brossard, QC J4X 1C2
450-466-0036, Fax: 450-466-9019
info@journaldesainthubert.qc.ca
www.journaldesainthubert.qc.ca
Circulation: 28 000 *Frequency: Mercredi*
Léo Gagnon, Rédacteur

Buckingham: **Le Bullein de la Lièvre**
435, rue Principale, Buckingham, QC J8L 2G8
819-986-5089, Fax: 819-986-2073
Circulation: 11 351 *Frequency: Dimanche*
Michel Blais, Éditeur

Cantley: **L'Écho de Cantley**
188, montée de la Source, Boite 1, Comp. 9, Cantley, QC J8V 3J2
819-827-3496, Fax: 819- -
echo.cantley@sympatico.ca
Circulation: 2 400
Steve Harris

Cap-aux-Meules: **Le Radar**
CP 8183, Cap-aux-Meules, QC G4T 1R3
418-986-2345, Fax: 418-986-6358, 866-986-2345
leradar@lino.com
www.leradar.qc.ca
Circulation: 3 000 *Frequency: Vendredi; français*
Achille Hubert, Éditeur
Marielle Ouellet, Rédactrice-en-chef

Chambly: **Le Journal de Chambly**
CP 175, 1685, rue Bourgogne, Chambly, QC J3L 4B3
450-658-6516, Fax: 450-658-3785
info@journaldechambly.com
www.hebdos.net/jdc/
Circulation: 21 237 *Frequency: Mardi*
Carole Pronovost, Rédactrice-en-chef

Châteauguay: **Le Soleil du Samedi**
82, rue Salaberry sud, Châteauguay, QC J6J 4J6
450-692-8552, Fax: 450-692-3460
info@ cybersoleil.com
www.cybersoleil.com
Circulation: 28 197 *Frequency: Samedi*

Chibougamau: **Le Jamesien**
CP 250, 317, 3e rue, Chibougamau, QC G8P 2K7
418-748-6406, Fax: 418-748-2421
www.hebdosquebecor.com
Circulation: 10,000 *Frequency: Samedi*

Chicoutimi: **Le Progrès Dimanche**
1051, boul Talbot, Chicoutimi, QC G7H 5C1
418-690-8800, Fax: 418-690-8805
Circulation: 44 500 *Frequency: Dimanche*
Claude Gagnon, Éditeur

Coaticook: **Le Progrès de Coaticook**
72, rue Child, Coaticook, QC J1A 2B1
819-849-9846, Fax: 819-849-1041
progres@leprogres.net
www.leprogres.net
Circulation: 8 600 *Frequency: Samedi*
Henri Gérin, Éditrice

Cookshire: **Le Haut Saint-François**
CP 976, 212, rue Principale est, Cookshire, QC J0B 1M0
819-875-5501, Fax: 819-875-5327
jourhsf@globetrotter.net
www.microtec.net/~jourhsf
Circulation: 17 500 *Frequency: 20 fois par an*
Maxime Doyon, Président

Courcelette: **Journal Adsum**
CP 1000 Forces, Garnison Valcartier, bâtisse 200, local 102, Courcelette, QC G0A 4Z0
418-844-5000, Fax: 418-844-6934
tadsum@forces.gc.ca
Circulation: 5 500
Col. erry Champagne, Éditeur

Cowansville: **Le Guide/The Guide**
121, rue Principale, Cowansville, QC J2K 1J3
450-263-5288, Fax: 450-263-9435
leguide@canadafrancais.com
www.journal-leguide.com
Circulation: 17 884 *Frequency: Samedi*
Martine Chagnon, Directrice general

Daveluyville: **Le Causeur**
539, rte Principale, Daveluyville, QC G0Z 1C0
819-367-2210, Fax: 819-367-4011
lecauseur@yahoo.ca
Circulation: 1 100
Lucie Boulanger, Coordonnatrice

Delson: **Le Reflet**
11, rte 132, Delson, QC J0L 1G0
450-635-9146, Fax: 450-635-4619
info@lereflet.qc.ca
www.lereflet.qc.ca

Circulation: 31 700 *Frequency: Samedi*
Robert Fichaud, Éditeur
Hélène Gingras, Rédactrice-en-chef

Disraéli: **Le Cantonnier**
888, St-Antoine, Disraéli, QC G0N 1E0
418-449-1888, Fax: 418-449-1889
lecantonnier@lino.com
www.lecantonnier.com
Jean-Denis Grimard, Rédacteur en chef

Dolbeau-Mistassini: **Nouvelles Hebdo**
1741, des Pins, Dolbeau-Mistassini, QC G8L 1M9
418-276-6211, Fax: 418-276-6166
nh@destination.ca
www.nouvelles-hebdo.qc.ca
Circulation: 13 369
Michel Aubé, Éditeur

Dolbeau-Mistassini: **Le Point**
1570, boul Wallberg, Dolbeau-Mistassini, QC G8L 1H4
418-276-5110, Fax: 418-276-5354
atelierlepoint@qc.aira.com
www.lepoint.ca
Circulation: 12 375 *Frequency: Dimanche*
Diane Audet, Directrice générale

Dollard-Des Ormeaux: **Le Messager Lachine Dorval**
3677, boul. des Sources, Dollard-Des Ormeaux, QC H9B 2K4
514-685-4690, Fax: 514-685-3923
www.messagerlachine.com
Circulation: 23 100 *Frequency: Sun.; English & French*
Michel Bessette, Éditeur

Dollard-des-Ormeaux: **The Chronicle**
3677, boul des Sources, Dollard-des-Ormeaux, QC H9B 2T6
514-685-4690, Fax: 514-685-3452
www.westislandchronicle.com
Circulation: 14 800 *Frequency: Wed.*
Albert Kramberger, Éditeur

Dollard-des-Ormeaux: **Cités Nouvelles / City News**
3677, boul des Sources, Dollard-des-Ormeaux, QC H9B 2T6
514-685-4690, Fax: 514-685-3923
www.citesnouvelles.com
Circulation: 55 000 *Frequency: Sun.; English & French*

Donnacona: **Le Courrier de Portneuf**
CP 1030, 276, rue Notre-Dame, Donnacona, QC G3M 1G7
418-285-0211, Fax: 418-285-2441
www.courrierdeportneuf.com
Circulation: 31 953 *Frequency: Samedi*
Josee-Anne Fiset, Directrice general

Drummondville: **L'Express**
1050, rue Cormier, Drummondville, QC J2C 2N6
819-478-8171, Fax: 819-478-4306
lorraine.paquet@transcontinental.ca
www.expressparole.com
Circulation: 46 089 *Frequency: Dimanche*
Jean-Claude Bonneau, Rédacteur-en-chef
Johanne Marceau, Éditeur

Drummondville: **La Parole**
1050, rue Cormier, Drummondville, QC J2C 2N6
819-478-8171, Fax: 819-478-4306
lorraine.paquet@transcontinental.ca
www.expressparole.com
Circulation: 43 070 *Frequency: Mercredi*
Jean-Claude Bonneau, Rédacteur-en-chef
Johanne Marceau, Éditeur

Farnham: **L'Avenir & des Rivières**
322A, rue Principale est, Farnham, QC J2N 1L7
450-293-3138, Fax: 450-293-2093
lavence@canadafrancais.com
avenir-rivieres.com
Circulation: 14 390 *Frequency: Samedi*

Fermont: **Le Trait d'Union du Nord**
1 Centre L.J. Patterson, CP 561, Fermont, QC G0G 1J0
418-287-3655, Fax: 418-287-3874
journalisteTDN@.diffusionfermont.ca
Circulation: 1 700
Eric Cyr, Rédacteur-en-chef

Forestville: **Journal Haute Côte-Nord Ouest**
#100, 31 rte 138 ouest, Forestville, QC G0T 1E0
418-587-2090, Fax: 418-587-6407
journhcn@globetrotter.net
www.journalhautecotenord.com
Circulation: 6 285 *Frequency: Vendredi*
Luc Brisson

Fort-Coulonge: **Fort Coulonge/Pontiac Journal / Le Journal de Pontiac**
PO Box 279, 289, Hwy. 148, Fort-Coulonge, QC J0X 1V0
819-683-3583, Fax: 819-683-2977
journalpontiac@bellnet.ca
Circulation: 9,855 *Frequency: Every other Wed.; English & French*
Dana Bertrand, Circulation Manager
Fred Ryan, Publisher & Editor

Gatineau: **Aylmer Bulletin**
#C-10, 181, rue Principale, Gatineau, QC J9H 6A6
819-684-4755, Fax: 819-684-6428, 800-486-7678
abawqp@videotron.ca
www.bulletinaylmer.com
Circulation: 17,645 *Frequency: Wed.*
Lynne Lavery, General Manager
Fred Ryan, Publisher

Gatineau: **Le Régional Aylmer/Hull**
#30, 160, boul de l'Hopital, Gatineau, QC J8T 8J1
819-568-7736, Fax: 819-568-8728
www.info07.com/
Circulation: 10 650 *Frequency: Mercredi*

Gatineau: **Le Régional d'Aylmer**
#30, boul de l'Hopital, Gatineau, QC J8T 8J1
819-684-0097, Fax: 819-776-1668
regional@magma.ca
Circulation: 11,905
Jacques Blais, Éditeur
Bryan Kirk, Rédacteur-en-chef

Gatineau: **La Revue de Gatineau**
#106, 430, boul de l'Hôpital, Gatineau, QC J8V 1T7
819-568-7736, Fax: 819-568-7038
www.info07.com
Circulation: 41 174 *Frequency: Mercredi*
Yves Blondin, Éditeur

Gatineau: **Week-end Outaouais**
#106, 430, boul de L'Hôpital, Gatineau, QC J8V 1T7
819-568-7736, Fax: 819-568-7038
Circulation: 50 903 *Frequency: Samedi*
Sylvain Dupras, Editeur-en-chef

Gatineau: **West Québec Post**
#C-10, 181, rue Principale, Gatineau, QC J9H 6A6
819-684-4755, Fax: 819-684-6428, 800-486-7678
abawqp@videotron.ca
Circulation: 5,238 *Frequency: Fri.*
Lynne Lavery, General Manager
Fred Ryan, Publisher

Granby: **Le Citoyen**
#2, 189, rue Dufferin, Granby, QC J2G 4X2
450-777-1636, Fax: 450-378-4980
Circulation: 17 500 *Frequency: Samedi*
Charles Gagnon, Éditeur

Granby: **Journal l'Express**
#5, 398, rue Principale, Granby, QC J2G 2W6
450-777-4515, Fax: 450-777-4516
monjournalexpress.com
Circulation: 39 500 *Frequency: Hebdomadaire*
Claude Hébert, Redactrice-en-chef

Granby: **La voix de l'est plus**
76, rue Dufferin, Granby, QC J2G 9L4
450-375-6850, Fax: 450-777-4865
Circulation: 47 222 *Frequency: Samedi*
Pierre Gobeil, Éditeur

Grande-Vallée: **Le Phare, l'autre vision**
3, Saint-François-Xavier est, Grande-Vallée, QC G0E 1K0
418-393-2161, Fax: 418-393-2274
journallephare@chez.com
www.chez.com/journallephare
Circulation: 1 325
Noël-Denis Samson, Président

Grosse Isle: **First Informer**
2-246 Ch. Principale, Grosse Isle, QC G4T 6A8
418-985-2100, Fax: 418-985-2274
first@duclos.net
www.firstinformer.com
Circulation: 619 *Frequency: Fri.*
Joy Davies, Publisher

Hudson: **Hudson/St. Lazare Gazette**
PO Box 70, Hudson, QC J0P 1H0
450-458-5482, Fax: 450-458-3337
hudsongazette@videotron.ca
www.hudsongazette.com
Circulation: 16,000 *Frequency: Wed.*
Was Lake of Two Mountains Gazette. First English Quebec weekly on the web.
G. Jones, Publisher & Editor

Huntingdon: **The Gleaner**
66 Chateauguay, Huntingdon, QC J0S 1H0
450-264-5364, Fax: 450-264-9521
info@gleaner-source.com
www.gleaner-source.com
Circulation: 3,328 *Frequency: Wed.; English & French*
Patrice Laflamme, French Editor,
plaflamme@gleaner-source.com
Andre Castagnier, Publisher, acastagnier@gleaner-source.com
Susanne J. Brown, Editor, editorial@gleaner-source.com

Joliette: **L'Action**
342, Beaudry nord, Joliette, QC J6E 6A6
450-759-3664
infolanaudiere@transcontinental.ca
www.laction.com
Circulation: 46 700 *Frequency: Dimanche*

Joliette: **L'Action Montcalm**
262, boul l'Industrie, Joliette, QC J6E 3Z1
450-759-3664, Fax: 450-759-9828
André Nadeau, Éditeur
Francine Rainville, Rédactrice-en-chef

Joliette: **L'Expression de Lanaudière**
342, Beaudry nord, Joliette, QC J6E 6A6
450-752-0447, Fax: 450-759-0945
Circulation: 45 195 *Frequency: Dimanche*
Jean-Pierre Malo, Éditeur
André Lafrenière, Rédacteur-en-chef

Jonquière: **Le Réveil**
CP 520, 3388, boul St-François, Jonquière, QC G7X 7W4
418-695-2601, Fax: 418-695-0530, 800-387-2601
atelier.reveil@hebdosquebecor.com
www.lereveil.com
Circulation: 70 529 *Frequency: Dimanche*
Diane Audet, Directrice générale

Jonquière: **Le Réveil**
CP 520, 3388, boul St-François, Jonquière, QC G7X 7W4
418-695-2601, Fax: 418-695-1391, 800-387-2601
atelier.reveil@hebdosquebecor.com
www.lereveil.com
Circulation: 71 416 *Frequency: Dimanche; aussi Le Point (samedi, 13 067)*
Diane Audet, Contact

Knowlton: **Brome County News**
88-A Lakeside St., Knowlton, QC J0E 1V0
450-242-1188, Fax: 450-243-5155, 800-463-9525
newsroom@sherbrookerecord.com
www.sherbrookerecord.com
Circulation: 12,307 *Frequency: Wed.*
Elanor Brown, Editor
Randy Kinnear, Publisher

L'Islet: **Le Hublot**
CP 347, 62, ave 5, L'Islet, QC G0R 2C0
418-247-7345, Fax: 418-247-5085
lehublot@caramail.com
Circulation: 1 735 *Frequency: Last Thurs. of the month*
Jean-François Pelletier, Président

La Malbaie: **Le Plein Jour Charlevoix**
#110, 249, rue Nairn, La Malbaie, QC G5A 1M4
418-665-6121, Fax: 418-665-3105
redaction@pleinjour.com
www.hebdosquebecor.com
Circulation: 12 725 *Frequency: Vendredi*
Benoit Paré

La Salle: **Magazine Ile des Soeurs / Nuns Island Magazine**
420 rue Lafleur, La Salle, QC H8R 3H6
514-363-5656, Fax: 514-363-3895
pierre.vigneault@transcontinental.ca
www.lemagazineids.com
Circulation: 8 091 *Frequency: Wed.; English & French*
Pierre Vigneault, Éditeur

La Salle: **Le Messager Verdun**
420, rue Lafleur, La Salle, QC H8R 3H6
514-363-5656, Fax: 514-363-3895
lussierp@transcontinental.ca
www.messagerverdun.com
Circulation: 24 500 *Frequency: Sun.; English & French*

La Salle: **La Voix Populaire**
420, rue Lafleur, La Salle, QC H8R 3H6
514-363-5656, Fax: 514-363-3895
,arilyse.hamelin@transcontinental.ca
www.lavoixpopulaire.com
Circulation: 23 500 *Frequency: Dimanche*
Mathieu Robert-Perron, Directeur de l'information,
mathieu.robert-perron@transcontinental.c

La Tuque: **L'Echo de La Tuque**
324, rue St-Joseph, La Tuque, QC G9X 1L2
819-523-6141
www.lechodelatuque.com/
Circulation: 6 802

Lac-Etchemin: **La Voix du Sud**
1516A, rte 277, Lac-Etchemin, QC G0R 1S0
418-625-7471, Fax: 418-625-5200, 866-325-8649
production_lacetchemin@transcontinental.ca
www.lavoixdusud.com
Circulation: 22 434 *Frequency: Samedi*
Caroline Gilbert, Éditeur
André Poulin, Rédacteur-en-chef

Lac-Mégantic: **L'Echo de Frontenac**
5040, boul des Vétérans, Lac-Mégantic, QC G6B 2G5
819-583-1630, Fax: 819-583-1124, 866-583-1630
hebdo@echodefrontenac.com
www.echodefrontenac.com
Circulation: 9 134 *Frequency: Dimanche; français*
Gaétan Poulin, Éditeur
Rémi Tremblay, Rédacteur-en-chef

Lachenaie: **Le Trait d'Union**
#210, 1300, Grande Allée, Lachenaie, QC J6W 4M4
450-964-4400
www.letraitdunion.com

Lachute: **L'Argenteuil**
52, rue Principale, Lachute, QC J8H 3A8
450-562-2494, Fax: 450-562-1434
roger@eap.on.ca
www.largenteuil.ca
Circulation: 15 000 *Frequency: Mercredi; français*
Evelyne Bergeron, Rédacteur-en-chef

Lachute: **Progrès Watchman**
52, rue Principale, Lachute, QC J8H 3A8
450-562-8593, Fax: 450-562-1434, 800-561-5738
www.progres-watchman.ca
Circulation: 13 000 *Frequency: Samedi*
Evelyne Bergeron, Editor

Lasalle: **Le Messager de LaSalle**
420, Lafleur, Lasalle, QC H8R 3H6
514-363-5656, Fax: 514-363-3895
boulangerp@transcontinental.ca
www.messagerlasalle.com
Circulation: 32 200 *Frequency: Sun.; English & French*
Jean-Guy Marceau, Éditeur

Lasalle: **Weekly Post/L'Hebdo de Ville Mount-Royal**
#70, 410, rue Lafleur, Lasalle, QC H8R 3H6
514-739-3302, Fax: 514-739-3304
Frequency: Thur.; English & French

Laurier-Station: **Le Peuple Lotbinière**
CP 130, 1000, ch St-Joseph, Laurier-Station, QC G0S 1N0
418-728-2131, Fax: 418-728-4819
redaction.lotbiniere@hebdosquebecor.com
www.peuplelotbiniere.com
Circulation: 12 390 *Frequency: Dimanche; français*
Denys Simoneau, Éditeur

Laval: **The Chomedey News**
250, 657, boul Curé-Labelle, Laval, QC H7V 2T8
450-978-9999, Fax: 450-687-6330
www.chomedeynews.ca
Circulation: 28,965 *Frequency: Thu.*
George Bakoyannis, Publisher

Laval: **Courrier Laval**
189, av Laval, Laval, QC H7N 3V8
450-667-4360, Fax: 450-667-9498
www.courrierlaval.com
Circulation: 108 375 *Frequency: Dimanche; aussi Courrier du Jeudi*
François Charbonneau, Éditeur

Laval: **Vivre**
828 - 79 av, Laval, QC H7V 3J1
450-973-8787, Fax: 450-973-8414
ccvm@videotron.ca
www.ccvm.org

Circulation: 5 000
Johane Papineau, Directrice

***Lennoxville:* The Townships Sun**
PO Box 28, 7 Conley St., Lennoxville, QC J1M 1Z3
819-566-7424, Fax: 819-566-7424
townsun@abacom.com
Circulation: 696 *Frequency: Monthly*
David Wright, Editor

***Lévis:* Le Peuple**
CP 1200, 421, rue Dorimene Des Jardins, Lévis, QC G6V 6R8
418-833-9398, Fax: 418-833-8177
bertrand.picard@hebdosquebecor.com
www.peuplelevis.com
Circulation: 57 087 *Frequency: Samedi*

***Lingwick:* Le Reflet du Canton de Lingwick**
#306, 72, rte 108, Lingwick, QC J0B 2Z0
819-877-3560
refletgt@axion.ca
www.axion.ca/~reflet
Frequency: 9/an
Daniel Pezat, Président

***Longueuil:* Point Sud**
#200, 24, rue De Gentilly, Longueuil, QC J4H 1Y8
450-677-2626, Fax: 450-442-2663
info@pointsud.ca
www.pointsud.ca

***Louiseville:* L'Echo d'Autray et de Maskinongé**
43, St-Louis, Louiseville, QC J5V 2C7
819-228-5532, Fax: 819-228-9379, 877-228-5532
lyne.baribeau@transcontinental.ca
www.lechoam.com
Circulation: 27 200 *Frequency: Dimanche*
Lyne Baribeau, Éditrice

***Magog:* Le Reflet du Lac**
#104, 101, rue Du Moulin, Magog, QC J1X 4A1
819-843-3500, Fax: 819-843-3085
www.lerefletdulac.com
Circulation: 23 359 *Frequency: Samedi*

***Malartic:* Le Courrier de Malartic**
CP 4020, Malartic, QC J0Y 1Z0
819-757-4712, Fax: 819-757-4712
Circulation: 1 200 *Frequency: Mardi; français*
Denyse Roberge, Éditrice

***Maniwaki:* La Gatineau**
114, rue de la Ferme, Maniwaki, QC J9E 3J9
819-449-1725, Fax: 819-449-5108
Circulation: 11 100 *Frequency: Vendredi; français*
Marguette Ceré, Directrice

***Matane:* La Voix Gaspesienne**
#107, 305, rue de la Gare, Matane, QC G4W 3J2
418-562-4040, Fax: 418-562-4607
www.hebdosquebecor.com/vxg/index_vxg.asp
Circulation: 5 013 *Frequency: Mercredi; aussi La Voix du dimanche*
Romain Pelletier, Rédacteur-en-chef

***Mont-Joli:* L'Information**
135, rue Doucet, Mont-Joli, QC G5H 1R6
418-775-4381, Fax: 418-775-7768
www.hebdosquebecor.com/ifm/index_ifm.asp
Circulation: 10 500 *Frequency: Dimanche*

***Mont-Laurier:* Le Choix d'Antoine-Labelle**
369, boul Paquette, Mont-Laurier, QC J9L 1K5
819-623-3112, Fax: 819-623-6224, 888-484-8181
www.journallechoix.qc.ca
Circulation: 16 890 *Frequency: Vendredi*
Luc Bélanger, Éditeur

***Mont-Laurier:* L'Echo de la Lievre**
534, de la Madonne, Mont-Laurier, QC J9L 1S5
819-623-5250, Fax: 819-623-7148
www.hebdosquebecor.com/edl/index_edl.asp
Circulation: 16 000 *Frequency: Samedi*

***Mont-Royal:* Greek Canadian Reportage**
PO Box 54025, Mont-Royal, QC H3P 3H4
514-279-7772,
Circulation: 15,000 *Frequency: Weekly; Greek*
Anthony Bartzakos, Publisher & Editor

***Mont-Tremblant:* L'Information du Nord**
1107, rue de Saint-Jovite, Mont-Tremblant, QC J8E 3J9
819-425-8658, Fax: 819-425-7713
info.nord@hebdoqquebecor.com
www.hebdosquebecor.com/ifj/i ndex_ifj.asp

Circulation: 14 300 *Frequency: Vendredi*
Daniel Deslauriers, Rédacteur-en-chef

***Montmagny:* L'Oie Blanche**
70, rue de l'Anse, Montmagny, QC G5V 3S7
418-248-8227, Fax: 418-248-4033
oieblanc@globetrotter.net
www.oieblanc.com/oie3/index.asp
Circulation: 19 672 *Frequency: Samedi*
France Fortin

***Montmagny:* Le Peuple de la Côte-du-Sud**
80, boul Taché est, Montmagny, QC G5V 3S7
418-248-0415, Fax: 418- -
www.hebdosquebecor.com/pcs/index_pcs.asp
Circulation: 21 073 *Frequency: Samedi*

***Montréal:* Le Couac**
CP 222, Montréal, QC H3K 3G5
info@lecouac.org
www.lecouac.org

***Montréal:* Courrier Ahuntsic**
1569, rue Fleury est, Montréal, QC H2C 1S7
514-381-4414, Fax: 514-381-1278
www.courrierahuntsic.com
Frequency: Dimanche

***Montréal:* Échos du Vieux-Montréal**
234, rue St-Paul ouest, Montréal, QC H2Y 1Z9
514-844-2133, Fax: 514-844-5858
echos@pubrde.com
Circulation: 15 000
Denise Di Candido, Chief Editor
Vincent Di Candido, Président

***Montréal:* Le Journal de Mont-Royal**
6965 6e ave., Montréal, QC H2A 3E3
514-270-8088
www.expressoutrement.com
Frequency: also Le Point d'Outremont, L'Etoile du Plateau & Mile End

***Montréal:* Journal de Rosemont**
6965, 6e Avenue, Montréal, QC H2A 3E3
514-270-8088, Fax: 514-270-8368
cerasis@transcontinental.ca
www.journalderosemont.com
Circulation: 59 588
Sylvia Cerasi, Rédactrice-en-chef
Sylviane Lussier, Éditrice

***Montréal:* Journal L'Itinéraire**
2103, rue Sainte-Catherine est, 3e étage, Montréal, QC H2K 2H9
514-597-0238, Fax: 514-597-1544
itineraire@itineraire.ca
www.itineraire.ca
Circulation: 13 000 *Frequency: bimensuel*
Jocelyne Sénécal, Directrice des ressources humines
Serge Lareault, Directeur général

***Montréal:* Le Monde**
CP 201 St-Michel, Montréal, QC H2A 3L8
514-722-7708, Fax: 514-722-3667
lemonde@arobas.net
Circulation: 22 000 *Frequency: Monthly*
Raymond Gagnon, President

***Montréal:* National Review of Medicine**
400 McGill St., 3rd Fl., Montréal, QC H2Y 2G1
514-397-8833, Fax: 514-397-0228, 800-663-7403
editor@nationalreviewofmedicine.com
www.nationalreviewofmedicine.com
Circulation: 41,761 *Frequency: 21 times a year*
David Elkins, Executive Editor

***Montréal:* Nouvelles de l'Est**
6965, 6e Ave., Montréal, QC H2A 3E3
514-270-8088, Fax: 514-270-8368
pinely@transcontinental.ca
www.nouvellesdelest.com
Circulation: 24 629
Yannick Pinel, Rédacteur-en-chef
Sylviane Lussier, Éditrice & Directrice

***Montréal:* Nouvelles Parc-Extension News**
#250, 657, boul Curé-Labelle, Montréal, QC H7V 2T8
450-978-9999, Fax: 450-687-6330
http://px-news.com/
Frequency: Sat.; English & French
George Bakoyannis, Co-Publisher, General Director

***Montréal:* Place Publique**
3516, Place du Parc, Montréal, QC H2X 2H7
514-844-6917
placepub@cam.org
Circulation: 25 000
Alex Frettier, Rédacteur en chef

***Montréal:* Le Plateau**
6965, 6e av, Montréal, QC H2A 3E3
514-270-8088, Fax: 514-270-8368
lussiers@transcontinental.ca
www.leplateau.com
Circulation: 34 132
Sylviane Lussier, Éditeur
Alain Perron, Rédacteur-en-chef

***Montréal:* Progrès Saint-Léonard**
#212, 8770, boul Langelier, Montréal, QC H1P 3C6
514-899-5888, Fax: 514-899-5984
www.progresstleonard.com
Circulation: 30 592 *Frequency: Mercredi*
Jean Touchette, Éditeur
Jacques Boulanger, Éditeur

***Montréal:* Progrés Villeray**
6965, 6e Ave., Montréal, QC H2A 3E3
514-270-8088, Fax: 514-270-8368
www.leprogresvilleray.com
Circulation: 22 576
Alain Perron, Rédacteur-en-chef
Sylviane Lussier, Éditrice

***Montréal:* Reflet de Société/Le Journal de la rue**
4237, rue Ste-Catherine est, Montréal, QC H1V 1X4
514-256-9000, Fax: 514-256-9444
journal@journaldelarue.ca
www.cafegraffiti.net
Circulation: 60 000 *Frequency: 6 fois par an*
Raymond Viger, Redacteur en chef

***Montréal:* Le Soi-disant**
4240, rue Ontario est, Montréal, QC H1V 1K1
514-257-9028, Fax: 514-252-7425
Circulation: 5 000
Richard Aubry, Président

***Montréal:* Le Ville-Marie**
6965, 6e av, Montréal, QC H2A 3E3
514-270-8088, Fax: 514-270-8368
www.leville-marie.com

***Montréal:* Visions Voisins / Neighbour Visions**
770 Rachel east (3rd Fl), Montréal, QC H2W 2M5
514-277-7801, Fax: 514-277-8919
afarrell@cdn-news.com
Circulation: 4 000
Ann Farrell, Rédactrice

***Montréal:* Vue sur la Bourgogne**
755, rue des Seigneurs, Montréal, QC H3J 1K2
514-596-4978, Fax: 514-596-4981
Circulation: 5 500
Miriam Rouleau-Perez, Responsable

***Napierville:* Coup D'Oeil**
350, rue St-Jacques, Napierville, QC J0J 1L0
450-245-3344, Fax: 450-245-7419, 800-363-4542
coupdoeil@canadafrancois.com
www.journal-coupdoeil.com
Circulation: 12 072 *Frequency: Samedi*
Claude Trahan, Directeur de la publication
Charles Couture, Directeur édition et distribution

***Natashquan:* Le Portageur**
CP 40, 50, ch d'en haut, Natashquan, QC G0G 2E0
418-726-3736, Fax: 418-726-3714
secom@globetrotter.net
Circulation: 548 *Frequency: Mercredi*
Nicole Lessard

***New Carlisle:* The Gaspé Spec**
CP 99, 128, boul Gerard D. Levesque, New Carlisle, QC G0C 1Z0
418-752-5400, Fax: 418-752-6932
specs@globetrotter.net
www.gaspespec.com/
Circulation: 3,022 *Frequency: Sun.*
Sharon Farrell, Publisher

***New Richmond:* L'Echo de la Baie**
140, boul Perron ouest, New Richmond, QC G0C 1B0
418-392-5083, Fax: 418-392-6605
www.hebdosquebecor.com/eba/index_eba.asp
Frequency: Dimanche

Alain St-Amand, Directeur général régional

Nicolet: Le Courrier du Sud
3255 Marie-Victorin, Nicolet, QC J3T 1X5
450-646-3333, Fax: 450-674-0205, 866-646-3332
journal@courrierdusud.com
www.lecourrierdusud.com
Circulation: 127 350 *Frequency: Samedi aussi Longueuil Extra (mercredi, tirage 50 000)*
Lucie Masse

Nicolet: Le Courrier-Sud
Medias Trancontinental, 3255, rue Marie Victorin, Nicolet, QC J3T 1X5
819-293-4551, Fax: 819-293-8758
nancy.allaire@transcontinental.ca
www.lecourriersud.com
Circulation: 21 105 *Frequency: Dimanche*
Emilie Vallée, Rédactrice
Nancy Allaire, Editrice
Suzanne Blanchette, Secrétaire de direction

Outremont: L'Express d'Outremont/de Mont-Royal
6965 6e ave., Outremont, QC H2V 2K8
514-270-8088
redactionexpress@transcontinental.ca
www.expressoutremont.com
Circulation: 28 748 *Frequency: Jeudi, hebdo*
Mario Marois, Éditeur
Marilaine Bolduc-Jacob, Rédactrice en chef

Port-Cartier: Le Port-Cartois
10, des Pins, Port-Cartier, QC G5B 2A5
418-766-5322, Fax: 418-766-5329
redaction.portcartois@hebdosquebecor.com
www.hebdosquebecor.com
Circulation: 3 600 *Frequency: Dimanche*
Jean-Guy Gougeon

Préissac: L'Alliance
180, av du Lac, Préissac, QC J0Y 2E0
819-759-4141, Fax: 819-759-4142
journalalliance@cablevision.qc.ca
Circulation: 1 000 *Frequency: Mensuel*
Estelle Gelot, Présidente

Québec: L'Actuel
#900, 1265, boul Charest ouest, Québec, QC G1N 4V4
418-686-6400, Fax: 418-686-4841
www.quebechebdo.com
Circulation: 38 000 *Frequency: Samedi*
François Cattapan, Rédacteur en chef

Québec: L'Appel
#900, 1265, boul Charest ouest, Québec, QC G1N 4V4
418-686-6400, Fax: 418-686-4841
www.quebechebdo.com
Circulation: 52 000 *Frequency: Samedi*
François Cattapan, Rédacteur en chef

Québec: Beauport Express
Hebdos Transcontinental à Québec, #900, 1265, boul Charest ouest, Québec, QC G1N 4V4
418-686-6400, Fax: 418-686-1086
yvan.rancourt@transcontinental.ca
www.beauportexpress.com
Circulation: 38 700 *Frequency: Hebdomadaire*
Alain Lepage, Éditeur
Yvan Rancourt, Directeur des ventes

Québec: Charlesbourg Express
Médias-Transcontinental, #900, 1265, boul Charest ouest, Québec, QC G1N 4V4
418-686-6400, Fax: 418-686-4841
www.quebechebdo.com
Circulation: 30 100 *Frequency: Samedi*
François Cattapan, Rédacteur en chef

Québec: Journal Droit de Parole
412, 3e av, Québec, QC G1L 2W1
418-648-8043
cbv@oricom.ca
droitdeparole.org
Circulation: 15 000 *Frequency: bi-hebdomadaire*
Gilles Simard, Rédacteur-en-chef
Claude Giguère, Journaliste

Québec: Journal Jacques-Cartier
Médias-Transcontinental, #900, 1265, boul Charest ouest, Québec, QC G1N 4V4
418-686-3036
www.lejacquescartier.com
Circulation: 9,500 *Frequency: au 2 mois*
François Cattapan, Rédacteur en chef

Québec: Journal le Carrefour
#20, 580, Grande Allée est, Québec, QC G1R 2K2
418-649-0775, Fax: 418-649-7531
carrefour@webnet.qc.ca
Circulation: 72 500 *Frequency: Dimanche*
Martin Claveau, Éditeur
Nicolas Godbout, Rédacteur-en-chef

Québec: Journal Québec Express
#900, 1265, boul Charest ouest, Québec, QC G1N 4V4
418-686-6400
www.quebechebdo.com
Frequency: Dimanche

Québec: Quebec Chronicle-Telegraph
#101, 1248, che. Ste-Foy, Québec, QC G1X 2M5
418-650-1764, Fax: 418-650-5172
qct@videotron.ca
www.qctonline.com
Circulation: 1,854 *Frequency: Wed.*
Karen Macdonald, Publisher

Québec: Québec Express
Médias-Transcontinental, #900, 1265, boul Charest ouest, Québec, QC G1N 4V4
418-686-6400
www.quebechebdo.com
Circulation: 38 000
François Cattapan, Rédacteur en chef

Québec: La Quête
729, Côte d'Araham, Québec, QC G1R 1A1
418-649-2388, Fax: 418-649-7770
laquete@archipelentraide.com
www.archipelentraide.com
Circulation: 3 000
Bernard Hélie, Coordonnateur

Repentigny: L'Artisan
1004, rue Notre-Dame, Repentigny, QC J5Y 1S9
450-581-5120, Fax: 450-581-4515
www.journallartisan.com
Circulation: 46 432 *Frequency: Mardi; aussi Hebdo Rive-Nord (dimanche, tirage 39 900)*
Jacques Boulanger, Éditeur

Repentigny: Hebdo Rive-Nord
1004, rue Notre-Dame, Repentigny, QC J5Y 1S9
450-581-5120, Fax: 450-581-6509
boulangery@transcontinental.ca
www.hebdorivenord.com
Circulation: 46 457 *Frequency: Dimanche*
Yannick Boulanger, Éditeur

Richelain: Journal Servir
Garnison St-Jean, CP 100 Bureau Chef, Richelain, QC J0J 1R0
450-358-7099, Fax: 450-358-7423
journalservin@videotron.net
Circulation: 3 300 *Frequency: English & French*
Gaëtane Dion, Rédactrice-en-chef

Rimouski: L'Avantage Votre Journal
183, St-Germain ouest, Rimouski, QC G5L 4B8
418-722-0205, Fax: 418-723-4237
bgleeson@lavantage.qc.ca
www.lavantage.qc.ca
Circulation: 40 586 *Frequency: Vendredi*
Bill Gleeson

Rimouski: L'Avant-Poste Gaspesien
CP 410, 73, rue Saint-Germain est, Rimouski, QC G5L 7C4
418-723-4800, Fax: 418-722-4078
Frequency: Dimanche

Rimouski: Le Hâvre
CP 3217 A, 217, av Léonidas, Rimouski, QC G5L 9G6
418-689-4518, Fax: 418- -
Circulation: 8 430 *Frequency: Dimanche*
Karine Boudreau, Rédactrice-en-chef

Rimouski: Le Pharillon
CP 3217 A, 217, av Léonidas, Rimouski, QC G5L 9G6
418-368-3242, Fax: 418-368-1705
www.hebdosquebecor.com/pha/index_pha.asp
Circulation: 8 618 *Frequency: Dimanche*
Michèle Lemieux, Rédactrice-en-chef

Rimouski: Le Progrès Echo
CP 3217, 217, av Léonidas, Rimouski, QC G5L 9G6
418-721-1212, Fax: 418-723-1855
www.progresecho.com
Circulation: 30 492 *Frequency: Dimanche*
Ernie Wells, Rédacteur-en-chef

Rimouski: Le Rimouskois
CP 3217, 271, av Le¢nidas, Rimouski, QC G5L 9G6
418-721-1212, Fax: 418-723-1855
www.hebdosquebecor.com/rim/index_rim.asp
Circulation: 24 059 *Frequency: Mercredi*
Ernie Wells, Rédacteur-en-chef

Rimouski: Vision Terre et Forêt
CP 3217 A, 217, av Léonidas, Rimouski, QC G5L 9G6
418-721-1222, Fax: 418-721-1222
atelier.rimouski@editionsbelcor.com
www.hebdosquebecor.com/vis/index_vis .asp
Circulation: 6 500
Alice Roussell, Rédacteur-en-chef

Rivière-Portneuf: Nouvelles d'icitte
CP 310, Rivière-Portneuf, QC G0T 1P0
418-238-5566, Fax: 418-238-2793
Circulation: 800
Denise Fournier, Rédactrice-en-chef

Rivière-du-Loup: Info Dimanche
72, rue Fraser, Rivière-du-Loup, QC G5R 1C6
418-862-1911, Fax: 418-862-6165
journal@infodimanche.com
www.infodimanche.com
Circulation: 29 118 *Frequency: Dimanche*
Mario Pelletier, Rédacteur-en-chef
Michel Chalifour, Éditeur

Rivière-du-Loup: Info Dimanche
72, rue Fraser, Rivière-du-Loup, QC G5R 1C6
418-862-1911, Fax: 418-862-6165
journal@infodimanche.com
www.infodimanche.com
Circulation: 30 000 *Frequency: Dimanche*
Mario Pelletier, Rédacteur en chef

Rivière-du-Loup: Saint-Laurent Portage
16, rue du Domaine, Rivière-du-Loup, QC G5R 2P5
418-862-1774, Fax: 418-862-4387
grapho.ede_st@sympatico.ca
www.hebdosquebecor.com/slp/
Circulation: 39 000 *Frequency: Dimanche*
Richard Gauthier

Roberval: L'Etoile du Lac
#101, 797 boul. Saint-Joseph, Roberval, QC G8H 2L4
418-275-2911, Fax: 418-275-2834
production_roberval@transcontinental.ca
www.letoiledulac.com
Circulation: 14 158 *Frequency: Samedi*

Roberval: L'Horizon
#101, 797, boul St-Joseph, Roberval, QC G8H 2L4
418-236-4432, Fax: 418-236-9144
Circulation: 450

Rouyn-Noranda: Le Citoyen Rouyn-Noranda
CP 490, 25 rue Gamble est, Rouyn-Noranda, QC J9X 5C4
819-797-2450, Fax: 819-762-4361
Circulation: 18 760 *Frequency: Dimanche; supplement, Journal du Nord-Ouest*
Andre Renaud, Directeur, 819/762-4361

Rouyn-Noranda: La Frontière
CP 490, 25, rue Gamble est, Rouyn-Noranda, QC J9X 5C4
819-762-4361, Fax: 819-797-2450
www.hebdosquebecor.com/fro/index_fro.asp
Circulation: 5 626 *Frequency: Mercredi*

Saint-André-Avellin: La Petite Nation
CP 240, 70, rue Principale, Saint-André-Avellin, QC J0V 1W0
819-983-2725, Fax: 819-983-6844, 800-567-6898
Circulation: 9 600 *Frequency: Dimanche*
Michel Blais, Rédacteur

Saint-Anselme: Le Tour des ponts
#102, 134, rue Principale, Saint-Anselme, QC G0R 2N0
418-885-9867, Fax: 418-885-9834
Circulation: 1 425
Jacquelin Guillemette, Président

Saint-Basile-le-Grand: Journal L'Impact
#101, 155, Sir Wilfrid Laurier, Saint-Basile-le-Grand, QC J3N 1A9
450-441-7252, Fax: 450-441-4497
journallimpact@videotron.ca
www.journallimpact.com

Saint-Bruno: L'Écho de Saint-Bruno
1688, Place Seigneuriale, Saint-Bruno, QC J3V 4E4
450-653-5295, Fax: 450- -
Circulation: 10 000 *Frequency: Mensuel*

Saint-Bruno: **Le Journal de Saint-Bruno**
1507, rue Roberval, Saint-Bruno, QC J3V 3P8
450-653-3685, Fax: 450-653-6967
www.journaldest-bruno.qc.ca
Circulation: 14 900 *Frequency: Samedi*

Saint-Bruno: **Les Versants du Mont-Bruno**
1488, rue Montarville, Saint-Bruno, QC J3V 3T5
450-441-5300, Fax: 450-441-5450
www.versants.com
Circulation: 18 000

Saint-Bruno-Lac-Saint-Jea: **Le Brunois**
197, rue Jauvin, Saint-Bruno-Lac-Saint-Jea, QC G0W 2L0
418-343-3437, Fax: 418-343-2662
Circulation: 1 000
Jacques Demers, Rédacteur en chef

Saint-Bruno-de-Kamouraska: **Le Trait d'Union de St-Bruno**
CP 3, 4, rue du Couvent, Saint-Bruno-de-Kamouraska, QC G0L 2M0
418-492-7849, Fax: 418-492-2612
trdunion@globetrotter.net
Constance Gagné, Présidente

Saint-Denis-de-Brompton: **Le Saint-Denisien**
CP 244, 1495, route 222, Saint-Denis-de-Brompton, QC J0B 2P0
819-572-4445, Fax: 819-562-2888
stdenisi@abacom.com
Circulation: 1 175
Johanne Carrier, Président

Saint-Donat: **Journal Altitude**
CP 1350, 365, rue Principale, Saint-Donat, QC J0T 2C0
819-424-2610, Fax: 819-424-3615
journalaltitude@bellnet.ca
www.st-donat.com/journal.html
Circulation: 3,700 *Frequency: Vendredi; français*
Jean Lafortune, Rédacteur-en-chef

Saint-Eustache: **La Concorde**
53, rue St-Eustache, Saint-Eustache, QC J7R 2L2
450-472-3440, Fax: 450-472-1629
laconcorde@groupejcl.com
www.linfonet.com/concframe.cfm
Circulation: 45 300 *Frequency: Mercredi; aussi L'Eveil (dimanche; tirage 37 400)*
Jean-Claude Langlois, Éditeur
Rémi Binette, Rédacteur en chef

Saint-Eustache: **L'Éveil**
53, rue St-Eustache, Saint-Eustache, QC J7R 2L2
450-472-3440, Fax: 450-472-1638
Circulation: 45 720 *Frequency: Samedi*
Jean-Claude Langlois, Éditeur
Rémi Binette, Rédacteur-en-chef

Saint-Eustache: **Le Nord Info**
53, rue St-Eustache, Saint-Eustache, QC J4R 2L2
450-435-6537, Fax: 450-435-7968
pub@groupejcl.com
www.groupejcl.com
Circulation: 57 000 *Frequency: Samedi*
Jean-Claude Langlois, Éditeur

Saint-Hippolyte: **Le Sentier**
CP 135, Saint-Hippolyte, QC J8A 3P5
450-563-1975, Fax: 450-563-1059
journal.lesentier@videotron.ca
www.inter-actif.qc.ca/le-s entier/
Circulation: 4 000
Manon Dagenais, Présidente

Saint-Hyacinthe: **Le Clairon Regional de St-Hyacinthe**
655, av Ste-Anne, Saint-Hyacinthe, QC J2S 5G4
450-773-6028, Fax: 450-773-3115
publicite@courrierclairon.qc.ca
www.leclairon.qc.ca
Circulation: 33 985 *Frequency: Samedi*
Benoit Chartier, Editor, Ventes

Saint-Hyacinthe: **Le Courrier de Saint-Hyacinthe**
655, rue Ste-Anne, Saint-Hyacinthe, QC J2S 5G4
450-773-6028, Fax: 450-773-3115
info@lecourrier.qc.ca
www.lecourrier.qc.ca
Circulation: 13 605 *Frequency: Mercredi; français*
Martin Bourassa, Rédacteur-en-chef

Saint-Jean-sur-Richelieu: **Le Canada Français**
84, rue Richelieu, Saint-Jean-sur-Richelieu, QC J3B 6X3
450-347-0323, Fax: 450-347-4539
canadaf@canadafrancais.com
www.canadafrancais.com
Circulation: 18 955 *Frequency: Mercredi; aussi Le Richelieu Dimanche (dimanche)*
Robert Paradis, Éditeur

Saint-Jean-sur-Richelieu: **Le Richelieu Dimanche**
84, rue Richelieu, Saint-Jean-sur-Richelieu, QC J3B 6X3
450-347-0323, Fax: 450-347-4539
Circulation: 35 795
Robert Paradis, Éditeur

Saint-Jérome: **L'Echo du Nord**
179, rue St-Georges, Saint-Jérome, QC J7Z 4Z8
450-436-5887, Fax: 450-436-5904
www.hebdosquebecor.com/edl/index_edl.asp
Circulation: 7 500 *Frequency: Mercredi*
Andre Juteau, Éditeur
Claude Lamarche, Rédacteur-en-chef

Saint-Jérome: **Journal Le Mirabel**
179, rue St-Georges, Saint-Jérome, QC J7Z 4Z8
450-436-8200, Fax: 450-436-8912
Circulation: 39 430 *Frequency: Samedi*

Saint-Jérome: **Journal Le Nord**
393, boul des Laurentides, Saint-Jérome, QC J7Z 4L9
450-438-8383, Fax: 450-438-4174
editeur@journallenord.qc.ca
www.journallenord.com
Circulation: 40 012 *Frequency: Mercredi*
François Laferrière, Éditeur

Saint-Lambert: **Saint-Lambert Journal**
574, rue Victoria, Saint-Lambert, QC J4P 2J5
450-671-0014, Fax: 450- -
Circulation: 10,800 *Frequency: Wed.; English & French*

Saint-Laurent: **Les Nouvelles Saint-Laurent / Saint-Laurent News**
#304, 685, boul Décarie, Saint-Laurent, QC H4L 5G4
514-855-1292, Fax: 514-855-1855
gauthiera@transcontinental.ca
www.nouvellessaint-laurent. com
Circulation: 27 499 *Frequency: Sun.; English & French*
Alexandre Gauthier, Rédacteur-en-chef

Saint-Laurent: **The Suburban**
#105, 7575 Trans-Canada Hwy., Saint-Laurent, QC H4T 1V6
514-484-1107, Fax: 514-484-9616
suburban@thesuburban.com
www.thesuburban.com
Circulation: West End: 64,000; West Island: 41,000; East End: 25,000 *Frequency: Wed.: West End, West Island; Thu.: East End*
Michael Sochaczevski, Publisher
Sari Medicoff, Operations Manager

Saint-Malo: **L'Informalo**
50, ch Aukland, Saint-Malo, QC J0B 2Y0
819-658-3587, Fax: 819-658-1019
clevesque29@hotmail.com
Circulation: 450 *Frequency: Bimestrielle, 1er mardi à chaque 2 mois*

Saint-Pamphile: **L'Écho d'en Haut**
#209, 25, rue Principale, Saint-Pamphile, QC G0R 3X0
418-356-5491, Fax: 418-356-5491
Circulation: 2 915
Claudel Pelletier, Président

Saint-Pascal: **Le Placoteux**
491, av d'Anjou, Saint-Pascal, QC G0L 3Y0
418-492-2706, Fax: 418-492-9706
association@leplacoteux.qc.ca
www.leplacoteux.qc.ca
Circulation: 17 469 *Frequency: Dimanche*
Bruno Lacroix, Editeur

Saint-Pierre-Ile-d'Orléan: **Autour de l'île**
CP 124, Saint-Pierre-Ile-d'Orléan, QC G0A 4E0
418-828-0330, Fax: 418-828-0741
autourdelile@videotron.ca
Circulation: 3 400 *Frequency: 6/an*
Léo- Desaulniers, Président

Saint-Siméon: **Le Goéland**
CP 250, 127, boul Perron ouest, Saint-Siméon, QC G0C 3A0
418-534-2026, Fax: 418-534-4353
Circulation: 610
Antoinette Arsenault, Éditrice

Saint-Tite: **L'Hebdo Mekinac/des Chenaux**
CP 4057, Saint-Tite, QC G0X 3H0
819-537-5111, Fax: 819-537-5471
gilles.guay@transcontinental.ca
www.lhebdomekinacdeschenaux.com
Circulation: 13 081 *Frequency: Samedi; français*
Gilles Guay, Éditeur

Sainte-Adèle: **Le Journal des Pays D'en Haut**
102, rue Morin, Sainte-Adèle, QC J8B 2P7
450-229-6664, Fax: 450-229-6063
www.hebdosquebecor.com/pdh/index_pdh.asp
Circulation: 23 000 *Frequency: Mercredi*
Kim Nymark, Directrice générale

Sainte-Anne: **Le Point d'Impact**
194B, boul Sainte-Anne, Sainte-Anne, QC J0N 1H0
Circulation: 6 000 *Frequency: Samedi*

Sainte-Anne-de-Beaupré: **L'Autre Voix**
#230, 9749, boul Ste-Anne, Sainte-Anne-de-Beaupré, QC G0A 3C0
418-827-1511, Fax: 418-827-1513
info@lautrevoix.com
www.lautrevoix.com
Mathieu Tremblay, Éditeur

Sainte-Anne-des-Monts: **Le Riverain**
21-A, boul. Ste-Anne Est, Sainte-Anne-des-Monts, QC G4V 1M4
418-763-7777, Fax: 418-763-7778
atelier.matane@hebdoquebecor.com
www.hebdosquebecor.com/riv/index_riv.as p
Circulation: 5,749 *Frequency: Dimanche*
Allen Cormier, Rédacteur-en-chef

Sainte-Brigitte-de-Laval: **Le Lavalois**
CP 1020, Sainte-Brigitte-de-Laval, QC G0A 3K0
418-907-7172, Fax: 418-907-7172
lelavalois@ccapcable.com
pages.ccapcable.com/lavalois/?page=100
Circulation: 1 300 *Frequency: 10/an*
Lucille Thomassin, Présidente

Sainte-Geneviève-de-Batis: **Le Bulletin des Chenaux**
#220, 44, Rivière-à-Vaeillette, Sainte-Geneviève-de-Batis, QC G0X 2R0
418-362-2134, Fax: 418-362-2861
redaction@lebulletindeschenaux.com
www.lebulletindescheneaux.com
Circulation: 9 000
Fanny Prince, Directrice générale

Sainte-Julie: **L'Information Ste-Julie**
#2, 566, rue Jules-Choquet, Sainte-Julie, QC J3E 1W6
450-649-0719, Fax: 450-649-7748
info@infodeste-julie.qc.ca
www.hebdos.net/isj/
Circulation: 19 363 *Frequency: Samedi*
Serge Landry, Éditeur
Yves Bélanger, Rédacteur-en-chef

Sainte-Marie: **Beauce Media**
CP 400, 1147, boul Vachon, Sainte-Marie, QC G0S 2Y0
418-387-8000, Fax: 418-387-4495
www.hebdosquebecor.com/bem/index_bem.asp
Circulation: 16 807 *Frequency: Lundi*

Sainte-Marie: **Beauce Week-End**
450, 2e av, Sainte-Marie, QC G6E 1B6
418-387-6969, Fax: 418-387-5223, 877-387-6969
bweekend@dynamiques.com
www.dynamiques.com/dynamiques/bwe.html
Circulation: 19 400 *Frequency: Vendredi*
Nicolas Lapointe, Directeur

Sainte-Thérèse: **Le Courrier de Groulx**
#204, 190, rue Curé Labelle, Sainte-Thérèse, QC J7E 2X5
450-434-4144, Fax: 450-434-3142
Circulation: 54 072 *Frequency: Samedi*
Donald Brouillette, Rédacteur-en-chef

Sainte-Thérèse: **Journal Le Courrier**
#204, 190, boul Labelle, Sainte-Thérèse, QC J7E 2X5
450-434-4144, Fax: 450-434-3142, 866-434-4144
louis.sauvageau@transcontinental.ca
www.journallecourrier.com
Circulation: 55 472 *Frequency: Samedi*
Louis Sauvageau, Editor
Linda Veilleux, Directrice de tirage

Sainte-Thérèse: **La Voix des Milles-Iles**
50B, rue Turgeon, Sainte-Thérèse, QC J7E 3H4

450-435-6537, Fax: 450-435-0588
pubnordinfo@groupejcl.com
www.linfonet.com; www.groupejcl.com
Circulation: 57 000 *Frequency: Mercredi*
Jean-Claude Langlois, Éditeur

***Saint-Élie-d'Orford:* L'Info**
CP 157, Saint-Élie-d'Orford, QC J0B 2S0
819-829-9639, Fax: 819-566-5218
Circulation: 3 000
Jean Charron, Directeur

***Saint-Étienne-des-Grès:* Le Stéphanois**
CP 282, 1260, rue St-Alphonse, Saint-Étienne-des-Grès, QC G0X 2P0
819-535-2089, Fax: 819-535-5118
lestephanois@cgocable.ca
www.lestephanois.ca/
Circulation: 1 700
Gilbert Bournival, Président

***Sept-Iles:* Le Nord-Est**
365, boul Laure, Sept-Iles, QC G4R 2X1
418-962-4100, Fax: 418-962-0439
www.hebdosquebecor.com/nes/index_nes.asp
Circulation: 13 510 *Frequency: Dimanche; aussi Le Nord-Est Plus (mercredi)*

***Shawinigan:* L'Hebdo du St-Maurice**
CP 10, 2102, av Champlain, Shawinigan, QC G9N 6T8
819-537-5111, Fax: 819-537-5471
michel.matteau@transcontinental.ca
www.lhebdodustmaurice.com
Circulation: 30 511 *Frequency: Samedi; français*
Michel Matteau, Éditeur

***Shawville:* The Equity**
PO Box 4300, 133 Centre St., Shawville, QC J0X 2Y0
819-647-2204, Fax: 819-647-2206
news@theequity.ca
www.theequity.ca
Circulation: 3,362 *Frequency: Upd from CCNA*
Heather Dickson, Publisher

***Sherbrooke:* Entrée Libre**
#317, 187, rue Laurier, Sherbrooke, QC J1H 4Z4
819-821-2270, Fax: 819-566-2664
Circulation: 9 000
Normand Gilbert, Président

***Sherbrooke:* La Nouvelle de Sherbrooke**
1950, rue Roy, Sherbrooke, QC J1K 2E8
819-566-8022, Fax: 819-563-1977
Circulation: 47 000 *Frequency: Mercredi*
Céline Maheu, Éditrice
Denis Duchaine, Rédacteur-en-chef

***Shipshaw:* La Vie d'Ici**
4681, rue Saint-Léonard, Shipshaw, QC G7P 1J4
418-542-6252, Fax: 418-542-0850
Circulation: 1 200 *Frequency: Mensuel*
Claire Duchesne, Présidente

***Sorel:* Les 2 Rives**
77, rue George, Sorel, QC J3P 1C2
450-742-9408, Fax: 450-742-2493
les2rives@les2rives.com
www.hebdos.net/drs
Circulation: 28 000 *Frequency: Mardi*
Pierre Plante, Éditeur
Louise Grégoire-Racicot, Rédactrice-en-chef

***Sorel-Tracy:* Journal La Voix**
58, rue Charlotte, Sorel-Tracy, QC J3P 1G3
450-743-8466, Fax: 450-742-8567
info@journallavoix.net
www.journallavoix.net
Circulation: 29 125 *Frequency: Hebdomadaire, samedi*
Johanne Berthiaume, Éditrice/Dir. gén., j.berthiaume@journallavoix.net
Hélène Goulet, Rédactrice, h.goulet@journallavoix.net

***St-Charles-de-Bellechasse:* Au fil de la Boyer**
CP 316, 8B ave Commerciale, St-Charles-de-Bellechasse, QC G0R 2T0
418-882-4242, Fax: 418-887-5050
laboyer@laboyer.com
www.laboyer.com
Circulation: 1 000
Jean-Pierre Paré, Éditeur

***St-Fabien-de-Panet:* Le Réveil**
199B, rue Bilodeau, St-Fabien-de-Panet, QC G0R 2J0
418-249-2128, Fax: 418-249-2138
lereveil@sogetel.net
Frequency: Mensuel
Thérèse Bilodeau, Présidente

***St-François:* L'Echo de St-François**
534, ch St-François ouest, St-François, QC G0R 3A0
418-259-2177, Fax: 418-259-2177
echosf@globetrotter.net
Circulation: 675 *Frequency: Mensuel*
Lorraine Lamonde, Présidente

***St-Georges:* Éclaireur Progrès/Beauce Nouvelle**
12625, 1e av, St-Georges, QC G5Y 2E4
418-228-8858, Fax: 418-227-0268
eclaprog@globetrotter.net
www.hebdosquebecor.com/ecl/index_ecl.asp
Circulation: 28 700 *Frequency: Mercredi, Vendredi*
Michel Roy, Directeur de l'information

***St-Jean:* L'Attisée**
CP 847, 318, rue Verreault, 2e étage, St-Jean, QC G0R 3G0
418-598-9590, Fax: 418-598-7588
journalattisee@videotron.ca
Circulation: 2 250
Benoit Lévesque, Éditeur

***St-Laurent:* Courrier Bordeaux/Cartierville**
#304, 685, boul, Décarie, St-Laurent, QC H4L 5G4
514-855-1292, Fax: 514-381-1278
www.courrierbc.com
Circulation: 17 237 *Frequency: Dimanche*
Jacques Dion, Éditeur

***St-Léonard:* L'Avenir de l'Est**
 # 210, 8770 boulevard Langelier, St-Léonard, QC H1P 3C6
514-899-5888, Fax: 514-899-5001
www.avenirdelest.com
Circulation: 42 314

***St-Léonard:* Le Flambeau de l'Est**
#210, 8770, boul Langelier, St-Léonard, QC H1P 3C6
514-899-5888, Fax: 514-899-5001
www.flambeaudelest.com

***St-Léonard:* Guide de Montréal-Nord**
#210, 8770, boul Lanaelier, St-Léonard, QC H1P 3C6
514-899-5888, Fax: 514-899-5001
www.guidemtlnord.com
Circulation: 32 841
Sylviane Lussier, Éditrice
Marie-Josée Chouinard, Rédactrice-en-chef

***St-Léonard:* Le Guide Montréal-Nord**
#210, 8770, boul Langelier, St-Léonard, QC H1P 3C6
514-899-5888, Fax: 514-899-5001
www.guidemtlnord.com

***St-Léonard:* L'Informateur de Rivières-Des-Prairies**
#210, 8770 boul. Langelier, St-Léonard, QC H1P 3C6
514-899-5888, Fax: 514-899-5001
www.linformateurrdp.com

***St-Pierre-du-Sud:* Le Pierr'Eau**
645, 2e av, St-Pierre-du-Sud, QC G0R 4B0

***St-Sauveur:* Journal La Vallée**
#104, 94, de la Gare, St-Sauveur, QC J0R 1R6
450-227-4646, Fax: 450-227-8144
www.hebdosquebecor.com/jlv/index_jlv.asp
Circulation: 28,000
André Guillemette, Editeur

***St-Sauveur-des-Monts:* Le Journal de la Vallée**
#104, 94, de la Gare, St-Sauveur-des-Monts, QC J0R 1R0
Circulation: 31 300 *Frequency: Vendredi*

***Stanstead:* Stanstead Journal**
269 Dufferin St., Stanstead, QC J0B 3E2
819-876-7514, Fax: 819-876-7515, 800-567-1259
journal@stansted.journal.com
www.stanstead-journal.com
Circulation: 2 700 *Frequency: Wed.*
Jean-Yves Durocher, Publisher & Editor

***Témiscaming:* Contact**
CP 566, 32, rue Simon, Témiscaming, QC J0Z 3R0
819-627-9050, Fax: 819-627-1794
contact@cablevision.qc.ca
Circulation: 1 000 *Frequency: Bilingual*
Elaine Ouellet, Rédactrice-en-chef

***Terrebonne:* La Revue de Terrebonne**
231, rue Ste-Marie, Terrebonne, QC J6W 3E4
450-964-4444, Fax: 450-471-1023
ventes@larevue.qc.ca
www.larevue.qc.ca
Other information: Montréal: 514/990-7314
Circulation: 50 800 *Frequency: Mercredi*
Gilles Bordonado, Propriétaire

***Thetford Mines:* Le Courrier Frontenac**
CP 789, 541, boul Smith nord, Thetford Mines, QC G6G 5V3
418-338-5181, Fax: 418-338-5482
publicite@courrierfrontenac.com
www.courrierfrontenac.com
Circulation: 20 750 *Frequency: Vendredi; aussi Courrier Affaires & Économie (bimensuel)*
Danie Blais, Rédacteur-en-chef

***Trois-Rivières:* La Gazette Populaire**
942, rue Ste-Geneviève, Trois-Rivières, QC G9A 3X6
819-375-4012, Fax: 819-375-9670
info@lagazettepopulaire.com
www.lagazettepopulaire.com
Circulation: 75 000 *Frequency: Mensuel*
Jean-Marc Lord, Rédacteur

***Trois-Riviéres:* L'Hebdo-Journal**
#205, 525, rue Barkoff, Trois-Riviéres, QC G8T 2A5
819-379-1490, Fax: 819-379-0705
redaction.hj@transcontinental.ca
www.lhebdojournal.com
Circulation: 48 900 *Frequency: Samedi*

***Trois-Rivières:* Le Tour d'y voir**
991, rue Champflour, Trois-Rivières, QC G9A 1Z8
819-375-0484, Fax: 819-371-3827
tdv@tr.cgocable.ca
www.tdv.qc.ca
Circulation: 1 000
Sonia Lavergne, Directrice

***Val-David:* Ski-se-dit**
2600, rue Monty, Val-David, QC J0T 2N0
819-322-7969, Fax: 819-322-7904
ski-se-dit@bellnet.ca
Circulation: 3 000 *Frequency: Mensuel*
Françoise Gilbert, Présidente

***Val-d'Or:* Le Citoyen de la Vallée de l'Or**
1462, rue de la Québécoise, Val-d'Or, QC J9P 5H4
819-874-4545, Fax: 819-874-4547
citoyens@cablevision.qc.ca
www.hebdosquebecor.com/cvo/index_cvo.asp
Frequency: Dimanche
André Renaud, Directeur général régional

***Val-d'Or:* Les Echos Abitibiens**
1462, rue de la Québécoise, Val-d'Or, QC J9P 5H4
819-825-3755, Fax: 819-825-0361
Circulation: 17 700 *Frequency: Mercredi; (Amos, Lasarre, Malartic, Matagami)*

***Val-des-Monts:* Journal l'Envol**
12, Potvin, Val-des-Monts, QC J8N 7B2
819-671-1502, Fax: 819-671-7463
envol.desmonts@sympatico.ca
Circulation: 11 500 *Frequency: Mensuel*
Nicole A. Thibodeau, Contact

***Valleyfield:* Journal Le Suroît**
#201, 52, rue Nicholson, Valleyfield, QC J6T 4M8

***Valleyfield:* Le Journal St-François**
55, rue Jacques Cartier, Valleyfield, QC J6T 4R4
450-371-6222, Fax: 450-371-7254
info@st-francois.com
www.st-francois.com
Circulation: 31 000
Diane Dumont, Directrice générale

***Valleyfield:* Le Soleil de Salaberry-de-Valleyfield**
20, rue Académie, Valleyfield, QC J6T 6M9
450-373-8555, Fax: 450-373-8666
redacval@lesoleil.qc.ca
www.hebdos.net/lsv/default.asp
Circulation: 30 200
Andre Mooney, a.mooney@lesoleil.qc.ca

***Vaudreuil-Dorion:* L'Etoile de l'Outaouais**
469, av St-Charles, Vaudreuil-Dorion, QC J7V 2N4
450-455-6111, Fax: 450-455-0596
Circulation: 34 324 *Frequency: Mercredi*
Angèle Marcoux Prévost, Éditrice

***Vaudreuil-Dorion:* 1ère Édition du Sud-Ouest**
469, av St-Charles, Vaudreuil-Dorion, QC J7V 2N4

514-597-2231, Fax: 514-597-1932
peinfo@hebdosdusuroit.com
Circulation: 48 770 *Frequency: Sat.; English & French*
Isabelle Boutin

Victoriaville: L'Avenir de l'Erable
43, rue Notre-Dam, Victoriaville, QC G6P 3Z4
819-758-6211, Fax: 819-362-2216
www.lanouvelle.net
Circulation: 11 049 *Frequency: Dimanche*
Normand Poulin, Rédacteur-en-chef

Victoriaville: La Nouvelle de Victoriaville
CP 130, 43, rue Notre-Dame est, Victoriaville, QC G6P 3Z4
819-758-6211, Fax: 819-758-0417
www.lanouvelle.net
Circulation: 42 074 *Frequency: Dimanche*
Sylvie Côté, Éditrice
Manon Samson, Rédactrice-en-chef

Victoriaville: L'Union
43, rue Notre-Dame est, Victoriaville, QC G6P 3Z4
819-759-6211, Fax: 819-758-2759
www.lanouvelle.net
Circulation: 25 968 *Frequency: Mercredi*
Sylvie Côté, Éditrice
Manon Samson, Rédactrice-en-chef

Ville LaSalle: Westmount Examiner
420, LaFleur, Ville LaSalle, QC H8R 3H6
514-363-5656, Fax: 514-937-6365
larsenw@transcontinental.ca
www.westmountexaminer.com
Circulation: 9,800 *Frequency: Thur.*

Ville-Marie: Le Reflet
Le Reflet Témiscamien inc., 22, rue Ste-Anne, Ville-Marie, QC J9V 2B7
819-622-1313, Fax: 819-622-1333
le.reflet@cablevision.qc.ca
www.journallereflet.com
Circulation: 9 700 *Frequency: Vendredi*
Karen LaChapelle, Directrice

Ville-Marie: Le Témiscamien
22, rue Sainte-Anne, Ville-Marie, QC J9V 2B7
819-622-1313, Fax: 819-622-1333
www.journallereflet.com
Circulation: 8 500 *Frequency: Mercredi*

Wakefield: The Low Down to Hull & Back News
PO Box 99, Wakefield, QC J0X 3G0
819-459-2222, Fax: 819-459-3831
thelowdown@earthlink.net
www.lowdownonline.com
Circulation: 2,990 *Frequency: Wed.*
Nikki Mantell, Publisher

Windsor: L'Etincelle
193, rue St-Georges, Windsor, QC J1S 1J7
819-845-2705, Fax: 819-845-5520
journal@letincelle.qc.ca
www.letincelle.qc.ca
Circulation: 10 093 *Frequency: Samedi*
Claude Frenette, Éditeur

Évain: Ensemble pour bâtir
CP 424, 200, rue Côté ouest, Évain, QC J0Z 1Y0
819-768-2495,
Circulation: 1 400
Jocelyne Maynard, Présidente

Saskatchewan

Daily Newspapers in Saskatchewan

Moose Jaw: Times-Herald
44 Fairford St. West, Moose Jaw, SK S6H 1V1
306-692-6441, Fax: 306-692-2101
moose.jaw.times@sasknet.sk.ca
www.mjtimes.sk.ca
Circulation: 10,500 *Frequency: Evening*
Rob Clark, Publisher
Rob Clark, Publisher/General Manager

North Battleford: Battlefords News-Optimist
Battlefords Publishing Ltd., PO Box 1029, 892 - 104th St., North Battleford, SK S9A 3E6
306-445-7261, Fax: 306-445-3223, 866-549-9979
battlefords.publishing@sasktel.net
Circulation: 2,997 *Frequency: Wed.; also Regional Optimist/Advertiser-Post, Fri.*
Alana Schweitzer, Contact

Prince Albert: Daily Herald
30 - 10th St. East, Prince Albert, SK S6V 0Y5
306-764-4276, Fax: 306-763-3119
editorial@paherald.sk.ca
www.paherald.sk.ca
Circulation: 8,784 *Frequency: Evening*
Ian Jensen, Publisher & General Manager

Regina: The Leader-Post
PO Box 2020, 1964 Park St., Regina, SK S4P 3G4
306-565-8211, Fax: 306-565-8812
www.leader-post.sk.ca/
Circulation: 70,203 *Frequency: Afternoon*
Greg MacLean, Publisher
Bob Hughes, Editor

Saskatoon: The StarPhoenix
204 - 5th Ave. North, Saskatoon, SK S7K 2P1
306-657-6231, Fax: 306-657-6437, 800-667-2002
spnews@sp.canwest.com
www.thestarphoenix.com
Circulation: 54,093 Mon.-Thu., 62,117 Fri., 51,199 Sat.
Frequency: Morning
Steve Gibb, Editor
Dale Brin, Publisher

Other Newspapers in Saskatchewan

Assiniboia: Assiniboia Times
PO Box 910, 410 - 1st Ave. East, Assiniboia, SK S0H 0B0
306-642-5901, Fax: 306-642-4519
Circulation: 2,413 *Frequency: Fri.*
Glen Hall, Publisher

Biggar: Biggar Independent
PO Box 40, 102 - 3rd Ave. West, Biggar, SK S0K 0M0
306-948-3344, Fax: 306-948-2133
Circulation: 1,891 *Frequency: Mon.*
Daryl Hasein, Publisher

Canora: Canora Courier
PO Box 746, Canora, SK S0A 0L0
306-563-5131, Fax: 306-563-6144
Circulation: 1,639 *Frequency: Wed.*
Brant Kersey, Publisher

Canora: Kamsack Times
PO Box 746, Canora, SK S0A 0L0
306-563-5131, Fax: 306-563-6144
Circulation: 1,260 *Frequency: Thu.*
Brant Kersey, Publisher

Canora: Norquay North Star
PO Box 746, Canora, SK S0A 0L0
306-563-5131, Fax: 306-563-6144
Circulation: 599 *Frequency: Wed.*
Brant Kersey, Publisher

Canora: Preeceville Progress
PO Box 746, Canora, SK S0A 0L0
306-563-5131, Fax: 306-563-6144
Circulation: 1,169 *Frequency: Thur.*
Brant Kersey, Publisher

Carlyle: Carlyle Observer
PO Box 160, 132 Main St., Carlyle, SK S0C 0R0
306-453-2525, Fax: 306-453-2938
observer@saskte.net
www.carlyleobserver.com
Circulation: 3,076 *Frequency: Fri.*
Cindy Moffatt, General Manager

Carnduff: Carnduff Gazette-Post News
PO Box 220, 106 Broadway St., Carnduff, SK S0C 0S0
306-482-3252, Fax: 306-482-3373
www.sasknews.com/info/carnduff.shtml
Circulation: 1,246 *Frequency: Mon.*
Bill Grass, Publisher

Coronach: Triangle News
PO Box 689, Coronach, SK S0H 0Z0
306-267-3381, Fax: 306-267-3381
Circulation: 1,000 *Frequency: Mon.*
Randall Burns, Publisher

Craik: Craik Weekly News
PO Box 360, 221 - 3rd St., Craik, SK S0G 0V0
306-734-2313, Fax: 306- -
Circulation: 880 *Frequency: Tues.*
Harve Friedel, Publisher

Cut Knife: Highway 40 Courier
PO Box 639, 200 Steel St., Cut Knife, SK S0M 0N0
306-398-4901, Fax: 306-398-4909
ckcouriernews@sasktel.net
Circulation: 579 *Frequency: Wed.*
Lorie Gibson, Publisher

Davidson: Davidson Leader
PO Box 786, 205 Washington Ave., Davidson, SK S0G 1A0
306-567-2047, Fax: 306-567-2900
lmt@sasktel.net
Circulation: 1,319 *Frequency: Mon.*
Tara de Ryk, Publisher & Editor

Esterhazy: Esterhazy Miner-Journal
PO Box 1000, 606 - 2nd Ave., Esterhazy, SK S0A 0X0
306-745-6669, Fax: 306-745-2699
miner.journal@sasktel.net
www.minerjournal.com
Circulation: 1,627 *Frequency: Mon.*
Brenda Matchett, Publisher

Estevan: Estevan Lifestyles
PO Box 783, Estevan, SK S4A 2A6
306-634-5112, Fax: 306-634-2588
lifestyles@sasktel.net
www.sasklifestyles.com
Circulation: 7,918 *Frequency: Fri.*
Teresa Howie, Publisher
Teresa Howie, Editor

Estevan: Estevan Mercury
PO Box 730, 68 Souris Ave. North, Estevan, SK S4A 2A6
306-634-2654, Fax: 306-634-3934
www.estevanmercury.ca
Circulation: 3,308 *Frequency: Wed.*
Peter Ng, Publisher

Estevan: Estevan Southeast Trader Express
PO Box 730, Estevan, SK S4A 2A6
306-634-2654
www.estevanmercury.ca
Circulation: 8,661 *Frequency: Fri.*
Andrea Heath, Publisher
Robert Heath, Publisher

Estevan: The Southeast Trader Express
PO Box 730, 68 Souris Ave. North, Estevan, SK S4A 2A6
306-634-2654, Fax: 306-634-3934
mercury_merc1@sasktel.net
www.estevanmercury.ca
Circulation: 8,661 *Frequency: Fri.*
Peter Ng, Publisher

Eston: Eston Press Review
PO Box 787, 112 Main St. West, Eston, SK S0L 1A0
306-962-3221, Fax: 306-962-4445
Circulation: 1,042 *Frequency: Tue.*
Stuart Crump, Publisher
Tim Crump, Editor

Foam Lake: Foam Lake Review
PO Box 550, 325 Main St., Foam Lake, SK S0A 1A0
306-272-3262, Fax: 306-272-4521
Circulation: 1,582 *Frequency: Mon.*
Bob Johnson, Publisher

Fort Qu'appelle: Fort Qu'Appelle Times
PO Box 940, 141 Broadway St. West, Fort Qu'appelle, SK S0G 1S0
306-332-5526, Fax: 306-332-5414
forttimes@sasktel.net
Circulation: 1,462 *Frequency: Tue.*
Sandra Huber, Publisher

Gravelbourg: Gravelbourg Tribune
PO Box 1017, 611 Main St., Gravelbourg, SK S0H 1X0
306-648-3479, Fax: 306-648-2520
gravelbourgtribune@sasktel.net
Circulation: 1,221 *Frequency: Mon.*
Paul Boisvert, Publisher

Grenfell: Broadview Express
PO Box 189, 813 Desmond St., Grenfell, SK S0G 2B0
306-697-2722, Fax: 306-697-2689
stoneprint@sasktel.net
Circulation: 526 *Frequency: Tue.*
Dwayne Stone, Publisher

Grenfell: Grenfell Sun
PO Box 189, 813 Desmond St., Grenfell, SK S0G 2B0
306-697-2722, Fax: 306-697-2689
stoneprint@sasktel.net
Circulation: 1,114 *Frequency: Tue.*
Dwayne Stone, Publisher

Gull Lake: Gull Lake Advance
PO Box 628, 1462 Conrad, Gull Lake, SK S0N 1A0

306-672-3373, Fax: 306-672-3573
gladvance@sasktel.net
glcn.com/town/business/peters/peters.htm
Circulation: 1,245 *Frequency: Tue.*
John Peters, Publisher

***Herbert:* Herbert Herald**
PO Box 399, 716 Herbert Ave., Herbert, SK S0H 2A0
306-784-2422, Fax: 306-784-3246
Circulation: 1,663 *Frequency: Tue.*
Rhonda Ens, Publisher & Editor

***Hudson Bay:* Hudson Bay Post Review**
PO Box 10, 20 Railway Ave., Hudson Bay, SK S0E 0Y0
306-865-2771, Fax: 306-865-2340
post.review@sasktel.net
Circulation: 1,243 *Frequency: Wed.*
Larry Mitchell, Publisher

***Humboldt:* Humboldt Journal**
PO Box 970, Humboldt, SK S0K 2A0
306-682-2561, Fax: 306-682-3322
journal.ads@sasktel.net
Circulation: 10,650 *Frequency: Sun. & Wed; also, Humboldt Trader Regional (Sun.)*
Kent Peters, Publisher

***Indian Head:* Indian Head-Wolseley News**
PO Box 70, 311 Grand Ave., Indian Head, SK S0G 2K0
306-695-3565,
Circulation: 1,735 *Frequency: Tue.*
Ken McCabe, Publisher

***Ituna:* The Ituna News**
PO Box 413, Ituna, SK S0A 1N0
306-795-2412, Fax: 306-795-3621
Circulation: 822 *Frequency: Mon.*
Bob Johnson, Publisher

***Kindersley:* Kerrobert Citizen Dispatch**
PO Box 1150, 919 Main St., Kindersley, SK S0L 1S0
306-463-4611, Fax: 306-463-6505
Circulation: 611 *Frequency: Wed.*
Tim Crump, Editor
Barry Malindine, Manager, Sales
Stewart Crump, General Manager

***Kindersley:* Kindersley Clarion**
PO Box 1150, 919 Main St., Kindersley, SK S0L 1S0
306-463-4611, Fax: 306-463-6505
Circulation: 2,308 *Frequency: Wed.*
Stewart Crump, Publisher

***Kindersley:* The Leader News**
PO Box 1150, 919 Main St., Kindersley, SK S0L 1S0
306-463-4611, Fax: 306-463-6505
Circulation: 1,025 *Frequency: Wed.*

***Kindersley:* The Luseland Dispatch**
PO Box 1150, 919 Main St., Kindersley, SK S0L 1S0
306-463-4611, Fax: 306-463-6505
Circulation: 846

***Kindersley:* West Central Crossroads**
PO Box 1150, 919 Main St., Kindersley, SK S0L 1S0
306-463-4611, Fax: 306-463-6505
Circulation: 14,886 *Frequency: Monday*
Stewart Crump, Publisher

***Kipling:* Kipling Citizen**
PO Box 329, Kipling, SK S0J 2S0
306-736-2535, Fax: 306-736-8445
www.kiplingcitizen.com
Circulation: 1,547 *Frequency: Fri.*
Michael Kearns, Publisher

***La Ronge:* La Ronge Northerner**
PO Box 1350, 715 La Ronge Ave., La Ronge, SK S0J 1L0
306-425-3344, Fax: 306-425-2827
Circulation: 1,485 *Frequency: Thurs.*
Brenda Fitch, Publisher

***Langenburg:* Langenburg Four-Town Journal**
PO Box 68, Langenburg, SK S0A 2A0
306-743-2617, Fax: 306-743-2299
Circulation: 1,463 *Frequency: Wed.*
Bill Johnston, Publisher

***Lanigan:* Lanigan Advisor**
PO Box 1029, 80 Downing Dr., Lanigan, SK S0K 2M0
306-365-2010, Fax: 306-365-3388
Circulation: 1,072 *Frequency: Mon.*
Linda Mallett, Publisher

***Lumsden:* New Waterfront Press**
PO Box 507, 635 James St. North, Lumsden, SK S0G 3C0
306-731-3143, Fax: 306-731-2277
watpress@sasktel.net
Circulation: 3,795 *Frequency: Thurs.; 4 supplements (Agriculture, Farm Progress Show, Remembrance Day, Christmas)*
Lucien Chouinard, Publisher
Jacqueline Chouinard, Publisher

***Macklin:* Macklin Mirror**
PO Box 100, Macklin, SK S0L 2C0
306-753-2424, Fax: 306-753-2424
macklinmirror@sasktel.net
Circulation: 990 *Frequency: Wed.*
Robert Brost, Editor

***Maidstone:* Maidstone Mirror**
PO Box 1029, 892-104 St., Maidstone, SK S9A 3T6
306-445-7261, Fax: 306-445-3223, 866-549-9979
battlefords.publishing@sasktel.net
Circulation: 533 *Frequency: Wed.*
Alana Schweitzer, Manager, Sales
Becky Doig, Editor

***Maple Creek:* Maple Creek & Southwest Advance Times**
PO Box 1328, Maple Creek, SK SON 1NO
306-662-2100, Fax: 306-662-5005
www.maplecreektimes.ca
Circulation: 2,278 *Frequency: Tues.*
Mike Hertz, Publisher

***Maple Creek:* Maple Creek News**
PO Box 1328, 116 Harder St., Maple Creek, SK S0N 1N0
306-662-2133, Fax: 306-662-3092
www.maplecreeknews.com
Circulation: 2,500 *Frequency: Thurs.*
Mike Hertz, Publisher

***Meadow Lake:* Meadow Lake Progress**
PO Box 879, 311 Centre St., Meadow Lake, SK S9X 1Y6
306-236-5265, Fax: 306-236-3130
editor@meadowlakeprogress.com
www.meadowlakeprogress.com
Circulation: 2,703 *Frequency: Sun.*
Donna Ritco, Publisher

***Meadow Lake:* Northern Pride**
205A - 3rd Ave. East, Meadow Lake, SK S9X 1Z4
306-236-5353, Fax: 306-236-5962
Circulation: 4,281 *Frequency: Tue.*
Terry Villeneuve, Publisher

***Melfort:* Kinistino/Birch Hills Post Gazette**
PO Box 1300, Melfort, SK S0E 1A0
306-752-5737, Fax: 306-752-5358
Circulation: 1,257 *Frequency: Wed.*
Ken Sorenson, Publisher

***Melfort:* Melfort Journal**
PO Box 1300, 901 Main St., Melfort, SK S0E 1A0
306-752-5737, Fax: 306-752-5358, 800-752-9559
journal@melfortjournal.com
www.melfortjournal.com
Circulation: 2,774 *Frequency: Tue.*
Ken Sorenson, Publisher, Advertising
Ken Sorenson, General Manager
Greg Wiseman, Editor

***Melville:* Melville Advance**
PO Box 1420, Melville, SK S0A 2P0
306-728-5448, Fax: 306-728-4004
editor@melvilleadvance.com
www.melvilleadvance.com
Circulation: 2,818 *Frequency: Wed.*
Mark Orosz, Publisher
Lin Orosz, Publisher

***Moose Jaw:* Moose Jaw This Week**
44 Fairford St. West, Moose Jaw, SK S6H 6E4
306-692-6441, Fax: 306-692-2101
Circulation: 19,478 *Frequency: Sun.*
Rob Clark, Publisher

***Moosomin:* Moosomin World-Spectator**
PO Box 250, 624 Main St., Moosomin, SK S0G 3N0
306-435-2445, Fax: 306-435-3969
world_spectator@sasktel.net
www.world-spectator.com
Circulation: 3,128 *Frequency: Mon.*
Kevin Weedmark, Publisher & Editor

***Nipawin:* Nipawin Journal**
PO Box 2014, 220 Centre St., Nipawin, SK S0E 1E0
306-862-4618, Fax: 306-862-4566
njournal@sk.sympatico.ca
www.nipawinjournal.com
Circulation: 3,115 *Frequency: Wed.*
Ryan Kiedowski, Editor
Kathy McAuley, Publisher

***Nokomis:* Southey, The Market Connection**
PO Box 340, 103 First Ave. West, Nokomis, SK S0G 3R0
306-528-2020, Fax: 306-528-2090
lmt@sasktel.net
Circulation: 10,700
Lyle Emmons, Publisher

***Nokomis:* Strasbourg, Last Mountain Times**
PO Box 340, Nokomis, SK S0G 3R0
306-528-2020, Fax: 306-528-2090
lmt@sasktel.net
Circulation: 1,323 *Frequency: Tue.; also The Market Connection (10,700)*
Lyle Emmons, Publisher

***North Battleford:* News-Optimist Sunday Edition**
PO Box 1029, North Battleford, SK S9A 3E6
306-445-7261, Fax: 306-445-3223, 866-549-9979
battlefords.publishing@sasktel.net
Circulation: 2,997 *Frequency: Wed.*
Alana Schweitzer, Manager, Sales
Becky Doig, Editor

***North Battleford:* Regional Optimist**
PO Box 1029, 892 - 104 St., North Battleford, SK S9A 3E6
306-445-7261, Fax: 306-445-3223, 866-549-9979
battlefords.publishing@sasktel.net
Circulation: 14,056 *Frequency: Fri.*
Alana Schweitzer, Publisher

***North Battleford:* Turtleford Northwest Neighbours**
PO Box 1029, North Battleford, SK S9A 3E6
306-445-7261, Fax: 306-445-3223, 866-549-9979
battlefords.publishing@sasktel.net
Circulation: 819 *Frequency: Wed.*
Alana Schweitzer, Manager, Sales
Becky Doig, Editor

***Outlook:* The Outlook**
PO Box 1717, 108 Saskatchewan Ave. East, Outlook, SK S0L 2N0
306-867-8262, Fax: 306-867-9556
www.theoutlook.ca
Circulation: 2,170 *Frequency: Mon.*
Terry Jenson, Publisher

***Oxbow:* Oxbow Herald**
PO Box 420, Oxbow, SK S0C 2B0
306-483-2323, Fax: 306-483-5258
oxbow.herald@sasktel.net
www.oxbowherald.com
Circulation: 1,329 *Frequency: Mon.*
Ken Pedlar, Publisher

***Pierceland:* The Beaver River Banner**
PO Box 700, Pierceland, SK S0M 2K0
306-839-4496, Fax: 306-839-2306
br.banner@sasktel.net
Circulation: 1,715 *Frequency: Tue.*
Robin Harrison, Publisher
Brad Harrison, Publisher

***Radville:* Radville Star**
PO Box 370, Radville, SK S0C 2G0
306-869-2202, Fax: 306-869-2533
radstar@hotmail.com
Circulation: 1,128 *Frequency: Wed.*
George Hay, Publisher

***Redvers:* The Optimist**
PO Box 490, Redvers, SK S0C 2H0
306-452-3363, Fax: 306-452-6408
Circulation: 1,577 *Frequency: Sat.*
Bruce Schwanke, Publisher

***Regina:* Journal L'eau vive**
410, av Victoria, Regina, SK S4N 0P6
306-347-0481, Fax: 306-565-3450
direction@accesscomm.ca
www.leauvive.net
Circulation: 1,400 *Frequency: Thurs.*
Réjeanne Geoffrion-Flichel, Directrice générale

***Regina:* Regina Sun**
PO Box 2020, 1964 Park St., Regina, SK S4P 3G4

306-565-8250, Fax: 306-565-8350
Circulation: 67,318 Wed.; 68,212 Sun. city, 20,528 Sun. rural
Frequency: Wed., Sun.

***Rosetown:* Rosetown Eagle**
PO Box 130, Rosetown, SK S0L 2V0
306-882-4202, Fax: 306-882-4204
rosetown.eagle@sasktel.net
Circulation: 2,190 *Frequency:* Mon.
Danny Pagé, Publisher

***Rosthern:* Saskatchewan Valley News**
PO Box 10, Rosthern, SK S0K 3R0
306-232-4865, Fax: 306-232-4694
valleynews@sasktel.net
Circulation: 2,785 *Frequency:* Wed.
Renay Kowalczyk, Editor

***Saskatoon:* Saskatoon Sun**
204 - 5th Ave. North, Saskatoon, SK S7K 2P1
306-657-6231, Fax: 306-657-6437, 800-667-2002
spnews@sp.canwest.com
Circulation: 96,200 *Frequency:* Sun.
Wayne Roberts, Editor
Dale Brin, Publisher

***Shaunavon:* Shaunavon Standard**
PO Box 729, Shaunavon, SK S0N 2M0
306-297-4144, Fax: 306-297-3357
standard@sk.sympatico.ca
Circulation: 1,700 *Frequency:* Tue.
Leslie Corrins, Publisher

***Shellbrook:* Shellbrook Chronicle**
PO Box 10, Shellbrook, SK S0J 2E0
306-747-2442, Fax: 306-747-3000
www.shellbrookchronicle.com
Circulation: 4,478 *Frequency:* Fri.
Clark Pepper, Publisher

***Shellbrook:* Spiritwood Herald**
PO Box 10, Shellbrook, SK S0J 2E0
306-747-2442, Fax: 306-747-3000
www.spiritwoodherald.com
Circulation: 2,770 *Frequency:* Fri.
Clark Pepper, Publisher

***Swift Current:* The Southwest Booster**
PO Box 1330, 30 - 4th Ave. NW, Swift Current, SK S9H 3X4
306-773-9321, Fax: 306-773-9136
boosternews@swbooster.com
www.swbooster.com
Circulation: 19,100 *Frequency:* Sat.
Bob Watson, Publisher
Scott Anderson, Editor

***Tisdale:* Tisdale Recorder**
PO Box 1660, Tisdale, SK S0E 1T0
306-873-4515, Fax: 306-873-4712
Circulation: 1,554 *Frequency:* Wed.
Larry Mitchell, Publisher

***Unity:* The Northwest Herald**
PO Box 309, Unity, SK S0K 4L0
306-228-2267, Fax: 306-228-2767
northwest.herald@sasktel.net
Circulation: 1,793 *Frequency:* Mon.
Dan Feser, Co-Publisher
Lisa Feser, Co-Publisher

***Unity:* Press**
PO Box 309, 304 Main St., Unity, SK S0K 4L0
306-228-2267, Fax: 306-228-2767
northwest.herald@sasktel.net
Circulation: 672 *Frequency:* Mon.
Joanne Urlacher, Publisher

***Wadena:* Kelvington Radio**
PO Box 100, Wadena, SK S0A 4J0
306-338-2231, Fax: 306-338-3421
wadena.news@sasktel.net
Circulation: 988 *Frequency:* Wed.
Bruce Squires, Co-Publishers
Alison Squires, Co-Publishers

***Wadena:* Wadena News**
PO Box 100, 101 1st St. N.E., Wadena, SK S0A 4J0
306-338-2231, Fax: 306-338-3421
wadena.news@sasktel.net
Circulation: 3,114 *Frequency:* Wed.
Bruce Squires, Co-Publisher
Alison Squires, Co-Publisher

***Wakaw:* Wakaw Recorder**
PO Box 9, Wakaw, SK S0K 4P0
306-233-4325, Fax: 306-233-4386
Circulation: 2,159 *Frequency:* Wed.
Dwayne Biccum, Publisher

***Warman:* The Country Press**
PO Box 880, Warman, SK S0K 4S0
306-934-6191, Fax: 306-668-8250
countrypress@sasktel.net
Circulation: 11,351 *Frequency:* Wed.
C. Lynn Handford, General Manager

***Watrous:* Watrous Manitou**
PO Box 100, 309 Main St., Watrous, SK S0K 4T0
306-946-3343, Fax: 306-946-2026
watrous.manitou@sasktel.net
Circulation: 1,827 *Frequency:* Mon.
Nicole Lay, Publisher
Robin Lay, Publisher

***Watson:* East Central Connection**
#100-102 Main St., Watson, SK S0E 1T0
306-287-4388, Fax: 306-287-3308
eastcentral@sk.sympatico.ca
Circulation: 9,139 *Frequency:* Fri.
Karen Mitchell, Publisher

***Watson:* The Naicam News**
PO Box 576, #100, 102 Main St., Watson, SK S0K 4V0
306-287-4388, Fax: 306-287-3308
Circulation: 330 *Frequency:* Fri.
Karen Mitchell, Publisher

***Watson:* Watson Witness**
PO Box 129, 313 Railway Ave. West, Watson, SK S0K 4V0
306-287-3245, Fax: 306-287-4333
Circulation: 1,562 *Frequency:* Wed.
Ken Sopkow, Publisher

***Weyburn:* Weyburn Review**
PO Box 400, Weyburn, SK S4H 2K4
306-842-7487, Fax: 306-842-0282
production@weyburnreview.com
www.weyburnreview.com
Circulation: 4,139 *Frequency:* Wed.; also Weyburn Booster (Mon.; Circ. 12,990; Sat.; Circ.7,698)
Darryl Ward, Publisher
Patricia Ward, Editor-in-chief

***Weyburn:* Weyburn This Week**
19 - 11th St. NE, Weyburn, SK S4H 1J1
306-842-3900, Fax: 306-842-2515
weyburnthisweek@sasktel.net
www.weyburnthisweek.com
Circulation: 6,048 *Frequency:* Fri.
Penny Tochor, General Manager
Troy Kramm, Editor

***Whitewood:* Whitewood Herald**
PO Box 160, Whitewood, SK S0G 5C0
306-735-2230, Fax: 306-735-2899
www.whitewoodherald.sk.ca
Circulation: 812 *Frequency:* Mon.
Elaine Ashfield, Publisher

***Wolseley:* The RTown News**
PO Box 89, 219 Poplar St., Wolseley, SK S0G 5H0
306-698-2271, Fax: 306-698-2808
unos@sasktel.net
www.saskfarmnews.com
Circulation: 2,200 *Frequency:* Fri. (50 times a year)
Rick Dahlman, Editor/Publisher

***Wolseley:* The Wolseley Bulletin**
PO Box 89, 284 Oak St., Wolseley, SK S0G 5H0
306-698-2271, Fax: 306-698-2808
www.saskfarmnews.com
Circulation: 273 *Frequency:* Fri.
Eleanor Dahlman, Publisher

***Wynyard:* Wynyard Advance/Gazette**
Bowes Publishers Limited, PO Box 10, 117 Ave. B East, Wynyard, SK S0A 4T0
306-554-2224, Fax: 306-554-3226
w.advance@sasktel.net
www.wynyardadvance.com
Circulation: 1,757 *Frequency:* Mon.
Bob Johnson, Publisher

***Yorkton:* The News Review Extra**
18 - 1st Ave. North, Yorkton, SK S3N 1J4
306-783-7355, Fax: 306-783-9138
info@yorktonnews.com
www.yorktonnews.com
Circulation: 6,575 *Frequency:* Thurs.
Ken Chyz, Publisher

***Yorkton:* Yorkton This Week**
PO Box 1300, 20 Third Ave., Yorkton, SK S3N 2X3
306-782-2465, Fax: 306-786-1898
www.yorktonthisweek.com
Circulation: 4,680 *Frequency:* Wed.
Neil Thom, Publisher

Yukon Territory

Daily Newspapers in Yukon Territory

***Whitehorse:* The Whitehorse Star**
2149 - 2nd Ave., Whitehorse, YT Y1A 1C5
867-668-2060, Fax: 867-668-7130
star@whitehorsestar.com
www.whitehorsestar.com
Circulation: Mon.-Thu. 2,900; Fri. 4,200 *Frequency:* Weekdays
Jackie Pierce, Publisher
Jim Butler, Editor, 403/667-4481

Other Newspapers in Yukon Territory

***Whitehorse:* L'Aurore boréale**
302, rue Strickland, Whitehorse, YT Y1A 2K1
867-667-2931, Fax: 867-667-2932
auroredir@afy.yk.ca
www.afy.ca/aurore
Circulation: 945 *Frequency:* Bi-mensuel; français
Marie-Hélène Comeau, Journaliste
Odette Poirier, Coordonatrice, Publicité
Cécile Girard, Directrice

***Whitehorse:* Yukon News**
211 Wood St., Whitehorse, YT Y1A 2E4
867-667-6285, Fax: 867-668-3755
stever@yukon-news.com
www.yukon-news.com
Circulation: Mon 5,248 Wed. 5,613, Fri 7,243; Total 18,104.
D.S. Robertson, Publisher
Richard Mostyn, Editor

Magazine Name Index

D

E

M

N

O

Magazines

Business

Advertising, Marketing, Sales

Adnews Insight Magazine
#1463, 1011 Upper Middle Rd., Oakville, ON L6H 5Z9
416-252-9400, Fax: 416-252-8002
info@adnews.com
www.adnews.com
Frequency: 4 times a year
Robert A. Bale, Publisher
Derek Winkler, Editor

Adnews Online Daily
#1463, 1011 Upper Middle Rd. East, Oakville, ON L6H 5Z9
416-252-9400, Fax: 416-252-8002
info@adnews.com
www.adnews.com
Circulation: 33,000 *Frequency:* Daily
Robert Bale, Publisher

Blitz Magazine Inc
#544, 1489 Marine Dr., West Vancouver, BC V7T 1B8
604-921-8735, Fax: 604-921-8738, 866-632-5489
editor@blitzmagazine.com
www.blitzmagazine.com
Circulation: 10,000 *Frequency:* 6 times a year
Louise Aird, Publisher & Editor-in-chief

Boards
#500, 366 Adelaide St. West, Toronto, ON M5V 1R9
416-408-2300, Fax: 416-408-0870, 866-262-7371
drankin@brunico.com
www.boardsmag.com
Circulation: 11,250
Russell Goldstein, Publisher, rgoldstein@brunico.com
Rae Ann Fera, Editor, raeann@boardsmag.com

Canadian Advertising Rates & Data
1 Mount Pleasant Rd., 7th Fl., Toronto, ON M4Y 2Y5
416-764-2000, Fax: 416-764-1709, 800-265-3561
www.cardonline.ca
Circulation: 2,100 *Frequency:* Monthly
Bruce Richards, Publisher,
bruce.richards@cardonline.rogers.com
Bruce Richards, Publisher

Canadian Direct Marketing News
#302, 137 Main St. North, Markham, ON L3P 1Y2
905-201-6600, Fax: 905-201-6601, 800-688-1838
home@dmn.ca
www.dmn.ca
Circulation: 8,058 *Frequency:* Monthly, plus annual directory of suppliers & annual directories The List of Lists...The DM Industry Sourcebook & the Canadian Call Centre Industry Directory
Ron Glen, Editor
Mark Henry, Ad Sales
Steve Lloyd, Publisher & President

The Chronicle of Healthcare Marketing
905-273-9116, Fax: 905-273-4322, 866-633-4766
health@chronicle.org
www.chronicle.ca
Circulation: 2,159 *Frequency:* 9 times a year
Mitchell Shannon, Publisher
R. Allan Ryan, Editorial Director

Contact
Canadian Professional Sales Assn., #800, 310 Front St., Toronto, ON M5V 3B5
416-408-2685, Fax: 416-408-2684
www.cpsa.com
Circulation: 37,125 *Frequency:* 6 times a year
Bernadette Johnson, Editor
Harvey Copeman, Vice-President, Sales & Marketing

Direct Marketing News
#302, 137 Main St. North, Markham, ON L3P 1Y2
905-201-6600, Fax: 905-201-6601
www.dmn.ca
Ron Glen, Editor

Ethnic Media & Markets
1 Mount Pleasant Rd., 7th Fl., Toronto, ON M4Y 2Y5
416-764-1606, Fax: 416-764-1709
bruce.richards@cardonline.rogers.com
www.cardonline.ca
Circulation: 1,500 *Frequency:* 2 times a year
Bruce Richards, Publisher

Imprint Canada
#16, 190 Marycroft Ave., Woodbridge, ON L4L 5Y2

905-856-2600, Fax: 905-856-2667, 877-895-7022
feedback@imprintcanada.com
www.imprintcanada.com
Circulation: 6,700
Tony Muccilli, Publisher

Infopresse

514-842-5873, Fax: 514-842-2422
redaction@infopresse.com
www.infopresse.com
Circulation: 7 500 *Frequency: 10 fois par an*
Charles Grandmont, Rédacteur-en-chef
Bruno Gautier, Éditeur

Kidscreen
#500, 366 Adelaide St. West, Toronto, ON M5V 1R9
416-408-2300, Fax: 416-408-0870, 800-543-4512
dmacneil@brunico.com
www.kidscreen.com
Circulation: 11,500 *Frequency: Monthly*
Donna MacNeil, Vice-President & Group Publisher, dmacneil@brunico.com
Jocelyn Christie, Editor

Marketing Magazine

416-596-5853, Fax: 416-596-3482
www.marketingmag.ca
Circulation: 10,187 *Frequency: Weekly*
Richard Elliott, Executive Publisher

Marketwire
48 Yonge St., 8 Fl., Toronto, ON M5E 1G6
416-362-0885, Fax: 416-955-0705, 888-299-0338
www.marketwirecanada.com
Other information: Toll Free Fax: 1-800-363-9296
Michael J. Nowlan, President & CEO

The National List of Advertisers
1 Mount Pleasant Rd., 7th Fl., Toronto, ON M4Y 2Y5
416-764-2000, Fax: 416-764-1709
bruce.richards@cardonline.rogers.com
www.cardonline.ca
Circulation: 1,467 *Frequency: Annually, Dec.*
Bruce Richards, Publisher

Publication Profiles
1 Mount Pleasant Rd., 7th Fl., Toronto, ON M4Y 2Y5
416-764-2000, Fax: 416-764-1709, 800-265-3561
bruce.richards@cardonline.rogers.com
www.cardonline.ca
Circulation: 1,432 *Frequency: Annually, Apr.*
Bruce Richards, Publisher

Sales Promotion

905-634-2100, Fax: 905-634-2238
www.sp-mag.com
Circulation: 14,000 *Frequency: 6 times a year*
Jackie Roth, Publisher
Nathan Mallet, Editor

Sign Media

905-771-7333, Fax: 905-771-7336, 800-409-8688
editor@kenilworth.com
www.signmedia.ca
Circulation: 13,200 *Frequency: 6 times a year*
Ellen Kral, Publisher
Blair Adams, Editorial Director
Erik Tolles, Sales Manager

Silver Screen
383 Lawrence Ave. West, Toronto, ON M5M 1B9
416-488-3393, Fax: 416-488-5217
malcolm@msilver.com
www.msilver.com
Circulation: 1,800
Malcolm Silver, Publisher

Strategy

416-408-2300, Fax: 416-408-0870
cmacdonald@brunico.com
www.strategymag.com
Circulation: 13,152 *Frequency: 12 times a year*
Claire MacDonald, Associate Publisher

Architecture

Award Magazine
4180 Lougheed Hwy., Burnaby, BC V5C 6A7
604-299-7311, Fax: 604-299-9188
cwm@canadawide.com
www.canadawide.com
Circulation: 8,500 *Frequency: 6 times a year*
Les Wiseman, Editor
Peter Legge, Publisher

Canadian Architect
#800, 12 Concord Place, Toronto, ON M3C 4J2
416-510-6845, Fax: 416-510-5140, 800-268-7742
editors@canadianarchitect.com
www.canadianarchitect.com
Circulation: 10,323 *Frequency: Monthly*
Tom Arkell, Publisher

Construction Canada

905-771-7333, Fax: 905-771-7336, 800-409-8688
sales@constructioncanada.net
www.constructioncanada.net
Circulation: 12,109 *Frequency: 6 times a year*
Ellen Kral, Publisher
Blair Adams, Editorial Director
Cora Golden, Sales Director

Info-Link
#270, 3044 Bloor St. West, Toronto, ON M8X 2Y8
416-604-7552
info@infolinkcanada.com
www.infolinkcanada.com
Frequency: 4 times a year

Perspectives
c/o Canadian Association Publishers, PO Box 90510, 230 Markham Rd., Toronto, ON M1J 3N7
416-955-1550, Fax: 416-955-1391
jeaton@capmagazines.ca
www.capmagazines.ca
Circulation: 6,200 *Frequency: 4 times a year*
Kelly Chase, Production
Jim Eaton, Publisher
Gordon Grice, Editor

Automobile, Cycle, & Automotive Accessories

L'Automobile

514-630-5955, Fax: 514-630-5980, 800-363-1327
garbour@lautomobile.ca
Circulation: 12 829 *Frequency: 6 fois par an; français*
Guy Arbour, Éditeur et Rédacteur-en-chef

Automotive Parts & Technology
c/o Newcom Business Media Inc., 451 Attwell Dr., Toronto, ON M9W 5C4
416-614-0955, Fax: 416-614-2781
info@aptmag.ca
www.aptmag.ca
Jim Glionna, Publisher

Automotive Service Data Book

416-445-6641, Fax: 416-442-2261
Frequency: Annually, Dec.
David Booth, Editor

Bike Trade Canada
#200, 260 Spadina Ave., Toronto, ON M5T 2E4
416-977-2100, Fax: 416-977-9200, 866-977-3325
info@pedalmag.com
www.pedalmag.com
Circulation: 5,000 *Frequency: 3 times a year*
Benjamin A. Sadavoy, Publisher & Editor
Sarah Carlin, Circulation

Bodyshop

416-510-6763, Fax: 416-442-2213
www.bodyshopbiz.com
Circulation: 11,917 *Frequency: 6 times a year*
Andrew Ross, Publisher, aross@bodyshopbiz.com
JD Ney, Editor, jdney@bodyshopbiz.com

Canadian Auto World
c/o Formula Media Group, #4, 447 Speers Rd., Oakville, ON L6K 3S7
905-842-6591, Fax: 905-842-4432
www.wheels.ca
Circulation: 4,529 *Frequency: 6 times a year*
Joseph Knycha, Editor-in-chief
J. Scott Robinson, Publisher

Canadian Technician
451 Attwell Dr., Toronto, ON M9W 5C4
416-614-0955, Fax: 416-614-2781
www.canadiantechnician.com
Mark Vreugdenhill, Publisher
Allan Janssen, Editor

Collision Quarterly
Automotive Retailer Publishing Company Ltd., #1, 8980 Fraserwood Ct., Burnaby, BC V5J 5H7
604-432-7987, Fax: 604-432-1756
publish@ara.bc.ca
www.ara.bc.ca
Circulation: 6,179 *Frequency: 4 times a year*
Kara Cunningham, Publisher & Editor
Kelly Johnston, Circulation Manager

Collision Repair Magazine
86 John St., Thornhill, ON L3T 1Y2
905-889-3544, Fax: 905-889-4680
collisionrepair@rogers.com
www.collisionrepairmag.com
Darryl Simmons, Publisher
Mike Davey, Editor

Jobber News

416-445-5600, Fax: 416-442-2213
www.autoserviceworld.com
Circulation: 11,136 *Frequency: Monthly*
Andrew Ross, Publisher

Octane
Fulcrum Publications, #201, 508 Lawrence Ave. West, Toronto, ON M5A 1A1
416-504-0504, Fax: 416-256-3002
info@fulcrum.ca
www.fulcrum.ca
Circulation: 9,000 *Frequency: 6 times a year*

Revue Le Garagiste
Publications Rousseau et associés, 2938, Terrasse Abenaquis, Longueuil, QC J4M 2B3
450-448-2220, Fax: 450-448-1041, 888-748-2220
admin@p-rousseau.com
www.legaragiste.com
Circulation: 18 200 *Frequency: 8 fois par an*
Rémy L. Rousseau, Éditeur

Service Station & Garage Management

416-442-2275, Fax: 416-442-2213, 800-268-7742
rtelford@ssgm.com
www.autoserviceworld.com
Other information: 1-800-387-0273 (U.S.)
Circulation: 31,200 *Frequency: Monthly*
Robert Telford, Publisher

Taxi News
38 Fairmount Cres., Toronto, ON M4L 2H4
416-466-2328, Fax: 416-466-4220
taxinews@the-wire.com
www.taxinews.com
Circulation: 9,800 *Frequency: Monthly*
John Duffy, Publisher
William McOuat, Editor

Aviation & Aerospace

Airforce
c/o Airforce Productions Ltd., PO Box 2460 D, #400, 222 Somerset St. West, Ottawa, ON K1P 5W6
613-232-2303, Fax: 613-232-2156, 866-351-2322
vjohnson@airforce.ca
www.airforce.ca
Circulation: 16,526 *Frequency: 4 times a year*
Vic Johnson, Editor

Aviation Business Directory - Eastern Directory
#900, 1080 Howe St., Vancouver, BC V6Z 2T1
604-606-4644, Fax: 604-687-1925, 800-656-7598
markyelic@oppublishing.com
www.aviatormag.com
Frequency: annual
Jack Scholfield, Publisher
Katherine Kjaer, Manager, Sales

Aviation Business Directory - Western Directory
#900, 1080 Howe St., Vancouver, BC V6Z 2T1
780-643-3962, Fax: 604-687-1925, 800-656-7598
markyelic@oppublishing.com
www.aviationbusinessdirectories.com
Frequency: annual
Mark Yelic, Publisher, myelic@outdoorgroupmedia.com
Russ Niles, Editor, canadianaviator@xplornet.com

Canadian Aviator Magazine
#213, 3347 Oak St., Victoria, BC V8X 1R2
250-658-6575, Fax: 250-658-6576, 800-656-7598
sales@canadianaviatormagazine.com
www.canadianaviatormagazine.com
Circulation: 16,000 *Frequency: 6 times a year*
Mark Yelic, Publisher
Katherine Kjaer, Advertising Sales, pilotpresssale@shaw.ca
Garth Eichel, Editor, 250/386-6575, pilotpressedit@shaw.ca

Canadian Flight
#207, 75 Albert St., Ottawa, ON K1P 5E7
613-236-4901, Fax: 613-236-8646
editorial@copanational.org
www.copanational.org
Circulation: 18,000 *Frequency: Monthly; includes: Canadian Homebuilt Aircraft News, Canadian Ultralight News, Executive Flight News, Seaplane News, Aircraft Maintenance Engineers News, Canadian Plane Trade, Aviation Museum News*
Michel Hell, Publisher

Helicopters
PO Box 530, 105 Donly Dr. South, Simcoe, ON N3Y 4N5
519-428-3471, Fax: 519-429-3094
www.helicoptersmagazine.com
Frequency: 4 times a year

ICAO Journal
International Civil Aviation Organization, 999, rue University, Montréal, QC H3C 5H7
514-954-8222, Fax: 514-954-6376
icaohq@icao.int
www.icao.int
Circulation: 15,000 *Frequency: 6 issues a year; English, French & Spanish editions*
Eric MacBurnie, Editor

Western & Eastern Canada - Aviation Business Directory
#900, 1080 Howe St., Vancouver, BC V6Z 2T1
604-606-4644, Fax: 604-687-1925
markyelic@oppublishing.com
www.canadianaviatormagazine.com
Frequency: annual
Katherine Kjaer, Manager, Sales
Mark Yelic, Publisher

Wings
888-599-2228
www.wingsmagazine.com
Frequency: 6 times a year
Drew McCarthy, Editor

Baking & Bakers' Supplies

Bakers Journal
105 Donly Drive S., Simcoe, ON N3Y 4N5
888-599-2228
editor@bakersjournal.com
www.bakersjournal.com
Circulation: 6,800 *Frequency: 10 times a year*
Martin McAnulty, Publisher, mmcanulty@annexweb.com
Brian Hartz, Editor, bhartz@annexweb.com

La Fournée
Les Éditions Comestibles inc., 615, av Notre-Dame, Saint-Lambert, QC J4P 2K8
514-990-6967, Fax: 514-990-6967
Circulation: 4 718 *Frequency: 4 fois par an; français*
Lyne Gosselin, Editor

Barbers & Beauticians

Canadian Hairdresser Magazine
11 Spadina Rd., Toronto, ON M5R 2S9
416-923-1111, Fax: 416-968-1031, 800-588-5221
info@canhair.com
www.canhair.com
Circulation: 30,112 *Frequency: 10 times a year*
Joan Harrison, Managing Editor

Salon Magazine
416-869-3131, Fax: 416-869-3008, 800-720-6665
frontdesk@beautynet.com
www.beautynet.com
Circulation: 35,000 *Frequency: 8 times a year; English (circ. 25,000) & French (circ. 10,000) editions*
Brian Light, President
Gregory Robins, Website Producer

Boating & Yachting

Boating Business
905-842-6591, Fax: 905-842-6843
Circulation: 5,375 *Frequency: 6 times a year*
J. Scott Robinson, Publisher
Valerie Tryer, Circulation Coordinator

Books

Access
c/o Ontario Library Association, #201, 50 Wellington St., Toronto, ON M5E 1C8
416-363-3388, Fax: 416-941-9581, 866-873-9867
info@accessola.com
www.accessola.com
Circulation: 4,500 *Frequency: 4 times a year*
Lori Knowles, Editor

Canadian Bookseller
Canadian Booksellers Association, #700, 789 Don Mills Rd., Toronto, ON M3C 1T5
416-467-7883, Fax: 416-467-7886, 866-788-0790
enquiries@cbabook.org
www.cbabook.org
Circulation: 2,500 *Frequency: 6 times a year*
Susan Dayus, Publisher & Executive Director

Feliciter
c/o Canadian Library Association, 328 Frank St., Ottawa, ON K2P 0X8
613-232-9625, Fax: 613-563-9895
publishing@cla.ca
www.cla.ca
Circulation: 3,000 *Frequency: 6 times a year*
Don Butcher, Executive Director

Quill & Quire
111 Queen St. East, 3rd Fl., Toronto, ON M5C 1S2
416-364-3333, Fax: 416-595-5415
info@quillandquire.com
www.quillandquire.com
Circulation: 5,265 *Frequency: Monthly; supplement, Canadian Publishers' Directory (June & Dec.); ISSN: 0033-6491*
Alison Jones, Publisher, 416/364-3333, ext.31

Teacher Librarian
The Scarecrow Press, Inc., 15200 NBN Way, Blue Ridge Summit, PA 17214
717-794-3800, Fax: 717-794-3833
admin@teacherlibrarian.com
www.teacherlibrarian.com
Circulation: 7,500-10,000 *Frequency: 5 times a year; ISSN: 1481-1782*
Kim Tabor, Managing Editor
David V. Loertscher, Co-Editor
Esther Rosenfeld, Co-Editor
Edward Kurdyla, Publisher

Brides, Bridal

Weddings & Honeymoons
65 Helena Ave., Toronto, ON M6G 2H3
416-653-4986, Fax: 416-653-2291
barwed@interlog.com
www.weddingshoneymoons.com
Circulation: 30,000 *Frequency: 3 times a year; ISSN: 1192-764X*
Joyce Barshow, Publisher & Editor-in-chief

Broadcasting

Broadcast Dialogue
18 Turtle Path, Site 1, Box 150, Brechin, ON L0K 1B0
705-484-0752
broadcastdialogue@rogers.com
www.broadcastdialogue.com
Circulation: 7,200
Howard Christensen, Publisher, howard@broadcastdialogue.com
Barry Hamelin, Executive Director, barry@broadcastdialogue.comm

Broadcaster
416-510-6871, Fax: 416-510-5134, 800-268-7742
jcook@broadcastermagazine.com
www.broadcastermagazine.com
Circulation: 7,670 *Frequency: monthly*
James A. Cook, Publisher

Mediacaster
416-510-6878, Fax: 416-510-5140
www.mediacastermagazine.com
Circulation: 6,800 *Frequency: 12 times a year*
Grenville Pinto, Publisher

Playback
#500, 366 Adelaide St. West, Toronto, ON M5V 1R9
416-408-2300, Fax: 416-408-0870, 888-278-6426
www.playbackmag.com
Circulation: 9,052 *Frequency: 25 times a year*
Peter Vamos, Publisher

Building & Construction

Alberta Construction Magazine
#300, 5735 - 7 St. NE, Calgary, AB T2E 8V3
403-265-3700, Fax: 403-265-3706, 888-563-2946
marketing@junewarren.com
www.junewarren.com
Circulation: 8,500 *Frequency: 6 times a year; also Alberta Constuction Association Membership Roster & Buyers' Guide (annual, May)*
Chaz Osburn, Editor

Alberta Construction Service & Supply Directory
6111 - 91 St. NW, Edmonton, AB T6E 6V6
780-944-9333, Fax: 780-944-9500, 800-563-2946
theath@junewarren.com
www.junewarren.com
Circulation: 10,000 *Frequency: Annually*
Agnes Zalewski, Publisher

Atlantic Construction Journal
Transcontinental Specialty Publications, #609, 1888 Brunswick St., Dartmouth, NS B3J 3J9
902-468-8027, Fax: 902-468-2425, 800-537-5507
acj@hfnews.ca
Circulation: 15,000 *Frequency: 4 times a year*
Naster Tracz, Senior Account Executive
Ken Partridge, Editor

BSDA Newsmagazine
Building Supply Dealers Assn. of BC, #2, 19299 - 94th Ave., Surrey, BC V4N 4E6
604-513-2205, Fax: 604-513-2206
bsdabc@telus.net
www.bsdabc.com
Circulation: 1,000 *Frequency: 4 times a year*
George Tracy

Building & Construction Trades Today
PO Box 186, 27 St. Clair Ave. East, Toronto, ON M4T 2M1
416-944-1217, Fax: 416-944-0133
hize@earthlink.net
Circulation: 2,000-2,500 *Frequency: 8 times a year*
Alan Heisey, Publisher
Jason Kieffer, Editor

Building Magazine
#800, 12 Concorde Place, Toronto, ON M3C 2J4
416-442-5600, Fax: 416-442-2191, 800-668-2374
www.building.ca
Circulation: 10,737 *Frequency: 6 times a year*
Tom Arkell, Senior Publisher, 416-510-6806, tomarkell@canadianarchitect.com

Canadian Apartment Magazine
Circulation: 7,000 *Frequency: 6 times a year*
Ellie Chesnutt, Editor

Canadian Contractor
416-764-1656, Fax: 416-764-1484
dchestnut@rmpublishing.com
canadiancontractormagazine.com
Circulation: 45,000 *Frequency: 4 times a year*
David Chestnut, Associate Publisher

Canadian Property Management
416-512-8186, Fax: 416-512-8344
Circulation: 12,504 *Frequency: 8 times a year*
Tony Robinson, Publisher

Canadian Renovator Magazine
PO Box 7400, London, ON N5Y 4X3
519-471-8412, Fax: 519-473-7859, 877-707-3639
drawlings@bowesnet.com
renopub.com
Circulation: 13,200 *Frequency: 5 times a year*
Don Rawlings, Publisher & Editor

Canadian Roofing Contractor & Design
3 Kennett Dr., Whitby, ON L1P 1L5
905-430-7267, Fax: 905-430-6418, 877-880-4877
mike@perkspub.com
www.perkspub.com
Circulation: 6,000 *Frequency: 4 times a year*
Michael Nosko, Publisher

Canadian Window & Door Manufacturer
519-657-2088, Fax: 519-657-2796
Frequency: 2 times a year
Bruce Munro, Editor

CondoBusiness
416-512-8186, Fax: 416-512-8344
info@mediaedge.ca
www.mediaedge.ca
Circulation: 2,500 *Frequency: 8 times a year*
Angela Altass, Editor
Tracy Ryan, Publisher

Construire
L'Association de la Construction du Québec, #205, 7400, boul des Galeries-d'Anjou, Anjou, QC H1M 3M2
450-963-4339, Fax: 450-625-6065, 888-868-3424
communication@acq.org
www.rep-comm.ca
Circulation: 27 400 *Frequency: 6 fois par an; français*
Monique Thomas, Rédactrice
Pierre Leduc, Directeur, ventes

Daily Commercial News
Reed Construction Data, 500 Hood Rd., 4th Fl., Markham, ON L3R 9Z3
905-752-5547, Fax: 905-752-5448
sonia.kalraali@reedbusiness.com
www.dailycommercialnews.com
Circulation: 4,000 *Frequency: Daily*
Mark Casaletto, Publisher

Equipment Journal
Pace Publishing Limited, #6, 5160 Explorer Dr., Mississauga, ON L4W 4T7
905-629-7500, Fax: 905-629-7988, 800-667-8541
ej@equipmentjournal.com
www.equipmentjournal.com
Circulation: 23,500 *Frequency: 17 issues a year, every 3 weeks*
John Baker, Publisher

Formes
6718, rue Chambord, Montréal, QC H2G 3C3
514-736-7637, Fax: 514-272-3477
info@formes.ca
www.formes.ca
Frequency: 6 fois par an

Heavy Construction News On-Site
416-764-2000, Fax: 416-764-1733
www.on-sitemag.com
Circulation: 22,984 *Frequency: 7 times a year*
Jim Barnes, Editor
Peter Leonard, Publisher

Heavy Equipment Guide
604-291-9900, Fax: 604-291-1906
www.baumpub.com
Circulation: 26,575 *Frequency: 10 times a year*
Engelbert J. Baum, Publisher
Lawrence Buser, Editor

Home Builder Magazine
4819 St. Charles Blvd., Pierrefonds, QC H9H 3C7
514-620-2200, Fax: 514-620-6300
homebuilder@work4.ca
www.homebuildercanada.com
Circulation: 26,418 *Frequency: 6 times a year*
Nachmi Artzy, Publisher

HPAC Magazine/Buyer's Guide
1 Mount Pleasant Rd., Toronto, ON M4Y 2Y5
416-764-2000, Fax: 416-764-1746
bruce.meacock@hpacmag.rogers.com
www.hpacmag.com
Circulation: 16,379 *Frequency: annually (August)*
Bruce Meacock, Publisher

Journal Constructo
#200, 1500, boul Jules-Poitras, Saint-Laurent, QC H4N 1X7
514-745-5720, Fax: 514-339-2267, 800-363-0910
groupeconstructo@transcontinental.ca
www.constructo.ca
Circulation: 2 611 *Frequency: 80 fois par an; français*
Anik Girard, Éditeur
Marie Vaillancourt, Chef de L'Information

Le Journal de L'Habitation
Médias-Transcontinental, #900, 1265, boul Charest ouest, Québec, QC G1N 4V4
418-686-6400, Fax: 418-686-4841
www.journalhabitation.com
Circulation: 28 000 *Frequency: 2 times a month*
François Cattapan, Rédacteur en chef

Journal of Commerce
#101, 4299 Canada Way, Burnaby, BC V5G 1H3
604-433-8164, Fax: 604-433-9549, 888-878-2121
jocinfor@reelbusiness.com
www.joconl.com
Circulation: 1,800 *Frequency: 2 times a week*

LBMAO Reporter
#27, 5155 Spectrum Way, Mississauga, ON L42 5A1
905-625-1084, Fax: 905-625-3006
reporter@lbmao.on.ca
www.lbmao.on.ca
Circulation: 1,750 *Frequency: 6 times a year*
David Campbell, President

Ontario Home Builder
1074 Cooke Blvd., Burlington, ON L7T 4A8
905-634-8003, Fax: 905-634-7661, 800-387-0109
info@ohba.ca
www.homesontario.com
Circulation: 8,084 *Frequency: 5 times a year*
Wayne Nanciso, Publisher

Ottawa Construction News
#202, 1 Cleopatra Dr., Ottawa, ON K2G 3W9
613-224-3460, Fax: 613-224-1076, 888-432-3555
editor@constructionnrgroup.com
www.ottawaconstructionnews.com
Circulation: 12,000 *Frequency: 12 times a year*
Mark Buckshon, Publisher
Terry Tinkess, Editor

Québec Habitation
5930, boul Louis-H.-Lafontaine, Anjou, QC H1M 1S7
514-353-9960, Fax: 514-353-0835, 800-468-8160
quebec-hab@apchq.com
www.quebec-habitation.com
Circulation: 30 000 *Frequency: 6 fois par an; français*
Lise Plante, Éditeur
Jean Garon, Rédactrice-en-chef

Sanitation Canada
3 Kennett Dr., Whitby, ON L1P 1L5
905-430-7267, Fax: 905-430-6418, 877-880-4877
mike@perkspub.com
www.perkspub.com
Circulation: 5,134 *Frequency: 6 times a year*
Michael Nosko, Publisher

Toronto Construction News
Reed Construction Data, 500 Hood Rd., 4th Fl., Markham, ON L3R 9Z3
905-752-5539, Fax: 905-750-5450, 800-465-6475
www.dailycommercialnews.com
Circulation: 4,000 *Frequency: 7 times a year*
Patrick McConnell, Publisher

Business & Finance

Advisor's Edge
One Mount Pleasant Rd., Toronto, ON M4Y 2Y5
416-764-3859, Fax: 416-764-3943
service@advisor.ca
www.advisor.ca
Circulation: 40,000 *Frequency: 12 times a year*
Advisor's Edge magazine is an independent Canadian publication focused solely on the information needs of Canadian retail financial advisors (brokers, financial planners, insurance specialists, mutual fund salespeople and bank-based consultants). With a strong emphasis on practice management, the magazine helps advisors stay on top of industry trends, investment insurance products and strategies, as well as marketing and client relationship best practices
Donna Kerry, Publisher, donna.kerry@rci.rogers.com
Philip Porado, Executive Editor, philip.porado@rci.rogers.com

Les Affaires
1100, boul René-Lévesque ouest 24e étage, Montréal, QC H3B 4X9
514-392-9000, Fax: 514-392-1586, 800-361-5479
lesaffaires.redaction@transcontinental.ca
www.lesaffaires.com
Circulation: 90 000 *Frequency: 52 fois par an; français; aussi Affaires 500, PME, Affaires plus (10 fois par an, 93 288)*
Principal journal d'affaires de langue française au Canada, fondé en 1928. Ce tabloïd tout en couleur paraît le samedi et a un tirage de 88 000 exemplaires, surtout vendus au Québec. Il est publié par les Publications Transcontinental Inc. Il est reconnu pour sa couverture des grandes sociétés canadiennes, des petites et moyennes entreprises québécoises, de l'économie canadienne et des affaires publiques. La moitié de son contenu est consacrée aux finances personnelles et aux placements avec diverses pages spécialisées, des tableaux et des graphiques
Michel Lord, Éditeur
Jean-Paul Gagné, Rédacteur-en-chef, pierre.marcoux@transcontinental.ca

Affaires Plus Magazine
1100, boul René-Lévesque 24e étage, Montréal, QC H3B 4X9
514-392-9000, Fax: 514-392-4726
aplus@transcontiental.ca
www.lesaffaires.com
Circulation: 88 806 *Frequency: 12 fois par an; français*
Créé en 1978, le magazine Affaires PLUS est le magazine d'affaires au plus fort tirage et au plus fort lectorat au Québec. C'est aussi la plus personnelle des publications d'affaires de Médias Transcontinental. Le magazine est bâti autour de trois axes: mon argent, ma carrière, ma vie, qui déterminent à la fois le positionnement et le contenu d'Affaires PLUS
Stéphane Labrèche, Rédacteur en chef, stephane.labreche@transcontinental.ca

Alberta Venture
10259 - 105 St., Edmonton, AB T5J 1E3
780-990-0839, Fax: 780-425-4921, 866-227-4276
admin@albertaventure.com
www.albertaventure.com
Circulation: 40,800 *Frequency: 10 times a year*
Alberta Venture is the only province-wide magazine that keeps you informed about Alberta's business community. Covers trends, issues, people and events that set the pace for Canada's fastest growing economy
Ruth Kelly, Editor

Atlantic Business Magazine
PO Box 2356 C, 197 Water St., St. John's, NL A1C 6E7
709-726-9300, Fax: 709-726-3013
www.atlanticbusinessmagazine.com
Circulation: 33,000 *Frequency: 6 times a year*
Founded in 1989, Atlantic Business Magazine is an independently owned, bi-monthly glossy publication that covers all areas of business within the four Atlantic provinces.
Hubert Hutton, Publisher, hhutton@atlanticbusinessmagazine.com
Dawn Chafe, Editor, dchafe@atlanticbusinessmagazine.com

Avantages
#800, 1200, ave McGill College, Montréal, QC H3B 4G7
514-843-2510, Fax: 514-843-2182
www.revueavantages.ca
Circulation: 5 159 *Frequency: 8 fois par an; français*
Avantages is a French-language pension and benefits publication produced to meet the needs of the Quebec marketplace. Avantages provides information and analysis on pensions, benefits, healthcare and investments to key decision-makers who manage employer-sponsored pension and benefits plans in Quebec
Alexandre Daudelin, Rédacteur-en-chef, alexandre.daudelin@avantages.rogers.com
Jean Goulet, Éditeur, jean.goulet@rci.rogers.com

Backbone Magazine
c/o Publimedia Communications Inc., 187 Rondoval Cres., North Vancouver, BC V7N 2W6
905-918-0567, Fax: 604-986-5309
info@backbonemag.com
www.backbonemag.com
Circulation: 115,000 *Frequency: 6 times per year*
Backbone magazine's aim is to provide business people with a tangible tool to enhance the way they do business in Canada's New Economy
Steve Dietrich, Publisher, sdietrich@backbonemag.com
Peter Wolchak, Editor, pwolchak@backbonemag.com

Le Banquier/Canadian Banker
Canadian Bankers Association, CP 348, Commerce Ct. West, 30th Fl., Toronto, ON M5L 1G2
416-362-6092, Fax: 416-362-7705, 800-263-0231
cbacallcentre@cba.ca
www.cba.ca

Circulation: 8 400 *Frequency: 4 fois par an; français/anglais*
Canadian Banker and Le Banquier are published four times annually by the Canadian Bankers Association. The magazines aim to keep their readers informed about the broad trends and changes in banking and the financial-services industry

BCBusiness Magazine
4180 Lougheed Hwy. 4th Fl., Burnaby, BC V5C 6A7
604-299-7311, Fax: 604-299-9188, 800-663-0518
ttjaden@canadawide.com
www.bcbusinessmagazine.com
Circulation: 26,000 *Frequency: Monthly; ISSN: 0849-481X*
An authoritative voice on the province's business scene, BCBusiness goes beyond the headlines to give readers valuable, relevant insights into today's trends and issues
Peter Legge, Publisher, ttjaden@canadawide.com
Matt O'Grady, Editor, mogrady@canadawide.com
John Bucher, Editor, jbucher@canadawide.com

Benefits & Pensions Monitor
#501, 245 Fairview Mall Dr., Toronto, ON M2J 4T1
416-494-1066, Fax: 416-494-2536
info@powershift.ca
www.bpmmagazine.com
Circulation: 22,850 *Frequency: 12 times a year*
Benefits and Pensions Monitor is published eight times a year. Benefits and Pensions Monitor had to be different from the other industry magazine to succeed. It had to provide a unique editorial focus on issues that affect the industry. Monitor delivers. Today, Monitor has the industry's highest audited circulation.
John McLaine, Publisher & Editorial Director, jmclaine@powershift.ca
Joe Hornyak, Executive Editor, jhornyak@powershift.ca

Benefits Canada
One Mount Pleasant Rd. 12th Floor, Toronto, ON M4Y 2Y5
416-764-3915, Fax: 416-764-3938
paulb.williams@rci.rogers.com
www.benefitscanada.com
Circulation: 17,000 *Frequency: 12 times a year; English & French*
Provides information and analysis on pensions, benefits, healthcare and investments to key decision-makers who manage employer-sponsored pension and benefits plans. The publication targets the plan sponsor community, particularly those employers with more than 500 employees
Paul Williams, Publisher & Vice President, 416-764-3848, PaulO.williams@rci.rogers.com
Alyssa Hodder, Editor, 416-764-3823, alyssa.hodder@rci.rogers.com

BIZ Magazine
1074 Cooke Blvd, Hamilton, ON L7T 4A8
905-522-6117, Fax: 905-529-2242
info@townmedia.ca
Circulation: 24,000 *Frequency: 4 times a year*
Business publication in the Hamilton/Burlington region, with award-winning features, profiles, real-life photography and controversial opinions
Arend Kirsten, Editor

The Bottom Line
#700, 123 Commerce Valley Dr. East, Markham, ON L3T 7W8
905-415-5804, Fax: 905-479-3758
tbl@butterworths.ca
www.thebottomlinenews.com
Circulation: 30,428 *Frequency: 16 times a year*
The Bottom Line is an independent and specialized business periodical that keeps accredited professional accountants, financial managers, and consultants abreast of news, trends, and technology within the industry
Robert Kelly, Managing Editor
Gary P. Rodrigues, Publisher

Business Bulletin
Mississauga Board of Trade, #701, 77 City Centre Dr., Mississauga, ON L5B 1M5
905-273-6151, Fax: 905-273-4937
info@mbot.com
www.mbot.com
Circulation: 22,000 *Frequency: 11 times a year*
Business Bulletin has been replaced by the mbot magazine. mbot magazine is our dynamic business resource and reference tool. It provides an array of practical articles and advice that address the issues, news and trends important to businesses of all sizes and scopes in Mississauga as well as companies located outside the City. mbot magazine replaces our tabloid-style newspaper Business Bulletin.
Naveen Atwal, External Communications, 905-273-3523, naveena@mbot.com

Business Central Magazine
#304, 4820 Gaetz Ave., Red Deer, AB T4N 4A4
403-309-5587, Fax: 403-346-3044
Circulation: 5,000 *Frequency: 6 times a year*
Donald C. Sylvester, Publisher & Editor

Business Examiner - North
777B Poplar St., Nanaimo, BC V9S 2H7
250-754-8344, Fax: 250-754-8304, 800-332-7355
merv@businessexaminer.net
www.businessexaminer.net
Circulation: 14,000 *Frequency: Monthly*
Steve Weatherbee, Editor

Business Examiner - South Island Edition
818 Broughton St., Victoria, BC V8W 1E4
250-381-3926, Fax: 250-381-5606
www.businessexaminer.net
Circulation: 14,400 *Frequency: 24 times a year*
Bill MacAdam, Publisher
Simon Lindley, Publisher/Sales Manager, simon@businessexaminer.net
Steve Weatherbee, Editor, editor@businessexaminer.net

The Business Executive
#220, 466 Speers Rd., Oakville, ON L6K 3W9
905-845-8300, Fax: 905-845-9086
wpeters@busexec.com
www.busexec.com
Circulation: 30,000 *Frequency: 12 times a year*
The Business Executive is Southern Ontario's only business-to-business newspaper published on a monthly basis. The Business Executive is divided into sections to allow the readers to pick and choose subjects of most interest to them. Some of the sections include: Real Estate & Construction, Finance, Business News, People and Lifestyles, Computers and Technology, International Trade & Travel.
Thomas Peters, Publisher, t.peters@busexec.com
Wendy Peters, Editor, wpeters@busexec.com

Business in Calgary
#1025, 101 - 6th Ave. SW, Calgary, AB T2P 3P4
403-264-3270, Fax: 403-264-3276, 800-465-0322
info@businessincalgary.com
www.businessincalgary.com
Circulation: 30,735 *Frequency: Monthly*
A monthly publication dedicated to producing intelligent, colorful articles about the people, trends and events that make Calgary a prominent business centre in the west.
Camie Leard, Editor, editor@businessincalgary.com
Pat Ottmann, Publisher, pat@businessincalgary.comcom
Tim Ottmann, Publisher, tim@businessincalgary.comcom

Business London
PO Box 7400, London, ON, ON N5Y 4X3
519-472-7601, Fax: 519-473-7859
editorial@businesslondon.ca
www.businesslondon.ca
Circulation: 12,000 *Frequency: Monthly*
The Magazine provides unparalleled behind-the-scenes coverage, chronicling companies on the move and putting faces to faceless events.
Gord Delamont, Publisher, editorial@businesslondon.ca

Business Trends
1383 Confederation St., Sarnia, ON N7S 5P1
519-336-1100, Fax: 519-336-1833
businesstrends@cogeco.net
www.sarniabusinesstrends.com
Circulation: 6,300 *Frequency: 12 times a year*
Covers business trends in the Sarnia area
Gord Bowes, Editor
Kirsten Anderson, Account Manager

Business Voice
1300 Hollis St., Halifax, NS B3J 1T6
902-420-9943, Fax: 902-429-9058
publishers@metroguide.ca
www.metroguidepublishing.ca/bv.php
Circulation: 7,500 *Frequency: 10 times a year*
Business Voice is Halifax's leading business magazine, offering unrivalled access to Metro's decision-makers. Business Voice is the official voice of the Halifax Chamber of Commerce: 95% of members read most or every issue. It keeps readers updated on Chamber policies and activities, plus develop-ments in the business community
Sheila Blair, Publisher

BusinessWoman Canada Magazine
PO Box 31010, Barrie, ON L4N 0B3
705-722-9692, Fax: 705-722-7268, 877-251-7226
Circulation: 20,000 *Frequency: 4 times a year*
Donna Messer, Editor

Businest
#800, 625 boul René-Lévesque Ouest, Montréal, QC H3B 1R2
514-866-3131, Fax: 514-866-3030, 800-361-7262
infos@reseauselect.com
www.reseauselect.com
Circulation: 20 100 *Frequency: Mensuel; français*
Publication qui couvre de domaine des affaires, et dessert les professionnels, les entreprises et les gens d'affaires le territoire de La Pocatière aux les-de-la-Madeleine, et la Côte-Nord
Ernie Wells, Rédacteur-en-chef

CA Magazine
277 Wellington St. West, Toronto, ON M5V 3H2
416-977-3222, Fax: 416-204-3409
CAmagazine@cica.ca
www.camagazine.com
Circulation: 72,500 *Frequency: 10 times a year; English & French*
CAmagazine is published by the Canadian Institute of Chartered Accountants (CICA) ten times a year. Articles about careers in chartered accounting are featured while current issues are discussed and explained. The magazine also deals with a wide variety of business topics from the Chartered Accountant's perspective
Christian Bellavance, Editor-in-chief

Canada Japan Journal
Japan Advertising Ltd., #410, 1199 West Pender St., Vancouver, BC V6E 2R1
604-688-2486, Fax: 604-688-1487, 888-245-2549
japanad@telus.net
www.canadajournal.com
Circulation: 15,750 *Frequency: Monthly; Japanese*
Taka Aoki, Editor

Canadian Association Publishers
PO Box 90510, 230 Markham Rd., Scarborough, ON M1J 3N7
416-955-1550, Fax: 416-955-1391
info@capmagazines.ca
www.capmagazines.ca
Circulation: 30,650 *Frequency: Semi-annual*
Business Resources Canada is Canada's premier Small Business Resource Directory for Owners and Entrepreneurs. Published quarterly, Business Resources Canada, with its combined directory and magazine format, guides and inspires Canadians who are starting or growing a business as their career.
Kelly Chase, Production, production@capmagazines.ca
Jim Eaton, Publishing Enquiries, jeaton@capmagazines.ca
Adrienne Ramsay, Advertising

Canadian Business
One Mount Pleasant Rd. 11th Floor, Toronto, ON M4Y 2Y5
416-764-1200, Fax: 416-764-1404
adsales@canadianbusiness.com
www.canadianbusiness.com/can adian_business_magazine
Circulation: 84,000 *Frequency: 24 times a year; ISSN: 0008-3100*
Canadian Business, Canada's best-selling business magazine, captures the attention of Canada's business leaders with topical, timely stories that matter to corporate managers and executives. Written for an audience with an orientation to the future, its compelling insight inspires readers to capitalize on change
Joe Chidley, Editor
Deborah Rosser, Publisher

Canadian Business Franchise/L'entreprise
c/o Kenilworth Media Inc., #710, 15 Wertheim Ct., Richmond Hill, BC L4B 3H7
905-771-7333, Fax: 905-771-7336, 800-409-8688
info@kenilworth.com
www.cgb.ca
Frequency: Bi-monthly
Canadian Business Franchise Magazine is a bi-monthly publication that features articles on franchise advice from bankers, lawyers and franchise specialists. The magazine is in its eleventh year of production and is the best selling Franchise magazine in Canada
Colin Bradbury, Publisher & Editor
Tuesday Royko, Editorial Assistant

Canadian German Trade
#1500, 480 University Ave., Toronto, ON M5G 1V2
416-598-3355, Fax: 416-598-1840
info@germanchamber.ca
www.germanchamber.ca
Circulation: 2,500 *Frequency: 6 times a year*
Covers news concerning the Canadian and German economy, special articles which are of interest to the Canadian and German business community, as well as updated economic datanews concerning the Canadian and German economy,

special articles which are of interest to the Canadian and German business community, as well as updated economic data
Sonya Deevy, Contact

Canadian Investment Review
One Mount Pleasant Ave., 12th Fl., Toronto, ON M4Y 2Y5
416-764-3867, Fax: 416-764-3934
www.investmentreview.com
Frequency: 4 times a year
Canada's leading forum for academics, institutional investors and industry practitioners to exchange ideas on the capital markets, investment and economic theory, and the related sociology and demographics.
Caroline Cakebread, Editor, caroline.cakebread@rogers.com
Paul Williams, Publisher, VP, Healthcare and Financial, don.bisch@rogers.comogers.com

The Canadian Manager
Canadian Institute of Management, 15 Collier St., Lower Level, Barrie, ON L4M 1G5
705-725-8926, Fax: 705-725-8196, 800-387-5774
office@cim.ca
www.cim.ca
Circulation: 4,500 *Frequency: 4 times a year*
The Canadian Manager is published 4 times per year by the Canadian Institute of Management, with a readership over 12,000 (approx.)
Anna Victoria Wong, Editor/Manager, awong@baseconsulting.ca

Canadian Not-For-Profit News
One Corporate Plaza, 2075 Kennedy Rd., Toronto, ON M1T 3V4
416-609-8000, Fax: 416-298-5094
www.carswell.com
Frequency: Monthly
Source of current information on the tax implications and practical considerations relating to the most relevant and timely issues surrounding registered charities and other non-profit organizations

The Canadian Taxpayer
416-609-8000, Fax: 416-298-5082, 800-387-5164
carswell.orders@thomson.com
www.carswell.com
Circulation: 1,000 *Frequency: 24 times per year*
The Taxpayer is the flagship publication of the Canadian Taxpayers Federation (CTF). It is published six times a year and contains comprehensive updates on CTF happenings and accomplishments around the country. It features articles written by CTF researchers and spokespersons. Guest editorial writers also contribute to this publication.
Robert Freeman, Vice-President

Canadian Treasurer
c/o Treasury Management Association of Canada, #1010, 8 King St. East, Toronto, ON M5C 1B5
416-367-8500, Fax: 416-367-3240, 800-449-8622
info@tmac.ca
www.tmac.ca
Circulation: 5,313 *Frequency: 6 times a year*
TMAC's bimonthly magazine, Canadian Treasurer, brings directly to you the latest trends in treasury management. Canadian Treasurer reaches treasury professionals of major corporate and government organizations throughout Canada. It is also distributed to other organizations within the Canadian financial community, the U.S. and around the world. Circulation includes the top 1,000 companies in Canada.
Bruce McDougall, Managing Editor
Mike Whiston, Executive Director

Central Nova Business News
Advocate Print & Publishing Ltd., PO Box 1000, 181 Brown's Point Rd., Pictou, NS B0K 1H0
902-893-0375, Fax: 902-893-1353
Circulation: 1,500 *Frequency: Monthly*
The official Publication of the Truro and District Chamber of Commerce
Jason Warren, Editor

CGA Magazine
#800, 1188 Georgia St. West, Vancouver, BC V6E 4A2
604-669-3555, Fax: 604-689-5845, 800-663-1529
jward@cga-canada.org
www.cga-online.org/canada
Circulation: 60,000 *Frequency: 6 times a year; English & French*
CGA Magazine profiles current issues relevant to professional accountancy and discusses news and trends in the business and regulatory environment. Printed 6 times a year, this glossy publication is distributed to 68,000 CGA students, members, and leaders in the business, government, education and regulatory communities.
Barbara Cameron, Publisher
Peggy Homan, Associate Publisher/Editor

China's Wired!
#400, 1235 Bay St., Toronto, ON M5R 3K4
416-966-9391, Fax: 416-699-1165
www.flyingarmchair.com
Frequency: 12 times a year (internet)
China's Wired! Your Guide to the Internet in China, is the first book written on the Internet and its use and potential in the People's Republic of China. China's Wired! is designed to be the Internet guide on the PRC for investors and entrepreneurs

CMA Management Magazine
c/o Society of Management Accountants of Canada, Miss. Exec., #1400, One Robert Speck Pkwy., Mississauga, ON L4Z 3M3
905-949-4200, Fax: 905-949-0888, 800-263-7622
info@cma-canada.org
www.managementmag.com
Circulation: 48,000 *Frequency: 9 times a year; English & French*
Management is an outstanding business magazine specifically tailored to help you make informed business decisions and give you a strategic advantage. It provides effective, practical solutions to your most pressing business challenges. It features the latest trends in management strategies with sharp, fresh editorial and attention-grabbing design.
David Fletcher, Publisher
Robert Colman, Editor-in-chief

Commerce & Industry
1740 Wellington Ave., Winnipeg, MB R3H 0E8
204-954-2085, Fax: 204-954-2057
mp@mercury.mb.ca
www.mercury.mb.ca
Circulation: 18,154 *Frequency: 6 times a year*
A national publication focused on the industrial, manufacturing, resource, transportation and construction sectors. Each issue offers a large variety of sector analysis, in-depth company profiles and reports on key areas of interest to the magazine's target audience.
Al Kaglik, National Account Manager, al@mercury.mb.ca
Frank Yeo, Publisher
Edna Saito, Production Manager

Commerce News
Edmonton Chamber of Commerce, #700, 9990 Jasper Ave., Edmonton, AB T5J 1P7
780-426-4620, Fax: 780-424-7946
info@edmontonchamber.com
www.edmontonchamber.com
Circulation: 36,000 *Frequency: 11 times a year*
Published by the Edmonton Chamber of Commerce, reaches an estimated audience of over 150,000 business readers per issue. It is direct mailed eleven times per year to every Chamber member and subscriber (4,500 copies), to all Edmonton area businesses, government and association leaders around the region, and to all Alberta Chambers of Commerce (25,500 copies).
Martin Salloum, Publisher
Chris O'Brien, Editor
Rita Boyce, Ad Sales
Kimberly Nishikaze, Managing Editor

Corporate Ethics Monitor
Lawrence Plaza, PO Box 54034, Toronto, ON M6A 3B7
416-783-6776, Fax: 416-783-7386
info@ethicscan.ca
www.ethicscan.ca
Circulation: 400 *Frequency: Bi-monthly*
Each sixteen page issue of the bi-monthly Corporate Ethics Monitor ($297 Canadian for one year, $456 CDN for foreign subscriptions) is laden with articles and stories that deal with recognizing and enhancing ethics in the workplace. Expect to find original research, timely articles, provocative perspectives, and practical ideas. The reporting on comparative business practices reflects dozens of hours of interviews, data base retrieval, fact checking and preparation of tables, charts and profiles. All this, plus insightful articles from regular columnists, an OPEN FORUM for executives, a Face to Face debate section, and lively book reviews.

Defined Benefit Monitor
#501, 245 Fairview Mall Dr., Toronto, ON M2J 4T1
Frequency: 2 times a year
John McLaine, Publisher

Defined Contribution Monitor
#501, 245 Fairview Maill Dr., Toronto, ON M2J 4T1
Frequency: 2 times a year
John McLaine, Publisher

EDGE
#302, 55 World Town Centre Ct., Scarborough, ON M1P 4X4
416-290-0240, 800-387-5312
info@itbusiness.ca
www.itbusiness.ca
Circulation: 16,640 *Frequency: 12 times a year*
EDGE (Executives in a Digital Global Economy) is a non-technical, monthly magazine for CEOs, CFOs, CIOs and other senior executives who want to know how information technology can be used to transform their business. Through a combination of case studies, executive profiles and a look at best practices, EDGE not only demystifies IT, it shows how organizations can achieve competitive advantage.
Martin Slofstra, Editorial Director
Joe Tersigni, Publisher
Dave Web, Writer and Editor

L'Edition Le Journal des Gens d'Affaires
514-257-1000, Fax: 514-257-7505
Circulation: 29 700
Carole Le Hirez, Rédacteur-en-chef
Lise Thériault, Éditeur

Entreprendre
Editions Qualité Performante inc., #660, 1600, boul St-Martin est, Laval, QC H7G 4R8
450-669-8373, Fax: 450-669-9078, 800-479-1777
message@entreprendre.ca
www.entreprendre.ca
Circulation: 45 000 *Frequency: 10 fois par an; français*
Le magazine Entreprendre rejoint un auditoire exceptionnel de décideurs du monde des affaires. Outil d'information qui développe des références et éclaire la nature profonde de l'entrepreneurship au Québec
Edmond Bourque, Publisher

Exchange Magazine for Business
#10, 160 Frobisher Dr., Waterloo, ON N2V 2B1
519-886-0298, Fax: 519-886-6409
editor@exchangemagazine.com
www.exchangemagazine.com
Circulation: 17,500 *Frequency: 8 times a year*
Covers business news in the Kitchener-Waterloo area
Jon Rohr, Editor-in-chief

Finance et Investissement
514-392-9000, Fax: 514-392-4726, 800-361-5479
www.finance-investissement.com
Circulation: 18,000 *Frequency: 14 times a year*
Depuis son lancement en novembre 1999, le journal Finance et Investissement est devenu la source d'information privilégiée des représentants en épargne collective, des conseillers en valeurs mobilières, des conseillers en sécurité financière et des planificateurs financiers
Sylvain Bedard, Publisher, sylvain.bedard@transcontinental.ca

Financial Post Business
#300, 1450 Don Mills Rd., Toronto, ON M3B 3R5
416-383-2300, Fax: 416-386-2836
editorial@nationalpostbusiness.com
www.nationalpostbusiness.com
Circulation: 289,000 *Frequency: 12 times a year*
Brian Banks, Editor

FlashFinance
#100, 321, rue de la Commune, Montréal, QC H2Y 2E1
514-289-9595, Fax: 514-289-9527
flash@flashfinance.ca
www.flashfinance.ca
Circulation: 2 000 *Frequency: Weekly*
Outil privilégié d'information du monde de l'assurance et de la finance, FlashFinance.ca joint des milliers de dirigeants de compagnies d'assurance, de propriétaires de cabinets, de directeurs de courtage, et de conseillers financiers
Serge Therrien, Publisher

The FP Survey of Industrials
Financial Post Data Group, 1450 Don Mills Rd., 2nd Fl., Toronto, ON M3B 2X7
416-442-2121, Fax: 416-442-2968
fpdg@canwest.com
Circulation: 3,870 *Frequency: Annually, Aug.*
Financial and operational information on publicly traded Canadian companies

Franchise Canada Directory
Canadian Franchise Association, #300, 2585 Skymark Ave., Mississauga, ON L4W 4L5
905-625-2896, Fax: 905-625-9076, 800-665-4232
jschofield@cfa.ca
www.cfa.ca

Frequency: Annually
John Schofield, Editor

Franchise Canada Magazine
Canadian Franchise Association, #116, 5399 Eglinton Ave. West, Toronto, ON M9C 5K6
416-695-2896, Fax: 416-695-1950, 800-665-4232
info@cfa.ca
www.cfa.ca
Circulation: 6,000 *Frequency: 6 times a year*
A bi-monthly magazine geared at entrepreneurs interested in acquiring a franchise. Franchise Canada Magazine will contain top-notch editorial from leading authorities in the industry as well as countless tips on how to establish a successful franchise.
John Scofield, Editor

Gestion
3000, ch de la Côte-Sainte-Catherine, Montréal, QC H3T 2A7
514-340-6677, Fax: 514-340-6975
revue.gestion@hec.ca
revue.hec.ca/gestion
Circulation: 3 500 *Frequency: 4 fois par an; français*
La Revue Gestion a pour but de favoriser la diffusion des connaissances dans tous les domaines de la gestion en français. Particulièrement populaire au Québec, la revue est également lue dans d'autres régions francophones. Offre à ses lecteurs des articles inédits présentant les dernières recherches, des analyses critiques, des synthèses et des réflexions originales dans le domaine de la gestion en Amérique du nord
Michel Vézina, Rédacteur-en-chef

GST & Commodity Tax
One Corporate Plaza, 2075 Kennedy Rd., Toronto, ON M1T 3V4
416-609-8000, Fax: 416-298-5094
www.carswell.com

The exclusive source for what leading experts are saying about the latest developments in GST, federal and provincial sales and commodity taxes, and customs and excise duties

Halton Business Times
#1, 5040 Mainway, Burlington, ON L7L 7G5
905-632-4444, Fax: 905-632-9162
thepost@worldchat.com
Circulation: 12,000 *Frequency: 12 times a year*
Ian Oliver, Publisher
Karen Smith, Editor

Huronia Business Times
Kozlov Centre, #243, 400 Bayfield St., Barrie, ON L4M 5A1
705-728-3090, Fax: 705-734-9600
businesstimes@simcoe.com
www.huroniabusinesstimes.com
Circulation: 12,000 *Frequency: 12 times a year*
Purchased by Metroland Business Publications in September of 1998, Huronia Business Times, and its sister publication the Mississauga Business Times, was formerly owned by North Island Publishing from 1992-1998. Metroland also publishes five other Business Times newspapers in southern Ontario
Martin Melbourne, Editor
Shaun Sauve, General Manager

In Business Windsor
1775 Sprucewood, La Salle, ON N9J 1X7
519-250-2880, Fax: 519-250-2881
gbaxter@inbusinesswindsor.com
www.inbusinesswindsor.com
Circulation: 10,500 *Frequency: 12 times a year*
Monthly publication which highlights business news in the Windsor area
Jenine Fry, Associate Editor
Gary Baxter, Publisher

Info-ACAIQ
Association des courtiers et agents immobilier du Québec, #300, 6300, rue Auteuil, Brossard, QC J4Z 3P2
450-676-4800, Fax: 450-676-7801, 800-440-5110
info@acaiq.com
www.acaiq.com
Circulation: 16 000
L'Info ACAIQ est le journal des professionnels du courtage immobilier du Québec. Il couvre divers sujets relatifs à l'application de la Loi sur le courtage immobilier, aux règlements de la profession, au marché immobilier en plus de questions d'ordre juridique et déontologique reliées à la pratique du courtage immobilier

Investment Executive
#100, 25 Sheppard Ave. West, Toronto, ON M2N 6S7
416-733-7600, Fax: 416-218-3544
twilmott@investmentexecutive.com
www.investmentexecutive.com
Circulation: 50,200 *Frequency: 16 times a year*
Investment Executive is Canada's national newspaper for financial service industry professionals. Investment Executive is published 16 times a year and reaches more than 120,000 financial advisors. Investment Executive has gained the respect of its readers by offering intelligent, informed coverage of the financial services industry and providing insightful information for advisors on topics as diverse as mutual funds, investment research, technology, estate planning, tax, building relationships with clients and developing products and services for the client of the future.
Tessa Wilmott, Editor-in-chief, twilmott@investmentexecutive.com

Investor's Digest of Canada
#700, 133 Richmond St. West, Toronto, ON M5H 3M8
416-869-1177, Fax: 416-869-0616, 800-504-8846
customers@mplcomm.com
www.adviceforinvestors.com
Circulation: 42,912 *Frequency: 24 times a year*
Devoted to uncovering profitable opportunities in every area of investing, using the insights of Canada's leading investment professionals
Michael Popovich, Editor
Barrie Martland, Publisher

Italcommerce
Italian Chamber of Commerce in Canada, #1150, 550, rue Sherbrooke ouest, Montréal, QC H3A 1B9
514-844-4249, Fax: 514-844-4875, 800-263-4372
info.montreal@italchambers.net
www.italchamber.qc.ca
Frequency: 3 times a year; French, English & Italian
A pour mission de promouvoir et soutenir les échanges commerciaux entre le Québec, le Canada et l'Italie. Le magazine est diffusé au Canada, en Italie ainsi que dans 60 autres pays où on retrouve des chambres de commerce italiennes
Pasquale Iacobacci, Managing Editor

ITBusiness Report
#302, 55 Town Ct., Scarborough, ON M1P 4X4
416-290-0240
info@itbusiness.ca
www.itbusiness.ca
Circulation: 20,000 *Frequency: 12 times a year*
Covers Canada's IT industry: the key players, the important issues, the decision-making processes. Provides informative, incisive and unbiased coverage examining Canadian case studies, news stories and applications. It provides an overview of trends and technologies, and looks at Canadian product availability and costs
Joe Tersigni, Publisher, jtersigni@itworldcanada.com
Neil Sutton, Editor

Ivey Business Journal
c/o Richard Ivey School of Business, University of Western O, London, ON N6A 3K7
519-661-3208, Fax: 519-661-3882
www.iveybusinessjournal.com
Circulation: 12,013 *Frequency: 6 times a year; ISSN: 1481-8248*
For more than 70 years, the Ivey Business Journal has delivered incisive, practical articles about managing. Covers articles about e-business, managing uncertainty, knowledge management, marketing, strategy and other topics that managers need to know more about to steer their firms to success
Ed Pearce, Publisher
Stephen Bernhut, Editor

Journal Économique de Québec
#900, 1265, boul Charest ouest, Québec, QC G1N 4V4
418-686-6400, Fax: 418-868-1086, 888-293-0999
redacjeq@transcontinental.ca
Circulation: 19 000 *Frequency: Hebdomadaire*
Yvon Giroux, Rédacteur-en-chef

Kootenay Business Magazine

250-426-7253, Fax: 250-426-4125, 800-663-8555
info@kpimedia.com
www.kootenaybiz.com
Circulation: 9,400 *Frequency: 6 times a year*
Kootenay Business magazine is free to businesses within the Kootenay/ Columbia/ Boundary/ Revelstoke area
Keith Powell, Publisher, keith@kpimedia.com

Le lien économique
#2, 500, rue Somerset ouest, Ottawa, ON K1R 5J8
613-858-1336, Fax: 613-234-1148
sara.grenier@lelieneconomique.com
Circulation: 13 500 *Frequency: 6 fois par an*
Le Lien économique est lu par des décideurs de tous les secteurs de l'économie: Propriétaires et gestionnaires d'entreprises dans tous les secteurs d'activité commerciale : manufactures, institutions financières, services de santé, vente au détail, services et haute technologie
Réjean Grenier, Éditeur et rédacteur en chef

Magazine PME
1100, boul René-Lévesque 24e étage, Montréal, QC H3B 4X9
514-392-9000, Fax: 514-392-2026
Circulation: 35 922 *Frequency: 10 fois par an; français*
Couvre les petites et moyennes entreprises au Québec
Marie Quinty, Rédactrice en chef
Pierre Duhamel, Editeur

The Manitoba Broker
#3C, 2020 Portage Ave., Winnipeg, MB R3J 0K4
204-985-9785, Fax: 204-985-9795
info@kelman.mb.ca
Circulation: 1,300 *Frequency: 4 times a year*
Has timely industry releated articles by feature writers and advertisements of interest to Manitoba brokers
Terry Ross, Editor-in-chief

Manitoba Business Magazine
#508, 294 Portage Ave., Winnipeg, MB R3C 0B9
204-943-2931, Fax: 204-943-2942, 888-477-4620
mbm@mts.net
www.manitobabusinessmagazine.com
Circulation: 8,000 *Frequency: 10 times a year*
Ritchie Gage, Editor

Marketplace Magazine
PO Box 523, 910 Queen St., Kincardine, ON N2Z 2Y9
519-396-9142, Fax: 519-396-3555, 877-396-9142
marketplace@bmts.com
Circulation: 13,000 *Frequency: 12 times a year*
James Pannell, Publisher
Linda Pannell, General Manager

mbot Magazine
Mississauga Board of Trade, 701-77 City Dr., Mississauga, ON L5B 1M5
905-273-6151, Fax: 905-273-4937
info@mbot.com
www.mbot.com
Circulation: 5,000 *Frequency: 11 times a year*
Sheryl McKean, President & CEO

Mississauga Business Times
3145 Wolfedale Rd., Mississauga, ON L5C 3A9
905-273-8111, Fax: 905-273-8219
www.mississauganews.com
Circulation: 40,000 *Frequency: Monthly*
The News is a perennial newspaper award winner, including best newspaper in Ontario and Canada, on several occasions. The Mississauga News is delivered three times a week to houses.
Rick Drennan, Editor, rdrennan@mississauga.net
Ron Lenyk, Publisher

Monday Report on Retailers
One Mount Pleasant Rd., 7th Fl., Toronto, ON M4Y 2Y5
416-764-1463, Fax: 416-764-1711
www.mondayreport.ca
Frequency: Weekly
Canada's premier information resource for people seeking in-depth, up to-date data on the retail, food service and shopping centre industries in Canada
Don Douloff, Managing Editor

MoneySense
One Mount Pleasant Rd., 11th Fl., Toronto, ON M4Y 2Y5
416-764-1400, Fax: 416-764-1404
adsales@moneysense.com
www.canadianbusiness.com/moneysense_magazine
Circulation: 106,600 *Frequency: 6 times a year*
MoneySense is Canada's leading personal finance magazine. Each issue contains insightful and informative columns and articles to help you make the most of your money. MoneySense magazine is published seven times a year by Rogers Media.
Ian McGugan, Editor
Deborah Rosser, Publisher

National Post Business, FP 500
#300, 1450 Don Mills Rd., Toronto, ON M3B 3R5
416-383-2300, Fax: 416-386-2836, 800-668-7678
feedback@canada.com
www.nationalpostbusiness.com
Circulation: 289,000 *Frequency: Annually, June*
Ranking of Canada's largest corporations
Brian Banks, Editor

North Country Business
PO Box 180, Bracebridge, ON P1L 1T6
705-646-1314, Fax: 705-645-6424
info@muskokamagazine.com
http://ospreymediagroup.com

Circulation: 5,259 *Frequency:* 12 times a year
Donald Smith, Publisher

Northern Ontario Business
Laurentian Publishing Co., 158 Elgin St., Sudbury, ON P3E 3N5
705-673-5705, Fax: 705-673-9542, 800-757-2766
info@nob.on.ca
www.northernontariobusiness.com
Circulation: 10,000 *Frequency:* Monthly
Northern Ontario Business is printed every month and is the only publication devoted to the region's business community
Patricia Mills, Publisher, pmills@nob.on.ca
Kelly Louiseize, Managing Editor, kellyl@nob.on.ca

Northwest Business Magazine
Dakota Design & Advertising Ltd., 3907 - 3A St. NE, Bay 114, Calgary, AB T2E 6S7
403-250-1128, Fax: 403-250-1194
dakotade@telusplanet.net
Circulation: 15,000 *Frequency:* 10 times a year
Regional business magazine that focuses on developments affecting the resource sectors in Northern BC, Alberta, Northwest Territories
Kathryn Engel, Editor

Nova Scotia Business Journal
Transontinental Specialty Publications, #609, 1888 Brunswick St., Halifax, NS B3J 3J8
902-468-8027, Fax: 902-468-1775
info@transcontinental.ca
www.novascotiabusinessjournal.com
Circulation: 15,000 *Frequency:* Monthly
This established business-to-business journal, published 12 times a year, features coverage of premier events, local success stories, issues affecting Nova Scotia's many business sectors, and sought-after special features.
Barbt McCay Cashin, Editor

Office@Home
PO Box D-79, Bowen Island, BC V0N 1G0
604-947-2275, Fax: 604-947-0633
officeathome@dowco.com
Frequency: 4 times a year
Dave Sharrock, Publisher
Dale Gagne, Editor

Okanagan Business Magazine
Byrne Publishing Group Inc., #10, 1753 Dolphin Ave., Kelowna, BC V1Y 8A6
250-861-5399, Fax: 250-868-3040, 888-311-1119
info@okanaganlife.com
www.okanaganlife.com
Circulation: 25,000 *Frequency:* 10 times a year
Okanagan Life captures the essence of life and lifestyles in the Okanagan with informative and entertaining stories on Okanagan food and wine, Okanagan travel, Valley music and entertainment, Okanagan real estate, fashion trends, Okanagan personalities, Okanagan business profiles, community activism, and much more. Okanagan Life Magazine is distributed to 24,460 Okanagan Valley homes, businesses, newsstands and subscribers making it the only city or regional magazine in North America to match or exceed the circulation of the region's largest daily newspaper.
Paul Byrne, Publisher

Ontario Industrial Magazine
#1159, 1011 Upper Middle Rd. East, Oakville, ON L6H 5Z9
416-446-1404, Fax: 416-446-0502, 800-624-2776
sales@oim-online.com
www.oim-online.com
Circulation: 20,000 *Frequency:* Monthly
OIM provides the very latest information about manufacturing technology, material handling products, industrial equipment & services, financial management and general business news
Keith Laverty, Publisher
Bill Bryson, Editorial Advisor

L'Opportuniste
450, 2e av, Sainte-Marie, QC G6E 1B6
418-387-6969, Fax: 418-387-5223, 877-387-6969
redactionopp@dynamiques.com
www.dynamiques.com
Frequency: Mensuel

Ottawa Business Journal
Transcontinental Media, #30, 5300 Canotek Rd., Ottawa, ON K1J 8R7
613-744-4800, Fax: 613-744-8232
obj@transcontinental.ca
www.ottawabusinessjournal.com
Circulation: 16,300 *Frequency:* 51 times a year
Ottawa Business Journal is the leading source of local business news and information for Canada's national capital region. Every Monday, the newspaper provides authoritative and in-depth news coverage on the sectors that comprise Ottawa's vibrant business scene, ranging from technology to commercial real estate and corporate finance to hospitality.
Michael Curran, Publisher

Partners, Italy & Canada
Italian Chamber of Commerce of Toronto, #1502, 80 Richmond St. West, Toronto, ON M5H 2A4
416-789-7169, Fax: 416-789-7160
info.toronto@italchambers.net
www.italchambers.ca
Circulation: 12,000 *Frequency:* 4 times a year
partners is the official publication of the Italian Chamber of Commerce of Toronto. Published quarterly, the magazine features editorials and special reports written by international experts and tackles themes such as business ethics, design, multiculturalism, foreign trade, arts and entertainment. Through interviews and company profiles, partners is the voice of the Canadian, Italian and international business community.
Corrado Paina, Editorial Director, paina@italchambers.ca
Emily Saso, Managing Editor, saso@italchambers.ca

Port of Halifax
1300 Hollis St., Halifax, NS B3J 1T6
902-420-9943, Fax: 902-429-9058
swhite@metroguide.ca
www.metroguidepublishing.ca/port.php
Circulation: 20,000
Port of Halifax Magazine features information about the Port of Halifax along with stories of interest to the international shipping community
Sheila Blair, Publisher

Profit: The Magazine for Canadian Entrepreneurs
One Mount Pleasant Rd., 11th Fl., Toronto, ON M4Y 2Y5
416-764-1402, Fax: 416-764-1404
www.canadianbusiness.com
Circulation: 102,600 *Frequency:* 6 times a year; ISSN: 1183-1324
Published six times per year and boasting circulation of 101,000 and readership of 373,000, PROFIT delivers the highest composition of business decision-makers and managers / owner / professionals amongst all PMB measured English-language magazines in Canada
Deborah Rosser, Publisher

Progress
Penthouse, #1201, 1660 Hollis St., Halifax, NS B3J 1V7
902-494-0999, Fax: 902-494-0997
progress@progresscorp.com
www.progresscorp.com
Circulation: 26,513 *Frequency:* 10 times a year; ISSN: 0046-6735
Pamela Scott Crace, Editor

Québec Enterprise
#200, 5, Place du Commerce, Ile des Soeurs, Montréal, QC H3E 1M8
514-842-5492, Fax: 514-842-5375, 866-303-5492
magazine@quebecenterprise.com
www.quebecentreprise.com
Circulation: 25,000 *Frequency:* 5 fois par an; français
Magazine d'affaires couvrant les activités industrielles de toutes les régions du Québec
Daniel Boisvert, Président-éditeur

Québec Franchise & Occasions d'Affaires
CP 57, Youville, QC H2P 2V2
514-383-0034, Fax: 514-383-0057
info@quebec-franchise.qc.ca
www.quebec-franchise.qc.ca
Circulation: 10 000 copies *Frequency:* 6 times a year, French, 25% English
Spécialisé dans la franchise et les opportunités d'affaires au Québec et au Canada
Jacques Desforges, Editor

Québec inc
#100, 321, rue de la Commune ouest, Montréal, QC H2Y 2E1
514-289-9595, Fax: 514-289-9527
quebecinc@quebecinc.ca
www.quebecinc.ca/
Circulation: 33 231 *Frequency:* 8 fois par an
Magazine pour gens d'affaires du Québec
Claude Breton, Rédacteur en chef
Serge Therrien, Éditeur

Report on Business Magazine (ROB)
c/o The Globe and Mail, 444 Front St. West, Toronto, ON M5V 2S9
416-585-5000, Fax: 416-585-3327
newsroom@globeandmail.com
www.theglobeandmail.com
Frequency: 11 times a year
Canada's premier business magazine is distributed nationwide with The Globe and Mail to targeted circulation. The thought-provoking and important business stories reach an influential and educated audience. As a pro-business, pro-Canada and pro-reader magazine, it charts the path of business like no other publication in this country
Philip Crawley, Publisher and CEO

Revue Commerce
1100, boul René-Lévesque ouest, 24e étage, Montréal, QC H3B 4X9
514-392-9000, Fax: 514-392-2026
www.lesaffaires.com/publications/commerce.fr.html
Circulation: 37,766 *Frequency:* Mensuel; français; ISSN: 0380-9811
Magazine d'actualité qui couvre le monde des affaires
Diane Bérar, Rédactrice en chef

Senior Executive
Beacon Publishing Inc., 2150 Fillmore Cres., Ottawa, ON K1J 6A4
613-747-1138, Fax: 613-747-7319
!publisher@seniorexec.ca!
www.seniorexec.ca
Circulation: 20,000 *Frequency:* 6 times a year
Senior Executive magazine features informative articles on topics such as: management techniques; service improvement;business developments; success stories; best practices; IM and IT; innovative use of technology; financial management; personal finance; innovative organizational approaches; modern comptrollership; risk management; policy issues; personnel and retention issues; stress management; transformations; horizontal management;and partnering innovations/successes/challenges between business and government.
John Kiska, Associate Editor
Jonathan Calof, Associate Editor
Chris MacLean, Managing Editor, !cmaclean@seniorexec.ca!
John Kiska, Associate Editor

SOHO Business Report
439A Marmont St., Coquitlam, BC V3K 4S4
604-936-5815, Fax: 604-936-5805, 888-963-5815
info@SOHObusinessreport.com
www.sohobusinessreport.com
Circulation: 40,000 *Frequency:* 4 times a year
SOHO Business Report is a quarterly magazine begun in 1989, when the SOHO-based business phenomenon was just a "blip" on the screen of public consciousness. It originated in Abbotsford, British Columbia, Canada from the home of founding publisher Barbara Mowat. Starting as a small newsletter, it first started as The B.C. Home Business Report, and was designed to help link home-based businesses across the province, providing the lone entrepreneur with practical tips and sensible advice on running their business. The newsletter was in demand, and soon other regional editions followed in Alberta and Ontario. Then in 1994, Home Business Report went national. After all these years, it was time for the magazine to enter its teenage growth spurt and the SOHO Business Report emerged as a celebration of over a decade and a half of helping entrepreneurs
Chad Thiessen, Publisher

Sounding Board
World Trade Center, #400, 999 Canada Pl., Vancouver, BC V6C 3E1
604-681-2111, Fax: 604-681-0437
contactus@boardoftrade.com
www.boardoftrade.com
Circulation: 12,000 *Frequency:* 10 times a year
As the official monthly publication of The Vancouver Board of Trade, the Sounding Board newspaper provides analysis and discussion of regional and national issues facing the business community. The paper has a primary circulation of 12,000 and a conservatively estimated total readership of 30,000. Sounding Board is published 10 times per year by The Board, Vancouver's chamber of commerce.
Darcy Rezac, Managing Director, 604-641-1255
Tracy Campbell, Editor

Thompson's World Insurance News
PO Box 1027, Waterloo, ON N2J 4S1
519-579-2500, Fax: 519-745-7321
mpub@sympatico.ca
www.thompsonsnews.com
Frequency: Weekly
Canada's only independent weekly for p&c insurance professionals, has been the industry's most trusted news source for more than a decade
Mark Publicover, Managing Editor

Thunder Bay Business
1145 Barton Street, Thunder Bay, ON P7B 5N3

807-623-2348, Fax: 807-623-7515
nspinc@tbaytel.net
www.thunderbaybusiness.ca
Circulation: 5,000 *Frequency: Monthly*
Northwestern Ontario business publication
Scott Sumner, Publisher & Editor

Toronto Business Magazine
11966 Woodbine Ave., Gormley, ON L0H 1G0
905-887-5048, Fax: 905-887-0764
Circulation: 48,085 *Frequency: 6 times a year*
Janet Gardiner, Publisher

The Toronto Stock Exchange Daily Record
130 King St. West, 3rd Fl., Toronto, ON M5X 1J2
416-947-4655, Fax: 416-814-8811
Circulation: 1,000 *Frequency: Daily*
Toronto Stock Exchange publishes the names of conditionally approved companies in the Daily Record, a daily TSX publication
Catherine McGravey, Publisher & Editor

The Toronto Stock Exchange Monthly Review
130 King St., 3rd Fl., Toronto, ON M5X 1J2
416-947-4655, Fax: 416-814-8811
Circulation: 2,000 *Frequency: 12 times a year*
Monthly bulletin containing market information for companies traded on the Toronto Stock Exchange
Catherine McGravey, Publisher & Editor

Trade & Commerce
1700 Church Ave., Winnipeg, MB R2X 3A2
204-632-2606, Fax: 204-694-3040
tcommerce@wpgsun.com
www.tradeandcom.com
Circulation: 10,000 *Frequency: 4 times a year*
Trade & Commerce magazine produces annual "Market Surveys" on all Canadian provinces and territories, that review overall economic performance and highlight investment and growth opportunities in specific communities. Each of the year's five issues also profiles leading companies operating within the surveyed regions. The Access Americas section features attractive U.S. and international locations for Canadian business and industrial expansion. Distributed nationally to top managers in Canada fastest growing companies
George Mitchell, Publisher

YorkU
York University, West Office Bldg., 4700 Keele St., Toronto, ON M3J 1P3
416-736-5058, Fax: 416-736-5681
editor@yorku.ca
www.yorku.ca/yorku
Circulation: 180,000 alumni editions *Frequency: 5 times a year; includes 3 for alumni*
YorkU is the magazine of York University
Berton Woodward, Publications Director

Camping & Outdoor Recreation

Camping Canada's Dealer News
Camping Canada Ltd., #5, 1020 Brevik Pl., Mississauga, ON L4W 4N7
905-624-8218, Fax: 905-624-6764
Circulation: 56,000
William E. Taylor, Publisher
Peter Tasler, Editor-in-chief

Chemicals & Chemical Process Industries

Canadian Chemical News / L'Actualité chimique canadienne
c/o The Chemical Institute of Canada, #550, 130 Slater St., Ottawa, ON K1P 6E2
613-232-6252, Fax: 613-232-5862
editorial@accn.ca
www.accn.ca
Circulation: 5,500 *Frequency: 10 times a year*
Michelle Piquettee, Editor-in-chief
Heather Dana Munroe, Managing Editor

Canadian Process Equipment & Control News
#29, 588 Edward Ave., Richmond Hill, ON L4C 9Y6
905-770-8077, Fax: 905-770-8075
cpe@cpecn.com
www.cpecn.com
Circulation: 24,127 *Frequency: 6 times a year*
Mike Overment, Editor

Industrial Process Products & Technology
#1235, 1011 Upper Middle Rd. East, Oakville, ON L6H 5Z9
905-475-4231, Fax: 905-475-3512, 800-572-4231
mswan@ippt.ca
www.ippt.ca
Circulation: 24,190 *Frequency: 6 times a year*
Michael Swan, Publisher

Clothing & Accessories

Canadian Apparel Magazine
Canadian Apparel Federation, #504, 124 O'Connor St., Ottawa, ON K1P 5M9
613-231-3220, Fax: 613-231-2305, 800-661-1187
info@apparel.ca
www.apparel.ca
Circulation: 25,466 *Frequency: 6 times a year*
Bob Kirke, Publisher
Marsha Ross, Managing Editor

Kids Creations
c/o Children's Apparel Manufacturers' Association, #3110, 6900, boul Decarie, Montréal, QC H3X 2T8
514-731-7774, Fax: 514-731-7459
cama@apparel.org
www.cama-apparel.org
Circulation: 12,000 *Frequency: 4 times a year; English & French*
Patrick Thomas, Business Manager & Executive Director
Andrea Taylor, Editor

Style
#701, 555 Richmond St. West, Toronto, ON M5V 3B1
416-203-6737, Fax: 416-203-1057
rod@style.ca; leslie@style.ca
www.style.ca
Circulation: 12,000 *Frequency: 5 times a year*
Rod Morris, Publisher
Leslie Wu, Editor

Computing & Technology

CIO Canada
#302, 55 Town Centre Ct., Toronto, ON M1P 4X4
416-290-0240, Fax: 416-290-0238
www.itworldcanada.com
Circulation: 8,000 *Frequency: 12 times a year*
David Carrey, Editor

Communications & Networking
416-733-7600
info@itbusiness.ca
www.itbusiness.ca
Circulation: 18,053 *Frequency: 12 times a year*
Joe Tersigni, Publisher

Computer Dealer News
416-733-7600
cdnsales@itbusiness.ca
www.itbusiness.ca
Circulation: 18,859 *Frequency: 18 times a year*
Paolo Del Nibletto, Editor

Computer World Canada
#302, 55 Town Centre Ct., Toronto, ON M1P 4X4
416-290-0240, Fax: 416-290-0238
computerworld_canada@itworldcanada.com
www.itworldcanada.com
Circulation: 40,000 *Frequency: 25 times a year*
Dan McLean, Publisher
Greg Enright, Editor

Computing Canada
416-733-7600, Fax: 416-227-8300
info@itbusiness.ca
www.itbusiness.ca
Circulation: 40,000 *Frequency: 26 times a year*
Joe Tersigni, Publisher

ConnectIT
17 Moodie Dr., Richmond Hill, ON L4C 8C9
905-763-1200, Fax: 905-886-6216
swexler@integratedmar.com
www.integratedmar.com

Direction Informatique
416-733-7600, Fax: 416-227-8324, 800-387-5012
directioninformatique@transcontinental.ca
www.directioninformatique.com
Circulation: 17 939 *Frequency: 10 fois par an; français*
Stephanie Manseau, Coordonnatrice de Production
Patrice-Guy Martin, Rédacteur
Marc Meloche, Directeur des Ventes

eChannelLine
17 Moodie Dr., Richmond Hill, ON L4C 8C9
905-763-1200, Fax: 905-886-6216, 800-465-2059
swexler@integratedmar.com
www.integratedmar.com
Circulation: 36,000 *Frequency: daily*
Steve Wexler, Editor-in-chief, Special Projects

HUB: Digital Living Magazine
c/o Piccolo Publishing Inc., 775 B The Queensway, Toronto, ON M8Z 1N1
416-348-9666, Fax: 416-348-9553, 800-465-3517
www.hubcanada.com

IT for Industry
1 Mount Pleasant Rd., 7th Fl., Toronto, ON M4Y 2Y5
416-764-1546, Fax: 416-764-1742, 800-268-9119
Joe.Terrett@plant.rogers.com
www.itforindustry.com
Circulation: 20,100 *Frequency: 6 times a year*
Dan Bordun, Publisher
Joe Terrett, Editor

Network Cabling
905-727-0077, Fax: 905-727-0017
www.networkcabling.ca
Circulation: 9,200 *Frequency: 6 times a year*
Peter Young

Network World Canada
#302, 55 Town Centre Ct., Toronto, ON M1P 4X4
416-290-0240, Fax: 416-290-0238
www.itworldcanada.com
Circulation: 16,000 *Frequency: 24 times a year*
Michael Martin, Editor

Technologies for Worship Magazine
3891 Holborn Rd., Queensville, ON L0G 1R0
905-473-9822, Fax: 905-473-9928
info@tfwm.com
www.tfwm.com
Circulation: 30,000 *Frequency: bi-monthly*
Shelagh Rogers, Founder
Kevin Rogers Cobus, Editor

Technology in Government
416-733-7600, Fax: 416-227-8300
info@itbusiness.ca
www.itbusiness.ca
Circulation: 19,437 *Frequency: Monthly*
Joe Tersigni, Publisher

Conventions & Meetings

Conventions Meetings Canada
1 Mount Pleasant Rd., 7th Fl., Toronto, ON M4Y 2Y5
416-764-1635, Fax: 416-764-1419
steve.dempsey@mtg.rogers.com
www.meetingscanada.com
Circulation: 10,586 *Frequency: Annually*
Stephen Dempsey, Publisher

Meeting Places
BIV Media Group, #500, 1155 West Pender St., Vancouver, BC V6E 2P4
604-688-2398, Fax: 604-688-6058
Circulation: 13,000
Paul Harris, Editor
Gail Clark, Publisher

Meetings & Incentive Travel (M&IT)
416-764-1635, Fax: 416-764-1419
Circulation: 10,764 *Frequency: 6 times a year*
Steven Dempsey, Publisher

Cosmetics

Cosmetics Magazine
416-764-1664, Fax: 416-764-1704
Circulation: 12,000 *Frequency: 6 times a year; also Cosmetiques (3 fois par an; français)*
James R. Hicks, Publisher

Credit

The Atlantic Co-operator
Atlantic Co-operative Publishers, 123 Halifax St., Moncton, NB E1C 8N5
506-858-6617, Fax: 506-858-6615
editor@theatlanticco-opoerator.coop
www.theatlanticco-operator.coop
Circulation: 17,500 English; 3,500 French *Frequency: 9 times a year; English & French*

The Atlantic Co-operator is a monthly newspaper covering all aspects of co-operation values and principles in Atlantic Canada and around the world. We are published 9 times a year in both French and English by the Atlantic Co-operative Publishers and distributed throughout Atlantic Canada and les Iles-de-la-Madeleine, in Québec.
Jennifer MacLeod, Publisher
Mark Higgins, Editor, 506-858-6614
Jennifer MacLeod, Publisher

Dentistry

Canadian Journal of Dental Hygiene
c/o Canadian Dental Hygienists Assn., 96 Centrepointe Dr., Ottawa, ON K2G 6B1
613-224-5515, Fax: 613-224-7283, 800-267-5235
info@cdha.ca
www.cdha.ca
Circulation: 11,400 *Frequency: 6 times a year*
Susan A. Ziebarth, Executive Director
Susanne Sunell, Scientific Editor

Denturism Canada - The Journal of Canadian Denturism / Denturologie Canada
204-985-9780, Fax: 204-985-9795, 866-985-9780
info@kelman.ca
www.kelman.ca
Other information: Toll Free Fax: 1-866-985-9799
Circulation: 1,909 *Frequency: 4 times a year*
Kevin Hill, Editor

Journal de l'Ordre des dentistes du Québec
Ordre des dentistes du Québec, 625, boul René-Lévesque ouest, 15e étage, Montréal, QC H3B 1R2
514-875-8511, Fax: 514-875-9049
journal@odq.qc.ca
www.odq.qc.ca
Circulation: 5 300 *Frequency: 10 fois par an; French*
Dr. Denis Forest, Rédacteur

Journal of the Canadian Dental Association / Journal de l'Association Dentaire Canadienne
1815 Alta Vista Dr., Ottawa, ON K1G 3Y6
613-523-1770, Fax: 613-523-7736, 800-267-6354
reception@cda-adc.ca
www.cda-adc.ca
Circulation: 19,600 *Frequency: 11 times a year; English & French*
Dr. John O'Keefe, Editor

Manitoba Dentist
Cutting Edge Communications, #2, 1248 Pembina Hwy., Winnipeg, MB
204-669-2377, Fax: 204-669-2336
Circulation: 1,700 *Frequency: Annual*
Jamie Parcells, Publisher

Ontario Dentist
4 New St., Toronto, ON M5R 1P6
416-922-3900, Fax: 416-922-9005
www.oda.on.ca
Circulation: 7,000 *Frequency: 10 times a year*
Julia Kuipers, Managing Editor

Oral Health
416-510-6785, Fax: 416-510-5140, 800-268-7742
msummerfield@oralhealthjournal.com
www.oralhealthjournal.com
Other information: Toll Free: U.S. 1-800-387-0273
Circulation: 17,200 *Frequency: Monthly*
Melissa Summerfield, Publisher

Directories & Almanacs

Almanach du Peuple
#213, 3100, boul de la Concorde Est, Laval, QC H7E 2B8
450-665-0271
adv-pub.media@videotron.ca
Circulation: 125 000 *Frequency: Annuellement; français*
Luc Lemay, Éditeur
Robert Ferland, Directeur, Marketing

Buildcore
Reed Construction Data, 500 Hood Rd., 4th Fl., Markham, ON L3R 9Z3
905-752-5450, Fax: 866-309-5774, 800-465-6475
buildcore@reedbusiness.com
www.buildcore.com
Other information: Toll Free Fax: 1-800-570-5399
Circulation: 8,500 *Frequency: Quarterly*
Denise Holtby, Editor
David Dehaas, Publisher

Canadian Forces Base Kingston Official Directory
PO Box 1352, #205, 11 Princess St., Kingston, ON K7L 5C6
613-549-8442, Fax: 613-549-4333
editorial@kingstonpublications.com
Circulation: 3,000 *Frequency: Annually, March; English & French*
Liza Nelson, Publisher

Frasers
416-764-1467, Fax: 416-764-1710
suzanne.mccauley@frasers.rogers.com
www.frasers.com
Circulation: 6,000; 15,000 CD-Rom *Frequency: Annually, Mar.*
Gloria Gallagher, Publisher

Sources
#305, 489 College St., Toronto, ON M6G 1A5
416-964-7799, Fax: 416- -
www.sources.com
Circulation: 14,000 *Frequency: 2 times a year*
Ulli Diemer, Publisher

Drugs

L'actualité pharmaceutique
514-843-2105, Fax: 514-843-2183
caroline.belisle@rci.rogers.com
www.pharmacyconnects.com
Circulation: 6 000 *Frequency: 12 fois par an; français*
Caroline Bélisle, Éditeur
Caroline Baril, Rédacteur

The Canadian Journal of Hospital Pharmacy / Le Journal canadien de la pharmacie hospitalière
The Cdn. Society of Hospital Pharmacists, #3, 30 Concourse Gate., Ottawa, ON K2E 7V7
613-736-9733, Fax: 613-736-5660
cjhpedit@cshp.ca
www.cshp.ca
Circulation: 3,200 *Frequency: 7 times a year; English & French*
Mary Ensom, Editor

Canadian Pharmaceutical Journal
1785 Alta Vista Dr., Ottawa, ON K1G 3Y6
613-523-7877, Fax: 613-523-2332, 800-917-9489
cpj@pharmacists.ca
www.pharmacists.ca
Circulation: 18,076 *Frequency: 6 times a year*
Leesa D. Bruce, Publisher
Renée Dykeman, Managing Editor
Rosemary R. Killeenn, Editor

Le Pharmactuel
L'Association des pharmaciens des établissements de santé, #320, 4050, rue Molson, Montréal, QC H1VH3A 1T1
514-286-0776, Fax: 514-286-1081
apes@globetrotter.net
www.pharmactuel.com
Circulation: 1 800 *Frequency: 5 fois par an*
Louise Mallet, ADES Editor

Pharmacy Post
416-764-2000, Fax: 416-764-3931
www.pharmacyconnects.com
Circulation: 18,800 *Frequency: 12 times a year; OTC Report (Apr.)*
Janet Smith, Executive Publisher
Vicki Wood, Editor

Pharmacy Practice
416-764-3926, Fax: 416-764-3931
rosalind.stefanac@pharmacygroup.rogers.com
www.pharmacyconnects.com
Circulation: 20,387 *Frequency: 12 times a year*
Rosalind Stefanac, Editor

Québec Pharmacie
#800, 1200, av McGill College, Montréal, QC H3B 4G7
514-843-2569, Fax: 514-843-2183
www.quebecpharmacie.org
Circulation: 7 350 *Frequency: 10 fois par an; français*
Hélène Blanchette, Editor

Education

Agenda
c/o Ontario English Catholic Teachers' Association, #400, 65 St. Clair Ave. East, Toronto, ON M4T 2Y8
416-925-2493, Fax: 416-925-7764, 800-268-7230
a.oconnor@oecta.on.ca
www.oecta.on.ca
Circulation: 46,000 *Frequency: Sept.-June monthly (7 times during school year)*
Aleda O'Connor, Director, Communications

The ATA Magazine
The Alberta Teachers' Association, 11010 - 142 St., Edmonton, AB T5N 2R1
780-447-9400, Fax: 780-455-6481
www.teachers.ab.ca
Circulation: 42,000 *Frequency: 4 times a year*
Timothy Johnston, Editor
Raymond Gariépy, Managing Editor

Canadian Vocational Journal
Canadian Vocational Association, 645, rue Labonté, Longueuil, QC J4H 2R5
450-442-2353, Fax: 450-442-2353
cva_acfp@ca.inter.net
cva-acfp.ca/journal/vol37no1_cover.htm
Frequency: 4 times a year electronically; English & French

CAUT Bulletin ACPPU
2675 Queensview Dr., Ottawa, ON K2B 8K2
613-820-2270, Fax: 613-820-2417
duhaime@caut.ca
www.caut.ca
Circulation: 41,000 *Frequency: 10 times a year*
Greg Allain, President
James Turk, Executive Director
Liza Duhaime, Managing Editor

Education Forum
c/o Ontario Secondary School Teachers' Federation, 60 Mobile Dr., Toronto, ON M4A 2P3
416-751-8300, Fax: 416-751-3875, 800-267-7867
claytom@osstf.on.ca
www.osstf.on.ca
Circulation: 49,323 *Frequency: 3 times a year*
Renate Brandon, Advertising Director
Marianne Clayton, Assistant Editor
Janice Grant, Traffic Coordinator
Pierre Côté, Editor

Education Today
Ontario Public School Boards Assn., 439 University Ave. 18th Fl., Toronto, ON M5G 1Y8
416-340-2540, Fax: 416-340-7571
webmaster@opsba.org
www.opsba.org
Circulation: 3,500 *Frequency: 3 times a year; ISSN: 0843-5081*
Catherine Watson, Editor

Educational Digest
11966 Woodbine Ave., Gormley, ON L0H 1G0
905-887-5048, Fax: 905-887-0764
Circulation: 76,216 *Frequency: 4 times a year*
Janet Gardiner, Publisher

ESL in Canada Directory
PO Box 75117, 20 Bloor St. East, Toronto, ON M4W 3T3
416-608-4194, Fax: 416-513-0026
info@eslincanada.com
www.eslincanada.com
Frequency: 2 times a year
Ross McBride, Production Manager

Green Teacher: Education for Planet Earth
95 Robert St., Toronto, ON M5S 2K5
416-960-1244, Fax: 416-925-3474
info@greenteacher.com
www.greenteacher.com
Circulation: 7,200 *Frequency: 4 times a year; ISSN: 1192-1285*
Tim Grant, Co-Editor
Gail Littlejohn, Co-Editor

The Manitoba Teacher
The Manitoba Teachers' Society, 191 Harcourt St., Winnipeg, MB R3J 3H2
204-888-7961, Fax: 204-831-0877, 800-262-8803
gstephenson@mbteach.org
www.mbteach.org/mbteacher.htm
Circulation: 17,000 *Frequency: 7 times a year*
George Stephenson, Editor

OPC Register
180 Dundas St. West, Toronto, ON M5G 1Z8
416-322-6600, Fax: 416-322-6618
Frequency: 4 times a year

Professionally Speaking / Pour parler profession
Ontario College of Teachers, 121 Bloor St. East, Toronto, ON M4W 3M5
416-961-8800, Fax: 416-961-8822, 888-534-2222
ps@oct.ca
www.oct.ca
Circulation: 218,570 *Frequency: 4 times a year*
Richard Lewko, Publisher
Philip Carter, Editor

Quebec Home & School News
Québec Federation of Home & School Associations, #560, 3285, boul Cavendish, Montréal, QC H4B 2L9
514-481-5619, Fax: 514-481-5610, 888-808-5619
info@qfhsa.org
www.qfhsa.org
Circulation: 7,600 distribution; 5,900 paid distribution *Frequency: 4 times a year*
Notorized publications data as of Sept. 2005
Donna Norris, President
Helen Koeppe, Editor

Teach Magazine
#206, 258 Wallace Ave., Toronto, ON M6P 3M9
416-537-2103, Fax: 416-537-3491
info@teachmag.com
www.teachmag.com
Circulation: 22,000 *Frequency: 5 times a year*
Wili Liberman, Publisher & Editor

The Teacher
c/o Nova Scotia Teachers Union, 3106 Joseph Howe Dr., Halifax, NS B3L 4L7
902-477-5621, Fax: 902-477-3517, 800-565-6788
theteacher@nstu.ca
www.nstu.ca
Circulation: 13,000 *Frequency: 10 times a year; Sept. to June*
Angela Murray, Editor
Wayne Noseworthy, Executive Director
Mary-Lou Donnelly, President

University Affairs / Affaires universitaires
c/o Assn. of Universities & Colleges of Canada, #600, 350 Albert St., Ottawa, ON K1R 1B1
613-563-1236, Fax: 613-563-9745
ua@aucc.ca
www.aucc.ca; www.universityaffairs.ca;
www.affairesuniversitaires.ca
Circulation: 18,153 *Frequency: 10 times a year; English & French; ISSN: 0041-9257*
Christine Tausig Ford, Publisher
Peggy Berkowitz, Editor

Electrical Equipment & Electronics

CNS Cabling Networking Systems
#800, 12 Concorde Place, Toronto, ON M3C 4J2
416-510-5111, Fax: 416-510-5134, 800-268-7742
mlevy@cnsmagazine.com
www.cablingsystems.com
Circulation: 10,313 *Frequency: 6 times a year*
Maureen Levy, Publisher
Paul Barker, Editor

Electrical Business
www.ebmag.com
Circulation: 18,500 *Frequency: Monthly*
Bill Begin, Publisher

Electrical Line
3105 Benbow Rd., West Vancouver, BC V7V 3E1
604-922-5516, Fax: 604-922-5312
info@electricalline.com
www.electricalline.com
Circulation: 20,789 *Frequency: 6 times a year*
Ken Buhr, Editor
Kevin Buhr, Publisher

Électricité Québec
5925, boul Decarie, Montréal, QC H3W 3C9
514-738-2184, Fax: 514-738-2192
info@cmeq.org
www.cmeq.org
Circulation: 9 834 *Frequency: 6 fois par an; français*
Hélène Rioux, Éditrice et rédactrice-en-chef

Electricity Today
Hurst Communications, #215, 1885 Clements Rd., Pickering, ON L1W 3V4
905-686-1040, Fax: 905-509-4451
hq@electricityforum.com
www.electricityforum.com
Circulation: 12,255 *Frequency: 8 times a year*
Randolph Hurst, Publisher

EP&T
LVP Media Inc., #27, 1200 Aerowood Dr., Mississauga, ON L4W 2S7
905-624-8100, Fax: 905-624-1760
info@ept.ca
www.ept.ca
Circulation: 24,000 *Frequency: 8 times a year; also EP&T's Electrosource Product Reference Guide & Telephone Directory (annually, Jan.)*
Robert Luton, Publisher

Report on Wireless
#1800, 160 Elgin St., Ottawa, ON K2P 2P7
613-230-1984, Fax: 613-230-3793
phoffman@decima.ca
www.decima.ca
Frequency: Weekly
Perry Hoffman, Editor

Emergency Services

Canadian Emergency News
1121 Newscastle Rd., Drumheller, AB T0J 0Y2
403-823-2290, 800-567-0911
cen@emsnews.com
www.emsnews.com
Circulation: 4,000 *Frequency: 6 times a year*
Lyle Blumhagen, Publisher/Editor

Engineering

Aggregates & Roadbuilding Magazine
105 Donly Drive South, Simcoe, ON N3Y 4N5
514-487-9868, Fax: 514-487-9276
www.rocktoroad.com
Circulation: 11,400 *Frequency: 6 times a year*
Andy Bateman, Editor, abateman1@cogeco.ca
Scott Jamieson, Group Publisher, sjamieson@annexweb.com

Annuaire Téléphonique de la Construction du Québec
CP 590, 22, rue St-Charles, Sainte-Thérèse, QC J7E 2A4
450-437-1600, Fax: 450-437-0723
optilog@optilog.com
www.optilog.com
Circulation: 7 200 *Frequency: Annuellement; français*
Michel Vaudrin, Éditeur & Rédacteur

Canadian Consulting Engineer
#800, 12 Concorde Place, Toronto, ON M4C 4J2
416-510-5111, Fax: 416-510-5134, 800-268-7742
bparsons@ccemag.com
www.canadianconsultingengineer.com
Circulation: 8,476 *Frequency: 7 times a year*
Maureen Levy, Publisher
Bronwen Parsons, Editor, 416/510-5119

Construction Alberta News
#50, 22 Rowland Cres., St Albert, AB T8N 5B3
780-460-8004,
Frequency: 2 times a year

Engineering Dimensions
#1000, 25 Sheppard Ave. West, Toronto, ON M2N 6S9
416-224-1100, Fax: 416-224-8168, 800-339-3716
webmaster@peo.on.ca
www.peo.on.ca
Other information: Toll Free Fax: 1-800-268-0496
Circulation: 68,000 *Frequency: 6 times a year*
Connie Mucklestone, Publisher

Geomatica
#400, 1390 Prince of Wales Dr., Ottawa, ON K2C 3N6
613-224-9851, Fax: 613-224-9577
editgeo@magma.ca
www.cig-acsg.ca
Circulation: 1,059 *Frequency: 4 times a year; English & French*
Kelly Dean, Editor

Innovation
c/o Assn. of Professional Engineers & Geoscientists of BC, #200, 4010 Regent St., Burnaby, BC V5C 6N2
604-430-8035, Fax: 604-430-8085, 888-430-8035
apeginfo@apeg.bc.ca
www.apeg.bc.ca
Circulation: 22,000 *Frequency: 6 times a year*
Melinda Lau, Publications Specialist & Managing Editor
Derek Doyle, Executive Director & Registrar

Ontario Professional Surveyor
1043 McNicoll Ave., Toronto, ON M1W 3W6
416-491-9020, Fax: 416-491-2576, 800-268-0718
admin@aols.org
www.aols.org
Circulation: 1,400 *Frequency: 4 times a year*
Maureen Mountjoy, Editor

The Ontario Technologist
CLB Media Inc., 240 Edward St., Aurora, ON L4G 3S9
905-727-0077, Fax: 905-727-0017
arush@clbmedia.ca
www.oacett.org
Circulation: 21,240 *Frequency: 6 times a year*
Angela Rush, Sales Representative

The PEGG
APEGGA, Scotia One, #1500, 10060 Jasper Ave. NW, Edmonton, AB T5J 4A2
780-426-3990, Fax: 780-425-1722, 800-661-7020
email@apegga.org
www.apegga.org
Circulation: 47,000 *Frequency: 10 times a year*
George Lee, Managing Editor

PLAN
Ordre des ingenieurs du Québec, Gare Windsor, #350, 1100, rue de la Gauchetière ouest, Montréal, QC H3B 2S2
514-845-6141, Fax: 514-845-1833, 800-461-6141
plan@oiq.qc.ca
www.oiq.qc.ca
Circulation: 49 000 *Frequency: 9 fois par an; français*
Daniel Boismenu, Editeur
Geneviève Terreault, Coordonatrice
France Cadieux, Publicité

Plan Canada
Canadian Institute of Planners, #801, 116 Albert St., Ottawa, ON K1P 5G3
613-237-7526, Fax: 613-237-7045, 800-207-2138
general@cip-icu.ca
www.cip-icu.ca
Circulation: 4,715 *Frequency: 4 times a year*
Michele Garneau, Publisher
Mark Seasons, Chair, Editorial Board

Publiquip Inc.
490, Gilles Villeneuve, Berthierville, QC J0C 1A0
450-836-3666, Fax: 450-836-7401
ftrepanier@publiquip.com
www.publiquip.com
Circulation: 43 506 *Frequency: Mensuel; français*
Gilles Chevigny, Éditeur

Supply Post
#105, 26730 - 56th Ave., Langley, BC V4W 3X5
604-607-5577, Fax: 604-607-0533, 800-663-4802
robert.watson@supplypost.com
www.supplyline.com
Circulation: 14,436 *Frequency: 11 times a year*
Robert Watson, General Manager

Environment & Nature

Eco Week.ca
#800, 12 Concorde Pl., Toronto, ON M3C 4J2
416-442-5600, Fax: 416-510-5148
dorchard@ecolog.com
www.ecoweek.ca
Frequency: weekly
Formally EcoLog Week, this publication aims to show its readers how to live a green lifestyle, as well keeping the public up-to-date on environmental issues of the day, including the environmental regulatory programs, new developments in waste-treatment, and how to get involved with local environmentalist organizations.
Deborah Orchard, Editor

EcoCompliance.ca
#800, 12 Concorde Place, Toronto, ON M3C 4J2
416-422-5600, Fax: 416-510-5148, 888-702-1111
llubka@ecolog.com
www.ecocompliance.ca
Frequency: Monthly
A monthly national newsletter that examines the developments and amendments in Canadian environmental law. It gives its readers commentary on new legislation, proposed environmental bills, changing environmental legislation, and all other issues affecting enviromental law policies in Canada.
Lidia Lubka, Associate Publisher

Ecoforestry
Ecoforestry Institute Society, PO Box 5070 B, Victoria, BC V8R 6N3

250-595-0655, Fax: 250- -
journal@ecoforestry.ca
ecoforestry.ca

Frequency: quarterly
Journal looks at issues relating to the forestry industry using a low-impact approach to forest management. Its goal is to increase public awareness of ecoforestry by working with community organizations, offering workshops to the public and providing information.

EnviroLine
PO Box 77042 Chinatown, 4905 - 23 Ave. NW, Calgary, AB T2G 5J8
403-263-3272, Fax: 403-263-3280
enviroline@shaw.ca; enviroca@cadvision.com
Circulation: 500 *Frequency: 20 times a year*
Provides Western Canadian resource industries with reviews of important and up-to-date environmental issues.
Mark Lowey, Publisher & Editor

Environmental Reviews
M-55, 1200 Montreal Rd., Ottawa, ON K1A 0R6
613-993-9101, Fax: 613-952-9907, 877-672-2672
pubs@nrc-cnrc.gc.ca; info@nrc-cnrc.gc.ca
pubs.nrc-cnrc.gc.ca
Circulation: 300 *Frequency: Annually ISSN: 1208-6053*
Publication presents reviews on a range of environmental issues and topics, emphasizing the effects humans have on natural and manmade ecosystems. Topics investigated in this publication include climate change, air and marine pollution, erosion and agroforestry.
Bruce P. Dancik, Editor
Bushra Waheed, Managing Editor
Cameron Macdonald, Director

Recycling Canada
PO Box 378, Campbellford, ON K0L 1L0
705-653-1112, Fax: 705-653-1113
dbp@personainternet.com
Mark Sabourin, Publisher & Editor

Recycling Product News
#201, 2323 Boundary Rd., Vancouver, BC V5M 4V8
604-291-9900, Fax: 604-291-1906
ebaum@baumpub.com
www.baumpub.com
Circulation: 18,000 *Frequency: 8 times a year*
Publication focuses on products, technologies services and industry news in recycling and waste management, ranging from composting to scrap metal.
Engelbert J. Baum, Publisher
Keith Barker, Editor

Vecteur Environnement
#220, 911, rue Jean-Talon est, Montréal, QC H2R 1V5
514-270-7110, Fax: 514-270-7154
info@reseau-environnement.com
www.reseau-environnement.co m
Circulation: 4 000 *Frequency: 5 fois par an; français*
Revue de l'industrie, des sciences et techniques de l'environnement du Québec; publiée par RÉSEAU environnement
Martine Boivin, Rédactrice-en-chef

European

Gateway to Czech Trade
#1006, 909 Bay St., Toronto, ON M5S 3G2
416-929-3432, Fax: 416-929-3432
trade@ccrcc.net
www.ccrcc.net
Circulation: 4,500
L.J. Novotny, Publisher & Editor

Fire Protection

Atlantic Firefighter
Hilden Publishing Ltd., #456, 6 - 295 Queen St. East, Brampton, NS L6W 4S6
800-555-2514
info@atlanticfirefighter.ca
www.atlanticfirefighter.ca
Circulation: 6,200 *Frequency: 11 times a year*
Jennifer Brown, Publisher & Editor

Canadian Firefighter & EMS Quarterly
105 Donly Dr. South, Simcoe, ON N3Y 4N5
800-265-2827
firefightcan@annexweb.com
www.firefightingincanada.com
Circulation: 7,500 *Frequency: 4 times a year*
Martin McAnulty, Publisher
Jim Haley, Editor

Fire Fighting in Canada
800-265-2827
fire@annexweb.com
www.firefightingincanada.com
Circulation: 5,200 *Frequency: 8 times a year*
James Haley, Editor
Martin J. McAaulty, Publisher

The Fire Services Journal
6 Hillman Dr., Ajax, ON L1S 6X9
905-428-8465, Fax: 905-683-9572
fire@interlog.com
www.fsj.on.ca
Circulation: 14,185 *Frequency: 6 times a year*
David Ross, Editor-in-chief
Sue Wells, Editor
Dan Haden, Publisher

Fisheries

Atlantic Fisherman
130 Wright Ave., Dartmouth, NS B3B 1R6
902-422-4990, Fax: 902-422-4278
Circulation: 3,818 *Frequency: Monthly*
Ian Ross, Editor

The Fisherman
326 - 12th St., 1st Fl., New Westminster, BC V3M 4H6
604-519-3638, Fax: 604-524-6944
fisherman@ufawu.org
Circulation: 7,700 *Frequency: 4 times a year*
Sean Griffin, Editor

Northern Aquaculture
4623 William Head Rd., Victoria, BC V9J 1R3
250-478-3973, Fax: 250-478-3979
editor@naqua.com
www.naqua.com
Circulation: 3,600 *Frequency: 12 times a year*
Peter Chettleburgh, Publisher

The Sou'Wester
Transcontinental Media, #609, 1888 Brunswick St., Halifax, NS B3J 3J8
902-425-8255, Fax: 902-468-1775
Circulation: 10,500 *Frequency: 12 times a year*
Jeff Nearing, Publisher

Floor Coverings

Coverings
Mayville Publishing (Canada) Ltd., 990 County Rd. 18, Cherry Valley, ON K0K 1P0
613-476-4244, Fax: 613-476-5233
coverings@floorpage.com
www.floorpage.com
Circulation: 7,100 *Frequency: 8 times a year*
Peter Spragg, Publisher
Gillian Spragg, Administration

Surface
2105, rue de Salaberry, St-Bruno-de-Montarville, QC J3V 4N7
450-441-4243, Fax: 450-441-6997
soury@biz.videotron.ca
soury.ca/surface
Circulation: 5 500 *Frequency: 5 fois par an; français*
Marcel Soury, Rédacteur-en-chef

Florists

Canadian Florist
PO Box 530, 105 Donly Dr. South, Simcoe, ON N3Y 4N5
Fax: 519-429-3094, 888-599-2228
dmccarthy@annexweb.com
florist.hortport.com
Circulation: 5,394 *Frequency: 6 times per year*
Drew McCarthy, Editorial Director
Sue Fredericks, Publisher

Food & Beverage

L'Actualité Alimentaire
615, Notre-Dame, Saint-Lambert, QC J4P 2K8
514-990-6967, Fax: 514-990-6967
mlemire@editionscomestibles.com
www.actualitealimentaire.com
Circulation: 5 000
Martin Lemire, Rédacteur

Canadian Pizza Magazine
PO Box 530, 105 Donly Dr. South, Simcoe, ON N3Y 4N5
519-429-5177, Fax: 519-429-3094, 888-599-2228
dgeerlinks@annexweb.com
www.canadianpizzamag.com
Circulation: 9,500 *Frequency: 8 times a year*
Diane Kleer, Publisher
Cam Wood, Editor

Food in Canada
416-764-1503, Fax: 416-764-1755
www.foodincanada.com
Circulation: 9,200 *Frequency: 9 times a year*
Ingrid Eilbracht, Publisher

Footwear

Canadian Footwear Journal
241, rue Senneville, Senneville, ON H9X 3X5
514-457-8787, Fax: 514-457-5832
cfj@shoetrades.com
www.shoetrades.com
Circulation: 7,000 *Frequency: 8 times a year; plus Retail Buyers' Guide (annual), Shoemaking Buyers' Guide (annual)*
Shirley Boake, Associate Publisher
Barbara McLeish, Editor

Forest & Lumber Industries

Canadian Forest Industries
#14, rue 90 Morgan, Baie-d'Urfé, QC H9X 3A8
514-457-2211, Fax: 514-457-2558
jcft@qc.aira.com
www.forestcommunications.com
Circulation: 14,600 *Frequency: 8 times a year*
Tim Tolton, Publisher
Guy Fortin, Publisher
Scott Jamieson, Editor

Canadian Wood Products
514-457-2211, Fax: 514-457-2558
info@forestecommunications.com
www.forestcommunications.c om/cwp/
Circulation: 7,340 *Frequency: 6 times a year*
Tim Tolton, Publisher
Scott Jamieson, Editor

Directory of Ontario Lumber & Building Materials Retailers, Buyers' Guide & Product Directory
Lumber & Building Materials Association of Ontario, #27, 5155 Spectrum Way, Mississauga, ON L4W 5A1
905-625-1084, Fax: 905-625-3006
www.lbmao.on.ca
Frequency: Annually, Oct.

The Forestry Chronicle
Canadian Institute of Forestry, #504, 151 Slater St., Ottawa, ON K1P 5H3
613-234-2242, Fax: 613-234-6181
cif@cif-ifc.org
www.cif-ifc.org
Circulation: 2,800 *Frequency: 6 times a year*
Roxanne M. Comeau, Publisher

Logging & Sawmilling Journal
PO Box 86670, 211 East 1st St., North Vancouver, BC V7L 1B4
604-990-9970, Fax: 604-990-9971, 866-405-6462
stanhope@forestnet.com
www.forestnet.com
Circulation: 16,200 *Frequency: 10 times a year*
Robert Stanhope, Publisher

Logging Management
604-298-3005, Fax: 604-298-3966
Circulation: 20,000 *Frequency: 4 times a year*
Heri R. Baum, Publisher

Madison's Canadian Lumber Directory
PO Box 2486, #209, 980 West 1st St., Vancouver, BC V6B 3W7
604-984-6838, Fax: 604-984-6572
madrep@direct.ca
www.madisonsreport.com
Circulation: 1,200 *Frequency: Annually, Spring*
Laurence Cater, Publisher

Mid-Canada Forestry & Mining
204-985-9780, Fax: 204-985-9795
info@kelman.mb.ca
Circulation: 3,400 *Frequency: 4 times a year*
Terry Ross, Editor

Le Monde forestier

418-877-4583, Fax: 418-877-6449
journal@lemondeforestier.ca
www.lemondeforestier.ca
Circulation: 18 500 *Frequency: 10 fois par an; français*
Alain Castonguay, Rédacteur-en-chef

Opérations forestières et de scierie
#14, 90, rue Morgan, Baie d'Urfe, QC H9X 3A8
514-457-2211, Fax: 514-457-2558
info@forestcommunications.com
www.forestcommunications.co m/of/
Circulation: 5 436 *Frequency: 4 fois par an; français*
Guy Fortin, Éditeur/Rédacteur

Yardstick
100 Southerland Ave., Winnipeg, MB R2W 3C7
204-947-0222, Fax: 204-947-2047, 800-665-2456
www.naylor.com
Circulation: 1,669 *Frequency: 6 times a year; also WRLA Directory & Buyers' Guide (annually, Jan.)*
Jonah O'Neill, Editor

Funeral Service

The Canadian Funeral Director Magazine
HPL Publishers, 1 Hanlan Ct., Whitby, ON L1N 9X4
905-686-7161, Fax: 905-686-2159
info@thefuneralmagazine.com
www.thefuneralmagazine.com
Frequency: Monthly
Scott Hillier, Publisher & Editor

Canadian Funeral News
#1025, 101 - 6th Ave. SW, Calgary, AB T2P 3P4
403-264-3270, Fax: 403-264-3276, 800-465-0322
info@otcommunications.com
www.otcommunications.com/cfnindex.html
Frequency: Monthly
Patrick Ottmann, Publisher
Cammie Leard, Editor

Network
#1025, 101 - 6th Ave. SW, Calgary, AB T2P 3P4
403-264-3270, Fax: 403-264-3276, 800-465-0322
info@otcommunications.com
www.otcommunications.com/networkcontact.html
Frequency: 6 times a year
Patrick Ottman, Publisher
Cammie Leard, Editor

Fur Trade

The Canadian Trapper
Coyote Communications Inc., 32 Willoughby Dr., St Albert, AB T8N 3R3
780-459-4734, Fax: 780-459-4731
Circulation: 5,778 *Frequency: 6 times a year; also Alberta Trapper, 4 times a year (circ. 1,800); BC Trapper Magazine, 4 times a year (circ. 1,500)*
Becky McIntosh, Publisher

Gardening & Garden Equipment

Canadian Garden Centre & Nursery

519-429-3966, Fax: 519-429-3094
Circulation: 4,000 *Frequency: 6 times a year*
Anja Sonnenberg, Editor
Diane Geerlinks, Publisher

Greenhouse Canada
PO Box 530, 105 Donly Dr. South, Simcoe, ON N3Y 4N5
519-235-2400, Fax: 519-235-0798, 888-599-2228
pdarbishire@annexweb.com
www.greenhousecanada.com
Circulation: 5,500 *Frequency: Monthly*
Peter Darbishire, Publisher

Gifts

CGTA Retail News
Canadian Gift & Tableware Association, 42 Voyager Ct. South, Toronto, ON M9W 5M7
416-679-0170, Fax: 416-679-1868, 800-611-6100
retailnews@cgta.org
www.cgta.org
Circulation: 16,529 *Frequency: 6 times a year*
Tom Foran, Publisher
Erica Kirkland, Editor

Gifts & Tablewares
#800, 12 Concord Place, Toronto, ON M3C 4J2
416-510-6826, Fax: 416-510-5134, 800-268-7742
bbishop@gifts-and-tablewares.com
www.gifts-and-tablewares.com
Circulation: 15,010 *Frequency: 7 times a year*
Brenda Bishop, Publisher
Lori Smith, Editor

Glass

Glass Canada

519-235-2400, Fax: 519-235-0798
ais@aiscommunications.net
Circulation: 5,800 *Frequency: 6 times a year*
Chris Skalkos, Editor
Peter Phillips, Publisher

Government

Forum
Federation of Canadian Municipalities, 24 Clarence St., Ottawa, ON K1N 5P3
613-241-5221, Fax: 613-241-7440
www.fcm.ca
Frequency: 6 times a year; English & French
Robert Ross, Managing Editor

Government Purchasing Guide
Kenilworth Media Inc., #710, 15 Wertheim Ct., Richmond Hill, ON L4B 3H7
905-771-7333, Fax: 905-771-7336, 800-409-8688
sales@gpgmag.ca
www.gpgmag.ca
Circulation: 10,220 *Frequency: 6 times a year*
Ellen Kral, Publisher
Cora Golden, Director, Sales
Blair Adams, Editorial Director

MERX
#1000, 38 Antares Dr., Nepean, ON K2E 7V2
800-964-6379, Fax: 888-235-5800, 800-964-6379
merx@merx.com
www.merx.com

Municipal Redbook

604-433-8164, Fax: 604-433-9549, 888-878-2121
jocinfo@reedbusiness.com
www.journalofcommerce.com
Circulation: 2,000 *Frequency: Annual*

Municipal World
PO Box 399 Main, St Thomas, ON N5P 3V3
519-633-0031, Fax: 519-633-1001
mwadmin@municipalworld.com
www.municipalworld.com
Circulation: 7,500 *Frequency: Monthly*
Susan Gardner, Executive Editor

Optimum Online: The Journal of Public Sector Management
The Summit Group, #100, 263 Holmwood Ave., Ottawa, ON K1S 2P8
613-688-0763, Fax: 613-688-0767, 800-575-1146
info@optimumonline.ca
www.optimumonline.ca
Circulation: 10,000
Gilles Paquet, Editor

Parliamentary Names & Numbers
Sources, #305, 489 College St., Toronto, ON M6G 1A6
416-964-7799, Fax: 416- -
www.sources.com
Circulation: 500 *Frequency: 2 times a year*
Ulli Diemer, Publisher

Scott's Government Index
#800, 12 Concorde Place, Toronto, ON M3C 4J2
416-442-2010, Fax: 416-510-6870, 800-408-9431
pstuckey@scottsdirectories.com
www.scottsgi.ca
Paul Stuckey, Group Publisher
Barb Peard, Editor

Urba
Union des municipalitiés de Québec, #680, 680, rue Sherbrooke ouest, Montréal, QC H3A 2M7
514-282-7700, Fax: 514-282-8893
lpmenard@umq.qc.ca
www.umq.qc.ca
Circulation: 6 600 *Frequency: 6 fois par an; français*
Laurent Paul Ménard, Rédacteur

Graphic Arts

Applied Arts
#411, 18 Wynford Dr., Toronto, ON M3C 3S2
416-510-0909, Fax: 416-510-0913
art@appliedartsmag.com
www.appliedartsmag.com
Circulation: 12,000 *Frequency: 6 times a year; ISSN: 1196-1775*
Roberta Heckhausen, Publisher, rosetta@appliedartsmag.com
Peter Giffen, Editor, editor@appliedartsmag.com

The Graphic Exchange
Brill Communications Inc., 25 Elm Ave., Toronto, ON M4W 1M9
416-961-1325, Fax: 416-961-0941
Circulation: 13,394 *Frequency: 6 times a year*
Dan Brill, Publisher & Editor

Grocery Trade

L'Alimentation
Les Editions du marchand québécois, 1298, rue St-Zotique est, Montréal, QC H2S 1N7
514-271-6922, Fax: 514-271-1308
dbeaudin@l-alimentation.com
www.l-alimentation.com
Circulation: 15 700 *Frequency: 10 fois par an; français*
Diane Beaudin, Éditrice

Canadian Grocer

416-764-2000, Fax: 416-764-1523
www.bizlink.com/cangrocer.htm
Circulation: 20,000 *Frequency: 10 times a year*
Karen James, Publisher

Grocer Today
4189 Lougheed Hwy., 4th Fl., Burnaby, BC V5C 6A7
604-299-7311, Fax: 604-299-9188
cwm@canadawide.com
www.canadawide.com
Circulation: 14,812 *Frequency: 10 times a year*
Les Wiseman, Editor
Peter Legge, Publisher

Western Grocer

204-954-2085, Fax: 204-954-2057
mp@mercury.mb.ca
www.mercury.mb.ca
Circulation: 16,005 *Frequency: 6 times a year*
Frank Yeo, Publisher
Kelly Gray, Editor

Hardware Trade

Hardware & Home Centre Magazine
#800, 12 Concorde Place, Toronto, ON M3C 4J2
416-510-5106, Fax: 416-510-5140
eopasini@centremagazine.com
www.centremagazine.com
Circulation: 15,167 *Frequency: 8 times a year*
Greg Paliouras, Publisher
Elena Opasini, Editor

Hardware Merchandising

416-764-1672, Fax: 416-764-1484
stephen.payne@rci.rogers.com
www.bizlink.com/hardwaremerc handising.htm
Circulation: 14,881 *Frequency: 6 times a year*
Stephen Payne, Publisher

Home Improvement Retailing
Powershift Communications Inc., #501, 245 Fairview Mall Dr., Toronto, ON M2J 4T1
416-494-1066, Fax: 416-494-2536
info@powershift.ca
www.hirmagazine.com
Circulation: 15,500 *Frequency: 6 times a year*
Dante Piccinin, Publisher

Quart de Rond
Assn. des détaillants de matériaux de construction du Québec, 474, rue Trans-Canada, Longueuil, QC J4G 1N8
450-646-5842, Fax: 450-646-6171, 877-723-6220
information@admacq.qc.ca
www.admacq.qc.ca
Circulation: 3 200 *Frequency: 8 fois par an; français*
Donald O'Hara, Éditeur

Health & Medical

L'Actualité Médicale

514-843-5141, Fax: 514-843-2183
Circulation: 18 258 *Frequency: 40 fois par an; français*
Catherine Choquette, Rédactrice

The Alberta Doctors' Digest
Alberta Medical Association, 12230 - 106 Ave. NW, Edmonton, AB T5N 3Z1
780-482-2626, Fax: 780-482-5445, 800-270-9680
amamail@albertadoctors.org
www.albertadoctors.org
Circulation: 8,300 *Frequency: 6 times a year*
Dr. Dennis W. Jirsch, Editor

British Columbia Medical Journal
c/o BC Medical Association, #115, 1665 West Broadway, Vancouver, BC V6J 5A4
604-638-2815, Fax: 604-638-2917, 800-972-2262
journal@bcma.bc.ca
www.bcma.org/public/bc_medical_journal/overview.htm;
www.bcmj.org
Circulation: 10,500 *Frequency: 10 times a year*
Jay Draper, Managing Editor M.D., JDraper@bcma.bc.ca

Canadian Association of Radiologists Journal (CARJ/JACR) / Journal l'assn canadienne des radiologistes
Department of Radiology, HHSC - MUMC Site, 1200 Main St. West, Hamilton, ON L8N 3Z5
Fax: 905-521-1390
carj@mcmaster.ca
www.carj.ca
Circulation: 1,800 *Frequency: 5 times a year; English & French*
Emphasizes medical education and continuing professional development fo r radiologists
Dr. Craig Coblentz, Editor-in-chief

Canadian Chiropractor
519-429-5174, Fax: 519-429-3094
www.canadianchiropractor.ca
Circulation: 5,800 *Frequency: 7 times a year*
David Stubbs, Editor
Diane Geerlinks, Publisher

Canadian Family Physician
College of Family Physicians of Canada, 2630 Skymark Ave., Mississauga, ON L4W 5A4
905-629-0900, Fax: 905-629-0893, 800-387-6197
www.cfpc.ca/cfp
Circulation: 35,000 *Frequency: Monthly*
Dr. Diane Kelsall, Scientific Editor

Canadian Healthcare Manager
416-764-2000, Fax: 416-764-3930
www.chmonline.ca
Circulation: 19,000 *Frequency: 8 times a year*
Kim Laudrum, Editor
Alison Webb, Publisher

Canadian Healthcare Technology
#207, 1118 Centre St., Thornhill, ON L4J 7R9
905-709-2330, Fax: 905-709-2258
info2@canhealth.com
www.canhealth.com
Circulation: 12,715 *Frequency: 8 times a year*
Jerry Zeidenberg, Publisher

Canadian Journal of Anesthesia / Journal Canadien d'Anesthésie
c/o Canadian Anesthesiologists' Society, #208, 1 Eglinton Ave. East, Toronto, ON M4P 3A1
416-480-0602, Fax: 416-480-0320
cja@cas.ca
www.cas.ca
Circulation: 5,000 *Frequency: Monthly*
Dr. Donald R. Miller, Editor
Phillipe Ménard, Managing Editor

Canadian Journal of Cardiology
2902 South Sheridan Way, Oakville, ON L6J 7L6
905-829-4770, Fax: 905-829-4799
pulsus@pulsus.com
www.pulsus.com
Circulation: 15,500 *Frequency: 14 times a year*
Robert B. Kalina, Publisher
Dr. E.R. Smith, Editor-in-chief

Canadian Journal of Cardiology
Circulation: 15,500 *Frequency: 14 times a year*
Dr. E. Smith, Editor

Canadian Journal of Continuing Medical Education (CME)
514-695-7623, Fax: 514-695-8554
cme@sta.ca
www.stacommunications.com
Circulation: 35,544 *Frequency: 12 times a year*
Robert E. Passaretti, Publisher

The Canadian Journal of Diagnosis
514-695-7623, Fax: 514-695-8554
diagnosis@sta.ca
www.stacommunications.com
Circulation: 35,266 *Frequency: Monthly*
Robert Passaretti, Publisher

Canadian Journal of Dietetic Practice & Research / Revue canadienne de la pratique et de la recherche en diété
#5, 500 Cochrane Dr., Markham, ON L3R 8E2
905-940-0200, Fax: 905-940-0204
www.dietitians.ca
Circulation: 5,305 *Frequency: 4 times a year; French & English*
Marsha Sharp, CEO

Canadian Journal of Emergency Medicine (CJEM/JCMU) / Journal canadien de la médecine d'urgence
Canadian Association of Emergency Physicians, #104, 1785 Alta Vista Dr., Ottawa, ON K1G 3Y6
613-523-3343, Fax: 613-523-0190, 800-463-1158
cjem@caep.ca
www.caep.ca
Circulation: 4,000 *Frequency: 6 times a year*
Grant Innes, Editor-in-chief

Canadian Journal of Gastroenterology
905-829-4770, Fax: 905-829-4799
pulsus@pulsus.com
www.pulsus.com
Circulation: 13,700 *Frequency: Monthly*
Robert B. Kalina, Publisher
Dr. P. Adams, Editor-in-chief

Canadian Journal of Geriatrics
#220, 115 King St. West, Dundas, ON L9H 1V1
905-628-4309, Fax: 905-628-6847
brobinson@andrewjohnpublishing.com
www.andrewjohnpublishing.com
Circulation: 15,500 *Frequency: 4 times a year*
John D. Birkby, Publisher

Canadian Journal of Infectious Diseases & Medical Microbiology
905-829-4770, Fax: 905-829-4799
pulsus@pulsus.com
www.pulsus.com
Circulation: 8,800 *Frequency: 6 times a year*
Robert B. Kalina, Publisher
Dr. L.E. Nicolle, Editor-in-chief

Canadian Journal of Infectious Diseases & Medical Microbiology
Circulation: 9,600 *Frequency: 6 times a year*
Dr. L. Nicolle, Editor

Canadian Journal of Medical Laboratory Science (CJMLS)
Cdn. Society for Medical Laboratory Science, PO Box 2830 LCD 1, Hamilton, ON L8N 3N8
905-528-8642, Fax: 905-528-4968, 800-263-8277
Alison@csmls.org
www.csmls.org
Circulation: 16,000 *Frequency: 6 times a year; English & French editions*
Alison McLennan, Publisher

Canadian Journal of Medical Radiation Technology / Le Journal Canadien des Techniques en Radiation Médicale
Canadian Assn. of Medical Radiation Technologists, 85 Albert St., 10th Fl., Ottawa, ON K1P 6A4
613-234-0012, Fax: 613-234-1097, 800-463-9729
www.camrt.ca/english/publications/journal.asp
Circulation: 10,468 *Frequency: 4 times a year; English & French*
Christiane Ménard, Director of Communications

Canadian Journal of Neurological Sciences
#709, 7015 MacLeod Trail SW, Calgary, AB T2H 2K6
403-229-9575, Fax: 403-229-1661
journal@cjns.org
www.cjns.org
Circulation: 1,600 *Frequency: 4 times a year; English & French*
G. Bryan Young, Editor
Dan Morin, CEO

The Canadian Journal of Occupational Therapy / Revue canadienne d'ergothérapie
Carleton Technology & Training Centre, #3400, 1125 Colonel By Dr., Ottawa, ON K1S 5R1
613-523-2268, Fax: 613-523-2552, 800-434-2268
publications@caot.ca
www.caot.ca
Circulation: 7,000 *Frequency: 5 times a year; English & French*
Marcia Finlayson, Editor

Canadian Journal of Ophthalmology
Canadian Ophthalmological Society, #610, 1525 Carling Ave., Ottawa, ON K1Z 8R9
613-729-6779, Fax: 613-729-7209, 800-267-5763
cos@eyesite.ca
www.eyesite.ca
Circulation: 1,300 *Frequency: 7 times a year*
Dr. Graham E. Trope, Editor in Chief

The Canadian Journal of Plastic Surgery / Journal canadien de chirurgie plastique
2902 South Sheridan Way, Oakville, ON L6J 7L6
905-829-4770, Fax: 905-829-4799
pulsus@pulsus.com
www.pulsus.com
Circulation: 5,200 *Frequency: 4 times a year; English with French abstracts*
Dr. P.E. Wyshynski, Editor-in-chief
Robert B. Kalina, Publisher

Canadian Journal of Plastic Surgery
Circulation: 13,000 *Frequency: 4 times a year*
Dr. P. Wyshynski, Editor

Canadian Journal of Public Health (CJPH) / Revue canadienne de santé publique
Canadian Public Health Association, #400, 1565 Carling Ave., Ottawa, ON K1Z 8R1
613-725-3769, Fax: 613-725-9826
cjph@cpha.ca
www.cpha.ca
Circulation: 2,300 *Frequency: Bi-monthly; English & French*
Patricia Huston, Hon. Scientific Editor
Elinor Wilson, Executive Managing Editor

Canadian Journal of Rural Medicine (CJRM) / Journal canadien de la médecine rurale
613-731-9331, Fax: 613-523-0937
pubs@cma.ca
www.cma.ca/cjrm
Circulation: 7,000 *Frequency: 4 times a year*
John Wootton, Editor-in-chief M.D.
Suzanne Kingsmill

Canadian Journal of Surgery (CJS/JCC) / Journal canadien de chirurgie
613-731-9331, Fax: 613-523-0937, 800-267-9703
pubs@cma.ca
www.cma.ca/cjs
Circulation: 2,900 *Frequency: 6 times a year; English & French*
A peer reviewed journal meeting the medical education needs of Canada's surgical specialists
Garth L. Warnick, Co-Editor M.D.
J.P. Waddell, Co-Editor M.D.

Canadian Medical Association Journal (CMAJ/JAMC) / Journal de l'Association médicale canadienne
613-731-9331, Fax: 613-565-5471, 800-663-7336
pubs@cma.ca
www.cmaj.ca
Circulation: 62,000 *Frequency: 25 times a year; English; some French*
For canadian physicians; reflects the complexities of modern medical practice through concise reports on original research, peer commentaries and review articles

Canadian Nursing Home
c/o Health Media, 14453 - 29A Ave., White Rock, BC V4P 1P7

604-535-7933, Fax: 604-535-9000
www.nursinghomemagazine.ca
Circulation: 3,000 *Frequency: 4 times a year*
Agnes Forster, Managing Editor
Frank Fagan, Editor

Canadian Respiratory Journal

905-829-4770, Fax: 905-829-4799, 866-879-4770
pulsus@pulsus.com
www.pulsus.com
Circulation: 15,600 *Frequency: 8 times a year*
Robert B. Kalina, Publisher
Dr. N. Anthonisen, Editor-in-chief

The Chronicle of Cardiovascular & Internal Medicine

905-273-9116, Fax: 905-273-4322
health@chronicle.org
www.chronicle.ca
Circulation: 5,843 *Frequency: 6 times a year*
Mitchell Shannon, Publisher
R. Allan Ryan, Editorial Director

The Chronicle of Neurology & Psychiatry

905-273-9116, Fax: 905-273-4322, 866-633-4766
health@chronicle.org
www.chronicle.ca/neuro.htm
Circulation: 6,189 *Frequency: 9 times a year*
Mitchell Shannon, Publisher
R. Allan Ryan, Senior Editor

The Chronicle of Skin & Allergy

905-273-9116, Fax: 905-273-4322, 866-633-4766
health@chronicle.org
www.chronicle.ca
Circulation: 7,045 *Frequency: 9 times a year*
R. Allan Ryan, Senior Editor
Mitchell Shannon, Publisher

The Chronicle of Urology & Sexual Medicine

905-273-9116, Fax: 905-273-4322, 866-633-4766
health@chronicle.org
www.chronicle.ca
Circulation: 5,020 *Frequency: 6 times a year*
Mitchell Shannon, Publisher
R. Allan Ryan, Senior Editor

Clinical & Investigative Medicine (CIM) / Médecine clinique et expérimentale
Canadian Society for Clinical Investigation, 774 Echo Dr., Ottawa, ON K1S 5N8
613-730-6240, Fax: 613-730-1116
csci@rcpsc.edu
www.csci-scrc.medical.org
Circulation: 1,000 *Frequency: 6 times a year*
David Bevan, Editor

Clinical & Refractive Optometry

514-331-4561, Fax: 514-336-1129
info@mediconcept.ca
www.mediconcept.ca
Circulation: 3,065 *Frequency: 12 times a year*
Lawrence Goldstein, Publisher
Dr. Barbara Caffery, Editor-in-chief

Clinical & Surgical Ophthalmology

514-331-4561, Fax: 514-336-1129
info@mediconcept.ca
www.mediconcept.ca
Circulation: 1,500 *Frequency: 12 times a year*
Dr. Steve Arshinoff, Editor
Lawrence Goldstein, Publisher

Le Clinicien
#306, 955 Boul. St. John, Pointe-Claire, QC H9R 5K3
514-695-7623, Fax: 514-695-8554
clinicien@sta.ca
www.stacommunications.com
Circulation: 12 149 *Frequency: Mensuel; français*
Robert Passaretti, Éditeur

Coup d'oeil
Breton Communications Inc., #202, 495, boul St-Martin ouest, Laval, QC H7M 1Y9
450-629-6005, Fax: 450-629-6044, 888-462-2112
breton.com@bretoncom.com
www.bretoncom.com
Circulation: 4,055 *Frequency: 6 fois par an*
Martine Breton, President

CrossCurrents: The Journal of Addiction & Mental Health
Centre for Addiction & Mental Health, 33 Russell St., Toronto, ON M5S 2S1
416-595-6714, Fax: 416-593-4694
hema_zbogar@camh.net
www.camh.net/publications
Circulation: 3,000 *Frequency: 4 times a year*
Hema Zbogar, Editor

Dental Practice Management

416-510-6785, Fax: 416-510-5140, 800-268-7742
cwilson@oralhealthjournal.com
www.oralhealthjournal.com
Other information: Toll Free: U.S. 1-800-387-0273
Circulation: 18,700 *Frequency: 4 times a year*
Catherine Wilson, Editor

Dermatology Times of Canada
#102, 155A Matheson Blvd. West, Mississauga, ON L5R 3L5
905-286-9800, Fax: 905-286-9811, 800-561-7516
info@ctccomm.com
www.ctccomm.com
Circulation: 6,800 *Frequency: 6 times a year*
M.E. Farley, Publisher
K. Pearsall, Managing Editor
Karen Tousignant, Advertising

Doctor's Review
400 McGill, 3rd Fl., Montréal, QC H2Y 2G1
514-397-8833, Fax: 514-397-0228, 800-663-7403
drletters@parkpub.com
www.doctorsreview.com
Circulation: 40,000 *Frequency: Monthly*
David Elkins, Publisher
Annarosa Sabbadini, Editor

doctorNS
Doctors Nova Scotia, 5 Spectacle Lake Dr., Dartmouth, NS B3B 1X7
902-468-1866, Fax: 902-468-6578
kelly.stoddard@doctorsns.com
www.doctorsns.com
Circulation: 3,000 *Frequency: 10 times a year*
Kelly Stoddard, Editor

Fitness Business Canada
30 Mill Pond Dr., Georgetown, ON L7G 4S6
905-873-0850, Fax: 905-873-8611
www.fitnet.ca
Graham Longwell, Publisher
Barb Gormley, Managing Editor

FMWC Newsletter
Federation of Medical Women of Canada, 780 Echo Dr., Ottawa, ON K1S 5R7
613-569-5881, Fax: 616-569-4432, 877-771-3777
fmwcmain@fmwc.ca
www.fmwc.ca
Other information: Toll Free Fax: 1-877-772-5777
Circulation: 1,000 *Frequency: 3 times a year*
Gail Beck, President

Gastroenterology Canada

Circulation: 10,041 *Frequency: 4 times a year*
Michael E. Farley, Publisher

Geriatrics & Aging
#300, 162 Cumberland St., Toronto, ON M5R 3N5
416-480-9478, Fax: 416-480-2740
www.geriatricsandaging.ca
Circulation: 25,270 *Frequency: 10 times a year*
Michael Yasny, Publisher
Kristin Casady, Editorial Director

Guide to Canadian Healthcare Facilities
c/o Canadian Healthcare Association, 17 York St., Ottawa, ON K1N 9J6
613-241-8005, Fax: 613-241-9481
custserv@cha.ca
www.cha.ca
Circulation: 1,300 *Frequency: annual*
Eleanor Sawyer, Director, Publishing
Nola Haddadian, Managing Editor

HEALTHbeat
#319, 9768 - 170 St., Edmonton, AB T5T 5L4
780-413-9342, Fax: 780-413-9328, 800-727-0782
info@mccronehealthbeat.com
www.mccronehealthbeat.com
Circulation: 40,000 *Frequency: 12 times a year*
Jan Henry, Publisher

Healthcare Management FORUM / Forum gestion des soins de santé
Canadian College of Health Service Executives, 292 Somerset St. West, Ottawa, ON K2P 0J6
613-235-7218, Fax: 613-235-5451, 800-363-9056
cchse@cchse.org
www.cchse.org
Circulation: 3,500 *Frequency: 4 times a year*
Patricia Brown, Managing Editor

Hospital News, Canada
Trader Media Corp, 15 Apex Rd., Toronto, ON M6A 2V6
416-781-5516, Fax: 416-781-5499
editor@hospitalnews.com
www.hospitalnews.com
Circulation: 32,650 *Frequency: Monthly*
Julie Abelsohn, Publisher

Journal of Otolaryngology

905-522-7017, Fax: 905-522-7839
info@bcdecker.com
www.bcdecker.com
Circulation: 1,113 *Frequency: 6 times a year*

Journal of Psychiatry & Neuroscience (JPN) / Revue de psychiatrie & de neuroscience

613-731-9331, Fax: 613-523-0937, 800-267-9703
pubs@cma.ca
www.cma.ca/jpn
Circulation: 7,200 *Frequency: 6 times a year, English & French*
R.T. Joffe, Co-Editor M.D.
S.N. Young, Co-Editor M.D.

The Journal of Rheumatology
Journal of Rheumatology Publishing Co. Ltd., #901, 365 Bloor St. East, Toronto, ON M4W 3L4
416-967-5155, Fax: 416-967-7556
jrheum@jrheum.com
www.jrheum.com
Circulation: 3,500 *Frequency: Monthly*
Duncan A. Gordon, Editor-in-chief

Journal of the Canadian Chiropractic Association
1396 Eglinton Ave. West, Toronto, ON M6C 2E4
416-781-5656, Fax: 416-781-7344
Circulation: 5,384 *Frequency: 4 times a year*
Dr. Allan Gotlib, Editor

Journal SOGC
Society of Obstetrician & Gynaecology of Canada, 780 Echo Dr., Ottawa, ON K1P 5J3
613-730-4192, Fax: 613-730-4314, 800-561-2416
helpdesk@sogc.com
www.sogc.org/jogc
Circulation: 9,970 *Frequency: 13 times a year; English with French abstracts*
Timothy Rowe, Editor in Chief

Long Term Care
Ontario Long Term Care Association, #202, 345 Renfrew Dr., Markham, ON L3R 9S9
905-470-8995, Fax: 905-470-9595
info@oltca.com
www.oltca.com
Circulation: 6,000 *Frequency: 4 times a year*

Medactuel-FMC
c/o Éditions Santé Rogers media, 1001, boul de Maisonneuve ouest, 10e étage, Montréal, QC H3A 3E1
514-843-2539,
Circulation: 11 158 *Frequency: 15 fois par an*
Catherine Choquette, Rédactrice-en-chef

Le Médecin du Québec
Quebec Federation of General Practitioners, #1000, 1440, rue St-Catherine ouest, Montréal, QC H3G 1R8
514-878-1911, Fax: 514-878-4455, 800-361-8499
info@fmoq.org
www.fmoq.org
Circulation: 17 900 *Frequency: Mensuel; français*
Louise Roy, Rédacteur M.D.

Médecine/sciences
#800, 500, Sherbrooke ouest, Montréal, QC H3A 3C6
514-288-2247, Fax: 514-288-0520
medecine.sciences@bellnet.caa

Circulation: 2 007 *Frequency: 10 fois par an*
Michel Bergeron, Directeur général

The Medical Post

416-764-3887, Fax: 416-764-1207
info@medicalpost.rogers.com
www.mdpassport.com
Circulation: 47,755 *Frequency: 48 times a year*
Nancy Kent, Associate Publisher

Nutrition - Science en Evolution
#1220, 2155, rue Guy, Montréal, QC H3H 2R9
514-393-3733, Fax: 514-393-3582, 888-393-8528
opdq@opdq.org
www.opdq.org
Circulation: 2,500 *Frequency: 3 times a year; French*
Paul-Guy Duhamel, President

Obesity Surgery
PO Box 1002, 5863 Leslie St., Toronto, ON M2H 1J8
416-224-5055, Fax: 416-224-5455
journal@obesitysurgery.com
www.obesitysurgery.com
Circulation: 2,300 *Frequency: 12 times a year*
Frances Deitel, Publisher

Obstetrics & Gynaecology Canada

Circulation: 10,000 *Frequency: 4 times a year*
Michael E. Farley, Publisher
Kathy Pearsall, Managing Editor

Occupational Therapy Now / Actualités ergothérapiques
CTTC Bldg., #3400, 1125 Coloney By Dr., Ottawa, ON K1S 5R1
613-523-2268, Fax: 613-523-2552, 800-434-2268
subscriptions@caot.ca
www.caot.ca
Circulation: 6,500 *Frequency: 6 times a year*
Fern Swedlove, Editor

Oncology Exchange
400 McGill St., 3rd Fl., Montréal, QC H2Y 2G1
514-397-8833, Fax: 514-397-0228, 800-663-7403
www.oncologyex.com
Circulation: 6,000 *Frequency: 6 times a year*

Ontario Medical Review
Ontario Medical Assn., #300, 525 University Ave., Toronto, ON M5G 2K7
416-599-2580, Fax: 416-340-2232, 800-268-7215
kim_secord@oma.org
www.oma.org
Circulation: 27,000 *Frequency: 11 times a year*
Jeff Henry, Editor
Elizabeth Petruccelli, Managing Editor
Kim Secord, Circulation Manager

Optical Prism
Nusand Publishing Inc., #1113, 250 the East Mall, Toronto, ON M9B 6L3
416-233-2487, Fax: 416-233-1746
info@opticalprism.ca
www.opticalprism.ca
Circulation: 10,609 *Frequency: 10 times a year*
Robert May, Publisher
Kim Edwards, Editor

Opti-Guide
Breton Communications Inc., #202, 495, boul St-Martin ouest, Laval, QC H7M 1Y9
450-629-6005, Fax: 450-629-6044, 888-462-2112
breton.com@bretoncom.com
www.opti-guide.com
Circulation: 5,481 *Frequency: Annual*
Martine Breton, President

L'Optométriste
#740, 1265, rue Berri, Montréal, QC H2L 4X4
514-288-6272, Fax: 514-288-7071, 888-505-6786
aoq@aoqnet.qc.ca
Circulation: 4 400 *Frequency: 6 fois par an; français*

Paediatrics & Child Health

905-829-4770, Fax: 905-829-4799, 866-879-9770
pulsus@pulsus.com
www.pulsus.com
Circulation: 14,500 *Frequency: 10 times a year*
Robert Kalina, Publisher
Dr. E. Ford-Jones, Editor
Dr. N. MacDonald, Editor

Pain Research & Management

905-829-4770, Fax: 905-829-4799, 866-879-4770
pulsus@pulsus.com
www.pulsus.com
Circulation: 15,300 *Frequency: 4 times a year*
Robert Kalina, Publisher
Dr. K. Craig, Editor

Parkhurst Exchange
400, rue McGill, 3e étage, Montréal, QC H2Y 2G1
514-397-8833, Fax: 514-397-0228, 800-663-7403
parkex@parkpub.com
www.parkpub.com
Circulation: 39,453 *Frequency: 12 times a year*
Madeleine Pantais, Publisher

Patient Care

416-764-2000, Fax: 416-764-1207, 888-766-7043
Circulation: 27,256 *Frequency: 12 times a year*
Golda Goldman, Editor

Perspectives in Cardiology
#306, 955 Boul. St. Jean, Pointe-Claire, QC H9R 5K3
514-695-7623, Fax: 514-695-8554
cardio@sta.ca
www.stacommunications.com
Circulation: 15,270 *Frequency: 10 times a year*
Robert Passaretti, Publisher

Physicians' Computing Chronicle

905-273-9116, Fax: 905-273-4322, 866-633-4766
health@chronicle.org
www.chronicle.ca
Circulation: 33,682 *Frequency: 6 times a year*
Mitchell Shannon, Publisher
R. Allan Ryan, Senior Editor

Physiotherapy Canada

905-522-7017, Fax: 905-522-7839, 800-387-8679
www.physiotherapy.ca
Circulation: 9,500 *Frequency: 4 times a year*
Dr. Susan R. Harris, Scientific Editor
Kathy Hay, Journal Coordinator

Psychology Ontario
Ontario Psychological Association, #221, 730 Yonge St., Toronto, ON M4Y 2B7
416-961-5552, Fax: 416-961-5516
info@psych.on.ca
www.psych.on.ca
Circulation: 1,450 *Frequency: 4 times a year*
Dr. Mario Cappelli, Editor
Sandra Traub, Publication Manager

Rehab & Community Care Medicine
BCS Communications Ltd., 101 Thorncliffe Park Dr., Toronto, ON M4H 1M2
416-421-7944, Fax: 416-421-0966, 800-798-6282
reception@bcsgroup.com
www.bscgroup.com
Circulation: 20,500 *Frequency: 4 times a year*
Caroline Tapp-McDougall, Publisher

Stitches: The Journal of Medical Humour
240 Edward St., Aurora, ON L4G 3S9
905-727-0077, Fax: 905-727-0017, - - 0
stitches@stitchesmagazine.com
www.stitchesmagazine.com
Circulation: 38,652 *Frequency: Bi-monthly*
Michael Moriarty, Publisher
Randall Willis, Editor

Strategy: The Financial Digest for Physicians
Canadian Medical Association, 1867 Alta Vista Dr., Ottawa, ON K1G 3Y6
613-731-4552, Fax: 613-736-5367
Circulation: 41,500
Stephen Prudhomme, Publisher

Synergie
#400, 505, boul de Maisonneuve ouest, Montréal, QC H3A 3C2
514-282-4251, Fax: 514-282-4289
michel.lauzier@ssss.gouv.qc.ca
www.aqesss.qc.ca
Circulation: 6 212 *Frequency: 10 fois par an; français*
Marie-Hélène Juneau, Rédactrice
Michel Lauzier, Directeur commercial, Publicité

Urology Times of Canada
#102, 155A Matheson Blvd. West, Mississauga, ON L5R 3L5
905-712-3636, Fax: 905-712-2935, 800-561-7516
info@ctccomm.com
www.ctccomm.com
Circulation: 4,800 *Frequency: 6 times a year*
Mike Farley, Publisher
K. Pearsall, Managing Editor
Karen Tousignant, Advertising

Heating, Plumbing, Air Conditioning

Contracting Canada Magazine
1697 Kelsey Ct., Mississauga, ON L5L 3J8
905-569-2777, Fax: 905-569-2444
don.beaulieu@rogers.com
www.contractingcanada.com
Circulation: 30,000 *Frequency: 4 times a year*
Don B. Beaulieu, Publisher

Heating Plumbing Air Conditioning

416-764-2000, Fax: 416-764-1746
www.hpacmag.com
Circulation: 16,312 *Frequency: 7 times a year; also Buyers Guide (annually, Aug.)*
W. Bruce Meacock, Publisher
Kerry Turner, Editor

Inter-mécanique du bâtiment (CMMTQ)
8175, boul St-Laurent, Montréal, QC H2P 2M1
514-382-2668, Fax: 514-382-1566, 800-465-2668
cmmtq@cmmtq.org
www.cmmtq.org
Circulation: 6 000 *Frequency: 10 fois par an; français*
André Dupuis, Rédacteur-en-chef

Plumbing & HVAC Product News

416-242-8088, Fax: 416-242-8085
rshuker@nytek.ca
www.plumbingandhvac.ca
Circulation: 17,982 *Frequency: 6 times a year*
Simon Blake, Editor, sblake@nytek.ca
Ronald H. Shuker, Executive Editor, rshuker@nytek.ca

Hotels & Restaurants

Atlantic Restaurant News
#301, 2065 Dundas St. West, Mississauga, ON L4X 2W1
905-206-0150, Fax: 905-206-9972, 800-201-8596
www.can-restaurantnews.com
Circulation: 5,500 *Frequency: 6 times a year*
Steve Isherwood, Publisher, sisherwood@can-restaurantnews.com

Bar & Beverage Business

204-954-2085, Fax: 204-954-2057
mp@mercury.mb.ca
www.barandbeverage.com
Circulation: 17,063 *Frequency: 6 times a year*
Frank Yeo, Publisher
Kelly Gray, Editor

BC Restaurant News
British Columbia Restaurant & Foodservices Association, 439 Helmcken St., Vancouver, BC V6B 2E6
604-669-2239, Fax: 604-669-6175, 877-669-2239
info@bcrfa.com
www.bcrfa.com
Frequency: 8 times a year
Jason McRobbie, Editor

Canadian Lodging News

905-206-0150, Fax: 905-206-9972, 800-201-8596
mandrews@can-lodgingnews.com
Circulation: 9,000 *Frequency: 4 times a year*
Steven Isherwood, Publisher

Le Chef du service alimentaire
252, St-André, Saint-Étienne-de-Lauzon, QC G6J 1E8
418-831-5317, Fax: 418-831-5172, 800-363-1727
lechef@magazinelechef.com
www.magazinelechef.com
Circulation: 20 286 *Frequency: 6 fois par an; français*
Maurice LeBlanc, Publisher
Christiane Rioux, Editor-in-chief

Foodservice & Hospitality

416-447-0888, Fax: 416-447-5333
mkostuch@foodservice.ca
www.foodserviceworld.com
Circulation: 25,120 *Frequency: 12 times a year*
Mitch Kostuch, President/Publisher
Rosanna Caira, Associate Publisher/Editor

Foodservice News
#1000, 5255 Yonge St., Toronto, ON M2N 6P4
416-512-8186, Fax: 416-512-8344, 866-216-0860
Circulation: 21,347 *Frequency: 9 times a year*
Arthur Mensher, Publisher

Hotelier
#101, 23 Lesmill Rd., Toronto, ON M3B 3P6
416-447-0888, Fax: 416-447-5333
rcaira@foodservice.ca
www.foodserviceworld.com
Circulation: 9,000 *Frequency: 8 times a year*
Mitch Kostuch, President
Rosanna Caira, Editor & Publisher

Ontario Restaurant News
#201, 2065 Dundas St. East, Mississauga, ON L4X 2W1
905-206-0150, Fax: 905-206-9972, 800-201-8596
info@can-restaurantnews.com
www.can-restaurantnews.com
Circulation: 16,500 *Frequency: 12 times a year*
Steven Isherwood, Publisher

Pacific/Prairie Restaurants
905-206-0150, Fax: 905-206-9972, 800-201-8596
cisherwood@can-restaurantnews.com
www.can-restaurantnews.com
Circulation: 14,500 *Frequency: 6 times a year*
Steven Isherwood, Publisher
Colleen Isherwood, Editor

Western Hotelier
204-954-2085, Fax: 204-954-2057
mp@mercury.mb.ca
www.mercury.mb.ca
Circulation: 5,200 *Frequency: 5 times a year*
Frank Yeo, Publisher
Kelly Gray, Editor, editorial@mercury.mb.ca
Kristi Balon, Editorial Coordinator, editorial@mercury.mb.ca

Western Restaurant News
204-954-2085, Fax: 204-954-2057
mp@mercury.mb.ca
www.mercury.mb.ca
Circulation: 14,523 *Frequency: 6 times a year*
Frank Yeo, Publisher
Kelly Gray, Editor, editorial@mercury.mb.ca

Housewares

Canadian Home Style Magazine
Lorell Communication Inc., 146 Cavendish Ct., Oakville, ON L6J 5S2
905-338-0799, Fax: 905-338-5657
homestylemag@home.com
Frequency: 6 times a year
Laurie O'Halloran, Publisher & Editor

Human Resources

Canadian HR Reporter
1 Corporate Plaza, 2075 Kennedy Rd., Toronto, ON M1T 3V4
416-609-8000, Fax: 416-298-5031
john.hobel@thomson.com
www.hrreporter.com
Circulation: 10,800 *Frequency: 22 times a year*
John Hobel, Publisher & Editor

Human Resources Professional
204-947-0222, Fax: 204-947-2047, 800-665-2456
wayne@naylor.com
Circulation: 12,000 *Frequency: 6 times a year*
Martin Rissin, Publisher

Workplace News
905-841-6472, Fax: 905-841-5078
shughes@clbmedia.ca
www.wpnonline.com
Circulation: 10,000 *Frequency: Monthly*
Jackie Roth, Publisher
Nathan Mallett, Editor

Industrial & Industrial Automation

Advanced Manufacturing
240 Edward St., Aurora, ON L4G 3S9
905-727-0077, Fax: 905-727-0017
www.advancedmanufacturing.com
Circulation: 17,363 *Frequency: 6 times a year*
Klaus B. Pirker, Publisher
Andre Voshart, Acting Editor, avoshart@clbmedia.ca

Canadian Electronics
905-727-0077, Fax: 905-727-0017
ce@clbmedia.ca
www.canadianelectronics.ca
Circulation: 23,393 *Frequency: 6 times a year; also annual web & product directory*
Roger Heritage, Publisher, rheritage@clbmedia.ca

Canadian Industrial Equipment News
416-442-5600, Fax: 416-442-2214
mking@cienmagazine.com
CIENMagazine.com
Circulation: 21,293 *Frequency: Monthly*
Michael King, Publisher
Olga Markovich, Editor
Dianne Rakoff, Circulation Manager

Industrial Sourcebook
905-727-0077, Fax: 905-727-0017
www.industrialsourcebook.com
Circulation: 18,000 *Frequency: Annual*
Frank Shoniker, Publisher

Le Journal Industriel du Québec
2370, rue Henri-Bourassa Est, Montréal, QC H2B 1T6
514-388-8801, Fax: 514-388-7871
ygauthier@industriel.qc.ca
www.industriel.qc.ca
Circulation: 20 000 *Frequency: 10 fois par an; français*
Yvan Gauthier, Publisher

Manufacturing Automation
905-727-0077, Fax: 905-727-0017
www.automationmag.com
Circulation: 20,300 *Frequency: 7 times a year*
Klaus Pirker, Senior Publisher

MCI
P.A.P. Communications Inc., 1627, boul Bastien, Québec, QC G2K 1H1
418-623-3383, Fax: 418-623-5033, 800-387-3383
info@magazinemci.com
www.magazinemci.com
Circulation: 23 000 *Frequency: 6 fois par an; français*
Andre Pageau, Editor

PEM: Plant Engineering & Maintenance (PEM)
905-727-0077, Fax: 905-727-0017
www.pem-mag.com
Circulation: 18,494 *Frequency: 7 times a year*
Frank Schoniker, Publisher

Plant
416-764-2000, Fax: 416-764-1742
www.plant.ca
Circulation: 30,000 *Frequency: 12 times a year*
Joe Terrett, Editor

Produits pour l'industrie québécoise
905-727-0077, Fax: 905-727-0017
tgouldson@clbmedia.ca
www.pig-mag.ca
Frequency: 6 fois par an; français
Linda Nadon, Éditeur
Tim Gouldson, Rédacteur

Industrial Safety

Accident Prevention
Industrial Accident Prevention Assn (IAPA)., #300, 5110 Creekbank Rd., Mississauga, ON L4W 0A1
905-614-4272, Fax: 905-614-1414, 800-316-4272
apmag@iapa.ca
www.iapa.ca
Circulation: 12,500 *Frequency: 5 times a year*
Scott Williams, Editor

Canadian Occupational Safety
905-727-0077, Fax: 905-727-0017
www.cos-mag.com
Circulation: 14,000 *Frequency: 6 times a year*
Cocoe Horsley, Publisher
Jennifer Brown, Editor

OHS Canada Magazine (OH&S Canada)
416-442-2122, Fax: 416-442-2191, 800-668-2374
astelmakowich@ohscanada.com
www.ohscanada.com
Circulation: 10,587 *Frequency: 8 times a year*
Peter Boxer, Publisher
Angela Stelmakowich, Editor

Travail et santé
CP 1089, Napierville, QC J0J 1L0
450-245-7285, Fax: 450-245-0593
travail.sante@sympatico.ca
www.travailetsante.net
Frequency: 4 fois par an; français
Robert Richards, Rédacteur

Insurance

Alberta Insurance Directory
PO Box 3311 Terminal, 661 Market Hill, Vancouver, BC V5Z 4B5
604-874-1001, Fax: 604-874-3922
manager@insurancewest.ca
www.insurancewest.ca
Circulation: 1,555 *Frequency: Annually*
The directory, started in 1982, is considered the recognized reference authority. It contains full, accurate and up-to-date listings in Alberta of 600 general insurance broker offices, 100 independent adjusting offices, 280 general and life insurer offices, and 50 insurance association and government-related offices. In addition, 2700 senior insurance personnel are listed and cross-referenced; 100 trades and suppliers also included. The 230-page coil-bound book is used primarily by general insurance brokers, adjusters and insurers in Alberta.
Linda Helme, Publisher & Editor & Advertising Sales
Bill Earle, Publisher & Editor & Advertising Sales

The BC Broker
PO Box 3311 Terminal, 661 Market Hill, Vancouver, BC V5Z 4B5
604-874-1001, Fax: 604-874-3922
manager@insurancewest.ca
www.insurancewest.ca
Circulation: 3,500 *Frequency: 6 times a year*
The official publication of the Insurance Brokers Association of British Columbia (IBABC), the magazine is published six times a year - February, April, June, August, October and December. Circulation is 3500 of which 2600 is to member insurance brokers, the balance going to insurance companies, adjusters and suppliers to the industry. The BC Broker is an ideal medium for advertisers who wish to reach a target audience of all or part of the B.C. general insurance industry market. Not only does its circulation cover virtually all the key decision makers, it is also widely recognized as the best provincial insurance publication in Canada.
Bill Earle, Publisher & Managing Editor & Advertising Sales
Jim Bensley, Publisher & Managing Editor & Advertising Sales

British Columbia Insurance Directory
PO Box 3311 Terminal, 661 Market Hill, Vancouver, BC V5Z 4B5
604-874-1001, Fax: 604-874-3922
manager@insurancewest.ca
www.insurancewest.ca
Circulation: 2,563 *Frequency: Annually, Apr.*
The directory, started in 1964, is considered the recognized reference authority. It contains full, accurate and up-to-date listings in B.C. of 950 general insurance broker offices, 160 independent adjusting offices, 250 general and life insurer offices, and 60 insurance association and government-related offices. In addition, 5000 senior insurance personnel are listed and cross-referenced; 200 trades and suppliers also included. The 340-page coil-bound book is used primarily by general insurance brokers, adjusters and insurers in B.C.
Bill Earle, Editor & Publisher & Advertising Sales
Jim Bensley, Editor & Publisher & Advertising Sales

Canadian Insurance
#500, 111 Peter St., Toronto, ON M5V 2H1
416-599-0772, Fax: 416-599-0867
info@cdnins.com
www.cdnins.com
Circulation: 11,600 *Frequency: Monthly*
Canadian Insurance magazine provides leading coverage of the

news, events and trends that shape the p&c insurance industry. Focus is on the issues of claims management, information technology; global & commercial risks, reinsurance, loss prevention, adjusters, risk management, brokers & underwriters, environment, and financial services
Barbara Aarsteinsen, Editor, baarsteinsen@cdnins.com
John D. Wyndham, Publisher, jwyndham@cdnins.com

Canadian Insurance Claims Directory
#700, 10 St Mary St., Toronto, ON M4Y 2W8
416-978-2239, Fax: 416-978-4738, 800-565-9523
publishing@utpress.untoronto.ca
www.utppublishing.com
Circulation: 1,500 *Frequency: Annually, May*
This directory is published yearly to facilitate the forwarding of insurance claims throughout Canada and the United States. Its subscribers are adjusters, firms specializing in counsel to the insurance industry, insurance companies, and industrial and government offices. Listed are a total of 1600 independent adjusting offices, which offer dependable service to claims forwarders, as well as some 100 insurance counsel, who are experienced in insurance defense litigation.
Gwen Peroni, Editor

Canadian Underwriter
#800, 12 Concorde Pl., Toronto, ON M3C 4J2
Fax: 416-510-6809, 800-268-7742
www.cdnunderwriter.com
Circulation: 10,061 *Frequency: Monthly; also Rehabilitation & Medical Services Guide, Litigation Services Guide, Insurance Marketer, Annual Statistical Issue, Ontario Insurance Directory*
Canadian Underwriter is a professional Insurance and Risk Management magazine covering all aspects of Canada's property and casualty Insurance Market. Covers all the insurance news and insight into the issues, events and people affecting this $30 billion market. Reporting on all sectors of the market, including: brokers; insurers; reinsurance; claims; risk management; associations; legislation; legal; technology; insurer statistical review and all other related Insurance topics
David Gambrill, Editor, 416-510-6796, david@canadianunderwriter.ca
Steve Wilson, Senior Publisher, 416-510-6800, steve@canadianunderwriter.ca

Forum
c/o Advocis, 350 Bloor St. East, 2nd Fl., Toronto, ON M4W 3W8
416-444-5251, Fax: 416-444-8031
info@advocis.ca
www.advocis.ca
Circulation: 18,100 *Frequency: 12 times a year*
Peter Wilmshurst, Publisher
Kristin Doucet, Editor

General Insurance Register
416-599-0772, Fax: 416-599-0867
info@cdnins.com
www.cdnins.com
Circulation: 5,500 *Frequency: Annually, Jan.*
Lists insurance Adjusters, Appraisers, Legal firms in Canada; Consultants, Engineering, Investigation, Rehabilitation, Replacement, Restoration and other services companies; also lists Brokers, Intermediaries and Managing Agents
J. Wyndham, Publisher & Editor

The Insurance Journal
#100, 321 Rue de la Commune West, Montreal, QC H2Y 2E1
514-289-9595, Fax: 514-289-9527
idesk@insurance-journal.ca
www.insurance-journal.ca
Circulation: 15 500 *Frequency: 10 times a year*
The Insurance Journal targets financial advisors, life insurance producers, financial planners, and general insurance brokers in Canada. The magazine publishes news and examines trends in the development of insurance and financial products, such as group and individual insurance, disability insurance, mutual funds, segregated funds, health care management, and information technology. Published 10 times per year.
Serge Therrien, Publisher, serge.therrien@insurance-journal.ca
Donna Glasgow, Editor in Chief, donna.glasgow@insurance-journal.ca

Insurancewest
PO Box 3311 Terminal, 661 Market Hill, Vancouver, BC V5Z 4B5
604-874-1001, Fax: 604-874-3922
manager@insurancewest.ca
www.insurancewest.ca
Circulation: 6,000 *Frequency: 6 times a year*
Launched in 1996, this bi-monthly magazine (formerly a quarterly) circulates to 6000 in Canada's four western provinces - virtually every insurance industry decision-maker in the west. Insurancewest is about insurance people and companies
Bill Earle, Publisher & Editor & Advertising Sales
Jim Bensley, Publisher & Editor & Advertising Sales

Le Journal de l'Assurance
#100, 321, Rue de la Commune West, Montreal, QC H2Y 2E1
514-289-9595, Fax: 514-289-9527
Circulation: 26 000 *Frequency: 10 times a year; français; ISSN: 1198-4678*
Journal de l'assurance is a French-language news magazine that targets life insurance producers, general insurance brokers, financial planners, and financial advisors in Quebec
Serge Therrien, Publisher, serge.therrien@insurance-journal.ca
Donna Glasgow, Editor-in-Chief, donna.glasgow@insurance-journal.ca

Ontario Insurance Directory
#800, 12 Concorde Place, Toronto, ON M3C 4J2
416-442-2122, Fax: 416-442-2191, 800-668-2374
Circulation: 3,500 *Frequency: Annually, Dec.*
Personal address and telephone book dedicated solely to the Ontario insurance industry
Steve Wilson, Senior Publisher
Cathy Donaghy, Associate Editor

Interior Design & Decor

Azure
#601, 460 Richmond St. West, Toronto, ON M5V 1Y1
416-203-9674, Fax: 416-203-9842
azure@azureonline.com
www.azuremagazine.com
Circulation: 30,000 *Frequency: 8 times a year; ISSN: 0829-982X*
Sergio Sgaramella, Publisher
Catherine Osborne, Senior Editor
Nelda Rodger, Editor

Canadian Facility Management & Design
#338, 4195 Dundas St. West, Toronto, ON M8X 1Y4
416-236-5856, Fax: 416-236-5219
Circulation: 6,538 *Frequency: 6 times a year*
Arvid Stonkus, Publisher & Production Manager

Canadian Interiors
800, 12 Concorde Place, Toronto, ON M3C 4J2
416-442-5600, Fax: 416-442-2191, 800-668-2374
www.canadianinteriors.com
Circulation: 11,847 *Frequency: 6 times a year*
Martin Spreer, Publisher, 416-510-6766, mspreer@canadianinteriors.com

Ontario Design
905-479-4663, Fax: 905-479-4482, 800-363-4663
info@ontariodesigntrade.com
www.ontariodesigntrade.com
Circulation: 12,000 *Frequency: Annually*
Michael Rosset, Publisher

Jewellery & Giftware

Canadian Jeweller
Style Communications, #701, 555 Richmond St. West, Toronto, ON M5V 3B1
416-203-6737, Fax: 416-203-1057, 877-789-5315
canjewel@style.ca
www.canadianjeweller.com
Circulation: 5,400 *Frequency: 7 times a year*
John Peters, Publisher
Carol Besler, Editor

Journalism

L'edition Nouvelles
8030, rue Marie Lefranc, Laval, QC H7Y 2C2
450-962-7610, Fax: 450-962-7092, 866-639-7226
dcoggins@newscanada.com
www.newscanada.com
Circulation: 1 451 *Frequency: mensuel*
Ruth Douglas, President & Publisher

Media
Canadian Association of Journalists, #B224, 1385 Woodroffe Ave., Ottawa, ON K2G 1V8
613-526-8061, Fax: 613-521-3904
caj@igs.net
www.eagle.ca/caj
Circulation: 4,000 *Frequency: 4 times a year*
David McKie, Publisher

News Canada / L'Édition Nouvelles
416-599-9900, Fax: 416-599-9700
www.newscanada.com
Frequency: Monthly
Ruth Douglas, President/Publisher

Press Review
PO Box 368 A, Toronto, ON M5W 1C2
416-368-0512, Fax: 416-366-0104
info@pressreview.ca
www.pressreview.ca
Circulation: 8,500 *Frequency: 4 times a year*
Jana Cassidy, Publisher

Ryerson Review of Journalism
School of Journalism, Ryerson University, 350 Victoria St., Toronto, ON M5B 2K3
416-979-5000, Fax: 416-979-5216
reynolds@ryerson.ca
www.rrj.ca
Circulation: 4,500 *Frequency: 2 times a year; ISSN: 0838-0651*
Paul Knox, Publisher
Bill Reynolds, Editorial Instructor

Landscaping

GreenMaster
905-771-7333, Fax: 905-771-7336, 800-409-8688
editor@kenilworth.com
www.kenilworth.com
Circulation: 4,948 *Frequency: 6 times a year*
Ellen Kral, Publisher
Blair Adams, Editorial Director
Cora Golden, Director, Advertising Sales

Horticulture Review: The Voice of Landscape Ontario
905-875-1805, Fax: 905-875-0183
Circulation: 2,837 *Frequency: Monthly*
Lee Ann Knudson, Publisher
Sarah Wills, Editorial Director

Hortwest
c/o BC Landscape & Nursery Association, #102, 5783 - 176A St., Surrey, BC V3S 6S6
604-574-7772, Fax: 604-574-7773, 800-421-7963
bnelson@bclna.com
www.canadanursery.com; www.gardenwise.bc.ca
Circulation: 1,250 *Frequency: 10 times a year*
Karen DeJong, Managing Editor
Barb Nelson, Manager, Advertising, b-nelson@telus.net

Landscape Trades
7856 5th Line South, RR #4, Milton, ON L9T 2X8
905-875-1805, Fax: 905-875-0183, 800-265-5656
sarahw@landscapeontario.com
www.hort-trades.com
Circulation: 8,226 *Frequency: 9 times a year*
Sarah Willis, Editorial Director

Landscaping & Groundskeeping
604-291-9900, Fax: 604-291-1906
www.baumpub.com
Circulation: 14,229 *Frequency: 6 times a year*
Engelbert Baum, Publisher
Lawrence Buser, Editor

Prairie Landscape Magazine
Aurora Design, PO Box 85127 APPO, Calgary, AB T2A 7R7
403-273-6917, Fax: 403-313-6917
prairielandscape@shaw.ca
Circulation: 1,050 *Frequency: 6 times a year*
Jennett Jackson, Publisher

Québec Vert
1320, boul. Saint-Joseph, Québec, QC G2K 1G2
418-628-8690, Fax: 418-628-0524, 800-463-1576
editions@versicolores.ca
www.quebecvert.com
Circulation: 3 167 *Frequency: 8 fois par an; français*
Claire Bélisle, Éditeur

Turf & Recreation
275 James St., Delhi, ON N4B 2B2
519-582-8873, Fax: 519-582-8877, 800-525-6825
turf@on.aibn.com
www.turfandrec.com
Circulation: 15,000 *Frequency: 7 times a year*
Bart Crandon, Publisher

Laundry & Dry Cleaning

Fabricare Canada
Todd's Your Answer Ltd., PO Box 968, Oakville, ON L6J 5E8
905-337-0516, Fax: 905-337-0525
martodd@cogeco.ca
www.fabricarecanada.com
Circulation: 6,300 *Frequency: 6 times a year*
Marcia Todd, Publisher & Editor

Legal

The Advocate
Editorial Office, #1600, 925 West Georgia St., Vancouver, BC V6C 3C2
604-685-3456, Fax: 604-631-9190
tswoods@lawsonlundell.com
Circulation: 11,000 *Frequency: 6 times a year*
The periodical's observation of its theme "Of interest to the lawyer and in the lawyer's interest" has made it a welcome and invaluable resource for lawyers throughout British Columbia
Thomas S. Wood, Editor

Canadian Bar Review / La Revue du Barreau canadien
c/o Canadian Bar Foundation, #500, 865 Carling Ave., Ottawa, ON K1S 5S8
613-237-2925, Fax: 613-237-0185, 800-267-8860
info@cba.org
www.cba.org
Circulation: 36,200 on-line *Frequency: 3 times a year; English & French*
The official, bilingual learned legal journal of the CBA, the Canadian Bar Review is published online three times a year. Fully searchable archives of the Bar Review, dating back to 1923, are available in PDF format. The Review directly meets the educational objective of the CBA. It is frequently cited in the Supreme Court of Canada and boasts an international reputation for quality and excellence.
Prof. Beth Bilson, Editor-in-chief

Canadian Lawyer
240 Edward St., Aurora, ON L4G 3S9
905-841-6480, Fax: 905-841-5078
cleditor@clbmedia.ca
www.canadianlawyermag.com
Circulation: 28,000 *Frequency: 11 times a year; ISSN: 0703-2129*
Canadian Lawyer is the first national consumer-style magazine devoted exclusively to lawyers. It's the magazine that Canada's legal professionals turn to the most for coverage of the news, events and issues that are continually shaping the profession
Karen Lorimer, Publisher, klorimer@clbmedia.ca
Jim Middlemiss, Editor, cleditor@clbmedia.ca

Le Journal du Barreau
445, boul St-Laurent, Montréal, QC H2Y 3T8
514-954-3440, Fax: 514-954-3477, 800-361-8495
journaldubarreau@barreau.qc.ca
www.barreau.qc.ca
Circulation: 26 000 *Frequency: 12 fois par an; français*
Le Journal du Barreau, édité par le Service des communications, est la publication phare du monde juridique québécois. Il traite de l'évolution de l'exercice de la profession d'avocat, de différents domaines du droit, du système judiciaire et des aspects du droit liés aux enjeux de société
Virginie Savard, Assistante en communications

Law Times
240 Edward St., Aurora, ON L4G 3S9
905-841-6481, Fax: 905-727-0017
gcohen@clbmedia.ca
www.lawtimesnews.com
Circulation: 12,700 *Frequency: 40 times a year*
Ontario's source of legal affairs news and commentary. News Flash: Our weekly coverage offers analysis and insight into the legal profession's key players, news events and court rulings. Focus Sections: Each issue explores in detail a topic of compelling interest to Ontario's legal profession. Our focus sections cover topics as diverse as computer software, private investigators and forensic services
Kimberlee Pascoe
Gail Cohen, Editor, gcohen@clbmedia.ca
Karen Lormier, Publisher, klorimer@clbmedia.ca

LawNow
c/o University of Alberta, 174 University Campus NW, #4-36, 8303 - 112 St., Edmonton, AB T6G 2T4
780-492-1751, Fax: 780-492-6180
lawnow@ualberta.ca
www.lawnow.org
Circulation: 2,500 *Frequency: 6 times a year; ISSN: 0841-2626*
Each issue of LawNow magazine includes articles on a featured THEME, as well as a SPECIAL REPORT section. Upcoming Themes include Family Law, and Landmark Cases. Upcoming Special Reports include Administrative Law, and Law and the Disadvantaged.
Lois Gander, Publisher

The Lawyers Weekly
#700, 123 Commerce Valley Dr., Markham, ON L3T 7W8
905-479-2665, Fax: 905-479-6460, 800-668-6481
tlw@lexisnexis.ca
www.thelawyersweekly.ca
Circulation: 21,400 *Frequency: 48 times a year*
Published since 1983, The Lawyers Weekly was the first newspaper for the Canadian legal profession. It serves the national market with bureaus in Ottawa and Toronto and correspondents across the country. Published 48 times a year, The Lawyers Weekly provides lawyers with information essential to maintaining and building a successful practice in today's competitive business environment.
Tim Wilbur, Managing Editor
Gary Rodrigues, Publisher

McGill Law Journal / Revue de droit de McGill
3644 Peel St., Montréal, QC H3A 1W9
514-398-7397, Fax: 514-398-7360
journal.law@mcgill.ca
lawjournal.mcgill.ca
Circulation: 1,330 *Frequency: 4 times a year; English & French*
The McGill Law Journal is an academic legal journal established in 1952 by the students of the McGill University Faculty of Law. More than fifty years later, and still entirely student-run, we remain committed to the advancement of legal scholarship in both the common and civil law. Amongst university law journals, McGill's is especially unique as a result of its bilingual, bijuridical character, and its success as the most frequently quoted university law journal by the Supreme Court of Canada.
Christine Stecura, Managing Editor

Le Monde Juridique
6050, av de L'Authion, Montréal, QC H1M 2S4
514-353-3549, Fax: 514-353-4159
agmonde@videotron.ca
Circulation: 10 000 *Frequency: 10 fois par an; français*
Magazine des juristes du Québec
André Gagnon, Éditeur & Rédacteur

National
416-764-3910, Fax: 416-764-3933
Circulation: 38,400 *Frequency: 8 times a year; English & French*
National is the official magazine of the Canadian Bar Association. It tracks and analyzes the latest trends and developments in the law, provides practice and career information to lawyers, informs members of CBA activities and explores issues of importance to Canadian law practitioners
Jim Farley, Publisher

Ontario Legal Directory
University of Toronto Press, #700, 10 St. Mary St., Toronto, ON M4Y 2W8
416-978-2239, Fax: 416-978-4738, 800-565-9523
publishing@utpress.utoronto.ca
www.utppublishing.com
Circulation: 5,500 *Frequency: Annually, Feb.*
Accuracy and completeness of detail have characterized the Ontario Legal Directory since 1925, when the first annual edition of the Toronto Legal Directory was published. With over 30,000 listings of lawyers, law firms, federal and provincial courts and government offices, each complete with names, addresses, telephone and fax numbers, and e-mail and web addresses, the Ontario Legal Directory places all the information you need right at your fingertips. The Blue Pages put governments and courts information right up front, organized in easy-to-find categories with thumb-tab indexing.
Lynn N. Browne, Editor

The Ontario Reports
#700, 123 Commerce Valley Dr. East, Markham, ON L3T 7WB
905-479-2665, Fax: 905-479-3758, 800-668-6481
Frequency: Weekly
Published by the Law Society of Upper Canada through LexisNexis Canada, the Ontario Reports, Third Series provides in full text, leading cases decided at all levels of Ontario courts. Published 52 times per year, the soft cover parts also contain official Law Society notices (i.e., Practice Directions), government notices of interest to the legal profession, fee schedules, lawyers announcements and advertising. A personally addressed copy is sent to each of the Law Society's members each Friday.
Sarojini Pillay, Editor

Osgoode Hall Law Journal
Osgoode Hall Law School of York University, 4700 Keele St., Toronto, ON M3J 1P3
416-736-5354, Fax: 416-736-5869
journal@osgoode.yorku.ca
www.ohlj.ca
Circulation: 1,500 *Frequency: 4 times a year, plus index; English or French*
The Journal has acquired a reputation for excellence in publishing scholarly articles that represent a wide range of perspectives about law and legal institutions
Jamie Cameron, Editor-in-chief
John Boadway, Managing Editor
Yvonne Massop, Journal Coordinator
Val Culp, Managing Editor

The Scrivener Magazine
PO Box 44, #1220, 625 Howe St., Vancouver, BC V6C 2T6
604-681-4516, Fax: 604-681-7258, 800-663-0343
scrivener@notaries.bc.ca
www.notaries.bc.ca
Circulation: 6,000 *Frequency: 4 times a year*
The Scrivener is published quarterly by The Society of Notaries Public of British Columbia. Celebrates the Notary's role in drafting, communicating, authenticating, and getting the facts straight. Strives to publish articles about points of law and the Notary profession for the education and enjoyment of its members, their Allied Professionals, and the public
Val Wilson, Editor-in-chief

Lighting

Professional Lighting & Production
905-641-1512, Fax: 905-641-1648, 877-746-4692
info@nor.com
www.professional-lighting.com
Circulation: 10,200 *Frequency: 4 times a year*
Jim Norris, Publisher

Machinery Maintenance

Machinery & Equipment MRO
416-510-5600, Fax: 416-510-5134, 800-387-0273
broebuck@mromagazine.com
www.mro-esource.com
Circulation: 19,000 *Frequency: 6 times a year*
Nick Naunheimer, Publisher
William Roebuck, Editor

Materials Handling & Distribution

Gestion & Logistique
450-435-3131, Fax: 450-435-3884
gestionlogistique@bomartgroup.com
www.bomartgroup.com
Circulation: 10 104 *Frequency: 10 fois par an*
Ginette Marsolais, Directrice générale
Pierre Gravel, Éditeur
Elanka A. Todorov, Rédacteur-en-chef
André Perreault, Gestion, Circulation

Materials Management & Distribution
416-764-1537, Fax: 416-764-1739
emily.atkins@mmd.rogers.com
www.mmdonline.com
Circulation: 19,000 *Frequency: Monthly; also Data Capture Communication & Commerce (4 times a year)*
Supply chain magazine covering information management & transportation
Emily Atkins, Editor
Warren Patterson, Publisher

Metalworking

Canadian Machinery & Metalworking
1 Mount Pleasant Rd., 7th Fl., Toronto, ON M4Y 2Y5
416-764-1540, Fax: 416-764-1735
larry.bonikowsky@rci.rogers.com
www.canadianmetalworking.com
Circulation: 20,500 *Frequency: 10 times a year*
Larry Bonikowsky, Publisher
Mary Scianna, Editor

Metalworking Production & Purchasing
905-727-0077, Fax: 905-727-0017
mpp@clbmedia.ca
www.metalworkingcanada.com
Circulation: 20,129 *Frequency: 6 times a year; also The Canadian Machine Tool Dealer*

Nigel Bishop, Publisher

Military

Canadian Defence Review
PO Box 305, 21 Main St., Markham, ON L3P 3J8
905-472-2801, Fax: 905-472-3091
info@canadiandefencereview.com
www.canadiandefencereview. com
Circulation: 10,470 *Frequency: 6 times a year*
Peter A. Kitchen, Publisher
Nick Stephens, Managing Editor
Dianne Osadchuk, Circulation Manager

Mining

Canadian & American Mines Handbook
416-442-5600, Fax: 416-510-5187, 800-668-2374
mineshandbook@northernminer.com
www.northernminer.com
Frequency: Annually, Nov.
Doug Donnelly, Publisher
Diane Giancola, Editor

Canadian Miner
285 Lynn Ave., North Vancouver, BC V7J 2C3
604-980-0794, Fax: 604-980-7123, 800-570-3366
subscriptions@canadianminer.com
Circulation: 3,250 *Frequency: 4 times a year*
Michael J. McGrath, Editor

Canadian Mining Journal
416-510-6891, Fax: 416-510-5138, 800-268-7742
www.canadianminingjournal.com
Circulation: 10,045 *Frequency: 9 times a year*
Jane Werniuk, Editor
Ray Perks, Publisher

CIM Bulletin
514-939-2710, Fax: 514-939-2714
cim@cim.org
www.cim.org
Circulation: 10,213 *Frequency: 10 times a year*
H. Ednie, Editor

CIM Directory
#855, 3400 de Maisonneuve Blvd. West, Montréal, QC H3Z 3B8
514-939-2710, Fax: 514-939-2714
cim@cim.org
www.cim.org
Circulation: 10,531 *Frequency: Annual*
Perla Gantz, Editor
Yvan Jacques, Publisher

CIM Reporter
#855, 3400 de Maisonneuve Blvd. West, Montréal, QC H3Z 3B8
514-939-2710, Fax: 514-939-2714
cim@cim.org
www.cim.org
Circulation: 6,582
H. Ednie, Editor
Yvan Jacques, Publisher

FP Survey-Mines & Energy
416-442-2121, Fax: 416-442-2968
helpdesk@canwest.com
www.fpinfomart.ca
Circulation: 4,300 *Frequency: Annually, Aug.*

Mineral Exploration
4180 Lougheed Hwy., 4th Fl., Burnaby, BC V5C 6A7
604-299-7311, Fax: 604-299-9188
cwm@canadawide.com
www.canadawide.com; www.amebc.ca/mineralexploration.htm
Circulation: 3,000 *Frequency: 4 times a year*
Peter Legge, Publisher/President

Mining Sourcebook
416-510-6891, Fax: 416-510-5138
www.canadianminingjournal.com
Circulation: 5,861 *Frequency: Annually, Nov.*
Ray Perks, Publisher, rperks@canadianminingjournal.com

The Northern Miner
416-510-6768, Fax: 416-510-5137
tnm@northernminer.com
www.northernminer.com
Circulation: 16,874 *Frequency: Weekly*
Doug Donnelly, Publisher

The Prospector Investment and Exploration News
#360, 7360 - 137th St., Surrey, BC V3R 1A3
604-580-1844, Fax: 604-580-1019
info@miningandinvestment.com
www.miningandinvestment.com
Circulation: 25,000 *Frequency: 6 times a year*
Kasey Gordon, Publisher
Samantha D. Amara, Editor

Motor Trucks & Buses

L'Echo du Transport
450-435-3131, Fax: 450-435-3884
editions@bomartgroup.com
www.lechodutransport.com
Circulation: 19 063 *Frequency: 10 fois par an; français*
Pierre Gravel, Éditeur
Eric Bérard, Rédacteur-en-chef
Manon Laviolette, Directrice, Ventes

highwaySTAR
451 Attwell Dr., Toronto, ON M9W 5C4
416-614-2200, Fax: 416-614-8861
rolf@highwaystar.ca
highwaystarmagazine.com
Circulation: 40,470 *Frequency: 12 times a year*
Rolf Lockwood, Publisher/Editorial Director
Jim Park, Editor

Manitoba Ship-by-Truck Directory
204-985-9780, Fax: 204-985-9795
info@kelman.mb.ca
Circulation: 1,000 *Frequency: Annually*

Motor Truck
416-510-5123, Fax: 416-510-5143
www.trucknews.com
Circulation: 20,477 *Frequency: 6 times a year*
Lou Smyrlis, Editorial Director
Julie Kuzeljevich, Managing Editor

Over the Road
18 Parkglen Dr., Ottawa, ON K2G 3G9
613-224-9947, Fax: 613-224-8825
otr@otr.on.ca
www.overtheroad.ca
Frequency: 12 times a year
Steve Jenkins, Editor

Today's Trucking
New Communications Group Inc., 451 Attwell Dr., Toronto, ON M9W 5C4
416-614-2200, Fax: 416-614-8861
rolf@todaystrucking.com
www.todaystrucking.com
Circulation: 30,000 *Frequency: 10 times a year*
Rolf Lockwood, Publisher
Peter Carter, Editor

Truck News
416-510-5123, Fax: 416-510-5143
www.trucknews.com
Circulation: 71,824 *Frequency: Monthly*
Rob Wilkins, Publisher
Lou Smyrlis, Editorial Director

Truck West
416-510-5123, Fax: 416-510-5143
www.trucknews.com
Circulation: 20,782 *Frequency: 12 times a year*
Rob Wilkins, Publisher
Lou Smyrlis, Editorial Director

La Voix du vrac
#235, 670, rue Bouvier, Québec, QC G2J 1A7
418-623-7923, Fax: 418-623-0448
revue@ancai.com
www.ancai.com
Circulation: 9 491 *Frequency: 6 fois par an; français*
Alain Simard, Éditeur

Western Canada Highway News
204-985-9785, Fax: 204-985-9795, 866-985-9780
info@kelman.ca
Circulation: 4,000 *Frequency: 4 times a year*
Craig Kelman, Publisher
T. Ross, Editor

Music

Canadian Music Trade
905-641-1512, Fax: 905-641-1648, 877-746-4692
mail@nor.com
www.canadianmusictrade.com
Circulation: 3,500 *Frequency: 6 times a year*
Jim Norris, Publisher

Music Directory Canada
905-641-1512, Fax: 905-641-1648, 800-265-8481
info@nor.com
www.musicdirectorycanada.com
Circulation: 6,000
Jim Norris, Publisher

Professional Sound
905-641-1512, Fax: 905-641-1648, 877-746-4692
info@nor.com
www.professional-sound.com
Circulation: 10,400 *Frequency: 6 times a year*
Jim Norris, Publisher

Nursing

Alberta RN
College & Association of Registered Nurses of Alberta, 11620 - 168 St., Edmonton, AB T5M 4A6
780-451-0043, Fax: 780-452-3276, 800-252-9392
carna@nurses.ab.ca
www.nurses.ab.ca
Circulation: 28,000 *Frequency: 9 times a year*
Margaret Ward-Jack, Managing Editor
Rachel Champagne, Editor

Canadian Journal of Cardiovascular Nursing
c/o Canadian Council of Cardiovascular Nurses, 84 Isabella St., Pembroke, ON K8A 5S5
613-735-0952, Fax: 613-735-7983
heather@pappin.com
www.CardiovascularNurse.com
Circulation: 700 *Frequency: 4 times a year*
Bruce Pappin, Managing Editor

Canadian Nurse
Canadian Nurses Assn., 50 Driveway, Ottawa, ON K2P 1E2
613-237-2133, Fax: 613-237-3520, 800-361-8404
info@canadian-nurse.com
www.canadian-nurse.com
Circulation: 120,815 *Frequency: 9 times a year*
Muriel Hurst, Editor-in-chief

Canadian Oncology Nursing Journal
The Victoria Centre, 84 Isabella St., Pembroke, ON K8A 5S5
613-735-0952, Fax: 613-735-7983
www.pappin.com
Circulation: 1,000 *Frequency: 4 times a year; English & French*
Bruce M. Pappin, Managing Editor
Dr. Heather Porter, Editor-in-chief

Infirmière canadienne
Canadian Nurses Assn., 50 Driveway, Ottawa, ON K2P 1E2
613-237-2159, Fax: 613-237-3520, 800-361-8404
redaction@infirmiere-canadienne.com
www.infirmiere-canadienne.com
Circulation: 3 000 *Frequency: 9 fois par an*
Lucille Auffrey, Editor-in-chief

Newsbulletin
Saskatchewan Registered Nurses' Association, 2066 Retallack St., Regina, SK S4S 7X5
306-359-4200, Fax: 306-525-0849, 800-667-9945
info@srna.org
www.srna.org
Circulation: 10,000 *Frequency: 5 times a year*
Shirley McKay, Director Registrar

Nursing B.C.
2855 Arbutus St., Vancouver, BC V6J 3Y8
604-736-7331, Fax: 604-738-2272
nursingbc@crnbc.ca
www.crnbc.ca
Circulation: 34,454 *Frequency: 5 times a year*
Bruce Wells, Editor, wells@crnbc.ca

Perspective Infirmière
4200, boul Dorchester ouest, Montréal, QC H3Z 1V4

514-935-2501, Fax: 514-935-2055, 800-363-6048
revue@oiiq.org
www.oiiq.org
Circulation: 66 913 *Frequency: 6 fois par an; français*
Marlène Lavoie, Secrétaire de rédaction
Colette Pilon-Bergman, Rédactrice

Registered Nurse Journal
#1600, 438 University Ave., Toronto, ON M5G 2K8
416-599-1925, Fax: 416-599-1926, 800-268-7199
smackinnon@rnao.org
www.rnao.org
Circulation: 24,000 *Frequency: 6 times a year*
Sine MacKinnon, Publisher

The Registered Practical Nursing Journal
Bldg. 4, #200, 5025 Orbitor Dr., Mississauga, ON L4W 4Y5
905-602-4664, Fax: 905-602-4666, 877-602-4664
info@rpnao.org
www.rpnao.org
Circulation: 5,500 *Frequency: 4 times a year*
Joanne Young Evans, Executive Director

Santé Québec
Ordre des infirmières & infirmiers auxiliaires du Québec, 531, rue Sherbrooke est, Montréal, QC H2L 1K2
514-282-9511, Fax: 514-282-0631, 800-283-9511
oiiaq@oiiaq.org
www.oiiaq.org
Circulation: 23 000 *Frequency: 3 fois par an; français et anglais*
Catherine-Dominique Nantel, Rédactrice-en-chef & Éditrice

Packaging

Canadian Packaging
1 Mount Pleasant Rd., 7th Fl., Toronto, ON M4Y 2Y5
416-764-1497, Fax: 416-764-1755
stephen.dean.@packaging.rogers.com
www.canadianpackaging.com
Circulation: 13,626 *Frequency: 9 times a year*
Stephen Dean, Publisher
George Guidoni, Editor

Paint, Finishes, Coatings

Coatings Magazine
416-764-1554, Fax: 416-764-1740, 800-382-4957
pete.wilkinson@coatings.rogers.com
www.coatingsmagazine.com
Circulation: 8,400 *Frequency: 7 times a year*
Pete Wilkinson, Publisher

Petroleum, Oil & Gas

Alberta Oil & Gas Directory
780-429-1073, Fax: 780-425-5844
armadale@nucleus.com
www.global-serve.net
Circulation: 10,000 *Frequency: Annually*
Haloshini Naidoo, Manager
Winston Mohabir, Publisher

Canada-Z Oil Gas Mining Directory
780-429-1073, Fax: 780-425-5844
armadale@nucleus.com
www.global-serve.net
Circulation: 10,000 *Frequency: Annually*
Haloshini Naidoo, Manager
Winston Mohabir, Publisher

Canadian Oil Register
#300, 999 - 8 St. SW, Calgary, AB T2R 1N7
403-209-3500, Fax: 403-245-8666
www2.canadianoilregister.com
Frequency: Annually, Sept.
Doreen McArthur, Manager

Canadian Oilfield Gas Plant Atlas
6111 - 91 St. NW, Edmonton, AB T6E 6V6
780-944-9333, Fax: 780-944-9500, 800-563-2946
www.junewarren.com
Circulation: 4,000 *Frequency: Bi-annual*
Agnes Zalewski, Publisher

Canadian Oilfield Service & Supply Directory
780-944-9333, Fax: 780-944-9500
Frequency: Annually
Bill Whitelaw, Publisher

Energy Processing/Canada
403-263-6881, Fax: 403-263-6886, 800-526-4177
energy@northernstar.ab.ca
www.northernstar.ab.ca
Circulation: 9,866 *Frequency: 6 times a year*
Scott Jeffrey, Publisher
Heather DeSimone, Sales Manager

The Journal of Canadian Petroleum Technology
The Petroleum Society, #425, 500 - 5 Ave. SW, Calgary, AB T2P 3L5
403-237-5112, Fax: 403-262-4792
info@petsoc.org
www.petsoc.org
Circulation: 3,800 *Frequency: 12 times a year*
Nancy Hawthorne, Editor

Nickle's New Technology Magazine
#300, 999 - 8 St. SW, Calgary, AB T2R 1N7
403-209-3500, Fax: 403-245-8666
www.nickles.com
Frequency: 8 times a year
Maurice Smith, Editor

Ocean Resources
162 Trider Cres., Dartmouth, NS B3B 1R6
902-422-4990, Fax: 902-422-4728
www.ocean-resources.com
Frequency: 8 times a year
Joanne Elliott, Editor

Oil & Gas Inquirer
6111 - 91 St. NW, Edmonton, AB T6E 6V6
780-944-9333, Fax: 780-944-9500, 800-563-2946
marketing@junewarren.com
www.junewarren.com
Circulation: 10,000 *Frequency: Monthly*
Janet Howes, Editor

The Oil & Gas Magazine
#201, 1062 Topsail Rd., Mount Pearl, NF A1N 5E6
709-722-5444, Fax: 709-722-4555
Info@oilandgasmagazine.ca
www.oilworks.com
Frequency: Bi-monthly
Bill Abbott, Editor

Oil & Gas Network
#300, 840 - 6th Ave. SW, Calgary, AB T2P 3E5
403-539-1165, Fax: 403-206-7753
www.oilgas.net
Frequency: 6 times a year
Shelly Brimble, Editor

Oil & Gas Product News
604-291-9900, Fax: 604-291-1906
www.baumpub.com
Circulation: 10,708 *Frequency: 6 times a year*
Engelbert J. Baum, Publisher
Morena Zanotto, Editor

Oilsands Review
#300, 5735 - 7 St. NE, Calgary, AB T2E 8V3
403-265-3700, Fax: 403-265-3706
Circulation: 12,000 *Frequency: Monthly*
Deborah Jaremko, Editor

Oilweek
9915 - 56 Ave. NW, Edmonton, AB T6E 5L7
780-944-9333, Fax: 780-944-9500
marketing@junewarren.com
Circulation: 10,000 *Frequency: 12 times a year Oil Week Magazine; 52 times a year Oilweek Newsletter*
Darrell Stonehouse, Managing Editor
Bill Whitelaw, Publisher

Propane-Canada
403-263-6881, Fax: 403-263-6886, 800-526-4177
propane@northernstar.ab.ca
www.northernstar.ab.ca
Circulation: 8,800 *Frequency: 6 times a year*
Scott Jeffrey, Publisher
Lisa McGuire, Advertising Sales
Alister Thomas, Editor

The Roughneck
#500, 900 - 6th Ave. SW, Calgary, AB T2P 3K2
780-263-6881, Fax: 780-423-6886
Circulation: 6,527 *Frequency: 12 times a year*
Scott Jeffrey, Publisher

Photography

Master Guide
185 St-Paul St., Québec, QC G1K 3W2
418-692-2110, Fax: 418-692-3392, 800-905-7468
www.photolife.com
Other information: Toll Free Fax: 1-800-644-2739
Circulation: 6,500 *Frequency: Annually*
Guy J. Poirier, Publisher
Xavier Bonaccasi, Editor

Photo Life Buyers' Guide
185, rue St-Paul, Québec, QC G1K 3W2
800-905-7468
sales@photolife.com
www.photolife.com
Other information: Toll Free Fax: 1-800-664-2739
Circulation: 65,000 *Frequency: Annual*
Xavier Bonaconsi, Editor
Guy Poirier, Publisher

Photo Sélection
185, rue St-Paul, Québec, QC G1K 3W2
418-692-2110, Fax: 418-692-3392, 800-905-7468
info@photoselection.com
www.photoselection.com
Circulation: 10 000 *Frequency: 6 fois par an; français*
Xaviar Bonacorsi, Rédacteur en Chef
Xavier Bonacorsi, Rédacteur

Plastics

Canadian Plastics
416-442-5600, Fax: 416-510-5143
www.canplastics.com
Circulation: 10,402 *Frequency: 12 times a year*
Judith Nancekivell, Senior Publisher, 416/442-2067

Canadian Plastics Directory & Buyer's Guide
#800, 12 Concorde Place, Toronto, ON M3C 4J2
416-442-5600, Fax: 416-510-5134, 800-268-7742
cmacdonald@canplastics.com
www.canplastics.com
Circulation: 10,959 *Frequency: Annual*
Judith Nancekivell, Publisher
Bill Young, Associate Publisher

Plastics in Canada Magazine
416-764-1514, Fax: 416-764-1740
www.bizlink.com/plasticsincanada.htm
Circulation: 10,500 *Frequency: 6 times a year*
Nick Passingham, Publisher
Edward Mason, Editor

Police

Blue Line Magazine
#254, 12A - 4981 Hwy. 7 East, Markham, ON L3R 1N1
905-640-3048, Fax: 905-640-7547
blueline@blueline.ca
www.blueline.ca
Circulation: 12,000 *Frequency: 10 times a year*
Morley S. Lymburner, Publisher/Editor
Mark Reesor, Senior Editor

Tour of Duty
Toronto Police Assn., 180 Yorkland Blvd., Toronto, ON M2J 1R5
416-491-4301, Fax: 416-494-4948
editor@tpassn.com
Circulation: 9,245 *Frequency: Monthly*

Power & Power Plants

Nuclear Canada Yearbook
Canadian Nuclear Association, #1610, 130 Albert St., Ottawa, ON K1P 5G4
613-237-4262, Fax: 613-237-0989
huntc@cna.ca
www.cna.ca
Circulation: 3,500 *Frequency: Annually*
Colin Hunt, Publisher & Editor

Printing & Publishing

Canadian Printer
416-764-1509, Fax: 416-764-1738
www.canadianprinter.com
Circulation: 11,500 *Frequency: 8 times a year*
Susan Ritcey, Publisher
Doug Picklyk, Editor

Estimators' & Buyers' Guide

905-625-7070, Fax: 905-625-4856

Frequency: Annually
Alexander Donald, Publisher

Grafika

514-842-5873, Fax: 514-842-2422
redaction@infopresse.com
www.infopresse.com

Circulation: 6 000 *Frequency: 10 fois par an*
Bruno Gautier, Éditeur
Mélanie Rudel-Tessier, Rédactrice en chef

Graphic Arts Magazine

#202, 1180 Kingdale Rd., Newmarket, ON L3Y 4W1
905-830-4394, Fax: 905-830-9345
joe@graphicartsmagazine.com
www.graphicartsmagazine.com

Circulation: 11,200 *Frequency: 10 times a year*
Joe Mulcahy, Publisher
Scott Bury, Editor

Graphic Monthly

905-625-7070, Fax: 905-625-4856, 800-331-7408
www.graphicmonthly.ca

Circulation: 10,372 *Frequency: 6 times a year*
Alexander Donald, Publisher

Livre d'ici

#55, 222, Cours Dominion, Montréal, QC H3J 2X1
514-933-8033, Fax: 514-933-7958
livredici.com

Circulation: 1,600
Jacques Therriault, Publisher

Le Maître Imprimeur

5400, rue Chemin, Saint-Laurent, QC H4S 1P6
514-388-9311, Fax: 514-388-0188

Circulation: 5 000 *Frequency: 10 fois par an; français*
Christine Veznia, Éditeur

Masthead

905-625-7070, Fax: 905-625-4856
wshields@masthead.ca
www.mastheadonline.com

Circulation: 2,800 *Frequency: 6 times a year; ISSN 0832-512X*
Doug Bennet, Publisher

The Publisher

#300, 8 Market St., Toronto, ON M5E 1M6
416-482-1090, Fax: 416-482-1908, 877-305-2262
publisher@ccna.ca
www.communitynews.ca; www.ccna.ca

Circulation: 750 *Frequency: 10 times a year*
Lyne Hennigar, Publisher
John Hinds, Editor

Second Impressions

35 Mill Dr., St Albert, AB T8N 1J5
780-458-9889, Fax: 780-458-9839
secondimpressions@second-impressions.com
www.second-impressions.com

Circulation: 9,000 *Frequency: 6 times a year*
Loretta Puckrin, Publisher

Product Engineering & Design

Design Engineering

1 Mount Pleasant Rd., 7th Fl., Toronto, ON M4Y 2Y5
416-764-1534, Fax: 416-764-1735
alan.macpherson@de.rogers.com
www.design-engineering.com

Circulation: 19,000 *Frequency: 8 times a year*
Alan Macpherson, Associate Publisher
Mike Mcleod, Editor

Design Product News

905-727-0077, Fax: 905-727-0017
dpn@clbmedia.ca
www.clbmedia.ca

Circulation: 20,407 *Frequency: 6 times a year*
Nigel Bishop, Publisher
Mike Edwards, Editor
James Zammit, Circulation Manager

Pulp & Paper

Mill Product News

604-298-3005, Fax: 604-298-3966
www.baumpub.com

Circulation: 20,137 *Frequency: 6 times a year*
Heri R. Baum, Publisher
Gunnar Mardon, Editor

Les Papetières du Québec

Business Information Group, #705, Tour Est, 1, rue Holiday, Pointe-Claire, QC H9R 5N3
514-630-5955, Fax: 514-630-5980, 800-363-1327
jbussiere@pulpandpapercanada.com
www.pulpandpapercanada.com

Circulation: 4 348 *Frequency: 5 fois par an; français*
Jim Bussiere, Éditeur-en-chef
Jaclin Ouellet, Rédacteur-en-chef

Pulp & Paper Canada

Business Information Group, #705, Tour Est, 1, rue Holiday, Pointe-Claire, QC H9R 5N3
514-630-5955, Fax: 514-630-5980, 800-363-1327
jbussiere@pulpandpapercanada.com
www.pulpandpapercanada.com

Circulation: 9,698 *Frequency: Monthly; also Annual Directory (Dec.)*
Jim Bussiere, Publisher
Anya Orzechowska, Editor

Purchasing

Canadian Trade Index

#208, 2085 Hurontario St., Mississauga, ON L5A 4G1
905-290-1818, Fax: 905-290-1760, 877-463-6284
owenmediainfocti@owen-media.com
www.ctidirectory.com

Frequency: Annually, May
Hugh Owen, President

Purchasing B2B

416-764-1499, Fax: 416-764-1740
www.purchasingb2b.ca

Circulation: 19,292 *Frequency: 10 times a year*
Tim Dimopoulos, Publisher

Real Estate

Canadian Appraiser / L'Évaluateur Canadien

#3C, 2020 Portage Ave., Winnipeg, MB R3J 0K4
204-985-9780, Fax: 204-985-9795
info@kelman.ca
www.kelman.ca

Circulation: 5,961 *Frequency: 4 times a year*
Craig Kelman, Editor

Canadian Office Guide

2014 Stavebank Rd., Mississauga, ON L5C 1T2
905-273-7950, Fax: 905-273-3816
www.factorygroup.com/magaz.htm

Frequency: Annual

Canadian Property Guide

#1000, 33 Yonge St., Toronto, ON M5E 1S9
416-359-2550, Fax: 416-359-2538
cmildon@royallepage.com
www.canadianpropertyguide.com

Circulation: 70,000 *Frequency: Bi-annual*
Caroline Mildon

Espace Montréal

#9235, 800, rue de la Gauchetière ouest, Montréal, QC H5A 1K6
514-879-1559, Fax: 514-879-1556, 800-232-9846
espace@espacequebec.com
www.espacepublications.com

Circulation: 10 000 *Frequency: 4 fois par an*
Andrew Cross, Publisher & Editor

Espace Québec

#9235, 800, de la Gauchetière ouest, Montréal, QC H5A 1K6
514-879-1559, Fax: 514-879-1556, 800-232-9846
andrew@espacequebec.com
www.espacepublications.com

Circulation: 5 000 *Frequency: 2 fois par an*
Andrew Cross, Éditeur/Rédacteur

REM: Canada's Magazine for Real Estate Professionals

House Magazine Inc., 808 Coxwell Ave., Toronto, ON M4C 3E4
416-425-3504, Fax: 416-406-0882
www.remonline.com

Circulation: 50,000 *Frequency: 12 times a year*
Heino Molls, Publisher
Jim Adair, Editor, jim@remonline.com

The Western Investor

Business in Vancouver Media Group, #501, 1155 West Pender St., Vancouver, BC V6E 2P4
604-669-8500, Fax: 604-669-2154
www.westerninvestor.com

Circulation: 16,000 *Frequency: Monthly*
Cheryl Carter, Publisher
Frank O'Brien, Editor

Rental & Leasing Equipment

Canadian Rental Service

519-235-2400, Fax: 519-235-0798

Circulation: 3,543 *Frequency: 9 times a year*
Chris Skalkos, Editor

Contractors Magazine

604-291-9900, Fax: 604-291-1906
www.baumpub.com

Circulation: 14,021 *Frequency: 6 times a year*
Engelbert Baum, Publisher
Keith Barker, Editor

Retailing

Canadian Retailer

#800, 1255 Bay St., Toronto, ON M5R 2A9
416-922-6678, Fax: 416-922-8011, 888-373-8245
www.retailcouncil.org/cdnretailer

Circulation: 15,000 *Frequency: 6 times a year*
Theresa Rogers, Editor-in-chief
Diane Brisebois, Publisher

Science, Research & Development

Bio Business

#202, 30 Beaver Creek Rd. East, Richmond Hill, ON L4B 1J2
905-886-5040, Fax: 905-886-6615, 800-613-6353
cforbes@jesmar.com
www.biobusinessmag.com

Circulation: 15,000 *Frequency: 4 times a year*
Christopher Forbes, Publisher

Biochemistry & Cell Biology / Biochimie & biologie cellulaire

National Research Council of Canada, Ottawa, ON K1A 0R6
613-993-0362, Fax: 613-952-7656
pubs@nrc-cnrc.gc.ca
pubs.nrc-cnrc.gc.ca

Circulation: 1,150 *Frequency: Bi-monthly; English & French*
Cameron Macdonald, Director
Bruce P. Dancik, Editor
Judy Busnarda, Managing Editor

Camford Chemical Report

38 Groomsport Cres., Toronto, ON M1T 2K9
416-740-5604, Fax: 416-291-3406
ccr@camfordinfo.com
www.camfordinfo.com

Frequency: 50 times a year
Bob Douglas, Publisher

Canadian Biotech News

Canadian Biotech News Service, 110 Ebb Tide Dr., Winnipeg, MB R3X 2H9
415-591-5474, Fax: 415-591-5401
canadianbiotech@yahoo.com
www.canadianbiotechnews.com

Circulation: 3,500 *Frequency: 12 times a year; ISSN: 1188-455X*
Peter Winter, Editor-in-chief
Jeff Miller, Publisher

Canadian Geotechnical Journal / Revue canadienne de géotechnique

National Research Council of Canada, Ottawa, ON K1A 0R6
613-993-0362, Fax: 613-952-7656
pubs@nrc-cnrc.gc.ca
pubs.nrc-cnrc.gc.ca

Circulation: 2,600 *Frequency: 6 times a year; English & French*
Cameron Macdonald, Director
Bruce P. Dancik, Editor
Bushra Waheed, Managing Editor

Canadian Journal of Botany / Revue canadienne de botanique

National Research Council of Canada, Ottawa, ON K1A 0R6
613-993-0362, Fax: 613-952-7656
pubs@nrc-cnrc.gc.ca
pubs.nrc-cnrc.gc.ca

Circulation: 1,550 *Frequency: Monthly; English & French*
Cameron Macdonald, Director
Bruce P. Dancik, Editor

Cecily Pearson, Managing Editor

Canadian Journal of Chemistry / Revue canadienne de chimie
National Research Council of Canada, Ottawa, ON K1A 0R6
613-993-0362, Fax: 613-952-7656
pubs@nrc-cnrc.gc.ca
pubs.nrc-cnrc.gc.ca
Circulation: 1,700 *Frequency: Monthly; English & French*
Cameron Macdonald, Director
Dr. R.H. Lipson, Editor
Judy Buscarda, Managing Editor

Canadian Journal of Civil Engineering / Revue canadienne de génie civil
National Research Council of Canada, Ottawa, ON K1A 0R6
613-993-0362, Fax: 613-952-7656
pubs@nrc-cnrc.gc.ca
pubs.nrc-cnrc.gc.ca
Circulation: 3,200 *Frequency: 6 times a year; English & French*
Cameron Macdonald, Director
Bruce P. Dancik, Editor
Bushra Waheed, Managing Editor

Canadian Journal of Earth Sciences / Revue canadienne des sciences de la Terre
National Research Council of Canada, Ottawa, ON K1A 0R6
613-993-0362, Fax: 613-952-7656
pubs@nrc-cnrc.gc.ca
pubs.nrc-cnrc.gc.ca
Circulation: 2,400 *Frequency: Monthly; English & French*
Cameron Macdonald, Director
Bruce P. Dancik, Editor
Bushra Waheed, Managing Editor

Canadian Journal of Fisheries & Aquatic Science / Journal canadien des sciences halieutiques et aquatiques
National Research Council of Canada, Ottawa, ON K1A 0R6
613-993-0362, Fax: 613-952-7656
pubs@nrc-cnrc.gc.ca
pubs.nrc-cnrc.gc.ca
Circulation: 2,400 *Frequency: Monthly*
Bruce P. Dancik, Editor
Cecily Pearson, Managing Editor
Cameron Macdonald, Director

Canadian Journal of Forest Research / Revue canadienne de recherche forestière
National Research Countil of Canada, Ottawa, ON K1A 0R6
613-993-0362, Fax: 613-952-7656
pubs@nrc-cnrc.gc.ca
pubs.nrc-cnrc.gc.ca
Circulation: 900 *Frequency: Monthly; English & French*
Cameron Macdonald, Director
Bruce P. Dancik, Editor
Donald S. Mavinic, Assistant Editor
Cecily Pearson, Managing Editor

Canadian Journal of Microbiology / Revue canadienne de microbiologie
National Research Council of Canada, Ottawa, ON K1A 0R6
613-993-0362, Fax: 613-952-7656
pubs@nrc-cnrc.gc.ca
pubs.nrc-cnrc.gc.ca
Circulation: 1,675 *Frequency: Monthly; English & French*
Bruce P. Dancik, Editor
Cameron Macdonald, Director
Donald S. Mavinic, Assistant Editor
Judy Busnarda, Managing Editor

Canadian Journal of Physics / Revue canadienne de physique
National Research Council of Canada, Ottawa, ON K1A 0R6
613-993-0362, Fax: 613-952-7656
pubs@nrc-cnrc.gc.ca
pubs.nrc-cnrc.gc.ca
Circulation: 850 *Frequency: Monthly; English & French*
Cameron MacDonald, Director
Bushra Waheed, Managing Editor
Bruce P. Dancik, Editor

Canadian Journal of Physiology & Pharmacology / Revue canadienne de physiologie & pharmacologie
Natioanl Research Council of Canada, Ottawa, ON K1A 0R6
613-993-0362, Fax: 613-952-7656
pubs@nrc-cnrc.gc.ca
pubs.nrc-cnrc.gc.ca
Circulation: 975 *Frequency: Monthly; English & French*
Cameron Macdonald, Director
Bruce P. Dancik, Editor
Donald S. Mavinic, Assistant Editor
Judy Busnarda, Managing Editor

Canadian Journal of Zoology / Revue canadienne de zoologie
National Research Council of Canada, Ottawa, ON K1A 0R6
613-993-0362, Fax: 613-952-7656
pubs@nrc-cnrc.gc.ca
pubs.nrc-cnrc.gc.ca
Circulation: 1,250 *Frequency: Monthly; English & French*
Cameron Macdonald, Director
Bruce P. Dancik, Editor
Cecily Pearson, Managing Editor

Genome / Génome
National Research Council of Canada, Ottawa, ON K1A 0R6
613-993-0362, Fax: 613-952-7656
pubs@nrc-cnrc.gc.ca
pubs.nrc-cnrc.gc.ca
Circulation: 1,350 *Frequency: 6 times a year; English & French*
Cameron MacDonald, Director
Cecily Pearson, Managing Editor
Bruce P. Dancik, Editor

LAB Business
#202, 30 East Beaver Creek Rd., Richmond Hill, ON L4B 1J2
905-886-5040, Fax: 905-886-6615
cforbes@jesmar.com
www.labbusinessmag.com
Circulation: 30,250 *Frequency: 5 times a year*
Christopher Forbes, Publisher

Laboratory Buyers Guide
416-510-6835, Fax: 416-510-5140
lburt@labcanada.com
www.labcanada.com
Circulation: 20,000 *Frequency: Annually*
Leslie Burt, Publisher/Editor

Laboratory Product News
416-510-6835, Fax: 416-510-5140, 800-268-7742
lburt@labcanada.com
www.labcanada.com
Circulation: 20,000 *Frequency: 6 times a year*
Leslie Burt, Publisher/Editor

The Microscopical Society of Canada Bulletin
c/o Dept. of Physics, Acadia University, Wolfville, NS B4P 2R6
902-585-1318
michael.robertson@acadiau.ca
msc.rsvs.ulaval.ca/english/pages/bulletin.html
Circulation: 650 *Frequency: 4 times a year; ISSN 0383-1825*
Dr. Michael Robertson, Editor

OSMT Advocate
#402, 234 Eglinton Ave. East, Toronto, ON M4P 1K5
416-485-6768, Fax: 416-485-7660, 800-461-6768
osmt@osmt.org
www.osmt.org
Circulation: 3,000 *Frequency: 4 times a year*
Blanca McArthur, Executive Director

Physics in Canada / La Physique au Canada
#112, McDonald Bldg., 150 Louis Pasteur Ave., Ottawa, ON K1N 6N5
613-562-5614, Fax: 613-562-5615
cap@physics.uottawa.ca
www.cap.ca
Circulation: 1,623 *Frequency: 6 times a year; French & English*
Béla Jo¢s, Editor

Security

Canadian Security
905-727-0077, Fax: 905-727-0017
sfenninger@clbmedia.ca
www.canadiansecuritymag.com
Circulation: 16,000 *Frequency: 9 times a year*
Jennifer Brown, Editor

Security Products & Technology News
905-727-0077, Fax: 905-727-0017
www.sptnews.ca
Circulation: 12,000 *Frequency: 10 times a year*
Frank Shoniker, Publisher
Jennifer Brown, Editor

Shipping & Marine

Canadian Sailings
#200, 5165, rue Sherbrooke ouest, Montréal, QC H4A 1T6
514-934-0373, Fax: 514-934-4708
www.canadiansailings.com
Circulation: 9,000 *Frequency: Weekly*
Joyce Hammock, Publisher & Editor

Harbour & Shipping
#200, 1865 Marine Dr., West Vancouver, BC V7V 1J7
604-922-6717, Fax: 604-922-1739
harbour_shipping@bc.sympatico.ca
Circulation: 2,200 *Frequency: Monthly*
Murray D. McLellan, President/Publisher
Allison Smith, Editor

Sporting Goods & Recreational Equipment

Golf Business Canada
#105, 955 Green Valley Cres., Ottawa, ON K1C 3V4
613-226-3616, Fax: 613-226-4148
ngcoa@ngcoa.ca
www.ngcoa.ca
Circulation: 4,000 *Frequency: 4 times a year*
Pamela Stewart, Editor

Jim Rennie's Sports Letter
PO Box 1000, 101 Pretty River Pkwy. South, Collingwood, ON L9Y 4L4
705-445-7161, Fax: 705-445-8650
rennies@rennies.net
Circulation: 2,000 *Frequency: Weekly*
Jim Rennie, Publisher & Editor

Motorsport Dealer & Trade
Point One Media Inc., #3, 2232 Wilgress Rd., Nanaimo, BC V9S 4N4
Fax: 250-758-8665, 877-755-8665
info@pointonemedia.com
www.mdtcanada.net
Circulation: 3,500 *Frequency: 6 times a year*
Jim Aikins, Editor
Lara Perraton, Group Publisher

Pool & Spa Marketing
Hubbard Marketing & Publishing Ltd., #12, 270 Esna Park Dr., Markham, ON L3R 1H3
905-513-0090, Fax: 905-513-1377, 800-268-5503
richard@poolspamarketing.com
www.poolspamarketing.com
Circulation: 8,000 *Frequency: 7 times a year*
Richard Hubbard, Publisher

Telecommunications

Canadian New Media
#1800, 160 Elgin St., Ottawa, ON K2P 2P7
613-230-1984, Fax: 613-230-3793
jlewis@decima.com
www.decima.com
James Lewis, Editor

Wireless Telecom
#1110, 130 Albert St., Ottawa, ON K1P 5G4
613-233-4888, Fax: 613-233-2032
info@cwta.ca
www.cwta.ca
Circulation: 7,273 *Frequency: 3 times a year*

Television, Radio, Video & Home Appliances

Marketnews
Bomar Publishing Inc., #102, 701 Evans Ave., Toronto, ON M9C 1A3
416-667-9945, Fax: 416-667-0609
jtomson@marketnews.ca
www.marketnews.ca
Circulation: 11,200 *Frequency: Monthly*
John Thomson, Associate Publisher, jtomson@marketnews.ca
Bob Grierson, Publisher, bgrierson@marketnews.ca
Robert Franner, Editor, rfranner@marketnews.ca
Erik Devantier, Creative Director

Media Names & Numbers
Sources, #305, 489 College St., Toronto, ON M6G 1A5
416-964-7799, Fax: 416- -
www.sources.com
Circulation: 500 *Frequency: annually*
Ulli Diemer, Publisher

Première Video Magazine
#100, 102 Atlantic Ave., Toronto, ON M6K 1X9
416-539-8800, Fax: 416-539-8511
Circulation: 7,900 *Frequency: 12 times a year*
Salah Bachir, President

Textiles

Canadian Textile Journal
#3000, rue Boullé, Saint-Hyacinthe, QC J2S 1H9
450-778-1870, Fax: 450-778-9016, 877-288-8878
rleclerc@gcttg.com
www.textilejournal.ca
Circulation: 2,500 *Frequency: 7 times a year*
Daniel Bertrand, Editor-in-chief

The Textile Journal
3000, rue Boulle, Saint-Hyacinthe, QC J2S 1H9
450-778-1870, Fax: 450-778-9016
rleclerc@ctt.ca
www.textilejournal.ca
Roger Leclerc

Toys

Toys & Games
Chelsie Communications Inc., #216, 61 Alness St., Toronto, ON M3J 2H2
416-663-9229, Fax: 416-663-2353
cantoymag@look.ca
www.toysandgamesmag.com
Circulation: 5,000 *Frequency: 6 times a year*
Graham Kennedy, Publisher

Transportation, Shipping & Distribution

Atlantic Construction & Transportation Journal
#609, 1888 Brunswick St., Halifax, NS B3J 3J8
902-468-8027, Fax: 902-425-8118
ken.partridge@transcontinental.ca
Circulation: 12,500 *Frequency: 4 times a year*
Jeff Nearing, General Manager

Canadian Automotive Fleet
#110, 295 The West Mall, Toronto, ON M9C 4Z4
416-383-0302, Fax: 416-383-0313
caf@fleetbusiness.com
www.fleetbusiness.com
Circulation: 12,474 *Frequency: 7 times a year*
Jake McLaughlin, Publisher & Editor

Canadian Transit Forum
#710, 15 Wertheim Ct., Richmond Hill, ON L4B 3H7
905-771-7333, Fax: 905-771-7336
ellenkrai@kenilworth.com
www.kenilworth.com
Circulation: 1,800 *Frequency: 6 times a year*
Ellen Krai, Publisher

Canadian Transportation Logistics
#800, 12 Concorde Place, Toronto, ON M3C 4J2
416-510-5108, Fax: 416-510-5134
nick@ctl.ca
www.ctl.ca
Circulation: 17,665 *Frequency: 11 times a year*
Nick Krukowski, Publisher
Lou Smyrlis, Editorial Director

Guide du Transport par Camion
450-435-3131, Fax: 450-435-3884
guidedutransport@bomartgroup.com
www.bomartgroup.com
Circulation: 3 000 *Frequency: annuel; français*
Pierre Gravel, Président et éditeur
Ginette Marsolais, Conception

Logistics Magazine
#115, 916, boul Ste-Adèle, Sainte-Adèle, QC J8B 2N2
450-229-7777, Fax: 450-229-3233
www.logistics-mag.com
Frequency: Bi-monthly
Michel Trudeau, Editor

Maritime Magazine
418-692-3779, Fax: 418-692-5198, 877-595-3779
pterrien@maritimemag.com
Circulation: 11,000 *Frequency: 4 times a year; French & English*
Covers Marine Transport Industry
Léo YRyanen, Rédacteur en chef

Routes et Transports
A.Q.T.R., #200, 1255, rue University, Montréal, QC H3B 3B2
514-523-6444, Fax: 514-523-2666
info@aqtr.qc.ca
www.aqtr.qc.ca
Circulation: 3 500 *Frequency: 4 fois par an; français*
Jean Auden, Editor

Travel

Bulletin Voyages
78 boul Saint-Joseph Ouest, Montréal, QC H2T 2P4
514-287-9773, Fax: 514-842-6180
Circulation: 9 062 *Frequency: Hebdomadaire; français*
Jean-Pierre Kerten, Éditeur

Canada Journal
KLR Communications, 44 Cameron Cres., Toronto, ON M4G 1Z8
416-487-0166, Fax: 416-487-2452
mail@canadajournal.ca
www.canadajournal.ca
Circulation: 27,000 *Frequency: bi-weekly; German*
Klaus Ruland, Publisher/Editor

Canadian Travel Press
310 Dupont St., Toronto, ON M5R 1V9
416-968-7252, Fax: 416-968-2377
dmcclung@baxter.net
www.travelpress.com
Circulation: 13,000 *Frequency: Thu.- weekly; summer - bi-weekly*
David McClung, President
Edith Baxter, Editor

Canadian Traveller
ACT Communications Inc., #203, 1104 Hornby St., Vancouver, BC V6Z 1V8
604-699-9990, Fax: 604-699-9993
info@canadiantraveller.net
www.canadiantraveller.net
Circulation: 14,782 *Frequency: Monthly*
Rex Armstead, Publisher
Stephen Fountaine, Associate Publisher
Janice Strong, Associate Editor

GSA: The Travel Magazine for Western Canada
604-689-2909, Fax: 604-689-2989, 888-286-6148
sales@gsa.publishing.com
www.gsapublishing.com
Circulation: 5,100 *Frequency: 26 times a year*
Frank Cumming, Publisher
Lynda Cumming, Editor

Le Magazine l'agent de voyages inc.
CP 38, Anjou, QC H1K 4G5
514-881-9637, Fax: 514-881-8292
info@planisphere.qc.ca
Circulation: 8 500 *Frequency: 7 fois par an; français*
Michel Villeneuve, Éditeur

Personnel Guide to Canada's Travel Industry
416-968-7252, Fax: 416-968-2377
sales@baxter.net
www.personnelguide.ca
Circulation: 4,500 *Frequency: 2 times a year*
David McClung, President

Tourisme Plus
#301, 11800, 5e av, Montréal, QC H1E 7C1
514-881-8583, Fax: 514-881-8292
production@planisphere.qc.ca
Circulation: 9 200 *Frequency: 46 fois par an; français*
Michel Villeneuve, Rédacteur-en-chef

Travel Courier
310 Dupont St., Toronto, ON M5R 1V9e
416-968-7252, Fax: 416-968-2377
www.travelpress.com
Circulation: 11,191 *Frequency: Weekly, Thu.*
Edith Baxter, Editor-in-chief

Travelweek
Concepts Travel Media Ltd., #100, 282 Richmond St. East, Toronto, ON M5A 1P4
416-365-1500, Fax: 416-365-1504, 800-727-1429
travelweek@travelweek.ca
www.travelweek.ca
Circulation: 12,420 *Frequency: Weekly*
Patrick Dineen, Editor

Voyage en Groupe / Group Travel
590, ch St-Jean, La Prairie, QC J5R 2L1
450-444-5870, Fax: 450-444-4720
voyageengroupe@bellnet.ca
www.revue-voyage-groupe.com
Circulation: 13 000 *Frequency: 6 fois par an; français*
Monique Papineau, Éditrice

Vending & Vending Equipment

Canadian Vending & Coin Box Amusement News
PO Box 530, 105 Donly Dr. Aouth, Simcoe, ON N3Y 4N5
519-429-5177, Fax: 519-429-3094, 888-599-2228
dkleer@annexweb.com
www.canadianvending.com
Circulation: 3,900 *Frequency: 10 times a year*
Diane Geerlinks, Publisher

Veterinary

The Canadian Veterinary Journal / La Revue Vétérinaire Canadienne
c/o Canadian Veterinary Medical Association, 339 Booth St., Ottawa, ON K1R 7K1
613-236-1162, Fax: 613-236-9681, 800-567-2862
admin@cvma-acmv.org
canadianveterinarians.net/publications-journal-issue .aspx
Circulation: 5,500 *Frequency: Monthly; English & French*
Dr. W.C.D. Hare, Editor-in-chief

Le Vétérinarius
#200, 800, av Sainte-Anne, Saint-Hyacinthe, QC J2S 5G7
450-774-1427, Fax: 450-774-7635, 800-267-1427
omvq@omvq.qc.ca
www.omvq.qc.ca
Circulation: 2 500 *Frequency: 6 fois par an; français*
Mathieu Bilodeau, Rédacteur-en-chef

Water & Wastes Treatment

Canadian Environmental Protection
604-291-9900, Fax: 604-291-1906
ebaum@baumpub.com
www.baumpub.com
Circulation: 20,127 *Frequency: 8 times a year*
Morena Zanotto, Editor
Engelbert J. Baum, Publisher

Environmental Science & Engineering Magazine
Environmental Science & Engineering Publications Inc., #30, 220 Industrial Pkwy. South, Aurora, ON L4G 3V6
905-727-4666, Fax: 905-841-7271, 888-254-8769
steve@esemag.com
www.esemag.com
Circulation: 19,000 *Frequency: 6 times a year; ISSN 0835-605X*
Steve Davey, Publisher & Editor

Ground Water Canada
519-235-2400, Fax: 519-235-0798
cskalkos@annexweb.com
Circulation: 3,842 *Frequency: 4 times a year*
Chris Skalkos, Editor

Hazardous Materials Management Magazine
#800, 12 Concorde Pl., Toronto, ON M3C 4J2
416-442-5600, Fax: 416-510-5133, 888-702-1111
gcrittenden@solidwastemag.com
www.hazmatmag.com
Circulation: 14,048 *Frequency: Bi-monthly; ISSN 0843-9303*
Guy Crittenden, Editor
Brad O'Brien, Publisher

Maritime Provinces Water & Wastewater Report
Transcontinental Media, #609, 1888 Brunswick St., Halifax, NS B3J 3J8
902-468-8027, Fax: 902-468-2425
barb.cashin@transcontinental.ca
www.mpwwa.ca/newsletter.asp
Circulation: 2,567 *Frequency: 4 times a year*
Barb McCay Cashin, Editor

Solid Waste & Recycling Magazine
416-510-6798, Fax: 416-510-5133
cvitello@solidwastemag.com
www.solidwastemag.com
Circulation: 10,000 *Frequency: 6 times a year; ISSN: 1206-0879*
Brad O'Brien, Publisher & Sales Manager
Guy Crittenden, Editor

Woodworking

2 x 4
Editions C.R. Inc., PO Box 1010, Victoriaville, QC G6P 8Y1
819-752-4243, Fax: 819-382-2970
c-roy@ivic.qc.ca
www.2x4.net
Circulation: 8,000 *Frequency: 4 times a year; English & French*
Claude Roy, Publisher
Bernard Gauthier, Editor, info@bernardgauthier.com

Woodworking
240 Edward St., Aurora, ON L4G 3S9
905-272-0077, Fax: 905-272-0017
woodworking@clbmedia.ca
www.woodworkingcanada.com
Circulation: 11,190 *Frequency: 6 times a year; also Woodworking Sourcer (annually)*
Bert Kleiser, Publisher
Adam Freill, Editor

Consumer

Advertising, Marketing, Sales

Adbusters
1234 - West 7th Ave., Vancouver, BC V6H 1B7
604-736-9401, Fax: 604-737-6021, 800-663-1243
info@adbusters.org
www.adbusters.org
Circulation: 120,000 *Frequency: 6 times a year; ISSN: 0847-9097*
Kalle Lasn, Publisher

Airline Inflight

enRoute
#707, 4200 boul. St-Laurent, Montréal, QC H2W 2R2
514-844-2001, Fax: 514-844-6001
info@enroutemag.net
www.enroutemag.com
Circulation: 149,478 *Frequency: Monthly; English & French*

Animals

Animals' Voice
Ontario SPCA, 16586 Woodbine Ave., RR#3, Newmarket, ON L3Y 4V8
905-898-7122, Fax: 905-853-8643
info@ospca.on.ca
www.ospca.on.ca
Circulation: 100,000 *Frequency: 2 times a year*
Vicki Quigley, Editor, vquigley@ospca.on.ca

Canine Review
PO Box 40215 Highfield, Calgary, AB T2G 5G6
403-236-0557, Fax: 403-236-3271, 866-236-0557
editor@canine-review.com
www.canine-review.com
Circulation: 2,000 *Frequency: 10 times a year*
Karen Milne, Editor
Merla Thomson, Publisher

Dog Sport
131 McElderry Rd., Guelph, ON N1G 4J8
519-837-9257, Fax: 519-837-4976
www.dogsportmagazine.com
Anne B. Douglas, Editor

Dogs in Canada
Apex Publishing Ltd., #200, 89 Skyway Ave., Toronto, ON M9W 6R4
416-798-9778, Fax: 416-798-9671
info@dogsincanada.com
www.dogsincanada.com
Circulation: 40,000 *Frequency: Monthly (13 issues a year, including Dogs in Canada Annual)*
Ann McDonagh, Publisher

Dogs in Canada Annual
Apex Publishing Ltd., #200, 89 Skyway Ave., Toronto, ON M9W 6R4
416-798-9778, Fax: 416-798-9671
info@dogsincanada.com
www.dogsincanada.com
Circulation: 120,000 *Frequency: Annual*
Ann McDonagh, Publisher

Dogs, Dogs, Dogs!
PO Box 157 Brooklin, Toronto, ON L1M 1B5
416-203-8186, Fax: 905-620-0805
info@dogsx3.com
www.dogsx3.com
Frequency: 6 times a year
Jackie Lindsay, Publisher & Editor

Magazine Animal
141, rue des Perce Neige, Otterburn Park, QC J3H 5V1
450-467-0064, Fax: 450-467-0060
www.magazineanimal.com
Frequency: 10 fois par an
France Philippon, Éditrice

Modern Dog
#202, 343 Railway St., Vancouver, BC V6A 1A4
604-734-3131, Fax: 604-734-3031
info@moderndogmagazine.com
www.moderndogmagazine.com
Frequency: 4 times a year
Connie Wilson, Editor-in-chief

Pets Magazine
905-771-7333, Fax: 905-771-7336, 877-738-7624
editor@petsmagazine.ca
www.petsmagazine.ca
Circulation: 36,565 *Frequency: 6 times a year*
Cora Golden, Director, Advertising Sales
Blair Adams, Editor-in-chief
Ellen Kral, Publisher

Pets Quarterly Magazine
PO Box 90510, 230 Markham Rd., Scarborough, ON M1J 3N7
416-955-1550, Fax: 416-955-1391
jeaton@capmagazines.ca
www.capmagazines.ca/petsquarterly/index.html
Circulation: 53,800 *Frequency: 4 times a year*
Kelly Chase, Editor
Adrienne Ramsay, Manager, Advertising
Jim Eaton, Publisher

Arts, Art & Antiques

Border Crossings
#500, 70 Arthur St., Winnipeg, MB R3B 1G7
204-942-5778, Fax: 204-949-0793, 866-825-7165
bordercrossings@mts.net
bordercrossingsmag.com
Circulation: 5,500 *Frequency: 4 times a year; ISSN: 0831-2559*
Meeka Walsh, Editor
Robert Enright, Editor-at-large

C international contemporary art magazine
C The Visual Arts Foundation, PO Box 5 B, Toronto, ON M5T 2T2
416-539-9495, Fax: 416-539-9903, 800-745-6312
general@cmagazine.com
www.cmagazine.com
Circulation: 3,000 *Frequency: 4 times a year; ISSN: 1480-5472*

Canadian Art
#210, 51 Front St. East, Toronto, ON M5E 1B3
416-368-8854, Fax: 416-368-6135, 800-222-4762
info@canadianart.ca
www.canadianart.ca
Circulation: 23,500 *Frequency: 4 times a year; ISSN: 0825-3854*
Melony Ward, Publisher, mward@canadianart.ca
Richard Rhodes, Editor, rhodes@canadianart.ca

Capers Aweigh Annual Anthology
142 Lornest, Sydney, NS B1P 4H4
902-849-0822, Fax: 902-564-4144
capersaweigh@hotmail.com
Circulation: 500 *Frequency: Annually*
John MacNeil, Publisher

Cityart Magazine
PO Box 1063 F, Toronto, ON M4Y 2T7
416-925-5564, Fax: 416-925-2972
info@artfocus.com
www.artfocus.com/cityart.html
Circulation: 8,000 *Frequency: 3 times a year*
Pat Fleisher, Publisher/Editor

Dance International
The Vancouver Ballet Society, Level 6, 677 Davie St., Vancouver, BC V6B 2G6
604-681-1525, Fax: 604-681-7732
danceint@direct.ca
www.danceinternational.org
Circulation: 4,000 *Frequency: 4 times a year; ISSN: 1189-9816*
Maureen Riches, Editor

Downhomer Magazine
43 James Lane, St. John's, NL A1E 3H3
709-726-5113, Fax: 709-726-2135
mail@downhomer.com
www.downhomer.com
Circulation: 35,180 *Frequency: Monthly*
Ron Young, Publisher

ETC Montréal
#250, 1435, rue St-Alexandre, Montréal, QC H3A 2G4
514-848-1125, Fax: 514-848-0071
etcmtl@dsuper.net
www.etcmontreal.com
Circulation: 2 500 *Frequency: 4 fois par an*
Isabelle Lelarge, Rédacteur-en-chef

Galleries West
#301, 690 Princeton Way SW, Calgary, AB T2P 5J9
403-234-7097, Fax: 403-243-4649
www.gallerieswest.ca
Frequency: 3 times a year
Jennifer MacLeod, Editor

Inter
Les Éditions intervention, 345, rue du Pont, Québec, QC G1K 6M4
418-529-9680, Fax: 418-529-6933
infos@inter-lelieu.org
www.inter-lelieu.org
Circulation: 1 200 *Frequency: 3 fois par an*

Inter, art actuel
345, rue du Pont, Québec, QC G1K 6M4
418-529-9680, Fax: 418-529-6933
edinter@total.net
Circulation: 1 200 *Frequency: 3 times a year; ISSN: 0825-8708*
Nathalie Perreault, Coordinator

Inuit Art Quarterly
Inuit Art Foundation, 2081 Merivale Rd., Ottawa, ON K2G 1G9
613-224-8189, Fax: 613-224-2907
iaq@inuitart.org
www.inuitart.org
Circulation: 3,500 *Frequency: 4 times a year; ISSN: 0831-6708*
Marybelle Mitchell, Editor

Jump Magazine
#306, 6021 Yonge St., Toronto, ON M2M 3W2
416-657-8884, Fax: 416-658-5385
info@blackpages.ca
www.blackpages.ca
Circulation: 50,000 *Frequency: quarterly*
Lynrod Douglas, Publisher

Muse
Canadian Museums Assn., #400, 280 Metcalfe St., Ottawa, ON K2P 1R7
613-567-0099, Fax: 613-233-5438
info@museums.ca
www.museums.ca
Circulation: 2,500 *Frequency: 6 times a year; English & French; ISSN: 0820-0165*

Muzik Etc./Drums Etc.
753, rue Ste-Hélène, Longueuil, QC J4K 3R5
450-651-4257, Fax: 450-670-8683
montrealdrumfest.com
Circulation: 30,000 *Frequency: 6 times a year*
Serge Gamache, Publisher
Ralph Anelillo, Editor

The National Ballet of Canada Souvenir Magazine
#101, 5397 Eglinton Ave. West, Toronto, ON M9C 5K6
416-928-2909, Fax: 416-966-1181, 800-320-6420
debby@scoregolf.com
Circulation: 6,000 *Frequency: Annual*
Kim Locke, Publisher

Ontario Craft
Designers Walk, #300, 170 Bedford Rd., Toronto, ON M5R 2K9
416-925-4222, Fax: 416-925-4223
ontariocraftscouncil@craft.on.ca
www.craft.on.ca
Circulation: 2,500 *Frequency: 2 times a year; ISSN: 0229-1320*
Deborah Kirkegaard, Program & Development Officer

Parachute
#501, 4060, boul St-Laurent, Montréal, QC H2W 1Y9
514-842-9805, Fax: 514-842-9319
info@parachute.ca
www.parachute.ca
Circulation: 4,000 *Frequency: 4 times a year; ISSN: 0318-7020*
C. Pontbriand, Rédacteur

Qui Fait Quoi
#200, 3430, rue Saint-Denis, Montréal, QC H2X 3L3
514-842-5333, Fax: 514-842-6717
info@qfq.com
www.qfq.com
Other information: n7
Circulation: 7,000 *Frequency: 9 times a year*
Claude Desjardins, Publisher

Rotunda
c/o Royal Ontario Museum, 100 Queen's Park, Toronto, ON M5S 2C6

416-586-5758, Fax: 416-586-5649
sandrap@rom.on.ca
www.rom.on.ca
Circulation: 27,000 *Frequency: 3 times a year; ISSN: 0035-8495*
Sandra Piller, Executive Editor

Sequences
CP 26 Haute-Ville, Québec, QC G1R 4M8
418-656-5040, Fax: 418-656-7282
revue.cap-aux-diamants@hst.ulaval.ca
www.revuesequences.com
Circulation: 1 400 *Frequency: 6 fois par an*
Elie Castiel, Rédacteur-en-chef
Yves Beauregard, Directeur

Slate
155 King St. East, Kingston, ON K7L 2Z9
613-542-3717, Fax: 613-542-1447, 800-871-8093
info@slateartguide.com
www.slateartguide.com
Circulation: 12,000 *Frequency: 8 times a year*
Allan Lochhead, Publisher

Spirale
6742, rue Saint-Denis, Montréal, QC H3K 1G6
514-934-5651, Fax: 514-934-6390
spiralemagazine@yahoo.com
www.spiralemagazine.com
Circulation: 1 500
Pierre L'Hérault, Direction

Storyteller Magazine
TYO Communications, 3687 Twin Falls Pl., Ottawa, ON K1V 1W6
613-521-9734, Fax: 613-521-1753
info@storytellermagazine.com
www.storytellermagazine.com
Circulation: 2,000 *Frequency: 4 times a year*
Terry Tyo, Publisher

Take One
#482, 283 Danforth Ave., Toronto, ON M4K 1N2
416-944-1096, Fax: 416-465-4356
takeone@interlog.com
www.takeonemagazine.ca
Circulation: 5,000 *Frequency: 4 times a year; ISSN: 1192-5507*
Wyndham Wise, Publisher

Vie des Arts
#400, 486, rue Sainte-Catherine ouest, Montréal, QC H3B 1A6
514-282-0205, Fax: 514-282-0235
arts@qc.aira.com
www.viedesarts.com
Circulation: 3 386 *Frequency: 4 fois par an; français avec section en anglais; ISSN: 0042-5435*
Bernard Lévy, Rédacteur

Westbridge Art Market Report
1737 Fir St., Vancouver, BC V6J 5J9
604-736-1014, Fax: 604-734-4944
info@westbridge-fineart.com
www.westbridge-fineart.com

Published free online only
Anthony R. Westbridge, Publisher & Editor

Automobile, Cycle, & Automotive Accessories

Canadian Biker
735 Market St., Victoria, BC V8T 2E2
250-384-0333, Fax: 250-384-1832, 800-667-5667
canbike@canadianbiker.com
www.canadianbiker.com
Circulation: 20,000 *Frequency: 10 times a year; ISSN: 1196-7218*
Len Creed, Editor & Publisher
Marilyn Piercey, Circulation Manager

Canadian Classics & Performance
PO Box 342, O'Leary, PE C0B 1V0
902-859-3869, Fax: 902-859-1539, 877-859-1539
dale@lidstonepub.pe.ca
www.canadianclassicsmag.com
Circulation: 11,000 *Frequency: 12 times a year*
Dale Lidstone, Publisher, dale@lidstonepub.pe.ca

Canadian International Auto Show Program
#4, 447 Speers Rd., Oakville, ON L6K 3S7
905-842-6591, Fax: 905-842-6843
Circulation: 50,000 *Frequency: Annual*
J. Scott Robinson, Publisher

Carguide/Le Magazine Carguide
905-842-6591, Fax: 905-842-6843
mailbox@FormulaPublications.com
www.CarguideMagazine.com
Circulation: 333,043 *Frequency: 6 times a year, English & French editions*
Joe Knycha, Editor-in-chief
J. Scott Robinson, Publisher

Cycle Canada
450-444-5773, Fax: 514-444-6773, 866-522-5656
www.cyclecanadamagazine.net
Circulation: 38,000 *Frequency: 10 issues a year; ISSN: 0319-2822*
Costa Mouzouris, Editor
Jean Lemieux, Publisher

Lemon-Aid Magazine / Roulez sans vous faire rouler
c/o Automobile Protection Association, 292, boul St-Joseph ouest, Montréal, QC H2V 2N7
514-272-5555, Fax: 514-273-0797
apamontreal@apa.ca
www.apa.ca

Luxury Vehicles Magazine
3 Ainsley Gardens, Toronto, ON M9A 1M5
416-233-2171,
Circulation: 177,405 *Frequency: Quarterly*
John D. Duncan, Publisher
Bob English, Editor, 519/833-2089

Le Monde de l'Auto
LC Media inc., 4105, boul Matte, Brossard, QC J4Y 2P4
450-444-5773, Fax: 450-444-6773, 866-522-5656

Le Monde du VTT
215, rue Principale, Saint-Amable, QC J0L 1N0
450-922-9010, Fax: 450-922-8211
info@motomag.qc.ca
Circulation: 9 560 *Frequency: 6 times a year*
Richard Jetté, Éditeur

Moto Journal
514-738-9439, Fax: 514-738-4929, 800-561-0318
turbocirculation@qc.aibn.com
www.motojournalmagazine.net
Circulation: 12 644 *Frequency: 10 fois par an; ISSN: 0319-2865*
Didier Constant, Éditeur
Claude Leonard, Rédacteur

Motocycliste
Fédération Motocycliste du Québec, #208, 4875, boul Métropolitan est, Montréal, QC H1R 3J2
514-252-8121, Fax: 514-252-7857
fmq@fmq.qc.ca
www.fmq.qc.ca
Circulation: 15 500 *Frequency: 5 fois par an*

MOTOMAG
1730 - 55e av, Lachine, QC H8T 3J5
514-631-6550, Fax: 514-631-0591
Circulation: 11 234 *Frequency: 6 fois par an*
Genevieve Pepin, Chief Editor
Michel Crepault, Publisher

Old Autos
PO Box 250, 348 Main St., Bothwell, ON N0P 1C0
519-695-2303, Fax: 519-695-3716, 800-461-3457
www.oldautos.ca
Circulation: 19,263 *Frequency: 24 times a year*
Murray McEwan, Publisher/Editor

Ottawa-Gatineau International Auto Show Program
#4, 447 Speers Rd., Oakville, ON L6K 3S7
905-842-6591, Fax: 905-842-6843
jknycha@formulapublications.com
www.formulamediagroup.com
Circulation: 10,000 *Frequency: Annual*
J. Scott Robinson, Publisher

Performance Racing News
1009678 Ontario Inc., 593 Yonge St., Toronto, ON M4Y 1Z4
416-922-7223, Fax: 416-922-8001, 800-667-7223
editor@prn.com
www.prnmag.com
Circulation: 11,691 *Frequency: 12 times a year*
Frank Spezzano, Group Publisher
Neal Jones, Editor-in-chief

Pole Position
553, rue Calixa-Lavallée, Beloeil, QC J3G 4B6
450-464-4076, Fax: 450-464-7742
info@poleposition.ca
www.poleposition.ca
Circulation: 16,625 *Frequency: 8 times a year*
Philippe Brasseur, Editor

Vancouver International Auto Show Program
Carling Media, #70, 10551 Shellbridge Way, Richmond, BC V6X 2W9
604-214-9964, Fax: 604-214-9965
autoshowinfo@newcardealers.ca
www.bcautoshow.com
Circulation: 50,000
Glen Ringdal, Publisher

Vélo Mag
514-521-8356, Fax: 514-521-5711, 800-567-8356
velomag@velo.qc.ca
www.velomag.com
Circulation: 15 000 *Frequency: 6 fois par an; français*
Jacques Sennechael, Rédacteur-en-chef

World of Wheels
1 Yonge St., Toronto, ON M5E 1P9
416-869-4010, Fax: 416-869-4183
editor@wheels.ca, torstar@torstar.ca
www.wheels.ca
Circulation: 26,099 *Frequency: 6 times a year; ISSN: 0824-5487*
Michael Bettencourt, Managing Editor
J. Scott Robinson, Publisher

Aviation & Aerospace

Canadian Aviation Historical Society Journal
PO Box 705 P, Toronto, ON M5S 2Y4
416-410-9774, Fax: 416-923-3425
cahsnatmem@sympatico.ca
www.cahs.com
Circulation: 1,100 *Frequency: 4 times a year*
W. Wheeler, Editor

Babies & Mothers

The Baby & Child Care Encyclopaedia
416-537-2604, Fax: 416-538-1794
admin@parentscanada.com
Circulation: 100,000 *Frequency: 2 times a year (May & Nov.).*
Donald G. Swinburne, Publisher

Best Wishes
416-537-2604, Fax: 416-538-1794, 866-457-3320
admin@parentscanada.com
www.parentscanada.com
Circulation: 142,260 *Frequency: 2 times a year (May & Nov.)*
Donald G. Swinburne, Publisher
Susan Pennell-Sebekos, Editor, susanp@parentscanada.com

C'est Pour Quand? Revue prénatale
2260, des Patriotes, Laval, QC H7L 3K8
450-622-0091, Fax: 450-622-0099
mlemoyne@qc.aira.com
Circulation: 43 000 *Frequency: 2 fois par an; français*
Manon Le Moyne, Éditrice & Rédactrice-en-chef

The Compleat Mother - The Magazine of Pregnancy, Birth & Breastfeeding
PO Box 38033, Calgary, AB T3K 5G9
403-255-0246, Fax: 403- -
thecompleatmother@shaw.ca
www.thecompleatmother.com
Circulation: 8,000 *Frequency: 4 times a year*
Angela van Son, Publisher & Editor

Expecting Magazine
416-537-2604, Fax: 416-538-1794
admin@parentscanada.com
www.parentscanada.com
Circulation: 146,649 *Frequency: 3 times a year*
Donald G. Swinburne, President

Grossesse
468, boul Roland-Thierrien, Longueuil, QC J4H 4E3
450-677-2556, Fax: 450-677-4097
Circulation: 20 000 *Frequency: 2 fois par an*
Richard Desmarais, Rédacteur

Mère Nouvelle
1 Mount Pleasant Rd., 8th Fl., Toronto, ON M4Y 2Y5
416-764-2850, Fax: 416-764-2894
maria.paguirigan@tpg.rogers.com
toronto.todaysparent.com

Circulation: 35 700 *Frequency: 2 fois par an*
Holly Bennett, Rédactrice

Mon Bébé Revue Postnatale
2260, des Patriotes, Laval, QC H7L 3K8
450-622-0091, Fax: 450-622-0099
mlemoyne@qc.aira.com
Circulation: 43 000 *Frequency: 2 fois par an; français*
Manon Le Moyne, Éditrice & Rédactrice-en-chef

Newborn
1 Mount Pleasant Rd., 8th Fl., Toronto, ON M4Y 2Y5
416-764-2844, Fax: 416-764-2894
Tiziana.Roberts@tpg.rogers.com
toronto.todaysparent.com
Circulation: 132,875 *Frequency: 2 times a year; English & French editions*
Holly Bennett, Editor
Tiziana Roberts, Publisher

Spécial Bébé
186, rue Val Chenaie, Rosemère, QC J7A 4B6
514-331-0661, Fax: 514-331-8821
Circulation: 38 000 *Frequency: 2 fois par an*
Ronald Lapierre, Rédacteur

Today's Parent Pregnancy & Birth
1 Mount Pleasant Rd., 8th Fl., Toronto, ON M4Y 2Y5
416-764-2883, Fax: 416-764-2801
askus@todaysparent.com
www.todaysparent.com
Circulation: 132,875 *Frequency: 2 times a year*
Holly Bennett, Editor
Tiziana Roberts, Publisher

Boating & Yachting

Boat Guide
905-842-6591, Fax: 905-842-6843
boatbiz@idirect.ca
www.carguideca.com
Circulation: 60,000 *Frequency: 2 times a year*
Scott Robinson, Publisher
Lizanne Madigan, Editor

Boating East Ports & Cruising Guide
Marble Rock Rd., RR#2, Gananoque, ON K7G 2V4
613-382-5735, Fax: 613-382-8326
boateast@kos.net
Circulation: 20,000 *Frequency: Annually, May*
K. Christensen, Contact

Boats & Places
#13, 130 Saunders Rd., Barrie, ON L4N 9A8
705-725-4669, Fax: 705-725-4669
info@boatsandplaces.com
www.boatsandplaces.com
Circulation: 24,692 *Frequency: 6 times per year*
Brian Minton, Publisher
Amanda Dyer Comission, Editor

Canadian Yachting
Kerrwil Publications Limited, #201, 49 Bathurst St., Toronto, ON MV5 2P2
416-703-7167, Fax: 416-703-1330
www.cymagazine.ca
Circulation: 24,500 *Frequency: 6 times a year; ISSN: 0384-0999*
Elizabeth Kerr, Publisher

DIY Boat Owner
PO Box 118, Lindsay, ON K9V 4R8
705-359-2094, Fax: 705-359-2097, 888-658-2628
info@diy-boat.com
www.diy-boat.com
Circulation: 20,000 *Frequency: 4 times a year*
Jan Mundy, Publisher & Editor

L'Escale Nautique
418-863-5055, Fax: 418-692-5198
redaction@escalenautique.qc.ca
www.escalenautique.qc.ca
Circulation: 12 000 *Frequency: 4 fois par an, plus guide nautique; français*
Michel Sacco, Rédacteur-en-chef

Gam on Yachting
#202, 250 The Esplanade, Toronto, ON M5A 1J2
416-368-1559, Fax: 416-368-2831
gam@passport.ca
www.gamonyachting.com
Circulation: 13,500 *Frequency: 8 times a year*
Craig M. Green, Manager, Sales
Karin Larson, Publisher & Editor

Ontario Sailor Magazine
91 Hemmingway Dr., Courtice, ON L1E 2C2
905-434-7409, Fax: 905-434-1654
sails@istar.ca
www.ontariosailormagazine.ca
Circulation: 8,000/issue *Frequency: 7 times a year*
Sandra McDowell, Publisher
Greg McDowell, Managing Editor

Pacific Yachting
#900, 1080 Howe St., Vancouver, BC V6Z 2T1
604-606-4644, Fax: 604-687-1925, 800-816-0747
info@oppublishing.com
www.oppublishing.com
Circulation: 16,975 *Frequency: Monthly*
Mark Yelic, Publisher
Peter Robson, Editor

Les Plaisanciers
#310, 970, Montée de Liesse, Saint-Laurent, QC H4T 1W7
514-856-0788, Fax: 514-856-0790
roy@magazinelesplaisanciers.com
Circulation: 20 000 *Frequency: 5 fois par an; français*
Roy Baird, Sr., Publisher
Claude Leonard, Editor

Port Hole / Le Hublot
c/o Canadian Power & Sail Squadrons, 26 Golden Gate Ct., Toronto, ON M1P 3A5
416-293-2438, Fax: 416-293-2445, 888-277-2628
hqg@cps-ecp.ca
www.cps-ecp.ca
Circulation: 28,000 *Frequency: 4 times a year; English & French*
Joan Eyolfson Cadham, Editor-in-chief

Power Boating Canada
#5, 1020 Brevik Pl., Mississauga, ON L4W 4N7
905-624-8218, Fax: 905-624-6764
www.powerboating.com
Frequency: 7 times a year
William Taylor, Publisher
Steve Fennel, Editor

Québec Yachting
912, rue Bellerive, Longueuil, QC J4J 1A7
450-670-0377, Fax: 450-670-5262
quebecyachting@videotron.ca
Circulation: 10 500 *Frequency: 6 fois par an; français*
Pierre Hudon, Co-Editor
Henri R. de Cotret, Co-Editor

Windsport Magazine
SBC Media Inc., #3266, 2255B Queen St. East, Toronto, ON M4E 1G3
416-406-2400, Fax: 416-406-0656
info@windsport.com
www.windsport.com
Circulation: 26,000 *Frequency: 4 times a year*
John Bryja, Editor

Books

Amphora
c/o Alcuin Society, PO Box 3216, Vancouver, BC V6B 3X8
604-937-3293
info@alcuinsociety.com
www.alcuinsociety.com
Circulation: 340 *Frequency: Quarterly; ISSN: 0003-200x*
Rollin Milroy, amphora@alcuinsociety.com

BC BookWorld
A.R.T. BookWorld Productions, 3516 West 13th Ave., Vancouver, BC V6R 2S3
604-736-4011, Fax: 604-736-4011
bookworld@telus.net
www.bcbookworld.com
Circulation: 100,000 *Frequency: 4 times a year; ISSN 0847-7728*
Alan Twigg, Publisher
David Lester, Editor

Brides, Bridal

Mariage Québec
#1301, 1155, rue Université, Montréal, QC H3B 3A7
514-284-2552, Fax: 514-284-4492
info@mariagequebec.com
www.mariagequebec.com
Circulation: 22 915 *Frequency: 2 fois par an; français*
Denyse Clermont, Éditrice
Claude LaFramboise, Directeur de la direction

Sposa Magazine
c/o Jasmin Publishing, #202, 55 York St., Toronto, ON M5J 1R7
416-364-5899, Fax: 416-364-5996
editor@sposa.com
www.sposa.com
Circulation: 50,000 *Frequency: 2 times a year*
Gulshan Sippy, Editor

Today's Bride
416-537-2604, Fax: 416-538-1794
Circulation: 99, 361 *Frequency: 2 times a year*
Donald G. Swinburne, Publisher

WeddingBells
#320, 111 Queen St. East, Toronto, ON M5C 1S2
416-364-3333, Fax: 416-594-3374
feedback@weddingbells.ca
www.weddingbells.ca
Circulation: 103,500 *Frequency: 2 times a year; ISSN: 1203-0392*
Alethea Wakefield, Associate Publisher

Business & Finance

The Bay Street Bull
#208, 80 Park Lawn Rd., Toronto, ON M8Y 3H8
416-252-4356, Fax: 416-252-0838
info@thebaystreetbull.com
www.thebaystreetbull.com

Magazine for men and women who make up Canada's leading business community
Stephen Petherbridge, Publisher

Business in Vancouver
102 East 4th St., Vancouver, BC V5T 1G2
604-688-2398, Fax: 604-688-1963
www.biv.com
Circulation: 16,000 *Frequency: Weekly, Tue.*
Business in Vancouver is an award-winning weekly newspaper serving Greater Vancouver since 1989. Targeted at business decision-makers, it provides local business news and information every Tuesday and reaches more than 62,000+ readers a week.
Tom Siba, Publisher

Business Niagara Magazine
159 York St., St Catharines, ON L2R 6E9
905-682-4509, Fax: 905-682-8219
www.bizniagara.com
Circulation: 20,000
Released bi-monthly by Osprey Media Group Inc., Business Niagara Magazine reaches over 20,000 registered businesses and is geared to everyone from a one-person operation to a large publicly traded organization.
Mishka Balsom, Publisher

Canadian MoneySaver
PO Box 370, 5540 Loyalist Pkwy., Bath, ON K0H 1G0
613-352-7448, Fax: 613-352-7700
moneyinfo@canadianmoneysaver.ca
www.canadianmoneysaver.ca
Circulation: 69,700 *Frequency: 9 times a year*
Canadian MoneySaver is an acclaimed investment advisory with a recognized reputation for providing a trustworthy and down-to-earth service since 1981. Canadian MoneySaver publishes monthly with three double issues (July/August, November/December and March/April).
Dale Ennis, Publisher/Editor-in-Chief

Canadian Shareowner Magazine
#806, 4 King St. West, Toronto, ON M5H 1B6
416-595-9600, Fax: 416-595-0400, 800-268-6881
magazine@ShareOwner.com
www.shareowner.com
Circulation: 20,876 *Frequency: 6 times a year; ISSN: 0836-0960*
Periodical offering a proprietary Stock Selection Guide to find stocks in which subscribers ought to consider investing
John T. Bart, Publisher & Editor

Pensez-y bien!
Les Éditions EJS, 13, ch du Pied-de-Roi, Lac Beaufort, QC G0A 2C0
418-686-1940, Fax: 418-871-0972
info@ejs.qc.ca
www.ejs.qc.ca
Circulation: 150 000 *Frequency: 4 fois par an; français*
Les articles présentent et expliquent les services et les produits financiers
France Bégin, Éditeur

Votre Avoir: La revue de vos Finances Personnelles
#2001, 1500, rue Notre Dame, Montréal, QC H8S 2E3

514-639-5355, Fax: 514-639-8880
info@votreavoir.com
www.votreavoir.com
Circulation: 34,000 *Frequency: 6 times a year*
Revue de finances personnelles
Roger Déry, Éditeur

Camping & Outdoor Recreation

Camping Caravaning
Communication Camping Caravaning, CP 1000 M, 4545, av Pierre de Coubertin, Montréal, QC H1V 3R2
514-252-3003, Fax: 514-254-0694, 866-237-3722
communication@fqcc.qc.ca
www.campingquebec.com
Circulation: 46 000 *Frequency: 8 fois par an*
Paul Laquerre, Rédacteur-en-chef

Camping in Ontario
Ontario Private Campground Assn., #8, 220 Royal Crest Ct., Markham, ON L43 9Y2
Fax: 905-947-9501, 877-672-2226
opca@campinginontario.ca
www.campinginontario.ca
Circulation: 200,000 *Frequency: Annually, Jan.*
Beth Potter, Executive Director

explore
Quarto Communications, 54 St. Patrick St., Toronto, ON M5T 1V1
416-599-2000, Fax: 416-599-0800, 877-874-5253
explore@explore-mag.com
www.explore-mag.com
Circulation: 30,000 *Frequency: 6 times a year; 0714-816X*
Al Zikovitz, Publisher
James Little, Editor

Kanawa: Canada's Paddling Magazine
Paddle Canada, PO Box 20069 Taylor-Kidd, Kingston, ON K7P 2T6
613-521-7267, Fax: 613-547-6292, 888-252-6292
info@paddlingcanada.com
www.paddlingcanada.com
Circulation: 21,000 *Frequency: 4 times a year; ISSN: 1198-9580*
Anne Baxter, Managing Director
Richard Alexander, President, Canadian Recreational Canoeing Association

RV Gazette
Explorer RV Club, #6, 328 Mill St., Beaverton, ON L0K 1A0
705-426-1419, Fax: 705-426-1403, 800-999-0819
info@rvgazette.com
www.rvgazette.com
Circulation: 13,304 *Frequency: 6 times a year*
Marcia Anderson, General Manager

Vie en Plein Air
#310, 970, Montée de Liesse, Saint-Laurent, QC H4T 1W7
514-856-0787, Fax: 514-856-0790
Circulation: 20 000 *Frequency: 4 fois par an; français*
Claude Leonard, Éditeur

Children's

ChickaDEE
#400, 10 Lower Spadina Ave., Toronto, ON M5V 2Z2
416-340-2700, Fax: 416-340-9769, 800-551-6957
chickadee@owlkids.com
www.owlkids.com
Circulation: 95,000 *Frequency: 10 times a year; ISSN: 0707-4611*
Mary Vincent, Publisher

Chirp
#400, 10 Lower Spadina Ave., Toronto, ON M5V 2Z2
416-340-2700, Fax: 416-340-9769, 800-551-6957
chirp@owlkids.com
www.owlkids.com
Circulation: 75,000 *Frequency: 10 times a year; ISSN: 1206-4580*
Sarah Trusty, Assistant Editor

Les Débrouillards
4475, rue Frontenac, Montréal, QC H2H 2S2
514-844-2111, Fax: 514-278-3030
scientifix@lesdebrouillards.qc.ca
www.lesdebrouillards.qc.ca
Circulation: 37 000 *Frequency: 10 fois par an; français*
Félix Maltais, Éditeur
Isabelle Vaillancourt, Rédactrice-en-chef

Les Explorateurs
Les Publications BLD, 4475, rue Frontenac, Montréal, QC H2H 2S2
514-844-2111, Fax: 514-278-3030
lesexplorateurs@lesdebrouillards.qc.ca
www.lesexplos.qc.ca
Félix Maltais, Éditeur
Sarah Perreault, Rédactrice en chef

Famous Kids
#100, 102 Atlantic Ave., Toronto, ON M6K 1X9
416-539-8800, Fax: 416-539-8511
Frequency: 4 times a year
Salah Bachir, Publisher

J'Aime Lire
4475, rue Frontenac, Montréal, QC H2H 2S2
514-844-2111, Fax: 514-278-3030, 800-313-3020
redaction@bayardpresse.qc.ca
www.bayardjeunesse.ca
Circulation: 23 000
Suzanne Spino, Directrice générale

Kids Tribute
71 Barber Greene Rd., Toronto, ON M3C 2A2
416-445-0544, Fax: 416-445-2894
generalinfo@tribute.ca
www.tribute.ca
Circulation: 300,000 *Frequency: 4 times a year*
Sandra Stewart, Publisher & Editor

kidsworld Magazine
#301, 177 Danforth Ave., Toronto, ON M4K 1N2
416-466-4956, Fax: 416-466-5002
kidsworld@kidsworld-online.com
www.kidsworld-online.com
Circulation: 300,000 *Frequency: 5 times a year*
Michael Sheasgreen, Publisher

The Magazine not for Adults / Le Magazine Interdit aux Adultes
643 Queen St. East, Toronto, ON M4M 1G4
416-778-8727, Fax: 416-778-8726
letters@themagazine.ca
www.themagazine.ca
Circulation: 3,800,000 *Frequency: 12 times a year*
Eric Conroy, Publisher

OWL Magazine
#400, 10 Lower Spadina Ave., Toronto, ON M5V 2Z2
416-340-2700, Fax: 416-340-9769, 800-551-6957
owl@owlkids.com
www.owlkids.com
Circulation: 75,000 *Frequency: 10 times a year; ISSN: 0382-6627*
Craig Battle, Associate Editor

Planète 912
#301, 177 Danforth Ave., Toronto, ON M4K 1N2
416-466-4956, Fax: 416-466-5002
Circulation: 75,000 *Frequency: 5 times a year*
Michael Sheasgreen, Publisher
Martine Becquet, Editor

YES Mag: Canada's Science Magazine For Kids
#501, 3960 Quadra St., Victoria, BC V8X 4A3
250-477-5543, Fax: 250-477-5390
info@yesmag.ca
www.yesmag.ca
Circulation: 18,000 *Frequency: bi-monthly*
David Garrison, Publisher

City Magazine

Avenue
RedPoint Media Group Inc., #105, 1210 - 20th Ave. SE, Calgary, AB T2G 1M8
403-240-9055, Fax: 403-240-9059
info@redpointmedia.ca
www.avenuemagazine.ca
Circulation: 27,000 *Frequency: 10 times a year*
Gary Davies, Publisher, gdavies@redpointmedia.ca
Jennifer Hamilton, Managing Editor, jhamilton@redpointmedia.ca
Kathe Lemon, Editor, klemon@redpointmedia.ca

eye
625 Church St., 6th Fl., Toronto, ON M4Y 2G1
416-596-4393, Fax: 416-504-4341
www.eye.net
Circulation: 95,893 *Frequency: Weekly*
Peter Burke, Publisher

Fast Forward Weekly
Great West Publishing, #206, 1210 - 20th Ave. SE, Calgary, AB T2G 3G2
403-244-2235, Fax: 403-244-1431
info@ffwd.greatwest.ca
www.ffwdweekly.com
Circulation: 24,000 *Frequency: Weekly*

The Georgia Straight
1701 West Broadway St., Vancouver, BC V6J 1Y3
604-730-7000, Fax: 604-730-7010
info@straight.com
www.straight.com
Circulation: 115,238 *Frequency: Weekly*
Dan McLeod, Publisher/Editor, 604/730-7088

Le Guide Prestige Montréal
#700, 2160, de la Montagne, Montréal, QC H3G 2T3
514-982-9823, Fax: 514-289-9160
tamara@prestipresse.com
Circulation: 150,000 *Frequency: 4 times a year; English & French*
Peter Weiss, Publisher
André Ducharme, Editor-in-chief

Hamilton Magazine
905-634-8003, Fax: 905-634-7661
info@townmedia.ca
www.hamiltonmagazine.com
Circulation: 39,901 *Frequency: 5 times a year*
Wayne Narciso, Publisher
David Young, Editor

HighGrader
PO Box 624, Timmins, ON P4N 1E9
705-266-4950
: highgrader@nt.net
www.highgradermagazine.com
Circulation: 2,500
Brit Griffin, Publisher

Hour
Communications Voir Inc., 355, rue Ste-Catherine ouest, 7e étage, Montréal, QC H3B 1A5
514-848-0777, Fax: 514-848-9004
info@hour.ca
www.hour.ca
Circulation: 49,000 *Frequency: 52 times a year*
Jamie O'Meara, Editor-in-chief

In Montréal
1, Carré Cummings Sq., Montréal, QC H3W 1M6
514-345-2645, Fax: 514-345-2655
info@inmontreal.com
Frequency: 6 times a year

International Guide, Banff
403-760-3484
igpub@telusplanet.net
www.igpublications.com
Circulation: 18,000
Wayne Kehoe, Publisher
Cherie Rautio, Editor

Kingston Life Magazine
PO Box 1352, Kingston, ON K7L 5C6
613-549-8442, Fax: 613-549-4333
Frequency: 4 times a year
Mary Laflamme, Publisher

Legacy
9667 - 87th Ave., Edmonton, AB T6C 1K5
780-439-0705, Fax: 780-439-0549
legacy@legacymagazine.ab.ca
www.legacymagazine.ab.ca
Circulation: 8,700 *Frequency: 4 times a year; ISSN: 1203-5769*
Barbara Dacks, Publisher

Lethbridge Living
PO Box 22005 Henderson Lake, 1518 - 3rd Ave. S, Lethbridge, AB T1K 6X5
403-381-1454, Fax: 403-329-0264
editor@lethbridgeliving.com
lethbridgeliving.com
Circulation: 15,000 *Frequency: 4 times a year*
Martin Oordt, Editor
Mary Oordt, Managing Editor

London City Life Magazine
1147 Gainsborough Rd., London, ON N6H 5L5
519-471-2907, Fax: 519-473-7859
Circulation: 31,000 *Frequency: 6 times a year*
Gord Delamont, Publisher & Editor

Monday Magazine
Island Publisher Ltd., 818 Broughton St., Victoria, BC V8W 1E4
250-382-6188, Fax: 250-382-6014
publisher@mondaymag.com
www.mondaymag.com
Circulation: 40,000 *Frequency: Weekly*
Jim Parker, Publisher

Montreal Mirror
Communications Gratte-Ciel ltée, 465 McGill St., 3rd Fl., Montréal, QC H2Y 4B4
514-393-1010, Fax: 514-393-3173
letters@mtl-mirror.com
www.montrealmirror.com
Circulation: 70,000 *Frequency: Weekly, Thu.*
Alastair Sutherland, Editor-in-charge

Montréal Scope
#202, 4416, boul St-Laurent, Montréal, QC H2W 1Z5
514-933-3333, Fax: 514-933-4286
info@montrealscope.com
Circulation: 40,000 *Frequency: 15 times a year*
Priscilla Baritte, Head Editor & Coordinator

Moving to Magazines.. / Emménager-à
905-479-0641, Fax: 905-479-1286
info@movingto.com
www.movingto.com
Circulation: 240,000 *Frequency: Annually, or bi-annual issues cover all major Canadian cities & areas; 2 bilingual issues, Montréal, Ottawa/Hull*
Michael Rosset

Niagara Life Magazine (a division of Downtowner Publications Inc.)
#1, 3550 Schmon Pkwy., Thorold, ON L2V 4Y5
905-641-1984, Fax: 905-641-0682
niagaralife@on.aibn.com
www.niagaralifemag.com
Circulation: 45,000 *Frequency: 8 times a year*
Ian Oliver, Publisher
Gail Todd, Managing Editor

Northword Magazine
PO Box 817, Smithers, BC V0J 2N0
250-847-4600, Fax: 250-847-4668
www.northword.ca
Frequency: 4 times a year

Now
189 Church St., Toronto, ON M5B 1Y7
416-364-1300, Fax: 416-364-1168
alice@nowtoronto.com
www.nowtoronto.com
Circulation: 108,779 *Frequency: Weekly - Thu.*
Alice Klein, Editor/CEO
Michael Hollett, Editor/Publisher

Off-Centre Magazine
PO Box 1384, Vernon, BC V1T 7H4
250-558-3979, Fax: 250-558-3912
info@off-centre.ca
www.off-centre.ca
Circulation: 17,000 *Frequency: Monthly*
Leanne Allen, Publisher

Okanagan Life Magazine
Byrne Publishing Group Inc., #10, 1753 Dolphin Ave., Kelowna, BC V1Y 8A6
250-861-5399, Fax: 250-868-3040, 888-311-1119
info@okanaganlife.com
www.okanaganlife.com
Circulation: 25,000 *Frequency: 10 times a year*
J. Paul Byrne, Publisher

Ottawa City Magazine
MacKenzie Publishing, #300, 111 Sparks St., Ottawa, ON K1P 5B5
613-688-5433, Fax: 613-688-1994
olife@magma.ca
Circulation: 35,500 *Frequency: 6 times a year*
Dan Donovan, Publisher
Harvey Chartrand, Editor

Ottawa Life Magazine
1A Springfield Rd., Ottawa, ON K1M 1C8
613-688-5433, Fax: 613-688-1994
info@ottawalife.com
www.ottawalife.com
Circulation: 40,000 *Frequency: 6 times a year*
Harvey Chartrand, Editor

The Ottawa X Press
Communications Voir Inc., #204, 396 Cooper St., Ottawa, ON K2P 2H7
613-237-8226, Fax: 613-237-8220, 877-632-8647
info@ottawaexpress.ca
www.ottawaxpress.ca
Circulation: 29,344 *Frequency: Weekly, Thu.*
Matthew Harrison, Editor-in-chief

Pique Newsmagazine
#202, 1390 Alpha Lake Rd., Whistler, BC V0N 1B1
604-938-0202, Fax: 604-938-0201
mail@piquenewsmagazine.com
www.piquenewsmagazine.com
Circulation: 16,500 *Frequency: Weekly, Fri.*
Kathy Barnett, Publisher
Darren ROberts, Director, Advertising
Bob Barnett, Editor

the prairie dog
#201, 1836 Scarth St., Regina, SK S4P 2G3
306-757-8522, Fax: 306-352-9686
reception@prairiedogmag.com
prairiedog.inregina.com
Circulation: 16,000 *Frequency: Bi-weekly*
April Bourgeois, Publisher
Stephen Whitworth, Editor

Profile Kingston
PO Box 91, Kingston, ON K7L 4V6
613-546-6723, Fax: 613-546-0707
editor@profilekingston.com
www.profilekingston.com
Circulation: 16,000 *Frequency: 6 times a year*
Bonnie Golomb, Publisher

Pulse Niagara
Dynasty Communications Inc., #208, 243 Church St., St Catharines, ON L2R 3E8
905-682-5999, Fax: 905-682-1414
www.pulseniagara.com
Circulation: 18,000 *Frequency: Weekly*
Ron Kilpatrick, Publisher/Editor

Thunder Bay Guest Magazine
87 North Hill St., Thunder Bay, ON P7A 5V6
807-345-2625, Fax: 807-345-9923
info@thunderbaypost.com
Circulation: 12,469 *Frequency: 9 times a year*
Richard Sadick, Publisher

Toronto Events Calendar
#460, 20 Eglinton Ave. East, Toronto, ON M4P 1A9
416-782-3322, Fax: 416-787-9299
info@torontoeventscalendar.com
www.torcalendar.com
Frequency: 2 times a year, Jan., June
R.S. Diamond, Editor
Sybil Levine, Publisher

Toronto Life
#320, 111 Queen St. East, Toronto, ON M5C 1S2
416-364-3333, Fax: 416-861-1169
editorial@torontolife.com
www.torontolife.com
Circulation: 91,692 *Frequency: Monthly; ISSN: 0049-4194*
John Macfarlane, Editor

UPtown Magazine
Rosebud Publications Ltd., 1465 St. James St., Winnipeg, MB R3H 0W9
204-949-4370, Fax: 204-949-4376
source@uptownmag.com
www.uptownmag.com
Circulation: 17,000 *Frequency: Weekly*
John Kendle, Editor

Vancouver Magazine
Transcontinental Publishing, #500, 2608 Granville St., Vancouver, BC V6H 3V3
604-877-7732, Fax: 604-877-4823
mail@vancouvermagazine.com
www.vancouvermagazine.com
Circulation: 48,000 *Frequency: 11 times a year*
Kim Peacock, Publisher
Gary Stephen Ross, Editor-in-chief

Victoria Boulevard
PO Box 5417 LCD 9, Victoria, BC V8R 6S4
250-598-8111, Fax: 250-598-3183
baypub@telus.net
www.victoriaboulevard.com
Circulation: 45,000 *Frequency: Bi-monthly*
Evelyn Butler, Publisher

Visitor's Choice, Vancouver
#500, 1155 West Pender St., Vancouver, BC V6E 2P4
604-608-5180, Fax: 604-608-5181, 800-867-5141
info@visitorschoice.com
www.visitorschoice.com
Circulation: 795,000
Pierre Pelletier, Publisher

Voilà Québec
1255, rue Maguire, Sillery, QC G1T 1Z2
418-694-1272, Fax: 418-694-1119
info@voilaquebec.com
Circulation: 70,000 *Frequency: 4 times a year; English & French*
Curtis J. Sommerville, Publisher
Lynn Magee, Editor

Voir Gatineau-Ottawa
#200, 396, rue Cooper, Ottawa, ON K2P 2H7
613-237-8226, Fax: 613-237-8220
www.voir.ca
Frequency: Hebdomadaire, français
Jean-François Landré, Directeur général
Mélissa Proulx, Rédactrice-en-chef

Voir Montréal
375, rue Ste-Catherine ouest, 7e étage, Montréal, QC H3B 1A5
514-848-0805, Fax: 514-848-9004
www.voir.ca
Circulation: 102 000
Christophe Bergeron, Rédacteur-en-chef

Voir Québec
470, rue de la Couronne, Québec, QC G1K 6G2
418-522-7777, Fax: 418-522-7779
info@qc.voit.ca
www.voir.ca
Circulation: 41 725 *Frequency: Hebdomadaire; français, aussi Voir Québec City; 52 par an*
Benoit Paré, Directeur général
David Desjardins, Rédacteur-en-chef

Vue Weekly
10303 - 108th St., Edmonton, AB T5J 1L7
780-426-1996, Fax: 780-426-2889
chris@vueweekly.com
www.vueweekly.com
Circulation: 24,274 *Frequency: Weekly*
Ross Moroz, Managing Editor
Ron Garth, Publisher & Editor

What's Happening Magazine
553 Morrison Point Rd., RR#2, Milford, ON KOK 2P0
613-476-6175, Fax: 613-476-1050
whatshappening@primus.ca
Circulation: 6,000 *Frequency: 4 times a year*
Gudrun Gallo, Editor

Where Calgary
St. Joseph Media Inc., #250, 125 - 9 Ave. SE, Calgary, AB T2G 0P6
403-299-1888, Fax: 403-299-1899
info_calgary@where.ca
www.where.ca/calgary
Circulation: 46,500 *Frequency: Bi-monthly*
Brian French, Publisher

Where Edmonton
Tanner Publishing Ltd., #4, 9343 - 50 St., Edmonton, AB T6B 2L5
780-465-3362, Fax: 780-448-0424
info@whereedmonton.com
www.whereedmonton.com
Circulation: 33,240 *Frequency: 6 times a year*
Rob Tanner, Publisher

Where Halifax
902-420-9943, Fax: 902-429-9058
publishers@metroguide.ca
www.where.ca/halifax
Circulation: 220,000 *Frequency: 10 times per year*
Sheila Blair-Reid, Publisher

Where Ottawa
St. Joseph Media, 226 Argyle Ave., Ottawa, ON K2P 1B9
613-230-0333, Fax: 613-230-4441
dianne@capitalpublishers.com
www.where.ca/ottawa
Circulation: 19,081 *Frequency: Monthly*
Melanie Scott, Editor
Dianne Wing, Publisher

Where Toronto
111 Queen St. East, Toronto, ON M5C 1S2
416-364-3333, Fax: 416-594-3375
editorial@wheretoronto.com
www.wheretoronto.com
Circulation: 74,988 *Frequency: Monthly*
Anne Gibson, Editor-in-chief

Where Victoria
818 Broughton St., Victoria, BC V8W 1E4
250-383-3633, Fax: 250-480-3233
info@wherevictoria.com
www.where.ca/victoria
Circulation: 64,320 *Frequency: 6 times a year*
Anna Scolnick, Publisher

Where Winnipeg
Fanfare Magazine Group, #400, 112 Market Ave., Winnipeg, MB R3B 0P4
204-943-4439, Fax: 204-947-5463
www.wherewinnipeg.com
Circulation: 33,708 *Frequency: 6 times a year*
Brad Hughes, Editor-in-chief
Laurie Hughes, Publisher

Windsor Life Magazine
#318, 5060 Tecumseh Rd. East, Windsor, ON N8T 1C1
519-979-5433, Fax: 519-979-9237
publisher@windsorlife.com
www.windsorlife.com
Circulation: 79,373 Windsor & Essex County *Frequency: 8 times a year*
Robert E. Robinson, Publisher
Hal Sullivan, Editor

YVR Skytalk
#306, 5400 Airport Rd. South, Richmond, BC V7B 1B4
604-736-6754, Fax: 604-736-6750
jstewart@westerndriver.com
www.yvr.ca/authority/news/skytalk.asp
Circulation: 68,000 *Frequency: Monthly*
Patrick Stewart, Publisher

Computing & Technology

Atout Micro
CP 240, Saint-Isidore, QC G0S 2S0
418-882-5214, 866-826-1089
atout@atoutmicro.ca
www.atoutmicro.ca
Other information: Sans frais: 1-866-826-1089
Circulation: 8 000
François Picard, Éditeur & Rédacteur en chef

INFORMATION Highways: The Magazine about Online Information
e-Content Institute, 60 Waterloo Ave., Toronto, ON M3H 3Y2
416-488-7372, Fax: 416-488-7078
info@econtentinstitute.org
www.econtentinstitute.org
Circulation: 5,000 *Frequency: 6 times a year*
David Shinwell, Publisher

We Compute
483 Kennedy Rd., Toronto, ON M1K 2B1
416-264-6938, Fax: 416-266-3614
editors@we-compute.com
Circulation: 150,000 *Frequency: 12 times a year*
Eric Macmillan, Editor
George Bachir, Publisher

Culture, Current Events

Edges: New Planetary Patterns
655 Queen St. East, Toronto, ON M4M 1G4
416-691-2316, Fax: 416-691-2491, 877-691-1422
ica@icacan.ca
www.icacan.ca
Circulation: 12,000 *Frequency: 3 times a year*
Fred Simons, Executive Director
Leah Taylor, Editor

Fuse
#454, 401 Richmond St. West, Toronto, ON M5V 3A8
416-340-8026, Fax: 416-340-0494
info@fusemagazine.org
www.fusemagazine.org
Circulation: 3,300 *Frequency: 4 times a year; ISSN: 0838-603X*
Michael Maranda, Associate Publisher
Izida Zorde, Associate Editor

MIX: Independent Art & Culture Magazine
Parallélogramme Artist-Run Culture & Publishing Inc., #446, 401 Richmond St. West, Toronto, ON M5V 3A8
416-506-1012, Fax: 416-506-0141
editor@mixmagazine.com
www.mixmagazine.com
Circulation: 120,000 *Frequency: 4 times a year; English & French; ISSN: 1204-5349*
Claudia McKoy, Editor-in-Chief

The Newfoundland Herald
PO Box 2015, St. John's, NL A1C 5R7
709-726-7060, Fax: 709-726-6971
www.nfldherald.com
Circulation: 23,913 *Frequency: Weekly*
Mark Dwyer, Managing Editor

Saltscapes Publishing Inc.
#501, 40 Alderney Dr., Dartmouth, NS B2Y 2N5
902-464-7258, Fax: 902-464-3755, 877-311-5877
subscriptions@saltscapes.com
www.saltscapes.com
Circulation: 40,000 *Frequency: 6 times a year*
Jim Gourlay, Publisher
Heather White, Editor

This Magazine
Red Maple Foundation, #396, 401 Richmond St. West, Toronto, ON M5V 3A8
416-979-9429, Fax: 416-979-1143
info@thismagazine.ca
www.thismagazine.ca
Circulation: 8,000 *Frequency: 6 times a year; ISSN: 1491-2678*
Jessica Johnston, Editor
Lisa Whittington-Hill, Publisher

Education

Life Learning Magazine
Life Media, #508, 264 Queen's Quay West, Toronto, ON M5J 1B5
416-260-0303, 800-215-9574
publisher@lifelearningmagazine.com
www.lifelearningmagazine.com
Circulation: 35,000
Wendy Priesnitz, Editor
Rolf Priesnitz, Publisher

Entertainment

CineAction: Radical Film Criticism & Theory
#705, 40 Alexander St., Toronto, ON M4Y 1B5
416-964-3534, Fax: 416- -
smorr@the-wire.com
Circulation: 4,000 *Frequency: 3 times a year; ISSN: 0826-9866*
Robin Wood
Susan Morrison

Cinema Scope
465 Lytton Blvd., Toronto, ON M5N 1S5
www.cinema-scope.com
Mark Peranson, Publisher & Editor
Andrew Tracy, Managing Editor

En Primeur
71 Barber Greene Rd., Toronto, ON M3C 2A2
416-445-0544, Fax: 416-445-2894
www.enprimeur.ca
Circulation: 105,000
Sandra I. Stewart, Publisher

En Primeur Jeunesse
416-445-0544, Fax: 416-445-2894
www.enprimeur.ca
Circulation: 50 000 *Frequency: 4 fois par an; français*

Famous Magazine
1303 Yonge St., Toronto, ON M4T 2Y9
416-539-6600, Fax: 416-539-6616
customerservice@cineplex.com
Circulation: 500,000 *Frequency: 12 times a year*

Festival Cinemas
2236 Queen St. East, Toronto, ON M4E 1G2
416-691-7330,
Circulation: 85,000

Inside Entertainment
134 Peter St., 3rd Fl., Toronto, ON M5V 2H2
416-367-7658
www.insideeonline.com
Frequency: 9 times a year
Kendon Polak, Editor-in-chief

Magazine Le Clap
#370, 2360, ch Ste-Foy, Sainte-Foy, QC G1V 4H2
418-653-2470, Fax: 418-653-6018
leclap@clap.qc.ca
www.clap.qc.ca
Circulation: 100 000 *Frequency: 7 fois par an; français*

Marquee
Marquee Media Inc., 1325 Burnhamthorpe Rd. East, Mississauga, ON L4Y 3V8
905-274-7174, Fax: 905-274-9799
marquee@marquee.ca
Circulation: 150,000 *Frequency: 7 times a year*
David Haslam, Publisher
Michael Bukovac, President

The Mosaic
PO Box 130, 105 Garafraxa St. North, Durham, ON N0G 1R9
519-369-2716, Fax: 519-369-2311
Circulation: 3,000
Vi Bland, Publisher

Playboard
Arch-Way Publishers, #3, 11720 Voyageur Way, Richmond, BC V6X 3G9
604-278-5881, Fax: 604-278-5813
theatre@shawbiz.ca
Circulation: 15,000 *Frequency: 10 times a year*
Alan Slater, Publisher & Editor

Preview
1700 Church Ave., Winnipeg, MB R2X 3A2
204-694-2022, Fax: 204-694-2347
www.canoe.ca/winnipegsun
Circulation: 70,700
Ed Huculak, Publisher

Satellite Direct
1420 Parsons Rd. SW, Edmonton, AB T6X 1M5
780-424-6222, Fax: 780-426-0279, 800-661-3203
info@captivemultimedia.com
www.satguide.com
Circulation: 19,397 *Frequency: 12 times a year*
Steven R. Vogel, Publisher
Gene Kosowan, Editor

Scene Magazine
PO Box 2302, London, ON N6A 4E3
519-642-4780, Fax: 519-642-0737
bret@scenemagazine.com
www.scenemagazine.com
Circulation: 18,500 *Frequency: 25 times a year*
Bret Downe, Editor-in-chief

SEE Magazine
#200, 10275 Jasper Ave., Edmonton, AB T5J 1X8
780-430-9003, Fax: 780-432-1102
info@see.greatwest.ca
www.seemagazine.com
Circulation: 24,000 *Frequency: Weekly, Thu.*
Gord Nielsen, Publisher
Zoltan Varadi, Music Editor
Kevin Wilson, News Editor

Teen Tribute
416-445-0544, Fax: 416-445-2894
advertising@tribute.ca
www.tribute.ca
Circulation: 300,000 *Frequency: 4 times a year*
Robin Stevenson, Editor
Sandra Stewart, Publisher

Teleguide
9185 Commercial St., New Minas, NS B4N 3G1
902-681-2121, Fax: 902-681-0830
Circulation: 28,000
Caroline Andrews, Publisher

Tribute Magazine
416-445-0544, Fax: 416-445-2894
generalinfo@tribute.ca
www.tribute.ca
Circulation: 500,450 *Frequency: 9 times a year*
Sandra Stewart, Editorial Director

TV Channels
44 Fairford St. West, Moose Jaw, SK S6H 6E4
306-692-6441, Fax: 306-692-2101
timesads@sk.sympatico.ca
www.mjtimes.sk.ca
Circulation: 10,500
Rob Clark, Publisher

View Weekly
370 Main St. West, Hamilton, ON L8P 1K3

905-527-3343, Fax: 905-527-3721
info@viewmag.com
www.viewmag.com
Circulation: 30,000 *Frequency: Weekly*
Sarah Cairns, Editor-in-chief
Marcus Rosen, Publisher

Visitor Magazine
PO Box 41030, Waterloo, ON N0K 3K0
519-886-2831, Fax: 519-886-6409
jonr@visitor.on.ca
www.visitor.on.ca
Circulation: 100,000
John Rohr, Publisher

Environment & Nature

Alternatives Journal: Canadian Environmental Ideas & Action
c/o Faculty of Environmental Studies, University of Waterloo, 200 University Ave. West, Waterloo, ON N2L 3G1
519-888-4442, Fax: 519-746-0292, 866-437-2587
infoalternativesjournal.ca
www.alternativesjournal.ca
Circulation: 4,500 *Frequency: 6 times a year; ISSN: 1205-7398*
A theme-based publication dedicated to illustrating the relationships between the environment and social justice, politics and the economy. It looks at the challenges and issues related to the interaction of humanity and the environment, and the responses to those issues.
Nicola Ross, Executive Editor

The Atlantic Salmon Journal
Atlantic Salmon Federation, PO Box 5200, St Andrews, NB E5B 3S8
506-529-1033, Fax: 506-529-4438
tiffinic@nb.aibn.com
www.asf.ca
Circulation: 11,000 *Frequency: 4 times a year*
This magazine is the world's oldest publication regarding conservation-minded salmon angling, covering issues related to fly-fishing for Atlantic salmon and the over-all protection of the species.
Martin Silverstone, Editor

British Columbia Environmental Report
c/o British Columbia Environmental Network, #122, 718-333 Brooksbank Ave., North Vancouver, BC V7J 3V6
604-515-1969
editor@ecobc.org; network@bcen.bc.ca
www.ecobc.org
The British Columbia Environmental Report is a journal which features news, analysis, events, & reviews about British Columbia environmental topics.
Dave Stevens, Chair, Board of Directors
Chris Blake, Executive Coordinator

Canadian Environmental Protection
#201, 2323 Boundary Rd., Vancouver, BC V5M 4V8
604-291-9900, Fax: 604-291-1906
ebaum@baumpub.com
www.baumpub.com
Circulation: 20,000 *Frequency: 8 times a year*
This publication is one of Canada's most popular environmental trade publications, with four marketplace issues, an internet version and industry supplements. Some issues this magazine covers are bio-fuels, specialty gasses and air pollution.

Canadian Geographic
c/o Royal Canadian Geographical Society, 39 McArthur Ave., Ottawa, ON K1L 8L7
613-745-4629, Fax: 613-744-0947
editorial@canadiangeographic.ca
www.canadiangeographic.ca
Circulation: 222,000 *Frequency: 6 times a year; ISSN: 0706-2168*
Publication aims to promote Canada both to Canadians and around the world. It looks at issues relating to the nature and wildlife within Canada, and what can be done to preserve the natural Canadian landscape.
John L. Thomson, CEO & Publisher
Rick Boychuk, Editor

Canadian Wildlife
350 Michael Cowpland Dr., Kanata, ON K2M 2W1
613-599-9594, Fax: 613-599-4428, 800-563-9453
info@cwf-fcf.org
www.cwf-fcf.org
Frequency: 6 times a year
Aimed at both teenagers and adults, this magazine covers issues relating to Canadian and international wildlife, and reports on the work of the Canadian Wildlife Federation.

Environmental Science & Engineering Magazine
#30, 220 Industrial Parkway South, Aurora, ON L4G 3V6
905-727-4666, Fax: 905-841-7271
sandra@esemag.com
www.esemag.com
Circulation: 19,000 *Frequency: 6 times a year*
This publicationis the largest documentary magazine in Canada and has articles on various environmental issues, including air pollution, water filtration, hazerdous waste, alternative energy, greenhouse gasses, among others.

EnviroZine
70 Crémazie St., 7th Fl., Gatineau, QC K1A 0H3
819-997-2800, Fax: 819-994-1412, 800-668-6767
enviroinfo@ec.gc.ca
www.ec.gc.ca/envirozine
Circulation: available online only *Frequency: monthly ISSN: English ed. ISSN 1499-1411; French ed. 1499-142X*
This webzine covers a wide range of environmental issues that are of importance to Canadians. It provides information in several categories, such as Air, Climate Change, Environmental Action, Nature and Wildlife, Pollution, Science & Technology, Water, and Weather, and attracts readers from 58 countries.

Green Living Magazine
Key Publishers Company Ltd., #400, 70 the Esplanade, Toronto, ON M5E 1R2
416-360-0044, Fax: 416-362-2387
info@green-living.ca
www.greenlivingmagazine.ca
Circulation: 150,000 *Frequency: quarterly*
Green Living Magazine attempts to promote living a green lifestyle to its readers by providing information about organics, health, the environment and eco-consumer products. They support sustainable and healthy living and publicizing the green message.
Laurie Simmonds, Publisher

Journal of Environmental Engineering and Science
M-55, 1200 Montreal Rd., Ottawa, ON K1A 0R6
613-993-9084, Fax: 613-952-7656, 800-668-1222
pubs@nrc-cnrc.gc.ca
pubs.nrc-cnrc.gc.ca
Frequency: 6 times a year ISSN: 1496-256X
This publication provides a forum for the discussion of environmental engineering and science research. Topics this journal explores include environmental engineering, physical and analytical sciences, life sciences related to environmental issues, health sciences, and oceanography.

La Maison du 21e siècle
2955, lac Lucerne, Sainte-Adèle, QC J8B 3K9
450-228-1555, Fax: 450-228-1555
info@21esiecle.qc.ca
www.21esiecle.qc.ca
Frequency: 4 fois par an
André Fauteux, Éditeur

Natural Life
Life Media, #508, 264 Queens Quay West, Toronto, ON M5J 1B5
416-260-0303, 800-215-9574
natural@life.ca
www.life.ca
Circulation: 35,000 *Frequency: 6 times a year; ISSN 0701-8002*
This independently owned magazine has an international focus on providing intelligent and in-depth practical information on issues such as healthy cooking, organic gardening, sustainable homes, natural parenting, wellness and natural healing, eco-leisure and eco-travel and sustainable business.
Wendy Priesnitz, Editor
Rolf Priesnitz, Publisher

Nature Canada
c/o Nature Canada, #900, 84 Albert St., Ottawa, ON K1P 6A4
613-562-3447, Fax: 613-562-3371, 800-267-4088
info@naturecanada.ca
naturecanada.ca
Circulation: 26,400 *Frequency: 4 times a year; ISSN: 0374-9894*
The mission of this magazine is to protect nature, its diversity and the processes that sustain it, and does this by providing information regarding several environmental topics including bird conservation, wilderness protection, endangered species and national parks. The publication supports community-based efforts to protect wildlife; encourages the development of an effective network of parks and protected areas across Canada; and promoting biodiversity in Canada and abroad.

ON Nature
Federation of Ontario Naturalists, #201, 366 Adelaide St. West, Toronto, ON M5V 1R9
416-444-8419, Fax: 416-444-9866, 800-440-2366
onnature@ontarionature.org
www.ontarionature.org
Circulation: 14,500 *Frequency: 4 times a year; ISSN: 0227-793X*
ON Nature attempts to bring its readers closer to nature by providing information about Ontario's natural areas and wildlife, and by providing insight into current environmental issues. Magazine features articles by nature specialists, colour photography, information regarding wilderness travel and up-to-date news on conservation battles.
Caroline Schultz, Executive Director
Victoria Foote, Editor

Québec Oiseaux
1251, rue Rachel est, Montréal, QC H2S 2J9
514-521-8356, Fax: 514-521-5711
quebecoiseaux@aqgo.qc.ca
www.quebecoiseaux.qc.ca
Circulation: 7 928 *Frequency: 4 fois par an*
Michel Préville, Rédacteur-en-chef

Shared Vision
#301, 873 Beatty St., Vancouver, BC V6B 2M6
604-733-5062, Fax: 604-731-1050
publisher@shared-vision.com
www.shared-vision.com
Circulation: 42,000 *Frequency: 12 times a year*
This publication attempts to help its readers live healthy, happy lives while creating and maintaining a sustainable society. The magazine features information on topics including green living, natural wellness, and organic food.
Rebecca Edhraim, Publisher

Solid Waste & Recycling
#800, 12 Concorde Place, Toronto, ON M3C 4J2
416-510-6798, Fax: 416-510-5133, 888-702-1111
bobrien@solidwastemag.com
www.solidwastemag.com
Circulation: 9,426 *Frequency: 6 times a year*
This publication dicusses all issues and topics pertaining to recyling and waste management.

The Sustainable Times
1225 Prospect Bay Rd., Prospect Village, NS B3T 2A6
902-850-2510
times@chebucto.ns.ca
www.sustainabletimes.ca
Circulation: online only
A webzine that discusses and publicizes global issues including environmetalism, the Third World, and Fair Trade. The webzine is published by CUSO, which works for sustainable development in places such as Africa, Asia, Latin America and the Caribbean.
Sean Kelly, Editor

Watershed Sentinel
c/o Watershed Sentinel Educational Society, PO Box 39, Whaletown, BC V0P 1Z0
250-935-6992, Fax: 250-935-6992
editor@watershedsentinel.ca
www.watershedsentinel.ca
Circulation: 5,000 *Frequency: 6 times a year*
This West Coast based publication focuses on how humanity affect the environment around them, by looking at issues such as logging and fishing practices and air and water pollution. It covers both bioregional and global perspectives on topics such as the environment, health and sustainability.
Delores Broten, Publisher & Editor

Women & Environments International Magazine
HNES Building, room 234, York University, 4700 Keele St., Toronto, ON M3J 1P3
416-736-2100, Fax: 416-736-5679
weimag@yorku.ca
www.weimag.com
Circulation: 2,000 *Frequency: 2 times a year*
Publication examines the relationships between women and the environment from a feminist perspective. It provides a forum for academic research and theory, professional practice and community experience and covers topics such as ecology and environmental activism, community development, childcare, and urban and rural agriculture.
Prabha Khosla
Reggie Modlich

Families

BC Parent Magazine
PO Box 72086, Sasamat RPO, Vancouver, BC V6R 4P2
604-221-0366
bcparent@shaw.ca
www.bcparent.ca
Circulation: 50,000 *Frequency: 9 times a year*

Elizabeth Shaffer, Editor, eshaffer@telus.net

Calgary's Child Magazine
#723, 105-150 Crowfoot Cres. NW, Calgary, AB T3G 3T2
403-241-6066, Fax: 403-286-9731
calgaryschild@shaw.ca
www.calgaryschild.com
Circulation: 70,000 *Frequency: 6 times a year*
Ellen Percival, Publisher

City Parent
Torstar Direct Services, #600, 625 Church St., Toronto, ON M4Y 2G1
416-596-4347, Fax: 416-596-4360, 800-265-3673
cityparent@torstardirect.com
www.cityparent.com
Circulation: 77,785 *Frequency: 12 times a year*
Neil Oliver, Publisher
Jane Muller, Editor-in-chief

Divorce Magazine
#1179, 2255B Queen St. East, Toronto, ON M4E 1G3
416-368-8853, Fax: 416-368-4978
danc@divorcemag.com
www.divorcemagazine.com
Circulation: 170,000 *Frequency: 4 times a year*
Dan Couvrette, Publisher

Edmonton's Child Magazine
#208, 14218 Stony Plain Rd., Edmonton, AB T5N 3R3
780-484-3360, Fax: 780-486-1844, 866-484-3360
edmchild@telus.net
www.edmontonschild.com
Circulation: 30,000 *Frequency: 6 times a year*
Jane Martin, CEO/Publisher

Island Parent Magazine
#A-10, 830 Pembroke St., Victoria, BC V8T 1H9
250-388-6905, Fax: 250-388-6920, 888-372-0862
mail@islandparent.ca
www.islandparent.ca
Circulation: 20,000 *Frequency: Monthly*
Paul Abra, Publisher
Mada Johnson, Editor

Junior
Versant Média Inc., 468, boul Rolland-Therrien, Longueuil, QC J4H 4E3
450-677-2556, Fax: 450-677-4099
Circulation: 23 579 *Frequency: 4 fois par an; français*
Richard Desmarais, Rédacteur

Le Magazine Enfants Québec
300, rue Arran, Staint-Lambert, QC J4R 1K5
450-875-9612, Fax: 450-672-5448
magazineenfants@editionsheritage.com
www.enfantsquebec.com
Circulation: 60 600 *Frequency: 12 fois par an; français*
Eve Christian, Rédactrice
Sylvie Payette, Éditrice

Our Kids Go to Camp
4242 Rockwood Rd., Mississauga, ON L4W 1L8
905-272-1843, Fax: 905-272-0474
fun@ourkids.net
www.ourkids.net
Circulation: 200,000 *Frequency: Annual*
Agatha Stawicki, Managing Editor

Our Kids Go to School
4242 Rockwood Rd., Mississauga, ON L4W 1L8
905-272-1843, Fax: 905-272-0474
fun@ourkids.net
www.ourkids.net
Circulation: 250,000 *Frequency: Annual*
Agatha Stawicki, Managing Editor

Owl Canadian Family
#400, 10 Lower Spadina Ave., Toronto, ON M5V 2Z2
416-340-2700, Fax: 416-340-9769
owlfamily@m-v-p.com
www.owlkids.com/owl/
Circulation: 66,768 *Frequency: 6 times a year*
Mary Beth Leatherdale, Editor

Pomme d'Api Québec
4475, rue Frontenac, Montréal, QC H2H 2S2
514-844-2111, Fax: 514-278-3030, 800-313-3020
redaction@bayardpresse.qc.ca
www.bayardjeunesse.ca
Circulation: 16 000
Suzanne Spino, Directrice générale

7 Jours
7, ch Bates, Montréal, QC H2V 4V7
514-848-7000, Fax: 514-848-7070, 800-367-0667
7jours@tva-publications.com
Circulation: 121 540 *Frequency: Hebdomadaire*
Jocelyn Poirier, Président

Today's Parent
1 Mount Pleasant Rd., 8th Fl., Toronto, ON M4Y 2Y5
416-764-2883, Fax: 416-764-2801
www.todaysparent.com
Circulation: 175,000 *Frequency: 11 times a year; also Prenatal Class Guide (annual); ISSN: 0823-9258*
Linda Lewis, Editor

Fashion

Clin d'oeil
514-848-7164, Fax: 514-270-7079
clindoeil@publicor.ca
Circulation: 60 372 *Frequency: Mensuel; français*
Claire Syril, Éditeur
Mitsou Gélinas, Directeur de la publication

Dolce Magazine
#1, 60 Winges Rd., Woodbridge, ON L4L 6B1
905-264-6789, Fax: 905-264-3787
dolce.ca
Michelle Zerillo-Sosa, Publisher & Editor-in-chief

Fashion Magazine
St. Joseph Media, #320, 111 Queen St. East, Toronto, ON M5C 1S2
416-364-3333, Fax: 416-594-3374
www.fashionmagazine.com
Circulation: 124,927 *Frequency: 10 times a year; ISSN: 0049-4194*
Ceri Marsh, Editor-in-chief
Michelle Bilodeau, Assoc. Editor
Giorgina Bigioni, Publisher

Flare
416-764-2871, Fax: 416-764-2864, 800-268-6823
david.hamilton@rci.rogers.com
www.flare.com
Circulation: 158,904 *Frequency: Monthly; ISSN: 0708-4927*
David Hamilton, Publisher

Glow
416-764-2886, Fax: 416-764-2488
mail@glow.rogers.com
www.glow.ca
Frequency: 6 times a year; English & French

Good Life Connoisseur
#317, 1489 Marine Dr., West Vancouver, BC V7T 1B8
604-925-0313
www.goodlifecanada.com
Frequency: 4 times a year
Terry Tremaine, Publisher & Editor

LOULOU
#1700, 1200 McGill College Ave., Montréal, QC H3B 4G7
514-843-2189, Fax: 514-843-2189
loulou.infoweb@rci.rogers.com
www.louloumagazine.com
Circulation: 8 times a year; English & French
Marie-Joseé Desmarais, Publisher/Editor
Claude LaFramboise, Executive Editor

Nuvo Magazine
#200, 460 Nanaimo St., Vancouver, BC V5L 4W3
604-899-9380, Fax: 604-899-1450
www.nuvomagazine.com
Frequency: 4 times a year
Jim Tobler, Editor

VMM
303, av Saint-Denis, Saint-Lambert, QC J4P 2G5
450-465-0009, Fax: 450-465-2110
info@imagellan.com
www.imagellan.com
Circulation: 50 000 *Frequency: 4 fois par an; français*
Marie-Claude Guérin, Rédactrice

Fifty-Plus Adults

Active Adult
178 Main St., Unionville, ON L3R 2G9
905-479-4663, Fax: 905-479-4482, 800-363-4663
nsicilia@homesmag.com
www.activeadultmag.com
Circulation: 100,000 *Frequency: 3 times a year*
Michael Rosset, Publisher
Patrick Tivy, Editor

Bel Age
514-499-0561, Fax: 514-499-9112
belage@transcontinental.ca
Circulation: 145 872 *Frequency: 11 fois par an; français*
Lucie Desaulniers, Éditrice

CARP Magazine
Kemur Publishing, #702, 27 Queen St. East, Toronto, ON M5C 2M6
416-363-5562, Fax: 416-363-7394
magazine@kemur.ca
www.50Plus.com
Circulation: 219,506 *Frequency: 9 times a year*
Gord Poland, Publisher
Bonnie Baker-Cowan, Editor

Choices After 50
EMC Marketing Associates Ltd., PO Box 1291, Saint John, NB E2L 4H8
506-658-0754, Fax: 506-633-0868
emc@nb.aibn.com
Circulation: 20,000 *Frequency: Bi-monthly*
Carol Maber, Editor

Comfort Life
905-272-1843, Fax: 905-272-0474
info@comfortlife.ca
www.comfortlife.ca
Circulation: 250,000 *Frequency: Annual*
Hugh Wesley, Executive Director

Community Resource Directory
250-765-3886, Fax: 250-765-7346
Frequency: Annual
Joel A. Rickard, Publisher

The Edmonton Senior
780-429-1610, Fax: 780-421-7677
abrnews@shaw.ca
seniorsgotravel.com
Circulation: 60,000 *Frequency: 12 times a year*
Lorne Silverstein, Publisher
Colin Smith, Editor

Fifty-Five Plus
c/o Coyle Publishing Inc., #220, 362 Terry Fox Dr., Kanata, ON K2K 2P5
613-271-8903, Fax: 613-271-8905
publisher@fifty-five-plus.com
www.fifty-five-plus.com
Circulation: 45,000 *Frequency: 8 times a year*
George Coyle, Publisher
Pat den Boer, Editor

Focus 50+
#13-215, 4 Alliance Blvd., Barrie, ON L4M 5J1
705-735-2144, Fax: 705-735-6002
focusplus@csolve.net
Circulation: 11,500 *Frequency: 12 times a year*
Taylor Ledden, Editor
Jeanneke Van Hattem, Publisher

Gold Mine Manitoba
#202, 63 Albert St., Winnipeg, MB R3B 1G4
204-949-4371, Fax: 204-949-4818
prime.editorial@uptownmag.com
Circulation: 15,000 *Frequency: Quarterly*
Dianne Biggs, Publisher
John Ross, General Manager

Good Times
Transcontinental Media, #100, 25 Sheppard Ave., Toronto, ON M2N 6S7
416-733-7600, Fax: 416-218-3630, 888-290-1466
goodtimes.pub@mail.transcontinental.ca
www.goodtimes.ca
Circulation: 157,086 *Frequency: 11 times a year*
Francine Tremblay, Publisher

The Independent Times
K.W. Publishing Ltd., #360, 7360 - 137 St., Surrey, BC V3W 1A3
604-580-1844, Fax: 604-580-1019
kweditor@telus.net
Circulation: 50,000 *Frequency: 10 times a year*
K. Gordon, Publisher
Wanda Boyd, Editor

Le Journal du Bel Age
Senior Publications, #900, 2001, rue University, Montréal, QC H3A 2A6
514-499-0561, Fax: 514-499-9112
Circulation: 70,000 *Frequency: 10 fois par an; français*
Francine Tremblay, Éditrice

Kerby News
1133 - 7th Ave. SW, Calgary, AB T2P 1B2
403-265-0661, Fax: 403-264-7047
kerbynews@kerbycentre.com
www.kerbynews.com
Circulation: 25,000 *Frequency: Monthly*
Barry Whitehead, Editor

Mainly for Seniors Lambton-Kent
140 South Front St., Sarnia, ON N7T 7M8
519-882-1770, Fax: 519-882-3212
Circulation: 4,400 *Frequency: Monthly*

The Montrealer
342 Ballantyne North, Montreal Lake, QC H4X 2C5
514-369-7000, Fax: 514-369-1362
foryoung@mlink.net
www.themontrealeronline.com
Circulation: 30,000 *Frequency: Monthly*
Peter Kerr, Publisher

Our World 50+
PO Box 68034 Crowfoot NW, Calgary, AB T3G 3N8
403-208-1235, Fax: 403-208-0004
ow@ow50.com
www.ow50.com
Circulation: 20,000 *Frequency: 6 times a year*
Karen Cottingham, Publisher

Prime Time
Metroland Printing, Publishing & Distributing Ltd., 884 Ford St., Peterborough, ON K9J 5V3
705-749-3383, Fax: 705-749-0074
bdanford@mykawartha.com
Circulation: 7,100 *Frequency: Monthly*
Bruce Danford, Publisher & General Manager
Paul Relinger, Editor

Prime Times News
Rosebud Publications Ltd., 1465 St. James St., Winnipeg, MB R3H 0W9
204-789-0800, Fax: 204-953-4300
Circulation: 10,000 *Frequency: 24 times a year*
John Proven, Publisher
John Kendle, Editor

The Saskatchewan Senior
PO Box 1010, Regina, SK S4P 3B2
306-525-8988, Fax: 306-525-8031
clay@sasksenior.com
www.sasksenior.com
Circulation: 18,529 *Frequency: 11 times a year*
Clay Stacey, Publisher & Editor

The Seniors Choice
PO Box 41075, South RPO, Lake Country, BC V4V 1Z7
250-765-6065, Fax: 250-765-7346, 800-866-2755
ads@seniorschoice.com
www.seniorschoice.com
Circulation: 15,000 *Frequency: Monthly*
James E. Archibald, Publisher
Patricia Archibald, Editor

The Seniors Review
#B2, 11 Bond St., St Catharines, ON L2R 4Z4
905-687-9861, Fax: 905-687-6911, 800-627-3111
seniorsreview@seniorsreview.com
Circulation: 40,000
David Irwin, Publisher
Carol Anderson, Editor

The Silver Pages
24 Cherryhill Dr., Grimsby, ON L3M 3B5
905-309-1525, Fax: 905-309-1524
info@thesilverpages.ca
www.thesilverpages.ca
Circulation: 50,000 *Frequency: 6 times a year*
John Bauslaugh, Publisher
Tim Miller, Editorial Director

Virage
CP 1000 M, 4545, av Pierre-de-Coubertin, Montréal, QC H1V 3R2
514-252-3017, Fax: 514-252-3154
fadoq@fadoq.ca
www.fadoq.ca
Circulation: 215 027 *Frequency: 4 fois par an*
Martine Langlois, Éditrice
Lyne Rémillard, Rédacteur-en-chef

Fishing & Hunting

Alberta Fishing Guide
#6C, 5571 - 45 St., Red Deer, AB T4N 1L2
403-347-5079, Fax: 403-341-5454
Circulation: 27,825 *Frequency: Annually, March*
Barry Mitchell, Publisher

Aventure chasse et pêche
332, rue Veilleux, Saint-Simon-les-Mines, QC G0M 1K0
418-774-4443, Fax: 418-774-4444
cregimbald@qacp.com
www.qacp.com
Circulation: 50,600 *Frequency: 4 times a year*
Claude Regimbald, Marketing Manager
Denis Lapointe, Production Manager

Bateaux de pêche
#310, 970, Montée de Liesse, Saint-Laurent, QC H4T 1W7
514-856-0787, Fax: 514-856-0790
Circulation: 18,000
Roy Baird, Publisher

BC Fishing Recreation Guide & Atlas
#900, 1080 Howe St., Vancouver, BC V6Z 2T1
604-606-4644, Fax: 604-687-1925, 800-816-0747
info@oppublishing.com
www.oppublishing.com
Circulation: 15,000 *Frequency: Annually, Saltwater (Jan.); Freshwater (Jan.)*
Mark Yelic, Publisher
Mike Mitchell, Editor

BC Outdoors Hunting & Shooting
#900, 1080 Howe St., Vancouver, BC V6Z 2T1
604-606-4644, Fax: 604-687-1925, 800-816-0747
info@oppublishing.com
www.oppublishing.com
Circulation: 25,000 *Frequency: 2 times a year*
Mark Yelic, Publisher
Mike Mitchell, Editor

BC Sport Fishing Magazine
#900, 1080 Howe St., Vancouver, BC V6Z 2T1
604-606-4644, Fax: 604-687-1925, 800-816-0747
info@oppublishing.com
www.oppublishing.com
Circulation: 23,195 *Frequency: 6 times a year*
Mark Yelic, Publisher
Mike Mitchell, Editor

The Canadian Fly Fisher
256 1/2 Front St., 2nd Fl., Belleville, ON K8N 2Z2
613-966-8017, Fax: 613-966-4192, 888-805-5608
info@canflyfish.com
www.canflyfish.com
Chris Marshall, Editor

Eastern Woods & Waters
#501, 40 Alderney Dr., Dartmouth, NS B2Y 2N5
902-464-3757, Fax: 902-464-3755
Circulation: 13,681 *Frequency: 6 times a year*
Jim Gourlay, Publisher & Editor

Island Angler
30 Acacia Ave., Nanaimo, BC V9R 3L4
250-753-2227, Fax: 250-753-2295
editor@islandangler.net
www.islandangler.net
Circulation: 15,000
Andrew Kolasinski, Publisher

Newfoundland Sportsman
PO Box 13754 A, 36 Pippy Pl., St. John's, NL A1B 4G5
709-754-3515, Fax: 709-454-2490
www.newfoundlandsportsman.com
Circulation: 17,692 *Frequency: 6 times a year*
Dwight J. Blackwood, Publisher
Gordon Follet, Editor

Ontario Out of Doors
416-764-1652, Fax: 416-764-1751
mail@ontariooutofdoors.com
www.fishontario.com
Circulation: 92,026 *Frequency: 10 times a year*
Matt Nicholls, Editor/Associate Publisher
Alison de Groot, Publisher

Outdoor Canada
#100, 25 Sheppard Ave. West, Toronto, ON M2N 6S7
416-733-7600, Fax: 416-227-8296
walsh@outdoorcanada.ca
www.outdoorcanada.ca
Circulation: 82,574 *Frequency: 8 times a year; ISSN: 0315-0542*
Patrick Walsh, Editor
Jaqueline Howe, Publisher

The Outdoor Edge
c/o Keywest Marketing Ltd., PO Box 173, Debden, SK
306-724-2233, Fax: 306-724-4448
odedge@sasktel.net
Circulation: 54,517 *Frequency: 6 times a year*
Mark Yelic, Publisher

Saskatchewan Fishing & Hunting
Tourism Saskatchewan, 1922 Park St., Regina, SK S4P 3V7
306-787-9685, Fax: 306-787-0715, 877-237-2273
belva.schlosser@sasktourism.com
www.sasktourism.com
Circulation: 85,000 *Frequency: Annual*

Sentier Chasse-Pêche
450-665-0271, Fax: 450-665-2974, 800-563-6738
redaction@sentierchassepeche.com
www.sentierchassepeche.com
Circulation: 80 000 *Frequency: 11 fois par an; français*
Luc Lemay, Éditeur
Jeannot Ruel, Rédacteur

Western Sportsman
#900, 1080 Howe St., Vancouver, BC V6Z 2T1
604-606-4644, Fax: 604-687-1925, 800-816-0747
info@oppublishing.com
www.oppublishing.com
Circulation: 25,933 *Frequency: 6 times a year; ISSN: 0709-1532*
Dave Webb, Editor
Mark Yelic, Publisher

Food & Beverage

Appeal
604-299-7311, Fax: 604-299-9188
cwm@canadawide.com
www.canadawide.com
Circulation: 230,000 *Frequency: 2 times a year*
Kim Mah, Editor
Peter Legge, Publisher

La Barrique
#414, 5165, rue Sherbrooke Ouest, Montréal, QC H4A 1T6
514-481-5892, Fax: 514-481-9699
labarrique@majesticlaser.com
Circulation: 12 000 *Frequency: 6 fois par an; français*
Aldo Parise, Rédacteur-en-chef adjoint
Nick Hamilton, Rédacteur-en-chef
Marylin Barker, Directrice de tirage

BC Wine Trails
2250 Camrose St., Penticton, BC V2A 8R1
250-492-3636,
Circulation: 15,000 *Frequency: 4 times a year*
Dani Greene, Manager

Coffee & Beverage Magazine
2C Fairfield Rd., Toronto, ON M4P 1T1
416-932-2743, Fax: 596-979-3
coffee@primus.ca
www.coffeeandbeverage.ca
Circulation: 10,000 *Frequency: 5 times a year*
Vida Radovanovic, Publisher

Coup de Pouce Cuisine
Transcontinental Publications, #900, 2001, rue University, Montréal, QC H3A 2A6
514-499-0561, Fax: 514-499-1844
Frequency: 5 fois par an; français
Francine Tremblay, Éditrice
France Lefebvre, Rédacteur

Elite Wine, Food & Travel Magazine
PO Box 37, #5, 23 McCleary Ct., Concord, ON L4K 1B2
905-760-1724, Fax: 905-760-1718
editor@elitewinefoodtravel.com
www.elitewinefoodtravel.co m
Circulation: 10,000 *Frequency: 4 times a year; ISSN: 72906-86110*
Anna Cavaliere, Editor

Flavours
www.flavoursmagazine.ca

Frequency: 4 times a year
Brandon Boone, Editor-in-chief

Food & Drink
Liquor Control Board of Ontario, 55 Lakeshore Blvd. East, Toronto, ON M5E 1A4
416-365-5900, Fax: 416-365-5935, 800-668-5226
foodanddrink@lcbo.com
www.lcbo.com/fooddrink
Circulation: 500,000 *Frequency: 6 times a year; English & French*
Judy Dunn, Editor
Wayne Leek, Publisher

Le Guide Cuisine
Communication Duocom Inc., #203, 90, rue Sainte-Anne, Sainte-Anne-de-Bellevue, QC H9X 1L8
514-457-0144, Fax: 514-457-0226
info@leguidecuisine.com
www.leguidecuisine.com
Circulation: 47 000 *Frequency: 5 times a year*
Nicolas Vallée, Éditeur

Tidings
514-481-5892, Fax: 514-481-9699
editor@tidingsmag.com
www.tidingsmag.com
Circulation: 29,200 *Frequency: 8 times a year; ISSN: 0228-6157*
Aldo Parise, Editor-in-chief

Toronto Wine & Cheese Show Guide
467 Speers Rd., Oakville, ON L6K 3S4
905-815-0017, Fax: 905-887-0764, 800-265-3673
marti.milks@sympatico.ca
www.towineandcheese.com
Circulation: 33,500 *Frequency: 1 times a year*
Janet Gardiner, Publisher

Fraternal, Service Clubs, Associations

KIN Magazine
c/o Kin Canada (Kinsmen & Kinette Clubs of Canada), Cambridge, ON N3H 5C6
519-653-1920, Fax: 519-650-1091, 800-742-5546
mrickard@kinclubs.ca
www.kinclubs.ca
Circulation: 10,000 *Frequency: 3 print (Feb., June, Oct.); 3 online (April, Aug. & Dec.)*
Michelle Rickard, Editor

Mensa Canada Communications
Mensa Canada Society, PO Box 1570, Kingston, ON K7L 5C8
613-547-0824, Fax: 613-531-0626
mensa@eventsmgt.com
www.canada.mensa.org
Circulation: 2,100 *Frequency: 6 times a year*
Phyrne Parker, President

Papyrus
c/o Rameses Temple, A.A.O.N.M.S., 3100 Keele St., Toronto, ON M3M 2H4
416-633-6317, Fax: 416-633-6345
Circulation: 7,200 *Frequency: 6 times a year*
Otto Yoworski, Editor

The Sentinel
c/o Loyal Orange Association, 94 Sheppard Ave. West, Toronto, ON M2N 1M5
416-223-1690, Fax: 416-223-1324
sentinel@orange.ca
www.orange.ca
Circulation: 4,000 *Frequency: 4 times a year*
Jeremy Dowdell, Editor

Gardening & Garden Equipment

Canadian Gardening
#100, 25 Sheppard Ave. West, Toronto, ON M2N 6S7
416-218-3570, Fax: 416-227-8298
satterthwaite@canadiangardening.com
www.canadiangardening.com
Circulation: 153,000 *Frequency: 8 times a year; ISSN: 0847-3463*
Aldona Satterthwaite, Editor-in-chief
Jacqueline Howe, Publisher

Canadian Organic Grower
323 Chapel St., Ottawa, ON K1N 7Z2
613-216-0741, Fax: 613-236-0743, 888-375-7383
office@cog.ca
www.cog.ca/magazine.htm
Circulation: 2,600 *Frequency: 4 times a year*
Janet Wallace, Editor, janet@cog.ca

Fleurs, plantes et jardins
418-686-3036, Fax: 418-628-0524, 800-463-1576
Circulation: 55 506 *Frequency: 9 fois par an; français*
Francine Tremblay, Éditeur
Sophie Banford, Rédacteur

Gardening Life
#120, 511 King St. West, Toronto, ON M5V 2Z4
416-593-0204, Fax: 416-591-1630, 800-559-8868
mail@canhomepub.com
www.gardeninglife.ca
Circulation: 95,797 *Frequency: 6 times a year; ISSN: 1203-858X*
Giorgina Bigioni, Publisher
Caren Watkins, Editor-in-chief

Gardens West
Cornwall Publishing Co. Ltd., PO Box 2680, Vancouver, BC V6B 3W8
604-879-4991, Fax: 604-879-5110, 800-263-1088
grow@gardenswest.com
www.gardenswest.com
Circulation: 40,000 *Frequency: 9 times a year*
Dorothy Horton, Publisher/Editor

GardenWise Magazine
4180 Lougheed Hwy., 4th Fl., Burnaby, BC V5C 6A7
604-299-7311, Fax: 604-299-9188, 800-663-0518
cwm@canadawide.com
www.canadawide.com
Circulation: 35,000 *Frequency: 6 times a year*
Peter Legge, Publisher
Karen Foss, Associate Publisher
Carol Pope, Editor

Manitoba Gardener
130A Cree Cres., Winnipeg, MB R3J 3W1
204-940-2700, Fax: 204-940-2727, 888-680-2008
ddobbie@pegasuspublications.net
www.localgardener.net
Circulation: 6,628 *Frequency: 6 times a year*
Dorothy Dobbie, Publisher
Joan Cohen, Editor

Ontario Gardener
#107A, 219 Dufferin St., Toronto, ON M6K 3J1
416-963-3434, Fax: 416-963-5929
www.localgardener.net/ontario/
Frequency: 6 times a year
Shauna Dobbie, Publisher & Editor

Gay/Lesbian

Capital Xtra
#503, 251 Bank St., Ottawa, ON K2P 1X3
613-237-7133, Fax: 613-237-6651
capxtra@capital.xtra.ca
Circulation: 20,000 *Frequency: monthly*
Brandon Matheson, Publisher & Editor-in-chief

Gaiety.ca
#1, 438 Parliament St., Toronto, ON M5A 3A5
416-944-2963, Fax: 416-944-9013
gaiety.ca
Frequency: 3 times a year
Joanna M. Valius, Editor

Perceptions
PO Box 8581, Saskatoon, SK S7K 6K7
306-244-1930, Fax: 306-665-1280
perceptions@shaw.ca
Circulation: 1,500
Gens Hellquist, Publisher

XTRA West!
#501, 1033 Davie St., Vancouver, BC V6E 1M7
604-684-9696, Fax: 604-684-9697
xtrawest@xtra.ca
www.xtra.ca
Circulation: 30,000 *Frequency: Bi-weekly*
Ken Hickling, Publisher, ken.hickling@xtra.ca

Xtra!
#200, 491 Church St., Toronto, ON M4Y 2C6
416-925-6665, Fax: 416-925-6674
info@xtra.ca
www.xtra.ca
Circulation: 42,000
Brandon Matheson, Publisher & Editor-in-chief

General Interest

Access Magazine
Trafalgar Publications, 79 Portsmouth Dr., Toronto, ON M1C 5C8
416-335-0747, Fax: 416-335-0748
crossfire@accessmag.com
www.accessmag.com
Circulation: 150,000 *Frequency: 10 times a year*
Sean Plummer, Editor

Active Living
2276 Rosedene Rd., St Ann's, ON L0R 1Y0
905-957-6016, Fax: 905-957-6017
activeliv@aol.com
www.activelivingmagazine.com
Circulation: 50,000 *Frequency: 4 times a year, plus Active Living's Buyers' Guide Product & Service Directory (annual)*
Kimberley Barrada, Editor
Jeffrey Tiessen, Publisher

L'Agora
CP 96, Ayer's Cliff, QC J0B 1C0
819-849-6360
agora.qc.ca
Circulation: 10 000
Hélène Laberge, Rédactrice-en-chef
Jacques Dufresne, Éditeur

Alberta Views
#208, 320 - 23 Ave. SW, Calgary, AB T2S 0J2
403-243-5334, Fax: 403-243-8599, 877-212-5334
avadmin@albertaviews.ab.ca
www.albertaviews.ab.ca
Circulation: 20,000 *Frequency: 8 times a year*
Jackie Flanagan, Publisher & Editor

Angus Magazine
PO Box 306, 298 Main St., Mattawa, ON P0H 1V0
705-744-4954, Fax: 705-744-4955
www.angusmagazine.com
Kevin J. Pecore, Editor-in-chief

CAA Magazine
Redwood Custom Communications, 37 Front St. East, Toronto, ON M5E 1B3
416-360-7339, Fax: 416-640-6164
caamagazine@redwoodcc.com
redwoodcc.com
Frequency: 4 times a year
Tracy Howard, Editor

The Canadian Forum
5502 Atlantic St., Halifax, NS B3H 1G4
902-421-7022, Fax: 902-425-0166
Frequency: 10 times a year; ISSN: 0008-3631
Robert Chodos, Editor

Canadian Immigrant Magazine
#228, 4401 Still Creek Dr., Burnaby, BC V5C 6G9
604-872-0102, Fax: 604-709-0102
www.thecanadianimmigrant.com

Canadian Newcomer
222 Parkview Hill Cres., Toronto, ON M4B 1R8
416-406-4719, Fax: 416-757-7086
cnmag@rogers.com
www.cnmag.ca
Dale Sproule, Publisher

Contact
Cité Universitaire, Université Laval, 3577, Pavillon Alphonse-Desjardins, Québec, QC G1K 7P4
418-656-7266, Fax: 418-656-2809
magazine.contact@dap.ulaval.ca
Circulation: 37 125 *Frequency: 3 fois par an; français*
Louise Desautels, Manager/Editor

Continuité
82, Grande-Allée ouest, Québec, QC G1R 2G6
418-647-4525, Fax: 418-647-6483
continuite@cmsq.qc.ca
www.cmsq.qc.ca/continuite
Circulation: 5 000 *Frequency: 4 fois par an; français*
Sophie Marcotte, Rédactrice en chef

The Country Connection
PO Box 100, Boulter, ON K0L 1G0
613-332-3651, 866-332-3651
magazine@pinecone.on.ca
www.pinecone.on.ca
Circulation: 5,000 *Frequency: 4 times a year; ISSN: 1486-0643*
Gus Zylstra, Publisher & Managing Editor

Dernière heure
7, chemin Bates, Outremont, QC H2V 4V7
514-848-7000, Fax: 514-270-9079
Circulation: 26 798 *Frequency: Hebdomadaire; français*
Isabelle Clément, Éditrice

Digital Journal Magazine
PO Box 1046, Toronto, ON M5C 2K4
416-410-9675
www.digitaljournal.com
Christopher A. Hogg, Editor-in-chief

Eye for the Future
493 Markham St., Toronto, ON M6G 2L1
416-654-5858, Fax: 416-654-5898
Circulation: 50,000 *Frequency: 10 times a year*
Elizabeth Rizzuto, Publisher

fab Magazine
511 Church St., 2nd Fl., Toronto, ON M4Y 2C9
416-925-5221, Fax: 416-925-4817
Circulation: 31,000 *Frequency: 26 times a year*
Michael Schwarz, Publisher

The Family Herald Magazine
PO Box 1042, Chatham, ON N7M 5L6
519-352-4359,
Circulation: 10,000 *Frequency: quarterly*
Lorn LeDrew, Publisher

The Flag & Banner
International Flag & Banner Inc., 1755 - 4th Ave. West, Vancouver, BC V6J 1M2
604-736-8161, Fax: 604-736-6439, 800-663-8681
editor@flagshop.com
www.flagshop.com
Circulation: 14,000 *Frequency: 2 times a year*
Doreen Braveman, Editor
Dan Bogdon, Production Assistant

Focus Magazine
Campbell Communicatons Inc., PO Box 5310, Victoria, BC V8R 6S4
250-388-7231, Fax: 250-383-1140
focusadmin@shaw.ca
www.focusonline.ca
Circulation: 35,000 *Frequency: Monthly*
Leslie Campbell, Publisher

Fugues
1212, St-Hubert, Montréal, QC H2L 3Y7
514-848-1854, Fax: 514-845-7645
www.fugues.com
Circulation: 50,000 *Frequency: 14 times a year*
Maurice Nadeau, Publisher

Georgian Bay Today
PO Box 186, 27 St. Clair Ave. East, Toronto, ON M4T 2M1
416-944-1217, Fax: 416-944-0133
hize@earthlink.net
Circulation: 2,000 *Frequency: 4 times a year*
Michael Ufford, Editor
Alan Heisey, Publisher

Going Natural
Federation of Canadian Naturists, PO Box 186 D, Toronto, ON M9A 4X2
905-304-4836
editor@fcn.ca
www.fcn.ca/GN.html
Circulation: 2,500 *Frequency: 4 times a year*
Dr. Paul Rapoport, Editor

Harrowsmith Country Life
#213, 3100 de la Concorde East Blvd., Laval, QC H7E 2B8
450-665-0271, Fax: 450-665-2974, 800-563-6738
hclmag.media@videotron.ca
www.harrowsmithcountrylife.ca
Circulation: 129,000 *Frequency: 6 times a year; ISSN: 1190-8416*
Tom Cruickshank, Editor
Michel Paradis, Vice-President & Group Publisher

Humanist in Canada
PO Box 943, Duncan, BC V9L 3Y2
250-748-0962, Fax: 250-746-6672
editor@humanistincanada.com
www.humanistincanada.com
Circulation: 1,500 *Frequency: 4 times a year; ISSN: 0018-7402*
Gary Bauslaugh, Editor

ICI Montreal
Communications Gratte-Ciel ltée, 465, rue McGill, 3e étage, Montréal, QC H2Y 4B4
514-393-1010, Fax: 514-393-3756
ici@ici-mirror.com
Circulation: 80,154 *Frequency: Weekly, Thu.*
Pierre Thibeault, Editor-in-charge

Kindred Spirits of PEI
#3, 5 Gerald McCarville Dr., Kensington, PE C0B 1M0
902-836-5502
kws@annesociety.org
www.annesociety.org
Circulation: 5,000 *Frequency: 4 times a year; English*
George Campbell, Publisher & Editor

Legion Magazine
Canvet Publications Ltd., 86 Aird Pl., Ottawa, ON K2L 0A1
613-235-8741, Fax: 613-233-7159
magazine@legion.ca
www.legionmagazine.com
Circulation: 313,217 *Frequency: 6 times a year*
Mac Johnston, Editor & General Manager

Lifestyles
A.T.E. Publishing Co. Ltd., PO Box 1000, #24, 155 East Beaver Creek Rd., Richmond Hill, ON L4B 2N1
905-881-3070, Fax: 905-731-6000
atopmag@aol.com
Frequency: 6 times a year
Gabriel Erem, Publisher
P.S. Henley, Managing Editor

Living Safety / Famille Avertie
c/o Canada Safety Council, 1020 Thomas Spratt Place, Ottawa, ON K1G 5L5
613-739-1535, Fax: 613-739-1566
csc@safety-council.org
www.safety-council.org
Circulation: 25,000 *Frequency: 4 times a year*
Jack A. Smith, General Manager

Le Lundi
514-848-7164, Fax: 514-270-7079
Circulation: 27 589 *Frequency: Hebdomadaire; français*
Sylvie Bourgeault, Publisher

Magazine Prestige
305, boul René-Lévesque ouest, Québec, QC G1S 1S1
418-683-5333, Fax: 418-683-2899
info@magazineprestige.com
www.magazineprestige.com
Frequency: 11 fois par an
Jean Frenette, Rédacteur-en-chef

Muskoka Magazine
PO Box 180, Bracebridge, ON P1L 1T6
705-646-1314, Fax: 705-645-6424
info@muskokamagazine.com
www.muskokamagazine.com
Circulation: 14,550 *Frequency: 7 times a year*
Jenny Cressman, Editor
Richard Everett, Manager, Sales
Donald Smith, Publisher & Editor

Nouvelles CSQ
Centrale des syndicats du Québec, 9405, rue Sherbrooke est, Montréal, QC H1L 6P3
514-356-8888, Fax: 514-356-9999
allaire.luc@csq.qc.net
www.csq.qc.net
Circulation: 103 000 *Frequency: 5 fois par an; français*
Louise Rochefort, Directrice

On the Bay Magazine
#201, 186 Hurontario St., Collingwood, ON L9Y 4T4
705-444-9192, Fax: 705-444-5658
www.onthebaymagazine.com
Frequency: 6 times a year
Janet Lees, Editor

Our Canada
1100, boul René Levesque ouest, Montréal, QC H3B 5H5
514-940-0751, Fax: 514-940-0751
Frequency: 6 times a year

Pacific Rim Magazine
100 West 49th Ave., Vancouver, BC V5Y 2Z6
604-323-5648, Fax: 604-323-5393
erains@langara.bc.ca
www.langara.bc.ca/publishing/prm
Circulation: 18,000
Elizabeth Rains, Publisher, erains@langara.bc.ca
Keith Murray, Manager, Advertising Sales, kmurray@langara.bc.ca

Profile Markting & Publishing
#201, 212 East Miles St., Thunder Bay, ON P7C 1J6
807-621-0400, Fax: 807-767-7352
santacom@tbaytel.net
Circulation: 40,000 *Frequency: Monthly*
Gillian Hamilton, Editor-in-chief
Orville Santa, Publisher

Protégez-Vous
#305, 2120, rue Sherbrooke est, Montréal, QC H1T 1C2
514-873-3000, Fax: 514-223-7160
courrier@pv.qc.ca
www.pv.qc.ca
Circulation: 151 145 *Frequency: 12 fois par an; français*
David Clerk, Contact

R.G.
CP 915 C, Montréal, QC H2L 4V2
514-523-9463, Fax: 514-523-2214
info@rgmag.com
www.rgmag.com
Circulation: 11 500
Alain Bouchard, Éditeur

Reader's Digest / Sélection du Reader's Digest
1100, boul René Lévesque ouest, Montréal, QC H3B 5H5
514-940-0751, Fax: 514-940-3637, 800-465-0780
customerservice@readersdigest.ca
www.rd.ca; www.selection.ca
Circulation: 1,200,000 *Frequency: Monthly; English & French editions*
Andrea C. Martin, President & CEO
Antoni Cioffi, Vice-President & CFO
Mathieu Péloquin, Vice-President, Marketing
Linda Melrose, Production Manager

Safarir
#501, 407, St-Laurent, Montréal, QC H2Y 2Y5
514-396-5179
www.safarir.com
Frequency: 12 fois par an; français
Sylvain Bolduc, Éditeur

Sélection du Reader's Digest
1100, boul René-Lévesque ouest, Montréal, QC H3B 5H5
514-940-0751, Fax: 514-940-3637, 888-459-3333
www.selectionrd.ca
Circulation: 242,970 *Frequency: Monthly*
Robert Goyette, Rédacteur-en-chef

Shunpiking, Nova Scotia's Discovery Magazine
6211 North St., Halifax, NS B3L 1P4
902-444-4922, Fax: 902-444-7599
shunpike@shunpiking.com
www.shunpiking.com
Circulation: 25,000
Tony Seed, Publisher
Richard LeBlanc, Marketing Director

Times 10
#402, 10175 - 114 St., Edmonton, AB T5K 2L4
780-415-5616, Fax: 780-455-6540
www.times10.org
Frequency: 10 times a year
Dennis Cambly, On Line Editor

Touring: Travel, Automobile, Lifestyle Magazine
c/o Medias Transcontinental S.E.N.C., 1100 René Lévesque Blvd., 24th Fl., Montréal, QC H3B 4X9
514-392-9000, Fax: 514-392-1489
ghislaine.mercille@transcontinental.ca
Circulation: 625,000 *Frequency: 4 times a year; English & French*
Jean-Louis Gauthier, Editor-in-chief
Ghislaine Mercille, Sales Manager

University of Toronto Magazine
University of Toronto, Div. of University Advancement, 21 King's College Circle, Toronto, ON M5S 3J3
416-946-7575, Fax: 416-978-3958
uoft.magazine@utoronto.ca
www.magazine.utoronto.ca
Circulation: 252,000 *Frequency: 4 times a year*
Scott Anderson, Editor & Manager

Up Here: Explore Canada's Far North
PO Box 1350, Yellowknife, NT X1A 2N9
867-766-6711, Fax: 867-873-9876, 800-661-0861
kathy@uphere.ca
www.uphere.ca
Circulation: 24,827 *Frequency: 8 times a year; ISSN: 0828-4253*
Jake Kennedy, Editor
Marion LaVigne, Publisher

Western Living
Transcontinental Media, #560, 2608 Granville St., Vancouver, BC V6H 3V3
604-877-7732, Fax: 604-877-4849
wlmail@westernlivingmagazine.com
www.westernlivingmagazine.com
Circulation: 195,500 *Frequency: 10 times a year; ISSN: 0824-0604*
Lance Neale, Publisher
Jim Sutherland, Editor

Westworld Alberta
4180 Lougheed Hwy., 4th Fl., Burnaby, BC V5C 6A7
604-299-7311, Fax: 604-299-9188
cwm@canadawide.com
www.canadawide.com
Circulation: 413,479 *Frequency: 5 times a year*
Peter Legge, Publisher
Anne Rose, Editor

Westworld British Columbia
4180 Lougheed Hwy., 4th Fl., Burnaby, BC V5C 6A7
604-299-7311, Fax: 604-299-9188
cwm@canadawide.com
www.canadawide.com
Circulation: 502,239 *Frequency: 4 times a year; also Westworld Saskatchewan (circ. 106,607, 4 times a year), Westworld Alberta (circ. 413,479, 5 times a year)*
Peter Legge, Publisher
Anne Rose, Editor

Westworld Saskatchewan
1480 Lougheed Hwy., 4th Fl., Burnaby, BC V5C 6A7
604-299-7311, Fax: 604-299-9188
cwm@canadawide.com
www.canadawide.com
Circulation: 110,000 *Frequency: 4 times a year*
Peter Legge, Publisher
Sheila Hansen, Editor

Yours for Fun
PO Box 518, 185 Ontario St., Burks Falls, ON P0A 1C0
705-382-3943, Fax: 705-382-3440
news@almaguinnews.com
www.almaguinnews.com
Circulation: 60,000
Peter Barr, Publisher

Health & Medical

Abilities Magazine
c/o Canadian Abilities Foundation, #401, 340 College St., Toronto, ON M5T 3A9
416-923-1885, Fax: 416-923-9829
info@abilities.ca
www.abilities.ca
Circulation: 45,000 *Frequency: 4 times a year; ISSN: 0845-4469*
Jaclyn Law, Managing Editor
Raymond D. Cohen, Editor-in-chief

Alive Magazine
Alive Publishing Group Inc., #100 - 12751 Vulcan Way, Richmond, BC V6V 3C8
800-663-6580
editorial@alive.com
www.alive.com
Circulation: 250,000 *Frequency: 12 times a year*

beyond fitness
#502, 3535 St. Charles Blvd., Kirkland, QC H9H 5B9
514-697-5888, Fax: 514-693-0833
beyondfit@bellnet.ca
Circulation: 150,000 *Frequency: 11 times a year*
Pierre Martineau, President & Publisher
Laura Warf, Fitness Editor
Amanda Vogel, Fashion Editor
André Thibault, Administration & Circulation Manager

Canada's Family Guide to Home Health Care & Wellness Solutions
BCS Communications Ltd., 101 Thorncliffe Park Dr., Toronto, ON M4H 1M2
416-421-7997, Fax: 416-421-0966
www.bcsgroup.com
Circulation: 30,000 *Frequency: 4 times a year*
Caroline Tapp-McDougall, Publisher

Capital Santé
514-499-0317, Fax: 514-849-9779
capitalsantepub@mail.transcontinental.ca
Circulation: 49 594 *Frequency: 10 fois par an; français*
Francine Tremblay, Éditrice
Jean-Louis Gauthier, Rédacteur

Common Ground Magazine
#204, 4381 Fraser St., Vancouver, BC V5V 4G4
604-733-2215, Fax: 604-733-4415, 800-365-8897
admin@commonground.ca
www.commonground.ca
Circulation: 70,000 *Frequency: 12 times a year*
Joseph Roberts, Publisher

Diabetes Dialogue
#1400, 522 University Ave., Toronto, ON M5G 2R5
416-363-3373, Fax: 416-363-7067, 800-226-8464
Membership@diabetes.ca.
www.diabetes.ca
Circulation: 45,510 *Frequency: 4 times a year*
Amir Hanna, Editor-in-chief

Family Health
PO Box 2421, Edmonton, AB T5J 2S6
780-429-5189, Fax: 780-498-5661
Circulation: 120,000 *Frequency: 4 times a year; ISSN 0830-0305*
Robert Clarke, Publisher

Future Health
c/o Canadians for Health Research, PO Box 126, Westmount, QC H3Z 2T1
514-398-7478, Fax: 514-398-8361
info@chrcrm.org
www.chrcrm.org
Circulation: 2,000 *Frequency: 4 times a year; English, some French*
Heather Pengelley, Editor

The Health Journal: Canada's Authorative Health Forum
Gemini Communications Inc., #2200, 4950 Yonge St., Toronto, ON M2N 6K1
416-218-5568, Fax: 416-221-4668
thehealthjournal@sympatico.ca
Circulation: 214,572 *Frequency: 5 times a year*
Chantal Goudreau, Publisher

Health'N Vitality
#502, 3535, St-Charles, Kirkland, QC H9H 5B9
514-697-5888, Fax: 514-693-0833
vitalitemag@qc.aira.com
Circulation: 200,000 *Frequency: 6 times a year*
Pierre Martineau, President
Kate Tompkins, Editor-in-chief
André Thibault, Circulation Manager

Healthcare Information Management & Communications Canada
5782 - 172 St., Edmonton, AB T6M 1B4
780-489-4521, Fax: 780-489-3290
healthcare@shaw.ca
www.hcccinc.com
Circulation: 6,000 *Frequency: 5 times a year*
Steven A. Huesing, Publisher & Editor

HeartBeat
PO Box 1, Site 100, RR#1, Carvel, AB T0E 0H0
780-380-2, Fax: 780-892-3401
pnewman@xplornet.com
www.heartbeatangels.com
Circulation: 4,600 *Frequency: 4 times a year*
Pauline Newman, Publisher

Impact Magazine
2007 - 2nd St. SW, Calgary, AB T2S 1S4
403-228-0605, Fax: 403-228-0627
info@impactmagazine.ca
www.impactmagazine.ca
Frequency: Bi-monthly
Elaine Kupser, Publisher
Louise Hodgson-Jones, Editor

Lifestyle & Wellness
2813 Victoria Park Ave., Toronto, ON M1W 1A1
416-492-6598, Fax: 416-492-6725
landwmag@rogers.com
Circulation: 30,000 *Frequency: 4 times a year*
Sheila McKenzie-Barnswell

Magazine Vie et santé
#200, 5 Place du Commerce, Verdun, QC H3E 1M8
514-842-5492, Fax: 514-842-5375
info@vie-sante.com
vieetsante.branchez-vous.com
Frequency: 8 fois par an
Veronique Tremblay, Rédactrice-en-chef

Synchronicity
PO Box 63118, 2604 Kensington Rd., NW, Calgary, AB T2N 4S5
403-270-9544, Fax: 403-270-7407
info@synchronicitymagazine.ca
www.synchronicitymagazine.c a
Circulation: 37,000 *Frequency: 6 times a year; ISSN: 1198-760X*
Doreen Nystrom, Editor/President
Joy Nystrom, Publisher/Secretary

Vision Magazine
Breton Communications Inc., #202, 495, boul St-Martin ouest, Laval, QC H7M 1Y9
450-629-6005, Fax: 450-629-6044, 888-462-2112
breton.com@bretoncom.com
www.bretoncom.com
Circulation: 11,435 *Frequency: 6 times a year*
Martine Breton, Présidente

Vitalité Québec Mag
#502, 3535, boul St-Charles, Kirkland, QC H9H 5B9
514-697-5888, Fax: 514-693-0833
vitalitemag@qc.aira.com
Circulation: 40 000 *Frequency: 10 fois par an; français*
André Thibault, Directeur, Administration et diffusion
Monick Juliette Élie, Rédacteur-en-chef
Pierre Martineau, Président

Vitality Magazine: Toronto's Monthly Wellness Journal
356 Dupont St., Toronto, ON M5R 1V9
416-964-0528, Fax: 416- -
advertising@vitalitymagazine.com
www.vitalitymagazine.com; www.wholelifecanada.com
Circulation: 52,000 *Frequency: 10 times a year*
Julia Woodford, Editor

WHOLifE JOURNAL
#15, 2301 St. Henry Ave., Saskatoon, SK S7M 0P6
306-653-1283, Fax: 306-653-3291, 800-780-3564
editor@wholife.com
www.wholife.com
Circulation: 17,000 *Frequency: 6 times a year*
Covers natural health & wellness for body, mind & spririt, plus environmental issues
Melva Armstrong, Publisher

History & Genealogy

Canada's History Magazine
Canada's National History Society, #478, 167 Lombard Ave., Winnipeg, MB R3B 0T6
204-988-9300, Fax: 204-988-9309, 800-816-6777
thebeaver@historysociety.ca
www.canadashistory.ca
Circulation: 45,000 *Frequency: 6 times a year; ISSN: 0005-7517*
Deborah Morrison, President/CEO

Family Chronicle
416-491-3699, Fax: 416-491-3996, 888-326-2476
publisher@familychronicle.com
www.familychronicle.com
Frequency: 6 times a year
Halvor Moorshead, Publisher

Heritage/Patrimoine
5 Blackburn Ave., Ottawa, ON K1N 8A2
613-237-1066, Fax: 613-237-5987
heritagecanada@heritagecanada.org
www.heritagecanada.org
Frequency: 4 times a year; ISSN: 1480-6924
Carolyn Quinn, Editor

Kayak: Canada's History Magazine for Kids
Canada's National History Society, #478, 167 Lombard Ave., Winnipeg, MB R3B 0T6
204-988-9300, Fax: 204-988-9309, 800-816-6777
info@kayakmag.ca
www.kayakmag.ca
Circulation: 16,000 *Frequency: 6 times a year; ISSN: 1712-3984*
Deborah Morrison, President/CEO

The Loyalist Gazette
#202, 50 Baldwin St., Toronto, ON M5T 1L4
416-591-1783, Fax: 416-591-7506
uela@becon.org
www.uelac.org
Circulation: 2,500 *Frequency: 2 times a year*
Robert McBride, Editor

Newfoundland and Labrador Studies
Memorial University of Newfoundland, St. John's, NL A1C 5S7

709-737-7474, Fax: 709-737-7560
nlstudies@mun.ca
www.mun.ca/nls/

Bi-annual, interdisciplinary journal about the society & culture of Newfoundland & Labrador
Al Potter

OHS Bulletin
34 Parkview Ave., Toronto, ON M2N 3Y2
416-226-9011, Fax: 416-226-2740
bulletin@ontariohistoricalsociety.ca
www.ontariohistoricalsociety.ca
Circulation: 2,500 *Frequency: 5 times a year*
Sheila Creighton, Editor
Patricia K. Neal, Executive Director

Hobbies

The Canadian Amateur
CARF Publications, #217, 720 Belfast Rd., Ottawa, ON K1G 0Z5
613-244-4367, Fax: 613-244-4369, 877-273-8304
rachq@rac.ca
www.rac.ca
Circulation: 7,200 *Frequency: 6 times a year*
Alan Griffin

Canadian Coin News
PO Box 28103 Lakeport, St. Catherines, ON L2N 7P8
905-646-7744, Fax: 905-646-0995, 800-408-0352
bret@trajan.ca
www.canadiancoinnews.com
Circulation: 8,500 *Frequency: 26 times a year; ISSN: 0702-3162*
Bret Evans, Managing Editor & Associate Publisher
Hans Niedermair, News Editor

Canadian Railway Modeller
c/o North Kildonan Publications, PO Box 99 F, 355 Henderson Hwy., Winnipeg, MB R2L 2A5
204-668-0168, Fax: 204-669-9821
morgant@cdnrwymod.com
www.cdnrwymod.com
Circulation: 25,000 *Frequency: 6 times a year*
Morgan B. Turney, Editor
John Longhurst, Editor

Canadian Sports Collector
PO Box 28103 Lakeport, 600 Ontario St., St. Catherines, ON L2N 7P8
905-646-7744, Fax: 905-646-0995, 800-408-0352
pwinkler@trajan.ca
www.sportscollector.ca
Circulation: 7,500 *Frequency: Monthly; ISSN: 1492-3513*
Paul Winkler, Publisher

Canadian Stamp News
PO Box 28103 Lakeport, St. Catherines, ON L2N 7P8
905-646-7744, Fax: 905-646-0995, 800-408-0352
bret@trajan.ca
www.canadianstampnews.ca
Circulation: 5,000 *Frequency: 26 times a year; ISSN: 0702-3145*
Paul Winkler, Publisher
Bret Evans, Editor

ÉCHEC+
c/o La Fédération Québécoise des Échecs, CP 640 C, Montréal, QC H2L 4L5
514-252-3034, Fax: 514-251-8038
info@fqechecs.qc.ca
www.fqechecs.qc.ca
Circulation: 2 000 *Frequency: 6 fois par an; français*
Louis Morin, Rédacteur

Metalcraft
345 Munster Ave., Toronto, ON M8Z 3C6
416-232-0330, Fax: 416-234-1516
info@metalcraftmag.com
www.metalcraftmag.com
Frequency: 4 times a year
Nestor Gula, Editor

Model Aviation Canada
#9, 5100 South Service Rd., Burlington, ON L7L 6A5
905-632-9808, Fax: 905-632-3304
maachq@on.aibn.com
www.maac.ca
Circulation: 12,600 *Frequency: 6 times a year*
Keith Morison, Editor, 403/282-0837

Philatélie Québec
275, rue Bryant, Sherbrooke, QC J1J 3E6
819-252-3035, Fax: 819-563-6482
sdu@videotron.ca
Circulation: 1 500 *Frequency: 6 fois par an; français*
Guy Desrosiers, Editeur

Homes

ARIDO Journal
#220, 6 Adelaide St. East, Toronto, ON M5C 1H6
416-921-2127, Fax: 416-921-3660, 800-334-1180
ltheoret@arido.on.ca
www.arido.on.ca
Circulation: 4,000
Lori Theoret, Publisher

Canadian Home & Country
#100, 25 Sheppard Ave. West, Toronto, ON M2N 6S7
416-733-7600, Fax: 416-227-8298
editorial@canadianhomeandcountry.com
www.canadianhomeandcountry.com
Circulation: 140,000 *Frequency: 7 times a year; ISSN: 0838-9330*
Erin McLaughlin, Editor

Canadian Home Workshop
c/o Quarto Communications, 54 St. Patrick St., Toronto, ON M5T 1V1
416-599-2000, 800-465-6183
www.canadianhomeworkshop.com
Frequency: 6 times a year; ISSN: 1485-8509
Canadian Home Workshop magazine provides information about woodworking & home improvement. Features include do-it-yourself projects & reviews of tools & products.
Douglas Thomson, Editor
Randy Craig, Director, Advertising & Marketing
Amy McCleverty, Art Director
Jodi Brooks, Manager, Production
Heather Maxwell-Tufford, Manager, Circulation

Canadian Homes & Cottages
The In-Home Show, #4, 2650 Meadowvale Blvd., Mississauga, ON L5N 6M5
905-567-1440, Fax: 905-567-1442, 888-830-6696
sgriffin@homesandcottages.com
www.homesandcottages.com
Circulation: 79,099 *Frequency: 6 times a year*
Steven Griffin, Publisher
Janice Naisby, Editor-in-chief

Canadian House & Home
Canadian Home Publishers, #120, 511 King St. West, Toronto, ON M5V 2Z4
416-593-0204, Fax: 416-591-1630, 800-559-8868
advertising@hhmedia.com
www.canadianhouseandhome.com
Circulation: 249,124 *Frequency: 10 times a year; ISSN: 0826-7642*
Lynda Reeves, Publisher
Cobi Ladner, Editor

Canadian Living
#100, 25 Sheppard Ave. West, Toronto, ON M2N 6S7
905-733-7600, Fax: 905- -
letters@canadianliving.com
www.canadianliving.com
Circulation: 533,370 *Frequency: 12 times a year; ISSN: 0382-4624*
Debbie Gibson, Publisher

Classic Homestyles Home Plans
102 Ellis St., Penticton, BC V2A 4L5
250-493-0942, Fax: 250-493-7526
plan@westhomeplanners.com
Circulation: 10,000 *Frequency: Annually*
G.T. Giroux, Publisher
Michael A. Giroux, Editor

Condo Life Magazine
178 Main St., Unionville, ON L3R 2G9
905-479-4663, Fax: 905-479-4482, 800-363-4663
info@homesmag.com
www.condolifemag.com
Circulation: 140,000
Michael Rosset, Publisher
Patrick Tivy, Editor

Cottage Life
54 Patrick St., Toronto, ON M5T 1V1
416-599-2000, Fax: 416-599-0800, 877-874-5253
clmag@cottagelife.com
www.cottagelife.com
Circulation: 70,000 *Frequency: 6 times a year*
Al Zikovitz, Publisher
Penny Caldwell, Editor

Cottage Magazine
#900, 1080 Howe St., Vancouver, BC V6Z 2T1
604-606-4644, Fax: 604-687-1925, 800-816-0747
info@oppublishing.com
www.oppublishing.com
Circulation: 13,195 *Frequency: 6 times a year*
Mark Yelic, Publisher
Desiree Daniel, Editor

The Cottager
PO Box 40, Victoria Beach, MB R0E 2C0
204-756-8381, Fax: 204-756-2662
magazine@thecottager.mb.ca
www.thecottager.com
Circulation: 10,000
Glenn Halgren
Cathy Halgren, Circulation

Décoration Chez-Soi

514-848-7164, Fax: 514-270-7079
Circulation: 74 174 *Frequency: 10 fois par an; français*
Pierre Deschènes, Directeur

Décormag
Trancontinental Media, 1100, boul. René-Lévesque Ouest, 24e étage, Montréal, QC H3A 4X9
514-392-9000, Fax: 514-848-9779
redaction@decormag.com
www.decormag.com
Circulation: 84 542 *Frequency: 11 fois par an; français*
Marie-Christine Tremblay, Édimestre
Michèle Dubreuil, Directrice

Del Condominium Life
4800 Dufferin St., Toronto, ON M3H 5S9
416-739-5143, Fax: 416-661-4538
pmackellar@delcondo.com
delpropertymanagement.com
Circulation: 32,500 *Frequency: 3 times a year*
Patricia MacKellar, Editor/Production Manager

Designer Showcase
1300 Hollis St., Halifax, NS B3J 1T6
902-420-9943, Fax: 902-429-9058
publishers@metroguide.ca
www.metroguide.ca
Circulation: 8,000
Trevor Adams, Editor
Sheila Blair, Publisher

Designers' Best Home Plans

250-493-0942, Fax: 250-493-7526
plan@westhomeplanners.com
www.westhomeplanners.com
Circulation: 10,000 *Frequency: Annually*
G.T. Giroux, Publisher
Michael A. Giroux, Editor-in-chief

East Coast Living
1300 Hollis St., Halifax, NS 3J 1T6
902-420-9943, Fax: 902-429-9058
publishers@metroguide.ca
www.metroguidepublishing.ca
Circulation: 34,100 *Frequency: 2 times a year*
Sheila Blair, Publisher

Home Digest
1416 Stonehampton Ct., Pickering, ON L1V 7C9
905-509-9900, Fax: 905-509-9990
homedigest@sympatico.ca
www.homedigest.ca
Circulation: 700,000 *Frequency: 4 times a year*
Barry Holmes, Publisher
William Roebuck, Editor

Homes Magazine

905-479-4663, Fax: 905-479-4482, 800-363-4663
info@homesmag.com
www.homesmag.com
Circulation: 100,000 *Frequency: 9 times a year*
Michael Rosset, Publisher
Patrick Tivy, Editor

Les Idées de ma maison
7, Chemin Bates, Outremont, QC H2V 4V7
514-848-7000, Fax: 514-270-7079
Circulation: 65 493 *Frequency: 10 fois par an; français*
Béatrix Marik, Rédactrice

Les idées Réno-Dépôt

514-848-7164, Fax: 514-270-7079
Circulation: 120 000 *Frequency: 2 fois par an*
Michel Blain, Rédacteur

Maison d'Aujourd'hui
3390, boul Métropolitain est, Montréal, QC H2A 1A4
514-729-0000, Fax: 514-729-2552
courriel@maisonmax.com
www.maisondirect.com
Circulation: 50 000 *Frequency: semi-annuel*
Phillippe Massé, Président

Planimage Magazines
#105, 1501, rue Ampere, Boucherville, QC J4B 5Z5
450-641-7526, Fax: 450-641-6688, 800-752-6744
info@planimage.com
www.planimage.com
Circulation: 30 000 *Frequency: 6 times a year*
Daniel Therrien, Publisher & Editor

Plans de Maisons du Québec
514-848-7164, Fax: 514-848-7079
Frequency: 4 fois par an; français
Claude Leclerc, Rédacteur

Practical Homes Home Plans
250-493-0942, Fax: 250-493-7526
plan@westhomeplanners.com
www.westhomeplanners.com
Circulation: 10,000 *Frequency: Annually*
G.T. Giroux, Publisher
Michael A. Giroux, Editor-in-chief

Proven & Popular Home Plans
250-493-0942, Fax: 250-493-7526
plan@westhomeplanners.com
www.westhomeplanners.com
Circulation: 10,000 *Frequency: Annually*
G.T. Giroux, Publisher
Michael A. Giroux, Editor-in-chief

Real Estate News
1400 Don Mills Rd., Toronto, ON M3B 3N1
416-443-8113, Fax: 416-443-9185
ren@thestar.ca
www.toronto.com/realestatenews
Circulation: 99,442 *Frequency: Weekly*
Mirella Torchia, General Manager

Real Estate Victoria
Monday Publications, 818 Broughton St., Victoria, BC V8W 1E4
250-381-9171, Fax: 250-381-9172
rev@revweekly.com
www.revweekly.com
Circulation: 20,000 *Frequency: Weekly*
Glenda Turner, Publisher, gturner@monday.com

Renovation & Decor Magazine
178 Main St., Unionville, ON L3R 2G9
905-479-4663, Fax: 905-479-4482, 800-363-4663
nsicilia@homesmag.com
www.homespublishinggroup.com
Circulation: 75,000
Michael Rosset, Publisher

Rénovation Bricolage
7, ch Bates, Outremont, QC H2V 4V7
514-848-7164, Fax: 514-270-6918
renobrico@tva-publications.com
Circulation: 33 270 *Frequency: 9 fois par an; français*
Claude Leclerc, Éditeur/Rédacteur

Select Home Designs
#102, 9440 - 202 St., Langley, BC V1M 4A6
604-881-1124, Fax: 604-881-2114
sales@selecthomedesigns.com
www.selectaplan.com
Circulation: 82,500 *Frequency: 3 times a year*
Steve Riley, Publisher

Sounder Profiles Newsmagazine
#6A, 17675 - 66 Ave., Surrey, BC V3S 7X1
604-574-6530, Fax: 604-574-6529
Circulation: 40,000 *Frequency: monthly*
Arlie McClurg, Publisher

Style at Home: Canada's Decorating Magazine
#100, 25 Sheppard Ave. West, Toronto, ON M2N 6S7
416-733-7600, Fax: 416-218-3632
letters@styleathome.com
styleathome.com
Circulation: 235,000 *Frequency: 12 times a year; ISSN: 1206-5870*
Jacqueline Howe, Publisher
Gail Johnston Habs, Editor

Horses, Riding & Breeding

Atlantic Horse & Pony
PO Box 1509, Liverpool, NS B0T 1K0
902-354-5411, Fax: 902- -
Circulation: 4,000 *Frequency: 6 times a year*
Dirk van Loon, Editor

Canadian Arabian Registry/News
#113, 37 Athabascan Ave., Sherwood Park, AB T8A 4H3
780-416-4990, Fax: 780-416-4860
editor@cahr.ca
www.cahr.ca
Circulation: 2,200 *Frequency: 4 times a year*
Nicole Toren, Editor
Shari Christie, Administrator/Registrar

The Canadian Sportsman
PO Box 129, 25 Old Plank Rd., Straffordville, ON N0J 1Y0
519-866-5558, Fax: 519-866-5596
gfoerster@canadiansportsman.ca
www.canadiansportsman.ca
Frequency: Bi-weekly
Gary Foerster, Publisher
Dave Briggs, Editor

Canadian Thoroughbred
905-727-0107, Fax: 905-841-1530, 800-505-7428
info@horse-canada.com
www.horse-canada.com
Circulation: 4,500 *Frequency: 6 times a year*
Jennifer Anstey, Publisher
Lee Benson, Editor

The Corinthian/Horse Sport
905-727-0107, Fax: 905-841-1530, 800-505-7428
info@horse-canada.com
www.horse-canada.com
Circulation: 10,000 *Frequency: 12 times a year*
Jennifer Anstey, Publisher

Courrier Hippique
CP 1000 M, 4545, av Pierre-de-Coubertin, Montréal, QC H1V 3R2
514-252-3030, Fax: 514-252-3165
courrier@hippique.qc.ca
www.hippique.qc.ca
Circulation: 7 000 *Frequency: 6 times a year*
Laure Chazerand, Rédactrice-en-chef

Horse & Country Canada
PO Box 203, #23, 845 Dakota St., Winnipeg, MB R2M 5M3
204-256-7467, Fax: 204-257-2467
horsecountry@mts.net
www.horsecountry.ca
Circulation: 12,000 *Frequency: 6 times a year*
Linda Hazelwood, Publisher & Editor

Horse-Canada.com
PO Box 670, 225 Industrial Pkwy. South, Aurora, ON L4G 4J9
905-727-0107, Fax: 905-841-1530, 800-505-7428
info@horse-canada.com
www.horse-canada.com
Circulation: 17,000 *Frequency: 6 times a year*
Jennifer Anstey, Publisher
Lee Benson, Editor

Horsepower: Magazine for Young Horse Lovers
PO Box 670, Aurora, ON L4G 4J9
905-727-0107, Fax: 905-841-1530, 800-505-7428
janstey@horse-canada.com
www.horse-canada.com
Circulation: 16,000 *Frequency: 6 times a year*
Jennifer Anstey, Publisher
Susan Stafford, Editor

Horses All
629 Evermeadow Rd. SW, Calgary, AB T2Y 4W8
403-249-8770, Fax: 403-249-8769
www.horsesall.com
Circulation: 7,000 *Frequency: Monthly*
Steve Mark, Publisher
Cindy Mark, Editor

Pacific & Prairie Horse Journal
PO Box 2190, Sidney, BC V8L 3S8
250-655-8883, Fax: 250-655-8913, 800-299-3799
editor@horsejournals.com
www.horsejournals.com
Circulation: 20,000 *Frequency: 12 times a year*
Kathy Smith, Publisher/Editor

The Rider
PO Box 10072, 487 Book Rd. West, Ancaster, ON L9K 1P2
905-648-2035, Fax: 905-648-6977, 877-743-3715
therider@worldchat.com
www.therider.com
Circulation: 7,000 *Frequency: Monthly*
Aidan Finn, Editor

Trot
c/o Standardbred Canada, 2150 Meadowvale Blvd., Mississauga, ON L5N 6R6
905-858-3060, Fax: 905-858-3089
trotmagazine@standardbredcanada.ca
Frequency: Monthly
Chris Roberts, Manager & Editor

Interior Design & Decor

Homefront
BCS Communications Ltd., 101 Thorncliffe Park Dr., Toronto, ON M4H 1M2
416-421-7944, Fax: 416-421-0966, 800-298-6282
dostal@bcsgroup.com
www.homefrontmagazine.ca
Circulation: 35,000 *Frequency: 4 times a year*
Helmut Dostal, Publisher

Plaisirs de Vivre/Living in Style
#1703, 1115 Sherbrooke St. West, Montréal, QC H3A 1H3
514-982-9823, Fax: 514-289-9160
pdv@prestipresse.com
Circulation: 70,198 *Frequency: 6 times a year; English & French*
Peter Weiss, Publisher
Céline Tremblay, Editor-in-chief
Steve Robins, Associate Publisher

Labour, Trade Unions

Our Times
#407, 15 Gervais Dr., Toronto, ON M3C 1Y8
416-703-7661, Fax: 416-703-9094, 800-648-6131
office@ourtimes.ca
www.ourtimes.ca
Circulation: 8,000 *Frequency: 4 times a year*

Socialist Worker
PO Box 339 E, Toronto, ON M6H 4E3
416-972-6391, Fax: 416-972-6319
sworker@sympatico.ca
www.socialist.ca
Circulation: 2,000 *Frequency: 24 times a year; ISSN 0836-7094*
Paul Kellogg, Editor

Literary

The Antigonish Review
PO Box 5000, St. Francis Xavier University, Antigonish, NS B2G 2W5
902-867-3962, Fax: 902-867-5563
tar@stfx.ca
www.antigonishreview.com
Circulation: 900 *Frequency: 4 times a year; ISSN: 0003-5661*
Bonnie McIsaac, Office Manager
Gerald Trites, Editor

ARC: Canada's National Poetry Magazine
PO Box 81060, Ottawa, ON K1P 1B1
613-729-3550
arc@arcpoetry.ca
www.arcpoetry.ca
Circulation: 1,200 *Frequency: 2 times a year; ISSN: 0705-6397*
Anita Lahey, Editor
Pauline Conley, Managing Editor

Brick: A Literary Journal
PO Box 537 Q, Toronto, ON M4T 2M5
416-593-9684, Fax: 416- -
info@brickmag.com
www.brickmag.com
Circulation: 2,200 *Frequency: 2 times a year; ISSN: 0382-8565*
M. Redhill

Canadian Notes & Queries
The Porcupine's Quill, 68 Main St., Erin, ON N0B 1T0
519-833-9158, Fax: 519-833-9845
pql@sentex.net
www.sentex.net/~pql
Circulation: 500 *Frequency: 2 times a year; ISSN: 0576-5803*
Tim Inkster, Publisher

John Metcalf, Editor

The Capilano Review
2055 Purcell Way, North Vancouver, BC V7J 3H5
604-984-1712, Fax: 604-990-7837
tcr@capcollege.bc.ca
www.capcollege.bc.ca/thecapilanoreview/
Circulation: 900 *Frequency: 3 times a year; ISSN: 0315-3754*
Jenny Pennberthy, Editor

The Claremont Review
Claremont Review Publishers, 4980 Wesley Rd., Victoria, BC V8Y 1Y9
250-658-5221, Fax: 250-658-5387
editor@theclaremontreview.ca
www.theclaremontreview.ca
Circulation: 1,000 *Frequency: 2 times a year; ISSN: 1188-5068*
Susan Stenson, Editor
Lucy Bashford, Managing Editor

Contemporary Verse 2
 # 207, 100 Arthur St., Winnipeg, MB R3B 1H3
204-949-1365, Fax: 204-942-5754
cv2@mts.net
www.contemporaryverse2.ca
Circulation: 650 *Frequency: 4 times a year; ISSN: 0831-9502*
Clarise Foster, Managing Editor

The Dalhousie Review
Dalhousie University, 6209 University Ave., Halifax, NS B3H 4R2
902-494-2541, Fax: 902-494-3561
dalhousie.review@dal.ca
dalhousiereview.dal.ca
Circulation: 700 *Frequency: 3 times a year*
Jennifer Lambert, Production Manager
Anthony Stewart, Editor

Descant
Descant Arts & Letters Foundation, PO Box 314 P, Toronto, ON M5S 2S8
416-593-2557, Fax: 416-593-9362
info@descant.on.ca
www.descant.on.ca
Circulation: 1,200 *Frequency: 4 times a year; ISSN: 0382-909X*
Karen Mulhallen, Editor

Exile
134 Eastbourne Ave., Toronto, ON M5P 2G6
416-485-4885
exq@exilequarterly.com
www.exilequarterly.com
Circulation: 1,200 *Frequency: 4 times a year*
Michael Callaghan, Publisher

The Fiddlehead
Campus House, PO Box 4400 A, 11 Garland Ct., Fredericton, NB E3B 5A3
506-453-3501, Fax: 506-453-5069
fiddlehd@unb.ca
www.Lib.unb.ca/Texts/Fiddlehead
Circulation: 1,000 *Frequency: 4 times a year; ISSN: 015-0630*
Ross Leckie, Editor

Geist
#200, 341 Water St., Vancouver, BC V6B 1B8
604-681-9161, Fax: 604-669-8250, 800-434-7834
geist@geist.com
www.geist.com
Circulation: 8,000 *Frequency: 4 times a year; ISSN: 1181-6554*
Stephen Osborne, Editor

Grain
PO Box 67, Saskatoon, SK S7K 3K1
306-244-2828, Fax: 306-244-0255
grainmag@sasktel.net
www.grainmagazine.ca
Circulation: 1,700 *Frequency: 4 times a year; ISSN: 1491-0497*
Kent Bruyneel, Editor

The Malahat Review
University of Victoria, PO Box 1700 CSC, Victoria, BC V8W 2Y2
250-721-8524, Fax: 250-472-5051
malahat@uvic.ca
www.malahatreview.ca
Circulation: 1,000 *Frequency: 4 times a year; ISSN: 0025-1216*
John Barton, Editor

Matrix
#502, 1400, boul de Maisonneuve ouest, Montréal, QC H3G 1M8
514-848-2357, Fax: 514-848-4501
matrix@alcor.concordia.ca
alcor.concordia.ca/~matrix
Circulation: 1,500 *Frequency: 4 times a year; ISSN 0318-3610*
R.E.N. Allen, Editor

The New Quarterly
c/o St. Jerome's University, 290 Westmount Rd. North, Waterloo, ON N2L 3G3
519-884-8111, Fax: 519-884-5759
editor@newquarterly.net
newquarterly.net
Circulation: 1,000 *Frequency: 4 times a year; ISSN: 0227-0455*
Covers Canadian writers & writing
Kim Jernigan, Editor

Nuit blanche
#403, 1026, rue St-Jean, Québec, QC G1R 1R7
418-692-1354, Fax: 418-692-1355
nuitblanche@nuitblanche.com
www.nuitblanche.com
Circulation: 2 800 *Frequency: 4 fois par an; français*
Anne-Marie Guérineau, Directrice

On Spec Magazine
The Copper Pig Writers' Society, PO Box 4727, Edmonton, AB T6E 5G6
780-413-0215, Fax: 780-413-1538
onspec@onspec.ca
www.onspec.ca
Circulation: 2,000 *Frequency: 4 times a year; ISSN: 0843-476X*
Diane Walton, Managing Editor

paperplates
19 Kenwood Ave., Toronto, ON M6C 2R8
416-651-2551, Fax: 416-651-2910
magazine@paperplates.org
www.paperplates.org
Frequency: 4 issues a year; ISSN: 1183-3742, online
Bernard Kelly, Publisher & Editor

Prairie Fire
Prairie Fire Press Inc., #423, 100 Arthur St., Winnipeg, MB R3B 1H3
204-943-9066, Fax: 204-942-1555
prfire@mts.net
www.prairiefire.ca
Circulation: 1,500 *Frequency: 4 times a year; ISSN: 0821-1124*
Janine Tschuncky, Operations Manager
Andris Taskans, Editor
Heidi Harms, Associate Editor

Prairie Journal
Prairie Journal Press, PO Box 61203 Brentwood, Calgary, AB T2L 2K6
prairiejournal@yahoo.com
www.geocities.com/prairiejournal
Circulation: 600 *Frequency: 2 times a year; ISSN: 0827-2921*
A. Burke

Prism International
Buch., #E462, Dept. of Creative Writing, UBC, 1866 Main Mall, Vancouver, BC V6T 1Z1
604-822-2514, Fax: 604-822-3616
prism@interchange.ubc.ca
www.prism.arts.ubc.ca
Circulation: 1,200 *Frequency: 4 times a year; ISSN: 0032-8790*
Jamella Hagen, Executive Editor
Kellee Ngan, Executive Editor

Rampike Magazine
c/o Dept. of English, University of Windsor, 401 Sunset Ave., Windsor, ON N9B 3P4
519-253-3000, Fax: 519-971-3676
jirgins@uwindsor.ca
Circulation: 4,000 *Frequency: 2 times a year; ISSN: 0711-7647*
Karl E. Jirgins, Editor/Publisher

The Readers Showcase
780-413-6163, Fax: 780-413-6185, 877-784-4488
www.suggitt.com
Circulation: 380,895 *Frequency: 6 times a year*

sub-TERRAIN Magazine
PO Box 3008 MPO, Vancouver, BC V6B 3X5
604-876-8710, Fax: 604-879-2667
subter@portal.ca
www.subterrain.ca
Circulation: 3,500 *Frequency: 3 issues a year; ISSN: 0840-7533*
Brian Kaufman, Editor

TickleAce
PO Box 5353, St. John's, NL A1C 5W2
709-754-6610, Fax: 709-754-5579
tickleace@nfld.com
Circulation: 1,000 *Frequency: 2 times a year; ISSN: 0823-6399*
Bruce Porter, Editor

West Coast Line
2027 East Annex, Simon Fraser University, 8888 Universi, Burnaby, BC V5A 1S6
604-291-4287, Fax: 604-291-4622
wcl@sfu.ca
Circulation: 800 *Frequency: 3 times a year; ISSN: 1182-4271*
Michael Barnholden, Managing Editor

White Wall Review
63 Gould St., Toronto, ON M5B 1E9
416-977-9924, Fax: 416-977-7709
Frequency: Annually; ISSN: 0712-8991

Men's

Highrise Magazine
83 Clansman Blvd., Toronto, ON M2H 1X7
info@highrisemag.com
www.highrisemag.com
Frequency: 4 times a year
Cynthia Cully, Editor-in-chief

Military

Esprit de Corps
#204, 1066 Somerset St. West, Ottawa, ON K1Y 4T3
613-725-5060, Fax: 613-725-1019, 800-361-2791
espritdecorp@idirect.com
www.espritdecorps.ca
Circulation: 15,000
Scott Taylor, Publisher

Music

Beatlology Magazine
#90, 260 Adelaide St. East, Toronto, ON M5A 1N1
www.beatlology.com
Andrew Croft, Publisher, publisher@beatlology.com
Charles Iscove, Editor, editor@beatlology.com

Canadian Musician
905-641-3471, Fax: 905-641-1648, 877-746-4692
mail@nor.com
www.canadianmusician.com
Circulation: 27,000 *Frequency: 6 times a year*
Jim Norris, Publisher

Chart
Chart Communications Inc., #200, 41 Britain St., Toronto, ON M5A 1R7
416-363-3101, Fax: 416-363-3109
chart@chartattack.com
www.chartattack.com
Circulation: 40,000 *Frequency: Monthly; ISSN: 1198-7235*
Edward Skira, Co-Publisher
Nada Laskovski, Co-Publisher

Country Music News
PO Box 7323 Vanier Terminal, Ottawa, ON K1L 8E4
613-745-6006, Fax: 613-745-0576
Larry@CountryMusicNews.ca
www.countrymusicnews.ca
Circulation: 6,500 *Frequency: Monthly*
Larry Delaney, Publisher & Editor, Larry@CountryMusicNews.ca

Crescendo
Toronto Musicians' Assn., #500, 15 Gervais Dr., Toronto, ON M3C 1Y8
416-421-1020, Fax: 416-421-7011, 800-463-6333
info@torontomusicians.org
www.torontomusicians.org
Circulation: 4,000 *Frequency: 3 times a year*
Allan MacMillan, Publisher
Brian Blain, Managing Editor

Exclaim!
#966, 7-B Pleasant Blvd., Toronto, ON M4T 1K2
416-535-9735, Fax: 416-535-0566
exclaim@exclaim.ca
www.exclaim.ca
Circulation: 102,000 *Frequency: Monthly*
Ian Danzig, Publisher

Musicworks: The Journal of Sound Explorations
#358, 401 Richmond St. West, Toronto, ON M5V 3A8

416-977-3546
sound@musicworks.ca
www.musicworks.ca
Circulation: 3,000 *Frequency: 3 times a year; English & French; ISSN: 0225-686X*
Gayle Young, Editor

Opera Canada
#244, 366 Adelaide St. East, Toronto, ON M5A 3X9
416-363-0395, Fax: 416-363-0396
Circulation: 5,575 *Frequency: 5 times a year; ISSN: 0030-3577*
Wayne Gooding, Editor

Opus
161 Frederick St., Toronto, ON M5A 4P3
416-596-1480, Fax: 416-596-9793
www.warwickgp.com/opus/main/main.htm
Frequency: 4 times a year
Rick MacMillan, Editor-in-chief

La Scena Musicale
5409, rue Waverly, Montréal, QC H2T 2X8
514-274-1128, Fax: 514-274-9456, 877-948-2520
info@scena.org
www.scena.org
Circulation: 42,000 *Frequency: monthly*
Wah Keung Chan, Publisher/Editor

TRIBE Magazine
PO Box 65053, 358 Danforth Ave., Toronto, ON M4K 3Z2
416-778-4115, Fax: 416-405-9473
editor@tribe.ca
www.tribemagazine.com
Circulation: 35,000 *Frequency: 10 times a year*
Alex Dordevic, Publisher/Editor

WHOLENOTE: Toronto's Music, Classical & New
#503, 720 Bathurst St., Toronto, ON M5S 2R4
416-603-3786, Fax: 416-603-4791
info@thewholenote.com
www.thewholenote.com
Circulation: 36,000
Allan Pulker, Publisher

News

L'Actualité
#800, 1200 av. McGill College, Montréal, QC H3B 4G7
514-843-2564, Fax: 514-843-2186
redaction@lactualite.rogers.com
www.lactualite.com
Circulation: 187 700 *Frequency: 20 fois par an; français; ISSN: 03830-8714*
Carole Beaulieu, Rédactrice

Behind the Headlines
Canadian Institute of International Affairs, #302, 205 Richmond St. West, Toronto, ON M5V 1V3
416-977-9000, Fax: 416-977-7521, 800-668-2442
mailbox@ciia.org
www.ciia.org
Frequency: 4 times a year
The Hon. Barbara McDougall
Robert Johnstone, Editor

Broken Pencil
PO Box 203 P, Toronto, ON M5S 2S7
416-204-1700
editor@brokenpencil.com
www.brokenpencil.com
Circulation: 3,000 *Frequency: 3 times a year; ISSN: 1201-8996*
Anna Bowness, Editor

Columbia Journal
PO Box 2633 Main, Vancouver, BC V6B 3W8
604-266-6552, Fax: 604-267-3342
cjournal@telus.net
www.columbiajournal.ca
Circulation: 20,000 *Frequency: 12 times a year*
Jim Lipkovits, Publisher
Marco Procaccini, Editor

Le Courrier Parlementaire
30 Grande-Allée ouest, Québec, QC G1R 2G6
418-640-4211, Fax: 418- -
editeur@courrierparlementaire.com
www.courrierparlementaire.com
Denis Massicotte, Publisher

Inroads
3777 Kent Ave., #A, Montréal, QC H3S 1N4
514-731-8383, Fax: 514- -
inroads@canada.com
www.inroadsjournal.ca

Frequency: 2 times a year; ISSN: 0315-7911
Robert Chodos, Managing Editor

Maclean's
1 Mount Pleasant Rd., 11th Fl., Toronto, ON M4Y 2Y5
416-764-1300, Fax: 416-764-1332, 800-268-9119
service@macleans.ca
www.macleans.ca
Circulation: 401,080 *Frequency: Weekly*
Ken Whyte, Publisher/Editor-in-Chief

Northwest Compass
PO Box 21034, Prince Rupert, BC V8J 2P4
250-627-7777, Fax: 250-627-7756
www.northwestcompass.com
Rob Ritchie, Publisher
Bob Colebrook, Editor

TIME
Time Canada Ltd., North Tower, #602, 175 Bloor St. East, Toronto, ON M4W 3R8
416-929-1115, Fax: 416-929-0019, 800-668-9934
joan_brehl@timeinc.com
www.timecanada.com
Circulation: 225,000 *Frequency: Weekly*
Joan Brehl, Managing Director
George Russell, President

Photography

Blackflash
Buffalo Berry Press, PO Box 7381 Main, 12 - 23rd St. East, 2nd Fl., Saskatoon, SK S7K 4J3
306-374-5115, Fax: 306-665-6568
editor@blackflash.ca
www.blackflash.ca
Circulation: 1,300 *Frequency: 3 times a year; ISSN: 0826-3922*
John Shelling, Managing Editor

Photo Life
Apex Publications, 185, rue St-Paul, Québec, QC G1K 3W2
800-905-7468
editor@photolife.com
www.photolife.com
Other information: Toll Free Fax: 1-800-664-2739
Circulation: 55,000 *Frequency: 6 times a year; ISSN: 0700-3021*
Guy Poirier, Publisher
Anita Dammer, Editor-in-chief

Productions Ciel Variable
#204, 661, rue Rose-de-Lima, Montréal, QC H4C 2L7
514-390-1193, Fax: 514-390-8802
info@cielvariable.ca
www.ceilvariable.ca
Circulation: 1,850 *Frequency: 4 times a year; English & French; ISSN: 0831-3091*
Jacques Doyen, Directeur

Political

bout de papier
#412, 47 Clarence St., Ottawa, ON K1N 9K1
613-241-1391, Fax: 613-241-5911
boutdepapier@pafso.com
Circulation: 2,800 *Frequency: 4 times a year; English & French; ISSN: 305-500*
Debra Hulley, Managing Editor

Briarpatch
2138 McIntyre St., Regina, SK S4P 2R7
306-525-2949, Fax: 306-565-3430
info@briarpatchmagazine.com
www.briarpatchmagazine.com
Circulation: 2,000 *Frequency: 8 times a year; ISSN 0703-8968*
Shayna Stock, Publisher, publisher@briarpatchmagazine.com
Dave Oswald Mitchell, Managing Editor, editor@briarpatchmagazine.com

Canadian Dimension
#2B, 91 Albert St., Winnipeg, MB R3B 1G5
204-957-1519, Fax: 204-943-4617, 800-737-7051
www.canadiandimension.mb.ca
Circulation: 3,500 *Frequency: 6 times a year; ISSN: 0008-3402*
Cy Gonick, Publisher & Coordinating Editor

Dialogue Magazine
Gabriel Communications, 6227 Groveland Dr., Nanaimo, BC V9V 1B1
250-758-9877, Fax: 250-758-9855
dialogue@dialogue.ca
www.dialogue.ca
Circulation: 1,000 *Frequency: 6 times a year*
Maurice J. King, Publisher
Janet Hicks, Editor

Peace Magazine
PO Box 248 P, Toronto, ON M5S 2S7
416-588-8748, Fax: 416-789-4508
office@peacemagazine.org
www.peacemagazine.org
Circulation: 2,500 *Frequency: 4 times a year; ISSN: 0826-9521*
Metta Spencer, Chair
Verda McDonald, Treasurer

Printing & Publishing

Devil's Artisan: A Journal of the Printing Arts
c/o The Porcupine's Quill, 68 Main St., Erin, ON N0B 1T0
519-833-9158, Fax: 519-833-9845
pql@sentex.net
www.sentex.net/~pql
Circulation: 800 *Frequency: 2 times a year; ISSN: 0225-7874*
Tim Inkster, Publisher
Don McLeod, Editor

Religious & Denominational

The Anglican
135 Adelaide St. East, Toronto, ON M5C 1L8
416-363-6021, Fax: 416- -
Frequency: Monthly
Stuart Mann, Editor

Anglican Journal
c/o Anglican Church of Canada, 80 Hayden St., Toronto, ON M4Y 3G2
416-924-9192, Fax: 416-921-4452
editor@national.anglican.ca
www.anglicanjournal.com
Circulation: 215,000 *Frequency: 10 times a year*
Steven Brickenden, Editorial Assistant
Leanne Larmontoin, Editor

BC Christian News
#200, 20316 - 56th Ave., Langley, BC V3A 3Y7
604-534-1444, Fax: 604-534-2970
admin@canadianchristianity.com
www.canadianchristianity.c om
Circulation: 37,000 *Frequency: Monthly*
Flyn Ritchie, Publisher & Editor, editor@canadianchristianity.com
David Dawes, Managing Editor, ddawes@canadianchristianity.com

Canada Lutheran
#302, 393 Portage Ave., Winnipeg, MB R3B 3H6
204-984-9172, Fax: 204-984-9185, 888-786-6707
canaluth@elcic.ca
www.elcic.ca
Circulation: 14,000 *Frequency: 8 times a year*
Trina Gallop, Managing Editor

Canadian Jewish News
#205, 1500 Don Mills Rd., Toronto, ON M4B 3K8
416-391-1836, Fax: 416-391-0949
www.cjnews.com
Circulation: 50,000 *Frequency: Weekly*
Mordechai Ben-Dat, Editor
Gary Laforet, General Manager

Canadian Mennonite
#C5, 490 Dutton Dr., Waterloo, ON N2L 6H7
519-884-3810, Fax: 519-884-3331, 800-378-2524
editor@canadianmennonite.org
canadianmennonite.org
Circulation: 17,000 *Frequency: 24 times a year*
Timothy Miller Dyck, Editor

The Canadian Messenger
c/o Jesuit Fathers, 661 Greenwood Ave., Toronto, ON M4J 4B3
416-466-1195, Fax: 416- -
Circulation: 14,000 *Frequency: 11 times a year*
Rev. F.J. Power, Editor

Catholic Insight
PO Box 625 Adelaide, 31 Adelaide St. East, Toronto, ON M5C 2J8
416-204-9601, Fax: 416-204-1027
reach@catholicinsight.com
www.catholicinsight.com
Circulation: 3,700 *Frequency: 11 times a year; ISSN: 1192-5671*
Fr. Alphonse de Valk, Publisher

Catholic New Times
80 Sackville St., Toronto, ON M5A 3E5
416-361-0761, Fax: 416-361-0796
editor@catholicnewtimes.org
www.catholicnewtimes.org

Frequency: 20 times a year
Diane Bisson, Publisher/Editor

The Catholic Register
#401, 1155 Yonge St., Toronto, ON M4T 1W2
416-934-3410, Fax: 416-934-3409
news@catholicregister.org
www.catholicregister.org
Circulation: 33,000 *Frequency: 47 times a year*
Joseph Sinasac, Editor

Christian Courier
c/o Reformed Faith Witness, 1 Hiscott St., St Catharines, ON L2R 1C7
905-682-8311, Fax: 905-682-8313, 800-969-4838
editor@christiancourier.ca
www.christiancourier.ca
Circulation: 3,500 *Frequency: bi-weekly*
Harry DerNederlanden, Editor-in-chief

ChristianCurrent
PO Box 725, Winnipeg, MB R3C 2K3
204-982-2060, Fax: 204-947-5632
www.christiancurrent.com
Brian Koldyk, Publisher
Robert White, Managing Editor

ChristianWeek
#204, 424 Logan Ave., Winnipeg, MB R3A 0R4
204-982-2060, Fax: 204-947-5632, 800-263-6695
admin@christianweek.org
www.christianweek.org
Circulation: 5,000 *Frequency: Every other Tue., except every 3 weeks in Dec.*
Doug Koop, Editorial Director

Clarion
1 Beghin Ave., Winnipeg, MB R2J 3X5
204-663-9000, Fax: 204-633-9202
premier@premierprinting.ca
www.premierprinting.ca
Circulation: 3,000 *Frequency: Bi-weekly*
W. Gortemaker, Publisher

Edmonton Jewish Life
7200 - 156 St. NW, Edmonton, AB T5R 1X3
780-488-7276, Fax: 780-484-4978
ejlife@shaw.ca
Circulation: 1,500 *Frequency: Monthly*
John Bresler, Publisher
Neil Loomer, Editor

Edmonton Jewish News
#300, 10036 Jasper Ave., Edmonton, AB T5J 2W2
780-421-7966, Fax: 780-424-3951
Circulation: 2,000
David Moser, Publisher

Faith Today
c/o The Evangelical Fellowship of Canada, PO Box 3745, Markham, ON L3R 0Y4
905-479-5885, Fax: 905-479-4742
ft@efc-canada.com
www.faithtoday.ca
Circulation: 20,000 *Frequency: 6 times a year*
Gail Reid, Managing Editor
Bruce Clemenger, Publisher

Gospel Herald
c/o Gospel Herald Foundation, 4904 King St., Beamsville, ON L0R 1B6
905-563-7503, Fax: 905-563-7503, 866-722-2264
maxc@strathmorecofc.ca
www.gospelherald.org
Circulation: 1,320 *Frequency: Monthly*
Wayne Turner, Editor
Max E. Craddock, Managing Editor

Huron Church News
190 Queens Ave., London, ON N6A 6H7
519-434-6893, Fax: 519-673-4151
Bishop Bruce Howe, Publisher
David Parson, Editor

Island Catholic News
PO Box 5424 LCD 9, Victoria, BC V8R 6S4
250-727-9420, Fax: 250-727-3647
icn@islandnet.com
Circulation: 2,000 *Frequency: Monthly*
Marnie Butler, Senior Editor
Patrick Jamieson, Managing Editor

Jewish Free Press
8411 Elbow Dr. SW, Calgary, AB T2V 1K8
403-252-9423, Fax: 403-255-5640
jewishfp@telus.net
Circulation: 2,000 *Frequency: Semi-monthly*
Richard Bronstein, Publisher

The Jewish Tribune
15 Hove St., Toronto, ON M3H 4Y8
416-633-6224, Fax: 416-630-2159
editor@jewishtribune.ca
www.jewishtribune.ca/TribuneV2/
Circulation: 60,000 *Frequency: weekly*
Norm Gordner, Editor

Living Light News
#200, 5306 - 89th St., Edmonton, AB T6E 5P9
780-468-6397, Fax: 780-468-6872
shine@livinglightnews.org
www.livingnews.org
Circulation: 50,000 *Frequency: Bi-Monthly*
Jeff Caporale, Editor-in-chief

London Jewish Community News
536 Huron St., London, ON N5Y 4J5
519-673-3310, Fax: 519-673-1161
Frequency: quarterly

Mennonite Brethren Herald
Canadian Mennonite Brethren Conference, 1310 Taylor Ave., Winnipeg, MB R2M 3Z6
204-654-5760, Fax: 204-654-1865, 888-669-6575
mbherald@mbconf.ca
www.mbherald.com
Circulation: 17,500 *Frequency: Monthly*
Dora Dueck, Assistant Editor
Laura Kalmar, Editor
Helga Kasdorf, Manager, Circulation & Advertising

The New Brunswick Anglican
773 Glengarry Place, Fredericton, NB E3B 5Z8
506-459-5358, Fax: 506- -
awatts@nbnet.nb.ca
fredericton.anglican.org
Circulation: 10,000 *Frequency: 10 times a year*
Rt. Rev. Claude Miller, Publisher

The New Freeman
1 Bayard Dr., Saint John, NB E2L 3L5
506-653-6806, Fax: 506-653-6818
tnf@nbnet.nb.ca
Circulation: 7,480 *Frequency: Weekly*
Margie Trafton, Editor

Niagara Anglican
c/o Anglican Diocese of Niagara, Cathedral Place, 252 James St. North, Hamilton, ON L8R 2L3
905-573-0962, Fax: 905- -
dihutton@mountaincable.com
Circulation: 16,175 *Frequency: Monthly exc. July & Aug.*
Christopher Grabiec, Editor

L'Oratoire / The Oratory
3800, ch Queen Mary, Montréal, QC H3V 1H6
514-733-8211, Fax: 514-733-9735
revue@osj.qc.ca
www.saint-joseph.org
Circulation: 7,500 English; 42,000 French *Frequency: 6 fois par an; français*
Nathalie Dumas, Rédactrice-en-chef

Ottawa Jewish Bulletin
21 Nadolny Sachs, Ottawa, ON K2A 1R9
613-798-4696, Fax: 613-798-4730
bulletin@jccottawa.com
www.ottawajewishbulletin.com
Circulation: 2,500 *Frequency: 19 times a year*

Outlook
#3, 6184 Ash St., Vancouver, BC V5Z 3G9
604-324-5101, Fax: 604-325-2470
outlook@vcn.bc.ca
www.vcn.bc.ca/outlook/
Frequency: 6 times a year; ISSN: 0834-0242
Carl Rosenberg, Editor-in-chief

Prairie Messenger
Benedictine Monks of St. Peter's Abbey, PO Box 190, Muenster, SK S0K 2Y0
306-682-1772, Fax: 306-682-5285
pm.ads@stpeterspress.ca
www.stpeters.sk.ca/prairie_messenger
Circulation: 7,000 *Frequency: 46 times a year*
Rev. Peter Novecosky, Editor OSB

Presbyterian Record
50 Wynford Dr., Toronto, ON M3C 1J7
416-441-1111, Fax: 416-441-2825, 800-619-7301
record@presbyterianrecord.ca
www.presbyterianrecord.ca
Circulation: 42,000 *Frequency: Monthly exc. Aug.*
David Harris, Editor

Présence Magazine
2715, ch Côte Ste-Catherine, Montréal, QC H3T 1B6
514-739-9797, Fax: 514-739-1664
presence@presencemag.qc.ca
www.presencemag.qc.ca
Circulation: 2,000 *Frequency: 8 times a year*
Marie-Thérèse Guilbault, Editor-in-chief
Gilles Leblanc, Director

Shalom
#508, 5670 Spring Garden Rd., Halifax, NS B3J 1H6
902-422-7491, Fax: 902-425-3722
atlanticjewishcouncil@theajc.ns.ca
www.theajc.ns.ca
Circulation: 1,400 *Frequency: 3 times a year*
Jon Goldberg, Editor

Studies in Religion / Sciences Religieuses
#347 Arts, University of Alberta, Edmonton, AB T6G 2E6
780-492-2879, Fax: 780-492-2715
willi.braun@ualberta.ca
www.ccsr.ca
Circulation: 1,400 *Frequency: 4 times a year*
Marc Dumas, Editor-in-chief
Willi Braun, Managing Editor

Sunday Magazine
PO Box 53529, PO Box 53529, Broadmead RPO, Victoria, BC V8X 5K2
250-592-6026, Fax: 250-592-8217, 877-992-6071
info@sundaymagazine.org
www.sundaymagazine.org
Circulation: 11,000
Tony Reynolds, Publisher & Editor

Testimony
The Penetecostal Assemblies of Canada, 2450 Milltower Ct., Mississauga, ON L5N 5Z6
905-542-7400, Fax: 905-542-7313
testimony@paoc.org
www.paoc.org/testimony
Circulation: 14,000 *Frequency: Monthly*
Stacey McKenzie, Editor

The United Church Observer
478 Huron St., Toronto, ON M5R 2R3
416-960-8500, Fax: 416-960-8477
general@ucobserver.org
www.ucobserver.org
Circulation: 80,000 *Frequency: 11 times a year; ISSN: 0041-7238*
Muriel Duncan, Editor

La Voix Sépharade
#216, 1, carré Cummings, Montréal, QC H3W 1M6
514-733-4998, Fax: 514-733-3158
info@csq.qc.ca
Frequency: 5 fois par an
Élie Benchetrit, Directeur
Daniel N. Sebban, Rédacteur-en-chef

The War Cry
2 Overlea Blvd., Toronto, ON M4H 1P4
416-422-6117, Fax: 416-422-6120
warcry@can.salvationarmy.org
warcry.salvationarmy.ca
Circulation: 20,000 *Frequency: Monthly*
Maj. Ken Smith, Editor

Western Catholic Reporter
8421 - 101 Ave., Edmonton, AB T6A 0L1
780-465-8030, Fax: 780-465-8031
wcr@wcr.ab.ca
www.wcr.ab.ca
Circulation: 37,015 *Frequency: 44 times a year*
Glen Argan, Managing Editor

Science, Research & Development

Découvrir: La revue de la recherche
425, rue de la Gauchetière est, Montréal, QC H2L 2M7
514-849-0045, Fax: 514-849-5558
decouvrir@acfas.ca
www.acfas.ca/decouvrir
Circulation: 10 000 *Frequency: 6 fois par an; français*
Danielle Ouellet, Éditrice & Rédactrice

Québec Science
#300, 4388, rue St-Denis, Montréal, QC H2J 2L1
514-843-6888, Fax: 514-843-4897
courrier@quebecscience.qc.ca
www.cybersciences.com
Circulation: 32 000 *Frequency: 10 fois par an; français*
Raymond Lemieux, Rédacteur-en-chef

Spectre Magazine
#259, 7400, boul St-Laurent, Montréal, QC H2R 2Y1
514-948-6422, Fax: 514-948-6423
diane.apsq@videotron.ca
www.apsq.org
Circulation: 3,000
Diane Poulin, Editor-in-chief

Social Welfare

Canadian Social Work & CASW Bulletin / Travail social canadien et Bulletin de l'ACTS
Myropen Publications Ltd., #402, 383 Parkdale Ave., Ottawa, ON K1Y 4R4
613-729-6668, Fax: 613-729-9608
casw@casw-acts.ca
www.casw-acts.ca
Circulation: 16,000 *Frequency: English/French; 3 times a year*
Eugenia Repetur Moreno, Executive Director

Community Action: Canada's Community Service Newspaper
41 Marbury Cres., Toronto, ON M3A 2G3
416-449-6766, Fax: 416-444-5850
Circulation: 12,010 *Frequency: 11 times a year*
Leon Kumove, Publisher

Human Rights TRIBUNE
#301, One Nicholas St., Ottawa, ON K1N 7B7
613-789-7407, Fax: 613-789-7414
tribune@hri.ca
www.hri.ca/tribune
Circulation: 2,000 *Frequency: 3 times a year; ISSN: 1192-3822*
Gemma Richardson, Editor

Perception
Canadian Council on Social Development, #100, 190 O'Connor St., Ottawa, ON K2P 2R3
613-236-8977, Fax: 613-236-2750
council@ccsd.ca
www.ccsd.ca
Frequency: 2 times a year; English & French
Nancy Perkins, Communications Coordinator

WhyNot Magazine
Canadian Foundation for Physically Disabled Persons, 731 Runnymede Ave., Toronto, ON M6N 3V7
416-760-7351, Fax: 416-760-9405
whynot@sympatico.ca
www.cfpdp.com
Frequency: 3 times a year
Bill McQuat, Editor
Vim Kochhar, Publisher
Larry Allen, Editor

Sports & Recreation

Athletics: Canada's National Track & Field/Running Magazine
#211, 3 Concorde Gate, Toronto, ON M3C 3N7
416-426-7215, Fax: 416-426-7358
ontrack@eol.ca
www.otfa.ca
Circulation: 4,000 *Frequency: 8 times a year; ISSN 0229-4966*
John Craig, Editor
Cecil Smith, Managing Director

Atlantic Snowmobiler
#510, 527 Beaverbrook Ct., Fredericton, NB E3B 1X6
506-444-6489, Fax: 506-444-6453
Circulation: 20,000 *Frequency: 4 times a year*
Terrence D. Kehoe, Publisher

BC Hockey Now
#300, 92 Lonsdale Ave., North Vancouver, BC V7M 2E6
604-990-1432, Fax: 604-990-1433
www.bchockey.com
Frequency: 18 times a year; also Alberta Hockey Now & Ontario Hockey Now
Don McIntosh, Publisher, dmcintosh@hockeynow.ca
Andrew Chong, Editor, andrewchong@hockeynow.ca

Below the Belt Boxing Magazine
#1712, 1478 Pilgrims Way, Oakville, ON L6M 3G7
416-336-1947
dameon@belowthebelt.tv
www.belowthebelt.tv

Canadian Cyclist
7 Barker St., Paris, ON N3L 2H4
519-442-7905, Fax: 519-442-5259
news@canadiancyclist.com
www.canadiancyclist.com
Circulation: 8,000
Tracy Harkness, Publisher
Robert Jones, Editor

Canadian Rodeo News
#223, 2116 - 27 Ave. NE, Calgary, AB T2E 7A6
403-250-7292, Fax: 403-250-6926
editor@rodeocanada.com
www.rodeocanada.com
Circulation: 4,000 *Frequency: Monthly*
Darell Hartlen, Editor

Diver Magazine
241 East 1st St., North Vancouver, BC V7K 1B4
604-988-0711, Fax: 604-988-0747
mail@divermag.com
www.divermag.com
Circulation: 7,000 *Frequency: 8 times a year*
Phil Nuytten, Publisher
Virginia Cowell, Editor

Flagstick Golf Magazine
8197 Parkway Rd., Metcalfe, ON K0A 2P0
613-821-0888, Fax: 613-821-4888
info@flagstick.com
www.flagstick.com
Circulation: 20,000 *Frequency: 6 times a year*
Jeff Bauder, Publisher

Golf Guide
16410 - 137 Ave., Edmonton, AB T5L 4H8
780-447-2128, Fax: 780-447-1933
Frequency: Annually, April
Paul McCracken, Publisher

Golf International
c/o Media Transcontinental, 1100, boul René Lévesque ouest, 24e étage, Montréal, QC H3B 4X9
514-392-9000, Fax: 514-392-1489, 800-361-5479
www.transcontinental-gtc.com
Circulation: 40 000 *Frequency: 6 fois par an; français*
Luc Desjardins, President & CEO

Golf West
250-426-7253, Fax: 250-426-4125, 800-663-8555
info@kpimedia.com
www.mygolfwest.com
Circulation: 30,000 *Frequency: Annually, spring*
Jooy Jacob, Writer
Keith G. Powell, Publisher
Amber Cowie, Writer

Hockey News
Transcontinental Media Inc., #100, 25 Sheppard Ave. West, Toronto, ON M2N 6S7
416-227-8237, Fax: 416-340-2786
Circulation: 103,350 *Frequency: 42 times a year*
Gerald McGroarty, Publisher & Editor-in-chief

Hot Sled
#5, 1020 Brevik Pl., Mississauga, ON L4W 4N7
905-624-8218, Fax: 905-624-6764
info@hotsled.com
www.hotsled.com
Circulation: 75,000
William E. Taylor, Publisher

Le Journal Québec Quilles / Bowling Québec
CP 126 Anjou, Montréal, QC H1L 4N7
514-351-5224, Fax: 514-351-6818
qcquilles@videotron.ca
Frequency: 5 fois par an; français
Yves Larocque, Éditeur

The Leader
#100, 1345 Baseline Rd., Ottawa, ON K2C 0A7
613-224-5131, Fax: 613-224-5982
smuehlherr@scouts.ca
www.scouts.ca
Circulation: 38,000 *Frequency: 10 times a year; ISSN: 0711-5377*
Susan Muehlherr, Executive Editor

MARCHE-Randonnée
CP 1000 M, 4545, ave. Pierre-De Coubertin, Montréal, QC H1V 3R2
514-252-3157, Fax: 514-252-5137, 866-252-2065
revuemarche@fqmarche.qc.ca
www.fqmarche.qc.ca/revue.asp
Circulation: 8 225 *Frequency: 4 fois par an*
Raymond Dulude, Advertising
Daniel Pouplot, Production Manager
Louise Giroux, Co-ordinatrice

Motoneige Québec
4545, av Pierre-de-Coubertin, Montréal, QC H1V 3R2
514-252-3163, Fax: 514-254-2066
michel.garneau@fcmq.qc.ca
Circulation: 60 000 *Frequency: 4 fois par an; français*
Michel Garneau, Directeur de la rédaction

MX Performance
593 Yonge St., Toronto, ON M4Y 1Z4
416-922-7223, Fax: 416-922-8001
Frequency: Bi-monthly
Noel Simpson, Managing Editor

National Rugby Post
13228 - 76 St., Edmonton, AB T5C 1B6
780-476-0268, Fax: 780-473-1066
hector@oanet.com
www.rugbypost.com
Circulation: 6,000 *Frequency: 6 times a year*
David C. Graham, Publisher

Northwestern Ontario Golfing News
807-623-2348, Fax: 807-623-7515
nspinc@tbaytel.net
Circulation: 2,000 *Frequency: 5 times a year*
Scott Sumner, Publisher & Editor

Northwestern Ontario Snowmobile News
807-623-2348, Fax: 807-623-7515
nspinc@tbaytel.net
Circulation: 2,000 *Frequency: 7 times a year*
Scott A. Summer, Publisher & Editor

Ontario Golf
Town Media, 1074 Cooke Blvd., Burlington, ON L7T 4A8
905-634-8003, Fax: 905-634-7661
info@townmedia.ca
www.golfontario.ca
Circulation: 55,000 *Frequency: 4 times a year*
Wayne Narcisco, Publisher

Ontario Snowmobiler
78 Main St. South, Newmarket, ON L3Y 3Y6
905-898-8585, Fax: 905-898-8071, 888-661-7469
ontariosnowmobile@bellnet.ca
www.ontariosnowmobiler.com
Circulation: 70,000 *Frequency: 5 times a year*
Raymond D. Kehoe, Publisher
Terrence D. Kehoe, CEO

Ontario Tennis
Ontario Tennis Association, #200, 1 Shoreham Dr., Toronto, ON M3N 3A7
416-514-1100, Fax: 416-514-1112, 800-387-5066
ota@tennisontario.com
www.tennisontario.com
Circulation: 20,000 *Frequency: 3 times a year*

Outdoor Sportsman
PO Box 13754 A, 36 Pippy Pl., St. John's, NL A1B 4G5
709-754-3515, Fax: 709-754-7490
customerservice@newfoundlandsportsman.com
newfoundlandsportsman.com
Circulation: 14,621 *Frequency: 6 times a year*
Dwight J. Blackwood, Publisher
Gordon Follett, Editor

Pacific Golf Magazine
604-299-7311, Fax: 604-299-9188
cwm@canadawide.com
www.canadawide.com
Circulation: 25,000 *Frequency: 4 times a year*
Peter Legge, Publisher
Stephen Thomas, General Sales Manager

Pedal Magazine
#703, 317 Adelaide St. West, Toronto, ON M5V 1P9
416-977-2100, Fax: 416-977-9200
info@pedalmag.com
www.pedalmag.com

Circulation: 18,000 *Frequency: 6 times a year; ISSN: 1191-2685*
Benjamin Sadavoy, Publisher & Editor

Physical Education Digest
11 Cerilli Cres., Sudbury, ON P3E 5R3
Fax: 705-523-3331, 800-544-8782
pedigest@cyberbeach.net
www.pedigest.com
Circulation: online only *Frequency: website database*
Dick Moss, Publisher

Québec Soccer
6900, rue St-Denis, 3e étage, Montréal, QC H2S 2S2
514-278-6399, Fax: 514-278-9737
journal@quebecsoccer.com
www.quebecsoccer.com
Circulation: 40 000 *Frequency: 12 fois par an; français*
Pascal Cifarelli, Publisher
Matthias Van Halst, Editor-in-chief

SBC Skateboard Magazine
#3266, 2255B Queen St. East, Toronto, ON M4E 1G3
416-406-2400, Fax: 416-406-0656
info@sbcskateboard.com
www.sbcskateboard.com
Circulation: 25,000 *Frequency: 5 times a year*
Steve Jarrett, Publisher
Ryan Stutt, Managing Editor

SCORE - Canada's Golf Magazine
416-928-2909, Fax: 416-928-1181, 800-320-6420
info@scoregolf.com
www.scoregolf.com
Circulation: 142,438 *Frequency: 6 times a year*
Bob Weeks, Managing Editor
Kim Locke, Publisher

SCORE Golf for Women
416-928-2909, Fax: 416-966-1181
Frequency: Annually

SCORE Golf Québec
#101, 5397 Eglinton Ave. West, Toronto, ON M9C 5K6
416-928-2909, Fax: 416-966-1181
scoresls@idirect.com
Circulation: 35,000 *Frequency: 4 fois par an*
Peter Robinson, Editor, robinson@scoregolf.com
Kim Locke, Publisher

Ski Canada
47 Soho Sq., Toronto, ON M5T 2Z2
416-595-1252, Fax: 416-595-7255, 888-666-9754
info@skicanadamag.com
www.skicanadamag.com
Circulation: 40,733 *Frequency: 6 times a year*
Iain MacMillan, Editor
Paul Green, Publisher

Ski Press/Ski Presse
1395, rue Marie-Victorin, Saint-Bruno, QC J3V 6B7
450-653-1033, Fax: 450-653-1038, 888-854-3121
info@skipressmag.com
www.skipressworld.com
Circulation: 182,000 *Frequency: 4 times a year*
Jean Marc Blais, Publisher
Jules Older, Editor-in-chief, English version

Ski& Ride West
250-426-7253, Fax: 250-426-4125, 800-663-8555
info@kpimedia.com
www.koocanusapublications.com
Circulation: 30,000 *Frequency: Annually, fall*
Jeff Cummings, Editor
Keith G. Powell, Publisher

SkiTrax
#703, 317 Adelaide St. West, Toronto, ON M5V 1P9
416-977-2100, Fax: 416-977-9200
info@skitrax.com
www.skitrax.com
Circulation: 30,000 *Frequency: 4 times a year; ISSN: 1191-2677*
Benjamin Sadavoy, Publisher

Sno Riders West
250-426-7253, Fax: 250-426-4125, 800-663-8555
info@kpimedia.com
www.snoriderswest.com; www.riderswestmag.com
Frequency: 5 times a year; fall (41,000), winter (30,000), mid-winter (32,000), spring (32,000), summer (32,000)
Jeff Cummings, Editor
Keith G. Powell, Publisher

Snowboard Canada Magazine
SBC Media, #3266, 2255B Queen St. East, Toronto, ON M4E 1G3
416-406-2400, Fax: 416-406-0656
info@snowboardcanada.com
Circulation: 73,000 *Frequency: 4 times a year*
Steve Jarrett, Publisher

Sporting Scene
22 Maberley Cres., West Hill, ON M1C 3K8
416-284-0304
sportingscene@yahoo.com
Circulation: 24,000 *Frequency: 11 times a year*
Peter Martens, Publisher & Editor-in-chief

Squash Life
c/o Squash Ontario, 1185 Eglinton Ave. East, Toronto, ON M3C 3C6
416-426-7201, Fax: 416-426-7393
www.squashontario.com
Circulation: 5,000 *Frequency: 3 times a year*
Sherry Funston, Executive Director & Managing Editor

Supertrax International
#187, 762 Upper James St., Hamilton, ON L9C 3A2
905-286-2135, Fax: 905-286-6308
info@supertraxmag.com
www.supertraxmag.com
Circulation: 76,520 *Frequency: 4 times a year; English & French*
Mark Lester, Publisher
Kent Lester, Executive Editor

Sweep! Curling's Magazine
#12, 6655 Kitimat Rd., Mississauga, ON L5N 6J4
905-542-0539, Fax: 905-567-8920
sweep@sweepmag.com
www.sweepmag.com
Circulation: 8,000 *Frequency: 6 times a year*
Bob Garvin, Editor

Swim News
356 Sumach St., Toronto, ON M4X 1V4
416-963-5599, Fax: 416- -
swimnews@swimnews.com
www.swimnews.com
Circulation: 4,300 *Frequency: 10 times a year*
N.J. Thierry, Publisher

Volleyball Canada Magazine
#202, 5510 Canotek Rd., Gloucester, ON K1J 9J5
613-748-5681, Fax: 613-748-5727
info@volleyball.ca
www.volleyball.ca
Circulation: 35,000 *Frequency: 4 times a year*
Greg Smith, Publisher

Wakeboard SBC Magazine
#3266, 2255B Queen St. East, Toronto, ON M4E 1G3
416-406-2400, Fax: 416-406-0656
info@sbcmedia.com
www.sbcmedia.com
Circulation: 36,000 *Frequency: 2 times a year*
Steve Jarrett, Publisher

WaveLength Magazine
1773 El Verano Dr., Gabriola Island, BC V0R 1X6
250-247-9093, Fax: 250-247-9083, 800-668-8806
RMumford@WavelengthMagazine.com
www.wavelengthmagazine.com
Circulation: 22,000 *Frequency: 6 times a year*
Ron Mumford, Publisher
Diana Mumford, Editor

Television, Radio, Video & Home Appliances

Audio Ideas Guide
#12, 860 Dufferin St., King City, ON L7B 1K5
905-833-7177, Fax: 905-833-7178
mail@audio-ideas.on.ca
www.audio-ideas.com
Frequency: Quarterly
Andrew Marshall, Editor/Publisher, andrew@audio-ideas.com

The Brandon Sun TV Book
501 Rosser Ave., Brandon, MB R7A 5Z6
204-727-2451, Fax: 204-725-0976
Circulation: 14,843 *Frequency: Weekly*
Bill Chester, General Manager

Feature (Your Premium Entertainment Magazine)
514-939-5024, Fax: 514-939-8027
editor@feature.ca
www.featuremagazine.com
Circulation: 930,000 *Frequency: Monthly*
Marvin Boisvert, Publisher
David Sherman, Editor

Globe Television
Globe & Mail, 444 Front St. West, Toronto, ON M5V 2S9
416-585-5567, Fax: 416-585-5599
Frequency: Weekly
Andrew Ryan, Editor

The Inner Ear Report
Disticor Magazines, #14, 695 Westney Rd. South, Ajax, ON L1S 6M9
905-619-6565, Fax: 905-619-2903
Circulation: 16,000 *Frequency: 4 times a year*

Post TV
The National Post Company, 1450 Don Mills Rd., Toronto, ON M3B 3R5
416-383-2300, Fax: 416-442-2212
Circulation: 104,000 *Frequency: 52 times a year*

Primeurs
514-939-5024, Fax: 514-939-8027
editor@feature.ca
www.featuremagazine.com
Circulation: 409 000 *Frequency: Mensuel; français*
Marvin Boisvert, Éditeur
Mireille Duhamel, Rédactrice
Nathalie Abitbol, Directrice de tirage

StarWeek Magazine
c/o Toronto Star, One Yonge St., Toronto, ON M5E 1E6
416-869-4244, Fax: 416-869-4103
Circulation: 645,181 *Frequency: Weekly*
Gord Stimmell, Editor

Sunday Sun Television Magazine
Calgary Sun, 2615 - 12 St. NE, Calgary, AB T2E 7W9
403-250-4220, Fax: 403-250-4258
Circulation: 63,794 *Frequency: Weekly*
Guy Huntingford, Publisher
Chris Nelson, Editor-in-chief

Sunday Sun Television Magazine
c/o Edmonton Sun, #250, 4990 - 92 Ave., Edmonton, AB T6B 3A1
780-468-0100, Fax: 780-468-0233
Circulation: 95,860 *Frequency: Weekly*
Graham Delziel, Editor

Sunday Sun Television Magazine
c/o Ottawa Sun, 6 Antares Dr., Ottawa, ON K1G 5H7
613-739-7000, Fax: 613- -
Circulation: 54,267 *Frequency: Weekly*
Rick Gibbons, Publisher

Sunday Sun Television Magazine
c/o Toronto Sun, 333 King St. East, Toronto, ON M5A 3X5
416-947-2000, Fax: 416-947-2441
Circulation: 400,652 *Frequency: Weekly*

Télé Horaire
c/o Le Journal de Montréal, 4545, rue Frontenac, Montréal, QC H2H 2R7
514-521-4545, Fax: 514-525-5442
www.journalmtl.com
Circulation: 326 440 *Frequency: Hebdomadaire; français*
Raymond Fortin, Director, Special Projects & Sections

Télé Horaire (Québec)
c/o Le Journal de Québec, 450, rue Bechard, Vanier, QC G1M 2E9
418-683-1573, Fax: 418-683-1027
www.journaldequebec.com
Circulation: 126 689 *Frequency: Hebdomadaire; français*
Jean-Claude L'Abbée, Éditeur

Téléromans
Trustmedia, 7, ch Bates, Outremont, QC H2V 4V7
514-848-7000, Fax: 514-843-7079
Circulation: 46 000 *Frequency: 2 fois par an; français*
Clair Syril, Vice-President & General Manager

TV 7 Jours
514-848-7164, Fax: 514-270-7079
Circulation: 92 361 *Frequency: Hebdomadaire; français*

TV Guide
Transcontinenal Media Inc., #100, 25 Sheppard Ave. West, Toronto, ON M2N 6S7
416-733-7600, Fax: 416-733-3568, 800-387-1163
www.tvguide.ca
Circulation: 281,955 *Frequency:* Weekly; *ISSN:* 1191-5315
Jamie Hubbard, Editor

TV Hebdo
514-848-7000, Fax: 514-270-7079
Circulation: 123 670 *Frequency:* Hebdomadaire
Claire Syril, Président

TV Scene, Fort McMurray
8550 Franklin Ave., Bag 4008, Fort McMurray, AB T9H 3G1
780-743-8186, Fax: 780-790-1006
today@bowesnet.com
www.fortmcmurraytoday.com
Circulation: 8,205 *Frequency:* Weekly
Tim O'Rourke, Publisher

TV This Week
6 Louise St., Truro, NS B2N 5C3
902-893-9405, Fax: 902-893-0518
Circulation: 11,000
Peter Padbury, Publisher

TV Times, Calgary
PO Box 2400 M, 215 - 16th St. SE, Calgary, AB T2P 0W8
403-235-7100, Fax: 403-235-7379
www.calgaryherald.com
Circulation: 150,000

TV Times, Edmonton
10006 - 101 St., Edmonton, AB T5J 0S1
780-429-5100, Fax: 780-429-5500
www.edmontonjournal.com
Circulation: 150,000
Linda Hughes, Publisher
Allan Mayer, Editor-in-chief

TV Times, St. Catharines
17 Queen St., St Catharines, ON L2R 5G5
905-684-7251, Fax: 905-684-8011
Circulation: 44,600
Paul McCraig, Publisher

TV Times, Windsor
167 Ferry St., Windsor, ON N9A 4M5
519-255-5711, Fax: 519-255-5515
Circulation: 87,275
Jim McCormack, Publisher

TV Week Magazine
4180 Lougheed Hwy., 4th Fl., Burnaby, BC V5C 6A7
604-299-7311, Fax: 604-299-9188, 800-663-0518
cwm@canadawide.com
www.canadawide.com
Circulation: 80,000 *Frequency:* Weekly
Peter Legge, Publisher
Brent Furdyk, Editor

TV Week Stratford
PO Box 430, 16 Packham Rd., Stratford, ON N5A 6T6
519-271-2220, Fax: 519-271-1026, 800-265-8577
jkastner@bowesnet.com
stratfordbeaconherald.com
Circulation: 11,475 *Frequency:* Weekly
John Kastner, Editor
Dave Carter, Publisher

TVOntario Magazine
TV Ontario, PO Box 200 Q, 2180 Yonge St., 5th Fl., Toronto, ON M4T 2T4
416-484-2600, Fax: 416-484-6285
Frequency: 10 times a year
Angela Garde, Editor

Voila
c/o GESCA, 7, rue St-Jacques, Montréal, QC H2Y 1K9
514-285-7306, Fax: 514-845-8129
Frequency: Hebdomadaire; français

The Winnipeg Sun TV Magazine
1700 Church Ave., Winnipeg, MB R2X 3A2
204-694-2022, Fax: 204-632-8709
wpgsun@wpgsun.com
Circulation: 44,337 *Frequency:* Weekly
Ed Huculak, Publisher

Travel

Above & Beyond Magazine
PO Box 13142, Kanata, ON K2K 1X3
613-599-4190, Fax: 613-599-4191, 877-227-2842
info@arcticjournal.ca
Circulation: 20,000 *Frequency:* 6 times a year
Tom Koelbel, Publisher & Editor

Bear Country
1475 West Walsh St., Thunder Bay, ON P7E 4X6
807-474-2636, Fax: 807-474-2658
pgresham@bearskinairlines.com
bearskinairlines.com
Circulation: 10,000 *Frequency:* 4 times a year
Patti Gresham, Production Manager & Editor

British Columbia Magazine
1803 Douglas St., 3rd Fl., Victoria, BC V8T 5C3
250-356-5860, Fax: 250-356-5896, 800-663-7611
orders@bcmag.ca
www.bcmag.ca
Other information: Toll Free Fax: 1-800-308-4533
Circulation: 125,000 *Frequency:* 4 times a year
Don Foxford, Publisher
Anita Willis, Editor, editor@bcmag.ca

Dreamscapes Travel & Lifestyle Magazine
3 Bluffwood Dr., Toronto, ON M2H 3L4
416-497-5353, Fax: 416-497-0871, 888-700-4464
gtm@ca.inter.net
www.dreamscapes.ca
Circulation: 110,000 *Frequency:* 8 times a year
Sandra Kitchen, Publisher
Donna Vieira, Editor
Joe Turkel, President & Group Publisher

Espaces
#205, 911, rue Jean-Talon est, Montréal, QC H2R 1V5
514-277-3477, Fax: 514-277-3822
info@espaces.qc.ca
www.espaces.qc.ca
Circulation: 50 000 *Frequency:* 6 times a year
Marie Eisenmann, Rédactrice en chef

Family Getaways
4242 Rockwood Rd., Mississauga, ON L4W 1L8
905-272-1843, Fax: 905-272-0474
fun@ourkids.net
www.ourkids.net
Circulation: 100,000 *Frequency:* annual
Agatha Stawicki, Managing Editor

Geo Plein Air
514-521-8356, Fax: 514-521-5711, 800-567-8356
geopleinair@velo.qc.ca
www.geopleinair.com
Circulation: 25 358 *Frequency:* 7 fois par an; français
Magazine québécois de la nature et de l'aventure
Pierre Hamel, Éditeur
Nathalie Schneider, Rédactrice en chef

Great Getaways Guide
Vancouver, Coast & Mountains Tourism, #250, 1508 West 2nd Ave., Vancouver, BC V6J 1H2
604-739-9011, Fax: 604-739-0153, 800-667-3306
info@vcmbc.com
www.vcmbc.com/greatgetaways/
Jennifer Huitema, Director, Communications

Greater Halifax Visitor Guide
1300 Hollis St., Halifax, NS B3J 1T6
902-420-9943, Fax: 902-429-9058
publishers@metroguide.ca
www.metroguidepublishing.ca
Circulation: 240,000 *Frequency:* Annual
Sheila Blair, Publisher

HolidayMaker
Wild Boar Publications, PO Box 10, 23260 - 88 Ave., Fort Langley, BC V1M 2R4
604-888-4037, Fax: 604-888-6663
holidaymaker@telus.net
www.cwtleisure.ca/holidaymaker/
Circulation: 86,500 *Frequency:* 2 times a year
Chris Potter, Publisher & Editor

Horizon Travel Magazine
#303, 65 Front St. East, Toronto, ON M5E 1B5
416-603-8900, Fax: 416-603-8901
horizon@horizontravelmag.com
www.horizontravelmag.com
Frequency: 6 times a year
Amir Shirazi, Publisher
Denise Shirazi, Editor-in-chief

Key to Kingston
Osprey Media, PO Box 1352, 11 Princess St., Kingston, ON K7L 5C6
613-549-8442, Fax: 613-549-4333
Circulation: 22,500 *Frequency:* 8 times a year
Mary Laflamme, Publisher

The Laurentians Tourist Guide / Les Laurentides Guide Touristique
#14, 142, rue de la Chapelle, Mirabel, QC J7J 2C8
450-436-8532, Fax: 450-436-5309
info-tourisme@laurentides.com
www.laurentides.com
Circulation: 73,000, English edition; 202,000, French edition
Frequency: Annually; English & French editions
Diane Leblond, General Manager

müv
#202, 3863, boul Saint-Laurent, Montréal, QC H2W 1Y1
514-286-9696, Fax: 514-284-9152
info@muvmag.com
www.muvmag.com
Frequency: 4 fois par an
Julie Boisvert, Rédactrice-en-chef

99 North Magazine
4180 Lougheed Hwy., Burnaby, BC V5C 6A7
604-299-7311, Fax: 604-299-9188
cwm@canadawide.com
www.canadawide.com
Circulation: 100,000 *Frequency:* 2 times a year
Samantha Legge, General Manager

Outpost: Canada's Travel Magazine
#201, 425 Queen St. West, Toronto, ON M5V 2A5
416-972-6527, Fax: 416-972-6645
www.outpostmagazine.com
Circulation: 28,000 *Frequency:* Bi-monthly
Matthew Robinson, Publisher
Larry Frolick, Editor

Presse Voyages
19, rue La Gallois, Gatineau, QC J8V 2H3
819-246-9855
tvcanada@videotron.ca
Circulation: 5,000 *Frequency:* Bi-monthly
Ynes De Lara, Publisher

La Revue Voil à Québec
#201, 735, boul. Wilfrid-Hamel, Québec, QC G1M 2R1
418-694-1272, Fax: 418-694-1119, 888-694-1272
Circulation: 265 000
Curtis J. Sommerville, Éditeur
Lynn Magee, Rédactrice-en-chef

Rocky Mountain Visitor's Magazine
250-426-7253, Fax: 250-426-4125, 800-663-8555
info@kpimedia.com
koocanusapublications.com
Circulation: 40,000 May; 30,000 Nov. *Frequency:* Semi-annual
Jeff Cummings, Editor
Keith G. Powell, Publisher

Saskatchewan Vacation Guide
Tourism Saskatchewan, 1922 Park St., Regina, SK S4P 3V7
306-787-9685, Fax: 306-787-0715, 877-237-2273
www.sasktourism.com
Circulation: 195,000 *Frequency:* annually

The Travel Society Magazine
#218, 1033 Bay St., Toronto, ON M5S 3A5
416-926-0111, Fax: 416-926-0222
brit@thetravelsociety.com
www.thetravelsociety.com
Circulation: 7,000
Nigel D. Raincock, Publisher
Ann Wallace, Editor

Where Canadian Rockies
#250, 125 - 9 Ave. SE, Calgary, AB T2G 0P6
403-299-1897, Fax: 403-299-1899
info@whererockies.com
www.wherecanadianrockies.com
Circulation: 240,000 summer, 145,000 winter *Frequency:* 2 times a year; English with some Japanese
Jack Newton, Publisher

Where Vancouver
2208 Spruce St., Vancouver, BC V6H 2P3
604-736-5586, Fax: 604-736-3465
infovancouver@where.ca
www.where.ca
Circulation: 53,000 *Frequency:* Monthly

Peggie Terry, Publisher

Women's & Feminist

L'Actuelle
1043, rue Tiffin, Longueuil, QC J4P 3G7
450-442-3983, Fax: 450-442-4363
cerfer@videotron.ca
www.cfq.qc.ca
Circulation: 50 000 *Frequency: 5 fois par an; français*
Publication officielle des Cercles de Fermières du Québec

Canadian Guider
c/o Girl Guides of Canada, 50 Merton St., Toronto, ON M4S 1A3
416-487-5281, Fax: 416-487-5570
bryantc@girlguides.ca
www.girlguides.ca
Circulation: 30,891 *Frequency: 3 times a year*
Deborah Del Duca

Canadian Woman Studies / Les Cahiers de la Femme
210 Founders College, York University, 4700 Keele St., Toronto, ON M3J 1P3
416-736-5356, Fax: 416-736-5765
cwscf@yorku.ca
www.yorku.ca/cwscf
Circulation: 5,000 *Frequency: 4 times a year; ISSN: 0713-3235*
Luciana Ricciutelli, Editor

Chatelaine
1 Mount Pleasant Rd., 8th Fl., Toronto, ON M4Y 2Y5
416-764-1888, Fax: 416-764-2891, 800-268-6812
lise.ravary@chatelaine.com
www.chatelaine.com
Circulation: 675,016 *Frequency: Monthly; ISSN 0009-1995*
Sara Angel, Editor-in-Chief
Lise Ravary, Editorial Director

Châtelaine
514-845-5141, Fax: 514-843-2183
www.chatelaine.qc.ca
Circulation: 203 014 *Frequency: Mensuel; français; ISSN: 0317-2635*
Lise Ravary, Éditeur

City Woman Magazine
Capital Publishers, 226 Argyle St., Ottawa, ON K2E 6Z5
613-230-0333, Fax: 613-230-4441
www.capitalpublishers.com
Circulation: 30,000 *Frequency: 4 times a year*
Dianne Wing
Steve Ball

Coup de Pouce
#900, 2001, rue University, Montréal, QC H3A 2A6
514-499-0317, Fax: 514-848-9779
www.transcontinental.com
Circulation: 228 071 *Frequency: 12 fois par an; ISSN: 0822-3033*
Francine Tremblay, Éditeur
France Lefebvre, Rédacteur-en-chef

Edmonton Woman
780-424-1221, Fax: 780-421-7677
abrnews@shaw.ca
www.edmontonwoman.com
Circulation: 25,000 *Frequency: 6 times a year*
Lorne Silverstein, Publisher
Colin Smith, Editor-in-chief

elevate magazine
#1902, 365 Bloor St. East, Toronto, ON M4W 3L4
416-869-3131, Fax: 416-869-3008
www.elevatemagazine.com
Brian Light, Publisher
Chantel Simmons, Editor-in-chief

Elle Canada
Transcontinental Media, #100, 25 Sheppard Ave. West, Toronto, ON M2N 6S7
416-218-3604
www.ellecanada.com
Jacqueline Howe, Publisher
Noreen Flanagan, Sr. Editor

Elle Québec
Publications Transcontinental-Hachette, #900, 2001, rue University, Montréal, QC H3A 2A6
514-499-0491, Fax: 514-848-9779
Circulation: 88 398 *Frequency: Mensuel; français*
Francine Tremblay, Éditrice
Sylvie Poirier, Rédactrice-en-chef

Femme d'Aujourd'hui
514-848-7164, Fax: 514-270-7079
Circulation: 47 000 *Frequency: Mensuel; français*
Sandra Cliche, Editorial Director

Femme Plus
514-270-1100, Fax: 514-270-7079
femmeplus@publicor.ca
Circulation: 52 204 *Frequency: Mensuel; français*
Claire Syril, Éditrice
Hélène Matteau, Directrice

FQ Magazine
134 Peter St., 3rd Fl., Toronto, ON M5V 2H2
416-367-7664, Fax: 416-367-7659
Frequency: 5 times a year
Jeanne Beker, Editor-in-chief

Homemaker's Magazine / Madame
Transcontinental Media, #100, 25 Sheppard Ave. West, Toronto, ON M2N 6S7
416-733-7600, Fax: 416-733-8683
Circulation: 512,000 *Frequency: 8 times a year*
Kathy Ullyott, Editor-in-chief

The Look
St. Joseph Media, #320, 111 Queen St. East, Toronto, ON M5C 1S2
416-364-3333, Fax: 416-595-7217
thelook@thelookmagazine.ca
www.thelookmagazine.ca
Circulation: 199,718 *Frequency: 4 times a year*
David Livingstone, Editor-in-chief

Madame
Transcontinental Media, #900, 2001, rue Université, Montréal, QC H3A 2A6
514-499-0317, Fax: 514-848-9779
Circulation: 109 634 *Frequency: 9 fois par année*
Jean-Louis Gauthier, Rédacteur

Magazine les Ailes de la mode
Les Editions San Francisco inc., 50, rue de Lauzon, Boucherville, QC J4B 1E6
450-449-1313, Fax: 450-449-1317
Circulation: 29 751 *Frequency: 6 fois par an*
Claude Fortin, Éditeur
Julie Brisson, Rédactrice-en-chef
Camille Roberge, Rédactrice

Orah Magazine
Canadian Hadassah-WIZO, #900, 1310, av Greene, Westmount, QC H3Z 2B8
514-937-9431, Fax: 514-933-6483
natoff@canadian-hadassah-wizo.org
www.canadian-hadassah-wizo.org
Circulation: 14,000 *Frequency: 2 times a year*
Rochelle Levinson, Editor-in-chief
Lily Frank, National Exec. Vice-President

Room of One's Own
PO Box 46160 D, Vancouver, BC V6J 5G5
contactus@roommagazine.com
www.roommagazine.com
Circulation: 1,100 *Frequency: 4 times a year; ISSN: 0316-1609*

Youth

The Canadian Leader
Canyouth Publications, #100, 1345 Baseline Rd., Ottawa, ON K2C 0A7
613-224-5131, Fax: 613-224-3571
leader@scouts.ca
www.scouts.ca/leader
Circulation: 37,000 *Frequency: 10 times a year*
Ross Francis, Executive Editor

Cool! Le magazine qui bouge
514-848-7164, Fax: 514-270-7079
cool@tva-publications.com
Circulation: 62 000 *Frequency: 12 fois par an*
Marie-Claude Bonneau, Director

Fashion 18
St. Joseph Media, 111 Queen St. East, Toronto, ON M5C 1S2
416-364-3333
www.fashion18.com
Frequency: 4 times a year
Giorgina Bigioni, Publisher

Faze Magazine
#2400, 4936 Yonge St., Toronto, ON M2N 6S3
416-222-3060, Fax: 416-222-2097
letters@fazeteen.com
www.fazeteen.com
Frequency: 5 times a year
Paul Zander, Publisher

Filles Clin d'oeil
514-848-7000, Fax: 514-270-7079
fillescool.canoe.com
Frequency: Mensuel; français

Filles d'aujourd'hui
7, Chemin Bates, Outremont, QC H2V 4V7
514-270-1100, Fax: 514-270-7079
fillesdaujourdhui@publicor.ca
tva.canoe.com
Circulation: 56 030 *Frequency: Mensuel; français*
Claire Sgril, Éditrice
Isabelle Jomphe, Rédactrice-en-chef
Francine Trudeau, Directrice

Fuel
#245, 401 Richmond St. West, Toronto, ON M5V 1X3
416-595-1313, Fax: 416-595-1312
kay@youthculture.com
www.fuelpowered.com
Circulation: 119,268 *Frequency: 7 times a year*
Sara Graham, Editor

Magazine Adorable
#102, 50, rue Queen, Montréal, QC H3C 2N5
514-761-0556, Fax: 514-761-0085
www.adorable.qc.ca
Circulation: 13 173 *Frequency: 10 fois par année; français*
Patrice Demers, Éditeur
Violaine Trudeau, Rédactrice-en-chef

Vervegirl
#245, 401 Richmond St. West, Toronto, ON M5V 1X3
416-595-1313, Fax: 416-595-1312, 888-292-5559
nigel@youthculture.com
www.vervegirl.com
Circulation: 178,851 *Frequency: 8 times a year*
Sara Graham, Associate Editor
Jaishree Drepaul, Editor-in-chief

What's Hers Magazine
#108, 93 Lombard Ave., Winnipeg, MB R3B 3B1
204-985-8160, Fax: 204-943-8991, 800-665-9428
www.whatshers.com
Circulation: 180,000 *Frequency: 5 times a year*
Nancy Moore, Publisher
Barbara Chabai, Editor-in-chief

What's His Magazine
#106, 93 Lombard Ave., Winnipeg, MB R3B 3B1
204-985-8160, Fax: 204-943-8991
letters@whatshis.com
www.whatshis.com
Circulation: 100,000 *Frequency: 5 times a year*
Barbara Chabai, Editor-in-chief
Nancy Moore, Publisher

Youthink
1275 West 6th Ave, 2nd Fl., Vancouver, BC V6H 1A6
604-732-6397, Fax: 604-732-6390, 866-370-6462
andrew@youthink.ca
www.youthink.ca
Circulation: 69,987 *Frequency: 10 times a year*
Andrew Sloan, Publisher

Ethnic

Aboriginal

Alberta Native News
#207, 11460 Jasper Ave., Edmonton, AB T5K 0M1
780-421-7966, Fax: 780-424-3951
editor@albertanativenews.com
www.albertanativenews.com
Circulation: 14,000 *Frequency: 12 times a year*
David Moser, Publisher

Alberta Sweetgrass
13245 - 146 St., Edmonton, AB T5L 4S8
780-455-2700, Fax: 780-455-7639
market@ammsa.com
www.ammsa.com/sweetgrass/
Circulation: 7,000 *Frequency: Monthly*

Bert Crowfoot, Publisher
Laura Suthers, Editor

The Drum
Taiga Communications, #554, 70 Arthur St., Winnipeg, MB R3B 1G7
204-943-1500, Fax: 204-943-1160
staff@taiga-communications.com
www.firstperspective.ca
Circulation: 15,000 *Frequency: monthly*
James Wastasecoot, Publisher
Joseph Quesnel, Editor

First Nations Free Press
363 Sioux Rd., Sherwood Park, AB T8A 4W7
780-449-1803, Fax: 780-449-1807, 800-830-1803
fnfp@telus.net
Frequency: Monthly
Flo Baker, Publisher

The First Perspective & The Drum
Taiga Communications Inc., #554, 70 Arthur St., Winnipeg, MB R3B 1G7
204-943-1500, Fax: 204-943-1160
staff@taiga-communications.com
www.taiga-communications.c om
Circulation: 10,000 *Frequency: Monthly*
James Wastasecoot, Publisher
Len Kruzenga, Editor

Ha-Shilth-Sa
PO Box 1383, Port Alberni, BC V9Y 7M2
250-724-5757, Fax: 250-723-0463, 877-677-1131
hashilthsa@nuuchahnulth.org
www.nuuchahnulth.org
Circulation: 3,100
Denise Ambrose, Regional Reporter
Annie Watts, Office Manager

Inuvik Drum
PO Box 2820, 5108 - 50 St., Yellowknife, NT X1A 2R1
867-777-4545, Fax: 867-777-4412
inuvikdrum@nnsl.com
www.nnsl.com
Circulation: 1,634
Jack Sigvaldson, Publisher
Bruce Valpy, Managing Editor
Petra Ehrke, National/Territorial Manager

Journal of Aboriginal Tourism
PO Box 1240 M, Calgary, AB T2P 2L2
403-228-9984, Fax: 403-229-3598
eao@telusplanet.net
Circulation: 7,800 *Frequency: Annual Directory of Canadian Aboriginal Tourism (Jan.-Feb.); annual directory of Cultural Heritage Tourism (Sept.-Oct.)*
Edmund A. Oliverio, Editorial Director

Kahtou News: The Voice of B.C.'s First Nations
PO Box 192, 5526 Sinku Dr., Sechelt, BC V0N 3A0
604-885-7391, Fax: 604-885-7397, 800-561-4311
kahtou@dcc.net
www.kahtou.com
Circulation: 12,431 *Frequency: Monthly*
Stan Dixon, Publisher & Editor

Ktuqcqakyam Newsletter
7468 Mission Rd., Cranbrook, BC V1C 7E5
250-417-4022, Fax: 250-489-2438
dlalande@ktunaxa.org
www.ktunaxa.com
Circulation: 700 *Frequency: Bi-monthly*
Donna Kraus-Hagerman, Contact

Mi'kmaq-Maliseet Nation News
PO Box 1590, 57 Martin Cres., Truro, NS B2N 5V3
902-895-2038, Fax: 902-893-3030
marketing@cmmns.com
Frequency: Monthly
Don Julien, Publisher
Art Stevens, Managing Editor

The Nation: The News & Cultural Magazine of the James Bay Cree
#3018, 5505, boul St. Laurent, Montréal, QC H2T 1S6
514-272-3077, Fax: 514-278-9914
beesum@beesum-communications.com
www.beesum-communications.com
Circulation: 6,730 *Frequency: 26 times a year; English & James Bay Cree*
Aaron MacDevitt, Sales Representative

Native Journal
#57096, 2020 Sherwood Dr., Sherwood Park, AB T8A 5L7
780-448-9693, Fax: 780-448-9694, 866-526-8688
elaine@nativejournal.ca
www.nativejournal.ca
Frequency: Monthly
Elaine Shuflita, Publisher
Lisa Doucet, Publisher

Native Youth News
363 Sioux Rd., Sherwood Park, AB T8A 4W7
780-449-1803, Fax: 780-449-1807, 800-830-1803
fnfpltd@telusplanet.net
Frequency: Monthly
Flo Baker, Publisher

Natotawin
PO Box 10880, Opaskwayak, MB R0B 2J0
204-627-7066
gabriel.constant@opaskwayak.ca
www.opaskwayak.mb.ca/natotawin
Circulation: 1,000 *Frequency: Weekly*
Gabriel Constant, Editor

New Breed Magazine
c/o Gabriel Dumont Institute, #2, 604 - 22nd St. West, Saskatoon, SK S7M 5W1
306-657-5716, Fax: 306-244-0252
darren.prefontaine@gdi.gdins.org
www.metismuseum.ca
Circulation: 1,000 *Frequency: 3 times a year*
Darren Préfontaine
David Morin
Karon Shmon

Nunavut News/North
c/o Northern News Services Ltd., PO Box 2820, Yellowknife, NT X1A 2R1
867-979-5990, Fax: 867-979-6010
editor@nunavutnews.com
www.nnsl.com
Frequency: Weekly
J.W. (Sig) Sigvaldason, Publisher
Mike Scott, General Manager

Raven's Eye
13245 - 146 St., Edmonton, AB T5L 4S8
780-455-2700, Fax: 780-455-7639
market@ammsa.com
www.ammsa.com/raven
Circulation: 6,500 *Frequency: Monthly*
Bert Crowfoot, Publisher

Saskatchewan Sage
13245 - 146 St., Edmonton, AB T5L 4S8
780-455-2700, Fax: 780-455-7639, 800-661-5469
market@ammsa.com
www.ammsa.com/sage/
Circulation: 6,000 *Frequency: Monthly*
Bert Crowfoot, Publisher
Cheryl Petten, Editor

Secwepemc News, The Voice of the Shuswap Nation
Secwepemc Cultural Education Society, #311, 355 Yellowhead Hwy., Kamloops, BC V2H 1H1
250-828-9783, Fax: 250-372-1127
communic@secewemc.org
www.secwepemc.org
Circulation: 5,000 *Frequency: Monthly*
Kathy Manuel, Managing Editor

Turtle Island News
PO Box 329, Ohsweken, ON N0A 1M0
519-445-0868, Fax: 519-445-0865
news@theturtleislandnews.com
www.theturtleislandnews.com
Circulation: 10,000 *Frequency: Weekly*
Lynda Powless, Publisher & Editor

Western Native News Ltd.
#330, 10115 - 100A St., Edmonton, AB T5J 2W2
780-421-7966, Fax: 780-424-3941
nativenews@telus.net
David Moser, Publisher
Deborah Shatz, Editor

Windspeaker
13245 - 146 St., Edmonton, AB T5L 4S8
780-455-2700, Fax: 780-455-7639
market@ammsa.com
www.ammsa.com/windspeaker
Circulation: 25,500 *Frequency: Monthly*
Bert Crowfoot, Publisher
Debora Steel, Managing Editor

African-Canadian & Caribbean Canadian Communi

Caribbean Camera
#212, 55 Nugget Ave., Toronto, ON M1S 3L1
416-412-2905, Fax: 416-412-2134
caribbeancamera@aol.com
www.thecaribbeancamera.com
Circulation: 35,000 *Frequency: Weekly; 2 editions: Montreal & Toronto*
Raynier Maharaj, Editor

Equality News
1646 Victoria Park Ave., Toronto, ON M1R 1P7
416-759-6397,
Circulation: 37,000 *Frequency: Weekly*
Bhaskar Sharma, Publisher & Managing Editor

The Jamaican Weekly Gleaner
1390 Eglinton Ave. West, Toronto, ON M6C 2E4
416-784-3002, Fax: 416-784-5719, 800-565-3961
gleanercan@gleanerna.com
www.jamaica-gleaner.com
Circulation: 110,000 *Frequency: Weekly; also The Jamaican Weekly Star, The Black Pages Directory*
Maxwell Wynter, General Manager
Yulanda Gordon, Editor

Pride News Magazine
#304, 5200 Finch Ave., Toronto, ON M1S 4Z5
416-335-1719, Fax: 416-335-1723
pridenews@bellnet.ca
www.pridenewsmagazine.com
Circulation: 25,000
Michael Van Cooten, Publisher & Editor

Somali Press
PO Box 30097, 2141 Kipling Ave., Toronto, ON M9W 6T1
416-242-7777, Fax: 416-242-3603
Axmed M.I. Barkhadle, Editor-in-chief

Word: Toronto's Urban Culture Magazine
Working Word Cooperative Ltd., #123, 4-2880 Queen St. East, Brampton, ON L6S 6H4
905-799-1630, Fax: 905-799-2788
editor@wordmag.com
www.wordmag.com
Circulation: 50,000 *Frequency: 9 times a year*
Angela Baldassarre, Editor
Phillip Vassell, Publisher

Arabic

Al-Mughtarib Weekly Newspaper
PO Box 48113, 60 Dundas St. East, Mississauga, ON L5A 4G8
Fax: 905-949-0117, 866-771-9358
Frequency: Weekly
Saleh Rafai, Editor-in-chief

Al-Mustakbal
#6, 1305, Mazurette, Montréal, QC H4N 1G8
514-334-0909, Fax: 514-332-5419
info@almlustakbal.com
www.almustakbal.com
Circulation: 12,000
Joseph Nakhlé, Editeur
Ibrahim Ghorqyebo, Rédacteur-en-chef

Arab Guide
368 Queen St. East, 2nd Fl., Toronto, ON M5A 1T1
416-362-0304, Fax: 416-861-0238
Circulation: 5,000
E. Elgamal, Editor
F. Ahmed, Publisher

Arab News International
602 Millwood Rd., Toronto, ON M5A 1K8
416-362-0307, Fax: 416-861-0238
info@arabnews.ca
Frequency: Bi-weekly
Salah Allam, Publisher
Eynass El Masri, Managing Editor

Arabbusiness International
368 Queen St. East, 2nd Fl., Toronto, ON M5A 1T1
416-362-0304, Fax: 416-861-0238
allam@octoline.com
Circulation: 6,000
S. Allam, Publisher
N. Soliman, Editor & Manager, Advertising

ARC Arabic Journal
368 Queen St. East, Toronto, ON M5A 1T1
416-362-0304, Fax: 416-861-0238
Circulation: 5,000

Emad Nafeh, Editor

Canada & the Arab World
602 Millwood Rd., Toronto, ON M5A 1K8
416-362-0307, Fax: 416-861-0238
info@arabnews.ca
Circulation: 5,000
Salah Allam, Publisher
Ibrahim Salama, Editor

Egypt & the Arab World in Canada
#521, 1117, rue Ste-Catherine, Montréal, QC H3B 1H9
514-288-0188, Fax: 514-288-1944
georgesaad@videotron.ca
Frequency: 4 times a year
George Saad, Editor-in-chief

El-Mahroussa Magazine
Egyptian Canadian Friendship Association Inc., 879, av St-Charles, Chomedey, QC H7V 3T5
450-687-0273, Fax: 450-505-1880
masri1993@hotmail.com
www.el-mahrousaonline.com
Circulation: 12,000 *Frequency: 12 issues a year; Arabic & French*
Nancy Youssef, Chief of Staff

El-Masri Newspaper
879, av St-Charles, Laval, QC H7V 3T5
450-687-0273, Fax: 450-505-1880
ads@el-masrionline.com
www.el-masrionline.com
Circulation: 12,000 *Frequency: Bi-weekly; Arabic & French*
Adel Iskander, General Director

The Iran Star
#205, 72 Steeles Ave. West, Thornhill, ON L4J 1A1
905-763-9770, Fax: 905-763-9771
iranstar@iranstar.com
www.iranstar.com
Circulation: 12,500
Bijan Binesh, Editor-in-chief
Shahram Binesh, Editor & Coordinator

Middle East Report
368 Queen St. East, 2nd Fl., Toronto, ON M5A 1T1
416-362-0304, Fax: 416-861-0238
allam@idirect.com
Circulation: 5,000
N. Soliman, Editor & Manager, Advertising

Armenian

Abaka
Tekeyan Armenian Cultural Association of Montréal, 825, rue Manoogian, Saint-Laurent, QC H4N 1Z5
514-747-6680, Fax: 514-747-6162
abaka@bellnet.ca
Circulation: 1,000 *Frequency: Weekly; Tabloid; Armenian, French & English*
Arsène Mamourian, Editor

Horizon
3401, rue Olivar-Asselin, Montréal, QC H4J 1L5
514-332-3757, Fax: 514-332-4870
manager.horizonweekly@bellnet.ca
Circulation: 2,000
Vahakn Karakashian, Editor

Lradou Newsletter
3401, rue Olivar-Asselin, Montréal, QC H4J 1L5
514-333-1616, Fax: 514-333-1612
ars-canada@bellnet.ca
www.ars-canada.ca
Frequency: Annual

Pourastan
Parish Council of St. Gregory, 615, av Stuart, Outremont, QC H2V 3H2
514-279-3066, Fax: 514-279-8008
sounpkr.kor@qc.aira.com
www.armeniancathedral.ca
Circulation: 700
Father Boyajan

Bulgarian

Bulgarian Horizons
#7, 648A Yonge St., Toronto, ON M4Y 2A6
416-962-7100, Fax: 416-962-7101
maksim1@mail.com
www.bulgarianhorizons.com
Circulation: 2,000
Maxim Bozhilov, Editor

Celtic

Celtic Heritage
PO Box 8805 A, #204, 1454 Dresden Row, Halifax, NS B3K 5M4
902-835-6244, Fax: 902-835-0080
editorial@celticheritage.ns.ca
www.celticheritage.ns.ca
Circulation: 5,800 *Frequency: 6 times a year; ISSN: 1202-7553*
Angus M. MacQuarrie, Publisher
Alexa Thompson, Editor

Chinese

The Capital Chinese News
#203, 1390 Prince of Wales Dr., Ottawa, ON K2C 3N6
613-837-3564, Fax: 613-834-1193
Frequency: Monthly
Ping J. Chiu, Publisher & Editor-in-chief

Chinese Canadian Community News
80 Florence St., Ottawa, ON K1R 7W6
613-232-8403, Fax: 613-232-4953
cccny.g@cyberus.ca
Yu Qin Guo, Publisher
King Wan Wu, Editor

The Chinese Journal
10553A - 97 St., Edmonton, AB T5H 2L4
780-424-0213, Fax: 780-428-7117
chinesejournal@telusplanet.net
Circulation: 7,000 *Frequency: Weekly*
Vicki Lim, Publisher
Grace Chi, Editor

Chinese News
#11, 50 Weybright Ct., Toronto, ON M1S 5A8
416-504-0761, Fax: 416-504-4928
Frequency: Weekly
Jack Jia, Publisher

The Chinese Press
1123, rue Clark, 2e étage, Montréal, QC H2Z 1K3
514-397-9969, Fax: 514-397-9929
cpreader@chinesepress.com
www.chinesepress.com
Circulation: 25,000 *Frequency: Weekly*
Crescent Chau, Publisher/Editor

Herald Monthly
#205, 3325 Victoria Park Ave., Toronto, ON M1W 2R8
416-492-4578, Fax: 416-492-6570
toronto@cchc.org
www.cchc.org
Circulation: 75,000 *Frequency: Monthly*
Helena Lee, Chief Editor

Jasmine
218 Viewmount Ave., Toronto, ON M6B 1T8
416-901-5201, Fax: 416-901-5202
info@jasminemagazine.com
www.jasminemagazine.com
Circulation: 4 times a year
English print - 18-34 years old Asian female
Amy Lan, Publisher

Ming Pao Daily News
1355 Huntingwood Dr., Toronto, ON M1S 3J1
416-321-0088, Fax: 416-321-5377
Circulation: 73,000, Mon.; 62,000, Tue.; 71,000, Wed.-Thu.; 66,000, Fri.; 97,000, Sat.; 102,0 *Frequency: Daily; Chinese*
Jeannie Lee, Regional General Manager
Frankie Chow, Manager, Advertising

Ming Pao Daily News, Western Edition
5368 Parkwood Pl., Richmond, BC V6V 2N1
604-231-8992, Fax: 604-231-9882
Frequency: Daily
Agnes Wong, Manager, Advertising
Lydia Yu, Manager, Sales Service

Modesty Magazine
#115, 18 Crown Steel Dr., Markham, ON L3R 9X8
905-513-1232, Fax: 905-513-0483
modestygroup@rogers.com
www.modestymagazine.com
Circulation: 10,000-20,000 annually
Ivy Lee, Publisher & Editor

Popular Lifestyle & Entertainment Magazine
3248 Cambie St., Vancouver, BC V5Z 2W4
604-872-1285, Fax: 604-872-0677
info@plem.com
www.plem.com
Circulation: 75,953 *Frequency: Monthly*
Patrick Wong, President & Editor-in-chief
Amanda Pi, Managing Editor
Lorna Chan, Account Executive

Les Presses Chinoises
1123, rue Clark, 2e étage, Montréal, QC H2Z 1K3
514-397-9969, Fax: 514-397-9929
cpmarket@chinesepress.com
www.chinesepress.com
Circulation: 25 000 *Frequency: Weekly*
Amy Tsang

Rice Paper
PO Box 74174 Hillcrest, Vancouver, BC V5V 5C8
604-879-5962
info@ricepaperonline.com
www.ricepaperonline.com
Circulation: 3,000 *Frequency: 4 times a year*
Jessica Gin-Jade, Editor-in-chief

Shing Wah News
#203, 1252 Lawrence Ave. East, Toronto, ON M3A 1C3
416-778-1854, Fax: 416-778-6340
willywecheng@hotmail.com
Frequency: Monthly
W. Cheng, President

Sing Pao Vancouver Chinese News
1296 Kingsway, Vancouver, BC V5V 3E1
604-872-6968, Fax: 604-872-1608
Circulation: 50,000 *Frequency: Daily*
Shing Pao, Publisher

Sing Tao Daily
417 Dundas St. West, Toronto, ON M5T 1G6
416-596-8140, Fax: 416-599-6688
Frequency: Daily
Robert Lang, Chief Editor

World Journal (Toronto)
415 Eastern Ave., Toronto, ON M4M 1B7
416-778-0889, Fax: 416-778-1037
editorial@worldjournal.net
www.worldjournal.com
Circulation: 30,000 *Frequency: Daily*
Paul Chang, Editor-in-chief
David Ting, President

World Journal (Vancouver)
2288 Clark Dr., Vancouver, BC V5N 3G8
604-876-1338, Fax: 604-876-3728
Frequency: Daily; Chinese
Kuo-Liang Swei, Editor
Richard Lin, President

Croatian

Glasnik Hrvatske Seljacke Stranke
PO Box 82187, Burnaby, BC V5C 5P2
604-524-2813, Fax: 604-521-0030
georged@smart.com
Circulation: 800 *Frequency: Monthly*
George Durkovich, Editor

Dutch

De Nederlandse Courant
1945 Four Seasons Dr., Burlington, ON L7P 2Y3
905-333-3615
courant@sympatico.cadsecourant.com
www.denederlandsecourant.com
Circulation: 5,800 *Frequency: 25 times a year; Dutch & English*
Theo Luykenaar, Publisher

The Windmill Herald
PO Box 3006 LCD1, Langley, BC V3A 4R3
604-532-1733, Fax: 604-532-1734
windmill@godutch.com
www.godutch.com
Circulation: 12,500

Estonian

Eesti Elu/Estonian Life
3 Madison Ave., Toronto, ON M5R 2S2
416-733-4550, Fax: 416-733-0944
eetoimetus@eestielu.ca
www.eesti.ca
Circulation: 2,300 *Frequency: Weekly; Estonian*
Elle Puusaag, Editor
Juri Laansoo, General Manager

Filipino

Filipiniana News
1531 Queen St. West, Toronto, ON M6R 1A5
416-534-7836, Fax: 416-535-9491
filipiniananews@rogers.com
Circulation: 10,000 *Frequency: Monthly*

Filipino Journal
46 Pincarrow Rd., Winnipeg, MB R3Y 1E3
204-489-8894, Fax: 204-489-1575
info@filipinojournal.com
filipinojournal.com
Circulation: 4,500 *Frequency: 24 times a year*
Linda Natividad-Cantiveros, Publisher/Editor-in-chief

The North American Filipino Star
4950, rue Queen Mary, Penthouse, Montréal, QC H3W 1X3
514-485-7861, Fax: 514-485-3076
filipinostar@yahoo.com
Circulation: 5,000 *Frequency: Monthly*
Zenaida Ferry-Kharroubi, Publisher & Chief Editor

The Philippine Reporter
807 Queen St. East, Toronto, ON M4M 1H8
416-461-8694, Fax: 416-461-7399
thephilreporter@on.aibn.com
www.philreporter.com
Circulation: 10,000 *Frequency: 24 times a year*
Hermie Garcia, Publisher & Editor

Finnish

Vapaa Sana
#308, 191 Eglinton Ave. East, Toronto, ON M4P 1K1
416-321-0808, Fax: 416-321-0811
markus@vapaasana.com
www.vapaasana.com
Circulation: 2,500 *Frequency: Weekly*
Matti Termiseva, Editor
Markus Ratty, General Manager

German

Albertaner
3635 - 28th St., Edmonton, AB T6T 1N4
780-465-7526, Fax: 780-465-3140
ajoop@planet.eon.net
Circulation: 3,500
Arnim Joop, Publisher & Editor

Der Bote
Mennonite Church Canada, 600 Shaftesbury Blvd., Winnipeg, MB R3P 0M4
204-888-6781, Fax: 204-831-5675, 866-888-6785
ijamzenlamp@mennonitechurch.ca
Circulation: 3,300 *Frequency: Bi-weekly*
Ingrid Jamzen, Editor

Deutsche Presse
#303, 455 Spadina Ave., Toronto, ON M5S 2G8
416-595-9714, Fax: 416-595-9716
Frequency: Weekly
Rolf Meyer, Publisher

Deutsche Zeitung
85 Inglis St., Ayr, ON N0B 1E0
519-632-7700, Fax: 519-632-8700, 888-749-0606
deutschezt@golden.net
Circulation: 7,500 *Frequency: Weekly; German*
Erhard Matthaes, Editor

Die Mennonitische Post
383 Main St., Steinbach, MB R5G 1Z4
204-326-6790,
Circulation: 5,000 *Frequency: 23 times a year*

Echo Germanica
383 Vaughan Rd., Toronto, ON M6C 2N8
416-652-1332, Fax: 416-658-6909
editor@echoworld.com
www.echoworld.com
Circulation: 16,000
Sybille Forster-Rentmeister, Publisher/Editor-in-chief

Freundschaft/Friendship
Central-Organization of German-Sudeten-Clubs in Canada, 20 Banff Rd., Toronto, ON M4S 2V5
416-483-8240, Fax: 416- -
Circulation: 200
Rolf Lorenz

German Canadian Business & Trade Directory
2255B Queen St. East, Box 106, Toronto, ON M4E 1G3
416-465-9957, Fax: 416-465-8169
directory@germancanadian.com
www.germancanadian.com
Circulation: 5,000
Eva Wazda, Publisher

Mennonitische Rundschau
1310 Taylor Ave., Winnipeg, MB R3M 3Z6
204-669-6575, Fax: 204-654-1865
mr@mbconf.ca
www.rundschau.ca
Circulation: 2,200 *Frequency: Monthly; German*
Marianne Dulder, Editor

Greek

Courier Grec
765, rue Jean-Talon ouest, Montréal, QC H3N 1S3
514-278-9299, Fax: 514-278-4572
Frequency: Weekly
Iraklis Theodorakopoulos, Editor

drassis/Greek Canadian Action
#250, 657, boul Curé Labelle, Laval, QC H7V 2T8
450-978-0070, Fax: 514-687-6330
Circulation: 44,300 *Frequency: Weekly*
George Guzmas, Publisher

Greek Canadian Tribune / Ellinokanadiko Vima
7835, av Wiseman, Montréal, QC H3N 2N8
514-272-6873, Fax: 514-272-3157
info@bhma.net
www.bhma.net
Circulation: 13,000 *Frequency: Weekly; Greek & English*
Christos Manikis, Publisher & Editor

Greek Press
6 Chester Ave., Toronto, ON M4K 2Z9
416-465-3243, Fax: 416-604-2480
info@greekpress.ca
www.greekpress.ca
Circulation: 6,000 *Frequency: Bi-weekly*
Constantine Kranias, Publisher/Editor

H Poh
2975, Brighton, Montréal, QC H3S 1T7
514-342-0808
hpoh@videotron.ca
Circulation: 20,000 *Frequency: Weekly*
Kostas Georgoulis, Publisher

Hellenic Hamilton News
#2, 8 Morris Ave., Hamilton, ON L8L 1X7
905-549-9208, Fax: 905-549-7935
Circulation: 5,300 *Frequency: Monthly; Greek*
Panos Andronidis, Publisher & Editor

The Hellenic News
Alpha Omega Communications, 37 Hillsmount Rd., London, ON N6K 1W1
519-472-4807, Fax: 519-471-6116
alpha_omega_com@hotmail.com
Frequency: Monthly
George N. Drossos, Managing Editor

Hellenic-Canadian Chronicles
Ledra Publishing Co. Ltd., 437 Danforth Ave., Toronto, ON M4K 1P1
416-465-4628, Fax: 416-465-6592
Circulation: 6,000 *Frequency: Weekly; English & Greek*
Peter Maniatakos, Editor

Patrides, A North American Review
PO Box 266 O, Toronto, ON M4A 2N3
416-921-4229, Fax: 416-921-0723
saras@patrides.com
www.patrides.com
Circulation: 160,000 *Frequency: Bi-weekly*
Kathy Saras, Publisher
Thomas Saras, Editor-in-chief

Hungarian

Kanadai Magyarsag
74 Advance Rd., Toronto, ON M8Z 2T7
416-233-3131, Fax: 416-233-5984
Frequency: Weekly
Csaba Gaal, Editor & Manager

Menorah-Egyenloseg
PO Box 54017 Lawrence Plaza, #312, 1089 Bathurst St., Toronto, ON M6A 3B7
416-780-9168, Fax: 416-780-9167
Circulation: 4,500 *Frequency: bi-weekly, Fri.*
William Koseras, Publisher & Editor

Icelandic

Logberg-Heimskringla
The Sterling Bldg., #100, 283 Portage Ave., Winnipeg, MB R3B 2B5
204-284-5686, Fax: 204-284-7099, 866-564-2374
lh@lh-inc.ca
www.lh-inc.ca
Circulation: 2,000 *Frequency: 24 issues a year; Fri.; English & Icelandic*

Italian

Corriere Canadese
101 Wingold Ave., Toronto, ON M6B 1P8
416-785-4300, Fax: 416-781-4329, 877-503-5077
corriere@corriere.com
www.corriere.com
Circulation: 29,500 *Frequency: Mon.-Sat.*
Paola Bernardini, Managing Editor
Lori Abittan, General Manager/COO
Elena Caprile, Editor-in-chief

Corriere Italiano
6900, rue St-Denis, Montréal, QC H2S 2S2
514-279-4536, Fax: 514-279-3900
pubital@biz.videotron.ca
Circulation: 20 500 *Frequency: Weekly*
Carole Gagliardi, President & Editor

Donna
#100, 166 Woodbridge Ave., Woodbridge, ON L4L 2S7
905-856-2823, Fax: 905-856-2825
lospecchio@msn.com
Circulation: 18,500 *Frequency: 4 times a year*
Giovanna Tozzi, Managing Editor

L'Eco D'Italia
Marco Polo World News, #302, 3680 East Hastings St., Vancouver, BC V5K 2A9
604-294-8707, Fax: 604-291-1707
marcopolonews@shaw.ca
Circulation: 5,900 *Frequency: Weekly*
Rino Vultaggio, Editor/Publisher

La Gazzetta
909 Howard Ave., Windsor, ON N9A 1S3
519-253-8883, Fax: 519-253-3280
Frequency: Weekly; Italian & English
Rita Bison, Managing Editor

Il Cittadino Canadese
#209, 5960, rue Jean Talon est, Saint-Léonard, QC H1S 1M2
514-253-2332, Fax: 514-253-6574
Circulation: 38,000 *Frequency: Weekly*
Basilio Giordano, Publisher

Il Congresso
Cura Enterprises Ltd., 9227 - 169 Ave., Edmonton, AB T5Z 1X3
780-424-3010, Fax: 780-424-3037
ilcongresso@shaw.ca
Circulation: 7,500 *Frequency: 12 times a year; Italian*
Alessandro Urso, Publisher & Editor

Il Rincontro / La Recontre
6675, av Wilderton, Montréal, QC H3S 2L8
514-739-4213, Fax: 514-344-8238
tony.vellone@videotron.ca
Circulation: 11,500 *Frequency: Monthly; Italian*
Tony Vellone, Editor

Insieme
4358, rue Charleroi, Montréal, QC H1H 1T3
514-328-2062, Fax: 514-328-6562
insieme@multimedianova.com
Circulation: 38,000 *Frequency: Weekly; Italian*
Lori Abittan, Publisher
Mimmo Forte, Editor

Lo Specchio/Vaughan
#100, 166 Woodbridge Ave., Woodbridge, ON L4L 2S7
905-856-2823, Fax: 905-856-2825
editorial@lospecchio.com
www.lospecchio.com
Circulation: 28,000 *Frequency: Weekly*
Sergio Tagliavini, Editor

L'Ora Di Ottawa
203 Louisa St., Ottawa, ON K1R 6Y9
613-232-5689, Fax: 613-563-2573
info@loradiottawa.ca
Circulation: 2,115 *Frequency: Weekly*
Donatella Votano
Luciano Gonella, Editor

Tandem
101 Wingold Ave., Toronto, ON M6B 1P8
416-785-4300, Fax: 416-781-4329, 877-503-5077
corriere@corriere.com
www.tandemnews.com
Circulation: 55,000 *Frequency:* Weekly
Angela Baldassarre, Managing Editor
Lori Abittan, General Manager/COO
Elena Caprile, Editor-in-chief

Vita Italiana
PO Box 1098, Toronto, ON M9L 2R8
416-656-2050, Fax: 416-780-0208
mcvarano@hotmail.com
Frequency: 24 times per year
Dr. Mario Caligure Varano, Editor

Japanese

Japanese Canadian National Museum (JCNM)
#120, 6688 Southoaks Cres., Vancouver, BC V5S 4M7
807-777-8000, Fax: 807-777-7001
jcnmas@telus.net
www.jcnm.ca
Grace Eiko Thomson, Executive Director

The Montreal Bulletin
8155, rue Rousselot, Montréal, QC H2E 1Z7
514-723-5551
bulletin@dsuper.net
Circulation: 500
Mary Burke, Managing Editor

Nikkei Voice
6 Garamond Ct., Toronto, ON M3C 1Z5
416-386-0287, Fax: 416-386-0136
nikkeivoice@bellnet.com
Frequency: Monthly
Frank Moritsugu, Publisher

Korean

Korea Central Daily
655 Bloor St. West, Toronto, ON M6G 1L1
416-533-5533, Fax: 416-533-5500
toronto.koreadaily.com
Hyo Kim, Publisher
James Lim, Editor-in-Chief

The Korea Times Daily
287 Bridgeland Ave., Toronto, ON M6A 1Z6
416-787-1111, Fax: 416-781-7777
www.koreatimes.net
Circulation: 17,000 *Frequency:* 6 times a week; Korean
Woon Y. Kim, Editor-in-chief
Lawrence M. Kim, Publisher

Latin American

El Mundo Latino News
3050 Kirwin Ave., Mississauga, ON L5A 2K6
905-306-7929, Fax: 905-279-2702
info@elmundolatinonews.ca
www.elmundolatinonews.ca
Circulation: 10,000 *Frequency:* Weekly
Ana Griselda Romero, Publisher

El Popular
2413 Dundas St. West, Toronto, ON M6P 1X3
416-531-2495, Fax: 416-531-7187
editor@diarioelpopular.com
Frequency: Weekly
Eduardo Uruena, Publisher

Reporte Latino
PO Box 1098, Toronto, ON M9L 2R8
416-656-2050, Fax: 416-780-0208
Frequency: Monthly
Dr. Mario Caligiure Varano, Editor

Lithuanian

Teviskes Ziburiai/Lights of Homeland
2185 Stavebank Rd., Mississauga, ON L5C 1T3
905-275-4672, Fax: 905-290-9802
tevzib@pathcom.com
Circulation: 2,800 *Frequency:* Weekly
P. Gaida, Editor-in-chief
J. Kuras, Chair

Macedonian

Macedonia
PO Box 97589, 364 Old Kingston Rd., Toronto, ON M1C 4Z1
416-288-7673, Fax: 416-286-0712
Tanas Jovanovska, Editor

Roots
2145 Danforth Ave., Toronto, ON M4C 1K2
416-691-7184, Fax: 416-691-3439

Multicultural

Community Digest
#216, 1755 Robson St., Vancouver, BC V6G 3B7
604-875-8313, Fax: 604-875-0336
digestnews@yahoo.com
Circulation: 25,000 *Frequency:* Weekly
N. Ebrahim, Publisher

Ethno-Cultural Networker
c/o 129 Browning Blvd., Winnipeg, MB R3K 0L1
204-774-3569,
Frequency: Monthly

FACES: Canada's Multicultural Magazine
Multicultural Council of Saskatchewan, 369 Park St., Regina, SK S4N 5B2
306-721-2769, Fax: 306-721-3342
mcos@accesscomm.ca
mcos.sask.com
Circulation: 1,500 *Frequency:* 4 times a year
Wade Luzny, CEO

New Canada Weekly
#500, 120 Eglinton Ave. East, Toronto, ON M4P 1E2
416-481-7793, Fax: 416- -
humanrights@sympatico.ca
hrrrc.ca
Circulation: 10,000 *Frequency:* Weekly; English & Urdu
Hasanat Ahmad Syed, Publisher & Editor

Peel Multicultural Scene
Peel Multicultural Council, 6630 Turner Valley Rd., Mississauga, ON L5N 2P1
905-819-1144, Fax: 905-542-3950
pmcgeneral@peelmc.com
www.peelmc.com
Circulation: 400
Naveed Chaudhey

Persian

Sarmayeh/Investment
Sarmayeh Publications, #415, 5795 Yonge St., Toronto, ON M2M 4J3
416-221-1400, Fax: 416-221-1451
sarmayeh@idirect.com
Circulation: 7,000
Arman Parsi, Editor/Sales Manager

Shahrvand
#208, 4610 Dufferin St., Toronto, ON M3H 5S4
905-739-1086, Fax: 905-739-6418
www.shahrvand.com
Circulation: 30,000 *Frequency:* Tues., Fri.
Hassan Zerehi, Editor-in-chief

Polish

Czas Polish Times
207 Cathedral Ave., Winnipeg, MB R2W 0X2
204-582-4392
czaspol@mts.net
Circulation: 651 *Frequency:* Weekly
Krystyna Gajda, President

Glos Polski/Polish Voice
71 Judson St., Toronto, ON M8Z 1A4
416-201-9601, Fax: 416-201-9602
info@glospolski.com
Circulation: 6,000
Czeslaw Zacharski, Editor-in-chief

Polish Business Directory
777C The Queensway, Toronto, ON M8Z 1N4
416-255-9182, Fax: 416-255-9893, 877-742-9455
mail@master.on.ca
www.przewodnikhandlowy.com
Circulation: 40,000 *Frequency:* annually
Martin Chlapowski
Robert Wagner

The Polish Canadian Courier/Nowy Kurier
12 Foch Ave., Toronto, ON M8W 3X1
416-259-4353, Fax: 416-259-4353
zkopc549@rogers.com
www.nowykurier.com
Circulation: 20,000 *Frequency:* Weekly; Polish & English
Jolanta Kowalewska-Cabaj, Publisher & Editor-in-chief

Zwiazkowiec
c/o Polonia Media Ltd., 22 Roncesvalles Ave., Toronto, ON M6R 2K3
416-531-2491, Fax: 416-531-5153
Frequency: Weekly

Portuguese

Alem-Fronteiras
585 Queen St. South, Kitchener, ON N2G 1W9
519-745-3233, Fax: 519-745-3395
legacytr@golden.net
Circulation: 1,000

Correio Português/Portuguese Mail
793 Ossington Ave., Toronto, ON M6G 3T8
416-532-9894, Fax: 416-532-1475
correioportugues@tht.net
Circulation: 122,000 *Frequency:* 24 times a year
Antonio Ribeiro, Publisher

Gente Modesta
256B Lansdowne Ave., Toronto, ON L6T 3Z8
416-531-0833, Fax: 416-531-0770
sino@interlog.com
Circulation: 4,950 *Frequency:* Monthly
Severiano Da Silva, Editor & Publisher

Golo/Goal
977 College St., Toronto, ON M6H 1A6
416-538-1788, Fax: 416-538-7953
golo@solnet.com
www.solnet.com
Circulation: 12,000 *Frequency:* Weekly
Antonio Perinu, Publisher
Alice Perinu, Editor-in-chief

O Mundial
1148 Ellice Ave., Winnipeg, MB R3G 0E6
204-786-7689, Fax: 204-775-6549
omundial@shaw.ca
Circulation: 2,000 *Frequency:* Monthly
Manuel Guerra, Editor-in-chief

Sol Portugues/Portuguese Sun
977 College St., Toronto, ON M6H 1A6
416-538-1788, Fax: 416-538-7953
sol@solnet.com
www.solnet.com
Circulation: 12,000 *Frequency:* Weekly
Antonio Perinu, Publisher
Alice Perinu, Editor-in-chief

Voice Luso-Canadian Newspaper
428 Ossington Ave., Toronto, ON M6J 3A7
416-534-3177, Fax: 416-534-6441
voice@ftn.net
Frequency: Weekly
Joaquim R. Baptista, Publisher & Editor

A Voz de Portugal
4231, boul St-Laurent, Montréal, QC H2W 1Z4
514-284-1813, Fax: 514-284-6150, 866-684-1813
jornal@avozdeportugal.com
www.avozdeportugal.com
Circulation: 10,000 *Frequency:* Weekly
Sylvio Martins, Editor, sylviomartins@avozdeportugal.com

Romanian

Romanian Voice
PO Box 78010 Westcliffe, Hamilton, ON L9C 7N5
905-387-1832, Fax: 905-388-4651
Frequency: Monthly
George Balasu, Director
Eugene Barasan, Chief Editor
Mihaela Moisin, Manager

Russian

Gazeta Plus
#108, 5987 Bathurst St., Toronto, ON M2R 1Z3
416-226-4777, Fax: 416-226-0374, 877-877-5240
info@infogazeta.com
Circulation: 12,000 *Frequency:* Weekly
Boris Nusenbaum
Eugene Koutcher

ISKRA: Voice of the Doukhobors
PO Box 3024, Castlegar, BC V1N 3H4
250-365-3613, Fax: 250-365-5477
info@iskra.ca
iskra.ca
Circulation: 1,100
Lisa Poznikoff, Editor

Nasha Gazeta
592 Champagne Dr., Toronto, ON M3J 2T9
416-725-8337, Fax: 416-757-9713
info@exo.ca
Circulation: 10,000 *Frequency: Weekly*
G. Kukuy, President
T. Sergeeva, Managing Editor
I. Toutchinski, Editor-in-chief

Russian Canadian INFO
#108, 5987 Bathurst St., Toronto, ON M2R 1Z3
416-226-4777, Fax: 416-226-0374, 877-877-5240
info@infogazeta.com
www.ruscanada.com
Circulation: 15,000 *Frequency: Weekly*
Boris Nusenbaum
Eugene Koutcher

The Voice of Community
308 Blue Haven, Dollard-des-Ormeaux, QC H9G 2K3
514-696-8955, Fax: 514-696-9493
Circulation: 9,000
Mark Groysberg, Publisher & Editor

Serbian

Kanadski Srbobran
Serbian League of Canada, 335 Britannia Ave., Hamilton, ON L8H 1Y4
905-549-4079, Fax: 905-549-8552
Circulation: 755 *Frequency: Bi-monthly*
Dragan Ciric, Manager

Kisobran
#368, 3495 Cambie St., Vancouver, BC V5Z 4R3
604-731-9446
kisobran@telus.net; redakcija@kisobran.com
www.kisobran.com
Circulation: 4,000 *Frequency: monthly*
Dragan Andrejevic, Publisher

Serbia
269 Glover Rd., Stoney Creek, ON L8E 5H6
905-643-3341, Fax: 905-643-3341
serbrad@sympatico.ca
Frequency: Monthly
David Damjanovic, Publisher & Editor

Srpsko Bratsvo
1 Secroft Cres., Toronto, ON M3N 1R5
416-663-3409, Fax: 416-665-3564
Frequency: Monthly
William Durovic, Editor-in-chief
Drag D. Georgevic, Editor

Voice of Canadian Serbs
c/o Serbian National Shield Society of Canada, #303, 1900 Sheppard Ave. East, Toronto, ON M2J 4T4
416-496-7881, Fax: 416-493-0335
Circulation: 1,500 *Frequency: Monthly; Serbian & English*
Bora Dragasevich, Editor

Slovak, Czech

Kanadske Listy / Canadian Pages
388 Atwater Ave., Mississauga, ON L5G 2A3
905-278-4116, Fax: 905- -
mirko388@allstream.net
Circulation: 2,200 *Frequency: Bi-monthly; Czech*
Mike Janecek, Publisher & Editor
Jana Janeckova-Bayerova, Secretary

Novy Domov
Masaryk Memorial Institute Inc., 450 Scarborough Golf Club Rd., Toronto, ON M1G 1H1
416-439-9557
novydom@sympatico.ca
Frequency: Bi-weekly
Jan Rotbauer, Editor

Satellite 1-416
PO Box 176 E, Toronto, ON M6H 4E2
416-530-4222, Fax: 416-530-0069
satellite1-416@rogers.com
www.satellite1-416.com
Circulation: 1,600
Ales Brezina, Publisher & Editor

South Asian

Ahmadiyya Gazette Canada
10610 Jane St., Maple, ON L6A 3A2
905-303-4000, Fax: 905-832-3220
gazette@ahmadiyya.ca
www.ahmadiyya.ca
Frequency: English, French & Urdu
Hasan Muhammad Khan, Editor-in-chief,
editor@ahmadiyyagazette.ca
S.H. Hadi, Urdu Editor
M. Nadeem A. Siddiq, Editor

Al-Hilal/Crescent
338 Hollyberry Trail, Toronto, ON M2H 2P6
416-493-4374, Fax: 416-493-4374
lowaisi@rogers.com
Circulation: 4,200 *Frequency: Bi-monthly*
M.L. Owaisi, Publisher
Farida Abdullah, Editor

Bazm
4248, rue Hugo, Pierrefonds, QC H9H 2V7
514-620-2041, Fax: 419-828-7613
bazm1989@yahoo.ca
Frequency: Monthly
Saira Watsy, Publisher & Chief Editor
Itaat Wasty, Sr. Editor

Canadian Times of India
7 Axsmith Cres., Main Fl., Toronto, ON M2J 3K2
416-490-0091, Fax: 416-490-9592
umeshvijaya@msn.com
Circulation: 22,500
Umesh Vijaya, Publisher & Editor

Charhdi Kala
#6, 7743 - 128th St., Surrey, BC V3W 4E6
604-590-6397, Fax: 604-591-6397
cknewsgroup@telus.net
Circulation: 15,000 *Frequency: Weekly; Punjabi & English*
Gurpreet Singh Sahota, Editor

Desi News
37 Firestone Rd., Toronto, ON M9C 4N1
416-695-4357, Fax: 416-621-2691
desinews@rogers.com
www.e-desinews.com
Circulation: 30,000 *Frequency: Monthly*
G.A. Easwar, Publisher
Shagorika Easwar, Editor

Eastern News
5790 Riverside Pl., Mississauga, ON L5M 4W9
905-858-7525, Fax: 905-858-7951
mkhan@theeasternnews.com
Circulation: 7,500 *Frequency: 24 times a year*
Alia Sultana, Publisher
Masood Khan, Editor

Gujarat Express
20 Eldwood Pl., Brampton, ON L6V 3N3
905-890-6919, Fax: 905-457-7096
Circulation: 7,500 *Frequency: Weekly*
Amit Bhatt, Publisher

Gujarat Vartman
250 Norfinch Dr., Toronto, ON M3N 1Y4
416-736-1640, Fax: 416-736-0848
Frequency: Monthly; Gujarti
J.D. Shah, Editor

India Calling
#1908, 41 Mabelle Ave., Toronto, ON M9A 5A9
416-233-9577,
Sanyogta Singh, Publisher
Sonia Singh, Publisher & Editor-in-chief

India Journal
#11, 2355 Derry Rd. East, Mississauga, ON L5S 1V6
905-405-0420, Fax: 905-405-0428
indiajournal@indiajournal.ca
www.indiajournal.ca
Circulation: 22,000
Harjinder Singh, Publisher

Indo Caribbean World
312 Brownridge Dr., Thornhill, ON L4J 5X1
905-738-5005, Fax: 905-738-3927
Circulation: 30,000 *Frequency: 2 times per month*
Harry Ramkhelawan, Publisher & Editor

Indo-Canadian Awaaz
#200, 12732 - 80 Ave., Surrey, BC V3W 3A3
604-502-6100, Fax: 604-501-6111
new@voiceonline.com
Circulation: 10,000 *Frequency: weekly*
Vinnie Combow, Editor
Rajesh Gupta, Publisher

Journal Apna Watan
4021, boul Notre Dame, Laval, QC H7W 1S8
450-681-3108
apnawatan2002@yahoo.com
Circulation: 5,000 *Frequency: Monthly*
Arshad Randhawa, Editor

Kerala Express
18 Greenbrook Dr., Toronto, ON M6M 2J9
416-654-0431, Fax: 416- -
Circulation: 2,000 *Frequency: Bi-weekly; Malayalam*
J.P. George, Publisher

Pakeeza International
905-337-3030, Fax: 905-338-1364
pakeeza@mansoor.com
Circulation: 8,000 *Frequency: Wed.; Urdu*
Sabih Mansoor, Publisher & Editor

Sangam
7 Axsmith Cres., Toronto, ON M3J 3K2
416-490-0091, Fax: 416-490-9592
umeshvijaya@msn.com
Circulation: 22,500
Umesh Vijaya, Publisher/Editor

Sanjh Savera/Dust and Dawn
#2, 2575 Steeles Ave. East, Brampton, ON L6T 5T1
905-789-7787, Fax: 905-789-7717
info@sanjhsavera.com
www.sanjhsavera.com
Circulation: 15,000
Nirmal Hansa, Publisher

Shama/Flame
5790 Riverside Pl., Mississauga, ON L5M 4W9
905-826-6397, Fax: 905-858-7951
nkhan@theeasternnews.com
Circulation: 5,000 *Frequency: Semi-monthly; Urdu*
Alia Sultana, Publisher & Editor

The South Asian Voice
905-337-3030, Fax: 905-338-1364
southasianvoice@mansoor.com
Circulation: 8,000 *Frequency: Wed.; English & Urdu*
Sabih Mansoor, Publisher

Thamilar Thakaval
PO Box 3 F, Toronto, ON M4Y 2L4
416-920-9250, Fax: 416-921-6576
tamilsinfo@sympatico.ca
Circulation: 5,000 *Frequency: Monthly*
Thiru S. Thiuchelvam, Editor-in-chief

The Times of Sri Lanka
58 Sundial Cres., Toronto, ON M4A 2J8
416-445-5390, Fax: 416-285-8494
timeslanka@rogers.com
Circulation: 5,000
Upali Obeyesekere, Managing Editor

The Weekly Voice
#212, 6705 Tomken Rd., Mississauga, ON L5T 2J6
905-795-8282, Fax: 905-795-9801
info@weeklyvoice.com
www.weeklyvoice.com
Circulation: 50,000
Binoy Thomas, Editor

Spanish

Noticero De Norte a Sur
295 Vaughan Rd., Toronto, ON M6C 2N3
416-653-8942, Fax: 416-653-6441
denorteasur@on.aibn.com
www.denorteasur.com
Circulation: 60,000 *Frequency: Monthly*
Emilia Modolo, Editor

La Voz de Montreal
#112, 6225, Place North Crest, Montréal, QC H3S 2T5
514-253-2739, Fax: 514-343-9697
lavoz@sympatico.ca
Circulation: 15,000 *Frequency: 12 times a year*
Gilberto Miranda, Director

Swedish

Scandinavian Press
1294 - 7th Ave. West, Vancouver, BC V6H 1B6
604-731-6381, Fax: 604-731-2292
office@nordicway.com
www.nordicway.com
Frequency: 4 times a year; ISSN: 1201-3447
Anders Neumuller, Publisher & Editor

Swedish Press
1294 - 7th Ave. West, Vancouver, BC V6H 1B6
604-731-6381, Fax: 604-731-2292
office@nordicway.com
www.nordicway.com
Circulation: 6,000 *Frequency: Monthly; English & Swedish; ISSN: 0839-2323*
Anders Neumuller, Publisher & Editor

Ukrainian

Homin Ukrainy
83 Christie St., Toronto, ON M6G 3B1
416-516-2443, Fax: 416-516-4033
homin@on.aibn.com
Circulation: 1,000 *Frequency: Weekly; Ukrainian & English*
M. Shepetyk, Publisher
O. Romanyshyn, Editor

Moloda Ukraina
12 Minstrel Dr., Toronto, ON M8Y 3G4
416-255-8604, Fax: 416-961-9609
Walentina Rodak, Contact

Novy Shliakh/New Pathway
New Pathway Publishers Ltd., 145 Evans Ave., Toronto, ON M5Z 5X8
416-960-3424, Fax: 416-960-1442
npweekly@look.ca
www.infoukes.com/newpathway
Circulation: 4,500 *Frequency: Weekly; also New Pathway Almanac (annual)*
Leslie Salnick, President

Progress Ukrainian Catholic News
233 Scotia St., Winnipeg, MB R2V 1V7
204-338-7801, Fax: 204-339-4006
progress@archeparchy.ca
www.archeparchy.ca/progress/
Circulation: 4,900
Rev. Mikhail Kouts, Associate Editor
Lydia Firman, Business Manager
Most Rev. Richard Soo, Managing Editor SJ

Promin
PO Box 57268 Jackson, Hamilton, ON L8P 4X1
905-572-9626, Fax: 905-524-5362
promin@networx.on.ca
Circulation: 1,600
Orysia Sushko, Editor-in-chief

Ukrainian News
c/o Edmonton Lasergraphics, #1, 12227 - 107 Ave., Edmonton, AB T5M 1Y9
780-488-3860, Fax: 780-488-3859
ukrnews@interbaun.com
Circulation: 3,274 *Frequency: Bi-weekly; English & Ukrainian*
Marco Levytsky, Publisher & Editor
Vitaly Shevchenko, Chief, KYIV Bureau
Irene Hladki, Manager, Advertising & Production

Ukrainsky Holos
842 Main St., Winnipeg, MB R2W 3N8
204-589-5871, Fax: 204-586-3618
presstr@mbsympatico.ca
Circulation: 2,100 *Frequency: Bi-Weekly; Ukrainian & English*
Maria Bosak

Visnyk/The Herald
9 St. John's Ave., Winnipeg, MB R2W 1G8
204-582-0996, Fax: 204-582-5241, 877-586-3093
visnyk@uocc.ca
www.uocc.ca
Circulation: 10,000 *Frequency: Monthly; English & Ukrainian*
Rev. Andrew Jarmus, Editor-in-chief

Zhinochy Svit / Woman's World
Ukrainian Women's Organization of Canada, 145 Evans Ave., Toronto, ON M8Z 5X8
416-960-5297, Fax: 416-960-1442
Circulation: 2,000 *Frequency: 4 issues a year; English & Ukrainian*
Lesia Panko, Editor

Vietnamese

Lang Van
PO Box 218 U, Toronto, ON M8Z 5P1
905-607-8010, Fax: 905-607-8011
langvan@ilap.com
Circulation: 5,000
Nguyen Huu Nghia, Publisher/Editor-in-chief

Thôi Bâo/Time News
1114 College St., Toronto, ON M6H 1B6
416-925-8607, Fax: 416-925-0695
mails@thoibao.com
www.thoibao.com
Circulation: 14,500 *Frequency: Weekly*
Lee Nguyen, Manager
Dave Nguyen, Publisher

Vietnam Time Magazine Edmonton
PO Box 284 Main, Edmonton, AB T5J 2J1
780-429-4781, Fax: 780-429-4781
thoibao@telus.net
Circulation: 1,500
Thanh Nguyen, Publisher

Farm

Farm Publication

The Ad-Viser
Farm Press Ltd., 1320 - 36th St. North, Lethbridge, AB T1H 5H8
403-328-5114, Fax: 403-328-5443, 877-328-0048
adsales@farmpressltd.com
www.farmpressgroup.com
Circulation: 20,159 *Frequency: Every other Thu.*
Jeff Sarich, Publisher

Agri Digest
Site 26, Comp. 32, RR#2, Chase, BC V0E 1M0
250-679-5362, Fax: 250-675-6851, 800-555-7102
meaghen@elltel.net
www.agridigest.com
Circulation: 10,546 *Frequency: 12 times a year; Aug. issue - Agri Digest Directory (annual)*
Fran Kay, Publisher
Jodi Houghton, Editor

Agricom
2474 Champlain St., Clarence Creek, ON K0A 1N0
613-488-2651, Fax: 613-488-2541
info.agricom@lavoieagricole.ca
www.lavoieagricole.ca/agri _com.cfm
Circulation: 5 000 *Frequency: 22 times a year*
Pierre Glaude, Publisher

Alberta Beef
#202, 2915 - 19 St. NE, Calgary, AB T2E 7A2
403-250-1090, Fax: 403-291-9546
info@beefnews.com
www.albertabeef.ca
Circulation: 8,700 *Frequency: 12 times a year*
Garth McClintock, Publisher

Alberta Farmer Express
1666 Dublin Ave., Winnipeg, MB R3H OH1
204-954-1400, Fax: 204-954-1422
www.albertafarmexpress.ca
Circulation: 29,500 *Frequency: 12 times per year*
Will Verboven, Editor, will.verboven@fbcpublishing.com
Dave Bedard, Daily News Editor, daveb@fbcpublishing.com

Barley Country
c/o Alberta Barley Commission, #200, 3601A - 21 St. NE, Calgary, AB T2E 6T5
403-291-9111, Fax: 403-291-0190, 800-265-9111
abbarley@albertabarley.com
www.albertabarley.com
Circulation: 35,000 *Frequency: 4 times a year*
Terry Bullick, Editor, tbullick@telusplanet.net
Nikki Barnes, Advertising, Project Coordinator

BC Dairy Directory
PO Box 724, Summerland, BC V0H 1Z0
250-496-5707, Fax: 250-496-5132, 888-324-7347
info@bcdairydirectory.com
www.bcdairydirectory.com
Circulation: 1,450 *Frequency: Annually, June*
Karin McCarty, Editor

Beef in B.C. Inc.
c/o B.C. Cattlemen's Association, #4, 10145 Dallas Dr., Kamloops, BC V2C 6T4
250-573-3611, Fax: 250-573-5155
beefinbc@kamloops.net
www.cattlemen.bc.ca
Circulation: 2,200 *Frequency: 7 times a year*
Bob France, Editor

Better Farming
ON
519-763-4044, Fax: 519-763-4482
publisher@betterfarming.com
www.betterfarming.com
Circulation: 43,000
Paul Nolan, Publisher & Advertising Director
Don Stoneman, Senior Staff Editor, 519-654-9106, Fax: 519-654-9357, dstoneman@betterfarming.com
Robert Irwin, Managing Editor, 613-678-2232, Fax: 613-678-5993, rirwin@betterfarming.com

Better Pork
519-763-4044, Fax: 519-763-4482
Circulation: 6,403 *Frequency: 6 times a year*

Le Bulletin des Agriculteurs
#800, 1200, av McGill College, Montréal, QC H3B 4G7
514-845-5141, Fax: 514-843-2180
info@lebulletin.rogers.com
www.lebulletin.com
Circulation: 24 000 *Frequency: Mensuel; français*
Simon M. Guertin, Éditeur
Yvon Thérien, Rédacteur-en-chef

CAAR Communicator
#107, 1090 Waverley St., Winnipeg, MB R3T 3P4
204-989-9300, Fax: 204-989-9306, 800-463-9323
www.caar.org
Circulation: 4,700 *Frequency: 5 times a year*
J. Ryrie

Canada's Who's Who Of The Poultry Industry
519-429-3966, Fax: 516-429-3094, 888-599-2228
jbauslaugh@annexweb.com
www.canadianpoultrymag.com
Circulation: 5,300 *Frequency: Annually, July*
John Bauslaugh, Publisher
Kristy Nudds, Editor

Canadian Ayrshire Review
4865, boul Laurier ouest, Saint-Hyacinthe, QC J2S 3V4
450-778-3535, Fax: 451-778-3531
info@ayrshire-canada.com
www.ayrshire-canada.com
Circulation: 1,500 *Frequency: Bi-monthly; English & French*
Linda Ness, Business Manager

Canadian Cattlemen: The Beef Magazine
PO Box 9800, Winnipeg, MB R3C 3K7
204-944-5753, Fax: 204-942-8463
gren@fbcpublishing.com
www.agcanada.com
Circulation: 26,825 *Frequency: Monthly*
Gren Winslow, Editor

Canadian Guernsey Journal
Canadian Guernsey Assn., RR#5, Guelph, ON N1H 6J2
519-836-2141, Fax: 519-763-6582
guernsey@gencor.ca
www.guernseycanada.ca
Circulation: 250 *Frequency: annual*
Vivianne M. Macdonald, Managing Editor

Canadian Hereford Digest
5160 Skyline Way NE, Calgary, AB T2E 6V1
403-274-1734, Fax: 403-275-4999
info@herefordddigest.com
www.herefordddigest.com
Circulation: 2,500; 8,000 (commercial issue) *Frequency: 7 times a year; English & French*
Kurt Gilmore, Publisher & Editor

The Canadian Horsetrader
PO Box 219, Dutton, ON N0L 1J0
519-762-3993, Fax: 519-762-0572
pams@wwdc.com
www.horsetradermagazine.com
Circulation: 10,000

Canadian Jersey Breeder
#9, 350 Speedvale Ave. West, Guelph, ON N1H 7M7
519-821-1020, Fax: 519-821-2723
info@jerseycanada.com
www.jerseycanada.com
Circulation: 1,400 *Frequency: 5 times a year*
Ryan Barrett, Editor

Canadian Poultry Magazine
519-429-3966, Fax: 519-429-3094, 888-599-2228
jbauslaugh@annexweb.com
www.canadianpoultrymag.com
Circulation: 5,300 *Frequency: 12 times a year*
Kristy Nudds, Editor
John Bauslaugh, Advertising Manager

Canola Country
Saskatchewan Canola Growers Association, #210, 111 Research Dr., Saskatoon, SK S7N 3R2
306-668-2380, Fax: 306-975-1126
lkuchenski@innovationplace.com
Circulation: 1,100 *Frequency: 4 times a year*
Lanette Kuchenski, Editor

Canola Digest
315 Pacific Ave., Winnipeg, MB R3A 0M2
204-947-6912, Fax: 204-947-9136
www.canola-council.org
Circulation: 50,405 *Frequency: 4 times a year*
Kelly Funke, Editor

Canola Guide
204-944-5569, Fax: 204-944-5562
www.agcanada.com
Circulation: 26,012 *Frequency: 4 times a year*
Cory Bourdeau'hui, Editor

Central Alberta Farmer
780-986-2271, Fax: 780-986-6397
cafarmer@ccinet.ab.ca
www.albertafarmer.com
Circulation: 32,800 *Frequency: 12 times a year*
Neil Sutcliffe, Publisher

Central Alberta Life
PO Box 5200, 2950 Bremner Ave., Red Deer, AB T4N 5G3
403-343-2400, Fax: 403-342-4051
Circulation: 38,460 *Frequency: Twice weekly*
Fred Gorman, Publisher

Charolais Banner
#1, 2241 Alberts St., Regina, SK S4P 2V5
306-546-3940, Fax: 306-546-3942
charolaisbanner@sasktel.net
www.charolaisbanner.com
Circulation: 1,900 *Frequency: 5 times a year*
Candace By, Managing Editor

Le Coopérateur Agricole
#200, 9001, boul de l'Acadie, Montréal, QC H4N 3H7
514-384-6450, Fax: 514-858-2025
cooperateur@lacoop.coop
www.lacoop.coop/cooperateur
Circulation: 20 718 *Frequency: 10 fois par an; français*
André Léger, Advertising Manager
Patrick Dupuis, Rédacteur-en-chef

Country Guide
204-944-5754, Fax: 204-942-8463
jay@fbcpublishing.com
www.agcanada.com
Circulation: 42,000 (West & East editions) *Frequency: 11 times a year; also Corn-Soy Guide*
Jay Whetter, Editor

Dairy Contact
PO Box 549, 4914 - 50th St., Onoway, AB T0E 1V0
780-967-2929, Fax: 780-967-2930
dccontact@icrossroads.com
Frequency: Monthly
Allen Parr, Editor

Dairy Update
204-944-5569, Fax: 204-944-5562
www.agcanada.com
Circulation: 44,405 *Frequency: 9 times a year*
G. Winslow, Editor

Drainage Contractor
519-235-2400, Fax: 519-235-0798
pdarbishire@annexweb.com
drainagecontractor.com
Circulation: 8,000 *Frequency: Annual*
Peter Darbishire, Editor

Eastern Ontario Agrinews
PO Box 368, 7 King St., Chesterville, ON K0C 1H0
613-448-2321, Fax: 613-448-3260
rm@agrinewsinteractive.com
agrinewsinteractive.com
Circulation: 14,000 *Frequency: Monthly*
Robin R. Morris, Publisher

Farm Focus
Optipress Publishing, PO Box 128, 2 Second St., Yarmouth, NS B5A 4B1
902-742-7111, Fax: 902-742-2311
www.atlanticfarmfocus.ca
Circulation: 5,990 *Frequency: 24 times a year*
Mark Richardson, Publisher

Farm Market
930 Richmond St., Chatham, ON N7M 5J5
519-351-7331, Fax: 519-351-2452
farmmarketnew@bowesnet.com
Circulation: 12,518 *Frequency: 25 times a year*
Peter Epp, Editor
Dean Muharren, Publisher

Farming for Tomorrow
#204, 2114 Robinson St., Regina, SK S4T 2P7
888-213-9999
info@farmingfortomorrow.ca
www.farmingfortomorrow.ca
Other information: Toll Free Fax: 1-888-213-9999
Circulation: 67,400 *Frequency: 2 times a year*
Tom Bradley, Editor/Publisher

Feather Fancier Newspaper
5739 Telfer Rd., Sarnia, ON N7T 7H2
519-542-6859, Fax: 519-542-4168
featherfancier@ebtech.net
www.featherfancier.on.ca
Circulation: 1,800 *Frequency: 11 times a year*
Paul Monteith, Editor/Publisher

Fruit & Vegetable Magazine
519-429-3966, Fax: 519-429-3094, 800-265-2827
fruitedit@annexweb.com
www.fruitandveggie.com
Circulation: 7,000 *Frequency: 8 times a year*
Peter Darbishire, Publisher
Marg Land, Editor

Germination
Issues Ink, #203, 897 Corydon Ave., Winnipeg, MB R3M 0W7
204-453-1965, Fax: 204-475-5247
issues@issuesink.com
www.germination.ca
Circulation: 5,000 *Frequency: 5 times a year*
Robynne Anderson, Editor

Gestion et Technologie Agricoles
655, av Sainte-Anne, Saint-Hyacinthe, QC J2S 5G4
450-773-6028, Fax: 450-773-3115
publicite@courrierclarion.qc.ca
www.lecourrier.qc.ca
Circulation: 20 000 *Frequency: 11 fois par an; français*
Guy Roy, Directeur

Grainews
204-944-5567, Fax: 204-944-5562, 800-665-1362
cory@fbcpublishing.com
www.agcanada.com
Circulation: 28,771 *Frequency: 18 times a year*
Cory Bourdeaud'hui, Editor

Holstein Journal
#210, 30 East Beaver Creek Rd., Richmond Hill, ON L4B 1J2
905-886-4222, Fax: 905-866-0037
peter@holsteinjournal.com
www.holsteinjournal.com
Circulation: 4,900 *Frequency: Monthly; English & French*
G. Peter English, Publisher
Bonnie Cooper, Editor

Island Farmer
PO Box 790, 567 Main St., Montague, PE C0A 1R0
902-838-2515, Fax: 902-838-4392, 800-806-5443
pmacneill@islandpress.ca
www.peicanada.com
Circulation: 2,244 *Frequency: 26 times a year*
Paul MacNeill, Publisher
Andy Walker, Editor

The Limousin Leader
Bollum Marketing, PO Box 10, Site 11, RR#1, Airdrie, AB T4B 2A3
403-948-4768, Fax: 403-948-7531
rhonda@limousinleader.com
www.limousinleader.com
Frequency: 4 times a year
Randy Bollum, Editor

Ma Revue de machinerie agricole
Section Rouge Média Inc., 468, boul Roland-Therrien, Longueuil, QC J4H 4E3
450-677-2556, Fax: 450-677-4099
info@marevueagricole.com
www.marevueagricole.com
Circulation: 35 000 *Frequency: 11 fois par an; français*
Louise Gionet, Directeure des ventes publicitaires

The Manitoba Co-Operator
PO Box 9800 Main, 220 Portage Ave., Winnipeg, MB R3C 3K7
204-944-5569, Fax: 204-944-5562
www.agcanada.com
Circulation: 11,939 *Frequency: Weekly; supplements Seed Manitoba (annual); Yield Manitoba (annual); ISSN: 0025-2239*
Andy Sirski, Editorial Director

Manitoba Farmers' Voice
Frequency: 4 times a year
Kevin Hill, Editor

Manitoba FarmLIFE
#300, 2050 Cume Blvd., Brandon, MB R7A 5Y1
204-727-5459, Fax: 204-729-8965, 888-756-7770
farmlife@mts.net
www.farmpressgroup.com
Circulation: 28,000 *Frequency: 26 times a year*
Dale Coulter, Manager

Niagara Farmers' Monthly
PO Box 52, 131 College St., Smithville, ON L0R 2A0
905-957-3751, Fax: 905-957-0088
editor@niagarafarmers.com
Circulation: 21,078 *Frequency: 11 times a year*
Maribeth Fitts, Editor

The Northern Horizon
901 - 100th Ave., Dawson Creek, BC V1G 1W2
250-782-4888, Fax: 250-782-6300
Circulation: 29,000 *Frequency: Bi-weekly*

Northern Horse Review
403-250-1128, Fax: 403-250-1194
ingrids@telusplanet.net
www.northernhorsereview.com
Circulation: 15,000 *Frequency: Monthly*
Ingrid Schulz, Co-Publisher & Editor, ingrid@telusplanet.net
Ruth Dunbar, Co-Publisher

Northwest Farmer/Rancher
PO Box 1029, 892 - 104th St., North Battleford, SK S9A 3E6
306-445-7621, Fax: 306-445-3223, 866-549-9979
battlefords.publishing@sasktel.net
Circulation: 16,800 *Frequency: 6 times a year*
Alana Schweitzer, General Manager
Doug Collie, Editor

Ontario Beef
Ontario Cattlemen's Assn., 130 Malcolm Rd., Guelph, ON N1K 1B1
519-824-0334, Fax: 519-824-9101
ontbeef@cattle.guelph.on.ca
www.cattle.guelph.on.ca
Circulation: 20,000 *Frequency: 5 times a year*
Lianne Appleby, Editor
Donna Corbet, Circulation Manager

Ontario Beef Farmer
519-473-0010, Fax: 519-473-2256
Circulation: 10,310 *Frequency: 5 times a year*
Mervyn J. Hawkins, Publisher
Paul Mahon, Editor

Ontario Corn Producer
c/o Ontario Corn Producers Assn., 90 Woodlawn Rd. West, Guelph, ON N1H 1B2
519-837-1660, Fax: 519-837-1674
ontcorn@ontariocorn.org
www.ontariocorn.org/magazine.html
Circulation: 22,000 *Frequency: 9 times a year*
Brenda Miller-Sanford, Editor

Ontario Dairy Farmer
519-473-0010, Fax: 519-473-2256, 800-567-3276
www.ontariofarmer.com
Circulation: 7,445 *Frequency: 8 times a year*
Mervyn J. Hawkins, Publisher

Ontario Farmer

519-473-0010, Fax: 519-473-2256
www.ontariofarmer.com
Circulation: 32,127 *Frequency: Weekly, Tue.*
Mervyn J. Hawkins, Publisher
Paul Mahon, Editor

Ontario Hog Farmer

519-473-0010, Fax: 519-473-2256
www.ontariofarmer.com
Circulation: 4,830 *Frequency: 8 times a year*
Mervyn J. Hawkins, Publisher

Ontario Milk Producer
Dairy Farmers of Ontario, 6780 Campobello Rd., Mississauga, ON L5N 2L8
905-821-8970, Fax: 905-821-3160
Circulation: 10,791 *Frequency: Monthly*
Bill Dimmick, Editor

Porc Québec - Québec Hog Industry Magazine
555, boul Roland Therrien, Longueuil, QC J4H 4E9
450-679-0530, Fax: 450-679-0102
rloiseau@upa.qc.ca
Circulation: 3 000 *Frequency: 5 times a year*
Dominique Blanchard, Production Manager

Prairie Farmer
PO Box 1356, 500 Main St., Winkler, MB R6W 4B3
204-325-4771, Fax: 204-325-5059, 888-565-8357
Circulation: 26,000 *Frequency: 25 times a year*
Rick Reimer, Publisher

Prairie Hog Country
PO Box 5536, Leduc, AB T9E 2A1
780-986-0962, Fax: 780-980-9640
hogcountry@shaw.ca
www.prairiehogcountry.ca
Circulation: 4,800 *Frequency: 6 times a year*
Calvin Daniels, Copy Editor
Laurie Brandly, Publisher

Le Producteur de lait québécois
Fédération des producteurs de lait du Québec, 555, boul Roland Thérrien, Longueuil, QC J4H 3Y9
450-679-0530, Fax: 450-670-4788
rloiseau@laterre.ca
www.lait.org
Circulation: 9 338 *Frequency: 10 fois par an; français*
Jean Vigneault, Éditeur-en-chef

Producteur Plus
CP 147, Farnham, QC J2N 2R4
450-293-8282, Fax: 450-293-8554
leonard.pigeon@producteurplus.com
Circulation: 18 644 *Frequency: 8 fois par an; français*
Léonard Pigeon, Éditeur et Rédacteur-en-chef

Pro-farm
#300, 2216 Lorne St., Regina, SK S4P 2M7
306-586-5866, 888-776-3276
wcwga@wcwga.ca
Circulation: 9,000 *Frequency: 4 times a year*
Shannon McArton, Editor
Shelley Collins, Circulation Manager

Québec Farmers' Advocate
Maison l'UPA, 555, boul Roland-Therrien, Longueuil, QC J4H 3Y9
450-679-0530, Fax: 450-463-5291
qfa@upa.qc.ca
www.quebecfarmers.org
Circulation: 3,722 *Frequency: 11 times a year*

Regional Country News
115 Queen St. East, St Marys, ON N4X 1B7
519-284-2440, 888-270-1604
editor@regionalcountrynews.com
www.regionalcountrynews.co m
Circulation: 18,000 *Frequency: Monthly*
Stew Slater, Editor
Bill Huether, Publisher

Richelieu Agricole
#800, 625 boul Rene-Levesque, Montréal, QC H3B 1R2
514-866-3131, Fax: 514-866-3030, 800-361-7262
infos@reseauselect.com
www.reseauselect.com
Circulation: 15 700 *Frequency: 12 fois par an*
Gilles Lévesque, Rédacteur-en-chef
Lucie Leduc, General Manager

Rural Roots
30 - 10th Ave. East, Prince Albert, SK S6V 0Y5
Fax: 306-922-4237
rural.roots@paherald.sk.ca
www.paherald.sk.ca
Circulation: 31,992 *Frequency: 52 times a year*
Ian Jensen, Publisher
Ruth Griffiths, Editor

The Rural Voice

519-523-4311, Fax: 519-523-9140
Circulation: 13,293 *Frequency: Monthly; ISSN: 0703-7724*
Keith Roulston, Publisher

Saskatchewan Farm Life
2206A Ave. C North, Saskatoon, SK S7L 6C3
306-242-5723, Fax: 306-668-6164, 888-924-6367
Circulation: 56,200 *Frequency: 26 times a year*
Dan Moores, Publisher

Sheep Canada
1489 Rte. 560, Deerville, NB E7K 1W7
506-328-3599, Fax: 506-328-8165, 888-241-5124
gallivan@sheepcanada.com
www.sheepcanada.com
Frequency: 4 times a year
Dr. Cathy Gallivan, Editor

Simmental Country
#13, 4101 - 19 St. NE, Calgary, AB T2E 7C4
403-250-5255, Fax: 403-250-5121
country@simmental.com
www.simmental.com
Circulation: 1,800 *Frequency: Monthly*

Specialty Farms
PO Box 530, 105 Donly Dr. South, Simcoe, ON N3Y 4N5
519-429-5190, Fax: 519-429-3094, 888-599-2228
mland@annexweb.com
www.specialtyfarms.ca
Other information: Toll-Free Fax: 1-888-404-1129
Circulation: 3,500 *Frequency: 6 times a year*
Peter Darbishire, Publisher
Sharon Kauk, Advertising Manager
Marg Land, Editor

La Terre de chez nous
555, boul Roland Therrien, Longueuil, QC J4H 3Y9
450-679-8483, Fax: 450-670-4788
lhamon@laterre.ca
laterre.ca
Circulation: 38 620 *Frequency: Hebdomadaire; français*
Loïc Hamon, Rédacteur-en-chef

Union Farmer Quarterly
National Farmers Union, 2717 Wentz Ave., Saskatoon, SK S7K 4B6
306-652-9465, Fax: 306-664-6226
nfu@nfu.ca
www.nfu.ca
Circulation: 5,000 *Frequency: 4 times a year*
Terry Pugh, Editor

Voice of the Farmer
PO Box 490, 254 Main St., Dresden, ON N0P 1M0
519-683-4485, Fax: 519-683-4355
Frequency: Biweekly; also - Voice of the: Huron Farmer, Kent Farmer, Lambton Farmer, Middlesex Farmer, Elgin Farmer, Perth Farmer, Oxford Farmer, Waterloo Farmer; monthly Voice of: York Farmer, Durham Farmer, Vi
Mary Baxter, Editor

Western Dairy Farmer Magazine

780-986-2271, Fax: 780-986-6397
editor-wdf-caf@webcoleduc.com
www.westerndairyfarmer.com
Circulation: 6,962 *Frequency: 6 times a year*
Diana MacLeod, Editor
Neil Sutcliffe, Publisher

Western Hog Journal
Alberta Pork Producers Development Corp., 4828 - 89 St., Edmonton, AB T6E 5K1
780-474-8288, Fax: 780-479-5128
Circulation: 4,315 *Frequency: 4 times a year, 1 special Banff pork seminar edition*
Jody Wacowich, Editor

The Western Producer
PO Box 2500, 2310 Millae Ave., Saskatoon, SK S7K 2C4
306-665-3544, Fax: 306-934-2401, 800-667-6978
newsroom@producer.com
www.producer.com
Circulation: 70,000 *Frequency: Weekly*
Ken Zacharias, Publisher
Barb Glen, Editor

Scholarly

Literary

Event
c/o Douglas College, PO Box 2503, New Westminster, BC V3L 5B2
604-527-5293, Fax: 604-527-5095
event@douglas.bc.ca
event.douglas.bc.ca
Circulation: 1,250 *Frequency: 3 times a year; ISSN: 0315-3770*
Billeh Nickerson, Editor
Ian Cockfield, Managing Editor
Rick Maddocks, Editor

Scholarly Publication

Acadiensis: Journal of the History of the Atlantic Region / Revue d'Histoire de la Région Atlantique
Campus House, University of New Brunswick, PO Box 4400 A, Fredericton, NB E3B 5A3
506-453-4978, Fax: 506-453-5068
acadiensis@unb.ca
www.lib.unb.ca/Texts/Acadiensis
Circulation: 900 *Frequency: 2 times a year; English & French; ISSN: 0044-5851*
Bill Parenteau, Editor
Nicole Lang, Editor, nlang@umce.ca
Stephen Dutcher, Managing Editor, nlang@umce.ca

Annals of Air & Space Law / Annales de droit aérian et spatial
Institute & Centre of Air & Space Law, McGill University, 3661, rue Peel, Montréal, QC H3A 1X1
514-398-5095, Fax: 514-398-8197
edannals.law@mcgill.ca
www.mcgill.ca/iasl/annals
Circulation: 1,000 *Frequency: annually*
Prof.Dr. Paul S. Dempsey, Editor

Anthropologica
Wilfrid Laurier University Press, 2-139 DAWB, 75 University Ave. West, Waterloo, ON N2L 3C5
519-884-0710, Fax: 519-725-1399
press@wlu.ca
www.anthropologica.ca
Circulation: 625 *Frequency: 2 times a year*
Dr. Leslie Jermyn, Managing Editor, ljermyn@chass.utoronto.ca
Andrew Lyons, Editor-in-chief, andrewpaullyons@gmail.com

Arctic
c/o Arctic Institute of North America, University of Calgary, 2500 University Dr. NW, Calgary, AB T2N 1N4
403-220-7515, Fax: 403-282-4609
kmccullo@ucalgary.ca
www.artic.ucalgary.ca
Circulation: 1,500 *Frequency: 4 times a year; ISSN: 0004-0843*
Dr. Karen McCullough, Editor, 403/220-4049
Dr. Benoît Beauchamp, Executive Director, 403/220-7516

ARIEL - A Review of International English Literature
Dept. of English, University of Calgary, 2500 University Dr. NW, Calgary, AB T2N 1N4
403-220-4657, Fax: 403-289-1123
ariel@ucalgary.ca
Circulation: 850 *Frequency: 4 times a year*
Pamela McCallum, Editor

Atlantis: A Women's Studies Journal
Institute for the Study of Women, Mount Saint Vincent Univer, Halifax, NS B3M 2J6
902-457-6319, Fax: 902-443-1352
atlantis@msvu.ca
www.msvu.ca/atlantis
Circulation: 500 *Frequency: 2 times a year*
Linda Kealey, General Editor
Annalee Lepp, General Editor
Katherine Side, General Editor

BC Studies: The British Columbian Quarterly
Buchanan E, #162, 1866 Main Mall, Vancouver, BC V6T 1Z1
604-822-3727, Fax: 604-822-0606
info@bcstudies.com
www.bcstudies.com
Circulation: 700 *Frequency: 4 times a year*
Leanne Coughlin, Editor

Canadian Children's Literature (CCL) / Littérature Canadienne pour la Jeunesse
Centre for Research in Young People's Texts and Cultures, University of Winnipeg, 515 Portage Ave., Winnipeg, MB R3B 2E9
204-786-9351, Fax: 204-774-4134
ccl@uwinnipeg.ca
ccl.uwinnipeg.ca
Circulation: 900 *Frequency: 4 times a year; English & French; ISSN 0319-0080*
Perry Nodelman, Editor
Marie Davis, Associate Editor
Anne Rusnak, Associate Editor

Canadian Ethnic Studies / Études Ethniques au Canada
University of Calgary, 2500 University Dr. NW, Calgary, AB T2N 1N4
403-220-7257, Fax: 403-210-8764
ces@ucalgary.ca
www.ss.ucalgary.ca/ces
Circulation: 1,800 *Frequency: 3 times a year; ISSN: 0008-3496*
Dr. James Frideres, Editor

Canadian Foreign Policy / La Politique étrangère du Canada
2116 Dunton Tower, Carleton University, 1125 Colonel By Dr., Ottawa, ON K1S 5B6
613-520-6696, Fax: 613-520-3981
cfp@carleton.ca
www.carleton.ca/cfpj
Frequency: 3 times a year
Maureen Molot, Editor
Sarah Geddes, Managing Editor

The Canadian Historical Review
5201 Dufferin St., Toronto, ON M3H 5T8
416-667-7810, Fax: 416-667-7881
journals@utpress.utoronto.ca
www.utpjournals.com/chr/chr. html
Circulation: 1,700 *Frequency: 4 times a year; English & French; ISSN: 0008-3755*
Ken Cruikshank, Co-Editor
Sylvie Dépatie, Co-Editor

Canadian Journal of Development Studies / Revue canadienne d'études du développement
c/o University of Ottawa, 542 King Edward Ave., Ottawa, ON K1N 6N5
613-562-5800, Fax: 613-562-5361
cjds@uottawa.ca
www.cjds.ca
Circulation: 500 *Frequency: 4 times a year, plus 1 special issue; English & French*
Henry Veltmeyer, Co-Editor
Scott Simon, Co-Editor

Canadian Journal of Economics / Revue canadienne d'economique
CIREQ, Université de Montréal, PO Box 6128 Centre Ville, #C-6086, 3150, Jean-Brillant, Montréal, QC H3C 3J7
514-343-2104, Fax: 514-343-5831
cje@umontreal.ca
economics.ca/cje
Circulation: 3,200 *Frequency: 4 times a year*
Dwayne Benjamin, Managing Editor

Canadian Journal of Higher Education / La Revue canadienne d'enseignement supérieur
c/o The Canadian Society for the Study of Higher Education, 220 Sinnot Building, 70 Dysart St., Winnipeg, MB R3T 2N2
204-474-8309, Fax: 204-474-7607
csshe@cc.umanitoba.ca
www.umanitoba.ca/csshe
Circulation: 550 *Frequency: 3 times a year*
Keith Archer, Editor

Canadian Journal of History (CJH) / Annales canadiennes d'histoire
Dept. of History, University of Saskatchewan, 9 Campus Dr., Saskatoon, SK S7N 5A5
306-966-5794, Fax: 306-966-5852
cjh@duke.usask.ca
www.usask.ca/history/cjh
Circulation: 725 *Frequency: 3 times a year; ISSN: 0008-4107*
John McCannon, Editor
Linda Dietz, Managing Editor

The Canadian Journal of Information & Library Science
5201 Dufferin St., Toronto, ON M3H 5T8
416-667-7810, Fax: 416-667-7881
journals@utpress.utoronto.ca
www.utpjournals.com/cjils/cj ils.html
Circulation: 400 *Frequency: 4 times a year*
Lynne McKechnie, Editor

Canadian Journal of Law & Society (CJLS/RCDS) / Revue Canadienne Droit et Société
Dept des sciences juridiques, UQAM, CP 8888 Centre-Ville, Montréal, QC H3C 3P8
514-987-3000, Fax: 514-987-4784
www.acds-clsa.org/en/rcds
Circulation: 700 *Frequency: Biennially; English & French*
Ruth Murbach, Editor

Canadian Journal of Linguistics / Revue Canadienne de Linguistique
5201 Dufferin St., Toronto, ON M3H 5T8
416-667-7810, Fax: 416-667-7881
journals@utpress.utoronto.ca
www.utpjournals.com/cjl/cjl. html
Circulation: 900 *Frequency: 4 times a year*
Rose-Marie Dechaine, Editor

Canadian Journal of Mathematics
CMS, 5201 Dufferin St., Toronto, ON M3H 5T8
416-667-7810, Fax: 416-667-7881
journals@utpress.utoronto.ca
www.utpjournals.com/cjm/cjm. html
Circulation: 1,225 *Frequency: 6 times a year*
James B. Carrell, Editor
Nassif Ghoussoub, Editor

Canadian Journal of Philosophy
403-220-3514, Fax: 403-282-0085
ucpmail@ucalgary.ca
www.uofcpress.com/UCP/CJP.html
Circulation: 875 *Frequency: 4 times a year plus supplementary volume*
Dr. M. Stingl, Editorial Board Coordinator

Canadian Journal of Program Evaluation / La Revue canadienne d'évaluation de programme
PO Box 450 A, 145 Jean-Jacques-Lussier, Ottawa, ON K1N 6N5
613-562-5800, Fax: 613-562-5146
cjpe@uottawa.ca
www.evaluationcanada.ca
Circulation: 1,900 *Frequency: Bi-annually; English & French*
Prof. J. Bradley Cousins, Editor

Canadian Journal of Psychiatry
#701, 141 Laurier Ave. West, Ottawa, ON K1P 5J3
613-234-2815, Fax: 613-234-9857
subscriptions@cpa-apc.org
www.cpa-apc.org/Publications/cjpHome.asp
Circulation: 6,100 *Frequency: 12 times a year*
Dr. Joel Paris, Editor-in-chief

Canadian Journal of Psychoanalysis / Revue canadienne de psychanalyse
7000, Côte-des-Neiges, Montréal, QC H3S 2C1
514-738-9847, Fax: 514-738-6393
cjp-rcp@qc.aira.com
Circulation: 650 *Frequency: Bi-annually; ISSN 1195-3330*
Brian M. Robertson, Editor

The Canadian Journal of Sociology / Cahiers canadiens de sociologie
5201 Dufferin St., Toronto, ON M3H 5T8
416-667-7810, Fax: 416-667-7881
journals@utpress.utoronto.ca
www.utpjournals.com/cjs/cjs. html
Circulation: 1,100 *Frequency: 4 times a year; English with French abstracts; ISSN: 0318-6431*
Kevin D. Haggerty, Editor

Canadian Journal of Women & The Law (CJWL/RFD) / Revue Femmes et Droit
University of Toronto Press - Journals Division, 5210 Dufferin St., Toronto, ON M3H 5T8
416-667-7810, Fax: 416-667-7881
www.utpjournals.com/cjwl
Frequency: 2 times a year; English & French

Canadian Journal on Aging / La Revue Canadienne du Vieillissement
5201 Dufferin St., Toronto, ON M3H 5T8
416-667-7810, Fax: 416-667-7881
journals@utpress.utoronto.ca
www.utpjournals.com/cja/cja. html
Circulation: 1,600 *Frequency: 4 times a year; English & French; ISSN: 0714-9808*
Mark W. Rosenberg, Editor

Canadian Literature
c/o University of British Columbia, Buchanan E158, 1866 Main Mall, Vancouver, BC V6T 1Z1
604-822-2780, Fax: 604-822-5504
can.lit@ubc.ca
www.canlit.ca
Circulation: 1,200 *Frequency: 4 times a year*
Donna Chin, Managing Editor
Laurie Ricou, Editor

Canadian Mathematical Bulletin
5201 Dufferin St., Toronto, ON M3H 5T8
416-667-7810, Fax: 416-667-7881
journals@utpress.utoronto.ca
www.utpjournals.com/cmb/cmb. html
Circulation: 775 *Frequency: 4 times a year*
Maung Min-Oo, Editor-in-chief
Andrew J. Nicas, Editor-in-chief

Canadian Modern Language Review (CMLR/RCLV) / Le Revue canadienne des langues vivantes
5201 Dufferin St., Toronto, ON M3H 5T8
416-667-7810, Fax: 416-667-7881
journals@utpress.utoronto.ca
www.utpjournals.com/cmlr/cml r.html
Circulation: 1,000 *Frequency: 4 times a year; English & French; ISSN: 0008-4506*
Larry Vandergrift, Co-Editor
Tracey Derwing, Co-Editor

Canadian Poetry: Studies, Documents, Reviews
Dept. of English, University of Western Ontario, Richmond St. North, London, ON N6A 3K7
519-673-1164, Fax: 519-661-3776
dbentley@uwo.ca
www.canadianpoetry.ca
Circulation: 400 *Frequency: 2 times a year*
D.M.R. Bentley, Editor

Canadian Public Administration (CPA/APC) / Administration publique du Canada
#401, 1075 Bay St., Toronto, ON M5S 2B1
416-924-8787, Fax: 416-924-4992
ntl@ipac.ca; ntl@iapc.ca
www.ipac.ca; www.iapc.ca
Circulation: 3,600 *Frequency: 4 times a year; ISSN: 008-4840*
Barbara Wake Carroll, Editor

Canadian Public Policy / Analyse de Politique
CIREQ - Université de Montréal, PO Box 6128 Centre-Ville, Montréal, QC H3C 3J7
514-343-2104, Fax: 514-343-5831
cpp@umontreal.ca
economics.ca/cpp
Circulation: 1,500 *Frequency: 4 times a year; English & French; ISSN: 0317-0861*
James B. Davis, Managing Editor

Canadian Review of American Studies
5201 Dufferin St., Toronto, ON M3H 5T8
416-667-7810, Fax: 416-667-7881
journals@utpress.utoronto.ca
www.utpjournals.com/cras/cra s.html
Circulation: 400 *Frequency: 3 times a year; English & French*
Priscilla Walton, Editor

Canadian Review of Sociology & Anthropology / Revue canadienne de sociologie et d'anthropologie
SB-323, 1455, boul de Maisonneuve West, Montréal, QC H3G 1M8
514-848-8780, Fax: 514-848-8780
info@csaa.ca
www.csaa.ca
Circulation: 1,428 *Frequency: 4 times a year; French & English*
Harley Dickinson, Managing Editor

Canadian Theatre Review
5201 Dufferin St., Toronto, ON M3H 5T8
416-667-7810, Fax: 416-667-7881
journals@utpress.utoronto.ca
www.utpjournals.com/ctr
Circulation: 650 *Frequency: 4 times a year; ISSN: 0315-0836*
Ann Wilson, Co-Editor
Rick Knowles, Co-Editor
Harry Lane, Co-Editor
Reid Gilbert, Co-Editor
Catherine Graham, Co-Editor
Andrew Houston, Co-Editor

Cartographica
5201 Dufferin St., Toronto, ON M3H 5T8

416-667-7810, Fax: 416-667-7881
journals@utpress.utoronto.ca
www.utpjournals.com/carto/ca rto.html
Circulation: 900 *Frequency: 4 times a year*
Jeremy Crampton, Co-Editor
Roger Wheate, Co-Editor
Clifford Wood, Co-Editor

Economics Working Papers
Dept. of Economics, McMaster University, #426, Kenneth Taylor Hall, Hamilton, ON L8S 4M4
905-525-9140, Fax: 905-521-8232
econ@mcmaster.ca
socserv2.socsci.mcmaster.ca/~econ/rsrch/index.html
Frequency: 4 times a year

Eighteenth-Century Fiction

416-667-7810, Fax: 416-667-7881
journals@utpress.utoronto.ca
www.utpjournals.com
Circulation: 750 *Frequency: 4 times a year*
Jacqueline Langille, Managing Editor
Peter Walmsley, Co-Editor
Julie Park, Co-Editor

Energy Studies Review
c/o MIES, KTH 330, McMaster University, Hamilton, ON L8S 4M4
905-525-9140, Fax: 905-777-8344
mies@mcmaster.ca
www.socsci.mcmaster.ca/mies/
Frequency: 2 times a year; ISSN: 0843-4379
Prof. Joseph A. Doucet, Editor

Environments: A Journal of Interdisciplinary Studies
Geography & Environmental Studies, Wilfred Laurier University, Waterloo, ON N2L 3C5
519-884-0710, Fax: 519-725-1342
www.fes.uwaterloo.ca/research/environments/
Circulation: 400 *Frequency: 3 times a year; ISSN: 0711-6780*
D. Scott Slocombe, Editor, sslocomb@wlu.ca

Essays on Canadian Writing (ECW)
#200, 2120 Queen St. East, Toronto, ON M4E 1E2
416-694-3348, Fax: 416-698-9906
info@ecwpress.com
www.ecw.ca
Circulation: 1,200 *Frequency: 3 times a year; ISSN: 0313-0300*
Jack David, Publisher & Editor

Exceptionality Education Canada
c/o Lindsey Leenaars, Uni. of Alberta, #6, 102 Education North, Edmonton, AB T6G 2G5
780-492-0800, Fax: 780-492-1318
eecj@ualberta.ca
www.uofaweb.ualberta.ca/eec
Circulation: 250 *Frequency: 3 times a year*
Judy Lupart, Editor
Christina M. Rinaldi, Editor
Jessica Whitley, Associate Editor
Lindsey Leenaars, Editorial Assistant

Infor
5201 Dufferin St., Toronto, ON M3H 5T8
416-667-7810, Fax: 416-667-7881
journals@utpress.utoronto.ca
www.utpjournals.com/infor/in for.html
Circulation: 400 *Frequency: 4 times a year*
Bernard Gendron, Editor

Interculture
4917, rue Saint-Urbain, Montréal, QC H2T 2W1
514-288-7229, Fax: 514-844-6800
info@iim.qc.ca
www.iim.qc.ca
Circulation: 900 *Frequency: 2 times a year; English & French editions; ISSN: 0828-797X (English), 0712-1571 (French)*
Robert Vachon, Publisher

International Journal
c/o Canadian Institute of International Affairs, #302, 205 Richmond St. West, Toronto, ON M5V 1V3
416-997-9000, Fax: 416-977-7521
mailbox@ciia.org
www.ciia.org
Circulation: 1,300 *Frequency: 4 times a year; ISSN: 0020-7020*
David Haglund, Co-Editor
Joseph Jodcel, Co-Editor

Intersections : Canadian Journal of Music/Revue canadienne de musique
PO Box 507 Q, Toronto, ON M4T 2M5
416-483-7282, Fax: 416-489-1713
journals@interlog.com
www.cums-smuc.ca
Circulation: 400 *Frequency: 2 times a year; ISSN 1911-0146; French*
Prof. Mary Woodside, Editor
François de Médicis, Rédacteur

Journal of Baha'i Studies / La Revue des Études Bahá'¡es/La Revista des Estudios Bahá'¡
34 Copernicus St., Ottawa, ON K1N 7K4
613-233-1903, Fax: 613-233-3644
editor@bahai-studies.ca
www.bahai-studies.ca
Circulation: 2,000 *Frequency: biannual; English, French & Spanish; ISSN: 0838-0430*
Anne Furlong, Editor

Journal of Canadian Art History / Annales d'histoire de l'art canadien
c/o EV-3.819, Concordia University, 1455, boul de Maisonneuve ouest, Montréal, QC H3G 1M8
514-848-2424, Fax: 514-848-4584
jcah@vax2.concordia.ca
art-history.concordia.ca/JCAH/index.html
Circulation: 550 *Frequency: 2 times a year; English & French*
Sandra Paikowsky, Publisher

Journal of Canadian Poetry
Dept. of English, University of Ottawa, Ottawa, ON K1N 6N5
613-562-5800, Fax: 613-562-5975
dstaines@uottawa.ca
Circulation: 350 *Frequency: Annually*
David Staines, Editor

Journal of Canadian Studies / Revue d'Études Canadiennes
c/o Trent University, 1600 West Bank Dr., Peterborough, ON K9J 7B8
705-748-1279, Fax: 705-748-1110
jcs_rec@trentu.ca
Circulation: 1,300 *Frequency: 4 times a year; English & French*
Robert M. Campbell
Kerry Cannon, Managing Editor

Journal of Law & Social Policy / Revue des lois et des politiques sociales
Clinic Resource Office, Legal Aid Ontario, #41, 425 Adelaide St. West, Toronto, ON M5V 3C1
416-204-5408, Fax: 416-204-5422, 800-668-8258
jlsp@lao.on.ca
www.legalaid.on.ca
Circulation: 230 *Frequency: Annually; ISSN 0829-3929*
Margaret Capes, Editor
Andrew Bolter, Editor

Journal of Scholarly Publishing
5201 Dufferin St., Toronto, ON M3H 5T8
416-667-7810, Fax: 416-667-7881
journals@utpress.utoronto.ca
www.utpjournals.com/jsp/jsp. html
Circulation: 800 *Frequency: 4 times a year; ISSN: 1198-9742*
Tom Radko, Editor

Journal of Ukrainian Studies
CIUS Press, #125, 10 Orde St.res., Toronto, ON M5T 1N7
416-978-6934, Fax: 416-978-2672
zakydalsky@sympatico.ca
www.utoronto.ca/cius/
Circulation: 250
Taras Zakydalsky, Managing Editor, zakydalsky@sympatico.ca

Labour, Capital & Society: A Journal on the Third World / Travail, capital et société
c/o Dr. Suzanne Dansereau, Intl. Development Studies Program, Saint Mary's University, Halifax, NS B3H 3C3
902-420-5793
journallcs-tcs@smu.ca
www.marua.com/journallcs/index.html
Circulation: 700 *Frequency: 2 times a year; English & French*
Dr. Suzanne Dansereau, Editor

Labour/Le Travail
FM 2005, Faculty of Arts Publications, Memorial University of Newfoundland, St. John's, NL A1C 5S7
709-737-2144, Fax: 709-737-4342
cclh@mun.ca
www.mun.ca/cclh
Circulation: 1,000 *Frequency: 2 times a year; English & French; ISSN: 0700-3862*
Bryan D. Palmer, Editor-in-chief
Irene Whitfield, Managing Editor, 709/737-3453

Material Culture Review
c/o University of Cape Breton, PO Box 5300, Sydney, NS B1P 6L2
902-563-1604, Fax: 902-563-1177
www.uccbpress.ca/MCReview.htm
Circulation: 400 *Frequency: 2 times a year; ISSN: 1183-1073*
Richard McKinnon, Managing Editor

McGill Journal of Education / Revue des sciences de l'éducation McGill
c/o Faculty of Education, McGill University, 3700, rue McTavish, Montréal, QC H3A 1Y2
514-398-4246, Fax: 514-398-4529
ann.keenan@mcgill.ca
Circulation: 500 *Frequency: 3 times a year; English & French*
Anthony Paré, Editor
Ann Keenan, Managing Editor

McMaster Journal of Theology & Ministry
c/o McMaster Divinity College, McMaster University, 1280 Main St. West, Hamilton, ON L8S 4K1
905-525-9140, Fax: 905-577-4782
mjtm@mcmaster.ca
www.mcmaster.ca/mjtm
Frequency: annual
Wendy J. Porter, Editor

Le Médecin Vétérinaire du Québec
Ordre des médecins vétérinaires du Québec, #200, 800, av Ste-Anne, Saint-Hyacinthe, QC J2S 5G7
450-774-1427, Fax: 450-774-7635, 800-267-1427
omvq@omvq.qc.ca
www.omvq.qc.ca
Circulation: 2 500 *Frequency: 4 fois par an; français*
Jean Piérard, Rédacteur-en-chef d.m.v.

Modern Drama
5201 Dufferin St., Toronto, ON M3H 5T8
416-667-7810, Fax: 416-667-7881
journals@utoronto.ca
www.utpjournals.com/md/md.html
Circulation: 1,700 *Frequency: 4 times a year; ISSN: 0026-7694*
Alan Ackerman, Editor

The Monograph - Journal of the Ont. Assn. for Geographic & Environmental Education
Ontario Association for Geographic & Environmental Education, PO Box 507 Q, Toronto, ON M4T 2M5
416-483-7282, Fax: 416-489-1713
journals@interlog.com
www.oagee.org
Circulation: 800 *Frequency: 4 times a year; ISSN 0048-1973*
Gary Birchall, Editor

Mosaic: A Journal for the Interdisciplinary Study of Literature
#208, Tier Bldg., University of Manitoba, Winnipeg, MB R3T 2N2
204-474-9763, Fax: 204-474-7584
mosaic_journal@umanitoba.ca
www.umanitoba.ca/mosaic
Circulation: 900 *Frequency: 4 times a year; ISSN: 0027-1276*
Lisa Muirhead, Production Manager
Donna Danyluk, Manager, Subscriptions
Jackie Pantel, Business, Submissions & Systems Manager
Dawne McCance, Editor

Mouseion, Journal of the Classical Association of Canada/ Revue de la Societé canadienne des ét
Department of Classics, Memorial University of Newfoundland, St. John's, NF A1C 5S7
709-737-7914,
Frequency: 3 times a year; English & French
Dr. Mark Joyal, Editor
Dr. J. Butrica, Editor, jbutrica@mun.ca
Dr. L. Stirling, Editor

Newfoundland and Labrador Studies
Faculty of Arts Publications, Memorial University of Newfoun, FM 2005, St. John's, NL A1C 5S7
709-737-2144, Fax: 709-737-4342
nlstudies@mun.ca
www.mun.ca/nls
Circulation: 350 *Frequency: 2 times a year; English & French; ISSN: 0823-1737*
Ron Rompkey, Chair
Irene Whitfield, Managing Editor

Ontario History

416-226-9011, Fax: 416-226-2740
ohs@ontariohistoricalsociety.ca
www.ontariohistoricalsociety.ca

Circulation: 1,200 *Frequency: 2 times a year*
Thorald J. Tronrud, Editor
Patricia K. Neal, Executive Director

Pacific Affairs
c/o University of British Columbia, #164, 1855 West Mall, Vancouver, BC V6T 1Z2
604-822-4534, Fax: 604-822-9452
enquiry@pacificaffairs.ubc.ca
pacificaffairs.ubc.ca
Circulation: 1,600 *Frequency: 4 times a year; ISSN: 0030-851X*
Jacquelilne Garnett, Managing Editor
Pittman Potter, Chair, Editorial Board
Timothy Cheek, Editor

The Philantropist / Le Philanthrope
The AGORA Foundation, PO Box 507 Q, Toronto, ON M4T 2M5
416-483-7282, Fax: 416-489-1713
journals@interlog.com
www.thephilanthropist.ca
Circulation: 450 *Frequency: 4 times a year*
Donald Bourgeois, Editor

Policy Options / Options politiques
Inst. for Research on Public Policy, #200, 1470, rue Peel, Montréal, QC H3A 1T1
514-985-2461, Fax: 514-985-2559
irpp@irpp.org
www.irpp.org
Circulation: 2,000 *Frequency: 10 times a year; ISSN: 0226-5893*
L. Ian MacDonald, Editor

Prairie Forum: Journal of the Canadian Plains Research Center
Canadian Plains Research Center, University of Regina, Regina, SK S4S 0A2
306-585-4795, Fax: 306-585-4699
brian.mlazgar@uregina.ca
www.cprc.ca
Circulation: 300 *Frequency: 2 times a year; ISSN: 0317-6282*
Dr. Patrick Douaud, Editor

Public Sector Management et Secteur Publique
#401, 1075 Bay St., Toronto, ON M5S 2B1
416-924-8787, Fax: 416-924-4992
ntl@ipac.ca; ntl@iapc.ca
www.ipac.ca; www.iapc.ca
Circulation: 4,000 *Frequency: 3 times a year; ISSN: 1183-1081*
Patrice Dutil, Editor

Queen's Quarterly
Queen's University, Kingston, ON K7L 3N6
613-533-2667, Fax: 613-533-6822
qquarter@post.queensu.ca
www.queensu.ca/quarterly
Circulation: 3,000 *Frequency: 4 times a year; ISSN: 0033-6041*
Dr. Boris Castel, Editor
Penny Roantree, Business Manager

Relational Child & Youth Care Practice
School of Child & Youth Care, Ryerson University, SHE Bldg., 350 Victoria St., Toronto, ON M5B 2K3
416-598-5923, Fax: 416-979-5209
rcycp@ryerson.ca
Circulation: 450 *Frequency: 4 times a year*
Gerry Fewster, Founding Editor
Carol Stuart, Managing Editor
Dr. T. Garfat, Co-Editor

Renaissance & Reformation / Renaissance et réforme
CRRS Publications, Victoria University, 71 Queen's Park Cres. East, Toronto, ON M5S 1K7
416-585-4465, Fax: 416-585-4430
crrs.publications@utoronto.ca
www.RenRef.ca
Circulation: 700 *Frequency: 4 times a year; ISSN 0034-429X*
Michael O'Connor, Managing Editor

Resources for Feminist Research
Ontario Institute for Studies in Education/University of Tor, 252 Bloor St. West, Toronto, ON M5S 1V6
416-923-6641, Fax: 416-926-4725
rfrdrf@oise.utoronto.ca
www.oise.utoronto.ca/rfr
Circulation: 2,000 *Frequency: 2 times a year; ISSN: 0707-8412*
Philinda Masters, Editor

Revue canadienne de linguistique appliquée / Canadian Journal of Applied Linguistics
Institut des langues secondes, Université d'Ottawa, 600 King Edward, Ottawa, ON K1N 6N5
613-562-5743, Fax: 613-562-5126
hknoerr@uottawa.ca
www.aclacaal.org
Frequency: 2 fois par an
Hélène Knoerr, Editor

Russell: The Journal of Bertrand Russell Studies
The Bertrand Russell Research Centre, TSH #619, McMaster Uni, Main St. West, Hamilton, ON L8S 4M2
905-525-9140, Fax: 905-577-6930
blackwk@mcmaster.ca
www.humanities.mcmaster.ca/~russell/journal.htm
Circulation: 400 *Frequency: 2 times a year*
Kenneth Blackwell, Editor

Science Fiction Studies
c/o Veronica Hollinger, Cultural Studies Program, Trent University, Peterborough, ON K9J 7B8
705-748-1011, Fax: 705-748-1826
vhollinger@trentu.ca
www.depauw.edu/sfs
Circulation: 800 *Frequency: 3 times a year*
Arthur B. Evans, Managing Editor

Scientia Canadensis - Journal of the History of Cdn. Science, Technology & Medicine
Canadian Science & Technology Historical Association, PO Box 8509 T, Ottawa, ON K1G 3H9
Circulation: 200 *Frequency: Annually; ISSN 0829-2507*
Stéphane Castonguay, Editor-in-chief

Scrivener Creative Review
c/o McGill University, 853, rue Sherbrooke ouest, Montréal, QC H3A 2T6
514-398-6588, Fax: 514-398-8146
scrivener.review@gmail.com
arts.mcgill.ca/english/scrivener/
Circulation: 500 *Frequency: Annually; ISSN: 0227-5090*
Lisa Guimond, Editor
Andrew Cleland, Editor

Seminar
5201 Dufferin St., Toronto, ON M3H 5T8
416-667-7810, Fax: 416-667-7881
journals@utpress.utoronto.ca
www.utpjournals.com/seminar/ seminar.html
Circulation: 770 *Frequency: 4 times a year*
Raleigh Whitinger, Editor

Social History / Histoire Sociale
5201 Dufferin St., Toronto, ON M3H 5T8
416-667-7810, Fax: 416-667-7881
journals@utpress.utoronto.ca
www.utpjournals.com/hssh/hss h.html
Circulation: 500 *Frequency: 2 times a year*
Chad Gaffield, Editor
Gordon Darroch, Editor

Studies in Canadian Literature / Études en littérature canadienne
Campus House, PO Box 4400, 11 Garland Ct., Fredericton, NB E3B 5A3
506-453-3501, Fax: 506-453-5069
scl@unb.ca
www.Lib.unb.ca/Texts/SCL
Circulation: 500 *Frequency: 2 times a year*
J.C. Ball, Editor
S.R. Campbell, Managing Editor
J. Andrews, Editor

Studies in Political Economy
Carleton University, Colonel By Dr., Ottawa, ON K1S 5B6
613-520-2600, Fax: 613-520-3713
spe@carleton.ca
www.carleton.ca/spe
Circulation: 600 *Frequency: 2 times a year*
Hélène Pellerin

Tessera
Études littéraires, UQAM, CP 8888 Centre-Ville, Montréal, QC H3C 3P8
514-987-3000, Fax: 514-987-8218
delvaux.martine@uqam.ca
Circulation: 500 *Frequency: 2 times a year; ISSN: 0840-4631*
Martine Delvaux, Co-Editor

Theatre Research in Canada / Recherches théâtrales au Canada
Graduate Centre for Study of Drama, University of Toronto, 214 College St., 3rd Fl., Toronto, ON M5T 2Z9
416-978-7984, Fax: 416-971-1378
tric.rtac@utoronto.ca
www.lib.unb.ca/Texts/TRIC/
Circulation: 350 *Frequency: 2 times a year; English & French*
Bruce Barton, Editor

The Tocqueville Review / La Revue Tocqueville
5201 Dufferin St., Toronto, ON M3H 5T8
416-667-7781, Fax: 416-667-7881
journals@utpress.utoronto.ca
www.utpjournals.com/ttr/ttr. html
Circulation: 400 *Frequency: 2 times a year; English & French*
Michel Forsé, Co-Editor
Françoise Mélonio, Co-Editor
Laurence Gullec, Co-Editor
Cheryl Welch, Co-Editor

Topia: A Canadian Journal of Cultural Studies
c/o 3013 Tel Centre, York University, 4700 North Keele St., Toronto, ON M3J 1P3
416-736-2100, Fax: 416-736-5392
topia@yorku.ca
www.yorku.ca/topia
Circulation: 300 *Frequency: 2 times a year; ISSN: 1206-0143*
Jody Berland, Editor

Transcultural Psychiatry
Psychiatry Dept., McGill University, 1033, av des Pins ouest, Montréal, QC H3A 1A1
514-398-7302, Fax: 514-398-4370
Laurence.Kirmayer@mcgill.ca
www.mcgill.ca/tcpsych/publica tions
Circulation: 500 *Frequency: 4 times a year*
Laurence J. Kirmayer, Editor M.D.
Sing Lee, Associate Editor M.D.
Roland Littlewood, Associate Editor M.D., PhD
Leslie Swartz, Associate Editor PhD

Ultimate Reality & Meaning
5201 Dufferin St., Toronto, ON M3H 5T8
416-667-7810, Fax: 416-667-7881
journals@utpress.utoronto.ca
www.utpjournals.com/uram/ura m.html
Circulation: 380 *Frequency: 4 times a year*
John F. Perry, Editor
J. Patrick Mohr, Executive Editor

University of Toronto Law Journal
5201 Dufferin St., Toronto, ON M3H 5T8
416-667-7810, Fax: 416-667-7881
journals@utpress.utoronto.ca
www.utpjournals.com/utlj/utl j.html
Circulation: 700 *Frequency: 4 times a year*
Karen Knop, Editor

University of Toronto Quarterly
5201 Dufferin St., Toronto, ON M3H 5T8
416-667-7810, Fax: 416-667-7881
journals@utpress.utoronto.ca
www.utpjournals.com/utq/utq. html
Circulation: 1,100 *Frequency: 4 times a year*
Brian Corman, Editor

Urban History Review / Revue d'Histoire Urbaine
416-483-7282, Fax: 416-489-1713
subscribe@urbanhistoryreview.ca
www.urbanhistoryreview.ca
Circulation: 400 *Frequency: 2 times a year; ISSN 0703-0428*
Michèle Dagenais, Co-Editor
Robert Lewis, Co-Editor

Windsor Review
c/o Dept. of English, University of Windsor, #2, 104 Chrysler Hall North, Windsor, ON N9B 3P4
519-253-3000, Fax: 519-971-3676
uwrevu@uwindsor.ca
athena.uwindsor.ca/units/english/English.nsf
Circulation: 500 *Frequency: 2 times a year; ISSN: 0042-0352*

University

Student Guides

Acces Media
#31, 1124, ch Marie-Anne est, Montréal, QC H2J 2B7
514-524-1182, Fax: 514-524-7771, 800-391-1182
info@accesmedia.com
www.accesmedia.com
Circulation: 300,000
Edgar Donelle

The Student Traveller
The Canadian Federation of Students - Services, #100, 45 Charles St. East, Toronto, ON M4Y 1S2

416-966-2887, Fax: 416-966-4043
suben@travelcuts.com
www.travelcuts.com
Circulation: 130,000 *Frequency: 2 times a year*
Lisa Trainor, Editor

Welcome Back Student Magazine
Osprey Media Group, PO Box 1352, #205, 111 Princess St., Kingston, ON K7L 5C6
613-549-8442, Fax: 613-549-4333
kingmags@kos.net
Circulation: 18,500 *Frequency: Annually*
Mary Laflamme, Publisher & Editor

University & Student Publications

Algonquin Times
1385 Woodroffe Ave., Ottawa, ON K2G 1V8
613-727-4723, Fax: 613-727-7743
times@algonquincollege.com
www.algonquincollege.com
Kris Lapenskie, Online Editor

L'Alinéa
781, rue Notre Dame, Repentigny, QC J5Y 1B4
450-470-0911, Fax: 450-581-1567
infocom@collanaud.qc.ca
www.collanaud.qc.ca

antiThesis
99 University Ave., Kingston, ON K7L 3N6
613-533-2000, Fax: 613-533-6300
antithesis@sgps.ca
www.queensu.ca

Aquinian
Fredericton, NB E3B 5G3
506-452-0532, Fax: 506-452-0617
www.stu.ca

Argosy Weekly
62A York St., Sackville, NB E4L 1H3
506-364-2300
argosy@mta.ca
www.mta.ca
Dan Wortman, Managing Editor
Julie Stephenson, Editor

The Argus
955 Oliver Rd., Thunder Bay, ON P7B 5E1
807-343-8110, Fax: 807-343-8023
www.lakeheadu.ca

Arthur
#104, 751 George St., Peterborough, ON K9H 7P5
705-745-3535, Fax: 705-745-3534
editors@trentarthur.ca
www.trentu.ca
James Burrows, Editor
Ariel Sharratt, Editor

At Guelph
50 Stone Rd. East, Guelph, ON N1G 2W1
519-824-4120, Fax: 519-767-1693
www.uoguelph.ca
Barbara Chance, Editor

The Athenaeum
Wolfville, NS B4P 2R6
902-542-2201, Fax: 902-585-1072
www.acadiau.ca

L'Attribut
9155, rue St-Hubert, Montréal, QC H2M 1Y8
514-389-5921, Fax: 514-389-5762
www.collegeahuntsic.qc.ca

Bandersnatch
CP 2000, 21275, rue Lakeshore, Sainte-Anne-de-Bellevue, QC H9X 3L9
514-457-6610, Fax: 514-457-1655
bandersnatch@johnabbott.qc.ca
www.johnabbott.qc.ca

Bricklayer
PO Box 5005, 100 College Blvd., Red Deer, AB T4N 5H5
403-342-3300, Fax: 403-340-8940
www.rdc.ab.ca

Brock Press
500 Glenridge Ave., St Catharines, ON L2S 3A1
905-688-5550, Fax: 905-688-2789
www.brocku.ca

Brunswickan
PO Box 4400 A, Fredericton, NB E3B 5A3
506-453-4666, Fax: 506-453-5158
trudya@unb.ca
www.unb.ca

The Buzz
c/o Newnham Campus, 1750 Finch Ave. East, Toronto, ON M2J 2X5
416-491-5050
www.senecac.on.ca/

The Cadre
550 University Ave., Charlottetown, PE C1A 4P3
902-566-0439, Fax: 902-566-0420
www.upei.ca

Le Calvaire
60, rue de l'Évêché ouest, Rimouski, QC G5L 4H6
418-723-1880, Fax: 418-724-4061
infoscol@cegep-rimouski.qc.ca
www.cegep-rimouski.qc.ca

The Campus
PO Box 5000, Lennoxville, QC J1M 1Z7
819-822-9600, Fax: 819-822-9661, 1 8-0 5-7 27
liaison@ubishops.ca
www.ubishops.ca

Campus Times
Vancouver, BC V6T 1Z2
604-822-2211
www.ubc.ca

Capilano Courier
2055 Purcell Way, North Vancouver, BC V7J 3H5
604-986-1911, Fax: 604-984-4985
switchboard@capcollege.bc.ca
www.capcollege.bc.ca

CAS
1455, boul de Maisonneuve ouest, Montréal, QC H3G 1M8
514-848-2424, Fax: 514-848-2621
communications@concordia.ca
www.concordia.ca

Cascade
33844 King Rd., Abbotsford, BC V2S 7M8
604-504-7441, Fax: 604-855-7614
www.ucfv.ca

The Charlatan
1125 Colonel By Dr., Ottawa, ON K1S 5B6
613-520-7400
www.carleton.ca

The Chronicle
PO Box 385, 2000 Simcoe St. North, Oshawa, ON L1H 7L7
905-721-2000, Fax: 905-721-3113
www.durhamcollege.ca

Cityside
3737 Wascana Pkwy., Regina, SK S4S 0A2
306-585-4402, Fax: 306-585-4997
www.uregina.ca

The Cord Weekly
75 University Ave. West, Waterloo, ON N2L 3C5
519-884-0710
www.wlu.ca

La Criée
616, av St-Rédempteur, Matane, QC G4W 1L1
418-562-1240, Fax: 418-566-2115
comcegep@cgmatane.qc.ca
www.cegep-matane.qc.ca

La Crise
1660, boul de l'Entente, Québec, QC G1S 4S3
418-688-8310, Fax: 418-688-1539
communications@cegep-fxg.qc.ca
www.cegep-fxg.qc.ca

The Crown
777 Garner Rd. East, Ancaster, ON L9K 1J4
905-648-2131, Fax: 905-648-2134
mvanbev@redeemer.ca
www.redeemer.ca

D'Épiderme
175, rue De La Vérendrye, Sept-Iles, QC G4R 5B7
418-962-9848, Fax: 418-962-3852
info@cegep-sept-iles.qc.ca
www.cegep-sept-iles.qc.ca

D.E.C. express
537, boul Blanche, Baie-Comeau, QC G5C 2B2
418-589-5707, Fax: 418-589-9842, 1 8-0 4-3 20
www.cegep-baie-comeau.qc.ca

de Fouille-moi
235, rue Saint-Jacques, Granby, QC J2G 3N1
450-372-6614, Fax: 450-372-6565
www.cegepgranby.qc.ca

Dialog Newspaper
PO Box 1015 B, Toronto, ON M5T 2T9
416-415-2000, Fax: 416-415-4493, 1 8-0 2-5 20
info@gbrownc.on.ca
www.gbrownc.on.ca

The Echo
821, av Ste-Croix, Saint-Laurent, QC H4L 3X9
514-744-7500, Fax: 514-744-7023
info@vaniercollege.qc.ca
www.vaniercollege.qc.ca

Eclosion
2410, ch Ste-Foy, Sainte-Foy, QC G1V 1T3
418-659-6630, Fax: 418-659-7576
www.cegep-ste-foy.qc.ca

L'Ecorché
100, rue Duquet, Sainte-Thérèse, QC J7E 3G6
450-430-3120, Fax: 450-971-7872
info@clg.qc.ca
www.clg.qc.ca

L'Électic
3000, av Boullé, Saint-Hyacinthe, QC J2S 1H9
450-773-6800, Fax: 450-773-9971
info@cegepsth.qc.ca
www.cegepsth.qc.ca

The Emery Weal
1301 - 16 Ave. NW, Calgary, AB T2M 0L4
403-284-8110, Fax: 403-284-7112
www.sait.ca
Canada's premier technical institute by 2010

The Endeavour
3000 College Dr. South, Lethbridge, AB T1K 1L6
403-320-3200, Fax: 403-320-1461, 1 8-0 5-2 01
info@lethbridgecollege.ab.ca
www.lethbridgecollege.ab.ca

L'Entremetteur
333, boul Cité-des-Jeunes, Hull, QC J8Y 6M5
819-770-4012, Fax: 819-770-8167
www.coll-outao.qc.ca

Etcetera
North Campus, 205 Humber College Blvd., Toronto, ON M9W 5L7
416-675-5005, Fax: 416-675-2427
enquiry@humber.ca
www.humber.ca

L'Exemplaire
3000, boul Tracy, Sorel-Tracy, QC J3R 5B9
450-742-6651, Fax: 450-742-1878
info@cegep-sorel-tracy.qc.ca
www.cegep-sorel-tracy.qc.ca

Express This
299 College Dr. SE, Medicine Hat, AB T1A 3Y6
403-529-3811, Fax: 403-504-3517
info@mhc.ab.ca
www.mhc.ab.ca

Folio
114 St. - 89 Ave., Edmonton, AB T6G 2E1
780-492-3111
www.ualberta.ca

Le Forcep
205, rue Mgr Bourget, Lévis, QC G6V 6Z9
418-833-5110, Fax: 418-833-7323
www.clevislauzon.qc.ca

Free Forum
3330 - 22nd Ave., Prince George, BC V2N 1P8
250-562-2131, Fax: 250-561-5816, 1 8-0 3-1 81
askcnc@cnc.bc.ca
www.cnc.bc.ca

Le Front
Moncton, NB E1A 3E9

506-858-4000, Fax: 506-858-4379
www.umoncton.ca

Gargoyle
15 King's College Circle, Toronto, ON M5S 3H7
416-978-3170, Fax: 416-978-6019

The Gauntlet
2500 University Dr. NW, Calgary, AB T2N 1N4
403-220-5110, Fax: 403-282-8413
www.ucalgary.ca

Gazette
1459 Oxford St., Halifax, NS B3H 4R2
902-494-2211, Fax: 902-494-2319
www.dal.ca

The Georgian Eye
One Georgian Dr., Barrie, ON L4M 3X9
705-728-1968, Fax: 705-722-5123
inquire@georgianc.on.ca
www.georgianc.on.ca

La Gifle
CP 97, 3500, rue De Courval, Trois-Rivières, QC G9A 5E6
819-376-1721, Fax: 819-693-4663
dir.generale@cegeptr.qc.ca
www.cegeptr.qc.ca

Golden Ram
PO Box 550, Truro, NS B2N 5E3
902-893-6722, Fax: 902-895-5529
www.nsac.ns.ca/

The Gradzette
134 Services Building, 97 Dafoe Rd., Winnipeg, MB R3T 2N2
204-474-8880
www.umanitoba.ca

Le Grafitti
3200, ch Côte Ste-Catherine, Montréal, QC H3T 1C1
514-342-9342, Fax: 514-342-6607
mapril@brebeuf.qc.ca
www.brebeuf.qc.ca

Great Northern Way Campus
3700 Willingdon Ave., Burnaby, BC V5G 3H2
604-434-5734, Fax: 604-431-6917
www.bcit.ca

L'Hermes
CP 1018, 30, boul du Séminaire nord, Saint-Jean-sur-Richelieu, QC J3B 7B1
450-347-5301, Fax: 450-358-9350
communications@cstjean.qc.ca
www.cstjean.qc.ca

Impact Campus
Cité universitaire, Québec, QC G1K 7P4
418-656-3333, Fax: 418-656-2809
sg@sg.ulaval.ca
www.ulaval.ca

in Extremis
475, rue du Parc, Sherbrooke, QC J1E 4K1
819-564-6350, Fax: 819-564-1579
communications@cegepsherbrooke.qc.ca
www.cegepsherbrooke.qc.ca

L'Infomane
10555, av de Bois-de-Boulogne, Montréal, QC H4N 1L4
514-332-3000, Fax: 514-332-5857
www.bdeb.qc.ca

The Intercamp
City Centre Campus, 10700 - 104 Ave., Edmonton, AB T5J 4S2
780-497-5401, Fax: 780-497-5405
www.macewan.ca

L'Interdit
1300, 8e av, Québec, QC G1J 5L5
418-647-6600, Fax: 418-647-6798
info@climoilou.qc.ca
www.climoilou.qc.ca

L'Interêt
3000, ch de la Côte-Sainte-Catherine, Montréal, QC H3T 2A7
514-340-6000, Fax: 514-340-6411
www.hec.ca

The Interrobang
PO Box 7005, 1460 Oxford St. East, London, ON N5Y 5R6
519-452-4430, Fax: 519-452-4420
www.fanshawec.ca

Jargon
166 Bedford Hwy., Halifax, NS B3M 2J6
902-457-6117, Fax: 902-457-6498
www.msvu.ca

Le Jets
1100, rue Notre-Dame ouest, Montréal, QC H3C 1K3
514-396-8800, Fax: 514-396-8950
www.etsmtl.ca

The Journal
923 Robie St., Halifax, NS B3H 3C3
902-420-5400, Fax: 902-420-5566
www.smu.ca

Journal l'actif
CP 610, Shawinigan, QC G9N 6V8
819-539-6401, Fax: 819-539-2435
information@collegeshawinigan.qc.ca
www.collegeshawinigan.qc.ca

Kwantlen Chronicle
12666 - 72 Ave., Surrey, BC V3W 2M8
604-599-2100, Fax: 604-599-2068
www.kwantlen.bc.ca

Lion's Tale
1457 London Rd., Sarnia, ON N7S 6K4
519-542-7751, Fax: 519-541-2418
www.lambton.on.ca

MacMedia (McLaughlin College)
4700 Keele St., Toronto, ON M3J 1P3
416-736-2100, Fax: 416-736-5700
www.yorku.ca

Magnetic North
PO Box 60, 443 Northern Ave., Sault Ste Marie, ON P6A 5L3
705-759-6774, Fax: 705-759-3273, 1 8-0 4-1 22
www.saultc.on.ca/

Le Majeur
675, boul Auger ouest, Alma, QC G8B 2B7
418-668-2387, Fax: 418-668-7336
college@calma.qc.ca
www.calma.qc.ca

Mars' Hill
7600 Glover Rd., Langley, BC V2Y 1Y1
604-888-6158, Fax: 604-888-5729

Le Matulu
10748, boul Saint-Vital, Montréal-Nord, QC H1H 4T3
514-322-8111, Fax: 512- -
dg@marievictorin.qc.ca
www.marievictorin.qc.ca

The Medium
3359 Mississauga Rd., Mississauga, ON L5L 1C6
905-828-5399, Fax: 905-569-4301
www.erin.utoronto.ca/

The Meliorist
4401 University Dr., Lethbridge, AB T1K 3M4
403-329-2201, Fax: 403-329-2097
www.uleth.ca

The Mike
81 St. Mary St., Toronto, ON M4S 1J4
416-926-1300, Fax: 416-926-7266

La Minerve
625, av Ste-Croix, Saint-Laurent, QC H4L 3X7
514-747-6521, Fax: 514-748-1249
www.cegep-st-laurent.qc.ca

Le Motdit
945, ch de Chambly, Longueuil, QC J4H 3M6
450-679-2631, Fax: 450-679-5570
www.collegeem.qc.ca

Mouton Noir
960, rue St-Georges, Drummondville, QC J2C 6A2
819-478-4671, Fax: 819-478-8823
dg@cdrummond.qc.ca
www.cdrummond.qc.ca/cegep/index.htm

The Muse
PO Box 4200, 230 Elizabeth Ave., St. John's, NL A1C 5S7
709-737-8000, Fax: 709-737-4569
www.mun.ca

Navigator
900 Fifth St., Nanaimo, BC V9R 5S5
250-753-3245, Fax: 250-740-6473
www.mala.bc.ca

Le Nénu phare
534, rue Jacques-Cartier est, Chicoutimi, QC G7H 1Z6
418-549-9520, Fax: 418-549-1315
dirgene@cegep-chicoutimi.qc.ca
www.cegep-chicoutimi.qc.ca

news@niagara
Welland Campus, 300 Woodlawn Rd., Welland, ON L3C 7L3
905-735-2211, Fax: 905-736-6000
webmaster@niagarac.on.ca
www.niagarac.on.ca

Nexus
Lansdowne Campus, 3100 Foul Bay Rd., Victoria, BC V8P 5J2
250-370-3550, Fax: 250-370-3551
www.camosun.bc.ca

NightViews
350 Victoria St., Toronto, ON M5B 2K3
416-979-5000
inquire@ryerson.ca
www.ryerson.ca

Nomad
King & Portsmouth, 100 Portsmouth Ave., Kingston, ON K7L 5A6
613-544-5400, Fax: 613-545-3923
www.sl.on.ca

Le Nordet
140, 4e av, La Pocatière, QC G0R 1Z0
418-856-1525, Fax: 418-856-4589
information@cglapocatiere.qc.ca
www.cglapocatiere.qc.ca/cg

The Nugget
11762 - 106 St., Edmonton, AB T5G 2R1
780-471-7400, Fax: 780-471-8583
registrar@nait.ca
www.nait.ca

Opus
PO Box 398, 1450 Nakina Dr., Thunder Bay, ON P7C 4W1
807-475-6110, Fax: 807-623-4512, 1 8-0 4-5 54
www.confederationc.on.ca/

L'Original déchainé
Ramsey Lake Rd., Sudbury, ON P3E 2C6
705-675-1151, Fax: 705-675-4891
admissions@laurentian.ca
www.laurentian.ca

Teaching is in French & English. Certain faculties offer parallel programs in both languages.

Other Press
PO Box 2503, New Westminster, BC V3L 5B2
604-527-5400, Fax: 604-527-5095
registrar@douglas.bc.ca
www.douglas.bc.ca/

Over the Edge
3333 University Way, Prince George, BC V2N 4Z9
250-960-5555, Fax: 250-960-5794
www.unbc.ca

The Papercut
3880, Côte-des-Neiges, Montréal, QC H3H 1W1
514-931-8792, Fax: 514-931-8790
www.marianopolis.edu

Pars ailleurs
169, rue Champlain, Salaberry-de-Valleyfield, QC J6T 1X6
450-373-9441, Fax: 450-377-6035
courrier@colval.qc.ca
www.colval.qc.ca

The Peak
8888 University Dr., Burnaby, BC V5A 1S6
604-291-3111
www.sfu.ca

La Petite Caisse
555, boul de l'Université, Chicoutimi, QC G7H 2B1
418-545-5011, Fax: 418-545-5012
www.uqac.uquebec.ca

The Phoenix
1000 KLO Rd., Kelowna, BC V1Y 4X8
www.okanagan.bc.ca

La Pige
2505, rue St-Hubert, Jonquière, QC G7X 7W2

418-547-2191, Fax: 418-547-6965
cegep@cjonquiere.qc.ca
www.cjonquiere.qc.ca

The Pioneer
PO Box 4200, Belleville, ON K8N 5B9
613-969-1913, Fax: 613-962-1376
liaison@loyalistc.on.ca
www.loyalistcollege.com

Plant
3040, rue Sherbrooke ouest, Montréal, QC H3Z 1A4
514-931-8731, Fax: 514-931-5181
www.dawsoncollege.qc.ca

Le Polyscope
CP 6079 Centre-ville, Montréal, QC H3C 3A7
514-340-4711
www.polymtl.ca

Le Profane
425, boul du Collège, Rouyn-Noranda, QC J9X 5E5
819-762-0931, Fax: 819-762-2071
cegepat.qc.ca

Quartier Libre
CP 6128 Centre-Ville, Montréal, QC H3C 3J7
514-343-6111, Fax: 514-343-2098
www.umontreal.ca

Quill
270 - 18th St., Brandon, MB R7A 6A9
204-728-9520, Fax: 204-726-4573
www.brandonu.ca

Reflector
4825 Richard Rd. SW, Calgary, AB T3E 6K6
403-440-6111, Fax: 403-440-5938
slscalia@mtroyal.ca
www.mtroyal.ca

La Répliqué
475, rue Notre-Dame est, Victoriaville, QC G6P 4B3
819-758-6401, Fax: 819-758-8126
www.cgpvicto.qc.ca

Le Republique
255, rue Ontario est, Montréal, QC H2X 1X6
514-982-3437, Fax: 514-982-3400
www.cvm.qc.ca

République étudiante
6400, 16e av, Montréal, QC H1X 2S9
514-376-1620, Fax: 514-376-1440
mdionne@crosemont.qc.ca
www.crosemont.qc.ca

Réseau/U.Q. Network
475, rue de l'Église, Québec, QC G1K 9H7
418-657-3551, Fax: 418-657-2132
cscuq@uqss.uquebec.ca
www.uquebec.ca

Le Réveil
200, av de la Cathédrale, Winnipeg, MB R2H 0H7
204-233-0210,

The Ring
PO Box 1700 CSC, Victoria, BC V8W 2Y2
250-721-7211, Fax: 250-721-7212
www.uvic.ca

La Rotonde
550 Cumberland St., Ottawa, ON K1N 6N5
613-562-5700, Fax: 613-562-5103, 1 8-7 8-8 82
www.uottawa.ca

The Satellite
PO Box 2034, Hamilton, ON L8N 3T2
905-575-1212, Fax: 905-575-2378
www.mohawkcollege.ca

Le Script
9, rue Monseigneur Gosselin, Lévis, QC G6V 5K1
418-833-1249, Fax: 418-833-1974
lvezina@collegedelevis.qc.ca

Le Sentier
CP 7300, Saint-Félicien, QC G8K 2R8
418-679-5412, Fax: 418-679-0238
www.cstfelicien.qc.ca

The Sheaf
105 Admin. Place, Saskatoon, SK S7N 5A2
306-966-4343, Fax: 306-966-4530
www.usask.ca

The Sheridan Sun
Trafalgar Road Campus, 1430 Trafalgar Rd., Oakville, ON L6H 2L1
905-845-9430, Fax: 905-815-4148
infosheridan@sheridaninstitute.ca
www.sheridaninstitute.ca

The Shield
1400 Barrydowne Rd., Sudbury, ON P3A 3V8
705-566-8101
info@cambrianc.on.ca
www.cambrianc.on.ca

The Silhouette
1280 Main St. West, Hamilton, ON L8S 4K1
905-525-9140, Fax: 905-521-1504
www.mcmaster.ca

Siren
PO Box 631 A, Scarborough, ON M1K 5E9
416-289-5000, Fax: 416-439-7358
www.centennialcollege.ca

The 60th Meridian
PO Box 5300, 1250 Grand Lake Rd., Sydney, NS B1P 6L2
902-539-5300, Fax: 902-562-0119, 1 8-0 4-4 72
www.capebretonu.ca

Sommets
2500, boul de l'Université, Sherbrooke, QC J1K 2R1
819-821-7686
information@usherbrooke.ca
www.usherbrooke.ca

Spoke
299 Doon Valley Dr., Kitchener, ON N2G 4M4
519-748-5220, Fax: 519-748-3505
www.conestogac.on.ca/

Strand
73 Queen's Park Cres. East, Toronto, ON M5S 1K9
416-585-4524, Fax: 416-585-4584
www.vicu.utoronto.ca

Student Connection
8115 Franklin Ave., Fort McMurray, AB T9H 2H7
780-791-4800, Fax: 780-791-1555, 1 8-0 2-1 14
registrar@keyano.ca
www.keyano.ca

Suites
CP 8888 Centre-Ville, Montréal, QC H3C 3P8
514-987-3000
www.uqam.ca

The Surveyor
Administrative Services, 140 Weymouth St., Charlottetown, PE C1A 4Z1
902-629-4217, Fax: 902-629-4239
info@hollandc.pe.ca
www.hollandc.pe.ca/

The Tablet
845, rue Sherbrooke ouest, Montréal, QC H3A 2T5
514-398-4455, Fax: 514-398-4455
www.mcgill.ca

The Three Penny Beaver
Sutherland Campus, 599 Brealey Dr., Peterborough, ON K9J 7B1
705-749-5530, Fax: 705-749-5540
copeland@flemingc.on.ca
www.flemingc.on.ca/

The Toike Oike
21 King's College Circle, Toronto, ON M5S 1A1
416-978-2011
www.utoronto.ca

Le Trait d'Union
3800, rue Sherbrooke est, Montréal, QC H1X 2A2
514-254-7131, Fax: 514-253-7637
communic@cmaisonneuve.qc.ca
www.cmaisonneuve.qc.ca

L'Ulcère
80, rue Frontenac, Rivière-du-Loup, QC G5R 1R1
418-862-6903, Fax: 418-862-4959
sercom@cegep-rdl.qc.ca
www.cegep-rdl.qc.ca

Underground
1265 Military Trail, Toronto, ON M1C 1A4
905-287-8872, Fax: 905-287-7525
www.scar.utoronto.ca/

The Uniter
401 Sunset Ave., Windsor, ON N9B 3P4
519-253-3000, Fax: 519-973-7050
www.uwindsor.ca

The Uniter
515 Portage Ave., Winnipeg, MB R3B 2E9
204-786-7811, Fax: 204-786-8983
adm@uwinnipeg.ca
www.uwinnipeg.ca

Uquarium
300, allée des Ursulines, Rimouski, QC G5L 3A1
418-723-1986
uqar@uqar.qc.ca
www.uqar.qc.ca

UW Gazette
200 University Ave. West, Waterloo, ON N2L 3G1
519-885-1211, Fax: 519-884-8009
www.uwaterloo.ca/

V.C.C. Voice
1155 East Broadway, Vancouver, BC V5T 4V5
604-871-7000, Fax: 604-871-7100
www.vcc.ca

Le Virus
Pavillion Alexandre-Taché, CP 1250 Hull, 283, boul Alexandre-Taché, Gatineau, QC J8X 3X7
819-595-3900, Fax: 819-595-3924
www.uqo.ca

The Voice
1 University Dr., Athabasca, AB T9S 3A3
780- -, Fax: 780-675-6437, 1 8-0 7-8 90
www.athabascau.ca

The Voice
100 West 49th Ave., Vancouver, BC V5Y 2Z6
604-323-5511, Fax: 604-323-5555
geninfo@langara.bc.ca
www.langara.bc.ca

Vox-Populi
1111, rue Lapierre, Lasalle, QC H8N 2J4
514-364-3320, Fax: 514-364-7130
courrier@claurendeau.qc.ca
www.claurendeau.qc.ca

Le Voyeur
445, boul de l'Université, Rouyn-Noranda, QC J9X 5E4
819-762-0971, Fax: 819-797-4727
www.uqat.ca

Le Voyeur
CP 500 Bureau-chef, 3351, boul des Forges, Trois-Rivières, QC G9A 5H7
819-376-5011, Fax: 819-376-5012
www.uqtr.ca

Wallaceburg Campus
2000 Talbot Rd. West, Windsor, ON N9A 6S4
519-966-1656, Fax: 519-972-3811
info@stclaircollege.ca
www.stclaircollege.ca

Watch
6350 Coburg Rd., Halifax, NS B3H 2A1
902-422-1271, Fax: 902-423-3357
www.ukings.ns.ca

Western News
#2, 1151 Richmond St., London, ON N6A 5B8
519-661-2111
www.uwo.ca

Window
300 Huron, Toronto, ON M5S 3J6
416-978-2460, Fax: 416-978-0554

Xaverian Weekly
PO Box 5000, Antigonish, NS B2G 2W5
902-863-3300, Fax: 902-867-5153
www.stfx.ca

Le Zèle
475, boul de l'Avenir, Laval, QC H7N 5H9
450-975-6100, Fax: 450-975-6116
cmontmorency.qc.ca

SECTION 14
RELIGION

Broad Faith Based Associations

Action des Chrétiens pour l'abolition de la torture (ACAT) / Action by Christians for the Abolition of Torture
15, rue de Castelnau ouest, Montréal QC H2R 2W3
Tél: 514-890-6169; *Téléc:* 514-890-6484
Courriel: info@acatcanada.org
URL: www.acatcanada.org
Également appelé: ACAT Canada
Aperçu: *Dimension:* moyenne; *Envergure: nationale; Organisme sans but lucratif; fondée en 1984*
Membre(s) du bureau directeur:
Raoul Lincourt, Président
Célene Dupuis, Directeur
Finances: *Budget de fonctionnement annuel:* $50,000-$100,000
Personnel: 2 membre(s) du personnel; 30 bénévole(s)
Membre: 600; *Montant de la cotisation:* 30 $-80 $; *Critères d'admissibilite:* ouvert; *Comités:* Commission des interventions; Financement; Relations publiques; Ressourcement
Activités: Campagne annuelle; *Listes de destinataires:* Oui *Bibliothèque:* Oui rendez-vous
Description: Dans un but d'engagement évangélique, encourager les différentes communautés Chrétiennes du Canada à porter ensemble, par la prière, les souffrances des victimes de la torture; dans un but éducatif, sensibiliser particulièrement les Chrétiens au scandale de la torture (par l'information et la formation aux droits de la personne); dans un but de soulager la misère des victimes de la torture, apporter une aide concrète par l'envoi de lettres et pétitions aux responsables de torture et des lettres d'encouragement aux victimes; Affiliation(s): Fédération internationale de l'action des Chrétiens pour l'abolition de la torture (FIACAT)

Adventive Cross Cultural Initiatives (ACCI)
89 Auriga Dr., Nepean ON K2E 7Z2
Tel: 613-298-1546; *Fax:* 613-225-7455
e-mail: lauren@adventive.ca
URL: www.adventive.ca
Previous Name: New Life League
Overview: A small national charitable organization founded in 1986
Chief Officer(s):
John Haley, Executive Director
Lauren Carrion, Canadian National Director
Finances: *Annual Operating Budget:* Less than $50,000; *Funding Sources:* Donations
Staff: 4 staff member(s); 1 volunteer(s)
Activities: *Internships:* Yes
Description: International, interdenominational Christian missionary organization ministering through printing & literature, children's homes, national workers, evangelism & church planting; *Member of:* Canadian Council of Christian Charities

Alcoholics for Christ Canada
1277 Fennell Ave. East, Hamilton ON L8T 1T3
Tel: 905-383-4160
e-mail: afc@execulink.com
URL: www.alcoholicsforchrist.ca
Overview: A small national organization
Description: Direct & restore the alcoholic or substance abuser, the family member & the adult child to a sincere & dedicated relationship with Jesus Christ

American Academy of Religion (AAR)
#300, 825 Houston Mill Rd., Atlanta GA 30329-4205 USA
Tel: 404-727-3049; *Fax:* 404-727-7959
e-mail: aaw@aarweb.org; membership@aarweb.org
URL: www.aarweb.org
Overview: A medium-sized national charitable organization founded in 1909
Chief Officer(s):
John R. Fitzmier, Executive Director & Treasurer
jfitzmier@aarweb.org
Emilie M. Townes, President
Michel Desjardins, Secretary
Membership: 10,000+; *Fees:* Schedule available; *Member Profile:* Teachers; Research scholars; *Committees:* Academic Relations; Executive; Finance; Graduate Student; International Connections; Nominations; Program; Publications; Public Understanding of Religion; Regions; Status of Racial & Ethnic Minorities in the Profession; Status of Women in the Profession; Teaching & Learning; Theological Education Steering Committee
Activities: Governance Task Force; Job Placement Task Force; Religion in the Schools Task Force; Sustainability Task Force; Status of Lesbian, Gay, Bisexual, & Transgendered Persons in the Profession; Awards for Excellence in the Study of Religion Book Award Juries; History of Religions Jury; Research Grants Jury; *Speaker Service:* Yes
Description: The American Academy of Religion promotes research, teaching & scholarship in the field of religion.; *Member of:* American Council of Learned Societies

The Apostolic Church in Canada
c/o New Life Centre, 220 Adelaide St. North, London ON N6B 3H4
Tel: 519-852-7755
e-mail: nlt@apostolic.ca
URL: www.apostolic.ca
Overview: A small national organization founded in 1934
Chief Officer(s):
D. Karl Thomas, National Leader
Finances: *Annual Operating Budget:* $500,000-$1.5 Million
Staff: 15 staff member(s)
Membership: 500-999
Activities: *Internships:* Yes

Associated Gospel Churches (AGC) / Association des églises évangéliques (AEE)
1500 Kerns Rd., Burlington ON L7P 3A7
Tel: 905-634-8184; *Fax:* 905-634-6283
e-mail: admin@agcofcanada.com
URL: www.agcofcanada.com
Overview: A medium-sized national charitable organization founded in 1925
Chief Officer(s):
Bill Fietje, President
bill@agcofcanada.com
Susan Page, Church Relations Coordinator
sue@agcofcanada.com
Finances: *Annual Operating Budget:* $250,000-$500,000
Staff: 5 staff member(s)
Membership: 21,400 members; 140+ churches; *Fees:* 4% of revenue minus missions support; *Committees:* Doctrine & Credentials; Finance & Administration; Communication; Church Growth; Church Renting
Description: To glorify God by partnering together in obedience to the Great Commandment & the Great Commission; to become a movement of healthy, reproducing churches; Affiliation(s): World Relief; World Team; UFM International; Evangelical Fellowship of Canada

Association of Unity Churches (Canada)
2631 Kingsway Dr., Kitchener ON N2C 1A7
Tel: 519-894-0810
e-mail: info@unitycanada.org
URL: www.unitycanada.org
Overview: A small national charitable organization founded in 1978
Chief Officer(s):
Doris Lewis, Chair
Finances: *Annual Operating Budget:* $50,000-$100,000
Membership: 20 churches
Activities: *Internships:* Yes; *Speaker Service:* Yes
Description: To serve God by serving the people of Canada through the support & expansion of Unity ministries; Affiliation(s): Association of Unity Churches USA

Atlantic Episcopal Assembly (AEA) / Assemblée des évêques de l'Atlantique
Diocesan Centre, 60 Bouchard St., Edmundston NB E3V 3K1
Tel: 506-735-5578; *Fax:* 506-735-4271
Overview: A small local organization founded in 1967
Chief Officer(s):
Léo Grégoire, I.V.Dei, Secretary-Treasurer
François Thibodeau, C.F.M., President
Terrence Prendergast, S.J.
Finances: *Annual Operating Budget:* Less than $50,000
Membership: 12; *Committees:* Exécutif; Affaires sociales
Description: Proposer l'évangile de Jésus Christ dans les diverses situations de la vie ainsi que ses implications pratiques de notre temps; echange d'information pour les évêques

The Bible League of Canada / Société canadienne pour la distribution de la Bible
PO Box 5037, Burlington ON L7R 3Y8
Tel: 905-319-9500; *Fax:* 905-319-0484
Toll-Free: 800-363-9673
e-mail: admin@thebibleleague.ca
URL: www.thebibleleague.ca
Previous Name: World Home Bible League
Overview: A large international charitable organization founded in 1949
Chief Officer(s):
Dick Kranendonk, Executive Director
J. Ellens, President
Finances: *Annual Operating Budget:* $3 Million-$5 Million; *Funding Sources:* Donations
Staff: 15 staff member(s)
Activities: *Speaker Service:* Yes *Library:* Yes
Description: To introduce people to Jesus Christ; to spread God's Word worldwide; *Member of:* Canadian Council of Christian Charities; International Association of Bible Leagues; Affiliation(s): The Bible League

Brethren in Christ
2700 Bristol Circle, Oakville ON L6H 6EH
Tel: 905-339-2335; *Fax:* 905-337-2120
e-mail: biccanada@bellnet.ca
URL: www.bic-church.org
Overview: A medium-sized international charitable organization founded in 1788
Chief Officer(s):
Brad Fisher, Treasurer
Trish Hogg, Secretary
Darrell Winger, Bishop
Finances: *Annual Operating Budget:* $500,000-$1.5 Million; *Funding Sources:* Congregational giving
Staff: 8 staff member(s)
Membership: 3,450 + 43 congregations in Canada; *Member Profile:* North American membership is about 20,000 with significant churches in other countries including India, Japan, Zambia, Zimbabwe, Nicaragua, Cuba, Venezuela, Columbia, South Africa
Activities: *Speaker Service:* Yes; *Rents Mailing List:* Yes
Member of: Evangelical Fellowship of Canada; Affiliation(s): Mennonite Central Committee; Canadian Holiness Federation

British Israel World Federation (Canada) Inc. (BIWF)
313 Sherbourne St., Toronto ON M5A 2S3
Tel: 416-921-5996; *Fax:* 416-921-9511
e-mail: info@british-israel-world-fed.ca
URL: www.british-israel-world-fed.ca
Overview: A small international charitable organization founded in 1929
Chief Officer(s):
Douglas C. Nesbit, President
Membership: 1,200; *Fees:* $10
Activities: Meetings; *Speaker Service:* Yes
Description: To proclaim the Gospel of the Kingdom of God as contained in the Holy Bible

Canada's National Bible Hour (CNBH)
PO Box 1210, St Catharines ON L2R 7A7
Tel: 905-684-1401
e-mail: joblackwood@globaloutreachmission.org
URL: www.missiongo.org/ministries.html
Overview: A small national organization founded in 1925
Chief Officer(s):
Ernest C. Manning, Founder
Len Lane
Description: Canada's oldest religious broadcast. They are committed to teaching the "infallible Word Of God", while also creating and partaking in local and international missionary programs.; *Member of:* Global Outreach Mission

Canadian Association for Pastoral Practice & Education (CAPPE) / Association canadienne pour la pratique et l'éducation pastorales (ACPEP)
660 Francklyn St., Halifax NS B3H 3B5
Tel: 902-820-3085; *Fax:* 902-820-3087
Toll-Free: 866-442-2773
e-mail: office@cappe.org
URL: www.cappe.org
Overview: A medium-sized national organization founded in 1965
Chief Officer(s):
Walton Brian, President, 306-655-5827
brian.walton@saskatoonhealthregion.ca
Tony Sedfawi, Executive Director
office@cappe.org
Dawn Dyer, Secretary, 519-646-6000 42551
Dawn.Dyer@sjhc.london.on.ca
King Harold, Treasurer, 204-889-8931
hjking@mts.net
Kathy Greig, Office Manager
kathy.greig@cappe.org
Finances: *Funding Sources:* Membership dues
Fees: $200 associate members, with any amount of CPE or PCE training, & corporate members; $400 certified specialists or teaching supervisors; *Member Profile:* Persons involved in a variety of ministries, in settings such as parishes, prisons & correctional facilities, pastoral counselling centres, health care facilities, & industrial facilities
Activities: Offering educational programs for both clergy & lay persons; Providing certification for supervisors & specialists; Creating networking opportunities
Description: To support persons involved in pastoral care & pastoral counselling in Canada; To set standards & monitor professional practice; To accredit educational centres in a range of settings

Canadian Bible Society / Société biblique canadienne

10 Carnforth Rd., Toronto ON M4A 2S4
Tel: 416-757-4171; *Fax:* 416-757-3376
Toll-Free: 800-465-2425
e-mail: info@biblesociety.ca
URL: www.biblesociety.ca

Overview: A large national charitable organization founded in 1804
Chief Officer(s):
Ted Seres, National Director
Hart Wiens, Director, Scripture Translation, 519-741-8285, Fax: 519-741-8351
hwiens@biblesociety.ca
Serge Rhéaume, Director, Secteur francophone, 514-524-7873, Fax: 514-524-6116
srheaume@biblesociety.ca
Finances: *Annual Operating Budget:* Greater than $5 Million; *Funding Sources:* Donations
Staff: 130 staff member(s)
Activities: *Speaker Service:* Yes *Library:* Yes (Open to Public) by appointment
Description: To promote & encourage, without doctrinal note or comment, the translation, publication, distribution & use of the Scriptures throughout Canada & Bermuda, & to cooperate with the United Bible Societies in its worldwide work; *Member of:* United Bible Societies

Canadian Foodgrains Bank Association Inc. (CFGB) / Association de la banque canadienne de grains inc.

PO Box 767, #400, 280 Smith St., Winnipeg MB R3C 2L4
Tel: 204-944-1993; *Fax:* 204-943-2597
Toll-Free: 800-665-0377
e-mail: cfgb@foodgrainsbank.ca
URL: www.foodgrainsbank.ca

Also Known As: Foodgrains Bank
Overview: A large international charitable organization founded in 1983
Chief Officer(s):
Jim Cornelius, Executive Director
j_cornelius@foodgrainsbank.ca
Sol Janzen, Administrator
s_janzen@foodgrainsbank.ca
Finances: *Funding Sources:* Donations; Fundraising
Membership: 15; *Member Profile:* Canadian church agencies
Activities: Improving community development; Protecting & building sustainable economic livelihoods; Encouraging peace-building; Strengthening Canadian & international policy & action towards hunger issues; Increasing public awareness & engagement; Collecting grain & cash donations from donors
Description: To provide a Christian response to hunger; to share resources with & support hungry populations outside Canada to achieve food security; to reduce hunger in developing countries

The Canadian Orthodox Church (COC) / L'Église Orthodoxe canadienne (EOC)

37323 Hawkins Pickle Rd., Dewdney BC V0M 1H0
Tel: 604-826-9336; *Fax:* 604-820-5247
e-mail: synaxis@new-ostrog.org
URL: www.orthodoxcanada.org

Overview: A medium-sized national organization founded in 1970
Chief Officer(s):
Lazar Puhalo, Archbishop
Finances: *Funding Sources:* Publications; candle factory sales
Membership: 2,000
Activities: *Speaker Service:* Yes *Library:* Yes (Open to Public) by appointment
Description: Approximately 20 parishes & missions exist in Canada presently; *Member of:* Ukrainian Orthodox Church, Kiev, Ukraine; Affiliation(s): The Nemanjic Institute for Serbo-Byzantine Studies; Centre for Canadian Orthodox Studies

Canadian Society for the Study of Religion (CSSR) / Société canadienne pour l'étude de la religion (SCER)

c/o Dr. Mark D. Chapman, #100, 30 Carrier Dr., Toronto ON M9W 5T7
e-mail: mchapman@alumni.uwaterloo.ca
URL: www.ccsr.ca/cssr

Overview: A small national organization founded in 1966
Chief Officer(s):
Michel Desjardins, President
mdesjardins@wlu.ca
Mark Chapman, Membership Secretary
mchapman@alumni.uwaterloo.ca
Richard Mann, Treasurer
Richard_mann@carleton.ca
Fees: $50 students; $60 part-time & retired persons; $90 regular; *Member Profile:* Scholars engaged in various academic approaches to the study of religion
Description: To promote research in the study of religion, with particular reference to Canada; to encourage a critical examination of the teaching of the discipline; *Member of:* International Association for the History of Religions (IAHR); Affiliation(s): Canadian Federation for the Humanities & Social Sciences (CFHSS)

Canadian Society of Biblical Studies (CSBS) / Société canadienne des études bibliques (SCEB)

c/o Prof. Robert A. Derrenbacker, Jr., Regent College, 5800 University Blvd., Vancouver BC V6T 2E4
e-mail: rderrenbacker@regent-college.edu
URL: www.ccsr.ca/csbs

Overview: A small national organization founded in 1933
Chief Officer(s):
Terry Donaldson, President
terry.donaldson@utoronto.ca
Francis Landy, Vice-President
francis.landy@ualberta.ca
Robert A. Derrenbacker, Jr., Treasurer & Membership Secretary
rderrenbacker@regent-college.edu
Richard S. Ascough, Officer, Communications
rsa@queensu.ca
Fees: $35 students & retired & unemployed persons; $72 full membership; *Member Profile:* Individuals interested in all aspects of the academic study of the Bible
Description: To stimulate the critical investigation of the classical biblical literature & related literature

Canadian Society of Patristic Studies (CSPS) / Association canadienne des études patristiques

c/o Membership, 45 Inkerman Dr., Charlottetown PE C1A 2P4
e-mail: lturcesc@alcor.concordia.ca
URL: www.ccsr.ca/csps

Overview: A small national organization founded in 1975
Chief Officer(s):
Steven Muir, Treasurer
Lucien Turcescu, President
Lorraine Buck, Secretary
Finances: *Annual Operating Budget:* Less than $50,000; *Funding Sources:* Membership dues
Membership: 60; *Fees:* $17-$40; *Member Profile:* Open to all who share the objectives of the Society. They encourage university faculty, students, and private scholars who work in the field.
Description: To encourage & contribute to the study in Canada of everything to do with the era of the "church fathers".; *Member of:* Canadian Federation for the Humanities and Social Sciences; Affiliation(s): Canadian Corporation for the Study of Religion

Canadian Theological Society (CTS) / Société théologique canadienne

c/o N. Jesson, St. Thomas More College, University of Saskatchewan, 1437 College Dr., Saskatoon SK S7N 0W6
URL: www.ccsr.ca/cts/

Overview: A small national organization founded in 1955
Chief Officer(s):
Michael Bourgeois, President, 416-585-4534, Fax: 416-585-4516
michael.bourgeois@utoronto.ca
Bob McKeon, Treasurer
rmckeon@shaw.ca
Nicholas Jesson, Officer, Communications, 306-652-1595
jesson@ecumenism.net
Fees: $86 full members; $61 associate members; $45 student, retired, & unwaged members; *Member Profile:* Theologians, clergy, scholars, & students from universities, seminaries, & churches; Lay people
Activities: *Awareness Events:* Annual Student Essay Contest
Description: To promote theological reflection & writing in Canada; *Member of:* Canadian Corporation for the Study of Religion (CCSR); Affiliation(s): Congress of the Humanities & Social Sciences

Canadian Theosophical Society Inc. / Association théosophique canadienne inc.

27 Northmount Cr. NW, Calgary AB T2K 2V6
Tel: 403-275-7817
e-mail: office@theosophical.ca
URL: www.theosophical.ca

Overview: A medium-sized national charitable organization founded in 1924
Chief Officer(s):
Lorraine Christensen, President
Finances: *Annual Operating Budget:* Less than $50,000; *Funding Sources:* Memberships; Donations
Membership: 100-499; *Fees:* $25; *Member Profile:* From all across Canada & all backgrounds
Activities: Promotion of Theosophy or wisdom, whatever the source
Description: To form a nucleus of the Universal Brotherhood of Humanity, without distinction of race, creed, sex, caste, or colour; to encourage the study of comparative religion, philosophy, & science; to investigate unexplained laws of nature & the powers latent in man; *Member of:* Theosophical Society, India; Affiliation(s): 70 other countries

Canadian Tract Society

PO Box 2156, Stn. LCD 1, Brampton ON L6T 3S4
Tel: 905-457-4559; *Fax:* 905-457-0529
e-mail: cts@ctstracts.com
URL: www.ctstracts.com

Overview: A small national charitable organization founded in 1970
Description: To proclaim the One who is the centre of the Word of God, Jesus Christ; to make Him known in His redeeming grace & to promote the interests of vital godliness & sound morality.

Carrefour Humanisation Santé

1870, boul Pie-IX, 1er étage, Montréal QC H1V 2C6
Tel: 514-527-4595; *Fax:* 514-527-4475
e-mail: carrefour.humanisation@ssss.gouv.qc.ca
URL: www.carrefourhumanisationsante.org

Previous Name: Carrefour des Chrétiens du Québec pour la Santé
Overview: A small provincial organization
Chief Officer(s):
M. Michel Delorme, Président
Description: Promouvoir l'humanisation des soins de santé.

Centre for Faith & the Media

PO Box 5694, Stn. A, Calgary AB T2H 1Y1
Toll-Free: 877-210-0077
e-mail: info@faithandmedia.org
URL: www.faithandmedia.org

Overview: A small national organization
Chief Officer(s):
Richelle Wiseman, Executive Director
Description: To inform, advise & help media & the general public achieve a stronger understanding of spiritual history, practices & values in Canadian society

Chosen People Ministries (Canada)

PO Box 897, Stn. B, 291 Sheppard Ave. West, Toronto ON M2K 2R1
Tel: 416-250-0177; *Fax:* 416-250-9235
Toll-Free: 888-442-5535
e-mail: info@cpmcanada.ca
URL: www.cpmcanada.ca

Also Known As: Beth Sar Shalom Mission
Overview: A medium-sized national charitable organization founded in 1967
Chief Officer(s):
Joseph Gray, Director
Finances: *Annual Operating Budget:* $500,000-$1.5 Million; *Funding Sources:* Donations
Staff: 11 staff member(s)
Activities: *Speaker Service:* Yes
Description: To bring the Gospel of Jesus to Jewish people

Christ for the Nations (Canada) Inc. (CFNI)

19533 - 64 Ave., Surrey BC V4N 3G6
Tel: 604-514-2364; *Fax:* 604-514-2604
Toll-Free: 888-999-2364
e-mail: info@cfnc.ca
URL: www.cfni.bc.ca

Also Known As: Christ for the Nations Bible College
Overview: A small national charitable organization founded in 1978
Chief Officer(s):
Gerald Nussbaum, President
Patty Moreno, Secretary
Membership: 1-99
Description: To prepare spiritually mature servant leaders who are competent in Ministry & who influence their world by living as Jesus did; *Member of:* The Christ for the Nations Association of Bible Schools; Affiliation(s): Association for Biblical Higher Education

Christian Medical & Dental Society of Canada (CMDS)

246 Main St., #B, Steinbach MB R5G 1Y8
Tel: 204-326-2523; *Fax:* 204-326-3098
Toll-Free: 888-256-8653
e-mail: office@cmdscanada.org
URL: www.cmdscanada.org

Overview: A medium-sized provincial organization founded in 1971
Chief Officer(s):

Roger Gingerich, Executive Director
Abraham Ninan, President
Rudy W. Hamm, Treasurer
Sue McLoughlin, Secretary
Finances: *Funding Sources:* Dues; Donations
Fees: $325 Full-time Medical & Dental Practitioners; $165 Part-time Practitioners; $50 Residents; $25 Medical or Dental Students or Missionaries; *Member Profile:* Christian physicians, dentists, & students who wish to integrate faith with professional practice
Activities: Offers workshops & conferences; supports a toll-free helpline for medical & dental trainees; publishes a Members Directory & other literature; offers mission opportunities; provides investment services
Description: CMDS has the following mission: to uphold a Christian view of medicine & dentistry; to understand & minister to the spiritual needs of patients & colleagues; to create educational materials about public policy & health; to develop programs that promote a Christian view of medical ethics; & to support local group activities, plan conferences, & locate mentorship & other opportunities.; *Member of:* Practitioners Christian Medical & Dental Association

Christos Metropolitan Community Church
427 Bloor St. West, Toronto ON M5S 1X7
Tel: 416-435-1211; *Fax:* 416-922-8587
e-mail: christosmcc@hotmail.com
URL: www.christosmcc.com
Also Known As: Christos MCC
Overview: A small local charitable organization founded in 1984
Chief Officer(s):
Deana Dudley, Pastor
Judi Bonner, Secretary
Finances: *Annual Operating Budget:* Less than $50,000
Staff: 1 staff member(s); 8 volunteer(s)
Membership: 30
Activities: Weekly worship services; spirituality-based study groups; social events
Member of: Universal Fellowship of Metropolitan Community Churches

Church Council on Justice & Corrections (CCJC) / Conseil des églises pour la justice et la criminologie
507 Bank St., 2nd Fl., Ottawa ON K2P 1Z5
Tel: 613-563-1688; *Fax:* 613-237-6129
e-mail: info@ccjc.ca
URL: www.ccjc.ca
Overview: A medium-sized national charitable organization founded in 1974
Chief Officer(s):
Lorraine Berzins, Communication Chair of Justice, 613-563-1688 2
lberzins@ccjc.ca
Finances: *Annual Operating Budget:* $250,000-$500,000
Staff: 3 staff member(s)
Membership: 46 directors + 292 supporting; *Fees:* $40 individuals; $200 organizations; *Committees:* Steering
Activities: *Internships:* Yes; *Speaker Service:* Yes *Library:* Yes
Description: To strengthen churches' ministry in fields of crime prevention, justice & corrections; to initiate, encourage & support programs which sensitize congregations & educate volunteer groups to participate in development of community responses to crime, justice & corrections; to promote a healing justice; to examine & respond to policy concerns with assistance of churches; to call on churches to address issues; to provide resources to churches & other related organizations.; *Member of:* National Associations Active in Criminal Justice; Affiliation(s): The Network - Interaction for Conflict Resolution

The Church Lads' Brigade (CLB)
PO Box 28126, St. John's NL A1B 4J8
Tel: 709-722-1737
e-mail: clb@nf.aibn.com
URL: www.theclb.ca
Overview: A medium-sized national organization founded in 1892
Chief Officer(s):
Keith Arns, Chair
Sterling Pritchett, Secretary
Finances: *Annual Operating Budget:* $50,000-$100,000; *Funding Sources:* Donations; building rentals; fundraising
Staff: 1 staff member(s); 200 volunteer(s)
Membership: 800; *Fees:* $20; *Member Profile:* Boys & girls of all religious affiliations
Activities: Youth activities; recreational, educational & social; *Internships:* Yes *Library:* CLB Archives (Open to Public) by appointment
Description: The advancement of Christ's kingdom among youth, the promotion of Christian charity, reverence, discipline, self-respect, respect for others & all that lends towards true Christian character; Affiliation(s): The Church Lads' & Church Girls' Brigade (UK)

Church of the Good Shepherd
116 Queen St. North, Kitchener ON N2H 2H7
Tel: 519-743-3845; *Fax:* 519-743-3375
e-mail: secretary@churchofthegoodshepherd.ca
URL: www.churchofthegoodshepherd.ca
Also Known As: Swedenborgian Church
Overview: A small local organization
Chief Officer(s):
John Maine, Minister
Membership: 140 individual

Community of Christ - Canada East Mission
390 Speedvale Ave. East, Guelph ON N1E 1N5
Tel: 519-822-4150; *Fax:* 519-822-1236
Toll-Free: 888-411-7537
e-mail: info@communityofchrist.ca
URL. www.communityofchrist.ca/east/east.htm
Also Known As: Saints' Church
Previous Name: Reorganized Church of Jesus Christ of Latter Day Saints (Canada)
Overview: A medium-sized local charitable organization founded in 1830
Chief Officer(s):
Ken Barrows, Canada East Mission President
ken@communityofchrist.ca
Jim Poirier, Canadian Bishop & Financial Officer
jim@communityofchrist.ca
Description: To promote communities of joy, hope, love, & peace

Community of Christ - Canada West Mission
6415 Ranchview Dr. NW, Calgary AB T3G 1B5
Tel: 403-239-8070; *Fax:* 403-239-3542
Toll-Free: 877-411-2632
e-mail: darrell@communityofchrist.ca
URL: www.communityofchrist.ca/west/west.htm
Overview: A medium-sized local organization
Chief Officer(s):
Darrell Belrose, Mission President
Description: To promote communities of joy, hope, love, & peace

The Coptic Orthodox Church (Canada)
St. Mark's Coptic Orthodox Church, 41 Glendinning Ave., Toronto ON M1W 3E2
Tel: 416-494-4449; *Fax:* 416-494-4196
e-mail: mail@coptorthodox.ca
URL: www.stmark.toronto.on.coptorthodox.ca
Overview: A small national organization
Chief Officer(s):
M.A. Marcos, Protopriest
Membership: 45,000
Member of: The Canadian Council of Churches; Coptic Orthodox Patriarchate

Council on Homosexuality & Religion (CHR) / Conseil de l'homosexualité et la religion
PO Box 1912, Winnipeg MB R3C 3R2
Tel: 204-772-8215; *Fax:* 204-478-1160
Toll-Free: 888-399-0005
e-mail: cvogel@mts.net
Overview: A small national charitable organization founded in 1976
Chief Officer(s):
Chris Vogel, Sec.-Treas., 204-945-6660
cvogel@nr.gov.mb.ca
A.E. Millward, President
Finances: *Annual Operating Budget:* Less than $50,000; *Funding Sources:* Donations
Staff: 5 volunteer(s)
Membership: 40 individuals + 21 organizations; *Fees:* Schedule available
Activities: Administers the Manitoba Gay & Lesbian Legal Defense Fund & the Victims of Homophobic Violence Memorial; distributes publications; provides referrals for union ceremonies & the like; *Internships:* Yes; *Speaker Service:* Yes *Library:* Yes
Description: To foster the welfare of homosexually-oriented persons & promote the understanding & acceptance of homosexuality within religious institutions; to provide counselling & referral services; to conduct workshops, seminars & lectures; to provide a library & a range of publications on homosexuality & religion; to assist others in the same activities; *Member of:* Association for Manitoba Archives; Manitoba Library Association; Social Planning Council

Creation Science Association of British Columbia
PO Box 39577, White Rock BC V4B 5L6
Tel: 604-535-0019
e-mail: info@creationbc.org
URL: www.creationbc.org
Overview: A small provincial charitable organization founded in 1968
Chief Officer(s):
George Pearce, President
Finances: *Annual Operating Budget:* Less than $50,000
Staff: 25 volunteer(s)
Membership: 125 individual; *Fees:* $15 individual
Activities: *Speaker Service:* Yes *Library:* Yes by appointment
Description: To compile scientific as well as Biblical evidence which supports creation & contradicts evolution & to communicate this information to schools, churches & the general public

Creation Science of Saskatchewan Inc. (CSSI)
PO Box 26, Kenaston SK S0G 2N0
Tel: 306-252-2842; *Fax:* 306-252-2842
e-mail: gbmiller@sasktel.net
URL: www.creation-science.sk.ca
Overview: A small provincial charitable organization founded in 1978
Chief Officer(s):
Rudi Fast, President
Finances: *Annual Operating Budget:* Less than $50,000; *Funding Sources:* Donations
Staff: 13 volunteer(s)
Membership: 15 institutional + 140 individual; *Fees:* $10 institutional; $10 individual
Activities: Meetings; speakers; book tables; tours; summer camp; *Speaker Service:* Yes *Library:* Yes by appointment
Description: To share scientific & scriptural evidence for special creation & the Creator

CrossTrainers Canada
PO Box 1426, Bradford ON L3Z 2B7
Tel: 905-778-2048; *Fax:* 905-775-0444
e-mail: ct@crosstrainersyto.com
URL: www.crosstrainersyto.com
Overview: A small local organization
Chief Officer(s):
Jodi Greenstreet
Patti LaRose
Brian Langford, Program Director
Description: Christian ministry organization serving the Bradford community

Diocèse militaire du Canada
USFC (O), Site Uplands, Édifice 469, Ottawa ON K1A 0K2
Tél: 613-990-7824; *Téléc:* 613-991-1056
Courriel: rc.milord@on.aibn.com
URL: www.missa.org
Aperçu: *Dimension:* petite; *Envergure: nationale; Organisme sans but lucratif; fondée en 1987*
Membre(s) du bureau directeur:
A. Asselin, Chancelier
Donald Thériault, Évêque
R. Marchand, Aumônier principal
Activités: *Bibliothèque:* Centre d'entraînement des aumôniers de Borden
Description: Fournir une dimension spirituelle et morale à toutes les activités affectant le moral et le bien-être des membres catholiques des Forces canadiennes, leurs familles et les employés civils du Ministère de la Défense nationale; *Membre de:* La Conférence des évêques catholiques du Canada

Direction Chrétienne Inc.
#520, 1450, rue City Councillors, Montréal QC H3A 2E6
Tél: 514-878-3035; *Téléc:* 514-878-8048
Courriel: info@direction.ca
URL: www.direction.ca
Également appelé: Christian Direction
Aperçu: *Dimension:* petite; *Envergure: provinciale; Organisme sans but lucratif; fondée en 1964*
Finances: *Budget de fonctionnement annuel:* $500,000-$1.5 Million
Personnel: 13 membre(s) du personnel; 3 bénévole(s)
Membre: 1-99
Description: Rendre visite aux communautés chrétiennes locales et particulièrement celles des grands centres urbains afin de se faire connaître et partager son mandat

Edmonton & District Council of Churches (EDCC)
c/o Garneau United Church, #123, 11148 - 84 Ave., Edmonton AB T6G 0V8
Tel: 780-439-2501; *Fax:* 780-439-3067
e-mail: garneau@uccedm.org
Overview: A small local organization founded in 1942
Chief Officer(s):
Cliff Guebert, President
Finances: *Annual Operating Budget:* Less than $50,000

Staff: 1 staff member(s); 7 volunteer(s)
Membership: 22; *Fees:* $60 denominational member; $30 individual member; *Member Profile:* Christian denominations; *Committees:* Ecumenical Coordinators; Week of Prayer for Christian Unity Service Planning Committee; Way of the Cross Planning Committee; No Room in the Inn Planning Committee
Activities: Organization of events; distribution of information; participation in interdenominational projects; *Awareness Events:* Week of Prayer for Christian Unity, Jan.; Good Friday Way of the Cross; No Room in the Inn Fundraising for Low Income Housing, Dec.
Description: To express through fellowship, consultation, cooperation, & service, the essential unity of the Christian church; to maintain open relationships & foster dialogue with other faith groups & inter-faith organizations; to provide support & monitoring for chaplaincy programs; Affiliation(s): Canadian Council of Churches

Église Réformée St-Jean
3407A, av du Musee, Montréal QC H4E 4L7
Tél: 514-767-3165
Courriel: info@erq.qc.ca
URL: www.stjean.erq.qc.ca
Aperçu: *Dimension:* moyenne; *Envergure: provinciale*
Membre(s) du bureau directeur:
Jean Zoellner, Pastor
Description: The majority of our members are French-speaking Québecers practising various occupations in society, blue and white collared workers. People coming from a wide range of cultural, regional and national backgrounds also contribute to a rich diversity. People of all ages can be found amongst us: young children, adolescents, students, the middle-aged and the retired. The dynamic nature of our church can be seen in the presence of many young families. We recognise that the Lord Jesus Christ, head of the Church, has assembled us, with our children in a community which holds one vision, one love, one faith and one hope: to live for His Glory and to serve Him where He has placed us.; Affiliation(s): Christian Reformed Church; Presbyterian Church of North America

Fédération nationale du MFC - Mouvement des Femmes Chrétiennes (MFC)
CP 174, 49, boul Lanaudière, Sainte-Anne-de-la-Pérade QC G0X 2J0
Tél: 418-325-2338; *Téléc:* 418-325-2255
Courriel: mfcnational@sympatico.ca
URL: www.mfcnational.com
Aperçu: *Dimension:* grande; *Envergure: nationale; Organisme sans but lucratif; fondée en 1962*
Membre(s) du bureau directeur:
Claire Duchesneau, Secrétaire
Finances: *Budget de fonctionnement annuel:* Moins de $50,000
Personnel: 1 membre(s) du personnel; 700 bénévole(s)
Membre: 8000; *Montant de la cotisation:* 15$; *Critères d'admissibilite:* Femmes de tout âge, condition et culture
Activités: Rencontre mensuelle sur le programme d'action; formation
Description: Un mouvement d'action catholique générale, il forme des femmes efficaces et dynamiques sur le plan familial, paroissial, social, et chrétien afin de transformer le milieu de vie par des projects concrets et en utilisant la méthode de l'action catholique; *Membre de:* Regroupement des Organismes Volontaires d'Éducation Populaire

Focus on the Family Canada
#200, 20486 - 64 Ave., Langley BC V2Y 2V5
Tel: 604-539-7900; *Fax:* 604-539-7999
Toll-Free: 800-661-9800
e-mail: letters@fotf.ca
URL: www.fotf.ca
Overview: A large national charitable organization founded in 1982
Chief Officer(s):
Terence Rolston, President
Finances: *Annual Operating Budget:* Greater than $5 Million; *Funding Sources:* Donations
Staff: 72 staff member(s); 250 volunteer(s)
Activities: Community Impact Seminars; *Library:* Yes
Description: To strengthen & encourage the Canadian family through education & resources; *Member of:* Canadian Council of Christian Charities

Fondation Père-Eusèbe-Ménard
1195, rue Sauvé est, Montréal QC H2C 1Z8
Tél: 514-274-7645; *Téléc:* 514-274-7647
Ligne sans frais: 800-665-7645
Courriel: info@fondationperemenard.org
URL: www.fondationperemenard.org
Aperçu: *Dimension:* petite; *Envergure: internationale; Organisme sans but lucratif; fondée en 1970*
Membre(s) du bureau directeur:
Nicole Bernard, Directrice générale
Finances: *Budget de fonctionnement annuel:* $1.5 Million-$3 Million
Personnel: 3 membre(s) du personnel; 10 bénévole(s)
Membre: 15 000+
Activités: La Fondation travaille en partenariat avec les Missionnaires de Saints-Apôtres présents dans les pays d'intervention pour assurer la croissance des Églises locales en contribuant particulièrement à la formation de futurs prêtres et agents de pastorale, et pour améliorer les conditions de vie inhumaines de nos frères et soeurs dans ces pays
Description: Encourager les personnes qui le désirent à appuyer les efforts de développement et d'évangélisation des populations défavorisées dans le Tiers-Monde

Foursquare Gospel Church of Canada
#307, 2099 Lougheed Hwy., Port Coquitlam BC V3B 1A8
Tel: 604-941-8414; *Fax:* 604-941-8415
e-mail: info@foursquare.ca
URL: www.foursquare.ca
Overview: A medium-sized national charitable organization founded in 1981
Chief Officer(s):
Barry Buzza, President/General Supervisor
Finances: *Annual Operating Budget:* $250,000-$500,000
Staff: 3 staff member(s)
Membership: 67 churches
Member of: Evangelical Fellowship of Canada

Full Gospel Business Men's Fellowship in Canada (FGBMFI)
#403, 50 Gervais Dr., Toronto ON M3C 1Z3
Tel: 416-449-7272; *Fax:* 416-449-9743
e-mail: fgbmfi@allstream.net
URL: www.fgbmfi.ca
Overview: A medium-sized national charitable organization founded in 1964
Finances: *Annual Operating Budget:* $100,000-$250,000
Staff: 2 staff member(s); 2 volunteer(s)
Membership: 1,000-4,999; *Fees:* $60 individual
Activities: National convention; *Internships:* Yes; *Speaker Service:* Yes
Description: To reach men at all levels of our modern society, calling them to God, & releasing them into their respective gifts & talents through the Holy Spirit; *Member of:* Full Gospel Business Men's Fellowship International

General Church of the New Jerusalem in Canada
c/o Olivet Church of the New Jerusalem, 279 Burnhamthorpe Rd., Toronto ON M9B 1Z6
Tel: 416-239-3054; *Fax:* 416-239-4935
e-mail: olivetchurch@on.aibn.com
URL: www.newchurch.org/societies/toronto
Overview: A small national organization
Chief Officer(s):
James Cooper, Pastor
Jon Lee, Assistant Pastor
Member of: General Church of the New Jerusalem

General Conference of the Canadian Assemblies of God / Conférence générale des assemblées de dieu canadiennes
6724, rue Fabre, Montréal QC H2G 2Z6
Tel: 514-279-1100; *Fax:* 514-279-1131
e-mail: info@caogonline.org
URL: www.caogonline.org
Previous Name: Italian Pentecostal Church of Canada
Overview: A small national charitable organization founded in 1912
Chief Officer(s):
David Quackenbush, General Treasurer
Alberico DeVito, Overseer Emeritus
David Mortelliti, General Superintendent
David DiStaulo, General Secretary
Mario Catalano, Overseer
Finances: *Annual Operating Budget:* $100,000-$250,000
Staff: 2 staff member(s); 3 volunteer(s)
Membership: 6,000 + 21 affiliated churches
Activities: Annual Conference, Thanksgiving Weekend; *Internships:* Yes
Description: Distinctive ministry to the Italian community extending to all Canadians, regardless of language, nationality, or race, that proclaims the gospel of Jesus Christ in the power of the Holy Spirit throughout Canada & the world, based on the biblical standard of ministry in the New Testament; *Member of:* The Evangelical Fellowship of Canada; Canadian Council of Christian Charities

Global Outreach Mission Inc.
PO Box 1210, St Catharines ON L2R 7A7
Tel: 905-684-1401; *Fax:* 905-684-3069
Toll-Free: 866-483-5787
e-mail: glmiss@on.aibn.com
URL: www.missiongo.org/contact.html
Previous Name: European Evangelistic Crusade, Inc.
Overview: A small international organization founded in 1943
Chief Officer(s):
Len Lane, Vice-President, Candidates/Personnel
Affiliation(s): Interdenominational Foreign Mission Association

Good News Broadcasting Association of Canada
#3 Lower, 40 Centre Street, Chatham ON N7M 5W3
Toll-Free: 800-663-2425
e-mail: bttb@backtothebible.ca
URL: www.backtothebible.ca
Also Known As: Back to the Bible Canada
Overview: A small local charitable organization
Chief Officer(s):
Byron Reaume, CFO & Director of Stewardship
Bob Beasley, CEO
Member of: Canadian Council of Christian Charities; Evangelican Fellowship of Canada

Greek Orthodox Metropolis of Toronto (Canada)
86 Overlea Blvd., Toronto ON M4H 1C6
Tel: 416-429-5757; *Fax:* 416-429-4588
e-mail: metropolis@gocanada.org
URL: www.gocanada.org
Previous Name: Greek Orthodox Church (Canada)
Overview: A large national organization
Chief Officer(s):
Haralambos Elles, Administrative Assistant
Membership: 50,000 Plus
Description: There are 76 Greek Orthodox Communities in Canada under the jurisdiction of the Greek Orthodox Metropolis of Toronto (Canada); *Member of:* The Canadian Council of Churches

Habitat for Humanity Canada (HFHC) / Habitat pour l'Humanité Canada
40 Albert St., Waterloo ON N2L 3S2
Tel: 519-885-4565; *Fax:* 519-885-5225
Toll-Free: 800-667-5137
e-mail: habitat@habitat.ca
URL: www.habitat.ca
Overview: A medium-sized national charitable organization founded in 1985
Chief Officer(s):
Stewart Hardacre, President & CEO
Finances: *Annual Operating Budget:* $3 Million-$5 Million; *Funding Sources:* Corporate & individual donations of cash & building materials
Staff: 20 staff member(s); 15 volunteer(s)
Membership: 72 local affiliates
Activities: Ed Schreyer Work Project; All Women Build Project; *Speaker Service:* Yes *Library:* Yes (Open to Public)
Description: To provide affordable & adequate housing for God's people in need by mobilizing local communities, volunteers & material & financial resources in wide-ranging, inclusive partnerships; to support, encourage, facilitate & empower those affiliates to build affordable homes in partnership with needy families.; *Member of:* Habitat for Humanity International

Holy Face Association
CP 1000, Succ A, Montréal QC H3C 2W9
Tel: 514-747-0357; *Fax:* 514-747-9147
e-mail: holyface@holyface.com
Overview: A small national charitable organization founded in 1975
Chief Officer(s):
Gordon Deery, Contact
Finances: *Annual Operating Budget:* $250,000-$500,000; *Funding Sources:* Donations
Staff: 20 volunteer(s)
Membership: 15,000-49,999
Activities: *Speaker Service:* Yes *Library:* Yes by appointment
Description: The goal of this apostolate is reparation to God (Father, Son and Holy Spirit) through contemplative devotion to the Holy Face of Jesus

Independent Assemblies of God International - Canada
PO Box 653, Chatham ON N7M 5K8
Tel: 519-352-1743; *Fax:* 519-351-6070
e-mail: pmcphail@ciaccess.com
URL: www.iaogcan.com
Also Known As: IAOGI Canada
Overview: A small national charitable organization founded in 1918
Chief Officer(s):
Paul McPhail, General Secretary
Finances: *Annual Operating Budget:* $100,000-$250,000; *Funding Sources:* Membership fees; offerings

Staff: 2 staff member(s); 12 volunteer(s)
Membership: 500 churches/ministries; *Fees:* $100; *Member Profile:* Must be called by God to preach His Word
Activities: *Awareness Events:* National Convention, May; *Speaker Service:* Yes
Member of: Independent Assemblies of God International

Institut Séculier Pie X (ISPX) / Pius X Secular Institute

CP 7731, Succ. Succ. Charlesbourg, 1645, 80e rue Est, Québec QC G1G 5W6
Tél: 418-626-5882; *Téléc:* 418-624-2277
Courriel: info@ispx.org
URL: www.ispx.org
Aperçu: *Dimension:* petite; *Envergure: internationale; Organisme sans but lucratif; fondée en 1939*
Membre(s) du bureau directeur:
Gérald Cyprien Lacroix, Directeur général
Finances: *Budget de fonctionnement annuel:* $100,000-$250,000
Membre: 17 consacrés + 250 associés
Activités: Apostolat catholique; évangélisation; présence au monde; *Service de conférenciers:* Oui
Description: Évangéliser les milieux populaires par la présence et par des activités apostoliques; *Membre de:* Conférence canadienne des instituts séculiers; Conférence mondiale des instituts séculiers

Institut Voluntas Dei / Voluntas Dei Institute

7385, boul. Parent, Trois-Rivières QC G9A 5E1
Tel: 819-375-7933; *Fax:* 819-691-1841
e-mail: ivd.cent@cgocable.ca
URL: www.voluntasdei.org
Also Known As: I.V. Dei
Overview: A small international charitable organization founded in 1958
Finances: *Annual Operating Budget:* $100,000-$250,000
Staff: 3 staff member(s)
Membership: 752; *Member Profile:* Clerics & laymen who commit their lives to the service of Jesus Christ; married people as associate members who live out the same ideal & same apostolic project as the celibate members
Activities: *Internships:* Yes
Description: To make known & communicate God's love for all to all people; to be present in every milieu; apostolic objective is "to create peace & brotherhood in Jesus Christ"; *Member of:* Roman Catholic Church

Integrity/Calgary

1121 - 14th Ave. SW, Calgary AB T2R 0P3
Tel: 403-276-9266
e-mail: calgary@integritycanada.org
URL: members.aol.com/DWFrancis/integrity.html
Overview: A small local organization
Member Profile: Gay & lesbian Anglicans & their friends

Integrity/Toronto

PO Box 873, Stn. F, Toronto ON M4Y 2N9
Tel: 416-925-9872
e-mail: toronto@integritycanada.org
URL: www.toronto.integritycanada.org
Overview: A small local organization founded in 1975
Finances: *Annual Operating Budget:* Less than $50,000; *Funding Sources:* Donations
Staff: 6 volunteer(s)
Membership: 100 individual; *Fees:* $15
Description: International organization of gay & lesbian Anglicans & their friends; to help its members discover & affirm that we can be both Christian & gay/lesbian/bisexual/transgender; Affiliation(s): Integrity Inc. - USA

Integrity/Vancouver

PO Box 2797, Stn. Main, Vancouver BC V6B 3X2
Tel: 604-432-1230
e-mail: vancouver@integritycanada.org
URL: www.vancouver.integritycanada.org
Overview: A small local charitable organization
Finances: *Annual Operating Budget:* Less than $50,000
Staff: 14 volunteer(s)
Membership: 50-100; *Fees:* $20; *Member Profile:* Gay, lesbian, bisexual, transgendered Anglicans
Activities: Monthly services on first Sunday, St. Paul's Anglican Church; monthly potluck dinners at members' homes; *Speaker Service:* Yes
Affiliation(s): Integrity Inc. - USA

International Institute of Integral Human Sciences (IIIHS) / Institut international des sciences humaines intégrales

PO Box 1445, Stn. H, Montréal QC H3G 2N3
Tel: 514-937-8359; *Fax:* 514-937-5380
e-mail: iiihs@iiihs.org
URL: www.iiihs.org
Overview: A medium-sized international organization
Chief Officer(s):
John Rossner
jrossner@iiihs.org
Marilyn Rossner
mrossner@iiihs.org
Membership: 10,000; *Fees:* $15
Activities: Corporate Divisions: SSF-IIIHS National & Regional Chapters; International College of Human Sciences; International Academy for Research & Advanced Studies; International Council of World Religions & Cultures; The Order of the Transfiguration
Description: An interdisciplinary, professional association for scientists, scholars, and spiritual leaders worldwide, who are involved in the sciences of human consciousness & healing, paradigms for the convergence of science, spirituality & humane values in the world, & new insights into the potential of the human spirit.

International Society for Krishna Consciousness (Toronto Branch) (ISKCON) / Subuddhi Deri Dasi

243 Avenue Rd., Toronto ON M5R 2J6
Tel: 416-922-5415; *Fax:* 416-922-1021
e-mail: toronto@pamho.net
URL: www.iskcon.com
Also Known As: ISKCON Toronto - Hare Krishna Movement
Overview: A medium-sized local charitable organization founded in 1966
Chief Officer(s):
Subuddhi Dasi, President
Finances: *Annual Operating Budget:* $3 Million-$5 Million; *Funding Sources:* Donations from congregations & festivals
Staff: 10 staff member(s); 20 volunteer(s)
Membership: 700 institutional; 2,000 individual; *Fees:* $1,100
Activities: Distribution of free food; taking care of seniors & youth; *Internships:* Yes *Library:* Yes (Open to Public)
Description: To preach Krishna Consciousness around the world, following in the footsteps of the founder & spiritual master, His Divine Grace A.C. Bhaktivedanta Swami Prabhupada.

International Society of Toronto for Hungarian Church History

Regis College, 15 St. Mary St., Toronto ON M4Y 2R5
Tel: 416-922-2476; *Fax:* 416-922-2773
e-mail: t.horvath@utoronto.ca
Also Known As: METEM
Overview: A small international charitable organization founded in 1990
Chief Officer(s):
Emma Perlaky, Information Technology, 905-764-3859
Magda Szegvary, Secretary, 416-630-7516
Levente Diosady, President, 416-978-4137
Finances: *Annual Operating Budget:* Less than $50,000; *Funding Sources:* Charitable organizations & funds; fundraising
Staff: 3 staff member(s); 50 volunteer(s)
Membership: 400; *Fees:* $36; *Member Profile:* Scholarship & interest in Hungarian church history; *Committees:* Canadian; Hungarian; International
Activities: Congress banquets; *Library:* Yes by appointment
Description: To promote research in Hungarian church history by preparing & publishing an encyclopedia, collecting documents & sources; to support publications related to the purpose of the Society; to promote public interest in the history of places related to church history in Canada & Hungary; to establish & maintain suitable quarters & facilities to hold meetings & exhibitions for discussing problems related to church history in general; to establish funds & scholarships for university students studying church history; to promote historical & archaeological research; Affiliation(s): METEM - Hungary

Jeunes canadiens pour une civilisation chrétienne

880, av Louis Frechette, Québec QC G1S 3N3
Tél: 418-683-5222
Aperçu: *Dimension:* petite; *Envergure: locale; fondée en 1977*
Membre(s) du bureau directeur:
Sébastien Bolduc
Description: Travailler avec la jeunesse pour préserver les principes catholiques et éducatifs

Jews for Jesus

#402, 1315 Lawrence Ave. East, Toronto ON M3A 3R3
Tel: 416-444-7020; *Fax:* 416-444-1028
e-mail: toronto@jewsforjesus.ca
URL: www.jewsforjesus.ca
Overview: A small local charitable organization
Chief Officer(s):
Andrew Barron, Canadian Director
Member of: Canadian Council of Christian Charities; Evangelical Fellowship of Canada; Interdenominational Foreign Mission Association

Latin American Mission Program (LAMP)

81 Prince St., Charlottetown PE C1A 4R3
Tel: 902-368-7337; *Fax:* 902-368-7180
Overview: A small international organization
Finances: *Annual Operating Budget:* $50,000-$100,000; *Funding Sources:* Share Lent collections taken up annually in all parishes
Membership: 20
Activities: Educational events; orientation & support for missionaries
Description: To send out & receive back missionaries; to learn from the dispossessed & oppressed & to stand with them in building a society of justice; to develop & encourage a Faith response based on the life & struggle of dispossessed peoples; to participate in "return mission" by working with groups committed to social justice in Canada & developing education programs in PEI which analyze the causes of exploitation of the poor & which exposes the reality of their lives; Affiliation(s): Les missionnaires du Sacre-Coeur; Scarboro Foreign Mission Society

Missionaires de la Royauté du Christ / Missionaries of the Kingship of Christ

5750, boul Rosemont, Montréal QC H1T 2H2
Tél: 514-259-2542
Aperçu: *Dimension:* petite; *Envergure:* locale

Les Missions des Soeurs Missionnaires du Christ-Roi

4730, boul Lévesque ouest, Chomedey QC H7W 2R4
Tél: 450-687-2100
Courriel: missionsmcr@hotmail.com
Également appelé: Missions MCR
Aperçu: *Dimension:* moyenne; *Envergure: internationale; Organisme sans but lucratif; fondée en 1979*
Membre(s) du bureau directeur:
S. Evva Melanson, Contact
Finances: *Budget de fonctionnement annuel:* Moins de $50,000
Personnel: 1 membre(s) du personnel
Membre: 213 institutionnel
Activités: *Bibliothèque:* Oui (Bibliothèque publique)
Description: Organiser, administrer, maintenir une oeuvre dont les fins sont la religion, la charitépromouvoir l'éducation et le bien-être, particulièrement en ce qui a trait aux différents buts qu'il s'est fixéaide internationale

Multifaith Action Society (MAS)

305 - 41 Ave. West, Vancouver BC V5Y 2S5
Tel: 604-321-1302; *Fax:* 604-321-1370
e-mail: admin@multifaithaction.org
URL: www.multifaithaction.org
Previous Name: Canadian Ecumenical Action
Overview: A small national charitable organization founded in 1973
Chief Officer(s):
Barry F.H. Cooke, Executive Director
Charles Feinberg, President
Finances: *Annual Operating Budget:* Less than $50,000
Staff: 3 staff member(s)
Membership: 200; *Fees:* $25; *Member Profile:* Members come from many religious faiths: Aboriginal, Baha'i, Buddhist, Christian, Hindu, Muslim, Jain, Jewish, Sikh, Unitarian, Zoroastrian; *Committees:* Program; Calendar; Development; Personnel; Advocacy
Activities: Lectures & conferences promoting interreligious dialogue; forums on faith; environmental awareness programs within religious communities; faith centre visits; *Speaker Service:* Yes
Description: To promote interreligious understanding; to provide information & resources on world religions for the community; to encourage people of all religions to dialogue on community issues; to promote community service programs.; *Member of:* Affiliation of Multicultural Societies & Service Agencies of BC; Vancouver Multicultural Society

Les Oblates missionnaires de Marie Immaculée (OMMI) / Oblate Missionaries of Mary Immaculate

#100, 7535, boul Parent, Trois-Rivières QC G9A 5E1
Tél: 819-375-7317; *Téléc:* 819-691-1769
Courriel: ommi@ommi-is.org
URL: www.ommi-is.org
Aperçu: *Dimension:* petite; *Envergure: internationale; fondée en 1952*
Membre(s) du bureau directeur:
Claire Nantel, Presidente-directrice générale

OMF International - Canada (OMF)

5155 Spectrum Way, Bldg. 21, Mississauga ON L4W 5A1

Tel: 905-568-9971; Fax: 905-568-9974
Toll-Free: 888-657-8010
e-mail: omfcanada@omf.ca
URL: www.ca.omf.org
Also Known As: Overseas Missionary Fellowship
Previous Name: China Inland Mission
Overview: A medium-sized international organization founded in 1865
Chief Officer(s):
Ron Adams, Director, Administration & Finance
Richard J. Konieczny, National Director
Membership: 1,300 missionaries worldwide; *Member Profile:* Four years post-secondary education
Member of: Interdenomination Foreign Mission Association; Affiliation(s): Evangelical Fellowship of Canada

Ontario Consultants on Religious Tolerance (OCRT)
PO Box 27026, Stn. Frontenac, Kingston ON K7M 8W5
Fax: 613-547-9015
e-mail: ocrt4@religioustolerance.org
URL: www.religioustolerance.org
Overview: A small provincial organization founded in 1995
Chief Officer(s):
B.A. Robinson, Coordinator
Finances: *Annual Operating Budget:* Less than $50,000; *Funding Sources:* Lecture fees; donations; banner ads
Staff: 1 staff member(s); 5 volunteer(s)
Membership: 1-99
Activities: *Speaker Service:* Yes
Description: To promote religious tolerance & expose religious hatred & misinformation

Pioneer Clubs Canada Inc.
#100, 3350 South Service Rd., Burlington ON L7N 3M6
Tel: 905-681-2883; Fax: 905-681-3256
Toll-Free: 800-465-5437
e-mail: info@pioneerclubs.ca
URL: www.pioneerclubs.ca
Also Known As: Pioneer Girls/Pioneer Boys
Overview: A large national licensing charitable organization founded in 1974
Chief Officer(s):
Jessica Breski, Executive Director
jbreski@pioneerclubs.ca
Finances: *Annual Operating Budget:* $250,000-$500,000
Staff: 9 staff member(s)
Membership: 216 institutional; 16,000 individual; *Fees:* $12 child
Activities: *Speaker Service:* Yes
Description: To serve God by assisting churches & other ministries in helping children & youth make Christ Lord in every aspect of life; Affiliation(s): Canadian Council of Christian Charities

Presbyterian Church in Canada (PCC) / Église presbytérienne au Canada
50 Wynford Dr., Toronto ON M3C 1J7
Tel: 416-441-1111; Fax: 416-441-2825
Toll-Free: 800-619-7301
e-mail: hamilton@presbyterian.ca
URL: www.presbyterian.ca
Overview: A large national organization founded in 1875
Chief Officer(s):
John Vissers, Principal, Presbyterian College
M. Jean Morris, Moderator
Tony Plomp, BA, BD, DD, Deputy Clerk
Sarah Kim, Executive Director, Women's Missionary Society
Margaret McGillvary, WMS President
Donald Muir, BA, M.Div., Deputy Clerk
S. Kendall, B.Eng., M.Dw., Principal Clerk
Richard Fee, BA, MDiv., DD, General Secretary, Life & Mission Agency
Stephen Roche, CFO
Dorcas J. Gordon, Principal, Knox College, Toronto
Helen Humphreys, AMS President
Finances: *Funding Sources:* Congregations
Membership: 125,509; *Member Profile:* Presbyteries; congregations; communicants on roll; ministers
Activities: *Library:* Knox College & Presbyterian College Libraries (Open to Public)
Member of: The Canadian Council of Churches; World Alliance of Reformed Churches; World Council of Churches; Action By Churches Together; Ecumenical Advocacy Alliance

Prison Fellowship Canada / Fraternite des prisons du Canada
PO Box 19510 RPO Manulife, Toronto ON M4W 3T9
Tel: 416-848-4793; Fax: 416-961-7190
Toll-Free: 888-470-2748
e-mail: info@prisonfellowship.ca
URL: www.prisonfellowship.ca
Overview: A small national organization
Chief Officer(s):
Eleanor Clitheroe, President/CEO
Jim Cavanagh, Contact, Kingston Office, 613-530-1205
Description: To challenge, equip, & serve the body of Christ in its ministry to prisoners, ex-prisoners, their families, & victims; to promote the advancement of restorative justice; *Member of:* Prison Fellowship International

The Reformed Episcopal Church of Canada - Diocese of Central & Eastern Canada (REC)
PO Box 2532, 320 Armstrong St., New Liskeard ON P0J 1P0
Tel: 705-647-4565; Fax: 705-647-1340
e-mail: trinityfed@hotmail.com
URL: recus.org; www.reccec.homestead.com
Overview: A medium-sized provincial charitable organization founded in 1886
Chief Officer(s):
Alison Buffet, Secretary
Michael Fedechko, Bishop Ordinary
Finances: *Annual Operating Budget:* Less than $50,000; *Funding Sources:* Donations
Staff: 4 volunteer(s)
Membership: 210 + 6 churches; *Committees:* Standing; Constitution & Canons; Church Extension
Activities: Synodical Council, 3rd week of Sept.; *Library:* Yes (Open to Public) by appointment
Description: We believe the Bible to be the inspired, the only infallible, inerrant, authoritative Word of God

The Reformed Episcopal Church of Canada - Diocese of Western Canada & Alaska (RECWCAN)
2604 Quadra St., Victoria BC V8T 4E4
Tel: 250-727-3722; Fax: 250-727-3722
e-mail: recwcan@islandnet.com
URL: www.recwcan.ca
Overview: A small national licensing charitable organization founded in 1874
Chief Officer(s):
John Boudewyn, Treasurer, 250-544-0098
Jack Cryderman, Secretary, 250-339-4014
Charles W. Dorrington, Diocesan Bishop, 250-652-8850
Finances: *Annual Operating Budget:* Less than $50,000; *Funding Sources:* Offerings; bequests; church assessments
Staff: 2 staff member(s)
Membership: 300; *Fees:* Church offerings; *Committees:* Council; Vestry; Executive; Standing; Synod
Activities: Douglas House Retirement Home Ministry; Victoria Prayer Counselling; Healing Rooms; *Internships:* Yes; *Speaker Service:* Yes *Library:* Diocesan Office Library by appointment
Description: To reach out to those outside the existing congregation; establish new churches; assist congregations within the Diocese; receive congregations wishing to affiliate with the Reformed Episcopal Church; ordain candidates into the ministry; Affiliation(s): Common Cause Network

Religious Freedom Council of Christian Minorities
PO Box 223, Stn. A, Vancouver BC V6C 2M3
Tel: 250-492-3376
Also Known As: Bible Holiness Movement
Overview: A small local organization founded in 1979
Chief Officer(s):
Wesley H. Wakefield, Chair
Finances: *Annual Operating Budget:* Less than $50,000
Staff: 4 volunteer(s)
Activities: *Speaker Service:* Yes *Library:* Bible Holiness Movement by appointment
Description: To act as a sponsored organization of the Bible Holiness Movement

Romanian Orthodox Church in America (Canadian Parishes)
St. Demetrios Romanian Orthodox Church, 103 Furby St., Winnipeg MB R3C 2A4
Tel: 204-775-6472
e-mail: malancav@mts.net
Overview: A small national organization
Chief Officer(s):
Victor Malanca, Priest
Victor Malanca, Contact

Saint Swithun's Society
427 Lynett Cres., Richmond Hill ON L4C 2V6
Tel: 905-883-0984
e-mail: norman@stswithunssociety.ca
URL: www.stswithunssociety.ca
Overview: A small local organization founded in 1974
Chief Officer(s):
Norman McMullen, KStG, President
Kevin Dark, KStG, Vice-President
Elisabeth Stenson, Sec.-Treas.
Finances: *Annual Operating Budget:* Less than $50,000
Staff: 3 staff member(s)
Membership: 300; *Member Profile:* Non-denominational, non-political/sectarian & inclusive
Activities: Annual Celebration; *Library:* Yes (Open to Public)
Description: To promote feelings of goodwill; to encourage the celebration of Saint Swithun's Day (July 15) & to pattern members' lives after the example of our Patron; Affiliation(s): Friends of Winchester Cathedral (England)

The Salvation Army in Canada
Territorial Headquarters, Canada & Bermuda, 2 Overlea Blvd., Toronto ON M4H 1P4
Tel: 416-425-2111
Toll-Free: 800-725-2769
URL: www.salvationarmy.ca
Overview: A large international charitable organization founded in 1882
Chief Officer(s):
Gail Cook-Bennett, Chair
Don Copple, Chief Secretary
Jim Champ, Liaison Officer
Finances: *Annual Operating Budget:* $3 Million-$5 Million
Staff: 152 staff member(s)
Membership: 343 Corps (congregations); 165 social institutes across Canada
Activities: *Speaker Service:* Yes
Description: To preach the Gospel of Jesus Christ; to supply basic human needs; to provide personal counselling & undertake the spiritual & moral regeneration & physical rehabilitation of all persons in need who come within its sphere of influence regardless of race, colour, creed, sex or age; *Member of:* Evangelical Fellowship of Canada

Samaritan House Ministries Inc.
630 Rosser Ave., Brandon MB R7A 0K7
Tel: 204-726-0758; Fax: 204-729-9951
e-mail: exec@samaritanhouse.net
URL: samaritanhouse.net
Overview: A small local charitable organization founded in 1987
Chief Officer(s):
Marla Somersall, Executive Director
Activities: *Internships:* Yes; *Speaker Service:* Yes
Description: To provide support & services to at-risk populations - the homeless, those living in poverty, people with literacy challenges or persons leaving abusive relationships

Seicho-No-Ie Toronto Centre
662 Victoria Park Ave., Toronto ON M4C 5H4
Tel: 416-690-8686; Fax: 416-690-3917
URL: www.snitoronto.ca
Also Known As: Home of Infinite Growth
Previous Name: Seicho-No-Ie Canada Truth of Life Centre
Overview: A small national organization founded in 1963
Chief Officer(s):
Nana Ishii, Contact
Fees: $60
Description: Provides a place of worship for those who believe in the Seicho-No-Ie Humanity Enlightenment Movement, which says that all religions emanate from one universal god.; *Member of:* Seicho-No-Ie (Canada)

Serbian Orthodox Church in the United States of America & Canada - Diocese of Canada
7470 McNiven Rd., RR#3, Campbellville ON L0B 1B0
Tel: 905-878-0043; Fax: 905-878-1909
e-mail: vladika@istocnik.com
URL: www.istocnik.com
Overview: A medium-sized national charitable organization founded in 1983
Chief Officer(s):
Davor Milicevic, Episcopal Secretary, 905-878-3438
Finances: *Annual Operating Budget:* $500,000-$1.5 Million; *Funding Sources:* Donations; parish taxes; dispensations
Staff: 23 staff member(s)
Membership: 150,000; *Committees:* Diocesan Executive Board; Diocesan Assembly
Activities: *Library:* Holy Transfiguration (Open to Public) by appointment
Description: To serve the Serbian Orthodox community & teach the Orthodox faith & culture

Seventh-day Adventist Church in Canada (SDACC) / Église adventiste du septième jour au Canada
1148 King St. East, Oshawa ON L1H 1H8
Tel: 905-433-0011; Fax: 905-433-0982
e-mail: communications@sdacc.org
URL: www.sdacc.org
Overview: A large national charitable organization founded in 1901
Chief Officer(s):
Dan Jackson, President
djackson@sdacc.org

Finances: *Annual Operating Budget:* $3 Million-$5 Million; *Funding Sources:* Donations
Staff: 23 staff member(s)
Membership: 55,000
Activities: Adventist Development & Relief Agency (ADRA); It Is Written Canada; Christian Record Services
Description: To be a significant Christian movement that recognizes the unique role to which Christ has called it & the urgency of the message of salvation & judgment; to lead people to salvation in Jesus; to teach them the biblical faith & discipline of the Christian life; to equip them to serve with their God-given abilities through the leadership of our various administrative & ministry teams; to proclaim Christ; to nurture believers; to serve humanity

Société internationale de sociologie des religions (SISR) / International Society for the Sociology of Religion (ISSR)
Bremveldstraat 16, Herent B-3020 Belgium
Tél: 32-16-230-398
Courriel: sisr@soc.kuleuven.be
URL: www.sisr.org
Aperçu: *Dimension:* petite; *Envergure: internationale; fondée en 1948*
Membre(s) du bureau directeur:
Hilde Van Meerbeek-Cravillon, Secrétaire générale
Finances: *Budget de fonctionnement annuel:* Moins de $50,000; *Fonds:* Cotisations des membres
Personnel: 2 bénévole(s)
Membre: 300; *Montant de la cotisation:* 106 E; *Critères d'admissibilite:* En sciences sociales des religions

Société québécoise pour l'étude de la religion
Bureau R303, Université Concordia, 1455, rue de Maisonneuve ouest, Montréal QC H3G 1M8
Tél: 514-848-2076; *Téléc:* 514-848-4541
URL: www.er.uqam.ca/nobel/sqer/
Aperçu: *Dimension:* petite; *Envergure: provinciale; fondée en 1989*
Membre(s) du bureau directeur:
Alain Bouchard, Président
alain.bouchard@ftsr.ulaval.ca
Description: Promouvoir la recherche, l'enseignement et la diffusion des connaissances dans les disciplines ayant pour objet l'étude de la religion

Spiritual Science Fellowship/International Institute of Integral Human Sciences (SSF-IIIHS)
PO Box 1445, Stn. H, 1974, rue de Maisonneuve ouest, Montréal QC H3G 2N3
Tel: 514-937-8359; *Fax:* 514-937-5380
e-mail: info@iiihs.org
URL: www.iiihs.org
Overview: A small local charitable organization
Chief Officer(s):
Marilyn Z. Rossner
Membership: 10,000; *Fees:* $15; gifts
Activities: *Internships:* Yes; *Speaker Service:* Yes
Description: An inter-faith fellowship providing spiritual services, educational programs, & pastoral ministrations for persons, regardless of religious background, who desire to understand experiences of psyche & spirit, & to dedicate themselves to personal spiritual growth & psychic development, in an atmosphere of informed free-thought & enquiry

Taoist Tai Chi Society of Canada
134 Darcy St., Toronto ON M5T 1K3
Tel: 416-656-2110; *Fax:* 416-654-3937
e-mail: headoffice@taoist.org
URL: www.taoist.org
Overview: A medium-sized national organization founded in 1970
Finances: *Funding Sources:* Membership fees
Staff: 20 staff member(s)
Membership: 15,000; *Fees:* $20; *Member Profile:* Open to everyone
Activities: *Awareness Events:* National Taoist Tai Chi Awareness Day, first Sat. after Labour Day
Description: To make Taoist Tai Chi available to all &, through its teaching & practice, promote health improvement, cultural exchange & helping others

TEAM of Canada Inc. (TEAM)
2635 - 32 St. SW, Calgary AB T3E 2R8
Tel: 403-248-2344; *Fax:* 403-207-6025
Toll-Free: 800-295-4160
e-mail: team@teamcanada.org
URL: www.teamcanada.org
Also Known As: The Evangelical Alliance Mission of Canada Inc.
Overview: A medium-sized international charitable organization founded in 1969
Chief Officer(s):
Robert Hodge, Chairman
Jim Couture, Vice Chairman
Finances: *Annual Operating Budget:* $1.5 Million-$3 Million
Staff: 6 staff member(s)
Membership: 1-99
Activities: *Internships:* Yes; *Speaker Service:* Yes *Library:* Resource Centre
Description: To help churches send missionaries to establish reproducing churches among the nations, to the Glory of God; *Member of:* Canadian Council of Christian Charities

Teamwork Children's Services International
5983 Ladyburn Cres., Mississauga ON L5M 4V9
Tel: 905-542-1047
e-mail: jchacha@teamworkchildrenservices.com
URL: www.teamworkchildrenservices.com
Overview: A small international charitable organization
Chief Officer(s):
Joel Chacha, Program Director
Finances: *Funding Sources:* donations
Description: Non-profit organization that works to provide orphaned and disadvantaged children in rural areas of Africa a safe and secure faith-based home environment; and provide them with good health, education and vocational training, enabling them to become self-supporting and productive citizens.

Ukrainian Orthodox Church of Canada
Ecumenical Patriarchate, 9 St. Johns Ave., Winnipeg MB R2W 1G8
Tel: 204-586-3093; *Fax:* 204-582-5241
Toll-Free: 877-586-3093
e-mail: consistory@uocc.ca
URL: www.uocc.ca
Overview: A large national organization founded in 1918
Chief Officer(s):
John Stinka, Archbishop
Yurij Kalistchuk, Archbishop
Victor Lakusta, Acting Chancellor
Membership: 120,000
Activities: *Speaker Service:* Yes *Library:* Yes (Open to Public) by appointment

Union mondiale des organisations féminines catholiques (UMOFC) / World Union of Catholic Women's Organizations (WUCWO)
37, rue Notre-Dame des Champs, Paris F-75006 France
Tél: 33-1-45-44-27-65; *Téléc:* 33-1-42-84-04-80
Courriel: wucwoparis@wanadoo.fr
URL: www.wucwo.org
Aperçu: *Dimension:* grande; *Envergure: internationale; fondée en 1910*
Membre(s) du bureau directeur:
Gillian Badcock, Secrétaire générale
Membre: 50,000 Plus; *Critères d'admissibilite:* Organisation féminine catholique ayant 3 ans d'existance; *Comités:* Commissions Permanentes - Droits Humains; Développement et Coopération; Femmes et Église; Famille; Oecuménisme; Comités permanents - International; Finances; Procédures; Liturgie
Activités: Groupe de travail sur la violence contre les femmes, santé et prises de décisions; éducation; droits humains
Description: Promouvoir l'apport des femmes catholiques à la communauté ecclésiale et humaine; étudier et encourager la participation des femmes dans la mission d'évangélisation de l'Église; promouvoir une action qui rend les femmes capables de mieux remplir leur rôle dans l'Église et dans la société*Membre de:* Conférence des Organisations Internationales Catholiques (OIC); Affiliation(s): Catholic Women's League of Canada; Ukrainian Catholic Women's League of Canada; Association féminine d'éducation d'action sociale; Mouvement des femmes chrétiennes - Inter-Montréal

Union of Spiritual Communities of Christ
PO Box 3024, Castlegar BC V1N 3H4
Tel: 250-365-5477
e-mail: info@iskra.ca
URL: iskra.ca
Overview: A small national organization
Chief Officer(s):
Lisa Poznikoff, Contact
Description: The Union of Spiritual Communities of Christ (USCC) is a registered Canadian charitable society dedicated to the sustainability and enrichment of the Doukhobor Life-Concept based on the Law of God and the Teachings of Jesus Christ

The United Brethren Church in Canada
501 Whitelaw Rd., Guelph ON N1K 1E7
Tel: 519-836-0180; *Fax:* 519-821-8385
e-mail: brian.magnus@ubcanada.org
URL: www.ubcanada.org
Previous Name: Ontario Conference, Church of the United Brethren in Christ
Overview: A small national charitable organization founded in 1856
Chief Officer(s):
Brian K. Magnus, Bishop
Finances: *Annual Operating Budget:* $50,000-$100,000; *Funding Sources:* Donations
Staff: 1 staff member(s)
Membership: 12 churches; *Fees:* Schedule available; *Member Profile:* Personal knowledge of God through faith in Christ; desire to live a life conforming to biblical principles
Activities: *Library:* At Emmanuel Bible College Library
Description: To organize groups of people into congregations to worship God; to make effective application of principles of righteousness in the Society; *Member of:* Church of the United Brethren in Christ, International; Affiliation(s): Evangelical Fellowship of Canada

VISION TV
#230, 171 East Liberty St., Toronto ON M6K 3P6
Tel: 416-368-3194; *Fax:* 416-368-9774
Toll-Free: 888-321-2567
e-mail: visiontv@visiontv.ca
URL: www.visiontv.ca
Overview: A medium-sized national charitable organization founded in 1988
Chief Officer(s):
William D. Roberts, President & CEO
Peter Miller, Chief Operating Officer, Programming
Gail Thomson, Dir., Audience, Brand & Marketing, Communications & Marketing
Mark Prasuhn, Chief Content Officer
Finances: *Annual Operating Budget:* Greater than $5 Million; *Funding Sources:* Sale of airtime; advertising; cable fees
Staff: 70 staff member(s); 3 volunteer(s)
Description: To reflect & illuminate the full spectrum of faith & religious belief which make up Canada's diverse society; to build bridges of knowledge & understanding between faiths & cultures; licenced to provide paid access to all eligible religious & faith communities & broadcast ministries; also mandated to broadcast non-sectarian programs based on values, ethics & spirituality on a wide variety of issues & themes; *Member of:* Canadian Association of Broadcasters; North American Interfaith Network; Affiliation(s): North American Broadcasters Association

Watch Tower Bible & Tract Society of Canada
PO Box 4100, Halton Hills ON L7G 4Y4
Tel: 905-873-4100; *Fax:* 905-873-4554
URL: www.watchtower.org
Also Known As: Jehovah's Witnesses
Overview: A medium-sized national organization
Chief Officer(s):
Kenneth Little, President
Description: Serving Jehovah's Witnesses in Canada

The Wesleyan Church of Canada - Atlantic District
229 Beulah Rd., Browns Flat NB E5M 2R5
Tel: 506-468-2286; *Fax:* 506-468-2004
e-mail: office@atlanticdistrict.com
URL: www.atlanticdistrict.com
Overview: A medium-sized local organization
Chief Officer(s):
David W. LeRoy, District Superintendent

The Wesleyan Church of Canada - Central Canada District
17 St. Paul St., Belleville ON K8N 1A4
Tel: 613-966-7527; *Fax:* 613-968-6190
e-mail: ccd@on.aibn.com
URL: www.ccdwesleyan.com
Also Known As: The Wesleyan Methodist Church of Canada
Overview: A medium-sized national charitable organization founded in 1897
Chief Officer(s):
Donald E. Hodgins, District Superintendent
Finances: *Annual Operating Budget:* $500,000-$1.5 Million; *Funding Sources:* District churches
Staff: 3 staff member(s)
Membership: 1,736; *Member Profile:* Covenant members & community members
Activities: *Internships:* Yes
Description: To create a context that produces healthy churches; Affiliation(s): Tyndale Seminary; World Hope International; World Relief Canada; Bethany Bible College; Outreach Canada; Evangelical Fellowship of Canada

Women's Inter-Church Council of Canada (WICC) / Conseil oecuménique des chrétiennes du Canada
47 Queen's Park Cres. East, Toronto ON M5S 2C3

Tel: 416-929-5184; *Fax:* 416-929-4064
e-mail: wicc@wicc.org
URL: www.wicc.org
Overview: A medium-sized national organization founded in 1918
Chief Officer(s):
Janet Anstead, President
Finances: *Funding Sources:* World Day of Prayer offerings
Member Profile: Representatives from the Anglican Church of Canada, the Canadian Baptist Ministries, the Christian Church (Disciples of Christ), the Evangelical Lutheran Church in Canada, the Mennonite Central Committee, the Presbyterian Church in Canada, the Religious Society of Friends, the Roman Catholic Church, the Salvation Army, & the United Church of Canada; Membership is by appointment & election; *Committees:* Program; Communications; Membership & Nominating; Finance
Activities: Establishing the Ecumenical Network for Women's Justice; Preparing policy statements on issues such as racial justice & health care; Granting funds for a variety of projects that benefit women & children in Canada & around the world; Coordinating the Fellowship of the Least Coin program in Canada; Providing education, such as theology workshops
Description: To focus on national & international issues affecting women, growth in ecumenism, action for social justice, & the sharing of spirituality & prayer

World Conference on Religion & Peace (Canada) (WCRP)
#490-1, 333 Queen Mary Rd., Montréal QC H3Z 1A2
Tel: 514-343-7869
e-mail: patrice.brodeur@umontreal.ca
URL: www.wcrp.org
Also Known As: Religions for Peace (Canada)
Overview: A medium-sized national organization founded in 1975
Chief Officer(s):
Patrice Claude Brodeur, President
Membership: 100-499; *Fees:* $100 institutional; $10 student; $25 individual; $15 senior
Activities: Meetings; occasional conferences; newsletter
Description: To establish peace & justice at the local, national & international levels; to encourage members to work together with like-minded organizations on issues of social & economic justice, human rights, ecological harmony, arms limitation & nuclear disarmament; to aim for world peace through interfaith dialogue & applied ethics; Affiliation(s): World Conference on Religion & Peace (International)

World Council of Churches
PO Box 2100, 150, rte de Ferney, Geneva CH-1211 Switzerland
Tel: 41-22-791-6111; *Fax:* 41-22-791-0361
URL: oikoumene.org
Overview: A medium-sized international organization
Chief Officer(s):
Luzia Wehrle, Administrative Assistant, General Secretariat
Affiliation(s): International Council of World Religions & Cultures

World-Wide Bible Study Association
PO Box 98590, 873 Jane St., Toronto ON M6N 4C0
Tel: 416-766-1855
e-mail: richard.kruse@sympatico.ca
URL: www.ibcschool.ca
Also Known As: International Bible Correspondence School
Overview: A small local organization founded in 1968
Chief Officer(s):
Richard Kruse, Director

Worldwide Church of God Canada
#101, 5660 - 192 St., Surrey BC V3S 2V7
Tel: 604-575-2705; *Fax:* 604-575-2758
e-mail: info@wcg.ca
URL: www.wcg.ca
Overview: A small national organization
Description: To proclaim the gospel of Jesus Christ around the world & to help members grow spiritually

Wycliffe Bible Translators of Canada, Inc. (WBT)
4316 - 10th St. NE, Calgary AB T2E 6K3
Tel: 403-250-5411; *Fax:* 403-250-2623
Toll-Free: 800-463-1143
e-mail: info@wycliffe.ca
URL: www.wycliffe.ca
Also Known As: Wycliffe Canada
Overview: A large national charitable organization founded in 1968
Chief Officer(s):
David Ohlson, Executive Director
Finances: *Annual Operating Budget:* Greater than $5 Million; *Funding Sources:* Charitable donations; CIDA funding for literacy projects
Staff: 146 staff member(s); 50 volunteer(s)
Membership: 501 individual
Activities: Monthly newsletter on website; *Internships:* Yes; *Speaker Service:* Yes *Library:* Resource Centre (Open to Public)
Description: To empower indigenous peoples worldwide for spiritual, personal & social growth through Bible translations & other language-related ministries; *Member of:* Evangelical Fellowship of Canada; Canadian Council of Christian Charities; Affiliation(s): Wycliffe Bible Translators International; Summer Institute of Linguistics; Canada Institute of Linguistics; Wycliffe Associates Canada

Yasodhara Ashram Society
PO Box 9, Kootenay Bay BC V0B 1X0
Tel: 250-227-9224; *Fax:* 250-227-9494
Toll-Free: 800-661-8711
e-mail: yashram@netidea.com
URL: www.yasodhara.org
Overview: A small international charitable organization founded in 1963
Finances: *Annual Operating Budget:* $500,000-$1.5 Million
Staff: 15 volunteer(s)
Membership: 125; *Fees:* $25
Activities: *Internships:* Yes; *Speaker Service:* Yes *Library:* Yes by appointment
Description: To maintain a centre for adults engaged in a life of spiritual intent; to provide instruction in & opportunities for religious & spiritual practice

Yonge Street Mission (YSM)
270 Gerrard St. East, Toronto ON M5A 2G4
Tel: 416-929-9614; *Fax:* 416-929-7204
Toll-Free: 800-416-5111
e-mail: ysm@ysm.on.ca
URL: www.ysm.on.ca
Overview: A medium-sized local charitable organization founded in 1896
Chief Officer(s):
Rick Tobias, Executive Director
Finances: *Annual Operating Budget:* Greater than $5 Million; *Funding Sources:* Donations; churches; individuals; businesses; foundations; grants
Staff: 80 staff member(s); 500 volunteer(s)
Activities: Recreation; education; social & family events; relief; housing; *Internships:* Yes; *Speaker Service:* Yes
Description: To bring God's peace, dignity & justice to the poor & needy in downtown Toronto

Youth for Christ - Canada
PO Box 93008, #135, 19705 Fraser Highway, Langley BC V3A 8H2
Tel: 604-595-2498; *Fax:* 604-595-2473
Toll-Free: 800-899-9322
e-mail: info@yfccanada.com
URL: www.yfccanada.com
Overview: A medium-sized national organization
Chief Officer(s):
Dave Brereton, National Director
Shirley Loewen, Office Manager
Activities: Responsible, effective & culturally sensitive evangelism of youth, communicating & caring in ways that are relevant to this generation
Description: To impact every young person in Canada with the person, work & teachings of Jesus Christ & discipling them into the Church

Yukon Church Heritage Society (YCHS)
PO Box 31461, Whitehorse YT Y1A 6K8
Tel: 867-668-2555; *Fax:* 867-667-6258
e-mail: logchurch@yknet.yk.ca
Also Known As: Old Log Church Museum
Overview: A small provincial charitable organization founded in 1982
Chief Officer(s):
Susan Twist, Director/Curator
L. Thistle, President
Finances: *Annual Operating Budget:* $50,000-$100,000
Staff: 1 staff member(s); 8 volunteer(s)
Membership: 25; *Fees:* $10
Activities: Operates Old Log Church Museum; *Library:* Yes (Open to Public) by appointment
Description: To promote & preserve church history in the Yukon; *Member of:* Yukon Historical & Museums Association; Affiliation(s): Canadian Museums Association

Zoroastrian Society of Ontario (ZSO)
3590 Bayview Ave., Toronto ON M2M 3S6
Tel: 416-733-4586
e-mail: info@zso.org
URL: www.zso.org
Overview: A small provincial charitable organization founded in 1971
Chief Officer(s):
Sam M. Vesuna, President
Kevin Mancherjee, Exec. Vice-President
Fram Sethna, Treasurer
Mehroo Chothia, Secretary
Finances: *Annual Operating Budget:* $100,000-$250,000; *Funding Sources:* Membership fees; donations; investment income
Staff: 1 staff member(s); 200 volunteer(s)
Membership: 1,000; *Fees:* $70 family; $40 individual; $20 seniors & students; *Member Profile:* Zoroastrians living in Ontario; *Committees:* 15 sub-committees reporting to elected executive committee
Activities: Religious, cultural, youth, religious classes, seniors activities; sponsors 100th Scout Group; *Library:* ZSO Library by appointment
Description: Meeting the religious & cultural needs of the Zoroastrian community of Ontario; Affiliation(s): Federation of North American Zoroastrian Associations

Specific Faith Based Associations

Anglican

The Anglican Church of Canada (ACC) / L'Église anglicane du Canada
80 Hayden St., Toronto ON M4Y 3G2
Tel: 416-924-9192; *Fax:* 416-968-7983
e-mail: information@national.anglican.ca
URL: www.anglican.ca
Previous Name: Church of England in Canada
Overview: A large national charitable organization founded in 1893
Chief Officer(s):
Michael Pollesel, General Secretary
Fred Hiltz, Primate, Anglican Church of Canada
Peter Blachford, CA, Treasurer & Director, Financial Management & Development
Membership: 717,708 members; 2,346 churches
Activities: *Library:* Yes by appointment
Description: To proclaim & celebrate the gospel of Jesus Christ in worship & action, as a partner in the world-wide Anglican Communion & the universal church; to value our heritage of faith, reason, liturgy, tradition, bishops & synods, & the rich variety of life in community; to acknowledge that God calls us to greater diversity of membership, wider participation in ministry & leadership, better stewardship in God's creation & a strong resolve in challenging attitudes & structures which cause injustice; *Member of:* Canadian Council of Churches

Anglican Foundation of Canada
Anglican Church House, 80 Hayden St., Toronto ON M4V 3G2
Tel: 416-924-9199; *Fax:* 416-924-8672
e-mail: foundation@anglicanfoundation.org
URL: www.anglicanfoundation.org
Overview: A small national charitable organization founded in 1957
Chief Officer(s):
John Wright, Executive Director
jwright@anglicanfoundation.org
Kavitha Gunaseelan, Executive Assistant
kgunaseelan@anglicanfoundation.org
Activities: *Speaker Service:* Yes
Description: To assist parishes, dioceses & programs of Anglican Church of Canada with low interest loans &/or grants; Affiliation(s): World Council of Churches

The Church Army in Canada
105 Mountain View Dr., Saint John NB E2J 5B5
Tel: 506-642-2210; *Fax:* 506-657-8217
Toll-Free: 888-316-8169
e-mail: hello@churcharmy.com
URL: www.churcharmy.com
Overview: A medium-sized national charitable organization founded in 1929
Chief Officer(s):
Bruce Smith, National Director
Finances: *Annual Operating Budget:* $500,000-$1.5 Million; *Funding Sources:* Individuals; churches; foundations
Staff: 50 staff member(s)
Membership: 1-99
Activities: *Speaker Service:* Yes *Library:* Cowan Memorial Library
Description: A society of evangelists within the Anglican Communion dedicated to bringing people from all walks of life into a living relationship with Jesus Christ; Affiliation(s): Anglican Church of Canada

Baha'i Faith

Association for Baha'i Studies (ABS) / Association d'études Baha'is
34 Copernicus St., Ottawa ON K1N 7K4
Tel: 613-233-1903; *Fax:* 613-233-3644
e-mail: abs-na@bahai-studies.ca
URL: www.bahai-studies.ca
Previous Name: Canadian Association for Studies in the Baha'i Faith
Overview: A medium-sized international charitable organization founded in 1975
Chief Officer(s):
Martha Schweitz, Chair
Finances: *Annual Operating Budget:* $100,000-$250,000; *Funding Sources:* Grants; Conference & Literature revenue; Membership fees
Staff: 2 staff member(s)
Membership: 2,000; *Fees:* $50 adult; $60 couple; $25 student/senior; $60 institution; $999 life
Activities: *Library:* Yes (Open to Public) by appointment
Description: To foster Baha'i scholarship & to demonstrate the value of this scholarly approach; to promote courses of study on the Baha'i faith; to foster relationships with various leaders of thought & persons of capacity; to publish scholarly materials examining the Baha'i faith, especially on its application to the concerns & needs of humanity; to organize annual meetings & develop chapters of the Association around the world

Baha'i Community of Ottawa
211 McArthur Ave., Ottawa ON K1L 6P6
Tel: 613-297-9406
Toll-Free: 800-433-3284
URL: www.bahai-ottawa.org
Overview: A small local organization
Membership: 9 sectors
Description: To support the development of the Baha'i Faith Community in Ottawa, Ontario.

The Baha'i Faith in Canada
Baha'i National Centre, 7200 Leslie St., Thornhill ON L3T 6L8
Tel: 905-889-8168; *Fax:* 905-889-8184
e-mail: info@bahai.org
URL: www.ca.bahai.org
Overview: A large national charitable organization founded in 1844
Chief Officer(s):
Gerald Filson, PhD, Director, Office of External Affairs
gfilson@cdnbnc.org
Finances: *Annual Operating Budget:* Greater than $5 Million; *Funding Sources:* Contributions from members
Staff: 30 staff member(s)
Membership: 30,000
Activities: *Awareness Events:* Unity in Diversity Week, Nov.; *Speaker Service:* Yes *Library:* Yes (Open to Public) by appointment
Description: An independent religion based on the writings of Baha'u'llah, 1817-1892, teaching the oneness of humanity, the common divine source of all the great religions, equality of the sexes & eventual world government; headquarters in Haifa, Israel; 5-6 million adherents in 214 countries & territories; Canada's 30,000 Baha'is are located in some 1,500 centres, 261 of which elect local governing councils called Spiritual Assemblies; National Spiritual Assembly of Baha'is of Canada incorporated by Act of Parliament in 1949; Affiliation(s): Baha'i International Community

Baptists

Association d'églises baptistes évangéliques au québec
7415, boul Gouin ouest, Montréal QC H4K 1B8
Tél: 514-337-2555; *Téléc:* 514-337-8892
Courriel: association@aebeq.qc.ca
URL: www.aebeq.qc.ca
Aperçu: *Dimension:* moyenne; *Envergure:* nationale
Membre(s) du bureau directeur:
Michel M. Habbib, Secrétaire général
Membre: 65 000
Activités: Camps de jeunes; retraites; congrès; cohortes; *Stagiaires:* Oui; *Service de conférenciers:* Oui
Description: Aider les églises à: communiquer l'évangile de Jésus-Christ à tous les Québécois; former des disciples et des leaders; devenir plus solides et se reproduire; *Membre de:* Fellowship of Evangelical Baptist Churches in Canada

Baptist Convention of Ontario & Québec (BCOQ)
#100, 304 The East Mall, Toronto ON M9B 6E2
Tel: 416-622-8600; *Fax:* 416-622-2308
e-mail: bcoq@baptist.ca
URL: www.baptist.ca
Overview: A large local organization founded in 1887
Chief Officer(s):
Ken Bellous, Executive Minister
Finances: *Annual Operating Budget:* $3 Million-$5 Million; *Funding Sources:* Member churches
Staff: 15 staff member(s)
Membership: 375
Activities: *Internships:* Yes *Library:* Yes (Open to Public)
Description: A family of churches building Christ's kingdom; supports & enables member churches to be healthy, mission congregations as we serve God together; Affiliation(s): Baptist Women of Ontario and Quebec; McMaster Divinity College; Canadian Council of Churches; Evangelical Fellowship of Canada; Canadian Council of Christian Charities

Canadian Baptist Ministries
Canadian Baptist Place, 7185 Millcreek Dr., Mississauga ON L5N 5R4
Tel: 905-821-3533; *Fax:* 905-826-3441
e-mail: info@cbmin.org
URL: www.cbmin.org
Merged from: Canadian Baptist International Ministries; Canadian Baptist Federation
Overview: A medium-sized national organization founded in 1912
Chief Officer(s):
Gary V. Nelson, General Secretary
Finances: *Annual Operating Budget:* Greater than $5 Million; *Funding Sources:* Member churches; individuals; CIDA
Staff: 112 staff member(s); 540 volunteer(s)
Membership: 250,000 + 1,000 churches; *Member Profile:* Members of churches affiliated with the four conventions/unions; *Committees:* Public Affairs
Activities: Partners in Mission - 75 missionaries serving in Asia, Africa, Latin America, Europe & Canada; The Sharing Way - relief & development ministries in 13 countries, working in areas of agricultural & community development, community health, etc.; Canadian Baptist Volunteers - short-term ministry opportunities; Canada Caucus - consensus building among the churches in Canada; *Library:* Daniel Global Mission Resource Room
Description: To unite, encourage & enable Canadian Baptist Churches in their national & international endeavor to fulfill the commission of our Lord Jesus Christ, in the power of the Holy Spirit, proclaiming the gospel & sharing the love of God to all people.; *Member of:* Canadian Council of Christian Charities; Affiliation(s): Baptist World Alliance

Canadian Baptists of Western Canada (CBWC)
#1100, 550 - 11 Ave. SW, Calgary AB T2R 1M7
Tel: 403-228-9559; *Fax:* 403-228-9048
Toll-Free: 800-820-2479
e-mail: info@cbwc.ca
URL: www.cbwc.ca
Previous Name: The Baptist Union of Western Canada
Overview: A medium-sized local charitable organization founded in 1908
Chief Officer(s):
Jeremy Bell, PhD, Executive Minister
jbell@cbwc.ca
Finances: *Funding Sources:* Church congregations
Staff: 12 staff member(s)
Membership: 178 congregations representing 100,000 worshippers; *Committees:* Western Canada Missions; Evangelism; Finance; Youth
Activities: *Internships:* Yes
Affiliation(s): Baptist World Alliance

Canadian Convention of Southern Baptists (CCSB) / Convention canadienne des baptistes du Sud
100 Convention Way, Cochrane AB T4C 2G2
Tel: 403-932-5688; *Fax:* 403-932-4937
Toll-Free: 888-442-2272
e-mail: office@ccsb.ca
URL: www.ccsb.ca
Overview: A medium-sized national charitable organization founded in 1985
Chief Officer(s):
Gérald J. Taillon, Executive Director
Alan Braun, President
Finances: *Funding Sources:* Member churches
Staff: 8 staff member(s); 4 volunteer(s)
Membership: 10,189
Activities: *Library:* Resource Centre (Open to Public)
Description: To help churches build the Kingdom of God; a church for every person across Canada & around the world; Affiliation(s): Southern Baptist Convention

Convention of Atlantic Baptist Churches (CABC) / Convention des Églises Baptistes de l'Atlantique
1655 Manawagonish Rd., Saint John NB E2M 3Y2
Tel: 506-635-1922; *Fax:* 506-635-0366
URL: www.baptist-atlantic.ca
Also Known As: Atlantic Baptist Convention
Previous Name: United Baptist Convention of the Maritime Provinces
Overview: A medium-sized local charitable organization founded in 1905
Chief Officer(s):
Malcolm Beckett, Interim Executive Minister
Bruce Fawcett, Rev. Dr., Associate Executive Minister
Activities: Providing seminars, conferences, stewardship education, & retreats; *Speaker Service:* Yes
Description: To resource pastors, churches, & people; to facilitate a shared mission on behalf of churches; to establish & maintain professional standards & ethics for clergy

Buddhism

Buddhist Association of Canada
1330 Bloor St. West, Toronto ON M6H 1P2
Tel: 416-537-1342
e-mail: hongfatemple@netzero.net
URL: www.buddhistassoc.ca
Overview: A small national organization founded in 1974
Finances: *Annual Operating Budget:* Less than $50,000
Staff: 10 volunteer(s)
Membership: 200; *Fees:* $20
Activities: *Speaker Service:* Yes

Jodo Shinshu Buddhist Temples of Canada
11786 Fentiman Pl., Richmond BC V7E 6M6
Tel: 604-272-3330; *Fax:* 604-272-6865
e-mail: jsbtcheadquarters@shaw.ca
URL: www.bcc.ca
Previous Name: Buddhist Churches of Canada
Overview: A medium-sized national charitable organization founded in 1933
Chief Officer(s):
Leslie Kawamura, Director, Living Dharma Centre
Finances: *Annual Operating Budget:* $100,000-$250,000
Staff: 9 staff member(s)
Membership: 2,500; *Fees:* $45
Activities: *Speaker Service:* Yes *Library:* Yes by appointment
Description: Propagation of Buddhism; Affiliation(s): Jodo Shinshu Hongwanji, Kyoto

The Palyul Foundation of Canada
c/o Orgyan Osal Cho Dzong, Buddhist Monastery & Retreat Centre, 1755 Lingham Lake Rd., RR#3, Box 68, Madoc ON K0K 2K0
Tel: 613-967-7432; *Fax:* 416-604-8101
e-mail: palyul@ca.inter.net
URL: www.palyulcanada.org
Overview: A small local charitable organization founded in 1981
Activities: Classes on Buddhism, meditation, ritual practices; retreats; empowerments; celebration of Buddhist holy days & festivals;
Description: Dedicated to the preservation & advancement of the teachings of the Nyingma lineage of Vajrayana Buddhism

Union of Vietnamese Buddhist Churches in Canada
229 Ave. Y South, Saskatoon SK S7M 3J4
Tel: 306-978-0085
URL: www.buddhismcanada.com/sask.html
Previous Name: The General Committee Vietnamese Buddhism in Canada
Overview: A medium-sized national organization founded in 1983
Finances: *Funding Sources:* Membership dues
Staff: 9 staff member(s); 7 volunteer(s)
Activities: *Speaker Service:* Yes *Library:* Bibliothèque Tam Bao Som (Open to Public) by appointment
Description: To preach Buddhism; to preserve traditional culture of the Vietnamese

Catholicism

Alberta Catholic Health Corporation (ACHC)
9810 - 165 St., Edmonton AB T5P 3S7
Tel: 780-481-9900; *Fax:* 780-455-4150
e-mail: info@achc.ab.ca
URL: www.achc.ab.ca
Overview: A small provincial organization
Chief Officer(s):
Michael Shea, CEO

Alberta Catholic School Trustees Association
#325, 9940 - 106 St., Edmonton AB T5K 2N2
Tel: 780-484-6209; *Fax:* 780-484-6248
e-mail: admin@acsta.ab.ca
URL: www.acsta.ab.ca
Overview: A medium-sized provincial organization
Chief Officer(s):
Stefan Michniewski, Executive Director

Affiliation(s): Canadian Catholic School Trustees Association

Assemblée des évêques catholiques du Québec (AEQ) / Assembly of Québec Catholic Bishops
3331, rue Sherbrooke Est, Montréal QC H1W 1C5
Tél: 514-274-4323; *Téléc:* 514-274-4383
Courriel: aeq@eveques.qc.ca
URL: www.eveques.qc.ca
Nom précédent: Assemblée des Évêques du Québec
Aperçu: *Dimension:* moyenne; *Envergure: provinciale; Organisme sans but lucratif; fondée en 1871*
Membre(s) du bureau directeur:
Pierre Gaudette, Secrétaire général
Finances: *Budget de fonctionnement annuel:* $500,000-$1.5 Million
Personnel: 8 membre(s) du personnel
Membre: 37; *Critères d'admissibilite:* Évêque diocésain; évêque auxiliaire; *Comités:* Éducation; Laicat; Ministères; Missions; Affaires sociales; Théologie; Communications; Prospective; Législation; Administration; Relations interculturelles; Pastorale des Autochtones
Description: Ôtre un lieu d'échange et de concertation où ses membres s'entraident dans la recherche d'actions à entreprendre pour rendre l'Église au Québec toujours plus vivante et engagée dans la société et la culture contemporaines; Affiliation(s): Conférence des évêques catholiques du Canada

Association des parents catholiques du Québec (APCQ)
#406, 7400, boul Saint-Laurent, Montréal QC H2R 2Y1
Tél: 514-276-8068; *Téléc:* 514-948-2595
Ligne sans frais: 866-376-8068
Courriel: apcq406@bellnet.ca
URL: www.apcqc.net
Aperçu: *Dimension:* grande; *Envergure: provinciale; Organisme sans but lucratif; fondée en 1966*
Membre(s) du bureau directeur:
Jean Morse-Chevrier, Présidente
Finances: *Budget de fonctionnement annuel:* $50,000-$100,000
Personnel: 2 membre(s) du personnel; 25 bénévole(s)
Membre: 4 000; *Montant de la cotisation:* 12$; *Critères d'admissibilite:* Familles; *Comités:* Éducation de la foi; comité provincial d'enseignement privécarrefour famille-Québec
Activités: Secrétariat permanent; périodique; colloques; conférences; cours; congrès parents-jeunes; pétitions; rédactions de mémoires; *Service de conférenciers:* Oui
Description: Regroupe des parents catholiques pour promouvoir et défendre leurs droits et leurs intérêts selon les valeurs catholiques en matière d'éducation, de famille et de culture par l'information et la représentation de ses membres auprès de la population et des autorités civiles et religieuses; *Membre de:* Regroupement Inter-Organismes pour une politique familiale au Québec; Affiliation(s): Organisation internationale de l'enseignement catholique (OIEC)

Association of Canadian Catholic Students
47 Queen's Park Cres. East, Toronto ON M5S 2C3
Tel: 416-506-0183
Overview: A small national organization
Chief Officer(s):
Melinda Szilva, National Coordinator
Rick Benson, National Chaplain, 506-849-4885, Fax: 506-849-4895
rbenson@cccm.ca
Finances: *Annual Operating Budget:* Less than $50,000
Staff: 3 staff member(s)
Membership: 1-99
Member of: Canadian Catholic Campus Ministry; Affiliation(s): Mouvement international des étudiants catholiques/International Catholic Students Movement

Augustines de la Miséricorde de Jésus
2285, ch Saint-Louis, Sillery QC G1H 1R5
Tél: 418-681-4651; *Téléc:* 418-683-7969
Courriel: secretaire@augustines.org
URL: www.augustines.org
Aperçu: *Dimension:* petite; *Envergure: locale*
Membre(s) du bureau directeur:
Claire Gagnon, Supérieure générale
Description: Les trois dimensions de la vie spirituelle des Augustines d'hier et de demain sont: communion fraternelle; louange et intercession; et miséricorde

Auxiliaires du clergé catholique
12350, rue Fort Lorette, Montréal QC H2C 3C8
Tél: 514-384-0880
Aperçu: *Dimension:* moyenne; *Envergure: provinciale; fondée en 1939*
Membre(s) du bureau directeur:
Odette Desmarteau, Présidente
Finances: *Budget de fonctionnement annuel:* Moins de $50,000
Membre: 150

Benedictine Sisters of Manitoba (OSB)
225 Masters Ave., Winnipeg MB R4A 2A1
Tel: 204-338-4601; *Fax:* 204-339-8775
e-mail: stbens@mts.net
URL: www.mts.net/~stbens/
Also Known As: Sisters of the Order of St. Benedict
Overview: A small provincial charitable organization founded in 1912
Chief Officer(s):
Virginia Evard, Director, Communications
Irene Burzynski, OSB, Prioress
Finances: *Funding Sources:* Donations
Staff: 35 staff member(s); 30 volunteer(s)
Membership: 33
Activities: Programs in spirituality, personal growth & a variety of retreats; *Library:* St. Benedict's Monastery Library by appointment
Description: To witness Jesus Christ, through community life & prayer, contemplative living, hospitality, service to the people of God & stewardship of all God's gifts; *Member of:* Federation of St. Gertrude

Calgary Catholic Immigration Society (CCIS)
120 - 17th Ave., 3rd Fl., Calgary AB T2S 2T2
Tel: 403-262-2006; *Fax:* 403-262-2033
e-mail: contact@ccis-calgary.ab.ca
URL: www.ccis-calgary.ab.ca
Overview: A small international organization
Chief Officer(s):
F. Birjandian, Executive Director
Activities: Immigrant services
Description: Provides settlement and integration services to all immigrants and refugees in Southern Alberta.

Canadian Catholic Historical Association - English Section (CCHA) / Société canadienne d'histoire de l'église catholique - Section anglaise
c/o St. Michael's College, 81 St. Mary St., Toronto ON M5S 1J4
Tel: 905-893-9754; *Fax:* 416-934-3444
e-mail: revedjackman@rogers.com
URL: www.umanitoba.ca/colleges/st_pauls/ccha/ccha.html
Overview: A medium-sized national organization founded in 1933
Chief Officer(s):
Edward Jackman, Secretary General
Finances: *Annual Operating Budget:* Less than $50,000; *Funding Sources:* Membership fees; donations
Staff: 11 volunteer(s)
Membership: 100-499; *Fees:* $50 Canadian; US$50 American; $30 student; $60 French-English
Activities: Annual scholarly conference at the Canadian Congress
Description: To promote interest in history of Canadian Catholics; divided into English & French sections.

Canadian Catholic School Trustees' Association (CCSTA) / Association canadienne des commissaires d'écoles catholique
Catholic Education Centre, 570 West Hunt Club Rd., Nepean ON K2G 3R4
Tel: 613-224-4455; *Fax:* 613-224-3187
e-mail: ccsta@ottawacatholicschools.ca
URL: www.ccsta.ca
Overview: A medium-sized national organization founded in 1960
Chief Officer(s):
Greg McNally, Executive Director
gmcnally@xplornet.com
Regis O'Connor, President
roconnor@hscdsb.on.ca
Paula Peroni, Vice-President
peronip@vianet.ca
Finances: *Funding Sources:* Sponsoships
Membership: 7 associations; *Member Profile:* Provincial & territorial Catholic school trustees' associations in Canada
Activities: Promoting Catholic education; Providing professional development opportunities for trustees; Collaborating with the Canadian Conference of Catholic Bishops; Liaising with Canadian government agencies & other Catholic education organizations; *Awareness Events:* Catholic Education Week
Description: To protect the right to Catholic education in Canada; to promote excellence in Catholic education across Canada

Canadian Conference of Catholic Bishops (CCCB) / Conférence des évêques catholiques du Canada (CECC)
2500 Don Reid Dr., Ottawa ON K1H 2J2
Tel: 613-241-9461; *Fax:* 613-241-9048
e-mail: cecc@cccb.ca
URL: www.cccb.ca
Previous Name: Canadian Catholic Conference
Overview: A small national charitable organization founded in 1943
Chief Officer(s):
Mario Paquette, PH, General Secretary
gensec@cccb.ca
Member Profile: Diocesan bishops in Canada; Coadjutor Bishops; Auxiliary Bishops; Titular Bishops of any rite within the Catholic Church
Activities: Providing aid to developing countries & Christian education; Offering a forum for bishops to share experiences & insights
Description: To exercise pastoral functions for Catholics in Canada

Canadian Jesuits International (CJI)
#100, 1325 Bay St., Toronto ON M5R 2C4
Tel: 416-962-4500; *Fax:* 416-962-4501
Toll-Free: 800-448-2148
URL: www.canadianjesuitsinternational.ca
Also Known As: Canadian Jesuit Missions
Overview: A medium-sized national charitable organization founded in 1955
Chief Officer(s):
Jenny Cafiso, Director
Membership: 100-499
Activities: Support projects in Africa, India, Nepal, Jamaica, & Ukraine
Description: Committed to the service of faith & the promotion of justice for the poor of the world; especially dedicated to the educational needs of women, children, elderly & indigenous people at home & abroad

Canadian Latvian Catholic Association
34 Edenvale Cres., Toronto ON M9A 4A4
Tel: 416-244-4576; *Fax:* 416-244-1513
Overview: A medium-sized national organization founded in 1949
Finances: *Annual Operating Budget:* Less than $50,000
Staff: 10 volunteer(s)
Membership: 3,000 individual; *Fees:* $10 individual

Carrefour des mouvements d'action catholique
435, rue du Roi, Québec QC G1K 2X1
Tél: 418-525-6187; *Téléc:* 418-525-6081
Nom précédent: Comité diosésain d'action catholique
Aperçu: *Dimension:* petite; *Envergure: locale*
Membre(s) du bureau directeur:
Bernadette Dubuc, Contact
Description: Groupe de coordination des associations d'action catholique dans le diocèse de Québec

Catholic Biblical Association of Canada (CBAC)
#1407, 2300 Confederation Pkwy., Mississauga ON L5B 1R5
Tel: 416-406-4398; *Fax:* 416-406-5139
URL: www.cbac.org
Previous Name: Canadian Catholic Biblical Association
Overview: A medium-sized national charitable organization founded in 1974
Chief Officer(s):
Jocelyn Monette, NDS, Executive Director
jocelyn@cbac.org
Elizabeth M. Davis, RSM, President
Finances: *Annual Operating Budget:* $100,000-$250,000
Fees: $30; *Committees:* Media & Communications; Resource; Program; Finance
Activities: *Rents Mailing List:* Yes *Library:* Resource Centre (Open to Public)
Description: To foster knowledge & love of the Word of God as found in the Scriptures, through provision of a variety of sources, primarily to the Catholic community.; Affiliation(s): World Catholic Biblical Federation

Catholic Biblical Federation (CBF) / Fédération biblique catholique (FBC)
St. Ottilien 86941 Germany
Tel: 49-8193-716900; *Fax:* 49-8193-716999
e-mail: gensec@c-b-f.org
URL: www.c-b-f.org
Overview: A small international charitable organization founded in 1969
Chief Officer(s):
Alexander Schweitzer, General Secretary
Membership: 300+ in 130 countries
Activities: Workshops; Plenary Assembly
Affiliation(s): Catholic Biblical Association of Canada

Catholic Charities of The Archdiocese of Toronto
#400, 1155 Yonge St., Toronto ON M4T 1W2
Tel: 416-934-3401; *Fax:* 416-934-3402
e-mail: info@catholiccharitiestor.org
URL: www.catholiccharitiestor.org
Previous Name: Council of Catholic Charities

Overview: A medium-sized local licensing charitable organization founded in 1913
Chief Officer(s):
Maryann Burton, Association Administrator
Finances: *Annual Operating Budget:* $250,000-$500,000
Staff: 1 staff member(s); 10 volunteer(s)
Activities: *Speaker Service:* Yes
Description: Catholic Charities of the Archidiocese of Toronto is dedicated to ensuring the provision of health and social sciences and to provide leadership and advocacy on behalf of the member agencies and those in need. The people served live and work throughout the Greater Toronto Area, as well as, in Simcoe, Durham, Peel, and York.; Affiliation(s): Catholic Family Services of Toronto & 26 member agencies

Catholic Children's Aid Society
26 Maitland St., Toronto ON M4Y 1C6
Tel: 416-395-1500; *Fax:* 416-395-1581
e-mail: pr@ccas.toronto.on.ca
URL: www.ccas.toronto.on.ca
Previous Name: Catholic Children's Aid Society of Metropolitan Toronto
Overview: A medium-sized local organization
Chief Officer(s):
Mary A. McConville, Executive Director
Activities: Central Adoption Centre/Public Relations Fax 416/395-1616
Description: On behalf of the Catholic community, this organization is committed to provide social services that protect children and strengthen family life.; *Member of:* Catholic Charities of the Archdiocese of Toronto

Catholic Children's Aid Society of Hamilton (CCAS)
735 King St. East, Hamilton ON L8M 1A1
Tel: 905-525-2012; *Fax:* 905-525-5606
e-mail: karen.dolyniuk@hamiltonccas.on.ca
URL: www.hamiltonccas.on.ca
Overview: A small local charitable organization founded in 1954
Chief Officer(s):
Cathy Wellwood, President
Ersilia DiNardo, Executive Director
Finances: *Annual Operating Budget:* Greater than $5 Million; *Funding Sources:* Ontario Ministry of Community & Social Services
Staff: 180 staff member(s); 191 volunteer(s)
Membership: 100-499; *Fees:* $10
Activities: Annual general meeting; *Awareness Events:* Serendipity Auction, Nov.; *Internships:* Yes; *Speaker Service:* Yes
Description: To provide child welfare services to the Roman Catholic population of the City of Hamilton; *Member of:* Ontario Association of Children's Aid Societies; Affiliation(s): Council of Catholic Service Organziations

Catholic Community Services Inc. (CCS) / Services communautaires catholiques inc.
1857, boul de Maisonneuve ouest, Montréal QC H3H 1J9
Tel: 514-937-5351; *Fax:* 514-937-5548
e-mail: info@ccs-montreal.org
URL: www.ccs-montreal.org
Overview: A medium-sized local organization founded in 1974
Chief Officer(s):
Bruno J. Mital, Managing Director
brunom@ccs-montreal.org
Finances: *Annual Operating Budget:* $1.5 Million-$3 Million
Staff: 33 staff member(s); 1104 volunteer(s)
Membership: 65; *Fees:* $10
Activities: Youth groups; home sharing; administrative & support services; community organization & development; family support programs; personal development & support groups; camping services; Almage Senior Centre; Teapot Senior Centre; Good Shepherd Community Centre; Home Support Program; volunteer coordination; Home Day Care Program; *Speaker Service:* Yes
Description: A private sector social agency providing a broad spectrum of social services on behalf of the English-speaking Catholic community of the Diocese of Montréal; as a Catholic agency, it is an expression of the mission of charity & social justice of the English-speaking Catholic sector of the community

Catholic Education Foundation of Ontario (CEFO)
80 Sheppard Ave. East, Toronto ON M2N 6E8
Tel: 416-229-5326; *Fax:* 416-229-5345
Overview: A small provincial charitable organization founded in 1976
Chief Officer(s):
John J. Flynn, Executive Secretary
Description: To foster & promote the principles of Catholic education; to support parents in their role as primary educators; to assist the Church in its pastoral responsibilities to the schools; to encourage the establishment of Catholic schools; to promote equity of educational funding in Ontario

Catholic Family Life Centre of South Simcoe
#5, 20 Bell Farm Rd., Barrie ON L4M 6E4
Tel: 705-726-2503; *Fax:* 705-726-2570
Toll-Free: 888-726-2503
e-mail: cathfamlife@interhop.net
URL: www.catholicfamilylife.ca
Overview: A small local charitable organization founded in 1979
Chief Officer(s):
Stuart MacMillan, Executive Director
Finances: *Annual Operating Budget:* $250,000-$500,000; *Funding Sources:* Charities; United Way
Staff: 13 staff member(s)
Membership: 1-99
Activities: Family, individual & group counselling; family life education
Description: To offer professional social services to all residents of Simcoe South; services will be directed to the treatment of troubled families & individuals, as well as to strengthening & enriching family life & individual functioning in all their dimensions & contexts

Catholic Family Service of Ottawa-Carleton / Service familial catholique d'Ottawa-Carleton
219 Argyle St., 3rd Fl., Ottawa ON K2P 2H4
Tel: 613-233-8478; *Fax:* 613-233-9881
e-mail: cfssfc@magma.ca
URL: www.cfssfc-ottawa.org
Overview: A small local charitable organization founded in 1940
Chief Officer(s):
Franca DiDiomete, Executive Director
Finances: *Annual Operating Budget:* $1.5 Million-$3 Million
Staff: 34 staff member(s); 15 volunteer(s)
Membership: 50; *Member Profile:* Residents of Ottawa-Carleton who agree with our mission statement
Activities: Counselling services; family violence/sexual abuse support services; support to the community; information & referral; *Internships:* Yes *Library:* Yes (Open to Public)
Description: To offer a range of social services in English & French to all residents of Ottawa-Carleton; services are provided by professional qualified staff through a variety of programs designed to strengthen & empower individuals & families; *Member of:* Family Service Canada; United Way

Catholic Family Services of Hamilton (CFS)
#201, 447 Main St. East, Hamilton ON L8N 1K1
Tel: 905-527-3823; *Fax:* 905-546-5779
Toll-Free: 877-527-3823
e-mail: intake@cfshw.com
URL: www.cfshw.com
Previous Name: Catholic Family Services of Hamilton-Wentworth
Overview: A small local organization founded in 1944
Chief Officer(s):
Linda Dayler, Executive Director & Secretary
Teresa Hartnett, Chair
Kathleen Leach, Vice-Chair
Carol James, Treasurer
Paula Forbes, Associate Director
Mary Jefferson, Associate Director
Finances: *Funding Sources:* Government of Canada; Province of Ontario; City of Hamilton; United Way of Burlington & Greater Hamilton; Foundations such as ON Trillium Foundation
Activities: Offering programs, such as the Employee Assistance Program, Debt Management Program, K.I.D.S. (Kids in Divorced / Separated Situations), Men's Anti-Violence & Abuse Program, & the Senior's Intervention & Support Program; Providing mediation services, in areas such as the workplace, credit, estates, & commerce; Offering consumer credit education to the general public; Offering money management coaching
Description: To provide individual, marriage, family, & credit counselling services in the Hamilton & Burlington communities; *Member of:* Ontario Association of Credit Counselling Service; Affiliation(s): Ontario Community Support Association; ONTCHILD; Family Services Ontario; Canadian Association for Community Care; Continuing Gerontological Education Cooperative; Older Persons' Mental Health & Addictions Network; Ontario Association on Developmental Diabilities; Ontario Case Managers Association; Ontario Gerontology Association; Ontario Partnership on Aging Development Disabilities

Catholic Family Services of Peel Dufferin (CFSPD)
#D8, 18 King St. East, Bolton ON L7E 1E8
Tel: 905-450-1608; *Fax:* 905-450-8902
Toll-Free: 888-940-0584
e-mail: info@cfspd.com
URL: www.cfspd.com
Previous Name: Peel Dufferin Catholic Services
Overview: A small local charitable organization founded in 1981
Finances: *Annual Operating Budget:* $500,000-$1.5 Million
Staff: 30 staff member(s); 85 volunteer(s)
Activities: *Internships:* Yes; *Speaker Service:* Yes
Description: To strengthen individual families & the community of Peel Dufferin in a manner that reflects the traditions & values of the Catholic faith; to provide effective individual, marital & family counselling; to provide effective counselling for survivors of woman abuse, the children who witness the abuse & the men who commit the abuse but who want to stop; to provide effective counselling for adult survivors of childhood abuse; to provide community development services; to assist parishes in the region & their local neighbourhood; *Member of:* Catholic Charities; Archdiocese of Toronto; United Way of Peel Region

Catholic Family Services of Toronto / Services familiaux catholiques de Toronto
Catholic Pastoral Centre, #200, 1155 Yonge St., Toronto ON M4T 1W2
Tel: 416-921-1163; *Fax:* 416-921-1579
e-mail: info@cfsofto.org
URL: www.cfsofto.org
Previous Name: Catholic Welfare Bureau
Overview: A medium-sized local charitable organization founded in 1964
Chief Officer(s):
Gladys McMullin, Executive Director
Finances: *Annual Operating Budget:* $1.5 Million-$3 Million
Staff: 35 staff member(s); 18 volunteer(s)
Activities: *Library:* Yes
Description: Committed to providing innovative, relevant & the highest quality family services to the entire community within the context of Catholic beliefs, values & teaching, & affirming the cultural, racial & special differences of families & individuals; *Member of:* Catholic Charities of the Archdiocese of Toronto; Affiliation(s): Family Service Canada; Family Service Ontario

Catholic Family Services of Windsor-Essex County
6038 Empress St., Windsor ON N8T 1B5
Tel: 519-254-5164; *Fax:* 519-254-0611
e-mail: intake@cfswindsor-essex.com
URL: www.cfswindsor-essex.com
Previous Name: Windsor Catholic Family Service Bureau
Overview: A small local charitable organization founded in 1947
Chief Officer(s):
Mary Reaume, Executive Assistant
Tim Ellard, Executive Director
Finances: *Annual Operating Budget:* $250,000-$500,000; *Funding Sources:* United Way; government; fees
Staff: 8 staff member(s); 2 volunteer(s)
Activities: *Speaker Service:* Yes
Description: To strengthen the ability of individuals, families & communities to reach their potential within the context of Catholic beliefs, values & teachings, while affirming the cultural, racial & specific differences of people; *Member of:* Family Service Canada; Family Service Ontario

The Catholic Foundation of Manitoba / Fondation catholique du Manitoba
#5, 434 Archibald St., Winnipeg MB R2J 0X5
Tel: 204-233-4268; *Fax:* 204-233-1800
e-mail: cfmb@mts.net
URL: catholicfoundation.mb.ca
Overview: A medium-sized provincial organization founded in 1964
Chief Officer(s):
Peter Muzyka, President
Description: The vision of the Catholic Foundation is to provide for the needy, better the situation of the underprivileged, promote cultural advancement and scientific research, and promote the cultural life of the Catholic community of Manitoba by encouraging the funding of endowments and by providing prudent management of funds and responsible distribution of the derived revenue

Catholic Health Association of British Columbia (CHABC)
9387 Holmes St., Burnaby BC V3N 4C3
Tel: 604-524-3427; *Fax:* 604-524-3428
e-mail: smhouse@shawlink.ca
URL: chabc.bc.ca
Overview: A medium-sized provincial organization founded in 1940
Chief Officer(s):
Dianne Doyle, President
Membership: 114; *Committees:* Mission Intergration; Pastral Care; Ethics
Description: To witness to the healing ministry and abiding presence of Jesus. Inspired by the Gospel, this Association strives to have a universal concern for health as a condition for full human development.; *Member of:* Catholic Health Association of Canada; Health Employers Association of British Columbia; Affiliation(s): Euthanasia Prevention Coalition; Canadian Association of Parish Nurse Ministries

Catholic Health Association of Canada (CHAC) / Association catholique canadienne de la santé (ACCS)
1247 Kilborn Pl., Ottawa ON K1H 6K9
Tel: 613-731-7148; *Fax:* 613-731-7797
e-mail: info@chac.ca
URL: www.chac.ca
Previous Name: Catholic Hospital Association of Canada
Overview: A large national charitable organization founded in 1939
Chief Officer(s):
Dianne Doyle, Chair
Gerard Lewis, President/CEO
glewis@chac.ca
Joan Lawrence, Administrator & Coordinator, Member Services
jlawrence@chac.ca
Finances: *Funding Sources:* Membership dues
Membership: 7 provincial associations + 23 sponsors & owners of health care organizations + 96 hospitals, long-term care organizations & health care professionals; *Fees:* $750 corporate member; $250 associate member; $50 individual member; *Member Profile:* Membership includes provincial associations, sponsors & owners of health care organizations, hospitals, long-term care organizations, health care professionals, affiliate organizations, & individuals.
Description: The Association strengthens & supports the ministry of Catholic health care organizations & providers through advocacy & governance.

Catholic Health Association of Manitoba (CHAM) / Association catholique manitobaine de la santé (ACMS)
SBGH Education Bldg., #N5067, 409 Taché Ave., Winnipeg MB R2H 2A6
Tel: 204-235-3136; *Fax:* 204-235-3811
e-mail: executivedirector@cham.mb.ca
URL: www.cham.mb.ca
Overview: A medium-sized provincial charitable organization founded in 1943
Chief Officer(s):
Wilmar Chopyk, Executive Director
Daniel Lussier, Chair
Julie Turenne-Maynard, Vice-Chair
Charles Gagné, Secretary-Treasurer
Fees: $20 personal members; $100 associate members; *Member Profile:* Organizations; Health care facilities; Individuals
Activities: Promoting collaboration in health care services; Providing education to health care professionals, parish workers, & volunteers; Engaging in advocacy activities for the needs of the vulnerable & disadvantaged; Promoting the dignity & sacredness of each person; *Awareness Events:* CHAC World Day of the Sick
Description: To carry out the healing ministry of the Catholic Church in the delivery of both health & social services in Manitoba; to treat the people of Manitoba with compassion & respect for all; to recognize the spiritual dimension integral to health & healing; Affiliation(s): Bishops of Manitoba; Diocese of Churchill-Hudson Bay, Northwest Territories

Catholic Health Association of Saskatchewan (CHAS)
1702 - 20 St. West, Saskatoon SK S7M 0Z9
Tel: 306-655-5330; *Fax:* 306-655-5333
e-mail: cath.health@sasktel.net
URL: www.chassk.ca
Overview: A medium-sized provincial charitable organization founded in 1943
Chief Officer(s):
Edwin Hoffart, President
Bert Yakichuk, Vice-President
Fenton Yeo, Secretary-Treasurer
Fees: $25 person members; $75 associations; *Member Profile:* Institutions, groups, & individuals who are interested in Catholic health care & support the work of the association
Activities: Providing education & resources to members; Offering programs, such as the Parish Home Ministry of Care Program & the Catholic Health Leadership Program; Engaging in advocacy activities with government; Providing both provincial & national networking opportunities; *Awareness Events:* Mission Week; World Day of the Sick *Library:* Catholic Health Association of Saskatchewan Resource Library
Description: To provide leadership in mission, ethics, spiritual care, & social justice in Saskatchewan; to promote the sanctity of life & the dignity of all

Catholic Health Corporation of Ontario (CHCO)
PO Box 1879, 712 College Ave. West, Guelph ON N1H 7A1
Tel: 519-767-5600; *Fax:* 519-767-5602
e-mail: chco@chco.ca
URL: www.chco.ca
Overview: A medium-sized provincial organization
Chief Officer(s):
Don McDermott, President
Sarah Quackenbush, Vice-President
squackenbush@hrsrh.on.ca
Description: Sponsors member institutions and thereby continues and strengthens Catholic health care in Ontario

Catholic Missions in Canada (CMIC) / Missions catholiques au Canada
#201, 1155 Yonge St., Toronto ON M4T 1W2
Tel: 416-934-3424
Toll-Free: 866-937-2642
e-mail: info@cmic.info
URL: www.cmic.info
Previous Name: Catholic Church Extension Society of Canada
Overview: A large national charitable organization founded in 1908
Chief Officer(s):
Thomas C. Collins, Apostolic Chancellor & Chair, Executive Committee
Philip J. Kennedy, President
John P. McGrath, Secretary
Finances: *Funding Sources:* Donations; Fundraising
Activities: Supporting over 600 missionaries who serve in home mission communities throughout Canada
Description: To keep the Catholic faith in remote & poor communities throughout Canada

Catholic Organization for Life & Family (COLF) / Organisme catholique pour la vie et la famille (OCVF)
2500 Don Reid Dr., Ottawa ON K1H 2J2
Tel: 613-241-9461; *Fax:* 613-241-9048
e-mail: colf@colf.ca
URL: www.colf.ca
Overview: A small national organization founded in 1996
Chief Officer(s):
Jean Gagnon, Chair
Michèle Boulva, Director
Lea Singh, Assistant Director
Jocelyne Pagé, Administrative Assistant
Finances: *Funding Sources:* Donations
Activities: Promoting the teaching of the Catholic Church in circumstances from conception to natural death; Preparing & providing educational resources; Strengthening the role of the family; Participating in public debate about the family & respect for life; Collaborating with the Canadian Conference of Catholic Bishops & the Knights of Columbus
Description: To build a civilization of love; to promote respect for human life & the important role of the family

The Catholic Principals' Council of Ontario (CPCO)
#400, 161 Eglinton Ave. East, Toronto ON M4P 1J5
Tel: 416-483-1556; *Fax:* 416-483-2554
Toll-Free: 888-621-9190
e-mail: info@cpco.on.ca
URL: www.cpco.on.ca
Overview: A small provincial organization
Chief Officer(s):
Clara Pitoscia, Executive Director
director@cpco.on.ca
Paul Lacalamita, President
president@cpco.on.ca
Finances: *Annual Operating Budget:* $1.5 Million-$3 Million
Staff: 6 staff member(s); 6 volunteer(s)
Membership: 2,000 members who are principals & vice-principals in more than 1,300 elementary & secondary separate schools across Ontario; *Committees:* Communications; Member Security; Professional Development; Finance; Issues in Catholic Education
Activities: Advocacy, professional development; legal services; *Speaker Service:* Yes
Description: CPCO is a voluntary, professional association that serves more than 2,100 principals and vice-principals in twenty-nine Catholic school boards across Ontario

Congrégation de Sainte-Croix - Les Frères de Sainte-Croix / Congregation of Holy Cross
3745, ch Queen Mary, Montréal QC H3V 1A7
Tél: 514-737-6660; *Téléc:* 514-341-0739
Courriel: saintecroixcsc@yahoo.ca
Aperçu: *Dimension:* petite; *Envergure:* locale
Membre(s) du bureau directeur:
Réjean Charette, Supérieur provincial
Description: Congrégation religieuse catholique qui oeuvre en éducation, en milieu paroissial et dans divers autres secteurs de la société

Congregation of St-Basil (Basilian Fathers) (CSB)
95 St. Joseph St., Toronto ON M5S 3C2
Tel: 416-921-6674; *Fax:* 416-920-3413
e-mail: basilian@basilian.org
URL: www.basilian.org
Also Known As: Basilian Fathers
Overview: A small international organization founded in 1822
Chief Officer(s):
Michael P. Cerretto, CSB, Secretary General
Ronald P. Fabbro, CSB, Superior General
Finances: *Annual Operating Budget:* Less than $50,000
Staff: 3 volunteer(s)
Membership: 325; *Member Profile:* Priests; students for the priesthood
Activities: *Library:* Yes by appointment
Description: Roman Catholic congregation of priests whose primary apostolate is education, parishes & Hispanic ministry in Canada, USA, Mexico, Colombia, & France; *Member of:* RC Church

Council of Catholic School Superintendents of Alberta
e-mail: superintendents@ccssa.ab.ca
URL: www.ccssa.ab.ca
Overview: A small provincial organization
Chief Officer(s):
George Zeigner, Executive Director
Description: Provides a forum for discussion regarding the direction & development of Catholic Education in Alberta

Development & Peace / Développement et paix
1425, boul René-Lévesque ouest, 3e étage, Montréal QC H3G 1T7
Tel: 514-257-8711; *Fax:* 514-257-8497
Toll-Free: 888-234-8533
e-mail: info@devp.org
URL: www.devp.org
Also Known As: Canadian Catholic Organization for Development & Peace
Overview: A large international charitable organization founded in 1967
Chief Officer(s):
Michael Casey, General Manager
Margie Noonan, President
Finances: *Annual Operating Budget:* Greater than $5 Million; *Funding Sources:* Donations; CIDA (Canadian International Development Agency) provides grants for projects & programs
Staff: 70 staff member(s); 5000 volunteer(s)
Membership: 3 000; *Fees:* 5$
Activities: Financial support of projects in the developing world; emergency relief; advocacy on crises/issues in developing countries
Description: The official organization of the Canadian Catholic Church for international development which aims to promote & foster solidarity & understanding with people of developing countries. Offices in Toronto & Montreal; *Member of:* Caritas Internationalis; Conseil canadien pour la coopération internationale/Canadian Council for International Cooperation; Affiliation(s): Asia Partnership for Human Development; Coopération internationale pour le développement et la solidarité

Dignity Canada Dignité
PO Box 2102, Stn. D, Ottawa ON K1P 5W3
Tel: 613-746-7279
e-mail: info@dignitycanada.org
URL: www.dignitycanada.org
Overview: A medium-sized national organization
Chief Officer(s):
Dennis Benoit, President, 604-669-3677
pilgrim8220@hotmail.com
Frank Testin, Sec.-Treas., 780-990-1696
trainlvr@compusmart.ab.ca
Finances: *Funding Sources:* Donations
Activities: Encouraging spiritual development, education, & social involvement
Description: To voice the concerns of Roman Catholic sexual minorities; To promote the development of sexual theology, justice, & acceptance of the lesbian & gay community; To reinforce a sense of dignity & to encourage gay men & lesbian women to become more active members in the Church & society

Dignity Toronto Dignité
175 Windermere Ave., Toronto ON M6S 3J8
Tel: 416-925-9872
e-mail: dignity-toronto@canada.com
URL: www.dignitycanada.org/dtd.html
Overview: A small local organization founded in 1974
Chief Officer(s):
M. Heuer, Coordinator
B. Golong, Coordinator
Finances: *Annual Operating Budget:* Less than $50,000
Membership: 20; *Fees:* $30
Activities: Monthly liturgical meeting to support gay & lesbian Roman Catholics; social gatherings

Description: To support & affirm gay & lesbian Roman Catholics through spiritual development, education, social involvement, equity issues, social events; *Member of:* Dignity Canada Dignité

Dignity Vancouver Dignité
PO Box 3016, Vancouver BC V6B 3X5
Tel: 604-669-3677
e-mail: info@dignitycanada.org
URL: www.dignitycanada.org
Overview: A small local organization founded in 1977
Dennis Benoit, Contact
Finances: *Annual Operating Budget:* Less than $50,000
Membership: 12; *Fees:* $35 individual; *Member Profile:* Gays; lesbians; friends from the Roman Catholic tradition
Description: Support group for gay & lesbian Catholics & their friends emphasizing educational, spiritual, social & justice activities; *Member of:* Dignity Canada Dignité

Dignity Winnipeg Dignité
PO Box 1912, Winnipeg MB R3C 3R2
Tel: 204-779-6446; *Fax:* 204-284-0132
e-mail: dignitywinnipeg@yahoo.ca
URL: www.dignitycanada.org/chapters.html#winnipeg
Overview: A small provincial organization founded in 1970
Finances: *Annual Operating Budget:* Less than $50,000
Staff: 3 volunteer(s)
Membership: 20; *Fees:* $25 (optional); *Member Profile:* Gay & lesbian people; non-gay men & women, encompassing a broad spectrum of professions, political beliefs, ethnic & linguistic backgrounds & economic levels
Activities: Regular liturgies/discussion groups; annual retreat; social events; brochures; *Speaker Service:* Yes
Description: International movement to bring together gay & lesbian Catholics & their friends; to encourage a process of self-understanding & personal integration with respect to issues including spirituality & sexuality; *Member of:* Dignity Canada Dignité

Foundation of Catholic Community Services Inc (FCCS)
#310, 1857, boul de Maisonneuve ouest, Montréal QC H3H 1J9
Tel: 514-934-1326; *Fax:* 514-934-0453
e-mail: foundationcathcom@yahoo.ca
Overview: A small local organization founded in 1932
Chief Officer(s):
Mary Ellen Bayard, Adminstrator
Membership: 100 individual

Frères de Notre-Dame de la Miséricorde / Brothers of Our Lady of Mercy
1149, ch Tour du Lac nord, Lac-Sergent QC G0A 2J0
Tél: 418-875-2792; *Téléc:* 418-875-4829
Courriel: fndm@cite.net
Aperçu: *Dimension:* petite; *Envergure: internationale; Organisme sans but lucratif; fondée en 1839*
Membre(s) du bureau directeur:
Omer Beaulieu, Délégué du Supérieur général
Finances: *Budget de fonctionnement annuel:* Moins de $50,000
Personnel: 1 membre(s) du personnel; 6 bénévole(s)
Membre: 9
Description: Rassembler des personnes en vue d'un travail apostolique auprès des jeunes et particulièrement auprès des personnes éprouvant des difficultés

Holy Childhood Association (HCA)
3329 Danforth Ave., #D, Toronto ON M1L 4T3
Tel: 416-699-7077; *Fax:* 416-699-9019
Toll-Free: 800-897-8865
e-mail: hca@missionsocieties.ca
URL: www.missionsocieties.ca
Also Known As: Children Helping Children
Overview: A medium-sized international charitable organization founded in 1843
Chief Officer(s):
Mary Jo Mahon-Oakes, National Secretary
hca@missionsocities.ca
Description: To develop mission awareness through a school program for elementary Catholic school children; to provide aid to children in developing countries.; *Member of:* Pontificial Mission Societies

Jesuit Development Office (JDO)
c/o Jesuit in English Canada, Provincial Office, 43 Queen's Park Cres. East, Toronto ON M5S 2C3
Tel: 416-481-9154; *Fax:* 416-920-5799
URL: www.jesuits.ca
Overview: A medium-sized international charitable organization founded in 1940
Chief Officer(s):
Winston Rye, SJ, National Director
wrye@jesuits.ca
Barbara DeCarlo, Director, Development & Administration
bdecarlo@jesuits.ca
Membership: under 200
Description: To raise & provide the funds necessary for the support of Jesuit brothers & priests in formation, in ministry & in their senior years; *Member of:* Jesuit Fathers & Brothers of Upper Canada

LAUDEM, L'Association des musiciens liturgiques du Canada
1085, rue de la Cathédrale, Montréal QC H3B 2V3
Tél: 514-866-1661; *Téléc:* 514-767-1168
Courriel: info@laudem.org
URL: www.laudem.org
Nom précédent: L'Association des organistes liturgiques du Canada
Aperçu: *Dimension:* petite; *Envergure: nationale; fondée en 1992*
Membre(s) du bureau directeur:
Hélène Dugal, Présidente
Membre: 117; *Critères d'admissibilite:* Laudem accueille parmi ses membres actifs les organistes professionnels, amateurs et étudiants, titulaires, assistants, ou remplaçants dans les paroisses, sanctuaires, dessertes et communautés religieuses d'expression française de l'Église canadienne; Laudem accueille en outre parmi ses membres donateurs toutes les personnes intéressées à promouvoir les buts pour lesquels l'association a été créé
Description: De réunir les organistes liturgiques pour la promotion et le développement de leur ministère dans l'Église catholique romaine; *Membre de:* Fédération francophone des amis de l'orgue

Little Brothers of the Good Shepherd / Petits Frères du Bon-Pasteur
Good Shepherd Centre, PO Box 1003, 135 Mary St., Hamilton ON L8N 3R1
Tel: 905-528-9109; *Fax:* 905-528-6967
e-mail: info@goodshepherdcentres.ca
URL: www.goodshepherdcentres.ca
Overview: A small local organization founded in 1964
Chief Officer(s):
Richard MacPhee, Executive Director
Finances: *Annual Operating Budget:* $500,000-$1.5 Million
Activities: Housing for battered women & children; residence for homeless youth; men's hostel; food bank & food line; speakers on topics dealing with violence & abuse; *Speaker Service:* Yes

Messagères de Notre-Dame de l'Assomption (MNDA)
1671, ch de Château-Bigot, Charlesbourg QC G2L 1H4
Tél: 418-626-7492
Aperçu: *Dimension:* petite; *Envergure: locale; Organisme sans but lucratif; fondée en 1964*
Membre(s) du bureau directeur:
Lucie Dorval, Présidente
Finances: *Budget de fonctionnement annuel:* Moins de $50,000
Membre: 200 membres auxiliaires; 10 membres engagés, célibataires et veuves; *Montant de la cotisation:* 100$

Missionary Sisters of The Precious Blood
685 Finch Ave. West, Toronto ON M2R 1P2
Tel: 416-630-3298
e-mail: srkatericps@hotmail.com
URL: www.cpsmissionarysisters.com
Overview: A small international organization founded in 1885
Finances: *Funding Sources:* donations
Staff: 60 staff member(s)
Description: Involved in early childhood education and teaching at the elementary, secondary, and college levels. Also work in health care services as nurses, doctors, administrators, physical and occupational therapists, hospital chaplains, caregivers for the elderly, with AIDs patients and in nutrition education. Serves in social work, parish ministry, domestic work, gardening, religious education, work with the mentally and physically handicapped, retreat work, art, and in ministry to the Hispanic and First Nations people.

Mosaic Counselling & Family Services
400 Queen St. South, Kitchener ON N2G 1W7
Tel: 519-743-6333
e-mail: info@mosaiconline.ca
URL: www.mosaiconline.ca
Previous Name: Catholic Family Counselling Centre; Catholic Social Services; Catholic Welfare Bureau
Overview: A small local charitable organization founded in 1952
Chief Officer(s):
Cathy Brothers, Executive Director, 519-743-6333 232
Jennifer Berry, Director, Communications, 519-743-6333 303
Megan Conway, Director, Pathways to Education, 519-743-6333 306
Peter Fisher, Director, Clinical Services, 519-743-6333 223
Sandy Hoy, Director, Research & Evaluation, 519-743-6333 267
Nancy Kyle, Director, Community Services, 519-743-6333 229
Kathie Must, Director, Workplace Programs, 519-743-6333 231
Judy Nairn, Director, Business, 519-743-6333 328
Karin Voisin, Director, Volunteers & Community Relations, 519-743-6333 243
Andrew Wilding, Director, Resource Development, 519-743-6333 307
Heather Cudmore, Manager, Credit Counselling Program, 519-743-6333 236
Finances: *Annual Operating Budget:* $3 Million-$5 Million; *Funding Sources:* United Way; Government of Canada; Province of Ontario; Regional Municipality of Waterloo; Foundations, such as Pathways to Education Canada
Activities: Offering individual, group, & credit counselling; Providing workplace & employee assistance programs; Offering community outreach services; *Library:* Mosaic Counselling & Family Services Library
Description: To provide full-service professional counselling services in Kitchener & the surrounding region; *Member of:* Canadian Association of Credit Counselling Services; Ontario Association of Credit Counselling Services; United Way of Kitchener-Waterloo & Area; Family Service Ontario

New Brunswick Catholic Health Association (NBCHA)
1773 Water St., Miramichi NB E1N 1B2
Tel: 506-778-5302; *Fax:* 506-778-5303
e-mail: nbcha@nb.aibn.com
URL: www.chanb.com/chanb/
Also Known As: Catholic Health Association of New Brunswick
Overview: A small provincial organization founded in 1986
Chief Officer(s):
Robert Stewart, Executive Director
rstewart@health.nb.ca
Membership: 300
Description: The New Brunswick Catholic Health Association is a provincial Christian organization promoting health care in the tradition of the Catholic Church. The Association fosters healing in all its aspects: Physical, psychological, social and spiritual

Newman Foundation of Toronto
89 St. George St., Toronto ON M5S 2E8
Tel: 416-979-2468; *Fax:* 416-596-6920
e-mail: secretary@newmantoronto.com
URL: www.newmantoronto.com
Overview: A small local charitable organization
Chief Officer(s):
W.F. Morneau, President
Patrick O'Dea, Director
Description: To maintain & support Roman Catholic chaplaincy on University of Toronto campus

Ontario Conference of Catholic Bishops / Conférence des évêques catholiques de l'Ontario
#800, 10 St. Mary St., Toronto ON M4Y 1P9
Tel: 416-923-1423; *Fax:* 416-923-1509
e-mail: occb@occb.on.ca
URL: www.occb.on.ca
Overview: A small provincial organization
Chief Officer(s):
Alphonse Ainsworth, General Secretary
ainswortha@occb.on.ca
Richard Smith, D.D., President, 613-732-7933, Fax: 613-732-1697
Description: The Ontario Conference of Catholic Bishops is the association of the Catholic bishops of the Province of Ontario in the service of Catholics of Ontario. Involved in providing information and instruction about the principles and moral positions of the Church on all aspects of life

Ontario English Catholic Teachers' Association (CLC) (OECTA)
#400, 65 St. Clair Ave. East, Toronto ON M4T 2Y8
Tel: 416-925-2493; *Fax:* 416-925-7764
Toll-Free: 800-268-7230
e-mail: a.oconnor@oecta.on.ca
URL: www.oecta.on.ca
Overview: A large provincial organization founded in 1944
Chief Officer(s):
Greg Pollock, General Secretary
Donna Marie Kennedy, President
Membership: 36,000; *Fees:* $950
Description: Committed to the advancement of Catholic education; to provide professional services, support, protection & leadership; *Member of:* Canadian Teachers' Federation; Canadian Labour Congress; Ontario Federation of Labour; Affiliation(s): Ontario Teachers' Federation

Orthodox Church in America Archdiocese of Canada (OCA ADOC)
Office of the Bishop, PO Box 179, Spencerville ON K0E 1X0

Tel: 613-925-5226; *Fax:* 613-925-1521
e-mail: zoe@ripnet.com
URL: www.archdiocese.ca/home.htm
Also Known As: Orthodox Church in Canada
Previous Name: Russian Orthodox Greek Catholic Church (Metropolia)
Overview: A medium-sized international organization founded in 1902
Chief Officer(s):
Seraphim Storheim, Bishop of Ottawa
Dennis Pihach, Chancellor, 514-481-0109
Membership: 10,000+
Description: A component of the Orthodox Church in America, an autocephalous (self-governing) church with territorial jurisdiction in Canada, the USA & Mexico; its doctrine & worship are those of the world-wide One Holy Catholic & Apostolic Church; *Member of:* Canadian Council of Churches; Churches of Manitoba; Orthodox Clergy Association of Québec

Pax Romana
CP 374, 15, rue du Grand-Bureau, Geneva 24 CH-1211 Switzerland
Tél: 41-22-823-0707; *Téléc:* 41-22-823-0708
Courriel: international_secretariat@paxromana.org
URL: www.paxromana.org
Également appelé: International Catholic Organization
Nom précédent: International Movement of Catholic Students; International Catholic Movement for Intellectual & Cultural Affairs
Aperçu: *Dimension:* grande; *Envergure: internationale; fondée en 1921*
Membre(s) du bureau directeur:
Bernard Hyon, Secretary General
Activités: Pax Romana has consultative status with the United Nations Economic & Social Council, UNESCO & the European Council, & has accredited representatives to those organisations in New York, Vienna, Paris, Geneve & Strasbourg
Description: Aims, through its various professional & intellectual commitments in society & the Church, to engage in pro-active dialogue between Christian faith & cultures in order to promote the evangelization of cultures & the inculturation of the Gospel for the realization of the Kingdom of God; Affiliation(s): Mouvement d'étudiants chrétiens du Québec; Association of Canadian Catholic Students

Religious of The Sacred Heart / Religieuses du Sacré-Coeur
#811, 325 Dalhousie St., Ottawa ON K1N 7G2
Tel: 613-241-4050; *Fax:* 613-241-3142
e-mail: sshcph@on.aibn.com
URL: www.sshc.ca
Also Known As: Society of the Sacred Heart
Overview: A small local charitable organization founded in 1800
Chief Officer(s):
Mary Finlayson, Provincial Superior
Membership: 1-99
Activities: *Library:* Provincial Archives (Open to Public) by appointment
Description: To make known the love of Jesus in the world, through educaton & social justice activities

St. John's Cathedral Polish Catholic Church
186 Cowan Ave., Toronto ON M6K 2N6
Tel: 416-532-8249; *Fax:* 416-532-4653
e-mail: stjohnscathedralcc@sympatico.com
Previous Name: Polish National Catholic Church of Canada
Overview: A small national organization
Chief Officer(s):
Joris Vercammen, Bishop Administrator
Finances: *Annual Operating Budget:* $100,000-$250,000
Membership: 300
Member of: The Canadian Council of Churches

ShareLife
1155 Yonge St., Toronto ON M4T 1W2
Tel: 416-934-3400; *Fax:* 416-934-3412
Toll-Free: 800-263-2595
e-mail: slife@archtoronto.org
URL: www.sharelife.org
Overview: A large international charitable organization founded in 1976
Chief Officer(s):
Arthur Peters, Executive Director
Bill Steinburg, Communications Manager
Finances: *Annual Operating Budget:* $500,000-$1.5 Million
Membership: 34 organizations
Activities: *Awareness Events:* Kickoffs; *Speaker Service:* Yes
Description: ShareLife is the Catholic Community's response to helping the whole community through Catholic agencies by effectively raising & allocating funds; *Member of:* International Catholic Stewardship Council; Affiliation(s): Canadian Centre for Philanthropy

Sisters Adorers of the Precious Blood / Soeurs Adoratrices du Précieux Sang
301 Ramsay Rd., London ON N6G 1N7
Tel: 519-473-2499; *Fax:* 519-473-6590
e-mail: sremwalsh@pbsisters.on.ca
URL: www.vocations.ca
Overview: A small local charitable organization founded in 1861
Chief Officer(s):
Eileen Mary Walsh, General Superior

Sisters of Charity of Halifax (SC)
215 Seton Rd., Halifax NS B3M 0C9
Tel: 902-406-8077; *Fax:* 902-457-3506
e-mail: communications@schalifax.ca
URL: www.schalifax.ca
Overview: A small local organization founded in 1849
Chief Officer(s):
Carrie Flemming, Advancement Associate
advancement@schalifax.ca
Ruth Jeppesen, Director, Communications
Membership: 500
Description: To develop a sensitivity to the oppressed through presence, prayer & ministry to others

Sisters of Mary of The Miraculous Medal
81 Lunness Rd., Toronto ON M8W 4M7
Tel: 416-259-2808; *Fax:* 416-259-2808
Overview: A small local charitable organization
Chief Officer(s):
Mirta Rezar, Sr. Superior
Finances: *Annual Operating Budget:* Less than $50,000
Staff: 3 staff member(s)
Membership: 100-499
Activities: Nursing order

Sisters of Saint Joseph of Pembroke (CSJ)
1127 Pembroke St. West, Pembroke ON K8A 5R3
Tel: 613-735-5650; *Fax:* 613-732-1788
e-mail: csjadmin@csjpembroke.ca
URL: www.csjpembroke.ca
Overview: A small local organization founded in 1921
Chief Officer(s):
Mary McGuire, General Superior
Membership: 1-99
Description: The Sisters of St. Joseph of Pembroke are a group of fifty Roman Catholic women religious based in eastern Ontario

Sisters of Saint Joseph of Peterborough (CSJ)
PO Box 566, Mount Saint Joseph, Peterborough ON K9J 6Z6
Tel: 705-750-1688; *Fax:* 705-745-1377
e-mail: csjteamtwo@nexicom.net
Overview: A small local charitable organization founded in 1890
Chief Officer(s):
Helen Russell, Vocation Director
Membership: 90
Description: To respond to the poor & most needy, particularly where the need is not already met

Sisters of Saint Joseph of Sault Ste Marie
2025 Main St. West, North Bay ON P1B 2X6
Tel: 705-474-3800; *Fax:* 705-495-3028
e-mail: csjnbay@ontera.net
URL: www.csjssm.ca
Overview: A small local organization
Description: Lives and works that all people may be united with God and with one another

Sisters of the Child Jesus (SEJ) / Soeurs de l'Enfant-Jésus
318 Laval St., Coquitlam BC V3K 4W4
Tel: 604-939-7545; *Fax:* 604-939-7549
e-mail: gpainchaud@shaw.ca
URL: members.shaw.ca/gmlamy
Also Known As: Sisters of Instruction of the Child Jesus
Overview: A small local charitable organization founded in 1667
Chief Officer(s):
Gilberte Painchaud, Provincial Superior
Description: To be a presence of love to the Father & to others for the definite purpose of awakening & deepening the faith; to enable people to grow in the uniqueness of their person as created by God & to liberate themselves from all that prevents their being truly human; to bring hope & direction to contemporaries; to be at the service of the least favoured, the marginalized & those who have no voice in society

Sisters of the Sacred Heart / Suore del Sacro Cuore di Ragusa
1 Edward St., Welland ON L3C 5H2
Tel: 905-732-4542
Overview: A small local charitable organization founded in 1889
Membership: 600 worldwide
Activities: Day care, schools, orphanages, retirement homes for the elderly, parish work, home visits, missions, nursing
Description: To live an apostolic life in the church & society through the works of beneficence among the poor & needy; to instruct & educate youth; to collaborate in parish pastoral work, especially through the teaching of catechism

Société canadienne d'histoire de l'Église Catholique - Section française (SCHEC) / Canadian Catholic Historical Association - French Section
SCHEC, Université du Québec à Trois-Rivières, 3351, boul des Forges, Trois-Rivières QC G9A 5H7
Tél: 819-376-5011; *Téléc:* 819-376-5179
URL: www.cieq.ca/schec
Aperçu: *Dimension:* moyenne; *Envergure: nationale; fondée en 1933*
Membre(s) du bureau directeur:
René Hardy, Président
Finances: *Budget de fonctionnement annuel:* Moins de $50,000
Personnel: 4 bénévole(s)
Membre: 150 individu; 100 institutionnel; *Montant de la cotisation:* 30$ individu; 40$ institutionnel; *Critères d'admissibilite:* La Société compte des membres dans toutes les parties du Canada de même qu'en Europe et aux États-Unis; les membres peuvent être des individus, ou des institutions publiques ou privées, tels des dépôts d'archives, bibliothèques, diocèses, communautés religieuses
Description: Grouper les personnes intéressées à l'histoire de l'Église catholique au Canada; stimuler l'intérêt pour cette histoire dans le grand public; tenir des congrès annuels dans diverses régions du Canada afin de susciter un dialogue entre chercheurs participants et de promouvoir les travaux d'histoire régionale

Société catholique de la Bible (SOCABI) / Catholic Bible Society
#608, 7400, boul St-Laurent, Montréal QC H2R 2Y1
Tél: 514-274-4381; *Téléc:* 514-274-5184
Courriel: socabi@bellnet.ca
URL: www.interbible.org/socabi
Aperçu: *Dimension:* moyenne; *Envergure: nationale; Organisme sans but lucratif; fondée en 1940*
Membre(s) du bureau directeur:
Yvon Forgues, Directeur général
Finances: *Budget de fonctionnement annuel:* $100,000-$250,000
Personnel: 6 membre(s) du personnel; 3 bénévole(s)
Membre: 130; *Montant de la cotisation:* 45$ tous les trois ans; *Critères d'admissibilite:* Implication dans le pastorale biblique; *Comités:* Administration; Financement
Activités: Service de librairie; conférences sur cassettes; cours par correspondance; cours d'initiation et formation; voyage en Israël; retraites; publication d'articles; *Bibliothèque:* Oui (Bibliothèque publique) rendez-vous
Description: Rendre la bible accessible au plus grand nombre de personnes possible, en facilitant la lecture et la compréhension; *Membre de:* Association canadienne des périodiques catholiques; Affiliation(s): World Catholic Federation for the Biblical Apostolate

The Society of St. Peter the Apostle
3329 Danforth Ave., Toronto ON M1L 4T3
Tel: 416-699-7077; *Fax:* 416-699-9019
Toll-Free: 800-897-8865
e-mail: missions@missionsocieties.ca
URL: www.missionsocieties.ca
Overview: A small national charitable organization founded in 1889
Finances: *Annual Operating Budget:* $500,000-$1.5 Million
Activities: Funds the training of local clergy & religious missions; *Speaker Service:* Yes
Description: A Roman Catholic society that educates local clergy & religious men & women in developing countries

Soeurs Auxiliatrices
1637, rue St-Christophe, Montréal QC H2L 3W7
Tél: 514-522-4452; *Téléc:* 514-524-1448
Courriel: auxiqc@point-net.com
Aperçu: *Dimension:* petite; *Envergure: provinciale; fondée en 1856*
Membre(s) du bureau directeur:
Maria-Paule Lebél
Suzanne Loiselle
Andrée Brosseau

Les Soeurs de Sainte-Anne
#22, 1950, rue Provost, Lachine QC H8S 1P7
Tél: 514-637-3783; *Téléc:* 514-637-5400
Courriel: accueil@ssacong.org
URL: www.ssacong.org/
Aperçu: *Dimension:* petite; *Envergure: internationale; Organisme sans but lucratif; fondée en 1850*

Membre(s) du bureau directeur:
Marie Ellen King, Supérieure générale
Madeleine Lanoue, Secrétaire générale
Finances: *Budget de fonctionnement annuel:* $100,000-$250,000
Description: Impliquée dans l'éducation, les soins de santé, l'animation pastorale et sociale en divers milieux

Soeurs de Sainte-Marie de Namur / Sisters of Saint Mary of Namur

156, voul. Lorrain, Gatineau QC J8P 2G2
Tél: 819-663-5736
Courriel: cdjeunes@comnet.ca
Aperçu: *Dimension:* petite; *Envergure: internationale; Organisme sans but lucratif; fondée en 1819*
Membre(s) du bureau directeur:
Réjeanne Roussel, Secrétaire-trésorière
Françoise Sabourin, Supérieure provinciale
Suzanne Martineau, Secrétaire-trésorière, 613-725-3427
ssmnproc@sympatico.ca
Finances: *Budget de fonctionnement annuel:* $250,000-$500,000
Membre: 1-99

Soeurs de Saint-Joseph de Saint-Vallier (SSJ)

860, av Louis-Fréchette, Québec QC G1S 3N3
Tél: 418-683-9653; *Téléc:* 418-681-8781
Courriel: ssjvallier1903@videotron.ca
Aperçu: *Dimension:* petite; *Envergure: locale; fondée en 1683*
Membre(s) du bureau directeur:
Berthe Fortin, Supérieure générale, 418-681-2989
Membre: 165

Soeurs missionnaires Notre-Dame des Anges / Missionary Sisters of Our Lady of the Angels

323, rue Queen, Lennoxville QC J1M 1K8
Tél: 819-569-9248; *Téléc:* 819-569-9180
Courriel: mindalen@videotron.ca
Aperçu: *Dimension:* petite; *Envergure: internationale; Organisme sans but lucratif; fondée en 1919*
Membre(s) du bureau directeur:
Fernande Leblanc, Contact
Membre: 142
Description: The congregation is exclusively at the service of the missionary Church. Its specific mission is the formation of religious sisters, catechists and committed lay people. In addition, they respond to the needs of the local churches by working in the medical, social and educational fields when it is possible

Sovereign Military Hospitaller Order of St-John of Jerusalem of Rhodes & of Malta - Canadian Association / Ordre souverain militaire hospitalier de St-Jean de Jérusalem, de Rhodes et de Malte - Association canadienne

#302, 1247 Kilborn Pl., Ottawa ON K1H 6K9
Tel: 613-731-8897; *Fax:* 613-731-1312
e-mail: wgs@bellnet.ca
URL: www.orderofmaltacanada.org
Previous Name: Association of Canadian Knights of the Sovereign Military Order of Malta
Overview: A medium-sized national charitable organization founded in 1953
Chief Officer(s):
Peter Quail, Q.C., President
Finances: *Annual Operating Budget:* $100,000-$250,000; *Funding Sources:* Donations
Staff: 1 staff member(s); 259 volunteer(s)
Membership: 100-499
Description: To act as a Roman Catholic religious, chivalric & charitable organization; To provide assistance for: Good Shepherd Refuge, St. Francis, Second Mile Club, Providence Centre in Toronto, Czech Republic, Safe Motherhood Project, Nigeria, & ambulance brigades, Montréal, Cap-de-la-Madeleine, Ste. Anne de BeaupréAffiliation(s): Sovereign Military Order of Malta

Spiritans, the Congregation of the Holy Ghost

Laval House, 121 Victoria Park Ave., Toronto ON M4E 3S2
Tel: 416-691-9319; *Fax:* 416-698-1884
e-mail: communications@spiritans.com
URL: www.spiritans.com
Overview: A medium-sized national organization
Chief Officer(s):
Pat Fitzpatrick, Contact
Description: Roman Catholic religious congregation specializing in education & mission

Christian

The Antiochan Orthodox Christian Archdiocese of North America

Antiochian Orthodox Christian Archdiocese, PO Box 5238, Englewood NJ 07631-5238 USA
Tel: 201-871-1355; *Fax:* 201-871-7954
e-mail: archdiocese@antiochian.org
URL: www.antiochian.org
Overview: A small national organization founded in 1875
Chief Officer(s):
Philip Saliba, Archpriest
Membership: 275 parishes, 19 in Canada
Description: The Antiochan Orthodox Community in Canada is under the jurisdiction of the Patriarch of Antioch & all the East, with headquarters in Damascus, Syria. There are five churches in Canada & eight missions. The headquarters for all churches in North America is the Antiochan Orthodox Christian archdiocese, in Englewood, New Jersey, under Archbishop Philip Salica; Affiliation(s): Canadian (Can-Am) Region

Armenian Holy Apostolic Church - Canadian Diocese (AHAC)

615, av Stuart, Outremont QC H2V 3H2
Tel: 514-276-9479; *Fax:* 514-276-9960
e-mail: adiocese@armenianchurch.ca
URL: www.armenianchurch.ca
Overview: A medium-sized national charitable organization founded in 1984
Chief Officer(s):
Bagrat V. Galstanian, Bishop
Silva Mangassarian, Executive Secretary
Finances: *Annual Operating Budget:* $250,000-$500,000; *Funding Sources:* Donations; parish dues
Staff: 6 staff member(s)
Membership: 50,000 Plus; *Member Profile:* Baptized in the Armenian faith; *Committees:* Endowment Fund
Activities: Humanitarian Aid to Armenia; *Library:* Yes (Open to Public) by appointment
Description: To preserve & promote Christian & national heritage; humanitarian aid to Armenia; Affiliation(s): Canadian Council of Churches

Association of Christian Churches in Manitoba (ACCM) / Association des églises chrétiennes du Manitoba

151 de la Cathedrale Ave., Winnipeg MB R2H 0H6
Tel: 204-237-9851
Previous Name: Ecumenical Committee of Manitoba
Overview: A medium-sized provincial organization founded in 1990
Finances: *Annual Operating Budget:* Less than $50,000
Description: To bring Christian churches into living encounter with one another; to provide a network of news & events which can help member churches act together in all matters except those in which deep differences compel us to act separately; to act as common Christian voice & media contact on issues of spiritual & social concern in the Province

Association of Christian Schools International - Eastern Canada Office

1 Wenden Ct., RR#2, Minesing ON L0L 1Y2
Tel: 705-728-7344; *Fax:* 705-728-4401
e-mail: acsiec@sympatico.ca
URL: www.acsi.org
Overview: A small international organization
Chief Officer(s):
Mark Kennedy, Regional Director

Association of Christian Schools International - Western Canada Office (ACSI)

PO Box 3460, 44 Willow Brook Dr. NW, Airdrie AB T4B 2J5
Tel: 403-948-2332; *Fax:* 403-948-2395
e-mail: phills@asciwc.org
URL: www.acsi.org
Overview: A medium-sized local organization founded in 1989
Chief Officer(s):
Philip Hills, Regional Director
Finances: *Annual Operating Budget:* $250,000-$500,000; *Funding Sources:* Membership fees
Staff: 5 staff member(s)
Membership: 94 schools/colleges; *Fees:* Schedule available; *Member Profile:* Christian school; affirmation of ACSI statement of faith; *Committees:* Convention Planning; Student Leadership; Musical; Administrators
Activities: Teacher conferences; student leadership conferences; board/administrator conferences; district principals meetings; music events; professional development days; *Speaker Service:* Yes
Description: To enable Christian educators & schools worldwide to effectively prepare students for life; Affiliation(s): Association of Christian Schools International

Canadian Church Press (CCP)

8 MacDonald Ave., Hamilton ON L8P 4N5
Tel: 905-521-2240
e-mail: info@canadianchurchpress.com
URL: www.canadianchurchpress.com
Overview: A small national organization founded in 1957
Chief Officer(s):
Glen Argan, President
wcr@wcr.ab.ca
Trina Gallop, Vice-President
tgallop@elcic.ca
Pamela Richardson, Treasurer
pamela_richardson@can.salvationarmy.org
Finances: *Funding Sources:* Sponsorships
Activities: Offering fellowship for members; Supporting members; Conducting professional development workshops
Description: To promote high standards of religious journalism; to encourage a positive Christian influence on contemporary society

Canadian Council of Christian Charities (CCCC)

#1, 43 Howard Ave., Elmira ON N3B 2C9
Tel: 519-669-5137; *Fax:* 519-669-3291
e-mail: mail@cccc.org
URL: www.cccc.org
Overview: A medium-sized national licensing charitable organization founded in 1972
Chief Officer(s):
John Pellowe, CEO
Finances: *Annual Operating Budget:* $500,000-$1.5 Million
Staff: 14 staff member(s); 56 volunteer(s)
Membership: 3,000; *Fees:* $185-$500
Activities: Education; training on legal, financial & leadership issues
Description: To encourage the Canadian Christian community to a biblical stewardship of all He has entrusted to us by integrating practical concepts of administration, development & accountability with the spiritual concerns of ministry

The Canadian Council of Christians & Jews (CCCJ) / Conseil canadien des chrétiens et des juifs

PO Box 17, 4211 Yonge St., Toronto ON M2P 2A9
Tel: 416-597-9693; *Fax:* 416-597-9775
Toll-Free: 800-663-1848
e-mail: info@cccj.ca
URL: www.cccj.ca
Overview: A medium-sized national charitable organization founded in 1947
Finances: *Annual Operating Budget:* $250,000-$500,000; *Funding Sources:* Private; corporate; government for special projects
Staff: 4 staff member(s)
Membership: 100-499
Activities: Educational workshops/forums; research; public service announcements; *Awareness Events:* Brotherhood/Sisterhood Week, 3rd week of Feb. *Library:* Yes by appointment
Description: Non-sectarian organization that builds on our common heritage in pursuit of our goal to eradicate discrimination, prejudice & bigotry in Canadian society through education, research, communication & community building. The CCCJ promotes religious, racial & cultural equality through programming for young people; Affiliation(s): International Council of Christians & Jews

Canadian Society of Church History (CSCH) / Société canadienne d'histoire de l'Église

c/o Robynne R. Healey, Dept. of History, Trinity Western University, 7600 Glover Rd., Langley BC V2Y 1Y1
e-mail: robynne.healey@twu.ca
URL: www.augustana.ab.ca/csch/
Overview: A small national organization founded in 1960
Chief Officer(s):
Todd Webb, President
Marguerite Van Die, Vice-President & Program Chair
Robynne Rogers Healey, Administrative Secretary
John H. Young, Treasurer
Fees: $36 students; $53 retired academics; $60 individuals; *Member Profile:* Historians of Christianity in Canada & the United States
Description: To encourage research in the history of Christianity, especially the history of Christianity in Canada; *Member of:* Canadian Corporation for Studies in Religion; Congress of Social Sciences & Humanities

Christian Blind Mission International (CBMI)

PO Box 800, 3844 Stoufville Rd., Stouffville ON L4A 7Z9
Tel: 905-640-6464; *Fax:* 905-640-4332
Toll-Free: 800-567-2264
e-mail: cbmi@cbmcanada.org
URL: www.cbmi-can.org

Overview: A medium-sized international charitable organization founded in 1978
Chief Officer(s):
Ed Epp, Executive Director
Finances: *Annual Operating Budget:* Greater than $5 Million
Staff: 28 staff member(s); 45 volunteer(s)
Activities: Talking Book Library; Craft Store; works with nearly 600 mission agencies, local churches, Christian relief organizations & self-help groups overseas; *Rents Mailing List:* Yes *Library:* Talking Book Library (Open to Public)
Description: To serve the blind & disabled in the developing world, irrespective of nationality, race, sex, or religion; to prevent & treat blindness & other disabilities through medical care, rehabilitation training & integration programs; to help people to help themselves; *Member of:* Canadian Council of Christian Charities

Christian Brethren Churches of Québec (CBCQ) / Églises de frères chrétiens du Québec (EFCQ)
#101, 1520, rue King ouest, Sherbrooke QC J1J 2G2
Tel: 819-820-1693; *Fax:* 819-821-9287
Also Known As: Plymouth Brethren
Overview: A medium-sized provincial charitable organization founded in 1942
Chief Officer(s):
Richard Strout, Secretary
Finances: *Annual Operating Budget:* Less than $50,000; *Funding Sources:* Dues from local churches
Staff: 2 volunteer(s)
Description: To handle affairs for local affiliated churches regarding government & affairs of civil status

Christian Catholic Church Canada (CCRCC) / Église catholique-chrétien Canada
PO Box 2043, Stn. Hull, Gatineau QC J8X 3Z2
Tel: 613-738-2942; *Fax:* 613-738-7835
e-mail: info@ccrcc.ca
URL: www.ccrcc.ca
Previous Name: Canadian Chapter of the International Council of Community Churches
Overview: A large international charitable organization founded in 1858
S.A. Thériault, Ph.D, Th.D, Bishop Ordinary
Finances: *Annual Operating Budget:* Less than $50,000; *Funding Sources:* Clergy; churches; benefactors
Staff: 15 staff member(s); 25 volunteer(s)
Membership: 1,000-4,999; *Fees:* $200 church; $50 clergy; *Committees:* Order of the Crown of Thorns
Activities: Church Ministry; Seminary Program; counselling & mediation services; *Library:* Archives (Open to Public) by appointment
Description: Advancing the kingdom of God through worship, pastoral work & fellowship. Parishes in Ottawa-Gatineau, North Bay, Montreal; Affiliation(s): International Council of Community Churches (ICCC), ICCC Canada, World Council of Churches

Christian Children's Fund of Canada (CCFC)
1200 Denison St., Markham ON L3R 8G6
Tel: 905-754-1001
Toll-Free: 800-263-5437
e-mail: supporter-services@ccfcanada.ca
URL: www.ccfcanada.ca
Overview: A large international organization founded in 1960
Chief Officer(s):
Bruce Herzog, CEO
Finances: *Annual Operating Budget:* Greater than $5 Million
Staff: 100 staff member(s); 200 volunteer(s)
Membership: 30,000+; *Fees:* $35/month suggested donation
Activities: International development; working to help those affected by HIV/AIDS; water & sanitation; health & nutrition; gender issues; poverty; micro-enterprise development; education; environmental sustainability; *Internships:* Yes; *Speaker Service:* Yes
Description: A child-centred international development organization, the CCFC focusses on community development ministry, starting with basic assistance & leading to programs stressing self-help & eventual independence. Working with colleagues & partners in developing countries, CCFC reaches out to children & families of all faiths; *Member of:* Canadian Council for International Cooperation; Affiliation(s): Canadian Direct Marketing Association; National Society of Fundraising Executives

Christian Church (Disciples of Christ) in Canada (DISCAN) / Église chrétienne (Disciples du Christ) au Canada
PO Box 25087, London ON N6C 6A8
Tel: 519-472-9083
e-mail: ccicl@eastlink.ca
URL: www.disciplesofchrist.ca
Previous Name: All-Canada Committee of the Christian Church (Disciples of Christ)
Overview: A small national charitable organization founded in 1922
Chief Officer(s):
Tom Rutherford, Regional Minister
Finances: *Annual Operating Budget:* $100,000-$250,000; *Funding Sources:* Donations
Staff: 2 staff member(s)
Membership: 4,000 + 30 churches; *Committees:* Archives; Biennial Convention; Christian Nurture, Service, Witness; Church Development; College; Ministry
Activities: *Internships:* Yes; *Speaker Service:* Yes *Library:* Resource Centre
Member of: The Canadian Council of Churches; Affiliation(s): The Christian Church (Disciples of Christ) in USA

Christian Episcopal Church of Canada (CECC)
St. Saviour's Anglican Church, 9280 #2 Rd., Richmond BC V6E 3C8
Tel: 604-275-7422
Also Known As: Traditional Anglican Church in Canada
Overview: A small national charitable organization founded in 1991
Chief Officer(s):
Robert D. Redmile
Finances: *Annual Operating Budget:* $100,000-$250,000; *Funding Sources:* Donations
Staff: 12 staff member(s); 40 volunteer(s)
Membership: 450; *Fees:* Free-will offerings; *Member Profile:* Baptised & confirmed Anglican Christians; *Committees:* Parochial Church Council, Assembly & Consistory; Diocesan Synod & Diocesan Council
Activities: Traditional Anglican faith & worship according to the Book of Common Prayer
Member of: Anglican Communion; Affiliation(s): Christian Episcopal Church in the USA

Christian Health Association of Alberta (CHAA)
132 Warwick Rd., Edmonton AB T5X 4P8
Tel: 780-488-8074; *Fax:* 780-475-7968
e-mail: chaaa@compusmart.ab.ca
URL: www.chaaa.ab.ca
Previous Name: Catholic Health Care Conference of Alberta
Overview: A medium-sized provincial charitable organization founded in 1943
Chief Officer(s):
Glyn J. Smith, Administrator
Finances: *Annual Operating Budget:* $50,000-$100,000
Staff: 1 staff member(s); 13 volunteer(s)
Membership: 22 health facilities + 29 associate + 48 personal + 10 life; *Fees:* $25 individual; $75 associate
Description: Represents the shared vision & values of those seeking to make visible Jesus the Healer; provides support & leadership to members & the community through education, advocacy & collaboration

Christian Record Services Inc.
PO Box 31119, #119, 1300 King St. East, Oshawa ON L1H 8N9
Tel: 905-436-6938; *Fax:* 905-436-7102
Toll-Free: 888-899-0006
e-mail: crs-ncb@hotmail.com
URL: www.crsblindservices.ca
Also Known As: National Camps for the Blind
Previous Name: Christian Record Braille Foundation Inc.
Overview: A medium-sized national charitable organization founded in 1899
Chief Officer(s):
Patricia L. Page, Executive Director
ppage@christianrecordservices.ca
Finances: *Annual Operating Budget:* $500,000-$1.5 Million; *Funding Sources:* Public contribution
Staff: 14 staff member(s)
Activities: Magazines in braille, large print & on audio cassette; full-vision books (a combination of print & braille for blind parents with sighted children); Bible Correspondence School (Bible study guides available in braille, in large print, on audio cassettes & in easy English for the deaf); National Camps for the Blind; personal visitation; glaucoma screenings; deaf services.; *Library:* Lending Library for the Blind (Open to Public)
Description: To enrich the lives of blind, deaf, visually, physically & hearing impaired persons regardless of race, creed, economic status or sex.; *Member of:* Christian Camping International; Canadian Camping Association

Christian Reformed Church in North America (CRCNA)
PO Box 5070, Stn. LCD 1, 3475 Mainway, Burlington ON L7R 3Y8
Tel: 905-336-2920; *Fax:* 905-336-8344
Toll-Free: 800-730-3490
e-mail: crcna@crcna.org
URL: www.crcna.org
Overview: A large international organization founded in 1857
Chief Officer(s):
Bruce Adema, Director, Canadian Ministries
Finances: *Annual Operating Budget:* Greater than $5 Million; *Funding Sources:* Gifts & donations
Staff: 225 staff member(s)
Membership: In US & Canada: 275,000 members in more than 1,000 congregations; *Committees:* Abuse Prevention; Back to God Hour; Calvin College; Calvin Theological Seminary; CRC Publications; Home Missions; World Missions; World Relief; Chaplaincy Ministries; CRC Loan Fund; Disability Concerns; Fund for Smaller Churches; Pastor-Church Relations; Pensions & Insurance; Race Relations; Historical; Interchurch Relations; Sermons for Reading Services
Activities: *Awareness Events:* Sea to Sea Celebration Rally; *Speaker Service:* Yes
Description: The Denominational Office in Canada coordinates the work of the Church in Canada, overseeing the Committee for Contact with the Government (social justice issues), urban Aboriginal Ministry Centres (Edmonton, Regina, Winnipeg), & ecumenical involvement in KAIROS task forces (KAIROS: Canadian Ecumenical Justice Initiatives); Affiliation(s): National Association of Evangelicals; Reformed Ecumenical Council; World Alliance of Reformed Churches; Canadian Council of Churches; Evangelical Fellowship of Canada

Christian Reformed World Relief Committee of Canada (CRWRC)
PO Box 5070, 3475 Mainway, Burlington ON L7R 3Y8
Tel: 905-336-2920; *Fax:* 905-336-8344
Toll-Free: 800-730-3490
e-mail: crwrc@crcna.ca
URL: www.crwrc.org
Overview: A large international charitable organization founded in 1962
Chief Officer(s):
Ida Mutoigo, Director
Kristen VanderBerg, Coordinator of Communications
Finances: *Annual Operating Budget:* Greater than $5 Million; *Funding Sources:* Christian Reformed Churches; CIDA; other denominations
Staff: 40 staff member(s)
Membership: 15,000-49,999
Activities: *Awareness Events:* World Hunger Week, 1st week of Nov.; *Internships:* Yes; *Speaker Service:* Yes *Library:* CRWRC Development Education Library (Open to Public)
Description: To engage God's people in redeeming resources & developing gifts in collaborative activities of love, mercy, justice & compassion.; *Member of:* Canadian Foodgrains Bank; Canadian Council of Christian Charities; Canadian Council for International Cooperation.; Affiliation(s): Christian Reformed Church in North America

Christian Science / La Première Église du Christ, Scientiste
The First Church of Christ, Scientist, 175 Huntington Ave., Boston MA 02115-3195 USA
Tel: 617-450-2000; *Fax:* 617-450-3790
Toll-Free: 800-775-2775
e-mail: info@churchofchristscientist.org
URL: www.tfccs.com; www.csmonitor.com; www.marybakereddy.org
Also Known As: The Mother Church
Overview: A large international organization founded in 1879
Chief Officer(s):
Phil Davis, Manager, Committee on Publication
Judy Wolff, Chairman
Victor Westberg, Manager, The Christian Science Publishing Society, 1 8-0 2-8 70
sales@cspc.com
Finances: *Annual Operating Budget:* Greater than $5 Million; *Funding Sources:* Donations
Staff: 850 staff member(s)
Membership: 2,200 churches in over 70 countries; *Fees:* Per capita tax of not less than 1$; *Member Profile:* Open to anyone 12 years or older who is "a believer in the doctrines of Christian Science textbook: Science & Health with Key to the Scriptures, by Rev. Mary Baker Eddy."; members come from all walks of life, backgrounds, & ethnicity; they may not be members of another denomination
Activities: Sunday worship services & Wednesday testimonial meetings at branch churches worldwide; Sunday School for children up to 20; worldwide speakers bureau; retail book stores; Christian Science Reading Rooms; Christian Science programs & Weekly Bible Lessons are broadcast on television & radio.; *Internships:* Yes; *Speaker Service:* Yes *Library:* Mary Baker Eddy Library for the Betterment of Humanity (Open to Public) by appointment
Description: To commemorate the word & works of our master (Christ Jesus), which should reinstate primitive Christianity & its lost element of healing; the Church dedicates its resources to

responding to the world's growing demand for a means to achieve effective spiritual healing & living.

Christian Stewardship Services (CSS)
#214A, 500 Alden Rd., Markham ON L3R 5H5
Tel: 905-947-9262; *Fax:* 905-947-9263
Toll-Free: 800-267-8890
e-mail: admin@csservices.ca
URL: www.csservices.ca
Overview: A medium-sized national charitable organization founded in 1976
Chief Officer(s):
Henry Eygenraam, CFP, CLU, CH.F., Executive Director
Chris Platteel, BSc, MDiv, Administrator, Finance & Systems
Rick DeGraaf, M.Sc, Coordinator, Stewardship Education, 519-620-2242
Finances: *Funding Sources:* Christian charities, including churches & schools; Social service organizations
Activities: Providing advice about will & estate planning; Offering the Growing & Giving program, featuring presentations & workshops
Description: To connect families, faith, & finances for efficient estate & gift planning; To promote Biblical stewardship; *Member of:* Canadian Council of Christian Charities; Affiliation(s): Diaconal Ministries of the Christian Reformed Church

Christians Concerned for Racial Equality
PO Box 223, Stn. A, Vancouver BC V6C 2M3
Tel: 250-492-3376
Overview: A small national organization founded in 1979
Chief Officer(s):
Wesley H. Wakefield, Chair
Finances: *Annual Operating Budget:* Less than $50,000
Staff: 4 volunteer(s)
Membership: 1-99
Activities: Against slavery & racism; *Speaker Service:* Yes *Library:* Bible Holiness Movement by appointment
Description: To act as a sponsored organization of The Bible Holiness Movement; *Member of:* The Bible Holiness Movement

Citizens for Public Justice (CPJ)
#501, 309 Cooper St., Ottawa ON K2P 0G5
Fax: 613-232-1275
Toll-Free: 800-667-8046
e-mail: cpj@cpj.ca
URL: www.cpj.ca
Overview: A medium-sized national organization
Chief Officer(s):
Joe Gunn, Executive Director
Membership: 1500; *Fees:* $50 individual; $25 low income; $10 student
Activities: *Internships:* Yes
Description: To promote public justice in Canada by shaping key public policy debates through research and analysis, publishing and public dialogue. CPJ encourages citizens, leaders in society and governments to support policies and practices which reflect God's call for love, justice and stewardship.

Congregational Christian Churches in Canada (CCCC)
Dunsdon Plaza, #405, 241 Dunsdon St., Brantford ON N3R 7C3
Tel: 519-751-0606; *Fax:* 519-751-0852
Toll-Free: 866-868-8702
e-mail: admincccc@bellnet.ca
URL: www.cccc.ca
Overview: A small national charitable organization founded in 1821
Chief Officer(s):
David Schrader, National Pastor
nationalpastor@bellnet.ca
George Wilson, Chair
ChairofBoard@cccc.ca
Kim Adeniran, Administrative Assistant
Finances: *Annual Operating Budget:* $100,000-$250,000
Staff: 2 staff member(s)
Membership: 8,000 + 100 churches across Canada
Activities: *Internships:* Yes
Description: To celebrate & serve Jesus Christ in the 21st century through shared concern for others.

Gospel Tract & Bible Society
PO Box 180, Ste. Anne MB R5H 1R1
Tel: 204-355-4975
e-mail: info@gospeltract.ca
Overview: A small national organization
Description: Publishes Christian religious tracts; affiliated with Church of God in Christ, Mennonite.

Hamilton & District Christian Churches Association
147 Chedoke Avenue, Hamilton ON L8P 4P2
Overview: A small local organization founded in 1890
Chief Officer(s):
John Johnston, Contact
Membership: 13+; *Fees:* Proportional; *Member Profile:* Mainline denominations in Hamilton
Activities: Pre-ordinating ecumenical work of denominations in Hamilton
Description: To strengthen the work & witness of Jesus Christ by fostering cooperation among Christians of different traditions; *Member of:* The Canadian Council of Churches

Indian Métis Christian Fellowship (IMCF)
3131 Dewdney Ave., Regina SK S4T 0Y5
Tel: 306-359-1096; *Fax:* 306-359-0103
e-mail: imcfr@sasktel.net
URL: metfel.sasktelwebsite.net
Overview: A small local organization founded in 1978
Chief Officer(s):
Bert Adema, Director, 306-359-1096
Finances: *Annual Operating Budget:* $100,000-$250,000
Membership: 30 individual
Description: To serve spiritual & social needs; Affiliation(s): Canadian Ministry Board; Christian Reformed Church in North America

Intercede International
201 Stanton St., Fort Erie ON L2A 3N8
Tel: 905-871-1773; *Fax:* 905-871-5165
Toll-Free: 800-871-0882
e-mail: friends@intercedenow.ca
URL: www.intercedenow.ca
Previous Name: Christian Aid Mission
Overview: A medium-sized international charitable organization founded in 1953
Chief Officer(s):
James S. Eagles, President
Finances: *Annual Operating Budget:* $500,000-$1.5 Million; *Funding Sources:* Private donations
Staff: 10 staff member(s); 50 volunteer(s)
Membership: 10; *Committees:* Audit Review
Activities: Sponsorship programs; relief aid; equipment & materials provisions; Missions cafe held in major cities; *Speaker Service:* Yes *Library:* Yes (Open to Public) by appointment
Description: To aid, encourage & strengthen indigenous new testament Christianity, particularly where Christians are impoverished, few, or persecuted; to encourage Christian witness & ministry to the international community in North America; *Member of:* Canadian Council of Christian Churches; Affiliation(s): Evangelical Fellowship of Canada

Inter-Varsity Christian Fellowship of Canada (IVCF)
64 Prince Andrew Pl., Toronto ON M3C 2H4
Tel: 416-443-1170
Toll-Free: 800-668-9766
e-mail: inquiries@ivcf.ca; donorservices@ivcf.ca
URL: www.ivcf.ca
Overview: A medium-sized national charitable organization founded in 1929
Chief Officer(s):
Geri Rodman, President/CEO
Finances: *Funding Sources:* Donations
Activities: Offering Pioneer Camps across Canada; Providing ministry at university & college campuses; Offering travel opportunities through Inter-Varsity's World Services' Global Partnerships; Participating in the Urbana Student Mission Convention
Description: To help young people live a transformed life in Jesus Christ

Lifewater Canada
#194, 307 Euclid Ave., Thunder Bay ON P7E 6G6
Tel: 807-622-4848; *Fax:* 807-577-9798
Toll-Free: 888-543-3426
e-mail: gehrelji@yahoo.com
URL: www.lifewater.ca
Overview: A small international organization
Chief Officer(s):
Jim Gehrels, President
Member Profile: Hydrogeologists, well drillers, educators, engineers, environmental scientists, businessmen & many other people with diverse skills & training
Description: Christian organization dedicated to ensuring that people everywhere have access to adequate supplies of safe water; to train & equip Nationals with drill rigs & hand pumps so they can solve their own water problems; to place as many technical documents on-line as possible so they can benefit people everywhere, regardless of affiliation

M2/W2 Association - Restorative Christian Ministries (M2/W2)
#208, 2825 Clearbrook Rd., Abbotsford BC V2T 6S3
Tel: 604-859-3215; *Fax:* 604-859-1216
Toll-Free: 800-298-1777
e-mail: info@m2w2.com
URL: www.m2w2.com
Also Known As: Man-to-Man/Woman-to-Woman
Overview: A small provincial charitable organization founded in 1966
Chief Officer(s):
Wayne Northey, Co-Director
Bernie Martens, Co-Director
Finances: *Annual Operating Budget:* $250,000-$500,000; *Funding Sources:* 65% community fundraising; 35% federal & provincial government contracts
Staff: 11 staff member(s); 400 volunteer(s)
Membership: 190; *Fees:* $10; *Member Profile:* Wide range of people whose common interest is the focus of M2/W2; *Committees:* Finance/Promotion; Program/New Initiatives; Personnel
Activities: Annual Promotion Dinners; *Speaker Service:* Yes
Description: Mutually transforming lives - one relationship at a time; to see individuals & communities in British Columbia safer, transformed, reconciled & restored through justice, accountability, partnerships, mutual support, mediation, education & prevention; to provide one-to-one volunteers for men & women in BC prisons, combined with pre- & post-release support & resources; counselling for prisoners, ex-prisoners & their families; crime prevention through one-to-one support for parents of young children at risk; *Member of:* Canadian Council of Christian Charities

Micah House
c/o 333 King St. East, Hamilton ON L8N 1C1
Tel: 905-296-4387
e-mail: info@micahhouse.ca
URL: www.micahhouse.ca
Overview: A small local organization founded in 2005
Chief Officer(s):
Ian Innis, Chair
Scott Jones, Executive Director
Finances: *Funding Sources:* Donations
Staff: 6 staff member(s)
Activities: *Awareness Events:* Walkathon
Description: Micah House is the work of a group of Christians from a variety of churches and organizations in Hamilton with the goal of demonstrating God's love to newly arrived refugees in Hamilton.

National Christian School Association
PO Box 26005, Saskatoon SK S7K 8C1
Tel: 306-280-9991
e-mail: lbrunelle@aceministries.com
URL: www.aisca.ab.ca/associations.htm
Also Known As: School of Tomorrow Canada
Previous Name: Canadian National Accelerated Christian Education Association
Overview: A small national organization founded in 1991
Chief Officer(s):
Lou Brunelle, President
Finances: *Annual Operating Budget:* Less than $50,000; *Funding Sources:* Provincial dues
Staff: 24 volunteer(s)
Membership: 100-499
Description: To continue to assure Canadians of the freedom to choose alternative Christian education; Affiliation(s): Federation of Independent Schools in Canada

New Apostolic Church Canada
319 Bridgeport Rd. East, Waterloo ON N2J 2K9
Tel: 519-884-2862
Toll-Free: 866-622-7828
e-mail: info@naccanada.org
URL: www.newapostolicchurch.com
Overview: A medium-sized international organization
Chief Officer(s):
E. Wagner, President
T. Witt, Treasurer
Membership: 4,283,287 internationally
Description: The New Apostolic Church comprises a world-wide community of Christian worshippers that are growing into the future together. We take a balanced approach to our bible-based faith and enjoy life and the many benefits that come from faith, family and friendship.; *Member of:* New Apostolic Church (International)

Ontario Alliance of Christian Schools (OACS)
790 Shaver Rd., Ancaster ON L9G 3K9
Tel: 905-648-2100; *Fax:* 905-648-2110
e-mail: oacs@oacs.org
URL: www.oacs.org
Overview: A medium-sized provincial organization founded in 1952
Chief Officer(s):
Adrian Guldemond, B.A., M.A., M.E, Executive Director

Finances: *Annual Operating Budget:* $500,000-$1.5 Million; *Funding Sources:* Membership dues
Staff: 15 staff member(s); 200 volunteer(s)
Membership: 1-99; *Fees:* Schedule available; *Committees:* Finance; Education; PR; Planning; Government Relations; Personnel
Activities: *Speaker Service:* Yes; *Rents Mailing List:* Yes
Description: To promote independent schools in Ontario; to promote Christian education in Canada; to provide educational services for member schools; to lobby government for educational choice. Canada's largest & oldest independent school organization, representing 79 schools with approximately 14,000 students.; Affiliation(s): Christian Schools International; Christian Schools Canada

Ontario Christian Music Assembly
90 Topcliff Ave., Toronto ON M3N 1L8
Tel: 416-636-9779; *Fax:* 905-775-2230
Overview: A small provincial organization founded in 1961
Chief Officer(s):
Érick De Bellefeuille, Président
Membership: 130 individual
Activities: Spring & Christmas concerts series; annual christian festival concert;

Prairie Association of Christian Librarians (PACL)
Briercrest College & Seminary, 510 College Dr., Caronport SK S0H 0S0
Tel: 306-756-3262; *Fax:* 306-756-5588
e-mail: library@briercrest.ca
URL: www.pacl.ca
Overview: A small local organization
Chief Officer(s):
Brad Doerksen, Sec.-Treas.
bdoerksen@briercrest.ca
Finances: *Annual Operating Budget:* Less than $50,000
Membership: 1-99

Project Peacemakers
745 Westminster Ave., Winnipeg MB R3G 1A5
Tel: 204-775-8178; *Fax:* 204-784-1339
e-mail: info@projectpeacemakers.org
URL: www.projectpeacemakers.org
Overview: A small international charitable organization founded in 1982
Finances: *Annual Operating Budget:* Less than $50,000; *Funding Sources:* Member donations; church grants
Staff: 2 staff member(s); 30 volunteer(s)
Membership: 200; *Fees:* $25 one year $40 two year individual; $8 low income
Activities: Building peace through play; land mines; child soldiers; nuclear abolition; military spending; violent video game regulation; curriculum kits; *Speaker Service:* Yes *Library:* Yes (Open to Public)
Description: To activate peacemaking that goes beyond the absence of war to justice, wholeness & love for all creation; to empower the Christian community & community at large to respond to local & global peace issues as they emerge; *Member of:* Project Ploughshares; Affiliation(s): Canadian Centre for Arms Control & Disarmament; Manitoba Environmental Network; Project Ploughshares; Mennonite Central Committee; Peace Alliance Winnipeg

REHOBOTH Christian Ministries
3920 - 49th Ave., Stony Plain AB T7Z 2J7
Tel: 780-963-4044; *Fax:* 780-963-3075
e-mail: stonyplain@ rehoboth.ab.ca
URL: rehoboth.ab.ca
Also Known As: Christian Association for the Mentally Handicapped of Alberta
Overview: A medium-sized provincial charitable organization founded in 1976
Chief Officer(s):
Wally Mulder, Executive Director
Finances: *Annual Operating Budget:* Greater than $5 Million; *Funding Sources:* Provincial government; membership fees; donations; church offerings
Staff: 411 staff member(s); 950 volunteer(s)
Membership: 4,600; *Fees:* $10; *Member Profile:* Everybody accepting our mission statement; *Committees:* Regional Advisory
Activities: Residential, vocational & recreational support for individuals who live with disabilities; summer camp program; fundraising golf tournament
Description: To convey God's love to persons with disabilities through support, advocacy & public education, & by providing opportunities for personal growth & meaningful participation in society; *Member of:* Alberta Association of Rehabilitation Centres; Canadian Council of Christian Charities; Canadian Centre for Philanthropy; Affiliation(s): Christian Stewardship Services

Samaritan's Purse Canada
20 Hopewell Way NE, Calgary AB T3J 5H5
Tel: 403-250-6565; *Fax:* 403-250-6567
Toll-Free: 800-663-6500
e-mail: canada@samaritan.org
URL: www.samaritanspurse.ca
Also Known As: Operation Christmas Child
Overview: A large international charitable organization founded in 1973
Chief Officer(s):
Jeff Adams, Communications Director
Franklin Graham, President & CEO
Sean P. Campbell, Executive Director
Finances: *Annual Operating Budget:* Greater than $5 Million; *Funding Sources:* Donations
Staff: 60 staff member(s); 1300 volunteer(s)
Activities: Operation Christmas Child packages; Turn on the Tap access to safe water program; *Internships:* Yes; *Speaker Service:* Yes
Description: A nondenominational evangelical Christian international relief organization with projects around the globe, meeting both physical & spiritual needs of people who are victims of war, poverty, natural disasters, disease & famine. Focus is on emergency relief & development programs, medical projects. International offices in Canada, Australia, Germany, Ireland, the Netherlands, the U.S. & the U.K.; *Member of:* Canadian Council of Christian Charities; Affiliation(s): Samaritan's Purse USA

Society of Christian Schools in BC (SCSBC)
7600 Glover Rd., Langley BC V2Y 1Y1
Tel: 604-888-6366; *Fax:* 604-888-2791
e-mail: contact@scsbc.ca
URL: www.scsbc.ca
Overview: A small international organization founded in 1976
Chief Officer(s):
Henry Contant, Executive Director
Joanne Den Boer, Director of Curriculum
Finances: *Annual Operating Budget:* $100,000-$250,000
Staff: 4 staff member(s)
Membership: 45; *Fees:* Schedule available
Activities: *Library:* Yes by appointment
Description: To provide assistance to Christian schools in British Columbia in connection with curriculum, pedagogy, legal, promotion, & employee-related issues; *Member of:* Federation of Independent Schools in Canada; Christian Schools International; Affiliation(s): Ontario Alliance of Christian Schools; Federation of Independent School Associations; Christian Schools Canada; Christian Schools International

Strathcona Christian Academy Society
1011 Cloverbar Rd., Sherwood Park AB T8A 4V7
Tel: 780-449-2787; *Fax:* 780-449-3954
e-mail: sca@ei.educ.ab.ca
URL: www.ei.educ.ab.ca/sch/sca/
Overview: A small local organization
Chief Officer(s):
Robert McCoy, Director, Advancement
Finances: *Annual Operating Budget:* $3 Million-$5 Million; *Funding Sources:* Regional Government
Staff: 47 staff member(s); 120 volunteer(s)
Description: To challenge students, through Christ-centred education, to know Jesus Christ as Savior & Lord in order to pursue a life of Godly character, personal & academic excellence & service to others

World Fellowship of Orthodox Youth - Syndesmos
Syndesmos General Secretariat, PO Box 66051, Holargos 15510 Greece
Tel: 30-210-656-0991; *Fax:* 30-210-656-0992
e-mail: syndesmos@syndesmos.org
URL: www.syndesmos.org
Also Known As: Syndesmos
Overview: A small international organization founded in 1953
Chief Officer(s):
Christopher D'Aloisio, President
christophedaloisio@hotmail.com
Tony El Soury, Vice-President
telsoury@Tidm.net.lb
Tsimouris Spyros, Secretary General
Finances: *Annual Operating Budget:* $50,000-$100,000; *Funding Sources:* Orthodox churches; Orthodox church organisations; council of Eurpoe; European Christina Diakonia age
Staff: 2 staff member(s); 4 volunteer(s)
Membership: 121 organizations in 42 countries; *Fees:* $500 affiliated; *Member Profile:* Christian Orthodox youth organizations & theological schools; *Committees:* Publications
Activities: Orthodox youth camps, festivals, encounters, seminars, consultations, conferences, training courses, workshops; *Internships:* Yes *Library:* Yes (Open to Public)
Description: To serve as a bond of unity among Orthodox youth movements, organisations & theological schools around the world, promoting a consciousness of the catholicity of the Orthodox faith; to foster relations, coordination & mutal aid among them; to promote among young people a full understanding of the Orthodox faith & the mission of the Church in the contemporary world & an active participation of youth in ecclesial life; to promote a way of life founded in eucharistic communion, in the Gospel & in patristic teaching, for witness & service to the world; to assist & promote Orthodox effocrts for visible Christian unity & for positive relations with people of other faiths; to encourage reflection & action on issues affecting the lives of Orthodox Christians & the local churches; to be an instrument for furthering cooperation & deeper communion between the Orthodox Church & the Oriental Orthodox Churches

Ecumenism

The Canadian Churches' Forum for Global Ministries / Le forum des églises canadiennes pour les ministères globaux
47 Queens Park Cres. East, Toronto ON M5S 2C3
Tel: 416-924-9351; *Fax:* 416-978-7821
e-mail: director@ccforum.ca
URL: www.ccforum.ca
Previous Name: Ecumenical Forum of Canada
Overview: A medium-sized international charitable organization founded in 1921
Chief Officer(s):
Jonathan Schmidt, Co-director
Alice Schuda, Co-director
Finances: *Annual Operating Budget:* $100,000-$250,000; *Funding Sources:* Churches; religious orders; individuals
Staff: 2 staff member(s); 30 volunteer(s)
Membership: 1-99
Activities: Mission Personnel Programs, Jan., July & Sept.; Annual Katherine Hockin Award & Dinner; International Visitor; *Library:* Yes by appointment
Description: To provide ecumenical orientation & re-entry programs for mission personnel; to stimulate ecumenical dialogue on issues of mission, global concerns & social justice; to prepare individuals to serve faithfully in mission in an ever-changing world; *Member of:* International Association for Mission Studies; Forum on International Personnel; Forum on Mutuality in Mission; Affiliation(s): Canadian Council of Churches

The Canadian Council of Churches (CCC) / Le Conseil canadien des églises
47 Queen's Park Crescent East, Toronto ON M5S 2C3
Tel: 416-972-9494; *Fax:* 416-927-0405
Toll-Free: 866-822-7645
e-mail: admin@ccc-cce.ca
URL: www.ccc-cce.ca
Overview: A large national charitable organization founded in 1944
Chief Officer(s):
James Christie, President
Finances: *Annual Operating Budget:* $250,000-$500,000; *Funding Sources:* Member churches
Staff: 4 staff member(s); 2 volunteer(s)
Membership: 10 original member churches, 4 affiliates
Activities: Sponsor of Project Ploughshares; maintains dialogue with all faith groups
Description: To engage in ecumenical education & training; to address issues of justice, liberty, peace, human rights in keeping with principals inherent in the Christian Gospel; to promote understanding among member churches & with other Christian churches & religious organizations in Canada; to provide coordinating services for preparation of statements, programs, activities & resources; to aid in development of ecumenism in Canada; to provide a forum in which members & interested parties can discuss, study & act on issues of faith & worship; Affiliation(s): Anglican Church of Canada; Baptist Convention of Ontario & Québec; Canadian Conference of Catholic Bishops; British Methodist Episcopal Church; Canadian Diocese of the Armenian Orthodox Church; Christian Church (Disciples of Christ); Christian Reformed Church in North America; Coptic Orthodox Church; Ethiopian Orthodox Church; Greek Orthodox Church; Evangelical Lutheran Church in Canada; Mennonite Church Canada; Orthodox Church in America; Polish National Catholic Church of Canada; Presbyterian Church in Canada; Reformed Church in America; Religious Society of Friends; Salvation Army

The Churches' Council on Theological Education in Canada: an Ecumenical Foundation (CCTE) / Le Conseil des Églises pour l'éducation théologique au Canada: une fondation oecuménique
47 Queen's Park Cres., Toronto ON M5S 2C3

Tel: 416-928-3223; *Fax:* 416-928-3563
e-mail: director@ccte.ca
URL: www.ccte.ca
Overview: A small national organization founded in 1962
Chief Officer(s):
Robert Faris, Executive Director
Robert Smith, President
Finances: *Annual Operating Budget:* $100,000-$250,000
Staff: 2 staff member(s); 24 volunteer(s)
Membership: 24 individual
Description: To provide for the coordination of consultation, research, & administration of grants awarded by the Council, in order to promote the development of theological education for ministry; Affiliation(s): Association of Theological Schools

Student Christian Movement of Canada (SCM) / Mouvement d'étudiant(e)s chrétien(ne)s
310 Danforth Ave., Toronto ON M4K 1N6
Tel: 416-463-4312; *Fax:* 416-463-9410
e-mail: info@scmcanada.org
URL: www.scmcanada.org
Overview: A medium-sized national charitable organization founded in 1921
Chief Officer(s):
David Ball, National Coordinator
Finances: *Annual Operating Budget:* $50,000-$100,000
Staff: 2 staff member(s)
Membership: 500; *Member Profile:* Groups at Canadian universities
Description: National, ecumenical student organization; to encourage members in theological/social reflection & in actions for social change. Offices in Toronto & Winnipeg; *Member of:* World Student Christian Federation

World Association for Christian Communication (WACC) / Association mondiale pour la communication
308 Main St., Toronto ON M4C 4X7
Tel: 416-691-1999; *Fax:* 416-691-1997
e-mail: wacc@waccglobal.org
URL: www.waccglobal.org
Overview: A small international charitable organization founded in 1975
Chief Officer(s):
Randy Naylor, General Secretary
rn@waccglobal.org
Musimbi Kanyoro, President
Young-Cheol Cheon, Treasurer
Membership: 1,000-4,999; *Fees:* US$120 corporate; US$40 personal; US$10 student; *Member Profile:* Individuals, churches, church-related agencies, media producers, educational institutions, secular communication organizations, & persons who share WACC's mission
Activities: *Speaker Service:* Yes *Library:* Yes by appointment
Description: Communication for social change is promoted by WACC through advocacy, education, training, & the creation & sharing of knowledge. Areas of chief concern include media diversity, equal & affordable access to communication & knowledge, media & gender justice, & the relationship between communication & power.; *Member of:* UNESCO; ECOSOC

Evangelism

Africa Inland Mission International (Canada) (AIM) / Mission à l'intérieur de l'Afrique (Canada)
1641 Victoria Park Ave., Toronto ON M1R 1P8
Tel: 416-751-6077; *Fax:* 416-751-3467
Toll-Free: 877-407-6077
e-mail: general.can@aimint.net
URL: www.aimcanada.org
Also Known As: AIM Canada
Overview: A medium-sized international charitable organization founded in 1895
Finances: *Annual Operating Budget:* $1.5 Million-$3 Million; *Funding Sources:* Donations from churches & individuals
Staff: 8 staff member(s); 3 volunteer(s)
Membership: 135; *Committees:* Finance; Personnel; Projects
Description: Evangelization of people within Eastern & Central Africa & Islands around India Ocean; to plant & establish churches; to train leadership for those churches; to provide medical, educational & agricultural services; *Member of:* Africa Inland Mission International, Bristol, England; Interdenominational Foreign Mission Association

Baptist Foundation, Alberta, Saskatchewan & the Territories, Inc. (B-FAST)
14323 - 107A Ave. NW, Edmonton AB T5N 1G2
Tel: 780-451-4878; *Fax:* 780-451-0413
e-mail: info@febcast.com
Overview: A small local organization founded in 1982
Chief Officer(s):
Nanja Reynolds, Office Manager
Membership: 15 individual
Description: Funding capital projects for Fellowship of Evangelical Baptist Churches in Alberta, Saskatchewan & the Territories

Baptist General Conference of Canada (BGCC)
#205, 15824 - 131 Ave., Edmonton AB T5V 1J4
Tel: 780-438-9127; *Fax:* 780-435-2478
e-mail: info@bgc.ca
URL: www.bgc.ca
Overview: A large national charitable organization founded in 1981
Chief Officer(s):
Jamey McDonald, Executive Director
Finances: *Funding Sources:* Churches; individuals; BGC Stewardship Foundation
Staff: 5 staff member(s); 12 volunteer(s)
Membership: 7,000+ individuals + 106 churches; *Member Profile:* Agreement with our Affirmation of Faith, Distinctives & ministry goals; *Committees:* Global Ministries; Equipping Ministries; Women; Youth; Regents - Canadian Baptist Seminary; Finance
Activities: Global Ministries; new church development; leadership training; youth programs; women's ministries; international development consulting; *Library:* BGC Canada Archives by appointment
Description: To unite churches in a fellowship that is scriptual in doctrine, evangelical in character & irenic (peaceful) in spirit, & seeking to fulfil the Great Commission of Christ (Mt.28: 19-20) in Canada & abroad; *Member of:* Evangelical Fellowship of Canada

Billy Graham Evangelistic Association of Canada (BGEAC)
20 Hopewell Ave. NE, Calgary AB T3J 5H5
Tel: 403-219-2300; *Fax:* 403-250-6567
Toll-Free: 800-293-3717
URL: www.billygraham.ca
Overview: A small national charitable organization founded in 1968
Chief Officer(s):
Fred Weiss, Executive Director
Steve Wile, Director, Ministry
Finances: *Funding Sources:* Donations
Staff: 21 staff member(s)
Activities: Television & radio broadcasts; schools of evangelism; evangelistic crusades; teaching seminars
Description: The goal is to expose those who are searching to the message of Christ; to help edify the Christian body in Canada; Affiliation(s): Bill Graham Evangelistic Association USA

Child Evangelism Fellowship of Canada (CEF) / Association de l'évangelisation des enfants (AEF)
PO Box 165, Stn. Main, 189 Henderson Highway, Winnipeg MB R3C 2G9
Tel: 204-943-2774; *Fax:* 204-943-9967
Toll-Free: 866-943-2774
e-mail: info@cefcanada.org
URL: www.cefcanada.org
Also Known As: CEF of Canada
Overview: A medium-sized national charitable organization founded in 1937
Chief Officer(s):
Jerry Hanson, National Director
jhanson@cefcanada.org
Finances: *Annual Operating Budget:* $500,000-$1.5 Million; *Funding Sources:* Individual, corporate & church donations
Staff: 45 staff member(s); 200 volunteer(s)
Membership: 8
Activities: Working in more than 150 countries providing programs, materials & training for Christian education among children
Description: To help local churches reach out to children; *Member of:* Canadian Council of Christian Charities; Evangelical Fellowship of Canada; Affiliation(s): Child Evangelism Fellowship Inc.; CEF of Nations

The Christian & Missionary Alliance in Canada (C&MA) / L'Alliance chrétienne et missionnaire au Canada
#100, 30 Carrier Dr., Toronto ON M9W 5T7
Tel: 416-674-7878; *Fax:* 416-674-0808
e-mail: info@cmacan.org
URL: www.cmacan.org
Also Known As: The Alliance Church
Overview: A large national charitable organization founded in 1972
Chief Officer(s):
Franklin Pyles, President
Finances: *Annual Operating Budget:* Greater than $5 Million; *Funding Sources:* Donations
Staff: 1200 staff member(s)
Membership: 430 churches + 300 missionaries + 43,700 baptized + 127,000 inclusive members
Description: To proclaim the truth of God's Word & to disciple people of all nations, particularly where Christ has not been named, emphasizing the Lordship of Jesus Christ & the person & work of the Holy Spirit, & looking for the coming of the Lord; to establish & nurture churches related in fellowship with C&MA around the world, dedicated to evangelism & missions; to establish local churches throughout Canada; to teach & train believers for the work of the ministry of Christ; to provide fellowship for individual believers of kindred spirit with one another without affecting their denominational relations; to encourage the cooperation of such evangelical groups of churches or Christians as may be disposed to send their missionaries through C&MA & contribute their missionary offerings through the general treasury; *Member of:* Alliance World Fellowship; Affiliation(s): Evangelical Fellowship of Canada

Emmanuel International (Canada) (EIC)
PO Box 4050, 3967 Stouffville Rd., Stouffville ON L4A 8B6
Tel: 905-640-2111; *Fax:* 905-640-2186
e-mail: info@e-i.org
URL: www.e-i.org
Overview: A large national charitable organization founded in 1975
Chief Officer(s):
Andrew Atkins, General Director
Finances: *Annual Operating Budget:* $1.5 Million-$3 Million; *Funding Sources:* Government; donations
Staff: 14 staff member(s); 3 volunteer(s)
Membership: 1-99
Activities: *Internships:* Yes
Description: To encourage, strengthen & assist churches worldwide to meet the spiritual & physical needs of the poor in accordance with the Holy Scriptures through programs of relief, rehabilitation, community development, evangelism & church planting; *Member of:* Canadian Council of Christian Charities

Evangelical Covenant Church of Canada (ECCC)
PO Box 34025, RPO Fort Richmond, Winnipeg MB R3T 5T5
Tel: 204-269-3437; *Fax:* 204-269-3584
Toll-Free: - - 020
e-mail: messengr@escape.ca
URL: www.canadacovenantchurch.org
Overview: A medium-sized national charitable organization founded in 1904
Chief Officer(s):
Jeff Anderson, ECCC Conference Superintendent
Finances: *Funding Sources:* Donations
Member Profile: Evangelical Covenant Churches in Canada
Member of: World Relief Canada; The Evangelical Fellowship of Canada; The Canadian Council of Christian Charities

Evangelical Fellowship of Canada (EFC) / Alliance évangélique du Canada
PO Box 3745, Stn. MIP, Markham ON L3R 0Y4
Tel: 905-479-5885; *Fax:* 905-479-4742
e-mail: efc@evangelicalfellowship.ca
URL: www.evangelicalfellowship.ca
Overview: A medium-sized national charitable organization founded in 1964
Chief Officer(s):
Bruce J. Clemenger, President
Finances: *Annual Operating Budget:* $1.5 Million-$3 Million; *Funding Sources:* General & corporate donations; member & subscriber fees
Staff: 20 staff member(s); 90 volunteer(s)
Membership: 32 evangelical denominations + 110 organizations + 1,200 churches
Activities: Task forces: Evangelism; Women in Ministry; Aboriginal; Global Mission; Commissions: Education; Religious Liberty; Social Action; *Speaker Service:* Yes
Description: To be a public advocate of the gospel of Jesus Christ; to provide an evangelical identity which unites Canadian Christians of diverse backgrounds; to express biblical views on the critical issues of our time; to assist individuals & groups in proclaiming the gospel & advancing Christian values in our nation & around the world; *Member of:* World Evangelical Fellowship

Evangelical Medical Aid Society (EMAS)
PO Box 820, Stn. Main, 3967 Stouffville Road, Stouffville ON L4A 7Z9
Tel: 905-642-4661; *Fax:* 905-640-2186
Toll-Free: 866-648-0664
e-mail: info@emascanada.org
URL: www.emascanada.org
Overview: A small international charitable organization founded in 1948
Chief Officer(s):
Hendrik Visser, M.D., Chair

Finances: *Annual Operating Budget:* $500,000-$1.5 Million
Staff: 1 staff member(s); 175 volunteer(s)
Membership: 25 individual
Description: A global medical ministry, revealing Christ's love; to work with national groups to provide assistance in healing & teaching

The Evangelical Order of Certified Pastoral Counsellors of America (EOCPCA)
#210, 3017 St. Clair Ave., Burlington ON L7N 3P5
Tel: 905-639-0137; *Fax:* 905-333-8901
e-mail: admin@eocpc.com
URL: www.eocpc.com
Previous Name: Order of Certified Pastoral Counsellors of America
Overview: A medium-sized national organization founded in 1982
Chief Officer(s):
Stephen Hambly, Contact
shambly@eocpc.com
Finances: *Annual Operating Budget:* $500,000-$1.5 Million
Staff: 3 staff member(s)
Membership: 1,200 individual; *Fees:* $75-250
Description: To promote a Christian-oriented order; to certify & accredit pastoral counsellors by federal charter; *Member of:* Canadian Christian Counsellors Association; Canadian Christian Clinical Counsellors College; Affiliation(s): California State Christian University

Evangelical Tract Distributors
PO Box 146, Stn. Main, 12151 - 67 St. NW, Edmonton AB T5J 2G9
Tel: 780-477-1538; *Fax:* 780-477-3795
Overview: A small national organization
Chief Officer(s):
John Harder, President/Managing Director
Description: To print & distribute gospel tracts free of charge to missionaries & Christian workers

Fellowship of Evangelical Baptist Churches in Canada
PO Box 457, 351 Elizabeth St., Guelph ON N1H 6K9
Tel: 519-821-4830; *Fax:* 519-821-9829
e-mail: president@fellowship.ca
URL: www.fellowship.ca
Overview: A large national organization
Chief Officer(s):
John Kaiser, President
Finances: *Annual Operating Budget:* Greater than $5 Million
Staff: 16 staff member(s)
Membership: 501 churches
Activities: *Library:* Archives
Description: To glorify God & to proclaim the good news of Jesus Christ, evangelizing our generation & producing healthy, growing churches in Canada & around the world

Gideons International in Canada
501 Imperial Rd. North, Guelph ON N1H 7A2
Tel: 519-823-1140; *Fax:* 519-767-1913
Toll-Free: 888-482-4253
e-mail: info@gideons.ca; tcg@gideons.ca
URL: www.gideons.ca
Overview: A medium-sized international charitable organization founded in 1911
Chief Officer(s):
Paul Mercer, Executive Director
Finances: *Funding Sources:* Membership fees; voluntary donations
Membership: 1,000-4,999; *Member Profile:* Christian business & professional people
Activities: Sharing faith; Placing Bibles & New Testaments in institutions; Distributing New Testaments to selected groups
Description: The interdenominational lay association communicates God's Word in Canada & around the world.

Jack West Evangelistic Association
#401, 76 Rochampton Ave., St Catharines ON L2M 7W5
Overview: A small local charitable organization founded in 1966
Chief Officer(s):
Jack West, Contact
Membership: 100 individual
Activities: *Speaker Service:* Yes

Lighthouse Mission
669 Main St., Winnipeg MB R3B 1E3
Tel: 204-943-9669
Overview: A small local organization founded in 1911
Chief Officer(s):
Scott Miller, Contact
Activities: Operates a soup kitchen; distributes clothing to the needy
Description: Provides food and services to the needy in Winnipeg.

Living Bible Explorers (LBE)
600 Burnell St., Winnipeg MB R3G 2B7
Tel: 204-786-8667; *Fax:* 204-775-7525
Toll-Free: 866-786-8667
e-mail: lbe1@mts.net
URL: livingbibleexplorers.com
Overview: A small local charitable organization founded in 1969
Chief Officer(s):
Lainie Loiselle, Chair
George Hill, General Manager
Finances: *Annual Operating Budget:* $250,000-$500,000; *Funding Sources:* Provincial government; individual churches; foundations
Staff: 7 staff member(s); 100 volunteer(s)
Membership: 700 individual; *Member Profile:* Manitobans who have a tangible interest by working, volunteering or giving to the work
Activities: Boys & Girls Clubs; summer camps; weekend camps; weekly kids church; teens church; food distribution; weekly home visitation; annual banquet, Mar.; *Internships:* Yes; *Speaker Service:* Yes *Library:* Resource Library (Open to Public)
Description: To develop relationships with children & teens from inner city homes in an effort to evangelize them & to promote discipleship with a view to integrating them into the life & care of Bible-believing churches; *Member of:* Canadian Council of Christian Charities

Society for International Ministries (SIM Canada)
10 Huntingdale Blvd., Toronto ON M1W 2S5
Tel: 416-497-2424; *Fax:* 416-497-2444
Toll-Free: 800-294-6918
e-mail: info@sim.ca
URL: www.sim.ca
Overview: A small international organization founded in 1893
Chief Officer(s):
Gregg Bryce, Executive Director
Finances: *Annual Operating Budget:* $3 Million-$5 Million
Staff: 30 staff member(s)
Membership: 300
Description: To evangelize the unreached & minister to human need

Solbrekken Evangelistic Association of Canada
PO Box 44220, Stn. Garside, Edmonton AB T5V 1N6
Tel: 780-460-8444
e-mail: mswm@telusplanet.net
URL: www.mswm.org
Also Known As: Max Solbrekken World Mission
Overview: A small national charitable organization founded in 1961
Chief Officer(s):
Max Solbrekken, President
Donna Solbrekken, Secretary
Description: To promote the gospel; Affiliation(s): Europa for Kristus, Oslo, Norway

Friends

Canadian Friends Service Committee (CFSC) / Secours Quaker Canadien
60 Lowther Ave., Toronto ON M5R 1C7
Tel: 416-920-5213; *Fax:* 416-920-5214
e-mail: cfsc-office@quaker.ca
URL: www.cfsc.quaker.ca
Also Known As: Religious Society of Friends (Quakers)
Overview: A medium-sized national charitable organization founded in 1931
Chief Officer(s):
Jane Orion Smith, General Secretary
Svetlana MacDonald, Clerk
Finances: *Annual Operating Budget:* $500,000-$1.5 Million; *Funding Sources:* Individuals; meetings
Staff: 7 staff member(s); 40 volunteer(s)
Activities: Peace & social justice work; *Internships:* Yes; *Speaker Service:* Yes *Library:* Friends House Library (Open to Public)
Description: To unify & expand the concerns of Friends (Quakers); *Member of:* The Canadian Council of Churches; Kairos: Canadian Ecumenical Justice Initiatives; Project Ploughshares; Canadian Council for Refugees; War Resistors Support Campaign

Friends Historical Association (FHA)
Quaker Collection, Haverford College, 370 Lancaster Ave., Haverford PA 19041-1392 USA
Tel: 610-896-1161; *Fax:* 610-896-1102
e-mail: fha@haverford.edu
URL: www.haverford.edu/library/fha/fha.html
Overview: A medium-sized international charitable organization founded in 1873
Chief Officer(s):
Kenneth Carroll, President
Joelle Bertolet, Office Manager
Finances: *Annual Operating Budget:* Less than $50,000; *Funding Sources:* Membership dues; subscriptions; donations
Staff: 1 staff member(s); 21 volunteer(s)
Membership: 800; *Fees:* $15; *Member Profile:* Friends & interested historians; *Committees:* Membership; Publication; Historical Research; Finance; Curatorial; Development
Activities: Pilgrimages to historic Friends Meetings; lectures; *Rents Mailing List:* Yes
Description: To promote the study, preservation & publication of material relating to the history of the Religious Society of Friends; Affiliation(s): Conference of Quaker Historians & Archivists

Friends Historical Society - London (FHS)
c/o Friends House, 173 Euston Rd., London NW1 2BJ United Kingdom
Tel: 44 020 7663 1094; *Fax:* 44 020 7663 1001
Overview: A small international organization founded in 1903
Finances: *Funding Sources:* Membership fees
Membership: 400
Description: To encourage the study of Quaker history; *Member of:* Association of Denominational Historical Societies & Cognate Libraries

Hinduism

Hindu Society of Alberta
14225 - 133 Ave., Edmonton AB T5L 4W3
Tel: 780-451-5130; *Fax:* 780-451-5130
e-mail: webmaster@hindusociety.ab.ca
URL: www.hindusociety.ab.ca
Overview: A small provincial organization
Chief Officer(s):
Rajiv Ranjan, President
Membership: 500

Islam/Muslim

Ahmadiyya Movement in Islam (Canada) (AMI) / Mouvement Ahmadiyya en Islam (Canada)
Bai'tul Islam Mosque, 10610 Jane St., Maple ON L6A 3A2
Tel: 905-303-4000; *Fax:* 905-832-3220
e-mail: info@ahmadiyya.ca
URL: www.ahmadiyya.ca
Overview: A large international charitable organization founded in 1966
Chief Officer(s):
Syed Muhammad Aslam Daud, Secretary
Naseem Mahdi, President & Missionary-in-Charge
Finances: *Annual Operating Budget:* $500,000-$1.5 Million; *Funding Sources:* Contributions from members
Staff: 5 staff member(s); 30 volunteer(s)
Membership: 200 million+ followers in 170 countries
Activities: *Speaker Service:* Yes *Library:* Reference Library (Open to Public) by appointment
Description: Seeks to establish, maintain & conduct mosques & to carry on the teachings of the Holy Koran; to establish, maintain, organize & unify Muslims & particularly the members of Ahmadiyya Movement in Islam; to conduct public or private meetings of a religious nature & to establish, maintain & conduct classes for Islamic education & to employ instructors; to employ, send out & direct Muslim missionaries to preach the Holy Koran & its principles highlighting peaceful co-existence of adherents of different religions; *Member of:* Horizon Interfaith Council

Ahmadiyya Muslim Centre
525 Kylemore Ave., Winnipeg MB R3L 1B5
Tel: 204-475-2642; *Fax:* 204-452-2455
URL: www.ahmadiyya.ca
Overview: A small local organization founded in 1979
Membership: 1-99
Activities: *Library:* Yes

Association des Projets charitables Islamiques / Association of Islamic Charitable Projects
6691, av du Parc, Montréal QC H2V 4J1
Tél: 514-274-6194; *Téléc:* 514-274-0011
Aperçu: *Dimension:* petite; *Envergure:* locale
Membre(s) du bureau directeur:
Bassam Derbas, 514-945-1549
Maher Bissany, 514-892-2295
Description: Dénonce tout acte de terrorisme et promouvoit le support envers la communauté musulmane

Canadian Council of Muslim Women (CCMW) / Conseil canadien des femmes musulmanes
PO Box 154, Gananoque ON K7G 2T7

Tel: 613-383-2847
e-mail: info@ccmw.com
URL: www.ccmw.com

Overview: A medium-sized national organization founded in 1982
Chief Officer(s):
Alia Hogben, Executive Director, 613-382-2847
Razia Jaffer, President, 403-243-7995
razia_jaffer@shaw.ca
Nuzhat Jafri, Board Media & Communications, 416-487-8037
nuzhat.jafri@rogers.com
Finances: *Annual Operating Budget:* Less than $50,000; *Funding Sources:* Fundraising; public funds
Staff: 20 volunteer(s)
Membership: 100-499; *Fees:* Schedule available; *Member Profile:* Practising Muslim women
Activities: Affirmative Action/Women's Issues; Community Associations; Cultural Diversity; Education/Islamic; Gender Equality; Gender Issues; Immigrant Women; Inter-Faith Relations; International Islamic Affairs; Islam; Islamic Activities; Islamlc Information; Islamic Religious Matters; Minority Women's Issues; Mosques/Islamic Centres; Muslim Community; Muslims; Religion; Religious Activities; Religious Publications; Religious Tolerance; Status of Women; Women's Associations/Advocacy Groups; Women's Image Development; Women's Issues; *Speaker Service:* Yes
Description: To assist Muslim women in participating effectively in Canadian society & to promote mutual understanding with women of other faiths; our goals: Equity, Equality, Empowerment

Council on American-Islamic Relations Canada (CAIR-CAN)
PO Box 13219, Ottawa ON K2K 1X4
Tel: 613-254-9704; *Fax:* 613-254-9810
e-mail: canada@cair-net.org
URL: www.caircan.ca
Overview: A small international organization
Description: To educate Canadians & empower Canadian Muslims

International Development & Relief Foundation (IDRF)
#210, 2 Berkeley St., Toronto ON M5A 4J5
Tel: 416-497-0818; *Fax:* 416-497-0686
Toll-Free: 866-497-4373
e-mail: office@idrf.ca
URL: www.idrf.ca
Overview: A small international organization founded in 1985
Chief Officer(s):
Cassim Degani, MD, Chair
Finances: *Annual Operating Budget:* $500,000-$1.5 Million
Staff: 5 staff member(s)
Activities: Provided aid worth more than $8 million to people in 15 countries
Description: Dedicated to empowering the disadvantaged peoples of the world through emergency relief & participatory development programs based on the Islamic principles of human dignity, self-reliance & social justice; Affiliation(s): Canadian Council for International Cooperation

Islamic Affairs Council of Québec (IACQ)
1830, Thierry, Brossard QC J4W 2M8
Tel: 450-672-8027
e-mail: naseer@library.mcgill.ca
Overview: A small local organization founded in 1991
Chief Officer(s):
Syed Naseer, President
Finances: *Annual Operating Budget:* Less than $50,000
Staff: 5 volunteer(s)
Description: Seeks effective cooperation among Islamic organizations & Muslims of all nationalities or schools of thought; seeks better understanding of Islam; assists media by open discussion; takes part in multicultural activities

Islamic Association of Nova Scotia (IANS)
42 Leaman Dr., Dartmouth NS B3A 2K9
Tel: 902-469-9490
e-mail: info@islamnovascotia.ca
URL: www.islamnovascotia.ca
Previous Name: Islamic Association of the Maritimes
Overview: A small local organization
Chief Officer(s):
Mohsin Rashid, President
rashid@eastlink.ca
Mohammed Amin Aliyar, Secretary
Fees: $50 single; $100 family; $25 student

Islamic Association of Saskatchewan (Saskatoon)
222 Copland Cres., Saskatoon SK S7H 2Z5
Tel: 306-665-6424
e-mail: info@islamiccenter.sk.ca
URL: www.islamiccenter.sk.ca
Overview: A small provincial organization founded in 1968
Chief Officer(s):
Khalil-Ur Rehman, President
Shakeel Akhtar, Secretary
Activities: Operates Islamic Centre; represents Muslims; provides activities; responsible for Muslim Cemetery Affiliation(s): Multi-Faith Group; Saskatchewan Organization for Heritage Language; Saskatchewan Intercultural Association; Saskatchewan Forum for "Racialized" Canadians; Saskatchewan Council for International Cooperation

Islamic Foundation of Toronto
441 Nugget Ave., Toronto ON M1S 5E1
Tel: 416-321-0909; *Fax:* 416-321-1995
e-mail: info@islamicfoundation.ca
URL: www.islamicfoundation.ca
Also Known As: Nugget Mosque
Overview: A small local charitable organization founded in 1969
Chief Officer(s):
Shakil Akhter, Administrator
Zaib Mirza, Social Services Coordinator
Finances: *Annual Operating Budget:* $3 Million-$5 Million
Staff: 72 staff member(s)
Membership: 1,000-4,999; *Committees:* DAwah; Library; School Board; Social Services
Activities: Full time Islamic school, JK to Grade 10; part-time evening Islamic school; Arabic language centre for adults; Friday & Sunday schools; *Library:* Yes (Open to Public)

Islamic Information Centre (IIC)
312 Lisgar St., Ottawa ON K2P 0E8
Tel: 613-232-0210; *Fax:* 613-232-0210
e-mail: mail@islamottawa.com
URL: www.islamottawa.com
Also Known As: Daw'ah Centre
Overview: A small national organization founded in 1993
Chief Officer(s):
Sulaiman Khan, Director
Finances: *Annual Operating Budget:* $50,000-$100,000
Staff: 2 staff member(s); 10 volunteer(s)
Membership: 35; *Fees:* $50; *Committees:* Business; Conference; Daw'ah; Membership; Newsletter
Activities: *Speaker Service:* Yes *Library:* Islamic Information (Open to Public)
Member of: Muslim Community Council of Ottawa; Affiliation(s): Islam Care Centre

Islamic Information Foundation (IIF)
8 Laurel Lane, Halifax NS B3M 2P6
Tel: 902-445-2494; *Fax:* 902-445-2494
Overview: A small national charitable organization founded in 1981
Chief Officer(s):
Jamal Badawi, Chairperson
Finances: *Annual Operating Budget:* $100,000-$250,000; *Funding Sources:* Sale of religious material; donations
Staff: 4 volunteer(s)
Membership: 40 individuals
Activities: *Speaker Service:* Yes
Description: To promote better understanding of Islam among Muslims & Christians through information provided in print, audio & video forms & through lecture, seminars & interfaith dialogues

Islamic Propagation Centre International (Canada) (IPCI (Canada))
5761 Coopers Ave., Mississauga ON L4Z 1R9
Tel: 905-507-3323; *Fax:* 905-507-3323
e-mail: zsyed@ipci-canada.com
URL: www.ipci-canada.com
Also Known As: Jama Masjid Mississauga
Overview: A small local charitable organization founded in 1984
Finances: *Annual Operating Budget:* $50,000-$100,000
Staff: 2 staff member(s); 100 volunteer(s)
Membership: 100 student; 1,000 individual; *Fees:* $200 individual; *Committees:* Fundraising; Eid & Ramadhan; Executive
Activities: Congregation; marriages; family counselling; summer & evening school for kids; *Speaker Service:* Yes *Library:* IPC Office Library (Open to Public) by appointment
Description: Promoting harmony & understanding between Muslims & others

Manitoba Islamic Association (MIA)
247 Hazelwood Ave., Winnipeg MB R2M 4W1
Tel: 204-256-1347
e-mail: editorialboard@miaonline.org
URL: www.miaonline.org
Overview: A small provincial organization founded in 1976
Chief Officer(s):
G. Joundi, President
Khaled Al-Nahar, Office Manager
Fees: $30; *Member Profile:* Muslim persons in Manitoba who abide by the association's rules & regulations; Associate members are non-Muslim persons in Manitoba; *Committees:* Takaful Fund
Activities: Accepting applications for financial assistance, through the Takaful Fund; Providing funeral services to the Muslim community, through partnership with Cropo Funeral Services; Offering services for marriage; Conducting Sunday Qur'an classes for children & the MIA Al Nur Weekend Islamic School; Sponsoring the Al-Hamd Learning Center, which offers an Arabic & Islamic educational program for preschoolers

Muslim Association of Canada (MAC)
#332, 1568 Merivale Rd., Ottawa ON K2G 5Y7
Tel: 613-321-5000; *Fax:* 613-321-5001
e-mail: mac@macnet.ca
URL: www.macnet.ca
Overview: A medium-sized national organization
Activities: Schools & community centres; educational & other projects; youth projects; outreach
Description: Seeks to promote a balanced, constructive & integrated Islamic presence in Canada; operates in 11 Canadian cities

Muslim Association of New Brunswick (MANB)
1100 Rothesay Rd., Saint John NB E2H 2H8
Tel: 506-633-1675
e-mail: info@manb.ca
URL: www.manb.ca
Overview: A medium-sized provincial organization
Chief Officer(s):
Tareq Shah, President
Description: The Muslim Association of New Brunswick (MANB) is a Saint John-based, nonprofit organization found to present, serve and educate the Muslim community in the Saint John Area. MANB aims to; strengthen access to Islamic education, facilitate community outreach and interaction with other religious organizations and community groups, consolidate the social fabric of the community, and sustain Islamic work by encouraging and building endowments.

Muslim Community of Québec (MCQ) / Communauté musulmane du Québec
7445, av Chester, Montréal QC H4V 1M4
Tel: 514-484-2967; *Fax:* 514-484-3802
Also Known As: Mosque of Montréal
Overview: A small local organization founded in 1979
Chief Officer(s):
Mohammed M. Amin, Founder
Finances: *Annual Operating Budget:* $500,000-$1.5 Million
Membership: 500
Activities: *Speaker Service:* Yes
Description: To facilitate Muslim religious life

Muslim Education & Welfare Foundation of Canada (MEWFC)
2580 McGill St., Vancouver BC V5K 1H1
Tel: 604-255-9941; *Fax:* 604-255-9941
Also Known As: Almuassasatul Islamiyah Lit-Tarbiyah War-Riaayah (Canada)
Overview: A medium-sized national charitable organization founded in 1987
Chief Officer(s):
Nazih Hammad, Librarian, Jannat Bibi Library
Activities: *Library:* Jannat Bibi Library
Description: To provide for the educational, religious & welfare needs of the Muslim community

Muslim World League
#220, 2550 Argentia Rd., Mississauga ON L5N 5R1
Tel: 905-542-1050; *Fax:* 905-542-1054
e-mail: mwl@mwlcanada.org
URL: www.mwlcanada.org
Overview: A small international organization founded in 1985
Chief Officer(s):
Mohamad Khatib, Director
abusinan@yahoo.com
Member Profile: Muslims
Activities: *Rents Mailing List:* Yes *Library:* Yes (Open to Public)
Description: To serve the religious needs of Muslims in Canada.

Ottawa Muslim Community Circle (OMCC)
PO Box 29105, Stn. Barrhaven, Nepean ON K2J 4A9
Tel: 613-825-7059; *Fax:* 613-825-4667
e-mail: omcc@magma.ca
URL: www.magma.ca/~omcc
Overview: A small local organization founded in 1984
Chief Officer(s):
Mahmood Rasheed, President
Finances: *Annual Operating Budget:* Less than $50,000
Staff: 15 volunteer(s)

Membership: 400
Activities: Social services; seminars & conferences
Description: To foster unity among various Muslims; to promote better understanding of Muslims & Islam among Canadians of other faiths; to maintain cultural identity

Scarborough Muslim Association (SMA)
2665 Lawrence Ave. East, Toronto ON M1P 2S2
Tel: 416-750-2253; *Fax:* 416-750-1616
e-mail: info@smacanada.ca
URL: www.smacanada.ca
Overview: A small local organization
Chief Officer(s):
Yakub Hatia, President

Windsor Islamic Association (WIA)
c/o Windsor Mosque, 1320 Northwood Dr., Windsor ON N9W 1A4
Tel: 519-966-2355
e-mail: presidentwia@yahoo.com
URL: www.wiao.org
Overview: A small local organization founded in 1964
Chief Officer(s):
Ismail Peer, President
Hussein Khalaf, Vice-President
Abdelkader Tayebi, Secretary
Description: Serves a population of over 25,000 Muslims in the Windsor locality; Affiliation(s): World Muslim League

Judaism

Canadian Council for Reform Judaism
#301, 3845 Bathurst St., Toronto ON M3H 3N2
Tel: 416-630-0375; *Fax:* 416-630-5089
Toll-Free: 800-560-8242
e-mail: ccrj@urj.org
URL: urj.org/ccrj/
Previous Name: Canadian Council of Reform Rabbis
Overview: A medium-sized national organization
Chief Officer(s):
Sharon L. Sobel, Executive Director
Description: The CCRJ is the Canadian region of the Union for Reform Judasim Congregations, and serves as the umbrella organization for Reform Judaism in Canada, representing about 10,000 households in 26 affiliated congregations.; *Member of:* Union for Reform Judaism

Congregation Beth Israel - British Columbia
4350 Oak St., Vancouver BC V6H 2N7
Tel: 604-731-4161; *Fax:* 604-731-4989
e-mail: info@bethisrael.ca
URL: www.bethisrael.ca
Overview: A small local organization
Chief Officer(s):
Shannon Etkin, Executive Director
Description: Dedicated to the strengthening of all aspects of Jewish life, including worship and Torah study, religious, educational and social activities for all ages, and the observance of life cycle events.

National Council of Jewish Women of Canada
#118, 1588 Main St., Winnipeg MB R2V 1Y3
Tel: 204-339-9700; *Fax:* 204-334-3779
e-mail: info@ncjwc.org
URL: www.ncjwc.org
Overview: A medium-sized national charitable organization founded in 1897
Description: To further human welfare in the Jewish & general communities; to help fulfill unmet needs & to serve the individual & the community.; *Member of:* UNESCO Canadian Subcommission of the Status of Women; Jewish Women Against Domestic Violence; Coalition for Agunot Rights; Affiliation(s): International Council of Jewish Women

Orthodox Rabbinical Council of British Columbia
#401, 1037 West Broadway, Vancouver BC V6H 1E3
Tel: 604-731-1803; *Fax:* 604-731-1804
e-mail: info@bckosher.org
URL: www.bckosher.org
Also Known As: BC Kosher
Overview: A small provincial charitable organization founded in 1983
Finances: *Annual Operating Budget:* $100,000-$250,000
Staff: 4 staff member(s); 6 volunteer(s)
Membership: 1-99
Activities: *Speaker Service:* Yes
Description: Kashruth (kosher food) organization; kashruth symbol BCK

Shaare Zion Congregation
5575 Côte St. Luc Rd., Montréal QC H3X 2C9
Tel: 514-481-7727; *Fax:* 514-481-1219
e-mail: Webmaster@shaarezion.org
URL: www.shaarezion.org
Overview: A small local charitable organization
Chief Officer(s):
David Moscovitch, Executive Director
Gerry Silverman, President
Affiliation(s): United Synagogue of Conservative Judaism

Toronto Association of Synagogue & Temple Administrators
1445 Eglinton Ave. West, Toronto ON M6C 2E6
Tel: 416-783-6103; *Fax:* 416-783-9923
Overview: A small local organization
Chief Officer(s):
Barbara Berke, President
Finances: *Annual Operating Budget:* Less than $50,000
Membership: 12; *Fees:* $50; *Member Profile:* Executive directors of synagogues & temples

Vaad Harabonim (Orthodox Rabbinical Council)
3600 Bathurst St., Toronto ON M6A 2C9
Tel: 416-787-1631; *Fax:* 416-785-5378
Also Known As: Rabbinical Council of Ontario
Overview: A small provincial organization founded in 1982
Finances: *Annual Operating Budget:* Less than $50,000
Membership: 40
Description: To serve & guide the Jewish community

Lutheran

Canadian Lutheran World Relief (CLWR)
1080 Kingsbury Ave., Winnipeg MB R2P 1W5
Tel: 204-694-5602; *Fax:* 204-694-5460
Toll-Free: 800-661-2597
e-mail: clwr@clwr.mb.ca
URL: www.clwr.org
Overview: A large national charitable organization founded in 1946
Chief Officer(s):
Robert Granke, Executive Director
Finances: *Annual Operating Budget:* Greater than $5 Million; *Funding Sources:* Lutheran churches; Canadian International Development Agency; Province of Saskatchewan
Staff: 20 staff member(s)
Activities: We Care kits & quilts; study tours; *Speaker Service:* Yes
Description: To provide development programming in Africa, Asia, Latin America & the Middle East, to provide emergency relief in case of disaster, to enable sponsorships for refugee resettlement in Canada. Focus is on development, peace building, alternative approaches to trade, education & community building. Offices in Winnipeg, Toronto, Burnaby, Bolivia & Zambia; *Member of:* Canadian Council for International Cooperation; Manitoba Council for International Cooperation; Affiliation(s): Canadian Foodgrains Bank; Inter-Church Action

Estonian Evangelical Lutheran Church Consistory (EELK)
383 Jarvis St., Toronto ON M5B 2C7
Tel: 416-925-5465; *Fax:* 416-925-5688
e-mail: e.e.l.k@eelk.ee
URL: www.eelk.ee/EELCabroad.html
Overview: A small national organization founded in 1950
Chief Officer(s):
Jaan Kiivit, Dr.h.c., Archbishop
Membership: 7,200 + 13 churches
Description: Part of the 165 congregations in the EELC.; Affiliation(s): Lutheran World Federation; World Council of Churches

Evangelical Lutheran Church in Canada (ELCIC)
#302, 393 Portage Ave., Winnipeg MB R3B 3H6
Tel: 204-984-9150; *Fax:* 204-984-9185
Toll-Free: 888-786-6707
URL: www.elcic.ca
Overview: A medium-sized national charitable organization founded in 1986
Chief Officer(s):
Susan Johnson, Bishop
Donald Storch, Secretary
Ken Hartviksen, Treasurer
Finances: *Annual Operating Budget:* $1.5 Million-$3 Million; *Funding Sources:* Benevolence
Staff: 20 staff member(s)
Membership: 162,000 individuals; 613 congregations; *Member Profile:* Membership in one of our congregations
Description: To share the gospel of Jesus Christ with people in Canada & around the world through the proclamation of the Word, celebration of the sacraments, & through service in Christ's name; *Member of:* The Canadian Council of Churches; The Lutheran Council in Canada; The Lutheran World Federation; World Council of Churches

Lutheran Association of Missionaries & Pilots (LAMP)
4966 - 92 Ave. NW, Edmonton AB T6B 2V4
Tel: 780-466-8507; *Fax:* 780-466-6733
Toll-Free: 800-307-4036
e-mail: office@lampministry.org
URL: www.lampministry.org
Overview: A small international organization founded in 1970
Chief Officer(s):
Ron Ludke, Executive Director
Finances: *Annual Operating Budget:* $500,000-$1.5 Million
Staff: 300+ volunteer(s)
Activities: *Speaker Service:* Yes *Library:* Yes (Open to Public)
Description: A cross-cultural ministry sharing Jesus Christ with God's people in remote areas of Canada; Affiliation(s): Lutheran Church Canada; Evangelical Lutheran Church in Canada

Lutheran Bible Translators of Canada Inc. (LBTC)
PO Box 934, Kitchener ON N2G 4E3
Tel: 519-742-3361; *Fax:* 519-742-5989
Toll-Free: 866-518-7071
e-mail: info@lbtc.ca
URL: www.lbtc.ca
Overview: A small international charitable organization founded in 1974
Finances: *Annual Operating Budget:* $250,000-$500,000
Staff: 5 staff member(s)
Membership: 1-99
Activities: *Speaker Service:* Yes
Description: To bring people to faith in Jesus Christ through Bible translations & literacy work; Affiliation(s): Canadian Council of Christian Charities

Mennonites

Calgary Mennonite Centre for Newcomers
#125, 920 - 36th St. NE, Calgary AB T2A 6L8
Tel: 403-569-3325; *Fax:* 403-248-5041
e-mail: newcomer@cmcn.ab.ca
URL: www.cmcn.ab.ca
Overview: A small local organization founded in 1988
Chief Officer(s):
Dale Taylor, Executive Director
Description: To assist refugees & immigrants arriving in Calgary in meeting their settlement needs

Canadian Conference of Mennonite Brethren Churches
1310 Taylor Ave., Winnipeg MB R3M 3Z6
Tel: 204-669-6575; *Fax:* 204-654-1865
Toll-Free: 888-669-6575
URL: www.mbconf.ca
Overview: A medium-sized national organization founded in 1945
Chief Officer(s):
David Wiebe, Executive Director
Finances: *Funding Sources:* Donations
Staff: 19 staff member(s)
Membership: 31,264; *Committees:* Mennonite Central Committee; Mennonite Disaster Service; Manitoba Missions/Service
Activities: *Library:* Centre for M.B. Studies (Open to Public)
Description: To glorify God, to nurture & equip members to live the Christian life, & to mobilize them for ministry

Evangelical Mennonite Conference (EMC)
440 Main St., Steinbach MB R5G 1Z5
Tel: 204-326-6401; *Fax:* 204-326-1613
e-mail: messenger@emconf.ca
URL: www.emconf.ca
Overview: A medium-sized national charitable organization founded in 1812
Chief Officer(s):
Tim Dyck, General Secretary
Finances: *Annual Operating Budget:* $1.5 Million-$3 Million; *Funding Sources:* Donations
Membership: 7,300
Activities: *Library:* EMC Archives
Description: To encourage local churches to work together on missions in Canada & around the world

Evangelical Mennonite Mission Conference (EMMC)
PO Box 52059, Stn. Niakwa, Winnipeg MB R2M 5P9
Tel: 204-253-7929; *Fax:* 204-256-7384
e-mail: info@emmc.ca
URL: www.emmc.ca
Previous Name: Rudnerweider Mennonite Church
Overview: A medium-sized national charitable organization founded in 1959

Chief Officer(s):
Jake Friesen, Executive Director & Moderator
Al Kehler, Conference Pastor
al@emmc.ca
Gin Thiessen, Secretary
Henry Derksen, Treasurer
Activities: *Library:* EMMC Resource Centre; EMMC Media Library
Affiliation(s): Mennonite Central Committee of Canada; Mennonite World Conference; Mennonite Foundation of Canada; Mennonite Foundation of Canada

MBMS International (MBMSI) / Mennonite Brethren Mission & Service International
(Manitoba/Ontario/Sask.), 1310 Taylor Ave., Winnipeg MB R3M 3Z6
Tel: 204-478-2690; *Fax:* 204-654-1865
Toll-Free: 888-866-6267
e-mail: winnipeg@mbmsi.org
URL: www.mbmsi.org
Also Known As: Board of Missions & Services of the Mennonite Brethren Churches of North America
Overview: A medium-sized local charitable organization founded in 1900
Chief Officer(s):
Randy Friesen, General Director
Finances: *Annual Operating Budget:* Greater than $5 Million; *Funding Sources:* Voluntary contributions; grants
Staff: 2 staff member(s)
Activities: Cross-cultural mission agency of Mennonite Brethren churches in Canada & the US; *Internships:* Yes; *Speaker Service:* Yes
Description: To make disciples & plant churches globally through church planting & envangelism, discipleship & leadership training & social ministry; *Member of:* Evangelical Fellowship of Mission Agencies

Mennonite Central Committee Canada (MCCC)
134 Plaza Dr., Winnipeg MB
Tel: 204-261-6381; *Fax:* 204-269-9875
Toll-Free: 888-622-6337
e-mail: canada@mennonitecc.ca
URL: www.mcc.org/canada
Overview: A large international charitable organization founded in 1920
Description: Mennonite Central Committee Canada (MCCC) is the Canadian arm of Mennonite Central Committee (MCC). MCC is a relief and development service agency. As the name indicates, the organization reflects joint ownership by various Mennonite and Brethren in Christ Churches in Canada and the United States. MCC Canada's core values are to promote relief, development, and peace; *Member of:* Mennonite Central Committee

Mennonite Church Canada (MC Canada)
600 Shaftesbury Blvd., Winnipeg MB R3P 0M4
Tel: 204-888-6781; *Fax:* 204-831-5675
Toll-Free: 866-888-6785
e-mail: office@mennonitechurch.ca; resources@mennonitechurch.ca
URL: www.mennonitechurch.ca
Also Known As: Conference of Mennonites in Canada
Overview: A medium-sized national charitable organization founded in 1903
Chief Officer(s):
Robert J. Suderman, General Secretary
rjsuderman@mennonitechurch.ca
Finances: *Funding Sources:* Donations
Staff: 40 staff member(s)
Membership: 33,000 baptized believers in 225 congregations & 5 area conferences
Activities: *Library:* Resource Centre
Description: To form a people of God; To become a global church; To grow leaders

Mennonite Economic Development Associates Canada
#I-106, 155 Frobisher Dr., Waterloo ON N2V 2E4
Tel: 519-725-1633; *Fax:* 519-725-9083
Toll-Free: 800-665-7026
e-mail: meda@meda.org
URL: www.meda.org
Also Known As: MEDA Canada
Overview: A medium-sized international charitable organization founded in 1953
Chief Officer(s):
Allan Sauder, President
Finances: *Annual Operating Budget:* $1.5 Million-$3 Million
Membership: 3,000 Canada & US
Activities: *Library:* Yes by appointment
Description: An association of persons committed to the nurture & expression of their Christian faith in a business setting; to enable members to integrate biblical values & business principles in their daily lives & to address the needs of the disadvantaged through programs of economic development

Mennonite Foundation of Canada (MFC)
#12, 1325 Markham Rd., Winnipeg MB R3T 4J6
Tel: 204-488-1985; *Fax:* 204-488-1986
Toll-Free: 800-772-3257
e-mail: contact@mennofoundation.ca
URL: www.mennofoundation.ca
Overview: A medium-sized national charitable organization founded in 1973
Chief Officer(s):
Erwin Warkentin, General Manager
Lloyd Plett, Board Chair
Finances: *Annual Operating Budget:* $500,000-$1.5 Million
Staff: 12 staff member(s)
Membership: 24; *Member Profile:* Representatives of 7 conferences
Activities: *Speaker Service:* Yes *Library:* Yes (Open to Public)
Description: To accumulate, manage & distribute financial resources exclusively for charitable purposes; to provide stewardship education & service from an Anabaptist perspective; Affiliation(s): Mennonite Church Canada; Evangelical Mennonite Mission Conference; Mennonite Church Eastern Canada; Northwest Mennonite Conference; Evangelical Mennonite Conference; Chortitzer Mennonite Conference; Evangelical Missionary Church of Canada

Northwest Mennonite Conference
PO Box 1316, 2025 - 20 Ave., Didsbury AB T0M 0W0
Tel: 403-335-9805; *Fax:* 403-335-9548
URL: www.nwmc.ca
Overview: A medium-sized local organization
Chief Officer(s):
Carol Gelleny, Contact
Membership: 14 congregations; *Committees:* Congregational Ministries; Congregational Leadership; Missions & Service; Stewardship
Member of: Mennonite Church North America

Methodists

The Bible Holiness Movement / Mouvement de sainteté biblique
PO Box 223, Stn. A, Vancouver BC V6C 2M3
Tel: 250-492-3376
URL: www.bible-holiness-movement.com
Previous Name: The Bible Holiness Mission
Overview: A medium-sized international charitable organization founded in 1949
Chief Officer(s):
Wesley H. Wakefield, Bishop-General
Finances: *Annual Operating Budget:* $100,000-$250,000; *Funding Sources:* Unsolicited gifts from Christian believers
Staff: 16 staff member(s); 6 volunteer(s)
Membership: 93,658 worldwide in 89 countries; 954 Canadian; *Fees:* None
Activities: *Internships:* Yes; *Speaker Service:* Yes *Library:* Yes by appointment
Description: To emphasize the original Methodist faith of salvation & scriptural holiness, with principles of discipline, non-conformity, & non-resistance, & to administer overseas indigenous missionary centres in West Africa, the Philippines, East Africa & the West Indies; South Korea, India; *Member of:* Christian Holiness Partnership; National Black Evangelical Association; Anti-Slavery International; Affiliation(s): Religious Freedom of Council of Christian Minorities; Christians Concerned for Racial Equality

Free Methodist Church in Canada (FMCIC) / Église méthodiste libre du Canada
4315 Village Centre Ct., Mississauga ON L4Z 1S2
Tel: 905-848-2600; *Fax:* 905-848-2603
e-mail: ministrycentre@fmc-canada.org
URL: www.fmc-canada.org
Overview: A medium-sized national organization founded in 1880
Chief Officer(s):
Daniel Sheffield, Director, Global & Intercultural Ministries
Jared Siebert, Director, Growth Ministries
Mark Molczanski, Director, Administrative Services
Keith A. Elford
Alan Retzman, Director, Personnel
retzmana@fmc-canada.org
Finances: *Annual Operating Budget:* $1.5 Million-$3 Million
Staff: 11 staff member(s)
Membership: 12,000+ attendees at 144 churches
Activities: *Internships:* Yes; *Speaker Service:* Yes
Description: To make known to people everywhere God's call to wholeness through forgiveness & holiness in Jesus Christ & to invite into membership & to equip for ministry all who respond in faith; to see healthy churches within the reach of all people in Canada & beyond.; *Member of:* Free Methodist World Conference; Affiliation(s): Evangelical Fellowship of Canada; Canadian Council of Christian Charities; World Relief Canada

Mormonism

Church of Jesus Christ of Latter-day Saints (Mormons)
c/o Toronto Ontario Temple, 10060 Bramalea Rd., Brampton ON L6R 1A1
Tel: 905-799-1122
URL: www.lds.org
Overview: A medium-sized national organization founded in 1830
Membership: 178,000 members + 324 congregations in Canada
Activities: *Speaker Service:* Yes *Library:* Family History Library by appointment
Description: Brampton Church.

Pentecostal

Apostolic Church of Pentecost of Canada Inc. (ACOP) / Église apostolique de Pentecôte du Canada inc.
International Office, #119, 2340 Pegasus Way NE, Calgary AB T2E 8M5
Tel: 403-273-5777; *Fax:* 403-273-8102
e-mail: acop@acop.ca
URL: www.acop.ca
Overview: A small national licensing charitable organization founded in 1921
Wes Mills, President & National Director
Finances: *Annual Operating Budget:* $1.5 Million-$3 Million; *Funding Sources:* Donations
Staff: 30 staff member(s)
Membership: 155 affiliated churches + 436 members; *Fees:* Varies
Activities: *Internships:* Yes; *Speaker Service:* Yes *Library:* Yes by appointment
Description: To provide fellowship, encouragement & accountability in the proclamation of the Gospel of Jesus Christ by the Power of the Holy Spirit; Affiliation(s): Evangelical Fellowship of Canada

Church of God of Prophecy in Canada
Eastern Canada Head Office, 5145 Tomken Rd., Mississauga ON L4W 1P1
Tel: 905-625-1278; *Fax:* 905-625-1316
e-mail: info@cogop.ca
URL: www.cogop.ca
Overview: A medium-sized national charitable organization
Finances: *Annual Operating Budget:* $100,000-$250,000
Staff: 3 staff member(s)
Membership: 31 churches
Activities: *Internships:* Yes; *Speaker Service:* Yes
Description: The Church of God of Prophecy has its roots in the Holiness/Pentecostal tradition and has felt a special burden to call attention to the principle of unity in the body of Christ, while faithfully proclaiming the gospel of Jesus Christ before a watching world.

The Pentecostal Assemblies of Canada (PAOC) / Les Assemblées de la Pentecôte du Canada
2450 Milltower Ct., Mississauga ON L5N 5Z6
Tel: 905-542-7400; *Fax:* 905-542-7313
e-mail: info@paoc.org
URL: www.paoc.org
Overview: A large national charitable organization founded in 1919
Chief Officer(s):
David Hazzard, Assistant Superintendent, Fellowship Services
David Wells, General Superintendent
Murray Cornelius, Assistant Superintendent, International Missions
George Werner, Divisional Director, Missions in Canada
Finances: *Annual Operating Budget:* Greater than $5 Million; *Funding Sources:* Local churches; individuals
Staff: 50 staff member(s)
Membership: 1,100 churches, 3,500 pastors representing 235,000 parishoners; *Committees:* General Executive; Administrative; Overseas Missions
Activities: Task Force; Work Force; Volunteers in Mission; Short-Term Missions; Volunteers in Special Assignment; ERDO (Emergency Relief & Development Overseas); Child Care Plus; *Library:* The PAOC Archives (Open to Public) by appointment
Description: To make disciples everywhere by the proclamation & practice of the gospel of Christ in the power of the Holy Spirit; to establish local congregations & to train spiritual leaders;

Affiliation(s): World Pentecost; Pentecostal/Charismatic Churches of North America; Pentecostal World Fellowship; World Assemblies of God Fellowship; Focus on the Family; Canadian Foodgrains Bank; Pentecostal European Mission; Seeds International; VisionLEDD; Canadian Council of Christian Charities; Every Home for Christ; Evangelical Missiological Society; Evangelical Fellowship of Canada; Canadian Children's Ministries Network; Canadian Bible Society; Family Life Ministries; Society of Pentecostal Studies

The Pentecostal Assemblies of Newfoundland & Labrador (PAON)
PO Box 8895, Stn. A, 57 Thorburn Rd., St. John's NL A1B 3T2
Tel: 709-753-6314; *Fax:* 709-753-4945
e-mail: info@paonl.ca
URL: www.paonl.ca
Overview: A medium-sized provincial charitable organization founded in 1911
Chief Officer(s):
H. Paul Foster, General Superintendent
Finances: *Annual Operating Budget:* $1.5 Million-$3 Million
Membership: 40,000
Activities: *Internships:* Yes; *Speaker Service:* Yes *Library:* Yes by appointment
Description: To promote evangelism, world missions, famine relief, & education; Affiliation(s): Pentecostal Fellowship of North America

Protestants

Grand Orange Lodge of Canada
94 Sheppard Ave. West, Toronto ON M2N 1M5
Tel: 416-223-1690; *Fax:* 416-223-1324
Toll-Free: 800-565-6248
e-mail: secretary@grandorangelodge.ca
URL: www.grandorangelodge.ca
Also Known As: Loyal Orange Association
Previous Name: The Grand Orange Lodge of British America
Overview: A large national organization founded in 1830
Chief Officer(s):
John Chalmers, Grand Secretary
Finances: *Annual Operating Budget:* Less than $50,000; *Funding Sources:* Membership dues
Staff: 8 staff member(s)
Membership: 100,000; *Fees:* Schedule available; *Member Profile:* Protestant faith
Activities: *Awareness Events:* Annual Golf Tournament
Description: To encourage its members to actively participate in the Protestant church of their choice; to actively support the Canadian system of government; to anticipate legislation & its impact on the civil & religious liberties of all Canadians; to provide social activities which will enrich the lives of its members; to participate in benevolent activities which will enrich our communities & our country; *Member of:* Imperial Orange Council of the World

Operation Mobilization Canada (OM)
84 West St., Port Colborne ON L3K 4C8
Tel: 905-835-2546; *Fax:* 905-835-2533
Toll-Free: 877-487-7777
e-mail: info@cdn.om.org
URL: www.omcanada.org
Overview: A small international charitable organization founded in 1966
Chief Officer(s):
Harvey Thiessen, Executive Director
Finances: *Annual Operating Budget:* $1.5 Million-$3 Million
Staff: 25 staff member(s)
Activities: *Speaker Service:* Yes *Library:* Yes
Description: Missionary training movement operating in 80 countries with 6,000 people in program every year; mobilizes & trains young Protestant believers for mission fields.; *Member of:* Evangelical Fellowship of Canada; Canadian Council of Christian Charities

Taoism

Fung Loy Kok Institute of Taoism
1376 Bathurst St., 2nd Fl., Toronto ON M5R 3J1
Tel: 416-656-2110; *Fax:* 416-654-3937
e-mail: fungloykok@ttcs.org
Overview: A small international organization

Unitarian

Canadian Unitarian Council (CUC) / Conseil unitarien du Canada
#018, 1179A King St. West, Toronto ON M6K 3C5
Tel: 416-489-4121; *Fax:* 416-489-9010
e-mail: info@cuc.ca
URL: www.cuc.ca
Also Known As: Unitarian Church
Overview: A medium-sized national charitable organization founded in 1961
Chief Officer(s):
Philip Strapp, Financial Administrator, 416-489-4121
phil@cuc.ca
Mary Bennett, Executive Director, 416-489-4121
mary@cuc.ca
Finances: *Annual Operating Budget:* $250,000-$500,000; *Funding Sources:* Donations; membership dues
Staff: 6 staff member(s); 20 volunteer(s)
Membership: 50 institutional + 25 individual; *Fees:* $80 individual; congregations - assessment per member; *Committees:* Lay & Chaplaincy; Social Responsibility
Activities: *Library:* CUC Library by appointment
Description: To enhance, nurture & promote Unitarian & Universalist religion in Canada; to provide support for religious exploration, spiritual growth & social responsibility; Affiliation(s): International Association for Religious Freedom; International Council of Unitarians & Universalists

First Unitarian Congregation of Toronto
175 St.Clair Ave. West, Toronto ON M4V 1P7
Tel: 416-924-9654; *Fax:* 416-924-9655
e-mail: administrator@firstunitariantoronto.org
URL: www.firstunitariantoronto.org
Overview: A small national charitable organization founded in 1845
Chief Officer(s):
Shawn Newton, Minister
Finances: *Annual Operating Budget:* $250,000-$500,000
Staff: 9 staff member(s); 25 volunteer(s)
Membership: 306 individual
Activities: *Internships:* Yes *Library:* Yes by appointment
Description: To serve the religious needs of those who embrace Unitarian Universalist principles, who respect the free exercise of private judgment in all matters of belief & who live in the Metropolitan Toronto area; *Member of:* Canadian Unitarian Council

USC Canada
#705, 56 Sparks St., Ottawa ON K1P 5B1
Tel: 613-234-6827; *Fax:* 613-234-6842
Toll-Free: 800-565-6872
e-mail: info@usc-canada.org
URL: www.usc-canada.org
Also Known As: Unitarian Service Committee of Canada
Overview: A medium-sized international charitable organization founded in 1945
Chief Officer(s):
Jackie Boisvenue, Media Relations Officer
Lise Latrémouille, Director, International Programs
Ron Cross, Communications Officer
Francine Longtin, Director, Finance and Administration
Susan Walsh, Executive Director
Finances: *Annual Operating Budget:* Greater than $5 Million; *Funding Sources:* Support from the general public; bequests; foundations & corporations; investment income; government
Staff: 22 staff member(s)
Membership: 1,000; *Member Profile:* Membership is offered to individuals supporting USC through volunteer or financial means; *Committees:* Finance; Executive; Programs
Activities: Communications/Media Program; Development Education Program to raise awareness about development issues & their impact on our lives in Canada; Fundraising & Volunteer Program; Overseas Program to work in partnership with people in the developing world to build self-reliant communities; *Speaker Service:* Yes; *Rents Mailing List:* Yes *Library:* Yes by appointment
Description: Committed to enhancing human development through an international partnership of people linked in the challenge to reduce poverty; *Member of:* Canadian Council for International Cooperation

United Church of Christ

Affirm United/S'affirmer ensemble / S'affirmer ensemble/Affirm United
PO Box 57057, Somerset Stn, Ottawa ON K1R 1A1
e-mail: affirmunited@affirmunited.ca
URL: www.affirmunited.ca
Overview: A medium-sized national organization founded in 1982
Chief Officer(s):
Read Sherman, Communications Coordinator
Finances: *Annual Operating Budget:* Less than $50,000
Staff: 20 volunteer(s)
Membership: 500 individual; *Fees:* $40 individual/household; $100 institutional
Activities: *Speaker Service:* Yes
Description: To affirm gays, lesbian, bisexual & transgender people & their friends, within The United Church of Canada; to provide a network of supports among affirming ministries & regional groups; to act as a point of contact for individuals; to speak to the church in a united fashion encouraging it to act prophetically & pastorally both within & beyond the church structure; Affiliation(s): United Church of Canada

Boys & Girls Clubs of Alberta
J. Percy Page Centre, 11759 Groat Rd., Edmonton AB T5M 3K6
Tel: 780-415-1734; *Fax:* 780-415-1737
e-mail: info@bgcalberta.com
URL: www.bgcalberta.com
Overview: A medium-sized provincial organization
Chief Officer(s):
Jane Hirst, Regional Executive Director
jhirst@bgcalberta.com
Finances: *Annual Operating Budget:* $100,000-$250,000
Staff: 2 staff member(s)
Membership: 15,000-49,999
Description: To provide a safe, supportive place where children & youth can experience new opportunities, overcome barriers, build positive relationships & develop confidence & skills for life; *Member of:* Boys & Girls Clubs of Canada

KAIROS: Canadian Ecumenical Justice Initiatives / Initiatives canadiennes oecuméniques pour la justice
#200, 310 Dupont St., Toronto ON M5R 1V9
Tel: 416-463-5312; *Fax:* 416-463-5569
Toll-Free: 877-403-8933
e-mail: info@kairoscanada.org
URL: www.kairoscanada.org
Previous Name: Ecumenical Coalition for Economic Justice; GATT-Fly
Overview: A small national organization founded in 1973
Chief Officer(s):
Mary Corkery, Executive Director
Adiat Junaid, Communications Coordinator
Finances: *Annual Operating Budget:* $100,000-$250,000
Staff: 4 staff member(s)
Fees: $100
Activities: *Speaker Service:* Yes
Description: To undertake a program of research & action with churches & popular groups emphasizing coalition-building & social transformation; five churches have participated in the Coalition since its inception: the Anglican Church of Canada, the Canadian Conference of Catholic Bishops, the Evangelical Lutheran Church in Canada, the Presbyterian Church in Canada, the United Church of Canada; *Member of:* Action Canada Network; Affiliation(s): Canadian Council of Churches

Manitoba CGIT Association
PO Box 52073, Winnipeg MB R2M 5P9
Tel: 204-254-2378
e-mail: cgit@cgitmanitoba.ca
Also Known As: Canadian Girls in Training - Manitoba
Previous Name: National CGIT Association - Manitoba & Northwestern Ontario
Overview: A small local organization

Maritime Regional CGIT Committee
PO Box 383, Pictou NS B0K 1H0
Tel: 902-485-4011
e-mail: g.cmacdonald@ns.sympatico.ca
Also Known As: Canadian Girls in Training - Maritimes
Previous Name: National CGIT Association - Maritime Regional Committee
Overview: A small local organization
Chief Officer(s):
Chris MacDonald, Contact

National Alliance of Covenanting Congregations (NACC)
489 East Osborne Rd., North Vancouver BC V7N 1M4
Tel: 604-987-9876; *Fax:* 604-987-9835
e-mail: geoff@unitedrenewal.org
URL: www.unitedrenewal.org
Overview: A large national charitable organization founded in 1991
Chief Officer(s):
Geoff Wilkins, Chair
Finances: *Annual Operating Budget:* $50,000-$100,000; *Funding Sources:* Donations
Staff: 1 volunteer(s)
Membership: 100 congregations; 15,000 members; *Member Profile:* All congregational members; spectrum of congregations rural to urban, coast to coast
Activities: *Speaker Service:* Yes *Library:* NACC Resources/Yoke Study Centre (Open to Public)
Description: To offer support & fellowship to United Churches wishing to uphold traditional theology & to work for reform &

renewal in the United Church of Canada; Affiliation(s): United Church of Canada

Ontario CGIT Association

PO Box 371, Norwich ON N0J 1P0
Tel: 519-863-6760; *Fax:* 519-863-6760
e-mail: ontario@cgit.ca
URL: www.cgit.ca
Also Known As: Canadian Girls in Training - Ontario
Previous Name: National CGIT Association - Ontario
Overview: A small provincial charitable organization founded in 1915
Finances: *Annual Operating Budget:* Less than $50,000
Staff: 1 staff member(s); 150 volunteer(s)
Membership: 350; *Member Profile:* Teen girls & adult women; *Committees:* Leadership Training; Camps; Publicity & Promotion
Activities: Leadership training weekend; camp council leadership training for senior girls; Red Maple Leaf Program Affiliation(s): The United Church of Canada; The Presbyterian Church in Canada

Provincial CGIT Board of BC

c/o J. Grinnell, 13780 Hill Rd., Ladysmith BC V9G 1G7
Tel: 250-245-4016
e-mail: grinncon@nanaimo.ark.com
Also Known As: Canadian Girls in Training - BC
Previous Name: National CGIT Association - BC Provincial Board
Overview: A small provincial organization

Saskatchewan CGIT Committee

3624 - 28th Ave., Regina SK S4S 2N6
e-mail: saskcgit@accesscomm.ca
URL: www.cgit.ca/saskatchewan
Also Known As: Canadian Girls in Training - Saskatchewan
Previous Name: National CGIT Association - Saskatchewan Committee
Overview: A small provincial organization
Chief Officer(s):
Alice Monks, Chair

SECTION 15
SPORTS

Associations & Organizations

Archery

Alberta Bowhunters Association (ABA)
c/o Mark Walliser, #8, 7957 - 49 Ave., Red Deer AB T4P 2V5
URL: www.bowhunters.ca
Brent Watson, President
Gun Lemke, Secretary

Archers Association of Nova Scotia (AANS)
NS
e-mail: president@aans.ca
URL: www.aans.ca
Lindsey Poehl, President

Archery Association of New Brunswick (AANB)
1003 Duckcove Lane, Saint John NB E2M 3G3
Tel: 506-617-5766
e-mail: contact@archerynb.ca
URL: www.archerynb.ca
Robert McIntyre, Provincial President

Fédération de tir à l'arc du Québec (FTAQ)
CP 1000, Succ. M, 4545, av Pierre-de Coubertin, Montréal QC H1V 3R2
Tél: 514-252-3054; *Téléc:* 514-252-3165
Courriel: ftaq@ftaq.qc.ca
URL: www.ftaq.qc.ca
Gabriela Cosovan, Directrice technique

Federation of Canadian Archers Inc. (FCA) / Fédération canadienne des archers inc.
#108, 2255 St. Laurent Blvd., Ottawa ON K1G 4K3
Tel: 613-260-2113; *Fax:* 613-260-2114
e-mail: information@fca.ca
URL: www.fca.ca
Kathleen Millar, Executive Director
Roger Murray, President

International Archery Federation (IAF) / Fédération internationale de tir à l'arc (FITA)
Maison du Sport International, Avenue de Rhodanie 54, Lausanne 1007 Switzerland
Tel: 41-21-614-3050; *Fax:* 41-21-614-3055
e-mail: info@archery.org
URL: www.archery.org
Affiliation(s): Federation of Canadian Archers Inc.
Ugur Erdener, President
Tom Dielen, Secretary General

Moncton Archers & Bowhunters Association
99 West Lane, Coal Branch NB E4T 4K1
Tel: 506-785-9806
e-mail: spencers@nb.sympatico.ca
Affiliation(s): New Brunswick Archery Association; Canadian Archery Association
Charles Spencer, President

Ontario Association of Archers Inc. (OAA)
PO Box 45, Stn. Caledon Village, Caledon ON L7K 3L3
Tel: 519-927-3256; *Fax:* 519-927-9137
e-mail: info@oaa-archery.on.ca
URL: www.oaa-archery.on.ca
Adam Thomas, President
Cathy Fischer, Secretary

Saskatchewan Archery Association (SAA)
PO Box 5, RR#2, Site 6, Craven SK SOG 0W0
Tel: 306-775-0385
e-mail: rlakeman.coram@sasktel.net
URL: www.saskarchery.com
Robert Lakeman, President

Athletics

Association régionale du sport collégial de l'Ile de Montréal (ARSCIM)
a/s FQSE, CP 1000, Succ. M, 4545, av Pierre-de-Coubertin, Montréal QC H1V 3R2
Tél: 514-252-3300; *Téléc:* 514-254-3292
Courriel: infos@arscim.qc.ca
URL: www.arscim.qc.ca
Robert Dussault, Directeur général

Association régionale du sport étudiant de l'Abitibi-Témiscamingue (ARSEAT)
375, ave. Centrale, Val-d'Or QC J9P 1P4
Tél: 819-825-2047; *Téléc:* 819-825-0125
Ligne sans frais: 866-626-2047
Courriel: mlangelier@ulsat.qc.ca
URL: www.ulsat.qc.ca/lsat/pages/sportetudiant.php
Affiliation(s): Fédération québécoise du sport étudiant
Pierre Boulerice, Président
Serge Hurtubise, Vice-président

Association régionale du sport étudiant de la Côte-Nord (ARSECN)
110, rue Comeau, Sept-Iles QC G4R 1J4
Tél: 418-968-3731; *Téléc:* 418-968-4033
Ligne sans frais: 866-968-3731
Courriel: sport.etudiant.cn@globetrotter.net
Yvette Cyr, Directrice

Association régionale du sport étudiant de la Mauricie (ARSEM)
260, rue Dessureault, Trois-Rivières QC G8T 9T9
Tél: 819-693-5805; *Téléc:* 819-693-1189
URL: www.arsem.qc.ca
Micheline Guillemette, Directrice générale

Association régionale du sport étudiant de Laval
#221, 3235, St-Martin Est, Laval QC H7E 5G8
Tél: 450-664-1917; *Téléc:* 450-664-7832
Courriel: info@sportslaval.qc.ca
URL: www.sportslaval.qc.ca
Richard Courteau, Directeur général

Association régionale du sport étudiant de Québec et Chaudière-Appalaches (ARSEQCA)
2450, ch Ste-Foy, Québec QC G1V 1T2
Tél: 418-657-7678; *Téléc:* 418-657-1367
Courriel: mleclerc@sportetudiant.qc.ca
URL: www.sportetudiant.qc.ca
Daniel Veilleux, Directeur général

Association régionale du sport étudiant du Richelieu (ARSER)
École secondaire Gérard-Filion, 1330, boul. Curé-Poirier Ouest, Longueuil QC J4K 2G8
Tél: 450-463-4055; *Téléc:* 450-463-4229
Courriel: sport_etudiant@csmv.qc.ca
URL: www.arser.qc.ca/site/index.html
Sylvie Cornellier, Directrice générale

Association régionale du sport étudiant Lac Saint-Louis
2900, rue Lake, Dollard-des-Ormeaux QC H9B 2P1
Tél: 514-855-4230; *Téléc:* 514-685-4643
Courriel: administration@arselsl.qc.ca
URL: www.arselsl.qc.ca
Serge Bélanger, Directeur général

Association régionale du sport étudiant Laurentides-Lanaudière
430, boul. Arthur-Sauvé, Saint-Eustache QC J7R 6V6
Tél: 450-419-8786; *Téléc:* 450-419-8892
Courriel: ginette.laforest@cssmi.qc.ca
URL: www7.cssmi.qc.ca/sportell
Jacinthe Lussier, Directrice générale

Association régionale du sport scolaire / Greater Montreal Athletic Association
#101, 5925, av Monkland, Montréal QC H4A 1G7
Tel: 514-482-8555; *Fax:* 514-487-0121
e-mail: gmaa@gmaa.ca
URL: www.gmaa.ca
Don McEwen, Executive Director

Athletics Alberta
Percy Page Centre, 11759 Groat Rd., Edmonton AB T5M 3K6
Tel: 780-427-8792; *Fax:* 780-427-8899
e-mail: info@athleticsalberta.com
URL: www.athleticsalberta.com
Peter Ogilvie, Executive Director
Sheryl Mack, Office Manager

Athletics Manitoba
#214, 200 Main St., Winnipeg MB R3C 4M2
Tel: 204-925-5743; *Fax:* 204-925-5792
e-mail: office@athleticsmanitoba.com
URL: www.athleticsmanitoba.com
Rob Guy, Managing Director

Athletics New Brunswick (ANB) / Athlétisme du Nouveau-Brunswick
Tel: 506-457-4122; *Fax:* 506-325-9420
e-mail: ncactm@nb.aibn.com
URL: www.anb.ca
Annette Wetmore, Secretary
Harold Nicholson, President

Athletics Nova Scotia
5516 Spring Garden Rd, 4th Fl, Halifax NS B3J 1G6
Tel: 902-425-5450; *Fax:* 902-425-5606
e-mail: athletics@sportnovascotia.ca
URL: www.athleticsnovascotia.ca
Peter Lord, Executive Director

Athletics PEI
55 Villa Ave., Charlottetown PE C1A 2B2
Tel: 902-566-6861; *Fax:* 902-368-4548
Barrie Stanfield, Treasurer

Athletics Yukon
4061 - 4th Ave., Whitehorse YT Y1A 1H1
Tel: 867-668-2545
e-mail: info@athleticsyukon.ca
URL: www.athleticsyukon.ca
Chris Locke, President

British Columbia Athletics
#120, 3820 Cessna Dr., Richmond BC V7B 0A2
Tel: 604-333-3550; *Fax:* 604-333-3551
e-mail: bcathletics@bcathletics.org
URL: www.bcathletics.org
Brian McCalder, President & CEO

Canadian Wheelchair Basketball Association (CWBA) / Association canadienne de basketball en fauteuil roulant (ACBFR)
#B2, 2211 Riverside Dr., Ottawa ON K1H 7X5
Tel: 613-260-1296; *Fax:* 613-260-1456
Toll-Free: 877-843-2922
e-mail: info@wheelchairbasketball.ca
URL: www.wheelchairbasketball.ca
Affiliation(s): Canada Basketball
Wendy Gittens, Executive Director
Steven Bach, President

Fédération québécoise d'athlétisme (FQA)
CP 1000, Succ. M, 4545, av Pierre-de Coubertin, Montréal QC H1V 3R2
Tél: 514-252-3041; *Téléc:* 514-252-3042
Courriel: fqa@athletisme.qc.ca
URL: www.athletisme.qc.ca
Jean-Paul Baert, Directeur général

National Association of Collegiate Directors of Athletics (NACDA)
PO Box 16428, 24651 Detroit Rd., Westlake, Cleveland OH 44116 USA
Tel: 440-892-4000; *Fax:* 440-892-4007
URL: www.nacda.com
Mike Cleary, Executive Director

Newfoundland & Labrador Athletics Association (NLAA)
PO Box 21406, RPO MacDonald Dr., St. John's NL A1A 5G6
Tel: 709-576-1303; *Fax:* 709-576-7493
e-mail: athletics@nlaa.ca
URL: www.nlaa.ca
Affiliation(s): Athletics North-East; Mariners Athletics Club; Nautilus Running Club; New World Running Club; Pearlgate T&F Club; Trappers Running Club; Trinity-Conception Athletics Club; Westerland Track Club
Bob Walsh, President
Alison Walsh, Treasurer
George Stanoev, Technical Director

Ontario Track & Field Association (OTFA)
#211, 3 Concorde Gate, Toronto ON M3C 3N7
Tel: 416-426-7215; *Fax:* 416-426-7358
e-mail: ontrack@eol.ca
URL: www.otfa.ca
Bill Stephens, Chair

Saskatchewan Athletics
2020 College Dr., Saskatoon SK S7N 2W4
Tel: 306-664-6744; *Fax:* 306-664-6761
e-mail: athletics@sasktel.net
URL: www.saskathletics.ca
Bob Reindl, Executive Director
Janine Platana, Admin Assistant

World Masters Athletics
Via Padre Leopoldo da Castel-Nuovo 1, Assenza di Brenzon I-370 10 Italy
e-mail: info@world-masters-athletics.org
URL: www.world-masters-athletics.org

Automobile Racing

Motorsport Club of Ottawa (MCO) / Club des sports moteur d'Ottawa
PO Box 65006, RPO Merivale Mall, Nepean ON K2G 5Y3

Tel: 613-788-0525
e-mail: registrar@mco.org
URL: www.mco.org
Affiliation(s): ASN Canada FIA; CASC-OR; Rallysport Ontario
Pat McDermott, President

Toronto Autosport Club (TAC)
#1214, 2267 Lakeshore Dr. West, Toronto ON M8V 3X2
e-mail: president@torontoautosportclub.ca
URL: www.torontoautosportclub.ca
Dietmar Seelemnayer, President

Aviation

Canada's Aviation Hall of Fame (CAHF)
c/o Reynolds-Alberta Museum, PO Box 6360, Wetaskiwin AB T9A 2G1
Tel: 780-361-1351; Fax: 780-361-1239
e-mail: info@cahf.ca
URL: www.cahf.ca
Justin Cuffe, Curator
John Holding, Chair
Victor Bennett, Vice-Chair

Badminton

Badminton Alberta
c/o Alberta Badminton Centre, 60 Patterson Blvd SW, Calgary AB T3H 2E1
Tel: 403-297-2722; Fax: 403-297-2706
Toll-Free: 888-397-2722
e-mail: info@badmintonalberta.ca
URL: www.badmintonalberta.ca
Jeff Bell, Executive Director

Badminton BC
#252, 3820 Cessna Dr., Richmond BC V7B 0A2
Tel: 604-333-3595; Fax: 604-333-3594
Toll-Free: 800-483-2473
e-mail: info@badmintonbc.com
URL: www.badmintonbc.com
Brock Turner, Executive Director
Ken Thiesen, Operations & Programs Manager

Badminton Canada
#99, 2201 Riverside Dr., Ottawa ON K1H 8K9
Tel: 613-569-2424; Fax: 613-569-3232
e-mail: badminton@badminton.ca
URL: www.badminton.ca
Affiliation(s): International Badminton Federation
Sonia Blanchard, Office Administrator
Kyle Hunter, Executive Director

Badminton New Nouveau Brunswick
PO Box 355, Stn. Main, Bathurst NB E2A 3Z3
Tel: 506-783-4654
e-mail: badminton@bnnb.ca
URL: www.bnnb.ca
Bernard Duguay, Administration
Diane MacLeod, President

Badminton Newfoundland & Labrador Inc.
PO Box 21248, #213, 810 East White Hills Rd., St. John's NL A1A 5B2
Tel: 709-576-7606; Fax: 709-576-7493
e-mail: badminton@sportnf.com
URL: www.badmintonnl.ca/
Janice Reid-Boland, Executive Director
Mike Alexander, President

Badminton Québec
4940, rue Hochelaga est, Montréal QC H1V 1E7
Tél: 514-252-3066; Téléc: 514-252-3175
Courriel: badmintonquebec@videotron.ca
URL: www.badmintonquebec.com
Maryse Bellavance, Directrice générale

International Badminton Federation (IBF)
Stadium Badminton Kuala Lumpur, Batu 3 «, Jalan Cheras, Kuala Lumpur 56000 Malaysia
Tel: 603-9283 7155; Fax: 603-9284 71553
e-mail: bwf@internationalbadminton.org
URL: www.internationalbadminton.org
Kang Young Joong, President

Manitoba Badminton Association
200 Main St., Winnipeg MB R3C 4M2
Tel: 204-925-5679; Fax: 204-925-5703
Toll-Free: 888-243-0890
e-mail: badminton@shawbiz.ca
URL: www.badminton.mb.ca
Ron Waterman, President

Connie Blamie, Executive Director

Nova Scotia Badminton Association
5516 Spring Garden Road, Halifax NS B3J 1G6
Tel: 902-425-5450; Fax: 902-425-5606
e-mail: nsbadminton@sportnovascotia.ca
URL: www.nsba.ca
Jennifer Petrie, Executive Director
Linda Pride, President

NWT Badminton Association
4407 School Draw Ave., Yellowknife NT X1A 2K2
Tel: 867-669-2606
e-mail: jimu@ssimicro.com
URL: www.nwtbadminton.yk.com
Jim Umpherson, President

Ontario Badminton Association (OBA)
#209, 3 Concorde Gate, Toronto ON M3C 3N7
Tel: 416-426-7192; Fax: 416-426-7346
e-mail: info@ontariobadminton.on.ca
URL: www.ontariobadminton.on.ca
Affiliation(s): Badminton Canada; Badminton World Federation
Val Butler, Executive Director

Prince Edward Island Badminton Association
c/o Sport PEI, PO Box 302, Charlottetown PE C1A 7K7
Tel: 902-368-4262; Fax: 902-368-4548
Dawna Woodside, President

Saskatchewan Badminton Association (SBA)
3615 Pasqua St., Regina SK S4S 6W8
Tel: 306-780-9368; Fax: 306-780-9369
e-mail: saskbadminton@sasktel.net
URL: www.saskbadminton.ca
Frank Gaudet, Executive Director

Yukon Badminton Association
4061 - 4th Ave., Whitehorse YT Y1A 1H1
Tel: 867-668-4821
e-mail: bluestone@northwestel.net
Michael Muller, President
Randy Carlson, Vice-President

Ball Hockey

British Columbia Ball Hockey Association (BCBHA)
1302 Cliveden Ave., Delta BC V3M 6G4
Tel: 604-812-6720; Fax: 604-588-7760
URL: www.bcbha.com
Affiliation(s): Canadian Ball Hockey Association
Wade Traversy, President
Kris Little, Vice-President
Rob Moxness, Secretary
Roger Sidhu, Treasurer

Canadian Ball Hockey Association / Association canadienne de hockey-balle
#5, 56 Pennsylvania Ave, Concord ON L4K 3V9
Tel: 905-832-6200; Fax: 905-856-1331
e-mail: info@cbha.com
URL: www.cbha.com
Domenic de Gironimo, President

Manitoba Ball Hockey Association
200 Main St., Winnipeg MB R3C 4M2
Tel: 204-925-5602
e-mail: mbha1@hotmail.com
URL: www.manitobaballhockey.com
Jeff Dzikowcz, President

New Brunswick Ball Hockey Association (NBBHA)
16 Reflection Lane, Quispamsis NB E2E 6E7
Tel: 506-333-7772; Fax: 506-847-8585
e-mail: sheila@committedtoyourgoals.com
Sheila Elliott, Contact

Newfoundland & Labrador Ball Hockey Association (NLBHA)
PO Box 2579, Stn. C, St. John's NL A1C 6K1
Tel: 709-729-0689
e-mail: paulbarron@gov.nl.ca
Paul Barron, President

Nova Scotia Ball Hockey Association
100 Auburn Drive, Dartmouth NS B2W 3S6
Tel: 902-462-5433; Fax: 902-477-0243
Affiliation(s): Canadian Ball Hockey Association; Sport Nova Scotia
Bill Davidson, Contact

Ontario Ball Hockey Association (OBHA)
#5, 56 Pennsylvania Ave., Concord ON L4K 3V9
Tel: 905-738-3320; Fax: 905-738-3321
URL: www.ontarioballhockey.ca
Affiliation(s): Canadian Ball Hockey Association; International Street & Ball Hockey Association; Sport Canada; Canadian Hockey Association
Mauro Cugini, Executive Director

Québec Ball Hockey Association
#203, 5960 Jean-Talon E, St. Leonard QC H1S 1M2
Tel: 514-251-9346; Fax: 514-251-8285
e-mail: info@ballhockeynews.ca
URL: www.ballhockeynews.ca
Tony Iannitto

Wild Rose Ball Hockey Association
7604 - 182 St., Edmonton AB T5T 1Y9
Tel: 780-970-0637; Fax: 780-484-9957
e-mail: info@wrbha.com
URL: www.wrbha.com
Craig Thiessen, Contact

Baseball

Baseball Alberta (BA)
Percy Page Centre, 11759 Groat Rd., Edmonton AB T5M 3K6
Tel: 780-427-8943; Fax: 780-427-9032
e-mail: bradwolansky@baseballalberta.com
URL: www.baseballalberta.com
Affiliation(s): Alberta Amateur Baseball Council

Baseball BC
#310, 15225 - 104th Ave., Surrey BC V3R 6Y8
Tel: 604-586-3310; Fax: 604-586-3311
e-mail: info@baseball.bc.ca
URL: www.baseball.bc.ca

Baseball Canada / Fédération canadienne de baseball amateur
2212 Gladwin Cres., #A7, Ottawa ON K1B 5N1
Tel: 613-748-5606; Fax: 613-748-5767
e-mail: info@baseball.ca
URL: www.baseball.ca
Affiliation(s): Canadian Olympic Association
Jim Baba, Director General
Ray Carter, President

Baseball New Brunswick (BNB) / Baseball Nouveau-Brunswick
#13, 900 Hanwell Rd., Fredericton NB E3B 6A2
Tel: 506-451-1329; Fax: 506-451-1325
e-mail: baseballnb2003@nb.aibn.com
URL: www.baseballnb.ca
Affiliation(s): Sport New Brunswick; Baseball Atlantic

Baseball Nova Scotia (BNS)
5516 Spring Garden Rd., 4th Fl., Halifax NS B3J 1J
Tel: 902-425-5450; Fax: 902-425-5606
URL: www.baseballnovascotia.com
Brad Lawlor, Executive Director

Baseball Ontario
#3, 131 Sheldon Dr., Cambridge ON N1R 6S2
Tel: 519-740-3900; Fax: 519-740-6311
e-mail: baseball@baseballontario.com
URL: www.baseballontario.com
Affiliation(s): Little League Ontario
Mary-Ann Smith, Administrative Director

Fédération du baseball amateur du Québec
CP 1000, Succ. M, 4545, av Pierre-de Coubertin, Montréal QC H1V 3R2
Tél: 514-252-3075; Téléc: 514-252-3134
Courriel: info@baseballquebec.qc.ca
URL: www.baseballquebec.qc.ca

Little League Canada / Petite ligue Canada
235 Dale Ave., Ottawa ON K1G 0H6
Tel: 613-731-3301; Fax: 613-731-2829
e-mail: canada@littleleague.org
URL: www.littleleague.ca
Roy Bergerman, President & Chair
Marthe Dubroy, Secretary
Bruce Campbell, Treasurer

Manitoba Baseball Association
200 Main St., Winnipeg MB R3C 4M2
Tel: 204-925-5763; Fax: 204-925-5928
e-mail: info.baseball@sport.mb.ca
URL: www.baseballmanitoba.ca
Morgan de Pe¤a, Executive Director

Newfoundland Baseball
83 Ashford Dr., Mount Pearl NL A1N 3N7

Tel: 709-368-2819; Fax: 709-368-6080
e-mail: nlbaseball@nl.rogers.com
URL: www.sport.ca/nlbaseball
John Janes, President

Prince Edward Island Amateur Baseball Association
PO Box 302, Charlottetown PE C1A 7K7
Tel: 902-368-4208; Fax: 902-368-4548
Toll-Free: 800-235-5687
e-mail: kmcintosh@sportpei.pe.ca
URL: www.baseballpei.ca
Kelsey McIntosh, Executive Director

Saskatchewan Baseball Association (SBA)
1870 Lorne St., Regina SK S4P 2L7
Tel: 306-780-9237; Fax: 306-352-3669
e-mail: mramage@sasktel.net
URL: www.saskbaseball.ca
Mike Ramage, Executive Director

Basketball

Basketball Alberta
Percy Page Centre, 11759 Groat Rd., Edmonton AB T5M 3K6
Tel: 780-427-9044; Fax: 780-427-9124
e-mail: bballab@basketballalbert.ab.ca
URL: www.basketballalberta.ca
Bob Mitchell, President
Brian Anstice, Vice President

Basketball BC
#310, 7155 Kingsway, Burnaby BC V5E 2V1
Tel: 604-718-7852; Fax: 604-525-7762
e-mail: hoopsbc@basketball.bc.ca
URL: www.basketball.bc.ca
Michael Hind, Executive Director

Basketball Manitoba
200 Main St., Winnipeg MB R3C 4M2
Tel: 204-925-5775; Fax: 204-925-5929
Toll-Free: 800-282-8069
e-mail: info@basketball.mb.ca
URL: www.basketball.mb.ca
Adam Wedlake, Executive Director

Basketball New Brunswick (BNB) / Basketball Nouveau-Brunswick
53D Clark Rd., Rothesay NB E2E 2K9
Tel: 506-849-4667; Fax: 506-849-4668
e-mail: info@basketball.nb.ca
URL: www.basketball.nb.ca
Affiliation(s): New Brunswick Association of Approved Basketball Officials; New Brunswick Interscholastic Athletic Association
Marg Jones, Executive Director
Chuck Beyea, President

Basketball Nova Scotia
5516 Spring Garden Rd., 4th Fl., Halifax NS B3J 1G6
Tel: 902-425-5450; Fax: 902-425-5606
e-mail: bnsadmin@basketball.ns.ca
URL: www.basketball.ns.ca
Affiliation(s): Sport Nova Scotia
Donnie Ehler, Executive Director
Mike Brien, President

Basketball PEI
PO Box 302, 40 Enman Cres., Charlottetown PE C1A 7K7
Tel: 902-368-4208; Fax: 902-368-4208
Toll-Free: 800-247-6712
e-mail: info@basketballpei.ca
URL: www.basketballpei.ca
Stephen Marchbank, Executive Director

Basketball Saskatchewan Inc. (BSI)
2205 Victoria Ave., Regina SK S4P 0S4
Tel: 306-780-9264; Fax: 306-525-4009
e-mail: mbarr@basketballsask.com
URL: www.basketballsask.com
Affiliation(s): Sask Sport
Marg Barr, Executive Director

Canada Basketball
#11, 1 Westside Dr., Toronto ON M9C 1B2
Tel: 416-614-8037; Fax: 416-614-9570
e-mail: info@basketball.ca
URL: www.basketball.ca
Affiliation(s): 10 provincial + 2 territorial associations; Canadian Interuniversity Athletic Union; Canadian Colleges Athletic Association; Canadian School Sports Federation; Toronto Raptors; Canadian Wheelchair Basketball Association; Canadian Association of Basketball Officials; National Association of Basketball Coaches of Canada; Women's Basketball Coaches Association
Wayne Parrish, Executive Director & CEO

Fédération de basketball du Québec (FBBQ) / Québec Basketball Federation
CP 1000, Succ. M, 4545, av Pierre-De Coubertin, Montréal QC H1V 3R2
Tél: 514-252-3057; Téléc: 514-252-3357
Ligne sans frais: 866-557-3057
Courriel: basket@basketball.qc.ca
URL: www.basketball.qc.ca
Daniel Méthot, Directeur général

Newfoundland & Labrador Basketball Association
PO Box 21029, St. John's NL A1A 5B2
Tel: 709-576-0247; Fax: 709-576-8787
e-mail: nlba@sportnf.com
URL: www.nlba.nf.ca
Bill Murphy, Executive Director
Roger Head, Secretary-Treasurer
Bas Kavanagh, President

Ontario Basketball
#311, 3 Concorde Gate, Toronto ON M3C 3N7
Tel: 416-426-7200; Fax: 416-426-7360
e-mail: info@basketball.on.ca
URL: www.basketball.on.ca
Affiliation(s): Provincial Sports Organizations Council; Canada Basketball; Toronto Raptors Basketball Club; NBA Canada; Coaches Association of Ontario; Canadian Sports Centre; and other provincial basketball organizations
Michele O'Keefe, Executive Director
Ken Urbach, President
Greg Verner, Vice President

STARS Sports Association
PO Box 15, Okotoks AB T1S 1A4
Tel: 403-938-3475; Fax: 403-938-3625
e-mail: info@starsvolleyball.ca; info@starsbasketball.com

Biathlon

Biathlon Alberta
818 - 16 Ave. NW, Calgary AB T2M 0K1
Tel: 403-297-2719; Fax: 403-297-2702
e-mail: info@biathlon.ca
URL: www.biathlon.ca
Alan Ball, Sport Development

Biathlon Canada
#111, 2197 Riverside Dr., Ottawa ON K1H 7X3
Tel: 613-748-5608; Fax: 613-748-5762
e-mail: jthomson@biathloncanada.ca
URL: www.biathloncanada.ca
Affiliation(s): International Biathlon Union; Canadian Olympic Committee
Joanne Thomson, Executive Director
Chris Lindsay, Coordinator, Technical Programs

Bicycling

Alberta Bicycle Association (ABA)
Percy Page Centre, 11759 Groat Rd., Edmonton AB T5M 3K6
Tel: 780-427-6352; Fax: 780-427-6438
Toll-Free: 877-646-2453
e-mail: office@albertabicycle.ab.ca
URL: www.albertabicycle.ab.ca
Kipp Kaufmann, Executive Director

Bicycle Newfoundland & Labrador
PO Box 2127, Stn. C, St. John's NL A1C 5R6
Tel: 709-753-5788; Fax: 709-753-3301
e-mail: bnl@bnl.nf.ca
URL: www.bnl.nf.ca/
Leon Organ, President

Bicycle Nova Scotia (BNS)
5516 Spring Garden Rd., 4th Fl., Halifax NS B3J 1G6
Tel: 902-425-5454; Fax: 902-425-5606
e-mail: staff@bicycle.ns.ca
URL: www.bicycle.ns.ca
Simon Myatt, President

Bicycle Trade Association of Canada (BTAC) / Association canadienne de l'industrie du vélo (ACIV)
17 Main St. North, Newmarket ON L3Y 3Z6
Tel: 905-853-5031; Fax: 905-853-7632
Toll-Free: 866-528-2822
e-mail: info@btac.org
URL: www.btac.org
Janet O'Connell, Executive Director

Canadian Cycling Association (CCA) / Association cycliste canadienne
#203, 2197 Riverside Dr., Ottawa ON K1H 7X3
Tel: 613-248-1353; Fax: 613-248-9311
e-mail: general@canadian-cycling.com
URL: www.canadian-cycling.com/
Lorraine Lafrenière, CEO

Cycling Association of the Yukon
4061, 4th Avenue, Whitehorse YT Y1A 1H1
Tel: 867-668-4990; Fax: 867-668-8212
e-mail: sue.richards@gov.yk.ca
Sue Richards, President

Cycling British Columbia (CBC)
#201, 210 West Broadway, Vancouver BC V5Y 3W2
Tel: 604-737-3034; Fax: 604-737-3141
e-mail: assist@cycling.bc.ca
URL: www.cycling.bc.ca
Ryan Keith, Chief Executive Officer

Cycling PEI (CPEI)
Sport PEI, PO Box 302, 40 Enman Cresent, Charlottetown PE C1A 7K7
Tel: 902-368-4985; Fax: 902-368-4548
e-mail: mconnolly@sportpei.pe.ca
URL: www.cpei.ca
Mike Connolly, Executive Director

Edmonton Bicycle & Touring Club (EBTC)
PO Box 52017, Stn. Garneau, Edmonton AB T6G 2T5
Tel: 780-424-2453
URL: www.bikeclub.ca
Affiliation(s): Alberta Bicycle Association

Fédération québécoise des sports cyclistes (FQSC) / Québec Cycling Sports Federation
4545, av Pierre-de-Coubertin, Montréal QC H1V 3R2
Tél: 514-252-3071; Téléc: 514-252-3165
Courriel: reception@fqsc.net
URL: www.fqsc.net
Affiliation(s): Association cycliste canadienne; Union cycliste internationale; Sports-Québec; Regroupement loisir Québec
Simon Thériault, Directeur technique
Louis Barbeau, Directeur général
André Michaud, Président

Ontario Cycling Association (OCA) / Association cycliste ontarienne
#307, 3 Concorde Gate, Toronto ON M3C 3N7
Tel: 416-426-7416; Fax: 416-426-7349
e-mail: info@ontariocycling.org; ocamagazine@ontariocycling.org
URL: www.ontariocycling.org
Affiliation(s): Canadian Cycling Association
Duncan Vipond, President
Malcolm Eade, Vice-President, Administration & Finance
Glenn Meeuwisse, Vice-President, High Performance
Matthias Schmidt, Vice-President, Development
Jim Crosscombe, Executive Director
Denise Kelly, Director, Provincial Coaching
Chris Baskys, Coordinator, Membership
Nicky Pearson, Coordinator, BMX Growth & Development

Saskatchewan Cycling Association
2205 Victoria Ave., Regina SK S4P 0S4
Tel: 306-780-9299; Fax: 306-525-4009
e-mail: cycling@accesscomm.ca
URL: www.saskcycling.ca
Wayne Walker, President

Toronto Bicycling Network
PO Box 279, #200, 131 Bloor St. West, Toronto ON M5S 1R8
Tel: 416-760-4191
e-mail: info@tbn.ca
URL: www.tbn.ca
Brian Mclean, President

Vélo New Brunswick
536 McAllister Rd., Riverview NB E1B 4G1
Tel: 506-474-0214
e-mail: christine.martin@velo.nb.ca
URL: www.velo.nb.ca
Affiliation(s): Sport New Brunswick
Kelly Murray, President
Michelle Chase, Vice-President
Sheila Colbourne, Executive Director

Vélo Québec
1251, rue Rachel est, Montréal QC H2J 2J9
Tél: 514-521-8356; Téléc: 514-521-5711
Ligne sans frais: 800-567-8356

Courriel: velo_quebec@velo.qc.ca
URL: www.velo.qc.ca
Jean-François Pronovost, Directeur général

Blindness

Blind Sports Nova Scotia
c/o CNIB, 6136 Almon St., Halifax NS B3K 1T8
Tel: 902-453-1480; *Fax:* 902-454-6570
e-mail: blindsports@yahoo.ca
URL: www.blindsportnovascotia.ca
Yvon Clement, President

Boating

Canadian International Dragon Boat Festival Society
110 Keefer St., Vancouver BC V6A 1X4
Tel: 604-688-2382; *Fax:* 604-677-2147
URL: www.adbf.com
Ann Phelps, General Manager

Canadian Power & Sail Squadrons (Canadian Headquarters) (CPS) / Escadrilles canadiennes de plaisance (ECP)
26 Golden Gate Ct., Toronto ON M1P 3A5
Tel: 416-293-2438; *Fax:* 416-293-2445
Toll-Free: 888-277-2628
e-mail: hgg@cps-ecp.ca
URL: www.cps-ecp.ca
Alain Brière, Executive Director
John Gullick, Manager, Government & Special Programs

Bobsledding & Luge

Alberta Bobsleigh Association
Bob Niven Training Centre, #205, 88 Canada Olympic Rd. SW, Calgary AB T3B 5R5
Tel: 403-297-2721; *Fax:* 403-286-7213
e-mail: slide@albertabobsleigh.com
URL: www.albertabobsleigh.com
Devin Findlay, Technical Director

Alberta Luge Association (ALA)
Rm 201, BNTC, 88 Canada Olympic Rd. SW, Calgary AB T3B 5R5
Tel: 403-202-6570; *Fax:* 403-247-5497
e-mail: admin@albertaluge.com
URL: www.albertaluge.com
Affiliation(s): Canadian Luge Association
Darryl Gunn, President

Bobsleigh Canada Skeleton
140 Canada Olympic Rd. SW, Calgary AB T3B 5R5
Tel: 403-247-5950; *Fax:* 403-247-5951
e-mail: ddreher@bobsleigh.ca
URL: www.bobsleigh.ca/
Affiliation(s): Fédération internationale de bobsleigh et de tobogganing
Shane Pearsall, Managing Director

Canadian Luge Association / Association canadienne de luge
88 Canada Olympic Rd. SW, Calgary AB T3B 5R5
Tel: 403-202-6581; *Fax:* 403-247-8820
e-mail: tfarstad@coda.ca
URL: www.luge.ca
Tim Farstad, Executive Director

Fédération internationale de bobsleigh et de tobogganing
Via Piranesi, 44/B, Milan 120137 Italy
Tél: 39-02-757-3319; *Téléc:* 39-02-757-3384
Courriel: egarde@tin.it
URL: www.fibt.com
Affiliation(s): Canadian Amateur Bobsleigh & Tobogganing Association
Robert H. Storey, Président
Ermanno Gardella, Secrétaire général

Fédération Internationale de Luge de Course (FIL) / International Luge Federation
Rathausplatz 9, Berchtesgaden 83471 Germany
Tél: 49-86-526-6960; *Téléc:* 49-86-526-6969
Courriel: office@fil-luge.org
URL: www.fil-luge.org
Affiliation(s): Canadian Luge Association
Josef Fendt, Président
Svein Romstad, Secrétaire général

Bowling

Alberta 5 Pin Bowlers' Association (A5-PBA)
432 - 14 St. South, Lethbridge AB T1J 2X7
Tel: 403-320-2695; *Fax:* 403-320-2676
Toll-Free: 800-762-3075
e-mail: a5pba@telusplanet.net
URL: www.alberta5pin.com
Annette Bruneau, President

Bowling Federation of Canada / Fédération des quilles du Canada
c/o Administrator, #206, 720 Belfast Rd., Ottawa ON K1G 0Z5
Tel: 613-744-5090; *Fax:* 613-744-2217
e-mail: info@canadabowls.ca
URL: www.canadabowls.ca
Affiliation(s): Bowling Proprietors Association of Canada; Canadian 5-pin Bowlers Association; Canadian Tenpin Federation.
Sheila Carr, Interim Administrator

Bowling Federation of Saskatchewan
#101, 1805 - 8th Ave., Regina SK S4R 1E8
Tel: 306-780-9412; *Fax:* 306-780-9455
e-mail: bowling@sasktel.net
URL: saskbowl.com
Rhonda Sereda, Executive Director

Bowling Proprietors' Association of BC
#209, 332 Columbia St., New Westminster BC V3L 1A6
Tel: 604-522-2990; *Fax:* 604-522-2055
e-mail: bowl4fun@bowlbc.com
URL: www.bowlbc.com
Sheilagh Meyers, Executive Director

Bowling Proprietors' Association of Canada (BPAC)
#10A, 250 Shields Ct., Markham ON L3R 9W7
Tel: 905-479-1560; *Fax:* 905-479-8613
e-mail: bowling@bpac.ca
URL: www.bpac.ca
Paul Oliveira, Executive Director
Claude Rhéaume, President

Bowling Proprietors' Association of Ontario (BPAO)
#202, 500 Alden Road, Markham ON L3R 5H5
Tel: 905-940-8200
e-mail: bpao@bpao.ca
URL: www.bpao.ca
Affiliation(s): Bowling Proprietors' Association of Canada
Walter J. Valentan, Secretary
Don Gorman, President/Chair
Margaret Gorman, Administrative Assistant

Canadian 5 Pin Bowlers' Association (C5PBA) / Association canadienne des cinq quilles (AC5Q)
#206, 720 Belfast Rd., Ottawa ON K1G 0Z5
Tel: 613-744-5090; *Fax:* 613-744-2217
e-mail: c5pba@c5pba.ca
URL: www.c5pba.ca
Affiliation(s): Bowling Federation of Canada
Sheila Carr, Executive Director
Mel Osmond, President
Don MacIver, Corporate Sec.-Treas.

Canadian Tenpin Federation, Inc. (CTF) / Fédération canadienne des dix-quilles, inc.
916 3 Ave. N., Lethbridge AB T1H 0H3
Tel: 403-381-2830; *Fax:* 403-381-6247
URL: www.gotenpinbowling.ca
Affiliation(s): Fédération internationale des quilleurs
Stan May, Executive Director

Fédération de pétanque du Québec
CP 1000, Succ. M, 4545, av Pierre-de Coubertin, Montréal QC H1V 3R2
Tél: 514-252-3077
Courriel: petanque@loisirquebec.qc.ca
URL: www.petanque.qc.ca
Denise Coutu, Secrétaire administrative

Manitoba Five Pin Bowling Federation, Inc.
#219, 200 Main Street, Winnipeg MB R3C 4M2
Tel: 204-925-5766; *Fax:* 204-925-5767
Toll-Free: 800-282-8069
URL: www.mfpbf.org
Deanne Zilinsky, Executive Director

National Youth Bowling Council
#10A, 250 Shields Ct., Markham ON L3R 9W7
Tel: 905-479-1560; *Fax:* 905-479-8613
e-mail: bpac@bpac.ca
URL: www.bpac.ca/YBC.html
Paul Oliveira, Executive Director

New Brunswick Candlepin Bowlers Association
PO Box 4315, 11 Sawyer Rd., Woodstock NB E7M 6B7
Tel: 506-328-8418
Bill Hamilton, Contact

Northwest Territories 5 Pin Bowlers' Association (NWT5PBA)
PO Box 2643, Yellowknife NT X1A 2P9
Tel: 867-873-8189; *Fax:* 867-873-8237
e-mail: gary@nwt5pba.ca
URL: www.nwt5pba.ca
Gary Black, President

Ontario 5 Pin Bowlers' Association (O5PBA)
#302, 3 Concorde Gate, Toronto ON M3C 3N7
Tel: 416-426-7167; *Fax:* 416-426-7364
e-mail: o5pba@o5pba.ca
URL: www.o5pba.ca
Rhonda Gifford, Program Coordinator
Harold Stoddart, Technical Director
Al Hong, Executive Director

Prince Edward Island Five Pin Bowlers Association Inc.
c/o Sport PEI, PO Box 302, Charlottetown PE C1A 7K7
Tel: 902-368-4110; *Fax:* 902-368-4548
Toll-Free: 800-247-6712
e-mail: sports@sportpei.pe.ca
URL: www.pei5pba.com
Sue MacPherson, President

Saskatchewan 5 Pin Bowlers' Association
#100, 1805 - 8th Ave., Regina SK S4R 1E8
Tel: 306-780-9412; *Fax:* 306-780-9455
e-mail: bowling@sasktel.net
URL: saskbowl.com
Affiliation(s): Bowling Federation of Saskatchewan
Rhonda Sereda, Executive Director

Boxing

Boxing Alberta
Percy Page Centre, 11759 Groat Rd., Edmonton AB T5M 3K6
Tel: 780-427-6515; *Fax:* 780-427-1205
e-mail: dbelair@telus.net
URL: www.boxingalberta.com
Tom Daly, President
Dennis Belair, Executive Director

Boxing BC Association
250 Willingdon Ave., Burnaby BC V5C 5E9
Tel: 604-291-7921; *Fax:* 604-291-7927
e-mail: boxingbc@telus.net
URL: www.boxing.bc.ca
Affiliation(s): Canadian Amateur Boxing Association
Scotty Jackson, President

Boxing Ontario
#207, 1185 Eglinton Ave. East, Toronto ON M3C 3C6
Tel: 416-426-7250; *Fax:* 416-426-7367
e-mail: info@boxingontario.com
URL: www.boxingontario.com
Doug Hannum, Executive Director

Boxing Saskatchewan
PO Box 4711, Regina SK S4P 3Y3
Tel: 306-525-6678; *Fax:* 306-569-3454
e-mail: skboxing@accesscomm.ca
URL: www.saskboxing.com
Affiliation(s): Canadian Amateur Boxing Association
Graham Craig, Executive Director

Calgary Boxing & Wrestling Commission (CBWC)
PO Box 2100, Stn. M #63, Calgary AB T2P 2M5
Tel: 403-268-5367
e-mail: cscchair@tooks.net
Candy S. Schacter, Chair

Canadian Amateur Boxing Association (CABA) / Association canadienne de boxe amateur (ACBA)
888 Belfast Rd., Ottawa ON K1G 0Z6
Tel: 613-238-7700; *Fax:* 613-238-1600
e-mail: caba@boxing.ca
URL: www.boxing.ca
Affiliation(s): International Amateur Boxing Association
Robert G. Crête, Executive Director
Daniel Trépanier, Coordinator, Technical
Michelle Ethier, Registrar & Accountant

City of Edmonton Combative Sports Commission
PO Box 82079, Stn. Yellowbird, Edmonton AB T6J 7E6
Tel: 780-915-3239
e-mail: ozmyndak@telusplanet.net

Affiliation(s): Association of Boxing Commissions
Orest Zmyndak, Executive Director

Fédération québécoise de boxe olympique (FQBO)
CP 1000, Succ. M, 4545, av Pierre-de Coubertin, Montréal QC H1V 3R2
Tél: 514-252-3047; *Téléc:* 514-254-2144
Ligne sans frais: 866-241-3779
Courriel: info@fqbo.qc.ca
URL: www.fqbo.qc.ca
Kenneth Piché, Directeur général
Victoria Sullivan-Smith, Adjointe administrative

Manitoba Amateur Boxing Association
#302, 200 Main St., Winnipeg MB R3C 4M2
Tel: 204-925-5658
Rosemary Broadbent

Manitoba Boxing Commission
#420, 213 Notre Dame Ave., Winnipeg MB R3B 1N3
Tel: 204-945-8954; *Fax:* 204-945-1675
e-mail: mansport@sport.mb.ca
Henry Janzen, Chair
Dan Vandal, Contact

Broomball

Alberta Broomball Association
Percy Page Centre, 11759 Groat Rd., Edmonton AB T5M 3K6
Tel: 780-459-7668; *Fax:* 780-460-0527
e-mail: neigel@telus.net
Greg Mastervick, President

British Columbia Broomball Society
Rick Przybysz, 5356 Lochside Dr., Victoria BC V8Y 2G7
Tel: 250-658-4406
e-mail: president@broomballbc.com
URL: www.broomballbc.com
Rick Przybysz, President

Broomball Newfoundland & Labrador
734 Birch St., Labrador City NL A2V 1C8
Tel: 709-944-5780; *Fax:* 709-944-5780
e-mail: clarkep@nf.sympatico.ca
Harold Clarke, President

Canadian Broomball Federation / Fédération canadienne de ballon sur glace
#302, 200 Main St., Winnipeg MB R3C 4M2
Tel: 204-925-5656; *Fax:* 204-925-5703
e-mail: cbfbroomball@shaw.ca
URL: www.broomball.ca

Federation of Broomball Associations of Ontario
515 Gascon St., Russell ON K4R 1C6
Tel: 613-445-0904; *Fax:* 613-445-9844
e-mail: gerry.wever@ontariobroomball.ca
URL: www.ontariobroomball.ca
Gerry Wever, President

Fédération québécoise de ballon sur glace
CP 1000, Succ. M, 4545, av Pierre-de Coubertin, Montréal QC H1V 3R2
Tél: 514-252-3078; *Téléc:* 514-252-3051
Courriel: info@fqbg.net
URL: www.fqbg.net
Richard Mimeau, Président

Manitoba Amateur Broomball Association (MABA)
#305, 200 Main St., Winnipeg MB R3C 4M2
Tel: 204-925-5668; *Fax:* 204-925-5703
Toll-Free: 866-792-7666
e-mail: info@mbbroomball.com
URL: www.mbbroomball.com
Alan Park, President
Scott Marohn, Vice President

Northwest Territories Broomball Association
Stn. 529 Range Lake Road, Yellowknife NT X1A 3Y1
e-mail: nwtbroomball@yahoo.ca
URL: www.nwtbroomball.com
Jan Vallillee, President

Saskatchewan Broomball Association (SBA)
2205 Victoria Ave., Regina SK S4P 0S4
Tel: 306-780-9215; *Fax:* 306-525-4009
e-mail: saskbroomball@sasktel.net
URL: www.saskbroomball.ca
Greg Perreaux, Executive Director

Canoeing & Rafting

Alberta Sprint Racing Canoe Association
11759 Groat Rd., Edmonton AB T5M 3K6
Tel: 780-203-3987
e-mail: arsca@shaw.ca
URL: www.albertasprintcanoe.com
Rick Hill, President

Association québécoise de canoë-kayak de vitesse (AQCKV)
CP 1000, Succ. M, 4545, av Pierre-de Coubertin, Montréal QC H1V 3R2
Tél: 514-252-3086; *Téléc:* 514-252-3094
Courriel: directeur.technique@aqckv.qc.ca
URL: www.aqckv.qc.ca
Luc Therrien, Président

Canoe Kayak New Brunswick
PO Box 263, Moncton NB E1C 8K9
Toll-Free: 800-363-6060
e-mail: president@canoenb.org
URL: www.canoekayaknb.org
Evan Young, President

Canoe Kayak Nova Scotia (CKNS)
5516 Spring Garden Rd., 4th Fl., Halifax NS B3J 1G6
Tel: 902-425-5454; *Fax:* 902-425-5606
e-mail: canoens@sportnovascotia.ca
URL: www.ckns.ca
Ike Whitehead, Administrator

Canoe Newfoundland & Labrador
PO Box 23072, Stn. Churchill Sq., Saint John's NL A1B 4J9
Tel: 709-364-1601; *Fax:* 709-368-8357
e-mail: tumblehomecanoeclub@hotmail.com
URL: www.canoenfld.ca
Frank Galway, President

Canoe Ontario
c/o OCSRA, 570 Blenheim Cres., Oakville ON L6J 6P6
Tel: 905-337-8314
e-mail: jorlando1@cogeco.ca
URL: www.canoeontario.ca
Affiliation(s): Ontario Canoe Sprint Racing Affiliation; Ontario Marathon Canoe Racing Association; Whitewater Ontario
John Orlando, Treasurer

CanoeKayak BC
20585 - 124A Ave., Maple Ridge BC V2X 0M6
Tel: 604-465-5268; *Fax:* 604-460-0587
e-mail: info@canoekayakbc.ca
URL: www.canoekayakbc.ca
Mary Jane Abbot, Executive Director

CanoeKayak Canada (CKC)
#705, 2197 Riverside Dr., Ottawa ON K1H 7X3
Tel: 613-260-1818; *Fax:* 613-260-5137
e-mail: christine@canoekayak.ca
URL: www.canoekayak.ca
Anne Merklinger, Director General
Christine Lafontaine, Administrative Coordinator

CanoeKayak Canada - Atlantic Division
c/o Sport NS, 5516 Spring Garden Rd., 4th Fl., Halifax NS B3J 3G6
Tel: 902-425-5450; *Fax:* 902-425-5606
e-mail: ccaatlantic@sportnovascotia.ca
URL: www.ccaatlantic.ca
Liz Orton, Program Coordinator

Fédération québécoise du canot et du kayak (FQCK)
CP 1000, Succ. M, 4545, av Pierre-de Coubertin, Montréal QC H1V 3R2
Tél: 514-252-3001; *Téléc:* 514-252-3091
Courriel: info@canot-kayak.qc.ca
URL: www.canot-kayak.qc.ca
Pierre Trudel, Directeur général

Ikaluktutiak Paddling Association
PO Box 125, Cambridge Bay NU X0B 0C0
Tel: 867-983-2068
e-mail: ipanorth69@gmail.com
Rob Harmer, President

Manitoba Paddling Association Inc. (MPA)
200 Main St., Winnipeg MB R3C 4M2
Tel: 204-925-5678; *Fax:* 204-925-5703
e-mail: mpa@sport.mb.ca; dragonboat@sport.mb.ca
URL: www.mpa.mb.ca
Jeff Dzikowicz, Executive Director
Robin McClure, President
Marcia Hrechkosy, Secretary
Bob Hunter, Treasurer

Manitoba Recreational Canoeing Association (MRCA)
PO Box 2663, Winnipeg MB R3C 4B3
Tel: 204-338-6722
URL: www.paddle.mb.ca
Affiliation(s): Manitoba Paddling Association
Cameron White, President

New Brunswick Competitive Canoe Association
c/o Sport New Brunswick, 181 Kennebecasis River Rd., Hampton NB E5N 6L1
e-mail: nbcca_m@hotmail.com
J. Timothy Flood, President

Newfoundland & Labrador Paddling Association (NLPA)
103« Forest Rd., St. John's NL A1A 1E4
Affiliation(s): Kayak Newfoundland & Labrador; Tumblehome Recreational Canoe Club
Allan Goodridge, President
Brian Hemeon, Vice-President, Canoeing
Darren MacDonald, Vice-President, Kayaking
Neil Burgess, Secretary
Alex Mcgruer, Treasurer

Prince Edward Island Canoe Kayak Association
RR#4, Alliston, Montague PE C0A 1R0
Tel: 902-962-3883; *Fax:* 902-962-3883
e-mail: justin.heidi@windsinc.com
URL: www.windsinc.com/canoekayak/canoekayak.htm
Justin Richard Batten, President

Prince Edward Island Recreational Canoeing Association
PO Box 5604, RR#5, Charlottetown PE C1A 7J8
Tel: 902-368-6355; *Fax:* 902-368-6186
Shawn Shea, Chair

Recreational Canoeing Association BC (RCABC)
1755 East 7th Ave., Vancouver BC V5N 1S1
Tel: 604-253-5410; *Fax:* 604-253-5490
e-mail: sec@bccanoe.com
URL: www.bccanoe.com
Alan Thomson, President
Jean Chandler, Secretary

Whitewater Kayaking Association of British Columbia (WKABC)
PO Box 91549, Stn. West Vancouver, Vancouver BC V7V 3P2
Tel: 604-515-6376
e-mail: admin@whitewater.org
URL: www.whitewater.org
Affiliation(s): Outdoor Recreation Council of BC
Don Butler, President

Whitewater Ontario
411 Carnegie Beach Rd., Port Perry ON L9L 1B6
Tel: 905-985-4585; *Fax:* 905-985-5256
Toll-Free: 888-322-2849
e-mail: info@whitewaterontario.ca
URL: www.whitewaterontario.ca
Claudia Kerkoff, Vice-President

Yukon Canoe & Kayak Club
PO Box 40080, 3 Sitka Cres., Whitehorse YT Y1A 6M6
Tel: 867-456-4827
e-mail: current@yckc.ca
URL: www.yckc.ca
Eyvi Smith, President

Cerebral Palsy

Canadian Cerebral Palsy Sports Association (CCPSA) / Association canadienne de sport pour paralytiques cérébraux (ACPSA)
PO Box 41009, 1910 St. Laurent Blvd., Ottawa ON K1G 5K9
Tel: 613-748-1430; *Fax:* 613-748-1355
Toll-Free: 866-247-9934
e-mail: ccpsa@bellnet.ca
URL: www.ccpsa.ca
Affiliation(s): Canadian Paralympic Committee; Cerebral Palsy International Sport & Recreation Association
Sandy Hermiston, President

Cerebral Palsy Sports Association of British Columbia (CPSABC)
6235A - 136th St., Surrey BC V3X 1H3
Tel: 604-599-5240; *Fax:* 604-599-5241
Toll-Free: 877-711-3111

e-mail: sportinfo@telus.net
URL: www.cpsports.com
Affiliation(s): Sport BC
Terri Moore, Executive Director

Manitoba Cerebral Palsy Sports Association (MCPSA)
200 Main St., Winnipeg MB R3C 1A8
Tel: 204-925-5682; *Fax:* 204-925-5703

Sport Ability Alberta
Percy Page Centre, 11759 Groat Rd., Edmonton AB T5M 3K6
Tel: 780-422-2904; *Fax:* 780-422-2663
Toll-Free: 866-282-4356
e-mail: acpsa@telusplanet.net
Sandy Hermiston, President
Norma Lorincz, Executive Director

Coaching

Coaches Association of British Columbia (CABC)
#200, 3820 Cessna Drive, Richmond BC V7B 0A2
Tel: 604-333-3600; *Fax:* 604-333-3450
e-mail: info@coaches.bc.ca
URL: www.coaches.bc.ca
Gordon May, CAE, Executive Director

Coaches Association of PEI (CAPEI)
PO Box 302, Charlottetown PE C1A 7K7
Tel: 902-569-0583; *Fax:* 902-368-4548
Toll-Free: 800-247-6712
e-mail: cgcrozier@sportpei.pe.ca
URL: www.coachespei.ca
Cheryl G. Crozier, Executive Director

Coaching Association of Canada (CAC) / Association canadienne des entraîneurs
#300, 141 Laurier Ave. West, Ottawa ON K1P 5J3
Tel: 613-235-5000; *Fax:* 613-235-9500
e-mail: coach@coach.ca
URL: www.coach.ca
Affiliation(s): Professional Arm: Canadian Professional Coaches Association
John Bales, CEO
Gaëtan Robitaille, COO

Commonwealth Games

The Commonwealth Games Association of Canada Inc. (CGAC) / Association canadienne des jeux du Commonwealth inc.
#120, 2255 St. Laurent Blvd., Ottawa ON K1G 4K3
Tel: 613-244-6868; *Fax:* 613-244-6826
e-mail: info@commonwealthgames.ca
URL: www.commonwealthgames.ca
Affiliation(s): Commonwealth Games Federation - London, England
Kelly Laframboise, Administrative Coordinator
Thomas Jones, CEO

Croquet

Fédération des clubs de croquet du Québec
CP 1000, Succ. M, 4545, av Pierre-de Coubertin, Montréal QC H1V 3R2
Tél: 514-252-3032
Courriel: croquet@fqjr.qc.ca
URL: www.fqjr.qc.ca/croquet.html
Suzanne Hébert, Présidente

Curling

Alberta Curling Federation (ACF)
11759 Groat Rd., Edmonton AB T5M 3K6
Tel: 780-643-0809; *Fax:* 780-427-8103
e-mail: jim@albertacurling.ab.ca
URL: www.albertacurling.ab.ca
J.W. (Jim) Pringle, Executive Director
Kathy Odegard, Office Manager

Canadian Curling Association (CCA) / Association canadienne de curling
1660 Vimont Ct., Cumberland ON K4A 4J4
Tel: 613-834-2076; *Fax:* 613-834-0716
Toll-Free: 800-550-2875
e-mail: cca@curling.ca
URL: www.curling.ca
Affiliation(s): World Curling Federation
Greg Stremlaw, CEO

Curl BC
#320, 1367 West Broadway, Vancouver BC V6H 4A9
Tel: 604-737-3040; *Fax:* 604-737-1476
Toll-Free: 800-667-2875
e-mail: curling@curlbc.ca
URL: www.curlbc.ca
Scott Braley, Executive Director & CEO
Terry Vandale, President

Curling Québec
CP 1000, Succ. M, 4545, av Pierre-de Coubertin, Montréal QC H1V 3R2
Tél: 514-252-3088; *Téléc:* 514-252-3342
Ligne sans frais: 888-292-2875
Courriel: info@curling-quebec.qc.ca
URL: www.curling-quebec.qc.ca
Marco Berthelot, Directeur général

Manitoba Curling Association (MCA)
#208, 200 Main St., Winnipeg MB R3C 4M2
Tel: 204-925-5723; *Fax:* 204-925-5720
Toll-Free: 800-706-1486
e-mail: mca@curlmanitoba.org
URL: www.curlmanitoba.org
Affiliation(s): Canadian Curling Association
Ian Staniloff, Executive Director
Kyla Denisuik, Event/Media Coordinator
Dale Brooks, President

New Brunswick Curling Association (NBCA) / Association de Curling du Nouveau-Brunswick (ACNB)
PO Box 812, Moncton NB E1C 8N6
Tel: 506-854-9143; *Fax:* 506-388-5708
Toll-Free: 800-592-2875
e-mail: nbca@nb.sympatico.ca
URL: www.nbcurling.nb.ca
Affiliation(s): Curl Atlantic
Tradina Meadows-Forgeron, Executive Director
Jerry McCann, President
Catherine MacLean, Treasurer

Newfoundland & Labrador Curling Association
c/o Bob Osborne, 54 Hoyles Ave., St. John's NL A1B 1E3
Tel: 709-738-3640
URL: www.curlingnl.ca
Bob Osborne, President
Roy Hodder, Vice-President
Baxter House, Secretary
Carl C. Loughlin, Treasurer
Jean Blackie, Coordinator, Technical
Len Kostaszek, Coordinator, Tournament

Northern Alberta Curling Association (NACA)
#110, 9440 - 49 St., Edmonton AB T6B 2M9
Tel: 780-440-4270; *Fax:* 780-463-4519
e-mail: naca@planet.eon.net
URL: northernalbertacurling.com
Marylynn Morris, Executive Director

Northern Ontario Curling Association
PO Box 940, Unit #4, 214 Main St. West, Atikokan ON P0T 1C0
Tel: 807-597-8730; *Fax:* 807-597-4241
Toll-Free: 888-597-8730
e-mail: info@curlnoca.ca
URL: www.curlnoca.ca
Leslie Kerr, Executive Director
Al Gemmell, President

Northwest Territories Curling Association
c/o PO Box 11089, Yellowknife NT X1A 3X7
e-mail: nwtca@auroranet.nt.ca
URL: www.curlingnwt.ssimicro.com
Jennifer Keith, Secretary

Northwestern Ontario Curling Association (NWOCA)
433 Catherine St., Thunder Bay ON P7E 1K9
Tel: 807-622-8254; *Fax:* 807-626-9622
URL: www.norontcurl.tripod.com
Colleen Syrja, Sec.-Treas.
Don R. MacLeod, President

Northwestern Québec Curling Association (NWQCA) / Association de curling du Nord-Ouest québécois
281, 3e rue est, Amos QC J9T 2A7
Tel: 819-732-2089; *Fax:* 819-732-1617
Claude Noel, Secretary

Ontario Curling Association (OCA)
Office Mall 2, #2B, 1400 Bayly St., Pickering ON L1W 3R2
Tel: 905-831-1757; *Fax:* 905-831-1083
Toll-Free: 877-668-2875
e-mail: doug@ontcurl.com
URL: www.ontcurl.com
Affiliation(s): Curl Ontario
Doug Bakes, General Manager

Ottawa Valley Curling Association (OVCA)
PO Box 40129, Ottawa ON K1V 0W8
Tel: 613-521-5822; *Fax:* 613-521-5344
Toll-Free: 800-385-6621
e-mail: events@ovca.com
URL: www.ovca.com
Affiliation(s): Curling Quebec
Perry Anderson, President
Lily Ooi, Coordinator, Events

Peace Curling Association (PCA)
PO Box 265, Grande Prairie AB T8V 3A4
Tel: 780-532-4782; *Fax:* 780-538-2485
Toll-Free: 800-567-0171
e-mail: peaccurl@telusplanet.net
URL: www.peacecurl.org
Elaine Muceniek, President

Prince Edward Island Curling Association (PEICA)
PO Box 302, 40 Enman Cres., Charlottetown PE C1A 7K7
Tel: 902-368-4986; *Fax:* 902-368-4548
e-mail: glucas@sportpei.pe.ca
URL: www.peicurling.com
Affiliation(s): Sports PEI, Curl Atlantic
Ray McCourt, President

Saskatchewan Curling Association (SCA)
613 Park St., Regina SK S4N 5N1
Tel: 306-780-9202; *Fax:* 306-780-9404
Toll-Free: 877-722-2875
e-mail: saskcurling@sasktel.net
URL: www.saskcurl.com/sca/scahome.htm
Del Jones, President

Southern Alberta Curling Association (SACA)
#720, 3 St. NW, Calgary AB T2N 1N9
Tel: 403-246-9300; *Fax:* 403-246-9349
e-mail: curling@saca.ca
URL: www.saca.ca
Brent Syme, General Manager

Temiskaming & Northern Ontario Curling Association
c/o Stephen Chenier, PO Box 735, Englehart ON P0J 1H0
Tel: 705-647-2589; *Fax:* 705-544-8525
e-mail: jcdhh@ntl.sympatico.ca
URL: www.tnoca.curlingclub.ca
Stephen Chenier, Secretary/Treasurer

World Curling Federation (WCF)
74 Tay St., Perth PH2 8N Scotland
Tel: 44-173-845-1630; *Fax:* 44-173-845-1641
e-mail: wcf@dial.pipex.com
URL: www.worldcurling.net
Lester Harrison, President
Kate Caithness, Vice-President
Mike Thomson, Secretary General

Yukon Curling Association (YCA)
4061 - 4th Ave., Whitehorse YT Y1A 1H1
Tel: 867-668-7121; *Fax:* 867-667-4237
e-mail: yca@sportyukon.com
URL: yukoncurling.inthehack.com
Affiliation(s): Watson Lake Curling Club; Mayo Curling Club
Gord Zealand, President

Deafness

Alberta Deaf Sports Association (ADSA)
11404 - 142 St., Edmonton AB T5M 1V1
e-mail: adsa@shaw.ca
URL: adsa.deafalberta.org
Arista Haas, President
Ryan Bercier, Vice-President
Brenda Hillcox, Secretary

Diabetes

Diabetes Exercise & Sports Association (DESA)
8001 Montcastle Dr., Nashville TN 37221 USA
Fax: 615-673-2077
Toll-Free: 800-898-4322
e-mail: desa@diabetes-exercise.org
URL: www.diabetes-exercise.org
Paula Harper, President

Diving

Alberta Diving
426 Reeves Cres., Edmonton AB T6R 2A4
Tel: 780-988-5571; *Fax:* 780-988-7753
URL: www.albertadiving.ca
Cindy Casper, President
Susan Zwaenepoel, Vice-President
Barb Bush, Executive Director
Jim MacDonald, Secretary
Curtis Yano, Treasurer

British Columbia Diving
2630 Dogwood Dr., Surrey BC V4A 3K5
Tel: 604-541-9332; *Fax:* 604-541-9303
e-mail: info@bcdiving.ca
URL: www.bcdiving.ca
Bev Boys, Executive Director
Joyne MacDonald, Manager, Operations

Dive Ontario
#207, 1185 Eglinton Ave. East, Toronto ON M3C 3C6
Tel: 416-426-7040; *Fax:* 416-426-7367
e-mail: info@diveontario.com
URL: www.diveontario.com
Bev Lauder, Executive Director

Diving Plongeon Canada (DPC) / Association canadienne du plongeon amateur Inc.
#703, 2197 Riverside Dr., Ottawa ON K1H 7X3
Tel: 613-736-5238; *Fax:* 613-736-0409
e-mail: cada@diving.ca
URL: www.diving.ca
Affiliation(s): Aquatics Federation of Canada; Swimming Natation Canada; Synchronized Swimming; Water Polo Canada
Penny Joyce, Chief Operating Officer
Mitch Geller, Chief Technical Officer
Nancy Brawley, Director, National Team
Kathy Seaman, President

Fédération du plongeon amateur du Québec (FPAQ)
CP 1000, Succ. M, 4545, av Pierre-de-Coubertin, Montréal QC H1V 3R2
Tél: 514-252-3096; *Téléc:* 514-252-3094
Courriel: fpaq@plongeon.qc.ca
URL: www.plongeon.qc.ca
Isabelle Cloutier, Directrice exécutive

Fédération québécoise des activités subaquatiques (FQAS)
CP 1000, Succ. M, 4545, av Pierre-de Coubertin, Montréal QC H1V 3R2
Tél: 514-252-3009; *Téléc:* 514-254-1363
Ligne sans frais: 866-391-8835
Courriel: info@fqas.qc.ca
URL: www.fqas.qc.ca
Affiliation(s): Confédération mondiale des activités subaquatiques
Jean-Sébastien Naud, Directeur général

Manitoba Diving Association
Sport Manitoba Building, 200 Main St., Winnipeg MB R3C 1A8
Tel: 204-925-5654; *Fax:* 204-925-5703
e-mail: headcoach@panamdiving.com
URL: www.manitobadiving.com
Jim Lambie, Head Coach

Manitoba Underwater Council (MUC)
PO Box 711, Winnipeg MB R3C 2K3
Tel: 204-632-8508
e-mail: info@manunderwater.com
URL: www.manunderwater.com

Ontario Underwater Council (OUC)
#104, 1185 Eglinton Ave. East, Toronto ON M3C 3C6
Tel: 416-426-7033; *Fax:* 416-426-7280
e-mail: ouc@underwatercouncil.com
URL: www.underwatercouncil.com
Raimund Krob, President

Saskatchewan Diving
1870 Lorne St., Regina SK S4P 2L7
Tel: 306-780-9405; *Fax:* 306-781-6021
e-mail: skdiving@accesscomm.ca
URL: www.saskdiving.ca
Karen Swanson, Provincial Administrator
Carol Lunn, President

Equestrian Sports & Activities

Alberta Equestrian Federation (AEF)
#100, 251 Midpark Blvd. SE, Calgary AB T2X 1S3
Tel: 403-253-4411; *Fax:* 403-252-5260
Toll-Free: 877-463-6233
e-mail: execdir@albertaequestrian.com
URL: www.albertaequestrian.com
Sonia Meyer, Executive Director

Atlantic Canada Trail Riding Association
Sylvia Gillies, #344 Route 875, Belleisle Creek NB E5P 1C8
Roy Drinnan, Chair

British Columbia Competitive Trail Riders Association (BCCTRA)
c/o 2980 Giovando Road, Nanaimo BC V9X 1K5
Tel: 250-245-4405
e-mail: nicole.vaugeois@viu.ca
URL: www.bcctra.ca
Nicole Vagueois, Sec.-Treas.

Canadian Sport Horse Association (CSHA)
PO Box 970, 7904 Franktown Rd., Richmond ON K0A 2Z0
Tel: 613-686-6161; *Fax:* 613-686-6170
e-mail: csha@canadian-sport-horse.org
URL: www.canadian-sport-horse.org
Paul Morgan, President
David Lancaster, Treasuerer

Distance Riders of Manitoba (DRM)
PO Box 36, RR#2, Dugald MB R0E 0K0
Tel: 204-444-2314
e-mail: maura.leahy@mts.net
URL: www.kucera.mb.ca/drma/
Affiliation(s): American Endurance Ride Conference
Maura Leahy, Membership Director

Drive Canada
PO Box 2062, Vancouver BC V6B 3S3
Tel: 604-875-1905; *Fax:* 604-857-9582
e-mail: drivecanada@shaw.ca
URL: www.drivecanada.org
Affiliation(s): American Driving Society
Simon Rosenman, President

Endurance Riders Association of British Columbia (ERABC)
c/o 1624 Duncan Dr., Delta BC V4L 1S2
Affiliation(s): Canadian Long Distance Riding Association
Terre O'Brennan

Endurance Riders of Alberta (ERA)
c/o President, PO Box 418, Seba Beach AB T0E 2B0
Tel: 780-797-5404
URL: www.enduranceridersofalberta.com
Affiliation(s): Canadian Long Distance Riding Association
Carol Wadey, Treasurer
Owen Fulcher, President

Equestrian Association for the Disabled
8360 Leeming Rd., RR#3, Mount Hope ON L0R 1W0
Tel: 905-679-8323; *Fax:* 905-679-1705
URL: www.tead.on.ca
Jim Sykes, Chair & President
Patrick Warner, Vice-President
Hilary Webb, Executive Director
Gord Hyland, Treasurer
Trish Brakewell, Coordinator
Pat Bullock, Instructor, Riding

Equine Canada (EC) / Canada Hippique
#100, 2685 Queensview Dr., Ottawa ON K2B 8K2
Tel: 613-248-3433; *Fax:* 613-248-3484
Toll-Free: 866-282-8395
e-mail: inquiries@equinecanada.ca
URL: www.equestrian.ca
Affiliation(s): Provincial Partners: Horse Council of B.C., Alberta Equestrian Federation, Saskatchewan Horse Federation, Manitoba Horse Council, Ontario Equestrian Federation, Fédération Équestre du Quebec, New Brunswick Equestrian Association, PEI Horse Council, Nova Scotia Equestrian Federation, Newfoundland Equestrian Association, Canadian Pony Club
Akaash Maharaj, CEO

Fédération équestre du Québec inc. (FEQ)
CP 1000, Succ. M, 4545, av Pierre-de-Coubertin, Montréal QC H1V 3R2
Tél: 514-252-3053; *Téléc:* 514-252-3165
Courriel: infocheval@feq.qc.ca
URL: www.feq.qc.ca
Richard Mongeau, Directeur général

Horse Council British Columbia (HCBC)
27336 Fraser Hwy., Aldergrove BC V4W 3N5
Tel: 604-856-4304; *Fax:* 604-856-4302
Toll-Free: 800-345-8055
e-mail: reception@hcbc.ca; membership@hcbc.ca; education@hcbc.ca
URL: www.hcbc.ca
Lisa Laycock, Executive Director
Sarah Bradley, President
Susan Harrison, Secretary
Gary Patterson, Treasurer

Horse Trials New Brunswick
c/o Donna Lee Cole, 7515 Rte.102, Browns Flat NB E5M 2N8
Tel: 506-468-2098
URL: www.htnb.org
Affiliation(s): Horse Trials Canada
Donna Lee Cole, President
Louise McSheffrey, Secretary

Horse Trials Nova Scotia (HTNS)
60 Rockwell Drive, Mount Uniacke NS B0N 1Z0
Tel: 902-866-3889
URL: www.htns.org
Affiliation(s): Horse Trials Canada; Nova Scotia Equestrian Federation
Kim Elliott-Foster, President

Island Horse Council (IHC)
PO Box 1887, Charlottetown PE C1A 7N5
e-mail: islandhorsecouncil@yahoo.ca
URL: www.islandhorsecouncil.ca
Affiliation(s): Equine Canada
Ken Smith, Chair
Bobbi Jo Duffy, Treasurer

Manitoba Horse Council Inc.
#207, 200 Main St., Winnipeg MB R3C 4M2
Tel: 204-925-5718; *Fax:* 204-925-5792
e-mail: admin@manitobahorsecouncil.ca
URL: www.manitobahorsecouncil.ca
Dave Myers, President
Sheilagh Antoniuk, Executive Director

Manitoba Trail Riding Club Inc.
838 Alfred Ave., Winnipeg MB R2X 0T6
e-mail: Kelli.Hayhurst@pwgsc.gc.ca
URL: www.mbtrailridingclub.ca
Affiliation(s): Canadian Long Distance Riding Association
Kelli Hayhurst, President
Mary Anne Kirk, Treasurer

New Brunswick Equestrian Association (NBEA)
c/o Sport NB, #13, 900 Hanwell Rd., Fredericton NB E3B 6A3
Tel: 506-454-2353; *Fax:* 506-454-2363
e-mail: generalinfo@equestrian.nb.ca
URL: www.equestrian.nb.ca
Jeremy Hoyt, President
Jennifer Everett, Secretary

Newfoundland Equestrian Association (NEA)
PO Box 372, Stn. C, St. John's NL A1C 5J9
URL: www.horsenewfoundland.com
Katrina Butler, President
Sheila Anstey, Vice-President & Director, Competitions
Katie Murray, Secretary
Cathy Favre, Treasurer

North American Riding for the Handicapped Association (NARHA)
PO Box 33150, Denver CO 80233 USA
Tel: 303-452-1212; *Fax:* 303-252-4610
Toll-Free: 800-369-7433
e-mail: narha@narha.org
URL: www.narha.org
Carol Nickell, CEO

Nova Scotia Distance Riding Association (NSDRA)
RR#3, Site 802, Newport NS B0N 2A0
Affiliation(s): Canadian Long Distance Riding Association

Nova Scotia Equestrian Federation
5516 Spring Garden Rd., 4th Fl., Halifax NS B3J 1G6
Tel: 902-425-5450; *Fax:* 902-425-5606
e-mail: nsef@sportnovascotia.ca
URL: www.horsenovascotia.ca
Heather Myrer, Executive Director

Ontario Competitive Trail Riding Association Inc. (OCTRA)
R.R.#4, Tottenham ON L0G 1W0
Tel: 905-936-3362
e-mail: webmaster@octra.on.ca
URL: www.octra.on.ca
Affiliation(s): Horse Ontario; Ontario Equestrian Federation
Mark Ford, President
Joe Mezenberg, Vice-President
Marg Murray, Secretary

Kelly Corbyn, Treasurer

Ontario Equestrian Federation (OEF)
#203, 9120 Leslie St., Richmond Hill ON L4B 3J9
Tel: 905-709-6545; *Fax:* 905-709-1867
Toll-Free: 877-441-7112
e-mail: horse@horse.on.ca
URL: www.horse.on.ca
Affiliation(s): Equine Guelph; Ontario Trails Council; Ontario Federation of Agriculture
Deborah Thompson, Executive Director
Gary Yaghdjian, President
Kathy Fremes, Secretary

Ontario Horse Trials Canada (OHTC)
#186, 3-304 Stone Rd. West, Guelph ON N1G 4W4
e-mail: Roseanne.Corbett@gmail.com
URL: www.horsetrials.on.ca
Robin Winn, President
Vickie Witherspoon, Secretary

Ontario Trail Riders Association (OTRA)
PO Box 3038, Elmvale ON L0L 1P0
URL: www.otra.ca
Affiliation(s): Ontario Trails Council; Ontario Equestrian Federation
Janice Clegg, President

Saskatchewan Horse Federation (SHF)
2205 Victoria Ave., Regina SK S4P 0S4
Tel: 306-780-9244; *Fax:* 306-525-4009
e-mail: sk.horse@sasktel.net
URL: www.saskhorse.ca
Affiliation(s): Sask Sport; Western College Veterinary Medicine; SK Agriculture & Food (SAF)
Mae Smith, Executive Director

Saskatchewan Long Riders
C/O Diane Trundle, Stn. 429, Balgonie SK S0G 0E0
Tel: 306-978-1225; *Fax:* 306-230-1224
e-mail: bsutherland@shaw.ca
URL: www.sasklongriders.com
Affiliation(s): Canadian Long Distance Riding Association
Rachel Croskery, President

Trail Riding Alberta Conference (TRAC)
738 Wheeler Road, Edmonton AB T6M 2E8
Tel: 403-486-0957
e-mail: shanharms@shaw.ca
URL: www.trailriding.ab.ca
Affiliation(s): Canadian Long Distance Riding Association
Brent Seufert, President

Fencing

Alberta Fencing Association (AFA)
Percy Page Centre, 11759 Groat Rd., Edmonton AB T5M 3K6
Tel: 780-427-9474; *Fax:* 780-447-5959
e-mail: abfence@telus.net
URL: www.fencing.ab.ca
Vanessa Bjerreskov, Executive Director

British Columbia Fencing Association (BCFA)
Sport BC Building, #302, 1367 West Broadway, Vancouver BC V6H 4A9
Tel: 604-737-3044; *Fax:* 604-738-7175
e-mail: president.bcfa@gmail.com
URL: www.fencing.bc.ca
Jeffery Bowman, President

Canadian Fencing Federation (CFF) / Fédération canadienne d'escrime
10 Masterson Dr., St. Catharines ON L2T 3P1
Tel: 647-476-2401; *Fax:* 647-476-2402
e-mail: cff@fencing.ca
URL: www.fencing.ca
Affiliation(s): Fédération internationale d'escrime
Stephen Symons, President
Ron Dewar, Vice-President

Fédération d'escrime du Québec
CP 1000, Succ. M, 4545, av Pierre-de-Coubertin, Montréal QC H1V 3R2
Tél: 514-252-3045; *Téléc:* 514-254-3451
Courriel: info@escrimequebec.qc.ca
URL: www.escrimequebec.qc.ca
Maître Dominique Teisseire, Directeur, technique et administratif

Fencing Association of Nova Scotia (FANS) / Association d'escrime de la Nouvelle-Écosse
C/O Sport Nova Scotia, 5516 Spring Garden Rd., 4th Fl., Halifax NS B3J 3G6
Tel: 902-425-8946; *Fax:* 902-473-4425
e-mail: Ron.dewar@ccns.nshealth.ca
URL: www.chebucto.ns.ca/SportFit/Fencing
Ron Dewar, President

Manitoba Fencing Association (MFA)
200 Main St., Winnipeg MB R3C 4M2
Tel: 204-925-5696; *Fax:* 204-925-5703
e-mail: fencingmb@shawbiz.ca
URL: www.fencing.mb.ca
Marian McLennan, Executive Director
Paul Smith, President
Chris Whitmore, Vice-President, Technical
Kathy Borgfjord, Vice-President, Finance
Michel Allard, Vice-President, Athlete Programs
Dave Dessens, Vice-President, Sport Development

New Brunswick Fencing Association (NBFA)
c/o 20 Glenburn Ct., Saint John NB E2K 3Y9
Tel: 506-633-7047
e-mail: execdir@fencingnb.ca
URL: www.fencingnb.ca
Jane Corey, President
Tammy Crowley, Secretary

Newfoundland & Labrador Fencing Association (N&LFA)
#168, Unit 50 Hamlyn Road Plaza, St. John's NL A1E 5X7
Fax: 709-368-8830
e-mail: nlfencing@gmail.com
URL: sites.google.com/site/nlfencing/
Justin So, President

Ontario Fencing Association (OFA) / Association d'escrime de l'Ontario
984 Main St. West, Hamilton ON L8S 1B2
Tel: 905-525-6693
e-mail: info@fencingontario.ca
URL: fencingontario.ca/cms
Ranil Sonnadara, President
June McGuire, Executive Director

Prince Edward Island Fencing Association (PEIFA)
c/o Sport PEI, PO Box 302, 40 Enman Cres., Charlottetown PE C1A 7K7
Tel: 905-368-4110; *Fax:* 905-386-4548
Toll-Free: 800-247-6712
e-mail: sports@sportpei.pe.ca
URL: www.upei.ca/~fencing

Saskatchewan Fencing Association (SFA)
510 Cynthia St., Saskatoon SK S7L 7K7
Tel: 306-975-0823; *Fax:* 306-242-8007
e-mail: saskfencing@shaw.ca
URL: saskfencing.com
Affiliation(s): Saskatchewan Sport
Lynn Seguin, Executive Assistant

Field Hockey

Fédération de hockey sur gazon Québec / Québec Field Hockey Federation
CP 1000, Succ. M, 4545, av Pierre-de Coubertin, Montréal QC H1V 3R2
Tél: 514-426-8405; *Téléc:* 514-426-9418
Courriel: hockeysurgazon@yahoo.com
Affiliation(s): Field Hockey Canada; Sports Canada
Harbir Bhamrah, Président

Field Hockey Alberta (FHA)
#1, 2135 Westmount Rd. NW, Calgary AB T2N 3N3
Tel: 403-670-0014; *Fax:* 403-670-0018
Toll-Free: 888-670-0018
e-mail: info@fieldhockey.ab.ca
URL: fieldhockey.ab.ca
Liz Allan, Executive Director

Field Hockey Canada (FHC) / Hockey sur gazon Canada
#240, 1101 Prince of Wales Dr., Ottawa ON K2C 3W7
Tel: 613-521-8774; *Fax:* 613-521-0261
e-mail: fhc@fieldhockey.ca
URL: www.fieldhockey.ca
Mary Cicinelli, President
Suzzanne Nicholson, Executive Director
Ian Clark, Administrative Coordinator

Field Hockey Manitoba (FHM)
200 Main St., Winnipeg MB R3C 4M2
Tel: 204-925-5794; *Fax:* 204-925-5703
e-mail: fieldhockeymb@shawbiz.ca
URL: www.fieldhockeymb.org
Alex Chiborak, Contact

Field Hockey Nova Scotia
NS
Tel: 902-479-0207; *Fax:* 902-455-7638
e-mail: president@fieldhockey.ns.ca
URL: www.fieldhockey.ns.ca
Mario DeMello, President

Field Hockey Ontario (FHO)
PO Box 1037, Erin ON N0B 1T0
Tel: 905-492-1680
e-mail: fhoboard@gmail.com
URL: www.fieldhockeyontario.netfirms.com
Ann Doggett, President

New Brunswick Field Hockey Association (NBFHA)
c/o 2341 Golden Grove Rd., Saint John NB E2N 1Z8
Tel: 506-634-1241
e-mail: sara.hayward@nbed.nb.ca
Sara Hayward, President

Saskatchewan Field Hockey Association
1860 Lorne St., Regina SK S4P 2L7
Tel: 306-780-9256; *Fax:* 306-781-6021
e-mail: sfha@sasktel.net
URL: www.saskfieldhockey.ca
Stefanie Sloboda, Technical Director

Firearms

Buckskinners Muzzleloading Association, Limited
PO Box 4127, Stn. Champlain Mall, Moncton NB E1C 8L4
Tel: 506-576-1959; *Fax:* 506-859-1249
e-mail: wdj@fox.nstn.ca
Affiliation(s): New Brunswick Wildlife Federation
Shirley Stuart, Contact

Football

Alberta Amateur Football Association (AAFA)
Percy Page Centre, 11759 Groat Rd., Edmonton AB T5M 3K6
Tel: 780-427-8108; *Fax:* 780-427-0524
e-mail: bfryer@telus.net
URL: www.footballalberta.ab.ca
Neil Gerritsen, President
Brian Fryer, Executive Director

Canadian Football Hall of Fame & Museum
58 Jackson St. West, Hamilton ON L8P 1L4
Tel: 905-528-7566; *Fax:* 905-528-9781
e-mail: info@footballhof.com
URL: www.footballhof.com
Janice Smith, Managing Director

Canadian Football League (CFL) / Ligue canadienne de football (LCF)
50 Wellington St. East, 3rd Fl., Toronto ON M5E 1C8
Tel: 416-322-9650; *Fax:* 416-322-9651
e-mail: info@cfl.ca
URL: www.cfl.ca
Brent Scrimshaw, Chief Marketing Officer
Michael Copeland, Chief Operating Officer
Mark Cohon, Commissioner
Alexis Redmond, Director, Communications

Canadian Football Officials Association
c/o Ontario Region, 73 Alpaca Dr., Toronto ON M1J 2Z9
Tel: 416-431-7887
e-mail: webcommittee@cfoa-acof.ca
URL: www.cfoa-acof.ca
Mike Groleau, President

Canadian Junior Football League (CJFL)
9611 RR#1, Richmond BC V7E 1R8
Tel: 604-277-8133; *Fax:* 604-277-8136
e-mail: ronald_white@telus.net
URL: www.cjfl.ca
Ron Osterkampf, Commissioner

Canadian University Football Coaches Association (CUFCA)
c/o Huskies Football, St. Mary's University, Halifax NS B3H 3C3
Tel: 902-420-5550
Affiliation(s): Canadian Interuniversity Athletic Union
Blake Nill, President

Football BC
10605 - 135 St., Surrey BC V3T 4C8
Tel: 604-583-9363; *Fax:* 604-583-9939
e-mail: footballbc@footballbc.org
URL: www.playfootball.bc.ca

Football Canada
#100, 2255 St. Laurent Blvd., Ottawa ON K1G 4K3
Tel: 613-564-0003; *Fax:* 613-564-6309
e-mail: info@footballcanada.com
URL: footballcanada.com
Richard Munro, CEO
Bob Swan, Technical Consultant
Cara Lynch, Manager, Non-Contact Programs
Josh Sacobie, Technical Coordinator
Christine Piché, Administrative Coordinator

Football Nova Scotia Association
5516 Spring Garden Rd., Halifax NS B3J 1G6
Tel: 902-880-2816; *Fax:* 902-477-3535
URL: www.footballnovascotia.ca
Affiliation(s): Canadian Amateur Football Association
Richard MacLean, President
Todd Van Ritchie, Vice-President

Football Québec (FFAQ) / Fédération de football amateur de Québec
CP 1000, Succ. M, 4545, av Pierre-de-Coubertin, Montréal QC H1V 3R2
Tél: 514-252-3059; *Téléc:* 514-252-5216
Courriel: jeancharles@football.qc.ca
URL: www.football-quebec.com
Affiliation(s): National Football Federation of Canada
René Robillard, Président

Ontario Football Alliance
#B11, 100 Crimea St., Guelph ON N1H 2Y6
Tel: 519-780-0200; *Fax:* 519-780-0705
e-mail: otf@on.aibn.com
URL: www.ontariotacklefootball.com
Peter Repac, President

Foundations

Dr. James Naismith Basketball Foundation / La fondation de basketball Dr James Naismith
PO Box 1030, 14 Bridge St., Almonte ON K0A 1A0
Tel: 613-256-0492; *Fax:* 613-256-7883
e-mail: naismith@trytel.com
Affiliation(s): Basketball Canada
John Gosset, Executive Director
Allen G. Rae, President

Royal Canadian Golf Association Foundation
#1, 1333 Dorval Dr., Oakville ON L6M 4X7
Tel: 905-849-9700; *Fax:* 905-845-7040
Toll-Free: 800-263-0009
e-mail: khewson@rcga.org
URL: www.rcga.org
Karen Hewson, Executive Director

Fundraising

Calgary Olympic Development Association
88 Canada Olympic Rd. SW, Calgary AB T3B 5R5
Tel: 403-247-5452; *Fax:* 403-286-7213
e-mail: info@coda.ca
URL: www.coda.ab.ca
John P. Mills, President

Golf

Alberta Golf Association (AGA)
#22, 11410 - 27 St. SE, Calgary AB T2Z 3R6
Tel: 403-236-4616; *Fax:* 403-236-2915
Toll-Free: 888-414-4849
e-mail: info@albertagolf.org
URL: www.albertagolf.org
Brent Ellenton, Executive Director

Association des golfeurs professionnels du Québec (AGP)
435, boul. Saint-Luc, Saint-Jean-sur-Richelieu QC J2W 1E7
Tél: 450-349-5525; *Téléc:* 450-349-6640
Courriel: agpinfo@agp.qc.ca
URL: www.agp.qc.ca
Jean Trudeau, Directeur général

Association des surintendants de golf du Québec (ASGQ) / Québec Golf Superintendents Association (QSGA)
CP 642, Succ. B, Montréal QC H3B 3K3
Tél: 514-285-4874; *Téléc:* 514-282-4292
Courriel: info@asgq.org
URL: www.asgq.org
Christian Pilon, Président

British Columbia Golf Association (BCGA)
#2105, 21000 Westminster Hwy., Richmond BC V6V 2S9
Tel: 604-279-2580; *Fax:* 604-207-9535
Toll-Free: 888-833-2242
e-mail: info@bcga.org
URL: www.bcga.org
Affiliation(s): Canadian Golf Foundation; Professional Golf Association of BC; Canadian Ladies Golf Association of BC; Golf Course Superintendents Association of BC; International Association of Golf Administrators; National Golf Foundation; Pacific Coast Golf Association; Pacific Northwest Golf Association
George Faithfull, President
Kris Jonasson, Executive Director

British Columbia Golf Superintendents Association (BCGSA)
PO Box 807, 231 Nootka Cres., Lake Cowichan BC V0R 2G0
Tel: 250-749-6703; *Fax:* 250-749-6702
e-mail: admin@bcgsa.com
URL: www.bcgsa.com
Ginny Tromp, Executive Administrator
Rob Wilke, BCGSA President
Jerry Rousseau, Treasurer

British Columbia Professional Golfers Association
3540 Morgan Creek Way, Surrey BC V3C 0J7
Tel: 604-536-7878; *Fax:* 604-536-7879
Toll-Free: 800-667-4653
e-mail: brian@pgabc.org
URL: www.bcpga.org
Brian Butters, Executive Director
Troy Peverley, President

Canadian Caribbean Amateur Golfers Association (CCAGA)
#718, 7305 Woodbine Ave, Markham ON L3R 3V7
Fax: 905-420-8421
e-mail: info@ccaga.ca
URL: www.ccaga.ca

Canadian Golf Industry Association / Association canadienne de l'industrie du golf
7 Aspendale Dr., Toronto ON M1P 4J5
Tel: 416-289-1305; *Fax:* 416-289-1412
e-mail: cgiacgi@bellnet.ca
Chuck Fitzpatrick, Executive Director

Canadian Golf Superintendents Association (CGSA) / Association canadienne des surintendants de golf
#205, 5520 Explorer Dr., Mississauga ON L4W 5L1
Tel: 905-602-8873; *Fax:* 905-602-1958
Toll-Free: 800-387-1056
e-mail: cgsa@golfsupers.com
URL: www.golfsupers.com
Kenneth S. Cousineau, CAE, Executive Director
Bob Burrows, President
Patrick Moir, Vice-President
Greg Holden, Secretary-Treasurer

Canadian Professional Golfers' Association (CPGA) / Association canadienne des golfeurs professionnels
13450 Dublin Line, RR#1, Acton ON L7J 2W7
Tel: 519-853-5450; *Fax:* 519-853-5449
Toll-Free: 800-782-5764
e-mail: cpga@cpga.com
URL: www.cpga.com
Gary Bernard, Interim Executive Director

Canadian Society of Club Managers (CSCM) / La Société canadienne des directeurs de club
2943 Bloor St. West, #B, Toronto ON M8X 1B3
Tel: 416-979-0640; *Fax:* 416-979-1144
Toll-Free: 877-376-2726
e-mail: national@cscm.org
URL: www.cscm.org
Elizabeth Di Chiara, Executive Director

Golf Association of Ontario (GAO)
PO Box 970, Uxbridge ON L9P 1N3
Tel: 905-852-1101; *Fax:* 905-852-8893
Toll-Free: 800-668-2949
e-mail: administration@gao.ca
URL: www.gao.ca
Stephen James, President
David Mills, Executive Director

Golf Manitoba Inc.
200 Main St., Winnipeg MB R3C 4M2
Tel: 204-925-5730; *Fax:* 204-925-5731
e-mail: golfmb@golfmanitoba.mb.ca
URL: golfmanitoba.mb.ca
Dave Comaskey, Executive Director

Golf Newfoundland & Labrador (GNL)
77 Morgan Dr., Gander NL A1V 2K3
Tel: 709-722-2470; *Fax:* 709-722-8104
e-mail: golf@hnl.ca
URL: www.golfnewfoundland.ca
Greg Hillier, President

Golf Québec
#110, 415, rue Bourke, Dorval QC H9S 3W9
Tél: 514-633-1088; *Téléc:* 514-633-1074
Courriel: golfquebec@golfquebec.org
URL: www.golfquebec.org
Diane Dunlop-Hébert, President
Jean-Pierre Beaulieu, Directeur général

National Golf Course Owners Association Canada (NGCOA)
#105, 955 Green Valley Cres., Ottawa ON K2C 3V4
Tel: 613-226-3616; *Fax:* 613-226-4148
Toll-Free: 866-626-4262
e-mail: ngcoa@ngcoa.ca
URL: www.ngcoa.ca
Jeff Calderwood, CEO
Nathalie Lavallée, Director, Communications & Member Services

New Brunswick Golf Association (NBGA) / Association de golf du nouveau brunswick
PO Box 1555, Stn. A, Fredericton NB E3B 1G2
Tel: 506-451-1324; *Fax:* 506-451-1348
e-mail: nbgolf@nbnet.nb.ca
URL: www.nbga.nb.ca
Pierre Arsenault, Executive Director

Nova Scotia Golf Association (NSGA)
#4, 24 Simmonds Dr., Dartmouth NS B3B 1R3
Tel: 902-468-8844; *Fax:* 902-484-5327
e-mail: adminexec@ns.aliantzinc.ca
URL: www.nsga.ns.ca
David Campbell, Executive Director
Shelley Pineault, Executive Assistant

Prince Edward Island Golf Association
PO Box 51, Charlottetown PE C1A 7K2
Tel: 902-393-3293; *Fax:* 902-628-2260
e-mail: peiga@peiga.ca
URL: www.peiga.ca
Don Chandler, Executive Director
Jean Kelly, President

Royal Canadian Golf Association (RCGA) / Association royale de golf du Canada
Golf House, #1, 1333 Dorval Dr., Oakville ON L6M 4X7
Tel: 905-849-9700; *Fax:* 905-845-7040
e-mail: cboag@rcga.org
URL: www.rcga.org
Affiliation(s): World Amateur Golf Council
Scott Simmons, Executive Director
Peter Beresford, COO
Rick Desrochers, Senior Director, Corporate Planning

Saskatchewan Golf Association
510 Cynthia St., Saskatoon SK S7L 7K7
Tel: 306-975-0850; *Fax:* 306-975-0840
e-mail: info@saskgolf.ca
URL: www.saskgolf.ca
Daniel Rauckman, Executive Director

Gymnastics

Alberta Gymnastics Federation (AGF)
#207, 5800 - 2 St. SW, Calgary AB T2H 0H2
Tel: 403-259-5500; *Fax:* 403-259-5588
Toll-Free: 800-665-1010
e-mail: info@abgym.ab.ca
URL: www.abgym.ab.ca
Scott Hayes, President & CEO

Fédération de gymnastique du Québec (FGQ) / Québec Gymnastics Federation
CP 1000, Succ. M, 4545, av Pierre-de-Coubertin, Montréal QC H1V 3R2
Tél: 514-252-3043; *Téléc:* 514-252-3169
Courriel: info@gymnastique.qc.ca
URL: www.gymnastique.qc.ca
Robert Paquin, Directeur général
Claude Aubertin, Président

Raymond Paquin, Vice-président

Gymnastics B.C. (GBC)
#230, 3820 Cessna Drive, Richmond BC V3B 0A2
Tel: 604-333-3496; *Fax:* 604-333-3499
Toll-Free: 800-556-2242
e-mail: info@gymnastics.bc.ca
URL: www.gymnastics.bc.ca
Moira Gooksetter, CEO
Twyla Ryan, President

Gymnastics Canada Gymnastique (GCG)
#120, 1900 City Park Dr., Ottawa ON K1J 1A3
Tel: 613-748-5637; *Fax:* 613-748-5691
e-mail: info@gymcan.org
URL: www.gymcan.org
Affiliation(s): Fédération internationale de gymnastique
Jean-Paul Caron, President & CEO

Gymnastics Newfoundland & Labrador Inc.
PO Box 21248, Stn. MacDonald Dr., St. John's NL A1A 5B2
Tel: 709-576-0146; *Fax:* 709-576-7493
e-mail: gymnastics@sportnl.ca
Pat Jenkins, Executive Director

Gymnastics Nova Scotia (GNS)
5516 Spring Garden Rd., 4th Fl., Halifax NS B3J 1G6
Tel: 902-425-5450; *Fax:* 902-425-5606
e-mail: gns@sportnovascotia.ca
URL: www.gymns.ca
Angela Gallant, Executive Director
Jan Chipman, President
Louise Hawkins, Vice-President

Gymnastics PEI
Sport PEI, PO Box 302, Charlottetown PE C1A 7K7
Tel: 902-368-4262; *Fax:* 902-368-4548
e-mail: gflood@sportpei.pe.ca
URL: www.sportpei.pe.ca
Glen Flood, Executive Director

Gymnastics Saskatchewan
1870 Lorne St., Regina SK S4P 2L7
Tel: 306-780-9229; *Fax:* 306-780-9475
e-mail: info@gymsask.com
URL: www.gymsask.com
Klara Miller, Executive Director

Manitoba Gymnastics Association
200 Main St., Winnipeg MB R3C 4M2
Tel: 204-925-5781; *Fax:* 204-925-5932
e-mail: mangym@sport.mb.ca
URL: www.gymnastics.mb.ca
Kathy Stoesz, Executive Director

New Brunswick Gymnastics Association (NBGA) / Association gymnastique du Nouveau-Brunswick
110 Rivercrest Ave., Riverview NB E1B 1M7
Tel: 506-384-6242; *Fax:* 506-384-6244
e-mail: nbga@gym.nb.ca
URL: user.fundy.net/nbga/
Reid Middleton, President
Nathalie Colpitts, Executive Director

Ontario Gymnastic Federation (OGF)
#504, 1185 Eglinton Ave. East, Toronto ON M3C 3C6
Tel: 416-426-7100; *Fax:* 416-426-7377
Toll-Free: 866-565-0650
e-mail: info@ogf.com
URL: www.ogf.com
Holly Abraham, CEO
Angel Crossman, President
Ruth Uren, Secretary

Rhythmic Gymnastics Alberta (RGA)
c/o Percy Page Centre, 11759 Groat Rd., 3rd Fl., Edmonton AB T5M 3K6
Tel: 780-427-8152; *Fax:* 780-427-8153
Toll-Free: 800-881-2504
e-mail: rga@rgalberta.com
URL: www.rgalberta.com
Joan Jack, President
Odette Lindstrom, Treasurer
Helen Marchak, Vice-President

Yukon Gymnastics Association
4061 - 4th Ave., Whitehorse YT Y1A 1H1
Tel: 867-668-4794; *Fax:* 867-667-4237
e-mail: polarett@internorth.com
URL: www.polarettes.org
Kelly Mock, Technical Director

Halls of Fame

Alberta Sports Hall of Fame & Museum (ASHFM)
#30, Riverview Park, Red Deer AB T4N 1E3
Tel: 403-341-8614; *Fax:* 403-341-8619
e-mail: postmaster@albertasportshalloffame.com
URL: www.albertasportshalloffame.com
Donna Hateley, Managing Director

British Columbia Sports Hall of Fame & Museum
Gate A, BC Place Stadium, 777 Pacific Blvd. South, Vancouver BC V6B 4Y8
Tel: 604-687-5520; *Fax:* 604-687-5510
e-mail: sportsinfo@bcsportshalloffame.com
URL: www.bcsportshalloffame.com
Affiliation(s): International Association of Sports Museums & Halls of Fame
Colin Brown, Chair

Canada's Sports Hall of Fame / Temple de la renommée des sports du Canada
Exhibition Place, 115 Princes' Blvd., Toronto ON M6K 3C3
Tel: 416-260-6789; *Fax:* 416-260-9347
e-mail: info@cshof.ca
URL: www.cshof.ca
Sheryn Posen, COO
J. Trevor Eyton, Chair

Canadian Golf Hall of Fame & Museum (CGHF) / Musée et Temple canadien de la renommée du golf
Glen Abbey Gold Club, 1333 Dorval Dr., Oakville ON L6J 4Z3
Tel: 905-849-9700; *Fax:* 905-845-7040
e-mail: cghf@cghf.org
URL: www.rcga.org
Karen E. Hewson, Director
Meggan Pacheco, Archivist
Paul Stone, Curator

Canadian Lacrosse Hall of Fame
302 Royal Ave., New Westminster BC V3L 1H7
Tel: 604-527-4640; *Fax:* 604-527-4641
e-mail: allan@lacrosse.ca
Allan Blair, Curator

Canadian Olympic Hall of Fame / Temple de la renommée olympique du Canada
c/o COC, #1400, 85 Albert St., Ottawa ON K1P 6A4
Tel: 613-244-2020; *Fax:* 613-244-0169
URL: www.olympic.ca/EN/hof/index.shtml
Sue Holloway, Contact

Manitoba Sports Hall of Fame & Museum (MSHF&M)
200 Main St., 2nd Fl., Winnipeg MB R3C 4M2
Tel: 204-925-5735; *Fax:* 204-925-5792
URL: halloffame.mb.ca
Affiliation(s): Sport Manitoba
Rick Brownlee, Executive Director

New Brunswick Sports Hall of Fame / Temple de la renommée sportive du N.-B.
Clark Bldg., PO Box 6000, 503 Queen St., Fredericton NB E3B 5H1
Tel: 506-453-3747; *Fax:* 506-459-0481
e-mail: deborah.williams@gnb.ca
URL: www.nbsportshalloffame.nb.ca
Affiliation(s): International Sports Heritage Association
Jamie Wolverton, Executive Director

Northwestern Ontario Sports Hall of Fame & Museum
219 May St. South, Thunder Bay ON P7E 1B5
Tel: 807-622-2852; *Fax:* 807-622-2736
e-mail: nwosport@tbaytel.net
URL: www.nwosportshalloffame.com
Kathryn Dwyer, Curator
Diane Imrie, Executive Director

Nova Scotia Sport Heritage Centre
#446, 1800 Argyle Street, Halifax NS B3J 3N8
Tel: 902-421-1266; *Fax:* 902-425-1148
Bill Robinson, Executive Director

Ottawa Sports Hall of Fame Inc. (OSHOF) / Temple de la renommée des sports d'Ottawa
Ottawa ON
Tel: 613-562-6515
e-mail: frank.lambros@NBPCD.com
URL: www.ottawasportshalloffame.com
Tom Deacon, Chair

Prince Edward Island Sports Hall of Fame & Museum Inc.
PO Box 1523, Summerside PE C1N 4K4
Tel: 902-436-0423; *Fax:* 902-436-0960
e-mail: publicrelations@sportpei.pe.ca
URL: www.peisportshalloffame.ca
Clair Sudsbury, Chair

Saskatchewan Sports Hall of Fame & Museum (SSFHM)
2205 Victoria Ave., Regina SK S4P 0S4
Tel: 306-780-9232; *Fax:* 306-780-9427
e-mail: sshfm@sasktel.net
URL: www.sshfm.com
Sheila Kelly, Executive Director

Handball

Alberta Team Handball Federation (ATHF)
Percy Page Centre, 11759 Groat Rd., Edmonton AB T5M 3K6
Tel: 780-415-2666; *Fax:* 780-422-2663
e-mail: Handballalberta@gmail.com
URL: www.teamhandball.ab.ca
Rick Ryll, President/CEO
Amber Smart, Chief Information Officer

Balle au mur Québec (BAMQ) / Québec Handball Association
CP 1000, Succ. M, 4545, av Pierre-de-Coubertin, Montréal QC H1V 3R2
Tél: 514-252-3062
Courriel: info@sports-4murs.qc.ca
URL: www.balleaumur.qc.ca
Affiliation(s): Association canadienned de Balle au mur
Michel Foster, Directeur général
Danny Bell, Président

Canadian Handball Association (CHA) / Fédération de balle au mur du Canada
30 Melwood Ave., Halifax NS B3N 1E3
Tel: 902-477-2902; *Fax:* 902-431-3145
e-mail: handball@cdnhandball.ca
URL: www.cdnhandball.ca
Brian Goto, President
Mike Wilson, Treasurer

Canadian Team Handball Federation (CTHF) / Fédération canadienne de handball olympique (FCHO)
453, rue Jacob-Nicol, Sherbrooke QC J1J 4E5
Tel: 819-563-7937; *Fax:* 819-563-5352
e-mail: f.lebeau@videotron.ca
URL: www.handballcanada.ca
Affiliation(s): International Handball Federation; Pan American Team Handball Federation; Commonwealth Handball Federation
François LeBeau, COO
Ward Hrabi, President

Fédération québécoise de handball olympique
CP 1000, Succ. M, 4545, av Pierre-de-Coubertin, Montréal QC H1V 3R2
Tél: 514-252-3067; *Téléc:* 514-251-8882
Courriel: handball@handball.qc.ca
URL: www.handball-elite.com
Michelle Lortie, Contact

Manitoba Team Handball Federation
#311, 200 Main St., Winnipeg MB R3C 4M2
Tel: 204-925-5652; *Fax:* 204-925-5703
e-mail: NancyKarpinsky@hotmail.com
URL: www.handballmanitoba.com
Nancy Karpinsky, President

New Brunswick Team Handball Association
585, Pointe des Ferguson, Tracadie-Sheila NB E1X 1C6
Tél: 506-395-7722; *Téléc:* 506-395-3809
Ernest Ferguson, President

Newfoundland & Labrador Handball Federation
c/o School of Human Kinetics, Memorial Univ., St. John's NL A1C 5S7
Tel: 709-737-8684
e-mail: rwheeler@mun.ca
Ralph Wheeler, Contact

Team Handball Federation of British Columbia
Vancouver BC
e-mail: info@vancouverhandball.ca
URL: www.vancouverhandball.ca
Deborah Magdee, President

Hang Gliding

British Columbia Hang Gliding/Paragliding Association (BCHPA)
PO Box 41, Heffley Creek BC V0E 1Z0
Tel: 250-767-6717
e-mail: confusedone@uniserve.ca
URL: www.bchpa.org
Mike Miller, President

Hang Gliding & Paragliding Association of Atlantic Canada (HPAAC)
General Delivery, Diligent River NS B0M 1H0
Tel: 902-254-2972
e-mail: jnewman@eastlink.ca
URL: www.hpaac.ca
Affiliation(s): Hang Gliding & Paragliding Association of Canada
Judith Newman, Contact

Hang Gliding & Paragliding Association of Canada (HPAC) / Association canadienne de vol libre (ACVL)
5 Millennium Dr., Stratford PE C1B 2H2
Fax: 902-367-3358
Toll-Free: 877-370-2078
e-mail: admin@hpac.ca
URL: www.hpac.ca
Domagoj Juretic, President
Sam Jeyes, Business Manager

Health

Island Fitness Council
#2, 1216 Sand Cove Rd., Saint John NB E2M 5V8
Tel: 506-672-1993; *Fax:* 506-672-8762
Toll-Free: 888-790-1411
e-mail: membershipservices@fitnessnb.ca
URL: www.fitnessnb.ca
Affiliation(s): National Fitness Leadership Alliance

Physical & Health Education Canada / Éducation physique et santé Canada
#301, 2197 Riverside Dr., Ottawa ON K1H 7X3
Tel: 613-523-1348; *Fax:* 613-523-1206
Toll-Free: 800-663-8708
e-mail: info@phecanada.ca
URL: www.phecanada.ca
Mark Jones, President
Andrea Grantham, Executive Director
Sharon May, Director, Programs

Hearing

Canadian Deaf Ice Hockey Federation (CDIHF)
c/o C. Cooper, #137, 201 Queen Victoria Dr., Hamilton ON L8W 1W7
e-mail: cdihf@rogers.com
URL: www.cdihf.deafhockey.com
Affiliation(s): Canadian Hockey Association; Ontario Deaf Sports Association, Inc.; Canadian Deaf Sports Association
Danny Daniels, President
Eugene Franciosi, Vice-President
Brenda Stanley, Secretary
Raymond Patterson, Treasurer

Hiking

Federation of Mountain Clubs of British Columbia
PO Box 19673, 130 West Broadway, Vancouver BC V5T 4E7
Tel: 604-873-6096; *Fax:* 604-873-6086
e-mail: fmcbc@mountainclubs.bc.ca
URL: www.mountainclubs.bc.ca
Patrick R. Harrison, President
Ron Ford, Registrar
Brian Jones, Manager
Peter Rothermel, Vice-President

Hockey

British Columbia Amateur Hockey Association (BCAHA) / Association de hockey amateur de la Colombie-Britannique
6671 Oldfield Rd., Saanichton BC V8M 2A1
Tel: 250-652-2978; *Fax:* 250-652-4536
e-mail: info@bchockey.net
URL: www.bchockey.net
Barry Petrachenko, Executive Director
Ed Mayert, President

Canadian Adult Recreational Hockey Association (CARHA)
#610, 1420 Blair Pl., Ottawa ON K1J 9L8
Tel: 613-244-1989; *Fax:* 613-244-0451
Toll-Free: 800-267-1854
e-mail: hockey@carhahockey.ca
URL: www.carhahockey.ca
Mike Peski, President

Canadian Hockey League
#201, 305 Milner Ave., Toronto ON M1B 3V4
Tel: 416-332-9711; *Fax:* 416-332-1477
URL: www.chl.ca
Tim Van Overbeek, Contact

Fédération internationale de hockey (FIH) / International Hockey Federation
Résidence du Parc, Rue du Valentin 61, Lausanne 1004 Switzerland
Tél: 41-21-641-0606; *Téléc:* 41-21-641-0607
Courriel: nicole.delaloye@worldhockey.org
URL: www.worldhockey.org
Affiliation(s): Field Hockey Canada
Leandro Negre, President

Hockey Canada
#N204, 801 King Edward Ave., Ottawa ON K1N 6N5
Tel: 613-562-5677; *Fax:* 613-562-5676
Toll-Free: 800-667-2242
e-mail: nsouliere@hockeycanada.ca
URL: www.hockeycanada.ca
Affiliation(s): International Ice Hockey Federation
Bob Nicholson, President
Al Morris, Chairman

Hockey Development Centre for Ontario (HDCO)
#312, 3 Concorde Gate, Toronto ON M3C 3N7
Tel: 416-426-7252; *Fax:* 416-426-7348
Toll-Free: 888-843-4326
e-mail: hockey@hdco.on.ca
URL: www.hdco.on.ca
Wayne Dillon, Executive Director
Wayne Salatino, Chair

Hockey Manitoba
#217, 200 Main St., Winnipeg MB R3C 4M2
Tel: 204-925-5755; *Fax:* 204-925-5761
e-mail: info@hockeymanitoba.mb.ca
URL: www.hockeymanitoba.mb.ca
Affiliation(s): Hockey Canada
Peter Woods, Executive Director
Brian Franklin, President
Bernie Reichardt, Director, Hockey Development

Hockey New Brunswick (HNB) / Hockey Nouveau-Brunswick
PO Box 456, 861 Woodstock Rd., Fredericton NB E3B 4Z9
Tel: 506-453-0089; *Fax:* 506-453-0868
URL: www.hnb.ca
Brian Whitehead, Executive Director
Tom Donovan, President
Pat MacFadzen, Director, Administration

Hockey Newfoundland & Labrador (NLHA) / Association de hockey de Terre-Neuve et Labrador
PO Box 176, 13B High St., Grand Falls-Windsor NL A2A 2J4
Tel: 709-489-5512; *Fax:* 709-489-2273
e-mail: office@hockeynl.ca
URL: www.hockeynl.ca
Craig Tulk, Executive Director
Tamar Hobbs, Administrative Assistant

Hockey North
47 Pine Cres., Hay River NT X0E 0R5
Tel: 867-874-6903; *Fax:* 867-874-4603
Cheryl Carriere, Executive Director

Hockey Northwestern Ontario (HNO)
#100, 216 Red River Rd., Thunder Bay ON P7B 1A6
Tel: 807-623-1542; *Fax:* 807-623-0037
John Pucci, General Manager
Ron MacKinnon, Development Coorindator

Hockey Nova Scotia
#200, 6300 Lady Hammond Rd., Halifax NS B3K 2R6
Tel: 902-454-9400; *Fax:* 902-454-3883
URL: www.hockeynovascotia.ca
Darren Cossar, Executive Director

Hockey Québec (FQHG)
CP 1000, Succ. M, 4545, av Pierre-de-Coubertin, Montréal QC H1V 3R2
Tél: 514-252-3079; *Téléc:* 514-252-3158
Courriel: info@hockey.qc.ca
URL: www.hockey.qc.ca
Sylvain B. Lalonde, Directeur général
Claude Allain, Président

International Hockey Hall of Fame & Museum (IHHOF)
PO Box 82, 277 York St., Kingston ON K7L 4V6
Tel: 613-544-2355; *Fax:* 613-544-2844
e-mail: info@ihhof.com
URL: www.ihhof.com
Mark Potter, President

International Hockey Heritage Centre
c/o MacDonnell Group Consulting Ltd., #1100, 1505 Barrington St., Halifax NS B3J 3K5
Tel: 902-425-3980; *Fax:* 902-423-7593
e-mail: info@hockeyland.ca
URL: www.hockeyland.ca
Ralston MacDonnell, Project Manager
Wayne Russell, Chair

International Ice Hockey Federation (IIHF)
Brandschenkestrasse 50, Zurich CH-8027 Switzerland
Tel: 41-1-562-2200; *Fax:* 41-1-562-2229
e-mail: office@iihf.com
URL: www.iihf.com
Affiliation(s): Hockey Canada
Horst Lichtner, General Secretary
René Fasel, President

Minor Hockey Alliance of Ontario
71 Albert St., Stratford ON N5A 3K2
Tel: 519-273-7209; *Fax:* 519-273-2114
e-mail: alliance@alliancehockey.com
URL: www.alliancehockey.com
Tony Martindale, Executive Director

Northern Ontario Hockey Association (NOHA)
108 Lakeshore Dr., North Bay ON P1A 2A8
Tel: 705-474-8851; *Fax:* 705-474-6019
e-mail: noha@noha.on.ca
URL: www.noha.on.ca
Affiliation(s): Ontario Hockey Federation
Chris May, Executive Director
Bryce Kulik, President

Nova Scotia Minor Hockey Council
#910, 6080 Young St., Halifax NS B3K 5L2
Tel: 902-455-8320; *Fax:* 902-454-3883
Toll-Free: 800-313-8320
Affiliation(s): Nova Scotia Hockey Association
Cliff Pottie, Executive Director
Tom O'Keefe, Chairman

Ontario Hockey Federation (OHF)
Sport Alliance of Ontario Bldg., #212, 3 Concorde Gate, Toronto ON M3C 3N7
Tel: 416-426-7249; *Fax:* 416-426-7347
e-mail: info@ohf.on.ca
URL: www.ohf.on.ca
Affiliation(s): Minor Hockey Alliance of Ontario; Greater Toronto Hockey League; Northern Ontario Hockey Association; Ontario Minor Hockey Association; Ontario Hockey Association; Ontario Hockey League; Ontario Women's Hockey Association
Joe Drago, Executive Director
Bill Bowman, 1st Vice-President
Frank Pindar, 2nd Vice-President
Phil McKee, Executive Director
Wayne Tod, Secretary-Treasurer
Ryan Berg, Coordinator, Hockey Development
Cheryl Boston, Coordinator, Communications, Marketing, & Events

Ontario Minor Hockey Association (OMHA)
#3, 25 Brodie Dr., Richmond Hill ON L4B 3K7
Tel: 905-780-6642; *Fax:* 905-780-0344
e-mail: omha@omha.net
URL: www.omha.net
Affiliation(s): Ontario Hockey Federation
Marg Ensoll, President
Richard Ropchan, Executive Director
Kevin Boston, Director, Marketing & Events
Ian Taylor, Director, Development
Bill Rowney, Treasurer
Mark Dickie, Manager, Communications & IT

Ontario Women's Hockey Association (OWHA) / Association de hockey féminin de l'Ontario
#3, 5155 Spectrum Way, Mississauga ON L4W 5A1

Tel: 905-282-9980; *Fax:* 905-282-9982
e-mail: info@owha.on.ca
URL: owha.on.ca
Fran Rider, President

Ottawa & District Hockey Association (ODHA) / Association de hockey du district d'Ottawa
#D 300, 1247 Kilborn Pl., Ottawa ON K1H 6K9
Tel: 613-224-7686; *Fax:* 613-224-6079
e-mail: rts-ed@odha.com
URL: www.odha.com
Richard T. Sennott, Executive Director

Pan American Hockey Federation (PAHF)
46 Barton St., Ottawa ON K1S 4R7
Tel: 819-956-8023; *Fax:* 819-956-8019
e-mail: info@panamhockey.org
URL: www.panamhockey.org

Prince Edward Island Hockey Association / Association de hockey de l'Île-du-Prince-Edouard
40 Enman Cres., Charlottetown PE C1A 7K7
Tel: 902-368-4334; *Fax:* 902-368-4337
e-mail: peiha@pei.sympatico.ca
Mike Whelan, Secretary/Manager

Saskatchewan Hockey Association (SHA) / Association de hockey de la Saskatchewan
#2, 575 Park St., Regina SK S4N 5B2
Tel: 306-789-5101; *Fax:* 306-789-6112
URL: www.sha.sk.ca
Greg Camp, President
Kelly McClintock, General Manager

Sledge Hockey of Canada (SHOC)
c/o Hockey Canada, #N204, 801 King Edward Ave., Ottawa ON K1N 6N5
Tel: 613-562-5677; *Fax:* 613-562-5676
e-mail: cchampagne@hockeycanada.ca
URL: www.hockeycanada.ca
Adam Crockatt, Manager

Western Hockey League (WHL)
#1, 3030 Sunridge Way NE, Calgary AB T1Y 7K4
Tel: 403-693-3030; *Fax:* 403-693-3031
e-mail: info@whl.ca
URL: www.whl.ca
Ron Robison, Commissioner

Horse Racing

Alberta Horse Trials Association
c/o Joanne Cameron, 21 Greenbrier Cres., St Albert AB T8N 1A2
Tel: 780-922-3170
e-mail: mgaglione@xplornet.com
URL: www.albertahorsetrials.com
Affiliation(s): Canadian Equestrian Federation
George Balogh, President

Association Trot & Amble du Québec (ATAQ)
#230, 5375, rue Paré, Montréal QC H4P 1P7
Tél: 514-731-9484; *Téléc:* 514-731-7687
Ligne sans frais: 800-731-9484
Courriel: courses@qc.aira.com
URL: www.trotetamble.ca/fr/index.html
Michel St-Louis, Président

Jockey Club of Canada / Jockey Club du Canada
PO Box 66, Stn. B, Toronto ON M9W 5K9
Tel: 416-675-7756; *Fax:* 416-675-6378
e-mail: jockeyclub@bellnet.ca
URL: www.jockeyclubcanada.com
Richard Bonnycastle, Steward
Bridget Bimm, Executive Director

Jockeys Benefit Association of Canada (JBAC)
c/o Thoroughbred Race Office, 555 Rexdale Blvd., Toronto ON M9W 5L2
Tel: 416-798-8715
e-mail: jbacmanager@mac.com
URL: jbac.ca/trainers/jbac
Chad Hoverson, President
Robert King, Secretary-Manager

Ontario Horse Racing Industry Association (OHRIA)
PO Box 456, 555 Rexdale Blvd., Toronto ON M9W 5L4
Tel: 416-679-0741; *Fax:* 416-679-9114
e-mail: ohria@ohria.com
URL: www.ohria.com
Hector Clouthier, Executive Director

Horses

Saskatchewan Standardbred Horsemen's Association
PO Box 4122, Regina SK S4P 3W5
Tel: 306-757-4755
Ron McLeod, President

Kayaking

Canoe Kayak Saskatchewan (CKS)
1870 Lorne St., Regina SK S4P 2L7
Tel: 306-729-4220; *Fax:* 306-729-4216
e-mail: cks@accesscomm.ca
URL: www.saskcanoe.ca
Jan Hanson, Executive Director
Fiona Vincent, President
Jeanette Hamilton, Treasurer

Fédération québécoise de canoë-kayak d'eau vive
CP 1000, Succ. M, 4545, av Pierre-de Coubertin, Montréal QC H1V 3R2
Tél: 514-252-3099; *Téléc:* 514-252-3094
Courriel: fqckev@kayak.qc.ca
URL: www.kayak.qc.ca
Patrick Lévesque, Coordonnateur

Ontario Recreational Canoeing and Kayaking Association (ORCKA)
#411, 1185 Eglinton Ave. East, Toronto ON M3C 3C6
Tel: 416-426-7016; *Fax:* 416-426-7363
e-mail: info@orca.on.ca
URL: www.orca.on.ca
Gordon Haggert, President

Paddle Canada (PC) / Pagaie Canada
PO Box 20069, Stn. RPO Taylor-Kidd, Kingston ON K7P 2T6
Tel: 613-547-3196; *Fax:* 613-547-4880
Toll-Free: 888-252-6292
e-mail: info@paddlingcanada.com
URL: www.paddlingcanada.com
Affiliation(s): Active Living Alliance for Canadians with a Disability; Canadian Heritage Rivers System; Girl Guides of Canada
Sue J. Hopson, Business Manager

Wilderness Canoe Association (WCA)
PO Box 91068, 2901 Bayview Ave., Toronto ON M2K 2Y6
Tel: 416-223-4646
e-mail: info@wildernesscanoe.ca
URL: www.wildernesscanoe.ca
Aleks Gusev, Chair

Labour Unions

Canadian Football League Players' Association (CFLPA) / Association des joueurs de la ligue de football canadienne
#207, 603 Argus Rd., Oakville ON L6J 6G6
Tel: 905-844-7852; *Fax:* 905-844-5127
Toll-Free: 800-616-6865
e-mail: admin@cflpa.com
URL: www.cflpa.com
Stu Laird, President
Mike O'Shea, 1st Vice-President
Jay McNeil, 2nd Vice-President
Sean Fleming, Member-at-Large
Edward Molstad, Legal Counsel
Fred James, Benefits Chairman
Deanne Mitchell, Executive Assistant

Major League Baseball Players' Association (Ind.) / Association des joueurs de la Ligue majeure de baseball (ind.)
12 East 49th St., 24th Fl., New York NY 10017 USA
Tel: 212-826-0808; *Fax:* 212-752-4378
e-mail: feedback@mlbpa.org
URL: www.majorleaguebaseball.com/
Donald M. Fehr, Executive Director
Gene Orza, Chief Operating Officer

Professional Hockey Players' Association (PHPA)
#701, 1 St Paul St., St Catharines ON L2R 7L2
Tel: 905-682-4800; *Fax:* 905-682-4822
e-mail: phpa@phpa.com
URL: www.phpa.com
Larry Landon, Executive Director

Lacrosse

British Columbia Lacrosse Association (BCLA)
4041B Remi Pl., Burnaby BC V5A 4J8
Tel: 604-421-9755; *Fax:* 604-421-9775
e-mail: info@bclacrosse.com
URL: www.bclacrosse.com
Rochelle Winterton, Executive Director

Canadian Lacrosse Association (CLA) / Association canadienne de crosse (ACC)
#B4, 2211 Riverside Dr., Ottawa ON K1H 7X5
Tel: 613-260-2028; *Fax:* 613-260-2029
e-mail: info@lacrosse.ca
URL: www.lacrosse.ca
Affiliation(s): International Lacrosse Federation; International Federation of Women's Lacrosse Associations; Fédération internationale d'Inter-crosse; Canadian Lacrosse Foundation; Sport Canada; Coaching Association of Canada
David Miriguay, CLA General Manager

Fédération de crosse du Québec (FCQ)
CP 1000, Succ. M, 4545, av Pierre-de Coubertin, Montréal QC H1V 3R2
Tél: 514-252-3058; *Téléc:* 514-251-8038
Courriel: crosse@crosse.qc.ca
URL: www.crosse.qc.ca
Affiliation(s): Sports Québec; Regroupement Loisir Québec
Joe Cambria, Président

Lacrosse Nova Scotia
PO Box 3010 South, Halifax NS B3J 3G6
Tel: 902-233-1783; *Fax:* 902-425-5606
e-mail: bill.brydon@rcmp-grc.gc.ca
URL: www3.ns.sympatico.ca/hami/
Affiliation(s): Canadian Lacrosse Association; Sport Nova Scotia
Stephen Brown, Vice-President, Administration
Wayne Finck, Vice-President, Technical Development
Brian Thompson, Vice-President, Finance

Ontario Lacrosse Association
#607, 1185 Eglinton Ave. East, Toronto ON M3C 3C6
Tel: 416-426-7068; *Fax:* 416-426-7382
e-mail: info@ontariolacrosse.com
URL: www.ontariolacrosse.com
Stan Cockerton, Executive Director

Saskatchewan Lacrosse Association
2205 Victoria Ave., Regina SK S4P 0S4
Tel: 306-780-9216; *Fax:* 306-525-4009
e-mail: lacrosse@sasktel.net
URL: www.sasklacrosse.net
Dale Measner, Executive Director

Lawn Bowling

Bowls BC (BBC)
#148, 5525 West Blvd., Vancouver BC V6M 3W6
URL: www.bowlsbc.ca
Affiliation(s): World Bowls Board; World Indoor Bowls Board
Keith Terlson, President
Pat Cutt, Vice-President
Marjorie Mitchell, Treasurer
Juanita Tucker, Secretary

Bowls Canada Boulingrin (BCB)
#207, 720 Belfast Rd., Ottawa ON K1G 0Z5
Tel: 613-244-0021; *Fax:* 613-244-0041
Toll-Free: 800-567-2695
e-mail: office@bowlscanada.com
URL: www.bowlscanada.com
Affiliation(s): Commonwealth Games Association of Canada
Kevin Penny, Executive Director

Bowls Manitoba
200 Main St., Winnipeg MB R3C 4M2
Tel: 204-925-5694; *Fax:* 204-925-5703
e-mail: bowls@shawbiz.ca
URL: www.bowls.mb.ca
Cathy Derewianchuk, Executive Director

Bowls Saskatchewan Inc.
#102, 1860 Lorne St., Regina SK S4P 2L7
Tel: 306-780-9426; *Fax:* 306-781-6021
e-mail: bowlsask@sasktel.net
URL: www.bowls.sk.ca
Karen Swanson, Executive Director
Jean Roney, President

Lawn Bowls Association of Alberta
Percy Page Centre, 11759 Groat Rd., 3rd Fl., Edmonton AB T5M 3K6

Tel: 780-427-8119; Fax: 780-422-2663
e-mail: lawnbowl@telusplanet.net
URL: www.bowls.ab.ca
Neil Douglas, Treasurer
Betty Mertens, Secretary

New Brunswick Lawn Bowling Association
929A Cloverdale Rd., Riverview NB E1B 5E6
e-mail: rkhm118@aol.com
Dugald Richford, Executive Secretary

Ontario Lawn Bowls Association
c/o Elaine Stevenson, 23018 Lakeridge Rd., RR#2, Sunderland ON L0C 1H0
Tel: 705-228-8058
e-mail: olba@olba.ca
URL: www.olba.ca
Arja Nesbitt, President
Elaine Houtby, Vice-President
Alan Dean, 2nd Vice-President
Bob O'Neil, Executive Director
Edith Pedden, Secretary
Richard Peart, Treasurer

Prince Edward Island Lawn Bowling Association
Sport PEI, PO Box 302, Charlottetown PE C1A 7K7
e-mail: sharonrenner@eastlink.ca
Sharon Renner, President

Québec Lawn Bowling Federation / Fédération de Boulingrin du Québec
c/o #662 Oak Ave., Saint-Lambert QC J4P 2R6
URL: www.qlbf.org
Shirley Ahern, Contact

Libraries

North American Sport Library Network (NASLIN)
c/o University of Calgary Law Library, 2500 University Dr. NW, Calgary AB T2N 1N4
Tel: 403-220-6097; Fax: 403-282-6837
e-mail: gghent@ucalgary.ca
URL: www.naslin.org
Affiliation(s): International Association for Sports Information
Gretchen Ghent, Chair

Martial Arts

Association de taekwondo du Québec
CP 1000, Succ. M, 4545, av Pierre-de Coubertin, Montréal QC H1V 3R2
Tél: 514-252-3198; Téléc: 514-254-7075
Ligne sans frais: 800-762-9565
Courriel: info@taekwondo-quebec.ca
URL: www.taekwondo-quebec.ca
Jean Faucher, Président
Richard Gagné, Vice-président

Canadian Chito-Ryu Karate-Do Association
89 Curlew Ave., Toronto ON M3A 2P8
Tel: 416-444-5310
URL: www.canadianchitoryu.ca
David Smith, President
Derek J. Ryan, Vice-President

Canadian Jiu-jitsu Association Inc. / Association canadienne du jiu-jitsu inc.
c/o Pro Spar Martial Arts Centre, #10, 4 Alliance Blvd., Barrie ON L4M 5J1
Tel: 705-725-9186
Toll-Free: 800-352-1338
e-mail: info@canadianjiujitsu.com
URL: www.canadianjiujitsu.com
Affiliation(s): World Council of Jiu-Jitsu Organizations
Gary Pilon, Vice-President/Treas.
Terry Yanke, President

Canadian Kendo Federation (CKF) / Fédération canadienne de kendo
8013 Hunter St., Burnaby BC V5A 2B8
Tel: 604-420-0438; Fax: 604-420-1971
e-mail: hokusa@kendo-canada.com
URL: www.kendo-canada.com
Hiro Okusa, President
Yoshiaki Taguchi, Vice-President
Christian d'Orangeville, 2nd Vice-President
Kim Taylor, Secretary
John Maisonneuve, Treasurer

Confederation of Canadian Wushu Organizations
#22-25B, 2370 Midland Ave., Toronto ON M1S 5C6
Tel: 416-321-5913; Fax: 416-321-5068
e-mail: cdnwushu@rogers.com
URL: www.canadawushu.com
Sunny Tang, National President

Judo Alberta
11759 Groat Rd., Edmonton AB T5M 3K6
Tel: 780-427-8379; Fax: 780-447-1915
Toll-Free: 866-919-5836
e-mail: judo@judoalberta.com
URL: www.judoalberta.com
Affiliation(s): International Judo Federation
Garry Yamashita, President

Judo British Columbia
4421 Prince Albert St., Vancouver BC V5V 4K1
Tel: 604-734-3197; Fax: 604-251-3197
e-mail: info@judobc.ca
URL: www.judobc.ca
Renée Hock, Executive Director

Judo Manitoba
c/o Sport Manitoba, #310, 200 Main St., Winnipeg MB R3C 4M2
Tel: 204-925-5691; Fax: 204-925-5703
e-mail: judomb@sport.mb.ca
URL: www.judomanitoba.mb.ca
John Wenham, Executive Director
David Minuk, President

Judo New Brunswick / Judo Nouveau Brunswick
#13, 900 Hanwell Rd., Fredericton NB E3B 6A2
Tel: 506-451-1322; Fax: 506-451-1325
e-mail: judonb@nb.aibn.com
URL: www.sport.nb.ca/judonb/
Jean Pierre Cantin, Executive Director

Judo Newfoundland
#112, Hamlyn Rd. Plaza, Unit 50, St. John's NL A1E 5X7
Fax: 709-722-2573
Toll-Free: 877-879-5836
e-mail: judo@nfld.com
URL: www.judonl.ca
Blair Bradbury, President

Judo Nova Scotia
224 Victoria Rd., Bridgewater NS B4V 2P1
Tel: 902-543-2836; Fax: 902-527-4847
e-mail: tim.lohnes@abitibibowater.com
URL: www.judons.ca
Tim Lohnes, President

Judo Ontario
1185 Eglinton Ave. East, Toronto ON M3C 3C6
Tel: 416-426-7006; Fax: 416-426-7390
Toll-Free: 866-553-5836
e-mail: info@judoontario.ca
URL: www.judoontario.ca
Ron Wilson, Executive Director
Charles Formosa, President
Mohamad Hassani, Secretary General

Judo Prince Edward Island
40 Enman Cres., Charlottetown PE C1E 1E6
Tel: 902-368-4262; Fax: 902-368-4548
e-mail: gflood@sportpei.pe.ca
URL: sites.townsquare.ca/JudoPEI/index.cfm
John Wilbert, President

Judo Saskatchewan
c/o Registrar, 3130 Parkland Dr., Regina SK S4V 1W5
Tel: 306-789-7395
e-mail: abyuen@sasktel.net
URL: www.judosask.ca
Affiliation(s): International Judo Federation
T.V. Taylor, President
Bev Yuen, Registrar

Judo-Québec inc
CP 1000, Succ. M, 4545, av Pierre-de-Coubertin, Montréal QC H1V 3R2
Tél: 514-252-3040; Téléc: 514-254-5184
Courriel: info@judo-quebec.qc.ca
URL: www.judo-quebec.qc.ca
Affiliation(s): Fédération internationale de Judo; Union panaméricaine du Judo
Daniel De Angelis, Président
Patrick Esparbès, Directeur général
Patrick Vesin, Coordonnateur technique

Karate BC (KBC)
#225, 3820 Cessna Dr., Richmond BC V7B 0A2
Tel: 604-333-3610; Fax: 604-333-3612
e-mail: info@karatebc.org
URL: www.karatebc.org
Affiliation(s): National Karate Association; Sport BC; Sport Canada; Canadian Olympic Association
Dan Wallis, President
Robert G. Tuss, Executive Director
Ken Corrigan, Treasurer

Karate Manitoba
200 Main St., Winnipeg MB R3C 4M2
Tel: 204-925-5682; Fax: 204-925-5703
e-mail: colettem@highspeedcrow.ca
URL: www.karatemanitoba.ca
Meron Solonynka, President
Cindy Glacken, Treasurer
Bill Murray, Secretary

Karate New Brunswick
294 Water St., St Andrews NB E5B 1B7
e-mail: david.langley@gnb.ca
URL: karatenb.com
Rick MacMichael, Treasurer
Joe Hatfield, Secretary
Paul Oliver, President

Karate Ontario
#160, 2 County Ct. Blvd., Brampton ON L6W 4V1
Tel: 905-455-2170
e-mail: info@karateontario.org
URL: www.karateontario.org
Affiliation(s): World Karate Federation; Sport Alliance of Ontario; Coaches Assocation of Ontario
Joshua Drury, Secretary

Karaté Québec
CP 1000, Succ. M, 4545, rue Pierre de Coubertin, Montréal QC H1V 3R2
Tél: 514-252-3161; Téléc: 514-252-3036
Courriel: info@karatequebec.com
URL: www.karatequebec.com
Mohamed Jelassi, Coordonnateur général

Manitoba Tae Kwon-Do Association
200 Main St., Winnipeg MB R3C 4M2
Tel: 204-925-5682; Fax: 204-925-5703
e-mail: tkd-exec@rainyday.mb.ca
K.S. Cho, President

National Tae Kwon-Do Federation
c/o Whitecroft Hall, #314, 52313 Range Rd. 232, Sherwood Park AB T8B 1B5
Tel: 780-468-3418
URL: www.ntf.ca
Wilfred Ho, President & Founder

Newfoundland & Labrador WTF (World Taekwondo Federation) Tae Kwon Do Association
PO Box 28083, 48 Kenmount Rd., St. John's NL A1B 4J8
URL: www.nltkd.ca
Affiliation(s): WTF Canada; Sport Canada; Sport NL; Kukkiwon
Neil Tucker, President
Paul Gosse, Vice-President
Sheila McGrath, Secretary
Lisa Collette, Treasurer

Ontario Taekwondo Association
#201, 2355 Keele Street, North York ON M6M 4A2
Tel: 416-245-8582
e-mail: otasecretarygeneral@yahoo.com
URL: www.taekwondo.on.ca
Hwa Sun Myung, President
Yoneh Chae, Secretary General

Police Martial Arts Association
PO Box 7303, Sub. #12, Riverview NB E1B 4T9
Tel: 506-387-5126
e-mail: pmaa@nbnet.nb.ca
URL: www.policemartialarts.org
Rannie MacDonald
Foster MacLeod

Prince Edward Island Karate Association (PEIKA)
PO Box 640, Montague PE C0A 1R0
Tel: 902-892-3640
URL: www.karatepei.ca
Affiliation(s): Sport PEI; National Karate Association
Erick A. Silva, Treasurer
Ken Roper, President
Lori Beck, Secretary

Yukon Judo
4061 - 4th Ave., Whitehorse YT Y1A 1H1

Tel: 867-668-4236; *Fax:* 867-667-4237
e-mail: jessup@klondiker.com
Penny Prysnuk, President

Massage Therapy

Canadian Sport Massage Therapists Association (CSMTA) / Association canadienne des massothérapeutes du sport
#306, 50 Eccleston Dr., Toronto ON M4A 1K8
Tel: 416-285-1745; *Fax:* 416-285-1914
e-mail: natoffice@csmta.ca
URL: www.csmta.ca
Affiliation(s): Canadian Olympic Committee; Expert Provider Group
Trish Scheidel, President
Joanne Baker, National Office Coordinator
Aurel Hamran, President, Alberta Chapter
Kim Mark-Goldsworthy, President, BC Chapter
Johanna Thackwray, President, Ontario Chapter
Al Bodnarchuk, President, Saskatchewan Chapter

Mediation

Sport Dispute Resolution Centre of Canada
#950, 1080 Beaver Hall Hill, Montréal QC H2Z 1S8
Tel: 450-686-1245; *Fax:* 450-686-1246
Toll-Free: 866-733-7767
e-mail: info@adrsportred.ca
URL: www.adrsportred.ca
Allan J. Stitt, President
Benoit Girardin, Executive Director

Motorcycles

Association des motocyclistes gais du Québec (AMGQ)
CP 36, Succ. C, Montréal QC H2L 4J7
Tél: 514-247-9564
Courriel: info@amgq.org
URL: www.amgq.org
Adam Roy, Président

Canadian Motorcycle Association (CMA) / Association motocycliste canadienne
PO Box 448, Hamilton ON L8L 8C4
Tel: 905-522-5705; *Fax:* 905-522-5716
e-mail: registration@canmocycle.ca
URL: www.canmocycle.ca
Affiliation(s): Fédération internationale motocycliste; Canadian Olympic Association; North American Motorcycle Union
Marilyn Bastedo, General Manager
Joseph Godsall, President

Fédération motocycliste du Québec (FMQ) / Quebec Motorcyclist Federation
#208, 4875, boul Métropolitain est, Montréal QC H1R 3J2
Tél: 514-252-8121; *Téléc:* 514-252-7857
Courriel: fmq@fmq.qc.ca
URL: www.fmq.qc.ca
Jacques Lafontaine, Président

Mountaineering

The Alpine Club of Canada (ACC) / Club alpin du Canada
PO Box 8040, Indian Flats Rd., Canmore AB T1W 2T8
Tel: 403-678-3200; *Fax:* 403-678-3224
e-mail: info@alpineclubofcanada.ca
URL: www.alpineclubofcanada.ca
Affiliation(s): International Union of Alpinist Associations
Lawrence White, Executive Director
Peter Muir, President

Association of Canadian Mountain Guides (ACMG) / Association des guides de montagne canadiens
PO Box 8341, Canmore AB T1W 2V1
Tel: 403-678-2885; *Fax:* 403-609-0070
e-mail: acmg@acmg.ca
URL: www.acmg.ca
Peter Tucker, Executive Director
Scott Davis, President

British Columbia Mountaineering Club
PO Box 2674, Vancouver BC V6B 3W8
Tel: 604-268-9502
e-mail: info@bcmc.ca
URL: www.bcmc.ca
Affiliation(s): Federation of Mountain Clubs of BC
David Hughes, President

Native Peoples

Aboriginal Sport & Recreation Association of BC (ASRA)
#4, 2475 Mt. Newton X Rd., Saanichton BC V8M 2B7
Tel: 250-544-8172; *Fax:* 250-544-8173
e-mail: asra@asra.ca
URL: www.asra.ca
Alex Nelson, President & CEO
Patrick Chénier, General Manager
Gordon Celesta, Operations Manager
Karen Henry, Program Manager
Linda Bristol, Office Manager

Aboriginal Sport Circle
Roundpoint Memorial Bldg., #7, 34 McCumber Rd., Akwesasne Mohawk Territory, Cornwall Island ON K6H 5R7
Tel: 613-938-1176; *Fax:* 613-938-9181
e-mail: rbrant@aboriginalsportcircle.ca
URL: www.aboriginalsportcircle.ca
Viginia Doucett, Executive Director

Netball

British Columbia Netball Association
3468 Triumph St., Vancouver BC V5K 1T8
Tel: 604-293-1820; *Fax:* 604-293-1851
e-mail: netball_info@bcnetball.net
URL: www.bcnetball.net

Fédération de Netball du Québec / Québec Amateur Netball Federation
5617, av Jellicoe, Montréal QC H4W 1Z5
Tél: 514-486-2769
Courriel: quebecnetball@yahoo.ca
URL: www.netballquebec.com
Avice Roberts-Joseph, Présidente

Netball Alberta
PO Box 270, 7620 Elbow Dr. SW, Calgary AB T2V 1K2
Tel: 403-238-8041
e-mail: info@albertanetball.com
URL: www.netballalberta.com
Affiliation(s): International Federation of Netball Associations
Paula MacWilliam, President

Obesity

Active Healthy Kids Canada / Jeunes en forme Canada
#1804 - 2 Bloor St. E, Toronto ON M4W 1A8
Tel: 416-913-0238; *Fax:* 416-913-1541
e-mail: info@activehealthykids.ca
URL: www.activehealthykids.ca
Michelle Brownrigg, Chief Executive Officer

Olympic Games

Canadian Olympic Committee (COC) / Comité olympique canadien
#900, 21 St Clair Ave. East, Toronto ON M4T 1L9
Tel: 416-962-0262; *Fax:* 416-967-4902
URL: www.olympic.ca
Chris Rudge, CEO

Vancouver Organizing Committee for the 2010 Olympic & Paralympic Winter Games
#400, 1095 West Pender St., Vancouver BC V6E 2M6
Tel: 778-328-2010; *Fax:* 778-328-2011
Toll-Free: 877-408-2010
URL: www.vancouver2010.com
John Furlong, CEO

Orienteering

Alberta Orienteering Association (AOA)
#128, 4307 - 130 Ave. SE, Calgary AB T2Z 3V8
Tel: 403-697-5750
e-mail: pascale@orienteeringalberta.ca
URL: www.orienteeringalberta.ca
Don Riddle, President
J.P. Buysschaert, Treasurer
Pascale Levesque, Executive Director

Canadian Orienteering Federation (COF) / Fédération canadienne de course d'orientation
1239 Colgrove Ave. NE, Calgary AB T2C 5C3
Tel: 403-283-0807; *Fax:* 403-451-1681
e-mail: info@orienteering.ca
URL: www.orienteering.ca
Affiliation(s): International Orienteering Federation
Charlotte MacNaughton, President

Manitoba Orienteering Association Inc. (MOA)
200 Main St., Winnipeg MB R3C 4M2
Tel: 204-925-5706; *Fax:* 204-925-5792
e-mail: info@orienteering.mb.ca
URL: www.orienteering.mb.ca
Affiliation(s): Sports Manitoba
Jennifer Hamilton, President
Dave Graupner, Treasurer

Orienteering Association of British Columbia (OABC)
4337 San Cristo Pl., Victoria BC V8N 5G5
URL: www.orienteeringbc.ca
Affiliation(s): Canadian Orienteering Federation (COF); Coaching Association of Canada
John Rance, President
Alex Kerr, Secretary

Orienteering Association of Nova Scotia (OANS)
c/o Andrew Harding, 5516 Spring Garden Rd., 4th Fl., Halifax NS B3J 1G6
Tel: 902-446-2295; *Fax:* 902-425-5606
e-mail: info@orienteeringns.ca
URL: www.orienteeringns.ca
Andrew Harding, Executive Director
Michael Price, President
Dale Ellis, Vice-President
Ian Folkins, Treasurer

Orienteering Ontario Inc.
2163 Third Side Rd., Campbellville ON L0P 1B0
Tel: 416-284-5580
Toll-Free: 888-810-9990
e-mail: admin@orienteering.on.ca
URL: www.orienteering.on.ca

Orienteering Québec (OQ) / Fédération québécoise de course d'orientation
Tel: 450-433-3624
e-mail: orientering_quebec@orienteringquebec.ca
URL: www.orienteringquebec.ca
Michael MacConaill, President
Randall Kemp, Vice-President
Colin Kirk, Treasurer

Yukon Orienteering Association (YOA)
4061 - 4th Ave., Whitehorse YT Y1A 1H1
e-mail: info@yukonorienteering.ca
URL: www.yukonorienteering.ca
Barbara Scheck, President
Jean-François Roldan, Vice-President

Parachuting

Alberta Sport Parachuting Association (ASPA)
#63, 2505 - 42 St., Edmonton AB T6L 7G8
e-mail: admin@aspa.ca
URL: www.aspa.ca
Phil Perry, President

Canadian Sport Parachuting Association (CSPA) / Association canadienne du parachutisme sportif (ACPS)
300 Forced Rd., Russell ON K4R 1A1
Tel: 613-445-1881; *Fax:* 613-445-2698
e-mail: office@cspa.ca
URL: www.cspa.ca
Judy Donnelly, Executive Secretary
Tim Grech, President

Manitoba Sport Parachute Association (MSPA)
#309, 200 Main St., Winnipeg MB R3C 4M2
Tel: 204-925-5682; *Fax:* 204-925-5703
e-mail: president@mspa.mb.ca
URL: www.mspa.mb.ca
Jill Forbes, President

Sport Parachute Association of Saskatchewan
PO Box 37056, Regina SK S4S 7K3
Tel: 306-934-8528
URL: www.skydive.sk.ca
Craig Skihar, President
Burk Reiman, Vice-President

Pentathlon

Alberta Modern Pentathlon Association
e-mail: info@albertapentathlon.com
URL: albertapentathlon.com
Joanne Willis, President

Canadian Modern Pentathlon Association (CAMPA) / Association canadienne du pentathlon moderne
70 Como Gardens, Hudson QC J0P 1H0
Tel: 450-458-7974; *Fax:* 450-458-1746
e-mail: president@pentathloncanada.ca
URL: www.pentathloncanada.ca
Affiliation(s): Union internationale de pentathlon moderne et biathlon
Angela Ives, President

Physical Education & Training

Association régionale du sport étudiant de l'Est du Québec (ARSEEQ)
60, rue de L'Evêché ouest, Rimouski QC G5L 4H6
Tél: 418-723-1880; *Téléc:* 418-722-0457
Courriel: marcboud@cegep-rimouski.qc.ca
URL: www.arseeq.net
Affiliation(s): Fédération québécoise du sport étudiant
Marc Boudreau, Directeur

Association régionale du sport étudiant de Montréal (ARSEM)
#200, 7800, boul. Métropolitain Est, Montréal QC H1K 1A1
Tél: 514-645-6923; *Téléc:* 514-354-8632
Courriel: secretariat@arsemontreal.com
URL: www.arsemontreal.com
Jacques Desrochers, Directeur général
Dominique Blanc, Secrétaire

Fédération des éducateurs et éducatrices physiques enseignants du Québec (FEEPEQ)
2500, boul de l'Université, Sherbrooke QC J1K 2R1
Tél: 819-821-8000; *Téléc:* 819-821-7970
Courriel: feepeq.information@usherbrooke.ca
URL: www.feepeq.com
Affiliation(s): Sports Québec; Fédération québécoise du sport étudiant
Dav Bergeron, Président
Nathalie Morneau, Directrice, Opérations

Ontario Physical & Health Education Association (OPHEA)
#608, 1 Concorde Gate, Toronto ON M3C 3N6
Tel: 416-426-7120; *Fax:* 416-426-7373
Toll-Free: 888-446-7432
e-mail: info@ophea.org
URL: www.ophea.org
Mark Seaton, President
Chris Markham, Executive Director & CEO
Jennifer Cowie Bonne, Director, Marketing & Development
Gwen Slauenwhite, Director, Finance & Administration
Brenda Whitteker, Director, Programs

Saskatchewan Physical Education Association (SPEA)
#306, 104 - 5th St. NE, Weyburn SK S4H 0Z1
Tel: 306-842-0978; *Fax:* 306-842-2465
e-mail: spea@xplornet.com
URL: www.speaonline.ca
Affiliation(s): Canadian Association for Health, Physical Education, Recreation, & Dance; Saskatchewan Teachers' Federation
Holly Stevens, Executive Director
Vic Stynsky, President

Physical Fitness

Alberta Fitness Leadership Certification Association (AFLCA)
Percy Page Bldg., 11759 Groat Rd., 3rd Fl., Edmonton AB T5M 3K6
Tel: 780-492-4435; *Fax:* 780-455-2264
Toll-Free: 866-348-8648
e-mail: general@provincialfitnessunit.ca
URL: www.provincialfitnessunit.ca
Katherine MacKeigan, Executive Director

The Canadian Association of Fitness Professionals / Association canadienne des professionnels en conditionnement physique
#110, 255 Consumers Rd., Toronto ON M2J 1R4
Tel: 416-493-3515; *Fax:* 416-493-1756
Toll-Free: 800-667-5622
e-mail: info@canfitpro.com
URL: www.canfitpro.com
Maureen Hagan, Executive Director
Kathy Ash, Contact, Administration

Canadian Fitness & Lifestyle Research Institute (CFLRI) / Institut canadien de la recherche sur la condition physique et le mode de vie
#201, 185 Somerset St. West, Ottawa ON K2P 0J2
Tel: 613-233-5528; *Fax:* 613-233-5536
e-mail: info@cflri.ca
URL: www.cflri.ca
Lawrence Brawley, Chair
Cora Lynn Craig, President & Chief Scientist

Canadian Society for Exercise Physiology (CSEP) / Société canadienne de physiologie de l'exercice (SCPE)
#202, 185 Somerset St. West, Ottawa ON K2P 0J2
Tel: 613-234-3755; *Fax:* 613-234-3565
Toll-Free: 877-651-3755
e-mail: info@csep.ca
URL: www.csep.ca
Affiliation(s): Active Living Coalition for Older Adults; Canadian Federation of Biological Societies; Canadian Fitness & Lifestyle Research Institute; Canadian Association of Cardiac Rehabilitation; American College of Sports Medicine; Public Health Agency of Canada - Physical Activity Unit; Canadian Ethnocultural Council; Active Living Alliance for Canadians with a Disability; Coalition for Active Living
Phillip Gardiner, Executive Director
Mary Duggan, Manager, Administration
Brian MacIntosh, President
Panagiota Klentrou, Treasurer

Certified Professional Trainers Network (CPTN)
122 D'Arcy St., Toronto ON M5T 1K3
Tel: 416-979-1654; *Fax:* 416-979-1466
e-mail: info@cptn.com
Susan Lee, Executive Director

National Association of Physical Activity & Health (NAPAH)
Tel: 416-879-2348; *Fax:* 416-879-1905
Toll-Free: 866-228-3492
e-mail: info@napah.ca
URL: www.napah.ca

Physical Culture Association of Alberta
Percy Page Centre, 11759 Groat Rd., Edmonton AB T5M 3K6
Tel: 780-415-1744
e-mail: physicalculture@hotmail.com
URL: www.physicalculture.ca
Lesley McEwan, Executive Director

The Recreation Association / L'Association récréative
2451 Riverside Dr., Ottawa ON K1H 7X7
Tel: 613-733-5100; *Fax:* 613-736-6234
e-mail: racentre@racentre.com
URL: www.racentre.com
Rick Baker, General Manager
John Ossowski, President

Polo

Canadian Polo Association (CPA)
#301, 250 Consumers Rd., Toronto ON M2J 4V6
Tel: 416-494-0724; *Fax:* 416-495-8723
Toll-Free: 888-494-0724
e-mail: info@polocanada.ca
URL: www.polocanada.ca
Affiliation(s): Canadian Amateur Athletic Association (RCAAA); Federation of International Polo (FIP); Equine Canada; Ontario Equestrian Federation (OEF); International Olympic Committee (IOC)
Justin R. Fogarty, President
Don. B. Pennycook, Vice-President
Wayne Venhuizen, Secretary
Dave Offen, Treasurer

Powerlifting

Canadian Powerlifting Organization (CPO)
PO Box 51180 RPO Beddington, Calgary AB T3K EV9
Fax: 403-698-2434
e-mail: powerlifting@gmail.com; info@wpc-canada.com
URL: www.worldpowerlifting.com/cpo

Canadian Powerlifting Union (CPU)
#17, 1063 Coteau St. W, Moose Jaw SK S6H 5G3
Tel: 306-694-6116; *Fax:* 306-693-3301
e-mail: jbutt@sasktel.net
URL: www.powerlifting.ca
Affiliation(s): International Powerlifting Federation
Jeff Butt, President

Nova Scotia Powerlifting Association
Sydney NS B1P 3W7
Tel: 902-567-0893
e-mail: president@nspowerlifting.org
URL: www.nspowerlifting.org
Cliff Samms, Vice-President
John Fraser, President

Ontario Powerlifting Association
412 Big Creek Rd., Caledonia ON N3W 2G9
Tel: 905-765-5345
e-mail: info@ontariopowerlifting.org
URL: www.ontariopowerlifting.org
Bill Jamison, President

Racquetball

Association québécoise de racquetball (AQR)
CP 1000, Succ. M, 4545, av Pierre-de-Coubertin, Montréal QC H1V 3R2
Tél: 514-252-3062
Courriel: info@sports-4murs.qc.ca
URL: www.sports-4murs.qc.ca/racquetball/
Michel Gagnon, Président

British Columbia Racquetball Association (BCRA)
1282 - 7th Ave. West, Vancouver BC V6H 1B6
Tel: 604-737-1786; *Fax:* 604-737-1786
e-mail: bcracquetball@hotmail.com
URL: www.racquetballbc.ca
Cheryl McKeeman, President, Memberships
Cal Smith, Vice-President, Officiating & Communication
David Serra, Secretary, Junior Development
Diana Hambley, Treasurer, Ranking

Canadian Racquetball Association (CRA) / Association canadienne de racquetball
25 Golflinks Dr., Ottawa ON K2J 4Y1
Tel: 613-692-5394
e-mail: emlane@rogers.com
URL: www.racquetball.ca
Affiliation(s): Canadian Sport Council; Canadian Olympic Association; Coaching Association of Canada
Usher Barnoff, President

New Brunswick Racquetball Association (NBRA)
24 Baxter St., Lower Coverdale NB E1J 1B4
Tel: 506-387-4196
e-mail: moorbar@rogers.com
Barry Moore, NB Provincial Representative, Racquetball Canada

Newfoundland Racquetball Association
16 Fairhaven Pl., St. John's NL A1W 4S2
Tel: 709-364-9151; *Fax:* 709-364-9151
e-mail: measton@roadrunner.nf.net
Eric Easton, Vice-President
Dino Sauntuccione, Secretary

Racquetball Manitoba
#304, 200 Main St., Winnipeg MB R3C 4M2
Tel: 204-925-5666; *Fax:* 204-925-5703
e-mail: rball@shawbiz.ca
URL: members.shaw.ca/racquetball
Jennifer Saunders, Executive Director

Racquetball Ontario (RO)
5591 Mc Adam Road, Mississauga ON L4Z 1N4
Tel: 519-584-0235
e-mail: info@racquetballontario.ca
URL: www.racquetballontario.ca
John Ursino, President

Racquetball PEI
c/o Sport PEI, PO Box 302, Charlottetown PE C1A 7K7
Tel: 902-368-4110; *Fax:* 902-368-4548
e-mail: postie@vapordragon.ca
Allan Postie, President

Recreation

Canadian Volkssport Federation (CVF) / Fédération canadienne volkssport (FCV)
PO Box 2668, Stn. D, Ottawa ON K1P 5W7

Tel: 613-234-7333
e-mail: cvffcv@bellnet.ca
URL: www.walks.ca
Benoît Pinsonneault, President

Coalition for Active Living
#301, 2197 Riverside Dr., Ottawa ON K1H 7X3
Tel: 613-277-9979
e-mail: info@activeliving.ca
URL: www.activeliving.ca
Christa Costas-Bradstreet, Co-Chair
Nancy Dubois, Co-Chair

Fitness New Brunswick (NBCFAL) / Conditionnement physique Noueau-Brunswick (CCPVANB)
#2, 1216 Sand Cove Rd., Saint John NB E3M 5V8
Tel: 506-672-1993; *Fax:* 506-672-8762
Toll-Free: 888-790-1411
e-mail: membershipservices@fitnessnb.ca
URL: www.fitnessnb.ca
Affiliation(s): Atlantic Canadian Society for Exercise Physiology (CSEP) Health & Fitness Program (H&FP); National Fitness Leadership Alliance (NFLA)
Gina Simpson, Executive Director
Lauren Rogers, BPE, MA(SRA), President

International Masterathlete Federation (IMAF)
PO Box 185, Richmond Hill ON L4B 4R5
Tel: 905-473-9714; *Fax:* 905-473-9715
Toll-Free: 888-883-3315
Liz Roach, President
Iain Douglas, Vice-President

International Orienteering Federation (IOF)
Radiokatu 20, Slu FI-00093 Finland
Tel: 358-9-3481-3112; *Fax:* 358-9-3481-3113
e-mail: iof@orienteering.org
URL: www.orienteering.org
Affiliation(s): Canadian Orienteering Federation
Barbro Rönnberg, Secretary General
Anna Zeelig, Assistant to the Secretary General

Paralympics PEI
c/o Royalty Center House Of Sport, PO Box 841, 40 Enman Cres., Charlottetown PE C1A 7L9
Tel: 902-368-4540; *Fax:* 902-368-4548
e-mail: info@website.paralympicspei.pe.ca
URL: www.paralympicspei.pe.ca
Tracy Stevenson, Executive Director

Sport Alliance of Ontario
3 Concorde Gate, Toronto ON M3C 3N7
Tel: 416-426-7000; *Fax:* 416-426-7381
e-mail: jjoseph@sportalliance.com
URL: www.sportalliance.com
Jim Bradley, CEO
Larry Rudner, Interim CFO

Rhythmic Sportive Gymnastics

Canadian Rhythmic Sportive Gymnastic Federation (CRSGF) / Fédération canadienne de gymnastique rythmique sportive
c/o 2288 Covington Place, Victoria BC V8N 5N6
Tel: 250-472-3322; *Fax:* 250-472-2659
e-mail: dfrattaroli@shaw.ca
Danielle Frattaroli, GCG-RG Program Coordinator

Rhythmic Gymnastics Manitoba Inc. (RGM)
Sport Manitoba Bldg., 200 Main St., Winnipeg MB R3C 4M2
e-mail: rhythmic@sport.mb.ca
URL: www.rgmanitoba.com
Affiliation(s): Sport Manitoba; Rhythmic Gymnastics Canada; Gymnastics Canada; International Gymnastics Federation; Canadian Sport Centre - Manitoba; Coaching Manitoba; Gymnastics Manitoba
Zlatica Stauder, Executive Director
Raymond Chu, President
Susan Yurkiw, Vice-President

Rifles

British Columbia Rifle Association (BCRA)
43583 Bracken Dr., Chilliwack BC V2R 4A3
Tel: 604-793-0300; *Fax:* 604-793-4385
e-mail: contact@bcrifle.org
URL: www.bcrifle.org
Affiliation(s): Responsible Firearms Owners Coalition of British Columbia
Robert Pitcairn, Secretary

British Columbia Target Sports Association
PO Box 496, Kamloops BC V2C 5L2
Tel: 250-374-6705
e-mail: targetsports@bctsa.bc.ca
URL: www.bctsa.bc.ca

Manitoba Provincial Rifle Association Inc. (MPRA)
795 Valour Rd., Winnipeg MB R3G 3B3
Tel: 204-783-0768
URL: www.manitobarifle.ca
Affiliation(s): Sports Manitoba
John C. Chapman, President

Nova Scotia Rifle Association (NSRA)
PO Box 482, Dartmouth NS B2Y 3Y8
Tel: 902-456-7468
e-mail: nsrifle@ns.sympatico.ca
URL: www.nsrifle.org
Affiliation(s): Shooting Federation of Canada
A.S. Webber, President
D.G. Beaulieu, Secretary

Province of Québec Rifle Association (PQRA) / Association de tir de la province de Québec (ATPQ)
PO Box 141, St Augustin de Desmaures QC G2N 1W5
Tel: 418-878-4195
e-mail: jacques.denis@globetrotter.net
URL: www.pqra.org
Jacques Denis, President

Shooting Federation of Canada (SFC) / Fédération de tir du Canada (FTC)
45 Shirley Blvd., Nepean ON K2K 2W6
Tel: 613-727-7483; *Fax:* 613-727-7487
e-mail: info@sfc-ftc.ca
URL: www.sfc-ftc.ca
Affiliation(s): Canadian Shooting Sports Association
Reg Potter, President

Ringette

British Columbia Ringette Association (BCRA) / Association de ringuette de Colombie-Britannique
#319, 789 West Pender Street, Vancouver BC V6C 1H2
Fax: 604-629-0876
URL: www.bcringette.org
Glen Ritchie, President
Donna Mihalcheon, Vice President

Fédération sportive de ringuette du Québec
CP 1000, Succ. M, 4545, av Pierre-de-Coubertin, Montréal QC H1V 3R2
Tél: 514-252-3085; *Téléc:* 514-254-1069
Courriel: ringuette@ringuette-quebec.qc.ca
URL: www.ringuette-quebec.qc.ca
Florent Gravel, Président

International Ringette Federation
#201, 5510 Chemin Canotek Rd., Gloucester ON K1J 9J4
Tel: 613-748-5655; *Fax:* 613-748-5860
e-mail: ringette@ringette.ca
URL: www.ringette.ca
David Patterson, Executive Director

Manitoba Ringette Association (MRA) / Association de ringuette du Manitoba
Sport Manitoba, #309, 200 Main St., Winnipeg MB R3C 4M2
Tel: 204-925-5710; *Fax:* 204-925-5925
e-mail: ringette@sport.mb.ca
URL: www.manitobaringette.ca
Affiliation(s): Sport Manitoba
Cheryl Adlard, Executive Director
Melanie Perkins, Technical Director

Northwest Territories Ringette / Association de ringuette des Territoires Nord-Ouest
#2, 496 Range Lake Road, Yellowknife NT X1A 3R5
Tel: 867-920-7419; *Fax:* 867-920-2843
e-mail: nwt_ringette@yahoo.com
Affiliation(s): Ringette Alberta
Miles Harris, President

Ontario Ringette Association (ORA) / Association de ringuette de l'Ontario
#207, 3 Concorde Gate, Toronto ON M3C 3N7
Tel: 416-426-7204; *Fax:* 416-426-7359
e-mail: info@ontario-ringette.com
URL: www.ontario-ringette.com
Ellorie Hanson, President
Mike Beaton, Executive Director

Ringette Association of Saskatchewan (RAS) / Association de ringuette de Saskatchewan
#204, 1860 Lorne St., Regina SK S4P 2L7
Tel: 306-780-9432; *Fax:* 306-780-9460
e-mail: executivedirector@ringettesask.com
URL: www.ringettesask.com
Darrell Liebrecht, President
Crystal Gellner, Executive Director

Ringette Canada (RC) / Ringuette Canada
#201, 5510 Canotek Rd., Ottawa ON K1J 9J4
Tel: 613-748-5655; *Fax:* 613-748-5860
e-mail: ringette@ringette.ca
URL: www.ringette.ca
Jim Dawson, President
David Patterson, Executive Director

Ringette New Brunswick (RNB) / Ringuette Nouveau-Brunswick
c/o Marise Aufrey, Administrative Assistant, 940 Centrale St., Memramcook NB E4K 3T4
Tel: 506-758-2546
e-mail: MariseA@rrsb.nb.ca
URL: www.sport.nb.ca/ringette/
Ron Richard, President
Hélène L. Beaulieu, Q.C., Vice-President

Ringette Nova Scotia
5516 Spring Garden Rd., 4th Fl., Halifax NS B3J 1G6
Tel: 902-425-5450; *Fax:* 902-425-5606
e-mail: ringette@sportnovascotia.ca
URL: www.ringette.ns.ca
Lindsay Bennett, Executive Director
Dennis Barnhart, President

Ringette PEI
PO Box 302, Charlottetown PE C1A 7K7
Tel: 902-368-4208; *Fax:* 902-362-4548
URL: www.ringettepei.ca
Kelsey McIntosh, Executive Director
Ian MacIsaac, President
Dan Delaney, Vice-President
Susan McInnis, Treasurer

Rowing

Alberta Rowing Association (ARA)
Percy Page Centre, 11759 Groat Rd., Edmonton AB T5M 3K6
Tel: 780-427-8154; *Fax:* 780-422-2663
e-mail: albertarows@can.rogers.com
URL: www.albertarowing.ca
Carol Hermansen, President

Association québécoise d'aviron (AQA)
CP 1000, Succ. M, 4545, av Pierre-de Coubertin, Montréal QC H1V 3R2
Tél: 514-252-3191; *Téléc:* 514-252-3094
Courriel: info@avironquebec.ca
URL: www.avironquebec.ca
Matteo Cendamo, Président

Ontario Rowing Association (ORA)
#210, 3 Concorde Gate, Toronto ON M3C 3N7
Tel: 416-426-7002; *Fax:* 416-426-7309
e-mail: admin@rowontario.ca
URL: www.rowontario.ca
Affiliation(s): Ontario Sport Council
Derek Ventor, Executive Director

Rowing Canada Aviron (RCA) / Association canadienne d'aviron amateur
100 - 4636 Elk Lake Dr., Victoria BC V8Z 5M1
Fax: 250-361-4211
Toll-Free: 877-722-4769
e-mail: rca@rowingcanada.org
URL: www.rowingcanada.org
Affiliation(s): Fédération Internationale des Sociétés d'Aviron; Canadian Olympic Association
Donna Atkinson, Executive Director

Rowing Newfoundland
PO Box 50536, SS#3, St. John's NL A1B 4M2
Tel: 709-753-8515
Adrian Miller, President

Saskatchewan Rowing Association
510 Cynthia St., Saskatoon SK S7L 7K7
Tel: 306-975-0876; *Fax:* 306-242-8007
e-mail: saskrowing@sasktel.net
URL: www.saskrowing.ca
Affiliation(s): Rowing Aviron Canada, Saskatchewan Sports Hall of Fame & Museum, Saskatchewan Coaches Association

Siobhan McLaughlin, Head Coach/Executive Director
Bruce Acton, President

Rugby

Alberta Rugby Football Union
Percy Page Centre, 11759 Groat Rd., Edmonton AB T5M 3K6
Tel: 780-415-1773; *Fax:* 780-422-5558
Toll-Free: 866-784-2922
e-mail: rugbyab@telus.net
URL: www.rugbyalberta.com
Bert Radford, President

British Columbia Rugby Union
#203, 210 West Broadway, Vancouver BC V5Y 3W2
Tel: 604-737-3065; *Fax:* 604-737-3916
e-mail: bcrugby@telus.net
URL: www.bcrugby.com
Louise Wheeler, Manager, Member Services
Jeff Sauvé, CEO

Fédération de rugby du Québec (FRQ) / Quebec Rugby Union
CP 1000, Succ. M, 4545, av Pierre-de Coubertin, Montréal QC H1V 3R2
Tél: 514-252-3189; *Téléc:* 514-252-3159
Courriel: rugbyquebec@rugbyquebec.qc.ca
URL: www.rugbyquebec.qc.ca
Nicholas Clapinson, Directeur

Newfoundland & Labrador Rugby Union
349 Old Broad Cove Rd., St. Phillips NL A1M 3N2
Tel: 709-895-2608; *Fax:* 709-895-0214
e-mail: tjacobs@nl.rogers.com
URL: www.rockrugby.ca
Tom Jacobs, President

Nova Scotia Rugby Football Union
5516 Spring Garden Rd., Halifax NS B3J 1G6
Tel: 902-425-5450; *Fax:* 902-425-5606
e-mail: rugby@sportnovascotia.ca
URL: www.rugbyns.ns.ca
Affiliation(s): International Rugby Board
Marty Williams, CEO

Ontario Rugby Union (ORU)
#702A, 1185 Eglinton Ave. East, Toronto ON M3C 3C6
Tel: 416-426-7050; *Fax:* 416-426-7369
e-mail: rugbyregistration@osrc.com
URL: www.rugbyontario.com
Affiliation(s): Canadian Rugby Union
Allen Piggott, Executive Director

Saskatchewan Rugby Union (SRU)
510 Cynthia St., Saskatoon SK S7L 7K7
Tel: 306-975-0895; *Fax:* 306-242-8007
e-mail: sru@sasktel.net
URL: www.saskrugby.com

Sailing

Alberta Sailing Association (ASA)
4915 Graham Dr. SW, Calgary AB T3E 4L3
Tel: 403-617-9092
e-mail: info@albertasailing.com
URL: www.albertasailing.com
Peter MacDougal, Executive Director & Head Coach
Ron Hewitt, President

Association maritime du Québec (AMQ)
#500, 621, rue Stravinski, Brossard QC J4X 1Y7
Tél: 450-466-1777; *Téléc:* 450-466-6056
Ligne sans frais: 877-560-1777
Courriel: info@nautismequebec.com
URL: www.nautismequebec.com
Walter Timmerman, Président
Yves Paquette, Directeur général
Walter Timmerman, Vice-président

British Columbia Sailing Association
#223, 3820 Cessna Dr., Richmond BC V7B 0A2
Tel: 604-333-3628; *Fax:* 604-333-3626
e-mail: crew@bcsailing.bc.ca
URL: www.bcsailing.bc.ca
Affiliation(s): Canadian Yachting Association; International Sailing Federation; Sport BC
Tine Moberg-Parker, Executive Director

Canadian Albacore Association (CAA)
PO Box 81085, 47A Harbour Sq., Toronto ON M5J 2V3
e-mail: info@albacore.ca
URL: www.albacore.ca
Teresa Miolla, Commodore
Jason G. Roth, Treasurer

Canadian Yachting Association (CYA) / Association canadienne de yachting
Portsmith Olympic Harbour, 53 Yonge St., Kingston ON K7M 6G4
Tel: 613-545-3044; *Fax:* 613-545-3045
Toll-Free: 877-416-4720
e-mail: sailcanada@sailing.ca
URL: www.sailing.ca
Affiliation(s): International Sailing Federation; International Sailing Schools Association
Gerry Giffin, President

Manitoba Sailing Association Inc. (MSA)
#406, 200 Main St., Winnipeg MB R3C 4M2
Tel: 204-925-5650; *Fax:* 204-925-5624
e-mail: sailing@sport.mb.ca
URL: www.sailmanitoba.com
Ivan McMorris, President
Brigitte Smutny, Executive Director

Ontario Sailing / Association de voile de l'Ontario
65 Guise St. East, Hamilton ON L8L 8B4
Tel: 905-572-7245; *Fax:* 905-572-6056
Toll-Free: 888-672-7245
e-mail: info@ontariosailing.ca
URL: www.ontariosailing.ca
Glenn Lethbridge, Executive Director

S.A.L.T.S. Sail & Life Training Society (SALTS)
PO Box 5014, Stn. B, Victoria BC V8R 6N3
Tel: 250-383-6811; *Fax:* 250-383-7781
e-mail: info@saltsociety.com
URL: www.saltsociety.ca
Loren Hagerty, Executive Director

Tanzer 22 Class Association
PO Box 11122, Stn. H, Nepean ON K2H 7T9
Fax: 613-828-4636
e-mail: president@tanzer22.com
URL: www.tanzer22.com
Affiliation(s): Canadian Yachting Association; United States Sailing Association

Schools

Prince Edward Island School Athletic Association (PEISAA)
PEISAA, 109 Water St., Summerside PE C1N 1A8
Tel: 902-888-8037; *Fax:* 902-569-7530
URL: www.edu.pe.ca/peisaa
Garth Turtle, Executive Director
Lona Ryan, Game Reporting
Gerald MacCormack, Sec.-Treas.

Senior Citizens

Alberta Senior Citizens Sport & Recreation Association (ASCSRA)
#101, 525 - 11 Ave. SW, Calgary AB T2R 0C9
Tel: 403-297-2703; *Fax:* 403-297-6669
e-mail: ascsra@telus.net
URL: www.alberta55plus.ca
Affiliation(s): Alberta Sport, Recreation, Parks & Wildlife Foundation

Shooting Sports

Alberta Federation of Shooting Sports (AFSS)
Percy Page Centre, 11759 Groat Rd., Edmonton AB T5M 3K6
Tel: 780-415-1775; *Fax:* 780-422-2663
e-mail: afss@abshooters.org
URL: www.abshooters.org
Brenda Shewaga, Executive Director

Alberta Metallic Silhouette Association
2306 - 22nd St. South, Lethbridge AB T1K 2K2
Tel: 403-327-7552
Affiliation(s): Shooting Federation of Canada; Alberta Federation of Shooting Sports
Ralph Oler, President
Kathy Oler, Sec.-Treas.

Atlantic Marksmen Association
PO Box 181, Stn. Dartmouth Main, Dartmouth NS B2Y 3Y3
Tel: 902-469-2062
e-mail: boudreau@chebucto.ns.ca
URL: www.atlanticmarksmen.ca
Edward Doane, President

Calgary & District Target Shooters Association
PO Box 56, Site 6, RR#5, Calgary AB T2P 2G6
Tel: 403-275-3257; *Fax:* 403-291-5579
e-mail: president@cdtsa.org
URL: www.cdtsa.org
Affiliation(s): Alberta Fish & Game Association; Alberta Black Powder Association; Alberta Metallic Silhouette Association

Canadian Shooting Sports Association
#106, 3 Director Ct., Vaughan ON L4L 4S5
Tel: 905-265-0692; *Fax:* 905-265-9794
Toll-Free: 888-873-4339
e-mail: info@cdnshootingsports.org
URL: www.cdnshootingsports.org
Affiliation(s): Ontario Council of Shooters; Shooting Federation of Canada

Canadian Trapshooting Association (CTA)
RR#1, Penhold AB T0M 1R0
Tel: 403-886-2600; *Fax:* 403-886-2600
Bob Brown, President

Dominion of Canada Rifle Association (DCRA) / L'Association de tir dominion du canada
45 Shirley Blvd., Ottawa ON K2K 2W6
Tel: 613-829-8281; *Fax:* 613-829-0099
e-mail: office@dcra.ca
URL: www.dcra.ca
Jim Thompson, Executive Director
Stan E. Frost, Executive Vice-President
T.F. deFaye, President

Fédération québécoise de tir (FQT) / Québec Shooting Federation
CP 1000, Succ. M, 4545, av Pierre-De Coubertin, Montréal QC H1V 3R2
Tél: 514-252-3056; *Téléc:* 514-252-3060
Courriel: fqt@fqtir.qc.ca
URL: www.fqtir.qc.ca
Affiliation(s): Regroupment Loisir Québec; Sports Québec
Yvon Morissette, Directeur exécutif
Gérald Tousignant, Président

Manitoba Provincial Handgun Association
200 Main St., Winnipeg MB R3C 4M2
Tel: 204-925-5682; *Fax:* 204-925-5703
e-mail: mpha@handgun.mb.ca
URL: www.handgun.mb.ca
Randy Myrdal, President

Ontario Muzzle Loading Association (OMLA)
c/o Irene Wardell, 372 Beattie St., Strathroy ON N7G 2X6
URL: www.omla.ca
Irene Wardell, President
Russ Moore, Vice-President
Vivian Moore, Secretary
George Wortner, Treasurer

Ontario Provincial Trapshooting Association
c/o 273 Bousfield Cres., Milton ON L9T 3N5
Tel: 905-878-5669
e-mail: info@trapshooting.on.ca
URL: www.trapshooting.on.ca
Smokey Smith, President
Gord Kerr, Secretary-Treasurer

Ontario Rifle Association
PO Box 60, Locust Hill ON L0H 1J0
Tel: 905-294-8266; *Fax:* 905-294-1213
e-mail: jimc.thompson@sympatico.ca
URL: www.ontariorifleassociation.org
Affiliation(s): Dominion of Canada Rifle Association

Ontario Skeet Shooting Association (OSSA)
PO Box 96, Hampton ON L0B 1J0
Tel: 905-263-8174; *Fax:* 905-263-4870
e-mail: info@ontarioskeet.com
URL: www.ontarioskeet.com
Bill Marsh, Secretary
Brad McRae, President

Saskatchewan Black Powder Association (SBPA)
PO Box 643, Saskatoon SK S7K 3L7
URL: www.sbpa.ca

Saskatchewan Provincial Rifle Association Inc. (SPRA)
20 Acadia Bay, Regina SK S4S 4T6
Tel: 306-586-0617; *Fax:* 306-586-7547
e-mail: fullbore.rifle@saskrifle.ca
URL: www.saskrifle.ca

Shooting Federation of Nova Scotia (SFNS)
PO Box 28023, Dartmouth NS B2W 6E2

Tel: 902-462-7048; Fax: 902-462-7048
e-mail: marcom79@ns.sympatico.ca
Ray Fisher, President

Shooting Federation of PEI (SFPEI)
c/c 21 Euston St., Charlottetown PE C1A 1V7
Tel: 902-892-2938
Affiliation(s): Provincial Rifle Association; Charlottetown Handgun Club; Charlottetown Trap & Skeet Club; Historical Arms Society; Sport PEI

Yellowknife Shooting Club (YKSC)
PO Box 2931, Yellowknife NT X1A 2R2
Tel: 867-873-3212; Fax: 867-873-9008
e-mail: mail@yellowknifeshootingclub.ca
URL: yellowknifeshootingclub.ca
Affiliation(s): NWT Federation of Shooting Sports; Shooting Federation of Canada; NRA
Barry Taylor, President
Jim Robinson, Vice-President

Skating

Alberta Amateur Speed Skating Association (AASSA)
2500 University Dr. NW, Calgary AB T2N 1N4
Tel: 403-220-7911; Fax: 403-220-9226
e-mail: info@albertaspeedskating.ca
URL: www.albertaspeedskating.ca
Wendy Walker, Office Administrator

British Columbia Speed Skating Association
33844 King Rd., Abbotsford BC V2S 7M8
Tel: 604-557-4020; Fax: 604-853-4629
e-mail: speedskating@ucfv.ca
URL: www.speed-skating.bc.ca/
Lorna Holbech, Office Administrator

Fédération de patinage artistique du Québec (FPAQ)
CP 1000, Succ. M, 4545, av Pierre-de-Coubertin, Montréal QC H1V 3R2
Tél: 514-252-3073; Téléc: 514-252-3170
Courriel: patinage@patinage.qc.ca
URL: www.patinage.qc.ca
Josée Beauséjour, Directeur exécutif

Fédération de Patinage de Vitesse du Québec
930, av Roland Beaudin, Sainte-Foy QC G1V 4H8
Tél: 418-651-1973; Téléc: 418-651-1977
Courriel: fpvq@fpvq.org
URL: www.fpvq.org
Hélène Savard, Adjointe administrative

International Skating Union (ISU) / Union Internationale de Patinage
Chemin de Primerose 2, Lausanne 1007 Switzerland
Tel: 41-21-612-6666; Fax: 41-21-612-6677
e-mail: info@isu.ch
URL: www.isu.org
Fredi Schmid, General Secretary

Manitoba Speed Skating Association
200 Main St., Winnipeg MB R3C 4M2
Tel: 204-925-5657; Fax: 204-925-5703
Toll-Free: 888-628-9921
e-mail: mssa@shawbiz.ca
URL: www.mbspeedskating.org
Nicolle Masken, Office Administrator

New Brunswick Speed Skating Association
246 St. Pierre East Blvd., Caraquet NB E1E 1B1
Tel: 506-727-6334; Fax: 506-727-6334
e-mail: speedskates@nb.aibn.com
URL: www.homestead.com/ssnb
Chantal Brideau, Office Administrator

Newfoundland Speed Skating Association
75 Carter Ave., Corner Brook NL A2H 2P9
Tel: 709-637-8215
e-mail: vic.simmons@aliant.ca
Vic Simmons, Office Coordinator

Nova Scotia Speed Skating Association
10 Thistle Dr., North Sydney NS B2A 3R1
Tel: 902-794-8954
e-mail: laurolea@ns.sympatico.ca
Judith Brown, President

Nunavut Speed Skating Association
PO Box 761, Iqaluit NU X0A 0H0
Tel: 867-979-1226; Fax: 867-975-3384
e-mail: jtmaurice@northwestel.net
John Maurice, Branch President

NWT Speed Skating Association
PO Box 2664, Yellowknife NT X1A 2P9
e-mail: pamela@ssimicro.com
URL: www.nwtspeedskating.ca
Pam Dunbar, President

Prince Edward Island Speed Skating Association
PO Box 383, Charlottetown PE C1A 7K7
Tel: 902-569-3701; Fax: 902-368-7347
e-mail: speedskate@hotmail.com
URL: www.isn.net/speedskating/contacts.html
Fred Foster, Executive Director (Sport PEI)
Glenn Holmes, President

Saskatchewan Amateur Speed Skating Association (SASSA)
2205 Victoria Ave., Regina SK S4P 0S4
Tel: 306-780-9400; Fax: 306-525-4009
e-mail: sassa@sasktel.net
URL: www.saskspeedskating.ca
Affiliation(s): Sask Sport Inc.
Shawn MacLennan, Executive Director

Skate Canada / Patinage Canada
865 Shefford Rd., Ottawa ON K1J 1H9
Tel: 613-747-1007; Fax: 613-748-5718
Toll-Free: 888-747-2372
e-mail: skatecanada@skatecanada.ca
URL: www.skatecanada.ca
William Thompson, CEO
Brenda Gorman, Chief Communications Officer
Benoît Lavoie, Chair

Skate Ontario
99 Cabot Cr., Sault Ste Marie ON P6C 5X8
Tel: 705-949-9219
e-mail: skateontario@sympatico.ca
URL: www.skateontario.org
John Greenwood, President

Speed Skating Canada (SSC) / Patinage de vitesse Canada
#402, 2781 Lancaster Rd., Ottawa ON K1B 1A7
Tel: 613-260-3669; Fax: 613-260-3660
e-mail: ssc@speedskating.ca
URL: www.speedskating.ca
Affiliation(s): International Skating Union
Jean R. Dupré, Director General
Brian Rahill, Director of Sport
Mylène Croteau, Manager of Communications

Yukon Speed Skating Association
11 Buttercup Pl., Whitehorse YT Y1A 5V1
Tel: 867-668-4591; Fax: 867-393-8101
Bruce Henry, Branch President

Skiing

Alberta Freestyle Ski Association (AFSA)
88 Canada Olympic Rd. SW, Calgary AB T3B 5R5
Tel: 403-297-2718; Fax: 403-202-2522
e-mail: info@abfreestyle.com
URL: www.abfreestyle.com
Affiliation(s): Canadian Feestyle Ski Association
Gord Campbell, Executive Director
Larry Bilton, Chair
Al Ulsifer, Vice-Chair
Neil Orr, Treasurer

Alpine Canada ALPIN
#153, 401 - 9th Ave. SW, Calgary AB T2P 3C5
Tel: 403-777-3200; Fax: 403-777-3213
e-mail: info@canski.org
URL: www.canski.org
Gary Allan, President
Jennifer Duggan, Manager, National Services

Association des stations de ski du Québec (ASSQ)
#100, 7665, rue Larrey, Anjou QC H1J 2T7
Tél: 514-493-1810; Téléc: 514-493-3975
Courriel: lbissonnette@assq.qc.ca
URL: www.quebecskisurf.com
Claude Péloquin, Président-directeur général

British Columbia Alpine Ski Association
#306, 1367 West Broadway, Vancouver BC V6H 4A9
Tel: 604-678-3070; Fax: 604-678-8073
e-mail: info@bcalpine.com
URL: www.bcalpine.com
Bruce Goldsmid, General Manager

Canadian Association of Nordic Ski Instructors (CANSI)
Secrétariat, CANSI National Office, 8 Douglas Rd., Chelsea QC J9B 1K4
Tel: 819-360-6700; Fax: 819-827-1800
e-mail: office@cansi.ca; membership@cansi.ca; communications@cansi.ca
URL: www.cansi.ca
Paul Graner, President
Keith Payne, First Vice-President
Henry Madsen, Secretary-Treasurer

Canadian Freestyle Ski Association / Association canadienne de ski acrobatique
808 Pacific St., Vancouver BC V6Z 1C2
Tel: 604-714-2233; Fax: 604-714-2232
e-mail: info@freestyleski.com
URL: www.freestyleski.ca
Affiliation(s): Canadian Ski & Snowboard Association
Peter Judge, CEO

Canadian Masters Cross-Country Ski Association (CMCSA) / Association canadienne des maîtres en ski de fond
2 MacNeil Crescent, Stephenville NL A2N 3E3
Tel: 709-643-3259
e-mail: bruce.legrow@nf.sympatico.ca
URL: www.canadian-masters-xc-ski.ca/en_index.htm
Affiliation(s): World Masters Cross-Country Ski Association; Cross-Country Canada
Bruce Legrow, National Director

Canadian Ski Coaches Federation (CSCF) / Fédération des entraîneurs de ski du Canada
#220, 4900 Jean Talon ouest, Montréal QC H4P 1W9
Tel: 514-748-2648; Fax: 514-748-2476
Toll-Free: 800-811-6428
e-mail: national@snowpro.com
URL: www.snowpro.com/csia/e
Michel Lamothe, Chief Executive Officer

Canadian Ski Council (CSC) / Conseil canadien du ski
21 Fourth St. East, Collingwood ON L9Y 1T2
Tel: 705-445-9140; Fax: 705-445-0525
e-mail: info@skicanada.org
URL: www.skicanada.org
Affiliation(s): Canadian Association for Disabled Skiing; Canadian Association of Nordic Ski Instructors; Canadian Ski Area Operators' Association; Canadian Ski Association; Canadian Ski Instructors' Alliance; Canadian Ski Coaches Federation; Canadian Ski Patrol System; Canadian Association of Snowboard Instructors; National Snow Industries Association
Colin S. Chedore, President

Canadian Ski Instructors' Alliance (CSIA) / Alliance des moniteurs de ski du Canada
#220, 4900, Jean Talon ouest, Montréal QC H4P 1W9
Tel: 514-748-2648; Fax: 514-748-2476
Toll-Free: 800-811-6428
e-mail: national@snowpro.com
URL: www.snowpro.com/csia/e
Affiliation(s): International Ski Instructors Association
Martin Jean, National Program Director
Michel Lamothe, CEO

Canadian Ski Marathon (CSM) / Marathon canadien de ski
#200, 81 Jean-Prolux, Gatineau QC J8Z 1W2
Tel: 819-770-6556; Fax: 819-770-7428
Toll-Free: 877-770-6556
e-mail: ski@csm-mcs.com
URL: www.csm-mcs.com
Affiliation(s): Tourisme Outaouais; Tourisme Laurentides
Gregory Koegl, President

Canadian Ski Patrol System (CSPS) / Patrouille canadienne de ski (OPCS)
4531 Southclark Pl., Ottawa ON K1T 3V2
Tel: 613-822-2245; Fax: 613-822-1088
Toll-Free: 900-565-2777
e-mail: info@skipatrol.ca
URL: www.csps.ca
John Leu, Executive Director
Brian Low, Chair
Bill Powell, Corporate Secretary

Canadian Snowsports Association (CSA) / L'Association canadienne des sports d'hiver (ACSH)
#202, 1451 West Broadway, Vancouver BC V6H 1H6

Tel: 604-734-6800; Fax: 604-669-7954
e-mail: lillianalderton@hotmail.com
URL: www.canadaskiandsnowboard.net
Chris Robinson, President
David Pym, Managing Director

Cross Country Alberta (CCA)
Percy Page Centre, 11759 Groat Rd., Edmonton AB T5M 3K6
Tel: 780-415-1738; Fax: 780-427-0524
e-mail: manager@xcountryab.net
URL: www.xcountryab.net
Ken Hewitt, Chair
Michael Neary, Manager, Sport

Cross Country British Columbia
#106, 3003 - 30th St., Vernon BC V1T 9J5
Tel: 250-545-9600; Fax: 250-545-9614
e-mail: office@crosscountrybc.ca
URL: www.crosscountrybc.ca

Cross Country Canada (CCC) / Ski de fond Canada (SFC)
c/o Bill Warren Training Centre, #100, 1995 Olympic Way, Canmore AB T1W 2T6
Tel: 403-678-6791; Fax: 403-678-3644
Toll-Free: 877-609-3215
e-mail: info@cccski.com
URL: www.cccski.com
Affiliation(s): Canadian Ski & Snowboard Association
Jim McCarthy, President
Davin MacIntosh, Executive Director
Cathy Sturgeon, Director, Administration & Communication

Cross Country New Brunswick / Ski de fond Nouveau-Brunswick
1450 Maria Street, Bathurst NB E2A 3G2
Tel: 506-548-5707; Fax: 506-542-2638
e-mail: skis@nbnet.nb.ca
URL: www.xcski-nb.ca
Marie-Eve Cyr, Contact

Cross Country Ontario
738 River Street, Thunder Bay ON P7A 3S8
Tel: 807-768-4617; Fax: 807-768-8368
e-mail: admin@xco.org
URL: www.xco.org
Liz Inkila, Administrator

Cross Country PEI
RR#1, Belle River PE C0A 1B0
e-mail: keuper@pei.sympatico.ca
Anne Keuper, Contact

Cross Country Saskatchewan (CCS)
1860 Lorne St., Regina SK S4P 2L7
Tel: 306-780-9240; Fax: 306-780-9462
e-mail: ccs@sasktel.net
URL: www.crosscountrysask.ca
Dave Martinuk, President
Alana Ottenbreit, Executive Director

Cross Country Ski Association of Manitoba
#206, 200 Main St., Winnipeg MB R3C 4M2
Tel: 204-925-5639; Fax: 204-231-0297
e-mail: ccsam@shawcable.com
URL: www.ccski.mb.ca
Karin McSherry

Cross Country Ski Nova Scotia (CCSNS)
5516 Spring Garden Rd., 4th Fl., Halifax NS B3J 1G6
Tel: 902-425-5450; Fax: 902-425-5606
e-mail: ccsns@sportnovascotia.ca
URL: www.crosscountryskins.com
Kenzie MacDonald, Treasurer

Cross Country Yukon (CCY)
4061 - 4th Ave., Whitehorse YT Y1A 1H1
Tel: 867-334-9220; Fax: 867-667-4237
e-mail: xcyukon@northwestel.net
URL: www.crosscountryyukon.com
Alain Masson, Coordinator

Fédération québécoise de la montagne et de l'escalade (FQME)
CP 1000, Succ. M, 4545, av Pierre-de-Coubertin, Montréal QC H1V 3R2
Tél: 514-252-3004; Téléc: 514-252-3201
Ligne sans frais: 866-204-3763
Courriel: fqme@fqme.qc.ca
URL: www.fqme.qc.ca
Affiliation(s): Union internationale des associations d'alpinisme
André St-Jacques, Directeur des opérations

National Snow Industries Association (NSIA) / Association nationale des industries de la neige
#810, 245, av Victoria, Montréal QC H3Z 2M6
Tel: 514-939-7370; Fax: 514-939-7371
Toll-Free: 800-263-6742
e-mail: central.station@nsia.ca
URL: www.nsia.ca
Anna Di Meglio, President
Nicole Garand, Administration & Customer Service

Northwest Territories Ski Division
c/o PO Box 682, Yellowknife NT X1A 2N5
Tel: 867-873-4782
e-mail: cygnus@theedge.ca
Brenda Hans

Ontario Track 3 Ski Association
PO Box 67, Stn. D, #4, 61 Advance Rd., Toronto ON M9A 4X1
Tel: 416-233-3872; Fax: 416-233-7862
Toll-Free: 877-308-7225
e-mail: track3@track3.org
URL: www.track3.org
Henk Engels, Executive Director

Ski Hawks Ottawa
522 Hillcrest Ave., Ottawa ON K2A 2M9
Tel: 613-725-2472
Affiliation(s): Canadian Association for Disabled Skiing; Canadian Association for Disabled Skiers-National Capital Division
Bruce Meredith, Treasurer

Ski-Québec
CP 1000, Succ. M, 4545, av Pierre de Coubertin, Montréal QC H1V 3R2
Tél: 514-252-3089; Téléc: 514-252-5282
Courriel: johanne@skiquebec.qc.ca
URL: www.skiquebec.qc.ca
Sylvie Halou, Directrice générale

Snowbound
#1, 733 Ross Ave. East, Timmins ON P4N 8S8
Tel: 705-264-4700; Fax: 705-268-3585
Toll-Free: 800-575-3210
Chantal Pépin, Contact

Union internationale des associations d'alpinisme (UIAA) / International Union of Alpine Associations
c/o International Mountaineering & Climbing Federation, Monbijoustrasse 61/Postfach, 23, Bern CH-3000 Switzerland
Tel: 41-(0)31-370-18-28; Fax: 41-(0)31-370-18-38
e-mail: office@uiaa.ch
URL: www.uiaa.ch
Affiliation(s): Alpine Club of Canada; Fédération québecoise de la montagne
Judith Safford, Executive Director

Snowboarding

Canadian Association for Disabled Skiing (CADS) / Association canadienne pour les skieurs handicapés (ACSH)
91 Nelson St., Barrie ON L4M 4K4
Tel: 705-725-4845; Fax: 705-725-4804
e-mail: michelle.bavington@sympatico.ca
URL: www.disabledskiing.ca
David O'Brien, Executive Director
Al Matile, President
Helen Grimm, Secretary
Jeff Laidlaw, Treasurer

Canadian Association of Snowboard Instructors (CASI) / Association canadienne des moniteurs de surf des neiges (ACMS)
#220, 4900, Jean-Talon ouest, Montréal QC H4P 1W9
Tel: 514-748-2648; Fax: 514-748-2476
Toll-Free: 800-811-6428
e-mail: national@casi-acms.com
URL: www.casi-acms.com
Affiliation(s): Canadian Ski Instructors Alliance; Canadian Snowboard Federation
Dan Genge, Executive Director

HeliCat Canada
#102, 810 Waddington Dr., Vernon BC V1T 8T3
Tel: 250-542-9020; Fax: 250-542-5070
e-mail: info@helicatcanada.com
URL: www.helicatcanada.com
John Forrest, President

Snowmobiles

Alberta Snowmobile Association (ASA)
11759 Groat Rd., Edmonton AB T5M 3K6
Tel: 780-427-2695; Fax: 780-415-1779
e-mail: info@altasnowmobile.ab.ca
URL: www.altasnowmobile.ab.ca
Affiliation(s): Canadian Council of Snowmobile Organizations
Louise A. Sherren, Executive Director

British Columbia Snowmobile Federation (BCSF)
Stn. 400, 2439 Poulton Ave., Houston BC V0Y 1Z0
Tel: 250-845-7705; Fax: 250-845-7715
Toll-Free: 877-537-8716
e-mail: office@bcsf.org
URL: www.bcsf.org
Affiliation(s): International Snowmobile Council; Canadian Council of Snowmobile Organizations
Les Auston, Executive Director

Canadian Council of Snowmobile Organizations (CCSO) / Conseil canadien des organismes de motoneige (CCOM)
PO Box 21059, Thunder Bay ON P7A 8A7
Tel: 807-345-5299
e-mail: ccso.ccom@tbaytel.net
URL: www.ccso-ccom.ca
Kevin Sweetland, President
Patrick McGrath, 1st Vice-President, Communications
Brenda R. Welsh, Secretary-Treasurer
Craig Giles, National Coordinator, Safety

Fédération des clubs de motoneigistes du Québec (FCMQ)
CP 1000, Succ. M, 4545, av Pierre-de-Coubertin, Montréal QC H1V 3R2
Tél: 514-252-3076; Téléc: 514-254-2066
Courriel: info@fcmq.qc.ca
URL: www.fcmq.qc.ca
Mario Côté, Président

Great Slave Snowmobile Association
4209 - 49A Ave., Yellowknife NT X1A 1B3
Tel: 867-766-4353
URL: www.yktrailriders.com
Affiliation(s): Canadian Council of Snowmobile Organizations; International Snowmobile Council
Dave Abernethy, President

Klondike Snowmobile Association
PO Box 9034, 29 Wann Rd., Whitehorse YT Y1A 4A2
Tel: 867-667-7680
e-mail: klonsnow@yknet.ca
URL: www.ksa.yk.ca
Affiliation(s): Trans Canada Trail - Yukon

Ontario Federation of Snowmobile Clubs (OFSC)
#9, 501 Welham Rd., Barrie ON L4N 8Z6
Tel: 705-739-7669; Fax: 705-739-5005
URL: www.ofsc.on.ca

Saskatchewan Snowmobile Association Inc. (SSA)
PO Box 533, 221 Centre St., Regina Beach SK S0G 4C0
Tel: 306-729-3500; Fax: 306-729-3505
Toll-Free: 800-499-7533
e-mail: sasksnow@sasktel.net
URL: www.sasksnowmobiling.sk.ca
Barry Bradshaw, Chair
George Belchamber, Co-Chair

Snowmobilers Association of Nova Scotia (SANS)
5516 Spring Garden Rd., 4th Fl., Halifax NS B3J 3G6
Tel: 902-425-5450; Fax: 902-425-5606
e-mail: info@snowmobilersNS.com
URL: www.snowmobilersns.com
John Cameron, General Manager

Snowmobilers of Manitoba Inc.
2121 Henderson Hwy., Winnipeg MB R2G 1P8
Tel: 204-940-7533; Fax: 204-940-7531
e-mail: info@snoman.mb.ca
URL: www.snoman.mb.ca
Affiliation(s): Canadian Council of Snowmobile Organizations
Duncan Stokes, Executive Director

Thunder Bay Adventure Trails
PO Box 29190, Thunder Bay ON P7B 6P9
Tel: 807-939-7533
e-mail: tbat_den@hotmail.com
URL: www.tbat.ca

Soaring

Aéro Club des Outardes
1455, de Biencourt, Montréal QC H4E 1T1
Tél: 514-465-7806
Courriel: francisco45@gmail.com
URL: aeroclubdesoutardes.iquebec.com
Jacques Fairpault, Président

Air Sailing Club
144 Maple St., Guelph ON N1G 2G7
Tel: 519-836-7049
e-mail: stephen.szikora@sympatico.ca
Stephen Szikora

Alberta Soaring Council
PO Box 13, Black Diamond AB T0L 0H0
Tel: 403-933-4968
e-mail: asc@platinum.ca
URL: www.soaring.ab.ca
Phil Stade, Executive Director

Association de vol à voile Champlain
10, 745 de Martigny, Montréal QC H2B 2N1
Tél: 450-771-0500
Courriel: champlain@videotron.ca
URL: www.avvc.qc.ca

Base Borden Soaring
PO Box 286, Borden ON L0M 1C0
Tel: 705-424-1200
URL: users.csolve.net/~ourplace/
Ray Leiska

Bonnechere Soaring Club
PO Box 1081, Deep River ON K0J 1P0
Tel: 613-584-4636; *Fax:* 613-584-4636
Iver Theilmann

Central Alberta Gliding Club
4309 Grandview Blvd., Red Deer AB T4N 3E7
Tel: 403-227-0543
e-mail: shane-o@telusplanet.net
URL: www.cagcsoaring.ca
Affiliation(s): Alberta Soaring Council
Shane Cockriell, President

Club de vol à voile de Québec
CP 9276, Sainte-Foy QC G1V 4B1
Tél: 418-337-4905
URL: www.cvvq.net
Richard Noël, Président

Cu Nim Gliding Club
113 Midridge Pl. SW, Calgary AB T2X 1E4
Tel: 403-630-4332
URL: www.soaring.ab.ca/exec.html
Affiliation(s): Alberta Soaring Council
Danny Russell

Edmonton Soaring Club (ESC)
PO Box 472, Edmonton AB T5J 2K1
Tel: 780-363-3860
e-mail: groupten@hotmail.com
URL: www.edmontonsoaringclub.com

Gatineau Gliding Club
PO Box 8145, Stn. T, Ottawa ON K1G 3H6
Tel: 613-673-5386
e-mail: ggc@gatineauglidingclub.ca
URL: www.gatineauglidingclub.ca

Grande Prairie Soaring Society
PO Box 64, Hythe AB T0H 2C0
Tel: 780-354-8769
e-mail: lsherk@telusplanet.net
URL: soaring.ab.ca/gpss/
Lloyd Sherk, President
Terry Hatfield, Sec.-Treas.

London Soaring Club
130 Holcroft Street West, Ingersoll ON N5C 2B8
Tel: 519-661-7844
e-mail: info@londonsoaringclub.ca
URL: www.londonsoaringclub.ca
Cal Gillett, Treasurer

Manitoba Soaring Council
200 Main St., Winnipeg MB R3C 4M2
Tel: 204-925-5682; *Fax:* 204-925-5703
URL: www.wgc.mb.ca/msc/Manitoba_Soaring_Council_Home_Page.htm

Montréal Soaring Council (MSC) / Club de Vol à Voile MSC
PO Box 1804, Hawkesbury Airfield, Saint-Laurent QC H4L 4W6
Tel: 613-632-5438
e-mail: alainlaprade@hotmail.com
URL: www.flymsc.org
Arvind K. Jain, Administration

Ontario Soaring Association
10 Courtwood Pl., Toronto ON M2K 1Z9
Tel: 416-223-6487
Walter Chmela, Contact

Pemberton Soaring Centre
Pemberton BC V0N 2L1
Tel: 604-894-5727; *Fax:* 604-894-5776
Toll-Free: 800-831-2611
e-mail: info@pembertonsoaring.com
URL: www.pembertonsoaring.com
Rudy Rozsypalek

Prince Albert Gliding & Soaring Club (PAG&SC)
219 Scissons Ct., Saskatoon SK S7S 1B7
Tel: 306-249-1859
URL: www.soar.sk.ca/pagsc
Affiliation(s): Soaring Association of Saskatchewan; Soaring Association of Canada
Keith Andrews, President
Don Klassen, Treasurer

Regina Gliding & Soaring Club
PO Box 4093, Regina SK S4P 3W5
Tel: 306-536-4119
e-mail: fly@soar.regina.sk.ca
URL: www.soar.regina.sk.ca

Saskatoon Soaring Club
510 Cynthia St., Saskatoon SK S7L 7K7
Tel: 306-975-0844
e-mail: j.toles@sasktel.net
URL: www.ssc.soar.sk.ca
John Toles, Secretary

Soaring Association of Canada (SAC) / Association canadienne de vol à voile (ACVV)
#107, 1025 Richmond Rd., Ottawa ON K2B 8G8
Tel: 613-829-0536; *Fax:* 613-829-9497
e-mail: sac@sac.ca
URL: www.sac.ca
Affiliation(s): Aero Club of Canada; International Gliding Commission of the Fédération Aéronautique Internationale
John Toles, President
James F. McCollum, Executive Director

Soaring Nova Scotia
c/o Charles Yeates, #110, 105 Dunbrack St., Halifax NS B3M 3G7
Tel: 902-443-0094
URL: www.soarns.ca
Larry Bogan, Chair
Charles Yeates, Sec-Treas.

SOSA Gliding Club
PO Box 81, Rockton ON L0R 1X0
Tel: 519-740-9328
e-mail: sosa@sosaglidingclub.com
URL: www.sosaglidingclub.com
Dave Springford, President/Treasurer

Toronto Soaring Club
c/o President, 58 River Ridge Rd., Barrie ON L4N 7E8
Tel: 705-735-4422
e-mail: dellis@rogers.com
URL: www.toronto-soaring.ca
Dave Ellis, President

Winnipeg Gliding Club (WGC)
PO Box 1255, Winnipeg MB R3C 2Y4
Tel: 204-735-2868
e-mail: info@wgc.mb.ca
URL: www.wgc.mb.ca

York Soaring Association
10 Courtwood Pl., Toronto ON M2K 1Z9
Tel: 416-223-6487; *Fax:* 416-223-6487
e-mail: robertocentazzo@yorksoaring.com
URL: www.yorksoaring.com
Walter Chmela, President

Soccer

Alberta Soccer Association
Commonwealth Stadium, 1100 Stadium Rd., Edmonton AB T5H 4E2
Tel: 780-474-2200; *Fax:* 780-474-6300
Toll-Free: 866-250-2200
URL: www.albertasoccer.com
Ron Axelson, Executive Director

British Columbia Soccer Association
#510, 375 Water St., Vancouver BC V6B 5C6
Tel: 604-299-6401; *Fax:* 604-299-9610
e-mail: bcsoccer@gmail.com
URL: www.bcsoccer.net
Bjorn Osieck, Executive Director

Canadian Soccer Association (CSA) / Association canadienne de soccer
237 Metcalfe St., Ottawa ON K2P 1R2
Tel: 613-237-7678; *Fax:* 613-237-1516
e-mail: info@soccercan.ca
URL: www.canadasoccer.com
Affiliation(s): Féderation Internationale de Football Association, FIFA; Football Confederation; Canadian Olympic Association
Dominic Maestracci, President
Richard Scott, Director, Communications

Fédération de soccer du Québec
955, av Bois-de-Boulogne, Laval QC H7N 4G1
Tél: 450-975-3355; *Téléc:* 450-975-1001
Courriel: courriel@federation-soccer.qc.ca
URL: www.federation-soccer.qc.ca
Brigitte Frot, Directrice générale

Newfoundland & Labrador Soccer Association
PO Box 21029, St. John's NL A1A 5B2
Tel: 709-576-0601; *Fax:* 709-576-0588
e-mail: nlsa@sportnl.ca
URL: www.nlsa.ca
Doug Redmond, President
Dragan Mirkovic, Technical Director

Northwest Territories Soccer Association (NWTSA)
PO Box 11089, Yellowknife NT X1A 3X7
Tel: 867-669-8326; *Fax:* 867-669-8327
Toll-Free: 800-661-0797
URL: www.nwtkicks.ca
Affiliation(s): Sport North Federation
Melanie Kornacki, Sport Consultant
Ryan Fequet, President

Ontario Soccer Association (OSA)
7601 Martin Grove Rd., Vaughan ON L4L 9E4
Tel: 905-264-9390; *Fax:* 905-264-9445
e-mail: TheOSA@soccer.on.ca
URL: www.soccer.on.ca
Colin Linford, President
Dan Tomlinson, Secretary
Brian Avey, Executive Director

Prince Edward Island Soccer Association (PEISA)
House of Sports, Holland College Royalty Centre, PO Box 1863, Charlottetown PE C1A 7N5
Tel: 902-368-6251; *Fax:* 902-569-7693
e-mail: admin@peisoccer.com
URL: www.peisoccer.com
Dianne Bishop, Executive Administrator
Colleen Arsenault, Treasurer
Gerald MacDonald, President

Saskatchewan Soccer Association Inc. (SSA)
1870 Lorne St., Regina SK S4P 2L7
Tel: 306-780-9225; *Fax:* 306-780-9480
e-mail: coo@sasksoccer.com
URL: www.sasksoccer.com
Boyd Clark, Executive Director

Soccer New Brunswick
#2, 125 Russ Howard Dr., Moncton NB E1C 0L7
Tel: 506-382-7529; *Fax:* 506-382-5621
e-mail: office@soccernb.org
URL: www.soccernb.org
Jeff Salvis, Executive Director

Soccer Nova Scotia
210 Thomas Raddall Dr., Halifax NS B3S 1K3
Tel: 902-445-0265; *Fax:* 902-445-0258
e-mail: soccerns@ns.sympatico.ca
URL: www.soccerns.ns.ca
George Athanasiou, Executive Director

Yukon Soccer Association
4061 - 4th Ave., Whitehorse YT Y1A 1H1
Tel: 867-633-4625; *Fax:* 867-667-4237
e-mail: yukonsoccer@sportyukon.com
URL: www.yukonsoccer.yk.ca
Kim King, Administrator

Softball

Alberta Amateur Softball Association (AASA)
9860 - 33 Ave., Edmonton AB T6N 1C6
Tel: 780-461-7735; *Fax:* 780-461-7757
e-mail: calie@softballalberta.ca
URL: www.softballalberta.ca
Affiliation(s): Western Canada Softball Association
Michele Patry, Executive Director

British Columbia Amateur Softball Association (BCASA)
PO Box 45570, Stn. Sunnyside Mall, 2201 - 148th St., Surrey BC V4A 9N3
Tel: 604-531-0044; *Fax:* 604-531-8831
e-mail: info@softball.bc.ca
URL: www.softball.bc.ca
Dennis Bidin, President

Ontario Rural Softball Association
RR#1, Innerkip ON N0J 1M0
Tel: 519-469-3593
URL: www.ontarioruralsoftball.ca/index.php
Carl Littlejohns, Secretary
Dennis Wilson, President

Softball Canada
#212, 223 Colonnade Rd., Ottawa ON K1H 7X3
Tel: 613-523-3386; *Fax:* 613-523-5761
e-mail: info@softball.ca
URL: www.softball.ca
Hugh Mitchener, CEO
Kevin Quinn, President

Softball Manitoba
200 Main St., Winnipeg MB R3C 4M2
Tel: 204-925-5673; *Fax:* 204-925-5703
e-mail: softball@softball.mb.ca
URL: www.softball.mb.ca
Bill Finch, President

Softball NB Inc. (SNB) / Softball Nouveau-Brunswick Inc.
4242 Water St., Miramichi NB E1N 4L2
Tel: 506-773-3507; *Fax:* 506-773-5630
e-mail: softball@softballnb.ca
URL: www.softballnb.ca
Bev Adams, President
Réjean Léger, Sec.-Treas.
Peter McLean, Executive & Technical Director

Softball Newfoundland & Labrador
PO Box 21165, St. John's NL A1A 5B2
Tel: 709-576-7231; *Fax:* 709-576-7081
e-mail: softball@sportnl.ca
URL: www.softball.nf.ca
Lloyd Power, President

Softball Ontario
#305, 1185 Eglinton Ave. East, Toronto ON M3C 3C6
Tel: 416-426-7150; *Fax:* 416-426-7368
e-mail: info@softballontario.ca
URL: www.softballontario.ca
Wendy Cathcart, Executive Director

Softball Québec
CP 1000, Succ. M, 4545, av Pierre-de Coubertin, Montréal QC H1V 3R2
Tél: 514-252-3061; *Téléc:* 514-252-3134
Courriel: cgagnon@softballquebec.com
URL: www.softballquebec.com
Sophie Bédard, Présidente

Softball Saskatchewan
2205 Victoria Ave., Regina SK S4P 0S4
Tel: 306-780-9235; *Fax:* 306-780-9483
e-mail: info@softball.sk.ca
URL: www.softball.sk.ca
Guy Jacobson, Executive Director

Softball Yukon
18 Stewart Rd., Whitehorse YT Y1A 3S3
e-mail: sbyukon@whtvcable.com
URL: www.softballyukon.com
Rob Andison, President

Sport Medicine

Alberta Athletic Therapists Association
c/o University Of Calgary Sport Medicine Centre, 2500 University Dr. NW, Calgary AB T2N 1N4
Tel: 403-220-8957
e-mail: info@aata.ca
URL: www.aata.ca
Jocelyn Hines, Secretary

Athletic Therapists' Association of British Columbia (ATABC)
c/o Coast Sport Therapy, #170, 5640 Hollybridge Way, Richmond BC V7C 4N3
Tel: 604-233-1850; *Fax:* 604-233-1852
e-mail: mail@athletictherapybc.ca
URL: www.athletictherapybc.ca
Jonathan Sun, President

Atlantic Provinces Athletic Therapists Association
c/o Memorial University, PO Box 4200, 2300 Elizabeth Ave., St. John's NL A1C 5S7
Tel: 709-737-3442
e-mail: contact@apata.ca
URL: www.apata.ca
Shauna Stone, President

Canadian Academy of Sport Medicine (CASM) / Académie canadienne de médecine du sport (ACMS)
#4, 5330 Canotek Rd., Ottawa ON K1J 9C1
Tel: 613-748-5851; *Fax:* 613-748-5792
Toll-Free: 877-585-2394
e-mail: bfalardeau@casm-acms.org
URL: www.casm-acms.org
Affiliation(s): World Federation of Sport Medicine
Dawn Haworth, Executive Director

Canadian Athletic Therapists Association (CATA) / Association canadienne des thérapeutes du sport
#402, 1040 - 7th Ave. SW, Calgary AB T2P 3G9
Tel: 403-509-2282; *Fax:* 403-509-2280
e-mail: info@athletictherapy.org
URL: www.athletictherapy.org
Grant Slessor, Executive Director

Corporation des thérapeutes du sport du Québec (CTSQ)
Concordia University, #SP165.04, 7141, rue Sherbrooke ouest, Montréal QC H4B 1R6
Tél: 514-848-2424
Courriel: admin@ctsq.qc.ca
URL: www.ctsq.qc.ca
Christina Grace, President
Diana Berardi, General Manager

Manitoba Athletic Therapists Association Inc. (MATA)
University of Manitoba, 233 Investors Group Athletic Centre, 75 Sidney Smith St., Winnipeg MB R3T 2N2
Tel: 204-474-6004; *Fax:* 204-474-7680
e-mail: mail@mata.mb.ca
URL: www.mata.mb.ca
Mike Hutton, President

Ontario Athletic Therapists Association
283 Danforth Avenue, Toronto ON M4K 1N2
Tel: 416-845-4993
e-mail: president@athletictherapist.on.ca
URL: www.athletictherapist.on.ca
Drew Laskoski, President

Saskatchewan Athletic Therapists Association (SATA)
Tel: 306-291-6069
e-mail: karihiebert@yahoo.ca
URL: www.smscs.ca/sata.htm
Kari Hiebert, Bsc (Kin), CAT(, President

Sport Medicine Council of Alberta (SMCA)
Percy Page Centre, 11759 Groat Rd., Edmonton AB T5M 3K6
Tel: 780-415-0812; *Fax:* 780-422-3093
e-mail: smca@sportmedab.ca
URL: www.sportmedab.ca
Dwayne Laing, President

Sport Medicine Council of British Columbia
1325 Keith Road, North Vancouver BC V7J 1J3
Tel: 604-903-3880; *Fax:* 604-929-3877
Toll-Free: 888-755-3375
e-mail: info@sportmedbc.com
URL: www.sportmedbc.com
Lynda Cannell, President/CEO

Sport Medicine Council of Manitoba Inc.
#403, 200 Main St., Winnipeg MB R3C 4M2
Tel: 204-925-5750; *Fax:* 204-925-5624
e-mail: cbaker@sport.mb.ca
URL: sportmed.mb.ca
Scott Leckie, Presidnet

Sports Medicine Council of Nova Scotia (SMCNS)
50 West Porters Lake Rd., Porters Lake NS B3E 1K2
Fax: 902-435-4491
e-mail: kelliott@smcns.ca
URL: www.smcns.ca
Affiliation(s): Sport Medicine & Science Council of Canada
Kate Elliott, President

Sport Sciences

Canadian Society for Psychomotor Learning & Sport Psychology (CSPLSP) / Société canadienne d'apprentissage psychomoteur et de psychologie du sport (SCAPPS)
c/o College of Kinesiology, University of Saskatchewan, Saskatoon SK S7N 5B2
e-mail: webmaster@scapps.org
URL: www.scapps.org
Affiliation(s): International Society of Sport Psychology
Lybbert Larry, President
Gordon Binstead, Sec.-Treas.

Ontario Association of Sport & Exercise Sciences (OASES)
295 Broadway, Orangeville ON L9W 1L2
Tel: 519-925-2265; *Fax:* 519-925-9853
Affiliation(s): Canadian Society for Exercise Physiology
Patricia Clark, Executive Director

Sports

Alberta Schools' Athletic Association (ASAA)
Percy Page Centre, 11759 Groat Rd., Edmonton AB T5M 3K6
Tel: 780-427-8182; *Fax:* 780-415-1833
e-mail: info@asaa.ca
URL: www.asaa.ca
Affiliation(s): National Federation of State High School Associations
John F. Paton, Executive Director
Dave M. Jones, President

Amateur Athletic Union (AAU)
PO Box 22049, 1910 Hotel Plaza Blvd., Lake Buena Vista FL 32830 USA
Tel: 407-934-7200; *Fax:* 407-934-7242
Toll-Free: 800-228-4872
e-mail: anita@aausports.org
URL: www.aausports.org
Bobby Dodd, President/CEO
Mike Killpack, Director, Sports

Arctic Winter Games International Committee (AWGIC)
#400, 5201 - 50 Ave., Yellowknife NT X1A 3S9
Tel: 867-873-7245; *Fax:* 867-920-6467
URL: www.awg.ca
Lloyd Bentz, Secretary
Gerry Thick, President
Wendell Shiffler, Vice-President
Ian D. Legaree, Technical Director

Association régionale du sport étudiant du Saguenay-Lac St-Jean (ARSESLSJ)
CEGEP de Chicoutimi, 534, rue Jacques Cartier Est, Chicoutimi QC G7H 1Z6
Tél: 418-543-3532; *Téléc:* 418-693-0503
Courriel: arse@arseslsj.qc.ca
URL: www.arseslsj.qc.ca
Éric Benoit, Directeur général

Athletes CAN
#301, 1376 Bank St., Ottawa ON K1H 7Y3
Tel: 613-526-4025; *Fax:* 613-526-9735
Toll-Free: 888-832-4222
e-mail: info@athletescan.com
URL: www.athletescan.com
Guy Tanguay, CEO
Claire Carver-Dias, President

Athletes International
#2702, 3550 Jeanne Mauce, Montréal QC H2X 3P7
Tel: 514-982-9989; *Fax:* 514-982-0111
Toll-Free: 800-344-1810

e-mail: info@athletes-int.com
URL: www.athletes-int.com
Peter Schleicher, President

Atlantic University Sport Association (AUSA)
#403, 5657 Spring Garden Rd., Halifax NS B3J 3R4
Tel: 902-425-4235; *Fax:* 902-425-7825
e-mail: feedback@atlanticuniversitysport.com
URL: www.atlanticuniversitysport.com

The Boomerang Association of Canada (BAC)
URL: www.canboom.org
Andy Cross, Contact

British Columbia Games Society
#200, 990 Fort St., Victoria BC V8V 3K2
Tel: 250-387-1375; *Fax:* 250-387-4489
e-mail: info@bcgames.org
URL: www.bcgames.org
Kelly Mann, President & CEO

British Columbia School Sports (BCSS)
#100, 4585 Canada Way, Burnaby BC V5G 4L6
Tel: 604-737-3066; *Fax:* 604-737-9844
e-mail: info@bcschoolsports.ca
URL: www.bcschoolsports.ca
Affiliation(s): USA National Federation of State High Schools
Sue Keenan, Executive Director
Raj Puri, President

Canada Games Council (CGC) / Conseil des jeux du Canada
#701, 2197 Riverside Dr., Ottawa ON K1H 7X3
Tel: 613-526-2320; *Fax:* 613-526-4068
e-mail: canada.games@canadagames.ca
URL: www.canadagames.ca
Sue Hylland, President/CEO
Kelly Dearborn, Director of Sport and Games

Canadian Centre for Ethics in Sport (CCES) / Centre canadien pour l'éthique dans le sport
#350, 955 Green Valley Cr., Ottawa ON K2C 3V4
Tel: 613-521-3340; *Fax:* 613-521-3134
e-mail: info@cces.ca
URL: www.cces.ca
Affiliation(s): True Sport Foundation
Roger Jackson, Chair
Paul Melia, CEO

Canadian Colleges Athletic Association / Association canadienne du sport collégial
c/o St. Lawrence College, 2 Belmont St., Cornwall ON K6H 4Z1
Tel: 613-937-1508; *Fax:* 613-937-1530
e-mail: sandra@ccaa.ca
URL: www.ccaa.ca
Affiliation(s): Atlantic Colleges Athletic Association; Fédération québécoise du sport étudiant; Ontario Colleges Athletic Association; Alberta Colleges Athletic Conference; British Columbia Colleges Athletic Association
Sandra Murray-MacDonell, Executive Director

Canadian Paintball Association
92 Arlington Ave., Oshawa ON L1G 2N6
e-mail: admin@canadianpaintball.ca
URL: www.canadianpaintball.ca
Jody L.E. McLeod, Contact

Canadian Sport Tourism Alliance (CSTA)
#600, Lisgar St., Ottawa ON K2P 0C2
Tel: 613-688-5843; *Fax:* 613-238-3878
e-mail: info@canadiansporttourism.com
URL: www.canadiansporttourism.com
Ursula Gobel, President
Rick Traer, CEO

Canadian Ultimate Players Association (CUPA)
200 Main St., Winnipeg MB R3C 4M2
Toll-Free: 888-691-1080
e-mail: info@canadianultimate.com
URL: www.canadianultimate.com
Danny Saunders, Executive Director

Fédération québécoise du sport étudiant (FQSE)
CP 1000, Succ. M, 4545, av Pierre-De Coubertin, Montréal QC H1V 3R2
Tél: 514-252-3300; *Téléc:* 514-254-3292
URL: www.fqse.qc.ca; www.sportetudiant.com
Yves Paquette, Président

Fraser Valley Soccer Referees' Association (FVSRA)
10945B River Rd, Delta BC V4C 2R8
Tel: 604-588-3959
URL: www.fraservalleysoccerreferees.com
David Miller, President

International Curling Information Network Group (ICING)
73 Appleford Rd., Hamilton ON L9C 6B5
Tel: 905-389-7781
e-mail: psmith@icing.org
URL: www.icing.org
Peter M. Smith, Contact

Judo Canada
#212, 1725 St. Laurent, Ottawa ON K1G 3V4
Tel: 613-738-1200; *Fax:* 613-738-1299
e-mail: info@judocanada.org
URL: www.judocanada.org
Affiliation(s): International Judo Federation
Andrzej Sadej, Director General
Phil Moreau, Administrative Coordinator

Manitoba High Schools Athletic Association (MHSAA)
#405, 200 Main St., Winnipeg MB R3C 4M2
Tel: 204-925-5640; *Fax:* 204-925-5624
e-mail: info@mhsaa.ca
URL: www.mhsaa.mb.ca
Morris Glimcher, Executive Director
Don Hurton, President

Nova Scotia School Athletic Federation
PO Box 3010, Stn. South, 5516 Spring Garden Rd., Halifax NS B3J 3G6
Tel: 902-425-8662; *Fax:* 902-425-5606
e-mail: dweston@sportnovascotia.ca (D.Weston Secretary)
URL: nssaf.ednet.ns.ca
Tom Fahie, Executive Director
Dianne Weston, Secretary

Ontario Federation of School Athletic Associations (OFSAA) / Fédération des associations du sport scolaire de l'Ontario
#204, 3 Concorde Gate, Toronto ON M3C 3N7
Tel: 416-426-7391; *Fax:* 416-426-7317
e-mail: lindsey@ofsaa.on.ca (Newsletter)
URL: www.ofsaa.on.ca
Martin Ritsma, President
Lynn Kelman, Vice-President
Doug Gellatly, Executive Director
Lindsey Evanoff, Coordinator, Marketing & Communications

Orienteering New Brunswick (ONB)
34 Fairview Dr., Moncton NB E1E 3C7
Tel: 506-389-8091
URL: www.orienteering.nb.ca
Affiliation(s): International Orienteering Federation
David Ross, President
Paul Looker, Secretary

Ottawa Carleton Ultimate Association (OCUA)
PO Box 142, 99 Fifth Ave., Ottawa ON K1S 5P5
Tel: 613-860-6282
e-mail: board@ocua.ca
URL: www.ocua.ca
Marci Morris, Executive Director
Neil Saravanamuttoo, President
Shawn Roussy, Treasurer

Sarnia Highland Games
PO Box 713, 137 Davis St., Sarnia ON N7S 7J7
Tel: 519-336-5054; *Fax:* 519-336-5564
Toll-Free: 888-772-8170
e-mail: highland@rivernet.net
URL: www.sarniahighlandgames.com
Shirley Kelly, Director
John W. Stewart, Chair

Sask Sport Inc.
1870 Lorne St., Regina SK S4P 2L7
Tel: 306-780-9300; *Fax:* 306-781-6021
e-mail: sasksport@sasksport.sk.ca
URL: www.sasksport.sk.ca
Don MacAulay, President

School Sports Newfoundland & Labrador (SSNL)
PO Box 8700, Bldg. 810, Pleasantville NL A1B 4J6
Tel: 709-729-2795; *Fax:* 709-729-2705
e-mail: ssnl@sportnl.ca
URL: www.schoolsportsnl.ca
Karen Richard, Executive Director

Société des Jeux de l'Acadie inc. (SJA)
#210, 702, rue Principale, Petit-Rocher NB E8J 1V1
Tél: 506-783-4207; *Téléc:* 506-783-4209
Courriel: sja1@nbnet.nb.ca
URL: www.jeuxdelacadie.org
Stéphane Hachey, Président
Mario Doucet, Directeur général

Sport BC
#260, 3820 Cessna Dr., Richmond BC V7B 0A2
Tel: 604-333-3400; *Fax:* 604-333-3401
e-mail: info@sport.bc.ca
URL: www.sport.bc.ca
Paul Varian, President/CEO

Sport Manitoba
200 Main St., Winnipeg MB R3C 4M2
Tel: 204-925-5600; *Fax:* 204-925-5916
Toll-Free: 866-774-2220
e-mail: info@sport.mb.ca
URL: www.sportmanitoba.ca
Jeff Hnatiuk, President/CEO
Tara Skibo, Communications/Public Relations

Sport New Brunswick / Sport Nouveau-Brunswick
#13, 900 Hanwell Rd., Fredericton NB E3B 6A2
Tel: 506-451-1320; *Fax:* 506-451-1325
e-mail: director@sportnb.com
URL: www.sportnb.com
Jason Dickson, Executive Director

Sport North Federation
Don Cooper Building, PO Box 11089, 4908-49 St., Yellowknife NT X1A 3X7
Tel: 867-669-8326; *Fax:* 867-669-8327
Toll-Free: 800-661-0797
URL: www.sportnorth.com
Doug Rentmeister, Executive Director

Sport Nova Scotia (SNS)
PO Box 3010, Stn. South, 5516 Spring Garden Rd., Halifax NS B3J 1G6
Tel: 902-425-5450; *Fax:* 902-425-5606
e-mail: sportns@sportnovascotia.ca
URL: www.sportnovascotia.ca
Jamie Ferguson, CEO

Sport PEI Inc.
PO Box 302, Charlottetown PE C1A 7K7
Tel: 902-368-4110; *Fax:* 902-368-4548
Toll-Free: 800-247-6712
e-mail: sports@sportpei.pe.ca
URL: www.sportpei.pe.ca
Lyall Huggan, Special Projects
Gemma Koughan, Executive Director
Wendy Reid, President
Nick Murray, Communications
Lisa MacKay, Finance & Administration

Sport Yukon
4061 - 4 Ave., Whitehorse YT Y1A 1H1
Tel: 867-668-4236; *Fax:* 867-667-4237
e-mail: news@sportyukon.com
URL: www.sportyukon.com
George Arcand, President

Sports-Québec
CP 1000, Succ. M, 4545, av Pierre-De Coubertin, Montréal QC H1V 3R2
Tél: 514-252-3114; *Téléc:* 514-254-9621
Courriel: sports@sportsquebec.com
URL: www.sportsquebec.com
André-François Lafond, Directeur général

True Sport Foundation / Fondation sport pur
#350, 955 Green Valley Crescent, Ottawa ON K2C 3V4
Tel: 613-526-6043; *Fax:* 613-521-3134
Toll-Free: 888-995-8899
e-mail: info@truesport.ca
URL: www.truesportfoundation.ca
Victor Lachance, Executive Director

Sports for the Disabled

Active Living Alliance for Canadians with a Disability (ALACD) / Alliance de vie active pour les canadiens/canadiennes ayant un handicap
#104, 720 Belfast Rd., Ottawa ON K1G 0Z5
Tel: 613-244-0052; *Fax:* 613-244-4857
Toll-Free: 800-771-0663; *TTY:* 888-771-0663
e-mail: info@ala.ca
URL: www.ala.ca
Affiliation(s): Canadian Amputee Sports Association; Canadian Association for Disabled Skiing; Canadian Association for Health, Physical Education, Recreation & Dance; Canadian Blind Sports Association; Canadian Cerebral Palsy Sports Association; Canadian Deaf Sports Association; Canadian Intramural Recreation Association; Canadian National Institute

for the Blind; Canadian Paralympic Committee; Canadian Paraplegic Association; Canadian Parks/Recreation Association; Canadian Red Cross Society; Canadian Special Olympics; Learning Disabilities Association of Canada; National Network for Mental Health
Jane Arkell, Director

Alberta Amputee Sports & Recreation Association (AASRA)
PO Box 708, Stn. M, Calgary AB T2P 2J3
Tel: 403-201-0507; *Fax:* 403-256-7611
Toll-Free: 800-501-0507
e-mail: info@aasra.ab.ca
URL: www.aasra.ab.ca
Gwen Davies, Executive Director

Alberta Northern Lights Wheelchair Basketball Society
6788 - 99th St., Edmonton AB T6E 5B8
Tel: 780-433-4310; *Fax:* 780-431-1764
Toll-Free: 800-465-2992
e-mail: info@albertanorthernlights.com
URL: www.albertanorthernlights.com

Alberta Sports & Recreation Association for the Blind (ASRAB)
#007, 15 Colonel Baker Pl. NE, Calgary AB T2E 4Z3
Tel: 403-262-5332; *Fax:* 403-265-7221
Toll-Free: 888-882-7722
e-mail: marilyn@asrab.ab.ca
URL: www.asrab.ab.ca
Marilyn McIntosh, Executive Director
Peter Wettlaufer, President

Association des sports pour aveugles de Montréal (ASAM)
CP 95, Succ. M, Montréal QC H1V 3L6
Tél: 514-252-3178; *Téléc:* 514-254-1303
Courriel: infoasam@sportsaveugles.qc.ca
URL: www.sportsaveugles.qc.ca/asam
Affiliation(s): Association sportive des aveugles du Québec
Gérald Cousineau, Président
Guillaume Thibault, Vice-président

Association québécoise des sports en fauteuil roulants (AQSFR)
CP 1000, Succ. M, 4545, rue Pierre-de-Coubertin, Montréal QC H1V 3R2
Tél: 514-252-3108; *Téléc:* 514-254-9793
Courriel: aqsfr@aqsfr.qc.ca
URL: www.aqsfr.qc.ca
José Malo, Directrice générale

Association sportive des aveugles du Québec inc.
CP 1000, Succ. M, 4545, av Pierre-de Coubertin, Montréal QC H1V 3R2
Tél: 514-252-3178; *Téléc:* 514-254-1303
URL: www.sportsaveugles.qc.ca
Robert Deschênes, Président

Blind Sailing Association of Canada (BSAC)
45 Brahms Ave., Toronto ON M2H 1H3
Tel: 416-489-2433; *Fax:* 416-489-2433
e-mail: info@blindsailing.ca
URL: www.blindsailing.ca
David Brown, President
Grant Robinson, Vice-President
Randy Nelson, Treasurer

British Columbia Blind Sports & Recreation Association (BCBSRA)
#330, 5055 Joyce St., Vancouver BC V5R 6B2
Tel: 604-325-8638; *Fax:* 604-325-1638
e-mail: info@bcblindsports.bc.ca
URL: www.bcblindsports.bc.ca
Affiliation(s): International Blind Sports Association; BC Sport & Fitness Council for the Disabled
Brian Cowie, President
Tami Grenon, Vice President

British Columbia Deaf Sports Federation (BCDSF)
#254, 3820 Cessna Dr., Richmond BC V7B 0A2
Fax: 604-738-7175; *TTY:* 604-333-3606
e-mail: bcdeafsports@telus.net
URL: www.bcdeafsports.bc.ca
Affiliation(s): BC Sport & Fitness Council for the Disabled
Roger Chan, President
Mandy Harker, Media/Programming

British Columbia Disability Sports (BCDS)
#217, 12837 - 76th Ave., Surrey BC V3W 2V3
Tel: 604-598-7890; *Fax:* 604-598-7892; *TTY:* 604-598-7890
e-mail: info@disabilitysport.org
URL: www.disabilitysport.org
Affiliation(s): Sportability BC; Deaf Sports Federation of BC; Disabled Skiers Association of BC; Canadian Amputee Sports Association BC Division; BC Blind Sports & Recreation Association; BC Therapeutic Riding Association; Disabled Sailing Association of BC; BC Sledge Hockey & Ice Picking; Wheeling Eights Square Dance Club; BC Wheelchair Basketball Society
Jane Samletzki, Executive Director

British Columbia Wheelchair Sports Association (BCWSA)
#210 - 3820 Cessna Drive, Richmindr BC V7B 0A2
Tel: 604-333-3520; *Fax:* 604-333-3450
Toll-Free: 877-737-3090
e-mail: info@bcwheelchairsports.com
URL: www.bcwheelchairsports.com
Kathy Newman, Executive Director

Canadian Amputee Golf Association (CAGA)
PO Box 6091, Stn. A, Calgary AB T2H 2L4
e-mail: canamps@caga.ca
URL: www.caga.ca
Gwen Davies, President

Canadian Amputee Sports Association (CASA) / Association canadienne des sports pour amputés
1399 Weslemkoon Lake Rd., Gilmour ON K0L 1W0
Tel: 613-474-1397
e-mail: bobfox1@hotmail.com
URL: www.canadianamputeesports.ca
Affiliation(s): Canadian Paralympic Committee; Hockey Canada
Robert Fox, President

Canadian Association for Disabled Skiing - Alberta (CADS - Alberta)
11759 Groat Rd., Edmonton AB T5M 3K6
Tel: 780-427-8104; *Fax:* 780-427-0524
e-mail: info@cadsalberta.ca
URL: www.cadsalberta.ca
Peter Quaiattini, President
Allyson Szafranski, Executive Coordinator

Canadian Association for Disabled Skiing - Newfoundland Division
6 Albany Pl., St. John's NL A1E 1Y2
Tel: 709-753-3625; *Fax:* 709-777-4884
e-mail: margaret.tibbo@easternhealth.ca
Marg Tibbo, Secretary

Canadian Association for Disabled Skiing Nova Scotia
c/o Alpine Ski Nova Scotia, 5516 Spring Garden Rd., Halifax NS B3J 1G6
Tel: 902-425-5450; *Fax:* 902-425-5606
e-mail: alpinens@sportnovascotia.ca
Lorraine Burch

Canadian Blind Sports Association Inc. / Association canadienne des sports pour aveugles inc.
#325, 5055 Joyce St., Vancouver BC V5R 6B2
Tel: 604-419-0480; *Fax:* 604-419-0481
Toll-Free: 866-604-0480
e-mail: jane@canadianblindsports.ca
URL: www.canadianblindsports.ca
Affiliation(s): International Blind Sports Association; Canadian Paralympic Committee; Active Living Alliance
Jane D. Blaine, Executive Director

Canadian Deaf Sports Association (CDSA) / Association des sports des sourds du Canada (ASSC)
#202A, 10217 boul Pie IX, Montréal-Nord QC H1H 3Z5
Tel: 514-321-4520; *Fax:* 514-321-2937
Toll-Free: 800-855-0511
e-mail: office@assc-cdsa.com
URL: www.assc-cdsa.com
Affiliation(s): International Committee of Sports for the Deaf
Kimberley D. Rizzi, Executive Director
Bradford Bentley, External Relations Director
Greg Desrosiers, President

Canadian Electric Wheelchair Hockey Association (CEWHA)
#920, 200 Yorkland Blvd., Toronto ON M2J 5C1
Tel: 416-757-8544; *Fax:* 416-490-9334
e-mail: info@cewha.ca
URL: www.cewha.ca

Canadian Paralympic Committee (CPC) / Comité paralympique canadien
#1401, 85 Albert St., Ottawa ON K1P 6A4
Tel: 613-569-4333; *Fax:* 613-569-2777
e-mail: reachus@paralympic.ca
URL: www.paralympic.ca
Affiliation(s): International Paralympic Committee
Brian MacPherson, Director General
Manali Haridas, Coordinator, Office and Leadership

Canadian Wheelchair Sports Association (CWSA) / Association canadienne des sports en fauteuil roulant (ACSFR)
#108, 2255 St. Laurent Blvd., Ottawa ON K1G 4K3
Tel: 613-523-0004; *Fax:* 613-523-0149
e-mail: info@cwsa.ca
URL: www.cwsa.ca
Affiliation(s): International Stoke Mandeville Wheelchair Sports Federation
Cathy Cadieux, Executive Director
Donald Royer, President

Commission de Ski pour Personnes Handicapées du Québec (CSPHQ)
165 Place Lilas, Pincourt QC J7V 5B6
Tél: 514-425-8894; *Téléc:* 514-425-8894
Courriel: hwohler@yahoo.com
Henry Wohler, President

Disabled Sailing Association of BC
#207, 3077 Granville Street, Vancouver BC V6H 3J9
Tel: 604-668-6464; *Fax:* 604-688-6463
e-mail: dsa@disabilityfoundation.org
URL: www.disabilityfoundation.org/dsa
Affiliation(s): BC Sport & Fitness Council for the Disabled
Kirk Duncan, Program Coordinator

Disabled Skiers Association of BC (DSABC)
#220, 3820 Cessna Dr., Richmond BC V7B 0A2
Tel: 604-333-3630; *Fax:* 604-333-3450
e-mail: disabledskiers@telus.net
URL: www.disabledskiingbc.com
Brian Forrester, Executive Director
Kevin ter Kuile, President

International Committee of Sports for the Deaf (ICSD) / Comité international des Sports des Sourds (CISS)
528 Trail Ave., Frederick MD 21701 USA
Fax: 301-620-2990
e-mail: info@ciss.org
URL: www.ciss.org; www.deaflympics.com
Affiliation(s): Canadian Deaf Sports Association
Craig A. Crowley, President

Manitoba Amputee Sport & Recreation Association
286 Harvard Ave., Winnipeg MB R3M 0K8
Tel: 204-489-9278; *Fax:* 204-488-1094
e-mail: rootel@shaw.ca
Raquel Godin, Contact

Manitoba Blind Sport Association
#311, 200 Main St., Winnipeg MB R3C 4M2
Tel: 204-925-5694; *Fax:* 204-925-5703
e-mail: blindsport@shawbiz.ca
URL: www.blindsport.mb.ca
Cathy Drewianchuk, Executive Director

Manitoba Wheelchair Sports Association
200 Main St., Winnipeg MB R3C 4M2
Tel: 204-925-5790; *Fax:* 204-925-5792
e-mail: mwsa@sport.mb.ca
URL: www.mwsa.ca
Tricia Klassen, Executive Director

National Capital Sports Council of the Disabled Inc. (NCSCD) / Le Conseil des sports des handicapées de la capitale nationale inc. (CSHCN)
#104, 720 Belfast Rd., Ottawa ON K1G 0Z5
Tel: 613-569-7632; *Fax:* 613-244-4857
e-mail: ncscd@ncscd.ca
URL: www.ncscd.ca

New Brunswick Deaf Sports Association
#902, 656 Brunswick Dr., Saint John NB E2L 3S5
Tel: 506-642-3903
Eugene Frost, President

Ontario Amputee & Les Autres Sports Association (OALASA)
#102, 1185 Eglinton Ave. East, Toronto ON M3C 3C6
Tel: 519-659-7452
URL: www.oalasa.org

Rodney Reimer, President
Douglas Walker, Treasurer
Archie Watts, Secretary

Ontario Blind Sport Association (OBSA)
#102, 1185 Eglinton Ave. East, Toronto ON M3C 3C6
Tel: 416-426-7191; *Fax:* 416-426-7361
e-mail: mary@blindsports.on.ca
URL: www.blindsports.on.ca
Shirley Shelby, President

Ontario Deaf Sports Association
219 Carlton St., Toronto ON M5A 2L2
Tel: 416-413-0299
e-mail: office@ontariodeafsports.on.ca
URL: www.ontariodeafsports.on.ca
Rohan Smith, President

Ontario Wheelchair Sports Association (OWSA)
#102, 1185 Eglinton Ave. East, Toronto ON M3C 3C6
Tel: 416-426-7189; *Fax:* 416-426-7361
e-mail: info@ontwheelchairsports.org
URL: www.ontwheelchairsports.org
Affiliation(s): Canadian Wheelchair Sports Association
Barb Montemurro, President
Michael Suraci, Executive Director

Paralympic Sports Association (Alberta) (PSA)
10024 - 79 Ave., Edmonton AB T6E 1R5
Tel: 780-439-8687; *Fax:* 780-432-0486
e-mail: info@parasports.net
URL: www.parasports.net
Affiliation(s): Wheelchair Sports Alberta
Kim McDonald, Executive Director

Paralympics Ontario
1185 Eglinton Ave. East, Toronto ON M3C 3C6
Tel: 416-426-7187; *Fax:* 416-426-7361
Toll-Free: 800-265-1539
e-mail: info@paralympicsontario.ca
URL: www.paralympicsontario.ca
Affiliation(s): Ontario Amputee & Les Autres Sports Association; Ontario Blind Sports Association; Ontario Cerebral Palsy Sports Association; Ontario Wheelchair Sports Association
Cathy Vincelli, Executive Director

Saskatchewan Blind Sports Association Inc.
510 Cynthia St., Saskatoon SK S7L 7K7
Tel: 306-975-0888; *Fax:* 306-242-8007
Toll-Free: 877-772-7798
e-mail: sbsa.sk@shaw.ca
URL: www.saskblindsports.ca
Darren Newberry, Executive Director
Terry Parsons, President

Saskatchewan Deaf Sports Association
511 Main St. East, Saskatoon SK S7N 0C2
Tel: 306-787-3432; *Fax:* 306-924-1421
Toll-Free: 800-855-0511
e-mail: lbirley@cableregina.com
Affiliation(s): Regina Deaf Athletic Club; Saskatoon Deaf Athletic Club
Kenneth Dittrick, President

Saskatchewan Ski Association - Skiing for Disabled (SASKI)
17 Clark Cres., Saskatoon SK S7H 3L8
Tel: 306-374-7745; *Fax:* 306-955-5979
e-mail: sask.ski@sasktel.net
URL: www.saski.ca
Alana Ottenbreit, Executive Director
Pat Prokopchuk, Contact, Skiing for Disabled
Doug Sylvester, Contact, Biathlon

Saskatchewan Wheelchair Sports Association (SWSA)
510 Cynthia St., Saskatoon SK S7L 7K7
Tel: 306-975-0824; *Fax:* 306-975-0825
e-mail: info@swsa.ca
URL: www.swsa.ca
Judy Peddle, Executive Director

Special Olympics Alberta (SOA)
Percy Page Centre, 11759 Groat Rd., Edmonton AB T5M 3K6
Tel: 780-415-0719; *Fax:* 780-422-2663
Toll-Free: 800-444-2883
e-mail: info@specialolympics.ab.ca
URL: www.specialolympics.ab.ca
Carmen Wyton, President & CEO

Wheelchair Sports Alberta
Percy Page Center, 11759 Groat Rd., Edmonton AB T5M 3K6
Tel: 780-427-8699; *Fax:* 780-427-8723
Toll-Free: 888-453-6770
e-mail: wsa1@telusplanet.net
URL: www.abwheelchairsport.ca

Wheelchair Sports Association of Newfoundland & Labrador (WSANL)
40 Imogene Cr., Paradise NL A1L 1H5
Tel: 709-782-0487
e-mail: gpower@cwsa.ca
Gary Power, President

Sports, Amateur

Alberta Amateur Wrestling Association (AAWA)
Percy Page Centre, 11759 Groat Rd., Edmonton AB T5M 3K6
Tel: 780-415-0140; *Fax:* 780-427-0524
e-mail: aawa@ocii.com
URL: www.albertawrestling.ab.ca
Tammie Bradley, Program Director

Hockey Alberta / Hockey l'Alberta
#1, 7875 - 48 Ave., Red Deer AB T4P 2K1
Tel: 403-342-6777; *Fax:* 403-346-4277
e-mail: operations@hockeyalberta.ca
URL: www.hockey-alberta.ca
Rob Litwinski, General Manager
Brad Robbins, Senior Manager, Operations & Member Services
Tim Leer, Senior Manager, Hockey Development

Ontario Speed Skating Association (OSSA)
Memorial Hall, PO Box 1179, 2 Queen St., 2nd Fl., Lakefield ON K0L 2H0
Tel: 705-652-0653; *Fax:* 705-652-1227
e-mail: jdeschenes@speedskatingontario.org
URL: www.speedskatingontario.org
Jackie Deschenes, Executive Director
Bill Allen, Director of Sport

Sport Newfoundland & Labrador
PO Box 8700, St. John's NL A1B 4J6
Tel: 709-576-4932; *Fax:* 709-576-7493
e-mail: sportnl@sportnl.ca
URL: www.sportnl.ca
Troy Croft, Executive Director

Squash

Squash Alberta
3415 - 3 Ave. NW, Calgary AB T2N 0M4
Tel: 403-270-7344; *Fax:* 403-270-8445
Toll-Free: 877-646-6566
e-mail: lynn@squashalberta.com
URL: squash.ab.ca

Squash British Columbia
4867 Ontario St., Vancouver BC V5H 3H4
Tel: 604-737-3084; *Fax:* 604-736-3527
e-mail: info@squashbc.com
URL: www.squashbc.com
John Roche, President

Squash Canada
#401, 2197 Riverside Dr., Ottawa ON K1H 7X3
Tel: 613-731-7385; *Fax:* 613-731-6291
e-mail: squash.canada@squash.ca
URL: www.squash.ca
Linda MacPhail, Executive Director
Robert Wyma, President

Squash Manitoba
#303, 200 Main St., Winnipeg MB R3C 4M2
Tel: 204-925-5661; *Fax:* 204-925-5703
e-mail: squashmb@shawbiz.ca
URL: www.squashmb.org

Squash New Brunswick
276 Parkhurst Dr., Fredericton NB E3B 2J9
Tel: 506-457-0877; *Fax:* 506-443-0830
e-mail: russky@unb.ca
URL: www.squashnb.ca

Squash Nova Scotia
PO Box 3010, Stn. Park Lane Centre, #401, 5516 Spring Garden Rd., Halifax NS B3J 3G6
Tel: 902-425-5450; *Fax:* 902-425-5606
e-mail: sdavies@thirdwaveconsulting.ca
URL: www.squashns.ca

Squash Ontario
#308, 3 Concorde Gate, Toronto ON M3C 3N7
Tel: 416-426-7201; *Fax:* 416-426-7393
Toll-Free: 888-741-5111
e-mail: info@squashontario.com
URL: www.squashontario.com
Tom Craig, President
Sherry Funston, Executive Director
Geoffrey Johnson, Program Coordinator
Laura Mauer, Administrative Coordinator

Squash P.E.I.
C/O Sport PEI, PO Box 302, Stn. Enman Cres., Charlottetown PE C1A 7K7
Tel: 902-566-0338
e-mail: meleclair@edu.pe.ca
URL: www.squashpei.org
Steven Banks, President
Nicole Blanchard, Secretary
Des Lecky, Treasurer

Squash Québec
CP 1000, Succ. M, 4545, av Pierre-de Coubertin, Montréal QC H1V 3R2
Tél: 514-252-3062; *Téléc:* 514-252-3103
Courriel: info@sports-4murs.qc.ca
URL: www.squash.qc.ca
Barry Faguy, Président

Squash Yukon
PO Box 31226, Whitehorse YT Y1A 5P7
Tel: 867-667-7071; *Fax:* 867-668-6442
e-mail: squashyukon@yknet.yk.ca
URL: www.squashyukon.yk.ca
Jim Gilpin, President

Swimming

Fédération de natation du Québec
CP 1000, Succ. M, 4545, av Pierre-de-Coubertin, Montréal QC H1V 3R2
Tél: 514-252-3200; *Téléc:* 514-252-3232
Courriel: fnq@fnq.qc.ca
URL: www.fnq.qc.ca
Bernard Charron, directeur général

International Amateur Swimming Federation (IASF) / Fédération internationale de natation amateur (FINA)
Av. de l'Avant-Poste 4, Lausanne 1005 Switzerland
Tel: 41-21-310-4710; *Fax:* 41-21-312-6610
URL: www.fina.org
Bartolo Consolo, Hon. Secretary
Mustapha Larfaoui, President
Cornel Marculescu, Executive Director

Solo Swims of Ontario Inc. (SSO)
32 Coxwell Cres., Brantford ON N3P 1Z1
URL: www.soloswims.com
Greg Taylor, President & Secretary

Swim Alberta
Percy Page Centre, 11759 Groat Rd., Edmonton AB T5M 3K6
Tel: 780-415-1780; *Fax:* 780-415-1788
e-mail: office@swimalberta.ca
URL: www.swimalberta.ca
Doug Bird, President
James Hood, General Manager

Swim BC
#204, 4475 Viewmont Ave., Victoria BC V8Z 6L8
Tel: 250-479-2069; *Fax:* 250-479-3021
e-mail: markschuett@swim.bc.ca
URL: www.swim.bc.ca
Mark Hahto, Executive Director

Swim Manitoba / Natation Manitoba
#224, 200 Main St., Winnipeg MB R2C 4M2
Tel: 204-925-5778; *Fax:* 204-925-5792
e-mail: office@swimmanitoba.mb.ca
URL: www.swimmanitoba.mb.ca
Cathie Pickerl, President
Michael McMullen, Vice-President
Sharra Hinton, Treasurer

Swim Nova Scotia (SNS)
5516 Spring Garden Rd., Halifax NS B3J 1G6
Tel: 902-425-5450; *Fax:* 902-425-5606
e-mail: swimming@sportnovascotia.ca
URL: www.swimnovascotia.com
Lynn Sitland, President
Bette El-Hawary, Executive Director

Swim Ontario
#206, 3 Concorde Gate, Toronto ON M3C 3N7

Tel: 416-426-7220; *Fax:* 416-426-7356
e-mail: info@swimontario.com
URL: www.swimontario.com
John Vadeika, Executive Director

Swim Saskatchewan
2205 Victoria Ave., Regina SK S4P 0S4
Tel: 306-780-9291; *Fax:* 306-525-4009
e-mail: marjwalton@swimsask.ca
URL: www.swimsask.ca
Marj Walton, Executive Director

Swimming New Brunswick
#13, 900 Hanwell Rd., Fredericton NB E3B 6A3
Tel: 506-451-1323; *Fax:* 506-451-1325
e-mail: swimnb@nbnet.nb.ca
URL: www.swimnb.ca
Maurice Leger, President

Swimming Newfoundland & Labrador
PO Box 21248, Stn. Macdonald Dr., St. John's NL A1A 5B2
Tel: 709-576-7946; *Fax:* 709-576-7493
e-mail: swimnl@sportnl.ca
URL: www.swimnl.nfld.net
Corina Hartley, Executive Director

Swimming Prince Edward Island
PO Box 302, Charlottetown PE C1A 7K7
Tel: 902-569-0583; *Fax:* 902-368-4548
e-mail: cgcrozier@sportpei.pe.ca
URL: www.swimpei.com
Cheryl Crozier, Executive Director

Swimming/Natation Canada
#700, 2197 Riverside Dr., Ottawa ON K1H 7X3
Tel: 613-260-1348; *Fax:* 613-260-0804
e-mail: natloffice@swimming.ca
URL: www.swimming.ca
Affiliation(s): Aquatic Federation of Canada
Pierre Lafontaine, CEO/National Coach
Mark Hahto, COO
Larry Clough, CFO
Martin Richard, Communications Director

Synchro Alberta
The Percy Page Centre, 11759 Groat Rd., Edmonton AB T5M 3K6
Tel: 780-415-1789; *Fax:* 780-415-0056
e-mail: syncro@synchroalberta.com
URL: www.synchroalberta.com
Chris Hampshire, President

Synchro BC
#301, 1367 West Broadway, Vancouver BC V6H 4A9
Tel: 604-737-3169; *Fax:* 604-738-7175
e-mail: synchrobc@telus.net
URL: www.synchro.bc.ca
Twyla Ryan, Executive Director
Cathy Chapell, Office Coordinator

Synchro Canada / Association canadienne de nage synchronisée amateur
#200, 1010 Polytek St., Unit 14, Gloucester ON K1J 9H9
Tel: 613-748-5674; *Fax:* 613-748-5724
e-mail: catherine@synchro.ca
URL: www.synchro.ca
Catherine Gosselin-Desprès, Chief Operations Officer
Diane Oligny, Chief Technical Officer

Synchro Manitoba
200 Main St., Winnipeg MB R3C 4M2
Tel: 204-925-5693; *Fax:* 204-925-5703
e-mail: info@synchromb.ca
URL: www.synchromb.ca
Affiliation(s): Manitoba Sports Federation
Allison Gervais, Executive Director

Synchro Newfoundland & Labrador
1 Pine Bud Pl., St. John's NL A1B 1N1
Tel: 709-722-0439
Lorna Proudfoot, Contact

Synchro Ontario
#303, 1185 Eglinton Ave. East, Toronto ON M3C 3C6
Tel: 416-426-7110; *Fax:* 416-426-7376
e-mail: lmakins@osrc.com
URL: www.synchroontario.com
Leslie Makins, Executive Director

Synchro PEI
PO Box 302, Charlottetown PE C1A 7K7
Tel: 902-892-1873
e-mail: lucillecarter@aol.com
URL: www.sportpei.pe.ca
Lucille Carter, President

Synchro Saskatchewan
#209, 1860 Lorne St., Regina SK S4P 2L7
Tel: 306-780-9227; *Fax:* 306-780-9445
e-mail: synchro.sk@sasktel.net
URL: www.synchrosask.com
Kathleen Reynolds, Executive Director

Synchro-Québec
CP 1000, Succ. M, 4545, av Pierre-de Coubertin, Montréal QC H1V 3R2
Tél: 514-252-3087; *Téléc:* 514-252-5658
Ligne sans frais: 866-537-3164
Courriel: fnsq@synchroquebec.qc.ca
URL: www.synchroquebec.qc.ca

Table Soccer

Canadian Table Soccer Federation
8311, rue Ouimet, Brossard QC J4Y 3B3
Tel: 514-668-2326
e-mail: secretary@canadafoos.com
URL: www.canadafoos.com
Eric Dunn, President
Adam Imanpoor, Secretary

Ontario Table Soccer Association & Tour
Tel: 905-812-9994
Toll-Free: 866-247-7702
e-mail: info@ontariotablesoccer.com
URL: www.ontariotablesoccer.com
Mario Recupero, Executive Director

Table Tennis

Alberta Table Tennis Association (ATTA)
Percy Page Centre, 11759 Groat Rd., Edmonton AB T5M 3K6
Tel: 780-427-8588; *Fax:* 866-273-6708
e-mail: atta@abtabletennis.com
URL: www.abtabletennis.com
Affiliation(s): International Table Tennis Federation
Joseph Chan, President
Judy Ellefson, Program Coordinator

British Columbia Table Tennis Association
#227 - 3820 Cessna Drive, Richmond BC V7B 0A2
Tel: 604-333-3655; *Fax:* 604-333-3450
e-mail: bctta@hotmail.com
URL: www.bctta.ca
Amelia Ho, President

Canadian Table Tennis Association (CTTA) / Association canadienne de tennis de table
#400, 2211 Riverside Dr., Ottawa ON K1H 7X5
Tel: 613-733-6272; *Fax:* 613-733-7279
e-mail: ctta@ctta.ca
URL: www.ctta.ca
Affiliation(s): Sports Council of Canada
Manali Haridas, Office Administrator
Tony Kiesenhofer, Director General

Fédération de tennis de table du Québec (FTTQ)
CP 1000, Succ. M, 4545, av Pierre-de Coubertin, Montréal QC H1V 3R2
Tél: 514-252-3064; *Téléc:* 514-251-8038
URL: www.tennisdetable.ca/
Jacques Plamandon, Directeur général

Manitoba Table Tennis Association (MTTA)
200 Main St., Winnipeg MB R3C 4M2
Tel: 204-925-5690; *Fax:* 204-925-5703
e-mail: mtta@shawbiz.ca
URL: www.mtta.ca
Affiliation(s): International Table Tennis Federation
Ron Edwards, Executive Director
Darek Mikita, President
Ryan Szajkowski, Vice-President, Administration
Dan Racicot, Vice-President, Technical

Ontario Table Tennis Association (OTTA)
PO Box 42040, Stn. Conestoga, 550 King St. North, Waterloo ON N2L 6K5
Toll-Free: 877-396-6601
e-mail: larry.laughlen@ottacanada.com
URL: www.ottacanada.com
Larry Laughlen, President

Prince Edward Island Table Tennis Association (PEITTA)
3 Hurry Rd., RR#10, Charlottetown PE C1E 1Z4
Tel: 902-368-2360
e-mail: nchishti@biovectra.com
Todd Gaudin, Vice-President
Lorne Clow, Secretary
Wade Gregory, Treasurer
Najam Chishti, President

Saskatchewan Table Tennis Association Inc. (STTA)
John V. Remai Centre, 510 Cynthia St., Saskatoon SK S7N 7K7
Tel: 306-975-0835
e-mail: info@sasktabletennis.ca
URL: www.sasktabletennis.ca
Dwayne Yachiw, Program Coordinator
Joseph Chan, President
Edward Hung, Vice-President

Teaching

British Columbia Physical Education Provincial Specialist Association
c/o B.C. Teachers' Federation, #100, 550 West 6th Ave., Vancouver BC V5Z 4P2
Tel: 604-871-2283; *Fax:* 604-871-2286
URL: www.bctf.bc.ca/pebc
Debbie Keel, President

Tennis

Alberta Tennis Association (ATA)
11759 Groat Rd., Edmonton AB T5M 3K6
Tel: 780-415-1661; *Fax:* 780-415-1693
e-mail: info@tennisalberta.com
URL: www.tennisalberta.com
Darryl Szafranski, Chief Executive Officer
Eva Wolicki, Technical Director

International Tennis Federation (ITF)
Bank Lane, Roehampton, London SW15 5XZ United Kingdom
Tel: 44-20-8878-6464; *Fax:* 44-20-8392-4744
URL: www.itftennis.com
Affiliation(s): Tennis Canada
Francesco Ricci Bitti, President
Juan Margets, Executive Vice-President

Nova Scotia Tennis Association
5516 Spring Garden Rd., Halifax NS B3J 1G6
Tel: 902-425-5450; *Fax:* 902-425-5606
e-mail: tennisns@sportnovascotia.ca
URL: www.tennisnovascotia.ca
Roger Keating, Executive Director

Ontario Tennis Association (OTA)
#200, 1 Shoreham Dr., Toronto ON M3N 3A7
Tel: 416-514-1100; *Fax:* 416-514-1112
Toll-Free: 800-387-5066
e-mail: ota@tennisontario.com
URL: www.tennisontario.com
Michel Lecavalier, President
Jim Boyce, Executive Director
Simon Bartram, Vice-President
Scott Fraser, Vice-President, Finance & Administration
Glenna Poick, Vice-President, Marketing & Communications
Liz Wood, Vice-President, Membership & Regional Development

Prince Edward Island Tennis Association
PO Box 302, 40 Enman Cres., Charlottetown PE C1A 7K7
Tel: 902-368-4208; *Fax:* 902-368-4548
e-mail: brianhall@peitennis.ca
URL: www.peitennis.ca
Fred Foster, Executive Director
Brian Hall, Contact

Tennis BC
#204, 210 West Broadway, Vancouver BC V5Y 3W2
Tel: 604-737-3086; *Fax:* 604-737-3124
e-mail: tbc@tennisbc.org
URL: tennisbc.org
Ryan Clark, Chief Executive Officer

Tennis Canada
Rexall Centre, #100, 1 Shoreham Dr., Toronto ON M3N 3A6
Tel: 416-665-9777; *Fax:* 416-665-9017
Toll-Free: 877-283-6647
e-mail: info@tenniscanada.com
URL: www.tenniscanada.com
Michael S. Downey, President & CEO
Tony Eames, Chair

Tennis Manitoba
#303, 200 Main St., Winnipeg MB R3C 4M2

Tel: 204-925-5660; *Fax:* 204-925-5703
e-mail: tennismb@shawbiz.ca
URL: www.tennismanitoba.com
Rick Bochinski, Executive Director
Brigitte Epp, Administrative Assistant

Tennis New Brunswick
PO Box 604, Fredericton NB E3B 5A6
Tel: 506-444-0885
e-mail: tnb@tennisnb.net
URL: www.tennisnb.net

Tennis Newfoundland & Labrador
Bldg. 810, PO Box 8700, Stn. Pleasantville, St. John's NL A1B 4J6
Tel: 709-765-0426; *Fax:* 709-722-1670
e-mail: tennis@sportnl.ca
URL: www.tennisnl.ca
Ryan Maarschalk, Technical Director

Tennis Northwest Territories
PO Box 671, Yellowknife NT X1A 2N5
Tel: 867-873-2018
e-mail: eastarm@ssimicro.com
URL: www.tennisnwt.ca
Fran Hurcomb, President

Tennis Québec (TQ)
285, rue Faillon ouest, Montréal QC H2R 2W1
Tél: 514-270-6060; *Téléc:* 514-270-2700
Courriel: courrier@tennis.qc.ca
URL: www.tennis.qc.ca
Jean François Manibal, Directeur général
Réjean Genois, Président

Tennis Saskatchewan
2205 Victoria Ave., Regina SK S4P 0S4
Tel: 306-780-9410; *Fax:* 306-525-4009
e-mail: tennissask@sasktel.net
URL: www.tennissask.com
Affiliation(s): Sask Sport Incorporated
Rory Park, Executive Director

Therapeutic Riding

Antigonish Therapeutic Riding Association
50 The Heights, Antigonish NS B2G 1K5
Tel: 902-863-1479
URL: www.nsnet.org/riding/

British Columbia Therapeutic Riding Association (BCTRA)
25768 - 128th Ave., Maple Ridge BC V4R 1C4
Tel: 604-462-9884; *Fax:* 604-462-9597
e-mail: supremehm@shaw.ca
URL: vcn.bc.ca/bctra
Affiliation(s): Horse Council BC; Sports & Fitness Council for the Disabled
Jane James, President

Canadian Therapeutic Riding Association / Association canadienne d'équitation thérapeutique
#11, 5420 Hwy. 6 North, RR#5, Guelph ON N1H 6J2
Tel: 519-767-0700; *Fax:* 519-767-0435
e-mail: ctra@golden.net
URL: www.cantra.ca
Lisa Burd, President
Donna Naylor, Executive Director

Cavalier Riding Club Ltd. (CRC)
c/o Ashton Ridge Equestrian Centre, 711 Pine Glen Rd., Pine Glen NB E1J 1S1
Tel: 506-386-2596
e-mail: mgs500@gmail.com
URL: ashton-ridge.com/cavalier.htm
Mark G. Stevens, President

Central Ontario Developmental Riding Program (CODRP)
Pride Stables, 584 Pioneer Tower Rd., Kitchener ON N2P 2H9
Tel: 519-653-4686; *Fax:* 519-653-5565
e-mail: codrp@sentex.net
URL: www.codrp.com; www.pridestables.com
Affiliation(s): Ontario Therapeutic Riding Association (ONTRA)
Heather Mackneson, Contact

Community Association for Riding for the Disabled (CARD)
4777 Dufferin St., Toronto ON M3H 5T3
Tel: 416-667-8600; *Fax:* 416-739-7520
e-mail: card.info@sympatico.ca
URL: www.card.ca
Affiliation(s): Ontario Therapeutic Riding Association
Abbey Simbrow, Executive Director

Comox Valley Therapeutic Riding Society (CVTRS)
PO Box 3666, Courtenay BC V9N 7P1
Tel: 250-338-1968; *Fax:* 250-338-4137
e-mail: cvtrs@telus.net
URL: www.cvtrs.com
Affiliation(s): North American Handicapped Riding Association
Margaret Hind, Coordinator

Errington Therapeutic Riding Association (ETRA)
PO Box 462, Parksville BC V9P 2G6
e-mail: etrainfo@shaw.ca
URL: islandpages.com/etra/
Affiliation(s): BC Therapeutic Riding Association; Canadian Therapeutic Riding Association
Tom Roy, President

Halifax Area Leisure & Therapeutic Riding
1690 Bell Rd., Halifax NS B3H 2Z3
Tel: 902-860-0697
e-mail: haltr@bengallancers.com
URL: www.bengallancers.ca/haltr.html
Lisa Burd, President

Lanark County Therapeutic Riding Programme (LCTRP)
103 Judson St., Carleton Place ON K7C 2S5
Tel: 613-257-7121; *Fax:* 613-257-2675
Toll-Free: 800-667-2617
e-mail: info@therapeuticriding.ca
URL: www.therapeuticriding.ca
Susan Cressy, Contact

Lethbridge Handicapped Riding Association
RR#8-24-6, Lethbridge AB T1J 4P4
Tel: 403-328-2165
e-mail: lhra@telusplanet.net
Nancy Conan, Contact
Cory Conan, Contact

Little Bits Therapeutic Riding Association
PO Box 29016, Stn. Lendrum, Edmonton AB T6H 5Z6
Tel: 780-476-1233
e-mail: info@littlebits.ca
URL: www.littlebits.ca

Manitoba Riding for the Disabled Association Inc. (MRDA)
200 Main St., 2nd Fl., Winnipeg MB R3C 4M2
Tel: 204-925-5905; *Fax:* 204-925-5792
e-mail: mrda@shawcable.com
URL: www.mrda.cc
Peter Manastyrsky, Executive Director

Mirabel Morgan Special Riding Centre
1201 - 2nd Line South, RR#1, Bailieboro ON K0L 1B0
Tel: 705-939-6485
e-mail: mirabel.ms@sympatico.ca
Colleen Baptist, Contact

Mount View Special Riding Association (MVSRA)
5629 - 49 Ave., Olds AB T4H 1G5
Tel: 403-556-7247

New Brunswick Therapeutic Riding
860 Mitchell St., Fredericton NB E3B 6C5
Tel: 506-455-1621
Carol Morrison

Nova Scotia Riding for the Disabled Association (NSRDA)
608 West Lawrencetown Road, Lawrencetown NS B2Z 1S5
Tel: 902-435-9344; *Fax:* 902-434-0545
e-mail: salliemurphy@hotmail.com
Affiliation(s): Nova Scotia Equestrian Federation; Recreation Council on Disability in Nova Scotia
Sallie Murphy, Sec.-Treas.

Ontario Therapeutic Riding Association (ONTRA) / Association ontarienne d'équitation thérapeutique
PO Box 50058, 660 Eglinton Avenue E, Toronto ON M4G 4G1
URL: www.ontra.ca
Karen Sibbald, President

Pacific Riding for Developing Abilities (PRDA)
1088 - 208 St., Langley BC V2Z 1T4
Tel: 604-530-8717; *Fax:* 604-530-8617
e-mail: admin@prda.ca
URL: www.prda.ca
Affiliation(s): United Way of the Lower Mainland
Carla Robin, Executive Director

PARD Therapeutic Riding (PARD)
PO Box 1654, Peterborough ON K9J 5S4
Tel: 705-742-6441
e-mail: info@pard.ca
URL: www.pard.ca
Joanna Primavesi, President

Peace Area Riding for the Disabled (PARDS)
PO Box 2, Site 24, RR#1, Grande Prairie AB T8V 2Z8
Tel: 780-538-3211; *Fax:* 780-538-3683
e-mail: pards@telusplanet.net
URL: www.pards.ca
Jennifer Douglas, Executive Director

Quinte Therapeutic Riding Association (QUINTRA)
PO Box 22129, Belleville ON K8N 5V7
Tel: 613-395-4472
e-mail: barbara.davis@sympatico.ca
URL: www.quintra.org
Affiliation(s): United Way of Quinte
Barb Davis, Contact

SARI Therapeutic Riding
12659 Medway Rd., RR#1, Arva ON N0M 1C0
Tel: 519-666-1123; *Fax:* 519-666-1971
e-mail: office@sari.ca
URL: www.sari.ca
Affiliation(s): Ontario Therapeutic Riding Association
Heather Zak, Executive Director

Saskatchewan Therapeutic Riding Association
PO Box 1072, North Battleford SK S9A 3E6
Tel: 306-398-2889
Ed Gendall, Contact

Sunrise Therapeutic Riding & Learning Centre
6920 Concession 1, RR#2, Puslinch ON n0B 2J0
Tel: 519-837-0558; *Fax:* 519-837-1233
e-mail: info@sunrise-therapeutic.ca
URL: www.sunrise-therapeutic.ca
Affiliation(s): Ontario's Promise
Ann Caine, Executive Director
Suzy Bender, Head Instructor

Therapeutic Ride Algoma
188 Upton Rd., Sault Ste Marie ON P6A 3W4
Tel: 705-759-2935; *Fax:* 705-541-5700
Toll-Free: 877-526-4438
e-mail: slavik@sympatico.ca
URL: www.ridealgoma.com

Victoria Riding for Disabled Association (VRDA)
PO Box 43032, Stn. Victoria North, Victoria BC V8X 3G2
Tel: 250-658-6272
e-mail: vrda@shaw.ca
URL: www.members.shaw.ca/vrda
Affiliation(s): B.C. Therapeutic Riding Association; Horse Council of British Columbia

Windsor Essex Therapeutic Riding Association (WETRA) / Association d'équitation thérapeutique Windsor-Essex
4465 Huron Church Line Rd., Windsor ON N9H 1H3
Tel: 519-969-1261; *Fax:* 519-969-4016
e-mail: wetra@on.aibn.com
URL: www.wetra.ca
Affiliation(s): Ontario Therapeutic Riding Association
Sue Klotzer, Program Director

Track & Field Sports

Achilles Canada
119 Snowden Ave., Toronto ON M4N 2A8
Tel: 416-485-6451; *Fax:* 416-485-0823
e-mail: bmclean@idirect.com
URL: www.achillestrackclub.ca
Brian McLean, Contact

Athletics Canada / Athlétisme Canada
#B1-110, 2445 St-Laurent Blvd, Ottawa ON K1G 6C3
Tel: 613-260-5580; *Fax:* 613-260-0341
e-mail: athcan@athletics.ca
URL: www.athletics.ca
Affiliation(s): International Amateur Athletic Federation
Joanne Mortimore, CEO

Canadian Masters Athletic Association (CMAA)
426 Valermo Dr., Toronto ON M8W 2L9
Tel: 416-252-7047
e-mail: masters@sympatico.ca
URL: www.canadianmastersathletics.com
Brian Keaveney, President
Joan Christiensen, Membership

Northwest Territories Track & Field Association
PO Box 11089, Yellowknife NT X1A 3X7
Fax: 867-669-8327
Toll-Free: 800-661-0797
Joe LeBlanc, President

Ontario Masters Track & Field Association (OMTFA)
1185 Eglinton Ave. East, Toronto ON M3C 3C6
Tel: 416-426-4427; *Fax:* 416-426-7358
e-mail: douglasj.smith@sympatico.ca
URL: www.ontariomasters.ca
Doug Smith, President
Paul Osland, Vice-President

Ontario Roadrunners Association
#158, 2255B Queen St. East, Toronto ON M4E 1G3
Tel: 416-691-9556
e-mail: info@ontarioroadrunners.com
URL: www.ontarioroadrunners.com

Transportation

Toronto Cycling Committee (TCC)
850 Coxwell Ave., 2nd Fl., Toronto ON M4C 5R1
Tel: 416-392-7592
e-mail: btww@toronto.ca
URL: www.toronto.ca/cycling
Adrian A. Heaps, Chair

Triathlon

Alberta Triathlon Association (ATA)
11759 Groat Rd., Edmonton AB T5M 3K6
Tel: 780-427-8616; *Fax:* 780-427-8628
Toll-Free: 866-888-7448
e-mail: info@triathlon.ab.ca
URL: www.triathlon.ab.ca
Bradly Babiak, Executive Director

Ontario Association of Triathletes (OAT)
#304, 1185 Eglinton Ave. East, Toronto ON M3C 3C6
Tel: 416-426-7025; *Fax:* 416-426-7303
e-mail: info@triathlonontario.com
URL: www.triathlonontario.com
Linda Kirk, Executive Director
Andrew Armstrong, President

Triathlon Canada
#106, 3 Concorde Gate, Toronto ON M3C 3N7
Tel: 416-426-7180; *Fax:* 416-426-7294
e-mail: info@triathloncanada.com
URL: www.triathloncanada.com
Alan Trivett, Executive Director

Triathlon Newfoundland & Labrador
PO Box 113, 1 Union St., Corner Brook NL A2H 6C3
Tel: 709-634-9570; *Fax:* 709-634-9417
e-mail: triathlon@nf.sympatico.ca
Affiliation(s): International Triathlon Union
Allen Vansen, President

Triathlon Québec
CP 1000, Succ. M, 4545, av Pierre-de-Coubertin, Montréal QC H1V 3R2
Tél: 514-252-3121; *Téléc:* 514-252-5328
Courriel: info@triathlonquebec.org
URL: www.triathlonquebec.org
Affiliation(s): Triathlon Canada
Benoît-Hugo St-Pierre, Directeur

Universities & Colleges

Alberta Colleges Athletic Conference (ACAC)
Percy Page Centre, 11759 Groat Rd., Edmonton AB T5M 3K6
Tel: 780-427-8068; *Fax:* 780-427-9289
e-mail: office@acac.ab.ca
URL: www.acac.ab.ca
Robert D. Day, Executive Director
Wade Kolmel, President
Alan Rogan, Vice-President, Operations
Leigh Goldie, Vice-President, Finance
Laurie de Grace, Coordinator, Marketing & Communications

British Columbia Colleges' Athletic Association (BCCAA)
100 West 49th Ave., Vancouver BC V5X 2X6
Tel: 604-439-9325; *Fax:* 604-439-9245
URL: www.bccaa.ca
Affiliation(s): Canadian Colleges Athletics Association (CCAA)
Clayton Munro, President
Bruce Hunter, Chair, Discipline
Elise Le Brun, Chair, Eligibility

Canadian Council of University Physical Education & Kinesiology Administrators (CCUPEKA) / Conseil canadien des administrateurs universitaires en éducation physique et kinésiologie (CCAUEPK)
c/o Dr. J. Starkes, Department of Kinesiology, McMaster University, Hamilton ON L8S 4K1
URL: www.ccupeka.ca
Janet Starkes, Coordinator, Accreditation Council

Canadian Interuniversity Sport (CIS) / Sport interuniversitaire canadien (SIC)
#N205, 801 King Edward, Ottawa ON K1N 6N5
Tel: 613-562-5670; *Fax:* 613-562-5669
e-mail: cisoffice@universitysport.ca
URL: www.cis-sic.ca
Affiliation(s): Atlantic University Sport; Québéc Student Sport Federation; Ontario University Athletics; Canada West Universities Athletic Association
Marg McGregor, CEO

Ontario Colleges Athletic Association (OCAA)
#201m 3 Concorde Gate, North York ON M3C 3N7
Tel: 416-426-7043; *Fax:* 416-426-7308
e-mail: admin@ocaa.com
URL: www.ocaa.com
Mark Couch, Sport Services Coordinator
Lindsay Bax, Marketing/Communications
Blair Webster, Executive Director
Ron Fearon, President

Ontario University Athletics (OUA) / Sports universitaires de l'Ontario
#230, 1119 Fennell Ave. East, Hamilton ON L8T 1S2
Tel: 905-540-5148; *Fax:* 905-574-2840
e-mail: info@oua.ca
URL: www.oua.ca
Ward Disle, Executive Director

Volleyball

Alberta Volleyball Association (AVA)
Percy Page Centre, 11759 Groat Rd., Edmonton AB T5M 3K6
Tel: 780-415-1703; *Fax:* 780-415-1700
e-mail: info@albertavolleyball.com
URL: www.albertavolleyball.com
Affiliation(s): Federation of Outdoor Volleyball Associations
Terry Gagnon, Executive Director
Gail Senkiw, Office Manager

Fédération de volleyball du Québec (FVBQ)
CP 1000, Succ. M, 4545, av Pierre-de Coubertin, Montréal QC H1V 3R2
Tél: 514-252-3065; *Téléc:* 514-252-3176
Courriel: info-fvbq@volleyball.qc.ca
URL: www.volleyball.qc.ca
Affiliation(s): Sports Québec; Regroupement loisirs Québec
Alain D'Amboise, Directeur général
Charles H. Cardinal, Président

International Volleyball Association / Fédération Internationale de Volleyball (FIVB)
Edouard-Sandoz 2-4, Lausanne 1006 Switzerland
Tel: 41-21-345-3535; *Fax:* 41-21-345-3545
e-mail: info@fivb.org
URL: www.fivb.ch
Affiliation(s): Canadian Volleyball Association
Jizhong Wei, President

Manitoba Volleyball Association (MVA)
200 Main St., Winnipeg MB R3C 4M2
Tel: 204-925-5783; *Fax:* 204-925-5786
e-mail: mbvolley@sport.mb.ca
URL: www.manitobavolleyball.com
Affiliation(s): Volleyball Canada
Greg Jarvis, Executive Director
Leanne Leskiw, President
Pat Alexander, Vice-President & Treasurer
Colin Glass, Secretary

Newfoundland & Labrador Volleyball Association (NLVA)
PO Box 21248, St. John's NL A1A 5B2
Tel: 709-576-0817; *Fax:* 709-576-7493
e-mail: nlvaruss@sportnl.ca
URL: www.nlva.net
Russell Jackson, Executive Director
Eric Hiscock, President
Mike Murrran, Elite Development Chair

Northwest Territories Volleyball Association (NWTVA)
Tel: 867-920-2712
e-mail: terrel_hobbs@nwtvolleyball.ca
URL: www.nwtvolleyball.ca
Terrell Hobbs, President & Regl Official Chair
Micher Haener, Vice-President
Ryan Nichols, Secretary
Kim Weir, Treasurer

Ontario Volleyball Association (OVA)
#304, 3 Concorde Gate, Toronto ON M3C 3N7
Tel: 416-426-7316; *Fax:* 416-426-7109
Toll-Free: 800-563-5938
e-mail: ova@ontariovolleyball.org
URL: www.ontariovolleyball.org
Kristine Drakich, President
Orest Stanko, Executive Director
Jason Trepanier, Technical Director

Saskatchewan Volleyball Association
1758 McAra St., Regina SK S4N 6L4
Tel: 306-780-9250; *Fax:* 306-780-9288
Toll-Free: 800-321-1685
e-mail: officemanager@saskvolleyball.ca
URL: www.saskvolleyball.ca
Dalene Phillips, President
Sandra Sandbeck, Program Coordinator
Dennis Pomeroy, Executive Director

Volleyball BC
Harry Jerome Sports Centre, 7564 Barnet Hwy., Burnaby BC V5A 1E7
Tel: 604-291-2007; *Fax:* 604-291-2602
e-mail: contact@volleyballbc.ca
URL: www.volleyballbc.ca
Tom Caverly, Executive Director

Volleyball Canada (VC)
#202, 5510 Canotek Rd., Gloucester ON K1J 9J5
Tel: 613-748-5681; *Fax:* 613-748-5727
e-mail: info@volleyball.ca
URL: www.volleyball.ca
Affiliation(s): International Volleyball Federation; Canadian Olympic Association; Coaching Association of Canada
John-Paul Cody-Cox, Executive General
Hugh Wong, President

Volleyball New Brunswick
#13, 900 Hanwell Rd., Fredericton NB E3B 6A3
Tel: 506-451-1346; *Fax:* 506-451-1325
e-mail: vnb@nb.aibn.com
URL: www.vnb.nb.ca
James Cress, Executive Director
John Richard, President

Volleyball Nova Scotia
5516 Spring Garden Rd., 4th Floor, Halifax NS B3J 1G6
Tel: 902-425-5450; *Fax:* 902-425-5606
e-mail: vns@sportnovascotia.ca
URL: www.volleyballnovascotia.ca
Liam Blanchard, Executive Director
Steve Stuart, Treasurer
Eugene Tan, President

Volleyball Prince Edward Island
PO Box 302, Charlottetown PE C1N 7K7
Tel: 902-569-0583; *Fax:* 902-368-4548
Toll-Free: 800-247-6712
e-mail: cgcrozier@sportpei.pe.ca
URL: www.volleyballpei.com
Affiliation(s): Sport PEI
Cheryl Crozier, Executive Director
Krista Walsh, President
Harvey Mazerolle, Vice-President

Volleyball Yukon
4061 - 4th Ave., Whitehorse YT Y1A 1H1
Tel: 867-334-4592; *Fax:* 867-667-4237
e-mail: bunpalamar@whtvcable.com
URL: www.volleyballyukon.com
Tara Wardle, President
Bunne Palamar, Executive Director

Water Polo

Alberta Water Polo Association (AWPA)
PO Box 54, 2225 Macleod Trail South, Edmonton AB T2G 5B6
Tel: 403-475-6747; *Fax:* 403-475-6748
e-mail: office@albertawaterpolo.ca
URL: www.albertawaterpolo.ca
Mike Erickson, President

British Columbia Water Polo Association (BCWPA)
#227, 3820 Cessna Dr., Richmond BC V7B 0A2
Tel: 604-333-3480; *Fax:* 604-333-3450
e-mail: bcwaterpolo@telus.net
URL: www.bcwaterpolo.com
Dave Soul, Executive Director

Fédération de Water-Polo du Québec (FWPQ) / Water Polo Québec
CP 1000, Succ. M, 4545, Pierre de Coubertin, Montréal QC H1V 3R2
Tél: 514-252-3098; *Téléc:* 514-252-5658
Courriel: waterpolo@waterpolo-quebec.qc.ca
URL: www.waterpolo-quebec.qc.ca
Jean Thomas, Directeur général
Guy Lapointe, Président

Manitoba Water Polo Association Inc.
#304, 200 Main St., Winnipeg MB R3C 4M2
Tel: 204-925-5777; *Fax:* 204-925-5730
e-mail: mwpa@shaw.ca
URL: www.mbwaterpolo.com
Marilyn Thorington, President
Joy Halliday, Secretary

Ontario Water Polo Association (OWPA) / L'Association de water polo d'Ontario
#206, 3 Concorde Gate, Toronto ON M3C 3N7
Tel: 416-426-7028; *Fax:* 416-426-7356
e-mail: info@ontariowaterpolo.ca
URL: www.ontariowaterpolo.ca
Ross McDonald, Technical Director

Water Polo Saskatchewan Inc.
1860 Lorne St., Regina SK S4P 2L7
Tel: 306-780-9260; *Fax:* 306-780-9467
e-mail: admin@wpsask.ca
URL: www.wpsask.ca
Jymmi Kaye-Demchuk, Executive Director

Water Skiing

Fédération québécoise de ski nautique (FQSN)
CP 1000, Succ. M, 4545, av Pierre-de Coubertin, Montréal QC H1V 3R2
Tél: 514-252-3092; *Téléc:* 514-252-3186
Courriel: louissimard@skinautiquequebec.qc.ca
URL: www.skinautiquequebec.qc.ca/
Louis Simard, Président

Nova Scotia Water Ski Association (NSWSA)
PO Box 783, Dartmouth NS B2Y 3Z3
e-mail: nswsa@aol.com
URL: www.nswsa.com
Gary Allen, President

Ontario Water Ski Association (OWSA)
#307, 1185 Eglinton Ave. East, Toronto ON M3C 3C6
Tel: 416-426-7092; *Fax:* 416-426-7378
e-mail: info@wswo.ca
URL: www.wswo.ca
Paul Roberts, President

Water Ski - Wakeboard Manitoba
200 Main St., Winnipeg MB R3C 4M2
Tel: 204-925-5700; *Fax:* 204-925-5703
e-mail: waterski@waterski.mb.ca
URL: www.waterski.mb.ca
Katja Smutny, Executive Director
Kevin Polley, President

Water Ski & Wakeboard Alberta (WSWA)
Percy Page Centre, 11759 Groat Rd., Edmonton AB T5M 3K6
Tel: 780-415-0088; *Fax:* 780-422-2663
Toll-Free: 866-258-2754
e-mail: info@wswa.ca
URL: www.wswa.ca
Affiliation(s): Water Ski Canada; International Water Ski Federation
Rose Dufty, President
Dallas Harrop, Executive Director

Water Ski & Wakeboard British Columbia (WSWBC)
PO Box 42049, Stn. RPO North, Lake Country BC V4V 1Z8
Toll-Free: 888-696-6677
e-mail: info@wswbc.org
URL: www.wswbc.org
Kim McKnight, Executive Director
Dale Erb, President
Ian Kellow, Vice-President

Water Ski & Wakeboard Canada / Ski nautique et planche Canada
#210, 223 Colonnade Rd. South, Ottawa ON K2E 7K3
Tel: 613-526-0685; *Fax:* 613-526-4380
e-mail: wswc@waterski-wakeboard.ca
URL: www.waterski-wakeboard.ca
Glenn Bowie, President
Dan Wolfenden, Executive Director

Water Ski & Wakeboard Saskatchewan
PO Box 202, Warman SK S0K 4S0
Tel: 306-931-2901; *Fax:* 306-249-3062
e-mail: sheri@wswsask.com
URL: www.wswsask.com
Sheri Seiferling, Executive Director
Berk Summach, President

Women in Sports

Canadian Association for the Advancement of Women & Sport & Physical Activity (CAAWS) / Association canadienne pour l'avancement des femmes du sport et de l'activité physique (ACAFS)
#202N, 801 King Edward Ave., Ottawa ON K1N 6N5
Tel: 613-562-5667; *Fax:* 613-562-5668
e-mail: caaws@caaws.ca
URL: www.caaws.ca
Karin Lofstrom, Executive Director
Sydney Millar, Manager, National Program
Stéphanie Legault, Manager, Marketing & Projects
Jessica Lowe, Administrator & Office Coordinator

Field Hockey BC (FHBC) / Hockey sur gazon C-B
#202, 210 Broadway West, Vancouver BC V5Y 3W2
Tel: 604-737-3046; *Fax:* 604-737-6488
e-mail: info@fieldhockeybc.com
URL: www.fieldhockeybc.com
Mark Saunders, Executive Director

Ladies' Golf Union (LGU)
The Scores, St. Andrews, Fife KY16 9AT United Kingdom
Tel: 44-13-34-475811; *Fax:* 44-13-34-472818
e-mail: info@lgu.org
URL: www.lgu.org
Affiliation(s): Canadian Ladies' Golf Association
Maureen Lockett, President
Shona Malcolm, CEO

Nova Scotia Curling Association (NSCA)
5516 Spring Garden Rd., 4th Fl., Halifax NS B3J 1G6
Tel: 902-421-2875; *Fax:* 902-425-5606
e-mail: nsca@sportnovascotia.ca
URL: www.nscurl.com
Affiliation(s): Canadian Curling Association
Jeremiah Anderson, Executive Director
Shirley Osborne, President

Wrestling

British Columbia Wrestling Association (BCWA)
#208, 1367 West Broadway, Vancouver BC V6H 4A9
Tel: 604-737-3092; *Fax:* 604-737-6043
e-mail: info@bcwrestling.com
URL: www.bcwrestling.com
Affiliation(s): BC School Sports
MaryAnn DeCorby, Executive Director

Canadian Amateur Wrestling Association (CAWA) / Association canadienne de lutte amateur
#7, 5370 Canotek Rd., Gloucester ON K1J 9E6
Tel: 613-748-5686; *Fax:* 613-748-5756
e-mail: info@wrestling.ca
URL: www.wrestling.ca
Tamara Medwidsky, Executive Director
Doug Cox, President
Clint Kingsbury, Manager, Domestic Development
Dave Mair, Manager, High Performance
Dave McKay, National Coach, Senior Men
Leigh Vierling, National Coach, Senior Women

Lutte NB Wrestling
e-mail: gdouc5110@rogers.com
URL: www.luttenbwrestling.ca
Greg Doucette, Vice-President, Administration
Don Ryan, President

Manitoba Freestyle Wrestling Association
200 Main St., Winnipeg MB R3C 4M2
Tel: 204-925-5670; *Fax:* 204-925-5703
e-mail: mbfreewr@mb.sympatico.ca
Nat Brigante, Executive Director/Coach

Newfoundland & Labrador Amateur Wrestling Association (NLAWA)
1 Wade's Ln., Flatrock NL A1K 1C3
Fax: 709-643-5103
e-mail: contact@nlawa.com
URL: www.nlawa.com
Randy Ralph, President

Ontario Amateur Wrestling Association (OAWA)
#213, 3 Concorde Gate, Toronto ON M3C 3N7
Tel: 416-426-7274; *Fax:* 416-426-7343
e-mail: admin@oawa.ca
URL: www.oawa.ca
Affiliation(s): International Amateur Wrestling Association; Canadian Amateur Wrestling Association
Tim MaGarrey, Provincial Director

Saskatchewan Amateur Wrestling Association (SAWA)
510 Cynthia St., Saskatoon SK S7L 7K7
Tel: 306-975-0822; *Fax:* 306-242-8007
e-mail: sk.wrestling@shaw.ca
URL: www.saskwrestling.com
Anna-Beth Zulkowkey, Executive Director

Wrestling Nova Scotia
General Delivery, Bear River NS B0S 1B0
Tel: 902-857-1761
e-mail: wrestlingns@canada.com
URL: www.wrestlingnovascotia.ca
Peter Coulthard, President
Scott Aldridge, Vice-President
Debbie MacDonald, Sec.-Treas.

Wrestling PEI
Sport PEI, PO Box 302, Charlottetown PE C1A 7K7
Tel: 902-368-4110; *Fax:* 902-368-4548
Toll-Free: 800-247-6712
e-mail: gflood@sportpei.pe.ca
URL: www.sportpei.pe.ca
Glen Flood, Executive Director

Leagues & Teams

Baseball, Professional: Major League

Major League Baseball/MLB
245 Park Avenue
31st Floor
New York, NY 10167
212-931-7800
866-800-1275
Fax: 212-945-5654
www.mlb.com
Allan (Bud) H. Selig, Baseball Commissioner
Bob DuPuy, President/Chief Operating Officer
Jimmie Lee Solomon, Baseball Operations Executive VP
Tim Brosnan, Executive Vice President, Business
Rob Manfred, Executive VP, Labor Relations & HR
John McHale, Jr., Executive VP, Administration, & Chief Information Officer
Jonathan Mariner, Executive VP, Finance
Nature of Service:
Administrates professional baseball. Established and enforces rules regarding franchise operation. Supervises national radio and television contracts. Handles publicity and marketing of baseball and legal matters pertaining to baseball as an industry. Operates the World Series and All-Star games.
Membership Requirements:
Teams operating in the American or National Leagues.
Year Founded:
1920
Sponsors:
Ameriquest Mortgage; Anheuser Busch; Baby Ruth; Bank of America; DHL; FIA Card Services, NA; Gatorade; General Motors/Chevrolet; Gillette; Intercontinental Hotels Group/Holiday Inn; MasterCard International; Nestle; Nike; Pepsi-Cola; Sharp; Taco Bell; Wheaties; XM Satellite Radio.

Teams:

Toronto Blue Jays
Rogers Centre
One Blue Jays Way
Suite 3200
Toronto, On, CANADA M5V 1J1
416-341-1000
888-654-6529
Fax: 416-341-1250
http://toronto.bluejays.mlb.com

J.P. Ricciardi, SVP, Baseball Operations/General Manager
Richard Wong, SVP, Stadium Operations
Howard Starkman, Vice President of Special Projects
Jay Stenhouse, Vice President Communications
George Poulis, Head Trainer
Matthew Shuber, Director of Business Affairs
Wilna Behr, VP Stadium Initiatives
Jon Lalonde, Director, Scouting
Stephen Brooks, VP of Finance & Administration
Jason Diplock, VP of Ticket Sales & Service
Mario R. Coutinho, Vice President Stadium Operations/Security
Scott Hext, Manager, Box Office
Cito Gaston, Team Manager
Stadium:
Rogers Centre.
Stadium Seating Capacity:
50,516
Publications:
Inside Pitch newsletter.

Baseball, Professional: Minor League

Canadian American Association of Professional Baseball
1415 Hwy 54 West, Suite 210
Durham, NC 27707
919-401-8150
Fax: 919-401-8152
www.canamleague.com

Teams:

Quebec Capitals
Le Stade De Québec
100 Rue Du Cardinal Maurice-Roy
Quebec, QC, CANADA G1K 8Z1
418-521-2255
Fax: 418-521-2266
baseball@capitalesdequebec.com
www.capitalesdequebec.com
Miles Wolff, President
Alex Harvey, General Manager
Michel Laplante, Field Manager
Ballpark:
La Stade de Québec.
Ballpark Description:
Opened in 1939. Seating Capacity: 4,800
Team History:
Eastern Canada League - 1923; Quebec-Ontario-Vermont League - 1924; Quebec Provincial League - 1940; Canadian-American League - 1941-42, 1946-50, 2005-present; Provincial League - 1951-55; Eastern League - 1971-77; Northern League - 1999-2002; Northeast League - 2003-04.
Publications:
Le Journal de Québec; Le Soleil; Media Matin Québec
Media Broadcast:
CHRC 800 AM

Northwest League
P.O. Box 1645
Boise, Idaho 83701
208-429-1511
Fax: 208-429-1525
mail@northwestleague.com
http://www.northwestleague.com
Bob Richmond, NWL President
Rob Richmond, NWL Publicist

Teams:

Vancouver Canadians
4601 Ontario St
Vancouver, BC, CANADA V5V 3H4
604-872-5232
Fax: 604-872-1714
staff@canadianbaseball.com
www.canadianbaseball.com
Jake Kerr, Owner
Jeff Mooney, Owner
Andy Dunn, President
Years in League:
1967-71, 1979-present.
Ballpark:
Nat Bailey Stadium.
Ballpark Description:
Opened in 1951. Seating Capacity: 6,500
Media Broadcast:
The TEAM Sports Radio 1040-AM.

Basketball, Professional

National Basketball Association/NBA
2 Penn Plaza
Suite 2430
New York, NY 10121
212-655-0800
Fax: 212-754-6414
info@nba.com
www.nba.com

David Stern, Commissioner
Adam Silver, Deputy Commissioner, & Chief Operating Officer
Heidi Ueberroth, President, Global Marketing Partnerships & International Business Operations

Description:
The premier professional basketball league in North America. Many of the world's best players play in the NBA, and the overall standard of the competition is considerably higher than any other professional competition. The NBA was founded in New York City on June 6, 1946 as the Basketball Association of America (BAA). It adopted the name National Basketball Association in the fall of 1949 after adding several teams from the rival National Basketball League.
Business Ventures:
NBA City (Restaurants) - A partnership with Ralph Burnet/RWB Financial.
Publications:
Official NBA Guide, annual; NBA Register, annual; NBA Basketball Encyclopedia.
Membership Requirements:
Approval of the franchise by Board of Governors.

Teams:

Toronto Raptors
Air Canada Center
40 Bay Street
Suite 400
Toronto,ON, CANADA M5J 2X2
416-815-5600
Fax: 416-359-9758
www.raptors.com
Richard Peddie, President/Chief Executive Officer
Tom Anselmi, Executive VP/Chief Operating Officer
Ian Clarke, Executive VP/Chief Financial Officer
Jay Triano, Head Coach
Robert Hunter, Executive VP, Venues & Entertainment
Bryan Colangelo, President and General Manager
Alex English, Director Player Development/Assistant Coach
History:
Founded in 1995 in Toronto.
Arena:
Air Canada Center. Seating Capacity: 19,800

Football, Professional

Canadian Football League/CFL
50 Wellington Street East
3rd Floor
Toronto, ON, CANADA M5E 1C8
416-322-9650
Fax: 416-322-9651
www.cfl.ca

Mark Cohon, Commissioner
Michael Copeland, Chief Operating Officer
Rob Assimakopoulos, SVP, Marketing & Commercial Assets
Matt Maychak, VP, Communications
Jamie Nishino, VP, Marketing & Broadcast
Douglas Allison, Director, Finance and Administration
Kevin McDonald, Director, Football Operations
Tom Higgins, Director, Officiating
Adrian Sciarra, Director, Partnerships

Teams:

B.C. Lions
765 Pacific Boulevard
Vancouver, BC V6B 4Y9
604-661-3626
Fax: 604-661-3616
www.bclions.com
David Braley, Owner/President/CEO
Wally Buono, General Manager/Head Coach
Roy Shivers, Director of Player Personnel
George Chayka, Vice President, Business
Phil Adams, Director, Corporate Partnerships
Jamie Taras, Director, Community Relations
Jamie Cartmell, Director, Communications
Jordan Eshpeter, Manager, Ticket Sales

Calgary Stampeders
Calgary Stampeder Football Club
McMahon Stadium
1817 Crowchild Trail NW
Calgary, AB, CANADA T2M 4R6
403-289-0205
Fax: 403-289-7850
stampeder@stampeders.com
www.stampeders.com
John Forzani, Chairman
Ted Hellard, Managing Partner/President/Alternate Governor
Doug Mitchell, Governor
Stan Schwartz, EVP/Consultant to the Executive Committee
Jim Brent, Vice-President, Club Operations
Chris Poffenroth, Director of Finance/Administration
chrisp@stampeders.com
Stefan Kalenchuk, Director, Marketing
Jane Mawby, Director, Football Administration
John Hufnagel, Head Coach/General Manager
Jim Barker, SVP, Football Operations/Director, Player Personnel

Edmonton Eskimos
Edmonton Eskimo Football Club
9023-111 Avenue
Edmonton, AB, CANADA T5B 0C3
780-448-1525
Fax: 780-429-3452
comments@esks.com
www.esks.com
Douglas Goss, Chairman
Rick LeLacheur, President/Chief Executive Officer
Allan Sawin, Treasurer
Danny Maciocia, General Manager & Director of Football Operations
Dave Jamieson, Marketing & Communications Manager
Richie Hall, Head Coach
Greg Treble, Director of Business Operations
Cathy Presniak, Director of Finance & Administration

Hamilton Tiger-Cats
1 Jarvis Street
Hamilton, ON L8R 3J2
905-547-2287
Fax: 905-547-8423
www.ticats.com
Robert F. Young, Owner
Bob, O'Billovich, General Manager
Adam Provost, Executive Vice President
Scott Mitchell, President
Jim Edmands, VP, Sales & Marketing
Mark Bowden, VP, Business Affairs
Dan Deighton, VP, Finance
Scott McNaughton, Manager, Media Relations
Marcel Bellefeuille, Head Coach
Bob Young, Caretaker

Montreal Alouettes
4545 Pierre-De-Coubertin
Montreal, PQ H1V 3L6
514-871-2266
Fax: 514-871-2277
info@montrealalouettes.com
www.montrealalouettes.com
Robert Wetenall, Owner
Paul Harris, Director
L. Jacques Ménard, O.C., Director
Philippe de Gaspé Beaubien III, Director
Larry Smith, President/Chief Executive Officer
Laurie Bennett, VP, Business Operations
lbennett@montrealalouettes.com
Richard Blais, VP, Corporate Partnerships
rblais@montrealalouettes.com
Jim Popp, VP/GM/Director, Football Operations & Player Personnel
jpopp@montrealalouettes.com
Claude Rochon, VP, Marketing/Communications
crochon@montrealalouettes.com
Mark Weightman, VP, Operations & Events
Olivier Poulin, Director of Communications
Marc Trestman, Head Coach

Saskatchewan Roughriders
Mosaic Stadium
1910 Piffles Taylor Way, Box 1966
Regina, SK S4P 3E1
306-569-2323
888-474-3377
Fax: 306-566-4280
www.saskriders.com

Rob Pletch, Chairman
Jim Hopson, President/CEO
Steve Mazurak, VP, Marketing/Sales
Shannon Chinn, Manager Corporate Partnerships/Game Day Operations
Eric Tillman, GM/Director of Football Operations
Craig Reynolds, Chief Financial Officer
Hugh McKay, Manager Facilities and Stadium Operations
Gail Mund, Manager, Ticket Operations
gailm@saskriders.com
Ryan Whippler, Director, Communications
Mark Habicht, Director, Retail Sales
Ken Miller, Head Coach

Toronto Argonauts
355 King Street West, 6th Floor
Toronto, ON M5V 1J6
416-341-2700
Fax: 416-341-2714
www.argonauts.ca
David Cynamon, Owner
Howard Sokolowski, Owner
Bob Nicholson, President/CEO
Michael 'Pinball' Clemons, Vice-Chair
Matt Afinec, VP, Partnerships & Corporate Hospitality
Alexandra Felix, VP, Marketing & Events
Joey Nalevka, VP, Business Operations
Daniel Steinfeld, VP, Finance
Adam Rita, GM & VP, Football Operations
Beth Waldman, Director, Communications
Bart Andrus, Head Coach

Winnipeg Blue Bombers
1465 Maroons Road
Winnipeg, MB R3G 0L6
204-784-2583
Fax: 204-783-5222
bbombers@bluebombers.com
www.bluebombers.com
Lyle Bauer, President/Chief Executive Officer
Ken Hildhal, Chairperson Board of Directors
Jerry Maslowsky, VP, Marketing
Jim Bell, VP, Finance/Administration
Shirlee Preteau, VP, Event Operations
Ross Hodgkinson, Director, Football Operations
John Murphy, Director of Player Personnel
Mike Kelly, Head Coach

Hockey, Professional (NHL)

National Hockey League/NHL
1251 Avenue of the Americas
47th Floor
New York, NY 10020
212-789-2000
Fax: 212-789-2020
www.nhl.com

Gary Bettman, Commissioner
Bill Daly, Deputy Commissioner
John Collins, Chief Operating Officer
Brian Jennings, Executive Vice President of Marketing
Keith Ritter, SVP New Business Development
(212)789-2000
Doug Perlman, SVP Television/Media Ventures
(212)789-2000
Terry Gregson, SVP & Director of Officiating
Jim Haskins, VP Consumer Products/Marketing
Adam Acone, VP Broadcasting/Programming
Scott Carmichael, Vice President Club Marketing
Andrew Judelson, Group VP Corporate Marketing
Ken Yaffe, Group VP/Managing Director
Ed Home, President NHL Enterprises
Lisa Schoeck, Director Human Resources

Year Founded:
1917
Description:
League of professional hockey teams
Membership Requirements:
Approval by NHL Board of Governors
Publications:
NHL Rule Book, annual; NHL Schedule, annual; NHL MEDIA DIRECTORY, annual; NHL Official Guide and Record Book, annual
Additional Offices:
75 International Blvd, Ste 300, Rexdale, Ont, Canada M9W 6L9. 416 798-0809; FAX: 416 798-0819. Montreal Office: 1800 McGill College Ave, Ste 2600, Montreal, P.Q., Canada H3A 3J6. 514 288-9220; FAX: 514 284-0300

Teams:

Calgary Flames
Po Box 1540
Station M
Calgary, AB, CANADA T2P 3B9
403-777-2177
888-5-FLAMES
Fax: 403-777-2171
www.calgaryflames.com
N. Murray Edwards, Owner
Harley N. Hotchkiss, Owner
Alvin G. Libin, Owner
Allan P. Markin, Owner
Jeffrey L. McCaig, Owner
Clayton H. Riddell, Owner
Byron J. Seaman, Owner
Daryl K. Seaman, Owner
Ken King, President/Chief Executive Officer
Michael Holditch, VP Hockey Administration/CFO
Mike Sands, Director Amateur Scouting
Darryl Sutter, General Manager
Brent Sutter, Head Coach
Ryan McGill, Assistant Coach
Dave Lowry, Assistant Coach
Rob Cookson, Assistant Coach
Jamie McLennan, Assistant Coach
Year Founded:
1972
Description:
The Calgary Flames are a National Hockey League team based in Calgary, Alberta
Home Arena:
Pengrowth Saddledome

Edmonton Oilers
11230 110th Street
2nd Floor
Edmonton, Ab, CANADA T5G 3H7
780-414-4000
Fax: 780-409-5848
www.edmontonoilers.com
Patrick LaForge, President/Chief Executive Officer
Kevin Lowe, President, Hockey Operations
Darryl Boessenkool, VP Finance/Chief Financial Officer
Allan Watt, VP Communications/Broadcast
Steve Tambellini, General manager
Kevin Prendergast, Assistant General Manager
Mike Sillinger, Director of Player Development
Pat Quinn, Head Coach
Tom Renney, Assistant Coach
Kelly Buchberger, Assistant Coach
Wayne Fleming, Assistant Coach
Year Founded:
1972
Description:
The Edmonton Oilers are a National Hockey League twam based in Edmontn, Alberta
Home Arena:
Rexall Place

Montreal Canadiens
1260 De La Gauchetiere Quest
Montreal, Qc, CANADA H3B 5E8
514-932-2582
Fax: 514-932-8285
www.canadiens.com
George N. Gillette, Jr., Owner
Pierre Boivin, President
Bob Gainey, Executive Vice President & General Manager
Fred Steer, Chief Financial Officer
Trevor Timmins, Director of Player Recruitment and Development
Jacques Martin, Head Coach
Perry Pearn, Assistant Coach
Kirk Muller, Assistant Coach
Pierre Groulx, Assistant Coach
Year Founded:
1909
Description:
The Montreal Canadiens are the oldest established National Hockey League team
Home Arena:
Centre Bell

Ottawa Senators
1000 Palladium Drive
Kanata, ON, CANADA K2V 1A5
613-599-0250
Fax: 613-599-0358
info@ottawasenators.com
www.ottawasenators.com
Eugene Melnyk, Owner/Chairman/Governor
Cyril Leeder, President/Alternate Governor
Bryan Murray, Executive Vice-President/General Manager
Erin Crowe, Executive Vice-President/Chief Financial Officer/Alternate Governor
Phil Legault, VP, Communications
Tom Conroy, VP/Executive Director, Scotiabank Place
Chad Schella, Director of Player Services
Cory Clouston, Head Coach
Greg Carvel, Assistant Coach
Tim Pattyson, Video Coach
Eli Wilson, Goaltending Coach
Year Founded:
1992
Description:
The Ottawa Senators are a National Hockey League team based in Ottawa, Ontario Canada
Home Arena:
Scotiabank Place

Toronto Maple Leafs
40 Bay Street
Suite 400
Toronto, ON, CANADA M5J 2X2
416-815-5700
Fax: 416-359-9331
www.torontomapleleafs.com
Richard A. Peddie, President/CEO, MLSE
Tom Anselmi, Executive Vice President/COO, MLSE
Ian Clarke, Executive Vice President/CFO, Business Development, MLSE
Bob Hunter, Executive Vice President, Venues & Entertainment, MLSE
Brian Burke, President & General Manager
Pat Park, Director Media Relations
Ron Wilson, Head Coach
Keith Acton, Assistant Coach
Tim Hunter, Assistant Coach
Rob Zettler, Assistant Coach
Jim Hughes, Director of Player Development
Corey Hirsch, Goaltending Coach
Year Founded:
1917
Description:
The Toronto Maple Leafs are a National Hockey League team based in Toronto, Ontario
Home Arena:
Air Canada Centre

Vancouver Canucks
800 Griffiths Way
Vancouver, BC, CANADA V6B 6G1
604-899-4600
888-663-9311
Fax: 604-899-7401
info@canucks.com
www.canucks.com
Francesco Aquilini, Chairman & Governor
Todd Kobus, Vice President, Finance/Chief Financial Officer
Mike Gillis, President/General Manager
Victor de Bonis, Chief Operating Officer
Lorne Henning, VP Player Personnel/Assistant General Manager
Laurence Gilman, VP Hockey Operations/Assistant General Manager
Jon Festinger, Executive Vice President, Business/General Counsel
Janeil Mackay, Director, Retail & Consumer Product Marketing
Alain Vigneault, Head Coach
Rick Bowness, Associate Coach
Ryan Walter, Assistant Coach
Darryl Williams, Assistant Coach
Ian Clark, Goaltending Consultant
Year Founded:
1970
Description:
The Vancouver Canucks are a National Hockey League team based in Vancouver, British Columbia
Home Arena:
GM Place

Hockey, Professional: Minor League

American Hockey League/AHL
1 Monarch Place, Suite 2400
Springfield, MA 01144
413-781-2030
Fax: 413-733-4767
info@theahl.com
www.theahl.com

David A. Andrews, President/CEO
Rod Pasma, Executive VP, Hockey Operations
Chris Nikolis, Executive VP, Marketing & Business Development
Sean Lavoine, VP, Licensing and Corporate Sales
Jason Chairmovitch, VP, Communications
Drew Griffin, Director, Finance & Administration
Year Founded:
1936
Description:
Promotes and operates the sport of professional ice hockey
Membership Requirements:
Purchase of a franchise
Publications:
Official guide and record book; Rule book; Schedule; Year End Statistical Package

Teams:

Hamilton Bulldogs
101 York Boulevard
Hamilton, ON, CANADA L8R 3L4
905-529-8500
Fax: 905-777-2360
info@hamiltonbulldogs.com
www.hamiltonbulldogs.com
Michael Andlauer, Majority Owner/Chairman
Glenn Stanford, President/Governor
Derek Wills, Director, Broadcasting & Communications
Robert Jefferies, Director, Finance
Paul Giordano, Director, Brand Marketing
Julien BriseBois, General Manager
Guy Boucher, Head Coach
Daniel Lacroix, Assistant Coach
Martin Raymond, Assistant Coach
Home Ice:
Copps Coliseum

Manitoba Moose
260 Hargrave
Winnipeg, MB, CANADA R3C 5S5
204-987-7825
Fax: 204-926-5555
www.moosehockey.com
Mark Chipman, Chairman/Governor
Jim Ludlow, President/CEO
John Offert, Chief Operating Officer
Audrey Ma, Controller
Craig Heisinger, SVP/General Manager
Norva Riddell, SVP, Sales & Marketing
Scott Brown, Director, Corporate Communications & Hockey Operations
Robert Thorsten, VP, People & Patron Services
Scott Arniel, Head Coach
Keith McCambridge, Assistant Coach
Rick St.Croix, Assistant Coach
Bruce Southern, Director, Player Personnel
Home Ice:
MTS Centre

Toronto Marlies
100 Princess Boulevard
Toronto, On, CANADA M6K 3C3
416-263-3900
Fax: 416-263-3901
www.torontomarlies.com
Jeff Jackson, General Manager/Governor
Jennifer Millard, Director, Business Operations
Nathan McFadden, Manager, Hockey & Team Operations
Ashley Kane, Manager, Marketing, Promotions & Game Operations
Dallas Eakins, Head Coach
Gord Dineen, Assistant Coach
Derek King, Assistant Coach

Home Ice:
Ricoh Coliseum

ECHL
116 Village Blvd, Suite 304
Princeton, NJ 08540

609-452-0770
Fax: 609-452-7147
www.echl.com

Brian McKenna, Commissioner
Patrick J. Kelly, Commissioner Emeritus
Todd Corliss, Director of Finance
Ryan Crelin, Director of Business Operations
Mike Murray, Vice President of Hockey Operations
Joe Ernst , Director of Officiating
Brent Garbutt, Manager of Hockey Operations
Jack Carnefix, SVP of Communications/New Media

Teams:

Victoria Salmon Kings
1925 Blanshard Street
Victoria, BC, CANADA V8T 4J2
250-220-7888
Fax: 250-220-7887
info@saveonfoodsmemorialcentre.com
www.salmonkings.com
Graham Lee, Owner/Governor
Dave Darkers, President/Alternate Governor
Mark Morrison, General Manager/Head Coach
Cheri Youden, Controller
Jeff Harris, Assistant General Manager & Director, Media and Community Relations
Troy Sauer, Assistant Director of Media and Community Relations
Ryan Wade Assistant Coach
Home Ice:
Save-On Foods Memorial Centre

Ontario Hockey League
305 Milner Avenue
Suite 200
Scarborough, ON, CANADA M1B 3V4

416-299-8700
Fax: 416-299-8787
ohl@chl.ca
www.ontariohockeyleague.com

David E. Branch, Commissioner
Ted Baker, Vice President
Ray Hollowell, Director of Finance
Herb Morell, Director of Administration
Ian Ellis, Director of Marketing and Special Events
Aaron Bell, Director of Media/Information Services and Publications
Conrad Hache, Director of Officiating
Rob Kitamura, Director of Central Scouting & Player Development
Joe Birch, Director of Recruitment and Education Services
Year Founded:
1896

Teams:

Barrie Colts
555 Bayview Drive
Barrie, On, CANADA L4N 8Y2
705-722-6587
Fax: 705-721-9709
operations@barriecolts.com
www.barriecolts.com
Howie Campbell, President
Jim Payetta, VP of Business Development and Marketing
Jason Ford, Assistant General Manager
Terry Wilson, Manager of Corporate Relations
Andrew Wells, Media Relations Coordinator
Marty Williamson, Head Coach
David Bell, Assistant Coach
Brad Brown, Assistant Coach
Home Ice:
Barrie Molson Centre

Belleville Bulls
265 Cannifton Road
Belleville, ON, CANADA K8N 4V8
613-966-8338
Fax: 705-966-8761
hockey@bellevillebulls.com
www.bellevillebulls.com
Gord Simmonds, Owner/Governor
George Burnett, General Manager/Head Coach
Robert L. Vaughan, Founder
Barclay Branch, Assistant General Manager/Director of Player Personnel
Dave Steenburgh, Director of Business Operations
Jake Grimes, Assistant Coach
Jason Supryka, Assistant Coach
Home Ice:
Yardmen

Brampton Battalion
7575 Kennedy Road South
Brampton, ON, CANADA L6W 4T2
905-874-2393
Fax: 905-874-2394
info@battalionhockey.com
www.battalionhockey.com
C. Scott Abbott, Owner/Governor
Michael Griffin, President
Stan Butler, Director Hockey Operations & Head Coach
Phil Ercolani, Marketing, Sales & Media Relations
Gord Smith, Player Development
Jamie Allison, Assistant Coach
Kelly Harper, Assistant Coach
Mike Tamburro, Goaltending Coach
Binne Brouwer, Head Trainer
Greg Phillips, Assistant Trainer
Home Ice:
Brampton Centre

Guelph Storm
55 Wyndham Street North
Guelph, ON, CANADA N1H 7T8
519-837-9690
Fax: 519-837-9692
info@guelphstorm.com
www.guelphstorm.com
Rick Hoyle, President
Rick Gaetz, Governor
Matt Newby, Director Business Operations
Lindsay Pink, Media Relations
Jason Brooks, General Manager/Head Coach
Chris Hajt, Assistant Coach
Dave Milek, Assistant Coach
Brad Maxwell, Assistant Coach
Shane Mabey, Athletic Therapist
Home Ice:
Guelph Sports Entertainment Centre

Kingston Frontenacs
Po Box 665
Kingston, ON, CANADA K7l 4X1
613-542-4042
Fax: 613-542-2834
kgnfront@kos.net
www.kingstonfrontenacs.com
Doug Springer, President/Governor
Jeff Stilwell, Director Sales/Marketing
Larry Mavety, General Manager
Doug Gilmour, Head Coach
Tony Cimellaro, Assistant Coach
Darren Keily, Assistant Coach
Craig Belfer, Head Trainer
Brenda Mavety, Administrator
Michelle Skolnick, Director of Business & Community Development
Home Ice:
Kingston Memorial Centre

Kitchener Rangers
Po Box 43013
Eastwood Square
Kitchener, ON, CANADA N2H 6S9
519-576-3700
Fax: 519-576-7571
info@kitchenerrangers.com
www.kitchenerrangers.com
Steve Bienkowski, Chief Operating Officer
Michael Lannan, President
Murray Hiebert, Director of Player Development/Scout
Steve Spott, General Manager/Head Coach
Paul Fixter, Associate Coach & Assistant General Manager
Troy Smith, Assistant Coach
Mike Torchia, Goaltending Coach
Jim Brown, Assistant Coach
Dan Lebold, Head Trainer
Home Ice:
Kitchener Memorial Auditorium

London Knights
99 Dundas Street
London, ON, CANADA N6A 6K1
519-681-0800
Fax: 519-668-7291
info@londonknights.com
www.londonknights.com
Dale Hunter, President/Head Coach
Mark Hunter, Vice President/General Manager
Trevor Whiffen, Governor
Jim McKellar, Assistant General Manager
Stefanie Turnball, Senior Marketing Director
Jacques Beaulieu, Assistant Coach
Dave Rook, Goaltender Coach
Lyle Dennis, Strength Coach
Andrew Scott, Head Trainer
Home Ice:
John Labatt Centre

Mississauga St. Michael's Majors
5500 Rose Cherry Place
Mississauga, ON, CANADA L4Z 4B6
905-502-7788
Fax: 905-502-0169
administration@majors.ca
www.stmichaelsmajors.com

Eugene Melnyk, Owner
Duncan Stauth, Executive Vice President
Rick Radovski, Vice President Marketing/Sales
Jason Harding, Manager, Sponsorship/Group Sales
Ben Hodge, Manager, Game Day Operations/Special Events
Joel Roberts, Manager, New Business Development
Ankie Yip, Manager, Public Relations and Community Initiatives
Dave Cameron, General Manager / Head Coach
James Boyd, Co-Coach
Jim Cassidy, Director of Player Personnel
Ivan Bokanovic, Head Athletic Therapist
Jon Elkin, Goaltending Coach
Home Ice:
Hershey Centre

Oshawa Generals
99 Athol Street East
Oshawa, ON, CANADA L1H 1J8
905-433-0900
Fax: 905-433-0868
admin@oshawagenerals.com
www.oshawagenerals.com
Rocco Tullio, Owner
John Davies, Co-Owner
Chris DePiero, General Manager/Head Coach
Rich Ricci, Assistant General Manager/Associate Coach
Randy Fitzgerald, Assistant Coach
Ron Tugnutt, Goalie Coach
Elio Capizzano, Dir Player Development
Joe Kantor, VP, Business Operations
Roger Lajoie, Director of Communications
Home Ice:
Civic Auditorium

Ottawa 67's
Lansdowne Park
1015 Bank Street
Ottawa, ON, CANADA K1S 3W7
613-232-6767
Fax: 613-232-5582
ottawa67s@chl.ca
www.ottawa67s.com
Jeff Hunt, Owner/Governor
Patrick Whalen, President/CEO
Randy Burgess, Vice-President
Brian Kilrea, General Manager
Chris Byrne, Head Coach
Mark Grady, Assistant Coach
Bert O'Brien, Advisor, Hockey Operations
Neil Hoch, Head Trainer
Home Ice:
Ottawa Civic Centre

Owen Sound Attack
1900 - 3rd Avenue East
Owen Sound, ON, CANADA N4K 2M6
519-371-7452
Fax: 519-371-7990
attack@bmts.com
www.attackhockey.com
Bob Severs, Owner/President
Dale DeGray, General Manager
Mark Reeds, Head Coach
Home Ice:
Harry Lumley Bayshore Community Centre

Peterborough Petes
151 Landsdowne Street West
Peterborough, ON, CANADA K9J 1Y4
705-743-3681
Fax: 705-743-5497
petes@gopetesgo.com
www.gopetesgo.com
Ken Jackman, President
Bob Neville, Governor
Jeff Twohey, General Manager
Aaron Garfat, Assistant General Manager
Don Sharp, Director of Merchandise, Community Relations, & Ticket Sales
Ken McRae, Head Coach
Ryan Barnes, Assistant Coach
Jon Elkin, Goalie Coach
Brian Miller, Head Trainer
Home Ice:
Peterborough Memorial Centre

Sarnia Sting
1455 London Road
Sarnia, ON, CANADA N7S 6K7
519-542-4494
Fax: 519-542-2388
buzz@sarniasting.com
www.sarniasting.com
Larry Ciccarelli, President
Bill Abercrombie, VP Operations
Dino Ciccarelli, Director Hockey Operations
Paula McKinlay, Groups Coordinator and Marketing Representative
Marla Doyle, Office Manager
Mark Glavin, PR/Marketing Coordinator
Dave MacQueen, Head Coach
Greg Walters, Assistant Coach
Tim Bacik, Assistant Coach
Home Ice:
Sarnia Sports Entertainment Centre

Sault Ste. Marie Greyhounds
269 Queen Street East
Sault Ste. Marie, ON, CANADA P6A 1Y9
705-253-5976
Fax: 705-945-9458
info@soogreyhounds.com
www.soogreyhounds.com
Lou Lukenda, President/Chairman of the Board
George Shunock, Governor
Gerry Liscumb, Public Relations Manager
Dave Torrie, General Manager
Denny Lambert, Head Coach
Mike Stapleton, Assistant Coach
Nick Warriner, Assistant Coach
Peter Sljivic, Director of Player Development
Home Ice:
Sault Memorial Gardens

Sudbury Wolves
240 Elgin Street South
Sudbury, ON, CANADA P3E 3N6
705-675-3941
Fax: 705-675-7951
info@sudburywolves.com
www.sudburywolves.com
Mark Burgess, CEO/Chairman of the Board
Blaine Smith, President/Governor
Curtis Hall, Director Marketing
Mike Foligno, General Manager
Bryan Verreault, Head Coach
Jeff Beukeboom, Assistant Coach
Glen Burke, Head Trainer
Home Ice:
Sudbury Community Arena

Windsor Spitfires
334 Wyandotte Street East
Windsor, ON, CANADA N9A 3H6
519-254-9256
Fax: 519-254-9257
frontoffice@windsorspitfires.com
www.windsorspitfires.com
Bob Boughner, President/Head Coach
Warren Rychel, Vice President/General Manager
Peter Dobrich, Governor/Treasurer
Steve Horne, Director of Business Development
Bob Jones, Assistant Coach
D.J. Smith, Assistant Coach
Mark Turner, Video Coach
Home Ice:
Windsor Arena

Quebec Major Junior Hockey League
1205 Ampère
Suite 101
Boucherville, QC, CANADA J4B 7M6
450-650-0500
Fax: 450-650-0510
hockey@lhjmq.qc.ca
www.lhjmq.qc.ca
Gilles Courteau, Commissioner
Pierre Daoust, Vice-President Administration
Marcel Patenaude, Vice-President Hockey
Karl Jahnke, Director Communications & Marketing Services
Jean Hould, Coordinator, Officiating
Pierre Leduc, Director Hockey Operations
Description:
Member of Canadian Hockey League

Teams:

Acadie-Bathurst Titan
850 St. Anne Street
Bathurst, NB, CANADA E2A 6X2
506-549-3300
Fax: 506-549-3355
letitan@nbnet.nb.ca
www.letitan.com
Annie Morrissette, Co-Owner
Stéphane Morrissette, Co-Owner
John Greene, Governor
Luc Foulem, Director Marketing & Public Relations
Sylvain Courturier, General Manager
Ron Choules, Head Coach
Charles LeBlanc, Assistant Coach
Leo Luongo, Goalie Coach
Home Ice:
K.C. Irving Regional Centre

Baie-Comeau Drakkar
70 Avenue Michel-Hémon
Baie-Comeau, QC G4Z 2A5
418-296-2522
Fax: 418-296-0011
drakkar@globetrotter.net
www.le-drakkar.com
Paul Joncas, President
Steve Ahern, General Manager
Pierre Lebreux, Governor
Stéphane Hains, Head Coach
Jean Cormier, Assistant Coach
Dominic Boucher, Goalie Coach
Michel Larocque, Head Trainer
Home Ice:
Henry Leonard Center

Cape Breton Screaming Eagles
479 George Street
Sydney, NS, CANADA B1P 6G9
902-567-6378
Fax: 902-567-6303
admin@capebretoneagles.com
www.capebretoneagles.com
Richard Morency, Governor
Paul MacDonald, President & Director of Business Operations
Peter MacDonald, Director of Marketing
Bill Sidney, Director of Sales
Mario Durocher, General Manager/Head Coach
John Hanna, Assistant Coach
Blair Joseph, Assistant Coach
John Kibyuk, Assistant Coach
Alain Chabbert, Head Trainer
Home Ice:
Centre Georges Vezina

Chicoutimi Saguenéens
643 Bégin
C.P. 323
Chicoutimi, QC, CANADA G7H 5C2
418-549-9489
Fax: 418-549-1645
sagueneens@videotron.ca
www.sagueneens.com
Gervais Munger, Governor
Michael Bolvin, Vice President Marketing
Pierre Cardinal, Sales/Promotions Manager
Richard Martel, General Manager/Head Coach
Marc-Etienne Hubert, Assistant Coach
Rénald Nepton, Head Trainer
Guy Carbonneau, President
Home Ice:
Centre Georges Vezina

Drummondville Voltigeurs
300 Cockburn Street
Drummondville, QC, CANADA J2C 4L6
819-477-9400
Fax: 819-477-0561
info@voltigeurs.ca
www.voltigeurs.ca
Louis Brousseau, Governor
Eric Verrier, President
Daniel Gagnon, VP Marketing
Stéphan Leblanc VP Operations
Dominic Ricard, General Manager
Mario Duhamel, Head Coach
Danny Brooks, Assistant Coach
Frédéric Malette, Goalie Coach
Alain Couturier, Head Trainer
Home Ice:
Centre Marcel Dionne

Gatineau Olympiques
Station Hull
125 Carillon Street
Po Box 1251
Gatineau, QC, CANADA J8X 3X7
819-777-0661
Fax: 819-777-6933

hockey@lesolympiques.net
www.lesolympiques.net
Alain Sear, President
Charles Henry, General manager
Daniel Brunet, Marketing Manager
Jérome Dupont, Head Coach
Guy Lalonde, Assistant Coach
Guy Desjardins, Assistant Coach
Michel Vallière, Goalie Coach
Serge Haché, Head Trainer
Home Ice:
Robert Gatineau Arena

Halifax Mooseheads
5284 Duke Street
Halifax, NS, CANADA B3J 3L2
902-496-5993
Fax: 902-423-6413
mooseheads@halifaxmooseheads.ca
www.halifaxmooseheads.ca
Cam Russell, General Manager/Head Coach
Tipper Leblanc, Assistant General Manager
Brian Urquhart, Vice President, Business Operations
Chris Donnelly, Associate Coach
Jeff MacLeod, Assistant Coach
Jason Troini, Assistant Coach
Ian Cox, Head Trainer
Home Ice:
Halifax Metro Center

Moncton Wildcats
100 Midland Drive
Dieppe, NB, CANADA E1A 6X4
506-382-5555
Fax: 506-858-2222
info@moncton-wildcats.com
www.moncton-wildcats.com
Bill Schurman, General Manager
Amy Richard, Manager, Sponsorship & Sales
Danny Flynn, Dir Hockey Operations/Head Coach
Fabian Joseph, Associate Coach
Darryl Seward, Assistant Coach
Frantz Bergevin-Jean, Goalie Coach
Serge Leblanc, Head Trainer
Home Ice:
Moncton Coliseum

Montreal Juniors
4110, boul LaSalle
Montréal, QC, CANADA H4G 2A5
514-670-2100
Fax: 514-670-2258
info@juniordemontreal.com
www.juniordemontreal.com
Farrel Miller, Governor
Martin Routhier, President
Éric Tessier, Tickets Director
Jérôme Burke, Controller
Valérie Clément, Director of Communications
Sonya Lamoureux, Director of Corporate Relations
Pascal Vincent, General Manager/Head Coach
Dominique Ducharme, Assistant Coach
Joel Bouchard, Assistant Coach
Alain Grenier, Goaltending Coach
Dominic Boudriau, Head Trainer
Home Ice:
Auditorium de Verdun

P.E.I. Rocket
46 Kensington Road
Charlottetown, PE, CANADA C1A 5H7
902-892-7349
Fax: 902-892-7350
administration@peirocket.com
www.peirocket.com
Serge Savard, Jr., President/Governor
Kent Hudson, General Manager
Nathan Baker, Director of Sales & Marketing
Tom Tessier, Media Relations Manager
Guy Chouinard, Head Coach & Director of Hockey Operations
Corrado Micalef, Assistant Coach
Jamie Blanchard, Goalie Coach
Andrew MacNeill, Trainer
Home Ice:
Charlottetown Civic Centre

Quebec Remparts
250 boul. Wilfrid Hamel
Quebec, QC, CANADA G1L 5A7
418-525-1212
Fax: 418-525-2242
info@remparts.qc.ca
www.remparts.qc.ca
Julien Gagnon, Governor
Claude Rousseau, President
Lucie Cloutier, Director Communications/Marketing
Michel Cloutier, Director of Finances
Myriam Raby, Controller
Louis Painchaud, General Manager
Patrick Roy, Head Coach
Martin Laperriere, Assistant Coach
Claude Lefebvre, Assistant Coach
Benoit Fortier, Goalie Coach
Stéphane Savard, Head Trainer
Home Ice:
Colisee Pepsi

Rimouski Oceanic
111 2nd Street West
Po Box 816
Rimouski, QC, CANADA G5L 7C9
418-723-4444
Fax: 418-725-0944
hockey@oceanic.qc.ca
www.oceanic.qc.ca
Camille Leblanc, Governor
Henri Martin, President
André Jolicoeur, VP Hockey Operations
Yannick Dumais, General Manager
Mario Arsenault, Director of Administration
Clément Jodoin, Head Coach
Nicolas Chabot, Assistant Coach
Donald Dufresne, Assistant Coach
Eric Lévesque, Head Trainer
Home Ice:
Rimouski Coliseum

Rouyn-Noranda Huskies
218 Murdoch Avenue
Rouyn-Noranda, QC, CANADA J9X 1E6
819-797-3022
Fax: 819-797-4311
admin@huskies.qc.ca
www.huskies.qc.ca
Pierre Cloutier, Governor
Jacques Blais, President
Ian Clermont, Director of Administration
Andre Tourigny, General Manager/Head Coach
Garry Parke, Assistant Coach
Mario Pouliot, Assistant Coach
Matt Doyle, Head Trainer
Home Ice:
Dave Keon Arena

Saint John Sea Dogs
99 Station Street
Suite 200
Saint John, NB, CANADA E2L 4X4
506-657-3647
Fax: 506-696-0611
info@saintjohnseadogs.com
www.saintjohnseadogs.com
Joe Richard, Governor
Wayne Long, President
Mike McGraw, Vice President
Scott McCain, Chief Executive Officer
Mike Kelly, Director of Hockey Operations
Gérard Gallant, Head Coach
Marc Hussey, Assistant Coach
Yvon Vautour, Assistant Coach
David Kelly, Head Trainer
Home Ice:
Harbour Station

Shawinigan Cataractes
1200, rue des Cèdres
Shawinigan, QC, CANADA G9N 1P6
819-537-6327
Fax: 819-537-3538
cats@cataractes.qc.ca
www.cataractes.qc.ca
Mario Clermont, Governor
Martin Mondou, General Manager
Réal Marineau, Jr., Director of Hockey Operations
Kim Lajoie, Director Marketing
Eric Veilleux, Head Coach
Danny Dupont, Assistant Coach
Sylvain St-Hilaire, Assistant Coach
Patrick Léonard, Head Trainer
Home Ice:
Arena Jacques-Plante

Val D'Or Foreurs
810 6th Avenue
Val-D'or, QC, CANADA J9P 1B4
819-824-0093
Fax: 819-824-7602
admin@foreurs.qc.ca
www.foreurs.qc.ca
Glenn J. Mullan, Governor
Louis Blanchette, President
Mario Carrière, Director Hockey Operations
Marc-André Dumont, Head Coach
Patrice Lefebvre, Assistant Coach
Joel Duguay, Goalie Coach
Phillippe Desrosiers, Head Trainer
Home Ice:
Palais des Sports

Victoriaville Tigers
400 boul. Jutras Est
PO Box 857
Victoriaville, QC, CANADA G6P 7W7
819-752-6353
Fax: 819-758-2846
info@tigresvictoriaville.com
www.tigersvictoriaville.com
Jean Marcotte, Governor
Eric Bernier, President
Gervais Laroche, VP Finance
Pierre Sansoucy, VP Marketing
Jérôme Mésonéro, General Manager
Yanick Jean, Head Coach
Simon Olivier, Assistant Coach
Daniel Fréchette, Assistant Coach
Patrick Villeneuve, Head Trainer
Home Ice:
Colisee des Bois-Francs

Western Hockey League
1 - 3030 Sunridge Way NE
Calgary, AB, CANADA T1Y 7K4
403-693-3030
Fax: 403-693-3031
info@whl.ca
www.whl.ca
Ron Robison, Commissioner
Richard Doerksen, VP Hockey
Yvonne Bergmann, VP Operations
Corey Flett, Director Communications
Jesse Watts, Communications Assistant
Kevin Muench, Director Officiating
Jim Donlevy, Director, Education Services
Dianne Hayes, Manager, Accounting
Dallas Kitt, Manager, Marketing & Events
Jeff Hubert, Coordinator, Hockey Operations & WHL Web TV
Sarah Poberznick, Administrative Assistant, Hockey

Teams:

Brandon Wheat Kings
#2 1175 - 18th Street
Brandon, MB, CANADA R7A 7C5
204-726-3535
Fax: 204-726-3540
office@wheatkings.com
www.wheatkings.com
Kelly McCrimmon, General Manager/Head Coach
Rick Dillabough, Director of Sales and Marketing
Al MacPherson, Director of Player Personnel
Dwayne Glywoychuck, Assistant Coach
Darren Ritchie, Assistant Coach
Cam McGhee, Athletic Trainer
Home Ice:
Keystone Arena

Calgary Hitmen
Po Box 1540
Station M
Calgary, AB, CANADA T2P 3B9
403-571-2200
Fax: 403-571-2211
info@hitmenhockey.com
www.hitmenhockey.com
Ken King, Governor/President/CEO
Kelly Kisio, General Manager/Alternate Governor
Bernie Bajnok, Assistant to the General Manager
Mike Moore, Director of Business Operations
Mike Williamson, Head Coach
Joel Otto, Assistant Coach
Brent Kisio, Assistant Coach
Will McMillan, Head Trainer
Home Ice:
Pengrowth Saddledome

Chilliwack Bruins
45323 Hodgins Avenue
Chilliwack, BC, CANADA V2P 8G1
604-792-4625
Fax: 604-795-4656
info@chilliwackbruins.com
www.chilliwackbruins.com
Brian Burke, Owner
Jim Bond, Owner
Moray Keith, Owner
Darryl Porter, Owner
Glen Sather, Owner
Marc Habscheid, General Manager/Head Coach
Bob Rouse, Assistant Coach/Assistant General Manager
Peter Hay, Assistant Coach
Brady Robinson, Goaltender Coach
Matt Auerbach, Head Trainer
Home Ice:
Prospera Centre

Edmonton Oil Kings
11913 Wayne Gretzky Drive South
Edmonton, AB, CANADA T5B 1Z7
780-409-3700
Fax: 780-409-3701
www.oilkings.ca
Patrick LaForge, Governor
Nick Wilson, Alternate Governor & VicPresident of Business Operations
Bob Green, General Manager
Kelly Row, Manager, Communications
Steve Pleau, Head Coach
Rocky Thompson, Assistant Coach
Darryl Weinberger, Assistant Coach
Terrill Lobo, Head Trainer
Home Ice:
Prospera Centre

Kamloops Blazers
300 Lorne Street
Kamloops, BC, CANADA V2C 1W1
250-828-1144
Fax: 250-828-7822
info@blazerhockey.com
www.blazerhockey.com
Tom Gaglardi, President/Governor
Craig Bonner, Vice President/General Manager
Matt Recchi, Director Player Personnel
Barry Smith, Head Coach
Scott Ferguson, Assistant Coach
Geoff Smith, Assistant Coach
Dan De Palma, Goalie Coach
Colin "Toledo" Robinson, Head Trainer
Angie Mercuri, Executive Director of Business Operations
Dave Chyzowski, Director of Sales Marketing
Home Ice:
Interior Savings Centre

Kelowna Rockets
#101-1223 Water Street
Kelowna, BC, CANADA V1Y 9V1
250-860-7825
Fax: 250-860-7880
info@kelownarockets.com
www.kelownarockets.com
Bruce Hamilton, President/General Manager
Lorne Frey, Assistant GM/Director Player Personnel
Ryan Huska, Head Coach
Ryan Cuthbert, Assistant Coach
Dan Lambert, Assistant Coach
Jeff Thorburn, Athletic Therapist
Home Ice:
Prospera Place

Kootenay Ice
#2 - 1777 2nd Street North
Cranbrook, BC, CANADA V1C 7G9
250-417-0322
Fax: 250-417-0323
info@kootenayice.net
www.kootenayice.net
Ed Chynoweth, President/ General Manager
Tiffany Harris, Director of Marketing
Geoff Davidson, Director of Sales
Mark Holick, Head Coach
Scott Beattie, Assistant Coach
Kris Knoblauch, Assistant Coach
Brad Shaw, Head Trainer
Home Ice:
Cranbrook Rec Plex

Lethbridge Hurricanes
Enmax Centre
2510 Scenic Drive S
Lethbridge, AB, CANADA T1J 7J1
403-328-1986
Fax: 403-329-1622
admin@lethbridgehurricanes.com
www.lethbridgehurricanes.com
Herman Elfring, Governor
Brian Wichers, Vice President
Rich Preston, General Manager/Head Coach
Matt Kabayama, Assistant Coach
Chris Chisamore, Assistant Coach
Home Ice:
Enmax Center

Medicine Hat Tigers
155 Ash Avenue SE
Medicine Hat, AB, CANADA T1A 7G2
403-526-2666
Fax: 403-526-3072
admin@tigershockey.com
www.tigershockey.com
Darrell Maser, Governor/President
Brent Maser, Vice President
Dave Andjelic, Director of Marketing & Public Relations
Willie Desjardins, General Manager/Head Coach
Shaun Clouston, Associate Coach
Darren Kruger, Assistant Coach
Mikki Lanuk, Head Trainer
Home Ice:
The Arena

Moose Jaw Warriors
PO Box 74
Moose Jaw, SK, CANADA S6H 4N7
306-694-5711
Fax: 306-692-7833
warriors1@mjwarriors.com
www.mjwarriors.ca
Darin Chow, Governor
Chad Taylor, President
Corey Nyhagen, Director, Corporate Sales and Marketing
Marnel Rasmussen, Director, Community Relations
Jeff Truitt, Director of Hockey Operations
Dave Hunchak, Head Coach
Kevin Higo, Assistant Coach
Curtis Amiot, Head Trainer
Home Ice:
Moose Jaw Civic Center

Prince Albert Raiders
690 - 32nd Street East
Prince Albert, SK, CANADA S6V 2W8
306-764-4263
Fax: 306-764-5454
info@raiderhockey.com
www.raiderhockey.com
Dale McFee, President
Bob MacDonald, Governor
Bruno Campese, General Manager/Head Coach
Gord Broda, Vice President
Sharon Martin, Business Manager
Bruce Vance, Director of Marketing/Media Relations
Steve Young, Assistant General Manager/Assistant Coach
Craig Bedard, Assistant Coach
Duane Bartley, Head Trainer
Home Ice:
Art Hauser Centre

Prince George Cougars
#102, 2187 Ospika Boulevard South
Prince George, BC, CANADA V2N 6Z1
250-561-0783
Fax: 250-561-0743
cougars@mag-net.com
www.pgcougars.com
Rick Brodsky, President
Dallas Thompson, General Manager
Brandi Brodsky, Vice President
Wade Klippenstein, Assistant General Manager/Director of Player Personnel
Dean Clark, Head Coach
Jeff Battah, Assistant Coach
Brent Arsenault, Assistant Coach
Ramandeep (Chico) Singh Dhanjal, Head Trainer
Home Ice:
CN Center

Red Deer Rebels
4847-19th Street, Unit C
Red Deer, AB, CANADA T4R 2N7
403-341-6000
Fax: 403-341-6009
rebels@telusplanet.net
www.reddeerrebels.com
Brent Sutter, Owner/President/Governor
Jerry Van Someren, VP of Business Operations
Greg McConkey, VP of Business Development
Randy Peterson, Director of Scouting & Player Development
Jesse Wallin, VP of Hockey Operations/Head Coach
Dallas Gaume, Assistant Coach
Bryce Thoma, Assistant Coach
Andy Nowicki, Goalie Coach
Dave Horning, Head Trainer
Home Ice:
Enmax Centrium

Regina Pats
PO Box 104
Regina, SK, CANADA S4P 2Z5
306-522-5604
Fax: 306-569-1021
pats@reginapats.com
www.reginapats.com
Russ Parker, Owner/President/Governor
Diane Parker, Owner/President/Governor
Brent Parker, General Manager
Cliff Mapes, Vice President of Business Operations
Dan Plaster, Director of Communications and Media Relations
Chris Hutchinson, Corporate Sales
Curtis Hunt, Head Coach
Shaun Sutter, Assistant Coach
Greg Mayer, Head Trainer/Equipment Manager
Home Ice:
Brandt Centre

Saskatoon Blades
201-3515 Thatcher Avenue
Saskatoon, SK, CANADA S7R 1C4
306-975-8844
Fax: 306-934-1097
info@saskatoonblades.com
www.saskatoonblades.com
Jack Brodsky, Owner/Governor
Trent Coghill, Director of Business Operations
Mike Scissons, Manager of Corporate Development
Lorne Molleken, General Manager/Head Coach
Jarrod Brodsky, Assistant General Manager
Dave Struch, Associate Coach
Jerome Engele, Associate Coach
Steve Hildebrand, Head Trainer
Home Ice:
Credit Union Centre

Swift Current Broncos
PO Box 2345
Swift Current, SK, CANADA S9H 4X6
306-773-1509
Fax: 306-773-5406
s.c.broncos@sasktel.net
www.scbroncos.com
Ben Wiebe, Governor
Al Stewart, Alternate Governor/Chairman
Jordan Wall Director of Business Operations
Keegan Goodrich, Public/Media Relations Director
Mark Lamb, General Manager/Head Coach
Tim Kehler, Assistant Coach
Jamie LeBlanc, Head Trainer
Sheldon Ferguson, Assistant General Manager/Director of Hockey Operations
Home Ice:
Centennial Civic Centre

Vancouver Giants
100 North Renfrew Street
Vancouver, BC, CANADA V5K 3N7
604-444-2687
Fax: 604-254-2687
info@vancouvergiants.com
www.vancouvergiants.com
Ron Toigo, Owner
Gordie Howe, Owner
Pat Quinn, Owner
Sultan Thiara, Owner
Dale Saip, VP Business Development
Tony Hall, VP Finance & Administration
Paul Lucrezi, Director of Ticket Sales & Marketing
Scott Bonner, General Manager
Jason Ripplinger, Director of Player Personnel
Don Hay, Head Coach
Chad Scharff, Assistant Coach
Yogi Svejkovsky, Assistant Coach
Ian Gallagher, Strength & Conditioning Coach

Home Ice:
Pacific Coliseum

Lacrosse

National Lacrosse League
9 East 45th Street
5th Floor
New York, NY 10017
212-764-1390
Fax: 917-510-9890
www.nll.com

George Daniel, Interim Commissioner
Tatia Mays-Russell, Chief Financial Ocer
Brian Lemon, VP Operations
Doug Frills, VP Communications
Scott Neiss, Director of Operations
Jason Lai, Director of Team Business Development
Description:
Founded 1997. Professional Indoor Lacrosse League.

Teams:

Calgary Roughnecks
6120 - 2nd Street S.E.
Building A, Unit 9B
Calgary, AB T2H 2L8
403-294-9244
Fax: 403-206-4888
info@calgaryroughnecks.com
www.calgaryroughnecks.com
Brad Banister, Owner/General Manager
Miranda Barrett, Director of Media Relations
Mark Goodwin, Director of Corporate Sales
Troy Cordingley, Head Coach
Terry Sanderson, Assistant Coach
Dave Pym, Assistant Coach
Neil Hergott, Athletic Therapist
Description:
Arena: Pengrowth Saddledome

Edmonton Rush
137 Turbo Drive
Sherwood Park, AB T8H 2J6
780-732-7874
Fax: 780-467-7854
info@edmontonrush.com
www.edmontonrush.com
Bruce Urban, Owner/Governor
Gord Sawyer, President
Kail Schofield, Director of Marketing & Promotions
Pauline Hughes, Director Communications
Derek Keenan, General Manager/Head Coach
Todd Lorenz, Offensive Coach
Jeremy Tallevi, Defensive Coach
Description:
Arena: Rexall Place

Toronto Rock
416 North Service Road East
Suite 100
Oakville, ON L6H 5R2
416-596-3075
Fax: 905-339-3473
info@torontorock.com
www.torontorock.com
Brad Watters, President
bwatters@torontorock.com
Terri Workman, Public Relations Manager
Mike Kloepfer, Director Lacrosse Operations
Troy Cordingley, Head Coach
John Lovell, Assistant Coach
Matt Sawyer, Assistant Coach
Terry Sanderson, General Manager
Description:
Air Canada Centre

Soccer

Canadian Soccer League
1690 Bonhill Road
Mississauga, ON, CANADA L5T 1C8
905-564-2297
Fax: 905-564-4881
brobinson@canadiansoccerleague.ca
www.canadiansoccerleague.ca

Cary Kaplan, Commissioner
Stan Adamson, Executive Director
Tony Camacho, Director of Officials
Clifford Dell, Director of Discipline

Teams:

Brampton Lions
8820 Jane Street
Vaughan, ON L4K 2M9
905-760-2241
Fax: 905-760-2820
pionadi@bramptonlionsfc.ca
www.bramptonlionsfc.ca
Phil Ionadi, VP of Operations
Armando Costa, Director of Soccer Operations/Head Coach
Michael A. Trichilo, Director of Marketing & Public Relations
Victor Cameira, Manager

Italia Shooters
10200 Keele Street
Maple, On, CANADA L6A 1R2
905-303-9241
Fax: 905-889-1802
info@vaughanshooters.ca
www.italiashooters.ca
John Pacione, General Manager
Rob Pugliese, Head Coach
Tony De Thomasis, Assistant Coach

London City
PO Box 125
Station B
London, ON N6A 4V6
519-672-5425
Fax: 519-438-4625
Markus Gauss, President
Ryan M. Gauss, C.E.O/Vice President/General Manager
Andrew Loague, Head Coach

North York Astros
1589 Weston Road
Toronto, ON M9N 1T4
416-240-1718
Fax: 416-240-1648
astros@northyorkastros.ca
www.northyorkastros.ca
Bruno Ierullo, General Manager
Jordan Grossman, Director, Sponsorship & Sales
Vladimir Klinovsky, Head Coach

Portugal FC
964 The Queensway
Toronto, ON, CANADA M6H 1A2
416-417-2349
Fax: 416-731-9501
info@portugalfc.ca
www.portugalfc.ca
Isac Cambas, President
Juan Carlos Ramirez Gaston, Director of Soccer
Daniel Amaral, Head Coach

Serbian White Eagles
30 Titan Road, Unit 15
Toronto, ON, CANADA M8Z 5Y2
416-252-4762
Fax: 416-252-4668
ingo@serbianwhiteeagles.ca
www.serbianwhiteeagles.ca
Dragan Bakoc, President
Rafael Carbajal, Head Coach

St Catharines Wolves
125 Vansickle Road
St. Catharines, ON, CANADA L2S 3X5
(905-682-7621
Fax: 905-682-8811
armanddifruscio@hotmail.com
www.romasoccer.com
Armand Di Fruscio, General Manager
James McGilivary, Head Coach

TFC Academy
BMO Field
170 Princes' Blvd.
Toronto, On, CANADA M6K 3C3
416-815-5400
Fax: 416-815-5452
http://toronto.fc.mlsnet.com/t280/youth/academy/
Earl Cochrane, General Manager
Stuart Neely, Head Coach

Toronto Croatia
89 Queen Street South
Mississauga, On, CANADA L5M 2K7
905-812-7868
Fax: 905-828-7753
P.jazbec@likro.com
www.torontocroatia.com
Joe Pavicic, President
Velimir Crljen, Head Coach

Trois-Rivières Attak
6455 Notre-Dame-Ouest, Bureau 1
Trois-Rivières, QC, CANADA G9A 5A6
819-374-0044
Fax: 819-374-0044
cquesnel@attakfc.com
www.attakfc.com
Tony Iannitto, President
Philippe Eullaffroy, Head Coach

Major League Soccer
420 Fifth Avenue, Seventh Floor
New York, NY 10018
212-450-1200
Fax: 212-450-1300
feedback@mlsnet.com
www.mlsnot.com

Don Garber, Commissioner
Ivan Gazidis, Deputy Commissioner
Sean Prendegast, Chief Financial Officer
Dan Courtemanche, Senior Vice President, Marketing & Communications

Teams:

Toronto FC
BMO Field
170 Princes' Blvd.
Toronto, ON, CANADA M6K 3C3
416-360-4625
http://web.mlsnet.com/t280/
Mo Johnston, Manager, Director of Soccer
Chris Cummins, Interim Head Coach

United Soccer Leagues
14497 N. Dale Mabry Hwy
Ste 201
Tampa, FL 33618
813-963-3909
Fax: 813-963-3807
jason.minnick@uslsoccer.com
www.uslsoccer.com

Rob Hoskins, Chairman
Tim Holt, President
Neels Van Wyk, Director Financial Services
Lee Cohen, Director, PDL Operations
Gerald Barnhart, Director Public Relations

Teams:

Montreal Impact
Stade Saputo
4750 Sherbrooke Est
Montreal, QC, CANADA H1V 3S8
514-328-3668
Fax: 514-328-1287
info@montralimpact.com
www.montrealimpact.com
Joey Saputo, President
Richard Legendre, Executive Vice President
John Di Terlizzi, Vice President, Corporate Sales & Development
Marc Dos Santos, Head Coach

Ottawa Fury
458 Maclaren Street
Floor 2
Ottawa, ON, CANADA K1R 5K6
613-235-3879
Fax: 613-567-3879
www.ottawafury.com
John Pugh, Owner/CEO
Melanie Rutherford, Director of Operations
Stephen O'Kane, Head Coach

Thunder Bay Chill
191 Hazelwood Drive
Thunder Bay, ON, CANADA P7G 1Y5
807-623-5911
Fax: 807-344-7177
tbchill@tbaytel.net
www.thunderbaychill.com
John Marrello, General Manager
Tony Colistro, Head Coach

Toronto Lynx Soccer Club
100 Westmore Drive
Suite 8
Toronto, ON, CANADA M9V 5C3
416-251-4625
Fax: 416-251-7054

lynx@lynxsoccer.com
www.lynxsoccer.com
Bruno Hartrell, Chief Financial Officer
Duncan Wilde, Head Coach

Vancouver Whitecaps
The Landing
375 Water Street
Suite 550
Vancouver, BC, CANADA V6B 5C6
604-669-9283
Fax: 604-684-5173
info@whitecapsfc.com
www.whitecapsfc.com
Bob Lenarduzzi, President
Teitur Thordarson, Men's Head Coach
Alan Koch, Women's Head Coach

Facilities

Arenas & Stadiums

Air Canada Centre
40 Bay St
Suite 400
Toronto, On, CANADA M5J 2X2
416-815-5500
Fax: 416-359-9332
www.theaircanadacentre.com
Bob Hunter, SVP / General Manager
Seating Capacity:
Basketball-19,800; Hockey-18,800; Concerts-19,800; Theatre-5,200; also 1020 Club Seats, 40 Platinum Lounges, 65 Executive Suites, and 32 Theatre Suites.
Tenant(s):
NBA - Toronto Raptors basketball, NHL - Toronto Maple Leafs hockey, NLL - Toronto Rock lacrosse.
Seating Capacity:
Basketball-19,800; Hockey-18,800; Concerts-19,800; Theatre-5,200; also 1020 Club Seats, 40 Platinum Lounges, 65 Executive Suites, and 32 Theatre Suites.
Tenant(s):
NBA - Toronto Raptors basketball, NHL - Toronto Maple Leafs hockey, NLL - Toronto Rock lacrosse.

BC Place Stadium
777 Pacific Boulevard
Vancouver, Bc, CANADA V6B 4Y8
604-669-2300
Fax: 604-661-3412
stadium@bcpavco.com
www.bcplacestadium.com
Howard Crosley, General Manager
Brian Griffin, Director, Operations Division
Graham Ramsay, Director, Business Development Division
Bob Starkey, Director, Business Administration Division
Seating Capacity:
60,000
Description:
Future host of the 2010 Winter olympic Games Opening/Closing Ceremonies.

Bell Centre
1260 De La Gauchetiere Ouest
Montreal, Quebec, CANADA H3B 5E8
514-790-1245
Fax: 514-932-8571
services@bellcentre.ca
www.bellcentre.ca
Eric Molson, Chairman
Daniel O'Neill, Chief Executive Officer
Pierre Boivin, Team President
Aldo Giampaolo, EVP
Tenant(s):
NHL - Montreal Canadiens Hockey, NLL - Montreal Express Lacrosse.
Permanent Seating Capacity:
21,500
Tenant(s):
NHL - Montreal Canadiens Hockey, NLL - Montreal Express Lacrosse.
Permanent Seating Capacity:
21,500

BMO Field
210 Princes' Boulevard
Toronto, On, CANADA M6K 363
Seating Capacity:
20,000
Description:
Home of the Toronto FC. Held the FIFA U-20 World Championships in July of 2007.

Calgary Exhibition & Stampede
1410 Olympic Way Se
Alberta, CANADA T2P-2K8
403-261-0101
800-661-1260
Fax: 403-265-7197
reception3@calgarystampede.com
www.calgarystampede.com
Vern Kimball, Chief Operating Officer
Bvkimball@calgarystampede.com
Vern Kimball, Chief Operating Officer
Bvkimball@calgarystampede.com
David Beck, Senior Marketing Sales/Facilities
beck@calgarystampede.com
David Beck, Senior Marketing, Sales and Facilties
beck@calgarystampede.com
Keith Marrington, Senior Marketing Race
Keith Marrington, Senior Marketing, Race
Robin Burwash, Manager Rodeo
Robin Burwash, Manager, Rodeo

Canad Inns Stadium
1430 Maroons Road
Winnipeg, Mb, CANADA R3G 0L5
204-784-2583
Seating Capacity:
29,503
Playing Surface:
Artificial
Teams:
Winnipeg Blue Bombers

Canwest Global Park
One Portage Avenue East
Manitoba, CANADA R3B 3N3
204-982-2273
Fax: 204-982-2274
goldeyes@goldeyes.com
www.goldeyes.com
Scott Horn, Facility Manager
Tom Thiessen, Box Office Manager
Sport:
Baseball
Team:
Winnipeg Goldeyes
Capacity:
6,266
Sport:
Baseball
Team:
Winnipeg Goldeyes
Capacity:
6,266

Colisee Pepsi De Quebec
250, Boulevard Wilfrid-Hamel
Quebec, CANADA G1L 5A7
418-691-7110
Fax: 418-691-7249
info@expocite.com
www.expocite.com
Denis Jobin, Manager
(418)619-7242
djobin@expocite.com
Arena Seating Capacity:
15,399.00
Year Founded:
1950
Arena Seating Capacity:
15,399.00
Year Founded:
1950

Commonwealth Stadium
11000 Stadium Road
Po Box 2359
Edmonton, Ab, CANADA T5J 2R7
780-944-7561
Seating Capacity:
60,217
Playing Field:
Grass
Teams:
Edmonton Eskimos

Copps Coliseum
101 York Boulevard
Hamilton, ONTARIO L8R 3L4
905-546-4040
Fax: 905-527-6856
www.hecfi.on.ca/copps
Description:
Seats 19,000

Enmax Centre
2510 Scenic Drive South
Lethbridge, Alberta, CANADA T1K 1N2
403-320-4040
Fax: 403-327-3620
enmaxcentre@lethbridge.ca
www.lethbridge.ca
Ashley M Matthews, General Manager

Exhibition Place
200 Princes' Boulevard
Toronto, Ontario, CANADA M6K 3C3
416-263-3600
Fax: 416-263-3690
information@explace.on.ca
www.explace.on.ca
Gordon R Walker, General Manager
Stadium Seating Capacity:
55,000
Arena Seating Capacity:
5,777
Stadium Seating Capacity:
55,000
Arena Seating Capacity:
5,777

Frank Clair Stadium
1015 Bank Street
Ottawa, On, CANADA K1S 3W7
Seating Capacity:
30,927
Playing Surface:
Artificial
Teams:
Ottawa Renegades

General Motors Place
800 Griffith Way
Vancouver, Bc, CANADA V6B 6G1
604-899-7400
Fax: 604-899-7401
www.canucks.com
Steven H Bellringer, President
Leila Bell-Irving, Business Development VP
Valerie Lewis, Suites
Owned by:
Orca Bay Sports & Entertainment
Tenant(s):
NHL - Vancouver Canucks Hockey, NLL - Vancouver Ravens Lacrosse.
Permanent Seating Capacity:
20,000
Owned by:
Orca Bay Sports & Entertainment
Tenant(s):
NHL - Vancouver Canucks Hockey, NLL - Vancouver Ravens Lacrosse.
Permanent Seating Capacity:
20,000

Halifax Metro Centre
1800 Argyle St
Suite 416, Po Box 955
Halifax, Ns, CANADA B3J 2V9
902-421-8000
Fax: 902-422-2922
judith@wtcchmc.com
www.halifaxmetrocentre.com
Scott D Ferguson, Operations VP
(902)421-1302
scott@wtechmc.com
Deanna A Sperry, Marketing Manager
(902)421-1302
deanna@halifaxmetrocentre.com
Ralph J Williams, Events Booking Manager
(902)421-1302
ralph@halifaxmetrocentre.com
Robert Logan, Corporate Sales Manager
(902)421-1302
robertl@halifaxmetrocentre.com
Arena Seating Capacity:
10,000.00
Arena Seating Capacity:
10,000.00

Hamilton Entertainment & Convention Facilities, Inc.
10 MacNab St, S.
Hamilton, On, CANADA L8P 4Y3
905-546-3100
Fax: 905-521-0924
hectemp@hamilton.ca
www.hecfi.on.ca
Brad Calder, Acting Manager Director/Chief Executive
Debra Vivian, Marketing/Public Relations Manager
Rick Difilippo, Business Services Director
John Elder, Programming Manager
Permanent Seating Capacity:
17,500
Permanent Seating Capacity:
17,500

Harbour Station
99 Station St
Saint John, Nb, CANADA E2L 4X4
506-632-6103
Fax: 506-632-6121
mail@harbourstation.nb.ca
www.harbourstation.nb.ca
Michael Caddell, General Manager
Ewan Cameron, Operations Director
Kelly Lamont, Box Office Manager

Ivor Wynne Stadium
75 Balsam Avenue North
Hamilton, On, CANADA L8L 8C1
905-546-4246
Seating Capacity:
35,000
Playing Surface:
Artificial
Teams:
Hamilton Tigercats

John Labatt Centre
99 Dundas Street
Ontario, CANADA N6A 6K1
519-667-5700
Fax: 519-432-3386
info@johnlabattcentre.com
www.johnlabattcentre.com
Brian Ohl, General Manager
Dave Harris, Marketing Director
(519)667-5733
Vince Vella, Operations Director
(519)667-5746
Paul Brock, Sales Director
Arena Seating Capacity:
10,000.00
Clients:
Harlem Globetrotters, Stars on Ice, US Hot Rod Monster Jam, Sesame Street, Disney on Ice, various concerts.
Nature of Service:
Multi-purpose Sports, Entertainment Facility.
Arena Seating Capacity:
10,000.00
Clients:
Harlem Globetrotters, Stars on Ice, US Hot Rod Monster Jam, Sesame Street, Disney on Ice, various concerts.
Nature of Service:
Multi-purpose Sports, Entertainment Facility.

Landsdowne Park
1015 Bank St
Ottawa, Ontario, CANADA K1S 3W7
613-580-2429
Fax: 613-564-1619
lansdowne@ottawa.ca
www.lansdownepark.ca
Richard W Haycock, General Manager
Patrick Desrosiers, Booking Supervisor
Arena Seating Capacity:
10,000
Stadium Seating Capacity:
30,000
Arena Seating Capacity:
10,000
Stadium Seating Capacity:
30,000

Le Stade De Quebec
100 Rue Du Cardinal Maurice-Roy
Quebec City, CANADA G1K 8Z1
418-521-2255
Fax: 418-521-2266
baseball@capitalesdequebec.com
www.capitalesdequebec.com
Sport:
Baseball
Team:
Capitales de Quebec
Capacity:
4,800
Sport:
Baseball
Team:
Capitales de Quebec
Capacity:
4,800

Lynx Stadium
300 Coventry Rd
Ottawa, On, CANADA K1K 4P5
613-747-5969
Fax: 613-747-0003
lynx@ottawalynx.com
www.ottawalynx.com
Melissa Rumble, Director Ticket Operations
(613)747-5969
rumble@ottawalynx.com
Steve Benhott, Head Groundskeeper
(613)747-5969
lynxcrew@hotmail.com
Matt Horan, Head Groundskeeper
(613)747-5969
lynxcrew@hotmail.com
Seating Capacity
10,332.00
Track Type
Natural grass
Track Size
325 feet LF and RF, 404 feet CF
Seating Capacity
10,332.00
Track Type
Natural grass
Track Size
325 feet LF and RF, 404 feet CF

McMahon Stadium
1817 Crowchild Trail Nw
Calgary, Ab, CANADA T2M 4R6
403-282-2044
Fax: 403-282-2018
mcmahonstadium@shaw.ca
www.mcmahonstadium.ca
John Haverstock, Manager
Year Opened:
1960
Seating Capacity:
36,000 permanent with 10,000 additional seats available.
Description:
Home to the Calgary Stampeders and the University of Calgary Dinos.
Events:
Held the opening and closing ceremonies of the 1988 Olympic Winter Games. Opening ceremonies of the 1997 World Police/Fire Games. CFL Grey Cup Championship games in 1975, 1993, and 2000.

Molson Stadium
475 Pine Avenue West
Montreal, Qc, CANADA H2W 1S4
514-398-7017
www.athletics.mcgill.ca/facilities
Phil Quintal, Manager, Recreation/Facilities
(514)398-7000
philip.quintall@mcgill.ca
Playing Surface:
FieldTurf

Northlands Park
Box 1480
Edmonton, Alberta, CANADA T5J 2N5
780-471-7210
888-800-7275
Fax: 780-471-8195
info@northlands.com
www.northlands.com
Dale Leschuitta, President
Ken Knowles, Designate General Manager
Gerry Stoll, Entertainment/Booking Manager
Duane Vienneau, Sales Business Unit Manager
Permanent Seating Capacity:
17,099
Permanent Seating Capacity:
17,099
Facility:
Edmonton Coliseum.
Facility:
Edmonton Coliseum.
Permanent Seating Capacity:
17,099
Permanent Seating Capacity:
17,099
Facility:
Edmonton Coliseum.
Facility:
Edmonton Coliseum.

Olympic Stadium
4141 Pierre De Coubertin Ave
Montreal, Quebec, CANADA H1V 3N7
514-252-4614
Fax: 514-252-4440
rio@rio.gouv.qc.ca
www.rio.gouv.qc.ca
Michel Aird, Project Manager
(514)252-4614
marketing@rio.gouv.qc.ca
Stadium Seating Capacity:
55,389
Stadium Seating Capacity:
55,389

Pacific Coliseum
2901 East Hasting Street
Vancouver, British Columbia, CANADA V5K 5J1
604-253-2311
Fax: 604-251-7761
sales@pne.bc.ca
www.pne.bc.ca
Mike McDaniel, President/Chief Executive Officer
Peter Male, Sales VP
(604)251-7787
peterm@pne.bc.ca
Shelley Frost, Marketing VP
Oliver Wong, Beverage Operations Director
Arena Seating Capacity:
17,300.00
Clients:
Boys Basketball, Old Timers Hockey, Slam City Jam.
Nature of Service:
Ice Hockey Services, Catering, Event Concessions, Arena Configurations, Video, Scoreboard.
Tenant(s):
Vancouver Giants, Weston Hockey League.
Arena Seating Capacity:
17,300.00
Clients:
Boys Basketball, Old Timers Hockey, Slam City Jam.
Nature of Service:
Ice Hockey Services, Catering, Event Concessions, Arena Configurations, Video, Scoreboard.
Tenant(s):
Vancouver Giants, Weston Hockey League.

Pengrowth Saddledome
555 Saddledome Rise Se
Calgary, Alberta, CANADA T2G 2W1
403-777-4636
Fax: 403-777-3695
customerservice@calgaryflames.com
www.pengrowthsaddledome.com
Libby Raines, General Manager
Garry McKenzie, Marketing VP
George Greenwood, Operations Manager
John Vidalin, Advertising/Promotions Director
Owned by:
Calgary Flames Ltd. Partnership (20 year lease from Saddledome Foundation, City of Calgary).
Tenant(s):
NHL - Calgary Flames hockey; NLL - Calgary Roughnecks lacrosse; WHL - Calgary Hitmen hockey.
Permanent Seating Capacity:
18,800
Owned by:
Calgary Flames Ltd. Partnership (20 year lease from Saddledome Foundation, City of Calgary).
Tenant(s):
NHL - Calgary Flames hockey; NLL - Calgary Roughnecks lacrosse; WHL - Calgary Hitmen hockey.
Permanent Seating Capacity:
18,800

Ricoh Coliseum
100 Princes' Blvd
Exhibition Place
Ontario, CANADA M6K 3C3

416-263-3001
Fax: 416-263-3029
www.ricohcoliseum.com

Bob Papke, Booking Consultant
(416)263-3022
bpapke@ricohcoliseum.com
Jennifer Pym, Marketing Coordinator
(416)236-3011
jpym@ricohcoliseum.com
Food & Beverage:
Centerplate Inc.
Management Firm:
O&Y/SMG Canada
Permanent Seating Capacity:
10,000
Tenant(s):
AHL - Toronto Roadrunners hockey
Food & Beverage:
Centerplate Inc.
Management Firm:
O&Y/SMG Canada
Permanent Seating Capacity:
10,000
Tenant(s):
AHL - Toronto Roadrunners hockey

Roger Centre
One Blue Jays Way
Toronto, CANADA M5V 1J1

416-341-3663
Fax: 416-341-3101
guestservices@rogerscentre.com
www.rogerscentre.com

Silvio D'Addario, Chief Operating Officer
Mario Coutinho, Director Operations
Paul So, Manager Guest Relations
Owned by:
Sportsco International, L.P.
Tenants:
MLB - Toronto Blue Jays baseball, CFL - Toronto Argonauts football.
Permanent Seating Capacity:
53,506 - Football; 51,517 - Baseball.
Owned by:
Sportsco International, L.P.
Tenants:
MLB - Toronto Blue Jays baseball, CFL - Toronto Argonauts football.
Permanent Seating Capacity:
53,506 - Football; 51,517 - Baseball.

Sarnia Sports and Entertainment Centre
1455 London Road
Ontario, CANADA N7S 1P6

519-541-1000
info@ssec.on.ca
www.ssec.on.ca

Mike Richardson, General Manager
richardson@ssec.on.ca
Charlene Lockhart, Business Manager
lockhart@ssec.on.ca
Sue Baert, Marketing Manager
baert@ssec.on.ca
Frank Fanelli, Building/Operations Manager
fanelli@ssec.on.ca
Tenant(s):
OHL - Sarnia Sting hockey.
Permanent Seating Capacity:
5,500
Tenant(s):
OHL - Sarnia Sting hockey.
Permanent Seating Capacity:
5,500

Saskatchewan Place
101-3515 Thatcher Ave
Saskatoon
Saskatchewan, CANADA S7R 1C4

306-975-3155
Fax: 306-975-2907
Info@creditunioncentre.com
www.saskatchewanplace.com

Kenneth H Wood, General Manager
Will Antonishyn, Finance Manager
Brian Swidrovich, Business Development Manager
Scott Ford, Marketing/Events Manager
Description:
Saskatchewan Place is the province's premier, multi-purpose trade, sports and entertainment facility. 110,000 sq.ft. of trade show space; free parking for over 3000 vehicles, 13,000 seating space.
Permanent Seating Capacity:
11,301
Description:
Saskatchewan Place is the province's premier, multi-purpose trade, sports and entertainment facility. 110,000 sq.ft. of trade show space; free parking for over 3000 vehicles, 13,000 seating space.
Permanent Seating Capacity:
11,301

Saskatoon Kinsmen/Henk Ruys Soccer Centre
219 Primrose Drive
Saskatoon
Saskatchewan, CANADA S7K 2J9

306-975-3400
Fax: 306-975-3407
www.saskatoonsoccer.com

John Tomchuk, General Manager
Grace Kachur, Administrative Assistant
DeAnn Eckdahl, Financial Administrator
deann.eckdahl@sk.sympatico.ca
Murray Waters, Food/Beverage Manager
Nature of Sports Service:
A multi-purpose facility dedicated to soccer, including four indoor pitches, internal restaurant, concession and lounge. 84,000 sq. feet.
Nature of Sports Service:
A multi-purpose facility dedicated to soccer, including four indoor pitches, internal restaurant, concession and lounge. 84,000 sq. feet.

Scotiabank Place
1000 Palladium Dr
Kanata, Ontario, CANADA K2V 1A5

613-599-0100
Fax: 613-599-0101
feedback@Scotiabankplace.com
www.corelcentre.com

Tom Conroy, VP/Executive Director
Krista Pogue, Director Media/Marketing
Owned by:
Palladium Corp.
Tenant(s):
NHL - Ottawa Senators hockey.
Permanent Seating Capacity:
18,500
Owned by:
Palladium Corp.
Tenant(s):
NHL - Ottawa Senators hockey.
Permanent Seating Capacity:
18,500

Skyreach Center
7424 118th St.
Alberta, CANADA T5B 4M9

780-471-7210
Fax: 780-414-4301

Jack Doff, VP Executive Director
Gerry Stoll, Entertainment Manager
Sara Adamski, Operations Manager

Taylor Field
2940-10th Avenue
Regina, Sk, CANADA S4P 3B8

306-569-2323

Seating Capacity:
27,637
Playing Surface:
Artificial
Teams:
Saskatchewan Roughriders and Regina Rams High School Football

Telus Field
10233 96 Ave. N.W.
Alberta, CANADA T5K OA5

780-414-4450
Fax: 780-414-4475
www.eks.com

Heather Sayers, Ticket Manager
Don Benson, Stadium Operations Manager
Sport:
Baseball.
Team:
Edmonton Trappers.
Capacity:
9,200
Sport:
Baseball.
Team:
Edmonton Trappers.
Capacity:
9,200

Winnipeg Arena
1430 Maroons Rd
Winnipeg, Mb, CANADA R3G 0L5

204-982-5400
888-780-7328
Fax: 204-774-4332

Kevin Donnelly, President/Chief Executive Officer
Jim Wakeham, VP
Dianne Gabbs, General Manager
Ed Metzlaff, Director Facility Operations
Seating Capacity:
13,758 - 15,380.
Seating Capacity:
13,758 - 15,380.

Race Tracks

Clinton Raceway
147 Beech Street
P.O. Box 897
Clinton, Ontario, CANADA N0M 1LO

519-482-5270
Fax: 519-482-1489
www.clintonraceway.com

Ian Fleming, Racing Secretary
Murray Watt, President
Description:
Horse race track.
Description:
Horse race track.

Flamboro Downs
967 Highway #5 West
P.O. Box 8220
Hamilton, On, CANADA L9H 6Y6

905-627-3561
Fax: 905-627-0480
info@flamborodowns.com
www.flamborodowns.com

Neil McCoag, Racing Secretary
Ron Barr, Marketing Manager

Mosport International Raceway
3233 Concession Road #10, Rr #5
Bowmanville, Ontario, CANADA L1C 3K6

905-983-9141
Fax: 905-983-5195
info@mosports.com
www.mosport.com

Myles Brandt, President/General Manager
Andrew Foxman, Sales Director
Glenn Butt, Marketing Director
Janet Brandt, Food Service Manager
Notes:
Purchased by Panoz Motorsports.
Description:
Motor Speedway.
Notes:
Purchased by Panoz Motorsports.
Description:
Motor Speedway.

Sanair International Raceway
669 Petit Rang St.-Francois
Po Box 222
St.-Pie,(Quebec), CANADA J0H 1W0

450-772-6400
Fax: 450-772-2236
www.sanairracing.com

Description:
Auto race track.
Description:
Auto race track.

Shannonville Motorsport Park
7047 Old Hwy #2
Po Box 259
Shannonville, On, CANADA K0K 3A0

613-969-1906
Fax: 613-966-6890
info@shannonville.com
www.shannonville.com

Jean Gauthier, Owner
Description:
Auto Race Track.
Long Track:
4.03km.
Pro Track:
2.47km

Fabi Circuit:
2.23km.
Description:
Auto Race Track.
Long Track:
4.03km.
Pro Track:
2.47km
Fabi Circuit:
2.23km.

Stampede Park
2300 Stampede Trail S.E
P.O. Box 1060
2300 Stampede Trail Se
Calgary, CANADA T2P 2K8

403-261-0214
Fax: 403-265-7009
www.stampede-park.com

Gail Poole, Race Manager
Patti Hunt, Publicity and Marketing Manager

Sudbury Downs
2070 Old Burwash Rd
Sudbury, On, CANADA P3E 4Z4

705-855-9001
Fax: 705-855-5434
suddowns@vianet.ca
www.sudburydowns.com

Patrick Macisaac, President
Ken M. Le Drew, General Manager
Year Founded:
1974
Nature of Sports Service:
Harness horse race track.
Year Founded:
1974
Nature of Sports Service:
Harness horse race track.

Western Fair Raceway
316 Rectory St
P.O. Box 7550
London, On, CANADA N5Y 3V9

519-438-7203
800-619-4629
Fax: 519-679-3124
info@westernfair.com
www.westernfair.com

Gary McRae, General Manager
Dave Taylor, Senior Marketing Manager
dtaylor@westernfair.com
Ian Fleaming, Acting Raceway Manager
ifleaming@westernfair.com
Pam Kelly, Assistant Raceway Manager
pkelly@westernfair.com
Description:
Founded 1960. Harness horse race track.
Seating capacity:
4,500
Description:
Founded 1960. Harness horse race track.
Seating capacity:
4,500

Windsor Raceway
5555 Ojibway Parkway
P.O. Box 998
Windsor, On, CANADA N9A 6P6

519-969-8311
Fax: 519-969-0780
info@windsorraceway
www.windsorraceway.com

Joe McGorisk, VP, Operations
Pat Soulliere, EVP/Chief Financial Officer
Bill Carter, President/Chief Executive Officer
Description:
Horse race track.
Description:
Horse race track.

Woodbine Racetrack
555 Rexdale Blvd
Rexdale, On, CANADA M9W 5L2

416-675-7223
888-675-7223
Fax: 416-213-2129
www.woodbine-racetrack.com

Hugh Mitchell, SVP, Racing
Nick Eaves, SVP Marketing/Gaming
Bruce Murray, Senior Manager, Media & Community Relati
Barry Hewson, Director, Racing/Standardbred

Woodstock Raceway
875 Nellis St
P.O. Box 234
Woodstock, On, CANADA N4S 7W8

519-537-5717
Fax: 519-421-7374
wdstock@windsorraceway.com
www.windsorraceway.com

Sharon Taylor, General Manager
Ian Fleming, Racing Secretary

SECTION 16
TRANSPORTATION

Associations

Aerospace Industries Association of Canada (AIAC) / Association des industries aérospatiales du Canada
#1200, 60 Queen St., Ottawa ON K1P 5Y7
Tel: 613-232-4297; *Fax:* 613-232-1142
e-mail: info@aiac.ca
URL: www.aiac.ca
Previous Name: Air Industries Association of Canada
Overview: A large national organization founded in 1962
Membership: 400; *Committees:* Airworthiness; International Exhibition; Technology Council; Defence Procurement Council; Suppliers Council; Space Council
Description: To promote & facilitate the continued success & growth of this strategic industry; to establish & maintain a public policy environment that enables sustained aerospace industry growth; to strengthen the international competitiveness of all aerospace firms in Canada; to strengthen Canadian aerospace SME capabilities & position them as "suppliers of choice"; to represent & involve the full range of aerospace companies that operate in Canada

Air Canada Pilots Association (ACPA) / L'Association des pilotes d'Air Canada
#205, 6299 Airport Rd., Mississauga ON L4V 1N3
Tel: 905-678-9008; *Fax:* 905-678-9016
Toll-Free: 800-634-0944
e-mail: info@acpa.ca
URL: acpa.ca
Overview: A medium-sized national organization founded in 1995
Finances: *Annual Operating Budget:* $3 Million-$5 Million
Staff: 20 staff member(s); 50 volunteer(s)
Membership: 3,100
Affiliation(s): Association of Star Alliance Pilots

Air Line Pilots Association, International - Canada (ALPA)
#1301, 155 Queen St., Ottawa ON K1P 6L1
Tel: 613-569-5668; *Fax:* 613-569-5681
URL: www.alpa.org
Previous Name: Canadian Air Line Pilots Association
Overview: A large national organization founded in 1931
Finances: *Funding Sources:* Membership dues
Staff: 10 staff member(s); 360 volunteer(s)
Membership: 2,200 + 19 locals in Canada; *Member Profile:* Active airline pilots employed by airlines in Canada; *Committees:* Air Safety; Aeromedical; Insurance
Activities: In Québec call 1-888-337-2033;
Description: To promote & represent the interests of the airline pilot profession & to safeguard the rights of individual members; to promote & maintain the highest standards of flight safety; to function as trade union & professional association
Affiliation(s): International Federation of Air Line Pilots' Associations; Canadian Labour Congress

Air Transport Association of Canada (ATAC) / Association du transport aérien du Canada
#1100, 255 Albert St., Ottawa ON K1P 6A9
Tel: 613-233-7727; *Fax:* 613-230-8648
e-mail: atac@atac.ca
URL: www.atac.ca
Overview: A medium-sized national organization founded in 1934
Finances: *Annual Operating Budget:* $500,000-$1.5 Million; *Funding Sources:* Member contributions
Staff: 11 staff member(s)
Membership: 300; *Committees:* Tax; Faciliation; Labour; Security; Engineering; Environment; Flight Operations; Air Traffic Services; Flight Training; Helicopter; Dangerous Goods; Industry Monetary Affairs
Description: To support our members in their pursuit of a safe, world-leading & competitive Canadian air transport industry
Affiliation(s): Aviation Alberta; BC Aviation Council; Canadian Business Aviation Association; Helicopter Association International; National Air Transportation Association; Northern Air Transport Association; Saskatchewan Aviation Council; Federation of Canadian Municipalities; Canadian Owners & Pilots Association; Flight Safety Foundation; Manitoba Aviation Council

Airport Management Conference of Ontario
10 Geddes Cres., Barrie ON L4N 7B3
Tel: 705-726-2626; *Fax:* 705-739-8520
Toll-Free: 877-636-2626
e-mail: amco@amco.on.ca
URL: www.amco.on.ca
Overview: A small provincial organization founded in 1985
Membership: 65 airports + 30 businesses
Activities: *Speaker Service:* Yes

Alberta Construction Trucking Association (ACTA)
PO Box 4520, Stn. C, Calgary AB T2T 5N3
Tel: 403-244-4487; *Fax:* 403-244-2340
Previous Name: Alberta Gravel Truckers Association
Overview: A medium-sized provincial organization
Description: To develop & promote the business of transporting construction & construction-related material

Alberta Motor Transport Association (AMTA)
3660 Blackfoot Trail SE, Calgary AB T2G 4E6
Tel: 403-243-4161; *Fax:* 403-243-4610
Toll-Free: 800-267-1003
e-mail: amtamsc@amta.ca
URL: www.amta.ca
Merged from: Alberta Trucking Industry Safety Association; Alberta Trucking Association
Overview: A medium-sized provincial organization
Membership: 12,000; *Member Profile:* All sectors of the highway transportation industry; *Committees:* Injury Reduction & Training; Compliance & Regulatory Affairs; Member Services
Activities: Six regional meetings;
Description: To take a leadership role in fostering a healthy, vibrant industry. PUBLICATIONS: Quaterly Newsletter; Annual Source Book; Western Canada Highway News Magazine.; *Member of:* Canadian Council of Motor Transport Administrators

Alberta Pioneer Railway Association
PO Box 70014, Stn. Londonderry, Edmonton AB T5C 3R6
Tel: 780-472-6229; *Fax:* 780-968-0167
e-mail: hdixon@incentre.net
URL: www.railwaymuseum.ab.ca
Also Known As: Alberta Railway Museum
Overview: A small provincial charitable organization founded in 1968
Finances: *Annual Operating Budget:* $50,000-$100,000; *Funding Sources:* Grants; donations
Membership: 50; *Fees:* $30 regular; $35 family; $20 senior; $10 associate; *Member Profile:* Railway enthusiasts; retired railway workers
Activities: Operates Alberta Railway Museum; *Library:* John Rechner Memorial Library (Open to Public) by appointment
Description: To collect, preserve, restore, exhibit & interpret artifacts which represent the history & social impact of the railways in Western Canada, with emphasis on Canadian National Railways & Northern Alberta Railways & their predecessors in northern & central Alberta; *Member of:* Alberta Museums Association; Museums Canada
Affiliation(s): Heritage Canada

Amalgamated Transit Union (AFL-CIO/CLC) / Syndicat uni du transport (FAT-COI/CTC)
5025 Wisconsin Ave. NW, Washington DC 20016 USA
Tel: 202-537-1645; *Fax:* 202-244-7824
URL: www.atu.org
Overview: A medium-sized international organization

Association des propriétaires d'autobus du Québec (APAQ)
#107, 225, boul Charest est, Québec QC G1K 3G9
Tél: 418-522-7131; *Téléc:* 418-522-6455
Courriel: apaq@apaq.qc.ca
URL: www.apaq.qc.ca
Aperçu: *Dimension:* moyenne; *Envergure: provinciale; Organisme sans but lucratif; fondée en 1926*
Finances: *Budget de fonctionnement annuel:* $500,000-$1.5 Million
Personnel: 11 membre(s) du personnel
Membre: 250 sociétés; *Montant de la cotisation:* Barème (entre 240$ et 8 000$); *Critères d'admissibilite:* Transportateurs par autocars; vendeurs de produits touristiques pour les groupes; *Comités:* Scolaire; Interurbain; Nolise
Activités: Congrès annuel, Bienvenue Québec, Golf;
Description: Défendre les intérêts des enterprises offrant des services de transport collectif de personnes par autobus et autocars; *Membre de:* Association de l'industrie touristique du Canada

Association du camionnage du Québec inc. (ACQ) / Québec Trucking Association Inc.
#200, 6450, rue Notre Dame ouest, Montréal QC H4C 1C4
Tél: 514-932-0377; *Téléc:* 514-932-1358
Ligne sans frais: 800-361-5813
Courriel: info@carrefour-acq.org
URL: www.carrefour-acq.org
Aperçu: *Dimension:* moyenne; *Envergure: provinciale; Organisme sans but lucratif; fondée en 1951*
Finances: *Budget de fonctionnement annuel:* $500,000-$1.5 Million
Personnel: 13 membre(s) du personnel
Membre: 600 sociétés + 251 associés; *Critères d'admissibilite:* transporteurs et locateurs publics & privés
Activités: *Stagiaires:* Oui
Description: Favoriser l'amélioration des normes de sécurité, d'efficacité et d'éthique dans l'industrie du camionnage; maintenir un contact avec l'autorité gouvernementale, les usagers des services de camionnage et le public en général; soutenir le perfectionnement professionnel; soutenir les entreprises dans la défense de leurs intérêts.
Affiliation(s): Union Internationale des Transports Routiers - Genève; American Trucking Association - Washington, DC

Association du transport écolier du Québec (ATEQ)
#300, 5300, boul des Galeries, Québec QC G2K 2A2
Tél: 418-622-6544; *Téléc:* 418-622-6595
Ligne sans frais: 877-622-6544
Courriel: courrier@ateq.qc.ca
URL: www.ateq.qc.ca
Aperçu: *Dimension:* moyenne; *Envergure: provinciale; fondée en 1962*
Membre: 700 transporteurs scolaires; *Montant de la cotisation:* Barème

Association du transport urbain du Québec (ATUQ)
#8090, 800, rue de la Gauchetière, Montréal QC H5A 1J6
Tél: 514-280-4640; *Téléc:* 514-280-7053
Courriel: info@atuq.com
URL: www.atuq.com
Aperçu: *Dimension:* moyenne; *Envergure: provinciale; fondée en 1983*
Description: Organisme de concertation et de représentation politique qui a pour mandat d'assurer la promotion du transport en commun et la défense des intérêts de ses membres auprès des partenaires de l'industrie et des différentes instances gouvernementales

Association nationale des camionneurs artisans inc. (ANCAI)
#235, 670, rue Bouvier, Québec QC G2J 1A7
Tél: 418-623-7923; *Téléc:* 418-623-0448
Courriel: infos@ancai.com
URL: www.ancai.com
Aperçu: *Dimension:* moyenne; *Envergure: provinciale; fondée en 1966*
Finances: *Budget de fonctionnement annuel:* $500,000-$1.5 Million
Personnel: 10 membre(s) du personnel
Membre: 5 000; *Montant de la cotisation:* 185$; *Critères d'admissibilite:* Camionneur propriétaire de son véhicule
Activités: Congrès annuel; Tirage camion;
Description: Défendre les intérêts des transporteurs en vrac (gravier et forêts) auprès des gouvernements, organismes patronaux et entreprises privées

Association of Canadian Port Authorities (ACPA)
#1502, 85 Albert St., Ottawa ON K1P 6A4
Tel: 613-232-2036; *Fax:* 613-232-9554
e-mail: leroux@acpa-ports.net
URL: www.acpa-ports.net
Previous Name: Canadian Port & Harbour Association
Overview: A medium-sized national organization founded in 1958
Finances: *Annual Operating Budget:* $50,000-$100,000; *Funding Sources:* Membership fees; seminars
Staff: 1 staff member(s)
Membership: 18 corporate + 17 associate; *Fees:* $750 associate & affiliate; $100 individual; *Committees:* Constitution; Finance & Administration; Marketing; Public Relations; Operations & Environment; Past Presidents; Real Property Management
Activities: Annual conferences where papers are given by experts in the field of port operations & where members inspect the host port's dock & industrial facilities; port-related research; special seminars; *Speaker Service:* Yes
Description: To encourage, mentor & stimulate the development of excellence within Canadian ports
Affiliation(s): American Association of Port Authorities

Association québécoise du transport aérien (AQTA)
Aéroport international Jean-Lesage, 600, 6e av de l'Aéroport, Québec QC G2G 2T5
Tél: 418-871-4635; *Téléc:* 418-871-8189
Courriel: aqta@aqta.ca
URL: www.aqta.ca
Aperçu: *Dimension:* moyenne; *Envergure: provinciale; Organisme sans but lucratif; fondée en 1975*
Membre: 130; *Montant de la cotisation:* Barème; *Critères d'admissibilite:* Transporteurs aériens et fournisseurs de produits et services liés à l'aviation
Description: Voué à la défense et la promotion des intérêts de tous les secteurs du transport aérien

Association québécoise du transport et des routes inc. (AQTR)
#200, 1255, rue University, Montréal QC H3B 3B2

Tél: 514-523-6444; *Téléc:* 514-523-2666
Courriel: info@aqtr.qc.ca
URL: www.aqtr.qc.ca

Aperçu: *Dimension:* grande; *Envergure: provinciale; fondée en 1965*
Finances: *Budget de fonctionnement annuel:* $500,000-$1.5 Million
Personnel: 7 membre(s) du personnel; 100+ bénévole(s)
Membre: 950; *Montant de la cotisation:* 270 $; *Critères d'admissibilite:* Secteur privé - Ingénieur conseils; Entrepreneurs; Fournisseurs et manufacturiers; Laboratoires; Transporteurs; Architectes et urbanistes; Étudiants; Spécialistes en environnement; Secteur public et parapublic - Ministères; Municipalités; Maisons d'enseignement; Sociétés de transport; Autres sociétés, départements et services publics; *Comités:* Directions techniques - Infrastructures de transport; Transport des personnes; Circulation; Sécurité dans les transports; Transport aérien; Recherche et développement; Comités - Transport des marchandises; Environnement; Revue; Congrès; Activités municipales
Activités: Regrouper les personnes impliquées dans les techniques du transport; encourager les échanges multidisciplinaires et favoriser la collaboration entre différents secteurs; recommander toute mesure permettant de développer des techniques du transport; *Listes de destinataires:* Oui
Description: Assumer un leadership technique; définir des règles en matière de sécurité et d'environnement; favoriser l'échange international des expertises; promouvoir la recherche et le développement des expertises et des produits en transport; promouvoir la formation dans le domaine des transports; assumer la représentativité de l'AQTR par la participation aux principaux forums sur les transports; contribuer à servir la société par l'éducation et l'information du grand public.

Association Sectorielle Transport Entreposage (ASTE)

#301, 6455, boul Jean-Talon est, Montréal QC H1S 3E8
Tél: 514-955-0454; *Téléc:* 514-955-0449
Ligne sans frais: 800-361-8906
Courriel: info@aste.qc.ca
URL: www.aste.qc.ca

Aperçu: *Dimension:* moyenne; *Envergure: provinciale; fondée en 1983*
Membre: 1-99
Description: L'Association Sectorielle Transport Entreposage est une organisme en prèvention, autonome et paritaire, sans but lucratif, fondé et administré par des reprétants des employeurs et des syndicats.

Atlantic Provinces Trucking Association (APTA)

#400, 725 Champlain St., Dieppe NB E1A 1P6
Tel: 506-855-2782; *Fax:* 506-853-7424
Toll-Free: 866-866-1679
e-mail: apta@apta.ca
URL: www.apta.ca

Overview: A medium-sized local organization founded in 1950
Membership: 400 corporate & individual; *Member Profile:* Open to anyone having an interest in the trucking industry in Atlantic Canada, including common carriers, owner-operators & private fleets; *Committees:* Accident Review; Associated Trades Council; Broker; Common Carrier; Group Insurance; Marine; Membership; New Brunswick Legislative; Newfoundland Legislative; Nova Scotia Legislative; Prince Edward Island Legislative; Safety Council; Workers Compensation
Activities: Infrastructure improvements; complete twinning of the highway between Halifax & Saint John; elimination of motor carrier plates & fees; simplification of multiple registration & other tax collection systems in North America to allow for "one-stop shipping"; establishment of training programs; Annual Meeting & Convention; Atlantic Truck Show; Spring Maintenance Seminar; *Rents Mailing List:* Yes
Description: To promote an efficient, safe & environmentally sound trucking industry in Atlantic Canada. PUBLICATIONS: Atlantic Trucking Magazine (quaterly); Atlantic Report Newsletter (monthly) (only to members).

British Columbia Aviation Council (BCAC)

4360 Agar Dr., Richmond BC V7B 1A3
Tel: 604-278-9330; *Fax:* 604-278-8210
e-mail: bcac@telus.net
URL: www.bcaviation.org

Overview: A small provincial organization founded in 1938
Finances: *Funding Sources:* Membership fees
Description: A self-sustaining organization with the mission to "promote the safe and orderly development of aviation and aviation services to the province of British Columiba".

British Columbia Ferry & Marine Workers' Union (CLC) (BCFMWU) / Syndicat des travailleurs marins et de bacs de la Colombie-Britannique (CTC)

1511 Stewart Ave., Nanaimo BC V9S 4E3
Tel: 250-716-3454; *Fax:* 250-716-3455
Toll-Free: 800-663-7009
e-mail: mailroom@bcfmwu.com
URL: www.bcfmwu.com

Also Known As: Ferry Workers' Union
Overview: A medium-sized provincial organization founded in 1977
Finances: *Annual Operating Budget:* $1.5 Million-$3 Million; *Funding Sources:* Union dues
Staff: 9 staff member(s)
Membership: 4,400; *Fees:* $60 initiation fee; 1.5% of gross monthly income
Description: To unite in the Union all workers eligible for membership; to seek the best possible wage standards & improvements in the conditions of employment for these workers & to represent members in protecting & maintaining their rights; to act as the representative of the membership; to establish free child day care for all individuals; to engage in educational, legislative, political, civic, social, welfare, community & other activities to safeguard & promote economic & social benefits & justice for all workers, unionized & non-unionized.
Affiliation(s): BC Federation of Labour; National Union of Public & General Employees (NUPGE)

British Columbia Railway Historical Association (BCRHA)

1148 Balmoral Rd., Victoria BC V8T 1B1
Tel: 250-383-7063
e-mail: bcrha@shaw.ca
URL: www.trainweb.org/bcrha

Overview: A small provincial charitable organization founded in 1961
Finances: *Annual Operating Budget:* Less than $50,000; *Funding Sources:* Donations; book sales; membership dues
Staff: 30 volunteer(s)
Membership: 5 associate + 1 senior/lifetime + 30 individual; *Fees:* $15 full; $4 associate; *Member Profile:* Interest in BC railway history; *Committees:* Acquisitions; Book Sales; New Book Review; Financial
Activities: Research & publication of books on BC railway history; *Library:* Yes (Open to Public)
Description: To preserve railway exhibits, manuscripts & film of BC railways; *Member of:* Heritage Society of BC

British Columbia Supercargoes' Association

#206, 3711 Delbrook Ave., North Vancouver BC V7N 3Z4
Tel: 604-878-1258; *Fax:* 604-904-6545
e-mail: admin@supercargoes.bc.ca; president@supercargoes.bc.ca
URL: www.supercargoes.bc.ca

Overview: A medium-sized provincial organization founded in 1952
Finances: *Annual Operating Budget:* $50,000-$100,000; *Funding Sources:* Membership dues
Staff: 8 volunteer(s)
Membership: 12; *Member Profile:* Marine professionals in the shipping industry
Description: To provide expert marine cargo planning & onsite management & supervision of shiploading & discharge of all types of cargoes & vessels on the west coast of North America

British Columbia Trucking Association (BCTA)

#100, 20111 - 93A Ave., Langley BC V1M 4A9
Tel: 604-888-5319; *Fax:* 604-888-2941
Toll-Free: 800-565-2282
e-mail: bcta@bctrucking.com
URL: www.bctrucking.com

Previous Name: BC Motor Transport Association
Overview: A large provincial organization founded in 1913
Finances: *Annual Operating Budget:* $500,000-$1.5 Million; *Funding Sources:* Membership dues
Staff: 8 staff member(s)
Membership: 1,000 corporate; *Fees:* $325-$400; *Member Profile:* Trucking company operating in BC or supplier to trucking industry; *Committees:* Convention; Insurance; International; Labour; Freight Claims & Hazardous Goods; Safety; Truxpo; Vehicle Standards
Activities: *Speaker Service:* Yes; *Rents Mailing List:* Yes *Library:* Yes by appointment
Description: To act as the recognised voice of the commercial road transportation industry in British Columbia, by consulting & communicating with the industry, government & the public; to promote a prosperous, safe, efficient & responsible road transportation industry; to provide programs & services to members

Bytown Railway Society (BRS)

PO Box 47076, Ottawa ON K1B 5P9
Tel: 613-745-1201; *Fax:* 613-745-1201
e-mail: info@bytownrailwaysociety.ca
URL: www.bytownrailwaysociety.ca

Overview: A medium-sized national charitable organization founded in 1969
Finances: *Annual Operating Budget:* $100,000-$250,000; *Funding Sources:* Publications sale; memberships
Staff: 60 volunteer(s)
Membership: 20 corporate + 3 senior/lifetime + 1,225 individual; *Fees:* $40/year plus $2.00 GST or $5.20 HST; *Committees:* Publications
Activities: Restoration/preservation of owned railway equipment; *Library:* Yes (Open to Public) by appointment
Description: To promote an interest in railways & railway history, with particular emphasis on Canadian railways. PUBLICATIONS: Canadian Trackside Guide, The Quebec Railway Light and Power Company, Montreal Streetcars- Vol.2. People and Places, Montreal and Southern Counties Railway Co., The Ottawa Streetcar Company, Hamilton's Other Railway.

Canadian Aeronautics & Space Institute (CASI) / Institut aéronautique et spatial du Canada

#104, 350 Terry Fox Dr., Ottawa ON K2K 2W5
Tel: 613-591-8787; *Fax:* 613-591-7291
e-mail: casi@casi.ca; membership@casi.ca
URL: www.casi.ca

Previous Name: Canadian Aeronautical Institute (CAI)
Merged from: Institute of Aircraft Technicians; Ottawa Aeronautical Society; US Institute of Aeronautical Science
Overview: A medium-sized national licensing organization founded in 1954
Membership: 1,600; *Fees:* $36.75 juniors; $63 seniors; $94.50 associates & individuals
Activities: Facilitating communications among the Canadian aeronautics & space community; Developing members' skills;
Description: To advance the art, science, engineering, & applications of aeronautics & associated technologies in Canada; to promote Canadian competence & international competitiveness
Affiliation(s): Canadian Air Cushion Technology Society; Canadian Navigation Society; Canadian Remote Sensing Society

Canadian Airports Council (CAC) / Conseil des aéroports du Canada

#706, 350 Sparks St., Ottawa ON K1R 7S8
Tel: 613-560-9302; *Fax:* 613-560-6599
e-mail: sharon.redden@cacairports.ca
URL: www.cacairports.ca

Overview: A medium-sized national organization founded in 1991
Finances: *Funding Sources:* Sponsorships
Membership: 48; *Member Profile:* Canadian airports (CAC members are also members of Airports Council International - North America)
Activities: Preparing submissions to governmental bodies & agencies;
Description: To act as the voice for Canadian airports on a great range of important issues; *Member of:* Airports Council International - North America (ACI-NA)
Affiliation(s): Air Transport Association of Canada (ATAC); Canadian International Freight Forwarders Association (CIFFA); Canadian Chamber of Commerce; Canadian Tourism Commission; Tourism Industry Association of Canada (TIAC)

Canadian Association of Movers (CAM) / Association canadienne des déménageurs (ACD)

#525, 2085 Hurontario St., Mississauga ON L5A 4G1
Tel: 905-848-6579; *Fax:* 905-848-8499
Toll-Free: 866-860-0065
e-mail: admin@mover.net
URL: www.mover.net

Overview: A small national organization
Membership: 100-499
Activities: Government & political affairs; membership development; volunteer participation & recognition; van lines; public affairs & publications; research & development; education & training; professional ethics & standards; organizational competency;
Description: To further the interests of the owner-managed moving & storage companies by providing for its members leadership, motivation, research, education, programs of mutual benefit, consultation & technical advice
Affiliation(s): American Moving & Storage Association

Canadian Association of Railway Suppliers / Association canadienne des fournisseurs de chemins de fer

#901, 99 Bank St., Ottawa ON K1P 6B9
Tel: 613-237-3888; *Fax:* 613-237-4888
e-mail: info@railwaysuppliers.ca
URL: www.railwaysuppliers.ca

Previous Name: Canadian Railway & Transit Manufacturers Association

Overview: A medium-sized national organization
Membership: 18 organizations; *Fees:* Schedule available

Canadian Automobile Association (CAA) / Association canadienne des automobilistes
National Office, #200, 1145 Hunt Club Rd., Ottawa ON K1V 0Y3
Tel: 613-247-0117; *Fax:* 613-247-0118
e-mail: info@national.caa.ca
URL: www.caa.ca
Overview: A large national organization founded in 1913
Finances: *Funding Sources:* Membership dues
Staff: 25 staff member(s)
Membership: 5+million; *Member Profile:* CAA British Columbia; Alberta Motor Association; CAA Saskatchewan; CAA Manitoba; CAA Mid-Western Ontario; CAA South Central Ontario; CAA Niagara; CAA Central Ontario; CAA North & East Ontario; CAA Québec; CAA Maritimes
Activities: *Speaker Service:* Yes *Library:* Yes
Description: To promote, develop & implement programs & information relating to the rights, responsibilities & needs of the motorist as a consumer
Affiliation(s): Alliance internationale de tourisme; Fédération internationale de l'automobile; Federacion interamericana de touring y automovil-clubes; Commonwealth Motoring Conference; American Automobile Association

Canadian Aviation Historical Society (CAHS)
National Headquarters, PO Box 705, Stn. P, Toronto ON M5S 2Y4
e-mail: cahsnatpres@cahs.ca
URL: www.cahs.com
Overview: A small national charitable organization founded in 1962
Finances: *Funding Sources:* Donations
Fees: $40 Canadian members; $50 USA members; $60 overseas members; *Member Profile:* Individuals with an interest in the history of aviation
Activities: Supporting research in Canadian aeronautical history;
Description: To celebrate, preserve, & document Canada's flying heritage

Canadian Aviation Maintenance Council (CAMC) / Conseil canadien de l'entretien des aéronefs (CCEA)
#155, 955 Green Valley Cres., Ottawa ON K2C 3V4
Tel: 613-727-8272; *Fax:* 613-727-7018
Toll-Free: 800-448-9715
e-mail: secretariat@camc.ca
URL: www.camc.ca
Overview: A medium-sized national organization founded in 1992
Finances: *Annual Operating Budget:* $250,000-$500,000; *Funding Sources:* Aviation maintenance industry; Human Resources Development Canada; federal government
Staff: 5 staff member(s)
Membership: 1,000-4,999; *Fees:* Initial: $84/2 yrs; Renewal $59.50/2 yrs; Certified $89.49/2 yrs
Activities: *Internships:* Yes
Description: To develop occupational training standards & facilitate the implementation of a human resources strategy for the Canadian Aviation Maintenance Industry.

Canadian Bus Association (CBA) / Association canadienne de l'autobus
c/o #2001, 45 O'Connor St., Ottawa ON K1P 1A4
Tel: 613-238-1800; *Fax:* 613-241-4936
e-mail: mresnick@rothwellgroup.ca
Previous Name: Canadian Motor Coach Association
Overview: A medium-sized national organization founded in 1936
Membership: 100 companies
Description: To act as the national voice of the Canadian bus industry; to act as a national forum for the discussion of bus-related issues & the establishment of positions in relation to industry-wide areas of concern; to function as a technical & operational information gathering & exchange mechanism; to further the objectives of safety, convenience & quality of the motor coach industry.

Canadian Business Aviation Association (CBAA) / Association canadienne de l'aviation d'affaires (ACAA)
#430, 55 Metcalfe St., Ottawa ON K1P 6L5
Tel: 613-236-5611; *Fax:* 613-236-2361
e-mail: info@cbaa.ca
URL: www.cbaa.ca
Previous Name: Canadian Business Aircraft Association Inc.
Overview: A medium-sized national organization founded in 1962
Finances: *Annual Operating Budget:* $500,000-$1.5 Million; *Funding Sources:* Membership dues; convention/tradeshow
Staff: 9 staff member(s)
Membership: 150 business + 5 commercial + 108 associate + 12 affiliate + 9 affiliated organizations; *Member Profile:* Business: owns or operates a Canadian privately or state registered aircraft as an aid to conduct its business; Commercial: owns or operates Canadian commercially registered aircraft whose aims are consistent with the principles & interests of the association; Associate: businesses primarily concerned with aviation activities, including the manufacture of aircraft whose aims are consistent with the principles & interests of the association; Affiliate: owns or operates aircraft exclusively registered in a nation other than Canada who are engaged in a field of endeavour consistent with the principles & interests of the association
Activities: Leadership; excellence; collaboration; ethics;
Description: To represent & promote the Canadian business aviation community globally, advocating safety, security & efficiency.
Affiliation(s): National Business Aviation Association; International Business Aviation Council; European Business Aircraft Association

Canadian Council of Motor Transport Administrators (CCMTA) / Conseil canadien des administrateurs en transport motorisé (CCATM)
2323 St. Laurent Blvd., Ottawa ON K1G 4J8
Tel: 613-736-1003; *Fax:* 613-736-1395
e-mail: ccmta-secretariat@ccmta.ca
URL: www.ccmta.ca
Overview: A medium-sized national charitable organization founded in 1940
Finances: *Funding Sources:* Member assessments; special projects; membership fees
Membership: 100-499; *Member Profile:* Members include representatives of provincial, territorial, & federal governments, & associate members from transportation related organizations.; *Committees:* Drivers & Vehicles; Compliance & Regulatory Affairs; Road Safety Research & Policies
Activities: Developing strategies & programs; Managing a communications network, called the Interprovincial Record Exchange system; *Rents Mailing List:* Yes
Description: CCMTA coordinates operational matters dealing with the administration, regulation, & control of motor vehicle transportation & highway safety.

Canadian Federation of AME Associations (CFAMEA)
837 Charlotte St., Fredericton NB E3B 1M7
Tel: 506-452-1809; *Fax:* 506-452-8251
Also Known As: Aircraft Maintenance Engineers Association
Overview: A medium-sized national organization
Finances: *Annual Operating Budget:* Less than $50,000; *Funding Sources:* Membership dues
Staff: 6 volunteer(s)
Membership: 1,000-4,999
Activities: Liaison with government concerning aircraft maintenance & AME licensing;

Canadian Ferry Operators Association (CFOA) / Association canadienne des opérateurs de traversiers
c/o Anthonie A. de Hoog, CFOA Executive Director, 21 Meredith Dr., Sussex Corner NB E4E 2T8
Tel: 506-433-4810; *Fax:* 506-432-9505
e-mail: adehoog@cfoa.ca
URL: www.cfoa.ca
Overview: A small national organization founded in 1987
Finances: *Funding Sources:* Sponsorships
Membership: 37; *Member Profile:* Major ferry owners & operators in Canada
Activities: Providing opportunities for discussion of matters of interest to members; Promoting the safety, reliability, & efficiency of Canadian ferry operators; Providing representation at regulatory forums such as CMAC;
Description: To establish & maintain a standard of professional & technical excellence in the operation of Canadian ferries; to promote & protect the interests of members of the association

Canadian Flight Instructors Association
579 Kingston Rd., Ajax ON L1S 6M1
Tel: 905-683-8986; *Fax:* 905-683-6977
e-mail: bill@jsdavidson.ca
Overview: A small national organization

Canadian Heartland Training Railway
PO Box 1174, Camrose AB T4V 1X2
Tel: 780-679-4008; *Fax:* 780-672-4032
URL: www.chtr.ca
Overview: A small national organization
Description: To support the practical training needs of the railway industry in Canada & around the world; *Member of:* Railway Association of Canada; Railway Suppliers Association of Canada

Canadian Industrial Transportation Association (CITA) / Association canadienne de transport industriel (ACTI)
#405, 580 Terry Fox Dr., Ottawa ON K2L 4C2
Tel: 613-599-3283; *Fax:* 613-599-1295
e-mail: info@cita-acti.ca
URL: www.cita-acti.ca
Overview: A medium-sized national organization
Finances: *Annual Operating Budget:* $250,000-$500,000; *Funding Sources:* Membership dues
Staff: 3 staff member(s)
Membership: 400 major shippers
Activities: Advocacy; education; *Speaker Service:* Yes *Library:* Yes (Open to Public)
Description: CITA-ACTI actively promotes a competitive and cost effective North American transportation system serving Canada and its NAFTA allies. Their vision is to be recognized as the "National Voice" of industrial transportation in Canada through increased membership and member representation in all regions of the county.

Canadian Institute of Traffic & Transportation (CITT) / Institut canadien du trafic et du transport
#400, 10 King St. East, Toronto ON M5C 1C3
Tel: 416-363-5696; *Fax:* 416-363-5698
e-mail: info@citt.ca
URL: www.citt.ca
Overview: A medium-sized national organization founded in 1958
Membership: 2,000; *Fees:* $275; *Member Profile:* Members must complete course of study to hold the designation, CITT
Activities: Offers the CITT Diploma Program;
Description: Designation granting body in logistics management.

Canadian International Freight Forwarders Association, Inc. (CIFFA) / Association des transitaires internationaux canadiens, inc. (ATIC)
#480, 170 Attwell Dr., Toronto ON M9W 5Z5
Tel: 416-234-5100; *Fax:* 416-234-5152
Toll-Free: 866-282-4332
e-mail: ciffa@ciffa.com
URL: www.ciffa.com
Overview: A large international organization founded in 1948
Finances: *Annual Operating Budget:* $500,000-$1.5 Million; *Funding Sources:* Membership dues; education fees
Staff: 5 staff member(s); 20 volunteer(s)
Membership: 188 regular + 94 associate; *Fees:* Schedule available; *Committees:* AGM; Bylaws; Counsel; Education; Electronic Data Interchange; Ethics/Standards; FIATA; Judicial; Logistics Institute; Membership; Public Relations; Road & Rail; Sea Freight; Ways & Means
Activities: CIFFA Professional Training Program; education courses; dangerous goods courses, topical workshops;
Description: To represent & support members of the Canadian international freight forwarding industry in providing the highest level of quality & professional services to their clients.; *Member of:* Federation internationale des associations de transitaires et assimiles
Affiliation(s): International Federation of Freight Forwarders Associations

Canadian Marine Pilots' Association (CLC) / Association des pilotes de la marine canadienne (CTC)
1150 Morrison Dr., Ottawa ON K2H 8S9
Tel: 613-829-9531; *Fax:* 613-596-6079
Overview: A small national organization founded in 1918

Canadian National Railways Police Association (Ind.) (CNRPA) / Association des policiers des chemins de fer nationaux du Canada (ind.)
6479 Miller's Grove, Mississauga ON L5N 3E5
Tel: 905-824-0856; *Fax:* 905-824-4584
e-mail: fjmorgan@ica.net
URL: www.cnrpa.ca
Also Known As: CNR Police Association
Overview: A small national organization founded in 1923
Membership: 159 + 7 locals

Canadian Northern Society (CNoS)
PO Box 1174, Camrose AB T4V 1X2
Tel: 780-672-3099
e-mail: canadiannorthern@telus.net
URL: www.canadiannorthern.ca
Overview: A small local charitable organization founded in 1987
Finances: *Funding Sources:* Donations
Fees: $20 full members; $10 associate; *Committees:* Camrose Railway Station Park & Morgan Railway Garden; Meeting Creek Grain Elevator & Railway Station Heritage Site; Big Valley

Railway Station & Roundhouse Interpretive Park; Fundraising; Canora Chronicle; Finance & Audit
Description: To preserve prairie heritage

Canadian Owners & Pilots Association (COPA)
#207, 75 Albert St., Ottawa ON K1P 5E7
Tel: 613-236-4901; *Fax:* 613-236-8646
e-mail: copa@copanational.org
URL: www.copanational.org
Overview: A medium-sized national charitable organization founded in 1954
Finances: *Annual Operating Budget:* $500,000-$1.5 Million; *Funding Sources:* Membership dues; advertising
Staff: 9 staff member(s); 20 volunteer(s)
Membership: 17,000; *Fees:* $50 individual; $250 corporate; *Member Profile:* Pilots & aircraft owners; corporate members; *Committees:* Air Navigation Services National Advisory Group; Canadian Aviation Regulation Advisory Committee
Activities: COPA Flight Chapters located across Canada; *Library:* Yes (Open to Public)
Description: The recognized voice of general aviation in Canada

Canadian Parking Association (CPA)
#350, 2255 St. Laurent Blvd., Ottawa ON K1G 4K3
Tel: 613-727-0700; *Fax:* 613-727-3183
e-mail: info@canadianparking.ca
URL: www.canadianparking.ca
Also Known As: Association canadienne du stationnement
Overview: A medium-sized national organization founded in 1983
Membership: 320; *Fees:* $475 full
Description: The Association is the national organization that represents the parking industry & provides a dynamic forum for learning & sharing to enhance member's ability to serve the public & improve the economic vitality of communities.

Canadian Ports Clearance Association
#500, 101 Syndicate Ave. North, Thunder Bay ON P7C 3V4
Tel: 807-623-8491; *Fax:* 807-623-2676
Previous Name: British Columbia Grain Shippers Clearance Association; Lake Shippers Clearance Association
Overview: A small national organization
Description: Shipping agent

Canadian Professional Logistics Institute / Institut canadien des professionnels de la logistique
#200, 160 John St., Toronto ON M5V 2E5
Tel: 416-363-3005; *Fax:* 416-363-5598
Toll-Free: 877-363-3005
e-mail: loginfo@loginstitute.ca
URL: www.loginstitute.ca
Also Known As: The Logistics Institute
Previous Name: Professional Logistics Institute of Canada
Overview: A medium-sized national organization founded in 1990
Finances: *Annual Operating Budget:* $500,000-$1.5 Million; *Funding Sources:* Membership dues; training tuition
Staff: 4 staff member(s); 5 volunteer(s)
Membership: 1,400 professional + 60 institutional + 50 associate; *Fees:* $395 professional; $99 associate; $875 corporate; *Member Profile:* Members must meet a professional standard developed & maintained by the Institute; *Committees:* Administration; Admissions; Legal; Marketing; Policy Development; Professional Development; R & D; Rules
Activities: *Internships:* Yes; *Speaker Service:* Yes
Description: To establish professional standards, certification & a program of professional development for the Logistics community.
Affiliation(s): Canadian Institute of Traffic & Transportation; Canadian International Freight Forwarders Association

Canadian Railroad Historical Association (CRHA) / Association canadienne d'histoire ferroviaire
110, rue St-Pierre, Saint-Constant QC J5A 1G7
Tel: 450-632-2410; *Fax:* 450-638-1563
e-mail: info@exporail.org
URL: www.exporail.org
Overview: A medium-sized national charitable organization founded in 1932
Membership: 1,100; *Fees:* $36
Activities: *Library:* Yes (Open to Public) by appointment
Description: To collect, preserve & disseminate information/items relating to the history of railways in Canada

Canadian Seaplane Pilots Association (CSPA)
#1001, 75 Albert St., Ottawa ON K1P 5E7
Tel: 613-236-4901; *Fax:* 613-236-8646
Overview: A medium-sized national organization
Finances: *Annual Operating Budget:* $50,000-$100,000
Staff: 2 staff member(s); 10 volunteer(s)
Membership: 400; *Fees:* US$28
Activities: Fly-ins; safety seminars;
Description: To maintain communications among seaplane pilots; to represent them at all levels of government; to help develop regulations conducive to safe & pleasurable flying; to prepare & disseminate educational material; to advance among its members information & knowledge of seaplane flying.
Affiliation(s): Seaplane Pilots Association International

Canadian Shipowners Association (CSA) / Association des armateurs canadiens (AAC)
#705, 350 Sparks St., Ottawa ON K1R 7S8
Tel: 613-232-3539; *Fax:* 613-232-6211
e-mail: csa@shipowners.ca
URL: www.shipowners.ca
Previous Name: Dominion Marine Association
Overview: A medium-sized national organization founded in 1903
Membership: 8 corporate
Activities: Monitors Canadian & US government legislative/regulatory actions, initiatives by various international marine organizations, political trends, public policy relating to navigation, safety & the Canadian shipping environment; executes strategic communications & public relations campaigns to effectively represent the interests of member companies;
Description: To promote an economic & competitive Canadian marine transportation industry; to support a national policy conducive to the development & maintenance of the Canadian flag merchant fleet in the inland, coastal & Arctic waters of Canada & foster the growth of a Canadian flag deep sea merchant fleet.; *Member of:* International Chamber of Shipping; International Shipping Federation; Chamber of Maritime Commerce; Canada Maritime Law Association

Canadian Transport Lawyers Association
c/o S.S.T. Thibault, Heenan Blaikie LLP, #600, 900, rue René-Lévesque ouest, Québec QC G1R 2B5
URL: www.ctla.ca
Overview: A small national organization
Fees: $100 - $195; *Member Profile:* Lawyers engaged in transportation law, regulatory policy, procedure, & related legal interests

Canadian Transport Workers Union (Ind.) (CTWU) / Syndicat canadien des travailleurs du transport (ind.)
c/o Local #213, 73 Misty St., Kitchener ON N2B 3V6
Tel: 519-896-2671
Overview: A small national organization
Membership: 90 + 2 locals

Canadian Transportation Equipment Association (CTEA) / Association d'équipement de transport du canada (AETC)
#3B, 16 Barrie Blvd., St Thomas ON N5P 4B9
Tel: 519-631-0414; *Fax:* 519-631-1333
e-mail: transportation@ctea.on.ca
URL: www.ctea.ca
Overview: A medium-sized national organization founded in 1963
Membership: 544; *Member Profile:* Commercial vehicle & component manufacturers; Dealers & distributors; Service providers
Activities: Lobbying; Providing access to technical & regulatory information; Offering networking opportunities; Encouraging research;
Description: To promote excellence in commercial vehicle manufacturing; to develop standard practices

Canadian Transportation Research Forum (CTRF) / Groupe de recherches sur les transports au Canada
PO Box 23033, Woodstock ON N4T 1R0
Tel: 519-421-9701; *Fax:* 519-421-9319
e-mail: feedback@ctrf.ca, cawoudsma@ctrf.ca
URL: www.ctrf.ca
Overview: A medium-sized national charitable organization founded in 1967
Finances: *Annual Operating Budget:* Less than $50,000
Staff: 21 volunteer(s)
Membership: 320; *Fees:* $129; *Member Profile:* Open to anyone interested in any aspect of transportation; membership is individual rather than corporate; present membership is drawn from carriers, shippers, consultants & suppliers in the commercial sector, the policy, regulatory, planning & research environments at all levels of government, students & professors at universitites & community colleges
Description: To promote the development of research in transportation & related fields; to publish research papers through media & through national & regional forum meetings.

Canadian Trucking Alliance (CTA) / L'Alliance canadienne du camionnage (ACC)
324 Somerset St. West, Ottawa ON K2P 0J9
Tel: 613-236-9426; *Fax:* 866-823-4076
e-mail: info@cantruck.ca
URL: www.cantruck.com
Overview: A medium-sized national organization founded in 1937
Member Profile: Motor carriers & associated trades
Activities: *Speaker Service:* Yes
Description: To promote business excellence in trucking; to participate in the development of public policy which supports the economic growth, safety & prosperity of the industry; to provide services, including research, development, products & information to meet the needs of the industry.
PUBLICATIONS: Dangerous Goods: A Trucker's Guide; Crossing International Borders:A Trucker's Guide; National Safety Code: A Trucker's Guide.

Canadian Trucking Human Resources Council (CTHRC) / Conseil canadien des ressources humaines en camionnage
#203, 720 Belfast Rd., Ottawa ON K1G 0Z5
Tel: 613-244-4800; *Fax:* 613-244-4535
e-mail: info@cthrc.com
URL: www.cthrc.com
Overview: A medium-sized national organization
Activities: Conducting research; Training; Offering advice; Liaising with industry members;
Description: To respond to the human resource needs of the trucking industry
Affiliation(s): CCA Truck Driver Training Ltd.; Capilano Truck Driver Training Institute; JVI Provincial Transportation & Safety Academy; Mountain Transport Institute Ltd.; Red Deer College; SK Driver Training Ltd.; Wheels On Ltd. / Training & Driver Training

Canadian Urban Transit Association (CUTA) / Association canadienne du transport urbain (ACTU)
#1401, 55 York St., Toronto ON M5J 1R7
Tel: 416-365-9800; *Fax:* 416-365-1295
e-mail: transit@cutaactu.ca
URL: www.cutaactu.ca
Overview: A large national organization founded in 1904
Finances: *Annual Operating Budget:* $1.5 Million-$3 Million
Staff: 16 staff member(s)
Membership: 120 transit system; 15 government; 250 business; 50 affiliate; *Fees:* Schedule available; *Member Profile:* Providers of urban transit services, suppliers & related organizations
Activities: Conferences; training programs; statistics; *Library:* Yes (Open to Public) by appointment
Description: To promote the role of urban transit in enhancing mobility.

Canadians for Responsible & Safe Highways (CRASH)
PO Box 1042, Stn. B, Ottawa ON K1P 5R1
Tel: 613-860-0529; *Fax:* 613-567-6204
Toll-Free: 800-530-9945
e-mail: crash@web.net
URL: www.web.net/~crash/about.html
Overview: A small national organization
Description: To ensure that safety, environmental & economic concerns are fully considered by governments when the latter establish & administer regulations pertaining to trucking operations on public highways

Carefree Society Transportation Service
2832 Queensway St., Prince George BC V2L 4M5
Tel: 250-562-1394; *Fax:* 250-562-1393
e-mail: carefree_society@telus.net
Also Known As: Carefree Society
Overview: A small local charitable organization founded in 1971
Finances: *Annual Operating Budget:* $250,000-$500,000; *Funding Sources:* Provincial government; regional government
Staff: 12 staff member(s); 10 volunteer(s)
Membership: 15; *Fees:* $6; *Committees:* Accessible Transportation Awareness
Description: To provide transportation services for the disabled in our community
Affiliation(s): BC Transit

Central British Columbia Railway & Forest Industry Museum Society
850 River Rd., Prince George BC V2L 5S8
Tel: 250-563-7351; *Fax:* 250-563-3697
e-mail: trains@pgrfm.bc.ca
URL: www.pgrfm.bc.ca
Also Known As: Railway & Forestry Museum
Overview: A small local charitable organization founded in 1983
Finances: *Annual Operating Budget:* $50,000-$100,000
Staff: 6 staff member(s); 15 volunteer(s)
Membership: 75; *Fees:* $15-$40
Activities: *Awareness Events:* Steam Day; Forester Day; Family Carnival *Library:* Canfor Library by appointment

Description: Administers Prince George Railway & Forest Industry Museum; *Member of:* Canadian Railway Historical Association; Canadian Museum Association; British Columbia Museum Association; American Railway Museum Association

Chamber of Maritime Commerce (CMC) / Chambre du commerce maritime (CCM)

#700, 350 Sparks St., Ottawa ON K1R 7S8
Tel: 613-233-8779; *Fax:* 613-233-3743
e-mail: email@cmc-ccm.com
URL: www.cmc-ccm.com
Previous Name: Great Lakes Waterways Development Association
Overview: A large national organization founded in 1959
Finances: *Annual Operating Budget:* $250,000-$500,000; *Funding Sources:* Membership dues
Staff: 4 staff member(s)
Membership: 180+ institutional; *Member Profile:* Major Canadian & American shippers, ports & marine service providers, domestic & international shipowners
Activities: *Speaker Service:* Yes
Description: To bring together all sectors of the economy that rely on a cost efficient & safe marine transportation system

Chartered Institute of Logistics & Transport (CILT)

Earlstrees Court, Earlstrees Rd., Corbyn NN17 4Ax United Kingdom
Tel: 44-0-1536-740-100; *Fax:* 44-0-1536-740-101
e-mail: enquiry@ciltuk.org.uk
URL: www.cilt-international.com
Previous Name: Chartered Institute of Transport
Overview: A medium-sized international charitable organization founded in 1919
Finances: *Annual Operating Budget:* Greater than $5 Million; *Funding Sources:* Membership dues
Staff: 21 staff member(s)
Membership: 23,000 in UK; 33,000 worldwide; *Fees:* Schedule available; *Member Profile:* Professionals in transport & logistics; *Committees:* Membership; Education
Activities: Education Programs; Lecture Meetings; Training; Transport Reports; *Speaker Service:* Yes *Library:* Yes (Open to Public)
Description: Largest organization of transportation professionals in the world; to promote, encourage & coordinate the study & advancement of the science & art of transportation in all its branches
Affiliation(s): Integrated in UK with Institute of Logistics UK section now titled Institute of Logistics & Transport

Chartered Institute of Logistics and Transport in North America (CILT) / Institut agréé de la logistique et des transports Amérique du Nord

#900, 275 Slater St., Ottawa ON K1P 5H9
Tel: 613-688-1438; *Fax:* 613-688-0966
e-mail: ghonima@ciltna.com
URL: www.ciltna.com
Also Known As: CILT in North America
Previous Name: Chartered Institute of Transport in Canada
Overview: A medium-sized international organization founded in 1919
Finances: *Funding Sources:* Membership fees
Staff: 1 staff member(s); 15 volunteer(s)
Membership: 460; *Member Profile:* Individuals with experience, interest & education in the transportation field.; *Committees:* Regional
Description: To promote, encourage, coordinate study & advancement of science & art of transportation.; *Member of:* Chartered Institute of Transport

Chatham Railroad Museum Society

PO Box 434, 2 McLean Street, Chatham ON N7M 5K5
Tel: 519-352-3097
Overview: A small local charitable organization founded in 1989
Membership: 1-99
Description: Located in a retired CN baggage car

Club de trafic de Québec

CP 72, Saint-Jean-Chrysostome QC G6Z 2L3
Tél: 418-654-5446; *Téléc:* 418-619-1044
Courriel: jcoulombe@videotron.ca
URL: www.clubtraficqc.org
Aperçu: *Dimension:* moyenne; *Envergure: provinciale; Organisme sans but lucratif; fondée en 1960*
Finances: *Budget de fonctionnement annuel:* $100,000-$250,000
Membre: 235; *Montant de la cotisation:* 75$
Description: Regrouper les représentants oeuvrant dans le domaine du transport de la grande région de Québec

The Company of Master Mariners of Canada

c/o Tom Kearsey, 5 Averill St., Dartmouth NS B3A 2H1
e-mail: postmaser@mastermariners-capital.ca
URL: www.mastermariners.ca
Overview: A medium-sized national organization founded in 1967
Finances: *Funding Sources:* Membership dues
Membership: 520; *Fees:* $70-$140; *Member Profile:* Master Mariners
Activities: *Speaker Service:* Yes
Description: To further the efficiency of the Sea Service; to uphold the status, dignity, prestige of Master Mariners; will act as advisors on technical matters pertaining to ships & marine operations. PUBLICATIONS: From the Bridge Newsletter.
Affiliation(s): Master Mariner organizations in the UK, USA, South Africa, Australia & NZ

Dewdney-Alouette Railway Society (DARS)

22520 - 116 Ave., Maple Ridge BC V2X 0S4
Tel: 604-463-5311
e-mail: ras1@uniserve.com
Overview: A small local organization founded in 1979
Finances: *Annual Operating Budget:* Less than $50,000
Staff: 25 volunteer(s)
Membership: 2 senior/lifetime + 27 individual; *Fees:* $30; *Member Profile:* 20 hour apprenticeship
Activities: *Library:* Yes
Description: To preserve railway history of Maple Ridge; to foster, promote, stimulate & encourage arts & crafts of railroading; to educate persons engaged in model railroading, building & operating in a prototypical manner
Affiliation(s): National Model Railway Association; Pacific Northwest Region 7th Division Society; BC Heritage Society; Maple Ridge Historical Society; Maple Ridge Museum

Edmonton Radial Railway Society

PO Box 45040, Stn. Lansdowne, Edmonton AB T6H 5Y1
Tel: 780-437-7721; *Fax:* 780-457-9315
e-mail: info@edmonton-radial-railway.ab.ca
URL: www.edmonton-radial-railway.ab.ca
Overview: A small national charitable organization founded in 1979
Finances: *Annual Operating Budget:* $50,000-$100,000
Staff: 100 volunteer(s)
Membership: 100; *Fees:* $20
Activities: Operates two street railway systems within Edmonton from May to Oct.; *Library:* Yes
Description: To collect, preserve, restore, & operate vintage streetcars, primarily those from 1908-1951; *Member of:* Canadian Museum Association
Affiliation(s): Association of Railway Museums; Alberta Museums Association

Electric Vehicle Council of Ottawa Inc. (EVCO)

PO Box 4044, Stn. E, Ottawa ON K1S 5B1
e-mail: info@evco.ca
URL: www.evco.ca
Overview: A small local organization founded in 1980
Finances: *Annual Operating Budget:* Less than $50,000; *Funding Sources:* Memberships
Membership: 80; *Fees:* $5 student; $25 electronic; $30 paper
Description: To provide information about electric road vehicles, in Canada & worldwide

Electric Vehicle Society of Canada (EVS)

21 Burritt Rd., Toronto ON M1R 3S5
Tel: 416-755-4324; *Fax:* 416-755-4324
e-mail: info@evsociety.ca
URL: www.evsociety.ca
Overview: A medium-sized national organization
Member Profile: Engineers; Environmentalists; Enthusiasts for electric energy for propulsion
Activities: Providing a forum for member discussions; Examining modes of electric transportation; Encouraging electric vehicle conversions in high schools;
Description: To investigate & promote clean transportation technologies

Freight Carriers Association of Canada (FCA)

#3-4, 427 Garrison Rd., Fort Erie ON L2A 6E6
Tel: 905-994-0560; *Fax:* 905-994-0117
Toll-Free: 800-559-7421
e-mail: info@fca-natc.org
URL: www.fca-natc.org
Previous Name: Canadian Transport Tariff Bureau Association
Overview: A medium-sized national organization founded in 1939
Finances: *Annual Operating Budget:* $1.5 Million-$3 Million; *Funding Sources:* Membership fees; sales of publications & software
Staff: 17 staff member(s)
Membership: 100; *Fees:* Based on revenues; *Member Profile:* For-hire motor carriers; *Committees:* Tariff Advisory; Québec Comité Consultatif
Activities: Carrier meetings; seminars; research; info gathering & dissemination; *Speaker Service:* Yes
Description: To provide quality information, products & services to users, providers & third parties involved in motor carrier transportation. PUBLICATIONS: Fuel Price and Surcharge Information Bulletin (weekly); Currency Exchange Bulletin (2X/month -14th and last day of the month).
Affiliation(s): North American Transportation Council

Hope Air / Vols d'espoir

Procter & Gamble Bldg., #703, 4711 Yonge St., Toronto ON M2N 6K8
Tel: 416-222-6335; *Fax:* 416-222-6930
Toll-Free: 877-346-4673
e-mail: mail@hopeair.org
URL: www.hopeair.org
Previous Name: Mission Air Transportation Network
Overview: A small national charitable organization founded in 1985
Finances: *Annual Operating Budget:* $250,000-$500,000; *Funding Sources:* Corporate; private donations; government
Staff: 4 staff member(s); 30 volunteer(s)
Membership: 1-99; *Committees:* Air Coordination; Funding; Finance; Office Administrations; Planning; Public Relations
Description: To provide free air transportation to Canadians in financial need who must travel between their own communities & recognized facilities for medical care

Huntsville & Lake of Bays Railway Society

26 Centre St. North, Huntsville ON P1H 1X4
Tel: 705-635-2227; *Fax:* 705-635-2227
e-mail: nicholls@vianet.ca
URL: www.portageflyer.org
Also Known As: The Portage Railway
Overview: A small local charitable organization founded in 1984
Finances: *Annual Operating Budget:* Less than $50,000; *Funding Sources:* Fundraising; Rotary Club; local industry; donations
Staff: 15 volunteer(s)
Membership: 145; *Fees:* $35
Activities: A fully functional operating railway;
Description: Maintains & displays original artifacts of the old Huntsville & Lake of Bays Railway, plus vintage railway equipment of the turn of the century
Affiliation(s): Muskoka Heritage Place

Industrial Truck Association (ITA)

#460, 1750 K St. NW, Washington DC 20006 USA
Tel: 202-296-9880; *Fax:* 202-296-9884
URL: www.indtrk.org
Overview: A medium-sized international organization
Finances: *Annual Operating Budget:* $1.5 Million-$3 Million
Staff: 5 staff member(s)
Membership: 100; *Fees:* Varies; *Member Profile:* Manufacturers of forklifts & suppliers
Description: Represents the manufacturers of lift trucks & their suppliers who do business in Canada, the United States or Mexico

INFORM Inc.

5 Hanover Square, 19th Floor, New York NY 10004 USA
Tel: 212-361-2400; *Fax:* 212-361-2412
e-mail: inform@informinc.org
URL: www.informinc.org
Overview: A medium-sized international charitable organization founded in 1974
Finances: *Annual Operating Budget:* $1.5 Million-$3 Million; *Funding Sources:* Individual donors; foundations; government; corporate contributions; book sales
Staff: 25 staff member(s); 5-10 volunteer(s)
Membership: 1,000; *Fees:* $35
Activities: Research currently focuses on strategies to prevent chemical hazards, to develop sustainable products & practices; *Internships:* Yes; *Speaker Service:* Yes
Description: Examines the effects of business practices on the environment & human health; our goal is to identify ways of doing business that ensure environmentally sustainable economic growth; *Member of:* Earthshare

Intermodal Association of North America (IANA)

#1100, 11785 Beltsville Dr., Calverton MD 20705 USA
Tel: 301-982-3400; *Fax:* 301-982-4815
e-mail: iana@intermodal.org
URL: www.intermodal.org
Overview: A medium-sized international organization founded in 1991
Finances: *Annual Operating Budget:* $3 Million-$5 Million
Staff: 21 staff member(s)
Membership: 700; *Committees:* Conference Planning; Education & Training; Electronic Business Solutions; Maintenance & Repair, Operations & P.R.

Description: IANA is the leading industry trade association representing the combined interests of intermodal freight transportation companies & their suppliers

International Air Transport Association / Association du transport aérien international
800, Place Victoria, CP 113, Montréal QC H4Z 1M1
Tel: 514-874-0202; *Fax:* 514-874-9632
URL: www.iata.org

Overview: A small international organization founded in 1945
Description: To promote safe, regular & economical air transport for the benefit of the peoples of the world; to foster air commerce; to study the problems connected with air transport; to provide a means for collaboration among the air transport enterprises engaged directly or indirectly in international air transport service; to cooperate with the International Civil Aviation Organization & other international organizations; to furnish for governments a forum for developing industry working standards &, as appropriate, coordinating international fares & rates; to simplify the travelling process for the general public
Affiliation(s): International Civil Aviation Organization

International Association of Ports & Harbours (IAPH)
7F South Tower, New Pier Takeshiba, 1-16-1 Kaigan, Minato-Ku, Tokyo 105-0022 Japan
Tel: 81-3-5403-2770; *Fax:* 81-3-5403-7651
e-mail: info@iaphworldports.org
URL: www.iaphworldports.org

Overview: A large international organization founded in 1955
Finances: *Annual Operating Budget:* $1.5 Million-$3 Million; *Funding Sources:* Membership fees
Staff: 7 staff member(s)
Membership: 360; *Fees:* Schedule available; *Member Profile:* 90 maritime countries are represented; *Committees:* Finance, Constitution & By-Laws; Long Range Planning/Review; Port Safety, Environment & Marine Operations; Dredging Task Force; Legal Protection; Trade Facilitation; Cargo Operations; Ship Trends; Combined Transport & Distribution; Port Planning & Construction; Trade Policy; Membership; Communication & Networking; Human Resources Development
Activities: *Library:* Yes (Open to Public)
Description: To promote the development of the international port & maritime industry by fostering cooperation among members in order to build a more cohesive partnership among the world's ports & harbors, thereby promoting peace in the world & the welfare of mankind; to ensure that the industry's interests & views are represented before international organizations involved n the regulation of international trade & transportation & incorporated in the regulatory initiatives of these organizations; & to collect, analyse, exchange & distribute information on developing trends in international trade, transportation, ports & the regulations of these industries
Affiliation(s): International Maritime Organization; United Nations Conference on Trade & Development; United Nations Economic & Social Council; Permanent International Association of Navigation Congresses; International Cargo Handling Coordination Association; International Maritime Pilots Association; International Association of Independent Tanker Owners; Baltic & International Martime Council

International Industry Working Group (IIWG)
International Air Transport Association, PO Box 113, 800, Place Victoria, Montréal QC H4Z 1M1
Tel: 514-874-0202; *Fax:* 514-874-9632
e-mail: obrienm@iata.org
URL: www.iata.org

Overview: A small international organization founded in 1970
Membership: 50; *Member Profile:* Aircraft & aeroengine manufacturers; airlines & airport authorities
Description: To promote & develop an open exchange of information to minimize interface problems through well-informed design, development & operation of both aircraft & airports; to study jointly solutions to major problems which impede the development of the air transport system

International Maritime Organization (IMO) / Organisation maritime internationale
4 Albert Embankment, London SE1 7SR United Kingdom
Tel: 44-20-7735-7611; *Fax:* 44-20-7587-3210
e-mail: info@imo.org
URL: www.imo.org

Overview: A large international organization founded in 1948
Finances: *Annual Operating Budget:* Greater than $5 Million; *Funding Sources:* Government
Staff: 300 staff member(s)
Membership: 166 governments; *Fees:* Based on shipping fleet tonnage; *Committees:* Maritime Safety; Marine Environment Protection; Legal; Technical Cooperation; Facilitation
Activities: *Library:* Yes by appointment
Description: To encourage the adoption of high standards in matters concerning maritime safety, security, efficiency of navigation & control of marine pollution from ships

Locomotive & Railway Historical Society of Western Canada
#4104, 2120 Southland Dr. SW, Calgary AB T2V 4W3
Tel: 403-265-9229; *Fax:* 403-261-1057
e-mail: laniganj@telus.net

Overview: A small local charitable organization founded in 1985
Finances: *Annual Operating Budget:* Less than $50,000
Staff: 9 volunteer(s)
Membership: 9
Activities: Preservation & restoration of important historic Canadian railway equipment; *Speaker Service:* Yes
Description: To promote the preservation of railway equipment integral to the history of Western Canada; to act in a consultative capacity on heritage rail projects; *Member of:* Canadian Council for Railway Heritage

Manitoba Trucking Association
25 Bunting St., Winnipeg MB R2X 2P5
Tel: 204-632-6600; *Fax:* 204-694-7134
e-mail: info@trucking.mb.ca
URL: www.trucking.mb.ca

Overview: A medium-sized provincial organization founded in 1932
Finances: *Funding Sources:* Membership dues & fundraising through services
Staff: 5 staff member(s)
Membership: 350 organizations; *Member Profile:* PSV Carriers; City Transportation; Private Fleet; Household Goods Carriers; Associated Trades; Vehicle Maintenance; *Committees:* Associated Trades (Members, Executive); Vehicle Maintenance Council; Maintenace Council Executive
Activities: *Library:* Yes by appointment
Description: Serves the needs of the trucking industry & its interested parties by promoting a healthy business environment & advocating safety, education, & responsibility.
Affiliation(s): Canadian Trucking Alliance; Canadian Council of Motor Transport Administrators; Canadian Trucking Human Resource Council; Winnipeg Chamber of Commerce; Manitoba Chamber of Commerce; Infrastructure Council of Manitoba; Employers' Task Force on Workers' Compensation; Manitoba Employers' Council

Motorcycle & Moped Industry Council (MMIC) / Le Conseil de l'industrie de la motocyclette et du cyclomoteur (CIMC)
#100, 716 Gordon Baker Rd., Toronto ON M2H 3B4
Tel: 416-491-4449; *Fax:* 416-493-1985
Toll-Free: 877-470-6642
e-mail: info@mmic.ca
URL: www.mmic.ca

Overview: A small national organization founded in 1971
Finances: *Annual Operating Budget:* $500,000-$1.5 Million
Staff: 2 staff member(s); 15 volunteer(s)
Membership: 150 corporate; 500 individual; *Fees:* Schedule available

National Association of Railroad Passengers (NARP)
#308, 900 - 2 St. NE, Washington DC 20002-3557 USA
Tel: 202-408-8362; *Fax:* 202-408-8287
e-mail: narp@narprail.org
URL: www.narprail.org

Overview: A medium-sized international charitable organization founded in 1967
Finances: *Annual Operating Budget:* $250,000-$500,000; *Funding Sources:* Membership dues
Staff: 4 staff member(s)
Membership: 23,000; *Fees:* $35 individual; $45 family; $25 senior
Activities: *Rents Mailing List:* Yes *Library:* Yes (Open to Public)
Description: To encourage & promote a more balanced US transporation system including promotion of federal & state policies beneficial to all forms of rail service, urban rail transit, rural public transporation & intermodal terminals
Affiliation(s): Transport 2000 Ltd.

National Transportation Brokers Association
PO Box 238, Markham ON L3P 3J7
Tel: 416-798-7211
e-mail: info@ntba-brokers.com
URL: www.ntba-brokers.com

Overview: A medium-sized national organization
Fees: $200; *Member Profile:* Freight brokerage services providers
Description: Promotes and continually improves business relationships among shippers, carriers, government and freight brokers

New Brunswick Potato Shippers Association
8824 Route 2, Grand-Sault/Grand Falls NB E3Z 1P8
Tel: 506-473-5520; *Fax:* 506-473-6701
e-mail: tatered@nbnet.nb.ca

Overview: A small provincial organization
Description: The shippers association monitors industry growth

The Ninety-Nines Inc./International Organization of Women Pilots
4300 Amelia Earhart Rd., Oklahoma City OK 73159 USA
Tel: 405-685-7969; *Fax:* 405-685-7985
Toll-Free: 800-994-1929
e-mail: 99s@ninety-nines.org
URL: www.ninety-nines.org

Also Known As: 99's
Overview: A small international charitable organization founded in 1929
Finances: *Annual Operating Budget:* $250,000-$500,000
Staff: 4 staff member(s); 4 volunteer(s)
Membership: 5,400 worldwide; *Fees:* US$65 for US; US$57 Canadian; US$44 other countries; *Member Profile:* Women pilots
Activities: *Speaker Service:* Yes *Library:* 99s Museum of Women Pilots
Description: To promote world fellowship through flight; to provide networking & scholarship opportunities for women & aviation education in the community; to preserve the unique history of women in aviation

North America Railway Hall of Fame
RPO Centre, PO Box 20040, St Thomas ON N5P 4H4
Tel: 519-633-2535; *Fax:* 519-633-3087
e-mail: info@narhf.org
URL: www.narhf.org

Overview: A small national charitable organization founded in 1996
Description: To establish a tribute to those who have made significant contributions relating to the railway industry in North America; honour railway organizations, related innovations & technical accomplishments; preserve & display a collection of library materials & railway heritage artifacts related to the Hall of Fame inductees; to educate the public about the impact of railway transportation on history & the development of communities, nations & international relations

Northern Air Transport Association (NATA)
PO Box 2457, Yellowknife NT X1A 2P8
Tel: 867-920-2985; *Fax:* 867-920-2983
e-mail: nata-yzf@theedge.ca
URL: www.nata-yzf.ca

Overview: A small local organization founded in 1977
Member Profile: Northern air carriers
Activities: Advocating for Northern air transport; Establishing partnerships with governments & within the transportation industry; *Speaker Service:* Yes
Description: To promote safe & effective Northern air transportation

Northwestern Ontario Air Carriers Association (NOACA)
PO Box 4075, 143 Cedar Point Dr., Sioux Lookout ON P8T 1J9
Tel: 807-737-7470; *Fax:* 807-583-2812

Overview: A small local organization

Ontario Community Transit Association (OCTA)
#306, 4141 Yonge St., Toronto ON M2P 2A8
Tel: 416-229-6222; *Fax:* 416-229-6281
URL: www.octa.on.ca

Previous Name: Ontario Urban Transit Association
Overview: A medium-sized provincial organization founded in 1997
Fees: Annual fees for transportation service providers & suppliers based on transportation operating budget or net sales; $160 non-profit organizations; *Member Profile:* Representatives of public transit systems; Health & social service agency transportation providers; Government representatives; Suppliers to the industry; Consultants
Activities: Engaging in advocacy activities; Sharing information;
Description: To strengthen & improve public transit services in Ontario; To ensure excellence & sustainability in public transit

Ontario Good Roads Association (OGRA)
#2, 6355 Kennedy Rd., Mississauga ON L5T 2L5
Tel: 905-795-2555; *Fax:* 905-795-2660
e-mail: info@ogra.org
URL: www.ogra.org

Overview: A medium-sized provincial organization founded in 1894
Finances: *Funding Sources:* Membership fees; Sponsorships
Membership: 445 Ontario municipalities; *Member Profile:* Ontario municipalities; First Nations communities; Corporations; *Committees:* Executive; Policy; Member Services; Nominating; Combined Conference; Companions Program
Activities: Advocating for the collective interests of municipal transportation & works departments; Analyzing policies;

Reviewing legislation Consulting with stakeholders & partners; Offering education & training opportunities;
Description: To represent the transportation & public works-related interests of Ontario's municipalities & First Nation communities; To deliver programs & services that meet the needs of members; To support municipalities in the provision of effective & efficient transportation systems throughout Ontario

Ontario Milk Transport Association (OMTA)
#301, 660 Speedvale Ave. West, Guelph ON N1K 1E5
Overview: A medium-sized provincial organization founded in 1967
Membership: 60 companies; *Member Profile:* Transporters of milk, such as producer-owned co-operatives, which collect raw milk from Ontario farms & take it to processing plants in Ontario, Quebec, & Manitoba

Ontario Traffic Conference (OTC)
#2, 6355 Kennedy Rd., Mississauga ON L5T 2L5
Tel: 647-346-4050; *Fax:* 647-346-4060
e-mail: info@otc.org
URL: www.otc.org
Overview: A medium-sized provincial organization
Description: To improve traffic conditions & traffic safety in municipalities of Ontario

Ontario Trucking Association (OTA)
555 Dixon Rd., Toronto ON M9W 1H8
Tel: 416-249-7401; *Fax:* 416-245-6152
e-mail: info@ontruck.org
URL: www.ontruck.org
Overview: A large provincial organization founded in 1926
Finances: *Funding Sources:* Membership fees
Membership: 1,700 member companies; *Committees:* Axle Weight; Credit; Education; Executive; Social/Labour; Tech./Ops; Convention; Dues; Membership; Insurance; Finance; Environmental Issues
Activities: Drug Testing Consortium; training courses & seminars; Trucking Industry Compensation & Benefits Report; *Speaker Service:* Yes *Library:* Yes
Description: Canada's largest trade association representing companies & industry suppliers; provides political advocacy, education & information services to North American freight transport companies with operations in Ontario.

Ontario Trucking Association Education Foundation Inc.
555 Dixon Rd., Toronto ON M9W 1H8
Tel: 416-249-7401; *Fax:* 416-245-6152
e-mail: education.foundation@ontruck.org
Overview: A small provincial charitable organization
Finances: *Annual Operating Budget:* Less than $50,000
Staff: 1 staff member(s); 5 volunteer(s)
Membership: 18

Operation Lifesaver (OL) / Opération Gareautrain
#1401, 99 Bank St., Ottawa ON K1P 6B9
Tel: 613-564-8100; *Fax:* 613-567-6726
e-mail: admin@operationlifesaver.ca
URL: www.operationlifesaver.ca
Overview: A small national organization founded in 1981
Finances: *Annual Operating Budget:* $250,000-$500,000; *Funding Sources:* Transport Canada; Railway Association of Canada
Staff: 2 staff member(s); 150 volunteer(s)
Activities: *Awareness Events:* OL Rail Safety Week, April
Description: To create an awareness by the general public of the potential hazards of rail/highway crossings; to improve drivers' & pedestrians' behaviour at these intersections; to inform the public of the dangers associated with trespassing on railway property; & to reduce the number of accidents resulting in fatalities, injuries & monetary losses

Pharmaceutical & Personal Care Logistics Association (PPCLA) / Association de logistique des soins personnels et pharmaceutiques
PO Box 40598, Stn. Six Points Plaza, Toronto ON M9B 6K8
Tel: 416-232-6817; *Fax:* 416-232-6818
Toll-Free: 866-293-1238
e-mail: ppcla@ppcla.org
URL: www.ppcla.org
Previous Name: Pharmaceutical & Toilet Preparations Traffic Association
Overview: A medium-sized national organization founded in 1958
Finances: *Annual Operating Budget:* Less than $50,000
Staff: 1 volunteer(s)
Membership: 47 institutional; *Fees:* $350; *Member Profile:* Logistics managers in the pharmaceutical & personal care industries
Description: To develop & promote the interchange of ideas & information concerning traffic & transportation matters of the pharmaceutical & toilet preparations industry; to foster fair dealings & cordial relationships among members & between representatives of the various modes of transportation employed by members

Private Motor Truck Council of Canada (PMTC) / Association canadienne du camionnage d'entreprise (ACCE)
#11, 1155 North Service Rd. West, Oakville ON L6M 3E3
Tel: 905-827-0587; *Fax:* 905-827-8212
Toll-Free: 877-501-7682
e-mail: info@pmtc.ca
URL: www.pmtc.ca
Overview: A medium-sized national organization founded in 1977
Finances: *Annual Operating Budget:* $250,000-$500,000; *Funding Sources:* Seminars; social events; membership fees
Staff: 4 staff member(s)
Membership: 400; *Member Profile:* Private truck fleets or suppliers to same; private truck fleets operated by companies whose principal business is other than transportation, but that use their own truck fleets to further their business
Activities: Seminars; annual conference; topical seminars; National Vehicle Graphics Design Competition
Description: Is recognized as the leader of the private trucking community; represents the varied interests of that community with integrity & sound business practices. PUBLICATIONS: The Counsellor, Quaterly News Magazine, News Briefs Newsletter.; *Member of:* North American Private Truck Council
Affiliation(s): National Private Truck Council

The Railway Association of Canada (RAC) / L'Association des chemins de fer du Canada (ACFC)
#901, 99 Bank St., Ottawa ON K1P 6B9
Tel: 613-567-8591; *Fax:* 613-567-6726
e-mail: rac@railcan.ca
URL: www.railcan.ca
Overview: A large national organization founded in 1917
Finances: *Annual Operating Budget:* Greater than $5 Million; *Funding Sources:* Members fees
Staff: 23 staff member(s)
Membership: 55 railways & 40 associates; *Fees:* $2,000 minimum; *Member Profile:* Railway companies operating in Canada; *Committees:* Policy; Accounting; Finance; Human Resources; Safety & Operations Management; Taxation
Activities: Operation Lifesaver;
Description: To promote the commercial viability & the safe & efficient operation of the Canadian railway industry; to act on behalf of, or work jointly with, member companies to promote public policy & regulation that provides equitable treatment between shipping modes; to provide factual information on the railway industry for the public, government & industry, & to provide the views of the industry on public policy issues. PUBLICATIONS: Interchange; Canadian Railway Medical Rules Handbook; Locomotive Emissions Monitoring Program 2009; Canada's Railway Lead North America.
Affiliation(s): Association of American Railroads

Recreational Aircraft Association (RAA) / Réseau aéronefs amateur
Brampton Airport, RR#1, Cheltenham ON L0P 1C0
Tel: 905-838-1357; *Fax:* 905-838-1359
Toll-Free: 800-387-1028
e-mail: raa@zing-net.ca
URL: www.raa.ca
Previous Name: Experimental Aircraft Association of Canada
Overview: A medium-sized national organization founded in 1983
Finances: *Annual Operating Budget:* $100,000-$250,000; *Funding Sources:* Membership dues
Staff: 1 staff member(s); 150 volunteer(s)
Membership: 2,000; *Fees:* $40; *Committees:* 12 regional
Activities: Fly-ins across Canada; *Speaker Service:* Yes
Description: To be a national leader in the development & advancement of recreational aviation; to promote recreational flying & building of amateur built aircraft, restorations of classic & antique aircraft
Affiliation(s): Recreational Aviation Foundation

Saskatchewan Trucking Association (STA)
1335 Wallace St., Regina SK S4N 3Z5
Tel: 306-955-7833; *Fax:* 306-569-1008
Toll-Free: 800-563-7623
e-mail: sta@sasktrucking.com
URL: www.sasktrucking.com
Overview: A medium-sized provincial licensing organization founded in 1937
Finances: *Annual Operating Budget:* $250,000-$500,000; *Funding Sources:* Membership fees; sponsorship of programs
Staff: 8 staff member(s)
Membership: 300
Activities: Truck Driver Roadeos;
Description: Helps the industry fight its battles in everything from deregulation to weights and measures. Represents the industry in discussions with government

The Shipping Federation of Canada / La Fédération maritime du Canada
#326, 300, rue St-Sacrement, Montréal QC H2Y 1X4
Tel: 514-849-2325; *Fax:* 514-849-8774
Toll-Free: 877-534-7367
e-mail: info@shipfed.ca
URL: www.shipfed.ca
Overview: A medium-sized national organization founded in 1903
Finances: *Funding Sources:* International shipping
Staff: 8 staff member(s)
Membership: 83; *Member Profile:* Direct involvement in steamship business; *Committees:* Customs; Dangerous Goods; EDI; Immigration; Pilotage; Railways; Tanker Safety
Activities: To protect members in all matters affecting the operation of shipping from & to Eastern Canada, the St. Lawrence River, the Great Lakes & Arctic ports; areas of concern include pilotage, pollution, navigation aids, port operations, port charges, & federal government legislation & regulation;

Shipyard General Workers' Federation of British Columbia (CLC) / Fédération des ouvriers des chantiers navals de la Colombie-Britannique (CTC)
#130, 111 Victoria Dr., Vancouver BC V5L 4C4
Tel: 604-254-8204; *Fax:* 604-254-7447
e-mail: office@bcshipyardworkers.com
URL: www.bcshipyardworkers.com
Overview: A medium-sized provincial organization
Membership: 1,100 + 3 locals
Affiliation(s): Machinists, Fitters & Helpers Industrial Union #3, Marine Workers & Boilerworkers' Industrial Union #1, Shipwrights, Joiners & Caulkers' Industrial Union #9

Société des traversiers du Québec (STQ)
250, rue Saint-Paul, Québec QC G1K 9K9
Tél: 418-643-2019; *Téléc:* 418-643-7308
Ligne sans frais: 877-787-7483
Courriel: stq@traversiers.gouv.qc.ca
URL: www.traversiers.gouv.qc.ca
Aperçu: *Dimension:* petite; *Envergure: provinciale; fondée en 1971*
Finances: *Budget de fonctionnement annuel:* Plus de $5 Million
Membre: 100-499
Description: Contribuer à la mobilité des personnes et des marchandises en assurant des services de transport maritime de qualité, sécuritaires et fiables, favorisant ainsi l'essor social, économique et touristique du Québec

Sydney & Louisburg Railway Historical Society / Le Musée de chemin de fer de Sydney à Louisburg
7330 Main St., Louisbourg NS B1C 1P5
Also Known As: S&L Museum
Overview: A small local organization founded in 1973
Finances: *Annual Operating Budget:* Less than $50,000
Staff: 6 volunteer(s)
Membership: 210; *Fees:* $10
Activities: Annual reunion, Sept.; *Awareness Events:* Samuel B. Morse - Museum Day, July 1 *Library:* Resource Centre (Open to Public) by appointment
Description: To commemorate the history of the S&L Railway by preserving & displaying the artifacts & documents which survive; to commemorate the people who worked for the S&L Railway; to explain the local & commercial history of the area which relates to the S&L Railway; to explain & commemorate the general themes of railway & transportation history & technology; *Member of:* Federation of the Nova Scotian Heritage; Heritage Canada

Teamsters Canada Rail Conference (TCRC) / Conference ferroviaire de Teamsters Canada (CFTC)
#1710, 130 Albert St., Ottawa ON K1P 5G4
Tel: 613-235-1828; *Fax:* 613-235-1069
e-mail: info@teamstersrail.ca
URL: www.teamstersrail.ca
Previous Name: Brotherhood of Locomotive Engineers
Overview: A medium-sized national organization
Membership: 16,000 in 21 divisions; *Fees:* $15
Activities: *Library:* Yes (Open to Public)

Toronto Transportation Society (TTS)
PO Box 5187, Stn. A, Toronto ON M5W 1N5
e-mail: ttswebmaster@torontotransportationsociety.org
URL: www.torontotransportationsociety.org
Overview: A small local organization founded in 1973
Finances: *Funding Sources:* Membership dues
Staff: 7 volunteer(s)

Membership: 131; *Fees:* $20; *Committees:* Executive; Trips & Excursions
Activities: *Library:* Yes
Description: To afford persons interested in transportation by land, facilities for discussion & exchange of information

Transport Action Canada
Bronson Centre, PO Box 858, Stn. B, #303, 211 Bronson Ave., Ottawa ON K1P 5P9
Tel: 613-594-3290; *Fax:* 613-594-3271
e-mail: info@transport-action.ca
URL: www.transport-action.ca
Previous Name: Transport 2000 Canada
Overview: A medium-sized national charitable organization founded in 1976
Finances: *Annual Operating Budget:* $50,000-$100,000; *Funding Sources:* Donations
Staff: 15 volunteer(s)
Membership: 1,500; *Fees:* $35 regular; $30 senior; $50 family; $75 affiliate non-profit; $170corporate
Activities: Research, public education & advocacy, representation of the consumer interests before federal, provincial, municipal public hearings & regulatory bodies, direction of consumer complaints to public carriers; *Speaker Service:* Yes *Library:* Yes (Open to Public)
Description: National federation of environmental & consumer groups concerned about the importance of transportation on our environment & quality of life; to inform Canadians of the need for a coherent national transport policy which recognizes that conservation of resources must be a priority & that access to good public transportation is a right of all Canadians; to work for the improvement & greater use of bus & rail transportation in the interests of public safety, social equity & the protection of the environment; to press for the coordination of all transport services for the benefit of users; to demand more attention to the needs of pedestrians, cyclists & public transport users; to maximize the use of the energy-efficient rail & marine modes for the shipment of freight. PUBLICATIONS: National Transport Newsletter.
Affiliation(s): Transport 2000 International

Transportation Association of Canada (TAC) / Association des transports du Canada (ATC)
2323 St. Laurent Blvd., Ottawa ON K1G 4J8
Tel: 613-736-1350; *Fax:* 613-736-1395
e-mail: secretariat@tac-atc.ca
URL: www.tac-atc.ca
Previous Name: Roads & Transportation Association of Canada
Overview: A large national organization founded in 1970
Finances: *Annual Operating Budget:* Greater than $5 Million
Staff: 30 staff member(s); 500 volunteer(s)
Membership: 550 corporate; *Fees:* Schedule available; *Committees:* Technical & Research; Editing & Publications; Rules of the Road; Project; Technical Steering; Asphalts Advisory; Operations; Pavements; Structures; Aviation; Conference Technical Program; Geometric Design; Goods Movement; Soils & Materials; Traffic; Transit Planning; Technology
Activities: *Library:* Technical Information Centre by appointment
Description: To promote the provision of safe, efficient, effective & environmentally sustainable transportation services in support of Canada's social & economic goals; to act as a neutral forum for the discussion of transportation issues & matters; to act as a technical focus in the highway transportation area. PUBLICATIONS: TAC News.

Transportation Health & Safety Association of Ontario (THSAO)
#101, 555 Dixon Rd., Toronto ON M9W 1H8
Tel: 416-242-4771; *Fax:* 416-242-4714
Toll-Free: 800-263-5016
e-mail: info@thsao.on.ca
URL: www.thsao.on.ca
Previous Name: Transportation Safety Association of Ontario
Overview: A large provincial organization founded in 1942
Finances: *Annual Operating Budget:* $1.5 Million-$3 Million; *Funding Sources:* Workers' Compensation Board
Staff: 23 staff member(s); 425 volunteer(s)
Membership: 15,000-49,999
Activities: *Speaker Service:* Yes *Library:* Film & Video Library (Open to Public)
Description: To educate employers & employees on the work of accident & occupational illness prevention in industries covered under Class 20 of WCB Act

Truck Training Schools Association of Ontario Inc. (TTSAO)
Fax: 519-858-0920
Toll-Free: 866-475-9436
e-mail: training@ttsao.com
URL: www.ttsao.com
Overview: A small national licensing organization founded in 1992
Finances: *Annual Operating Budget:* $100,000-$250,000
Staff: 7 staff member(s)
Membership: 75; *Fees:* Schedule available
Activities: *Internships:* Yes
Description: To provide the trucking industry with the highest quality driver training programs for entry level individuals that earn & maintain public confidence, adhering to sound & ethical business practices
Affiliation(s): Ontario Trucking Association; Ministry of Education, Ministry of Transportation

Truckers Association of Nova Scotia
PO Box 1527, 184 Arthur St., Truro NS B2N 5V2
Tel: 902-895-7447; *Fax:* 902-897-0487
Toll-Free: 800-232-6631
e-mail: contact@tans.ca
URL: www.tans.ca
Overview: A medium-sized provincial organization founded in 1968
Description: Promotes all matters aiding the development and improvement of the trucking industry and the allied trades in Nova Scotia, including social, recreational, benevolent, educational and charitable activities. In addition, the Truckers Association of Nova Scotia makes presentations to government and other regulatory bodies in relation to the economic welfare of the trucking industry and is the main proponent in gaining access to the provincial haul rates and beneficial changes to the contract specifications used by the contractors

Ultralight Pilots Association of Canada (UPAC) / Association canadienne des pilotes d'avions ultra-légers
907289 Township Road 12, RR#4, Bright ON N0J 1B0
Tel: 519-684-7628
URL: www.upac.ca
Overview: A small national organization
Finances: *Annual Operating Budget:* Less than $50,000; *Funding Sources:* Membership fees
Staff: 10 volunteer(s)
Membership: 500+; *Fees:* $40; *Member Profile:* Interest in ultralight aviaton
Activities: Video library for members; *Library:* Video Library (Open to Public)
Description: To promote ultralight aviation in Canada

Union of Canadian Transportation Employees (UCTE) / Union canadienne des employés des transports (UCET)
#702, 233 Gilmour St., Ottawa ON K2P 0P2
Tel: 613-238-4003; *Fax:* 613-236-0379
e-mail: ucte_webmaster@psac.com
URL: www.ucte.com
Overview: A medium-sized national organization
Membership: 7,500 + 90 locals
Description: The Union represents members working in the public & private sectors of the Canadian transportation industry (ports, airports, NAV Canada, pilotage authorities, transportation companies, canals, the Dept. of Transport, lighthouses, ships and Canadian Coast Guard bases)

United Transportation Union (AFL-CIO/CLC) - Canada
71 Bank St., 7th Fl., Ottawa ON K1P 5N2
Tel: 613-747-7979; *Fax:* 613-747-2815
Overview: A medium-sized national organization
Membership: 8,500 + 79 locals
Member of: United Transportation Union (AFL-CIO/CLC), Cleveland USA

University of Toronto Institute for Aerospace Studies
Faculty of Applied Science & Engineering, 4925 Dufferin St., Toronto ON M3H 5T6
Tel: 416-667-7700; *Fax:* 416-667-7799
e-mail: info@utias.utoronto.ca
URL: www.utias.utoronto.ca
Overview: A medium-sized national organization founded in 1949
Membership: 68
Activities: *Library:* Yes
Description: UTIAS is a graduate studies and research institute, forming part of the faculty of Applied Science and Engineering at the University of Toronto.
Affiliation(s): Canadian Aeronautics & Space Institute; Institute for Space & Terrestrial Science; Canadian Space Agency; Intelligent Sensing for Innovative Structures Canada

Upper Canada Railway Society
PO Box 122, Stn. A, Toronto ON M5W 1A2
Tel: 416-921-4023
e-mail: ucrs@btinternet.com
Overview: A small national organization founded in 1941
Membership: 600; *Fees:* $29
Description: To work to preserve history & railways of Canada; *Member of:* Community Heritage Project

The Van Horne Institute for International Transportation & Regulatory Affairs
#620 Earth Sciences Bldg., 2500 University Dr. NW, Calgary AB T2N 1N4
Tel: 403-220-8455; *Fax:* 403-282-4663
e-mail: vanhorne@ucalgary.ca
URL: www.vanhorne.info/
Overview: A small international organization founded in 1991
Finances: *Annual Operating Budget:* Less than $50,000; *Funding Sources:* Private sector
Staff: 4 staff member(s)
Membership: 60; *Member Profile:* Government; industry; education; *Committees:* Centre for Transportation; Centre for Regulatory Affairs; Centre for Innovation & Communication
Activities: Transporation research & education; programs to assist in improving the efficiency & equity of transportation & regulated industries; *Speaker Service:* Yes; *Rents Mailing List:* Yes *Library:* Yes (Open to Public)
Description: To contribute to public policy development & education in the areas of transportation & regulated industries. PUBLICATIONS: On-Trac.
Affiliation(s): University of Calgary; University of Alberta; Southern Alberta Institute of Technology

Vintage Locomotive Society Inc.
PO Box 33021, RPO Polo Park, Winnipeg MB R3G 3N4
Tel: 204-832-5259; *Fax:* 866-751-2348
e-mail: info@pdcrailway.com
URL: www.pdcrailway.com
Also Known As: Prairie Dog Central Steam Train
Overview: A small local charitable organization founded in 1968
Finances: *Annual Operating Budget:* $250,000-$500,000
Staff: 170 volunteer(s)
Membership: 170 individuals; *Fees:* $25 full; $15 junior; $40 family; *Committees:* Restoration-Locomotive; Restoration-Coaches; Painting; Sign Work; Public Relations; Advertising; Photography; Operations & Maintenance
Activities: *Speaker Service:* Yes
Description: To collect, restore for operation & maintain steam locomotives & rolling stock of early part of twentieth-century; to provide source of historical information relating to origin & past operation of acquired equipment & buildings

West Coast Railway Association (WCRA)
PO Box 2790, Vancouver BC V6B 3X2
Tel: 604-524-1011; *Fax:* 604-876-4104
Toll-Free: 800-722-1233
e-mail: info@wcra.org
URL: www.wcra.org
Overview: A small local charitable organization founded in 1961
Finances: *Annual Operating Budget:* $500,000-$1.5 Million; *Funding Sources:* Tours; government grants; donations; fundraising; foundation
Staff: 12 staff member(s); 150 volunteer(s)
Membership: 600 individual; *Fees:* Schedule available; *Member Profile:* Interest in railways past & present; *Committees:* Museum; Tours; Collections; Motive Power; Children; Education
Activities: Develops & operates West Coast Railway Heritage Park in Squamish B.C. - collection of over 60 locomotives, freight & passenger cars; operates tour progrm; other community event; Day out with Thoma, June; *Speaker Service:* Yes *Library:* Archives (Open to Public) by appointment
Description: Collects, preserves, restores, operates & exhibits artifacts relating to the history of railways, especially those of BC; the West Coast Railway Heritage Park in Squamish BC develops educational exhibits on railway heritage for all age groups; the tour program encourages the public to travel today's railways to see Canada; *Member of:* Association of Rail Museums; Tourist Railroad Association

Western Transportation Advisory Council (WESTAC)
#1140, 800 Pender St. West, Vancouver BC V6C 2V6
Tel: 604-687-8691; *Fax:* 604-687-8751
e-mail: infoservices@westac.com
URL: www.westac.com
Overview: A small local organization founded in 1973
Finances: *Annual Operating Budget:* $500,000-$1.5 Million; *Funding Sources:* Membership fees; project fees; professional services fees
Staff: 4 staff member(s)
Membership: 52 corporate; *Fees:* Revenue-related scale; *Member Profile:* Carriers; shippers; ports & terminals; labour unions; government
Activities: *Library:* Yes by appointment

Description: To advance Western Canadian economy through the improvement of the region's transportation system.

Companies

Airline Companies

ACE Aviation Holdings Inc.
5100, boul de Maisonneuve ouest, Montréal, QC H4A 3T2
www. aceaviation.com; www.aircanada.ca
Profile: Air Canada, Aeroplan, Jazz, and ACTS are subsidiaries of ACE Aviation.
Monte R. Brewer, President & CEO, Air Canada
Duncan Dunne, EVP/CFO
Sydney Isaacs, SVP Corporate Affairs/Cheif Administrative Officier
Greg Cote, SVP Corporate Development/Chief Legal Officer
Jack McLean, Controller

Aer Lingus
Suite 130, 300 Jericho Quadrangle, Jericho, NY 11753
516-622-4022 Fax: 516-752-2045 866-886-8844
groupsusa@aerlingus.com
www.flyaerlingus.com

Aeroflot - Russian Airlines
PO Box 61, #1908, 1 Queen St. East, Toronto, ON M5C 2C5
416-642-1653 Fax: 416-642-1658
info@aeroflotcanada.com
www.aeroflotcanada.com
Gelena Bakholdina, Marketing and advertising events
omosheva@aeroflot.ru

Aerolineas Argentinas
Rm. 1600, 51 East 42nd St., New York, NY
212-542-8880 Fax: 212-542-8881 800-333-0276
salesnyc@usaerolinesas.aero
www.aerolineas.com.ar
Vilma Castellino, Manager, Rep World

Air Canada
7373, boul de la Côte-Vertu ouest, Montréal, QC H4S 1Z3
514-422-5000 Fax: 514-422-5789
www.aircanada.ca
Ticker Symbol: AC
Profile: Scheduled air transportation; Travel agencies; Arrangement of transportation of freight & cargo
Lise Fournel, Sr. Vice-President, E-Commerce
Joseph D. Randell, President, Air Canada Jazz
Joshua Koshy, CFO & Exec. Vice-President
Duncan Dee, Sr. Vice-President, Corporate Affairs

Air Canada Jazz
c/o Halifax International Airport, 310 Goudey Dr., Enfield, NS B2T 1E4
902-873-5000 Fax: 902-873-2098
websupport@flyjazz.ca
Profile: At Jazz, their priorities include safe, efficient, and on-time operations and have over 4,300 employees. They have a fleet of 36 planes.

Air Creebec
PO Box 430, 101, 7th St., Val-d'Or, QC J9P 4P4
819-825-8355 Fax: 418-748-6030
www.aircreebec.ca
Profile: Air Creebec aims to provide safe, reliable, and efficient air transportation within Eeyou Istchee and beyond.
Albert Diamond, President

Air France
1510, 2000 rue Mansfield, Montreal, QC H3A 3A3
514-847-1106 Fax: 514-847-5013 800-667-2747
www.airfrance.ca
Jean-Cyril Spinette, Chairman and CEO
Pierre-Henri Gourgeon, President and Chief Operating Officier
Philippe Calavia, CEO
Alain Bassil, EVP- Air France Industries
Francois Brousse, SVP Corporate Communications
Pascal de Izaguirre, EVP Ground Operations
Bruno Matheu, EVP Marketing/Network Management
Bruno Matheu, EVP Marketing/Network Management
Edouard Odier, EVP Information Technology
Gilbert Rovetto, EVP Flight Operations

Air India Ltd.
#218, 5955 Airport Rd., Mississauga, ON L4V 1R9
905-405-2160 Fax: 905-405-2169 800-625-6424
yyz@airindiacanada.ca
www.airindia.com
V. Thulasidas, Chairman and Managing Director, Air India
M. Kacker, Chief Vigiliance Officer/Offg. Executive Director-Secur
Amod Sharma, Director Finance
K.M. Unni, Director Engineering
V.K. Verma, Director Commercial
Jitender Bhargava, Executive Director-Coordination
S. Ranganathan, Executive Director Ground Services
Deepak Anand, Executive Director Operations
Paul Lakra, Executive Director-Mumbai Airport
I.S. Vhatkar, General Manager Properties/Facilities

Air Nootka
PO Box 19, Gold River, BC V0P 1G0
250-283-2255 Fax: 250-283-2256
info@airnootka.com
http://www.airnootka.com/
Profile: Air Nootka takes pride in providing the best service to new and longtime customers. A floatplane operation based out of Cold River, British Columbia. They service all of Vancouver Island, including Victoria, Nanaimo, Comox, Campbell River, and Kyuquot, as well as Vancouver.

Air North Airlines
Fax: 867-393-4601
office@flyairnorth.com
www.flyairnorth.com
Profile: Frequent departures from all supported aiports; Great Value Cargo service at the price of general freight (ground service); Cargo Friendly Cargo can be taken directly to the Airport and quickly processed while you wait.

Air St-Pierre
c/o Air Saint-Pierre, PO Box 1660, 1 Bell Blvd., Enfield, NS B2T 1K2
902-873-3566 Fax: 902-873-3567
halifax@airsaintpierre.com
www.airsaintpierre.com

Air Transat
5959 Côte-Vertu Blvd., Montréal, QC H4S 2E6
514-636-3630 866-435-0011
information@airtransat.com
www.airtransat.com
Profile: Air Transat is a wholly owned subsidiary of Transat A.T. Inc. They specialize in both scheduled and charter flights from Canada to vacation destinations. In the winter months, the majority of flights are between Canada to vacation desintations. In the winter months, the majority of flights are between Canada and the Caribbean/USA and in the summer between Canada and many European countries. Year-round schedule services operate between Europe and Canada. The Air Transat fleet of 15 aircraft serves over 90 destinations in 25 countries.
Pierre Ménard, Vice-President, Operations

Alitalia
#202, 5915 Airport Rd., Mississauga, ON L4V 1T1
905-673-2442 Fax: 905-673-6089 800-268-9277
atitaliasupport@alicos.net
www.alitalia.ca
Berardino Libonati, Chairman

American Airlines Inc.
Lester B. Pearson Airport, PO Box 6005, Stn Toronto AMF, Mississauga, ON L5P 1B6
905-612-7266 Fax: 905-612-0144 800-433-7300
www.aa.com
A.W. Pliszka, General Manager, Toronto

Austrian Airlines
2085, Union St., Montréal, QC H3A 2C3
514-842-2500 Fax: 514-842-3300 888-817-4444
www.aua.com
Pierre Doueihi, Manager

Avianca
#1102, 1 St. Clair Ave. West, Toronto, ON M4V 1K6
416-969-8817 Fax: 416-969-9926 800-387-8667
www.avianca.com

British Airways
c/o British Airways Customer Relations, USA, East Elmhurst, NY 11369-0098
www.british-airways.com
Bernie Herenberg

BWIA West Indies Airways
#401, 40 Holly St., Toronto, ON M4S 3C3
800-920-4225
mail@caribbean-airlines.com
www.caribbean-airlines.com
Peter Davies, CEO
Ian Brunton, EVP Operations
Anne Cole, VP Human Resource Services
Roy Harrypersad, VP Finance
Derek De Gannes, VP Information Services
Rachel Laquis, VP Legal/Corporate Services
Robert Bodish, Regional Director North America
Mark Garcia, Director Quality Assurance
Francois Pariseau, Director Marketing
Arthur Lok Jack, Chairman

CanJet Airlines
PO Box 980, Enfield, NS B2T 1R6
902-873-7800 Fax: 902-873-6580 800-809-7777
www.canjet.com

Central Mountain International
PO Box 998, 6431 Airport Rd., Smithers, BC V0J 2N0
250-877-5000 Fax: 250-874-3744
info@flycma.com
Profile: 300+ employees. Centreal Mountain Air is pleased to offer selected cargo services to a majority of our route network destinations. we endeavor to provide our cusomters with a convenient and economical cargo product. Established in 1987 Central Mountain Air (CMA) is a Western Canadian privately owned and operated company offering scheduled and charter flights to over 17 British Columbia and Alberta communities.

CHC Helicopter Corporation
4740 Agar Dr., Richmond, BC V7B 1A3
604-276-7500
communications@chc.ca
www.chc.ca
Ticker Symbol: FLY
Profile: Nonscheduled & scheduled air transportation; Airports, flying fields & airport terminal services; Vocational schools
Sylvain A. Allard, CEO
Jo Mark Zurel, CFO & Sr. Vice-President

Continental Airlines
PO Box 4607, Houston, TX 77210-4607
Fax: 832-235-1806 800-346-3133
www.continental.com
Profile: Subsidary company: Continental Mirconesia, Inc.
Larry Kellner, Chairman/CEO
Jeffery Smisek, President Continental Airlines
Jim Compton, EVP Marketing
Jeff Misner, EVP/CFO
Mark Moran, EVP Operations
Ron Anderson-Lehman, SVP/CIO
Rebecca Cox, SVP Government Affairs
Dave Hilfman, SVP Sales

Cubana
620, rue St-Jacques, Montréal, QC H3C 1C7
514-871-1222 Fax: 514-871-1227 888-667-1222
ventas@qc.aira.com
www.cubana.cu
Ramon Valdivia

Czech Airlines
#1510, 401 Bay St., Toronto, ON M5H 2Y4
416-363-3174 Fax: 416-363-0239 800-641-0641
www.czechairlines.com
Ladislav Slipka, Regional Director

El Al Israel Airlines
#701, 151 Bloor St. West, Toronto, ON M5S 1S4
416-967-4222 Fax: 416-967-1643 800-361-6174
www.elal.co.il

Finnair G.S.A Canada
Vista Centre, Core C, #235, 6500 Silver Dart Dr., Mississauga, ON L5P 1B2
416-222-0740 Fax: 416-678-8949 800-461-8651
feedback@ca.finnair.com
www.finnair.com
Tommi Mormonen, Managing Director

First Air
20 Cope Dr., Kanata, ON K2M 2V8
613-254-6200 Fax: 613-254-6398 800-267-1247
reservat@firstair.ca
www.firstair.ca
Profile: Specializes in travel to Northern Canada. First Air operates a versatile fleet of 17 aircraft for regularly scheduled passenger and air cargo services. The fellt of well-maintained, modern aircraft also provides First Air with the size and flexibility to meet your air charter services requirements. First Air offers scheduled service to 28 destinations in Nunavut, Northwest Territories, Manitoba, Alberta, Yukon, Quebec, and Ontario operating a fleet of 20 aircraft. The Inuit owned airline has over 1,000 employees, of which more than 450 work and live in the north.

Rick Lefebvre, Director Sales, Eastern Region
Mike Olsen, Director Sales, Western Region
Scott Bateman, VP Commercial Operations
Don Orr, VP Flight Operations/Maintenance
Jim Ballingall, VP Marketing/Sales
Jan Traversy, VPVP Finance

Harbour Air Seaplanes
1095 West Waterfront Rd., Vancouver, BC
604-274-1277 Fax: 604-274-1200 800-665-0212
rreid@harbourair.com
www.harbour-air.com

Harmony Airways, Inc.
Corporate Office, 3600 Lysander Lane, Richmond, BC V7B 1C2
604-248-7800 Fax: 604-248-7800 866-868-6789

Helijet International
c/o Vancouver International Airport, 5911 Airport Rd. South, Richmond, BC V7B 1B5
604-273-4688 Fax: 604-273-5301
passengerServices@helijet.com
www.helijet.com

Profile: Helijet are the first scheduled helicopter service in Canada and since their inception in 1986, they now have a fleet of 10 helicopters and airplanes with a staff of over 100 employees. They also have cargo services which ship time sensitive envelops and packages with speed and reliability.

Icelandair
#410, 5950 Symphony Woods Rd., Columbia, MD
410-715-1600 Fax: 410-715-3547 800-223-5500
america@icelandair.is
www.icelandair.com

J¢n Karl ¢lafsson, CEO/President, The Americas
Andri Ass Grétarsson, SVP Finance/Resource Management
Guòjòn Arngr¡msson, VP Corporate Communications
Guòmundur Pálsson, SVP Operations
Gunnar Már Sigurfinnsson, SVP Marketing/Sales
Hjörtur Porgilsson, VP Information Technology
Jens Bjarnason, SVP Technical Services
Una Eyp¢rsd¢ttir, VP Human Resources

Japan Airlines
#2515, 1075 West Georgia St., Vancouver, BC V6E 3C9
800-525-3663
www.japanair.com

Haruka Nishimatsu, President/CEO

Korean Air
1813 Wilshire Blvd., Los Angeles, CA 90057
905-676-8440 Fax: 213-484-5790 800-438-5000
www.koreanair.com

LanChile
#902, 18 King St. East, Toronto, ON M5C 1C4
416-862-0807 Fax: 416-862-5453
www.lanchile.cl

LOT Polish Airlines
Clarica Centre Tower, 10th Fl., #3080, 3300 Bloor St. West., Toronto, ON M8X 2X3
416-236-4242 Fax: 416-776-3152 800-668-5928
lotyto@lot.com
www.lot.com

Wojciech Maciszewski, General Manager

Lufthansa German Airlines
PO Box 939, 31 Adelaide St. E, Toronto, ON M5K 2K3
905-612-5000 Fax: 416-360-3605 800-563-5954
www.lufthansa.com

Justin Gosling, General Manager, Passenger Sales, Canada

Malev Hungarian Airlines
#909, 175 Bloor St. East, Toronto, ON M4W 3R8
416-944-0093 Fax: 416-944-0095 866-379-7313
toronto@malev.hu
www.malev.hu

Attila Gogh

Martinair Holland
#1503, 111 Richmond St. West, Toronto, ON M5H 2G4
416-364-3672 Fax: 800-561-8083
www.martinair.ca

Mexicana
1315 Skyway Dr., Bakersfield, CA 93308
661-387-9755
www.mexicana.com

Erika Flores, "Person in Charge"
Manuel Borja Chico, CEO

Northern Thunderbird Air Inc.
#101, 4245 Hangar Rd., Prince George, BC V2N 4M6
250-963-9611 Fax: 250-963-8422 800-963-9611
infoWntair.ca
www.ntair.ca

Bill Hesse, General Manager
Bernice Hesse, Operations Manager
Ed Goodkey, Controller
Shawna Finch, Maintenance Manager

Northwest/KLM Royal Dutch Airlines
Passgenger Refund Department MS C6455, 7500 Airline Dr., Minneapolis, MN 55450-1101
612-726-2422
www.nwa.com

Olympic Airways
#503, 80 Bloor St. West, Toronto, ON M5S 2V1
416-964-2720 Fax: 416-920-3686
sales.yyz@olympicairlines.ca
www.olympic-airways.gr

Pacific Coastal Airlines
c/o Vancouver International Airport, Unit 2, 4440 Cowely Crest., Richmond, BC V7B 1B8
604-214-2358 Fax: 604-273-4485
www.pacific-coastal.com

Daryl Smith, CEO/Director

PIA Pakistan International Airlines
#500, 131 Bloor St. West, Toronto, ON M5S 1P7
416-926-8747 Fax: 416-926-0507 800-387-1375
www.piac.com.pk

Zaffar A. Khan, Chairman

Purolator Courier Ltd.
#100, 5995 Avebury Rd., Mississauga, ON L5R 3T8
905-712-1251 Fax: 905-712-6696
suggestions@purolator.com
www.purolator.com

Profile: Air courier services
Robert C. Johnson, President/CEO
Sheldon Bell, Sr. Vice-President & CFO

Royal Jordanian
#940, 1801, av McGill College, Montréal, QC H3A 2N4
514-288-1655 Fax: 514-288-7572 800-363-0711
yultbrj@rja.com.jo
www.rja.com.jo/

Omar Kamal, Area Manager, Canada

Skyservice Airlines Inc.
c/o Corporate Office, 31 Fasken Dr., Etobicoke, ON M9W 1K6
416-679-5700 Fax: 416-678-5654 888-571-0094
customer_service@skyservice.com
www.skyservice.com

Swiss International Air Lines
#800, 1555, rue Peel, Montréal, QC H3A 3L8
514-954-5600 Fax: 514-954-5619 877-359-7947
www.swiss.com

Olivier Schlegel, General Manager

Tango
Air Canada Centre, 7373, boul Côte-Vertu ouest, Montréal, QC H4Y 1H4
514-422-5000
www.flytango.com

Trans North Helicopters
PO Box 8, 115 Range Rd., Whitehorse, YK Y1A 5X9
867-668-2177 Fax: 867-668-3420
email@tntaheli.com
http://www.tntaheli.com

Arden Meyer, General Manager
Rob Fletcher, Operations Manager
Charlie Hoeller, Director of Maintenance
Doug Kerley, Chief Pilot
Diane Barnhart, Accountant

Transat A.T. Inc.
Place du Parc, #600, 300, rue Léo-Pariseau, Montréal, QC H2X 4C2
514-987-1660 Fax: 514-987-8035
info@transat.com
www.transat.com
Ticker Symbol: TRZ

Profile: Offices of holding companies; Air transportation, scheduled; Travel agencies; Airports, flying fields, & airport terminal services; Tour operators
Jean-Marc Eustache, President/CEO
Nelson Gentiletti, CFO & Vice-President, Finance & Administration
Jean-Marc Bélisle, Vice-President/Chief Information Officer

United Airlines
77 W. Wacker Dr., Chicago, IL 60601
847-700-4000 Fax: 847-700-4081 800-241-6522
www.ual.com

Varig
#1108, 77 Bloor St. West, Toronto, ON M5S 1M2
416-926-7500 Fax: 416-926-1536 800-898-2744
www.varig.com.br

WestJet
5055 - 11 St. NE, Calgary, AB T2E 8N4
403-444-2600 Fax: 403-444-2301 888-2 W-STJE
customercare@westjet.com
www.westjet.com

Profile: Their fleet is the most modern of any large commercial airline which is comprised of 62 Boeing Next-Generation 737 aircrafts equipped with more legroom, leather seats and live seatback televisions on more than 85% of its fleet.
Sean Durfy, President
Donald Bell, Executive VP of Culture

WestJet Airlines Ltd.
5055 - 11 St. NE, Calgary, AB T2E 8N4
403-444-2600 Fax: 403-444-2301
investor_relations@westjet.com
www.westjet.com
Ticker Symbol: WJA

Profile: Scheduled air transportation throughout North America
Clive J. Beddoe, President & Chair
Alexander (Sandy) Campbell, CFO/Sr. Vice President, Finance
Russ Hall, Exec. Vice-President, Guest Service & Information Technology

Zip Air Inc.
8050 - 22 St. NE, Calgary, AB T2E 7H6
604-270-5676 Fax: 604-276-3433

Zoom Airlines Inc.
#200, 380 Hunt Club Rd., Ottawa, ON K1V 1C1
613-235-9666 Fax: 613-231-7340
custrel@flyzoom.com
www.flyzoom.com

Kris Dolinky, President & CEO

Maritime Shipping

Admiral Marine Inc.
#207-7035 Maxwell Rd., Mississauga, ON L5S 1R5
905-564-8788 Fax: 905-564-1440
admiral@admiralmarine.ca
www.admiralmarine.ca

Profile: Canstar Ocean Line through Admiral Marine operate a regular break-bulk/conventional service from North America to Europe with transshipment via Antwerp to Eastern Europe, the Middle East and Africa. Canstar is a full service transportation consulting company that specializes in the shipment of over-dimensional, ro.ro, break-bulk, heavy lift, and project cargoes.

Algoma Central Corporation
#1000, 103 Church St., St Catharines, ON L2R 3C4
905-687-7888 Fax: 905-687-7882
gdwight@algonet.com
www.algonet.com
Ticker Symbol: ALC

Profile: Algoma Central Corporation operates vessels throughout the Great Lakes-St. Lawrence Waterway from the Gulf of St. Lawrence, through all 5 Great Lakes. The corporation owns 19 Canadian-flagged dry-bulk vessels. The operational and commercial activities of the Canadian-flag dry-bulk team are managed by Seaway Marine Transport, a partnership with Upper Great Lakes Shipping Inc., an unrelated company. The Corporation also has an interest in one tug and one barge.
Tim S. Dool, President/CEO
G.D. Wight, Vice-President, Finance
Robert Cook, Director, Information Services
Kevin Reid, Director, Safety

American President Lines Ltd.
#728, 185 The West Mall, Etobicoke, ON M9C 5L5
416-620-7790 Fax: 416-620-7723
www.apl.com

Profile: APL provides customers around the world with container transportation services through a network combining high-quality intermodal operations with state-of-the-art information technology.
David Goodwin, Vice President, Corporate Affairs
Mike Zampa, Director, Corporate Communications

Anglo-Eastern Ship Management Ltd.

www.angloeasterngroup.com
Profile: Currently the Anglo-Eastern Group looks after a varied fleet and crew base trading and operates worldwide.
Peter Cremers, President

Canada Steamship Lines Inc.
759 Victoria Square, Montreal, QC H2Y 2K3
514-982-3800 Fax: 514-982-3802
ships@cslmtl.com
csl.ca/new/
Profile: Since 1945 Canada Steamship Lines and its affiliates have been part of the lifeblood of the Canadian economy. Throughout the years, Canada Steamship lines has consistently fulfilled the needs of its clients by providing the supply lines necessary to ensure the survival and prosperity of many industry sectors. Today, Canada Steamship Lines is considered a visionary pioneer in its field and a commendable success story for Canada.
Gerald Carter, President
Claude Dumais, Vice President, Technical Operations
Kirk Jones, Director, Transportation Services

Celtic Maritime
1066 Thierry, La Salle, QC H8N 2Y6
514-932-6464 Fax: 514-932-6565
info@celticmaritime.com
www.celticmaritime.com
Anthony Morahan, Administrative Contact

CSL Group Inc.
759, carré Victoria, Montréal, QC H2Y 2K3
514-982-3800 Fax: 514-982-3802
ships@cslmtl.com
www.thecslgroup.ca
Profile: Specializes in bulk transportation & self-loading technology
Meredith (Sam) Hayes, President/CEO
Pierre Richard, Vice-President, Finance & Administration

F.K. Warren Ltd.
Cogswell Tower, #209, 2000 Barrington St., Halifax, NS B3J 2X1
902-423-8136 Fax: 902-429-1326
www.fkwarren.ca
Profile: F.K. Warren brings together technological, human, and material resources to ensure we meet our of supplying efficient and quality service to those in the Marine and Offshore industries. Provides a comprehensive range of Marine Agency Services at all porst throughout Atlantic Canada.
Gordon Smith, President
gsmith@fkwarren.ca
Richard Danells, Vice President
rdanells@fkwarren.ca

Fednav Limited
#3500, 1000, rue de la Gauchetière ouest, Montréal, QC H3B 4W5
514-878-6500 Fax: 514-878-6642
info@fednav.com
www.fednav.com
Profile: Deep sea foreign transportation of freight; Freight transportation on the Great Lakes-St.Lawrence Seaway; Marine cargo handling
Laurence F. Pathy, President/CEO

Groupe Desgagnés Inc.
21 Marché-Champlain St., Québec, QC G1K 8Z8
418-692-1000 Fax: 418-692-6044
info@degagnes.com
www.groupedesgagnes.com
Profile: Groupe Desgagnés' entire history has been marked by sustained, carefully orchestrated efforts that have helped ensure its growth and maintain its position as a shipping industry leader. Purchasing vessels, creating subsidiaries, forming partnerships - this strategy of diversification and combining strengths has helped keep us growing. The fleet includes 14 vessels and 1 barge; 6 vessels for the transportation of general and dry bulk cargo; 7 tankers and 1 barge for the transportation of liquid bulks; 1 passenger and cargo vessels serving the Middle and Lower North shore.
Louis-Marie Beaulieu, CEO

Holmes Maritime Inc.
1345 Hollis St., Halifax, NS B3J 1T8
902-422-0400 Fax: 902-422-9439
info@holmesmaritime.com
www.holmesmaritime.com
Profile: Holmes Maritime Inc. is a privately owned Canadian headquartered in Halifax, Nova Scotia, providing port agency and logistics services to international ship owners and operators throughout eastern Canada and along the Great Lakes.
Louis Homes, President

Logistec Corporation
#1500, 360, rue Saint-Jacques, Montréal, QC H2Y 1P5
514-844-9381 Fax: 514-843-5217
corp@logistec.com
www.logistec.com
Ticker Symbol: LGT
Profile: Deep sea foreign transportation of freight; Freight transportation on the Great Lakes & the St. Lawrence Seaway; Marine cargo handling; Various water transportation services; Refuse systems
Madeleine Paquin, President/CEO
Jean-Claude Dugas, Assistant Sec./Treasurer & Vice-President, Finance
Nicole Paquin, Vice-President, Information Systems

Marine Atlantic Inc.
Baine Johnston Centre, #802, 10 Fort William Pl., St. John's, NL A1C 1K4
709-772-8957 Fax: 709-772-8956 800-341-7981
info@marine-atlantic.ca
www.marine-atlantic.ca
Profile: Deep sea domestic transportation of freight; Ferries; Various water transportation of passengers
Sidney J. Hynes, Chair/CEO
Murray Hupman, Chief Information Officer
Anthony deHoog, Sr. Technical Manager

Montship Inc.
Purdy's Wharf Tower 1, #1502, 1959 Upper Water St., Halifax, NS B3J 3N2
902-420-9184 Fax: 902-422-6010
ops@montshipmaritime.com
www.montship.ca
Profile: Montship Maritime Inc.'s objective is to ensure the outgoing competitiveness of our Maritime operation, and to continue to provide top quality service for our valued Principals.
Kirk Tyler, General Manager
902-420-9184, ktyler@montship.ca
Dennis Merner, Port Superintendent
902-420-9184, dmerner@montship.ca

N.M. Paterson & Sons Limited
PO Box 24, GRP 210, RR2 ., Winnipeg, MB R3C 2E6
204-694-4445 Fax: 204-694-4446
winnipeg_terminal@patersongrain.com
www.patersongrain.com
Profile: Freight transportation on the great lakes-st.lawrence seaway; Wholesales-grain and field beans
Andrew B. Paterson, CEO
J.B. Gresham, Treasurer/CFO

Oceanex Inc.
#2550, 630 René-Lévesque Blvd. West, Montreal, QC H3B 1S6
514-875-9244 Fax: 514-877-0226
www.oceanex.com
Profile: With our modern fleet, state-of-the-art technology and hands-on experience, Oceanex ensures you of prompt, relieable and cost-effective pick-up, handling and delivery of any of the industry's cargo needs. From full-load or LTL, the Oceanex track record for outstanding intermodal freight service and customer satisfaction remains second to none. To Newfoundland from anywhere in North America and just in time...every time. That's what you can count on from Oceanex, your Newfoundland connection.
Peter Henrico, President & CEO
Daniel Bélisle, Vice President, Finance & Administration
Glenn Etchegary, Vice President, Operations
Peter Grayton, Sales Manager

Rigel Shipping Canada
PO Box 5151, 3521 Route 134, Shediac, NB E4P 8T9
506-533-9000 Fax: 506-533-9010
www.rigelcanada.com
Profile: Dedicated to being a quality, technology driven company that provides safe, efficient, environmentally friendly, corteous, and cost-effective marine transportation to our partners and clients.
Brian Ritchie, President
Scott Lewis, General Manager
Shirley Cripps, Human Resources Manager

Robert Redford
2 Place Alexis Nihon, #1777, 3500 de Maisonneuve West, Montreal, QC H3Z 3C1
514-845-5201 Fax: 514-845-6490
info@redford.ca
www.robertredford.com
Profile: Since 1945, the company has acted exclusively as General Steamship Agents. The company is the oldest Canadian steamship agency organization. It is a wholly owned Canadian company.

Ross Kennedy, President
514-887-5201
Donny Coelho, Operations Manager
514-924-5209
Andrew Digby, Vice President, Operations
514-928-5203

Seaway Marine Transport
#300, 20 Corporate Park, St. Catharines, ON L2S 3W2
905-988-2600 Fax: 905-988-1803
www.seawaymarinetransport.com
Profile: Seaway Marine Transport Manages the largest and most versatile fleet of self-unloading vessels and the largest fleet of gearless bulk carriers operating on the Great Lakes, St. Lawrence River and the waters of eastern Canada. This is comprised of 22 self-unloading vessels and 12 gearless bulk cargo vessels.
Allister Paterson, President & CEO
Dennis McPhee, Director, Marketing

Senator Lines
#1000, 465 rue St. Jean, Montreal, QC H2Y 2R6
514-845-9800 Fax: 514-845-8182
www.senatorlines.com
Profile: Our company is motivated by a multi-national team spirit. With our fast and reliable scheduled container services, we can provide your goods with excellent connections to people in the strong-growth markets - Europe-the Middle and Far East, Asia, Canada, South America and the whole Mediterranean region.
Hans-Hermann Mohr, CEO
Jong-Seong Hahm, Vice President

Upper Lakes Group Inc.
49 Jackes Ave., Toronto, ON M4T 1E2
416-920-7610 Fax: 416-922-6159
inquiries@upperlakes.com
www.upperlakes.com
Profile: Upper Lakes Group Inc. is a client focused full service provider, moving, handling, and storing wet and dry bulk commodities and dry bulk commodities and containerized cargoes in the Great Lakes, across Canada, and around the world. We manage an integrated group of companies offering innovative solutions to our customers, and growth, sustainability, and profitability to our shareholders.
Pat Loduca, President & CEO
ploduca@upperlakes.com
Sam Amendola, Vice President & CFO, Finance
samendola@upperlakes.com
Ewa Chudecki, Vice President, Human Resources
eshudecki@upperlakes.com

Wallenius Wilhelmsen Logistics
#1700, 1959 Upper Water St., Halifax, NS B3J 3N2
902-425-2873 Fax: 902-425-9820
www.wwlamericas.com
Profile: We shall create business success for our customers by providing logistics solutions for the distribution of rolling and selected static cargo in a changing global market - with maximum reliability, quality, and cost-effectiveness.
Andrea Farrison, Manager, Public Relations
Elana Brennan, Manager, Marketing Communications

Railroad Companies

Agence métropolitaine de transport
500, Place d'Armes, 25e étage, Montréal, QC H2Y 2W2
514-287-2464 Fax: 514-287-2460
tram@amt.qc.ca
www.amt.qc.ca
Joël Gauthier, Président/CEO

Alberta Prairie Railway
PO Box 1600, Stettler, AB T0C 2L0
403-742-2811 Fax: 403-742-2844
info@absteamtrain.com
www.absteamtrain.com
Don Gillespie

Alberta RailNet Inc.
9410 - 92 Ave., Grande Prairie, AB T8V 7A6
780-831-0407
railnet1@telusplanet.net
www.albertarailnet.com

Algoma Central Railway Inc.
PO Box 130, 129 Bay St., Sault Ste Marie, ON P6A 6Y2
705-946-7300 Fax: 705-541-2989 800-242-9287
www.agawacanyontourtrain.com
Profile: "Rail service, Sault Ste Marie to Hearst, Ont."

BC Rail Ltd.
#660-221 West Esplanade, North Vancouver, BC V7M 3J3
604-678-4735 Fax: 604-678-4736
www.bcrproperties.com/bcrco/
Profile: "Full & intermodal service with CP & CN connections; 1,388 miles of track; 125 locomotives; 10,050 freight cars"
Kevin Mahoney, President/CEO

British Columbia Railway Company
#400, 221 West Esplanade Ave, North Vancouver, BC V7M 3J3
604-678-4735 Fax: 604-678-4736
www.bcrco.com
Profile: Offices of holding companies; Real estate operators of nonresidential buildings; Real estate agents & managers; Railroads, line-haul operating; Marine cargo handling
Kevin Mahoney, President/CEO
Michael Kaye, CFO & Vice-President, Finance

Burlington Northern Santa Fe (Manitoba) Inc.
963 Lindsay St., Winnipeg, MB R3N 1X6
204-453-4415 Fax: 204-477-0046

Burlington Northern Sante Fe Railway
PO Box 961056, 2650 Lou Menk Dr., Fort Worth, TX 76161-0056
800-795-2673
www.bnsf.com
Profile: "31,000 miles (70 miles in Canada); 200,000 railcars; 4,000 locomotives"
Matthew K. Rose, Chair/President/CEO

Canadian National Railway Company
935, rue de la Gauchetière ouest, Montréal, QC H3B 2M9
514-399-0052 Fax: 514-399-5985 888-888-5909
contact@cn.ca
www.cn.ca
Ticker Symbol: CNR
Profile: Railroads & line-haul operating; Railroad switching & terminal establishments. Founded in 1919; 21,685 employees.
E. Hunter Harrison, President/CEO
Claude Mongeau, CFO & Exec. Vice-President
Fred Grigsby, Sr. Vice-President & Chief Information Officer
J.V. Raymond Cyr, Chair, Environment, Safety & Security Committee

Canadian National Railway Company
935 de La Gauchetiere St. West, Montreal, QC H3B 2M9
888-888-5909
contact@cn.ca
www.cn.ca
Hunter Harrison, President & CEO

Canadian Pacific Railway
401 - 9th Ave. SW, Calgary, AB T2P 4Z4
403-319-7000 Fax: 403-319-7567 800-716-9132
www.cpr.ca
Fred J. Green, President & CEO

Canadian Pacific Railway Limited
#500, 401 - 9th Ave. SW, Calgary, AB T2P 4Z4
403-319-7000 888-333-6370
investor@cpr.ca
www.cpr.ca
Ticker Symbol: CP
Profile: Transcontinental carrier; Rail network operates in Canada & the USA. Founded in 1881; over 15,000 employees
Fred J. Green, CEO
Michael R. Lambert, Exec. Vice-President/CFO
Allen H. Borak, Vice-President, Information Services

Cando Contracting Ltd.
740 Rosser Ave., 4th Fl., Brandon, MB R7A 0K9
204-725-2627 Fax: 204-725-4100
info@candoltd.com
www.candoltd.com
Profile: "Operates 4 shortlines: Barrie/Collingwood Railway, Central Manitoba Railway Inc., Athabasca Northern, Orangeville-Brampton"
Gord Peters, President

Cape Breton & Central Nova Scotia Railway
PO Box 2240, 121 King St., Stellarton, NS B0K 1S0
902-752-3357 Fax: 902-752-2713 800-565-5715
Jim Ryan, General Manager

Cartier Railway Company
Rte. 138, Port Cartier, QC G5B 2H3
514-285-2064 Fax: 514-285-1978
Profile: "416 km; 21 locomotives; 1,365 cars"
Guy Dufresne, President/CEO

Central Western Railway
Associated Centre, #306, 13220 St-Albert Trail, Stettler, AB T5L 5W1
780-448-5877 Fax: 780-742-1477
www.railamerica.com
Shawn Smith, General Manager
shawn.smith@railamerica.com

CN
935, rue de la Gauchetière ouest, Montréal, QC H3B 2M9
Fax: 204-987-9310 888-888-5909
cn@wpg.fanfuil.com
www.cn.ca
Profile: "17,544 route miles of track in Canada & the US.; 1,450 diesel locomotives; 61,500 freight cars"
E. Hunter Harrison

Consolidated Rail Corporation
PO Box 41416, 2001 Market St., 29th Fl., Philadelphia, PA 19103
215-209-2000 Fax: 215-209-4819
info@conrail.com
www.conrail.com
Profile: "66 route miles in Québec, from New York-Québec border to Montréal. Includes owned lines, leased lines & trackage rights. Total route miles US & Canada, 13,068"
T.T. O'Toole, President

CSX Transportation Inc.
500 Water St., Jacksonville, FL 33202
904-359-3200
www.csxt.com
Profile: 166 miles in Canada
Michael J. Ward, Chair/President/CEO

E&N Railway
PO Box 581, 23 Esplanade, Nanaimo, BC V9R 5L3
250-754-9222

Essex Terminal Railway Co.
PO Box 24025, 1601 Lincoln Rd., Windsor, ON N8Y 4Y9
519-973-8222 Fax: 519-973-7234
www.essexterminalrailway.com
Profile: Freight only; 24 miles of main track (CN CP CSX NS connect); 5 locomotives; 5 cars
B.G. McKeown, President

GO Transit
#600, 20 Bay St., Toronto, ON M5J 2W3
416-869-3200 Fax: 416-869-3525 888-438-6646
publicrelations@gotransit.com
www.gotransit.com
Gary W. McNeil, Managing Director

Goderich-Exeter Railway Company Ltd.
#2, 126 Weber St. West, Kitchener, ON N2H 3Z9
519-749-8000 Fax: 519-749-8088
www.railamerica.com
Cheryl Ford, General Manager

Greater Winnipeg Water District Railway
598 Plinguet St., Winnipeg, MB R2J 2W7
204-986-4118 Fax: 204-986-3562
Profile: Express Co.-None~92 miles; 3 locomotives; 150 cars
T. Hutchinson, Railway Supervisor

Huron Central Railway Inc.
30 Oakland Ave., Sault Ste Marie, ON P6A 2T3
705-254-4511 Fax: 705-254-5056
Garth E. Rushton, General Manager

Kelowna Pacific Railway Ltd.
2806 - 27 Ave., Vernon, BC V1T 9K4
250-549-1473 Fax: 250-549-1589
kenf@smartt.com
Kenneth Fitzgerald, Chairman & CEO

Mackenzie Northern Railway
#306, Associated Centre, 13220 St. Albert Trail, Edmonton, AB T5L 4W1
780-448-5855 Fax: 780-448-5658

New Brunswick Southern Railway Company Limited
11 Gifford Rd., Saint John, NB E2M 4X7
506-632-4654 Fax: 506-632-5818
www.nbsouthern.com
Ian Simpson, General Manager

Norfolk Southern Corporation
Three Commercial Place, Norfolk, VA 23510-9241
757-629-2600 Fax: 757-629-2607
www.nscorp.com
Profile: "Operating Subsidiary: Norfolk Southern Railway Co.~Track miles 21,500 (245 miles in Canada); 3,000 locomotives; 19,000 road haul equipment"
Charles Moorman, Chairman/President/CEO

OC Transpo
1500 St. Laurent Blvd., Ottawa, ON K1G 0Z8
613-741-6440 Fax: 613-230-6543
ocinfo@octranspo.com
www.octranspo.com
Alex Cullen, Chairman

Ontario Northland Transportation Commission
555 Oak St. East, North Bay, ON P1B 8L3
705-472-4500 Fax: 705-476-5598 800-363-7512
info@ontc.on.ca
www.ontc.on.ca
Profile: (Owned by Province of Ontario)~700 miles; 26 locomotives; 700 cars
Steve Carmichael, President & CEO

Ontario Southland Railway Inc.
383 Everglade Cres., London, ON N6H 4M8
519-471-9606 Fax: 519-471-7334
info@osrinc.ca
www.osrinc.ca

Québec North Shore & Labrador Railway Company
PO Box 1000, Sept-Iles, QC G4R 4L5
418-968-7497 Fax: 418-968-7926
robitaim@ironore.ca
www.ironore.ca
M. Robitaille, General Manager

Québec Railway Corporation
#525, 1010, rue Sherbrooke ouest, Montréal, QC H3A 2R7
514-982-0917 Fax: 514-849-2319
cnplus.cn.ca
Profile: "Operates the following shortlines: Ottawa Central Railway (OCRR), New Brunswick East Coast Railway (NBEC), Chemin de fer Charlevoix (CFC), Chemin de fer de la Matapédia et du Golfe inc. (CFMG)"
Marc Laliberté, President

Roberval & Saguenay Railway Company
PO Box 1277, Jonquière, QC G7S 4K8
418-699-3685 Fax: 418-699-2069
Profile: Express Co.-None (Canadian National Railway connects)~54 miles; 11 locomotives; 189 cars
Claude Chamberland, Vice President

Rocky Mountaineer Rail
#100, 1150 Station St., Vancouver, BC V6A 2X7
604-606-7245 Fax: 604-606-7250 877-460-3200
reservations@rockymountaineer.com
www.rockymountaineer.com
Peter Armstrong, President & CEO

South Simcoe Railway
PO Box 186, Tottenham, ON L0G 1W0
905-936-5815
info@steamtrain.com
www.steamtrain.com
Eric Smith, President

Southern Manitoba Railway
PO Box 253, #2, 156 Boyne, Morris, MB R0G 1K0
204-746-2722 Fax: 204-746-2749
cnplus.cn.ca
Steve Van Wagenen, General Manager

Southern Ontario Railway
PO Box 953, 241 Stuart St. West, Hamilton, ON L8N 3P9
905-777-1234
www.railamreica.com
Stuart Thomas, General Manager

Southern Railway of British Columbia Limited
2102 River Dr., New Westminster, BC V3M 6S3
604-521-1966 Fax: 604-526-0914
www.sryraillink.com
Profile: (freight only)~75 miles; 19 locomotives; 475 cars
John van der Burch, President

Toronto Terminals Railway Company Ltd.
#402, Union Station, 65 Front St. West, Toronto, ON M4J 1E6
416-864-3440
www.ttrly.com
S.L. Spares, Director of Operations

Trillium Railway
PO Box 218, 265 King St., Port Colborne, ON L3K 5V8
905-835-2772 Fax: 905-835-8943
wayne.ettinger@trilliumrailway.com
www.trilliumrailway.com
Wayne Ettinger, President & CEO

VIA Rail Canada Inc.
PO Box 8116 A, #500, 3, Place Ville Marie, Montréal, QC H3C 3N3
514-871-6000 Fax: 514-871-6619
www.viarail.ca
Profile: Railroads, line-haul operating; Local & suburban transit
Paul Côté, President/CEO
J. Roger Paquette, CFO
Paul Raynor, Director, Corporate Communications
Michael Greenberg, Vice-President, Procurement, Real Estate & Environment

Via Rail Canada Inc.
#500, 3, Place Ville-Marie, Montréal, QC H3B 2C9
514-871-6000 Fax: 514-871-6117
www.viarail.ca
Profile: (passenger services only)
Paul Côté, President & CEO

Wabush Mines
PO Box 878, Sept-Iles, QC G4R 4L4
418-964-3000 Fax: 418-962-9876
Profile: Wabush Mines represents both the Arnaud Railway Company & the Wabush Lake Railway
D. Lebel, General Manager

West Coast Express Ltd.
#295, 601 West Cordova, Vancouver, BC V6B 1G1
604-488-8906 Fax: 604-689-3896
www.westcoastexpress.com
Doug Kelsey, President & CEO

White Pass & Yukon Route
PO Box 435, 231 Second Ave., Skagway, AK 99840-0435
907-983-2214 Fax: 907-983-2734 800-343-7373
info@whitepass.net
www.whitepassrailroad.com
Profile: Express Co.-None 40 miles; 20 locomotives; 59 cars
Gary C. Danielson, President

Windsor & Hantsport Railway Co.
PO Box 578, 2 Water St., Windsor, NS B0N 2T0
902-798-0798
cnplus.cn.ca
James Taylor, General Manager

Public Transit Systems

100 Mile House Transit System (Paratransit)
c/o LDN Transportation, 6119 Reita Cres., 100 Mile House, BC V0K 2E0
250-395-2834
lnieson@telus.net
www.bctransit.com/regions/one
Profile: The 100 Mile House Transit System has many routes which offer service to major residenial areas of 100 Mile House, 103 Mile and 108 Ranch. It also has several accessible services, including rural transit service, HandyDART and priority seating.

Agence métropolitaine de transport
500, Place d'Armes, 25e étage, Montréal, QC H2Y 2W2
514-287-8726 Fax: 514-276-2460 888-702-8726
www.amt.qc.ca
Profile: AMT's mission is to improve the efficiency of personal travel in the metropolitan area by promoting the use of public transit. AMT is therefore responsible for the planning, coordination, integration and promotion of public transit services (bus, metro, taxi-bus, commuter trains and adapted transit), as well as for improving the efficiency of roads of metropolitan significance.
Joel Gauthier, Président/CEO

Barrie Transit
24 Maple Ave., Barrie, ON L4N 7W4
705-739-4209
Profile: The City of Barrie offers both conventional bus service with Barrie Transit and specialized transit services for people with mobility restrictions with Barrie Accessible Community Transportation Service (BACTS)

BC Transit
520 Gorge Rd. East, Victoria, BC V8W 2P3
250-385-2551 Fax: 250-995-5639
nancy_longphee@bctransit.com
www.bctransit.com
Profile: BC Transit provides planning, marketing, fleet and funding support for all transit services in BC, except for the Greater Vancouver region. BC Transit's fleet of 20 fuel cell buses will be the world's first to be placed in regular transit operation.

Belleville Transit
City Hall, 169 Front St., Belleville, ON K8N 2Y8
613-962-1925
Profile: Belleville Transit operates 6 days a week, Monday to Saturday, inclusive with 9 routes servicing the urban area of the city. The fleet consists of 14 coaches travelling approximately 2,300 kilometers per day and carries 3,000 riders daily

Boundary Transit System
c/o Interior Health Authority, Hardy View Lodge, PO Box 2647, 2320 - 78 Ave., Grand Forks, BC V0H 1H0
250-443-2080 Fax: 250-442-8331
trish.hallstrom@interiorhealth.ca
www.bctransit.com/regions/bdy
Profile: The Boundary Transit System has many routes within Grand Forks, with trips to and from Greenwood on Fridays. It also has several accessible services, including HandyDART and priority seating.

Brampton Transit
185 Clark Blvd., Brampton, ON L6T 4G6
905-874-2750
www.brampton.ca/transit/home.taf
Profile: Brampton Transit provides approximately 583,000 transit service hours per year

Brandon Transportation Services
900 Richmond Ave. East, Brandon, MB R7A 6A2
204-729-2300 Fax: 204-729-2485
Profile: Brandon City Transit offers many services to the community, including Handi-Transit, an environmentally friendly way of traveling, and specialized schedules.
Bob MacDonald, City Transportation Manager

Brantford Transit
64 Darling St., Brantford, ON N3T 6G6
519-753-3847 Fax: 519-750-0491
mspicer@brantford.ca
www.city.brantford.on.ca/transit
Profile: Operated by the Engineering Department of the Corporation of the City of Brantford. The fleet consists of 25 buses

British Columbia Ferry Services Inc.
1112 Fort St., Victoria, BC V8V 4V2
250-386-3431 Fax: 250-388-7754
www.bcferries.com
Profile: Ferries
David Hahn, President/CEO

British Columbia Rapid Transit Company Ltd. (SkyTrain
6800 - 14 Ave., Burnaby, BC V3N 4S7
604-520-3641 Fax: 604-521-2818
www.skytrain.info/index.html
Profile: The SkyTrain in Vancouver, British Columbia, Canada is an advanced light rapid transit system operating fully automated trains on two lines. Built for the Expo 86 World's Fair, it has since become the world's longest automated light rapid transit system. The system uses the same family of linear induction motor-driven trains as the Scarborough RT line in Toronto, the Putra LRT in Kuala Lumpur, Malaysia, and the JFK AirTrain in New York.

Burlington Transit
3332 Harvester Rd., Burlington, ON L7N 3M8
905-639-0550 Fax: 905-335-7878
transit&traffic@burlington.ca

Calgary Transit
c/o City of Calgary, PO Box 2100 M, Calgary, AB T2P 2M5
TPCT043@calgary.ca
www.calgarytransit.com
Profile: Calgary Transit serves a population of 991,759 with the help of 960 vehicles on more than 161 routes
John Hubbell, Director

Campbell River Transit System
1050 - 9 Ave., Campbell River, BC V9W 4C2
250-287-7433 Fax: 250-287-7488
transit@oberon.ark.com
www.bctransit.com/regions/cam
Profile: The Campbell River Transit System has several services available to the community, including three types of Accessible Service, including Low Floor Busses, handyDART and the Taxi Saver Program. It has routes to most major destinations in Campbell River, and to Willow Point and Oyster Bay.

Cape Breton Transit
320 Esplanade, Sydney, NS B1P 7B9
902-539-8124 Fax: 902-564-0481
epw@cbrm.ns.ca
www.cbrm.ns.ca
Profile: Transit Cape Breton offers the community travel within Industrial Cape Breton, including Loonie Days every Saturday, and discounted tickets.

Castlegar Regional Transit System
c/o Trail Transit Services Inc., 8170 Old Waneta Rd., Trail, BC V1R 4W9
250-365-3100 Fax: 250-364-2418
dennis.trailtransit@shawlink.ca
www.bctransit.com/regions/cas
Profile: The Castlegar Regional Transit system has routes to Downtown and the College. It also has several accessible services, including rural transit services, HandyDART and priority seating.

Central Fraser Valley Transit System
c/o Township Transit Services Inc., 1225 Riverside Rd., Abbotsford, BC V2S 7P1
604-854-3232 Fax: 604-854-3598
inquiries@townshiptransit.com
www.busonline.ca/regions/cfv
Profile: The Central Fraser Valley Transit System has several services available to the community, including routes to most major destinations in the City of Abbotsford and the District of Mission, as well as accessible services such as low floor busses, HandyDART and a taxi saver program.

Chatham Transit
c/o Municipality of Chatham-Kent, PO Box 640, 315 King St. West, Chatham, ON N7M 5K8
519-360-1998

Chilliwack Transit
44580 Yale Rd. West, Chilliwack, BC V2R 4H1
604-795-3838 Fax: 604-795-5110
inquiries@townshiptransit.com
www.bctransit.com/regions/chw
Profile: The Chilliwack Transit System has several routes available to the community, which go to most major destinations in the City of Chilliwack, and to Rosedale, Popkum, Agassiz and Harrison Hot Springs, including service to Minter Gardens, Bridal Falls and Dusty's Dino Town. It also has accessible services including low floor busses, HandyDART, a specializex HandyDART flex route and a taxi saver program.

Clearwater & Area Transit System (Paratransit)
c/o Yellowhead Community Services, 612 Park Dr., Clearwater, BC V0E 1N0
250-674-3935
jack.k@yellowheadcs.ca
www.bctransit.com/regions/clr
Profile: The Clearwater & Area transit system services an area that covers Vavenby, Birch Island, Clearwater and Blackpool. On the last Thursday of every month the bus goes to Kamloops and back to Clearwater. It has several accessible services including door-to-door services and priority seating.

Coast Mountain Bus Company
13401 - 108 Ave., Surrey, BC V3T 5T4
604-953-3000
info@coastmountainbus.com
www.coastmountainbus.com
Profile: Coast Mountain Bus Company (CMBC) is a vital link in the Greater Vancouver multi-modal public transportation network. You experience our service when you ride a CMBC bus, or cross Vancouver harbour on SeaBus ferry service. Coast Mountain Bus Company (CMBC) operates conventional buses, smaller community shuttles, SeaBus and, soon, a fleet of state-of-the-art trolley buses in Greater Vancouver, in the largest single transit service area in Canada.

Cobourg Transit
c/o Town of Cobourg, 55 King St. West, Cobourg, ON K9A 2M2
905-373-0582
Profile: Cobourg Transit is a fully accessible community transit system that combines a fixed route service with the flexibility of door-to-door service for eligible riders

Codiac Transit Commission
140 Millennium Blvd., Moncton, NB E1E 2G8
506-857-2008 Fax: 506-859-2680
www.codiactransit-moncton.com
Profile: Transit system for Moncton with express routes, charters and airport routes.

Comox Valley Transit System
1635 Knight Rd., Comox, BC V9N 5N1
250-339-5426 Fax: 250-339-2797
karen_sankey@hotmail.com
www.bctransit.com/regions/com
Profile: Comox Valley Transit has several routes available to the community, which go to Cumberland, Royston/Buckley Bay, Courtenay, Comox, and BC Ferries and the airport. It has

accessible services including low floor busses, HandyDART and a taxi saver program.

Cornwall Transit
PO Box 877, 863 Second St. West, Cornwall, ON K6J 1H5
613-930-2636 Fax: 613-932-9906
cityhall@city.cornwall.on.ca
Profile: The City operated transit system transports approximately 525,000 passengers annually
Gerry Godard, Senior Supervisor

Cowichan Valley Regional Transit System
#8, 180 Central Rd., Duncan, BC V9L 4X3
250-746-4841
rick.salewski@greyhound.ca
www.transitbc.com/regions/cow/
Profile: The Cowichan Valley Regional Transit System has several routes to the Duncan/North Cowichan area, including Quamichan, Mt Prevost and Maple Bay; the Cowichan Lake area, including Youbou and Honeymoon Bay; and the South End communities including Mill Bay, Shawnigan Lake, Cobble Hill and Cowichan Bay. It also has accessible services including low floor busses and priority seating.

Cranbrook Transit System
C/O Gray Line of Victoria, 1229 Crambrook St. North, Cranbrook, BC V1C 3S6
250-426-3331 Fax: 250-426-5101
john.darula@suncity.bc.ca
www.bctransit.com/regions/cra
Profile: Cranbrook Transit System has several routes available to the community, and many services, such as low-floor busses, HandyDART, etc. for those who are in need of them.

Creston Valley Transit System
c/o Grouse Mountain Transportation, 1607 Canyon St., Creston, BC V0B 1G5
250-428-5533 Fax: 250-428-2658
crestonchamber@kootnay.com
www.bctransit.com/regions/cre
Profile: The Creston Valley Transit System has routes that go to most of the major destinations in the area. It also has several accessible services including door to door service and priority seating.

Dawson Creek Transit System
10105 - 13A St., Dawson Creek, BC V1G 3V7
250-784-3600 Fax: 250-782-3203
jchute@dawsoncreek.ca
www.bctransit.com/regions/daw
Profile: Dawson Creek Transit system has several routes available to the community, which go to most of the major destinations in Dawson Creek. It has several low floor busses and priority seating.

Durham Region Transit
605 Rossland Rd. East, Whitby, ON L1N 6A3
905-668-7711 Fax: 905-668-1567
www.durhamregiontransit.com
Profile: Durham Region Transit (DRT) is an integrated transit system serving all communities in Durham Region. The service area is divided into West, East, Centre and North service sectors. Door to door transit for disabled passengers is provided by Specialized Services

Edmonton Transit System
PO Box 2610 Main, Edmonton, AB T5J 3R5
780-496-1611 Fax: 780-496-1670
etransit@edmonton.ca
Profile: Today, Edmonton Transit's fleet encompasses over 847 diesel and trolley buses, and 29 community buses. The system covers more than 150 routes, including a Light Rail Transit (LRT) system with 37 vehicles and 11 stations. ETS also offers transportation to persons with disabilities, called the Disabled Adult Transit Service (DATS)

Fort St. John Transit System
c/o Nordbo Services Ltd., 10404 - 87 Ave., Fort St John, BC V1J 5K7
250-787-9373
nordbo@awink.com
www.bctransit.com/regions/fsj/
Profile: The Fort St. John Transit system has many routes available to the community, reaching most of the major destinations in the city. It has low floor busses for easy accessibility, and priority seating.

Fredericton Transit
PO Box 130, Fredericton, NB E3B 4Y7
506-460-2200 Fax: 506-460-2211
transit@fredericton.ca
www.fredericton.ca
Profile: The City of Fredericton Transit Division operates 27 buses on eight routes, Monday to Saturday, 6:30 am until 11:00 pm, providing safe, affordable mobility to those in the community who do not have access to or choose not to use a private vehicle. In addition we operate chartered busing to various school, tour, and conference groups in and around Fredericton, and a parallel service , Dial-A-Bus, for persons with a disability.
Alex MacNeill, Contact

GO Transit
#600, 20 Bay St., Toronto, ON M5J 2W3
416-869-3600 Fax: 416-869-3525
www.gotransit.com
Profile: GO Transit is Canada's first, and Ontario's only, interregional public transit system, linking Toronto with the surrounding regions of the Greater Toronto Area (GTA). The system began operating in May 1967 and carries 49 million passengers a year by train & bus

GP Transit
City Hall, PO Bag 4000, Grande Prairie, AB T8V 6V3
780-538-0337 Fax: 780-538-667
gptransit@cityofgp.com
Profile: For over 24 years, GP transit has served the citizens of Grand Prairie, Alberta. Fares range from $1.50 to $2.00 per ride, and children under 12 ride free when accompanied by a paying passenger.

Grand River Transit
250 Strasburg Rd., Kitchener, ON N2E 3M6
519-585-7555
www.grt.ca/web/transit.nsf/fmFrontPage?openform

Greater Sudbury Transit
c/o City of Sudbury, PO Box 5000 A, Sudbury, ON P3A 593
705-675-3333 Fax: 705-560-4571
Profile: Operates a fleet of 42 buses
Roger Sauvé, Director
roger.sauve@city.greatersudbury.on.c

Greater Vancouver Transportation Authority (TransLink
#1600, 4720 Kingsway, Burnaby, BC V5H 4N2
604-453-4500
www.translink.bc.ca
Profile: TransLink, the Greater Vancouver Transportation Authority, is a small organization involved with transportation planning, administration of service contracts with subsidiary companies and contractors, the management of capital projects, financial management and planning, public affairs and supporting business functions.

Guelph Transit
City Hall, 59 Carden St., Guelph, ON N1H 3A1
519-822-1811 Fax: 519-822-1322
transit@guelph.on.ca
Profile: Guelph Transit has 20 low-floor conventional buses in its fleet and guarantees accessible service on ten of its transit routes

The Hamilton Street Railway Company
2200 Upper James St., Hamilton, ON L0R 1W0
905-528-4200 Fax: 905-679-7305
hsrserve@hamilton.ca
www.myhamilton.ca/myhamilton/CityandGovernment/City
Profile: Operates over 30 bus routes serving Hamilton, Stoney Creek, Dundas, Ancaster and Burlington. Buses run seven days a week on most routes, from around 5:30 a.m. to 1:00 a.m. the next morning
Don Hull, Director

Hazeltons' Regional Transit System
c/o Farwest Bus Lines Ltd., 5251 First Ave., New Hazelton, BC V0J 1Y0
250-847-2134 877-842-2131
phil.malnis@farwestgroup.com
www.bctransit.com/regions/haz
Profile: The Hazeltons' Regional Transit System has routes to most communities within the Hazeltons', as well as major destinations like Wrinch Memorial Hospital, Northwest Community College, First Nations Education Centre and the historic Village of 'Ksan. It also has routes to Moricetown and Smithers on Tuesday and Thursdays. It has accessible services which include door to door service and priority seating.

Kamloops Transit System
1550 Ord Rd., Kamloops, BC V2B 7V4
250-376-6373 Fax: 250-376-7398
coordinators@farwestgroup.com
www.bctransit.com/regions/kam
Profile: The Kamloops Transit System has several routes available to the public which go to all regions of Greater Kamloops. It also has several services available, including low floor busses, HandyDART, a Taxi Saver Program and priority seating.

Kaslo Transit System (Paratransit)
c/o Arrow & Slocan Lakes Community Services, PO Box 100, 205 - 6 Ave. North, Nakusp, BC V0G 1R0
250-265-3674 Fax: 250-265-3378
jbrown@aslcs.com

Kelowna Regional Transit System
c/o Farwest Transit Services Inc., 1494 Hardy St., Kelowna, BC V1Y 8H2
250-860-8140
m.docherty@kelownatransit.com
www.busonline.ca/regions/kel
Profile: The Kelowna Transit System has several routes available to the public, which go to all regions of Greater Kelowna. It also has many accessible services, including low floor busses, HandyDART, a Taxi Saver program and priority seating.

Kimberley Transit System
260 - 4 Ave., Kimberley, BC V1A 2R6
250-423-2015
carole.rausch@interiorhealth.ca
www.bctransit.com/regions/kim
Profile: The Kimberley Transit System has routes within the City of Kimberley, and makes a round-trip to Cranbrook every 1st and 3rd Monday of the month. It also has several accessible services, including door to door service and priority seating.

Kings Transit Authority
PO Box 100, Kentville, NS B4N 3W3
902-678-7310 Fax: 902-678-2545 888-546-4442
info@kingstransit.ns.ca
www.kingstransit.ns.ca
Profile: King Transit Authority is a public tranist system that operates in teh Annapolis Country between the towns of Bridgetown, Annapolis Royal and Greenwood. Their service also extends to Cornwallis Park and Upper Clements Park, as well as Digby County to Weymouth.
Andrew A. Paterson, General Manager

Kitimat Transit System
c/o Coastal Bus Lines Ltd., 780 Lahakas Blvd. South, Kitimat, BC V8C 1T9
250-632-4444
phil.malnis@farwestgroup.com
www.bctransit.com/regions/kit
Profile: The Kitimat Transit System has many routes that go to most of the major destinations in Kitimat. It also has several accessible services, including low floor busses, HandyDART, and priority seating.

Kootenay Boundary Transit System
8170 Old Waneta Rd., Trail, BC V1R 4W9
250-364-3262 Fax: 250-364-2418
dennis.trailtransit@shawlink.ca
www.bctransit.com/regions/kob
Profile: The Kootenay Transit System has several routes available to the community that go to most of the major destinations in Trail. It also has many accessible services, including low floor busses, HandyDART, and priority seating.

Lethbridge Transit
619 - 4 Ave. North, Lethbridge, AB T1H 0K4
403-320-3885 Fax: 403-380-3876
wbest@lethbridge.ca
Profile: Lethbridge Transit's mission is to provide a safe and efficient public transportation system that allows community access to economic, social, educational or leisure opportunities.

London Transit Commission
450 Highbury Ave. North, London, ON N5W 5L2
519-451-1347
www.londontransit.ca
Profile: L.T.C. services 32 routes (19 accessible). Annual ridership reaches 18.3 million
Larry E. Ducharme, General Manager

Medicine Hat Transit
333 - 6 Ave. SE, Medicine Hat, AB T1A 2S6
403-529-8214 Fax: 403-527-5844
transit_dept@medicinehat.ca
Profile: The City of Medicine Hat operates a public transportation system, which is available and accessible to all residents of the community. Medicine Hat Transit makes every attempt to be responsive to the needs of residents and other community partners. Efficient use of human and physical resources, customer service and satisfaction, and a leadership role in providing a integrated transit system which meets the needs of our community, are just some of the objectives of our Transit Operations Plan.

Metro Transit
c/o Transit Services, Halifax Regional Municipalit, 200 Ilsley Ave., Dartmouth, NS B3B 1V1
709-490-4000
contactHRM@halifax.ca
www.region.halifax.ns.ca/metrotransit
Profile: Metro Transit has many services available to the community, including Accessible Low-Floor Buses, Charter Services, FRED (Free Rides Everwhere in Dowtown Halifax) as well as using more environmentally friendly biodiesal fuel.

Metrobus
245 Freshwater Rd., St. John's, NL A1B 1B3
709-570-2020 Fax: 866-843-5287
infoservices@metrobus.com
www.metrobus.com
Profile: St. John's Metrobus System has recently been revitalized and is now offering more frequent services, more direct routes, reduced travel times and more express routes.

Mississauga Transit
975 Central Parkway West, Mississauga, ON L5C 3B1
905-615-4636
transit.info@mississauga.ca
www.mississauga.ca/portal/residents/publictransit
Profile: City operated since 1974 with a fleet of over 300 buses

Moose Jaw Transit System
City Hall, 228 Main St. North, Moose Jaw, SK S6H 3J8
306-694-4488 Fax: 306-694-4022
transit@city.moose-jaw.sk.ca
Profile: The City of Moose Jaw Transit System offers bus service to all areas of the community. Routes are designed to provide the most efficient service possible to the citizens of Moose Jaw. Charter Service is also available, as is a Special Needs Service.

Nakusp Transit System (Paratransit)
c/o Arrow & Slocan Lakes Community Services, PO Box 100, 205 - 6 Ave. North, Nakusp, BC V0G 1R0
250-265-3674 Fax: 250-265-3378
jbrown@aslcs.com

Nanaimo Regional Transit System
6300 Hammond Bay Rd., Nanaimo, BC V9T 6N2
250-390-4531 Fax: 250-390-2757 877-604-4111
transprt@rdn.bc.ca
www.rdn.bc.ca
Profile: Nanaimo Regional Transit System provides both regular transit and HandyDART custom transit service. Regional Transit is operated by the Regional District of Nanaimo in partnership with BC Transit. We serve the area from Cedar in the south of the Regional District to Qualicum Beach in the north.
Anita Wajouda

Nelson/Slocan Valley Transit
c/o City of Nelson Public Works, #101, 310 Ward St., Nelson, BC V1L 5S4
250-352-8228
rod@city.nelson.bc.ca
www.bctransit.com/regions/nel
Profile: The Nelson/Slocan Valley Transit System has several routes which go to most of the major destinations in the area, as well as many rural stops in Taghum, Blewett, Beasley, Bonnington, South Slocan, Playmor, Shore Acres, Crescent Valley, Slocan Park, Passmore, Winlaw and Appledale. It also has accessible services including low floor busses, HandyDART and priority seating.

Niagara Transit Commission
4320 Bridge St., Niagara Falls, ON L2E 2R7
905-356-1179 Fax: 905-356-5576 866-336-1119
info@niagaratransit.com
www.niagaratransit.com
Profile: Niagara Transit has supplied public transportation for the City of Niagara Falls since 1960. Presently supplies the city with 10 bus routes
Terry Librock, General Manager

North Bay Transit
PO Box 360, 200 McIntyre St. East, North Bay, ON P1B 8H8
705-474-0419 Fax: 705-476-5308
Profile: Operates a fleet of 25 buses
Peter Reid, Transit Manager
705-474-0626, peter.reid@cityofnorthbay.ca

Oakville Transit
c/o Town of Oakville, PO Box 310, Oakville, ON L6J 5A6
905-815-2020 Fax: 905-338-4166
transit-info@oakville.ca
www.oakvilletransit.com
Profile: Oakville Transit has been providing bus service to Oakville since 1972

Osoyoos Transit System
c/o South Okanagan Transit Society - Osoyoos Bapti, 8606 - 92nd Ave., Osoyoos, BC V0H 1V2
250-495-8054 888-706-9752
obc@cablerocket.com
www.busonline.ca/regions/oso
Profile: Osoyoos Transit System operates Monday through Thursday, with Monday catering to destinations between Osoyoos and Kelowna Airport, including Oliver, Okanagan Falls, Penticton, Summerland, Peachland, Westbank and Kelowna, and Tuesday through Thursday servicing all destinations between Osoyoos and Summerland, including Oliver, Okanagan Falls and Penticton. It also has accessible services including handyDART and priority seating.

Ottawa Carleton Regional Transit Commission
1500 St. Laurent Blvd., Ottawa, ON K1G 0Z8
613-741-6440
ocinfo@ottawa.ca
www.octranspo.com
Profile: Has 911 buses in fleet; covers 225 routes and has over 2,200 employees
Janet Stavinga, Chair

Penticton Transit System
301 Warren Ave. East, Penticton, BC V2A 3M1
250-492-4042
mattb@berryandsmith.com
www.bctransit.com/regions/pen
Profile: The Penticton Transit System has many routes available both in the community and in rual areas. It also has several accessible services, including low floor busses, HandyDART, a taxi saver program and priority seating.

Peterborough Transit
c/o City of Peterborough, 190 Simcoe St., Peterborough, ON K9H 2H7
705-745-0525
jkimble@city.peterborough.on.ca
www.peterborough.ca/Living/City_Services/Transporta
Profile: Services the City of Peterborough, Ontario with regular and Handi-Van transit services. All regular Peterborough Transit routes now have fully accessible buses
Jim Kimble, Manager

Port Alberni/Clayoquot Transit
c/o Western Bus Lines, 4521 - 10 Ave., Port Alberni, BC V9Y 4X9
250-723-3341 Fax: 250-723-8115
wbl@telus.net
www.bctransit.com/regions/pta
Profile: The Port Alberni/Clayoquot Transit System has several routes that go to most of the major destinations in the area, as well as many accessible services, including low floor busses, handyDART and priority seating.

Powell River Regional Transit System
c/o Powell River Municipal Transportation, 6910 Duncan St., Powell River, BC V8A 1W2
604-485-4287 Fax: 604-485-4219
bprice@cdpr.bc.ca
www.bctransit.com/regions/pow
Profile: The Powell River Transit System has many routes available to the community, which go to most of the major destinations in the area. It also has several accessible services, including a rural transit service, low floor busses, HandyDART and priority seating.

Prince George Transit System
1041 Great St., Prince George, BC V2N 2K8
250-563-0011 Fax: 250-564-4901
rick@bc.pwt.ca
www.bctransit.com/regions/prg
Profile: The Prince George Transit System has many routes that go to most of the major regions in the area. It also has several accessible services available to the community, including community travel training, low floor busses, HandyDART, a taxi saver program and priority seating.

Prince Rupert/Port Edward Transit
c/o Coastal Bus Lines Ltd., 225 - 2 Ave. West, Prince Rupert, BC V8J 1G4
250-624-6400 Fax: 250-624-6432
bart.carrigan@farwestgroup.com
www.bctransit.com/regions/prr
Profile: The Prince Rupert/Port Edward Transit system has several routes available to the community that go to most of the major destinations in the area, as well as many accessible services, including low floor busses, HandyDART, a taxi saver program and door to door service.

Princeton & Area Transit System (Paratransit)
c/o Princeton & District Community Services, PO Box 1960, 47 Harold Ave., Princeton, BC V0X 1W0
250-295-6666 Fax: 250-295-6214 800-291-0911
pcomserv@cablerocket.com
Profile: The Princeton and Area Transit System runs Monday through Friday, with door-to-door trips within Princeto and to and from Penticton, Hedley, Keremeos and Coalmont.
Lynn Pelly, Contact

Quesnel Transit System
c/o Five Five Transport, 355C Vaughan St., Quesnel, BC V2J 2T1
250-992-1109
fivefive@quesnelbc.ca
www.busonline.ca/regions/que
Profile: Quesnel Transit has several routes that go to most of the major destinations in the area, as well as many accessible services, including HandyDART and priority seating.

Red Deer Transit
PO Box 5008, Red Deer, AB T4N 3T4
403-342-8225 Fax: 403-342-8222
transit@reddeer.ca
Profile: Red Deer Transit has several services available to the community, including Low Floor Buses, Overload Busses, Charter Bus Services, and a Citizen's Action Bus.

Regina Transit
PO Box 1790, 333 Winnipeg St., Regina, SK S4P 3C8
306-777-7726 Fax: 306-949-7211
www.reginatransit.com
Profile: The City of Regina Transit System has several services available to the community, including a charter service, a safebus, night stops, and paratransit.

Réseau de transport de la capitale (RTC-Québec)
720, rue des Rocailles, Québec, QC G2J 1A5
418-627-2351 Fax: 418-641-6716
www.stcuq.qc.ca

Le Réseau de transport de Longueuil
Centre administratif, 1150, boul Marie-Victorin, Longueuil, QC J4G 2M4
450-463-0131
www.rtl-longueuil.qc.ca
Profile: Le Réseau de transport de Longueuil's (RTL) mission is to improve the quality of life of citizens in the territory served by the RTL by meeting their evolving transportation needs through the promotion and cost-effective operation of various quality and environmentally friendly public transportation means."
Pierre Del Fante, Dir.-gén.

Saint John Transit Commission
PO Box 3860 B, 951 Fairville Blvd., Saint John, NB E2M 5C2
506-658-4700 Fax: 506-658-4704
Profile: The Saint John Transit Commission was established in 1979 to provide scheduled transit service to the city. It is the largest public transit system in New Brunswick in terms of both mileage and passengers. Saint John Transit's ridership is approximately 50 percent higher than the average for Canadian cities with a population of between 50,000 and 150,000.

St. Albert Transit
235 Carnegie Dr., St Albert, AB T8N 5A7
780-418-6060 Fax: 780-459-4050
transit@st-albert.net
Profile: St-Albert Transit (StAT) local routes serve all neighbourhoods within the City of St. Albert, connecting with StAT commuter services to Edmonton destinations at either (or both) the Village Transit Station or St. Albert Centre Exchange. Edmonton destinations include downtown, the University of Alberta, MacEwan, NAIT, Government Centre and West Edmonton Mall.

St Catherines Transit Commission
2012 First St. Louth, RR#3, St Catharines, ON L2S 3V9
905-687-5555
phil@yourbus.com
www.yourbus.com

Sarnia Transit
1169 Michener Rd., Sarnia, ON N7S 4W3
519-336-3271 Fax: 519-336-3361
transit@city.sarnia.on.ca
www.sarnia.ca/visit.asp?sectionid=53
Profile: Operates and maintains a fleet of 25 buses on the conventional transit system and 6 specialized vehicles on their Care-a-Van service (provided to people with disabilities)
Jim Stevens, Director

Saskatchewan Transportation Company
2041 Hamilton St., Regina, SK S4P 2E2

306-787-3340
info@stcbus.com
www.stcbus.com
Profile: Saskatchewan Transit has been providing passenger and freight transportation services for over 60 years, and provides passenger transportation and parcel express services throughout Saskatchewan operating main terminals in Regina, Saskatoon and Prince Albert with an additional 206 rural agencies in the Province.

Saskatoon Transit Services
c/o City of Saskatoon, 222 - 3rd Ave. North, Saskatoon, SK S7K 0J5
306-975-3100 Fax: 306-975-7532
transit.services@saskatoon.ca
Profile: Saskatoon Transit's mission is to provide cost-effective, safe and affordable public transit services using clean and enviornmentally friendly equipment that enables all residents to access work, education, health care, shopping, social and recreational opportunities.

Sault Ste. Marie Transit
111 Huron St., Sault Ste Marie, ON P6A 5P9
705-759-5848 Fax: 705-759-5834
d.scott@cityssm.on.ca
Profile: The Sault Ste. Marie Transit has a fleet of 28 regular Transit vehicles, 7 Para Transit buses, and 1 Community Bus
Don Scott, Transit Manager
d.scott@cityssm.on.ca

Société de transport de l'Outaouais
111, rue Jean-Proulx, Gatineau, QC J8Z 1T4
819-770-7900 Fax: 819-770-5987
www.sto.ca
Profile: The mission of the Société de transport de l'Outaouais is to provide residents of the municipalities in its area, which includes the Gatineau urban area as well as Cantley and Chelsea, with a reliable public transit system that meets their needs at a reasonable cost for users, taxpayers and these municipalities. They have 246 busses, 259 shelters, 11 million kilometers travelled each ear, 56 bus routes, comprised of 41 regular, 13 express and 2 interzone routes).

Société de transport de Laval
2250, av Francis-Hughes, Laval, QC H7S 2C3
450-662-5400 Fax: 450-662-5459
pgiard@stl.laval.qc.ca
www.stl.laval.qc.ca
Profile: The Société de transport de Laval ha 34 bus routes, covering a total distance of 627 km, has approx. 22 hours of daily service on weekdays, and 21 hours on weekends, and covers 13.4 million km in a year. It has 463 drivers, 225 busses, 281 bus shelters and 2300 bus stops.
Pierre Giard, Directeur général

Société de transport de Montréal
800, rue de la Gauchetière ouest, Montréal, QC H5A 1J6
514-786-4636
www.stm.info
Profile: Transport Montreal, or STM, has both a bus, para-transit and metro system. It provides 1.3 million trips on its system every day, with 1503 busses, 89 mini paratransit busses and 759 metro cars.

Société de transport de Sherbrooke
895, rue Cabana, Sherbrooke, QC J1K 2M3
819-564-2687 Fax: 819-564-1069
service.clientele@sts.qc.ca
www.sts.qc.ca

Squamish Transit System
c/o Whistler Transit Ltd., #101, 1055 Millar Creek Rd., Whistler, BC V0N 1B0
604-938-0388
scott@whistlertransit.pwt.ca
www.bctransit.com/regions/squ
Profile: The Squamish Transit System has many routes that go to Valleycliffe, Brackendale, Highlands, Downtown, Woodfibre Ferry, Garibaldi Highlands and most major destinations in Squamish. It also has accessible services including low floor busses, HandyDART and priority seating.

Stratford Transit
60 Corcoran St., Stratford, ON N5A 1V7
519-271-0250

Strathcona Transit
2001 Sherwood Dr., Sherwood Park, AB T8A 3W7
780-417-7187 Fax: 780-417-7176
transit@strathcona.ab.ca
Profile: Strathcona's Transit's mission is to provide an effective, efficient and customer-focused transit service that aligns with the County's three pillars of sustainability: environmental, economic and social.

Sunshine Coast Transit System
5920 Mason Rd., Sechelt, BC V0N 3A0
604-885-6899
transit@scrd.bc.ca
www.bctransit.com/regions/sun
Profile: The Sunshine Coast Transit System has many routes that go to the most built-up residential neighbourhoods between the Langdale, Gibsons and Sechelt. In addition, there is service to Halfmoon Bay and limited service on Saturday, Sunday and holidays to Secret Cove in the summertime.

Terrace Regional Transit System
c/o Coastal Bus Lines Ltd., 4904 Hwy. 16 West, Terrace, BC V8G 1L8
250-635-4991 Fax: 250-635-6417
phil.malnis@farwestgroup.com
www.bctransit.com/regions/ter
Profile: The Terrace Regional Transit System has many routes through the City of Terrace and the Regional District of Kitimat-Stikine. It also has several accessible services including low floor busses, Handy-DART and priority seating.

Thunder Bay Transit
570 Fort William Rd., Thunder Bay, ON P7B 2Z8
807-684-3744 Fax: 807-345-5744
www.thunderbay.ca/index.cfm?fuse=html&pg=728
Profile: Operates with a fleet of 49 buses on 17 routes
Alex Grant, Manager

Timmins Transit
220 Algonquin Blvd. East, Timmins, ON P4N 1B3
705-360-2654 Fax: 705-360-2698
transit@timmins.ca
www.timminstransit.ca/new
Profile: Timmins Transit is a service operated by the City of Timmins. They operate a fleet of over 25 buses, low floor buses, and accessible mini-buses
David Onodera, Transit Superintendent
david.onodera@city.timmins.on.ca

Toronto Transit Commission
1900 Yonge St., Toronto, ON M4S 1Z2
416-393-4000 Fax: 416-338-0210
www.city.toronto.on.ca/ttc
Profile: Operates a subway system which is linked with buses, streetcars, and light rail transit. The TTC dates to 1892

Transit Windsor
3700 North Service Rd. East, Windsor, ON N8W 5X2
519-944-4141 Fax: 519-944-5121
tw@city.windsor.on.ca
www.citywindsor.ca/transitwindsor
Profile: Fleet consists of 99 transit coaches, including 49 low floor vehicles

Trius Tours Ltd.
PO Box 2288, 22 Garfield St., Charlottetown, PE C1A 8C1
902-566-5664 Fax: 902-566-3497
trius.tours@pei.aibn.com
Profile: Trius Tours has 2-54 passenger motor coaches, 12-47 passenger motor coaches and 5-15 passenger vans which provide scenic tours of Prince Edward Island.
George M. Brookins, Contact

Vernon Regional Transit System
4210 - 24 Ave., Vernon, BC V1T 1M2
250-545-7286
vernontransit@shawcable.ca
www.bctransit.com/regions/ver
Profile: The Vernon Regional Transit System has many routes available to the community which go to to most major destinations in the City of Vernon, to the District of Coldstream, and Spallumcheen, Armstrong, Endergy, Lavington, Whitevale and Lumby. It has accessible services including community travel training, a taxi saver program, low floor busses and HandyDART.

Victoria Regional Transit Commission
c/o BC Transit, 520 Gorge Rd. East, Victoria, BC V8W 2P3
250-385-2551 Fax: 250-995-5639
nancy_longphee@bctransit.com
www.bctransit.com/regions/vic
Profile: The Victoria Regional Transit System began operation on 22 February 1890 with a fleet of four street cars. The system now serves approximately 312,000 persons and operates in a 400-square-kilometre area. The peak fleet in operation is 178 buses operating on 36 conventional routes, and 40 vans providing custom door-to-door service for people who cannot ride the conventional buses.
Barbara Harris, Contact

WAVE Whistler & Valley Express
#101, 1055 Millar Creek Rd., Whistler, BC V0N 1B0
604-932-4020
scott@whistlertransit.pwt.ca
www.bctransit.com/regions/whi
Profile: The Whistler and Valley Express, or WAVE, runs through Emerald Estates, Alpine Meadows, Spruce Grove, White Gold, Nesters, Tapleys Farm, Blueberry Hill, Whistler Village, the Upper Village, Alta Vista, Nordic Whistler Creek, Tamarisk, Function Junction and Pemberton. It has racks on which you can attach your bicycles or skis, and runs from 5:30 am to 3:00 am, 365 days a year.

Welland Transit
c/o City Hall, 60 East Main St., Welland, ON L3B 3X4
905-735-1700
transit@welland.ca
www.city.welland.on.ca/Transit/wTransit.html
Margaret Fortin, Office Coordinator

West Coast Express Ltd.
#295, 601 West Cordova, Vancouver, BC V6B 1G1
604-488-8906 Fax: 604-689-3896
wcecustomerservice@translink.bc.ca
www.westcoastexpress.com
Profile: West Coast Express (WCE) is an efficient commuter rail service linking Mission, Port Haney, Maple Ridge, Pitt Meadows, Port Coquitlam, Coquitlam and Port Moody with downtown Vancouver. They operate ten trains and two TrainBuses per day, Monday to Friday. There are five trains westbound from Mission to Vancouver in the morning peak commuter period and five trains eastbound from Vancouver to Mission in the afternoon. There is a morning TrainBus from Mission to Vancouver and an evening bus from Vancouver to Mission. West Coast Express does not run on weekends or statutory holidays.
Doug Kelsey, President & CEO

Whitehorse Transit
139 Tlingit St., Whitehorse, YT Y1A 2Y6
867-668-8394
transit@city.whitehorse.yk.ca
Profile: Whitehorse Transit runs six days a week, with no service on Sundays or holidays. There is also a Handy Bus which provides door-to-door service for those who are unable to use regular transit.
Dave Muir, Transit Manager

Winnipeg Transit
421 Osborne St., Winnipeg, MB R3L 2A2
204-986-5717
transit@winnipeg.com
winnipegtransit.com
Profile: Winnipeg Transit has 68 fixed routes throughout the city, including main line routes, express routes and suburban feeders, as well as a 'Handi-Transit' system.

Wood Buffalo Transit
9909 Franklin Ave., Fort McMurray, AB T9H 2K4
780-743-4157 Fax: 780-799-5899
transit@woodbuffalo.ab.ca
Profile: The Fort McMurray Public Transit System provides efficient bus service on a fixed route, fixed schedule basis. Offering eight regular routes and service five days a week, it carries 900,000 riders annually and links all of Fort McMurray's subdivisions through direct or feeder connections. The service is reduced on weekends and not available on some statutory holidays. It is free for seniors and children under five years of age.

York Region Transit
50 High Tech Rd., 5th Fl., Richmond Hill, ON L4B 4N7
905-762-2100
transitinfo@york.ca
www.yorkregiontransit.com
Profile: YRT offers more than 100 routes including conventional services, GO Shuttles, Express services, community buses and high school, college and university services

Trucking Companies

American Cartage Ltd.
#101-9366 200A St., Langley, BC V1M 4B3
604-513-3681 Fax: 604-513-3677
www.americancartage.com
Profile: To ensure prompt, safe delivery of marine containers to and from Vancouver's busy waterfront terminals.
Gloria Vander Schaaf, President

AMJ Campbell Inc.
1445 Courtneypark Dr., Mississauga, ON L5T 2E3

905-795-3785 Fax: 905-670-3787
www.amjcampbell.com
Ticker Symbol: AMJ
Profile: Local trucking with storage; Trucking, except local
Bruce Bowser, President/CEO
Richard Smith, CFO

Bulk Carriers (PEI) Ltd.
PO Box 153, 779 Bannockburn Rd., Cornwall, PE C0A 1H0
902-675-2600 Fax: 902-675-3100
info@bulkcarrierspei.com
www.bulkcarrierspei.com
Profile: With a fleet made up of reefer trailers, we haul primarily food products throughout 48 States and all the Canadian Provinces.
Jack Kelly, President

Canadian American Transportation Inc.
4 rue du Transport, Coteau-du-Lac, QC J0P 1B0
450-763-6363 Fax: 450-763-2400 800-363-5313
cat@cat.ca
www.cat.ca
Profile: For over 25 years, we have listened to our customers and responded to their needs with services that met their requirements. As a result, our efforts have awarded us the reputation of being a leader in the transportation industry. C.A.T. also offers logistics services and a partnership program with other transportation companies enabling opportunities to serve you better.
Daniel Goyette, President

Canadian Freightways
Lake City Industrial Park, 7867 Express St., Burnaby, BC V5A 1S8
604-420-4044 Fax: 604-420-4312
http://cf.cfmvmt.com
Profile: North American Coverage: Canadian Freightways provides services to 25,000 points across Canada and the U.S. through an integrated network of regional carriers including sister companies Epic Express and Click Express and strategic partners Averitt Express, New England Motor Freight, Midwest Motor Express and the Connection Company. Regional Expertise: Each partner in their North American network is a regional specialist providing overnight and second day service within their region. Partners operate local Service Centers and are represented by professional drivers and sales teams in key economic communities.
Ralph Wettstein, Vice President

Can-Truck Inc.
655 Bloor St. West, Oshawa, ON L1J 5Y6
905-404-6622 Fax: 905-404-6620
donf@can-truck.com
www.can-truck.com
Profile: Concentrates mainly on truckload freight including consolation and distribution throughout North America
Don Flesch, President
Frank Cassano, General Manager

Challenger Motor Freight Inc.
300 Maple Grove Rd., Cambridge, ON N3E 1B7
519-653-6226 Fax: 519-653-9810 800-265-6358
info1@challenger.com
www.challenger.com
Profile: Challenger transports goods between Canada and anywhere in North America. Has a full range of transportation, warehousing and logistics services
Dan Einwechter, Chairman & CEO

Challenger Motor Freight Inc.
300 Maple Grove Rd., Cambridge, ON N3E 1B7
519-653-6226 Fax: 519-653-9810 800-265-6358
info1@challenger.com
www.challenger.com
Profile: Constantly challenging ourselves to set new standards of quality and performance through leadership, respect and commitment.
Dan Einwechter, Chairman & CEO

Contrans Income Fund
PO Box 1210, 1179 Ridgeway Rd., Woodstock, ON N4S 8P6
519-421-4600 Fax: 519-539-9220
info@contrans.ca
www.contrans.ca
Ticker Symbol: CSS
Profile: Offices of holding companies; Long-distance trucking
Stan G. Dunford, Chair/CEO
Gregory W. Rumble, President/COO
James S. Clark, CFO & Vice-President, Finance
Kim Barnes, Manager, Management Information Systems

CRS-Express Inc.
2100, 95e rue, Saint-Georges, QC G5Y 8J3
418-227-7379 Fax: 418-227-7381 800-807-7379
www.crs-express.com
Profile: CRS Express is dedicated to excellence in the transportation industry. Pur customers will receive high quality services by a professional and complete transport.

Essen Transport Ltd.
PO Box 2229, Winkler, MB R6W 4B9
204-325-5200 Fax: 204-325-5252 800-760-3776
www.essentransport.com
Profile: Their focus on teamwork continues to satisfy new customers with effective supply chain management that consistently delivers on time. Essen Transport's team uses cutting edge logistics to track inbound and outbound shipments for over 100 reputable companies in Canada and the US .

Ghost Transportation Services
715E-46th St. West, Saskatoon, SK S7L 6A1
306-249-3515 Fax: 306-249-3335
customerservice@ghosttrans.com
www.ghosttrans.com
Profile: Ghost Transportation Services' diversity and flexibility are the keys. Whether it be warehousing, the shipment of raw materials, transportation or distribution of finished products, our dedication to satisfy our customer's needs and wants provides mutual success.
Clay Dowling, President

GN Transport
163 Bowes Rd., Concord, ON L4K 1H3
905-760-2888 Fax: 905-760-2040
info@gntransport.com
www.gntransport.com
Profile: With deregulation firmly in place, GN Transport Ltd. has expanded to serve our customers more effectively and to generate business opportunities within Ontario, and cross border into the United States.

Go Transport Ltd.
88 Golden Dr., Coquitlam, BC V3K 6T1
604-945-8300 Fax: 604-945-8305 888-363-6699
dispatch@gotransport.ca
www.gotransport.ca
Mark Maarsman, President

Grimshaw Trucking LP
11510-151 St., Edmonton, AB T5M 3N6
780-414-2880 Fax: 780-455-7818 888-414-2850
www.grimshaw-trucking.com
Profile: A highly respected transportation company in Western Canada.
Graham McDonald, Vice President

Group Express Inc.
170 Main St. N., Alexandria, ON K0C 1A0
613-525-1275 Fax: 613-525-1278
traffic@groupexpress.ca
www.groupexpress.ca
Profile: Groupex will provide our customers with quality transportation services of the highest value while emphasizing sustainable growth and public safety as measures of corporate strength and security for our employees.
Reynald Blais, President
Jeff ManKinnon, Traffic Manager

Harold Newell & Son Trucking Ltd.
R.R. #1, Barrington, NS B0W 1E0
902-637-2243 Fax: 902-637-1563
trucking@ns.sympatico.ca
www.tcfb.com/trucking

International Truck and Engine Corporation Canada
5500 North Service Rd., 4th Fl., Burlington, ON L7L 5H7
905-332-3323 Fax: 905-332-2965
www.internationaldelivers.com
Profile: Dealers of trucks, buses, vans: engines, parts, services & financing
James J. Schumacher, President

Kindersley Transport Inc.
660 Alford Ave., Delta, BC V3M 6X1
604-522-4002 Fax: 604-525-2955
customerservice@kindersleytransport.com
www.kindersleytransport.com
Profile: One of the largest, most modern fleets based in Western Canada providing truckload and less-than-truckload services through a network of strategically located service centers in Canada and the U.S.
Erwen Siemens, President

KO Transport Inc.
651 Burlington St. E., Hamilton, ON L8L 4J5
905-544-9000
info@kotransport.com
www.kotransport.com
Profile: KO Transport is a family-owned and operated business. Established in 1933, KO Transport has been in business since 1933, servicing the Southern Ontario region and points well beyond.

Kooi Trucking Inc.
PO Box 70, Scotland, ON N0E 1R0
519-446-3333 Fax: 519-446-3999
info@kooitruckinginc.com
www.kooitruckinginc.com
Profile: Kooi Trucking Inc. is an experienced freight company, specializing in the transportatoin needs of North American importers and exporters since 1993.
Sue Kooi, President

Lark Transport Inc.
2880 Saskatchewan Ave. W., Portage la Prarie, MB R1N 3B9
888-444-5257 Fax: 888-246-9365
www.larktransport.com
Profile: Lark Transport Inc. is proud to be a Canadian based freight transportation company.
Reynold Plett, Contact, Sales
reynold@larktransport.com
Rene Painchaud, Contact, Dispatch
rene@larktransport.com

Lighthouse Transport Services Ltd.
PO Box 38010, #2-150 Wright Ave., Dartmouth, NS B3B 1X2
902-468-3696 Fax: 902-468-5267 800-770-5457
colleen@lighthousetransport.com
www.lighthousetransport.com
Profile: Offers FTL and LTL transport, container transport, warehousing and crating, oversized cargo moves, pilot car services, flatbed moves, deconsolidations, in bond warehousing, exclusive deliveries, in bond transport.
Ernest O'Toole, President

Motrux Inc.
731 Belgrave Way, Delta, BC V3M 5R8
604-527-1000 Fax: 604-527-1002 800-663-3436
info@motrux.com
www.motrux.com
Profile: Over the years Motrux has evolved from a designated carrier, serving only a few specific customers in Western Canada, to one that now serves many customers across a variety of industries - throughout North America.

Mullen Transportation Inc.
PO Box 87, 1 Maple Leaf Rd., Aldersyde, AB T0L 0A0
403-652-8888 Fax: 403-601-8301
ir@mullentransportation.com
www.mullen-trans.com
Ticker Symbol: MTL
Profile: Offices of holding companies; Long-distance trucking; Local trucking with storage; Various oil & gas fields services
Murray K. Mullen, CEO/Chair
Stephen H. Lockwood, President & Co-CEO
David E. Olsen, CFO & Vice-President, Finance

Overland Freight Courrier
#300-10362 King George Hwy., Surrey, BC V3T 2W5
604-580-4600 Fax: 604-580-4601 800-698-2111
admin@overland.ca
www.welightentheload.com
Profile: We are a diverse group of Canadian individuals who try to provide our customers with no surprises LTL-freight-courier service in British Columbia Canada, Alberta Canada, and the Western United States of America.

Pacific Coast Express Ltd.
#220-185 Golden Dr., Coquitlam, BC V3K 6T1
800-667-6061
www.pcx.ca/pacificcoast.htm
Profile: Pacific Coast Express Ltd. is a wholly owned operating unit of Landtran Systems Inc., Western Canada's largest integrated regional distribution company. The primary service offered by the company is expedited LTL/TL, dry van motor freight service between all points in Western Canada and core markets in Arizona, California, Oregon Washington and Mexico. We also provide selected service to points in the Idaho and Utah markets from British Columbia and Alberta, as well as domestic transportation to and from Vancouver Island.
Al Turner, President

Phantom Freightlines
5300 86 Ave. SE, Calgary, AB T2C 47L
403-219-1008 Fax: 403-219-1016
www.phantomfreightlines.com
Profile: Phantom Freightlines is a family-owned, Alberta based business that specializes in the transportation of time sensitive

and delicate materials for over 25 years. From meat and produce, to flowers and plants, we understand the unique needs of temperature controlled cargo and pride ourselves on providing safe, hassle-free delivery 365 days a year across Canada and the United States.
Scott Decker, Director, Corporate Development
Lindsey Kydd, Vice President, Sales and Marketing

Polar Express Transportation Ltd.
#4, 10097-201 St., Langley, BC V1M 3G4
604-888-3729 Fax: 604-888-3759
jplowman@polarexpresstrans.com
www.polarexpresstrans.com
Profile: Starting January 2000 with one 10 ton and one tractor/trailer we began hauling refrigerated goods to/from Seattle/Tacoma, WA and Vancouver, BC. Using this foundation we have grown to become the West's best choice for handling refrigerated goods moving between the US and Canada.

Premium Trucknig Ltd.
PO Box 39, 449 Lower Rd., Arichat, NS B0E 1A0
902-226-3474 Fax: 902-226-0026
www.premiumseafoods.ns.ca/ptrucking.php
Profile: Premium Trucking Ltd. provides world-class transportation services at a fair price. The company owns and operates a fleet of high-quality vehicles, which includes five delivery trucks and two tractor-trailers.
Edgar Sampson, President

Redline Transport
PO Box 22, R.R. #4, Brandon, MB R7A 5Y4
204-727-1673 Fax: 204-725-3548 800-367-0375
redline@escape.ca
www.redlinetransport.com
Profile: Redline Transport has remained an important part of the rural economy. Redline Transport changed ownership in September 2005, when it was bought be Robert & Lynda Moffatt in Strathclair. Redline continues to grow with more than 20 trucks on the road and offices in both Rivers and Brandon.
Ron Bouchardd, General Manager

Rockman Transport
10765 Cote de Lisse #56, Dorval, QC H9P 1A7
514-422-1085 Fax: 514-422-1083
www.rockmantransport.com
Profile: A bonded transport company with facilities at Montreal and Ottawa, serving the CL and LCL container deliveries for the major Maritime Companies for over 20 years, Rockman Trucking is equipped with recent and well kept equipment to ensure prompt and timely deliveries. We can deliver any size container; from 20' to 53'. Whether regular, High Cube, Open top or Reefer containers for Imports as well as Exports purposes.

Rolls Right Industry
2961 Norland Ave., Burnaby, BC V5B 3A9
604-298-0080 Fax: 604-298-1366
info@rollsright.ca
www.rollsright.ca
Profile: At Rolls Right Industries, we understand that our customers depend on timely deliveries to maintain proper inventory levels, fully-stocked shelves and secure sales. Whether your are a local supplier to the retail sector or a custom broker moving containers, with a wide range of time sensitive freight transportation services, Rolls Right will get you there.

Shadow Lines Transportation Group
9818 198B St., Langley, BC V1M 2X5
604-888-2976 Fax: 604-888-2459
www.shadowlines.com
Profile: Shadow Lines has over 35 years experience as a service based transportation company. We operate in Canada from British Columbia to Ontario and throughout the 48 states of the continental USA.

Swift Dispatch Service Ltd.
32 West 5th Ave., Vancouver, BC V5Y 1H5
604-873-5422 Fax: 604-879-2311
info@swiftdispatch.com

TLI FlatDecks Inc.
1260 Cliveden Ave., Delta, BC V3M 6Y1
877-517-1177 Fax: 604-527-1175
www.tliflatdecks.net
Profile: We are an international flat deck specialized carrier, based in Delta BC, servicing all of North America. As a bonded carrier with terminals across Canada, we offer cross dock and reload services at all our locations. We have 24-hour dispatch and all types of trailers, including heavy haul units. Continuous improvement is the cornerstone of a growing, innovative company.
John Stokes, Contact

TMT Freight System
14 Cadetta Rd., Brampton, ON L6T 3Z8
905-794-9845 Fax: 905-794-9846 888-817-4410
info@tmtfreight.com
www.tmtfreight.com
Profile: TMT Freight System was emerged as an innovative company in the year 1993 and over our nearly 13 year history; we have dedicated our efforts to being a container carrier with a strong motto of on time delivery with care and safety.
Bobby Mahal, President
Jasbir Sanghera, Vice Prestident

Trailmobile Canada Limited
455 Gibraltar Dr., Mississauga, ON L5T 2S9
905-565-9500 Fax: 905-565-9525
hq@trailmobile.com
www.trailmobile.com
Profile: Manufacturers of truck trailers
Tom Wiseman, President
Bert Clay, Vice-President, Sales & Marketing

TransForce Income Fund
6600, ch St-François, Montréal, QC H4S 1B7
514-856-7500 Fax: 514-332-9527
administration@transforce.ca
www.transforce.ca
Ticker Symbol: TFI
Profile: Long-distance trucking; Local trucking without storage
Alain Bedard, President/CEO & Chair
Salvatore Vitale, CFO

TransForce Income Fund
#300, 8585 Trans-Canada Highway, Saint-Laurent, QC H4S 1Z6
514-331-4000 Fax: 514-337-4200
administration@transforce.ca
www.transforce.ca
Profile: TransForce Income Fund creates value for unitholders by managing and investing in a growing network of independent operating companies. The Fund, through these subsidiaries, is the leader in Canada's transportation and logistics industry.
Alain Bedard, President & CEO

Trappers Transport Ltd.
2475 Day St., Winnipeg, MB R2C 2Z2
204-697-7647 Fax: 204-633-5569
www.trapperstransport.com
Profile: We specialize in the transportation of refrigerated LTL or Full Loads throughout North America. Our maintenance shop services or repairs all makes and models of trucks, trailers, heavy equipment and reefer units.
Dan Omeniuk, President & CEO
Pankaj Sharma, Vice President & CFO, Finance

Trimac Corporation
PO Box 3500 M, #1700, 800 - 5th Ave. SW, Calgary, AB T2P 2P9
403-298-5100 Fax: 403-298-5146
info@trimac.com
www.trimac.com
Ticker Symbol: TMA.UN
Profile: The company provides services in highway transportation of bulk commodities.
Terry Owen, President/CEO
416-298-5101, Fax: 416-298-5355, tjowen@trimac.com
Ed Malysa, Vice-President/CFO
416-298-5176, Fax: 416-298-5146, emalysa@trimac.com

Vitran Corporation Inc.
#701, 185 The West Mall, Toronto, ON M9C 5L5
416-596-7664 Fax: 416-596-8039
webmaster@vitran.com
www.vitran.com
Ticker Symbol: VTN
Profile: Long-distance trucking; Arrangement of transportation of freight & cargo; General warehousing & storage; Refuse systems
Rick E. Gaetz, President/CEO
Sean P. Washchuk, CFO & Vice-President, Finance

West Arm Truck Lines
1077 Columbia Rd., Castlegar, BC V1N 4K5
250-365-2127 Fax: 250-365-5658 800-363-9247
info@westarm.com
www.westarm.com
Profile: West Arm Truck Lines is the premier freight service provider in Southern British Columbia and Alberta. We provide overnight LTL service to all major centres in these areas. Well maintained, late model equipment and the most up to date computer technology allow the people of West Arm Truck Lines to deliver on commitments to our customers.
Michael Revane, Contact
michael_revane@westarm.com

Yanke Group of Companies
2815 Lorne Ave., Saskatoon, SK S7J 0S5
306-955-4221 Fax: 306-955-5663 800-667-7988
yanke_sales@yanke.ca
www.yanke.ca
Profile: During the last 30 years, our founder has seen Yanke expand from a mere two trucks to a fleet of more than 400, and flourish from 33 employees to over 700. Cancom satellite systems. Instant shipment tracking. National weather monitoring system. Why does Yanke do all of this? We strive to stay ahead of our time to make sure that we are always on time.

Zeena Transport
PO Box 759, Morden, MB R6M 1A7
204-822-4915 Fax: 204-822-4687
www.zeenatransport.com
Profile: We are proud to offer our customers the best refrigerated and dry van service possible. We accomplish this by utilizing dependable, up-to-date equipment and well trained, dependable employees.
Henry Giesbrecht, President
Reynold Hildebrand, Operations Manager

Transportation Manufacturers & Services

Atlas Cold Storage Income Trust
5255 Yonge St., Toronto, ON M2N 5P8
416-512-2352 Fax: 416-512-2353 888-642-3333
inquiries@atlascold.com
www.atlascold.com
Ticker Symbol: FZR
Profile: Refrigerated warehousing & storage
J. David Williamson, President/CEO
Kevin Glass, Sr. Vice-President & CFO
Robert Lockie, Vice-President, Information Technology Operations

Bombardier Inc.
800, boul René-Lévesque ouest, Montréal, QC H3B 1Y8
514-861-9481 Fax: 514-861-7053
www.bombardier.com
Ticker Symbol: BBD
Profile: Manufacturers of railroad equipment, aircraft, aircraft engines & engine parts, aircraft parts & auxiliary equipment, various transportation equipment; Personal credit institutions; Real estate land subdividers & developers
Laurent Beaudoin, Chair/CEO
Pierre Beaudoin, President/COO, Bombardier Aerospace
Pierre Alary, Sr. Vice-President/CFO

Dynetek Industries Ltd.
4410 - 46 Ave. SE, Calgary, AB T2B 3N7
403-720-0262 Fax: 403-720-0263
invest@dynetek.com
www.dynetek.com
Ticker Symbol: DNK
Profile: Manufacturers of cylinders, fuel cell storage systems
Robb D. Thompson, President/CEO
Karen Y. Minton, Vice-President, Finance & Administration

Glendale International Corp.
353 Iroquois Shore Rd., Oakville, ON L6H 1M3
905-844-2870 Fax: 905-844-2907
info@glendaleint.com
www.glendaleint.com
Ticker Symbol: GIN
Profile: Manufacturers of motor homes, travel trailers & campers, radio & television broadcasting & communications equipment, printed circuit boards, & various electronic components
Edward C. Hanna, President/CEO & Chair
Philip L. Szabo, Vice-President/CFO & Secretary

Greyhound Canada Transportation Corp.
877 Greyhound Way SW, Calgary, AB T3C 3V8
403-260-0877 Fax: 403-260-0779
canada.info@greyhound.ca
www.greyhound.ca
Profile: Intercity & rural bus transportation; travel agencies; courier services
Dave Leach, Sr. Vice President, Canada

Héroux-Devtek inc
Tour est, #658, 1111, rue St-Charles, Longueuil, QC J4K 5G4
450-679-3330 Fax: 450-679-3666
ir@herouxdevtek.com
www.herouxdevtek.com
Ticker Symbol: HRX
Profile: Manufacturers of aircraft parts & auxiliary equipment; Wholesalers of transportation equipment & supplies; Airports, flying fields & airport terminal services
Gilles Labbé, President/CEO

Réal Bélanger, CFO & Exec. Vice-President

Intier Automotive Inc.
521 Newpark Blvd., Newmarket, ON L3Y 4X7
905-898-5200 Fax: 905-898-4178
info@intier.com
www.intier.com
Ticker Symbol: IAI.A
Profile: Develops & manufactures vehicle interiors; Consumer research
Donald J. Walker, President/CEO
Michael E. McCarthy, CFO & Exec. Vice-President
Georg Kirchbaumer, Chief Technology Officer

Lear Canada Ltd.
PO Box 9758, 530 Manitou Dr., Kitchener, ON N2G 4C2
519-895-1600 Fax: 519-895-3248
www.lear.com
Profile: Designs, tests & produces automotive interiors
Donald J. Stebbins, President/COO, Americas
David C. Wajsgras, CFO & Sr. Vice-President, Lear Corporation

Linamar Corporation
287 Speedvale Ave. West, Guelph, ON N1H 1C5
519-836-7550 Fax: 519-836-9175
investorrelations@linamar.com
www.linamar.com
Ticker Symbol: LNR
Profile: Manufacturers of motor vehicle parts & accessories, fabricated plate work, carburetors, pistons, piston rings, valves, farm machinery equipment, aircraft parts & auxiliary equipment, pumps & pumping equipment; Wholesalers of farm & garden machinery & equipment
Linda Hasenfratz, President/CEO
Csaba Havasi, Group President, Europe
Peggy Mulligan, CFO/ Exec. Vice-President & Treasurer
Mark Stoddart, Chief Technology Development Officer & Vice-President, Marketing

Magellan Aerospace Corporation
3160 Derry Rd. East, Mississauga, ON L4T 1A9
905-677-1889 Fax: 905-677-5658
info@aerospace.com
www.magellanaerospace.com
Ticker Symbol: MAL
Profile: Manufacturers of aircraft parts & auxiliary equipment, aircraft engines & engine parts
Richard A. Neill, President/CEO
John B. Dekker, Secretary/Vice-President, Finance
Donald C. Lowe, Chair, Risk Management & Environmental Committee

Magna International Inc.
337 Magna Dr., Aurora, ON L4G 7K1
905-726-2462 Fax: 905-726-7164
www.magnaint.com
Ticker Symbol: MG
Profile: Manufacturers of motor vehicle parts & accessories, automotive stampings, various fabricated metal products, motor vehicles & passenger car bodies, vehicular lighting equipment, various fabricated textile products, public building & related furniture; Wholesalers of motor vehicle supplies & new parts; Racing, including track operation; Various amusement & recreation services
Siegfried Wolf, Co-CEO
Vincent J. Galifi, CFO & Exec. Vice-President, Finance

NAV Canada
PO Box 3411 D, 77 Metcalfe St., Ottawa, ON K1P 5L6
613-563-5588 Fax: 613-563-3426 800-876-4693
service@navcanada.ca
www.navcanada.ca
Profile: Provides, maintains & enhances an air navigation service
John W. Crichton, President/CEO
R.A. (Sandy) Morrison, Chair
William G. Fenton, Treasurer/CFO & Vice-President, Finance
John Morris, Director, Communications
Sidney Koslow, Vice-President/Chief Technology Officer

Northstar Aerospace
105 Bedford Rd., Toronto, ON M5R 2K4
416-364-5852 Fax: 416-362-5334
www.northstar-aerospace.com
Ticker Symbol: NAS
Profile: Manufacturers of motor vehicle parts & accessories, aircraft parts & auxiliary equipment, speed changers, industrial high-speed drives, gears, aircraft engines & engine parts; Airports, flying fields & airport terminal services
Mark Emery, President/CEO
Thomas E. Connerty, CFO

Pratt & Whitney Canada Corp.
1000, boul Marie-Victorin, Longueuil, QC J4G 1A1
450-677-9411 Fax: 450-647-3620
communications@pwc.ca
www.pwc.ca
Profile: Manufacturers of aircraft engines & engine parts; Wholesalers of transportation equipment & supplies
Alain M. Bellemare, President
Miguel C. Doyon, Vice-President, Finance
Amal M. Girgis, Chief Information Officer
John Saabas, Exec. Vice-President

Prevost Car Inc.
35, boul Gagnon, Sainte-Claire, QC G0R 2V0
418-883-3391 Fax: 418-883-4157
www.prevostcar.com
Profile: Manufacturers of intercity coaches & coach shells for motorhomes & specialty conversion
Gaetan Bolduc, President/CEO

Public Storage Canadian Properties
First Canadian Place, #6600, 100 King St. West, Toronto, ON M5X 1B8
866-772-2623
investor@publicstorage.ca
www.publicstoragecanada.com
Ticker Symbol: PUB
Profile: General warehousing & storage
David P. Singelyn, President
Vincent R. Chan, Vice-President/Controller

Rolls-Royce Canada ltée
9500, ch de la Côte-de-Liesse, Montréal, QC H8T 1A2
514-636-0964 Fax: 514-636-9969
www.rolls-royce.com
Profile: Airports, flying fields & airport terminal services; Manufacturers of steam, gas, hydraulic turbines & turbine generator units
Pierre Racine, President/CEO
Stephane Guerin, CFO

Spar Aerospace Limited
Edmonton International Airport, PO Box 9864, Edmonton, AB T5J 2T2
780-890-6300 Fax: 780-890-6652
www.spar.ca
Profile: Aviation services: aircraft programs; Component maintenance, repair & operation; Support services
Patrice M. Pelletier, President

ThyssenKrupp Budd Canada Inc.
PO Box 1204, Kitchener, ON N2G 4G8
519-895-1000 Fax: 519-895-0099
Ticker Symbol: BUD
Profile: Manufacturers of motor vehicle parts & accessories; Wholesalers of motor vehicle supplies & new parts
Micheal Balavich, President
David A. Robinson, CFO & Controller

The Toronto Transit Commission
1900 Yonge St., Toronto, ON M4S 1Z2
416-393-4000 Fax: 416-482-0478
www.ttc.ca
Profile: Operates & maintains urban transit system: buses, subways, streetcars & trolleys
R. Ducharme, CEO
Mike Roche, CFO
John Cannon, Chief Information Officer

Tri-White Corporation
#1400, 1 University Ave., Toronto, ON M5J 2P1
416-367-6877 Fax: 416-367-6890
www.tri-white.com
Ticker Symbol: TWH
Profile: Local & suburban transit; Local passenger transportation
K. (Rai) Sahi, Chair/CEO
Donald W. Turple, CFO
Beverley Flynn, Corporate Counsel & Secretary

Uniglobe Travel International L.P.
#900, 1199 West Pender St., Vancouver, BC V6E 2R1
604-718-2600 Fax: 604-718-2678
info@uniglobetravel.com
www.uniglobetravel.com
Profile: Travel franchise specializing in corporate travel services for small to medium accounts as well as individual travelers.
U. Gary Charlwood, Chair/CEO
Tracy Bartram, CFO & Exec. Vice-President

Vector Aerospace Corporation
#300, 105 Bedford Rd., Toronto, ON M5R 2K4
416-925-1143 Fax: 416-925-7214
investorinfo@vectoraerospace.ca
www.vectoraerospace.ca
Ticker Symbol: RNO
Profile: Manufacturers of aircraft parts & auxiliary equipment; Electrical & electronic repair shops; Various repair shops & related services
Donald Jackson, President/CEO
Randal L. Levine, Sr. Vice-President/CFO & Corporate Secretary

Versacold Income Fund
2115 Commissioner St., Vancouver, BC V5L 1A6
604-255-4656 Fax: 604-255-4330
info@versacold.com
www.versacold.com
Ticker Symbol: ICE
Profile: Refrigerated logistics services: storage & transportation
H. Brent Sugden, Chair/President & CEO
Joel M. Smith, CFO & Exec. Vice-President

Wescast Industries Inc.
150 Savannah Oaks Dr., Brantford, ON N3T 5L8
519-750-0000 Fax: 519-720-1629
investor.relations@wescast.com
www.wescast.com
Ticker Symbol: WCS
Profile: Manufacturers of motor vehicle parts & accessories; Wholesalers of motor vehicle supplies & new parts
Edward G. Frackwiak, Chair/CEO
Dave Dean, Vice-President, Finance

World Point Terminals Inc.
#303, 407 - 8th Ave. SW, Calgary, AB T2P 1E5
403-261-3700 Fax: 403-282-3323
Ticker Symbol: WPO
Profile: Various transportation services; Special warehousing & storage; Manufacturers of petroleum refining
Bruce N. Calvin, President
Steven G. Twele, CFO

Government Agency Guide

AIRPORTS & AVIATION
See Also: Transportation

Canadian Air Transport Security Authority, 99 Bank St., 13th Fl., Ottawa, ON K1P 6B9
Fax: 613-991-6726, 888-294-2202

Institute for Aerospace Research, 1200 Montreal Rd., Ottawa, K1A 0R6 ON
613-991-5738, Fax: 613-952-7214

Transport Canada, Place de Ville, 330 Sparks St., Tower C, Ottawa, K1A 0N5 ON
613-990-2309, Fax: 613-954-4731, minTC@tc.gc.ca

Transportation Appeal Tribunal of Canada, 333 Laurier Ave. West, 12th Fl., Ottawa, ON K1A 0N5
613-990-6906, Fax: 613-990-9153, info@tatc.gc.ca

Newfoundland & Labrador
Department of Transportation & Works, Confederation Bldg., West Block, 6th Fl., PO Box 8700, St. John's, A1B 4J6 NL
709-729-3679, Fax: 709-729-4285, twminister@gov.nl.ca

Northwest Territories
Airports, YK Centre, 4922 - 28th St., 4th fl., PO Box 1320, Yellowknife, X1A 2L9 NT
867-873-7725, Fax: 867-873-0297

Department of Transportation, Lahm Ridge Bldg., 4501 50 Ave., PO Box 1320, Yellowknife, X1A 2L9 NT
867-920-3460, Fax: 867-873-0363

Nunavut
Department of Community & Government Services, J.G. Brown Bldg., PO Box 1000 700,Iqaluit, X0A 0H0 NU
867-975-5400, Fax: 867-975-5305

Ontario
Ministry of Transportation, Ferguson Block, 77 Wellesley St. West, 3rd Fl., Toronto, M7A 1Z8 ON
416-235-4686, Fax: 416-327-9185, 800-268-4686

Saskatchewan
Saskatchewan Highways & Infrastructure, 1855 Victoria Ave., Regina, S4P 3T2 SK
306-787-4800,

Yukon Territory
Yukon Highways & Public Works, PO Box 2703, Whitehorse, Y1A 2C6 YT
867-393-7193, Fax: 867-393-6218, 800-661-0408, hpw-info@gov.yk.ca

RAIL TRANSPORTATION
See Also: Transportation

Transportation Safety Board of Canada, 200 Promenade du Portage, 4th Fl., Ottawa, K1A 1K8 ON
819-994-3741, Fax: 819-997-2239, 800-387-3557
Via Rail Canada Inc., #500, 3, Place Ville-Marie, Montréal, H3B 2C9 QC
514-871-6000, Fax: 514-871-6768

Manitoba
Manitoba Infrastructure & Transportation, Legislative Building, #203, 450 Broadway Ave., Winnipeg, R3C 0V8 MB
204-945-3723, Fax: 204-945-7610

New Brunswick
Department of Transportation, Kings Pl., 440 KingSt., PO Box 6000, Fredericton, E3B 5H8 NB
506-453-3939, Fax: 506-453-2900, Transportation.Web@gnb.ca

Newfoundland & Labrador
Department of Transportation & Works, Confederation Bldg., West Block, 6th Fl., PO Box 8700, St. John's, A1B 4J6 NL
709-729-3679, Fax: 709-729-4285, twminister@gov.nl.ca

Nova Scotia
Department of Transportation & Infrastructure Renewal, Johnston Bldg., 1672 Granville St., 2nd Fl., PO Box 186, Halifax, B3J 2N2 NS
902-424-2297, Fax: 902-424-0171, 888-432-3233, tpwpaff@gov.ns.ca

Ontario
GO Transit, #600, 20 Bay St., Toronto, ON M5J 2W3
416-869-3600, Fax: 416-869-1755, 888-438-6646

Quebec
Société du port ferroviaire Baie-Comeau-Hauterive, 18, rte Maritime, Baie-Comeau, QC G4Z 2L6
418-296-6785, Fax: 418-296-2377, soport@globetrotter.qc.ca
Ministère des Transports, 700, boul René-Lévesque est, 27e étage, Québec, G1R 5H1 QC
Fax: 514-643-1269, 888-355-0511, communications@mtq.gouv.qc.ca

Saskatchewan
Saskatchewan Highways & Infrastructure, 1855 Victoria Ave., Regina, S4P 3T2 SK
306-787-4800

TRANSPORTATION

Atlantic Pilotage Authority Canada, #910, 2000 Barrington St., Halifax, B3J 3K1 NS
902-426-2550, Fax: 902-426-4004
Canadian Air Transport Security Authority, 99 Bank St., 13th Fl., Ottawa, ON K1P 6B9
Fax: 613-991-6726, 888-294-2202
Canadian Coast Guard, Centennial Towers, #6S018, 200 Kent St., Ottawa, K1A 0E6 ON
613-998-1573, Fax: 613-990-2780
Canadian Transportation Agency, Les Terrasses de la Chaudière, 15, rue Eddy, Gatineau, K1A 0N9 QC
819-997-0344, Fax: 819-997-6727, 888-222-2592, info@otc-cta.gc.ca
Centre for Surface Transportation Technology, 2320 Lester Rd., Ottawa, K1V 1S2 ON
613-998-9639, Fax: 613-957-0831, inquiries.cstt@nrc-cnrc.gc.ca
Federal Bridge Corporation Limited, #1210, 55 Metcalfe St., Ottawa, ON K1P 6L5
613-993-6880, Fax: 613-993-6945, info@federalbridge.ca
Great Lakes Pilotage Authority, 202 Pitt St., 2nd fl., PO Box 95, Cornwall, K6H 5R9 ON
613-933-2991, Fax: 613-932-3793, administration@glpa-apgl.com
Institute for Aerospace Research, 1200 Montreal Rd., Ottawa, K1A 0R6 ON
613-991-5738, Fax: 613-952-7214
Laurentian Pilotage Authority Canada, #1501, 555, boul René-Lévesque ouest, Montréal, H2Z 1B1 QC
514-283-6320, Fax: 514-496-2409, administration@apl.gc.ca
Marine Atlantic Inc., Baine Johnston Centre, #802, 10 Fort William Place, St. John's, A1C 1K4 NL
709-772-8957, Fax: 709-772-8956, 800-341-7981, info@marine-atlantic.ca
Old Port of Montréal Corporation Inc., 333, rue de la Commune ouest, Montréal, H2Y 2E2 QC
514-283-5256, Fax: 514-283-8423
Pacific Pilotage Authority Canada, #1000, 1130 Pender St. West, Vancouver, V6E 4A4 BC
604-666-6771, Fax: 604-666-1647, info@ppa.gc.ca
Parc Downsview Park Inc., #1, 35 Carl Hall Rd., Toronto, M3K 2B6 ON
613-952-2222, Fax: 613-952-2225, info@pdp.ca
St. Lawrence Seaway Management Corporation, 202 Pitt St., Cornwall, K6J 3P7 ON
613-932-5170, Fax: 613-932-7286, marketing@seaway.ca
Transport Canada, Place de Ville, 330 Sparks St., Tower C, Ottawa, K1A 0N5 ON
613-990-2309, Fax: 613-954-4731, minTC@tc.gc.ca
Transportation Appeal Tribunal of Canada, 333 Laurier Ave. West, 12th Fl., Ottawa, ON K1A 0N5
613-990-6906, Fax: 613-990-9153, info@tatc.gc.ca
Transportation Safety Board of Canada, 200 Promenade du Portage, 4th Fl., Ottawa, K1A 1K8 ON
819-994-3741, Fax: 819-997-2239, 800-387-3557
Via Rail Canada Inc., #500, 3, Place Ville-Marie, Montréal, H3B 2C9 QC
514-871-6000, Fax: 514-871-6768

Alberta
Automobile Insurance Rate Board, Terrace Bldg., #200, 9515 - 107 St. NW, Edmonton, AB T5K 2C3
780-427-5428, Fax: 780-644-7771, airb@gov.ab.ca
Alberta Infrastructure & Transportation, Twin Atria Bldg., 4999 - 98 Ave., Edmonton, T6B 2X3 AB
780-427-2731, Fax: 780-466-3166,-310-0000
Transportation Safety Board, Twin Atria Bldg., 4999 - 98 Ave., Edmonton, AB T6B 2X3
780-427-7178, Fax: 780-422-9739

British Columbia
British Columbia Ferry Commission, PO Box 1497, Comox, BC V9M 8A2
250-339-2714, info@bcferrycommission.com
British Columbia Transit, 520 Gorge Rd. East, PO Box 610, Victoria, BC V8W 2P3
250-385-2551, Fax: 250-995-5639
British Columbia Ferry Services Inc., 1112 Fort St., Victoria, V8V 4V2 BC
250-381-1401, 888-223-3779
Passenger Transportation Board, #202, 940 Blanshard St., PO Box 9850 Prov Govt, Victoria, BC V8W 9T5
250-953-3777, Fax: 250-953-3788, ptboard@gov.bc.ca
Ministry of Transportation & Infrastructure, 940 Blanshard St., PO Box 9850 Prov Govt,Victoria, V8W 9T5 BC
250-387-3198, Fax: 250-356-7706, tran.webmaster@gov.bc.ca
Transportation Planning & Policy Department, #5C, 940 Blanshard St., PO Box 9850 Prov Govt,Victoria, V8W 9T5 BC
250-387-5062, Fax: 250-387-6431

Manitoba
Highway Traffic Board/Motor Transport Board, #200, 301 Weston St., Winnipeg, MB R3E 3H4
204-945-8912, Fax: 204-783-6529
Manitoba Infrastructure & Transportation, Legislative Building, #203, 450 Broadway Ave., Winnipeg, R3C 0V8 MB
204-945-3723, Fax: 204-945-7610
License Suspension Appeal Board/Medical Review Committee, #200, 301 Weston St., Winnipeg, MB R3E 3H4
204-945-7350, Fax: 204-948-2682
Taxicab Board, #200, 301 Weston St., Winnipeg, MB R3E 3H4
Fax: 204-948-2315

New Brunswick
New Brunswick Transportation Authority, Kings Place, 440 King St., PO Box 6000, Fredericton, NB E3B 5H1
506-453-3939, Fax: 506-453-2900
Department of Transportation, Kings Pl., 440 KingSt., PO Box 6000, Fredericton, E3B 5H8 NB
506-453-3939, Fax: 506-453-2900, Transportation.Web@gnb.ca

Newfoundland & Labrador
Department of Transportation & Works, Confederation Bldg., West Block, 6th Fl., PO Box 8700, St. John's, A1B 4J6 NL
709-729-3679, Fax: 709-729-4285, twminister@gov.nl.ca

Northwest Territories
Highways, 4510 - 50 Ave., 2nd fl., PO Box 1320, Yellowknife, X1A 2L9 NT
867-920-8771, Fax: 867-873-0288
Department of Transportation, Lahm Ridge Bldg., 4501 50 Ave., PO Box 1320, Yellowknife, X1A 2L9 NT
867-920-3460, Fax: 867-873-0363

Nova Scotia
Department of Transportation & Infrastructure Renewal, Johnston Bldg., 1672 Granville St., 2nd Fl., PO Box 186, Halifax, B3J 2N2 NS
902-424-2297, Fax: 902-424-0171, 888-432-3233, tpwpaff@gov.ns.ca

Nunavut
Department of Community & Government Services, J.G. Brown Bldg., PO Box 1000 700,Iqaluit, X0A 0H0 NU
867-975-5400, Fax: 867-975-5305
Department of Economic Development & Transportation, #1104 Inuksugait Plaza, PO Box 1000 1500,Iqaluit, X0A 0H0 NU
867-975-7800, Fax: 867-975-7870, 888-975-5999, edt@gov.nu.ca

Ontario
GO Transit, #600, 20 Bay St., Toronto, ON M5J 2W3
416-869-3600, Fax: 416-869-1755, 888-438-6646
Licence Appeal Tribunal (LAT), 1 St. Clair Ave. West, 12th Fl., Toronto, ON M4V 1K6
416-314-4260, Fax: 416-314-4270, 800-255-2214
Niagara Falls Bridge Commission, PO Box 395, Niagara Falls, L2E 6T8 ON
905-354-5641, Fax: 905-353-6644
Ontario Highway Transport Board, 151 Bloor St. West, 10th Fl., Toronto, ON M5S 2T5
416-326-6732, Fax: 416-326-6738, ohtb@mto.gov.on.ca
Owen Sound Transportation Company Ltd., RR#5, Hwy 6 & 21, Owen Sound, ON N4K 5N7
519-376-8740
Road User Safety Division, #191, Bldg A, 1201 Wilson Ave., Toronto, M3M 1J8 ON
416-235-2999, Fax: 416-235-4153
Ministry of Transportation, Ferguson Block, 77 Wellesley St. West, 3rd Fl., Toronto, M7A 1Z8 ON
416-235-4686, Fax: 416-327-9185, 800-268-4686

Prince Edward Island
Department of Transportation & Public Works, Jones Bldg., 11 Kent St., PO Box 2000, Charlottetown, C1A 7N8 PE
902-368-5100, Fax: 902-368-5395

Quebec
Abitibi-Témiscamingue-Nord-du-Québec, 80, av Québec, Rouyn-Noranda, J9X 6R1 QC
819-763-3271, Fax: 819-763-3493, datnq@mtq.gouv.qc.ca
Bas-Saint-Laurent-Gaspésie-Iles-de-la-Madeleine, #101, 92, 2e rue ouest, Rimouski, G5L 8E6 QC
418-727-3674, Fax: 418-727-3673, dtbgi@mtq.gouv.qc.ca
Capitale-Nationale, 475, boul de l'Atrium, 2e étage, Québec, G1H 7H9 QC
418-643-1911, Fax: 418-646-0003, dcnat@mtq.gouv.qc.ca
Chaudière-Appalaches, 1156, boul de la Rive-Sud, Saint-Romuald, G6W 5M6 QC
418-839-5581, Fax: 418-834-7338, dtca@mtq.gouv.qc.ca
Commission des transports du Québec, 200, ch Sainte-Foy, 7e étage, Québec, QC G1R 5V5
Fax: 418-644-8034, 888-461-2433, courrier@ctq.gouv.qc.ca
Côte-Nord, #110, 625, boul Laflèche, Baie-Comeau, G5C 1C5 QC
418-295-4765, Fax: 418-295-4766, dtcn@mtq.gouv.qc.ca
Est-de-la-Montérégie, 201, place Charles-Lemoyne, 5e étage, Longueuil, J4K 2T5 QC
450-677-3413, Fax: 450-442-1317, dtem@mtq.gouv.qc.ca
Estrie, #2.02, 200, rue Belvédère nord, Sherbrooke, J1H 4A9 QC
819-820-3280, Fax: 819-820-3118, dte@mtq.gouv.qc.ca
Ile-de-Montréal, 440, boul René-Lévesque ouest, 10e étage, Montréal, H2Z 2A6 QC
514-873-7781, Fax: 514-864-3867, dtim@mtq.gouv.qc.ca
Laurentides-Lanaudière, 222, rue Saint-Georges, 2e étage, Saint-Jérôme, J7Z 4Z9 QC
450-569-3057, Fax: 450-569-3072, dll@mtq.gouv.qc.ca
Laval-Mille-Iles, 1725, boul Le Corbusier, Laval, H7S 2K7 QC
450-680-6330, Fax: 450-973-4959, dtlmi@mtq.gouv.qc.ca
Mauricie-Centre-du-Québec, 100, rue Laviolette, 4e étage, Trois-Rivières, G9A 5S9 QC
819-371-6896, Fax: 819-371-6136, dmcq@mtq.gouv.qc.ca
Ouest-de-la-Montérégie, #200, 180, boulevard d'Anjou, Châteauguay, J6K 1C4 QC
450-698-3400, Fax: 450-698-3452, dtom@mtq.gouv.qc.ca
Outaouais, #5.110, 170, rue de l'Hôtel-de-Ville, Gatineau, J8X 4C2 QC
819-772-3849, Fax: 819-772-3338, dto@mtq.gouv.qc.ca
Saguenay-Lac-Saint-Jean-Chibougamau, 3950, boul Harvey, Jonquière, G7X 8L6 QC
418-695-7916, Fax: 418-695-7926, dt.slsjc@mtq.gouv.qc.ca
Société de l'assurance automobile du Québec, 333, boul Jean-Lesage, CP 19600 Terminus, Québec, QC G1K 8J6
418-643-7620, Fax: 418-644-0339, 800-361-7620, courrier@saaq.gouv.qc.ca
Société des traversiers du Québec, 250, rue Saint-Paul, Québec, QC G1K 9K9
418-643-2019, Fax: 418-643-7308, stq@traversiers.gouv.qc.ca
Société du port ferroviaire Baie-Comeau-Hauterive, 18, rte Maritime, Baie-Comeau, QC G4Z 2L6
418-296-6785, Fax: 418-296-2377, soport@globetrotter.qc.ca
Ministère des Transports, 700, boul René-Lévesque est, 27e étage, Québec, G1R 5H1 QC
Fax: 514-643-1269, 888-355-0511, communications@mtq.gouv.qc.ca

Saskatchewan

Saskatchewan Highways & Infrastructure, 1855 Victoria Ave., Regina, S4P 3T2 SK
306-787-4800

Saskatchewan Highway Traffic Board, 1550 Saskatchewan Dr., Regina, SK S4P 0E4
306-775-6674

Yukon Territory

Yukon Community Services, PO Box 2703, Whitehorse, Y1A 2C6 YT
867-667-5811, Fax: 867-393-6295, 800-661-0408, inquiry@gov.yk.ca

Driver Control Board, 308 Steele St., PO Box 2703, Whitehorse, YT Y1A 2C6
867-667-3774, Fax: 867-393-6483, dcb@gov.yk.ca

Yukon Highways & Public Works, PO Box 2703, Whitehorse, Y1A 2C6 YT
867-393-7193, Fax: 867-393-6218, 800 661 0408, hpw-info@gov.yk.ca

Yukon Motor Transport Board, PO Box 2703, Whitehorse, YT Y1A 2C6
867-667-5782, Fax: 867-393-6408, Laurie.Hrynuik@gov.yk.ca

Port Authorities

Halifax Port Authority
1215 Marginal Rd., Halifax, NS B3H 4P8
902-426-8222 Fax: 902-426-7335 www.portofhalifax.ca @PROFILE = **Profile:** Cargo: Bulk Cargo (Oil, Fuel, Gypsum) - 8.8 million metric tones Breakbulk Cargo (Iron/Steel, Machinery, Rubber) - 136,000 metric tones Roll-on, Roll-off Cargo (Cars and Trucks) - 216,000 metric tones Containerized Cargo - 4.6 million metric tones

Fraser River Port Authority
400 - 625 Agnes St., New Westminster, BC V3M 5Y4
604-524-6655 Fax: 604-524-1127
info@frpa.com
www.fraserportauthority.com @PROFILE = **Profile:** The Fraser River Port Authority is a federally mandated port authority operating under the Canada Marine Act. It administers Fraser River Port, a major deep-sea port located on the main arm of the Fraser River, south of Vancouver, British Columbia

Hamilton Port Authority
605 James St. North, 6th Floor, Hamilton, ON L8L 1K1
905-525-4330 Fax: 905-528-6554 800-263-2131
cargo@hamiltonport.ca
www.hamiltonport.ca @ORG = Nanaimo Port Authority
104 Front St., Nanaimo, BC V9R 5H7
250-753-4146 Fax: 250-753-4899
info@npa.ca
www.npa.ca/en/index.htm @PROFILE = **Profile:** The NPA administers the federal harbour from the Nanaimo Assembly Wharf to the Petro-Canada dock on Newcastle Channel and extending to Newcastle and Protection Islands

North Fraser Port Authority
7911 Grauer Rd., Richmond, BC V7B 1N4
604-273-1866 Fax: 604-273-3772 www.nfpa.ca/engindex.html @PROFILE = **Profile:** Our mission is to provide innovative and responsible leadership in the administration of the North Arm's river highway and to ensure that all development enhances the economic opportunity, recreational potential and environmental integrity of the area

Port Alberni Port Authority
2750 Harbour Rd., Port Alberni, BC V9Y 7X2
250-723-5312 Fax: 250-723-1114
www.portalberniportauthority.ca/english/index.html @PROFILE = **Profile:** Committed to the continued waterfront development of the Alberni Inlet and the economic sustainability of the Alberni Valley

Prince Rupert Port Authority
200 - 215 Cow Bay Rd., Prince Rupert, BC V8J 1A2
250-627-8899 Fax: 250 627 8980
pcorp@rupertport.com
www.rupertport.com @PROFILE = **Profile:** Significant changes in world trade patterns have shifted the focus of the Prince Rupert Port Authority (PRPA) and have already resulted in new initiatives, including a cruise and container port. Significant opportunities for industrial development mark the next phase in development potential at the port

Quebec Port Authority
PO Box 2268, 150 rue Dalhousie, Québec, QC G1K 7P7
418-648-3640 www.portquebec.ca @PROFILE = **Profile:** The mission of the Québec Port Authority is to promote and develop maritime trade, to serve the economic interests of the Quebec area and of Canada and to ensure that it is profitable while respecting both its community and the environment

Saguenay Port Authority
6600, rue Quai-Marcel-Dionne, La Baie, QC G7B 3N9
418-697-0250 Fax: 418-697-0243
info@portsaguenay.ca
www.portsaguenay.ca @PROFILE = **Profile:** The Port of Saguenay is the only public port in the Saguenay-Lac-St-Jean area. It is a port recognized for its strategic importance to the country's trade and economy. This international seaport is also part of the essential infrastructures of the municipality and the region and generates several hundred jobs. The port is the cornerstone of the community of Saguenay-Lac-St-Jean. It is an element of Canada's transportation infrastructure and offers a marine gateway to global markets

Saint John Port Authority
133 Prince William St., 5th Floor, Saint John, NB E2L 2B5
506-636-4869 Fax: 506-636-4443
port@sjport.com
www.sjport.com @ORG = Sept-Iles Port Authority
1 Quai Mgr-Blanche, Sept-Iles, QC G4R 5P3
418-968-1231 Fax: 418-962-4445
www.portsi.com/eg/default.htm @ORG = Toronto Port Authority
60 Harbour St., Toronto, ON M5J 1B7
416-863-2000 Fax: 416-863-4830 www.torontoport.com @PROFILE = **Profile:** Maintains a paved facility of over 50 acres centrally located, adjacent to downtown Toronto. The yard provides convenience, with excellent access to the railroads, as well as all major highways. This facility is fully bonded and has 24-hour security

Windsor Port Authority
#502, 251 Goyeau St., Windsor, ON N9A 6V2
519-258-5741 Fax: 519-258-5905
wpa@portwindsor.com
www.portwindsor.com @PROFILE = **Profile:** The mission of the Windsor Port Authority is to manage, develop, and promote the Port of Windsor for the benefit of its stakeholders and ensure the general security of the port while remaining sensitive to the need for a high degree of safety and environmental responsibility

Port of Belledune
112, Shannon Dr., Belledune, NB E8G 2W2
506-522-1200 Fax: 506-522-0803
info@portofbelledune.ca
www.portofbelledune.ca @PROFILE = **Profile:** To develop to the fullest, the services and facilities of the port, to enable it to become the anchor of economic development in Northern New Brunswick. Existing infrastructures can handle any product & merchandise, We can handle Bulk, break bulk, containers, trailer, liquid, RoRo, Space and storage available for available for lease, Low storage and rental cost, Customize rate available, Custom Bonded available, Space available for break cargo, Industrial location

Vancouver Port Authority
100 The Pointe, 999 Canada Pl., Vancouver, BC V6C 3T4
604-665-9000 Fax: 604-665-9007 888-767-8826
public_affairs@portvancouver.com
www.portvancouver.com @PROFILE = **Profile:** Marine cargo handling; Regulation & administration of transportation programs. The Port of Vancouver handled 79.4 million tonnes in 2006, up 4% from 2005's 76.5 million tonnes

Montreal Port Authority
Édifice du port de Montréal, Aile N§ 1, Cité du Havre, Montréal, QC H3C 3R5
514-283-7011 Fax: 514-283-0829
info@port-montreal.com
www.port-montreal.com @PROFILE = **Profile:** The Montreal Port Authority's mandate is to facilitate domestic and international trade and thereby contribute to the attainment of local, regional and national socioeconomic objectives

SECTION 17
UTILITIES

Associations

American Public Works Association (APWA)
#700, 2345 Grand Blvd., Kansas City MO 64108-2625 USA
Tel: 816-472-6100; *Fax:* 816-472-1610
Toll-Free: 800-848-2792
e-mail: apwa@apwa.net
URL: www.apwa.net
Overview: A medium-sized international organization founded in 1938
Chief Officer(s):
Peter King, Executive Director, 202-218-6700
pking@apwa.net
Kaye Sullivan, Deputy Executive Director/COO, 816-595-5233
ksullivan@apwa.net
Finances: *Annual Operating Budget:* Greater than $5 Million; *Funding Sources:* Membership dues; federal grants; products
Staff: 50 staff member(s); 250+ volunteer(s)
Membership: 26,000; *Fees:* Schedule available; *Member Profile:* Public works professionals; *Committees:* Transportation; Solid Waste; Water Resources; Engineering & Technology; Management & Leadership; Emergency Management; Fleet Services; Facilities & Grounds; Utility & Public Right of Way
Description: Educational & professional association of public agencies, private sector companies & individuals dedicated to providing high quality public works goods & services

Association de l'industrie électrique du Québec (AIEQ)
#320, 2000, rue Mansfield, Montréal QC H3A 2Y9
Tél: 514-281-0615; *Téléc:* 514-281-7965
Courriel: aieq@aieq.net
URL: www.aieq.net
Nom précédent: Club d'électricité du Québec inc.
Aperçu: *Dimension:* moyenne; *Envergure: provinciale; Organisme sans but lucratif; fondée en 1916*
Membre(s) du bureau directeur:
Jean-François Samray, Président et directeur général
Finances: *Budget de fonctionnement annuel:* $500,000-$1.5 Million
Personnel: 7 membre(s) du personnel
Membre: 152; *Montant de la cotisation:* Selon le nombre d'employés au Québec; *Critères d'admissibilite:* Membres industriels; *Comités:* Consultatif; Finances; Services aux membres; Promotion; Débats projects
Activités: Déjeuners; conférences; activités sociales; *Service de conférenciers:* Oui
Description: Etre porte parole de l'industrie 'électrique au Québec; favoriser la circulation de toute information et intérêt pour les membres et l'industrie électrique en général; contribuer au développement de nos membres et à la promotion de leurs intérêts par des initiatives de concertation et de représentation; encourager l'utilisation rationnelle des ressources dans une perspective de développement

Association of Major Power Consumers in Ontario (AMPCO)
Sterling Tower, 372 Bay St., Toronto ON M5H 2W9
Tel: 416-260-0280; *Fax:* 416-260-0442
e-mail: info@ampco.org
URL: www.ampco.org
Overview: A large provincial organization founded in 1975
Chief Officer(s):
John Lemay, Chair
Adam White, President
Fareeda Heeralal, Contact
Finances: *Funding Sources:* Membership fees
Staff: 1 staff member(s)
Membership: 42; *Fees:* Based on electrical energy usage; *Member Profile:* Companies that are major manufacturers, employers, & power consumers (represents key industries - mining, pulp & paper, automobile manufacturing, petro-chemicals, metals, consumer products, steel, etc.); *Committees:* Transition Issues; Executive
Description: To represent Ontario's electricity-intensive companies; to ensure reliability of power supply to support the economy of Ontario & to advocate a fair & equitable pricing system for electricity; to present views on energy matters to such groups as the Ontario Energy Board, the Ontario Government, Ontario Hydro, the news media, & the general public; to provide decision makers with recommendations on resolving issues

Association québécoise du gaz naturel (AQGN)
#207, 560, boul. Henri-Bourassa Ouest, Montréal QC H3L 1P4
Tél: 514-339-9399; *Téléc:* 514-339-9353
Courriel: aqgn@aqgn.com
URL: www.aqgn.com
Aperçu: *Dimension:* petite; *Envergure: provinciale*
Membre(s) du bureau directeur:
Ginette Gamache, Directrice générale
Montant de la cotisation: 450$ régulier; 2 500$ aviseur
Description: L'Association Québécoise du Gaz Naturel regroupe les gens d'affaires intéressés par le développement de l'industrie du gaz naturel au Québec

Canadian Association of Members of Public Utility Tribunals (CAMPUT) / Association canadienne des membres des tribunaux d'utilité publique
#646, 200 North Service Rd. West, Oakville ON L6M 2Y1
Tel: 905-827-5139; *Fax:* 905-827-3260
e-mail: info@camput.org
URL: www.camput.org
Previous Name: Canadian Association of Utility Commissioners
Overview: A small national organization founded in 1976
Chief Officer(s):
Terry Rochefort, Executive Director
rochefort@camput.org
Peter Gurnham, QC, Chair
gurnhapw@gov.ns.ca
Alison Rhodes, Secretary-Treasurer
alison.rhodes@bcuc.com
Member Profile: Federal, provincial, & territorial boards & commissions which regulate electric, water, gas, & pipeline utilities in Canada; *Committees:* Regulatory Affairs; Education
Activities: Educating & training commissioners & staff of public utility tribunals; Communicating with members; Liaising with parallel regulatory organizations;
Description: To improve public utility regulation in Canada

Canadian Association of Petroleum Producers (CAPP) / Association canadienne des producteurs pétroliers
#2100, 350 - 7 Ave. SW, Calgary AB T2P 3N9
Tel: 403-267-1100; *Fax:* 403-261-4622
e-mail: communication@capp.ca; membership@capp.ca; publications@capp.ca
URL: www.capp.ca
Merged from: Canadian Petroleum Association; Independent Petroleum Association of Canada
Overview: A large national organization founded in 1992
Chief Officer(s):
David Collyer, President
dave.collyer@capp.ca
Janet Annesley, Vice-President, Communications
janet.annesley@capp.ca
Tom Huffaker, Vice-President, Policy & Environment
tom.huffaker@capp.ca
David Pryce, Vice-President, Operations
pryce@capp.ca
Nick Schultz, Vice-President, Pipeline Regulation
schultz@capp.ca
Greg Stringham, Vice-President, Oil Sands & Markets
stringham@capp.ca
Membership: 100+ producer members + 150 associate members; *Member Profile:* Producer members range from two person operations to internationally recognized corporations employing thousands; Associate members provide services, such as drilling, baniking, & computing, for Canada's oil & gas industry
Activities: Reviewing, analyzing, & recommending industry policy positions; Participating in regulatory change dialogues; Representing the industry on multi-sector international, federal, & provincial consultation bodies; Communicating with governments, regulators, stakeholders, & the public; Offering seminars & workshops; Providing industry trends, statistics, & research information; Informing members of industry standards & guidelines; Monitoring pipeline expansions; Improving coordinated land use planning processes
Description: To represent companies that produce Canada's natural gas & crude oil; To enhance the economic sustainability of the Canadian upstream petroleum industry; To ensure work is conducted in a safe & environmentally & socially responsible manner; To work with government to develop regulatory requirements

Canadian Clean Power Coalition (CCPC)
c/o Bob Stobbs, Executive Director, 2901 Powerhouse Dr., Regina SK S4N 0A1
URL: www.canadiancleanpowercoalition.com
Overview: A medium-sized national organization
Chief Officer(s):
Bob Stobbs, Executive Director, 306-566-3326
bstobbs@saskpower.com
David Lewin, Chair, 780-412-3196
dlewin@epcor.ca
Member Profile: Canadian coal & coal-fired electricity producers
Activities: Addressing environmental issues with governments & stakeholders
Description: To secure a future for coal-fired electricity generation, along with a mix of fuels such as solar, wind, hydro, & nuclear; to research & develop clean coal technology

Canadian Electricity Association (CEA) / Association canadienne de l'électricité (ACE)
#907, 350 Sparks St., Ottawa ON K1R 7S8
e-mail: info@canelect.ca
URL: www.canelect.ca
Overview: A medium-sized national organization founded in 1891
Chief Officer(s):
Pierre Guimond, President/CEO, 613-230-4762
Francis Bradley, Vice-President, Corporate & Communications, 613-230-5027
bradley@canelect.ca
Member Profile: Corporate utility & consulting companies; Electrical manufacturers
Activities: Analyzing national & international business issues; Providing a national forum for the electricity business; Advocating industry views; Helping companies in evolving markets
Description: To act as the voice of the Canadian electricity business

Canadian Energy Workers Association (CEWA)
#202, 10707 - 100 Ave., Edmonton AB T5J 3M1
Tel: 780-420-7887
e-mail: cewa@cewa.ca
URL: www.cewa.ca
Previous Name: Canadian Utilities & Northland Utilities Employees' Association; Alberta Power Employees' Association
Overview: A small national organization founded in 1969
Activities: Engaging in problem solving between members & management; Creating programs for members in the areas of safety, security, & skills development; Offering an annual bursary program
Description: To represent the interests of members, by serving as a bargaining agent for matters related to working relations with employers

Canadian Gas Association (CGA) / Association canadienne du gaz
#809, 350 Sparks St., Ottawa ON K1R 7S8
Tel: 613-748-0057; *Fax:* 613-748-9078
e-mail: info@cga.ca
URL: www.cga.ca
Overview: A large national organization founded in 1907
Chief Officer(s):
Michael Cleland, President/CEO
Finances: *Annual Operating Budget:* $1.5 Million-$3 Million
Staff: 22 staff member(s)
Membership: 125+ organizations & individuals; *Fees:* Based on formula; *Member Profile:* Energy industry organizations; *Committees:* Corporate Affairs; Sustainable Growth; Operations; Public Affairs; Manufacturers Section; Canadian Energy Partnership for Environmental Innovation (CEPEI)
Activities: *Speaker Service:* Yes
Description: To provide leadership in the development of Canada's natural gas industry
Affiliation(s): International Gas Union; Canadian Gas Research Institute

Canadian Hydropower Association (CHA) / Association canadienne de l'hydroélectricité
#1300, 340 Albert St., Ottawa ON K1R 7Y9
Tel: 613-751-6655; *Fax:* 613-751-4465
e-mail: info@canhydropower.org
URL: www.canhydropower.org
Overview: A small national organization founded in 1998
Membership: 16 generators; 21 industry; 8 associate; *Member Profile:* Hydroelectric generation; hydroelectric industry; Associated associations and organizations
Description: To provide leadership for the responsible growth & prosperity of the Canadian hydropower industry

Canadian Petroleum Law Foundation
PO Box 4143, Stn. C, Calgary AB T2T 5M9
Tel: 403-237-2423
e-mail: lara.h.pella@esso.ca
URL: www.cplf.org
Overview: A small national organization founded in 1963
Chief Officer(s):
Ben Rogers, President
ben.rogers@blakes.com
Miles Pittman, Treasurer
miles.pittman@fmc-law.com
Description: To study oil & gas laws

Canadian Public Works Association (CPWA) / Association Canadienne des Travaux Publics
#191, 253 College St., Toronto ON M5T 1R5
Tel: 202-408-9541; *Fax:* 202-408-9542
e-mail: cpwa@cpwa.net
URL: www.cpwa.net

Overview: A medium-sized national organization founded in 1938
Chief Officer(s):
W. Gary Losier, P.Eng, President
glosier@quispamsis.ca
Membership: 1,800
Description: Their mission statement is to be recognized as the "voice of public works" in Canada; to create a forum for public works professionals in Canada to exchange inforamation, develop ideas, and share skills, knowledge, and technologies on issues unique to Canada; to increase membership and participation.

Compressed Gas Association, Inc. (CGA)
4221 Walney Rd., 5th Fl., Chantilly VA 20151-2923 USA
Tel: 703-788-2700; *Fax:* 703-961-1831
e-mail: cga@cganet.com
URL: www.cganet.com
Overview: A small international organization founded in 1913
Chief Officer(s):
Carl T. Johnson, President/CEO
Finances: *Funding Sources:* Membership dues
Staff: 14 staff member(s)
Membership: 150; *Fees:* Schedule available
Description: To promote, develop & coordinate technical & standardization activities in compressed gas industries in interest of public safety

Electrical & Utilities Safety Association of Ontario (EUSA)
#400, 5110 Creekbank Rd., Mississauga ON L4W 0A1
Tel: 905-625-0100; *Fax:* 905-625-8998
Toll-Free: 800-263-5024
e-mail: info@eusa.on.ca
URL: www.eusa.on.ca
Previous Name: Electric Employers Association
Overview: A medium-sized provincial organization founded in 1915
Chief Officer(s):
Ted Vandevis, CET, MBA, CUSA, President/CEO & Sec.-Treas.
tvandevis@eusa.on.ca
B.A. (Brian) Weber, Chair
Finances: *Annual Operating Budget:* Greater than $5 Million
Staff: 40+ staff member(s)
Activities: Developing skills; Implementing ergonomic changes; Conducting audits; Researching & developing health & safety methods & products; Assessing training needs; Offering seminars & workshops
Description: To build sustainable health & safety systems; To work towards zero injuries; To promote internal responsibility, best practices, health & safety cultures, & risk management

Electricity Distributors Association (EDA)
#1100, 3700 Steeles Ave. West, Vaughan ON L4L 8K8
Tel: 905-265-5300; *Fax:* 905-265-5301
Toll-Free: 800-668-9979
e-mail: email@eda-on.ca
URL: www.eda-on.ca
Previous Name: Municipal Electric Association
Overview: A large provincial organization founded in 1986
Chief Officer(s):
Mara Ostby, Director, Administration
Tanya Fobear, Coordinator, Communications & Member Relations
Charlie Macaluso, President & CEO
Finances: *Annual Operating Budget:* Greater than $5 Million; *Funding Sources:* Membership dues
Staff: 18 staff member(s); 100 volunteer(s)
Membership: 256; *Fees:* $750 commercial member; *Member Profile:* Public & privately owned electricity distributors
Description: To be the voice of Ontario's electricity distributors, the publicly & privately owned companies that deliver electricity to Ontario homes, businesses & public institutions. Focus is on advocacy & representation to government, analysis of legislation & market regulations, communication & networking among members & industry colleagues

Electro-Federation Canada Inc. (EFC)
#200, 5800 Explorer Dr., Mississauga ON L4W 5K9
Tel: 905-602-8877; *Fax:* 905-602-5686
Toll-Free: 866-602-8877
e-mail: info@electrofed.com
URL: www.electrofed.com
Overview: A medium-sized national organization founded in 1995
Chief Officer(s):
Milos Jancik, President/CEO
mjancik@electrofed.com
Ken Frankum, Chair
Harald Henze, Treasurer
Larry Moore, Vice-President, Consumer Councils
lmoore@electrofed.com
Joseph Neu, Vice-President, Engineering, Codes & Standards
jneu@electrofed.com
Membership: 300 companies; *Member Profile:* Companies that manufacture, distribute, & service electrical, electronics, & telecommunications products; *Committees:* Canadian Appliance Manufacturers Association; Consumer Electronics Marketers of Canada; Electrical Equipment Manufacturers Association of Canada; Supply & Manufacturers' Reps Councils; Installation Maintenance & Repair Sector Council & Trade Association; Electro-Federation Canada Alumni Association
Activities: Collecting & disseminating market data; Providing networking opportunities; Hosting annual conferences; Researching; Offering educational programs; Communicating with members; Promoting the industry; Conducting surveys
Description: To represent members provincially, federally, & internationally on issues affecting the electro-technical business

Gas Processing Association Canada (GPAC)
#505, 900 - 6th Avenue SW, Calgary AB T2P 3K2
Tel: 403-705-0223; *Fax:* 403-263-6886
e-mail: info@gpacanada.com
URL: www.gpacanada.com
Previous Name: Canadian Gas Processors Association
Overview: A medium-sized national organization founded in 1960
Chief Officer(s):
Richard Bosomworth, President
Joel Hayes, Secretary
Finances: *Annual Operating Budget:* Less than $50,000; *Funding Sources:* Membership dues
Staff: 17 volunteer(s)
Membership: 450 individual; *Fees:* $75 Regular, $9 Retired; *Member Profile:* Open to those employed in companies processing gaseous & liquid hydrocarbons; *Committees:* Safety; Research; Environment; Membership; Publications
Activities: *Library:* Yes
Description: To promote interaction & exchange of ideas & technology that will add value to those who are involved with or affected by the hydrocarbon processing industry
Affiliation(s): Gas Processors Association (USA)

Independent Power Producers Association of British Columbia
#26, 181 Ravine Dr., Port Moody BC V3H 4T3
Tel: 604-461-4778; *Fax:* 604-469-3717
e-mail: steve.davis@ippbc.com
URL: www.ippbc.com
Overview: A small provincial organization
Chief Officer(s):
Steve Davis, President
Description: To develop a viable independent power industry in British Columbia that serves the public interest by providing cost-effective electricity through the efficient & environmentally responsible development of the Province's energy resources

Independent Power Producers Society of Alberta (IPPSA)
#400, 505 - 8th Ave. SW, Calgary AB T2P 1G2
Tel: 403-282-8811; *Fax:* 403-256-8342
e-mail: Evan.Bahry@ippsa.com
URL: www.ippsa.com
Overview: A small provincial organization
Chief Officer(s):
Evan Bahry, Executive Director
Membership: 185; *Fees:* $250-$10,000; *Member Profile:* Power suppliers, retailers & supporting industries

Industrial Gas Users Association Inc. (IGUA) / Association des consommateurs industriels de gaz (ACIG)
#1201, 99 Metcalfe St., Ottawa ON K1P 6L7
Tel: 613-236-8021; *Fax:* 613-230-9531
URL: www.igua.ca
Overview: A medium-sized national organization founded in 1973
Chief Officer(s):
Murray Newton, President
mnewton@igua.ca
Finances: *Annual Operating Budget:* $500,000-$1.5 Million; *Funding Sources:* Membership dues
Staff: 3 staff member(s)
Membership: 39 corporate; *Fees:* Based on gas consumption, $1,200-$36,099; *Member Profile:* Open to end users of natural gas
Description: To provide a coordinated & effective voice for industrial firms depending on natural gas as fuel or feedstock; to represent industrial users of natural gas before regulatory boards & governments

Municipal Equipment & Operations Association (Ontario) Inc.
38 Summit Ave., Kitchener ON N2M 4W5
Tel: 519-741-2780; *Fax:* 519-741-2750
e-mail: admin@meoa.org
URL: www.meoa.org
Overview: A medium-sized provincial organization
Chief Officer(s):
Don Miller, Treasurer
Bill Barr, President, 519-837-5628, Fax: 519-822-8714
bill.barr@guelph.ca
Membership: 270
Description: A network of individuals working directly with equipment & operations, to exchange information, promote high standards in the field & cost effective public service in Ontario.

Natural Gas Employees' Association
#100, 10612 - 124th St. NW, Edmonton AB T5N 1S4
Tel: 780-483-9330; *Fax:* 780-469-2504
Overview: A small national organization
Chief Officer(s):
Brad Crocker, President

NOIA
Atlantic Place, #602, 215 Water St., St. John's NL A1C 6C9
Tel: 709-758-6610; *Fax:* 709-758-6611
URL: www.noianet.com
Also Known As: Newfoundland & Labrador Oil & Gas Industries Association
Overview: A medium-sized provincial organization founded in 1977
Chief Officer(s):
Robert Cadigan, President & CEO
Finances: *Annual Operating Budget:* $500,000-$1.5 Million; *Funding Sources:* Membership fees; conferences, seminars & special events
Staff: 10 staff member(s); 100 volunteer(s)
Membership: 450; *Fees:* Schedule available; *Member Profile:* Those who develop, manufacture & market products & services in the oil & gas industry, both offshore & onshore; *Committees:* Board of Directors; Petroleum Research & Information; Membership Services & Internal Communications; External Relations; Finance & Human Resources; Policy & Positions
Activities: Promotes development of East Coast Canada's hydrocarbon resources & facilitates its membership's participation in oil & gas industries; *Library:* Yes by appointment
Description: To assist, promote & facilitate the participation of members in ocean industries, with particular emphasis on oil & gas, to enhance their growth & development; to promote the growth of ocean industry; to act as a focal point for representations to government bodies & agencies; to act as a source of information & education for members

Offshore/Onshore Technologies Association of Nova Scotia (OTANS)
#400, 1718 Argyle St., Halifax NS B3J 3N6
Tel: 902-425-4774; *Fax:* 902-422-2332
e-mail: otans@otans.com
URL: www.otans.com
Overview: A small provincial organization founded in 1982
Chief Officer(s):
Paul McEachern, Managing Director
Finances: *Funding Sources:* Membership dues
Staff: 5 staff member(s); 19 volunteer(s)
Membership: 346; *Fees:* $475-$950
Description: To identify, promote & support the development of opportunities both offshore & onshore in the oil & gas industry

Ontario Municipal Water Association (OMWA)
c/o Doug Parker, 43 Chelsea Cres., Belleville ON K8N 4Z5
Tel: 613-966-1100; *Fax:* 613-966-3024
Toll-Free: 888-231-1115
e-mail: dparker@omwa.org
URL: www.omwa.org
Overview: A medium-sized provincial organization
Chief Officer(s):
Peter Veltheer, President
Douglas Parker, Executive Director, 613-966-1100, Fax: 613-966-3024
dparker@omwa.org
Membership: 180+ public drinking water authorities in Ontario; *Fees:* Schedule available, based upon population; *Member Profile:* Ontario's public water supply authorities
Activities: Reviewing policy, & legislative, & regulatory issues; Liaising with government, agencies, & associations to maintain safe & sustainable water sources; Lobbying to improve conditions; Promoting high standards of treatment, infrastructure, & operations; Offering technical training for operating authorities, operators, & owners of drinking water systems; Encouraging dissemination of information for public education
Description: To act as the voice of municipal water supply in Ontario; To ensure the safety, quality, reliability, & sustainability of drinking water in Ontario

Affiliation(s): Ontario Water Works Association (a section of the American Water Works Association)

Ontario Petroleum Institute Inc. (OPI)

#104, 555 Southdale Rd. East, London ON N6E 1A2
Tel: 519-680-1620; *Fax:* 519-680-1621
e-mail: opi@ontpet.com
URL: www.ontpet.com
Overview: A medium-sized provincial organization founded in 1963
Chief Officer(s):
Bill Fay, President, 519-436-5260
Joe Van Overberghe, Executive Director
Ray Neal, Treasurer, 519-243-2870
Scott Tompkins, Secretary
Fran McCallum, Executive Assistant
Finances: *Funding Sources:* Sponsorships
Member Profile: Geologists in Ontario; Geophysicists, Explorationists; Producers; Contractors; Petroleum engineers; Companies involved in the oil & gas, hydrocarbon storage, & solution mining industries
Activities: Liaising with government agencies; Disseminating information to members; Increasing public awareness of the importance of the industry in Ontario
Description: To promote responsible exploration & development by Ontario's oil, gas, hydrocarbon storage, & solution-mining industries

Ontario Propane Association

#11, 1155 North Service Rd. West, Oakville ON L6M 3E3
Tel: 905-469-1941; *Fax:* 905-469-1942
e-mail: opa@propane.ca
URL: www.propane.ca
Overview: A medium-sized provincial licensing organization founded in 1996
Chief Officer(s):
René Chartier, President & Secretary
Finances: *Annual Operating Budget:* $100,000-$250,000
Staff: 55 volunteer(s)
Membership: 100-499; *Member Profile:* Producers; wholesalers; retailers; equipment suppliers & trainers; *Committees:* Responsible Management Plan; Emergency Response Assistance Plan; Member Services; Technical, Standards & Training
Activities: Annual conference; regional meetings
Description: To promote the safe handling & increased use of propane; to work toward a favourable environment for propane; to serve as a resource centre for its members; to act as the principal voice of the propane industry in Ontario

Petrolia Discovery Foundation Inc.

PO Box 1480, Petrolia ON N0N 1R0
Tel: 519-882-0897; *Fax:* 519-882-4209
e-mail: petdisc@xcelco.on.ca
URL: www.petroliadiscovery.com
Overview: A small national charitable organization founded in 1980
Finances: *Annual Operating Budget:* $100,000-$250,000
Staff: 2 staff member(s); 35 volunteer(s)
Membership: 35 individual
Activities: *Speaker Service:* Yes
Description: To preserve & conserve oil heritage

Pipe Line Contractors Association of Canada (PLCAC)

#201, 1075 North Service Rd. West, Oakville ON L6M 2G2
Tel: 905-847-9383; *Fax:* 905-847-7824
e-mail: plcac@pipeline.ca
URL: www.pipeline.ca
Overview: A small national organization founded in 1954
Chief Officer(s):
Barry L. Brown, Executive Director
Sylvia Simmons, Secretary
Finances: *Annual Operating Budget:* $500,000-$1.5 Million; *Funding Sources:* Membership dues
Staff: 3 staff member(s)
Membership: 35 regular + 63 associate + 4 honorary; *Member Profile:* Open to pipe line contractors or suppliers

Propane Gas Association of Canada Inc. (PGAC) / Association canadienne du gaz propane inc.

#800, 717 - 7th Ave. SW, Calgary AB T2P 3C4
Tel: 403-543-6500; *Fax:* 403-543-6508
Toll-Free: 877-784-4636
e-mail: info@propanegas.ca
URL: www.propanegas.ca
Overview: A medium-sized national licensing organization founded in 1967
Chief Officer(s):
Ann Marie Hann, President, 403-543-6504
Tracy Walden, Manager, Communications, 613-321-2276
Bill Egbert, General Manager, Propane Training Institute, 403-543-6506
Membership: 270+; *Member Profile:* Members include producers, wholesalers, retailers, transporters, manufacturers of appliances, cylinders & equipment, & associates.
Activities: Providing industry related training & emergency response; Promoting the interests of the industry; Engaging in regulatory relations
Description: Acting as the national voice of the Canadian propane industry, PGAC supports its members in the development of a safe, environmentally responsible Canadian propane industry.
Affiliation(s): Propane Training Institute, a division of the PGAC; Liquefied Petroleum Gas Emergency Response Corporation, a wholly owned subsidiary of the PGAC

Small Explorers & Producers Association of Canada (SEPAC)

#1060, 717 - 7th Ave. SW, Calgary AB T2P 0Z3
Tel: 403-269-3454; *Fax:* 403-269-3636
e-mail: info@sepac.ca
URL: www.sepac.ca
Overview: A small national organization founded in 1986
Chief Officer(s):
Jim Screaton, Chair
Gary Leach, Executive Director
Membership: 387 corporate; *Fees:* $500-$3,335
Description: To represent & promote the interests of small producers & explorers, not only to government & regulatory bodies, but to other sectors of the conventional oil & gas industry; to educate the public at large about the importance of emerging companies in resource development in Western Canada, & investment opportunities available in the growing segment of the oilpatch; to propose long-term, effective fiscal & operating strategies for the ongoing health & vitality of this important sector of the Canadian economy

The Society of Energy Professionals

#300, 425 Bloor St. East., Toronto ON M4W 3R4
Tel: 416-979-2709; *Fax:* 416-979-5794
Toll-Free: 866-288-1788
e-mail: society@society.on.ca
URL: www.thesociety.ca
Previous Name: Society of Ontario Hydro Professional & Administrative Employees
Overview: A medium-sized provincial organization founded in 1944
Chief Officer(s):
Rodney Sheppard, President
Finances: *Annual Operating Budget:* $1.5 Million-$3 Million; *Funding Sources:* Membership dues
Staff: 14 staff member(s); 300 volunteer(s)
Membership: 7,000 + 265 locals; *Fees:* $10 per week; *Member Profile:* Professional, administrative, & associated personnel of Ontario Hydro; *Committees:* Operations; Negotiating; Health & Safety; Training; Member Services; External Relations; Communications
Description: To represent the interests of the professional, administrative, & associated employees in all aspects of their employment with Ontario Hydro
Affiliation(s): Canadian Court of Utility Professionals & Associated Societies (CCUPAS)

Society of Petroleum Engineers (SPE)

PO Box 833836, Richardson TX 75083-3836 USA
Tel: 972-952-9393; *Fax:* 972-952-9435
Toll-Free: 800-456-6863
e-mail: spedal@spe.org
URL: www.spe.org
Overview: A large international organization founded in 1957
Chief Officer(s):
Mark A. Rubin, Executive Director
Finances: *Annual Operating Budget:* $3 Million-$5 Million
Staff: 87 staff member(s)
Membership: 79,000+ (active operations in some 50 countries); *Member Profile:* Managers, engineers, operating personnel & scientists engaged in the exploration, drilling & production sectors of the global oil & gas industry
Activities: *Internships:* Yes; *Speaker Service:* Yes *Library:* Yes (Open to Public)
Description: To collect, disseminate & exchange technical knowledge concerning the exploration, development & production of oil & gas resources & related technologies for the public benefit; provide opportunities for professionals to enhance their technical & professional competence

United Utility Workers' Association of Canada (UUWA)

1207 - 20 Ave. NW, Calgary AB T2M 1G2
Tel: 403-284-4521; *Fax:* 403-282-1598
URL: www.uuwac.org
Overview: A small provincial organization
Chief Officer(s):
Grace Thostenson, Business Manager
Finances: *Annual Operating Budget:* $500,000-$1.5 Million
Staff: 3 staff member(s); 60 volunteer(s)
Membership: 900; *Member Profile:* Employees of TransAlta Utilities, Fortis, AltaLink, Dataco, SNC-Lavalin ATP Inc, TransAlta Corporation

Utility Contractors' Association of Ontario Inc. (UCA)

#201, 1075 North Service Rd. West, Oakville ON L6M 2G2
Tel: 905-847-7305; *Fax:* 905-847-7824
e-mail: info@pipeline.ca
URL: www.uca.on.ca
Overview: A medium-sized provincial organization founded in 1968
Chief Officer(s):
Barry L. Brown, General Manager
Finances: *Annual Operating Budget:* $100,000-$250,000; *Funding Sources:* Membership dues
Membership: 35

World Petroleum Congress (WPC) / Congrès mondiaux du pétrole

#1, 1 Duchess St., 4th Fl., London W1W 6AN United Kingdom
Tel: 44-20-7637-4958; *Fax:* 44-20-7637-4965
e-mail: secretariat@world-petroleum.org
URL: www.world-petroleum.org
Overview: A medium-sized international organization founded in 1933
Chief Officer(s):
Pierce Riemer, Director General
pierce@world-petroleum.org
Ulrike von Lonski, Director of Communications
ulrike@world-petroleum.org
Finances: *Funding Sources:* Membership dues; royalties; levy on registration
Staff: 4 staff member(s)
Membership: 57 countries; *Fees:* Schedule available; *Member Profile:* Major oil producing & consuming nations of the world; each country has a National Committee made up of representatives of the oil industry, academic & research institutions, & government departments; *Committees:* Permanent Council; Executive Board; Scientific Program; Congress Arrangements; Environmental Affairs; Development
Description: To help the oil industry in the development of petroleum resources & the use of petroleum products for the benefit of mankind; to promote petroleum science & technology; to encourage the application of scientific advances & the transfer of technology
Affiliation(s): IEA; OPEN; United Nations

Government Agency Guide

CONSERVATION & ECOLOGY

See Also: Heritage Resources; Natural Resources

Canadian Heritage, 15 Eddy St., Gatineau, K1A 0M5 QC
819-997-0055, 866-811-0055

Canadian Polar Commission, Constitution Square, #1710, 360 Albert St., Ottawa, K1R 7X7 ON
613-943-8605, Fax: 613-943-8607, 888-765-2701, mail@polarcom.gc.ca

Environment Canada, 10 Wellington St., Gatineau, K1A 0H3 QC
819-997-2800, Fax: 819-994-1412, 800-668-6767, enviroinfo@ec.gc.ca

Commission for Environmental Cooperation, Secretariat, #200, 393, rue St-Jacques ouest, Montréal, H2Y 1N9 QC
514-350-4300, Fax: 514-350-4314, info@cec.org

Fisheries Resource Conservation Council, PO Box 2001 D, Ottawa, ON K1P 5W3
613-998-0433, Fax: 613-998-1146, info@frcc-ccrh.ca

Natural Resources Canada, 580 Booth St., Ottawa, K1A 0E4 ON
613-995-0947, Fax: 613-992-7211

Parks Canada, 25 Eddy St., Gatineau, K1A 0M5 QC
888-773-8888, information@pc.gc.ca

Alberta

Alberta Environmental Appeal Board, Peace Hills Trust Tower, #306, 10011 - 109 St. NW, Edmonton, AB T5J 3S8
780-427-6207, Fax: 780-427-4693

Alberta Special Areas Board, 212 - 2nd Ave. West, PO Box 820, Hanna, AB T0J 1P0
403-854-5600, Fax: 403-854-5527, specarea@telusplanet.net

Alberta Used Oil Management Association, Scotia One, Scotia Place, #1050, 10060 Jasper Ave., Edmonton, AB T5J 3R8
780-414-1510, Fax: 780-414-1519, reception@usedoilrecycling.ca

Beverage Container Management Board, #1010, 10707 - 100 Ave., Edmonton, AB T5J 3M1
780-424-3193, Fax: 780-428-4620, 888-424-7671, info@bcmb.ab.ca

Clean Air Strategic Alliance, Centre West Bldg, 10035 - 108 St., 10th Fl., Edmonton, AB T5J 3E1
780-427-9793, Fax: 780-422-3127, casa@casahome.org
Alberta Environment, South Tower, Petroleum Plaza, 9915 - 108 St., Main Fl., Edmonton, T5K 2G8 AB
780-427-2700, Fax: 780-422-4086,-310-0000, env.infocent@gov.ab.ca
Natural Resources Conservation Board, Sterling Place, 9940 - 106 St., 4th Fl., Edmonton, AB T5K 2N2
780-422-1977, Fax: 780-427-0607, 866-383-6722

British Columbia
British Columbia Assessment Authority, 1537 Hillside Ave., Victoria, BC V8T 4Y2
250-595-6211, Fax: 250-595-6222, info@bcassessment.ca
Ministry of Environment, PO Box 9339 Prov Govt,Victoria, V8W 9M1 BC
250-387-1161, Fax: 250-387-5669, www.envmail@gov.bc.ca
Environmental Appeal Board, 747 Fort St., 4th Fl., PO Box 9425 Prov Govt, Victoria, BC V8W 9V1
250-387-3464, Fax: 250-356-9923, eabinfo@gov.bc.ca
Environmental Stewardship Division, 2975 Jutland Rd., 5th Fl., PO Box 9339 Prov Govt,Victoria, V8T 5J9 BC
250-356-0121, Fax: 250-953-3414
Forest Practices Board, 1675 Douglas St., 3rd Fl., PO Box 9905 Prov Govt, Victoria, BC V8W 9R1
250-387-7964, Fax: 250-387-7009, 800-994-5899, fpboard@gov.bc.ca
Fraser Basin Council, Central Office, 470 Granville St., 1st Fl., Vancouver, BC V6C 1V5
604-488-5350, Fax: 604-488-5351, info@fraserbasin.bc.ca
Mediation & Arbitration Board, #310, 9900 - 100 Ave., Fort St John, BC V1J 5S7
250-787-3403, Fax: 250-787-3228, mab.office@gov.bc.ca
Northern Interior, 1011 - 4 Ave., 5th Fl., Prince George, V2L 3H9 BC
250-565-6100, Fax: 250-565-6671, www.for.gov.bc.ca/rni

Manitoba
Clean Environment Commission, #305, 155 Carlton St., Winnipeg, MB R3C 3H8
204-945-0594, Fax: 204-945-0090
Manitoba Conservation, 200 Saulteaux Cres., Winnipeg, R3J 3W3 MB
204-945-6784, 800-214-6497, mincon@leg.gov.mb.ca
Ecological Reserves Advisory Committee, c/o Manitoba Conservation, Parks & Natural Areas Branch, 200 Saulteaux Cres., Winnipeg, MB R3J 3W3
204-945-4148, Fax: 204-945-0012, hhernandez@gov.mb.ca
Manitoba Conservation Districts Commission, Secretariat c/o Planning & Coordination Branch, 123 Main St., PO Box 20000, Neepawa, MB R0J 1H0
204-476-7033, Fax: 204-476-7539, whildebran@gov.mb.ca

New Brunswick
Assessment & Planning Appeal Board, #201, 435 King St., PO Box 6000, Fredericton, NB E3B 5H1
506-453-2126, Fax: 506-444-4881,
Department of the Environment, Marysville Place, 20 McGloin St., PO Box 6000, Fredericton, E3B 5H1 NB
506-453-2690, Fax: 506-457-4991

Newfoundland & Labrador
Department of Environment & Conservation, Confederation Bldg., West Block, 4th Fl., PO Box 8700, St. John's, A1B 4J6 NL
709-729-2664, Fax: 709-729-6639, 800-563-6181, info@gov.nl.ca

Northwest Territories
Department of Environment & Natural Resources, PO Box 1320, Yellowknife, X1A 2L9 NT

Nova Scotia
Environmental & Natural Areas Management, PO Box 697, Halifax, B3J 3T8 NS
902-424-3571
Department of Natural Resources, Founder's Square, 1701 Hollis St., 3rd Fl., PO Box 698, Halifax, B3J 2T9 NS
902-424-5935, Fax: 902-424-0594, 800-565-2224

Ontario
Ministry of Environment, 135 St. Clair Ave. West, Toronto, M4V 1P5 ON
416-325-4000, Fax: 416-325-3159, 800-565-4923
Ministry of Natural Resources, Whitney Block, #6630, 99 Wellesley St. West, 6th Fl., Toronto, M7A 1W3 ON
800-667-1940
Niagara Escarpment Commission, 232 Guelph St., Georgetown, L7G 4B1 ON
905-877-5191, Fax: 905-873-7452

Prince Edward Island
Department of Environment, Energy & Forestry, Jones Bldg., 11 Kent St., 4th & 5th Fl., PO Box 2000, Charlottetown, C1A 7N8 PE
902-368-5000, Fax: 902-368-5830
Environmental Advisory Council, 11 Kent St., PO Box 2000, Charlottetown, PE C1A 7N8
Department of Tourism, PO Box 2000, Charlottetown, C1A 7N8 PE
800-463-4734

Quebec
Comité consultatif de l'environnement Kativik, CP 930, Kuujjuaq, QC J0M 1C0
819-964-2961, Fax: 819-964-0694, ndea@krg.ca
Ministère du Développement durable, de l'Environnement et des Parcs, Édifice Marie-Guyart, 675, boul René-Lévesque est, 29e étage, Québec, G1R 5V7 QC
418-521-3830, Fax: 418-646-5974, 800-561-1616, info@mddep.gouv.qc.ca
Fondation de la faune du Québec, Place Iberville II, #420, 1175, av Lavigerie, Québec, QC G1V 4P1
418-644-7926, Fax: 418-643-7655, 877-639-0742, ffq@riq.qc.ca
Société de développement de la Baie James, 110, boul Matagami, CP 970, Matagami, QC J0Y 2A0
819-739-4717, Fax: 819-739-4329
Société québécoise de récupération et de recyclage, Siège social, #200, 420, boul Charest est, Québec, QC G1K 8M4
418-643-0394, Fax: 418-643-6507, 866-523-8290, info@recyc-quebec.gouv.qc.ca

Saskatchewan
Saskatchewan Assessment Management Agency, #200, 2201 - 11 Ave., Regina, S4P 0J8 SK
306-924-8000, Fax: 306-924-8070, 800-667-7262, info.request@sama.sk.ca
Saskatchewan Environment, 3211 Albert St., 2nd Fl., Regina, S4S 5W6 SK
306-953-3750, Fax: 306-787-9544, 800-567-4224, inquiry@serm.gov.sk.ca
Saskatchewan Conservation Data Centre, 3211 Albert St., Regina, SK S4S 5W6
306-787-9038, Fax: 306-787-9544
Saskatchewan Watershed Authority, 111 Fairford St. East, Moose Jaw, SK S6H 7X9
306-694-3900, Fax: 306-694-3465, comm@swa.ca

Yukon Territory
Alsek Renewable Resource Council, PO Box 2077, Haines Junction, YT Y0B 1L0
867-634-2524, Fax: 867-634-2527
Carmacks Renewable Resource Council, PO Box 122, Carmacks, YT Y0B 1C0
867-863-6838, Fax: 867-863-6429, carmacksrrc@lscfn.ca
Dawson District Renewable Resource Council, PO Box 1380, Dawson City, YT Y0B 1G0
867-993-6976, Fax: 867-993-6093, dawsonrrc@yknet.yk.ca
Yukon Environment, PO Box 2703, Whitehorse, Y1A 2C6 YT
867-667-5652, Fax: 867-393-6213, 800-661-0408, environmentyukon@gov.yk.ca
Mayo District Renewable Resources Council, PO Box 249, Mayo, YT Y0B 1M0
867-996-2942, Fax: 867-996-2948, mayorrc@yknet.yk.ca
North Yukon Renewable Resources Council, PO Box 80, Old Crow, YT Y0B 1N0
vgrrc@yknet.yk.ca
Selkirk Renewable Resources Council, PO Box 32, Pelly Crossing, YT Y0B 1P0
867-537-3937, Fax: 867-537-3939, selkirkrre@yknet.yk.ca
Teslin Renewable Resource Council, PO Box 186, Teslin, YT Y0A 1B0
867-390-2323, Fax: 867-390-2919, teslinrrc@yknet.yk.ca
Yukon Land Use Planning Council, #201, 307 Jarvis St., Whitehorse, YT Y1A 2H3
867-667-7397, Fax: 867-667-4624, ylupc@planyukon.ca

ENERGY

See Also: Natural Resources

Atomic Energy of Canada Limited, Head Office, 2251 Speakman Dr., Mississauga, L5K 1B2 ON
905-823-9040, webmaster@aecl.ca
Canadian Nuclear Safety Commission, 280 Slater St., PO Box 1046 B,Ottawa, K1P 5S9 ON
613-995-5894, Fax: 613-995-5086, 800-668-5284, info@cnsc-ccsn.gc.ca
Indian Oil & Gas Canada, #100, 9911 Chula Blvd., Tsuu T'ina (Sarcee), AB T2W 6H6
Fax: 403-292-5618
National Energy Board, 444 - 7 Ave. SW, Calgary, T2P 0X8 AB
403-292-4800, Fax: 403-292-5503, 800-899-1265, info@neb-one.gc.ca

Alberta
Alberta Energy & Utilities Board, 640 - 5 Ave. SW, Calgary, AB T2P 3G4
403-297-8311, Fax: 403-297-7336
Alberta Energy Research Institute, AMEC Place, #2540, 801 - 6 Ave. SW, Calgary, AB T2P 3W2
403-297-8650, Fax: 403-297-3638, aeri@gov.ab.ca
Alberta Energy, North Petroleum Plaza, 9945 - 108 St., 7th Fl., Edmonton, T5K 2G6 AB
780-427-7425, Fax: 780-422-0698, 780-310-0000

British Columbia
Ministry of Energy, Mines & Petroleum Resources, PO Box 9318 Prov Govt,Victoria, V8W 9N3 BC
250-952-0241
British Columbia Hydro, 333 Dunsmuir St., 18th Fl., Vancouver, V6B 5R3 BC
604-224-9376, Fax: 604-623-4467, 800-224-9376
Oil & Gas Commission, #100, 10003 - 110 Ave., Fort St John, BC V1J 6M7
250-261-5700, 800-663-7867
Powerex Corp., #1400, 666 Burrard St., Vancouver, BC V6C 2X8
604-891-5000, Fax: 604-891-6060, 800-220-4907, customer.service@bchydro.com
Powertech Labs Inc., 12388 - 88 Ave., Surrey, BC V8W 7R7
604-590-7500, Fax: 604-590-5347, info@powertechlans.com
British Columbia Utilities Commission, 900 Howe St., 6th Fl., PO Box 250, Vancouver, V6Z 2N3 BC
604-660-4700, Fax: 604-660-1102, 800-663-1385, commission.secretary@bcuc.com

Manitoba
Manitoba Hydro, PO Box 815 Main,Winnipeg, R3C 2P4 MB
204-474-3311, Fax: 204-475-0069, publicaffairs@hydro.mb.ca
Petroleum, #360, 1395 Ellice Ave., Winnipeg, R3G 3P2 MB
204-945-6577, Fax: 204-945-0586
Manitoba Science, Technology, Energy & Mines, #333, 450 Broadway, Winnipeg, R3C 0V8 MB

New Brunswick
Efficiency NB, #101, 33 Charlotte St., Saint John, NB E2L 2H3
506-643-7826, Fax: 506-643-7835, 866-643-8833
Department of Energy, Brunswick Square, #100M, 1 Germain St., PO Box 5001, Saint John, E2L 4Y9 NB
506-658-3180, Fax: 506-658-3191
Department of Natural Resources, PO Box 6000, Fredericton, E3B 5H1 NB
506-453-2510, Fax: 506-444-5839, dnrweb@gnb.ca
New Brunswick Power Group of Companies, 515 King St., PO Box 2000, Fredericton, E3B 4X1 NB
506-458-4444, Fax: 506-458-4000, questions@nbpower.com

Newfoundland & Labrador
Canada-Newfoundland Offshore Petroleum Board, TD Place, 140 Water St., 5th Fl., St. John's, NL A1C 6H6
709-778-1400, Fax: 709-778-1473, postmaster@cnlopb.nl.ca
Churchill Falls (Labrador) Corporation Limited, Hydro Place, 500 Columbus Dr., PO Box 12500, St. John's, A1B 4K7 NL
709-737-1859, Fax: 709-737-1816
Newfoundland & Labrador Hydro, Hydro Place, Columbus Dr., PO Box 12400, St. John's, A1B 4K7 NL
709-737-1400, Fax: 709-737-1800
Newfoundland & Labrador Board of Commissioners of Public Utilities, PO Box 21040, St. John's, A1A 5B2 NL
709-726-8600, Fax: 709-726-9604, 866-782-0006, ito@pub.nf.ca
Twin Falls Power Corporation, PO Box 12500, St. John's, A1B 3T5 NL

Northwest Territories
Department of Environment & Natural Resources, PO Box 1320, Yellowknife, X1A 2L9 NT
Northwest Territories Power Corporation, 4 Capital Dr., Hay River, X0E 1G2 NT
867-874-5200, Fax: 867-874-5229, info@ntpc.com

Nova Scotia
Canada-Nova Scotia Offshore Petroleum Board, TD Centre, 1791 Barrington St., 6th Fl., Halifax, NS B3J 3K9
902-422-5588, Fax: 902-422-1799, postmaster@cnsopb.ns.ca
Department of Energy, Bank of Montreal Bldg., #400, 5151 George St., PO Box 2664, Halifax, B3J 3P7 NS
902-424-4575, Fax: 902-424-0528, energyinfo@gov.ns.ca
Nova Scotia Utility & Review Board, 1601 Lower Water St., 3rd Fl., PO Box 1692 M,Halifax, B3J 3S3 NS
902-424-4448, Fax: 902-424-3919, uarb.board@gov.ns.ca

Ontario
Ministry of Energy and Infrastructure, Hearst Block, 900 Bay St., 4th Fl., Toronto, M7A 2E1 ON
416-327-6758, Fax: 416-327-0033, 888-668-4939

Ministry of Environment, 135 St. Clair Ave. West, Toronto, M4V 1P5 ON
416-325-4000, Fax: 416-325-3159, 800-565-4923
Hydro One Inc., North Tower, 483 Bay St., Toronto, M5G 2P5 ON
416-345-5000, 877-955-1155, webmaster@HydroOne.com
Independent Electricity System Operator, PO Box 4474 A,Toronto, M5W 4E5 ON
905-403-6900, Fax: 905-403-6921, 888-448-7777, customer.relations@ieso.ca
Ontario Energy Board, #2700, 2300 Yonge St., Toronto, ON M4P 1E4
416-481-1967, Fax: 416-440-7656, 888-632-6273
Ontario Power Authority, #1600, 120 Adelaide St. West, Toronto, ON M5H 1T1
416-967-7474, Fax: 416-967-1947, info@powerauthority.on.ca
Ontario Power Generation, 700 University Ave., Toronto, M5G 1X6 ON
416-592-2555, 877-592-2555

Prince Edward Island

Department of Environment, Energy & Forestry, Jones Bldg., 11 Kent St., 4th & 5th Fl., PO Box 2000, Charlottetown, C1A 7N8 PE
902-368-5000, Fax: 902-368-5830
PEI Energy Corporation, Jones Bldg., 11 Kent St., 4th Fl., PO Box 2000, Charlottetown, PE C1A 7N8
902-894-0288, Fax: 902-368-0290

Quebec

Agence de l'efficacité énergétique, #B-405, 5700, 4e av ouest, Québec, QC G1H 6R1
418-627-6379, Fax: 418-643-5828, 877-727-6655, aee@aee.gouv.qc.ca
Hydro-Québec, 75, boul René-Lévesque ouest, 20e étage, Montréal, H2Z 1A4 QC
514-289-2211
Régie de l'énergie, Tour de la Bourse, #255, 800, Place Victoria, CP 1, Montréal, QC H4Z 1A2
514-873-2452, Fax: 514-873-2070, 888-873-2452, secretariat@regie-energie.qc.ca
Société d'énergie de la Baie-James, 888, de Maisonneuve est, 2e étage, Montréal, H2L 5B2 QC
514-286-2020

Saskatchewan

Saskatchewan Energy & Resources, #300, 2103 - 11th Ave., Regina, S4P 3Z8 SK
306-787-2528, Fax: 306-787-8447, 866-727-5427
Saskatchewan Power Corporation (SaskPower), 2025 Victoria Ave., Regina, S4P 0S1 SK
306-566-2121, Fax: 306-566-2330, 800-667-4749
SaskEnergy Incorporated, 1777 Victoria Ave., Regina, S4P 4K5 SK
306-777-9225, Fax: 306-777-9200, 800-567-8899

Yukon Territory

Yukon Energy, Mines & Resources, PO Box 2703, Whitehorse, Y1A 2C6 YT
867-667-5466, Fax: 867-667-8601, 800-661-0408, emr@gov.yk.ca

HYDRO ELECTRIC POWER

National Energy Board, 444 - 7 Ave. SW, Calgary, T2P 0X8 AB
403-292-4800, Fax: 403-292-5503, 800-899-1265, info@neb-one.gc.ca

Alberta

Alberta Energy & Utilities Board, 640 - 5 Ave. SW, Calgary, AB T2P 3G4
403-297-8311, Fax: 403-297-7336
Alberta Utilities Consumer Advocate, TD Tower, 10088 - 102 Ave., Edmonton, T5J 2Z1 AB
780-644-5130, Fax: 780-644-5129, 866-714-4455, UtilitiesConsumerAdvocate@gov.ab.

British Columbia

British Columbia Hydro, 333 Dunsmuir St., 18th Fl., Vancouver, V6B 5R3 BC
604-224-9376, Fax: 604-623-4467, 800-224-9376
Powertech Labs Inc., 12388 - 88 Ave., Surrey, BC V8W 7R7
604-590-7500, Fax: 604-590-5347, info@powertechlans.com

Manitoba

Manitoba Hydro, PO Box 815 Main,Winnipeg, R3C 2P4 MB
204-474-3311, Fax: 204-475-0069, publicaffairs@hydro.mb.ca

New Brunswick

New Brunswick Electric Finance Corporation, #376, 670 King St., PO Box 6000, Fredericton, NB E3B 5H1
506-453-3952, Fax: 506-453-2053
New Brunswick Power Group of Companies, 515 King St., PO Box 2000, Fredericton, E3B 4X1 NB
506-458-4444, Fax: 506-458-4000, questions@nbpower.com

Newfoundland & Labrador

Churchill Falls (Labrador) Corporation Limited, Hydro Place, 500 Columbus Dr., PO Box 12500, St. John's, A1B 4K7 NL
709-737-1859, Fax: 709-737-1816
Newfoundland & Labrador Hydro, Hydro Place, Columbus Dr., PO Box 12400, St. John's, A1B 4K7 NL
709-737-1400, Fax: 709-737-1800
Twin Falls Power Corporation, PO Box 12500, St. John's, A1B 3T5 NL

Northwest Territories

Northwest Territories Power Corporation, 4 Capital Dr., Hay River, X0E 1G2 NT
867-874-5200, Fax: 867-874-5229, info@ntpc.com

Nova Scotia

Nova Scotia Utility & Review Board, 1601 Lower Water St., 3rd Fl., PO Box 1692 M,Halifax, B3J 3S3 NS
902-424-4448, Fax: 902-424-3919, uarb.board@gov.ns.ca

Ontario

Hydro One Inc., North Tower, 483 Bay St., Toronto, M5G 2P5 ON
416-345-5000, 877-955-1155, webmaster@HydroOne.com
Independent Electricity System Operator, PO Box 4474 A,Toronto, M5W 4E5 ON
905-403-6900, Fax: 905-403-6921, 888-448-7777, customer.relations@ieso.ca
Ontario Power Authority, #1600, 120 Adelaide St. West, Toronto, ON M5H 1T1
416-967-7474, Fax: 416-967-1947, info@powerauthority.on.ca
Ontario Power Generation, 700 University Ave., Toronto, M5G 1X6 ON
416-592-2555, 877-592-2555

Quebec

Hydro-Québec, 75, boul René-Lévesque ouest, 20e étage, Montréal, H2Z 1A4 QC
514-289-2211
Société d'énergie de la Baie-James, 888, de Maisonneuve est, 2e étage, Montréal, H2L 5B2 QC
514-286-2020

Saskatchewan

Saskatchewan Power Corporation (SaskPower), 2025 Victoria Ave., Regina, S4P 0S1 SK
306-566-2121, Fax: 306-566-2330, 800-667-4749

OIL & NATURAL GAS RESOURCES

See Also: Energy; Natural Resources

Indian Oil & Gas Canada, #100, 9911 Chula Blvd., Tsuu T'ina (Sarcee), AB T2W 6H6
Fax: 403-292-5618
National Energy Board, 444 - 7 Ave. SW, Calgary, T2P 0X8 AB
403-292-4800, Fax: 403-292-5503, 800-899-1265, info@neb-one.gc.ca

Alberta

Alberta Energy & Utilities Board, 640 - 5 Ave. SW, Calgary, AB T2P 3G4
403-297-8311, Fax: 403-297-7336
Alberta Energy, North Petroleum Plaza, 9945 - 108 St., 7th Fl., Edmonton, T5K 2G6 AB
780-427-7425, Fax: 780-422-0698, 780-310-0000

British Columbia

Ministry of Energy, Mines & Petroleum Resources, PO Box 9318 Prov Govt,Victoria, V8W 9N3 BC
250-952-0241
Oil & Gas Commission, #100, 10003 - 110 Ave., Fort St John, BC V1J 6M7
250-261-5700, 800-663-7867
British Columbia Utilities Commission, 900 Howe St., 6th Fl., PO Box 250, Vancouver, V6Z 2N3 BC
604-660-4700, Fax: 604-660-1102, 800-663-1385, commission.secretary@bcuc.com

Manitoba

Petroleum, #360, 1395 Ellice Ave., Winnipeg, R3G 3P2 MB
204-945-6577, Fax: 204-945-0586
Surface Rights Board, #360, 1395 Ellice Ave., Winnipeg, MB R3G 3P2
204-945-0731, Fax: 204-948-2578, 800-282-8069, bmiskimmin@gov.mb.ca

Newfoundland & Labrador

Canada-Newfoundland Offshore Petroleum Board, TD Place, 140 Water St., 5th Fl., St. John's, NL A1C 6H6
709-778-1400, Fax: 709-778-1473, postmaster@cnlopb.nl.ca

Nova Scotia

Canada-Nova Scotia Offshore Petroleum Board, TD Centre, 1791 Barrington St., 6th Fl., Halifax, NS B3J 3K9
902-422-5588, Fax: 902-422-1799, postmaster@cnsopb.ns.ca
Nova Scotia Utility & Review Board, 1601 Lower Water St., 3rd Fl., PO Box 1692 M,Halifax, B3J 3S3 NS
902-424-4448, Fax: 902-424-3919, uarb.board@gov.ns.ca

Nunavut

Department of Environment, PO Box 1000 1300,Iqaluit, X0A 0H0 NU
867-975-7700, Fax: 867-975-7742, 866-222-9063, environment@gov.nu.ca

Ontario

Ministry of Natural Resources, Whitney Block, #6630, 99 Wellesley St. West, 6th Fl., Toronto, M7A 1W3 ON
800-667-1940

Saskatchewan

SaskEnergy Incorporated, 1777 Victoria Ave., Regina, S4P 4K5 SK
306-777-9225, Fax: 306-777-9200, 800-567-8899,

PUBLIC UTILITIES

Alberta

Alberta Energy & Utilities Board, 640 - 5 Ave. SW, Calgary, AB T2P 3G4
403-297-8311, Fax: 403-297-7336
Alberta Utilities Consumer Advocate, TD Tower, 10088 - 102 Ave., Edmonton, T5J 2Z1 AB
780-644-5130, Fax: 780-644-5129, 866-714-4455, UtilitiesConsumerAdvocate@gov.ab.

British Columbia

British Columbia Hydro, 333 Dunsmuir St., 18th Fl., Vancouver, V6B 5R3 BC
604-224-9376, Fax: 604-623-4467, 800-224-9376
British Columbia Transmission Corporation, Four Bentall Centre, #1100, 1055 Dunsmuir St., PO Box 49260, Vancouver, V7X 1V5 BC
604-699-7300, Fax: 604-699-7333, 866-647-3334, contact.us@bctc.com
British Columbia Utilities Commission, 900 Howe St., 6th Fl., PO Box 250, Vancouver, V6Z 2N3 BC
604-660-4700, Fax: 604-660-1102, 800-663-1385, commission.secretary@bcuc.com

Manitoba

Manitoba Hydro, PO Box 815 Main,Winnipeg, R3C 2P4 MB
204-474-3311, Fax: 204-475-0069, publicaffairs@hydro.mb.ca
Public Utilities Board, #400, 330 Portage Ave., Winnipeg, MB R3C 0C4
204-945-2638, Fax: 204-945-2643, 866-854-3698, publicutilities@gov.mb.ca

New Brunswick

NB Board of Commissioners of Public Utilities, #1400, 15 Market Sq., PO Box 5001, Saint John, NB E2L 4Y9
506-658-2504, Fax: 506-643-7300, 866-766-2782, general@pub.nb.ca
New Brunswick Power Group of Companies, 515 King St., PO Box 2000, Fredericton, E3B 4X1 NB
506-458-4444, Fax: 506-458-4000, questions@nbpower.com

Newfoundland & Labrador

Churchill Falls (Labrador) Corporation Limited, Hydro Place, 500 Columbus Dr., PO Box 12500, St. John's, A1B 4K7 NL
709-737-1859, Fax: 709-737-1816
Newfoundland & Labrador Hydro, Hydro Place, Columbus Dr., PO Box 12400, St. John's, A1B 4K7 NL
709-737-1400, Fax: 709-737-1800
Newfoundland & Labrador Board of Commissioners of Public Utilities, PO Box 21040, St. John's, A1A 5B2 NL
709-726-8600, Fax: 709-726-9604, 866-782-0006, ito@pub.nf.ca

Northwest Territories

Northwest Territories Power Corporation, 4 Capital Dr., Hay River, X0E 1G2 NT
867-874-5200, Fax: 867-874-5229, info@ntpc.com
Northwest Territories Water Board, 5114 - 49th St., PO Box 1326, Yellowknife, X1A 1N9 NT
867-765-0106, Fax: 867-765-0114, info@nwtwb.com

Nova Scotia

Nova Scotia Utility & Review Board, 1601 Lower Water St., 3rd Fl., PO Box 1692 M,Halifax, B3J 3S3 NS
902-424-4448, Fax: 902-424-3919, uarb.board@gov.ns.ca

Ontario

Hydro One Inc., North Tower, 483 Bay St., Toronto, M5G 2P5 ON
416-345-5000, 877-955-1155, webmaster@HydroOne.com

Independent Electricity System Operator, PO Box 4474 A,Toronto, M5W 4E5 ON
905-403-6900, Fax: 905-403-6921, 888-448-7777, customer.relations@ieso.ca

Ontario Power Generation, 700 University Ave., Toronto, M5G 1X6 ON
416-592-2555, 877-592-2555

Prince Edward Island

Island Regulatory & Appeals Commission, National Bank Tower, #501, 134 Kent St., PO Box 577, Charlottetown, C1A 7L1 PE
902-892-3501, Fax: 902-566-4076, 800-501-6268, irac@irac.pe.ca

Quebec

Hydro-Québec, 75, boul René-Lévesque ouest, 20e étage, Montréal, H2Z 1A4 QC
514-289-2211

Régie de l'énergie, Tour de la Bourse, #255, 800, Place Victoria, CP 1, Montréal, QC H4Z 1A2
514-873-2452, Fax: 514-873-2070, 888-873-2452, secretariat@regie-energie.qc.ca

Saskatchewan

Saskatchewan Power Corporation (SaskPower), 2025 Victoria Ave., Regina, S4P 0S1 SK
306-566-2121, Fax: 306-566-2330, 800-667-4749

Saskatchewan Water Corporation (SaskWater), #200, 111 Fairford St. East, Moose Jaw, S6H 1C8 SK
306-694-3098, Fax: 306-694-3207, 888-230-1111, comm@saskwater.com

SaskEnergy Incorporated, 1777 Victoria Ave., Regina, S4P 4K5 SK
306-777-9225, Fax: 306-777-9200, 800-567-8899

Yukon Territory

Yukon Utilities Board, #19, 1114 - 1st Ave., PO Box 31728, Whitehorse, YT Y1A 6L3
867-667-5058

Companies

Alberta

AltaGas Income Trust
#1700, 355 - 4th Ave. SW, Calgary, AB T2P 0J1
403-691-7575 Fax: 403-691-7576 888-890-2715
feedback@altagas.ca
www.altagas.ca
Ticker Symbol: ALA
Profile: The energy infrastructure organization acquires, grows, & optimizes gas & power infrastructure. AltaGas Income Trust focuses upon renewable energy sources.

AltaGas Income Trust
#1700, 355 - 4th Ave. SW, Calgary, AB T2P 0J1
403-691-7575 Fax: 403-691-7576 888-890-2715
feedback@altagas.ca
www.altagas.ca
Ticker Symbol: ALA
Profile: The energy infrastructure organization acquires, grows, & optimizes gas & power infrastructure. AltaGas Income Trust focuses upon renewable energy sources.
David W. Cornhill, B.Sc.(Hons), MBAChair/CEO
Richard M. Alexander, BBM, CFA, CMAPresident/COO
David Wright, B.Sc., M.Sc., LLBExec. Vice-President, Strategy & Corporate Development
Deborah S. Stein, CFO & Vice-President, Finance
James (Jim) Bracken, CASr. Vice-President, Major Projects
Gregory A. Aarssen, B.Sc.(Hons), MBA, LLBVice-President, Corporate Affairs
Denis C. Fonteyne, Chair, Environment Occupational Health & Safety Committee
David W. Cornhill, B.Sc.(Hons), MBAChair/CEO
Richard M. Alexander, BBM, CFA, CMAPresident/COO
David Wright, B.Sc., M.Sc., LLBExec. Vice-President, Strategy & Corporate Development
Deborah S. Stein, CFO & Vice-President, Finance
James (Jim) Bracken, CASr. Vice-President, Major Projects
Gregory A. Aarssen, B.Sc.(Hons), MBA, LLBVice-President, Corporate Affairs
Denis C. Fonteyne, Chair, Environment Occupational Health & Safety Committee

AltaGas Utility Group Inc.
#540, 355 - 4 Ave. SW, Calgary, AB T2P 0J1
403-806-3310 Fax: 403-806-3311
information@altagasutility.com
www.altagasutilitygroup.com
Ticker Symbol: AUI
Profile: AltaGas Utility Group Inc. is involved in the natural gas distribution marketplace. The company invests in infrastructure-based utility & related businesses. It holds interest in the following companies: AltaGas Utilities Inc., Inuvik Gas Ltd., Heritage Gas Limited, & Ikhil Joint Venture.

AltaGas Utility Group Inc.
#540, 355 - 4 Ave. SW, Calgary, AB T2P 0J1
403-806-3310 Fax: 403-806-3311
information@altagasutility.com
www.altagasutilitygroup.com
Ticker Symbol: AUI
Profile: AltaGas Utility Group Inc. is involved in the natural gas distribution marketplace. The company invests in infrastructure-based utility & related businesses. It holds interest in the following companies: AltaGas Utilities Inc., Inuvik Gas Ltd., Heritage Gas Limited, & Ikhil Joint Venture.
Patricia Newson, CAPresident/CEO
403-806-3330, patricia.newson@altagasutility.com
Jared Green, Vice-President, Controller, & Corporate Secretary
403-806-3320, jared.green@altagasutility.com
Patricia Newson, CAPresident/CEO
403-806-3330, patricia.newson@altagasutility.com
Jared Green, Vice-President, Controller, & Corporate Secretary
403-806-3320, jared.green@altagasutility.com

Aquila Networks Canada
#700, 801 - 7th Ave. SW, Calgary, AB T2P 3P7
403-514-4000 Fax: 403-514-4001
Profile: Electric services
Fauzia Lalani, President/CEO
Bill Van Yzerloo, CFO
Denis Painchaud, General Manager, Corporate Communications
Andrew McQuattie, Director, Environment, Health & Safety
Fauzia Lalani, President/CEO
Bill Van Yzerloo, CFO
Denis Painchaud, General Manager, Corporate Communications
Andrew McQuattie, Director, Environment, Health & Safety

ATCO Ltd.
#1400, 909 - 11th Ave. SW, Calgary, AB T2R 1N6
403-292-7500 Fax: 403-292-7623
info@atco.com
www.atco.com
Ticker Symbol: ACO
Profile: The management holding company consists of the following main divisions: utilities, which includes natural gas & electricity transmission & distribution; power generation, which features the operation of hydroelectric, coal, & natural gas fired power plants; & global enterprises, which comprises ATCO Frontec, ATCO Midstream, ATCO Structures, ATCO Travel, ATCO I-Tek, & ATCO Noise Management.

ATCO Ltd.
#1400, 909 - 11th Ave. SW, Calgary, AB T2R 1N6
403-292-7500 Fax: 403-292-7623
info@atco.com
www.atco.com
Ticker Symbol: ACO
Profile: The management holding company consists of the following main divisions: utilities, which includes natural gas & electricity transmission & distribution; power generation, which features the operation of hydroelectric, coal, & natural gas fired power plants; & global enterprises, which comprises ATCO Frontec, ATCO Midstream, ATCO Structures, ATCO Travel, ATCO I-Tek, & ATCO Noise Management.
Nancy C. Southern, President/CEO
Karen M. Watson, Sr. Vice-President/CFO
Michael M. Shaw, Managing Director, ATCO Ltd., Global Enterprises, Corp. Dev., & ATCO Group
Siegfried W. Kiefer, Chief Information Officer & Managing Director, Utilities
Nancy C. Southern, President/CEO
Karen M. Watson, Sr. Vice-President/CFO
Michael M. Shaw, Managing Director, ATCO Ltd., Global Enterprises, Corp. Dev., & ATCO Group
Siegfried W. Kiefer, Chief Information Officer & Managing Director, Utilities

BP Canada Energy Company
240-4th Ave., SW, Calgary, AB T2P 2H8
403-233-1313 www.bp.com
Profile: BP is an energy company which provides its customers with fuel for transportation, energy for heat & light, retail services, & petrochemical products.

BP Canada Energy Company
240-4th Ave., SW, Calgary, AB T2P 2H8
403-233-1313 www.bp.com
Profile: BP is an energy company which provides its customers with fuel for transportation, energy for heat & light, retail services, & petrochemical products.
Tony Howard, Group Chief Executive
Tony Hayward, Group Chief Executive

Canadian Hydro Developers, Inc.
#500, 1324 - 17 Ave. SW, Calgary, AB T2T 5S8
403-269-9379 Fax: 403-244-7388
canhydro@canhydro.com
www.canhydro.com
Ticker Symbol: KHD
Profile: Canadian Hydro Developers, Inc. owns, develops, & operates generating facilities, which are certified, or slated for certification, under Environment Canada's EcoLogo Program. Renewable power generation facilities are situated in Quebec, Ontario, Alberta, & British Columbia. The renewable generation portfolio includes water, wind, & biomass technologies. The company's wholly-owned subsidiary is Canadian Renewable Energy Corporation.

Canadian Hydro Developers, Inc.
#500, 1324 - 17 Ave. SW, Calgary, AB T2T 5S8
403-269-9379 Fax: 403-244-7388
canhydro@canhydro.com
www.canhydro.com
Ticker Symbol: KHD
Profile: Canadian Hydro Developers, Inc. owns, develops, & operates generating facilities, which are certified, or slated for certification, under Environment Canada's EcoLogo Program. Renewable power generation facilities are situated in Quebec, Ontario, Alberta, & British Columbia. The renewable generation portfolio includes water, wind, & biomass technologies. The company's wholly-owned subsidiary is Canadian Renewable Energy Corporation.
John D. Keating, CAChief Executive Officer
jkeating@canhydro.com
Ross Keating, P.EngPresident, Operations & Development
Kent Brown, CAExec. Vice-Presidnet/CFO
kbrown@canhydro.com
Keith O'Regan, P.Eng, B.B.A.Exec. Vice-President/COO
Steve O'Gorman, Manager, Marketing & Communications
403-298-0262
John D. Keating, CAChief Executive Officer
jkeating@canhydro.com
Ross Keating, P.EngPresident, Operations & Development
Kent Brown, CAExec. Vice-Presidnet/CFO
kbrown@canhydro.com
Keith O'Regan, P.Eng, B.B.A.Exec. Vice-President/COO
Steve O'Gorman, Manager, Marketing & Communications
403-298-0262

Canadian Utilities Limited
#1400, 909 - 11th Ave. SW, Calgary, AB T2R 1N6
403-292-7500 Fax: 403-292-7623
investors@canadian-utilities.com
www.canadian-utilities.com
Ticker Symbol: CU
Profile: Part of the ATCO Group of Companies, Canadian Utilities Limited is engaged in natural gas & electricity transmission & distribution, as well as technology, logistics, & energy services.

Canadian Utilities Limited
#1400, 909 - 11th Ave. SW, Calgary, AB T2R 1N6
403-292-7500 Fax: 403-292-7623
investors@canadian-utilities.com
www.canadian-utilities.com
Ticker Symbol: CU
Profile: Part of the ATCO Group of Companies, Canadian Utilities Limited is engaged in natural gas & electricity transmission & distribution, as well as technology, logistics, & energy services.
Nancy C. Southern, President/CEO
Karen M. Watson, Sr. Vice-President/CFO
Siegfried W. Kiefer, Chief Information Officer & Managing Director, Utilities
Susan R. Werth, Sr. Vice-President & Chief Administration Officer
Nancy C. Southern, President/CEO
Karen M. Watson, Sr. Vice-President/CFO
Siegfried W. Kiefer, Chief Information Officer & Managing Director, Utilities
Susan R. Werth, Sr. Vice-President & Chief Administration Officer

CU Inc.
#1600, 909 - 11 Ave. SW, Calgary, AB T2R 1N6
403-292-7500 Fax: 403-292-7532 www.canadian-utilities.com
Ticker Symbol: CIU.PR.A
Profile: A wholly owned subsidiary of Canadian Utilities Limited, CU Inc. is involved in natural gas & electricity transmission &

distribution, as well as power generation. CU Inc.'s subsidiaries include CU Water Limited, ATCO Gas & Pipelines Ltd., ATCO Electric Ltd., & Alberta Power (2000) Ltd.

CU Inc.
#1600, 909 - 11 Ave. SW, Calgary, AB T2R 1N6
403-292-7500 Fax: 403-292-7532 www.canadian-utilities.com
Ticker Symbol: CIU.PR.A
Profile: A wholly owned subsidiary of Canadian Utilities Limited, CU Inc. is involved in natural gas & electricity transmission & distribution, as well as power generation. CU Inc.'s subsidiaries include CU Water Limited, ATCO Gas & Pipelines Ltd., ATCO Electric Ltd., & Alberta Power (2000) Ltd.
N.C. Southern, President/CEO & Chair
K.M. (Karen) Watson, Sr. Vice-President/CFO
403-292-7502
N.C. Southern, President/CEO & Chair
K.M. (Karen) Watson, Sr. Vice-President/CFO
403-292-7502,

Enbridge Income Fund
Fifth Avenue Place, #3000, 425 - 1st St. SW, Calgary, AB T2P 3L8
403-231-3900 Fax: 403-231-3920
webmaster@enbridgeincomefund.com
www.enbridgeincomefund.com
Ticker Symbol: ENF.UN
Profile: The unincorporated, open-ended trust is the owner of the following organizations: Enbridge Pipelines (Saskatchewan) Inc. (Saskatchewan System); NRGreen Power Limited Partnership (50% interest); wind power projects; & Alliance Canada Pipeline (50% interest). Enbridge is also developing electrical generation opportunities with waste heat. Operations are conducted in western Canada.

Enbridge Income Fund
Fifth Avenue Place, #3000, 425 - 1st St. SW, Calgary, AB T2P 3L8
403-231-3900 Fax: 403-231-3920
webmaster@enbridgeincomefund.com
www.enbridgeincomefund.com
Ticker Symbol: ENF.UN
Profile: The unincorporated, open-ended trust is the owner of the following organizations: Enbridge Pipelines (Saskatchewan) Inc. (Saskatchewan System); NRGreen Power Limited Partnership (50% interest); wind power projects; & Alliance Canada Pipeline (50% interest). Enbridge is also developing electrical generation opportunities with waste heat. Operations are conducted in western Canada.
James A. Schultz, President
John K. Whelen, CFO & Vice-President, Business Development
David K. Wudrick, Treasurer
James E.R. Lord, Corporate Secretary
Jennifer Varey, Manager, Corporate Communications
403-508-6568, jennifer.varey@enbridge.com
Kurtis Griffeth, Sr. Advisor, Investor Relations
403-266-7924, kurtis.griffeth@enbridge.com
James A. Schultz, President
John K. Whelen, CFO & Vice-President, Business Development
David K. Wudrick, Treasurer
James E.R. Lord, Corporate Secretary
Jennifer Varey, Manager, Corporate Communications
403-508-6568, jennifer.varey@enbridge.com
Kurtis Griffeth, Sr. Advisor, Investor Relations
403-266-7924, kurtis.griffeth@enbridge.com

ENMAX Corporation
141 - 50 Ave. SE, Calgary, AB T2G 4S7
403-514-3000 Fax: -310-2010 877-571-7111
customercare@enmax.com
www.enmax.com
Profile: ENMAX Corporation provides electricity & natural gas energy services in Alberta.

ENMAX Corporation
141 - 50 Ave. SE, Calgary, AB T2G 4S7
403-514-3000 Fax: 403-310-2010 877-571-7111
customercare@enmax.com
www.enmax.com
Profile: ENMAX Corporation provides electricity & natural gas energy services in Alberta.
Gary Holden, President/CEO
Kim Hubick, CFO & Exec. Vice-President, Finance
Gary Holden, President/CEO
David Halford, CFO & Exec. Vice-President, Finance

EPCOR Power Equity Ltd.
Investor Relations, EPCOR Centre, 10065 Jasper Ave., Edmonton, AB T5J 3B1
780-412-4297 Fax: 780-412-3808 866-896-4636
InvestorInquiries@epcorpowerlp.ca
www.epcor.ca
Ticker Symbol: EPP.PR.A
Profile: EPCOR's business & power generation assets, plus other assets in the United States, are indirectly held by EPCOR Power Equity Ltd.

EPCOR Power Equity Ltd.
Investor Relations, EPCOR Centre, 10065 Jasper Ave., Edmonton, AB T5J 3B1
780-412-4297 Fax: 780-412-3808 866-896-4636
InvestorInquiries@epcorpowerlp.ca
www.epcor.ca
Ticker Symbol: EPP.PR.A
Profile: EPCOR's business & power generation assets, plus other assets in the United States, are indirectly held by EPCOR Power Equity Ltd.
Don Lowry, President/CEO
Mark Wiltzen, Sr. Vice-President/CFO
Brian Vaasjo, Exec. Vice-President/COO
Denise Carpenter, Sr. Vice-President, Public & Government Affairs
Peter Arnold, Sr. Vice-President, Human Resources & Corporate Health & Safety
Don Lowry, President/CEO
Mark Wiltzen, Sr. Vice-President/CFO
Brian Vaasjo, Exec. Vice-President/COO
Denise Carpenter, Sr. Vice-President, Public & Government Affairs
Peter Arnold, Sr. Vice-President, Human Resources & Corporate Health & Safety

EPCOR Power L.P.
EPCOR Centre, 10065 Jasper Ave., 20th Fl., Edmonton, AB T5J 3B1
780-412-4297 Fax: 780-412-3808 866-896-4636
investorinquiries@epcorpowerlp.ca
www.epcorpowerlp.ca
Ticker Symbol: EP.UN
Profile: EPCOR Power L.P. is a limited partnership, which is involved in the generation of electricity & steam, through it ownership & operation of a portfolio power plants. Earnings & cash flows are derived from this activity. The Partnership's wholly-owned power generation assets are situated in Canada & the United States. The General Partner of the Partnership, EPCOR Power Services Ltd., is responsible for management of the Partnership.

EPCOR Power L.P.
EPCOR Centre, 10065 Jasper Ave., 20th Fl., Edmonton, AB T5J 3B1
780-412-4297 Fax: 780-412-3808 866-896-4636
investorinquiries@epcorpowerlp.ca
www.epcorpowerlp.ca
Ticker Symbol: EP.UN
Profile: EPCOR Power L.P. is a limited partnership, which is involved in the generation of electricity & steam, through it ownership & operation of a portfolio power plants. Earnings & cash flows are derived from this activity. The Partnership's wholly-owned power generation assets are situated in Canada & the United States. The General Partner of the Partnership, EPCOR Power Services Ltd., is responsible for management of the Partnership.
Brian T. Vaasjo, President, EPCOR Power Services Ltd.
Stuart Lee, Chief Financial Officer, EPCOR Power Services Ltd.
Kathryn Chisholm, Sr. Vice-President, General Counsel & Corporate Secretary, EPCOR Power Services Ltd.
Tim LeRiche, Contact, Media Inquiries
780-969-8238
Randy Mah, Contact, Unitholder & Analyst Inquiries
Brian T. Vaasjo, President, EPCOR Power Services Ltd.
Stuart Lee, Chief Financial Officer, EPCOR Power Services Ltd.
Kathryn Chisholm, Sr. Vice-President, General Counsel & Corporate Secretary, EPCOR Power Services Ltd.
Tim LeRiche, Contact, Media Inquiries
780-969-8238
Randy Mah, Contact, Unitholder & Analyst Inquiries

FortisAlberta
320 17th Avenue SW, Calgary, AB T2S 2V1
403-514-4000 Fax: 403-514-4001
866-717-3113www.fortisalberta.ca
Profile: FortisAlberta provides power to various communities in Alberta. It is affliated with the Fortis Family of Companies.

FortisAlberta
320 17th Avenue SW, Calgary, AB T2S 2V1
403-514-4000 Fax: 403-514-4001
866-717-3113www.fortisalberta.com
Profile: FortisAlberta provides power to various communities in Alberta. It is affliated with the Fortis Family of Companies.
Cynthia Johnston, Vice-President, Customer Service, Corp. Services
Karl W. Smith, President and CEO
Nipa Chakravarti, Vice-President, Customer Service
Karl W. Smith, President and CEO

Keyera Facilities Income Fund
#600, 144 - 4 Ave. SW, Calgary, AB T2P 3N4
403-205-8300 Fax: 403-205-8303
ir@keyera.com
www.keyera.com
Ticker Symbol: KEY.UN
Profile: The Keyera Facilities Income Fund is an unincorporated open-ended trust. It owns 100% interest in Keyera Energy Canada Partnership. Keyera is engaged in the following activities: gathering & processing natural gas; storing & transporting natural gas liquids & crude oil; & marketing natural gas liquids.

Keyera Facilities Income Fund
#600, 144 - 4 Ave. SW, Calgary, AB T2P 3N4
403-205-8300 Fax: 403-205-8303
ir@keyera.com
www.keyera.com
Ticker Symbol: KEY.UN
Profile: The Keyera Facilities Income Fund is an unincorporated open-ended trust. It owns 100% interest in Keyera Energy Canada Partnership. Keyera is engaged in the following activities: gathering & processing natural gas; storing & transporting natural gas liquids & crude oil; & marketing natural gas liquids.
Jim V. Bertram, President/CEO
Dean Setoguchi, Vice-President/CFO
Graham Balzun, Vice-President, Engineering & Corporate Responsibility
Ron Daniels, Manager, Manager, Information Technology
403-205-7635
Tanis Fiss, Manager, Financial Communications
Murray Selle, Manager, Health & Safety
Rod Sikora, Manager, Environment
403-205-8335
W. John Cobb, Director, Investor Relations
403-205-7673
Jim V. Bertram, President/CEO
Dean Setoguchi, Vice-President/CFO
Graham Balzun, Vice-President, Engineering & Corporate Responsibility
Ron Daniels, Manager, Manager, Information Technology
403-205-7635
Tanis Fiss, Manager, Financial Communications
Murray Selle, Manager, Health & Safety
Rod Sikora, Manager, Environment
403-205-8335
W. John Cobb, Director, Investor Relations
403-205-7673

MAXIM Power Corp.
#1210, 715 - 5th Ave. SW, Calgary, AB T2P 2X6
403-263-3021 Fax: 403-263-9125
maxim@maximpowercorp.com
www.maximpowercorp.com
Ticker Symbol: MXG
Profile: MAXIM Power Corp. is an independent power producer. The company is involved in the acquisition, development, ownership, & operation of environmentally responsible power projects. Its assets include coal & natural gas powered generators in western Canada, the United States, & France.

MAXIM Power Corp.
#1210, 715 - 5th Ave. SW, Calgary, AB T2P 2X6
403-263-3021 Fax: 403-263-9125
maxim@maximpowercorp.com
www.maximpowercorp.com
Ticker Symbol: MXG
Profile: MAXIM Power Corp. is an independent power producer. The company is involved in the acquisition, development, ownership, & operation of environmentally responsible power projects. Its assets include coal & natural gas powered generators in western Canada, the United States, & France.
John R. Bobenic, President/CEO
Xavier Embroise, President, COMAX France S.A.S.
Michael R. Mayder, CFO & Vice-President, Finance
Ian Sanchez, Vice-President, Corporate Development
Jamie Urquhart, Vice-President, Operations
John R. Bobenic, President/CEO
Xavier Embroise, President, COMAX France S.A.S.
Michael R. Mayder, CFO & Vice-President, Finance
Ian Sanchez, Vice-President, Corporate Development
Jamie Urquhart, Vice-President, Operations

Medicine Hat Electric
2172 Brier Park Place NW, Medicine Hat, AB T1C 1S6
403-529-8262 Fax: 403-502-8060
elecdist@medicinehat.ca

Profile: Responsible for providing electrical power, natural gas, water treatment & supply, and waste management services to the city of Medicine Hat

Medicine Hat Electric
2172 Brier Park Place NW, Medicine Hat, AB T1C 1S6
403-529-8262 Fax: 403-502-8060
elecdist@medicinehat.ca
Profile: Responsible for providing electrical power, natural gas, water treatment & supply, and waste management services to the city of Medicine Hat

Pristine Power
#1450, 645 - 7th Avenue SW, Calgary, AB T2P 4G8
403-444-6401 Fax: 403-444-6784
gkrause@pristinepower.ca
www.pristinepower.ca
Ticker Symbol: PPX
Profile: Develops, owns, and operates independent power plants to produce and sell electricity

Pristine Power
#1450, 645 - 7th Avenue SW, Calgary, AB T2P 4G8
403-444-6401 Fax: 403-444-6784
gkrause@pristinepower.ca
www.pristinepower.ca
Ticker Symbol: PPX
Profile: Develops, owns, and operates independent power plants to produce and sell electricity
Jeffry Myers, President/CEO
Geoffrey D. Krause, CFO
Jeffry Myers, President/CEO
Geoffrey D. Krause, CFO

TransAlta Corporation
PO Box 1900 M, 110 - 12 Ave. SW, Calgary, AB T2P 2M1
403-267-7110 Fax: 403-267-2590
investor_relations@transalta.com
www.transalta.com
Ticker Symbol: TA
Profile: TansAlta Corporation is engaged in coal & gas-fired generation. The company carries out its activities in Canada, the United States, Mexico, & Australia.

TransAlta Corporation
PO Box 1900 M, 110 - 12 Ave. SW, Calgary, AB T2P 2M1
403-267-7110 Fax: 403-267-2590
investor_relations@transalta.com
www.transalta.com
Ticker Symbol: TA
Profile: TansAlta Corporation is engaged in coal & gas-fired generation. The company carries out its activities in Canada, the United States, Mexico, & Australia.
Stephen G. Snyder, President/CEO
Brian Burden, Exec. Vice-President/CFO
William D.A. Bridge, Exec. Vice-President, Generation Technology & Procurement
Dawn Farrell, Exec. Vice-President, Commercial Operations & Development
Mike Williams, Exec. Vice-President, Human Resources, Information Technology & Communication
Ken Stickland, Exec. Vice-President, Legal, SD, & Environmental Health & Safety
Stephen G. Snyder, President/CEO
Brian Burden, Exec. Vice-President/CFO
William D.A. Bridge, Exec. Vice-President, Generation Technology & Procurement
Dawn Farrell, Exec. Vice-President, Commercial Operations & Development
Mike Williams, Exec. Vice-President, Human Resources, Information Technology & Communication
Ken Stickland, Exec. Vice-President, Legal, SD, & Environmental Health & Safety

TransAlta Power, L.P.
PO Box 1900 M, 110 - 12 Ave. SW, Calgary, AB T2P 2M1
403-267-7110 Fax: 403-267-2590
investor_relations@transalta.com
www.transalta.com
Ticker Symbol: TPW
Profile: Unit investment trusts, certificate/closed-end management offices; Electric services

TransAlta Power, L.P.
PO Box 1900 M, 110 - 12 Ave. SW, Calgary, AB T2P 2M1
403-267-7110 Fax: 403-267-2590
investor_relations@transalta.com
www.transalta.com
Ticker Symbol: TA
Profile: Unit investment trusts, certificate/closed-end management offices; Electric services
Ian A. Bourne, President
Marvin J. Waiand, Vice-President & Treasurer
Stephen G. Snyder, President & CEO
Brian Burden, Chief Financial Officer

TransCanada Corp.
450 - 1 St. SW, Calgary, AB T2P 5H1
403-920-2000 Fax: 403-920-2200
communications@transcanada.com
www.transcanada.com
Ticker Symbol: TRP
Profile: TransCanada Corporation is engaged in the pipelines & energy business. Pipelines are located in Canada, the United States, & Mexico. Power operations & natural gas storage are part of the energy segment.

TransCanada Corp.
450 - 1 St. SW, Calgary, AB T2P 5H1
403-920-2000 Fax: 403-920-2200
communications@transcanada.com
www.transcanada.com
Ticker Symbol: TRP
Profile: TransCanada Corporation is engaged in the pipelines & energy business. Pipelines are located in Canada, the United States, & Mexico. Power operations & natural gas storage are part of the energy segment.
Harold N. Kvisle, President/CEO
Alexander J. Pourbaix, President, Energy
Russell K. Girling, President, Pipelines
Gregory A. Lohnes, Exec. Vice-President/CFO
Sarah E. Raiss, Exec. Vice-President, Corporate Services
Sean McMaster, General Counsel & Exec. Vice-President, Corporate
Don Wishart, Exec. Vice-President, Operations & Engineering
Harold N. Kvisle, President/CEO
Alexander J. Pourbaix, President, Energy
Russell K. Girling, President, Pipelines
Gregory A. Lohnes, Exec. Vice-President/CFO
Sarah E. Raiss, Exec. Vice-President, Corporate Services
Sean McMaster, General Counsel & Exec. Vice-President, Corporate
Don Wishart, Exec. Vice-President, Operations & Engineering

British Columbia

Atlantic Power Corp.
#1900, 355 Burrard Street, Vancouver, BC V6L 2G8
617-977-2700 Fax: 617-977-2410
info@atlanticpowercorporation.com
www.atlanticpowercorporation.com
Ticker Symbol: ATP.UN

Atlantic Power Corp.
#1900, 355 Burrard Street, Vancouver, BC V6L 2G8
617-977-2700 Fax: 617-977-2410
info@atlanticpowercorporation.com
www.atlanticpowercorporation.com
Ticker Symbol: ATP.UN
Barry Welch, President & CEO
Patrick Welch, Secretary & CFO
Barry Welch, President & CEO
Patrick Welch, Secretary & CFO

Atlantic Power Corporation
#1900, 355 Burrard St., Vancouver, BC V6L 2G8
617-977-2700 Fax: 617-977-2410
info@atlanticpowercorporation.com
www.atlanticpowercorporation.com

Atlantic Power Corporation
#1900, 355 Burrard St., Vancouver, BC V6L 2G8
617-977-2700 Fax: 617-977-2410
info@atlanticpowercorporation.com
www.atlanticpowercorporation.com
Barry Welch, President/CEO
Patrick Welch, Secretary & CFO
Barry Welch, President/CEO
Patrick Welch, Secretary & CFO

British Columbia Hydro
6911 Southpoint Dr., Burnaby, BC V3N 4X8
604-224-9376 Fax: 604-528-3137
800-224-9376www.bchydro.com
Profile: Electric services

British Columbia Hydro
6911 Southpoint Dr., Burnaby, BC V3N 4X8
604-224-9376 Fax: 604-528-3137
800-224-9376www.bchydro.com
Profile: Electric services
Robert G. Elton, President/CEO
Valerie C. Lambert, Treasurer
Robert J. Steele, Chief Information Officer
Glen S. Smyrl, Vice-President, Engineering
Bev Van Ruyven, Acting President/CEO
Charles Reid, Exec. Vice President/CFO
Robert J. Steele, Chief Information Officer
Chris O'Riley, Vice-President, Engineering

British Columbia Utilities Commission
PO Box 250, 900 Howe St., Vancouver, BC V6Z 2N3
604-660-4700 Fax: 604-660-1102 800-663-1385
commission.secretary@bcuc.com
www.bcuc.com
Profile: The British Columbia Utilities Commission is an independent regulatory agency of the Provincial Government. The Commission's primary responsibility is the regulation of British Columbia's natural gas & electricity utilities. It also regulates intra-provincial pipelines & universal compulsory automobile insurance.

British Columbia Utilities Commission
PO Box 250, 900 Howe St., Vancouver, BC V6Z 2N3
604-660-4700 Fax: 604-660-1102 800-663-1385
commission.secretary@bcuc.com
www.bcuc.com
Profile: The British Columbia Utilities Commission is an independent regulatory agency of the Provincial Government. The Commission's primary responsibility is the regulation of British Columbia's natural gas & electricity utilities. It also regulates intra-provincial pipelines & universal compulsory automobile insurance.
Robert Hobbs, Chair
Len Kelsey, Chair

EarthFirst Canada Inc.
2960 B Jutland Road, Victoria, BC V8T 5K2
250-381-1208 Fax: 250-381-1298
dnewell@earthfirstcanada.com
www.earthfirstcanada.com
Ticker Symbol: EF
Profile: Developer, builder, owner and operator of windpower projects throughout Canada

EarthFirst Canada Inc.
2960 B Jutland Road, Victoria, BC V8T 5K2
250-381-1208 Fax: 250-381-1298
dnewell@earthfirstcanada.com
www.earthfirstcanada.com
Ticker Symbol: EF
Profile: Developer, builder, owner and operator of windpower projects throughout Canada
Derren Newell, Chief Financial Officer
Derren Newell, Chief Financial Officer

Plutonic Power Corp.
#600, 888 Dunsmuir Street, Vancouver, BC V6C 3K4
604-669-4999 Fax: 604-682-3727
elisha.moreno@plutonic.ca
www.plutonic.ca
Ticker Symbol: PCC
Profile: Clean energy company focused on hydroelectric projects in British Columbia

Plutonic Power Corp.
#600, 888 Dunsmuir Street, Vancouver, BC V6C 3K4
604-669-4999 Fax: 604-682-3727
elisha.moreno@plutonic.ca
www.plutonic.ca
Ticker Symbol: PCC
Profile: Clean energy company focused on hydroelectric projects in British Columbia
Donald A. McInnes, Chief Executive Officer
Peter G. Wong, Chief Financial Officer
Donald A. McInnes, Chief Executive Officer
Peter G. Wong, Chief Financial Officer

Powerex
1400-666 Burrad St., Vancouver, BC V6C 2X8
604-891-5000 Fax: 604-891-6060 800-220-4907
sheena.macdonald@powerex.com
www.powerex.com
Profile: Powerex is the wholly-owned power marketing subsidiary of BC Hydro. It has grown to be a leading marketer of wholesale energy products & services in western Canada & the western United States, & a growing niche player in other markets in North America.

Powerex Corp.
#1400, 666 Burrard St., Vancouver, BC V6C 2X8
604-891-5000 Fax: 604-891-6060 800-220-4907
Brian.Moghadam@powerex.com (Business Dev)
www.powerex.com
Profile: As a wholly-owned subsidiary of BC Hydro, Powerex markets BC Hydro's surplus electricity. Powerex is a participant in energy markets across North America, where it supplies &

buys wholesale power, natural gas, ancillary services, & environmental products.
Brian Moghadam, Contact (Business Development)
604-891-5058
Amit Budhwar, Director, Risk Management
604-891-5041
Deb Armour, Director, Compliance
604-891-5063
Bernice Crick, Manager, Credit Risk Management
604-895-7093
Andrew Newell, Manager, Market Risk Management
604-891-6093
Jay Ratzlaff, Manager, Contract Management
604-895-7067

Primary Energy Recycling Corp.
#129, 2000 York Road, Oak Brook, IL
630-371-0505 Fax: 630-371-0673
investorinfo@primaryenergy.com
www.primaryenergyrecycling.com
Ticker Symbol: PRI.UN
Profile: Owns and operates recycled energy projects
V. Michael Alverson, Vice-President & CFO
V. Michael Alverson, Vice-President & CFO

Duke Energy Canada Exchangeco Inc.
1333 West Georgia St., Vancouver, BC V6E 3K9
604-488-8000 Fax: 604-488-8500
investduk@duke-energy.com
www.duke-energy.com
Ticker Symbol: DK
Profile: Natural gas transmission & distribution; Electric services; Crude petroleum, natural gas & natural gas liquids extraction; Natural gas transmission; Special warehousing & storage.

Spectra Energy Inc.
#1000, 1055 West Georgia St., Vancouver, BC V6E 3K9
604-488-8000 Fax: 604-488-8500 www.duke-energy.com
Profile: Natural gas transmission & distribution; Electric services; Crude petroleum, natural gas & natural gas liquids extraction; Natural gas transmission; Special warehousing & storage.
Paul M. Anderson, Chair/CEO
Fred J. Fowler, President/COO
David L. Hauser, Sr. Vice-President/Acting CFO
Gregory L. Ebel, President/CEO
John Patrick Reddy, Chief Financial Officer

Terasen Gas
PO Box 6666 Terminal, Vancouver, BC V6B 6M9
250-979-4900 Fax: 888-224-2720 888-224-2710
customerservice@tersengas.com
www.terasengas.com
Profile: Tersan Gas delivers natural gas & piped propane to homes & businesses throughout BC. It has approximately 900,000 customers in 125 communities & provides service to 95% of BC's natural gas customers.

Terasen Gas
PO Box 6666 Terminal, Vancouver, BC V6B 6M9
250-979-4900 Fax: 888-224-2720 888-224-2710
customerservice@tersengas.com
www.terasengas.com
Profile: Tersan Gas delivers natural gas & piped propane to homes & businesses throughout BC. It has approximately 900,000 customers in 125 communities & provides service to 95% of BC's natural gas customers.

Manitoba

Manitoba Hydro
PO Box 815 Main, 820 Taylor Ave., Winnipeg, MB R3C 2P4
204-474-3311 Fax: 204-475-0069 888-624-9376
publicaffairs@hydro.mb.ca
www.hydro.mb.ca
Profile: Manitoba Hydro is a Crown Corporation & the province's major energy utility. It exports electricity to over 30 electric utilities through its participation in four wholesale markets in Canada & the mid-western USA.

Manitoba Hydro
PO Box 815 Main, 360 Portage Ave., Winnipeg, MB R3C 2P4
204-480-5900 Fax: 204-475-0069 888-624-9376
publicaffairs@hydro.mb.ca
www.hydro.mb.ca
Profile: Manitoba Hydro is a major energy utility. It serves electric & natural gas customers in Manitoba.
Robert B. Brennan, President/CEO
Vince Warden, CFO & Vice-President, Finance & Administration
Bob Brennan, President & Chief Executive Officer
Vince Warden, Chief Financial Officer & Senior Vice-President, Finance & Administration
Ken Adams, Senior Vice-President, Power Supply
Ed Tymofichuk, Vice-President, Transmission
Gerry Rose, Vice-President, Customer Care & Marketing
Lyn Wray, Vice-President, Corporate Planning & Strategic Analysis
Brad Ireland, Contact, Corporate Health & Safety

New Brunswick

Bell Aliant Regional Communications Income Fund
1 Brunswick Sq., 5th Fl., Saint John, NB E2L 4L4
877-248-3113 Fax: 877-498-2464
investors@bell.aliant.ca
www.bell.aliant.ca
Ticker Symbol: BA.UN
Profile: The wireline company operates in Atlantic Canada, Quebec, & Ontario.

Bell Aliant Regional Communications Income Fund
1 Brunswick Sq., 5th Fl., Saint John, NB E2L 4L4
877-248-3113 Fax: 877-498-2464
investors@bell.aliant.ca
www.bell.aliant.ca
Ticker Symbol: BA.UN
Profile: The wireline company operates in Atlantic Canada, Quebec, & Ontario.
Karen H. Sheriff, President/CEO
Glen LeBlanc, Exec. Vice-President/CFO
Fred Crooks, Chief Legal Officer & Exec. Vice-President, Corporate Services
David Rathbun, Exec. Vice-President, Bell Aliant, & President, xwave (Bell Alliant's Information Technology Division)
Chuck Hartlen, Sr. Vice-President, Customer Experience, Chief Information Office
Karen H. Sheriff, President/CEO
Glen LeBlanc, Exec. Vice-President/CFO
Fred Crooks, Chief Legal Officer & Exec. Vice-President, Corporate Services
David Rathbun, Exec. Vice-President, Bell Aliant, & President, xwave (Bell Alliant's Information Technology Division)
Chuck Hartlen, Sr. Vice-President, Customer Experience, Chief Information Office

Fortis Inc.
Fortis Bldg., PO Box 8837, #1201, 139 Water St., St. John's, NL A1B 3T2
709-737-2800 Fax: 709-737-5307
investorrelations@fortisinc.com
www.fortisinc.com
Ticker Symbol: FTS
Profile: Fortis Inc. is an international distribution utility holding company, which serves gas & electricity customers. The company also owns hotels & commercial real estate in Canada.

Fortis Inc.
Fortis Bldg., PO Box 8837, #1201, 139 Water St., St. John's, NL A1B 3T2
709-737-2800 Fax: 709-737-5307
investorrelations@fortisinc.com
www.fortisinc.com
Ticker Symbol: FTS
Profile: Fortis Inc. is an international distribution utility holding company, which serves gas & electricity customers. The company also owns hotels & commercial real estate in Canada.
H. Stanley Marshall, President/CEO
Barry V. Perry, CFO & Vice-President, Finance
Ronald W. McCabe, General Counsel & Corporate Secretary
H. Stanley Marshall, President/CEO
Barry V. Perry, CFO & Vice-President, Finance
Ronald W. McCabe, General Counsel & Corporate Secretary

New Brunswick Power Corporation
PO Box 2000, 515 King St., Fredericton, NB E3B 4X1
506-458-4444 Fax: 506-458-4000 800-663-6272
questions@nbpower.com
www.nbpower.com
Profile: NB Power is preparing to meet the electricity demands of NB in a deregulated industry. It recently reorganized into separate companies.

New Brunswick Power Distribution & Customer Svs. Corp
PO Box 2000, 515 King St., Fredericton, NB E3B 4X1
506-458-4444 Fax: 506-458-4000 800-663-6272
customerservices@nbpower.com
www.nbpower.com
Profile: NB Power provides safe & sustainable energy services to homes, businesses, & facilities in New Brunswick. Electricity is generated at sixteen facilities.
David D. Hay, President & CEO
Francis Mcguire, Chairman of the Board of Directors
David D. Hay, President & Chief Executive Officer
Darrell Bishop, Executive Vice-President, Strategic Planning
Darren Murphy, Vice-President, Transmission, Distribution, & Customer Service
Wayne Snowdon, Vice-President, Generation (Conventional)
Gaëtan Thomas, Vice-President, Nuclear

Newfoundland & Labrador Hydro
PO Box 12400, 500 Columbus Dr., St.John's, NL A1B 4K7
709-737-1335 Fax: 709-737-1795
hydro@nlh.nl.ca
www.nlh.nl.ca/hydroweb/hydroweb.nsf
Profile: Newfoundland & Labrador Hydro generates, trasmits, & distributes electrical power & energy to utility, residential, & industrial customers throughout the province. It is part of the Hydro Group of Companies.

Newfoundland & Labrador Hydro
Hydro Place, PO Box 12400, 500 Columbus Dr., St.John's, NL A1B 4K7
709-737-1400 Fax: 709-737-1800 888-737-1296
hydro@nlh.nl.ca; tenders@nlh.nl.ca
www.nlh.nl.ca
Profile: Newfoundland & Labrador Hydro is the primary generator of safe & reliable electricity to residents, utilities, & industries across the province. The company's assets include hydroelectric generating stations, high-voltage terminal stations, lower-voltage interconnected distribution stations, diesel plants, gas turbines, transmission & distribution lines, & an oil-fired plant.
Dean MacDonald, Chair
Ed Martin, President/CEO
Jim Haynes, Vice-President, Regulated Operations
Ed Martin, President & Chief Executive Officer
Derrick Sturge, Chief Financial Officer & Vice-President, Finance
Jim Haynes, Vice-President, Regulated Operations
John Mallam, Vice-President, Engineering Services
Gerard McDonald, Vice-President, Human Resources & Organizational Effectiveness

Newfoundland Power Inc.
PO Box 8910, St. John's, NL A1B 3P6
709-737-5600 Fax: 709-737-5300
contactus@newfoundlandpower.com
www.newfoundlandpower.com
Profile: The company is engaged in electric services.

Newfoundland Power Inc.
PO Box 8910, 55 Kenmout Rd., St. John's, NL A1B 3P6
709-737-2802 Fax: 709-737-2903 800-663-2802
contactus@newfoundlandpower.com
www.newfoundlandpower.com
Profile: Newfoundland Power Inc. is engaged in the operation of an integrated generation, transmission, & distribution system. Safe, reliable electricity is supplied to the island portion of Newfoundland & Labrador.
Karl Smith, President/CEO
Bernard Ryan, Director, Environment
Jocelyn Perry, Vice-President, Finance
Peter Collins, Manager, Information Services
Earl Ludlow, President & Chief Executive Officer
Peter Alteen, Vice-President, Regulation & Planning
Jocelyn Perry, Chief Financial Officer & Vice-President, Finance
Gary Smith, Vice-President, Customer Operations & Engineering
Peter Collins, Manager, Customer Relations & Information Technology

Saint John Energy
PO Box 850, Saint John, NB E2L 4C7
506-658-5252 Fax: 506-658-0868
877-907-5550www.sjenergy.com
Profile: Responsible for providing electricity to the city of Saint John. Other services include tree trimming, rental of water heaters, street light repair

Saint John Energy
PO Box 850, Saint John, NB E2L 4C7
506-658-5252 Fax: 506-658-0868
877-907-5550www.sjenergy.com
Profile: Responsible for providing electricity to the city of Saint John. Other services include tree trimming, rental of water heaters, street light repair
Eric Marr, President/CEO
Eric Marr, President/CEO

Nova Scotia

Emera Incorporated
Barrington Tower, Scotia Square, PO Box 910, 1894 Barrington St., 18th Fl., Halifax, NS B3J 2W5

902-450-0507 Fax: 902-428-6112 888-450-0507
investors@emera.com
www.emera.com
Ticker Symbol: EMA

Profile: The holding company is involved in the energy sector. Emera Inc.'s subsidiaries include Bangor Hydro-Electric Company, Nova Scotia Power Inc., Emera Energy, Maritimes & Northeast Pipeline, Brunswick Pipeline, Emera Utility Services, & Grand Bahama Power Ltd.

Emera Incorporated
Barrington Tower, Scotia Square, PO Box 910, 1894 Barrington St., 18th Fl., Halifax, NS B3J 2W5
902-450-0507 Fax: 902-428-6112 888-450-0507
investors@emera.com
www.emera.com
Ticker Symbol: EMA

Profile: The holding company is involved in the energy sector. Emera Inc.'s subsidiaries include Bangor Hydro-Electric Company, Nova Scotia Power Inc., Emera Energy, Maritimes & Northeast Pipeline, Brunswick Pipeline, Emera Utility Services, & Grand Bahama Power Ltd.
Christopher Huskilson, President/CEO
Rob Bennett, President/CEO, Nova Scotia Power Inc.
Robert Hanf, President/COO, Bangor Hydro Electric Company
Robin McAdam, President, Brunswick Pipeline Company Ltd.
Nancy Tower, F.C.A.Chief Financial Officer
902-429-6991, nancy.tower@emera.com
Wayne Crawley,, CAVice-President, Corporate Strategy & Development
James Spurr, General Counsel & Vice-President, Government Relations
Jennifer Nicholson, CADirector, Investor Relations & Strategic Development
902-428-6347, jennifer.nicholson@emera.com
Christopher Huskilson, President/CEO
Rob Bennett, President/CEO, Nova Scotia Power Inc.
Robert Hanf, President/COO, Bangor Hydro Electric Company
Robin McAdam, President, Brunswick Pipeline Company Ltd.
Nancy Tower, F.C.A.Chief Financial Officer
902-429-6991, nancy.tower@emera.com
Wayne Crawley,, CAVice-President, Corporate Strategy & Development
James Spurr, General Counsel & Vice-President, Government Relations
Jennifer Nicholson, CADirector, Investor Relations & Strategic Development
902-428-6347, jennifer.nicholson@emera.com

Northwest Territories Power Corporation
4 Capital Dr., Hay River, NT X0E 1G2
867-874-5200 Fax: 867-874-5229
info@ntpc.com
www.ntpc.com

Profile: The following services are offered: electric, water, sewer, pipeline, communications & power line construction.

Northwest Territories Power Corporation
4 Capital Dr., Hay River, NT X0E 1G2
867-874-5200
info@ntpc.com
www.ntpc.com

Profile: Northwest Territories Power Corporation generates & delivers power across the Northwest Territories. The corporation operates 28 separate power systems. Northwest Territories Power Corporation attempts to reduce its environmental impact with natural gas engines in Inuvik, rather than shipping in diesel.
Leon Courneya, President/CEO
867-874-5245, lcourneya@ntpc.com
Judith Goucher, CFO & Director, Finance
867-874-5234, jgoucher@ntpc.com
John Locke, Director, Information Technology
jlocke@ntpc.com
Leon Courneya, FCAPresident & Chief Executive Officer
Judith Goucher, MAChief Financial Officer & Director, Finance
John Locke, Chief Information Officer & Director, Information Technology
Brian Willows, Chief Operating Officer
Stephen Kerrows, Director, Engineering
Robert Schmidt, Director, Hydro Region

Nova Scotia Power Inc.
PO Box 910, #1800, 1894 Barrington St., Halifax, NS B3J 2W5
902-450-0507 Fax: 902-428-6112 800-428-6230
investors@emera.com
www.nspower.ca
Ticker Symbol: NSI

Profile: Nova Scotia Power Inc. is engaged in the generation, transmission, & distribution of electric power across Nova Scotia.

Nova Scotia Power Inc.
PO Box 910, #1800, 1894 Barrington St., Halifax, NS B3J 2W5
902-450-0507 Fax: 902-428-6112 800-428-6230
investors@emera.com
www.nspower.ca
Ticker Symbol: NSI

Profile: Nova Scotia Power Inc. is engaged in the generation, transmission, & distribution of electric power across Nova Scotia.
Rob Bennett, President/CEO
Sarah MacDonald, President/COO, Emera Utility Services & Vice-President Human Resources
Rick Janega, Exec. Vice-President, Business Infrastructure & Optimization
Greg Blunden, CATreasurer & Vice-President, Finance
Mark Savory, Vice-President, Technical & Construction Services
Gerald Weseen, General Manager, Communications & Public Affairs
James Taylor, General Manager, Environmental Planning & Monitoring
Rob Bennett, President/CEO
Sarah MacDonald, President/COO, Emera Utility Services & Vice-President Human Resources
Rick Janega, Exec. Vice-President, Business Infrastructure & Optimization
Greg Blunden, CATreasurer & Vice-President, Finance
Mark Savory, Vice-President, Technical & Construction Services
Gerald Weseen, General Manager, Communications & Public Affairs
James Taylor, General Manager, Environmental Planning & Monitoring

Ontario

Algonquin Power Income Fund
2845 Bristol Circle, Oakville, ON L6H 7H7
905-465-4500 Fax: 905-465-4514
apif@algonquinpower.com
www.algonquinpower.com
Ticker Symbol: APF

Profile: Algonquin Power Income Fund is an open-ended investment trust. It owns or has interests in a portfolio of renewable power & sustainable infrastructure assets throughout Canada & the United States. The Trust's facilities include the following: hydroelectric generation, wind energy, energy from waste, landfill gas, biomass-fired generation, natural gas cogeneration, water distribution, & wastewater treatment.

Algonquin Power Income Fund
2845 Bristol Circle, Oakville, ON L6H 7H7
905-465-4500 Fax: 905-465-4514
apif@algonquinpower.com
www.algonquinpower.com
Ticker Symbol: APF

Profile: Algonquin Power Income Fund is an open-ended investment trust. It owns or has interests in a portfolio of renewable power & sustainable infrastructure assets throughout Canada & the United States. The Trust's facilities include the following: hydroelectric generation, wind energy, energy from waste, landfill gas, biomass-fired generation, natural gas cogeneration, water distribution, & wastewater treatment.
Chris K. Jarrat, Managing Director, Development
David Bronicheski, CFO & Managing Director, Administration
David C. Kerr, Managing Director, Power Generation & Corporate Services
Ian E. Robertson, Managing Director, Utilities
Chris K. Jarrat, Managing Director, Development
David Bronicheski, CFO & Managing Director, Administration
David C. Kerr, Managing Director, Power Generation & Corporate Services
Ian E. Robertson, Managing Director, Utilities

American Eco Corporation
154 University Ave Suite 200, Toronto, ON M5H 3Y9
416-340-2727 Fax: 416-340-2457
investorrelations@americaneco.
Ticker Symbol: ECX

Profile: Offices of holding companies; Refuse systems; Management services; Mfrs-industrial & commercial machinery & equipment (various)
C. Brewer, Chief Executive Officer
T.J. Gardner, Pres. & Chief Liquidating Off.
C. Brewer, Chief Executive Officer
T.J. Gardner, Pres. & Chief Liquidating Off.

Atomic Energy of Canada Limited
2251 Speakman Dr., Mississauga, ON L5K 1B2
905-823-9040 Fax: 905-823-1290 866-886-2325
info@aecl.ca
www.aecl.ca

Profile: Manufacturers of various industrial inorganic chemicals, measuring & controlling devices, special industry machinery; Commercial physical & biological research; Management services; Electric services

Atomic Energy of Canada Limited
2251 Speakman Dr., Mississauga, ON L5K 1B2
905-823-9040 Fax: 905-823-1290 866-886-2325
info@aecl.ca
www.aecl.ca

Profile: Manufacturers of various industrial inorganic chemicals, measuring & controlling devices, special industry machinery; Commercial physical & biological research; Management services; Electric services
Robert Van Adel, President/CEO
Michael C. Burns, Chair of the Board
Allan A. Hawryluk, Sr. Vice-President, Corporate Affairs, General Counsel, and Corporate Sec.
Hugh MacDiarmid, President/CEO
Glenna Carr, Chair of the Board
Jonathan Lundy, Sr. Vice-President, General Counsel and Corporate Secretary

Brantford Power Inc.
84 Market St. 3rd Fl., Brantford, ON N3T 5N8
519-751-3522 Fax: 519-753-6130
brantfordpower@brantford.ca
www.brantfordpower.com

Profile: Brantford Power strives to provide safe, reliable, & competitively priced services to customers, while providing value for municipal shareholder.

Brantford Power Inc.
84 Market St. 3rd Fl., Brantford, ON N3T 5N8
519-751-3522 Fax: 519-753-6130
brantfordpower@brantford.ca
www.brantfordpower.com

Profile: Brantford Power strives to provide safe, reliable, & competitively priced services to customers, while providing value for municipal shareholder.
George Mychailenko, CEO/General Manager
519-751-3522, gmychailenko@brantford.ca
Ann Elwood, Administrative Coordinator
aelwood@brantford.ca
Brian D'Amboise, Chief Financial Officer
damboise@brantford.ca
George Mychailenko, CEO/General Manager
519-751-3522, gmychailenko@brantford.ca
Ann Elwood, Administrative Coordinator
aelwood@brantford.ca
Brian D'Amboise, Chief Financial Officer
damboise@brantford.ca

Cambridge & North Dumfries Hydro Inc.
PO Box 1060, 1500 Bishop St., Cambridge, ON N1R 5X6
519-621-3484 Fax: 519-621-7420
customercare@camhydro.com

Profile: Cambridge & North Dumfries Hydro Inc. is a local distribution company which delivers electricity to the community on a not-for-profit basis. Local distribution rates are approved by the Ontario Energy Board.

Cambridge & North Dumfries Hydro Inc.
PO Box 1060, 1500 Bishop St., Cambridge, ON N1R 5X6
519-621-3530 Fax: 519-621-0383

Profile: Cambridge & North Dumfries Hydro Inc. is a local distribution company which delivers electricity to the community on a not-for-profit basis. Local distribution rates are approved by the Ontario Energy Board.
Grotheer President/CEO
jgrotheer@camhydro.com
Jeff Brown, Director of Operations
jbrown@camhydro.com
M.Jane Hale-MacDonald, Director, Human Resources
jhalemcdonald@camhydro.com
Grotheer President/CEO
jgrotheer@camhydro.com
Jeff Brown, Director of Operations
jbrown@camhydro.com
M.Jane Hale-MacDonald, Director, Human Resources
jhalemcdonald@camhydro.com

Countryside Power Income Fund
#920, 495 Richmond St., London, ON N6A 5A9
519-435-0298 Fax: 519-435-0396
www.countrysidepowerfund.com

Profile: Indirectly invested in the U.S. Energy Biogas Corporation loans & royalty interest; Has a direct ownership of the District Energy Systems

Countryside Power Income Fund
#920, 495 Richmond St., London, ON N6A 5A9
519-435-0298 Fax: 519-435-0396

Profile: Indirectly invested in the U.S. Energy Biogas Corporation loans & royalty interest; Has a direct ownership of the District Energy Systems
Goran Mornhed, President & CEO

Edward M. Campana, Chief Financial Officer
Goran Mornhed, President & CEO
Edward M. Campana, Chief Financial Officer

Creststreet Power & Income Fund LP
#1450, 70 University Ave., Toronto, ON M5J 2M4
416-864-6330 Fax: 416-862-8950
info@creststreet.com
www.creststreet.com
Ticker Symbol: CRS.DB
Profile: Owns & operates two wind energy projects in Quebec & Nova Scotia

Creststreet Power & Income Fund LP
#1450, 70 University Ave., Toronto, ON M5J 2M4
416-864-6330 Fax: 416-862-8950
info@creststreet.com
www.creststreet.com
Ticker Symbol: CRS.DB
Profile: Owns & operates two wind energy projects in Quebec & Nova Scotia
Eric C. McFadden, President & CEO
Derren Newell, CFO & Vice-President, Finance
Eric C. McFadden, President & CEO
Derren Newell, CFO & Vice-President, Finance

Energy Savings Income Fund
#2630, 100 King St. West, Toronto, ON M5X 1E1
416-367-2998 Fax: 416-367-4749
fundinfo@energysavingsincomefund.com
www.esif.ca
Ticker Symbol: SIF
Profile: The open-ended, limited purpose trust is involved in the sale of natural gas & electricity to both residential & commercial customers. Operating affiliates inlcude Ontario Energy Savings L.P., Energy Savings (Manitoba) L.P., Energy Savings (Quebec) L.P., ES (B.C.) Limited Partnership, Alberta Energy Savings L.P., Illinois Energy Savings Corp., New York Energy Savings Corp., Indiana Energy Savings Corp., & Energy Savings Texas Corp.

Energy Savings Income Fund
#2630, 100 King St. West, Toronto, ON M5X 1E1
416-367-2998 Fax: 416-367-4749
fundinfo@energysavingsincomefund.com
www.esif.ca
Ticker Symbol: SIF
Profile: The open-ended, limited purpose trust is involved in the sale of natural gas & electricity to both residential & commercial customers. Operating affiliates inlcude Ontario Energy Savings L.P., Energy Savings (Manitoba) L.P., Energy Savings (Quebec) L.P., ES (B.C.) Limited Partnership, Alberta Energy Savings L.P., Illinois Energy Savings Corp., New York Energy Savings Corp., Indiana Energy Savings Corp., & Energy Savings Texas Corp.
Ken Hartwick, CAPresident/CEO
Peter Bloch, CAChief Financial Officer
905-795-4206, pbloch@energysavings.com
Scott Gahn, Exec. Vice-President, U.S. Energy Savings
Ken Hartwick, CAPresident/CEO
Peter Bloch, CAChief Financial Officer
905-795-4206, pbloch@energysavings.com
Scott Gahn, Exec. Vice-President, U.S. Energy Savings

Enersource Hydro Mississauga
3240 Mavis Rd., Mississauga, ON L5C 3K1
905-273-9050 Fax: 905-566-2731
info@enersource.com
www.enersource.com
Profile: Provides electricity to the City of Mississauga

Enersource Hydro Mississauga
3240 Mavis Rd., Mississauga, ON L5C 3K1
905-273-9050 Fax: 905-566-2731
info@enersource.com
www.enersource.com
Profile: Provides electricity to the City of Mississauga
Roland Herman, Exec. Vice-President/COO
Ray Rauber, Vice-Presiednt, Engineering & Operations
Roland Herman, Exec. Vice-President/COO
Ray Rauber, Vice-Presiednt, Engineering & Operations

FortisOntario
PO Box 1218, 1130 Bertie St., Fort Erie, ON L2A 5Y2
905-871-0330 www.cornwallelectric.com
Profile: FortisOntario is an innovative growth company with core businesses focused on electricity distribution, transmission, & generation. It is 100% Canadian owned & is affliated with the Fortis Family of Companies.

FortisOntario
PO Box 1218, 1130 Bertie St., Fort Erie, ON L2A 5Y2
905-871-0330 www.cornwallelectric.com
Profile: FortisOntario is an innovative growth company with core businesses focused on electricity distribution, transmission, & generation. It is 100% Canadian owned & is affliated with the Fortis Family of Companies.
Bill Daley, President and CEO
905-994-3631, Fax: 905-994-2202
Glen King, Vice President, Finance and CFO
905-994-3643, Fax: 905-994-2200
Bill Daley, President and CEO
905-994-3631, Fax: 905-994-2202
Glen King, Vice President, Finance and CFO
905-994-3643, Fax: 905-994-2200

Grimsby Power Incorporated
231 Roberts Rd., Grimsby, ON L3M 5N2
905-945-5437 Fax: 905-945-9933
info@grimsbypower.com
www.grimsbypower.com
Profile: Grimsby Power Incorporated provides customers in Grimsby with electricity.

Grimsby Power Incorporated
231 Roberts Rd., Grimsby, ON L3M 5N2
905-945-5437 Fax: 905-945-9933
info@grimsbypower.com
www.grimsbypower.com
Profile: Grimsby Power Incorporated provides customers in Grimsby with electricity.
Brian Weber, President
Vacant, President

Guelph Hydro Electric Systems Inc.
395 Southgate Dr., Guelph, ON N1G 4Y1
519-822-3010 Fax: 519-822-0960
bbagley@guelphhydro.com
www.guelphhydro.com
Profile: Guelph Hydro Electric Systems Inc. is Guelph's and Rockwood's electricity distribution company. They deliver electricity, maintain the lines to homes and businesses provide 24-hr emergency service and ensure that the local distribution system meets Guelph's and Rockwood's growing needs.

Hydro One Inc.
483 Bay St., 15th Fl., Toronto, ON M5G 2P5
416-345-6867 Fax: 416-345-6225 877-955-1155
investor.relations@hydroone.com
www.hydroone.com
Profile: HydroOne is the largest electricity delivery company in Ontario. It is a holding company for various subsidiaries. It provides electric services in Toronto.

Hydro One Inc.
483 Bay St., 15th Fl., Toronto, ON M5G 2P5
416-345-6867 Fax: 416-345-6225 877-955-1155
investor.relations@hydroone.com
www.hydroone.com
Profile: HydroOne is the largest electricity delivery company in Ontario. It is a holding company for various subsidiaries. It provides electric services in Toronto.
Larua Forumusa, President/CEO (Acting)
Beth Summers, CFO
Maureen Wareham, Secretary
Myles D'Arcey, Customer Operations
Peter Gregg, Corporate and Regulatory Affairs
Larua Forumusa, President/CEO
Sandy Struthers, CFO
Maureen Wareham, Secretary
Myles D'Arcey, Customer Operations
Peter Gregg, Corporate and Regulatory Affairs

Independent Electricity System Operator
PO Box 4474 A, Toronto, ON M5W 4E5
905-403-6900 Fax: 905-403-6921
customer.relations@ieso.ca
www.ieso.ca
Profile: The IESO balances the supply of & demand for electricity in Ontario & then directs its flow across the province's transmission lines. The IESO works at the heart of Ontario's power system, connecting all participants that produce electricity, transmitters that send it across the province, retailers that buy & sell it, industries & businesses that use it in large quantities, & local distribution companies that deliver it to homes.

Independent Electricity System Operator
PO Box 4474 A, Toronto, ON M5W 4E5
905-403-6900 Fax: 905-403-6921
customer.relations@ieso.ca
www.ieso.ca
Profile: The IESO balances the supply of & demand for electricity in Ontario & then directs its flow across the province's transmission lines. The IESO works at the heart of Ontario's power system, connecting all participants that produce electricity, transmitters that send it across the province, retailers that buy & sell it, industries & businesses that use it in large quantities, & local distribution companies that deliver it to homes.
Paul Murphy, B.Sc., P.Eng.President and CEO
paul.murphy@ieso.ca
Paul Murphy, B.Sc., P.Eng.President and CEO
paul.murphy@ieso.ca

Kenora Hydro Electric Corp. Ltd
City Hall, 1 Main St. South, Kenora, ON P9N 3X2
807-467-2000
service@kenora.ca
Profile: Distributes electricity to the towns of Kenora and Keewatin; has 12 employees dedicated to the delivery of electricity to its customers

Kenora Hydro Electric Corp. Ltd
City Hall, 1 Main St. South, Kenora, ON P9N 3X2
807-467-2000
service@kenora.ca
Profile: Distributes electricity to the towns of Kenora and Keewatin; has 12 employees dedicated to the delivery of electricity to its customers
Dave Sinclair, President/CEO
Dave Sinclair, President/CEO

London Hydro
111 Horton St., London, ON N6A 4J8
519-661-5503 Fax: 519-661-5838
admin@londonhydro.com
www.londonhydro.com
Profile: The City of London is the sole shareholder of London Hydro. It is responsible for providing London residents & business owners with electricity.

London Hydro
111 Horton St., London, ON N6A 4J8
519-661-5503 Fax: 519-661-5838
admin@londonhydro.com
www.londonhydro.com
Profile: The sole shareholder of London Hydro is the City of London. London Hydro provides London residents & businesses with electricity, through a network of overhead & underground power lines.
Bernie Watts, Chief Executive Officer
Peter Johnson, Chair
Vinay Sharma, Chief Executive Officer

Macquarie Power & Infrastructure Income Fund
Brookfield Place, #3100, 181 Bay St., Toronto, ON M5J 2T3
416-848-3500 Fax: 416-607-5073
mpt@macquarie.com
www.macquarie.com/mpt
Ticker Symbol: MPT.UN
Profile: Macquarie Power & Infrastructure Income Fund makes investments in essential infrastructure assets. It focuses upon power infrastructure.

Macquarie Power & Infrastructure Income Fund
Brookfield Place, #3100, 181 Bay St., Toronto, ON M5J 2T3
416-848-3500 Fax: 416-607-5073
mpt@macquarie.com
www.macquarie.com/mpt
Ticker Symbol: MPT.UN
Profile: Macquarie Power & Infrastructure Income Fund makes investments in essential infrastructure assets. It focuses upon power infrastructure.
Gregory Smith, President/CEO, MPT
Harry Atterton, Vice-President/CFO
416-607-5198, harry.atterton@macquarie.com
Sarah Borg-Olivier, Vice-President, Investor Relations
416-607-5009, sarah.borg-olivier@macquarie.com
Gregory Smith, President/CEO, MPT
Harry Atterton, Vice-President/CFO
416-607-5198, harry.atterton@macquarie.com
Sarah Borg-Olivier, Vice-President, Investor Relations
416-607-5009, sarah.borg-olivier@macquarie.com

Peninsula West Utilities Limited
4548 Ontario St. - Unit #2, Beamsville, ON L0R 1B5
905-563-5550 Fax: 905-563-0383
judith@penwest.on.ca
www.penwest.on.ca
Profile: Peninsula West Utilities Limited provides consumers in Lincoln, Pelham, & West Lincoln with electricity.

Niagara Peninsula Energy Inc.
PO Box 120, 7447 Pin Oak Dr., Niagara Falls, ON L2E 6S9
905-356-2681 Fax: 905-356-0118 877-270-3938
info@npei.ca
www.npei.ca
Profile: Niagara Peninsula Energy Inc. provides local electricity distribution & related services in the Township of West Lincoln, the City of Niagara Falls, the Town of Pelham, & the Town of Lincoln. It serves both business & residential customers.
Brian Wilkie, President & Chief Executive Officer

Margaret Battista, Vice-President, Customer Service & Information Technology
Margaret Battista, Vice-President, Customer Service & Information Technology
Tom Sielicki, Vice-President, Engineering
Suzanne Wilson, Vice-President, Finance

Ontario Power Generation Inc.
700 University Ave., Toronto, ON M5G 1X6
416-592-2555 877-592-2555
webmaster@opg.com
www.opg.com, www.mypowercareer.com
Profile: Electricity generation company

Ontario Power Generation Inc.
700 University Ave., Toronto, ON M5G 1X6
416-592-2555 877-592-2555
investor.relations@opg.com; media@opg.com
www.opg.com; mypowercareer@opg.com
Profile: The electricity generation company operates in a safe & environmentally responsible manner to generate & sell electricity throughout Ontario. Assets include sixty-five hydroelectric generating stations, five fossil generating stations, & three nuclear generating stations.
James F. Hankinson, President/CEO
Donn Hanbidge, Chief Financial Officer
Pierre Charlebois, Chief Nuclear Officer
John Murphy, Chief Ethics Officer & Exec. Vice-President, Human Resources
Tom Mitchell, President & Chief Executive Officer
John Murphy, Executive Vice President, Hydro
Janice Dunlop, Chief Ethics Officer & Senior Vice-President, Human Resources
Donn Hanbidge, Chief Financial Officer & Senior Vice-President
Wayne Robbins, Chief Nuclear Officer
Robert Boguski, Senior Vice-President, Business Services & Information Technology
Charles Pautler, Vice-President, Public Affairs

Oshawa PUC Networks Inc.
100 Simcoe St. South, Oshawa, ON L1H 7M7
905-723-4623 877-997-2899
contactus@opuc.on.ca
www.opuc.on.ca
Profile: Oshawa PUC Networks Inc. is the electricity distributor for all homes & businesses in the City of Oshawa.

Oshawa PUC Networks Inc.
100 Simcoe St. South, Oshawa, ON L1H 7M7
905-723-4623 Fax: 905-743-5222
contactus@opuc.on.ca
www.opuc.on.ca
Profile: Oshawa PUC Networks distributes electricity to homes & businesses in Oshawa.
Jeff Rosenthal, President and CEO
Atul Mahajanal, President & Chief Executive Officer
Mike Leslie, P. Eng.Vice-President, Engineering & Operations
Phil Martin, Vice-President, Finance & Regulatory Compliance
Nadeige Carter, Coordinator, Conservation Project

Peterborough Utilities Services Inc.
PO Box 4125 Main, 1867 Ashburnham Dr., Peterborough, ON K9J 6Z5
705-748-9300 Fax: 705-748-6761
puc@puc.org
www.puc.org
Profile: Peterborough Utilities Services Inc. provides utility services for residents of Peterborough, Lakefield, & Norwood, Ontario.

Peterborough Utilities Group
PO Box 4125 Main, 1867 Ashburnham Dr., Peterborough, ON K9J 6Z5
705-748-9300 Fax: 705-748-6761
info@peterboroughutilities.ca
www.peterboroughutilities.ca
Profile: Peterborough Utilities Group delivers & sells utility-related products & services.
Larry Doran, President & Chief Executive Officer
John Stephenson, Chief Financial Officer, Secretary-Treasurer & Vice-President, Corporate Service
Larry Franks, Vice-President, Information Technology Services
Jeff Guilbeault, Vice-President, Electric Utility Services
Wayne Stiver, Vice-President, Water Utility Services
John Wynsma, Vice-President, Generation & Retail Services
Carrissa McCaw, Director, Human Resources & Safety

Toronto Hydro Corporation
14 Carlton St., Toronto, ON M5B 1K5
416-542-3000 Fax: 416-542-3452
contactus@torontohydro.com
www.torontohydro.com
Profile: Offices of holding companies; Electric services; Natural gas distribution.

Toronto Hydro Corporation
14 Carlton St., Toronto, ON M5B 1K5
416-542-3100 Fax: 416-542-3452
contactus@torontohydro.com
www.torontohydro.com
Profile: Offices of holding companies; Electric services; Natural gas distribution.
David S. O'Brien, President/CEO
David Dobbin, President, Toronto Hydro Telecom
Jean-Sebastien Couillard, CFO
Blair H. Peberdy, Vice-President, Communications & Public Affairs
Anthony M. Haines, President
Ave Lethbridge, Vice-President, Organizational Effectiveness
Lawrence Wilde, Vice-President and General Counsel
David S. O'Brien, President/CEO
David Dobbin, President, Toronto Hydro Telecom
Jean-Sebastien Couillard, CFO
Blair H. Peberdy, Vice-President, Communications & Public Affairs
Anthony M. Haines, President
Ave Lethbridge, Vice-President, Organizational Effectiveness
Lawrence Wilde, Vice-President and General Counsel

Universal Energy Group Ltd.
#1700, 25 Sheppard Avenue West, Toronto, ON M2N 6S6
416-673-1162 Fax: 416-673-4790
splummer@uegl.ca
www.universalenergygroup.ca
Ticker Symbol: UEG
Profile: Electricity and natural gas company focused in Ontario and Michigan

Universal Energy Group Ltd.
#1700, 25 Sheppard Avenue West, Toronto, ON M2N 6S6
416-673-1162 Fax: 416-673-4790
splummer@uegl.ca
www.universalenergygroup.ca
Ticker Symbol: UEG
Profile: Electricity and natural gas company focused in Ontario and Michigan
Mark Silver, President
Stephen Plummer, Chief Financial Officer
Mark Silver, President
Stephen Plummer, Chief Financial Officer

UPI Energy LP
200-105 Silvercreek Parkway North, Guelph, ON N1H 8M1
519-821-2667 Fax: 519-821-4919
info@upi.on.ca
www.upienergylp.com
Profile: UPI Energy LP provides energy products in rural Ontario.
Robert P. Sicard, President & Chief Executive Officer

Utilities Kingston
PO Box 790, Kingston, ON K7L 4X7
613-456-0000
info@utilitieskingston.com
www.utilitieskingston.com
Profile: Utilities Kingston is responsible for supplying, distributing and metering electricity and natural gas in the City Central. Also responsible for supplying, distributing and metering water and for collecting, pumping and treating sewage for the entire city of Kingston

Utilities Kingston
PO Box 790, Kingston, ON K7L 4X7
613-456-0000
info@utilitieskingston.com
www.utilitieskingston.com
Profile: Utilities Kingston is responsible for supplying, distributing and metering electricity and natural gas in the City Central. Also responsible for supplying, distributing and metering water and for collecting, pumping and treating sewage for the entire city of Kingston

Wellington North Power Inc.
290 Queen St West, Mont Dorest, ON N0G2L3
519-323-1710
wnp@wellingtonnorthpower.com
www.wellington-north.com
Profile: Wellington North Power supplies hydro services to the urban areas of the Township.

Wellington North Power Inc.
PO Box 359, 290 Queen St. West, Mount Forest, ON N0G 1A0
519-323-1710 Fax: 519-323-2425
wnp@wellingtonnorthpower.com
www.wellingtonnorthpower.com
Profile: The distribution company delivers electricity & maintains service to residents & businesses. Wellington North Power Inc. serves the areas of Arthur, Mount Forest, & Holstein in Ontario.
Judy Rosebrugh, President & Chief Executive Officer
jrosebrugh@wellingtonnorthpower.com

Westario Power
24 Eastridge Rd., RR#2, Walkerton, ON N0G 2V0
519-507-6937 Fax: 519-507-6887
customer.service@westario.com
www.westario.com
Profile: Westario is committed to providing the safest, most reliable, & cost-effective electric services possible to customers. It is a local distribution company (LDC), which supplies electricity to various Ontario communities including Clifford, Elmwood, Hanover, Kincardine.

Westario Power Inc.
24 Eastridge Rd., RR#2, Walkerton, ON N0G 2V0
519-507-6937 866-978-2746
customer.service@westario.com
www.westario.com
Profile: Westario Power Inc. is engaged in the safe & reliable delivery of electricity. It is owned by the municipalities it serves. FortisOntario also has a 10% interest in Westario Power.
Guy Cluff, President and CEO
Lisa Milne, CGAPresident & Chief Executive Officer
Patrick Protomanni, P. Eng.Manager, System Reliability

Prince Edward Island

Maritime Electric
PO Box 1328, 180 Kent St., Charlottetown, PE C1A 7N2
902-629-3799 800-670-1012
customerservice@maritimeelectric.com
www.maritimeelectric.com
Profile: Serving approximately 66,000 customers throughout PEI, the company owns & operates a fully integrated system providing for the generation, transmission, & distribution of electricity throughout the Island. Its energy delivery system is linked to the NB Power grid via two submarine cables.

Maritime Electric
c/o Island Customer Service Centre, PO Box 1328, 180 Kent St., Charlottetown, PE C1A 7N2
Fax: 902-629-3630 800-670-1012
customerservice@maritimeelectric.com
www.maritimeelectric.com
Profile: Maritime Electric operates according to the Electric Power Act & the Renewable Energy Act to deliver electricity on Prince Edward Island.
Fred J. O'Brien, President & Chief Executive Officer
J. William Geldert, CFO, Corporate Secretary, & Vice-President, Finance & Administration
John D. Gaudet, Vice-President, Corporate Planning & Energy Supply
Kim A. Griffin, Manager, Corporate Communications & Public Affairs
Gil A. Jubainville, Manager, Information Technology

Québec

Boralex Inc.
36, rue Lajeunesse, Kingsey Falls, QC J0A 1B0
819-363-5860 Fax: 819-363-5866
info@boralex.com
www.boralex.com
Ticker Symbol: BLX
Profile: The electricity producer provides the following types of power generation: natural gas cogeneration, hydroelectric, wind power, & wood-residue.

Boralex Inc.
36, rue Lajeunesse, Kingsey Falls, QC J0A 1B0
819-363-5860 Fax: 819-363-5866
info@boralex.com
www.boralex.com
Ticker Symbol: BLX
Profile: The electricity producer provides the following types of power generation: natural gas cogeneration, hydroelectric, wind power, & wood-residue.
Patrick Lemaire, President/CEO
Jean-François Thibodeau, Vice-President/CFO
Claude Audet, Vice-President/Chief Operating Officer
Patricia Lemaire, Director, Public Affairs & Communications
514-985-1353, Fax: 514-985-1355,
patricia.lemaire@boralex.com
Gabriel Ouellet, Technical Director, Biomass, Quebec & USA
Gilles Shooner, Environmental Consultant & Member, Environmental, Health, & Safety Committee
Patrick Lemaire, President/CEO

Jean-François Thibodeau, Vice-President/CFO
Claude Audet, Vice-President/Chief Operating Officer
Patricia Lemaire, Director, Public Affairs & Communications
514-985-1353, Fax: 514-985-1355,
patricia.lemaire@boralex.com
Gabriel Ouellet, Technical Director, Biomass, Quebec & USA
Gilles Shooner, Environmental Consultant & Member, Environmental, Health, & Safety Committee

Boralex Power Income Fund
36 Lajeunesse Street, Kingsey Falls, QC J0A 1B0
819-363-5860 Fax: 819-363-5866
info@boralex.com
www.boralex.com/trust
Ticker Symbol: BPT.UN
Profile: Open-ended limited purpose trust; owns hydroelectricity, wood residue and natural gas power stations in Quebec and New York

Boralex Power Income Fund
36 Lajeunesse Street, Kingsey Falls, QC J0A 1B0
819-363-5860 Fax: 819-363-5866
info@boralex.com
www.boralex.com/trust
Ticker Symbol: BPT.UN
Profile: Open-ended limited purpose trust; owns hydroelectricity, wood residue and natural gas power stations in Quebec and New York

Gaz Métro inc
1717, rue du Havre, Montréal, QC H2K 2X3
514-598-3444 Fax: 514-598-3144
info@gazmetro.com
www.gazmetro.com
Ticker Symbol: GZM
Profile: Offices of holding companies; Natural gas transmission & distribution; Retail in household appliance stores; Equipment rental & leasing

Gaz Métro inc
1717, rue du Havre, Montréal, QC H2K 2X3
514-598-3444 Fax: 514-598-3144 800-361-4005
info@gazmetro.com
www.gazmetro.com
Ticker Symbol: GZM
Profile: Offices of holding companies; Natural gas transmission & distribution; Retail in household appliance stores; Equipment rental & leasing
Robert Tessier, President/CEO
Pierre Despars, Vice-President, Finance & Corporate Affairs
Stéphanie-Hélène Leclerc, Contact, Public & Governmental Affairs
E. Morin, Director, Engineering, Geomatics & Technology
J.-P. Noël, Director, Regulatory Matters, Rates & Environment
Sophie Brochu, President/CEO
Pierre Despars, Vice-President, Finance & Corporate Affairs
Stéphanie-Hélène Leclerc, Contact, Public & Governmental Affairs
E. Morin, Director, Engineering, Geomatics & Technology
J.-P. Noël, Director, Regulatory Matters, Rates & Environment

Gaz Métro Limited Partnership
1717, rue du Havre, Montréal, QC H2K 2X3
514-598-3444 Fax: 514-598-3144
investors@gazmetro.com
www.gazmetro.com
Ticker Symbol: GZM
Profile: Gaz Métro Limited Partnership focuses upon the distribution of natural gas, through its interests in natural gas transmission companies. The company is also engaged in the sale of goods in the energy & fiber optics fields, as well as the diagnosis & rehabilitation of drinking water & wastewater infrastructures. In order to reduce greenhouse gas emissions, Gaz Métro has adopted an environmental policy, an environmental management system, & energy efficiency programs.

Gaz Métro Limited Partnership
1717, rue du Havre, Montréal, QC H2K 2X3
514-598-3444 Fax: 514-598-3144
investors@gazmetro.com
www.gazmetro.com
Ticker Symbol: GZM
Profile: Gaz Métro Limited Partnership focuses upon the distribution of natural gas, through its interests in natural gas transmission companies. The company is also engaged in the sale of goods in the energy & fiber optics fields, as well as the diagnosis & rehabilitation of drinking water & wastewater infrastructures. In order to reduce greenhouse gas emissions, Gaz Métro has adopted an environmental policy, an environmental management system, & energy efficiency programs.
Sophie Brochu, President/CEO
Pierre Despars, Exec. Vice-President/CFO
Martin Imbleau, Vice-President, Operations & Major Projects
Marc Lemieux, Corporate Secretary & Vice-President, Legal Affairs
Sophie Brochu, President/CEO
Pierre Despars, Exec. Vice-President/CFO
Martin Imbleau, Vice-President, Operations & Major Projects
Marc Lemieux, Corporate Secretary & Vice-President, Legal Affairs

Great Lakes Hydro Income Fund
#200, 480, boul de la Cité, Gatineau, QC J8T 8R3
819-561-2722 Fax: 819-561-7188 888-327-2722
unitholderenquiries@greatlakeshydro.com
www.greatlakeshydro.com
Ticker Symbol: GLH
Profile: Electric services; Open-ended management investment offices.

Great Lakes Hydro Income Fund
#200, 480, boul de la Cité, Gatineau, QC J8T 8R3
819-561-2722 Fax: 819-561-7188 888-327-2722
unitholderenquiries@greatlakeshydro.com
www.greatlakeshydro.com
Ticker Symbol: GLH
Profile: Electric services; Open-ended management investment offices.
Richard Legault, President/CEO
Donald Tremblay, CFO & Vice-President
Harry A. Goldgut, Chairman of the Board and Director
Richard Legault, President/CEO
Donald Tremblay, CFO & Vice-President
Harry A. Goldgut, Chairman of the Board and Director

Hydro-Québec
75, boul René-Lévesque ouest, Montréal, QC H2Z 1A4
514-289-2211 Fax: 514-289-5773
800-790-2424www.hydroquebec.com
Profile: Electricity services in Quebec

Hydro-Québec
75, boul René-Lévesque ouest, Montréal, QC H2Z 1A4
514-289-2211 Fax: 514-289-5773
800-790-2424www.hydroquebec.com
Profile: Electricity services in Quebec
Thierry Vandal, President/CEO
Joseph Benarrosh, President, JJDS Capital inc.
Daniel Garant, CFO & Exec. Vice-President, Finance
Marie-José Nadeau, Secretary General/Exec. Vice-President, Corporate Affairs
Thierry Vandal, President/CEO
Joseph Benarrosh, President, JJDS Capital inc.
Daniel Garant, CFO & Exec. Vice-President, Finance
Marie-José Nadeau, Secretary General/Exec. Vice-President, Corporate Affairs

Innergex Renewable Energy Inc.
#1255, 1111, rue Saint-Charles ouest, Longueil, QC J4K 5G4
450-928-2550 Fax: 450-928-2544
jtrudel@innergex.com
www.innergex.com
Ticker Symbol: INE
Profile: Innergex Renewable Energy develops & operates renewable power generating facilities. If focuses upon the wind power & hydroelectric sectors.

Innergex Renewable Energy Inc.
#1255, 1111, rue Saint-Charles ouest, Longueil, QC J4K 5G4
450-928-2550 Fax: 450-928-2544
jtrudel@innergex.com
www.innergex.com
Ticker Symbol: INE
Profile: Innergex Renewable Energy develops & operates renewable power generating facilities. If focuses upon the wind power & hydroelectric sectors.
Michel Letellier, MBAPresident/CEO
Jean Perron, Vice-President/CFO
Michèle Beauchamp, LL.B., LL.M.,Corporate Secretary & Vice-President, Legal Affairs
Guy Dufort, Vice-President, Public Affairs
Peter Grover, Eng.Vice-President, Project Management
Jean Trudel, MBAVice-President, Finance & Investor Relations
Michel Letellier, MBAPresident/CEO
Jean Perron, Vice-President/CFO
Michèle Beauchamp, LL.B., LL.M.,Corporate Secretary & Vice-President, Legal Affairs
Guy Dufort, Vice-President, Public Affairs
Peter Grover, Eng.Vice-President, Project Management
Jean Trudel, MBAVice-President, Finance & Investor Relations

Saskatchewan

Saskatoon Light & Power
322 Brand Rd., Saskatoon, SK S7K 0J5
306-975-2414 Fax: 306-975-3057
www.city.saskatoon.sk.ca/org/electrical
Profile: Founded in 1906, Saskatoon Light & Power distributes electrical services to citizens & businesses of the Saskatoon area that lies roughly within the 1958 boundary. The utility is also responsible for the street light system for the city.

Saskatoon Light & Power
322 Brand Rd., Saskatoon, SK S7K 0J5
306-975-2414 Fax: 306-975-3057
www.city.saskatoon.sk.ca/org/electrical
Profile: Founded in 1906, Saskatoon Light & Power distributes electrical services to citizens & businesses of the Saskatoon area that lies roughly within the 1958 boundary. The utility is also responsible for the street light system for the city.

SaskEnergy Incorporated
1601 Winnipeg St., Regina, SK S4P 4E7
306-777-9225 Fax: 306-777-9223
800-567-8899www.saskenergy.com
Profile: Natural gas transmission & distribution

SaskEnergy Incorporated
1777 Victoria Ave., Regina, SK S4P 4K5
306-777-9225 800-567-8899www.saskenergy.com
Profile: The natural gas distribution company is a provincial Crown corporation. SaskEnergy Incorporated delivers safe & environmentally friendly natural gas to customers throughout Saskatchewan. The company also works with independent natural gas retailers to offer natural gas appliances, maintenance, & financing.
Doug Kelln, President/CEO
Dean Reeve, Executive Vice-President, SaskEnergy
Daryl Posehn, Senior Vice-President, TransGas
Berney Ryma, Director, Environmental Affairs
Doug Kelln, President & Chief Executive Officer
Dennis Terry, Chief Financial Officer & Vice-President, Finance
Dean Reeve, Executive Vice-President
Daryl Posehn, Senior Vice-President, Gas Supply & Business Development
Mark Guillet, Vice-President, General Counsel, & Corporate Secretary

Yukon Territory

Yukon Electrical Company Limited
100-1100 1st Ave., Whitehorse, YT Y1A 3T4
867-633-7000 Fax: 867-668-6692 800-661-0513
cynthia.malchow@atco.com
www.yukonelectrical.com
Profile: The Yukon Electrical Company Limited has been providing electrical service to Yukoners for over a century. It currently serves 14,900 customers in 19 communities from south of the Yukon border to north of the Arctic Circle. As a private, investor-owned utility, Yukon Electrical is a member of the ATCO Group of Companies.

Yukon Electrical Company Limited
#100, 1100 - 1st Ave., Whitehorse, YT Y1A 3T4
867-633-7000 Fax: 867-668-6692
800-661-0513www.yukonelectrical.com
Profile: The Yukon Electrical Company Limited is a private, investor-owned utility which provides electrical services to Yukoners. The company works to design & construct its facilities in a way that reduces pollution & the impact of operations upon the environment.
Cynthia Malchow, Contact
800-661-0513, cynthia.malchow@atco.com
Jerome Babyn, General Manager

ENTRY NAME INDEX

A

B

C

D

E

F

H

J

K

L

M

N

O

P

Q

R

T

U

V

W

X

Y

Z

Canada Info Desk

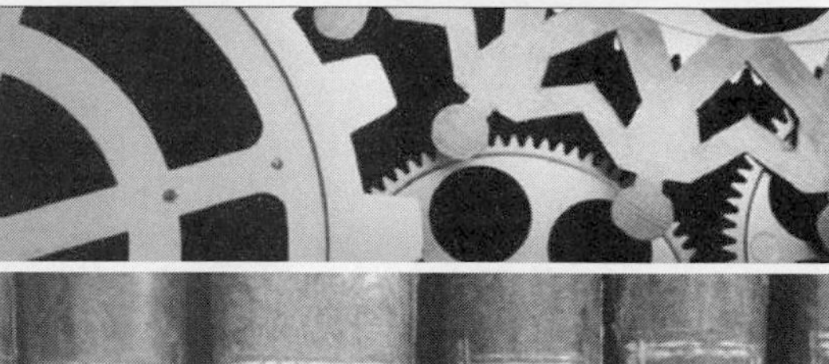

Canada Info Desk integrates Grey House Canada's best-selling directories into a single online Canadian resource—making it the most comprehensive directory database in Canada. The easy-to-use Web interface gives users instant access to thousands of organizations, contacts, facts and figures about Canadian business, government and society.

Start your search here

Canada Info Desk can be found on the desktops of Canada's finest libraries and institutions and on desks and shelves in libraries and institutions all accross Canada. Professional researchers can search by fielded data to pinpoint information on the spot. Students can quickly track down organizations or people, locate addresses, analyze activities or even job hunt using the extensive listings. Invaluable to business professionals, Canada Info Desk is an excellent tool to pinpoint contacts or prospects, identify partner groups, search for promotional opportunities and export custom lists in seconds.

Design your own custom lists, why wait?

Save time and money with this unique and valuable resource. Canada Info Desk database gives you the option to define and extract your own lists in seconds. Whether you need contact, mail or e-mail lists, Canada Info Desk can pull together the information quickly and export it in a variety of formats to where you need it most… your desktop.

Innovative interface with enhanced functionality

Canada Info Desk gives users the ability to limit their search many different ways including the original database source, subject category and location. Researchers can choose between a complex Expert Search or a simple Quick Search.

KEY ADVANTAGES OF CANADA INFO DESK:

- seamlessly cross-database search all database content or content subsets
- generate and export customized lists for contact data, marketing, or research collection
- regular ongoing changes are added to the Web version on a monthly basis.
- conduct a quick search with fields common to all databases, or build a complex Boolean expert search query
- customize results by searching for records that are head offices, have e-mail, phone, fax or Web sites, promote conferences, produce publications, or are mailing list compliant
- save time by saving search results for future reference
- mark records in the results list or full record and then view, print, e-mail or export
- link directly to Web sites or e-mail addresses

Subscribers can search based on more general record categorization, including:

- arts and culture
- awards
- business and finance
- Canadians and society
- communications
- education
- environment
- governments
- health
- industry
- labour
- law and justice
- meetings
- public services
- religion
- science and nature
- sports and recreation
- transportation
- utilities

For more information please contact Grey House Publishing Canada by Tel.: 1-866-433-4739 or (416) 644-6479
Fax: (416) 644-1904 or via E-mail: info@greyhouse.ca • www.greyhouse.ca

INFORMATION FORM

PHOTOCOPY THIS FORM FOR CONVENIENCE

CHANGE TO LISTING

PAGE NUMBER: DIRECTORY:

NAME OF ORGANIZATION:

PLEASE CHANGE OUR LISTING TO REFLECT THE FOLLOWING:

NEW LISTING:

WE ARE NOT REPRESENTED IN THE DIRECTORY. HERE IS THE INFORMATION ON OUR ASSOCIATION/ORGANIZATION/ GOVERNMENT BODY: (Please examine the guidelines in the front of the directory and the entries of similar organizations for an indication of how best to present your data).

WE WOULD LIKE TO SEE MORE INFORMATION ON:

MAIL INFORMATION TO:
GREY HOUSE PUBLISHING CANADA
555 RICHMOND ST., W, SUITE 301
TORONTO, ONTARIO M5V 3B1

E-MAIL TO:
INFO@GREYHOUSE.CA

FAX INFORMATION TO:
THE EDITOR
(416) 644-1904

Mailing List Services

As a boutique provider of mailings lists, Grey House Canada specializes in the areas below to ensure a ***high level*** of accuracy. Our clients return time to us time and time again because of the reliability and customer service. We'll work with you to develop a campaign that provides results. No other list services will work as closely as we do to meet your unique needs.

Grey House Canada Custom Mailing Lists:

- ***Associations*** - the most extensive list of Canadian Associations available, featuring all professional, trade and business organizations together with not-for profit groups.
- ***Arts & Culture*** - the definitive source of key prospects in various Canadian arts and cultural outlets.
- ***Education*** - the most comprehensive list of educational institutions and organizations in Canada.
- ***Health Care / Hospitals*** - includes all major medical facilities with chief executives.
- ***Lawyers*** - key prospects for a number of direct mail offers.
- ***Media*** - the definitive source of key prospects in various Canadian media outlets, offering the top business managers and/or publishers.
- ***Environmental*** - a complete profile of the Canadian Environmental scene, constantly revised for the annual Canadian Environmental Directory.
- ***Financial Services*** - a list of key contacts from the full range of Canada's financial services industry.
- ***Government Key Contacts*** - a list of key Government contacts, maintained by the Canadian Almanac & Directory, Canada's standard institutional reference for over 160 years.
- ***Libraries*** - the most unique and complete list of government, special and public libraries available.
- ***Major Canadian Companies*** - listings of Canada's largest private, public and crown corporations with major key contacts of the top business decision-makers.

Availability

Lists are available on CD, labels, and via e-mail. They are provided on a one-time use basis or for a one year lease.
For a quotation on tailor made lists to suit your needs, inquire using the contact information listed below.

For more information please contact Grey House Publishing Canada by Tel.: 1-866-433-4739 or (416) 644-6479
Fax: (416) 644-1904 or via E-mail: info@greyhouse.ca • www.greyhouse.ca

CANADIAN DIRECTORIES ORDER FORM

QTY	TITLE	PRINT	ONLINE
	CANADIAN ALMANAC & DIRECTORY 2011	$350.00	*Please call for quote*
	ASSOCIATIONS CANADA 2011	$375.00	*Please call for quote*
	CANADIAN PARLIAMENTARY GUIDE 2011	$229.00	*Please call for quote*
	FINANCIAL SERVICES CANADA 2010/11	$350.00	*Please call for quote*
	CANADIAN ENVIRONMENTAL RESOURCE GUIDE 2010/11	$350.00	*Please call for quote*
	LIBRARIES CANADA 2010/11	$255.00	*Please call for quote*
	GOVERNMENTS CANADA *(updated monthly)*	*N/A*	*Please call for quote*
	CANADA INFO DESK *(updated monthly)*	*N/A*	*Please call for quote*

PLEASE NOTE:
- Prices are listed in Canadian dollars. All prices are subject to change without notice. N/A = Not Available
- To purchase print directories online visit our Web site – www.greyhouse.ca
- Orders shipped outside Canada are charged in US dollars

COMMENTS:

METHOD OF PAYMENT:

❑ CHEQUE/MONEY ORDER

Please make cheque/money order payable to Grey House Publishing Canada for total amount including shipping & handling and all applicable taxes. (Please call to confirm total)

❑ CREDIT CARD

❑ VISA ❑ MASTERCARD ❑ AMEX

CARD NUMBER:

EXPIRY DATE:

SIGNATURE:

❑ BILL MY COMPANY/ORGANIZATION

PO # IF APPLICABLE

BILL TO INFORMATION:

NAME

TITLE/DEPT.

ORGANIZATION

ADDRESS

CITY

PROV

BUSINESS PHONE POSTAL CODE

E-MAIL FAX NUMBER

SHIP TO INFORMATION: *(if different from above)*

NAME

TITLE/DEPT.

ORGANIZATION

ADDRESS

CITY

PROV

BUSINESS PHONE POSTAL CODE

E-MAIL FAX NUMBER

❑ STANDING ORDER PLAN

Please book my standing order for future annual print editions. With an automatic renewal, I'll save 10% off subsequent orders.

APPLICABLE TAXES
- 5% GST applies to AB, MB, SK, QC, YT, NT, NU & PE
- 12% HST applies to BC
- 13% HST applies ON, NB and NL
- 15% HST applies to NS

SHIPPING & HANDLING

$15.50 for a single directory
$4.00 each additional directory
(Canadian & US Orders).

International Orders – call for rates. Subject to customs duty tax at customer expense.

555 Richmond St. W
Suite #301, PO Box 1207
Toronto, Ontario M5V 3B1

PHONE
(866) 433-4739

FAX
(416) 644-1904

E-MAIL
info@greyhouse.ca